ALABAMA · COLORADO · ARIZONA · MAINE · TEXAS · UTAH · ALASKA · GEORGIA · DELAWARE · ILLINOIS · KANSAS · NORTH CAROLINA · OREGON · NEBRASKA · KENTUCKY · OHIO · WYOMING · VERMONT · VIRGINIA · WASHINGTON · HAWAII · CALIFORNIA · MICHIGAN · MINNESOTA · MISSISSIPPI · MISSOURI · WEST VIRGINIA · NEW YORK · NEVADA

IOWA · LOUISIANA · WISCONSIN · TENNESSEE · IDAHO · NEW HAMPSHIRE · NEW JERSEY · NEW MEXICO · CONNECTICUT · FLORIDA · MASSACHUSETTS · MONTANA · RHODE ISLAND · OKLAHOMA · INDIANA · NORTH DAKOTA · PENNSYLVANIA · SOUTH CAROLINA · SOUTH DAKOTA · MARYLAND · ARKANSAS

1817  2023

The Official Catholic Directory

Anno Domini 2023

Published Annually by

P. J. Kenedy & Sons

The Official Catholic Directory®

P.J. Kenedy & Sons, Publisher

FOREWORD

It is with great pleasure that we present the 2023 edition of *The Official Catholic Directory*. For over 200 years *The Official Catholic Directory* has provided comprehensive coverage of all the charitable organizations and clergy within the Catholic Church in the United States. To complement this coverage, we have included the "2022 Highlights", our annual recap of the key events from the past year, along with an insightful tribute to the late Pope Benedict XVI written by Archbishop Salvatore Cordileone.

This edition maintains several recent format/layout enhancements for **a)** improved readability and navigation, making it easier for users to locate entities and the clergy, brothers, sisters, and laity that serve those entities; and to **b)** reduce redundancies that increase the page count unnecessarily and causes book binding problems. Among the changes are:

- **Larger Font and Increased "leading" (i.e., vertical space between lines of text)** – These two key changes alone dramatically improve the readability of the OCD.
- **Bolded Entity Names** – Parish, School, Convent, Hospital, etc. names now display in distinctive bold font, and all are left aligned for easier identification.
- **Indented Sub-Orgs** – Sub-orgs are now indented a few spaces, making them more easily distinguished from their parent entities.
- **Enhanced Placement/Grouping** – entities are now consistently grouped by state and city placement headers in all dioceses rather than the less intuitive county groupings used in some dioceses.
- **Underlined Placement Headers** – underlined state and city placement headers make locating entities easier and faster.
- **Standardized Headers** – in Curia and Institutions sections, headers enable the grouping together of like entities. Standardized headers make finding organizations quicker and easier.
- **Closed/Merged Parishes** – Parishes closed within the current or previous year will compose in the directory along with the month/year of closure/merger and any relevant notes.
- **Deacons Index** – a new deacons index will appear online only until we are able to reduce the size of OCD enough to include the deacons index and still meet the maximum page count requirement for binding.
- **Chaplains at non-Catholic Institutions (formerly CPI) / Miscellaneous Assignments** – These sections have been removed from within each diocesan section and are now tracked within the Priests index (i.e., chaplain and miscellaneous assignments will be notated within a priest's index entry).

Although the Catholic Church in the United States has changed significantly over the past two hundred years, our core mission remains the same: to constantly update and annually publish an accurate listing of all the charitable organizations and clergy of the Catholic Church in the United States. This mission cannot be completed without the help of the United States Conference of Catholic Bishops, other ecclesiastical authorities, and countless diocesan staff members. We owe each a debt of gratitude and would like to conclude this foreword by thanking them for their longstanding cooperation and invaluable assistance to *The Official Catholic Directory*.

Sincerely,

Robert J. Docherty
Publisher

220 College Ave., Ste. 618, Athens, GA 30601-9801
info@nrpdirect.com

The Seal of P.J. Kenedy & Sons The Official Catholic Directory

Significance

The shield is the central part of a heraldic device, which is more commonly known as a coat of arms. If that shield is enclosed within a body of text, or other type of surrounding configuration, the device becomes known as a seal, yet it is the shield portion of the design that is the most important, and that which is described technically as the blazon. As the design is examined, it must be remembered that by heraldic tradition the design is described (blazoned) as if being done by the bearer with the shield being worn on the arm. Therefore, the terms dexter and sinister will be reversed as the design is viewed from the front.

The shield of the seal for **The Official Catholic Directory** has been designed to reflect the character and heritage of this publication of P.J. Kenedy & Sons.

The shield is in two major portions. The right half (sinister impalement) is composed of the blue shield on which are seen a silver tree, two candles (in silver or white) in their candleholders (of gold or yellow) and an open book, edged in gold and with a red bookmark. These symbols have been used over the years as the sign of the P.J. Kenedy & Sons publishing organization. These are the traditional symbols of knowledge and learning, so appropriate to a publisher.

The other side of the shield (the dexter impalement) is composed of a silver (white) field on which is seen a red cross, throughout, and a gold eagle. These symbols, combined with the field of the sinister impalement, are represented in the color of the flag of the United States of America and the eagle, the symbol of the United States. The cross represents Christianity and all of this combines to signify that **The Official Catholic Directory** annually reports on the Catholic Church in the United States.

The shield is surrounded by a laurel wreath of excellence and is enclosed within the legend that states the name of the company, the name of the publication and date (1817) of its founding.

— ***Paul J. Sullivan***

Liturgical Design • Construction Management • Painting & Decoration • Marble Appointments & Flooring

St. Paul Catholic Church - Arcadia Florida
Bishop Frank J. Dewane

Converting a Grocery Store into a Catholic Church

Renovation Project Highlights

Complete Transformation
New roof and HVAC System
New Facade
New Custom Wood Reredos with Marble Inlays
Custom Marble Altar, Ambo and Tabernacle Throne
New Marble Floors and Sanctuary with Coordinated Inlays
New Porcelain Tiles in the Nave with Marble Inlays
Custom Millwork for Wrapping Beams
All New LED Lighting Design and Fixtures
New Side Shrines
New Electronic Sound System
Custom 13 Ft. Bronze Statues from Italy
Beautiful Custom Stained Glass Windows
New Pews and Kneelers

Baker Liturgical Art, LLC
Church Restoration Church Renovation

Brian T. Baker
President/Liturgical Designer

HARA-ARCH, LLC
Wojciech Harabasz
Architectural Liturgical Designer

1210 Meriden-Waterbury Tpke., Plantsville, CT 06479 • P: 860-621-7471 • F: 860-621-7607 • info@bakerart.net
9427 South Ocean Drive • Jensen Beach, FL 34957 • P: 860-919-2119 • www.bakerliturgicalart.com

Mural & Mosaic Restoration • Stained Glass • Audio & Video Systems • Marble & Wood Carved Statues • Millwork

U.S. Catholic Church 2022 Highlights

BY KELSEY S. WICKS

Marked by the momentous questions surrounding the dignity of life and the sorrow associated with death, beginning with the March for Life through the start of the war in Ukraine on Feb. 24, crescendoing through the summer as the Supreme Court overturned Roe v. Wade on Jun. 24, and finally concluding with the passage of Pope Benedict XVI on Dec. 31, the year 2022 was replete with moments of epochal change as well as moments of cultural levity, including the joyful public witness of football coaches and players and the rise of several possible U.S. women saints.

The headlines for 2022 began with a fire on Jan. 9 in New York City–one of the city's deadliest in decades–that claimed the lives of 19, including nine children.

Pope Francis prayed for the victims and offered his "heartfelt condolences" to the families of the deceased via a telegram to Cardinal Timothy Dolan.

Shortly after that, the church bade farewell to Catholic philosopher and professor Alice Von Hildebrand, who went to her eternal rest on Jan. 14 at age 98 after a brief illness. Awarded the college's Presidential Award for excellence in teaching, Von Hildebrand is best known for her book *The Privilege of Being a Woman*.

With the questions surrounding womanhood and motherhood at the forefront of American consciousness and a decision pending in the Dobbs v. Jackson Women's Health case before the Supreme Court, enthusiasm was at a premium during the 49th annual March for Life, whose theme was "Equality Begins in the Womb." According to Students for Life of America, 150,000 marched past its elevated camera.

The event took place amidst an uptick in vandalism against Catholic Churches, including the defacement of the marble statue of Our Lady of Fatima outside the Basilica the week prior, a trend that would continue and heighten throughout 2022 in the wake of the leak of the Dobbs opinion on May 2.

Questions of life continued to magnify in the public square and the Catholic Church when Russia launched a full-scale invasion of Ukraine. The conflict, which began in 2014, dominated the headlines throughout 2022.

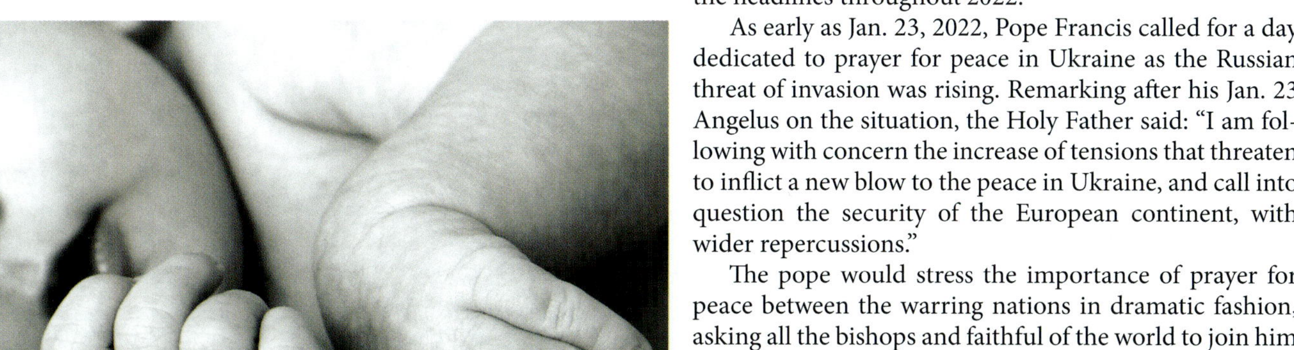

PIXABAY PHOTO

As early as Jan. 23, 2022, Pope Francis called for a day dedicated to prayer for peace in Ukraine as the Russian threat of invasion was rising. Remarking after his Jan. 23 Angelus on the situation, the Holy Father said: "I am following with concern the increase of tensions that threaten to inflict a new blow to the peace in Ukraine, and call into question the security of the European continent, with wider repercussions."

The pope would stress the importance of prayer for peace between the warring nations in dramatic fashion, asking all the bishops and faithful of the world to join him on the Solemnity of the Annunciation, Mar. 25, 2022, in consecrating Ukraine and Russia to the Immaculate Heart of Mary.

Ukraine's Latin Rite Catholic bishops also requested Pope Francis to "publicly perform the act of consecration to the Immaculate Heart of Mary of Ukraine and Russia, as requested by the Blessed Virgin in Fatima."

While several Popes have already consecrated the church and the entire world to the Blessed Virgin, the timing made the pope's actions at the end of the penitential service on Mar. 25 especially significant.

The papal almoner, Cardinal Konrad Krajewski, simultaneously performed the consecration at the Sanctuary of Our Lady of Fatima.

All bishops, priests, and lay faithful worldwide were given the text, which could be inserted into Mass or prayed separately.

"God changed history by knocking at the door of Mary's heart," Pope Francis said during the penitential service. "Today, renewed by God's forgiveness, may we too knock at the door of her immaculate heart. In union with the bishops and faithful of the world, I desire in a solemn way to bring all that we are presently experiencing to the Immaculate Heart of Mary."

Touched by its own violence on May 24, the deadliest shooting in Texas history took the lives of 21 in Uvalde, Texas, at Robb Elementary School. Nearby Sacred Heart Church hosted funeral Masses for 11 of the victims.

In the wake of the tragedy, Catholic Extension funded 30 scholarships to the local Catholic school to ease the trauma of students returning to the place of the crime. "We're very encouraged by the kind of loving, joyful, faithful environment that they are creating at Sacred Heart School in Uvalde and it really gives us hope that it will be a place where these children can begin the long process of healing after the atrocities that they witnessed," Joe Boland, vice president of missions at Catholic Extension told Catholic News Agency.

Eleven of the 30 students now attending the Catholic school were wounded in the shooting at Robb Elementary.

In October, the students sent letters to Pope Francis, who promised to "remember the students, their families, and all of those suffering from the recent act of violence in Uvalde," according to a letter sent by the Holy See's substitute for general affairs of the Secretariat of State.

A little over a month later, the Supreme Court's decision in Dobbs v. Jackson Women's Health came down on Jun. 24, 2022–the solemnity of the Sacred Heart of Jesus and the last Friday of the term–and returned the question of legal abortion to individual U.S. States, opening new avenues for the protection of the unborn, including automatic bans in at least eight states should Roe v. Wade be overturned.

Five justices signed the majority opinion, written by Justice Samuel Alito, with Chief Justice John Roberts filing a concurring judgment, moving the 6-3 decision away from constitutional recognition of abortion.

"The Constitution does not confer a right to abortion. Roe and Casey are overruled; and the authority to regulate abortion is returned to the people and their elected representatives," the opinion holds.

Although the decision does not ban or criminalize abortion, the overturning of both Roe and Casey, which affirmed Roe, allows new pathways at the local or constitutional level to progress, according to pro-life advocates.

Archbishop Jose H. Gomez of Los Angeles, President of the U.S. Conference of Catholic Bishops, and Archbishop William E. Lori of Baltimore, Chair of the Committee on Pro-Life Activities, reacted in a joint statement: "Today's decision is also the fruit of the prayers, sacrifices, and advocacy of countless ordinary Americans from every walk of life. Over these long years, millions of our fellow citizens have worked together peacefully to educate and persuade their neighbors about the injustice of abortion, to offer care and counseling to women, and to work for alternatives to abortion, including adoption, foster care, and public policies that truly support families."

The summer was also characterized by the response of the Catholic Church to an influx of immigrants crossing the southern border who didn't have adequate places to rest. Sister Norma Pimentel, President of the Rio Grande Valley Catholic Charities, explained that the Humanitarian Crisis Relief was an effort that began during the summer of 2022. With the help of the Sacred Heart Church, the city of McAllen, and volunteers and donations, the group opened the doors to the Respite Center. The center provides a place for the countless men, women, children, and infant refugees to rest, have a warm meal, shower, and change into clean clothing as well as receive medicine and other supplies before continuing on their journey. In only six months, the Respite Center was able to help tens of thousands of individuals.

On Aug. 27, the Catholic Church in the United States received a new red hat when Pope Francis elevated Bishop Robert E. McElroy to the rank of cardinal with 19 others. Ordained to the priesthood in 1980, he was named an auxiliary bishop of San Francisco

"God changed history by knocking at the door of Mary's heart," Pope Francis said during the penitential service. "Today, renewed by God's forgiveness, may we too knock at the door of her immaculate heart. In union with the bishops and faithful of the world, I desire in a solemn way to bring all that we are presently experiencing to the Immaculate Heart of Mary."

in 2010 and, in 2015, was named bishop of the diocese of San Diego, where he still resides.

"I'm deeply honored by this appointment, and deeply pleased I'm remaining here in San Diego, allowing me to continue in ministry here in a beautiful city," said McElroy at a May 31 press conference.

Thanks to his elevation, the United States will now have ten cardinal electors under age 80 eligible to vote in the next conclave, placing it behind only Italy in the number of cardinal electors per country.

During the late summer, Catholics also flocked to the theaters to see special screenings of "Mother Teresa: No Greater Love," a documentary film produced by the Knights of Columbus that chronicles her life and mission to found a religious order dedicated to serving the poor with love: the Missionaries of Charity. The movie generated $1.2 million in ticket sales in just two nights of its premiere.

PEXEL FREE PHOTO/MARIA ORLOVA

"Saint Michael: Meet the Angel" was also given special showings in theaters in 2022. With expert commentators that include Father Donald Calloway of the Marian Fathers of the Immaculate Conception, and Father Wolfgang Seitz of Opus Angelorum, the movie explores the providence of St. Michael's role in the battle against evil and darkness.

By far the biggest Catholic movie of the year, however, was the story of Father Stuart Long, a priest of the Diocese of Helena. Starring Mark Wahlberg and Mel Gibson, the 2022 motion picture tells the story of a wayward soul whose great ambition for cursing, boxing, and acting is crushed after a motorcycle accident that will lead to his conversion, ordination, and ultimately draw out the power of redemptive suffering as it chronicles the disease that leads to Fr. Stu's early and painful death.

A raw and intensely dramatic film, a PG-13 version was re-released later in the year.

In the podcast space, Dominican Father Sergio Serrano, director of the Hispanic Apostolate for the Archdiocese of New Orleans, launched the wildly successful "La Biblia en un año" on Jan. 1 in the Spanish language.

In September, as the college football season began to swing into high gear, the new head coach for the University of Notre Dame, Marcus Freeman, swam the Tiber.

Freeman began his head coaching tenure at the University of Notre Dame by restoring the Fighting Irish tradition of game day Masses to the football program.

He wasn't the only one whose football fame would allow him to witness to others about the faith.

Kansas State University's senior wide receiver, Landry Weber, finished his career with a victory in the Texas Bowl and a ticket to the seminary. The sports media complex was astounded when the announcer revealed his post-graduation plans.

Heisman Trophy winner Caleb Williams also made headlines concerning the Catholic education he received from Gonzaga College High School in Washington, D.C.

"Coach, you may not know this, but the Gonzaga mantra that you drilled into us, 'men for others,' has helped inspire me to create the Caleb Cares Foundation, which is all about giving back, so thank you coach, thank you Gonzaga," said Williams about the Jesuit-run all boys school.

As part of the worldwide process of the Synod on Synodality, the United States Conference of Catholic Bishops released on Sept. 19, a "national synthesis" of the diocesan synod phase.

In an introduction to the 16-page official summary, Bishop Daniel Flores of Brownsville, chair of the USCCB's committee on doctrine, revealed that some 700,000 people in 178 dioceses out of an estimated 66.8 million U.S. Catholics were involved in the process.

"As Pope Francis frequently reminds us, synodality is not a one-time event, but an invitation to an ongoing style of Church life. We have taken the first steps of this path, and we have learned much; we have more to learn and more to do. Let us pray that this National Synthesis will in some way serve to deepen our communion as a Church," he wrote.

The U.S. document was then submitted to a "continental" phase, aimed at preparing the two-phase General Assembly of the Synod of Bishops to take place at the Vatican in October 2023 and 2024, respectively.

In November, the U.S. Bishops voted to advance the cause for the beatification and canonization of three U.S. women. They include the middle of the 20th century Mormon convert and mystic Cora Evans, who Jesus reportedly asked to promulgate the mystical humanity of Christ as "a way of prayer that encourages people to live with a heightened awareness of the indwelling presence of Jesus in their daily lives."

Fellowship of Catholic University Students missionary and adult faith formation director Michelle Duppong's cause also advanced. A North Dakota native who died of ovarian cancer on Christmas day at age 31, she devoted her life to evangelization.

Mother Margaret Mary Healy Murphy, foundress of the Sisters of the Holy Spirit and Mary Immaculate, who died in 1907 after a life of service in Texas as both a religious and laywoman, was also forwarded by the bishops.

On the last day of 2022, Catholics worldwide bid farewell to Benedict XVI after the Vatican announced his death on Dec. 31.

Pope for just shy of eight years from Apr. 19, 2005, until his resignation on Feb. 28, 2013, Benedict XVI lived as Pope Emeritus for ten years, carving out a new role in the modern papacy.

Considered by many as one of the greatest theologians of the 20th century, his pontificate was known for its intellectual precision and his person for his extraordinary meekness.

Just before his election to the papacy, he delivered a pre-conclave homily about the dangers of the "dictatorship of relativism." His pontificate would continue to battle this dictatorship; he decried, as well, the growing secularism of the age.

Benedict XVI visited the United States as Pope in April of 2008, acknowledging the pain that the sexual abuse crisis inflicted upon its victims and the entire church in America, and called for renewal within it. He also complimented what he saw as the unique history of the United States.

"From the dawn of the Republic, America's quest for freedom has been guided by the conviction that the principles governing political and social life are intimately linked to a moral order based on the dominion of God the Creator. The framers of this nation's founding documents drew upon this conviction when they proclaimed the 'self-evident truth' that all men are created equal and endowed with inalienable rights grounded in the laws of nature and of nature's God," he said during the welcoming ceremony at the White House, on Apr. 16, 2008.

The trip changed the perception of many to a "more favorable" opinion of the Pontiff, according to a Pew Research Center survey conducted in 2008 after the trip.

Hundreds of thousands of pilgrims paid homage to his body as it laid in state at St. Peter's Basilica, and a similarly large crowd joined for his funeral as Catholics around the world mourned the gentle Bavarian Pope who steered them so eloquently to Truth.

He was 95 at the time of his passing.

"As Pope Francis frequently reminds us, synodality is not a one-time event, but an invitation to an ongoing style of Church life. We have taken the first steps of this path, and we have learned much; we have more to learn and more to do."— Bishop Daniel Flores of the Diocese of Brownsville

KELSEY S. WICKS is the Executive Director of the ACI Group.

Pope Benedict XVI: The Great Defender of Vatican II

He was a gentleman and a scholar, a brilliant mind with a servant's heart.

BY MOST REVEREND SALVATORE J. CORDILEONE

As Joseph Ratzinger, he is known as one of the great Catholic thinkers of the 20th and 21st centuries, dubbed by some "the Mozart of theology," or the "Doctor of the Logos." To many of us, Pope Benedict XVI was the great defender of the Catholic faith under attack by an increasingly hostile and secular world. The same firm fidelity led his critics inside and outside the Church to mislabel Pope Benedict "God's Rottweiler." [1] In truth, as those who knew him testify, a man more committed to listening, to dialogue in the midst of disagreement, and to service could hardly be found.

The essence of Christian teaching, as he reminded us in his first papal encyclical *Deus Caritas Est*, is that God is love. "Only if I serve my neighbour can my eyes be opened to what God does for me and how much he loves me. The saints—consider the example of Blessed Teresa of Calcutta—constantly renewed their capacity for love of neighbour from their encounter with the Eucharistic Lord, and conversely this encounter acquired its realism and depth in their service to others." [2]

Pope Benedict XVI loved being a professor. He gathered and mentored many students, befriended many theologians and scholars, but never tried to create a circle of theology centered around his own insights. Pope Benedict XVI left behind and sought to leave behind no ingenious new philosophical system: "[T]he essence of Christianity is not an idea, not a system of thought, not a plan of action. The essence of Christianity is a person: Jesus Christ Himself. That which is essential is the one who is essential." [3]

In this sense, Pope Benedict XVI shared Pope Francis's distrust of rigid, human-crafted ideologies that threaten to overwhelm both faith and reason. As a boy, Pope Benedict XVI watched an evil ideology sweep over his beloved Germany, reject the living God, attack the Church, and end up murdering millions of Jews and others (including his own cousin who had Down's Syndrome, who was killed as part of a so-called eugenics campaign).

To his other epithets it should be added that Pope Benedict XVI was the great defender of Vatican II. His call for reform of the reform, for a hermeneutic of reform and continuity rather than rupture, was rooted in defending what the fathers of Second Vatican Council actually said and did, rather than attempting to justify so much damage that has been done over the past half century since the Council by others in their name.

Father Ratzinger was one of the young theologians who attended and was inspired by the Second Vatican Council. The goal was not rupture, but *ressourcement*: a deeper grounding of the Catholic faith in Scripture, the Church fathers and the other deep sources of the Tradition.

SHUTTERSTOCK/MARCO IACOBUCCI EPP

In a book-length interview published in 2016, Pope Benedict XVI named himself as one of the Vatican II "progressives" but with this important caveat: "At that time progressive did not mean that you were breaking out of the faith, but that you wanted to understand it better, and more accurately, how it lives from its origins. I was of the opinion then that that was what we all wanted." Pope Benedict XVI recalled this youthful enthusiasm a half century later, even calling himself with regard to Pope John XXIII, "a real fan, you might say"[4]: "We wanted a new era of piety, which formed itself from the liturgy, its sobriety and its greatness, which drew on the original sources—and was new and contemporary precisely because of this," he recalled.[5]

Precisely because of this deep appreciation for the actual work of Vatican II, Cardinal Ratzinger emerged as one of the early voices warning against damage done by the so-called spirit of Vatican II, especially in matters liturgical. When Pope Paul VI issued the new, re-ordered Roman Missal to replace what came before, then-Professor Ratzinger publicly criticized the move. But his forthright criticism did not prevent Pope Paul VI from naming Joseph Ratzinger the Archbishop of Munich and Freising. "He was safe in the knowledge that he and I were fundamentally in alignment," Pope Benedict XVI noted many years later.[6]

His sensitivity to the importance of the liturgy in Catholic renewal grounded his resistance to deformations of what Vatican II intended. Pope Benedict XVI will likely be remembered longest for these powerful contributions to our understanding of the liturgy and its significance for the Christian life.

In 1997, Cardinal Ratzinger wrote: "The Church stands and falls with the liturgy. When the adoration of the divine Trinity declines, when the faith no longer appears in its fullness in the liturgy of the Church,...then faith will have lost the place where it is expressed and where it dwells. For that reason, the true celebration of the sacred liturgy is the center of any renewal of the Church whatever."[7]

This was not just a theoretical insight. A journalist once asked him *"Your students say that they were able to observe, over decades, that your celebration of the Eucharist was never stale, but that you wholly devoted yourself to the full change in the elements on every occasion, as if it were for the first time."*

"Well," he replied, "it is so exciting that one meets it repeatedly. I mean, it is something completely extraordinary, that the Lord is here Himself. That is no longer bread, but the body of Christ—of course this permeates someone."[8] Asked what spiritual experiences led to his vocation, Pope Benedict said, "I would say it was my entering ever more deeply into the liturgy."[9] This was very much my own experience with responding to the call to Priesthood as well. I still have fond and vivid childhood memories of attending Sunday Mass at my parish. Something very different happened; it was unlike anything else we did the rest of the week. The reverential silence very much mediated sensitivity to the presence of God. It was not the result of rigid doctrines and disciplines, but of the ordinary faithful's awareness of the sacredness of the Eucharist, their encounter with the Real Presence of Christ at the Mass. This was not a matter of head knowledge but of instinct; there was much more of a Catholic instinctual sensitivity to the Eucharist as a breaking through of the Divine into our ordinary world that lifted hearts and stirred souls.

And from this experience of the love of the living God—Pope Benedict reminds us—Christians must be moved to serve the poor, the needy, the marginalized, giving them not only the things they need but "the look of love which they crave."[10]

Of Pope Benedict XVI's many insights into the liturgy, let me pull out three that are key:

First: the liturgy is authoritative. The rites we have received are part and parcel of the apostolic tradition, given to us by a God who acted in history, decisively.

"The authority of the liturgy can certainly be compared to that of the great confessions of faith of the early Church. Like these, it developed under the guidance of the Holy Spirit," Pope Benedict XVI pointed out.[11] All the families of liturgical rites descend to us through the great historic Apostolic Sees, "the central places of the apostolic tradition, and that this connection with apostolic origins is essential to what defines them. From this it follows there can be no question of creating totally new rites."[12]

Second: the liturgy is a gift from God, not a thing manufactured by human ingenuity for human purposes.

The liturgy grows and develops, slowly and organically, over time. The different liturgical families grounded in the great historic Apostolic Sees influence each other. Elements of local culture may be elevated into the liturgy.[13] But the rite itself is a gift from God, revealed in history through the authority of the apostolic fathers. One of the most unfortunate consequences of recent history is the abandonment of this profound sense of the givenness, of the gift, of the liturgy.

"After the Second Vatican Council, the impression arose that the pope really could do anything in liturgical matters, especially if he were acting on the mandate of an ecumenical council. Eventually the idea of the givenness of the liturgy, the fact that one cannot do with it what one will, faded from the public consciousness of the West."[14]

He went on to note the problem today:

"[A] not insignificant number of people today are trying to construct the liturgy afresh on the basis of *sola scriptura.* In these reconstructions, they identify Scripture with the prevailing exegetical opinions, thus confusing faith with opinion. Liturgy 'manufactured' in this way is based on human words and opinions. It is a house built on sand...The life of the liturgy does not come from what dawns upon the minds of individuals and planning groups. On the contrary, it is God's descent upon our world...".[15]

The liturgy is what reveals to us the givenness and therefore the solidity of our own truest identity as children of God.

In the book-length interview published in English as *The Ratzinger Report*, then-Cardinal Ratzinger said, "Many no longer believe that what is at issue is a reality willed by the Lord Himself. Even with some theologians, the church appears to be a human construction, an instrument created by us and one that we ourselves can freely reorganize according to the requirements of the moment." [16]

The authentic Catholic view, by contrast, provides a secure anchor in an otherwise seething and turbulent world.

"For a Catholic…the fundamental structures are willed by God Himself, and therefore they are inviolable. Behind the *human* exterior stands the mystery of a *more than human* reality, in which reformers, sociologists, organizers have no authority whatsoever." [17]

Third: the primary purpose of the liturgy is to worship God in the way He has revealed to us that He wants. If the ceremony brings the primary focus on the priest or the community, it is not offering the spirit of liturgy. The Mass brings us into communion with each other, only in so far as it brings us into a shared communion with our Creator and Redeemer, transforming us into His body and prompting us to offer, 'Thy will be done.'

In my own view, the liturgical abuses and the lack of reverence and beauty in the celebration of too many Masses has contributed greatly to the loss of understanding and faith in the Real Presence in the Eucharist we now face in the Church.

Pope Benedict's great hope in issuing *Summorum Pontificum* was that the two forms of the Roman rite would organically and naturally influence each other, bringing us closer to the liturgical vision of Vatican II. His great achievement with *Summorum Pontificum* was to enact a cease fire, at least temporarily, in the liturgy wars then riving the Church. His primary concern in doing so, as he repeatedly stated, was not healing any external schism, but healing the inner rift in Catholic identity such a liturgical polarization threatened to create. "I have always said, and even still say, that it was important that something which was previously the most sacred thing in the Church to people should not suddenly be completely forbidden. A society that considers now to be forbidden what it once perceived as the central core—that cannot be. The inner identity it has with the other must remain visible. So for me it was not about tactical matters and God knows what, but about the inward reconciliation of the Church with itself," Pope Benedict XVI said in 2016. [18]

Today, Pope Francis calls us to find other ways to improve the beauty and reverence of the Novus Ordo Mass so that in each Mass the ordinary faithful meet Jesus.

In his last days, Pope Benedict XVI published a short, one-page final spiritual testament [19] which sums up the essence of this great and holy man. It was not a philosophical treatise. Pope Benedict XVI's last words to us are mostly expressions of gratitude for the gifts he was given. For me, his list of thank yous is nothing less than a roadmap to the things that really matter in this life.

First, gratitude to God, "the giver of all good gifts, who has given me life and guided me through all kinds of confusion; who has always picked me up when I began to slip, who has always given me anew the light of his countenance." [20]

Second, a grateful thanks to his family, his brother and sister and his mother and father:

"I thank my parents, who gave me life in difficult times and prepared a wonderful home for me with their love, which shines through all my days as a bright light until today. My father's clear-sighted faith taught us brothers and sisters to believe and stood firm as a guide in the midst of all my scientific knowledge; my mother's heartfelt piety and great kindness remain a legacy for which I cannot thank her enough." [21]

You who are in the middle of the messy challenge of making homes, raising children in a world which tells you money, power and status are more important, take heart from this great man's testimony: After nearly a century of living, it is these simple loving joys that he remembered and that sustained him. May your children and grandchildren, bodily and spiritual, confer such a blessing on you.

Pope Benedict XVI thanks God as well for his friends and co-workers. And then again for a blessing which is there for all of us if we only have eyes to see: the blessing of beauty, which Pope Benedict XVI knew intimately connects us with God:

"And I would like to thank the Lord for my beautiful home in the Bavarian foothills of the Alps, in which I was able to

SHUTTERSTOCK/ FRIPPITAUN

see the splendour of the Creator Himself shining through time and again. I thank the people of my homeland for allowing me to experience the beauty of faith time and again. I pray that our country will remain a country of faith and I ask you, dear compatriots, not to let your faith be distracted. Finally, I thank God for all the beauty I was able to experience during the various stages of my journey, but especially in Rome and in Italy, which has become my second home."[22]

Of the many important insights, big thoughts, intellectual and scholarly breakthroughs he has given us, he left us as his final word, this one great thought, borne of being a witness to a tumultuous century of change in the Church and in the world:

"Stand firm in the faith! Do not be confused! Often it seems as if science—on the one hand, the natural sciences; on the other, historical research (especially the exegesis of the Holy Scriptures)—has irrefutable insights to offer that are contrary to the Catholic faith. I have witnessed from times long past the changes in natural science and have seen how apparent certainties against the faith vanished, proving themselves not to be science but philosophical interpretations only apparently belonging to science—just as, moreover, it is in dialogue with the natural sciences that faith has learned to understand the limits of the scope of its affirmations and thus its own specificity. For 60 years now, I have accompanied the path of theology, especially biblical studies, and have seen seemingly unshakeable theses collapse with the changing generations, which turned out to be mere hypotheses: the liberal generation (Harnack, Jülicher, etc.), the existentialist generation (Bultmann, etc.), the Marxist generation. I have seen, and see, how, out of the tangle of hypotheses, the reasonableness of faith has emerged and is emerging anew."[23]

Let us thank God for the blessing he gave us in Pope Benedict XVI and let us join our dear departed brother in proclaiming:

"Jesus Christ is truly the Way, the Truth, and the Life—and the Church, in all her shortcomings, is truly His Body."[24]

[1] See e.g. https://www.ncronline.org/news/vatican/gods-rottweiler-silenced-many-head-doctrinal-congregation

[2] Pope Benedict XVI, Deus est Caritas, 18. (December 25, 2005). https://www.vatican.va/content/benedict-xvi/en/encyclicals/documents/hf_ben-xvi_enc_20051225_deus-caritas-est.html

[3] Pope Benedict XVI, "Guardini on Christ in Our Century" in John F. Thornton and Susan B. Varenne (eds.) *The Essential Pope Benedict XVI: His Central Writings and Speeches* (New York: Harper One, 2007) page 55.

[4] Benedict XVI (with Peter Seewald) *Last Testament in His Own Words*, Page 127.

[5] Benedict XVI (with Peter Seewald) *Last Testament in His Own Words*, Page 78.

[6] Benedict XVI (with Peter Seewald) *Last Testament in His Own Words*, page 136.

[7] Preface to Franz Breid, ed. *Die Heilige Liturgie*, papers from the "Internationale Theologische Sommerakademie 1997" of the Priest's Circle of Linz, Ennsthaler, Verlag, Steyr 1997. Quoted by Cardinal Sarah in his preface to the 2018 commemorative edition of *The Spirit of the Liturgy*, Cardinal Ratzinger Ignatius p13-14

[8] Benedict XVI (with Peter Seewald) *Last Testament in His Own Words*, page 88.

[9] Benedict XVI (with Peter Seewald) *Last Testament in His Own Words*, page 55.

[10] Pope Benedict XVI, Deus est Caritas, 18. (December 25, 2005). https://www.vatican.va/content/benedict-xvi/en/encyclicals/documents/hf_ben-xvi_enc_20051225_deus-caritas-est.html

[11] Joseph Cardinal Ratzinger, *The Spirit of the Liturgy* (commemorative edition), (San Francisco: Ignatius Press 2020 paperback edition) Page 181.

[12] Joseph Cardinal Ratzinger, *The Spirit of the Liturgy* (commemorative edition), (San Francisco: Ignatius Press 2020 paperback edition) Page 183. Benedict points out the very first Council of Nicaea identifies three "primatial sees" (Rome, Alexandria and Antioch, which become close to Byzantium as "the new Rome") each giving birth to a family of liturgical rites tracing their authority back to the Apostles themselves including (in addition to the Latin rite(s)) the Syro-Malankar rite, the Maronite Rite and the Chaldean rites associated with Antioch, the Coptic and Ethiopian rites associated with Alexandria, the Armenian rites in the Byzantine family of liturgical rites. pages 174-184.

[13] Pope Benedict XVI pointed to the Zaire rite as an adaptation of the Roman rite, its processions which some misdescribe as dancing, properly understood as a "rhythmically ordered procession, very much in keeping with the dignity of the occasion." Joseph Cardinal Ratzinger, *The Spirit of the Liturgy* (commemorative edition), (San Francisco: Ignatius Press 2020 paperback edition). Page 213.

[14] Joseph Cardinal Ratzinger, The Spirit of the Liturgy (commemorative edition), (San Francisco: Ignatius Press 2020 paperback edition). Page 179-180.

[15] Joseph Cardinal Ratzinger, The Spirit of the Liturgy (commemorative edition), (San Francisco: Ignatius Press 2020 paperback edition). Page 182.

[16] Pope Benedict XVI "At the Root of the Crisis: The Idea of Church: Vittoria Messori Interviews 1985" (published in English as *The Ratzinger Report*) in The Essential Pope Benedict XVI: *His Central Writings and Speeches* p. 63.

[17] Pope Benedict XVI "At the Root of the Crisis: The Idea of Church: Vittoria Messori Interviews 1985" (published in English as *The Ratzinger Report*) in The Essential Pope Benedict XVI: *His Central Writings and Speeches* p. 64.

[18] Benedict XVI (with Peter Seewald). *Last Testament in His Own Words*. Page 201.

[19] Pope Benedict XVI, "My Spiritual Testament" Dated August 29, 2006 and released December 31, 2022. https://www.vatican.va/content/benedict-xvi/en/elezione/documents/testamento-spirituale-bxvi.html

[20] Pope Benedict XVI, "My Spiritual Testament" Dated August 29, 2006 and released December 31, 2022. https://www.vatican.va/content/benedict-xvi/en/elezione/documents/testamento-spirituale-bxvi.html

[21] Pope Benedict XVI, "My Spiritual Testament" Dated August 29, 2006 and released December 31, 2022. https://www.vatican.va/content/benedict-xvi/en/elezione/documents/testamento-spirituale-bxvi.html

[22] Pope Benedict XVI, "My Spiritual Testament" Dated August 29, 2006 and released December 31, 2022. https://www.vatican.va/content/benedict-xvi/en/elezione/documents/testamento-spirituale-bxvi.html

[23] Pope Benedict XVI, "My Spiritual Testament" Dated August 29, 2006 and released December 31, 2022. https://www.vatican.va/content/benedict-xvi/en/elezione/documents/testamento-spirituale-bxvi.html

[24] Pope Benedict XVI, "My Spiritual Testament" Dated August 29, 2006 and released December 31, 2022. https://www.vatican.va/content/benedict-xvi/en/elezione/documents/testamento-spirituale-bxvi.html

The Official Catholic Directory

for the Year of Our Lord

2023

CHARITABLE STATUS OF THE CATHOLIC CHURCH AS OF JANUARY 1, 2023

Containing Ecclesiastical Statistics of

THE UNITED STATES, PUERTO RICO,
THE VIRGIN ISLANDS, AGANA, CAROLINE AND MARSHALL ISLANDS,
AND FOREIGN MISSIONARY ACTIVITIES.

The information contained in this Directory is derived from reports submitted to the publishers by the ecclesiastical authorities of the countries concerned, and neither the publishers nor the ecclesiastical authorities assume responsibility for any errors or omissions.

P.J. KENEDY & SONS

Publishers of the Holy Apostolic See

For inquiries email: info@nrpdirect.com or write:
NRP Direct, 220 College Ave., Ste. 618
Athens, GA 30601-9801

THE OFFICIAL CATHOLIC DIRECTORY®

Published by P.J. Kenedy & Sons in association with NRP Direct

President R. Brett Grayson

Publisher Robert J. Docherty

EDITORIAL

Managing Editor Eileen Fanning

Content Editors Linda Hummer
Ian Sidney O'Blenis
Patrick O'Dowd

MARKETING

Creative Services Manager Kathleen F. Stein

SALES

Sales Manager April Tann

Printed and bound in the United States of America
International Standard Book Number: 978-0-87217-134-3
International Standard Serial Number: 0078-3854
Library of Congress Catalog Card Number: 81-30961

CONTENTS

ARCHDIOCESES AND DIOCESES

APOSTOLATES

PRELATURE OF THE HOLY CROSS AND OPUS DEI

EASTERN CHURCHES

TERRITORIAL SEES1385

RELIGIOUS INSTITUTION SECTION

THE ARCHDIOCESES AND DIOCESES OF THE UNITED STATES—BY STATES

A—Indicates Archdiocese. The Archdiocese of Washington includes the District of Columbia and five counties of Maryland. Dioceses traverse state lines in the following instances only: Cheyenne includes all of Yellowstone National Park; South Norwich includes Fisher's Island; Wilmington includes the eastern shores of Maryland; and Gallup includes parts of Arizona and New Mexico.

United States Conference of Catholic Bishops

Address—3211 Fourth St., N.E., Washington, DC 20017-1194. Tel: 202-541-3000; Web Site: www.usccb.org.

The United States Conference of Catholic Bishops is a permanent institute composed of Catholic bishops of the United States of America in and through which the bishops exercise in a communal or collegial manner the pastoral mission entrusted to them by the Lord Jesus of sanctification, teaching, and leadership, especially by devising forms and methods of the apostolate suitably adapted to the circumstances of the times. Such exercise is intended to offer appropriate assistance to each bishop in fulfilling his particular ministry in the local Church, to effect a commonality of ministry addressed to the people of the United States of America, and to foster and express communion with the Church in other nations within the Church universal, under the leadership of its chief pastor, the Pope.

OFFICE

President—Archbishop Timothy P. Broglio
Vice President—Archbishop William E. Lori
Treasurer—Bishop James F. Checchio
Secretary—Archbishop Paul S. Coakley

GENERAL SECRETARIAT

General Secretary—Rev. Michael J. K. Fuller, S.T.D.
Associate General Secretary—Rev. Paul B.R. Hartmann
Mr. Anthony R. Picarello, Jr., Esq.
Ms. Theresa Ridderhoff
Director of Strategic Planning—Mr. Robert Yates

STAFF OFFICES

Chief Communications Officer—Mr. James L. Rogers
Finance & Accounting—Mrs. Joyce L. Jones
General Counsel—Mr. Anthony R. Picarello, Jr., Esq.
General Services—Mr. Keith Manley
Government Relations—Ms. Lauren McCormack
Human Resources—Ms. Allison McGinn
Information Technology—Mr. John A. Galotta
Child & Youth Protection—Deacon Bernard V. Nojadera

USCCB COMMITTEES
I. EXECUTIVE LEVEL
ADMINISTRATIVE COMMITTEE

Chairman—Archbishop Timothy P. Broglio
Members—Cardinal Timothy M. Dolan
Archbishop Borys Gudziak
Archbishop Nelson J. Pérez
Archbishop Alexander K. Sample (Region XII)
Archbishop Jerome E. Listecki
Bishop Mario Avilés, C.O. (Region X)
Bishop Robert E. Barron
Bishop Juan Miguel Betancourt, S.E.M.V. (Region I)
Bishop Steven Biegler (Region XIII)
Bishop Earl A. Boyea
Bishop Mark E. Brennan (Region IV)
Bishop Michael F. Burbidge
Bishop Arturo Cepeda
Bishop Andrew H. Cozzens
Bishop Thomas A. Daly
Bishop Daniel E. Flores
Bishop Timothy E. Freyer (Region XI)
Bishop James V. Johnston, Jr.
Bishop Steven J. Lopes
Bishop David J. Malloy
Bishop Steven J. Raica (Region V)
Bishop Robert Reed
Bishop Michael A. Saporito (Region III)
Bishop Edward B. Scharfenberger (Region II)
Bishop Mark J. Seitz
Bishop Bernard E. Shlesinger, III (Region XIV)
Bishop Joseph M. Siegel (Region VII)
Bishop David P. Talley
Bishop David J. Walkowiak (Region VI)
Bishop James S. Wall
Bishop Abdallah Elias Zaidan, M.L.M. (Region XV)
Bishop Thomas Zinkula (Region IX)
Vice President: Archbishop William E. Lori
Treasurer: Bishop James F. Checchio
Secretary: Archbishop Paul S. Coakley
Past President: Archbishop José H. Gomez
General Secretary: Rev. Michael J. K. Fuller, S.T.D.
Staff— Rev. Paul B.R. Hartmann
Mr. Anthony R. Picarello, Jr., Esq.
Ms. Theresa Ridderhoff
Mrs. Joyce L. Jones
Mr. James L. Rogers

ADMINISTRATIVE COMMITTEE-REGIONAL ALTERNATES

Alternate (Region I)—Bishop Peter J. Uglietto
Alternate (Region II)—Bishop Peter J. Byrne
Alternate (Region III)—Bishop Kevin J. Sweeney
Alternate (Region IV)—Bishop Adam J. Parker
Alternate (Region V)—Bishop Michael G. Duca
Alternate (Region VI)—Bishop Jeffrey M. Monforton
Alternate (Region VII)—Bishop Ronald A. Hicks
Alternate (Region VIII)—Bishop Donald E. DeGrood
Alternate (Region IX)—Bishop W. Shawn McKnight
Alternate (Region X)—Bishop Robert Coerver
Alternate (Region XI)—Bishop Alejandro Aclan
Alternate (Region XII)—Bishop Austin A. Vetter
Alternate (Region XIII)—Bishop Eduardo A. Nevares
Alternate (Region XIV)—Bishop Luis R. Zarama
Alternate (Region XV)—Bishop Kurt R. Burnette

EXECUTIVE COMMITTEE

President—Archbishop Timothy P. Broglio
Vice President—Archbishop William E. Lori
Treasurer—Bishop James F. Checchio
Secretary—Archbishop Paul S. Coakley
General Secretary—Rev. Michael J. K. Fuller, S.T.D.
Staff—Rev. Paul B.R. Hartmann
Mr. Anthony R. Picarello, Jr., Esq.
Ms. Theresa Ridderhoff

COMMITTEE ON BUDGET AND FINANCE

Chairman—Bishop James F. Checchio
Members—Archbishop Paul D. Etienne
Bishop Roy E. Campbell
Bishop Enrique Delgado
Bishop David J. Malloy
Bishop Robert J. McClory
Bishop Daniel H. Mueggenborg
Bishop W. Michael Mulvey
Bishop Thomas John Paprocki
Bishop Gregory L. Parkes
Consultant—Rev. Michael J. K. Fuller, S.T.D.
Staff—Ms. Raquel Dean
Mrs. Joyce L. Jones
Ms. Sonja Sweetney-Ransome

Audit Subcommittee

Chairman—Bishop Gregory L. Parkes
Members—Bishop Michael A. Saporito
Bishop Joseph M. Siegel
Consultant—Bishop John M. LeVoir
Staff—Mrs. Joyce L. Jones
Ms. Sonja Sweetney-Ransome

COMMITTEE ON PRIORITIES AND PLANS

Chairman—Archbishop Paul S. Coakley
Vice Chairman—Bishop James F. Checchio
Members— Archbishop Alexander K. Sample (Region XII)
Bishop Mario Avilés, C.O. (Region X)
Bishop Juan Miguel Betancourt, SEMV (Region I)
Bishop Steven Biegler (Region XIII)
Bishop Mark E. Brennan (Region IV)
Bishop Steven J. Raica (Region V)
Bishop Timothy E. Freyer (Region XI)
Bishop Michael A. Saporito (Region III)
Bishop Edward B. Scharfenberger (Region II)
Bishop Bernard E. Shlesinger, III (Region XIV)
Bishop Joseph M. Siegel (Region VII)
Bishop David J. Walkowiak (Region VI)
Bishop Abdallah Elias Zaidan, M.L.M. (Region XV)
Bishop Chad Zielinski (Region VIII)
Bishop Thomas Zinkula (Region IX)
Consultant—Rev. Michael J. K. Fuller, S.T.D.
Staff—Rev. Paul B.R. Hartmann
Mr. Anthony R. Picarello, Jr., Esq.
Ms. Theresa Ridderhoff
Mrs. Joyce L. Jones
Mr. James L. Rogers
Dr. Siobhan M. Verbeek
Mr. Robert Yates

II. GENERAL MEMBERSHIP LEVEL STANDING COMMITTEES CANONICAL AFFAIRS AND CHURCH GOVERNANCE

Chairman—Archbishop Jerome E. Listecki
Chairman-Elect—Bishop Thomas John Paprocki
Members—Archbishop Salvatore J. Cordileone
Archbishop Bernard A. Hebda
Bishop Mark L. Bartchak
Bishop Robert P. Deeley
Bishop Edward C. Malesic
Bishop Peter L. Smith
Bishop Kevin W. Vann
Consultants—Rev. Msgr. Ronny E. Jenkins
Rev. Sean Sheridan, T.O.R.
Prof. Kurt Martens
Staff—Rev. Paul B.R. Hartmann
Ms. Siobhan M. Verbeek

CATHOLIC EDUCATION

Chairman—Bishop Thomas A. Daly
Members—Bishop Donald J. Hying
Bishop William M. Joensen
Bishop Gerald F. Kicanas
Bishop James Massa
Bishop Michael F. Olson
Bishop Larry Silva
Bishop Edmund J. Whalen
Consultants–Mr. Thomas Carroll
Ms. Nicole Garnett, Esq.
Sr. Mary Agnes Greiffendorf, O.P.
Rev. Dennis Holtschneider
Ms. Kathryn Page
Mr. Shawn Peterson
Mr. Lincoln Snyder
Mr. John Zimmer
Staff—Ms. Jennifer Daniels
Dr. Marc DelMonico
Ms. Mary Pat Donoghue
Ms. Barbara Humphrey McCrabb

Subcommittee on Certification for Ecclesial Ministry and Service

Chairman—Bishop Gerald F. Kicanas
Members—Archbishop Alfred C. Hughes
Bishop Earl A. Boyea
Bishop Jorge H. Rodríguez
Members-at-Large—Bishop James Golka
Bishop Michael A. Saporito
Consultants— Bishop George J. Rassas
Very Rev. James J. Greenfield, O.S.F.S.
Rev. Wayne Cavalier, O.P.
Ms. Linda Couri
Sr. Maria Theresa Lara, O.P.
Ms. Dorothy Mensah-Aggrey
Dr. C. Vanessa White
Staff—Dr. Marc DelMonico

CLERGY, CONSECRATED LIFE, AND VOCATIONS

Chairman—Bishop Earl A. Boyea
Members—Archbishop Charles C. Thompson
Bishop Juan Miguel Betancourt, S.E.M.V.
Bishop François Beyrouti
Bishop Ronald A. Hicks
Bishop David L. Toups
Bishop Austin A. Vetter
Bishop William Wack, C.S.C.
Consultants— Rev. Frank Donio, S.A.C.
Deacon Dennis Dorner, Jr.
Sr. Sharon A. Euart, R.S.M.
Rev. Michael Patella, O.S.B.
Mrs. Rosemary Sullivan
Staff—Ms. Casey Brusnahan
Rev. Jorge Torres

COMMUNICATIONS

Chairman—Bishop Robert Reed
Members—Archbishop Gregory J. Hartmayer, O.F.M.Conv.
Bishop William D. Byrne
Bishop Joel M. Konzen, S.M.
Bishop John J. McIntyre
Bishop Louis Tylka
Bishop Kevin W. Vann
Rev. J. Mark Spalding
Consultants—Mr. Phil Alongi
Ms. Kelsey Cronin
Ms. Elizabeth Solsburg
Staff—Mr. David Felber
Ms. Mary McDonald
Ms. Maura Moser
Ms. Chieko Noguchi
Mr. James L. Rogers
Ms. Dana Sealy

Subcommittee on the Catholic Communications Campaign
Chairman—Archbishop Gregory J. Hartmayer, O.F.M.Conv.
Bishop Christopher J. Coyne
Bishop Joel M. Konzen, S.M.
Bishop John J. McIntyre
Bishop J. Mark Spalding
Bishop William Wack, C.S.C.
Bishop Edward J. Weisenburger
Bishop Luis R. Zarama
Staff—Ms. Maura Moser
Mr. James L. Rogers
Ms. Dana Sealy

CULTURAL DIVERSITY IN THE CHURCH

Chairman—Bishop Arturo Cepeda
Members—Archbishop Nelson J. Pérez
Archbishop Charles C. Thompson
Bishop Oscar Cantú
Bishop Eusebio L. Elizondo, M.Sp.S.
Bishop Joseph N. Perry
Bishop Larry Silva
Bishop Chad Zielinski
Consultants—Ms. Cecilia Flores
Dr. Young Hoang
Ms. Patricia Maldonado
Ms. Kathleen A. Merritt
Staff—Mr. Alejandro Aguilera-Titus
Rev. Michael Carson
Ms. Donna Toliver Grimes
Mrs. María del Mar Muñoz-Visoso
Sr. Joanna Okereke, H.H.C.J.
Sr. Myrna Tordillo, M.S.C.S.
Ms. Madeline Watkins

Subcommittee on African American Affairs
Chairman—Bishop Joseph N. Perry
Members—Bishop Brendan J. Cahill
Bishop Roy E. Campbell
Bishop Jerome Feudjio
Bishop Jeffrey Haines
Bishop Barry C. Knestout
Bishop Denis J. Madden
Consultants—Rev. Anthony Bozeman, S.S.J.
Ms. Valerie Jennings
Mr. Ashley Morris
Sr. Odessa Stanford, C.C.C.
Rev. Stephen Thorne
Staff—Ms. Donna Toliver Grimes

Subcommittee on Asian and Pacific Island Affairs
Chairman—Bishop Larry Silva
Members—Bishop Alejandro Aclan
Bishop Joy Alappatt
Bishop Kevin M. Birmingham
Bishop Italo Dell'Oro, C.R.S.
Bishop Witold Mroziewski
Bishop Thanh Thai Nguyen
Bishop Oscar Azarcon Solis
Consultants—Bishop Ryan P. Jimenez
Rev. Linh Hoang, O.F.M., Ph.D.
Ms. Josie Howard
Dr. Jem Sullivan
Staff—Sr. Myrna Tordillo, M.S.C.S.

Subcommittee on Hispanic Affairs
Chairman—Bishop Oscar Cantú
Members—Archbishop Mitchell Thomas Rozanski
Bishop Mark A. Bartosic
Bishop Ramon Bejarano
Bishop Roy E. Campbell
Bishop Enrique Delgado
Bishop Jorge H. Rodríguez
Bishop Alberto Rojas
Bishop Joseph J. Tyson
Consultants—Ms. Yazmín Maní
Mr. Edwin Ferrera
Dr. Dora Tobar
Staff—Mr. Alejandro Aguilera-Titus

Subcommittee on Native American Affairs
Chairman—Bishop Chad Zielinski
Members—Bishop John T. Folda
Bishop Terry R. LaValley
Bishop Peter M. Muhich
Bishop Stephen D. Parkes
Bishop Alberto Rojas
Bishop Austin A. Vetter
Consultants—Ms. Jenny Blackbear
Mr. Ben Blackbear
Mr. Juanatano Cano
Ms. Joanie Denemy
Deacon Mike Leman
Rev. Maurice Henry Sands
Staff—Rev. Michael Carson

Subcommittee on Pastoral Care of Migrants, Refugees, and Travelers
Chairman—Bishop Eusebio L. Elizondo, M.Sp.S.
Members—Archbishop Thomas G. Wenski
Bishop Kevin M. Birmingham
Bishop Brendan J. Cahill
Bishop Edgar M. da Cunha, S.D.V.
Bishop Frank J. Dewane
Bishop Jacques E. Fabre-Jeune, C.S.
Bishop Jerome Feudjio
Bishop Philipos Mar Stephanos Thottathil
Bishop Joseph J. Tyson
Consultants—Mr. Donald Kerwin
Rev. Tony Massad
Rev. Msgr. Anselm Nwaorgu
Rev. Jean Yvon Pierre
Staff—Sr. Joanna Okereke, H.H.C.J.
Ms. Madeline Watkins

DIVINE WORSHIP

Chairman—Bishop Steven J. Lopes
Members—Archbishop Samuel J. Aquila
Archbishop Paul S. Coakley
Bishop Mario Avilés, C.O.
Bishop Christopher J. Coyne
Bishop John T. Folda
Bishop Mark J. Seitz
Bishop Timothy C. Senior
Bishop Michael G. Woost
Consultants—Archbishop Leonard P. Blair
Ms. Laura Bertone
Mr. Christopher J. Carstens
Dr. Jennifer Donelson-Nowicka
Abbot Jeremy Driscoll, O.S.B.
Ms. Maria Perez-Rudisill
Abbot Gregory J. Polan, O.S.B.
Rev. Ryan T. Ruiz
Mrs. Rita Thiron
Staff—Ms. Silvina Cerezo
Rev. Dustin P. Dought
Rev. Andrew Menke

Subcommittee on Divine Worship in Spanish
Chairman—(Vacant)
Members—Bishop Mario Avilés, C.O.
Bishop Juan Miguel Betancourt, S.E.M.V.
Bishop Daniel E. Garcia
Bishop Jorge H. Rodríguez
Bishop Alberto Rojas
Bishop Luis M. Romero Fernandez, M. ID.
Consultants—Rev. Heliodoro Lucatero
Rev. Juan J. Sosa
Staff—Ms. Silvina Cerezo

DOCTRINE

Chairman—Bishop Daniel E. Flores
Members—Bishop Michael C. Barber, S.J.
Bishop Steven J. Lopes
Bishop James Massa
Bishop Robert J. McManus
Bishop Michael F. Olson
Bishop Kevin C. Rhoades
Coadjutor Bishop Richard G. Henning
Consultants—Archbishop William E. Lori
Dr. John C. Cavadini
Rev. Msgr. Michael Heintz
Dr. Margaret McCarthy
Staff—Rev. Ronald T. Kunkel
Dr. James LeGrys
Ms. Siobhan M. Verbeek

Subcommittee on Health Care Issues
Chairman—Bishop Michael F. Olson
Members—Bishop Donald J. Hying
Bishop David Konderla
Bishop Michael G. McGovern
Bishop Robert J. McManus
Bishop Timothy C. Senior
Bishop George Leo Thomas
Consultants—Dr. Marie Hilliard, Philadelphia, PA
Dr. John F. Brehany
Mr. William J. Cox
Sr. Mary Haddad, R.S.M.
Dr. Paul Scherz
Dr. Steven White
Staff—Mr. Daniel Balserak
Mr. Richard Coll
Mr. Tom Grenchik
Rev. Ronald T. Kunkel
Dr. James LeGrys
Mrs. Lauren McCormack
Mr. Michael O'Rourke
Ms. Siobhan M. Verbeek

Subcommittee on the Translation of Scripture Text
Chairman—Bishop Richard G. Henning
Members—Bishop Juan Miguel Betancourt, S.E.M.V.
Bishop Steven R. Biegler
Bishop Daniel H. Mueggenborg
Consultants—Dr. Thomas Bolin
Rev. Pablo Gadenz
Rev. Kevin Zilverberg
Dr. Mary Healy
Staff— Rev. Ronald T. Kunkel
Dr. James LeGrys

DOMESTIC JUSTICE AND HUMAN DEVELOPMENT

Chairman—Archbishop Borys Gudziak
Members—Archbishop Paul S. Coakley
Archbishop Thomas G. Wenski
Bishop Frank J. Dewane
Bishop David J. Malloy
Bishop David G. O'Connell
Bishop Richard E. Pates
Bishop Timothy C. Senior
Bishop David P. Talley
Bishop James S. Wall
Consultants—Archbishop Shelton J. Fabre
Bishop Mario E. Dorsonville-Rodríguez
Sr. Mary Bendyna, R.S.M.
Mr. Ray Boshara
Very Rev. Frank Donio, S.A.C.
Mr. James Ennis
Sr. Mary Haddad, R.S.M.
Mr. Jason Hall
Dr. Joseph P. Kaboski
Dr. Michael J. Naughton
Dr. Peter Kilpatrick
Sr. Donna Markham, O.P.
Ms. Debra Soltis, Esq.
Dr. W. Bradford Wilcox
Sr. Carol Zinn, S.S.J.
Staff—Ms. Julie M. Bodnar
Mr. Richard Coll
Ms. Ingrid Delgado
Mr. Michael O'Rourke
Ms. Jill Rauh

Subcommittee on the Catholic Campaign for Human Development
Chairman—Bishop David G. O'Connell

Members—Bishop Fernand Cheri, III, O.F.M.
Bishop John P. Dolan
Bishop Timothy E. Freyer
Bishop Gerald F. Kicanas
Bishop Mark O'Connell
Bishop John Stowe, O.F.M.Conv.
Bishop David P. Talley
Consultants— Mr. Matthew Brower
Sr. Judy Donovan, C.S.J.
Rev. Ty S. Hullinger
Rev. J. Daniel Mindling, O.F.M.Cap
Staff—Mr. Juan Aranda
Ms. Alexandra Carroll
Mr. Richard Coll
Mr. Gene Giannotta
Mr. W. Randy Keesler
Mr. Ralph McCloud
Mr. Ian Mitchell
Mr. Michael O'Rourke
Ms. Jill Rauh
Ms. Jessica Zurcher

ECUMENICAL AND INTERRELIGIOUS AFFAIRS

Chairman—Bishop David P. Talley
Members—Archbishop Mitchell Thomas Rozanski
Bishop David D. Kagan
Bishop Denis J. Madden
Bishop Michael Mulvey
Bishop Alfred A. Schlert
Bishop Peter L. Smith
Rev. Jeffrey M. Monforton
Consultant—Rev. Dennis McManus
Staff—Dr. Anthony Cirelli
Ms. Rebecca Cohen
Rev. Walter F. Kedjierski
Rev. Ronald G. Roberson, C.S.P.

EVANGELIZATION AND CATECHESIS

Chairman—Bishop Andrew H. Cozzens
Chairman-Elect—Archbishop Charles C. Thompson
Members—Archbishop Alfred C. Hughes
Bishop Frank J. Caggiano
Bishop Thomas A. Daly
Bishop Daniel E. Flores
Bishop Joseph G. Hanefeldt
Bishop Jeffrey M. Monforton
Bishop Michael J. Sis
Bishop David L. Toups
Consultants—Mr. Timothy Glemkowski
Dr. Mary Healy
Mr. Curtis Martin
Sr. M. Johanna Paruch, F.S.G.M.
Ms. Julianne Stanz
Dr. Jonathan J. Reyes
Staff—Dr. Zachary Keith
Ms. Marylin Santos
Dr. David Spesia
Mr. Carlos Taja

Subcommittee on the Catechism

Chairman—Bishop Frank J. Caggiano
Members—Archbishop Alfred C. Hughes
Bishop Juan Miguel Betancourt, S.E.M.V.
Bishop Christopher J. Coyne
Bishop Felipe J. Estévez
Bishop Elias Lorenzo, O.S.B.
Bishop James Massa
Staff—Dr. Zachary Keith
Dr. David Spesia
Mr. Carlos Taja

INTERNATIONAL JUSTICE AND PEACE

Chairman—Bishop David J. Malloy
Members— Archbishop Borys Gudziak
Archbishop Nelson J. Pérez
Bishop Joseph C. Bambera
Bishop Frank J. Dewane
Bishop W. Michael Mulvey
Bishop William F. Murphy
Bishop Alberto Rojas
Consultants—Mr. Sean Callahan
Ambassador Mary Ann Glendon
Dr. Maryann Cusimano Love
Rev. Msgr. Peter I. Vaccari
Dr. Thomas F. Farr
Staff—Mr. Richard Coll
Mrs. Virginia Farris
Mr. Stephen Hilbert
Mr. Lucas Koach
Mr. Christopher Ljunquist
Ms. Jill Rauh

LAITY, MARRIAGE, FAMILY LIFE AND YOUTH

Chairman—Bishop Robert Barron
Members—Archbishop Salvatore J. Cordileone
Archbishop Shelton J. Fabre
Bishop Edward J. Burns
Bishop James D. Conley
Bishop Donald J. Hying
Bishop David Konderla
Bishop Gregory John Mansour
Bishop Thomas John Paprocki
Consultants—Mr. Armando Cervantes
Mrs. Mary Hasson
Sr. Miriam James Hideland
Mrs. Lauren McCormack
Dr. Tom Neal
Mr. Jack Samour
Mr. Patrick Kelly
Staff—Mr. Andrew Buonopane
Ms. Julia Dezelski
Mr. Paul Jarzembowski
Mr. Dominic Lombardi
Dr. Theresa Notare
Ms. Katie Parker
Mr. Timothy Roder

MIGRATION

Chairman—Bishop Mark J. Seitz
Members—Cardinal Seán P. O'Malley, O.F.M.Cap.
Cardinal Joseph William Tobin, C.S.s.R.
Archbishop Gustavo García-Siller, M.Sp.S.
Archbishop Blase J. Cupich
Archbishop José H. Gomez
Archbishop Thomas G. Wenski
Bishop Mario E. Dorsonville-Rodríguez
Bishop Joseph J. Tyson
Consultants—Bishop Nicholas DiMarzio
Ms. Daniela Alulema
Mr. Sean Callahan
Mr. Dylan Corbett
Ms. Anna Marie Gallagher
Dr. Kristin Heyer
Sr. Donna Markham, O.P.
Staff—Ms. Jenny Cachaya
Mr. William Canny
Ms. Rachel Pollock
Mr. Todd Scribner
Mr. David Spicer

NATIONAL COLLECTIONS

Chairman—Bishop James S. Wall
Members—Archbishop Gregory J. Hartmayer, O.F.M.Conv.
Bishop Peter F. Christensen
Bishop Octavio Cisneros
Bishop W. Shawn McKnight
Bishop David G. O'Connell
Bishop Peter L. Smith
Bishop Jeffrey M. Monforton
Consultant—Mr. John Matthew Knowles
Staff—Ms. Mary Mencarini Campbell
Mr. Kevin Day
Ms. Jennifer M. Healy
Mr. Edward Kiely
Ms. Gina Laurent
Rev. Leo Perez, O.M.I.

Subcommittee on Catholic Home Missions

Chairman—Bishop W. Shawn McKnight
Members—Bishop Bohdan Danylo
Bishop Daniel H. Mueggenborg
Bishop Steven J. Raica
Bishop James A. Tamayo
Ms. Belinda Taylor
Bishop Michael W. Warfel
Bishop Chad Zielinski
Staff—Ms. Mary Mencarini Campbell
Mr. Kevin Day
Ms. Maria Lupiy
Mr. Kenneth Ong

Subcommittee on the Church in Africa

Chairman—Bishop Peter L. Smith
Members—Bishop John P. Dolan
Bishop Gregory W. Gordon
Bishop Gerald F. Kicanas
Bishop Barry C. Knestout
Bishop Edward B. Scharfenberger
Bishop David P. Talley
Bishop Gerald L. Vincke
Bishop Thomas Zinkula
Consultants—Cardinal Seán P. O'Malley, O.F.M.Cap.
Cardinal Joseph William Tobin, C.Ss.R.
Archbishop Nelson J. Pérez
Bishop John H. Ricard, S.S.J.
Rev. Msgr. Kieran E. Harrington
Mr. Patrick Markey
Mr. Don Rogers
Mr. Fritz Zuger
Staff—Ms. Mary Mencarini Campbell
Ms. Mireille Gbetholancy-Kun
Mr. Edward Kiely

Subcommittee on the Church in Central and Eastern Europe

Chairman—Bishop Jeffrey M. Monforton
Members—Cardinal Blase J. Cupich
Archbishop Borys Gudziak
Bishop Robert J. Fisher
Bishop Edward C. Malesic
Bishop Witold Mroziewski
Bishop Richard F. Stika
Bishop Gerald L. Vincke
Bishop Patrick J. Zurek
Consultants—Bishop John Michael Botean
Bishop Donald J. Hying
Mr. Patrick Markey
Staff—Ms. Mary Mencarini Campbell
Ms. Jennifer M. Healy
Mr. Andrew Kirkpatrick
Ms. Maria Lupiy

Subcommittee on the Church in Latin America

Chairman—Bishop Octavio Cisneros
Members—Archbishop Thomas G. Wenski
Bishop Oscar Cantú
Bishop Edgar M. da Cunha, S.D.V.
Bishop Eusebio L. Elizondo, M.Sp.S.
Bishop Alberto Rojas
Bishop Kevin J. Sweeney
Coadjutor Bishop Richard G. Henning
Consultants—Cardinal Seán P. O'Malley, O.F.M.Cap.
Bishop Mark J. Seitz
Mr. Jacques Liautaud
Staff—Ms. Mary Mencarini Campbell
Mr. David Corrales
Rev. Leo Perez, O.M.I.

PRO-LIFE ACTIVITIES

Chairman—Bishop Michael F. Burbidge
Members—Archbishop Bernard A. Hebda
Bishop Mark E. Brennan
Bishop Robert D. Gruss
Bishop Donald J. Hying
Bishop Stephen D. Parkes
Bishop Daniel E. Thomas
Bishop David A. Zubik
Dr. Kathleen Raviele
Consultants—Archbishop Shelton J. Fabre
Archbishop Joseph F. Naumann
Bishop Robert J. Brennan
Bishop Frank J. Dewane
Bishop Daniel H. Mueggenborg
Bishop Thomas J. Olmsted
Bishop Joe S. Vásquez
Mr. Carl A. Anderson
Mr. Sean Caine
Mother Agnes Mary Donovan, S.V.
Ms. Astrid Bennett Gutierrez
Dr. Margaret H. Hartshorn
Ms. Jennifer Kraska
Ms. Marianne Luthin
Ms. Jeanne Mancini
Dr. Joseph Meaney
Mr. O. Carter Snead
Mr. Patrick Kelly
Dr. Kathleen Raviele

Staff— Ms. Kimberly Baker
Ms. Anne Ferreira
Mr. Tom Grenchik
Mrs. Mary McClusky
Mr. Greg Schleppenbach
Ms. Francis Socrates
Ms. Katherine Talalas
Mr. Robert Vega
Ms Maria Zalot

PROTECTION OF CHILDREN AND YOUNG PEOPLE

Chairman—Bishop James V. Johnston, Jr.
Chairman-Elect—Bishop Barry C. Knestout
Members—Bishop Daniel Felton (Region VIII)
Bishop Joy Alappatt (Region XV)
Bishop David J. Bonnar (Region XI)
Bishop John S. Bonnici (Region VI)
Bishop Joseph V. Brennan (Region II)
Bishop Enrique Delgado (Region XIV)
Bishop Jeffrey S. Grob (Region VII)
Bishop John C. Iffert (Region V)
Bishop David Konderla (Region X)
Bishop Elias Lorenzo, O.S.B. (Region III)
Bishop Mark O'Connell (Region I)
Bishop Adam J. Parker (Region IV)
Bishop Edward J. Weisenburger (Region XIII)
Bishop Thomas Zinkula (Region IX)
Rev. Peter Schuster (Region XII)
Consultants—Dr. Heather Banis
Deacon Steve DeMartino
Mr. Rod Herrera
Ms. Regina Quinn
Staff—Rev. Paul B.R. Hartmann
Ms. Molly Fara
Mrs. Laura Garner
Ms. Chieko Noguchi
Deacon Bernard V. Nojadera
Mr. William Quinn
Rev. Jorge Torres
Ms. Siobhan M. Verbeek

RELIGIOUS LIBERTY

Chairman—Cardinal Timothy M. Dolan
Chairman-Elect—Bishop Kevin C. Rhoades
Members—Archbishop Paul S. Coakley
Bishop Andrew H. Cozzens
Bishop Mario E. Dorsonville-Rodríguez
Bishop David Konderla
Rev. Msgr. David Malloy
Deacon Maury Reed
Consultants—Archbishop Jerome E. Listecki
Archbishop William E. Lori
Archbishop Thomas G. Wenski
Bishop Robert Barron
Bishop Arturo Cepeda
Bishop Thomas A. Daly
Bishop David P. Talley
Mr. Jason Adkins, Esq.
Ms. Maria Alvarado
Mr. Carl A. Anderson
Mr. Kevin Baine, Esq.
Ambassador Mary Ann Glendon
Rev. Dominic Legge, O.P.
Mr. L. Martin Nussbaum, Esq.
Mrs. Gloria Purvis
Mr. Jason Shanks
Ms. Elise Ureneck
Mrs. Kim Daniels
Mr. Patrick Kelly
Staff—Rev. Michael J. K. Fuller, S.T.D.
Mr. Anthony R. Picarello, Jr., Esq.
Mr. Daniel Balserak
Mr. Kyle Burkhart
Mr. Richard Coll
Mr. Lucas Koach
Rev. Ronald T. Kunkel
Mrs. Lauren McCormack
Mr. James L. Rogers
Mr. Robert Vega
Mr. Aaron Weldon

NATIONAL ADVISORY COUNCIL

Chair—Ms. Lisa Weis, Winter Park, Florida, Region XIV
Chair-elect—Mr. Mark Berchem, West Saint Paul, Minnesota, Region VIII
Secretary—Mr. Armando Ruiz, Phoenix, Arizona, Region XIII
Members—
Bishops—Most Rev. David Bonnar, Diocese of Youngstown
Most Rev. Mark E. Brennan, Diocese of Wheeling-Charleston
Most Rev. Paul P. Chomnycky, O.S.B.M, Ukrainian Catholic Eparchy of Stamford
Most Rev. Edward Scharfenberger, Diocese of Albany
Diocesan Priests—Rev. Noel Reyes, Chicago, IL, Region VII
Rev. John Riley, Kansas City, KS, Region IX
Rev. Raymund Reyes, South San Francisco, CA, Region XI
Rev. Peter Short VG, Winslow, Arizona, Region XIII
Deacon—
Rev. Mr. Joseph Chebli Pharm.D., M.A., RPh, Belle Mead, NJ, Region XV
Men Religious—(Vacant)
Women Religious—Sr. Karen C. Dietrich, S.S.J., Ph.D., Philadelphia, PA
Sr. Mary-Jordan Hoover, O.P., Goodyear, AZ
Sr. Rose Marie Jasinski, C.B.S., Marriottsville, MD
Sr. Cecilia Ann Rezac, M.S., Springfield, MS
At Large—Mrs. Gail Thibaudeau Bellucci, North Haven, CT, Region I
Mr. Bernard (Bo) Garnek, Bobtown, PA, Region III
Mr. Mark Sadd, Esq., Charleston, WV, Region IV
Mr. Harry Albert Kemp, Royal Oak, MI, Region VI
Mr. Armando Ruiz, Phoenix, AZ, Region XIII
Ms. Lisa Weis, Winter Park, FL, Region XIV
Regional Representatives:
Region I—Mr. Gregg H. Ginn, Cape Elizabeth, ME
Ms. Marian Desrosiers, Fall River, MA
Region II—Dr. Joseph Dutkowsky, M.D., Cooperstown, NY
(Vacant)
Region III—Mr. Daniel Cellucci, Malvern, PA
(Vacant)
Region IV—Mr. Julius Caesar, Alexandria, VA
(Vacant)
Region V—
Mr. Robert Louis Hutton, Memphis, TN
Ms. Dina D. Dow, Baton Rouge, LA
Region VI—Mr. James P. Gulick, Strongsville, OH
Ms. Mary Ann Blakeley, Mentor, OH
Region VII—Mr. Walter Fountain, Green Bay, WI
(Vacant)
Region VIII—Mr. Mark Berchem, West Saint Paul, MN
(Vacant)
Region IX—
(Vacant)
(Vacant)
Region X—(Vacant)
Mrs. Maria Ruiz Scaperlanda, Oklahoma City, OK
Region XI—(Vacant)
(Vacant)
Region XII—Mr. Clinton Bentz, Scio, OR
Ms. Lana Mack-Worman, Volberg, MT
Region XIII— Honorable Robert Brack, Las Cruces, NM
(Vacant)
Region XIV—(Vacant)
Ms. Norely Soto, Niceville, FL
Region XV—(Vacant)
Ms. Ann M. Koshute MTS, Palmyra, PA
Staff— Mrs. Theresa Ridderhoff
Ms. Danilsa Reyes-Gonzalez
Mrs. Christina Zvir

NORTH AMERICAN COLLEGE, ROME

Chairman—Bishop Austin Vetter
Members—Cardinal Timothy M. Dolan
Bishop Leonard P. Blair
Archbishop Bernard A. Hebda
Bishop Earl A. Boyea
Bishop Yousif Habash
Bishop Jerry Vinke
Bishop Peter J. Jugis
Bishop Steven J. Lopes
Bishop Robert J. McClory
Bishop Glen J. Provost
Bishop Kevin W. Vann
Bishop Austin A. Vetter
Bishop William John Waltersheid
Secretary—Bishop Adam J. Parker
Staff—Rev. Michael J. K. Fuller, S.T.D.
Rev. David Schunk
Rev. Msgr. Thomas Powers
Mr. Mark Randall

BOARD OF DIRECTORS: CATHOLIC LEGAL IMMIGRATION NETWORK, INC.

Chairman—Bishop Jaime Soto
Members—Rev. Michael J. K. Fuller, S.T.D.
Archbishop Gregory J. Hartmayer, O.F.M.Conv.
Archbishop Thomas G. Wenski
Bishop Roy E. Campbell
Bishop Nicholas DiMarzio
Bishop Mario E. Dorsonville-Rodríguez
Bishop Eusebio L. Elizondo, M.Sp.S.
Bishop Jacques E. Fabre-Jeune, CS
Bishop Gerald F. Kicanas
Bishop George Leo Thomas
Mr. WIlliam Canny
Ms. Geraldine P. Carolan
Ms. Patricia Chappell
Ms. Marguerite Harmon
Mr. Francis J. Mulcahy
Mr. Mark Palmer
Mr. Vincent Pitta
Mr. D. Taylor
Vice President—Bishop Mark J. Seitz
Treasurer—Sr. Sally Duffy, S.C.
Secretary—Ms. Anna Marie Gallagher

BOARD OF DIRECTORS: CATHOLIC RELIEF SERVICES

Chairman—Archbishop Nelson J. Pérez
Vice-Chairman—Ms. Geraldine P. Carolan
Members—Cardinal Joseph William Tobin, C.Ss.R.
Archbishop Shelton J. Fabre
Archbishop Gregory J. Hartmayer, O.F.M.Conv.
Archbishop Bernard A. Hebda
Bishop Brendan J. Cahill
Bishop Octavio Cisneros
Bishop Daniel E. Garcia
Bishop Donald J. Hying
Bishop Mark J. Seitz
Bishop Oscar Azarcon Solis
Bishop Anthony B. Taylor
Bishop Luis R. Zarama
Ms. Helen Alvaré
Sr. Enelless Chimbali, S.B.V.M.
Ms. Christina Lamas
Mr. Matthew McKenna
Mrs. Karen Rauenhorst
Mr. John S. Scheid
Ms. Ann Thivierge
Dr. Reynold Verret
Mr. Brian Wenger
Dr. Richard Win Tun Kyi
Secretary—Rev. Michael J. K. Fuller, S.T.D.
Staff—Mr. Sean Callahan

BOARD OF TRUSTEES: CONFRATERNITY OF CHRISTIAN DOCTRINE, INC.

President—Archbishop Timothy P. Broglio
Members—Archbishop Paul S. Coakley
Bishop James F. Checchio
Bishop Daniel E. Flores
Archbishop William E. Lori
Staff—Ms. Mary Elizabeth Sperry

NATIONAL REVIEW BOARD

Chair—Ms. Suzanne Healy
Members—Mr. James Bogner
Mr. Steven Jubera
Mr. Thomas Mengler
Dr. Sarah Brennan
Hon. Elizabeth Hayden
Rev. Robert Leavitt
Mr. José Moreno
Dr. John Sheveland
Ms. Vivian Akel
Prof. Kurt Martens
Dr. Julie Hanlon Rubio

Staff—Ms. Molly Fara
Mrs. Laura Garner
Deacon Bernard V. Nojadera

AD HOC COMMITTEE AGAINST RACISM

Chairman—Bishop Shelton J. Fabre
Members—Archbishop William E. Lori
Cardinal Seán P. O'Malley, O.F.M.Cap.
Archbishop Paul S. Coakley
Archbishop Salvatore J. Cordileone
Archbishop Borys Gudziak
Bishop Gerard W. Battersby
Bishop Frank J. Caggiano
Bishop Arturo Cepeda
Bishop Frank J. Dewane
Bishop David G. O'Connell
Bishop Joseph N. Perry
Consultants—Cardinal Wilton D. Gregory
Cardinal Joseph William Tobin, C.Ss.R.
Archbishop José H. Gomez
Bishop James F. Checchio
Bishop Mario E. Dorsonville-Rodríguez
Bishop Daniel E. Flores
Bishop Martin D. Holley
Bishop John H. Ricard, S.S.J.
Bishop David P. Talley
Bishop James S. Wall
Ms. Jessica Murdoch, Collegeville, P.A.
Mr. James Ellis
Sr. Donna Markham, O.P.
Dr. Hosffman Ospino
Dr. C. Reynold Pichon, Ed.D.
Sr. Norma Pimentel, M.J.
Rev. Prentice A. Tipton
Dr. C. Reynold Verrett
Mr. Patrick Kelly
Rev. Maurice Henry Sands
Staff—Ms. Danielle M. Brown, Esq.
Mr. Richard Coll

NATIONAL RELIGIOUS RETIREMENT

National Religious Retirement Office
3211 Fourth St. NE, Washington, DC 20017-1194. Tel: 202-541-3215. Email: retirement@usccb.org. Sr. Stephanie Still, P.B.V.M., Exec. Dir. The Mission of the National Religious Retirement Office is to coordinate the National Collection for the Retirement Fund for Religious and to distribute these monies to eligible religious institutes for their retirement needs. The office also provides retirement planning and educational assistance to religious institutes. The National Religious Retirement Office is sponsored by the Conference of Major Superiors of Men, the Council of Major Superiors of Women Religious, the Leadership Conference of Women Religious and the United States Conference of Catholic Bishops.

REFUGEE TRAVEL ASSISTANCE PROGRAM LLC

Refugee Travel Assistance Program LLC
3211 Fourth St. NW Washington, DC 20017-1194. Tel: 202-541-3328. LLC's sole member: United States Conference of Catholic Bishops.
Managers—Rev. Michael J. K. Fuller, Bishop James F. Checchio, and Bishop Mark. J. Seitz.
Officers—Rev. Michael J. K. Fuller, William A. Canny and Gregory J. Scott.
The purpose of Refugee Travel Assistance Program LLC is to engage in and conduct any and all activities and transactions necessary, appropriate or incident to the servicing of refugee travel loans, pursuant to a memorandum of understanding with the International Organization for Migration, which are financed by The Bureau of Population, Refugees and Migration, United States Department of State, and made to refugees to assist them in resettling in the United States.

RELATED ORGANIZATIONS

***Catholic Legal Immigration Network, Inc.**
National Office, 8757 Georgia Ave., Ste 850 Silver Spring, MD 20910. Tel: 301-565-4829 Fax: 301-565-4824 Email: jatkinson@cliniclegal.org Web: www.cliniclegal.org
Board of Directors—Bishop Kevin W. Vann, Chm., Bishop Martin D. Holley, Vice Pres., Sr. Sally Duffy, S.C., Treas., Ms. Jeanne Atkinson, Exec. Dir., Rev. Msgr. Brian Bransfield, Gen. Sec., USCCB, William A. Canny, Bishop Edgar M. da Cunha, S.D.V., Bishop Nicholas A. DiMarzio, Sr. RayMonda DuVall, C.H.S., Bishop Eusebio L. Elizondo, M.Sp.S., Bishop Richard J. Garcia, Mr. Emilio Gonzalez, Ms. Marguerite (Peg) Harmon, Bishop Gerald F. Kicanas, Mr. Francis J. Mulcahy, Mr. Javier Palomarez, Bishop Joseph A. Pepe, Mr. Vincent Pitta, Bishop Mark J. Seitz, Bishop Jaime Soto, Mr. D. Taylor, Bishop Joe S. Vasquez, Archbishop Thomas G. Wenski
The Catholic Legal Immigration Network, Inc. (CLINIC), an independent agency founded by the United States Conference of Catholic Bishops (USCCB), operates a legal support agency for a rapidly growing national network of Catholic immigration programs. CLINIC advocates for transparent, fair and generous immigration policies, and expresses the Church's commitment to the full membership of migrants in U.S. society.

Catholic Relief Services
Catholic Relief Services-USCCB *CRS World Headquarters,* 228 W. Lexington St. Baltimore, MD 21201-3413. Tel: 877-435-7277; Web: www.crs.org; Mr. Sean Callahan, Pres.
Catholic Relief Services is the official international humanitarian agency of the Catholic community in the United States. CRS alleviates suffering and provides assistance to people in need in 116 countries, without regard to race, religion or nationality.
CRS was founded in 1943 by the bishops of the United States to assist the poor and disadvantaged outside this country — helping people in need for 80 years.
CRS is efficient and effective, directing 93 percent of the agency's expenditures directly to programs that benefit the poor overseas. Our agency touches more than 193 million lives, by addressing the root causes and effects of poverty, promoting human dignity, and helping to build more just and peaceful societies.
Our relief and development work is accomplished through programs of emergency response, health, agriculture, education, water and sanitation, social impact investing and peace building.
We serve Catholics in the United States by inviting them to live out their faith as part of one human family.
For more information, please visit www.crs.org.
Chairman—Archbishop Nelson J. Pérez
Vice Chair—Ms. Geraldine P. Carolan
Members—Prof. Helen Alvaré; Bishop Brendan J. Cahill; Sr. Enelless Chimbali, S.B.V.M.; Bishop Octavio Cisneros; Archbishop Shelton J. Fabre; Rev. Michael J. K. Fuller; Bishop Daniel E. Garcia; Archbishop Gregory J. Hartmayer, O.F.M.Conv.; Archbishop Bernard A. Hebda; Bishop Donald J. Hying; Ms. Christina Lamas; Mr. Matthew M. McKenna; Mrs. Karen Rauenhorst; Mr. John Scheid; Bishop Mark J. Seitz; Bishop Oscar A. Solis; Bishop Anthony B. Taylor; Ms. Ann Thivierge; Cardinal Joseph W. Tobin, C.Ss.R.; Mr. Brian Wenger; Dr. Richard Win Tun Kyi; Dr. Reynold Verret; Bishop Luis R. Zarama.
Staff—Mr. Sean Callahan, Pres. & CEO; Mr. James Bond, Exec. Vice Pres. & Chief Financial Officer; Mr. Mark Melia, Exec. Vice Pres., Charitable Giving; Mr. William O'Keefe, Exec. Vice Pres., Mission & Mobilization; Ms. Candace Osunsade, Exec. Vice Pres., Global Chief People & Diversity Officer; Ms. Annemarie Reilly, Chief of Staff & Exec. Vice Pres., Strategy, Technology & Communications; Mr. Schuyler Thorup, Exec. Vice Pres., Overseas Oper.; Rev. Robert A. Twele, O.F.M. Conv., Esq., Vice Pres. & Gen. Counsel.

NATIONAL ORGANIZATIONS

Listing in this category is not related to classification under Canon Law as a public juridic person.

American Catholic Historical Association (1919)
Fordham University, Dealy Hall, Rm. 637, 441 E. Fordham Bronx, NY 10458. Tel: 718-817-3830 Fax: 718-817-5690 Email: acha@fordham.edu Rev. Richard Gribble, C.S.C., Pres., Rev. R. Bentley Anderson, S.J., Sec. & Treas.
An academic and scholarly organization, founded to promote the study of Catholicism and Roman Catholic history understood in the broad sense.

The American College of the Roman Catholic Church of the United States
3211 Fourth St., N.E., Washington, DC 20017-1194. Tel: 202-541-5411 Fax: 202-722-8804 Email: pnacdc@pnac.org Most Rev. Robert Deeley, J.C.D., Chm., Rev. Peter C. Harman, S.T.D., Rector, Mark Randall, C.F.R.E, Exec. Dir., Institutional Advancement.
The American College is delegated by the Holy See to exercise oversight of the formational activities of the Pontifical North American College in Rome, and its Board of Governors is composed of one Bishop from each of the fifteen USCCB Regions. It was created by a Special Act of the Maryland Legislature in 1886, and its tax status is governed by Section 501(c)(3) of the United States Internal Revenue Code.

Apostleship of the Sea of the United States of America (AOSUSA)
1500 Jefferson Dr. Port Arthur, TX 77642-0646. Tel: 409-985-4545 Fax: 409-985-5945 Email: aosusa@sbcglobal.net Capt. George P. McShea, Jr., Pres., Rev. Sinclair Oubre, J.C.L., Immediate Past Pres., Ms. Doreen M. Badeaux, Sec. Gen.
AOSUSA is an association of the faithful of Catholic maritime chaplains, cruise ship priests, seafarers, deacons, religious, lay ecclesial ministers, and affiliates serving the people of the sea in ports throughout the USA.
Private Association of the Faithful.
Publication: *AOS USA Maritime E-News.*

Association for the Ongoing Formation of Priests, Inc. (AOFP) formerly NOCERCC
320 Cathedral St., Baltimore, MD 21201. Mailing address: P.O. Box 5977, Timonium, MD 21094. Tel. 410-978-3676. Email: office@aofpriests.org. Web: www.aofpriests.org. Rev. John McCrone, Pres. Rev. Julian Peters, O.S.B., M.S.A., Sec. Rev. Msgr. James Schillinger, S.T.L. Ex Officio: Patricia LeNoir, M.A., Mission Admin.
Founded in 1973, The National Organization for Continuing Education of Roman Catholic Clergy (NOCERCC), now known as The Association for the Ongoing Formation of Priests (AOFP), is a membership association of dioceses and religious communities and other interested organizations and individuals committed to the Church's mission to promote and support ongoing formation for priests and presbyterates. Professional and formational services offered include an annual convention; programs that dioceses and religious communities can host for clergy and other pastoral ministers; a monthly newsletter; a quarterly newsletter; and other practical resources in diverse media, such as sample policies, speaker and retreat leader listings, monthly books reviews, sabbatical information, etc.

Association of Catholic Diocesan Archivists
Diocese of Charleston Archives and Records Management Office, 114 Broad St., Charleston, SC 29401. Tel: 843-410-1720. Bishop Thomas J. Paprocki, D.D., J.C.D., S.T.D., Episcopal Moderator; Brian Fahey, Pres., Katherine Oubre, Vice Pres. & Pres.-Elect, Timothy Olson, Treas.; Ana-Elisa Arredondo, Sec.
The Association of Catholic Diocesan Archivists first met in 1979 and formally organized the Association of Catholic Diocesan Archivists in 1982. The organization promotes professionalism in the management of diocesan archives in

the United States and Canada, and fosters cooperation between diocesan archivists and others on regional, national and international levels. Membership information is available through the above address and telephone number.

***Bishops' Plan Insurance Company**
2386 Airport Rd., Barre, VT 05641.

Catholic Association of Diocesan Ecumenical and Interreligious Officers (CADEIO)
7600 Old Keene Mill Rd., Springfield, VA 22152. Email: frdonrooney@stbernpar.org Cell: 703-309-8719. Rev. Don Rooney, Pres., Rev. Joseph D. Wallace, Vice Pres., Mr. Rick Caporali, Treas., Rev. Phil Latronico, Sec.

CADEIO (formerly NADEO) is the Catholic Association of Ecumenical and Interreligious Officers who serve as delegates of dialogue on behalf of their bishops of (Arch)Dioceses and Eparchies in the United States: to promote collaboration which advances the work of Christian unity and interreligious understanding; to arrange programs for continuing formation and education of the membership; and to cooperate with the Bishops' Committee for Ecumenical and Interreligious Affairs of the United States Conference of Catholic Bishops, and with other ecumenical and interreligious networks and agencies.

Catholic Association of Teachers of Homiletics (CATH)
Mailing Address: CATH Secretary – Treasurer, 2402 Golf Links Court, Spicewood, TX 78669. Tel: 832-721-4259 Email: Cathomiletics@gmail.com.

CATH Executive Officers 2023-2024: Dr. Karla Bellinger, Pres., Rev. Benjamin A. Roberts, Vice Pres., Dr. Suzanne Nawrocki, D.Min., Sec. - Treas.

The Catholic Association of Teachers of Homiletics (CATH) is the professional guild of Catholic homileticians in North America. The non-profit is affiliated with the larger ecumenical society, the Academy of Homiletics. Internally, CATH provides peer support for members to strengthen the teaching of preaching. Through the mutual sharing of study, scholarship, and praxis, the organization bolsters the professional development of its members. To the broader Church community, CATH promotes the significance of Catholic preaching as integral to liturgy in proclaiming the Good News. The organization has also been a key contributor of resources and consultation to the USCCB in their responsibility for the continuing formation of preachers. Historically, CATH has developed programs in preaching for the preparation of priests, deacons and non-ordained ministers, as well as advocated for the development of advanced degree courses in homiletics within Catholic theological schools.

Catholic Campus Ministry Association
National Office, P.O. Box 3616, 650 South Greenwood Avenue, Easton, PA 18040-9800 Tel: 908-360-5110. Email: stpierre@ccmanetwork.org Web: www.ccmanetwork.org

Founded in 1969 by the United States Conference of Catholic Bishops, CCMA promotes the mission of the Church in higher education and implements the 1985 Pastoral Letter on Campus Ministry through the training, formation and networking of Catholic campus ministers. Membership is open to individuals involved in the campus ministry field.

Publications & Resources: Small Group Field Guide, Catholic Campus Ministry Directory, Ministry Evaluation Instrument, Affinity Groups, *One-Days, LAUNCH, Office Hours,* Thought LEADERS and CALLED.

Catholic Cemetery Conference
Office Headquarters, 1400 S. Wolf Rd., Bldg. 3 Hillside, IL 60162. Tel: 708-202-1242; Web: www.catholiccemeteryconference.org. Ralph A. Gervasi, CAE, Exec. Dir., Bishop Gerald F. Kicanas, D.D., Episcopal Moderator.

The Conference is an organization of Diocesan Directors of Cemeteries and parish cemetery administrators from throughout the United States, Canada, Australia, France, Ireland and Italy. Guided by the principle: "That burial of the dead is one of the Corporal Works of Mercy," the Conference promotes high standards of Catholic cemetery management, development, operation and maintenance consistent with Christian service to the Catholic community; and fosters and promotes the religious, charitable and educational interests of Catholic cemeteries and the people they serve.

Founded in 1949, the Catholic Cemetery Conference (CCC) helps cemetery staff enhance their skills in caring for the deceased and comforting their loved ones through ministry, education, networking and service opportunities.

Publications: monthly magazine, *Catholic Cemetery*; various booklets on cemetery management & evaluation services; funeral liturgy at the cemetery; event brochures; annual supplier catalog. Annual Convention; School of Leadership and Management Excellence at the University of Notre Dame, Exploring Catholic Cemetery Operations. Social Media: Instagram, LinkedIn, webinars, podcasts.

Catholic Charities USA
2050 Ballenger Ave., Ste. 400 Alexandria, VA 22314. Tel: 703-549-1390 Fax: 703-549-1656 Sr. Donna Markham, O.P., Ph.D., Pres. & CEO, Bishop Frank Dewane, Episcopal Liaison

Catholic Charities USA is a national network of more than 160 agencies that provide help and create hope for nearly 14 million people a year regardless of their religious, social, or economic backgrounds.

For more than 280 years, Catholic Charities agencies have been providing a wide range of vital services in their communities ranging from day care, adoption, and refugee resettlement to advocacy, counseling, and emergency food and housing. Today, the Catholic Charities network is made up of more than 70,000 staff and 260,000 volunteers. In addition, more than 5,000 individuals serve as volunteer members of local boards.

The national office, Catholic Charities USA, was founded in 1910 as the National Conference of Catholic Charities by the Most Rev. Thomas J. Shahan and Rt. Rev. Msgr. William J. Kerby in cooperation with lay leaders of the Society of St. Vincent De Paul.

Catholic Charities USA provides its members a national voice, networking opportunities, training and technical assistance, program development, and financial support.

Catholic Charities USA has been commissioned by the U.S. Catholic bishops to represent the Catholic community in times of domestic disaster. Catholic Charities USA also provides disaster preparedness training to dioceses and agencies to mitigate the disruption of business and services consequent to natural disasters.

Publications: Charities USA, a quarterly membership magazine; an annual report; an annual survey of Catholic Charities services nationwide; and various publications on issues of concern to Catholic Charities agencies.

The Catholic Health Association of the United States (1919)
4455 Woodson Rd. Saint Louis, MO 63134. Tel: 314-427-2500 Fax: 314-427-0029 Web: www. chausa. org. Sr. Mary Haddad, R.S.M., Pres. & CEO, Diarmuid Rooney, Interim Vice Pres. Sponsorship & Mission Svcs., Lisa Smith, Vice Pres. Advocacy & Public Policy, Loren Chandler, Chief Operations & Finance Officer, Catherine Hurley, Vice Pres. Gen. Counsel/Corporate Compliance, Brian Reardon, Vice Pres. Communications & Mktg.

CHA represents the combined strength of its members, more than 2,000 Catholic healthcare sponsors, systems, facilities, and related organizations. Founded in 1915, CHA unites members to advance selected strategic directions. Presents annual awards recognizing contribution to the health ministry by organizations and individuals. Sponsors continuing education for healthcare personnel.

Service Areas: Planning and Policy Development, Public Policy and Advocacy, Communications, Sponsorship, Ethics and Mission Services. Annual Assembly: Annual assembly and membership meeting for Catholic healthcare leaders.

Publications: 4 times-year, *Health Progress*; bimonthly, *Catholic Health World*; booklets, books & audiovisual on healthcare, Church-related subjects.

Catholic Kolping Society of America (1849)
(Please direct all correspondence to the National Administrator).

1223 Van Houten Clifton, NJ 07013. Patricia Farkas, Natl. Admin.

The Society was founded by Rev. Adolph Kolping in Cologne, Germany, and established in the United States in 1856. The Catholic Kolping Society of America is a part of the worldwide Kolping movement and belongs to the International Kolping Society. There are 11 branches in principal cities of the United States with a combined membership of approximately 2,000. The membership is open to men and women of all ages. The Society's mission statement reads: We, the members of the Catholic Kolping Society of America, extend the vision of our founder, Blessed Adolph Kolping, by promoting the development of the individual and family; we foster a sense of belonging and friendship through our program of spiritual, educational, charitable and social activities.

Catholic Medical Association
National Headquarters, 550 Pinetown Rd., Ste. 205, Ft. Washington, PA 19034. Tel: 484-270-8002 Fax: 866-714-0242. Email: info@cathmed.org Web: www.cathmed.org.

Officers—Mr. Mario R. Dickerson, M.T.S., Exec. Dir.; Craig L. Treptow, M.D., Pres.; Michelle K. Stanford, M.D., Vice Pres., David J. Hilger, M.D., Treas.; Jennifer Perone, M.D., Sec.

Upholding the principles of the Catholic faith in the science and practice of medicine.

Catholic Volunteer Network
6930 Carroll Ave., Ste. 500 Takoma Park, MD 20912-4423. Tel: 301-270-0900 Tel: 800-543- 5046 Email: info@catholicvolunteernetwork.org Web: www.catholicvolunteernetwork.org Bishop Oscar Solis, Episcopal Advisor

Catholic Volunteer Network promotes, recruits and refers volunteers to missions in the United States and overseas. We represent hundreds of faith-based volunteer programs worldwide and work with the U.S. dioceses, religious communities and the private sector to determine their needs for help. Catholic Volunteer Network (CVN) is committed to the goal that every Catholic man and woman be invited to consider a period of service in the missions, as a vital and important manifestation of the baptismal call of all Catholic people. Currently over 18,000 men and women are serving in CVN member mission programs offering their gifts and abilities in full-time service to people in need and living their Catholic faith more fully. These volunteers are serving domestically for a summer, six months, a year or more, and they are serving internationally for two or more years at a time. They are single and married, recent college graduates and early retirees, doctors and teachers, parish ministers and social workers, community organizers, computer programmers, legal aides and more. Gatherings: Annual Conference; Formation Workshop, Training Seminars.

Publications: annual, *Response: Directory of Volunteer Opportunities*; monthly, *How Can I Help?*

Awards: The Father George Mader Award, given annually to honor organizations and individuals who promote the value of lay mission service. The Bishop Joseph A. Francis Award to honor a former volunteer who has demonstrated exemplary service in his/her local community.

Catholic Media Association
205 W. Monroe St., Ste. 470 Chicago, IL 60606. Tel: 312-380-6789 Fax: 312-361-0256 Web: www. CatholicMediaAssociation.org.

Board of Directors—Amy Kawula, Pres., Most Rev. Michael F. Burbidge, Honorary Pres., Ed Langlois, Vice Pres., Joe Sinasac, Treas., Ana Rodriguez-Soto, Sec., Jennifer Brinker, Editorial Staff Member, Newspaper, Gretchen Crowe, Publisher Member, General, John Feister, Member-at-Large, Magazine, Janelle Gergen, Member-at-Large, Paula Gwynn Grant, Diocesan Communication Dir., Michael La Civita, Business Staff Member, Magazine, Antonio Enrique, Regional Rep., Eastern, Alton Pelowski, Editorial Staff Member, Magazine, Matthew Schiller, Publisher Member, Newspaper, Maria Wiering, Regional Rep., Midwest, JD Long-Garcia, Past Pres., Rob DeFrancesco, Exec. Dir.

The Catholic Press Association of the United States and Canada, Inc., is incorporated in New York state and now does business as the Catholic Media Association. It is the trade and professional association of Catholic newspapers, magazines, and general publishers in the U.S. and Canada and their staff personnel. The CPA was established in 1911. It serves a professional Catholic media market of nearly 2,000 persons working in more than 600 publications with a wide promotion and representation of Catholic press interests in social media, education, and professional development.

Catholic Rural Life

University of St. Thomas, 2115 Summit Ave. Mail 4080 St. Paul, MN 55105-1048. Tel: 651-962-5955 Fax: 651-962-5957 Email: info@catholicrurallife.org Web: www.catholicrurallife.org Bishop Brendan J. Cahill, Pres. Bd., Mr. James F. Ennis, Exec. Dir.

Catholic Rural Life is a membership-based organization focused on promoting Catholic life in rural America. CRL's vision is flourishing Catholic life in rural America—thriving families, farms and parishes—centered on faith community and care of creation. Our work in ethical agricultural and pastoral ministry & outreach supports and builds the rural Church by educating leaders—priests, religious and laity.

The Catholic Theological Society of America

c/o John Carroll University, 1 John Carroll Blvd. University Heights, OH 44118. Tel: 440-360-0816

Board Members—Francis X. Clooney, S.J., Pres., Cambridge, MA, Kristin Heyer, Pres.-Elect, Boston, MA, Nancy Pineda-Madrid, Vice Pres., Los Angeles, CA, Hosffman Ospino, Sec., Chestnut Hill, MA, Patrick Flanagan, C.M., Treas., Queens, NY, Christine Firer Hinze, Past Pres., Bronx, NY, Christina Astorga, Portland, OR, Edward Hahnenberg, University Heights, OH, Nancy Dallavalle, Fairfield, CT, Linh Hoang, Loudonville, NY, Mary Jane Ponyik, Exec. Dir., University Heights, OH.

An association of professional theologians. Its purpose is to promote studies and research in theology within the Roman Catholic tradition, to relate theological science to current problems, and to foster a more effective theological education by providing a forum for an exchange of views among theologians and with scholars in other disciplines.

Catholic Youth Foundation USA

415 Michigan Ave., Ste. 40 Washington, DC 20017-4503. Tel: 202-636-3825 Fax: 202-526-7544 Email: info@cyfusa.org Web: cyfusa.org. Ms. Christine Lamas, Exec. Dir.; Wayne Griffith, Chair.

Catholic Youth Foundation USA (CYFUSA) is a private, nonprofit organization, incorporated in the District of Columbia since 1989. It manages and provides financial resources to the National Federation for Catholic Youth Ministry in order to promote effective and innovative youth ministry and to ensure a faithful future of the Catholic church in the United States.

Conference for Catholic Facility Management

20 Archbishop May Dr. St. Louis, MO 63119. Tel: 314-792-7002 Email: info@ccfm.net Web: www.ccfm.net. Mary Tichy, Exec. Dir., Dave Prada, Bd. Pres., Jim Zielinkski, Bd. Vice Pres., Greg Hampson, Bd. Treas., Jo Ann Redmond, Bd. Sec., Most Rev. Roger Foys, Episcopal Moderator.

The mission of the Conference for Catholic Facility Management (CCFM) is to serve its members who work for the Roman Catholic Church in facility management, construction, real estate, and sustainability. CCFM seeks to promote the spiritual and professional development and provide a collaborative forum for its members to share knowledge and develop professional relationships.

The Conference of Major Superiors of Men of the United States, Inc.

7300 Hanover Dr., Ste. 304, Greenbelt, MD 20770. Tel: 301-588-4030 Fax: 240-650-3697. Web: www.cmsm.org. Very Rev. Jeffrey S. Kirch, C.PP.S., Pres., Rt. Rev. James Herring, O.Praem., Vice Pres., Very Rev. Christopher Fadok, O.P., Sec. & Treas., Rev. Frank S. Donio, S.A.C., Exec. Dir.

The canonical conference for major superiors of men's religious congregations, monastic communities, religious institutes, and societies of apostolic life in the United States. CMSM serves major superiors and their councilors in their role of leadership in their own communities and in the Conference as a whole.

The Confraternity of Christian Doctrine, Inc.

3211 Fourth St., N.E. Washington, DC 20017. Tel: 202-541-3098 Fax: 202-541-3089 Mary Elizabeth Sperry, Assoc. Dir. Email: msperry@usccb.org.

Members—Archbishop Timothy P. Broglio, Archbishop William E. Lori, Archbishop Paul S. Coakley, Bishop James F. Checchio, Bishop Daniel E. Flores.

The Confraternity is a distinct entity, separately incorporated and directed by a Board of Trustees from the United States Conference of Catholic Bishops. The purpose of the Corporation is to foster and promote the teachings of Christ as understood and handed down by the Roman Catholic Church. To this end it licenses use of the Lectionary for Mass and the New American Bible, translations made from the original languages.

Council of Major Superiors of Women Religious in the United States of America

415 Michigan Ave., N.E., Ste. 420, P.O. Box 4467, Washington, DC 20017-0467. Tel: 202-832-2575 Fax: 202-832-6325 Email: executivedirector@cmswr.org. Mother Anna Grace Neenan, O.P., Chairperson, Sr. Mary Bendyna, O.P., Exec. Dir.

A canonically erected conference of major superiors of institutes of apostolic women religious in the United States established in 1992 to promote mutual support and collaboration among them and to foster communication and cooperation with the Holy See, the United States Conference of Catholic Bishops, and individual Bishops.

Diocesan Fiscal Management Conference

National Office, 625 W. Deer Valley Rd., Ste. 103-410, Phoenix, AZ 85027. Tel: 602-992-2900 Email: jknowles@dfmconf.org Bishop Barry C. Knestout, Episcopal Moderator, Mr. John Matthew Knowles, J.D., Exec. Dir.

The mission of the Diocesan Fiscal Management Conference (DFMC) is to provide leadership in fiscal management to the Catholic Church. Mindful of its special ministry in the Church as the extension of the Diocesan Bishop in fiscal matters, the members of the Diocesan Fiscal Management Conference unite to be of service to the Church in the Ministry of Fiscal Management. In particular, this organization promotes the spiritual growth of its members; encourages the development of professional relationships of its members; facilitates the free exchange of ideas and information; and provides fiscal and administrative expertise and professional services to the local and national Church.

Diocesan Information Systems Conference

National Office, 1250 Connecticut Ave., N.W., Ste. 700 Washington, DC 20036. Tel: 512-949-2555 Email: info@discinfo.org Bishop Jeffrey M. Monforton, Episcopal Moderator, Jeffrey Hardy, Pres., Marcus Madsen, Vice Pres., Zachary Keninitz, Sec., Matthew Dolan, Treas.

DBA: Diocesan Information Solutions Community (DISC)

The members of DISC unite to serve the Roman Catholic Church in information systems matters. The DISC organization serves as a liaison among technology managers for Archdioceses, Dioceses and related entities.

This organization promotes the spiritual growth of its members, provides technical expertise in Information Technology, promotes professional technical services to the local and national church communities, encourages the development of professional relationships among its members and facilitates the free exchange of technical information and ideas.

Federation of Diocesan Liturgical Commissions

FDLC National Office, 415 Michigan Ave., N.E., Ste. 70 Washington, DC 20017. Tel: 202-635-6990; Web: www.FDLC.org Mrs. Rita A. Thiron, Exec. Dir., Ms. Laura Bertone, Chair, Board of Directors; Todd Williamson, Vice Chair; Ms. Leticia Thornton, Treas.

The FDLC was initiated by the Bishops' Committee on the Liturgy (BCL) in October, 1969, in order to assist and develop the liturgical apostolate in the dioceses of the USA. The FDLC is a national organization composed of members of diocesan liturgical commissions and directors of worship offices duly appointed by their local bishops. Its members may also include others who support the liturgical life of parishes and other Catholic institutions. As a pastoral and professional organization, the FDLC serves as an official collaborating agent between the local Churches and the BCDW. The Board of Directors is made up of fourteen representatives, one from each of the fourteen episcopal regions. The Executive Director leads the Federation's daily operations. The FDLC serves as a forum through which diocesan liturgy personnel may contribute responsibly and effectively in articulating the concerns of the local Church in liturgical matters; provides formation for parish and diocesan leadership; and aids the full implementation of the liturgical rites as envisioned by the Constitution on the Sacred Liturgy, subsequent post-conciliar documentation, and the praenotanda of the liturgical books.

Instituto Nacional Hispano de Liturgia, Inc.

St. Joseph Catholic Church, 8670 Byron Ave., Miami Beach, FL 33141. Tel: 305-866-6567 Email: Liturgia@liturgiahispana.com. Web: Liturgiahispana.com. Rev. Juan J. Sosa, Pres., Sr. Marilu Covani, S.P., Vice Pres., María Pérez-Rudisill, Treas.

The Instituto is a national organization committed to assisting the bishops of the country in promoting the liturgical reforms mandated by the Second Vatican Council, while it studies, reflects and celebrates more authentically the Catholic faith from the various religious traditions of Hispanics who reside in the United States. Instituto members assist the Church at the national, diocesan and parish levels by providing lectures, translations, and other Spanish and bilingual resources that may meet the liturgical needs of Hispanics whenever they surface. Membership to the organization is open to all persons and institutions interested in liturgy. Board members meet twice a year, members meet annually. National Conference every 2 years and/or symposium on liturgical topics.

International Catholic Migration Commission (ICMC) & ICMC, Inc.

31 Milk St., Ste. 315, Boston, MA 02109-5137. Rev. Msgr. Robert Vitillo, ICMC, Inc. Pres & Sec. Gen.; Kristen Lionetti, Head of U.S. Liaison Office; William Bagley, Development Officer.

Global network of Catholic Bishops' Conferences engaged in response to migrants and refugees; ICMC also sponsors direct humanitarian programs in several regions of the world, with headquarters in Geneva, Switzerland and affiliate offices include Washington, DC and Boston, Massachusetts.

International Catholic Stewardship Council, Inc. (ICSC)

National Office, 26300 Ford Rd., #317, Dearborn Heights, MI 48127. Tel: 800-352-3452 Fax: 313-446-8316 Email: icsc@catholicstewardship.org Web: www.catholicstewardship.com Most. Rev. Donald F. Hanchon, Auxiliary Bishop of Detroit, MI. Michael Murphy, Exec. Dir.

Through its annual conference, Stewardship and Development Institutes, publications and audio materials, ICSC allows people committed to Christian stewardship to gather, share ideas, and learn from each other. At one with the universal church, ICSC fosters solidarity of stewardship as a way of life in parishes and dioceses all over the world. Membership in ICSC is extended to several categories of Christian stewards: (Arch)dioceses, parishes, Catholic associations and professional firms from the United States and around the world. Members receive a number of essential benefits to enable them to live stewardship and bring this way of life to others in their communities and organizations.

ICSC encourages the growing professionalism of diocesan stewardship and development procedures and programs, as well as the development of parish-centered stewardship renewal aimed at increasing the time, talent and treasure contributed by parishioners. These principles of stewardship outlined in the 1992 USCCB Pastoral Letter: Stewardship: A Disciple's Response.

For a complete list of services and publications contact the ICSC office or visit the ICSC Website at www.catholicstewardship.org. Membership information is available upon request.

Jesuit Conference, Inc.

1016 16th St., N.W., Ste. 400 Washington, DC 20036. Tel: 202-462-0400 Fax: 202-328-9212 Very Rev. Timothy P. Kesicki, S.J., Pres., Rev. Sean D. Michaelson, S.J., Ph.D., Socius & Treas.

Ladies of Charity of the United States of America (LCUSA)

National Center, 2816 E. 23rd St., Kansas City, MO 64127. Tel: 816-260-3853 Email: office@ladiesofcharity.us Web: aic.ladiesofcharity.us Bishop David A. Zubik, D.D., Episcopal Chm., Debbie Chadwick, Pres. 2019-2021, Rev. Richard Gielow, C.M., Spiritual Advisor

Ladies of Charity in the United States of America (R) is a national organization with local associations of Ladies of Charity as its members. The Local Associations are dedicated to the service of poor & frail people in their communities in the spirit of St. Vincent de Paul, St. Louise de Marillac & St. Elizabeth Ann Seton. Nationally about 6,100 members contribute volunteer hours and financial support. LCUSA is a member of the International Association of Charities of St. Vincent de Paul (AIC) which traces its founding to St. Vincent de Paul in 1617. We are women acting together against all forms of poverty through service, education & advocacy.

Publications; triannual: *Servicette.*

Leadership Conference of Women Religious in the United States of America

Office, 8737 Colesville Rd., Suite 610, Silver Spring, MD 20910. Tel: 301-588-4955 Fax: 301-587-4575 Sr. Rebecca Ann Gemma, O.P., Pres., Sr. Mary Jane Herb, I.H.M., B.A., M.Ed., PhD., Past Pres., Sr. Maureen Geary, O.P., Pres.-Elect, Sr. Maureen O'Connor, O.S.F., B.S.N., M.S.N., M.B.A., Treas., Sr. Catherine Sheehan, D.W., B.A., B.S.N., M.P.H., Sec., Sr. Carol Zinn, C.S.J., B.A., PhD., Exec. Dir.

A conference of leaders of U.S. women religious congregations, founded in 1956, canonically approved in 1959 with a name change in 1972 and canonical approval of revised by-laws in 1972 and 1989, to promote a developing understanding and living of religious life, to assist members to carry out more collaboratively their service of leadership, to provide a vehicle for dialogue with the Bishops' Conference and other ecclesiastical authority, and to collaborate with other groups concerned with the needs of society in continuing the mission of Christ in the world today.

Lithuanian Roman Catholic Federation of America

4545 W. 63rd St. Chicago, IL 60629. Tel: 773-585-9500; Email: svkuprys@gmail.com. Saulius V. Kuprys, National Pres.

A not-for-profit corporation founded in 1906 in Wilkes-Barre, PA, to promote and coordinate religious, educational and charitable activities among Lithuanian American Catholics, their organizations, institutions, religious communities, and parishes (for detailed information regarding religious institutions please refer to the Apostolate for Lithuanians).

Mariological Society of America (1949)

Secretariat: Marian Library, University of Dayton Dayton, OH 45469-1390. Tel: 937-229-1431. MSA Web: http://mariologicalsociety.com MSA Email: gdodd1@udayton.edu Dr. Gloria Falcao Dodd, Sec.

The objects and purposes of this organization are to promote interest and research in the theology of the Virgin Mary. Professional and associate membership. Proceedings of annual meeting published in Marian Studies now available at https://ecommons.udayton.edu/marian_studies/. Annual convention in mid-May.

National Association of Black Catholic Deacons, Inc.

820 18th Ave. Seattle, WA 98122. Deacon Joseph E. Connor, Pres., Seattle, WA, Deacon Larry Chatman, Vice Pres., Oakland, CA, Deacon Leonard Chambliss, Sec., Atlanta, GA, Deacon Jerry M. Lett, Treas., Lithonia, GA, Deacon Paul E. Richardson, Immediate Past Pres. Yellow Springs, OH

Members At Large—Deacon Arthur L. Miller, Windsor, CT, Deacon Jimmie L. Boyd, Sr., Buffalo, NY, Deacon Keith McKnight, Jersey City, NJ, Deacon Ralph Cyrus, Ft. Washington, MD, Deacon Emith Fludd, St. Croix, VI, Deacon Dexter Watson, Chicago, IL, Deacon Oliver Washington, Cincinnati, OH, Deacon Dunn Cumby, Oklahoma City, OK, Deacon A. Stephen Pickett, Lenoir, SC

Wives Representatives—Magnolia Cumby, Oklahoma City, OK, Barbara Connor, Seattle, WA

To promote unity among Black Deacons by facilitating effective communication network on a national, regional and diocesan level. To Further the Professional and Spiritual Growth of its Members. To be a pro-active organization in promoting and contributing to the future of the Black family with emphasis on Black men. To nurture relationships with National Black Catholic Clergy Caucus and the Bishop's Committee on the Diaconate in matters that affect Black Deacons and their families...To promote justice, peace, equality, an end to racism, and the sharing of resources among all peoples in light of the social teachings of the Roman Catholic Church.

National Association of Catholic Chaplains

National Office, 4915 S. Howell Ave., Ste. 501 Milwaukee, WI 53207-5939. Tel: 414-483-4898 Fax: 414-483-6712; Email: info@nacc.org; Web: www.nacc.org. Bishop Jeffrey R. Haines, Diocese of Milwaukee, Episcopal Liaison, Deacon Jack R. Conrad, BCC, Chair Bd.; Ms. Erica Cohen Moore, Exec. Dir.

The National Association of Catholic Chaplains advocates for the profession of spiritual care and educates, certifies, and supports chaplains, clinical pastoral educators, and all members who continue the healing ministry of Jesus in the name of the Church.

Publication: Up to 6 times-year, journal-newsletter, *Vision*; 26 times-year (every other Monday), email newsletter, *NACC Now*.

The National Association of Catholic Family Life Ministers

P.O. Box 23, Alpha, OH 45301. Tel: 937-431-5443 Email: nacflm@gmail.com Web: www.nacflm.org. Jason Kidd, Pres., Jo Holt, Pres.-Elect

The National Association of Church Personnel Administrators (NACPA)

1727 King St., Ste. 105, Alexandria, VA 22314. Tel: 571-551-6064 Email: nacpa@nacpa.org Web: www.nacpa.org Maureen Fontenot, Bd. Pres., Regina Haney, Ed.D., Exec. Dir.

The National Association of Church Personnel Administrators (NACPA) is a membership association of lay, religious and clergy serving dioceses, parishes, religious congregations and other church-related institutions. The purpose of the Association is to promote justice in the workplace where the Church is the employer through ethical and just standards and to provide programs and resources that assist members in developing competencies in human resource management grounded in gospel values.

National Association of Diaconate Directors (1977)

National Office, 101945 State Bridge Road STE 401-122 Alpharetta, GA 30022. Tel: 404-274-9896 Email: info@nadd.org Web: www.nadd.org Deacon Dennis Dorner, Chm., Deacon Jim Caruso, Vice Chm., Deacon David Kushner, Sec. & Treas.

NADD serves formation directors, deacon directors, vicars for deacons, and other diocesan personnel who are responsible to their bishops for the formation of deacon candidates and the continued professional development and education of deacons following ordination. The Association takes a leadership role relating to national and regional issues of the diaconate and serves as a consultant to the USCCB Committee for Clergy, Consecrated Life and Vocations. The Association leadership is comprised of an Executive Director, Executive Committee and a Board of Directors representing each of the 14 USCCB regions. NADD promotes expertise through the National Directory Institute, Ministry and Life Institute, annual conventions, regional meetings, research, newsletters, and by providing consultation teams to evaluate formation programs upon request of the ordinary.

National Association of Pastoral Musicians

National Office, 962 Wayne Ave., Ste. 550, Silver Spring, MD 20910-4461. Tel: 240-247-3000 Fax: 240-247-3001 Email: npmsing@npm.org Web: www.npm.org. Jennifer Kluge, Exec. Dir., Bishop Mark J. Seitz, Episcopal Moderator

The National Association of Pastoral Musicians fosters the art of musical liturgy. The members of NPM serve the Catholic Church in the United States as musicians, clergy, liturgists, and other leaders of prayer. Three tiers of membership are available to meet the needs of clergy, religious, and lay pastoral musicians.

NPM programs include an annual national convention for musicians, clergy, and other leaders, as well as institutes for cantors, choir directors, youth, guitarists, and ensemble musicians in addition to programs in pastoral liturgy, chant and handbells and virtual training in liturgy and for cantors. NPM provides a Job Hotline to assist musicians seeking employment and parishes searching for musicians. The Association also sponsors certificate programs for organists, pianists, cantors, and those seeking additional information.

The Association is directed by a 7-member Board of Directors, advised by a 32-member NPM Council and served by a 5-person staff. NPM members serve the Association through 9 forums: affiliation & advocacy, certification, communications, cultural diversity, directors of music ministry, finance & development, membership, musical skills, and programming. Episcopal regions are represented by 14 regional representatives, elected by the members in their respective geographic areas.

Publications include *Pastoral Music* (five times annually); *Pastoral Music Notebook* (twice monthly newsletter by e-mail); *Sunday Word for Pastoral Musicians* (weekly by e-mail). The NPM website provides a wealth of free resources, including *Ministry Monday* (a weekly podcast), access to official church documents and recordings of the Chants of the Roman Missal (in English). Additionally, online resources for standard and premium members include a Planning Calendar, Choral Anthems, Choral Practice Tracks and Training Videos.

National Black Catholic Clergy Caucus

Resurrection Catholic Missions, Office, 2815 Forbes Dr. Montgomery, AL 36110.

Board of Directors—Rev. Kenneth Taylor, V.F., Pres., Rev. Clarence Williams, C.PP.S., Vice Pres., Rev. Manuel B. Williams, C.R., Sec., Deacon Jerry M. Lett, Treas., Lithonia, GA, Rev. Anthony M. Bozeman, S.S.J., Immediate Past Pres., Deacon Melvin Tardy, Deacon Larry Chatmon, Rev. Maurice J. Nutt, C.Ss.R., Rev. Norman Fischer, Bro. Douglas McMillan, O.F.M- .Conv., Men Religious Representative, Baltimore, MD, Deacon Joseph Connor, Pres., NABCD, Mr. Kareem Smith, Pres., NBCSA

The National Black Catholic Clergy Caucus serves as a fraternity for Black Catholic Clergy and Religious to support the spiritual, theological, educational and ministerial growth of its members. It is a vehicle to bring the contributions of the Black Community to fruition within the Catholic Church.

National Catholic Committee on Scouting Executive Committee (1934)

P.O. Box 949, Rociada, NM 87742. Tel. 214-714-6950. Bishop R. Daniel Conlon, Bishop of Joliet, IL, Episcopal Liaison, John Anthony, National Chairman (Ft. Worth, TX), Rev. Gerard Gentleman, National Chaplain (Massapequa, NY).

A voluntary organization of clergy and laymen, members include a chaplain and lay chairman from all the dioceses in the United States Conferences. It serves as an advisory committee to the Boy Scouts of America. It has the responsibility of promoting and guiding cooperative contracts between the proper authorities of the Catholic Church in the United States and the Boy Scouts of America.

National Catholic Educational Association (1904)

National Headquarters, 407 Bicksler Sq. SE, Leesburg, VA 20175. Tel: 800-711-6232 Fax: 703-243-0025. Bishop Gerald F. Kicanas, Bd. Chair; Lincoln Snyder, Pres./CEO.

The National Catholic Educational Association (NCEA) has been providing leadership to American Catholic school educators since 1904. NCEA's institutional and individual memberships represent Catholic school education in a variety of settings: preschools, elementary and secondary schools, diocesan offices and colleges and universities. NCEA is the professional membership organization for Catholic school educators. The association's vision: NCEA is a trusted partner that empowers all Catholic schools and their communities to flourish spiritually, academically and operationally; our mission: In service of the Gospel of Jesus Christ, NCEA strengthens Catholic school communities by convening all stakeholders and providing professional development, data, advocacy and resources to support faith and intellectual formation. It hosts an annual convention.

National Catholic Office for the Deaf (1971)

NCOD Office, 7202 Buchanan St. Landover Hills, MD 20784-2236. Tel: 301-577-1684, VP Tel: 301-841-8209 Email: info@ncod.org Web: www.ncod.org. Mrs. Joan Macy, NCOD Bd. Pres.; Rev. Msgr. Glenn L. Nelson, V.G., J.C.L.

The NCOD, established by the Catholic pastoral workers of the deaf in 1971 at Trinity College, Washington, DC is devoted to coordinating the Church's pastoral ministry to deaf and hard of hearing persons at the national level; developing special liturgies, catechetical texts and materials; organizing workshops, leadership programs, and national and regional pastoral workers meetings; coordinating a training program for ministers with the deaf; and serving as an information and referral center for all those involved in this special ministry as well as members of the deaf community and their families. Policy is established by a board of directors elected by the members.

Publication: pastoral journal, *Vision.*

National Catholic Partnership on Disability (NCPD)

415 Michigan Ave., N.E., Ste. 95 Washington, DC 20017-4501. Tel: 202-529-2933; Email: ncpd@ncpd.org; Web: www.ncpd.org. Charleen R. Katra, Exec. Dir., Michael J. Boyle, Ph.D., Chair.

Founded in 1982 to implement the U.S. Catholic Bishops' 1978 Pastoral Statement on Persons with Disabilities. NCPD trains diocesan and parish leadership nationally in disability ministry best practices, educates future pastoral leaders by working with universities and colleges, and develops advocacy resources for parishes and families. NCPD also collaborates with the USCCB and other national Catholic organizations to promote accessibility within the Church at large (e.g., catechesis, pro-life, liturgy, cultural diversity, youth ministry). NCPD's initiatives impact all disabilities at every stage of life. Mission is promoted through online courses, consultation, lectures, workshops, and conferences at regional, national, and international gatherings.

National Catholic Student Coalition (1988)

45 Lovett Ave. Newark, DE 19711. Tel: 302-368-4728 Email: ncsc@catholicstudent.org Web: www.catholicstudent.org

The National Catholic Student Coalition (NCSC) is a national coalition of Catholic student communities in institutes of higher education. The coalition provides a platform for Catholic students to reflect, speak, and act on issues within the university, the Church and society. The NCSC promotes the development of campus ministry and Catholic lay and religious leaders for the Church and society. The NCSC is a member of the International Movement of Catholic Students. Membership is open to groups or individuals associated with Catholic student groups in higher education. The NCSC holds an annual leadership conference.

Publication: *The Catholic Collegian.*

The National Center for Urban Ethnic Affairs (1971)

National Office, P.O. Box 20, Cardinal Station Washington, DC 20064. Tel: 202-319-5128 Tel: 202-319-6188 Dr. John A. Kromkowski, Pres., Rev. Msgr. Salvatore E. Polizzi, Chm.

"The great task incumbent on all men of good will is to restore the relations of the human family in truth, in justice, in love, and in freedom." (Pope John XXIII, Peace on Earth.) The independent program of this nonprofit organization has evolved from the efforts initiated by the former Task Force on Urban Problems of the United States Catholic Conference. Its aims and purposes are to continue the expression of the Catholic Church's concern for the problems facing our urban society. NCUEA promotes the celebration of cultural pluralism in America and bridges the gaps between groups of various ethnic and cultural traditions. The Center disseminates information, conducts research, develops and supports programs concerned with ethnic Americans and urban society. The Center in association with various community and church groups develops workshops, conferences, and programs related to the quality of human life, national priorities and the development of an urban mission strategy. The Center is also associated with public and private agencies in developing urban economic, social, and intercultural programs, etc.

In Word and Witness (formerly the National Conference for Catechetical Leadership)

810 7th St., NE, Washington, DC 20002. Tel: 202-750-4243; Web: inwordandwitness.org. Denise Utter, Pres.; Margaret Matijasevic, Exec. Dir.

In Word and Witness is a national Catholic community dedicated to evangelization and catechesis. Their inclusive membership consists of all who share their mission: to transform the work by reflecting Christ. They collaborate with and accompany their membership in their service to the Church by providing professional development resources, virtual and in-person gatherings, prayer experiences, and networking opportunities. In Word and Witness stands in solidarity with all God's people, seeks to authentically witness faith, and approaches organizational decision making with spirit of discernment.

National Conference of Catholic Airport Chaplains (NCCAC)

Chicago O'Hare International Airport, P.O. Box 66353 Chicago, IL 60666-0353. Tel: 773-686-2636 Fax: 773-280-5288 Email: office@nccac.us Web: www.nccac.us Rev. Fr. Michael G. Zaniolo, STL, CAC, Pres. (Chicago O'Hare & Midway International Airports), Rev. Canon Philip S. Majka, Vice Pres. (Washington Dulles International Airport), Ms. Susan E. Schneider, CAP, Sec. (Chicago O'Hare & Midway International Airport), Deacon Ray Oden, Treas. (Houston Bush Intercontinental Airport), Most Rev. Kevin Birmingham, Auxiliary Bishop of Chicago, Episcopal Liaison.

This Conference provides support and communication for all Catholics performing pastoral ministry to airport & airline workers, and travelers; in affiliation with USCCB Secretariat of Cultural Diversity in the Church, Subcommittee on Pastoral Care of Migrants, Refugees and Travelers.

National Council of Catholic Women

10335 Democracy Lane Unit 201, Fairfax VA 22030. Tel: 703-224-0990 Fax: 703-224-0991 Email: nccw01@nccw.org Web: www.nccw.org. Andrea Cecilli, Exec. Dir.

The National Council of Catholic Women acts through its members to support, empower, and educate all Catholic women in spirituality, leadership, and service. NCCW programs respond with Gospel values to the needs of the Church and society in the modern world.

Publications: quarterly, *Catholic Woman Magazine.*

National Federation for Catholic Youth Ministry, Inc. (NFCYM) (1981)

415 Michigan Ave., N.E., Ste. 40 Washington, DC 20017-4502. Tel: 202-636-3825 Email: info@nfcym.org Web: www.nfcym.org. Archbishop Nelson J. Pérez, Episcopal Advisor; Ms. Christina Lamas, Exec. Dir.; Mr. Paul Sifuentes, Chair.

NFCYM is a private, nonprofit membership organization, incorporated in the District of Columbia since 1981 (tax ID number 52-1260147) founded after a reorganization of the USCC Department of Education and the National CYO Federation. NFCYM's membership is comprised of dioceses, organizations, and individuals. Currently there are 24 members serving on the Board of Directors and seven staff members. NFCYM strives to support and strengthen those who accompany young people as they encounter and follow Jesus Christ. Members of NFCYM work through diocesan, regional and national structures to provide national leadership, resources and vision for adults and youth in youth ministry. Key services include the biennial; the annual National Catholic Youth Conference (for young people and their adult chaperones); the development of resources for parish leaders; religious recognitions for Catholic Girl Scouts/Camp Fire; forming/equipping/supporting parents, ministry leaders and other adults in their ministry to young people.

National Pastoral Center for the Chinese Apostolate, Inc.

Sacred Heart of Jesus, 4201 14th St. Plano, TX 75074. Tel: 972-516-8500 Rev. Vincent Lin Yu Ming, Dir.

North American Pastoral Center for Czech Catholics

235 S. Francisco Pl., Anaheim, CA 92807. Tel: 714-365-6503; Fax: 714-637-6789. Bishop Peter Esterka, Pres.

The Papal Foundation
Office, 2501 Seaport Dr., Ste. SH300, Chester, PA 19013. Tel: 610-535-6340; Fax: 610-535-6343. Mr. James V. Coffey, M.A., Vice Pres. Advancement
Cardinal Members—Cardinal Sean O'Malley, Chm., Cardinal Blase Cupich, Cardinal Daniel N. DiNardo, Cardinal Timothy M. Dolan, Cardinal Joseph Tobin, Cardinal Donald Wuerl. Lay Members: Robert Neal, Vice Chm. Carol Saeman. Cardinal Emeritus Members: Cardinal Roger Mahony, Cardinal Adam Maida, Cardinal Justin Rigali.
Trustees—Archbishop Samuel Aquila, Archbishop Gregory Aymond, Archbishop Wilton Gregory, Bishop Edward Burns, Bishop David Zubik, Eustace Mita, Pres., Timothy Busch, John Crowley, James Davis, William DeMucci, Dixon Doll, David Fischer, Ward Fitzgerald, Niall Gannon, Margie Hunter, Dennis Jilot, Sec., John Kennedy, Michael Mooney, Wayne Murdy, Treas., Robert Neal, Mark Rauenhorst, Carol Saeman, Michael Shannon, Michael Sullivan, Michael Shaughnessy, Dr. Tammy Carter Tenaglia, Eduardo Verastegui.

The Parish Evaluation Project
3073 S. Chase Ave., Ste. 320 Milwaukee, WI 53207. Tel: 414-483-7370; 414-520-3465 Fax: 414-483-7380 Email: pep@pitnet.net Web: www.pepparish.org Rev. Thomas P. Sweetser, S.J., Dir.
The Parish Evaluation Project, founded in 1973, is a nonprofit organization under the laws of Wisconsin, whose purpose is to provide religious and educational services to Catholic parishes in the United States in the areas of prayer and spiritual growth, leadership retreats, pastor guidance, staff development, pastoral council formation and other resources helpful in parish revitalization and renewal.

Pax Christi USA, National Catholic Peace Movement
415 Michigan Ave., N.E., Ste. 240, Washington, DC 20017-4502. Tel: 202-635-2741; Email: info@paxchristiusa.org. Johnny Zokovitch, Exec. Dir., Nadia Espinoza, Dir. of Administrative Operations, Lauren Bailey, National Field Organizer, Roxana Bendezu, Program Dir., Charlene Howard, Council Chair, Madeline Labriola, Vice-Chair, Diane Smith C.S.J., Sec., Rev. Fred Thelen, Treas., Bishop John Stowe, Bishop Pres.
Pax Christi USA is a national Catholic peace and justice movement, reaching more than half-a-million Catholics in the U.S. each year. Membership includes: individuals, state chapters, local groups, religious communities, parishes, college and high school chapters, U.S. bishops and clergy. Pax Christi USA is a section of Pax Christi International, with consultative status at the United Nations.
Publications: Peace Current, Advent & Lenten booklets along with peace education materials.

Religious Brothers Conference
National Office, 8819 Cross Island Pkwy., Bellerose, NY 11426. Tel: 917-780-5620; Email: rbc@todaysbrother.com; Web: www.todaysbrother.com
Board of Directors—Bro. David Eubank, M.S., Bro. John Skrodinsky, S.T., Bro. Peter O'Loughlin, C.F.C., Bro. Chris Patino, F.S.C., Bro. William Boslet, O.S.F., Exec. Sec., Bro. Allen Pacquing, S.M., Bro. Albert Rivera, F.M.S.; Bro. Thomas Sweeney, S.D.B., Bro. Bernie Dube, O.S.B.
Publications for members: Archival Editions of: Brothers' Voice; Reflections.

Religious Formation Conference
National Office, 5401 S. Cornell Ave., Ste. 304 Chicago, IL 60615. Tel: 773-675-8362. Sr. Ellen Dauwer, S.C., Ph.D., Exec. Dir.; Co-Chairs of the RFC Board: Nancy Gerth, SCN; Richard Hall, OMI.
A national Roman Catholic organization which assists women and men religious who are engaged in the ministry of initial and on-going formation in their congregations.

The Resource Center for Religious Institutes
8737 Colesville Rd., Ste. 610, Silver Spring, MD 20910. Tel: 301-589-8143 Fax: 301-589-2897 Email: trcri@trcri.org Web: www.trcri.org Sr. Sharon A. Euart, R.S.M., J.C.D., Exec. Dir. Lawrence J. Lundin, S.J., Assoc. Dir.; Christopher Fusco, J.D., Assoc. Dir.; Sabrina Hidalgo, Membership and Program Coord.
Serves its members institutes by providing integrated education, advocacy, consultation and collaborative initiatives to support religious institutes in meeting their current and emerging stewardship responsibilities.

The Slovak Catholic Federation (1911)
304 S. Elmer Ave. Sayre, PA 18840. Tel: 570-888-9641 Email: ahvoz87@gmail.com Web: www.slovakcatholicfederation.org, follow on facebook: Rev. Andrew S. Hvozdovic, V.F., Pres., Rev. Thomas Nasta, First Vice Pres., Rt. Rev. Gary A. Hoover, O.S.B., Mod., Dolores M. Evanko, Sec. & Treas.
Founded by Father Joseph Murgas at Wilkes-Barre, Pennsylvania as a nonprofit corporation to promote and coordinate religious and social activities among Slovak Catholic fraternal benefit societies, religious communities, Slovak parishes and individuals in order to address the pastoral needs of Slovak Catholics at home and abroad.

United States Catholic Mission Association
7300 Hanover Dr., Ste. 304, Greenbelt, MD 20770. Tel: 202-832-3112 Fax: 202-832- 3688 Email: uscma@uscatholicmission.org Web: www.uscatholicmission.org. Sr. Nancy Schramm, O.S.F., Pres.; Dr. Donald McCrabb, D.Min., Exec. Dir.
The USCMA was established September 1, 1981. Its members include U.S. missioners, mission organizations, missions, diocesan mission offices, and others concerned about the mission of the Church and global solidarity. It provides opportunities to convene, connect and collaborate on efforts to animate missionary disciples and accompany them through recruitment, preparation, service, integration and leadership. USCMA activities include webinars, video conferences and national meetings that highlight mission themes and issues and networking with other mission-related organizations.
Publications: monthly newsletter; study guides; educational programs.

NATIONAL ORGANIZATIONS WITH INDIVIDUAL I.R.S. RULINGS

Beginning Experience International Ministry Inc.
103 Biltmore St., Ste. 105, San Antonio, TX 78213-2260 Tel: 574-283-0279 Email: michelle.barrentine@beginningexperience.org; Web: www.beginningexperience.org. Bishop Patrick J. Zurek, D.D., Episcopal Moderator, Michelle Barrentine, Exec. Dir., JoAnne Paxton, Pres., Sandy Possehl, Treas., Dorothy DeGroot, Sec.
The Beginning Experience International Ministry offers copyrighted programs to help divorced, separated and widowed persons, as well as their families, work through the trauma of the loss of their spouse and make a new beginning in life. Its grief support programs were designed by and for Catholics and have their roots in sound Catholic tradition and the sacramental life of the Church. True to the ecumenical spirit in the Church since Vatican II, the programs have always been open to persons of all faiths. The Beginning Experience® Weekend originated in 1974 with the efforts of Sr. Josephine Stewart, SSMN & Mrs. Jo Lamia in Fort Worth, TX. It spread throughout the United States and other countries. Trained peer minister teams still offer the Beginning Experience® Weekend core program and other pre- and post-Weekend programs. Beginning in 2023, a weekly program will be available to dioceses and parishes for their use in grief support outreach.

Canon Law Society of America
415 Michigan Ave., N.E., Ste. 101 Washington, DC 20017. Tel: 202-832-2350 Fax: 202-832-2331 Email: generalsecretary@clsa.org. Rev. John Donovan, J.C.L., Pres.; Very Rev. Kenneth Riley, J.C.L., Vice Pres.; Rev. Gregory Luyet, J.C.L., Sec.; Very Rev. Jamin David, J.C.L., Treas.; Kathleen Butler, Gen. Sec.; Donna Miller, J.C.L., Exec. Coord.
A membership association of Bishops, Clergy, Religious and Laity for the purpose of promoting research and professional collaboration in the area of Canon Law.

Catholic Engaged Encounter, Inc.
4239 Shirley Rd. Richmond, VA 23225. Tel: 800-339-9790 Jim Dyk, Sandy Dyk, Rev. Jay Biber

Catholic Library Association
8550 United Plaza Blvd., Ste. 1001 Baton Rouge, LA 70809. Tel: 225-408-4417 Fax: 225-408-4422 Email: cla2@cathla.org Web: www.cathla.org

The Catholic Mutual Relief Society of America
10843 Old Mill Rd. Omaha, NE 68154-2600. Tel: 402-551-8765 Mr. Michael Intrieri, Pres. & CEO, Mr. Paul Peterson, Exec. Vice Pres. & COO

The Catholic Relief Insurance Company of America
76 St. Paul St., Ste. 500 Burlington, VT 05401. Tel: 402-551-8765 Mr. Michael Intrieri, Pres., Mr. Paul Peterson, Vice Pres.

Conference for Pastoral Planning and Council Development
P.O. Box 3523 Schenectady, NY 12303. Tel: 518-859-4506. Email: cppcd@cppcd.org Web: www.cppcd.org. Debra Trulli-Cassale, Admin. Dir.

National Association for Lay Ministry (NALM)
National Office, P.O. Box 256785, Chicago, IL 60625. Tel: 224-301-1968; Email: nalm@nalm.org Web: www.nalm.org
The National Association for Lay Ministry (NALM) is a collaborative organization of lay, vowed religious, and ordained ministers that empowers, advocates for, and develops lay pastoral leadership and promotes the growth of lay pastoral ministry in the Catholic Church. The organization also provides a national voice for Catholic lay ministry. NALM's membership is drawn from the more than 40,000 lay ecclesial ministers who devote their lives to the Church by working in parishes and dioceses. Other members are students preparing for ministry. Still others live out their baptismal call as generous volunteers to the Church. NALM has a long tradition of support from bishops, priests, deacons, publishers and academic institutions. Each, in its own way, collaborates with NALM to promote the empowerment of the laity in the Catholic Church.
NALM serves its members, and all lay ministers, through its national advocacy, professional standards for lay ecclesial ministers, an annual conference, kindred group discussions, seminars, listening sessions, and regular communication via email and social media. These sessions are presently offered virtually to support and provide on-going formation for lay ministers during covid. The ongoing work of NALM is done by its committees and working board.

The National Catholic Risk Retention Group, Inc.
National Office, 801 Warrenville Rd., Ste. 175 Lisle, IL 60532-4334. Tel: 630-725-0986 Tel: 877-486-2774 Fax: 630-725-1374 Dennis H. O'Hara, ARM, Pres. & CEO, Rev. Jay C. Haskin, M.Ch.A., Chm. Bd., Mr. John M. Scholl, C.P.C.U., A.I.M., Vice Pres., Mr. John J. Maxwell, CPA, Treas.
The Company is wholly owned by 52 Catholic (Arch) Dioceses and one Catholic Risk Pooling Trust. It underwrites excess liability insurance for Dioceses and other Church organizations listed in the Official Catholic Directory. Coverage is always subject to a minimum self-insured retention or underlying coverage of $250,000. Maximum limits of coverage available are $14,750,000. The company has the capability to underwrite insurance in all states, Territories and Possessions of the U.S.

National Catholic Young Adult Ministry Association

National Office, 415 Michigan Ave., N.E., Ste. 40 Washington, DC 20017. Email: info@ncyama.org Web: www.ncyama.org Amy McEntee, Exec. Dir.

Founded in 1982, NCYAMA is an organization supporting those who minister to and with single and married people in their late teens, twenties or thirties. We develop and promote programs and resources while providing opportunities for networking and communication. We advocate for the full integration of young adults in the life of the Catholic faith community in order to connect them with Jesus, the Church, the mission of the Church and their peers.

Publication: electronic newsletter.

National Conference of Diocesan Vocation Directors (1962)

National Office, 440 W. Neck Rd. Huntington, NY 11743. Tel: 631-645-8210 Email: office@ncdvd.org Web: www.ncdvd.org Rev. Brian Buettner, Pres., Rev. Neal Hock, Treas., Mrs. Rosemary C. Sullivan, Exec. Dir.

NCDVD is a professional organization that supports, educates and provides resources for diocesan vocation directors as they promote all Church vocations, but particularly diocesan priesthood. This organization serves all dioceses associated with the United States Conference of Catholic Bishops.

Online resources; documents of interest & training institutes; Meetings annually for Regional Conferences and a National Convention.

The National Federation of Priests' Councils (1968)

National Office, 333 N. Michigan Ave., Ste. 1114 Chicago, IL 60601-4002. Tel: 312-442-9700 Tel: 888-271-6372 Email: nfpc@nfpc.org Web: www.nfpc.org Rev. Anthony Cutcher, Pres., Mr. Terry Oldes, Financial Dir., Mr. Alan Szafraniec, Mng. Dir., Connie Awrey, Communications Dir.

The NFPC promotes the communion, brotherhood and solidarity of priests and bishops through the arch/diocesan priests' councils, offering services to support and facilitate communication between councils. NFPC is a clearinghouse for arch/dioceses promoting the sharing of knowledge and resources; offers advocacy for priests with the USCCB as a contributing organization to the Clergy, Consecrated Life and Vocations Committee; offers programs and publications on research and best practices; edits, condenses and shares information from Councils' minutes; partners with other national Catholic organizations; and offers an annual National Convocation of Priests to encourage fraternity, idea exchange, fellowship, and rejuvenation. All arch/diocesan priests' councils are members of NFPC; active members support NFPC financially. A Council of Consultors and a Board of Directors determine the direction of the organization, which is implemented by the NFPC President during a 5-year term.

Publications: NFPC This Week e-letter; Touchstone periodical; Income Tax for Priests Clergy (updated each year); and research results: Same Call Different Men and The Laborer is Worthy of His Hire.

National Service Committee of the Catholic Charismatic Renewal of the United States, Inc. (NSC)

10745 Babcock Blvd, Gibsonia, PA 15044. Mr. Ron Riggins, Chm., Alicia Hartle, Exec. Dir.

Over 70 Renewal Leaders from across the nation serve as elected Board Members and appointed Council Members in our work to foster baptism in the Holy Spirit in the life of the Church in the United States and throughout the world, to broaden and deepen the understanding that baptism in the Holy Spirit is the Christian inheritance of all, and to strengthen the Catholic Charismatic Renewal. The NSC recently launched a new name, "Pentecost Today USA," and a new mission in response to the CHARIS commission to: BRING baptism in the Holy Spirit to the whole Church, BUILD unity in the Body of Christ, and SERVE the Poor.

We support Renewal ministries, dioceses, parishes, universities, and seminaries in their work to raise up, connect, and equip Renewal Leaders through: 1) *regional and national events*; 2) *Pentecost Today Magazine and theological publications* on baptism in the Holy Spirit and the charismatic gifts; 3) *National Renewal Database* of over 2,800 Renewal Centers, Prayer Groups, Covenant Communities, Religious, and Diocesan Liaisons; 4) *support of Renewal Organizations* including CHARIS USA.

Our national headquarters are located at *The Ark* and *The Dove* in Pittsburgh, PA, and our new website is: **PentecostTodayUSA.org**.

Worldwide Marriage Encounter

275 W. Hospitality Ln., Ste. 203 San Bernardino, CA 92408. Tel: 909-332-7309; Fax: 909-332-7409; Email: wwmeoffice@wwme.com.

Secretariat Team—Joe Talarico; Sue Talarico; Rev. Salvador Ahumada.

Worldwide Marriage Encounter (WWME) is the largest and most popular faith-based marriage enrichment organization in the world. We proclaim the value of marriage and holy orders in the Church and in the world. We offer a peer-to-peer experience, typically over a weekend, where married couples, priest and religious can pause and reflect privately on the meaning of their vocations and are given the tools for nurturing their love.

WWME annually presents 2,000 experiences in nearly 100 countries. In North America, the Marriage Encounter experience is offered in English, Spanish, French and Korean by 1,600 "presenting team" couples and priests. There are Worldwide Marriage Encounter communities supporting couples and priests and religious in almost every diocese of USA and Canada.

Find more information at: www.wwme.org and www.facebook.com/worldwidemarriageencounter.

MISCELLANEOUS

Catholic Committee for Refugees & Children

3211 Fourth St., N.E. Washington, DC 20017-1194. Fax: 202-722-8755 Ambassador Johnny Young, Pres.

Incorporated since 1954, the Catholic Committee for Refugees and Children was founded to counsel and cooperate with European refugees during and after World War II. Since that time its mission has been expanded to include service to refugees worldwide. It has a special mandate from the bishops concerning its work with children through international child welfare, child care or placement, and international adoption. The USCCB Committee on Migration serves as the Board of Directors for CCRC.

Alphabetical List of Places in the United States

This comprehensive list includes all cities and towns in the United States in which a Catholic Institution is located.

The abbreviations identify each city or town to the corresponding Diocese or Archdiocese.

Abbeville, LA	LAF
SC	CHR
Abbott, TX	FWT
Abbottstown, PA	HBG
Aberdeen, MD	BAL
MS	JKS
SD	SFS
WA	SEA
Abernathy, TX	LUB
Abilene, KS	SAL
TX	SAN
Abingdon, IL	PEO
MD	BAL
VA	RIC
Abington, MA	BO
PA	PH
PA	SYM
Abiquiu, NM	SFE
Abita Springs, LA	NO
Absecon, NJ	CAM
Acme, MI	GLD
Acton, MA	BO
ME	PRT
Acushnet, MA	FR
Acworth, GA	ATL
Ada, MI	GR
MN	CR
OH	COL
OK	OKL
Adams, MA	SPR
MN	WIN
NY	OG
WI	LC
Adamsville, AL	BIR
Addison, IL	JOL
NY	ROC
Adel, GA	SAV
IA	DM
Adelanto, CA	SB
Adelphi, MD	WDC
Adena, OH	STU
Adrian, MI	LAN
MN	WIN
Advance, MO	SPC
Affton, MO	STL
Agawam, MA	SPR
Agua Dulce, TX	CC
Aguilar, CO	PBL
Ahoskie, NC	R
Aiea, HI	HON
Aiken, SC	CHR
Ainsworth, NE	GI
Aitkin, MN	DUL
Ajo, AZ	TUC
Akron, CO	DEN
NY	BUF
OH	CLV
OH	SJP
OH	NTN
Alakanuk, AK	FBK
Alameda, CA	OAK
Alamo, TX	BWN
Alamogordo, NM	LSC
Alamosa, CO	PBL
Albany, CA	OAK
GA	SAV
IL	RCK
KY	L
LA	BR
MN	SCL
NY	ALB
OR	P
TX	FWT
Albemarle, NC	CHL
Albers, IL	BEL
Albert Lea, MN	WIN
Albertville, MN	STP
Albia, IA	DAV
Albion, IN	FTW
MI	KAL
NE	OM
NY	BUF
PA	E
RI	PRO
Albuquerque, NM	HPM
NM	SFE
Alburgh, VT	BUR
Alcoa, TN	KNX
Alden, NY	BUF
Aledo, IL	PEO
TX	FWT
Alexander City, AL	BIR
Alexandria, IN	LFT
KY	COV
LA	ALX
MN	SCL
SD	SFS
VA	ARL
VA	WDC
Alexandria Bay, NY	OG
Alfred, ME	PRT
NY	BUF
Algoma, WI	GB
Algona, IA	SC
Algonquin, IL	RCK
Alhambra, CA	LA
Alice, TX	CC
Aliquippa, PA	PBR
PA	PIT
PA	SJP
Aliso Viejo, CA	ORG
Allegan, MI	KAL
Allegany, NY	BUF
Allen, TX	DAL
Allen Park, MI	DET
MI	PRM
Allendale, MI	GR
NJ	NEW
Allenspark, CO	DEN
Allenton, MI	DET
WI	MIL
Allentown, NJ	TR
PA	ALN
PA	OLD
PA	PSC
Alleyton, TX	VIC
Alliance, NE	GI
OH	Y
Allison Park, PA	PIT
Allston, MA	BO
Alma, MI	SAG
Alma Center, WI	LC
Almond, WI	LC
Aloha, OR	P
Alpena, MI	GLD
Alpha, NJ	MET
Alpharetta, GA	ATL
Alpine, AZ	GLP
CA	SD
TX	ELP
Alsip, IL	CHI
Alta Loma, CA	SB
Altadena, CA	LA
Altamont, IL	SFD
NY	ALB
Altamonte Springs, FL	ORL
Alton, IA	SC
IL	SFD
TX	BWN
Altona, NY	OG
Altoona, IA	DM
PA	ALT
PA	SJP
WI	LC
Alturas, CA	SAC
Altus, AR	LR
OK	OKL
Alva, OK	OKL
Alvin, TX	GAL
Alviso, CA	SJ
Ama, LA	NO
Amargosa Valley, NV	LAV
Amarillo, TX	AMA
Ambia, IN	LFT
Ambler, PA	PH
Amboy, IL	RCK
Ambridge, PA	PBR
PA	PIT
PA	SJP
Amelia, LA	HT
OH	CIN
Amenia, NY	NY
American Canyon, CA	SR
American Falls, ID	B
American Fork, UT	SLC
Americus, GA	SAV
Amery, WI	SUP
Ames, IA	DUB
Amesbury, MA	BO
Amherst, MA	SPR
NY	BUF
OH	CLV
VA	RIC
WI	LC
Amite, LA	BR
Amity, OR	P
Amityville, NY	RVC
Amory, MS	JKS
Amsterdam, NY	ALB
NY	STF
OH	STU
Anaconda, MT	HEL
Anacortes, WA	SEA
Anacostia, Washington, DC	WDC
Anadarko, OK	OKL
Anaheim, CA	HPM
CA	ORG
Anahuac, TX	BEA
Anamoose, ND	FAR
Anamosa, IA	DUB
Anchorage, AK	AJ
AK	HPM
Andale, KS	WCH
Andalusia, AL	MOB
IL	PEO
Anderson, CA	SAC
IN	LFT
SC	CHR
TX	GAL
Andover, KS	WCH
MA	BO
NJ	PAT
NY	BUF
OH	Y
Andrews, NC	CHL
TX	SAN
Angels Camp, CA	STO
Angleton, TX	GAL
Angola, IN	FTW
NY	BUF
Angus, MN	CR
Aniak, AK	FBK
Ankeny, IA	DM
Ann Arbor, MI	LAN
MI	OLL
Anna, IL	BEL
OH	CIN
Annandale, MN	STP
NJ	MET
VA	ARL
VA	PSC
Annapolis, MD	BAL
Annawan, IL	PEO
Anniston, AL	BIR
Annville, PA	HBG
Anoka, MN	STP
Anson, TX	LUB
Ansonia, CT	HRT
CT	STF
Anthem, AZ	PHX
Anthony, NM	LSC
Antigo, WI	GB
Antioch, CA	OAK
IL	CHI
TN	NSH
Anton Chico, NM	SFE
Antonito, CO	PBL
Anza, CA	SB
Apache Junction, AZ	TUC
Apalachicola, FL	PT
Apex, NC	R
NC	SYM
Apollo, PA	GBG
Apopka, FL	ORL
FL	SJP
Apple Creek, MO	STL
Apple Valley, CA	SB
Applegate, CA	SAC
Appleton, MN	NU
WI	GB
Appomattox, VA	RIC
Aptos, CA	MRY
Aransas Pass, TX	CC
Arbor Vitae, WI	SUP
Arcade, NY	BUF
Arcadia, CA	LA
FL	VEN
WI	LC
Arcata, CA	SR
Archbald, PA	SCR
Archbold, OH	TOL
Arcola, IL	SFD
Arden, NC	CHL
Ardmore, OK	OKL
PA	PH
Ardsley, NY	NY
PA	PH
Argo, IL	CHI
Argusville, ND	FAR
Argyle, MN	CR
MO	JC
TX	FWT
Arkadelphia, AR	LR
Arkansas City, KS	WCH
Arkansaw, WI	LC
Arlington, MA	BO
MN	NU
SD	SFS
TX	FWT
TX	POC
VA	ARL
VT	BUR
WA	SEA
Arlington Heights, IL	CHI
Arma, KS	WCH
Armada, MI	DET
Armonk, NY	NY
Armour, SD	SFS
Armstrong, IA	SC
Armstrong Creek, WI	GB
Arnaudville, LA	LAF
Arnold, MO	STL
PA	SJP
Arroyo Grande, CA	MRY
Arroyo Seco, NM	SFE
Artesia, CA	LA
NM	LSC
Arvada, CO	DEN
CO	SYM
Arvin, CA	FRS
Asbury Park, NJ	TR
Ash Fork, AZ	PHX
Ashaway, RI	PRO
Ashburn, VA	ARL
Ashburnham, MA	WOR
Ashdown, AR	LR
Asheboro, NC	CHL
Asherton, TX	LAR
Asheville, NC	CHL
Ashford, CT	NOR
Ashfork, AZ	PHX
Ashkum, IL	JOL
Ashland, IL	SFD
KS	DOD
KY	LEX
MA	BO
MT	GF
NE	LIN
OH	CLV
OR	P
PA	ALN
VA	RIC

WI SUP
Ashland City, TN NSH
Ashley, PA SCR
Ashtabula, OH Y
Ashton, IA SC
Aspen, CO DEN
Aspinwall, PA PIT
Assonet, MA FR
Assumption, IL SFD
Aston, PA PH
Astoria, NY BRK
OR P
Atascadero, CA MRY
CA NTN
Atchison, KS KCK
Atco, NJ CAM
Athens, AL BIR
GA ATL
NY ALB
OH STU
TN KNX
TX TYL
WI LC
WV WH
Atherton, CA SFR
Athol, MA WOR
Athol Springs, NY BUF
Atkins, AR LR
Atkinson, IL PEO
NE OM
Atlanta, GA ATL
GA NTN
GA SAM
TX TYL
Atlantic, IA DM
Atlantic Beach, FL STA
Atlantic City, NJ CAM
Atlantic Highlands, NJ TR
Atmore, AL MOB
Attica, IN LFT
NY BUF
OH TOL
Attleboro, MA FR
Attleboro Falls, MA FR
Atwater, CA FRS
Atwood, KS SAL
Au Sable Forks, NY OG
AuGres, MI SAG
Auburn, AL MOB
CA SAC
IA SC
IL SFD
IN FTW
KY OWN
MA WOR
ME PRT
MI SAG
NE LIN
NH MAN
NY ROC
WA SEA
Auburn Hills, MI DET
Auburndale, WI LC
Audubon, IA DM
PA PH
Augusta, GA NTN
GA SAV
KS WCH
KY COV
ME PRT
MI KAL
MO STL
Ault, CO DEN
Aumsville, OR P
Auriesville, NY ALB
Aurora, CO DEN
IL JOL
IL ROM
IL RCK
IN IND
MN DUL
MO SPC
NE LIN
NY ROC
OH Y
Austin, MN WIN
TX AUS
TX OLL
Austintown, OH Y
Ava, MO SPC
Avalon, CA LA
NJ CAM
Ave Maria, FL VEN
Avella, PA PBR
PA PIT
Avenal, CA FRS
Avenel, NJ MET
Avenue, MD WDC
Averill Park, NY ALB
Avilla, IN FTW
Aviston, IL BEL
Avoca, IA DM
PA SCR
Avon, CT HRT
MA BO
MN SCL
NY ROC
OH CLV
Avon By The Sea, NJ TR
Avon Lake, OH CLV
Avon Park, FL VEN
Avondale, AZ OLD
AZ PHX
CO PBL
LA NO
PA PH
Avonmore, PA GBG
Axtell, KS KCK
Ayrshire, IA SC
Aztec, NM GLP
Azusa, CA LA
Babbitt, MN DUL
Babylon, NY RVC
Bad Axe, MI SAG
Baden, PA PIT
Bagdad, AZ PHX
Bagley, MN CR
Bailey, CO COS
Baileys Harbor, WI GB
Baileyville, KS KCK
Bainbridge, GA SAV
NY SY
Bainbridge Island, WA SEA
Bairdford, PA PIT
Baker, MT GF
Baker City, OR BAK
Bakersfield, CA FRS
Bakerstown, PA PIT
Bala Cynwyd, PA PH
Baldwin, KS KCK
LA LAF
MI GR
NY RVC
Baldwin City, KS KCK
Baldwin Park, CA LA
Baldwinsville, NY SY
Baldwinville, MA WOR
Ball, LA ALX
Ballinger, TX SAN
Ballston Lake, NY ALB
Ballston Spa, NY ALB
Ballwin, MO STL
Bally, PA ALN
Balmorhea, TX ELP
Balsam Lake, WI SUP
Baltic, CT NOR
Baltimore, MD BAL
MD PHU
MD POC
MD SYM
MD PSC
Bancroft, IA SC
Bandera, TX SAT
Bandon, OR P
Bangor, ME PRT
MI KAL
PA ALN
WI LC
Banks, OR P
Bannister, MI SAG
Banquete, TX CC
Bantam, CT HRT
Baptistown, NJ MET
Bar Harbor, ME PRT
Baraboo, WI MAD
Barberton, OH CLV
OH PRM
Barbourville, KY LEX
Bardonia, NY NY
Bardstown, KY L
Bardwell, KY OWN
Barefoot Bay, FL ORL
Barhamsville, VA RIC
Bark River, MI MAR
Barker, NY BUF
Barling, AR LR
Barnegat, NJ TR
Barnesville, MD WDC
MN CR
OH STU
PA ALN
Barnwell, SC CHR
Barre, VT BUR
Barrett Station, TX GAL
Barrington, IL CHI
RI PRO
Barron, WI SUP
Barrow, AK FBK
Barryville, NY NY
Barstow, CA SB
Bartelso, IL BEL
Bartlesville, OK TLS
Bartlett, IL CHI
TN MEM
Barton, VT BUR
Bartonville, IL PEO
Bartow, FL ORL
Bascom, OH TOL
Basehor, KS KCK
Basile, LA LAF
Basking Ridge, NJ MET
Bassfield, MS BLX
Bastrop, LA SHP
TX AUS
Batavia, IL RCK
NY BUF
OH CIN
Batesburg–Leesville, SC CHR
Batesville, AR LR
IN IND
MS JKS
Bath, NY ROC
OH CLV
PA ALN
Bathgate, ND FAR
Baton Rouge, LA BR
LA LKC
Battle Creek, MI KAL
NE OM
Battle Ground, WA SEA
Battle Lake, MN SCL
Battle Mountain, NV RNO
Baudette, MN CR
Baxley, GA SAV
Bay City, MI PRM
MI SAG
TX VIC
Bay Head, NJ TR
Bay Minette, AL MOB
Bay Point, CA OAK
Bay Shore, NY RVC
Bay St. Louis, MS BLX
Bay Village, OH CLV
Bayard, NM LSC
Bayfield, WI SUP
Bayonne, NJ NEW
NJ OLD
NJ PSC
Bayou La Batre, AL MOB
Bayport, MN STP
Bayside, NY BRK
Baytown, TX GAL
Bayville, NJ TR
NY RVC
Beach, ND BIS
Beacon, NY NY
Beacon Falls, CT HRT
Bear, DE SYM
DE WIL
Bear Creek, PA SCR
Beardsley, MN NU
Beardstown, IL SFD
Beatrice, NE LIN
Beattie, KS KCK
Beattyville, KY LEX
Beaufort, SC CHR
Beaumont, CA SB
TX BEA
Beaver, PA PBR
PA PIT
Beaver Crossing, NE LIN
Beaver Dam, AZ PHX
KY OWN
WI MIL
Beaver Falls, PA PIT
Beaver Island, MI GLD
Beaver Meadows, PA PSC
Beavercreek, OH CIN
Beaverdale, PA PBR
Beaverton, OR P
OR OLL
Beaverville, IL JOL
Beckemeyer, IL BEL
Beckley, WV WH
Bedford, IN IND
MA BO
NH MAN
NY NY
OH CLV
OH PRM
PA ALT
TX FWT
VA RIC
Bee, NE LIN
Beebe, AR LR
Beech Grove, IN IND
Beemer, NE OM
Beeville, TX CC
Bel Air, MD BAL
Bel Aire, KS WCH
Belchertown, MA SPR
Belcourt, ND FAR
Belding, MI GR
Belen, NM SFE
Belfield, ND BIS
ND STN
Belgrade, MN SCL
MT HEL
Bell City, LA LKC
Bell Gardens, CA LA
Bella Vista, AR LR
Bellaire, MI GLD
OH STU
Belle, MO JC
WV WH
Belle Chasse, LA NO
Belle Fontaine, AL MOB
Belle Fourche, SD RC
Belle Glade, FL PMB
Belle Harbor, NY BRK
Belle Plaine, MN STP
Belle Rose, LA BR
Belle Vernon, PA GBG
Belleair, FL SP
Bellefontaine, OH CIN
Bellefonte, PA ALT
Bellerose, NY BRK
Belleview, FL ORL
Belleville, IL BEL
KS SAL
MI DET
NJ NEW
WI MAD
Bellevue, IA DUB
KY COV
NE OM
OH TOL
PA PIT
WA SEA
Bellflower, CA LA
Bellingham, MA BO
WA SEA
Bellmawr, NJ CAM
Bellmore, NY RVC
Bellows Falls, VT BUR
Bellport, NY RVC
Bellville, TX GAL
Bellwood, IL CHI
IL SYM
NE LIN
PA ALT
Belmar, NJ TR
Belmont, CA SFR
MA BO
MA OLN
MI GR
NC CHL
NH MAN
NY BUF
WI MAD
Beloit, KS SAL
WI MAD
WI MIL
Belpre, KS DOD
Belt, MT GF
Belton, MO KC
TX AUS
Beltsville, MD PSC
MD WDC
Belvidere, IL RCK
NJ MET
Belzoni, MS JKS
Bemidji, MN CR
Bemus Point, NY BUF
Ben Bolt, TX CC
Benavides, TX CC
Bend, OR BAK
Bendena, KS KCK
Benedict, MD WDC
Benedicta, ME PRT
Benet Lake, WI MIL
Benicia, CA SAC
Benkelman, NE LIN
Bennington, VT BUR
Bensalem, PA PH
Bensenville, IL JOL
IL SCL
IL SYM
Benson, AZ TUC
MN NU
Bentleyville, PA PIT
Benton, AR LR
IL BEL
LA SHP
MO SPC
TN KNX
WI MAD
Benton City, WA YAK
Benton Harbor, MI KAL
Bentonville, AR LR
Benwood, WV WH
Berea, KY LEX
OH CLV
Beresford, SD SFS

Bergen, NY BUF
Bergenfield, NJ NEW
Berkeley, CA OAK
Berkeley Heights, NJ NEW
Berkeley Springs, WV WH
Berkley, MI DET
MI SYM
Berlin, MA WOR
MD WDC
MD WIL
NH MAN
NJ CAM
WI MAD
Bernalillo, NM SFE
Bernardsville, NJ MET
Berryville, AR LR
VA ARL
Berthoud, CO DEN
Berwick, LA LAF
PA HBG
PA PHU
Berwyn, IL CHI
IL SYM
PA PH
Bessemer, AL BIR
MI MAR
Bethalto, IL SFD
Bethany, MO KC
WV WH
Bethany Beach, DE WIL
Bethel, AK FBK
CT BGP
OH CIN
VT BUR
Bethel Park, PA PIT
Bethesda, MD WDC
Bethlehem, CT HRT
PA ALN
PA PHU
PA PSC
Bethpage, NY RVC
Bettendorf, IA DAV
Beulah, ND BIS
Beverly, MA BO
OH STU
Beverly Hills, CA LA
CA SYM
FL SP
MI DET
Beverly Shores, IN GRY
Bicknell, IN EVN
Biddeford, ME PRT
Big Bear Lake, CA LA
CA SB
Big Bend, WI MIL
Big Lake, AK AJ
MN SCL
TX SAN
Big Pine Key, FL MIA
Big Rapids, MI GR
Big Spring, TX SAN
Big Stone City, SD SFS
Big Stone Gap, VA RIC
Big Sur, CA MRY
Big Timber, MT GF
Bigelow, AR LR
Bigfork, MN DUL
MT HEL
Billerica, MA BO
Billings, MO SPC
MT GF
Biloxi, MS BLX
Binghamton, NY SY
NY PSC
Birch Run, MI SAG
Bird Island, MN NU
Birmingham, AL BIR
AL NTN
AL OLL
MI DET
MI GLD
Birmingham (Hoover), AL BIR
Birnamwood, WI GB
Bisbee, AZ TUC
ND FAR
Biscoe, NC CHL
Bishop, CA FRS
TX CC
Bismarck, ND BIS
Bixby, OK TLS
Black Canyon City, AZ PHX
Black Creek, WI GB
Black Diamond, WA SEA
Black Mountain, NC CHL
Black River, NY OG
Black River Falls, WI LC
Blackfoot, ID B
Blacksburg, VA RIC
Blackstone, MA WOR
VA RIC
Blackwell, OK OKL
Blackwood, NJ CAM
Bladensburg, MD WDC
Blaine, MN STP
Blair, NE OM
Blairstown, NJ MET
Blairsville, GA ATL
PA GBG
Blakely, GA SAV
Blanco, NM GLP
TX AUS
Blasdell, NY BUF
Blauvelt, NY NY
NY CAM
Blenker, WI LC
Blessing, TX VIC
Block Island, RI PRO
Bloomer, WI LC
Bloomfield, CT HRT
IN EVN
NJ NEW
NJ PAT
NM GLP
Bloomfield Hills, MI DET
Bloomfield Township, MI EST
Blooming Prairie, MN WIN
Bloomingdale, IL JOL
NY OG
OH STU
Bloomington, CA SB
IL PEO
IN IND
MN STP
TX VIC
WI MAD
Bloomsburg, PA HBG
Bloomsbury, NJ MET
Bloomsdale, MO STL
Blountstown, FL PT
Blue Bell, PA PH
Blue Earth, MN WIN
Blue Grass, IA DAV
Blue Island, IL CHI
Blue Point, NY RVC
Blue Ridge, GA ATL
Blue Springs, MO KC
Bluefield, WV WH
Bluffton, IN FTW
MN SCL
OH TOL
SC CHR
Blythe, CA SB
Blytheville, AR LR
Blythewood, SC CHR
Boalsburg, PA ALT
Boardman, OH Y
OH ROM
OH PBR
OR BAK
Bobtown, PA PIT
Boca Grande, FL VEN
Boca Raton, FL PMB
Bode, IA SC
Boerne, TX SAT
Bogalusa, LA NO
Bogota, NJ NEW
Bohemia, NY RVC
Boise, ID B
Bokeelia, FL VEN
Bolingbrook, IL JOL
Bolivar, MO SPC
NY BUF
OH COL
PA GBG
TN MEM
Bolton, CT NOR
Bolton Landing, NY ALB
Bonduel, WI GB
Bonesteel, SD RC
Bonfield, IL JOL
Bonham, TX DAL
Bonifay, FL PT
Bonita, CA SD
Bonita Springs, FL VEN
Bonne Terre, MO STL
Bonner, MT HEL
Bonners Ferry, ID B
Bonnots Mill, MO JC
Boomer, WV WH
Boone, IA SC
NC CHL
Booneville, AR LR
MS JKS
Boonsboro, MD BAL
Boonton, NJ PAT
Boonville, IN EVN
MO JC
NC CHL
NY SY
Boothwyn, PA PH
Bordelonville, LA ALX
Bordentown, NJ TR
Borger, TX AMA
Borrego Springs, CA SD
Boscobel, WI MAD
Bossier City, LA SHP
Boston, MA BO
NY BUF
Boswell, PA ALT
Bothell, WA SEA
Botkins, OH CIN
Bottineau, ND FAR
Boulder, CO DEN
MT HEL
Boulder City, NV LAV
Boulder Creek, CA MRY
Boulder Junction, WI SUP
Bound Brook, NJ MET
Bountiful, UT SLC
Bourbonnais, IL JOL
Bourg, LA HT
Bovina, TX AMA
Bowdle, SD SFS
Bowie, MD WDC
Bowling Green, KY OWN
MO JC
OH TOL
Bowman, ND BIS
Bowmansville, NY BUF
Box Elder, MT GF
Boyce, LA ALX
Boyceville, WI LC
Boyd, WI LC
Boyertown, PA ALN
Boylston, MA WOR
Boyne City, MI GLD
Boynton Beach, FL PMB
Boys Town, NE OM
Bozeman, MT HEL
Brackettville, TX SAT
Braddock, PA PIT
Bradenton, FL VEN
Bradenville, PA PBR
Bradford, OH CIN
PA E
VT BUR
Bradley, IL JOL
Bradley Beach, NJ TR
Bradshaw, MD BAL
Brady, TX SAN
Brady's Bend, PA GBG
Braham, MN SCL
Braidwood, IL JOL
Brainard, NE LIN
Brainerd, MN DUL
Braintree, MA BO
Braithwaite, LA NO
Branchville, NJ PAT
Brandenburg, KY L
Brandon, FL SP
FL SYM
MN SCL
SD SFS
VT BUR
Brandywine, MD WDC
Branford, CT HRT
Branson, MO SPC
Brant Beach, NJ TR
Brasher Falls, NY OG
Brattleboro, VT BUR
Brawley, CA SD
Brazil, IN IND
Brazoria, TX GAL
Brea, CA ORG
Breaux Bridge, LA LAF
Breckenridge, MN SCL
TX FWT
Brecksville, OH CLV
OH PRM
Breda, IA SC
Breese, IL BEL
Bremen, IN FTW
OH COL
Bremerton, WA SEA
Bremond, TX AUS
Brenham, TX AUS
Brentwood, CA OAK
MO STL
NY RVC
TN NSH
Brevard, NC CHL
Brewerton, NY SY
Brewster, MA FR
MN WIN
NY NY
WA SPK
Brewton, AL MOB
Briarcliff Manor, NY NY
Briarwood, NY BRK
Brick, NJ TR
Brick Town, NJ TR
Bridal Veil, OR P
Bridge City, TX BEA
Bridgehampton, NY RVC
Bridgeport, CT BGP
CT STF
NE GI
NY SY
OH STU
PA PHU
PA POC
TX FWT
WV WH
Bridger, MT GF
Bridgeton, MO STL
NJ CAM
Bridgeview, IL CHI
Bridgeville, PA PIT
Bridgewater, MA BO
NJ MET
SD SFS
Bridgman, MI KAL
Bridgton, ME PRT
Brigantine, NJ CAM
Briggsville, WI MAD
Brigham City, UT SLC
Brighton, CO DEN
IL SFD
MA BO
MA ROM
MI DET
MI LAN
Brillion, WI GB
Brimfield, IL PEO
MA SPR
Brimley, MI MAR
Brinkley, AR LR
Bristol, CT HRT
IN FTW
PA PH
PA PHU
RI PRO
VA RIC
VT BUR
WI MIL
Bristow, IN IND
VA ARL
Britton, SD SFS
Broad Brook, CT HRT
Broadalbin, NY ALB
Broadus, MT GF
Broadview, IL CHI
Broadview Heights, OH CLV
Brockport, NY ROC
Brockton, MA BO
MA SAM
Brockway, PA E
Brodheadsville, PA SCR
Broken Arrow, OK TLS
Broken Bow, NE GI
Bromley, AL MOB
Bronson, MI KAL
Bronx, NY NY
NY STF
NY SYM
NY CHI
NY MCE
Bronxville, NY NY
Brook Park, OH CLV
Brookeville, MD WDC
Brookfield, CT BGP
IL CHI
MO JC
WI MIL
Brookhaven, MS JKS
PA PH
Brookings, OR P
SD SFS
Brookline, MA BO
MA ROM
Brooklyn, CT NOR
IA DAV
MI LAN
NY NY
NY BRK
NY NTN
NY STF
NY SAM
OH CLV
OH NTN
OH SJP
Brooklyn Center, MN STP
Brooklyn Park, MN STP
Brooksville, FL SP
FL SJP
KY COV
MS JKS
Brookville, IN IND
NY RVC
PA E
Broomall, PA PH
Broomfield, CO DEN
Brooten, MN SCL
Broussard, LA LAF

Place	Code
Browerville, MN	SCL
Brown Deer, WI	MIL
Brownfield, TX	LUB
Browning, MT	HEL
Browns Mills, NJ	TR
Browns Valley, MN	SCL
Brownsburg, IN	IND
Brownstown, MI	DET
Brownsville, PA	GBG
PA	PBR
TN	MEM
TX	BWN
Brownville, NY	OG
Brownwood, TX	SAN
Bruce, MS	JKS
Bruno, NE	LIN
Brunswick, GA	SAV
MD	BAL
ME	PRT
MO	JC
OH	CLV
OH	PRM
Brush, CO	DEN
Brushton, NY	OG
Brusly, LA	BR
Brussels, IL	SFD
WI	GB
Bryan, OH	TOL
TX	AUS
Bryant, IN	LFT
Bryantown, MD	WDC
Bryn Mawr, PA	PH
Bryson City, NC	CHL
Buchanan, MI	KAL
NY	NY
Buckeye, AZ	PHX
Buckeye Lake, OH	COL
Buckeystown, MD	BAL
Buckhannon, WV	WH
Buckley, WA	SEA
Buckner, MO	KC
Bucksport, ME	PRT
Bucyrus, KS	KCK
OH	TOL
Buda, TX	AUS
Budd Lake, NJ	PAT
Buena Park, CA	ORG
Buena Vista, CO	COS
Buffalo, IA	DAV
MN	STP
MO	SPC
NY	BUF
NY	STF
SD	RC
TX	TYL
WY	CHY
Buffalo Grove, IL	CHI
Buford, GA	ATL
Buhl, ID	B
MN	DUL
Bulger, PA	PIT
Bullhead City, AZ	PHX
Buna, TX	BEA
Bunkie, LA	ALX
Bunnell, FL	STA
Burbank, CA	LA
IL	CHI
Burgaw, NC	R
Burgettstown, PA	PIT
Burien, WA	SEA
Burkburnett, TX	FWT
Burke, SD	RC
VA	ARL
Burleson, TX	FWT
Burley, ID	B
Burlingame, CA	SFR
Burlington, CO	COS
IA	DAV
KS	KCK
KY	COV
MA	BO
NC	R
NJ	TR
TX	AUS
VT	BUR
WA	SEA
WI	MIL
Burnet, TX	AUS
Burney, CA	SAC
Burnham, IL	CHI
Burns, OR	BAK
Burnsville, MN	STP
Burr Ridge, IL	JOL
Burton, MI	LAN
OH	PRM
Burtonsville, MD	WDC
Bushnell, FL	ORL
IL	PEO
Bushton, KS	WCH
Bushwood, MD	WDC
Butler, AL	MOB
MO	KC
NJ	PAT
PA	PIT
WI	MIL
Butner, NC	R
Butte, MT	HEL
NE	OM
Butternut, WI	SUP
Buttonwillow, CA	FRS
Buxton, NC	R
Buzzards Bay, MA	FR
Byers, CO	DEN
Byron, CA	OAK
IL	RCK
MN	WIN
Byron Center, MI	GR
MI	KAL
Cable, WI	SUP
Cabot, PA	PIT
Cactus, TX	AMA
Cadet, MO	STL
Cadillac, MI	GLD
Cadiz, KY	OWN
OH	STU
Cadyville, NY	OG
Cahokia, IL	BEL
Cairo, IL	BEL
NY	ALB
Calais, ME	PRT
Caldwell, ID	B
KS	WCH
NJ	NEW
OH	STU
TX	AUS
Caledonia, MI	GR
MN	WIN
NY	ROC
WI	MIL
Calexico, CA	SD
Calhan, CO	COS
Calhoun, GA	ATL
KY	OWN
Caliente, NV	LAV
Califon, NJ	MET
California, KY	COV
MO	JC
PA	PIT
California City, CA	FRS
Calimesa, CA	SB
CA	HPM
Calipatria, CA	SD
Calistoga, CA	SR
Callahan, FL	STA
Callaway, MN	CR
Callicoon, NY	NY
Calmar, IA	DUB
Calumet, MI	MAR
Calumet City, IL	CHI
Calvert City, KY	OWN
Camanche, IA	DAV
Camarillo, CA	LA
Camas, WA	SEA
Cambria, CA	MRY
Cambria Heights, NY	BRK
Cambridge, MA	BO
MD	WIL
MN	SCL
NE	LIN
NY	ALB
OH	STU
VT	BUR
WI	MAD
Cambridge City, IN	IND
Cambridge Springs, PA	E
Camden, AL	MOB
AR	LR
ME	PRT
MS	JKS
NJ	CAM
NY	SY
OH	CIN
SC	CHR
TN	MEM
WV	WH
Camdenton, MO	JC
Cameron, LA	LKC
MO	KC
TX	AUS
Camillus, NY	SY
Camp Douglas, WI	LC
Camp Hill, PA	HBG
Camp Springs, KY	COV
MD	WDC
Camp Verde, AZ	PHX
Campbell, CA	SJ
CA	SPA
MO	SPC
NE	LIN
OH	Y
OH	PBR
Campbell Hall, NY	STF
Campbellsport, WI	MIL
Campbellsville, KY	L
Campo, CA	SD
Campti, LA	ALX
Campus, IL	PEO
Canaan, CT	HRT
Canadaigua, NY	ROC
Canadian, TX	AMA
Canal Fulton, OH	Y
Canal Winchester, OH	COL
Canandaigua, NY	ROC
Canaseraga, NY	BUF
Canastota, NY	SY
Canby, MN	NU
OR	P
Candler, FL	ORL
NC	CHL
Cando, ND	FAR
Candor, NC	CHL
Caney, KS	WCH
Canfield, OH	Y
Cankton, LA	LAF
Cannon Falls, MN	STP
Canoga Park, CA	LA
Canon City, CO	PBL
Canonsburg, PA	PBR
PA	PIT
Canterbury, CT	NOR
Canton, GA	ATL
IL	PEO
MA	BO
MI	DET
MI	LAN
MO	JC
MS	JKS
NY	OG
OH	Y
OH	ROM
PA	SCR
SD	SFS
TX	TYL
Cantonment, FL	PT
Canutillo, TX	ELP
Canyon, TX	AMA
Canyon Lake, TX	SAT
Capac, MI	DET
Cape Charles, VA	RIC
Cape Coral, FL	VEN
Cape Elizabeth, ME	PRT
Cape Girardeau, MO	SPC
Cape May, NJ	CAM
Cape May Court House, NJ	CAM
Cape May Point, NJ	CAM
Cape Vincent, NY	OG
Capitola, CA	MRY
Captain Cook, HI	HON
Capulin, CO	PBL
Carbondale, CO	DEN
IL	BEL
PA	PHU
PA	SCR
Cardington, OH	COL
Carefree, AZ	PHX
Carencro, LA	LAF
Carey, OH	TOL
Caribou, ME	PRT
Carle Place, NY	RVC
Carleton, MI	DET
Carlin, NV	RNO
Carlinville, IL	SFD
Carlisle, AR	LR
IA	DM
KY	LEX
MA	BO
PA	HBG
Carlos, MN	SCL
Carlsbad, CA	SD
CA	POC
NM	LSC
TX	SAN
Carlton, MN	DUL
OR	P
Carlyle, IL	BEL
Carmel, CA	MRY
IN	LFT
NY	NY
Carmel Valley, CA	MRY
Carmi, IL	BEL
Carmichael, CA	OLL
CA	SAC
Carmichaels, PA	PIT
Carnegie, PA	PIT
PA	SAM
PA	SJP
Carney's Point, NJ	CAM
Caro, MI	SAG
Carol Stream, IL	JOL
Carolina, RI	PRO
Carpentersville, IL	RCK
Carpinteria, CA	LA
Carrington, ND	FAR
Carrizo Springs, TX	LAR
Carrizozo, NM	LSC
Carroll, IA	SC
Carrollton, GA	ATL
IL	SFD
KY	COV
MI	SAG
MO	KC
OH	STU
TX	DAL
TX	FWT
Carrolltown, PA	ALT
Carson, CA	LA
ND	BIS
Carson City, MI	GR
NV	RNO
Carteret, NJ	MET
NJ	PSC
NJ	PHU
Cartersville, GA	ATL
Carterville, IL	BEL
Carthage, MO	SPC
MS	JKS
NY	OG
TX	TYL
Carthagena, OH	CIN
Caruthersville, MO	SPC
Carver, MA	BO
MN	STP
Cary, IL	RCK
NC	R
NC	PSC
Casa Grande, AZ	TUC
Cascade, CO	COS
IA	DUB
Casco, ME	PRT
WI	GB
Caseville, MI	SAG
Caseyville, IL	BEL
Cashion, AZ	PHX
Cashmere, WA	YAK
Cashton, WI	LC
Casper, WY	CHY
Caspian, MI	MAR
Cass City, MI	SAG
Cass Lake, MN	DUL
Casselberry, FL	ORL
Casselton, ND	FAR
Cassopolis, MI	KAL
Cassville, MO	SPC
WI	MAD
Castle Hayne, NC	R
Castle Rock, CO	COS
WA	SEA
Castleton, VT	BUR
Castleton On Hudson, NY	ALB
Castro Valley, CA	OAK
Castroville, CA	MRY
TX	SAT
Catasauqua, PA	ALN
Catawissa, MO	STL
PA	HBG
Catharine, KS	SAL
Cathedral City, CA	SB
Cato, WI	GB
Catonsville, MD	BAL
Catskill, NY	ALB
Cattaraugus, NY	BUF
Cavalier, ND	FAR
Cave Creek, AZ	PHX
Cayucos, CA	MRY
Cazenovia, NY	SY
WI	LC
Cecil, PA	PIT
WI	GB
Cecilia, LA	LAF
Cedar, MI	GLD
Cedar Bluffs, NE	OM
Cedar City, UT	SLC
Cedar Falls, IA	DUB
Cedar Grove, NJ	NEW
WI	MIL
Cedar Knolls, NJ	PAT
Cedar Lake, IN	GRY
Cedar Park, TX	AUS
Cedar Rapids, IA	DUB
NE	OM
Cedar Springs, MI	GR
Cedarburg, WI	MIL
Cedarhurst, NY	RVC
Cedartown, GA	ATL
Celebration, FL	ORL
Celestine, IN	EVN
Celina, OH	CIN
Centennial, CO	DEN
Center, CO	PBL
ND	BIS
TX	TYL
Center Harbor, NH	MAN
Center Line, MI	MCE
Center Moriches, NY	RVC

Place	Code
Center Ossipee, NH	MAN
Center Ridge, AR	LR
Center Valley, PA	ALN
Centereach, NY	RVC
Centerport, NY	RVC
Centerville, IA	DAV
LA	LAF
MA	FR
MN	STP
OH	CIN
SD	SFS
TN	NSH
TX	TYL
Central City, IA	DUB
KY	OWN
NE	OM
PA	ALT
Central Falls, RI	PRO
Central Islip, NY	RVC
Central Point, OR	P
Central Square, NY	SY
Central Valley, UT	SLC
Centralia, IL	BEL
MO	JC
WA	SEA
Centreville, MD	WIL
VA	SYM
Ceres, CA	SPA
CA	STO
Cerrillos, NM	SFE
Chadds Ford, PA	PH
Chadron, NE	GI
Chadwicks, NY	SY
Chaffee, MO	SPC
Chagrin Falls, OH	CLV
Chalfont, PA	PH
Chalmette, LA	NO
Chama, NM	SFE
Chamberino, NM	LSC
Chamberlain, SD	SFS
Chambersburg, PA	HBG
Chamblee, GA	ATL
Chamois, MO	JC
Champaign, IL	PEO
Champion, MI	MAR
Champlain, NY	OG
Chandler, AZ	PHX
OK	OKL
Chanhassen, MN	STP
Channahon, IL	JOL
Channelview, TX	GAL
Channing, MI	MAR
Chantilly, VA	ARL
Chanute, KS	WCH
Chaparral, NM	LSC
Chapel Hill, NC	R
Chapin, SC	CHR
Chapman, KS	SAL
Chappaqua, NY	NY
Chappell, NE	GI
Chappell Hill, TX	AUS
Chaptico, MD	WDC
Chardon, OH	CLV
Charenton, LA	LAF
Chariton, IA	DM
Charleroi, PA	PBR
PA	PIT
Charles City, IA	DUB
Charles Town, WV	WH
Charleston, AR	LR
IL	SFD
MO	SPC
MS	JKS
SC	CHR
SC	POC
WV	WH
Charlestown, IN	IND
MA	BO
NH	MAN
Charlevoix, MI	GLD
Charlotte, IA	DAV
MI	LAN
NC	CHL
NC	SYM
TX	SAT
VT	BUR
Charlotte Hall, MD	WDC
Charlottesville, VA	RIC
Charlton, MA	WOR
Charlton City, MA	WOR
Chaska, MN	STP
Chataignier, LA	LAF
Chateaugay, NY	OG
Chatfield, MN	WIN
Chatham, IL	SFD
MA	FR
NJ	PAT
NY	ALB
Chatom, AL	MOB
Chatsworth, CA	LA
Chattahoochee, FL	PT
Chattanooga, TN	KNX
Chauvin, LA	HT
Chazy, NY	OG
Chebanse, IL	JOL
Cheboygan, MI	GLD
Cheektowaga, NY	BUF
Chefornak, AK	FBK
Chehalis, WA	SEA
Chelan, WA	YAK
Chelmsford, MA	BO
Chelsea, MA	BO
MI	LAN
Cheltenham, PA	PH
Cheney, WA	SPK
Cheneyville, LA	ALX
Chenoa, IL	PEO
Chepachet, RI	PRO
Cheraw, SC	CHR
Cherokee, IA	SC
Cherokee Village, AR	LR
Cherry, IL	PEO
Cherry Hill, NJ	CAM
NJ	PHU
Cherry Valley, NY	ALB
Cherryvale, KS	WCH
Chesaning, MI	SAG
Chesapeake, OH	STU
VA	RIC
Cheshire, CT	HRT
MA	SPR
Chest Springs, PA	ALT
Chester, CT	NOR
IL	BEL
MD	WIL
MT	GF
NJ	PAT
NY	NY
PA	PH
SC	CHR
VT	BUR
WV	WH
Chesterfield, MO	STL
NJ	TR
VA	RIC
Chesterland, OH	CLV
OH	ROM
Chesterton, IN	GRY
Chestertown, MD	WIL
NY	ALB
Chestnut Hill, MA	BO
Chetek, WI	SUP
Chevak, AK	FBK
Cheverly, MD	WDC
Chewelah, WA	SPK
Cheyenne, WY	CHY
Cheyenne Wells, CO	COS
Chicago, IL	CHI
IL	STN
IL	SYM
IL	LIT
IL	DET
IL	JOL
IL	EST
Chicago Heights, IL	CHI
Chicago Ridge, IL	CHI
Chickasaw, AL	MOB
Chickasha, OK	OKL
Chico, CA	SAC
Chicopee, MA	SPR
Chicora, PA	PIT
Chiefland, FL	STA
Childress, TX	AMA
Childs, MD	WIL
Chillicothe, IL	PEO
MO	KC
OH	COL
Chillum, MD	WDC
Chiloquin, OR	BAK
Chilton, WI	GB
Chimayo, NM	SFE
China, TX	BEA
China Spring, TX	AUS
Chincoteague Island, VA	RIC
Chinle, AZ	GLP
Chino, CA	SB
Chino Hills, CA	SB
Chino Valley, AZ	PHX
Chinook, MT	GF
Chipley, FL	PT
Chippewa Falls, WI	LC
Chisholm, MN	DUL
Chittenango, NY	SY
Chokio, MN	SCL
Choteau, MT	HEL
Chowchilla, CA	FRS
Chrisney, IN	EVN
Christiansburg, VA	RIC
Christopher, IL	BEL
Christoval, TX	SAN
Chula Vista, CA	SD
Church Point, LA	LAF
Churchville, NY	ROC
Churdan, IA	SC
Churubusco, IN	FTW
Cibecue, AZ	GLP
Cicero, IL	CHI
IN	LFT
NY	SY
Cimarron, NM	SFE
Cincinnati, OH	CIN
OH	OLL
Cinnaminson, NJ	TR
Circle, MT	GF
Circleville, OH	COL
Citronelle, AL	MOB
Citrus Heights, CA	SAC
Citrus Springs, FL	SP
Claflin, KS	DOD
Clairton, PA	PBR
PA	PIT
Clanton, AL	BIR
Clara City, MN	NU
Clare, MI	SAG
Claremont, CA	LA
NH	MAN
Claremore, OK	TLS
Clarence, NY	BUF
PA	ALT
Clarendon, TX	AMA
Clarendon Hills, IL	JOL
Clarinda, IA	DM
Clarion, IA	DUB
PA	E
Clarissa, MN	SCL
Clark, NJ	NEW
SD	SFS
Clarkesville, GA	ATL
Clarklake, MI	LAN
Clarks Green, PA	SCR
Clarks Summit, PA	SCR
Clarksburg, CA	SAC
WV	WH
Clarksdale, MS	JKS
Clarkson, KY	OWN
NE	OM
Clarkston, MI	DET
WA	SPK
Clarksville, AR	LR
IN	IND
MD	BAL
PA	PIT
TN	NSH
TX	TYL
VA	RIC
Clawson, MI	DET
Claxton, GA	SAV
Clay Center, KS	SAL
Claymont, DE	WIL
Clayton, GA	ATL
MO	STL
NC	R
NJ	CAM
NM	SFE
NY	OG
Cle Elum, WA	YAK
Clear Lake, IA	DUB
MN	SCL
SD	SFS
Clearfield, PA	E
Clearlake, CA	SR
Clearville, PA	ALT
Clearwater, FL	SP
MN	STP
Clearwater Beach, FL	SP
Cleburne, TX	FWT
TX	POC
Clemmons, NC	CHL
Clemson, SC	CHR
Clermont, FL	ORL
IA	DUB
Cleveland, GA	ATL
MN	STP
MS	JKS
OH	CLV
OH	PRM
OH	SJP
OH	ROM
TN	KNX
TX	BEA
Cleveland Heights, OH	CLV
Clewiston, FL	VEN
Cliffside Park, NJ	NEW
NJ	NTN
Clifton, AZ	TUC
IL	JOL
NJ	PAT
TX	FWT
VA	ARL
Clifton Forge, VA	RIC
Clifton Heights, PA	PH
Clifton Park, NY	ALB
Clifton Springs, NY	ROC
Clint, TX	ELP
Clinton, AR	LR
CT	NOR
IA	DAV
IL	PEO
IN	IND
KY	OWN
MA	WOR
MD	WDC
MO	KC
MS	JKS
NC	R
NY	SY
OH	CLV
OK	OKL
SC	CHR
TN	KNX
WI	MAD
Clinton Township, MI	DET
MI	OLL
MI	PRM
Clintonville, WI	GB
Clintwood, VA	RIC
Clio, AL	MOB
MI	LAN
Cloquet, MN	DUL
Closter, NJ	NEW
Cloudcroft, NM	LSC
Cloutierville, LA	ALX
Cloverdale, CA	SR
OH	TOL
Cloverport, KY	OWN
Clovis, CA	FRS
NM	SFE
Clute, TX	GAL
Clyde, KS	SAL
MO	JC
MO	KC
NY	ROC
OH	TOL
Clymer, NY	BUF
PA	GBG
PA	PBR
Coachella, CA	SB
Coal City, IL	JOL
Coal Township, PA	HBG
Coal Valley, IL	PEO
Coalinga, CA	FRS
Coalport, PA	E
Coalton, WV	WH
Coatesville, PA	PH
PA	PSC
Cobden, IL	BEL
Cobleskill, NY	ALB
Cockeysville, MD	BAL
Cocoa, FL	ORL
Cocoa Beach, FL	ORL
Coconut Creek, FL	PSC
Coconut Grove, FL	MIA
Coden, AL	MOB
Cody, WY	CHY
Coeur d'Alene, ID	B
Coffeyville, KS	WCH
Coggon, IA	DUB
Cohasset, MA	BO
Cohoes, NY	ALB
NY	STF
Colbert, WA	SPK
Colby, KS	SAL
WI	LC
Colchester, CT	NOR
CT	STF
VT	BUR
Cold Spring, KY	COV
MN	SCL
NY	NY
Coldwater, KS	DOD
MI	KAL
OH	CIN
Colebrook, NH	MAN
Coleman, TX	SAN
Colerain, OH	STU
Coleraine, MN	DUL
Colfax, CA	SAC
IA	DAV
IL	PEO
LA	ALX
WA	SPK
College Park, MD	WDC
College Point, NY	BRK
College Station, TX	AUS
Collegeville, MN	SCL
PA	PH
Colleyville, TX	FWT
Collierville, TN	MEM
Collingdale, PA	PH
Collings Lakes, NJ	CAM
Collingswood, NJ	CAM
Collinsville, CT	HRT
IL	SFD
OK	TLS

Place	Code
Collyer, KS	SAL
Colma, CA	SFR
Colo, IA	DUB
Cologne, MN	STP
Colon, NE	LIN
Colona, IL	PEO
Colonia, NJ	MET
Colonial Beach, VA	ARL
Colonial Heights, VA	RIC
Colonie, NY	ALB
Colorado City, TX	SAN
Colorado Springs, CO	COS
CO	SYM
Colstrip, MT	GF
Colton, CA	SB
NY	OG
WA	SPK
Colts Neck, NJ	TR
Columbia, CT	NOR
IL	BEL
KY	L
MD	BAL
MO	JC
MS	BLX
PA	HBG
SC	CHR
TN	NSH
VA	RIC
Columbia City, IN	FTW
Columbia Falls, MT	HEL
Columbia Heights, MN	STP
Columbia Station, OH	CLV
Columbiana, OH	Y
Columbus, GA	SAV
IN	IND
KS	WCH
MS	JKS
MT	GF
NE	OM
OH	L
OH	COL
OH	PRM
OH	SYM
TX	VIC
WI	MAD
Columbus Grove, OH	TOL
Columbus Junction, IA	DAV
Colusa, CA	SAC
Colver, PA	ALT
Colville, WA	SPK
Colwich, KS	WCH
Combined Locks, WI	GB
Comfort, TX	SAT
Comfrey, MN	NU
Commack, NY	RVC
Commerce, CA	LA
TX	DAL
Commerce City, CO	DEN
Compton, CA	LA
Comstock Park, MI	GR
Conception, MO	KC
Conception Junction, MO	KC
Concord, CA	OAK
MA	BO
MI	LAN
NC	CHL
NH	MAN
Concord Twp., OH	CLV
Concordia, KS	SAL
Condon, OR	BAK
Conejos, CO	PBL
Conemaugh, PA	ALT
PA	PBR
Congers, NY	NY
Congress, AZ	PHX
Conifer, CO	DEN
Conklin, MI	GR
Conneaut, OH	Y
Conneaut Lake, PA	E
Conneautville, PA	E
Connell, WA	SPK
Connellsville, PA	GBG
Connersville, IN	IND
Conrad, MT	HEL
Conroe, TX	GAL
Conshohocken, PA	PH
Constable, NY	OG
Constableville, NY	OG
Continental, OH	TOL
Convent, LA	BR
Convent Station, NJ	PAT
Converse, TX	SAT
Conway, AR	LR
MI	GLD
MO	SPC
PA	PIT
SC	CHR
Conway Springs, KS	WCH
Conyers, GA	ATL
GA	SJP
Conyngham, PA	SCR
Cook, MN	DUL
Cookeville, TN	NSH
Coolidge, AZ	TUC
Coon Rapids, IA	SC
MN	STP
Coon Valley, WI	LC
Cooper City, FL	MIA
Coopersburg, PA	ALN
Cooperstown, ND	FAR
NY	ALB
Coopersville, MI	GR
Coos Bay, OR	P
Copake Falls, NY	ALB
Copemish, MI	GLD
Copenhagen, NY	OG
Copiague, NY	RVC
Coplay, PA	ALN
Copley, OH	CLV
Coppell, TX	DAL
TX	SYM
Copperas Cove, TX	AUS
Copperhill, TN	KNX
Copperopolis, CA	STO
Copperton, UT	SLC
Coquille, OR	P
Coral, PA	GBG
Coral Gables, FL	MIA
Coral Springs, FL	MIA
FL	SYM
Coralville, IA	DAV
Coram, NY	RVC
Coraopolis, PA	PIT
Corbin, KY	LEX
Corcoran, CA	FRS
MN	STP
Cordele, GA	SAV
Cordova, AK	AJ
TN	MEM
Corfu, NY	BUF
Corinth, MS	JKS
NY	ALB
Cornelius, OR	P
Cornell, WI	LC
Corning, AR	LR
CA	SAC
IA	DM
KS	KCK
NY	ROC
OH	COL
Cornucopia, WI	SUP
Cornwall, NY	NY
PA	HBG
Cornwall-on-Hudson, NY	NY
Corona, CA	SB
NY	BRK
Coronado, CA	SD
Corpus Christi, TX	CC
Corrales, NM	SFE
Corralitos, CA	MRY
Corry, PA	E
Corsicana, TX	DAL
Cortaro, AZ	TUC
Cortez, CO	PBL
Cortland, NE	LIN
NY	SY
OH	Y
Cortlandt Manor, NY	NY
Corvallis, OR	P
Corydon, IN	IND
Coshocton, OH	COL
Costa Mesa, CA	ORG
Cotati, CA	SR
Cottage City, MD	WDC
Cottage Grove, MN	STP
OR	P
WI	MAD
Cottonport, LA	ALX
Cottonwood, AZ	PHX
ID	B
MN	NU
Cotulla, TX	LAR
Coudersport, PA	E
Council Bluffs, IA	DM
Council Grove, KS	WCH
Country Club Hills, IL	CHI
Countryside, IL	CHI
Coushatta, LA	SHP
Coventry, CT	NOR
RI	PRO
Covina, CA	LA
Covington, GA	ATL
IN	LFT
KY	COV
LA	NO
OH	CIN
TN	MEM
VA	RIC
WA	SEA
Coweta, OK	TLS
Cowiche, WA	YAK
Cox's Creek, KY	L
Coxsackie, NY	ALB
Cozad, NE	GI
Crabtree, PA	GBG
Crafton, PA	PIT
Craig, CO	DEN
Cranberry Township, PA	PIT
Cranberry Twp, PA	PIT
Crandon, WI	GB
WI	SUP
Crane, TX	SAN
Cranford, NJ	NEW
Cranston, RI	PRO
RI	SAM
Crawford, NE	GI
Crawfordsville, IN	LFT
Crawfordville, FL	PT
Creighton, NE	OM
PA	PIT
Crescent, PA	PIT
Crescent City, CA	SR
FL	STA
Crescent Springs, KY	COV
Cresco, IA	DUB
PA	PSC
PA	SCR
Cresskill, NJ	NEW
Cresson, PA	ALT
Crest Hill, IL	JOL
Crestline, CA	SB
OH	TOL
Creston, IA	DM
Crestone, CO	PBL
Crestview, FL	PT
Crestview Hills, KY	COV
Crestwood, KY	L
MO	STL
NY	NY
Crete, NE	LIN
Creve Coeur, MO	STL
Crivitz, WI	GB
Crockett, CA	OAK
TX	TYL
Crofton, MD	BAL
NE	OM
Croghan, NY	OG
Cromwell, CT	NOR
Crookston, MN	CR
Cropwell, AL	BIR
Crosby, MN	DUL
ND	BIS
TX	GAL
Cross Plains, WI	MAD
Crossett, AR	LR
Crosslake, MN	DUL
Crossville, TN	KNX
Croton-on-Hudson, NY	NY
Crow Agency, MT	GF
Crowley, LA	LAF
TX	FWT
Crown, PA	E
Crown Point, IN	GRY
NY	OG
Crownpoint, NM	GLP
Crownsville, MD	BAL
Croydon, PA	PH
Crozet, VA	RIC
Crystal, MN	STP
Crystal City, MO	STL
TX	LAR
Crystal Falls, MI	MAR
Crystal Lake, IL	RCK
Crystal River, FL	SP
Crystal Springs, MS	JKS
Cuba, MO	JC
NM	GLP
NY	BUF
Cuba City, WI	MAD
Cudahy, CA	LA
WI	MIL
Cuero, TX	VIC
Cullman, AL	BIR
Cullom, IL	PEO
Culpeper, VA	ARL
Culver, IN	FTW
Culver City, CA	LA
Cumberland, KY	LEX
MD	BAL
RI	PRO
WI	SUP
Cumming, GA	ATL
Cunningham, KS	WCH
Cupertino, CA	SJ
Curdsville, KY	OWN
Currie, MN	WIN
Curtis, NE	LIN
Curwensville, PA	E
Cushing, OK	TLS
Custar, OH	TOL
Custer, MI	GR
SD	RC
WI	LC
Cut Bank, MT	HEL
Cut-Off, LA	HT
Cutchogue, NY	RVC
Cutler, CA	FRS
Cutler Bay, FL	MIA
Cuyahoga Falls, OH	CLV
Cynthiana, KY	COV
Cypress, CA	ORG
D'Hanis, TX	SAT
D'Iberville, MS	BLX
Dade City, FL	SP
Dahlgren, IL	BEL
Dahlonega, GA	ATL
Daingerfield, TX	TYL
Dakota Dunes, SD	SFS
Dale, IN	EVN
Dale City, VA	ARL
Dalhart, TX	AMA
Dallas, GA	ATL
OR	P
PA	SCR
TX	DAL
Dallastown, PA	HBG
Dalton, GA	ATL
MA	SPR
PA	SCR
Daly City, CA	SFR
Dalzell, IL	PEO
Damar, KS	SAL
Damascus, MD	WDC
Damiansville, IL	BEL
Damon, TX	GAL
Dana Point, CA	ORG
Danbury, CT	BGP
CT	SAM
CT	PSC
CT	NTN
TX	GAL
Dania, FL	MIA
Daniel Island, SC	CHR
Danielson, CT	NOR
Dannemora, NY	OG
Danvers, MA	BO
Danville, CA	OAK
IL	PEO
IN	IND
KY	LEX
OH	COL
PA	HBG
VA	RIC
Daphne, AL	MOB
Darby, PA	PH
Dardenne Prairie, MO	STL
Darien, CT	BGP
IL	JOL
Darien Center, NY	BUF
Darlington, PA	SAM
WI	MAD
Darnestown, MD	SYM
MD	WDC
Dartmouth, MA	SAM
Darwin, MN	NU
Dauphin, PA	HBG
Dauphin Island, AL	MOB
Davenport, CA	MRY
IA	DAV
WA	SPK
Davey, NE	LIN
David, KY	LEX
David City, NE	LIN
Davidsonville, MD	BAL
Davidsville, PA	ALT
Davie, FL	MIA
Davis, CA	SAC
Davis Park, NY	RVC
Davison, MI	LAN
Dawson, MN	NU
NE	LIN
Dawson Springs, KY	OWN
Dawsonville, GA	ATL
Dayton, KY	COV
KY	SYM
MN	STP
NV	RNO
OH	CIN
OH	OLL
OH	PRM
TN	KNX
TX	BEA
WA	SPK
Daytona Beach, FL	ORL
Dayville, CT	NOR
De Forest, WI	MAD
De Funiak Springs, FL	PT
De Motte, IN	LFT
De Pere, WI	GB
De Queen, AR	LR
De Ridder, LA	LKC
De Smet, SD	SFS
De Soto, MO	STL
De Witt, MI	LAN

Place	Code
DeBary, FL	ORL
DeKalb, IL	RCK
DeLand, FL	ORL
DePue, IL	PEO
DeQuincy, LA	LKC
DeSmet, ID	B
DeWitt, IA	DAV
NY	SY
Deal, NJ	TR
Dearborn, MI	DET
MI	STN
MI	ROM
Dearborn Heights, MI	DET
MI	STN
Decatur, AL	BIR
GA	ATL
IL	SFD
IN	FTW
MI	KAL
TX	FWT
Decherd, TN	NSH
Decorah, IA	DUB
Dedham, IA	SC
MA	BO
Deep River, CT	NOR
Deephaven, MN	STP
Deer Lodge, MT	HEL
Deer Park, NY	RVC
TX	GAL
WA	SPK
Deer River, MN	DUL
Deerbrook, WI	GB
Deerfield, IL	CHI
KS	DOD
MI	LAN
Deerfield Beach, FL	MIA
Defiance, IA	DM
MO	STL
OH	TOL
Del City, OK	OKL
Del Norte, CO	PBL
Del Rio, TX	SAT
Deland, FL	ORL
Delano, CA	FRS
MN	STP
Delanson, NY	ALB
Delavan, IL	PEO
WI	MIL
Delaware, OH	COL
Delaware City, DE	WIL
Delcambre, LA	LAF
Delhi, IA	DUB
NY	ALB
Dell Rapids, SD	SFS
Delmar, NY	ALB
Delphi, IN	LFT
Delphos, OH	TOL
Delran, NJ	TR
Delray Beach, FL	NTN
FL	PMB
Delta, CO	PBL
Delta Junction, AK	FBK
Delton, MI	KAL
Deltona, FL	ORL
Demarest, NJ	NEW
Deming, NM	LSC
Demopolis, AL	BIR
Demotte, IN	LFT
Denham Springs, LA	BR
Denison, IA	SC
TX	DAL
Denmark, WI	GB
Dennison, OH	COL
Dent, MN	SCL
Denton, NE	LIN
TX	FWT
Denver, CO	DEN
CO	STN
CO	HPM
NC	CHL
Denver City, TX	LUB
Denville, NJ	PAT
Depauw, IN	IND
Depew, NY	BUF
Dequincy, LA	LKC
Derby, CT	HRT
KS	WCH
NY	BUF
Derby Line, VT	BUR
Derry, NH	MAN
PA	GBG
Derwood, MD	WDC
Des Allemands, LA	NO
Des Moines, IA	DM
WA	SEA
Des Plaines, IL	CHI
Descanso, CA	SD
Desert Hot Springs, CA	SB
Deshler, OH	TOL
Destin, FL	PT
Destrehan, LA	NO

Place	Code
Detroit, MI	DET
MI	OLL
MI	ROM
MI	STN
Detroit Lakes, MN	CR
Deville, LA	ALX
Devils Lake, ND	FAR
Devine, TX	SAT
Devon, PA	PH
Dewey, OK	TLS
Dexter, ME	PRT
MI	LAN
MO	SPC
NM	LSC
Diamond Bar, CA	LA
Diamondhead, MS	BLX
Diberville, MS	BLX
Diboll, TX	TYL
Dickeyville, WI	MAD
Dickinson, ND	BIS
TX	GAL
Dickson, TN	NSH
Dickson City, PA	SCR
Dieterich, IL	SFD
Dighton, KS	DOD
MA	FR
Dilley, TX	SAT
Dillingham, AK	AJ
Dillon, MT	HEL
SC	CHR
Dilworth, MN	CR
Dime Box, TX	AUS
Dimmitt, TX	AMA
Dimock, SD	SFS
Dinuba, CA	FRS
Dittmer, MO	STL
Divide, CO	COS
Dix Hills, NY	BRK
NY	RVC
Dixon, CA	SAC
IL	RCK
MO	JC
NM	SFE
Dobbs Ferry, NY	NY
Dodge, NE	OM
WI	LC
Dodge Center, MN	WIN
Dodge City, KS	DOD
Dodgeville, WI	MAD
Dolan Springs, AZ	PHX
Dolgeville, NY	ALB
Dona Ana, NM	LSC
Donaldson, IN	FTW
Donaldsonville, LA	BR
Donegal, PA	GBG
Doniphan, MO	SPC
NE	LIN
Donna, TX	BWN
Donora, PA	PBR
PA	PIT
Doral, FL	ARL
FL	MIA
Doraville, GA	ATL
Dorchester, MA	BO
Dorr, MI	KAL
Dos Palos, CA	FRS
Dothan, AL	MOB
Douglas, AZ	TUC
GA	SAV
MA	WOR
MI	KAL
WY	CHY
Douglassville, PA	ALN
Douglaston, NY	BRK
Douglasville, GA	ATL
Dousman, WI	MIL
Dover, DE	WIL
MA	BO
NH	MAN
NH	SAM
NJ	PAT
OH	COL
TN	NSH
Dover Plains, NY	NY
Dowagiac, MI	KAL
Downers Grove, IL	JOL
Downey, CA	LA
Downieville, CA	SAC
Downingtown, PA	PH
Downs, IL	PEO
Doylesburg, PA	HBG
Doylestown, OH	CLV
PA	PH
WI	MAD
Dracut, MA	BO
Drake, ND	FAR
Draper, UT	SLC
Drayton, ND	FAR
Dresden, OH	COL
Drexel Hill, PA	PH
Dripping Springs, TX	AUS

Place	Code
Drummond, MT	HEL
Dryden, MI	DET
Du Bois, PA	E
PA	PBR
Du Quoin, IL	BEL
Dublin, CA	OAK
GA	SAV
OH	COL
Dubois, IL	BEL
IN	EVN
Dubuque, IA	DUB
Dudley, MA	WOR
PA	ALT
Dufur, OR	BAK
Dulac, LA	HT
Dulce, NM	GLP
Duluth, GA	ATL
MN	DUL
MN	SUP
Dumas, AR	LR
TX	AMA
Dumfries, VA	ARL
Dumont, NJ	NEW
Dunbar, PA	GBG
Duncan, OK	OKL
Duncansville, PA	ALT
Duncanville, TX	DAL
Dundas, IL	BEL
Dundee, IL	RCK
Dunedin, FL	SP
Dunellen, NJ	MET
NJ	PSC
Dunkerton, IA	DUB
Dunkirk, IN	LFT
NY	BUF
Dunlap, IA	DM
TN	KNX
Dunmore, PA	PSC
PA	SCR
Dunn, NC	R
Dunnellon, FL	ORL
Dunseith, ND	FAR
Dunsmuir, CA	SAC
Dunwoody, GA	ATL
Dupo, IL	BEL
Dupont, LA	ALX
PA	SCR
Duquesne, PA	PBR
PA	PIT
Durand, IL	RCK
MI	LAN
WI	LC
Durango, CO	PBL
Durant, OK	TLS
Durham, CT	NOR
NC	R
NH	MAN
Durhamville, NY	SY
Duryea, PA	SCR
Dushore, PA	SCR
Duson, LA	LAF
Dutton, MT	HEL
Duvall, WA	SEA
Duxbury, MA	BO
Dwight, IL	PEO
NE	LIN
Dyer, IN	GRY
Dyersburg, TN	MEM
Dyersville, IA	DUB
Dysart, PA	ALT
Eagan, MN	NU
MN	STP
Eagle, ID	B
WI	MIL
Eagle Butte, SD	RC
Eagle Harbor, MI	STN
Eagle Lake, TX	VIC
Eagle Pass, TX	LAR
Eagle River, AK	AJ
WI	SUP
Earlimart, CA	FRS
Earling, IA	DM
Earlington, KY	OWN
Earlville, IA	DUB
IL	PEO
Earth City, MO	STL
East Aurora, NY	BUF
East Berlin, CT	HRT
East Bernard, TX	VIC
East Boston, MA	BO
East Brady, PA	E
PA	GBG
East Bridgewater, MA	BO
East Brookfield, MA	WOR
East Brunswick, NJ	MET
NJ	PSC
East Carbon, UT	SLC
East Chicago, IN	GRY
IN	ROM
East China, MI	DET
East Dubuque, IL	RCK

Place	Code
East Elmhurst, NY	BRK
East Falmouth, MA	FR
East Freetown, MA	FR
East Glendale, NY	BRK
East Grand Forks, MN	CR
East Grand Rapids, MI	GR
East Greenbush, NY	ALB
East Greenwich, RI	PRO
East Hampton, CT	NOR
NY	RVC
East Hanover, NJ	PAT
East Hartford, CT	HRT
East Haven, CT	HRT
East Helena, MT	HEL
East Islip, NY	RVC
East Jordan, MI	GLD
East Lansdowne, PA	PH
East Lansing, MI	LAN
East Liverpool, OH	Y
East Longmeadow, MA	SPR
East Lyme, CT	NOR
East McKeesport, PA	PIT
East Meadow, NY	RVC
East Millinocket, ME	PRT
East Moline, IL	PEO
East Newark, NJ	NEW
East Norriton, PA	PH
East Northport, NY	RVC
East Orange, NJ	NEW
East Palo Alto, CA	SJ
CA	SFR
East Patchogue, NY	RVC
East Peoria, IL	PEO
IL	SFD
IL	RCK
East Providence, RI	PRO
East Rochester, NY	ROC
East Rockaway, NY	RVC
East Rutherford, NJ	NEW
East Saint Louis, IL	BEL
East Sandwich, MA	FR
East Stroudsburg, PA	SCR
East Syracuse, NY	SY
East Taunton, MA	FR
East Tawas, MI	GLD
East Templeton, MA	WOR
East Troy, WI	MIL
East Vandergrift, PA	GBG
East Walpole, MA	BO
East Wenatchee, WA	YAK
East Windsor, CT	HRT
Easthampton, MA	SPR
Eastlake, OH	CLV
Eastman, GA	SAV
WI	LC
Easton, CA	FRS
CT	BGP
KS	KCK
MD	WIL
MO	KC
PA	ALN
PA	SAM
Eastpointe, MI	DET
Eastport, NY	RVC
Eastvale, CA	SB
Eaton, OH	CIN
Eaton Rapids, MI	LAN
Eatontown, NJ	TR
NJ	CAM
Eau Claire, WI	LC
Eau Galle, WI	LC
Ebensburg, PA	ALT
Ebony, VA	RIC
Echo, LA	ALX
Ecorse, MI	DET
Edcouch, TX	BWN
Eddystone, PA	PH
Eddyville, KY	OWN
Eden, NC	CHL
NY	BUF
SD	SFS
TX	SAN
WI	MIL
Eden Prairie, MN	STP
Eden Valley, MN	SCL
Edenton, NC	R
Edgar, WI	LC
Edgard, LA	NO
Edgefield, SC	CHR
Edgeley, ND	FAR
Edgemere, MD	BAL
Edgerton, OH	TOL
WI	MAD
Edgewater, MD	BAL
NJ	NEW
Edgewood, IA	DUB
KY	COV
MD	BAL
Edina, MN	STP
MO	JC
Edinboro, PA	E

Edinburg, TX	BWN
TX	SYM
Edinburgh, IN	IND
Edison, NJ	MET
Edmond, OK	OKL
Edmonds, WA	SEA
Edmonton, KY	L
Edmore, MI	GR
Edna, TX	VIC
Edroy, TX	CC
Edwards, CO	DEN
Edwardsburg, MI	KAL
Edwardsville, IL	SFD
PA	PHU
Effingham, IL	SFD
KS	KCK
Egg Harbor, WI	GB
Egg Harbor Township, NJ	CAM
Eggertsville, NY	BUF
Egypt, OH	CIN
El Cajon, CA	SD
CA	OLD
CA	SPA
CA	OLL
El Campo, TX	VIC
El Centro, CA	SD
El Cerrito, CA	OAK
El Dorado, AR	LR
KS	WCH
El Dorado Hills, CA	SAC
El Dorado Springs, MO	SPC
El Mirage, AZ	PHX
El Monte, CA	LA
El Paso, IL	PEO
TX	ELP
TX	OLL
El Reno, OK	OKL
El Rito, NM	SFE
El Segundo, CA	LA
CA	NTN
El Sobrante, CA	OAK
Elberon, NJ	TR
Elberta, AL	MOB
Elbow Lake, MN	SCL
Elburn, IL	RCK
Elcho, WI	GB
Eldersburg, MD	BAL
Eldon, MO	JC
Eldora, IA	DUB
Eldorado, IL	BEL
TX	SAN
WI	MIL
Eldred, PA	E
Eldridge, IA	DAV
Elgin, IL	RCK
NE	OM
OK	OKL
OR	BAK
TX	AUS
Elizabeth, CO	COS
IL	RCK
MN	SCL
NJ	NEW
NJ	PSC
NJ	PHU
PA	PIT
Elizabeth City, NC	R
Elizabethton, TN	KNX
Elizabethtown, IL	BEL
KY	L
NY	OG
PA	HBG
Elk City, OK	OKL
Elk Grove, CA	SAC
Elk Grove Village, IL	CHI
Elk Mound, WI	LC
Elk Point, SD	SFS
Elk Rapids, MI	GLD
Elk River, MN	SCL
Elkader, IA	DUB
Elkhart, IA	DM
IN	FTW
KS	DOD
Elkhart Lake, WI	MIL
Elkhorn, NE	OM
WI	MIL
Elkins, WV	WH
Elkins Park, PA	PH
Elkland, PA	SCR
Elko, NV	RNO
Elko/New Market, MN	STP
Elkridge, MD	BAL
Elkton, FL	STA
KY	OWN
MD	WIL
VA	RIC
Elkview, WV	WH
Ellenburg Center, NY	OG
Ellendale, ND	FAR
Ellensburg, WA	YAK
Ellenville, NY	NY
Ellicott City, MD	BAL
Ellicottville, NY	BUF
Ellijay, GA	ATL
Ellington, CT	NOR
Ellinwood, KS	DOD
Ellis, KS	SAL
Ellis Grove, IL	BEL
Ellisville, MO	STL
Ellsworth, KS	SAL
ME	PRT
WI	LC
Ellwood City, PA	PIT
Elm Creek, NE	GI
Elm Grove, WI	MIL
Elma, IA	DUB
NY	BUF
WA	SEA
Elmendorf, TX	SAT
Elmer, NJ	CAM
Elmhurst, IL	JOL
NY	BRK
Elmhurst Twp., PA	SCR
Elmira, MI	GLD
NY	ROC
Elmira Heights, NY	STF
Elmont, NY	MCE
NY	RVC
Elmore, AL	MOB
OH	DET
Elmsford, NY	NY
Elmwood, IL	PEO
WI	LC
Elmwood Park, IL	CHI
NJ	NEW
Elon, NC	R
Eloy, AZ	TUC
Elrama, PA	PIT
Elrosa, MN	SCL
Elsa, TX	BWN
Elsberry, MO	STL
Elsmere, KY	COV
Elton, LA	LKC
Eltopia, WA	SPK
Elverson, PA	PH
Elwood, IN	LFT
Ely, MN	DUL
NV	LAV
Elyria, OH	CLV
Elyria Township, OH	CLV
Elysburg, PA	HBG
Elysian, MN	STP
Emerson, NE	OM
NJ	NEW
Emery, SD	SFS
Emeryville, CA	OAK
Emily, MN	DUL
Emlenton, PA	E
Emmaus, PA	ALN
Emmetsburg, IA	SC
Emmett, ID	B
MI	DET
Emmitsburg, MD	BAL
Emmonak, AK	FBK
Emory, TX	TYL
Empire, MI	GLD
Emporia, KS	KCK
VA	RIC
Emporium, PA	E
Encinal, TX	LAR
Encinitas, CA	SD
Encino, CA	LA
Enderlin, ND	FAR
Endicott, NY	SY
Endwell, NY	SY
Enfield, CT	HRT
IL	BEL
NH	MAN
England, AR	LR
Englewood, CO	DEN
FL	VEN
NJ	NEW
OH	CIN
Englewood Cliffs, NJ	NEW
Enid, OK	OKL
Ennis, TX	DAL
Enola, PA	HBG
Enosburg Falls, VT	BUR
Enterprise, AL	MOB
OR	BAK
Enumclaw, WA	SEA
Ephraim, UT	SLC
Ephrata, PA	HBG
WA	YAK
Epping, NH	MAN
Epworth, IA	DUB
Erath, LA	LAF
Erdenheim, PA	PH
Erie, CO	DEN
IL	RCK
KS	WCH
MI	DET
PA	E
PA	PBR
Erlanger, KY	COV
Ernest, PA	PBR
Erwin, TN	KNX
Escanaba, MI	MAR
Escondido, CA	SD
Esmond, ND	FAR
Esopus, NY	NY
Espanola, NM	SFE
Essex, CT	NOR
MD	BAL
Essex Junction, VT	BUR
Essexville, MI	SAG
Estacada, OR	P
Estes Park, CO	DEN
Estherville, IA	SC
Ettrick, WI	LC
Euclid, OH	CLV
OH	PRM
Eudora, KS	KCK
Eufaula, AL	MOB
Eugene, MO	JC
OR	P
Eunice, LA	LAF
Eureka, CA	SR
IL	PEO
KS	WCH
MO	STL
MT	HEL
NV	RNO
SD	SFS
Eureka Springs, AR	LR
Eustis, FL	ORL
Eutaw, AL	BIR
Evangeline, LA	LAF
Evans City, PA	PIT
Evans Mills, NY	OG
Evanston, IL	CHI
IL	MCE
WY	CHY
Evansville, IL	BEL
IN	EVN
WI	MAD
Evart, MI	GR
Eveleth, MN	DUL
Everett, MA	BO
PA	ALT
WA	SEA
Evergreen, CO	DEN
LA	ALX
Evergreen Park, IL	CHI
Everson, PA	GBG
Ewa, HI	HON
Ewa Beach, HI	HON
Ewen, MI	MAR
Ewing, MO	JC
NE	OM
Excelsior, MN	STP
Excelsior Springs, MO	KC
Exeter, CA	FRS
NE	LIN
NH	MAN
PA	SCR
RI	PRO
Export, PA	GBG
Exton, PA	PH
Fabens, TX	ELP
Fair Haven, NJ	TR
VT	BUR
Fair Lawn, NJ	NEW
Fair Oaks, CA	SAC
Fairbank, IA	DUB
Fairbanks, AK	FBK
Fairborn, OH	CIN
Fairbury, IL	PEO
NE	LIN
Fairchance, PA	GBG
Fairdale, KY	L
Fairfax, CA	SFR
MN	NU
OK	TLS
SD	RC
VA	ARL
VT	BUR
Fairfield, CA	SAC
CT	BGP
IA	DAV
IL	BEL
KY	L
MT	HEL
NJ	NEW
OH	CIN
PA	HBG
TX	TYL
VT	BUR
Fairfield Bay, AR	LR
Fairfield Glade, TN	KNX
Fairford, AL	MOB
Fairhaven, MA	FR
Fairhope, AL	MOB
Fairlawn, OH	CLV
OH	OLL
Fairless Hills, PA	PH
Fairmont, MN	WIN
WV	WH
Fairmont City, IL	BEL
Fairmount, ND	FAR
NY	SY
Fairport, NY	ROC
Fairport Harbor, OH	CLV
Fairview, NJ	NEW
PA	E
Fairview Heights, IL	BEL
Fairview Park, OH	CLV
OH	PRM
Faith, SD	RC
Falcon, CO	COS
Falconer, NY	BUF
Falfurrias, TX	CC
Fall Creek, WI	LC
Fall River, MA	FR
MA	STF
MA	SAM
Fallbrook, CA	SD
Fallentimber, PA	ALT
Fallon, NV	RNO
Falls, PA	SCR
Falls Church, VA	ARL
Falls City, NE	LIN
TX	SAT
Falls Creek, PA	E
Fallston, MD	BAL
Falmouth, KY	COV
MA	FR
ME	PRT
Fancy Farm, KY	OWN
Far Rockaway, NY	BRK
Fargo, ND	FAR
Faribault, MN	STP
Farley, IA	DUB
Farmer City, IL	PEO
Farmers Branch, TX	DAL
TX	SYM
Farmersville, IL	SFD
Farmingdale, NJ	TR
NY	RVC
Farmington, CT	HRT
IA	DAV
IL	PEO
ME	PRT
MI	DET
MI	OLN
MN	STP
MO	STL
NH	MAN
NM	GLP
PA	GBG
Farmington Hills, MI	DET
MI	OLD
MI	EST
Farmingville, NY	RVC
Farmville, NC	R
VA	RIC
Farnham, NY	BUF
Farrell, PA	E
Faulkner, MD	WDC
Faulkton, SD	SFS
Fayette, IA	DUB
MO	JC
MS	JKS
OH	TOL
Fayetteville, AR	LR
GA	ATL
IL	BEL
NC	R
NC	SAM
NY	SY
OH	CIN
TN	NSH
TX	AUS
Feasterville, PA	PH
Federal Way, WA	SEA
Feeding Hills, MA	SPR
Fellsmere, FL	PMB
Felton, CA	MRY
Fenelton, PA	PIT
Fennimore, WI	MAD
Fennville, MI	KAL
Fenton, LA	LKC
MI	LAN
MO	STL
Ferdinand, IN	EVN
Fergus Falls, MN	SCL
Ferguson, MO	STL
Fernandina Beach, FL	STA
Ferndale, CA	SR
WA	SEA
Fernley, NV	RNO
Ferriday, LA	ALX
Ferris, TX	DAL
Fertile, MN	CR

Place	Code
Fessenden, ND	FAR
Festus, MO	STL
Fife, WA	SEA
Fillmore, CA	LA
NY	BUF
Fincastle, VA	RIC
Findlay, OH	TOL
Finleyville, PA	PIT
Firebaugh, CA	FRS
Fisher, MN	CR
Fishers, IN	LFT
Fishers Island, NY	NOR
Fishkill, NY	NY
Fiskdale, MA	WOR
Fitchburg, MA	WOR
Flagler Beach, FL	STA
Flagstaff, AZ	PHX
Flanders, NJ	PAT
NJ	PSC
Flandreau, SD	SFS
Flasher, ND	BIS
Flat Rock, MI	DET
Flatonia, TX	AUS
TX	VIC
Fleming Island, FL	STA
Flemingsburg, KY	COV
Flemington, NJ	MET
Flint, MI	LAN
MI	OLL
MI	STN
TX	TYL
Flint Hill, MO	STL
Floodwood, MN	DUL
Flora, IL	BEL
Floral City, FL	SP
Floral Park, NY	BRK
NY	RVC
Florence, AL	BIR
AZ	TUC
CO	PBL
KY	COV
OR	P
SC	CHR
TX	AUS
WI	GB
Floresville, TX	SAT
Florham Park, NJ	PAT
Florida, NY	NY
Florida City, FL	MIA
Florissant, MO	STL
Flossmoor, IL	CHI
Flourtown, PA	PH
Flowery Branch, GA	ATL
Flowood, MS	JKS
Floydada, TX	LUB
Floyds Knobs, IN	IND
Flushing, MI	LAN
MI	PRM
NY	BRK
Foley, AL	MOB
MN	SCL
Follansbee, WV	WH
Folly Beach, SC	CHR
Folsom, CA	SAC
LA	NO
Fond Du Lac, WI	MIL
Fond du Lac, WI	MIL
Fonda, IA	SC
NY	ALB
Fontana, CA	SB
CA	HPM
WI	MIL
Footville, WI	MAD
Force, PA	E
Ford City, PA	GBG
PA	SJP
Fords, NJ	MET
Fordsville, KY	OWN
Fordyce, AR	LR
NE	OM
Foreman, AR	LR
Forest, MS	JKS
Forest City, IA	DUB
NC	CHL
PA	SCR
Forest Grove, OR	P
Forest Hill, MD	BAL
Forest Hills, NY	BRK
Forest Lake, MN	STP
Forest Park, IL	CHI
Forestburgh, NY	NY
Foreston, MN	SCL
Forestport, NY	SY
Forestville, CT	HRT
MD	MCE
MD	WDC
Forked River, NJ	TR
Forks, WA	SEA
Forman, ND	FAR
Forney, TX	DAL
Forrest City, AR	LR

Place	Code
Forsyth, MO	SPC
MT	GF
Fort Ann, NY	ALB
Fort Ashby, WV	WH
Fort Atkinson, WI	MAD
Fort Benton, MT	GF
Fort Bragg, CA	SR
Fort Branch, IN	EVN
Fort Calhoun, NE	OM
Fort Collins, CO	DEN
Fort Covington, NY	OG
Fort Davis, TX	ELP
Fort Defiance, AZ	GLP
Fort Dodge, IA	SC
Fort Edward, NY	ALB
Fort Gratiot, MI	DET
Fort Hancock, TX	ELP
Fort Jennings, OH	TOL
Fort Jones, CA	SAC
Fort Kent, ME	PRT
Fort Lauderdale, FL	MIA
FL	SAM
FL	SYM
Fort Leavenworth, KS	KCK
Fort Lee, NJ	NEW
Fort Loramie, OH	CIN
Fort Lupton, CO	DEN
Fort Madison, IA	DAV
Fort Mc Clellan, AL	BIR
Fort Mill, SC	CHR
Fort Mitchell, AL	MOB
KY	COV
Fort Monroe, VA	RIC
Fort Morgan, CO	DEN
Fort Myers, FL	VEN
Fort Myers Beach, FL	VEN
Fort Oglethorpe, GA	ATL
Fort Payne, AL	BIR
Fort Pierce, FL	PMB
FL	PSC
Fort Pierre, SD	RC
Fort Plain, NY	ALB
Fort Recovery, OH	CIN
Fort Riley, KS	SAL
Fort Scott, KS	WCH
Fort Shaw, MT	GF
Fort Smith, AR	LR
Fort Stockton, TX	SAN
Fort Sumner, NM	SFE
Fort Thomas, KY	COV
Fort Thompson, SD	SFS
Fort Totten, ND	FAR
Fort Walton Beach, FL	PT
Fort Washington, MD	WDC
Fort Wayne, IN	FTW
Fort Worth, TX	FWT
TX	POC
Fort Wright, KY	COV
Fort Yates, ND	BIS
Fortuna, CA	SR
Fortville, IN	IND
Fosston, MN	CR
Foster, RI	PRO
Foster City, CA	SFR
Fostoria, OH	TOL
Fountain City, WI	LC
Fountain Hill, PA	ALN
Fountain Hills, AZ	PHX
Fountain Valley, CA	ORG
Fowler, CA	FRS
IN	LFT
KS	DOD
MI	LAN
Fowlerville, MI	LAN
Fox Chase Manor, PA	PH
PA	PHU
Fox Lake, WI	MIL
Fox Point, WI	MIL
Foxborough, MA	BO
Foxfield, CO	DEN
Foxholm, ND	BIS
Frackville, PA	ALN
PA	PHU
Framingham, MA	BO
MA	SYM
Francis Creek, WI	GB
Frankenmuth, MI	SAG
Frankfort, IL	JOL
IN	LFT
KS	KCK
KY	LEX
MI	GLD
NY	ALB
Franklin, IN	IND
KY	OWN
LA	LAF
MA	BO
MN	NU
NC	CHL
NH	MAN
NJ	PAT

Place	Code
OH	CIN
PA	E
TN	NSH
TX	AUS
VA	RIC
WI	MIL
WV	WH
Franklin Furnace, OH	STU
Franklin Lakes, NJ	NEW
Franklin Park, IL	CHI
Franklin Square, NY	RVC
Franklinton, LA	NO
Franklinville, NY	BUF
Frankston, TX	TYL
Franktown, CO	OKL
Fraser, MI	DET
Frazee, MN	CR
Frazier Park, CA	FRS
Frederic, WI	SUP
Frederick, CO	DEN
MD	BAL
Fredericksburg, TX	SAT
VA	ARL
Fredericktown, MO	SPC
PA	PIT
Fredonia, KS	WCH
NY	BUF
WI	MIL
Free Soil, MI	GR
Freeburg, IL	BEL
MO	JC
Freedom, PA	PIT
WI	GB
Freehold, NJ	TR
Freeland, MI	SAG
PA	PSC
PA	SCR
Freeport, IL	RCK
MN	SCL
NY	RVC
PA	GBG
TX	GAL
Freer, TX	CC
Freeville, NY	ROC
Fremont, CA	OAK
CA	SYM
MI	GR
NE	OM
OH	TOL
French Lick, IN	IND
French Settlement, LA	BR
Frenchburg, KY	LEX
Frenchtown, MT	HEL
Frenchville, ME	PRT
PA	E
Fresh Meadows, NY	BRK
NY	STF
Fresno, CA	FRS
Friday Harbor, WA	SEA
Fridley, MN	STP
Friend, NE	LIN
Friendship, WI	LC
Friendsville, PA	SCR
Friendswood, TX	GAL
Friona, TX	AMA
Frisco, CO	DEN
TX	DAL
TX	FWT
Front Royal, VA	ARL
Frontenac, KS	WCH
MN	STP
MO	STL
Frostburg, MD	BAL
Fruita, CO	PBL
Fruitland, ID	B
Fryburg, PA	E
Frydek, TX	GAL
Fulda, MN	WIN
Fullerton, CA	ORG
NE	OM
Fulshear, TX	GAL
Fulton, IL	RCK
KY	OWN
MD	BAL
MO	JC
NY	SY
Fultonville, NY	ALB
Fuquay–Varina, NC	R
Gadsden, AL	BIR
Gaffney, SC	CHR
Gahanna, OH	COL
Gaines, MI	LAN
Gainesville, FL	STA
GA	ATL
TX	FWT
VA	ARL
Gaithersburg, MD	WDC
Galena, AK	FBK
IL	RCK
MD	WIL
Galena Park, TX	GAL

Place	Code
Gales Ferry, CT	NOR
Galesburg, IL	PEO
Galeton, PA	E
Galion, OH	TOL
Gallatin, MO	KC
TN	NSH
Galliano, LA	HT
Gallipolis, OH	STU
Gallitzin, PA	ALT
Galloway, NJ	CAM
Gallup, NM	GLP
Galt, CA	SAC
Galva, IL	PEO
Galveston, TX	GAL
Gambrills, MD	BAL
Ganado, AZ	GLP
TX	VIC
Garberville, CA	SR
Garciasville, TX	BWN
Garden, MI	MAR
Garden City, KS	DOD
MI	DET
NY	RVC
TX	SAN
Garden Grove, CA	ORG
Garden Plain, KS	WCH
Gardena, CA	LA
Gardendale, AL	BIR
Gardiner, NY	NY
Gardner, KS	KCK
MA	WOR
Gardnerville, NV	RNO
Garfield, NJ	NEW
NM	LSC
Garfield Heights, OH	CLV
Garland, TX	DAL
TX	SYM
Garner, IA	DUB
NC	R
NC	SJP
Garnerville, NY	NY
Garnett, KS	KCK
Garretson, SD	SFS
Garrett, IN	FTW
Garrett Park, MD	WDC
Garrettsville, OH	Y
Garrison, MN	DUL
ND	BIS
NY	NY
Garwood, NJ	NEW
Gary, IN	GRY
Garyville, LA	NO
Gas City, IN	LFT
Gassaway, WV	WH
Gastonia, NC	CHL
Gate City, VA	RIC
Gates Mills, OH	CLV
Gatesville, TX	AUS
Gatlinburg, TN	KNX
Gautier, MS	BLX
Gaylord, MI	GLD
MN	NU
Gays Mills, WI	LC
Geddes, SD	SFS
Genesee Depot, WI	MIL
Geneseo, IL	PEO
ND	FAR
NY	ROC
Geneva, AL	MOB
IL	RCK
IN	FTW
NE	LIN
NY	ROC
OH	Y
Genoa, IL	RCK
NE	OM
OH	TOL
WI	LC
George West, TX	CC
Georgetown, CA	SAC
CT	BGP
DE	WIL
IL	PEO
IN	IND
KY	LEX
MA	BO
MN	CR
OH	CIN
SC	CHR
TX	AUS
Gering, NE	GI
Germantown, IL	BEL
MD	WDC
NY	ALB
OH	CIN
TN	MEM
WI	MIL
Gervais, OR	P
Gettysburg, PA	HBG
SD	SFS
Getzville, NY	BUF

Place	Code
Ghent, MN	NU
Gibbon, MN	NU
Gibbsboro, NJ	CAM
Gibbstown, NJ	CAM
Gibson, LA	HT
Gibson City, IL	JOL
Gibsonburg, OH	TOL
Gibsonia, PA	PBR
PA	PIT
Giddings, TX	AUS
Gig Harbor, WA	SEA
Gilbert, AZ	HPM
AZ	PHX
MN	DUL
Gilberts, IL	RCK
Gilbertville, IA	DUB
MA	WOR
Gillespie, IL	SFD
Gillett, WI	GB
Gillette, WY	CHY
Gilman, IL	JOL
MN	SCL
WI	SUP
Gilmer, TX	TYL
Gilroy, CA	SJ
Girard, IL	SFD
KS	WCH
OH	Y
PA	E
PA	PBR
Gladewater, TX	TYL
Gladstone, MI	MAR
MO	KC
NJ	PAT
Gladwin, MI	SAG
Gladwyne, PA	PH
Glandorf, OH	TOL
Glasgow, KY	L
MO	JC
MT	GF
Glassboro, NJ	CAM
Glassport, PA	PIT
Glastonbury, CT	HRT
CT	STF
Glen Allen, VA	RIC
VA	SAM
Glen Burnie, MD	BAL
Glen Carbon, IL	SFD
Glen Cove, NY	RVC
NY	STF
Glen Dale, WV	WH
Glen Echo, MD	WDC
Glen Ellyn, IL	JOL
Glen Head, NY	RVC
Glen Lyon, PA	SCR
Glen Mills, PA	PH
Glen Rock, NJ	NEW
Glen Rose, TX	FWT
Glen Ullin, ND	BIS
Glenburn, ND	BIS
Glencoe, MN	NU
Glendale, AZ	PHX
CA	LA
CA	OLN
NY	BRK
WI	MIL
Glendale Heights, IL	JOL
Glendive, MT	GF
Glendora, CA	LA
CA	MCE
Glenmora, LA	ALX
Glennallen, AK	AJ
Glenolden, PA	PH
Glenrock, WY	CHY
Glens Falls, NY	ALB
Glenshaw, PA	PIT
Glenside, PA	PH
Glenview, IL	CHI
IL	SYM
Glenville, NY	ALB
WV	WH
Glenwood, AR	LR
IA	DM
IL	CHI
MN	SCL
Glenwood City, WI	SUP
Glenwood Springs, CO	DEN
Glidden, IA	SC
WI	SUP
Globe, AZ	TUC
Gloucester, MA	BO
NJ	CAM
VA	RIC
Glouster, OH	STU
Gloversville, NY	ALB
Gloverville, SC	CHR
Gluckstadt, MS	JKS
Glyndon, MD	BAL
Gobles, MI	KAL
Goddard, KS	WCH
Godfrey, IL	SFD
Goetzville, MI	MAR
Goffstown, NH	MAN
Gold Hill, OR	P
Golden, CO	DEN
Golden Meadow, LA	HT
Golden Valley, MN	STP
Goldendale, WA	YAK
Goldsboro, NC	R
Goldthwaite, TX	AUS
Goleta, CA	LA
Goliad, TX	VIC
Gonic, NH	MAN
Gonzales, CA	MRY
LA	BR
TX	SAT
Goodhue, MN	STP
Gooding, ID	B
Goodland, KS	SAL
Goodman, WI	GB
Goodrich, MI	LAN
Goodyear, AZ	PHX
AZ	TUC
Goose Creek, SC	CHR
Gordon, NE	GI
Gorham, KS	SAL
NH	MAN
Goshen, CT	HRT
IN	FTW
NY	NY
Gould, AR	LR
Gouldsboro, PA	SCR
Gouverneur, NY	OG
Gowanda, NY	BUF
Gower, MO	KC
Graceville, MN	NU
Graford, TX	FWT
Grafton, IL	SFD
MA	WOR
ND	FAR
OH	CLV
WI	MIL
WV	WH
Graham, TX	FWT
Grambling, LA	SHP
Grampian, PA	E
Granada Hills, CA	LA
Granbury, TX	FWT
Granby, CO	DEN
CT	HRT
MA	SPR
Grand Bay, AL	MOB
Grand Blanc, MI	EST
MI	LAN
Grand Canyon, AZ	PHX
Grand Chenier, LA	LKC
Grand Coteau, LA	LAF
Grand Coulee, WA	YAK
Grand Forks, ND	FAR
Grand Haven, MI	GR
Grand Island, NE	GI
NY	BUF
Grand Isle, LA	HT
Grand Junction, CO	PBL
IA	SC
Grand Ledge, MI	LAN
Grand Marais, MI	MAR
MN	DUL
Grand Meadow, MN	WIN
Grand Mound, IA	DAV
Grand Prairie, TX	DAL
TX	FWT
Grand Rapids, MI	GR
MI	STN
MN	DUL
OH	TOL
Grand Rivers, KY	OWN
Grand Ronde, OR	P
Grand Terrace, CA	SB
Grandview, MO	KC
WA	YAK
Grandville, MI	GR
Granger, IA	DM
IN	FTW
TX	AUS
WA	YAK
Grangeville, ID	B
Granite Bay, CA	SAC
Granite City, IL	SFD
Granite Falls, MN	NU
Graniteville, VT	BUR
Grant, NE	LIN
Grants, NM	GLP
Grants Pass, OR	P
Granville, IA	SC
IL	PEO
NY	ALB
OH	COL
Grapevine, TX	FWT
Grass Lake, MI	LAN
Grass Valley, CA	SAC
Gray, LA	NO
LA	PBR
Grayling, MI	GLD
Grayslake, IL	CHI
Grayson, KY	LEX
Great Barrington, MA	SPR
Great Bend, KS	DOD
PA	SCR
Great Falls, MT	GF
VA	ARL
Great Meadows, NJ	MET
NJ	PHU
Great Mills, MD	WDC
Great Neck, NY	RVC
Greeley, CO	DEN
KS	KCK
Green Bay, WI	GB
Green Isle, MN	NU
Green Lake, WI	MAD
Green Pond, NJ	PAT
Green River, WY	CHY
Green Valley, AZ	TUC
Greenacres, FL	PMB
FL	SAM
Greenbelt, MD	WDC
Greenbrae, CA	SFR
Greenbush, MN	CR
Greencastle, IN	IND
PA	HBG
Greendale, WI	MIL
Greene, IA	DUB
NY	SY
Greeneville, TN	KNX
Greenfield, CA	MRY
IA	DM
IL	SFD
IN	IND
MA	SPR
OH	CIN
WI	MIL
Greenfield Center, NY	ALB
Greenlawn, NY	RVC
Greenleaf, WI	GB
Greenport, NY	RVC
Greensboro, GA	ATL
NC	CHL
Greensburg, IN	IND
KS	DOD
PA	GBG
PA	PBR
Greenup, IL	SFD
Greenville, AL	MOB
IL	SFD
IN	IND
ME	PRT
MI	GR
MS	JKS
NC	R
NH	MAN
NY	ALB
OH	CIN
PA	E
RI	PRO
SC	CHR
SC	POC
TX	DAL
WI	GB
Greenwald, MN	SCL
Greenwell Springs, LA	BR
Greenwich, CT	BGP
NY	ALB
Greenwood, IN	IND
MS	JKS
SC	CHR
Greenwood Lake, NY	NY
Greenwood Village, CO	DEN
Greer, SC	CHR
SC	SAM
Gregory, SD	RC
TX	CC
Grenada, MS	JKS
Grenora, ND	BIS
Grenville, SD	SFS
Gresham, OR	P
WI	GB
Gretna, LA	NO
NE	OM
Grey Eagle, MN	SCL
Greybull, WY	CHY
Gridley, CA	SAC
Griffin, GA	ATL
Griffith, IN	GRY
Grinnell, IA	DAV
KS	SAL
Griswold, CT	NOR
IA	DM
Groom, TX	AMA
Grosse Ile, MI	DET
Grosse Pointe, MI	DET
Grosse Pointe Farms, MI	DET
Grosse Pointe Park, MI	DET
Grosse Pointe Woods, MI	DET
Grosse Tete, LA	BR
Groton, CT	NOR
NY	ROC
SD	SFS
Grove, OK	TLS
Grove City, MN	NU
OH	COL
PA	E
Grove Hill, AL	MOB
Groveport, OH	COL
Groves, TX	BEA
Groveton, NH	MAN
Grovetown, GA	SAV
Grulla, TX	BWN
Guadalupe, AZ	PHX
CA	LA
Guerneville, CA	SR
Guernsey, WY	CHY
Gueydan, LA	LAF
Guilderland, NY	ALB
Guilford, CT	HRT
IN	IND
Gulf Breeze, FL	PT
Gulf Shores, AL	MOB
Gulfport, FL	SP
MS	BLX
Gun Barrel City, TX	TYL
Gunnison, CO	PBL
Guntersville, AL	BIR
Gurnee, IL	CHI
Gustine, CA	FRS
Guthrie, KY	OWN
OK	OKL
Guthrie Center, IA	DM
Guttenberg, IA	DUB
Guymon, OK	OKL
Guys Mills, PA	E
Gwinn, MI	MAR
Gwynedd Valley, PA	PH
Hacienda Heights, CA	LA
Hackberry, LA	LKC
Hackensack, MN	DUL
NJ	NEW
Hackettstown, NJ	MET
Haddon Heights, NJ	CAM
Haddonfield, NJ	CAM
Hadley, MA	SPR
Hagaman, NY	ALB
Hagerstown, MD	BAL
Hague, ND	BIS
Hahnville, LA	NO
Haiku, HI	HON
Hailey, ID	B
Haines, AK	AJ
Haines City, FL	ORL
Haines Falls, NY	ALB
Hainesport, NJ	TR
NJ	CAM
Halbur, IA	SC
Haledon, NJ	PAT
Hales Corners, WI	MIL
Halethorpe, MD	BAL
Half Moon Bay, CA	SFR
Halifax, MA	BO
Hallandale Beach, FL	MIA
Hallettsville, TX	VIC
Hallock, MN	CR
Halstead, KS	WCH
Ham Lake, MN	STP
Hamburg, IA	DM
NJ	PAT
NY	BUF
PA	ALN
Hamden, CT	HRT
Hamel, MN	STP
Hamilton, AL	BIR
MA	BO
MO	KC
MT	HEL
NJ	TR
NY	SY
OH	CIN
TX	AUS
Hamilton Square, NJ	TR
Hamlet, IN	GRY
NC	CHL
Hamlin, NY	ROC
Hammond, IN	GRY
IN	NTN
LA	BR
WI	SUP
Hammondsport, NY	ROC
Hammonton, NJ	CAM
Hampden, MA	SPR
Hampshire, IL	RCK
Hampstead, NC	R
NH	MAN
Hampton, IA	DUB
MN	STP
NH	MAN
NJ	MET

VA	RIC
Hampton Bays, NY	RVC
Hamptonville, NC	CHL
Hamtramck, MI	DET
MI	STN
Hana, HI	HON
Hanahan, SC	CHR
Hanceville, AL	BIR
Hancock, MD	BAL
MI	MAR
NY	ALB
Hanford, CA	FRS
Hankinson, ND	FAR
Hannibal, MO	JC
NY	SY
Hanover, IL	RCK
KS	SAL
MA	BO
MD	BAL
NH	MAN
PA	HBG
Hanover Park, IL	CHI
Hanover Township, PA	SCR
Hanson, MA	BO
Hapeville, GA	ATL
Happy, TX	AMA
Harahan, LA	NO
Harbor Beach, MI	SAG
Harbor Springs, MI	GLD
Harborcreek, PA	E
Hardin, IL	SFD
KY	OWN
MT	GF
Hardinsburg, KY	OWN
Hardwick, VT	BUR
Hardyston, NJ	PAT
Harker Heights, TX	AUS
Harlan, IA	DM
KY	LEX
Harlingen, TX	BWN
Harlowton, MT	HEL
Harmony, MN	WIN
Harper, KS	WCH
TX	SAT
Harpers Ferry, IA	DUB
Harrah, OK	OKL
Harriman, NY	NY
TN	KNX
Harrington Park, NJ	NEW
Harrisburg, IL	BEL
PA	HBG
PA	PSC
Harrison, AR	LR
MI	SAG
NJ	NEW
NY	NY
OH	CIN
Harrison City, PA	GBG
Harrison Township, MI	DET
Harrisonburg, VA	RIC
Harrisonville, MO	KC
Harrisville, MI	DET
MI	GLD
NY	OG
RI	PRO
WV	WH
Harrodsburg, KY	LEX
Hart, MI	GR
Hartford, CT	HRT
CT	STF
MI	KAL
SD	SFS
WI	MIL
Hartford City, IN	LFT
Hartington, NE	OM
Hartland, WI	MIL
Hartsdale, NY	NY
Hartshorne, OK	TLS
Hartsville, SC	CHR
Hartwell, GA	ATL
Harvard, IL	RCK
MA	WOR
NE	LIN
Harvey, IL	CHI
LA	NO
ND	FAR
Harvey Cedars, NJ	TR
Harveys Lake, PA	SCR
Harwick, PA	PIT
Harwinton, CT	HRT
Harwood Heights–Norridge, IL	CHI
Hasbrouck Heights, NJ	NEW
Haskell, NJ	PAT
Hastings, MI	KAL
MN	STP
NE	LIN
PA	ALT
Hastings–on–Hudson, NY	NY
Hatboro, PA	PH
Hatch, NM	LSC
Hatfield, MA	SPR
PA	PH
Hatley, WI	LC
Hattiesburg, MS	BLX
Hattieville, AR	LR
Haubstadt, IN	EVN
Hauppauge, NY	RVC
Havana, IL	PEO
Havelock, NC	R
Haverford, PA	PH
Haverhill, MA	BO
Haverstraw, NY	NY
Havertown, PA	PH
Havre, MT	GF
Havre de Grace, MD	BAL
Hawaiian Gardens, CA	LA
Hawarden, IA	SC
Hawesville, KY	OWN
Hawi, HI	HON
Hawk Point, MO	STL
Hawk Run, PA	PBR
Hawley, MN	CR
PA	SCR
Haworth, NJ	NEW
Hawthorne, CA	LA
NJ	PAT
NV	RNO
NY	NY
Hayden, AZ	TUC
Haydenville, MA	SPR
Hayfield, MN	WIN
Hays, KS	SAL
MT	GF
Haysville, KS	WCH
Hayward, CA	OAK
WI	SUP
Hazard, KY	LEX
Hazel Crest, IL	CHI
Hazel Green, WI	MAD
Hazel Park, MI	DET
Hazelton, ND	BIS
Hazelwood, MO	STL
Hazen, ND	BIS
Hazleton, PA	PSC
PA	SCR
Healdsburg, CA	SR
Healdton, OK	OKL
Healy, AK	FBK
Hearne, TX	AUS
Heart Butte, MT	HEL
Heath, OH	COL
Hebbronville, TX	LAR
Heber Springs, AR	LR
Hebron, CT	NOR
IN	GRY
ND	BIS
NE	LIN
Hecker, IL	BEL
Hector, MN	NU
Hedgesville, WV	WH
Helena, AR	LR
MT	HEL
OH	TOL
Helenwood, TN	KNX
Hellertown, PA	ALN
Helmetta, NJ	MET
Helmville, MT	HEL
Helotes, TX	SAT
TX	SYM
Helper, UT	SLC
Hemet, CA	SB
Hemlock, MI	SAG
Hemphill, TX	TYL
Hempstead, NY	RVC
NY	STF
TX	GAL
Henderson, KY	OWN
MN	NU
NC	R
NV	LAV
TX	TYL
Hendersonville, NC	CHL
TN	NSH
Hennepin, IL	PEO
Hennessey, OK	OKL
Henniker, NH	MAN
Henning, MN	SCL
Henrico, VA	RIC
Henrietta, NY	POC
NY	ROC
TX	FWT
Henry, IL	PEO
SD	SFS
Henryetta, OK	TLS
Heppner, OR	BAK
Herculaneum, MO	STL
Hercules, CA	OAK
Hereford, AZ	TUC
TX	AMA
Herington, KS	SAL
Herkimer, NY	ALB
Herman, MN	SCL
Hermann, MO	JC
Herminie, PA	GBG
PA	PBR
Hermiston, OR	BAK
Hermitage, MO	JC
PA	E
PA	PBR
Hermosa Beach, CA	LA
Hernando, MS	JKS
Herndon, VA	ARL
Heron Lake, MN	WIN
Herreid, SD	SFS
Herrin, IL	BEL
Herron, MI	GLD
Herscher, IL	JOL
Hershey, PA	HBG
Hesperia, CA	SB
Hessmer, LA	ALX
Hettinger, ND	BIS
Heuvelton, NY	OG
Hewitt, NJ	PAT
WI	LC
Hewlett, NY	RVC
Hialeah, FL	MIA
Hiawatha, IA	DUB
KS	KCK
Hibbing, MN	DUL
Hickman, KY	OWN
Hickory, NC	CHL
Hickory Hills, IL	CHI
Hicksville, NY	RVC
OH	TOL
Hidalgo, TX	BWN
Higganum, CT	NOR
Higgins Lake, MI	GLD
Higginsville, MO	KC
High Bridge, NJ	MET
High Point, NC	CHL
High Ridge, MO	STL
High Springs, FL	STA
Highland, CA	SB
IL	SFD
IN	GRY
MI	DET
NY	NY
WI	MAD
Highland Beach, FL	PMB
Highland Falls, NY	NY
Highland Heights, KY	COV
OH	CLV
Highland Lakes, NJ	PAT
Highland Mills, NY	NY
Highland Park, IL	CHI
NJ	MET
Highland Springs, VA	RIC
Highlands, TX	GAL
Highlands Ranch, CO	COS
Highmore, SD	SFS
Hightstown, NJ	TR
Highwood, IL	CHI
Hilbert, WI	GB
Hill City, KS	SAL
SD	RC
Hillcrest Heights, MD	WDC
Hilliard, OH	COL
Hillman, MI	GLD
MN	SCL
Hills, IA	DAV
Hillsboro, IL	SFD
MO	STL
ND	FAR
OH	CIN
OR	P
TX	FWT
WI	LC
Hillsborough, NC	R
NH	MAN
NJ	MET
NJ	PHU
Hillsborough Township, NJ	PSC
Hillsdale, MI	LAN
NJ	NEW
Hillside, IL	CHI
NJ	NEW
Hillsville, PA	PIT
Hilltown, PA	PH
Hilmar, CA	FRS
Hilo, HI	HON
Hilton, NY	ROC
Hilton Head Island, SC	CHR
Hinckley, MN	DUL
OH	CLV
Hinesburg, VT	BUR
Hinesville, GA	SAV
Hingham, MA	BO
Hinsdale, IL	JOL
Hinton, WV	WH
Hitchcock, TX	GAL
Ho Ho Kus, NJ	NEW
Hobart, IN	GRY
Hobbs, NM	LSC
Hobe Sound, FL	PMB
Hoboken, NJ	NEW
Hobson, TX	SAT
Hockessin, DE	WIL
Hodge, LA	SHP
Hodgenville, KY	L
Hoffman Estates, IL	CHI
Hogansburg, NY	OG
Hohenwald, TN	NSH
Hoisington, KS	DOD
Holbrook, AZ	GLP
MA	BO
NY	RVC
Holden, MO	KC
Holdenville, OK	TLS
Holdingford, MN	SCL
Holdrege, NE	LIN
Holgate, OH	TOL
Holiday, FL	SP
Holland, MI	GR
NY	BUF
PA	PH
Holland Patent, NY	SY
Hollandale, WI	MAD
Holley, NY	BUF
Hollidaysburg, PA	ALT
Hollis, NY	BRK
NY	SYM
Hollis Hills, NY	BRK
Hollister, CA	MRY
Holliston, MA	BO
Holly, CO	PBL
MI	DET
Holly Lake Ranch, TX	TYL
Holly Springs, MS	JKS
Hollywood, CA	STN
FL	MIA
MD	WDC
Holmdel, NJ	TR
Holmen, WI	LC
Holstein, IA	SC
Holton, KS	KCK
Holts Summit, MO	JC
Holtville, CA	SD
Holy Cross, AK	FBK
IA	DUB
Holyoke, CO	DEN
MA	SPR
Homer, AK	AJ
NY	SY
Homer City, PA	PBR
Homer Glen, IL	JOL
IL	PRM
Homestead, FL	MIA
PA	PIT
Hometown, IL	CHI
Homewood, IL	CHI
IL	JOL
Homosassa, FL	SP
Hondo, TX	SAT
Honeoye, NY	ROC
Honeoye Falls, NY	ROC
Honesdale, PA	SCR
Honey Grove, TX	DAL
Honokaa, HI	HON
Honolulu, HI	HON
Hood River, OR	BAK
Hooksett, NH	MAN
Hoopa, CA	SR
Hooper, NE	OM
Hooper Bay, AK	FBK
Hoopeston, IL	PEO
Hoosick Falls, NY	ALB
Hooversville, PA	ALT
Hopatcong, NJ	PAT
Hope, AR	LR
Hope Mills, NC	R
Hope Valley, RI	PRO
Hopedale, MA	WOR
OH	STU
Hopelawn, NJ	MET
Hopewell, NJ	TR
VA	RIC
Hopewell Junction, NY	NY
Hopkins, MN	STP
Hopkinsville, KY	OWN
Hopkinton, IA	DUB
MA	BO
Horace, ND	FAR
Horicon, WI	MIL
Horizon City, TX	ELP
Hornell, NY	ROC
Horseheads, NY	ROC
Horseshoe Bay, TX	AUS
Horseshoe Bend, AR	LR
Horsham, PA	PH
Horton, KS	KCK
Hortonville, WI	GB
Hoschton, GA	ATL
Hospers, IA	SC
Hot Springs, AR	LR

Place	Code
SD	RC
VA	RIC
Hot Springs National Park, AR	LR
Hot Springs Village, AR	LR
Houck, AZ	GLP
Houghton, IA	DAV
MI	MAR
Houlton, ME	PRT
Houma, LA	HT
Housatonic, MA	SPR
House Springs, MO	STL
Houston, MN	WIN
MO	SPC
TX	GAL
TX	OLL
TX	POC
TX	STN
TX	PBR
Houtzdale, PA	E
Hoven, SD	SFS
Howard, SD	SFS
Howard Beach, NY	BRK
Howard City, MI	GR
Howardstown, KY	L
Howell, MI	LAN
NJ	TR
Howells, NE	OM
Howes, SD	RC
Howland, ME	PRT
Hoxie, KS	SAL
Hubbard, OH	Y
Huber Heights, OH	CIN
Hubertus, WI	MIL
Hudson, FL	SP
MA	BO
MI	LAN
NH	MAN
NY	ALB
NY	STF
OH	CLV
WI	SUP
Hudson Falls, NY	ALB
Huffman, TX	GAL
Hughson, CA	STO
Hugo, OK	TLS
Hugoton, KS	DOD
Hulbert, OK	TLS
Hull, MA	BO
Humble, TX	GAL
Humboldt, IA	SC
SD	SFS
TN	MEM
Humphrey, NE	OM
Hungerford, TX	VIC
Hunlock Creek, PA	SCR
Hunt Valley, MD	BAL
Hunter, NY	STF
Huntersville, NC	CHL
Huntingburg, IN	EVN
Huntingdon, PA	ALT
Huntingdon Valley, PA	PH
PA	SYM
Huntington, IN	FTW
NY	RVC
WV	WH
Huntington Beach, CA	ORG
Huntington Park, CA	LA
Huntington Station, NY	RVC
Huntingtown, MD	WDC
Huntley, IL	RCK
Huntsville, AL	BIR
AR	LR
OH	CIN
TX	GAL
UT	SLC
Hurley, NM	LSC
NY	NY
WI	SUP
Huron, CA	FRS
OH	TOL
SD	SFS
Hurricane, WV	WH
Hurst, TX	FWT
Hurt, VA	RIC
Hurtsboro, AL	MOB
Huslia, AK	FBK
Hutchinson, KS	WCH
MN	NU
Hutto, TX	AUS
Huttonsville, WV	WH
Hyannis, MA	FR
Hyattsville, MD	WDC
Hyde Park, MA	BO
NY	NY
UT	SLC
Hydes, MD	BAL
Iberia, MO	JC
Ida, MI	DET
Ida Grove, IA	SC
Idabel, OK	TLS
Idaho Falls, ID	B

Place	Code
Idaho Springs, CO	DEN
Idalou, TX	LUB
Idyllwild, CA	SB
Ignacio, CO	PBL
Ijamsville, MD	BAL
Ilion, NY	ALB
Imlay City, MI	DET
Immaculata, PA	PH
Immokalee, FL	VEN
Imogene, IA	DM
Imperial, CA	SD
MO	STL
NE	LIN
PA	PIT
Imperial Beach, CA	SD
Inchelium, WA	SPK
Incline Village, NV	RNO
Independence, IA	DUB
KS	WCH
KY	COV
LA	BR
MO	KC
OH	CLV
OH	OLL
OR	P
WI	LC
Indialantic, FL	ORL
Indian Creek, IL	CHI
Indian Head, MD	WDC
Indian Lake, NY	OG
Indian River, MI	GLD
Indian Rocks Beach, FL	SP
Indiana, PA	GBG
Indianapolis, IN	IND
IN	PRM
Indianola, IA	DM
MS	JKS
NE	LIN
Indiantown, FL	PMB
Indio, CA	SB
Inez, TX	VIC
Ingalls, KS	DOD
Ingleside, IL	CHI
TX	CC
Inglewood, CA	LA
Ingram, TX	SAT
Inkster, MI	DET
Interlachen, FL	STA
Interlaken, NY	ROC
International Falls, MN	DUL
Intervale, NH	MAN
Inver Grove Heights, MN	STP
Inverness, FL	SP
IL	CHI
Inwood, NY	RVC
WV	WH
Iola, KS	WCH
Ione, WA	SPK
Ionia, MI	GR
Iota, LA	LAF
Iowa, LA	LKC
Iowa City, IA	DAV
Iowa Falls, IA	DUB
Iowa Park, TX	FWT
Ipswich, MA	BO
SD	SFS
Ira Township, MI	DET
Ireland, IN	EVN
Irene, SD	SFS
Iron Mountain, MI	MAR
Iron River, MI	MAR
WI	SUP
Irondale, AL	BIR
Irons, MI	GR
Ironton, MO	SPC
OH	STU
Ironwood, MI	MAR
Irvine, CA	ORG
CA	POC
KY	LEX
Irving, TX	DAL
TX	PBR
Irvington, KY	OWN
NJ	NEW
NY	NY
Irwin, IL	JOL
PA	GBG
Irwindale, CA	LA
Isanti, MN	SCL
Iselin, NJ	MET
Ishpeming, MI	MAR
Island Park, NY	RVC
Isle La Motte, VT	BUR
Isleta Pueblo, NM	SFE
Isleton, CA	SAC
Islip, NY	RVC
Islip Terrace, NY	RVC
Issaquah, WA	SEA
Italy, TX	DAL
Itasca, IL	JOL
Ithaca, MI	SAG

Place	Code
NY	ROC
Ivanhoe, MN	NU
Ivesdale, IL	PEO
Jabor, Jaluit, MI	MI
Jackson, AL	MOB
CA	SAC
GA	ATL
KY	LEX
MI	LAN
MN	WIN
MO	SPC
MS	JKS
NE	OM
NJ	TR
OH	COL
TN	MEM
WY	CHY
Jackson Heights, NY	BRK
Jacksonville, AL	BIR
AR	LR
FL	OLD
FL	SYM
FL	STA
FL	SAM
IL	SFD
NC	R
NC	POC
TX	TYL
Jacksonville Beach, FL	STA
Jaffrey, NH	MAN
Jal, NM	LSC
Jamaica, NY	BRK
Jamaica Estates, NY	BRK
Jamaica Plain, MA	BO
MA	STF
MA	SAM
Jamesburg, NJ	MET
Jamestown, ND	FAR
NY	BUF
OH	CIN
RI	PRO
TN	KNX
Jamison, PA	PH
Jamul, CA	SD
Janesville, MN	WIN
WI	MAD
Jarrell, TX	AUS
Jasper, AL	BIR
GA	ATL
IN	EVN
TX	BEA
Jay, ME	PRT
Jeanerette, LA	LAF
Jeannette, PA	GBG
PA	SJP
Jefferson, GA	ATL
IA	SC
LA	NO
MA	WOR
NC	CHL
OH	Y
SD	SFS
TX	TYL
WI	MAD
Jefferson City, MO	JC
TN	KNX
Jefferson Hills, PA	PIT
Jeffersonville, IN	IND
NY	NY
Jemez Pueblo, NM	SFE
Jemez Springs, NM	SFE
Jena, LA	ALX
Jenison, MI	GR
Jenkins, KY	LEX
Jenkintown, PA	PH
PA	PHU
Jennings, LA	LKC
Jensen Beach, FL	PMB
Jermyn, PA	SCR
Jerome, ID	B
Jersey City, NJ	NEW
NJ	PSC
NJ	PHU
Jersey Shore, PA	SCR
Jerseyville, IL	SFD
Jessup, PA	PSC
PA	SCR
Jesup, GA	SAV
IA	DUB
Jetmore, KS	DOD
Jewett City, CT	NOR
Jim Falls, WI	LC
Jim Thorpe, PA	ALN
Joanna, SC	CHR
Jobstown, NJ	TR
Joelton, TN	NSH
Johannesburg, MI	GLD
John Day, OR	BAK
Johns Creek, GA	ATL
Johns Island, SC	CHR
Johnsburg, IL	RCK

Place	Code
Johnson City, NY	SY
NY	STF
TN	KNX
Johnsonburg, PA	E
Johnston, IA	DM
RI	PRO
Johnston City, IL	BEL
Johnstown, CO	DEN
NY	ALB
OH	COL
PA	ALT
PA	SJP
PA	PBR
Joliet, IL	JOL
Jolon, CA	MRY
Jonesboro, AR	LR
GA	ATL
Jonesburg, MO	JC
Jonestown, MS	JKS
Jonesville, VA	RIC
Joplin, MO	SPC
Joppa, MD	BAL
Jordan, MN	STP
NY	SY
Jordan Valley, OR	BAK
Jourdanton, TX	SAT
Julesburg, CO	DEN
Julian, CA	SD
Junction, TX	SAN
Junction City, KS	SAL
OR	P
WI	LC
Juneau, AK	AJ
Jupiter, FL	PMB
Justice, IL	CHI
Kahoka, MO	JC
Kahuku, HI	HON
Kahului, HI	HON
Kailua, HI	HON
Kailua–Kona, HI	HON
Kalaheo, HI	HON
Kalamazoo, MI	KAL
Kalaupapa, HI	HON
Kalida, OH	TOL
Kalispell, MT	HEL
Kalkaska, MI	GLD
Kalona, IA	DAV
Kalskag, AK	FBK
Kaltag, AK	FBK
Kamiah, ID	B
Kamuela, HI	HON
Kanab, UT	SLC
Kandiyohi, MN	NU
Kane, PA	E
Kaneohe, HI	HON
Kankakee, IL	JOL
Kannapolis, NC	CHL
Kansas City, KS	KCK
MO	KC
MO	PRM
Kansasville, WI	MIL
Kapaa, HI	HON
Kaplan, LA	LAF
Kapolei, HI	HON
Karnes City, TX	SAT
Kathleen, GA	SAV
Katonah, NY	NY
Katy, TX	GAL
Kaufman, TX	DAL
Kaukauna, WI	GB
Kaunakakai, HI	HON
Kayenta, AZ	GLP
Keams Canyon, AZ	GLP
Keansburg, NJ	TR
Kearney, MO	KC
NE	GI
Kearneysville, WV	WH
Kearns, UT	SLC
Kearny, AZ	TUC
NJ	NEW
Keene, NH	MAN
Keeseville, NY	OG
Keizer, OR	P
Kekaha, HI	HON
Keller, TX	FWT
WA	SPK
Kelliher, MN	CR
Kellnersville, WI	GB
Kellogg, ID	B
Kelly, KS	KCK
Kelso, MO	SPC
WA	SEA
Kemmerer, WY	CHY
Kenai, AK	AJ
Kenansville, NC	R
Kendall, WI	LC
Kendall Park, NJ	MET
Kendallville, IN	FTW
Kenedy, TX	SAT
Kenilworth, NJ	NEW
Kenmare, ND	BIS

Place	Code
Kenmore, NY	BUF
NY	STF
Kennebunk, ME	PRT
Kennebunkport, ME	PRT
Kenner, LA	NO
Kennesaw, GA	ATL
Kennett, MO	SPC
Kennett Square, PA	PH
Kennewick, WA	YAK
Kenosha, WI	MIL
WI	SYM
Kensington, CA	OAK
CT	HRT
MD	WDC
Kent, CT	HRT
MN	SCL
OH	Y
PA	GBG
WA	SEA
Kentfield, CA	SFR
Kentland, IN	LFT
Kenton, OH	COL
Kenyon, MN	STP
Keokuk, IA	DAV
Keota, IA	DAV
Kerens, TX	DAL
Kerhonkson, NY	STF
Kerman, CA	FRS
Kermit, TX	ELP
WV	WH
Kernersville, NC	CHL
Kerrville, TX	SAT
Kersey, PA	E
Keshena, WI	GB
Ketchikan, AK	AJ
Kettering, OH	CIN
Kew Gardens, NY	ROM
Kewanee, IL	PEO
Kewaskum, WI	MIL
Kewaunee, WI	GB
Key Biscayne, FL	MIA
Key Largo, FL	MIA
Key West, FL	MIA
Keyport, NJ	TR
Keyser, WV	WH
Keystone Heights, FL	STA
Kickapoo (Edwards), IL	PEO
Kiel, WI	GB
Kieler, WI	MAD
Kihei, HI	HON
Kilgore, TX	TYL
Killdeer, ND	BIS
Killeen, TX	AUS
Killingworth, CT	NOR
Kilmarnock, VA	ARL
Kiln, MS	BLX
Kimball, MN	SCL
NE	GI
SD	SFS
Kimberling City, MO	SPC
Kimberly, WI	GB
Kimberton, PA	PH
Kincaid, IL	SFD
Kinder, LA	LKC
Kindred, ND	FAR
King City, CA	MRY
King of Prussia, PA	PH
Kingfisher, OK	OKL
Kingman, AZ	PHX
KS	WCH
Kings Park, NY	RVC
Kingsburg, CA	FRS
Kingsford, MI	MAR
Kingsland, TX	AUS
Kingsley, IA	SC
MI	GLD
Kingsport, TN	KNX
Kingston, MA	BO
NY	NY
PA	PSC
PA	SCR
RI	PRO
Kingstree, SC	CHR
Kingsville, MD	BAL
OH	Y
TX	CC
Kingwood, WV	WH
Kinnelon, NJ	PAT
Kinsley, KS	DOD
Kinston, NC	R
Kiowa, KS	DOD
Kirkland, WA	SEA
Kirksville, MO	JC
Kirkwood, MO	STL
NY	SY
Kirtland, OH	CLV
Kissimmee, FL	ORL
Kittanning, PA	GBG
Kittery, ME	PRT
Kitty Hawk, NC	R
Klamath Falls, OR	BAK

Place	Code
Klawock, AK	AJ
Knights Landing, CA	SAC
Knightstown, IN	IND
Knottsville, KY	OWN
Knox, IN	GRY
Knox City, TX	FWT
Knoxville, IA	DAV
TN	KNX
TN	PBR
Kodiak, AK	AJ
Kohler, WI	MIL
Kokomo, IN	LFT
Koloa, HI	HON
Konawa, OK	OKL
Kosciusko, MS	JKS
Kotlik, AK	FBK
Kotzebue, AK	FBK
Kountze, TX	BEA
Kouts, IN	GRY
Koyukuk, AK	FBK
Krakow, WI	GB
Kranzburg, SD	SFS
Krebs, OK	TLS
Krotz Springs, LA	LAF
Kula, HI	HON
Kulpmont, PA	HBG
Kutztown, PA	ALN
Kyle, TX	AUS
L'Anse, MI	MAR
La Canada Flintridge, CA	LA
La Conner, WA	SEA
La Crescent, MN	WIN
La Crescenta, CA	LA
La Crosse, WI	LC
La Feria, TX	BWN
La Follette, TN	KNX
La Grande, OR	BAK
La Grange, IL	CHI
TX	AUS
TX	VIC
La Grange Park, IL	CHI
La Grulla, TX	BWN
La Habra, CA	ORG
La Jolla, CA	SD
La Joya, NM	SFE
TX	BWN
La Junta, CO	PBL
La Luz, NM	LSC
La Marque, TX	GAL
La Mesa, CA	SD
CA	STN
NM	LSC
La Mirada, CA	LA
La Moure, ND	FAR
La Pine, OR	BAK
La Place, LA	NO
La Plata, MD	WDC
La Porte, IN	GRY
TX	GAL
La Pryor, TX	LAR
La Puente, CA	LA
La Quinta, CA	SB
La Salle, IL	PEO
La Valle, WI	MAD
La Verne, CA	LA
La Vernia, TX	SAT
LaBelle, FL	VEN
LaCenter, KY	OWN
LaCoste, TX	SAT
LaCrosse, KS	DOD
LaGrange, GA	ATL
IN	FTW
KY	L
LaGrangeville, NY	NY
LaMoure, ND	FAR
Labadieville, LA	BR
Lac du Flambeau, WI	SUP
Lacey, WA	SEA
Laceyville, PA	SCR
Lackawanna, NY	BUF
NY	STF
Lacombe, LA	NO
Lacon, IL	PEO
Laconia, NH	MAN
Ladera Ranch, CA	ORG
Ladue, MO	STL
Lady Lake, FL	ORL
Ladysmith, VA	RIC
WI	SUP
Lafayette, CA	OAK
CO	DEN
IN	LFT
LA	LAF
MN	NU
NY	SY
TN	NSH
Lafayette Hill, PA	PH
Lafitte, LA	NO
Laflin, PA	SCR
Lago Vista, TX	AUS
Laguna, NM	GLP

Place	Code
Laguna Beach, CA	ORG
Laguna Heights, TX	BWN
Laguna Hills, CA	ROM
Laguna Niguel, CA	ORG
Laguna Woods, CA	ORG
Lagunitas, CA	SFR
Lahaina, HI	HON
Laingsburg, MI	LAN
Lake Almanor, CA	SAC
Lake Ariel, PA	SCR
Lake Arrowhead, CA	SB
Lake Arthur, LA	LKC
Lake Balboa, CA	LA
Lake Charles, LA	LKC
Lake City, FL	STA
IA	SC
MI	GLD
MN	WIN
SC	CHR
Lake Clear, NY	OG
Lake Dallas, TX	FWT
Lake Elmo, MN	STP
Lake Forest, CA	ORG
IL	CHI
Lake Geneva, WI	MIL
Lake George, NY	ALB
Lake Harmony, PA	ALN
Lake Havasu City, AZ	PHX
Lake Hopatcong, NJ	PAT
Lake Jackson, TX	GAL
Lake Katrine, NY	NY
Lake Leelanau, MI	GLD
Lake Linden, MI	MAR
Lake Mills, WI	MAD
Lake Milton, OH	Y
Lake Nebagamon, WI	SUP
Lake Odessa, MI	GR
Lake Orion, MI	DET
Lake Oswego, OR	P
Lake Ozark, MO	JC
Lake Park, MN	CR
Lake Placid, FL	VEN
NY	OG
Lake Providence, LA	SHP
Lake Ridge, VA	ARL
Lake Ronkonkoma, NY	RVC
Lake Saint Louis, MO	STL
Lake St. Croix Beach, MN	STP
Lake Station, IN	GRY
Lake Stevens, WA	SEA
Lake View, NY	BUF
Lake Villa, IL	CHI
Lake Village, AR	LR
IN	LFT
Lake Wales, FL	ORL
Lake Winola, PA	SCR
Lake Worth, FL	PMB
Lake Wylie, SC	CHR
Lake Zurich, IL	CHI
Lakehurst, NJ	TR
Lakeland, FL	ORL
GA	SAV
LA	BR
Lakemont, Altoona, PA	ALT
Lakeport, CA	SR
MI	DET
Lakeside, CA	SD
Lakeview, OR	BAK
Lakeville, CT	HRT
MA	BO
MN	STP
Lakeway, TX	AUS
Lakewood, CA	LA
CO	DEN
CO	OLL
NJ	TR
NY	BUF
OH	CLV
WA	SEA
WI	GB
Lakewood Ranch, FL	VEN
Lakin, KS	DOD
Lakota, ND	FAR
Lamar, CO	PBL
MO	SPC
TX	CC
Lamberton, MN	NU
Lambertville, NJ	MET
Lame Deer, MT	GF
Lamesa, TX	LUB
Lamont, CA	FRS
Lamoure, ND	FAR
Lampasas, TX	AUS
Lanai City, HI	HON
Lanark Village, FL	PT
Lancaster, CA	LA
KY	LEX
MA	WOR
NH	MAN
NY	BUF
NY	STF

Place	Code
OH	COL
PA	HBG
SC	CHR
TX	DAL
WI	MAD
Lancing, TN	KNX
Land O'Lakes, FL	SP
WI	SUP
Lander, WY	CHY
Landisville, NJ	CAM
Landover Hills, MD	WDC
Lanesville, IN	IND
Lanett, AL	BIR
Langdon, ND	FAR
Langhorne, PA	PH
Langley, OK	TLS
WA	SEA
Lanham, MD	WDC
Lansdale, PA	PH
Lansdowne, MD	BAL
PA	PH
Lanse, MI	MAR
Lansford, ND	FAR
PA	ALN
PA	PSC
Lansing, IA	DUB
IL	CHI
KS	KCK
MI	LAN
MI	NTN
NY	ROC
Lantana, FL	PMB
Laona, WI	GB
Lapeer, MI	DET
Laramie, WY	CHY
Larchmont, NY	NY
Larchwood, IA	SC
Laredo, TX	LAR
Largo, FL	SP
MD	WDC
Larimore, ND	FAR
Larkspur, CA	SFR
Larned, KS	DOD
Larose, LA	HT
Las Animas, CO	PBL
Las Cruces, NM	LSC
Las Vegas, NM	SFE
NV	HPM
NV	LAV
NV	OLL
NV	SPA
Lastrup, MN	SCL
Latham, NY	ALB
Lathrop, CA	STO
Laton, CA	FRS
Latrobe, PA	GBG
PA	SJP
PA	PBR
Lauderdale–by–the–Sea, FL	MIA
Laughlin, NV	LAV
Laupahoehoe, HI	HON
Laurel, MD	BAL
MD	WDC
MS	BLX
MT	GF
NE	OM
Laurence Harbor, NJ	MET
Laurens, IA	SC
Laurie, MO	JC
Laurinburg, NC	R
Lavallette, NJ	TR
Laveen, AZ	PHX
Laverock, PA	PH
Lavonia, GA	ATL
Lawrence, KS	KCK
KS	STN
MA	BO
MA	SAM
MA	NTN
NE	LIN
Lawrenceburg, IN	IND
KY	LEX
TN	NSH
Lawrenceville, GA	ATL
IL	BEL
NJ	TR
Lawtell, LA	LAF
Lawton, OK	OKL
Layton, UT	SLC
Le Center, MN	STP
Le Mars, IA	SC
Le Roy, NY	BUF
Le Sueur, MN	STP
LeClaire, IA	DAV
Lead, SD	RC
Leadville, CO	COS
League City, TX	GAL
Leavenworth, KS	KCK
WA	YAK
Leawood, KS	KCK
Lebanon, CT	NOR

Place	Code
IL	BEL
IN	LFT
KY	L
MO	SPC
NH	MAN
OH	CIN
OR	P
PA	HBG
TN	NSH
VA	RIC
Lebanon Junction, KY	L
Lebeau, LA	LAF
Lecanto, FL	SP
Lecompte, LA	ALX
Ledyard, IA	SC
Lee, IL	RCK
MA	SPR
Lee Center, NY	SY
Leechburg, PA	GBG
Leeds, AL	BIR
Lees Summit, MO	KC
Leesburg, FL	ORL
VA	ARL
Leesville, LA	ALX
Leetonia, OH	Y
Lefor, ND	BIS
Lehigh Acres, FL	VEN
Lehighton, PA	ALN
Leicester, MA	WOR
Leigh, NE	OM
Leipsic, OH	TOL
Leisenring, PA	PBR
Leisure City, FL	MIA
Leitchfield, KY	OWN
Leland, MS	JKS
Lemay, MO	STL
Lemhi, ID	B
Lemmon, SD	RC
Lemon Grove, CA	SD
Lemont, IL	CHI
IL	LFT
Lemoore, CA	FRS
Lena, IL	RCK
WI	GB
Lenexa, KS	KCK
Lenni, PA	PH
Lennox, SD	SFS
Lenoir, NC	CHL
Lenoir City, TN	KNX
Lenox, IA	DM
MA	SPR
Lenox Dale, MA	SPR
Leola, SD	SFS
Leominster, MA	WOR
Leon, IA	DM
Leonardtown, MD	WDC
Leonia, NJ	NEW
Leonville, LA	LAF
Leopold, IN	IND
MO	SPC
Leslie, MI	LAN
Levelland, TX	LUB
Levittown, NY	RVC
PA	PH
PA	PSC
Lewes, DE	WIL
Lewis Run, PA	E
Lewisburg, PA	HBG
TN	NSH
Lewisport, KY	OWN
Lewiston, ID	B
ME	PRT
MI	GLD
MN	WIN
NY	BUF
Lewistown, IL	PEO
MT	GF
PA	HBG
Lewisville, TX	FWT
TX	OLL
Lexington, KY	LEX
MA	BO
MA	OLN
MI	SAG
MO	KC
MS	JKS
NC	CHL
NE	GI
OH	TOL
SC	CHR
TN	MEM
TX	AUS
VA	RIC
Lexington Park, MD	WDC
Libby, MT	HEL
Liberal, KS	DOD
Liberty, IL	SFD
IN	IND
KY	L
MO	KC
NY	NY
TN	NSH
TX	BEA
Liberty Township, OH	CIN
Libertytown, MD	BAL
Libertyville, IL	CHI
Lidderdale, IA	SC
Lidgerwood, ND	FAR
Liebenthal, KS	DOD
Lighthouse Point, FL	MIA
Ligonier, IN	FTW
PA	GBG
Liguori, MO	STL
Lihue, HI	HON
Lilburn, GA	ATL
Lillian, AL	MOB
Lilly, PA	ALT
Lima, NY	ROC
OH	TOL
Lime Ridge, WI	MAD
Limerick, ME	PRT
Limon, CO	COS
Lincoln, CA	SAC
IL	PEO
KS	SAL
ME	PRT
NE	LIN
NH	MAN
RI	NTN
RI	PRO
Lincoln City, OR	P
Lincoln Park, MI	DET
NJ	PAT
Lincolnton, NC	CHL
Lincroft, NJ	TR
Lindale, TX	TYL
Linden, CA	STO
NJ	NEW
NJ	PSC
VA	ARL
Lindenhurst, NY	RVC
NY	STF
Lindenwold, NJ	CAM
Lindsay, CA	FRS
NE	OM
TX	FWT
Lindstrom, MN	STP
Linesville, PA	E
Linn, MO	JC
Lino Lakes, MN	STP
Linthicum Heights, MD	BAL
Linton, IN	EVN
ND	BIS
Linwood, MA	WOR
MI	SAG
NJ	CAM
Lisbon, ND	FAR
NY	OG
OH	Y
Lisbon Falls, ME	PRT
Lisle, IL	JOL
Litchfield, CT	HRT
IL	SFD
MN	NU
NH	MAN
OH	CLV
Lithia Springs, GA	ATL
Lithonia, GA	ATL
Lititz, PA	HBG
Little Canada, MN	STP
Little Chute, WI	GB
Little Compton, RI	PRO
Little Egg Harbor Twp, NJ	TR
Little Falls, MN	SCL
NJ	OLN
NJ	PAT
NY	ALB
Little Ferry, NJ	NEW
Little Hocking, OH	STU
Little Meadows, PA	NTN
Little River, KS	WCH
Little Rock, AR	LR
Littlefield, TX	LUB
Littlestown, PA	HBG
Littleton, CO	COS
CO	DEN
MA	BO
NH	MAN
Live Oak, FL	STA
Livermore, CA	OAK
IA	SC
Liverpool, NY	SY
Livingston, AL	BIR
CA	FRS
IL	SFD
MT	GF
NJ	NEW
TX	BEA
Livingston Manor, NY	NY
Livonia, LA	BR
MI	DET
MI	OLL
MI	PRM
MI	MCE
NY	ROC
Llano, TX	AUS
Lock Haven, PA	ALT
Lockeford, CA	STO
Lockhart, TX	AUS
Lockport, IL	JOL
LA	HT
NY	BUF
Locust Valley, NY	STF
Lodge Grass, MT	GF
Lodi, CA	STO
NJ	NEW
WI	MAD
Logan, IA	DM
KS	SAL
OH	COL
WV	WH
Logansport, IN	LFT
Loganville, GA	SYM
Loma Linda, CA	SB
Lombard, IL	JOL
IL	OLL
Lomira, WI	MIL
Lomita, CA	LA
Lompoc, CA	LA
London, KY	LEX
OH	COL
Londonderry, NH	MAN
Lone Pine, CA	FRS
Long Beach, CA	LA
MS	BLX
NY	RVC
Long Branch, NJ	TR
Long Grove, IA	DAV
Long Island City, NY	BRK
NY	STF
Long Lake, MN	STP
WI	GB
Long Prairie, MN	SCL
Long Valley, NJ	PAT
Longboat Key, FL	VEN
Longmeadow, MA	SPR
Longmont, CO	DEN
Longview, TX	TYL
WA	SEA
Longville, MN	DUL
Longwood, FL	ORL
Lonsdale, MN	STP
Loogootee, IN	EVN
Lookout Mountain, GA	ATL
Loomis, CA	SAC
Loose Creek, MO	JC
Lorain, OH	CLV
OH	PRM
OH	SJP
Lordsburg, NM	LSC
Loreauville, LA	LAF
Loretto, KY	L
MN	STP
PA	ALT
TN	NSH
Los Alamitos, CA	ORG
Los Alamos, NM	SFE
Los Altos, CA	SJ
Los Altos Hills, CA	SJ
Los Angeles, CA	LA
CA	OLN
CA	OLL
Los Banos, CA	FRS
Los Fresnos, TX	BWN
Los Gatos, CA	SJ
CA	MRY
CA	HPM
Los Lunas, NM	SFE
Los Nietos, CA	LA
Los Ojos, NM	SFE
Los Osos, CA	MRY
Lost Nation, IA	DAV
IA	DUB
Lott, TX	AUS
Loudonville, NY	ALB
OH	CLV
Louisa, KY	LEX
Louisburg, KS	KCK
NC	R
Louisiana, MO	JC
Louisville, CO	DEN
KY	L
KY	SYM
MS	JKS
OH	Y
Loup City, NE	GI
Loveland, CO	DEN
OH	CIN
Lovell, WY	CHY
Lovelock, NV	RNO
Loves Park, IL	RCK
Lovilia, IA	DAV
Loving, NM	LSC
Lovingston, VA	RIC
Lovington, NM	LSC
Lowell, IN	GRY
MA	BO
MI	GR
OH	STU
VT	BUR
Lowellville, OH	Y
Lower Brule, SD	RC
Lower Burrell, PA	GBG
Lowry, MN	SCL
Lowville, NY	OG
Loyal, WI	LC
Lubbock, TX	LUB
Lucan, MN	NU
Lucerne Valley, CA	SB
Lucinda, PA	E
Luck, WI	SUP
Ludington, MI	GR
Ludlow, KY	COV
MA	SPR
MA	STF
VT	BUR
Luebbering, MO	STL
Lufkin, TX	TYL
Lugoff, SC	CHR
Lukachukai, AZ	GLP
Luling, LA	NO
TX	AUS
Lumberton, MS	BLX
NC	R
NM	GLP
TX	BEA
Lunenburg, MA	WOR
Luray, VA	ARL
Lusk, WY	CHY
Lutherville, MD	BAL
Lutherville Timonium, MD	BAL
Lutz, FL	SP
Luverne, MN	WIN
Luxemburg, IA	DUB
WI	GB
Luzerne, PA	SCR
Lydia, LA	LAF
Lyford, TX	BWN
Lykens, PA	HBG
Lynbrook, NY	RVC
Lynch, NE	OM
Lynchburg, VA	RIC
Lynden, WA	SEA
Lyndhurst, NJ	NEW
OH	CLV
Lyndon Station, WI	LC
Lyndora, PA	PBR
PA	SJP
Lynn, MA	BO
Lynnfield, MA	BO
Lynnwood, WA	SEA
Lynwood, CA	LA
Lyon Mountain, NY	OG
Lyons, IL	CHI
KS	WCH
NE	OM
NY	ROC
WI	MIL
Lytle, TX	SAT
Mableton, GA	ATL
Mabton, WA	YAK
Macclenny, FL	STA
Macdona, TX	SAT
Macedon, NY	ROC
Macedonia, OH	CLV
Machias, ME	PRT
Mackinac Island, MI	MAR
Mackinaw City, MI	GLD
Macomb, IL	PEO
MI	DET
Macon, GA	SAV
MO	JC
Madawaska, ME	PRT
Madeira Beach, FL	SP
Madelia, MN	WIN
Madera, CA	FRS
Madill, OK	OKL
Madison, AL	BIR
CT	HRT
FL	PT
IL	SFD
IL	STN
IN	IND
MN	NU
MS	JKS
NE	OM
NJ	PAT
OH	CLV
SD	SFS
TN	NSH
VA	ARL
WI	MAD
WV	WH
Madison Heights, MI	DET

Place	Code
Madison Lake, MN	STP
MN	WIN
Madisonville, KY	OWN
LA	NO
TN	KNX
TX	TYL
Madras, OR	BAK
Madrid, IA	SC
NE	GI
NY	OG
Magee, MS	JKS
Maggie Valley, NC	CHL
Magna, UT	SLC
Magnolia, AR	LR
DE	WIL
TX	GAL
Magnolia Springs, AL	MOB
Mahanoy City, PA	ALN
PA	PSC
Mahnomen, MN	CR
Mahomet, IL	PEO
Mahopac, NY	NY
Mahtomedi, MN	STP
Mahwah, NJ	NEW
Maine, NY	SY
Makawao, HI	HON
Makoti, ND	BIS
Malakoff, TX	TYL
Malden, MA	BO
Malibu, CA	LA
Malone, NY	OG
WI	MIL
Malta, MT	GF
Malvern, AR	LR
PA	PH
Malverne, NY	RVC
Mamaroneck, NY	NY
Mammoth, AZ	TUC
Mammoth Lakes, CA	STO
Mamou, LA	LAF
Man, WV	WH
Manahawkin, NJ	TR
Manalapan, NJ	TR
NJ	MCE
Manasquan, NJ	TR
Manassas, VA	ARL
VA	PHU
Manawa, WI	GB
Mancelona, MI	GLD
Manchester, CT	HRT
IA	DUB
MA	BO
MD	BAL
MI	LAN
MO	STL
NH	MAN
NH	STF
NH	NTN
TN	NSH
Manchester Center, VT	BUR
Manchester Township, NJ	TR
Manchester by the Sea, MA	BO
Mandan, ND	BIS
Mandaree, ND	BIS
Manderson, SD	RC
Mandeville, LA	NO
Mangum, OK	OKL
Manhasset, NY	RVC
Manhattan, IL	JOL
KS	SAL
Manhattan Beach, CA	LA
Manheim, PA	HBG
Manistee, MI	GLD
Manistique, MI	MAR
Manitou Beach, MI	LAN
Manitowish Waters, WI	SUP
Manitowoc, WI	GB
WI	MIL
Mankato, KS	SAL
MN	WIN
Manley, NE	LIN
Manlius, NY	SY
Manly, IA	DUB
Manning, IA	SC
SC	CHR
Mannington, WV	WH
Manomet, MA	BO
Manor, TX	AUS
TX	SYM
Manorville, NY	RVC
Mansfield, LA	SHP
MA	FR
OH	TOL
PA	SCR
TX	FWT
Manson, IA	SC
Mansura, LA	ALX
Mantador, ND	FAR
Manteca, CA	STO
Manteno, IL	JOL
Mantua, NJ	CAM
OH	Y
Manvel, ND	FAR
TX	GAL
Manville, NJ	MET
RI	PRO
Many, LA	SHP
Maple City, MI	GLD
Maple Glen, PA	PH
Maple Grove, MN	STP
Maple Heights, OH	CLV
Maple Hill, KS	KCK
Maple Lake, MN	STP
Maple Mount, KY	OWN
Maple Park, IL	RCK
Maple Shade, NJ	TR
Mapleton, IA	SC
MN	WIN
Mapleville, RI	PRO
Maplewood, MN	STP
MO	STL
NJ	NEW
Maquoketa, IA	DUB
Marana, AZ	TUC
Marathon, FL	MIA
WI	LC
Marathon City, WI	LC
Marble Falls, TX	AUS
Marblehead, MA	BO
OH	PRM
OH	TOL
Marbury, AL	MOB
Marceline, MO	JC
Marcellus, NY	SY
Marco Island, FL	VEN
Marcus, IA	SC
Marengo, IA	DAV
IL	RCK
Marfa, TX	ELP
Margaretville, NY	ALB
Margate, FL	MCE
FL	MIA
FL	SYM
NJ	CAM
Margate City, NJ	CAM
Maria Stein, OH	CIN
Marianna, AR	LR
FL	PT
Maricopa, AZ	TUC
Marienthal, KS	DOD
Marietta, GA	ATL
NY	SY
OH	STU
Marina, CA	MRY
Marine City, MI	DET
Marine on St. Croix, MN	STP
Marinette, WI	GB
Maringouin, LA	BR
Marion, IA	DUB
IL	BEL
KS	WCH
KY	OWN
MA	FR
OH	COL
VA	RIC
Marionville, MO	SPC
Mariposa, CA	FRS
Marked Tree, AR	LR
Markham, IL	CHI
Marksville, LA	ALX
Marlboro, NJ	TR
NY	NY
Marlborough, CT	HRT
MA	BO
Marlin, TX	AUS
Marlinton, WV	WH
Marlton, NJ	TR
Marmarth, ND	BIS
Marmora, NJ	CAM
Marne, MI	GR
Marquette, MI	MAR
Marrero, LA	NO
Marriottsville, MD	BAL
Mars Hill, NC	CHL
Marseilles, IL	PEO
Marshall, AK	FBK
IL	SFD
MI	KAL
MN	NU
MO	JC
TX	TYL
Marshalltown, IA	DUB
Marshfield, MA	BO
MO	SPC
WI	LC
Mart, TX	AUS
Marthasville, MO	STL
Martin, KY	LEX
OH	TOL
SD	RC
TN	MEM
Martindale, TX	AUS
Martinez, CA	OAK
Martins Creek, PA	ALN
Martins Ferry, OH	STU
Martinsburg, MO	JC
WV	WH
Martinsville, IN	IND
NJ	MET
VA	RIC
Marty, SD	SFS
Mary Esther, FL	PT
Marydel, MD	WIL
Maryknoll, NY	NY
Maryland Heights, MO	STL
Marylhurst, OR	P
Marysville, CA	SAC
KS	KCK
MI	DET
OH	COL
PA	HBG
WA	SEA
Maryville, IL	SFD
MO	KC
Masaryktown, FL	SP
Mascoutah, IL	BEL
Mashpee, MA	FR
Mason, MI	LAN
OH	CIN
TX	AUS
Mason City, IA	DUB
Masontown, PA	GBG
Maspeth, NY	BRK
Massapequa, NY	RVC
Massapequa Park, NY	RVC
Massena, IA	DM
NY	OG
Massillon, OH	Y
Mastic Beach, NY	RVC
Masury, OH	Y
Matamoras, PA	SCR
Matawan, NJ	TR
NJ	MET
NJ	PSC
Mathews, VA	RIC
Mathis, TX	CC
Mattapan, MA	BO
Mattapoisett, MA	FR
Mattawa, WA	YAK
Mattawan, MI	KAL
Matteson, IL	CHI
Mattoon, IL	SFD
Mauldin, SC	CHR
Maumee, OH	TOL
Maurepas, LA	BR
Maurice, LA	LAF
Mauriceville, TX	BEA
Mauston, WI	LC
Maximo, OH	Y
Maybrook, NY	NY
Mayer, AZ	PHX
Mayetta, KS	KCK
Mayfield, KY	OWN
Maynard, MA	BO
Maynardville, TN	KNX
Mays Landing, NJ	CAM
Maysel, WV	WH
Maysville, KY	COV
Mayville, ND	FAR
WI	MIL
Maywood, CA	LA
IL	CHI
IL	SYM
NJ	NEW
Mazomanie, WI	MAD
Mc Intosh, SD	RC
Mc Kean, PA	E
Mc Lean, VA	ARL
Mc Leansboro, IL	BEL
McAdoo, PA	ALN
PA	PHU
PA	PSC
McAfee, NJ	PAT
McAlester, OK	TLS
McAllen, TX	BWN
McCall, ID	B
McCamey, TX	SAN
McComb, MS	JKS
McConnellsburg, PA	ALT
McCook, NE	LIN
McCormick, SC	CHR
McDonald, OH	Y
PA	PIT
McDonough, GA	ATL
McEwen, TN	NSH
McFarland, CA	FRS
WI	MAD
McGehee, AR	LR
McGrath, AK	FBK
McGregor, MN	DUL
TX	AUS
McHenry, IL	RCK
McKees Rocks, PA	PBR
PA	PIT
PA	SJP
McKeesport, PA	PBR
PA	PIT
PA	ROM
PA	SJP
McKenzie Bridge, OR	P
McKinleyville, CA	SR
McKinney, TX	DAL
McLaughlin, SD	RC
McLean, VA	ARL
VA	NTN
VA	WDC
McMechen, WV	WH
McMinnville, OR	P
TN	NSH
McMurray, PA	PIT
McNair, TX	GAL
McPherson, KS	WCH
McRae, GA	SAV
McSherrystown, PA	HBG
Mcnary, AZ	GLP
Mead, CO	DEN
NE	LIN
Meade, KS	DOD
Meadow Lands, PA	PIT
Meadowbrook, PA	PH
Meadville, PA	E
Mecca, CA	SB
Mechanicsburg, OH	CIN
PA	HBG
Mechanicsville, IA	DAV
MD	WDC
VA	RIC
Mechanicville, NY	ALB
Medfield, MA	BO
Medford, MA	BO
MN	WIN
NJ	TR
NY	RVC
OK	OKL
OR	P
WI	SUP
Media, PA	PH
Medical Lake, WA	SPK
Medicine Lodge, KS	DOD
Medina, NY	BUF
OH	CLV
Medway, MA	BO
Meeker, CO	DEN
Megargel, TX	FWT
Meherrin, VA	RIC
Melbourne, FL	ORL
KY	COV
Melbourne Beach, FL	ORL
Melcher, IA	DAV
Mellen, WI	SUP
Mellette, SD	SFS
Melrose, IA	DAV
MA	BO
MA	POC
MN	SCL
WI	LC
Melrose Park, IL	CHI
PA	PHU
Melville, LA	LAF
NY	RVC
Melvindale, MI	DET
Memphis, MI	DET
MO	JC
TN	MEM
TX	AMA
Mena, AR	LR
Menahga, MN	SCL
Menands, NY	ALB
Menard, TX	SAN
Menasha, WI	GB
Mendham, NJ	PAT
Mendocino, CA	SR
Mendon, MI	KAL
NY	ROC
Mendota, CA	FRS
IL	PEO
MN	STP
Mendota Heights, MN	OLL
MN	STP
Menlo Park, CA	SJ
CA	SFR
Menoken, ND	BIS
Menominee, MI	MAR
Menomonee Falls, WI	MIL
Menomonie, WI	LC
Mentor, MN	CR
OH	CLV
Mentor–on–the–Lake, OH	PRM
Mequon, WI	MIL
Meraux, LA	NO
Merced, CA	FRS
Mercedes, TX	BWN
Mercer, PA	E
WI	SUP

Mercer Island, WA	SEA
Merchantville, NJ	CAM
Meredith, NH	MAN
Meriden, CT	HRT
Meridian, ID	B
MS	JKS
Merion Station, PA	PH
Mermentau, LA	LAF
Merrick, NY	RVC
Merrill, IA	SC
OR	BAK
WI	SUP
Merrillville, IN	GRY
IN	PRM
Merrimack, NH	MAN
Merritt Island, FL	ORL
Mesa, AZ	PHX
ID	B
Mesilla, NM	LSC
Mesilla Park, NM	LSC
Mesquite, NV	LAV
TX	DAL
TX	MCE
Metairie, LA	NO
Metamora, IL	PEO
Methuen, MA	BO
MA	NTN
Metropolis, IL	BEL
Metuchen, NJ	MET
Mexia, TX	AUS
Mexico, ME	PRT
MO	JC
NY	SY
Mexico Beach, FL	PT
Meyersdale, PA	ALT
Meyersville, TX	VIC
Miami, AZ	TUC
FL	ARL
FL	PSC
FL	SAM
FL	SJP
FL	NTN
FL	MIA
OK	TLS
Miami Beach, FL	MIA
Miami Gardens, FL	MIA
Miami Lakes, FL	MIA
Miami Shores, FL	MIA
Miamisburg, OH	CIN
Michigan Center, MI	LAN
Michigan City, IN	GRY
Middle Village, NY	BRK
Middlebourne, WV	WH
Middleburg, FL	STA
VA	ARL
Middleburg Heights, OH	CLV
Middleburgh, NY	ALB
Middlebury, CT	HRT
VT	BUR
Middlefield, CT	NOR
Middlesboro, KY	LEX
Middlesex, NJ	MET
Middleton, MA	BO
WI	MAD
Middletown, CA	SR
CT	NOR
DE	WIL
MD	BAL
NJ	TR
NY	NY
NY	STF
OH	CIN
PA	HBG
RI	PRO
Middletown Springs, VT	BUR
Midland, MD	BAL
MI	SAG
PA	PIT
TX	SAN
Midland City, AL	MOB
Midland Park, NJ	NEW
Midlothian, IL	CHI
VA	RIC
Midvale, UT	SLC
Midway City, CA	ORG
Midwest City, OK	OKL
Mifflintown, PA	HBG
Milaca, MN	SCL
Milan, IL	PEO
IN	IND
MI	LAN
MO	JC
NM	GLP
OH	TOL
Milbank, SD	SFS
Miles, TX	SAN
Miles City, MT	GF
Milford, CT	HRT
DE	WIL
IA	SC
MA	WOR

MI	DET
NH	MAN
NJ	MET
OH	CIN
PA	SCR
UT	SLC
Mililani Town, HI	HON
Mill Creek, WA	SEA
Mill Valley, CA	SFR
Milladore, WI	LC
Millbrae, CA	OLL
CA	SFR
Millbrook, NY	NY
Millbury, MA	WOR
Milledgeville, GA	ATL
Millen, GA	SAV
Miller, SD	SFS
Miller City, OH	TOL
Millersburg, OH	COL
PA	HBG
Millersville, MD	BAL
Millington, TN	MEM
Millis, MA	BO
Millstadt, IL	BEL
Millstone Township, NJ	TR
Milltown, NJ	MET
Millville, MA	WOR
NJ	CAM
NJ	PHU
Milmont Park, PA	PH
Milnor, ND	FAR
Milpitas, CA	SJ
CA	SYM
Milroy, MN	NU
Milton, FL	PT
LA	LAF
MA	BO
PA	HBG
VT	BUR
WI	MAD
Milton Freewater, OR	BAK
Milwaukee, WI	MIL
WI	STN
WI	NTN
Milwaukie, OR	P
Mims, FL	ORL
Minden, LA	SHP
NE	LIN
Mineola, NY	RVC
TX	TYL
Mineral, VA	RIC
Mineral Point, WI	MAD
Mineral Ridge, OH	Y
Mineral Wells, TX	FWT
Minersville, PA	ALN
PA	PSC
PA	PHU
Minerva, OH	STU
Minetto, NY	SY
Mingo Junction, OH	PBR
OH	STU
Minneapolis, KS	SAL
MN	OLL
MN	STP
MN	STN
MN	PRM
Minneota, MN	NU
Minnetonka, MN	STP
Minong, WI	SUP
Minooka, IL	JOL
Minot, ND	BIS
Minster, OH	CIN
Minto, ND	FAR
Minturn, CO	DEN
Mio, MI	GLD
Miramar, FL	MIA
Miramar Beach, FL	PT
Mishawaka, IN	FTW
IN	STN
Mishicot, WI	GB
Misquamicut, RI	PRO
Mission, KS	KCK
SD	RC
TX	BWN
Mission Hills, CA	LA
Mission Viejo, CA	ORG
Missoula, MT	HEL
Missouri City, TX	GAL
TX	SYM
Missouri Valley, IA	DM
Mitchell, IN	IND
NE	GI
SD	SFS
Mitchellville, MD	WDC
Moab, UT	SLC
Moberly, MO	JC
Mobile, AL	MOB
AL	POC
Mobridge, SD	SFS
Mocanaqua, PA	SCR
Mocksville, NC	CHL

Modesto, CA	STO
Mogadore, OH	Y
Mohall, ND	BIS
Mohawk, NY	ALB
Mohnton, PA	ALN
Mokane, MO	JC
Mokena, IL	JOL
Molalla, OR	P
Moline, IL	PEO
KS	WCH
Momence, IL	JOL
Monaca, PA	PIT
Monahans, TX	ELP
Moncks Corner, SC	CHR
Mondovi, WI	LC
Monee, IL	JOL
Monessen, PA	GBG
PA	PBR
Moneta, VA	RIC
Monett, MO	SPC
Monkton, MD	BAL
Monmouth, IL	PEO
OR	P
Monmouth Beach, NJ	TR
Monmouth Junction, NJ	MET
Monona, IA	DUB
WI	MAD
Monongah, WV	WH
Monongahela, PA	PIT
Monroe, CT	BGP
GA	ATL
LA	SHP
MI	DET
NC	CHL
NY	NY
OH	CIN
WA	SEA
WI	MAD
Monroe City, MO	JC
Monroe Township, NJ	MET
Monroeville, AL	MOB
IN	FTW
OH	TOL
PA	PBR
PA	PIT
Monrovia, CA	LA
Monsey, NY	NY
Monson, MA	SPR
Mont Belvieu, TX	BEA
Mont Clare, PA	PSC
Montague, MI	GR
NJ	PAT
Montauk, NY	RVC
Montclair, CA	SB
NJ	NEW
Monte Vista, CO	PBL
Montebello, CA	LA
Montegut, LA	HT
Montello, WI	MAD
Monterey, CA	MRY
IN	LFT
Monterey Park, CA	LA
Montevallo, AL	BIR
Montevideo, MN	NU
Montezuma, OH	CIN
Montfort, WI	MAD
Montgomery, AL	MOB
IN	EVN
MN	STP
NY	NY
WV	WH
Montgomery City, MO	JC
Monticello, AR	LR
IA	DUB
IL	PEO
IN	LFT
KY	LEX
MN	STP
NY	NY
UT	SLC
Montoursville, PA	SCR
Montpelier, OH	TOL
VA	RIC
VT	BUR
Montrose, CA	LA
CA	OLN
CO	PBL
IL	SFD
MI	LAN
MO	KC
NY	NY
PA	SCR
SD	SFS
Montvale, NJ	NEW
Montville, NJ	PAT
Monument, CO	COS
Moodus, CT	NOR
Mooers, NY	OG
Mooers Forks, NY	OG
Moon Township, PA	PIT
Moore, OK	OKL

Moore Haven, FL	VEN
Moorefield, WV	WH
Moorestown, NJ	TR
Mooresville, IN	IND
NC	CHL
Mooreton, ND	FAR
Moorhead, MN	CR
Moorpark, CA	LA
Moose Lake, MN	DUL
Moosup, CT	NOR
Mora, MN	SCL
NM	SFE
Moraga, CA	OAK
Moreauville, LA	ALX
Morehead, KY	LEX
Morehead City, NC	R
Morenci, AZ	TUC
Moreno Valley, CA	SB
Morgan, MN	NU
TX	FWT
Morgan City, LA	HT
LA	LAF
Morgan Hill, CA	SJ
Morganfield, KY	OWN
Morganton, NC	CHL
Morgantown, KY	OWN
WV	WH
WV	PBR
Morganza, LA	BR
MD	WDC
Moriarty, NM	SFE
Morning View, KY	COV
Morrice, MI	LAN
Morrilton, AR	LR
Morris, IL	JOL
IN	IND
MN	SCL
NY	ALB
Morris Plains, NJ	PAT
Morrisdale, PA	E
Morrison, IL	RCK
Morrisonville, IL	SFD
NY	OG
Morristown, NJ	PAT
NY	OG
TN	KNX
Morrisville, NY	SY
PA	PH
VT	BUR
Morro Bay, CA	MRY
Morrow, LA	LAF
OH	CIN
Morse, LA	LAF
Morse Bluff, NE	LIN
Morton, IL	PEO
MN	NU
PA	PH
TX	LUB
WA	SEA
Morton Grove, IL	CHI
IL	MCE
IL	SYM
Moscow, ID	B
PA	SCR
Moses Lake, WA	YAK
Mosinee, WI	LC
Moss Beach, CA	SFR
Moss Bluff, LA	LKC
Moss Point, MS	BLX
Mott, ND	BIS
Moulton, AL	BIR
TX	VIC
Moultrie, GA	SAV
Mound, MN	STP
Mound Bayou, MS	JKS
Mound City, IL	BEL
Moundsville, WV	WH
Mount Airy, MD	BAL
Mount Angel, OR	P
Mount Arlington, NJ	PAT
Mount Calvary, WI	MIL
Mount Carmel, IL	BEL
PA	HBG
PA	PHU
Mount Carroll, IL	RCK
Mount Clemens, MI	DET
Mount Dora, FL	ORL
Mount Ephraim, NJ	CAM
Mount Holly, NJ	TR
Mount Hope, KS	WCH
Mount Horeb, WI	MAD
Mount Ida, AR	LR
Mount Jewett, PA	E
Mount Joy, PA	HBG
Mount Laurel, NJ	TR
Mount Morris, MI	LAN
Mount Olive, IL	SFD
NC	R
Mount Pleasant, IA	DAV
MI	SAG
PA	GBG

Place	Code
SC	CHR
TX	TYL
Mount Pocono, PA	SCR
Mount Rainier, MD	WDC
Mount Saint Francis, IN	IND
Mount Shasta, CA	SAC
Mount St. Francis, IN	IND
Mount St. Joseph, OH	CIN
Mount Sterling, IL	SFD
KY	LEX
Mount Union, PA	ALT
Mount Vernon, AL	MOB
IA	DUB
IL	BEL
IN	EVN
KY	LEX
MO	SPC
NY	NY
TX	TYL
WA	SEA
Mount Victoria, MD	WDC
Mount Washington, KY	L
Mountain City, TN	KNX
Mountain Grove, MO	SPC
Mountain Home, AR	LR
ID	B
TX	SAT
Mountain Home A F B, ID	B
Mountain Lakes, NJ	PAT
Mountain Top, PA	SCR
Mountain View, AR	LR
CA	SJ
HI	HON
MO	SPC
Mountain Village, AK	FBK
Mountainair, NM	SFE
Mountainside, NJ	NEW
Mountlake Terrace, WA	SEA
Moville, IA	SC
Moweaqua, IL	SFD
Moxee, WA	YAK
Mt. Airy, NC	CHL
Mt. Kisco, NY	NY
Mt. Lebanon, PA	PIT
Mt. Prospect, IL	CHI
Mt. Vernon, OH	COL
Mt. Zion, IL	SFD
Muenster, TX	FWT
Mukwonago, WI	MIL
Muleshoe, TX	LUB
Mullen, NE	GI
Mullens, WV	WH
Mullica Hill, NJ	CAM
Mulvane, KS	WCH
Muncie, IN	LFT
Muncy, PA	SCR
Munday, TX	FWT
Mundelein, IL	CHI
Munhall, PA	PBR
PA	PIT
Munich, ND	FAR
Munising, MI	MAR
Munjor, KS	SAL
Munnsville, NY	SY
Munster, IN	GRY
IN	STN
IN	PRM
Murdock, MN	NU
Murfreesboro, TN	NSH
Murphy, NC	CHL
Murphy Village, SC	CHR
Murphysboro, IL	BEL
Murray, KY	OWN
UT	OLL
UT	SLC
Murrells Inlet, SC	CHR
Murrieta, CA	SB
Murrysville, PA	GBG
Muscatine, IA	DAV
Muse, PA	PIT
Muskego, WI	MIL
Muskegon, MI	GR
Muskegon Heights, MI	GR
Muskogee, OK	TLS
Mustang, OK	OKL
Myerstown, PA	HBG
Myrtle Beach, SC	CHR
Myrtle Creek, OR	P
Mystic, CT	NOR
Naalehu, HI	HON
Naches, WA	YAK
Nacogdoches, TX	TYL
Nada, TX	VIC
Nadeau, MI	MAR
Nahant, MA	BO
Nampa, ID	B
Nanakuli, HI	HON
Nanticoke, PA	PHU
PA	SCR
Nantucket, MA	FR
Nanty–Glo, PA	ALT

Place	Code
PA	PBR
Nanuet, NY	NY
Napa, CA	SR
Naperville, IL	JOL
Naples, FL	VEN
Napoleon, IN	IND
ND	FAR
OH	TOL
Napoleonville, LA	BR
Naranja, FL	MIA
Narberth, PA	PH
Narragansett, RI	PRO
Narrowsburg, NY	NY
Nashotah, WI	MIL
Nashua, IA	DUB
NH	MAN
Nashville, AR	LR
IL	BEL
IN	IND
KS	WCH
TN	NSH
Nashwauk, MN	DUL
Nassau, NY	ALB
Natchez, LA	ALX
MS	JKS
Natchitoches, LA	ALX
Natick, MA	BO
National City, CA	SD
MI	GLD
Natrona Heights, PA	PIT
Naugatuck, CT	HRT
Nauvoo, IL	PEO
Navajo, NM	GLP
Navarre, FL	PT
OH	Y
Navasota, TX	GAL
Nazareth, KY	L
MI	KAL
PA	ALN
TX	AMA
Nebraska City, NE	LIN
Necedah, WI	LC
Nederland, TX	BEA
Needham, MA	BO
Needles, CA	SB
Needville, TX	GAL
Neenah, WI	GB
Neffs, OH	STU
Negaunee, MI	MAR
Neillsville, WI	LC
Nekoosa, WI	LC
Neligh, NE	OM
Nelsonville, OH	STU
Nenana, AK	FBK
Neodesha, KS	WCH
Neola, IA	DM
Neopit, WI	GB
Neosho, MO	SPC
Neptune, NJ	TR
Nerinx, KY	L
Nesbit, MS	JKS
Nesconset, NY	RVC
Nespelem, WA	SPK
Nesquehoning, PA	ALN
PA	PSC
Ness City, KS	DOD
Netcong, NJ	PAT
Nevada, MO	KC
Nevada City, CA	SAC
Nevis, MN	CR
New Albany, IN	IND
MS	JKS
OH	COL
New Alexandria, PA	GBG
New Almelo, KS	SAL
New Athens, IL	BEL
New Baden, IL	BEL
New Baltimore, MI	DET
MI	MCE
PA	ALT
New Bavaria, OH	TOL
New Bedford, MA	FR
MA	SAM
New Berlin, IL	SFD
NY	SY
WI	MIL
New Bern, NC	R
New Bethlehem, PA	E
New Blaine, AR	LR
New Bloomfield, PA	HBG
New Boston, MI	DET
OH	COL
TX	TYL
New Braunfels, TX	SAT
New Bremen, OH	CIN
New Brighton, MN	STP
PA	PIT
New Britain, CT	HRT
CT	STF
CT	PSC
New Brunswick, NJ	MET

Place	Code
NJ	PSC
New Buffalo, MI	KAL
New Cambria, MO	JC
New Canaan, CT	BGP
New Caney, TX	GAL
New Carlisle, IN	FTW
OH	CIN
New Castle, DE	WIL
IN	IND
PA	PIT
PA	SAM
VA	RIC
New City, NY	NY
New Cumberland, PA	HBG
WV	WH
New Cuyama, CA	LA
New Egypt, NJ	TR
New England, ND	BIS
New Fairfield, CT	BGP
New Franken, WI	GB
New Freedom, PA	HBG
New Hampton, IA	DUB
New Hartford, CT	HRT
NY	SY
New Haven, CT	HRT
CT	STF
IN	FTW
KY	L
MO	STL
New Hill, NC	R
New Holland, PA	HBG
New Holstein, WI	GB
New Hope, KY	L
MN	STP
PA	PH
New Hyde Park, NY	MCE
NY	RVC
New Iberia, LA	LAF
New Ipswich, NH	MAN
New Kensington, PA	GBG
New Lebanon, NY	ALB
New Leipzig, ND	BIS
New Lenox, IL	JOL
New Lexington, OH	COL
New Lisbon, WI	LC
New London, CT	NOR
MN	NU
NH	MAN
OH	TOL
WI	GB
New Lothrop, MI	SAG
New Madrid, MO	SPC
New Market, MN	STP
TN	KNX
New Martinsville, WV	WH
New Melle, MO	STL
New Middletown, OH	Y
New Milford, CT	HRT
NJ	NEW
New Monmouth, NJ	TR
New Munich, MN	SCL
New Munster, WI	MIL
New Orleans, LA	NO
LA	PBR
New Oxford, PA	HBG
New Paltz, NY	NY
New Philadelphia, OH	COL
PA	ALN
New Port Richey, FL	SP
FL	PSC
New Prague, MN	STP
New Providence, NJ	NEW
New Richland, MN	WIN
New Richmond, OH	CIN
WI	SUP
New Riegel, OH	TOL
New Ringgold, PA	ALN
New River, AZ	PHX
New Roads, LA	BR
New Rochelle, NY	NY
NY	MCE
New Rockford, ND	FAR
New Salem, ND	BIS
PA	PBR
New Smyrna Beach, FL	ORL
New Town, ND	BIS
New Trier, MN	STP
New Ulm, MN	NU
TX	VIC
New Vernon, NJ	PAT
New Vienna, IA	DUB
New Washington, OH	TOL
New Waverly, TX	GAL
New Windsor, NY	NY
New York, NY	NY
NY	PRO
NY	STF
NY	PSC
New York Mills, NY	SY
Newark, CA	OAK
DE	WIL

Place	Code
NJ	NEW
NJ	PSC
NJ	PHU
NY	ROC
OH	COL
VT	STF
Newaygo, MI	GR
Newberg, OR	P
Newberry, MI	MAR
SC	CHR
Newburg, MD	WDC
WI	MIL
Newburgh, IN	EVN
NY	NY
Newbury, OH	CLV
Newbury Park, CA	LA
Newburyport, MA	BO
Newcastle, WY	CHY
Newcomb, NY	OG
Newcomerstown, OH	COL
Newfane, NY	BUF
Newfield, NJ	CAM
Newington, CT	HRT
Newman, CA	STO
Newmarket, NH	MAN
Newnan, GA	ATL
Newport, KY	COV
MI	DET
NH	MAN
NY	ALB
OR	P
RI	PRO
TN	KNX
VT	BUR
WA	SPK
Newport Beach, CA	ORG
Newport News, VA	RIC
Newry, PA	ALT
Newtok, AK	FBK
Newton, IA	DAV
IL	BEL
IL	SFD
KS	WCH
MA	BO
MA	OLD
NC	CHL
NJ	PAT
WI	GB
Newton Falls, OH	Y
OH	PBR
Newton Grove, NC	R
Newtown, CT	BGP
PA	PH
Newtown Square, PA	PH
PA	SAM
Nez Perce, ID	B
Niagara, WI	GB
Niagara Falls, NY	BUF
NY	STF
Niagara University, NY	BUF
Niantic, CT	NOR
Niceville, FL	PT
Nicholasville, KY	LEX
Nicholson, PA	SCR
Nicktown, PA	ALT
Nicollet, MN	NU
Nightmute, AK	FBK
Niles, IL	CHI
MI	KAL
OH	Y
Nine Mile Falls, WA	SPK
Nipomo, CA	MRY
Nisswa, MN	DUL
Nitro, WV	WH
Nixa, MO	SPC
Nixon, TX	SAT
Noblesville, IN	LFT
Nogales, AZ	TUC
Nokomis, FL	VEN
IL	SFD
Nome, AK	FBK
Norco, CA	SB
LA	NO
Norcross, GA	ATL
GA	SYM
Norfolk, MA	BO
NE	OM
NY	OG
VA	RIC
Norge, VA	RIC
Normal, IL	PEO
Norman, OK	OKL
OK	OLL
Normandy, MO	STL
Norridge, IL	CHI
Norris, TN	KNX
Norristown, PA	PH
North Adams, MA	SPR
North Andover, MA	BO
North Arlington, NJ	NEW
North Attleboro, MA	FR

Place	Code
North Augusta, SC	CHR
North Aurora, IL	RCK
North Baltimore, OH	TOL
North Bay, NY	SY
North Beach, MD	WDC
North Bend, NE	OM
OH	CIN
OR	P
North Bennington, VT	BUR
North Bergen, NJ	NEW
North Bethesda, MD	WDC
North Branch, MI	DET
MN	STP
North Branford, CT	HRT
North Brookfield, MA	WOR
North Brunswick, NJ	MET
North Caldwell, NJ	NEW
North Canton, OH	Y
North Cape May, NJ	CAM
North Charleston, SC	CHR
North Chesterfield, VA	RIC
North Chili, NY	ROC
North Collins, NY	BUF
North Conway, NH	MAN
North Creek, NY	ALB
North Dartmouth, MA	FR
North Dighton, MA	FR
North East, PA	E
North Easton, MA	FR
North English, IA	DAV
North Falmouth, MA	FR
North Fond du Lac, WI	MIL
North Grafton, MA	WOR
North Grosvenordale, CT	NOR
North Guilford, CT	HRT
North Haledon, NJ	PAT
North Haven, CT	HRT
North Highlands, CA	SAC
North Hills, CA	LA
North Hollywood, CA	LA
CA	NTN
CA	OLD
CA	SPA
CA	MCE
North Huntingdon, PA	GBG
PA	PBR
North Jackson, OH	Y
OH	OLL
North Judson, IN	GRY
North Kingstown, RI	PRO
North Lake, WI	MIL
North Las Vegas, NV	LAV
North Lauderdale, FL	MIA
North Lewisburg, OH	CIN
North Lima, OH	Y
North Little Rock, AR	LR
North Manchester, IN	FTW
North Mankato, MN	NU
North Merrick, NY	RVC
North Miami, FL	MIA
North Miami Beach, FL	MIA
North Muskegon, MI	GR
North Myrtle Beach, SC	CHR
North Olmsted, OH	CLV
North Oxford, MA	WOR
North Palm Beach, FL	PMB
North Plainfield, NJ	MET
North Plains, OR	P
North Platte, NE	GI
NE	LIN
North Pole, AK	FBK
North Port, FL	SJP
FL	VEN
North Providence, RI	PRO
North Reading, MA	BO
North Richland Hills, TX	FWT
North Ridgeville, OH	CLV
North Riverside, IL	CHI
North Royalton, OH	CLV
OH	PRM
North Saint Paul, MN	STP
North Scituate, RI	PRO
North Smithfield, RI	PRO
North Stonington, CT	NOR
North Syracuse, NY	SY
North Tonawanda, NY	BUF
North Troy, VT	BUR
North Vernon, IN	IND
North Wales, PA	PH
North Wildwood, NJ	CAM
North Wilkesboro, NC	CHL
Northampton, MA	SPR
PA	ALN
PA	PHU
Northboro, MA	WOR
Northbridge, MA	WOR
Northbrook, IL	CHI
IL	EST
Northern Cambria, PA	ALT
PA	SJP
PA	PBR

Place	Code
Northfield, IL	CHI
MA	SPR
MN	STP
NJ	CAM
OH	CLV
VT	BUR
Northford, CT	HRT
Northglenn, CO	DEN
Northlake, IL	CHI
IL	NTN
Northport, NY	RVC
WA	SPK
Northridge, CA	LA
Northvale, NJ	NEW
Northville, MI	DET
NY	ALB
Northwood, OH	PRM
Norton, KS	SAL
MA	FR
OH	CLV
VA	RIC
Nortonville, KS	KCK
Norwalk, CA	LA
CT	BGP
CT	SYM
IA	DM
OH	TOL
Norway, ME	PRT
MI	MAR
Norwell, MA	BO
Norwich, CT	NOR
NY	SY
Norwichtown, CT	NOR
Norwood, MA	BO
MN	STP
NJ	NEW
NY	OG
PA	PH
Notre Dame, IN	FTW
Novato, CA	SFR
Novi, MI	DET
Nulato, AK	FBK
Nutley, NJ	NEW
Nyack, NY	NY
Nyssa, OR	BAK
O Fallon, IL	BEL
O'Donnell, TX	LUB
O'Fallon, MO	STL
O'Neill, NE	OM
Oak Brook, IL	JOL
Oak Creek, WI	MIL
Oak Forest, IL	CHI
Oak Grove, KY	OWN
LA	SHP
MN	STP
Oak Harbor, OH	TOL
WA	SEA
Oak Hill, WV	WH
Oak Lawn, IL	CHI
Oak Park, IL	CHI
MI	DET
MI	EST
Oak Park Heights, MN	STP
Oak Ridge, NJ	PAT
TN	KNX
Oak Ridge–Milton, NJ	PAT
Oakbrook Terrace, IL	JOL
IL	OLL
Oakdale, CA	STO
CT	NOR
IL	BEL
LA	LKC
MN	STP
NE	OM
NY	RVC
PA	PIT
Oakes, ND	FAR
Oakfield, NY	BUF
Oakhurst, CA	FRS
Oakland, CA	OAK
MD	BAL
NJ	NEW
Oakland City, IN	EVN
Oakland Gardens, NY	BRK
Oakland Park, FL	MIA
Oakley, CA	OAK
KS	SAL
Oaklyn, NJ	CAM
Oakmont, PA	PIT
Oakridge, OR	P
Oakville, CA	SR
CT	HRT
MO	STL
Oberlin, KS	SAL
LA	LKC
OH	CLV
Obernburg, NY	NY
Ocala, FL	ORL
Occidental, CA	SR
Ocean Beach, NY	RVC
Ocean City, MD	WIL

Place	Code
NJ	CAM
Ocean Grove, NJ	TR
Ocean Springs, MS	BLX
Oceanside, CA	SD
CA	POC
CA	NTN
NY	RVC
Oconee, IL	SFD
Oconomowoc, WI	MIL
Oconto, WI	GB
Oconto Falls, WI	GB
Odebolt, IA	SC
Odem, TX	CC
Odenton, MD	BAL
Odessa, MO	KC
TX	SAN
Oelwein, IA	DUB
Ogallala, NE	GI
Ogden, IA	SC
UT	SLC
Ogdensburg, NJ	PAT
NY	OG
Ogema, MN	CR
Oglala, SD	RC
Oglesby, IL	PEO
Ohio, IL	PEO
Ohkay Owingeh, NM	SFE
Oil City, PA	E
Ojai, CA	LA
Okanogan, WA	SPK
Okarche, OK	OKL
Okawville, IL	BEL
Okeechobee, FL	PMB
Okeene, OK	OKL
Okemos, MI	LAN
Oklahoma City, OK	OKL
OK	SYM
Oklee, MN	CR
Okmulgee, OK	TLS
Olathe, KS	KCK
Old Bethpage, NY	SYM
Old Bridge, NJ	MET
Old Forge, NY	OG
PA	PSC
PA	SCR
Old Hickory, TN	NSH
Old Lyme, CT	NOR
Old Mill Creek, IL	CHI
Old Monroe, MO	STL
Old Orchard Beach, ME	PRT
Old Saybrook, CT	NOR
Old Tappan, NJ	NEW
Old Town, ME	PRT
Old Westbury, NY	RVC
Oldenburg, IN	IND
Olean, NY	BUF
NY	SAM
NY	PSC
Olema, CA	SFR
Olive Branch, MS	JKS
Olive Hill, KY	LEX
Olivia, MN	NU
Olmito, TX	BWN
Olmitz, KS	DOD
Olmsted Falls, OH	CLV
Olney, IL	BEL
MD	WDC
Olpe, KS	KCK
Olton, TX	LUB
Olympia, WA	HPM
WA	ROM
WA	SEA
Olympia Fields, IL	CHI
Olyphant, PA	PHU
PA	SCR
Omaha, NE	OM
NE	STN
Omak, WA	SPK
Omro, WI	GB
Ona, WV	WH
Onaga, KS	KCK
Onalaska, WI	LC
Onamia, MN	SCL
Onawa, IA	SC
Onaway, MI	GLD
Oneida, NY	SY
WI	GB
Onekama, MI	GLD
Oneonta, AL	BIR
NY	ALB
Onida, SD	SFS
Onley, VA	RIC
Onset, MA	FR
Onsted, MI	DET
Ontario, CA	SB
NY	ROC
OR	BAK
Ontonagon, MI	MAR
Opelika, AL	MOB
Opelousas, LA	LAF
Oquossoc, ME	PRT

Place	Code
Oracle, AZ	TUC
Oradell, NJ	NEW
Oran, MO	SPC
Orange, CA	OLL
CA	ORG
CT	HRT
MA	SPR
NJ	NEW
TX	BEA
VA	ARL
Orange Beach, AL	MOB
Orange Cove, CA	FRS
Orange Grove, TX	CC
Orange Park, FL	STA
Orangeburg, NY	NY
SC	CHR
Orangevale, CA	SAC
CA	SPA
Orbisonia, PA	ALT
Orchard Lake, MI	DET
Orchard Park, NY	BUF
Ord, NE	GI
Orefield, PA	ALN
Oregon, IL	RCK
OH	TOL
WI	MAD
Oregon City, OR	P
Oreland, PA	PH
Orem, UT	SLC
Oriental, NC	R
Orinda, CA	OAK
Orion, IL	PEO
Oriska, ND	FAR
Oriskany Falls, NY	SY
Orland, CA	SAC
Orland Hills, IL	CHI
Orland Park, IL	CHI
Orlando, FL	ORL
FL	SAM
FL	SYM
FL	PSC
FL	POC
Orleans, MA	FR
NE	LIN
Ormond Beach, FL	ORL
Orofino, ID	B
Orono, ME	PRT
Oroville, CA	SAC
WA	SPK
Orr, MN	DUL
Orrtanna, PA	HBG
Orrville, AL	MOB
OH	CLV
Ortonville, MI	DET
MN	NU
Orwell, OH	Y
Orwigsburg, PA	ALN
Osage, IA	DUB
Osage City, KS	KCK
Osakis, MN	SCL
Osawatomie, KS	KCK
Osborne, KS	SAL
Osceola, AR	LR
IA	DM
NE	LIN
WI	SUP
Osceola Mills, PA	E
Oscoda, MI	GLD
Osgood, IN	IND
OH	CIN
Oshkosh, WI	GB
Oskaloosa, IA	DAV
Oslo, MN	CR
Osmond, NE	OM
Osprey, FL	VEN
Osseo, MN	STP
Ossineke, MI	GLD
Ossining, NY	NY
Osterville, MA	FR
Oswego, IL	JOL
KS	WCH
NY	SY
Osyka, MS	JKS
Othello, WA	SPK
Otis Orchards, WA	SPK
Otisville, MI	LAN
NY	NY
Oto, IA	SC
Otsego, MI	KAL
Ottawa, IL	PEO
KS	KCK
OH	TOL
Otter River, MA	WOR
Ottoville, OH	TOL
Ottsville, PA	PH
Ottumwa, IA	DAV
Ouray, CO	PBL
Overgaard, AZ	GLP
Overland, MO	STL
Overland Park, KS	KCK
Overton, NV	LAV

Ovid, MI LAN
NY ROC
Oviedo, FL ORL
Owasso, OK TLS
Owatonna, MN WIN
Owego, NY ROC
Owen, WI LC
Owensboro, KY OWN
Owensville, MO JC
OH CIN
Owings, MD WDC
Owings Mills, MD BAL
Owingsville, KY LEX
Owosso, MI LAN
Oxford, CT HRT
IA DAV
IN LFT
MA WOR
MI DET
MS JKS
NJ MET
NY SY
OH CIN
PA PH
Oxnard, CA LA
CA ROM
Oxon Hill, MD WDC
Oyster Bay, NY RVC
Ozark, AL MOB
AR LR
MO SPC
Ozona, TX SAN
Ozone, AR LR
Ozone Park, NY BRK
NY STF
Pacific, MO STL
Pacific Grove, CA MRY
Pacific Palisades, CA LA
Pacifica, CA SFR
Pacoima, CA LA
Paden City, WV WH
Paducah, KY OWN
Page, AZ GLP
Pagosa Springs, CO PBL
Pahala, HI HON
Pahoa, HI HON
Pahokee, FL PMB
Pahrump, NV LAV
Paia, HI HON
Paincourtville, LA BR
Painesville, OH CLV
Painesville Township, OH CLV
Paintsville, KY LEX
Pajaro, CA MRY
Pala, CA SD
Palacios, TX VIC
Palatine, IL CHI
IL STN
Palatka, FL STA
Palestine, TX TYL
Palisades Park, NJ NEW
Palm Bay, FL ORL
Palm Beach, FL PMB
Palm Beach Gardens, FL PMB
Palm City, FL PMB
Palm Coast, FL STA
Palm Desert, CA SB
Palm Harbor, FL SP
Palm Springs, CA SB
FL PMB
Palmdale, CA LA
Palmer, AK AJ
MA SPR
Palmerton, PA ALN
PA PHU
Palmetto, FL VEN
Palmetto Bay, FL MIA
Palmview, TX BWN
Palmyra, MO JC
NE LIN
PA HBG
VA RIC
WI MAD
Palo Alto, CA SJ
Palos Heights, IL CHI
Palos Hills, IL CHI
Palos Park, IL CHI
IL STN
Pampa, TX AMA
Pana, IL SFD
Panama, IA DM
Panama City, FL PT
Panama City Beach, FL PT
Panhandle, TX AMA
Panna Maria, TX SAT
Panora, IA DM
Panorama City, CA LA
Paola, KS KCK
Paoli, IN IND
PA PH
Paonia, CO PBL
Papaikou, HI HON
Papillion, NE OM
Paradis, LA NO
Paradise, CA SAC
MI MAR
Paradox, NY ALB
Paragould, AR LR
Paramount, CA LA
Paramus, NJ NEW
Parchment, MI KAL
Pardeeville, WI MAD
Paris, AR LR
IL SFD
KY LEX
TN MEM
TX TYL
Parisville, MI SAG
Park, KS SAL
Park City, UT SLC
Park Falls, WI SUP
Park Forest, IL CHI
IL JOL
Park Hills, KY COV
MO STL
Park Rapids, MN CR
Park Ridge, IL CHI
NJ NEW
Park River, ND FAR
Parker, AZ TUC
CO COS
SD SFS
Parkers Prairie, MN SCL
Parkersburg, WV WH
Parkesburg, PA PH
Parkland, FL MIA
Parkman, OH CLV
Parks, LA LAF
Parkston, SD SFS
Parkton, MD BAL
Parkville, MD BAL
Parlier, CA FRS
Parlin, NJ MET
Parma, OH CLV
OH SJP
OH PRM
Parma Heights, OH CLV
Parnell, MO KC
Parrish, FL VEN
Parshall, ND BIS
Parsippany, NJ PAT
Parsons, KS WCH
Pasadena, CA LA
MD BAL
TX GAL
Pascagoula, MS BLX
Pasco, WA SPK
Pascoag, RI PRO
Paso Robles, CA MRY
Pass Christian, MS BLX
Passaic, NJ PAT
NJ PHU
NJ PSC
Patagonia, AZ TUC
Patchogue, NY RVC
Paterson, NJ PAT
NJ SYM
Patterson, CA STO
LA LAF
NY NY
Pattison, TX GAL
Patton, PA ALT
PA PBR
Paulding, OH TOL
Paulina, LA BR
Pavilion, NY BUF
Paw Paw, MI KAL
Pawcatuck, CT NOR
Pawhuska, OK TLS
Pawleys Island, SC CHR
Pawling, NY NY
Pawnee Rock, KS DOD
Pawtucket, RI PRO
Paxton, IL JOL
MA WOR
Paynesville, MN SCL
Payneville, KY L
Payson, AZ PHX
AZ POC
AZ TUC
UT SLC
Pe Ell, WA SEA
Peabody, MA BO
Peachtree City, GA ATL
Peachtree Corners, GA ATL
Peapack, NJ MET
Pearce, AZ TUC
Pearisburg, VA RIC
Pearl, MS JKS
Pearl City, HI HON
Pearl River, LA NO
NY NY
Pearland, TX GAL
Pearsall, TX SAT
Pecatonica, IL RCK
Peckville, PA SCR
Pecos, NM SFE
TX ELP
Peebles, OH CIN
Peekskill, NY NY
NY PSC
Pekin, IL PEO
Pelham, NH MAN
NY NY
Pelham Manor, NY NY
Pelican Rapids, MN SCL
Pella, IA DAV
Pellston, MI GLD
Pembina, ND FAR
Pembine, WI GB
Pembroke, GA ATL
MA BO
Pembroke Pines, FL MIA
Pen Argyl, PA ALN
Pena Blanca, NM SFE
Penacook, NH MAN
Penasco, NM SFE
Pender, NE OM
Pendleton, OR BAK
Penelope, TX FWT
Penfield, IL PEO
NY ROC
Peninsula, OH CLV
Penitas, TX BWN
Penn Hills, PA PIT
Penn Yan, NY ROC
Penndel, PA PH
Penngrove, CA SR
Pennington, NJ TR
Pennsauken, NJ CAM
Pennsburg, PA PH
Pensacola, FL PT
Peoria, AZ PHX
IL OLL
IL PEO
Peoria Heights, IL PEO
Peosta, IA DUB
Peotone, IL JOL
Pepper Pike, OH CLV
Pepperell, MA BO
Pequannock, NJ PAT
Pequot Lakes, MN DUL
Peralta, NM SFE
Perham, MN SCL
Perkins, MI MAR
Perris, CA SB
CA SPA
Perry, FL PT
IA DM
KS KCK
MO JC
NY BUF
OH CLV
OK OKL
Perry Hall, MD BAL
Perryopolis, PA GBG
PA PBR
Perrysburg, OH TOL
Perryton, TX AMA
Perryville, MD WIL
MO STL
Perth Amboy, NJ MET
NJ PHU
NJ PSC
Peru, IL PEO
IN LFT
NY OG
Peshtigo, WI GB
Petal, MS BLX
Petaluma, CA SR
Peterborough, NH MAN
Petersburg, AK AJ
IL SFD
IN EVN
NE OM
VA RIC
WV WH
Petersham, MA SAM
MA WOR
Petoskey, MI GLD
Pevely, MO STL
Pewamo, MI GR
Pewaukee, WI MIL
Pewee Valley, KY L
Pflugerville, TX AUS
Pharr, TX BWN
Phelan, CA SB
Phenix City, AL MOB
Philadelphia, MS JKS
PA PH
PA SYM
PA SAM
PA PSC
PA MCE
PA PHU
Philip, SD RC
Philippi, WV WH
WV OLL
Philipsburg, PA ALT
Phillips, WI SUP
Phillipsburg, KS SAL
NJ MET
NJ PSC
Philo, IL PEO
Philpot, KY OWN
Phlox, WI GB
Phoenicia, NY NY
Phoenix, AZ HPM
AZ NTN
AZ OLL
AZ PHX
AZ SYM
AZ STN
NY SY
Phoenixville, PA PH
PA PHU
Picayune, MS BLX
Pickens, SC CHR
Pickerel, WI GB
Pickerington, OH COL
Pico Rivera, CA LA
Piedmont, CA OAK
MO SPC
OK OKL
SD RC
Pierce, NE OM
Pierce City, MO SPC
Pierceton, IN FTW
Piermont, NY NY
Pierre, SD SFS
Pierre Part, LA BR
Pierron, IL SFD
Pierz, MN SCL
Piffard, NY ROC
Pigeon Forge, TN KNX
Pikeville, KY LEX
Pilot Grove, MO JC
Pilot Point, TX FWT
Pilot Rock, OR BAK
Pilot Station, AK FBK
Pinckney, MI LAN
Pinckneyville, IL BEL
Pinconning, MI SAG
Pine Bluff, AR LR
Pine Bluffs, WY CHY
Pine Bush, NY NY
Pine City, MN DUL
NY ROC
Pine Island, MN STP
NY NY
Pine Mountain, GA SAV
Pine Plains, NY NY
Pine Prairie, LA LAF
Pine Ridge, SD RC
Pinecrest, FL MIA
Pinedale, WY CHY
Pinehurst, NC R
Pinellas Park, FL SP
Pinetop, AZ GLP
Pineville, LA ALX
Pinole, CA OAK
Pinon, AZ GLP
Pipestone, MN WIN
Piqua, OH CIN
Pirtleville, AZ TUC
Piscataway, NJ MET
Pisek, ND FAR
Pismo Beach, CA MRY
Pitman, NJ CAM
Pittsboro, NC R
Pittsburg, CA OAK
KS WCH
TX TYL
Pittsburgh, PA PBR
PA SJP
PA SYM
PA PIT
Pittsfield, IL SFD
MA SPR
MA STF
NH MAN
Pittsford, NY ROC
VT BUR
Pittston, PA PSC
PA SCR
Pittstown, NJ MET
Pittsville, WI LC
Placentia, CA NTN
CA ORG
Placerville, CA SAC
Plain, WI MAD
Plain City, OH COL
Plainfield, CT NOR
IL JOL

Place	Code
IN	IND
NJ	NEW
WI	GB
Plains, KS	DOD
MT	HEL
PA	SCR
Plainsboro, NJ	MET
Plainview, MN	WIN
NE	OM
NY	RVC
TX	LUB
Plainville, CT	HRT
KS	SAL
MA	BO
Plaistow, NH	MAN
Planada, CA	FRS
Plankinton, SD	SFS
Plano, IL	JOL
TX	DAL
Plant City, FL	SP
FL	SYM
Plantation, FL	MIA
Plantersville, TX	GAL
Plantsville, CT	HRT
Plaquemine, LA	BR
Platte, SD	SFS
Platte Center, NE	OM
Platte City, MO	KC
Plattekill, NY	NY
Platteville, CO	DEN
WI	MAD
Plattsburg, MO	KC
Plattsburgh, NY	OG
Plattsmouth, NE	LIN
Plaucheville, LA	ALX
Playa del Rey, CA	LA
Plaza, ND	BIS
Pleasant City, OH	PBR
Pleasant Grove, AL	BIR
Pleasant Hill, CA	OAK
MO	KC
Pleasant Mount, PA	SCR
Pleasant Prairie, WI	MIL
Pleasant Valley, NY	NY
Pleasanton, CA	OAK
CA	SAC
TX	SAT
Pleasantville, NJ	CAM
NJ	SAM
NY	NY
Plentywood, MT	GF
Plover, WI	LC
WI	SUP
Plum, PA	PIT
Plum City, WI	LC
Plymouth, IN	FTW
MA	BO
MI	DET
MI	LAN
MI	NTN
MN	STP
NC	R
NH	MAN
OH	TOL
PA	PHU
PA	SCR
WI	MIL
Plymouth Meeting, PA	PH
Pocahontas, AR	LR
IA	SC
Pocasset, MA	FR
Pocatello, ID	B
Pocomoke City, MD	WIL
Pocono Pines, PA	SCR
Pocono Summit, PA	PSC
Point Arena, CA	SR
Point Lookout, NY	RVC
Point Pleasant, NJ	TR
WV	WH
Point Pleasant Beach, NJ	TR
Point Richmond, CA	OAK
Pointe A La Hache, LA	NO
Poland, OH	Y
Polo, IL	RCK
Polson, MT	HEL
Pomeroy, OH	STU
WA	SPK
Pomfret, CT	NOR
MD	WDC
Pomona, CA	LA
NJ	CAM
Pompano Beach, FL	MIA
Pompey, NY	SY
Pompton Lakes, NJ	PAT
Pompton Plains, NJ	PAT
Ponca, NE	OM
Ponca City, OK	OKL
Ponchatoula, LA	BR
Ponte Vedra Beach, FL	STA
Pontiac, IL	BEL
IL	PEO
MI	DET
Pontotoc, MS	JKS
Poolesville, MD	WDC
Poplar, MT	GF
Poplar Bluff, MO	SPC
Poquonock, CT	HRT
Porcupine, SD	RC
Port Allen, LA	BR
Port Angeles, WA	SEA
Port Aransas, TX	CC
Port Arthur, TX	BEA
Port Austin, MI	SAG
Port Barre, LA	LAF
Port Carbon, PA	ALN
Port Charlotte, FL	VEN
Port Chester, NY	NY
Port Clinton, OH	TOL
Port Edwards, WI	LC
Port Ewen, NY	NY
Port Gibson, MS	JKS
Port Henry, NY	OG
Port Huron, MI	DET
Port Isabel, TX	BWN
Port Jefferson, NY	RVC
Port Jefferson Station, NY	RVC
Port Jervis, NY	NY
Port Lavaca, TX	VIC
Port Leyden, NY	OG
Port Murray, NJ	MET
Port Neches, TX	BEA
Port Orange, FL	ORL
Port Orchard, WA	SEA
Port Reading, NJ	MET
Port Richey, FL	SP
Port Saint Lucie, FL	PMB
Port Sanilac, MI	SAG
Port St. Joe, FL	PT
Port St. Lucie, FL	PMB
Port Sulphur, LA	NO
Port Tobacco, MD	WDC
Port Townsend, WA	SEA
Port Vue, PA	PIT
Port Washington, NY	RVC
WI	MIL
Port Wentworth, GA	SAV
Portage, IN	GRY
MI	KAL
PA	ALT
PA	PBR
WI	MAD
Portage Des Sioux, MO	STL
Portageville, MO	SPC
Portales, NM	SFE
Porter, TX	GAL
Porterfield, WI	GB
Porterville, CA	FRS
Portland, CT	NOR
IN	LFT
ME	PRT
MI	GR
OR	P
OR	OLL
OR	HPM
OR	BAK
TX	CC
Portola, CA	SAC
Portola Valley, CA	SFR
Portsmouth, IA	DM
NH	MAN
OH	COL
RI	PRO
VA	RIC
Posen, IL	CHI
MI	GLD
Poseyville, IN	EVN
Post, TX	LUB
Post Falls, ID	B
Poteau, OK	TLS
Poteet, TX	SAT
Poth, TX	SAT
Potomac, MD	WDC
Potomac Falls, VA	ARL
Potosi, MO	STL
WI	MAD
Pottstown, PA	PH
PA	PHU
PA	PSC
Pottsville, PA	ALN
Poughkeepsie, NY	NY
Poulsbo, WA	SEA
Poultney, VT	BUR
Poway, CA	SD
Powell, OH	COL
WY	CHY
Powers Lake, ND	BIS
Powhatan, VA	RIC
WV	WH
Poynette, WI	MAD
Prague, NE	LIN
OK	OKL
Prairie Du Chien, WI	LC
Prairie Village, KS	KCK
Prairie du Rocher, IL	BEL
Prairie du Sac, WI	MAD
Prairieville, LA	BR
Pratt, KS	DOD
Prattville, AL	MOB
Prayer Town, TX	AMA
Premont, TX	CC
Prescott, AZ	PHX
MI	GLD
WI	LC
Prescott Valley, AZ	PHX
Presho, SD	RC
Presidio, TX	ELP
Preston, CT	NOR
IA	DUB
Prestonsburg, KY	LEX
Price, UT	SLC
Prichard, AL	MOB
Priest River, ID	B
Primos, PA	PH
Prince Frederick, MD	WDC
Princess Anne, MD	WIL
Princeton, FL	MIA
IL	PEO
IN	EVN
KY	OWN
MA	WOR
MN	SCL
NJ	TR
WI	MAD
WV	WH
Princeton Jct., NJ	TR
Princeville, IL	PEO
Prineville, OR	BAK
Prior Lake, MN	STP
Proctor, MN	DUL
VT	BUR
WV	WH
Progreso, TX	BWN
Prophetstown, IL	RCK
Prospect, CT	HRT
KY	L
PA	PIT
Prospect Heights, IL	CHI
Prospect Park, NJ	PAT
Prosper, TX	FWT
Prosser, WA	YAK
Protivin, IA	DUB
Providence, RI	PRO
Provincetown, MA	FR
Prudenville, MI	GLD
Pryor, MT	GF
OK	TLS
Pueblo, CO	PBL
Pueblo West, CO	PBL
Pueblo of Acoma, NM	GLP
Pulaski, NY	SY
PA	PIT
TN	NSH
WI	GB
Pullman, WA	SPK
Punta Gorda, FL	VEN
Punxsutawney, PA	E
PA	PBR
Purcell, OK	OKL
Purcellville, VA	ARL
Put–In–Bay, OH	TOL
Putnam, CT	BUR
CT	NOR
Putney, VT	BUR
Puyallup, WA	SEA
Pylesville, MD	BAL
Quaker Hill, CT	NOR
Quakertown, PA	PH
Quarryville, PA	HBG
Queen Creek, AZ	PHX
Queens, NY	BRK
Queens Village, NY	BRK
Queensbury, NY	ALB
Questa, NM	SFE
Quincy, CA	SAC
FL	PT
IL	SFD
MA	BO
WA	YAK
Quinlan, TX	DAL
Quinque, VA	RIC
Quinton, VA	RIC
Raceland, LA	HT
Racine, WI	MIL
WI	SYM
Radcliff, KY	L
Radford, VA	RIC
Radnor, PA	PH
PA	OLN
Radom, IL	BEL
Raeford, NC	R
Raeville, NE	OM
Ragley, LA	LKC
Rahway, NJ	MCE
NJ	NEW
NJ	PSC
Rainelle, WV	WH
Rainier, OR	P
Raleigh, NC	R
NC	SJP
NC	SAM
Ralls, TX	LUB
Ralston, NE	OM
Ramah, NM	GLP
Ramey, PA	E
PA	SJP
Ramona, CA	SD
OK	TLS
Ramsey, IL	SFD
MN	STP
NJ	NEW
Rancho Cordova, CA	SAC
Rancho Cucamonga, CA	SB
Rancho Dominguez, CA	LA
Rancho Palos Verdes, CA	LA
Rancho Santa Fe, CA	SD
Rancho Santa Margarita, CA	ORG
Ranchos De Taos, NM	SFE
Rancocas, NJ	TR
Randall, MN	SCL
Randallstown, MD	BAL
Randolph, MA	BO
NE	OM
NJ	PAT
NY	BUF
VT	BUR
Random Lake, WI	MIL
Ranger, TX	FWT
Ransomville, NY	BUF
Rantoul, IL	PEO
Rapid City, SD	RC
Rapid River, MI	MAR
Rapids City, IL	PEO
Raritan, NJ	MET
Ratcliff, AR	LR
Raton, NM	SFE
Ravena, NY	ALB
Ravenna, KY	LEX
MI	GR
NE	GI
OH	Y
Ravenswood, WV	WH
Rawlins, WY	CHY
Ray Township, MI	DET
Raymond, IL	SFD
MS	JKS
WA	SEA
Raymondville, TX	BWN
Raymore, MO	KC
Rayne, LA	LAF
Raynham Center, MA	FR
Raytown, MO	KC
Rayville, LA	SHP
Raywick, KY	L
Raywood, TX	BEA
Reading, MA	BO
OH	CIN
PA	ALN
PA	PHU
Red Bank, NJ	TR
Red Bluff, CA	SAC
Red Bud, IL	BEL
Red Cloud, NE	LIN
Red Hook, NY	NY
Red Lake, MN	CR
Red Lake Falls, MN	CR
Red Lodge, MT	GF
Red Oak, IA	DM
Red Springs, NC	R
Red Wing, MN	STP
Redding, CA	SAC
CT	BGP
Redfield, SD	SFS
Redford, MI	DET
NY	OG
Redford Township, MI	DET
Redgranite, WI	GB
Redlands, CA	SB
Redmond, OR	BAK
WA	SEA
Redondo Beach, CA	LA
Redwood City, CA	SJ
CA	SFR
Redwood Falls, MN	NU
Redwood Valley, CA	STN
Reed, KY	OWN
Reed City, MI	GR
Reedley, CA	FRS
Reedsburg, WI	MAD
Reedsport, OR	P
Reese, MI	SAG
Reeseville, WI	MIL
Refugio, TX	CC
Regent, ND	BIS
Rego Park, NY	BRK

Place	Code
Rehoboth Beach, DE	WIL
Reidsville, NC	CHL
Reinbeck, IA	DUB
Remington, IN	LFT
Remsen, IA	SC
Remus, MI	GR
Renault, IL	BEL
Reno, NV	RNO
Renovo, PA	ALT
Rensselaer, IN	LFT
NY	ALB
Renton, WA	SEA
Renville, MN	NU
Republic, MI	MAR
WA	SPK
Reseda, CA	LA
Reserve, LA	NO
NM	GLP
Reston, VA	ARL
Revere, MA	BO
Revillo, SD	SFS
Reynolds, IN	LFT
ND	FAR
Reynoldsburg, OH	COL
Reynoldsville, PA	E
Rhame, ND	BIS
Rhinebeck, NY	NY
Rhineland, MO	JC
Rhinelander, WI	SUP
Rialto, CA	SB
Rib Lake, WI	SUP
Ribera, NM	SFE
Rice, MN	SCL
Rice Lake, WI	SUP
Riceville, IA	DUB
Rich Fountain, MO	JC
Richardson, TX	DAL
Richardton, ND	BIS
Richboro, PA	PH
Richfield, MN	STP
OH	CLV
Richford, VT	BUR
Richland, IA	DAV
NJ	CAM
NY	SY
WA	YAK
Richland Center, WI	LC
Richmond, CA	OAK
IL	RCK
IN	IND
KY	LEX
MI	DET
MN	SCL
MO	KC
OH	STU
TX	GAL
VA	RIC
VT	BUR
Richmond Heights, MO	STL
Richmond Hill, GA	SAV
NY	BRK
Richwood, TX	GAL
WV	WH
Richwoods, MO	STL
Riderwood, MD	BAL
Ridge, MD	WDC
Ridge Manor, FL	SP
Ridgecrest, CA	FRS
Ridgefield, CT	BGP
NJ	NEW
Ridgefield Park, NJ	NEW
Ridgeland, SC	CHR
Ridgely, MD	WIL
Ridgeway, WI	MAD
Ridgewood, NJ	NEW
NY	BRK
Ridgway, PA	E
Ridley Park, PA	PH
Riegelsville, PA	PH
Rifle, CO	DEN
Ringtown, PA	ALN
Ringwood, NJ	PAT
Rio Bravo, TX	LAR
Rio Grande, OH	STU
Rio Grande City, TX	BWN
Rio Hondo, TX	BWN
Rio Rancho, NM	SFE
Rio Rico, AZ	TUC
Rio Vista, CA	SAC
Ripley, MS	JKS
OH	CIN
Ripon, CA	STO
WI	MIL
Rittman, OH	CLV
Ritzville, WA	SPK
River Edge, NJ	NEW
River Falls, WI	LC
WI	SUP
River Forest, IL	CHI
River Grove, IL	CHI
River Ridge, LA	NO
Riverbank, CA	STO
Riverdale, CA	FRS
GA	ATL
IL	CHI
MD	WDC
NY	NY
Riverdale Park, MD	WDC
Riverhead, NY	RVC
NY	STF
Riverside, CA	SB
CA	OLL
CT	BGP
IA	DAV
IL	CHI
NJ	TR
RI	PRO
Riverton, IL	SFD
NJ	TR
UT	SLC
WY	CHY
Riverview, FL	SP
MI	DET
Riviera, TX	CC
Riviera Beach, FL	PMB
Roanoke, IL	PEO
IN	FTW
VA	RIC
VA	SAM
Roanoke Rapids, NC	R
Roaring Brook Twp., PA	SCR
Roaring Spring, PA	ALT
Robbinsdale, MN	STP
Robertsdale, AL	MOB
Robesonia, PA	ALN
Robinson, IL	SFD
Robinsonville, MS	JKS
Robstown, TX	CC
Rochelle, IL	RCK
Rochelle Park, NJ	NEW
Rochester, IL	SFD
IN	LFT
MI	DET
MN	WIN
NH	MAN
NY	NTN
NY	STF
NY	ROC
PA	PIT
Rochester Hills, MI	DET
Rock Creek, OH	Y
Rock Falls, IL	RCK
Rock Hill, SC	CHR
Rock Island, IL	PEO
Rock Rapids, IA	SC
Rock Springs, WY	CHY
Rock Valley, IA	SC
Rockaway, NJ	PAT
NY	BRK
OR	P
Rockaway Beach, NY	BRK
Rockaway Park, NY	BRK
Rockaway Point, NY	BRK
Rockdale, IL	JOL
TX	AUS
Rockford, IA	DUB
IL	RCK
MI	GR
OH	CIN
WA	SPK
Rockland, MA	BO
WI	LC
Rockledge, FL	ORL
Rocklin, CA	SAC
Rockport, IN	EVN
TX	CC
Rocksprings, TX	SAT
Rockville, CT	NOR
IN	IND
MD	WDC
MN	SCL
VA	RIC
Rockville Centre, NY	RVC
Rockwall, TX	DAL
Rockwell, IA	DUB
Rockwood, MI	DET
Rocky Ford, CO	PBL
Rocky Hill, CT	HRT
Rocky Mount, MO	STL
NC	R
VA	RIC
Rocky Point, NY	RVC
Rocky River, OH	CLV
Rodeo, CA	OAK
Roebling, NJ	TR
NJ	PSC
NJ	ROM
Roeland Park, KS	KCK
Rogers, AR	LR
MN	STP
TX	AUS
Rogers City, MI	GLD
Rogersville, MO	SPC
TN	KNX
Roggen, CO	DEN
Rohnert Park, CA	SR
Rolette, ND	FAR
Rolla, MO	JC
ND	FAR
Rolling Meadows, IL	CHI
Rolling Prairie, IN	GRY
Rollingstone, MN	WIN
Roma, TX	BWN
Rome, GA	ATL
NY	SY
Rome City, IN	FTW
Romeo, MI	DET
Romeoville, IL	JOL
Romney, WV	WH
Romulus, MI	DET
Ronan, MT	HEL
Ronceverte, WV	WH
Ronkonkoma, NY	RVC
Roosevelt, NY	RVC
UT	SLC
Roosevelt Island, NY	NY
Rootstown, OH	Y
Rosamond, CA	FRS
Roscoe, IL	RCK
PA	PIT
Roscommon, MI	GLD
Roseau, MN	CR
Rosebud, SD	RC
Roseburg, OR	P
Rosedale, MS	JKS
NY	BRK
Roseland, NE	LIN
NJ	NEW
Roselle, IL	JOL
NJ	NEW
Roselle Park, NJ	NEW
Rosemead, CA	LA
Rosemont, IL	CHI
PA	PH
Rosemount, MN	STP
Rosenberg, TX	GAL
Rosendale, NY	NY
Roseville, CA	SAC
MI	DET
MN	STP
Rosholt, SD	SFS
Roslindale, MA	BO
Roslyn, NY	RVC
PA	PH
Ross, CA	SFR
Rossford, OH	SJP
OH	TOL
Rossville, KS	KCK
Roswell, GA	ATL
GA	PSC
NM	LSC
Rotan, TX	LUB
Rothschild, WI	LC
Round Lake, IL	CHI
NY	ALB
Round Rock, TX	AUS
Roundup, MT	GF
Rouses Point, NY	OG
Rouseville, PA	E
Rowena, TX	SAN
Rowland Heights, CA	LA
Rowlett, TX	DAL
Roxboro, NC	R
Roxbury, MA	BO
Roy, NM	SFE
Royal, IA	SC
Royal City, WA	YAK
Royal Oak, MI	DET
Royal Palm Beach, FL	PMB
Royalton, MN	SCL
Royersford, PA	PH
Ruby, AK	FBK
Rudolph, WI	LC
Rudyard, MI	MAR
Rugby, ND	FAR
Ruidoso, NM	LSC
Rulo, NE	LIN
Rumford, RI	PRO
Rumson, NJ	TR
Runge, TX	SAT
Runnemede, NJ	CAM
Running Springs, CA	SB
Rupert, ID	B
Rush, NY	ROC
Rush City, MN	STP
Rushford, MN	WIN
Rushville, IL	PEO
IN	IND
Ruskin, FL	SP
Russell, KS	SAL
MA	SPR
Russells Point, OH	CIN
Russellton, PA	PIT
Russellville, AL	BIR
AR	LR
KY	OWN
MO	JC
Russia, OH	CIN
Ruston, LA	SHP
Ruth, MI	SAG
Rutherford, NJ	NEW
Ruthven, IA	SC
Rutland, MA	WOR
VT	BUR
Rutledge, TN	KNX
Rydal, PA	PH
Rye, NY	NY
Rye Beach, NH	MAN
Rye Brook, NY	NY
Sabattus, ME	PRT
Sabetha, KS	KCK
Sabinal, TX	SAT
Sac City, IA	SC
Saco, ME	PRT
Sacramento, CA	HPM
CA	SYM
CA	STN
CA	NTN
CA	SAC
Saddle Brook, NJ	NEW
Saddle River, NJ	NEW
Safety Harbor, FL	SP
Safford, AZ	TUC
Sag Harbor, NY	RVC
Saginaw, MI	SAG
Sahuarita, AZ	TUC
St. Agatha, ME	PRT
St. Albans, ME	PRT
NY	BRK
VT	BUR
WV	WH
St. Amant, LA	BR
St. Ann, MO	STL
St. Anne, IL	JOL
St. Anthony, ID	B
IN	EVN
MN	STP
ND	FAR
St. Augustine, FL	STA
St. Benedict, KS	KCK
LA	NO
OR	P
St. Bernard, LA	NO
St. Bonaventure, NY	BUF
St. Bonifacius, MN	STP
St. Catharine, KY	L
St. Charles, IL	RCK
MI	SAG
MN	WIN
MO	STL
St. Clair, MI	DET
MO	STL
PA	ALN
Saint Clair, PA	ALN
St. Clair Shores, MI	DET
St. Clairsville, OH	STU
St. Cloud, FL	ORL
MN	SCL
Saint Cloud, MN	SCL
St. Columbans, NE	OM
St. Croix, IN	IND
St. David, AZ	TUC
St. Edward, NE	OM
St. Elizabeth, MO	JC
St. Francis, KS	SAL
KY	L
SD	RC
WI	MIL
St. Francisville, LA	BR
St. Gabriel, LA	BR
St. George, UT	SLC
St. Hedwig, TX	SAT
St. Helen, MI	GLD
St. Helena, CA	SR
St. Helena Island, SC	CHR
St. Helens, OR	P
St. Henry, OH	CIN
St. Ignace, MI	MAR
St. Ignatius, MT	HEL
St. Inigoes, MD	WDC
St. James, LA	BR
MN	WIN
MO	JC
NY	RVC
St. John, FL	STA
IN	GRY
KS	DOD
ND	FAR
WA	SPK
St. Johns, AZ	GLP
FL	STA
MI	LAN
St. Johnsbury, VT	BUR
St. Joseph, LA	ALX

Place	Code
MI	KAL
MN	SCL
MO	KC
MO	STN
St. Leo, FL	SP
MN	NU
St. Libory, IL	BEL
NE	GI
St. Louis, MO	MIL
MO	STL
MO	STN
MO	PRM
MO	OLL
MO	WCH
MO	WIN
Saint Louis, MO	STL
St. Louis County, MO	STL
St. Louis Park, MN	STP
St. Maries, ID	B
St. Martin, MN	SCL
OH	CIN
St. Martinville, LA	LAF
St. Mary, MO	STL
St. Mary of the Woods, IN	IND
St. Mary's, MO	BEL
St. Mary's City, MD	WDC
St. Marys, AK	FBK
GA	SAV
IA	DM
KS	KCK
OH	CIN
PA	E
WV	WH
St. Meinrad, IN	IND
St. Michael, AK	FBK
MN	STP
ND	FAR
PA	ALT
St. Michaels, AZ	GLP
St. Nazianz, WI	GB
WI	ROM
St. Paul, KS	WCH
MN	STP
MN	SYM
MO	STL
NE	GI
OR	P
VA	RIC
St. Paul Park, MN	STP
St. Pete Beach, FL	SP
St. Peter, MN	NU
St. Peters, MO	STL
St. Petersburg, FL	SP
Saint Petersburg, FL	SP
St. Petersburg, FL	SJP
FL	PSC
St. Regis Falls, NY	OG
St. Robert, MO	JC
St. Rose, IL	BEL
St. Simons Island, GA	SAV
St. Stephen, MN	SCL
St. Stephens, WY	CHY
St. Theresa, WI	MIL
St. Thomas, MO	JC
St. Xavier, MT	GF
Salado, TX	AUS
Salamanca, NY	BUF
Salem, IL	BEL
IN	IND
MA	BO
MA	STF
MO	SPC
NH	MAN
NY	ALB
OH	Y
OR	P
SD	SFS
VA	RIC
WV	WH
Salida, CO	COS
Salina, KS	SAL
Salinas, CA	MRY
Saline, MI	LAN
Salisbury, MD	WIL
MO	JC
NC	CHL
PA	ALT
Sallisaw, OK	TLS
Salmon, ID	B
Salt Lake City, UT	SLC
Salt Point, NY	NY
Saltaire, NY	RVC
Sammamish, WA	SEA
San Andreas, CA	STO
San Angelo, TX	SAN
San Anselmo, CA	SFR
San Antonio, FL	SP
TX	OLL
TX	SYM
TX	SAT
San Benito, TX	BWN
San Bernardino, CA	SB
CA	NTN
San Bruno, CA	SFR
San Carlos, AZ	TUC
CA	SFR
San Clemente, CA	ORG
San Diego, CA	SD
CA	HPM
TX	CC
San Dimas, CA	LA
San Elizario, TX	ELP
San Fernando, CA	LA
CA	SYM
San Fidel, NM	GLP
San Francisco, CA	SFR
CA	STN
San Gabriel, CA	LA
San Isidro, TX	BWN
San Jacinto, CA	SB
San Jose, CA	SJ
CA	SYM
San Juan, TX	BWN
San Juan Bautista, CA	MRY
San Juan Capistrano, CA	ORG
San Leandro, CA	OAK
San Lorenzo, CA	OAK
San Luis, AZ	TUC
CO	PBL
San Luis Obispo, CA	HPM
CA	MRY
San Manuel, AZ	TUC
San Marcos, CA	SD
TX	AUS
San Marino, CA	LA
San Mateo, CA	SFR
San Miguel, CA	MRY
San Pablo, CA	OAK
San Patricio, NM	LSC
San Pedro, CA	LA
San Rafael, CA	SFR
San Ramon, CA	OAK
San Saba, TX	AUS
San Tan Valley, AZ	TUC
San Ysidro, CA	SD
Sanborn, IA	SC
MN	NU
Sanbornville, NH	MAN
Sand Lake, MI	GR
Sand Springs, OK	TLS
Sanderson, TX	SAN
Sandoval, IL	BEL
Sandpoint, ID	B
Sandstone, MN	DUL
Sandusky, MI	SAG
OH	TOL
Sandwich, IL	RCK
Sandy, OR	P
UT	SLC
Sandy Hook, KY	LEX
Sandyston, NJ	PAT
Sanford, FL	ORL
ME	PRT
MI	SAG
NC	R
Sanger, CA	FRS
Sanibel, FL	VEN
Santa Ana, CA	ORG
CA	SYM
CA	SPA
Santa Barbara, CA	LA
Santa Clara, CA	SJ
CA	STN
NM	LSC
Santa Clarita, CA	LA
Santa Cruz, CA	MRY
NM	SFE
Santa Fe, NM	SFE
Santa Fe Springs, CA	LA
Santa Margarita, CA	MRY
Santa Maria, CA	LA
Santa Monica, CA	LA
Santa Paula, CA	LA
Santa Rosa, CA	SR
NM	SFE
TX	BWN
Santa Rosa Beach, FL	PT
Santa Susana Knolls, CA	LA
Santa Ynez, CA	LA
Santa Ysabel, CA	SD
Santee, CA	SD
SC	CHR
Sapulpa, OK	TLS
Saranac, MI	GR
Saranac Lake, NY	OG
Sarasota, FL	VEN
Saratoga, CA	SJ
NY	ALB
WY	CHY
Saratoga Springs, NY	ALB
Sardinia, NY	BUF
Sarita, TX	CC
Sartell, MN	SCL
Satanta, KS	DOD
Saugerties, NY	NY
Saugus, MA	BO
Sauk Centre, MN	SCL
Sauk City, WI	MAD
Sauk Rapids, MN	SCL
Sauk Village, IL	CHI
Saukville, WI	MIL
Sault Sainte Marie, MI	MAR
Sausalito, CA	SFR
Savage, MN	STP
Savanna, IL	RCK
Savannah, GA	SAV
MO	KC
TN	MEM
Saxon, WI	SUP
Sayre, PA	PHU
PA	SCR
Sayreville, NJ	MET
Sayville, NY	RVC
Scales Mound, IL	RCK
Scammon Bay, AK	FBK
Scappoose, OR	P
Scarborough, ME	PRT
Scarsdale, NY	NY
Scenic, AZ	PHX
Schaller, IA	SC
Schaumburg, IL	CHI
Scheller, IL	BEL
Schenectady, NY	ALB
Schererville, IN	GRY
Schertz, TX	SAT
Schiller Park, IL	CHI
Schnellville, IN	EVN
Schriever, LA	HT
Schroon Lake, NY	OG
Schulenburg, TX	VIC
Schuyler, NE	OM
Schuylerville, NY	ALB
Schuylkill Haven, PA	ALN
Schwenksville, PA	PH
Scio, OR	P
Scituate, MA	BO
Scobey, MT	GF
Scotch Plains, NJ	NEW
Scotia, CA	SR
NY	ALB
Scotland, SD	SFS
Scott, LA	LAF
Scott AFB, IL	BEL
Scott City, KS	DOD
MO	SPC
Scott Twp., PA	SCR
Scottdale, PA	GBG
PA	PBR
Scotts Valley, CA	MRY
Scottsbluff, NE	GI
Scottsboro, AL	BIR
Scottsburg, IN	IND
Scottsdale, AZ	PHX
AZ	SPA
Scottsville, KY	OWN
NY	ROC
VA	RIC
Scranton, AR	LR
PA	NTN
PA	PHU
PA	POC
PA	PSC
PA	SCR
PA	SAM
Sea Cliff, NY	RVC
Sea Girt, NJ	TR
Sea Isle City, NJ	CAM
Seaford, DE	WIL
NY	RVC
Seahurst, WA	SEA
Seal Beach, CA	ORG
Sealy, TX	GAL
Searcy, AR	LR
Seaside, CA	MRY
OR	P
Seaside Heights, NJ	TR
Seaside Park, NJ	TR
Seat Pleasant, MD	WDC
Seattle, WA	HPM
WA	NTN
WA	SEA
WA	STN
Seaview, WA	SEA
Sebastian, FL	PMB
Sebastopol, CA	SR
Seboyeta, NM	GLP
Sebree, KY	OWN
Sebring, FL	VEN
OH	Y
Secane, PA	PH
Secaucus, NJ	NEW
Secretary, MD	WIL
Security, CO	COS
Sedalia, CO	COS
MO	JC
Sedan, KS	WCH
Sedona, AZ	PHX
Sedro Woolley, WA	SEA
Seekonk, MA	FR
Seffner, FL	SP
FL	SYM
Seguin, TX	SAT
Selah, WA	YAK
Selby, SD	SFS
Selden, KS	SAL
NY	RVC
Seligman, AZ	PHX
Selinsgrove, PA	HBG
Sellersburg, IN	IND
Sellersville, PA	PH
Selma, AL	MOB
CA	FRS
TX	SAT
Selmer, TN	MEM
Selz, ND	FAR
Seminole, FL	SP
TX	LUB
Semmes, AL	MOB
Senatobia, MS	JKS
Seneca, IL	PEO
KS	KCK
MO	SPC
SC	CHR
Sentinel Butte, ND	BIS
Sequim, WA	SEA
Sesser, IL	BEL
Setauket, NY	RVC
Severn, MD	BAL
Severna Park, MD	BAL
Seward, AK	AJ
KS	DOD
NE	LIN
PA	GBG
Sewell, NJ	CAM
Sewickley, PA	PIT
Seymour, CT	HRT
IL	PEO
IN	IND
TN	KNX
TX	FWT
WI	GB
Shady Cove, OR	P
Shadyside, OH	STU
Shafer, MN	STP
Shafter, CA	FRS
Shaker Heights, OH	CLV
Shakopee, MN	STP
Shallotte, NC	R
Shallowater, TX	LUB
Shamokin, PA	HBG
PA	PHU
Shamrock, TX	AMA
Shandon, OH	CIN
Shannon, IL	RCK
Sharon, CT	HRT
KS	DOD
MA	BO
PA	E
WI	MIL
Sharpsburg, PA	PIT
Sharpsville, PA	E
Shavano Park, TX	SAT
Shavertown, PA	SCR
Shaw, MS	JKS
Shaw Island, WA	SEA
Shawano, WI	GB
Shawnee, KS	KCK
OK	OKL
Shawnee Mission, KS	KCK
Shawneetown, IL	BEL
Sheboygan, WI	MIL
Sheboygan Falls, WI	MIL
Sheffield, IL	PEO
MA	SPR
OH	CLV
PA	E
PA	PBR
Sheffield Lake, OH	CLV
Shelbina, MO	JC
Shelburne, VT	BUR
VT	SAM
Shelburne Falls, MA	SPR
Shelby, MS	JKS
MT	HEL
NC	CHL
NE	LIN
OH	TOL
Shelby Twp., MI	DET
MI	EST
Shelbyville, IL	SFD
IN	IND
KY	L
TN	NSH
Sheldon, IA	SC

Place	Code
Shell Knob, MO	SPC
Shell Lake, WI	SUP
Shelter Island Heights, NY	RVC
Shelton, CT	BGP
WA	SEA
Shenandoah, IA	DM
PA	ALN
PA	PHU
Shepherd, MI	SAG
Shepherdstown, WV	WH
Shepherdsville, KY	L
Sherburne, NY	SY
Sheridan, AR	LR
CO	DEN
MT	HEL
OR	P
WY	CHY
Sherman, CT	BGP
IL	SFD
TX	DAL
Sherman Oaks, CA	LA
CA	HPM
CA	ROM
Sherrill, NY	SY
Sherwood, AR	LR
OR	P
WI	GB
Shieldsville, MN	STP
Shillington, PA	ALN
Shiloh, IL	BEL
Shiner, TX	VIC
Shinglehouse, PA	E
Shinnston, WV	WH
Shippensburg, PA	HBG
Shiprock, NM	GLP
Shirley, MA	BO
Shoemakersville, PA	ALN
Shohola, PA	SCR
Shoreham, NY	RVC
Shoreline, WA	SEA
Shoreview, MN	STP
Shorewood, IL	JOL
WI	MIL
Short Hills, NJ	NEW
Shoshone, ID	B
Show Low, AZ	GLP
Shreveport, LA	SHP
Shrewsbury, MA	WOR
MO	STL
Shrub Oak, NY	NY
Shullsburg, WI	MAD
Shumway, IL	SFD
Sibley, IA	SC
Sicklerville, NJ	CAM
Sidney, MT	GF
NE	GI
NY	ALB
OH	CIN
Sierra Madre, CA	LA
Sierra Vista, AZ	TUC
Sigel, IL	SFD
Signal Mountain, TN	KNX
Sigourney, IA	DAV
Sikeston, MO	SPC
Siler City, NC	R
Silex, MO	STL
Siloam Springs, AR	LR
Silsbee, TX	BEA
Silver Bay, MN	DUL
Silver City, NM	LSC
Silver Creek, NE	OM
NY	BUF
Silver Lake, MN	NU
Silver Spring, MD	PHU
MD	WDC
Silverado, CA	ORG
Silverthorne, CO	DEN
Silverton, CO	PBL
OR	P
TX	AMA
Simi Valley, CA	LA
CA	OLL
Simmesport, LA	ALX
Simpsonville, SC	CHR
Simsbury, CT	HRT
Sinking Spring, PA	ALN
Sinsinawa, WI	MAD
Sinton, TX	CC
Sioux Center, IA	SC
Sioux City, IA	SC
Sioux Falls, SD	SFS
Sioux Rapids, IA	SC
Siren, WI	SUP
Sisseton, SD	SFS
Sisters, OR	BAK
Sistersville, WV	WH
Sitka, AK	AJ
Skaneateles, NY	SY
Skiatook, OK	TLS
Skidmore, TX	CC
Skillman, NJ	MET

Place	Code
Skokie, IL	CHI
Skowhegan, ME	PRT
Slater, MO	JC
Slatersville, RI	PRO
Slatington, PA	ALN
Slaton, TX	LUB
Slayton, MN	WIN
Sleepy Eye, MN	NU
Sleepy Hollow, NY	NY
NY	SAM
Slickville, PA	GBG
Slidell, LA	NO
Slinger, WI	MIL
Slingerlands, NY	ALB
Slippery Rock, PA	PIT
Sloan, NY	BUF
Sloatsburg, NY	NY
NY	STF
Smethport, PA	E
Smiley, TX	SAT
Smithfield, NC	R
RI	PRO
VA	RIC
Smithton, IL	BEL
Smithtown, NY	RVC
Smithville, MO	KC
TN	NSH
TX	AUS
Smyrna, DE	WIL
GA	ATL
TN	NSH
Sneedville, TN	KNX
Snellville, GA	ATL
Snohomish, WA	SEA
Snoqualmie, WA	SEA
Snowflake, AZ	GLP
Snowmass, CO	DEN
Snyder, NE	OM
NY	BUF
TX	LUB
Sobieski, WI	GB
Socorro, NM	SFE
TX	ELP
Soda Springs, ID	B
Soddy Daisy, TN	KNX
Solana Beach, CA	SD
Soldotna, AK	AJ
Soledad, CA	MRY
Solomon, AZ	TUC
KS	SAL
Solomons, MD	WDC
Solon, IA	DAV
OH	CLV
OH	PRM
OH	SJP
Solon Springs, WI	SUP
Solvang, CA	LA
Solvay, NY	SY
Somers, NY	NY
Somers Point, NJ	CAM
Somerset, KY	LEX
MA	FR
NJ	MET
NJ	PSC
NJ	SYM
NJ	SAM
OH	COL
PA	ALT
TX	SAT
WI	SUP
Somersville, CT	NOR
Somersworth, NH	MAN
Somerton, AZ	TUC
Somerville, MA	BO
NJ	MET
TN	MEM
TX	AUS
Somonauk, IL	RCK
Sonoita, AZ	TUC
Sonoma, CA	SR
Sonora, CA	STO
TX	SAN
Soquel, CA	MRY
Sorrento, LA	BR
Sound Beach, NY	RVC
Sour Lake, TX	BEA
South Abington Township, PA	SCR
South Amboy, NJ	MET
South Amherst, OH	CLV
South Barre, MA	WOR
South Beloit, IL	RCK
South Bend, IN	FTW
South Boston, MA	BO
VA	RIC
South Bound Brook, NJ	MET
South Burlington, VT	BUR
South Charleston, OH	CIN
WV	WH
South Dartmouth, MA	FR
South Deerfield, MA	SPR
MA	STF

Place	Code
South Easton, MA	FR
South El Monte, CA	LA
South Euclid, OH	CLV
South Fork, PA	ALT
South Gate, CA	LA
South Glastonbury, CT	HRT
South Glens Falls, NY	ALB
South Grafton, MA	WOR
South Hadley, MA	SPR
South Haven, MI	KAL
South Heart, ND	BIS
South Hero, VT	BUR
South Hill, VA	RIC
South Holland, IL	CHI
South Houston, TX	GAL
South Huntington, NY	RVC
South Hutchinson, KS	WCH
South Kingstown, RI	PRO
South Lake Tahoe, CA	SAC
South Lyon, MI	DET
South Mantoloking, NJ	TR
South Milwaukee, WI	MIL
South Orange, NJ	NEW
South Ozone Park, NY	BRK
South Park, PA	PIT
South Pasadena, CA	LA
South Pittsburg, TN	KNX
South Plainfield, NJ	MET
South Portland, ME	PRT
South Prince George, VA	RIC
South Richmond Hill, NY	BRK
South Riding, VA	ARL
South River, NJ	MET
South San Francisco, CA	SFR
South Sioux City, NE	OM
South St. Paul, MN	STP
South Wilmington, IL	JOL
South Windsor, CT	HRT
South Yarmouth, MA	FR
Southampton, NY	RVC
PA	PH
Southaven, MS	JKS
Southborough, MA	WOR
Southbridge, MA	WOR
Southbury, CT	HRT
Southern Pines, NC	R
Southfield, MI	DET
MI	SYM
MI	EST
Southgate, KY	COV
MI	DET
Southington, CT	HRT
Southold, NY	RVC
Southport, NC	R
Southwest Ranches, FL	MIA
Southwick, MA	SPR
Spalding, MI	MAR
NE	GI
Sparkill, NY	NY
Sparks, MD	BAL
NV	RNO
Sparta, IL	BEL
MI	GR
NJ	PAT
TN	NSH
WI	LC
Spartanburg, SC	CHR
Spearfish, SD	RC
Spearman, TX	AMA
Spearville, KS	DOD
Speculator, NY	OG
Spencer, IA	SC
IN	IND
MA	WOR
WV	WH
Spencerport, NY	ROC
Spencerville, OH	TOL
Spicer, MN	NU
Spirit Lake, IA	SC
Splendora, TX	GAL
Spokane, WA	SPK
Spokane Valley, WA	HPM
WA	SPK
Spooner, WI	SUP
Spotswood, NJ	MET
Spotsylvania, VA	ARL
Spreckels, CA	MRY
Spring, TX	GAL
Spring Branch, TX	SAT
Spring City, PA	PH
Spring Green, WI	MAD
Spring Grove, IL	RCK
PA	HBG
Spring Hill, FL	SP
TN	NSH
Spring House, PA	PH
Spring Lake, MI	GR
NJ	TR
Spring Mills, PA	ALT
Spring Valley, CA	SD
IL	PEO

Place	Code
MN	WIN
NY	NY
NY	MCE
NY	STF
WI	LC
Springbrook, IA	DUB
NY	BUF
Springdale, AR	LR
PA	PIT
Springer, NM	SFE
Springerville, AZ	GLP
Springfield, CO	PBL
GA	SAV
IL	SFD
KY	L
MA	SAM
MA	SPR
MN	NU
MO	SPC
NE	OM
NJ	NEW
OH	CIN
OR	P
OR	STN
PA	PH
TN	NSH
VA	ARL
VA	WDC
VT	BUR
Springfield Gardens, NY	BRK
Springville, IA	DUB
NY	BUF
Spruce Pine, NC	CHL
Spur, TX	LUB
Stafford, TX	GAL
TX	SYM
TX	MCE
VA	ARL
Stafford Springs, CT	NOR
Stamford, CT	BGP
CT	STF
NY	ALB
TX	LUB
Stanberry, MO	KC
Standish, ME	PRT
MI	SAG
Stanford, CA	SJ
MT	GF
Stanley, ND	BIS
WI	LC
Stanton, CA	ORG
KY	LEX
MI	GR
NE	OM
TN	MEM
TX	SAN
Stanwood, WA	SEA
Staples, MN	SCL
Stapleton, NE	GI
Star City, AR	LR
IN	LFT
Star Lake, NY	OG
Starke, FL	STA
Starkville, MS	JKS
State College, PA	ALT
PA	PBR
Staten Island, NY	NY
NY	STF
Statesboro, GA	SAV
Statesville, NC	CHL
Staunton, IL	SFD
VA	RIC
Stayton, OR	P
Ste. Genevieve, MO	STL
Ste. Marie, IL	SFD
Steamboat Springs, CO	DEN
Stebbins, AK	FBK
Steele, ND	FAR
Steeleville, IL	BEL
Steelton, PA	HBG
Steger, IL	JOL
Steinauer, NE	LIN
Stella Niagara, NY	BUF
Stephan, SD	SFS
Stephen, MN	CR
Stephenson, MI	MAR
Stephenville, TX	FWT
Sterling, CO	DEN
IL	RCK
MA	WOR
VA	ARL
Sterling Heights, MI	DET
MI	PRM
MI	EST
Stetsonville, WI	SUP
Steubenville, OH	STU
Stevens Point, WI	LC
Stevenson, MD	BAL
Stevensville, MT	HEL
Stewart, MN	NU
Stewartsville, NJ	MET

Stewartville, MN	WIN
Stickney, IL	CHI
Still River, MA	WOR
Stillwater, MN	STP
NY	ALB
OK	TLS
Stirling, NJ	PAT
Stockbridge, MA	SPR
WI	GB
Stockdale, TX	SAT
Stockton, CA	STO
IL	RCK
Stone Harbor, NJ	CAM
Stone Lake, WI	SUP
Stone Mountain, GA	ATL
Stoneboro, PA	E
Stoneham, MA	BO
Stoneville, NC	CHL
Stonewall, TX	SAT
Stonewood, WV	WH
Stonington, CT	NOR
IL	SFD
Stony Point, NY	NY
Storm Lake, IA	SC
Storrs, CT	NOR
Stoughton, MA	BO
WI	MAD
Stow, OH	CLV
Stowe, PA	PH
VT	BUR
Strafford, PA	PH
Strandquist, MN	CR
Strasburg, ND	BIS
Stratford, CT	BGP
TX	AMA
WI	LC
Stratton, CO	COS
Strawberry Point, IA	DUB
Streamwood, IL	CHI
Streator, IL	PEO
Streetsboro, OH	Y
Strongsville, OH	CLV
Stroudsburg, PA	SCR
Struthers, OH	Y
Strykersville, NY	BUF
Stuart, FL	PMB
IA	DM
NE	OM
Sturgeon Bay, WI	GB
Sturgis, KY	OWN
MI	KAL
SD	RC
Sturtevant, WI	MIL
Stuttgart, AR	LR
Stuyvesant, NY	ALB
Suamico, WI	GB
Subiaco, AR	LR
Sublette, IL	RCK
Sublimity, OR	P
Succasunna, NJ	PAT
Sudbury, MA	BO
Suffern, NY	NY
Suffield, CT	HRT
Suffolk, VA	RIC
Sugar Creek, MO	KC
MO	PRM
Sugar Grove, IL	RCK
OH	COL
Sugar Land, TX	GAL
Sugar Notch, PA	SCR
Sugarloaf, PA	PSC
Suitland, MD	WDC
Sulligent, AL	BIR
Sullivan, IL	SFD
IN	EVN
MO	STL
WI	MAD
Sullivan's Island, SC	CHR
Sulphur, LA	LKC
Sulphur Springs, TX	TYL
Summerfield, FL	ORL
KS	KCK
Summerhill, PA	ALT
Summersville, WV	WH
Summerton, SC	CHR
Summerville, SC	CHR
Summit, IL	CHI
NJ	NEW
Summit Hill, PA	ALN
Sumner, IA	DUB
WA	SEA
Sumter, SC	CHR
Sun City, AZ	PHX
CA	SB
Sun City Center, FL	SP
Sun City West, AZ	PHX
Sun Lakes, AZ	PHX
Sun Prairie, WI	MAD
Sun Valley, CA	LA
ID	B
NV	RNO

Sunapee, NH	MAN
Sunbury, OH	COL
PA	HBG
Suncook, NH	MAN
Sunfish, KY	OWN
Sunland Park, NM	LSC
Sunman, IN	IND
Sunny Hills, FL	PT
Sunny Isles Beach, FL	MIA
Sunnyside, WA	YAK
Sunnyvale, CA	SJ
Sunrise, FL	MIA
Sunriver, OR	BAK
Sunset Hills, MO	STL
Superior, AZ	TUC
NE	LIN
WI	SUP
Suring, WI	GB
Surprise, AZ	PHX
Susanville, CA	SAC
Susquehanna, PA	SCR
Sussex, NJ	PAT
Sutton, MA	WOR
NE	LIN
Suttons Bay, MI	GLD
Swainsboro, GA	SAV
Swampscott, MA	BO
Swan Lake, MT	HEL
Swansboro, NC	R
Swansea, MA	FR
Swanton, OH	TOL
VT	BUR
Swanville, MN	SCL
Swarthmore, PA	PHU
Swartswood, NJ	PAT
Swartz Creek, MI	LAN
Swedesboro, NJ	CAM
Swedesburg, PA	PH
Sweeny, TX	GAL
Sweet Home, OR	P
TX	VIC
Sweetwater, TX	SAN
Swinomish, WA	SEA
Switzerland, FL	STA
Swormville, NY	BUF
Swoyersville, PA	SCR
Sybertsville, PA	PSC
Sycamore, IL	RCK
OH	TOL
Sykeston, ND	FAR
Sykesville, PA	E
PA	PBR
Sylacauga, AL	BIR
Sylmar, CA	LA
Sylva, NC	CHL
Sylvania, GA	SAV
OH	TOL
Syosset, NY	RVC
Syracuse, IN	FTW
KS	DOD
NE	LIN
NY	SY
NY	STF
Tabb, VA	RIC
Taberg, NY	SY
Tabernacle, NJ	TR
Tabor, SD	SFS
Tacoma, WA	SEA
Taft, CA	FRS
TX	CC
Taftville, CT	NOR
Tahlequah, OK	TLS
Tahoe City, CA	SAC
Takoma Park, MD	WDC
Talcott, WV	WH
Talkeetna, AK	AJ
Talladega, AL	BIR
Tallahassee, FL	PT
Tallassee, AL	MOB
Talleyville, DE	WIL
Tallmadge, OH	CLV
Tallulah, LA	ALX
Tama, IA	DUB
Tamaqua, PA	ALN
Tamarac, FL	MIA
Tamaroa, IL	BEL
Tampa, FL	SP
FL	SAM
Tampico, IL	RCK
Tanana, AK	FBK
Taneytown, MD	BAL
Tannersville, PA	SCR
Taos, NM	SFE
Tappahannock, VA	RIC
Tappan, NY	NY
Tarboro, NC	R
Tarentum, PA	PBR
PA	PIT
Tariffville, CT	HRT
Tarkio, MO	KC
Tarpon Springs, FL	SP

Tarrytown, NY	NY
Tarzana, CA	LA
Taunton, MA	FR
Tavernier, FL	MIA
Tawas City, MI	GLD
Taylor, MI	DET
TX	AUS
Taylor Mill, KY	COV
Taylors, SC	CHR
Taylors Falls, MN	STP
Taylorsville, UT	SLC
Taylorville, IL	SFD
Tazewell, VA	RIC
Tea, SD	SFS
Teaneck, NJ	NEW
Techny, IL	CHI
Tecumseh, MI	LAN
NE	LIN
Tehachapi, CA	FRS
Tekamah, NE	OM
Tekoa, WA	SPK
Tell City, IN	IND
Teller, AK	FBK
Telluride, CO	PBL
Temecula, CA	SB
CA	NTN
Tempe, AZ	PHX
Temperance, MI	DET
Temple, TX	AUS
Temple City, CA	LA
Temple Terrace, FL	SP
Tenafly, NJ	NEW
Tennessee Ridge, TN	NSH
Tequesta, FL	PMB
FL	SAM
Terre Haute, IN	IND
Terrell, TX	DAL
Terrytown, LA	NO
Terryville, CT	HRT
CT	STF
Teutopolis, IL	SFD
Tewksbury, MA	BO
MA	BUR
Texarkana, AR	LR
TX	TYL
Texas City, TX	GAL
Thatcher, AZ	TUC
The Colony, TX	FWT
TX	STN
The Dalles, OR	BAK
The Rock, GA	ATL
The Woodlands, TX	GAL
Theodore, AL	MOB
Theriot, LA	HT
Thermopolis, WY	CHY
Thibodaux, LA	HT
Thief River Falls, MN	CR
Thomas, WV	WH
Thomasboro, IL	PEO
Thomaston, CT	HRT
Thomasville, AL	MOB
GA	SAV
NC	CHL
Thompson, CT	NOR
ND	FAR
OH	CLV
Thompson Falls, MT	HEL
Thomson, GA	ATL
Thoreau, NM	GLP
Thornton, CO	DEN
Thornwood, NY	NY
Thorp, WI	LC
Thousand Oaks, CA	LA
Three Bridges, NJ	MET
Three Forks, MT	HEL
Three Lakes, WI	SUP
Three Oaks, MI	KAL
Three Rivers, CA	FRS
MA	SPR
MI	KAL
TX	CC
Throop, PA	SCR
Tiburon, CA	SFR
Tickfaw, LA	BR
Ticonderoga, NY	OG
Tidioute, PA	E
Tierra Amarilla, NM	SFE
Tiffin, OH	TOL
Tifton, GA	SAV
Tigard, OR	P
Tigerton, WI	GB
Tijeras, NM	SFE
Tilden, NE	OM
Tillamook, OR	P
Tiltonsville, OH	STU
Timber Lake, SD	RC
Timonium, MD	BAL
Tinley Park, IL	CHI
Tintah, MN	SCL
Tioga, ND	BIS
Tipp City, OH	CIN

Tipton, CA	FRS
IA	DAV
IN	LFT
KS	SAL
MO	JC
Tishomingo, OK	OKL
Tiskilwa, IL	PEO
Titusville, FL	ORL
NJ	TR
PA	E
Tiverton, RI	PRO
Tivoli, NY	NY
TX	CC
Toccoa, GA	ATL
Tohatchi, NM	GLP
Tok, AK	FBK
Toksook Bay, AK	FBK
Toledo, OH	SYM
OH	TOL
WA	SEA
Tolland, CT	NOR
Tolleson, AZ	PHX
Tolono, IL	PEO
Tomah, WI	LC
Tomahawk, WI	SUP
Tomales, CA	SFR
Tomball, TX	GAL
Tombstone, AZ	TUC
Tome, NM	SFE
Toms River, NJ	TR
NJ	PSC
NJ	PHU
Tonawanda, NY	BUF
Tonganoxie, KS	KCK
Tonica, IL	PEO
Tonkawa, OK	OKL
Tonopah, AZ	PHX
NV	LAV
Tontitown, AR	LR
Tooele, UT	SLC
Topawa, AZ	TUC
Topeka, KS	KCK
Toppenish, WA	YAK
Topping, VA	RIC
Topsfield, MA	BO
Toronto, OH	PBR
OH	STU
Torrance, CA	LA
Torrington, CT	HRT
CT	SAM
WY	CHY
Totowa, NJ	PAT
Towanda, PA	SCR
Tower, MN	DUL
Town and Country, MO	STL
Towner, ND	FAR
Townsend, MA	BO
MT	HEL
TN	KNX
Towson, MD	BAL
MD	POC
Tracy, CA	STO
MN	NU
Tracyton, WA	SEA
Traer, IA	DUB
Trafford, PA	GBG
Tranquillity, CA	FRS
Trappist, KY	L
Travelers Rest, SC	CHR
Traverse City, MI	GLD
Tremont, PA	ALN
Trempealeau, WI	LC
Trenary, MI	MAR
Trenton, IL	BEL
MI	DET
MO	KC
NE	LIN
NJ	TR
NJ	PHU
NJ	ROM
NJ	PSC
OH	CIN
Tres Pinos, CA	MRY
Trevorton, PA	HBG
Triangle, VA	ARL
Tribes Hill, NY	ALB
Tribune, KS	DOD
Trinidad, CO	PBL
Trinity, FL	SP
TX	TYL
Troy, AL	MOB
IL	SFD
KS	KCK
MI	DET
MI	EST
MI	OLD
MO	STL
NY	ALB
NY	STF
OH	CIN
Truckee, CA	SAC

Place	Code
Trumansburg, NY	ROC
Trumbull, CT	BGP
CT	PSC
Trussville, AL	BIR
Truth or Consequences, NM	LSC
Truxton, NY	SY
Tryon, NC	CHL
Tualatin, OR	P
Tuba City, AZ	GLP
Tubac, AZ	TUC
Tuckahoe, NY	NY
Tuckerton, NJ	TR
Tucson, AZ	HPM
AZ	TUC
AZ	STN
Tucumcari, NM	SFE
Tujunga, CA	LA
CA	OLN
Tukwila, WA	SEA
Tulare, CA	FRS
Tularosa, NM	LSC
Tulelake, CA	SAC
Tulia, TX	AMA
Tullahoma, TN	NSH
Tully, NY	SY
Tulsa, OK	OLL
OK	TLS
Tunkhannock, PA	SCR
Tununak, AK	FBK
Tupelo, MS	JKS
Tupper Lake, NY	OG
Turkey, TX	AMA
Turlock, CA	SPA
CA	STO
Turners Falls, MA	SPR
Turnersville, NJ	CAM
Turtle Creek, PA	PIT
Turton, SD	SFS
Tuscaloosa, AL	BIR
Tuscola, IL	SFD
Tuscumbia, AL	BIR
Tuskegee Institute, AL	MOB
Tustin, CA	ORG
CA	ROM
Tutwiler, MS	JKS
Tuxedo, NY	NY
Twain Harte, CA	STO
Twentynine Palms, CA	SB
Twin Falls, ID	B
Twin Lakes, WI	MIL
Twinsburg, OH	CLV
Twisp, WA	SPK
Two Harbors, MN	DUL
Two Rivers, WI	GB
Tybee Island, GA	SAV
Tyler, MN	NU
TX	TYL
Tyndall, SD	SFS
Tyngsborough, MA	BO
Tyringham, MA	SPR
Tyrone, GA	ATL
PA	ALT
Ubly, MI	SAG
Uhland, TX	AUS
Ukiah, CA	SR
CA	STN
Ulster Park, NY	NY
Ulysses, KS	DOD
NE	LIN
Umbarger, TX	AMA
Unalakleet, AK	FBK
Unalaska, AK	AJ
Uncasville, CT	NOR
Underhill Center, VT	BUR
Underwood, MN	SCL
ND	BIS
Union, KY	COV
MO	STL
NJ	NEW
OR	BAK
SC	CHR
Union City, CA	OAK
CT	HRT
IN	LFT
NJ	NEW
OK	OKL
PA	E
TN	MEM
Union Gap, WA	YAK
Union Grove, WI	MIL
Union Springs, AL	MOB
Uniondale, NY	RVC
Uniontown, KY	OWN
OH	Y
OH	CLV
PA	GBG
PA	SAM
PA	PBR
Unionville, CT	HRT
United, PA	GBG
University City, MO	STL
University Heights, OH	CLV
University Park, PA	ALT
Upland, CA	SB
Upper Arlington, OH	COL
Upper Darby, PA	PH
Upper Marlboro, MD	WDC
Upper Montclair, NJ	NEW
Upper Saddle River, NJ	NEW
Upper Sandusky, OH	TOL
Upper St. Clair, PA	PBR
Upsala, MN	SCL
Upton, MA	WOR
Urbana, IL	PEO
OH	CIN
Urbandale, IA	DM
Utica, IL	PEO
KY	OWN
MI	DET
NY	SY
NY	NTN
NY	STF
NY	SAM
OH	COL
Uvalde, TX	SAT
Uwchlan, PA	PH
Uxbridge, MA	WOR
Vacaville, CA	SAC
Vacherie, LA	BR
Vail, AZ	TUC
Valatie, NY	ALB
Valdez, AK	AJ
Valdosta, GA	SAV
Vale, NC	CHL
OR	BAK
Valentine, NE	GI
Valhalla, NY	NY
Valier, MT	HEL
Valinda, CA	LA
Vallejo, CA	SAC
Valley, NE	OM
Valley Center, CA	SD
KS	WCH
Valley City, ND	FAR
OH	CLV
Valley Lee, MD	WDC
Valley Park, MO	STL
Valley Stream, NY	RVC
Valmeyer, IL	BEL
Valparaiso, IN	GRY
NE	LIN
Valrico, FL	SP
Valyermo, CA	LA
Van Alstyne, TX	DAL
Van Buren, AR	LR
ME	PRT
Van Horn, TX	ELP
Van Horne, IA	DUB
Van Nuys, CA	LA
Van Wert, OH	TOL
Vanceburg, KY	COV
Vancleave, MS	BLX
Vancouver, WA	SEA
Vandalia, IL	SFD
MO	JC
OH	CIN
Vanderbilt, TX	VIC
Vandergrift, PA	GBG
Vanderwagen, NM	GLP
Vashon, WA	SEA
Vassar, MI	SAG
Vaughn, NM	SFE
Vega, TX	AMA
Velva, ND	FAR
Veneta, OR	P
Venice, CA	LA
FL	VEN
Ventnor, NJ	CAM
Ventura, CA	LA
CA	ROM
Verdigre, NE	OM
Vergennes, VT	BUR
Vermilion, OH	TOL
Vermillion, MN	STP
SD	SFS
Vernal, UT	SLC
Verndale, MN	SCL
Vernon, CA	LA
CT	NOR
NY	SY
TX	FWT
Vernonia, OR	P
Vero Beach, FL	PMB
Verona, NJ	NEW
NY	SY
PA	PIT
WI	MAD
Verplanck, NY	NY
Versailles, CT	NOR
KY	LEX
OH	CIN
Veseli, MN	STP
Vestal, NY	SY
Vicksburg, MI	KAL
MS	JKS
Victor, IA	DAV
NY	ROC
Victoria, KS	SAL
MN	STP
TX	VIC
Victorville, CA	SB
Vidalia, GA	SAV
LA	ALX
Vidor, TX	BEA
Vienna, IL	BEL
MO	JC
OH	Y
VA	ARL
WV	WH
Viera, FL	ORL
Villa Hills, KY	COV
Villa Maria, PA	PIT
Villa Park, IL	JOL
Villa Ridge, MO	STL
Villanova, PA	PH
Villanueva, NM	SFE
Ville Platte, LA	LAF
Vina, CA	SAC
Vincennes, IN	EVN
Vine Grove, KY	L
Vineland, NJ	CAM
Vineyard Haven, MA	FR
Vinita, OK	TLS
Vinton, IA	DUB
LA	LKC
Viola, KS	WCH
Violet, LA	NO
Virden, IL	SFD
Virgil, IL	RCK
Virginia, IL	SFD
MN	DUL
Virginia Beach, VA	RIC
Virginia City, NV	RNO
Virginia Dale, CO	DEN
Virginia Gardens, FL	MIA
Viroqua, WI	LC
Visalia, CA	FRS
Vista, CA	SD
Vivian, LA	SHP
Volga, IA	DUB
Volo, IL	CHI
Voluntown, CT	NOR
Von Ormy, TX	SAT
Voorheesville, NY	ALB
Vulcan, MI	MAR
WaKeeney, KS	SAL
Wabash, IN	FTW
Wabasha, MN	WIN
Wabasso, MN	NU
Wabeno, WI	GB
Waco, TX	AUS
Waconia, MN	STP
Waddington, NY	OG
Wadena, MN	SCL
Wading River, NY	RVC
Wadsworth, IL	CHI
OH	CLV
Waggaman, LA	NO
Wagner, SD	SFS
Wagon Mound, NM	SFE
Wagoner, OK	TLS
Wahiawa, HI	HON
Wahkon, MN	SCL
Wahoo, NE	LIN
Wahpeton, ND	FAR
Waialua, HI	HON
Waianae, HI	HON
Waihee, HI	HON
Wailuku, HI	HON
Waimanalo, HI	HON
Waipahu, HI	HON
Waite Park, MN	SCL
Wake Forest, NC	R
Wakefield, MA	BO
MI	MAR
RI	PRO
Wakeman, OH	TOL
Walbridge, OH	TOL
Walden, NY	NY
Waldorf, MD	WDC
Waldport, OR	P
Waldron, AR	LR
Walhalla, ND	FAR
Walker, IA	DUB
MN	DUL
Walkersville, MD	BAL
Walkerton, IN	FTW
IN	GRY
Wall, PA	PBR
SD	RC
TX	SAN
Walla Walla, WA	SPK
Wallace, ID	B
NC	R
NE	LIN
Walled Lake, MI	DET
Wallingford, CT	HRT
PA	PH
VT	BUR
Wallington, NJ	NEW
Wallis, TX	GAL
Walls, MS	JKS
Walnut, CA	LA
IL	PEO
Walnut Creek, CA	OAK
Walnut Grove, CA	SAC
MN	NU
Walnut Ridge, AR	LR
Walnutport, PA	ALN
Walpole, MA	BO
Walsenburg, CO	PBL
Walsh, IL	BEL
Walterboro, SC	CHR
Waltham, MA	BO
Walton, KY	COV
NY	ALB
Wamego, KS	KCK
Wanatah, IN	GRY
Wantagh, NY	RVC
Wapakoneta, OH	CIN
Wapato, WA	YAK
Wapella, IL	PEO
Wappingers Falls, NY	NY
Wapwallopen, PA	SCR
Ward, SC	CHR
Ware, MA	SPR
Wareham, MA	FR
Warminster, PA	PH
Warner, NH	MAN
Warner Robins, GA	SAV
Warren, AR	LR
IL	RCK
MA	WOR
MI	DET
MI	OLL
MI	STN
MI	EST
MI	NTN
MN	CR
NJ	MET
OH	Y
OH	PBR
PA	E
RI	PRO
Warrensburg, MO	KC
NY	ALB
Warrenton, MO	STL
VA	ARL
Warrenville, IL	JOL
Warrington, PA	PH
PA	PHU
Warroad, MN	CR
Warsaw, IL	PEO
IN	FTW
KY	COV
MO	JC
NY	BUF
Warson Woods, MO	STL
Warwick, NY	NY
RI	PRO
Wasco, CA	FRS
OR	BAK
Waseca, MN	WIN
Washburn, ND	BIS
WI	SUP
Washington, DC	PHU
DC	WDC
DC	SAM
DC	POC
GA	ATL
IA	DAV
IL	PEO
IN	EVN
KS	SAL
LA	LAF
MI	DET
MO	STL
NC	R
NJ	MET
NJ	SYM
PA	PIT
TX	AUS
VA	ARL
Washington Court House, OH	COL
Washington Depot, CT	HRT
Washington Township, NJ	NEW
Washingtonville, NY	NY
Wasilla, AK	AJ
Watchung, NJ	MET
Waterbury, CT	HRT
CT	SAM
CT	SYM
VT	BUR
Waterflow, NM	GLP

Place	Code
Waterford, CT	NOR
CT	NTN
MI	DET
NY	ALB
PA	E
WI	MIL
Waterloo, IA	DUB
IL	BEL
IN	FTW
NY	ROC
WI	MAD
Watersmeet, MI	MAR
Watertown, CT	HRT
MA	BO
MN	STP
NY	OG
SD	SFS
WI	MAD
Waterville, ME	PRT
ME	SAM
MN	STP
NY	SY
WA	YAK
Watervliet, MI	KAL
NY	ALB
NY	STF
NY	SAM
Watford City, ND	BIS
Wathena, KS	KCK
Watkins, MN	NU
MN	SCL
Watkins Glen, NY	ROC
Watonga, OK	OKL
Watseka, IL	JOL
Watsonville, CA	MRY
Waubun, MN	CR
Wauchula, FL	VEN
Wauconda, IL	CHI
Waukee, IA	DM
Waukegan, IL	CHI
Waukesha, WI	MIL
Waukon, IA	DUB
Waumandee, WI	LC
Waunakee, WI	MAD
Waupaca, WI	GB
Waupun, WI	MIL
Wauregan, CT	NOR
Wausau, WI	LC
Wausaukee, WI	GB
Wauseon, OH	TOL
Wautoma, WI	GB
Wauwatosa, WI	MIL
Wauzeka, WI	LC
Waveland, MS	BLX
Waverly, IA	DUB
KY	OWN
MN	STP
NE	LIN
OH	COL
Waxahachie, TX	DAL
Waycross, GA	SAV
Wayland, MA	BO
MI	KAL
NY	ROC
Waymart, PA	SCR
Wayne, IL	JOL
MI	DET
NE	OM
NJ	PAT
PA	PH
WV	WH
Waynesboro, GA	SAV
MS	BLX
PA	HBG
VA	RIC
Waynesburg, OH	Y
OH	STU
PA	PIT
Waynesville, NC	CHL
OH	CIN
Wayside, NJ	TR
Wayzata, MN	STP
Weatherford, OK	OKL
TX	FWT
Weatherly, PA	ALN
Weaverville, CA	SAC
Webb City, MO	SPC
Webster, MA	WOR
MN	STP
NY	ROC
SD	SFS
WI	SUP
Webster City, IA	DUB
Webster Groves, MO	STL
Webster Springs, WV	WH
Wedron, IL	PEO
Weed, CA	SAC
Weedsport, NY	ROC
Weehawken, NJ	NEW
Weimar, TX	VIC
Weiner, AR	LR
Weirton, WV	WH
WV	PBR
Weiser, ID	B
Welch, WV	WH
Wellesley, MA	BO
Wellesley Hills, MA	BO
Wellfleet, MA	FR
Wellington, FL	PMB
KS	WCH
OH	CLV
Wellman, IA	DAV
Wells, ME	PRT
MN	WIN
NV	RNO
Wellsboro, PA	SCR
Wellsburg, WV	WH
Wellston, OH	COL
Wellsville, NY	BUF
Wellton, AZ	TUC
Welsh, LA	LKC
Wenatchee, WA	YAK
Wendell, NC	R
Wendover, UT	SLC
Wenona, IL	PEO
Wentzville, MO	STL
Wernersville, PA	ALN
Weslaco, TX	BWN
Wesley, IA	SC
Wesley Hills, NY	NY
NY	SYM
Wessington Springs, SD	SFS
West, TX	AUS
West Allis, WI	MIL
West Babylon, NY	RVC
West Bend, IA	SC
WI	MIL
West Bloomfield, MI	DET
MI	EST
West Boylston, MA	WOR
West Branch, IA	DAV
MI	GLD
West Brandywine, PA	PH
West Bridgewater, MA	BO
West Brookfield, MA	WOR
West Brooklyn, IL	RCK
West Burke, VT	STF
West Burlington, IA	DAV
West Chazy, NY	OG
West Chester, OH	CIN
PA	PH
West Chicago, IL	JOL
West Clarksville, NY	BUF
West Covina, CA	LA
CA	OLL
West Deptford, NJ	CAM
West Des Moines, IA	DM
West Easton, PA	PHU
West End, NJ	TR
West Falls, NY	BUF
West Fargo, ND	FAR
West Frankfort, IL	BEL
West Greenwich, RI	PRO
West Grove, PA	PH
West Harrison, NY	NY
West Hartford, CT	HRT
West Harwich, MA	FR
West Haven, CT	HRT
CT	MCE
UT	SLC
West Hazleton, PA	SCR
West Hempstead, NY	RVC
West Hollywood, CA	LA
FL	MIA
West Hyattsville, MD	WDC
West Islip, NY	RVC
West Jefferson, OH	COL
West Jordan, UT	SLC
West Lafayette, IN	LFT
West Liberty, IA	DAV
KY	LEX
WV	WH
West Long Branch, NJ	TR
West Memphis, AR	LR
West Middlesex, PA	E
West Mifflin, PA	PIT
West Milford, NJ	PAT
West Milton, OH	CIN
West Milwaukee, WI	MIL
West Monroe, LA	SHP
West Mount Vernon, AL	MOB
West New York, NJ	NEW
West Newbury, MA	BO
West Newton, PA	GBG
West Nyack, NY	NY
West Orange, NJ	NEW
West Palm Beach, FL	PMB
West Park, NY	NY
West Paterson, NJ	NTN
West Peoria, IL	PEO
West Pittston, PA	SCR
West Plains, MO	SPC
West Point, IA	DAV
MS	JKS
NE	OM
NY	NY
VA	RIC
West Portsmouth, OH	COL
West Redding, CT	BGP
West River, MD	BAL
West Roxbury, MA	BO
MA	NTN
West Rutland, VT	BUR
West Sacramento, CA	SAC
West Salem, OH	CLV
WI	LC
West Sedona, AZ	PHX
West Seneca, NY	BUF
West Simsbury, CT	HRT
West Springfield, MA	SPR
West St. Paul, MN	STP
West Sunbury, PA	PIT
West Trenton, NJ	TR
West Union, IA	DUB
OH	CIN
West Valley, NY	BUF
West Valley City, UT	SLC
West Warren, MA	WOR
West Warwick, RI	PRO
West Winfield, NY	ALB
West Wyoming, PA	SCR
West Yellowstone, MT	HEL
Westampton, NJ	TR
Westborough, MA	WOR
Westbrook, CT	NOR
ME	PRT
MN	WIN
Westbury, NY	PSC
NY	RVC
Westchester, IL	CHI
Westcliffe, CO	PBL
Westerly, RI	PRO
Western Springs, IL	CHI
Westernport, MD	BAL
Westerville, OH	COL
OH	NTN
Westfield, IN	LFT
MA	SPR
NJ	NEW
NY	BUF
VT	BUR
Westford, MA	BO
Westhampton Beach, NY	RVC
Westlake, LA	LKC
OH	CLV
Westlake Village, CA	LA
Westland, MI	DET
Westminster, CA	ORG
CO	DEN
MA	WOR
MD	BAL
Westmont, IL	JOL
Westmorland, CA	SD
Weston, CT	BGP
FL	MIA
MA	BO
MO	KC
NE	LIN
PA	SCR
VT	BUR
WI	LC
WV	WH
Westphalia, IA	DM
MI	LAN
MO	JC
Westport, CT	BGP
MA	FR
SD	SFS
Westville, IL	PEO
Westville Grove, NJ	CAM
Westwego, LA	NO
Westwood, MA	BO
NJ	NEW
Wethersfield, CT	HRT
Wever, IA	DAV
Wexford, PA	PIT
Weyauwega, WI	GB
Weymouth, MA	BO
Wharton, NJ	PAT
TX	VIC
Wheat Ridge, CO	DEN
Wheatfield, IN	LFT
Wheatland, WY	CHY
Wheaton, IL	GB
IL	RCK
IL	IND
IL	JOL
MD	WDC
MN	SCL
Wheelersburg, OH	COL
Wheeling, IL	CHI
WV	WH
WV	OLL
WV	SJP
Whippany, NJ	PAT
NJ	PHU
Whistler, AL	MOB
White, SD	SFS
White Bear Lake, MN	STP
White Castle, LA	BR
White Deer, TX	AMA
White Hall, IL	SFD
White Haven, PA	SCR
White Lake, MI	DET
SD	SFS
WI	GB
White Mills, KY	L
White Oak, PA	PIT
White Pigeon, MI	KAL
White Pine, MI	MAR
White Plains, NY	NY
NY	PSC
White River, SD	RC
White River Junction, VT	BUR
White Salmon, WA	YAK
White Sulphur Springs, MT	HEL
WV	WH
White Swan, WA	YAK
Whitefish, MT	HEL
Whitefish Bay, WI	MIL
Whitehall, MT	HEL
NY	ALB
PA	ALN
WI	LC
Whitehouse, OH	TOL
TX	TYL
Whitehouse Station, NJ	MET
Whitelaw, WI	GB
Whiteriver, AZ	GLP
Whitesboro, NY	SY
Whitestone, NY	BRK
Whitesville, KY	OWN
Whitethorn, CA	SR
Whiteville, NC	R
Whitewater, WI	MIL
Whiting, IN	GRY
IN	PRM
NJ	TR
Whitinsville, MA	WOR
Whitman, MA	BO
Whitney, PA	GBG
Whitney Point, NY	SY
Whittemore, MI	GLD
Whittier, CA	LA
Wichita, KS	WCH
Wichita Falls, TX	FWT
Wickatunk, NJ	TR
Wickenburg, AZ	PHX
Wickford, RI	PRO
Wickliffe, OH	CLV
Wiggins, MS	BLX
Wilber, NE	LIN
Wilbraham, MA	SPR
Wilbur, WA	SPK
Wilburton, OK	TLS
Wilcox, PA	E
Wilder, KY	COV
Wildomar, CA	SB
Wildwood, FL	ORL
MO	STL
NJ	CAM
Wilkes–Barre, PA	PHU
PA	PSC
PA	SCR
PA	SAM
Willard, OH	TOL
WI	LC
Willcox, AZ	TUC
Williams, AZ	PHX
CA	SAC
IA	DUB
Williams Bay, WI	MIL
Williamsburg, IA	DAV
KY	LEX
PA	ALT
VA	PSC
VA	RIC
Williamson, WV	WH
Williamsport, IN	LFT
MD	BAL
PA	SCR
Williamston, MI	LAN
NC	R
Williamstown, KY	COV
MA	SPR
NJ	CAM
NJ	SYM
PA	HBG
Williamsville, NY	BUF
NY	SAM
Willimantic, CT	NOR
CT	STF
Willingboro, NJ	TR
Willington, CT	NOR

Place	Code
Williston, FL	STA
ND	BIS
VT	BUR
Williston Park, NY	RVC
Willits, CA	SR
Willmar, MN	NU
Willoughby, OH	CLV
Willoughby Hills, OH	CLV
Willow City, ND	FAR
Willow Grove, PA	PH
Willow River, MN	DUL
Willow Springs, IL	CHI
MO	SPC
Willowick, OH	CLV
Willows, CA	SAC
Wills Point, TX	TYL
Willsboro, NY	OG
Wilmerding, PA	PIT
Wilmette, IL	CHI
Wilmington, CA	LA
DE	PHU
DE	WIL
IL	JOL
MA	BO
NC	R
OH	CIN
VT	BUR
Wilmore, PA	ALT
Wilson, KS	SAL
NC	R
Wilsonville, OR	P
Wilton, CT	BGP
CT	SYM
IA	DAV
ND	BIS
ND	STN
Wimberley, TX	AUS
Wimbledon, ND	FAR
Winamac, IN	LFT
Winchendon, MA	WOR
Winchester, CA	SB
KY	LEX
MA	BO
VA	ARL
Winchester Center, CT	HRT
Wind Lake, WI	MIL
Windber, PA	ALT
PA	PBR
Winder, GA	ATL
Windham, CT	NOR
NH	MAN
NY	ALB
Windom, MN	WIN
Windsor, CA	SR
CO	DEN
CT	HRT
ME	PRT
NC	R
NY	SY
VT	BUR
Windsor Locks, CT	HRT
Windthorst, TX	FWT
Winfield, AL	BIR
IL	JOL
KS	WCH
Winlock, WA	SEA

Place	Code
Winn, MI	SAG
Winnebago, NE	OM
Winneconne, WI	GB
Winnemucca, NV	RNO
Winner, SD	RC
Winnetka, CA	LA
IL	CHI
Winnfield, LA	ALX
Winnie, TX	BEA
Winnsboro, LA	ALX
SC	CHR
TX	TYL
Winona, MN	WIN
Winooski, VT	BUR
Winslow, AR	LR
AZ	GLP
ME	PRT
Winsted, CT	HRT
MN	NU
Winston–Salem, NC	CHL
Winter, WI	SUP
Winter Garden, FL	ORL
Winter Haven, FL	ORL
Winter Park, FL	ORL
Winter Springs, FL	ORL
Winterhaven, CA	SD
Winters, CA	SAC
TX	SAN
Winterset, IA	DM
Wintersville, OH	STU
Winthrop, MA	BO
ME	PRT
MN	NU
Wisconsin Dells, WI	MAD
Wisconsin Rapids, WI	LC
WI	SUP
Wishek, ND	FAR
Wisner, NE	OM
Wittenberg, WI	LC
Wixom, MI	DET
Woburn, MA	BO
Wofford Heights, CA	FRS
Wolcott, CT	HRT
NY	ROC
Wolf Point, MT	GF
Wolfeboro, NH	MAN
Wolfforth, TX	LUB
Wonder Lake, IL	RCK
Wood Dale, IL	JOL
Wood Ridge, NJ	NEW
Wood River, IL	SFD
NE	GI
Woodbourne, NY	NY
Woodbridge, CT	HRT
NJ	MET
VA	ARL
Woodburn, OR	P
Woodbury, CT	HRT
MN	STP
NJ	CAM
NY	RVC
Woodbury Heights, NJ	CAM
Woodcliff Lake, NJ	NEW
Woodhaven, MI	DET
NY	BRK
Woodhull, IL	PEO

Place	Code
Woodinville, WA	SEA
Woodlake, CA	FRS
Woodland, CA	SAC
WA	SEA
Woodland Hills, CA	LA
Woodland Park, CO	COS
NJ	PAT
NJ	PSC
Woodlawn, VA	RIC
Woodridge, IL	JOL
Woodruff, WI	SUP
Woodsboro, TX	CC
Woodsfield, OH	STU
Woodside, NY	BRK
Woodstock, GA	ATL
IL	RCK
MD	BAL
NY	NY
VA	ARL
VT	BUR
Woodsville, NH	MAN
Woodville, FL	PT
MS	JKS
TX	BEA
Woodward, OK	OKL
Woodworth, LA	ALX
Woonsocket, RI	PRO
RI	STF
SD	SFS
Wooster, OH	CLV
Worcester, MA	NTN
MA	WOR
MA	SAM
NY	ALB
Worland, WY	CHY
Worthington, IA	DUB
MN	WIN
OH	COL
Wrangell, AK	AJ
Wray, CO	DEN
Wrentham, MA	BO
Wright, KS	DOD
Wrightsville Beach, NC	R
Wrightwood, CA	SB
Wurtsboro, NY	NY
Wyalusing, PA	SCR
Wyandanch, NY	RVC
Wyandotte, MI	DET
Wyckoff, NJ	NEW
Wylie, TX	DAL
Wymore, NE	LIN
Wynantskill, NY	ALB
Wyncote, PA	PH
Wyndmere, ND	FAR
Wyndmoor, PA	PH
Wynne, AR	LR
Wynnewood, PA	PH
PA	OLN
Wynot, NE	OM
Wyoming, IL	PEO
MI	GR
OH	CIN
PA	SCR
Wytheville, VA	RIC
Xenia, OH	CIN

Place	Code
Yakima, WA	YAK
Yakutat, AK	AJ
Yale, MI	DET
Yalesville, CT	HRT
Yamhill, OR	P
Yankton, SD	SFS
Yardley, PA	PH
Yardville, NJ	TR
Yarnell, AZ	PHX
Yatesboro, PA	GBG
Yazoo City, MS	JKS
Yellow Springs, OH	CIN
Yellville, AR	LR
Yelm, WA	SEA
Yerington, NV	RNO
Yoakum, TX	VIC
Yoder, IN	FTW
Yonges Island, SC	CHR
Yonkers, NY	NY
NY	MCE
NY	NTN
NY	SYM
NY	STF
Yorba Linda, CA	ORG
York, NE	LIN
PA	HBG
SC	CHR
York Haven, PA	HBG
Yorktown, TX	VIC
VA	RIC
Yorktown Heights, NY	NY
Yorkville, IL	JOL
Youngstown, NY	BUF
OH	Y
OH	OLL
OH	PBR
OH	SJP
Youngsville, LA	LAF
PA	E
Youngtown, AZ	PHX
Youngwood, PA	GBG
Yountville, CA	SR
Ypsilanti, MI	LAN
Yreka, CA	SAC
Yuba City, CA	SAC
Yucaipa, CA	SB
Yucca Valley, CA	SB
Yukon, OK	OKL
PA	GBG
Yulan, NY	NY
Yuma, AZ	TUC
CO	DEN
Zachary, LA	BR
Zaleski, OH	COL
Zanesville, OH	COL
Zapata, TX	LAR
Zelienople, PA	PIT
Zephyr Cove, NV	RNO
Zephyrhills, FL	SP
Zillah, WA	YAK
Zion–Beach Park, IL	CHI
Zionsville, IN	LFT
Zumbrota, MN	STP
Zuni, NM	GLP
Zwolle, LA	SHP

Diocesan Abbreviations

ARCHDIOCESES AND DIOCESES

(ALB) .... Albany (New York)
(ALN) .... Allentown (Pennsylvania)
(ALT) .... Altoona-Johnstown (Pennsylvania)
(ALX) .... Alexandria (Louisiana)
(AGN) .... Agana (Guam)
(AMA) .... Amarillo (Texas)
(AJ) .... Anchorage-Juneau (Alaska)
(ARE) .... Arecibo (Puerto Rico)
(ARL) .... Arlington (Virginia)
(ATH) .... Apostolate to Hungarians
(ATL) .... Atlanta (Georgia)
(AUS) .... Austin (Texas)
(B) .... Boise (Idaho)
(BAK) .... Baker (Oregon)
(BAL) .... Baltimore (Maryland)
(BEA) .... Beaumont (Texas)
(BEL) .... Belleville (Illinois)
(BGP) .... Bridgeport (Connecticut)
(BIR) .... Birmingham (Alabama)
(BIS) .... Bismarck (North Dakota)
(BLX) .... Biloxi (Mississippi)
(BO) .... Boston (Massachusetts)
(BR) .... Baton Rouge (Louisiana)
(BRK) .... Brooklyn (New York)
(BUF) .... Buffalo (New York)
(BUR) .... Burlington (Vermont)
(BWN) .... Brownsville (Texas)
(CAM) .... Camden (New Jersey)
(CC) .... Corpus Christi (Texas)
(CGS) .... Caguas (Puerto Rico)
(CHI) .... Chicago (Illinois)
(CHK) .... Chalan Kanoa
(CHL) .... Charlotte (North Carolina)
(CHR) .... Charleston (South Carolina)
(CHY) .... Cheyenne (Wyoming)
(CI) .... Caroline Islands
(CIN) .... Cincinnati (Ohio)
(CLV) .... Cleveland (Ohio)
(COL) .... Columbus (Ohio)
(COS) .... Colorado Springs (Colorado)
(COV) .... Covington (Kentucky)
(CR) .... Crookston (Minnesota)
(DAL) .... Dallas (Texas)
(DAV) .... Davenport (Iowa)
(DEN) .... Denver (Colorado)
(DET) .... Detroit (Michigan)
(DM) .... Des Moines (Iowa)
(DOD) .... Dodge City (Kansas)
(DUB) .... Dubuque (Iowa)
(DUL) .... Duluth (Minnesota)
(E) .... Erie (Pennsylvania)
(ELP) .... El Paso (Texas)
(EST) .... Saint Thomas the Apostle, Chaldean (Michigan)
(EVN) .... Evansville (Indiana)
(FAJ) .... Fajardo-Humacao (Puerto Rico)
(FAR) .... Fargo (North Dakota)
(FBK) .... Fairbanks (Alaska)
(FgM) .... Foreign Mission Section
(FR) .... Fall River (Massachusetts)
(FRS) .... Fresno (California)
(FTW) .... Fort Wayne-South Bend (Indiana)
(FWT) .... Fort Worth (Texas)
(GAL) .... Galveston-Houston (Texas)
(GLD) .... Gaylord (Michigan)
(GB) .... Green Bay (Wisconsin)
(GBG) .... Greensburg (Pennsylvania)
(GF) .... Great Falls-Billings (Montana)
(GI) .... Grand Island (Nebraska)
(GLP) .... Gallup (New Mexico)
(GR) .... Grand Rapids (Michigan)
(GRY) .... Gary (Indiana)
(HBG) .... Harrisburg (Pennsylvania)
(HEL) .... Helena (Montana)
(HON) .... Honolulu (Hawaii)
(HPM) .. Holy Protection of Mary Byzantine (Arizona)
(HRT) .... Hartford (Connecticut)
(HT) .... Houma-Thibodaux (Louisiana)
(IND) .... Indianapolis (Indiana)
(JC) .... Jefferson City (Missouri)
(JKS) .... Jackson (Mississippi)
(JOL) .... Joliet in Illinois
(KAL) .... Kalamazoo (Michigan)
(KC) .... Kansas City-St. Joseph (Missouri)
(KCK) .... Kansas City in Kansas
(KNX) .... Knoxville (Tennessee)
(L) .... Louisville (Kentucky)
(LA) .... Los Angeles (California)
(LAF) .... Lafayette (Louisiana)
(LAN) .... Lansing (Michigan)
(LAR) .... Laredo (Texas)
(LC) .... La Crosse (Wisconsin)
(LEX) .... Lexington (Kentucky)
(LFT) .... Lafayette in Indiana
(LIN) .... Lincoln (Nebraska)
(LIT) ..... Apostolate for Lithuanian Catholics (New York)
(LKC) .... Lake Charles (Louisiana)
(LR) .... Little Rock (Arkansas)
(LSC) .... Las Cruces (New Mexico)
(LUB) .... Lubbock (Texas)
(LAV) .... Las Vegas (Nevada)
(MAD) .... Madison (Wisconsin)
(MAN) .... Manchester (New Hampshire)
(MAR) .... Marquette (Michigan)
(MCE) .... St. Mary, Queen of Peace, Syro-Malankara (New York)
(MEM) .... Memphis (Tennessee)
(MET) .... Metuchen (New Jersey)
(MGZ) .... Mayaguez (Puerto Rico)
(MI) .... Marshall Islands
(MIA) .... Miami (Florida)
(MIL) .... Milwaukee (Wisconsin)
(MO) .... Military Services, U.S.A. (Maryland)
(MOB) .... Mobile (Alabama)
(MRY) .... Monterey in California
(NEW) .... Newark (New Jersey)
(NO) .... New Orleans (Louisiana)
(NOR) .... Norwich (Connecticut)
(NSH) .... Nashville (Tennessee)
(NTN) .... Newton, Melkite-Greek (Massachusetts)
(NU) .... New Ulm (Minnesota)
(NY) .... New York (New York)
(OAK) .... Oakland (California)
(OG) .... Ogdensburg (New York)
(OKL) .... Oklahoma City (Oklahoma)
(OLD) .... Our Lady of Deliverance-Syriac (Michigan)
(OLL) .... Our Lady of Lebanon of Los Angeles (California)
(OLN) .... Our Lady of Nareg-Armenian (California)
(OM) .... Omaha (Nebraska)
(ORG) .... Orange in California
(ORL) .... Orlando (Florida)
(OWN) .... Owensboro (Kentucky)
(P) .... Portland in Oregon
(PAT) .... Paterson (New Jersey)
(PBL) .... Pueblo (Colorado)
(PBR) .... Pittsburgh-Byzantine (Pennsylvania)
(PCE) .... Ponce (Puerto Rico)
(PEO) .... Peoria (Illinois)
(PH) .... Philadelphia (Pennsylvania)
(PHU) .... Philadelphia-Ukrainian (Pennsylvania)
(PHX) .... Phoenix (Arizona)
(PIT) .... Pittsburgh (Pennsylvania)
(PMB) .... Palm Beach (Florida)
(POC) .... Personal Ordnariate of the Chair of St. Peter (Texas)
(POD) .... Prelature of the Holy Cross and Opus Dei (New York)
(PRM) .... Parma-Byzantine of the Ruthenians (Ohio)
(PRO) .... Providence (Rhode Island)
(PRT) .... Portland (Maine)
(PSC) .... Passaic-Byzantine (New Jersey)
(PT) .... Pensacola-Tallahassee (Florida)
(R) .... Raleigh (North Carolina)
(RC) .... Rapid City (South Dakota)
(RCK) .... Rockford (Illinois)
(RIC) .... Richmond (Virginia)
(RNO) .... Reno (Nevada)
(ROC) .... Rochester (New York)
(ROM) .... St. George-Romanian (Ohio)
(RVC) .... Rockville Centre (New York)
(SAC) .... Sacramento (California)
(SAG) .... Saginaw (Michigan)
(SAL) .... Salina (Kansas)
(SAM) .... St. Maron (New York)
(SAN) .... San Angelo (Texas)
(SAT) .... San Antonio (Texas)
(SAV) .... Savannah (Georgia)
(SB) .... San Bernardino (California)
(SC) .... Sioux City (Iowa)
(SCL) .... St. Cloud (Minnesota)
(SCR) .... Scranton (Pennsylvania)
(SD) .... San Diego (California)
(SEA) .... Seattle (Washington)
(SFD) .... Springfield in Illinois
(SFE) .... Santa Fe (New Mexico)
(SFR) .... San Francisco (California)
(SFS) .... Sioux Falls (South Dakota)
(SHP) .... Shreveport (Louisiana)
(SJ) .... San Jose in California
(SJN) .... San Juan (Puerto Rico)
(SJP) .... St. Josaphat-Ukrainian(Ohio)
(SLC) .... Salt Lake City (Utah)
(SP) .... St. Petersburg (Florida)
(SPA) .... St. Peter the Apostle, Chaldean (California)
(SPC) .... Springfield-Cape Girardeau (Missouri)
(SPK) .... Spokane (Washington)
(SPP) .... Samoa-Pago Pago
(SPR) .... Springfield in Massachusetts
(SR) .... Santa Rosa in California
(STA) .... St. Augustine (Florida)
(STF) .... Stamford-Ukrainian (Connecticut)
(STL) .... St. Louis (Missouri)
(STN) .... St. Nicholas-Ukrainian (Illinois)
(STO) .... Stockton (California)
(STP) .... St. Paul and Minneapolis (Minnesota)
(STU) .... Steubenville (Ohio)
(STV) .... St. Thomas in the Virgin Islands
(SUP) .... Superior (Wisconsin)
(SY) .... Syracuse (New York)
(SYM) .... St. Thomas Syro-Malabar (Illinois)
(TLS) .... Tulsa (Oklahoma)
(TOL) .... Toledo (Ohio)
(TR) .... Trenton (New Jersey)
(TUC) .... Tucson (Arizona)
(TYL) .... Tyler (Texas)
(VEN) .... Venice (Florida)
(VIC) .... Victoria in Texas
(WCH) .... Wichita (Kansas)
(WDC) .... Washington (District of Columbia)
(WH) .... Wheeling-Charleston (West Virginia)
(WIL) .... Wilmington (Delaware)
(WIN) .... Winona-Rochester (Minnesota)
(WOR) .... Worcester (Massachusetts)
(Y) .... Youngstown (Ohio)
(YAK) .... Yakima (Washington)

Diocese of Albany

(Dioecesis Albanensis)

MOST REVEREND EDWARD B. SCHARFENBERGER

Bishop of Albany; ordained July 2, 1973; appointed Bishop of Albany February 11, 2014; ordained and installed April 10, 2014. Chancery Office: Pastoral Center, 40 N. Main Ave., Albany, NY 12203.

Chancery Office: Pastoral Center, 40 N. Main Ave., Albany, NY 12203. T: 518-453-6600; F: 518-453-6795.
www.rcda.org
chancery@rcda.org

ESTABLISHED APRIL 23, 1847.

Square Miles 10,419.

(Incorporated by a special act of the Legislature of the State of New York, April 12, 1941, with the title "The Roman Catholic Diocese of Albany, New York"). Comprises the entire Counties of Albany, Columbia, Delaware, Fulton, Green, Montgomery, Otsego, Rensselaer, Saratoga, Schenectady, Schoharie, Warren and Washington and that part of Herkimer and Hamilton Counties, south of the northern line of the townships of Ohio and Russia, as existing in 1872 in the State of New York.

For legal titles of parishes and diocesan institutions, consult the Chancery Office.

STATISTICAL OVERVIEW

Personnel
Bishop....1
Retired Bishops....1
Priests: Diocesan Active in Diocese....81
Priests: Diocesan Active Outside Diocese....3
Priests: Retired, Sick or Absent....68
Number of Diocesan Priests....152
Religious Priests in Diocese....22
Total Priests in your Diocese....174
Ordinations:
Diocesan Priests....2
Transitional Deacons....1
Permanent Deacons in Diocese....114
Total Brothers....60
Total Sisters....455

Parishes
Parishes....126
With Resident Pastor:
Resident Diocesan Priests....95
Resident Religious Priests....5
Without Resident Pastor:
Administered by Priests....6
Administered by Deacons....4
Administered by Religious Women....2
Administered by Lay People....7
Administered by Pastoral Teams, etc.....7
Missions....15

Professional Ministry Personnel:
Brothers....105
Sisters....56
Lay Ministers....520

Welfare
Catholic Hospitals....2
Homes for the Aged....1
Total Assisted....4
Residential Care of Children....2
Total Assisted....75
Day Care Centers....1
Total Assisted....27
Specialized Homes....6
Total Assisted....225
Special Centers for Social Services....80
Total Assisted....63,000
Residential Care of Disabled....20
Total Assisted....80

Educational
Seminaries, Diocesan....1
Students from This Diocese....20
Diocesan Students in Other Seminaries....13
Total Seminarians....33
Colleges and Universities....4
Total Students....8,000
High Schools, Diocesan and Parish....4
Total Students....800
High Schools, Private....3
Total Students....1,175
Elementary Schools, Diocesan and Parish....17
Total Students....3,225
Elementary Schools, Private....1
Total Students....150
Catechesis/Religious Education:
High School Students....4,000
Elementary Students....10,000
Total Students under Catholic Instruction....27,383
Teachers in Diocese:
Brothers....1
Lay Teachers....360

Vital Statistics
Receptions into the Church:
Infant Baptism Totals....1,714
Minor Baptism Totals....60
Adult Baptism Totals....33
Received into Full Communion....75
First Communions....1,632
Confirmations....1,713
Marriages:
Catholic....306
Interfaith....90
Total Marriages....396
Deaths....4,022
Total Catholic Population....316,275
Total Population....1,400,000

LEADERSHIP

Archivist - t) 518-453-6669 Amy Brozio-Andrews (archives@rcda.org);
Vicars General - t) 518-453-6612 Very Rev. David R. LeFort, Vicar; Very Rev. Robert Longobucco, Vicar (robert.longobucco@rcda.org);
Moderator of the Curia - t) 518-453-6612 Very Rev. Robert Longobucco (robert.longobucco@rcda.org);
Chancellor - t) 518-453-6612 Giovanni Virgiglio Jr., Chancellor (giovanni.virgiglio@rcda.org);
Diocesan College of Consultors - Very Rev. Anthony M. Barratt; Very Rev. James Belogi; Very Rev. Joseph G. Busch;
Finance Department - t) 518-453-6640 Loida Sarabia, CFO; Barbara Murin, Comptroller (barbara.murin@rcda.org); Sr. Teresa Grace Baillargeon, Parish Support Specialist (teresabaillargeon@rcda.org);
Insurance Office - t) 518-445-6250 Jon Rocco, Claims/ Risk Mgr. II (jrocco@catholicmutual.org); Kathleen Williams, Asst. Claims/Risk Mgr. (kwilliams@catholicmutual.org); Christine Pastino, Svc. Office Asst. (cpastino@catholicmutual.org);
Metropolitan Tribunal - t) 646-794-3200 tribunal@archny.org Rev. Robert Hospodar, Vicar;
Office of Human Resources and Safe Environment - t) 518-453-6635 diocesan.hr@rcda.org; safeenvironment.hr@rcda.org Ann Marie Carswell, Assoc. Dir.; Joyce C. Tarantino, Dir.;
Pastoral Center - t) 518-453-6600
Pastoral Planning - t) 518-453-6661 Dcn. Frank C. Berning, Dir. (frank.berning@rcda.org); Dcn. Al Censullo, Parish Demographics;
Presbyteral Council - Rev. Joseph Arockiasamy, Elected Member; Rev. Jay Atherton, Elected Member; Very Rev. Anthony M. Barratt, Appointed Member;
Regional Episcopal Vicars - Very Rev. James Belogi, Twin Rivers Vicariate; Very Rev. Joseph G. Busch, Adirondack Vicariate; Very Rev. Michael Cambi, Leatherstocking Vicariate;
The Tribunal - t) 518-453-6620 tribunal@rcda.org www.rcda.org/offices/tribunal
- **Assistants to the Tribunal** - Anna Colello; Anne Schmidt;
- **Auditors and Assessors** - Donna B. Haskins; Rev. Thomas J. Krupa; Rev. John L. Moyna;
- **Defender of the Bond** - Sr. Marilyn Vassallo, C.S.J.;
- **Judges** - Very Rev. Anthony M. Barratt; Rev. David V. Berberian; Very Rev. Matthew H. Frisoni;
- **Judicial Vicar** - Very Rev. Matthew H. Frisoni;
- **Promoter of Justice** - Rev. James I. Donlon;

OFFICES AND DIRECTORS

Acting Vicar for Religious - t) (518) 453-6612 Very Rev. David R. LeFort;
Apostleship of Prayer - t) 518-453-6643
Architecture and Building Commission - t) 518-453-6622 Rev. Randall P. Patterson, Chair; Roslyn Webber, Construction Project Coord. (roslyn.webber@rcda.org);
Assistance Coordinator - t) 518-453-6646 assistance.coordinator@rcda.org Frederick Jones;
Bishop's Appeal - t) 518-453-6680 stewardship@rcda.org thediocesanappeal.org/ Nancy Spadaro Bielawa, Exec.;
Black Catholic Apostolate of the Diocese of Albany/St. Joan of Arc Parish - t) 518-463-0378 Rev. Kofi Ntsiful-Amissah, Admin. (sjoa@nycap.rr.com);
Catholic Campaign for Human Development - t) 518-453-6650 Sr. Betsy VanDeusen, C.S.J., Dir.;
Catholic Charismatic Renewal (CCR) for the Diocesan Service Committee (DSC) - t) 518-334-6503; 518-663-5125 infor.dsc.albany@gmail.com www.albanyccr.org Jack Ellsbury, Co-Liaison to Bishop; Dian Seaver, Co-Liaison to Bishop;
Catholic Charities Agencies and Commissions - t) 518-453-6650 Dcn. Walter C. Ayres, Dir. (deaconayres@yahoo.com); Jackie Buff-Rogers, Dir.; Mary Carpenter, Dir.;
- **United Tenants of Albany** - t) 518-436-8997 K. Michelle Arthur, Exec. Dir.;

Catholic Charities of Diocese of Albany, Inc.; St. Vincent's Child Care Society, Inc. - t) 518-453-6650 Vincent W. Colonno, CEO; Michael Lawler, CFO/ COO;
Catholic Deaf Ministry - t) 518-453-6602 tobinr@rcda.org Rosemarie Tobin, Liaison (rosemarie.tobin@rcda.org);
Catholic Education and Faith Formation, Vicariate for - t) 518-453-6670 Very Rev. Robert Longobucco, Vicar (robert.longobucco@rcda.org); Giovanni Virgiglio Jr., Supt. (giovanni.virgiglio@rcda.org); Christopher Bott, Asst. Supt. (christopher.bott@rcda.org);
Catholic Relief Services - t) 518-453-6650 David Meyers, Dir. Immigration Services; Sr. Betsy VanDeusen, C.S.J., Dir.;
Catholic Women's Service League - t) 518-242-4731 Marcia Mahoney, Pres.;
Cemeteries - t) 518-730-0302 Emily Simmons, Exec. Dir. (Emily@ADCemeteries.org);
Censor Librorum - t) 518-453-6600
Communications Office - t) 518-453-6618 Kathy Barrans, Dir.;
Community Health Alliance - t) 518-453-6650 Vincent W. Colonno, Bishop's Rep.;
Consultation Center of the Diocese of Albany - t) 518-489-4431; 518-489-5189 consultation.center@rcda.org www.consultationcenteralbany.org Rev. Thomas E. Konopka, Exec.; Ginna Roeding, Dir.; Rev. Anthony Chiaramonte, Counselor;
Cursillo in Christianity - t) 518-326-3003 albanycursillo.org/ Eva Fitzgerald, Dir.; Sr. J. Elizabeth Van Deusen, C.S.J., Dir.; Joe Fitzgerald, Dir.;
Diocesan Pastoral Council - t) 518-453-6622 Roslyn Webber, Admin. (roslyn.webber@rcda.org);
Diocesan Stewardship Office - t) 518-453-6680 stewardship@rcda.org Nancy Spadaro Bielawa, Exec.;
Director Pastoral Care Ministry - t) 518-641-6823 Harley McDevitt (harley.mcdevitt@rcda.org);
Ecumenical and Interreligious Affairs of the Roman Catholic Diocese of Albany, Commission for - Rev. James Kane, Dir.; Dcn. Walter C. Ayres (deaconayres@yahoo.com); Sr. Betsy VanDeusen, C.S.J.;
Emmaus Retreat Ministry to College Age People - Maureen Athens, Co Dir. (momathens66@gmail.com); Chris O'Neill, Co Dir.;
The Evangelist - t) 518-453-6688 info@evangelist.org Mike Matvey, Editor;
Evangelization - t) (518) 453-6625 Thomas Cronin, Advisor (thomas.cronin@rcda.org);
The Foundation of the Roman Catholic Diocese of Albany - t) (518) 453-6657 www.foundationrcda.org Most Rev. Edward B. Scharfenberger, Pres.; Nancy Spadaro Bielawa, Exec.;
Health and Hospitals Office - t) 518-453-6650 Vincent W. Colonno, Bishop's Rep.;
Holy Name Societies - t) 518-453-6612 Very Rev. David R. LeFort, Contact;
Korean Catholic Apostolate of Albany - t) 518-438-1805 Rev. Jaeung Damian Lee, Chap.;
Ladies of Charity - t) 518-598-9697 www.localbany.org Mary Clinton, Pres.;
Ministers to Retired Priests - Rev. George St. John; Rev. Winston L. Bath; Rev. Paul C. Cox;
Office of Canonical Services - t) 518-453-6620 tribunal@rcda.org
- **Advocates** - Rev. Thomas Krupa; Rev. Joseph O'Brien; Rev. John L. Moyna;
- **Bishop's Delegate for Marriage Dispensations** - Rev. James I. Donlon; Very Rev. Matthew H. Frisoni;
- **Notaries** - Anne Schmidt; Anna Colello;

Office of Information Technology - t) 518-453-6685
Office of Parish Services - t) 518-453-6609 Renee Morgiewicz, Coord. Parish Svcs.;
Office of Prayer & Worship - t) 518-453-6645 Very Rev. Anthony M. Barratt, Dir.; Sarah Guerra, Administrative Asst. (prayer&worship@rcda.org);
Office of Real Property - t) 518-453-6623 Michael Kane, Dir.; Paula Bordis, Special Asst. to Dir. (paula.bordis@rcda.org);
Office of Respect Life Ministry - t) 518-453-6609 Renee Morgiewicz, Coord.;
Office of Vocations Diocese of Albany - t) 518-453-6690 Very Rev. Anthony F. Ligato, Vicar; Sarah Guerra, Admin. Asst. to Vicar;
Ongoing Formation and Continuing Education - Very Rev. Anthony M. Barratt; Very Rev. Mark G. Reamer, O.F.M.; Rev. Jay Atherton;
Permanent Deacons Office - t) 518-453-6643 Dcn. Joseph Brennan, Dir.;
Prevention Services - Catholic Schools Office - t) 518-453-6666 Jacquelyn Chiera, Dir. (jacquelyn.chiera@rcda.org);
Priests Placement Committee - t) 518-453-6643 Very Rev. James A. Ebert, Chair; Rev. John J. Bradley; Rev. David V. Berberian;
Priests Retirement Board - t) 518-452-1156 Rev. Thomas F. Berardi, Chair; Rev. David V. Berberian; Rev. John T. Provost;
St. Bernard's School of Theology and Ministry - t) 518-453-6760 stbernards@rcda.org Dr. Anthony Coleman, Dir.; Dr. Marco Stango, Campus Mgr.;
St. Luke's Guild of Catholic Physicians - t) 518-453-6612 stlukes.guild@rcda.org Very Rev. David R. LeFort;
Schools: Diocesan School Board - Mark Treanor, Pres.;
- **Directors** - Sr. Angela Leo, Business Support Spec.; Bridget Frament, Personnel Svcs. Coord.; Rosemarie Tobin, Persons with Disabilities Consultant;
- **Office of the Superintendent** - t) 518-453-6602; 518-453-6666 Patricia Welker, Executive Asst. to the Supt.; Giovanni Virgiglio Jr., Supt.; Christopher Bott, Asst. Supt.;
- **President** - Mark Treanor, Pres.;
- **Support Professionals** - t) 518-853-4001 James Bercharlie, Chief Data Officer; Sal Carbone, Occupational Safety Coord.; Daniel Jaromin, Accounting Assoc.;

Scouting - scouting@rcda.org Dcn. Peter R. Quinn, Chap.; Dcn. William H. Gaul Jr., Chap.; Greg Szczesny, Chair;
Society for the Propagation of the Faith - t) 518-453-6675 Very Rev. David R. LeFort, Dir.;
Society of St. Vincent de Paul - t) 518-937-0411 Paul J. Buehler Jr. (pbuehler@anscorporate.com);
Spanish Apostolate - t) 518-229-2634; 518-605-1814 Dcn. Ramon Bonifacio, Co-Dir.; Dcn. Miguel Fabian, Co-Dir.;
Spiritual Directors - t) 518-371-7372 Sr. J. Elizabeth Van Deusen, C.S.J., Spiritual Adv./Care Srvcs.; Rev. Christopher Walsh;
Vicar for Clergy - t) 518-453-6643 Very Rev. James A. Ebert;
Vietnamese Apostolate - t) 518-434-0680 sacredheartjesus.albany@rcda.org Rev. John T. Provost, Pst.; Giang (Johnny) Tran; Khiet Nguyen (sacredheartjesus.albany@rcda.org);

PARISHES, MISSIONS, AND CLERGY

STATE OF NEW YORK

ALBANY

Cathedral of the Immaculate Conception - 125 Eagle St., Albany, NY 12202 t) 518-463-4447 cathedraloftheimmaculateconception.albany@rcda.org cathedralic.com/ Very Rev. Anthony F. Ligato, Rector; Rev. Paul Mijas, Par. Vicar; Most Rev. Howard James Hubbard, In Res.; Dcn. James Agnew; Dcn. Timothy Kosto; Thomas Fowler, DRE;
- **Cathedral Social Services** - t) 518-463-2279 ciavardm@rcda.org Mark Ciavardoni, Contact;
- **Convent** - 93 Park Ave., Albany, NY 12202

t) 518-436-7697

All Saints Catholic Church - 16 Homestead St., Albany, NY 12203; Mailing: 12 Rosemont St., Albany, NY 12203 t) 518-482-4497 allsaintscatholicchurch.albany@rcda.org Dcn. Timothy J. McAuliffe; Dcn. Gary O'Connor; Rev. Thomas Lawless, Pst.;

All Saints Catholic Academy - (Grades N-8) 10 Rosemont St., Albany, NY 12203 t) 518-438-0066 principal@ascaalbany.org www.ascaalbany.org/ Traci Johnson, Prin.;

Blessed Sacrament - 607 Central Ave., Albany, NY 12206 t) 518-482-3375 blessedsacrament.albany@rcda.org; blessedsacramentalb@gmail.com www.blessedsacramentalbany.org Our Lady of the Americas Shrine Church Rev. Daniel J. Quinn, Pst.; Rev. Charles Onyeneke, Par. Vicar; Rev. Francis O'Connor, In Res.; CRP Stds.: 45

Blessed Sacrament School - (Grades PreK-8) 605 Central Ave., Albany, NY 12206 t) 518-438-5854 info@blessedsacramentschool.net www.blessedsacramentschool.net Maureen Daurio, Prin.;

Shrine of Our Lady of the Americas - 273 Central Ave., Albany, NY 12206 t) 518-465-3685 info@ourladyoftheamericas.org ourladyoftheamericas.org/

Sister Maureen Joyce Center - 369 Livingston Ave., Albany, NY 12208 t) 518-462-9885; 518-465-8262 Soup kitchen, food pantry, information and referrals.

Christ the King - 20 Sumter Ave., Albany, NY 12203 t) (518) 456-1644 ctkwestm@rcda.org www.ctkparishny.org/ Rev. Richard Lesser, Pst.; Dcn. Anthony G. Cortese; CRP Stds.: 235

St. Francis of Assisi Parish - 391 Delaware Ave., Albany, NY 12209 t) 518-434-4028 Very Rev. Anthony F. Ligato, Sacr. Min.; Rev. Sean O'Brien, Sacr. Min.;

St. Mary - 10 Lodge St., Albany, NY 12207-2196 t) 518-462-4254; 518-462-4255 smalbany@rcda.org www.hist-stmarys.org Rev. David Mickiewicz, Pst.; Rev. L. Edward Deimeke, In Res.; Dcn. Walter C. Ayres; Dcn. Aaron Tremblay;

Parish of Mater Christi - 40 Hopewell St., Albany, NY 12208 t) 518-489-3204 parishofmaterchristi.albany@rcda.org parishes.rcda.org/materchristi/ Rev. Brian Lehnert, Par. Admin.; Dcn. Bernard McConaghy;

Mater Christi School - (Grades PreK-8) 35 Hurst Ave., Albany, NY 12208 t) 518-489-3111 dtimmis@mcsalbany.org www.mcsalbany.org Sr. Deborah Timmis, Prin.;

Sacred Heart of Jesus - 33 Walter St., Albany, NY 12204 t) 518-434-0680 shjalban@rcda.org parishes.rcda.org/sacredheartofjesus/ Rev. Michael Flannery, Pst.; Dcn. Walter C. Ayres;

St. Vincent de Paul - 900 Madison Ave., Albany, NY 12208 t) 518-489-5408 www.stvincentalbany.org Rev. Thomas J. Hayes, Sacr. Min.; Rev. Leo P. O'Brien, Pastor Emer.; Elizabeth Simcoe, Parish Life Coord.;

ALTAMONT

St. Lucy/St. Bernadette - 113 Grand St., Altamont, NY 12009; Mailing: PO Box 678, Altamont, NY 12009 t) 518-861-8770 parishes.rcda.org/stlucystbernadettechurch/ Sr. Mary Lou Liptak, R.S.M., Parish Life Coord.; Sr. Patricia Davis, RSM, Pst. Assoc.; Rev. Paul Smith, Sacramental Min.;

Parish House - 109 Grand St., Altamont, NY 12009 slucys@nycap.rr.com

AMSTERDAM

The Parish of St. Joseph/St. Michael/Our Lady of Mount Carmel - 39 St. John St., Amsterdam, NY 12010; Mailing: PO Box 699, Amsterdam, NY 12010 t) 518-843-3250 Canonically merged in 1980 into St. Joseph-St. Michael-Our Lady of Mount Carmel. Rev. O. Robert De Martinis, Pst.; Dcn. Michael C. Ryba, Dir., Finance & Admin.;

St. Joseph-St. Michael-Our Lady of Mount Carmel - 39 St. John St., Amsterdam, NY 12010; Mailing: P.O. Box 699, Amsterdam, NY 12010 t) 518-843-3250 stjosephsstmichaelolmtcarmel.amsterdam@rcda.org Rev. O. Robert De Martinis, Pst.; Dcn. Michael C. Ryba, Dir., Finance & Admin.;

St. Mary - 156 E. Main St., Amsterdam, NY 12010 t) 518-842-4500 www.stmaryamsterdam.org/ Rev. Jeffrey L'Arche, Pst.; Dcn. Michael C. Ryba, Dir., Finance & Admin.;

St. Mary Institute - (Grades PreK-8) 10 Kopernik Dr., Amsterdam, NY 12010 t) 518-842-4100 luftn@smik8.org www.saintmarysinstitute.com Nicole Luft, Prin.;

St. Stanislaus - 50 Cornell St., Amsterdam, NY 12010; Mailing: 46 Cornell St., Amsterdam, NY 12010 t) 518-842-2771 ststanislaus.amsterdam@rcda.org parishes.rcda.org/ststanislaus/ Rev. O. Robert De Martinis, Pst.; Dcn. Michael C. Ryba, Dir., Finance & Admin.;

St. John Paul II Parish Center - 46 Cornell St., Amsterdam, NY 12010

ATHENS

St. Patrick - 24 N. Washington St., Athens, NY 12015; Mailing: 19 N. Franklin St., Athens, NY 12015 t) 518-943-3150 Rev. Jay Atherton, Pst.; Rev. Michael P. Melanson, Par. Vicar; CRP Stds.: 40

AVERILL PARK

St. Henry - 39 Old Rte. 66, Averill Park, NY 12018; Mailing: P.O. Box 550, Averill Park, NY 12018 t) 518-674-3818 www.sthenrysaverillpark.org Rev. Thomas F. Holmes, Pst.; Dcn. Frank S. Lukovits; Dcn. Robert Pasquarelli;

BALLSTON LAKE

Our Lady of Grace - 73 Midline Rd., Ballston Lake, NY 12019 t) 518-399-5713 www.olgchurchbl.org Rev. Thomas E. Konopka, Pst.; Dcn. Frank Thomas;

BALLSTON SPA

St. Mary - 167 Milton Ave., Ballston Spa, NY 12020; Mailing: 185 Milton Ave., Ballston Spa, NY 12020 t) 518-885-7411; 518-884-8479 (CRP) www.stmarysballstonspa.org/ Rev. Francis Vivacqua, Pst.; Allison Mendenhall, Music Min.; Rebecca Cronin, Youth Min.; Vicki Schuette, DRE; Dcn. Ronald T. Hogan; CRP Stds.: 370

St. Mary School - (Grades PreK-5) 40 Thompson St., Ballston Spa, NY 12020 t) 518-885-7300 principal@smsbspa.org www.smsbspa.org/ Lynn Fitzgerald, Prin.; Stds.: 186; Lay Tchrs.: 16

St. Mary's of Galway - 2113 East St., Galway, NY 12074 t) (518) 885-7411 stmarysballstonspa.org

BOLTON LANDING

Blessed Sacrament - 7 Goodman Ave., Bolton Landing, NY 12814; Mailing: 12 Goodman Ave., PO Box 266, Bolton Landing, NY 12814 t) 518-644-3861 blessedsacrament.boltonlanding@rcda.org Rev. John O'Kane, Assoc. Pst.; Dcn. Joseph Tyrrell, Parish Life Dir.;

BROADALBIN

St. Joseph's Church - North & N. Main Sts., Broadalbin, NY 12025; Mailing: P.O. Box 538, Broadalbin, NY 12025 t) 518-883-3774 parishes.rcda.org/stjosephstfrancis/ Very Rev. Anastacio Jun Segura, Pst.; Katy Ryan, DRE;

CAIRO

Sacred Heart - 35 Church St., Cairo, NY 12413 t) 518-622-3319 sacredheart.cairo@rcda.org www.sholk.weebly.com Rev. Jay Atherton, Pst.; Barbara Koerner-Fox, DRE;

Our Lady of Knock Shrine - 2052 Rt 145, East Durham, NY 12423; Mailing: 35 Church St, Cairo, NY 12413 sacredheartolok@gmail.com

CAMBRIDGE

St. Patrick - 17 S. Park St., Cambridge, NY 12816-1248 t) 518-677-2757 www.battenkillcatholic.org Rev. Peter Tkocz, Par. Vicar; Jeffrey C. Peck, Parish Life Dir.;

CASTLETON ON HUDSON

Sacred Heart - 3 Catholic Way, Castleton On Hudson, NY 12033-1543 t) 518-732-2155 www.sacredheartchurchcastletonny.org/ Rev. Thomas Krupa, Pst.; Dcn. Thomas Nash;

CATSKILL

St. Patrick - 66 William St., Catskill, NY 12414 t) 518-943-3150 stpatricks.catskill@rcda.org stpatrickathenscatskill.org/ Rev. Jay Atherton, Pst.; Rev. Michael P. Melanson, Par. Vicar; CRP Stds.: 40

CHATHAM

St. James - 117 Hudson Ave., Chatham, NY 12037 t) 518-392-4991 stjames.chatham@rcda.org www.stjameschatham.org/ Deborah Halpin, Pst. Assoc.; Rev. Steve Matthews, Sacr. Min.;

CHERRY VALLEY

St. Thomas the Apostle - 1 Church St., Cherry Valley, NY 13320; Mailing: P.O. Box 246, Cherry Valley, NY 13320 t) 607-264-3779 stthomas.cherryvalley@rcda.org www.turnpikecatholics.com Dcn. Richard J. Brown; Dcn. Randy Velez; Karen J. Walker, DRE;

CHESTERTOWN

Parish of St. Isaac Jogues - 86 Riverside Dr., Chestertown, NY 12817; Mailing: P.O. Box 471, 86 Riverside Dr., Chestertown, NY 12817 t) 518-824-1176 northernpointscluster.weebly.com/ Barbara Carlozzi, DRE; Rev. John O'Kane, Pst.;

CLIFTON PARK

St. Edward the Confessor - 569 Clifton Park Center Rd., Clifton Park, NY 12065-4838 t) 518-371-7372 www.stedwardsny.org/ Rev. Patrick J. Butler, Pst.; Dcn. Richard Dicaprio; Dcn. Walter J. MacKinnon;

COBLESKILL

St. Vincent de Paul - 138 Washington Ave., Cobleskill, NY 12043 t) 518-234-2892 stvincentdepaulcobleskillny.com/ Rev. Joseph Arockiasamy, Pst.; Dcn. Gary Surman; Greg Rys, Campus Min.;

COHOES

Holy Trinity - 122 Vliet Blvd., Cohoes, NY 12047-1842 t) 518-237-2373 holytrinity.cohoes@rcda.org www.holytrinitycohoes.org/ Rev. John Cronin, Pst.; Dcn. Paul LeBlanc;

St. Michael - Ontario St. at Page Ave., Cohoes, NY 12047; Mailing: 20 Page Ave., Cohoes, NY 12047 t) 518-357-5151 stmichaelsofcohoes.org/ Rev. John Cronin, Pst.; Dcn. Paul LeBlanc;

COLONIE

St. Clare - 1947 Central Ave., Colonie, NY 12205-4299 t) 518-456-3112 www.stclarescolonie.com/ Dcn. Richard J. Thiesen, Parish Life Coord.; Rev. James J. Kane, Sacr. Min.;

COOPERSTOWN

St. Mary - 31 Elm St., Cooperstown, NY 13326 t) 607-547-2213 stmarys.cooperstown@rcda.org www.stmaryscoop.org/ Very Rev. Michael Cambi, Pst.;

COPAKE FALLS

Parish of Our Lady of Hope - 8074 State Rte. 22, Copake Falls, NY 12517 t) 518-329-4711; 518-329-4240 ourladyofhope.copakefalls@rcda.org ourladyofhopecopakefalls.org/ Bruce Frishkoff, Parish Life Coord.; Rev. Joseph Mali, Sacr. Min.;

CORINTH

Holy Mother and Child Parish - 405 Palmer Ave., Corinth, NY 12822 t) (518) 654-2113 holymotherandchildparish.corinth@rcda.org; holymcparish@gmail.com parishes.rcda.org/holymotherandchildparish/ Dcn. Gary R. Picher, Interim Admin.; Rev. Kenneth J. Swain, Interim Priest;

COXSACKIE

St. Mary - Mansion St. at Washington Ave., Coxsackie, NY 12051; Mailing: 80 Mansion St., Coxsackie, NY 12051 t) 518-731-8800 stmarys.coxsackie@rcda.org stmaryscoxsackie.com/ Rev. Jay Atherton, Pst.; Rev. Joseph O'Brien, Par. Vicar; Dcn. Michael F. McDonald;

DELANSON

Our Lady of Fatima - 1735 Alexander Rd., Delanson, NY 12053-0219; Mailing: P.O. Box 219, Delanson, NY 12053-0219 t) 518-895-2788 parishes.rcda.org/ourladyoffatima/ Rev. Thomas Zelker, Pst.;

DELHI

St. Peter - 10 Cross St., Delhi, NY 13856; Mailing: 8 Franklin St., Delhi, NY 13753 t) 607-746-2503

catholicdelhi.com Rev. Edward Golding, Admin.; Dcn. Michael Freeman;

DELMAR

St. Thomas the Apostle (St. Thomas' Church of Delmar, N.Y.) - 35 Adams Pl., Delmar, NY 12054 t) 518-439-4951 office@stthomas-church.org www.stthomas-church.org/ Rev. F. Richard Lesser, Pst.; Rev. Daniel McHale, Par. Vicar; Dcn. Alfred R. Manzella;

St. Thomas the Apostle School - (Grades PreK-8) 42 Adams Pl., Delmar, NY 12054 t) 518-439-5573 info@stthomas-school.org www.stthomas-school.org Adam Biggs, Prin.; Stds.: 200; Lay Tchrs.: 16

DOLGEVILLE

St. Joseph - N. Helmer Ave. at W. State St., Dolgeville, NY 13329; Mailing: 31 N. Helmer Ave., Dolgeville, NY 13329 t) 315-429-8338 parishes.rcda.org/stjosephsdolgeville/ Rev. Brian K. Slezak, Pst.;

EAST GREENBUSH

Holy Spirit - 667 Columbia Tpke., East Greenbush, NY 12061 t) 518-477-7925 holyspiriteg.weconnect.com/ Rev. Quy Vo, Pst.;

Holy Spirit School - (Grades PreK-8) 54 Highland Dr., East Greenbush, NY 12061 t) 518-477-5739 principal@hsseg.org hsseg.com/ Michael Kosar, Prin.;

FONDA

St. Cecilia - 26 Broadway, Fonda, NY 12068; Mailing: P.O. Box 837, Fonda, NY 12068 t) 518-853-4195 stcecilias.fonda@rcda.org parishes.rcda.org/stcecilia&sacredheart/ Rev. Christopher Welch, Pst.;

FORT ANN

St. Ann's Roman Catholic Church - 85 George St., Fort Ann, NY 12827; Mailing: PO Box 226, Fort Ann, NY 12827 t) 518-639-5218 stannfortann@gmail.com olhstann.org/ Very Rev. Joseph G. Busch, Pst.; Rev. Zachariah Chichester, Par. Vicar; Gina Neron, Bus. Mgr.;

FORT EDWARD

St. Joseph - 166 Broadway, Fort Edward, NY 12828; Mailing: 164 Broadway, Fort Edward, NY 12828 t) 518-747-5117 Rev. Thomas Babiuch, Pst.;

FORT PLAIN

Parish of Our Lady of Hope - 115 Reid St., Fort Plain, NY 13339; Mailing: 119 Reid St., Fort Plain, NY 13339 t) 518-993-3822 Dcn. Joseph M. Cechnicki, Parish Life Coord.; Michaela Germond, DRE;

FRANKFORT

Our Lady Queen of Apostles - 412 Frankfort St., Frankfort, NY 13340; Mailing: 414 Frankfort St., Frankfort, NY 13340 t) 315-894-2360 olqoa.info/ Rev. Paul G. Catena, Pst.; Dcn. Michael Carbone;

GLENS FALLS

St. Mary - 62 Warren St., Glens Falls, NY 12801 t) 518-792-0989 stmarysglensfalls.org/ Rev. Scott VanDerveer, Pst.; Dcn. F. David Powers;

St. Mary's/St. Alphonsus Regional School - (Grades PreK-8) 10-12 Church St., Glens Falls, NY 12801 t) 518-792-3178 pblamer@smsarcs.org www.smsaschool.org Patricia Balmer, Prin.;

GLENVILLE

Immaculate Conception - 400 Saratoga Rd., Glenville, NY 12302 t) 518-399-9168 icglenvi@rcda.org www.icglenville.com Rev. Thomas E. Konopka, Pst.; Dcn. Craig Dempsey;

GLOVERSVILLE

Church of the Holy Spirit - 153 S. Main St., Gloversville, NY 12078; Mailing: 149 St. Main St., Gloversville, NY 12078 t) 518-725-3143 holyspirit.gloversville@rcda.org www.holyspirit12078.org/ Rev. Matthew Wetsel, Pst.; Rev. Donald Czelusniak, Pastor Emer.;

GRAFTON

Parish of Our Lady of the Snow - 31 Owens Rd., Grafton, NY 12082 t) 518-273-7602 A mission of Our Lady of Victory, Troy. Rev. Thomas Morrette, Pst.; Rev. Nathaniel Resila, Par. Vicar; Dcn. Brian Lewis; Dcn. Willis R. Wolfe;

GRANVILLE

St. Mary's Roman Catholic Church Roman Catholic Community of Granville - 23 Bulkley Ave., Granville, NY 12832 t) 518-642-1262 smgranvi@rcda.org St. Mary's, Granville, NY; Our Lady of Hope, Whitehall, NY; St. Ann's, Ft. Ann, NY; Chapel of the Assumption, Hulettes Landing, NY Very Rev. Joseph G. Busch, Pst.; Rev. Zachariah Chichester, Par. Vicar; CRP Stds.: 8

GREENFIELD CENTER

St. Joseph - 3159 Rte. 9N, Greenfield Center, NY 12833; Mailing: PO Box 547, Greenfield Center, NY 12833 t) 518-893-7680 stjosephs.greenfieldcenter@rcda.org www.stjosephschurchgreenfieldcenter.org/ Dcn. John Barone; Rev. Simon Udemgba, Admin.; Margie Carroll, Pst. Assoc.;

St. Paul - 771 Rte. 29, Rock City Falls, NY 12863

GREENVILLE

St. John the Baptist - 4987 Rt. 81, Greenville, NY 12083; Mailing: P.O. Box 340, Greenville, NY 12083 t) 518-966-8317 stjohnthebaptist.greenville@rcda.org sjbg.weebly.com/ Rev. Jay Atherton, Pst.;

GREENWICH

St. Joseph - 35 Hill St., Greenwich, NY 12834; Mailing: 36 Bleecker St., Greenwich, NY 12834 t) 518-692-2159 parishes.rcda.org/stjosephschurch/ Ron Derway, Pst. Assoc.;

HAGAMAN

St. Stephen - 51 Pawling St., Hagaman, NY 12086; Mailing: P.O. Box 81, Hagaman, NY 12086 t) 518-843-2951 www.ststephensofhagamanny.org/ Rev. Jeffrey L'Arche, Pst.; Dcn. Michael C. Ryba, Dir., Finance & Admin.;

HAINES FALLS

Sacred Heart-Immaculate Conception Church - N. Lake Rd., Haines Falls, NY 12436; Mailing: P.O. Box 379, Haines Falls, NY 12436 t) 518-589-5577 Rev. Jay Atherton, Pst.;

Wayside Shrine of the Immaculate Conception - Rt. 23-A, Haines Falls, NY 12436

HANCOCK

St. Paul the Apostle - 346 W. Main St., Hancock, NY 13783 t) 607-637-2571 spahanco@rcda.org stpaulshancock.org/ Rev. Christopher Welch, Pst.; Rev. James E. O'Rourke, Par. Vicar;

HERKIMER

St. Anthony-St. Joseph - 229 S. Main St., Herkimer, NY 13350; Mailing: 228 S. Main St., Herkimer, NY 13350 t) 315-866-6373 sasjherk@rcda.org; sts.anthonyandjoseph@gmail.com parishes.rcda.org/sts_anthony_joseph/ Dcn. James W. Bower, Parish Life Coord.; Rev. Terence P. Healy, Sacr. Min.;

St. Francis de Sales - 229 S. Main St., Herkimer, NY 13350; Mailing: 344 S. Washington St., Herkimer, NY 13350 t) 315-866-4282 Dcn. James W. Bower, Parish Life Coord.; Rev. Leo F. Potvin, Sacr. Min.;

Parish Center - 219 N. Bellinger St., Herkimer, NY 13350

St. Francis de Sales School - (Grades PreK-K) 220 Henry St., Herkimer, NY 13350 t) 315-866-4831 stfran@twcny.rr.com www.stfrancisherkimer.com Rebecca Marzeski, Prin.;

Convent - One Park Pl., Herkimer, NY 13350 t) 315-866-4492

HOOSICK FALLS

Immaculate Conception - 73 Main St., Hoosick Falls, NY 12090; Mailing: 67 Main St., Hoosick Falls, NY 12090-2003 t) 518-686-5064 icchoosickfalls.com/ Rev. Peter Tkocz, Par. Vicar; Jeffrey C. Peck, Parish Life Coord.;

HUDSON

Parish of the Holy Trinity - 429 E. Allen St., Hudson, NY 12534; Mailing: P.O. Box 323, Hudson, NY 12534 t) 518-828-1334 holytrinity.hudson@rcda.org holytrinityhudson.org/ Very Rev. Anthony M. Barratt, Pst.; Rev. Winston L. Bath, Pastor Emer.; Dcn. Richard Washburn;

Nativity -

HUDSON FALLS

Roman Catholic Community of Hudson Falls/Kingsbury - 11 Wall St., Hudson Falls, NY 12839 t) 518-747-4823 Church of St. Mary/St. Paul (Sandy Hill) Rev. Thomas Babiuch, Pst.; Dcn. William F. Bazinet;

ILION

Annunciation - 50 West St., Ilion, NY 13357; Mailing: 109 West St., Ilion, NY 13357 t) 315-894-3766 annunciation.ilion@rcda.org annunciationilion.org/ Rev. Paul G. Catena, Pst.; Dcn. Michael Carbone;

JOHNSTOWN

Holy Trinity Parish - E. Clinton St. and Glebe St., Johnstown, NY 12095; Mailing: 207 Glebe St., Johnstown, NY 12095 t) 518-762-2636 parishes.rcda.org/holytrinityjohnstown/ Rev. Matthew Wetsel, Pst.;

LAKE GEORGE

Sacred Heart - 50 Mohican St., Lake George, NY 12845 t) 518-668-2046 www.sacredheartlg.org/ Very Rev. Joseph G. Busch, Pst.; Rev. Peter Tkocz, Assoc. Pst.; Dcn. Frank D. Herlihy; Dcn. Ryan McNulty; Rev. Nellis Tremblay, Sacr. Min.; Torie Wattendorf, DRE;

LANSINGBURGH

St. Augustine - Fourth Ave. & 115th St., Lansingburgh, NY 12182; Mailing: 25 115th St., Troy, NY 12182 t) 518-235-3861 peggyr@nycap.rr.com staugchurchtroy.com Rev. Liam T. O'Doherty, O.S.A., Assoc. Pst.; Rev. David J Kelley, OSA, Pst.; Dcn. Gary Miles;

LATHAM

St. Ambrose - 347 Old Loudon Rd., Latham, NY 12110 t) 518-785-1351 salatham@rcda.org stambroselatham.com/ Rev. Brian Kelly, Pst.; Dcn. Frank Garceau; Dcn. Gerard F. Matthews;

St. Ambrose School - (Grades PreK-8) t) 518-785-6453 lily.spera@stambroselatham.com; kelly.sano@stambroselatham.com www.stambroselatham.com Lily Spera, Prin.;

Our Lady of the Assumption - 498 Watervliet-Shaker Rd., Latham, NY 12110 t) 518-785-0234 olalatham.org/ Rev. Geoffrey D. Burke, Pst.; Dcn. Paul Kisselback;

LITTLE FALLS

Holy Family - 763 E. Main St., Little Falls, NY 13365 t) 315-823-3410 holyfamily.littlefalls@rcda.org parishes.rcda.org/holy_family_parish Rev. Brian K. Slezak, Pst.; Mary Puznowski, Music Min.;

LOUDONVILLE

Christ Our Light Roman Catholic Church - 1 Maria Dr., Loudonville, NY 12211 t) 518-459-6635 christourlightchurch.loudonville@rcda.org www.christourlightchurch.org/ Dcn. Richard J. Thiesen, Parish Life Coord.;

St. Pius X - 23 Crumitie Rd., Loudonville, NY 12211 t) 518-462-1336 www.stpiusxloudonville.org/ Dcn. Martin Dinan; Rev. James J. Walsh, Pst.;

St. Pius X School - (Grades PreK-8) 79 Upper Loudon Rd., Loudonville, NY 12211 t) 518-465-4539 principal@nycap.rr.com www.stpiusx.nycap.rr.com Dennis Mullahy, Prin.;

MARGARETVILLE

Sacred Heart - 38 Academy St., Margaretville, NY 12455; Mailing: P.O. Box 909, Margaretville, NY 12455 t) 845-586-2665 sacredheartmargaretville.org/ Rev. Paul Mijas, Pst.; Doris Warner, DRE;

St. Ann -

MECHANICVILLE

Roman Catholic Community of All Saints on the Hudson - 52 William St., Mechanicville, NY 12118 t) 518-664-3354 allsaintsny.net/ Rev. George Fleming, Pst.; Rev. Martin J. Fisher, Sacr. Min.; Rev. Robert J. Hohenstein, Sacr. Min.;

St. Isaac Jogues - 716 Rte. 9P, Saratoga Lake, NY 12866 (Summer)

St. Paul Church - 121 N. Main St., Mechanicville, NY 12118

St. Peter Church - 895 Hudson Ave., Stillwater, NY 12170

MENANDS

St. Joan of Arc - 76 Menand Rd., Menands, NY 12204 t) 518-463-0378 Rev. Kofi Ntsiful-Amissah, Pst.;

MIDDLEBURGH

Parish of Our Lady of the Valley - Main St. at Wells Ave., Middleburgh, NY 12122; Mailing: 111 Wells Ave., PO Box 311, Middleburgh, NY 12122 t) 518-702-4385 ourladyofthevalley.middleburgh@rcda.org parishes.rcda.org/olvchurch/ Rev. Thomas Zelker, Pst.; Dcn. Gary J. Riggi;

MOHAWK

Blessed Sacrament - 71 E. Main St., Mohawk, NY 13407; Mailing: 54 E. Main St., Mohawk, NY 13407 t) 315-866-1752 blessedsacrament.mohawk@rcda.org Rev. Leo F. Potvin, Sacr. Min.; Sr. Mary Jo Tallman, C.S.J., Parish Life Coord.;

MORRIS

Holy Cross - 98 Main St., Morris, NY 13808; Mailing: 96 Main St., P.O. Box 118, Morris, NY 13808 t) 607-263-5143 Maureen E. Joy, Parish Life Coord.;

NASSAU

St. Mary - 26 Church St., Nassau, NY 12123; Mailing: P.O. Box 435, Nassau, NY 12123 t) 518-766-2701 stmarys.nassau@rcda.org stmarysnassau.org/ Rev. Thomas F. Holmes, Pst.; Rev. John Close, Sacr. Min.;

NEW LEBANON

Immaculate Conception - 732 U.S. Rte. 20, New Lebanon, NY 12125 t) 518-794-7651 immaculateconception.newlebanon@rcda.org parishes.rcda.org Rev. John Close, Pst.; Dcn. Peter R. Quinn;

St. Joseph's -

NEWPORT

St. John the Baptist - 7516 N. Main St., Newport, NY 13416; Mailing: 7514 N. Main St., P.O. Box 475, Newport, NY 13416 t) 315-845-8017 parishes.rcda.org/stjohnsnewport/ Dcn. James Bower, Parish Life Coord.; Rev. Terence P. Healy, Sacr. Min.;

NORTH CREEK

St. James - 237 Main St., North Creek, NY 12853; Mailing: 86 Riverside Dr., P.O. Box 471, Chestertown, NY 12817 t) 518-824-1176; 518-251-2518 stjames.northcreek@rcda.org northernpointscluster.weebly.com/ Rev. John O'Kane, Pst.; Barbara Carlozzi, DRE;

NORTHVILLE

St. Francis of Assisi - 501 Bridge St., Northville, NY 12134; Mailing: P.O. Box 126, Northville, NY 12134 t) 518-863-4736 stfrancisofassisi.northville@rcda.org parishes.rcda.org/stjosephstfrancis/ Very Rev. Anastacio Jun Segura, Pst.; Katy Ryan, DRE;

ONEONTA

St. Mary - 37 Walnut St., Oneonta, NY 13820; Mailing: 39 Walnut St., Oneonta, NY 13820 t) 607-432-3920 smoneont@rcda.org www.stmarysoneonta.org/ Rev. David Mickiewicz, Pst.; Dcn. Paul Cerosaletti;

QUEENSBURY

Our Lady of the Annunciation - 448 Aviation Rd., Queensbury, NY 12804 t) 518-793-9677 olaqueen@rcda.org www.olaqueensbury.org/ (Mission of St. Mary, Glens Falls from 1963-1970) Very Rev. Joseph G. Busch, Pst.; Patti Abbott, Bus. Mgr.; CRP Stds.: 117

RAVENA

St. Patrick - 21 Main St., Ravena, NY 12143 t) 518-756-3145 churchofsaintpatrick.wixsite.com Rev. Jay Atherton, Pst.; Rev. Joseph O'Brien, Par. Vicar; Dcn. Steve Young;

RENSSELAER

Parish of St. John the Evangelist and St. Joseph's - 54 Herrick St., Rensselaer, NY 12144; Mailing: P.O. Box 256, Rensselaer, NY 12144 t) 518-465-0482 churchofstjohnstjoseph.org Rev. Thomas F. Holmes, Pst.;

Church of St. Mary at Clinton Heights - 163 Columbia Tpke., Rensselaer, NY 12144-3521 t) 518-449-2232 www.stmaryny.org/ Rev. Thomas F. Holmes, Pst.; Dcn. Al Censullo, Pst. Assoc.; Dcn. Nicholas Ascioti, Pst. Assoc.;

ROUND LAKE

Corpus Christi - 2001 Rte. 9, Round Lake, NY 12151-1701 t) 518-877-8506 corpuschristi.roundlake@rcda.org; office@corpuschristichurch.net www.corpuschristichurch.net/ Rev. George Fleming, Pst.; Dcn. Andrew Haskins; CRP Stds.: 185

SALEM

Holy Cross - 249 Main St., Salem, NY 12865; Mailing: PO Box 357, Salem, NY 12865 t) 518-854-7626 holycross.salem@rcda.org battenkillcatholic.org/ Rev. Peter Tkocz, Par. Vicar; Jeffrey C. Peck, Parish Life Coord.;

SARATOGA SPRINGS

St. Clement - 231 Lake Ave., Saratoga Springs, NY 12866 t) 518-584-6122 stclementschurch.com/ Dcn. Frank C. Berning; Dcn. Lawrence Willette; Very Rev. James A. Ebert, Pst.; Rev. Kyle Gorenski, Par. Vicar; Randy Joseph Rivers, Admin.;

St. Clement School - (Grades PreK-5) t) 518-584-7350 stclem@stclementsschool.org www.stclementsschool.org Jane E. Kromm, Prin.;

Gansevoort, St. Therese - t) 518-587-3180

St. Peter - 241 Broadway, Saratoga Springs, NY 12866 t) 518-584-2375 www.stpetersaratoga.com/ Rev. Thomas H. Chevalier, Pst.; Dcn. Brian Levine; Dcn. Edward R. Solomon;

SCHAGHTICOKE

Transfiguration Parish - 17 S. Main St., Schaghticoke, NY 12154; Mailing: 50 Hillview Dr., Troy, NY 12182 t) 518-235-0337 transfigurationparish.troy@rcda.org transfigurationparish.net/ Rev. Dominic Ingemie, Assoc. Pst.; Dcn. Charles Valenti; Dcn. Christopher Keough, Parish Life Coord.;

North Site -

South Site -

SCHENECTADY

Church of St. Adalbert - 550 Lansing St., Schenectady, NY 12303 t) 518-346-4204 saschene@rcda.org www.churchofstadalbert.org Very Rev. Matthew H. Frisoni, Pst.; Stephen Mawn, Pst. Assoc.;

St. Anthony - Nott St. at Seward Pl., Schenectady, NY 12305; Mailing: 331 Seward Pl., Schenectady, NY 12305 t) 518-374-4591 stanthonys.schenectady@rcda.org stanthonyschurch.net Rev. Richard A. Carlino, Pst.; Sr. Maria Rose Querini, M.P.V., Pst. Assoc.;

Convent - 1834 Van Vranken Ave., Schenectady, NY 12308 t) 518-346-2060 Religious Venerini Sisters (M.P.V.)

St. Gabriel the Archangel - 3040 Hamburg St., Schenectady, NY 12303 t) 518-355-6600 parishes.rcda.org/st.gabriels_church/ Rev. Desmond Rossi, Par. Vicar; Rev. Leo F. Markert, Sacr. Min.; Very Rev. James Belogi, Pst.;

St. John the Evangelist - 812 Union St., Schenectady, NY 12308; Mailing: 806 Union St., Schenectady, NY 12308 t) 518-372-3381 sjechurch.com/ Rev. Richard A. Carlino, Pst.;

St. Joseph - 600 State St., Schenectady, NY 12305; Mailing: 225 Lafayette St., Schenectady, NY 12305 t) 518-374-4466 parishes.rcda.org Rev. Dominic P. Isopo, Pst.;

St. Kateri Tekakwitha Parish - 2216 Rosa Rd., Schenectady, NY 12309 t) 518-346-6137 stkateri.schenectady@rcda.org www.stkateriparish.org/ Very Rev. Robert Longobucco, Pst.; Dcn. Gregory Mansfield; Dcn. Donald Thomas Sharrow; CRP Stds.: 300

St. Kateri Tekakwitha Parish School - (Grades PreK-5) 1801 Union St., Schenectady, NY 12309 t) 518-382-8225 principal@stkaterischool.org www.stkaterischool.org Tosha Grimmer, Prin.;

St. Luke - 1235 State St., Schenectady, NY 12304; Mailing: 1241 State St., Schenectady, NY 12304 t) 518-346-3405 slschene@rcda.org www.stlukesschenectady.org/ Rev. Dominic P. Isopo, Pst.;

St. Madeleine Sophie - 3500 Carman Rd., Schenectady, NY 12303 t) 518-355-0421 www.smsparish.org/ Dcn. Thomas Poznanski; Very Rev. James Belogi, Pst.; Rev. Desmond Rossi, Par. Vicar; Donna Simone, Pst. Assoc.;

St. Madeleine Sophie School - (Grades PreK-5) 3510 Carman Rd., Schenectady, NY 12303 t) 518-355-3080 mainoffice@smsschool.org www.smsschool.org Kelly Sloan, Prin.;

Our Lady of Mt. Carmel - 1260 Pleasant St., Schenectady, NY 12303-1999; Mailing: 1255 Pleasant St., Schenectady, NY 12303 t) 518-393-4109 www.mountcarmelschdy.com Very Rev. Matthew H. Frisoni, Pst.; Stephen Mawn, Pst. Assoc.;

Roman Catholic Faith Formation - 2777 Albany St., Schenectady, NY 12304

Our Lady Queen of Peace - 210 Princetown Rd., Schenectady, NY 12306-1520 t) 518-346-4926 ourladyqueenofpeace.rotterdam@rcda.org www.olqprotterdam.org/ Very Rev. James Belogi, Par. Admin.; Dcn. Joseph Brennan;

Our Lady of the Assumption, Rotterdam - (Worship Site)

St. Margaret of Cortona - 1228 Main St., Rotterdam Junction, NY 12150

St. Paul the Apostle - 2733 Albany St., Schenectady, NY 12304; Mailing: 2777 Albany St., Schenectady, NY 12304 t) 518-377-8886 www.spacny.org/ Stephen Mawn, Pst. Assoc.; Rev. Matthew H. Frisoni, Pst.;

SCHUYLERVILLE

Notre Dame-Visitation - 18 Pearl St., Schuylerville, NY 12871 t) 518-695-3391; 518-695-3319 (CRP) ndvschuy@rcda.org; stephanieandrejcak@gmail.com ndv-schuylerville.weebly.com/ Very Rev. James A. Ebert, Pst.; Rev. Kyle Gorenski, Par. Vicar; Rev. Randall P. Patterson, Sacr. Min.; Stephanie Andrejcak, DRE; Juliana Bodensieck, Bus. Mgr.;

SCOTIA

St. Joseph Church - 231 Second St., Scotia, NY 12302; Mailing: 45 MacArthur Dr., Scotia, NY 12302 t) 518-346-2316; 518-374-3382 (CRP) www.stjosephschurchscotia.net/ Rev. Thomas E. Konopka, Pst.; Dcn. Stephen M. Lape;

Parish Center - 45 MacArthur Dr., Scotia, NY 12302

SIDNEY

Sacred Heart - 15 Liberty St., Sidney, NY 13838 t) 607-563-1591 parishes.rcda.org/sacredheartsidney/ Rev. Bernard Osei Ampong, Pst.; CRP Stds.: 30

SOUTH GLENS FALLS

St. Michael the Archangel - 80 Saratoga Ave., South Glens Falls, NY 12803 t) 518-792-5859 stmichaelschurchsgf.com/ Rev. Guy A. Childs, Pst.;

STAMFORD

Sacred Heart - 27 Harper St., Stamford, NY 12167 t) 607-652-7170 sacredheartstamford.org/ Dcn. Joseph M. Cechnicki, Parish Admin.; Rev. Martin J. Fisher, Interim Pastor;

St. Philip Neri -

STUYVESANT

Church of St. Joseph - 1820 State Rte. 9, Stuyvesant, NY 12173 t) 518-799-5411 Rev. Steve Matthews, Pst.; Deborah Halpin, Pst. Assoc.;

Worship Site - 2824 Atlantic Ave., Stottville, NY 12534 Rev. George Fleming, Pst.;

TRIBES HILL

Sacred Heart - 111 Third Ave., Tribes Hill, NY 12177; Mailing: P.O. Box 264, Tribes Hill, NY 12177 t) 518-829-7301 sacredheart.tribeshill@rcda.org Rev. Christopher Welch, Pst.;

TROY

St. Anthony of Padua - 28 State St., Troy, NY 12180-3916 t) 518-273-8622 parishes.rcda.org/stanthonyofpadua/ Holds records of St. Peter's; St. Patrick's; St. Anthony of Padua (territorial) Churches, Troy. Very Rev. Richard Donovan, O.F.M., Pst.; Dcn. Charles Z. Wojton; Rev. Primo Piscitello, In Res.;

St. Joseph - 416 Third St., Troy, NY 12180 t) 518-274-6720 stjosephcatholicchurch-troy.org Rev. Joseph Sheehan, O.Carm., In Res.; Rev. Joseph Phuong Ngo, O. Carm., Pst.;

St. Michael the Archangel - 175 Williams Rd., Troy, NY 12180 t) 518-283-6110 parishes.rcda.org/stmichaeltroy/ Rev. Patrick Rice, Pst.; Rev. James M. Mackey, Pastor Emer.; Dcn. Robert Sweeney, Dir., Pastoral Care; Dcn. Nicholas Ascioti;

Van Rensselaer Manor, County Nursing Home -

The Springs Nursing Home -

Our Lady of Victory - 55 N. Lake Ave., Troy, NY 12180

t) 518-273-7602 www.olvols.org/ Rev. Thomas Morrette; Dcn. Brian Lewis; Dcn. Willis R. Wolfe;

Our Lady of Victory Pre-K Program - 451 Marshland Ct., Troy, NY 12180 t) 518-274-6202 olvprek@nycap.rr.com Tiffany Crownover, Dir.;

Sacred Heart - 310 Spring Ave., Troy, NY 12180 t) 518-274-1363 sacredhearttroy.com/ Rev. John Yanas, Pst.; Mark Trudeau, Par. Admin.;

Sacred Heart School - (Grades PreK-6) 308 Spring Ave., Troy, NY 12180 t) 518-274-3655 www.sacredheartschooltroy.com/ Ernest Casile, Prin.;

VALATIE

St. John the Baptist - 1025 Kinderhook St., Valatie, NY 12184 t) 518-758-9401 www.stjohnsvalatie.org/ Deborah Halpin, Pst. Assoc.; Rev. Steve Matthews, Sacr. Min.;

VOORHEESVILLE

St. Matthew - 25 Mountainview St., Voorheesville, NY 12186-9551 t) 518-765-2805 stmatthewsfaithdevelopment@verizon.net; stmatthews.voorheesville@rcda.org www.stmatthewsvoorheesville.org/ Rev. F. Richard Lesser, Pst.; Rev. Daniel McHale, Par. Vicar; CRP Stds.: 80

WALTON

St. John the Baptist - 25 Benton Ave., Walton, NY 13856-0315; Mailing: 15 Benton Ave., Walton, NY 13856 t) 607-865-7394 www.catholicwalton.com/ Rev. Edward Golding, Admin.; Dcn. Michael Freeman;

Holy Family - 14918 State Hwy. 30, Downsville, NY 13755

WARRENSBURG

St. Cecilia - 3802 Main St., Warrensburg, NY 12885-1629 t) 518-623-3021 scwarren@rcda.org stceciliaschurch.com Rev. Paul C. Cox, Sacramental Min.;

WATERFORD

St. Mary of the Assumption - Broad and Sixth Sts., Waterford, NY 12188; Mailing: 119 Broad St., Waterford, NY 12188 t) 518-237-3131 stmaryswaterford.org Rev. David J. Kelley, O.S.A., Pst.; Rev. Liam O'Doherty, OSA, Par. Vicar;

St. Mary's Catholic School - (Grades PreK-8) 12 Sixth St., Waterford, NY 12188 t) 518-237-0652 principal@smswaterford.org www.smswaterford.org David E Evans, Prin.; Stds.: 237; Lay Tchrs.: 26

St. Mary's Church - 86 Church Hill Rd., Waterford, NY 12188 t) 518-371-9632 www.stmaryscrescent.com/ St. Mary's Church, Crescent Rev. David V. Berberian, Sacr. Min.; Rev. Joseph Cebula, Sacr. Min.; Dcn. Andrew Grebe;

WATERVLIET

Immaculate Heart of Mary - 2416 7th Ave., Watervliet, NY 12189 t) 518-273-6020 rcpw.weebly.com/ Rev. Samuel Bellafiore, Assoc. Pst.; Rev. Donald L. Rutherford, Pst.;

WEST WINFIELD

St. Joseph the Worker - 303 W. Main St., West Winfield, NY 13491 t) 315-822-3191 (West Winfield); 315-858-1682 (Richfield Springs) sjrichfi@rcda.org; stjosephsrichfield@verizon.net parishes.rcda.org/ stjosephtheworker/ Rev. Rendell Torres; Ruth Rowe, DRE; CRP Stds.: 27

WHITEHALL

Our Lady of Hope - Wheeler Ave. & Skene St., Whitehall, NY 12887; Mailing: 9 Wheeler Ave., Whitehall, NY 12887 t) 518-499-1656 olhwhite@rcda.org olhstann.org Very Rev. Joseph G. Busch, Pst.; Rev. Zachariah Chichester, Par. Vicar; Gina Neron, Bus. Mgr.; CRP Stds.: 25

Chapel of the Assumption - 2026 Lands End Rd., Huletts Landing, NY 12841 Rev. Rendell R. Torres, Contact;

WINDHAM

St. Theresa of Child Jesus - 5188 State Rte. 23, Windham, NY 12496 t) 518-734-3352 santtheresas.weebly.com/ Rev. Jay Atherton, Pst.; Rev. Kyle Eads, Assoc. Pst.; Dcn. Peter Sedlmeir;

St. Joseph's Chapel -

WORCESTER

St. Joseph - 201 Main St., Worcester, NY 12197 t) 607-397-9373 parishes.rcda.org/st.josephschurch/ Rev. Joseph Arockiasamy, Pst.;

WYNANTSKILL

St. Jude the Apostle - 43 Brookside Ave., Wynantskill, NY 12198-0347; Mailing: 42 Dana Ave., Wynantskill, NY 12198 t) 518-283-1162 stjudetheapostle.wynanstkill@rcda.org parishes.rcda.org/stjude/ Rev. Patrick Rice, Pst.; Dcn. Warren A. Safford;

St. Jude the Apostle School - (Grades PreK-6) 35 Dana Ave., Wynantskill, NY 12198 t) 518-283-0333 principal@sjsalbany.org www.sjsalbany.org Danielle Cox, Prin.;

SCHOOLS: PRESCHOOL THRU HIGH SCHOOL

SCHOOLS

STATE OF NEW YORK

GLENS FALLS

St. Mary's/St. Alphonsus Regional Catholic School - (PAR) (Grades PreK-8) 10-12 Church St., Glens Falls, NY 12801 t) 518-792-3178 www.smsaschool.org Patricia Balmer, Prin.;

LOUDONVILLE

Saint Gregory's School - (PRV) (Grades PreSchool-8) 121 Old Niskayuna Rd., Loudonville, NY 12211-1399 t) 518-785-6621 info@saintgregorysschool.org www.saintgregorysschool.org An independent Catholic day school. Kathryn Helm, Headmaster;

WATERFORD

St. Mary's School - (PAR) (Grades PreK-8) 12 Sixth St., Waterford, NY 12188 t) 518-237-0652 principalstmarys@smswaterford.org www.smswaterford.org Matthew Rucinski, Prin.;

HIGH SCHOOLS

STATE OF NEW YORK

ALBANY

Academy of the Holy Names Upper and Middle Schools - (PRV) (Grades 6-12) 1075 New Scotland Rd., Albany, NY 12208 t) 518-438-7895 centraladmin@ahns.org www.ahns.org Martin Kilbridge, Pres.; Michele Musto, Prin.; Stds.: 190; Lay Tchrs.: 26

Bishop Maginn High School - (DIO) 75 Park Ave., Albany, NY 12202 t) 518-463-2247 tolan@bishopmaginn.org www.bishopmaginn.org Michael Tolin, Prin.;

The Christian Brothers' Academy of Albany - (PRV) (Grades 5-12) 12 Airline Dr., Albany, NY 12205 t) 518-452-9809 www.cbaalbany.org JROTC College Prep. Program. Brothers of the Christian Schools. Dr. James Schlegel, Head of School; Charles Abba, Prin.;

SARATOGA SPRINGS

Saratoga Central Catholic High School - (DIO) (Grades 6-12) 247 Broadway, Saratoga Springs, NY 12866 t) 518-587-7070 lombard@saratogacatholic.org www.saratogacatholic.org Joseph Kilmeade, Interim Principal;

SCHENECTADY

Notre Dame-Bishop Gibbons School - (DIO) (Grades 6-12) 2600 Albany St., Schenectady, NY 12304 t) 518-393-3131 kiante_jones@nd-bg.org www.nd-bg.org (Coed) Kiante Jones, Prin.; Patrick Moran, Vice Prin.;

TROY

Catholic Central High School - (DIO) (Grades 7-12) 625 Seventh Ave., Troy, NY 12182 t) 518-235-7100 www.cchstroy.org Christopher Signor, Prin.;

LaSalle Institute - (PRV) (Grades 6-12) 174 Williams Rd., Troy, NY 12180 t) 518-283-2500 info@lasalleinstitute.org www.lasalleinstitute.org Brothers of the Christian Schools. Joseph B. Raczkowski, Prin.;

INSTITUTIONS LOCATED IN DIOCESE

ASSOCIATIONS [ASN]

HALFMOON

Catholic School Administrators' Association of New York State - 63 Westbury Ct, Halfmoon, NY 12065; Mailing: PO Box 5263, Halfmoon, NY 12065 t) 518-280-9807 csaanysoffice@twc.com; csaanys@twc.com www.csaanys.org Carol Hayes, Exec.;

CAMPUS MINISTRY / NEWMAN CENTERS [CAM]

ALBANY

University at Albany, State University of New York - 1400 Washington Ave., Albany, NY 12222 t) 518-489-8573 x22 creid@albany.edu Catherine Reid, Campus Min.;

COBLESKILL

State University of New York College of Agricultural & Technology at Cobleskill - St. Vincent de Paul Church, 138 Washington Ave., Cobleskill, NY 12043 t) 518-234-2892 Greg Rhys, Campus Min.;

LOUDONVILLE

Siena College - Office of the College Chaplain, 515 Loudon Rd., Loudonville, NY 12211 t) 518-783-2332 chaplainsoffice@siena.edu www.siena.edu Rev. Lawrence Anderson, O.F.M., Campus Min.; Dcn. Nicholas Ascioti, Asst. Campus Min.; Colleen Sheedy, Assoc. Campus Min.;

ONEONTA

Newman Clubs - SUNY Oneonta and Hartwick College - c/o St. Mary's Parish, 37 Walnut St, Oneonta, NY 13820 t) 607-432-3920 Corporate Title: Oneonta Newman Catholic Community. Matthew Houle, Campus Min.;

SARATOGA

Skidmore College - Case Center 227, 815 N. Broadway, Saratoga, NY 12866 t) 518-580-8340 kdiggory@skidmore.edu Parker Diggory, Dir.;

SCHENECTADY

Catholic Chaplain, Union College - 807 Union St., Schenectady, NY 12308-3152 t) 518-388-6087 stagliad@union.edu www.union.edu David Stagliano, Campus Min.;

TROY

Hudson Valley Community College - Siek Campus Center #220, 80 Vandenburgh Ave., Troy, NY 12180 t) 518-629-7168 m.thivierge@hvcc.edu www.hvcc.edu David Stagliano, Campus Min.; Catherine Reid, Campus Min.;

The Rensselaer Newman Foundation - 10 Tom Phelan Pl., Troy, NY 12180 t) 518-274-7793 rnf@rpi.edu renseealernewman.org Rev. Lawrence Rice, CSP, Chap.;

Chapel + Cultural Center - fred@rpi.edu Rev. Edward Kacerguis, Pst.;

University Parish of Christ Sun of Justice - 2125 Burdett Ave., Troy, NY 12180 t) (518) 274-7793 csjtroy@rcda.org rensselaernewman.org/christ-sun-of-justice-parish/ Rev. Thomas Morrette, Pst.;

Russell Sage College - McMurray-Spicer-Gale House (MSG), 65 1st St., Troy, NY 12180 t) 518-244-4507 Catherine Reid, Campus Min.; David Stagliano, Campus Min.;

CATHOLIC CHARITIES [CCH]

ALBANY
Catholic Charities of the Diocese of Albany, Inc. - 40 N. Main Ave., Albany, NY 12203 t) 518-453-6650 catholic.charities@ccrcda.org www.ccrcda.org Vincent W. Colonno, CEO; Michael Lawler, CFO & COO;

CEMETERIES [CEM]

ALBANY
Our Lady of Angels Cemetery - 1389 Central Ave., Albany, NY 12205; Mailing: 48 Cemetery Ave., Menands, NY 12204 t) 518-374-5319 info@rcdacemeteries.org www.capitaldistrictcemeteries.org Emily Simmons, Exec. Dir.;
COEYMANS
St. Patrick's Cemetery - Blaisdell Ave., Coeymans, NY 12045; Mailing: 48 Cemetery Ave., Menands, NY 12204 t) (518) 463-0134 info@adcemeteries.org www.capitaldistrictcemeteries.org/ Emily Simmons, Exec. Dir.;
COHOES
St. Agnes Cemetery - 79 St. Agnes Hwy., Cohoes, NY 12047; Mailing: 48 Cemetery Ave., Menands, NY 12204 t) 518-374-5319 info@rcdacemeteries.org www.capitaldistrictcemeteries.org Emily Simmons, Exec. Dir.;
COXSACKIE
St. Mary's Cemetery - Rte. 385, Coxsackie, NY 12051; Mailing: 48 Cemetery Ave., Menands, NY 12204 t) (518) 463-0134 info@adcemeteries.org www.capitaldistrictcemeteries.org/ Emily Simmons, Exec. Dir.;
GLENMONT
Calvary Cemetery - 481 Rte. 9 W., Glenmont, NY 12077; Mailing: 48 Cemetery Ave., Menands, NY 12204 t) 518-463-0134 info@rcdacemeteries.org www.capitaldistrictcemeteries.org Emily Simmons, Exec. Dir.;
Our Lady Help of Christians Cemetery - 41 Jolley Rd., Glenmont, NY 12077; Mailing: 48 Cemetery Ave., Menands, NY 12204 t) 518-463-0134 info@rcdacemeteries.org www.capitaldistrictcemeteries.org Emily Simmons, Exec. Dir.;
GLENVILLE
St. Anthony's Cemetery - 27 Glenridge Rd., Glenville, NY 12302; Mailing: 48 Cemetery Ave., Menands, NY 12204 t) 518-374-5319 info@rcdacemeteries.org www.capitaldistrictcemeteries.org Emily Simmons, Exec. Dir.;
MENANDS
St. Agnes Cemetery - 48 Cemetery Ave., Menands, NY 12204 t) 518-463-0134 info@rcdacemeteries.org www.capitaldistrictcemeteries.org Emily Simmons, Exec. Dir.;
NISKAYUNA
Most Holy Redeemer Cemetery - 2501 Troy Rd., Niskayuna, NY 12309; Mailing: 48 Cemetery Ave., Menands, NY 12204 t) 518-374-5319 info@rcdacemeteries.org www.capitaldistrictcemeteries.org Emily Simmons, Exec. Dir.;
RENSSELAER
Holy Sepulchre Cemetery - 3rd Ave. Ext., Rensselaer, NY 12144; Mailing: 48 Cemetery Ave., Menands, NY 12204 t) (518) 463-0134 info@adcemeteries.org www.capitaldistrictcemeteries.org/ Emily Simmons, Exec. Dir.;
ROTTERDAM
St. Cyril & St. Method Cemetery - 611 Duanesburg Rd., Rotterdam, NY 12306; Mailing: 48 Cemetery Ave., Menands, NY 12204 t) 518-374-5319 info@rcdacemeteries.org www.capitaldistrictcemeteries.org Emily Simmons, Exec. Dir.;
Holy Cross Cemetery - 1456 Dunnsville Rd., Rotterdam, NY 12306; Mailing: 48 Cemetery Ave., Menands, NY 12204 t) 518-374-5319 info@rcdacemeteries.org www.capitaldistrictcemeteries.org Emily Simmons, Exec. Dir.;
SCHENECTADY
St. John the Baptist Cemetery - Brandywine Ave., Schenectady, NY 12307; Mailing: 2501 Troy Rd., Niskayuna, NY 12309 t) (518) 374-5319 info@adcemeteries.org www.capitaldistrictcemeteries.org/ Emily Simmons, Exec. Dir.;
St. Mary's Cemetery - 738 McClellan St., Schenectady, NY 12304; Mailing: 48 Cemetery Ave., Menands, NY 12204 t) 518-374-5319 info@rcdacemeteries.org www.capitaldistrictcemeteries.org Emily Simmons, Exec. Dir.;
TROY
St. Jean Baptiste Cemetery - 968 Spring Ave. Ext., Troy, NY 12180; Mailing: 48 Cemetery Ave., Menands, NY 12204 t) 518-463-0134 info@rcdacemeteries.org www.capitaldistrictcemeteries.org Emily Simmons, Exec. Dir.;
St. John's Cemetery - 250 Cemetery Ave., Troy, NY 12180; Mailing: 48 Cemetery Ave., Menands, NY 12204 t) 518-463-0134 info@rcdacemeteries.org www.capitaldistrictcemeteries.org Emily Simmons, Exec. Dir.;
St. Mary's Cemetery of Troy, Inc. - 79 Brunswick Rd., Troy, NY 12180; Mailing: 48 Cemetery Ave., Menands, NY 12204 t) 518-463-0134 info@rcdacemeteries.org www.capitaldistrictcemeteries.org Emily Simmons, Exec. Dir.;
WATERFORD
St. Joseph's Cemetery - 40 Middletown Rd., Waterford, NY 12188; Mailing: 48 Cemetery Ave., Menands, NY 12204 t) 518-463-0134 info@rcdacemeteries.org www.capitaldistrictcemeteries.org Emily Simmons, Exec. Dir.;
WATERVLIET
Immaculate Conception Cemetery - 29 Delatour Rd., Watervliet, NY 12189; Mailing: 48 Cemetery Ave., Menands, NY 12204 t) 518-374-5319 info@rcdacemeteries.org www.capitaldistrictcemeteries.org Emily Simmons, Exec. Dir.;
St. Patrick Cemetery - 150 Troy Rd., Watervliet, NY 12189; Mailing: 48 Cemetery Ave., Menands, NY 12204 t) 518-374-5319 info@rcdacemeteries.org www.capitaldistrictcemeteries.org Emily Simmons, Exec. Dir.;

COLLEGES & UNIVERSITIES [COL]

ALBANY
St. Bernard's School of Theology and Ministry at Albany - 40 N. Main Ave., Albany, NY 12203 t) 518-453-6760 stbernards@rcda.org stbernards.edu Extension Program of St. Bernard's School of Theology and Ministry, Rochester, NY. Graduate School of Theology & Ministry Studies. Dr. Anthony Coleman, Dir.;
The College of Saint Rose - 432 Western Ave., Albany, NY 12203 t) 518-454-5111; 800-657-8556 admit@strose.edu www.strose.edu Founded by the Sisters of St. Joseph of Carondelet. Joan Horgan, Campus Min.; Marcia White, Pres.;
Maria College - 700 New Scotland Ave., Albany, NY 12208 t) 518-438-3111 bwales@mariacollege.edu mariacollege.edu Dr. Thomas J. Gamble, Pres.; Dr. John Kowal, VP, Academic Affairs; Frances Bernard, Dir., Business Affairs; Beth Wales, Dir., Mktg. & Comms.;
LOUDONVILLE
Siena College - 515 Loudon Rd., Loudonville, NY 12211 t) (518) 783-4147 www.siena.edu Founded by the Franciscan Friars, Order of Friars Minor, Province of the Most Holy Name of Jesus: Franciscan and Catholic college of higher education. Very Rev. Mark G. Reamer, O.F.M., Rel. Ord. Ldr.; Rev. Lawrence Anderson, O.F.M., Campus Min.; Bro. Brian C. Belanger, O.F.M.; Bro. George Camacho, O.F.M.; Rev. Julian A. Davies, O.F.M., In Res.; Rev. Daniel P. Dwyer, O.F.M., Prof.; Rev. Gregory Gebbia; Rev. Kenneth Himes, O.F.M., Prof.; Rev. Linh Hoang, O.F.M., Prof.; Rev. Louis Iasiello, Prof.; Rev. Daniel C. Nelson, O.F.M., Prof.; Rev. Sean O'Brien, O.F.M.; Rev. Kenneth Paulli, O.F.M., Prof.; Rev. Michael Perry, Prof.; Rev. Robert Sandoz; Rev. Roberto Serrano, Campus Min.; Rev. Ignatius Smith, O.F.M., In Res.; Rev. Dennis Tamburello, O.F.M., Prof.; Bro. Edgardo Zea, O.F.M., In Res.; Stds.: 3,400

CONVENTS, MONASTERIES, AND RESIDENCES FOR WOMEN [CON]

ALBANY
Daughters of Charity of St. Vincent de Paul - 96 Menand Rd., Albany, NY 12204-1499 t) 518-462-1811 tom.beck@doc.org Home for the senior Sisters. Sr. Margaret Palmer, D.C., Supr.; Srs.: 49
Religious of the Sacred Heart - 128 W. Lawrence St., Albany, NY 12203 t) 518-489-8280
Sisters of Mercy of the Americas - Northeast Community - 634 New Scotland Ave., Albany, NY 12208 t) 518-437-3000
Sisters of the Holy Names of Jesus and Mary, U.S. - Ontario Province - 360 Whitehall Rd., #122, Albany, NY 12208 t) 503-675-7123 www.snjmusontario.org (Corporate Name: Sisters of the Holy Names of Jesus and Mary of the New York Province, Inc.) Sr. Maureen Delaney, S.N.J.M., Prov.; Srs.: 18
CASTLETON ON HUDSON
Provincial House, Juniorate and Novitiate of the Sisters of the Resurrection - 35 Boltwood Ave., Castleton On Hudson, NY 12033-1097 t) 518-732-2226 crsister@resurrectionsisters.org www.resurrectionsisters.org Sr. Mary Krystyna Kobielus, C.R., Supr.; Sr. Danielle Marie Baran, C.R., Prov.; Sr. Dolores Palermo, C.R., Dir.;
Chaplain's Residence - 34 Boltwood Ave., Castleton On Hudson, NY 12033
Retreat and Vacation Home - 325 Madonna Lake Rd., Cropseyville, NY 12052-1819 t) 518-279-1673
CATSKILL
St. Anthony Friary - 24 Harrison St., Catskill, NY 12414-0487 t) (518) 943-3451 stanthonys@sistersoflife.org sistersoflife.org Order of Friars Minor. Sr. Brigid Ancilla Heisler, S.V., Supr.;
DELMAR
Mill Hill Sisters Franciscan House - 703 Derzee Ct., Delmar, NY 12054 t) 518-512-4362 jdever001@nycap.rr.com; sisterjudithd@gmail.com Regional House Sr. Judith Dever, F.M.S.J., Admin.;
GERMANTOWN
St. Teresa's Motherhouse - 600 Woods Rd., Germantown, NY 12526-5639 t) 518-537-5000 smrc@stmhcs.org; info@carmelitesisters.com www.carmelitesisters.com Motherhouse and Novitiate. Carmelite Sisters for the Aged and Infirm. Rev. James Hess, O.Carm., Chap.; Mother Mary Rose Heery, O.Carm., Pres.; Srs.: 24
Postulation Office - Dr. Giovanna Brizi, Postulator; Rev. Mario Esposito, O.Carm., Vice Postulator;
LATHAM
Sisters of St. Joseph of Carondelet (Albany Province) - St. Joseph's Provincial House, 385 Watervliet-Shaker Rd., Latham, NY 12110-4799 t) 518-783-3500; 518-783-3524 (Leadership Office) csjcarondelet.org/ Rev. Geoffrey D. Burke, Chap.; Sr. Joan Mary Hartigan, CSJ, Dir.; Sr. Rose Casaleno, CSJ, Prov. Leadership Team; Sr. Margaret M. Edic, CSJ, First Councilor & Prov. Treas.; Sr. Mary Catherine Ryan, CSJ, Prov. Leadership Team; Sr. Diane Zigo, CSJ, Prov. Exec. Committee; Srs.: 198
WATERVLIET
St. Colman's Convent - 11 Haswell Rd., Watervliet, NY 12189 t) 518-273-4911 mlouise@stcolmans.com www.sistersofthepresentationwatervlietny.com Motherhouse and Novitiate of Sisters of the Presentation of the B.V.M. Mother Mary Louise Kane, P.BV.M., Admin.; Srs.: 15

ENDOWMENTS / FOUNDATIONS / TRUSTS [EFT]

ALBANY

Bishop Broderick Apartments Housing Development Fund Co., Inc. - 50 Prescott St., Albany, NY 12205 t) 518-869-7441 bpaul@depaulhousing.com; jill.mclellanphelps@depaulhousing.com www.depaulhousing.com Affordable housing for seniors and people with mobility impairments. Jill McLellan Phelps, Dir.; Barbara J. Paul, Community Mgr.;

Care for Life Foundation - 40 N. Main Ave., Albany, NY 12203-1422 t) 518-453-6650 Joseph Profit, Contact;

The Community Hospice Foundation, Inc. - 310 S. Manning Blvd., Albany, NY 12208; Mailing: 315 S. Manning Blvd., Albany, NY 12208 t) 518-482-4433 smanny@communityhospice.org www.communityhospice.org Stephen J. Manny, Exec.;

Diocesan Investment and Loan Trust - 40 N. Main Ave., Albany, NY 12203-1422 t) 518-641-6948 Very Rev. David R. LeFort, Trustee;

The Foundation of the Roman Catholic Diocese of Albany, New York, Inc. - 40 N. Main Ave., Albany, NY 12203 t) 518-453-6657 Nancy Spadaro Bielawa, Dir.;

St. Peter's Hospital Foundation, Inc. - 310 S. Manning Blvd., Albany, NY 12208 t) 518-482-4433 shannon.galuski@sphp.com www.sphp.com Shannon Galuski, Exec.;

Support Fund Trust of the Province of St. Thomas of Villanova - c/o 40 N. Main Ave., Albany, NY 12203 t) 518-453-6600

St. Vincent Apartments Housing Development Fund Co., Inc. - 475 Yates St., Albany, NY 12208; Mailing: 41 N. Main Ave., Albany, NY 12208 t) 518-482-8915 lcaroccia@depaulhousing.com; jill.mclellanphelps@depaulhousing.com www.depaulhousing.com Affordable housing for seniors and mobility impairments. Jill McLellan Phelps, Dir.; Lorraine Caroccia, Community Mgr.;

CLIFTON PARK

Halfmoon Housing Development Fund Co., Inc. (Bishop Hubbard Senior Apartments) - 54 Katherine Dr., Clifton Park, NY 12065 t) 518-383-2705 cbeck@depaulhousing.com; jill.mclellanphelps@depaulhousing.com www.depaulhousing.com Affordable housing for seniors and people with mobility impairments. Jill McLellan Phelps, Dir.; Caitlin Beck, Sr. Community Mgr.;

DELMAR

Mill Hill Sisters Charitable Trust - 703 Derzee Ct., Delmar, NY 12054 t) 518-512-4362 jdever001@nycap.rr.com Sr. Judith Dever, F.M.S.J., Admin.;

GERMANTOWN

Carmelite Sisters of the Aged and Infirm Continuing Care Trust - 600 Woods Rd., Germantown, NY 12526 t) 518-537-5000 srvrobert@stmhcs.org Mother Mary Rose Heery, O.Carm., Rel. Ord. Ldr.;

LATHAM

The Sister M. Athanasia Gurry Trust Fund - 385 Watervliet-Shaker Rd., Latham, NY 12110-4799 t) 518-783-3500 lmb@csjalbany.org Sr. Eileen McCann, C.S.J., Treas.; Sr. Mary Anne Heenan, C.S.J., Pres.;

RENSSELAER

East Greenbush Housing Development Fund Co., Inc. (Branson Manor Senior Apartments) - 3 Grandview Dr., Rensselaer, NY 12144 t) 518-283-8280 bweatherwax@depaulhousing.com; jill.mclellanphelps@depaulhousing.com www.depaulhousing.com Affordable housing for seniors and people with mobility impairments. Jill McLellan Phelps, Dir.;

SCHENECTADY

LCS Housing Development Fund Company, Inc. (The Lawrence Commons) - 2660 Albany St., Schenectady, NY 12304 t) 518-393-2412 jill.mclellanphelps@depaulhousing.com www.depaulhousing.com Affordable housing for people with mobility impairments. Jill McLellan Phelps, Dir.;

Rotterdam Housing Development Fund Co., Inc. (Father Leo O'Brien Senior Community) - 3151 Marra Ln., Schenectady, NY 12303 t) 518-357-4424 jill.mclellanphelps@depaulhousing.com www.depaulhousing.com Affordable housing for seniors, 62 years+ Jill McLellan Phelps, Dir.;

VALATIE

Moreau Province Charitable Trust - 495 Maple Ln., Valatie, NY 12184 t) 203-937-3250 gcscsc@gmail.com Bro. George Schmitz, CSC, Chair;

WATERVLIET

C.S.C. Housing Development Fund Co., Inc. (Sanderson Court Senior Apts.) - 6 Carondelet Dr., Watervliet, NY 12189 t) 518-782-1123 jill.mclellanphelps@depaulhousing.com; topalka@depaulhousing.com www.depaulhousing.com Affordable housing for seniors. Jill McLellan Phelps, Dir.; Tina Opalka, Community Mgr.;

Delatour Housing Development Fund Company, Inc. (Carondelet Commons Senior Apartments) - 2 Carondelet Dr., Watervliet, NY 12189 t) 518-783-0444 cbeck@depaulhousing.com; jill.mclellanphelps@depaulhousing.com www.depaulhousing.com Affordable housing for seniors and people with mobility impairments. Jill McLellan Phelps, Dir.; Caitlin Beck, Senior Community Mgr.;

Fontbonne Manor Housing Development Fund Company, Inc. - 10 Carondelet Dr., Watervliet, NY 12189 t) 518-782-2780 jill.mclellanphelps@depaulhousing.com; topalka@depaulhousing.com www.depaulhousing.com Affordable housing for seniors. Jill McLellan Phelps, Dir.; Tina Opalka, Community Mgr.;

Italian-American Housing Development Fund Co., Inc. (Cabrini Acres Senior Apts.) - 4 Carondelet Dr., Watervliet, NY 12189 t) 518-785-0050 cbeck@rcda.org; jill.mclellanphelps@depaulhousing.com www.depaulhousing.com Affordable housing for seniors and mobility impairments. Jill McLellan Phelps, Dir.; Caitlin Beck, Sr. Community Mgr.;

WYNANTSKILL

S.J. Housing Development Fund Company, Inc. (St. Jude's Apartments) - 50 Dana Ave., Wynantskill, NY 12198 t) 518-283-5690 bweatherwax@depaulhousing.com; jill.mclellanphelps@depaulhousing.com www.depaulhousing.com Affordable housing for seniors and mobility impairments. Jill McLellan Phelps, Dir.; Barbara Weatherwax, Community Mgr.;

HOSPITALS / HEALTH SERVICES [HOS]

ALBANY

St. Clare's Corporation - 40 N. Main Ave., Albany, NY 12203-1422 t) 518-453-6650 Joseph Profiti, Pres.;

St. Clare's Holding Company, Inc. - 40 N. Main Ave., Albany, NY 12203-1422 t) 518-453-6650 www.stclares.org

St. Peter's Hospital of the City of Albany - 315 S. Manning Blvd., Albany, NY 12208 t) 518-525-1550 fineganm@trinity-health.org www.sphp.com Michael Finegan, Pres.; Bed Capacity: 442; Asstd. Annu.: 50,000; Staff: 4,000

Villa Mary Immaculate (St. Peter's Nursing & Rehabilitation Center) - 301 Hackett Blvd., Albany, NY 12208 t) 518-525-7600 helen.manganaro@sphp.com www.sphp.com Helen Manganaro, Dir.; Bed Capacity: 160; Asstd. Annu.: 500; Staff: 250

AMSTERDAM

St. Mary's Healthcare - 427 Guy Park Ave., Amsterdam, NY 12010 t) 518-842-1900 cortesej@ascension.org; giulianelliv@ascension.org www.ascension.org Sponsored by Ascension Health Ministries (Ascension Sponsor, a Public Juridic Person) Victor Giulianelli, Pres.;

The Foundation of St. Mary's at Amsterdam, Inc. - t) 518-841-7478

St. Mary's Hospital Auxiliary, Inc. - t) 518-841-7136 medwidc@smha.org Colleen Medwid, Dir.;

RENSSELAER

The Community Hospice, Inc. - 295 Valley View Blvd., Rensselaer, NY 12144; Mailing: 445 New Karner Rd., Albany, NY 12208 t) 518-724-0284 michelle.mazzacco@sphp.com www.communityhospice.org Michelle Mazzacco, Vice Pres. Community Svcs. and Hospice; Bed Capacity: 14; Asstd. Annu.: 4,000; Staff: 260

MISCELLANEOUS [MIS]

ALBANY

Assisi in Albany, Inc. - 646 State St., 2nd Fl., Albany, NY 12203 t) 518-391-2675 assisiinalbany@yahoo.com www.assisiinalbany.com Rev. Anthony Kall, O.F.M.Conv., Pst.; Pamela Bullock, Dir.;

Broderick Community Service Organization - 40 N. Main Ave., Albany, NY 12203-1422 t) 518-453-6623 paul.ehmann@rcda.org

Burke Community Service Corp., Inc. - 40 N. Main Ave., Albany, NY 12203 t) 518-453-6623 paul.ehmann@rcda.org Paul A. Ehmann, Contact;

The Cathedral Restoration Corp. - 40 N. Main Ave., Albany, NY 12203 t) 518-463-4447 ecathedra@nycap.rr.com Rev. William H. Pape, Secy.;

Crusade for Family Prayer, Inc. (Holy Cross Family Ministries Foundation) - 40 N. Main Ave., Albany, NY 12203; Mailing: 518 Washington St., North Easton, MA 02356 t) 508-238-4095 x2008 tmckenney@hcfm.org Sponsored by Congregation of Holy Cross (U.S. Province) Thomas McKenney, Exec.; Cynthia Slattery, Exec.; Rev. Wilfred Raymond, C.S.C.;

Cusack Community Service Corporation - 40 N. Main Ave., Albany, NY 12203 t) 518-459-0183 deborah.dammobrien@rcda.org Deborah Damm O'Brien, Exec.;

DePaul Housing Management Corp. - 41 N. Main Ave., Albany, NY 12203 t) 518-459-0183 www.depaulhousing.com Managing diocesan sponsored housing for persons who are elderly or mobility impaired. Jill McLellan Phelps, Dir.; Mary Beth Purcell, Exec. Dir.;

The Family Rosary, Inc. - 40 N. Main Ave., Albany, NY 12203; Mailing: 518 Washington St, North Easton, MA 02356 t) 508-238-4095 cslattery@hcfm.org www.familyrosary.org Sponsored by Congregation of Holy Cross (U.S. Province) Elizabeth Ponce, Exec.; Rev. Wilfred Raymond, C.S.C., Pres.; Cynthia Slattery, Exec.;

Family Theater Ministries - 40 N. Main Ave., Albany, NY 12203; Mailing: 518 Washington St., North Easton, MA 02356 t) 508-238-4095 cslattery@hcfm.org Sponsored by Congregation of Holy Cross (U.S. Province) Cynthia Slattery, Exec.; Rev. Wilfred Raymond, C.S.C.;

St. Francis Chapel (Albany), Franciscan Friars-Holy Name Province, Inc. - Wolf Road Shoppers Park, 515 Loudon Rd, Albany, NY 12211 t) 646-473-0265 mharlan@hnp.org Very Rev. Mark G. Reamer, O.F.M., Pres.;

Holy Cross International, Inc. - c/o Pastoral Center, 40 N. Main Ave., Albany, NY 12203 t) 518-463-1177 generalsteward@holycrossroma.org Rev. John Ryan, CSC, Treas.;

Korean Apostolate of the Roman Catholic Diocese of Albany - 15 Exchange St., Albany, NY 12202 t) 518-438-1805 Rev. Jaeung Damian Lee, Chap.;

LaSalle Albany, Inc., Christian Brothers Academy - 12 Airline Dr., Albany, NY 12205; Mailing: The Brothers of the Christian Schools District of Eastern North America, 444A Rte. 35 S., Eatontown, NJ 07724 t) 732-380-7296 x103 www.cbaalbany.org Bro. Joseph Juliano, F.S.C., Secy.; Bro. Joseph Schafer, FSC, Chair;

LaSalle School, Inc. - 391 Western Ave., Albany, NY 12203 t) 518-242-4731 information@lasalle-school.org www.lasalle-school.org Residential and day programs David Wallace, Exec. Dir.;

McCloskey Community Service Corporation - 41 N. Main Ave., Albany, NY 12203 t) 518-459-0183 charles.rockwell@rcda.org Charles Rockwell, Exec.;

New York State Catholic Conference - 465 State St., Albany, NY 12203 t) 518-434-6195 info@nyscatholic.org www.nyscatholic.org Dennis J Poust, Exec.;

Noonan Community Service Corporation - 40 N. Main Ave., Albany, NY 12203-1422 t) 518-453-6641

BALLSTON LAKE

Secular Order of Discalced Carmelites - 104 Midline Rd., Ballston Lake, NY 12019; Mailing: P.O. Box 408, Schenectady, NY 12301 t) 518-248-4291 secularcarmelit@gmail.com Joyce A. Panserella, Pres.;

CASTLETON ON HUDSON

Cooperative Christian Ministries of Schodack, Inc. (C.C.M. of Schodack) (CCMS The Anchor) - 92 S. Main St., Castleton On Hudson, NY 12033-0092 t) 518-732-4120

GERMANTOWN

Oneness in Peace Center, Inc. - 49 Main St., Germantown, NY 12526-5328 t) 518-537-5678 rccgtown@gmail.com

GLENVILLE

Albany, New York Chapter of Magnificat, Inc. - 5 Valleywood Dr., Glenville, NY 12302 t) 518-810-1310 albanymagnificat@gmail.com magnificat-ministry.org/ny-albany Diane Bigos, Contact;

MENANDS

Catholic Cemeteries of the Roman Catholic Diocese of Albany, New York - 48 Cemetery Ave., Menands, NY 12204 t) 518-432-4953 info@rcdacemeteries.org www.capitaldistrictcemeteries.org Emily Simmons, Exec. Dir.;

Medicus Christi, LTD - 16 MacAffer Dr., Menands, NY 12204-1208 t) 518-772-5119 marottaghana@aol.com

NORTH CREEK

North Country Ministry, Inc. - 32 Circle Ave., North Creek, NY 12853; Mailing: P.O. Box 111, North Creek, NY 12853 t) 518-251-4460 (North Creek); 518-623-2829 (Warrensburg) ncm32@frontier.com Bro. James Posluszny, C.S.C., Dir.;

RENSSELAER

Circles of Mercy, Inc. - 11 Washington St., Ste. A, Rensselaer, NY 12144 t) 518-462-0899 circlesofmercy@nycap.rr.com www.circlesofmercy.org Richard S. Zazycki, Dir.;

Franciscan Heights Community Service Corp. (Franciscan Heights Senior Community) - 1 St. Anthony Ln., Rensselaer, NY 12144 t) 518-432-3555 jill.mclellanphelps@depaulhousing.com www.depaulhousing.com Apartments and cottages for persons who are 55+ and income eligible. Jill McLellan Phelps, Dir.;

SCHENECTADY

Christ Child Society of Albany - 18 Terry Ave, Schenectady, NY 12303 c) (518) 810-7918 ccsalbany2020@gmail.com www.facebook.com/christchildalbany/ Volunteers who help children in need. Very Rev. James Belogi, Spiritual Adv./Care Srvcs.; Jeanette M. May, Pres.;

TROY

Eddy Licensed Home Care Agency - 433 River St., Troy, NY 12180 t) 518-274-6200 michelle.mazzacco@sphp.com www.sphp.com Michelle Mazzacco, Vice Pres. Community Svcs. & Hospice;

MONASTERIES AND RESIDENCES FOR PRIESTS AND BROTHERS [MON]

ALBANY

Vincentian Fathers Residence - 96 Menands Rd., Albany, NY 12204-1499 t) 518-462-1811 revlasma@yahoo.com Rev. Lawrence F. Asma, C.M.;

RENSSELAER

Franciscan Friars Conventual - 75 St. Francis Pl., Rensselaer, NY 12144-2142 t) (410) 531-1400; (518) 472-1007 www.olaprovince.org Immaculate Conception Friary Friar Joseph Angelini, OFM Conv.; Friar Edward Falsey, OFM Conv.; Friar Gregory Spuhler, OFM Conv.; Friar John Ruffo, OFM Conv., In Res.; Friar Joseph Freitag, OFM Conv., Guardian;

Franciscan Mission House - 517 Washington Ave., Rensselaer, NY 12144 t) (518) 472-1000 Order of Friars Minor Conventual Sandy Miller, Dir.;

Immaculate Conception Friary - Order of Friars Minor Conventual - 75 St. Francis Pl., Rensselaer, NY 12144; Mailing: P.O. Box 629, Rensselaer, NY 12144 t) 518-472-1007 provsec1@olaprovince.org www.olaprovince.org (Immaculate Conception Province), (Corporate Name: Order Minor Conventuals, Inc.) Bro. Andre Picotte, O.F.M.Conv., Vicar; Bro. Gerald Seipp, OFM Conv., In Res.; Rev. Alvin Somerville, O.F.M.Conv., In Res.; Rev. Giles Van Wormer, O.F.M.Conv., In Res.; Rev. Julian Zambanini, OFM Conv., In Res.; Friar Timothy Lyons, OFM Conv, Chap.; Rev. Anthony Kall, O.F.M.Conv., Guardian;

VALATIE

Brothers of Holy Cross of the Eastern Province of the United States of America, Inc. - 495 Maple Ln., Valatie, NY 12184 t) 512-442-7856 moreauprovinceoffices@gmail.com Bro. Thomas Dziekan, C.S.C., Pres.; Brs.: 6

St. Joseph Center - 495 Maple Ln., Valatie, NY 12184 t) 518-784-9481 x263 markbknightly@gmail.com Residence for retired Holy Cross Brothers and Priests. Bro. Mark Knightly, CSC, Dir.; Brs.: 20; Priests: 3

NURSING / REHABILITATION / CONVALESCENCE / ELDERLY CARE [NUR]

ALBANY

St. Joseph's Villa Senior Living Services - 40 N. Main Ave., Albany, NY 12203-1422 t) 518-453-6600

Our Lady of Hope Residence - 40 N. Main Ave., Albany, NY 12203 t) 518-453-6600 www.littlesistersofthepoor.org Sr. Alice Marie Jones, L.S.P., Prov.;

Teresian House - 200 Washington Ave. Ext., Albany, NY 12203 t) 518-456-2000 www.teresianhouse.com Corporate Title: Teresian House Nursing Home Co., Inc., Served by: Carmelite Sisters for the Aged and Infirm Rev. Jeffrey L'Arche, Chap.; Frank Yeboah, Admin.; Sandy Leboeuf, Dir., Pastoral Care; Asstd. Annu.: 550; Staff: 180

Teresian House Foundation -

Teresian House Housing Corporation (Avila) - 100 White Pine Dr., Albany, NY 12203 t) 518-640-9400 ffoley@avilaretirement.com www.avilaretirementcommunity.com Francis X. Foley Jr., CEO;

DELHI

Delhi Housing Development Fund Co., Inc. I and II - 7 Main St., Delhi, NY 13753 t) 607-746-8142 mary.thompson@depaulhousing.com; jill.mclellanphelps@depaulhousing.com www.depaulhousing.com Jill McLellan Phelps, Dir.; Mary Thompson, Community Mgr.; Asstd. Annu.: 45; Staff: 2

GERMANTOWN

Avila Institute of Gerontology, Inc. - 600 Woods Rd., Germantown, NY 12526 t) 518-537-5000 srpeter@avilainstitute.org www.avilainstitute.org (Educational Institute) Provides education and seminars and develops curricula, etc., on aging issues. Sr. M. Jeanne Francis Haley, O.Carm., Pres.; Sr. Peter Lillian, O.Carm., Dir.; Staff: 9

GUILDERLAND

Our Lady of Mercy Life Center - 2 Mercycare Ln., Guilderland, NY 12084 t) 518-464-8100 sandra.sullivansmith@sphp.com www.sphp.com Sandra Sullivan Smith, Dir.; Asstd. Annu.: 160; Staff: 240

SLINGERLANDS

Marie-Rose Manor HDFCI - 100 Marquis Dr., Slingerlands, NY 12159 t) 518-459-0204 jill.mclellanphelps@depaulhousing.com www.depaulhousing.com Affordable housing for seniors and persons with mobility impairments over 62 years of age. Jill McLellan Phelps, Dir.; Asstd. Annu.: 50; Staff: 2

PRESCHOOLS / CHILDCARE CENTERS [PRE]

ALBANY

St. Catherine's Center for Children - 40 N. Main Ave,, Albany, NY 12203 t) 518-453-6700 iandrea@st-cath.org www.st-cath.org Residential and day treatment, group homes and foster family programs for children with special needs. Community based prevention programs. Frank Pindiak, Exec.; Stds.: 45; Lay Tchrs.: 9

NISKAYUNA

Villa Fusco Child Day Care (Pre-K) - 955 Balltown Rd., Niskayuna, NY 12309 t) 518-377-1613 fcppschaloux@gmail.com Daughters of Charity of the Most Precious Blood. Sr. Sharmila Mathew, Supr.;

TROY

Troy CYO Day Camp - 237 Fourth St., Troy, NY 12180; Mailing: Box 867, Troy, NY 12180 t) 518-274-2630 rpisci2624@aol.com Sponsored by Troy Youth Organization, Inc. for Boys and Girls, ages 5-12 yrs. Raymond R. Piscitelli, Exec.;

WYNANTSKILL

Camp Scully - 24 Camp Scully Way, Wynantskill, NY 12198; Mailing: PO Box 28, Rensselaer, NY 12144 t) 518-283-1617 campscully@ccalbany.org www.campscully.camp/ Day & resident camp for children 5-17. Under direction of Catholic Charities of the Diocese of Albany. Colin Stewart, Dir.;

RETREAT HOUSES / RENEWAL CENTERS [RTR]

FULTONVILLE

Shrine of Our Lady of Martyrs - Rte. 5S, Fultonville, NY 12072; Mailing: 136 Shrine Rd., Suite 2, Fultonville, NY 12072 t) 518-630-9922 friendsofauriesville@gmail.com www.auriesvilleshrine.com/ National Shrine of the Jesuit Martyrs of North America. Julie Baaki, Exec. Dir.;

LAKE GEORGE

St. Mary's of the Lake - 3535 St. Rte. 9L, Lake George, NY 12845 t) 518-668-5594 frankd@paulist.org paulist.org/location/st-marys-of-the-lake/ Summer retreat of the Paulist Fathers. Rev. Frank Desiderio, Dir.;

MIDDLEBURGH

Bethany Ministries - 104 Grove St., Apt. 2, Middleburgh, NY 12212; Mailing: PO Box 432, Middleburgh, NY 12122 t) 518-827-4699 bethmin@midtel.net www.bethmin.org Sr. Anna Tantsits, IHM, Treas.; Rev. Peter Chepaitis, O.F.M., Dir.;

PARADOX

Pyramid Life Center - 1 Pyramid Rd., Paradox, NY 12858; Mailing: Box 103, Paradox, NY 12858 t) 518-585-7545 www.pyramidlife.org Corporation Name: Albany Catholic Youth Association, Inc. Brian P. Evers, Dir.;

QUEENSBURY

Wellsprings Outreach - 230 Robert Gardens N., #5, Queensbury, NY 12804 t) 518-745-1617 laratondafms@yahoo.com www.wellspringsoutreach.org Programs in Spirituality Bro. Michael Laratonda, Dir.;

SCHENECTADY

Dominican Retreat and Conference Center - 1945 Union St., Schenectady, NY 12309 t) 518-393-4169 dslcny@nybiz.rr.com www.dslcny.org Sr. Susan M. Zemgulis, O.P., Admin.;

VALATIE

St. Joseph Center - 495 Maple Ln., Valatie, NY 12184 t) 518-784-9481 x263 sjcval@gmail.com Bro. Mark Knightly, CSC, Admin.;

SHRINES [SHR]

FONDA

The National Shrine of Saint Kateri Tekakwitha and Friary - 3636 State Hwy. 5, Fonda, NY 12068; Mailing: PO Box 627, Fonda, NY 12068-0627 t) 518-853-3646 nationalkaterishrine@gmail.com www.katerishrine.com Friar Timothy Lyons, OFM Conv, Chap.; Rita Gullion, Dir.;

SPECIAL CARE FACILITIES [SPF]

ALBANY

Saint Anne Institute - 160 N. Main Ave., Albany, NY

12206 t) 518-437-6500 acortese@s-a-i.org www.stanneinstitute.org Residential, Educational, and Community-Based Counseling services Dcn. Anthony G. Cortese, CEO;

Diocesan AIDS Services - 100 Slingerland St., Albany, NY 12202 t) 518-449-3581 Candace Ellis, Exec.;

Emmaus House - 45 Trinity Pl., Albany, NY 12202 t) 518-482-4966 Albany Catholic Worker Community. Fred Boehrer, Dir.; Diana Conroy, Dir.;

Hospitality House Therapeutic Community Inc. - 271 Central Ave., Albany, NY 12206 t) 518-434-6468 www.hospitalityhousetc.org A private, not-for-profit, intensive residential treatment program for males, 18 years or older, with a history of drug and/or substance abuse. Young Do, Exec. Dir.; Linda Smith, Dir., Opers.;

CLIFTON PARK

Seton Health at Schuyler Ridge Residential Healthcare - One Abele Dr., Clifton Park, NY 12065 t) 518-371-1400 marc.walker@sphp.com www.sphp.com Marc Walker, Dir.; Bed Capacity: 120; Asstd. Annu.: 120; Staff: 190

GERMANTOWN

The Carmelite System, Inc. - 646 Woods Rd., Germantown, NY 12526-5617 t) 518-537-7500 pmacgiffert@carmelitesystem.org carmelitesystem.org Mother M. Mark Louis Anne Randall, O.Carm., Mem.;

WATERVLIET

St. Colman's Home - 11 Haswell Rd., Watervliet, NY 12189 t) 518-273-4911 mlouise@stcolmans.com www.stcolmans.com/ Sisters of the Presentation of the B.V.M. Sr. S. Joseph Mary, P.B.V.M., Dir., Social Svc.;

An asterisk (*) denotes an organization that has established tax-exempt status directly with the IRS and is not covered by the USCCB Group Ruling.

Diocese of Alexandria

(Dioecesis Alexandrina in Louisiana)

MOST REVEREND ROBERT W. MARSHALL, JR.

Bishop of Alexandria; ordained June 10, 2000; appointed Bishop of Alexandria April 21, 2020; installed August 20, 2020. Chancery Office: 4400 Coliseum Blvd., Alexandria, LA 71306.

Chancery Office: 4400 Coliseum Blvd., P.O. Box 7417, Alexandria, LA 71306. T: 318-445-2401 (Receptionist); T: 318-445-6424 (Auto Attendant); F: 318-448-6121. www.diocesealex.org

ERECTED AS DIOCESE OF NATCHITOCHES JULY 29, 1853.

Square Miles 11,108.

Transferred to Alexandria August 6, 1910 and became Diocese of Alexandria.

Redesignated Diocese of Alexandria-Shreveport on January 12, 1977; split, forming two Dioceses, the Diocese of Alexandria and the Diocese of Shreveport as of June 16, 1986. Comprises the Counties (parishes) of Rapides, Avoyelles, Concordia, Catahoula, LaSalle, Grant, Natchitoches, Vernon, Tensas, Caldwell, Winn, Franklin and Madison.

For legal titles of parishes and diocesan institutions, consult the Chancery Office.

STATISTICAL OVERVIEW

Personnel

Bishop.....1
Priests: Diocesan Active in Diocese.....39
Priests: Diocesan Active Outside Diocese.....2
Priests: Retired, Sick or Absent.....21
Number of Diocesan Priests.....62
Religious Priests in Diocese.....3
Total Priests in your Diocese.....65
Extern Priests in Diocese.....13
Ordinations:
Transitional Deacons.....1
Permanent Deacons in Diocese.....36
Total Brothers.....2
Total Sisters.....15

Parishes

Parishes.....50
With Resident Pastor:
Resident Diocesan Priests.....44
Resident Religious Priests.....3
Without Resident Pastor:
Administered by Priests.....3
Missions.....21

Professional Ministry Personnel:
Brothers.....2
Sisters.....15
Lay Ministers.....17

Welfare

Catholic Hospitals.....1
Total Assisted.....255,349
Homes for the Aged.....1
Total Assisted.....104
Residential Care of Disabled.....1
Total Assisted.....202

Educational

Diocesan Students in Other Seminaries.....7
Total Seminarians.....7
High Schools, Diocesan and Parish.....3
Total Students.....768
Elementary Schools, Diocesan and Parish.....7
Total Students.....1,920
Catechesis/Religious Education:
High School Students.....701
Elementary Students.....1,386
Total Students under Catholic Instruction.....4,782
Teachers in Diocese:
Priests.....2
Sisters.....9
Lay Teachers.....190

Vital Statistics

Receptions into the Church:
Infant Baptism Totals.....367
Minor Baptism Totals.....44
Adult Baptism Totals.....28
Received into Full Communion.....71
First Communions.....448
Confirmations.....317
Marriages:
Catholic.....86
Interfaith.....35
Total Marriages.....121
Deaths.....648
Total Catholic Population.....36,505
Total Population.....379,872

LEADERSHIP

Moderator of the Curia - t) 318-445-6424 x204
Vicar General - t) 318-445-6424 x204 Very Rev. Michael Craig Scott (frcscott@diocesealex.org);
Chancellor - t) 318-445-6424 x228 Rev. Chad A. Partain, Chancellor (frcpartain@diocesealex.org);
Vice Chancellor - t) 318-445-6424 x206 Dcn. Richard Mitchell (dcnrmitchell@diocesealex.org);
Director of Catholic Charities and Special Ministries - t) 318-445-6424 x500 www.cccenla.org Rev. John K. Brocato, Exec. Dir. (frjbrocato@cccenla.org);
Superintendent of Catholic Schools - t) 318-445-6424 x224 Thomas Roque (troque@diocesealex.org);
Director of Development and Public Affairs - t) 318-445-6424 x206 Dcn. Richard Mitchell, Dir. (dcnrmitchell@diocesealex.org);
Chief Financial Officer - t) 318-445-6424 x214 David Brook, CFO (dbrook@diocesealex.org);
Director of Religious Formation and Training - t) (318) 445-6424 x207 Dcn. Jason Lavergne, Dir. (dcnjlavergne@diocesealex.org);
Secretary to the Bishop - t) 318-445-6424 x201 Deborah Deorosan (ddeorosan@diocesealex.org);
St. Joseph Catholic Center - t) 318-445-2401 (Receptionist); 318-445-6424 (Auto-Attendant)

MISCELLANEOUS / OTHER OFFICES

Administrator and Assessor, Code of Pastoral Conduct - t) 318-445-6424 x204 Very Rev. Michael Craig Scott (frcscott@diocesealex.org);
Archivist - t) 318-445-6424 x228 Rev. Chad A. Partain, Archivist (frcpartain@diocesealex.org);
Boy Scouts of America -
Diocesan, Region 5 & Louisiana Purchase Council Chaplain - t) 318-473-0010 x2543 Rev. Stephen J. Brandow, Chap.;
Region 5 Chaplain (Vacant) -
Catholic Charismatic Renewal of Cenla - t) 318-419-1547 Diane Ardoine (dianeardoine@yahoo.com);
Catholic Medical Association of Central Louisiana - t) 318-922-3131 Rev. Martin L. Laird (frmlaird@diocesealex.org);
Catholic Relief Services (Vacant) -
College of Consultors - Rev. Stephen Scott Chemino (frchemino@diocesealex.org); Rev. Wade DeCoste (Canada) (frwdecoste@diocesealex.org); Rev. Anthony Dharmaraj, M.S.F.S. (India) (fradharmaraj@diocesealex.org);
Communications - Cari Terracina, Publications (cterracina@diocesealex.org); Joan Ferguson, Multi-Media (jferguson@diocesealex.org);
Continuing Education of the Clergy - t) 318-379-2521 Rev. Charles Ray (frcray@diocesealex.org);
Coordinator for Religious - t) 318-985-2772 Sr. Sandra Norsworthy, O.L.S. (srsandraols@yahoo.com);
Deans - Rev. Dwight De Jesus (Philippines), Avoyelles Deanery (frddejesus@diocesealex.org); Rev. John O'Brien (Canada), Natchitoches Deanery (frjobrien@diocesealex.org); Rev. John Pardue, Eastern Deanery (frjpardue@diocesealex.org);
Defender of the Bond and Promoter of Justice - t) 318-445-6424 x265 Rev. James A. Ferguson (frjferguson@diocesealex.org);
Diaconate Program - t) 318-445-6424 x206 Dcn. Richard Mitchell, Dir. (dcnrmitchell@diocesealex.org);
Diocesan Tribunal - t) (318) 445-6424 x263 Patricia Thomas, Moderator (pthomas@diocesealex.org);
Hispanic Ministry - t) 318-445-6424 x217 Very Rev. Peter A. Faulk (frpfaulk@diocesealex.org);
Holy Childhood Association - t) 318-445-6424 x228 Rev. Chad A. Partain, Dir. (frcpartain@diocesealex.org);
Judges - Very Rev. Peter A. Faulk (frpfaulk@diocesealex.org); Rev. Stephen Scott Chemino (frchemino@diocesealex.org); Rev. Taylor Reynolds (frtreynolds@diocesealex.org);
Life and Justice (Vacant) -
Liturgy Commission - t) 318-445-6424 x206 Dcn. Richard Mitchell (dcnrmitchell@diocesealex.org);
Louisiana Interchurch Council - t) (318) 346-7274 Rev. Stephen Scott Chemino, Ecumenical Liaison (frchemino@diocesealex.org);
Maryhill Renewal Center - t) 318-542-1707 Dcn. Luther "Luke" White, Facility Mgr. (dcnlwhite@diocesealex.org);
Notary - Kathy Cole (kcole@diocesealex.org);
Presbyteral Council - Rev. Wade DeCoste (Canada) (frwdecoste@diocesealex.org); Rev. Anthony Dharmaraj, M.S.F.S. (India) (fradharmaraj@diocesealex.org); Very Rev. Peter A. Faulk (frpfaulk@diocesealex.org);
Propagation of the Faith and Foreign Mission Education - t) (318) 445-6424 x228 Rev. Chad A. Partain, Dir. (frcpartain@diocesealex.org);
Protection of Children -
Program Director - t) 318-445-6424 x213 Pam Delrie;
Victim Assistance Minister - t) 318-445-6424 x229 Dr. Lee Kneipp, Clinical Psychologist;
Vicar for Clergy (Vacant) -
Vocations and Seminarians - t) 318-445-6424 x260 Rev. Luke LaFleur, Dir. (frllafleur@diocesealex.org);

PARISHES, MISSIONS, AND CLERGY

STATE OF LOUISIANA

ALEXANDRIA

St. Francis Xavier Cathedral - 626 Fourth St., Alexandria, LA 71301-8424 t) 318-445-1451 frjferguson@diocesealex.org www.sfxcathedral.org Rev. James A. Ferguson, Rector; Rev. William Gearheard, Par. Vicar; Dcn. Richard Mitchell; Dcn. Jason Lavergne; Mary Lou Maples, DRE; CRP Stds.: 23
St. Frances Xavier Cabrini - 2211 E. Texas Ave., Alexandria, LA 71301-4207 t) 318-445-4588 www.cabrinichurch.com Rev. Chad A. Partain, Pst.; Rev. Robert Johnson, Par. Vicar; Dcn. Lawrence Feldkamp; Jonathan Brooks, DRE; CRP Stds.: 37
St. Frances Xavier Cabrini School - (Grades PreK-8) 2215 E. Texas Ave., Alexandria, LA 71301 t) 318-448-3333 www.cabrinischool.com Sr. Nina Vincent, O.L.S., Prin.; Stds.: 313; Sr. Tchrs.: 2; Lay Tchrs.: 20
St. James Memorial - 714 Winn St., Alexandria, LA 71301 t) 318-487-9512 frcscott@diocesealex.org Very Rev. Michael Craig Scott, Pst.; Dcn. Tommy Robichaux; Natile Nelson, DRE; CRP Stds.: 28
St. Juliana - 900 Daspit St., Alexandria, LA 71302-5343 t) 318-445-6700 frllafleur@diocesealex.org www.stjulianaccf.org Rev. Luke LaFleur, Admin.; Dcn. Luther "Luke" White; Angela Lee, DRE; CRP Stds.: 28
Our Lady of Prompt Succor - 2120 Elliott St., Alexandria, LA 71301-6548; Mailing: 401 21st St., Alexandria, LA 71301-6548 t) 318-445-3693 julie.bayone@olpschurch.org; frrusty@olpschurch.org www.olpschurch.org Rev. Rusty P. Rabalais, Pst.; Rev. Thomas Kennedy, Par. Vicar; Rev. Joy Retnazihamoni Antony (India), In Res.; Dcn. Michael L. Young; Dcn. Leslie "Les" Glankler; Shelly Michiels, DRE; CRP Stds.: 124
Our Lady of Prompt Succor School - (Grades PreK-6) 420 21st St., Alexandria, LA 71301 t) 318-487-1862 olpsoffice@promptsuccor.org www.promptsuccor.org Megan Beck, Prin.; Stds.: 419; Lay Tchrs.: 30
St. Rita - 4401 Bayou Rapides Rd., Alexandria, LA 71303; Mailing: 4401Bayou Rapides Rd., Bldg. C, Alexandria, LA 71303 t) 318-445-7120 strita@strita.org; etta@strita.org www.strita.org Rev. Anthony Dharmaraj, M.S.F.S. (India), Pst.; Rev. David J. Braquet, Sacr. Min.; Dcn. Kenneth Sayes; Courtney Brinkman, DRE; CRP Stds.: 97

BALL

Immaculate Heart of Mary - 1220 Tioga Rd., Ball, LA 71405 t) 318-640-9446 tara@ihmarychurch.org; dcnroger@ihmarychurch.org www.ihmarychurch.org Rev. Rick Gremillion, Pst.; Dcn. Roger Christopher; CRP Stds.: 71

BORDELONVILLE

St. Peter - 4702 Hwy. 451, Bordelonville, LA 71320-0031; Mailing: PO Box 31, Bordelonville, LA 71320 t) 318-997-2151 saintpeter@centurytel.net Rev. Louis E. Sklar, Pst.; Terri Guillory, DRE; CRP Stds.: 28

BOYCE

St. Margaret - 402 Ryan St., Boyce, LA 71409 t) 318-793-8811 frpfaulk@diocesealex.org Very Rev. Peter A. Faulk, Admin.; Dcn. Alexander Mangini Jr.; Robert Williams, DRE;
St. Cyril - Hwy. 8, Flatwoods, LA 71427; Mailing: 402 Ryan St., Boyce, LA 71409 t) (318) 793-8811
St. Margaret Mary - Hwy. 119, Gorum, LA 71434; Mailing: 402 Ryan St., Boyce, LA 71409 t) (318) 793-8811

BUNKIE

St. Anthony of Padua - 409 St. John St., Bunkie, LA 71322; Mailing: P.O. Box 719, Bunkie, LA 71322-0719 t) 318-346-7274 frchemino@diocesealex.org stanthonyscathol@bellsouth.net Carol Steckler, DRE; Rev. Stephen Scott Chemino, Pst.; CRP Stds.: 41
St. Anthony of Padua School - (Grades PreK-8) 116 S. Knoll St., Bunkie, LA 71322 t) 318-346-2739 sassecure@bellsouth.net www.sasbunkie.com Joel Desselle, Prin.; Stds.: 178; Lay Tchrs.: 13

CAMPTI

Nativity of the Blessed Virgin Mary - 119 Tally St., Campti, LA 71411-4007 t) 318-476-2116 nativityofbvmcampti@gmail.com Rev. Gus Voltz III, Pst.; Dcn. Chad A. Thibodeaux; Daisy LaBorde, DRE; CRP Stds.: 10
St. Joseph - 2443 Hwy. 1226, Natchitoches, LA 71457; Mailing: 119 Tally St., Campti, LA 71411 t) (318) 476-2116
Our Lady of the Holy Rosary - 131 Pardee Rd., Campti, LA 71411; Mailing: 119 Tally St., Campti, LA 71411 t) (318) 476-2116

CHENEYVILLE

St. Joseph - 301 Stanley, Cheneyville, LA 71325-0446; Mailing: P. O. Box 446, Cheneyville, LA 71325-0446 t) 318-279-2394 frddejesus@diocesealex.org Rev. Dwight De Jesus (Philippines), Pst.; Dcn. L.G. Deloach;

CLOUTIERVILLE

St. John the Baptist - 423 Hwy. 495, Cloutierville, LA 71416-0040; Mailing: P.O. Box 40, Cloutierville, LA 71416-0040 t) 318-379-2231 stjohnthebaptist_catholicchurch@yahoo.com Rev. Christian Iheanyichukwu Ogbonna (Nigeria), Pst.; Jannie LaCour, DRE; CRP Stds.: 2
Holy Rosary - 2262 Emmanuel Rd., Emmanuel, LA 71416; Mailing: PO Box 40, Cloutierville, LA 71416 t) (318) 379-2231
Holy Family - 17398 Hwy. 1, Monet Ferry, LA 71446 t) (318) 379-2231

COLFAX

St. Joseph - 139 Second St., Colfax, LA 71417-0243; Mailing: P.O.Box 243, Colfax, LA 71417 t) 318-627-3952 frjbrocato@diocesealex.org Rev. John K. Brocato, Admin.; Dcn. Emile Barre III; Rachel Bruce, DRE; CRP Stds.: 16
St. Patrick - 624 Rowena St., Montgomery, LA 71454 t) (318) 627-3952

COTTONPORT

St. Mary Assumption - 820 Front St., Cottonport, LA 71327-1123; Mailing: P.O. Box 1123, Cottonport, LA 71327-1123 t) 318-876-3681 stmary@diocesealex.org www.stmaryscottonport.com Dcn. Doug Moreau; Rev. John Wiltse, Pst.; CRP Stds.: 130
St. Mary Assumption School - (Grades PreK-8) 850 Front St., Cottonport, LA 71327-1123 t) 318-876-3651 principal@stmaryscottonport.com smsangels.org/ Blaine Dauzat, Prin.; Stds.: 234; Lay

Tchrs.: 13

DEVILLE

Sts. Francis and Anne Catholic Church - 143 Booner Miller Rd., Deville, LA 71328; Mailing: P O Box 3147, Pineville, LA 71361-3147 t) 318-767-2078 kmh50@bellsouth.net Rev. Binochan Pallipparambil (India), Pst.; Dcn. Gregory LeBlanc; R. J. Mitchel, DRE; CRP Stds.: 74

St. John the Baptist - 1024 Hwy. 1207, Deville, LA 71328; Mailing: PO Box 7, Deville, LA 71328 t) 318-466-5587 sheripaulstjohn@gmail.com Rev. Albi Mulloth (India), Pst.; Sheri Paul, DRE; CRP Stds.: 68

St. Winifred - 2644 Hwy. 107, Effie, LA 71328 t) (318) 466-5587

St. John the Baptist - 334 Community Center Rd., Moncla, LA 71328 t) (318) 466-5587

DUPONT

Immaculate Conception - 5765 Hwy. 107 S., Dupont, LA 71329-0385; Mailing: P. O. Box 385, Dupont, LA 71329-0385 t) 318-922-3243 frjdesimone@diocesealex.org Rev. Joseph C. Desimone, Admin.; Cynthia Dixon, DRE; CRP Stds.: 19

ECHO

St. Francis de Sales - 104 Echo St., Echo, LA 71330; Mailing: P.O. Box 37, Echo, LA 71330-0037 t) 318-563-4530 stfrancisdesalescatholicchurch@outlook.com Rev. Dwight De Jesus (Philippines), Pst.; Dcn. L.G. Deloach; CRP Stds.: 60

EVERGREEN

Little Flower - 2912 Main St., Evergreen, LA 71333-0020; Mailing: PO Box 20, Evergreen, LA 71333 t) 318-346-2840 litflowr@bellsouth.net Rev. Shouraiah Ramji (India), Pst.;

St. Charles - Hwy. 361, Goudeau, LA 71333 t) (318) 346-2840

FERRIDAY

St. Patrick - 601 Florida Ave., Ferriday, LA 71334; Mailing: P O Box 369, Ferriday, LA 71334 t) 318-757-3834 stpatrickchurch@bellsouth.net Rev. John Pardue, Pst.; Mary Wilson, DRE;

St. Gerard - 303 Willow St., Jonesville, LA 71343; Mailing: P.O. Box 863, Jonesville, LA 71343 t) 318-339-6143

GLENMORA

St. Louis - 826 8th St., Glenmora, LA 71433; Mailing: P.O. Box 636, Glenmora, LA 71433 t) 318-748-8324 stlouisglenmora@yahoo.com Rev. Kenneth Obiekwe (Nigeria), Pst.; Ellen Jennings, DRE; CRP Stds.: 6

St. Peter - 6684 Hwy. 112, Elmer, LA 71424 t) (318) 748-8324

St. Jude - 78 Price Rd., Sieper, LA 71472 t) (318) 748-8324

HESSMER

St. Alphonsus - 3645 Main St., Hessmer, LA 71341; Mailing: P.O. Box 66, Hessmer, LA 71341-0066 t) 318-563-4550 fredwinrod@yahoo.com Rev. Edwin Rodriguez-Hernandez, Pst.; Tina Laborde, DRE; CRP Stds.: 107

St. Martin of Tours - 1981 Hwy. 114, Hessmer, LA 71341 t) 318-563-9097 frkzachariah@diocesealex.org Rev. Kurian Zachariah (India), Pst.; Rev. Daniel Corkery (Ireland), In Res.; Dcn. Darrell Dubroc;

JENA

St. Mary - 1571 N. 2nd St., Jena, LA 71342 t) (318) 709-9092 (Leave msg); (318) 992-1019 stsmaryedward@gmail.com Rev. Daniel Hart, Pst.; CRP Stds.: 9

St. Edward - 2711 Hwy. 8, Pollock, LA 71432; Mailing: 1571 N. Second St., Jena, LA 71342

KLEINWOOD

St. Michael - 142 Rexmere Ln., Kleinwood, LA 71320; Mailing: P. O. Box 31, Bordelonville, LA 71320-0031 t) 318-997-2151 saintpeter@centurytel.net Rev. Louis E. Sklar, Pst.; Terri Guillory, DRE;

LECOMPTE

St. Martin - 1815 St. Martin St., Lecompte, LA 71346-0459; Mailing: P.O. Box 459, Lecompte, LA 71346-0459 t) 318-776-9480 stmartin@diocesealex.org Rev. Marc A. Noel (Canada), Pst.; Robyn Carrington, DRE; CRP Stds.: 81

Our Lady of Guadalupe - 10 Butter Cemetery Rd., Forest Hill, LA 71430 t) (318) 776-9480

LEESVILLE

St. Michael - 604 S. Fifth St., Leesville, LA 71446; Mailing: 105 W. South St., Leesville, LA 71446 t) 337-239-2656 stmichaelschurch@bellsouth.net Rev. Kenneth J. Michiels, Pst.; Dcn. Fidel Andrade; Dcn. William Endris; Dcn. Stephen Gramigna; Tara Rindahl, DRE; CRP Stds.: 107

MANSURA

Our Lady of Prompt Succor - 1910 Escude St., Mansura, LA 71350-0067; Mailing: P.O. Box 67, Mansura, LA 71350 t) 318-964-2654 frbdeshautelle@diocesealex.org Rev. Blake Paul Deshautelle, Pst.;

St. Paul the Apostle - 1879 Leglise St., Mansura, LA 71350; Mailing: P. O. Box 130, Mansura, LA 71350-0130 t) 318-597-2231 stpaulmansura@yahoo.com Rev. Blake Paul Deshautelle, Pst.; Amie Smith, DRE; CRP Stds.: 39

MARKSVILLE

St. Genevieve - 4052 Hwy. 452, Marksville, LA 71351-3530 t) 318-253-9237 st.genevievebrou@yahoo.com Rev. Abraham Palakkattuchira, CMI (India), Pst.; Don Brevelle, DRE;

Holy Ghost Catholic Church - 121 S. Preston St., Marksville, LA 71351-3034 t) 318-253-7131 holyghostchur783@bellsouth.net Rev. Abraham Varghese (India), Pst.; Dcn. Ted Moulard; Rose Noel, DRE; CRP Stds.: 28

St. Richard - 265 St. Richards Loop Rd., Marksville, LA 71351; Mailing: 121 S. Preston St., Marksville, LA 71351-3033 t) (318) 253-7131

St. Joseph's - 141 S. Washington St., Marksville, LA 71351-3021 t) 318-253-7561 frdan@stjosephmarksville.com www.stjosephmarksville.com Rev. Daniel O'Connor, Pst.; Dcn. Ken Primeaux; Dcn. Gary Schupbach; Nancy Desselle, DRE; CRP Stds.: 160

Our Lady of Lourdes - 1315 Eggbend Rd., Marksville, LA 71351-4223 t) 318-253-9936 lourdeschurch@bellsouth.net www.ollsjbchurch.org Rev. Kurian Zachariah (India), Pst.; Dcn. Darrell Dubroc; Sondra Andes, DRE; CRP Stds.: 68

MOREAUVILLE

Our Lady of Sorrows - 524 Main St., Moreauville, LA 71355-0247; Mailing: P.O. Box 247, Moreauville, LA 71355 t) 318-985-2968 Rev. Brian Seiler, Pst.; Andre Spruill, DRE;

Sacred Heart - 9986 Bayou Des Glaises St., Moreauville, LA 71355-9702 t) 318-985-2774 shc_moreauville@yahoo.com; shcmoreauville@gmail.com www.shcmoreauville.org/ Rev. Brian Seiler, Pst.; Monique Mayeux, DRE; Andre Spruill, DRE; CRP Stds.: 67

Sacred Heart School - (Grades PreK-8) 9968 Bayou Des Glaises, Moreauville, LA 71355; Mailing: P.O. Box 179, Moreauville, LA 71355 t) 318-985-2772 sacredheart@kricket.net www.shsmoreauville.com Sr. Sandra Norsworthy, O.L.S., Prin.; Michelle Daigrepont, Librn.; Stds.: 342; Pr. Tchrs.: 1; Sr. Tchrs.: 3; Lay Tchrs.: 23

NATCHEZ

St. Augustine's - 2262 Hwy. 484, Natchez, LA 71456-3622 t) 318-379-2521 staugustine1803@gmail.com staugustinecaneriver.com Rev. Charles Ray, Pst.; Dcn. Harlan Mark Guidry; Deloris Jones, DRE; CRP Stds.: 38

St. Anne - 3659 Old River Rd., Natchitoches, LA 71457; Mailing: 2262 Hwy. 484, Natchez, LA 71456 t) (318) 379-2521 staugustinechrch@hughes.net

NATCHITOCHES

St. Anthony of Padua - 911 Fifth St., Natchitoches, LA 71457; Mailing: P.O. Box 432, Natchitoches, LA 71458-0432 t) 318-352-2559 stanthysec@hotmail.com stanthonyofpaduanatchitoches.com Rev. John O'Brien (Canada), Pst.; Dcn. Steven Newbury; Rev. Wade DeCoste (Canada), In Res.; Rev. Peter Kuligowski (Poland), In Res.; Rev. Thomas Elmus Paul, In Res.; CRP Stds.: 114

Holy Cross - 129 Second St., Natchitoches, LA 71457 t) 318-352-2615 holycross129@gmail.com www.nsucatholic.org Rev. Jose Pallipurath (India), Pst.; Janice Ebert, DRE; CRP Stds.: 4

Immaculate Conception - 145 Church St., Natchitoches, LA 71457 t) 318-352-3422 office@minorbasilica.org minorbasilica.org Rev. Irion St. Romain, Pst.; Rev. Derek Ducote, Par. Vicar; Dcn. John Whitehead; Kathleen Hicks, DRE; CRP Stds.: 47

St. Mary's Catholic School - (Grades PreK-12) 1101 E. Fifth St., Natchitoches, LA 71458-2070 t) 318-352-8394 jlachica@smstigers.org smstigers.org Jason Lachica, Prin.; Krista Sklar, Librn.; Stds.: 326; Lay Tchrs.: 36

PINEVILLE

Sacred Heart - 600 Lakeview, Pineville, LA 71360-7519 t) 318-445-2497; 318-445-2496 (CRP) rgraham@jesusinpineville.com www.jesusinpineville.com Rev. Hershal Dale Meade, Pst.; Dcn. Lee Moreau; Melanie Dubre Delahoussaye, DRE; CRP Stds.: 167

PLAUCHEVILLE

Mater Dolorosa - 3458 Hwy. 107 S., Plaucheville, LA 71362-0009; Mailing: P.O. Box 9, Plaucheville, LA 71362-0009 t) 318-922-3131 materdolorosa@parish.diocesealex.org www.materdolorosaplaucheville.com Rev. Martin L. Laird, Pst.; Angela Dixon, DRE; CRP Stds.: 31

St. Joseph Elementary School - (Grades PreK-8) 3406 Hwy. 107 S., Plaucheville, LA 71362; Mailing: P.O. Box 59, Plaucheville, LA 71362-0059 t) 318-922-3401 adesoto@sjsplaucheville.org; balbritton@sjsplaucheville.org www.sjsplaucheville.org Billy Albritton, Prin.; Stds.: 212; Pr. Tchrs.: 1; Sr. Tchrs.: 4; Lay Tchrs.: 10

St. Joseph High School - (Grades 9-12) 3406 Hwy. 107 S., Plaucheville, LA 71362-0059; Mailing: P.O. Box 59, Plaucheville, LA 71362-0059 t) 318-922-3401 adesoto@sjsplaucheville.org; balbritton@sjsplaucheville.org www.sjsplaucheville.org Billy Albritton, Prin.; Stds.: 79; Lay Tchrs.: 6; Pr. Tchrs.: 1

POWHATAN

St. Francis of Assisi - 179 LA Hwy. 485, Powhatan, LA 71457; Mailing: P.O. Box 964, Natchitoches, LA 71457 t) 318-352-8819 frtpaul@diocesealex.org Rev. Thomas Elmus Paul, Admin.; Ashley Berry, DRE;

St. Anne - 4310 Hwy. 485, Robeline, LA 71457 t) (318) 352-8819

SIMMESPORT

Christ the King - 705 Main St., Simmesport, LA 71369; Mailing: P.O. Box 186, Simmesport, LA 71369-0186 t) 318-941-2381 christtheking186@gmail.com Rev. Paul Kunnumpuram, M.S.F.S. (India), Pst.; CRP Stds.: 14

ST. JOSEPH

St. Joseph - 919 Plank Rd., St. Joseph, LA 71366; Mailing: P.O. Box 198, St. Joseph, LA 71366-0198 t) 318-766-3565 stjosephinstjoe@gmail.com Rev. Taylor Reynolds, Pst.; Michael Vizard, DRE; CRP Stds.: 29

St. Francis of Assisi - 142 Main St, Waterproof, LA 71375; Mailing: PO Box 198, St. Joseph, LA 71366-0198 t) (317) 766-3565 frtreynolds@diocesealex.org

TALLULAH

St. Edward - 204 Hwy. 80 E., Tallulah, LA 71282-1308; Mailing: P.O. Box 1308, Tallulah, LA 71284-1308 t) 318-574-1677 saintedwardtallulah.church Rev. Ryan P. Humphries, Pst.;

VIDALIA

Our Lady of Lourdes - 503 Texas St., Vidalia, LA 71373; Mailing: P.O. Box 460, Vidalia, LA 71373-0460 t) 318-336-5450 ollourdesv@yahoo.com Rev. Joseph Xavier Vethamanickam (India), Pst.; Maria Bordelon, Music Min.; Phyllis Parker, DRE; Brigid Martin, CRE;

WINNFIELD

Our Lady of Lourdes - 772 Country Club Rd., Winnfield, LA 71483-1412; Mailing: P.O. Box 1412,

Winnfield, LA 71483-1412 t) 318-628-2561 Rev. Wade DeCoste (Canada), Pst.; Laurie Derr, DRE;

St. William - 4580 Main St., Olla, LA 71465; Mailing: P.O. Box 1232, Olla, LA 71465 t) (318) 435-5658 saintmaryscc@bellsouth.net Rev. Jason E. Gootee, Pst.;

WINNSBORO

St. Mary - 1712 West St., Winnsboro, LA 71295-3240; Mailing: P.O. Box 58, Winnsboro, LA 71295 t) 318-435-5658 saintmaryscc@bellsouth.net Rev. Jason E. Gootee, Pst.; Cindy Futch, DRE; Katie Hillestad, DRE; CRP Stds.: 36

St. John - 7900 Hwy. 165, Columbia, LA 71295 t) (318) 435-5658

WOODWORTH

Congregation of Mary, Mother of Jesus Roman Catholic Church, Woodworth, Louisiana - 9323 Hwy. 165 S., Woodworth, LA 71485; Mailing: P.O. Box 408, Woodworth, LA 71485 t) 318-487-9894 mmjwoodworth@suddenlinkmail.com www.mmjchurch.org Brinda Edwards, DRE; Rev. Paul M. LaPalme, Pst.; CRP Stds.: 56

SCHOOLS: PRESCHOOL THRU HIGH SCHOOL

HIGH SCHOOLS

STATE OF LOUISIANA

ALEXANDRIA

Holy Savior Menard Central - (DIO) (Grades 7-12) 4603 Coliseum Blvd., Alexandria, LA 71303 t) 318-445-8233 dskelly@holysaviormenard.com www.holysaviormenard.com Junior & High School. Chris Gatlin, Prin.; Monica De Lacerda, Librn.; Stds.: 373; Lay Tchrs.: 34

INSTITUTIONS LOCATED IN DIOCESE

CAMPUS MINISTRY / NEWMAN CENTERS [CAM]

ALEXANDRIA

Louisiana State University at Alexandria - 8100 Hwy. 71-S, Alexandria, LA 71302-9633 t) 318-473-6494 abordelon@diocesealex.org Amelia Bordelon, Campus Min.;

NATCHITOCHES

Northwestern State University - 120 Second St., Natchitoches, LA 71457; Mailing: 129 Second St., Natchitoches, LA 71457 t) 318-352-2615 holycross129@gmail.com www.nsucatholic.org Rev. Jose Pallipurath (India), Pst.;

CATHOLIC CHARITIES [CCH]

ALEXANDRIA

Catholic Charities and Special Ministries - 4400 Coliseum Blvd., Alexandria, LA 71303; Mailing: P.O. Box 7417, Alexandria, LA 71306 t) 318-445-6424 x533 (Dir., Opers); (318) 445-6424 x500 (Exec. Dir.) frjbrocato@cccenla.org; jgilchrist@cccenla.org www.cccenla.org Rev. John K. Brocato, Exec. Dir.; Jennifer Gilchrist, Dir., Opers.; Heidi Wampler, Mgr. Fin. & Devel.; Asstd. Annu.: 240; Staff: 3

CEMETERIES [CEM]

ALEXANDRIA

Lecompte Cemetery - 4400 Coliseum Boulevard, Alexandria, LA 71303; Mailing: P.O. Box 7417, Alexandria, LA 71306-0417 t) 318-445-2401 x215 dbrook@diocesealex.org David Brook, Contact;

PINEVILLE

Maryhill Cemetery for Clergy - 600 Maryhill Rd., Pineville, LA 71360 t) 318-445-2401 x202 frcpartain@diocesealex.org Rev. Chad A. Partain, Chancellor;

CONVENTS, MONASTERIES, AND RESIDENCES FOR WOMEN [CON]

ALEXANDRIA

Sisters of Our Lady of Sorrows - 440 Browns Bend Rd., Alexandria, LA 71303 t) 318-787-5513 stjoe97@aol.com Sr. Linda Norsworthy, O.L.S., Supr.; Srs.: 3

Sisters of the Holy Family - 3000 Elliott St., Alexandria, LA 71301 t) 318-483-9480 eholmes@cabrinischool.com sistersoftheholyfamily.com Sr. Gloria Lewis, S.S.F., Supr.; Srs.: 3

MOREAUVILLE

Sisters of Our Lady of Sorrows - 9968 Bayou Des Glaises, Moreauville, LA 71355 t) 318-985-2994 www.ols.org/ Sr. Sandra Kay Norsworthy, OLS, Supr.; Srs.: 3

ENDOWMENTS / FOUNDATIONS / TRUSTS [EFT]

ALEXANDRIA

Catholic Charitable Endowment of Alexandria - 4400 Coliseum Blvd., Alexandria, LA 71303; Mailing: P.O. Box 7417, Alexandria, LA 71306-0417 t) 318-445-2401 x215 dbrook@diocesealex.org; ncoody@diocesealex.org David Brook, Secy.;

The Catholic Foundation of North-Central Louisiana, Inc. - 4400 Coliseum Blvd., Alexandria, LA 71303; Mailing: P.O. Box 12833, Alexandria, LA 71315 t) 318-487-9222 cfnclouisiana@gmail.com Joseph L. Hebert, Dir.;

HOSPITALS / HEALTH SERVICES [HOS]

ALEXANDRIA

Christus Health Central Louisiana (Christus St. Frances Cabrini Hospital) - 3330 Masonic Dr., Alexandria, LA 71301 t) (318) 528-6701 kim.kelsch@christushealth.org www.cabrini.org Monte Wilson, CEO; Patrick Braquet, Vice. Pres.; Rev. Joy Retnazihamoni Antony (India), Chap.; Dcn. William Aldridge, Chap.; Dcn. Jason Lavergne, Chap.; Dcn. Richard Mitchell, Chap.; Bed Capacity: 291; Asstd. Annu.: 255,349; Staff: 1,576

Christus St. Frances Cabrini Hospital Foundation of Alexandria, Inc. - 3330 Masonic Dr., Alexandria, LA 71301 t) 318-448-6580 www.christuscabrinifoundation.org Ashley Walker, Dir.;

MISCELLANEOUS [MIS]

ALEXANDRIA

Manna House - 2655 Lee St., Alexandria, LA 71303; Mailing: P.O. Box 6011, Alexandria, LA 71307 t) 318-445-9053 cenlamannahouse@gmail.com www.givetomannahouse.com Chris Soprano, Chair; Jessica Viator, Exec. Dir.;

Tekakwitha Conference National Center - 2225 N. Bolton Ave., Alexandria, LA 71303-4408; Mailing: P. O. Box 121, Forest Hill, LA 71430 t) 318-483-3908 info@tekconf.org www.tekconf.org Scotty S Durio, Bus. Mgr.;

JONESVILLE

Magnificat - Central Louisiana Chapter of the Diocese of Alexandria - 4569 Parhams Rd., Jonesville, LA 71343; Mailing: P.O. Box 37, Hessmer, LA 71341 c) (318) 359-7735 marykwilson51@gmail.com Mary Wilson, Central Service Team;

MONASTERIES AND RESIDENCES FOR PRIESTS AND BROTHERS [MON]

PLAUCHEVILLE

Brothers of the Holy Eucharist - 168 St. Paul St., Plaucheville, LA 71362; Mailing: P.O. Box 25, Plaucheville, LA 71362 t) 318-922-3630 dmetoyer@diocesealex.org Bro. Augustine Brian Kozdroj, F.S.E., Supr.; Brs.: 2

NURSING / REHABILITATION / CONVALESCENCE / ELDERLY CARE [NUR]

ALEXANDRIA

Our Lady's Manor, Inc. - 402 Monroe St., Alexandria, LA 71301 t) (318) 473-2063 ourladysmanor@olpschurch.org HUD subsidized apartment complex for independent living for elderly Cindy Burr, Admin.; Asstd. Annu.: 104; Staff: 5

RETREAT HOUSES / RENEWAL CENTERS [RTR]

PINEVILLE

Maryhill Renewal Center - 600 Maryhill Rd., Pineville, LA 71360 t) 318-640-1378 dbrook@diocesealex.org; ncoody@diocesealex.org www.diocesealex.org David Brook, Contact;

SPECIAL CARE FACILITIES [SPF]

ALEXANDRIA

Our Lady of Sorrows Community Homes (Congregation of the Sisters of Our Lady of Sorrows of the U.S.A., Inc.) - 347 Browns Bend Rd., Alexandria, LA 71303 t) 318-487-8897 ols.homes.office@gmail.com Karen J. Coor, Admin.; Bed Capacity: 20; Asstd. Annu.: 20; Staff: 24

BOYCE

St. Mary's Residential Training School, Inc. - 6715 Hwy. 1 N., Boyce, LA 71409; Mailing: P.O. Drawer 7768, Alexandria, LA 71306 t) 318-445-6443 x2102 christi.guillot@stmarys-rts.org; info@stmarys-rts.org www.stmarysalexandria.org Christi Guillot, Admin.; Bed Capacity: 202; Asstd. Annu.: 202; Staff: 350

Diocese of Allentown

(Dioecesis Alanopolitana)

MOST REVEREND ALFRED A. SCHLERT, D.D., J.C.L.

Bishop of Allentown; ordained September 19, 1987; appointed Bishop of Allentown June 27, 2017; ordained and installed August 31, 2017. Office: 4029 W. Tilghman St., Allentown, PA 18104.

Chancery Office: 4029 W. Tilghman St., Allentown, PA 18104. Mailing Address: P.O. Box F, Allentown, PA 18105-1538. T: 610-437-0755; F: 610-433-7822.

ESTABLISHED JANUARY 28, 1961.

Square Miles 2,773.

Comprises the Counties of Berks, Carbon, Lehigh, Northampton and Schuylkill in the Commonwealth of Pennsylvania.

Legal Title: The Diocese of Allentown, each parish in the diocese, and each regional Catholic elementary school are organized as separate Unincorporated Religious Associations under Pennsylvania law, each with one or more supporting Pennsylvania Charitable Trusts. The formal name of each of those Charitable Trusts generally coincides with the name of the Diocese of Allentown, applicable parish, or applicable regional Catholic elementary school, respectively, and does include the phrase "Charitable Trust" and, for the purposes of this listing, it is understood that the phrase is part of each trust's name.

For legal titles of parishes and diocesan institutions, consult the Chancery Office.

STATISTICAL OVERVIEW

Personnel	
Bishop	1
Retired Bishops	1
Priests: Diocesan Active in Diocese	82
Priests: Diocesan Active Outside Diocese	2
Priests: Retired, Sick or Absent	52
Number of Diocesan Priests	136
Religious Priests in Diocese	37
Total Priests in your Diocese	173
Extern Priests in Diocese	2
Ordinations:	
Diocesan Priests	1
Transitional Deacons	1
Permanent Deacons in Diocese	166
Total Brothers	8
Total Sisters	227
Parishes	
Parishes	80
With Resident Pastor:	
Resident Diocesan Priests	65
Resident Religious Priests	4
Without Resident Pastor:	
Administered by Priests	11

Professional Ministry Personnel:	
Sisters	5
Welfare	
Catholic Hospitals	2
Total Assisted	291,345
Homes for the Aged	12
Total Assisted	686
Specialized Homes	4
Total Assisted	150
Special Centers for Social Services	5
Total Assisted	51,546
Educational	
Diocesan Students in Other Seminaries	15
Total Seminarians	15
Colleges and Universities	2
Total Students	7,216
High Schools, Diocesan and Parish	7
Total Students	2,471
Elementary Schools, Diocesan and Parish	29
Total Students	6,631
Non-residential Schools for the Disabled	3
Total Students	116

Catechesis/Religious Education:	
High School Students	61
Elementary Students	6,414
Total Students under Catholic Instruction	22,924
Teachers in Diocese:	
Sisters	10
Lay Teachers	710
Vital Statistics	
Receptions into the Church:	
Infant Baptism Totals	1,421
Adult Baptism Totals	70
First Communions	1,596
Confirmations	1,751
Marriages:	
Catholic	61
Interfaith	316
Total Marriages	377
Deaths	2,797
Total Catholic Population	215,601
Total Population	1,301,308

LEADERSHIP

Vicar General - t) 610-437-0755 Rev. Msgr. David L. James;

Chancellor - t) 610-332-0442 Rev. Eugene P. Ritz;

Assistant in the Diocesan Curia - t) 610-437-0755 Rev. Keith A. Mathur;

The A.D. Times - t) 610-871-5200 Jill M. Caravan, Editor;

Director of Communications - t) 610-871-5200 Matthew Kirby, Dir.;

Office of Rite of Christian Initiation of Adults (RCIA) - t) 610-437-0755 kmathur@allentowndiocese.org Rev. Keith A. Mathur;

Council of Priests/Diocesan Consultors - t) 610-437-0755

Appointed Members - Rev. Andrew N. Gehringer; Rev. Christopher M. Zelonis; Rev. Msgr. Joseph A. DeSantis;

College of Consultors - Rev. Msgr. David L. James; Rev. Msgr. Joseph A. DeSantis; Rev. Andrew N. Gehringer;

Elected Members - Rev. Robert T. Finlan; Rev. Brendon M. Laroche; Rev. Msgr. James J. Reichert;

Ex Officio Members - Rev. Msgr. David L. James; Very Rev. Adam C. Sedar; Rev. Eugene P. Ritz;

Vicar for Clergy - Very Rev. Adam C. Sedar;

Finance Council - t) 610-437-0755 Most Rev. Alfred A. Schlert; Rev. Msgr. David L. James; Dennis Domchek;

Censor of Books - Rev. Msgr. Michael J. Chaback;

Diocesan Tribunal - t) 610-434-3200 Rev. Msgr. Victor F. Finelli, Vicar;

Advocates - Rev. Msgr. Robert J. Biszek; Rev. Msgr. John J. Grabish; Rev. Msgr. David L. James;

Defenders of the Bond - Rev. Msgr. David L. James; Rev. David J. Kozak;

Judges - Rev. Msgr. David J. Morrison, Judge Emeritus; Rev. Msgr. Thomas P. Koons; Rev. Eugene P. Ritz;

Notaries - Patricia Dewain;

Promoter of Justice - Rev. Eugene P. Ritz;

Vicar for Religious - t) 610-434-3200 Rev. Msgr. Thomas P. Koons (tkoons@allentowndiocese.org);

Vicars Forane - Rev. Msgr. John G. Chizmar, Carbon Deanery; Very Rev. Thomas P. Bortz, Berks Deanery; Rev. Msgr. Daniel J. Yenushosky, Lehigh Deanery;

Secretariat for Clergy - t) 610-437-0755 Very Rev. Adam C. Sedar, Vicar (asedar@allentowndiocese.org);

Holy Family Villa for Priests - t) 610-694-0395 Rev. E. Michael Camilli, M.S.C., Spiritual Dir.; Christina Shupe, Admin.;

Office for Permanent Diaconate Formation - t) 610-332-0442 diaconate@allentowndiocese.org Rev. Eugene P. Ritz, Dir.;

Office of Vocations - t) 610-437-0755 Rev. Mark R. Searles, Dir.;

Priest Personnel Office - Very Rev. Adam C. Sedar, Dir.; Christina Shupe, Dir.;

Secretariat for Evangelization, Education and Formation - Philip J. Fromuth, Supt. (pfromuth@allentowndiocese.org);

Assistant Superintendent of Curriculum, Professional Development and Government Programs - t) 610-866-0581 Emily J. Kleintop, Asst. Supt.;

Bishop's Delegate to Hispanic Community - t) 610-289-8900 Ana Hidalgo;

Catholic Youth Organization - t) 610-289-8900 Daniel Jones, Coord.;

Deputy Superintendent, Secondary Education and Special Education (VACANT) - t) 610-866-0581

Director of School Marketing and Enrollment - t) 610-866-0581 Sarah Kerins;

Ecumenical and Interreligious Dialogue - t) 610-838-7045 Rev. John A. Krivak;

Executive Director of the Office of Evangelization and Formation - t) 610-289-8900 Magdalene Riggins;

Office of Young Adult and College Campus Ministry - Robert Johnson, Dir.;

Office of Adult Catechesis and Evangelization and Formation - Kristin Osenbach, Dir.;

Program Manager for Scholarships - t) 610-866-0581 Amy Impellizerri;

Secretariat for Administration - t) 610-871-5200 x2205 Kim Viti Fiorentino, Secy. (kfiorentino@allentowndiocese.org);

Accounting Services - Sean Werner, CFO; Jeffrey K. Buck, Controller;

Catholic Mutual Group - t) 610-871-5211 Karen Messics;

Cemeteries - Rev. Msgr. William F. Baver, Dir.;

Diocesan Cemetery Perpetual Care Trust - t) 610-866-2372 Brian Palma, Supt.;

Forward with Christ Allocations Committee - Rev. Msgr. William F. Baver; Paul Domalakes; Francis Hartnett;

Information Technology - Michael Doolittle, Exec. Dir.;

Human Resources - Michael Doolittle, Exec. Dir.; Jill Weaver, Dir.;

Human Resources Coordinator - Amy Bober;

Benefits and Payroll Manager (VACANT) -

Parish and School Support Services - Leslie Shirock;

Properties, Facilities, and Real Estate - David Wong, Mgr.;

Stewardship and Development - Paul Acampora, Exec. Dir.;

Secretariat for Catholic Health and Human Services and Youth Protection - t) 610-871-5200 x2204 prusso@allentowndiocese.org Pamela J. Russo, Secy.;

Catholic Charities of the Diocese of Allentown - t) 610-435-1541 Robert Nicolella, Exec.;

Charter Compliance Officer - Pamela J. Russo;

Diocesan Medical Ethicist - t) 610-838-7045 Rev. John A. Krivak;

Victim Assistance Coordinator - t) 800-791-9209 Wendy S. Krisak;

Holy Family Grace Mansion Personal Care - www.holyfamilysl.org Nora Alba, Admin.;

Holy Family Manor - t) 610-865-5595 Joseph Shadid, Admin.;

Holy Family Senior Living - Joseph Shadid, CEO; Randall Wadsworth, Dir.;

Ministry with Persons with Disabilities - t) 610-870-5200 Pamela J. Russo;

ORGANIZATIONS

American Catholic Overseas Aid Fund - t) 610-437-0755

Catholic Daughters of the Americas - Dcn. Kevin C. Wasielewski, Diocese Committee Chap.;

Ashland - Court St. Joan of Arc #225 -

Easton - Court Easton #358 (Vacant) -

Frackville - Court St. James #1029 - Rev. Robert T. Finlan, Chap.;

Jim Thorpe - Court Ryan #911 - Rev. James J. Ward, Chap.;

Shenandoah - Court Annunciation #175 - Rev. Msgr. Ronald C. Bocian, Chap.;

Catholic Men of Good News (CMOGN) - t) 610-433-6102 Rev. Richard C. Brensinger;

Charismatic Renewal - Rev. George R. Winne;

Courage/Encourage - t) 610-683-8467 Dcn. Christopher May, Asst. Dir. (courage@allentowndiocese.org); Rev. Bernard J. Ezaki, Dir.;

Cursillo Movement - t) 610-867-8409 Rev. Martin F. Kern, Dir.;

Equestrian Order of the Holy Sepulchre of Jerusalem - t) 610-866-5582 Rev. Msgr. William F. Baver, Coord.;

Expectation of the Blessed Mother (Chapter #405) - John Tucker, Pres.;

Father Walter Ciszek Prayer League, Inc. (The) - t) 570-462-2270 Rev. Msgr. Ronald C. Bocian, Pres. (fwccenter@ciszek.org);

Holy Name Societies - Rev. Paul L. Rothermel;

Lay Fraternities of St. Dominic -

Legatus - Ray Bishop, Pres. (rbishop@bishopphoto.com); Rev. Christopher S. Butera, Chap.;

Legion of Mary - t) 610-301-5139 Joe Akkara, Pres.;

Operation Rice Bowl - t) 610-433-7413 Rev. Msgr. John P. Murphy, Dir.; Edward L. Liszka, Administrative Asst.;

Our Lady's Missionaries of the Eucharist - olme@olme.org www.olme.org Dcn. Don Libera, Contact;

St. Louis deMontfort Chapter 406 - Sandra Tucker, Pres.;

St. Thomas More Society - allentownstms@gmail.com www.stmsallentown.org Matthew J. Kloiber, Pres.; Rev. Msgr. Edward J. Coyle, Chap.;

Secular Franciscan Order - St. Francis Fraternity - t) 610-258-3053 Nancy Snyder, Min. (lmpnurpara@msn.com);

Serra Clubs -

Serra Club of Allentown - t) 610-349-4104 Rev. Msgr. Daniel J. Yenushosky, Chap.; Elizabeth Stehnach, Pres.;

Serra Club of Bethlehem - t) 610-867-5039 Rev. Anthony P. Mongiello, Chap.; Patricia Fielding, Pres.;

Serra Club of Reading - t) 610-779-0772 Paul T. Essig; Rev. Edward J. Essig, Chap.;

Third Order Secular Carmelites - t) 610-372-4010 Eileen Obrochta, Dir.;

PARISHES, MISSIONS, AND CLERGY

COMMONWEALTH OF PENNSYLVANIA

ALLENTOWN

Cathedral of St. Catharine of Siena - 1825 W. Turner St., Allentown, PA 18104 t) 610-433-6461; 610-432-7655 (PREP office) secretary@cathedral-church.org; prep@cathedral-church.org cathedral-church.org Rev. Donald W. Cieniewicz, Pst.; Rev. Stephan A. Isaac, Par. Vicar; Rev. Herman Pongantung, MSC (Indonesia), Par. Vicar; Dcn. Alex Brown; Dcn. Ricardo Ceballos; Dcn. William Hassler; Dcn. Joseph David Zubrovich; Donna Sciacca, DRE; CRP Stds.: 69

St. Francis of Assisi - 1046 W. Cedar St., Allentown, PA 18102-1304 t) 610-433-6102; 610-435-0364 (CRP) www.stfrancisallentown.org Rev. Richard C. Brensinger, Pst.; Rev. Kevin M. Gualano, In Res.; Dcn. Ricardo Reyes; Dcn. Robert P. Young; CRP Stds.: 55

Immaculate Conception - 501 Ridge Ave., Allentown, PA 18102 t) 610-433-4404 (Declared National Shrine of Our Lady of Guadalupe, Mother of the Americas 1974). Rev. John M. Gibbons, Pst.; Rev. George R. Winne, Assoc. Pst.; Dcn. Richard L. Benkovic; Rev. Harold F. Dagle, Pastor Emer.;

St. John the Baptist - 924 N. Front St., Allentown, PA 18102-1912 t) 610-432-0034 Rev. Speratus Kamanzi, Pst.;

Our Lady Help of Christians - 444 N. Jasper St., Allentown, PA 18109-2666 t) 610-432-9384 Rev. Msgr. William F. Baver, Pst.;

St. Paul - 920 S. Second St., Allentown, PA 18103 t) 610-797-9733 www.stpaulrc.com Rev. Michael E. Mullins, Pst.; Dcn. Jose F. DeCastro; Dcn. Gary Granato; Dcn. Saul Hernandez; Dcn. Cu T. Than; Angelino Rodriguez; Rev. Msgr. Robert J. Biszek, In Res.;

Sacred Heart of Jesus - 336 N. Fourth St., Allentown, PA 18102-3008 t) 610-434-5171 Dcn. Saul Hernandez; Dcn. Ramon Rodriguez; Dcn. Julian Corchado; Dcn. C. Miguel Vargas; Rev. John M. Gibbons, Pst.; Rev. George R. Winne, Assoc. Pst.;

St. Stephen of Hungary - 510 W. Union St., Allentown, PA 18101-2307 t) 610-439-0111 Rev. David Lopez, FSSP, Par. Vicar; Rev. Gregory Pendergraft, F.S.S.P., Pst.;

St. Thomas More - 1040 Flexer Ave., Allentown, PA 18103-5520 t) 610-433-7413 www.stmchurchallentown.org Rev. John S. Pendzick, Pst.; Rev. Jojappa Adagatla, MSC, Par. Vicar; Rev. Brendon M. Laroche, Par. Vicar; Rev. Msgr. John P. Murphy, Pastor Emer.; Dcn. James R. Duncan; Dcn. Christopher C. Kinsella Jr.; Dcn. Thomas F. Shubella; Dcn. James Toolan; Rev. Msgr. Francis P. Schoenauer, In Res.; Kevin Damitz, DRE;

St. Thomas More School - t) 610-432-0396 altlstm@ptd.com www.stmschoolpa.com Amanda Salovay, Prin.;

Convent - 992 Flexer Ave., Allentown, PA 18103-3664 t) 610-437-9520 stmbfs@ptd.net

ASHLAND

St. Charles Borromeo - 1104 Walnut St., Ashland, PA 17921; Mailing: 1115 Walnut St., Ashland, PA 17921-1844 t) 570-875-1521 catholicchurchashland@msn.com Rev. Giuseppe Esposito, Pst.;

St. Vincent de Paul - 260 N. 2nd St., Girardville, PA 17935 (Worship Site)

BALLY

Most Blessed Sacrament - 610 Pine St., Bally, PA 19503-1003; Mailing: Box C, Bally, PA 19503-1003 t) 610-845-2460 cindyr@mbsbally.org www.mbsbally.org Rev. Richard W. James, Admin.; Dcn. Michael J. Boyle;

BANGOR

Our Lady of Good Counsel - 436 S. Second St., Bangor, PA 18013-2514 t) 610-588-5445 www.ourladystvincent.com Rev. Simione Volavola, M.S.C., Pst.; Dcn. Ronald R. Pasquino; Rev. Stephen L. Maco, Pastor Emer.;

St. Vincent de Paul - 720 Delaware Ave., Portland, PA 18351

Our Lady of Mt. Carmel - 560 N. 6th St., Bangor, PA 18013 t) 610-588-2183 www.mtcarmel-roseto.org Rev. Daniel E. Kravatz, Par. Admin.; Rev. Remy Coly, MSC, Assoc. Pst.;

BARNESVILLE

St. Richard - 799 Barnesville Dr., Barnesville, PA 18214-2616 t) 570-467-2315 Rev. Robert T. Finlan, Par. Vicar; Dcn. John A. Setlock; Rev. Joseph T. Whalen, Pastor Emer.; Dcn. Edward J. Girard;

BATH

Sacred Heart of Jesus - 117 Washington St., Bath, PA 18014; Mailing: 210 E. Northampton St., Bath, PA 18014-1625 t) 610-837-7874 www.sacredheartbath.org Rev. Christopher S. Butera, Pst.; Dcn. Lewis T. Ferris; Dcn. Edward J. Saukulak; CRP Stds.: 44

BETHLEHEM

St. Anne - 450 E. Washington Ave., Bethlehem, PA 18017-5944 t) 610-867-5039 www.stannechurchbethlehem.org Rev. Anthony P. Mongiello, Pst.; Rev. Jerome A. Tauber, Chap.; Dcn. Stephen T. Gorbos Jr.; Dcn. Richard G. Scrak Jr.; CRP Stds.: 100

St. Anne School - (Grades PreK-8) 375 Hickory St., Bethlehem, PA 18017-5944 t) 610-868-4182; 610-868-7513 (Preschool) jkrupka@stannebethlehem.org www.stannebethlehem.org James Krupka, Prin.;

Assumption B.V.M. - 4101 Old Bethlehem Pike, Bethlehem, PA 18015-9097 t) 610-867-7424 abvmrect@ptd.net Rev. Msgr. Nevin J. Klinger, Pst.; Dcn. Donald W. Elliott; Dcn. Stewart T. Herman; Rev. Msgr. Robert J. Coll, Pastor Emer.; Dcn. Maurice E. Kelly; Christina Bigatel Durback, DRE; CRP Stds.: 180

Holy Ghost - 417 Carlton Ave., Bethlehem, PA 18015-1535 t) 610-867-9382 x3 www.holyghost-church.org Rev. David J. Kozak, Pst.; CRP Stds.: 6

Holy Infancy - 312 E. Fourth St., Bethlehem, PA 18015-1706 t) 610-866-1121; 610-866-1121 x5 (CRP) holyinfancybethlehem@gmail.com; holyinfancy.mrsgabby@gmail.com www.holyinfancychurch.com Rev. Andrew N. Gehringer, Pst.; Dcn. Isidro Gonzalez-Rivera; Dcn. Arcadio Leon; Dcn. Jose A. Ocampo; Rev. Keith A. Mathur, In Res.; Rev. Mark R. Searles, In Res.; Gabriela Colak, DRE; CRP Stds.: 106

Holy Infancy School - (Grades PreK-8) 551 Thomas St., Bethlehem, PA 18015 t) 610-868-2621 negronj@holyinfancy.k12.pa.us www.holyinfancyschool.org Jeanne Negron-Garcia, Prin.; Stds.: 122; Pr. Tchrs.: 1; Sr. Tchrs.: 1; Lay Tchrs.: 10

Incarnation of Our Lord Parish - Thomas and Buchanan Sts., Bethlehem, PA 18015; Mailing: 617 Pierce St., Bethlehem, PA 18015-3498 t) 610-866-3391 Rev. Andrew N. Gehringer, Pst.; Dcn. Jose A. Ocampo; Lisa Benedek, DRE;

Convent - 520 Buchanan St., Bethlehem, PA 18015-3499 t) 610-866-0275

Notre Dame of Bethlehem - 1861 Catasauqua Rd., Bethlehem, PA 18018-1298 t) 610-866-4371 notredamesec@gmail.com ndbethlehemchurch.org Rev. Msgr. Thomas D. Baddick, Pst.; Rev. Venatius T. Karobo, A.J., Chap.; Dcn. Richard T. Sewald Jr.; Dcn. William F. Urbine; Rev. Bernard J. Ezaki, In Res.;

Notre Dame of Bethlehem School - (Grades PreK-8) 1835 Catasauqua Rd., Bethlehem, PA 18018-1211 t) 610-866-2231 altlndb@ptd.net www.ndbethlehemschool.org Donna Hopper, Prin.;

Our Lady of Perpetual Help - 3219 Santee Rd., Bethlehem, PA 18020 t) 610-867-8409 Rev. Martin F. Kern, Pst.; Rev. Msgr. Edward R. Sacks, Pastor Emer.; Dcn. Leonard J. Mackesy; Dcn. Donald J. Dupont; Dcn. George C. Kelly Jr.; Dcn. Ralph K. Sullivan; Carol Salabsky, DRE;

Our Lady of Perpetual Help School - (Grades K-8) 3221 Santee Rd., Bethlehem, PA 18020 t) 610-868-6570 www.olphbeth.org Danielle Frio, Prin.;

Sacred Heart of Jesus - 1817 First St., Bethlehem, PA 18020 t) 610-865-5042 sacredheartrectory1936@gmail.com Rev. Frans J. Berkhout, Admin.; Dcn. Hugh Carlin; Dcn. Joseph B. Juhasz;

SS. Simon and Jude - 730 W. Broad St., Bethlehem, PA 18018 t) 610-866-5582 Rev. Msgr. William F. Baver, Pst.; Dcn. Reuben H. Hartzell Jr.; Dcn. Jeffrey R. Trexler;

BOYERTOWN

St. Columbkill - 200 Indian Spring Rd., Boyertown, PA 19512-2008 t) 610-367-2371 stcolumbkill.com Rev. Richard H. Clement, Pst.; Dcn. James A. Kochu; Dcn. Joseph L. Paschall Jr.; Dcn. Joseph Petrauskas;

CATASAUQUA

Annunciation B.V.M.-St. Mary's - 122 Union St., Catasauqua, PA 18032-1923 t) 610-264-0332 annunciationbvm.net Rev. Eric N. Tolentino, Admin.; Sharon Hontz, DRE; CRP Stds.: 20

St. John Fisher - 1229 3rd St., Catasauqua, PA 18032-2716 t) 610-264-1972 slchurch@rcn.com Rev. Eric J. Gruber, Admin.; Dcn. John C. O'Connell;

COOPERSBURG

St. Joseph - 5050 St. Joseph's Rd., Coopersburg, PA 18036-8920 t) 610-965-2877 stjoescoopersburg.org Rev. Thomas R. Buckley, Pst.; Dcn. Conrad Paulus; CRP Stds.: 111

COPLAY

St. Peter - 4 S. Fifth St., Coplay, PA 18037 t) 610-262-2417; 610-261-0144 (CRP) www.stpeterchurchcoplay.com Rev. Msgr. David L. James, Pst.; Dcn. Thomas B. Reimer;

DOUGLASSVILLE

Immaculate Conception - 905 Chestnut St., Douglassville, PA 19518-9006 t) 610-582-2411 www.icbvm.org Rev. Msgr. John B. McCann, Pst.; Dcn. James A. Bardi; Dcn. Paul J. Hiryak Jr.; Rev. Harold F. Dagle, In Res.;

Immaculate Conception Academy - (Grades K-8) 903 Chestnut St., Douglassville, PA 19518 t) 610-404-8645 lisa.forkin@icaknights.org www.icaberks.org Lisa Forkin, Prin.;

EASTON

St. Anthony of Padua - 9th and Lehigh Sts., Easton, PA 18042; Mailing: 900 Washington St., Easton, PA 18042 t) 610-253-7188 Rev. Keith R. Laskowski, Pst.; Dcn. Kenneth L. Weiland; Dcn. Jose M. Santos-Gonzalez;

St. Jane Frances de Chantal - 4049 Hartley Ave., Easton, PA 18045 t) 610-253-3553 info@stjanesofeastonpa.com www.stjanesofeastonpa.com Rev. Msgr. Stephen J. Radocha, Pst.; Rev. Guency Isaac, Par. Vicar; Rev. Jaya Kumar Francis, MSC, Par. Vicar; Dcn. Ranulfo Raymundo; Dcn. Robert W. Rodgers; Dcn. Gene G. Schroth Jr.; Dcn. Stephen J. Synoracki; Dcn. Kevin C. Wasielewski; Kelly DeRaymond, DRE; Kevin Kimmel, DRE; CRP Stds.: 295

St. Jane Frances de Chantal School - (Grades PreK-8) 1900 Washington Blvd., Easton, PA 18042-4619 t) 610-253-8442 principal@stjaneschool.com Marybeth Okula, Prin.;

Our Lady of Mercy Parish - 132 S. Fifth St., Easton, PA 18042 t) 610-252-7381 info@olomercy.com www.olomercy.com Rev. Keith R. Laskowski, Pst.; Rev. Elias Munyaneza, A.J., In Res.; Kelly DeRaymond, DRE; Dcn. Jose M. Santos-Gonzalez; Dcn. Kenneth L. Weiland; CRP Stds.: 69

EMMAUS

St. Ann - 415 S. Sixth St., Emmaus, PA 18049-3703 t) 610-965-2426 Rev. Msgr. Edward J. Coyle, Pst.; Rev. Abraham Ha, Pst. Assoc.; Dcn. Dominick F. Amedeo Jr.; Dcn. Richard A. Fenton; Rev. Msgr. Thomas E. Hoban, Pastor Emer.;

St. Ann School - (Grades PreK-8) 435 S. Sixth St., Emmaus, PA 18049-3703 t) 610-965-9220 dkile@stann-emmaus.org Diana Kile, Prin.;

FOUNTAIN HILL

St. Ursula - 1300 Broadway, Fountain Hill, PA 18015 t) 610-867-5122 Rev. David J. Kozak, Pst.; Dcn. David K. Rohner; Anne Korves, DRE; CRP Stds.: 28

FRACKVILLE

St. Joseph the Worker Parish - 49 N. Line St., Frackville, PA 17931; Mailing: 7 S. Broad Mtn. Ave., Frackville, PA 17931 t) 570-874-0610 frackvillerc3@verizon.net www.stjoesfrackville.com Rev. Giuseppe Esposito, Pst.;

HAMBURG

St. Mary - 94 Walnut Rd., Hamburg, PA 19526; Mailing: P.O. Box 189, Reading, PA 19526-0189 t) 610-562-7657 stmaryhamburg@aol.com www.stmaryhamburg.org Rev. David J. Loeper, Pst.; Dcn. Thomas B. Drogalis; Dcn. Henry G. Gordon;

HELLERTOWN

St. Theresa of the Child Jesus - 1408 Easton Rd., Hellertown, PA 18055-1127 t) 610-838-7045 sttheresacj@gmail.com www.sttheresaotcj.org Rev. John A. Krivak, Pst.; Dcn. Gerald R. Schmidt; Arokia Anita Vincent, DRE;

JIM THORPE

Immaculate Conception - 178 W. Broadway, Jim Thorpe, PA 18229; Mailing: 180 W. Broadway, Jim Thorpe, PA 18229 t) 570-325-2791 www.iccjimthorpe.org Rev. Ronald J. Minner, Pst.; Dcn. John J. Mroz; Rev. James J. Ward, Pastor Emer.; CRP Stds.: 70

KUTZTOWN

St. Mary - 14833 Kutztown Rd., Kutztown, PA 19530 t) 610-683-7443; 610-683-7466 parish@stmaryskutztown.com www.stmaryskutztown.com Rev. John C Maria, Pst.; Sr. Patrice Cosgrove, Pst. Assoc.; CRP Stds.: 91

LAKE HARMONY

St. Peter the Fisherman - 33 Trinity Cir., Lake Harmony, PA 18624-0237; Mailing: P.O. Box 237, Lake Harmony, PA 18624 t) 570-722-2034 Rev. Msgr. John G. Chizmar, Pst.; Denise Wettstein, DRE;

LEHIGHTON

SS. Peter and Paul - 260 N. Third St., Lehighton, PA 18235-1595 t) 610-377-3690 Rev. Christopher M. Zelonis, Pst.; Dcn. Joseph C. Wilhelm Jr., DRE;

MAHANOY CITY

St. Teresa of Calcutta Parish - 600 W. Mahanoy Ave., Mahanoy City, PA 17948; Mailing: 614 W. Mahanoy Ave., Mahanoy City, PA 17948 t) 570-773-2771 Rev. Kevin P. Gallagher, Pst.; Dcn. David J. Henninger; Lynn Minalda, DRE;

BTOC Education Center - 29 S. Catawissa St., Mahanoy City, PA 17948 t) 570-773-2668

MARTINS CREEK

St. Rocco - 6658 School St., Martins Creek, PA 18063-0010; Mailing: PO Box 421, Martins Creek, PA 18063-0010 t) 610-258-9059 strocco.org Rev. Joseph J. Kweder, Pst.; Rev. Msgr. James J. Reichert, Pastor Emer.; Dcn. Charles V. Palmeri;

MCADOO

All Saints Parish - 35 N. Cleveland St., McAdoo, PA 18237-1842 t) 570-929-1073 churchofallsaints@ptd.net google.com Rev. Msgr. William T. Baker, Pst.; Dcn. James M. Warnagiris; Grace Smith, DRE;

Our Lady of Lourdes - 318 Plane St., Weatherly, PA 18255 (Worship Site)

MINERSVILLE

Holy Family Parish - 538 Sunbury St., Minersville, PA 17954-1016 t) 570-544-4741 holyfamilyparishminersville@gmail.com www.minersvillecatholic.com Rev. Jason F. Stokes, Pst.; Dcn. James P. Henninger;

St. Vincent De Paul Center - 400 Church St., Minersville, PA 17954 t) 570-544-6484

Convent - 531 Sunbury St., Minersville, PA 17954-1016 t) 570-544-2016 ssjmin@comcast.net

MOHNTON

St. Benedict's - 2020 Chestnut Hill Rd., Mohnton, PA 19540 t) 610-856-1006 Rev. Msgr. Edward R. Domin, Pst.;

NAZARETH

Holy Family - 410 W. Center St., Nazareth, PA 18064-1300; Mailing: 23 Forest Dr., Nazareth, PA 18064 t) 610-759-0870 hfp23@rcn.com; elyd@holyfamily-edu.org www.holyfamilynazarethpa.com Rev. Jonas Tandayu, MSC, Pst.; Rev. Robert Alex Sander Anthony, MSC, Par. Vicar; Dcn. Richard Haddon; Dcn. Michael J. Toolan; Donna Ely, DRE; Dcn. Thomas J. Ely; CRP Stds.: 288

Holy Family School - (Grades PreK-8) 17 N. Convent Ave., Nazareth, PA 18064-1324 t) 610-759-5642 lauricatena@holyfamilynazareth.com holyfamilynazareth.com Derek Peiffer, Prin.; Stds.: 184; Lay Tchrs.: 16

NEW PHILADELPHIA

Holy Cross Parish - 99 Valley St., New Philadelphia, PA 17959-1243 t) 570-277-6800 hcchurch99@gmail.com Rev. Msgr. William F. Glosser, Pst.; CRP Stds.: 55

NORTHAMPTON

Assumption of the Blessed Virgin Mary - 22nd and Washington Ave., Northampton, PA 18067-1257; Mailing: 2174 Lincoln Ave., Northampton, PA 18067 t) 610-262-2559 bvm-northampton.com/ Rev. Msgr. Thomas P. Koons, Pst.; CRP Stds.: 56

Queenship of Mary Parish - 1308 Newport Ave., Northampton, PA 18067; Mailing: 1324 Newport Ave., Northampton, PA 18067-1442 t) 610-262-2227 info@queenshipmary.com queenshipofmary.weconnect.com Rev. Patrick H. Lamb, Pst.; Rev. Msgr. John S. Campbell, Pastor Emer.; Dcn. Michael W. Doncsecz;

OREFIELD

St. Joseph the Worker - 1879 Applewood Dr., Orefield, PA 18069-9507 t) 610-395-2876 www.stjw.org Rev. Msgr. Victor F. Finelli, Pst.; Rev. Francis Iroot, A.J., Par. Vicar; Dcn. Anthony L. Brasten; Dcn. Sherwood C. Readinger; Dcn. Bruno Schettini; Rev. Msgr. Joseph P.T. Smith, In Res.;

St. Joseph the Worker School - (Grades K-8) 1858 Applewood Dr., Orefield, PA 18069-9535 t) 610-395-7221 sjwadmin@ptd.net www.stjosephtheworkerschool.org Joseph Henrich, Prin.;

PALMERTON

Sacred Heart - 243 Lafayette Ave., Palmerton, PA 18071-1511 t) 610-826-2335 www.shcpalmerton.org Rev. Joseph S. Ganser, Par. Admin.; CRP Stds.: 30

PEN ARGYL

St. Elizabeth of Hungary - Babbitt and Heller Aves., Pen Argyl, PA 18072; Mailing: 300 W. Babbitt Ave., Pen Argyl, PA 18072-0126 t) 610-863-4777 Rev. Msgr. Vincent P. York, Pst.; Dcn. Francis A. Elchert;

Convent - 111-115 Lobb Ave., Pen Argyl, PA 18072 t) 610-881-4038

POTTSVILLE

St. John the Baptist - 913 Mahantongo St., Pottsville, PA 17901-3024 t) 570-622-5470 Rev. Kevin J. Bobbin, Pst.; Dcn. Lawrence J. Lonergan; CRP Stds.: 42

St. Patrick - Fourth and Mahantongo Sts., Pottsville, PA 17901-3012; Mailing: 319 Mahantongo St., Pottsville, PA 17901-3012 t) 570-622-1802 www.stpatrickpottsville.org Rev. Philip F. Rodgers, Pst.; Rev. Barnabas Shayo, A.J., Par. Vicar; Dcn. Lawrence J. Lonergan; Dcn. John E. Quirk; Kristine Barron, DRE; Lisa Arant, Bus. Mgr.;

READING

St. Catharine of Siena - 2427 Perkiomen Ave., Reading, PA 19606 t) 610-779-4005 Rev. Brian M. Miller, Pst.; Dcn. Craig A. Fry; Dcn. Gregory G. Schneider; Dcn. John J. Stapleton; Rev. Matthew J. Kuna, Par. Vicar;

Convent - 2328 Perkiomen Ave., Reading, PA 19606 t) 610-779-5583

St. Catharine of Siena School - (Grades PreK-8) 2330 Perkiomen Ave., Reading, PA 19606-2048 t) 610-779-5810 altbscs@ptd.net Marcella Kraycik, Prin.;

St. Mary Church - 250 S. 12th St., Reading, PA 19602 (Worship Site)

Holy Guardian Angels - 3121 Kutztown Rd., Reading, PA 19605-2659 t) 610-921-2729 www.hgaparish.com Rev. Allen J. Hoffa, Pst.; Rev. George Ababio (Ghana); Rev. E. Michael Camilli, M.S.C., Assoc. Pst.; Dcn. John B. Gallagher; Andrew Angstadt, DRE;

Holy Rosary - 237 Franklin St., Reading, PA 19602; Mailing: P.O. Box 6726, Reading, PA 19610 t) 610-373-5579 Rev. Msgr. Joseph A. DeSantis, Pst.; Rev. Samuel Yeboah (Ghana); Dcn. Christopher May;

Convent - t) 610-375-9072 srdivinezeal@hotmail.com Sr. Marietta Castellano, F.D.Z., Supr.;

St. Joseph - 1022 N. Eighth St., Reading, PA 19604; Mailing: 1018 N. Eighth St., Reading, PA 19604-2210 t) 610-376-2976 Rev. Msgr. John J. Grabish, Pst.; Rev. Quyet A. Pham, Assoc. Pst.; Dcn. Francisco De La Gracia Colon;

St. Margaret - 925 Centre Ave., Reading, PA 19601-2105 t) 610-376-2919 Rev. Angel L. Garcia-Almodovar, Pst.; Dcn. Ramon L. Rolon; Dcn. Gregory G. Schneider; Dcn. Bruce S. C. Swist; Juan Pedroza, DRE;

St. Margaret School - 235 Spring St., Reading, PA 19601-2121 t) 610-375-1882 stmargaretoffice@comcast.net www.smsreading.com Jeremy Kopp, Prin.;

Convent - 233 Spring St., Reading, PA 19601-2121 t) 610-372-1302 stmgrtconvent@holmail.com

St. Paul - 151 N. 9th St., Reading, PA 19601 t) 610-372-1531 Rev. Msgr. John J. Grabish, Pst.; Rev. Quyet A. Pham, Assoc. Pst.; Dcn. Francisco Najera-Ramirez; CRP Stds.: 213

St. Peter the Apostle - 322 S. Fifth St., Reading, PA 19602-2311 t) 610-372-9652 Rev. Msgr. Thomas J. Orsulak, Pst.; Rev. Juan Edwardo Rodriguez, Assoc. Pst.; Dcn. Howard J. Schultz; Dcn. Mariano Torres; Sr. Margaret Pavluchuk, I.H.M., DRE;

St. Peter the Apostle School - 225 S. Fifth St., Reading, PA 19602-1816 t) 610-374-2447 altbsp@ptd.com stpeterschoolreading.org Sr. Anna Musi, I.H.M., Prin.;

Convent - 218 S. Fifth St., Reading, PA 19602-1841 t) 610-373-6185 speter7@aol.com Sr. Joanne Ralph, I.H.M., Supr.;

SS. Cyril and Methodius - 449 S. 6th St., Reading, PA 19602 (Worship Site)

RINGTOWN

St. Mary - 82 N. Center St., Ringtown, PA 17967-9731; Mailing: 84 N. Center St., Ringtown, PA 17967-9731 t) 570-889-3850 smsjparishes@gmail.com www.stmarystjoseph.net Rev. Dominic Thao Pham, Pst.; CRP Stds.: 5

ROBESONIA

St. Francis de Sales - 320 N. Church St., Robesonia, PA 19551 t) 610-693-5851 www.stfrancisroby.org Very Rev. Thomas P. Bortz, Pst.; Rev. Philip James Maas, Assoc. Pst.; Dcn. Thomas J. Devaney; Dcn. Frederick J. Lanciano Jr.; Dcn. Edward L. Sanders; Alison Snyder, DRE; Rev. Zachary R. Wehr, Assoc. Pst.; CRP Stds.: 73

SAINT CLAIR

St. Clare of Assisi Parish - Mill and Hancock Sts., Saint Clair, PA 17970; Mailing: 250 E. Hancock St., Saint Clair, PA 17970 t) 570-429-0370 scassisi@ptd.net; stclareassisi250@gmail.com stclareassisi.weebly.com/ Rev. Msgr. William F. Glosser, Pst.; Dorothy Frie, DRE; CRP Stds.: 90

SCHUYLKILL HAVEN

St. Ambrose - 201 Randel St., Schuylkill Haven, PA 17972-1495 t) 570-385-1031 stambroseoffice@comcast.net stambrosehaven.com Rev. Msgr. Edward S. Zemanik, Pst.;

SHENANDOAH

Divine Mercy - 224 W. Cherry St., Shenandoah, PA 17976; Mailing: 108 W. Cherry St., Shenandoah, PA 17976-2207 t) 570-462-1968 x6 dmparish.com Rev. Msgr. Ronald C. Bocian, Pst.;

St. Casimir Church - 229 N. Jardin St., Shenandoah, PA 17976 (Worship Site)

SHEPPTON

St. Joseph - 14 E. Oak St., Sheppton, PA 18248; Mailing: 84 N. Center St., Ringtown, PA 17967-9731 t) 570-889-3850 smsjparishes@gmail.com www.stmarystjoseph.net Rev. Dominic Thao Pham, Pst.; CRP Stds.: 5

SHILLINGTON

St. John Baptist de la Salle - 42 Kerrick Rd., Shillington, PA 19607; Mailing: 420 Holland St., Shillington, PA 19607 t) 610-777-1697 st.jbdls@verizon.net www.stjohnsfamilyoffaith.com Rev. Edward J. Essig, Pst.; Bernadette H. Yohn, DRE; Dcn. Felix J. Lombardo;

SLATINGTON

Assumption B.V.M. - 649 W. Washington St., Slatington, PA 18080-1618; Mailing: 633 W. Washington St., Slatington, PA 18080-1618 t) 610-767-2214 abvm@ptd.net Rev. Eric A. Arnout, Admin.; Dcn. Fredric Bloom; Monica E. Prudente, DRE;

SUMMIT HILL

St. Joseph - 462 W. Ludlow St., Summit Hill, PA 18250-1108; Mailing: 118 N. Market St., Summit Hill, PA 18250-1108 t) 570-645-2664 lisassjpv@gmail.com; fatherbobsjpv@gmail.com www.stjscatholicchurch.org Rev. Robert J. George, Pst.; Dcn. Joseph T. Cannon; CRP Stds.: 67

Diocesan Shrine of St. Therese of Lisieux - 1 E. Garibaldi Ave., Nesquehoning, PA 18240 www.shrineofsainttherese.com

TAMAQUA

St. John XXIII - 307 Pine St., Tamaqua, PA 18252 t) 570-225-7410 secretary@sj23tamaqua.org www.sj23tamaqua.org Rev. Robert T. Finlan, Pst.;

SS. Peter & Paul - (Worship Site)

TREMONT

Most Blessed Trinity Parish - 113 Cherry St., Tremont, PA 17981 t) 570-695-3648 mostblessedtrinity.us Rev. George J. Kochuparambil, Pst.; CRP Stds.: 30

WALNUTPORT

St. Nicholas - 4412 Mountain View Dr., Walnutport, PA 18088-9728; Mailing: 1152 Oak Rd., Walnutport, PA 18088-9728 t) 610-767-3107 Very Rev. Adam C. Sedar, Pst.; Dcn. Michael W. Kudla;

WEST LAWN

St. Ignatius Loyola - 2600 St. Albans Dr., West Lawn, PA 19609; Mailing: 2810 St. Albans Dr., Sinking Spring, PA 19608-1028 t) 610-678-3767 www.stignatiusreading.org/ Very Rev. Thomas P. Bortz, Pst.; Rev. Philip James Maas, Assoc. Pst.; Rev. Zachary R. Wehr, Assoc. Pst.; Rev. Msgr. James A. Treston, Pastor Emer.; Dcn. Thomas J. Devaney; Dcn. Frederick J. Lanciano Jr.; Dcn. Edward L. Sanders;

St. Ignatius Loyola School - (Grades PreK-8) 2700 St.

Albans Dr., Reading, PA 19609 t) 610-678-0111 www.stignatiusvikings.org Carolyn Reed Wood, Prin.;

Convent - 2601 St. Alban's Dr., West Lawn, PA 19609 t) 610-750-5445

WEST READING

Sacred Heart - 740 Cherry St., West Reading, PA 19610-0217; Mailing: P.O. Box 6217, Reading, PA 19610-0217 t) 610-372-4010 secretary@shrcparish.org www.shrcparish.org Rev. Msgr. Joseph A. DeSantis, Pst.; Rev. Samuel Yeboah (Ghana), Par. Vicar; Dcn. William R. Kase; Dcn. Christopher May;

Sacred Heart School - (Grades PreK-8) 701 Franklin St., West Reading, PA 19611-1029 t) 610-373-3316 altbsh@ptd.net www.sacredheartreading.com Joan McNeil, Prin.;

WHITEHALL

St. Elizabeth of Hungary - 618 Fullerton Ave., Whitehall, PA 18052-6726 t) 610-266-0695; 610-266-0626 www.sercc.org Rev. Stanley M. Moczydlowski, Pst.; Dcn. Michael T. Meder; Rev. Robert J. Potts, In Res.; CRP Stds.: 93

Holy Trinity - 4456 Main St., Whitehall, PA 18052-2415; Mailing: 4102 S. Church St., Whitehall, PA 18052-2415 t) 610-261-0144 (CRP); 610-262-9315 holytrinitywhitehall.weconnect.com Rev. Msgr. Daniel J. Yenushosky, Pst.; Dcn. Arthur L. Chin-Fatt; Dcn. Michael J. Laroche; Dcn. Eugene J. Wyrwa; Linda Johnson, DRE; CRP Stds.: 61

St. John the Baptist - Ruch St. & Park Ave., Whitehall, PA 18052; Mailing: 3024 S. Ruch St., Whitehall, PA 18052 t) 610-261-0144 (CRP); 610-262-2260 Rev. Msgr. Gerald E. Gobitas, Pst.; Rev. Msgr. Albert J. Byrne, Pastor Emer.; Linda Johnson, DRE;

SCHOOLS: PRESCHOOL THRU HIGH SCHOOL

SCHOOLS

COMMONWEALTH OF PENNSYLVANIA

ALLENTOWN

St. John Vianney Regional School - (PAR) (Grades PreK-8) 210 N. 18th St., Allentown, PA 18104 t) 610-435-8981 principal@stjohnvianneyschool.org www.stjohnvianneyschool.org Beth Serrano, Prin.;

Mercy Special Learning Center, Inc. - 830 S. Woodward St., Allentown, PA 18103-3440 t) 610-797-8242 altlmslc@ptd.net mercyschool.org Ages 3 yrs to post 21. Elizabeth L. Grys, Prin.;

BALLY

St. Francis Academy - (DIO) 668 Pine St., Bally, PA 19503 t) 610-845-7364 chowald@mbsbally.org www.sfabally.org Serving Most Blessed Sacrament, Bally, St. Columbkill, Boyertown, and St. Mary, Kutztown. Cheryl Howald, Dir.;

BETHLEHEM

St. Michael the Archangel School - (DIO) (Grades PreK-8) 4121 Old Bethlehem Pike, Bethlehem, PA 18015 t) 610-867-8422 altlsma@ptd.net st-mikes.com Serving Assumption B.V.M., Bethlehem; St. Joseph, Coopersburg (Limeport) Harry Reese, Prin.;

St. Michael the Archangel School - (Grades PreK-8) 5040 St. Joseph's Rd., Coopersburg, PA 18036 t) 610-965-4441 www.st-mikes.com

Middle School - (Grades PreK-8) 4121 Old Bethlehem Pike, Bethlehem, PA 18015 t) (610) 867-8422 www.st-mikes.com

NORTHAMPTON

Good Shepherd Catholic School - (DIO) (Grades PreK-8) 1300 Newport Ave., Northampton, PA 18067 t) 610-262-9171 altngs@ptd.net www.gscatholic.com Serving Queenship of Mary, Assumption B.V.M., Northampton; St. John Fisher, Catasauqua; St. Peter, Coplay; St. John the Baptist & Holy Trinity. Susan Parker, Prin.;

PALMERTON

St. John Neumann Regional School - (DIO) (Grades K-8) 259 Lafayette Ave., Palmerton, PA 18071 t) 610-826-2354; 610-767-2935 altcsjn@ptd.net www.sjnrschool.org Serving St. Nicholas, Berlinsville; Sacred Heart, Palmerton; Assumption B.V.M., Slatington. Dr. Christopher Heery, Prin.;

PEN ARGYL

Immaculate Conception School - (DIO) (Grades K-6) 290 W. Babbitt Ave., Pen Argyl, PA 18072 t) 610-863-4816 altnics@ptd.net www.immaculateconceptionschool.net Regional school, Serving St. Elizabeth, Pen Argyl; St. Rocco, Martins Creek. Sr. Maria Luz, O.P., Prin.;

POTTSVILLE

Assumption BVM School - (DIO) (Grades K-8) 112 S. Seventh St., Pottsville, PA 17901-3079 t) 570-622-0106; 570-622-1765 altsabvm@ptd.net www.assumptionbvmschool.net Serving St. Patrick, St. John the Baptist, Pottsville, St. Matthew the Evangelist, St. Michael the Archangel, Minersville & Most Blessed Trinity. Teresa Keating, Prin.;

St. Joseph Center for Special Learning, Inc. - (PAR) 2075 W. Norwegian St., Pottsville, PA 17901-1907 t) 570-622-4638 altssjc@ptd.net www.stjosephctr.com Special learning program for students 4-21. Also offers an adult habilitation program. Robert Giba, Prin.;

READING

Holy Guardian Angels Regional School, Reading - (DIO) (Grades PreK-8) 3125 Kutztown Rd., Reading, PA 19605-2659 t) 610-929-4124 altbhga@ptd.net www.hgaschool.org Serving Holy Guardian Angels and St. Joseph, Reading. Kelly Prechtl, Prin.;

St. Ignatius Loyola School - (DIO) (Grades PreK-8) 2700 St. Albans Dr., Reading, PA 19609-1134 t) 610-678-0111 admin@stignatiusvikings.org www.stignatiusvikings.org Regional school, Serving St. Ignatius Loyola, Sinking Spring; St. Francis de Sales, Robesonia. Carolyn Reed Wood, Prin.;

The Aquinas Program St. Margaret School - (PAR) 233 Spring St., Reading, PA 19601-2121 t) 610-375-1882 altbsmg@ptd.net Jeremy Kopp, Prin.;

SHILLINGTON

John Paul II Center for Special Learning, Inc. - 1092 Welsh Rd., Shillington, PA 19607-0097 t) 610-777-0605 madams@johnpauliicenter.org www.johnpauliicenter.org Mary A. Adams, Prin.;

La Salle Academy - (Grades PreK-8) 440 Holland St., Shillington, PA 19607-3260 t) 610-777-7392 mickulik@lsabear.com www.lsabear.com Regional school, Serving St. John Baptist de La Salle, Shillington; St. Benedict, Mohnton; Stephen W Mickulik, Prin.;

TAMAQUA

St. Jerome Regional School - (DIO) 50 Meadow Ave., Tamaqua, PA 18252-4313 t) 570-668-2757 altssj@ptd.net www.sjrschool.com Serving St. John XXIII, Tamaqua, St. Richard, Barnesville, All Saints, McAdoo, St. Joseph, Summit, Hill. Amy Harris-Miskar, Prin.;

WHITEHALL

St. Elizabeth Regional School - (DIO) (Grades PreK-8) 433 Pershing Blvd., Whitehall, PA 18052 t) 610-264-0143 altlse@sercc.org www.sercc.org/school Serving St. Elizabeth, Whitehall; Annunciation, Catasauqua; St. John the Baptist, Immaculate Conception, Allentown, Our Lady Help of Christians. Kimberly Kocher, Prin.; Stds.: 182

HIGH SCHOOLS

COMMONWEALTH OF PENNSYLVANIA

ALLENTOWN

Allentown Central Catholic High School, Inc. - (DIO) 301 N. Fourth St., Allentown, PA 18102-3098 t) 610-437-4601 webmaster@acchs.info www.acchs.info Randy Rice, Prin.; Diane Young, Vice Prin.; Rev. Stephan A. Isaac, Chap.; Sr. Mathilde DeLucy, SCC, Campus Min.;

BATH

Kolbe Academy, Inc. - (DIO) (Grades 9-12) 115 Washington St., Bath, PA 18014 t) 610-419-3333 adangelo@kolbe-academy.com www.kolbe-academy.com Catholic recovery high school Andrew D'Angelo, Prin.; Rev. Christopher Butera, Chap.; Stds.: 5; Lay Tchrs.: 3

BETHLEHEM

Bethlehem Catholic High School, Inc. - (DIO) 2133 Madison Ave., Bethlehem, PA 18017-4699 t) 610-866-0791 altnbchs@ptd.net www.becahi.org Rev. Bernard J. Ezaki, Chap.; Lucas Wilde, Prin.; Thomas Vresics, Dir.;

EASTON

Notre Dame High School, Inc. - (DIO) 3417 Church Rd., Easton, PA 18045-2999 t) 610-868-1431 principal@ndcrusaders.org www.ndcrusaders.org Rev. Daniel E. Kravatz, Chap.; Jaclyn Friel, Prin.; Dena Farrell, Vice Prin.;

The Aquinas Program - Secondary Level Notre Dame High School, Inc. - 3417 Church St., Easton, PA 18045-2999 t) 610-868-1431 principal@ndcrusaders.org Jaclyn Friel, Prin.;

POTTSVILLE

Nativity B.V.M. High School, Inc. - (DIO) One Lawtons Hill, Pottsville, PA 17901-2795 t) 570-622-8110 nativitybvm@nativitybvm.net; lsabol@nativitybvm.net www.nativitybvm.net Lynn Sabol, Prin.; Rev. Kevin J. Bobbin, Chap.;

READING

Berks Catholic High School, Inc. - (DIO) 955 E. Wyomissing Blvd., Reading, PA 19611-1799 t) 610-374-8361 altbbchs@ptd.net William Hess, Prin.; Rev. Matthew J. Kuna, Chap.;

TAMAQUA

Marian High School, Inc. - (DIO) 166 Marian Ave., Tamaqua, PA 18252 t) 570-467-3335 altsmhs@ptd.net www.mariancatholicshs.org Jean M. Susko, Prin.; Rev. Robert J. George, Chap.;

INSTITUTIONS LOCATED IN DIOCESE

ASSOCIATIONS [ASN]

ALLENTOWN

Allentown Catholic Beneficial Association, Inc. - 4400 Walbert Ave., Allentown, PA 18104; Mailing: P.O. Box 1458, Allentown, PA 18105-1458 t) 610-871-5200 www.acbafunds.org Dennis Campbell, Chair;

CENTER VALLEY

Mission Vehicle Association, Inc. - 3300 Station Ave., Center Valley, PA 18034-9563 t) 610-737-5440 emcamilli@aol.com Rev. E. Michael Camilli, M.S.C., Contact;

CAMPUS MINISTRY / NEWMAN CENTERS [CAM]

ALLENTOWN

Muhlenberg College (Allentown) - 2339 Liberty St., Allentown, PA 18104-5586 t) 484-664-3122 blaroche@allentowndiocese.org Rev. John A. Frink, Chap.;

BETHLEHEM

Lehigh University (Bethlehem) - Newman Center at Lehigh University, 417 Carlton Ave., Bethlehem, PA 18015-1583 t) 610-758-4148 rjk5@lehigh.edu Ronald Koach, Campus Min.; Rev. Mark R. Searles, Chap.;

CENTER VALLEY

DeSales University (Center Valley) - 2755 Station Ave., Center Valley, PA 18034-9568 t) 610-282-1100 x1313

HELLERTOWN

Lafayette College (Easton) - 1408 Easton Rd.,

Hellertown, PA 18055-1127 dkravatz@allentowndiocese.org Rev. Daniel E. Kravatz, Chap.;

KUTZTOWN

Kutztown University (Kutztown) - 15207 Kutztown Rd., Kutztown, PA 19530-9218; Mailing: PO Box 632, Kutztown, PA 19530 t) 610-683-8467 catholicchaplain@kutztown.edu www.saintchristopher-ku.org Rev. John C Maria, Chap.;

READING

Alvernia College (Reading) - 400 St. Bernardine St., Reading, PA 19607 t) 610-796-8300 julianne.wallace@alvernia.edu Dr. Julianne Wallace, Campus Min.;

CATHOLIC CHARITIES [CCH]

ALLENTOWN

Catholic Charities, Inc. - 402 W. Chew St., Allentown, PA 18102 t) 610-435-1541 www.catholiccharityad.org Teri Dakuginow, Admin.;

Berks County Branch Office - 234 Grace St., Reading, PA 19611-1946 t) 610-376-7144 rnicolella@allentowndiocese.org

Lehigh-Northampton Counties Branch Office - rnicolella@allentowndiocese.org

Schuylkill-Carbon Counties Branch Office - 13 Westwood Ctr., Pottsville, PA 17901-1800 t) 570-628-0466 rnicolella@allentowndiocese.org

Catholic Charities of the Diocese of Allentown, Inc. - 402 W. Chew St., Allentown, PA 18102 t) 610-435-1541 rnicolella@allentowndiocese.org catholiccharityad.org Robert Nicolella, Dir.; Julie Scheck, Dir.;

CEMETERIES [CEM]

ALLENTOWN

Diocesan Cemetery Perpetual Care Trust - 547 N. Krocks Rd., Allentown, PA 18106-9732; Mailing: P.O. Box F, Allentown, PA 18105-1538 t) 610-395-3819 Rev. Msgr. William F. Baver, Dir.;

BETHLEHEM

Diocesan Cemetery Perpetual Care Trust - 2575 Linden St., Bethlehem, PA 18017-3842; Mailing: P.O. Box F, Allentown, PA 18105-1538 t) 610-866-2372 Rev. Msgr. William F. Baver, Dir.;

COLLEGES & UNIVERSITIES [COL]

CENTER VALLEY

DeSales University - 2755 Station Ave., Center Valley, PA 18034-9568 t) 610-282-1100 admiss@desales.edu www.desales.edu/ Administered by the Oblates of St. Francis de Sales. Rev. James J. Greenfield, O.S.F.S., Pres.; Gerard Joyce, Exec. Vice Pres.; Rev. Kevin M. Nadolski, O.S.F.S., Vice Pres., Mission; Rev. Douglas C. Burns, O.S.F.S., Prof.; Rev. Shaju K. Kanjiramparayil, O.S.F.S., Prof.; Rev. Daniel T. Lannen, O.S.F.S., Chap.; Mark Albert, CIO; Marc Albanese, Vice Pres., Campus Environ.; Cheryl Murphy, Vice Pres., Inst. Advancement; Robert J. Snyder, Vice Pres., Fin. & Admin.; Carolyn Steigleman, Assoc. Vice Pres., Mktg. & Comms.; Michael Sweetana, Dir., Fin. & Treas.; Derrick Wetzel, Assoc. Vice Pres., Enrollment Mgmt.; Linda Zerbe, Vice Pres. Student Life; Stds.: 4,112; Lay Tchrs.: 139; Pr. Tchrs.: 2; Sr. Tchrs.: 1

READING

Alvernia University - 400 St. Bernardine St., Reading, PA 19607 t) (484) 254-2121 president@alvernia.edu www.alvernia.edu Catholic Franciscan University offering undergraduate and graduate education. Bernardine Sisters of the Third Order of St. Francis. John Loyack, Pres.; Dr. Glynis Fitzgerald, SVP and Provost; Dr. John McCloskey Jr., SVP and Chief of Staff; Mary-Alice Ozechoski, SVP; Dr. Darryl Mace, Vice. Pres.; Thomas Minick, Vice. Pres.; Dr. Rodney Ridley, Vice. Pres.; Stds.: 3,104; Lay Tchrs.: 128; Sr. Tchrs.: 1

CONVENTS, MONASTERIES, AND RESIDENCES FOR WOMEN [CON]

BETHLEHEM

St. Joseph Convent - 2133 Madison Ave., Bethlehem, PA 18017-4642 t) 610-865-4691 srjoamssj@yahoo.com

Monocacy Manor - 395 Bridle Path Rd., Bethlehem, PA 18017 t) 610-866-2597 monocacyfranciscans@schoolsistersosf.org www.schoolsistersosf.org School Sisters of the Third Order Regular United States Prov. Sr. Barbara Brown, OSF, Supr.; Sr. Marian Sgriccia, OSF, Prov.; Srs.: 16

COOPERSBURG

Carmelite Monastery - 3551 Lanark Rd., Coopersburg, PA 18036-9324 t) 610-797-3721 carmelitemonasterylehighvalley@gmail.com www.carmelite-nuns.com St. Therese of the Child Jesus and St. Mary Magdalen de Pazzi, St. Therese's Valley. Sr. Mary Veronica, Prioress;

EASTON

Angelic Sisters of St. Paul - 3724 Knollcroft St., Easton, PA 18045-5067 t) 610-258-7792 lilia_asp@yahoo.com Sr. Pasqualina Pascarella, A.S.P., Supr.;

MAHANOY CITY

Missionaries of Charity - 536 W. South St., Mahanoy City, PA 17948-2422 t) 570-773-1420 Missionaries of Charity. Sr. M. Josephine, M.C., Supr.;

PEN ARGYL

Dominican Daughters of the Immaculate Mother - 115 Lobb Ave., Pen Argyl, PA 18072 t) 610-863-9214 Sr. Maria Luz, O.P., Supr.;

READING

The Bernardine Sisters of the Third Order of Saint Francis, Generalate, (aka Bernardine Franciscan Sisters) - 450 St. Bernardine St., Reading, PA 19607-1737 t) 484-334-6976 communications@bfranciscan.org www.bfranciscan.org Sr. John Ann Proach, OSF, Supr.;

Chevalier House - 43 Seminary Ave., Reading, PA 19605 t) 610-929-8348 jdecembrino@mscreading.org www.mscreading.org

St. Clare Convent - 750 Greenway Ter., Reading, PA 19607-1736 t) 484-755-5360 www.bfranciscan.org Bernardine Franciscan Sisters. Sr. Maria Bartos, OSF, Supr.; Srs.: 2

Hannibal House - Spiritual Center - 1526 Hill Rd., Reading, PA 19602-1410 t) 610-375-1738; 610-375-9072 srdivinezeal@hotmail.com

House of Nazareth (Casa Nazaret) - 532 Spruce St., Reading, PA 19602 t) 610-378-1947 casa_nazareth@aol.com Residence of the Poor Sisters of St. Joseph who work in Spanish Apostolate of Berks County. Sr. Marta Munoz, Supr.;

St. Ignatius Loyola Convent - 2601 St. Alban Dr., Reading, PA 19609-1132 t) 610-750-5445

St. Joseph Villa - 464 Bernardine St., Reading, PA 19607 t) 610-777-5556 administrator@saintjosephvilla.com www.saintjosephvilla.com Retirement Home of the Bernardine Sisters of the Third Order of St. Francis. Rev. Ronald P. Bowman, Chap.; Victoria L. Mitchell, Admin.; Sr. Mary Joseph Tirpak, OSF, Supr.;

MSC Province Center - 2811 Moyers Ln., Reading, PA 19605 t) 610-929-5944 usamsc@mscreading.org www.mscreading.org Provincial offices of Missionary Sisters of the Most Sacred Heart of Jesus.

Our Lady of the Sacred Heart Convent - t) 601-929-5944 mscsisters@aol.com

Precious Blood Convent - 1094 Welsh Rd., Reading, PA 19607-9363 t) 610-777-1624 pbcpatreas@comcast.net www.preciousbloodsisters.com Residence for Missionary Sisters of the Precious Blood. Sr. Christa-Mary Jones, C.P.S., Supr.; Sr. Monica Mary Ncube, C.P.S., Prov.;

Sacred Heart Convent - 460 St. Bernardine St., Reading, PA 19607-1737 t) 484-334-7000 localminister@bfranciscan.org www.bfranciscan.org Motherhouse, Residence for Bernardine Sisters of Third Order of St. Francis. Sr. Maria Korick, OSF, Admin.; Srs.: 46

WEATHERLY

Sisters Apostles of the Descent of the Holy Spirit - 484 Pump House Rd., Weatherly, PA 18255 t) 570-427-2467 sisters@peacepentecost.org Sr. Mary Jerome Kim, S.A.H.S., Supr.;

ENDOWMENTS / FOUNDATIONS / TRUSTS [EFT]

ALLENTOWN

Allentown Catholic Capital Campaign Charitable Trust - 1515 Martin Luther King Jr. Dr., Allentown, PA 18102-4500; Mailing: P.O. Box F, Allentown, PA 18102-4500 t) 610-871-5200 Paul Acampora, Contact;

The Allentown Catholic Unitized Investment Fund Charitable Trust - 1515 Martin Luther King Jr. Dr., Allentown, PA 18102-4500; Mailing: P.O. Box F, Allentown, PA 18102-4500 t) 610-871-5200 Most Rev. Alfred A. Schlert, Trustee;

Bishop's Annual Appeal Charitable Trust - 1515 Martin Luther King Jr. Dr., Allentown, PA 18102-4500; Mailing: P.O. Box F, Allentown, PA 18105-1538 t) 610-871-5200 becausewearecatholic.org/ Paul Acampora, Contact;

***Catholic Foundation of Eastern Pennsylvania, Inc.** - 1515 Martin Luther King Jr. Dr., Allentown, PA 18102-4500; Mailing: P.O. Box 1430, Allentown, PA 18105-1430 t) 610-439-7681 www.catholicfoundationep.org Paul E. Huck, Chair;

Clergy Third Age Charitable Trust - 1515 Martin Luther King Jr. Dr., Allentown, PA 18102-4500; Mailing: P.O. Box F, Allentown, PA 18105-1538 t) 610-871-5200 Very Rev. Adam C. Sedar, Contact;

Diocesan Cemetery Perpetual Care Charitable Trust - 1515 Martin Luther King Jr. Dr., Allentown, PA 18102-4500; Mailing: P.O. Box F, Allentown, PA 18105-1538 t) 610-871-5200 Rev. Msgr. William F. Baver, Contact;

Supplemental Health Care Benefits Trust, Lay Employees - 1515 Martin Luther King Jr. Dr., Allentown, PA 18102-4500; Mailing: P.O. Box F, Allentown, PA 18105-1538 t) 610-871-5200 Kim Viti Fiorentino, Contact;

BETHLEHEM

Eastern Pennsylvania Scholarship Foundation Charitable Trust - 1425 Mountain Dr. N., Bethlehem, PA 18015-4722 t) 610-866-0581 Phillip Fromuth, Admin.;

READING

Bernardine Franciscan Sisters Mission and Ministries Charitable Trust - 450 St. Bernardine St., Reading, PA 19607-1737 t) 484-334-6976 robertaann@bfranciscan.org www.bfranciscan.org Sr. John Ann Proach, OSF, Supr.;

HOSPITALS / HEALTH SERVICES [HOS]

ALLENTOWN

Sacred Heart Hospital - 421 Chew St., Allentown, PA 18102-3490 t) 610-776-4500 shh.org Rev. John G. Hilferty, Chap.; Sr. Josanne Huber, M.S.C., Chap.; Frank Ford, Pres.;

READING

Penn State Health Saint Joseph - 2500 Bernville Rd., Reading, PA 19603-0316; Mailing: P.O. Box 316, Reading, PA 19603-0316 t) 610-378-2000 James Bennett, COO; Joseph Frank, Pres.;

MISCELLANEOUS [MIS]

ALLENTOWN

Allentown Catholic Communications, Inc. - 1515 Martin Luther King Jr. Dr., Allentown, PA 18102-4500; Mailing: P.O. Box F, Allentown, PA 18102-1538 t) 610-871-5200 www.ad-today.com/ Paul Wirth, Contact;

Diocese of Allentown Independent Reconciliation and Compensation Tr - 4029 W. Tilghman St., Allentown, PA 18104 t) 610-437-0755 Most Rev. Alfred A. Schlert;

Diocese of Allentown Lay Employees Retirement Plan - 1515 Martin Luther King Jr. Dr., Allentown, PA 18102-4500; Mailing: P.O. Box F, Allentown, PA 18105-1538 t) 610-871-5200 Herman L. Rij, Trustee;

Retirement Plan for the Ordained Diocesan Priests of the Diocese of Allentown - 1515 Martin Luther King Jr. Dr., Allentown, PA 18102-4500; Mailing: P.O. Box F, Allentown, PA 18105-1538 t) 610-871-5200 Rev. Msgr.

John G. Chizmar;

BETHLEHEM

Lay Fraternities of St. Dominic, Expectations of the Blessed Mother Chapter 405 - 1861 Catasququa Rd., Bethlehem, PA 18018-1298; Mailing: 121 Nonemaker Rd., Kutztown, PA 19530 t) 610-285-2288 jptucker2@verizon.net John Tucker, Pres.;

Mary's Shelter, Inc., Cay Galgon Center - 714 W. Broad St., Bethlehem, PA 18018; Mailing: 736 Upland Ave., Reading, PA 19607 t) 610-867-9546 info@caygalgonlifehouse.org Christine Duddy, Dir.;

The Monocacy Farm Project - 395 Bridle Path Rd., Bethlehem, PA 18017 t) 610-867-8494 mfp-info@monocacyfarmproject.org monocacyfarmproject.org Sr. Bonnie Marie Kleinschuster, OSF, Dir.; Eli Stogsdill, Manager;

Stephen's Place, Inc. - 729 Ridge Ave., Bethlehem, PA 18015-3621 t) 610-861-7677 vlongcope@msn.com www.stephens-place.com A nonprofit residential community for adult non-violent offenders with a history of substance abuse. Sr. Virginia Longcope, M.S.C., Dir.;

EASTON

Secular Franciscan Fraternity, Secular Franciscan Order, St. Francis Retreat House, Inc. - 3918 Chipman Rd., Easton, PA 18045-3014 t) 610-252-5230 lmpnurpara@msn.com

NORTHAMPTON

***Apostles of Jesus** - 829 Main St., Northampton, PA 18067-1838 t) 610-502-1732 ajregionalusa@gmail.com www.apostlesofjesusmissionaries.com Rev. Simon Kimaryo, AJ, Chap.; Rev. Bruno Dongo, A.J., Secy.; Rev. Augustine L. Idra, A.J., Supr.; Rev. Odemary Bahati Kisaka, AJ, Secy. to Mission Office; Rev. Richard O'Nymawaro, A.J., Dir., Mission Office;

ORWIGSBURG

Seton Manor, Inc. - 1000 Seton Dr., Orwigsburg, PA 17961; Mailing: 4600 Edmundson Rd., St. Louis, MO 63134 t) 314-733-8000 www.ascension.org Ascension Health is the corporate member Craig Cordola, Exec. Vice Pres. & COO; Thomas VanOsdol, Exec. Vice Pres. & Chief Mission Integration Officer;

POTTSVILLE

Servants to All, Inc. (My Father's House) - 4 S. Centre St., Pottsville, PA 17901; Mailing: P.O. Box 1354, Pottsville, PA 17901-3001 t) 570-728-2917 servantstoall@comcast.net servantstoall.org Faith based program and homeless shelter. Jeanette S Triano, Exec.;

READING

Bernardine Center (Bernardine Franciscans, Delaware County) - 450 St. Bernardine St., Reading, PA 19607-1737 t) 484-334-6976 robertaann@bfranciscan.org www.bfranciscan.org Sr. John Ann Proach, OSF, Supr.;

Bernardine Franciscan Sisters Congregational Leadership Offices - 450 St. Bernardine St., Reading, PA 19607-1737 t) 484-334-6976 robertaann@bfranciscan.org www.bfranciscan.org Sr. John Ann Proach, OSF, Supr.;

***Clare of Assisi House** - 325 S. 12th St., Reading, PA 19602 t) 484-869-5483 pam.mills@clareofassisihouse.com www.clareofassisihouse.org Pamela A Mills, Exec.;

Dayspring Homes, Inc. - 430 Hazel St., Reading, PA 19607; Mailing: P.O. Box 158, Reading, PA 19607 t) 610-376-5648 dayspringhomes@dayspringhomes.org www.dayspringhomes.org Stacy Grube, CEO;

SHILLINGTON

***St. Francis Home** - 144 Hillside Dr., Shillington, PA 19607 t) 610-898-4242 information@stfrancishomereading.org www.stfrancishomereading.org Faith-based care facility for terminally ill. Mary Jo Bonner, Pres.;

MONASTERIES AND RESIDENCES FOR PRIESTS AND BROTHERS [MON]

BETHLEHEM

Holy Family Villa - 1325 Prospect Ave., Bethlehem, PA 18018-4916; Mailing: P.O. Box F, Allentown, PA 18018-1538 t) 610-694-0395 Very Rev. Adam C. Sedar, Vicar; Priests: 16

CENTER VALLEY

Oblates of St. Francis de Sales - Dijon House, 2755 Station Ave., Center Valley, PA 18034-9568 t) 610-282-3300 www.desales.edu Rev. Daniel T. Lannen, O.S.F.S., Supr.; Rev. Shaju K. Kanjiramparayil, O.S.F.S., Prof.; Rev. Douglas C. Burns, O.S.F.S., In Res.; Rev. James J. Greenfield, O.S.F.S., Pres.; Rev. Kevin M. Nadolski, O.S.F.S., Vice. Pres.;

Sacred Heart Villa, Missionaries of the Sacred Heart - 3300 Station Ave., Center Valley, PA 18034-9563 t) 610-282-1415 x35 jimmiller@misacor-usa.org www.misacor-usa.org Rev. Stephen Joseph Boland, MSC, Treas.; Rev. Vincent T. Freeh, M.S.C., Par. Vicar; Rev. Joseph Gleixner, M.S.C.; Rev. Joseph T. Muller, M.S.C.; Rev. Ioane I. Sigarara, M.S.C., Par. Vicar; Rev. Joseph F. Tobias, M.S.C.; Rev. Andrew Torma, M.S.C.; Rev. Leon Weisenberger, M.S.C.; Bro. Jmes Miller, MSC, Supr.; Bro. Francis Hung Nguyen, M.S.C., In Res.; Bro. Warren Perrotto, In Res.; Brs.: 3; Priests: 10

EASTON

St. Francis Friary (Franciscan Province of St. John the Baptist) - 3908 Chipman Rd., Easton, PA 18045-3014 t) 610-515-0867 Bro. Mark Ligett, O.F.M.; Bro. Edward Skutka, O.F.M.; Rev. Henry Beck, O.F.M., Vicar;

NURSING / REHABILITATION / CONVALESCENCE / ELDERLY CARE [NUR]

BETHLEHEM

Holy Family Senior Living - 1200 Spring St., Bethlehem, PA 18018 t) 610-865-5595 www.holyfamilysl.org Joseph Shadid, CEO;

EASTON

Antonian Towers, Inc. - 2405 Hillside Ave., Easton, PA 18042 t) 610-258-2033 xborja@holyfamilysl.org Catholic housing for the elderly. Ximena Borja, Dir.;

ORWIGSBURG

Holy Family Adult Day Care - 900 W. Market St., Orwigsburg, PA 17961 t) 570-366-2924 lherb@allentowndiocese.org Day care for the elderly. Linda Herb, Dir.;

POTTSVILLE

Queen of Peace Apartments of Catholic Housing Corporation of Schuylkill County - 777 Water St., Pottsville, PA 17901 t) 570-628-4504 dhess@holyfamilysl.org Catholic housing for the elderly. Randall Wadsworth, Dir.;

READING

Queen of Angels Apartments of Catholic Housing Corporation of Northern Berks County - 22 Rothermel St., Reading, PA 19605 t) 610-921-3115 mcampbell@holyfamilysl.org Catholic housing for the elderly. Randall Wadsworth, Dir.;

SAINT CLAIR

Holy Family Apartments of Catholic Housing Corporation of New Philadelphia - 25 N. Nichols St., Saint Clair, PA 17970 t) 570-429-0699 rwadsworth@holyfamilysl.org Randall Wadsworth, Dir.;

Neumann Apartments of Catholic Housing Corporation of St. Clair - 25 N. Nichols St., Saint Clair, PA 17970 t) 570-429-0699 dhess@holyfamilysl.org Catholic housing for the elderly. Diane Hess, Bus. Mgr.;

RETREAT HOUSES / RENEWAL CENTERS [RTR]

BARTO

***National Centre for Padre Pio** - 111 Barto Rd., Barto, PA 19504 t) (610) 845-3000 Nick Gibboni, Exec. Dir.;

BETHLEHEM

St. Francis Center for Renewal, Inc. (Monocacy Manor) - 395 Bridle Path Rd., Bethlehem, PA 18017 t) 610-867-8890 sfcr-info@stfrancisctr.org www.stfrancisctr.org Joanne Anderson, Dir.; Sr. M. Marguerite Stewart, O.S.F., Spiritual Dir.;

EASTON

St. Francis Retreat House, Inc. - 3918 Chipman Rd., Easton, PA 18045-3014 t) 610-258-3053 stfranrh@rcn.com www.stfrancisretreathouse.org Rev. Henry Beck, O.F.M., Admin.; Bro. Mark Ligett, O.F.M., Admin.; Sr. Regina Roskosny, O.S.F., Admin.; Rev. Loren Connel, OFM, In Res.; Bro. Scott Obrecht, OFM, In Res.; Bro. Edward Skutka, O.F.M., In Res.;

ORWIGSBURG

Holy Family Adult Day Care of Catholic Senior Housing and Health Care Services, Inc. - 900 W. Market St., Orwigsburg, PA 17961-1008 t) 570-366-2924 lherb@allentowndiocese.org Linda Herb, Dir.;

READING

Mariawald Renewal Center - 1094 Welsh Rd., Reading, PA 19607-9363 t) 610-777-0135 mariawaldcenter@gmail.com www.mariawaldrenewal.com

McGlinn Conference and Spirituality Center - 460 St. Bernardine St., Reading, PA 19607-1737 t) 484-334-6807 mcglinncc@bfranciscan.org Located in the Bernardine Franciscan Motherhouse. Sr. Shaun Kathleen Wilson, O.S.F., Dir.;

SPECIAL CARE FACILITIES [SPF]

BETHLEHEM

Grace Mansion Personal Care Home of Catholic Senior Housing and Health Care Services, Inc. - 1200 Spring St., Bethlehem, PA 18018 t) 610-865-5595 nalba@holyfamilysl.org www.holyfamilysl.org Personal care home for 28 elderly. Nora Alba, Admin.;

Holy Family Apartments of Catholic Housing Corporation of Bethlehem - 330-338 13th Ave., Bethlehem, PA 18018 t) 610-866-4603 rwadsworth@holyfamilysl.org Catholic housing for the elderly. Randall Wadsworth, Dir.;

Holy Family Manor of Catholic Senior Housing and Health Care Services, Inc. - 1200 Spring St., Bethlehem, PA 18018 t) 610-865-5595 jshadid@holyfamilysl.org www.hfmanor.org Skilled and intermediate nursing care facility. Rev. Venatius T. Karobo, A.J., Chap.; Joseph Shadid, CEO;

READING

Mary's Shelter, Inc. - 325 S. 12 St., Reading, PA 19607; Mailing: 736 Upland Ave., Reading, PA 19607 t) 610-603-8010 office@marysshelter.org www.marysshelter.org A residence for pregnant, homeless young women. Christine Folk, Exec.; Danielle Monahan, Exec.;

An asterisk (*) denotes an organization that has established tax-exempt status directly with the IRS and is not covered by the USCCB Group Ruling.

Diocese of Altoona-Johnstown

(Dioecesis Altunensis-Johnstoniensis)

MOST REVEREND MARK L. BARTCHAK, J.C.D.

Bishop of Altoona-Johnstown; ordained May 15, 1981; appointed Bishop of Altoona-Johnstown January 14, 2011; installed April 19, 2011. Pastoral Center: 2713 W. Chestnut Ave., Altoona, PA 16601.

Pastoral Center: 2713 W. Chestnut Ave., Altoona, PA 16601. T: 814-695-5579; F: 814-949-8234.
www.dioceseaj.org
tdegol@dioceseaj.org

ESTABLISHED DIOCESE OF ALTOONA, MAY 27, 1901.

Square Miles 6,674.

Redesignated Diocese of Altoona-Johnstown, October 9, 1957.

Comprises the Counties of Bedford, Blair, Cambria, Centre, Clinton, Fulton, Huntingdon and Somerset in the State of Pennsylvania.

For legal titles of parishes and diocesan institutions, consult the Pastoral Center.

STATISTICAL OVERVIEW

Personnel

Bishop	1
Priests: Diocesan Active in Diocese	42
Priests: Diocesan Active Outside Diocese	2
Priests: Retired, Sick or Absent	39
Number of Diocesan Priests	83
Religious Priests in Diocese	106
Total Priests in your Diocese	189
Ordinations:	
Diocesan Priests	1
Religious Priests	1
Transitional Deacons	1
Permanent Deacons	2
Permanent Deacons in Diocese	42
Total Brothers	21
Total Sisters	58

Parishes

Parishes	87
With Resident Pastor:	
Resident Diocesan Priests	42
Resident Religious Priests	16
Without Resident Pastor:	
Administered by Priests	29
Administered by Deacons	3
Missions	5

Welfare

Homes for the Aged	4
Total Assisted	425
Special Centers for Social Services	2
Total Assisted	7,229

Educational

Diocesan Students in Other Seminaries	5
Total Seminarians	5
Colleges and Universities	2
Total Students	5,424
High Schools, Diocesan and Parish	4
Total Students	940
Elementary Schools, Diocesan and Parish	13
Total Students	2,132
Catechesis/Religious Education:	
High School Students	1,461
Elementary Students	3,214
Total Students under Catholic Instruction	13,176
Teachers in Diocese:	
Priests	5
Brothers	1
Sisters	5
Lay Teachers	322

Vital Statistics

Receptions into the Church:	
Infant Baptism Totals	503
Minor Baptism Totals	32
Adult Baptism Totals	20
Received into Full Communion	43
First Communions	607
Confirmations	631
Marriages:	
Catholic	127
Interfaith	74
Total Marriages	201
Deaths	1,355
Total Catholic Population	68,561
Total Population	628,426

LEADERSHIP

Bishop - t) 814-695-5579 Most Rev. Mark Leonard Bartchak;
Vicar General - t) 814-695-5579 Very Rev. Alan E. Thomas (athomas@dioceseaj.org);
Judicial Vicar - t) 814-695-5579 Very Rev. John D. Byrnes (jbyrnes@dioceseaj.org);
Bishop's Vicar for Religious - t) 814-539-1632 Very Rev. Anthony Francis Spilka, O.F.M. Conv. (aspilka@dioceseaj.org);
Chancellor - t) 814-695-5579 Teresa M. Stayer (tstayer@dioceseaj.org);

OFFICES AND DIRECTORS

Building Commission (VACANT) -
Campus Ministry - t) 814-942-5503 Rev. Msgr. Michael A. Becker, Coord. (mbecker@dioceseaj.org);
Catholic Charities - t) 814-944-9388 Cindy O'Connor, Exec. Dir. (coconnor@dioceseaj.org);
Altoona Office - Cindy O'Connor, Exec. Dir.;
Emergency Homeless Shelter - Martha & Mary House - t) 814-254-4413 Jesse Trentini, Dir.;
Johnstown Office - t) 814-535-6538 Cindy O'Connor, Exec. Dir.;
State College Office - t) 814-944-9388 Cindy O'Connor, Exec. Dir.;
Catholic Relief Services & Foreign Mission Outreach - t) 814-695-5579 Andre McCarville, Dir. (amccarville@dioceseaj.org);
Cemetery Commission (VACANT) -
Children and Youth Protection - t) 814-695-5579 Michele Luciano, Dir. (mluciano@dioceseaj.org);
Commission for Life and Justice - t) 814-695-5579 lifeandjustice@dioceseaj.org Andre McCarville, Dir. (amccarville@dioceseaj.org);
Communications - t) 814-695-5579 Tony DeGol, Dir. (tdegol@dioceseaj.org); Alex Way, Multi-Media Coord. (away@dioceseaj.org); Justin Kirkland, Communications Coord. (jkirkland@dioceseaj.org);
Development - t) 814-695-5579 Heather Foor, Dir. (hfoor@dioceseaj.org); Shannon Warburton, Prog. Coord. (swarburton@dioceseaj.org);
Diocesan Liturgy Committee - t) 814-695-5579 George Pisula, Chair (ggpisula@atlanticbb.net);
Dmitri Manor - Priests' Residence - t) 814-696-4698
Ecumenical Minister - t) 814-942-5503 Rev. Msgr. Michael A. Becker (mbecker@dioceseaj.org);
Education - t) 814-695-5579 Jo-Ann Semko, Dir. (jsemko@dioceseaj.org);
Family Life Office - t) 814-695-5579 Andre McCarville, Dir. (amccarville@dioceseaj.org);
Finance - t) 814-695-5579 Matthew Stever, CFO (mstever@dioceseaj.org); Marsha Troxel, Comptroller (mtroxel@dioceseaj.org);
Fulton County Catholic Mission - t) 717-485-5917 Sr. Martha Burbulla, C.C.W., Dir. (mburbulla@dioceseaj.org);
Human Resources - t) 814-695-5579 Lynette McEvoy, Dir. (lmcevoy@dioceseaj.org);
Inter-Faith Minister - t) 814-535-7646 Very Rev. Mark S. Begly (mbegly@dioceseaj.org);
Liturgy - t) 814-695-5579 Jeanne H. Thompson (jthompson@dioceseaj.org);
Office of the Permanent Diaconate - St. Patrick's School - t) 814-361-2000 Dcn. Michael L. Russo, Dir. (mrusso@dioceseaj.org);
Ongoing Formation of the Clergy - t) 814-695-5579 Very Rev. Alan E. Thomas, Dir. (athomas@dioceseaj.org);
Parish Life Office - t) 814-695-5579 Jeanne H. Thompson, Coord. (jthompson@dioceseaj.org);
Adult Enrichment and Lay Ecclesial Ministry - St. Patrick's School Bldg. - t) 814-361-2000 Dcn. Michael L. Russo, Dir.;
Christian Initiation of Adults and Sacramental Preparation - t) 814-695-5579 Jeanne Thompson, Coord.;
Evangelization and Small Faith Sharing Groups - t) 814-742-7075 Sr. Linda LaMagna, C.C.W., Ministerial Coord.;
Youth Ministry and Religious Education - Francine M. Swope, Coord.;
Pastoral Center - t) 814-695-5579 Teresa M. Stayer, Chancellor (tstayer@dioceseaj.org);
Presbyteral Council - t) 814-443-6574 Very Rev. Angelo J. Patti, Chair (apatti@dioceseaj.org);
Priests' Personnel Board - t) 814-695-5579 Very Rev. Alan E. Thomas, Chair (athomas@dioceseaj.org);
Priests' Retirement Plan - t) 814-695-5579 Matthew Stever, CFO (mstever@dioceseaj.org);
Propagation of the Faith and Holy Childhood - t) 814-695-5579 Andre McCarville, Dir. (amccarville@dioceseaj.org);
St. John the Baptist Retreat Center - t) 814-733-2210 Rev. Mark Pattock, O.F.M.Cap., Dir. (mpattock@dioceseaj.org);
St. Vincent de Paul Society - t) 814-943-1981 Anthony Consiglio, Exec. Dir. (avcdepaul@atlanticbbn.net);
Scouting - t) 570-748-4594 Rev. Joseph T. Orr (jorr@dioceseaj.org);
Technology Services - t) 814-695-5579 David Eger, Dir. (deger@dioceseaj.org);
Technology Services Coordinator - Alison Link;
Technology Services Support Specialist - Mark Fetsko II;
Technology Services Support Technician - Gregory Clapper;
Temporalities - t) 814-695-5579 Matthew Stever, CFO (mstever@dioceseaj.org);
Tribunal - t) 814-695-5579 Very Rev. John D. Byrnes (jbyrnes@dioceseaj.org);
Victims' Advocate and Victim Assistance Coordinator - t) 814-944-9388 Jean Johnstone (jjohnstone@dioceseaj.org);
Vocations - t) 814-695-5579 Rev. Peter D. Crowe, Dir. (pcrowe@dioceseaj.org);

DEANERIES

Altoona Deanery - t) 814-943-8553 Very Rev. Lubomir J. Strecok (lstrecok@dioceseaj.org);
Johnstown Deanery - t) 814-535-7646 Very Rev. Mark S. Begly (mbegly@dioceseaj.org);
Northern Deanery - t) 814-542-4582 Very Rev. Joseph W. Fleming (jfleming@dioceseaj.org);
Prince Gallitzin Deanery - t) 814-736-4279 Very Rev. Thomas F. Stabile, T.O.R. (tstabile@dioceseaj.org);
Southern Deanery - t) 814-443-6574 Very Rev. Angelo J. Patti (apatti@dioceseaj.org);

PARISHES, MISSIONS, AND CLERGY

COMMONWEALTH OF PENNSYLVANIA

ALTOONA

Cathedral of the Blessed Sacrament - One Cathedral Sq., Altoona, PA 16601-3315 t) 814-944-4603 altcathedral@dioceseaj.org www.altoonacathedral.org Rev. Msgr. Stanley B. Carson, Admin.; CRP Stds.: 96
Holy Rosary - 900 N. 4th Ave., Altoona, PA 16601 t) 814-944-6676 holyrosaryaltoona@dioceseaj.org Rev. Nelson Javier, TOR (Philippines), Admin.; Suzanne L. Barry, DRE; CRP Stds.: 16
Immaculate Conception - 1405 Fifth Ave., Altoona, PA 16602 t) 814-942-2416 stmaryaltoona@dioceseaj.org stmaryschurchaltoona.wixsite.com/saintmarys (St. Mary's) Very Rev. Lubomir J. Strecok, Admin.; Debbie Bartley, DRE; CRP Stds.: 35
St. John the Evangelist - 309 Lotz Ave., Altoona, PA 16602 t) 814-942-5503 stjohnevangelistaltoona@dioceseaj.org www.stjohnsaltoona.org Rev. Msgr. Michael A. Becker, Pst.; Sr. Dcn. Gene P. Neral; CRP Stds.: 59
St. Mark - 416 Sixth Ave., Altoona, PA 16602 t) 814-942-0364 stmarkaltoona@dioceseaj.org www.churchofsaintmarks.org Rev. Nelson Javier, TOR (Philippines), Admin.; CRP Stds.: 19
Our Lady of Fatima - 2010 12th Ave., Altoona, PA 16601; Mailing: One Cathedral Square, Altoona, PA 16601 t) 814-942-0371 olof@dioceseaj.org www.ourladyoffatimaaltoona.org Rev. Msgr. Stanley B. Carson, Admin.; CRP Stds.: 7
Our Lady of Lourdes - 2716 Broad Ave., Altoona, PA 16601 t) 814-943-6185 www.ourladyoflourdesaltoona.com Rev. James M. Dugan, Admin.; CRP Stds.: 21
Our Lady of Mt. Carmel - 806 11th St., Altoona, PA 16602 t) 814-942-8501 www.mountcarmelaltoona.com Rev. Frank Scornaienchi, T.O.R., Pst.; Samantha Pope, DRE; Rev. Carl Vacek, T.O.R., Par. Vicar; CRP Stds.: 48
Our Lady of the Assumption - 1527 Adams Ave., Altoona, PA 16602 t) (814) 942-8501 (Our Lady of Mt. Carmel) Rev. Frank A Scornaienchi, TOR, Pst.;
St. Rose of Lima - 5514 Roselawn Ave., Altoona, PA 16602 t) 814-944-8509 strosealtoona@dioceseaj.org www.stroselima.com Rev. Msgr. Michael A. Becker, Pst.; Rev. Carl A. Spishak, In Res.; Dcn. James L. Woomer Sr.; CRP Stds.: 70
Sacred Heart - 511 20th St., Altoona, PA 16602 t) 814-943-8553 sacredheartaltoona@dioceseaj.org www.sacredheartaltoona.org Very Rev. Lubomir J. Strecok, Pst.; CRP Stds.: 46
Formation Center - 2009 Sixth Ave., Altoona, PA 16602 t) 814-944-3922
St. Therese of the Child Jesus - 2301 5th St., Altoona, PA 16601-3863 t) 814-942-4479 Rev. D. Timothy Grimme, Pst.; Dcn. Thomas J. McFee; Mary Beth Schmidhamer, DRE; CRP Stds.: 41

ASHVILLE

St. Thomas Aquinas - 159 Hickory St., Ashville, PA 16613; Mailing: 692 Glendale Valley Blvd., Fallentimber, PA 16639-6505 t) 814-943-5437 rreese@dioceseaj.org Rev. Robert P. Reese, Pst.; Renee Pettenati, DRE; CRP Stds.: 28

BEDFORD

St. Thomas the Apostle - 215 E. Penn St., Bedford, PA 15522-6661 t) 814-623-5526 stthomasbedford@dioceseaj.org www.webparish.com/aj/thomas Rev. Richard B. Tomkosky, Pst.; CRP Stds.: 51

BELLEFONTE

St. John the Evangelist - 134 E. Bishop St., Bellefonte, PA 16823 t) 814-355-3134 www.bellefontecatholicchurch.org Rev. Brian R. Saylor, Pst.; Dcn. Thomas E. Boldin; Mark Leskovansky, DRE; CRP Stds.: 200
St. John the Evangelist School - (Grades PreK-5) 116 E. Bishop St., Bellefonte, PA 16823 t) 814-355-7859 admin@saintjohnsch.net www.saintjohnsch.net Kristina Tice, Prin.; Stds.: 101; Lay Tchrs.: 7

BELLWOOD

St. Joseph - 623 E. Third St., Bellwood, PA 16617 t) 814-742-7075 stjosephbellwood@dioceseaj.org saintjosephbellwood.org Rev. Michael Pleva, Admin.; Sr. Linda LaMagna, C.C.W., DRE; CRP Stds.: 76

BOSWELL

All Saints - 325 Quemahoning St., Boswell, PA 15531 t) 814-629-5551 Rev. Aron M. Maghsoudi, Admin.; Sr. Dcn. Jay A. Pyle; CRP Stds.: 44

CARROLLTOWN

St. Benedict - 100 Main St., Carrolltown, PA 15722; Mailing: P.O. Box 447, Carrolltown, PA 15722 t) 814-344-6548 mgabler@dioceseaj.org; lbridgman@dioceseaj.org www.saintbenedictschurch.com Rev. Michael Gabler, O.S.B., Pst.; CRP Stds.: 150
St. Benedict's School - (Grades PreK-8) 119 S. Church St., Carrolltown, PA 15722; Mailing: P.O. Box 596, Carrolltown, PA 15722 t) 814-344-6512 jmaucieri@benedictpride.org Jeffery F. Maucieri, Prin.; Stds.: 66; Bro. Tchrs.: 1; Lay Tchrs.: 9

CENTRAL CITY
Our Lady Queen of Angels - 738 Sunshine Ave., Central City, PA 15926-1233 t) 814-754-5224 www.ladyqueenofangels.org Rev. Aron M. Maghsoudi, Pst.; CRP Stds.: 29
CHEST SPRINGS
St. Monica - 3037 Colonel Drake Hwy., Chest Springs, PA 16624; Mailing: P.O. Box 231, Chest Springs, PA 16624 t) 814-674-5613 akline@dioceseaj.org Rev. Jerzy Auguscik, O.F.M., Conv., Pst.; CRP Stds.: 65
CLARENCE
Queen of Archangels - 102 Church St., Clarence, PA 16829 t) 814-387-6762 queenofarchclarence@dioceseaj.org Rev. Michael A. Wolfe, Pst.; CRP Stds.: 60
Mission - 204 S. 4th St., Snow Shoe, PA 16874 mwolfe@dioceseaj.org
CLEARVILLE
Seven Dolors B.V.M. - 2174 Beans Cove Rd., Clearville, PA 15535-7901 t) 814-767-9504 mac@sevendolorsbvm.org; sevendolorsbeancove@dioceseaj.org Shelley Cessna, DRE; Rev. Richard B. Tomkosky, Pst.;
COLVER
Holy Family - 562 Fifth St., Colver, PA 15927-9999; Mailing: P.O. Box 543, Colver, PA 15927-9999 t) 814-748-7054 Rev. Christopher Lemme, T.O.R., Pst.; CRP Stds.: 23
CONEMAUGH
Church of the Transfiguration - 220 Oak St., Conemaugh, PA 15909; Mailing: 340 Second St., Conemaugh, PA 15909 t) 814-535-2250 Rev. Robert C. Hall, Pst.; Louise Brezovic, DRE; CRP Stds.: 5
CRESSON
St. Aloysius - 7911 Admiral Peary Hwy., Cresson, PA 16630 t) 814-886-2235 staloysiuscresson@dioceseaj.org www.saintaloysiuscresson.org Rev. Leo F. Arnone, Pst.; Deborah Baker, DRE; CRP Stds.: 45
St. Francis Xavier - 211 Powell Ave., Cresson, PA 16630 t) 814-886-2374 fxparish@dioceseaj.org www.saintfrancisxaviercressonpa.org Rev. Leo F. Arnone, Pst.; CRP Stds.: 28
DAVIDSVILLE
St. Anne - 205 Woodstown Hwy., Davidsville, PA 15928; Mailing: P.O. Box 500, Davidsville, PA 15928 t) 814-479-2664 sannep@atlanticbb.net; stannedavidsville@dioceseaj.org www.stannedavidsvillepa.org Rev. Karl Kolodziejski, O.F.M.Conv., Admin.; CRP Stds.: 32
DUDLEY
Immaculate Conception - 1416 Dudley Rd., Dudley, PA 16634; Mailing: PO Box 188, Dudley, PA 16634 t) 814-635-2919 iccdudley@dioceseaj.org www.iccdudley.com Rev. Mark R. Reid, Admin.; CRP Stds.: 5
DUNCANSVILLE
St. Catherine of Siena - 308 Old Rte. 22, Duncansville, PA 16635; Mailing: P.O. Box 88, Duncansville, PA 16635 t) 814-696-4126 stcatherinesienaduncansville@dioceseaj.org Rev. Msgr. Robert J. Saly, Pst.; CRP Stds.: 39
DYSART
St. Augustine - 803 St. Augustine Rd., Dysart, PA 16636 t) 814-674-8550 lthomas@dioceseaj.org Rev. Jerzy Auguscik, O.F.M., Conv., Pst.; CRP Stds.: 91
EBENSBURG
Holy Name - 500 N. Julian St., Ebensburg, PA 15931 t) 814-472-7244 holynameebg@dioceseaj.org www.holynameebg.org Rev. Brian Lee Warchola, Pst.; Dcn. Michael Condor Jr.; Nancy McCulley, DRE; CRP Stds.: 239
Holy Name School - (Grades PreK-8) Holy Name Elementary, 215 W. Horner St., Ebensburg, PA 15931 t) 814-472-8817 holynameelementary@comcast.net holynameschool.net Robin McMullen, Prin.; Stds.: 203; Lay Tchrs.: 18
EVERETT
St. John the Evangelist - 161 E. First Ave., Everett, PA 15537 t) 814-652-5854 stjohn022@comcast.net; stjohntheevangelisteverett@dioceseaj.org www.stjohneverettpa.org Rev. Derek Fairman, Pst.; CRP Stds.: 20
FALLENTIMBER
St. Joan of Arc - 692 Glendale Valley Blvd., Fallentimber, PA 16639-6505 t) 814-943-5437 stjoanofarcfrugality@dioceseaj.org Rev. Robert P. Reese, Pst.; CRP Stds.: 8
GALLITZIN
St. Demetrius - 811 Church St., Gallitzin, PA 16641-2001 t) 814-408-2371 stdemetriusgallitzin@dioceseaj.org Rev. Albert H. Ledoux, Pst.; CRP Stds.: 39
HASTINGS
St. Bernard - 148-Apt. 2 Seventh Ave., Hastings, PA 16646; Mailing: P.O. Box 497, Hastings, PA 16646 t) 814-247-6558 stbernardhastings@dioceseaj.org; ttrettger@comcast.net Rev. Thaddeus E. Rettger, O.S.B., Pst.; Dcn. Michael Anna; Dcn. Christopher Conner; Vickie Conner, DRE; CRP Stds.: 46
St. Boniface Chapel - 1278 Main St., St. Boniface, PA 16675
HOLLIDAYSBURG
St. Mary - 312 Clark St., Hollidaysburg, PA 16648 t) 814-695-0622 ecunningham@dioceseaj.org; athomas@dioceseaj.org www.webparish.com/aj/saintmarys Very Rev. Alan E. Thomas, Admin.; Sr. Dcn. Charles R. Ahearn; Dcn. Allan Duman; Sue Teske, DRE; CRP Stds.: 53
St. Michael the Archangel - 301 Spruce St., Hollidaysburg, PA 16648 t) 814-695-0912 stmichaelhburg@dioceseaj.org www.stmichael-hldg-pa.org Very Rev. Alan E. Thomas, Pst.; Susan M. Teske, DRE; CRP Stds.: 178
HOOVERSVILLE
Holy Family - 321 Sugar St., Hooversville, PA 15936; Mailing: P.O. Box 187, Hooversville, PA 15936 t) 814-798-2933 holyfamilyhooversville@dioceseaj.org holyfamilyparishhooversville,com Rev. Aron M. Maghsoudi, Pst.;
HUNTINGDON
Most Holy Trinity - 524 Mifflin St., Huntingdon, PA 16652 t) 814-643-0160 mhtcc@dioceseaj.org www.mhtcc.org Rev. Mark R. Reid, Admin.; Dcn. Donald Gibboney; Anita Roseborrough, DRE; CRP Stds.: 74
JOHNSTOWN
St. John Gualbert Cathedral - 117 Clinton St., Johnstown, PA 15907-0807; Mailing: PO Box 807, Johnstown, PA 15907-0807 t) 814-536-0117 johnstowncathedral@dioceseaj.org www.stjohngualbert.org Very Rev. Matthew B. Baum, Rector; CRP Stds.: 19
St. Andrew - 1621 Ferndale Ave., Johnstown, PA 15905 t) 814-288-4324 standrewjtown@dioceseaj.org www.standrewjohnstown.org Rev. Peter D. Crowe, Pst.; CRP Stds.: 22
St. Benedict - 2310 Bedford St., Johnstown, PA 15904-1127 t) 814-266-9718 saintbenedictjtown@dioceseaj.org www.stbenedictchurch.org Rev. Antony Sudherson, Par. Vicar; Rev. David S. Peles, Pst.; Dcn. Michael L. Russo; CRP Stds.: 163
Divine Mercy Catholic Academy East Campus - (Grades PreK-6) 2306 Bedford St., Johnstown, PA 15904 t) 814-961-3622 woodruff.ryan@dmcatholic.org www.dmcatholic.org Ryan Woodruff, Prin.; Stds.: 159; Lay Tchrs.: 9
St. Clare of Assisi - 124 Maple Ave., Johnstown, PA 15901-1422; Mailing: 110 Maple Ave., Johnstown, PA 15901 t) 814-535-1133 stclarejtown@dioceseaj.org www.webparish.com/aj/clare/ Rev. George M. Gulash, Admin.; CRP Stds.: 2
St. Clement - 114 Lindberg Ave., Johnstown, PA 15905 t) 814-255-4422 stclementchurch@atlanticbb.net; stclementjtown@dioceseaj.org www.stclementjohnstown.org Rev. William E. Rosenbaum, Pst.; Mandy Vigna, DRE; Rev. James F. Crookston, In Res.; CRP Stds.: 22
St. Francis of Assisi - 120 Barron Ave., Johnstown, PA 15906 t) 814-539-1632 sfassisich@atlanticbbn.net; stfrancisassisijtown@dioceseaj.org www.stfrancisofassisijohnstown.com Very Rev. Anthony Francis Spilka, Pst.; Dcn. Bruce L. Becker; CRP Stds.: 22
SS. Gregory & Barnabas - 120 Boltz St., Johnstown, PA 15902 t) 814-536-6818 www.ssgregbar.org Mary Helen Percinsky, DRE; Rev. Callistus Elue, Admin.; CRP Stds.: 46
St. Michael the Archangel - 180 Gilbert St., Johnstown, PA 15906 t) 814-535-7646 omos@dioceseaj.org www.omostoday.com Very Rev. Mark S. Begly, Pst.; CRP Stds.: 2
Our Mother of Sorrows - 407 Tioga St., Johnstown, PA 15905; Mailing: 415 Tioga St., Johnstown, PA 15905 t) 814-535-7646 omos@dioceseaj.org www.omostoday.com Very Rev. Mark S. Begly, Pst.; Anne DiFrancesco, Dir.; CRP Stds.: 165
St. Patrick - 609 Park Ave., Johnstown, PA 15902 t) 814-539-2186 stpats@floodcity.net; stpatrickjtown@dioceseaj.org www.stpats5.wixsite.com/spjtwn Very Rev. Matthew B. Baum, Pst.; Sr. Dcn. Joseph Dalla Valle; Rita Redden, DRE; CRP Stds.: 11
Resurrection Roman Catholic Church - 324 Chestnut St., Johnstown, PA 15906; Mailing: 408 8th Ave., Johnstown, PA 15906 t) 814-539-5788 resurrectionjtown@dioceseaj.org resurrectionparishjohnstown.com Rev. George M. Gulash, Pst.; CRP Stds.: 35
St. Therese of the Child Jesus - 536 Decker Ave., Johnstown, PA 15906 t) 814-539-7633 bkarmanocky@dioceseaj.org; sttheresejtown@dioceseaj.org Rev. Bernard Karmanocky, O.F.M., Pst.; CRP Stds.: 30
St. Anne - 533 Woodland Ave., Johnstown, PA 15902 t) (814) 539-7633 stannejtown@dioceseaj.org
St. Therese Convent - 702 Saybrook Pl., Johnstown, PA 15906-1271
Visitation of the B.V.M. - 1127 McKinley Ave., Johnstown, PA 15905-4323 t) 814-536-6110 visitationjtown@dioceseaj.org www.visitationbvmparish.org Rev. John Slovikovski, Pst.; CRP Stds.: 8
LILLY
Our Lady of the Alleghenies - 608 Main St., Lilly, PA 15938-1148 t) 814-886-2504 oloalilly@dioceseaj.org www.oloalilly.org Rev. Matthew A. Reese, Pst.; Dcn. Samuel F. Albarano Jr.; CRP Stds.: 86
LOCK HAVEN
Holy Spirit - 3 E. Walnut St., Lock Haven, PA 17745 t) 570-748-4594 holyspiritlockhaven.org Rev. Joseph T. Orr, Pst.; Sr. Dcn. Philip Gibson; Dcn. Calvin J. Young; Tammy Nesbitt, DRE; CRP Stds.: 32
Lock Haven Catholic School - (Grades K-8) 311 W. Water St., Lock Haven, PA 17745 t) 570-748-7252 principal@lhcs.org www.lhcs.org Kimberly Williamson, Prin.; Stds.: 166; Lay Tchrs.: 9
LORETTO
Basilica of St. Michael the Archangel - 321 St. Mary St., Loretto, PA 15940; Mailing: PO Box 10, Loretto, PA 15940 t) 814-472-8551 www.basilicasm-loretto.org Very Rev. John D. Byrnes, Pst.; Dcn. Richard T. Golden; CRP Stds.: 103
St. Michael School - (Grades K-8) 301 St. Elizabeth St., Loretto, PA 15940; Mailing: P.O. Box 67, Loretto, PA 15940 t) 814-472-9117 vkrug@st-michael-school.org www.st-michael-school.org Rhonda Seymour, Prin.; Stds.: 87; Lay Tchrs.: 9
MCCONNELLSBURG
St. Stephen - 303 Lincoln Way E., McConnellsburg, PA 17233 t) 717-485-3723 www.fultoncatholic.com Rev. Derek Fairman, Pst.; CRP Stds.: 9
MEYERSDALE
SS. Philip and James - 247 High St., Meyersdale, PA 15552 t) 814-634-8150 ssphilipjamesmeyersdale@dioceseaj.org; ssphilipandjames@aol.com Rev. Stephen Shin, O.F.M.Cap., Pst.; CRP Stds.: 23
St. Gregory - 137 Church St., Berlin, PA 15530;

Mailing: 247 High St., Meyersdale, PA 15552 sshin@dioceseaj.org

MOUNT UNION

St. Catherine of Siena - 205 W. Market St., Mount Union, PA 17066; Mailing: 203 W. Market St., Mount Union, PA 17066-1236 t) 814-542-4582 stcatherine@dioceseaj.org www.scosmu.org/ Very Rev. Joseph W. Fleming, Pst.; CRP Stds.: 28

MUNDY'S CORNER

St. John Vianney - 3513 William Penn Ave., Mundy's Corner, PA 15909 t) 814-322-4789 sjv@dioceseaj.org www.sjvcc.com Friar Timothy Harris, T.O.R., Pst.; Dcn. Thomas M. Buige; Sr. Karen Gruseck, CCW, DRE; CRP Stds.: 48

NANTY-GLO

Saint Mary's Church - 1020 Caroline St., Nanty-Glo, PA 15943 t) 814-749-9103 stmarynantyglo@dioceseaj.org stmarysnantyglo.org Rev. Leonard E. Voytek, Pst.; Dcn. James J. Janosik; CRP Stds.: 31

NEW BALTIMORE

St. John the Baptist - 101 Findley St., New Baltimore, PA 15553; Mailing: P.O. Box 10, New Baltimore, PA 15553 t) 814-733-2210 www.newbaltimorecatholic.com Rev. Mark Pattock, O.F.M.Cap., Pst.; Rev. Roman Kozacheson, O.F.M.Cap, In Res.; Rev. Stephen Shin, O.F.M.Cap., In Res.; CRP Stds.: 39

NEWRY

St. Patrick - 704 Patrick Ln., Newry, PA 16665; Mailing: P.O. Box 398, Newry, PA 16665-0398 t) 814-695-3413 stpatricknewry@dioceseaj.org www.stpatricknewry.org Rev. Allen P. Zeth, Admin.; CRP Stds.: 55

St. Patrick School - (Grades PreK-8) 731 Patrick Ln., Newry, PA 16665; Mailing: P.O. Box 400, Newry, PA 16665 t) 814-695-3819 tsteinbugl@stpatsnewry.org Tara Steinbugl, Prin.; Stds.: 68; Lay Tchrs.: 7

NICKTOWN

St. Nicholas - 1169 Alverda Rd., Nicktown, PA 15762; Mailing: P.O. Box 37, Nicktown, PA 15762 t) 814-948-9614 www.saintnicholasparish.org Rev. Jeremiah Lange, OSB, Pst.; CRP Stds.: 48

NORTHERN CAMBRIA

Prince of Peace - 811 Chestnut Ave., Northern Cambria, PA 15714-1461 t) 814-948-6842 popnc@dioceseaj.org www.popnc.net Rev. Mark Groeger, Admin.; Dcn. Gary F. Gill; Sr. Karen Gruseck, CCW, DRE; CRP Stds.: 43

ORBISONIA

St. Mary - 20896 Croghan Pike, Orbisonia, PA 17243-9000 t) 814-447-3172 stmaryorbisonia@dioceseaj.org www.stmarysinshadevalley.weebly.com Very Rev. Joseph W. Fleming, Pst.; Dcn. John Roth; CRP Stds.: 11

PATTON

Queen of Peace - 907 Sixth Ave., Patton, PA 16668 t) 814-674-8983 office@queenofpeacepatton.org www.queenofpeacepatton.org Rev. Ananias Buccicone, O.S.B., Pst.; Lisa Blake, CFO; CRP Stds.: 23

PHILIPSBURG

SS. Peter and Paul - 400 S. Fourth St., Philipsburg, PA 16866 t) 814-342-1700 www.sspeterandpaul.us Rev. Matthias Rendon, OFM; Dcn. Jerry Nevling; CRP Stds.: 66

PORT MATILDA

Church of the Good Shepherd - 867 Gray's Woods Blvd., Port Matilda, PA 16870 t) 814-238-2110 goodshepherd@dioceseaj.org www.goodshepherd-sc.org Rev. Jozef Kovacik, Pst.; Sr. Dcn. Michael A. Ondik Jr.; Dcn. Jack E. Orlandi; CRP Stds.: 176

PORTAGE

Holy Family - 509 Caldwell Ave., Portage, PA 15946 t) 814-736-4279 holyfamilyportage@dioceseaj.org www.holyfamilyportage.org Very Rev. Thomas Stabile, T.O.R., Pst.; CRP Stds.: 92

RENOVO

St. Joseph - 925 Huron Ave., Renovo, PA 17764 t) 570-923-0172 stjosephrenovo@dioceseaj.org www.stjosephchurchrenovopa.org Rev. Joseph T. Orr, Admin.; CRP Stds.: 36

ROARING SPRING

St. Thomas More - 619 E Main St., Roaring Spring, PA 16673 t) 814-224-4522 stthomasmoreroaringspring@dioceseaj.org Rev. Allen Zeth, Admin.; CRP Stds.: 25

SOMERSET

St. Peter - 433 W. Church St., Somerset, PA 15501 t) 814-443-6574 apatti@dioceseaj.org www.stpetersparish.com Very Rev. Angelo J. Patti, Pst.; Dcn. Mark Komula; CRP Stds.: 106

St. Peter School - (Grades K-6) t) 814-445-6662 principal@stpetersparish.com www.stpetersschoolsomerset.com Jill Harris, Prin.; Stds.: 102; Lay Tchrs.: 7

St. Peter in Chains - 1590 Walters Mill Rd., Somerset, PA 15510-0001 t) 814-443-8100 mbaum@dioceseaj.org Very Rev. Matthew B. Baum, Chap.;

SOUTH FORK

Most Holy Trinity - 550 Main St., South Fork, PA 15956 t) 814-495-4419 mostholytrinitysouthfork@dioceseaj.org Rev. Joseph C. Nale, Pst.; Betty Rosmus, DRE; CRP Stds.: 22

SPRING MILLS

St. Kateri Tekakwitha - 3503 Penns Valley Rd., Spring Mills, PA 16875; Mailing: P.O. Box 159, Spring Mills, PA 16875 t) 814-422-8983 saintkateri@dioceseaj.org www.stkaterichurch.org Rev. Brian R. Saylor, Pst.; CRP Stds.: 34

ST. MICHAEL

St. Michael's - 751 Locust St., St. Michael, PA 15951-0103; Mailing: Box 103, St. Michael, PA 15951-0103 t) 814-495-9640 stmichael@dioceseaj.org www.saintmichaelchurch.weebly.com Rev. Msgr. David A. Lockard, Admin.; Laurie Sloan, DRE; CRP Stds.: 113

STATE COLLEGE

Our Lady of Victory - 820 Westerly Pkwy., State College, PA 16801 t) 814-237-7832 office@ourladyofvictory.com; olovstatecollege@dioceseaj.org ourladyofvictory.com Rev. George I Jakopac, Pst.; Anne Bord, DRE; Dcn. David C. Lapinski; CRP Stds.: 355

Our Lady of Victory Pre-School - 810 Westerly Pkwy, State College, PA 16801 t) 814-238-6616 hoyj@olvcs.org; roganj@olvcs.org www.olvcatholicschool.org James Hoy, Prin.;

Our Lady of Victory School - (Grades K-8) 800 Westerly Pkwy., State College, PA 16801 t) 814-238-1592 hoyj@olvcs.org olvcatholicschool.org James Hoy, Interim Prin.; Stds.: 280; Lay Tchrs.: 24

SUMMERHILL

St. John the Baptist - 538 Main St., Summerhill, PA 15958; Mailing: P.O. Box 248, Summerhill, PA 15958 t) 814-495-5241 stjic@dioceseaj.org www.stjic.org Rev. Joseph C Nale, Pst.; Stephanie Partsch, DRE; CRP Stds.: 41

Immaculate Conception - jnale@dioceseaj.org Rev. Joseph C. Nale, Pst.;

TYRONE

St. Matthew - 1105 Cameron Ave., Tyrone, PA 16686 t) 814-684-1480 stmatthewtyrone@dioceseaj.org www.stmatthewtyrone.org Rev. Michael Pleva, Admin.; CRP Stds.: 95

St. Matthew School - (Grades PreK-6) t) 814-684-3510 Jennifer Casanave, Lead Teacher; Stds.: 44; Lay Tchrs.: 5

WEST SALISBURY

St. Michael - 1316 St. Paul Rd., West Salisbury, PA 15565 t) 814-662-2958 dmsaylor1@verizon.net Rev. Isaac Haywiaser, OSB, Sacr. Min.; Dcn. William R. Underhill, Par. Admin.; CRP Stds.: 12

St. Mary - 215 Warrens Mill Rd., Pocahontas, PA 15565; Mailing: PO Box 36, West Salisbury, PA 15565 t) (814) 662-2958 Dcn. William R. Underhill;

WILLIAMSBURG

St. Joseph the Worker - 628 W. First St., Williamsburg, PA 16693 t) 814-832-2137 stjosephwilliamsburg@dioceseaj.org Dcn. Kevin J. Nester, Admin.; CRP Stds.: 24

WILMORE

St. Bartholomew - 185 Church Hill Rd., Wilmore, PA 15962; Mailing: 550 Main St., South Fork, PA 15956 t) 814-495-4419 stbartholomewwilmore@dioceseaj.org Rev. Joseph C. Nale, Pst.; Diana Frantz, DRE; CRP Stds.: 37

WINDBER

St. Anthony of Padua - 2201 Graham Ave., Windber, PA 15963 t) 814-467-7292 stanthonywindber@dioceseaj.org; stanthonyswindber@msn.com www.stanthonyswindber.com Rev. Roderick N. Soha, T.O.R., Pst.; Rev. Lawrence L. Lacovic, In Res.; CRP Stds.: 67

Divine Mercy Catholic Academy East Campus - (Grades PreK-6) 2306 Bedford St., Johnstown, PA 15904 t) 814-961-3622 woodruff.ryan@dmcatholic.org www.dmcatholic.org Ryan Woodruff, Prin.; Stds.: 159; Lay Tchrs.: 10

SS. Cyril and Methodius - 604 Graham Ave., Windber, PA 15963; Mailing: c/o St. Anthony of Padua, 2201 Graham Ave., Windber, PA 15963 t) 814-467-7042; 814-467-9670 (CRP) sscyrilmethodius@yahoo.com; stscyrilmethodiuswindber@dioceseaj.org www.sscmwindber.com Rev. Roderick N. Soha, T.O.R., Pst.; Rev. Lawrence L. Lacovic, In Res.; Sr. Dcn. Thomas M. Papinchak; Roxanne Newcomer, DRE; CRP Stds.: 13

St. Elizabeth Ann Seton - 605 Graham Ave., Windber, PA 15963; Mailing: c/o St. Anthony of Padua, 2201 Graham Ave., Windber, PA 15963 t) 814-467-7191 stelizaseton@comcast.net; stelizaseton@dioceseaj.org Rev. Roderick N. Soha, T.O.R., Pst.; CRP Stds.: 46

SCHOOLS: PRESCHOOL THRU HIGH SCHOOL

SCHOOLS

COMMONWEALTH OF PENNSYLVANIA

ALTOONA

Holy Trinity Catholic School -- Middle School Campus - (PAR) (Grades 5-8) 5519 Sixth Ave., Altoona, PA 16602 t) 814-942-7835 spencer.elaine@holytrinitycatholic.school www.holytrinitycatholic.school Elaine Spencer, Prin.; Stds.: 114; Lay Tchrs.: 32

BOALSBURG

St. Joseph's Catholic Academy - (PAR) (Grades 9-12) 901 Boalsburg Pike, Boalsburg, PA 16827 t) 814-808-6118 www.stjoeacad.org Anna Rupprecht, Prin.; Stds.: 106; Lay Tchrs.: 7

CRESSON

All Saints Catholic School - (DIO) (Grades PreK-8) 220 Powell Ave., Cresson, PA 16630 t) 814-886-7942 allsaints@ascsknights.org www.allsaintscresson.org Kathleen L. Maurer, Prin.; Stds.: 107; Lay Tchrs.: 10

JOHNSTOWN

Divine Mercy Catholic Academy West Campus - (PAR) (Grades PreK-6) 430 Tioga St., Johnstown, PA 15905 t) 814-961-3622 woodruff.ryan@dmcatholic.org Ryan Woodruff, Prin.; Stds.: 158; Lay Tchrs.: 14

NICKTOWN

St. Nicholas Catholic School - (DIO) 3278 Blue Goose Rd., Nicktown, PA 15762; Mailing: P.O. Box 252, Nicktown, PA 15762-0252 t) 814-948-8900 nccs@northerncambriacatholic.org www.northerncambriacatholic.org Serves St. Nicholas & Prince of Peace. Theresa Burba, Prin.; Stds.: 142; Lay Tchrs.: 11

HIGH SCHOOLS

COMMONWEALTH OF PENNSYLVANIA

ALTOONA

***Bishop Guilfoyle Catholic High School** - (PRV) (Grades 6-12) 2400 Pleasant Valley Blvd., Altoona, PA 16602 t) 814-944-4014 jbutler@bguilfoyle.org www.bishopguilfoyle.org Joan Donnelly, Prin.; Michael Cacciotti, Vice Prin.; Joseph Adams, Pres.; Stds.: 274; Lay Tchrs.: 25

EBENSBURG

***Bishop Carroll Catholic High School** - (PRV) (Grades 9-12) 728 Ben Franklin Hwy., Ebensburg, PA 15931 t) 814-472-7500 cotchen.stephen@bishopcarroll.org bishopcarroll.com Rev. Jeremiah Lange, OSB, Chap.; Stephen Cotchen, Prin.; Lynn Weber, Bus. Mgr.; Stds.: 164; Pr. Tchrs.: 2; Lay Tchrs.: 16

JOHNSTOWN

***Bishop McCort Catholic High School** - (PRV) (Grades 7-12) 25 Osborne St., Johnstown, PA 15905 t) 814-536-8991 tsmith@mccort.org www.mccort.org Christopher Pfeil, Dean; Thomas A Smith, Prin.; Stds.: 366; Lay Tchrs.: 31

INSTITUTIONS LOCATED IN DIOCESE

CAMPUS MINISTRY / NEWMAN CENTERS [CAM]

ALTOONA

Office of Campus Ministry - 309 Lotz Ave., Altoona, PA 16602; Mailing: 2713 W. Chestnut Ave., Altoona, PA 16601 t) 814-942-5503 mbecker253@aol.com www.stjohnsaltoona.org Rev. Msgr. Michael A. Becker;

St. Francis University (Loretto) - 117 Evergreen Dr., Loretto, PA 15940; Mailing: P.O. Box 600, Loretto, PA 15940 t) 814-472-3172 vsoyka@francis.edu Rev. Stephen Waruszewski, TOR, Dir.;

Juniata College - 1700 More St., Huntington, PA 16652 t) 814-641-3362 baerl@juniata.edu Lisa Baer, Campus Min.; Rev. Mark R Reid, Sacr. Min.;

Lock Haven University (Lock Haven) - Newman Center, 445 W. Main St., Lock Haven, PA 17745 t) 570-748-8592 christopher.klopp@gmail.com Christopher Klopp, Campus Min.; Rev. Joseph Orr, Sacramental Min.;

Mount Aloysius College (Cresson) - 7373 Admiral Peary Hwy., Cresson, PA 16630 t) 814-886-6483 akanich@mtaloy.edu Amy Kanich, Dir.;

Penn State University, Altoona - Edith Davis Eve Chapel, 3000 Ivyside Park, Altoona, PA 16601 t) 814-695-5579 amccarville@dioceseaj.org Andre McCarville, Campus Min.; Very Rev. Alan E. Thomas, Sacramental Min.;

Penn State University, University Park - 205C Pasquerilla Spiritual Ctr., University Park, PA 16802 t) 814-865-4281 catholic@psu.edu www.psu.edu/catholic Rev. David R. Griffin, O.S.B., Campus Min.; Sr. Dcn. Laszlo P. Ivanits, Campus Min.; Rev. Matthew T. Laffey, O.S.B., Dir.;

University of Pittsburgh at Johnstown - 450 Schoolhouse Rd., Johnstown, PA 15904 t) 814-269-2007 lam220@pitt.edu LaDonna McCrary, Campus Min.; Rev. George M. Gulash, Sacr. Min.;

UNIVERSITY PARK

Penn State Catholic Community - 205C Pasquerilla Spiritual Ctr., University Park, PA 16802 t) 814-865-4281 catholic@psu.edu www.psu.edu/catholic Rev. Matthew T. Laffey, O.S.B., Dir.; Rev. David R. Griffin, O.S.B., Campus Min.; Sr. Dcn. Laszlo P. Ivanits, Campus Min.;

COLLEGES & UNIVERSITIES [COL]

CRESSON

Mount Aloysius College - 7373 Admiral Peary Hwy., Cresson, PA 16630 t) 814-886-4131 cnelen@mtaloy.edu www.mtaloy.edu John N. McKeegan, Pres.; Stds.: 2,924; Lay Tchrs.: 55

LORETTO

St. Francis University - 117 Evergreen Dr., Loretto, PA 15940; Mailing: P.O. Box 600, Loretto, PA 15940-0600 t) 814-472-3001 vsoyka@francis.edu www.francis.edu Rev. Malachi Van Tassell, T.O.R., Pres.; Jeffrey Savino, VP Fin. & Admin.; Stds.: 2,500; Bro. Tchrs.: 1; Lay Tchrs.: 117; Pr. Tchrs.: 1

CONVENTS, MONASTERIES, AND RESIDENCES FOR WOMEN [CON]

CRESSON

Sister Servants of the Most Sacred Heart of Jesus - Sacred Heart Province, 866 Cambria St., Cresson, PA 16630-1713 t) 814-886-4223 sscjusaprovince@gmail.com www.sacredheartsisters.org Sr. Mary Joseph Calore, SSCJ, Asst/Supr.; Srs.: 4

John Paul II Manor Personal Care Home - 856 Cambria St., Cresson, PA 16630 t) 814-886-7961 administrator@johnpaul2manor.org www.johnpaul2manor.org Linda A Long, Admin.; Sr. Mary Joan Greenburg, Local Supr.;

EBENSBURG

Carmelite Community of the Word - St. Therese Convent, 218 W. Lloyd St., Ebensburg, PA 15931 t) 814-472-9457 ebensburgccw@aol.com Srs.: 3

GALLITZIN

Carmelite Community of the Word-Incarnation Center - 394 Bem Rd., Gallitzin, PA 16641 t) 814-886-4098 newsccw@yahoo.com ccwsisters.org Sr. Marilyn Welch, CCW, Admin.; Srs.: 4

Little Sisters of Jesus - 347 Tunnel Hill St., Gallitzin, PA 16641 t) 814-886-4679 Sr. Mary Jo Byrne, Contact; Srs.: 2

LORETTO

Carmel of St. Therese of Lisieux - 2101 Manor Dr., Loretto, PA 15940; Mailing: P.O. Box 57, Loretto, PA 15940-0057 t) 814-472-8620 info@lorettocarmel.org www.lorettocarmel.org Discalced Carmelite Nuns. Mother John of the Cross Wagner, OCD, Prioress; Srs.: 11

MCCONNELLSBURG

Carmelite Community of the Word - Fulton County Mission, 110 S. Third St., McConnellsburg, PA 17223 t) 717-485-5917; 717-485-0661 mmonahan@dioceseaj.org Sr. Martha Burbulla, C.C.W., Dir.; Srs.: 2

PORTAGE

Sister Servants of the Most Sacred Heart of Jesus - St. Joseph Convent, 1872 Munster Rd., Portage, PA 15946 t) 814-886-4459 Sr. Maria Kotch, Local Supr.; Srs.: 4

ENDOWMENTS / FOUNDATIONS / TRUSTS [EFT]

ALTOONA

Diocese of Altoona-Johnstown Mutual-Aid-Plan Trust - 2713 W Chestnut Ave., Altoona, PA 16601 t) 814-695-5579 sbarry@dioceseaj.org Matthew Stever, CEO;

Second Century Scholarship Fund - 2713 W Chestnut Ave., Altoona, PA 16601 t) (814) 695-5579 www.secondcenturyfund.org Heather Foor, Dir.;

MISCELLANEOUS [MIS]

ALTOONA

Diocese of Altoona-Johnstown - 2713 W Chestnut Ave., Altoona, PA 16601 t) 814-695-5579 sbarry@dioceseaj.org www.dioceseaj.org Most Rev. Mark L Bartchak, Bishop; Teresa M Stayer, Chancellor; Rev. Alan E Thomas, Vicar Gen.; Rev. John D Byrnes, Judicial Vicar; Matthew Stever, CFO;

Office of Ongoing Formation of Clergy - 2713 W. Chestnut Ave., Altoona, PA 16601-1720 t) (814) 695-5579 athomas@dioceseaj.org Very Rev. Alan E. Thomas, Dir.;

Office of Vocations - 2713 W. Chestnut Ave., Altoona, PA 16601 t) (814) 695-5579 vocations@dioceseaj.org Rev. Peter D. Crowe, Dir.;

LORETTO

American Parish Youth Center, Inc. - 131 St. Francis Dr., Loretto, PA 15940; Mailing: P.O. Box 26, Loretto, PA 15940 t) 814-419-8885 www.franciscanfriarscresson.org Rev. Malachi Van Tassell, T.O.R., Pres.;

MONASTERIES AND RESIDENCES FOR PRIESTS AND BROTHERS [MON]

HOLLIDAYSBURG

St. Bernardine Monastery - 768 Monastery Rd., Hollidaysburg, PA 16648 t) 814-695-3992 www.thefranciscanfriars.org Rev. Anthony Criscitelli, T.O.R., Local Admin.; Rev. Robert D'Aversa, T.O.R., Vicar; Rev. Leonard J. Blostic, T.O.R., In Res.; Rev. Eugene Kubina, T.O.R., In Res.; Rev. A. Giles Schinelli, T.O.R., In Res.; Rev. Terrence T. Smith, T.O.R., In Res.; Rev. Vianney Cunningham, TOR, In Res.; Priests: 7

Franciscan Friars, T.O.R. Development Office and Mass Association - 788 Monastery Rd., Hollidaysburg, PA 16648; Mailing: P.O. Box 139, Hollidaysburg, PA 16648 t) 814-695-3802 kellie@thefranciscanfriars.org Kellie Wesner Bettwy, Dir.;

Province Econome's Office - 788 Monastery Rd., Hollidaysburg, PA 16648; Mailing: PO Box 117, Hollidaysburg, PA 16648 t) 814-696-3321 jen@thefranciscanfriars.org Jennifer Heck, Benefits Mgr.;

St. Joseph Friary - 501 Walnut St., Hollidaysburg, PA 16648 t) 814-695-5802 xtofertor@aol.com Rev. Christopher Panagoplos, T.O.R., In Res.; Bro. Tello Vu, T.O.R., In Res.; Brs.: 1; Priests: 1

LORETTO

St. Bonaventure Hall - 158 St. Francis Dr., Loretto, PA 15940; Mailing: P.O. Box 155, Loretto, PA 15940-0155 t) (814) 419-8860 Bro. Paul McMullen, Dir.; Rev. Joseph J. Lehman, T.O.R., Mem.; Rev. Peter Lyons, T.O.R., Mem.; Bro. Sean Fitzwater, T.O.R., Mem.; Bro. Richard Gates, T.O.R., Mem.; Bro. Shamus McGrenra, T.O.R., Mem.; Brs.: 4; Priests: 3

Saint Elizabeth Friary - 116 St. Elizabeth St., Loretto, PA 15940; Mailing: P.O. Box 136, Loretto, PA 15940 t) (814) 419-8901 Rev. Kevin Queally, T.O.R., Local Min.; Bro. Christopher Curliss, T.O.R., Mem.; Bro. Peter David Hoyer, T.O.R., Mem.; Bro. John Gregory Schratz, T.O.R., Mem.; Brs.: 3; Priests: 1

St. Francis Friary at Mount Assisi - 141 St. Francis Dr., Loretto, PA 15940-0040; Mailing: P.O. Box 40, Loretto, PA 15940-0040 t) (814) 419-8890 www.franciscanstor.org Rev. Terry Adams, T.O.R.; Rev. David Bonarrigo, T.O.R.; Rev. Joseph Chancler, T.O.R.; Rev. Richard L. Davis, T.O.R.; Rev. Christopher Dobson, Dir.; Rev. Andrew Draper; Rev. Terence Henry, T.O.R.; Rev. Joseph Janiszeski; Rev. Benjamin Medeiros; Rev. David Kraeger, T.O.R.; Rev. Francis Moyher, T.O.R.; Rev. Julio Rivero, T.O.R.; Rev. Samuel Vaccarella, T.O.R.; Rev. Joseph Yelenc, T.O.R.; Bro. Gabriel Mary Amato, T.O.R., Assoc. Dir.; Bro. Edward Bennett, T.O.R.; Bro. Callistus Gerardi, T.O.R.; Bro. John Paul McMahon; Bro. Norman McNelis; Rev. Daniel Sinisi; Bro. Michael Tripka, T.O.R.; Brs.: 6; Priests: 15

Sacred Heart Friary - 132 Franciscan Way, Loretto, PA 15940; Mailing: P.O. Box 600, Loretto, PA 15940 t) (814) 471-1322 Rev. Malachi Van Tassell, T.O.R., Vicar; Rev. Stephen Waruszewski, TOR, Local Econome; Bro. Dennis Snyder, T.O.R., Mem.; Bro. Kevin Smith, T.O.R., Mem.; Bro. Marius Strom, T.O.R., Local Min.; Friar Matthew Simons, T.O.R., Mem.; Friar Jason Wooleyhan, T.O.R., Mem.; Joseph Marie Krilich, T.O.R., Mem.; Brs.: 3; Priests: 5

NURSING / REHABILITATION / CONVALESCENCE / ELDERLY CARE [NUR]

HOLLIDAYSBURG

Dmitri Manor Priests' Residence - 162 Marian Heights Dr., Hollidaysburg, PA 16648; Mailing: Diocese of Altoona-Johnstown, 2713 W. Chestnut Ave., Altoona, PA 16601 t) 814-696-4698 dmitrimanor@dioceseaj.org Very Rev. Alan E. Thomas, Vicar General; Bed Capacity: 12; Asstd. Annu.: 12

Garvey Manor - 1037 S. Logan Blvd., Hollidaysburg, PA 16648 t) 814-695-5571 garveymanor@garveymanor.org www.garveymanor.org Senior Care Complex: Nursing, Personal Care, Independent Living. Sr. M. Joachim Anne Ferenchak, O.Carm., Admin.; Asstd. Annu.: 350; Staff: 250

St. Leonard's Home, Inc. - 601 N. Montgomery St., Hollidaysburg, PA 16648 t) 814-695-9581; 814-695-2920 www.stleonardshome.org Personal Care Home for seniors over 62 Sr. Cynthia Meyer, C.S.F.N., Pres.; Asstd. Annu.: 35; Staff: 15

RETREAT HOUSES / RENEWAL CENTERS [RTR]

EBENSBURG

Sisters of St. Ann Mother House - 1120 N. Center St., Ebensburg, PA 15931; Mailing: P.O. Box 328, Ebensburg, PA 15931 t) 814-472-9354 anthos1944@gmail.com; sistersann35@gmail.com www.suoredisantanna.org Retreat House. Sisters of St. Ann. Sr. Mary Kutty Vellaplamuriyil, Delegate Superior;

NEW BALTIMORE

St. John The Baptist Retreat Center - 101 Findley St., New Baltimore, PA 15553; Mailing: P.O. Box 10, New Baltimore, PA 15553 t) 814-733-2210 momhanknb@yahoo.com Rev. Mark Pattock, O.F.M.Cap., Dir.;

An asterisk (*) denotes an organization that has established tax-exempt status directly with the IRS and is not covered by the USCCB Group Ruling.

Diocese of Amarillo

(Dioecesis Amarillensis)

MOST REVEREND PATRICK J. ZUREK, D.D.

Bishop of Amarillo; ordained June 29, 1975; appointed Auxiliary Bishop of San Antonio and Titular Bishop of Tamugadi January 5, 1998; consecrated February 16, 1998; appointed Bishop of Amarillo January 3, 2008; installed Feb. 22, 2008.

Diocesan Pastoral Center: 4512 N.E. 24th Ave., Amarillo, TX 79107. T: 806-383-2243; F: 806-383-8452.
Mailing Address: P.O. Box 5644, Amarillo, TX 79117-5644.
www.amarillodiocese.org

ERECTED A DIOCESE BY POPE PIUS XI, AUGUST 25, 1926.

Square Miles 25,800.

Comprises that part of the State of Texas known as the Panhandle, and extending thence southward; bounded on the east by Oklahoma, and by the eastern county line of Childress and by the southern lines Childress, Hall, Briscoe, Swisher, Castro and Parmer Counties; the western boundary is the New Mexico state line from the southern line of Parmer County, Texas, northward to the northwestern corner of the Panhandle of Texas. There are 26 counties.

For legal titles of parishes and diocesan institutions, consult the Chancery Office.

STATISTICAL OVERVIEW

Personnel
Bishop ... 1
Priests: Diocesan Active in Diocese ... 32
Priests: Diocesan Active Outside Diocese ... 6
Number of Diocesan Priests ... 38
Religious Priests in Diocese ... 1
Total Priests in your Diocese ... 39
Extern Priests in Diocese ... 12
Permanent Deacons in Diocese ... 46
Total Sisters ... 84

Parishes
Parishes ... 38
With Resident Pastor:
Resident Diocesan Priests ... 24
Resident Religious Priests ... 1
Without Resident Pastor:
Administered by Priests ... 13
Missions ... 11
Pastoral Centers ... 1

Professional Ministry Personnel:
Sisters ... 7
Lay Ministers ... 22

Welfare
Day Care Centers ... 1
Total Assisted ... 140
Specialized Homes ... 1
Total Assisted ... 2,985
Special Centers for Social Services ... 1
Total Assisted ... 3,461

Educational
Diocesan Students in Other Seminaries ... 4
Total Seminarians ... 4
High Schools, Diocesan and Parish ... 1
Total Students ... 116
Elementary Schools, Diocesan and Parish ... 4
Total Students ... 600
Catechesis / Religious Education:
High School Students ... 968
Elementary Students ... 2,777
Total Students under Catholic Instruction ... 4,465
Teachers in Diocese:
Sisters ... 2
Lay Teachers ... 43

Vital Statistics
Receptions into the Church:
Infant Baptism Totals ... 628
Minor Baptism Totals ... 50
Adult Baptism Totals ... 96
Received into Full Communion ... 36
First Communions ... 613
Confirmations ... 729
Marriages:
Catholic ... 146
Interfaith ... 19
Total Marriages ... 165
Deaths ... 407
Total Catholic Population ... 42,235
Total Population ... 434,358

LEADERSHIP
Diocesan Pastoral Center - t) 806-383-2243
Vicar General - Very Rev. Francisco Perez;
Moderators of the Curia - Very Rev. Francisco Perez; Very Rev. Michael P. Colwell;
Vicar of Clergy - Rev. Hector Madrigal;
Vicars Forane - Rev. Tony Neusch, Central Deanery; Rev. Francisco Penez, East Deanery; Rev. Arokiaraj Malapady;

ADMINISTRATION
Chancellor - Very Rev. Lawrence John;

OFFICES AND DIRECTORS
Archivist - Susan Garner;
Diocesan Tribunal -
Advocates - Rev. Jose Gomez; Rev. Tony Neusch;
Defenders of the Bond - Very Rev. Lawrence John;
Judges - Very Rev. Michael P. Colwell; Very Rev. Francisco Perez; Very Rev. Jose Ricardo Zanetti;
Judicial Vicar - Very Rev. Jose Ricardo Zanetti;
Christian Formation Commission - Sr. Maria Elena Lopez-Ferrer, S.S.N.D.;
Deacon Director - Dcn. Blaine Westlake;
Department of Communications - Roman Asbill (rasbill@dioama.org); Cody Rose; Chris Albracht, Editor;
Department of Finances and Ecclesiastical Properties -
Administrative Services - Ivy Taylor, Risk Mgr., Real Estate Records & Asbestos Mgmt. in Schools; James Mitchell, CFO; Kathryn Brown, Secy.;
Fiscal Manager - t) 806-383-2243 x124 James Mitchell, CFO;
Director of Youth - Oscar Guzman;
Executive Assistant to the Bishop - Robert Aranda;
Family Life - James Schulte, Dir.;
Hispanic Ministry - Rev. Hector Madrigal (president@ncaddhm.org);
Natural Family Planning Coordinator - t) 806-379-9224 Faye Usala;
Office for the Permanent Diaconate - Dcn. Blaine Westlake, Coord.;
Promoter of Justice - Very Rev. Michael P. Colwell;
Rural Life Director - Rev. James Schmitmeyer;
Victim Assistance Coordinator - t) 806-372-7960 Sharon Delgado;
Vocation Development Team - Rev. Gabriel Garcia, O.F.M., Vocation Dir.; Rev. Jose Gomez; Rev. Canon Nicholas J. Gerber;

ADVISORY BOARDS, COMMISSIONS, COMMITTEES, AND COUNCILS
Diocesan Council of Catholic Women - Rev. Msgr. Rex Nicholl, Mod.; Julie Neusch, Pres.;
Diocesan Pastoral Council (Vacant) -
Catholic Historical Society - t) 806-383-2243 x120 sgarner@dioama.org Susan Garner, Pres.;
Presbyteral Council - Very Rev. Jose Ricardo Zanetti, Mem.; Rev. Gabriel Garcia, O.F.M., Mem.; Rev. Canon Nicholas J. Gerber, Mem.;
Priests' Pension Plan Retirement Committee - Most Rev. Patrick J. Zurek; Rev. Antony Carl Neusch, Mem.; Rev. Hector Madrigal, Mem. (president@ncaddhm.org);

CATHOLIC CHARITIES
Downtown Women's Center Inc. - t) 806-373-3625 Diann Gilmore, Exec. Dir.; Stephanie Goins, Dir.; Jack Hilton, CFO;
Catholic Charities of the Texas Panhandle - t) 806-376-4571 Jeff Gulde, Dir.;

CLERGY AND RELIGIOUS SERVICES
Continuing Education of Clergy -

CONSULTATIVE BODIES
Charter Review Board - Louise Ross, Chair; Dorothy Guggemos; Charles Mestas;
College of Consultors - Rev. Gabriel Garcia, O.F.M.; Rev. Canon Nicholas J. Gerber; Rev. Hector Madrigal (president@ncaddhm.org);

DEVELOPMENT
Office of Development and Stewardship - Kim Richard, Dir.;
United Catholic Appeal - Kim Richard, Dir.;

EDUCATION
Office for the Catholic Schools - Angi Seidenberger, Supt.;

EVANGELIZATION
Propagation of the Faith - Rev. Mieczyslaw Przepiora;

FACILITIES
Bishop DeFalco Retreat Center -
Diocese of Amarillo Museum -

FAMILY LIFE
Engaged Encounter - James Schulte, Dir.; Molly Villegas; Cody Rose;
Marriage Encounter - Very Rev. Michael P. Colwell;
Scouting - Dcn. Robert Smith;

ORGANIZATIONS
A.C.T.S. Movement - Dcn. Bob Birkenfeld, Chap.; Shelley Sample, Pres.;
Cursillo Movement - Rev. Marco Antonio Gonzalez, Spiritual Adv./Care Srvcs.; Lupe Gomez, Contact; Marisol Castanon;
National Catholic Association of Diocesan Directors of Hispanic Ministry (NCADDHM) - t) 806-355-5621 Rev. Hector Madrigal, Pres. (president@ncaddhm.org);
Neocatechumenite - t) 806-202-5812 Antonio Barba; Lourdes Barba;
Serra Club - Joe Shehan;

PASTORAL SERVICES
Catholic Student Center at West Texas A & M University - t) 806-655-4345 Rev. Canon Grant Spinhirene, Dir.; Betty Aragon, Asst. Dir.;
Director of Prison Ministry - t) 806-364-8432 Dcn. Andres Gonzalez;

MISCELLANEOUS / OTHER OFFICES
Diocesan Attorney - Frederick J. Griffin;

PARISHES, MISSIONS, AND CLERGY

STATE OF TEXAS

AMARILLO

St. Mary's Cathedral - 1200 Washington St., Amarillo, TX 79102 t) 806-376-7204; 806-376-7204 x3001 (CRP) sjones@stmarysamarillo.com; stmarysamarillo@gmail.com www.stmarysamarillo.com Rev. Antony C Neusch, Rector; Dcn. Robert Aranda; Dcn. Patrick Griffin; Dcn. Ronald Herr; Dcn. Kevin Morris; Dcn. Robert Smith; Yvonne Vasquez, DRE; CRP Stds.: 240
Blessed Sacrament - 4112 S.E. 25th St., Amarillo, TX 79103 t) 806-374-1132; (806) 367-2395 blessedsacramentamarillo@gmail.com Rev. Nicholas Gerber, Pst.; Dcn. Mark Seidlitz; Dcn. Rene Perez; Dcn. Baltazar Montoya; CRP Stds.: 150
St. Francis - 5005 Klinke Rd., Amarillo, TX 79108-9628 t) 806-335-1872 stfrancischurchamarillo@gmail.com stfrancisamarillo.org Rev. Jose Ricardo Zanetti, J.C.L., Pst.; Dcn. Louis Paul Artho; CRP Stds.: 54
St. Hyacinth's - 4500 Westhills Tr., Amarillo, TX 79106 t) 806-358-1351 office@sthama.org sthyacinthamarillo.org Rev. J. Guadalupe Mayorga, Pst.; Dcn. Arnold Schwertner; Dcn. Henry Wilhelm; CRP Stds.: 133
St. Joseph's - 4122 S. Bonham St., Amarillo, TX 79110 t) 806-355-5621 parish.office@stjosephamarillo.com www.stjosephamarillo.com Rev. Hector Madrigal, Pst.; Dcn. Jose Joaquin Castaneda; Dcn. John Renteria; Sr. Rita Campos, DRE; CRP Stds.: 116
St. Joseph's Day Care Center - 4108 S. Bonham St., Amarillo, TX 79110 t) 806-353-7043 gail.accdc@yahoo.com Gail Sainz, Dir.;
St. Laurence Church - 2300 N. Spring St., Amarillo, TX 79107 t) 806-383-2261 stlaurenceamarillotx@gmail.com Rev. Haider Quintero, Pst.; Rev. Taylor J Elzner, Vicar; Dcn. Alfredo Alarcon; Dcn. David Duenes; Dcn. Pablo Morales; Dcn. Miguel Tovar; Patricia Guerra, DRE; CRP Stds.: 249
St. Martin De Porres Mission - 1507 N. Adams St., Amarillo, TX 79107 t) 806-376-8771 rex.nicholl@yahoo.com Rev. Msgr. Rex Nicholl, Pst.; CRP Stds.: 30
Our Lady of Guadalupe - 1210 S.E. 11th Ave., Amarillo, TX 79102 t) 806-372-1128 ourladyofguadalupeamarillo@gmail.com Rev. Jose Gomez, Pst.; Dcn. Andres Gonzalez; Dcn. Tino Frausto; CRP Stds.: 81
Our Lady of Vietnam - 3334 N.E. 20th Ave., Amarillo, TX 79107; Mailing: 2001 N. Grand St., Amarillo, TX 79107 t) 806-383-8669 paulchaucmc@yahoo.com Rev. Paul Nuyen, Pst.; CRP Stds.: 78
St. Thomas the Apostle - 4100 S. Coulter Dr., Amarillo, TX 79109 t) 806-358-2461 rwalker@amarillo.church www.amarillo.church Rev. John Valdez, Pst.; Dcn. Blaine Westlake; Dcn. Darryl Dixon; Dcn. Mark White; Kerry Acker, DRE; CRP Stds.: 428

BORGER

St. John the Evangelist - 201 St. John's Rd., Borger, TX 79007 t) 806-274-7064; 806-316-0509 (CRP) stjohntx@gmail.com saintjohntx.org April Ramos, DRE; Rev. Shane Wieck, Pst.; CRP Stds.: 104
St. Ann's -

BOVINA

St. Ann's - 3rd. St., Bovina, TX 79009; Mailing: Box 660, Bovina, TX 79009 t) 806-251-1511; 806-250-2871 (CRP) Rev. Gregory Bunyan, Pst.; Dcn. Teodoro Chavez; CRP Stds.: 96

CACTUS

Our Lady of Guadalupe - 1501 Center Dr., Cactus, TX 79013; Mailing: PO Box 118, Cactus, TX 79013 t) 806-310-0438 (CRP) stjoeolg@gmail.com Rev. Victor Hugo Andrade, Pst.; CRP Stds.: 124

CANADIAN

Sacred Heart - 804 Kingman Ave., Canadian, TX 79014; Mailing: P. O Box 938, Canadian, TX 79014 t) 806-323-6608 shcanadiantx.org Dcn. Jose Jesus Gutierrez; CRP Stds.: 97

CANYON

St. Ann's - 605 38th St., Canyon, TX 79015; Mailing: P.O. Box 59, Canyon, TX 79015 t) 806-655-3302 parish@stannsofcanyon.org www.stannsofcanyon.org Rev. Scott Raef, Pst.; Dcn. Brian Lewis; Dcn. Eldon Beck Knox; Dcn. Gabriel Rivas; Dcn. John David Rausch; Dcn. Joseph Roder; Adrian Johnson, DRE; CRP Stds.: 264

CHILDRESS

Holy Angels - 308 Ave. B, S.W., Childress, TX 79201; Mailing: P.O. Box 608, Childress, TX 79201 t) 940-937-3946 johnsudhakar333@gmail.com www.holyangelchildresstx.com Rev. John Sudhatar Sangabathini, Pst.; Elizabeth Gamboa, DRE; CRP Stds.: 75

CLARENDON

St. Mary's - 815 McClelland St., Clarendon, TX 79226; Mailing: PO Drawer C, Clarendon, TX 79226-0090 t) 806-874-3910 samraj_1973@yahoo.co.in Rev. Arokia Raj Samala, Pst.; CRP Stds.: 6

DALHART

St. Anthony of Padua - 411 E. Texas Blvd., Dalhart, TX 79022; Mailing: P.O. Box 1029, Dalhart, TX 79022 t) 806-244-4128 jlawrence2002@gmail.com Dcn. Michael Anzaldua; Shay Batenhorst, Admin.; CRP Stds.: 230
St. Anthony of Padua School - (Grades PreK-6) 410 E.

13th, Dalhart, TX 79022; Mailing: P.O. Box 1329, Dalhart, TX 79022 t) 806-244-4811 batenhorst@mysapcs.net Sarah Pollard, Librn.; Stds.: 74; Lay Tchrs.: 6

St. Mary's - 305 E Pine St., Texline, TX 79087

DIMMITT

Immaculate Conception - 1001 W. Halsell St., Dimmitt, TX 79027; Mailing: 905 W. Halsell St., Dimmitt, TX 79027 t) 806-647-4219 iccdimmitt@windstream.net; iccdimmitt@gmail.com www.iccdimmitt.org Rev. Arokiaraj Malapady, Pst.; Dcn. Jose Garcia; Dcn. Paul Herrera Jr.; Dcn. John Nino; Dcn. Richard Martinez, RCIA Coord.; Gloria Hernandez, DRE; CRP Stds.: 193

St. John Nepomucene - 312 7th St., Hart, TX 79043; Mailing: P.O. Box 288, Hart, TX 79043 t) 806-938-2936 saintjohnhart@gmail.com

DUMAS

SS. Peter and Paul - 915 S. Maddox, Dumas, TX 79029; Mailing: Box 503, Dumas, TX 79029 t) 806-935-5002 stspeterandpaul@hotmail.com; cvaldez@sppdumas.org www.sppdumas.org Rev. Gabriel Garcia, O.F.M., Pst.; Dcn. Ricky DeLaRosa; Ofelia Garbalena, DRE; CRP Stds.: 371

FRIONA

St. Teresa of Jesus - 401 W. 17th, Friona, TX 79035-9601 t) 806-250-2871 Rev. Gregory Bunyan, Pst.; CRP Stds.: 102

GROOM

Immaculate Heart of Mary - 411 Ware Ave., Groom, TX 79039; Mailing: P.O. Box 130, Groom, TX 79039 t) 806-248-7584; 806-316-4146 (CRP) samraj_1973@yahoo.co.in immaculateheartgroomtx.com Rev. Arokia Raj Samala, Pst.; Nicole Kuehler, DRE; CRP Stds.: 29

HAPPY

Holy Name of Jesus - 317 W. Main, Happy, TX 79042; Mailing: 2610 4th Ave., Umbarger, TX 79015 t) 806-558-2871; 806-499-3531 Rev. Alvin Tshuma, Pst.; CRP Stds.: 4

HEREFORD

St. Anthony's - 115 N. 25 Mile Ave., Hereford, TX 79045; Mailing: 114 Sunset Dr., Hereford, TX 79045 t) 806-364-6150 stanthonyscatholicparish.com Rev. Grant Spinhirne, Pst.; CRP Stds.: 66

St. Anthony Catholic School - (Grades PreK-5) 120 W. Park Ave., Hereford, TX 79045 t) 806-364-1952 www.stanthonysaints.com Stds.: 90; Lay Tchrs.: 8

San Jose - 735 Brevard, Hereford, TX 79045 t) 806-364-5053; (806) 364-5057 (CRP) sanjosechurch@gmx.com Rev. Jose Ramon Molina, Admin.; Dcn. Richard Mendez; Elda Lucio, DRE;

MEMPHIS

Sacred Heart - 213 N. Third St., Memphis, TX 79245; Mailing: P.O. Box 239, Memphis, TX 79245 t) 806-437-2325; 940-937-3936 (CRP) www.sacredheartmemphistx.com Rev. John Sudhatar Sangabathini, Par. Vicar; CRP Stds.: 18

NAZARETH

Holy Family - 210 St. Joseph, Nazareth, TX 79063; Mailing: P.O. Box 100, Nazareth, TX 79063 t) 806-945-2616 holyfamilynaz@gmail.com www.hfpnaz.org Rev. Bhaskar Adusupalli, Admin.; Dcn. Bob Birkenfeld; Dcn. Joe Hochstein; Stephanie DeMoss, DRE; CRP Stds.: 148

PAMPA

St. Vincent de Paul - 810 W. 23rd Ave., Pampa, TX 79065 t) 806-665-8933; 806-665-8933 x4 (CRP) stvincentpampa.org Very Rev. Francisco Perez, Pst.; Rev. Luis Rene Lopez, Pst. Assoc.; Chrissie Silva, DRE; CRP Stds.: 223

PANHANDLE

St. Theresa - 125 Little Flower Way, Panhandle, TX 79068; Mailing: PO. Box 366, Panhandle, TX 79068 t) 806-537-3677 sgarner@dioama.org; sttheresachurchpanhandle@gmail.com www.theresacatholicchurchpanhandletexas.org Rev. Hrudaya Kondamudi, Pst.; Sr. Mary Katherine Dorsey, DRE; CRP Stds.: 3

PERRYTON

Immaculate Conception - 1000 S.W. 15th Ave., Perryton, TX 79070 t) 806-435-3802 icccptx@gmail.com Rev. Cesar Gomez, Pst.; Dcn. Estrada Guillermo; Dcn. Serigo Estrada; CRP Stds.: 203

St. Peter - Dcn. Felix Tudon;

SILVERTON

Our Lady of Loretto - 303 Pulitzer St., Silverton, TX 79257 t) 806-823-2548 arturomeza59@yahoo.com; aturomezago@gmail.com Rev. Msgr. Arturo Meza, Pst.;

St. Juan Diego - ; Mailing: P.O. Box 62, Quitaque, TX 79255

SPEARMAN

Sacred Heart - 901 S. Roland, Spearman, TX 79081; Mailing: P.O. Box 127, Spearman, TX 79081 t) 806-659-2166; 806-290-2190 (CRP) sacredheartspearmancatholic@gmail.com www.sacredheartspearman.com Rev. Anthony Raju Yanamala, Admin.; Dcn. Davin Winger; Olivia Mendoza, DRE; CRP Stds.: 174

Cristo Redentor - ; Mailing: P.O. Box 238, Gruver, TX 79040

STRATFORD

St. Joseph's - 515 S. Pearl St., Stratford, TX 79084; Mailing: PO Box 28, Stratford, TX 79084 t) 806-366-5687; 806-310-0438 (CRP) stjoeolg@gmail.com stjosephstratfordtx.com/ Rev. Victor Hugo Andrade, Pst.;

TULIA

Church of the Holy Spirit - 511 S. Austin St, Tulia, TX 79088; Mailing: P.O. Box 806, Tulia, TX 79088 t) 806-994-3511 holyspirit_saintpaul@hotmail.com holyspirittuliatx.com Rev. David Contreras, Pst.; Martha Rocha, DRE; CRP Stds.: 160

St. Paul the Apostle - 610 S Dudley St, Kress, TX 79052

TURKEY

Elizabeth Ann Seton - 902 Alexander Ave., Turkey, TX 79261; Mailing: P.O. Box 206, Turkey, TX 79261 t) 806-823-2548 arturomeza59@yahoo.com Rev. Msgr. Arturo Meza, Pst.;

UMBARGER

St. Mary's - 22830 Pondaseta Rd., Umbarger, TX 79091; Mailing: P.O. Box 105, Umbarger, TX 79091 t) 806-499-3531 stmarysumb@midplains.coop stmarysumbarger.com Rev. Alvin Tshuma, Pst.; CRP Stds.: 27

VEGA

Immaculate Conception - 905 S. Main St., Vega, TX 79092; Mailing: P.O. Box 250, Vega, TX 79092 t) 806-286-0149 immaculateconceptionvega.org/ Rev. Mieczyslaw Przepiora, Pst.; Mandi Brorman, DRE; CRP Stds.: 57

WELLINGTON

Our Mother of Mercy - 1108 Floydada St., Wellington, TX 79095; Mailing: P.O. Box 686, Wellington, TX 79095 t) 806-256-5358; 806-341-4354 (CRP) johnsudhakar333@gmail.com motherofmercywellingtontx.com Rev. John Sudhatar Sangabathini, Par. Vicar; Jennifer Lopez, DRE; CRP Stds.: 15

WHITE DEER

Sacred Heart Catholic Church - 500 N. Main St., White Deer, TX 79097; Mailing: P.O. Box 427, White Deer, TX 79097 t) 806-537-3677 sacredheartchurchwhitedeer@gmail.com Rev. Hrudaya Kondamudi, Pst.; Alberic Haiduk, DRE; CRP Stds.: 4

SCHOOLS: PRESCHOOL THRU HIGH SCHOOL

SCHOOLS

STATE OF TEXAS

AMARILLO

Amarillo Catholic Children's Development Centers - (PAR) 4108 Bonham St., Amarillo, TX 79110; Mailing: P.O. Box 19726, Amarillo, TX 79110 t) 806-353-7043 sgarner@dioama.org Gail Saiz, Contact; Stds.: 140; Lay Tchrs.: 7

St. Joseph Catholic Elementary and Montessori Preschool - 4118 S. Bonham St, Amarillo, TX 79110 t) 806-359-1604 office@stjosephlearning.com www.stjosephschoolamarillo.com Luis Hernandez, Prin.;

St. Joseph Catholic Elementary and Montessori Preschool - (PAR) (Grades PreK-5) 4118 S. Bonham St., Amarillo, TX 79110 t) 806-359-1604 office@stjosephlearning.com www.stjosephschoolamarillo.com Patricia Martinez, Prin.; Stds.: 65; Lay Tchrs.: 10

St. Mary's Cathedral School - (Grades PreK-5) 1200 S. Washington St., Amarillo, TX 79102 t) 806-376-9112 www.stmarysamarillo.org Lydia O'Rear, Prin.; Stds.: 175; Sr. Tchrs.: 2; Lay Tchrs.: 12

HIGH SCHOOLS

STATE OF TEXAS

AMARILLO

Holy Cross Catholic Academy - (DIO) (Grades 6-12) 4110 S. Bonham, Amarillo, TX 79110-1113 t) 806-355-9637 aseidenberger@holycrossama.org; clogan@holycrossama.org www.holycrossama.org (Coed) Stds.: 116; Scholastics: 4; Lay Tchrs.: 11

INSTITUTIONS LOCATED IN DIOCESE

ASSOCIATIONS [ASN]

AMARILLO

Association of Christ the King - 7108 Calumet Rd., Amarillo, TX 79106 t) 806-356-0337 mbernadetteblack@yahoo.com Order of Consecrated Virgins Mother Bernadette Black, Moderator;

CAMPUS MINISTRY / NEWMAN CENTERS [CAM]

CANYON

Catholic Student Center at West Texas A & M University - 2610 Fourth Ave., Canyon, TX 79015 t) 806-655-4345 csc@wtcsc.com www.wtcsc.org Rev. Grant Spinhirne, Dir.;

CATHOLIC CHARITIES [CCH]

AMARILLO

Catholic Charities of the Texas Panhandle - 2004 N. Spring St., Amarillo, TX 79107; Mailing: Box 15127, Amarillo, TX 79105-5127 t) 806-376-4571 jgulde@cctxp.org www.cctxp.org Jeff Gulde, Exec.; Asstd. Annu.: 3,461; Staff: 41

Downtown Women's Center, Inc. - 409 S. Monroe, Amarillo, TX 79101 t) 806-372-3625 diann@dwcenter.org www.dwcenter.org Diann Gilmore, Exec.; Asstd. Annu.: 2,985; Staff: 46

CONVENTS, MONASTERIES, AND RESIDENCES FOR WOMEN [CON]

AMARILLO

St. Francis Convent, Novitiate and U.S. Provincial House - 4301 N.E. 18th St., Amarillo, TX 79107 t) 806-383-5769 animationst.francis@outlook.com franciscansistersofmaryimmaculate.net Sr. Hilda Rodriguez, Vicar; Sr. Valentine A. Curry, F.M.I., Prov.; Srs.: 18

Madres Clarisas Capuchinas, Capuchin Nuns of St. Clare - 4201 N.E. 18th Ave., Amarillo, TX 79107 t) 806-383-9877; 806-383-6771 clarescap@gmail.com Convent of the Blessed Sacrament and Our Lady of

Guadalupe Sr. Frances de Maria Piceno, Abbess; Srs.: 11

PANHANDLE

Sancta Maria Convent (North American Region and Novitiate) - 119 Franciscan Way, Panhandle, TX 79068-0906; Mailing: P.O. Box 906, Panhandle, TX 79068 t) 806-537-3182 x3 schsrs@gmail.com www.panhandlefranciscans.org Sr. Mary Michael Husemam, OSF, Supr.; Sr. Maria Irina Teiner, OSF, Supr.; Srs.: 13

PRAYER TOWN

Disciples of the Lord Jesus Christ - 404 Holy Way, Prayer Town, TX 79010; Mailing: P.O. Box 64, Prayer Town, TX 79010 t) 806-534-2312 dljcsisters@gmail.com www.dljc.org Rev. Mieczyslaw Przepiora, Chap.; Mother Lucy Lukasiewicz, DLJC, Supr.; Srs.: 42

ENDOWMENTS / FOUNDATIONS / TRUSTS [EFT]

AMARILLO

Amarillo Scholarship Endowment and Assistance Fund - 4512 N. E. 24th Ave., Amarillo, TX 79117-5644 t) 806-383-2243 sgarner@dioama.org Most Rev. Patrick J. Zurek, Mem.;

Holy Family Parish of Nazareth, Texas Endowment Foundation - Diocese of Amarillo, 4512 N. E. 24th Ave., Amarillo, TX 79107 t) 806-383-2243 pwhitson@amarillodiocese.org Rev. Bhaskar Adusupalli; Most Rev. Patrick J. Zurek; James Mitchell, CEO;

Monsignor B.A. Erpen Trust Fund - Diocese of Amarillo, 4512 N. E. 24th Ave., Amarillo, TX 79107 t) 806-383-2243 pwhitson@dioama.org Most Rev. Patrick J. Zurek; James Mitchell, CEO;

Roman Catholic Diocese of Amarillo Deposit and Loan Fund - 4512 N. E. 24th Ave., Amarillo, TX 79107 t) 806-383-2243 pwhitson@amarillodiocese.org James Mitchell, CEO; Very Rev. Francisco Perez, Mem.; Most Rev. Patrick J. Zurek, Mem.;

Texas Panhandle Catholic Endowment Foundation - 4512 N. E. 24th Ave., Amarillo, TX 79107 t) 806-383-2243 pwhitson@amarillodiocese.org Most Rev. Patrick J. Zurek;

MISCELLANEOUS [MIS]

AMARILLO

Amarillo Catholic School System - 4512 N.E. 24th Ave., Amarillo, TX 79107 t) 806-383-2243 x110 sgarner@dioama.org Angie Seidenbeger, Supt.;

***Catholic Radio of the Texas High Plains** - 4037 S.W. 50th Ave., Ste. 101, Amarillo, TX 79109 t) 806-350-1360 stval@kdjw.org www.kdjw.org Dale Artho, Pres.;

Engaged Encounter - 4512 N.E. 24th Ave., Amarillo, TX 79107; Mailing: P.O. Box 5644, Amarillo, TX 79117-5644 t) 806-383-2243 x134 jschulte@dioama.org amarillodiocese.org James Schulte, Admin.;

Project Solidarity - Diocese of Amarillo, 4512 N. E. 24th Ave., Amarillo, TX 79107 t) 806-383-2243 mcolwell@amarillodiocese.org Rev. Christopher Schwind, Chancellor;

CANYON

Marriage Encounter - 2610 4th Ave., Canyon, TX 79015 t) 806-654-0066 s.c.schwind@gmail.com Patrick Kratochvil, Contact; Virginia Kratochvil, Contact;

RETREAT HOUSES / RENEWAL CENTERS [RTR]

AMARILLO

Bishop DeFalco Retreat Center - 2100 N. Spring St., Amarillo, TX 79107 t) 806-383-1811 general@bdrc.org www.bdrc.org Sr. Stella Maris, DLJC, Exec.;

Bishop DeFalco Retreat Center Foundation - Sr. Linda Astuto, Dir.;

PRAYER TOWN

Prayer Town Emmanuel Retreat House - 404 Holy Way, Prayer Town, TX 79010; Mailing: PO Box 64, Prayer Town, TX 79010 t) 806-534-2207; 806-534-2312 www.dljc.org Mother Lucy Lukasiewicz, DLJC, Supr.;

An asterisk (*) denotes an organization that has established tax-exempt status directly with the IRS and is not covered by the USCCB Group Ruling.

Archdiocese of Anchorage-Juneau

(Archidioecesis Ancoragiensis-Junellensis)

MOST REVEREND ANDREW E. BELLISARIO, C.M.

Archbishop of Anchorage-Juneau; ordained June 16, 1984; appointed Bishop of Juneau July 11, 2017; ordained and installed October 10, 2017; appointed Apostolic Administrator of Anchorage June 7, 2019; appointed first Archbishop of the Archdiocese of Anchorage-Juneau May 11, 2020; installed September 17, 2020.

Chancery Office - Anchorage: 225 Cordova St., Anchorage, AK 99501. T: 907-297-7700; F: 907-279-3041.
Chancery Office - Juneau: 415 Sixth St., Juneau, AK 99801. T: 907-586-2227; F: 907-463-3237.

www.aoaj.org

ESTABLISHED MAY 19, 2020.

Square Miles 176,551.

Comprises the First and Third Judicial Districts of the State of Alaska.

For legal titles of parishes and archdiocesan institutions, consult the Chancery Office.

STATISTICAL OVERVIEW

Personnel

Archbishops	1
Retired Archbishops	1
Priests: Diocesan Active in Diocese	19
Priests: Retired, Sick or Absent	8
Number of Diocesan Priests	27
Religious Priests in Diocese	12
Total Priests in your Diocese	39
Extern Priests in Diocese	7
Ordinations:	
Permanent Deacons	4
Permanent Deacons in Diocese	34
Total Brothers	1
Total Sisters	22

Parishes

Parishes	32
With Resident Pastor:	
Resident Diocesan Priests	14
Resident Religious Priests	8
Without Resident Pastor:	
Administered by Priests	8
Administered by Deacons	2
Missions	16
Pastoral Centers	1
Professional Ministry Personnel:	
Brothers	1
Sisters	14
Lay Ministers	22

Welfare

Catholic Hospitals	5
Total Assisted	124,332
Homes for the Aged	1
Total Assisted	42
Special Centers for Social Services	6
Total Assisted	17,968

Educational

Diocesan Students in Other Seminaries	1
Total Seminarians	1
High Schools, Diocesan and Parish	1
Total Students	96
Elementary Schools, Diocesan and Parish	4
Total Students	291
Catechesis/Religious Education:	
High School Students	341
Elementary Students	1,180
Total Students under Catholic Instruction	1,909
Teachers in Diocese:	
Lay Teachers	30

Vital Statistics

Receptions into the Church:	
Infant Baptism Totals	321
Minor Baptism Totals	36
Adult Baptism Totals	34
Received into Full Communion	46
First Communions	274
Confirmations	190
Marriages:	
Catholic	41
Interfaith	17
Total Marriages	58
Deaths	190
Total Catholic Population	25,634
Total Population	556,261

LEADERSHIP

Office of the Archbishop - t) (907) 297-7755

Vicar General - t) 907-297-7732 Rev. Patrick Travers (ptravers@aoaj.org);

Chancellor - t) 907-297-7732 Rev. Patrick Travers (ptravers@aoaj.org);

Vice Chancellor/Chief Operating Officer - t) (907) 297-7726 Matthew Meggs (mmeggs@aoaj.org);

Assistant to the Office of Archbishop Bellisario - t) 907-297-7755 Kimberly Bakic, Secy. (kbakic@aoaj.org);

Assistant to the Office of the Chancellor and Archbishop Emeritus Roger L. Schwietz, O.M.I. - t) 907-297-7720 Jessica Estes, Secy. (jestes@aoaj.org);

OFFICES AND DIRECTORS

Office of Stewardship & Communications - t) 907-297-7789 LeAndra Gee Childs, Dir. (lchilds@aoaj.org);

North Star Catholic - LeAndra Gee Childs, Dir.; Jay Luzardo, Editor;

Office of Deacons - t) (907) 297-7770 mfornelli@aoaj.org Dcn. James Fornelli, Dir.;

Deacon Formation - Dcn. David Van Tuyl, Dir.;

Office of Faith Formation and Catholic Schools - t) (907) 297-7723 lloeffler@aoaj.org Liz Loeffler, Dir.;

Office of Finance - t) (907) 297-7708 Danna Hoellering, Dir. (dhoellering@aoaj.org);

Office of Native Ministry - t) 907-297-7777 Sr. Frances Vista, D.C., Dir. (fvista@aoaj.org);

Office of Safe Environment and Victim Assistance Coordinators - t) 907-297-7736 Jennifer Michaelson, Dir. (jmichaelson@aoaj.org); Roberta Izzard, Victim Assistance Coord. (rizzard@aoaj.org);

Office of Seminarians - mgalbraith2121@gmail.com Rev. Michael D. Galbraith, Dir.;

Office of Vocations - roraff@gmail.com Rev. Arthur Roraff, Dir.;

ADVISORY BOARDS, COMMISSIONS, COMMITTEES, AND COUNCILS

Finance Council - Joe Moran, Chair;

Review Board for the Protection of Children and Young People - Destiny Sargeant, Chair;

TRIBUNAL

Judicial Vicar - t) 907-297-7724 Rev. Leo A. Walsh, Vicar (lwalsh@aoaj.org);

Administrator - t) 907-297-7724 Mary Nibbelink, Admin. (mnibbelink@aoaj.org);

Judge - t) 907-297-7724 Rev. Scott Garrett (tribunal@aoaj.org);

Defenders of the Bond - t) 907-297-7724 tribunal@aoaj.org Daniela Knepper (tribunal@aoaj.org);

Notaries - t) (907) 297-7724 tribunal@aoaj.org Mary Nibbelink (mnibbelink@aoaj.org); Angelina Cagle (acagle@aoaj.org); Charles Vankirk (cvankirk@aoaj.org);

Case Manager - t) 907-297-7710 Angelina Cagle (acagle@aoaj.org);

Auditor - t) (907) 297-7724 Charles Vankirk (cvankirk@aoaj.org);

PARISHES, MISSIONS, AND CLERGY

STATE OF ALASKA

ANCHORAGE

Cathedral of Our Lady of Guadalupe - 3900 Wisconsin St., Anchorage, AK 99517 t) 907-248-2000 olgakcocathedral.org/ Rev. Henry W Grodecki, C.M., Pst.; Rev. Humberto Aristizabal Sanchez, C.M., Pst. Min./Coord.; Carmen Ruiz, DRE; CRP Stds.: 167

Corp. of St. Andrew Kim Parish of the Korean Community - 7206 Lake Otis Pkwy., Anchorage, AK 99507 t) 907-333-5307 c) 907-227-3320 alaskakcc.com Rev. Joseph Ho-Sung Park, Pst.; CRP Stds.: 15

St. Anthony - 825 Klevin St., Anchorage, AK 99508-2656 t) 907-333-5544 office@stanthonyak.org www.stanthonyak.org Rev. Vincent Blanco, Pst.;

St. Benedict - 8110 Jewel Lake Rd., Anchorage, AK 99502 t) 907-243-2195; 907-273-1552 (CRP); (907) 273-1554 (CRP) parishsecretary@stbenedictsak.com; rmcmorrow@stbenedictsak.com www.stbenedictsak.com Rev. Thomas C. Lilly, Pst.; Robert McMorrow II, DRE; CRP Stds.: 91

St. Elizabeth Ann Seton - 2901 E. Huffman Rd., Anchorage, AK 99516 t) 907-345-4466 saintelizabeth.alaska@akseas.net www.akseas.net Rev. Scott Medlock, Pst.; Dcn. Kurt Adler; CRP Stds.: 156

Our Lady of the Snows - 370 Northface Rd., Girdwood, AK 99587 t) 907-783-1171 reservations@chapelourladyofthesnows.org www.chapelourladyofthesnows.org

Holy Cross - 2627 Lore Rd., Anchorage, AK 99507-5722 t) 907-349-8388 office@holycrossalaska.net www.holycrossalaska.net Rev. Patrick Travers, Pst.; Rev. Daniel J. Hebert, Parochial Admin.; Anna Schulten, DRE; CRP Stds.: 60

Holy Family Old Cathedral - 811 W. 6th Ave., Anchorage, AK 99501-2093 t) 907-276-3455 deacondave@holyfamilycathedral.org; frontdesk@holyfamilycathedral.org holyfamilycathedral.org Rev. Steve Maekawa, O.P., Pst.; Rev. Matthew Heynen, OP, Par. Vicar; Rev. Andy Opsahl, OP, Par. Vicar; Bro. Cassian Smyth, OP, DRE; Dcn. Gustavo Azpilcueta; Dcn. David Van Tuyl; CRP Stds.: 101

St. Patrick - 2111 Muldoon Rd., Anchorage, AK 99504-3612 t) 907-337-1538 www.st.patsak.org Rev. Leo A. Walsh, Pst.; Dcn. James Fornelli; Dcn. John A. Ostrom; Elizabeth Jones, DRE; Catherine A. Haslett, Youth Min.; John Peter Gagnon, Bus. Mgr.; CRP Stds.: 122

BIG LAKE

Our Lady of the Lake Church - 4275 S. Oscar Anderson Rd., Big Lake, AK 99652; Mailing: PO Box 520769, Big Lake, AK 99652 t) 907-892-6492 ourladyofc@mtaonline.net; kennelwood2000@yahoo.com Rev. Joseph McGilloway, Pst.; Rev. Madison Hayes, Par. Vicar; Rev. Armand Dice, Par. Vicar; Carol Hepler, Pst. Assoc.; CRP Stds.: 19

St. Christopher - ; Mailing: P.O. Box 412, Willow, AK 99688 t) 907-495-4500

CORDOVA

St. Joseph - 220 Adams Ave., Cordova, AK 99574; Mailing: P.O. Box 79, Cordova, AK 99574 t) 907-424-3637 Rev. Michael Hak Hyeon Kim, KMS, Pst.; Debbie Collins, DRE; CRP Stds.: 25

DILLINGHAM

Holy Rosary - 509 Airport Rd., Dillingham, AK 99576; Mailing: P.O. Box 810, Dillingham, AK 99576 t) 907-843-1277 www.holyrosaryalaska.org Rev. Scott Garrett, Pst.;

St. Theresa - Mile 8 Alaska Peninsula Hwy., Naknek, AK 99663; Mailing: P.O. Box 269, Naknek, AK 99633 t) 907-246-6652 sgarrett@caa-ak.org

EAGLE RIVER

St. Andrew - 16300 Domain Ln., Eagle River, AK 99577 t) 907-694-2170 parishsecretary@aksaintandrews.org www.aksaintandrews.org Rev. Arthur Roraff, Pst.; Most Rev. Roger L. Schwietz, O.M.I., In Res.; Dcn. Jim Lee; Dcn. Mark Merrill; Margaret Holtz, DRE; CRP Stds.: 192

GLENNALLEN

Holy Family - Aurora Dr./MP 187 Glenn Hwy., Glennallen, AK 99588; Mailing: P.O. Box 126, Glennallen, AK 99588 c) 907-350-8210 hermon@mtaonline.net Rev. Scott Medlock, Pst.; Dcn. Jon Hermon, Parish Life Coord.; CRP Stds.: 5

HAINES

Sacred Heart - 305 Dalton St., Haines, AK 99827; Mailing: Box 326, Haines, AK 99827 t) 907-766-2241 www.sacredhearthaines.org Rev. Michael Ko, K.M.S.; Dcn. Vincent G. Hansen, Pst. Assoc.;

St. Therese of the Child Jesus - 9th Ave. & State St., Skagway, AK 99840; Mailing: P.O. Box 496, Skagway, AK 99840 t) 907-983-2271 www.skagwaycatholicchurch.org/contact/

HOMER

St. John the Baptist - 255 Ohlson Ln., Homer, AK 99603 t) 907-235-8436 st.john@gci.net Rev. Jaime Mencias, Par. Admin.; CRP Stds.: 9

St. Peter the Apostle - 16145 Sterling Hwy., Ninilchik, AK 99639; Mailing: P.O. Box 39290, Ninilchik, AK 99639 t) 907-567-3490 st.peter136@gmail.com

JUNEAU

Co-Cathedral of the Nativity of the Blessed Virgin Mary - 416 Fifth St., Juneau, AK 99801 t) 907-586-1513; 907-586-1317 (CRP) cathedraladmin@dioceseofjuneau.org; cathedraldre@acsalaska.net www.juneaucathedral.org Rev. Patrick T. Casey, O.M.I., Pst.; Dcn. Steven B. Olmstead, Pst. Assoc.; Dcn. Charles H. Rohrbacher; Bridget Goertzen, DRE; CRP Stds.: 30

St. Paul the Apostle - 9055 Atlin Dr., Juneau, AK 99801 t) 907-789-7303 (CRP); 907-789-7307 x2 stpauls@ptialaska.net; stpcath@ptialaska.net www.stpaulsjuneau.org Rev. Michael D. Galbraith, Pst.; Rev. Steven P. Gallagher, Par. Vicar; Dcn. Mike Monagle; Kimberly Watt, DRE; CRP Stds.: 92

KENAI

Our Lady of the Angels - 225 S. Spruce Rd., Kenai, AK 99611 t) 907-283-4555 kenaicatholicchurch.org/ Rev. Patrick Brosamer, Pst.; Rev. Robert Whitney, Par. Vicar; Caroline Cordes, DRE; Rosemary Bird, Music Min.; Daniel Cordes, Youth Min.; CRP Stds.: 65

KETCHIKAN

Holy Name - 433 Jackson St., Ketchikan, AK 99901 t) 907-225-2570 churchoffice@holynamektn.org; dre@holynamektn.org holynamektn.com Rev. James Wallace, Par. Admin.; CRP Stds.: 15

Holy Name School - (Grades PreK-PreK) t) 907-225-2400 schooloffice@holynamektn.org www.holynameschoolketchikan.org Trish Nichols, Dir.; Stds.: 19; Lay Tchrs.: 2

Holy Family, Metlakatla -

KLAWOCK

St. John by the Sea - 6840 Michigan Ave., Klawock, AK 99925; Mailing: P.O. Box 245, Klawock, AK 99925 t) 907-755-2345 saintjohnbythesea@aoaj.org www.dioceseofjuneau.org Rev. Augustine Minn, KMS, Pst.; CRP Stds.: 14

KODIAK

St. Mary's - 2920 Mill Bay Rd., Kodiak, AK 99615; Mailing: 2932 Mill Bay Rd., Kodiak, AK 99615 t) 907-486-5411 saintmary@gci.net www.stmaryskodiak.org Rev. Mark Stronach, Par. Admin.; CRP Stds.: 56

PALMER

St. Michael - 432 E. Fireweed Ave., Palmer, AK 99645 t) 907-745-3229 frontdesk@st-mikesparish.org; joanner@st-mikesparish.org saintmichaelcatholicchurch.org Rev. Michael Shields, Pst.; Dcn. Curt Leuenberger; Dcn. Harry Moore; Michael Horvatin, Liturgy Dir.; Ashleigh Hecimovich, Music Min.; Margaret Giroux, Youth Min.; Joanne Rousculp, DRE; CRP Stds.: 130

PETERSBURG

St. Catherine of Siena - 306 N. Third St., Petersburg, AK 99833; Mailing: P.O. Box 508, Petersburg, AK 99833-0508 t) 907-772-3257 saintcatherine@aoaj.org www.stcatherineofsienapetersburg.com Rev. Jose Thomas, mcbs (India), Par. Admin.; CRP Stds.: 10

SEWARD

Sacred Heart - 409 Fifth Ave., Seward, AK 99664; Mailing: P.O. Box 207, Seward, AK 99664 t) 907-224-5414 sacredheartseward@gmail.com sacredheartseward.org Rev. Scott Medlock, Pst.; Rev. Richard Tero, Pastor Emer.; Dcn. Walter Corrigan;

Rev. William Hanrahan, In Res.; Celeste Lemme, DRE; CRP Stds.: 14

St. John Neumann Church - Snug Harbor Rd., Cooper Landing, AK 99572; Mailing: PO Box 737, Cooper Landing, AK 99572 t) 907-595-1300

SITKA

St. Gregory Nazianzen - 605 Lincoln St., Sitka, AK 99835; Mailing: P.O. Box 495, Sitka, AK 99835-0495 t) 907-747-8371 mail.stgregory@gmail.com sites.google.com/site/stgregorysitka/ Dcn. Ron Mathews; CRP Stds.: 20

SOLDOTNA

Our Lady of Perpetual Help - 222 W. Redoubt Ave., Soldotna, AK 99669 t) 907-262-4749; 907-262-5542 (CRP) www.olphak.org Rev. Patrick Brosamer, Pst.; Dcn. David Carey; Rev. Robert Whitney, Pst. Assoc.; CRP Stds.: 37

TALKEETNA

St. Bernard - 22036 S. F St., Talkeetna, AK 99676; Mailing: P.O. Box 510, Talkeetna, AK 99676 t) 907-733-2442; 907-223-3198 stbernardschurchtalkeetna@gmail.com Rev. Joseph McGilloway, Pst.;

St. Philip Benizi - Parks Hwy. Mile 114, Trapper Creek, AK 99683; Mailing: PO Box 510, Talkeetna, AK 99676 t) (907) 733-2442

UNALASKA

St. Christopher By the Sea - 107 Riverside Dr., Unalaska, AK 99685; Mailing: P.O. Box 405, Unalaska, AK 99685 t) 907-581-4022 stchrsea@yahoo.com Dcn. Daniel Winters; CRP Stds.: 10

VALDEZ

St. Francis Xavier - 357 Pioneer Dr., Valdez, AK 99686; Mailing: P.O. Box 908, Valdez, AK 99686 t) 907-835-4556 Rev. Frank Reitter, Pst.; Dcn. Daniel Stowe; CRP Stds.: 12

WASILLA

Sacred Heart - 1201 E. Bogard Rd., Wasilla, AK 99654-6523 t) 907-376-5087 shparish@mtaonline.net; frmadison@sacredheartwasilla.org www.sacredheartwasilla.org Rev. Joseph McGilloway, Pst.; Rev. Madison Hayes, Par. Vicar; Julie DeKreon, DRE; CRP Stds.: 100

WRANGELL

St. Rose of Lima - 120 Church St., Wrangell, AK 99929; Mailing: Box 469, Wrangell, AK 99929 t) 907-874-3771 strosewrg@gmail.com www.stroseoflimawrangell.com Rev. Jose Thomas, mcbs (India), Par. Admin.; CRP Stds.: 5

YAKUTAT

St. Ann - Forest Hwy. 10, Yakutat, AK 99689; Mailing: P.O. Box 323, Yakutat, AK 99689 t) 907-784-3287 Dcn. Mike Monagle;

SCHOOLS: PRESCHOOL THRU HIGH SCHOOL

SCHOOLS

STATE OF ALASKA

ANCHORAGE

St. Elizabeth Ann Seton School - (PAR) (Grades PreK-6) 2901 E. Huffman Rd., Anchorage, AK 99516 t) 907-345-3712 kathy@akseas.com www.akseas.com Kathy Gustafson, Admin.; Stds.: 190; Lay Tchrs.: 11

KODIAK

St. Mary's Catholic School - (PAR) (Grades PreK-K) 2932 Mill Bay Rd., Kodiak, AK 99615 t) 907-486-3513 www.smskodiak.org Teri Schneider, Prin.; Stds.: 25; Lay Tchrs.: 3

WASILLA

Our Lady of the Valley Catholic School - (PAR) (Grades PreK-8) 1201 E. Bogard Rd., Wasilla, AK 99654 t) 907-376-0883 ksmith@valleycatholicschool.org www.olvwasilla.com Joyce Lund, Prin.; Stds.: 57; Lay Tchrs.: 6

HIGH SCHOOLS

STATE OF ALASKA

ANCHORAGE

Lumen Christi High School - (PAR) (Grades 7-12) 8110 Jewel Lake Rd., Bldg. D., Anchorage, AK 99502 t) 907-245-9231 lchs@lumenchristiak.com www.lumenchristiak.org Brian Ross, Prin.; Stds.: 96; Lay Tchrs.: 8

CATHOLIC CHARITIES [CCH]

ANCHORAGE

Catholic Social Services Center - 3710 E. 20th Ave., Anchorage, AK 99508 t) 907-222-7300 info@cssalaska.org; rsmithson@cssalaska.org www.cssalaska.org Robin Dempsey, Exec.; Asstd. Annu.: 12,300; Staff: 260

Clare House - 4110 Spenard Rd., Anchorage, AK 99517; Mailing: 3710 E. 20th Ave., Anchorage, AK 99508 t) 907-563-4545 shughes@cssalaska.org; rdempsey@cssalaska.org www.cssalaska.org Temporary shelter for homeless women and women with children. Ministry of Catholic Social Service. Robin Dempsey, Exec.; Sharese Hughes, Dir.; Asstd. Annu.: 225; Staff: 14

JUNEAU

Catholic Community Service - 1803 Glacier Hwy., Juneau, AK 99801 t) 907-463-6100 info@ccsjuneau.org www.ccsak.org/ Catholic Community Service serves Southeast Alaska within the Diocese of Anchorage-Juneau Erin Walker-Tolles, Dir.; Asstd. Annu.: 3,200; Staff: 105

Society of St. Vincent de Paul - St. Therese Conference - 8617 Teal St., Juneau, AK 99801 t) 907-789-5535 info@svdpjuneau.org www.svdpjuneau.org Provide aid, shelter, and housing to the needy of Juneau. Dave Ringle, Dir.; Asstd. Annu.: 550; Staff: 23

CONVENTS, MONASTERIES, AND RESIDENCES FOR WOMEN [CON]

ANCHORAGE

Daughters of Charity - 3424 E. 15th Ave., Anchorage, AK 99508 t) 907-258-3424 Sr. Frances Virey Vista, Supr.; Srs.: 3

Sisters of Perpetual Adoration - 2645 E. 72nd Ave., Anchorage, AK 99507 t) 907-344-3330 adoratricesak@gmail.com Mother Evelia Alicia Martinez, Supr.; Srs.: 8

Sisters of St. Paul de Chartres - 7206 Lake Otis Pkwy., Anchorage, AK 99507; Mailing: 3005 W. 34th Ave., Apt. 4, Anchorage, AK 99517 t) 907-258-3273 andykwonak@gmail.com Sr. Youngae Ku, SPC, Contact; Srs.: 2

ENDOWMENTS / FOUNDATIONS / TRUSTS

INSTITUTIONS LOCATED IN DIOCESE [EFT]

ANCHORAGE

Archdiocese of Anchorage Priests Pension Trust - 225 Cordova St., Anchorage, AK 99501 t) 907-297-7755 kbakic@aoaj.org Jacque Briskey, Chair;

Catholic Foundation of Alaska - 225 Cordova St., Anchorage, AK 99501 t) 907-297-7755; 907-297-7732 kbakic@aoaj.org; ptravers@aoaj.org www.archdioceseofanchorage.org Matthew Meggs, Pres.; Danna Hoellering, Treas.;

Providence Alaska Foundation, Anchorage, Alaska - 3760 Piper St., Ste. 2021, Anchorage, AK 99508 t) 907-261-3600 suzanne.carte-cocroft@providence.org www.providence.org/alaska Suzanne Carte-Cocroft, Pres.;

HOSPITALS / HEALTH SERVICES [HOS]

ANCHORAGE

Providence Alaska Medical Center - 3200 Providence Dr., Anchorage, AK 99508; Mailing: P.O. Box 196604, Anchorage, AK 99519-6604 t) 907-212-2211 Properties, entities, and divisions owned or operated: Providence Health & Services-Washington; Providence Alaska Medical Center, Anchorage, AK. Ella Goss, CEO; Dr. Michael Bernstein, Chief Medical Officer; Bed Capacity: 401; Asstd. Annu.: 100,138; Staff: 2,339

KETCHIKAN

PeaceHealth Ketchikan Medical Center - 3100 Tongass Ave., Ketchikan, AK 99901 t) 907-225-5171 Liz Dunne, CEO; Bed Capacity: 25; Asstd. Annu.: 8,094; Staff: 481

KODIAK

Providence Kodiak Island Medical Center - 1915 E. Rezanof Dr., Kodiak, AK 99615 t) 907-486-3281 karl.hertz@providence.org Karl Hertz, Admin.; Timothy Hocum, CFO; Bonnie Neff, Exec. Dir., Nursing; Bed Capacity: 47; Asstd. Annu.: 9,698; Staff: 215

SEWARD

Providence Seward Medical & Care Center - 417 First Ave., Seward, AK 99664; Mailing: P.O. Box 365, Seward, AK 99664 t) 907-224-5205 robert.rang@providence.org alaska.providence.org Robert Rang, Admin.; Cole White, CFO; Bed Capacity: 46; Asstd. Annu.: 3,784; Staff: 138

VALDEZ

Providence Valdez Medical Center - 911 Meals Ave., Valdez, AK 99686; Mailing: P.O. Box 550, Valdez, AK 99686-0550 t) 907-835-2249 Matthew Wadsworth, Admin.; Lindsie King, CFO; Bed Capacity: 21; Asstd. Annu.: 2,618; Staff: 101

MISCELLANEOUS [MIS]

ANCHORAGE

Alaska Conference of Catholic Bishops - 225 Cordova St., Anchorage, AK 99501 t) 907-297-7744 mgore@aoaj.org www.akbishops.org Mary Gore, Exec.;

Providence Horizon House - 4140 Folker St., Anchorage, AK 99508 t) 907-212-5340 theresa.gleason@providence.org Assisted Living Theresa Gleason, Dir.;

Providence In-Home Services - 4001 Dale St., Ste. 101, Anchorage, AK 99507 t) 907-563-0130 sharon.bergstedt@providence.org Sharon Bergstedt, Dir.; Dr. Michael Bernstein, Region Chief Medical Officer;

JUNEAU

Archdiocesan Missions - 415 Sixth St., Ste. 300, Juneau, AK 99801 t) 907-586-2227 Dcn. Mike Monagle;

Elfin Cove - Dcn. Mike Monagle;

Excursion Inlet - Dcn. Mike Monagle;

St. Francis - Dcn. Vincent G. Hansen, Dir.;

Gustavus - Dcn. Mike Monagle;

Kake - t) 907-209-7005 Dcn. Steve Olmstead, Dir.;

Pelican - ; Mailing: 4115 6th St. #300, Juneau, AK 99801 Dcn. Mike Monagle;

Sacred Heart - Dcn. Steven B. Olmstead;

PALMER

Bishop's Attic II, Inc. - 840 S. Bailey St., Palmer, AK 99645 t) 907-745-4215 thebishopsattic2@hotmail.com Jack Williamson, Exec.;

NURSING / REHABILITATION / CONVALESCENCE / ELDERLY CARE [NUR]

ANCHORAGE

Providence Extended Care (Providence Health & Services-Washington) - 920 Compassion Cir., Anchorage, AK 99504 t) 907-212-9200 angela.lewis@providence.org Angela Lewis, Admin.; Asstd. Annu.: 42; Staff: 159

RETREAT HOUSES / RENEWAL CENTERS [RTR]

ANCHORAGE

Holy Spirit Center - 10980 Hillside Dr., Anchorage, AK 99507 t) 907-297-7700 hsc@holyspiritcenterak.org www.holyspiritcenterak.org Alan Muise, Dir.;

SHRINES [SHR]

JUNEAU

National Shrine of St. Therese - 21425 Glacier Hwy., Juneau, AK 99801; Mailing: 415 Sixth St., #300, Juneau, AK 99801 t) 907-789-9815 juneaushrine@aoaj.org shrineofsainttherese.org Joe Sehnert, Dir.;

SPECIAL CARE FACILITIES [SPF]

ANCHORAGE

Brother Francis Shelter - 1021 E. Third Ave., Anchorage, AK 99501; Mailing: 3710 E. 20th Ave., Anchorage, AK 99508 t) 907-277-1731 rdempsey@cssalaska.org; jstoehr@cssalaska.org www.cssalaska.org Overnight shelter for homeless men and women. A ministry of Catholic Social Services. Jennifer Stoehr, Dir.; Robin Dempsey, Exec.; Bed Capacity: 120; Asstd. Annu.: 440; Staff: 28

Covenant House Alaska - 755 A St., Anchorage, AK 99501; Mailing: PO Box 100620, Anchorage, AK 99510 t) 907-272-1255 akear@covenanthouseak.org; grants2@covenanthouseak.org Comprehensive services for homeless, trafficked, and at-risk youth ages 13-24. Alison Kear, CEO; Bed Capacity: 191; Asstd. Annu.: 1,253; Staff: 156

An asterisk (*) denotes an organization that has established tax-exempt status directly with the IRS and is not covered by the USCCB Group Ruling.

Diocese of Arlington

(Dioecesis Arlingtonensis)

MOST REVEREND MICHAEL F. BURBIDGE, ED.D., D.D.

Bishop of Arlington; ordained May 19, 1984; appointed Auxiliary Bishop of Philadelphia and Titular Bishop of Cluain Iraird June 21, 2002; consecrated September 5, 2002; appointed Fifth Bishop of Raleigh June 8, 2006; installed August 4, 2006; appointed Fourth Bishop of Arlington October 4, 2016; installed December 6, 2016. The Chancery: 200 N. Glebe Rd., Ste. 914, Arlington, VA 22203.

The Chancery: 200 N. Glebe Rd., Ste. 914, Arlington, VA 22203. T: 703-841-2500; F: 703-524-5028.

ESTABLISHED AUGUST 13, 1974.

Square Miles 6,541.

Comprises the following 21 Counties in Northern Virginia: Arlington, Clarke, Culpeper, Fairfax, Fauquier, Frederick, King George, Lancaster, Loudoun, Madison, Northumberland, Orange, Page, Prince William, Rappahannock, Richmond, Shenandoah, Spotsylvania, Stafford, Warren and Westmoreland and the 7 independent cities of Alexandria, Fairfax City, Falls Church, Fredericksburg, Manassas, Manassas Park and Winchester.

For legal titles of parishes and diocesan institutions, consult the Chancery Office.

STATISTICAL OVERVIEW

Personnel

Bishop....1
Retired Bishops....1
Abbots....1
Priests: Diocesan Active in Diocese....150
Priests: Diocesan Active Outside Diocese....15
Priests: Diocesan in Foreign Missions....2
Priests: Retired, Sick or Absent....31
Number of Diocesan Priests....198
Religious Priests in Diocese....61
Total Priests in your Diocese....259
Extern Priests in Diocese....30
Ordinations:
Diocesan Priests....8
Religious Priests....1
Transitional Deacons....9
Permanent Deacons in Diocese....89
Total Brothers....6
Total Sisters....97

Parishes

Parishes....70
With Resident Pastor:
Resident Diocesan Priests....61
Resident Religious Priests....9
Missions....6
Professional Ministry Personnel:
Brothers....4
Sisters....25

Welfare

Catholic Hospitals....1
Total Assisted....48,495
Health Care Centers....8
Total Assisted....40,845
Day Care Centers....38
Total Assisted....1,795
Specialized Homes....2
Total Assisted....58
Special Centers for Social Services....29
Total Assisted....24,917
Other Institutions....2
Total Assisted....488

Educational

Diocesan Students in Other Seminaries....48
Total Seminarians....48
Colleges and Universities....4
Total Students....5,444
High Schools, Diocesan and Parish....4
Total Students....3,799
High Schools, Private....3
Total Students....430
Elementary Schools, Diocesan and Parish....37
Total Students....11,722
Elementary Schools, Private....4
Total Students....612
Catechesis / Religious Education:
High School Students....1,724
Elementary Students....18,820
Total Students under Catholic Instruction....42,599
Teachers in Diocese:
Priests....14
Sisters....20
Lay Teachers....1,710

Vital Statistics

Receptions into the Church:
Infant Baptism Totals....4,931
Minor Baptism Totals....379
Adult Baptism Totals....317
Received into Full Communion....409
First Communions....4,939
Confirmations....5,003
Marriages:
Catholic....967
Interfaith....355
Total Marriages....1,322
Deaths....2,217
Total Catholic Population....433,401
Total Population....3,381,214

LEADERSHIP

The Chancery - t) 703-841-2500

Bishop - t) 703-841-2511 Most Rev. Michael F. Burbidge;

Vicar General - t) 703-841-2563 Very Rev. Jamie R. Workman;

Chancellor - t) 703-841-2763 Very Rev. Robert J. Rippy, Chancellor; Rev. Edward R. Horkan, Vice Chancellor;

General Counsel - t) 703-841-2524 Mark E. Herrmann;

Episcopal Vicar for Charitable Works - t) 703-841-3830 Very Rev. Robert C. Cilinski, Episcopal Vicar;

Episcopal Vicar for Clergy and Director of the Diaconate Formation Program - t) 703-841-3809 Very Rev. Paul D. Scalia, Episcopal Vicar;

Episcopal Vicar for Faith Formation - t) 703-841-8552 Very Rev. William P. Saunders, Episcopal Vicar;

Diocesan Finance Officer - t) 703-841-2543 Timothy R. Cotnoir;

Chief Operations Officer - t) 703-841-2563 Ward Jones;

OFFICES AND DIRECTORS

Campus Ministry - t) 540-373-6746 Rev. Christopher T. Vaccaro, Bishop's Liaison;

Catholic Charities of the Diocese of Arlington - t) 703-841-3895 Very Rev. Robert C. Cilinski, Episcopal Vicar; Stephen Carattini, Pres.;

Christ House Transitional Housing - t) 703-549-8644 John Croft, Prog. Dir.;

Christians Are Networking (CAN) Jobs Ministry - t) 703-841-3838 Debra Beard, Prog. Dir.;

Emergency Assistance - t) 703-443-2481 Sherri Longhill, Prog. Dir.;

Family Services - t) 703-425-0109 Lorenzo Resendez, Prog. Dir.;

Hogar Immigrant Services - t) 703-534-9805 Stacy Jones, Prog. Dir.;

Education Services - t) 571-208-1572 Jackeline Chavez, Prog. Dir.;

Migration and Refugee Services - t) 571-292-2259 Belayneh Loppisso, Prog. Dir.;

Mobile Response Center - t) 703-841-2581 Catherine Hassinger, Prog. Dir.;

Mother of Mercy Free Medical Clinic (Manassas) - t) 703-335-2779 Alexandra Luevano, Prog. Dir.;

Mother of Mercy Free Medical Clinic (Woodbridge) - t) 703-335-2779 Alexandra Luevano, Prog. Dir.;

Opioid Crisis Services - Dr. Michael Horne, Dir.;

Parish Liaison Network - t) 703-841-3838 Debra Beard, Prog. Dir.;

Pregnancy and Adoption Support - t) 703-425-0100 Meaghan Lane, Prog. Mgr.;

Prison Ministry - t) 703-841-3832 Bill Hall, Coord.;

Saint Lucy Food Distribution Program - t) 703-479-2975 Vince Cannava, Prog. Dir.;

Saint Margaret of Cortona Transitional Residences - t) 703-910-4845 Veronica Roth, Prog. Dir.;

Senior Services/St. Martin de Porres Senior Center - t) (703) 751-2766

Welcome Home Re-Entry Program - t) 703-841-3838 Debra Beard, Prog. Dir.;

Catholic Education, Office of Catechetics - Very Rev. William P. Saunders, Vicar; Ana Lisa Pinon, Dir.;

Office of Catholic Schools - t) 703-841-2519 catholicschools@arlingtondiocese.org Joseph E. Vorbach III, Supt.;

Child Protection and Safety - t) 703-841-3847 Dcn. R. Marques Silva, Dir.;

Communications Office - t) 703-841-2592 communications@arlingtondiocese.org Billy Atwell, Chief Communications Officer;

Development Office - t) 703-841-2545 Robert P. Mueller, Exec. Dir.;

Diaconal Formation Program - t) 703-841-3809 Very Rev. Paul D. Scalia, Episcopal Vicar;

Diocesan Offices -

Accounting Office - t) 703-841-2682 Laura Cayrampoma, Dir.;

Archives - t) 703-841-2340 archives@arlingtondiocese.org Lindsay Alukonis, Archivist;

Arlington Catholic Herald, Inc. - t) 703-841-2590 Kevin Schweers, Exec. Editor of Content;

Divine Worship Office - t) 703-224-1653 Rev. Michael D. Weston, Dir.; Richard Gibala, Coord.;

Ecumenical and Interreligious Affairs Commission - t) 703-451-8576 Rev. Donald J. Rooney, Chair;

Human Resources - t) 703-841-2522 Teresa D'Elia, Exec. Dir.;

Information Technology - t) 703-841-3825 Kimberly T. Murphy, Dir.;

Marriage, Family, and Respect Life Office - t) 703-841-2550 familylife@arlingtondiocese.org Therese Bermpohl, Exec. Dir.;

Gabriel Project-Pregnancy Assistance Program - t) 703-841-3812 gabrielproject@arlingtondiocese.org Sarah LaPierre, Dir.;

Marriage Preparation & Enrichment - t) 703-841-3807 cfe@arlingtondiocese.org Alex Wolfe, Prog. Specialist;

Project Rachel Post-Abortion Outreach - t) 703-841-2504 projectrachel@arlingtondiocese.org Sarah LaPierre, Dir.;

Respect Life/Pro-Life Activities - respectlife@arlingtondiocese.org Amy McInerny, Dir.;

Office of Charismatic Renewal - t) 703-224-1474

Office of Multicultural Ministries - t) 703-841-3888 mcm@arlingtondiocese.org Bridget Wilson, Dir.;

Planning, Construction and Facilities - t) 703-841-2572 Andrew Schulman, Dir.;

Pontifical Mission Societies and Propagation of the Faith - t) 703-532-8815 arlingtonmissions@arlingtondiocese.org Very Rev. Patrick L. Posey, Diocesan Dir.;

Spanish Apostolate - t) 703-841-3883 Joel de Loera, Dir.;

Risk Management, Office of - t) 703-841-2503 Mary Stewart, Dir.;

Victim Assistance Coordinator - t) 703-841-2530 victimassistance@arlingtondiocese.org Frank Moncher, Coord.;

Vocations, Office of - t) 703-841-2514 Rev. Michael C. Isenberg, Dir.; Mother Maria Gonzalez, Coord. Hispanic Women's Vocations;

Youth, Campus, and Young Adult Ministry, Office of - t) 703-841-2559 youthministry@arlingtondiocese.org Kevin Bohli, Exec. Dir.;

CONSULTATIVE BODIES

Clergy Personnel Board - t) 703-841-3809 Very Rev. Paul D. Scalia, Episcopal Vicar;

Diaconal Council - t) 703-969-1103 Dcn. Timothy H. Slayter, Chair;

Diocesan Finance Council - John Allen, Chair;

Pastoral Council - Most Rev. Michael F. Burbidge, Mem.;

Presbyteral Council - Most Rev. Michael F. Burbidge, Pres.; Rev. James R. Gould, Chair; Very Rev. Kevin B. Walsh, Vice Chmn.;

Sisters' Council - Sr. Judith Gebelein, F.S.E., Pres.; Sr. Elizabeth Ann Goltman, I.H.M., Vice. Pres.;

TRIBUNAL

Advocates for the Respondent - Rev. Michael C. Isenberg; Rev. Joseph D. Bergida; Sr. Paula Jean Miller, F.S.E.;

Defenders of the Bond - Rev. Paul A. Berghout; Rev. Thomas J. Lehning; Dcn. William J. Donovan;

Diocesan Judges - Very Rev. Robert J. Rippy; Rev. Thomas P. Ferguson; Rev. William B. Schardt;

Notaries - Rev. Kevin J. Dansereau; Claire Hilado; Rev. William Nyce;

The Tribunal - t) 703-841-2555 Very Rev. Robert J. Rippy, Judicial Vicar;

Judicial Vicar - t) 703-841-2556 Very Rev. Robert J. Rippy;

Promoter of Justice - Very Rev. Lee R. Roos;

PARISHES, MISSIONS, AND CLERGY

COMMONWEALTH OF VIRGINIA

ALDIE

Corpus Christi - 41677 Corpus Christi Dr., Aldie, VA 20105 t) 703-378-1037 info@corpuschristi.org Very Rev. Michael G. Taylor, Pst.; Rev. Charles W. Merkle III, Par. Vicar; Dcn. Peter A. Reyda; Rev. Stephen J. Schultz, In Res.; CRP Stds.: 536

ALEXANDRIA

Blessed Sacrament - 1427 W. Braddock Rd., Alexandria, VA 22302 t) 703-998-6100 parish_office@blessedsacramentcc.org Rev. John D. Kelly, Pst.; Rev. Peter J. St. George, Par. Vicar; Rev. Thomas M. Yehl, Y.A., Par. Vicar; CRP Stds.: 247

Blessed Sacrament School - (Grades PreK-8) 1417 W. Braddock Rd., Alexandria, VA 22302 t) 703-998-4170 schoolinfo@bssva.org bssva.org Katy Chelak, Prin.; Stds.: 242; Lay Tchrs.: 23

Good Shepherd - 8710 Mount Vernon Hwy., Alexandria, VA 22309 t) 703-780-4055 www.gs-cc.org Rev. Thomas P. Ferguson, Pst.; Rev. Lino Rico Rostro, Par. Vicar; Rev. Cedric M. Wilson, O.S.A., In Res.; Dcn. Julian Gutierrez; Dcn. Michael J. O'Neil; Dcn. Patrick A. Ouellette; Dcn. Thomas G. White Jr.; CRP Stds.: 830

St. Joseph's - 711 N. Columbus St., Alexandria, VA 22314 t) 703-836-3725 Rev. Donald M. Fest, S.S.J., Pst.; Dcn. Albert A. Anderson Jr.; CRP Stds.: 22

St. Lawrence - 6222 Franconia Rd., Alexandria, VA 22310 t) 703-971-4378 stlawrencealex.org Rev. Ronald J. Gripshover Jr., Pst.; Rev. Maurice M. Akwa, Par. Vicar; Rev. Joseph O. Ocran, In Res.; Dcn. Michael A. Waters; CRP Stds.: 93

St. Louis - 2907 Popkins Ln., Alexandria, VA 22306 t) 703-765-4421 saintlouisparish.org Rev. Keith M. O'Hare, Pst.; Rev. Mark Mullaney, Par. Vicar; Rev. Gregory S. Thompson, Par. Vicar; CRP Stds.: 264

St. Louis School - (Grades PreSchool-8) 2901 Popkins Ln., Alexandria, VA 22306 t) 703-768-7732 office@stlouisschool.org; kmcnutt@stlouisschool.org www.stlouisschool.org Anne Dyke, Prin.; Stds.: 465; Lay Tchrs.: 38

Basilica of St. Mary - 310 S. Royal St., Alexandria, VA 22314; Mailing: 313 Duke St., Alexandria, VA 22314 t) 703-836-4100 admin@stmaryoldtown.org www.stmaryoldtown.org Rev. Edward C. Hathaway, Rector; Rev. Peter J. Clem, Par. Vicar; Rev. Joseph B. Townsend, Par. Vicar; Rev. Noah C. Morey, In Res.; CRP Stds.: 186

St. Mary's School - (Grades PreK-8) 400 Green St., Alexandria, VA 22314 t) 703-549-1646 jcantwell@smsva.org www.smsva.org Robert Loia, Prin.; Stds.: 684; Lay Tchrs.: 48

Queen of Apostles - 4401 Sano St., Alexandria, VA 22312; Mailing: 4329 Sano Street, Alexandria, VA 22312 t) 703-354-8711 www.queenofapostles.org Rev. Alexander Diaz, Pst.; Rev. Paul A. Berghout, Par. Vicar; Dcn. Richard C. Caporiccio; Dcn. Vincent Kapral; CRP Stds.: 167

Queen of Apostles School - (Grades K-8) 4409 Sano St., Alexandria, VA 22312 t) 703-354-0714 info@queenofapostlesschool.org www.queenofapostlesschool.org Kristie Meyers, Prin.; Margaret Walker, Vice Prin.; Stds.: 200; Lay Tchrs.: 19

St. Rita - 3815 Russell Rd., Alexandria, VA 22305 t) 703-836-1640 www.strita-parish.net Rev. Christopher P. Christensen, Pst.; Rev. Nicholas J. Schierer, Par.

Vicar; Rev. Lukasz Duda, In Res.; Dcn. Stephen J. Dixon; CRP Stds.: 221

St. Rita School - (Grades PreSchool-8) 3801 Russell Rd., Alexandria, VA 22305 t) 703-548-1888 saintritaschool@me.com www.saintrita-school.org Bethany Hamm, Prin.; Stds.: 204; Lay Tchrs.: 23

Sisters of St. Joseph - 231 W. Glebe Rd., Alexandria, VA 22305 t) 703-683-1929 Mother Maria Gonzalez, Supr.;

ANNANDALE

St. Ambrose - 3901 Woodburn Rd., Annandale, VA 22003 t) 703-280-4400 www.stambroseva.org Very Rev. Andrew J. Fisher, Pst.; Rev. Joseph M. Rampino, Par. Vicar; Dcn. Edward O. Devlin; CRP Stds.: 138

St. Ambrose School - (Grades PreK-8) 3827 Woodburn Rd., Annandale, VA 22003 t) 703-698-7171 arowley@stambroseschool.org; cyaglou@stambroseschool.org stambroseschool.org Maria Tejada, Prin.; Stds.: 154; Lay Tchrs.: 16

Holy Spirit - 8800 Braddock Rd., Annandale, VA 22003; Mailing: 5121 Woodland Way, Annandale, VA 22003 t) 703-978-8074; 703-978-8925 (CRP) parish@holyspiritchurch.us; religious.ed@holyspiritchurch.us www.holyspiritchurch.us Rev. John M. O'Donohue, Pst.; Rev. Carroll L. Oubre, Par. Vicar; Rev. Jerry A. Wooton, Par. Vicar; Rev. Hagos Tesfagabir Haile, In Res.; Dcn. Malcolm L. D'Souza; Dcn. Thomas L. Grodek; Dcn. Nicholas J. LaDuca Jr.; CRP Stds.: 412

Holy Spirit School - (Grades PreK-8) t) 703-978-7117 mashby@holyspiritflames.org www.holyspiritflames.org Maureen Ashby, Prin.; Stds.: 417; Lay Tchrs.: 40

St. Michael - 7401 St. Michaels Ln., Annandale, VA 22003 t) 703-256-7822 www.stmichaelannandale.org Rev. Alexander R. Drummond, Pst.; Rev. Michael J. Folmar, Par. Vicar; Rev. Stefan P. Starzynski, In Res.; Dcn. David S. McCaffrey; CRP Stds.: 116

St. Michael School - (Grades K-8) 7401 A St. Michaels Ln., Annandale, VA 22003 t) 703-256-1222 annie.fernandez@stmikes22003.org www.stmikes22003.org Annie Fernandez, Prin.; Stds.: 184; Lay Tchrs.: 16

Sisters of Our Lady of La Salette (SNDS) - 7421 St. Michael's Ln., Annandale, VA 22003 t) 703-865-8767

ARLINGTON

Cathedral of St. Thomas More - 3901 Cathedral Ln., Arlington, VA 22203 t) 703-525-1300 www.cathedralstm.org Very Rev. Patrick L. Posey, Rector; Rev. Kevin J. Dansereau, Par. Vicar; Rev. Eliberto Garcia, Par. Vicar; Rev. Michael D. Weston, In Res.; CRP Stds.: 130

Cathedral of St. Thomas More School - (Grades PreK-8) 105 N. Thomas St., Arlington, VA 22203 t) 703-528-6781 stmoffice@stmschool.org; tashworth@stmschool.org www.stmschool.org Catherine Davis, Prin.; Stds.: 453; Lay Tchrs.: 31

St. Agnes - 1910 N. Randolph St., Arlington, VA 22207-3046; Mailing: 1914 N Randolph St., Arlington, VA 22207 t) 703-525-1166; 703-527-1129 (CRP) business@saintagnes.org; dff@saintagnes.org saintagnes.org/ Very Rev. William P. Saunders, Pst.; Rev. Andrew W. Haissig, Par. Vicar; Rev. Steven G. Oetjen, In Res.; Rev. Anthony J. Pinizzotto, In Res.; CRP Stds.: 142

St. Agnes School - (Grades PreK-8) 2024 N. Randolph St., Arlington, VA 22207-3031 t) 703-527-5423 jkuzdzal@saintagnes.org www.saintagnes.org Jennifer Kuzdzal, Prin.; Stds.: 413; Lay Tchrs.: 32

St. Ann - 5300 10th St. N., Arlington, VA 22205 t) 703-528-6276; 703-528-6199 (Faith Formation) www.stannchurch.org Rev. Ramel O. Portula, C.I.C.M., Pst.; Rev. Ange Masuta Mafuta, C.I.C.M., Par. Vicar; Dcn. William J. Donovan; Dcn. Forrest Wallace; CRP Stds.: 667

Saint Ann Catholic School - (Grades PreK-8) 980 N. Frederick St., Arlington, VA 22205 t) 703-525-7599 stann@stann.org www.stann.org Anthony Sahadi, Prin.; Stds.: 204; Lay Tchrs.: 18

St. Charles Borromeo - 3304 N. Washington Blvd., Arlington, VA 22201 t) 703-527-5500 www.stcharleschurch.org Rev. Donald J. Planty Jr., Pst.; Rev. David A. Dufresne, Par. Vicar; CRP Stds.: 425

St. Charles Borromeo School - (Grades PreK-8) 3299 N. Fairfax Dr., Arlington, VA 22201 t) 703-527-0608 office@stcharlesarlington.org www.stcharlesarlington.org Robin Baney, Dir.; Stds.: 147; Lay Tchrs.: 11

Holy Martyrs of Vietnam Catholic Church - 915 S. Wakefield St., Arlington, VA 22204 t) 703-553-0370 www.cttdva.com Rev. Joseph Q.A. Dang, O.P., Pst.; Rev. Joseph Tien Minh Vu, O.P., Par. Vicar; Rev. Peter Phuong Dinh Nguyen, O.P., Par. Vicar; Rev. Vincent Thao Ngoc Dinh, Par. Vicar; CRP Stds.: 156

Our Lady of La Vang Mission - 661 Cedar Spring Rd., Centreville, VA 20121

Our Lady of Lourdes - 830 23rd St. S., Arlington, VA 22202 t) 703-684-9261 dre@ololcc.net www.ololcc.net Rev. Frederick H. Edlefsen, Pst.; Rev. Joseph R. Kenna, Par. Vicar; Rev. Daniel L. Mode, In Res.; Rev. Steven R. Walker, In Res.; CRP Stds.: 84

Our Lady, Queen of Peace - 2700 19th St S., Arlington, VA 22204 t) 703-979-5580 www.olqpva.org Rev. Timothy J. Hickey, C.S.Sp., Pst.; Rev. Martin Tu Quoc Vu, Par. Vicar; Dcn. Antonio J. Remedios; Rev. Robert J. Richter, In Res.; CRP Stds.: 181

San Francisco de Asis, Banica - 200 N. Glebe Rd., Ste. 914, Arlington, VA 22203 t) 829-665-3687 frohare@yahoo.com www.banicamission.com Rev. Jeb S. Donelan, Pst.; Rev. Stephen F. McGraw, Par. Vicar;

San Jose, Pedro Santana - 200 N. Glebe Rd., Ste. 914, Arlington, VA 22203 t) 829-665-3687 frohare@yahoo.com www.banicamission.com Rev. Stephen F. McGraw, Pst.; Rev. Jeb S. Donelan, Par. Vicar;

ASHBURN

St. Theresa - 21370 St. Theresa Ln., Ashburn, VA 20147 t) 703-729-2287 www.sainttheresaparish.com Rev. James C. Hudgins, Pst.; Rev. Nicholas R. Barnes, Par. Vicar; Rev. Paul L. Dudzinski, Par. Vicar; Rev. John F. O'Farrell, Par. Vicar; Dcn. Paul Konold; Dcn. Matthew K. Noah; Dcn. Anthony J. Renzette; CRP Stds.: 984

St. Theresa School - (Grades K-8) t) 703-729-3577 schooloffice@stsashburn.com www.stsashburn.com Erin O'Malley, Prin.; Stds.: 453; Lay Tchrs.: 35

BERRYVILLE

St. Bridget of Ireland Parish - 1024 W. Main St., Berryville, VA 22611 t) 540-227-2943 office@stbridgetberryville.org stbridgetberryville.org Rev. Paul Grankauskas, Pst.; CRP Stds.: 120

BURKE

Church of the Nativity - 6400 Nativity Ln., Burke, VA 22015 t) 703-455-2400 abenson@nativityburke.org www.nativityburke.org Very Rev. Robert C. Cilinski, Pst.; Rev. Christopher H. Hayes, Par. Vicar; Rev. Edward J. Bresnahan, Par. Vicar; Dcn. Richard Kelly; CRP Stds.: 942

Church of the Nativity School - (Grades PreK-8) 6398 Nativity Ln., Burke, VA 22015 t) 703-455-2300 mkelly@nativityschool.org www.nativityschool.org Maria E. Kelly, Prin.; Stds.: 253; Lay Tchrs.: 19

Handmaids of Reparation of the Sacred Heart of Jesus - 6300 Capella Ave., Burke, VA 22015 t) 703-455-4180 Sr. Donatella Merulla, A.R., Supr.;

CHANTILLY

St. Timothy - 13807 Poplar Tree Rd., Chantilly, VA 20151 t) 703-378-7461; 703-378-7646 www.sttimothyparish.org Rev. David P. Meng, Pst.; Rev. Sunny Joseph, Par. Vicar; Rev. Charles C. Pavlick, Par. Vicar; Rev. James R. Searby, Par. Vicar; Dcn. James C. Hepler; CRP Stds.: 352

Saint Timothy School - (Grades K-8) 13809 Poplar Tree Rd., Chantilly, VA 20151 t) 703-378-6932 info@sainttimothyschool.org www.sainttimothyschool.org Michael Pryor, Prin.; Stds.: 642; Lay Tchrs.: 42

St. Veronica - 3460 Centreville Rd., Chantilly, VA 20151 t) 703-773-2000 info@stveronica.net; re@stveronica.net stveronica.net/ Rev. Dennis W. Kleinmann, Pst.; Rev. Richard E. Dyer Jr., Par. Vicar; Dcn. J. Paul Ochenkowski; CRP Stds.: 127

St. Veronica School - (Grades PreK-8) 3460B Centreville Rd., Chantilly, VA 20151 t) 703-773-2020 info@stveronicaschool.org www.stveronicaschool.org/ Michael Busekrus, Prin.; Stds.: 374; Lay Tchrs.: 42

CLIFTON

St. Andrew the Apostle - 6720 Union Mill Rd., Clifton, VA 20124 t) 703-817-1770 www.st-andrew.org Rev. Robert Wagner, Pst.; Rev. Jonathan M. Smith, Par. Vicar; Rev. Nicholas A. Thalakkottur, In Res.; CRP Stds.: 198

St. Andrew the Apostle School - (Grades PreK-8) 6720-B Union Mill Rd., Clifton, VA 20124-1115 t) 703-817-1774 office@standrew-clifton.org www.standrew-clifton.org Mary Baldwin, Prin.; Stds.: 175; Lay Tchrs.: 13

St. Clare of Assisi - 12409 Henderson Rd., Clifton, VA 20124 t) 703-266-1310; 703-266-7293 www.stclareclifton.org Rev. Michael J. Bazan, Pst.; Dcn. Michael J. Mochel, DRE; CRP Stds.: 37

COLONIAL BEACH

St. Elizabeth of Hungary - 11 Irving Ave., Colonial Beach, VA 22443 t) 804-224-7221 Very Rev. Francis M. de Rosa, Pst.; Rev. Eric L. Shafer, Par. Vicar;

St. Anthony's - t) 540-848-4785 stanthony@va.metrocast.net (King George)

CULPEPER

Precious Blood - 114 E. Edmondson St., Culpeper, VA 22701 t) 540-825-8945; 540-825-1339 (CRP) dre@preciousbloodcatholicchurch.com www.preciousbloodcatholicchurch.com Very Rev. Kevin B. Walsh, Pst.; CRP Stds.: 238

DALE CITY

Holy Family - 14160 Ferndale Rd., Dale City, VA 22193 t) 703-670-8161; 703-670-8161 x310 (CRP) parishoffice@holyfamilyva.org; re-ym@holyfamilyva.org www.holyfamilycatholicchurchdalecity.org Rev. Ramon A. Baez, Pst.; Rev. Daniel A. Rice, Par. Vicar; Rev. Christopher F. Tipton, In Res.; Dcn. Vincent Einsmann; Dcn. Helio A. Gomez; Dcn. Joseph L. Santiago; CRP Stds.: 373

Holy Family School - (Grades PreK-8) t) 703-670-3138 principal@holyfamilydalecity.org www.holyfamilydalecity.org Sarah Chevlin, Prin.; Stds.: 194; Lay Tchrs.: 17

FAIRFAX

St. Leo the Great - 3700 Blenheim Blvd., Fairfax, VA 22030 t) 703-273-5369 www.stleofairfax.com Rev. Juan Puigbo, Pst.; Rev. Jonathan R. Fioramonti, Par. Vicar; Rev. Thomas Nguyen, Par. Vicar; Dcn. Filipe Averia; Dcn. Jose J. Lopez; Dcn. R. Marques Silva; CRP Stds.: 322

St. Leo the Great School - (Grades PreK-8) 3704 Blenheim Blvd., Fairfax, VA 22030 t) 703-273-1211 ddipippa@saintleothegreatschool.org; office@saintleothegreatschool.org www.saintleothegreatschool.org Erica Palaza, Prin.; Stds.: 346; Lay Tchrs.: 37

St. Mary of Sorrows - 5222 Sideburn Rd., Fairfax, VA 22032-2640 t) 703-978-4141 stmaryofsorrows.org Very Rev. James S. Barkett, Pst.; Rev. Keith D. Cummings, Par. Vicar; Rev. Francis J. Peffley, Par. Vicar; Dcn. David M. Maurer; Dcn. Jeffrey M. Meyers; CRP Stds.: 210

St. Paul Chung - 4708 Rippling Pond Dr., Fairfax, VA 22033-5077 t) 703-818-9707 www.stpaulchung.org Rev. Tae Jin Kim, Pst.; Rev. Taeseop Lee, Par. Vicar; CRP Stds.: 202

FALLS CHURCH

St. Anthony - 3305 Glen Carlyn Rd., Falls Church, VA 22041 t) 703-820-7111 www.stanthonyparish.org Rev. Matthew H. Zuberbueler, Pst.; Rev. James F. Waalkes, Par. Vicar; Rev. Miguel A. Valle, Par. Vicar; Rev. Anthony Appiah, In Res.; Rev. David A. Whitestone, In

Res.; CRP Stds.: 677

St. Anthony of Padua Catholic School - 3301 Glen Carlyn Road, Falls Church, VA 22041 nbucaj@stanthonyschoolva.org stanthonyofpaduacommunity.com/school/ Amy Fry, Prin.; Stds.: 188; Lay Tchrs.: 20

St. James - 905 Park Ave., Falls Church, VA 22046 t) 703-532-8815 www.stjamescatholic.org Rev. Paul David Scalia, Pst.; Rev. John Paul Heisler, Par. Vicar; Rev. Joseph Q. Vu, Par. Vicar; Rev. Joel Yao Kwame, In Res.; Rev. Peter Michael McShurley, In Res.; Dcn. James A. Fishenden; CRP Stds.: 459

St. James School - (Grades PreK-8) 830 W. Broad St., Falls Church, VA 22046 t) 703-533-1182 x100 mainoffice@saintjamesschool.org Sr. Mary Sue Carwile, I.H.M., Prin.; Stds.: 460; Sr. Tchrs.: 1; Lay Tchrs.: 27

Sisters, Servants of the Immaculate Heart of Mary - 101 N. Spring St., Falls Church, VA 22046 t) 703-532-2388 Sr. Lorraine McGrew, IHM, Supr.;

St. Philip - 7500 St. Philip's Ct., Falls Church, VA 22042 t) 703-573-3808 stphilipsparish.com Rev. Denis M. Donahue, Pst.; Very Rev. Philip Briggs, Par. Vicar; Rev. Michael C. Isenberg, In Res.; Dcn. Vincent Cong T. Nguyen; CRP Stds.: 125

Franciscan Sisters of the Eucharist - 7504 St. Philip's Ct., Falls Church, VA 22042 t) 703-204-0837 Sr. Judith Gebelein, F.S.E., Supr.;

FREDERICKSBURG

Saint Jude - 9600 Caritas St., Fredericksburg, VA 22408 t) 540-891-7350 parishoffice@stjudechurch.us; religioused@stjudechurch.us www.stjudechurch.us Rev. J. Kevin O'Keefe, Pst.; Dcn. Richard A. Cronican; Dcn. Robert A. Lyons; Dcn. Aaron Zaccagnino; CRP Stds.: 119

St. Mary of the Immaculate Conception - 1009 Stafford Ave., Fredericksburg, VA 22401-5418 t) 540-373-6491; 540-373-6663 www.stmaryfred.org Rev. John P. Mosimann, Pst.; Rev. Phillip M. Cozzi, Par. Vicar; Rev. Sean T Koehr, Par. Vicar; Rev. Robert Renner, Par. Vicar; Rev. Scott Sina, Par. Vicar; Dcn. Alberto G. Bernaola; CRP Stds.: 634

Holy Cross Academy - (Grades PreK-8) 250 Stafford Lakes Pkwy., Fredericksburg, VA 22406 t) 540-286-1600 school@holycrossweb.com www.holycrossweb.com Sponsoring parish: St. Mary, Fredericksburg. Sephen Fry, Prin.; Stds.: 421; Pr. Tchrs.: 1; Lay Tchrs.: 31

St. Patrick - 9151 Elys Ford Rd., Fredericksburg, VA 22407 t) 540-785-5299 saintpatrickparish.org Rev. John A. Ziegler, Pst.; Rev. William B. Schierer, Par. Vicar; Dcn. Paul A. D'Antonio; Dcn. David E. Conroy; Dcn. Donald L. Perusi; Dcn. William D. Pivarnik; Dcn. James M. Stenstrom; CRP Stds.: 166

St. Patrick School - (Grades PreK-8) t) 540-786-2277 mmassad@saintpatrickschoolva.org; stpatschurch@comcast.net saintpatrickschool.com George Elliott, Prin.; Stds.: 196; Lay Tchrs.: 18

FRONT ROYAL

St. John the Baptist - 120 W. Main St., Front Royal, VA 22630 t) 540-635-3780 www.sjtb.org Rev. Daniel N. Gee, Pst.; Rev. Michael R. Duesterhaus, Par. Vicar; Rev. Thomas K. Shepanzyk, Par. Vicar; Dcn. Ralph A. Goldsmith; Dcn. Mark R. Jerge; Dcn. Gerald Solitario; CRP Stds.: 175

GAINESVILLE

Holy Trinity - 8213 Linton Hall Rd., Gainesville, VA 20155 t) 703-753-6700; 703-753-6700 x116 (CRP) religioused@holytrinityparish.net www.holytrinityparish.net Rev. Thomas P. Vander Woude, Pst.; Rev. Vincent D. Bork, Par. Vicar; Rev. Richard T. Carr, Par. Vicar; Dcn. Gerard-Marie Anthony; CRP Stds.: 701

GREAT FALLS

St. Catherine of Siena - 1020 Springvale Rd., Great Falls, VA 22066 t) 703-759-4350 office@saintcatherineschurch.org www.saintcatherineschurch.org Rev. Jerry Porkorsky, Pst.; CRP Stds.: 80

Siena Academy - t) 703-759-4129 office@sienamontessori.org Sr. Janet Siepker, F.S.E., Prin.; Stds.: 61; Sr. Tchrs.: 2; Lay Tchrs.: 8

HERNDON

St. Joseph - 750 Peachtree St., Herndon, VA 20170 t) 703-880-4300; 703-880-4332 (CRP) rruiz@sjcherndon.org www.sjcherndon.org Rev. Thomas G. Bourque, T.O.R., Pst.; Rev. David Dodd, T.O.R., Par. Vicar; Rev. Matthew Russick, T.O.R., Par. Vicar; CRP Stds.: 347

St. Joseph School - (Grades K-8) t) 703-880-4350 twesthues@sjcherndon.org sjschoolva.org Denise Rutledge, Prin.; Stds.: 505; Lay Tchrs.: 36

KILMARNOCK

St. Francis de Sales - 154 E. Church St., Kilmarnock, VA 22482-0759 t) 804-435-1511 www.stfranciskilmarnock.org Rev. Michael T. Orlowsky, Pst.; CRP Stds.: 11

St. Paul - 7808 Cople Hwy., Hague, VA 22469 t) 804-472-3090 saintpaulhague@gmail.com Rev. Andrew J. Heintz, Par. Vicar;

LAKE RIDGE

St. Elizabeth Ann Seton - 12807 Valleywood Dr., Lake Ridge, VA 22192 t) 703-494-4008; 703-494-3966 (CRP) c.ohearn@setonlakeridge.org www.setonlakeridge.org Rev. Brian Bashista, Pst.; Rev. Dort A. Bigg, Par. Vicar; Dcn. Robert Warner Jr.; CRP Stds.: 269

LEESBURG

St. John the Apostle - 101 Oakcrest Manor Dr., N.E., Leesburg, VA 20176-2221 t) 703-777-1317 church@stjohnleesburg.com saintjohnleesburg.org Rev. Kevin J. Larsen, Pst.; Rev. Edouard B. Guilloux, Par. Vicar; Rev. Michael J.R. Kelly, Par. Vicar; Dcn. Richard Napoli; CRP Stds.: 748

LURAY

Our Lady of the Valley - 200 Collins Ave., Luray, VA 22835 t) 540-743-4919 ourladyofthevalley@comcast.net ourladyofthevalleyluray.org Rev. Edwin E. Perez, Pst.; CRP Stds.: 16

MADISON

Our Lady of the Blue Ridge - 692 Lonnie Burke Rd., Madison, VA 22727 t) 540-948-4144 Rev. James C. Bruse, Pst.; CRP Stds.: 52

MANASSAS

All Saints - 9300 Stonewall Rd., Manassas, VA 20110 t) 703-368-4500; 703-393-2142 (CRP) parishoffice@allsaintsva.org www.allsaintsva.org Very Rev. Lee R. Roos, Pst.; Rev. Guillermo J. Gonzalez, Par. Vicar; Rev. Luis Quinones, Par. Vicar; Rev. Eugene L. Ngah Dzernjo, Par. Vicar; Rev. Daniel S. Reuwer, Par. Vicar; Dcn. Richard O'Connell; Dcn. Orlando J. Barros; Dcn. Brian R. Majewski; Dcn. James R. Van de Voorde; CRP Stds.: 1,129

All Saints School - (Grades PreK-8) 9294 Stonewall Rd., Manassas, VA 20110 t) 703-368-4400 schooloffice@allsaintsva.org www.allsaintsvaschool.org David E. Conroy Jr., Prin.; Stds.: 414; Lay Tchrs.: 30

St. Gabriel Mission - St. Gabriel Pastoral Ctr., 9110 Railroad Dr., Ste. 300, Manassas Park, VA 20111-7042 t) 703-366-3527 gabrielmanassaspark@gmail.com

Sacred Heart - 12975 Purcell Rd., Manassas, VA 20112-3217 t) 703-590-0030 office@shcva.org shcva.org Rev. Stephen Holmes, Pst.; Rev. Edwin Seh, Par. Vicar; Dcn. Alfred Caporaletti; Dcn. Gerald J. Moore; Dcn. Timothy H. Slayter; CRP Stds.: 224

MCLEAN

St. John the Beloved - 6420 Linway Ter., McLean, VA 22101 t) 703-356-7916 www.stjohncatholicmclean.org Rev. Christopher J. Pollard, Pst.; Rev. John H. Melmer, Par. Vicar; Rev. Ryan Alemeo, In Res.; CRP Stds.: 135

St. John the Beloved School - (Grades PreSchool-8) 6422 Linway Ter., McLean, VA 22101 t) 703-356-7554 rev.pastors@comcast.net www.stjohnacademy.org Jefffrey Presberg, Prin.; Stds.: 238; Lay Tchrs.: 24

St. Luke - 7001 Georgetown Pike, McLean, VA 22101 t) 703-356-1255; 703-356-8419 (Rel Ed) www.saintlukemclean.org Rev. Richard M. Guest, Pst.; Rev. Joseph Moschetto, Par. Vicar; Very Rev. Jamie R. Workman, In Res.; CRP Stds.: 250

St. Luke School - (Grades PreK-8) 7005 Georgetown Pike, McLean, VA 22101 t) 703-356-1508 frontoffice@stlukeschool.com www.stlukeschool.com Tanya Salewski, Prin.; Stds.: 225; Lay Tchrs.: 33

MIDDLEBURG

St. Stephen the Martyr - 23331 Sam Fred Rd., Middleburg, VA 20117-3221 t) 540-687-6433 office@saint-stephen.org www.saint-stephen.org Rev. Christopher D. Murphy, Pst.; CRP Stds.: 62

St. Katharine Drexel - 4100 Mill Creek Rd., Haymarket, VA 20169 t) 703-754-8444 www.katharinedrexelcc.org

ORANGE

St. Isidore the Farmer - 14414 St. Isidore Way, Orange, VA 22960-2573 t) 540-672-4933; 540-672-4933 x3 (CRP) panderson@saintisidorethefarmer.com; office@saintisidorethefarmer.com www.saintisidorethefarmer.com Rev. Terrence R. Staples, Pst.; CRP Stds.: 21

POTOMAC FALLS

Our Lady of Hope - 46639 Algonkian Pkwy., Potomac Falls, VA 20165 t) 703-433-6770; 703-433-6564 (CRP) hello@ourladyofhope.net www.ourladyofhope.net Rev. Anthony J. Killian, Pst.; Rev. Jordan M. Willard, Par. Vicar; Dcn. Marco Rajkovich; Dcn. Tom Wadolowski; CRP Stds.: 160

Our Lady of Hope School - (Grades K-8) 46633 Algonkian Pkwy., Potomac Falls, VA 20165 t) 703-433-6760 school@ourladyofhope.net www.ourladyofhopeschool.net Jeanne Canavan, Prin.; Stds.: 218; Lay Tchrs.: 11

PURCELLVILLE

St. Francis de Sales - 37730 St. Francis Ct., Purcellville, VA 20132 t) 540-338-6381 Rev. James R. Gould, Pst.; Rev. John F. Heisler, Par. Vicar; Dcn. Lawrence V. Hammel; CRP Stds.: 495

RESTON

St. John Neumann - 11900 Lawyers Rd., Reston, VA 20191-4299 t) 703-860-8510 www.saintjn.org Rev. Joseph T. Brennan, O.S.F.S., Pst.; Rev. Donald J. Heet, O.S.F.S., Par. Vicar; Rev. Michael S. Murray, Par. Vicar; Rev. John W. Crossin, In Res.; Dcn. Atanacio Sandoval; Dcn. John A. Wagner; CRP Stds.: 890

St. Thomas a Becket - 1421 Wiehle Ave., Reston, VA 20190 t) 703-437-7113 w.schardt@stbchurch.org www.stbchurch.com Rev. William B. Schardt, Pst.; CRP Stds.: 127

SPOTSYLVANIA

St. Matthew - 8200 Robert E. Lee Dr., Spotsylvania, VA 22551 t) 540-582-5575 stmatthewsec@comcast.net www.stmatthewspotsylvania.org Rev. Paul M. Eversole, Pst.; Dcn. Michael Strain; CRP Stds.: 100

SPRINGFIELD

St. Bernadette - 7600 Old Keene Mill Rd., Springfield, VA 22152-2022 t) 703-451-8576 www.stbernpar.org Rev. Donald J. Rooney, Pst.; Rev. Richard A. Miserendino, Par. Vicar; Dcn. Orlando Caicedo; CRP Stds.: 469

St. Bernadette School - (Grades PreSchool-8) 7602 Old Keene Mill Rd., Springfield, VA 22152-2099 t) 703-451-8696 school@stbernschool.org Darcie Girmus, Prin.; Stds.: 443; Lay Tchrs.: 34

St. Raymond of Penafort - 8750 Pohick Rd., Springfield, VA 22153 t) 703-440-0535 straymonds.org Rev. John C. De Celles, Pst.; Rev. Edward R. Horkan, In Res.; CRP Stds.: 221

STAFFORD

St. William of York - 3130 Jefferson Davis Hwy., Stafford, VA 22554 t) 540-659-1102 www.swoycc.org Rev. Robert J. DeMartino, Pst.; Rev. William Nyce, Par. Vicar; Dcn. James J. Benisek; CRP Stds.: 338

St. William of York School - (Grades PreK-8) t) 540-659-5207 bkeenan@stwillschool.org www.stwillschool.org Jennifer Schiller, Prin.; Stds.: 214; Lay Tchrs.: 17

STERLING

Christ the Redeemer - 46833 Harry Byrd Hwy., Sterling,

VA 20164 t) 703-430-0811 www.ctrcc.org Rev. Joel D. Jaffe, Pst.; Rev. Mark E. Moretti, Par. Vicar; Rev. Maurico Portillo, Par. Vicar; Dcn. Anthony J. Calderon; CRP Stds.: 777

TRIANGLE

St. Francis of Assisi - 18825 Fuller Heights Rd., Triangle, VA 22172 t) 703-221-4044 www.stfrncis.org Rev. John F. O'Connor, O.F.M., Pst.; Rev. George Corrigan Jr., Par. Vicar; Rev. Christopher J. Dunn, Par. Vicar; Rev. James Scullion, Par. Vicar; Dcn. Michael Gomes; CRP Stds.: 420

VIENNA

St. Mark - 9970 Vale Rd., Vienna, VA 22181 t) 703-281-9100 Rev. Patrick Holroyd, Pst.; Rev. Ghenghan B. Mbinkar, In Res.; Dcn. John P. Allen; Dcn. Charles Duck; CRP Stds.: 284

St. Mark School - (Grades PreK-8) 9972 Vale Rd., Vienna, VA 22181 t) 703-281-9103 gostmark@stmark.org Kimberly Parker, Prin.; Stds.: 369; Lay Tchrs.: 45

Our Lady of Good Counsel - 8601 Wolftrap Rd., Vienna, VA 22182-5026 t) 703-938-2828 info@olgcva.org www.olgcva.org Rev. Matthew J. Hillyard, OSFS, Pst.; Rev. Mathias Kumar, OSFS, Par. Vicar; Rev. Lewis S. Fiorelli, O.S.F.S., In Res.; Rev. Patrick J. Kifolo, O.S.F.S., In Res.; Rev. William J. Metzger, O.S.F.S., In Res.; Dcn. Christopher G. Moore; CRP Stds.: 566

Our Lady of Good Counsel School - (Grades PreK-8) t) 703-938-3600 admissions@olgcschool.org www.olgcschool.org Stds.: 467; Lay Tchrs.: 48

WARRENTON

St. John the Evangelist - 271 Winchester St., Warrenton, VA 20186 t) 540-347-2922; 540-347-2922 x209 (CRP) sjewarrentonvirginia@sjesva.org; smurphy@sje1.org www.sje1.org Rev. Charles C. Smith, Pst.; Rev. Nicholas Blank, Par. Vicar; Rev. Brian B. McAllister, Par. Vicar; Dcn. Kenneth Galvin; Dcn. Don Libera; Dcn. Jonathan A. Williams; CRP Stds.: 410

St. John the Evangelist School - (Grades PreK-8) 111 John E. Mann St., Warrenton, VA 20186 t) 540-347-2458 tmacdonald@sjesva.org; kgay@sjesva.org Temple MacDonald, Prin.; Stds.: 210; Lay Tchrs.: 19

WASHINGTON

St. Peter - 12762 Lee Hwy., Washington, VA 22747 t) 540-675-3432 stpeterschurch@comcast.net stpeterparishva.org/ Rev. Kevin J. Beres, Pst.; Rev. David H. Reinders, In Res.; Dcn. Robert E. Benyo; CRP Stds.: 40

WINCHESTER

Sacred Heart of Jesus - 120 Keating Dr., Winchester, VA 22601-2806; Mailing: 130 Keating Dr., Winchester, VA 22601-2806 t) 540-662-5858 sacredheartwinchester.org Rev. Bjorn C. Lundberg, Pst.; Rev. John J. Riley, Par. Vicar; Rev. Stephen M. Vaccaro, Par. Vicar; Dcn. Mark R. Maines; Dcn. Richard C. Vossler; CRP Stds.: 542

Sacred Heart of Jesus School - (Grades PreK-8) 110 Keating Dr., Winchester, VA 22601-2806 t) 540-662-7177 email@sacredheartva.org; epalaza@sacredheartva.org sacredheartva.org Anne Arias, Prin.; Stds.: 222; Lay Tchrs.: 36

WOODBRIDGE

Our Lady of Angels - 13752 Mary's Way, Woodbridge, VA 22191 t) 703-494-2444; 703-494-5015; 703-494-3696 (CRP) pastor@olacc.org www.ourladyofangelscatholicchurch.com Rev. Alvaro Montero, DCJM, Pst.; Rev. Juan Espino, D.C.J.M., Par. Vicar; Rev. Armando Marsal, D.C.J.M., Par. Vicar; Rev. Leopoldo M. Vives, D.C.J.M., Par. Vicar; Rev. Ignacio de Ribera, D.C.J.M., In Res.; Dcn. Emil P. Myskowski; CRP Stds.: 620

WOODSTOCK

St. John Bosco - 315 N. Main St., Woodstock, VA 22664 t) 540-459-4448 www.sjbwoodstock.org Rev. Augustine M. Tran, Admin.; Rev. Robert L. Ruskamp, Par. Vicar; CRP Stds.: 131

Our Lady of the Shenandoah - 240 Fritzel Way, Basye, VA 22810; Mailing: P.O. Box 654, Basye, VA 22810 t) 540-856-2411

SCHOOLS: PRESCHOOL THRU HIGH SCHOOL

SCHOOLS

COMMONWEALTH OF VIRGINIA

BRISTOW

Linton Hall - (PRV) (Grades PreK-8) 9535 Linton Hall Rd., Bristow, VA 20136 t) 703-368-3157 lhs@lintonhall.edu www.lintonhall.edu Adrianne Jewett, Prin.; Stds.: 198; Lay Tchrs.: 28

CULPEPER

Epiphany School - (PAR) (Grades PreK-8) 1211 E. Grandview Ave., Culpeper, VA 22701 t) 540-825-9017 office@epiphanycatholicschool.org www.epiphanycatholicschool.org Sponsoring parishes: Precious Blood, Culpeper; Our Lady of the Blue Ridge, Madison; St. Isidore the farmer, Orange and St. Peter, Washington, VA. Austin Poole, Prin.; Stds.: 167; Lay Tchrs.: 16

SPRINGFIELD

***Angelus Academy** - (PRV) (Grades PreK-8) 7644 Dynatech Ct., Springfield, VA 22153 t) 703-924-3996 headofschool@angelusacademy.org www.angelusacademy.org Raymond Joseph St. Pierre, Headmaster; Stds.: 153; Lay Tchrs.: 16

WOODBRIDGE

St. Thomas Aquinas Regional School - (PAR) (Grades PreK-8) 13750 Mary's Way, Woodbridge, VA 22191 t) 703-491-4447 office@aquinastars.org www.aquinastars.org Sponsoring parishes: Our Lady of Angels, Woodbridge; St. Elizabeth Ann Seton, Lake Ridge; and Sacred Heart, Manassas. Sr. Mary Sheila, O.P., Prin.; Stds.: 399; Sr. Tchrs.: 3; Lay Tchrs.: 25

HIGH SCHOOLS

COMMONWEALTH OF VIRGINIA

ALEXANDRIA

Bishop Ireton High School - (DIO) (Grades 9-12) 201 Cambridge Rd., Alexandria, VA 22314 t) 703-751-7606 info@bishopireton.org www.bishopireton.org Kathleen McNutt, Headmaster; Dr. Timothy Guy, Prin.; Rev. Noah C. Morey, Chap.; Stds.: 860; Sr. Tchrs.: 1; Lay Tchrs.: 75

ARLINGTON

Bishop Denis J. O'Connell High School - (DIO) (Grades 9-12) 6600 Little Falls Rd., Arlington, VA 22213 t) 703-237-1400 centeroffice@bishopoconnell.org www.bishopoconnell.org Coed College Prep Rev. Peter M. McShurley, Chap.; Jose Gonzalez, Dean; Sr. Catherine Hill, I.H.M., Dean; Meghan Lonergan, Dean; Frank Roque, Prin.; William T. Crittenberger, Headmaster; Stds.: 1,148; Pr. Tchrs.: 1; Sr. Tchrs.: 4; Lay Tchrs.: 111

CHANTILLY

Saint Paul VI Catholic High School - (DIO) 42341 Braddock Rd., Chantilly, VA 20152 t) 703-352-0925 www.paulvi.net Laura Swenson, Headmaster; Thomas G. Opfer, Prin.; Rev. Stephen J. Schultz, Chap.; Stds.: 1,193; Pr. Tchrs.: 1; Lay Tchrs.: 103

POTOMAC SHORES

Saint John Paul the Great Catholic High School - (DIO) (Grades 9-12) 17700 Dominican Dr., Potomac Shores, VA 22026 t) 703-445-0300 info@jpthegreat.org www.jpthegreat.org Rev. Christopher F. Tipton, Chap.; Shawn McNulty, Prin.; Sr. Mary Veronica Keller, O.P., Headmaster; Andrew Hawley, Bus. Mgr.; Stds.: 598; Pr. Tchrs.: 1; Sr. Tchrs.: 4; Lay Tchrs.: 50

CAMPUS MINISTRY / NEWMAN CENTERS [CAM]

ARLINGTON

Marymount University - 2807 N. Glebe Rd., Arlington, VA 22207 t) 703-284-1607 ministry@marymount.edu www.marymount.edu Campus Ministry Rev. Gabriel Muteru, Chap.;

FAIRFAX

George Mason University, Catholic Campus Ministry - 4515 Roberts Rd., Fairfax, VA 22032 t) 703-425-0022 chaplain@gmu.edu; gmuccm@gmail.com gmuccm.org Rev. Joseph W. Farrell, Chap.; Valeria Sierralta, Campus Min.; Michaela Robinson, Campus Min.; Justin Woodbury, Campus Min.;

St. Robert Bellarmine Chapel - George Mason University, 4515 Roberts Rd., Fairfax, VA 22032 Catholic Campus Ministry.

FREDERICKSBURG

University of Mary Washington - Catholic Campus Ministry, 1614 College Ave., Fredericksburg, VA 22401 t) 540-373-6746 fathervaccaro@umwccm.org umwcatholic.org Rev. Christopher T. Vaccaro, Chap.;

COLLEGES & UNIVERSITIES [COL]

INSTITUTIONS LOCATED IN DIOCESE

ALEXANDRIA

Notre Dame Graduate School of Christendom College - 4407 Sano St., Alexandria, VA 22312 t) 703-658-4304 www.graduate.christendom.edu Robert Matava, Dean; Timothy T. O'Donnell, Pres.; Stds.: 129; Lay Tchrs.: 6; Pr. Tchrs.: 4

ARLINGTON

***Divine Mercy University** - 2001 Jefferson Davis Hwy., Ste. 511, Arlington, VA 22202 t) 703-416-1441 communications@divinemercy.edu www.divinemercy.edu Development & promotion of approaches to mental health founded in the Catholic vision. Rev. Charles Sikorsky, L.C., Pres.; Stds.: 514; Lay Tchrs.: 49; Pr. Tchrs.: 3; Sr. Tchrs.: 1; Scholastics: 35

Marymount University - 2807 N. Glebe Rd., Arlington, VA 22207 t) 703-284-1598 mshank@marymount.edu; hphillip@marymount.edu www.marymount.edu Coed Irma Becerra, Pres.; Rev. Gabriel Muteru, Chap.; Stds.: 4,257; Lay Tchrs.: 166

FRONT ROYAL

Christendom College - 134 Christendom Dr., Front Royal, VA 22630 t) 540-636-2900 walter@christendom.edu www.christendom.edu Rev. Marcus Pollard, Chap.; Timothy T. O'Donnell, Pres.; Stds.: 544; Lay Tchrs.: 36

CONVENTS, MONASTERIES, AND RESIDENCES FOR WOMEN [CON]

ALEXANDRIA

Daughters of St. Paul - 1025 King St., Alexandria, VA 22314 t) 703-549-3806; 703-549-1323 (Convent) alexandria@pauline.org www.pauline.org Sr. Sophie Stewart, F.S.P., Supr.; Srs.: 5

Poor Clare Monastery of Mary, Mother of the Church - 2505 Stonehedge Dr., Alexandria, VA 22306 t) 703-768-4918 Observing the Primitive Rule of St. Clare. Mother Abbess Miriam, P.C.C., Abbess; Srs.: 14

Poor Sisters of St. Joseph, St. Gabriel Convent - 4319 Sano St., Alexandria, VA 22312 t) 703-354-0395 pssjalexandria@gmail.com Mother Maria Gonzalez, Supr.; Srs.: 6

ANNANDALE

Sisters of Our Lady of La Salette (Mary Mother of Life, USA Delegation Procure, Corporation) - 7421 St. Michael's Ln., Annandale, VA 22003 t) 703-865-8767 marijosnds@hotmail.com; sistersoflasalette@yahoo.com www.soeurs-lasalette.com

Sr. Maria Josephine Suarez Valenton, SNDS, Supr.; Srs.: 6

ARLINGTON

Religious of the Sacred Heart of Mary - 2807 N. Glebe Rd., Arlington, VA 22207-4299 t) 703-908-7526 jamx434@aol.com www.rshm.org Srs.: 1

Sisters, Servants of the Immaculate Heart of Mary - 2844 N. Rochester St., Arlington, VA 22213 t) 703-536-4531 ihmdjo@bishopconnell.org www.ihmimmaculata.org Sr. Lorraine McGraw, I.H.M., Supr.; Srs.: 5

BRISTOW

St. Benedict Monastery / Benedictine Sisters of Virginia - 9535 Linton Hall Rd., Bristow, VA 20136-1217 t) 571-428-2500; 703-361-0106 jburley@osbva.org; awestkamp@osbva.org www.osbva.org Sr. Joanna Burley, Prioress; Srs.: 28

FAIRFAX

Adorers of the Holy Cross - 10917 Marilta Ct., Fairfax, VA 22030 t) 703-591-0862 mtgdlva@yahoo.com Sr. Mary Trinh Nguyen, M.T.G., Supr.; Srs.: 6

FALLS CHURCH

Franciscan Sisters of the Eucharist - 7504 St. Philip's Ct., Falls Church, VA 22042 t) 703-204-0837 fallschurch@fsecommunity.org Sr. Judith Gebelein, F.S.E., Supr.; Srs.: 8

LINDEN

The Dominican Nuns, Saint Dominic's Monastery - 2636 Monastery Rd., Linden, VA 22642-5371 t) 540-635-3259 monastery@lindenopnuns.org www.lindenopnuns.org Sr. Mary Fidelis, O.P., Prioress; Srs.: 12

QUICKSBURG

Pax Christi Institute - 1769 Quicksburg Rd., Quicksburg, VA 22847 t) 540-740-9108 lauranieves98@yahoo.com Sr. Guadalupe Therese Licea, P.C.I., Supr.; Srs.: 3

WOODBRIDGE

Dominican Sisters Convent - 5009 Bobcat Ct., Woodbridge, VA 22193 t) 703-878-7823 (Congregation of St. Cecilia) Sr. Mary Veronica Keller, O.P., Supr.; Srs.: 8

ENDOWMENTS / FOUNDATIONS / TRUSTS [EFT]

ALEXANDRIA

***St. Luke Foundation for Haiti** - 3406 Sapphire Ct., Alexandria, VA 22310; Mailing: 8980 SW 56th St., Miami, FL 33165 c) (331) 643-5415 (Robin Forestal's Cell) robin.forestal@stlukehaiti.org; info@stlukehaiti.org stlukehaiti.org Frank Krafft, Treas.;

ARLINGTON

Catholic Investment Trust of Arlington - 200 N. Glebe Rd., Ste. 922, Arlington, VA 22203 t) (703) 841-2500 Most Rev. Michael F. Burbidge, Trustee; Timothy R. Cotnoir, Trustee; Kathy McKinless, Trustee;

Diocese of Arlington Scholarship Foundation, Inc. - 200 N. Glebe Rd., Ste. 914, Arlington, VA 22203 t) 703-841-2500 m.herrmann@arlingtondiocese.org Very Rev. Jamie R. Workman, Pres.;

The Foundation for the Catholic Diocese of Arlington, Inc. - 200 N. Glebe Rd., Ste. 914, Arlington, VA 22203 t) 703-841-2500 m.herrmann@arlingtondiocese.org Very Rev. Jamie R. Workman, Pres.;

MISCELLANEOUS [MIS]

ALEXANDRIA

***Pan American Catholic Health Care Network** - 8021 Lynnfield Dr., Alexandria, VA 22306 t) 646-320-2302 mary.healey-sedutto@hhh.us.org Mary Healey Sedutto, Dir.;

ANNANDALE

***Catholic Athletes For Christ** - 3703 Cameron Mills Rd., Annandale, VA 22305 t) 703-239-3070 info@catholicathletesforchrist.org; ray@catholicathletesforchrist.org www.catholicathletesforchrist.org Ray McKenna, Pres.;

ARLINGTON

Arlington Diocesan Investment and Loan Corp. - 200 N. Glebe Rd., Ste. 914, Arlington, VA 22203 t) 703-841-2500 m.herrmann@arlingtondiocese.org Very Rev. Jamie R. Workman, Pres.;

***Commissioned by Christ** - 200 N. Glebe Rd., Ste. 700, Arlington, VA 22203 t) 571-699-3339 info@commissionedbychrist.org www.cbc-missions.org Short term, international and domestic, Catholic mission trips for adults and families Michelle Haworth, Dir.;

Rooted in Faith-Forward in Hope, Inc. - 200 N. Glebe Rd., Ste. 914, Arlington, VA 22203 t) 703-841-2500 m.herrmann@arlingtondiocese.org Very Rev. Jamie R. Workman, Pres.;

FAIRFAX

Alpha Omega Clinic and Consultation Services - 3607A Chain Bridge Rd., Fairfax, VA 22030 t) 301-767-1733 alphaomegaclinic@verizon.net www.aoccs.org Rev. Frank Formolo; Kathleen Gallagher, Dir.;

***Divine Mercy Care** - 4001 Fair Ridge Dr., Ste. 305, Fairfax, VA 22033-2917 t) 703-934-5552 info@divinemercycare.org www.divinemercycare.org Rev. Gerald Weymes, Chap.; Will Waldron, Dir.;

FRONT ROYAL

***Human Life International** - 4 Family Life Ln., Front Royal, VA 22630 t) 540-635-7884 hli@hli.org www.hli.org Rev. Shenan J. Boquet, Pres.;

***Seton Home Study School** - 1350 Progress Dr., Front Royal, VA 22630 t) 540-636-9990 info@setonhome.org www.setonhome.org Bob Pennefather, Prin.;

HAYMARKET

The Women's Apostolate to Youth - 16810 Thunder Rd., Haymarket, VA 20169 t) 571-225-0044 womenofway@gmail.com www.waywomen.com Mary Camarca, Dir.; Sally Allman, Asst. Dir.;

MANASSAS

***Cardinal Newman Society** - 10432 Balls Ford Rd., Ste. 300, Manassas, VA 20109 t) 703-367-0333 governance@cardinalnewmansociety.org newmansociety.org Patrick J. Reilly, Pres.;

MCLEAN

***Institute of Catholic Culture** - ; Mailing: P.O. Box 10101, McLean, VA 22102 t) 540-635-7155 info@instituteofcatholicculture.org www.instituteofcatholicculture.org Rev. Hezekias Carnazzo, Dir.;

Secular Institute "Stabat Mater" - 2001 Great Falls St., McLean, VA 22101 c) 703-307-3466 aperezalca@cox.net www.stabatmater.net

SPOTSYLVANIA

St. Francis Catholic Worker (West) - 9631 Peppertree Rd., Spotsylvania, VA 22553 t) 540-972-3218 stfranciscw49@gmail.com John Mahoney, Dir.;

VIENNA

Mount Tabor Society, Inc. - 2363 Hunter Mill Rd., Vienna, VA 22181 t) 703-261-6857 provincial@missionhurst.org A House of Prayer and Christian Community. Rev. William G. Quigley, C.I.C.M., Rector;

MONASTERIES AND RESIDENCES FOR PRIESTS AND BROTHERS [MON]

ARLINGTON

Missionhurst, C.I.C.M.-Central House and Provincialate (American I.H.M. Province, Inc., Immaculate Heart Missions, Inc., Missionhurst, Inc.) - 4651 25th St. N, Arlington, VA 22207 t) 703-528-3800 provincial@missionhurst.org; provsec@missionhurst.org www.missionhurstcicm.org Congregation of the Immaculate Heart of Mary foreign and home missions. Rev. Andre Kazadi, Dir.; Rev. William G. Quigley, C.I.C.M., Mem.; Rev. Michael Hann, C.I.C.M., Mem.; Rev. Remy Kankolongo, Mem.; Rev. Pascal Ngboloma Kumanda, C.I.C.M., Mem.; Rev. Francis Mfesao, CICM, Mem.; Rev. Jean-Marie Mvumbi Phongo, Treas.; Rev. Terga Richard, CICM, Mem.; Rev. Celso Tabalanza, Prov.; Rev. William Wyndaele, C.I.C.M., Mem.; Brs.: 1; Priests: 31

BERRYVILLE

Community of Cistercians of the Strict Observance, Inc. - 901 Cool Spring Ln., Berryville, VA 22611-2700 t) 540-955-4383 holycross@hcava.org www.virginiatrappists.org Rev. Joseph Wittstock, O.C.S.O., Abbot; Brs.: 11; Priests: 4

PRESCHOOLS / CHILDCARE CENTERS [PRE]

ALEXANDRIA

Blessed Sacrament Grade School and Early Childhood Center - 1417 W. Braddock Rd., Alexandria, VA 22302 t) 703-998-4170 schoolinfo@blessedsacramentcc.org www.blessedsacramentcc.org Katy Chelak, Prin.; Stds.: 220; Lay Tchrs.: 10

St. Gabriel's (Poor Sisters of St. Joseph (Buenos Aires) - 4319 Sano St., Alexandria, VA 22312 t) 703-354-0395 stgdaycare@gmail.com stgdaycare.org Sr. Eneyda Martinez, Dir.; Stds.: 30; Lay Tchrs.: 6

MCLEAN

Youth Apostles Institute, An Association of Christian Faithful - 1600 Carlin Ln., McLean, VA 22101-4100 t) 703-556-0914 ya.opsmanager@gmail.com www.youthapostles.org Consecrated priests & laymen who work with volunteers to inspire the young. Rev. Thomas M. Yehl, Y.A.; Stds.: 1,000

RETREAT HOUSES / RENEWAL CENTERS [RTR]

BERRYVILLE

Retreat House, Holy Cross Abbey - 901 Cool Spring Ln., Berryville, VA 22611-2700 t) 540-955-4383 information@hcava.org www.virginiatrappists.org Rev. James Orthmann, O.C.S.O.;

WHITE POST

San Damiano Spiritual Life Center - 125 Old Kitchen Rd., White Post, VA 22663 t) 540-868-9220 sandamiano@arlingtondiocese.org www.arlingtondiocese.org Dcn. Mark R. Maines, Dir.;

An asterisk (*) denotes an organization that has established tax-exempt status directly with the IRS and is not covered by the USCCB Group Ruling.

Archdiocese of Atlanta

(Archidioecesis Atlantensis)

MOST REVEREND GREGORY J. HARTMAYER, OFM CONV.

Archbishop of Atlanta; ordained May 5, 1979; appointed Bishop of Savannah July 19, 2011; consecrated October 18, 2011; appointed Archbishop of Atlanta March 5, 2020; installed May 6, 2020.

Catholic Center Archdiocese of Atlanta: 2401 Lake Park Dr., S.E., Smyrna, GA 30080-8862. T: 404-920-7300; F: 404-920-7301. www.archatl.com

ESTABLISHED JULY 2, 1956.

Square Miles 21,445.

Canonically Erected November 8, 1956; created an Archdiocese February 21, 1962. Comprises the 69 Counties in the northern part of the State of Georgia, north of and including the following counties: Lincoln, McDuffie, Warren, Hancock, Baldwin, Putnam, Jasper, Monroe, Upson, Meriwether and Troup.

Patrons of the Archdiocese: I. Our Blessed Lady under the title of the Immaculate Heart of Mary; II. Saint Pius X.

For legal titles of parishes and archdiocesan institutions, consult the Archbishop's office.

MOST REVEREND BERNARD E. SHLESINGER, III
Auxiliary Bishop of Atlanta; ordained June 22, 1996; appointed Auxiliary Bishop of Atlanta and Titular Bishop of Naiera May 15, 2017; ordained July 19, 2017.

MOST REVEREND JOEL M. KONZEN, S.M.
Auxiliary Bishop of Atlanta; ordained May 19, 1979; appointed Auxiliary Bishop of Atlanta, Moderator of the Curia and Titular Bishop of Leavenworth February 5, 2018; ordained April 3, 2018.

MOST REVEREND JOHN NHAN TRAN
Auxiliary Bishop of Atlanta: ordained May 30, 1922; appointed Auxiliary Bishop of Atlanta and Titular Bishop of Tullia October 25, 2022; ordained January 23, 2023.

STATISTICAL OVERVIEW

Personnel	
Archbishops	1
Auxiliary Bishops	3
Abbots	1
Priests: Diocesan Active in Diocese	130
Priests: Diocesan Active Outside Diocese	8
Priests: Retired, Sick or Absent	46
Number of Diocesan Priests	184
Religious Priests in Diocese	90
Total Priests in your Diocese	274
Extern Priests in Diocese	12
Ordinations:	
Diocesan Priests	4
Religious Priests	1
Transitional Deacons	4
Permanent Deacons	8
Permanent Deacons in Diocese	306
Total Brothers	131
Total Sisters	105
Parishes	
Parishes	93
With Resident Pastor:	
Resident Diocesan Priests	73
Resident Religious Priests	15
Without Resident Pastor:	
Administered by Priests	5
Missions	10
Professional Ministry Personnel:	
Brothers	131
Sisters	105
Lay Ministers	236
Welfare	
Catholic Hospitals	4
Total Assisted	412,177
Homes for the Aged	6
Total Assisted	12
Specialized Homes	1
Total Assisted	12
Special Centers for Social Services	4
Total Assisted	61,800
Educational	
Diocesan Students in Other Seminaries	37
Total Seminarians	37
Colleges and Universities	1
Total Students	127
High Schools, Diocesan and Parish	3
Total Students	2,200
High Schools, Private	6
Total Students	2,061
Elementary Schools, Diocesan and Parish	15
Total Students	5,541
Elementary Schools, Private	3
Total Students	736
Catechesis / Religious Education:	
High School Students	11,288
Elementary Students	19,003
Total Students under Catholic Instruction	40,993
Teachers in Diocese:	
Priests	8
Brothers	3
Sisters	14
Lay Teachers	1,100
Vital Statistics	
Receptions into the Church:	
Infant Baptism Totals	7,081
Minor Baptism Totals	672
Adult Baptism Totals	445
Received into Full Communion	758
First Communions	6,166
Confirmations	5,639
Marriages:	
Catholic	1,126
Interfaith	254
Total Marriages	1,380
Deaths	1,997
Total Catholic Population	1,195,000
Total Population	7,805,239

LEADERSHIP

Vicars General - Most Rev. Joel M. Konzen, S.M., Auxiliary Bishop of Atlanta, Moderator of the Curia; Most Rev. Bernard E. Shlesinger III, Auxiliary Bishop of Atlanta (bishopshlesinger@archatl.com); Most Rev. John Nhan Tran, Auxiliary Bishop of Atlanta;
Chancellor - Dcn. Dennis J. Dorner Sr., Chancellor (ddorner@archatl.com); Kath Owens, Exec. Asst. (kowens@archatl.com); Lana Forbes, Admin. Asst. (lforbes@archatl.com);
Office of Divine Worship - t) 404-920-7339 Rev. Gerardo Ceballos-Gonzalez, Dir. (gerardoceballos@archatl.com); Dcn. William L. Bohn, Assoc. Dir. (wbohn01@archatl.com); Rene Ponce, Assoc. Dir.;
Judicial Vicar - t) 404-920-7500
Secretary for Finance - t) 404-920-7404 Bradley Wilson, CFO (bwilson@archatl.com);
Secretary for Catholic Charities Atlanta - t) 404-920-8862 Vanessa Russell, CEO (vrussell@ccatlanta.org);
Secretary for Communications - t) 404-920-7344 Maureen Smith (msmith@archatl.com);
Secretary for Schools - t) 404-920-7700 Dr. Diane Starkovich;
Secretary for Office of Evangelization and Discipleship - t) 404-920-7624 Andrew W. Lichtenwalner (alichtenwalner@archatl.com);
Secretary for Human Resources - t) 404-920-7482 Charles Thibaudeau, Secy. (cthibaudeau@archatl.com);
Archbishop's Office - Most Rev. Gregory J. Hartmayer, O.F.M. Conv.; Rev. Gerardo Ceballos-Gonzalez, Priest Asst. to the Archbishop; Master of Liturgical Ceremonies, Assoc. Vocations Dir. (gerardoceballos@archatl.com); Mardessa Smith, Sr. Exec. Asst. (mwsmith@archatl.com);
College of Consultors - Most Rev. Gregory J. Hartmayer, O.F.M. Conv., Pres.; Most Rev. Joel M. Konzen, S.M.; Most Rev. Bernard E. Shlesinger III (bishopshlesinger@archatl.com);
Deans - Very Rev. Henry Atem, Northeast Metro Deanery; Very Rev. Timothy A. Gadziala, Southwest Deanery; Very Rev. Jose Luis Hernandez-Ayala, Northeast Deanery;
Priest Personnel - Most Rev. Bernard E. Shlesinger III, Dir. (bishopshlesinger@archatl.com); Veronica Reyes, Exec. Asst. (vreyes@archatl.com); Yolanda Rivera, Admin. Asst. (yrivera@archatl.com);
Delegates for Clergy - Rev. Msgr. Henry C. Gracz; Rev. John Murphy; Rev. Francis Tran;
Delegate for Religious - t) 404-920-7653 Bro. Nicholas Wolfla, O.F.M.Conv. (secretaryolc@franciscansusa.org);

OFFICES AND DIRECTORS

Archives and Records - t) 404-920-7690 Angelique M. Richardson, Dir. (arichardson@archatl.com); Geoffrey Hetherington, Archivist (ghetherington@archatl.com); Lauren LeDesma, Records Mgr. (lledesma@archatl.com);
Campus & Young Adult Ministries - t) 404-920-7620 Allen Austin, Assoc. Dir. (aaustin@archatl.com);
Catholic Charities of Atlanta - t) 404-920-7725 www.catholiccharitiesatlanta.org Mike Dowdle, Chair (Mike@dowdle.net);
Catholic Construction Services, Inc. - t) 404-920-7860 John F. Schiavone, Dir. (jschiavone@archatl.com); Joseph LeDesma, Admin. Prog. Mgr. (jledesma@archatl.com); Vanessa Page, Office Mgr. & Exec. Asst. (vpage@archatl.com);
  Senior Program Managers - Randy Hood; Dennis W. Kelly;
Catholic Housing Initiatives, Inc. - t) 404-920-7729 Vanessa Russell;
  Catholic Retirement Facilities, Inc. - t) 404-346-0745 Keni Vanzant, Mgr.;
Catholic Schools - t) 404-920-7700 Dr. Diane Starkovich, Supt.; Julie Broom, Assoc. Supt. (jbroom@sjnrcs.org); Karen Vogtner, Assoc. Supt. (kvogtner@sjecs.net);
Chancery Facility Management (CFM) - t) 404-920-7875 Rob McKinnon, Dir.; Portia Riley, Office Mgr.; Arthur Glover, Facility Supvr.;
Child and Youth Protection - t) 888-437-0764 (24-Hr. Reporting Hotline); 404-920-7550 ocyp@archatl.com Jenni Weldin, Dir., Safe Environment (jweldin@archatl.com); Sue Stubbs, Dir., Victim Assistance (sstubbs@archatl.com); Gina Garcia, OCYP Prog. Asst. (ggarcia@archatl.com);
Communications - t) 404-920-7340 Maureen Smith, Dir. (msmith@archatl.com); David Pace, Creative Dir. (dpace@archatl.com); Allen Kinzly, Multimedia Specialist (akinzly@archatl.com);
  The Georgia Bulletin Newspaper - t) 404-920-7430 www.georgiabulletin.org Nichole Golden, Editor; Tom Aisthorpe, Advertising Mgr.; Andrew Nelson, Staff Reporter;
Finance Office - t) 404-920-7400 Bradley Wilson, CFO & Member of the Secretariat (bwilson@archatl.com); Brenda Leslie, Dir. Financial Svcs. (bleslie@archatl.com); Camtuyen Pham, Controller (cpham@archatl.com);
Human Resources - t) 404-920-7480 Charles Thibaudeau, Chief Human Resources Officer (cthibaudeau@archatl.com); Marquita Richburg, Director of Human Resources (mrichburg@archatl.com); Lily Gallagher, Director of Benefits (lgallagher@archatl.com);
Information Technology - t) 404-920-7450 support@archatl.zendesk.com help.archatl.com Thomas Hardy, Dir. (thardy@archatl.com); Tomasz Kasprzyk, Mgr. (tkasprzyk@archatl.com); Anthony Cotton, IT Support Specialist, Tier III (acotton@archatl.com);
Metropolitan Tribunal - t) 404-920-7500 tribunal@archatl.com www.archatl.com/offices/tribunal Very Rev. Daniel P. Ketter, Judicial Vicar (dketter@archatl.com); Rev. Paul A. Burke, Adjutant Judicial Vicar (pburke@archatl.com); Rev. Michael U. Onyekuru, Adjutant Judicial Vicar (monyekuru@archatl.com);
  Adjutant Judicial Vicar - Rev. Paul A. Burke; Rev. Michael U. Onyekuru;
  Advocate - Joseph Tovar, Chief Advocate;
  Archdiocesan Judges - Rev. Msgr. Edward J. Dillon; Rev. Pedro Poloche; Rev. Michael U. Onyekuru;
  Auditors - Rev. Ignacio Peres, Auditor; Sr. Crystal Payment, Auditor;
  Court Administrator - t) 404-920-7510 Dr. Felix Menendez;
  Court Expert - t) 404-920-7507 Ann G. Howe;
  Defenders of the Bond - Robert Brown; Elyn M. Macek;
  Judicial Vicar - Very Rev. Daniel P. Ketter;
  Notaries - Angela Pratt, Moderator of the Tribunal Chancery; Pablo Cepeda, Notary/Receptionist; Alondra Flores, Notary;
  Promoter of Justice - t) 404-920-7514 Robert Brown;
  Senior Office Administrator - t) 404-920-7509 Chris Martineck, Bus. Mgr.;
Office of Mission Advancement - t) (404) 920-7615 rmedina@archatl.com Dcn. Rick Medina, Dir.;
  Stewardship - t) 404-920-7600 www.appeal.archatl.com Nancy H. Stoehr, Annual Appeal Coord.; Tracy Zelczak, Oper. Mgr.; Julieta Sanchez, Database Asst.;
Office of Evangelization and Discipleship - t) 404-920-7620 oed@archatl.com Andrew W. Lichtenwalner, Dir. (alichtenwalner@archatl.com); Ivonne S. Vreeland, Oper. Mgr. (ivreeland@archatl.com); Patrick J. Metts, Assoc. Dir. (pmetts@archatl.com);
  LLASU-Llamados a Ser Uno - t) 678-327-6388 Carmen Saldana, Dir.; Lorena Mendez, Dir.;
Office of Intercultural Ministries - t) 404-920-7580 Ashley Morris, Dir., Black Catholics (amorris@archatl.com); Yolanda Munoz, Dir., Hispanic Catholics (ymunoz@archatl.com); Carmen L. Coya-Van Duijn, Asst. Dir. Intercultural Competencies & Communications (ccoya@archatl.com);
Office of Life, Dignity and Justice - Dcn. Dennis J. Dorner Sr., Dir. (ddorner@archatl.com);
  Disabilities Ministry - Maggie Rousseau, Dir.; Kathy Daykin, Coord. Deaf Svcs.;
  Justice and Peace - Kat Doyle, Dir.;
  Respect Life Ministry - t) 404-920-7362 Joey Martineck, Dir.;
  Restorative Justice - Jayna Hoffacker, Dir. Restorative Justice; Imelda Richard, Coord., Prison Ministry;
Office of Planning and Research - t) (404) 920-7852 Jennifer Miles, Mgr. (jmiles@archatl.com);
Permanent Diaconate - t) 404-920-7325 Dcn. Dennis J. Dorner Sr., Dir. (ddorner@archatl.com); Dcn. Jose G. Espinosa, Assoc. Co-Dir. Formation, Office of Permanent Diaconate (jespinosa@archatl.com); Penny Simmons, Assoc. Co-Dir. Formation, Office of Permanent Diaconate (psimmons@archatl.com);
Vocations - t) 404-920-7460 www.calledbychrist.com Rev. Reybert Pineda Avellanada, Dir. (rpineda@ctking.com); Rev. Gerardo Ceballos-Gonzalez, Assoc. Dir. (gerardoceballos@archatl.com); Pilar Castaneda, Intl. Liaison & Finance Analyst (pcastaneda@archatl.com);

ADVISORY BOARDS, COMMISSIONS, COMMITTEES, AND COUNCILS

Advisory Board on Sexual Abuse of Minors - Rev. Msgr. Edward J. Dillon, Promoter of Justice (edillon@archatl.com);
Archdiocesan School Advisory Council - John Cryer, Chair;
Atlanta Conference of Sisters - t) 404-920-7653 Sr. Rezan Mehanzel;
Audit Committee - John Nee, Chair;
Benefits Committee - Rochester Anderson, Chair;
Budget and Operations Committee - Ed Fisher, Chair;
Catholic Charities of the Archdiocese of Atlanta, Inc. - Mike Dowdle, Chair (Mike@dowdle.net); Jack Nichols, Vice Chair; Mike Flanagan, Secy.;
Compensation Committee - Rochester Anderson, Chair;
Council of Deacons - Dcn. Tom G. Walter, Chair;
Council of Priests - t) 770-532-6772 Rev. Mark Starr, Chair (mstarr@archatl.com);
Diaconate Formation Advisory Board - Dcn. Jose G. Espinosa (jespinosa@archatl.com); Penny Simmons (psimmons@archatl.com);
Eucharistic Congress Committee - Dcn. Dennis J. Dorner Sr., Chancellor (ddorner@archatl.com); Kath Owens, Exec. Asst. (kowens@archatl.com);
Finance Council - John A. Berry, Chair;
Investment Committee - Michael Mohr, Chair;
Project Review Committee - Steve Bachman;

MISCELLANEOUS / OTHER OFFICES

AACCW - t) 706-884-4224 Victoria Nimmo-Walters, Pres. (president@atlarchccw.org); Very Rev. Timothy A. Gadziala, Spiritual Adv./Care Svcs;
Archdiocese of Atlanta Catholic Committee on Scouting - t) 770-490-9436 Dcn. Thomas E. Gotschall, Chap. (tgotschall@maryourqueen.com);
Cursillo - c) 678-457-4410 Ylonne Swails (ylonne1@bellsouth.net);
Georgia Catholic Conference - t) 404-920-7367 Frank Mulcahy, Dir.;
Retrouvaille - Bob Botte, Secy.; Karen Botte, Secy. (bottekb@aol.com); Lucia Godshalk, Coord. (djgodshalk@comcast.net);

PARISHES, MISSIONS, AND CLERGY

STATE OF GEORGIA

ACWORTH

St. Clare of Assisi Catholic Church, Acworth, Inc. - 6301 Cedarcrest Rd., Acworth, GA 30101 t) 770-485-0825 frtim@stclarecc.org; office@stclarecc.org stclarecc.org Rev. Timothy E. Nadolski, Pst. & Pres.; Dcn. Dennis J. Dorner Sr., Secy.; CRP Stds.: 371

ALPHARETTA

St. Thomas Aquinas Catholic Church, Alpharetta, Inc. - 535 Rucker Rd., Alpharetta, GA 30004; Mailing: 575 Rucker Rd., Alpharetta, GA 30004 t) 770-475-4501 kkuczka@sta.org sta.org Rev. Fernando Molina-Restrepo, Pres.; Dcn. Dennis J. Dorner Sr., Secy.; Rev. Jaime Rivera, Par. Vicar; Rev. Paul W. Berny, In Res.; Dcn. Thomas F. McGivney; Dcn. Bernard J. Casey; Rev. Fernando Molina Restrepo, Pst.; Dcn. Geza Gereben; Dcn. Arthur Lerma; Dcn. Jesus Nerio; Dcn. Steven W. Shawcross; Dcn. John Strachan; Dcn. Kevin F. Tracy; CRP Stds.: 350

ATHENS

St. Joseph Catholic Church, Athens, Inc. - 958 Epps Bridge Pkwy., Athens, GA 30606 t) 706-548-6332 secretary@stjosephathens.com www.stjosephathens.com Very Rev. Paul Moreau, Pst. & Pres.; Rev. Bryan J. Kuhr, Par. Vicar; Rev. Avery Daniel, Par. Vicar; Dcn. Dennis J. Dorner Sr., Secy.; Dcn. Jim Gaudin; Dcn. Scott E. Medine; Lynn Langston, DRE; James Campbell, Youth Min.; Luis Candelario, Treas.; Ellyn Berg, Bus. Mgr.; CRP Stds.: 524

Catholic Student Center at The University of Georgia - 1344 S. Lumpkin St., Athens, GA 30605-1345 t) 706-543-2293 ccatuga.org Rev. Brian McNavish, Dir.; Rev. Michael Bremer, Assoc. Dir.; Lynn Renna, DRE; Sr. Uyen-Chi Dang, ACJ, Admin.; Sr. Catherine Kirwan-Avila, ACJ, CRE;

ATLANTA

Cathedral of Christ the King Catholic Church, Atlanta, Inc. - 2699 Peachtree Rd., N.E., Atlanta, GA 30305 t) 404-233-2145 ask@ctking.com www.cathedralctk.com Rev. Juan Carlos Villota Viteri, Par. Vicar; Rev. Joseph Wagner, Par. Vicar; Rev. Msgr. Francis G. McNamee, Rector & Pres.; Dcn. Dennis J. Dorner Sr., Secy.; Kim Sheppard, Treas.; Dcn. Christopher J. Andronaco; Dcn. Bruce Goodwin; Dcn. John J. McManus; Dcn. Whitney Robichaux; CRP Stds.: 892

Divine Mercy Mission - 3542 Clairmont Rd., Brookhaven, GA 30319 t) (404) 975-1765 info@divinemercyatl.com divinemercyatl.com Rev. Peeter Pedroza, C.M.F., Admin.;

St. Anthony of Padua Catholic Church, Atlanta, Inc. - 928 Ralph David Abernathy Blvd., S.W., Atlanta, GA 30310 t) 404-758-8861 www.stanthonyatlanta.org Very Rev. Victor A. Galier, Pst. & Pres.; Dcn. Dennis J. Dorner Sr., Secy.; Dcn. Leviticus Jelks; Dcn. William H. Simmons III; CRP Stds.: 30

St. Dominic - 5 Concourse Pkwy., #200, Atlanta, GA 30328 Rev. Robert B. Gramann, Pst.;

St. Joseph School - (Grades K-5) t) 770-828-4045 Brett Mason, Prin.;

Holy Cross Catholic Church, Atlanta, Inc. - 3773 Chamblee Tucker Rd., Atlanta, GA 30341; Mailing: 3175 Hathaway Ct., N.E., Atlanta, GA 30341 t) 770-939-3501 ftanzosch@holycrossatlanta.org www.holycrossatlanta.org Rev. Jude Michael Krill, O.F.M.Conv., Pst. & Pres.; Rev. Benedict Abugu, Par. Vicar; Rev. José Matus, Par. Vicar; Dcn. Dennis J. Dorner Sr., Secy.; Dcn. David Hernandez; CRP Stds.: 554

Holy Spirit Catholic Church, Atlanta, Inc. - 4465 Northside Dr., N.W., Atlanta, GA 30327 t) 404-252-4513 hsccatl.com Rev. Msgr. Edward J. Dillon, Pst. & Pres.; Rev. Roberto Suarez Barbosa, Par. Vicar; Rev. Tamiru Atraga, Par. Vicar; Dcn. Dennis J. Dorner Sr., Secy.; Dcn. Stephen G. Demko; Dcn. William F. McCarthy; Dcn. Mark D. Mitchell; Dcn. Allen Underwood; CRP Stds.: 232

Centro Catolico del Espiritu Santo - t) 404-303-9927 xcapinegro@hsccatl.com

Immaculate Conception Catholic Church, Atlanta, Inc. - 48 Martin Luther King, Jr. Dr., S.W., Atlanta, GA 30303-3599 t) 404-521-1866 contactus@catholicshrineatlanta.org www.catholicshrineatlanta.org Rev. Msgr. Henry C. Gracz, Pst. & Pres.; Rev. Dennis Dorner, Par. Vicar; Rev. Joseph E. Morris, Par. Vicar; Dcn. Dennis J. Dorner Sr., Secy.; Dcn. Randy Joseph Ortiz; CRP Stds.: 60

Immaculate Heart of the Blessed Virgin Mary Catholic Church, Atlanta, Inc. - 2855 Briarcliff Rd., N.E., Atlanta, GA 30329 t) 404-636-1418 ihmatlanta.org Rev. Msgr. Albert W. Jowdy, Pst. & Pres.; Rev. Robbie Cotta, Par. Vicar; Dcn. Dennis J. Dorner Sr., Secy.; Dcn. James Martin; Dcn. Robert J. Hauert; Dcn. Erik Wilkinson; Drew Denton, DRE; CRP Stds.: 442

Our Lady of Lourdes Catholic Church, Atlanta, Inc. - 25 Boulevard, N.E., Atlanta, GA 30312 t) 404-522-6776 info@lourdesatlanta.org www.lourdesatlanta.org Rev. Jeffery Ott, O.P., Pst. & Pres.; Dcn. Dennis J. Dorner Sr., Secy.; Dcn. Lennison Alexander; Dcn. Kenneth Bell; Dcn. Chester H. Griffin; Theresa Bowen, DRE; CRP Stds.: 111

St. Paul of the Cross Catholic Church, Atlanta, Inc. - 551 Harwell Rd., N.W., Atlanta, GA 30318 t) 404-696-6704 stpaulofthecrossatl@gmail.com saintpaulofthecross.org Rev. Jerome McKenna, C.P., Pst. & Pres.; Rev. Patrick Daugherty, Par. Vicar; Rev. Luis Alfredo Lopez-Galarza, C.P., Par. Vicar; Dcn. Dennis J. Dorner Sr., Secy.; Dcn. Joseph Goolsby; Dcn. George Smith; Jessica Darensbourg, Treas.; CRP Stds.: 149

Sacred Heart of Jesus Catholic Church, Atlanta, Inc. - 353 Peachtree St., N.E., Atlanta, GA 30308 t) 404-522-6800 sacredheartatlanta.org Very Rev. John T. Howren, Pst. & Pres.; Dcn. Dennis J. Dorner Sr., Secy.; Dcn. Michael K. Balfour; Dcn. Marino Gonzalez; CRP Stds.: 220

BLAIRSVILLE

St. Francis of Assisi Catholic Church, Blairsville, Inc. - 3717 Hwy. 515 E., Blairsville, GA 30512-3288 t) 706-745-6400 office@stfrancisblairsville.com www.stfrancisblairsville.com Rev. Mario A. Lopez, Pst. & Pres.; Dcn. Dennis J. Dorner Sr., Secy.; Dcn. Paul Dietz; Dcn. Loris Sinanian; CRP Stds.: 33

BLUE RIDGE

St. Anthony Catholic Church, Blue Ridge, Inc. - 967 E. Main St., Blue Ridge, GA 30513; Mailing: PO Box 1448, Blue Ridge, GA 30513 t) 706-632-5970 stanthony@tds.net www.saintanthonyblueridge.com Rev. John T. Conway, Pst. & Pres.; Dcn. Dennis J. Dorner Sr., Secy.; CRP Stds.: 20

BROOKHAVEN

Our Lady of the Assumption Catholic Church, Brookhaven, Inc. - 1406 Hearst Dr., N.E., Brookhaven, GA 30319 t) 404-261-7181 kkotara@olachurch.org www.olachurch.org Rev. James D. Duffy, S.M., Pst. & Pres.; Rev. Kevin J. Duggan, S.M., Par. Vicar; Rev. John M. Ulrich, S.M., Par. Vicar; Rev. Edward Sheehan, S.M., In Res.; Dcn. Dennis J. Dorner Sr., Secy.; Dcn. Antonius Anugerah; Dcn. Terry Biglow; Dcn. William John Kester; Dcn. Edward Patterson; Elizabeth Piper, DRE; Eric Johnson, Treas.; CRP Stds.: 235

CALHOUN

St. Clement Catholic Church, Calhoun, Inc. - 875 Hwy. 53, S.W., 875 Hwy 53 West SW, Calhoun, GA 30701 t) 706-629-2345 epalmerin@stclementsga.org www.stclementsga.org Rev. Carlos G. Ortega, Admin. & Pres.; Dcn. Dennis J. Dorner Sr., Secy.; CRP Stds.: 230

CANTON

Our Lady of LaSalette Catholic Church, Canton, Inc. - 2941 Sam Nelson Rd., Canton, GA 30114 t) 770-479-8923 accountingmanager@lasalettecanton.com; office@lasalettecanton.com lasalettecanton.com Rev. Mark Starr, Pst. & Pres.; Dcn. Dennis J. Dorner Sr., Secy.; Dcn. Charles E. Carignan; Jullian Guidry, DRE; Mary Ashley Diaz, Youth Min.; CRP Stds.: 189

CARROLLTON

Our Lady of Perpetual Help Catholic Church, Carrollton, Inc. - 210 Old Center Point Rd., Carrollton, GA 30117 t) 770-832-8977 www.olphcc.org Rev. Gaurav Manu Shroff, Pst. & Pres.; Dcn. Dennis J. Dorner Sr., Secy.; Dcn. James C. Harkins; Dcn. Jon Gary Atkinson; Joel M Daum, Bus. Mgr.; CRP Stds.: 342

Newman Center University of West Georgia - canolaura2016@gmail.com

CARTERSVILLE

St. Francis of Assisi Catholic Church, Cartersville, Inc. - 850 Douthit Ferry Rd., Cartersville, GA 30120 t) 770-382-4549 www.stfac.org Very Rev. Kevin J. Hargaden, Pst. & Pres.; Dcn. Dennis J. Dorner Sr., Secy.; Dcn. Thomas Coffey; Dcn. Miguel A. Echevarria; CRP Stds.: 312

CEDARTOWN

St. Bernadette Catholic Church, Cedartown, Inc. - 100 Evergreen Ln., Cedartown, GA 30125 t) 770-748-1517 parishoffice@stbernadettecc.org; frgallagher@stbernadettecc.org www.stbernadettecc.org Rev. Timothy Gallagher, Pst. & Pres.; Dcn. Jose M. Orellana; Dcn. Dennis J. Dorner Sr., Secy.; Laura Hernandez, DRE; Emmi Cruz, DRE; Cipriano Hernandez, RCIA Coord.; Jonathan Collado, Youth Min.;

CLARKESVILLE

St. Mark Catholic Church, Clarkesville, Inc. - 5410 Hwy. 197 S., Clarkesville, GA 30523 t) 706-754-4518 office.stmp@gmail.com Very Rev. Jose Luis Hernandez-Ayala, Pst. & Pres.; Dcn. Dennis J. Dorner Sr., Secy.; Dcn. William M. Brown; Dcn. Richard Marinchak; Dcn. Gary J. Roche; CRP Stds.: 278

Capilla Santo Domingo - 427 Cash St., Cornelia, GA 30531

CLAYTON

St. Helena Catholic Church, Clayton, Inc. - 137 Meadow Stream Ln., Clayton, GA 30525; Mailing: P.O. Box 534, Clayton, GA 30525 t) 706-782-5152 sthelenachurchclayton@windstream.net sthelenacc-clayton.org Rev. Luis E. Alvarez, Pst. & Pres.; Dcn. Dennis J. Dorner Sr., Secy.; CRP Stds.: 56

CLEVELAND

St. Paul the Apostle Catholic Church, Cleveland, Inc. - 1243 Hulsey Rd., Cleveland, GA 30528 t) 706-865-4474 cdelgado@stpaulcleveland.com stpaulcleveland.com Rev. Fabio Alvarez-Posada, Pst. & Pres.; Dcn. Dennis J. Dorner Sr., Secy.; CRP Stds.: 115

CONYERS

St. Pius X Catholic Church, Conyers, Inc. - 2621 Hwy. 20 S.E., Conyers, GA 30013-2424 t) 770-483-3660; 770-929-1017 (CRP) churchoffice@spxconyers.com spxconyers.com Rev. Juan F. Areiza, Pst. & Pres.; Rev. Javier Munoz, Par. Vicar; Dcn. Dennis J. Dorner Sr., Secy.; Dcn. John Yaeger; Dcn. Fred Johns; Dcn. Brian Kilkelly; Kevin York, Treas.; CRP Stds.: 243

COVINGTON

St. Augustine Catholic Church, Covington, Inc. - 11524 Hwy. 278 E., Covington, GA 30014 t) 770-787-1064 staugcc.weconnect.org Rev. Roberto Orellana, Pst. & Pres.; Dcn. Dennis J. Dorner Sr., Secy.; CRP Stds.: 91

Society of Our Lady of the Most Holy Trinity - 110 Aspen Dr., Covington, GA 30016-5824 t) 770-787-6468 soltgaoffice@ourladylovesyou.org Rev. James E. Blount, Dir.;

CUMMING

St. Brendan Catholic Church, Cumming, Inc. - 4633 Shiloh Rd., Cumming, GA 30040 t) 770-205-7969 info@stbrendansatl.com www.stbrendansatl.com Rev. Matthew Van Smoorenburg, L.C., Pst. & Pres.; Rev. Michael Shannon, Par. Vicar; Rev. Paul Alger, L.C., Par. Vicar; Dcn. Dennis J. Dorner Sr., Secy.; Dennis Mallon, Treas.; Dcn. Robert H. Grimaldi; Dcn. Luis C.

Lorza; CRP Stds.: 1,062

Good Shepherd Catholic Church, Cumming, Inc. - 3740 Holtzclaw Rd., Cumming, GA 30041 t) 770-887-9861 info@gsrcc.net www.gsrcc.net Rev. Diosmar Natad, Pst. & Pres.; Rev. Joseph Mullakkara, MSFS, Par. Vicar; Dcn. Dennis J. Dorner Sr., Secy.;

DAHLONEGA

St. Luke the Evangelist Catholic Church, Dahlonega, Inc. - 91 N. Park St., Dahlonega, GA 30533 t) 706-864-4779 www.stlukercc.org Rev. Matthew C. Dalrymple, Pst. & Pres.; Dcn. Dennis J. Dorner Sr., Secy.; Stanley Kunka, Treas.; CRP Stds.: 89

University of North Georgia Catholic Campus Ministry - college@stlukercc.org www.stlukercc.org/college

DALLAS

St. Vincent De Paul Catholic Church, Dallas, Inc. - 680 W. Memorial Dr., Dallas, GA 30132 t) 770-443-0566 ahew@svdpatl.com; church@svdpatl.com saintvincentdepaulchurch.org Rev. Adrian C.H. Pleus, Pst. & Pres.; Rev. Omar Loggiodice, In Res.; Dcn. Dennis J. Dorner Sr., Secy.; Dcn. James McDermott; Dcn. Jose Perez; CRP Stds.: 167

DALTON

St. Joseph Catholic Church, Dalton, Inc. - 968 Haig Mill Lake Rd., Dalton, GA 30720 t) 706-278-3107 www.sjcdalton.com Very Rev. Refugio Onate-Melendez, Pst. & Pres.; Rev. Salomon Garcia, Par. Vicar; Rev. Tuan Pham, Par. Vicar; Dcn. Dennis J. Dorner Sr., Secy.; CRP Stds.: 1,193

Capella Santo Toribio Romo - 2402 U.S. Hwy. 76, Chatsworth, GA 30705

Capilla San Juan Diego - 1609 E. Morris St., Dalton, GA 30720

DAWSONVILLE

Christ the Redeemer Catholic Church, Dawsonville, Inc. - 991 Kilough Church Rd., Dawsonville, GA 30534 t) 706-265-1361 office@ctrcc.net; religioused@ctrcc.net ctrcc.net/ Rev. Brian J. Higgins, Pst. & Pres.; Dcn. Dennis J. Dorner Sr., Secy.; Dcn. Joseph C. Anzalone; Dcn. Paul Lee Doppel; Anna Maria McCloy, DRE; Liz Cruz, Bus. Mgr.; CRP Stds.: 128

DECATUR

Sts. Peter and Paul Catholic Church, Decatur, Inc. - 2560 Tilson Rd., Decatur, GA 30032 t) 404-241-5862 www.stspandp.com Rev. Bryan D. Small, Pst. & Pres.; Rev. Carl Jean, Chap.; Dcn. Dennis J. Dorner Sr., Secy.; Dcn. James Anderson Jr.; Dcn. J. Tony King; Dcn. Jerry M. Lett; Dcn. Alfred Mitchell;

St. Thomas More Catholic Church, Decatur, Inc. - 636 W. Ponce de Leon Ave., Decatur, GA 30030 t) 404-378-4588 dwhiteley@stmga.org www.stmgaparish.org Rev. Robert Hussey, S.J., Pst. & Pres.; Dcn. Dennis J. Dorner Sr., Secy.; CRP Stds.: 125

DORAVILLE

Korean Martyrs Catholic Church, Doraville, Inc. - 6003 Buford Hwy., N.E., Doraville, GA 30340 t) 770-455-1380 kmccga.office@gmail.com www.kmccga.com Rev. Tonguk Ku, Pst. & Pres.; Rev. Sunghyun Kim, Par. Vicar; Dcn. Dennis J. Dorner Sr., Secy.; CRP Stds.: 90

DOUGLASVILLE

St. Theresa of the Child Jesus Catholic Church, Douglasville, Inc. - 4401 Prestley Mill Rd., Douglasville, GA 30135 t) 770-489-7115 www.ainttheresacatholicchurch.org Rev. Joseph Shaute, Pst. & Pres.; Dcn. Dennis J. Dorner Sr., Secy.; Dcn. Jose Facundo Maldonado; Dcn. Ronald A. St. Michel; Dcn. Carl A. Taylor; Dcn. Joseph Hrovat; Ivonne Oliveras, DRE; CRP Stds.: 258

DULUTH

St. Andrew Kim Korean Catholic Church, Norcross, Inc. - 2249 Duluth Hwy., Duluth, GA 30097 t) 770-622-2577 sakcga.office@gmail.com www.sakc.org Rev. Soo Young Park, S.J., Assoc. Pst.; Rev. Yongsop Yom, S.J. (Korea), Par. Vicar; Dcn. Dennis J. Dorner Sr., Secy.; CRP Stds.: 176

Mision del Divino Nino Jesus - 4400 Abbotts Bridge Rd., Duluth, GA 30097 t) 678-417-7912 barango@divinonino.org www.divinonino.org Rev. Carlos Quintero, Admin.; CRP Stds.: 180

St. Monica Catholic Church, Duluth, Inc. - 1700 Buford Hwy., Duluth, GA 30097 t) 678-584-9947 karen.lastufka@saintmonicas.com www.saintmonicas.com Rev. John F. Durkin Jr., Pst. & Pres.; Rev. Brian H. Baker, Par. Vicar; Rev. Augustine Tran, Par. Vicar; Dcn. Dennis J. Dorner Sr., Secy.; Dcn. Bob Tipton; CRP Stds.: 373

DUNWOODY

All Saints Catholic Church, Dunwoody, Inc. - 2443 Mount Vernon Rd., Dunwoody, GA 30338-3099 t) 770-393-3255 x139 www.allsaints.us Rev. Msgr. Hugh M. Marren, Pst. & Pres.; Rev. Daniel Rogaczewski, Assoc. Pst.; Dcn. Dennis J. Dorner Sr., Secy.; Dcn. Alan Sims; Dcn. Ricardo D. Medina;

ELLIJAY

Good Samaritan Catholic Church, Ellijay, Inc. - 55 Church St., Ellijay, GA 30540 t) 706-636-2772 office@goodsamaritanellijay.com goodsamaritanellijay.com Rev. Bradley A. Starr, Par. Admin. & Pres.; Dcn. Dennis J. Dorner Sr., Secy.; CRP Stds.: 103

FAYETTEVILLE

St. Gabriel Catholic Church, Fayetteville, Inc. - 152 Antioch Rd., Fayetteville, GA 30215-5702 t) 770-461-0492 www.stgabrielga.com Rev. Richard Anh Vu, Pst. & Pres.; Dcn. Dennis J. Dorner Sr., Secy.; CRP Stds.: 125

FLOWERY BRANCH

Prince of Peace Catholic Church, Flowery Branch, Inc. - 6439 Spout Springs Rd., Flowery Branch, GA 30542 t) 678-960-0040 www.popfb.org Rev. Ignacio Morales, Pst. & Pres.; Rev. Adam Blatt, Par. Vicar; Dcn. Dennis J. Dorner Sr., Secy.; Dcn. William A. Donohue; Dcn. Robert Perri; Dcn. Tom G. Walter; Dcn. Michael R. Jones; Dcn. John (Jack) Campbell; CRP Stds.: 889

FOREST PARK

San Felipe de Jesus - 925 Conley Rd., Forest Park, GA 30297 t) 404-675-0540 missionsanfelipe@bellsouth.net Rev. Vilmar Orsolin, Admin.; Rev. Jesus Antonio Manzo Madrigal, Par. Vicar; Rev. Walter Tonelotto, Par. Vicar; CRP Stds.: 950

FORT OGLETHORPE

St. Gerard Majella Catholic Church, Fort Oglethorpe, Inc. - 3049 LaFayette Rd., Fort Oglethorpe, GA 30742 t) 706-861-9410 secretary@saintgerardmajella.net; pastor@saintgerardmajella.net Rev. Brian J. Bufford, Pst. & Pres.; Dcn. Dennis J. Dorner Sr., Secy.; CRP Stds.: 28

GAINESVILLE

St. John Paul II Catholic Mission - 2410 S Smith Rd SW, Gainesville, GA 30504 t) 770-532-6772 stjohnpauliicatholicchurch.org/ Rev. Carlos E. Vargas, Admin.; Rev. Roberto Herrera, Vicar; CRP Stds.: 914

St. Michael Catholic Church, Gainesville, Inc. - 1440 Pearce Cir., N.E., Gainesville, GA 30501-2457 t) 770-534-3338 k.lampert@saintmichael.cc www.saintmichael.cc Rev. Timothy Hepburn, Pst. & Pres.; Dcn. Dennis J. Dorner Sr., Secy.; Dcn. William L. Bohn; Dcn. Kenneth W. Lampert, Bus. Mgr.; Dcn. Gilberto Perez; CRP Stds.: 450

St. John Paul II Catholic Mission - 622 Shallowford Rd., N.W., Ste. P, Gainesville, GA 30604 t) 770-532-6772 info.jp2tc@gmail.com

GREENSBORO

Christ Our King and Savior Catholic Church, Greensboro, Inc. - 6341 Lake Oconee, Greensboro, GA 30642 t) 706-453-7292 www.cokas.org Very Rev. Michael Silloway, Pst. & Pres.; Dcn. Dennis J. Dorner Sr., Secy.; Ana Pariselli, DRE; Laura Brennan, Youth Min.; John Steadman, Bus. Mgr.; CRP Stds.: 149

GRIFFIN

Sacred Heart Catholic Church, Griffin, Inc. - 1323 MacArthur Dr., Griffin, GA 30224 t) 770-227-2378 www.sacredheartofgriffin.org Rev. Dennis R. Juan, Pst. & Pres.; Dcn. Dennis J. Dorner Sr., Secy.; Dcn. Kenneth P. Bishop; CRP Stds.: 37

HAPEVILLE

St. John the Evangelist Catholic Church, Hapeville, Inc. - 230 Arnold St., Hapeville, GA 30354-1530 t) 404-768-5647 secretary@stjohnevangelist.net www.stjohnevangelist.net Parish and School Dcn. Dennis J. Dorner Sr., Secy.; Rev. Michael U. Onyekuru, Pst. & Pres.; Dcn. Nicholas Goodly; Dcn. Felix Morrero; Daphny Keel, Bus. Mgr.; CRP Stds.: 95

HARTWELL

Sacred Heart of Jesus Catholic Church, Hartwell, Inc. - 1009 Benson St., Hartwell, GA 30643 t) 706-376-4112 www.sacredheartofhartwell.com Rev. Rafael Castano Fernandez, Pst. & Pres.; Dcn. Dennis J. Dorner Sr., Secy.; Dcn. Barry S. Phillips, Admin.; Dcn. Jerry Korte; CRP Stds.: 160

Saint Mary's Catholic Church - 155 Forest Ave., Elberton, GA 30635

JACKSON

St. Mary Mother of God Catholic Church, Jackson, Inc. - 359 Old Griffin Rd., Jackson, GA 30233 t) 770-775-4162; 770-775-4174 szieg@stmaryjackson.org stmaryjackson.org/ Rev. Jose M. Kochuparampil, Admin. & Pres.; Dcn. Dennis J. Dorner Sr., Secy.; Jessica Scarbrough, DRE; CRP Stds.: 25

JASPER

Our Lady of the Mountains Catholic Church, Jasper, Inc. - 1908 Waleska Hwy. 108, Jasper, GA 30143 t) 706-253-3078 ladyofthemts@ellijay.com www.olmjasper.com Rev. Tri John-Bosco Nguyen, Pst.; Dcn. Dennis J. Dorner Sr., Secy.; CRP Stds.: 102

JEFFERSON

St. Catherine Laboure Catholic Church, Jefferson, Inc. - 180 Elrod Rd., Jefferson, GA 30549 t) 706-367-7220 info@stcatherinelabourega.org www.stcatherinelabourega.org Very Rev. Paul Moreau, Pst. & Pres.; Rev. Bryan J. Kuhr, Par. Vicar; Rev. Avery Daniel, Par. Vicar; Amy Friedman, Bus. Mgr.; Julie Ballman, DRE; Dcn. Dennis J. Dorner Sr., Secy.; David Boring, Treas.; Dcn. Pablo Perez; CRP Stds.: 96

JOHNS CREEK

St. Benedict Catholic Church, Johns Creek, Inc. - 11045 Parsons Rd., Johns Creek, GA 30097 t) 770-442-5903 www.stbenedict.net Rev. Paul A. Flood, Pst. & Pres.; Rev. Dairo Antonio Rico; Rev. Benjamin Thomsen; Dcn. Dennis J. Dorner Sr., Secy.; Dcn. John D. Puetz; Dcn. Gerard G. Kazin; Dcn. Timothy F. Dimond; Dcn. Derek Gant; Dcn. Jamie Morgan; CRP Stds.: 677

Mision del Divino Nino Jesus - 4400 Abbotts Bridge Rd., Duluth, GA 30097 t) 678-417-7912 Rev. Carlos Quintero, Admin.;

St. Brigid Catholic Church, Johns Creek, Inc. - 3400 Old Alabama Rd., Johns Creek, GA 30022 t) 678-393-0060 x111 office@saintbrigid.org; jrevell@saintbrigid.org www.saintbrigid.org Rev. Neil J. Herlihy, Pst. & Pres.; Rev. Darragh Griffith, Par. Vicar; Rev. William T. Hao, Par. Vicar; Dcn. Dennis J. Dorner Sr., Secy.; Dcn. Leo Gahafer; Dcn. Henry R. Hein; Dcn. Tom Huff; Dcn. Tim Tye; Dcn. James P. Wolf; Ron L. Leidenfrost; CRP Stds.: 311

JONESBORO

St. Philip Benizi Catholic Church, Jonesboro, Inc. - 591 Flint River Rd., Jonesboro, GA 30238-3452 t) 770-478-0178 mlanglois@stphilipbenizi.org www.stphilipbenizi.org Friar Paul Pantiru, OFM Conv., Par. Vicar; Rev. Calixto Salvatierra, OMF Conv., Par. Vicar; Rev. Martin Breski, O.F.M.Conv., In Res.; Friar Santo Cricchio, OFM Conv., Par. Vicar; Dcn. Thomas Nemchick; Melissa R. Langlois, Parish Life Coord.; Dcn. Peter B. Swan Sr., Pst. Assoc.; Dcn. Henry Ohaya; Dcn. Gregory L. Pecore; Dcn. Etienne Francisco Rodriguez; Dcn. James Windon; Dcn. Dennis J. Dorner Sr., Secy.; Darleine Arce, DRE; Nicholas Dragone, Liturgy Dir.; Ihuoma Ohaya, Treas.; CRP Stds.: 336

KENNESAW

St. Catherine of Siena Catholic Church, Kennesaw, Inc. - 1618 Ben King Rd., Kennesaw, GA 30144 t) 770-428-7139 stcatherinercc.org Very Rev. Neil Dhabliwala, Pst. & Pres.; Rev. Jose Duvan Gonzalez, Par. Vicar; Dcn. Dennis J. Dorner Sr., Secy.; Dcn. James A. Tramonte; Dcn. Jose G. Espinosa; Dcn. Bradford Young; Dcn. Rafael Cintron; Joan Hennes, DRE; CRP

Stds.: 526

LAGRANGE

St. Peter Catholic Church, LaGrange, Inc. - 200 LaFayette Pkwy., LaGrange, GA 30241 t) 706-884-4224 www.stplagrange.com Very Rev. Timothy A. Gadziala, Pst. & Pres.; Dcn. Dennis J. Dorner Sr., Secy.; CRP Stds.: 122

St. Elizabeth Seton - 2904 Judson Bulloch Rd., Warm Springs, GA 31830; Mailing: P.O. Box 638, Warm Springs, GA 31830

LAWRENCEVILLE

St. Lawrence Catholic Church, Lawrenceville, Inc. - 319 Grayson Hwy., Lawrenceville, GA 30046 t) 770-963-8992 www.saintlaw.org Very Rev. Henry Atem, Pst. & Pres.; Rev. Cristian Cossio Sepulveda, Par. Vicar; Dcn. Dennis J. Dorner Sr., Secy.; Dcn. Richard Hogan; Dcn. Terry D. Millinger; Dcn. Jose Ortiz-Velasquez; Dcn. Robert Riddett; Dcn. David Schreckenberger; CRP Stds.: 858

St. Marguerite d'Youville Catholic Church, Lawrenceville, Inc. - 85 Gloster Rd., N.W., Lawrenceville, GA 30044 t) 770-381-7337; 770-381-8062 admin@stmdy.org; frtomy@stmdy.org www.stmdy.org Rev. Tomy J. Puliyan, MSFS, Pst. & Pres.; Dcn. Peter Ranft; Dcn. Dennis J. Dorner Sr., Secy.; Dcn. George D. Angelich; CRP Stds.: 85

LILBURN

St. John Neumann Catholic Church, Lilburn, Inc. - 801 Tom Smith Rd., Lilburn, GA 30047-2299 t) 770-923-6633 www.sjnlilburn.com Rev. Sunny Joseph Punnakuziyil, M.S.F.S., Pst. & Pres.; Rev. Fredi Navarrete, M.S.F.S. (Chile), Par. Vicar; Dcn. Dennis J. Dorner Sr., Secy.; Dcn. Mike Byrne; Dcn. Manuel Echevarria; Dcn. Michael Hayward; Dcn. Joe Odom; CRP Stds.: 452

Our Lady of the Americas Catholic Mission - 4603 Lawrenceville Hwy., Lilburn, GA 30047 t) 770-717-1517 ljaramillo@oloacm.org www.oloacm.org Rev. Luis Guillermo Cordoba, Admin.; Rev. Carlos Bustamante, Par. Vicar; Dcn. John Martin; Leonardo Jaramillo-Giraldo, DRE; CRP Stds.: 1,789

St. Stephen the Martyr Catholic Church, Lilburn, Inc. - 5373 Wydella Rd., S.W., Lilburn, GA 30047 t) 770-381-7488 ststephenthemartyr.info Rev. Brian T. Lorei, Pst. & Pres.; Dcn. Dennis J. Dorner Sr., Secy.; Dcn. Evelio Garcia-Carreras; Dcn. Richard C. Kaszycki; Dcn. Richard Kren; CRP Stds.: 96

LITHIA SPRINGS

St. John Vianney Catholic Church, Lithia Springs, Inc. - 1920 Skyview Dr., Lithia Springs, GA 30122 t) 770-941-2807 parishoffice@sjvpar.net www.sjvpar.net Rev. John (Jack) Philp Knight, Pst. & Pres.; Rev. Peter-Elvis Moleke Akanang (Cameroon), Par. Vicar; Dcn. Dennis J. Dorner Sr., Secy.; Dcn. Francis Przybylek; Dcn. Felix Rentas; Dcn. Al Douglas Turner; CRP Stds.: 722

LITHONIA

Christ Our Hope Catholic Church, Lithonia, Inc. - 1786 Wellborn Rd., Lithonia, GA 30058 t) 770-482-5017 parish@christourhopeatl.org www.christourhopeatl.org Rev. Junot Nelvy, Pst. & Pres.; Dcn. Dennis J. Dorner Sr., Secy.; CRP Stds.: 50

LOOKOUT MOUNTAIN

Our Lady of the Mount Catholic Church, Lookout Mountain, Inc. - 1227 Scenic Hwy., Lookout Mountain, GA 30750 t) 706-820-0680 mthomas@olmcc.com; mvoges@olmcc.com www.olmcc.com Rev. Mark Edward Thomas, Admin. & Pres.; Dcn. Dennis J. Dorner Sr., Secy.; CRP Stds.: 28

St. Katharine Drexel - 140 New England Rd., Wildwood, GA 30757; Mailing: 1227 Scenic Hwy, Lookout Mountain, GA 30750

MABLETON

St. Francis de Sales Catholic Church, Mableton, Inc. - 587 Landers Dr., S.W., Mableton, GA 30126 t) 770-948-6888 secretary@fsspatl.com www.fsspatl.com Rev. Robert Dow, FSSP, Pst. & Pres.; Rev. Andrew Rapoport, FSSP, Par. Vicar; Rev. Brian Austin, FSSP, In Res.; Dcn. Dennis J. Dorner Sr., Secy.; Dcn. Douglas J. Anderson; Connor Nies, Treas.; CRP Stds.: 131

MADISON

St. James Catholic Church, Madison, Inc. - 562 Vine St., Madison, GA 30650 t) 706-342-9661 office@stjamesmadison.org stjamesmadison.catholicparish.info Rev. Liem Nguyen, Pst. & Pres.; Dcn. Dennis J. Dorner Sr., Secy.; CRP Stds.: 49

MARIETTA

St. Ann Catholic Church, Marietta, Inc. - 4905 Roswell Rd., N.E., Marietta, GA 30062 t) 770-552-6400 contact@st-ann.org www.st-ann.org Rev. Raymond G. Cadran, M.S., Pst. & Pres.; Rev. Robert Zaw Lwin, M.S., Assoc. Pst.; Rev. Andrews Kollannoor, MS (India); Dcn. Thomas Martin; Dcn. Dennis J. Dorner Sr., Secy.; Dcn. Thomas P. Badger; Dcn. Bobby Allen Jennings; Dcn. J. Nicholas Morning; Dcn. Randall Ory; Rev. Joseph G. Aquino, M.S., In Res.; Jenny Kiehl, DRE; CRP Stds.: 1,100

Transfiguration Catholic Church, Marietta, Inc. - 1815 Blackwell Rd., N.E., Marietta, GA 30066-2911 t) 770-977-1442 staff@transfiguration.com www.transfiguration.com Very Rev. Eric J. Hill, Pst. & Pres.; Rev. Miller Gomez-Ruiz, Par. Vicar; Dcn. Dennis J. Dorner Sr., Secy.; Dcn. David A. Fragale; Dcn. Paul Franklin; Dcn. Peter Harris; Dcn. Bruce C. Publicover; CRP Stds.: 1,247

Holy Family Catholic Church, Marietta, Inc. - 3401 Lower Roswell Rd., Marietta, GA 30068-3974 t) 770-973-0038 www.holyfamilycc.org Rev. Miguel Grave de Peralta, Pst. & Pres.; Rev. Vincent Sullivan, Par. Vicar; Very Rev. Daniel P. Ketter, In Res.; Dcn. Dennis J. Dorner Sr., Secy.; Dcn. Jim Grebe; Dcn. Randall Ory; CRP Stds.: 279

St. Joseph Catholic Church, Marietta, Inc. - 87 Lacy St., N.W., Marietta, GA 30060 t) 770-422-5633 www.saintjosephcc.org Rev. Msgr. John P. Walsh, Pst. & Pres.; Rev. Msgr. James A. Schillinger, Par. Vicar; Rev. Hernan Quevedo Rodriguez, Par. Vicar; Dcn. Dennis J. Dorner Sr., Secy.; Dcn. Francis Devereux; Dcn. Norman K. Keller; Dcn. Bruce Reed; Dcn. Thomas Shaver; Dcn. Phillip G. Smilski; Dcn. Kenneth Williams; CRP Stds.: 1,031

MCDONOUGH

St. James Catholic Church, McDonough, Inc. - 1000 Decatur Rd., Hwy. 155, McDonough, GA 30252 t) 770-957-5441 www.stjamesapostlecatholicchurch.com Rev. Liam Coyne, Pst. & Pres.; Rev. Msgr. Terry W. Young, In Res.; Dcn. Dennis J. Dorner Sr., Secy.; Dcn. Charles Iner; CRP Stds.: 176

MILLEDGEVILLE

Sacred Heart Catholic Church, Milledgeville, Inc. - 110 N. Jefferson St., Milledgeville, GA 31061; Mailing: P.O. Box 754, Milledgeville, GA 31061 t) 478-452-2421 sacredheartmilledgeville.org Rev. Dung Nguyen, Pst. & Pres.; Dcn. Dennis J. Dorner Sr., Secy.; Dcn. Cesar Basilio; Dcn. John W. Shoemaker; CRP Stds.: 41

MONROE

St. Anna Catholic Church, Monroe, Inc. - 1401 Alcovy St., Monroe, GA 30655 t) 770-267-7637 secretary@st-annas.com www.st-annas.com Rev. Randall Mattox, Pst. & Pres.; Dcn. Dennis J. Dorner Sr., Secy.; Victoria Reeves, DRE; CRP Stds.: 72

NEWNAN

St. George Catholic Church, Newnan, Inc. - 771 Roscoe Rd., Newnan, GA 30263 t) 770-251-5353 www.stgeorgenewnan.org Rev. Stephen J. Lyness, Pst. & Pres.; Dcn. Dennis J. Dorner Sr., Secy.; Dcn. Steve Beers; Dcn. Edward Buckley;

St. Mary Magdalene Catholic Church, Newnan, Inc. - 3 Village Rd., Newnan, GA 30265-6162 t) 770-253-1888 smmcc@smmcatholic.org www.smmcatholic.org Rev. Terence Crone, Pst. & Pres.; Dcn. Dennis J. Dorner Sr., Secy.; Dcn. Thomas Eden, Treas.; Dcn. Paul S. Swope Jr.; Dcn. Jim G. Weeks; CRP Stds.: 310

NORCROSS

Holy Name of Jesus Chinese Catholic Mission - 5395 Light Cir., N.W., Norcross, GA 30071 t) 678-691-3261 info@hnojatl.org; bhao@hnojatl.org hnojatl.org Rev. William T. Hao, Admin.; CRP Stds.: 9

Holy Vietnamese Martyrs Catholic Church, Norcross, Inc. - 4545 Timmers Way, Norcross, GA 30093 t) 770-921-0077 info@hvmatl.org www.hvmatl.org Rev. Tuan Quoc Tran, Pst. & Pres.; Rev. Dominic Tran, Assoc. Pst.; Dcn. Dennis J. Dorner Sr., Secy.; Dcn. Hoa (Joseph) V. Pham; Sr. Oanh Ngoc Do, DRE; Son Nguyen, CFO; CRP Stds.: 1,089

St. Patrick Catholic Church, Norcross, Inc. - 2140 Beaver Ruin Rd., Norcross, GA 30071 t) 770-448-2028 www.stpatricksga.org Rev. Pedro Poloche, Pst. & Pres.; Rev. Abel Guerrero-Oeta, Par. Vicar; Rev. Cyril Soo-Gil Chae, Par. Vicar; Dcn. Dennis J. Dorner Sr., Secy.; CRP Stds.: 800

PEACHTREE CITY

Holy Trinity Catholic Church, Peachtree City, Inc. - 101 Walt Banks Rd., Peachtree City, GA 30269 t) 770-487-7672 www.holytrinityptc.org Rev. John Murphy, Pst. & Pres.; Rev. Pavol Brenkus, Par. Vicar; Rev. Guyma Noel, Par. Vicar; Dcn. Dennis J. Dorner Sr., Secy.; Dcn. Rodney Arion; Dcn. Terry S. Blind; Dcn. Anthony F. Cuomo; Dcn. Mark F. Friedlein; Dcn. Ben Gross; Dcn. Michael K. Mobley Sr.; Dcn. Richard Schmidt; Dcn. Mark A. Sholander; CRP Stds.: 688

PEACHTREE CORNERS

Mary Our Queen Catholic Church, Peachtree Corners, Inc. - 6260 The Corners Pkwy., Peachtree Corners, GA 30092 t) 770-416-0002 office@maryourqueen.com www.maryourqueen.com Rev. Charles A. Byrd Jr., Pst. & Pres.; Dcn. Dennis J. Dorner Sr., Secy.; Dcn. Bill Boyd; Dcn. Thomas E. Gotschall; Dcn. Chris Waken; CRP Stds.: 238

RIVERDALE

Our Lady of Vietnam Catholic Church, Riverdale, Inc. - 91 Valley Hill Rd., Riverdale, GA 30274 t) 770-472-9963 www.giaoxuducmevietnam.org Rev. Peter Duc Vu, Pst. & Pres.; Rev. Tan Robert Pham, S.J., Par. Vicar; Dcn. Dennis J. Dorner Sr., Secy.; Dcn. Peter Hung Viet Huynh; Dcn. Joseph Phu Nguyen; CRP Stds.: 485

ROME

St. Mary Catholic Church, Rome, Inc. - 911 N. Broad St., Rome, GA 30161 t) 706-290-9000; 706-290-9054 (Res.) www.smcrome.org Very Rev. Rafael Carballo, Pst. & Pres.; Dcn. Dennis J. Dorner Sr., Secy.; Dcn. Stuart L. Neslin; Dcn. James S. Thacker; CRP Stds.: 380

ROSWELL

St. Andrew Catholic Church, Roswell, Inc. - 675 Riverside Rd., Roswell, GA 30075 t) 770-641-9720 www.standrewcatholic.org Very Rev. Juan Anzora, Pst. & Pres.; Dcn. Dennis J. Dorner Sr., Secy.; Dcn. Jose G. Campos; Dcn. Eduardo J. Rubio; Dcn. David Patterson;

St. Peter Chanel Catholic Church, Roswell, Inc. - 11330 Woodstock Rd., Roswell, GA 30075 t) 678-277-9424 mplachta@stpeterchanel.org www.stpeterchanel.org Rev. Msgr. Peter J. Rau, Pst. & Pres.; Rev. Paul Porter, Par. Vicar; Dcn. Michael Bickerstaff; Dcn. Joseph F. Crowley; Dcn. William Keen; Dcn. David J. Thomasberger; Dcn. John Wojcik; Dcn. Keith M. Kolodziej; David Dahm, Bus. Mgr.; Hugh Hayman, Treas.; Dcn. Dennis J. Dorner Sr., Secy.; Shannon Civetta, DRE; Jane Jackson, Music Min.; CRP Stds.: 649

SANDY SPRINGS

St. Jude the Apostle Catholic Church, Sandy Springs, Inc. - 7171 Glenridge Dr., N.E., Sandy Springs, GA 30328 t) 770-394-3896; 770-394-3896 x525 (CRP) www.judeatl.com Rev. Msgr. W. Joseph Corbett, Pst. & Pres.; Rev. Paul Matthew Nacey, Par. Vicar; Rev. Vanderley Oliveira (Brazil), Par. Vicar; Dcn. Dennis J. Dorner Sr., Secy.; Dcn. Gary E. Schantz; Dcn. Stanley Stewart; Colleen Tyner, Treas. & Dir. of Opers.; Kathleen Woods, Bus. Mgr.; Mike Higgins, Dir.; Bryan Archer, Music Min.; Roberta Meadows, DRE; Ann Sottile, RCIA Coord.; Lourdes Davis, Parish Life Coord.; CRP Stds.: 402

SMYRNA

St. Thomas the Apostle Catholic Church, Smyrna, Inc. - 4300 King Springs Rd., S.E., Smyrna, GA 30082 t) 770-432-8579 stthomastheapostle.org Rev. Brian R. Sheridan, M.S., Pst. & Pres.; Rev. Clemente Felix Mario, M.S., Par. Vicar; Rev. Jaime Molina-Juarez, M.N.M., Par. Vicar; Dcn. Dennis J. Dorner Sr., Secy.; Dcn. Michael Garrett; Dcn. Earl D. Jackson;

SNELLVILLE

St. Oliver Plunkett Catholic Church, Snellville, Inc. - 3200 Brooks Dr., Snellville, GA 30078 t) 770-979-2500; 770-978-6751 (CRP) www.stolivers.com Rev. Cyriac Mattathilanickal, Pst. & Pres.; Rev. Joseph Everton, MS, Par. Vicar; Rev. Robert Butler, MS, In Res.; Dcn. Dennis J. Dorner Sr., Secy.; Dcn. Michael S. Chavez; CRP Stds.: 409

SOUTH FULTON

Most Blessed Sacrament Catholic Church, Atlanta, Inc. - 2971 Butner Rd., South Fulton, GA 30331 t) 404-349-9263 www.mbschurch.com Rev. Desmond Drummer, Pst. & Pres.; Dcn. Dennis J. Dorner Sr., Secy.; Dcn. Frederick Toca;

STONE MOUNTAIN

Corpus Christi Catholic Church, Stone Mountain, Inc. - 600 Mountain View Dr., Stone Mountain, GA 30083 t) 770-469-0395 mcasnave@corpuschristicc.org www.corpuschristicc.org Rev. Paschal Amagba, C.M.F., Pst. & Pres.; Rev. Malachy Osunwa, CMF, Assoc. Pst.; Rev. Gregory D. Kenny, C.M.F., Pastor Emer.; Dcn. Dennis J. Dorner Sr., Secy.; Dcn. Ken W. Melvin; Marlice Casnave, Bus. Mgr.; Renay Ceasar, Dir., Faith Formation; CRP Stds.: 148

THOMASTON

St. Peter the Rock Catholic Church, The Rock, Inc. - 3594 Barnesville Hwy., Thomaston, GA 30286; Mailing: PO Box 280, The Rock, GA 30285 t) 706-648-2599 bluger@stpetertherock.com www.stpetertherock.com Rev. Thomas A. Zahuta, Pst. & Pres.; Dcn. Dennis J. Dorner Sr., Secy.; Dcn. Thomas Kretzmer; CRP Stds.: 62

THOMSON

Queen of Angels Catholic Church, Thomson, Inc. - 1326 Washington Rd., Thomson, GA 30824 t) 706-595-2913 qofa.office@gmail.com 32948.sites.ecatholic.com/ Rev. Mark White, Par. Admin. & Pres.; Dcn. Dennis J. Dorner Sr., Secy.; CRP Stds.: 31

TOCCOA

St. Mary Catholic Church, Toccoa, Inc. - 231 Rothell Rd. Ext., Toccoa, GA 30577 t) 706-886-2819 www.stmarystoccoaga.com Rev. Thang M. Pham, Pst. & Pres.; Dcn. Dennis J. Dorner Sr.; Dcn. Gregory Ollick; Jessica Burger, DRE; CRP Stds.: 35

TYRONE

St. Matthew Catholic Church, Tyrone, Inc. - 215 Kirkley Rd., Tyrone, GA 30290-9549 t) 770-964-5804 www.saintmatthew.us Rev. Valery Akoh, Par. Admin. & Pres.; Dcn. Dennis J. Dorner Sr., Secy.; Dcn. King E. Cooper; Dcn. William Hampton; Dcn. Gayle P. Peters; Dcn. Harold Leon Roberts; CRP Stds.: 260

WASHINGTON

St. Joseph Catholic Church, Washington, Inc. - 1015 N. By Pass Hwy. 78 W., Washington, GA 30673 t) 706-678-2110 sjw.ga.office@gmail.com 32948.sites.ecatholic.com/ Rev. Mark White, Admin.; Dcn. Dennis J. Dorner Sr., Secy.; CRP Stds.: 30

WINDER

St. Matthew Catholic Church, Winder, Inc. - 25 Wilkins Rd., S.W., Winder, GA 30680-3878 t) 770-867-4876 busmgr@saintmatthewcc.org www.saintmatthewcc.org Rev. Gilbert Exume, Pst. & Pres.; Dcn. Dennis J. Dorner Sr., Secy.; Paul Hill, Treas.; Dcn. Michael P. Nungesser; Dcn. Earl D. Buckley; Dcn. Christopher Carroll; Dcn. Luis Londono; Dcn. Lawrence J. Welsh; CRP Stds.: 743

WOODSTOCK

St. Michael the Archangel Catholic Church, Woodstock, Inc. - 490 Arnold Mill Rd., Woodstock, GA 30188 t) 770-516-0009 www.saintmichaelcc.org Rev. Larry Niese, Pst. & Pres.; Rev. Fausto Marquez, Par. Vicar; Dcn. Dennis J. Dorner Sr., Secy.; Dcn. Jack Herndon; Dcn. Jose I. Pupo; Dcn. Victor L. Taylor; Dcn. Wayne E. Topper; Dcn. Kelly Stinson; Elizabeth Bonutti, DRE; CRP Stds.: 668

SCHOOLS: PRESCHOOL THRU HIGH SCHOOL

SCHOOLS

STATE OF GEORGIA

ATHENS

St. Joseph Catholic School - (PAR) (Grades PreK-8) 958 Epps Bridge Pkwy., Athens, GA 30606 t) 706-543-1621 theresa.bangert@sjsathens.org www.sjsathens.org Tina Bortle, Admin.; Theresa Napoli, Prin.; Stds.: 188; Lay Tchrs.: 13

ATLANTA

Christ the King Catholic School - (PAR) (Grades K-8) 46 Peachtree Way, N.E., Atlanta, GA 30305 t) 404-233-0383 www.christking.org (Co-ed) Melissa Lowry, Prin.; Nick Saporito, Vice Prin.; Stds.: 564; Lay Tchrs.: 40

***Holy Spirit Preparatory School, Inc.** - (PRV) (Grades PreK-12) 4449 Northside Dr., Atlanta, GA 30327 t) 678-904-2811 admissions@holyspiritprep.org www.holyspiritprep.org Rev. John Paul Duran, LC, Chap.; Stds.: 436; Pr. Tchrs.: 2; Lay Tchrs.: 48

Upper School Campus - (Grades PreK-12) 4449 Northside Dr., Atlanta, GA 30327 t) (678) 904-2811 mbertany@holyspiritprep.org Michelle Bertany, Prin.;

Lower School Campus - (Grades PreK-12) 4820 Long Island Dr., Atlanta, GA 30342 t) 404-255-0900 pradosta@holyspiritprep.org Peter Radosta, Prin.;

Preschool Campus - 4465 Northside Dr., Atlanta, GA 30327 t) 404-252-8008 gtate@holyspiritprep.org Georgia Tate, Dir.;

Immaculate Heart of Mary Catholic School - (PAR) (Grades PreK-8) 2855 Briarcliff Rd., N.E., Atlanta, GA 30329 t) 404-636-4488 lcichanski@ihmschool.org; lrhodes@ihmschool.org www.ihmschool.org Laura Cichanski, Prin.; Bob Baldonado, Vice Prin.; Stds.: 508; Lay Tchrs.: 33

St. Jude the Apostle Catholic School - (PAR) (Grades K-8) 7171 Glenridge Dr., N.E., Atlanta, GA 30328 t) 770-394-2880 pchilds@saintjude.net saintjude.net Patty Childs, Prin.; Eleneora Straub, Librn.; Stds.: 486; Lay Tchrs.: 36

Our Lady of the Assumption Catholic School - (PAR) (Grades PreK-8) 1320 Hearst Dr., N.E., Atlanta, GA 30319 t) 404-364-1902 office@olaschool.org www.olaschool.org/ Mandy Faletti Crock, Prin.; Stds.: 583; Lay Tchrs.: 52

CUMMING

***Pinecrest Academy, Inc.** - (PRV) (Grades PreK-12) 955 Peachtree Pkwy., Cumming, GA 30041 t) 770-888-4477 jmccabe@pinecrestacademy.org www.pinecrestacademy.org Jake Rodgers, Head of School; Amy Bowman, HS Prin.; Leonard Forti, Lower & Middle School Prin.; Joan McCabe, VP Fin. & CFO; Rev. Terrance Allen, LC, Chap.; Rev. Matthew A. Kaderabek, L.C., Chap.; Rev. Patrick O'Loughlin, LC, Chap.; Emily Roman, RC, Interim Dir. of Campus Min.; Stds.: 472; Pr. Tchrs.: 2; Sr. Tchrs.: 3; Lay Tchrs.: 58

DECATUR

St. Peter Claver Regional Catholic School - (DIO) (Grades PreK-8) 2560 Tilson Rd., Decatur, GA 30032 t) 404-241-3063 sgreenwood@spc-school.org www.spc-school.org Susanne Greenwood, Prin.; Alejandra Gordon, Bus. Mgr.; Stds.: 133; Lay Tchrs.: 11

St. Thomas More Catholic School - (PAR) (Grades PreK-8) 630 W. Ponce De Leon Ave., Decatur, GA 30030 t) 404-373-8456 stm@stmga.org www.stmga.org Shaun Bland, Prin.; Charlie Seamans, Vice Prin.; Eileen Maron, Registrar; Stds.: 475; Lay Tchrs.: 30

DULUTH

***Notre Dame Academy** - (PRV) (Grades PreK-12) 4635 River Green Pkwy., Duluth, GA 30096 t) 678-387-9385 jderucki@ndacademy.org; egillespie@ndacademy.org www.ndacademy.org International Baccalaureate program. Ken Willers, Pres.; Julia Derucki, Prin.; Julie Pack, DRE; Stds.: 293; Lay Tchrs.: 55

FAYETTEVILLE

St. Mary's Academy, Inc. - (DIO) (Grades PreK-12) 861 Hwy. 279, Fayetteville, GA 30214 t) 770-461-2202 mkomdat@smaschool.org www.smaschool.org JoAnn McPherson, Prin.; Cynthia Launay-Fallasse, Vice Prin.; Mark Komdat, Bus. Mgr.; Stds.: 329; Lay Tchrs.: 32

HAPEVILLE

St. John the Evangelist Catholic School - (PAR) (Grades PreK-8) 240 Arnold St., Hapeville, GA 30354 t) 404-767-4312 office@sjecs.net www.sjecs.org Bernadette Boisis, Prin.; Stds.: 278; Sr. Tchrs.: 1; Lay Tchrs.: 16

JOHNS CREEK

Holy Redeemer Catholic School - (DIO) (Grades K-8) 3380 Old Alabama Rd., Johns Creek, GA 30022 t) 770-410-4056 info@hrcatholicschool.org www.hrcatholicschool.org Jill Rice, Admin.; Lauren Schell, Prin.; Brenda Leslie, Controller; Stds.: 467; Lay Tchrs.: 27

KENNESAW

St. Catherine of Siena Catholic School - (PAR) (Grades K-8) 1618 Ben King Rd., Kennesaw, GA 30144 t) 770-419-8601 kwood@scsiena.org; mmong@scsiena.org www.scsiena.org Kelly Wood, Prin.; Stds.: 314; Sr. Tchrs.: 3; Lay Tchrs.: 17

LILBURN

St. John Neumann Regional Catholic School - (DIO) (Grades PreK-8) 791 Tom Smith Rd., S.W., Lilburn, GA 30047 t) 770-381-0557 mremshik@sjnrcs.org www.sjnrcs.org (Regional) Anna Abbott, Admin.; Stds.: 333; Lay Tchrs.: 20

MARIETTA

St. Joseph Catholic School - (PAR) (Grades PreK-8) 81 Lacy St., Marietta, GA 30060 t) 770-428-3328 rvillacura@stjosephschool.org stjosephschool.org Ramon Villacura, Prin.; Rita Hohman, Vice Prin.; Stds.: 375; Lay Tchrs.: 30

ROME

St. Mary's Catholic School - (PAR) (Grades PreK-8) 401 E. Seventh St. SE, Rome, GA 30161 t) 706-234-4953 jrittgers@smsrome.org www.smsrome.org Jennifer Rittgers, Prin.; Stds.: 198; Lay Tchrs.: 11

ROSWELL

Queen of Angels Catholic School - (DIO) (Grades K-8) 11340 Woodstock Rd., Roswell, GA 30075 t) 770-518-1804 jarthur@qaschool.org www.qaschool.org Danielle Montepare, Admin.; Dr. Jamie Arthur, Prin.; Brenda Leslie, Controller; Stds.: 488; Lay Tchrs.: 42

TYRONE

Our Lady of Victory Catholic School - (DIO) (Grades PreK-8) 211 Kirkley Rd., Tyrone, GA 30290 t) (404) 920-7700 dstarkovich@archatl.com

HIGH SCHOOLS

STATE OF GEORGIA

ATHENS

***Monsignor Donovan Catholic High School** - (PRV) (Grades 9-12) 590 Lavender Rd., Athens, GA 30606 t) 706-433-0223 pgessner@mdchs.org www.donovancatholichs.org Paul Gessner, Headmaster; Charles Auslander, Chair; Stds.: 105; Lay Tchrs.: 16

ATLANTA

Cristo Rey Atlanta Jesuit High School, Inc. - (PRV) (Grades 9-12) 222 Piedmont Ave., N.E., Atlanta, GA 30308 t) 404-637-2800 khackett@cristoreyatlanta.org

www.cristoreyatlanta.org David Fitzgerald, Chair; Camille Naughton, Pres.; Robert Anthony Harris, Prin.; Stds.: 483; Scholastics: 1; Pr. Tchrs.: 2; Lay Tchrs.: 28
***Marist School** - (PRV) (Grades 7-12) 3790 Ashford Dunwoody, N.E., Atlanta, GA 30319-1899 t) 770-457-7201 info@marist.com www.marist.com College Preparatory Day School conducted by The Marist Fathers and Brothers. Corporate Title: Marist School, Inc. Rev. Ralph F. Olek, S.M., Supr.; Rev. William F. Rowland, S.M., Pres.; Rev. Mark Kenney, S.M., Chap.; Rev. David D. Musso, S.M., Chap.; Rev. Thomas E. Ellerman, S.M., In Res.; Rev. Francis J. Kissel, S.M., In Res.; Stds.: 1,084; Pr. Tchrs.: 1; Lay Tchrs.: 118
St. Pius X Catholic High School - (DIO) (Grades 9-12) 2674 Johnson Rd., N.E., Atlanta, GA 30345 t) 404-636-3023 mfree@spx.org spx.org (Coed) Aaron Parr, Pres.; Edye Simpson, Prin.; LeyAnna Messick, Librn.; Stds.: 1,072; Lay Tchrs.: 104
ROSWELL
Blessed Trinity Catholic High School - (DIO) (Grades 9-12) 11320 Woodstock Rd., Roswell, GA 30075 t) 678-277-9083 clancaster@btcatholic.org www.btcatholic.org Cathy Lancaster, Prin.; Stds.: 954; Lay Tchrs.: 89

INSTITUTIONS LOCATED IN DIOCESE

ASSOCIATIONS [ASN]

ATLANTA
The Solidarity Association - 5 Concourse Pkwy., Ste. 200, Atlanta, GA 30328 t) 404-550-7961 www.solidarityassociation.com Frank J. Hanna III, Moderator;

CAMPUS MINISTRY / NEWMAN CENTERS [CAM]

SMYRNA
Campus Ministry - 2401 Lake Park Dr., Smyrna, GA 30080-8862 t) 404-920-7641 aaustin@archatl.com Andrew Lichtenwalner, Dir.; Allen Austin, Contact;
Berry College - 911 N. Broad St., Rome, GA 30161 t) 706-290-9000 Rev. Robert Frederick, Chap.;
Catholic Center Georgia State University - 4th Fl. Student Ctr. W., Rm. 483, Atlanta, GA 30302 t) 404-755-2646 lykehouse.org/ Rev. Urey P. Mark, S.V.D., Chap.;
Clark Atlanta - 809 Beckwith St., S.W., Atlanta, GA 30314 t) 404-755-2646 umark@archatl.com www.lykehouse.org/ Rev. Urey P. Mark, S.V.D., Chap.;
Emory University, Agnes Scott College - 1753 N. Decatur Rd., N.E., Atlanta, GA 30307 t) 404-636-7237 mzauche@emory.edu www.emory.edu Rev. John Joseph Blase Boll, O.P., Chap.; Michael Zauche, Campus Min.; Victoria Schwartz, Admin.;
Georgia College & State University (Milledgeville) - 211 W. Greene St., Milledgeville, GA 31061 t) 478-452-2421 deaconcesar@gmail.com gcsucampuscatholics.weebly.com/ Dcn. Cesar Basilio, Campus Min.;
Georgia Gwinnett College - 319 Grayson Hwy., Lawrenceville, GA 30046 t) 770-963-8992 Michelle Hamilton, Pres.; Very Rev. John T. Howren, Chap.;
Georgia Tech Catholic Center - 172 4th St., N.W., Atlanta, GA 30313 t) 404-892-6759 info@gtcatholic.org gtcatholic.org Rev. Branson S. Hipp, Chap.; Lisa Machado, Admin.; Madeline Zuniga, Admin.;
Kennesaw State University - 3487 Campus Loop Rd., N.W., Kennesaw, GA 30144 t) 770-423-9909 www.ccksu.org Rev. Joseph E. Morris, Chap.; Debra Bona, Admin.;
Morehouse College - 809 Beckwith St., S.W., Atlanta, GA 30314 t) 404-755-2646 umark@archatl.com www.lykehouse.org/ Rev. Urey P. Mark, S.V.D., Chap.;
Oglethorpe University - 1350 Hearst Dr., N.E., Atlanta, GA 30319 t) 404-261-7181 aknuckles@olachurch.org www.olachurch.org/youth-ministry Andrew Knuckles, Contact;
Spellman College - 809 Beckwith St., S.W., Atlanta, GA 30314 t) 404-755-2646 umark@archatl.com lykehouse.org Rev. Urey P. Mark, S.V.D., Chap.;
University of Georgia - Catholic Student Center - 1344 S. Lumpkin St., Athens, GA 30605 t) 706-543-2293 ccatuga.org/ (Athens) Rev. Fred Wendel, Chap.; Sr. Uyen-Chi Dang, ACJ, Admin.; Jessica Fox, Bus. Mgr.; Rev. Brian McNavish, Campus Min.;
University of North Georgia (Dahlonega) - 91 N. Park St., Dahlonega, GA 30533 t) 706-864-4779 ungcatholic.org Rev. Matthew C. Dalrymple, Chap.; Matt Hair, Campus Min.;
University of West Georgia - 1601 Maple St., Carrollton, GA 30118 t) 770-832-8977 uwgcampuscatholics@olphcc.org www.olphcc.org/?page_id=1935 Rev. Gaurav Manu Shroff, Chap.; Norma Rothschadl, Campus Min.;

CATHOLIC CHARITIES [CCH]

SMYRNA
Catholic Charities of the Archdiocese of Atlanta, Inc. - 2401 Lake Park Dr., S.E., Smyrna, GA 30080 t) (404) 920-7725 catholiccharitiesatlanta.org Vanessa Russell, CEO; Asstd. Annu.: 17,943; Staff: 95

CEMETERIES [CEM]

CARROLLTON
Our Lady of Perpetual Help - 210 Old Center Point Rd., Carrollton, GA 30117 t) 404-920-7800
CRAWFORDVILLE
Locust Grove - 976 Locust Grove Rd., S.E., Crawfordville, GA 30631; Mailing: 2401 Lake Park Dr., Smyrna, GA 30080 t) 404-920-7800
SMYRNA
Sparta - 2401 Lake Park Dr., Smyrna, GA 30080 t) 404-920-7800
WASHINGTON
Saint Patrick's Cemetery - U.S. Hwy. 78, Washington, GA 30673 t) 706-678-2110
Purification - U.S. Hwy. 78, Washington, GA 30673 t) 404-925-7800

COLLEGES & UNIVERSITIES [COL]

ATLANTA
Holy Spirit College, Inc. (Pontifex University) - 4465 Northside Dr., N.W., Atlanta, GA 30327 t) 678-904-4959 kschulman@holyspiritcollege.org www.pontifex.university/ Rev. Msgr. Edward J. Dillon, Chancellor; Gareth N. Genner, Pres.; Kim Schulman, Registrar; Stds.: 127; Lay Tchrs.: 1
Pontifex University - dclayton@pontifex.university www.pontifex.university/ David Clayton, Dean;

CONVENTS, MONASTERIES, AND RESIDENCES FOR WOMEN [CON]

ATLANTA
Missionaries of Charity - 995 St. Charles Ave., N.E., Atlanta, GA 30306-4211 t) 404-892-5111 Home for women with HIV/AIDS Sr. M. Jonathan, MC, Regl. Supr.; Sr. Aracelly M.C., Supr.; Srs.: 7
SNELLVILLE
Monastery of the Visitation - 2055 Ridgedale Dr., Snellville, GA 30078 t) 770-972-1060; 770-972-1062 superiormaryfield@gmail.com; vocationsmaryfield@gmail.com maryfieldvisitation.org (Maryfield), Strictly cloistered contemplative Office of First Federation. Vocation retreats for women interested in a religious vocation. Sr. Teresa Maria J. Kulangara, V.H.M., Supr.; Srs.: 9

ENDOWMENTS / FOUNDATIONS / TRUSTS [EFT]

ATHENS
St. Mary's Good Samaritan Foundation, Inc. - 1230 Baxter St., Athens, GA 30606 t) (706) 389-3000
ATLANTA
***The Catholic Foundation of North Georgia** - 5871 Glenridge Dr., Ste. 300, Atlanta, GA 30328 t) 404-497-9440 ncoveny@cfnga.org; lripoll@cfnga.org www.cfnga.org Helping Catholics make a lasting difference and managing endowment funds for parishes, schools, charities and other ministries. Nancy Dinka Coveny, Pres.;
***Mercy Care Foundation, Inc.** - 424 Decatur St., Atlanta, GA 30312 t) 678-843-8670 foundation@mercyatlanta.org www.mercyatlanta.org Steve Siler, Pres.;
The Sanctuary of Culture Foundation, Inc. - 5 Concourse Pkwy., Ste. 200, Atlanta, GA 30328; Mailing: 220 College Ave., Ste. 618, Athens, GA 30601 t) 404-550-7961 www.sanctuaryofculture.org Rev. Msgr. Laurence Spiteri, Dir.; R. Brett Grayson, Secy.;
SMYRNA
AoA Campus Ministries Trust - 2401 Lake Park Dr., S.E., Smyrna, GA 30080 t) 404-920-7404 bwilson@archatl.com Most Rev. Gregory J. Hartmayer, O.F.M. Conv., Trustee; Bradley Wilson, CFO;
AoA Canon 281.2 Trust - 2401 Lake Park Dr., S.E., Smyrna, GA 30080 t) 404-920-7404 bwilson@archatl.com Most Rev. Gregory J. Hartmayer, O.F.M. Conv., Trustee; Bradley Wilson, CFO;
AoA Common Trust Fund LLC - 2401 Lake Park Dr., S.E., Smyrna, GA 30080 t) 404-920-7404 bwilson@archatl.com Most Rev. Gregory J. Hartmayer, O.F.M. Conv., Trustee; Bradley Wilson, Pres.; Camtuyen Pham, Treas.; Dcn. Dennis J. Dorner Sr., Secy.;
AoA Parish Real Estate Trust - 2401 Lake Park Dr., S.E., Smyrna, GA 30080 t) 404-920-7404 bwilson@archatl.com Most Rev. Gregory J. Hartmayer, O.F.M. Conv., Trustee; Bradley Wilson, CFO;
The Roman Catholic Archdiocese of Atlanta Group Health Care Plan Trust (AoA Group Health Care Plan LLC) - 2401 Lake Park Dr., S.E., Smyrna, GA 30080 t) 404-920-7404 bwilson@archatl.com Most Rev. Gregory J. Hartmayer, O.F.M. Conv., Trustee; Charles Thibaudeau, Pres.; Bradley Wilson, Treas.; Dcn. Dennis J. Dorner Sr., Secy.;

HOSPITALS / HEALTH SERVICES [HOS]

ATHENS
St. Mary's Health Care System, Inc. (St. Mary's Hospital) - 1230 Baxter St., Athens, GA 30606-3791 t) (706) 389-2442 elizabeth.schoen@trinity-health.org www.stmarysathens.org David Allen Spivey, CEO; Bed Capacity: 196; Asstd. Annu.: 271,368; Staff: 1,644
St. Mary's Hospital Chapel - 1230 Baxter St., Athens, GA 30606-3791 t) 706-389-3000
FORT OGLETHORPE
CHI Memorial Hospital - Georgia - 100 Gross Crescent Cir., Fort Oglethorpe, GA 30742 t) 402-343-4413 angela.noel@alegent.org Lawrence Schumacher, CEO; Angela Noel, Dir.;
GREENSBORO
St. Mary's Good Samaritan Hospital - 5401 Lake Oconee Pkwy., Greensboro, GA 30642 t) 706-453-7331 tadcock@stmarysathens.org stmarysgoodsam.org Tanya Adcock, Pres.; Bed Capacity: 25; Asstd. Annu.: 71,857; Staff: 224
LAVONIA
St. Mary's Sacred Heart Hospital, Inc. - 367 Clear Creek Pkwy., Lavonia, GA 30553 t) 706-356-7800 jenglish@stmarysathens.org www.stmaryssacredheart.org Jeff English, Pres.; Bed Capacity: 56; Asstd. Annu.: 68,952; Staff: 352

MISCELLANEOUS [MIS]

ATLANTA
Catholic Metro Sports of Atlanta, Inc. - 1350 Hearst Dr., N.E., Atlanta, GA 30319 t) 404-465-4355 info@catholicmetrosports.com www.catholicmetrosports.com Parish and School Athletic and Sports Ministry for Youth and Adults. Pete Smith, Chair; Patricia Marmion, Dir.;
Catholic Retirement Facilities, Inc. (St. Joseph Place) - 2973 Butner Road, S.W., Atlanta, GA 30331; Mailing: 2401 Lake Park Dr., S.E., Smyrna, GA 30080 t) 404-920-7800 mchapman@ccatlanta.org Melissa Chapman, Treas.; Vanessa Russell, CEO;
Christ Child Society of Atlanta, Georgia, Inc. - ; Mailing: P.O. Box 88705, Atlanta, GA 30356 c) 404-312-9656 mdunn@christchildatlanta.org; treasurerchristchildatlanta@gmail.com www.christchildatlanta.org Karen Morakis, Pres.; Terri Wortham, Pres.; Annemarie Boehnlein, Treas.;
Georgia Patron of the Arts in the Vatican Museums, Inc. - 4933 Carol Ln., N.W., Atlanta, GA 30327 c) 404-769-4388 carolyn.johnson@canonburyhomes.com Carolyn Johnson, Contact;
Saint Joseph's Health System - 424 Decatur St., Atlanta, GA 30312 t) 678-843-8500 jwallace@mercyatlanta.org www.mercyatlanta.org Holding company: Trinity Health, Inc.; sponsored by Catholic Health Ministries Inc.; Saint Joseph's Health System (SJHS) operates: Mercy Care Found. Tom Andrews, CEO;
***Pope Francis School and Health Centre, Inc.** - 270 Pinecrest Rd, Atlanta, GA 30342; Mailing: P.O. Box 422155, Atlanta, GA 30342 c) 404-793-6857 mbarry@popefrancishome.org Michael Barry, Dir.;
Rebuilding Hope Missions, Inc. - 2566 Shallowford Rd., Ste. 104-108, Atlanta, GA 30345 c) 404-955-0684 rjortiz1966@gmail.com rebuildinghopemissions.com Dcn. Randy Joseph Ortiz, Pres.;
SJHS JOC Holdings, Inc. - 424 Decatur St., S.E., Atlanta, GA 30312 t) 678-843-8500 jwallace@mercyatlanta.org www.mercyatlanta.org Tom Andrews, CEO;
Treasures of History, Inc. - Five Concourse Pkwy., Ste. 200, Atlanta, GA 30328; Mailing: 220 College Avenue, Suite 618, Athens, GA 30601 t) 404-550-7961 Rev. Msgr. Laurence Spiteri, Dir.; R. Brett Grayson, Treas.;
CHAMBLEE
Good Shepherd Services of Atlanta, Inc. (Good Shepherd Corporation Atlanta) - 2426 Shallowford Terr., Chamblee, GA 30341 t) 770-986-8279; 770-455-9379 christshepherd51@yahoo.com (Incorporated as Good Shepherd Corporation) Sr. Christine Truong, Exec. Dir.;
Good Shepherd Outreach Center - t) (770) 455-9379 Sr. Madeleine Munday, Pres.;
Main Office - t) (770) 455-9379 shepherdatlanta@yahoo.com Sr. Christine Truong, M.S.W., Exec. Dir.;
CUMMING
Consecrated Women Inc. - 951 Peachtree Pkwy., Cumming, GA 30041 c) (214) 562-2565 www.consecratedwomen.org Allyson Wheeler, Treas.;
Consecrated Women of Regnum Christi NA Inc. - 951 Peachtree Pkwy., Cumming, GA 30041 c) 214-562-2565 www.consecratedwomen.org Allyson Wheeler, Treas.;
CRC Charitable, Inc. - 951 Peachtree Pkwy., Cumming, GA 30041 c) 708-638-2578 Sonia Baldwin, Treas.; Nancy Nohrden, Dir.;
CRC Dominus, Inc. - 951 Peachtree Pkwy., Cumming, GA 30041 c) 708-638-2578 Sonia Baldwin, Treas.; Nancy Nohrden, Dir.;
CRC NA Inc. - 951 Peachtree Pkwy., Cumming, GA 30041 c) 214-562-2565 www.consecratedwomen.org Allyson Wheeler, Treas.;
Domus Mariae Inc. - 951 Peachtree Pkwy., Cumming, GA 30041 c) 214-562-2565 www.consecratedwomen.org Allyson Wheeler, Treas.;
RC Federation, Inc. - 525 Tribble Gap Rd., Unit 1466, Cumming, GA 30028 t) 855-556-6872 Todd Brechbill, Secy.;
Vocation Action Circle, Inc. - 2820 Bordeaux Blvd., Cumming, GA 30041 t) (770) 828-4950 eramirez@arcol.org Rev. Frank Formolo, L.C., Secy.;
DECATUR
***Allegre Point Senior Residences, Inc.** - 3391 Flat Shoals Rd., Decatur, GA 30034 t) (303) 830-3300 www.mercyhousing.org James Alexander, Pres.;
PEACHTREE CITY
Magnificat - Joyful Visitation Chapter, Inc. - 203 Kelvington Way, Peachtree City, GA 30269 t) 770-486-1537 patforest@mindspring.com Pat Forest, Dir.;
PEMBROKE
***Mercy Housing Pembroke, Inc. (McFadden Place)** - 80 McFadden Pl., Pembroke, GA 31321; Mailing: 1600 Broadway, Ste. 2000, Denver, CO 80202 t) 303-830-3300 www.mercyhousing.org James Alexander, Pres.;
ROSWELL
***Amen Alleluia, Inc.** - 560 W. Crossville Rd., #101, Roswell, GA 30075 t) 678-585-7886 tom@amenalleluia.com amenalleluia.com evangelization and faith formation Tom Peterson, Pres.; Dr. Ryan Hanning, Dir. of Research;
***Atlanta Catholic Radio, Inc.** - 1802 Macy Dr., Roswell, GA 30076; Mailing: PO Box 88892, Atlanta, GA 30356 t) 470-508-1160 carol@thequestatlanta.com thequestatlanta.com/ Carol H. Tiarsmith, Pres.;
The Catholic Charismatic Renewal for the Archdiocese of Atlanta - 330 Wexford Glen, Roswell, GA 30075 t) 770-634-3642 deaconkmk@gmail.com www.atlccr.org Dcn. Keith M. Kolodziej;
Catholic Continuing Care Retirement Communities Inc. (St. George Village) - 11350 Woodstock Rd., Roswell, GA 30075 t) 770-645-2340 bwilson@archatl.com www.stgeorgevillage.org Bradley Wilson, CEO; Charles Thibaudeau, Vice. Pres.; Dcn. Dennis J. Dorner Sr., Secy.;
Catholic World Mission (GA), Inc. - 30 Mansell Ct., Ste. 103, Roswell, GA 30076 t) 770-828-4966 www.catholicworldmission.org Rev. Daniel Brandenburg, LC, Pres.;
Catholic Worldview Fellowship, Inc. - 30 Mansell Ct., Ste. 103, Roswell, GA 30076; Mailing: 1900 Preston Rd., Ste. 267-180, Plano, TX 75093 t) 469-750-3855 info@catholicworldview.com www.catholicworldview.com Nathan Sullivan, Bus. Mgr.; Rev. Ryan Richardson, LC, Dir.;
***Catholics Come Home** - 560 W. Crossville Rd., Ste. 101, Roswell, GA 30075 t) 678-585-7886 www.catholicscomehome.org apostolate for evangelization using media Tom Peterson, Pres.;
Home and Family, Incorporated - 30 Mansell Ct., Ste. 103, Roswell, GA 30076 t) 770-828-4950 office@missionnetworkatlanta.org Rev. Lino Otero, L.C., Secy.;
Horizons Institute, Inc. (CT), a Connecticut Non-Stock Corporation - 30 Mansell Ct., Ste. 103, Roswell, GA 30076 t) (770) 828-4950 Rev. Frank Formolo, L.C., Asst. Secy.;
Horizons Institute, Inc. (MA), a Massachusetts Non-Profit Corporation - 30 Mansell Ct., Ste. 103, Roswell, GA 30076 t) 770-828-4950 Rev. Frank Formolo, L.C., Asst. Secy.;
Human Resources ITA, Inc. - 30 Mansell Ct., Ste. 103, Roswell, GA 30076 t) 770-828-4950 Rev. Frank Formolo, L.C., Asst. Secy.;
LC RC Family Centers, Inc. - 30 Mansell Ct., Ste. 103, Roswell, GA 30076 t) 770-828-4950 eramirez@arcol.org Rev. Frank Formolo, L.C., Secy.;
LCNA Atlanta, Incorporated - 30 Mansell Ct., Ste. 103, Roswell, GA 30076 t) 770-828-4950 eramirez@arcol.org Rev. Frank Formolo, L.C., Asst. Secy.;
Legion of Christ, Atlanta, Inc. - 30 Mansell Ct., Ste. 103, Roswell, GA 30076 t) 770-828-4950 eramirez@arcol.org Rev. Frank Formolo, L.C., Secy.;
Lux et Vita, Inc. - 30 Mansell Ct., Ste. 103, Roswell, GA 30076 t) 678-938-4500 eramirez@arcol.org Rev. Frank Formolo, L.C., Secy.;
***Mission Network USA, Inc.** - 30 Mansell Ct., Ste. 103, Roswell, GA 30076; Mailing: P.O. Box 1466, Roswell, GA 30076 t) 770-828-4950 eramirez@arcol.org Rev. Frank Formolo, L.C., Secy.;
New Fire Evangelization Inc. - 30 Mansell Ct., 103, Roswell, GA 30076 t) 770-828-4950 Rev. Jorge Obregon, L.C., Dir.;
***Pregnancy Aid Clinic** - 281 S. Atlanta St., Roswell, GA 30075; Mailing: P.O. Box 92, Roswell, GA 30077 t) 404-763-4357 lregan@pregnancyaidclinic.org www.pregnancyaidclinic.com Operates 3 clinics throughout the Atlanta Archdiocese with life-affirming medical, educational and advocacy services. Lisa Regan, Exec. Dir.;
RC Education (GA), Inc. - 30 Mansell Ct., Ste. 103, Roswell, GA 30076 t) 770-828-4950 Rev. Frank Formolo, L.C., Secy.;
Sierra Madre, Inc. - 30 Mansell Ct., Ste. 103, Roswell, GA 30076 t) 770-828-4950 Rev. Frank Formolo, L.C., Secy.;
Sviluppo Risorse Umane, Inc. - 30 Mansell Ct., Ste. 103, Roswell, GA 30076 t) 678-938-4500 eramirez@arcol.org Rev. Frank Formolo, L.C., Asst. Sec.;
***Virtue Media, Inc.** - 560 W. Crossville Rd., Ste. 101, Roswell, GA 30075 t) 770-559-5533 tom@virtuemedia.org www.virtuemedia.org Pro life apostolate utilizing media to educate Tom Peterson, Pres.;
SMYRNA
AoA Deposit and Loan Fund LLC - 2401 Lake Park Dr., S.E., Smyrna, GA 30080 t) 404-920-7404 bwilson@archatl.com Most Rev. Gregory J. Hartmayer, O.F.M. Conv., Trustee; Bradley Wilson, Pres.; Camtuyen Pham, Treas.; Dcn. Dennis J. Dorner Sr., Secy.;
AoA Properties Holding, Inc. - 2401 Lake Park Dr. S.E., Smyrna, GA 30080 t) 400-920-7800 bwilson@archatl.com Most Rev. Gregory J. Hartmayer, O.F.M. Conv., Pres.; John Schiavone, Vice. Pres.; Bradley Wilson, Treas.; Dcn. Dennis J. Dorner Sr., Secy.;
Archdiocese of Atlanta Priests Payroll Services - 2401 Lake Park Dr., S.E., C/O Finance Office, Smyrna, GA 30080-8862 t) 404-920-7400 bwilson@archatl.com Neema Mollel-Mbonika, Contact; Bradley Wilson, Contact;
Catholic Education of North Georgia, Inc. - 2401 Lake Park Dr., S.E., Smyrna, GA 30080 t) 404-920-7800 bwilson@archatl.com Most Rev. Joel M. Konzen, S.M., Pres.; Dr. Diane Starkovich, CEO; Bradley Wilson, CFO & Treas.; Charles Thibaudeau, Vice Pres. HR; Dcn. Dennis J. Dorner Sr., Secy.;
Catholic Housing Initiatives, Inc. - 2401 Lake Park Dr., S.E., Smyrna, GA 30080 t) (404) 920-7778 Vanessa Russell, CEO; Melissa Chapman, Treas.;
G.R.A.C.E. Scholars, Inc. - 2401 Lake Park Dr. S.E., Smyrna, GA 30080 t) 404-920-7900 askgrace@gracescholars.org www.gracescholars.org Provides scholarships to assist with the tuition at Catholic schools in Georgia Elsa Rullan, Treas.; Bradley Wilson, CEO; Melissa Bassett, Exec.;
Nuestra Fe Catholic Broadcasting, Inc. - 2401 Lake Park Dr., S.E., Smyrna, GA 30080 t) 404-920-7344 msmith@archatl.com www.nuestrafeatlanta.com Angel R. Garcia, Pres.; Most Rev. Joel M. Konzen, S.M., Vice. Pres.; Neema Mollel, Treas.; Dcn. Dennis J. Dorner Sr., Secy.;
RCAA Administrative Services Inc. - 2401 Lake Park Dr., S.E., Smyrna, GA 30080 t) 404-920-7404 bwilson@archatl.com Bradley Wilson, Pres.; Brenda Leslie, Vice. Pres.; Charles Thibaudeau, Vice. Pres.; Camtuyen Pham, Treas.; Dcn. Dennis J. Dorner Sr., Secy.;
Roman Catholic Archdiocese of Atlanta, Inc. - 2401 Lake Park Dr., S.E., Smyrna, GA 30080 t) 404-920-7404 bwilson@archatl.com Most Rev. Gregory J. Hartmayer, O.F.M. Conv., Pres.; Bradley Wilson, CFO & Treas.; Most Rev. Joel M. Konzen, S.M., Vice. Pres.; Most Rev. Bernard E. Shlesinger III, Vice Pres.; Charles

Thibaudeau, Vice Pres. HR; Dcn. Dennis J. Dorner Sr., Secy.;

STONE MOUNTAIN

***Rosary Makers of America, Inc.** - 2300 W. Park Place Blvd., Ste. 142, Stone Mountain, GA 30087; Mailing: P.O. Box 870828, Stone Mountain, GA 30087 t) 678-345-0788 info@rosarymakersoa.org rosarymakersoa.org/ Training and Employment Center for Young Adults with Special Needs. Dr. Nicholas Ihenacho, Pres.; Cynthia Okoro, Admin.;

WOODSTOCK

Renovacion Carismatica Catolica Hispana De Atlanta - 490 Arnold Mill Rd., Woodstock, GA 30188 t) 678-213-0685

MONASTERIES AND RESIDENCES FOR PRIESTS AND BROTHERS [MON]

ATLANTA

Augustine House, Dominicans Friars of Atlanta (The Monastery on the Hill) - 780 Lakeview Ave., N.E., Atlanta, GA 30308-1845 c) 919-793-3325; 214-734-4491 bbsop@aol.com; boherlahan37@gmail.com Rev. Arthur Kirwin, O.P., Supr.; Rev. Jeffery Ott, O.P., Pst.; Rev. John Joseph Blase Boll, O.P., Chap.; Bro. Minlib Dallh, O.P., Scholar in Residence; Rev. Bruce Schultz, O.P., Par. Vicar; Brs.: 1

Marist Provincial Office, Society of Mary - Atlanta Province - 3790 Ashford-Dunwoody Rd., N.E., Atlanta, GA 30319; Mailing: P.O. Box 888263, Atlanta, GA 30356 t) 770-451-1316 maristprovincialoffice@gmail.com www.societyofmaryusa.org Society of Mary (Marists) (S.M) Rev. Joseph C. Hindelang, S.M., Prov.; Rev. Timothy G. Keating, S.M., Prov. Asst.; Rev. William F. Rowland, S.M., Vicar; Brs.: 6; Priests: 57

CONYERS

The Monastery of the Holy Spirit - 2625 Hwy. 212, S.W., Conyers, GA 30094-4044 t) 770-483-8705 monastery@trappist.net; info@trappist.net www.trappist.net Rev. Augustine Myslinski, O.C.S.O., Abbot; Rev. Francis Michael Stiteler, O.C.S.O., Abbot Emeritus; Bro. Mark Dohle, O.C.S.E., Prior; Bro. Philip Wodzinski, OCSO, Subprior; Bro. Nathanael Felarca, Treas.; Bro. Callistus Crichlow, O.S.C.O., Cellerar; Rev. Cassian Russell, OCSO, Novice Master; Rev. Peter Damian, OCSO, In Res.; Rev. John M. O'Brien, O.C.S.O., In Res.; Rev. Eduardo Rodriguez, O.C.S.O., In Res.; Rev. Thomas F. Smith, O.C.S.O., In Res.; Rev. Methodius Telnack, O.C.S.O., In Res.; Rev. Matt G. Torpey, O.C.S.O., In Res.; Rev. Gerard Gross, O.C.S.O., Music Min.; Brs.: 18; Priests: 10

CUMMING

Legionaries of Christ, Incorporated - 8825 Fulham Ct., Cumming, GA 30041 t) 770-828-4950 Rev. Shawn Aaron, LC, Territorial Dir.; Rev. Paul Alger, L.C., Par. Vicar; Rev. Terrance Allen, LC, Chap.; Rev. John Bartunek, Territorial Coun.; Rev. Daniel Brandenburg, LC, Chap., Lumen Inst.; Rev. David Daly, LC, Territorial Vicar; Rev. Frank Formolo, L.C., Territorial Admin.; Rev. Kevin Gillis, L.C., Asst. to Territorial Secy.; Rev. Matthew A. Kaderabek, L.C., Chap.; Rev. Lino Otero, L.C., Community Supr.; Rev. Patrick O'Loughlin, LC, ECyD Dir.; Rev. Steven Reilly, L.C., Territorial Coun.; Rev. Michael Shannon, Par. Vicar; Rev. Matthew Van Smoorenburg, L.C., Pst.; Priests: 23

Legionaries of Christ - 2595 Spalding Dr., Atlanta, GA 30350 t) 914-295-7780 www.legionariesofchrist.org Rev. Kevin Baldwin, L.C., Chap.; Rev. John Paul Duran, LC, Chap.; Rev. James Swanson, L.C., Chap.; Rev. Bruce Wren, L.C., Supr.; Rev. John Klein, LC, Youth Min.; Rev. Andrew Gronotte, Asst. Chap.; Rev. Edward Hopkins, LC, Vocations Dir.; Rev. John Vandorpe, Local Vocations Dir.;

DECATUR

Atlanta Jesuit Community, Inc. - 624 W. Ponce de Leon Ave., Decatur, GA 30030; Mailing: 636 W. Ponce de Leon Ave, Decatur, GA 30030 c) 762-323-1438 Rev. James R. Stormes, S.J., Supr.; Rev. James J Fleming, SJ, Treas.; Bro. Brian Engelhart, SJ, Mem.; Rev. Robert Hussey, S.J., Pst.; Rev. William A Noe, SJ, Spiritual Adv./Care Srvcs.; Rev. Ryan Maher, SJ, Mem.; Rev. Perard C Monestime, SJ, Mem.; Brs.: 1; Priests: 6

LOGANVILLE

The Missionaries of St. Francis de Sales - MSFS USA Vice Province - 3887 Rosebud Rd., Loganville, GA 30052-4656 t) 470-268-4069 msfsinc2011@hotmail.com www.fransaliansusa.com Rev. Anthony Bonela, MSFS (India), Prov.; Rev. Joseph Mullakkara, MSFS, Supr.; Rev. Tomy J. Puliyan, MSFS, Pst.; Rev. Sunny Joseph Punnakuziyil, M.S.F.S., Pst.; Rev. Fredi Navarrete, M.S.F.S. (Chile), Par. Vicar; Rev. Noble Dominic Ambalathuruthel, MSFS, Treas.; Rev. Mathew Thayil, Mem.; Rev. Joseph Mendes, MSFS, In Res.; Priests: 19

Fransalian House - 1641 Old Loganville Rd., Loganville, GA 30052 t) 770-972-0202 msfsbursarusa@gmail.com Rev. Joseph Pottemmel, M.S.F.S., In Res.;

ROSWELL

Norcross Pastoral Center, Inc. - 30 Mansell Ct., Ste. 103, Roswell, GA 30076 t) 770-828-4950 fformolo@legionaries.org Rev. Frank Formolo, L.C., Secy.; Priests: 23

NURSING / REHABILITATION / CONVALESCENCE / ELDERLY CARE [NUR]

ROME

Mercy Senior Care, Inc. (Mercy Care Rome, Inc.) - 300 Chatillon Rd. NE, Rome, GA 30161-4911; Mailing: P.O. Box 866, Rome, GA 30162-0866 t) 706-291-8496 emolina@mercyrome.org Elizabeth Molina, Exec. Dir.;

RETREAT HOUSES / RENEWAL CENTERS [RTR]

CONYERS

Monastery of the Holy Spirit - 2625 Hwy. 212, S.W., Conyers, GA 30094 t) 770-760-0959 retreat@trappist.net www.trappist.net Private retreats for men and women. Rev. Augustine Myslinski, O.C.S.O., Abbot; Rev. Francis Michael Stiteler, O.C.S.O., Abbot Emeritus; Bro. Mark Dohle, O.C.S.E., Retreat House Guest Master; Bro. Callistus Crichlow, O.S.C.O., Cellerar;

SANDY SPRINGS

Ignatius House Jesuit Retreat Center - 6700 Riverside Dr., Sandy Springs, GA 30328-2710 t) 404-255-0503 www.ignatiushouse.org Silent retreats in the Jesuit tradition; Spiritual direction; Spiritual Exercises of St. Ignatius of Loyola Maria Gaeta Cressler, Exec. Dir.; Rev. James J. Fleming, SJ, Rel. Ord. Ldr.; Rev. William A Noe, SJ, Retreat Dir.;

SEMINARIES [SEM]

ATLANTA

Aquinas Center of Theology at Emory University - 1531 Dickey Dr., Atlanta, GA 30322 t) 404-727-8860 acamer4@emory.edu aquinas.emory.edu Marie Marquardt, Chair; Alice Cameron, Dir.; Stds.: 5

SPECIAL CARE FACILITIES [SPF]

ATLANTA

Saint Joseph's Mercy Services, Inc. (Mercy Care) - 424 Decatur St., Atlanta, GA 30312-1848 t) 678-843-8500 abradford@mercyatlanta.org mercyatlanta.org Division of Saint Joseph's Health System. Alan Bradford, Pres.;

Our Lady of Perpetual Help Home - 760 Pollard Blvd., S.W., Atlanta, GA 30315 t) 404-688-9515 sistermiriam49@gmail.com olphhome.org Nursing Home for Free Care of Cancer Patients. Rev. Paul A. Burke, Chap.; Sr. Miriam Smith, O.P., Supr.;

An asterisk (*) denotes an organization that has established tax-exempt status directly with the IRS and is not covered by the USCCB Group Ruling.

Diocese of Austin

(Dioecesis Austiniensis)

MOST REVEREND JOE S. VASQUEZ

Bishop of Austin; ordained June 30, 1984; appointed Titular Bishop of Cova and Auxiliary Bishop of Galveston- Houston November 30, 2001; ordained January 23, 2002; appointed Bishop of Austin January 26, 2010; installed March 8, 2010. Office: 6225 E. US 290 Hwy. SVRD EB, Austin, TX 78723.

Pastoral Center: 6225 E. US 290 Hwy. SVRD EB, Austin, TX 78723. T: 512-949-2400; F: 512-949-2520.
www.austindiocese.org
info@austindiocese.org

ERECTED 1947.
Square Miles 21,066.

Comprises the Counties of Mills, Hamilton, San Saba, Lampasas, Coryell, McLennan, Limestone, Bell, Falls, Robertson, Mason, Llano, Burnet, Williamson, Milam, Brazos, Blanco, Travis, Bastrop, Lee, Burleson, Washington, Hays, Caldwell and the part of Fayette County north of the Colorado River in the State of Texas.

For legal titles of parishes and diocesan institutions, consult the Chancery Office.

STATISTICAL OVERVIEW

Personnel
Bishop....1
Priests: Diocesan Active in Diocese....109
Priests: Diocesan Active Outside Diocese....4
Priests: Retired, Sick or Absent....51
Number of Diocesan Priests....164
Religious Priests in Diocese....45
Total Priests in your Diocese....209
Extern Priests in Diocese....24
Ordinations:
Diocesan Priests....3
Permanent Deacons....16
Permanent Deacons in Diocese....241
Total Brothers....27
Total Sisters....80

Parishes
Parishes....102
With Resident Pastor:
Resident Diocesan Priests....84
Resident Religious Priests....18
Missions....22
Pastoral Centers....3
Professional Ministry Personnel:
Lay Ministers....311

Welfare
Catholic Hospitals....5
Total Assisted....1,482,146
Homes for the Aged....2
Total Assisted....437
Day Care Centers....10
Total Assisted....577
Specialized Homes....2
Total Assisted....58
Special Centers for Social Services....4
Total Assisted....15,958

Educational
Diocesan Students in Other Seminaries....28
Total Seminarians....28
Colleges and Universities....1
Total Students....6,840
High Schools, Diocesan and Parish....6
Total Students....754
High Schools, Private....2
Total Students....507
Elementary Schools, Diocesan and Parish....15
Total Students....3,641
Elementary Schools, Private....1
Total Students....513

Catechesis/Religious Education:
High School Students....6,654
Elementary Students....19,849
Total Students under Catholic Instruction....38,786
Teachers in Diocese:
Sisters....8
Lay Teachers....452

Vital Statistics
Receptions into the Church:
Infant Baptism Totals....5,700
Minor Baptism Totals....393
Adult Baptism Totals....359
Received into Full Communion....652
First Communions....4,961
Confirmations....4,488
Marriages:
Catholic....1,029
Interfaith....206
Total Marriages....1,235
Deaths....2,117
Total Catholic Population....652,966
Total Population....3,535,279

LEADERSHIP

Vicar General - Very Rev. James A. Misko;
Moderator of the Curia - Very Rev. James A. Misko;
Judicial Vicar - Very Rev. Christopher Ferrer; Rev. Douglas Jeffers, Adjutant Judicial Vicar;
Vicar for Priests - Very Rev. Timothy S. Nolt;
Chancellor - Dcn. Ron Walker, Chancellor; Dcn. Michael P. Forbes, Vice Chancellor;
Chief Financial Officer - Mary Beth Koenig;
Deans -
Austin Central - Very Rev. Basil Aguzie, M.S.P.;
Austin North - Very Rev. Keith Koehl;
Austin South - Very Rev. David Leibham;
Bastrop/Lockhart - Very Rev. Edward Karasek;
Brenham/La Grange - Very Rev. Miguel Duarte Duran;
Bryan/College Station - Very Rev. Albert Laforet Jr.;
Georgetown/Round Rock - Very Rev. Stephen Nesrsta;
Killeen/Temple - Very Rev. Richard O'Rourke, M.S.C.;
Lampasas/Marble Falls - Very Rev. Ruben M. Patino, C.S.P.;
San Marcos - Very Rev. Jairo Lopez;
Waco - Very Rev. James M. Ekeocha;
College of Consultors - Very Rev. James A. Misko;
Finance Council - Mary Beth Koenig;
Presbyteral Council - Rev. Payden Blevins; Rev. Ryan C. Higdon; Rev. Joseph Daheim;
Secretariats and Secretariat Directors -
Administration - t) 512-949-2452 Dcn. Ron Walker, Dir.;
Archives and Records - t) 512-949-2474 Olivia Herschel, Archivist;
Catholic Schools - t) 512-949-2499 Misty Poe, Supt.; Kelly Laster, Asst. Supt.;
Ethics and Integrity in Ministry - t) 512-949-2447 Abby Turner, Assoc. Dir.;
Human Resources - t) 512-949-2404 Claudia Chiquillo, Dir.;
Legal Services - t) 512-949-2400 Dcn. Ron Walker, Gen. Counsel;
Planning and Construction - t) 512-949-2418 Patrick Baker, Dir.;
Communications - t) 512-949-2456 Camille Garcia, Dir.;
Catholic Spirit Newspaper - t) 512-949-2443 catholic-spirit@austindiocese.org Shelley Metcalf, Editor;
Communications - Camille Garcia, Dir.;
Information Technology - t) 512-949-2555 Jeff Hardy, Dir.;
Finance - t) 512-949-2548 Mary Beth Koenig, CFO;
Controller - t) 512-949-2438 Terry Dumas;
Risk Management - t) 512-949-2425 Michael Scarpato;
Parish Business Services - t) 512-949-2544 Ione Voor;
Diocesan Facilities - t) 512-949-2425 Michael Scarpato; Veronica Tellez;
Formation and Spirituality - t) 512-949-2465 Alison Tate, Dir.;
Cedarbrake Retreat Center - t) 254-780-2436 Brian Egan, Dir.;
Evangelization & Catechesis - t) 512-949-2492 Russell Hoyt, Dir.;
Youth, Young Adult and Campus Ministry - Alison Tate, Dir.;
Life, Charity and Justice - t) 512-949-2471 F. DeKarlos Blackmon, Dir.;
Life, Marriage, and Family - t) 512-949-2487 Luisa de Poo, Dir.;
Hispanic Ministry - t) 512-949-2426 Lily Chhin;
Restorative Justice - t) 512-949-2460 Dcn. James (Tim) Hayden;
Black Ministry (Vacant) - t) 512-949-2449
Priestly and Consecrated Life - t) 512-949-2431 Very Rev. Timothy S. Nolt, Dir.;
Minister to Priests - t) 512-949-2431 Very Rev. Timothy S. Nolt;
Minister to Retired Priests - t) 512-784-8395 Dcn. Michael Aaronson;
Minister to Religious (Vacant) -
Stewardship and Development - t) 512-949-2441 Scott Whitaker, Dir.;
Stewardship - t) 512-949-2444 Margaret Kappel;
Planned Giving - t) 512-949-2496 Dan Wierzbowski;
Campaign Director - t) 320-493-1708
Annual Appeal (CSA) - t) 512-949-2450 Lisa Rosenberger;
Worship and Vocations - t) 512-949-2401 Very Rev. James A. Misko, Dir.;
Worship - t) 512-949-2400 Rebecca Spellacy, Dir.;
Vocations - t) 512-949-2405 Rev. Gregory Don Gerhart, Dir.;
Diaconal Vocations and Formation - t) 512-949-2452 Dcn. Michael P. Forbes, Dir.;

TRIBUNAL

Canonical and Tribunal Services - t) 512-949-2479 Very Rev. Christopher Ferrer, Judicial Vicar; Rev. Douglas Jeffers, Adjutant Judicial Vicar;
Advocate - Janie Cuellar;
Assessors - Fernanda Jaimes;
Auditor/Editor - Katie Koenig;
Defenders of the Bond - Rev. Zack Rodriguez; Paul Madrid;
Tribunal Judges - Rev. Thomas Reitmeyer; DeAnn Walker; Rev. Jozef Musiol, S.D.S.;
Notaries - James Sierra;

PARISHES, MISSIONS, AND CLERGY

STATE OF TEXAS

AUSTIN

St. Mary Cathedral - 203 E. 10th St., Austin, TX 78701 t) 512-476-6182 Very Rev. Daniel Liu, Rector; Rev. Jakob Hurlimann, Assoc. Pst.; Rev. Douglas Jeffers, Assoc. Pst.; Dcn. Hector Ortiz; CRP Stds.: 108
Cathedral School of St. Mary - (Grades PreK-8) 910 San Jacinto, Austin, TX 78701 t) 512-476-1480 principal@cssmaustin.org www.smcschoolaustin.org Robert LeGros, Prin.; Stds.: 173; Lay Tchrs.: 13
St. Albert the Great - 12041 Bittern Hollow, Austin, TX 78758 t) 512-837-7825 info@saintalbert.org www.saintalbert.org Rev. Charlie Garza, Pst.; Rev. Rito Davila, Par. Vicar; Dcn. Edward Rositas; Dcn. Dan Lanicek; Dcn. Phuc Thanh Phan; Dcn. David Ochoa; Dcn. Jose Trujillo; CRP Stds.: 748
St. Andrew Kim Taegon Korean Catholic Church - 6523 Emerald Forest, Austin, TX 78745 t) 512-326-3225 kcc.jlee@gmail.com Rev. Francis Chung, Pst.; Geumsoon Carter, DRE; CRP Stds.: 51
St. Austin - 2010 Guadalupe St., Austin, TX 78705; Mailing: St. Austin Catholic Parish, 500 W. MLK Blvd., Austin, TX 78701 t) 512-477-9471; 512-477-9471 x320 (CRP) rvaughn@staustin.org; dzbasnik@staustin.org www.staustin.org Rev. Charles Kullmann, C.S.P., Pst.; Rev. Paolo Puccini, C.S.P., Par. Vicar; Dcn. William Billy Atkins; Dcn. Dan Wright; Rev. Bruce Nieli, In Res.; CRP Stds.: 280
St. Austin School - (Grades PreK-8) 800 Herndon Ln., Austin, TX 78704 t) 512-477-3751 tcevallos@staustinschool.org www.staustinschool.org Tara Cevallos, Prin.; Kasey Buchanan, Librn.; Stds.: 198; Scholastics: 9; Lay Tchrs.: 20
St. Catherine of Siena - 4800 Convict Hill Rd, Austin, TX 78749 t) 512-892-2420 diane.bily@stcatherine-austin.org www.stcatherine-austin.org Rev. Patrick Coakley, M.S.C., Pst.; Rev. Ray Pothireddy, Par. Vicar; Dcn. Arthur Cavazos; Dcn. Christopher Schroeder; CRP Stds.: 600
Cristo Rey - 2208 E. 2nd St., Austin, TX 78702 t) 512-477-1099 cristoreycc@craustin.com Friar Guillermo Aguilar Alamilla, OFM Conv., Pst.; Friar John Calgaro, OFM Conv., Par. Vicar; Friar Calogero Drago, OFM Conv., Par. Vicar; Sr. Irene Tapia, DRE; CRP Stds.: 232
Holy Cross - 1610 E. 11th St., Austin, TX 78702 t) 512-472-3741 holycrossaustin@grandecom.net www.holycrossaustin.org Very Rev. Basil Aguzie, M.S.P., Pst.; Dcn. Donald Cooper; Jennifer Brooks, DRE; CRP Stds.: 68
Holy Vietnamese Martyrs Catholic Church - Austin, Texas - 1107 E. Yager Ln., Austin, TX 78753 t) 512-834-8483 hvmcc2020@gmail.com hvmcc.org Rev. Le-Minh Pham, Pst.; Dcn. Giao Duy Nguyen; Dcn. Hoa Mai; CRP Stds.: 476
St. Ignatius Martyr - 126 W. Oltorf St., Austin, TX 78704; Mailing: 2309 Euclid Ave., Austin, TX 78704 t) 512-442-3602; 512-442-8656 (CRP) office@st-ignatius.org st-ignatius.org Rev. John Dougherty, Pst.; Rev. Felipe Campos, CSC, Par. Vicar; Dcn. Richard Tucker; Dcn. Ron Walker; Isaac Garcia, DRE; CRP Stds.: 296
St. Ignatius Martyr School - (Grades PreK-8) 120 W. Oltorf St., Austin, TX 78704 t) 512-442-8547 school.st-ignatius.org JB Watters, Prin.;
St. Julia - 3010 Lyons Rd., Austin, TX 78702 t) 512-926-4186 sta.julia1957@gmail.com Rev. Efrain Villanueva, Pst.; CRP Stds.: 227
St. Louis - 7601 Burnet Rd., Austin, TX 78757 t) 512-454-0384; 512-454-0384 x209 (CRP) www.st-louis.org Rev. Craig DeYoung, Pst.; Rev. Zack Rodriguez, Par. Vicar; Rev. Jose Mena, Par. Vicar; Dcn. Rob Embry; Dcn. Javier Maldonado; Dcn. Luis Villa; Dcn. Victor Alvarado; Dcn. Mark Molchen; CRP Stds.: 409
St. Louis School - (Grades PreK-8) Dave Bauman, Prin.; Stds.: 291
Nuestra Senora De Dolores - 1111 Montopolis Dr., Austin, TX 78741 t) 512-385-4333 Rev. Bradford Hernandez Arriaga, Pst.; Dcn. Hector Rosales; CRP Stds.: 300
Our Lady of Guadalupe - 1206 E. 9th St., Austin, TX 78702 t) 512-478-7955 friarflorencio@olgaustin.org; annette@olgaustin.org olgaustin.org Rev. Florencio Rodriguez, T.O.R., Pst.; Friar Roque Ocampo Lopez, Par. Vicar; Sr. Claudia Galicia Castro, DRE; CRP Stds.: 510
St. Paul - 10000 David Moore Dr., Austin, TX 78748 t) 512-280-4460 administration@saintpaulaustin.org saintpaulaustin.org Rev. Johnson Nellissery, I.S.P. (India), Pst.; Rev. Hector Vega, I.S.P., Par. Vicar; Dcn. Rey Garza; Dcn. Salomon Villegas; Dcn. Michael Marchek; Mary Nieves, DRE; CRP Stds.: 221
St. Peter the Apostle - ; Mailing: P.O. Box 17575, Austin, TX 78760-7575 t) 512-442-0655; 512-442-2769 (CRP) st.peterapostle.dre@gmail.com Very Rev. Christopher Ferrer, Pst.; Dcn. Mark Bennett; Viola Duran, DRE; CRP Stds.: 116
Sacred Heart - 5909 Reicher Dr., Austin, TX 78723 t) 512-926-2552 sacredheartatx@gmail.com sacredheartchurchaustin.org/ Rev. Mark Hamlet, Pst.; Dcn. Oscar Gonzalez; Dcn. Francisco Federico; Sr. Olga Estrella Rivera, dj, Pst. Assoc.; Sr. Lucero Espitia, DJ, DRE; Bro. Alejandro Lopez Estrada, D.J.;
San Francisco Javier - 9110 Hwy. 183 S., Austin, TX 78747 t) 512-243-1404 Rev. Abraham Puentes Mejia, Pst.; Myra Maldonado, DRE; CRP Stds.: 432
San Jose - 2435 Oak Crest Ave., Austin, TX 78704 t) 512-444-7587 san-jose-office@sanjosechurch.org Rev. Jairo Sandoval Pliego, Pst.; Dcn. Agapito Lopez; Dcn. Jose Mendez; Rita Velasquez, DRE; CRP Stds.: 271
San Juan Diego - Stony Point - 9110 U.S. Hwy. 183 S., Austin, TX 78747 San Francisco Javier, Austin. Rev. Abraham Puentes Mejia, Pst.; CRP Stds.: 35
Santa Barbara Catholic Church - Austin, Texas - 13713 FM 969, Austin, TX 78724 t) 512-276-7718 santa_barbara@craustin.com Rev. Froylan Jerez

Rivera, Pst.; CRP Stds.: 363

St. Theresa - 4311 Small Dr., Austin, TX 78731 t) 512-451-5121 kari-cruz@sttaustin.org sttaustin.org Rev. Charles Covington, Pst.; Rev. Barry Cuba, Par. Vicar; Dcn. Peter Barger; Dcn. Keith Carter; Dcn. Tony Pynes; Amy Allert, DRE; CRP Stds.: 330

St. Theresa School - (Grades PreK-8) t) 512-451-7105 Brian Wheeler, Prin.; Stds.: 373

St. Thomas More - 10205 N. FM 620, Austin, TX 78726 t) 512-258-1161; 512-258-1944 (CRP) info@stmaustin.org www.stmaustin.org Very Rev. Keith Koehl, Pst.; Rev. Callan Sweeney, Par. Vicar; Rev. David Trahan II, Par. Vicar; Dcn. Daniel Lupo; Dcn. Thomas Mallinger; Dcn. Patrick Thomas O'Beirne; Dcn. Thomas Suniga; Cynthia Klaer-Jordan, DRE; CRP Stds.: 867

St. Vincent de Paul - 9500 Neenah Ave., Austin, TX 78717 t) 512-255-1389 josie@svdpparish.org www.svdpparish.org Rev. Thomas Reitmeyer, Pst.; Rev. Brian L. McMaster, Par. Vicar; Dcn. Al Cuevas; Dcn. Mark Fair; Dcn. Jose Rivera; Dcn. Christopher Sperling; Dcn. Manseung Han; Mhel Galaviz, DRE; CRP Stds.: 493

BASTROP

Ascension Catholic Church - 905 Water St., Bastrop, TX 78602 t) 512-321-3552 mainoffice@ascen.org ascensionbastrop.com Rev. Ramiro Tarazona, Pst.; Dcn. Corby Weiss; Dcn. Paul Cooke; Deborah Esquivel, DRE; CRP Stds.: 525

St. Mary of the Assumption - 4045 FM 535, Bastrop, TX 78602 t) 512-321-7991 shcrockne@hwtx.com Sacred Heart, Rockne. Rev. Dariusz Ziebowicz, S.D.S., Pst.; Dcn. Roger Muehr; Dcn. Alvin Frerich; Deanna Seidel, DRE; CRP Stds.: 100

Sacred Heart - 4045 FM 535, Bastrop, TX 78602 t) 512-321-7991 shcrockne@hwtx.com Rev. Dariusz Ziebowicz, S.D.S., Pst.; Dcn. Alvin Frerich; Dcn. Roger Muehr; Bill Kadura, DRE; CRP Stds.: 110

BELTON

Christ the King - 210 E. 24th Ave., Belton, TX 76513 t) 254-939-0806 secretary@ctkbelton.org ctkbelton.org/ Rev. Sang Ky Quan, Pst.; Dcn. Gustavo Escrueria; Krissie Lastovica, DRE; CRP Stds.: 294

BERTRAM

Holy Cross - 520 TX 29, Bertram, TX 78605; Mailing: 507 Buchanan Dr., Burnet, TX 78611 t) 512-756-4410 Our Mother of Sorrows, Burnet. Rev. Jose Luis Comparan, Pst.;

BLANCO

St. Ferdinand - 25 Main St., Blanco, TX 78606 t) 830-833-5227 admin@stferdinandblanco.org Rev. Brion Zarsky, Pst.; Susan Moore, DRE;

BREMOND

St. Mary - 715 N. Main St., Bremond, TX 76629-5173 t) 254-746-7789; 979-450-6194 (CRP) lindaantis@yahoo.com; justinbremond@yahoo.com catholicbremond.us Rev. Celso Yu, MF, Pst.; Rev. Richard Dee Du, MF, Par. Vicar; Linda Antis, DRE; CRP Stds.: 76

BRENHAM

St. Mary of the Immaculate Conception - 701 Church St., Brenham, TX 77833 t) 979-836-4441 www.stmarysbrenham.org Rev. Everardo Cazares, Pst.; Dcn. Steve Medina; Dcn. John Pelletier; Sr. Teresa Diaz, DRE; CRP Stds.: 340

BRYAN

St. Anthony - 401 S. Parker, Bryan, TX 77803 t) 979-823-8145 pastor@saintanthonys.org Rev. Rakshaganathan Selvaraj, Pst.; Dcn. Michael G. Beauvais; Dcn. Andy Perrone; Dcn. Bill Scarmardo; CRP Stds.: 118

St. Joseph - 507 E. 26th St., Bryan, TX 77803 t) 979-822-2721; 979-823-5568 (CRP); 979-485-9910 (CRP) frjohn@stjosephbcs.org; hmetzer@stjosephbcs.org www.stjosephbcs.org Rev. Brian Eilers, Pst.; Rev. William Rooney, Par. Vicar; Dcn. Patrick Gallagher; Dcn. Keith Comeaux; Dcn. Jeffrey Olsenholler; Lisa Storemski, DRE; CRP Stds.: 463

St. Joseph School - (Grades PreK-12) 600 S. Coulter Dr., Bryan, TX 77803 t) 979-822-6641 jrike@stjosephschoolbcs.org www.stjosephschoolbcs.org Julia Mishler, Prin.;

Santa Teresa - 1212 Lucky St., Bryan, TX 77803 t) 979-822-2932; 979-822-5714 santateresabryan.com Rev. Victor Mayorga (Colombia), Pst.; Rev. Cesar Jaime Guzman-Diaz, Assoc. Pst.; Dcn. Fred Molina; Dcn. Antonio de Jesus Jorge Julian; Martha Gallegos, DRE;

BUCKHOLTS

SS. Cyril and Methodius Catholic Church - Marak, Texas - 6633 FM 2269, Buckholts, TX 76518; Mailing: 20120 FM 485, Burlington, TX 76519 t) 254-985-2280 cyclone.marak@gmail.com marakchurch.org Attended from St. Joseph's, Cyclone. Rev. Ranjan Cletus, Pst.; Amy Tobias, DRE; CRP Stds.: 40

BUDA

Santa Cruz - 1100 Main St., Buda, TX 78610; Mailing: P.O. Box 187, Buda, TX 78610-0187 t) 512-312-2520 www.santacruzcc.org Rev. Jesse Martinez, Pst.; Dcn. Benjamin Garcia; Dcn. Larry Hiner; Dcn. John Kerrigan; Dcn. Vincent A. Boyle; Erik Diaz, DRE; CRP Stds.: 400

Santa Cruz School - (Grades PreK-8) t) 512-312-2137 mmcgettrick@sccstx.org Margaret McGettrick, Prin.; Stds.: 233

BURLINGTON

St. Joseph - 20120 FM 485, Burlington, TX 76519 t) 254-985-2280; 254-541-7950 (CRP) cyclone.marak@gmail.com; svwallace@hotmail.com Rev. Ranjan Cletus, Pst.; Shirley Hoelscher, DRE; CRP Stds.: 38

St. Michael - 85 Church Ave., Burlington, TX 76519 t) 254-869-2169 stmichaels85@windstream.net St. Ann, Rosebud. Rev. John Kelley, Pst.; Patsy Moeller, DRE;

BURNET

Our Mother of Sorrows - 507 Buchanan Dr., Burnet, TX 78611-2304 t) 512-756-4410 Rev. Jose Luis Comparan, Pst.; CRP Stds.: 135

CALDWELL

Holy Rosary - 8610 FM 2774, Caldwell, TX 77836-5574 t) 979-535-7559 www.holyrosaryfrenstat.com St. Mary's, Caldwell Rev. Melvin Dornak, Pst.; Dcn. Ernesto Valenzuela Sr.; Margaret Polansky, DRE; CRP Stds.: 13

St. Mary - 509 N Thomas, Caldwell, TX 77836 t) 979-567-3667 office-manager@stmaryscaldwell.com www.stmaryscaldwell.com Rev. Melvin Dornak, Pst.; Dcn. Ernesto Valenzuela Sr.; CRP Stds.: 113

San Salvador - 9203 CR 286, Caldwell, TX 77836 t) 979-823-8145 bscamardo@saintanthonys.org Mission of St. Anthony, Bryan Rev. Rakshaganathan Selvaraj, Pst.;

CAMERON

St. Monica - 306 S. Nolan, Cameron, TX 76520 t) 254-697-2107 soniaperez2005@att.net Rev. James Chamberlain, Pst.; Dcn. John (Jack) Murphy; Sonia Eva Vega-Perez, DRE; CRP Stds.: 168

CEDAR PARK

St. Margaret Mary - 1101 W. New Hope Dr., Cedar Park, TX 78613 t) 512-259-3126; 512-260-0162 (CRP) adrian@stmargaretmary.com Rev. Luis Alberto Caceres, Pst.; Rev. Anthony Xavier Velpula, Par. Vicar; Dcn. Brian James Hill; Dcn. Philip R. Roberge; Dcn. Paul Rodriguez; Dcn. John McCardle; Dcn. Dave Montoya; Sonia Eva Vega-Perez, DRE; CRP Stds.: 653

CHAPPELL HILL

St. Stanislaus Catholic Church - 9175 FM 1371, Chappell Hill, TX 77426 t) 979-836-3030 Rev. Thaddeus Tabak, SDS, Pst.; Peggy Husky, DRE; CRP Stds.: 24

CHINA SPRING

St. Philip Catholic Church - China Spring, Texas - ; Mailing: P.O. Box 430, China Spring, TX 76633 t) 254-836-1825; 254-733-8420 (CRP) stphilipcs@att.net Mission of St. Louis, Waco. Rev. Ryan C. Higdon, Pst.; Rev. Miguel Flores, Par. Vicar; CRP Stds.: 43

COLLEGE STATION

St. Mary - 603 Church Ave., College Station, TX 77840 t) 979-846-5717 www.aggiecatholic.org Rev. William Straten, Pst.; Rev. Andrew Dinh, Par. Vicar; Rev. Chris Smith, Par. Vicar; Dcn. David Reed; Dcn. John Manhire; Dcn. Glen Milton;

St. Thomas Aquinas Catholic Parish - 2541 Earl Rudder Fwy. S., College Station, TX 77845 t) 979-693-6994 www.stabcs.org Very Rev. Albert Laforet Jr., Pst.; Dcn. Frank Ashley; Dcn. Ronald Fernandes; Dcn. Dave Mayes; Dcn. Mark Nicholas Olivieri; Leanne Lewis Tirado, Bus. Mgr.; CRP Stds.: 762

COPPERAS COVE

Holy Family - 1001 Georgetown Rd., Copperas Cove, TX 76522 t) 254-547-3735 lmchugh@hf-cc.org hf-cc.org Rev. Augustine Ariwaodo, Pst.; Dcn. Timothy Dorsey; Dcn. James Hayden; Virginia Rodgers, DRE; CRP Stds.: 169

DIME BOX

St. Joseph - 8282 FM 141, Dime Box, TX 77853 t) 979-884-3100; 979-542-6161 (CRP) stjoedb@verizon.net www.stjosephdimeboxtx.com Rev. Joy J. Adimakkeel, Pst.; Ida Schuman, DRE; CRP Stds.: 29

DRIPPING SPRINGS

St. Martin de Porres - 230 Post Oak Dr., Dripping Springs, TX 78620; Mailing: PO Box 1062, Dripping Springs, TX 78620 t) 512-858-5667 formation@stmartindp.org stmartindp.org Rev. Justin M. Nguyen, Pst.; Dcn. Charles DeWitt; Dcn. Javier Herrera; Dcn. Daniel Pearson; Dcn. Geoffrey Robert Unger; Vicky Shelley, Bus. Mgr.; CRP Stds.: 455

ELGIN

Sacred Heart - 302 W. 11th St., Elgin, TX 78621 t) 512-281-3536 church@sacredheartofelgin.org www.sacredheartofelgin.org Rev. Paul Hudson, Pst.; Dcn. Larry Dunne; Dcn. Juan Jose Zepeda; Nancy Luna, DRE; CRP Stds.: 488

ELK

St. Joseph - 9656 Elk Rd., Elk, TX 76624 Rev. Walter Dhanwar, I.M.S., Pst.;

ELLINGER

St. Mary - 815 St Mary's Church Rd., Ellinger, TX 87940 Rev. Steven J. Sauser, Pst.;

St. Mary Catholic Church - 815 St. Mary's Church Rd., Ellinger, TX 78940; Mailing: P.O. Box 57, Fayetteville, TX 78940 t) 979-378-2277 stsjm@stjohnfayetteville.com; lmayorga@stjohnfayetteville.com www.stmaryellinger.com Mission of St. John Catholic Church, Fayetteville. Rev. Steven J. Sauser, Pst.; Dcn. Robert Jasek;

FAYETTEVILLE

St. John the Baptist - 207 E. Bell St., Fayetteville, TX 78940; Mailing: P.O. Box 57, Fayetteville, TX 78940 t) 979-378-2277 stsjm@stjohnfayetteville.com; lzika@stjohnfayetteville.com www.stjohnfayetteville.com Rev. Steven J. Sauser, Pst.; Dcn. Robert Jasek; Lexxus Zika, DRE; CRP Stds.: 113

FLATONIA

Sts. Peter and Paul - 210 Stolle Ln., Flatonia, TX 78941; Mailing: 204 Mills St., Smithville, TX 78957 Now a mission of St. Paul, Smithville. Rev. Bernard T. Hung, Pst.;

FLORENCE

Santa Rosa - 6571 FM 970, Florence, TX 76527-4473 t) 254-793-0273 srdl.business@gmail.com www.srdl-cc.org Rev. Larry Stehling, Pst.; Dcn. Steven Tedesco; Karen Kurtin, DRE; CRP Stds.: 184

FRANKLIN

St. Francis of Assisi - 1371 W. FM 1644, Franklin, TX 77856; Mailing: P.O. Box 543, Franklin, TX 77856 t) 979-828-1269 st.francis316@valornet.com; justinbremond@yahoo.com stfrancisofassisiparish.org Rev. Celso Yu, MF, Pst.; Rev. Richard Dee Du, MF, Par. Vicar; Dcn. Luis Doriocourt; Mary McNair, DRE; CRP Stds.: 75

GATESVILLE

Our Lady of Lourdes Catholic Church - Gatesville, Texas - 1108 W. Main St., Gatesville, TX 76528-1123 t) 254-865-6710 ourladygatesville@gmail.com Rev.

Jayaraju Polishetty, Pst.; Delilah Trejo-Martin, DRE; CRP Stds.: 80

GEORGETOWN

St. Helen - 2700 E. University Ave., Georgetown, TX 78626-7300 t) 512-863-3041 receptionist@sainthelens.org sainthelens.org/ Rev. Hai D. Nguyen, Admin.; Rev. Enrique Hernandez Montoya, OFM Conv, Par. Vicar; Dcn. John Evanoff; Dcn. Vern Dawson; Dcn. Joe Ruiz; Emily Triggs, Dir., Faith Formation; CRP Stds.: 459

St. Helen School - (Grades PreK-8) t) 512-868-0744 school@shcslions.org www.shcslions.org/ Mary Kay Sims, Prin.; Stds.: 196

GIDDINGS

St. Margaret - 485 S. Leon St,, Giddings, TX 78942 t) 979-542-0217 (CRP); 979-716-0051 (CRP) Very Rev. Miguel Duarte Duran, Pst.; Laura Orocio, DRE; CRP Stds.: 310

St. Mary - c/o St. Margaret Catholic Church, 485 S. Leon St., Giddings, TX 78942 t) 979-542-0217 St. Margaret, Giddings. Very Rev. Miguel Duarte Duran, Pst.;

GOLDTHWAITE

St. Peter, Mission of St. Mary, San Saba - 1212 Reynolds St., Goldthwaite, TX 76844; Mailing: P.O. Box 352, Goldthwaite, TX 76844 t) 325-648-3732 Mission of St. Mary, San Saba. Rev. Javier Toscano, Pst.; CRP Stds.: 8

GRANGER

SS. Cyril and Methodius - 100 N. Brazos, Granger, TX 76530; Mailing: PO Box 608, Granger, TX 76530 t) 512-859-2223 sscmchurch@gmail.com www.sscmchurch.org Rev. Hilario Guajardo, Pst.; Dcn. Mark White; Miriam Morales, DRE; CRP Stds.: 125

HAMILTON

St. Thomas Catholic Church - Hamilton, Texas - 843 N. Nicholson Dr., Hamilton, TX 76531 t) 254-865-6724 stthomashamilton@gmail.com Our Lady of Lourdes, Gatesville Rev. Jayaraju Polishetty, Pst.; CRP Stds.: 35

HARKER HEIGHTS

St. Paul Chong Hasang - 1000 E. FM 2410 Road, Harker Heights, TX 76548; Mailing: P.O. Box 2414, Harker Heights, TX 76548 t) 254-698-4110 www.stpaulchonghasang.org Very Rev. Richard O'Rourke, M.S.C., Pst.; Rev. Virchand Lakra, I.M.S. (India), Par. Vicar; Rev. Biju Chitteth, In Res.; Dcn. Klaus Adam; Dcn. Alfred Mojica Ponce; Michael Candelas, DRE; CRP Stds.: 117

HEARNE

St. Mary - 402 W. First St., Hearne, TX 77859 t) 979-279-2233 saintmarys402@aol.com stmaryhearne.org Rev. Ramon Frayna, Pst.; Dcn. Conception Luna; Becky Luza, DRE; CRP Stds.: 177

HORSESHOE BAY

Our Lady of the Lake - 304 Hillview Dr., Horseshoe Bay, TX 78657; Mailing: PO Box 1748, Kingsland, TX 78639 St. Charles Borromeo, Kingsland Rev. Uche Evaristus Obikwelu, Pst.; CRP Stds.: 49

St. Paul the Apostle - 201 Dalton Cir., Horseshoe Bay, TX 78657; Mailing: P.O. Box 8019, Horseshoe Bay, TX 78657 t) 830-598-8342 stpaul@zeecon.com Very Rev. Ruben M. Patino, C.S.P., Pst.; CRP Stds.: 18

HUTTO

St. Patrick - 2500 Limmer Loop, Hutto, TX 78634 t) 512-759-3712 info@stpatrickhutto.org; re@stpatrickhutto.org www.stpatrickhutto.org Rev. Paul-Michael Piega, Admin.; Dcn. Ralph Poyo; Dcn. Barry Ryan; Dcn. Robert Willem Van Til; Nancy Longo, DRE; CRP Stds.: 485

JARRELL

Holy Trinity Catholic Church - Corn Hill, Texas - 8626 FM 1105, Jarrell, TX 76537 t) 512-863-3020; 512-863-0401; 737-215-1042 (CRP) mainoffice@holytrinityofcornhill.org; religiouseducation@holytrinityofcornhill.org www.holytrinityofcornhill.org Very Rev. Stephen Nesrsta, Pst.; Monica Snook, Admin.; Virginia Loza-Lee, CRE; CRP Stds.: 76

JOHNSON CITY

Good Shepherd - 285 281 Loop Rd., Johnson City, TX 98636 Rev. Brion Zarsky, Pst.;

KILLEEN

St. Joseph - 2903 E. Rancier Ave., Killeen, TX 76543 t) 254-634-7878; 254-634-7878 x105 (CRP) pba@stjoseph.church stjosephkilleen.org Rev. Christopher J. Downey, Pst.; Rev. Gerardo Uribe, Par. Vicar; Dcn. Jesus Guerra; Dcn. James Rodgers; Maria Guerra, DRE; CRP Stds.: 365

St. Joseph School - (Grades PreK-6) 2901 E. Rancier Ave., Killeen, TX 76543 t) 254-634-7272 Dirk Steffens, Prin.;

KINGSLAND

St. Charles Borromeo Catholic Church - Kingsland, Texas - ; Mailing: P.O. Box 1748, Kingsland, TX 78639 Rev. Uche Evaristus Obikwelu, Pst.; Janie Collins, DRE; CRP Stds.: 50

KYLE

St. Anthony Marie De Claret - 801 N. Burleson St., Kyle, TX 78640; Mailing: P.O. Box 268, Kyle, TX 78640 t) 512-268-5311 Rev. Joseph Daheim, Pst.; Rev. Juan Pablo Barragan Mendoza, T.O.R. (Mexico), Par. Vicar; Dcn. Roy Briceno; Dcn. Hector Rodriguez; Dcn. Noel Caballero; Dcn. Louis Fernandez; CRP Stds.: 652

LA GRANGE

Sacred Heart of Jesus - 539 E. Pearl, La Grange, TX 78945; Mailing: P.O. Box 548, La Grange, TX 78945 t) 979-968-3430 mark@sacredheart-lg.org www.sacredheart-lg.org Rev. Brian Phillips, Pst.; Dcn. Mike Meismer; Debbie Greene, DRE; CRP Stds.: 172

Sacred Heart of Jesus School - (Grades PreK-6) t) 979-968-3223 LaDonna Voelkel, Prin.; Stds.: 100

LAGO VISTA

St. Mary, Our Lady of the Lake Catholic Church - Lago Vista, Texas - 6100 Lohman Ford Rd., Lago Vista, TX 78645 t) 512-267-2644 office@stmaryourlady.org www.stmaryourlady.org Rev. Edward Koharchik, Pst.; Christina Clem, DRE; CRP Stds.: 70

LAKEWAY

Church of the Resurrection, Emmaus - 1718 Lohman's Crossing, Lakeway, TX 78734 t) 512-261-8500 emmaus@emmausparish.org www.emmausparish.org Very Rev. David Leibham, Pst.; Rev. Richard Tijerina, Par. Vicar; Dcn. Terry Guilbert; Jennifer Torres, DRE;

Queen of Angels Chapel - 20600 Siesta Shores Rd., Spicewood, TX 78669 t) (512) 261-8500

LAMPASAS

St. Mary of the Immaculate Conception - 701 N. Key Ave., Lampasas, TX 76550-0866 t) 512-556-5544 smccltx3@gmail.com Rev. Boniface Onjefu, Pst.; Dcn. David Cardona; CRP Stds.: 128

LATIUM

Sacred Heart Catholic Church - Latium, Texas - 12800 Sacred Heart Rd., Latium, TX 77833; Mailing: 701 Church St., Brenham, TX 77833 t) 979-836-4441 St. Mary, Brenham. Rev. Everardo Cazares, Pst.;

LEXINGTON

Holy Family Catholic Church - Lexington, Texas - 1027 FM 696 E., Lexington, TX 78947; Mailing: PO Box 541, Lexington, TX 76567 t) 979-773-2500 holyfamilylex@verizon.net Mission of St. Joseph, Dime Box. Rev. Joy J. Adimakkeel, Pst.; Kristen Bryan, DRE; CRP Stds.: 47

LLANO

Holy Trinity Catholic Church - Llano, Texas - 708 Bessemer, Llano, TX 78643; Mailing: 700 Bessemer Ave., P.O. Box 698, Llano, TX 78643 t) 325-247-4481 office@holytrinityllano.org holytrinityllano.org/ Rev. Payden Blevins, Pst.; Jan Pedersen, DRE; CRP Stds.: 34

LOCKHART

St. Mary - 205 W. Pecan, Lockhart, TX 78644 t) 512-398-4649; 512-216-7794 (CRP) smvl.org Very Rev. Edward Karasek, Pst.; Sylvia V. Rodriguez, Bus. Mgr.; Eva Mendez, DRE; Scott Dillon; CRP Stds.: 48

LOMETA

Good Shepherd - 411 W. Main, Lometa, TX 76853; Mailing: 701 N. Key Ave., Lampasas, TX 76550 t) 512-556-5544 smccltx3@gmail.com; smccltx@gmail.com St. Mary, Lampasas. Rev. Boniface Onjefu, Pst.; Dcn. Dave Cardon; CRP Stds.: 30

LOTT

Church of the Visitation - 144 County Rd. 3000, Lott, TX 76656-3827 t) 254-584-4983 westphaliaparish@gmail.com www.churchofthevisitation.org Rev. Darrell Kostiha, Pst.; Dcn. Charlie Wright; CRP Stds.: 103

Sacred Heart - 213 N. 6th St., Lott, TX 76656; Mailing: P.O. Box 371, Marlin, TX 76661 t) 254-803-8888 stjosephmarlin@gmail.com St. Joseph, Marlin. Rev. Gregory McLaughlin, Pst.;

LULING

St. John the Evangelist - 500 E. Travis St., Luling, TX 78648 t) 830-875-5354 stjohn_luling@att.net www.stjohnluling.com Rev. Howard Goertz, Pst.; Marilyn Williams, DRE; CRP Stds.: 79

MANOR

St. Joseph - 1300 Old Hwy. 20, Manor, TX 78653; Mailing: P.O. Box 389, Manor, TX 78653 t) 512-272-4004 st_joseph_manor@sbcglobal.net Rev. Henry Cuellar Jr., Pst.; Dcn. Pedro Barrera III; Carmen Herrera, DRE; CRP Stds.: 432

MARBLE FALLS

St. John the Evangelist - 105 Hwy. 1431 E., Marble Falls, TX 78654 t) 830-693-5134 www.stjohnsmarblefalls.org Rev. Pedro Garcia-Ramirez, Pst.; Dcn. Curt Haffner; Dcn. Paul Lavallee; Dcn. Eraclio Solorzano; Amy Corley, DRE; CRP Stds.: 261

MARLIN

St. Joseph - 311 Oaks St., Marlin, TX 76661; Mailing: Box 371, Marlin, TX 76661 t) 254-803-8888 Rev. Gregory McLaughlin, Pst.; CRP Stds.: 150

MARTINDALE

Immaculate Heart of Mary - 312 Lockhart St., Martindale, TX 78655; Mailing: P.O. Box 117, Martindale, TX 78655 t) 512-357-6573; 512-357-9076 (CRP) Rev. Rafael Padilla Valdes, Pst.; Dcn. Eugene Wohlfarth; Jo Ann Zavala, DRE; CRP Stds.: 80

MASON

St. Joseph - 216 N. Ave. B, Mason, TX 76856; Mailing: P.O. Box 972, Mason, TX 76856 t) 325-347-6932 dtovar@stjosephmason.org www.stjosephmason.org Holy Trinity, Llano. Rev. Payden Blevins, Pst.; CRP Stds.: 54

St. Joseph - 216 Ave. B, Mason, TX 76856 Rev. Payden Blevins, Pst.;

MCGREGOR

St. Eugene Catholic Church - McGregor, Texas - 207 N. Johnson Dr., McGregor, TX 76657 t) 254-840-3174 stemcgregor@yahoo.com www.steugenemcgregor.com Rev. Albert Capello Ruiz, Pst.; Aurelia Montoya, DRE; CRP Stds.: 88

MEXIA

St. Mary - 606 N. Bonham St., Mexia, TX 76667 Rev. Moses Iyogwoya, Admin.; Dcn. Gordon Kenneth Lee; Dcn. Richard Johnson; Rick Schlitt, DRE; CRP Stds.: 313

MOODY

Our Lady of San Juan Catholic Mission Church - Moody, Texas - 401 2nd St., Moody, TX 76557; Mailing: 207 N. Johnson Dr., McGregor, TX 76657 t) 254-840-3174 ourladyofsanjuan@yahoo.com; stemcgregor@yahoo.com Mission of St. Eugene, McGregor. Rev. Albert Capello Ruiz, Pst.; Cindy Vega, DRE; CRP Stds.: 43

PFLUGERVILLE

St. Elizabeth - 1520 N. Railroad Ave., Pflugerville, TX 78660 t) 512-251-9838 info@stelizabethpf.org www.stelizabethpf.org Rev. Juan Carlos Lopez, Pst.; Rev. Enrique Sada-Coeto, Par. Vicar; Dcn. Emmanuel Nwokocha; Dcn. Rodrigo Reyna; Guadalupe Palacios, DRE; CRP Stds.: 703

PIN OAK

St. Mary - ; Mailing: 635 S. Leon St., Giddings, TX 78942 Rev. Miguel Duarte, Pst.;

ROCKDALE

St. Joseph - 234 San Gabriel, Rockdale, TX 76567; Mailing: P. O. Box 548, Rockdale, TX 76567

t) 512-446-2049 c) 512-429-3364 (Father); 512-429-3365 (Secretary) parishadmin@stjosephrockdale.org; father@stjosephrockdale.org stjosephrockdale.org Rev. Pedro Castillo (Colombia), Pst.; Dcn. Gus Coelho; Bonnie Holub, DRE; CRP Stds.: 155

ROGERS

St. Matthew - 14051 E. Hwy. 190, Rogers, TX 76569; Mailing: P.O. Box 69, Rogers, TX 76569 Rev. James Chamberlain, Pst.;

ROSEBUD

St. Ann, Rosebud - 511 S. Stallworth St., Rosebud, TX 76570; Mailing: 85 Church Ave., Burlington, TX 76519 t) 254-869-2169 stmichaels85@windstream.net; the-expert@msn.com Rev. John Kelley, Pst.; Patsy Moeller, DRE; CRP Stds.: 94

ROUND ROCK

St. John Vianney - 3201 Sunrise Rd., Round Rock, TX 78665 t) 512-218-1183 business@sjvroundrock.org www.sjvroundrock.org Rev. Patrick Ebner, Pst.; Dcn. Kapya Ngoy; Dcn. Gene Saienga; Dcn. Rodolfo Leandro Villarreal III; Dcn. Paul Yehl; CRP Stds.: 311

St. William - 620 Round Rock W. Dr., Round Rock, TX 78681-5017 t) 512-255-4473 www.st-william.org Rev. Francisco Rodriguez III, Pst.; Dcn. Guadalupe Rodriguez Jr.; Dcn. David Boren; Dcn. Michael P. Forbes; Dcn. Jaime Cervantes; Dcn. Richard Kotrola; Dcn. Victor Lara; Dcn. Terry Snell; Ana Arista, DRE; CRP Stds.: 897

ROUND TOP

St. Martin Catholic Church - Warrenton, Texas - 3490 S. Hwy. 237, Round Top, TX 78940; Mailing: P.O. Box 57, Fayetteville, TX 78940 t) 979-378-2277 stsjm@stjohnfayetteville.com Historic chapel, mission of St John, Fayetteville. Rev. Steven J. Sauser, Pst.;

SALADO

St. Stephen - 601 FM 2268, Salado, TX 76571; Mailing: P.O. Box 662, Salado, TX 76571 t) 254-947-8037 Rev. Jude Uche, M.S.P., Pst.; Dcn. Oscar Moreno; Dcn. Lewis Wald; Laura Snyder, DRE; CRP Stds.: 218

SAN MARCOS

St. John the Evangelist - 624 E. Hopkins, San Marcos, TX 78666 t) 512-353-8969; 512-353-5065 (CRP) www.sanmarcoscatholic.org Very Rev. Jairo Lopez, Pst.; Rev. Edwin Kagoo, Par. Vicar; Dcn. Roberto Gutierrez; Dcn. Jessie Mojica; Connie Ramirez, DRE; CRP Stds.: 691

Guadalupe Chapel - 218 Roosevelt, San Marcos, TX 78666

Our Lady of Wisdom University Parish (Our Lady of Wisdom Catholic Church - San Marcos, Texas) - 100 Concho St., San Marcos, TX 78666 t) 512-392-5925 admin@txstatecatholic.org www.txstatecatholic.org Rev. Jared Cooke, Admin.; Dcn. Cris Luna;

SAN SABA

St. Mary - 504 W. Wallace, San Saba, TX 76877; Mailing: P.O. Box 415, San Saba, TX 76877 t) 325-372-3679 stmarys@centex.net Rev. Javier Toscano, Pst.; CRP Stds.: 97

SMITHVILLE

St. Paul Catholic Church - 204 Mills St., Smithville, TX 78957 t) 512-237-3299 Rev. Bernard T. Hung, Pst.; Maria De Los Angeles Garza, DRE; CRP Stds.: 110

SOMERVILLE

St. Ann - 333 Thornberry Dr., Somerville, TX 77879; Mailing: P.O. Box 99, Somerville, TX 77879 t) 979-596-1966 secretary.stanns@gmail.com www.saintann-somerville.org Rev. Thaddeus Tabak, SDS, Pst.; CRP Stds.: 23

STRING PRAIRIE

Assumption of the Blessed Virgin Mary - 405 St. Mary's Rd., String Prairie, TX 78953 Rev. Dariusz Ziebowicz, S.D.S., Pst.;

TAYLOR

St. Mary of the Assumption - 301 E. 4th St., Taylor, TX 76574; Mailing: 408 Washburn St., Taylor, TX 76574 t) 512-352-2175; 512-352-2133 (CRP) church-office@stmarystaylor.org; kate.barta@stmarystaylor.org smtaylor.org Rev. Jungtack (John) Kim, Pst.; Dcn. Marc Griffin; Dcn. David Pustka; Aaron Barta, DRE; Kate Barta, DRE; CRP Stds.: 147

St. Mary of the Assumption School - (Grades PreK-8) 520 Washburn St., Taylor, TX 76574 t) 512-352-2313 principal@stmarystaylor.org smcst.org Heidi Altman, Prin.;

Our Lady of Guadalupe - 110 W. Rio Grande St., Taylor, TX 76574; Mailing: 111 W. Rio Grande St., Taylor, TX 76574 t) 512-365-2380 nsdguadalupe@att.net; nsdgred@att.net nsdguadalupe.org Rev. Alberto J. Borruel, Pst.; Dcn. Alfredo Torres; Carmelita Gonzales, DRE; CRP Stds.: 177

TEMPLE

St. Luke - 2807 Oakdale Dr, Temple, TX 76502 t) 254-773-1561 office@slparish.com; jordanna@slparish.com www.slparish.com Rev. John Guzaldo, Pst.; Rev. Vincent Tranh Nguyen, In Res.; Dcn. Robert Lindberg; Dcn. Timothy Daheim; Jordanna Richesin, DRE; CRP Stds.: 278

St. Mary Catholic Church - 1018 S. 7th St., Temple, TX 76504 t) 254-773-4541 stmaryoffice@stmarytempletx.org; patricia.stamour@stmarytempletx.org Rev. Kurtis Wiedenfeld, Pst.; Dcn. Bonifacio Rodriguez; Dcn. Matthew Hoelscher; Patricia St. Amour, DRE;

St. Mary Catholic Church School; - (Grades PreK-8) 1019 S. 7th St., Temple, TX 76504 t) 254-778-8141 Theresa Wyles, Prin.; Bernadette Hickman, Librn.; Stds.: 206

Our Lady of Guadalupe Catholic Church - Temple, Texas - 707 S. 6th St., Temple, TX 76504 t) 254-773-6779 pba@olgtemple.org Rev. Amado Ramos, Pst.; Dcn. Jesus Spindola; Betty Moreno, DRE; CRP Stds.: 311

TWIN SISTERS

St. Mary's Help of Christians - CR 473, Twin Sisters, TX 78606 Rev. Brion Zarsky, Pst.;

UHLAND

St. Michael - 80 S. Old Spanish Trl., Uhland, TX 78640 t) 512-398-7475 www.stmichaeluhlandtx.org Rev. Rafael Padilla Valdes, Pst.; Dcn. Tim Vande Vorde; Carolyn Martinez, DRE; CRP Stds.: 80

WACO

St. Francis on the Brazos - 315 Jefferson Ave., Waco, TX 76701 t) 254-752-1159 (CRP); 254-752-8434 (Office); 254-752-1012 (Rectory) jazotarin@stfrancistorwaco.org; churchoffice@stfrancistorwaco.org stfrancistorwaco.org Friar Jose Eduardo Jazo-Tarin, TOR, Pst.; Elena Carrizales, DRE; CRP Stds.: 405

Nursery & Kindergarten - 612 N. 3rd St., Waco, TX 76701 t) 254-753-5565 stfrancisdcwaco@gmail.com

Convent - 612 N. 3rd St., Waco, TX 76701

St. Jerome - 9820 Chapel Rd., Waco, TX 76712 t) 254-666-7722 (Parish); 254-666-6222 (CCE); 254-666-7764 (PDO); 254-666-4955 (YM) secretary@stjeromewaco.org; stjkids@stjeromewaco.org www.stjeromewaco.org Very Rev. James M. Ekeocha, Pst.; Dcn. Gregory George; Dcn. Raymond Jones; Dcn. Rae Carter; Betsy Wechter, DRE; CRP Stds.: 393

St. John the Baptist - 1312 Dallas St., Waco, TX 76703; Mailing: P.O. Box 585, Waco, TX 76704-0585 t) 254-313-2852 mina_lozano@gmail.com Rev. Cyril Ngbede Ejaidu, Pst.; Jessica Lozano, DRE;

St. Joseph - 1011 Boston St., Waco, TX 76705 t) 254-799-2531; 254-799-6646 (CRP) Rev. Fernando Saenz, Pst.; Esther Peine, DRE; CRP Stds.: 125

St. Louis - 2001 N. 25th St., Waco, TX 76708; Mailing: P.O. Box 5040, Waco, TX 76708 t) 254-754-1221 Rev. Ryan C. Higdon, Pst.; Rev. Miguel Flores, Par. Vicar; Zulma Diaz, DRE; CRP Stds.: 227

Bishop Louis Reicher Catholic School - 2208 N. 23rd St., Waco, TX 76708 t) 254-754-2041 (Lower School); 254-752-8349 (High School) bishopreicher.com Robert Whitworth, Prin.; Blake Evans, Pres.;

St. Mary of the Assumption - 1401 Washington Ave., Waco, TX 76701 t) 254-753-0146 pastor@stmarys-waco.org www.stmarys-waco.org Rev. Joseph Geleney Jr., Pst.; Julie Arensman, DRE; CRP Stds.: 31

Sacred Heart Catholic Church - Waco, Texas - 2621 Bagby Ave., Waco, TX 76711 t) 254-756-2656 sacredheartwaco@yahoo.com www.sacredheartwaco.com Rev. Carlo Benjamin Magnaye, M.F., Pst.; Dcn. Antonio Arocha; Dcn. Lorenzo Garcia; CRP Stds.: 524

WASHINGTON

Blessed Virgin Mary - 17370 Sweed Rd., Washington, TX 77880; Mailing: P.O. Box 485, Washington, TX 77880 t) 936-878-2910; 936-870-5579 St. Ann, Somerville. Rev. Thaddeus Tabak, SDS, Pst.; Dcn. Limas Sweed Sr.;

WEST

St. Joseph - 301 St. Martins Church Rd., West, TX 76691 t) 254-822-1145 St. Martin, Tours. Rev. Walter Dhanwar, I.M.S., Pst.; Leslie Moore, DRE; CRP Stds.: 26

St. Martin - 301 St. Martin's Church Rd., West, TX 76691-2135 t) 254-822-1145; 254-749-4605 (CRP) kkmidd@hotmail.com Rev. Walter Dhanwar, I.M.S., Pst.; Kayla Sinkule, DRE; CRP Stds.: 90

St. Mary's Church of the Assumption - 301 S. Harrison, West, TX 76691; Mailing: P.O. Box 276, West, TX 76691 t) 254-826-3705 office@assumptionwest.org assumptionwest.org Rev. Timothy V. Vaverek, Pst.; Rev. John Boiko, Par. Vicar; Dcn. Ron Sykora; Dcn. Robin Waters; Karen Tamayo-Rodarte, DRE; CRP Stds.: 136

St. Mary Church of the Assumption School - (Grades PreK-8) t) 254-826-5991 Ericka Sammon, Prin.; Stds.: 113

WESTLAKE HILLS

St. John Neumann - 5455 Bee Cave Rd., Westlake Hills, TX 78746 t) 512-328-3220 dwilhelm@sjnaustin.org sjnaustin.org Rev. Dean Wilhelm, Pst.; Rev. Kris Aneke, M.S.P., Par. Vicar; Dcn. Michael DeWayne Glenn; Dcn. Donald Prince, COO; Dcn. Manuel Torres; CRP Stds.: 461

WIMBERLEY

St. Mary - 14711 Ranch Rd. 12, Wimberley, TX 78676 t) 512-847-9181; 512-847-1662 (CRP) Rev. Christian Unachukwu, M.S.P., Pst.; Dcn. Thomas Gregory Sudderth; Morag Sell, Youth Min.; CRP Stds.: 107

SCHOOLS: PRESCHOOL THRU HIGH SCHOOL

SCHOOLS

STATE OF TEXAS

AUSTIN

St. Gabriel's Catholic School - (PRV) (Grades PreK-8) 2500 Wimberly Ln., Austin, TX 78735 t) 512-327-7755 cbutler@sgs-austin.org sgs-austin.org (Legal name: Southwest Austin Catholic School Inc.) Colleen Lynch, Head of School; Jacqui Glenn, Head of Lower School; Dr. Blanca Snyder, Head of Middle School; Stds.: 513

Holy Family Catholic School - (DIO) (Grades PreK-8) 9400 Neenah Ave., Austin, TX 78717 t) 512-246-4455 hfcs@holyfamilycs.org www.holyfamilycs.org Erin Vu, Prin.; Tim Cullen, Pres.; Stds.: 665

HIGH SCHOOLS

STATE OF TEXAS

AUSTIN

St. Dominic Savio Catholic High School - (DIO) 9300 Neenah Ave., Austin, TX 78717 t) 512-388-8846 Tim Cullen, Pres.; Dr. Enrique Garcia, Prin.; Stds.: 395

St. Michael's Catholic Academy - (PRV) 3000 Barton Creek Blvd., Austin, TX 78735 t) 512-328-2323 bhymson@smca.com www.smca.com Heidi Sloan, Head of School; Stds.: 409

San Juan Diego Catholic High School - (DIO) (Grades 9-12) 2512 S. 1st St., Austin, TX 78704 t) 512-804-1935 info@sjdchs.org; office@sjdchs.org sjdchs.org Blake Evans, Prin.; Pamela S. Jupe, Pres.; Stds.: 135; Lay Tchrs.: 10

BRYAN

St. Joseph High School - 600 S. Coulter, Bryan, TX 77803 t) 979-822-6641 jrike@stjosephschoolbcs.org Julia Mishler, Prin.; Stds.: 87

TEMPLE

Holy Trinity Catholic High School - (PRV) (Grades 9-12) 6608 W. Adams Ave., Temple, TX 76502 t) 254-771-0787 admissions@holytrinitychs.org; ibrogan@holytrinitychs.org www.holytrinitychs.org Isabelle Olwen Marie Brogan, Prin.; Stds.: 97

INSTITUTIONS LOCATED IN DIOCESE

ASSOCIATIONS [ASN]

BUDA

St. Mary's Academy Alumnae Association - 16005 Scenic Oak Trl., Buda, TX 78610 t) 512-312-0836 cbattal44@gmail.com Catherine Attal, Contact;

CAMPUS MINISTRY / NEWMAN CENTERS [CAM]

AUSTIN

University Catholic Center - 2010 University Ave., Austin, TX 78705 t) 512-476-7351 frontdesk@utcatholic.org www.utcatholic.org Rev. Fernando Ricaud, Par. Vicar; Rev. Jonathan Raia, Chap.;

BRYAN

Blinn College Catholic Student Union - 2423 Blinn Blvd., Bldg. E, Bryan, TX 77802 t) 979-209-7634

WACO

St. Peter Catholic Student Center at Baylor University - 1415 S. 9th St., Waco, TX 76706-0060; Mailing: PO Box 6060, Waco, TX 76706 t) 254-757-0636 general@baylorcatholic.org www.baylorcatholic.org For Catholic students attending Baylor University, Texas State Technical College, and McLennan Community College. Rev. Henry Finch, Rector; Katherine Audrey Groves, Campus Min.;

CATHOLIC CHARITIES [CCH]

AUSTIN

Catholic Charities of Central Texas - 1625 Rutherford Ln., Austin, TX 78754 t) 512-651-6100 sara-ramirez@ccctx.org Sara Ramirez, Exec.; Neal McMaster, Bus. Mgr.;

Immigration Legal Services - t) 512-651-6125 Sara Ramirez, Dir.;

COLLEGES & UNIVERSITIES [COL]

AUSTIN

St. Edward's University - 3001 S. Congress Ave., Austin, TX 78704-6489 t) 512-448-8400 presidentsoffice@stedwards.edu www.stedwards.edu Established in 1878 by the Congregation of Holy Cross and chartered by the state in 1885. Dr. Montserrat Fuentes, Pres.; Dr. Marianne Ward-Peradoza, Provost; Stds.: 3,470; Lay Tchrs.: 350

CONVENTS, MONASTERIES, AND RESIDENCES FOR WOMEN [CON]

AUSTIN

Congregation of the Sisters of the Holy Cross - La Casa Convent, 2213 Euclid Ave., Austin, TX 78704 t) 512-441-6693 Sr. Kathleen Moroney, C.S.C., Treas.;

Congregation of the Sisters of the Holy Cross - Our Lady of Victory Convent, 2215 Euclid Ave., Austin, TX 78704-5214 t) 512-441-2927 Sr. Kathleen Moroney, C.S.C., Treas.;

Daughters of Mary Help of Christians (Salesian Sisters of St. John Bosco) - St. Mary Mazzarello Convent, 2109 E. Second St., Austin, TX 78702 t) 512-474-2312 itapia@craustin.com

Franciscan Sisters Daughters of Mercy (Hermanas Franciscanas Hijas de la Misericordia) - 1207 Montopolis Dr., Austin, TX 78741 t) 512-385-5090 drmfhm1856@gmail.com Sr. Rose Moreno, F.H.M., Supr.; Srs.: 4

St. Francis Convent - 612 N. 3rd St., Waco, TX 76701 t) 254-753-5565

Missionary Sisters of the Immaculate Conception of the Mother of God - 4211-B Shoalwood, Austin, TX 78756 t) 512-451-2890 jreisch@prodigy.net Sr. Kathryn Conti, SMIC, Supr.;

Sinsinawa Dominican Sisters - 6008 Club Terr., Austin, TX 78741 t) 512-385-1719

Sisters of Charity of the Incarnate Word - 8233 Summer Side Dr., Austin, TX 78759 t) 512-451-0272; 512-231-9512 (Home)

Sisters, Servants of the Immaculate Heart of Mary - 2606 E. Side Dr., Austin, TX 78704 t) 512-442-5295

BRENHAM

Pax Christi Sisters - Pax Christi Institute - 9300 Hwy. 105, Brenham, TX 77833 t) 979-251-7450

BRYAN

Sisters of St. Francis of Our Lady of Lourdes - 2516 Clare Ct., Apt. B, Bryan, TX 77802 t) 979-219-0316 pdunn@st-joseph.org www.st-joseph.org

Sisters of St. Francis of Our Lady of Lourdes (O.S.F.) - 2514 Clare Ct., Apt. A, Bryan, TX 77802 t) 979-777-0578

GEORGETOWN

Dominican Sisters of Mary, Mother of the Eucharist - 5501 E. State Hwy. 29, Georgetown, TX 78626 t) 512-863-4826 secretary@sistersofmary.org Sr. Teresa Christi Balek, OP, Prioress; Srs.: 16

SOMERVILLE

Missionary Ecumenical - ; Mailing: P.O. Box 367, Somerville, TX 77879 t) 979-595-1494

WACO

Franciscan Sisters Daughters of Mercy - 612 N. Third St., Waco, TX 76701 t) 254-753-5565 rmfhm@yahoo.com (Franciscanas Hijas de la Misericordia) Sr. Rose Moreno, F.H.M., Supr.;

Franciscan Sisters Daughters of Mercy - 1207 Montopolis Dr., Austin, TX 78741

ENDOWMENTS / FOUNDATIONS / TRUSTS [EFT]

AUSTIN

Blue Ladies Minerals, Inc. - 1345 Philomena St., Austin, TX 78723 t) 512-324-1990 derek.covert@ascension.org William Davis, CEO; Derek Covert, Chief Mission Integration Officer;

Catholic Foundation - Diocese of Austin - 6225 E US 290 Hwy. SVRD EB, Austin, TX 78723 t) 512-949-2400 scott-whitaker@austindiocese.org www.catholicfdn.org Supports the future needs of Catholic ministries in the diocese Scott Whitaker, Exec.;

CMC Foundation of Central Texas (Dell Children's Medical Center Foundation) - 1345 Philomena St., Austin, TX 78723 t) 512-324-0170 derek.covert@ascension.org www.dellchildrens.net William Davis, CEO; Derek Covert, Chief Mission Integration Officer;

Diocese of Austin Pension Plan and Trust - 6225 Hwy. 290 E., Austin, TX 78723 t) 512-949-2400 krystal-reyes@austindiocese.org Rev. Payden Blevins, Chair; Rev. Mark Hamlet, Trustee; Very Rev. Edward Karasek, Trustee; Very Rev. Keith Koehl, Trustee; Very Rev. Albert Laforet Jr., Mem.; Rev. Le-Minh Pham, Trustee; Rev. Thomas Reitmeyer, Mem.; Rev. Dean Wilhelm, Mem.; Rev. Christopher J. Downey, Past Chmn.;

Fickett Health Legacy, Inc. - 1201 W. 38th St., Austin, TX 78705; Mailing: 1345 Philomena St., Austin, TX 78723 t) 512-324-1990 derek.covert@ascension.org William Davis, CEO; Derek Covert, Chief Mission Integration Officer;

Holy Family Catholic School Foundation - 9400 Neenah Ave., Austin, TX 78717 t) 512-246-4455 hfcs@holyfamilycs.org www.holyfamilycs.org Joan Wagner, Pres.;

Seton Fund of the Daughters of Charity of St. Vincent de Paul, Inc. - 1201 W. 38th St., Austin, TX 78705; Mailing: 1345 Philomena St., Austin, TX 78723 t) 512-324-1990 derek.covert@ascension.org www.setonfund.org William Davis, CEO; Derek Covert, Chief Mission Integration Officer;

Twenty-Six Doors, Inc. - 1345 Philomena St., Austin, TX 78723 t) 512-324-1990 derek.covert@ascension.org William Davis, CEO; Derek Covert, Chief Mission Integration Officer;

BRYAN

St. Joseph Memorial Endowment Fund - St. Joseph's, 507 E. 26th, Bryan, TX 77803 t) 979-822-2721 frjohn@stjosephbcs.org www.stjosephbcs.org Rev. Msgr. John A. McCaffrey;

St. Joseph's Foundation of Bryan - 2801 Franciscan Dr., Bryan, TX 77802 t) 979-774-4087 Thomas J. Pool, Exec.;

St. Joseph's School Memorial Endowment Fund - 507 E. 26th St., Bryan, TX 77803 t) 979-822-2721 frjohn@stjosephbcs.org www.stjosephschoolbcs.org Rev. Msgr. John A. McCaffrey;

KYLE

Seton Hays Foundation - 6001 Kyle Pkwy., Kyle, TX 78640; Mailing: 1345 Philomena St., Austin, TX 78723 t) 512-504-5061 derek.covert@ascension.org www.setonhaysfoundation.org William Davis, CEO; Derek Covert, Chief Mission Integration Officer;

LOCKHART

Clerical Endowment Fund - 205 W. Pecan, Lockhart, TX 78644 t) 512-398-4649 Very Rev. Edward Karasek;

RED ROCK

Father Bernard C. Goertz Scholarship Trust Fund - 136 Tucker Ln., Red Rock, TX 78662 t) 512-321-5735

ROUND ROCK

Seton Williamson Foundation - 201 Seton Pkwy., Round Rock, TX 78665; Mailing: 1345 Philomena St., Austin, TX 78723 t) 512-324-4090 derek.covert@ascension.org www.setonwilliamsonfdn.org William Davis, CEO; Derek Covert, Chief Mission Integration Officer;

WACO

***Providence Foundation, Inc.** - 6901 Medical Pkwy., Waco, TX 76712 t) 254-751-4762 derek.covert@ascension.org William Davis, CEO; Derek Covert, Chief Mission Integration Officer;

HOSPITALS / HEALTH SERVICES [HOS]

AUSTIN

Ascension Seton - 1345 Philomena St., Austin, TX 78723 t) 512-324-7074 healthcare.ascension.org/ DBA Dell Children's Medical Center; DBA Dell Seton Medical Center at The University of Texas. William Davis, CEO; Derek Covert, Chief Mission Integration Officer; Bed Capacity: 1,532; Asstd. Annu.: 867,393; Staff: 9,566

BRYAN

Burleson St. Joseph Health Center of Caldwell, Texas - 2801 Franciscan Dr., Bryan, TX 77802 t) 979-776-2599 bstanford@st-joseph.org www.st-joseph.org John Hughson, Admin.; James Schuessler, Pres.; Bed Capacity: 25; Staff: 57

CHI St. Joseph Health Center - 2801 Franciscan Dr., Bryan, TX 77802 t) 979-776-3777 rnapper@st-joseph.org www.st-joseph.org Jeb Blair, Chair; Rick Napper, Pres.; Bed Capacity: 235; Staff: 1,372

CHI St. Joseph Services Corp. - 2801 Franciscan Dr., Bryan, TX 77802 t) 979-776-3777 rnapper@st-joseph.org www.st-joseph.org Jeb Blair, Chair; Rick Napper, CEO;

WACO

Ascension Providence (Providence Health Services of

Waco) - 6901 Medical Pkwy., Waco, TX 76712; Mailing: P.O. Box 2589, Waco, TX 76712 t) 254-751-4000 derek.covert@ascension.org www.providence.net Ascension Providence -Medical/Surgical/OB/Pediatrics Acute Care; Ascension Providence DePaul Center - Psychiatric Care. William Davis, CEO; Derek Covert, Chief Mission Integration Officer; Bed Capacity: 234; Asstd. Annu.: 243,824; Staff: 1,230

MISCELLANEOUS [MIS]

AUSTIN

Ascension Texas - 1345 Philomena St., Austin, TX 78723 t) 512-324-0000 derek.covert@ascension.org William Davis, CEO; Derek Covert, Chief Mission Integration Officer;

Catholic Family Fraternal of Texas. KJZT - ; Mailing: P.O. Box 18896, Austin, TX 78760-8896 t) 512-444-9586 Loretta Stahl, Pres.;

Catholic Southwest - 6225 Hwy. 290 E., Austin, TX 78723 t) 512-476-6296 marian@txcatholic.org txcatholic.org/catholic-southwest/ Richard Fossey, Editor;

Juan Diego Missionary Society - 4606 E. St. Elmo, Austin, TX 78744 t) 512-731-8434 jdms1981@gmail.com Elias and Christina Limon, Dir.;

Juan Diego Work/Study Program, Inc. - 2512 S. 1st St., Austin, TX 78704 t) 512-804-1935 office@sjdchs.org; info@sjdchs.org www.sjdchs.org Phong Vu, Prin.; Pamela S. Jupe, Pres.;

Ladies of Charity of Austin, TX - ; Mailing: P.O. Box 9566, Austin, TX 78766 t) 512-416-7959 Anna LaFuente, Pres.;

***Mary's Touch** - ; Mailing: P.O. Box 341991, Austin, TX 78734 t) 512-965-4449 info@marystouch.org www.marystouch.org

North Central Catholic School Corporation - 9400 Neenah Ave., Austin, TX 78717 t) 512-246-4455 hfcs@holyfamilycs.org www.holyfamilycs.org Kelly Laster, Prin.; Joan Wagner, Pres.; Kelly Laster, Bus. Mgr.;

Seton Clinical Enterprise Corporation (Ascension Medical Group Texas) - 1345 Philomena St., Austin, TX 78723 t) 512-324-0000 derek.covert@ascension.org William Davis, CEO; Derek Covert, Chief Mission Integration Officer;

Seton Insurance Services Corporation - 1345 Philomena St., Austin, TX 78723 t) 512-324-1986 derek.covert@ascension.org William Davis, CEO; Derek Covert, Chief Mission Integration Officer;

Society of St. Katharine Drexel - 503 Vale St., Austin, TX 78746 t) 512-838-6142 Merlie Morales, Pres.;

***Society of St. Vincent de Paul, Diocesan Council of Austin** - 901 W. Braker Ln., Austin, TX 78758; Mailing: P.O. Box 81511, Austin, TX 78708 t) 512-251-6995 info@ssvdp.org ssvdp.org/ Roz Gutierrez, CEO;

Texas Catholic Conference of Bishops - 1600 N. Congress Ave., Ste. B, Austin, TX 78701; Mailing: P.O. Box 13285, Austin, TX 78711 t) 512-339-9882 info@txcatholic.org; jennifer@txcatholic.org www.txcatholic.org His Eminence Daniel DiNardo, Co-Chm.; Most Rev. Gustavo Garcia-Siller, M.Sp.S., Co-Chm.; Lisette Allen, Dir., Educ.; Selena Aleman, Archivist; Jennifer Carr Allmon, Exec. Dir.;

Catholic Archives of Texas - 6225 E. US 290 Hwy. SVRD EB, Austin, TX 78723 t) 512-476-6296 selena@txcatholic.org txcatholic.org/catholic-archives-of-texas/ Historical collection of the Church in the Southwest and Texas from 1519.

Texas Catholic Historical Society - 6225 E. US 290 Hwy. SVRD EB, Austin, TX 78723 t) 512-476-6296 selena@txcatholic.org txcatholic.org/historical-society/ Amanda Bresie, Pres.; Matthew Butler, Vice. Pres.;

BASTROP

Ladies of Charity of Bastrop, TX - ; Mailing: P.O. Box 1060, Bastrop, TX 78602 t) 512-321-9819

BRYAN

***Ablaze Ministries** - 201 W. Wm. J. Bryan Pkwy., Ste. 831, Bryan, TX 77803

Council of Catholic Women - 1315 Barak Ln., Bryan, TX 77802 t) 979-846-0617 judithl@suddenlink.net www.adccw.com Dianne Friend, Pres.;

COLLEGE STATION

The Apostles of the Interior Life - 603 Church Ave., College Station, TX 77840

GEORGETOWN

Christ Child Society of Texas, Capital Area, Inc. - 3610 Shell Rd., Georgetown, TX 78628; Mailing: P.O. Box 5953, Round Rock, TX 78683 c) 512-810-8248 texascapital@nationalchristchildsoc.org ccstxcapital.wordpress.com/ Margaret Beasley, Pres.;

JARRELL

Cursillo - 200 W. FM 487, Jarrell, TX 76537; Mailing: P.O. Box 65, Jarrell, TX 76537 Robin Spencer, Dir.; Silvia Villarreal, Dir.;

National Cursillo Movement, Inc. - 250 W. FM 487, Jarrell, TX 76537 t) 512-746-2020

LA GRANGE

Catholic Union of Texas, The K.J.T. - ; Mailing: P.O. Box 297, La Grange, TX 78945-0297 t) 979-968-5877 president@kjtnet.org www.kjtnet.org Christopher L. Urban, Pres.;

MART

Ladies of Charity of Waco, TX - 501 E. Navarro, Mart, TX 76664 t) 254-876-2277 imaginit@juno.com Lorraine Brooks, Secy.; Jeanne M. Arensman, Pres.;

SALADO

Catholic Vocation Advocates - Central Texas - 1417 Elizabeth Cir., Salado, TX 76571 t) 254-328-3708 cbroecker@live.com C. David Broecker, Pres.;

Serra Club - Austin - ; Mailing: P.O. Box 156, Salado, TX 76571 t) 512-330-1028 carrie@carrieweikert.com Carrie Weikert, Contact;

WACO

St. Francis Mission Center - 612 N. Third St., Waco, TX 76701 t) 254-753-5565 barbarajhtexas@hotmail.com Franciscan Sisters Daughters of Mercy. Sr. Jacinta Amengual, F.H.M., Supr.;

MONASTERIES AND RESIDENCES FOR PRIESTS AND BROTHERS [MON]

AUSTIN

Congregation of Holy Cross, Moreau Province - 1101 St. Edward's Dr., Austin, TX 78704-6512 t) 512-442-7856 moreauprovinceoffices@gmail.com www.holycrossbrothers.org Corporate Title: Congregation of Holy Cross, Moreau Province, Inc. Bro. Thomas Dziekan, C.S.C., Prov.; Bro. Donald Blauvelt, C.S.C., Vicar; Bro. Harold Ehlinger, C.S.C., Treas.; Bro. Richard Critz, C.S.C., Secy.; Brs.: 27; Priests: 3

Brother John Baptist Province Center -

Brother Vincent Pieau Residence - 921 St. Edward Dr., Austin, TX 78704 t) 512-493-0121 nick1040@gmail.com Bro. William Nick, C.S.C., Dir.;

Dominican Friars of Austin - 2502 Comburg Castle Way, Austin, TX 78748-5258 t) 512-282-3908 chiefop7@gmail.com Rev. Gerardo Guerra-Mayaudon, O.P.; Bro. Angel Mendez, O.P.;

Schoenstatt Fathers - 225 Addie Roy Rd. Ste C, Austin, TX 78746-4124 t) 512-301-8762 info@schoenstatt.us; mark.niehaus@schoenstatt.fathers.org schoenstatt-fathers.us Rev. Hector Vega, I.S.P.; Rev. Raimundo Costa, I.S.P.; Rev. Jesus Ferras; Rev. Johnson Nellissery, I.S.P.; Rev. Jeff Roedel, ISP, In Res.; Rev. Hugo Tagle, I.S.P., In Res.; Rev. Gonzalo Villaseca, In Res.; Rev. Cristobal Asenjo, I.S.P., Rector; Rev. Pushpa Antonysamy, I.S.P., In Res.; Rev. Christian Christensen, I.S.P., In Res.; Priests: 10

BREMOND

Clerical Congregation Missionaries of Faith - 715 N. Main St., Bremond, TX 76629-5173 t) 254-746-7789 yucelski@missionariesoffaith.us www.missionariesoffaith.us Rev. Celso Yu, MF, Registrar; Priests: 17

GEORGETOWN

Pope John Paul II, Residence for Priests - 2550 E. University Ave., #13, Georgetown, TX 78626 t) 512-868-3454

SALADO

Missionary Society of St. Paul, MSP - ; Mailing: P.O. Box 662, Salado, TX 76691 t) 254-947-8037 Rev. Jude Uche, M.S.P.;

NURSING / REHABILITATION / CONVALESCENCE / ELDERLY CARE [NUR]

BRYAN

St. Joseph Manor - 2333 Manor Dr., Bryan, TX 77802 t) 979-821-7330 ksims@st-joseph.org Kyle Sims, Admin.; James Schuessler, Pres.; Staff: 75

CALDWELL

CHI Burleson St. Joseph Manor - 1022 Presidential Corridore E., Hwy. 21, Caldwell, TX 77836; Mailing: 2801 Franciscan Dr., Bryan, TX 77802 t) 979-567-0920; 979-776-3777 jthreadgill@st-joseph.org Rick Napper, Pres.; Staff: 60

WACO

Ascension Living Providence Village (Providence Park, Inc.) - 300 W. Hwy. 6, Waco, TX 76712-7910 t) 314-292-9308 ahscm-mission@ascension.org www.ascensionliving.org/ Ryan Endsley, COO; Kenneth (Bob) Smoot, Chief Mission Integration Officer; Asstd. Annu.: 786; Staff: 172

RETREAT HOUSES / RENEWAL CENTERS [RTR]

TEMPLE

Cedarbrake Catholic Retreat Center - 5602 S. Hwy. 317 N., Temple, TX 76502 t) 254-780-2436 cedarbrake@austindiocese.org Rev. Harry Dean, Chap.;

An asterisk (*) denotes an organization that has established tax-exempt status directly with the IRS and is not covered by the USCCB Group Ruling.

Diocese of Baker

(Dioecesis Bakeriensis)

MOST REVEREND LIAM S. CARY

Bishop of Baker; ordained September 5, 1992; appointed Bishop of Baker March 8, 2012; installed May 18, 2012.

Diocesan Pastoral Office: 641 S.W. Umatilla Ave., Redmond, OR 97756. T: 541-388-4004; F: 541-388-2566.
chancellor1@dioceseofbaker.org

ESTABLISHED JUNE 19, 1903.

Square Miles 66,826.

Comprises the Counties of Baker, Crook, Deschutes, Gilliam, Grant, Harney, Hood River, Jefferson, Klamath, Lake, Malheur, Morrow, Sherman, Umatilla, Union, Wallowa, Wasco and Wheeler in the State of Oregon.

For legal titles of parishes and diocesan institutions, consult the Chancery Office.

STATISTICAL OVERVIEW

Personnel

Bishop	1
Priests: Diocesan Active in Diocese	16
Priests: Diocesan Active Outside Diocese	4
Priests: Retired, Sick or Absent	13
Number of Diocesan Priests	33
Religious Priests in Diocese	13
Total Priests in your Diocese	46
Extern Priests in Diocese	7
Ordinations:	
Transitional Deacons	1
Permanent Deacons in Diocese	8

Parishes

Parishes	36
With Resident Pastor:	
Resident Diocesan Priests	15
Resident Religious Priests	21
Missions	21
Pastoral Centers	1

Welfare

Catholic Hospitals	5
Total Assisted	234,229
Homes for the Aged	1
Special Centers for Social Services	7
Total Assisted	67,000

Educational

Diocesan Students in Other Seminaries	1
Total Seminarians	1
Elementary Schools, Diocesan and Parish	4
Total Students	636
Catechesis / Religious Education:	
High School Students	485
Elementary Students	1,694
Total Students under Catholic Instruction	2,816
Teachers in Diocese:	
Sisters	3
Lay Teachers	88

Vital Statistics

Receptions into the Church:	
Infant Baptism Totals	185
Minor Baptism Totals	359
Adult Baptism Totals	12
Received into Full Communion	67
First Communions	456
Confirmations	489
Marriages:	
Catholic	80
Interfaith	24
Total Marriages	104
Deaths	307
Total Catholic Population	31,211
Total Population	589,060

LEADERSHIP

Vicar General - Rev. Richard Owen Fischer;
Judicial Vicar and Chief Judge - Rev. Andrew Szymakowski;
Chancellor (Vacant) -
Diocesan Pastoral Office - t) 541-388-4004
Executive Secretary - Leah Bickett;
Diocesan Tribunal - t) 541-388-4004
Judge (Vacant) -
Defender of the Bond and Promoter of Justice (Vacant) -
Tribunal Assistant & Auditor - Marilyn Ransom;
Coordinator and Notary - Juliana Elliott;
Council of Priests - Most Rev. Liam S. Cary; Rev. Richard Owen Fischer; Rev. Andrew Szymakowski;
Diocesan Consultors - Most Rev. Liam S. Cary; Rev. Richard Owen Fischer; Rev. Andrew Szymakowski;
Deans - Rev. Robert Greiner; Rev. Bailey Clemens; Rev. Todd Unger;

OFFICES AND DIRECTORS

Board of Education - James Golden, Supt.; Rev. Todd Unger; Rev. Joseph P. Thomas;
Building Committee - Most Rev. Liam S. Cary; Rev. Richard Owen Fischer; Hope Burke;
Campus Ministry Apostolate -
Catholic Services -
Chief Operating Officer - Mark French;
Church Property, Administration of - Hope Burke;
Diocesan Attorney - Gregory Lynch;
Diocesan Development Office - t) 541-388-4004 Mark French;
Diocesan Finance Minister - Hope Burke;
Diocesan Financial Board - Most Rev. Liam S. Cary; Hope Burke; Gary Thompson;
Diocesan Scout Director - Janet Schwarz;
Diocesan Superintendent of Schools - t) 541-388-4004 James Golden;
Director of Campaign for Human Development (Vacant) -
Director of Catholic Hospitals - Rev. Richard Owen Fischer;
Director of Evangelization and Catechesis - Bryce Herrmann;
Director of Religious Education - t) 541-388-4004
Director of Youth Ministry - t) 541-388-4004
Executive Director of Legacy of Faith Foundation - Mark French;
Friends of the Catholic University of America (Vacant) -
Health and Retirement Board - Most Rev. Liam S. Cary; Rev. Todd Unger, Secy.; Rev. Robert Greiner;
Natural Family Planning - t) 541-388-4004
Office of Worship and Spirituality (Vacant) -
Priests' Continuing Education Committee -
R.C.I.A. Office - t) 541-388-4004
Victim Assistance Coordinator - t) 541-388-9271 Angelina Montoya;
Vocation Director - t) 541-798-5823 vocations@dioceseofbaker.org Rev. Tomy Chowaran;

PARISHES, MISSIONS, AND CLERGY

STATE OF OREGON

ARLINGTON

St. Francis - Main & Ivy, Arlington, OR 97812; Mailing: PO Box 485, Condon, OR 97823 t) 541-384-5271 stjohncondon@gmail.com Rev. Robert Greiner, Pst.;

BAKER CITY

Cathedral of St. Francis De Sales - 2235 First St., Baker City, OR 97814 t) 541-523-4521 office@sfdsc.org; ann.kniesel@sfdsc.org www.saintfranciscathedral.com Rev. Suresh Kumar Telagani, Pst.; Dawn Coles, Parish Life Coord.; Ann Kniesel, DRE; CRP Stds.: 14

St. Therese - 135 W. Bell St., Halfway, OR 97834 t) 541-742-4488 yvoriggs@pinetel.com Yvonne Riggs, Contact;

St. Anthony - 500 E. St., North Powder, OR 97867 t) 541-856-3475 Jackie Fritz, Contact;

BEND

St. Francis of Assisi Catholic Church of Bend, Inc. - 2450 N.E. 27th St., Bend, OR 97701 t) 541-382-3631 www.stfrancisbend.org Rev. Jose Thomas Mudakodiyil, Pst.; Rev. Rene Labrador, Vicar; Dcn. Stephen McGlone; Dcn. Steve Beard; Dcn. Philip McCarty; Janet Deppmeier, CRE; CRP Stds.: 189

St. Francis of Assisi School - (Grades PreK-8) t) 541-382-4701 saintfrancisschool.net/ Julie Manion, Prin.; Stds.: 183; Sr. Tchrs.: 3; Lay Tchrs.: 11

BOARDMAN

Our Lady of Guadalupe - 78922 Olson Rd., Boardman, OR 97818; Mailing: P.O. Box 1277, Boardman, OR 97818 t) 541-481-2024 guadalupeboardman@gmail.com Rev. Luis M. Flores-Alva, Pst.; CRP Stds.: 118

BURNS

Holy Family Catholic Church of Burns, Inc. - 678 N. Egan, Burns, OR 97720; Mailing: 685 N. Fairview Ave., Burns, OR 97720 t) 541-573-2613 office@jmjparish.org www.jmjparish.org Rev. Joseph Levine, Pst.; Lisa Marie Sceirine, DRE; CRP Stds.: 34

Our Lady of Loretto Catholic Church of Drewsey, Inc. - 78884 Drewsey Rd., Drewsey, OR 97904 t) (541) 573-2613 (Holy Family takes calls)

St. Thomas Aquinas Catholic Church of Crane - 64302 Main Ave., Crane, OR 97732 t) (541) 573-2613 (Holy Family contact.)

St. Charles Catholic Church of Juntura, Inc. - 5232 Hwy. 20, Juntura, OR 97911 t) (541) 573-2613 (Holy Family)

CHILOQUIN

Our Lady of Mount Carmel Catholic Church of Chiloquin, Inc. - 503 W. Chocktoot St., Chiloquin, OR 97624; Mailing: P.O. Box 396, Chiloquin, OR 97624 t) 541-783-2411 catholicrect037@centurytel.net Rev. Thomas Polimetla, Pst.; CRP Stds.: 1

St. James the Apostle - 61000 Hwy. 140 E., Bly, OR 97622; Mailing: PO Box 396, Chiloquin, OR 97624

CONDON

St. John - 412 W. Walnut St., Condon, OR 97823; Mailing: PO Box 485, Condon, OR 97823 t) 541-384-5271 c) 541-980-5660 stjohncondon@gmail.com Rev. Robert Greiner, Pst.; CRP Stds.: 10

St. Catherine - 675 Washington St., Fossil, OR 97823 t) (541) 384-5271 Very Rev. Robert Greiner;

DUFUR

St. Alphonsus - 425 N.E. Second St., Dufur, OR 97021; Mailing: P.O. Box 328, Dufur, OR 97021-0328 t) 541-467-2580 stalphonsuscc@ortelco.net; stalphonsusccdufur@gmail.com Rev. Roy Isac Elavungal, SDB (India), Admin.;

ELGIN

St. Mary - 92 S. 12th, Elgin, OR 97827; Mailing: PO Box 97, Elgin, OR 97827 t) 541-437-8101 garlitzj@eoni.com Rev. Noby Thomas, Pst.; Nancy Wheeling, DRE; CRP Stds.: 8

ENTERPRISE

St. Katherine's - 301 E. Garfield St., Enterprise, OR 97828; Mailing: PO Box 370, Enterprise, OR 97828 t) 541-426-4008; 541-426-3043 stkatherineenterprise@gmail.com www.stkatherineenterprise.org Rev. Thomas D'Souza, Pst.; Susan Joy Barcik, DRE; CRP Stds.: 14

St. Pius X - 407 S. Pine St., Wallowa, OR 97885

HEPPNER

St. Patrick's - 525 Gale St., Heppner, OR 97836; Mailing: P.O. Box 633, Heppner, OR 97836 t) 541-676-9462 saintpatschurch@gmail.com www.saintpatschurch.com Rev. Thankachan Joseph, Pst.; Laurie Wood, Youth Min.; Deborah Wryn, DRE;

HERMISTON

Our Lady of Angels - 565 Hermiston Ave., Hermiston, OR 97838 t) 541-567-5812; 541-567-3825 (CRP) kay@ourladyofangelscc.org; chuchy@ourladyofangelscc.org www.ourladyofangelscc.org Rev. Daniel J. Maxwell, Pst.; Rev. Arturo Jeronimo, Par. Vicar; Dcn. Jesus Esparaza; Kay Edwards, Pst. Assoc.; Rebecca Sanders, DRE; CRP Stds.: 386

HOOD RIVER

Immaculate Conception (St. Mary's Catholic Church) - 1501 Belmont Ave., Hood River, OR 97031; Mailing: P.O. Box 693, Hood River, OR 97031 t) 541-386-3373; 541-436-4333 (CRP) stmaryshroffice@gmail.com; stmaryformation@gmail.com stmaryshr.org/ Rev. Tomy Chowaran, Pst.; CRP Stds.: 196

IONE

St. William - 110 Main St., Ione, OR 97843; Mailing: P.O. Box 633, Heppner, OR 97836 t) 541-676-9462 Rev. Thankachan Joseph, Pst.; Jeri McElligott, DRE; CRP Stds.: 10

JOHN DAY

Saint Elizabeth of Hungary Catholic Church - 111 S.W. 2nd Ave., John Day, OR 97845 t) 541-575-1459 saintelizabeth1938@gmail.com Rev. Christie Tissera, Pst.; CRP Stds.: 12

St. Anne -

JORDAN VALLEY

St. Bernard - 208 Yturri Blvd., Jordan Valley, OR 97910; Mailing: P.O. Box 186, Jordan Valley, OR 97910 t) 541-586-2266 stbernardsjordanvalley.com Rev. Shaji Thomas, Admin.;

Holy Family - 3520 Arock Rd., Arock, OR 97902

KLAMATH FALLS

St. Pius X - 4880 Bristol Ave., Klamath Falls, OR 97603 t) 541-884-4242; 541-882-7593 (CRP) office@piusxkf.com; stpiusff@piusxkf.com www.piusxkf.com Rev. Shiju Thuruthiyil (India), Pst.; Tammra Lucht, CRE; CRP Stds.: 110

Sacred Heart - 815 High St, Klamath Falls, OR 97601 t) 541-884-4566 rsafari@sacredheartkf.org; sharla@sacredheartkf.org www.sacredheartkf.org Rev. Rogatian Urassa, Pst.; Sharla Bishop, Pst. Assoc.; Paul Chutikorn, DRE; CRP Stds.: 115

LA GRANDE

Our Lady of the Valley - 1002 L Ave., La Grande, OR 97850 t) 541-963-7341 www.olvcatholic.org (Under the title of the Immaculate Conception) Rev. Noby Thomas, Pst.; Jimmy Zamora, DRE; CRP Stds.: 48

LA PINE

Holy Redeemer Roman Catholic Parish - 16137 Burgess Rd., La Pine, OR 97739; Mailing: P.O. Box 299, La Pine, OR 97739 t) 541-536-3571 holyrdmr@msn.com www.holyredeemerparish.net Rev. Paul Antao, S.D.B., Pst.; Heather Meeuwsen, Finance Mgr.; CRP Stds.: 1

Our Lady of the Snows - 120 Mississippi Dr., Gilchrist, OR 97737 t) (541) 536-3571 Rev. Paul Antao, S.D.B., Pst.;

Holy Family - 57255 Fort Rock Rd., Fort Rock, OR 97735 t) (541) 536-3571 Rev. Paul Antao, S.D.B., Pst.;

Holy Trinity - 18143 Cottonwood Rd., Sunriver, OR 97707 t) (541) 536-3571 Rev. Paul Antao, S.D.B., Pst.;

LAKEVIEW

St. Patrick Catholic Church of Lakeview, Inc. - 12 N. G St., Lakeview, OR 97630; Mailing: P.O. Box 29, Lakeview, OR 97630 t) 541-947-2741; 541-947-2820 (CRP) saintpatrick1912@gmail.com www.stpatricklakeview.com Rev. Thomas Philip, O.S.H., Admin.;

St. Richard Catholic Church of Adel, Inc. - 17570 20 Mile Rd., Adel, OR 97620 saintpatrick1911@outlook.com

St. Thomas Catholic Church of Plush - 28163 Plush Ave., Plush, OR 97637 saintpatrick1911@outlook.com

St. John Catholic Church of Paisley, Inc. - 1115 Main St., Paisley, OR 97636 saintpatrick1911@outlook.com

MADRAS
St. Patrick - 341 S.W. J St., Madras, OR 97741 t) 541-475-2936; 541-325-7346 (CRP) office@stpatmadras.com; ym@stpatmadras.com stpatmadras.com Rev. Victor Manuel Mena Martinez, Pst.; Daisy Nunez-Palacios, Bus. Mgr.; Jacquelina Garcia, DRE; CRP Stds.: 118

St. Kateri Tekakwitha - 4190 Hwy. 26, Warm Springs, OR 97761 (Indian Reservation) Rev. Richard Owen Fischer, Pst.;

MERRILL
St. Augustine Catholic Church of Merrill, Inc. - 905 E. Front St., Merrill, OR 97633; Mailing: PO Box 340, Merrill, OR 97633 t) 541-798-5823 staugustine@fireserve.net; stabookkeeper@fireserve.net Rev. Francis Obijekwu, S.M.M.M. (Nigeria), Pst.; CRP Stds.: 24

St. Frances Cabrini - 31400 Hwy. 70, Bonanza, OR 97623 t) (541) 798-5823

MILTON FREEWATER
St. Francis of Assisi - 925 Vining St., Milton Freewater, OR 97862 t) 541-938-5436 stfrancismfw@gmail.com Very Rev. Charles Chika Nnabuife, Pst.; CRP Stds.: 76

NYSSA
St. Bridget of Kildare - 504 Locust Ave., Nyssa, OR 97913-3235 t) 541-372-3133 st.bridgetofkildare@yahoo.com Rev. Anish Philip, O.S.H, Pst.; Azucena Meza, Youth Min.; Lorena Meza, DRE; Christina Tuttle, Trustee; CRP Stds.: 110

ONTARIO
Blessed Sacrament - 829 S.W. Second Ave., Ontario, OR 97914-2695 t) 541-889-8469; 541-889-8404 (CRP) bsccparish@gmail.com; frptjoebscc@gmail.com www.blessedsacramentontario.org Rev. Joseph Puthiyath Thomas, Pst.; Judith Vazquez, DRE; CRP Stds.: 158

Saint Peter - (Grades PreK-6) 98 S.W. Ninth St., Ontario, OR 97914 t) 541-889-7363 ruiz@stpetercatholicschool.com www.stpetercatholicschool.com Kimberly Ruiz, Prin.; Stds.: 54; Lay Tchrs.: 8

PENDLETON
St. Andrew Catholic Mission of Pendleton, Inc. - 48022 St. Andrews Rd., Pendleton, OR 97801 t) (541) 276-0767 www.standrews.pendletown.com Rev. Michael J. Fitzpatrick, S.J., Pst.; Fern Oliver, DRE; CRP Stds.: 80

Sacred Heart - 5th & College Sts., Athena, OR 97813; Mailing: P.O. Box 665, Athena, OR 97813 t) 541-276-0767 Kim A Fitzpatrick, Admin.;

St. Mary - 800 S.E. Court Ave., Pendleton, OR 97801 t) 541-276-3615; 541-276-6163 (CRP) st.mary3615@outlook.com www.stmaryspendleton.com Rev. Kumar Udagandla, Pst.; Dcn. Martin Omar Tores; CRP Stds.: 87

PILOT ROCK
St. Helen - 740 S.W. Birch St., Pilot Rock, OR 97868; Mailing: PO Box V, Pilot Rock, OR 97868 t) 541-443-3151 byrneslaura@yahoo.com Rev. Stanislaus Strzyz, Pst.;

PRINEVILLE
St. Joseph - 150 E. First, Prineville, OR 97754; Mailing: 200 E. First St., PO Box 1315, Prineville, OR 97754 t) 541-447-6475 c) 541-420-4458 stjosephparish@bendbroadband.com stjosephsprineville.org Rev. Joseph T. Kunnelaya, Pst.; Barbara Dalton, DRE; CRP Stds.: 95

REDMOND
Saint Thomas Catholic Church of Redmond, Inc. - 1720 N.W. 19th St., Redmond, OR 97756 t) 541-923-3390; 541-923-0597 (CRP) fathertodd@stthomasredmond.com; stthomasministry@gmail.com www.stthomasredmond.com Rev. Todd Unger, Pst.; Rev. Alexandar Poulose (India), Par. Vicar; Noel Roy, DRE; CRP Stds.: 130

St. Thomas Academy - (Grades PreK-8) t) 541-548-3785 admin@redmondacademy.com www.redmondacademy.com Patty Schulte, Prin.; Stds.: 155; Sr. Tchrs.: 1; Lay Tchrs.: 11

SISTERS
St. Edward the Martyr - 123 Trinity Way, Sisters, OR 97759; Mailing: PO Box 489, Sisters, OR 97759-0489 t) 541-549-9391 stedward@bendbroadband.com Rev. Sibi Poulose, Pst.; CRP Stds.: 35

THE DALLES
St. Peter - 1222 W. 10th St., The Dalles, OR 97058; Mailing: P.O. Box 41, The Dalles, OR 97058 t) 541-296-2026 staff@stpeterstd.org; parishsecretary@stpeterstd.org stpeterstd.org Rev. Steve Garza, Pst.; Dcn. Ireneo Ledezma; Jamie Bailey, DRE; Maria Ledezma, Bus. Mgr.; CRP Stds.: 175

St. Mary's Academy - (Grades PreK-8) 1112 Cherry Heights Rd., The Dalles, OR 97058 t) 541-296-6004 office@smatd.org www.smatd.org Kim Koch, Prin.; Stds.: 180; Lay Tchrs.: 11

UNION
Sacred Heart - 340 S. 10th St., Union, OR 97883; Mailing: PO Box 473, Union, OR 97883 t) 541-562-5486 sacred.heart.cc@gmail.com Rev. Noby Thomas, Pst.;

VALE
St. Patrick - 690 A St. W., Vale, OR 97918; Mailing: P.O. Box J, Vale, OR 97918 t) 541-473-3906; 541-473-3848 (CRP) camifatima@yahoo.com Rev. Camillus Fernando (Sri Lanka), Pst.; Susan Seals, DRE; CRP Stds.: 43

St. Joseph -

WASCO
St. Mary - 807 Barnett St., Wasco, OR 97065; Mailing: P.O. Box 14, Wasco, OR 97065 t) 541-442-8560 stmarywasco@embarqmail.com Rev. Roy Isac Elavungal, SDB (India), Admin.; Cindy Brown, Youth Min.; Molly Belshe, DRE;

St. John the Baptist - t) (541) 442-8560 stmarywasco@yahoo.com

INSTITUTIONS LOCATED IN DIOCESE

ASSOCIATIONS [ASN]

REDMOND
The Health and Retirement Association of the Diocese of Baker, Oregon - 641 S.W. Umatilla Ave., Redmond, OR 97756 t) 541-388-4004 Rev. Todd Unger, Admin.;

CONVENTS, MONASTERIES, AND RESIDENCES FOR WOMEN [CON]

BEND
Sisters of Mary of Kakamega - 2863 N.E. Jill Ave., Bend, OR 97701 c) 509-607-7784 sistersofmary1932@gmail.com sistersofmaryofkakamega.org Sr. Angelicah Njuguna, Pres.; Srs.: 13

ENDOWMENTS / FOUNDATIONS / TRUSTS [EFT]

HOOD RIVER
Providence Hood River Memorial Hospital Foundation - 810 12th St., Hood River, OR 97031; Mailing: P.O. Box 149, Hood River, OR 97031 t) 541-387-6342 laurie.kelley@providence.org Susan Frost, Contact;

REDMOND
The Legacy of Faith Catholic Community Foundation of Oregon - 641 S.W. Umatilla Ave., Redmond, OR 97756 t) 541-388-4004 Mark W. French, Exec. Dir.;

HOSPITALS / HEALTH SERVICES [HOS]

BAKER CITY
Saint Alphonsus Medical Center - Baker City, Inc. - 3325 Pocahontas Rd., Baker City, OR 97814 t) 541-523-6461 dina.ellwanger@saintalphonsus.org Dina Ellwanger, Pres.; Bed Capacity: 25; Asstd. Annu.: 30,285; Staff: 127

HOOD RIVER
Providence Hood River Memorial Hospital - 810 12th St., Hood River, OR 97031; Mailing: 4400 N.E. Halsey St., Bldg. 2-Ste. 595, Portland, OR 97213 t) 541-386-3911 mark.thomas@providence.org www.providence.org Providence St. Joseph Health Jeanie Vieira, Exec.; Mark Thomas, Contact; Bed Capacity: 25; Asstd. Annu.: 198,000; Staff: 562

ONTARIO
Saint Alphonsus Medical Center - Ontario, Inc. - 351 S.W. Ninth St., Ontario, OR 97914 t) 541-881-7000 www.saintalphonsus.org/ontario Dina Ellwanger, Pres.; Bed Capacity: 49; Asstd. Annu.: 71,034; Staff: 252

PENDLETON
St. Anthony Hospital - 2801 St. Anthony Way, Pendleton, OR 97801 t) 541-276-5121 vonnisimonton@chiwest.com www.sahpendleton.org Harold Geller, Pres.; Bed Capacity: 25; Asstd. Annu.: 5,944; Staff: 360

MISCELLANEOUS [MIS]

HOOD RIVER
Providence Brookside Manor - 1550 Brookside Dr., Hood River, OR 97031 t) 541-387-6370 jamie.hanshaw@providence.org Jamie Hanshaw, Contact;

Providence Dethman House - 1205 Montello St., Hood River, OR 97031; Mailing: P.O. Box 4163, Portland, OR 97208 t) 541-386-8278 shannan.stickler@providence.org Shannan Stickler, Contact;

Providence Down Manor - 1950 Sterling Pl., Hood River, OR 97031 t) 541-387-8290 jamie.hanshaw@providence.org Jamie Hanshaw, Contact;

KLAMATH FALLS
St. Maurus Hanga Abbey - 4880 Bristol Ave., Klamath Falls, OR 97603 hangawater@gmail.com hangaabbey.org Rev. Ildefonce Mapara, O.S.B. (Tanzania), Dir.;

Archdiocese of Baltimore

(Archidioecesis Baltimorensis)

MOST REVEREND WILLIAM E. LORI, S.T.D.

Archbishop of Baltimore; ordained May 14, 1977; appointed Titular Bishop of Bulla and Auxiliary Bishop of Washington April 20, 1995; appointed Bishop of Bridgeport January 23, 2001; installed March 19, 2001; appointed Archbishop of Baltimore March 20, 2012; installed as sixteenth Archbishop of Baltimore May 16, 2012. 320 Cathedral St., Baltimore, MD 21201. T: 410-547-5437.

Chancery Office: 320 Cathedral St., Baltimore, MD 21201. T: 410-547-5446.
www.archbalt.org/chancery/
chancery@archbalt.org

Square Miles 4,801.

Established a Diocese November 6, 1789; Established an Archdiocese April 8, 1808.

Comprises the City of Baltimore and Allegany, Anne Arundel, Baltimore, Carroll, Frederick, Garrett, Harford, Howard and Washington Counties. By a Decree of the Sacred Congregation of the Propaganda, July 19, 1858, approved by His Holiness, Pius IX, July 25, 1858, "Prerogative of Place" was conferred on the Archdiocese of Baltimore. By the explicit words of this decree of the Holy See, the Archbishop of Baltimore takes precedence over all Archbishops of the United States (not Cardinals) in Councils, gatherings and meetings of whatever kind of the Hierarchy (in concillis, coetibus et comitiis quibuscumque) regardless of the seniority of other Archbishops in promotion or ordination. Decree signed by Cardinal Barnabo, August 15, 1858.

For legal titles of parishes and archdiocesan institutions, consult the Chancery Office.

Most Reverend Adam. J. Parker
Auxiliary Bishop of Baltimore; ordained May 27, 2000; appointed Titular Bishop of Tasaccora and Auxiliary Bishop of Baltimore December 5, 2016; installed January 19, 2017. Office: 320 Cathedral St., Baltimore, MD 21201. T: 410-547-5447.

Most Reverend Bruce A. Lewandowski, C.SS.R.
Auxiliary Bishop of Baltimore; ordained May 7, 1994; appointed Titular Bishop of Croae and Auxiliary Bishop of Baltimore June 10, 2020; installed August 18, 2020. Office: 320 Cathedral St., Baltimore, MD 21201. T: 410-547-5452.

STATISTICAL OVERVIEW

Personnel
Archbishops ... 1
Auxiliary Bishops ... 2
Retired Bishops ... 1
Priests: Diocesan Active in Diocese ... 110
Priests: Diocesan Active Outside Diocese ... 11
Priests: Retired, Sick or Absent ... 87
Number of Diocesan Priests ... 208
Religious Priests in Diocese ... 159
Total Priests in your Diocese ... 367
Extern Priests in Diocese ... 60
Ordinations:
Diocesan Priests ... 5
Religious Priests ... 1
Transitional Deacons ... 11
Permanent Deacons in Diocese ... 188
Total Brothers ... 12
Total Sisters ... 463

Parishes
Parishes ... 137
With Resident Pastor:
Resident Diocesan Priests ... 92
Resident Religious Priests ... 32
Without Resident Pastor:
Administered by Priests ... 6
Administered by Deacons ... 4
Administered by Lay People ... 2
Missions ... 8

Welfare
Catholic Hospitals ... 4
Total Assisted ... 803,385
Health Care Centers ... 1
Total Assisted ... 3,742
Homes for the Aged ... 31
Total Assisted ... 7,390
Residential Care of Children ... 4
Total Assisted ... 972
Day Care Centers ... 33
Total Assisted ... 1,965
Special Centers for Social Services ... 28
Total Assisted ... 1,830,973
Residential Care of Disabled ... 1
Total Assisted ... 191

Educational
Seminaries, Diocesan ... 2
Students from This Diocese ... 57
Students from Other Dioceses ... 215
Students, Religious ... 5
Total Seminarians ... 62
Colleges and Universities ... 4
Total Students ... 11,264
High Schools, Diocesan and Parish ... 6
Total Students ... 2,797
High Schools, Private ... 12
Total Students ... 6,520
Elementary Schools, Diocesan and Parish ... 32
Total Students ... 15,178
Elementary Schools, Private ... 6
Total Students ... 1,870
Non-residential Schools for the Disabled ... 1
Total Students ... 134
Catechesis / Religious Education:
High School Students ... 3,436
Elementary Students ... 13,729
Total Students under Catholic Instruction ... 54,990
Teachers in Diocese:
Priests ... 4
Brothers ... 1
Sisters ... 28
Lay Teachers ... 1,756

Vital Statistics
Receptions into the Church:
Infant Baptism Totals ... 4,355
Adult Baptism Totals ... 343
Received into Full Communion ... 326
First Communions ... 3,035
Confirmations ... 2,863
Marriages:
Catholic ... 630
Interfaith ... 203
Total Marriages ... 833
Deaths ... 3,617
Total Catholic Population ... 503,937
Total Population ... 3,368,757

LEADERSHIP

Office of the Archbishop - t) 410-547-5437 Most Rev. William E. Lori (archbishop@archbalt.org);

Priest Secretary to the Archbishop - t) 410-547-5568 Rev. Tyler G. Kline;

Office of the Cardinal Archbishop Emeritus, Edwin F. O'Brien -

Vicars General - Most Rev. Adam J. Parker, Moderator of the Curia (gvicar@archbalt.org);

Episcopal Vicars - Most Rev. Bruce Lewandowski, C.Ss.R., Episcopal Vicar for the Urban Vicariate (uvicar@archbalt.org); Rev. Msgr. Jay O'Connor, Episcopal Vicar for the Eastern Vicariate (evicar@archbalt.org);

Office of the Vicar General/Moderator of the Curia - t) 410-547-5447 Most Rev. Adam J. Parker, Moderator of the Curia (gvicar@archbalt.org);

Office of the Chancellor - t) 410-547-5446 Dr. Diane L. Barr, Chancellor;

Office of Child and Youth Protection - t) 866-417-7469 (Victim Assistance Hotline); 410-547-5567 (Main Office) Jerri Burkhardt, Dir. (jburkhardt@archbalt.org);

Communications Office - t) 410-547-5378 Christian Kendzierski, Exec. Dir. (communications@archbalt.org);

Catholic Review Media - t) 443-524-3150 Christopher Gunty, Assoc. Publisher/Editor;

Director of Community Affairs - t) 410-547-5341 Yvonne Wenger;

Office of Consecrated Life - t) 410-547-5584 Rev. Tom Dymowski, O.SS.T., Archbishop's Delegate for Religious (thdymowski@gmail.com);

Missions Office - t) 410-547-5498 Dr. Diane L. Barr, Interim Dir.;

Office of the Eastern Vicariate - evicar@archbalt.org

Episcopal Vicar for the Eastern Vicariate - t) 410-547-5527 evicar@archbalt.org Rev. Msgr. Jay O'Connor;

Pastoral Associate to the Eastern Vicar - t) 410-547-3148 Manuel Aliaga;

Office of the Urban Vicariate - uvicar@archbalt.org

Urban Vicar - t) 410-547-5452 Most Rev. Bruce Lewandowski, C.Ss.R.;

Episcopal Vicar for Black Catholic Ministries - Most Rev. Bruce Lewandowski, C.Ss.R.;

Office Black Catholic Ministries - t) 410-625-8472 obcm@archbalt.org Adrienne Curry, Dir.;

Episcopal Vicar for Hispanic Catholics - Most Rev. Bruce Lewandowski, C.Ss.R.;

Office of Hispanic Ministry - t) 410-547-5363 hispanicministry@archbalt.org Lia R. Salinas, Dir.;

Office of the Western Vicariate - wvicar@archbalt.org

Archbishop's Delegate for the Western Vicariate - t) 410-547-5456 Dcn. Christopher J. Yeung;

ADMINISTRATION

Department of Management Services - Office of the Executive Director - t) 410-547-5313 John M. Matera (mgmtserv@archbalt.org);

Division of Facilities and Real Estate Management - t) 410-547-5366 facserv@archbalt.org Nolan McCoy, Dir.;

Office of Cemetery Management - t) (410) 547-5375; (410) 566-7770 (New Cathedral Cemetery) cemetery@archbalt.org Rev. Patrick M. Carrion, Dir.; Nathan Nardi, Dir. New Cathedral Cemetery;

Division of Fiscal Services - fiscal@archbalt.org Mary Pat Stoval, Dir.;

Division of Information Technology - t) 410-547-5582 it@archbalt.org Marcus Madsen, Dir.;

CATHOLIC CHARITIES

Associated Catholic Charities - t) 667-600-2000 www.cc-md.org William J. McCarthy Jr., Exec. Dir.;

CLERGY AND RELIGIOUS SERVICES

Division of Clergy Personnel - t) 410-547-5550 clergy@archbalt.org Rev. James D. Proffitt, Vicar for Clergy;

Priestly Life and Ministry Board -

Office of Pastoral Service for Retired Priests - t) 410-547-5382 Rev. William P. Foley, Dir., Senior & Retired Priests;

Senior Priests' Retirement Board -

Office of the Diaconate - t) 410-547-5550 Rev. Michael Foppiano, Dir.; Dcn. Robert M. Shephard, Assoc. Dir., Deacon Personnel;

Deacon Formation Program - Rev. William Keown, Dir.;

Pastoral Service to Retired Deacons - Dcn. Kevin F. Reid;

Deacon Life and Ministry Board -

Office of Vocations - t) 410-547-5426 vocations@archbalt.org www.bmorevocations.org Rev. Stephen P. Roth, Dir.; Rev. Matthew T Himes, Assoc. Dir.;

CONSULTATIVE BODIES

Consultors - www.archbalt.org

See the webpage for a complete list of Consultors -

Presbyteral Council - www.archbalt.org

See webpage for a complete list of Presbyteral Council Members -

Board of Financial Administration - www.archbalt.org

See webpage for a complete list of members -

Archdiocesan Pastoral Council - www.archbalt.org

See webpage for complete list of members -

DEVELOPMENT

Department of Advancement - t) 888-202-5113 (Toll Free); 410-547-5356 giving@archbalt.org www.archbalt.org/giving Kim Montgomery, Interim Chief Advancement Officer & Dir., Catholic Community Foundation;

EDUCATION

Department of Catholic Schools -

Chancellor for Education (Open) - t) 410-547-5331

Office of the Superintendent - t) 410-547-5515 donna.hargens@archbalt.org Dr. Donna Hargens, Exec. Dir. & Supt. Catholic Schools;

EVANGELIZATION

Institute for Evangelization - Office of the Executive Director - t) 410-547-5405 www.archbalt.org/evangelization Edward P. Herrera (evangelization@archbalt.org);

Office of Divine Worship - t) 410-547-5403 www.archbalt.org Julie Grace Males, Dir.;

Office of Family, Youth and Young Adult Ministry - t) 410-547-5371 Stacy Golden, Dir.;

Office of Life, Justice & Peace - t) 410-547-5537 Erin Younkins, Dir.;

Office of Parish Renewal - t) 410-547-5488 officeofparishrenewal@archbalt.org www.archbalt.org/evangelization/ Julie St. Croix, Dir.;

Youth Retreat House, Monsignor O'Dwyer - t) 410-666-2400; 410-472-2400 odwyer@archbalt.org www.msgrodwyer.org Phil Howard, Dir.;

HUMAN RESOURCES

Department of Human Resources - t) 410-547-5432 www.archbalt.org/humanresources Joann Pelipesky, Exec. Dir. (Joann.Pelipesky@archbalt.org);

Lay Employees Retirement Board -

Division of Employee Benefits - t) 410-547-5512 Karen Funk, Dir.;

Division of Human Resources - Regina McCurdy, Dir. Oper.;

TRIBUNAL

Metropolitan Tribunal - t) 410-547-5533 mltribunalstaffall@archbalt.org www.archbalt.org/marriage-tribunal

Judicial Vicar - Rev. Jose Opalda, Judicial Vicar;

Adjutant Judicial Vicars - Rev. D. Reginald Whitt, O.P.;

Judges - Rev. Raymond L. Harris Jr.; Dcn. Anthony Norcio; Rev. John B. Ward;

Defenders of the Bond - Rev. Gonzalo Cadavid-Rivera;

Notaries - Teresa Ewen; Susan A. Smith; Christina Mahaley;

MISCELLANEOUS / OTHER OFFICES

Archives of the Archdiocese of Baltimore - St. Mary's Seminary & University - t) 410-864-4074 www.stmarys.edu/archives Tricia Pyne, Dir.; Alison Foley; Mary Shank;

Catholic Campaign For Human Development (CCHD) - t) 410-547-5446; 410-235-5136 www.cchdbaltimore.org Rev. Msgr. Richard J. Bozzelli, Archdiocesan Dir.;

Maryland Catholic Conference - t) 410-269-1155 www.mdcathcon.org Jenny Kraska, Exec.;

PARISHES, MISSIONS, AND CLERGY

STATE OF MARYLAND

ABERDEEN

St. Joan of Arc - 257 S. Law St., Aberdeen, MD 21001; Mailing: 222 S. Law St., Aberdeen, MD 21001 t) 410-272-6944 (CRP); 410-272-4535 parish@stjoanarc.org www.stjoanarc.org Rev. William F. Franken, Pst.;

St. Joan of Arc School - (Grades PreK-8) 230 S. Law St., Aberdeen, MD 21001 t) 410-272-1387 school@stjoanarc.org www.school.stjoanarc.org Dianne Kestler, Prin.;

ABINGDON

St. Francis de Sales - 1450 Abingdon Rd., Abingdon, MD 21009 t) 410-676-3354 (CRP); 410-676-5119 sfabing@archbalt.org www.stfrancisabingdon.org Rev. John Martinez, Admin.;

ANNAPOLIS

St. Andrew by the Bay - 701 College Pkwy., Annapolis, MD 21409 t) 410-974-4366 sabbanna@archbalt.org www.standrewbythebay.org Rev. Andrew T. DeFusco, Pst.;

St. Mary - 109 Duke of Gloucester St., Annapolis, MD 21401 t) 410-990-4779 (CRP); 410-990-4100 parishinfo@stmarysannapolis.org www.stmarysannapolis.org Rev. Patrick Woods, C.Ss.R., Pst.; Rt. Rev. Alistar Elias, C.Ss.R., Assoc. Pst.; Rev. Eric Hoog, C.Ss.R., Assoc. Pst.; Rev. Michael Houston, C.Ss.R., Assoc. Pst.; Rev. John McKenna, C.Ss.R., Assoc. Pst.; Rev. James O'Blaney, C.Ss.R., Assoc. Pst.; Rev. Hever Sanchez, C.Ss.R., Assoc. Pst.; Rev. Vang Cong Tran, C.Ss.R., Assoc. Pst.; Rev. Clement Vadakkedath, C.Ss.R., Assoc. Pst.;

St. Mary School - (Grades K-8) 111 Duke of Gloucester St., Annapolis, MD 21401 t) 410-263-2869 www.stmarysannapolis.org/es-homepage Megan Downs Back, Prin.;

St. Mary High School - 113 Duke of Gloucester St., Annapolis, MD 21401 t) 410-263-3294 www.stmarysannapolis.org/hs-homepage Mindi Imes, Prin.;

St. John Neuman - 620 N. Bestgate Rd., Annapolis, MD 21401 t) 410-266-2498

BALTIMORE

Cathedral of Mary Our Queen - 5200 N. Charles St., Baltimore, MD 21210-2098 t) 410-464-4000; 410-464-4010 (CRP) cathedral@archbalt.org www.cathedralofmary.org Rev. Louis A. Bianco, Rector; Rev. Justin Gough, Assoc. Pst.; Rev. Joseph F.

Breighner, In Res.; Rev. Matthew T Himes, In Res.; Rev. Stephen P. Roth, In Res.;

Cathedral of Mary Our Queen School - (Grades K-8) 111 Amberly Way, Baltimore, MD 21210-2098 t) 410-464-4100 scmoq@cmoq.org www.schoolofthecathedral.org Rosanna Czarnecki, Prin.; Kathleen Pendergast, Asst. Prin.;

St. Agnes - 5422 Old Frederick Rd., Baltimore, MD 21229 t) 410-744-2900 sagnes@archbalt.org www.saintsaw.org See School Section for St. Agnes Catholic School Rev. Isaac Makovo, Pst.;

St. Ambrose - 4502 Park Heights Ave., Baltimore, MD 21215 t) 410-367-9918 pastor@saintambrose.com www.saintambrose.com Rev. Paul Zaborowski, O.F.M.Cap., Pst.; Rev. Ignatius Okoye, OFM Cap., In Res.; Sr. Stella Kanu, O.S.P., DRE;

St. Ann - 2201 Greenmount Ave., Baltimore, MD 21218; Mailing: 528 E. 22nd St., Baltimore, MD 21218 t) 410-235-8169 stann528@comcast.net www.stannsofbaltimore.org Rev. Xavier Edet, S.S.J., Pst.;

St. Anthony of Padua - 4414 Frankford Ave., Baltimore, MD 21206 t) 410-488-0400; 410-254-1687 (CRP) dorris.vangaal@archbalt.org www.sapmpb.org Rev. Ty S. Hullinger, Pst.;

St. Athanasius - 4708 Prudence St., Baltimore, MD 21226 t) 410-355-5740; 410-355-2540 (CRP) athanasius5740@gmail.com www.starl.org Rev. Robert A. DiMattei Jr., Pst.;

Basilica of the National Shrine of the Assumption of the Blessed Virgin Mary - 408 N. Charles St., Baltimore, MD 21201 t) 410-727-3565 www.americasfirstcathedral.org (Co-Cathedral). Corporate Title: The Trustees of the Catholic Cathedral Church of Baltimore (The Basilica); Basilica of the Assumption Historic Trust. Rev. Brendan Fitzgerald, Rector; Most Rev. Denis J. Madden, Assisting Clergy; Rev. Tyler G. Kline, Assisting Clergy; Rev. William P. Foley, Assisting Clergy;

The Archbishop's Residence - t) 410-727-3564 Most Rev. William E. Lori, In Res.;

St. Benedict - 2612 Wilkens Ave., Baltimore, MD 21223 t) 410-947-4988 stbenedictbalto@gmail.com www.saintbenedict.org Rev. Paschal A. Morlino, O.S.B., Pst.;

St. Bernardine - 3800 Edmondson Ave., Baltimore, MD 21229; Mailing: 3812 Edmondson Ave., Baltimore, MD 21229 t) 410-362-8664; 410-362-8978 (CRP) stbernardine@archbalt.org www.stbernardinechurch.org Rev. Msgr. Richard J. Bozzelli, Pst.;

Blessed Sacrament Church - 4103 Old York Rd., Baltimore, MD 21218-1237 t) (410) 433-2300 www.stmatthewbaltimore.org Rev. Matthew T. Buening, Pst.;

St. Casimir - 2800 O'Donnell St., Baltimore, MD 21224 t) 410-276-1981 st.casimir@verizon.net www.stcasimir.org Rev. Dennis Grumsey, O.F.M.Conv., Pst.; Bro. Edward Handy, O.F.M. Conv., In Res.; Rev. Bartholomew A. Karwacki, O.F.M.Conv., In Res.;

St. Casimir Catholic School - (Grades PreK-8) 1035 S. Kenwood Ave., Baltimore, MD 21224 t) 410-342-2681 school@stcasimirschool.us www.stcasimirschool.us Noreen Heffner, Prin.;

Catholic Community of South Baltimore Roman Catholic Congregation, Inc. - 108 E. West St., Baltimore, MD 21230; Mailing: 110 E. West St., Baltimore, MD 21230 t) 410-752-8498 www.southbaltcatholic.org Holy Cross (1858); St. Mary, Star of the Sea (1868); and Our Lady of Good Counsel (1858) Rev. Joshua Laws, Pst.;

St. Cecilia - 3301 Windsor Ave, Baltimore, MD 21216; Mailing: 3300 Clifton Ave., Baltimore, MD 21216 t) 410-624-3600 office@churchofstcecilia.org www.churchofstcecilia.org Rev. Gemechu Y Raga, C.M., Pst.; Sr. Teresa Daily, D.C., Pst. Assoc.; Bro. William Stover, C.M., Pst. Assoc.;

Church of the Annunciation - 5212 McCormick Ave., Baltimore, MD 21206 t) 410-866-4020; 410-866-4706 (CRP) sites.google.com/site/churchoftheannunciation/home Rev. Hector Mateus-Ariza, Pst.; Rev. Macias Wency D. Serafica, Assoc. Pastor; Sr. Susan Engel, M.H.S.H., Pst. Assoc.;

St. Clare - 714 Myrth Ave., Baltimore, MD 21221-4898 t) 410-686-7693 (CRP); 410-687-6011 www.saintclare.org Rev. John Streifel, Pst.;

St. Clement Mary Hofbauer - 1212 Chesaco Ave., Baltimore, MD 21237 t) 410-391-5028 (CRP); 410-686-6188 parishoffice@stclementmh.org www.stclementmh.org Rev. Hector Mateus-Ariza, Pst.; Rev. Macias Wency D. Serafica, Assoc. Pastor;

Corpus Christi - 110 W. Lafayette Ave., Baltimore, MD 21217 t) 410-523-4161 corpus.christi@archbalt.org www.corpuschristibaltimore.org Rev. Martin H. Demek, Pst.;

St. Dominic - 5310 Harford Rd., Baltimore, MD 21214; Mailing: 4414 Frankford Ave., Baltimore, MD 21206 t) 410-426-0360 (CRP); 410-488-0400 dominicfaith@aol.com www.sapmpb.org Rev. Ty S. Hullinger, Pst.;

St. Edward - 901 Poplar Grove St., Baltimore, MD 21216-4350 t) 410-362-2000 stedwardsrccmd@gmail.com www.stedwardchurchmd.com Rev. Uju Patrick Okeahialam, C.S.Sp., Pst.; Rev. Kenny Udumka, C.S.Sp., Assoc. Pst.;

St. Francis of Assisi - 3615 Harford Rd., Baltimore, MD 21218 t) 410-235-5136 sfabalt@archbalt.org www.sfabalt.org Rev. Msgr. William F. Burke, Pastor Emer.; Dcn. Andrew Lacovara, Admin.;

St. Francis of Assisi School - (Grades PreK-8) 3617 Harford Rd., Baltimore, MD 21218 t) 410-467-1683 info@sfa-school.org www.sfa-school.org Dr. Karmen Collins, Prin.; Mary Carol Lidinsky, Asst. Prin.;

St. Francis Xavier - 1501 E. Oliver St., Baltimore, MD 21213 t) 410-837-0556 (CRP); 410-727-3103 stfrancisxavier@verizon.net www.historicfrancisxavier.org Rev. Xavier Edet, S.S.J., Pst.; Rev. Livinus Anweting, Assoc. Pst.;

St. Gregory the Great - 1542 N. Gilmor St., Baltimore, MD 21217-2304 t) 410-523-0061 sggreat@archbalt.org Rev. Uju Patrick Okeahialam, C.S.Sp., Pst.; Rev. Kenny Udumka, C.S.Sp., Assoc. Pst.;

Holy Korean Martyrs - 5801 Security Blvd., Baltimore, MD 21207 t) 410-265-8885 www.hkmcc.us Rev. Maurice Haechul Chung, Pst.;

Holy Rosary - 408 S. Chester St., Baltimore, MD 21231 t) 410-732-3960 holyrosarybalto@comcast.net www.holyrosarypl.org Rev. Ryszard Czerniak, S.Chr., Pst.;

St. Ignatius Church - 740 N. Calvert St., Baltimore, MD 21202; Mailing: 102 E. Madison St., Baltimore, MD 20202 t) 410-727-3848 parish@st-ignatius.net www.st-ignatius.net Rev. Brian B. Frain, S.J., Pst.; Rev. William J. Watters, S.J., Assisting Clergy;

Immaculate Conception - 1512 Druid Ave, Baltimore, MD 21217; Mailing: 3300 Clifton Ave, Baltimore, MD 21216 t) 410-624-3600 office@churchofstcecilia.org www.churchofstcecilia.org/ Rev. Gemechu Y Raga, C.M., Pst.; Sr. Teresa Daily, D.C., Pst. Assoc.; Bro. William Stover, C.M., Pst. Assoc.;

Immaculate Heart of Mary - 8501 Loch Raven Blvd., Baltimore, MD 21286 t) 410-668-7935 ihmparishoffice@imhchurchmd.org www.ihmchurchmd.org Rev. Jeffrey S. Dauses, Pst.;

Immaculate Heart of Mary School - (Grades PreK-8) t) 410-668-8466 school@ihmschoolmd.org www.ihmschoolmd.org Sr. Susan Louise Eder, O.S.F.S., Prin.; Marianne Kozlowski, Asst. Prin.;

St. Isaac Jogues - 9215 Old Harford Rd., Baltimore, MD 21234 t) 410-665-2561 (CRP); 410-668-3686 (CRP); 410-461-4888 sij@sij.org www.sij.org Rev. Brian P. Nolan, Pst.;

St. Joseph - 8420 Belair Rd., Baltimore, MD 21236 t) 410-256-1630 www.stjoefullerton.org Rev. Jesse L. Bolger, Pst.; Rev. Ross E. Conklin Jr., Assoc. Pst.; Rev. John C. Rapisarda, Assoc. Pst.;

St. Joseph School - (Grades PreK-8) 8416 Belair Rd., Baltimore, MD 21236 t) 410-256-8026 office@stjoefullerton.org www.stjoeschool.org Christina Ashby, Prin.;

St. Joseph Passionist Monastery Parish - 3801 Old Frederick Rd., Baltimore, MD 21229; Mailing: 251 S. Morley St., Baltimore, MD 21229 t) 410-566-0877 info@sjmp.com www.sjmp.org Rev. Michael A. Murphy, Pst.;

St. Jude Shrine - 308 N. Paca St., Baltimore, MD 21203; Mailing: P.O. Box 1455, Baltimore, MD 21203 t) 410-685-6026 info@stjudeshrine.org www.stjudeshrine.org Rev. Salvatore C. Furnari, S.A.C., Pst.; Rev. Vensus George, S.A.C., Assoc. Pst.;

St. Jude Shrine Corp. - 512 W. Saratoga St., Baltimore, MD 21203 t) (410) 685-6026

St. Leo the Great - 227 S. Exeter St., Baltimore, MD 21202-4451 t) 410-675-7275 saintleosoffice@gmail.com www.saintleorcc.com Rev. Bernie Carman, S.A.C., Pst.;

Little Flower, Shrine of - 3500 Belair Rd., Baltimore, MD 21213; Mailing: 2854 Brendon Ave, Baltimore, MD 21213 t) 410-483-1700 slflower@archbalt.org www.shrineofthelittleflower.org Dcn. Andrew Lacovara, Admin.;

St. Mary of the Assumption - 5502 York Rd., Baltimore, MD 21212 t) 410-435-5900 st.maryotag@archbalt.org www.stmarystpiusx.org Rev. Jose Opalda, Pst.; Rev. Samuel Lupico, In Res.; Rev. Joseph L. Muth Jr., In Res.;

St. Matthew - 5401 Loch Raven Blvd., Baltimore, MD 21239 t) 410-433-2300 www.stmatthewbaltimore.org Rev. Matthew T. Buening, Pst.;

Notre Dame Mission Volunteers - Americorps - t) 410-523-6844 natloffice@ndmva.org www.ndmva.org Lea Marshall, Contact;

Immigration Outreach Services Center, Inc. - t) 410-323-8564 info@ioscbaltimore.org www.ioscbaltimore.org Pat Shannon Jones, Exec. Dir.; Rev. Joseph L. Muth Jr., Founder & Chap.;

St. Michael - 10 Willow Ave., Baltimore, MD 21206 t) 410-665-1054 parish@smoverlea.org www.smoverlea.org Rev. Hector Mateus-Ariza, Pst.; Rev. Macias Wency D. Serafica, Assoc. Pst.;

St. Michael School - (Grades PreK-8) t) 410-668-8797 school@stmstc.org www.stmstc.org Paul Kristoff, Prin.; Christine Godlewski, Asst. Prin.;

Most Precious Blood - 5010 Bowleys Ln., Baltimore, MD 21206; Mailing: 4414 Frankford Ave., Baltimore, MD 21206 t) 410-488-0400 sapmpb@comcast.net www.sapmpb.org Rev. Ty S. Hullinger, Pst.;

The National Shrine of St. Alphonsus Liguori - 114 W. Saratoga St., Baltimore, MD 21201 t) 410-685-6090 www.stalphonsusbalt.org Rev. Ian Bozant, Pst.; Rev. Joseph Favole-Mihm, F.S.S.P., Assoc. Pst.;

New All Saints - 4408 Liberty Heights Ave., Baltimore, MD 21207 t) 410-542-0445 www.naschurch.org Rev. Uju Patrick Okeahialam, C.S.Sp., Pst.; Rev. Kenny Udumka, C.S.Sp., Assoc. Pst.;

Our Lady of Fatima - 6400 E. Pratt St., Baltimore, MD 21224; Mailing: 6420 E. Pratt St., Baltimore, MD 21224 t) 410-633-2828 www.olfmd.org Dcn. Alphonse C. Bankard III, Admin.; Rev. Giuliano Gargiulo; Sr. Sandra Montanez, MPS, Pst. Assoc.;

Our Lady of Hope - 7945 N. Boundary Rd., Baltimore, MD 21222; Mailing: 1727 Lynch Rd., Dundalk, MD 21222 t) 410-284-6600 www.olhstchurch.com Rev. Kevin A. Mueller, Pst.; Rev. Gregory Rapisarda, Assoc. Pastor;

Our Lady of Hope School - (Grades PreK-8) 8003 N. Boundary Rd., Baltimore, MD 21222 t) 410-288-2793 ipryle@archbalt.org www.olhsl.com Sr. Irene Mary Pryle, S.S.N.D., Prin.;

Convent - 8001 N. Boundary Rd., Baltimore, MD 21222 t) 410-282-3800 School Sisters of Notre Dame

Our Lady of La Vang - 335 Sollers Point Rd., Baltimore, MD 21222 t) 410-282-1496 olol_baltimore@yahoo.com www.olol-baltimore.net Rev. Joseph Chuc Tran, M.M., Pst.;

Our Lady of Pompei - 3600 Claremont St., Baltimore, MD 21224 t) 410-675-7790

ourladyofpompei@olpmd.org www.olpmd.org Rev. Claudio Piccolongo, Pst.; Rev. Matteo Dal Bianco Montagna, Assoc. Pst.;

Our Lady of Victory - 4414 Wilkens Ave., Baltimore, MD 21229 t) 410-242-9533 (CRP); 410-242-0131 parish@olvictory.org www.olvictory.org Rev. William Keown, Admin.;

Our Lady of Victory School - (Grades PreK-8) 4416 Wilkens Ave., Baltimore, MD 21229 t) 410-242-3688 kgreen@olvictory.org www.olvmd.org Ryan Hellem, Prin.;

St. Peter Claver - 1546 N. Fremont Ave., Baltimore, MD 21217 t) 410-669-0512 (Rectory); 410-728-1729 (Hall) www.claverpius.org Rev. Francis Asomkase, S.S.J., Pst.;

SS. Philip and James - 2801 N. Charles St., Baltimore, MD 21218 t) 410-235-2294 info@philipandjames.org www.philipandjames.org Rev. Michael Weibley, O.P., Pst.; Rev. Ambrose Arralde, O.P., Assoc. Pst.; Rev. Josemaría Guzmán-Dominguez, O.P., Assoc. Pst.; Rev. Michael Ciccone, O.P., In Res.; Rev. Innoncent Smith, O.P., In Res.; Rev. D. Reginald Whitt, O.P., In Res.;

St. Pius V - 1546 N. Fremont Ave., Baltimore, MD 21217-0550 t) (410) 696-0512 spiusv@verizon.net www.claverpius.org Rev. Francis Asomkase, S.S.J., Pst.;

St. Pius X - 6428 York Rd., Baltimore, MD 21212; Mailing: 6432 York Rd, Baltimore, MD 21212 t) 410-427-7500 info@stpius10.org www.stmarystpiusx.orrg Rev. Jose Opalda, Pst.;

St. Pius X School - -8) 6432 York Rd., Baltimore, MD 21212 t) 410-427-7400 jripley@stpius10school.org www.stpius10school.org Jennifer Ripley, Prin.;

St. Rita - 3 Dunmanway, Baltimore, MD 21222; Mailing: 6736 Youngstown Ave, Baltimore, MD 21222 t) 410-633-2828 office@shmstr.org shmstr.org Rev. John Harrison, C.Ss.R., Pst.;

St. Rose of Lima - 3803 4th St., Baltimore, MD 21225; Mailing: 4708 Prudence St., Baltimore, MD 21226 t) 410-355-8515 athanasius5740@gmail.com www.starl.org Rev. Robert A. DiMattei Jr., Pst.;

Sacred Heart of Jesus-Sagrado Corazon de Jesus - 600 S. Conkling St., Baltimore, MD 21224-4203 t) 410-342-4336 www.shjbaltimore.com Rev. Ako Walker, C.Ss.R., Pst.; Rev. Constancio Alipio Flores-Nina, C.Ss.R., Assoc. Pst.; Rev. Kenneth Gaddy, C.Ss.R., Assoc. Pst.; Rev. Leslie Mark Owen, C.Ss.R., Assoc. Pst.; Rev. John Kingsbury, C.Ss.R, In Res.;

St. Patrick - Bank St. & Broadway, Baltimore, MD 21231 www.shjbatlimore.com

St. John Neuman Residence - Stella Maris, 2300 Dulaney Valley Rd., Timonium, MD 21093 t) 410-427-7841 secprovince@redemptorists.net Rev. John Harrison, C.Ss.R., Admin.; Rev. Jack Jason Fiske, C.Ss.R., Asst. Supt.; Rev. Thomas Barrett, C.Ss.R.; Rev. John Bauer, C.Ss.R.; Rev. James Brennan, C.Ss.R.; Rev. Andrew Carr, C.Ss.R.; Bro. Bernard Colleran, C.Ss.R.; Rev. John Gauci, C.Ss.R.; Rev. Carl Hoegerl, C.Ss.R.; Rev. Timothy Keating, C.Ss.R.; Rev. John Francis Murray, C.Ss.R.; Rev. Anthony Russo, C.Ss.R.; Rev. Thomas Sullivan, C.Ss.R.; Rev. Arthur Wendel, C.Ss.R.; Bro. DeSales Zimpfer, C.Ss.R.; Rev. Philip Cabasino, C.Ss.R.;

Sacred Heart of Mary - 6736 Youngstown Ave, Baltimore, MD 21222 t) 410-633-2828 office@shmstr.org www.shmstr.org Rev. John Harrison, C.Ss.R., Pst.;

Shrine of the Sacred Heart - 5800 Smith Ave., Baltimore, MD 21209; Mailing: 1701 Regent Rd., Baltimore, MD 21209 t) 410-466-6884 x14 (CRP); 410-466-6884 office@theshrine.org www.theshrine.org Rev. William A. Au, Pst.;

St. Thomas Aquinas - 1008 W. 37th St., Baltimore, MD 21211 t) 410-366-4488 thomasaquinas@archbalt.org www.acquinasbmore.org Rev. Michael Ciccone, O.P., Admin.;

St. Thomas More - 6806 McClean Blvd., Baltimore, MD 21234 t) 410-444-6500 stmore@archbalt.org www.churchstmore.net Rev. Jeffrey S. Dauses, Pst.;

Transfiguration Catholic Community - 775 W. Hamburg St., Baltimore, MD 21230 t) 410-685-5044 transfigbalt@archbalt.org www.transfigurationbalt.org Rev. Augustine Etemma Inwang, M.S.P. (Nigeria), Pst.;

St. Ursula - 8801 Harford Rd., Baltimore, MD 21234 t) 410-665-2111; 410-661-0600 tursula@archbalt.org www.stursulaparish.org See School Section for St. Ursula Catholic School Rev. Jason Worley, Pst.; Rev. Msgr. Jay O'Connor, In Res.; Sr. Joan Kelly, S.N.D., Pst. Assoc.;

St. Veronica - 804 Cherry Hill Rd., Baltimore, MD 21225 t) 410-355-7466 stveronicas@gmail.com www.josephites.org/parish/md/sv/ Rev. Stephen Ositimehin, Pst.;

St. Vincent de Paul - 120 N. Front St., Baltimore, MD 21202-4804 t) 410-962-5078 parishoffice@stvchurch.org www.stvchurch.org Rev. Raymond C. Chase, Pst.; Rev. Charles Canterna, In Res.;

St. Vincent de Paul Church Historic Trust, Inc. -

St. Wenceslaus - 2111 Ashland Ave., Baltimore, MD 21205 t) 410-675-7304 swenceslaus@archbalt.org www.stwenceslausbaltimore.org/ Rev. Xavier Edet, S.S.J., Pst.;

St. William of York - 600 Cooks Ln., Baltimore, MD 21229; Mailing: 5422 Old Frederick Rd., Baltimore, MD 21229 t) 410-744-2900 sagnes@archbalt.org www.saintsaw.org Rev. Isaac Makovo, Pst.;

BEL AIR

St. Margaret - 141 N. Hickory Ave., Bel Air, MD 21014 t) 410-838-4224 (CRP); 410-879-2670; 410-838-6969 receptionist@stmargaret.org www.stmargaret.org Rev. Msgr. Kevin T. Schenning, Pst.; Rev. Ferdinand Ezenwachi, Assoc. Pst.; Rev. Michael Rubeling, Assoc. Pst.;

St. Margaret School - (Grades PreK-8) 205 Hickory Ave., Bel Air, MD 21014 t) 410-879-1113 smsch@archbalt.org www.smsch.org Anna Shanahan, Prin.; Anne Askey, Asst. Prin., Middle School; Lauren Kimmel, Asst. Prin., Elementary;

St. Mary Magdalen - 1716 Churchville Rd., Bel Air, MD 21015; Mailing: St. Margaret Parish, 141 Hickory Ave, Bel Air, MD 21014

BOONSBORO

St. James Boonsboro - 121 N. Main St., Boonsboro, MD 21713 t) 301-432-2887 www.cpswc.org Rev. John J. Jicha, Pst.; Rev. Jaime Garcia-Vazquez, Assoc. Pst.;

BRUNSWICK

St. Francis of Assisi - 113 First Ave., Brunswick, MD 21716 t) 301-473-4800 www.thepastorate.com Rev. Msgr. Robert J. Jaskot, Pst.;

St. Mary's - 4231 Catholic Church Rd., Petersville, MD 21758 t) (301) 473-4800

CATONSVILLE

St. Mark - 30 Melvin Ave., Catonsville, MD 21228 t) 410-744-6560 smcatons@archbalt.org www.stmarkchurch-catonsville.org Rev. Santhosh George, O.SS.T., Pst.; Rev. Tom Dymowski, O.SS.T., In Res.; Rev. Albert Michael Anuszewski, O.SS.T., In Res.;

St. Mark School - (Grades PreK-8) 26 Melvin Ave., Baltimore, MD 21228 t) (410) 744-6560 x2 info@stmark-school.org www.stmark-school.org Stephanie Rattell, Prin.; Terry Ferro, Asst. Prin.;

Our Lady of the Angels Catholic Community - 711 Maiden Choice Ln., Catonsville, MD 21228 t) 410-247-4779 llarrivee@archbalt.org Rev. Leo J. Larrivee, P.S.S., Pst.; Sr. Eileen McKeever, S.S.N.D., Pst. Assoc.;

CLARKSVILLE

St. Louis - 12500 Clarksville Pike, Clarksville, MD 21029 t) 410-531-6688 (CRP); 410-531-6040 www.stlouisparish.org Rev. Michael DeAscanis, Pst.; Rev. Kenneth Lukong, Assoc. Pst.;

St. Louis School - (Grades PreK-8) t) 410-531-6664 stlouisschool@stlouisparish.org www.stlouisparish.org/school Deborah Thomas, Prin.; Mary Ewachiw, Asst. Prin.;

COCKEYSVILLE

St. Joseph - 101 Church Ln., Cockeysville, MD 21030 t) 410-683-0600 www.sjpmd.org Rev. Msgr. Richard B. Hilgartner, Pst.; Rev. David Ray, Assoc. Pst.;

St. Joseph School - (Grades PreK-8) 105 Church Ln., Cockeysville, MD 21030 t) (410) 683-0600 www.sjpray.org Maggie Dates, Prin.; Janine Paetow, Asst. Prin.;

COLUMBIA

St. John the Evangelist - 10431 Twin Rivers Rd., Columbia, MD 21045 t) (410) 964-1425; 410-964-1440 (CRP) www.sjcolumbia.org Rev. Gerard J. Bowen, Pst.; Rev. Hilario Avendano, Assoc. Pst.; Rev. Marc L. Lanoue, Assoc. Pst.;

CROFTON

St. Elizabeth Ann Seton - 1800 Seton Dr., Crofton, MD 21114 t) 410-721-5774 (CRP); 410-721-5770 setonparish@seaseton.org www.seaston.org Rev. Msgr. Richard W. Woy, Pst.;

CUMBERLAND

Our Lady of the Mountains, Roman Catholic Congregation, Inc. - 300 E. Oldtown Rd. Ste. 2, Cumberland, MD 21502 t) 301-724-0288 (CRP); 301-777-1750 olmcumberland@archbalt.org www.olmcumberland.org Rev. Gregory Chervenak, O.F.M.Cap., Pst.; Rev. John Daya, O.F.M. Cap., Senior Parochial Vicar; Rev. Mark Carter, O.F.M. Cap., Par. Vicar;

Bishop Walsh School - (Grades PreK-12) 700 Bishop Walsh Rd., Cumberland, MD 21502 t) 301-724-5360 www.bishopwalsh.org Jennifer Flinn, Prin.; Joseph Carter, Pres.;

DAVIDSONVILLE

Holy Family - 826 W. Central Ave., Davidsonville, MD 21035-0130; Mailing: P.O. Box 130, Davidsonville, MD 21035-0130 t) 301-261-7399 www.holyfamilychurch.com Rev. Michael J. Jendrek, Pst.;

EDGEMERE

St. Luke - 7517 N. Point Rd., Edgemere, MD 21219-1499; Mailing: 1727 Lynch Rd., Baltimore, MD 21222 t) (410) 284-6600 stlukedgemere@yahoo.com www.olhstchurch.com Rev. Kevin A. Mueller, Pst.; Rev. Gregory Rapisarda, Assoc. Pst.;

EDGEWATER

Our Lady of Perpetual Help - 515 Loch Haven Rd., Edgewater, MD 21037 t) 443-203-1002 secretary@olph.net www.olph.net Rev. Richard Gray, Pst.;

EDGEWOOD

Prince of Peace - 2600 Willoughby Beach Rd., Edgewood, MD 21040-3412 t) 410-679-5912 princeofpeaceedgewood@archbalt.org www.princeofpeaceedgewoodmd.com Rev. John Martinez, Admin.;

ELKRIDGE

Catholic Community of Ascension and St. Augustine Roman Catholic Congregation, Inc. - 5976 Old Washington Rd., Elkridge, MD 21075 t) 410-242-2292; 410-796-1520 www.ccasta.org Church of the Ascension, Halethorpe (1913); St. Augustine Church, Elkridge (1844) See School Section for St. Augustine Catholic School Rev. Dale Picarella, Pst.;

ELLICOTT CITY

Our Lady of Perpetual Help - 4795 Ilchester Rd., Ellicott City, MD 21043-6898 t) 410-747-0131 (CRP); 410-747-4334 olphparish@archbalt.org www.olphparish.org Rev. Michael S. Triplett, Pst.; Rev. Anthony Abiamiri, Assoc. Pst.;

Our Lady of Perpetual Help School - (Grades PreK-8) 4801 Ilchester Rd., Elliott City, MD 21043 t) 410-744-4251 www.olphschool.org Tracy Underwood, Prin.;

St. Paul - 3755 St. Paul St., Ellicott City, MD 21043 t) 410-465-1670 office@stpaulec.org www.stpaulec.org Rev. Msgr. John A. Dietzenbach, Pst.; Rev. Scott Kady, Assoc. Pst.;

Resurrection - 3175 Paulskirk Dr., Ellicott City, MD 21042 t) 410-461-9111 x221 (CRP); 410-461-9112 www.resurrectionmd.org Rev. Msgr. John A. Dietzenbach, Pst.; Rev. Scott Kady, Assoc. Pst.;

Resurrection/St. Paul - (Grades PreK-8) 3155

Paulskirk Dr., Ellicott City, MD 21042-2698 t) (410) 461-9111 x214 www.resstpaul.org Ryan Hellem, Prin.;

EMMITSBURG

St. Anthony Shrine - 16150 St. Anthony Rd., Emmitsburg, MD 21727 t) 301-271-4099 (CRP); 301-447-2367 saolmc@archbalt.org www.sasolmc.org Rev. Alberto Barattero, IVE, Pst.; Rev. Andrés Ayala, IVE, Assoc. Pst.;

St. Joseph - 100 N. Seton Ave., Emmitsburg, MD 21727; Mailing: 47 DePaul St., P.O. Box 376, Emmitsburg, MD 21727 t) 301-447-2326 stjosephemmitsburg@comcast.net www.stjosephemmitsburg.org Rev. Alberto Barattero, IVE, Pst.; Rev. Andrés Ayala, IVE, Assoc. Pst.;

ESSEX

Our Lady of Mount Carmel - 1704 Old Eastern Ave., Essex, MD 21221 t) 410-686-4972 www.olmcessex.org See School Section for OLMC High School and OLMC Elementary School Rev. Msgr. Robert L. Hartnett, Pst.; Rev. Ernest P. Udoh, Assoc. Pastor;

FALLSTON

St. Mark - 2407 Laurel Brook Rd., Fallston, MD 21047 t) 410-879-1706 (CRP); 443-299-6489 parishoffice@saintmarkfallston.org www.saintmarkfallston.org Rev. Michael Foppiano, Pst.; Rev. William P. Foley, In Res.;

FOREST HILL

St. Ignatius - 533 E. Jarrettsville Rd., Forest Hill, MD 21050 t) 410-879-9390 (CRP); 410-879-1926 stignatiushickory@archbalt.org www.stignatiushickory.org Rev. Msgr. James Barker, Pst.; Rev. Peter Kiamo-oh, Assoc. Pst.; Rev. Roque G. Lim, In Res.; Rev. Stephen Sutton, In Res.;

FREDERICK

St. John the Evangelist - 112 E. Second St., Frederick, MD 21701 t) 301-662-6722 (CRP); 301-662-8288 parish@stjohn-frederick.org www.stjohn-frederick.org Rev. John A. Williamson, Pst.; Rev. Matthew DeFusco, Assoc. Pst.; Rev. Angel A. Marrero, Assoc. Pst.;

St. Joseph-on-Carrollton Manor - 5843 Manor Woods Rd., Frederick, MD 21717 t) 301-663-0907; 301-663-0907 x12 (CRP) office@sjcmmd.org www.sjcmmd.org Rev. John A. Williamson, Pst.; Rev. Matthew DeFusco, Assoc. Pst.; Rev. Angel A. Marrero, Assoc. Pst.; Rev. Lawrence K. Frazier, Pastor Emer.;

St. Katharine Drexel - 8428 Opossumtown Pike, Frederick, MD 21702 t) 301-360-9581 stkatharinedrexel@saintdrexel.org www.saintdrexel.org Rev. Keith W. Boisvert, Pst.;

FROSTBURG

Divine Mercy Parish - 44 E. Main St., Frostburg, MD 21532 t) 301-689-6767 divinemercy@archbalt.org www.divinemercymd.org St. Ann, Grantsville (1873); St. Gabriel, Barton (1862); St. Joseph, Midland (1891); St. Michael, Frostburg (1852); St. Peter, Westernport (1857) Rev. Edward S. Hendricks, Pst.; Rev. Eric Gauchat, O.F.M.Cap., Sacramental Min. & Health Care Min.;

FULTON

St. Francis of Assisi - 8300 Old Columbia Rd., Fulton, MD 20759 t) 410-792-0470 www.instrumentofpeace.org Rev. Michael DeAscanis, Pst.; Rev. Kenneth Lukong, Assoc. Pst.;

GLEN BURNIE

Christ the King Roman Catholic Congregation, Inc. - 7436 Baltimore-Annapolis Blvd., Glen Burnie, MD 20161; Mailing: 126 Dorsey Rd., Glen Burnie, MD 21061 t) 410-766-5070 info@ctkgb.org www.ctkgbandstb.org Rev. Austin Murphy, Pst.; Rev. Vincent Arisukwu, Assoc. Pst.; Rev. Robert Katafiasz, Assoc. Pst.; Rev. Diego Rivera, Assoc. Pst.;

GLYNDON

Sacred Heart - 65 Sacred Heart Ln., Glyndon, MD 21071-3672; Mailing: P.O. Box 3672, Reisterstown, MD 21136 t) 410-833-1696 parish@shgparish.org www.shgparish.org Rev. Gerard C. Francik, Pst.; Rev. Zachary Crowley, Assoc. Pst.; Rev. Leandro Fazolini, S.F., Assoc. Pst.;

Sacred Heart School - (Grades PreK-8) 63 Sacred Heart Ln., Glyndon, MD 21071-3672 t) 410-833-0857 info@shgschool.org www.shgschool.org John Keeley, Prin.; Amy Belz, Asst. Prin.; Lauren Noll, Asst. Prin., Middle School;

HAGERSTOWN

St. Ann - 1525 Oak Hill Ave., Hagerstown, MD 21742 t) 301-733-0410 x20 (CRP); 301-733-0410 church@stannchurch.com www.stannchurch.com Rev. Msgr. J. Bruce Jarboe, Pst.;

St. Joseph - 17630 Virginia Ave., Hagerstown, MD 21740 t) 301-790-1610 (CRP); 301-797-9445 www.cpswc.org Rev. John J. Jicha, Pst.; Rev. Jaime Garcia-Vazquez, Assoc. Pst.;

St. Mary - 224 W. Washington St., Hagerstown, MD 21740 t) 301-739-0390 x129 (CRP); 301-739-0390 x110 (Office) church@saintmarysonline.org www.saintmarysonline.org Rev. Ernest W. Cibelli, Pst.;

St. Mary School - (Grades PreK-8) 218 Washington St., Hagertown, MD 21740 t) 301-733-1184 www.stmarycatholicschool.org Michelle Smentanick, Prin.;

HANCOCK

St. Peter's - 16 E. High St., Hancock, MD 21750 t) 301-678-6339 www.stpeterpatrick.org Rev. John J. Lombardi, Pst.;

St. Patrick's - 12517 St. Patrick Rd., S.E., Little Orleans, MD 21766; Mailing: 16 E. High St., Hancock, MD 21750 t) 301-678-6336

HANOVER

St. Lawrence Martyr - 7850 Parkside Blvd., Hanover, MD 21076 t) 410-799-7790 (CRP); 410-799-1970 office@saintlawrencemartyr.org www.saintlawrencemartyr.org Rev. Victor J. Scocco, O.SS.T., Pst.; Rev. José Naralely, O.SS.T., Assoc. Pst.;

HAVRE DE GRACE

St. Patrick's - 615 Congress Ave., Havre de Grace, MD 21078 t) 410-939-2525 sphgrace@archbalt.org www.stpatrickhdg.org Rev. Francis Ouma, Admin.;

HUNT VALLEY

Catholic Community of St. Francis Xavier - 13717 Cuba Rd., Hunt Valley, MD 21030; Mailing: P.O. Box 407, Hunt Valley, MD 21030 t) 410-785-0356 info@ccfx.org www.ccsfx.org Rev. J. Kevin Farmer, Pst.;

HYDES

St. John the Evangelist-Long Green Valley - 13305 Long Green Pike, Hydes, MD 21082 t) 410-592-6206 office@sjehydes.org www.sjehydes.org Rev. Peter Literal, Pst.;

IJAMSVILLE

St. Ignatius of Loyola - 4103 Prices Distillery Rd., Ijamsville, MD 21754 t) 301-695-8845 www.e-stignatius.org Rev. Patrick M. Carrion, Pst.;

JOPPA

Church of the Holy Spirit - 540 Joppa Farm Rd., Joppa, MD 21085 t) 410-679-5912 (CRP); (410) 593-7162 hspiritchurch@comcast.net www.holyspiritjoppa.org Rev. George Gannon, Pst.; Rev. Maurice Sunde Afor, Assoc. Pastor; Rev. Samuel V. Young, Assoc. Pastor;

KINGSVILLE

St. Stephen - 8030 Bradshaw Rd., Kingsville, MD 21087 t) 410-592-7071 ststephen@archbalt.org www.ssparish.org Rev. George Gannon, Pst.; Rev. Samuel V. Young, Assoc. Pst.; Rev. Maurice Sunde Afor, Assoc. Pst.;

St. Stephen School - (Grades PreK-8) 8028 Bradshaw Rd., Kingsville, MD 21087 t) 410-592-7617 info@ssschool.org www.ssschool.org Marianne Kozlowski, Prin.; Deborah Liberto, Asst. Prin.;

LANSDOWNE

St. Clement - 2700 Washington Ave., Lansdowne, MD 21227 t) 410-242-1025 stclementoffice@archbalt.org www.stclementandstphilipneripastorate.org Rev. Andrew D. Aaron, Pst.; Rev. Lawrence Adamczyk, Assoc. Pst.; Rev. Claudio Piccolongo, Assoc. Pastor;

LAUREL

Resurrection of Our Lord - 8402 Brock Bridge Rd., Laurel, MD 20724 t) 301-498-9803 (CRP); 410-792-7982 www.roollaurel.org Rev. Victor J. Scocco, O.SS.T., Pst.; Rev. José Naralely, O.SS.T., Assoc. Pst.; Rev. Thomas J. Burke, O.SS.T., In Res.; Rev. William J. Moorman, O.SS.T., In Res.;

LINTHICUM HEIGHTS

St. Philip Neri - 6405 S. Orchard Rd., Linthicum Heights, MD 21090-2628 t) 410-859-0571 events@st.philip-neri.org www.saintphilipnerichurch.org Rev. Andrew D. Aaron, Pst.; Rev. Lawrence Adamczyk, Assoc. Pst.;

St. Philip Neri School - (Grades PreK-8) 6401 Orchard Rd., Linthicum Heights, MD 21090 t) 410-859-1212 spnschool@archbalt.org www.st.philip-neri.org Kate Daley, Prin.;

MANCHESTER

St. Bartholomew - 2930 Hanover Pike, Manchester, MD 21102; Mailing: 3071 Park Ave, Box 448, Manchester, MD 21102-0448 t) 410-239-8881 stbartholomewmanchester.org/ Rev. J. Collin Poston, Pst.;

MIDDLE RIVER

Our Lady, Queen of Peace - 10003 Bird River Rd., Middle River, MD 21220 t) 410-686-3085 x120 (CRP); 410-686-3085 qpeace@archbalt.org www.olqpmd.org Rev. Patrick E. Besel, Pst.; Rev. Gene Nickol, In Res.;

MIDDLETOWN

Holy Family Catholic Community - 7321 Burkittsville Rd., Middletown, MD 21769 t) 301-473-4800 info@hfccmd.org www.thepastorate.com Rev. Msgr. Robert J. Jaskot, Pst.;

MILLERSVILLE

Our Lady of the Fields - 1070 Cecil Ave. S., Millersville, MD 21108 t) 410-923-7060; 410-923-2195 (CRP) info@olfparish.com www.ourladyofthefields.org Rev. John B. Ward, Pst.; Rev. Paul Breczinski, Assoc. Pst.;

MOUNT AIRY

St. Michael - 1125 St. Michael's Rd., Mount Airy, MD 21771-3235 t) 410-489-7667 smpoplar@archbalt.org www.smpschurch.org Rev. Paul Sparklin, Pst.;

OAKLAND

St. Peter the Apostle - 208 S. Fourth St., Oakland, MD 21550 t) 301-334-2202 www.garrettstpeter.com Rev. Thomas Gills, Pst.; Bro. Arthur Wolf, OCD, Pst. Assoc.;

St. Peter at the Lake - 1140 Mosser Rd., Mc Henry, MD 21541 www.garrettstpeter.org

ODENTON

St. Joseph, Odenton - 1283 Odenton Rd., Odenton, MD 21113 t) 410-674-9238 info@stjosephodenton.org www.stjosephodenton.org Rev. James P. Kiesel, Pst.;

PARKTON

Our Lady of Grace - 18310 Middletown Rd., Parkton, MD 21120 t) 410-329-6826 www.ourladygrace.org Our Lady of Grace Preschool Rev. J. Kevin Farmer, Pst.;

PASADENA

St. Jane Frances de Chantal - 8499 Virginia Ave., Pasadena, MD 21122-3097 t) 410-437-4727 (CRP); 410-255-4646 ccummings@archbalt.org www.stjane.org Rev. Stephen E. Hook, Pst.; Rev. James Bors, Assoc. Pst.;

St. Jane Frances de Chantal School - (Grades PreK-8513 Saint Jane Dr., Pasadena, MD 21122 t) 410-255-4750 moreilly@stjaneschool.org www.stjaneschool.org Maureen O'Reilly, Dir.;

Our Lady of the Chesapeake - 8325 Ventnor Rd., Pasadena, MD 21122 t) 410-255-3677 info@olchesapeake.org www.olchesapeake.org Rev. Stephen E. Hook, Pst.; Rev. James Bors, Assoc. Pst.;

PIKESVILLE

St. Charles Borromeo - 101 Church Ln., Pikesville, MD 21208 t) 410-486-5400 charlesst@comcast.net www.ourstcharles.org Rev. Canisius T. Tah, Pst.; Rev. Thomas R. Malia, Assisting Clergy;

PYLESVILLE

St. Mary - 1021 St. Mary's Rd., Pylesville, MD 21132 t) 410-838-7471 smpylesv@archbalt.org www.stmaryspylesville.org Dcn. Phillip Seneschal, Admin.;

RANDALLSTOWN

Holy Family - 9531 Liberty Rd., Randallstown, MD 21133 t) 410-922-3800

holyfamilyrandallstown@archbalt.org www.holyfamilyrandallstown.org Rev. Raymond L. Harris Jr., Pst.;

SEVERN

St. Bernadette - 801 Stevenson Rd., Severn, MD 21144 t) 410-969-2786 (CRP); 410-969-2783 secretary@stbernadette.org www.stbernadette.org Rev. T. Austin Murphy Jr., Pst.; Rev. Robert Katafiasz, Assoc. Pst.; Rev. Diego Rivera, Assoc. Pst.; Rev. Vincent Arisukwu, Assoc. Pst.;

SEVERNA PARK

St. John the Evangelist - 689 Ritchie Hwy., S.E., Severna Park, MD 21146 t) 410-647-4892 (CRP); 410-647-4884 church@stjohnsp.org www.stjohnsp.org Rev. Erik J. Arnold, Pst.; Rev. Evan Ponton, Assoc. Pst.;

St. John the Evangelist School - (Grades PreK-8) 669 Ritchie Hwy., Severna Park, MD 21146 t) 410-647-2283 cbuckstaff@stjohnsp.org www.stjohnspschool.org J. Casey Buckstaff, Prin.;

SYKESVILLE

St. Joseph - 915 Liberty Rd., Sykesville, MD 21784 t) 410-920-9102 (CRP); 443-920-9191 parishoffice@saintjoseph.cc www.saintjoseph.cc Rev. John Worgul, Pst.; Rev. Armando Alejandro, Assoc. Pst.;

TANEYTOWN

St. Joseph - 44 Frederick St., Taneytown, MD 21787 t) 410-876-8108 (Baltimore Line); 410-756-2500 sjtaney@archbalt.org www.stjosephtaneytown.org Rev. Mark S. Bialek, Pst.; Rev. Leandro Fazolini, S.F., Assoc. Pst.; Rev. Rey D Landicho, Assoc. Pst.; Rev. Jude Okoye, Assoc. Pst.; Rev. Msgr. Martin E. Feild, Pastor Emer.;

THURMONT

Our Lady of Mount Carmel - 103 N. Church St., Thurmont, MD 21788; Mailing: 16150 Saint Anthonys Rd., Emmitsburg, MD 21727 t) 301-447-2367 saolmc@archbalt.org www.sasolmc.org Rev. Alberto Barattero, IVE, Pst.; Rev. Andrés Ayala, IVE, Assoc. Pastor;

TIMONIUM

Church of the Nativity - 20 E. Ridgely Rd., Timonium, MD 21093 t) 410-252-6080 welcome@churchnativity.com www.churchnativity.org Rev. Michael White, Pst.;

TOWSON

Church of the Immaculate Conception - 200 Ware Ave., Towson, MD 21204 t) 410-427-4700 www.theimmaculate.org Rev. Msgr. James P. Farmer, Admin.; Rev. Jeremy Smith, Assoc. Pst.; Rev. Msgr. Richard H. Tillman, In Res.;

Church of the Immaculate Conception School - (Grades PreK-8) 112 Ware Ave., Towson, MD 21204 t) 410-427-4801 www.theics.org Heather Cucuzzella, Prin.; Lisa Metzbower, Asst. Prin.;

UNION BRIDGE

St. Peter the Apostle - 9190 Church St., Union Bridge, MD 21791 t) 301-898-5111 www.stpeters-libertytown.org Rev. Charles M. Wible, Pst.;

WALKERSVILLE

St. Timothy - 8651 Briggs Ford Rd., Walkersville, MD 21793 t) 301-845-8043 ainttimothy@archbalt.org www.stimothys.org Rev. Juan Vazquez-Rubio, O.SS.T., Pst.;

WEST RIVER

Our Lady of Sorrows - 101 Owensville Rd., West River, MD 20778 t) 410-867-1941 (CRP); 410-867-2059 parishoffice@olos.us www.olos.us Rev. Richard Gray, Pst.;

WESTMINSTER

St. John - 43 Monroe St., Westminster, MD 21157 t) 410-848-8443 (CRP); 410-848-4744 sjwest@archbalt.org www.sjwest.org See School Section for St. John Catholic School Rev. Mark S. Bialek, Pst.; Rev. Leandro Fazolini, S.F., Assoc. Pst.; Rev. Rey D Landicho, Assoc. Pst.; Rev. Jude Okoye, Assoc. Pst.;

WILLIAMSPORT

St. Augustine - 32 E. Potomac St., Williamsport, MD 21795 t) 301-223-7959 jjicha@archbalt.org www.cpswc.org Rev. John J. Jicha, Pst.; Rev. Jaime Garcia-Vazquez, Assoc. Pst.;

WINDSOR MILL

St. Gabriel - 6950 Dogwood Rd., Windsor Mill, MD 21244-2697 t) 410-298-8888 www.stgabrielch.org Formerly St. Lawrence and Our Lady of Perpetual Help, Woodlawn. Rev. Msgr. Thomas L. Phillips, Pst.; Sr. Sonia Marie Fernandez, DRE;

WOODSTOCK

St. Alphonsus Rodriguez - 10800 Old Court Rd., Woodstock, MD 21163-1107 t) 410-461-5267 dee@stalchurch.org www.stalchurch.org Rev. Brian O'Donnell, S.J., Sacr. Min.; Dee Papania, Pastoral Life Dir.;

SCHOOLS: PRESCHOOL THRU HIGH SCHOOL

SCHOOLS

STATE OF MARYLAND

BALTIMORE

St. Agnes Roman Catholic Elementary School - (PAR) (Grades PreK-8) 603 St. Agnes Ln., Baltimore, MD 21229 t) 410-747-4070 www.stagnesschool.net Dr. Rahshida Wilson, Prin.;

Archbishop Borders School - (DIO) (Grades PreK-8) 3500 Foster Ave., Baltimore, MD 21224 t) 410-276-6534 principal@abbschool.com www.abbschool.com Language Immersion School Partner Language Spanish Valerie Sandoval, Prin.;

Cardinal Shehan School - (PAR) (Grades PreK-8) 5407 Loch Raven Blvd., Baltimore, MD 21239-2996 t) 410-433-2775 www.cardinalshehanschool.org Serving St. Matthew and St. Thomas More Parishes. Dr. Anika Logan, Prin.; Kevin Coons, Asst. Prin.;

St. Elizabeth School, Inc. - (Grades 1-12) 801 Argonne Dr., Baltimore, MD 21218-1998 t) 410-889-5054 info@stelizabeth-school.org www.stelizabeth-school.org Students with special needs. Michael Thorne, Pres.; Erin Upton, Prin.; Stds.: 134; Lay Tchrs.: 20

Holy Angels Catholic School, Inc. - (PAR) (Grades PreK-8) 1201 S. Caton Ave., Baltimore, MD 21227 t) 443-602-3200 www.hacschool.org Dr. Diane L. Barr, Resident Agent;

St. Ignatius Loyola Academy - (PRV) (Grades 5-8) 300 E. Gittings St., Baltimore, MD 21230 t) 410-539-8268 giving@saintignatius.org www.saintignatius.org Boys from low income families. Matt Ormiston, Prin.; John Ciccone, Pres.; Mike Conroy, Asst. Prin.; Stds.: 118

St. James and St. John School - (PAR) (Grades PreK-8) 1012 Somerset St., Baltimore, MD 21202 t) 410-342-3222 kcollins@ssjjschool.org www.ssjjschool.org Dr. Karmen Collins, Prin.;

The Loyola School, Inc. - (PRV) (Grades PreSchool-4) 801 Saint Paul St., Baltimore, MD 21202 t) 443-563-2589 office@loyolaearly.org www.loyolaschoolbaltimore.org Greta Rutstein, Prin.; Erica Carroll Meadows, Dir.; Rev. William Watters, S.J., Pres.; Stds.: 63; Lay Tchrs.: 16

Mother Mary Lange Catholic School, Inc. - 200 N. Martin Luther King Jr. Blvd., Baltimore, MD 21201 t) 414-884-9800 www.mmlcs.org Alisha Jordan, Prin.;

Mother Seton Academy - (PRV) (Grades 6-8) 2215 Greenmont Ave., Baltimore, MD 21218-5421 t) 410-563-2833 contact@mothersetonacademy.org www.mothersetonacademy.org Innovative Middle School for Inner City Youth. Dr. Gregory Sucre, Prin.; Sr. Margaret (Peggy) Juskelis, S.S.N.D., Pres.;

Sisters Academy of Baltimore, Inc. - (PRV) (Grades 5-8) 139 First Ave., Baltimore, MD 21227 t) 410-242-1212 ddowling@sistersacademy.org www.sistersacademy.org Dr. Jeanne Dolamore, Prin.; Sr. Delia Dowling, S.S.N.D., Pres.;

St. Ursula Roman Catholic Elementary School - (DIO) (Grades PreK-8) 8900 Harford Rd., Baltimore, MD 21234-4193 t) 410-665-3533 susoffice@stursula.org www.stursula.org Lisa Madgar, Prin.;

ELKRIDGE

St. Augustine School, Inc. - (Grades PreK-8) 5990 Old Washington Rd., Elkridge, MD 21075 t) 410-796-3040 www.staug-md.org Joseph Miller, Prin.;

ELLICOTT CITY

Resurrection St. Paul School, Inc. - (PAR) (Grades PreK-8) 3155 Paulskirk Dr., Ellicott City, MD 21042 t) 410-461-9111 www.resstpaul.org Ryan Hellem, Prin.;

Trinity School - (PRV) (Grades PreK-8) 4985 Ilchester Rd., Ellicott City, MD 21043 t) 410-744-1524 admintrin@trinityschoolmd.org www.trinityschoolmd.org K. Marguerite Conley, Prin.;

EMMITSBURG

Mother Seton School - (PRV) (Grades PreK-8) 100 Creamery Rd., Emmitsburg, MD 21727 t) 301-447-3161 office@mothersetonschool.org www.mothersetonschool.org Dr. Kathleen Kilty, Prin.; Stds.: 335; Sr. Tchrs.: 1; Lay Tchrs.: 21

ESSEX

Our Lady of Mount Carmel Catholic School - (DIO) (Grades PreK-12) 1702 Old Eastern Ave., Essex, MD 21221 t) 410-686-0859 olmchsch@archbalt.org www.olmcmd.org Ryan Kloetzer, Prin.; Larry Callahan, Pres.;

FREDERICK

St. John Regional Catholic School - (PAR) (Grades PreK-8) 8414 Opossumtown Pike, Frederick, MD 21702 t) 301-662-6722 www.sjrcs.org Dr. Annette Jones, Prin.; Kim Hanner, Asst. Prin.;

GAMBRILLS

School of the Incarnation, Inc. - (DIO) (Grades PreK-8) 2601 Symphony Ln., Gambrills, MD 21054 t) 410-519-2285 www.schooloftheincarnation.org Interparish school. Parishes: Our Lady of the Fields, Millersville; St. Joseph, Odenton; Our Lady Nancy Baker, Prin.; Kristin Jacobs, Asst. Prin.; Cameron Stehle, Asst. Prin.;

GLEN BURNIE

Monsignor Slade Catholic School - (PAR) (Grades PreK-8) 120 Dorsey Rd., Glen Burnie, MD 21061 t) 410-766-7130 mscs@msladeschool.com www.msladeschool.com Serving Glen Burnie, Pasadena, Hanover and Severn Parishes. Alexa A. Cox, Prin.;

HYDES

St. John the Evangelist School (Long Green Valley) - (DIO) (Grades PreK-8) 13311 Long Green Pike, Hydes, MD 21082 t) 410-592-9585 school@stjohnhydes.org www.stjohnschoollgv.org Suzanne Thomas, Prin.;

KINGSVILLE

St. Stephen School - (PAR) (Grades PreK-8) 8028 Bradshaw Rd., Kingsville, MD 21087-1807 t) 410-592-7617 info@ssschool.org www.ssschool.org Dr. Terrance Golden, Prin.; Susan Tobias, Asst. Prin.;

LINTHICUM HEIGHTS

St. Philip Neri School, Inc. - (Grades PreK-8) 6401 S. Orchard Rd., Linthicum Heights, MD 21090 t) 410-859-1212 info@st.philip-neri.org www.st.philip-neri.org Catherine Daley, Prin.;

PARKTON

Our Lady of Grace Preschool - (DIO) 18310 Middletown Rd., Parkton, MD 21120 t) 410-329-6956 slake@ourladygrace.org www.olgs.org Sally Lake, Dir.;

TIMONIUM

Villa Maria School at Dulaney Valley - 2300 Dulaney Valley Rd., Timonium, MD 21093 t) 667-600-3100 bhines@cc-md.org www.catholiccharities-md.org (Timonium Campus), Non-public special education for children with emotional/multiple disabilities, ages 3-15. Brenda Hines, Prin.;

WESTMINSTER

St. John School (Westminster) Roman Catholic Elementary School - (Grades PreK-8) 45 Monroe St., Westminster, MD 21157 t) 410-848-7455 jtolj@sjwestschool.org www.sjwestschool.org Jesse

Read, Prin.;

HIGH SCHOOLS

STATE OF MARYLAND

BALTIMORE

Archbishop Curley High School - (DIO) (Grades 9-12) 3701 Sinclair Ln., Baltimore, MD 21213 t) 410-485-5000 dgrzymski@archbishopcurley.org www.archbishopcurley.org Administered by Order of Friars Minor Conventual, Our Lady of Angels Province (USA). Rev. Christopher Dudek, O.F.M.Conv., Campus Min.; Rev. Donald Grzymski, O.F.M.Conv., Pres.; Jeremy Joseph, Prin.;

Calvert Hall - (PRV) (Grades 9-12) 8102 La Salle Rd., Baltimore, MD 21286 t) 410-825-4266 communications@calverthall.com www.calverthall.com Conducted by the Brothers of the Christian Schools (F.S.C.). Charles Stembler, Prin.; Bro. John Kane, F.S.C., Pres.; Stds.: 1,183; Bro. Tchrs.: 5; Lay Tchrs.: 103

The Catholic High School of Baltimore - (PRV) 2800 Edison Hwy., Baltimore, MD 21213 t) 410-732-6200 tchs@thecatholichighschool.org www.thecatholichighschool.org The Sisters of St. Francis of Philadelphia. Dr. Barbara Nazelrod, Pres.; Lisa Wetzel, Prin.; Bob Wuenschel, Asst. Prin.; Karen Mitchell, Dean of Students; Stds.: 295; Sr. Tchrs.: 1; Lay Tchrs.: 29

Cristo Rey Jesuit High School (Baltimore Jesuit Educational Initiative Inc.) - (PRV) 420 S. Chester St., Baltimore, MD 21231 t) 410-727-3255 www.cristoreybalt.org Walter Reap, Prin.; Dr. William Heiser, Pres.;

St. Frances Academy - (PRV) 501 E. Chase St., Baltimore, MD 21202 t) 410-539-5794 admissions@sfacademy.org www.sfacademy.org (Coed) Oblate Sisters of Providence. Melissa D'Adamo, Assoc. Head of School;

Mercy High School - (PRV) 1300 E. Northern Pkwy., Baltimore, MD 21239-1998 t) 410-433-8880 mercy@mercyhighschool.com www.mercyhighschool.com Sisters of Mercy of the Americas. Kathryn Adelsberger, Prin.; Mary Beth Lennon, Pres.; Stds.: 445; Lay Tchrs.: 38

Mount de Sales Academy - (PRV) 700 Academy Rd., Baltimore, MD 21228 t) 410-744-8498 mdsa@mountdesales.org www.mountdesalesacademy.org Sr. Mary Raymond Thye, O.P., Prin.; Theresa Greene, Vice Prin., Academics;

Mt. St. Joseph College High School - (PRV) 4403 Frederick Ave., Baltimore, MD 21229 t) 410-644-3300 www.msjnet.edu Xaverian Brothers. Francisco M. Espinosa Jr., Prin.; George E. Andrews Jr., Pres.;

BEL AIR

The John Carroll School - (PRV) 703 E. Churchville Rd., Bel Air, MD 21014 t) 410-879-2480 www.johncarroll.org Carl Patton, Prin.; Steve DiBiagio, Pres.; Jake Hollin, Asst. Prin.; Mark Ramsey, Bd. Chair; Stds.: 726; Lay Tchrs.: 64

BUCKEYSTOWN

Saint John's Catholic Preparatory - (PRV) 3989 Buckeystown Pike, Buckeystown, MD 21717; Mailing: P.O. Box 909, Buckeystown, MD 21717 t) 301-662-4210 www.saintjohnsprep.org (Coed) Will Knotek, Prin.; Dr. Thomas Powell, Pres.; Rev. Michael McDermott, Chap.; Patrick Crowley, Chmn., Bd of Trustees;

CUMBERLAND

Bishop Walsh School - (DIO) (Grades PreK-12) 700 Bishop Walsh Rd., Cumberland, MD 21502 t) 301-724-5360 www.bishopwalsh.org School Sisters of Notre Dame. Jennifer Flinn, Prin.; Joseph Carter, Pres.;

ESSEX

Our Lady of Mount Carmel Catholic School - (DIO) (Grades PreK-12) 1706 Old Eastern Ave., Essex, MD 21221 t) 410-686-0859 www.olmcmd.org Christopher M. Ashby, Prin.; Lawrence Callahan, Pres.;

HAGERSTOWN

St. Maria Goretti High School - (DIO) 1535 Oak Hill Ave., Hagerstown, MD 21742 t) 301-739-4266 admissions@goretti.org www.goretti.org (Coed) Dr. Shannon Storch, Prin.; Dr. Joseph Padasak, Pres.;

LUTHERVILLE TIMONIUM

Maryvale Preparatory School - (PRV) (Grades 6-12) 11300 Falls Rd., Lutherville Timonium, MD 21093 t) 410-252-3366 www.maryvale.com (Girls School) Tracey H. Ford, Pres.;

SEVERN

Archbishop Spalding High School - (DIO) 8080 New Cut Rd., Severn, MD 21144 t) 410-969-9105 info@archbishopspalding.org www.archbishopspalding.org Kathleen K. Mahar, Pres.; Brian Kohler, Prin.;

TOWSON

Loyola Blakefield - (PRV) (Grades 6-12) 500 Chestnut Ave., Towson, MD 21204; Mailing: P.O. Box 6819, Baltimore, MD 21285-6819 t) 410-823-0601 communications@loyolablakefield.org www.loyolablakefield.org Anthony I. Day, Pres.; Brian Marana, Upper School Prin.; John O'Hara, Middle School Prin.;

Notre Dame Preparatory School, Inc. - (PRV) (Grades 6-12) 815 Hampton Ln., Towson, MD 21286 t) 410-825-0590 admissions@notredameprep.com www.notredameprep.com Sr. Patricia McCarron, S.S.N.D., Headmistress; Stds.: 813; Lay Tchrs.: 106

INSTITUTIONS LOCATED IN DIOCESE

CAMPUS MINISTRY / NEWMAN CENTERS [CAM]

BALTIMORE

Division Of Campus Ministry For Universities And Colleges - Archdiocese of Baltimore, 320 Cathedral St., Baltimore, MD 21201 t) 410-547-5372 youngchurch@archbalt.org www.archbalt.org/campus-ministry Craig Gould, Dir.;

Coppin State University - 3300 Clifton Ave., Baltimore, MD 21216 t) 410-624-3600

Frostburg State University - 130 S. Broadway, Frostburg, MD 21532 t) 240-284-2079 sharon.bogusz@archbalt.org Sharon Bogusz, Dir., Campus Min.;

Goucher College/Hood College/UMAB -

Johns Hopkins University - 2801 N. Charles St., Baltimore, MD 21218 t) 410-235-2294 pastor@philipandjames.org

Loyola University - 4501 N. Charles St., Baltimore, MD 21210 t) 410-617-2444 campusministry@loyola.edu Sean Bray, Dir., Campus Min.;

McDaniel College - 43 Monroe St., Westminster, MD 21157 t) 410-259-7425 pgallagher@sjwest.org Kenneth DeMoll, Campus Min.;

Morgan State University - 5401 Loch Raven Blvd., Baltimore, MD 21239 t) 410-547-5405

Mount St. Mary's University - 16300 Old Emmitsburg Rd., Emmitsburg, MD 21727 t) 301-447-5223 d.ruiz@msmary.edu Rev. Diego Ruiz, I.V.E., Chap.; Brendon Johnson, Dir., Campus Min.;

Notre Dame of Maryland University - 4701 N. Charles St., Baltimore, MD 21210 t) 410-532-5565 mkerber@ndm.edu Rev. Joseph L. Muth Jr., Chap.; Julia Campagna, Dir., Campus Min.;

Stevenson University - 65 Sacred Heart Ln., Glyndon, MD 21071-3672; Mailing: P.O. Box 3672, Glyndon, MD 21071-3672

Towson University - 7909 York Rd., Towson, MD 21204 t) 410-828-0622 mbuening@towson.edu Rev. Kevin B. Ewing, Chap.;

University of Maryland, Baltimore County (UMBC) - 4795 Ilchester Rd., Ellicott City, MD 21043 t) 410-242-0131 sotoole@olvictory.org; wkeown@olvictory.org Rev. William Keown, Chap.; Shannon O'Toole, Campus Min.;

CATHOLIC CHARITIES [CCH]

BALTIMORE

Associated Catholic Charities, Inc. (Catholic Charities) - 320 Cathedral St., 3rd Fl., Baltimore, MD 21201-4421 t) 667-600-2000 www.catholiccharities-md.org/ William J. McCarthy Jr., Exec. Dir.;

661 Corporation - 123 Main St., Baltimore, MD 21022 t) 443-519-2383 website

Alternative Spring Break - 228 W. Lexington St., Ste. 220, Baltimore, MD 21201-3432; Mailing: 123 Main St, Balitmore, MD 20122 t) 410-261-6774

St. Ann Adult Day Services - 3308 Benson Ave., Baltimore, MD 21227-1001 t) 667-600-2681

Anna's House - 607 N. Tollgate Rd., Bel Air, MD 21014-0088

Answers for the Aging - 3300 Benson Ave., Baltimore, MD 21227-1035 t) 667-600-2100; 888-502-7587

Associated Catholic Charities Inc. - 320 Cathedral St., Baltimore, MD 21201-4421 t) 410-547-5469 www.cc-md.org Rev. Gerald L. Brown, P.S.S., CEO; Erin Bolles, Dir.;

Associated Catholic Charities Inc. - 228 W. Lexington St., Baltimore, MD 21201-3443 t) 667-600-3337 www.cc-md.org Amy Collier, Dir., Commun. Svcs.;

Associated Catholic Charities Inc. - 2300 Dulaney Valley Rd., Timonium, MD 21093-4164 t) 410-252-4700 x128 www.cc-md.org Ezra Buchdahl, Admin., St. Vincent's Villa Svcs. for Children & Families;

Associated Catholic Charities Inc. -

Associated Catholic Charities Inc. - 2300 Dulaney Valley Rd., Timonium, MD 21093 t) 667-600-2231 www.cc-md.org Diane Polk, Chief HR Officer; Scott Becker, CFO;

Associated Catholic Charities Inc. - 3320 Benson Ave., Baltimore, MD 21227-1035 t) 667-600-3265 www.cc-md.org Zachary Richards, Dir.;

Associated Catholic Charities Inc. - 2600 Pot Spring Rd., Timonium, MD 21093-2732 t) 410-252-4000 x1601 www.cc-md.org Kevin Keegan, Dir.;

Baltimore City Child and Adolescent Response (Foster/Kinship Care Stabilization Program) - 1118 S. Light St., #200, Baltimore, MD 21230-4152 t) 410-727-4800

Baltimore City Regional Expanded School Mental Health/Early Childhood Mental Health Services - 6999 Reisterstown Rd., Baltimore, MD 21215 t) 410-585-0598

The Bethany Community, Inc. - 2300 Dulaney Valley Rd., Timmonium, MD 21093 t) 667-600-2280

Brief Strategic Family Therapy - 2600 Pot Spring Rd., Lutherville Timonium, MD 21093-2739 t) 410-252-4000

Caritas House Assisted Living - 3308 Benson Ave., Baltimore, MD 21227-1035 t) 667-600-2660 rrich@cc-md.org

Carroll County, Head Start and Early Head Start and PreK School - 255 Clifton Blvd., Ste. 101, Westminster, MD 21157-4785 t) 410-871-2450

Catholic Charities Head Start of Baltimore City - 915 Sterrett St., Baltimore, MD 21230-2502 t) 410-685-1700

Catholic Charities Senior Community Application/Information Requests - 2300 Dulaney Valley Rd., Timonium, MD 21093 t) 667-600-2280

***Catholic Charities Senior Community at Aberdeen** - 901 Barnett La., Aberdeen, MD 21001-1748 t) 667-600-2175

Catholic Charities Senior Community at Abingdon - 3001 St. Clair Dr., Abingdon, MD 21009-3225 t) 677-600-2170 Debbie Seigle, Contact;

***Catholic Charities Senior Community at Arundel Woods (Glen Burnie Senior Housing, Inc.)** - 403 W. Ordnance Rd., Glen Burnie, MD 21061-6448

t) 667-600-3160

Catholic Charities Senior Community at Basilica Place (The Catholic Charities Housing, Inc.) - 124 W. Franklin St., Baltimore, MD 21201-4576 t) 667-600-3300

***Catholic Charities Senior Community at Coursey Station (Coursey Station Apartments, Inc.)** - 200 First Ave., Lansdowne, MD 21227-3031 t) 667-600-3155

Catholic Charities Senior Community at DePaul House (DePaul House, Inc.) - 3300 Benson Ave., Baltimore, MD 21227-1030 t) 667-600-2684

***Catholic Charities Senior Community at Friendship Station (Odenton Senior Housing, Inc.)** - 1212 Odenton Rd., Odenton, MD 21113-1629 t) 667-600-3370

Catholic Charities Senior Community at Friendship Village - 1212 Odenton Rd., Odenton, MD 21113-1629 t) 667-600-3380

***Catholic Charities Senior Community at Holy Korean Martyrs (Woodlawn Senior Housing, Inc.)** - 5500 Lexington Rd., Woodlawn, MD 21207-5600 t) 667-600-3150

Catholic Charities Senior Community at Our Lady of Fatima I & II - 6424 E. Pratt St., Baltimore, MD 21224-2818 t) 667-600-3301 www.cc-md.org

***Catholic Charities Senior Community at Owings Mills New Town (Owings Mills Senior Community, Inc.)** - 9773 Groffs Mill Dr., Owings Mills, MD 21117-6005 t) 667-600-3180

***Catholic Charities Senior Community at Reister's Clearing** - 304 Cantata Ct., Reisterstown, MD 21136-6471 t) 667-600-2190

***Catholic Charities Senior Community at Reister's View** - 306 Cantata Ct., Reisterstown, MD 21136-6472 t) 667-600-2180

Catholic Charities Senior Community at St. Charles House (St. Charles House, Inc.) - 11 Church Ln., Pikesville, MD 21208-6607 t) 667-600-3185

***Catholic Charities Senior Community at St. Joachim House (St. Joachim House, Inc.)** - 3310 Benson Ave., Baltimore, MD 21227-1075 t) 667-600-2685

***Catholic Charities Senior Community at St. Luke's Place (St. Luke's Apartments, Inc.)** - 2825 Lodge Farm Rd., Edgemere, MD 21219-1347 t) 667-600-3661

***Catholic Charities Senior Community at Starner Hill Apartments (Backbone Housing, Inc.)** - 25 N. Pennsylvania Ave., Grantsville, MD 21536-1390 t) 301-895-5842

***Catholic Charities Senior Community at Trinity House Apartments (Trinity House Apartments, Inc.)** - 409 Virginia Ave., Towson, MD 21286-5372 t) 667-600-3733

Catholic Charities Senior Housing at St. Mark's - 19 Winters Ln., Catonsville, MD 21228-4499 t) 667-600-3675

Center for Family Services - International Adoptions - 2300 Dulaney Valley Rd., Timmonium, MD 21093 t) 410-659-4050

Center for Family Services - Pregnancy, Parenting and Domestic Adoption Svcs. - 2300 Dulaney Valley Rd., Timmonium, MD 21093 t) 410-659-4050

Center for Family Services - Treatment Foster Care - 2601 N. Howard St., Ste. 200, Baltimore, MD 21218-4979 t) 410-685-2363

Center for Family Services - Therapeutic Alternative Shelter Care (TASC) - 2601 N. Howard St., Ste. 200, Baltimore, MD 21218-4979 t) 410-685-2363

***Cherry Hill Town Center (Cherry Hill Town Center, Inc.)** - 634 Cherry Hill Rd., Baltimore, MD 21225-1229 t) 410-354-0167

The Children's Fund, Inc. - 320 Cathedral St., Baltimore, MD 21201 t) 410-547-5469

Christopher Place Employment Academy - 725 Fallsway, Baltimore, MD 21202-4147 t) 443-986-9000

Congregate Housing Services Program - 2300 Dulaney Valley Rd., Timonium, MD 21093 t) 667-600-2280

Early Childhood Mental Health Screening - 2600 Pot Spring Rd., Timonium, MD 21093-2739 t) 410-252-4700

Employment Services - 725 Fallsway, Baltimore, MD 21202-4147 t) 443-986-9000

Esperanza Center - 430 S. Broadway, Baltimore, MD 21231-2409 t) 676-600-2900 esperanzainfo@cc-md.org www.catholiccharities-md.org

Everall Gardens - 6100 Everall Ave., Baltimore, MD 21206-1946 t) 667-600-2395

Family Support Groups and Resource Center - 2600 Pot Spring Rd., Timonium, MD 21093-2739 t) 410-252-4000 x1663

Family Systems Navigator - 2600 Pot Spring Rd., Timonium, MD 21093-2739 t) 410-252-4700 x265

Francis X. Gallagher Services - 2520 Pot Spring Rd., Timonium, MD 21093-2730 t) 667-600-2520 www.catholiccharities-md.org Programs include vocational, adult medical day & residential services.

GreenHouse Residences at Stadium Place - 1010 E. 33rd St., Baltimore, MD 21218-3780 t) 410-554-9890 www.cc-md.org Susan Stone, Admin.;

Harford County, Early Head Start - 422 S. Stokes St., Havre De Grace, MD 21078 t) 410-526-1940

Head Start Mental Health Consultation (Baltimore City, Harford and Carroll Counties) - 6999 Reisterstown Rd., Baltimore, MD 21215-1492 t) 410-585-0598

Holden Hall - 761 W. Hamburg St., Baltimore, MD 21230-2535 t) 410-347-9830

Home-Based Respite Program (Cecil, Harford, Baltimore County & Baltimore City) - 2601 N. Howard St., 2nd Fl., Baltimore, MD 21218-4979 t) 410-685-2363

In-Home Intervention Services - 2601 N. Howard St., Baltimore, MD 21218-4979 t) 410-685-2362

Kessler Park - 4230 Hollins Ferry Rd., Lansdowne, MD 21227-3468 t) 667-600-3670

Kinship Care Family Support Groups - t) 410-252-4000 x1515

Kinship Care Systems Navigations - 2903 Dunleer Rd., Dundalk, MD 21222-5113 t) 410-252-4000 x1515

Lansdowne Therapeutic After School Program - 2700 Washington Ave., Baltimore, MD 21227-3115 t) 410-368-3984

Making All the Children Healthy (M.A.T.C.H.)

Mental Health Assessment - 2601 N. Howard St., Ste. 200, Baltimore, MD 21218-4979 t) 410-659-4050

Mental Health Counseling for Deaf Clients (Fallstaff Outpatient Mental Health Clinic) - 6999 Resiterstown Rd., Baltimore, MD 21215-1492 t) 410-585-0598

My Sister's Place Lodge - 111 W. Mulberry St., Baltimore, MD 21201-3619 t) 410-528-9002

My Sister's Place Women's Center - 17 W. Franklin St., Baltimore, MD 21201-5005 t) 667-600-3700

The Neighborhoods at St. Elizabeth Rehabilitation and Nursing Center (Jenkins Memorial Nursing Home, Inc.) - 3320 Benson Ave., Baltimore, MD 21227-1035 t) 667-600-2601

Our Daily Bread Employment Center - 725 Fallsway, Baltimore, MD 21202-4147 t) 443-986-9000

Parish Social Ministry - 228 W. Lexington St., Ste. 220, Baltimore, MD 21201-3432 t) 410-261-6781

Parochial School Consultation Program - 2300 Dulaney Valley Rd., Timonium, MD 21093 t) 410-252-4700

Pastoral Care at the Jenkins Senior Living Community - 3320 Benson Ave., Baltimore, MD 21227-1035 t) 410-646-6513

Project BELIEVE - 725 Fallsway, Baltimore, MD 21202-4147 t) 443-986-6766

Project FRESH Start (Family Relocation, Empowerment, and Self-Help) - 228 W. Lexington St., Ste. 220, Baltimore, MD 21201-3432 t) 410-261-6766

Project SERVE (Service and Education through Residential Volunteer Experience) - 228 W. Lexington St., Ste. 220, Baltimore, MD 21201-3432 t) 410-261-6774

Safe Start - 1301 Continental Dr., Ste. 101, Abingdon, MD 21009-2338 t) 410-676-4002

Samaritan Center - 17 W. Franklin St., Baltimore, MD 21201-5005 t) 410-468-4632

Sarah's House - 2015 20th St., Fort Meade, MD 20755-1301 t) 410-551-7722

School Based Behavioral Health Services - 1220 E. Joppa Rd., Towson, MD 21286-5810 t) 410-705-4790 (Allegany, Anne Arundel, Baltimore, Baltimore City, Washington, Frederick and Harford County)

School-Based Mental Health Programs Baltimore County, Harford County, Baltimore City, Carroll County, Washington County, Allegany County, Frederick County, Anne Arundel County - 2600 Pot Spring Rd., Timonium, MD 21093-2739 t) 410-252-4700 Carl Fornoff, Contact; Lisa Serfass, Contact; Diane Shannon, Contact;

Social Concerns - 228 W. Lexington St., Ste. 220, Baltimore, MD 21201-3432 t) 410-261-6781

Therapeutic Mentoring Program - 2600 Pot Spring Rd., Timonium, MD 21093-2739 t) 410-252-4000 x1637

Timonium Out-Patient Mental Health Clinic - 1220 E. Joppa Rd., Towson, MD 21286-5810 t) 410-705-4790

Towson Therapeutic After School Program - 1220 E. Joppa Rd., Towson, MD 21286-5810 t) 410-705-4790

Treatment Foster Care HOPE Program - 2601 N. Howard St., Ste 200, Baltimore, MD 21218 t) 410-685-2363 x108

Villa Maria at Edgewood Middle School - 2311 Willoughby Beach Rd., Edgewood, MD 21040 t) 410-252-6343

Villa Maria at Lansdowne Behavioral Health Clinic - 2700 Washington Ave., Halethorpe, MD 21227-3115 t) 410-368-3984

Villa Maria Behavioral Health Clinic at Fallstaff - 6999 Reisterstown Rd., Ste. 4, Baltimore, MD 21215-1492 t) 410-585-0598

Villa Maria, Inc. - 2300B Dulaney Valley Rd., Timonium, MD 21093 t) 667-600-2231 www.cc.md.org Scott Becker, CFO;

Villa Maria of Anne Arundel Country Behavioral Health Clinic - 1111 Benfield Rd., #104, Millersville, MD 21108-3003 t) 410-729-8494

Villa Maria of Carroll County Behavioral Health Clinic - 1129 Business Pkwy. S., Ste. A, Westminster, MD 21157 t) 410-848-2037

Villa Maria of Frederick County Behavioral Health Clinic - 111 E. Church St., Frederick, MD 21701-5403 t) 301-694-6654; 301-898-7900 (Voicemail)

Villa Maria of Harford County Behavioral Health Clinic - 1301 Continental Dr., Ste. 101, Abingdon, MD 21009-2338 t) 410-676-4002

Villa Maria of Mountain Maryland Behavioral Health Clinic - 300 E. Oldtown Rd., Ste. 1, Cumberland, MD 21502-3600 t) 301-777-8685

Villa Maria of Washington County Behavioral Health Clinic - 229 N. Potomac St., Hagerstown, MD 21740-3812 t) 301-733-5858

Villa Maria School - 2300 Dulaney Valley Rd., Timonium, MD 21093-2739 t) 410-252-6343

Villa Maria School at St. Vincent's Center Type III Diagnostic Program - 2600 Pot Spring Rd., Timonium, MD 21093 t) 410-252-4000

Village Crossroads Senior Housing II, Inc. - 1966 Greenspring Dr., Ste. 200, Timonium, MD 21093 t) 443-798-3423 www.cc-md.org Aileen McShea Tinney, Vice Pres.;

St. Vincent's Villa Diagnostic Evaluation and Treatment Program - 2600 Pot Spring Rd., Timonium, MD 21093-2732 t) 410-252-4000

St. Vincent's Villa Residential Treatment Center - 2600 Pot Spring Rd., Timonium, MD 21093-2739 t) 410-252-4000

St. Vincent's Villa Therapeutic Weekend Respite Program - 2600 Pot Spring Rd., Timonium, MD 21093-2739 t) 410-252-4700 x107

White Oak Counseling (White Oak School) - 8401 Leefield Rd., Timonium, MD 21093 t) 410-252-4700 x126

CEMETERIES [CEM]

BALTIMORE
New Cathedral Cemetery - 4300 Old Frederick Rd., Baltimore, MD 21229 t) 410-566-7770 cemetery@archbalt.org www.newcathedralcemetery.org Rev. Patrick M. Carrion, Dir.;

COLLEGES & UNIVERSITIES [COL]

BALTIMORE
***Loyola University Maryland** - 4501 N. Charles St., Baltimore, MD 21210 t) 410-617-2000; 800-221-9107 officeofthepresident@loyola.edu www.loyola.edu Dr. Terrence M. Sawyer, Pres.; Randall Gentzler, Vice Pres. Finance, Treas.; Dr. Cheryl Moore Thomas, Acting Provost & Vice Pres., Academic Affairs; Robert D. Kelly, Vice Pres. & Special Asst., Pres.; Eric Nichols, Vice Pres., Enrollment Mngmt & Communs.; Dr. Bobby Waldrup, Acting Dean, Sellinger School of Bus. & Mngmt.; Dr. Afra Hersi, Acting Dean, School of Education; Dr. Stephen Fowl, Dean, College of Arts & Sciences; Stds.: 5,140; Lay Tchrs.: 443; Pr. Tchrs.: 9

Jesuit Community of Loyola University, Inc. - Ignatius House, 4603 Millbrook Rd., Baltimore, MD 21212-4721 t) 410-617-2318 Rev. John D. Savard, S.J., Rector; Rev. Charles Borges, S.J., In Res.; Rev. Timothy B. Brown, S.J., In Res.; Rev. John J. Conley, S.J., In Res.; Rev. Jack Dennis, S.J., In Res.; Rev. Christopher Duffy, S.J., In Res.; Rev. Lloyd D. George, S.J., In Res.; Brendan Gottschall, S.J., In Res.; Rev. Robert M. Hussey, S.J., In Res.; Rev. James J. Kelly, S.J., In Res.; Rev. Richard Malloy, S.J., In Res.; Rev. Sanil Mayilkunnel, S.J., In Res.; Rev. Richard McGowan, S.J., In Res.; Rev. Bao Nguyen, S.J., In Res.; Rev. Timothy O'Brien, S.J., In Res.; Melvin Rayappa, S.J., In Res.; Rev. Joseph S. Rossi, S.J., In Res.; Rev. Stephen F. Spahn, S.J., In Res.; Rev. Bruce A. Steggert, S.J., In Res.;

Loyola Graduate Center-Columbia Campus - 8890 McGaw Rd., Columbia, MD 21045-5245 t) 410-617-7600

Loyola Graduate Center-Timonium Campus - 2034 Greenspring Dr., Timonium, MD 21093 t) 410-617-1500

Notre Dame of Maryland University - 4701 N. Charles St., Baltimore, MD 21210 t) 410-435-0100; 410-532-5300 www.ndm.edu School Sisters of Notre Dame. Dr. Marylou Yam, Pres.; Scott Briell, Vice Pres., Enrollment Mngmt.; Sean Delaney, Vice Pres., Fin. & Admin.; Gregory FitzGerald, Chief of Staff & Assoc. Vice Pres., Planning & External Affairs; Kelley Kilduff, Vice Pres., Institutional Advancement & University Communs.; Sr. Sharon Slear, SSND, Provost/Vice Pres., Academic Affairs;

EMMITSBURG
Mount Saint Mary's University - 16300 Old Emmitsburg Rd., Emmitsburg, MD 21727 t) 301-447-6122 pr-communications@msmary.edu www.msmary.edu Timothy E. Trainor, Pres.; Kraig Sheetz, Exec. Vice Pres.; Rev. Msgr. Andrew R. Baker, Rector of Seminary & Vice Pres.; Rev. Martin O. Moran III, Chap.; William E. Davies, Vice Pres., Bus. & Fin.; Stds.: 2,806; Lay Tchrs.: 247

CONVENTS, MONASTERIES, AND RESIDENCES FOR WOMEN [CON]

BALTIMORE
***Carmelite Communities Assoc.** - 1318 Dulaney Valley Rd., Baltimore, MD 21286-1308 t) 845-831-5572 srmarjorie@gmail.com www.ccacarmels.org Sr. Marjorie Robinson, O.C.D., Pres.;

Carmelite Sisters of Baltimore - 1318 Dulaney Valley Rd., Baltimore, MD 21286-1399 t) 410-823-7415 info@baltimorecarmel.org www.baltimorecarmel.org Carmelite Sisters of Baltimore, Discalced Carmelite Nuns. Sr. Colette Ackerman, O.C.D., Prioress; Srs.: 16

Chesapeake Province of the Sisters of Notre Dame de Namur, Inc. - 305 Cable St., Baltimore, MD 21210-2511 t) 410-243-1993 patricia.chappell@sndden.org snddeneastwest.org/ Sr. Patricia Chappell, SNDdeN, EW Team Member; Srs.: 18

Comboni Missionary Sisters - 5401 Loch Raven Blvd., Baltimore, MD 21239-2902 t) 410-323-1469 usacomboni.deleg@gmail.com; andre.cms1964@gmail.com www.combonimissionarysistersusa.org Sr. Andre T. Rothschild, C.M.S., Supr.; Srs.: 4

Little Sisters of Jesus-Regional Residence - 400 N. Streeper St., Baltimore, MD 21224-1230 t) 410-327-7863 lsj.can.usa@gmail.com www.petitessoeursdejesus.eu Sr. Lynn Flear, L.S.J., Regl.; Srs.: 10

Little Sisters of the Poor, Baltimore Province, Inc. - 601 Maiden Choice Ln., Baltimore, MD 21228-3698 t) 410-949-6697 mpbaltimore@littlesistersofthepoor.org; cpbaltimore@littlesistersofthepoor.org www.littlesistersofthepoor.org Sr. Loraine Maguire, L.S.P., Prov.; Sr. Robert Tait, L.S.P., Prov. Asst.; Sr. Jeanne Mary Piché, L.S.P., Local Supr.; Rev. Michael J. Orchik, Chap.; Srs.: 16

Maria Health Care Center, Inc. - 6401 N. Charles St., Baltimore, MD 21212 t) 410-377-7774 ckrohe@amssnd.org Health Center for School Sisters of Notre Dame and other Religious Congregations. Sr. Charmaine Krohe, S.S.N.D., Prov.;

Mercy Villa Convent, Inc. (The Villa) - 2211 W. Rogers Ave., Baltimore, MD 21209 t) 443-810-2330 esebera@sistersofmercy.org Convent for Retired Sisters of Mercy. Sr. Elaine Sebera, R.S.M., Asst. Sister Life Min.; Srs.: 10

Mission Helper Center - 1001 W. Joppa Rd., Baltimore, MD 21204-3787 t) 410-823-8585 elangmead@missionhelpers.org www.missionhelpers.org Sr. Elizabeth Langmead, M.H.S.H., Pres.; Sr. Maria Luz Ortiz, M.H.S.H., Vice. Pres.; Sr. Marilyn Dunphy, M.H.S.H., Treas.; Sr. Barbara Baker, MHSH, Advisor; Srs.: 25

Missionaries of Charity - Gift of Hope Convent, 818 N. Collington Ave., Baltimore, MD 21205 t) 410-732-6056 Sr. Lia Ann, M.C., Supr. of House; Srs.: 5

Our Lady of Mt. Providence Convent-Motherhouse - 701 Gun Rd., Baltimore, MD 21227 t) 410-242-8500 info@oblatesisters.com Attended by Capuchin Franciscan Friars and Josephite Fathers. Sr. Rita Michelle Proctor, O.S.P., Supr.; Sr. Mary Crescentia Proctor, O.S.P., Secy.; Sr. Mary Alexis Fisher, O.S.P., Treas.; Sr. Mary Annette Beecham, O.S.P., Vicar General; Srs.: 40

The School Sisters of Notre Dame Atlantic-Midwest Province - 6401 N. Charles St., Baltimore, MD 21212 t) 410-377-7774 ckrohe@amssnd.org www.ssnd.org Sr. Charmaine Krohe, S.S.N.D., Prov.; Srs.: 354

Atlantic-Midwest Province Endowment Trust -

Atlantic-Midwest Province of the School Sisters of Notre Dame, Inc. - 6401 N. Charles St., Baltimore, MD 21212 t) (410) 377-7774

SSND Care, Inc. -

SSND Charitable Annuity Trust -

SSND Continuing Care Trust -

SSND Real Estate Holding Corporation -

SSND Real Estate Trust -

SSND Service Corporation -

School Sisters of Notre Dame in the City of Baltimore, Inc. - 6401 N. Charles St., Baltimore, MD 21212 t) 410-377-7774 ckrohe@amssnd.org; swall@amssnd.org ssnd.org Sr. Charmaine Krohe, S.S.N.D., Prov.; Srs.: 126

Sisters Servants of Mary Immaculate, Inc. - 1220 Tugwell Dr., Baltimore, MD 21228 t) 410-747-1353 www.ssmiusa.com Convent and Novitiate. Sr. Danuta Zielinska, S.S.M.I., Prov.; Srs.: 17

St. Clare of Assisi, Inc. - 3725 Ellerslie Ave., Baltimore, MD 21218; Mailing: 3221 S. Lake Dr., St. Francis, WI 53235 t) 414-747-7795 etcarr@msn.com www.lakeosfs.org Works with a non-profit developer of low-income housing to provide a multigenerational residential community. Sr. Lorraine McGraw, O.S.F., Admin.; Srs.: 7

CATONSVILLE
The Home of the All Saints Sisters of the Poor of Baltimore City - 1501 Hilton Ave., Catonsville, MD 21228-0127; Mailing: PO Box 3127, Baltimore, MD 21228 t) 410-747-4104 sremilyann@allsaintssisters.org; info@allsaintssisters.org www.allsaintssisters.org Mother Emily Ann Lindsey, A.S.S.P., Prioress; Srs.: 10

St. Gabriel's Retreat House - 1201 Hilton Ave., Catonsville, MD 21228-0127; Mailing: P.O. Box 3106, Catonsville, MD 21228-0127 t) 410-747-6767

EMMITSBURG
Daughters of Charity of St. Vincent de Paul, Province of St. Louise-St. Joseph House - 333 S. Seton Ave., Emmitsburg, MD 21727 t) 301-447-3121 tom.beck@doc.org www.daughtersofcharity.org Sr. Janet Keim, Supr.; Srs.: 63

LUTHERVILLE
Emmanuel Monastery - 2229 W. Joppa Rd., Lutherville, MD 21093-4601 t) 410-821-5792 bensrs@emmanuelosb.org www.emmanuelosb.org Benedictine Sisters of Baltimore. Sr. Kathleen McNany, O.S.B., Prioress; Srs.: 11

MARRIOTTSVILLE
Sisters of Bon Secours, USA, Leadership Office - 1525 Marriottsville Rd., Marriottsville, MD 21104 t) (410) 442-3110 elaine.davia@cbsparis.org www.bonsecours.us Sr. Elaine Davia, C.B.S., Pres.; Sr. Rose Marie Jasinski, C.B.S., Congregation Leader; Srs.: 17

STEVENSON
Maryland Province Center - 1531 Greenspring Valley Rd., Stevenson, MD 21153 t) 513-679-8107 ohprovoff@ohsnd.org www.sndden.org Additional Project Sponsored: Notre Dame Academy, Villanova, PA. Sr. Kathleen Harmon, S.N.D.deN., Prov.;

Villa Julie Residence - 1531 Greenspring Valley Rd., Stevenson, MD 21153 t) 410-486-6946 sndmd@aol.com www.sndden.org Residence for retired Sisters of Notre Dame de Namur Sr. Kathleen Harmon, S.N.D.deN., Prov.;

ENDOWMENTS / FOUNDATIONS / TRUSTS [EFT]

ANNAPOLIS
St. Andrew by the Bay Endowment Trust - 701 College Pkwy., Annapolis, MD 21409 t) 410-974-4366 andrew.defusco@archbalt.org Rev. Andrew T. DeFusco, Admin.;

BALTIMORE
St. Agnes Foundation, Inc. - 900 Caton Ave., Baltimore, MD 21229; Mailing: SAHC Box 123, Baltimore, MD 21229 t) 667-234-3155 kirstan.cecil@ascension.org www.stagnes.org Ed Lovern, Pres./CEO; Trevor Bonat, Chief Mission Integration Officer;

Archbishop Curley High School Endowment Trust - 3701 Sinclair Ln., Baltimore, MD 21213 t) 410-485-5000 Rev. Donald Grzymski, O.F.M.Conv., Pres.;

Basilica of the Assumption Historic Trust, Inc. - 409 Cathedral St., Baltimore, MD 21201 t) 410-727-3565 jboric@archbalt.org www.baltimorebasilica.org Rev. James E. Boric, Pst.;

The Catholic Community Foundation of the Archdiocese of Baltimore, Inc. - 320 Cathedral St., Baltimore, MD 21201 t) 410-547-5356 catholiccommunityfoundation@archbalt.org www.ccfmd.org Patrick Madden, Exec.;

***St. Elizabeth School Foundation, Inc.** - 801 Argonne Dr., Baltimore, MD 21218-1998 t) 410-889-5054 mthorne@stelizabeth-school.org www.stelizabeth-school.org Timothy Schere, Pres.; Michael Thorne, Exec.;

The Immaculate Heart of Mary School Endowment Trust - 8501 Loch Raven Blvd., Baltimore, MD 21286 t) 410-668-8466 Rev. Jeffrey S. Dauses, Pst.;

John Carroll Foundation of the Roman Catholic Archdiocese of Baltimore - 320 Cathedral St., Baltimore, MD 21201 t) 410-547-5446 Dr. Diane L. Barr, Chancellor;

St. Joseph Manor Foundation, Inc. - ; Mailing: P.O. Box 65010, Baltimore, MD 21209 t) 410-727-3386 josephite1@aol.com www.josephites.org Most Rev. John H Ricard, S.S.J., Supr.;

The Josephite Retirement and Disability Benefits Trusts - ; Mailing: P.O. Box 65010, Baltimore, MD 21209 t) 410-727-3386 josephite1@aol.com www.josephites.org Most Rev. John H Ricard, S.S.J., Supr.;

The Josephite Seminarian Education Trust - ; Mailing: P.O. Box 65010, Baltimore, MD 21209 t) 410-727-3386 josephite1@aol.com www.josephites.org Most Rev. John H Ricard, S.S.J., Supr.;

St. Luke Parish Education Endowment Trust - 7517 N. Point Rd., Baltimore, MD 21219 t) 410-477-5200 stlukedgemere@yahoo.com www.olhstchurch.com Purpose: to support the youth of the parish who attend catholic schools. Rev. Ross E. Conklin Jr., Pst.; Rev. Gregory Rapisarda, Pst. Assoc.;

St. Matthew's Parish Endowment Trust - 5401 Loch Raven Blvd., Baltimore, MD 21239 t) 410-433-2300 Rev. Joseph L. Muth Jr., Contact;

Mercy Health Foundation, Inc. - 301 St. Paul Pl., Baltimore, MD 21202 t) 410-332-9202 cchase@mdmercy.com mdmercy.com Dr. David N. Maine, Pres.;

Pallottine Charitable, Educational and Apostolic Ministry Trust - 512 W. Saratoga St., Baltimore, MD 21201 t) 410-685-3064 www.sacapostles.org Rev. Peter T. Sticco, S.A.C., Major Supr.;

The Paul Van Gerwin Religious & Charitable Trust - 4409 Frederick Ave., Baltimore, MD 21229 t) 410-644-0034 rtully@xaverianbrothers.org Bro. Arthur R Caliman, C.F.X., Trustee; Bro. Lawrence W Harvey, C.F.X., Trustee;

The Sacred Heart of Mary Cemetery Continuing Care Trust - 6736 Youngstown Ave., Baltimore, MD 21222 t) 410-633-2828 Rev. John Harrison, C.Ss.R., Admin.;

Serra Foundation - 320 Cathedral St., Baltimore, MD 21201 t) 410-547-5426 www.bmorevocations.org Rev. Stephen P. Roth, Vocations Dir.; John Jordan, Treas.;

The Seton Keough High School Endowment Trust - 320 Cathedral St., Baltimore, MD 21201 t) 410-547-5446 Dr. Diane L. Barr, Chancellor;

Society of St. Sulpice Foundation US, Inc. - 5408 Roland Ave., Baltimore, MD 21210 t) 410-323-5070 dmoore@sulpicians.org Very Rev. Daniel F. Moore, P.S.S., Acting Prov.;

St. Thomas Aquinas School Foundation Trust - 1008 W. 37th St., Baltimore, MD 21211 t) 410-889-4688 Dcn. Timothy D. Maloney, Pst. Admin.;

***The Thomas O'Neill Catholic Health Care Fund, Inc. -** 5601 Lock Raven Blvd., Baltimore, MD 21239 t) 410-772-6768

CATONSVILLE

***Faith Journeys Foundation, Inc. -** 38 Kimball Ridge Ct., Catonsville, MD 21228; Mailing: P.O. Box 1222, Ellicott City, MD 21041 t) 410-916-9677 fjourneys@aol.com; lynn@faithjourneys.org www.faithjourneys.org Lynn A. Cassella-Kapusinski, Pres.;

COCKEYSVILLE

St. Joseph, Texas Endowment Trust - 101 Church Ln., Cockeysville, MD 21030 t) 410-683-0600 rhilgartner@archbalt.org www.sjpmd.org Rev. Msgr. Richard B. Hilgartner, Pst.;

CUMBERLAND

The SS. Peter & Paul Parish Endowment Trust - 300 E. Oldtown Rd., Ste. 2, Cumberland, MD 21502 t) 301-777-1750 olmcumberland@archbalt.org Edward Jones, Admin.;

ELKRIDGE

St. Augustine School, Inc. - 5990 Old Washington Rd., Elkridge, MD 21075 t) 410-796-3040 www.staug-md.org Joseph Miller, Prin.;

ELLICOTT CITY

The St. Paul's Parish Endowment Trust - 3755 St. Paul St., Ellicott City, MD 21043 t) 410-465-1670 office@stpaulcc.org Rev. Msgr. John A. Dietzenbach, Pst.;

FROSTBURG

St. Peter's, Westernport, School Endowment Trust - 44 E. Main St., Frostburg, MD 21532 t) 301-689-6767 edward.jones@archbalt.org www.divinemercymd.org Rev. Edward S. Hendricks, Pst.; Edward Jones, Bus. Mgr.;

St. Joseph Midland Cemetery Continuing Care Trust - 44 E. Main St., Frostburg, MD 21532 t) 301-689-6767 edward.jones@archbalt.org www.divinemercymd.org Rev. Edward S. Hendricks; Edward Jones, Bus. Mgr.;

GLEN BURNIE

The Church of the Good Shepherd Parish Endowment Trust - 126 Dorsey Rd., Glen Burnie, MD 21061; Mailing: 1451 Furnace Ave., Glen Burnie, MD 21060 t) 410-766-5070 Rev. Austin Murphy, Pst.;

KINGSVILLE

St. Stephen School Endowment Trust - 8028 Bradshaw Rd., Kingsville, MD 21087-1807 t) 410-592-7617 www.ssschool.org/ Mary M. Patrick, Prin.;

LOTHIAN

Family of the Americas Foundation, Inc. - 5929 Talbot Rd., Lothian, MD 20711 t) 301-627-3346; 800-443-3395 nfo@familyoftheamericas.org www.familyplanning.net

MIDLAND

St. Joseph Midland Parish Endowment Trust - 19925 Church St., Midland, MD 21532; Mailing: 44 E. Main St., Frostburg, MD 21532 t) 301-689-6767 Rev. Edward S. Hendricks;

PASADENA

St. Jane Frances Educational Endowment Trust - 8499 Virginia Ave., Pasadena, MD 21122 t) 410-255-4646 stjane.org Rev. Msgr. Carl F. Cummings, Pst.;

SYKESVILLE

Cardinal Denhoff Trust - 1400 Underwood Rd., Sykesville, MD 21784 t) (410) 486-5171 treasurer.provincial@gmail.com Rev. Kurt J. Klismet, O.SS.T., Contact;

St. Joseph Catholic Community Endowment Trust - 915 Liberty Rd., Sykesville, MD 21784 t) 443-920-9191 parishoffice@saintjoseph.cc www.saintjoseph.cc Rev. John Worgul, Pst.;

TOWSON

The Immaculate Conception Elementary School Endowment Trust - 200 Ware Ave., Towson, MD 21204 t) 410-427-4801 www.theimmaculate.org Rev. Joseph F. Barr, Pst.;

Maryland Province of the Society of Jesus Aged and Infirm Trust - 8600 LaSalle Rd., Ste. 620, Towson, MD 21286 t) 443-921-1319 martreasurer@jesuits.org Rev. Richard McGowan, S.J., Treas.;

Maryland Province of the Society of Jesus Formation Trust - 8600 LaSalle Rd., Ste. 620, Towson, MD 21286 t) 443-921-1319 martreasurer@jesuits.org Rev. Richard McGowan, S.J., Treas.;

HOSPITALS / HEALTH SERVICES [HOS]

BALTIMORE

St. Agnes HealthCare, Ascension Health - 900 Caton Ave., Baltimore, MD 21229-5299 t) 667-234-6000 webmasterbal@ascension.org www.stagnes.org Rev. Livinus Anweting, Chap.; Jan McDonnell, Chap.; Trevor Bonat, Chief Mission Integration Officer; Ed Lovern, Pres./CEO; Bed Capacity: 280; Asstd. Annu.: 304,585; Staff: 2,057

St. Agnes Foundation, Inc. - trevor.bonat@ascension.org www.givesaintagnes.org

MedStar Good Samaritan Hospital - 5601 Loch Raven Blvd., Baltimore, MD 21239 t) 443-444-8000 www.medstargoodsamaritan.org Adult acute care teaching hospital. Bradley Chambers, Pres.; Joanie Carlson, Asst. Vice Pres., Mission Integration; Karen Owings, Vice Pres., Nursing; Rev. Emmanuel Acquaye, O.F.M. Conv., Chap.; Dan Cahill, Bd. Chm.;

Mercy Health Services Inc. - 345 St. Paul Pl., Baltimore, MD 21202 t) 410-332-9000 www.mdmercy.com Mercy Medical Center, Inc., St. Paul Place Specialists, Inc.; Maryland Family Care; Mercy Transitional Care; Stella Maris, Inc., Dr. David N. Maine, Pres.; Rev. Thomas R. Malia, Asst. to Pres. for Mission; Rev. Rodney Eugene (Haiti), Clergy; Rev. Augustine Etemma Inwang, M.S.P. (Nigeria), Clergy; Rev. Ernest P. Udoh, Clergy;

TOWSON

University of Maryland St. Joseph Medical Center - 7601 Osler Dr., Towson, MD 21204 t) 410-337-1000 www.umstjoseph.org Thomas B. Smyth, Pres.; Rev. Samuel Uzoukwu (Nigeria), Chap.; Rev. Livinus Anweting, Chap.; Rev. Sampson Etim, Chap.; Laura Richardson, Chap.;

MISCELLANEOUS [MIS]

BALTIMORE

Alhambra, International Order of - Supreme Headquarters, 4200 Leeds Ave., Baltimore, MD 21229; Mailing: 123 Main St., Dundalk, MD 21102 t) 410-242-0660 salaam@orderalhambra.org www.orderalhambra.org Nonprofit organization dedicated to assisting the developmentally disabled. Joe B Cortinaz, Exec.;

Bon Secours Baltimore Foundation (Bon Secours Community Works) - 1800 Washington Blvd., Ste. 822, Baltimore, MD 21230 t) 410-801-5216 sdschitter1@mercy.com bonsecours.com Julie Mercer, Pres.;

Bon Secours Baltimore Community Works, Inc. - 26 N. Fulton Ave., Baltimore, MD 21223 t) 410-801-7101 bonsecours.com Bon Secours Ministry. George Kleb, Dir.;

Bon Secours Baltimore Development, Inc. - 20 N. Fulton Ave., Baltimore, MD 21223 t) (410) 362-3000

Bon Secours Housing II, Inc - 20 N. Fulton Ave., Baltimore, MD 21223 t) (410) 801-5100

Bon Secours Housing, Inc. (aka Hollins Terrace) - 26 N. Fulton Ave., Baltimore, MD 21223 t) (410) 801-5100

Unity Properties, Inc. - t) (410) 801-5100

Bon Secours Family Support Center (Bon Secour of Maryland Foundation, Inc.) - 26 N. Fulton Ave., Baltimore, MD 21223 t) 410-362-3629 www.bonsecours.com Andrea Person, Dir.;

***Cardijn Associates, Inc. -** 4513 Bayonne Ave., Baltimore, MD 21206 t) 410-488-7936 nancyconrad@verizon.net Nancy Lee Conrad, Pres.; Rudy Dehaney, Prog. Coord.;

The Caroline Freiss Center, Inc. - 900 Somerset St., Baltimore, MD 21202 t) 410-563-1303 carolinecenter@caroline-center.org www.caroline-center.org Employment training education for low income women. Lynn M Selby, Exec.;

Cathedral Library - 5200 N. Charles St., Baltimore, MD 21210 t) 410-464-4041 cathedrallibrary@outlook.com Staffed by the Catholic Evidence League. Michele Hayes, Dir.;

The Catholic Charismatic Renewal in the Archdiocese of Baltimore, Inc. - 6 Oakridge Ct., Baltimore, MD 21093 t) 410-308-8962 thesawyers@archbalt.org www.holyspiritbaltimore.org Dr. Robert Sawyer, Pres. & Archdiocesan Liaison; Julie Sawyer, Archdiocesan Liaison; Lisa Sliker, Assoc. Liaison; Adam Novotny, Assoc. Liaison; Holly Novotny, Assoc. Liaison; Edward P. Herrera, Archbishop's Rep.;

Catholic Community at Relay - 5025 Cedar Ave., Baltimore, MD 21227 t) 410-247-4033 catholiccommunityatrelay@gmail.com www.ccrelay.org Maria Gamble-Farkas, Admin.; David Kraemer, Co-Coord.; William Marsh, Co-Coord.;

Catholic Evidence League of Baltimore - c/o Cathedral of Mary Our Queen, 5200 N. Charles St., Baltimore, MD 21210 t) 410-464-4041 To increase members knowledge of the history, teaching & laws of the Catholic Church. Rev. Jesse L. Bolger, Chap.; Sue Jones, Pres.;

Catholic Relief Services - United States Conference of Catholic Bishops - 228 W. Lexington St., Baltimore, MD 21201 t) 410-625-2220 info@crs.org www.crs.org For a more detailed explanation of this organization, please consult the A-pages located in the front of the Directory. Sean Callahan, Pres. & CEO;

Catholic Relief Services Foundation, Inc. - 228 W. Lexington St., Baltimore, MD 21201 t) 410-625-2220 ogc@crs.org Glenn Creamer, Chair; Sean Callahan, Pres.; Rev. Robert Twele, O.F.M. Conv., Corp. Secy.;

Chancery Office - 320 Cathedral St., Baltimore, MD 21201 t) 410-547-5446 chancery@archbalt.org www.archbalt.org See Schools Section for related schools. Dr. Diane L. Barr, Chancellor;

Archbishop of Baltimore Annual Appeal Trust/ Cardinal's Lenten Appeal - t) 410-547-5439

Archdiocesan General Insurance Program Trust - t) 410-547-5317

Archdiocesan Health Plan Trust Fund Agreement - t) 410-547-5317

Archdiocesan Priests Post-Retirement Benefits Plan Trust Fund - t) 410-547-5317 pphelps@archbalt.org Petra R. Phelps, Contact;

Cemetery Continuing Care Trust - St. Patrick's Havre de Grace, Cemetery Continuing Care Trust; Holy Cross Cemetery Continuing Care Trust; St. Joseph, Fullerton.

Christian Brothers Community Support Charitable Trust - 6001 Ammendale Rd., Beltsville, MD 20705; Mailing: 444A Rte. 35 S., Eatontown, NJ 07724 t) 732-380-7926 juliano@fscdena.org Bro. Joseph Juliano, F.S.C., Secy.;

Corpus Christi Jenkins Memorial Trust, Inc. - t) 410-523-4161

Dart, Inc. -

The Dr. Charles J. Foley Sr. and Mildred H. Foley Memorial Endowment Trust - t) 410-547-5322 Provides annual support for over 300 programs and agencies of the Archdiocese.

***G S Housing, Inc.** -

The Gallagher Family Fund - t) 410-547-5322

St. Gregory the Great Housing Committee, Inc. - t) 410-523-0061

St. Jane Frances Educational Endowment Trust - t) 410-255-4750

St. John Neumann Regional School, Inc. - t) 301-724-4055

St. John the Evangelist School Endowment Trust - 689 Ritchie Hwy., Severna Park, MD 21146 t) 410-647-2283

St. Jude Shrine Corporation - 512 W. Saratoga St., Baltimore, MD 21201 t) 410-685-6026 info@stjundeshrine.org Rev. Peter T. Sticco, S.A.C., Pres.;

Marianist Charitable Trust - t) 410-366-1300

Marion Burk Knott Scholarship Fund LLC - 5850 Waterloo Rd., Ste. 140, Columbia, MD 21045 t) 301-603-9501

St. Mark's Parish School Endowment Trust - t) 410-747-6613

Maryvale Educational Fund, Inc. - t) 410-252-3366

Mercy Primary Care Group, Inc. - t) 410-332-9000

The National Black Catholic Congress, Inc. - t) 410-547-8496 nbcc@nbccongress.org www.nbccongress.org

Neumann Early Childhood Center, Inc. - t) 410-547-5495

Our Lady of Good Counsel Historic Trust, Inc. - t) 410-752-0205

St. Peter's Cemetery Restoration Fund, Inc. - t) 410-547-5300

St. Pius V Housing Committee, Inc. - t) 410-523-1930

Plan of Self-Insurance Trust - t) 410-547-5317

The Priests Continuing Education and Formation Endowment Trust - t) 410-547-5317

Sacred Heart Community Health Services, Inc. - t) 301-723-5222

Sacred Heart Foundation, Inc. - t) 301-723-5222

Sacred Heart Hospital of the Sisters of Charity, Inc. - t) 410-723-5222

School Sisters of Notre Dame in the City of Baltimore Charitable Trust, Inc. - t) 410-377-7774

Sisters of Notre Dame de Namur Charitable Trusts - t) 410-255-1577

Sisters of Notre Dame de Namur, Maryland Province, Charitable Trust - t) 410-486-5382

St. Vincent De Paul Historic Trust, Inc. - t) 410-547-5377

Women's Auxiliary Board - t) 410-547-5356 Funds provide partial tuition for thousands of low income students in designated Baltimore City Catholic Schools.

ChristLife, Inc. - 600 Cooks Ln., Baltimore, MD 21229 t) 443-388-8910 info@christlife.org www.christlife.org Dave Nodar, Dir.;

Colombiere Jesuit Community - 5704 Roland Ave., Baltimore, MD 21210-1399 t) 410-532-1400 St. Claude La Colombiere Jesuit Community. Rev. Thomas M. McCoog, S.J., Supr.; Rev. Thomas R. Marciniak, S.J., Minister; Rev. Vincent C. Curtin, S.J.; Bro. Darrell J. Burns, S.J.; Bro. Paul Cawthorne, S.J.; Rev. John R. Donahue, S.J.; Rev. James N. Gelson, S.J.; Rev. F. Joseph Michini, S.J.; Rev. William J. Watters, S.J.; Rev. David Brooks; Rev. Lloyd D. George, S.J.; Rev. Aloysius P. Kelley, S.J.; Rev. Joseph J. Hayden, S.J.; Bro. Thomas S. Kretz, S.J.; Rev. Liborio J. LaMartina, S.J.; Rev. Robert B. Lawton, S.J.; Rev. John J. Madden, S.J.; Rev. Paul J. McCarren, S.J.; Rev. Thomas McDonnell; Rev. William C. McFadden, S.J.; Rev. Kenneth Meehan, S.J.; Rev. James O'Brien, S.J.; Rev. Ladislaus Orsy; Rev. James F. Salmon, S.J.; Rev. T. Howland Sanks, S.J.; Rev. Joseph A. Sobierajski, S.J.; Rev. Dominic J. Totaro, S.J.; Rev. Robert Yankevitch, S.J.;

Cristo Rey Corporate Internship Program, Inc. - 420 S. Chester St., Baltimore, MD 21231 t) 410-727-3255 Dr. William Heiser, Pres.; John Busse, Dir.; Leigh Profit, Dir., Fin.;

Esperanza Center Health Services Inc. - 320 Cathedral St., Baltimore, MD 21201 t) 443-825-3450 William J. McCarthy Jr., Dir.;

Food for Thought, Inc. - 1625 E. Baltimore, Baltimore, MD 21231 t) 410-563-0081 srmaryannh@aol.com Tutorial program for children & adult literacy. Sr. Mary Ann Hartnett, S.S.N.D., Dir.;

Franciscan Center, Inc. - 101 W. 23rd St., Baltimore, MD 21218 t) 410-467-5340 info@fcbmore.org www.fcbmore.org Sisters of St. Francis of Assisi. Jeffrey Griffin, Exec. Dir.;

***G S Properties, Inc.** - 5601 Loch Raven Blvd., Baltimore, MD 21239 t) 410-772-6768 www.medstarhealth.org

Ignatian Volunteer Corps - 740 N. Calvert St., Baltimore, MD 21202 t) 410-752-4686 info@ivcusa.org; seberle@ivcusa.org www.ivcusa.org Mary C. McGinnity, Pres./CEO; Becky Ehrman, Vice. Pres.; Rev. James R. Conroy, S.J., Founder - Ex Officio Bd. Mem.;

Inter Parish Loan Fund, Inc. - 320 Cathedral St., Baltimore, MD 21201 t) 410-547-5322 John Matera, Secy.;

Jesuit Volunteers - 740 N Calvert St., Baltimore, MD 21202 t) 410-244-1733 development@jesuitvolunteers.org www.jesuitvolunteers.org Tom Chabolla, Pres.;

St. Joseph's Society for Colored Missions - 1097-C W. Lake Ave., Baltimore, MD 21210 t) 410-727-3386 josephite1@aol.com www.josephites.org Most Rev. John H Ricard, S.S.J., Pres.;

Little Sisters of the Poor Service Corporation - 601 Maiden Choice Ln., Baltimore, MD 21228; Mailing: PO Box 21203, Catonsville, MD 21228 t) 410-744-9367 mpbaltimore@littlesistersofthepoor.org www.littlesistersofthepoor.org Sr. Loraine Maguire, L.S.P., Prov.; Sr. Robert Tait, L.S.P., Prov. Asst.;

Marian House, Inc. - 949 Gorsuch Ave., Baltimore, MD 21218 t) 410-467-4121 info@marianhouse.org www.marianhouse.org Katie Allston, Pres. & CEO;

Mother Mary Lange Support Corporation - 320 Cathedral St., Baltimore, MD 21201 t) 410-547-5587 John Matera, Admin.; Dr. Diane L. Barr, Resident Agent;

Mother Seton House on Paca Street, Inc. - 600 N. Paca St., Baltimore, MD 21201 t) 410-728-6464 info@stmaryspacast.org www.stmaryspacast.org

Mount Providence Reading Center - 701 Gun Rd., Baltimore, MD 21227 t) 410-247-0448 sisterconstance@oblatesisters.com www.oblatesisters.com Oblate Sisters of Providence. Sr. M. Constance Fenwick, O.S.P., Dir.; Asstd. Annu.: 25

My Sister's Place Women's Center Fund, Inc. - 320 Cathedral St., Baltimore, MD 21201-4421 t) 410-547-5490 wmccarth@cc-md.org William J. McCarthy Jr., Exec.;

Nigeria-Igbo Catholic Community - ; Mailing: P.O. Box 66027, Baltimore, MD 21239 t) 443-857-9991 igbomass@niccchurch.org www.niccchurch.org Ike Okwesili, Chair; Rev. Anthony Abiamiri, Archdiocesan Liaison; Felix Opara, Vice Chmn.;

Our Daily Bread Employment Center Fund, Inc. - 320 Cathedral St., Baltimore, MD 21201-4421 t) 410-547-5490 wmccarth@cc-md.org William J. McCarthy Jr., Exec.;

Partners in Excellence Scholarship Program - 320 Cathedral St., Baltimore, MD 21201 t) 410-625-8452 www.pieschools.org This Program provides partial tuition assistance to low income families wishing to send their children to a Catholic School in Baltimore City. Dr. Diane L. Barr, Chancellor;

Radio Mass of Baltimore, Inc. - St. Ignatius Church, 740 N. Calvert St., Baltimore, MD 21202 t) 410-727-3848

St. Mary's Seminary & University - 5400 Roland Ave., Baltimore, MD 21210-1994 t) 410-864-4000 Rev. Inniah Christy Arockiaraj, P.S.S.; Rev. Michael L. Barre, P.S.S.; Rev. Martin J. Burnham; Rev. Kasweka Joseph Chamwaza; Rev. Dominic Ciriaco, P.S.S.; Rev. Luis R. Corneli, P.S.S.; Rev. Robert J. Cro, P.S.S.; Rev. Emmanuel M. Ichidi, P.S.S.; Rev. Peter M. Kwaleyela, P.S.S.; Rev. Robert F. Leavitt, P.S.S.; Rev. Renato Lopez, P.S.S.; Rev. Geronimo A. Magat, P.S.S.; Rev. Victor Mwanamwambwa, P.S.S.; Rev. Eugene H. Mwanza, P.S.S.; Rev. Edward M. Mwepya; Rev. Jaime E. Robledo, P.S.S.; Rev. Shoba Nyambe, P.S.S., Rector; Rev. Gladstone H. Stevens, P.S.S., Pres.; Rebecca Hancock, Assoc. Dean of Administration, Ecumenical Institute;

Sarah's House Fund, Inc. - 320 Cathedral St., Baltimore, MD 21201-4421 t) 410-547-5490 wmccarth@cc-md.org William J. McCarthy Jr., Exec.;

Stella Maris Seafarers' Center - 320 Cathedral St., Baltimore, MD 21201 t) 443-845-7227 aosbalt@gmail.com www.aosbalt.org Apostleship of the Sea. Christian hospitality services. Rev. Msgr. John L. FitzGerald, Chap.; Andrew Middleton, Dir.;

The Benedictine Society of Baltimore, Inc. - 2612 Wilkens Ave., Baltimore, MD 21223 t) 410-947-4988 stbenedictbalto@gmail.com Rev. Martin Bartel, O.S.B., Pres.; Rev. Paschal A. Morlino, O.S.B., Vice President;

St. Thomas More Society of Maryland Inc. - 100 Light St., Baltimore, MD 21202 t) 410-576-4825 www.stmsms.org Rev. Msgr. James P. Farmer, Chap.; Kenneth Shaffrey, Pres.;

Union of Catholic Apostolate USA, Inc. - 512 W. Saratoga St., Baltimore, MD 21201 t) 302-956-0039 usncc@sacapostles.org Rev. Gregory P. Serwa, S.A.C., Pres.;

BOWIE

The Maryland State Council, Knights of Columbus - ; Mailing: P.O. Box 1468 B, Bowie, MD 20717 t) 443-968-0428 kofc-md@hotmail.com www.kofc-md.org Rev. Donald Grzymski, O.F.M.Conv., Chap.; Christopher L. Powers, State Deputy;

CATONSVILLE

Christian Life Community Regional Information Center - 615 Rest Ave., Catonsville, MD 21228 t) 410-465-1312 cazieba@yahoo.com www.clc-usa.com Lay organization that forms / sustains adults and youth, who commit themselves to the church & its mission. John Springer, Treas.; Lois Campbell, Regl. Chair; Carol A. Zieba, Regl. Rep.;

CROWNSVILLE

***Springhill Center for Family Development** - 1134 Bacon Ridge Rd., Crownsville, MD 21032 t) 410-923-8900 Enriching and strengthening family life in the community.

ELLICOTT CITY

The Baltimore Catholic League - 4725 Dorsey Hall Dr., Ste. A-610, Ellicott City, MD 21042 t) (443) 717-4786 John E. Degele Jr., Commissioner;

Fr. Justin Ministry Fund, Inc. - 12300 Folly Quarter Rd.,

Ellicott City, MD 21042 t) 410-531-1400 Order of Friars Minor Conventual Bro. Nicholas Romeo, OFM Conv., Secy.;

Franciscan Friars Conventual - Solidarity Fund, Inc. - 12300 Folly Quarter Rd., Ellicott City, MD 21042 t) 410-531-1400 Bro. Nicholas Romeo, OFM Conv., Secy.;

EMMITSBURG

National Shrine of St. Elizabeth Ann Seton/Seton Heritage Ministries, Inc. - 339 S. Seton Ave., Emmitsburg, MD 21727 t) 301-447-6606 office@setonshrine.org www.setonshrine.org Robert Judge, Exec. Dir.;

Seton Center, Inc. - 226 E. Lincoln Ave., Emmitsburg, MD 21727 t) 301-447-6102 setoncenterinc@doc.org www.setoncenter.org Social Services; Outreach; Seton Family Store. Daughters of Charity. Sr. Martha Beaudoin, D.C., Exec. Dir.; Asstd. Annu.: 855; Staff: 11

GLEN BURNIE

Friends of Ijebu-Ode Diocese, Inc. - 7811 Stonebriar Dr., Glen Burnie, MD 21060; Mailing: P.O. Box 2348, Glen Burnie, MD 21060 t) 202-460-9750 foid11@yahoo.com www.foidinc.org Rev. Augustine Adetola, Vice Prin.; Most Rev. John H Ricard, S.S.J., Pres.; Rev. Nelson A. Moreira, S.S.J., Treas.;

Mary's Center, Inc. - 898 Airport Park Rd., Ste. 109, Glen Burnie, MD 21061; Mailing: P.O. Box 1804, Pasadena, MD 21123-1804 t) (410) 761-8082 info@maryscentermd.org www.womenscaremc.org Pregnancy Support Services. Free pregnancy tests; limited obstetric ultrasound; material assistance to women and babies in need. Judith A. Crowninshield, Dir.; Asstd. Annu.: 467

PERRY HALL

Catholic Alumni Club of Baltimore - 4132 E. Joppa Rd., Ste. 11, Perry Hall, MD 21236; Mailing: P.O. Box 837, Perry Hall, MD 21236 t) 410-698-3889 info@cacbaltimore.org www.cacbaltimore.org Jason Bourne, CEO;

Catholic War Veterans USA, Inc. - 9511-P Kingscroft Ter., Perry Hall, MD 21128 t) 410-299-7283 cwvmd@yahoo.com www.cwvmd.org Rev. Michael J. Orchik, Chap.;

ROCKVILLE

Christ Child Society of Annapolis - 6110 Executive Blvd., Ste. 504, Rockville, MD 20852; Mailing: P.O. Box 1801, Annapolis, MD 21404 t) 443-534-4231 jamiekupstas@gmail.com Jamie Kupstas, Pres.;

Christ Child Society of Baltimore, Inc. - 6110 Executive Blvd., Ste. 504, Rockville, MD 20852; Mailing: P.O. Box 584, Riderwood, MD 21139 info@christchildbaltimore.org Natalie Shields, Pres.;

RUXTON

Reparation Society of the Immaculate Heart of Mary, Inc. - c/o 1 Riderwood Station, Ruxton, MD 21204 t) 973-220-6995 frmastroeni@icloud.com Purpose: To promote prayer and penance in reparation to the Immaculate Heart of Mary in accordance with the message of Fatima. Rev. Anthony Mastroeni, Pres.; Sr. Elias Margand, F.S.S.E., Secy./Treas.;

SEVERN

Baltimore Archdiocesan Holy Name Union - 1839 Montreal Rd., Severn, MD 21144 t) 410-336-7784 gemcknight55@hotmail.com Purpose: Promotes reverence for the Sacred Names of God and Jesus Christ, obedience and loyalty to the magisterium of the Catholic Church. Gregory McClain, Pres.;

STREET

Legion of Mary - 1431 Trappe Rd., Street, MD 21154 t) 410-916-8721 www.legionofmarybaltimore.org Baltimore Comitium, the governing body for the Legion of Mary in the Archdiocese of Baltimore. The objective of the Legion is Evangelization. Alice Armour, Pres.; Cassandra Boykin, Vice. Pres.;

TIMONIUM

Odenton Senior Housing II, Inc. - 1966 Greenspring Dr., Ste. 200, Timonium, MD 21093 t) 667-600-2280 www.cc-md.org Arnold Eppel, Vice Pres.;

***Rebuilt Parish, Inc.** - 101 W. Ridgely Rd., Ste. 7B, Timonium, MD 21093

TOWSON

Jesuit Jamshedpur Mission Society, Inc. - 8600 La Salle Rd., Ste. 620, Towson, MD 21286-2014 t) 443-921-1311 martreasurer@jesuits.org www.jesuitseast.org Rev. Richard McGowan, S.J., Treas.;

Jesuit Mission Bureau, Maryland Province Inc. - 8600 LaSalle Rd., Ste. 620, Towson, MD 21286-2014 t) 443-921-1311 martreasurer@jesuits.org www.jesuitseast.org Rev. Richard McGowan, S.J., Treas.;

Jesuit Seminary Guild, Maryland Province, Inc. - 8600 La Salle Rd., Ste. 620, Towson, MD 21286-2014 t) 443-921-1311 martreasurer@jesuits.org www.jesuitseast.org Rev. Richard McGowan, S.J., Treas.;

WOODSTOCK

Catholic Daughters of the Americas - 11150 Chambers Ct., Unit D, Woodstock, MD 21163 t) 410-499-8461 catholicdaughters.org/ Religious, charitable and educational to serve the needs of the Church and community through apostolate, renewal, community and youth. Rev. Christopher Moore, Chap.; Diana Bourne, State Regent;

MONASTERIES AND RESIDENCES FOR PRIESTS AND BROTHERS [MON]

BALTIMORE

St. Ambrose Friary - 4502 Park Heights Ave., Baltimore, MD 21215 t) 202-549-6591 pastor@saintambrose.com www.saintambrose.com Rev. Paul Zaborowski, O.F.M.Cap., Pst.; Rev. Ignatius Okoye, OFM Cap., Pastoral Supply; Chaplain; Priests: 3

Congregation of the Holy Spirit - 2846 W. Lafayette Ave., Baltimore, MD 21216 t) 412-831-0302 www.spiritans.org Rev. Donald J. McEachin, C.S.Sp., Prov.; Priests: 2

Jesuit Community of Loyola University Maryland, Inc. - Ignatius House, 4603 Millbrook Rd., Baltimore, MD 21212-4721 t) 410-617-2318 jsavard@loyola.edu Rev. Gregory Chisholm, S.S.J., Local Supr.; Rev. Brian F. Linnane, S.J., Univ. Pres.; Rev. John D. Savard, S.J., Rector; Rev. Charles Borges, S.J.; Rev. Timothy B. Brown, S.J.; Rev. John J. Conley, S.J.; Rev. Jack Dennis, S.J.; Rev. Christopher Duffy, S.J.; Rev. Lloyd D. George, S.J.; Rev. Robert M. Hussey, S.J.; Rev. James J. Kelly, S.J.; Rev. Richard Malloy, S.J.; Rev. Sanil Mayilkunnel, S.J.; Rev. Richard McGowan, S.J.; Rev. Bao Nguyen, S.J.; Rev. Timothy O'Brien, S.J.; Rev. Joseph S. Rossi, S.J.; Rev. Stephen F. Spahn, S.J.; Rev. Bruce A. Steggert, S.J.; Brs.: 1; Priests: 40

St. Joseph Society of the Sacred Heart House of Central Administration - 1097-C W. Lake Ave., Baltimore, MD 21210; Mailing: P.O. Box 65010, Baltimore, MD 21209 t) 410-727-3386 josephite1@aol.com www.josephites.org Most Rev. John H Ricard, S.S.J., Supr.; Rev. Raymond P. Bomberger, S.S.J., Vicar Gen.; Rev. Nelson A. Moreira, S.S.J., Treas.; Very Rev. Michael K. Saah-Buckman, S.S.J., Consultor Gen.; Priests: 5

Pallottine Center for Apostolic Causes - 512 W. Saratoga St., Baltimore, MD 21203 t) 410-685-3063 www.sacapostles.org Promotional Center for St. Jude Shrine. Rev. Peter T. Sticco, S.A.C., Dir.; Priests: 4

Society of St. Sulpice, Province of the United States - 5408 Roland Ave., Baltimore, MD 21210-1988 t) 410-323-5070 dmoore@sulpicians.org www.sulpicians.org Very Rev. Daniel F. Moore, P.S.S., Prov. Supr.; Rev. Inniah Christy Arockiaraj, P.S.S.; Rev. Michael L. Barre, P.S.S.; Rev. Melvin C. Blanchette, P.S.S.; Rev. Howard P. Bleichner, P.S.S.; Rev. Gerald L. Brown, P.S.S.; Rev. Phillip J. Brown, P.S.S.; Rev. Martin J. Burnham; Rev. Kasweka Joseph Chamwaza; Rev. Simon Cheba, P.S.S.; Rev. Timothy C. Chikweto, P.S.S.; Rev. Dominic Ciriaco, P.S.S.; Rev. Gerald D. Coleman, P.S.S.; Rev. Luis R. Corneli, P.S.S.; Rev. Robert J. Cro, P.S.S.; Rev. Frederick J. Cwiekowski, P.S.S.; Rev. Daniel J. Doherty, P.S.S.; Rev. Shawn D. Gould, P.S.S.; Rev. Peter W. Gray, P.S.S.; Rev. Richard M. Gula, P.S.S.; Rev. Cornelius Hankomoone, P.S.S.; Rev. Msgr. Fredrik Hansen; Rev. William E. Hartgen Jr., P.S.S.; Rev. Thomas R. Hurst, P.S.S.; Rev. Emmanuel M. Ichidi, P.S.S.; Rev. Enoch Kanjira; Rev. Nam J. Kim, P.S.S.; Rev. John S. Kselman, P.S.S.; Rev. Peter M. Kwaleyela, P.S.S.; Rev. Leo J. Larrivee, P.S.S.; Rev. Robert F. Leavitt, P.S.S.; Rev. Renato Lopez, P.S.S.; Rev. Geronimo A. Magat, P.S.S.; Rev. Paul A. Maillet, P.S.S.; Rev. Gerald D. McBrearity, P.S.S.; Rev. James L. McKearney, P.S.S.; Rev. John E. McMurry, P.S.S.; Rev. Neal M. N. Mulyata; Rev. Thomson Mwaba; Rev. Victor Mwanamwambwa, P.S.S.; Rev. Eugene H. Mwanza, P.S.S.; Rev. James E. Myers, P.S.S.; Rev. Alick-George Ngosa; Rev. Hy K. Nguyen, P.S.S.; Rev. Shoba Nyambe, P.S.S.; Rev. James P. Oberle, P.S.S.; Rev. Anthony J. Pogorelc, P.S.S.; Rev. Louis M. Reitz, P.S.S.; Rev. Jaime E. Robledo, P.S.S.; Rev. Victor S. Shikaputo, P.S.S.; Rev. Victor Simutonga, P.S.S.; Rev. Patrick Simutowe, P.S.S.; Rev. Gladstone H. Stevens, P.S.S.; Rev. J. Michael Strange, P.S.S.; Rev. Lawrence B. Terrien, P.S.S.; Rev. David D. Thayer, P.S.S.; Rev. Thomas R. Ulshafer, P.S.S.; Rev. Ronald D. Witherup, P.S.S.; Priests: 58

The Redemptorists - 600 S. Conkling St., Baltimore, MD 21224 t) 202-539-4410 provincial@redemptorists.net www.redemptorists.net Rev. Paul Borowski, C.Ss.R., Prov. Supr.; Brs.: 1; Priests: 26

Xaverian Brothers Generalate - 4409 Frederick Ave., Baltimore, MD 21229 t) 410-644-0034 development@xaverianbrothers.org www.xaverianbrothers.org Bro. Daniel E Skala, C.F.X, Gen. Supr.; Bro. Arthur R Caliman, C.F.X., Treas.; Bro. Lawrence W Harvey, C.F.X., Leadership Team; Bro. Paul J. Murray, C.F.X., Leadership Team; Shawn Lynch, Bus. Mgr.; Joshua Kinney, Communications; Brs.: 9

CHILLUM

St. Vincent's House - 706 Sargent Rd., Chillum, MD 20782; Mailing: P.O. Box 376, Emmitsburg, MD 21727 t) 301-447-2326 stjosephemmitsburg@comcast.net www.stjosephemmitsburg.org Rev. Alberto Barattero, IVE, Admin.; Priests: 7

CUMBERLAND

Our Lady of the Mountains Friary - 300 1/2 E. Oldtown Rd., Cumberland, MD 21502 t) 301-777-1750 olmcumberland@archbalt.org www.olmcumberland.org/ Province of St. Augustine of the Capuchin Order Rev. Paul Zaborowski, O.F.M.Cap., Pastor & Local Contact; Rev. Gregory Chervenak, O.F.M.Cap., Pst.; Rev. Mark Carter, O.F.M.Cap., Par. Vicar; Rev. Eric Gauchat, O.F.M.Cap., Chap.; Rev. John Daya, O.F.M.Cap., Sr. Par. Vicar; Priests: 5

ELLICOTT CITY

Franciscan Friars - Our Lady of the Angels Province, Inc. - 12300 Folly Quarter Rd., Ellicott City, MD 21042-1419 t) 410-531-1400 Rev. Michael Heine, OFM Conv., Major Supr.; Bro. Nicholas Romeo, OFM Conv., Secy.; Brs.: 6; Priests: 20

Order of Friars Minor Conventual - 12300 Folly Quarter Rd., Ellicott City, MD 21042-1419 t) 410-531-1400 provsec2@olaprovince.org www.olaprovince.org Rev. Michael Heine, OFM Conv., Prov.; Friar Gary Johnson, OFM Conv., Prov. Asst.; Bro. Nicholas Romeo, OFM Conv., Secy.; Brs.: 34; Priests: 127

Companions of St. Anthony - 12290 Folly Quarter Rd., Ellicott City, MD 21042 t) (844) 782-6846 info@companionsofstanthony.org companionsofstanthony.org Order of Friars Minor Conventual Joseph Hamilton, Dir.;

Shrine of St. Anthony - 12290 Folly Quarter Rd., Ellicott City, MD 21042 t) (410) 531-2800 info@shrineofstanthony.org shrineofstanthony.org Rev. Richard-Jacob Forcier, O.F.M.Conv., Dir.;

SYKESVILLE

Holy Trinity Monastery - 1400 Underwood Rd., Sykesville, MD 21784; Mailing: P.O. Box 1828, Sykesville, MD 21784 t) 410-486-5171 secretary@trinitarians.org www.trinitarians.org Rev. William Sullivan, O.SS.T., Prov.; Rev. Tom Dymowski, O.SS.T., Sec. Prov., Delegate for Rel.; Rev. Kurt J. Klismet, O.SS.T., Treas.; Rev. Luigi Buccarello, O.SS.T., Minister Gen.; Rev. Santhosh George, O.SS.T., Pst.; Rev. Victor J. Scocco, O.SS.T., Pst.; Rev. Albert Michael Anuszewski, O.SS.T.; Rev. Thomas J. Burke, O.SS.T.; Rev. Gerard Lynch, O.SS.T.; Rev. William J. Moorman, O.SS.T.; Bro. Ronald Francis Specht; Rev. Damian Anuszewski, O.SS.T., Assigned elsewhere; Rev. Michael Conway, O.SS.T., Assigned elsewhere; Rev. James R. Day, O.SS.T., Assigned Elsewhere; Rev. Richard Giner, O.SS.T., Assigned elsewhere; Rev. Daniel Houde, O.SS.T., Assigned Elsewhere; Bro. Kevin McGrady, O.SS.T., Assigned elsewhere; Rev. J. Edward Owens, O.SS.T., Assigned elsewhere; Rev. Joshua Trey Warshak, O.SS.T., Assigned elsewhere; Rev. Frank Whatley, O.SS.T., Assigned elsewhere; Brs.: 3; Priests: 21

TOWSON

Maryland Province of the Society of Jesus - 8600 LaSalle Rd., Ste. 620, Towson, MD 21286-2014 t) (443) 921-1311 www.jesuitseast.org See USA East Province of the Society of Jesus in the Archdiocese of New York. Rev. Richard McGowan, S.J., Treas.;

NURSING / REHABILITATION / CONVALESCENCE / ELDERLY CARE [NUR]

BALTIMORE

Belvedere Green/Woodbourne Woods at Medstar Good Samaritan - 1651 E. Belvedere Ave., Baltimore, MD 21239 t) 410-433-7255 Bradley Chambers, Pres.;

St. Charles Villa - 603 Maiden Choice Ln., Baltimore, MD 21228-3697 t) 410-747-1211 www.sulpicians.org AKA Villa Olier. Managed by the Society of the Priests of Saint Sulpice. Asstd. Annu.: 10; Staff: 4

St. Martin's Home for Aged, Little Sisters of the Poor, Baltimore Inc. - 601 Maiden Choice Ln., Baltimore, MD 21228 t) 410-744-9367 msbaltimore@littlesistersofthepoor.org www.littlesistersofthepoorbaltimore.org Rev. Michael J. Orchik, Chap.; Sr. Loraine Maguire, L.S.P., Prov.; Sr. Jeanne Mary Piché, L.S.P., Supr.; Asstd. Annu.: 72

The Neighborhoods at St. Elizabeth (St. Elizabeth Rehabilitation and Nursing Center) - 3320 Benson Ave., Baltimore, MD 21227-1035 t) 410-644-7100 info@catholiccharities-md.org www.catholiccharities-md.org Sponsored by Associated Catholic Charities. Rev. Raymond C. Chase, Chap.;

CATONSVILLE

St. Joseph's Nursing Home - 1222 Tugwell Dr., Catonsville, MD 21228 t) 410-747-0026 stjosephs@stjosephs.net www.stjosephs.net Sisters Servants of Mary Immaculate, Inc. Sr. Krystyna Mroczek, S.S.M.I., Admin.; Asstd. Annu.: 54

TIMONIUM

Stella Maris - 2300 Dulaney Valley Rd., Timonium, MD 21093 t) 410-252-4500 ljohnso2@stellamaris.org www.stellamaris.org Long-term care; sub-acute care; home health; rehabilitation services; in-patient and home hospice; skilled home care; personal care services. Crystal Hickey, Exec. Dir.; Rev. Lawrence M. Johnson, Dir., Pastoral Care; Asstd. Annu.: 4,527

PRESCHOOLS / CHILDCARE CENTERS [PRE]

BALTIMORE

Mount Providence Child Development Center - 701 Gun Rd., Baltimore, MD 21227 t) 410-247-0449 mpcdc@oblatesisters.com www.mpcdc.com Oblate Sisters of Providence. Sr. Brenda Cherry, O.S.P., Dir.; Stds.: 75; Lay Tchrs.: 16

TIMONIUM

Francis X. Gallagher Services - 2520 Pot Spring Rd., Timonium, MD 21093 t) 667-600-2520 www.cc-md.org/gallagher Residential, day habilitation, supported employment, respite care and medical day programs for the people with intellectual disabilities. Kathy Clemente, Admin.;

RETREAT HOUSES / RENEWAL CENTERS [RTR]

SPARKS

Msgr. Clare J. O'Dwyer Retreat House - 15523 York Rd., Sparks, MD 21152; Mailing: P.O. Box 310, Sparks, MD 21152 t) 410-472-2400 odwyer@archbalt.org www.msgrodwyer.org Cassandra Palmer, Contact;

SEMINARIES [SEM]

BALTIMORE

St. Mary's Seminary and University - 5400 Roland Ave., Baltimore, MD 21210-1994 t) 410-864-4000 info@stmarys.edu www.stmarys.edu Most Rev. William E. Lori, Chancellor, Chm. Bd. of Trustees; Rev. Phillip J. Brown, P.S.S., Pres. Rector/Vice Chancellor of Ecclesiastical Theological Faculty; Rev. Gladstone H. Stevens, P.S.S., Vice Rector; Dennis Castillo, Assoc. Dean, Assessment & Accreditation; Dr. Matthew Dugandzic, Dean of the School of Theology & Prases, the Ecclesiastical Theological Faculty; Michael J. Gorman, Special Asst. to Pres. for Faculty Devel.; Rebecca Hancock, Assoc. Dean of Admin., EI; Dr. D. Brent Laytham, Dean of St. Mary's Ecumenical Inst.; Rev. Paul A. Maillet, P.S.S., Dir., Spiritual Life Progs.; Leelamma Sebastian, Dir., Pastoral Formation; James Starke, Dir. Liturgy; Rev. Msgr. Fredrick Hansen, P.S.S., Prof.; Rev. William L. Burton, O.F.M., Prof.; Rev. Stephen P. Roth, Prof.; Rev. Dennis J. Billy, C.Ss.R., Prof.; Rev. Innoncent Smith, O.P., Prof.; Rev. Lawrence B. Terrien, P.S.S., Prof.; Stds.: 212; Lay Tchrs.: 14; Pr. Tchrs.: 10

Ecumenical Institute of Theology - 5400 Roland Ave., Baltimore, MD 21210-1994 t) 410-864-4200 ei@stmarys.edu www.stmarys.edu/ei

EMMITSBURG

Mount St. Mary's Seminary - 16300 Old Emmitsburg Rd., Emmitsburg, MD 21727 t) 301-447-5295 seminaryinfo@msmary.edu www.seminary.msmary.edu As an affiliate of Mount St. Mary's University, Mount St. Mary's Seminary is a 509(a)(3) Type 1 supporting organization to the University. Rev. Msgr. Andrew R. Baker, Rector/Vice Pres.; Rev. Msgr. Michael Heintz, Dean/Dir., Intellectual Formation; Rev. Lee W. Gross, Dean of Men/ Asst. Professor of Liturgy, Systematic Theology/Latin; Rev. Msgr. McLean A. Cummings, Dir., Spiritual Formation; Rev. John P. Trigilio, Dir., Pastoral Formation; Rev. Diego Ruiz, I.V.E., Asst. Spiritual Dir./Formation Advisor; Rev. Msgr. William J. King, Prof.; Rev. Dennis D. McManus, Prof.; Rev. J. Daniel Mindling, O.F.M.Cap., Prof.; Rev. Michael J. Roach, Prof.; Timothy E. Trainor, Pres.;

Diocese of Baton Rouge

(Dioecesis Rubribaculensis)

MOST REVEREND MICHAEL G. DUCA, J.C.L.

Bishop of Baton Rouge; ordained April 29, 1978; appointed Bishop of Shreveport April 1, 2008; consecrated and installed May 19, 2008; appointed Sixth Bishop of Baton Rouge June 26, 2018; installed August 24, 2018. Bishop's Office: P.O. Box 2028, Baton Rouge, LA 70821-2028. T: 225-242-0247; F: 225-336-8768; bishop@diobr.org.

Chancery Office: Catholic Life Center, 1800 S. Acadian Thruway, P.O. Box 2028, Baton Rouge, LA 70821-2028. T: 225-387-0561; F: 225-336-8789.
www.diobr.org
chancery@diobr.org

ESTABLISHED JULY 22, 1961.

Square Miles 5,513.

Comprises the civil parishes (counties) of Ascension, Assumption, East Baton Rouge, West Baton Rouge, Iberville, Pointe Coupee, East Feliciana, West Feliciana, St. Helena, Tangipahoa, Livingston and St. James in the State of Louisiana.

For legal titles of parishes and diocesan institutions, consult the Chancery Office.

STATISTICAL OVERVIEW

Personnel

Bishop	1
Retired Bishops	1
Priests: Diocesan Active in Diocese	45
Priests: Retired, Sick or Absent	26
Number of Diocesan Priests	71
Religious Priests in Diocese	34
Total Priests in your Diocese	105
Extern Priests in Diocese	10
Ordinations:	
Transitional Deacons	2
Permanent Deacons	4
Permanent Deacons in Diocese	81
Total Brothers	17
Total Sisters	65

Parishes

Parishes	64
With Resident Pastor:	
Resident Diocesan Priests	36
Resident Religious Priests	14
Without Resident Pastor:	
Administered by Priests	13
Administered by Deacons	1
Professional Ministry Personnel:	
Brothers	4
Sisters	5
Lay Ministers	423

Welfare

Catholic Hospitals	4
Total Assisted	588,351
Homes for the Aged	6
Total Assisted	792
Specialized Homes	5
Total Assisted	506
Special Centers for Social Services	7
Total Assisted	300,000

Educational

Diocesan Students in Other Seminaries	9
Total Seminarians	9
Colleges and Universities	1
Total Students	1,700
High Schools, Diocesan and Parish	5
Total Students	1,441
High Schools, Private	3
Total Students	2,346
Elementary Schools, Diocesan and Parish	22
Total Students	10,397
Non-residential Schools for the Disabled	1
Total Students	75
Catechesis / Religious Education:	
High School Students	4,887
Elementary Students	8,551
Total Students under Catholic Instruction	29,406
Teachers in Diocese:	
Priests	11
Brothers	3
Sisters	4
Lay Teachers	1,064

Vital Statistics

Receptions into the Church:	
Infant Baptism Totals	1,307
Minor Baptism Totals	467
Adult Baptism Totals	72
Received into Full Communion	153
First Communions	1,839
Confirmations	1,595
Marriages:	
Catholic	392
Interfaith	141
Total Marriages	533
Deaths	1,719
Total Catholic Population	199,248
Total Population	1,017,396

LEADERSHIP

Vicar General/Moderator of the Curia - Very Rev. Jamin S. David (jdavid@diobr.org);
Vicar General - Very Rev. Thomas C. Ranzino (tranzino@diobr.org);
Chancellor - Ann T. Boltin (aboltin@diobr.org);
Judicial Vicar - Very Rev. Paul D. Counce (pcounce@diobr.org);

ADMINISTRATION

Diocesan Corporation (The Roman Catholic Church of the Diocese of Baton Rouge) - diobr.org Most Rev. Michael G. Duca, Pres.; Very Rev. Jamin S. David, Vice. Pres. (jdavid@diobr.org); Glenn J. Landry Jr., Treas. (glandry@diobr.org);
Office of the Bishop & Vicars - t) 225-387-0561 bishop@diobr.org Very Rev. Jamin S. David, Vicar (jdavid@diobr.org); Very Rev. Thomas C. Ranzino, Vicar (tranzino@diobr.org); Mary B. Woodruff, Contact (mary.woodruff@diobr.org);
Chancery Office - Catholic Life Center - t) 225-387-0561 chancery@diobr.org Ann T. Boltin, Chancellor (aboltin@diobr.org); Mary B. Woodruff, Contact (mary.woodruff@diobr.org);
College of Consultors - Very Rev. Jamin S. David (jdavid@diobr.org); Very Rev. Thomas C. Ranzino (tranzino@diobr.org); Rev. Matthew J. Graham (mgraham@diobr.org);
Clergy Personnel Board - Very Rev. Jamin S. David (jdavid@diobr.org); Very Rev. Thomas C. Ranzino (tranzino@diobr.org); Rev. Christopher J. Decker;
Presbyteral Council - Very Rev. Jamin S. David (jdavid@diobr.org); Rev. Paul A. Gros (pgros@diobr.org); Rev. Matthew E. McCaughey (mmccaughey@diobr.org);

OFFICES AND DIRECTORS

Archives and Records Management - t) 225-242-0220 archives@diobr.org Ann T. Boltin, Chancellor (aboltin@diobr.org);
Catholic Schools Office - t) 225-336-8735 secretary@csobr.org csobr.org Dr. Patricia Davis, Supt. (pdavis@csobr.org); Claire Willis, Asst. Supt. (cwillis@csobr.org);
Child and Youth Protection Office - t) 225-242-0202 childprotection@diobr.org Amy J. Cordon, Dir.;
Finance - t) 225-387-0561 Glenn J. Landry Jr., Fiscal Officer (glandry@diobr.org);
Human Resources - t) 225-387-0561 Anita L. Krail, Dir. (akrail@diobr.org);
Propagation of the Faith - t) 225-387-0561 cberlinger@diobr.org Christine Berlinger, Contact;
Stewardship Office - t) 225-336-8790 stewardship@diobr.org Gwen Fairchild, Dir. (gfairchild@diobr.org);
Victim Assistance Coordinator - t) 225-242-0250 childprotection@diobr.org Amy J. Cordon;

CANONICAL SERVICES

Diocesan Tribunal - t) 225-336-8755 tribunal@diobr.org Claire E Breaux, Dir. (cbreaux@diobr.org);
Defenders of the Bond - Rev. Vincent J. Dufresne; Rev. Gerard R. Martin;
Judges - Very Rev. Jamin S. David; Rev. Michael J. Moroney; Rev. Frank M. Uter;
Judicial Vicar - t) 225-336-8755 Very Rev. Paul D. Counce;
Notaries - Ann T. Boltin; John Ladouceur; Mary B. Woodruff;
Promoter of Justice - Rev. Vincent J. Dufresne;

CATHOLIC CHARITIES

Catholic Charities of the Diocese of Baton Rouge, Inc. - t) 225-336-8700 info@ccdiobr.org ccdiobr.org David C. Aguillard, Exec. Dir. (daguillard@ccdiobr.org);

CLERGY AND RELIGIOUS SERVICES

Continuing Formation for Priests - Rev. Cary Bani, Dir. (cbani@diobr.org);
Permanent Diaconate, Office of -
Deacon Life & Ministry - t) 225-387-0561 Dcn. John Veron, Dir.; Dcn. Thomas D. Benoit, Assoc. Dir.; Dcn. Timothy T. Messenger Sr., Assoc. Dir.;
Diaconate Formation - t) 225-387-0561 Rev. Paul A. Gros, Dir.;
Vicar for Religious Men and Women - Sr. Joan LaPlace, C.S.J. (jlaplace@csjoseph.org);
Vocations and Seminarians - t) 225-336-8778 Rev. Andrew J. Merrick, Dir. (amerrick@diobr.org); Rev. Joshua D. Johnson, Dir. (jjohnson@diobr.org);
Worship, Office of - t) 225-387-0561 cberlinger@diobr.org Very Rev. Thomas C. Ranzino, Dir. (tranzino@diobr.org); Christine Berlinger, Contact;

COMMUNICATIONS

Catholic Life Television - t) 225-242-0218 television@diobr.org catholiclifetv.org Stephen Lee, Dir. (slee@diobr.org);
Digital Communications - t) 225-387-0561 communications@diobr.org Nicole Jones, Contact (njones@diobr.org);
Media Consultant - t) 225-387-0561 Kelly Alexander, Contact;
The Catholic Commentator- Diocesan Newspaper - t) 225-387-0983 tcc@diobr.org Richard Meek, Editor (rmeek@diobr.org);

EVANGELIZATION

Evangelization and Catechesis, Office of - t) 225-336-8760 formation@diobr.org Dina Dow, Dir. (ddow@diobr.org);
Marriage and Family Life - t) 225-242-0323 Darryl P. Ducote, Dir. (dducote@diobr.org);
Youth and Young Adult Ministry - t) 225-336-8751 Kathleen Higgins (khiggins@diobr.org);

ORGANIZATIONS

Serra Clubs - t) 225-336-8778 spayne@diobr.org Rev. Joshua D. Johnson, Spiritual Adv./Care Srvcs. (jjohnson@diobr.org);

PASTORAL SERVICES

Black Catholics, Office of - t) 225-562-3255; 225-562-3509 Dcn. Alfred P. Adams Sr., Dir. (aadams@diobr.org);
Catholic Charismatic Renewal - t) 225-636-2464 Dotty Loar, Dir. (loard2@hotmail.com);
Ecumenical Relations - t) 225-261-4650 Rev. Michael J. Moroney, Dir. (mmoroney@diobr.org);
Hispanic Apostolate - t) 225-927-8700 apostolado@diobr.org Rev. Emilio Gomez (El Salvador), Chap. (egomez@diobr.org); Julia Scarnato, Dir. (jscarnato@diobr.org);
Life, Peace and Justice, Office of - t) 225-387-0561 x1185 Dcn. Randall Waguespack, Dir. (rwaguespack@diobr.org);
Vietnamese Apostolate - t) 225-357-4800 Rev. Hieu Quang Nguyen, I.M.S., Dir. (pnguyen@diobr.org);

SOCIAL SERVICES

Society of St. Vincent De Paul - t) 225-383-7837 info@svdpbr.com svdpbr.org Michael J. Acaldo, CEO (macaldo@svdpbr.com); Sr. Joan LaPlace, C.S.J., Spiritual Adv./Care Srvcs. (jlaplace@csjoseph.org);

PARISHES, MISSIONS, AND CLERGY

STATE OF LOUISIANA

AMITE

Congregation of St. Helena's Roman Catholic Church, Amite, Louisiana - 122 S. First St., Amite, LA 70422-2701 t) 985-748-9057 laura@sthelenachurch.net sthelenachurch.net Rev. Mark B. Beard, Pst.; Rev. Howard R. Adkins, In Res.; CRP Stds.: 323

BATON ROUGE

Congregation of St. Joseph Roman Catholic Cathedral of Baton Rouge - 412 North St., Baton Rouge, LA 70802-5496 t) 225-387-5928 www.cathedralbr.org Rev. J. Cary Bani, Pst.; Dcn. Gary C. Mooney, Pst. Min./Coord.; Olga Johnson, DRE; CRP Stds.: 23
The Congregation of St. Agnes Roman Catholic Church - 749 East Blvd., Baton Rouge, LA 70802-6398 t) 225-383-4127 saintagnesbr2@gmail.com stagnesbr.com Rev. P. Brent Maher, Pst.; Rev. Joey F. Angeles, In Res.; Rev. Alex Harb, In Res.; Allen Taylor, DRE; CRP Stds.: 79
The Congregation of St. Aloysius Roman Catholic Church - 2025 Stuart Ave., Baton Rouge, LA 70808-3979 t) 225-343-6657 www.aloysius.org Rev. Randy M. Cuevas, Pst.; Rev. Nutan S. Minj, I.M.S., Par. Vicar; Dcn. P. Chauvin Wilkinson Jr.; Patricia Greely, DRE; CRP Stds.: 154
St. Aloysius School - (Grades PreK-8) 4001 Mimosa St., Baton Rouge, LA 70808-3998 t) 225-383-3871 ecandilora@aloysius.org Erin Candilora, Prin.; Stds.: 1,161; Lay Tchrs.: 85
Congregation Of St. Anthony Of Padua And Le Van Phung Roman Catholic Church, Baton Rouge, Louisiana - 2305 Choctaw Dr., Baton Rouge, LA 70805-7910 t) 225-357-4800 c) (346) 270-7509 phuonglanicm@yahoo.com www.stanthonybr.com Rev. Peter Hieu Quang Nguyen, IMS (Vietnam), Pst.; Sr. Lan Thi Nguyen, ICM, DRE; CRP Stds.: 314
Congregation of Christ the King Roman Catholic Church of the Diocese of Baton Rouge - 11 W. Fraternity Ln., Baton Rouge, LA 70803; Mailing: LSU Box 25131, Baton Rouge, LA 70803-0106 t) 225-344-8595 www.ctklsu.org Rev. Andrew J. Merrick, Pst.; Rev. Mathew Dunn, Par. Vicar; Elizabeth Grace Krause, DRE; Jennifer A. St. Cyr, Bus. Mgr.; CRP Stds.: 5
St. Francis Xavier Catholic Church - 1143 S. 11th St., Baton Rouge, LA 70802-4997 t) 225-383-3479 stfrancisxavierbr.org Rev. Edward Chiffriller, S.S.J., Pst.; CRP Stds.: 45
St. Francis Xavier School - (Grades K-8) 1150 S. 12th St., Baton Rouge, LA 70802-4997 t) 225-387-6639 pjohnson@sfxbr.org www.sfxbr.org Paula Johnson, Prin.; Stds.: 91; Sr. Tchrs.: 1; Lay Tchrs.: 7
Congregation Of St. George Roman Catholic Church, Baton Rouge, Louisiana - 7808 St. George Dr., Baton Rouge, LA 70809-4699 t) 225-293-2212 mollyr@st-george.org; karenf@st-george.org www.st-george.org Rev. Ju Hyung (Paul) Yi, Pst.; Rev. Bernard Banares, Par. Vicar; Dcn. Glenn Farnet; Karen Fawley, DRE; Molly Rose, DRE; Joseph Smaldino, Dir., Music & Liturgy; CRP Stds.: 78
St. George School - (Grades PreK-8) 7880 St. George Dr., Baton Rouge, LA 70809-4699 t) 225-293-1298 angele.fontenot@sgschoolbr.org www.st-georgeschool.com Angele Fontenot, Prin.; Stds.: 1,100; Lay Tchrs.: 60
Congregation Of St. Gerard Majella Roman Catholic Church, Parish Of East Baton Rouge, Louisiana - 5354 Plank Rd., Baton Rouge, LA 70805; Mailing: 3808 St. Gerard Ave., Baton Rouge, LA 70805-2834 t) 225-355-2553 stgerardmajellachurch.org Rev. Tat Thang Hoang, C.Ss R, Pst.; Rev. James C. Arrambide, C.Ss.R., Hispanic Min.; Rev. Timothy Watson, C.Ss.R., Hispanic Min.; Rev. John Fahey-Guerra, C.Ss.R., In Res.; Rev. Donald MacKinnon, C.Ss.R., In Res.; Rev. Lamar Partin, C.Ss.R., In Res.; Rev. John C. Vargas, C.Ss.R., In Res.;
Congregation of Immaculate Conception Roman Catholic Church Scotlandville LA - 1565 Curtis St., Baton Rouge, LA 70807-4906 t) 225-775-7067 www.immaculateconceptionbr.org Rev. Thomas F. Clark, S.J., Pst.; Rev. Alfred C Kammer, SJ, In Res.; CRP Stds.: 89
St. Isidore the Farmer (Congregation Of Saint Isidore Roman Catholic Church, Baker, Louisiana) - 5657

Thomas Rd., Baton Rouge, LA 70811-7356 t) 225-775-8850 stisidore@diobr.org stisidorecommunity.org Rev. Frank B. Bass, Pst.; Dcn. Thomas D. Benoit; Dcn. Micheal J. Joseph; Monice Oliphant, DRE; CRP Stds.: 52

Congregation of St. Jean Vianney Roman Catholic Church - 16166 S. Harrell's Ferry Rd., Baton Rouge, LA 70816-3199 t) 225-753-7950; 225-751-2926 (CRP) kferrara@stjeanvianney.org www.stjeanvianney.org Very Rev. Thomas C. Ranzino, Pst.; Dcn. Daniel S. Borne; Dcn. Richard Abbondante; Dcn. Jeff R. Easley; Dcn. Ricky Anthony Patterson; Kerry Ferrara, DRE; CRP Stds.: 73

St. Jean Vianney School - (Grades PreK-8) 16266 S. Harrell's Ferry Rd., Baton Rouge, LA 70816-3103 t) 225-751-1831 wross@stjeanvianneyschool.org www.stjeanvianneyschool.org Wendy Ross, Prin.; Stds.: 474; Lay Tchrs.: 46

SJV Early Learning and Growth Center - t) 225-752-5356 awilliams@stjeanvianney.org www.stjearlylearningcenter.org Amie Williams, Dir.;

The Congregation Of St. Jude The Apostle Roman Catholic Church Of Baton Rouge - 9150 Highland Rd., Baton Rouge, LA 70810-4096 t) 225-766-2431 www.stjudecatholic.org Rev. Caye A. Nelson III, Pst.; Dcn. Christopher Landry; Dcn. James J. Morrissey, Bus. Mgr.; Carmel Acosta, DRE; CRP Stds.: 109

St. Jude the Apostle School - (Grades PreK-8) t) 225-769-2344 mgardiner@stjudebr.org Michelle Gardiner, Prin.; Laura Favaloro, Vice Prin.; Stds.: 562; Lay Tchrs.: 37

Congregation Of The Most Blessed Sacrament Parish - 15615 Jefferson Hwy., Baton Rouge, LA 70817-6311 t) 225-752-6230 (Office); 225-751-5867 (CRP) churchoffice@mbsparish.org; mbspsr@gmail.com Rev. C. Todd Lloyd, Pst.; Rev. Amalraj Savarimuthu, IMS (India), Par. Vicar; Dcn. Mark Thomas Berard; Dcn. Donald J. Musso; Dcn. Mark Reynaud; CRP Stds.: 195

Most Blessed Sacrament School - (Grades K-8) 8033 Baringer Rd., Baton Rouge, LA 70817-6000 t) 225-751-0273 cgioe@mbsbr.org www.mbsbr.org Cheri Gioe, Prin.; Stds.: 551; Lay Tchrs.: 29

Congregation Of Our Lady Of Mercy Roman Catholic Church - 445 Marquette Ave., Baton Rouge, LA 70806-4497 t) 225-926-1883 cleo.milano@olomchurch.com; charbel.jamhoury@olomchurch.com www.olomchurch.com Rev. Cleo J. Milano, Pst.; Rev. Charbel Jamhoury, O.L.M., Par. Vicar; Dcn. Kirk Duplantis; Dcn. Richard H. Grant; CRP Stds.: 78

Our Lady of Mercy School - (Grades PreK-8) 400 Marquette Ave., Baton Rouge, LA 70806-4498 t) 225-924-1054 alaborde@olomschool.org www.olomschool.org Allyson Laborde, Prin.; Stds.: 965; Lay Tchrs.: 57

Congregation Of St. Patrick Roman Catholic Church - 12424 Brogdon Ln., Baton Rouge, LA 70816-4801 t) 225-753-5750 scolomb@stpatrickbr.org www.stpatrickbr.org Rev. Michael A. Miceli, Pst.; Dcn. J. Peter Walsh; Dcn. Alec Campbell; Melissa N. Harshbarger, DRE; CRP Stds.: 175

Congregation Of St Paul The Apostle Roman Catholic Church, East Baton Rouge Parish - 3912 Gus Young Ave., Baton Rouge, LA 70802-1727 t) 225-383-2537 stpaulbr@aol.com; stpaul@diobr.org stpaulbr.org Rev. Arockiam Arockiam, Pst.; Martha Davis, DRE; CRP Stds.: 66

The Congregation Of Sacred Heart Roman Catholic Church - 2250 Main St., Baton Rouge, LA 70802-3198 t) 225-387-6671 info@sacredheartbr.org; ccoulon@sacredheartbr.org www.sacredheartbr.org Rev. Joshua D. Johnson, Pst.; Rev. Timothy Grimes, Par. Vicar; Rev. Peter A. Dang, In Res.; Dcn. Clayton Hollier, Pst. Assoc.; Dcn. Eulis Simien, Pst. Assoc.; Clare Coulon, DRE; CRP Stds.: 22

Sacred Heart of Jesus School - (Grades PreK-8) 2251 Main St., Baton Rouge, LA 70802 t) 225-383-7481 info@sacredheartbr.com www.sacredheartbr.com Cecilia Methvin, Prin.; Stds.: 186; Lay Tchrs.: 18

Congregation Of St. Thomas More Roman Catholic Church, East Baton Rouge Parish - 11441 Goodwood Blvd., Baton Rouge, LA 70815-6299 t) 225-275-3940 www.stmbr.org Very Rev. Michael J. Alello, Pst.; Dcn. Paul Soileau; Dcn. Joseph Scimeca; CRP Stds.: 49

St. Thomas More School - (Grades PreK-8) 11400 Sherbrook Dr., Baton Rouge, LA 70815 t) 225-275-2820 info@stmbr.org Ashley Hebert McDaniel, Prin.; Stds.: 654; Lay Tchrs.: 49

BELLE ROSE

The Congregation Of St. Jules Roman Catholic Church - Louisiana 1, Belle Rose, LA 70341-0038; Mailing: P.O. Box 38, Belle Rose, LA 70341-0038 t) 225-473-8569 drek12@sesjchurch.com; deacon@sesjchurch.com www.sesjchurch.com Rev. Tomi Thomas, IMS, Pst.; Dcn. Ehren Oschwald; Lisa Landry, DRE; CRP Stds.: 10

Brusly/St. Martin, St. Martin - 6821 Hwy. 996, Belle Rose, LA 70341 t) (225) 473-8569 sesjchurch.com

BRUSLY

The Congregation Of St. John The Baptist Roman Catholic Church - 402 S. Kirkland Dr., Brusly, LA 70719; Mailing: P.O. Box 248, Brusly, LA 70719-0248 t) 225-749-2189; 225-749-3387 (CRP) stjohnbrusly@diobr.org; jhebert@sjbbrusly.com www.sjbbrusly.com/ Rev. Johny Injacka Pappu, Pst.; June Hebert, DRE; CRP Stds.: 310

CONVENT

St. Michael the Archangel (Congregation Of St. Michael Roman Catholic Church) - 6490 LA Hwy. 44, Convent, LA 70723; Mailing: P.O. Box 129, Paulina, LA 70763 t) 225-869-5751; 225-562-3255 office@rivrdcat.org www.rivrdcat.org Rev. Vincent J. Dufresne, Pst.; Dcn. Alfred P. Adams Sr.; CRP Stds.: 58

DARROW

St. Anthony of Padua (The Congregation Of St. Anthony Roman Catholic Church Of Darrow, Louisiana) - 37311 Hwy. 22, Darrow, LA 70725; Mailing: P.O. Box 9, Sorrento, LA 70778 t) 225-675-8126 stanne@eatel.net stannestanthony.org Rev. Keun-Soo Lee, Pst.; Dcn. Robert Templet Jr.;

DENHAM SPRINGS

Congregation Of The Immaculate Conception Roman Catholic Church, Denham Springs, Louisiana - 865 Hatchell Ln., Denham Springs, LA 70726; Mailing: P.O. Box 1609, Denham Springs, LA 70727-1609 t) 225-665-5359; 225-665-5926 (CRP) churchoffice@icc-msh.org www.icc-msh.org Rev. Matthew J. Graham, Pst.; Rev. Taylor Sanford, Assoc. Pst.; Dcn. Michael T. Chiappetta; Dcn. George J. Hooper; Dcn. Rudolph W. Stahl; Rozalyn Duplantis, CRE; CRP Stds.: 596

DONALDSONVILLE

Ascension of Our Lord Jesus Christ (The Congregation Of Ascension Roman Catholic Church, Of The Parish Of Ascension, State Of Louisiana) - 716 Mississippi St., Donaldsonville, LA 70346-0508; Mailing: P.O. Box 508, Donaldsonville, LA 70346-0508 t) 225-473-3176 susanj777@aim.com www.donaldsonvillecatholics.com Rev. Matthew C. Dupre, Pst.; Susan Jumonville, DRE; CRP Stds.: 19

St. Catherine of Siena - 421 Saint Patrick St., Donaldsonville, LA 70346-0428; Mailing: P.O. Box 428, Donaldsonville, LA 70346-0428 t) 225-473-8350; 225-348-2020 (CRP) stcatherinechurch@cox.net; risehir@yahoo.com www.saintcatherinechurch.weebly.com Rev. Raphael I. Asika, M.S.P., Pst.; Cassandra Brimmer, DRE; Dcn. Edward Joseph Gauthreaux; CRP Stds.: 58

The Congregation Of Saint Francis Of Assisi Roman Catholic Church - 818 W. Tenth St., Donaldsonville, LA 70346-9501; Mailing: P.O. Box 508, Donaldsonville, LA 70346-9501 t) 225-473-3176; 225-776-4131 (CRP) susanj777@aim.com www.donaldsonvillecatholics.com Rev. Matthew C. Dupre, Pst.; Susan Jumonville, DRE; CRP Stds.: 1

FRENCH SETTLEMENT

The Congregation Of Saint Joseph Roman Catholic Church Of The Parish Of Livingston, State Of Louisiana - 15710 LA Hwy. 16, French Settlement, LA 70733-9802 t) 225-698-3110 stjosephfs@eatel.net stjosephststephen.weconnect.com Rev. Jason P. Palermo, Pst.; Dcn. James A. Little; Dcn. Leon Roy Murphy Jr.; Barbara Berthelot, DRE; CRP Stds.: 140

GONZALES

Congregation Of St. Mark Roman Catholic Church - 42021 Hwy. 621, Gonzales, LA 70737-9354 t) 225-647-8461 stmark@diobr.org www.stmarkgonzales.org Rev. Rubin R. Reynolds, Pst.; CRP Stds.: 471

St. Theresa of Avila (Congregation Of St. Theresa Roman Catholic Church, Gonzales, Louisiana) - 1022 N. Burnside Ave., Gonzales, LA 70737-2551 t) 225-647-6588 www.st-theresa-of-avila.com Rev. Eric V. Gyan, Pst.; Dcn. Steven Carl Gonzales; Dcn. Jodi A. Moscona; Alice Blair, DRE; CRP Stds.: 252

St. Theresa Middle School (East Ascension/East Iberville Regional Catholic School Partnership, Inc.) - (Grades 4-8) 212 E. New River St., Gonzales, LA 70737-2499 t) 225-647-2803 michaballow@sta-sjp.org www.sjp-sta.org Micha Ballow, Prin.; Stds.: 362; Lay Tchrs.: 24

GRAMERCY

Most Sacred Heart of Jesus (Congregation Of Sacred Heart Roman Catholic Church Of Gramercy) - 616 E. Main St., Gramercy, LA 70052; Mailing: P.O. Box 129, Paulina, LA 70763 t) 225-869-5751 office@rivrdcat.org www.rivrdcat.org Rev. Vincent J. Dufresne, Pst.; Dcn. Alfred P. Adams Sr.; Melissa Laurent, DRE; Harriet Melancon, DRE; CRP Stds.: 225

GREENWELL SPRINGS

Congregation Of St. Alphonsus Liguori Roman Catholic Church - 14040 Greenwell Springs Rd., Greenwell Springs, LA 70739-3302 t) 225-261-4650; 225-261-4644 (CRP) dre@alphonsus.org alphonsus.org Rev. Michael J. Moroney, Pst.; Dcn. Ronald James Hebert; Dcn. Robert J. Kusch; Olga Johnson, DRE; CRP Stds.: 421

St. Alphonsus Liguori School - (Grades PreK-8) 13940 Greenwell Springs Rd., Greenwell Springs, LA 70739 t) 225-261-5299 cryals@stalphonsusbr.org www.stalphonsusbr.org Cynthia Ryals, Prin.; Stds.: 423; Lay Tchrs.: 29

GROSSE TETE

The Congregation Of St. Joseph Roman Catholic Church, Of The Parish Of Iberville, State Of Louisiana - 76940 Gum St., Grosse Tete, LA 70740-0008; Mailing: 11140 Hwy. 77, Maringouin, LA 70757 t) (225) 960-6833 pchampagne@triparishes.org www.triparishes.org Rev. David L. Dawson III, Pst.; Peggy Champagne, DRE; CRP Stds.: 16

HAMMOND

Congregation Of Holy Ghost Roman Catholic Church, Hammond, Louisiana - 601 N. Oak St., Hammond, LA 70401-2529 t) 985-345-3360 lsmith@hgchurch.org; tlabbe@hgchurch.org www.hgchurch.org Rev. Charles K. Johnson, O.P., Pst.; Rev. Cayet N. Mangiaracina, O.P., Assoc. Pst.; Dcn. Mauricio Salazar; Trisha Labbe, DRE; CRP Stds.: 104

Holy Ghost School - (Grades PreSchool-8) 507 N. Oak St., Hammond, LA 70401-2598 t) 985-345-0977 secretary@hgschool.org; info@hgschool.org www.hgschool.org Donna Wallette, Prin.; Stds.: 675; Lay Tchrs.: 40

St. Margaret Queen of Scotland (Congregation Of St. Margaret Roman Catholic Church) - 30300 Catholic Hall Rd., Hammond, LA 70403; Mailing: P.O. Box 100, Albany, LA 70711-0100 t) 225-567-3573; 225-567-2031 stmargaret@diobr.org stmargaretstthomas.com Very Rev. Jamin S. David, Pst.; Rev. Paul A. Gros, Par. Vicar; Dcn. William Corbett; Dcn. Timothy T. Messenger Sr.; Dcn. Randall Waguespack; CRP Stds.: 128

St. Thomas the Apostle Chapel - 32191 Hwy. 22, Springfield, LA 70462; Mailing: P. O. Box 100, Albany, LA 70711-0100 t) (225) 567-3573 stmargaretstthomas.com/

INDEPENDENCE

Congregation Of Mater Dolorosa Roman Catholic Church, Independence, Louisiana - 620 3rd St.,

Independence, LA 70443; Mailing: P.O. Box 349, Independence, LA 70443-0349 t) 985-878-9639 joyce@materdolorosa.net; shana@materdolorosa.net materdolorosa.net/ Rev. Reuben Dykes, Pst.; CRP Stds.: 59

Mater Dolorosa School - (Grades PreK-8) 509 Pine St., Independence, LA 70443-0380; Mailing: P.O. Box 380, Independence, LA 70443-0380 t) 985-878-4295 mcapadona@mdeagles.org mdeagles.org Melissa Capadona, Prin.; Stds.: 164; Lay Tchrs.: 9

Husser, St. Dominic - 55720 Hwy. 445, Husser, LA 70446; Mailing: 620 3rd St., P.O. Box 349, Independence, LA 70443-0349 rdykes@diobr.org www.materdolorosa.net

LABADIEVILLE

The Congregation Of Saint Philomena Roman Catholic Church - 118 Convent St., Labadieville, LA 70372-0099; Mailing: P.O. Box 99, Labadieville, LA 70372 t) 985-526-4247 philomena1847@gmail.com; dre.philomena1847@gmail.com Rev. Edwin J. Martin, Pst.; CRP Stds.: 84

LAKELAND

The Congregation Of Immaculate Conception Roman Catholic Church - 12364 LA Hwy. 416, Lakeland, LA 70752-0158; Mailing: P.O. Box 158, Lakeland, LA 70752-0158 t) 225-627-5124; 225-627-5819 (CRP) icclakeland@diobr.org www.immaculateconceptionlakeland.com Rev. Amrit Raj, I.M.S., Pst.; Dina Tunstall, DRE; CRP Stds.: 130

LIVONIA

Congregation Of St. Frances Xavier Cabrini Roman Catholic Church Of Livonia, Louisiana - 3523 Hwy. 78, Livonia, LA 70755; Mailing: 11140 Hwy. 77, Maringouin, LA 70757 t) (225) 960-6833 pchampagne@triparishes.org; ddawson@triparishes.org www.triparishes.org Rev. David L. Dawson III, Pst.; Peggy Champagne, DRE; CRP Stds.: 30

Fordoche, St. Catherine of Siena - 4324 N. Railroad Ave., Fordoche, LA 70732 t) 225-625-2438 ddawson@diobr.org

MARINGOUIN

Congregation Of Immaculate Heart Of Mary Roman Catholic Church Of Maringouin - 11140 Hwy. 77, Maringouin, LA 70757-3504 t) (225) 960-6833 pchampagne@triparishes.org; ddawson@triparishes.org www.triparishes.org Rev. David L. Dawson III, Pst.; Peggy Champagne, DRE; CRP Stds.: 14

MAUREPAS

St. Stephen the Martyr (Congregation Of St. Stephen's Roman Catholic Church Of Whitehall) - 22494 LA Hwy. 22, Maurepas, LA 70449-3404; Mailing: 15710 LA Hwy. 16, French Settlement, LA 70733 t) 225-698-3110 stjosephststephen.weconnect.com Rev. Jason P. Palermo, Pst.; Dcn. James A. Little; Dcn. Leon Roy Murphy Jr.; Kim Bourgeois, DRE; Dana Vicknair, DRE; CRP Stds.: 26

MORGANZA

Congregation Of St. Ann Roman Catholic Church Of Morganza - 182 Church St., Morganza, LA 70759-0128; Mailing: P.O. Box 128, Morgnza, LA 70759 t) 225-694-3781 www.goodsaintann.com Rev. Babu Nalkara Vereeth, Pst.; CRP Stds.: 42

Innis, St. Vincent De Paul - 6389 La. Hwy. 1, Innis, LA 70747 t) (225) 694-3781 Marietta Ramagos, Contact;

NAPOLEONVILLE

Congregation of St. Anne Roman Catholic Church - 405 Franklin St., Napoleonville, LA 70390-0090; Mailing: P.O. Box 99, Napoleonville, LA 70390 t) 985-369-6656 (CRP); 985-369-2130 stanne002@gmail.com; stanne033@gmail.com www.bayoulandchurches.com Rev. Edwin J. Martin, Pst.; Kathy Landry, DRE; CRP Stds.: 151

Assumption of the Blessed Virgin Mary (The Congregation Of The Assumption Roman Catholic Church Of Plattenville) - 5604 Royal St., Napoleonville, LA 70390-0099; Mailing: P.O. Box 58, Plattenville, LA 70393 t) 985-369-6656; 985-369-2103 (CRP) stanne002@gmail.com; stanne033@gmail.com www.bayoulandchurches.com Rev. Edwin J. Martin, Pst.; Kathy Landry, DRE; CRP Stds.: 151

St. Benedict the Moor - 5479 Hwy. 1, Napoleonville, LA 70390-2410; Mailing: P.O. Box 220, Napoleonville, LA 70390 t) 985-513-3470 stbenaug1911@gmail.com; pastor.benaug@gmail.com www.stbenaug.com Rev. Andrew A Toyinbo, MSP (Nigeria), Pst.; Tara Dupaty, DRE; Jerilyn S. Williams, DRE; CRP Stds.: 46

St. Augustine Church - 174 Hwy. 1003, Belle Rose, LA 70341 t) (985) 513-3470

NEW ROADS

The Congregation Of St. Augustine Roman Catholic Church - 809 New Roads St., New Roads, LA 70760-0548; Mailing: P.O. Box 548, New Roads, LA 70760-0548 t) 225-638-7553 Rev. Joseph Benjamin, S.S.J., Pst.;

The Congregation Of Saint Mary False River Roman Catholic Church Of The Parish Of Pte. Coupee, State Of Louisiana - 348 W. Main St., New Roads, LA 70760-3587; Mailing: 402 W. Main St., New Roads, LA 70760 t) 225-638-9665 info@stmarysfr.org; pastor@stmarysfr.org www.stmarysfr.org Rev. Christopher J. Decker, Pst.; Molly Cline, DRE; CRP Stds.: 130

St. Francis of Pointe Coupee Chapel - 10364 Pointe Coupee Rd., New Roads, LA 70760 t) (225) 638-9665 stmaryfalseriver@diobr.org stmarysfr.org

PAINCOURTVILLE

The Congregation Of Saint Elizabeth Roman Catholic Church - 119 Hwy. 403, Paincourtville, LA 70391; Mailing: P.O. Box 1, Paincourtville, LA 70391-0001 t) 225-473-8569 office@sesjchurch.com; drek12@sesjchurch.com www.sesjchurch.com Rev. Tomi Thomas, IMS, Pst.; Dcn. Ehren Oschwald; Lisa Landry, DRE; CRP Stds.: 30

PAULINA

Congregation Of St. Joseph's Roman Catholic Church - 2130 Rectory St., Paulina, LA 70763; Mailing: P.O. Box 129, Paulina, LA 70763 t) 225-869-5751 office@rivrdcat.org www.rivrdcat.org Rev. Vincent J. Dufresne, Pst.; Dcn. Alfred P. Adams Sr.; Melissa Laurent, DRE; CRP Stds.: 270

Lutcher, Our Lady of Prompt Succor - 2350 Louisiana Ave, Lutcher, LA 70071; Mailing: PO Box 129, Paulina, LA 70763

PIERRE PART

Congregation Of St. Joseph The Worker Roman Catholic Church Of Assumption, Louisiana - 3304 Hwy. 70 S., Pierre Part, LA 70339-0190; Mailing: P.O. Box 190, Pierre Part, LA 70339 t) 985-252-6633; 985-252-6008 office@sjworker.org; fral@sjworker.org www.sjworker.org Rev. Al M. Davidson, Pst.; CRP Stds.: 242

PLAQUEMINE

The Congregation Of Saint John The Evangelist Roman Catholic Church Of The Parish Of Iberville, State Of Louisiana - 57805 Main St., Plaquemine, LA 70764-2531 t) 225-687-2402 www.stjohnchurchplaq.org Rev. Gregory J. Daigle, Pst.; Dcn. Alfred J. Ricard; CRP Stds.: 89

PONCHATOULA

Congregation Of St. Joseph's Roman Catholic Church Ponchatoula, LA - 330 W. Pine St., Ponchatoula, LA 70454-0368; Mailing: P.O. Box 368, Ponchatoula, LA 70454-0368 t) 985-386-3749 aperrin@sjscrusaders.org www.stjosephsonline.com Rev. Paul A. McDuffie, Pst.; Dcn. Michael A. Agnello; Dcn. Ed Hanks; Dcn. Larry Melancon; CRP Stds.: 155

St. Joseph School - (Grades PreK-8) 175 N. Eighth St., Ponchatoula, LA 70454-3306 t) 985-386-6421; 985-386-8075 sjsoffice@sjscrusaders.org; dragusa@sjscrusaders.org sjscrusaders.org Danette Ragusa, Prin.; Stds.: 540; Lay Tchrs.: 33

PORT ALLEN

Congregation Of Holy Family Roman Catholic Church - 474 N. Jefferson, Port Allen, LA 70767-0290; Mailing: P.O. Box 290, Port Allen, LA 70767-0290 t) 225-383-1838; 225-336-4463 (CRP) holyfamilychurchpa.org Rev. James Singarayar (India), Admin.; Dcn. Minos Ponville Jr.; CRP Stds.: 38

Holy Family School - (Grades PreK-8) 335 N. Jefferson Ave., Port Allen, LA 70767-2798 t) 225-344-4100 aashford@hfspa.com holyfamilyschool.com Alise Ashford, Prin.; Stds.: 428; Lay Tchrs.: 33

Preschool - 415 N. Jefferson Ave., Port Allen, LA 70767 t) 225-343-6541 prek3@hfspa.com Leigh Le Blanc, Dir.;

PRAIRIEVILLE

The Congregation Of St. John The Evangelist Roman Catholic Church - 15208 Hwy. 73, Prairieville, LA 70769-3507 t) 225-673-8307; 225-673-8402 (CRP) khagendorfer@stjohnchurch.org Rev. Gerard R. Martin, Pst.; Rev. Lamar Partin, CsSR, Par. Vicar; Dcn. Randall A. Clement; Karen Hagendorfer, Contact; Marlene Bruce, DRE; CRP Stds.: 981

SORRENTO

Congregation Of St. Anne's Roman Catholic Church Of Sorrento - 7348 Main St., Sorrento, LA 70778-0009; Mailing: PO Box 9, Sorrento, LA 70778 t) 225-675-8126 stanne@eatel.net; stannepsr@eatel.net stannestanthony.org Rev. Keun-Soo Lee, Pst.; Anne Miller, DRE; CRP Stds.: 80

ST. AMANT

Congregation Of Holy Rosary Roman Catholic Church, St. Amant, Ascension Parish, Louisiana - 44450 Hwy. 429, St. Amant, LA 70774-4597 t) 225-647-5321; 225-647-3696 (CRP) holyrosary@diobr.org olohr.com Rev. Matthew P. Lorrain, Pst.; Dcn. Michael P. Parker; Jamie Lambert, DRE; Wendy Enloe, Spiritual Adv./Care Srvcs.; CRP Stds.: 467

Lake, Sacred Heart - 45049 Lake Martin Rd., Lake, LA 70774

ST. FRANCISVILLE

Congregation Of Our Lady Of Mt. Carmel Roman Catholic Church - 11485 Ferdinand St., St. Francisville, LA 70775; Mailing: P.O. Box 1249, St. Francisville, LA 70775-1249 t) 225-635-3630 marygodke@gmail.com; ourladyofmountcarmel@diobr.org www.felicianacatholic.org Rev. Bradley A. Doyle, Pst.; Mary Godke, DRE; CRP Stds.: 133

Jackson, Our Lady of Perpetual Help - 3147 Church St., Jackson, LA 70748 t) (225) 635-3630 Michelle Carter, Contact;

Our Lady of Perpetual Help Trust - t) (225) 635-3630

ST. GABRIEL

The Congregation Of Saint Gabriel Roman Catholic Church - 3625 Hwy. 75, St. Gabriel, LA 70776-9411 t) 225-642-8441 stgabrielcatholi@bellsouth.net www.stgabrielcatholicchurch.com Rev. Charles R. Landry, Pst.; Dcn. John Veron; Myra Tircuit, DRE; CRP Stds.: 18

ST. JAMES

The Congregation Of Saint James Roman Catholic Church - 6618 Hwy. 18, St. James, LA 70086; Mailing: 13281 Hwy. 644, Vacherie, LA 70090 t) 225-265-3953 stjameschurch@canecatholics.com; chymel@canecatholics.com www.canecatholics.com St. James is clustered with St. Philip and Our Lady of Peace form the cluster of Catholic Churches in West St. James. Rev. Matthew E. McCaughey, Pst.; Dcn. Glenn Michael Hymel; CRP Stds.: 50

TICKFAW

Congregation Of Our Lady Of Pompeii Roman Catholic Church, Tickfaw, LA - 14450 Hwy. 442, Tickfaw, LA 70466; Mailing: P.O. Box 276, Tickfaw, LA 70466-0276 t) 985-345-8957 Dcn. Albert Levy III, Parish Life Coord.; Rev. Michael A. Galea, Sacramental Min.; CRP Stds.: 18

VACHERIE

Our Lady Of Peace Roman Catholic Church - 13281 Hwy. 644, Vacherie, LA 70090-3102 t) 225-265-3953 office@canecatholics.com; kporet@canecatholics.com www.canecatholics.com Our Lady of Peace is clustered with St. James and St. Philip form the cluster of Catholic Churches in West St. James. Rev. Matthew E. McCaughey, Pst.; Dcn. Glenn Michael Hymel; Dcn. Ricky P. Oubre; CRP Stds.: 254

The Congregation Of Saint Philip Roman Catholic Church - 1175 Hwy. 18, Vacherie, LA 70090-9527; Mailing: 13281 Hwy 644, Vacherie, LA 70090 t) 225-265-3953 chymel@canecatholics.com; office@canecatholics.com www.canecatholics.com St. Philip is clustered with St. James and Our Lady of Peace forming the cluster of Catholic Churches in W. St. James Rev. Matthew E. McCaughey, Pst.; Dcn. Glenn Michael Hymel; CRP Stds.: 33

WHITE CASTLE

The Congregation Of Our Lady Of Prompt Succor Roman Catholic Church, Of The Parish Of Iberville, State Of Louisiana - 32615 Bowie St., White Castle, LA 70788; Mailing: P.O. Box 249, White Castle, LA 70788-0249 t) 985-252-6008; 225-545-3635 office@sjworker.org Rev. Al M. Davidson, Admin.; CRP Stds.: 5

ZACHARY

Congregation Of St. John The Baptist Roman Catholic Church Of Zachary - 4826 Main St., Zachary, LA 70791; Mailing: 4727 McHugh Dr., Zachary, LA 70791-3935 t) 225-654-5778; 225-654-5885 (CRP) religioused@sjb-ola.org sjb-ola.org Rev. M. Jeffery Bayhi, Pst.; Katie Myrick Hamilton, DRE; CRP Stds.: 137

Clinton, Our Lady of the Assumption - stjohnzachary@diobr.org

SCHOOLS: PRESCHOOL THRU HIGH SCHOOL

SCHOOLS

STATE OF LOUISIANA

BATON ROUGE

Redemptorist St. Gerard Elementary School - (Grades PreK-8) 3655 St. Gerard Ave., Baton Rouge, LA 70805-2898 t) 225-355-1437 redemptoristelem@csobr.org; cdomino@resbr.org resbr.org Cheryl Domino, Prin.; Stds.: 225; Lay Tchrs.: 20

NEW ROADS

Catholic Elementary School of Pointe Coupee (Pointe Coupee Catholic Interparochial School, Inc.) - (DIO) (Grades PreK-6) 304 Napoleon St., New Roads, LA 70760-3527 t) 225-638-9313 www.catholicpc.com Serving parishes in Lakeland, Livonia, Morganza, New Roads and Maringouin. Jason Christopher Chauvin, Prin.; Stds.: 345; Lay Tchrs.: 21

PAINCOURTVILLE

St. Elizabeth Interparochial School, Inc. - (DIO) (Grades PreK-8) 6051 Convent St, Paincourtville, LA 70391-0420; Mailing: P.O. Drawer M, Paincourtville, LA 70391 t) 985-369-7402 akling@sescubs.com geauxcubs.com/ Serving parishes in Belle Rose, Bertrandville, Napoleonville, Paincourtville, Pierre Part, Plattenville and Labadieville. Rev. Tomi Thomas, IMS, Admin.; Dr. Andy Kling, Prin.; Stds.: 155; Sr. Tchrs.: 2; Lay Tchrs.: 12

PAULINA

St. Peter Chanel Interparochial School (St. Peter Chanel Interparochial School Board, Inc.) - (DIO) (Grades PreK-8) 2590 LA Hwy. 44, Paulina, LA 70763 t) 225-869-5778 ppoche@stpchanel.org www.stpchanel.org Serving communities of Paulina, Gramercy, Convent, Vacherie, St. James, Lutcher and Grand Point. Paula Poche, Prin.; Amanda Duhon, Office Manager/Bookkeeper; Sandi Waguespack, Office Assistant/ Teacher; Stds.: 352; Scholastics: 352; Lay Tchrs.: 22

PRAIRIEVILLE

St. John Primary School (East Ascension/East Iberville Regional Catholic School Partnership) - (PAR) (Grades PreK-3) 37407 Duplessis Rd., Prairieville, LA 70769-4321 t) 225-647-2803 kimnaquin@sjp-sta.org www.sjp-sta.org Kim Naquin, Prin.; Stds.: 374; Lay Tchrs.: 24

HIGH SCHOOLS

STATE OF LOUISIANA

BATON ROUGE

Catholic High School - (PRV) (Grades 8-12) 855 Hearthstone Dr., Baton Rouge, LA 70806-5599 t) 225-383-0397 info@catholichigh.org www.catholichigh.org Lisa Harvey, Prin.; Gerald E. Tullier, Pres.; Stds.: 1,103; Bro. Tchrs.: 3; Lay Tchrs.: 135

CHS Foundation - t) (225) 383-0397

***St. Joseph's Academy** - (PRV) (Grades 9-12) 3015 Broussard St., Baton Rouge, LA 70808-1198 t) 225-383-7207 www.sjabr.org Stacia Andricain, Prin.; Jan Rhorer Breen, Pres.; Stds.: 1,080; Sr. Tchrs.: 1; Lay Tchrs.: 70

St. Michael the Archangel Diocesan Regional High School - (DIO) (Grades 9-12) 17521 Monitor Ave., Baton Rouge, LA 70817; Mailing: P.O. Box 86110, Baton Rouge, LA 70879-6110 t) 225-753-9782 www.smhsbr.org Ellen B. Lee, Prin.; Amy Donaldson, Librn.; Stds.: 588; Lay Tchrs.: 56

DONALDSONVILLE

Ascension Catholic Diocesan Regional School - (DIO) (Grades PreK-12) 311 St. Vincent St., Donaldsonville, LA 70346-2697 t) 225-473-9227 tammy.crochet@acbulldogs.org www.acbulldogs.org Serving parishes in Donaldsonville, St. James, Belle Rose, Vacherie, White Castle, Darrow, Gonzales, Convent, Paincourtville and Plattenville. Tammy Crochet, Prin.; Stds.: 424; Lay Tchrs.: 44

Ascension Catholic Interparochial School Endowment Fund - Rev. Matthew C. Dupre, Pst.;

HAMMOND

St. Thomas Aquinas Diocesan Regional Catholic High School - (DIO) (Grades 9-12) 14520 Voss Dr., Hammond, LA 70401-9801 t) 985-542-7662 will.johnson@stafalcons.org; brandi.cambre@stafalcons.org www.stafalcons.org Will Johnson, Prin.; Stds.: 312; Lay Tchrs.: 26

Veritas Foundation -

NEW ROADS

Catholic High School of Pointe Coupee (Pointe Coupee Catholic Interparochial School, Inc.) - (DIO) (Grades 7-12) 504 Fourth St., New Roads, LA 70760-3499 t) 225-638-9313 www.catholicpc.com Serving parishes in Lakeland, Livonia, Morganza, New Roads and Maringouin. Jason Christopher Chauvin, Prin.; Stds.: 240; Lay Tchrs.: 22

PLAQUEMINE

St John the Evangelist School - (DIO) (Grades PreK-12) 24250 Regina St., Plaquemine, LA 70764-3598 t) 225-687-3056 cschlatre@stjohnschool.org www.stjohnschool.org Serving parishes in Plaquemine, Brusly, Port Allen, Grosse Tete, St. Gabriel and White Castle. Cherie Schlatre, Prin.; Stds.: 454; Lay Tchrs.: 38

INSTITUTIONS LOCATED IN DIOCESE

CAMPUS MINISTRY / NEWMAN CENTERS [CAM]

BATON ROUGE

Christ the King Parish and Catholic Center (Congregation of Christ the King Roman Catholic Church of the Diocese of Baton Rouge) - 11 Fraternity Ln., Baton Rouge, LA 70803-0106; Mailing: PO Box 411, Baton Rouge, LA 70821-0411 t) 225-344-8595 adazzio@ctklsu.org www.ctklsu.org Rev. Andrew J. Merrick, Pst.; Rev. Mathew Dunn, Par. Vicar; Alison Dazzio, Admin.;

Martin Luther King, Jr. Catholic Student Center - 586 Harding Blvd., Baton Rouge, LA 70807-5301 t) 225-775-8691 mlkcatholiccenter@gmail.com www.immaculateconceptionbr.org Rev. Thomas F. Clark, S.J., Chap.;

HAMMOND

St. Albert the Great Catholic Student Center - 409 W. Dakota St., Hammond, LA 70401-2517 t) 985-345-7206 stalbertselu@gmail.com www.stalbertselu.org Serving Southeastern Louisiana University. Friar Michael James O'Rourke, OP, Dir.;

COLLEGES & UNIVERSITIES [COL]

BATON ROUGE

Franciscan Missionaries of Our Lady University - 5414 Brittany Dr., Baton Rouge, LA 70808 t) 225-768-1710 tina.holland@fmolhs.org www.franu.edu Tina Holland, Pres.; Stds.: 1,228; Scholastics: 97

CONVENTS, MONASTERIES, AND RESIDENCES FOR WOMEN [CON]

BATON ROUGE

Congregation of St. Joseph - 3134 Hundred Oaks Ave., Baton Rouge, LA 70808 t) 225-332-2999 pwarbritton@csjoseph.org; kroubique@csjoseph.org www.csjoseph.org Kristy Roubique, Contact; Srs.: 39

Franciscan Missionaries of Our Lady North American Province Inc. - 4200 Essen Ln., Baton Rouge, LA 70809-2196 t) 225-922-7443 ann.nguyen@fmolhs.org Srs.: 12

Maryville Novitiate and Provincial House - t) (225) 526-7443 www.fmolsisters.com

Missionaries of Charity - 737 East Blvd., Baton Rouge, LA 70802-6399 t) 225-383-8367 Convent with soup kitchen and Queen of Peace emergency night shelter for women Sr. M. Jesusla MC, MC, Supr.; Srs.: 7

ZACHARY

Hospitaler Sisters of Mercy - Mother of Mercy Convent - 4848 Lois Dr., Zachary, LA 70791 t) 225-999-5087 villaraffaella@msn.com Sr. Normita Nunez, SOM, Supr.; Srs.: 5

ENDOWMENTS / FOUNDATIONS / TRUSTS [EFT]

BATON ROUGE

St. Aloysius School Endowment Fund - 2025 Stuart Ave, Baton Rouge, LA 70808 t) 225-383-3871 info@aloysius.org school.aloysius.org Rev. Randy M. Cuevas, Pst.;

St. Joseph Cathedral Cemetery Fund - 412 North St., Baton Rouge, LA 70802 t) 225-387-5928 Rev. J. Cary Bani, Pst.;

Pamphile and Mabyn Donaldson Trust for St. Thomas More - 11441 Goodwood Blvd., Baton Rouge, LA 70815 t) 225-275-3940 Very Rev. Michael J. Alello, Pst.;

Sacred Heart School Endowment Fund - 2251 Main St., Baton Rouge, LA 70802-3144 t) 225-383-7481 Rev. Joshua D. Johnson, Pst.;

***SJA Foundation** - 3015 Broussard St., Baton Rouge, LA 70808 t) 225-383-7207 geraldm@sjabr.org; herringtonl@sjabr.org sjabr.org Jan Rhorer Breen, Exec.;

***The Society of St. Vincent de Paul Foundation** - 220 St. Vincent de Paul Pl., Baton Rouge, LA 70802; Mailing: P. O. Box 127, Baton Rouge, LA 70821-0127 t) 225-383-7837 macaldo@svdpbr.org svdpbr.org Michael J. Acaldo, CEO;

St. Joseph Cathedral Trust & Bettie Womack Dedicated Cathedral Trust Funds - 412 North St., Baton Rouge, LA 70802 t) 225-387-5928 Rev. J. Cary Bani, Pst.;

St. Thomas More School Endowment Trust - 11400 Sherbrook, Baton Rouge, LA 70815 t) 225-275-2820 mcdaniela@stmbr.org www.stmbr.org Ashley Hebert McDaniel, Prin.;

CONVENT

Hynes Fund - 5858 Louisiana Hwy. 44, Convent, LA 70723-0089; Mailing: P.O. Box 89, Convent, LA 70723-0089 t) 800-782-9431 manresahr@bellsouth.net Tim Murphy, Dir.;

GONZALES

St. Theresa of Avila Catholic School Educational Foundation - 212 E. New River St., Gonzales, LA 70737 t) 225-647-2803 michaballow@sjp-sta.org Micah Ballow, Prin.;

PORT ALLEN

Nim Pecquet Holy Family School Foundation - 335 N. Jefferson Ave., Port Allen, LA 70767 t) 225-344-4100 ashford@hfspa.org holyfamilyschool.com Alise Ashford, Prin.;

HOSPITALS / HEALTH SERVICES [HOS]

BATON ROUGE

Our Lady of the Lake Hospital, Inc. (Our Lady of the Lake Regional Medical Center; DBA Our Lady of the Lake Children's Hospital; DBA Our Lady of the Lake Ascension) - 5000 Hennessy Blvd., Baton Rouge, LA 70808-4398 t) 225-765-6565 chuck.spicer@fmolhs.org www.ololrmc.com Rev. Johnson Kuriapilly, Chap.; Sr. Barbara Arceneaux, FMOL, Supr.; Chuck Spicer, Pres.; Bed Capacity: 1,005; Asstd. Annu.: 574,005; Staff: 6,170

Our Lady of the Lake Foundation - 5000 Hennessy Blvd., Baton Rouge, LA 70808-4398 t) 225-765-5000 ann.marmandefrenzel@fmolhs.org Ann Marie Marmande, Vice. Pres.;

Tau Center - 8080 Margaret Ann Dr., Baton Rouge, LA 70809-3444 t) 225-767-1320 Bed Capacity: 47; Asstd. Annu.: 1,218; Staff: 204

NAPOLEONVILLE

Our Lady of the Lake Assumption Community Hospital, Inc. (Assumption Community Hospital) - 135 Hwy. 402, Napoleonville, LA 70390-2217 t) 985-369-3600 brian.tripode@fmolhs.org ololrmc.com Chuck Spicer, Exec.; Bed Capacity: 15; Asstd. Annu.: 12,490; Staff: 53

MISCELLANEOUS [MIS]

BATON ROUGE

Baton Rouge Chancery Office - 1800 S. Acadian Thwy., Baton Rouge, LA 70808-1698; Mailing: P.O. Box 2028, Baton Rouge, LA 70821-2028 t) 225-387-0561 chancery@diobr.org diobr.org/ Very Rev. Jamin S. David, Vicar; Very Rev. Thomas C. Ranzino, Vicar; Ann T. Boltin, Chancellor;

Bishop Stanley J. Ott Works of Mercy Trust - Glenn J. Landry Jr., Treas.;

Catholic Foundation of the Diocese of Baton Rouge - Glenn J. Landry Jr., Treas.;

Diocese of Baton Rouge Clergy Retirement Plan - Glenn J. Landry Jr., Treas.;

Diocese of Baton Rouge Lay Retirement Plan - Glenn J. Landry Jr., Treas.;

The Roman Catholic Church of The Diocese of Baton Rouge, Deposit and Loan Fund, Inc. - Glenn J. Landry Jr., CFO;

Bishop Stanley J. Ott Shelter Program - 220 St. Vincent de Paul Pl., Baton Rouge, LA 70802; Mailing: P.O. Box 127, Baton Rouge, LA 70821-0127 t) 225-383-7343; 225-383-7837 macaldo@svdpbr.com svdpbr.org Homeless shelter and services for men, women, children and families. Over 20,000 guest nights provided last year. Michael J. Acaldo, CEO;

Catholic Charities of the Diocese of Baton Rouge, Inc. - 1900 S. Acadian Thwy., Baton Rouge, LA 70808 t) 225-336-8700 info@ccdiobr.org www.ccdiobr.org David C. Aguillard, Exec.;

Child Nutrition Program - 1800 S. Acadian Thwy., Baton Rouge, LA 70808; Mailing: 3300 Hundred Oaks Ave., Baton Rouge, LA 70808 t) 225-387-6421 cnp@diobr.org www.cnpbr.org Lynda Carville, Dir.;

Closer Walk Catholic Communications - 4256 North Blvd., Baton Rouge, LA 70879-8279; Mailing: P.O. Box 87279, Baton Rouge, LA 70879-8279 t) 225-615-7085 admin@cwm.brcoxmail.com www.closerwalkcatholiccommunications.com Rev. M. Jeffery Bayhi, Pres.;

Franciscan Ministry Fund, Inc. - 4200 Essen Ln., Baton Rouge, LA 70809 t) 225-922-7443 peter.guarisco@fmolhs.org Sr. Barbara Arceneaux, FMOL, Contact;

Franciscan Missionaries of Our Lady Health System, Inc. - 4200 Essen Ln., Baton Rouge, LA 70809-2196 t) 225-923-2701 richard.vath1@fmolhs.org www.fmolhs.org Dr. Richard R Vath, CEO;

Franciscan PACE, Inc. - 4200 Essen Ln., Baton Rouge, LA 70809 t) 225-923-2701 karen.allen@fmolhs.org Karen B. Allen, Exec.;

Haiti Project, Inc. - 4200 Essen Ln., Baton Rouge, LA 70809-2196 t) 225-922-7443 martha.abshire@fmolhs.org Sr. Martha Abshire, FMOL, Exec.;

International Institute of Culture and Gender Studies - 6336 Snowden Dr., Baton Rouge, LA 70817 c) (504) 982-5729 contact@cultureandgender.com www.cultureandgender.com/ Rev. Alexander Albert, Dir.; Christina Uhlich, Secy.;

***Lebanese Maronite Order, Inc.** - 3915 Berkley Hill Ave., Baton Rouge, LA 70809

Louisiana Conference of Catholic Bishops - 2431 S. Acadian Thruway, Ste. 250, Baton Rouge, LA 70808-2365 t) 225-344-7120 admin@laccb.org Tom Costanza, Exec. Dir.;

Magnificat Diocese of Baton Rouge Chapter - 8825 Wakefield, Baton Rouge, LA 70806 t) 225-272-7607 Estella Champion, Treas.;

St. Michael's Home - 2305 Choctaw Dr., Baton Rouge, LA 70805-7999 t) 225-357-1204 nvhung@bellsouth.net (Vietnamese) Rev. Hung Viet Nguyen, I.C.M. (Vietnam), Supr.;

***Myriam's House** - 1141 W. Chimes St., Baton Rouge, LA 70802; Mailing: P. O. Box 127, Baton Rouge, LA 70821-0127 t) 225-383-7343; 225-383-7837 macaldo@svdpbr.com svdpbr.org A housing program for the homeless. Michael J. Acaldo, CEO;

***Particular Council of St. Vincent de Paul of Baton Rouge, Louisiana** - 220 St. Vincent de Paul Pl., Baton Rouge, LA 70802; Mailing: P. O. Box 127, Baton Rouge, LA 70821-0127 t) 225-383-7837 macaldo@svdpbr.org svdpbr.org Michael J. Acaldo, CEO;

Redemptorist Fathers of Baton Rouge, Inc. - 5354 Plank Rd., Baton Rouge, LA 70805 t) 225-355-2600 kmzubel@gmail.com Rev. Tat Thang Hoang, C.Ss R, Pst.; Rev. Samuel C. Maranto, C.Ss.R., Chap.; Rev. James C. Arrambide, C.Ss.R., Hispanic Min.; Rev. Timothy Watson, C.Ss.R., Hispanic Min.; Rev. Donald MacKinnon, C.Ss.R.; Rev. John C. Vargas, C.Ss.R.; Rev. John Fahey-Guerra, C.Ss.R., In Res.; Rev. Lamar Partin, C.Ss.R., In Res.;

Special Education Program - 1800 S. Acadian Thwy., Baton Rouge, LA 70808; Mailing: P.O. Box 2028, Baton Rouge, LA 70821 t) 225-336-8735 kmonsour@csobr.org www.csobr.org/specialeducation-1 Kristy Monsour, Admin.;

St. Vincent de Paul Baton Rouge Council - 220 St. Vincent de Paul Pl., Baton Rouge, LA 70802; Mailing: P.O. Box 127, Baton Rouge, LA 70821-0127 t) 225-383-7837 macaldo@svdpbr.com svdpbr.org Michael J. Acaldo, CEO;

***St. Vincent DePaul Community Pharmacy, Inc.** - 1647 Convention St., Baton Rouge, LA 70802; Mailing: P.O. Box 127, Baton Rouge, LA 70821-0127 t) 225-383-7450; 225-383-7837 macaldo@svdpbr.com svdpbr.org Charitable pharmacy serving the poor and homeless. Michael J. Acaldo, CEO;

St. Vincent DePaul Dining Room - 220 St. Vincent de Paul Pl., Baton Rouge, LA 70802; Mailing: P.O. Box 127, Baton Rouge, LA 70821-0127 t) 225-383-7837; 225-383-7439 macaldo@svdpbr.com svdpbr.org Providing meals to the poor & homeless. Michael J. Acaldo, CEO;

St. Vincent DePaul Stores - 1466 North St., Baton Rouge, LA 70802; Mailing: P.O. Box 127, Baton Rouge, LA 70821-0127 t) 225-267-5447; 225-383-7837 macaldo@svdpbr.com svdpbr.org Thrift stores. Michael J. Acaldo, CEO;

MONASTERIES AND RESIDENCES FOR PRIESTS AND BROTHERS [MON]

BATON ROUGE

Brothers of the Sacred Heart - 543 Baird Dr., Baton Rouge, LA 70808; Mailing: 4600 Elysian Fields Ave., New Orleans, LA 70122 t) 504-301-4758 unitedstatesprovince@gmail.com Bro. Lemoyne Roger, S.C., Dir.; Bro. Celestine Algero, S.C., In Res.; Bro. Ray Hebert, S.C., In Res.; Bro. John Hotstream, S.C., In Res.; Brs.: 4

Brothers of the Sacred Heart - 801 Hearthstone Dr., Baton Rouge, LA 70808; Mailing: 4600 Elysian Fields Ave., New Orleans, LA 70122 t) (504) 301-4758 Bro. Roland Champagne, S.C., Dir.; Bro. Robert Croteau, S.C., In Res.; Bro. Ramon Daunis, S.C., In Res.; Bro. Carl Evans, S.C., In Res.; Bro. Henry Gaither, S.C., In Res.; Bro. Harold Harris, S.C., In Res.; Bro. Malcolm Melcher, S.C., In Res.; Bro. Marcus Turcotte, S.C., In Res.;

Brothers of the Sacred Heart - 3437 Hundred Oaks Ave., Baton Rouge, LA 70808; Mailing: 4600 Elysian Fields Ave., New Orleans, LA 70122 t) (504) 301-4758 Bro. Michael Migacz, S.C., Vocations Dir.; Bro. Clifford King, S.C., In Res.; Bro. Paul Montero, S.C., In Res.;

St. Gerard Residence - 5354 Plank Rd., Baton Rouge, LA 70805 t) 225-355-2600 kmzubel@gmail.com Rev. Tat Thang Hoang, C.Ss.R., Pst.; Rev. Samuel C. Maranto, C.Ss.R., Chap.; Rev. James C. Arrambide, C.Ss.R., Hispanic Min.; Rev. Timothy Watson, C.Ss.R., Hispanic Min.; Rev. John Fahey-Guerra, C.Ss.R., In Res.; Rev. Donald MacKinnon, CSSR, In Res.; Rev. Lamar Partin, C.Ss.R., In Res.; Rev. John C. Vargas, C.Ss.R., In Res.; Priests: 8

Incarnatio Consecratio Missio - 2580 Tecumseh St., Baton Rouge, LA 70805-7999 t) 225-302-7457 nvhungicm@yahoo.com Society of Apostolic, Clerical Life for Men (Vietnamese) Rev. Francis Nguyen; Rev. Hung Viet Nguyen, I.C.M. (Vietnam), Supr.; Rev. Martin Thanh Nguyen, I.C.M.; Priests: 3

NURSING / REHABILITATION / CONVALESCENCE / ELDERLY CARE [NUR]

BATON ROUGE

Elderly HUD Housing of Our Lady of the Lake Hospital, Inc. - 5000 Hennessy Blvd., Baton Rouge, LA 70808-4398 t) 225-765-6565 karen.allen@fmolhs.org Karen B. Allen, Dir.; Asstd. Annu.: 300; Staff: 9

Assisi Village, Inc. - 7585 Bishop Ott Dr., Baton Rouge, LA 70806-8922 t) 225-926-5918 Housing facilities for elderly persons.

Calais House, Inc. - 7545 Bishop Ott Dr., Baton Rouge, LA 70806-8900 t) 225-927-1889 Housing facilities for elderly persons.

Chateau Louise - 7565 Bishop Ott Dr., Baton Rouge, LA 70806 t) 225-926-5918 Housing for elderly and handicapped persons.

Villa St. Francis, Inc. - 7575 Bishop Ott Dr., Baton Rouge, LA 70806-8906 t) 225-927-0070 Housing facilities for elderly and handicapped persons.

Hundred Oaks Center, Inc. - 3134 Hundred Oaks Ave., Baton Rouge, LA 70808 t) 225-332-2999 ahupp@csjinitiatives.org Sr. Patricia Warbritton, CSJ, Treas.; Asstd. Annu.: 15; Staff: 15

RETREAT HOUSES / RENEWAL CENTERS [RTR]

BATON ROUGE

Bishop Robert E. Tracy Center - 1800 S. Acadian Thwy., Baton Rouge, LA 70808; Mailing: P.O. Box 2028, Baton Rouge, LA 70821-2028 t) 225-336-8750 Dr. Susanna Greggio, Dir.;

CONVENT

Manresa House of Retreats - 5858 Louisiana Hwy. 44, Convent, LA 70723-0089; Mailing: P.O. Box 89, Convent, LA 70723-0089 t) 225-562-3596; 800-782-9431 info@manresala.org www.manresala.org Bro. Lawrence Huck, S.J., Dir.; Rev. Leonard E. Kraus, S.J., Supr.; Rev. Richard Buhler, S.J., Assoc. Dir.; Rev. Steve Kimmons, S.J., Assoc. Dir.;

SPECIAL CARE FACILITIES [SPF]

BATON ROUGE

Maternity Adoption & Behavioral Health - 1900 S. Acadian Thwy., Baton Rouge, LA 70808 t) 225-336-8708 adopt@ccdiobr.org www.adoptbatonrouge.com A department of Catholic Charities of the Diocese of Baton Rouge, Inc. Stephanie Sterling, Dir.; Bed Capacity: 8; Asstd. Annu.: 60; Staff: 8

Ollie Steele Burden Manor, Inc. - 4250 Essen Ln., Baton Rouge, LA 70809-2196 t) 225-926-0091 karen.allen@fmolhs.org Karen B. Allen, Exec.; Bed Capacity: 390; Asstd. Annu.: 191; Staff: 205

An asterisk (*) denotes an organization that has established tax-exempt status directly with the IRS and is not covered by the USCCB Group Ruling.

Diocese of Beaumont

(Dioecesis Bellomontensis)

MOST REVEREND DAVID LEON TOUPS, S.TH.D.

Bishop of Beaumont; ordained June 14, 1997; appointed Bishop of Beaumont June 9, 2020; consecrated and installed Sixth Bishop of Beaumont August 21, 2020.

Catholic Pastoral Center: 710 Archie St., Beaumont, TX 77701-2802. Mailing Address: P.O. Box 3948, Beaumont, TX 77704-3948. T: 409-924-4300; F: 409-838-4511. www.dioceseofbmt.org

ESTABLISHED SEPTEMBER 29, 1966.

Square Miles 7,878.

Comprises the counties of Chambers, Hardin, Jasper, Jefferson, Liberty, Newton, Orange, Polk and Tyler.

For legal titles of parishes and diocesan institutions, consult the Diocesan Chancellor at the Catholic Pastoral Center.

STATISTICAL OVERVIEW

Personnel
Bishop....1
Retired Bishops....1
Priests: Diocesan Active in Diocese....27
Priests: Retired, Sick or Absent....13
Number of Diocesan Priests....40
Religious Priests in Diocese....22
Total Priests in your Diocese....62
Extern Priests in Diocese....2
Permanent Deacons in Diocese....50
Total Sisters....21

Parishes
Parishes....42
With Resident Pastor:
Resident Diocesan Priests....25
Resident Religious Priests....17
Without Resident Pastor:
Administered by Priests....6
Missions....6
Pastoral Centers....1
Professional Ministry Personnel:
Sisters....21

Welfare
Catholic Hospitals....2
Total Assisted....253,261

Educational
Diocesan Students in Other Seminaries....12
Total Seminarians....12
High Schools, Diocesan and Parish....1
Total Students....331
Elementary Schools, Diocesan and Parish....4
Total Students....914
Catechesis/Religious Education:
High School Students....1,218
Elementary Students....4,066
Total Students under Catholic Instruction....6,541
Teachers in Diocese:
Priests....1
Sisters....3
Lay Teachers....117

Vital Statistics
Receptions into the Church:
Infant Baptism Totals....903
Minor Baptism Totals....12
Adult Baptism Totals....49
Received into Full Communion....98
First Communions....821
Confirmations....700
Marriages:
Catholic....145
Interfaith....37
Total Marriages....182
Deaths....772
Total Catholic Population....71,458
Total Population....646,856

LEADERSHIP

Catholic Pastoral Center - t) 409-924-4300 www.dioceseofbmt.org/

Office of the Bishop - t) 409-924-4310 Most Rev. David Leon Toups (bishop@dioceseofbmt.org); Larissa Martinez, Secy.;

Vicar General - t) 409-924-4303 Very Rev. M. Shane Baxter (sbaxter@dioceseofbmt.org); Heather Ripley, Secy. (hripley@dioceseofbmt.org);

Chancellor - t) (409) 924-4303 Dr. David Castronovo, Chancellor (chancellor@dioceseofbmt.org); Heather Ripley, Secy. (hripley@dioceseofbmt.org);

Judicial Vicar - Very Rev. Kevin Badeaux, Vicar;

Chief Financial Officer - t) 409-924-4313 Sabrina Vrooman;

Episcopal Vicar for Clergy - t) (409) 924-4303 Very Rev. James D. McClintock, Vicar; Heather Ripley, Secy. (hripley@dioceseofbmt.org);

Clergy Personnel Board - Rev. D. Stephen McCrate, Chair;

Episcopal Vicars -

Central Vicariate - Very Rev. Steven L. Leger, Vicar;

Eastern Vicariate - Very Rev. Sinclair Oubre, Vicar;

Northern Vicariate - Very Rev. Ronald B. Foshage, M.S., Vicar;

Southern Vicariate - Very Rev. Rejimon George, C.M.I., Vicar;

Western Vicariate - Very Rev. Joseph Khanh Ho, Vicar;

Presbyteral Council - Rev. Joseph R Sigur, Chair;

Diocesan Finance Council - Sam Parigi, Chair;

Diocesan College of Consultors - Very Rev. M. Shane Baxter, Chair (sbaxter@dioceseofbmt.org);

ADMINISTRATION

Human Resources - t) (409) 924-4364 Beverly Escamilla, Dir.; Cameron LaDay, Secy.;

Multimedia/Communications - t) 409-924-4352 Larry Jakobeit, Dir.;

East Texas Catholic Magazine - t) 409-924-4350 kgilman@dioceseofbmt.org Karen Gilman, Editor;

Information Technology - t) (409) 924-4339 Marisol Barajas, Dir.;

Director of Construction - t) (409) 924-4359 Dcn. Alan Bihm;

Diocesan Tribunal - t) 409-924-4319

Adjuant Judicial Vicar - Rev. Ernie Carpio;

Court Expert - Becky Richard;

Defenders of Bond - Rev. Martin Lester Nelson; Dr. David Castronovo;

Diocesan Judges - Rev. Ernie Carpio; Very Rev. Joseph Khanh Ho; Very Rev. Steven L. Leger;

Promoter of Justice - Very Rev. Sinclair Oubre;

Secretary-Notary - Alma Trevino;

Chief Administrator - Pastoral Offices - t) 409-924-4300 John Miller;

Office of Catholic Schools - t) 409-924-4322 Dr. Felicia Nichols;

OFFICES AND DIRECTORS

Apostleship of the Sea - aos-beaumont@dioceseofbmt.org Very Rev. Sinclair Oubre, Dir.;

Diaconate Formation - Very Rev. Sinclair Oubre, Dir.; Laura Dougharty, Secy. (ldougharty@dioceseofbmt.org);

Office of Permanent Diaconate - Dcn. Steve Obernuefemann, Dir. (sobernuefemann@dobcentral.org); Laura Dougharty, Secy. (ldougharty@dioceseofbmt.org);

Director of Seminarians/ Vocations - t) 409-924-4310 vocations@dioceseofbmt.org Rev. Rodel Faller, Dir.; Larissa Martinez, Secy.;

Multicultural Ministries - Jesus Abrego, Dir.; Morline Guillory, Dir.;

Office of Evangelization & Catechesis - t) 409-924-4323 Bryan Reising, Dir.;

Office of Family/Marriage/Youth Ministry - t) 409-924-4362 Robert Barbry;

Office of Stewardship & Development - t) 409-924-4302 Cindy Lockwood, Dir. (clockwood@dioceseofbmt.org); Rachel Johnson, Secy.;

Principal Master of Episcopal Ceremonies - t) 409-833-6433 Dcn. Flint Barboza;

Propagation of the Faith: Mission Co-op - t) 409-924-4302 Cindy Lockwood, Dir. (clockwood@dioceseofbmt.org);

ADVISORY BOARDS, COMMISSIONS, COMMITTEES, AND COUNCILS

Catholic Committee on Scouting - t) 409-727-3064 Mike Sigur, Chair;

Catholic Daughters of America - t) 409-883-3540 Susan Bayliss, Pres.;

Catholic Women, Council of - t) 409-828-0277 Melinda Turtledove, Pres.; Rev. Martin Lester Nelson, Moderator;

Charismatic Prayer Renewal - Rev. Polycarp Otieno, F.M.H., Group Liaison; Brenda Toups, Contact (btoups@att.net);

Commission for Continuing Education of Clergy & Religious - Very Rev. James D. McClintock;

Diocesan Building Commission - t) 409-924-4313 Hamil Cupero Jr., Chair;

Diocesan Review Board - Jim Clay, Chair;

Diocese of Beaumont Retirement Committee - Troy Domingue, Chair;

PARISHES, MISSIONS, AND CLERGY

STATE OF TEXAS

AMES

Our Mother of Mercy - 101 Donatto St., Ames, TX 77575; Mailing: P.O. Box 264, Liberty, TX 77575-0264 t) 936-336-3004 ourmotherofmercyames@yahoo.com Rev. Emmanuel Mbam, Pst.; Carolyn Victorian, DRE;

ANAHUAC

Our Lady of Light - 2207 S. Main, Anahuac, TX 77514 t) 409-296-4200 pastor@slcc-olol.org www.slcc-olol.org/our-lady-of-light Rev. Phillip Tran, Pst.; Dcn. Steve McGaha; CRP Stds.: 98

BEAUMONT

St. Anthony Cathedral Basilica - 700 Jefferson St., Beaumont, TX 77704-3309; Mailing: P.O. Box 3309, Beaumont, TX 77704-3309 t) 409-833-6433 support@stanthonycathedral.org; edu@stanthonycathedral.org www.stanthonycathedralbasilica.org Rev. Shane Baxter, Rector; Rev. Anthony McFarland, Par. Vicar; Dcn. Flint Barboza, Pst. Assoc.; Rev. Jaison Jacob, CMI, In Res.; Rev. Joseph Kattakkara, C.M.I., In Res.; Diane Barboza, Youth Min.; CRP Stds.: 200

St. Anthony Cathedral Basilica School - (Grades PreK-8) 850 Forsythe, Beaumont, TX 77701-2890 t) 409-832-3486 bnguyen@dobcentral.org www.sacbstx.org Sr. Bernadette Nguyen, Prin.; Stds.: 180; Lay Tchrs.: 14

St. Anne - 2715 Calder Ave., Beaumont, TX 77702; Mailing: P.O. Box 3429, Beaumont, TX 77704-3429 t) 409-832-9963 info@stannebmt.org; kknowles@stannebmt.org www.stannebmt.org Rev. Stephen McCrate, Pst.; Rev. Shiju Augustine, C.M.I., Par. Vicar; Dcn. Clint Elkins; Dcn. George Wood; Dcn. Ben Yett; Dcn. Joseph Scheurich; Kristine Knowles, DRE; CRP Stds.: 120

St. Anne School - (Grades PreK-8) 375 N. 11th St., Beaumont, TX 77702-1834 t) 409-832-5939 akiker@sasbmt.com www.sasbmt.com (Formerly St. Anne Tri-Parish School) Alison Kiker, Prin.; Stds.: 500; Sr. Tchrs.: 1; Lay Tchrs.: 45

Blessed Sacrament - 780 Porter St., Beaumont, TX 77701-7198 t) 409-833-6089 bsccatholic@gmail.com; pofoha@dobcentral.org Rev. Paul Ofoha, M.S.P., Pst.; CRP Stds.: 3

Cristo Rey - 767 Ave. A, Beaumont, TX 77701 t) 409-835-7788 mminifie@dobcentral.org; fperez@dobcentral.org Rev. Michael Minifie, Pst.; CRP Stds.: 244

St. Joseph - 1115 Orange St., Beaumont, TX 77701-4392 t) 409-835-5662 kbui@dobcentral.org; khuesibui@hotmail.com Rev. Khue Si Bui, Pst.; CRP Stds.: 78

St. Jude Thaddeus - 6825 Gladys, Beaumont, TX 77706-3239 t) 409-866-5088 stjude@stjudebmt.org www.stjudebmt.org Very Rev. Steven L. Leger, Pst.; Rev. Valentine Mayaka, Par. Vicar; Dcn. Randy Cashiola; Dcn. Frank Maida; CRP Stds.: 253

St. Martin de Porres Mission - 7467 Boyt Rd., Beaumont, TX 77705; Mailing: 9894 Gilbert, Beaumont, TX 77705 t) 409-794-2548; 409-794-1725 (CRP) stmarycc@hotmail.com stmaryandstmartin.com Rev. Eathan Oakes, Pst.; Dcn. Mirley Esprit;

St. Mary - 9894 Gilbert Rd., Beaumont, TX 77705-8878 t) 409-794-2548; 409-794-1725 (CRP) stmarycc@hotmail.com www.stmaryandstmartin.com Formerly St. Mary, Hamshire (1899). Rev. Eathan Oakes, Pst.; Dcn. Allan Santos; Debbie Peltier, DRE; CRP Stds.: 196

Our Lady of the Assumption - 4445 Avenue A, Beaumont, TX 77705-4998 t) 409-835-5343 apaulose@dobcentral.org www.assumptionbmt.org Very Rev. Kevin Badeaux, Pst.; Dcn. Harry Davis; Dcn. Senovio Sarabia; CRP Stds.: 51

Our Mother of Mercy - 3390 Sarah St., Beaumont, TX 77705-3098 t) 409-842-5533; 409-842-0112 (CRP) parish@omomcc.org; omomchurch@sbcglobal.net omomchurchbmt.com/ Rev. Joseph Ibiwoye, MSP, Pst.; CRP Stds.: 3

St. Pius X - 5075 Bigner Rd., Beaumont, TX 77708-5299 t) 409-892-3316; 409-892-6052 (CRP) stpiusxbmt@yahoo.com www.stpiusxbmt.org Rev. Gnanavoli Arulsamy, SVD, Pst.; CRP Stds.: 41

BRIDGE CITY

St. Henry - 475 W. Roundbunch Rd., Bridge City, TX 77611-0427; Mailing: P.O. Box 427, Bridge City, TX 77611-0427 t) 409-735-2422; 409-735-8642 (CRP) office@sthenrybctx.org Rev. Ernie Carpio, CMI, Pst.; Dcn. Steve Obernuefemann; CRP Stds.: 249

BROOKLAND

St. Raymond Mission - 283 FM 1007, Brookland, TX 75931; Mailing: P.O. Box 239, Jasper, TX 75951-0239 t) 409-698-9456 stmrectory@gmail.com Very Rev. Ronald B. Foshage, M.S., Pst.; Dcn. Glen Hebert; Dcn. William (Bill) Lawrence; Dcn. David Luther;

CHINA

Our Lady of Sorrows - 245 W. Hwy. 90, China, TX 77613; Mailing: P.O. Box 38, China, TX 77613-0038 t) 409-752-3571 olos1@sbcglobal.net ourladyofsorrowschina.com Rev. Polycarp Otieno, F.M.H.; CRP Stds.: 62

CLEVELAND

St. Mary - 702 E. Houston St., Cleveland, TX 77327; Mailing: P.O. Box 816, Cleveland, TX 77328-0816 t) 281-592-2985 stmarycleveland01@att.net www.stmaryscleveland tx.com/ Rev. Andy Dinh Vu, S.V.D., Pst.; Dcn. David Mueller; Dcn. Larry Terrell; CRP Stds.: 199

CORRIGAN

St. Martin de Porres Mission - 104 Gossett Rd., Corrigan, TX 75939; Mailing: P.O. Box 930, Livingston, TX 77351-0930 t) 936-967-8385; 936-581-3188 (CRP) viavitela@gmail.com; stjoe@eastex.net Rev. Anderson Luis De Souza, Pst.; Rev. Bartlomiej Jasilek, Par. Vicar; Sylvia Vitela, DRE; CRP Stds.: 45

DAYTON

St. Anne Mission - 804 S. Cleveland, Dayton, TX 77535-0640; Mailing: P.O. Box 640, Dayton, TX 77535-0640 t) 936-258-5735 stjosephdayton@comcast.net; officestjoseph@comcast.net Rev. Peter Phong Nguyen,

SVD, Pst.;
St. Joseph the Worker - 804 S. Cleveland, Dayton, TX 77535; Mailing: P.O. Box 640, Dayton, TX 77535-0640 t) 936-258-5735; 936-258-5735 (CRP) officestjoseph@comcast.net; stjosephdayton@comcast.net Rev. Peter Phong Nguyen, SVD, Pst.; CRP Stds.: 188

GROVES

Immaculate Conception-St. Peter - 6250 Washington, Groves, TX 77619 t) 409-962-0255; 409-962-8365 llawrence@dobcentral.org; jcoon@dobcentral.org immaculateconception-stpeterparish.com Rev. J.C. Coon, Pst.; Dcn. Willie Posey; CRP Stds.: 106

JASPER

St. Michael - 2898 U.S. Hwy. 190 W., Jasper, TX 75951; Mailing: P.O. Box 239, Jasper, TX 75951-0239 t) 409-384-2447; 409-384-2774 (CRP) stmrectory@gmail.com; rfoshage@dobcentral.org stmichaelsjasper.com Very Rev. Ronald B. Foshage, M.S., Pst.; Rev. David Lwin, Par. Vicar; Dcn. Glen Hebert; Dcn. William (Bill) Lawrence; Dcn. David Luther; Regina Lawrence, DRE; CRP Stds.: 95

Toledo Village - 163 S. Evergreen, Toledo Village, TX 75932

Our Lady of LaSalette - 1901 S. Margaret, Kirbyville, TX 75956

KOUNTZE

Holy Spirit Mission - 470 Monroe, Kountze, TX 77625-5414 t) 409-246-4457; 409-246-4457 (CRP) vfischer@dobcentral.org Rev. Andrew R. Moore, Pst.; Virginia Fischer, DRE; CRP Stds.: 3

LIBERTY

Immaculate Conception - 411 Milam, Liberty, TX 77575-4730 t) 936-336-7267 iccliberty@comcast.net; iccdre@comcast.net www.icclibertytx.org Rev. Paul Kahan, S.V.D., Pst.; Patty Lucas, DRE; CRP Stds.: 299

LIVINGSTON

St. Joseph - 2590 U.S. Hwy. 190 W., Livingston, TX 77351-0930; Mailing: P.O. Box 930, Livingston, TX 77351 t) 936-967-8385; 936-646-4685 (CRP) stjoe@eastex.net; tpuling@dobcentral.org stjoseph-livingston-tx.org/ Rev. Anderson Luis De Souza, Pst.; Rev. Bartlomiej Jasilek, Par. Vicar; Rosario Mendez, DRE; CRP Stds.: 280

LUMBERTON

Infant Jesus - 243 S. LHS Dr., Lumberton, TX 77657; Mailing: P.O. Box 8180, Lumberton, TX 77657-0180 t) 409-755-1734 infantjesus@gt.twcbc.com www.infantjesuscclumberton.com Rev. Andrew R. Moore, Pst.; Dcn. Bruce Grimes; Dcn. L.D. Keen; Dcn. Garry LeBlanc; Stacy Keen, DRE; CRP Stds.: 200

MONT BELVIEU

Holy Trinity - 3515 Trinity Dr., Mont Belvieu, TX 77580-0290; Mailing: P.O. Box 290, Mont Belvieu, TX 77580-0290 t) 281-576-4990 office@htcc-mb.org www.htcc-mb.org Very Rev. Joseph Khanh Ho, Pst.; Dcn. Eugene R. LeBlanc; CRP Stds.: 168

NEDERLAND

St. Charles Borromeo - 211 Hardy Ave., Nederland, TX 77627-7326; Mailing: 130 Hardy Ave., Nederland, TX 77627-7326 t) 409-722-3413; 409-722-0421 (CRP) stcharlesnederland@gmail.com www.stcharlesnederland.org Rev. John Hughes, Pst.; Rev. Eugen Nkardzedze, Par. Vicar; Dcn. Chris Penning; CRP Stds.: 359

ORANGE

St. Francis of Assisi - 4300 Meeks Dr., Orange, TX 77632-4508 t) 409-833-9153; 409-883-8232 (CRP) soubre@dobcentral.org stfrancisorangetx.org Very Rev. Sinclair Oubre, Pst.; Dcn. Tommy Ewing; Dcn. Keith Hebert; Dcn. Hector Maldonado; CRP Stds.: 187

St. Helen - 8105 FM 1442, Orange, TX 77630-8197 t) 409-735-2200 sthelenorange@gmail.com; mstrother@dobcentral.org sthelenorangefield.org Rev. Michael A. Strother, Pst.; Angela Hebert, DRE; CRP Stds.: 77

St. Mary - 912 W. Cherry St., Orange, TX 77630-5017 t) 409-883-2883; 409-886-0841 (CRP) debra@stmaryorange.org; jdaleo@dobcentral.org www.stmaryorange.org Rev. Antony Paulose, C.M.I., Pst.; Dcn. David Bonneaux; Dcn. Melvin Payne; CRP Stds.: 42

St. Mary School - (Grades PreK-8) 2600 Bob Hall Rd., Orange, TX 77630-2418 t) 409-883-8913 principal@stmaryschooltx.org www.stmaryschooltx.org Sr. Mary Benedicta, Prin.; Stds.: 85; Lay Tchrs.: 12

St. Maurice - 9079 Hwy. 62 N., Orange, TX 77632; Mailing: P.O. Box 940, Mauriceville, TX 77626-0940 t) 409-745-4060 stmaurice2@aol.com Rev. Michael A. Strother, Pst.;

St. Therese - 1409 N. Sixth St., Orange, TX 77630-3927 t) 409-883-3783 sttherese1350@yahoo.com Rev. Antony Paulose, C.M.I., Pst.; CRP Stds.: 6

PORT ARTHUR

St. Catherine of Siena - 3706 Woodrow Dr., Port Arthur, TX 77642-2320 t) 409-962-5715 afondren@stccpa.com; tbarrera@dobcentral.org www.stccpa.com/ Rev. Constantino Barrera, Pst.; Dcn. Keith Fontenot; Craig Bertrand, Youth Min.; Kim Tran, DRE; CRP Stds.: 18

St. Catherine of Siena School - (Grades PreK-8) 3840 Woodrow Dr., Port Arthur, TX 77642-2320 t) 409-962-3011 prios@stcats.org stcats.org/ Patricia Rios, Prin.; Stds.: 149; Bro. Tchrs.: 1; Sr. Tchrs.: 1; Scholastics: 17; Lay Tchrs.: 14

St. James - 3617 Gulfway Dr., Port Arthur, TX 77642-3675 t) 409-985-8865 stjamespa39@yahoo.com Rev. David A. Edwards, Pst.; CRP Stds.: 2

St. Joseph - 4600 Procter St., Port Arthur, TX 77642-1365 t) 409-982-6409 payala@dobcentral.org; kbadeaux@dobcentral.org www.stjosephportarthur.org Rev. Joseph R Sigur, Pst.; Dcn. Luis Javier Magana; CRP Stds.: 349

Our Lady of Guadalupe - 3648 S. Sgt. Lucian Adams Dr., Port Arthur, TX 77642-6403 t) 409-962-6777 olgsecretary@outlook.com; olgchurchpa@gmail.com www.olg-pa.org Rev. Urbano Saenz-Ramirez, O.S.A., Pst.; Rev. Jacob Mado, OSA, Par. Vicar; Maria Ortiz, Music Min.; Tatiana Owens, DRE; CRP Stds.: 349

Queen of Vietnam - 801 Ninth Ave., Port Arthur, TX 77642-3329 t) 409-983-7676 queenofvnchurch@hotmail.com Rev. Kha Philip Tran, C.R.M., Pst.; CRP Stds.: 45

Convent - 1148 Ninth Ave., Port Arthur, TX 77642 t) 409-985-5102 srmarydebradiep@gmail.com Sr. Mary Nguyen, Supr.;

Sacred Heart - St. Mary Parish - 920 Booker T. Washington Ave., Port Arthur, TX 77640-4923 t) 409-985-5104; 409-982-2900 (CRP) sacredheart@gt.rr.com sacredheartpa.org Rev. Anthony Afangide, MSP, Pst.; CRP Stds.: 49

St. Therese the Little Flower of Jesus - 6412 Garnet Ave., Port Arthur, TX 77640-1308 t) 409-736-1536 officelittleflower@gtbizclass.com www.littleflowerpa.org Very Rev. Rejimon George, C.M.I., Pst.; CRP Stds.: 88

PORT NECHES

St. Elizabeth - 2006 Nall St., Port Neches, TX 77651-3714 t) 409-727-8874; 409-722-5941 (CRP) donna@stepncatholic.org www.stepncatholic.org Very Rev. James D. McClintock, Pst.; Very Rev. Rejimon George, C.M.I., Par. Vicar; Rev. Msgr. Dan Malain, In Res.; Dcn. Ivan Watson; CRP Stds.: 337

RAYWOOD

Sacred Heart - 3730 FM 160 N., Raywood, TX 77582; Mailing: P.O. Box 429, Raywood, TX 77582 t) 936-587-4631 sacredheartchurchraywood@yahoo.com Rev. Emmanuel Mbam, Pst.; CRP Stds.: 17

SILSBEE

St. Mark the Evangelist - 905 N. Ninth St., Silsbee, TX 77656 t) 409-385-4498 mevangelist@sbcglobal.net; amoore@dobcentral.org Rev. Andrew R. Moore, Pst.; Dcn. Bruce Grimes; Dcn. L.D. Keen; Dcn. Garry LeBlanc; Kathy Watson, DRE; CRP Stds.: 72

SOUR LAKE

Our Lady of Victory - 210 W. Barkley, Sour Lake, TX 77659; Mailing: P.O. Box 1359, Sour Lake, TX 77659 t) 409-287-3287 olov1@att.net; rwaggoner@dobcentral.org olovcatholic.com Rev. Polycarp Otieno, F.M.H., Pst.; CRP Stds.: 27

Holy Spirit Mission - 470 Monroe, Kountze, TX 77625-5414 t) 409-246-4457 vfischer@dobcentral.org

VIDOR

Our Lady of Lourdes - 1600 N. Main, Vidor, TX 77662-3014 t) 409-769-2865; 409-769-6758 (CRP) ourladyoflourdes@sbcglobal.net; dreolol@sbcglobal.net olol.weconnect.com Rev. Ross E. Waggoner, Pst.; Dcn. Stephen Sellers; CRP Stds.: 27

WINNIE

St. Louis - 315 W. Buccaneer Dr., Winnie, TX 77665-9711 t) 409-296-4200 secretary@slcc-olol.org; pastor@slcc-olol.org Rev. Phillip Tran, Pst.; Dcn. Steve McGaha; Michelle Crone, DRE; CRP Stds.: 268

WOODVILLE

Our Lady of the Pines - 1601 N. Pine St., Woodville, TX 75979; Mailing: P.O. Box 2029, Woodville, TX 75979-2029 t) 409-283-5367 olopcc@sbcglobal.net www.ourladyofthepinescatholicchurch.com Very Rev. Ronald B. Foshage, M.S., Admin.; Rev. David Lwin, Par. Vicar; Diane Sanderson, DRE; Dcn. David Luther, Asst. Admin.; CRP Stds.: 54

SCHOOLS: PRESCHOOL THRU HIGH SCHOOL

HIGH SCHOOLS

STATE OF TEXAS

BEAUMONT

Monsignor Kelly Catholic High School - (DIO) 5950 Kelly Dr., Beaumont, TX 77707 t) 409-866-2351 fnichols@dioceseofbmt.org www.mkchs.com Dr. Tyrus Doctor, Prin.; Rev. Msgr. Dan Malain, Chap.; Rev. Anthony McFarland, Chap.; Dr. Felicia Nichols, Supt.; Stds.: 331; Pr. Tchrs.: 1; Sr. Tchrs.: 1; Lay Tchrs.: 32

INSTITUTIONS LOCATED IN DIOCESE

CAMPUS MINISTRY / NEWMAN CENTERS [CAM]

BEAUMONT

Lamar University-Catholic Student Center - 1010 E. Virginia St., Beaumont, TX 77704; Mailing: P.O. Box 3948, Beaumont, TX 77704-3948 t) 409-924-4361 rfaller@dobcentral.org www.dioceseofbmt.org Rev. Rodel Faller, Dir.;

CATHOLIC CHARITIES [CCH]

BEAUMONT

Catholic Charities of Southeast Texas - 2780 Eastex Fwy., Beaumont, TX 77703-4617 t) 409-924-4400 catholiccharities@catholiccharitiesbmt.org www.catholiccharitiesbmt.org Carolyn R. Fernandez, CEO; Asstd. Annu.: 13,120; Staff: 38

Asset Building Case Management - t) 409-924-4425 mhopson@catholiccharitiesbmt.org Matt Hopson, Dir.;

Disaster Response - t) (409) 924-4419 tduesler@catholiccharitiesbmt.org Teressa Duesler, Dir.;

Elijah's Place - t) 409-924-4433

rfertitta@catholiccharitiesbmt.org Children's grief support group. Randi Fertitta, Dir.;
Hospitality Center - 3959 Gulfway Dr., Port Arthur, TX 77642; Mailing: 2780 Eastex Freeway, Beaumont, TX 77703 t) 888-982-4842; 404-924-4406 Christina V. Green, Dir.;
Immigration Services - t) 409-924-4413 agarza@catholiccharitiesbmt.org Alma Garza-Cruz, Dir.;
Parish Social Ministry - t) (409) 924-4412 cfernandez@catholiccharitiesbmt.org

CEMETERIES [CEM]

BEAUMONT
Blessed Sacrament Cemetery - 780 Porter St., Beaumont, TX 77701 t) 409-833-6089 bsccatholic@gmail.com Rev. Paul Ofoha, M.S.P., Pst.;
Hebert Catholic Cemetery-Stivers Lane - Stivers Dr., Beaumont, TX 77705; Mailing: P.O. Box 3948, Beaumont, TX 77704-3948 t) 409-924-4313 svrooman@dioceseofbmt.org Sabrina Vrooman, Admin.;
DAYTON
St. Anne Cemetery - c/o St. Joseph, the Worker Church, Dayton, TX 77535-0640; Mailing: P.O. Box 640, Dayton, TX 77535-0640 t) 936-258-5735 stjosephdayton@comcast.net Rev. Peter Phong Nguyen, SVD, Pst.;
LIBERTY
Immaculate Conception Cemetery - 411 Milam, Liberty, TX 77575-4730 t) 936-336-7267 iccliberty@comcast.net Rev. Paul Kahan, S.V.D., Pst.;
Our Mother of Mercy Cemetery - c/o Our Mother of Mercy Church, Liberty, TX 77575-0264; Mailing: P.O. Box 264, Liberty, TX 77575-0264 t) 936-336-3004 ourmotherofmercyames@yahoo.com Rev. Andrew Toyinbo, MSP, Pst.;
ORANGE
St. Mary Cemetery - 912 W. Cherry St., Orange, TX 77630-5017 t) 409-883-7390 office@stmaryorange.org Rev. Joseph P. Daleo, Admin.;
PORT ARTHUR
Calvary Cemetery - 9th Ave. & 25th St., Port Arthur, TX 77642; Mailing: P.O. Box 3948, Beaumont, TX 77704-3948 t) (409) 924-4349 svrooman@dioceseofbmt.org Sabrina Vrooman, CFO;

ENDOWMENTS / FOUNDATIONS / TRUSTS [EFT]

BEAUMONT
St. Anthony School Foundation, Inc. - 850 Forsythe, Beaumont, TX 77701 t) 409-832-3486 gdixonpeters@sacbstx.org; rhubbell@sacbstx.org sacbstx.org Geneva Dixon-Peters, Admin.; Renee Hubbell, Secy.;
Catholic Clerical Student Fund - ; Mailing: P.O. Box 3948, Beaumont, TX 77704-3948 t) 409-924-4313 svrooman@dioceseofbmt.org Renella Primeaux, Coord.;
The Catholic Foundation of the Diocese of Beaumont, Inc. - ; Mailing: P.O. Box 3948, Beaumont, TX 77704-3948 t) 409-924-4313 svrooman@dioceseofbmt.org
CHRISTUS Health Foundation of Southeast Texas - 2830 Calder Ave., Beaumont, TX 77702 t) 409-236-7555 teri.hawthorne@christushealth.org; setx.foundation@christushealth.org www.christussoutheasttexasfoundation.org Teri Hawthorne, Dir.;
Monsignor Kelly Catholic High School Foundation, Inc. - 5950 Kelly Dr., Beaumont, TX 77707 t) 409-866-2351 fnichols@dioceseofbmt.org Dr. Felicia Nichols, Supt.;
ORANGE
St. Mary School Foundation, Inc. - 912 Cherry St., Orange, TX 77630 t) 409-883-2883 office@stmaryorange.org Rev. Joseph P. Daleo, Admin.;

HOSPITALS / HEALTH SERVICES [HOS]

BEAUMONT
CHRISTUS Southeast Texas Health System - St. Elizabeth - 2830 Calder St., Beaumont, TX 77702; Mailing: P.O. Box 5405, Beaumont, TX 77726-5405 t) 409-236-7171 x7107 daniel.ford@christushealth.org; deborah.tucker@christushealth.org www.christushospital.org Operated by CHRISTUS Health Southeast Texas. Rev. Emmanuel Chikezie (Nigeria), Chap.; Rev. Leonard Ogbonna (Nigeria), Chap.; Paul Trevino, CEO; Bed Capacity: 425; Asstd. Annu.: 205,020; Staff: 1,800
JASPER
CHRISTUS Southeast Texas Health System - Jasper Memorial - 1275 Marvin Hancock Dr., Jasper, TX 75951 t) 409-384-5461 daniel.ford@christushealth.org; deborah.tucker@christushealth.org Operated by CHRISTUS Health Southeast Texas Paul Trevino, CEO; Bed Capacity: 59; Asstd. Annu.: 48,590; Staff: 143

MISCELLANEOUS [MIS]

PORT ARTHUR
Apostleship of the Sea of the United States of America (AOSUSA) - 1500 Jefferson Dr., Port Arthur, TX 77642-0646 t) 409-985-4545 aosusa@sbcglobal.net www.aos-usa.org George P. McShea Jr., Pres.; Very Rev. Sinclair Oubre, Trustee;

MONASTERIES AND RESIDENCES FOR PRIESTS AND BROTHERS [MON]

WOODVILLE
Holy Cross Monastery - 521 County Rd. 2575, Woodville, TX 75979-2306 t) 409-899-3554 porter@holycrossmonks.org www.holycrossmonks.org Benedictine Monks. Bro. Michael Gallagher, Vice Pres.; Brs.: 2; Priests: 1

RETREAT HOUSES / RENEWAL CENTERS [RTR]

BEAUMONT
Abiding Place Catholic Charismatic Renewal Center - 4440 Chaison, Beaumont, TX 77705; Mailing: St. Anne Church, P.O. Box 3429, Beaumont, TX 77704 t) 409-832-9963 ncl890@aol.com; btoups@att.net Tammy Toups, Dir.; Brenda Toups, Dir.;
Holy Family Retreat Center - 9920 N. Major Dr., Beaumont, TX 77713-7618 t) 409-899-5617; 409-924-4370 retreatcenter@dioceseofbmt.org Sr. Theresa Ho, O.P., Dir.; Sr. Magdalene Tran, O.P., Asst. Dir.;

An asterisk (*) denotes an organization that has established tax-exempt status directly with the IRS and is not covered by the USCCB Group Ruling.

Diocese of Belleville

(Dioecesis Bellevillensis)

MOST REVEREND MICHAEL G. MCGOVERN, S.T.B., M.DIV.

Bishop of Belleville; ordained May 21, 1994; appointed Bishop of Belleville April 3, 2020; ordained and installed July 22, 2020.
Mailing Address: The Chancery, 222 S. Third St., Belleville, IL 62220-1985. T: 618-277-8181.

The Chancery: 222 S. Third St., Belleville, IL 62220-1985. T: 618-277-8181; F: 618-277-0387.
www.diobelle.org
info@diobelle.org

ERECTED JANUARY 7, 1887.

Square Miles 11,678.

Comprises Illinois south of the northern limits of the Counties of St. Clair, Clinton, Marion, Clay, Richland and Lawrence.

For legal titles of parishes and diocesan institutions, consult the Chancery Office.

STATISTICAL OVERVIEW

Personnel

Bishop	1
Retired Bishops	1
Priests: Diocesan Active in Diocese	32
Priests: Diocesan Active Outside Diocese	1
Priests: Retired, Sick or Absent	38
Number of Diocesan Priests	71
Religious Priests in Diocese	40
Total Priests in your Diocese	111
Extern Priests in Diocese	12
Ordinations:	
Diocesan Priests	1
Permanent Deacons in Diocese	40
Total Brothers	1
Total Sisters	90

Parishes

Parishes	103
With Resident Pastor:	
Resident Diocesan Priests	43
Resident Religious Priests	10
Without Resident Pastor:	
Administered by Priests	50
Completely vacant	2
Pastoral Centers	1
Professional Ministry Personnel:	
Sisters	41
Lay Ministers	11

Welfare

Catholic Hospitals	5
Homes for the Aged	2
Total Assisted	192
Day Care Centers	1
Total Assisted	35

Educational

Diocesan Students in Other Seminaries	6
Total Seminarians	6
High Schools, Diocesan and Parish	3
Total Students	858
Elementary Schools, Diocesan and Parish	25
Total Students	3,967
Catechesis/Religious Education:	
High School Students	995
Elementary Students	5,302
Total Students under Catholic Instruction	11,128
Teachers in Diocese:	
Lay Teachers	373

Vital Statistics

Receptions into the Church:	
Infant Baptism Totals	778
Minor Baptism Totals	89
Adult Baptism Totals	45
Received into Full Communion	117
First Communions	867
Confirmations	918
Marriages:	
Catholic	170
Interfaith	65
Total Marriages	235
Deaths	978
Total Catholic Population	79,643
Total Population	818,000

LEADERSHIP

Administrative Assistant to the Bishop - t) 618-722-5003 Judy Hoffmann;
Executive Administrative Assistant - t) (618) 722-5052 Mary Fournie;
Diocese of Belleville Chancery Office - t) 618-277-8181
Vicar General - t) (618) 722-5001 Very Rev. Steven L. Beatty;
Moderator of the Curia - t) 618-277-8181 x1061 Very Rev. Steven L. Beatty;
Office of the Chancellor and Canonical Affairs - t) 618-722-5002 Dcn. Douglas L. Boyer, Chancellor;
Vicar for Priests - t) (618) 722-5001 Very Rev. Steven L. Beatty, Vicar;
Vicar for Religious - t) 618-234-2068 Rev. Stanley J. Konieczny, Vicar;
Archivist - t) 618-722-5057 Sr. Mary Fran Flynn, S.S.N.D.;
Diocesan Tribunal - t) 618-722-5029 Rev. Paul R. Wienhoff; Very Rev. James Nall;
Advocates - Rev. Msgr. John T. Myler; Dcn. George G. Mills Jr.;
Defensores Vinculi - t) 618-722-5027 Rev. Msgr. Thomas D. Flach; Rev. Paul R. Wienhoff;
Judges - t) 618-722-5025 Rev. James M. Nall;
Judicial Vicar - t) 618-722-5025 Rev. James M. Nall;
Notary/Ecclesiastical Notary/Administrative Assistant for Tribunal - t) 618-722-5029 Joyce Jamison;
Promoter Justitiae - t) 618-722-5027 Rev. Paul R. Wienhoff;
Diocesan Consultors - t) 618-277-8181 x1061 Very Rev. Steven L. Beatty; Rev. Msgr. John T. Myler; Rev. James E. Deiters;
Diocesan Vicars Forane - Very Rev. Kenneth J. York, Vicar; Very Rev. Mark D. Reyling, Vicar; Rev. Msgr. Dennis R. Schaefer, Vicar;
Diocesan Finance Office - t) 618-722-5011 Michael Soete, CFO; Timothy Brendley, Comptroller, Chancery Office;
Building Commission - t) 618-233-1090 John Coers, Dir.;
Diocesan Finance Council - t) 618-722-5011 Most Rev. Michael G. McGovern; Rev. Eugene H. Wojcik (genewojcik@hotmail.com); Very Rev. Steven L. Beatty;
Diocesan Pastoral Council - Most Rev. Michael G. McGovern, Bishop of Belleville; Rev. Von C. Deeke; Marc Derwort;

OFFICES AND DIRECTORS

Catholic Campaign for Human Development - t) 618-722-5007 Judy Phillips;
Catholic Charities of Southern Illinois - t) 618-722-5002 Dcn. Douglas L. Boyer;
Chairperson of the Board -
Catholic Urban Programs - t) 618-398-5616 Toni Mohammad, Exec.;
Child Protection and Victim Assistance - t) 618-722-5028 Janet Hormberg, Dir.;
Child Protection Office - t) 618-722-5026 Lynn Muscarello, Dir.;
Clergymen's Aid Society - t) 618-722-5008 tbrendley@diobelle.org Most Rev. Michael G. McGovern, Chair; Rev. Edward F. Schaefer, Pres.;
Communications/Media - t) 618-722-5036 Kathleen Hunt (khunt@diobelle.org);
Daystar Community Program - t) 618-734-0178
Diaconate, Office of Permanent - t) 618-722-5042 Dcn. Thomas J. Helfrich, Coord. of Deacon;
Diocesan Board of Education - Debra Bunn, Pres.;
Diocesan Development Office; Catholic Service and Ministry Appeal; Planned Giving; Foundations & Corporations - t) 618-722-5007 Judy Phillips, Dir.;
Diocesan Liaison for International Priests & Seminarians - t) 618-539-3209 Rev. Von C. Deeke;
Diocesan Liturgical Commission - t) 618-588-4323 Rev. Msgr. David M. Darin, Chair;
Ecumenical and Interreligious Affairs - t) 618-457-4556 Rev. Robert B. Flannery;
Facilities and Risk Management - t) 618-233-1090 John Coers, Dir.;
Faith Formation - t) 618-722-5037 Mark Loyet, Dir.;
Formation of Priests - t) 618-632-3562 Rev. James R. Deiters, Chair;
Hispanic Ministry - t) 618-722-5050 Lucy Barragan, Dir.;
Insurance Commission - Michael Soete, CFO;
Newman Catholic Student Center - t) 618-529-3311 Tim Taylor, Dir. (tim@siucnewman.org);
Newspaper, "The Messenger" - t) 618-722-5044 Christopher Orlet, Editor;
Office of Pastoral Services - t) (618) 277-8181 Very Rev. Kenneth J. York;
Office of Deacon Formation - t) 618-722-5035 Rev. Steven Pautler, Dir.; Rev. Michaelsami Arockiam, Assoc. Dir.; Patti Warner, Assoc. Dir. Formation;
Office of Youth Ministry - t) 618-722-5037 Mark Loyet;
Propagation of the Faith - t) 618-234-1166 Rev. Msgr. John T. Myler;
Respect Life/Project Rachel Pastoral Center - t) 618-722-5048; 888-456-4673 (Project Rachel Hotline) Mary Fleming, Dir.;
Rural Life Conference - t) 618-722-5038 Rev. Robert J. Zwilling, Dir.;
St. Vincent de Paul Society - t) 618-394-0126 Charlie Cullen, Pres.; Patricia Hogrebe, Dir.;
Sick and Aged (Ministry) - t) 618-235-9991 Rev. Eugene J. Neff, Dir.;
Superintendent of Schools - t) 618-235-9601 Jonathan Birdsong, Supt.;
Vocation Office - t) 618-722-5035 x1482 Rev. Joel Seipp, Dir.; Very Rev. Nicholas G. Junker, Dir.; Patti Warner, Assoc. Dir. Formation;

PARISHES, MISSIONS, AND CLERGY

STATE OF ILLINOIS

ALBERS

St. Bernard - 202 N. Broadway, Albers, IL 62215; Mailing: PO Box 10, Albers, IL 62215 t) 618-248-5112; 618-248-5134 (CRP) st.bernard@charter.net www.stbernardandstdamian.org Very Rev. Steven L. Beatty, Pst.; Dcn. Glennon J. Netemeyer, DRE; Dcn. Kevin T. Templin; CRP Stds.: 88

ANNA

St. Mary - 402 Freeman, Anna, IL 62906; Mailing: 204 Church St., Anna, IL 62906 t) 618-833-5835; 618-833-3131 (CRP) st_marys@frontier.com Rev. Uriel Salamanca, Pst.; Jenna Sweitzer, DRE; CRP Stds.: 20

AVISTON

St. Francis of Assisi - 251 S. Clinton, Aviston, IL 62216-0093; Mailing: Box 93, Aviston, IL 62216-0093 t) 618-228-7219 parish@stfrancisav.org; dre@stfrancisav.org www.stfrancisav.org Rev. Daniel L. Friedman, Pst.; Connie Robben, DRE; Dcn. Stephen AuBuchon, RCIA Coord.; Amber N. Griesbaum, Bus. Mgr.; CRP Stds.: 253

BARTELSO

St. Cecilia - 304 S. Washington St., Bartelso, IL 62218; Mailing: P.O. Box 176, Bartelso, IL 62218 t) 618-765-2162 jbuerster@aol.com Rev. Msgr. James A. Buerster, Pst.; CRP Stds.: 148

BECKEMEYER

St. Anthony - 451 W. 3rd St., Beckemeyer, IL 62219; Mailing: P.O. Box 305, Beckemeyer, IL 62219 t) 618-227-8236; 618-526-7746 (CRP) www.stanthonybeckemeyer.org Rev. Charles W. Tuttle, Pst.; Dan Robben, DRE; CRP Stds.: 20

BELLEVILLE

Cathedral of St. Peter - 200 W. Harrison St., Belleville, IL 62220-2090 t) 618-234-1166 businessmanager@cathedralbelle.org www.cathedralbelle.org Rev. Godfrey Mullen, OSB, Rector; Dcn. David Fields; Dcn. Wayne L. Weiler; Sr. Theresa Markus, S.S.N.D., DRE; Josie Weiler, Bus. Mgr.; CRP Stds.: 117

Notre Dame Academy of Belleville, Illinois - (Grades PreK-8) 200 S. 2nd St., Belleville, IL 62220 t) 618-233-6414 linda.hobbs@notredamebelleville.org Linda Hobbs, Prin.; Stds.: 75; Lay Tchrs.: 8

St. Augustine of Canterbury - 1910 W. Belle St., Belleville, IL 62226 t) 618-233-3813; 618-722-2366 (CRP) maryz@stasaints.org; connie.woods@bellevillepsr.org www.stasaints.org Rev. Msgr. William P. McGhee, Pst.; Mary Zeveski, Bus. Mgr.; CRP Stds.: 21

Blessed Sacrament - 8707 W. Main St., Belleville, IL 62223 t) 618-397-2287 kahrens@bjpc.com bellevillecatholic.com/ Rev. Matthew J. Elie, Pst.; Greg Nowak, DRE; Karen Ferrara, Bus. Mgr.;

Blessed Sacrament School - (Grades PreK-8) 8809 W. Main St., Belleville, IL 62223 t) 618-397-1111 blsac@hotmail.com www.blessedsacramentbelleville.com/ Claire Hatch, Prin.; Stds.: 158; Lay Tchrs.: 13

St. Henry - 5315 W. Main St., Belleville, IL 62226 t) 618-233-2423 sthenryc@peaknet.net www.sthenrybelleville.com Very Rev. Kenneth J. York, Pst.; Dcn. James Law; Kim Ahrens, Dir.; CRP Stds.: 19

St. Luke - 301 N. Church St., Belleville, IL 62220 t) 618-236-1124 bwojcik@stteresabelleville.org www.stlukebelleville.org Rev. Joseph Oganda, Pst.; Dcn. Douglas L. Boyer; CRP Stds.: 9

St. Mary - 1706 W. Main St., Belleville, IL 62226 t) 618-233-2391 stmarychurch1893@sbcglobal.net; tmarkus@ssndcp.org www.stmaryparishbelleville.org Rev. Michaelsami Arockiam, Admin.; Dcn. Randall Riesenberger; Sr. Theresa Markus, S.S.N.D., DRE; CRP Stds.: 127

Our Lady Queen of Peace - 5923 N. Belt W., Belleville, IL 62223; Mailing: 8707 W. Main St., Belleville, IL 62223 t) 618-397-2287 qpparish@qofp.com; kahrens@bjpc.com bellevillecatholic.com Rev. Matthew J. Elie, Pst.; Karen Ferrara, Bus. Mgr.;

Our Lady Queen of Peace School - (Grades PreK-8) 5915 N. Belt W., Belleville, IL 62223 t) 618-234-1206 qpschool@qofp.com www.qofp.com Michelle Tidwell, Prin.; Stds.: 155; Lay Tchrs.: 11

St. Teresa of the Child Jesus - 1201 Lebanon Ave., Belleville, IL 62221 t) 618-233-3500 www.stteresabelleville.com (Little Flower) Rev. Joseph Oganda, Pst.; Dcn. Douglas L. Boyer; Dcn. Ron Tiberi; CRP Stds.: 237

St. Teresa of the Child Jesus School - (Grades PreK-8) 1108 Lebanon Ave., Belleville, IL 62221 t) 618-235-4066 www.stteresatigers.org Danielle Schnable, Prin.; Stds.: 185; Lay Tchrs.: 13

BENTON

St. Joseph - 506 W. Main, Benton, IL 62812 t) 618-438-9941; 618-200-4179 (CRP) www.catholicchurchesofrendlake.com Rev. Urban Osuji, C.M., Pst.; Vickie Simipson, DRE; CRP Stds.: 32

BREESE

St. Augustine - 525 S. Third St., Breese, IL 62230 t) 618-526-4362; 618-526-7746 (CRP) www.saintaugustinebreese.org Rev. Charles W. Tuttle; Dan Robben, DRE; CRP Stds.: 14

St. Dominic - 493 N. Second St., Breese, IL 62230 t) 618-526-7746 saintdominic@papadocs.com; dbrobben76@gmail.com www.saintdominicbreese.org Rev. Patrick N. Peter, Pst.; Daniel Robben, DRE; CRP Stds.: 112

All Saints Academy - (Grades PreK-8) 295 N. Clinton St., Breese, IL 62230 t) 618-526-4323 kgoetsch@asasaints.com www2.asasaints.com Kahiwalani Goetsch, Prin.; Stds.: 357; Lay Tchrs.: 24

CAHOKIA

Holy Family - 116 Church St., Cahokia, IL 62206 t) 618-337-4548 holyfamily1699.org Rev. Osang Idagbo, C.M. (Nigeria), Pst.; CRP Stds.: 3

CAIRO

St. Patrick - 312 9th St., Cairo, IL 62914 t) 618-734-2061 stpatrickcairo.com Rev. Michael Christopher Mujule (Uganda), Pst.;

CARBONDALE

St. Francis Xavier - 303 S. Poplar St., Carbondale, IL 62901-2709 t) 618-457-4556 www.stfx.org Rev. Robert B. Flannery, Pst.; Sr. Barbara Blesse, OP, DRE; CRP Stds.: 53

CARLYLE

St. Felicitas - 13322 Church Rd., Carlyle, IL 62231 t) 618-594-3040 stfelbp@whisperhome.com Rev. Edward F. Schaefer, Pst.; Deborah Raker, Admin.; CRP Stds.: 18

St. Mary - 1171 Jefferson St., Carlyle, IL 62231; Mailing: Box 179, Carlyle, IL 62231 t) 618-594-2225; 618-594-2284 (CRP) stmaryc@sbcglobal.net; rel_ed_stmary@yahoo.com www.stmarycarlyle.org (Immaculate Conception) Rev. George A. Mauck, Pst.; Ellen Knolhoff, DRE; CRP Stds.: 102

St. Teresa of Avila - 18021 Marydale Rd., Carlyle, IL 62231 t) 618-594-3266 stteresamarydale@gmail.com Rev. George A. Mauck, Pst.; Dcn. John Hempen;

CARMI

St. Polycarp (German) - 209 Fourth St., Carmi, IL 62821 t) 618-380-2262 Rev. Vincent J. Obi (Nigeria), Admin.; Julie Jackson, DRE; CRP Stds.: 14

CARTERVILLE

Church of the Holy Spirit - 300 N. Pine St., Carterville, IL 62918 t) 618-985-2900; 618-925-5099 www.holyspirit300.com Very Rev. Mark D. Reyling, Pst.; Bill Harper, DRE; Kimberly Booker, C.R.E.; CRP Stds.: 20

CASEYVILLE

St. Stephen - 901 S. Main St., Caseyville, IL 62232; Mailing: PO Box 458, Caseyville, IL 62232 t) 618-397-0666 office@ststephencaseyville.org; faithform@ststephencaseyville.org www.ststephencaseyville.org Rev. Harold Fisher, O.M.I., Pst.; Rev. James Fee, O.M.I.; CRP Stds.: 57

CENTRALIA

St. Mary - 424 E. Broadway, Centralia, IL 62801 t) 618-532-6291 fr.steve@stmarycentralia.org www.stmarycentralia.org Rev. Steven Pautler, Pst.; Vicki Laquet, DRE; CRP Stds.: 28

St. Mary School - t) 618-532-3473 mariapryor@stmarycentralia.org stmarycentralia.org Maria Pryor, Prin.; Stds.: 74; Lay Tchrs.: 6

CHESTER

St. Mary Help of Christians - 911 Swanwick St., Chester, IL 62233 t) 618-826-2444 We have a Parish Partnership with Mary of Divine Mercy in Ellis Grove and St. Joseph in Prairie du Rocher Rev. Sebastian Ukoh, C.M. (Nigeria), Pst.; Cheryl Gross, DRE; CRP Stds.: 22

St. Mary Help of Christians School - 835 Swanwick St., Chester, IL 62233 t) 618-826-3120 stmarychester@hotmail.com Janelle Robinson, Prin.; Stds.: 64; Lay Tchrs.: 8

CHRISTOPHER

St. Andrew - 412 E. Washington St., Christopher, IL 62822 t) 618-724-4114 Chapel status Rev. Urban Osuji, C.M., Pst.;

COBDEN

St. Joseph - 101 Centennial St., Cobden, IL 62920; Mailing: P.O. Box 237, Cobden, IL 62920 t) 618-893-2276; (618) 893-2289 (CRP) fr.uriel.salamanca@gmail.com; stjosephcobdenpsr@gmail.com www.stjosephcobden.com Rev. Uriel Salamanca, Admin.; Dcn. Patrick Patterson; Jill Skinner, Contact; CRP Stds.: 37

COLUMBIA

Immaculate Conception of the B.V.M. - 411 Palmer Rd., Columbia, IL 62236 t) 618-281-5105; 618-281-5105 x352 (CRP) www.icc-columbia-il.us Rev. Steven Thoma, CR, Pst.; Rev. Eric Wagner, CR, Par. Vicar; Hope Wienhoff, DRE; Lizanne Young, RCIA Coord.; CRP Stds.: 151

Immaculate Conception of the B.V.M. School - (Grades PreK-8) 409 Palmer Rd, Columbia, IL 62236 t) 618-281-5353 dgregson@icsmail.org David Gregson, Prin.; Stds.: 407; Lay Tchrs.: 23

DAMIANSVILLE

St. Damian - One W. Main St., Damiansville, IL 62215 t) 618-248-5134 www.stbernardandstdamian.org Very Rev. Steven L. Beatty, Pst.; Dcn. Glennon J. Netemeyer, Pst. Assoc.; Dcn. Kevin Templin; CRP Stds.: 59

DU QUOIN

Sacred Heart of Jesus - 100 W. Main St., Du Quoin, IL 62832; Mailing: 17 N. Walnut St., Du Quoin, IL 62832 t) 618-542-3423 jlhayden1@gmail.com Merged with Immaculate Conception Tamaroa Rev. Carl Schrage, Pst.; Janet Hayden, DRE; CRP Stds.: 37

DUBOIS

St. Charles Borromeo - 223 S. 3rd. St., Dubois, IL 62831; Mailing: P.O. Box 6, Dubois, IL 62831 t) 618-787-2781 Rev. Oliver Nwachukwu, Admin.; Judy Pieszchalski, DRE; CRP Stds.: 26

DUPO

Sacred Heart of Jesus - 124 S. 3rd St., Dupo, IL 62239; Mailing: P.O. Box 35, Dupo, IL 62239 t) 618-286-4373 sacredheartdupo@gmail.com Rev. Osang Idagbo, C.M. (Nigeria), Pst.;

EAST SAINT LOUIS

St. Augustine of Hippo - 408 Rev. Joseph Brown Blvd., East Saint Louis, IL 62205 t) 618-274-0655 staugustineofhippo@sbcglobal.net; cmofm1968@yahoo.com Rev. Carroll Mizicko, O.F.M., Pst.; CRP Stds.: 15

Sister Thea Bowman Chapel - 8313 Church Ln., East Saint Louis, IL 62203 t) 618-397-0316 nickerson.bowman@gmail.com Daniel Nickerson, Prin.;

Immaculate Conception - 1509 Baugh Ave., East Saint Louis, IL 62205 t) 618-274-0655 cmofm1968@yahoo.com Rev. Carroll Mizicko, O.F.M., Pst.;

ELDORADO

St. Mary - 1158 N. 2nd St., Eldorado, IL 62930 t) 618-253-7408 stmarys1@clearwave.com Rev. Christian Iwuagwu, Pst.; Megan Burris, DRE;

ELIZABETHTOWN

St. Joseph - 15 St. Joseph Rd., Elizabethtown, IL 62931-9711; Mailing: Box 190, Ridgway, IL 62979 t) 618-272-7059 gallatincatholic@gmail.com stkateri.net Rev. Vincent Mukasa, Assoc. Pst.; Debbie Soward, DRE; CRP Stds.: 6

ELLIS GROVE

Divine Maternity of the B.V.M. - 7362 Shawneetown Tr., Ellis Grove, IL 62241 t) 618-859-3541 vjbtmb@egyptian.net; ikennaukoh@yahoo.co.uk Rev. Sebastian Ukoh, C.M. (Nigeria), Pst.; Tammy Bert, DRE; CRP Stds.: 7

ENFIELD

St. Patrick - 1377 County Rd. 25, E., Enfield, IL 62835; Mailing: 209 4th St., Carmi, IL 62821 t) 618-380-2262 www.whitecountycatholic.org Rev. Vincent J. Obi (Nigeria), Admin.; Vince Mitchell, DRE; CRP Stds.: 16

EVANSVILLE

St. Boniface - 1007 Olive St., Evansville, IL 62242 t) 618-853-4435 Rev. Iuvenis N. Iheme, C.M., Pst.; Kurtis Gross, DRE; CRP Stds.: 18

FAIRFIELD

St. Edward - 300 N.W. 5th St., Fairfield, IL 62837 t) 618-847-7931 stedwardfairfield.com Rev. Charles Anyaoku, Admin.; CRP Stds.: 15

FAIRMONT CITY

Holy Rosary - 2716 N. 42nd St., Fairmont City, IL 62201 t) 618-274-3486 Rev. Harold Fisher, O.M.I., Pst.; Rev. James Fee, O.M.I., Par. Vicar; CRP Stds.: 109

FAIRVIEW HEIGHTS

Holy Trinity Catholic Church - 505 Fountains Pkwy., Fairview Heights, IL 62208 t) 618-628-8825 aklohr@holytrinityil.org www.holytrinityil.org Very Rev. James Nall, Pst.; Dcn. Arthur Hampton; Dcn. Tom Powers; CRP Stds.: 65

Holy Trinity Catholic Church School - 504 Fountains Pkwy., Fairview Heights, IL 62208 t) 618-628-7395 kfrawley@htcs.org Kristy Frawley, Prin.; Stds.: 278; Lay Tchrs.: 18

FLORA

St. Stephen - 812 N. Main St., Flora, IL 62839 t) 618-662-6261; 618-662-8121 (CRP) ststephen_flora@yahoo.com Rev. Charles Anyaoku, Pst.; CRP Stds.: 20

FREEBURG

St. Joseph - 6 N. Alton St., Freeburg, IL 62243; Mailing: P.O. Box 98, Freeburg, IL 62243 t) 618-539-3209 www.stjosephfreeburg.org Rev. Von C. Deeke, Pst.; Dcn. Corby Valentine; Cindy Ingold, DRE; CRP Stds.: 260

St. Joseph School - (Grades PreK-8) 2 N. Alton St., Freeburg, IL 62243 t) 618-539-3930 office@stjosephschoolfreeburg.org www.stjosephschoolfreeburg.org Kelly Schaaf, Prin.; Stds.: 101; Lay Tchrs.: 9

GERMANTOWN

St. Boniface - 402 Munster St., Germantown, IL 62245; Mailing: PO Box 280, Germantown, IL 62245 t) 618-523-4271 c) 618-210-4860 www.stbonifacechurch.net Rev. Msgr. James A. Buerster, Pst.; Danita Deerhake, PSR Dir.; CRP Stds.: 210

HARRISBURG

St. Mary - 2000 W. Poplar St., Harrisburg, IL 62946 t) 618-253-7408 Rev. Christian Iwuagwu, Admin.;

HECKER

St. Augustine of Canterbury - 310 N. Main St., Hecker, IL 62248; Mailing: PO Box 126, Hecker, IL 62248 t) 618-473-2217 staug@htc.net Rev. Linus Umoren, C.M., Pst.;

HERRIN

Our Lady of Mount Carmel - 316 W. Monroe St., Herrin, IL 62948; Mailing: 104 N. 17th St., Herrin, IL 62948 t) 618-942-3114 olmc@live.com; kweber.olmcpsr@gmail.com www.ourladyofmtcarmelherrin.com Very Rev. Mark D. Reyling, Pst.; Kristi Weber, DRE; CRP Stds.: 282

Our Lady of Mount Carmel School - (Grades PreK-8) 400 W. Monroe St., Herrin, IL 62948 t) 618-942-4484 jswann@olmcschool.net www.olmcschool.net Jason Swann, Prin.; Stds.: 262; Lay Tchrs.: 19

JACOB

St. Ann - 101 Raddle Church Ln., Jacob, IL 62950; Mailing: 724 Mulberry St., Murphysboro, IL 62966 t) 618-687-2012 Rev. Joel Seipp, Pst.; CRP Stds.: 23

JOHNSTON CITY

St. Paul - 1103 Washington Ave., Johnston City, IL 62951 t) 618-983-5073 stpaulsw47@gmail.com stjoseph-stpaul.com Rev. Brian Barker, Pst.; CRP Stds.: 6

KASKASKIA

Immaculate Conception - 203 First St., Kaskaskia, IL 62233; Mailing: 6450 Klein Ln, St. Mary, MO 63673 t) 618-615-5747 elyons@powrup.net (Independent Mission) Mary Brown, Treas.;

KINMUNDY

St. Elizabeth Ann Seton - 110 N. Madison St., Kinmundy, IL 62854; Mailing: 812 W. Main St., Salem, IL 62881-1407 t) 618-548-0899 www.sttheresaofavilaparish.com Rev. Jose R. Jacob (India); Anne Hoover, PSR Coord.; CRP Stds.: 9

LAWRENCEVILLE

St. Lawrence - 1006 Collins, Lawrenceville, IL 62439 t) 618-943-5255 rebbeca.ruppel@crawfordmh.org www.catholiccommunityofstlawrence.com Rev. Felix Chukwuma (Nigeria), Pst.; Very Rev. Mark D. Stec, Pst.; Dcn. Stephen P. Andrews; Rebecca Ruppel, PSR Dir.; CRP Stds.: 22

LEBANON

St. Joseph - 901 N. Alton St., Lebanon, IL 62254 t) 618-537-2575 lebstjoe@gmail.com; lebstjoepa@gmail.com www.stjosephlebanon.org Rev. Paul R. Wienhoff, Pst.; CRP Stds.: 20

MARION

St. Joseph - 600 N. Russell St., Marion, IL 62959 t) 618-993-3194 x1 secsjm@frontier.com; cpmsjm@frontier.com www.stjoseph-stpaul.com Rev. Brian Barker, Pst.; Cintia G. Yong, Pst. Min./Coord.;

Angela Lees, DRE; CRP Stds.: 78

MASCOUTAH

Holy Childhood of Jesus - 104 N. Independence St., Mascoutah, IL 62258 t) 618-566-2958 hcc@holychildhoodchurch.com holychildhoodchurch.com Rev. Nicholas Fleming, Admin.; Dcn. Daniel Cozzi; Wendy Uhl, DRE; CRP Stds.: 70

Holy Childhood of Jesus School - (Grades PreK-8) 215 N. John St., Mascoutah, IL 62258 t) 618-566-2922 hcs@holychildhoodschool.com www.holychildhoodschool.com Tim Keefe, Prin.; Stds.: 174; Lay Tchrs.: 12

MCLEANSBORO

St. John the Baptist - 7598 Piopolis Rd., McLeansboro, IL 62859 t) 618-648-2490; 618-838-4430 (CRP) hamiltoncountycatholic.org Rev. Slawomir Ptak (Poland), Admin.; Dcn. Archie L. Bowers Jr.; Megan Woodrow, DRE; CRP Stds.: 52

METROPOLIS

St. Rose of Lima - 315 E. Third St., Metropolis, IL 62960-2229 t) 618-524-8202 stroseoflimametropolis@gmail.com www.strosemetropolis.com Rev. Michael Christopher Mujule (Uganda), Admin.; CRP Stds.: 11

MILLSTADT

St. James - 405 W. Madison St., Millstadt, IL 62260 t) 618-476-3513 www.stjamesmillstadt.com Rev. Msgr. Marvin C. Volk, Pst.; Dcn. Ronald Karcher; Courtney Hasenstab, DRE; CRP Stds.: 45

St. James School - (Grades PreK-8) 412 W. Washington, Millstadt, IL 62260 t) 618-476-3510 Cindy Hasenstab, Prin.; Stds.: 92; Lay Tchrs.: 8

MOUNT CARMEL

St. Mary - 125 W. 5th St., Mount Carmel, IL 62863 t) 618-262-5337 www.stmarysparish.net Rev. Robert J. Zwilling, Pst.; Donna Sigler, CRE; Dcn. Stephen Lowe; CRP Stds.: 25

St. Mary School - (Grades PreK-8) 417 Chestnut St., Mount Carmel, IL 62863 t) 618-263-3183 www.smsrockets.net Christopher Lavely, Prin.; Stds.: 103; Lay Tchrs.: 12

St. Sebastian - 4921 N. 1400 Blvd., Mount Carmel, IL 62863 t) 618-298-2589 godislove333@hotmail.com Rev. Robert J. Zwilling, Pst.; Tamara Berberich, DRE; CRP Stds.: 18

MOUNT VERNON

St. Mary the Immaculate Conception - 1550 Main St., Mount Vernon, IL 62864 t) 618-244-1559 church@stmarymtvernon.org www.stmarymtvernon.org Very Rev. Nicholas G. Junker, Pst.; Rev. Benny George, C.M.I. (India), Pst. Assoc.; Dcn. Steven Eischens, DRE; CRP Stds.: 157

St. Mary the Immaculate Conception School - (Grades PreK-8) 1416 Main St., Mount Vernon, IL 62864 t) 618-242-5353 bheinzman@stmarymtvernon.org www.stmary.school Brett Heinzman, Prin.; Stds.: 106; Lay Tchrs.: 10

MURPHYSBORO

St. Andrew - 724 Mulberry St., Murphysboro, IL 62966 t) 618-687-2012 sec@sasmboro.org www.standrewmboro.org Rev. Joel Seipp, Pst.; Jennifer Craig, CRE; CRP Stds.: 5

St. Andrew School - 723 Mulberry St., Murphysboro, IL 62966 t) 618-687-2013 secretary@sasmboro.org saintandrew-school.org Jennifer Martin, Prin.; Stds.: 151; Lay Tchrs.: 9

NASHVILLE

St. Ann - 631 S. Mill St., Nashville, IL 62263 t) 618-327-3232 www.stannnashville.org Rev. Andrew J. Knopik, Pst.; Linda Williams, DRE; CRP Stds.: 18

St. Ann School - (Grades PreK-8) 675 S. Mill St., Nashville, IL 62263 t) 618-327-8741 principal@stannnashville.org Anthony Bodnar, Prin.; Stds.: 39; Lay Tchrs.: 5

Our Lady of Perpetual Help - 19824 Posen Rd., Nashville, IL 62263-6122 t) 618-327-3556; 618-327-3232 olph.posen@gmail.com; fatherandyk@gmail.com Rev. Andrew J. Knopik, Pst.; Brenda Spenner, DRE; CRP Stds.: 43

NEW ATHENS

St. Agatha - 205 S. Market St., New Athens, IL 62264 t) 618-475-2331 cmayfield@stagathaparish.com Rev. Von C. Deeke, Pst.; Dcn. Corby Valentine; Susan Colman, RCIA Coord.; CRP Stds.: 25

NEW BADEN

St. George - 200 N. 3rd St., New Baden, IL 62265 t) 618-588-4323 www.stgeorgefamily.org Very Rev. Steven L. Beatty, Admin.; Dcn. John C. Fridley; Jeff Mueth, DRE; CRP Stds.: 176

NEWTON

Holy Cross - 5782 Ingraham Ln, Newton, IL 62448 t) 618-752-5671 www.holycrosswendelin.com Rev. Felix Chukwuma (Nigeria), Pst.; Very Rev. Mark D. Stec, Pst.; CRP Stds.: 70

OAKDALE

St. Anthony - 6101 St. Anthony Church Rd., Oakdale, IL 62268 t) 618-824-6271 Rev. Christopher Anyanwu, Admin.; Christine Lintker, PSR Dir.; CRP Stds.: 37

O'FALLON

St. Clare of Assisi Parish - 1411 Cross St., O'Fallon, IL 62269 t) 618-632-3562 stclarechurch.org Rev. James E. Deiters, Pst.; Dcn. John J. Gomez; Dcn. Dennis W. Vander Ven; Jane Dotson, PSR Dir.; CRP Stds.: 179

St. Clare School - (Grades PreK-8) 214 W. 3rd St., O'Fallon, IL 62269 t) 618-632-6327 clarice.mckay@saintclareschool.org saintclareschool.org Clarice McKay, Prin.; Stds.: 382; Lay Tchrs.: 23

St. Nicholas - 625 St. Nicholas Dr., O'Fallon, IL 62269 t) 618-632-1797 busadmin@stnicholasofallon.org; dre@stnicholasofallon.org www.stnicholasofallon.org Rev. Msgr. William J. Hitpas, Pst.; Rev. Thomas Lugge, Assoc. Pst.; Dcn. Gary Mueller; Ann Daniels, Admin.; Beth Rheaume, DRE; Martha Rheaume, DRE; CRP Stds.: 421

OKAWVILLE

St. Barbara - 305 N. Front St., Okawville, IL 62271; Mailing: P.O. Box 494, Okawville, IL 62271 t) 618-243-6236 Rev. Christopher Anyanwu, Admin.; Robin Crouch, CRE; CRP Stds.: 18

OLNEY

St. Joseph - 220 S. Elliot St., Olney, IL 62450 t) 618-392-8181 stjosephchurch_olney@yahoo.com; ctrimblepa@gmail.com www.stjosephchurcholney.com Very Rev. Mark D. Stec, Pst.; Rev. Felix Chukwuma (Nigeria), Pst.; CRP Stds.: 14

St. Joseph School - (Grades PreK-8) 520 E. Chestnut St., Olney, IL 62450 t) 618-395-3081 office@stjoeolney.com Carol Potter, Prin.; Stds.: 259; Lay Tchrs.: 15

St. Joseph - 6342 N. Stringtown Rd, Olney, IL 62450; Mailing: P.O. Box 10, Dundas, IL 62425 t) 618-754-3676 stjoestringtown@hotmail.com; ctrimblepa@gmail.com www.stjosephstringtown.com Rev. Felix Chukwuma (Nigeria), Pst.; Very Rev. Mark D. Stec, Pst.; CRP Stds.: 21

PINCKNEYVILLE

St. Bruno - 204 N. Gordon St., Pinckneyville, IL 62274 t) 618-357-5510 stbsmm@yahoo.com www.stbrunostmarymagdalen.com Rev. Carl Schrage, Admin.; Kathy Sprehe, DRE; CRP Stds.: 31

St. Bruno School - (Grades PreK-8) 210 N. Gordon St., Pinckneyville, IL 62274 t) 618-357-8276 brittany.goldman@stbrunoschool.com Brittany Goldman, Prin.; Stds.: 115; Lay Tchrs.: 10

St. Mary Magdalen - 5047 Todds Mill Rd., Pinckneyville, IL 62274-2235; Mailing: 204 N. Gordon St., Pinckneyville, IL 62274 t) 618-357-5510 stbrunochurch@yahoo.com; stbsmm@yahoo.com www.stbrunostmarymagdalen.com Rev. Carl Schrage, Admin.;

PRAIRIE DU ROCHER

St. Joseph - 802 Middle St., Prairie du Rocher, IL 62277; Mailing: P. O. Box 365, Prairie du Rocher, IL 62277 t) 618-284-3314 www.stjoespdr.org/ Rev. Sebastian Ukoh, C.M. (Nigeria), Pst.; Marie Henry, DRE; Jill Whelen, PSR Dir.; CRP Stds.: 35

RADOM

St. Michael the Archangel - 52 S. Third St., Radom, IL 62876; Mailing: PO Box 128, Radom, IL 62876 t) 618-485-2265; 618-787-2781 (CRP) stmichaelsradom@frontier.com; stcharleschurch@wisperhome.com www.stmichaelradom.com Rev. Oliver Nwachukwu, Admin.; Judy Pieszchalski, DRE; CRP Stds.: 23

RED BUD

St. John the Baptist - 515 Locust St., Red Bud, IL 62278 t) 618-282-3222 drschaefer49@hotmail.com www.sjbcatholicredbud.com Rev. Msgr. Dennis R. Schaefer, Pst.; Amy Deterding, PSR Dir.; CRP Stds.: 80

St. John the Baptist School - (Grades PreSchool-8) 519 Hazel St., Red Bud, IL 62278 t) 618-282-3215 www.sjbcatholicschoolredbud.org Rhonda Niemeier, Prin.; Stds.: 74; Lay Tchrs.: 8

St. Patrick - #1 Pioneer Ln.-Ruma, Red Bud, IL 62278 t) 618-282-3176 stpatscatholicruma.weebly.com Rev. Msgr. Dennis R. Schaefer, Pst.; CRP Stds.: 7

RENAULT

Our Lady of Good Counsel - 2024 Washington St., Renault, IL 62279; Mailing: PO Box 98, Renault, IL 62279 t) 618-458-7710 olgcrenault@gmail.com Rev. John Kizhakedan, C.M.I., Pst.;

RIDGWAY

St. Kateri Tekakwitha - 211 W. Edwards St., Ridgway, IL 62979; Mailing: PO Box 190, Ridgway, IL 62979 t) 618-272-7059 gallatincatholic@gmail.com stkateri.net Rev. Vincent Mukasa, Assoc. Pst.; CRP Stds.: 40

ROYALTON

St. Aloysius/Sacred Heart - 212 S. Pecan St., Royalton, IL 62983; Mailing: 703 E. Main, West Frankfort, IL 62896 t) 618-932-2828 johnthebaptist@mchsi.com stalsacredheart.org Rev. Eusebius C. Mbidoaka, Admin.; CRP Stds.: 1

SALEM

St. Theresa of Avila - 812 W. Main St., Salem, IL 62881 t) 618-548-0899 www.sttheresaofavilaparish.com Rev. Jose R. Jacob (India), Pst.; Denise McCormack, PSR Coord.; CRP Stds.: 10

SANDOVAL

St. Lawrence - 311 W. Missouri St., Sandoval, IL 62882; Mailing: P.O. Box 278, Sandoval, IL 62882 t) 618-247-3300; 618-532-6291 (CRP) cre@stmarycentralia.org www.saintlawrencesandoval.org Rev. Steven Pautler, Pst.; Mary William, DRE; CRP Stds.: 2

SCHELLER

St. Barbara - 4281 N. Scheller Ln., Scheller, IL 62883; Mailing: 1550 Main St., Mount Vernon, IL 62864 t) 618-244-1559 frnick@stmarymtvernon.org Very Rev. Nicholas G. Junker, Pst.; Rev. Benny George, C.M.I. (India), Assoc. Pst.; CRP Stds.: 44

SESSER

St. Mary - 100 N. Poplar St., Sesser, IL 62884 t) 618-004-1792 Chapel status Rev. Urban Osuji, C.M., Pst.;

SHILOH

Corpus Christi - 205 Rasp St., Shiloh, IL 62269 t) 618-632-7614 corpuschristi1@sbcglobal.net; ccshilohym@sbcglobal.net www.corpuschristishiloh.com Rev. Paul R. Wienhoff, Pst.; Michele Stroot, DRE; CRP Stds.: 33

SMITHTON

St. John the Baptist - 10 S. Lincoln St., Smithton, IL 62285-1614 t) 618-234-2068 parish@stjohnsschool.us www.stjohnschool.us Rev. Stanley J. Konieczny, Pst.; Linda Bagsby, PSR Dir.; Phyllis Hanna, PSR Dir.; CRP Stds.: 80

St. John the Baptist School - t) 618-233-0581 principal@stjohnsschool.us stjohnsschool.wixsite.com/stjohnsschool Sarah Lanham, Prin.; Stds.: 116; Lay Tchrs.: 9

SPARTA

Our Lady of Lourdes - 611 W. Broadway St., Sparta, IL 62286 t) 618-443-2811 ollsparta@yahoo.com Rev. Iuvenis Iheme, CM, Pst.; CRP Stds.: 27

ST. LIBORY
St. Liborius - 911 Sparta St., St. Libory, IL 62282; Mailing: P.O. Box 331, St. Libory, IL 62282 t) 618-768-4921 Rev. Nicholas Fleming, Pst.; Dcn. Andrew Lintker; Helen Musenbrock, DRE;
ST. ROSE
St. Rose - 18010 St. Rose Rd., St. Rose, IL 62230-2506 t) 618-526-4118 belpsros@outlook.com www.strosechurchil.com Rev. Edward F. Schaefer, Pst.; Marilyn Bruggemann, DRE; CRP Stds.: 116
STEELEVILLE
St. Joseph - 501 Broadway, Steeleville, IL 62288; Mailing: P.O. Box 85, Steeleville, IL 62288 t) 618-853-4435 dboyer@diobelle.org Gary Cleland, Bus. Mgr.;
TAMAROA
Immaculate Conception - 533 W. 2nd North St., Tamaroa, IL 62888 t) 618-496-5867; 618-542-3423 Rev. Carl Schrage, Pst.; CRP Stds.: 3
TRENTON
St. Mary - 218 W. Kentucky St., Trenton, IL 62293 t) 618-224-9335 stmary@stmarytrenton.com; faithformation@stmarytrenton.com www.stmarytrenton.com Rev. Msgr. David M. Darin, Pst.; Kim Moss, DRE; CRP Stds.: 60
VALMEYER
Seven Dolors of the B.V.M. - 101 S. Meyer Ave., Valmeyer, IL 62295 t) 618-935-2247 Rev. John Kizhakedan, C.M.I., Pst.; Elissa Chausse, PSR Dir.; CRP Stds.: 32
VIENNA
St. Paul - 2020 State Rte. 146 E., Vienna, IL 62995 t) 618-658-4501 spccil@frontier.com www.stpaulvienna.org Rev. Christian Iwuagwu, Pst.; CRP Stds.: 15
WALSH
St. Pius V - 7681 Walsh Rd., Walsh, IL 62297 t) 618-853-4404 stpius@accessus.net Rev. Iuvenis Iheme, CM, Admin.;
WATERLOO
St. Michael - 4576 Buss Branch Rd., Waterloo, IL 62298 t) 618-473-2798 stmichaels4@aol.com stmichaelspaderborn.org Rev. Stanley J. Konieczny, Pst.; Karen Sue Walsh, DRE; Rev. James A. Voelker, In Res.; CRP Stds.: 22
St. Patrick - 5675 LL Rd., Waterloo, IL 62298 t) 618-458-6875 stpatrickstipton@gmail.com www.stpatrickstipton.org/ Rev. John Kizhakedan, C.M.I., Pst.;
SS. Peter and Paul - 204 W. Mill St., Waterloo, IL 62298 t) 618-939-6426; 618-939-6426 x24 (CRP) ssppcc.org Rev. Linus Umoren, C.M., Pst.; Rev. Evaristus Akabueze, Assoc. Pst.; Dcn. Thomas J. Helfrich; Catherine Burkart, PSR Dir.; CRP Stds.: 119
SS. Peter and Paul School - 217 W. Third St., Waterloo, IL 62298 t) 618-939-7217 Lori Matzenbacher, Prin.; Stds.: 224; Lay Tchrs.: 21
WEST FRANKFORT
St. John the Baptist - 703 E. Main St., West Frankfort, IL 62896 t) 618-932-2828 johnthebaptist@mchsi.com stjohnschurch-wf.org Rev. Eusebius C. Mbidoaka, Admin.; CRP Stds.: 5
St. John the Baptist School - 702 E. Poplar, West Frankfort, IL 62896 t) 618-937-2017 dpowell@stjohnswestfrankfort.com Kay Levanti, Prin.; Stds.: 70; Lay Tchrs.: 6

SCHOOLS: PRESCHOOL THRU HIGH SCHOOL

SCHOOLS

STATE OF ILLINOIS

EAST SAINT LOUIS
Sister Thea Bowman Catholic School - (DIO) (Grades K-8) 8213 Church Ln., East Saint Louis, IL 62203 t) 618-397-0316 sistertheabowmanschool@srthea.org; tkeefe@srthea.org www.stbcs.com Tim Keefe, Admin.; Stds.: 109; Lay Tchrs.: 12
FAIRVIEW HEIGHTS
Holy Trinity Catholic School - 504 Fountains Pkwy., Fairview Heights, IL 62208 t) 618-628-7395; 618-628-1570 office@holytrinityedu.org www.holytrinityedu.org Michael Oslance, Prin.; Stds.: 278; Lay Tchrs.: 18

HIGH SCHOOLS

STATE OF ILLINOIS

BELLEVILLE
Althoff Catholic High School - (DIO) (Grades 9-12) 5401 W. Main St., Belleville, IL 62226-4796 t) 618-235-1100 sgass@althoffcatholic.org www.althoffcatholic.org Dr. Sarah Gass, Prin.; Stds.: 317; Lay Tchrs.: 22
Althoff Catholic High School Educational Endowment Trust - 222 S. 3rd St., Belleville, IL 62220 t) 618-277-8181 enastoff@diobelle.org
BREESE
Mater Dei High School - (DIO) 900 N. Mater Dei Dr., Breese, IL 62230 t) 618-526-7216 knights@materdeiknights.org; dlitteken@materdeiknights.org www.materdeiknights.org Central Catholic High School for Clinton Co. Rev. Charles W. Tuttle, Chap.; Dennis Litteken, Prin.; Stds.: 360; Lay Tchrs.: 27
WATERLOO
Gibault Catholic High School - (DIO) 501 Columbia Ave., Waterloo, IL 62298 t) 618-939-3883 www.gibaultonline.com Steve Kidd, Prin.; Stds.: 181; Lay Tchrs.: 23

INSTITUTIONS LOCATED IN DIOCESE

CAMPUS MINISTRY / NEWMAN CENTERS [CAM]

CARBONDALE
The Newman Catholic Student Center - 715 S. Washington, Carbondale, IL 62901 t) 618-529-3311 office@siucnewman.org www.siucnewman.org Tim Taylor, Dir.;

CEMETERIES [CEM]

BELLEVILLE
Catholic Diocese of Belleville Cemetery Association - 10101 W. Main St., Belleville, IL 62223 t) 618-397-0181 cdbcemeteryassoc@gmail.com Covers: Mt. Carmel, Belleville; Immaculate Conception, Centreville; Holy Cross, Fairview Hts; St. Phillips, East St. Louis, IL Dee Dee Murray, Contact;
Green Mount Catholic Cemetery of the Cathedral Congregation of Belleville - 200 W. Harrison St., Belleville, IL 62220 t) 618-234-4858 businessmanager@cathedralbelle.org Nancy Lowe, Secy.;
BREESE
St. Dominic Roman Catholic Cemetery of Breese - Rt. 50, Breese, IL 62230; Mailing: 493 N. 2nd St., Breese, IL 62230 t) 618-526-7746 saintdominic@papadocs.com Rev. Patrick N. Peter, Pst.;
FAIRVIEW HEIGHTS
St. Adalbert Association (An Illinois Religious Corporation) -
O'FALLON
Mount Calvary Cemetery of St. Clare Roman Catholic Congregation -
VILLA RIDGE
Calvary Cemetery of St. Patrick Roman Catholic Church of Cairo - 312 Ninth St., Villa Ridge, IL 62914 t) (618) 734-2061 (Rectory Phone) George Belle, Trustee;

CONVENTS, MONASTERIES, AND RESIDENCES FOR WOMEN [CON]

BELLEVILLE
Hospital Sisters of The Third Order of St. Francis - 1000 Royal Heights Rd., Apt. 58, Belleville, IL 62226 t) 217-522-3386 www.springfieldfranciscans.org Amy Bulpitt, Admin.;
Poor Clare Monastery of Our Lady of Mercy - 300 N. 60th St., Belleville, IL 62223 t) 618-235-4407 mbmeyer1860@verizon.net www.poorclares-belleville.info Mother Giovanna Day, PCC, Abbess; Srs.: 12

ENDOWMENTS / FOUNDATIONS / TRUSTS [EFT]

BELLEVILLE
Catholic Community Foundation for the Diocese of Belleville - 222 S. 3rd St., Belleville, IL 62220-1985 t) 618-277-8181 enastoff@diobelle.org Very Rev. Steven L. Beatty, Vicar; Michael Soete, Treas.;
The Catholic Diocese of Belleville Parish & Agency Resource Fund - 222 S. Third St., Belleville, IL 62220 t) 618-277-8181 enastoff@diobelle.org Very Rev. Steven L. Beatty, Vicar; Michael Soete, Treas.;
Ministry Formation Fund, NFP - 222 S. Third St., Belleville, IL 62220 t) 618-277-8181 enastoff@diobelle.org Very Rev. Steven L. Beatty, Vicar; Michael Soete, Treas.;
Property & Liability Insurance Fund, NFP - 222 S. Third St., Belleville, IL 62220 t) 618-277-8181 enastoff@diobelle.org Very Rev. Steven L. Beatty, Vicar; Michael Soete, Treas.;
CENTRALIA
St. Mary's Hospital Foundation - 400 N. Pleasant Ave., Centralia, IL 62801 t) 618-899-1047 Kay Zibby-Damron, Dir.;
MOUNT VERNON
SSM Health Good Samaritan Hospital Foundation - 1 Good Samaritan Way, Mount Vernon, IL 62864 t) 618-899-1047 Kay Zibby-Damron, Dir.;

HOSPITALS / HEALTH SERVICES [HOS]

BREESE
St. Joseph Hospital of the Hospital Sisters of the Third Order of St. Francis (St. Joseph's Hospital Breese) - 9515 Holy Cross Ln., Breese, IL 62230; Mailing: P. O. Box 99, Breese, IL 62230 t) 618-526-4511 amy.bulpitt@hshs.org www.stjoebreese.com Aaron Puchbauer, CEO; Sr. Pam Falter, Pst. Min./Coord.; Bed Capacity: 44; Asstd. Annu.: 89,277; Staff: 240
CENTRALIA
***St. Mary's Hospital** - 400 N. Pleasant Ave., Centralia, IL 62801 t) 618-436-8000 www.smgsi.com John Kohler, Pres.; Bed Capacity: 108; Asstd. Annu.: 87,694; Staff: 656
MOUNT VERNON
***Good Samaritan Regional Health Center** - 1 Good Samaritan Way, Mount Vernon, IL 62864 t) 618-242-4600; 618-899-1002 www.ssmhealthillinois.com Member of SSM Health Care. Michael Baumgartner, Pres.; Bed Capacity: 134; Asstd. Annu.: 108,828; Staff: 1,405
MURPHYSBORO
St. Joseph Memorial Hospital - 2 S. Hospital Dr., Murphysboro, IL 62966 t) 618-684-3156 susan.odle@sih.net www.sih.net A service of Southern Illinois Healthcare. Adorers of the Blood of Christ Sue Odle, Admin.; Bed Capacity: 25; Asstd. Annu.: 10,777; Staff: 260
O'FALLON
St. Elizabeth Hospital - 1 St. Elizabeth's Blvd., O'Fallon, IL 62269 t) 618-234-2120 amy.bulpitt@hshs.org www.steliz.org Clinically Affiliated with St. Louis University School of Medicine. Hospital Sisters of the

Third Order of St. Francis Chris Klay, CEO; Bed Capacity: 144; Asstd. Annu.: 305,691; Staff: 1,107

MISCELLANEOUS [MIS]

BELLEVILLE

Ancient Order of Hibernians - 2012 Madison St., Belleville, IL 62226; Mailing: PO Box 247, O'Fallon, IL 62269 t) 618-257-2146 www.aohil1.com Patrick J. Hickey, Contact;

Catholic Committee on Scouting of the Diocese of Belleville - 1938 White Birch Ln., Belleville, IL 62220 t) 618-233-4303 rahermann417@gmail.com Daniel O'Keefe, Contact;

Catholic Diocese of Belleville General Fund - 222 S. Third St., Belleville, IL 62220 t) 618-277-8181 enastoff@diobelle.org Very Rev. Steven L. Beatty, Vicar; Michael Soete, Treas.;

Catholic Holy Family Society - 2021 Mascoutah Ave., Belleville, IL 62220; Mailing: P.O. Box 327, Mary Barbara Kurtz, Belleville, IL 62222 t) 618-233-0286 mbkurtz@chfsociety.org www.chfsociety.org Sandra Bouchard, COO;

Diocesan Council of Catholic Women - 222 S. Third St., Belleville, IL 62220 t) (618) 967-8050 Rev. Steven Pautler, Chap.;

Diocese of Belleville The Catholic Service and Ministry Appeal - 222 S. Third St., Belleville, IL 62220 t) (618) 277-8181 enastoff@diobelle.org Judy Phillips, Dir.; Very Rev. Steven L. Beatty, Vicar; Michael Soete, Treas.;

Engaged Encounter - 222 S. Third St., Belleville, IL 62220 t) (618) 277-8181 gerry.bach@sbcglobal.net www.eeofs-il.org Dcn. Gerald Bach Sr.; Ann Bach;

***Our Brothers' Keepers of Southern Illinois** - 222 S. Third St., Belleville, IL 62220; Mailing: P.O. Box 398, East Saint Louis, IL 62202 t) 618-482-5570 obkministry2@gmail.com; lslap@mindspring.com www.obkministry.org Louis Slapshak, Chap.;

Secular Franciscan Order of St. Peter Fraternity - 1830 Raab Ave., Belleville, IL 62226 t) 618-277-5147 dmrlmueller@sbcglobal.net Roger Mueller, OFS, Contact;

Serra Club of St. Clair County - 1333 Goldfinch Dr., Belleville, IL 62223 t) 618-473-3513 jtraney@me.com Jim Wachtel, Pres.;

TEC (Teens Encounter Christ) - 222 S. Third St., Belleville, IL 6222o t) (618) 977-0002 www.bellevilletec.com Michelle Biver, Chair;

Victorious Missionaries - 442 S. DeMazenod Dr., Belleville, IL 62223 t) 618-394-6281 truhmann@snows.org www.vmusa.org Spiritual Support Network for people with disabilities, chronic illness, and those who want to share the journey. Bro. Thomas Ruhmann, O.M.I., Dir.;

World Apostolate of Fatima, The Blue Army, U.S.A. - 2620 Lebanon Ave., Belleville, IL 62221 t) (618) 977-1698 jtm300@aol.com Rev. Msgr. John T. Myler, Spiritual Advisor;

CENTRALIA

***St. Mary's - Good Samaritan, Inc.** - 400 N. Pleasant Ave., Centralia, IL 62801 t) 618-436-8000 www.smgsi.com Co-Sponsored by the Franciscan Sisters of Mary and the Felician Sisters. John Kohler, Pres.;

FREEBURG

Catholic War Veterans - 3535 State Rte. 159, Freeburg, IL 62243; Mailing: P.O. Box 325, Belleville, IL 62222 t) 618-234-3074 rsatc82@att.net Rick Schmidt, Secy.;

O'FALLON

Worldwide Marriage Encounter - 118 Woodbourne Ct., O'Fallon, IL 62269 t) 618-622-8851 joepatkaiser@yahoo.com www.aweekendofdiscovery.org Joe Kaiser, Chair;

OREGON

Catholic Daughters of the Americas - 208 S. Fifth St., Oregon, IL 61061 t) 815-973-6753 dahead1@comcast.net www.catholicdaughters.org Patricia M Head, State Regent;

OZARK

Ondessonk, Camp - 3760 Ondessonk Rd., Ozark, IL 62972 t) 618-695-2489 camp@ondessonk.com ondessonk.com Summer camp Dan King, Exec. Dir.;

SCOTT AFB

Scott Air Force Base - Scott AFB Chapel, 375 AW/HC, 320 Ward Dr., Bldg. 1620, Scott AFB, IL 62225-5256 t) (618) 256-3303 Lisi Blake, Pst. Min./Coord.;

TROY

Daughters of Isabella - 208 Hazel St., Troy, IL 62294 t) 618-795-4641 insgirl2@gmail.com Angie Gerstenecker, State Regent;

MONASTERIES AND RESIDENCES FOR PRIESTS AND BROTHERS [MON]

BELLEVILLE

Missionary Association of Mary Immaculate- USA (MAMI-USA) - 9480 N. De Mazenod Dr., Belleville, IL 62223 t) 888-330-6264 duribe@omiusa.org www.oblatesusa.org Serving the missions of the Missionary Oblates, the National Shrine of Our Lady of the Snows, and the Tekakwitha Indian Missions. Rev. David Uribe, OMI, Dir.; Priests: 1

Missionary Oblates of Mary Immaculate - St. Henry's Oblate Residence - 200 N. 60th St., Belleville, IL 62223 t) 618-233-2991 sthenryomi@charter.net Rev. David A. Kalert, OMI, Supr.; Rev. James F. Allen, O.M.I.; Rev. Clyde Rausch, OMI; Rev. Walter Butor, O.M.I.; Rev. Gregory Cholewa, OMI; Rev. Thomas Hayes, O.M.I.; Rev. Joseph Hitpas, O.M.I.; Rev. Michael Hussey, O.M.I.; Rev. Thomas Killeen, O.M.I.; Rev. George Knab, O.M.I.; Rev. Allen J. Maes, O.M.I.; Rev. Robert Morin, OMI; Rev. Dale M. Schlitt, OMI; Rev. Sherman B. Wall, O.M.I.; Rev. Paul Wightman, OMI; Bro. Patrick McGee; Bro. Thomas Ruhmann, O.M.I.; Brs.: 2; Priests: 19

Shrine of Our Lady of the Snows - 442 S. DeMazenod Dr., Belleville, IL 62223-1023 t) 618-397-6700 info@snows.org www.snows.org Missionary Oblates of Mary Immaculate Central Province Rev. David Uribe, OMI, Dir.; Rev. Harold Fisher, O.M.I., Supr.; Rev. Juan Gaspar, O.M.I., Formation Dir.; Rev. Raul Salas, O.M.I., Pre-Novitiate Assoc.; Rev. Elvis Mwamba, OMI, Dir., Pilgrimages; Rev. Ronald Harrer, O.M.I., Attached; Benedictine Living Community; Rev. John R. Madigan, O.M.I., Attached; Benedictine Living Community; Rev. William H. Woestman, O.M.I., Attached; Benedictine Living Community; Rev. Terence J Figel, OMI, Attached; Benedictine Living Community; Rev. Norman Volk, OMI, Attached; Benedictine Living Community; Rev. Clarence Zachman, O.M.I., Attached; Benedictine Living Community; Rev. James Fee, O.M.I., In Res.; Priests: 6

EAST SAINT LOUIS

St. Benedict the Black Friary - 404 N. 14th St., East Saint Louis, IL 62201 t) 618-482-5570 cnreuter@yahoo.com Rev. Carroll Mizicko, O.F.M., Pst.; Rev. John Eaton, O.F.M., Dir.; Rev. Frank Coens, OFM, In Res.; Rev. Paul Gallagher, OFM, In Res.; Rev. William Spencer, OFM, In Res.; Priests: 5

WATERLOO

Vincentian Community (Province of Nigeria) - 204 W. Mill St., Waterloo, IL 62298 c) 313-819-0419 vincentianfathers1@gmail.com www.cmnigeria.org Rev. Linus Aniekan Umoren, C.M., Supr.; Priests: 6

NURSING / REHABILITATION / CONVALESCENCE / ELDERLY CARE [NUR]

BELLEVILLE

Apartment Community of Our Lady of the Snows (Benedictine Living Community | At The Shrine) - 726 Community Dr., Belleville, IL 62223 t) 618-394-6400 heather.stich@benedictineliving.org www.benedictineliving.org/belleville-il/ Heather Stich, Admin.; Rev. Terence J Figel, OMI; Rev. Ronald Harrer, O.M.I.; Rev. John R. Madigan, O.M.I.; Rev. Norman Volk, OMI; Rev. William H. Woestman, O.M.I.; Rev. Clarence Zachman, O.M.I.; Asstd. Annu.: 180; Staff: 125

Charles and Bertha Hincke Residence for Priests and Sense Residence - 2620 Lebanon Ave., Belleville, IL 62221 t) 618-234-5722 hinckehome@gmail.com Owned by Diocese of Belleville. Asstd. Annu.: 12; Staff: 8

PRESCHOOLS / CHILDCARE CENTERS [PRE]

BELLEVILLE

St. Henry Creative Learning Center - 5303 W. Main St., Belleville, IL 62226 t) 618-234-6061 st.henryclc1@yahoo.com; sthdaycare@peaknet.net www.sthenryclc.com Judy Shovlin, Dir.; Stds.: 35; Lay Tchrs.: 7

RETREAT HOUSES / RENEWAL CENTERS [RTR]

BELLEVILLE

King's House Retreat and Renewal Center - 700 N. 66th St., Belleville, IL 62223-3949 t) 618-397-0584 info@kingsretreatcenter.org www.kingsretreatcenter.org Rev. Salvador Gonzalez, O.M.I., Dir.; Rev. Mark Dean, O.M.I., Preaching Team;

An asterisk (*) denotes an organization that has established tax-exempt status directly with the IRS and is not covered by the USCCB Group Ruling.

Diocese of Biloxi

(Dioecesis Biloxiiensis)

MOST REVEREND LOUIS F. KIHNEMAN, III

Bishop of Biloxi; ordained November 18, 1977; appointed Bishop of Biloxi December 16, 2016; installed April 28, 2017. Office: 1790 Popps Ferry Rd., Biloxi, MS 39532-2118.

Chancery Office: 1790 Popps Ferry Rd., Biloxi, MS 39532-2118. T: 228-702-2100; F: 228-702-2178.

ESTABLISHED MARCH 1, 1977.

Square Miles 9,653.

Comprises 17 counties in southern Mississippi: Jackson, Harrison, Hancock, George, Stone, Pearl River, Greene, Perry, Forrest, Lamar, Marion, Walthall, Wayne, Jones, Covington, Jefferson Davis and Lawrence.

Legal Title: "Catholic Diocese of Biloxi".

For legal titles of parishes and diocesan institutions, consult the Chancery Office.

STATISTICAL OVERVIEW

Personnel
Bishop....1
Priests: Diocesan Active in Diocese....37
Priests: Retired, Sick or Absent....18
Number of Diocesan Priests....55
Religious Priests in Diocese....18
Total Priests in your Diocese....73
Extern Priests in Diocese....7
Ordinations:
Diocesan Priests....1
Transitional Deacons....1
Permanent Deacons....6
Permanent Deacons in Diocese....51
Total Brothers....10
Total Sisters....17

Parishes
Parishes....43
With Resident Pastor:
Resident Diocesan Priests....29
Resident Religious Priests....8
Without Resident Pastor:
Administered by Priests....6
Missions....8
Professional Ministry Personnel:
Sisters....1
Lay Ministers....18

Welfare
Homes for the Aged....9
Total Assisted....805
Special Centers for Social Services....7
Total Assisted....662,796
Other Institutions....1
Total Assisted....3,177

Educational
Diocesan Students in Other Seminaries....5
Total Seminarians....5
High Schools, Diocesan and Parish....4
Total Students....1,387
High Schools, Private....1
Total Students....343
Elementary Schools, Diocesan and Parish....9
Total Students....2,436
Catechesis / Religious Education:
High School Students....843
Elementary Students....2,149
Total Students under Catholic Instruction....7,163
Teachers in Diocese:
Lay Teachers....368

Vital Statistics
Receptions into the Church:
Infant Baptism Totals....576
Minor Baptism Totals....121
Adult Baptism Totals....73
Received into Full Communion....113
First Communions....763
Confirmations....652
Marriages:
Catholic....103
Interfaith....55
Total Marriages....158
Deaths....640
Total Catholic Population....54,520
Total Population....831,202

LEADERSHIP

Office of the Bishop - t) 228-702-2111 Most Rev. Louis F. Kihneman III;
Vicar General - t) 228-702-2114 Rev. Msgr. T. Dominick Fullam;
Moderator of Curia - t) 228-702-2114 Rev. Msgr. T. Dominick Fullam;
Chancery Office - t) 228-702-2100 Dcn. Karl Koberger, Chancellor (deaconkarl2013@gmail.com);
Deans - Rev. Godfrey Andoh, East Central Coast Deanery; Rev. Joseph M. Uko, Central Coast Deanery; Rev. Michael P. O'Connor, West Coast Deanery;
College of Consultors - Rev. Msgr. T. Dominick Fullam; Rev. Msgr. John R. McGrath; Rev. Msgr. Michael J. Thornton;

ADVISORY BOARDS, COMMISSIONS, COMMITTEES, AND COUNCILS

Diocesan Boards and Committees -
Association of Priests (Diocese of Biloxi and Jackson) - Most Rev. Louis F. Kihneman III, Chair; Most Rev. Joseph R. Kopacz, Bishop of Jackson & Co-Chm.; Rev. Thomas S. Conway, Pres.;
Board for the Formation, Life and Ministry of Permanent Deacons Class of 2025 - Rev. Daniel Martinez Patino; Rev. Patrick J. Mockler; Rev. Bernard J. Papania Jr.;
Building and Real Estate Committee - Rev. Michael P. Austin, Chair; Chuck Collins; Robert Starks;
Catholic Foundation-Diocese of Biloxi - Most Rev. Louis F. Kihneman III, Pres.; Rev. Msgr. T. Dominick Fullam, Vice. Pres.; David Wyrwich, Exec.;
Catholic Housing Board - Most Rev. Louis F. Kihneman III; Rev. Msgr. T. Dominick Fullam; Rev. Joseph M. Uko;
Communications and Systems Management Committee - Terrance P. Dickson; Rev. Dennis J. Carver; Rev. Braxton Necaise;
Consultative Committee for Safe Environment - Rev. Kenneth Ramon-Landry; Emily Cloud; Cindy Burnett;
Diocesan Liturgical Commission - Rev. Michael P. Austin, Chair; Rev. Msgr. T. Dominick Fullam; Dcn. William J. Vrazel;
Diocesan School Advisory Council - Dr. Matthew Buckley, Supt.; Rev. Braxton Necaise; Rev. Godfrey Andoh;
Finance Council - Most Rev. Louis F. Kihneman III; Rev. Msgr. T. Dominick Fullam; Rev. Msgr. John R. McGrath;
Governing Board for de l'Epee Deaf Center - Most Rev. Louis F. Kihneman III; Dcn. John R. Henderson; Greg Crapo, Dir.;
Insurance Committee - Rev. Msgr. T. Dominick Fullam; Greg Crapo; Dcn. John E. Jennings;
Mission Board - Most Rev. Louis F. Kihneman III; Rev. Michael P. Austin;
Priests Personnel Board - Rev. Msgr. T. Dominick Fullam; Rev. Msgr. John R. McGrath; Rev. Michael P. O'Connor;
Presbyteral Council - Rev. Msgr. T. Dominick Fullam; Rev. Msgr. John R. McGrath; Rev. Patrick J. Mockler;
Retired Priests' Committee - Most Rev. Louis F. Kihneman III; Rev. Msgr. T. Dominick Fullam; Rev. Msgr. John R. McGrath;

CATHOLIC CHARITIES

Twelve Baskets Food Bank - t) 228-822-0836 Jennifer Keegan, Prog. Dir.;
Disaster Relief and Recovery Office - t) 228-701-0555 Nancy Loftus, Prog. Dir.;
Western Deanery Outreach Center - t) 228-467-2600
Central and East Central Coast Deanery Outreach Center - t) 228-864-4221
East Coast Deanery Outreach Center - t) 228-567-0001
Northern Deanery Outreach Center - t) 601-408-3662
Catholic Relief Services - t) 228-897-2280 Gregory K. Crapo;
Office of Catholic Charities of South Mississippi - t) 228-701-0555 jwilliams@biloxidiocese.org Jennifer Williams, Dir.;

COMMUNICATIONS

Office of Social Media - t) 228-702-2121 pblanchard@biloxidiocese.org Paul Blanchard, Dir.;
Gulf Pine Catholic Newspaper - t) (228) 702-2126 Terrance P. Dickson, Editor;
Office of Communication - t) 228-702-2126 Terrance P. Dickson, Dir.;
Information Technology - t) (228) 702-2121 Paul Blanchard, Dir.;

DEVELOPMENT

Office of Stewardship and Development - t) 228-702-2113 dwyrwich@biloxidiocese.org David Wyrwich, Dir.;

EDUCATION

Department of Education - t) 228-702-2130 klingenfelder@biloxidiocese.org Katherine Lingenfelder, Admin. Asst.;
Office of Special Education - t) 228-702-2130 Dr. Matthew Buckley, Supt.;
Office of Superintendent of Catholic Schools - t) 228-702-2129 Dr. Matthew Buckley, Supt.;
Priests' Continuing Education and Retreat Programs - t) 228-863-1610 Rev. Cuthbert R. O'Connell;
Resource Center - t) 228-702-2131 ltrahan@biloxidiocese.org Leo Trahan;

FAITH FORMATION

Campus Ministry - t) 601-264-5192 Rev. Mark A. Ropel;
Cursillo and Retreats - t) 228-255-7560
Office of Faith Formation - t) 228-702-2131 ltrahan@biloxidiocese.org Leo Trahan, Diocesan D.R.E.;
Office of Youth Ministry - t) 228-702-2142 rlacy@biloxidiocese.org Ray Lacy, Dir.;
Propagation of the Faith - t) 228-452-4686 Rev. Michael P. Austin, Dir.;

FAMILY LIFE

Office of Marriage & Family Life - t) 228-872-4004 jgunkel@biloxidiocese.org Dcn. James Gunkel, Dir.;
Office of Pro-Life Ministries - t) (228) 424-0221 gnorris22@gmail.com Dcn. Gerald Norris, Co-Dir.; Sandra Norris, Co-Dir.;

FINANCE

Department of Finance - t) 228-702-2118 Tammy W. DiLorenzo, Dir. (tdilorenzo@biloxidiocese.org);

SPIRITUAL LIFE

Office of Evangelization and Pastoral Services - t) 228-702-2165 rsmith@biloxidiocese.org Dcn. Richard Smith, Dir.;
Office of Liturgy - t) 228-452-4686 Rev. Michael P. Austin, Dir.;
Office of Charismatic Ministry - c) (228) 860-4819 Dcn. Norbert Lloyd Jr., Coord.;

TRIBUNAL

Administrative Assistant and Ecclesiastical Notary - t) 228-702-2117 dbrown@biloxidiocese.org Donna Brown;
Special Delegate for Matrimonial Dispensations - t) 228-702-2117 Rev. Msgr. John R. McGrath;
Judicial Vicar - t) 228-702-2117 Rev. Msgr. John R. McGrath;
Promoter of Justice - Rev. Msgr. Michael J. Thornton;
Tribunal Judges - t) 228-702-2117 Rev. Msgr. John R. McGrath; Rev. Kevin Slattery; Rev. Msgr. Michael Flannery;
Defenders of the Bond - Rev. Msgr. T. Dominick Fullam; Rev. Thomas S. Conway;
Pro-Synodal Judge - Rev. Msgr. James P. McGough;
Advocates - Dcn. John R. Henderson; Dcn. Roberto Jimenez; David Wyrwich;

MISCELLANEOUS / OTHER OFFICES

Campaign for Human Development - t) 228-701-0555 Jennifer Williams;
Catholic Boy Scouts - t) 228-702-2142
Catholic University, Friends of - Rev. Msgr. T. Dominick Fullam;
***Deaf and Disabled, Office of the** - t) 228-897-2280; 228-206-6062 (Video) Gregory K. Crapo, Dir.;
Ecumenical & Interreligious Affairs - t) 228-702-2131 Leo Trahan, Contact;
Miscellaneous Apostolates -
Apostleship of the Sea - t) 228-209-6960 Dcn. John R. Henderson;
Hispanic Ministry - t) (228) 435-0007 Rev. Daniel Martinez Patino, Dir.;
Prison Apostolate - t) 228-861-6581 Dcn. Earl Saucier, Assoc. Dir.;
Vietnamese Apostolate - t) 228-374-1116 Rev. Thang John Pham;
Mission Office - t) 228-452-4686 Rev. Michael P. Austin;
Office of Diocesan Risk Management - t) 228-702-2104 jjennings@biloxidiocese.org Dcn. John E. Jennings, Dir.;
Ministry of the Diaconate - t) 228-702-2107 Dcn. Michael M. Harris, Dir.; Dcn. David W. Allen, Assoc. Dir. Continuing Educ.; Dcn. William J. Vrazel, Assoc. Dir. Liturgy & Devel.;
Pontifical Association of the Holy Childhood - t) 228-452-4686 Rev. Michael P. Austin, Dir.;
Diocesan Attorney - t) 228-388-7441 Christian Strickland;
Victim Assistance Coordinator - t) 228-424-7292 Emily Cloud (ecloud78@gmail.com);
Vocations - t) 228-762-1653 Rev. Adam Urbaniak, Dir.; Rev. Braxton Necaise;

PARISHES, MISSIONS, AND CLERGY

STATE OF MISSISSIPPI

BASSFIELD

St. Peter - 4135 Hwy. 42, Bassfield, MS 39421; Mailing: P.O. Box 10, Bassfield, MS 39421 t) 601-943-6688; (601) 943-5104 stpetersms@windstream.net stpeterbassfield.myfreesites.net/ Rev. Tomasz Golab, Par. Admin.; CRP Stds.: 36
St. Lawrence - 831 F.E. Sellers Hwy., Monticello, MS 39654; Mailing: P.O. Box 16, Monticello, MS 39654

BAY ST. LOUIS

St. Ann - 5858 Lower Bay Rd., Bay St. Louis, MS 39520 t) 228-467-5128 stanncathparish@gmail.com stannstjosephparish.org Rev. Truong Quang Trinh, Par. Admin.; CRP Stds.: 12
St. Joseph Chapel - 5383 Hwy. 604, Pearlington, MS 39572 t) (228) 467-5128
Holy Infant of Good Health Chapel - t) (228) 467-5128; (228) 332-3622
Our Lady of the Gulf - 228 S. Beach Blvd., Bay St. Louis, MS 39520 t) 228-467-6509 www.olgchurch.net Rev. Michael P. O'Connor, Pst.; Rev. James Michael Smith, Par. Vicar; Dcn. Michael M. Harris; Kathleen LeBlanc, Pst. Assoc.; Shelby Martin, Youth Min.; CRP Stds.: 99
Holy Trinity Catholic Elementary - (Grades 1-6) 301 S. Second St., Bay St. Louis, MS 39520 t) 228-467-5158 mroberts@holytrinitycatholic.net; dlizana@holytrinitycatholic.net www.holytrinitycatholic.net Desiree Lizana, Prin.;
St. Rose De Lima - 301 S. Necaise Ave., Bay St. Louis,

MS 39520 t) 228-467-7347; 228-467-7357; 228-342-5172 (CRP) www.srdla.org Rev. Anil Thomas, SVD, Par. Admin.; Joan Thomas, DRE; CRP Stds.: 37

BILOXI

Cathedral of the Nativity of the Blessed Virgin Mary - 870 Howard Ave., Biloxi, MS 39530 t) 228-374-1717 nativitybvmcathedral.org Rev. Godfrey Andoh, Rector; Rev. Bartosz T. Kunat, Par. Vicar; Dcn. John Williams; CRP Stds.: 29

Nativity BVM School - (Grades 1-6) 1046 Beach Blvd., Biloxi, MS 39530 t) 228-432-2269 nbvmbiloxi@aol.com www.nativitybvm.org Kelly Pennell, Librn.;

Blessed Francis Xavier Seelos - 356 Lameuse St., Biloxi, MS 39530; Mailing: P.O. Box 347, Biloxi, MS 39533-0347 t) 228-435-0007 blessedseeloscc@yahoo.com; bunwalq@yahoo.com www.seelosbiloxi.com Rev. Daniel Martinez Patino, Pst.; Dcn. Melvin J. Landry Jr.; Cheryl Thompson, DRE; CRP Stds.: 12

St. Mary - 8343 Woolmarket Rd., Biloxi, MS 39532 t) 228-392-1999 c) 228-731-2747 (Pastoral Assoc); 228-354-7900 (Pastor) www.stmarybiloxi.org Rev. Martin Joseph Gillespie, Pst.; Dcn. Al Stockert, Pst. Assoc.; Dcn. Gerald Pickich; Emily Cloud, Youth Min.; CRP Stds.: 55

St. Michael - 177 First St., Biloxi, MS 39533 t) 228-435-5578 stmichaelccbiloxi@gmail.com stmichaelchurchbiloxi.com/ Rev. Msgr. T. Dominick Fullam, Pst.; Dcn. Robert R. Wescovich; Dcn. Billy Shaidnagle;

Our Lady of Fatima - 2090 Pass Rd., Biloxi, MS 39531; Mailing: 2080 Pass Rd, Biloxi, MS 39531 t) 228-388-3887; 228-388-3891; 228-388-5737 (CRP) fatimabiloxi@gmail.com; fatimaccdchurch@gmail.com www.olfatima-biloxi.com Rev. Henry B. McInerney, Pst.; Rev. Charles Arthur, Par. Vicar; Rev. Daniel Martinez Patino, Hispanic Min.; Dcn. Ronald Alexander Jr.; Dcn. Paul G. Matherne; Dcn. Mardoqueo Magana, Hispanic Min.; CRP Stds.: 88

Our Lady of Fatima School - (Grades PreK-6) 320 Jim Money Rd., Biloxi, MS 39531 t) 228-388-3602 chahn@olfschool.org www.olfschool.org Cindy Hahn, Prin.; Marie Proctor, Librn.;

Our Mother of Sorrows - 803 Division St., Biloxi, MS 39530; Mailing: P.O. Box 347, Biloxi, MS 39533-0347 t) 228-435-0007 ourmotherofsorrowscc@yahoo.com; bunwalq@yahoo.com omsbiloxi.com Rev. Daniel Martinez Patino, Pst.; Dcn. Richard Smith; Cheryl Thompson, DRE; CRP Stds.: 5

Vietnamese Martyrs Church - 171 Oak St., Biloxi, MS 39530; Mailing: 172 Oak St., Biloxi, MS 39530 t) 228-374-1116 vnmartyrsblx@gmail.com Rev. Thang John Pham, Pst.; CRP Stds.: 152

COLUMBIA

Holy Trinity - 1429 N. Park Ave., Columbia, MS 39429 t) 601-736-3136 holytrinitycc@gmail.com Rev. Alwin Samy, H.G.N., Pst.;

St. Paul the Apostle - 702 Union Rd., Tylertown, MS 39667; Mailing: P.O. Box 470, Tylertown, MS 39667 t) 601-876-6422

D'IBERVILLE

Sacred Heart - 10446 LeMoyne Blvd., D'Iberville, MS 39540 t) 228-392-4526 www.sacredheartdiberville.org Rev. Dominic Pham, Pst.; Dcn. William Stentz; Mary Alexander, DRE; Christa Hedman, DRE; CRP Stds.: 104

Sacred Heart School - (Grades PreK-6) 10482 Lemoyne Blvd., D'Iberville, MS 39540 t) 228-392-4180 sgruich@shceschool.com www.sacredheartelementary.org Stephanie Gruich, Prin.;

GAUTIER

St. Mary - 809 De La Pointe Dr., Gautier, MS 39553 t) 228-497-2364 stmarygautier@yahoo.com www.saintmarygautier.com Rev. Arockia Doss (India), Pst.; Dcn. Robert E. Illanne; Dcn. Joseph Michael McIntyre; Becky Sparkman, DRE; CRP Stds.: 38

GULFPORT

St. Ann - 23529 Hwy. 53, Gulfport, MS 39503 t) 228-832-2560; 228-831-9452 (CRP) www.stannparishlizana.org Rev. David Milton Maria Augustin, HGN, Pst.; Robert Earl Lizana, DRE; CRP Stds.: 33

Our Lady of Chartres - Big Creek Rd., Gulfport, MS 39503; Mailing: 23529 Hwy. 53, Gulfport, MS 39503 t) (228) 832-2560 Rev. David Milton, H.G.N., Pst.;

St. James - 366 Cowan Rd., Gulfport, MS 39507 t) 228-896-6059 www.saintjamescc.com Rev. Ryan M. McCoy, Pst.; Dcn. Rick Conason; Dcn. John R. Henderson, Pst. Assoc.; Bridgett Bermond, Youth Min.; Sarah Rhodes, Youth Min.; Linda Arlene Hebert, DRE; Mara Russo, Family Life Coordinator; CRP Stds.: 242

St. James School - (Grades 1-6) 603 West Ave., Gulfport, MS 39507 t) 228-896-6631 jbroadus@stjamesgulfport.com www.stjamesgulfport.com Jennifer Broadus, Prin.; Connie Favret, Librn.; Stds.: 376

St. John the Evangelist - 2414 17th St., Gulfport, MS 39501 t) 228-864-2272 stjohngulfport.org Rev. Satish Baburao Adhav (India), Pst.; Dcn. David W. Allen; CRP Stds.: 9

St. Patrick High School - 18300 St. Patrick Rd., Biloxi, MS 39532-8655 t) 228-702-0500 www.stpatrickhighschool.net Dr. Matthew Buckley, Prin.;

St. Joseph Catholic Church - 12290 DePew Rd., Gulfport, MS 39503 t) 228-832-3244 stjosephgulfport@bellsouth.net; stjosephcatholiconline@gmail.com www.stjosephcc.com Rev. Joseph M. Uko, Pst.; Dcn. Karl Koberger; CRP Stds.: 63

St. Therese - 3521 19th St., Gulfport, MS 39501 t) 228-863-0624 Rev. Hyginus Boboh, SSJ, Pst.; Dcn. Gerald Norris; CRP Stds.: 20

HATTIESBURG

St. Fabian Catholic Parish - 9 St. Fabian Way, Hattiesburg, MS 39402 t) 601-467-5620 c) 601-554-6746 church@saintfabian.com; brandy@saintfabian.com www.saintfabian.com Rev. Thomas S. Conway, Pst.; CRP Stds.: 186

Holy Rosary - 900 Dabbs St., Hattiesburg, MS 39401 t) 601-584-6528 Rev. Kenneth Ramon-Landry, Par. Admin.;

Sacred Heart - 313 Walnut St., Hattiesburg, MS 39401; Mailing: P.O. Box 1027, Hattiesburg, MS 39401 t) 601-583-9404 sacheartchurch@aol.com; sacheartpastor@aol.com www.sacredhearthattiesburg.com Rev. Kenneth Ramon-Landry, Pst.; Rev. Tomasz Powroznik, Par. Vicar; Dcn. Calvin Authement; Dcn. Randy Duke; Dcn. Warren Goff; CRP Stds.: 46

Sacred Heart Elementary School - (Grades 1-6) 608 Southern Ave., Hattiesburg, MS 39401 t) 601-583-8683 vflanagan@shshattiesburg.com www.shshattiesburg.com Vicki Flanagan, Prin.; Karyn Walsh, Librn.;

Sacred Heart High School - (Grades 7-12) 510 W. Pine St., Hattiesburg, MS 39401 t) 601-450-5736 eyankay@shhattiesburg.com Elizabeth Yankay, Prin.;

St. Thomas Aquinas - 3117 W. Fourth St., Hattiesburg, MS 39401 t) 601-264-5192 church@stthomas-usm.org; admin@stthomas-usm.org stac.usm.web@gmail.com (University of Southern Mississippi-Student Parish) Rev. Mark A. Ropel, Pst.; Rev. Braxton Necaise, Par. Vicar; Dcn. Joe Lichtenhan; Dcn. Sean Fink; Renee Lichtenhan, DRE; CRP Stds.: 93

KILN

Annunciation - 5370 Kiln-DeLisle Rd., Kiln, MS 39556 t) 228-255-1800 annunciationkiln.com Rev. Sebastian Thekkedath, CMI, Admin.; CRP Stds.: 29

LAUREL

Immaculate Conception - 833 W. Sixth St., Laurel, MS 39440 t) 601-426-3473 laurelcatholic.com Rev. Ignacio Jimenez-Morales, Pst.; Rev. Marcin S. Wiktor, Par. Vicar; Dcn. Richard A. Hollingsworth; Dcn. David Hughes Sr.; CRP Stds.: 229

LONG BEACH

St. Thomas the Apostle - 720 E. Beach Blvd., Long Beach, MS 39560; Mailing: P.O. Box 1529, Long Beach, MS 39560 t) 228-863-1610; 228-868-3774 (CRP) secretary@saintthomaslb.org; religiouseducation@saintthomaslb.org www.saintthomaslb.org Rev. Cuthbert R. O'Connell, Pst.; Rev. Vincent Ajayi, Par. Vicar; Dcn. Ernest "Buddy" VanCourt; Dcn. Jerry Dubuisson; CRP Stds.: 234

St. Vincent de Paul Elementary - (Grades 1-6) 4321 Espy Ave., Long Beach, MS 39560 t) 228-222-6000 cchurch@svdpcatholicschool.org; mfairley@svdpcatholicschool.org www.svdpcatholicschool.org (Interparochial) Carol Church, Prin.;

LUMBERTON

Our Lady of Perpetual Help - 379 W. Seneca Rd., Lumberton, MS 39455-7728 t) 601-796-3053 Rev. Fintan J. Kilmurray, Pst.; CRP Stds.: 9

St. Joseph - 17 Bilbo Hill, Poplarville, MS 39470; Mailing: P.O. Box 202, Poplarville, MS 39470 t) 601-795-9164 stjosephcat4461@bellsouth.net

MOSS POINT

St. Joseph - 4114 First St., Moss Point, MS 39563; Mailing: P.O. Box 8549, Moss Point, MS 39562-8549 t) 228-475-0777 stjosephmosspoint.com Rev. Peter Varghese, C.M.I., Pst.; Dcn. Frank W. Martin; CRP Stds.: 6

St. Ann - 21424 Hwy. 613, Moss Point, MS 39562; Mailing: P.O. Box 244, Hurley, MS 39555 t) 228-588-0599

OCEAN SPRINGS

St. Alphonsus - 502 Jackson Ave., Ocean Springs, MS 39564 t) 228-875-5419 stalparishos@gmail.com www.osstalphonsus.org Rev. Michael E. Snyder, Pst.; Rev. Sahaya Kennedy Reelan Soosai, Par. Vicar; Dcn. James Gunkel; Dcn. Jesus Arellano; CRP Stds.: 114

St. Alphonsus School - (Grades 1-6) 504 Jackson Ave., Ocean Springs, MS 39564 t) 228-875-5329 school@stal.org Pamala Rogers, Prin.;

St. Elizabeth Ann Seton - 4900 Riley Rd., Ocean Springs, MS 39564 t) 228-875-0654 office@stelseton.com stelseton.com Rev. Sergio A. Balderas (Mexico), Pst.; Dcn. Michael Butler; Dcn. Martin Finnegan; CRP Stds.: 129

PASCAGOULA

Our Lady of Victories - 3109 Magnolia St., Pascagoula, MS 39567; Mailing: P.O. Box 368, 503 Convent Ave., Pascagoula, MS 39568 t) 228-762-1653; 228-762-1663 olvpasc@gmail.com www.olvpascagoula.com Rev. Adam Urbaniak, Pst.; Rev. Tomasz Golab, Par. Vicar; Dcn. Michael Gilly; Dcn. Gayden R. Harper; Dcn. Mark Stephen O'Brien; CRP Stds.: 12

St. Peter the Apostle - 1715 Telephone Rd., Pascagoula, MS 39568-0876; Mailing: P.O. Box 876, Pascagoula, MS 39568 t) 228-762-1759 www.stpeterparishpascagoula.org Rev. Emmanuel Awe, S.S.J., Pst.; CRP Stds.: 40

Sacred Heart - 3702 Quinn Dr., Pascagoula, MS 39581-2356 t) 228-762-1837 heartline@biloxidiocese.org; pastorsacredheartpascagoula@hotmail.com sacredheartpascagoula.com Rev. Everardo Mora-Torres, Pst.; Dcn. Jesus Arellano; CRP Stds.: 48

Resurrection School-Elementary - (Grades PreK-6) 3704 Quinn Dr., Pascagoula, MS 39581-2356 t) 228-762-7207 msprings@rcseagles.com www.rcseagles.com Sr. Marilyn Springs, Prin.; Bonnie Smith, Librn.;

PASS CHRISTIAN

Holy Family Parish - 22342 Evangeline Dr., Pass Christian, MS 39571 t) 228-452-4686; 228-222-6000 (CRP) holyfamilyparish.cc Rev. Michael P. Austin, Pst.; Dcn. William J. Vrazel; Linden Williams, DRE; CRP Stds.: 107

St. Vincent de Paul Elementary - (Grades PreK-6) 4321 Espy Ave., Long Beach, MS 39560 t) (228)

222-6000 svsoffice@svsknights.catholicschool.com svdpcatholicschool.org (Interparochial) Carol Church, Prin.; Stds.: 400; Lay Tchrs.: 24

Most Holy Trinity Parish - 9062 Kiln DeLisle Rd., Pass Christian, MS 39571 t) 228-255-1294 www.mhtcatholic.org Rev. Patrick J. Mockler, Pst.; Dcn. Norman Cantrelle; Dcn. Eduardo Ramos; Tina Balentine, DRE; CRP Stds.: 96

Our Mother of Mercy - 216 Saucier Ave., Pass Christian, MS 39571 t) 228-452-4514 (OMM Hall) ourmotherofmercy@bellsouth.net www.ourmotherofmercy.church Rev. Rofinus Jas, S.V.D., Pst.; CRP Stds.: 34

Sacred Heart - 14595 Vidalia Rd., Pass Christian, MS 39571 t) 228-255-7560 holygroundeagle@aol.com Rev. Khoa Phi Vo, Pst.; Dcn. Earl Saucier; CRP Stds.: 97

Cursillo Center - t) 228-255-0430 (Dedeaux)

PERKINSTON

St. Matthew the Apostle - 27074 St. Matthews Church Rd., Perkinston, MS 39573 c) 228-236-5878 lesleyhavard@live.com; st.matthew.white.cypress@gmail.com Rev. Emmanuel Subaar, Pst.; Lesley Havard, DRE; CRP Stds.: 52

PICAYUNE

St. Charles Borromeo - 1000 Goodyear Blvd., Picayune, MS 39466; Mailing: 1000 Fifth Ave., Picayune, MS 39466 t) 601-798-4779 www.scborromeo.org Rev. Bernard J. Papania Jr., Pst.; Rev. Jeyanthan Jordan (India), Par. Vicar; Dcn. Brian Klause; CRP Stds.: 110

VANCLEAVE

Holy Spirit Catholic Church - 6705 Jim Ramsey Rd., Vancleave, MS 39565 t) 228-283-5252 holyspiritcc@bellsouth.net holyspiritcc.com Rev. Piotr A. Kmiecik, Pst.; Dcn. John E. Jennings; Dcn. Norbert Lloyd Jr.; CRP Stds.: 58

Christ the King - 10601 Daisy Vestry, Latimer, MS 39565

WAVELAND

St. Clare - 236 S. Beach Blvd., Waveland, MS 39576 t) 228-467-9275 stclarecatholic@yahoo.com; paul@stclare-catholic.com www.stclarewaveland.com Rev. Jacob Mathew Smith, O.F.M., Pst.; Dcn. Michael Saxer; Paul Pitts Jr., DRE; CRP Stds.: 40

WAYNESBORO

St. Bernadette - 401 Mississippi Dr., Waynesboro, MS 39367 t) 601-735-9420 Rev. Ignacio Jimenez-Morales, Pst.; Rev. Marcin Wiktor, Par. Vicar; Dcn. Richard A. Hollingsworth; Dcn. David Hughes Sr.; CRP Stds.: 11

WIGGINS

St. Francis Xavier - 1026 Central Ave. E., Wiggins, MS 39577 c) 601-528-1393 stfxstl@gmail.com www.stfxstl.org Rev. Michael A. Marascalco, Pst.; Dcn. Steven Beckham; CRP Stds.: 6

St. Lucy - 125 Scott Rd., Lucedale, MS 39452; Mailing: 1026 Central Ave. E., Wiggins, MS 39577 Patricia Howell, DRE;

Perkinston Junior College -

Holy Trinity - 911 Jackson Ave., Leakesville, MS 39451; Mailing: 1026 Central Ave. E., Wiggins, MS 39577

SCHOOLS: PRESCHOOL THRU HIGH SCHOOL

HIGH SCHOOLS

STATE OF MISSISSIPPI

BAY ST. LOUIS

Our Lady Academy - (PAR) (Grades 7-12) 222 S. Beach Blvd., Bay St. Louis, MS 39520-4320 t) 228-467-7048 jennifer.seymour@ourladyacademy.com www.ourladyacademy.com Jennifer Seymour, Prin.; Stds.: 255; Lay Tchrs.: 20

Saint Stanislaus College - (PRV) (Grades 7-12) 304 S. Beach Blvd., Bay St. Louis, MS 39520-4301 t) 228-467-9057 admissions@ststan.com www.ststan.com Brothers of the Sacred Heart. Gary Blackburn, Prin.; Bro. Barry Landry, S.C., Pres.; Jeremy Clark, Dir.; Kyla Grace, Librn.; Stds.: 342; Bro. Tchrs.: 1; Lay Tchrs.: 25

Camp Stanislaus - camp@ststan.com www.campstanislaus.com Summer program for ages 8-15. Sam Doescher, Dir.;

BILOXI

St. Patrick Catholic High School - (DIO) (Grades 7-12) 18300 St. Patrick Rd., Biloxi, MS 39532 t) 228-702-0500 information@stpatrickhighschool.net www.stpatrickhighschool.net (Coed) Matt Buckley, Prin.; Stds.: 630; Lay Tchrs.: 38

PASCAGOULA

Resurrection Catholic High School - (PAR) (Grades 7-12) 520 Watts Ave., Pascagoula, MS 39567 t) 228-762-3353 ksisson@rcseagles.com www.rcseagles.com (Coed) Kristal Sisson, Prin.; Stds.: 445; Lay Tchrs.: 58

Resurrection Elementary School - (Grades 7-12) 3704 Quinn Dr., Pascagoula, MS 39581 t) 228-762-7207

INSTITUTIONS LOCATED IN DIOCESE

CAMPUS MINISTRY / NEWMAN CENTERS [CAM]

HATTIESBURG

University of Southern Mississippi - St. Thomas Aquinas Catholic Church, 3117 W. Fourth St., Hattiesburg, MS 39401 t) 601-264-5192 church@stthomas-usm.org www.stthomas-usm.org Rev. Mark A. Ropel, Chap.;

CONVENTS, MONASTERIES, AND RESIDENCES FOR WOMEN [CON]

BILOXI

Sisters of Mercy Convent - 11454 Spring Ln., Biloxi, MS 39532 t) 228-297-9097 klajoie@mercysc.org; klajoie@cableone.net Sr. Kim Marie Lajoie, R.S.M., Contact; Srs.: 3

GULFPORT

Community of Charity and Social Services - 2805 Oakridge Cir., Gulfport, MS 39507 t) 228-243-0784 Sr. Cecilia Nguyen, C.C.S.S., Contact; Srs.: 2

MISCELLANEOUS [MIS]

BAY ST. LOUIS

SSC Progression Corporation - 304 S. Beach Blvd., Bay St. Louis, MS 39520 t) 228-467-9057 bmurphy@ststan.com Brian Murphy, Dir., Advancement;

BILOXI

Catholic Foundation of the Diocese of Biloxi, Inc. - 1790 Popps Ferry Rd., Biloxi, MS 39532 t) (228) 702-2123 Most Rev. Louis F. Kihneman III, Pres.; Rev. Msgr. T. Dominick Fullam, Vice. Pres.; David Wyrwich, Dir.;

Catholic Social and Community Services, Inc. - 1790 Popps Ferry Rd., Biloxi, MS 39532 t) (228) 701-0555 Jennifer Williams, Dir.;

HATTIESBURG

***Wofford Park, Inc.** - 20 St. Claire Pkwy., Hattiesburg, MS 39401 t) 601-545-8953 woffordpark@sunstatesmgmt.com Dev Pugh, Mgr.;

OCEAN SPRINGS

***St. Vincent de Paul St. Maximilian Kolbe Conference, Inc. (St. Vincent de Paul Thrift Store)** - 2200 A Bienville Blvd, Ocean Springs, MS 39564 t) 228-334-5222 c) 228-215-6261 rgreuling@yahoo.com www.svdpos.com Robert Greuling, Pres.;

MONASTERIES AND RESIDENCES FOR PRIESTS AND BROTHERS [MON]

BAY ST. LOUIS

St. Augustine's Residence - 199 Seminary Dr., Bay St. Louis, MS 39520 t) 228-467-6414 svdbaysaintlouis@gmail.com www.divineword-uss.org Rev. Joseph Dang, Supr.; Rev. Michael Somers, Prov.; Rev. George Gormley, S.V.D., Treas.; Rev. James A. Pawlicki, S.V.D., Spiritual Adv./Care Srvcs.; Rev. Borgia Aubespin, S.V.D.; Rev. Joseph Vu Dao, S.V.D.; Bro. Richard Chambers, S.V.D.; Bro. James Heeb, S.V.D.; Bro. David Nikins, House Treas.; Brs.: 3; Priests: 7

Brothers of the Sacred Heart - 114 Bookter St., Bay St. Louis, MS 39520; Mailing: 4600 Elysian Fields Ave., New Orleans, LA 70122 t) 504-301-4758 unitedstatesprovince@gmail.com Bro. Barry Landry, S.C., Pres.; Bro. Dwight Kenney, S.C., Dir.; Bro. Jake Avergonzado, S.C., Novice; Bro. Patrick McGinity, S.C., In Res.; Bro. Paul Mulligan, S.C., In Res.; Bro. Eduardo Baldioceda, S.C., In Res.; Bro. Francis Fleming, S.C., In Res.; Brs.: 7

Media Production Center "In A Word" - 199 Seminary Dr., Bay St. Louis, MS 39520 t) 228-344-3166 inawordsvd@gmail.com www.inaword.com Rev. James Pawlicki, S.V.D., Dir.; Brs.: 3; Priests: 8

Southern Province of St. Augustine - Provincial Offices - 204 Ruella St., Bay St. Louis, MS 39520 t) 228-467-4322 gggormley864@yahoo.com www.divineword-uss.org Society of the Divine Word. Rev. Michael Somers, Prov.; Rev. George Gormley, S.V.D., Treas.; Brs.: 3; Priests: 62

Province Development Office - 199 Seminary Dr., Bay St. Louis, MS 39520 t) 228-467-3815 Rev. Thomas Potts, S.V.D., Dir.;

NURSING / REHABILITATION / CONVALESCENCE / ELDERLY CARE [NUR]

BAY ST. LOUIS

Notre Dame de la Mer Retirement Apartments - 292 Hwy. 90, Bay St. Louis, MS 39520 t) 228-467-2885 notredame@sunstatesmgmt.com Brittany VanBuskirk, Bus. Mgr.; Asstd. Annu.: 60; Staff: 2

BILOXI

Gabriel Manor - 2321 Atkinson Rd., Biloxi, MS 39531 t) 228-388-1013 gabrielmanor@sunstatesmgmt.com Cheryl Alexander, Community Mgr.; Kathy Necaise, Asst. Mgr.; Asstd. Annu.: 71; Staff: 3

Gabriel Manor II, Inc. -

Santa Maria Retirement Apartments - 1788 Medical Park Dr., Biloxi, MS 39532 t) 228-388-2495 aaguilar@sunstatesmgmt.com Andrea Aguilar, Bus. Mgr.; Asstd. Annu.: 209; Staff: 7

GULFPORT

Carlow Manor - 15195 Barbara Dr., Gulfport, MS 39503 t) 228-539-0707 carlowmanor@sunstatesmgmt.com Rhonda Evans, Mgr.; Asstd. Annu.: 40; Staff: 2

OCEAN SPRINGS

Samaritan House - 642 Jackson Ave., Ocean Springs, MS 39564 t) 228-875-1087 samaritanhouse@sunstatesmgmt.com Senior Housing Apartment Anna Harrison, Mgr.; Asstd. Annu.: 49; Staff: 3

Villa Maria Retirement Apartments - 921 Porter Ave., Ocean Springs, MS 39564 t) 228-875-8811 villamaria@sunstatesmgmt.com Jeanne Duplechin, Mgr.; Asstd. Annu.: 200; Staff: 7

PETAL

Caritas Manor - 145 W. 10th Ave., Petal, MS 39465 t) 601-545-7744 caritasmanor@sunstatesmgmt.com Theresa Sinclair, Mgr.; Asstd. Annu.: 33; Staff: 2

An asterisk (*) denotes an organization that has established tax-exempt status directly with the IRS and is not covered by the USCCB Group Ruling.

Diocese of Birmingham

(Dioecesis Birminghamiensis)

MOST REVEREND STEVEN J. RAICA, J.C.L., J.C.D.

Bishop of Birmingham; ordained October 14, 1978; appointed Bishop of Gaylord June 27, 2014; Episcopal ordination and installation August 28, 2014; appointed fifth Bishop of Birmingham March 25, 2020; installed June 23, 2020.

Chancery Office: Catholic Diocese of Birmingham, P.O. Box 12047, Birmingham, AL 35202-2047. T: 205-838-8322; F: 205-836-1910.
www.bhmdiocese.org

ESTABLISHED JUNE 28, 1969.

Square Miles 28,091.

Comprises the Counties of North Alabama in an irregular line between the Counties (west to east) of Sumter and Choctaw and following the base of the following Counties: Marengo, Perry, Chilton, Coosa, Tallapoosa and Chambers or comprising the Counties of: Bibb, Blount, Calhoun, Chambers, Cherokee, Chilton, Clay, Cleburne, Colbert, Coosa, Cullman, DeKalb, Etowah, Fayette, Franklin, Greene, Hale, Jackson, Jefferson, Lamar, Lauderdale, Lawrence, Limestone, Madison, Marengo, Marion, Marshall, Morgan, Perry, Pickens, Randolph, St. Clair, Shelby, Sumter, Talladega, Tallapoosa, Tuscaloosa, Walker and Winston.

Legal Title: The Catholic Bishop of Birmingham in Alabama, a Corporation Sole.

For legal titles of institutions, consult the Chancery Office.

STATISTICAL OVERVIEW

Personnel
Bishop....1
Retired Bishops....1
Abbots....1
Retired Abbots....2
Priests: Diocesan Active in Diocese....45
Priests: Retired, Sick or Absent....19
Number of Diocesan Priests....64
Religious Priests in Diocese....33
Total Priests in your Diocese....97
Extern Priests in Diocese....18
Ordinations:
Diocesan Priests....1
Religious Priests....1
Transitional Deacons....2
Permanent Deacons in Diocese....74
Total Brothers....26
Total Sisters....105

Parishes
Parishes....56
With Resident Pastor:
Resident Diocesan Priests....34
Resident Religious Priests....11
Without Resident Pastor:
Administered by Priests....10
Administered by Deacons....1
Administered by Lay People....1
Missions....18
Professional Ministry Personnel:
Sisters....6
Lay Ministers....56

Welfare
Catholic Hospitals....6
Total Assisted....1,241,210
Specialized Homes....1
Total Assisted....30
Special Centers for Social Services....10
Total Assisted....19,616

Educational
Diocesan Students in Other Seminaries....14
Students, Religious....3
Total Seminarians....17
High Schools, Diocesan and Parish....4
Total Students....1,077
High Schools, Private....2
Total Students....284
Elementary Schools, Diocesan and Parish....13
Total Students....3,049
Elementary Schools, Private....2
Total Students....267
Catechesis/Religious Education:
High School Students....2,127
Elementary Students....4,318
Total Students under Catholic Instruction....11,139
Teachers in Diocese:
Sisters....8
Lay Teachers....265

Vital Statistics
Receptions into the Church:
Infant Baptism Totals....1,980
Minor Baptism Totals....264
Adult Baptism Totals....145
Received into Full Communion....317
First Communions....1,891
Confirmations....1,659
Marriages:
Catholic....326
Interfaith....88
Total Marriages....414
Deaths....683
Total Catholic Population....113,241
Total Population....3,187,797

LEADERSHIP

Chancery Office - t) 205-838-8322 www.bhmdiocese.org Rev. Bryan W. Jerabek, Chancellor;

Office of the Bishop - t) 205-838-8322 x225; 205-838-8322 x219 www.bhmdiocese.org Kristin Sessions, Sec. to Bishop; Donna Mealer, Exec. Asst. to Bishop;

Diocesan College of Consultors - t) 205-838-8322 x219 Very Rev. Kevin M. Bazzel, Moderator (fatherbazzel@bhmdiocese.org); Most Rev. Steven J. Raica, Chair; Rev. Bryan W. Jerabek;

Diocesan College of Vicars - t) 205-838-8322 x219 Very Rev. Kevin M. Bazzel, Moderator (fatherbazzel@bhmdiocese.org); Very Rev. Robert J. Sullivan, Vicar; Rev. Joseph G. Culotta, Vicar;

Diocesan Pastoral Council - t) 205-838-8322 x225 Rev. Thomas Ackerman, Chair (office@stfrancisuofa.com); Rev. Jonathan Howell, Vice Chair; Rev. Vincent E. Bresowar, Secy.;

Diocesan Finance Council - t) 205-838-8322 x219 Very Rev. Kevin M. Bazzel, Moderator (fatherbazzel@bhmdiocese.org); Most Rev. Steven J. Raica, Pres.; Rev. Bryan K. Lowe, Chair;

Tribunal - t) 205-838-8322 x118 Rev. Bryan W. Jerabek, Judicial Vicar; Rev. Gregory T. Bittner, Judge; Dcn. Daniel J. Laurita, Defender of the Bond;

OFFICES AND DIRECTORS

Black Catholic Ministry - t) 205-838-8313 James Watts, Dir.;

Development and Stewardship - t) 205-838-8322 x200 R. Allen McClendon, Dir.; Fran Sisson, Asst. Dir. (fsisson@bhmdiocese.org);

Catholic Schools Office - t) 205-838-8322 x120 Margaret Dubose, Supt. (mdubose@bhmdiocese.org);

Religious Education and Faith Formation - t) 205-838-8322 x115 www.bhmdiocese.org David Anders, Chair;

New Evangelization and Family LIfe Ministries - John Martignoni, Dir.;

Discipleship and Mission - t) (205) 838-8322 Alex Kubik, Dir.;

Religious Education - t) (205) 838-8322 x112 Daniel McCormick, DRE;

Finance Office and Administration - t) 205-838-8322 x305 Rev. Bryan K. Lowe, Vicar of Finance; Bob M. Sellers Jr., CFO;

Hispanic Ministries - t) 205-838-8322 x218 Maria Jose Bonilla, Dir. (mbonilla@bhmdiocese.org); Krysthell Castillo, Youth Min. (kcastillo@bhmdiocese.org);

Hispanic Social Services - t) 205-987-4771 Sr. Rosa Cruz, Dir. (rcruz@bhmdiocese.org);

Human Resources - t) 205-838-8322 x323 Eugene Thibodeaux, Dir.;

Marriage Encounter - t) 256-882-2430 Steve Huffman; Janetta Huffman;

Office of Youth Protection and Victims Assistance - t) 205-597-9058 Albert Manzella, Dir.;

Priests' Retirement Fund - t) 205-838-8322 x305 Most Rev. Steven J. Raica, Chair; Very Rev. Robert J. Sullivan, Vice Chair;

Propagation of the Faith and Holy Childhood - t) 205-838-8322 x204 Rev. Raymond J. Remke, Dir.; Christina Wright, Asst. Dir.;

Sacred Liturgy - t) 205-838-8322 x105 Francisco Carbonell, Dir., Sacred Music (fcarbonell@bhmdiocese.org); Rev. Justin Ward, Vicar;

St. John Vianney Vocation Society of Birmingham - t) 205-936-9973 Bob Picou, Contact;

Victim Assistance Coordinator - t) 205-597-9058 Albert Manzella;

Vocations - t) 205-838-8322 x203 www.bhmdiocese.org Rev. Wyman Vintson, Vicar; Kristin Sessions, Coord. Vocations;

CATHOLIC CHARITIES

Apostolate with Persons Having Intellectual and Developmental Disabilities - t) 205-907-0287 rathmines.cullen@gmail.com Rev. Patrick P. Cullen, Dir.;

Catholic Centers of Concern - t) 205-786-4388 (Birmingham)

Catholic Family Services - t) 205-324-6561 (Birmingham); 256-236-7793 (Huntsville) Cathie McDaniel, Dir.;

Catholic Family Services Offices - t) 205-324-6561 Cathie McDaniel, Dir.;

Catholic Social Services & Emergency Services - t) 205-969-8947 Albert Manzella, Exec.; Sr. Gabrielle Ramirez, M.G.Sp.S., Dir.-Emergency Svcs. (gramirez@bhmdiocese.org);

COMMUNICATIONS

Communications and Media Relations - t) 205-838-8322 x209 Donald Carson, Dir. (dcarson@bhmdiocese.org);

One Voice - The Birmingham Catholic Press, Inc. - t) 205-838-8322 x210 Mary Dillard, Editor & Chief, Photojournalist, & Art Dir.; Ann Lanzi, Circulation;

COMMUNITY SERVICES

Catholic Scouting - t) 205-838-8322 x118 Donald Schwarzhoff, Dir.;

EVANGELIZATION

Campus Ministry - t) 205-776-7163 Rev. J. Thomas Ackerman, Contact;

HUMAN RESOURCES

Safe Environment and Youth Protection Training - t) (205) 838-8322 x118 www.bhmdiocese.org Donald Schwarzhoff, Dir.;

ORGANIZATIONS

Beginning Experience - Helen Bowers;

Catholic Women of the Diocese of Birmingham - t) 205-991-8870 Sally Springrose (sspringrose@gmail.com);

Cursillo Program - Mark Bonucchi, Dir.;

Engaged Encounter - t) 205-307-8316 Dan Catt; Terry Catt;

Natural Family Planning - t) 334-312-0000 Theresa Shirley;

PARISHES, MISSIONS, AND CLERGY

STATE OF ALABAMA

ADAMSVILLE

St. Patrick's - 301 Shamrock Tr., Adamsville, AL 35005 t) 205-798-5326 saintpat@catholicjewel.com saintpatrickcc.com Rev. Anthony J. Weis, Pst.; CRP Stds.: 35

ALEXANDER CITY

St. John the Apostle - 454 N. Central Ave., Alexander City, AL 35010 t) 256-307-3360; 256-409-9146 (CRP) stjohnsalexcity@gmail.com Rev. Gopu Thomas Reddy, Admin.; CRP Stds.: 52

St. Mark - 460 Country Club Rd., Ashland, AL 36251; Mailing: P. O. Box 98, Ashland, AL 36251 t) (256) 234-3631

ANNISTON

All Saints - 1112 W. 15th St., Anniston, AL 36201; Mailing: P.O. Box 4862, Anniston, AL 36204 t) 256-237-9230 bgreen5356@aol.com B. Dianne Green, Dir.; Rose Munford, DRE; CRP Stds.: 9

Sacred Heart of Jesus - 1301 Golden Springs Rd., Anniston, AL 36207 t) 256-237-3011 church@sacredheartanniston.org sacredheartanniston.org Rev. John G. McDonald, Pst.; CRP Stds.: 134

ATHENS

St. Paul's - 1900 Hwy. 72 W., Athens, AL 35611 t) 256-232-4191 secretary@stpaulathens.org; dre.stpauloffice@gmail.com stpaulcatholicchurchathens.org Rev. Tom John Velliyedathu, CMI, Admin.; Dcn. Charles L. Butler; Dcn. Dennis Kobs; Ann-Margaret Chapman, DRE; CRP Stds.: 263

BESSEMER

St. Aloysius Catholic Parish, Bessemer - 751 Academy Dr., Bessemer, AL 35022 t) 205 424 2984 staloysius@bellsouth.net www.staloysiuscc.org Rev. Reju Pynadath Johny (India), Admin.; CRP Stds.: 83

St. Francis of Assisi Catholic Parish, Bessemer - 2400 Seventh Ave. N., Bessemer, AL 35020 t) 205-428-4758 stfrancisbessemer@gmail.com Rev. Paul Asih, M.S.P., Pst.;

BIRMINGHAM

Cathedral of St. Paul Catholic Parish, Birmingham - 2120 Third Ave. N., Birmingham, AL 35203; Mailing: P.O. Box 10044, Birmingham, AL 35202-0044 t) 205-251-1279 krista@stpaulsbhm.org www.stpaulsbhm.org Rev. Bryan W. Jerabek, Rector; Rev. John Michael Adams; Dcn. Edward W. Zieverink; Dcn. Gerald Zuckaukas; CRP Stds.: 135

St. Stephen the Martyr Catholic University Chapel - 1515 12th Ave. S., Birmingham, AL 35205 t) 205-933-2500 Dcn. Daniel L. Rodgers;

St. Barnabas Catholic Parish, Birmingham - 7921 First Ave. N., Birmingham, AL 35206 t) 205-833-0334 stbarnabasbhm.com Rev. Balta Raju Reddy Pentareddy, Admin.; Adrianne Price, Music Min.; David Renda, Pst. Min./Coord.; Angie Dailey, DRE & Bus. Mgr.; CRP Stds.: 20

Blessed Sacrament Catholic Parish, Birmingham - 1460 Pearson Ave., S.W., Birmingham, AL 35211; Mailing: P.O. Box 110006, Birmingham, AL 35211 t) 205-785-9840 church@myblessedsacrament.org www.myblessedsacrament.org Rev. Jim W. Booth, Pst.;

Matt Talbot Mission House - 1472 Pearson Ave., S.W., Birmingham, AL 35211 t) 205-578-2988 franciscanspjcalabama@gmail.com Sr. Miracles of the Little Way, P.J.C., Prov.;

St. Francis Xavier Catholic Parish, Birmingham - 2 Xavier Cir., Birmingham, AL 35213; Mailing: P.O. Box 130669, Birmingham, AL 35213 t) 205-871-1153 saintfrancis@sfxbirmingham.com sfxbirmingham.com Rev. Joseph G. Culotta, Pst.; Rev. Jonathan Howell, Assoc. Pst.; Rev. Patrick P. Cullen, In Res.; Sr. Sara Burress, O.S.B., Pst. Min./Coord.; Shaun Byrne, DRE; CRP Stds.: 345

St. Francis Xavier School - (Grades PreK-8) t) 205-871-1687 office@sfxcatholic.com www.sfxcatholic.com Frances Ritchey Finney, Prin.; Stds.: 178; Lay Tchrs.: 17

Holy Family - 1910 19th St. Ensley, Birmingham, AL 35218 t) 205-780-3440 ppaxton@passionist.org www.holyfamilybirmingham.com Rev. Phil Paxton, C.P., Pst.; Rev. Robert Weiss, CP, In Res.; Dcn. Gerald Motherway; Dcn. Jacky M. Rodgers; Dcn. Peter V. Smith; Trudi Webb Stinson, DRE; Wade White, DRE; CRP Stds.: 2

Holy Family School - (Grades PreK-8) 1916 19th St. Ensley, Birmingham, AL 35218 t) 205-780-5858 principal@hfcatholicacademy.org Phyllis Rowser, Prin.; Stds.: 57; Lay Tchrs.: 11

St. Mary's - 6101 Dr. Martin Luther King Dr., Fairfield, AL 35064 t) 205-923-0202 stmaryscatholical.com Tammy Rogers, CFO;

Holy Rosary - 7414 Georgia Rd., Birmingham, AL 35212 c) (205) 266-3065 mhfgeerts@gmail.com www.holyrosarybirmingham.org Rev. Pentareddy Baltha Reddy (India), Admin.;

St. Joseph Catholic Parish, Birmingham - 3020 Ave. K, Birmingham, AL 35218-2448 t) 205-788-5721 stjosephbham@gmail.com Rev. Patricio Manosalvas, C.P., Pst.; CRP Stds.: 87

St. Luke Hwang - 759 Valley St., Birmingham, AL 35226 c) 205-881-7890 Rev. Jungjin Leo Choi, Admin.;

St. Mark the Evangelist Catholic Parish, Birmingham - 7340 Cahaba Valley Rd., Birmingham, AL 35242;

Mailing: P.O. Box 380396, Birmingham, AL 35238-0396 t) 205-980-1810 secretary@stmarkrc.org; pfboettcher@att.net stmarkrc.org Very Rev. Robert J. Sullivan, Pst.; Dcn. Philip F. Boettcher; Sr. Madeline Contorno, O.S.B., Pst. Assoc.; Sr. Margaret Mary Liang, Pst. Min./Coord.; Mary Beth Crumly, DRE; CRP Stds.: 219

Our Lady of Fatima - 708 First St. S., Birmingham, AL 35205 t) 205-322-1205; 205-251-8395 (CRP) Rev. Linus Gabriel Akpan (Nigeria), Admin.; Dcn. Douglas C. Moorer; Theresa Nalls, DRE;

Our Lady of La Vang Parish @ St. John Bosco Church - 5224 1st Ave. N., Birmingham, AL 35212; Mailing: 142 52nd Pl. N., Birmingham, AL 35212 t) (205) 847-0870 Rev. Douglas Michael Vu, Pst.;

Our Lady of Lourdes - 980 Huffman Rd., Birmingham, AL 35215 t) 205-836-2274 frbruce@bellsouth.net ollcbham.com/ Rev. Bruce Bumbarger, Pst.; CRP Stds.: 75

Our Lady of Sorrows Catholic Parish, Birmingham - 1730 Oxmoor Rd., Birmingham, AL 35209 t) 205-871-8121; 205-871-1431 (CRP) ourladyofsorrows.com Rev. Msgr. Martin M. Muller, Pst.; Rev. Eric Gami (Cameroon); Suzanne Corso, DRE; CRP Stds.: 300

Our Lady of Sorrows School - (Grades PreK-8) 1720 Oxmoor Rd., Homewood, AL 35209 t) 205-879-3237 mjdorn@olsschool.com Mary Jane Dorn, Prin.; Karen Sullivan, Librn.; Stds.: 365; Lay Tchrs.: 23

Our Lady of the Valley - 5514 Double Oak Ln., Birmingham, AL 35242 t) 205-991-5488; 205-991-5489 (CRP) www.olvbirmingham.com Rev. Thomas M. Kelly, Pst.; Dcn. Robert G. Long; Dcn. Robert A. Martin Jr.; Dcn. Dan Whitaker; Mark Woodard, DRE; Theresa Thienpont, Music Min.; CRP Stds.: 200

Our Lady of the Valley School - (Grades PreK-8) 5510 Double Oak Ln., Birmingham, AL 35242 t) 205-991-5963 olv@olvsch.com Andy Rothery, Prin.; Jennifer Elliott, Librn.; Stds.: 188; Lay Tchrs.: 16

Our Lady Queen of the Universe - 961 Center St. N., Birmingham, AL 35204 t) 205-328-7729 Rev. Richard E. Donohoe, Pst.; Dcn. Rufus N. Biggs; Angela Rembert, DRE; CRP Stds.: 15

Sacred Heart - 3401 27th Ct. N., Collegeville, AL 35207; Mailing: 961 Center St. N., Birmingham, AL 35204 t) (205) 328-7729

St. Peter the Apostle Catholic Parish, Birmingham - 2061 Patton Chapel Rd., Birmingham, AL 35216 t) 205-822-4480 stpeterapostle@bellsouth.net www.stpeterapostle.com Rev. Vernon F. Huguley, Pst.; Rev. Raymond J. Remke, Par. Vicar; Dcn. Sam Anzalone; Dcn. John H. Cooper; Dcn. Christopher J. Rosko; Dcn. Jose Vazquez; Janet Rubino, CRE; Steven L. Guilmet, Music Min.; CRP Stds.: 262

Prince of Peace Catholic Parish, Birmingham - 4600 Preserve Pkwy., Birmingham, AL 35226 t) 205-822-9125 (Church Office); 205-824-7886 (School main office) church.office@popcatholic.org; kelly.doss@popcatholic.org www.popcatholic.org Rev. Jon Chalmers, Pst.; Rev. Alfredo Quezada-Avila (Mexico), Assoc. Pst.; Rev. John Fallon, Pastor Emer.; Rev. Raymond A. Dunmyer, In Res.; Dcn. G. Rick DiGiorgio; Megan Everett, DRE; Kelly G. Doss, Bus. Mgr.; CRP Stds.: 749

Prince of Peace School - (Grades PreK-8) 4650 Preserve Pkwy., Birmingham, AL 35226 t) (205) 824-7886 (main office) cangstadt@popcatholic.org popcatholic.net Connie Angstadt, Prin.; Jennifer LeBlanc, Vice Prin.; Stds.: 488; Lay Tchrs.: 34

St. Stanislaus - 904 Indiana St., Birmingham, AL 35224 t) 205-785-9625 ststans@bellsouth.net Rev. Anthony J. Weis, Pst.;

CLANTON

Church of the Resurrection - 300 First Ave., Clanton, AL 35045 t) (334) 758-0219 rescath@gmail.com rescath.org Rev. Bradley Jantz, Pst.; Rev. Joseph Delano Lody Jr., Par. Vicar; Maria Hosmer, DRE; CRP Stds.: 168

CROPWELL

Our Lady of the Lake Catholic Parish, Pell City - 4609 Martin St. S., Cropwell, AL 35054 t) 205-525-5161 parish@ollpellcity.com; jimmathis.oll@gmail.com ollpellcity.com Rev. William P. Lucas, Pst.; Dcn. Serge L. Brazzolotto; Dcn. E. Lee Robinson Sr.; Dcn. Terrence L. Rumore; Jim Mathis, DRE; CRP Stds.: 33

CULLMAN

Sacred Heart of Jesus Catholic Parish, Cullman - 205 3rd Ave., S.E., Cullman, AL 35055 t) 256-734-3730 Rev. Patrick Egan, O.S.B., Pst.; Rev. Raul Posada Valencia, Assoc. Pst.; Dcn. Kenneth M. Kreps; Dcn. Peter C. Nassetta; Dcn. Ramon D. Rodriguez; Dcn. George M. Schaefers; Dcn. Craig R. Smith; Fharis Richter, DRE; CRP Stds.: 220

Sacred Heart School - (Grades PreK-6) 112 2nd Ave. S.E., Cullman, AL 35055 t) 256-734-4563 shsoffice@shscullman.org Shawna Norman, Prin.; Robin Skipper, Librn.; Stds.: 129; Sr. Tchrs.: 2; Lay Tchrs.: 13

St. Boniface - 301 Blountsville St., Hanceville, AL 35077; Mailing: 205 3rd Ave., S.E., Cullman, AL 35055 t) (256) 734-3730 price@shccullman.org www.sacredheartchurchcullman.org

DECATUR

Annunciation of the Lord Catholic Parish, Decatur (St. Ann Catholic Church) - 3910 Spring Ave., S.W., Decatur, AL 35603 t) 252-353-2667; 256-353-2667 x108 (CRP) parish@annunlord.com; religion@saintanndecatur.org www.annunlord.com Rev. Charles Merrill, Pst.; Rev. Charles Deering II, Par. Vicar; Dcn. Robert M. Catanach; Dcn. Richard A. Chenault Sr.; Dcn. Patrick W. Lappert; Dcn. Louis J. Sciaroni; Elizabeth Schroer, DRE; CRP Stds.: 424

St. Ann Catholic School - (Grades PreK-8) 3910A Spring Ave., S.W., Decatur, AL 35603 t) 256-353-6543 principal@saintanndecatur.org Brandi Lumley, Prin.; Stds.: 90; Lay Tchrs.: 9

DEMOPOLIS

St. Leo - 309 S. Main Ave., Demopolis, AL 36732; Mailing: P. O. Box 937, Demopolis, AL 36732 t) 334-289-2767 stleo.info Rev. George Maniangattu, Admin.; Mary McBride, DRE; CRP Stds.: 42

St. Mary - 274 Wilson Ave., Eutaw, AL 35462 t) (334) 289-2767

FLORENCE

St. Joseph Catholic Church - 203 Plum St., Florence, AL 35630 t) 256-764-3303 secretary@stjosephflorence.org www.stjosephflorence.org Rev. Joseph Kuzhichalil, C.M.I., Pst.; Dcn. Gregory J. Beam; CRP Stds.: 74

St. Joseph Catholic Church School - (Grades PreK-8) 115 Plum St., Florence, AL 35630 t) 256-766-1923 secretary@catholichill.com www.catholichill.com Courtney Magee, Prin.; Stds.: 126; Lay Tchrs.: 12

St. Michael - 2751 County Rd. 30, Florence, AL 35634 t) 256-764-1885 stmichaelcatholic.org Rt. Rev. Cletus D. Meagher, O.S.B., Pst.; Dcn. Stephen J. Kirkpatrick; CRP Stds.: 35

FORT PAYNE

Our Lady of the Valley Catholic Parish, Fort Payne - 2910 Gault Ave. N., Fort Payne, AL 35967; Mailing: P.O. Box 681446, Fort Payne, AL 35968 t) 256-845-4774 olvfp@farmerstel.com www.olvfortpayne.com Rev. Richard A. Chenault Jr., Pst.; Michael Speyrer, DRE; CRP Stds.: 379

GADSDEN

St. James Catholic Parish, Gadsden - 622 Chestnut St., Gadsden, AL 35901 t) 256-546-2975 x105 www.sjccgadsden.org/ Rev. Jose B. Chacko, Pst.; Dcn. Robert A. McCormick; Dcn. J. Fred Williams; Amy Sims, Youth Min.; CRP Stds.: 270

St. James School - (Grades PreK-8) 700 Albert Rains Blvd., Gadsden, AL 35901 t) 256-546-0132 jparker@stjamesgadsden.org www.stjamesgadsden.org John Parker, Prin.; Cynthia Hill, Librn.; Stds.: 143; Lay Tchrs.: 11

GARDENDALE

St. Elizabeth Ann Seton - 334 Main St., Gardendale, AL 35071; Mailing: P.O. Box 1027, Gardendale, AL 35071 t) 205-631-9398 seascc@yahoo.com www.seasgardendale.org Rev. Wyman Vintson, Admin.; Dcn. Timothy L. Vaughn; Kathy Stafford, DRE; CRP Stds.: 61

St. Henry - 211 5th St., Warrior, AL 35180; Mailing: P. O. Box 1027, Gardendale, AL 35071 t) (205) 631-9398 www.sthenrywarrior.org

GUNTERSVILLE

St. William - 929 Gunter Ave., Guntersville, AL 35976 t) 256-582-4245 laura@stwilliamchurch.com; fr.mark@stwilliamchurch.com www.stwilliamchurch.com Rev. Mark T. Spruill, O.B.S.B., Pst.; Dcn. Kenneth D. Hall; Laura Hodge, Admin.; Yolanda Nieto, DRE; CRP Stds.: 645

Chapel of the Holy Cross - 1534 Whitesville Rd., Albertville, AL 35950 t) 256-891-0550 juan@stwilliamchurch.com Juan Nunez, Contact;

HUNTSVILLE

Good Shepherd Catholic Parish, Huntsville - 13550 Chaney Thompson Rd., S.E., Huntsville, AL 35803-2326 t) 256-882-1844; 256-822-1844 (CRP) goodshep@goodshephsv.org; dre@goodshephsv.org www.goodshephsv.org Rev. Timothy Pfander, Pst.; Dcn. Paul T. Keil; Trina Maxwell, DRE; CRP Stds.: 261

Holy Spirit Catholic Parish, Huntsville - 625 Airport Rd., S.W., Huntsville, AL 35802 t) 256-881-4781 www.holyspirithsv.com Rev. Michael Mac Mahon, Pst.; Rev. Francisco Park, Pst.; Rev. Joshua Altonji, Assoc. Pst.; Dcn. Louis J. Citrano; Dcn. Robert J. Becher; Dcn. Lee G. Heckman; Dcn. Matthew J.S. Koh; Dcn. Antonio Moreno; Dcn. Michael P. Sudnik; Tracy Finke, DRE; CRP Stds.: 370

Holy Spirit School - (Grades PreK-8) 619 Airport Rd., S.W., Huntsville, AL 35802 t) 256-881-4852 vaquila@hstigers.org www.hstigers.org Vince Aquila, Prin.; Stds.: 452; Lay Tchrs.: 35

St. Joseph - 2300 Beasley Ave., N.W., Huntsville, AL 35816 t) 256-534-8459 www.saintjosephcc.com Rev. Joseph Lubrano, S.D.S., Pst.; Carmen Amato, DRE; CRP Stds.: 109

Holy Family School - (Grades PreK-8) t) 256-539-5221 www.holy-family-school.com James S. Bell, Prin.; Stds.: 187; Lay Tchrs.: 17

St. Mary of the Visitation - 222 Jefferson St. N., Huntsville, AL 35801 t) 256-536-6349 jennifer.kilroy@gmail.com; smvparish@smvparish.com smvparish.com Rev. Joy Thomas Nellissery (India), Pst.; Dcn. Jeffrey M. Montgomery; Jennifer Kilroy, DRE; CRP Stds.: 87

Our Lady, Help of Christians - 1201 Kingsbury Ave., Huntsville, AL 35801 t) 256-801-9157 ourladyhoc@icloud.com ourladyhelpofchristians-al.org Rev. Alan C. Mackey, Pst.; Jennifer Mackintosh, DRE; CRP Stds.: 105

Our Lady Queen of the Universe - 2421 Shady Ln. Dr. NW, Huntsville, AL 35810 t) 256-852-0788 www.olqu.org Rev. Charles Alookaran, Pst.; Dcn. James R. Multeri; Susan Turner, DRE; CRP Stds.: 102

JACKSONVILLE

St. Charles Borromeo - 308 Seventh St., N.E., Jacksonville, AL 36265 t) 256-435-3238 www.stcharlescatholicchurch.com Rev. Frankline Fomukong (Cameroon), Admin.; Dcn. A. B. King; Peggy Sugar, DRE; CRP Stds.: 24

St. Joachim - 555 Fagan Rd. at Babbling Brook Rd., Piedmont, AL 36272; Mailing: 308 7th St., N.E., Jacksonville, AL 36265 t) (256) 435-3238 stcharlesoffice@bellsouth.net

JASPER

St. Cecilia Catholic Church - 2159 Hwy. 195, Jasper, AL 35503-6235 t) 205-384-4800 secretary@stceciliajasper.com www.stceciliajasper.com/ Rev. Wayne Herpin, S.J., Pst.; Sr. Marie Leonard, Parish Life Coord.; Juan Hernandez Jaimes, Pst. Min./Coord.; Pedro Pablo Castro, Pst. Min./Coord.; Victor Ponce Batz, Pst. Min./Coord.; Maria Campsey, DRE; Doris Moody, Music Min.; CRP Stds.: 73

LANETT

Holy Family - 705 N. Third Ave., Lanett, AL 36863-0325 t) 334-644-4405 lanettcatholic@gmail.com facebook.com/lanettcatholic Rev. Gali Balaswamy,

Admin.; CRP Stds.: 25

Immaculate Conception - 506 County Rd. 1, Wedowee, AL 36278; Mailing: 300 Sheppard St., West Point, GA 31833 t) 256-357-2977 immaculateconceptional@gmail.com

LEEDS

St. Theresa Catholic Parish, Leeds - 1394 Ashville Ct., Leeds, AL 35094; Mailing: P.O. Box 525, Leeds, AL 35094 t) 205-352-3741 www.sttheresaleeds.org Rev. E. Gray Bean, Pst.; Dcn. Silverio Rubio Roman; CRP Stds.: 181

LIVINGSTON

St. Francis of Assisi - 101 Meadow Brook Dr., Livingston, AL 35470; Mailing: P. O. Box 937, Demopolis, AL 36732 t) 334-289-2767 Administered by The Catholic Church in West Central Alabama. Rev. George Maniangattu, Assoc. Pst.; Grace Neel, DRE;

MADISON

St. John the Baptist Catholic Parish, Madison - 1055 Hughes Rd., Madison, AL 35758 t) 256-722-0130 www.stjohnbchurch.org Rev. Bryan K. Lowe, Pst.; Rev. Antony Vadakara, CMI, Assoc. Pst.; Dcn. Kevin M. Brady; Dcn. Darrell Diem; Dcn. Daniel J. Laurita; Dcn. Gregory S. Thompson; CRP Stds.: 531

St. John the Baptist School - (Grades PreK-8) 1057 Hughes Rd., Madison, AL 35758 t) 256-722-0772 slewis@stjohnb.com Sherry Lewis, Prin.; Jeanne Crown, Librn.; Stds.: 385; Lay Tchrs.: 31

Most Merciful Jesus Catholic Church - 10509 Segers Rd., Madison, AL 35756 t) 256-325-0695 www.mercyparish.church Rev. Joy Chalissery, Pst.; Dcn. Derek D. Bothern; Dcn. Antolin Padron; Dcn. Richard E. Tuggle; CRP Stds.: 142

MONTEVALLO

St. Thomas the Apostle Catholic Parish, Montevallo - 80 St. Thomas Way, Montevallo, AL 35115 t) 205-663-3936 jlampton@stthomascatholic.com stthomascatholic.com Rev. Bradley Jantz, Pst.; Dcn. David M. Hicks; Dcn. William P. Alexiou; CRP Stds.: 430

MOULTON

Resurrection Catholic Chapel - 16335 Court St., Moulton, AL 35650; Mailing: P.O. Box 550, Moulton, AL 35650 t) 256-476-0134 rachen77@gmail.com www.moultoncatholic.com Dcn. Richard A. Chenault Sr., Admin.; Dcn. Robert M. Catanach; CRP Stds.: 80

ONEONTA

Corpus Christi - 32015 State Hwy. 75, Oneonta, AL 35121 t) 205-625-6078; 256-505-7324 (CRP) corpus@otelco.net corpusc.com Rev. James P. Hedderman, Pst.; CRP Stds.: 208

RUSSELLVILLE

Good Shepherd Catholic Parish, Russellville - 1706 N. Jackson Ave., Russellville, AL 35653; Mailing: 1700 N. Jackson Ave., P.O. Box 878, Russellville, AL 35653 t) 256-332-4861 www.russellvillecatholic.com Rev. Vincent E. Bresowar, Pst.; CRP Stds.: 211

SCOTTSBORO

St. Jude - 17205 AL Hwy. 35, Scottsboro, AL 35768; Mailing: P.O. Box 971, Scottsboro, AL 35768 t) 256-574-6156 Rev. Thomas F. Woods, Pst.; Ema Ortega-Soria, DRE; Victor Hugo Martinez, Bus. Mgr.; CRP Stds.: 116

SYLACAUGA

St. Jude - 310 W. Bay St., Sylacauga, AL 35150; Mailing: P.O. Box 111, Sylacauga, AL 35150 t) 256-245-7741 sjhn4life@catholicexchange.com Rev. Shobhan Singareddy, Admin.;

Holy Name of Jesus - 415 5th Ave., S.W., Childersburg, AL 35044; Mailing: 100 Crest Dr., Talladega, AL 35160 t) (256) 245-7741

TALLADEGA

St. Francis of Assisi - 722 East St. S., Talladega, AL 35161; Mailing: P.O. Box 1142, Talladega, AL 35160 t) 256-362-5372 Rev. Shobhan Singareddy, Admin.; Cindi Greene, DRE; CRP Stds.: 11

TRUSSVILLE

Holy Infant of Prague Catholic Parish, Trussville - 8090 Gadsden Hwy., Trussville, AL 35173; Mailing: P.O. Box 43, Trussville, AL 35173 t) 205-655-2541 hiopcc@aol.com; hiopccterry@aol.com hiopcc.org Rev. Gerald Holloway, Pst.; Dcn. Ed Pruet; Dcn. Danny W. McCay; Angela Grace Schauer, Admin.; Karen George, Music Min.; Terry Pruet, DRE; CRP Stds.: 173

TUSCALOOSA

St. Francis of Assisi Catholic Parish, Tuscaloosa - 811 Fifth Ave., Tuscaloosa, AL 35401 t) 205-758-5672 www.stfrancisuofa.com Rev. J. Thomas Ackerman, Pst.; Rev. Mugagga Epah, Assoc. Pst.; Dcn. William J. Remmert; CRP Stds.: 110

St. Robert - 407 Hwy 17 S., Reform, AL 35481; Mailing: P. O. Box 898, Reform, AL 35481 t) (205) 758-5672 Rev. Thomas Ackerman, Pst.;

Holy Spirit - 733 James I. Harrison Jr. Pkwy. E., Tuscaloosa, AL 35405 t) 205-553-9733 hsc@hschurch.com www.hschurch.com Rev. Msgr. Michael J. Deering, Pst.; Rev. Victor Salomon, Assoc. Pst.; Dcn. J. Adrian Straley; Jeanne Doyle, DRE; CRP Stds.: 438

Holy Spirit School - (Grades PreK-5) 711 James I. Harrison Jr. Pkwy. E., Tuscaloosa, AL 35405 t) 205-553-9630 jsaibini@holyspirit-al.com www.holyspirit-al.com Joshua Saibini, Prin.; Stds.: 318; Lay Tchrs.: 25

St. John - 800 Lurleen B. Wallace Blvd. N., Tuscaloosa, AL 35401; Mailing: 733 James I Harrison, Jr. Pkwy. E, Tuscalooosa, AL 35405 t) (205) 533-9733

TUSCUMBIA

Our Lady of the Shoals - 200 E. Commons St. N., Tuscumbia, AL 35674 t) 256-383-7207 www.ourladyoftheshoals.org Rev. Benny Karimalikkal (India), Admin.; Tena Flanagan, DRE;

WINFIELD

Holy Spirit - 2710 U.S. Hwy. 43 N., Winfield, AL 35594 t) 205-487-3616 our3churches@gmail.com Rev. Anil Thomas Puthussery, Admin.; CRP Stds.: 11

Holy Family - 423 19th St., N.W., Fayette, AL 35555; Mailing: 2710 Hwy 43 North, Winfield, AL 35594 t) (205) 487-3616 www.our3churches.com

Our Lady of Guadalupe - 485 Layne Hill Dr., Haleyville, AL 35565; Mailing: 2710 Hwy. 43 N., Winfield, AL 35594 t) (205) 487-3616

SCHOOLS: PRESCHOOL THRU HIGH SCHOOL

SCHOOLS

STATE OF ALABAMA

BIRMINGHAM

St. Rose Academy - (PRV) (Grades PreK-8) 1401 22nd St. S., Birmingham, AL 35205 t) 205-933-0549 smjuliana@saintroseacademyop.com www.saintroseacademy.com Dominican Sisters of Nashville, TN. Sr. Mary Juliana, Prin.; Stds.: 210; Sr. Tchrs.: 6; Lay Tchrs.: 11

HIGH SCHOOLS

STATE OF ALABAMA

BIRMINGHAM

Holy Family Cristo Rey Catholic High School - (PRV) (Grades 9-12) 1832 Center Way S., Birmingham, AL 35205; Mailing: P.O. Box 19577, Birmingham, AL 35219 t) 205-787-9937 bknighten@hfcristorey.org www.hfcristorey.org Bethany Knighten, Prin.; Stds.: 149; Lay Tchrs.: 17

John Carroll Catholic High School - (DIO) (Grades 9-12) 300 Lakeshore Pkwy., Birmingham, AL 35209 t) 205-940-2400 amontalto@jcchs.org; president@jcchs.org www.jcchs.org Anthony Montalto, Prin.; Rev. Jon Chalmers, Pres.; Very Rev. Robert J. Sullivan, Vicar; Stds.: 527; Scholastics: 44; Pr. Tchrs.: 1; Sr. Tchrs.: 2; Lay Tchrs.: 42

CULLMAN

St. Bernard Preparatory School - (PRV) (Grades 7-12) 1600 St. Bernard Dr., SE, Cullman, AL 35055 t) 256-739-6682 sbps@stbernardprep.com www.stbernardprep.com Rev. Joel W. Martin, O.S.B., Pres.; Bro. Thomas Jones, O.S.B., Librn.; Stds.: 135; Pr. Tchrs.: 1; Bro. Tchrs.: 4; Sr. Tchrs.: 3; Lay Tchrs.: 15

HUNTSVILLE

Saint John Paul II Catholic High School - (DIO) 7301 Old Madison Pike, Huntsville, AL 35806 t) 256-430-1760 www.jp2falcons.org Dr. Jeremiah Russell, Headmaster; Megan Ehemann, Librn.; Stds.: 327; Lay Tchrs.: 24

TUSCALOOSA

Holy Spirit Catholic High School - (DIO) (Grades 6-12) 601 James I. Harrison Jr. Pkwy. E., Tuscaloosa, AL 35405 t) 205-553-5606 jloper@holyspirit-al.com www.holyspirit-al.com Jonathan Loper, Prin.; Stds.: 223; Lay Tchrs.: 20

CAMPUS MINISTRY / NEWMAN CENTERS [CAM]

BIRMINGHAM

St. Stephen the Martyr Catholic University Chapel - 1515 12th Ave. S., Birmingham, AL 35205 t) 205-933-2500 stephenthemartyr.com Serves: University of Alabama at Birmingham, Samford University, Birmingham-Southern College. Dcn. Daniel L. Rodgers, Campus Min.; Rev. Bryan W. Jerabek, Contact;

FLORENCE

University of North Alabama - 1111 E. College St., Florence, AL 35630 t) 256-764-3303 secretary@stjosephflorence.org Rev. Joseph Kuzhichalil, C.M.I., Admin.;

INSTITUTIONS LOCATED IN DIOCESE

GADSDEN

Gadsden State Campus Ministry - St. James Church - 622 Chestnut St., Gadsden, AL 35901 t) 256-546-2975 sjccgadsden1@outlook.com www.sjccgadsden.org Rev. Jose B. Chacko, Pst.;

JACKSONVILLE

Jacksonville State University - 308 Seventh St., N.E., Jacksonville, AL 36265 t) 256-435-3238 Rev. Frankline Fomukong (Cameroon);

LIVINGSTON

University of West Alabama Campus Ministry - St. Francis-Livingston - 101 Meadow Brook Dr., Livingston, AL 35470; Mailing: P.O. Box 937, Demopolis, AL 36732 t) 334-289-2767 stleothegreatcatholic@gmail.com Rev. George Maniangattu, Admin.;

MADISON

Campus Ministry - University of Alabama in Huntsville - 1055 Hughes Rd., Madison, AL 35758 t) 256-722-0130 parishoffice@stjohnbchurch.org Rev. Bryan K. Lowe, Campus Min.;

MONTEVALLO

University of Montevallo Catholic Campus Ministry - St. Thomas the Apostle Catholic Campus Ministry, 80 St. Thomas Way, Montevallo, AL 35115 t) 205-663-3936 rdunmyer@stthomascatholic.com Rev. Brad Jantz, Campus Min.;

TALLADEGA

Talladega College Catholic Campus Ministry - 722 East St. S., Talladega, AL 35160; Mailing: P.O. Box 1142, Talladega, AL 35160 t) 256-362-5372 Rev. Reji Joseph Punnolil, CMI, Campus Min.;

TUSCALOOSA

Campus Ministry Office - University of Alabama - 811 Fifth Ave., Tuscaloosa, AL 35401 t) 205-758-5672 frtomackerman@stfrancisuofa.com www.stfrancisuofa.com/campusministries.html Rev. Thomas Ackerman, Pst.;

CATHOLIC CHARITIES [CCH]

ANNISTON

All Saints Interfaith Center of Concern - 1513 Noble St., Anniston, AL 36201 t) 256-236-7793 bhill@bhmdiocese.org Beverly Hill, Dir.; Asstd. Annu.: 3,600; Staff: 4

BIRMINGHAM

Catholic Center of Concern - 712 Fourth Ct. W., Birmingham, AL 35204 t) 205-786-4388 consolatabirmingham@gmail.com (Div. of Catholic Charities) Asstd. Annu.: 1,029; Staff: 6

Catholic Family Services - 1515 12th Ave. S., Birmingham, AL 35205 t) 205-324-6561 www.cfsbhm.org Cathie McDaniel, Dir.; Asstd. Annu.: 367; Staff: 5

EUTAW

Guadalupan Multicultural Services - 331 Boligee St., Eutaw, AL 35462; Mailing: P.O. Box 538, Eutaw, AL 35462 t) 205-372-3497 gmseutaw@gmail.com Sr. Marta Tobon, Dir.; Asstd. Annu.: 2,935; Staff: 3

GADSDEN

St. Martin de Porres Catholic Center of Concern - 612 Chestnut St., Gadsden, AL 35901 t) 256-546-0028 lbean@bhmdiocese.org Lee Bean, Dir.; Asstd. Annu.: 1,049; Staff: 2

HUNTSVILLE

Catholic Center of Concern - 1010 Church St., N.W., Huntsville, AL 35804; Mailing: P.O. Box 745, Huntsville, AL 35804 t) 256-963-9355 info@catholiccenterofconcernhsv.org catholiccenterofconcernhsv.org Kermit Elliott, Dir.; Asstd. Annu.: 6,292; Staff: 7

Catholic Family Services - 4920 Corporate Dr., N.W., Ste. J, Huntsville, AL 35805 t) 256-236-7793 cmcdaniel@bhmdiocese.org www.cfsbhm.org Cathie McDaniel, Dir.; Asstd. Annu.: 304; Staff: 4

TUSCALOOSA

Catholic Center of Concern - 608 James I. Harrison, Jr. Pkwy., Tuscaloosa, AL 35405; Mailing: P. O. Box 70187, Tuscaloosa, AL 35407 t) 205-759-1268 cwhite@bhmdiocese.org Sr. Maria Elena Mendez, M.G.Sp.S., Dir.; Asstd. Annu.: 4,040; Staff: 4

CONVENTS, MONASTERIES, AND RESIDENCES FOR WOMEN [CON]

CULLMAN

Sacred Heart Monastery - 916 Convent Rd., Cullman, AL 35055 t) 256-734-4622; 256-734-3835 treasurer@shmon.org; elisabethosb@shmon.org www.shmon.org Sr. Lynn Elisabeth Meadows, OSB, Prioress; Srs.: 32

HANCEVILLE

Our Lady of the Angels Monastery in Hanceville Alabama - 3222 County Rd. 548, Hanceville, AL 35077 t) 256-352-6267 secretary@olamnuns.com www.olamnuns.com Poor Clare Nuns of Perpetual Adoration Mother Mary Paschal, PCPA, Abbess; Sr. Mary Jacinta, PCPA, Vicar; Srs.: 13

IRONDALE

Sister Servants of the Eternal Word, Inc. - 3721 Belmont Rd., Irondale, AL 35210 t) 205-956-6760 info@sisterservants.org Mother Louise Marie Flanigan, Supr.; Srs.: 19

ENDOWMENTS / FOUNDATIONS / TRUSTS [EFT]

ADAMSVILLE

St. Michael Cemetery Fund - 301 Shamrock Trl., Adamsville, AL 35005 t) (205) 798-5326 www.saintpatrick.com Rev. Anthony J. Weis, Pst.; Bob M. Sellers Jr., CFO;

BIRMINGHAM

Anna C. Grace Liturgical Fund - 2121 Third Ave. N., Birmingham, AL 35203 t) 205-838-8322 bsellers@bhmdiocese.org

St. Barnabas Catholic Education Foundation - 7921 First Ave. N., Birmingham, AL 35206 t) 205-833-0334 www.barnabascatholic.com Rev. Pentareddy Baltha Reddy (India), Admin.; Bob M. Sellers Jr., CEO;

Birmingham Catholic Center of Concern Fund - 712 4th Ct. W., Birmingham, AL 35204 t) 205-786-4388 zmcordeiro@bhmdiocese.org Sr. Zelia M. Cordeiro, M.C., Dir.;

Bishop's Designated Fund - 2121 3rd Ave., N, Birmingham, AL 35203; Mailing: P.O. Box 12047, Birmingham, AL 35202-2047 t) 205-838-8322 x309 bsellers@bhmdiocese.org Bob M. Sellers Jr., Bus. Mgr.;

Blessed Sacrament Catholic Church Endowment Fund - 1460 Pearson Ave., S.W., Birmingham, AL 35211 t) 205-785-9840 church@myblessedsacrament.org Rev. Jim W. Booth, Pst.;

Burse Fund - 2121 3rd Ave., N, Birmingham, AL 35203; Mailing: P.O. Box 12047, Birmingham, AL 35202-2047 t) 205-838-8322 x309 bsellers@bhmdiocese.org Bob M. Sellers Jr., Bus. Mgr.;

Cathedral of St. Paul Columbarium Fund - 2120 3rd Ave., N., Birmingham, AL 35203 t) (205) 251-1279 (Cathedral Office) Rev. Bryan W. Jerabek, Rector;

Clergy Supplemental Retirement Fund - 2121 Third Ave. N., Birmingham, AL 35203 t) 205-838-8322 mshumate@bhmdiocese.org Bob M. Sellers Jr., CEO;

Deacon Joe Stephens Memorial Fund - 2121 3rd Ave., N, Birmingham, AL 35203; Mailing: P.O. Box 12047, Birmingham, AL 35202-2047 t) 205-838-8322 x309 bsellers@bhmdiocese.org Bob M. Sellers Jr., Exec.;

Deborah F. White Scholarship Fund - 2121 3rd Ave., N, Birmingham, AL 35203; Mailing: P.O. Box 12047, Birmingham, AL 35202-2047 t) 205-838-8322 x309 bsellers@bhmdiocese.org Bob M. Sellers Jr., Exec.;

Dr. Eric Wieschaus Fund - 2121 3rd Ave., N, Birmingham, AL 35203; Mailing: P.O. Box 12047, Birmingham, AL 35202-2047 t) 205-838-8322 x309 bsellers@bhmdiocese.org Bob M. Sellers Jr., Exec.;

Donald Scholber Memorial Fund - 2121 3rd Ave., N, Birmingham, AL 35203; Mailing: P.O. Box 12047, Birmingham, AL 35202-2047 t) 205-838-8322 x309 bsellers@bhmdiocese.org Bob M. Sellers Jr., Exec.;

Faith In Education Catholic Schools Fund - 2121 Third Ave. N, Birmingham, AL 35203 t) 205-838-8322 mdubose@bhmdiocese.org Margaret Dubose, Dir.;

St. Francis of Assisi University Parish Fund - 2121 3rd Ave., N, Birmingham, AL 35203; Mailing: P.O. Box 12047, Birmingham, AL 35202-2047 t) 205-838-8322 x309 bsellers@bhmdiocese.org Bob M. Sellers Jr., Exec.;

St. Francis Xavier Catholic School Education Foundation - 2 Xavier Cir., Birmingham, AL 35213 t) 205-871-1687 nwright@saintfrancisxavierschool.com; saintfrancis@sfxbirmingham.com www.sfxbirmingham.com Rev. Joseph G. Culotta, Pst.; Bob M. Sellers Jr., CFO;

St. Francis Xavier Columbarium - 2121 3rd Ave., N, Birmingham, AL 35203; Mailing: P.O. Box 12047, Birmingham, AL 35202-2047 t) 205-838-8322 x309 bsellers@bhmdiocese.org Bob M. Sellers Jr., Exec.;

Grace Lay Ministry Fund - 2121 Third Ave. N., Birmingham, AL 35203 t) 205-838-8322 bsellers@bhmdiocese.org

Holy Family Educational Foundation - 1910 19th St., Birmingham, AL 35218 t) 205-780-3440 lmlang@bellsouth.net www.passionist.org

Holy Name of Jesus Hospital Trust - c/o Regions Bank, Birmingham, AL 35202; Mailing: P.O. Box 1688, Birmingham, AL 35202 t) 205-264-5232 jennifer.foster@regions.com (Health and Medical Services) Jennifer Foster, Trustee; Bob M. Sellers Jr., Diocese of Birmingham CFO;

Investment Foundation of North Alabama - 2121 3rd Ave. N., Birmingham, AL 35203; Mailing: P.O. Box 12047, Birmingham, AL 35202-2047 t) (205) 838-8322 x309 www.bhmdiocese.org Bob M. Sellers Jr., CFO;

Jack Miller Education Foundation - 300 Lakeshore Pkwy., Birmingham, AL 35209 t) 205-940-2400 bsellers@bhmdiocese.org Very Rev. Robert J. Sullivan, Pres.;

John Carroll Catholic High School Educational Foundation, Inc. - 300 Lakeshore Pkwy., Birmingham, AL 35209 t) 205-940-2400 bsellers@bhmdiocese.org www.jcchs.org Very Rev. Robert J. Sullivan, Pres.;

John Carroll Catholic High School Endowed Choir Fund - 300 Lakeshore Pkwy., Birmingham, AL 35209 t) 205-940-2400 bsellers@bhmdiocese.org Very Rev. Robert J. Sullivan, Pres.;

John Carroll Catholic High School Endowment Scholarship Fund - 300 Lakeshore Pkwy., Birmingham, AL 35209 t) 205-940-2400 bsellers@bhmdiocese.org Very Rev. Robert J. Sullivan, Dir.;

St. John the Baptist Foundation - 2121 3rd Ave., N, Birmingham, AL 35203; Mailing: P.O. Box 12047, Birmingham, AL 35202-2047 t) 205-838-8322 x309 bsellers@bhmdiocese.org Bob M. Sellers Jr., Exec.;

St. John Vianney Memorial Fund - 2121 Third Ave. N., Birmingham, AL 35203 t) 205-838-8322 x309 bsellers@bhmdiocese.org

Knights of Columbus Council 635 - 2121 3rd Ave., N, Birmingham, AL 35203; Mailing: P.O. Box 12047, Birmingham, AL 35202-2047 t) 205-838-8322 x309 bsellers@bhmdiocese.org Bob M. Sellers Jr., Exec.;

Lay Incentive Fund - 2121 3rd Ave., N, Birmingham, AL 35203; Mailing: P.O. Box 12047, Birmingham, AL 35202-2047 t) 205-838-8322 x309 bsellers@bhmdiocese.org Bob M. Sellers Jr., Bus. Mgr.;

Lee Fisher Memorial Award - 300 Lakeshore Pkwy., Birmingham, AL 35209 t) 205-940-2400 bsellers@bhmdiocese.org Very Rev. Robert J. Sullivan, Prin.;

Loraine Cerfolio Memorial Award - 2121 Third Ave. N., Birmingham, AL 35203 t) 205-838-8322 bsellers@bhmdiocese.org

St. Mark the Evangelist Columbarium Fund - 7340 Cahaba Valley Rd., Birmingham, AL 35238; Mailing: P.O. Box 380396, Birmingham, AL 35238-0396 t) (205) 980-1810 www.stmarkrc.org Very Rev. Robert J. Sullivan, Pst.;

Michael Duquette Memorial Fund - 2121 3rd Ave., N, Birmingham, AL 35203; Mailing: P.O. Box 12047, Birmingham, AL 35202-2047 t) 205-838-8322 x309 bsellers@bhmdiocese.org Bob M. Sellers Jr., Exec.;

Nancy Goss Memorial Fund - 2121 3rd Ave., N, Birmingham, AL 35203; Mailing: P.O. Box 12047, Birmingham, AL 35202-2047 t) 205-838-8322 x309 bsellers@bhmdiocese.org Bob M. Sellers Jr., Exec.;

Nell H. and Robert J. Duquette Endowment Fund - 2121 3rd Ave., N, Birmingham, AL 35203; Mailing: P.O. Box 12047, Birmingham, AL 35202-2047 t) 205-838-8322 x209 bsellers@bhmdiocese.org Bob M. Sellers Jr., Exec.;

One Voice Endowment Fund - 2121 Third Ave. N., Birmingham, AL 35203 t) 205-838-8322 x210 bsellers@bhmdiocese.org Mary Dillard, Editor & Photojournalist;

Our Lady of Sorrows Educational School Foundation - 1730 Oxmoor Rd., Birmingham, AL 35209 t) 205-871-8121 Rev. Msgr. Martin M. Muller, Pst.;

Our Lady of the Valley Educational Foundation - 5514 Double Oak Ln., Birmingham, AL 35242 t) 205-991-5488 Rev. Thomas M. Kelly, Pst.;

St. Peter Child Development Center Fund - 2061 Patton Chapel Rd., Birmingham, AL 35216 t) 205-822-4480 stpeterapostle@bellsouth.net Rev. Vernon F. Huguley, Pst.;

Robert O'Sullivan Burse Fund - 2121 3rd Ave., N., Birmingham, AL 35203 t) (205) 838-8322 x309 www.bhmdiocese.org Bob M. Sellers Jr., CFO;

Roy and Linda Taylor Memorial Fund - 2121 3rd Ave., N, Birmingham, AL 35203; Mailing: P.O. Box 12047, Birmingham, AL 35202-2047 t) 205-838-8322 x309 bsellers@bhmdiocese.org Bob M. Sellers Jr., Exec.;

Sacred Heart School Endowment Foundation - 2121 3rd

Ave., N, Birmingham, AL 35203; Mailing: P.O. Box 12047, Birmingham, AL 35202-2047 t) 205-838-8322 x309 bsellers@bhmdiocese.org Bob M. Sellers Jr., Exec.;

St. Stephens University Chapel - 2121 3rd Ave., N, Birmingham, AL 35203; Mailing: P.O. Box 12047, Birmingham, AL 35202-2047 t) 205-838-8322 x309 bsellers@bhmdiocese.org Bob M. Sellers Jr., Exec.;

Thomas Scott Messina Memorial Endowment - 300 Lakeshore Pkwy., Birmingham, AL 35209 t) 205-940-2400 bsellers@bhmdiocese.org Very Rev. Robert J. Sullivan, Pres.; Bob M. Sellers Jr., Diocese of Birmingham CFO;

St. Vincent's Foundation of Alabama, Inc. - 1130 Twenty-Second St. S., Ste. 1000, Birmingham, AL 35205 t) 205-838-6151 jason.alexander@ascension.org; elizabeth.pautler@ascension.org www.stvfoundation.org Jason Alexander, CEO; Elizabeth Pautler, Chief Mission Integration Officer;

CULLMAN

St. Bernard Abbey Foundation - 1600 St. Bernard Dr., S.E., Cullman, AL 35055 t) 256-734-8291 abmarcus@stbernardabbey.com www.stbernardabbey.com Rt. Rev. Marcus J. Voss, O.S.B., Chair;

St. Bernard Preparatory School Educational Foundation - 1600 St. Bernard Dr., S.E., Cullman, AL 35055 t) 256-739-6682 abmarcus@stbernardabbey.com www.stbernardprep.com Rt. Rev. Marcus J. Voss, O.S.B., Chair;

***Clairvaux Society Foundation** - 1600 St. Bernard Dr., S.E., Cullman, AL 35055 t) (256) 734-8291 Rt. Rev. Marcus J. Voss, O.S.B., Abbot;

Friends of Sacred Heart School Endowment Foundation - 205 3rd Ave., S. E., Cullman, AL 35055 t) 256-734-3730 price@sacredheartchurchcullman.org Rev. Patrick Egan, O.S.B., Pst.;

Natalie Collier Memorial Scholarship Fund - 205 3rd Ave., S. E., Cullman, AL 35055 t) 256-734-3730 price@sacredheartchurchcullman.org Rev. Patrick Egan, O.S.B., Pst.;

Sacred Heart Monastery of Cullman, Alabama Foundation - 916 Convent Rd., Cullman, AL 35055-2019 t) 256-734-4622; 256-734-3835 development@shmon.org www.shmon.org Sr. Lynn Elisabeth Meadows, OSB, Pres.;

DECATUR

St. Ann's Educational Foundation - 3910 Spring Ave., S.W., Decatur, AL 35603 t) 256-353-2667 parish@annunlord.com Bob M. Sellers Jr., CEO;

FLORENCE

St. Joseph School Foundation, Florence - 115 Plum St., Florence, AL 35630 t) 256-766-1923 ceckleck@aol.com; info@stjosephschoolfoundation.org Rev. Joseph Kuzhichalil, C.M.I., Admin.;

GADSDEN

St. James Educational Foundation - 622 Chestnut St., Gadsden, AL 35904 t) 256-546-2975 Rev. Jose B. Chacko, Pst.;

HUNTSVILLE

The Bishop David E. Foley Endowed Scholarship - c/o St. John Paul II Catholic High School, 7301 Old Madison Pike, Huntsville, AL 35806 t) (256) 430-1760 Dr. Jeremiah Russell, Prin.; Bob M. Sellers Jr., CFO;

Father Francis Jordan Scholarship Fund - 2300 Beasley Ave., N.W., Huntsville, AL 35816 t) 256-539-5221 James S. Bell, Prin.;

Good Shepherd Parish Endowment Fund - 13550 Chaney Thompson Rd., S.E., Huntsville, AL 35803 t) (256) 882-1844 www.goodshephsv.org Rev. Timothy Pfander, Pst.;

Holy Spirit Haiti Foundation - 625 Airport Rd., S.W., Huntsville, AL 35802 t) (256) 881-4781 www.holyspirithsv.com Bob M. Sellers Jr., CFO;

Holy Spirit Regional School Foundation - 625 Airport Rd., S.W., Huntsville, AL 35802 t) 256-881-4852 foundation89@comcast.net www.hstigers.org Lee Dumbacher, Admin.;

The Kathleen Ganey Scholarship Fund - 135 Mill Stream Dr., Huntsville, AL 35806 t) (205) 838-8322 Bob M. Sellers Jr., CFO;

MADISON

St. John's Columbarium Perpetual Care Fund - 1055 Hughes Rd., Madison, AL 35758 t) (256) 722-0130 Rev. Bryan K. Lowe, Pst.; Bob M. Sellers Jr., CFO;

MONTEVALLO

St. Thomas Education Foundation - 80 St. Thomas Way, Montevallo, AL 35115 t) 205-663-3936 jlampton@stthomascatholic.com Rev. Brad Jantz, Pst.;

TUSCALOOSA

The Harrison Family Endowment Trust for the Benefit of Holy Spirit School - 711 James I. Harrison Jr. Pkwy. E., Tuscaloosa, AL 35405 t) 205-553-9630 sperry@holyspirital.com Rev. Msgr. Michael J. Deering;

Holy Spirit School of Tuscaloosa Endowment Foundation - 733 James I. Harrison, Jr. Pkwy. E, Tuscaloosa, AL 35405 t) 205-553-9733 hsc@hschurch.com www.hschurch.com Rev. Msgr. Michael J. Deering, Pst.; Bob M. Sellers Jr., Diocese of Birmingham CFO;

HOSPITALS / HEALTH SERVICES [HOS]

BIRMINGHAM

Holy Name of Jesus Medical Center, Inc. - 3102 Colony Park Dr., Birmingham, AL 35243; Mailing: P.O Box 430212, Birmingham, AL 35243 t) 256-880-7064 shgmsbtm30@aol.com Supports the health care ministries of the Missionary Servants of the Most Blessed Trinity Sr. Helen Gaffney, M.S.B.T., Pres.; Asstd. Annu.: 486; Staff: 1

St. Vincent's Health System (Ascension Health Ministries (Ascension Sponsorship) AJP) - 810 St. Vincent's Dr., Birmingham, AL 35205; Mailing: 102 Woodmont Blvd., Ste. 800, Nashville, TN 37205 t) 205-939-7688 jason.alexander@ascension.org; elizabeth.pautler@ascension.org www.stvhs.com Jason Alexander, CEO; Elizabeth Pautler, Chief Mission Integration Office; Bed Capacity: 868; Asstd. Annu.: 819,686; Staff: 4,188

St. Vincent's Birmingham (Ascension Health) - 810 St. Vincent's Dr., Birmingham, AL 35205 t) 205-939-7000 Jason Alexander, CEO; Bed Capacity: 439; Asstd. Annu.: 163,756; Staff: 1,932

St. Vincent's Blount (Ascension Health Ministries (Ascension Sponsor), A Public Juridic Person) - 150 Gilbreath Dr., Oneonta, AL 35121 t) 205-274-3000 Jason Alexander, CEO; Bed Capacity: 25; Asstd. Annu.: 64,517; Staff: 171

St. Vincent's East (Ascension Health Ministries (Ascension Sponsor), A Juridic Person) - 50 Medical Park E. Dr., Birmingham, AL 35235 t) 205-838-3000 Jason Alexander, CEO; Bed Capacity: 338; Asstd. Annu.: 106,111; Staff: 1,186

St. Vincent's St. Clair (Ascension Health Ministries (Ascension Sponsorship), A Public Juridic Person) - 7063 Veterans Pkwy., Pell City, AL 35125 t) 205-814-2429 Jason Alexander, CEO; Bed Capacity: 40; Asstd. Annu.: 52,935; Staff: 199

CLANTON

St. Vincent's Chilton (Ascension Health Ministries (Ascension Sponsor), A Public Juridic Person) - 2030 Lay Dam Rd., Clanton, AL 35405 t) 205-258-4400 jason.alexander@ascension.org; elizabeth.pautler@ascension.org www.stvhs.com Jason Alexander, CEO; Elizabeth Pautler, Chief Mission Integration Office; Bed Capacity: 26; Asstd. Annu.: 33,719; Staff: 143

MISCELLANEOUS [MIS]

BIRMINGHAM

Catholic Housing of Birmingham, Inc. - 2121 3rd Ave. N., Birmingham, AL 35203; Mailing: P.O. Box 12047, Birmingham, AL 35203 t) 205-838-8322 dmealer@bhmdiocese.org Bruce Hoagland, Pres.;

Congregation of the Passion: Holy Family Community, Inc. - 1910 19th St., Ensley, Birmingham, AL 35218 t) 205-780-3440 House of Religious Men, Corporation for Holy Family Church, & Holy Family Middle School, Birmingham, St. Mary's Church, Fairfield, and St. Joseph, BIR Rev. Phil Paxton, C.P., Pst.; Rev. Patricio Montsalvas Rizzo, C.P.; Rev. Robert Weiss, CP, In Res.;

Friends of Catholic Education - 2121 3rd Ave. N., Birmingham, AL 35203 t) (205) 838-8322 x309 Bob M. Sellers Jr., CFO;

Ladies of Charity of Central Alabama - 2843 Shook Hill Cir., Birmingham, AL 35223 t) 205-601-3973 cssauer@aol.com Carol Sauer, Contact;

Magnificat: Mary, Woman of Faith Chapter - 2121 3rd Ave. N., Birmingham, AL 35266-0136; Mailing: P.O. Box 660136, Birmingham, AL 35266-0136 t) 205-979-7645 carolinamaenza@gmail.com www.magnificat-birminghamal.org Virginia Springer, Contact;

St. Thomas More Society of Metro Birmingham - 2121 3rd Ave. N., Birmingham, AL 35203 t) 205-838-8322 x314 jwhitaker@bhmdiocese.org Dcn. G. Rick DiGiorgio, Chair; John Whitaker, Pres.;

Tuxedo Junction Catholic Community, Inc. - 1910 19th St., Ensley, Birmingham, AL 35218 t) 205-780-3440 kennethblckldg@aol.com Rev. Phil Paxton, C.P., Pst.;

Villa Maria I - 500 82nd St. S., Birmingham, AL 35206 t) 205-836-7839 villamariamgr@spm.net Sheila West, Contact;

Villa Maria II - 500 82nd St. S., Birmingham, AL 35206 t) 205-836-7839 villamariamgr@spm.net Elizabeth Johns, Contact;

CULLMAN

St. Scholastica Federation, Inc. - 916 Convent Rd., N.E., Cullman, AL 35055 t) (256) 734-4622 Sr. Lynn Marie McKenzie, OSB, Pres.;

FLORENCE

Society of St. Vincent de Paul, St. Joseph Conference - 659 S. Poplar St., Florence, AL 35630-6818 t) 256-718-0901 svdpflorence@gmail.com John B. Lehrter, Treas.;

HANCEVILLE

Shrine of the Most Blessed Sacrament (Our Lady of the Angels Monastery in Hanceville, Alabama) - 3224 County Rd. 548, Hanceville, AL 35077 t) 256-352-6267 pilgrimages@olamshrine.com www.olamshrine.com Rev. Paschal Mary Yohe, M.F.V.A., Admin.;

HUNTSVILLE

Society of St. Vincent de Paul, District Council of Huntsville - 625 Airport Rd., Huntsville, AL 35802 t) 256-883-0157 hsvsvdp@knology.net John Wolfsberger, Pres.; Patricia Schuessler, Treas.;

St. Vincent de Paul Thrift Store - 2140 Jonathan Dr., Huntsville, AL 35810-3453 t) 256-851-8881 Jim Jenkins, Pres.;

IRONDALE

***Eternal Word Television Network, Inc.** - 5817 Old Leeds Rd., Irondale, AL 35210 t) 205-271-2900 chairman@ewtn.com www.ewtn.com (EWTN Global Catholic Network) Michael P. Warsaw, Chair;

PLEASANT GROVE

***Bible Christian Society** - 544 Park Rd., Pleasant Grove, AL 35127-1613; Mailing: P.O. Box 424, Pleasant Grove, AL 35127-1613 t) 205-744-1856 admin@biblechristiansociety.com www.biblechristiansociety.com John Martignoni, Pres.;

Queen of Heaven Radio, Inc. - 544 Park Rd., Pleasant Grove, AL 35127-1613; Mailing: P.O. Box 483, Pleasant Grove, AL 35127-1613 t) 205-744-4456 info@queenofheavenradio.com John Martignoni, Pres.;

MONASTERIES AND RESIDENCES FOR PRIESTS AND BROTHERS [MON]

BIRMINGHAM

St. John Vianney Residence for Priests - 2724 Hanover Cir. S., Birmingham, AL 35205 t) 205-838-8322 x219 dmealer@bhmdiocese.org Most Rev. Steven J. Raica; Priests: 1

CULLMAN

St. Bernard Abbey - 1600 St. Bernard Dr., S.E., Cullman, AL 35055 t) 256-734-8291 abmarcus@stbernardabbey.com www.stbernardabbey.com (Corporate Title: Benedictine Society of Alabama, Inc.) Rt. Rev. Marcus J. Voss, O.S.B., Abbot; Rt. Rev. Victor J. Clark, O.S.B.; Rev. Patrick Egan, O.S.B.; Rev. Bede Marcy, O.S.B.; Rev. Joel W. Martin, O.S.B.; Rev. John O'Donnell, O.S.B.; Rev. Francis M. Reque, O.S.B.; Rev. Linus Klucsarits, O.S.B., Headmaster; Rt. Rev. Cletus D. Meagher, O.S.B., Abbot; Rev. Johnathan Denson, OSB, Student; Brs.: 16; Priests: 9

IRONDALE

Franciscan Missionaries of the Eternal Word, A Public Clerical Association of the Christian Faithful - 5821 Old Leeds Rd., Irondale, AL 35210 t) 205-271-2937 friars@mfvamedia.org www.franciscanmissionaries.com Rev. Patrick Mary Russell, M.F.V.A., Vicar; Rev. Matthew Bartow, Treas.; Rev. Leonard Mary Revilla, M.F.V.A., Community Servant; Brs.: 3; Priests: 10

RETREAT HOUSES / RENEWAL CENTERS [RTR]

CULLMAN

Benedictine Sisters Retreat Center - 916 Convent Rd., Cullman, AL 35055-2019 t) 256-734-8302 retreats@shmon.org www.shmon.org Sr. Janet Marie Flemming, OSB, Dir.;

IRONDALE

Casa Maria Retreat House - 3721 Belmont Rd., Irondale, AL 35210 t) 205-956-6760 retreats@sisterservants.com Mother Louise Marie Flanigan, Dir.;

SPECIAL CARE FACILITIES [SPF]

BIRMINGHAM

Contemplative Outreach Birmingham - 3416 River Tree Ln., Birmingham, AL 35223 t) 205-970-1892 calli.meredith@gmail.com centeringprayeralabama.wordpress.com Diana Tschache, Contact;

An asterisk (*) denotes an organization that has established tax-exempt status directly with the IRS and is not covered by the USCCB Group Ruling.

Diocese of Bismarck

(Dioecesis Bismarckiensis)

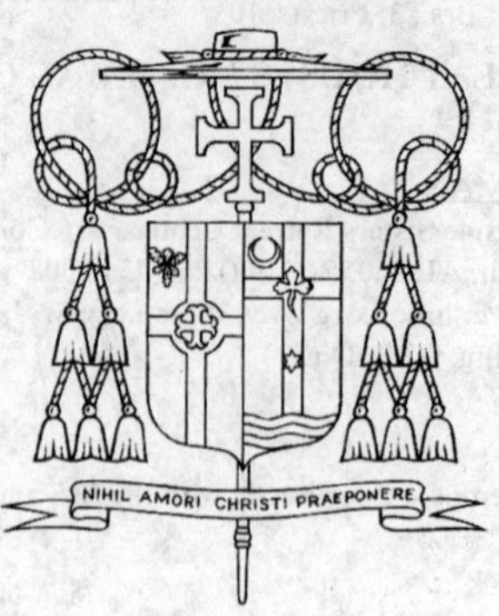

MOST REVEREND DAVID D. KAGAN, D.D., P.A., J.C.L.

Bishop of Bismarck; ordained June 14, 1975; named Prelate of Honor November 14, 1994; Protonotary Apostolic May 21, 2011; appointed Bishop of Bismarck October 19, 2011; installed November 30, 2011.

Chancery Office: P.O. Box 1575, Bismarck, ND 58502-1575. T: 701-223-1347; F: 701-223-3693.
Center for Pastoral Ministry Office, P.O. Box 1137, ND 58502-1137. T: 701-222-3035; F: 701-222-0269.
www.bismarckdiocese.com

ESTABLISHED DECEMBER 31, 1909.

Square Miles 34,268.

Comprises the Counties of Adams, Billings, Bowman, Burke, Burleigh, Divide, Dunn, Emmons, Golden Valley, Grant, Hettinger, McKenzie, McLean, Mercer, Morton, Mountrail, Oliver, Renville, Sioux, Slope, Stark, Ward and Williams in the State of North Dakota.

For legal titles of parishes and diocesan institutions, consult the Chancery Office.

STATISTICAL OVERVIEW

Personnel

Bishop	1
Abbots	1
Priests: Diocesan Active in Diocese	58
Priests: Diocesan Active Outside Diocese	5
Priests: Diocesan in Foreign Missions	1
Priests: Retired, Sick or Absent	12
Number of Diocesan Priests	76
Religious Priests in Diocese	10
Total Priests in your Diocese	86
Extern Priests in Diocese	4
Ordinations:	
Diocesan Priests	5
Transitional Deacons	3
Permanent Deacons	2
Permanent Deacons in Diocese	87
Total Brothers	17
Total Sisters	67

Parishes

Parishes	93
With Resident Pastor:	
Resident Diocesan Priests	40
Resident Religious Priests	3
Without Resident Pastor:	
Administered by Priests	50
Professional Ministry Personnel:	
Lay Ministers	47

Welfare

Catholic Hospitals	4
Total Assisted	326,393
Homes for the Aged	7
Total Assisted	1,166
Other Institutions	1
Total Assisted	97

Educational

Diocesan Students in Other Seminaries	13
Total Seminarians	13
Colleges and Universities	1
Total Students	3,800
High Schools, Diocesan and Parish	3
Total Students	611
Elementary Schools, Diocesan and Parish	10
Total Students	2,511
Catechesis/Religious Education:	
High School Students	802
Elementary Students	4,195
Total Students under Catholic Instruction	11,932
Teachers in Diocese:	
Priests	12
Sisters	9
Lay Teachers	255

Vital Statistics

Receptions into the Church:	
Infant Baptism Totals	832
Minor Baptism Totals	38
Adult Baptism Totals	27
Received into Full Communion	93
First Communions	805
Confirmations	826
Marriages:	
Catholic	131
Interfaith	70
Total Marriages	201
Deaths	818
Total Catholic Population	60,567
Total Population	347,876

LEADERSHIP

Moderator of the Curia - t) 701-204-7220 Rev. Msgr. Gene E. Lindemann;
Vicar General - t) 701-204-7220 Rev. Msgr. Gene E. Lindemann;
Censor Librorum - Rev. Greg Luger;
Chancellor - t) 701-204-7216 Dale Eberle;
Office of Canonical Services (Marriage Tribunal) Direct marriage papers to Bishop David D. Kagan - t) 701-222-3035
Associate Judges - Rev. Keith N. Streifel; Rev. David Richter; Rev. Shannon G. Lucht;
Defensor Vinculi - Rev. David L. Zimmer; Rev. Msgr. Gene E. Lindemann; Raphael Frackiewicz;
Judicial Vicar - t) 701-204-7204 Rev. Christopher J. Kadrmas; Rev. Doug S. Krebs, Adjutant Judicial Vicar;
Pro-Synodal Judges - Rev. Christopher J. Kadrmas;
Promoter of Justice - Rev. David L. Zimmer;
Auditor - Cheryl Hansen;
Ecclesiastical Notary - Sandra Breiner;
Presbyteral Council - Rev. Msgr. Gene E. Lindemann, Chair; Rev. Brian P. Gross; Rev. Todd Kreitinger;
Diocesan Corporate Board - Most Rev. David D. Kagan, Pres.; Rev. Msgr. Gene E. Lindemann, Vice. Pres.; Dale Eberle, Secy.;
Diocesan Finance Council - Most Rev. David D. Kagan, Pres.; Rev. Msgr. Gene E. Lindemann, Chair; Rev. Msgr. James B. Braaten;

OFFICES AND DIRECTORS

African Mission - t) 701-222-3035 Charles Reichert;
Archives - t) 701-204-7216 Dale Eberle;
Bishop's Delegate for Catholic Education - Rev. Justin P. Waltz;
Boy Scouts - c) 701-202-7190 deaconh@bis.midco.net Dcn. Harvey Hanel;
Catechesis and Youth - t) 701-204-7208 Christopher Kraft, Dir.;
Search Program - dean.johs@msd1.org Dean Johs;
Catholic Campaign For Human Development - t) 701-204-7202 Ronald Schatz, Dir.;
Catholic Charities North Dakota - t) 701-235-4457 Dianne Nechiporenko, Exec. Dir.;
Catholic Relief Services - t) 701-204-7202 Ronald Schatz, Dir.;
Communications Office - t) 701-204-7190 Sonia Mullally, Dir.;
Continuing Education for Clergy - t) 701-255-4600 Rev. Msgr. Patrick A. Schumacher;
Episcopal Vicar for Clergy - t) 701-204-7220 Rev. Msgr. Gene E. Lindemann;
Family Ministry - t) 701-204-7205 Amanda Jensen, Dir.;
Finance Officer - t) 701-204-7196 Laura J. Huber;
Internal Auditor - t) 701-425-0794 Dcn. Brent Naslund;
Newspaper Dakota Catholic Action - t) 701-204-7190 Sonia Mullally, Editor;
North Dakota Catholic Conference - t) 701-223-2519 Christopher Dodson, Exec. Dir.;
Office of Divine Worship - t) 701-471-5983 Rev. Nick L. Schneider, Dir.;
Office of Vocations - t) 701-516-4388 Rev. Jordan Dosch, Dir.;
Permanent Diaconate Office - t) 701-204-7210 Dcn. David Fleck, Dir.;
Episcopal Vicar for Deacons - t) 701-204-7220 Rev. Msgr. Gene E. Lindemann;
Priests' Benefit Association - Most Rev. David D. Kagan, Pres.; Rev. Shane Campbell, Secy.; Rev. Christopher J. Kadrmas, Chair;
Priests' Personnel Board - Rev. David Richter, Chair; Rev. William A. Ruelle; Rev. Chad Gion;
Propagation of the Faith - t) 701-204-7202 Ronald Schatz;
Safe Environment Coordinator - t) 701-204-7216 Dale Eberle;
Stewardship and Resource Development Office - t) 701-204-7202 Ronald Schatz, Dir.;
Victim Assistance Coordinator - victimassistance@bismarckdiocese.com

PARISHES, MISSIONS, AND CLERGY

STATE OF NORTH DAKOTA

ALEXANDER

Our Lady of Consolation - 3341 137th Ave., N.W., Alexander, ND 58831; Mailing: P.O. Box 670, Watford City, ND 58854-0670 t) 701-842-3505 wcepiphany@gmail.com; wcepiphanydre@gmail.com www.wcepiphany.com Served from Watford City. Rev. Brian P. Gross, Pst.; Erica Bohn, Youth Min.; Bob Nelson, DRE; Sara Millet, Bus. Mgr.; CRP Stds.: 1

ALMONT

St. Mary, Queen of Peace - 302 Margaret St., Almont, ND 58520; Mailing: PO Box C, New Salem, ND 58563-0429 t) 701-843-7061 stpiusv@westriv.com Served from New Salem. Rev. Stephen Folorunso, Pst.;

BEACH

St. John the Baptist - 162 2nd Ave., S.E., Beach, ND 58621; Mailing: Box 337, Beach, ND 58621-0337 t) 701-872-4153; 701-872-4154 (CRP) stjohn@midstate.net; wendy@triparishnd.org www.triparishnd.org Rev. Daniel J. Berg, Pst.; Dcn. James Wosepka; Dcn. Ronald J. Zachmann; Swenda Braden, DRE; Kim Thompson, DRE; Wendy Ekre, Bus. Mgr.; CRP Stds.: 56

BELFIELD

St. Bernard - 402 3rd Ave., N.E., Belfield, ND 58622; Mailing: PO Box 38, Belfield, ND 58622-0038 t) 701-575-4295 stbernardbelfield@ndsupernet.com; wendykordonowy@gmail.com saintbernardbelfield.com Rev. Shane Campbell, Pst.; Dcn. Loren Kordonowy; Wendy Kordonowy, DRE; CRP Stds.: 74

BERTHOLD

St. Ann - 217 Dewey St., N.W., Berthold, ND 58718; Mailing: PO Box 159, Stanley, ND 58784 t) 701-628-3405 holyrosarystanley.com Served from Stanley. Rev. Jason R. Signalness, Pst.; Elonda Davidson, DRE; Reann Bohrer, Bus. Mgr.;

BEULAH

St. Joseph - 115 3rd St., N.E., Beulah, ND 58523; Mailing: P.O. Box 146, Beulah, ND 58523 t) 701-873-5397 stjbeulah@westriv.com; stjk-12@westriv.com www.saints2b.org Rev. Thomas Grafsgaard, Pst.; Dcn. Daniel Wallach; Darlene Mellmer, DRE; CRP Stds.: 101

BISMARCK

Cathedral of the Holy Spirit - 519 Raymond St., Bismarck, ND 58501 t) 701-223-1033 dtrnka@cathedralparish.com www.cathedralparish.com Rev. Joshua Ehli, Rector; Rev. John Paul Gardner, Par. Vicar; Rev. Jake Magnuson, Par. Vicar; Dcn. Brent Naslund; Dcn. Les Noehre; Dcn. Randal Schmidt; Dcn. Anthony Ternes; Dianna Trnka, Bus. Mgr.; CRP Stds.: 201

Saint Anne - 1321 Braman Ave., Bismarck, ND 58501 t) 701-223-1549 mkorczak@stannesbismarck.org www.stannesbismarck.org Rev. Wayne V. Sattler, Pst.; Rev. Jeffrey A. Zwack, Par. Vicar; Rev. Kregg W. Hochhalter, Par. Vicar; Dcn. John Bachmeier; Dcn. David Fleck; Dcn. Wayne M. Jundt; Dcn. Joseph M. Krupinsky; Dcn. Jerry Volk; Holly Keller, DRE; Melanie Korczak, Bus. Mgr.; CRP Stds.: 172

Ascension - 1825 S. 3rd St., Bismarck, ND 58504; Mailing: 1905 S. 3rd St., Bismarck, ND 58504 t) 701-223-3606; 701-258-5692 ascension@midconetwork.com; bkathol@ascensionbismarck.org ascensionbismarck.org Rev. Msgr. James B. Braaten, Pst.; Dcn. John Paul Martin; Dcn. Doyle F. Schulz; Beth Kathol, Bus. Mgr.; CRP Stds.: 221

Church of Corpus Christi - 1919 N. Second St., Bismarck, ND 58501 t) 701-255-4600 info@corpuschristibismarck.com www.corpuschristibismarck.com Rev. Msgr. Patrick A. Schumacher, Pst.; Rev. Logan Obrigewitch, Par. Vicar; Dcn. Michael Fix; Dcn. Lonnie Grabowska; Dcn. Brian Lardy; Dcn. Rexford R. McDowell; Dcn. Robert Wingenbach; CRP Stds.: 632

St. Mary - 806 E. Broadway Ave., Bismarck, ND 58501; Mailing: 825 E. Broadway Ave., Bismarck, ND 58501 t) 701-223-5562 stmarysbismarck.org Rev. Jared Johnson, Pst.; Rev. Nicholas Vetter, Par. Vicar; Dcn. Daniel Brooke; Dcn. Michael Marback; Dcn. Terry Glatt; Meagan Kline, Dir.; Nancy Darling, Music Min.; Sheila Gilbertson, DRE; Olivia Richter, Bus. Mgr.; CRP Stds.: 248

BOWBELLS

St. Joseph (Bowbells) - 102 3rd St., N.W., Bowbells, ND 58721; Mailing: P.O. Box 488, Kenmare, ND 58746-0488 t) 701-385-4311 stagnes@restel.net Served from Kenmare Rev. Christy Pathiala, Pst.; CRP Stds.: 4

BOWMAN

St. Charles - 202 1st Ave., S.W., Bowman, ND 58623 t) 701-523-5292 stcharles2@ndsupernet.com; frfranchuk@stcharlesbowmannd.com www.stcharlesbowmannd.com Rev. Ben Franchuk, Pst.; Dcn. Leonard Fischer; Kathy Pauley, DRE; CRP Stds.: 123

BRADDOCK

St. Katherine - 200 1st Ave. N., Braddock, ND 58524; Mailing: 613 N. Broadway, Linton, ND 58552-7311 t) 701-254-4588 stanthony@bektel.com www.stanthonylinton.com Served from Linton. Rev. Mark Aune, Admin.; Dcn. Kenneth J. Wolbaum; Becky Small, DRE; CRP Stds.: 13

CANNON BALL

Oratory of St. Elizabeth, Cannon Ball - 7166 S. Big Lake Rd., Cannon Ball, ND 58528; Mailing: P.O. Box 394, Fort Yates, ND 58538-0394 t) 701-854-3473 www.catholicindianmission.com Served from Fort Yates. Rev. Chad Gion, Pst.; Sandy Gallagher, Bus. Mgr.; Bro. George Maufort, S.D.S.;

CARSON

St. Theresa the Child Jesus - 204 2nd Ave., N.E., Carson, ND 58529; Mailing: 421 Court St., Flasher, ND 58535-7216 t) 701-597-3228 www.catholic3nd.com Served from Flasher. Rev. Biju Antony, I.M.S. (India), Admin.; Valeria Noel Wax, DRE; CRP Stds.: 45

CENTER

St. Martin of Tours - 322 2nd St. E., Center, ND 58530; Mailing: P.O. Box 2766, Center, ND 58530-2766 t) 701-794-3601 stmartin@westriv.com; joleschm@westriv.com stmartinschurch-center.org Rev. Stephen Folorunso, Pst.; Joletta Schmidt, DRE; CRP Stds.: 43

CROSBY

St. Patrick - 205 1st St., N.W., Crosby, ND 58730; Mailing: PO Box 89, Crosby, ND 58730 t) 701-965-6537 stpatscr@nccray.com Rev. Patrick Ojedeji, Admin.; Vicki Haggin, DRE; CRP Stds.: 17

CROWN BUTTE

St. Vincent - 3182 36th St, Crown Butte, ND 58554; Mailing: PO Box 1137, c/o The Diocese of Bismarck, Bismarck, ND 58502 c) 701-202-0111; 701-471-5983 nschneider@bismarckdiocese.com Rev. Nick L. Schneider, Pst.; Dcn. Steve M. Brannan; Mary McHugh, DRE; CRP Stds.: 22

DICKINSON

St. Joseph - 240 E. Broadway, Dickinson, ND 58601 t) 701-483-2223 stjoseph@ndsupernet.com www.stjosephschurchdickinson.com Rev. Justin P. Waltz, Pst.; Rev. Benjamin Wanner, Par. Vicar; Dcn. Dallas Carlson; Dcn. Ross Reiter; Dcn. Alvin W. Schwindt; Tina Jassek, Bus. Mgr.; CRP Stds.: 109

St. Patrick - 310 2nd St. W., Dickinson, ND 58601; Mailing: 229 3rd Ave. W., Dickinson, ND 58601 t) 701-483-6700 stpatrick@ndsupernet.com stpatrickdickinson.com Rev. William A. Ruelle, Pst.; Rev. Christian Smith, Assoc. Pst.; Dcn. Ronald Keller;

CRP Stds.: 63

Queen of Peace Church - 725 12th St. W., Dickinson, ND 58601-3516 t) 701-483-2134 office@thequeenofpeace.com thequeenofpeace.com Rev. Msgr. Thomas J. Richter, Pst.; Rev. Grant Dvorak, Par. Vicar; Dcn. Leonard Krebs; CRP Stds.: 106

St. Wenceslaus - 525 Third St. E., Dickinson, ND 58601; Mailing: 505 3rd St. E., Dickinson, ND 58601-4504 t) 701-225-3972 www.stwenceslausnd.com Rev. Robert P. Shea, Pst.; Dcn. Robert Stockert; Dcn. Robert Zent; Nicole Berger, DRE; Nancy Woehl, Bus. Mgr.; CRP Stds.: 173

FLASHER

St. Lawrence - 421 Court St., Flasher, ND 58535 t) 701-597-3228 www.catholic3nd.com Rev. Biju Antony, I.M.S. (India), Admin.; Noel Wax, DRE; CRP Stds.: 42

FORT YATES

St. Peter - Catholic Indian Mission - 204 Church St., Fort Yates, ND 58538; Mailing: P.O. Box 394, Fort Yates, ND 58538 t) 701-854-3473 (Standing Rock Indian Reservation) Rev. Chad Gion, Pst.; Rev. Jolly George, Par. Vicar; Bro. George Maufort, S.D.S.; Sandy Gallagher, Bus. Mgr.; CRP Stds.: 29

St. Bernard Mission School - (Grades K-7) 1 Mission Ave., Fort Yates, ND 58538; Mailing: c/o St. Peter - Catholic Indian Mission, P.O. Box 394, Fort Yates, ND 58538-0394 t) 701-854-7413 www.catholicindianmission.com Lawrence Montclair, Prin.; Stds.: 33; Lay Tchrs.: 9

FOXHOLM

St. Mary - 17901 128th Ave., N.W., Foxholm, ND 58718-9643 t) 701-838-1026 office@stleothegreat.church www.stleosminot.com Rev. Todd Kreitinger, Admin.; Rev. Jadyn E. Nelson, Celebrate Mass & Sacraments; Rev. Gregory Crane, Assoc. Pst.; Paula Bachmeier, DRE; CRP Stds.: 31

GARRISON

St. Nicholas - 235 Second St., N.E., Garrison, ND 58540; Mailing: PO Box 870, Garrison, ND 58540-0870 t) 701-463-2327 www.stnicholaschurchgarrison.com Rev. Basil Atwell, O.S.B., Pst.; Stephanie Trautman, DRE; CRP Stds.: 56

GLADSTONE

St. Thomas the Apostle - 351 Cliff St, Gladstone, ND 58630; Mailing: 332 2nd St. N., Richardton, ND 58652 t) 701-974-3569 Served from Richardton. Rev. Thomas Wordekemper, O.S.B., Pst.; CRP Stds.: 2

GLEN ULLIN

St. Joseph - 6180 52nd St., S.W., Glen Ullin, ND 58631; Mailing: P.O. Box 609, Glen Ullin, ND 58631-0609 t) 701-348-3527 sacredheart@westriv.com www.sacredheartchurchglenullin.org Served from Sacred Heart of Jesus in Glen Ullin. Rev. Gary Benz, Pst.; CRP Stds.: 10

Sacred Heart of Jesus - 203 E. Ash Ave., Glen Ullin, ND 58631-0609; Mailing: PO Box 609, Glen Ullin, ND 58631-0609 t) 701-348-3527 sacredheart@westriv.com www.sacredheartchurchglenullin.org Rev. Gary Benz, Pst.; Dcn. Lance Gartner; Lisa Staiger, DRE; CRP Stds.: 34

GLENBURN

St. Philomena - 310 3rd Ave. N., Glenburn, ND 58740; Mailing: 218 1st St. S.E., Minot, ND 58701-3920 t) 701-838-1026 office@stleothegreat.church www.stleosminot.com Served from St. Leo in Minot. Rev. Todd Kreitinger, Admin.; Rev. Gregory Crane, Par. Vicar; Rev. Jadyn E. Nelson, Celebrate Mass & Sacraments; Kelly Zelinski, DRE; CRP Stds.: 6

GOLVA

St. Mary's Golva - 405 Gass St., Golva, ND 58632; Mailing: P.O. Box 337, Beach, ND 58621-0337 t) 701-872-4153; 701-872-4154 (CRP) stjohn@midstate.net; wendy@triparishnd.org www.triparishnd.org Served from Beach. Rev. Daniel J. Berg, Pst.; Dcn. James Wosepka; Dcn. Ronald J. Zachmann; Swenda Braden, DRE; Kim Thompson, DRE; Wendy Ekre, Bus. Mgr.; CRP Stds.: 20

GRENORA

St. Boniface - 300 East St., Grenora, ND 58845; Mailing: P.O. Box K, Williston, ND 58802-1115 t) 701-572-6731 (CRP) parishsecretary@stjparish.com; dre@stjparish.com www.stjparish.com Served from Williston Rev. Russell P. Kovash, Pst.; Rev. Greg Hilzendeger, Par. Vicar; Claudia Ortiz, DRE; Ray Urbi, Bus. Mgr.; CRP Stds.: 3

HAGUE

St. Mary - 210 S. 4th St., Hague, ND 58542; Mailing: PO Box 322, Strasburg, ND 58573 t) 701-336-7172 stspeterandpaul@bektel.com www.emmonscatholics.org Served from Strasburg. Rev. Shannon G. Lucht, Pst.; Joanne Ternes, DRE; CRP Stds.: 16

HALLIDAY

St. Paul - 31 3rd Ave.. N.E., Halliday, ND 58636; Mailing: PO Box 299, Killdeer, ND 58640 t) 701-764-5357 stjosephs-killdeer.com Served from Killdeer. Rev. Joseph A. Evinger, Pst.; Dcn. Dan Tuhy;

HAZELTON

St. Paul - 372 Harold St., Hazelton, ND 58544; Mailing: 613 N. Broadway St., Linton, ND 58552-7311 t) 701-254-4588 stanthony@bektel.com; stanthonybusadmin@bektel.com www.stanthonylinton.com Served by St Anthony Church in Linton Rev. Mark Aune, Admin.; Becky Small, DRE; Susan Schumacher, Bus. Mgr.; CRP Stds.: 14

HAZEN

St. Martin - 101 3rd Ave., S.W., Hazen, ND 58545; Mailing: P.O. Box 387, Hazen, ND 58545-0387 t) 701-748-2121 stmhazen@westriv.com; stmreled@westriv.com www.saints2b.org Rev. Thomas Grafsgaard, Pst.; Liz Lemer, Admin.; Michelle Reinhardt, DRE; CRP Stds.: 96

HEBRON

St. Ann - 204 Park St. S., Hebron, ND 58638-0012; Mailing: Box 12, Hebron, ND 58638-0012 t) 701-878-4658 www.stannshebron.com Sally Vogle, DRE; Eve Mollman, Bus. Mgr.; CRP Stds.: 68

HETTINGER

Holy Trinity - 405 3rd St. N., Hettinger, ND 58639 t) 701-567-2772 holytrinity@ndsupernet.com parishesofswnd.com Rev. Raphael Obotama, Par. Admin.; Dcn. Mike Mellmer; Sarah Dschaak, Bus. Mgr.; Joy Laufer, DRE; CRP Stds.: 45

HUFF

St. Martin - 5463 Huff St., Huff, ND 58554; Mailing: 801 1st St., S.E., Mandan, ND 58554-4470 t) 701-663-1660 office@myspiritoflife.com; stacey@myspiritoflife.com www.myspiritoflife.com Served from Spirit of Life, Mandan. Rev. Keith N. Streifel, Pst.; Stacey Bulcher, Bus. Mgr.; CRP Stds.: 1

KENMARE

St. Agnes - 409 E. Division, Kenmare, ND 58746-0488; Mailing: P.O. Box 488, Kenmare, ND 58746-0488 t) 701-385-4311 Rev. Christy Pathiala, Pst.; Nicole Michalenko, DRE; CRP Stds.: 29

KILLDEER

St. Joseph - 152 3rd Ave., N.W., Killdeer, ND 58640; Mailing: PO Box 299, Killdeer, ND 58640-0299 t) 701-764-5357 stjosephkilldeer.com Rev. Joseph A. Evinger, Pst.; Dcn. Dan Tuhy; Katlyn Steffan, DRE; CRP Stds.: 50

LANSFORD

St. John's Church of Lansford - 680 3rd Ave., Lansford, ND 58750; Mailing: P.O. Box 457, Mohall, ND 58761-0457 t) 701-756-6601 gluger@bismarckdiocese.com mlscatholic.com Served from Mohall. Rev. Greg Luger, Pst.;

LEFOR

St. Elizabeth - 5043 100D Ave., S.W., Lefor, ND 58641; Mailing: PO Box 369, New England, ND 58647 t) 701-579-4312 stmarychurchnewengland.com Served from New England Rev. Dennis R. Schafer, Pst.; Kris Ehlis, DRE; CRP Stds.: 6

LINTON

St. Anthony - 613 N. Broadway, Linton, ND 58552-7311 t) 701-254-4588 stanthony@bektel.com www.stanthonylinton.com Rev. Mark Aune, Admin.; Denice Kautz, DRE; Susan Schumacher, Bus. Mgr.; CRP Stds.: 102

St. Michael - 2155 76th St., S.E., Linton, ND 58552; Mailing: PO Box 322, Strasburg, ND 58573-0322 t) 701-336-7172; 701-782-4389 (CRP) stspeterandpaul@bektel.com; barbvetter@hotmail.com Served from Strasburg. Rev. Shannon G. Lucht, Admin.; Danielle Weigel, DRE; CRP Stds.: 16

MAKOTI

St. Elizabeth - 4th Ave. & Edwards St., Makoti, ND 58756; Mailing: P.O. Box 519, Parshall, ND 58770-0519 t) 701-862-3484 saintbridget@restel.com Served from Parshall. Rev. Terry Wipf, Pst.; Elizabeth Huus, Bus. Mgr.;

MANDAN

Christ the King - 505-10th Ave., N.W., Mandan, ND 58554-2552 t) 701-663-8842 katrina.kuntz@ctkmandan.com ctkmandan.com Rev. Frederick R. Harvey, Pst.; Dcn. Jim Belohlavek; Dcn. Bob Nutsch; Dcn. Dennis Rohr; CRP Stds.: 54

Christ the King School - (Grades PreSchool-6) t) 701-663-6200 derrick.nagel@ctkmandan.com www.ctkmandan.com Derrick Nagel, Prin.; Stds.: 176; Pr. Tchrs.: 1; Sr. Tchrs.: 1; Lay Tchrs.: 25

St. Joseph - 108 Third St., N.E., Mandan, ND 58554 t) 701-663-9562 lfriesz@stjosephmandan.com Rev. Joshua Waltz, Pst.; Dcn. Randall Frohlich; Laurie Friesz, Bus. Mgr.; CRP Stds.: 175

St. Joseph School - (Grades PreK-12) 410 Collins Ave., Mandan, ND 58554 t) 701-663-9563 www.stjosephmandan.com David Fleischacker, Prin.; Stds.: 153; Lay Tchrs.: 12

Spirit of Life - 801 1st St., S.E., Mandan, ND 58554-4470 t) 701-663-1660 stacey@myspiritoflife.com; karen@myspiritoflife.com myspiritoflife.com Rev. Keith N. Streifel, Pst.; Rev. Deacon Gary Mizeur; Rev. Deacon Kevin Leingang; Stacey Bulcher, Bus. Mgr.; Karen Eggers, DRE; CRP Stds.: 154

MANDAREE

St. Anthony - 9385 BIA Rte. 12, Mandaree, ND 58757 t) 701-759-3412 stanthonymandaree16@gmail.com saintanthonypadua.com Rev. Roger A. Synek, Pst.; Dcn. Jim Baker; Dcn. Daniel Barone; CRP Stds.: 34

MARMARTH

St. Mary - 30 5th St., S.W., Marmarth, ND 58643; Mailing: c/o St. Charles, 202 1st Ave., S.W., Bowman, ND 58623-4216 t) 701-523-5292 stcharles@ndsupernet.com; stcharles3@ndsupernet.com Served from Bowman. Rev. Ben Franchuk, Pst.;

MAX

Immaculate Conception - 401 Jacobson Ave., Max, ND 58759; Mailing: PO Box 870, Garrison, ND 58540-0870 t) 701-463-2327 stnicholas@restel.com stnicholaschurchgarrison.com Served from Garrison. Rev. Basil Atwell, O.S.B., Pst.; Peggy Bingham, DRE; CRP Stds.: 15

MEDORA

St. Mary (Medora) - 305 4th St., Medora, ND 58645; Mailing: P.O. Box 38, Belfield, ND 58622-0038 t) (701) 575-4295 stbernardbelfield@ndsupernet.com www.saintbernardbelfield Served from Belfield. Rev. Shane Campbell, Pst.;

MENOKEN

St. Hildegard - 17200 Hwy. 10, Menoken, ND 58558-9604 t) 701-673-3177 www.sthildegardmenoken.com Rev. Msgr. Gene E. Lindemann, Pst.; Denise Richter, DRE; CRP Stds.: 77

MINOT

St. John the Apostle - 2600 Central Ave. W., Minot, ND 58701 t) 701-839-7076 drestjohn@srt.com; businesssj@srt.com www.stjohnminot.com Rev. David A. Richter, Pst.; Lucas DeMers, Bus. Mgr.; Monica Perry, DRE; CRP Stds.: 67

St. Leo - 218 1st S., S.E., Minot, ND 58704 t) 701-838-1026 info@stleothegreat.church; faithformation@stleothegreat.church www.stleosminot.com Rev. Todd Kreitinger, Pst.; Rev.

Gregory Crane, Assoc. Pst.; Dcn. Lloyd E. Krueger; Rev. Jadyn E. Nelson, In Res.; Tamera Larson, DRE; Maurina Renda, Bus. Mgr.; CRP Stds.: 64

Our Lady of Grace - 707 16th Ave., S.W., Minot, ND 58701 t) 701-839-6834 admin@olgminot.org; education1@olgminot.org olgminot.org Rev. Adam Maus, Pst.; Rev. Jacob Degele, Par. Vicar; Dcn. Steven F. Streitz, Admin.; Dcn. Mohn Koble; Tanya Watterud, DRE; CRP Stds.: 333

St. Therese the Little Flower - 919 8th St., N.W., Minot, ND 58703; Mailing: 800 University Ave. W, Minot, ND 58703-2250 t) 701-838-1520 littleflowerminot@gmail.com; littleflowerfinance@srt.com littleflowerminot.com Rev. Kenneth Phillips, Pst.; Dcn. Steve Young; Kathy Wentz, Bus. Mgr.; Nancy Magnuson, DRE; CRP Stds.: 41

MOHALL

St. Jerome - 303 E. Main St., Mohall, ND 58761; Mailing: P.O. Box 457, Mohall, ND 58761-0457 t) 701-756-6601 gluger@bismarckdiocese.com mlscatholic.com Rev. Greg Luger, Pst.; Jodi Johnson, DRE; CRP Stds.: 30

MOTT

St. Vincent de Paul - 408 Iowa Ave., Mott, ND 58646 t) 701-824-2651 www.stvincentcatholicchurch.com Rev. Christopher J. Kadrmas, Pst.; Dcn. Ben Auch; Dcn. David M. Crane; CRP Stds.: 75

NEW ENGLAND

St. Mary - 437 Main St., New England, ND 58647; Mailing: PO Box 369, New England, ND 58647-0369 t) 701-579-4312 www.stmarychurchnewengland.com Rev. Dennis R. Schafer, Pst.; Dcn. Victor F. Dvorak; Kristina Ehlis, DRE; CRP Stds.: 76

NEW HRADEC

SS. Peter and Paul - 101 Lafayette Ave., New Hradec, ND 58601; Mailing: 240 E. Broadway St., Dickinson, ND 58601 t) (701) 483-2223 stjoseph@ndsupernet.com Served from St. Joseph's Church in Dickinson. Rev. Justin P. Waltz, Pst.; Rev. Benjamin Wanner, Par. Vicar;

NEW LEIPZIG

St. John the Baptist - 321 2nd Ave., S.E., New Leipzig, ND 58562; Mailing: 408 Iowa Ave., Mott, ND 58646 t) 701-824-2651 stvincentsmott@gmail.com www.stvincentcatholicchurch.com/ Served from the Tri-Parish of St. Vincent de Paul Catholic Church in Mott, North Dakota Rev. Christopher J. Kadrmas, Pst.; CRP Stds.: 7

NEW SALEM

St. Pius V - 202 N. 3rd. St., New Salem, ND 58563-0429; Mailing: P.O. Box C, New Salem, ND 58563-0429 t) 701-843-7061 stpiusv@westriv.com Rev. Stephen Folorunso, Pst.; Carrie Maier, DRE; CRP Stds.: 76

NEW TOWN

St. Anthony - 202 Eagle Dr., New Town, ND 58763; Mailing: P.O. Box 760, New Town, ND 58763 t) 701-627-4423 stanthony@restel.com www.saintanthonypadua.com Served from New Town Rev. Roger A. Synek, Pst.; CRP Stds.: 24

NOONAN

St. Luke - 300 Main St, Noonan, ND 58765; Mailing: P.O. Box 89, Crosby, ND 58730-0089 t) 701-965-6537 stpatscr@nccray.com Served from Crosby. Rev. Patrick Ojedeji, Admin.; Mary Dhuyvetter, DRE;

PARSHALL

St. Bridget - 12 First Ave., N.E., Parshall, ND 58770; Mailing: PO Box 519, Parshall, ND 58770-0519 t) 701-862-3484 saintbridget@restel.com Rev. Terry Wipf, Pst.; Maritza Garza, Bus. Mgr.;

PLAZA

Sacred Heart - 4th Ave. & Reserve St., Plaza, ND 58771; Mailing: P.O. Box 519, Parshall, ND 58770-0519 t) 701-862-3484 saintbridget@restel.com Served from Parshall. Rev. Terry Wipf, Pst.; CRP Stds.: 6

PORTAL

St. John the Baptist - 21 Dakota Ave., Portal, ND 58772; Mailing: P.O. Box 89, Crosby, ND 58730-0089 t) 701-965-6537; 701-933-2869 (CRP) stpatscr@nccray.com Served from Crosby. Rev. Patrick Ojedeji, Admin.; Mary Hawbaker, DRE;

POWERS LAKE

St. James - 400 Main St., Powers Lake, ND 58773; Mailing: P.O. Box 378, Powers Lake, ND 58773 t) 701-664-2445; 701-464-5012 (CRP) cnelson@bismarckdiocese.com stthomastioga.com Served from Tioga. Rev. Corey M. Nelson, Pst.; Sharon Anderson, DRE; CRP Stds.: 31

RALEIGH

St. Gertrude - 7785 St. Gertrude Ave., Raleigh, ND 58564 t) 701-597-3228 catholic3nd.com Served from Flasher Rev. Biju Antony, I.M.S. (India), Admin.; Valeria Noel Wax, DRE; CRP Stds.: 5

RAY

St. Michael - 216 West St., Ray, ND 58849; Mailing: PO Box 505, Ray, ND 58849-0505 t) 701-568-2252 cnelson@bismarckdiocese.com www.stthomastioga.com Served from Tioga. Rev. Corey M. Nelson, Pst.; Krista Becker, DRE; CRP Stds.: 18

REEDER

Sacred Heart - 402 E. 3rd Ave., Reeder, ND 58649; Mailing: 405 3rd St. N., Hettinger, ND 58639-7125 t) 701-567-2772 www.parishesofswnd.com Served from Hettinger. Rev. Raphael Obotama, Pst.; Ashley Fisher, DRE;

REGENT

St. Henry - 150 W. 5th St., Regent, ND 58650; Mailing: 408 Iowa Ave., Mott, ND 58646-7260 t) 701-824-2651 stvincentsmott@gmail.com Served from Mott Rev. Christopher J. Kadrmas, Pst.;

RHAME

St. Mel - 305 1st Ave. W., Rhame, ND 58651; Mailing: 202 1st Ave., S.W., Bowman, ND 58623-4216 t) 701-523-5292 stcharles2@ndsupernet.com Served from Bowman. Rev. Ben Franchuk, Pst.; CRP Stds.: 13

RICHARDTON

St. Mary - 332 2nd St. N., Richardton, ND 58652-7141 t) 701-974-3569 www.stmaryrichardton.com Rev. Thomas Wordekemper, O.S.B., Pst.; Dcn. Robert Bohn; Michelle Tormaschy, DRE; CRP Stds.: 83

St. Stephen, King of Hungary - Hwy. 8 S., Richardton, ND 58652; Mailing: 332 2nd St. N., Richardton, ND 58652-7141 t) 701-974-3569 www.marychurch.org Served from Richardton. Rev. Thomas Wordekemper, O.S.B., Pst.; Michelle Tormaschy, DRE; CRP Stds.: 15

SCRANTON

Sacred Heart - 408 Main St., Scranton, ND 58653; Mailing: 405 3rd St. N., Hettinger, ND 58639-7125 t) 701-567-2772 www.parishesofswnd.com Served from Hettinger. Rev. Raphael Obotama, Pst.; Ashley Fisher, DRE; CRP Stds.: 20

SHERWOOD

St. James - 220 4th Ave. E., Sherwood, ND 58782; Mailing: P.O. Box 457, Mohall, ND 58761-0457 t) 701-756-6601 gluger@bismarckdiocese.com mlscatholic.com Served from Mohall. Rev. Greg Luger, Pst.; CRP Stds.: 4

SOUTH HEART

St. Mary - 207 4th St., S.W., South Heart, ND 58655; Mailing: PO Box 189, South Heart, ND 58655-0189 t) 701-677-5886; 701-575-4295 (CRP) Rev. Shane Campbell, Pst.;

ST. ANTHONY

St. Anthony - 2362 County Rd. #136, St. Anthony, ND 58554; Mailing: 801 1st St., S.E., Mandan, ND 58554-4470 t) 701-663-1660 office@myspiritoflife.com; stacey@myspiritoflife.com www.myspiritoflife.com Served from Spirit of Life in Mandan. Rev. Keith N. Streifel, Pst.; Rev. Deacon Gary Mizeur; Rev. Deacon Kevin Leingang; Stacey Bulcher, Admin.; Karen Eggers, DRE; CRP Stds.: 12

STANLEY

Queen of the Most Holy Rosary - 426 2nd St., S.E., Stanley, ND 58784; Mailing: PO Box 159, Stanley, ND 58784-0159 t) 701-628-3405 www.holyrosarystanley.com Rev. Jason R. Signalness, Pst.; Elonda Davidson, DRE; Reann Bohrer, Bus. Mgr.; CRP Stds.: 85

STRASBURG

Sts. Peter and Paul - 505 N. 2nd St., Strasburg, ND 58573-0322; Mailing: PO Box 322, Strasburg, ND 58573-0322 t) 701-336-7172 stspeterandpaul@bektel.com www.emmonscatholics.org Rev. Shannon G. Lucht, Pst.; Joanne Ternes, DRE; CRP Stds.: 34

TIOGA

St. Thomas - 213 N. Gilbertson St., Tioga, ND 58852-0667; Mailing: PO Box 667, Tioga, ND 58852 t) 701-664-2445 cnelson@bismarckdiocese.com; saintthomasdre@gmail.com www.stthomastioga.com Rev. Corey M. Nelson, Pst.; Sheila E Sabinash, Bus. Mgr.; Kristal Sagaser, DRE; CRP Stds.: 33

TRENTON

St. John the Baptist - 205 2nd St., Trenton, ND 58853; Mailing: P.O. Box K, Williston, ND 58802-1115 t) 701-572-6731 www.sjparish.com Served from Williston. Rev. Russell P. Kovash, Pst.; Rev. Greg Hilzendeger, Par. Vicar; Ray Urbi, Bus. Mgr.; Claudia Ortiz, DRE;

TURTLE LAKE

St. Catherine - 401 Main St., Turtle Lake, ND 58575 t) 701-442-5229; 701-448-9289 (CRP) stcatherines@westriv.com www.centralmcleansaints.com Served from Underwood. Rev. Patrick M. Cunningham, Pst.; CRP Stds.: 10

TWIN BUTTES

St. Joseph - 8050 7th St., N.W., Twin Buttes, ND 58636; Mailing: PO Box 299, Killdeer, ND 58640-0299 t) 701-764-5357 stjosephs@ndsupernet.com stjosephkilldeer.com Served from Killdeer. Rev. Joseph A. Evinger, Pst.; Dcn. Dan Tuhy; CRP Stds.: 9

UNDERWOOD

St. Bonaventure - 505 Grant Ave., Underwood, ND 58576; Mailing: 503 Grant Ave., Underwood, ND 58576-4334 t) 701-442-5229 stbonaventureschurch@westriv.com www.centralmcleansaints.com/ Rev. Patrick M. Cunningham, Pst.; Tammy Sannes, DRE; CRP Stds.: 35

WASHBURN

St. Edwin's Church - 906 Northgate Rd., Washburn, ND 58577; Mailing: PO Box 65, Washburn, ND 58577 t) 701-462-3340 stedwins@westriv.com Served from Underwood. Rev. Patrick M. Cunningham, Pst.; CRP Stds.: 46

WATFORD CITY

Epiphany - 112 6th Ave., N.E., Watford City, ND 58854; Mailing: P.O. Box 670, Watford City, ND 58854 t) 701-842-3505 wcepiphany@gmail.com; wcepiphanydre@gmail.com www.wcepiphany.com Rev. Brian P. Gross, Pst.; Erica Bohn, Youth Min.; Bob Nelson, DRE; Sara Millet, Bus. Mgr.; CRP Stds.: 85

WHITE SHIELD

Sacred Heart - 1594 61st Ave., N.W., White Shield, ND 58540-0870; Mailing: P.O. Box 870, Garrison, ND 58540-0870 t) 701-463-2327 stnicholas@restel.com www.stnicholaschurchgarrison.com Served from Garrison. Rev. Basil Atwell, O.S.B., Pst.;

WILLISTON

St. Joseph - 106 6th St. W., Williston, ND 58802-1115; Mailing: PO Box K, Williston, ND 58802-1115 t) 701-572-6731 parishsecretary@stjparish.com; dre@stjparish.com stjparish.com Rev. Russell P. Kovash, Pst.; Rev. Greg Hilzendeger, Par. Vicar; Dcn. Gerald E. Martin; Claudia Ortiz, DRE; CRP Stds.: 110

St. Joseph School - (Grades PreK-6) 124 6th St. W., Williston, ND 58801 t) 701-572-6384 Narcel Clark, Prin.; Stds.: 217; Lay Tchrs.: 15

WILTON

Sacred Heart - 212 4th St. N., Wilton, ND 58579-0128; Mailing: PO Box 128, Wilton, ND 58579-0128 t) 701-734-8131 sacredht@bektel.com www.sacredhtwilton.com Rev. Msgr. Gene E. Lindemann, Pst.; Emily Hutzenbiler, DRE; CRP Stds.: 44

SCHOOLS: PRESCHOOL THRU HIGH SCHOOL

SCHOOLS

STATE OF NORTH DAKOTA

BISMARCK

Light of Christ Catholic Schools of Excellence - (PAR) (Grades PreK-12) 1025 N. 2nd St., Bismarck, ND 58501 t) 701-751-4883 gvetter@lightofchristschools.org www.lightofchristschools.org Michael Bichler, Prin.; Valerie Kuntz, Prin.; Michele Lind, Prin.; Jessica Pathroff, Prin.; Gerald Vetter, Pres.; Stds.: 1,434; Pr. Tchrs.: 2; Sr. Tchrs.: 1; Lay Tchrs.: 101

DICKINSON

Dickinson Catholic Schools (Trinity Catholic Schools) - (PAR) (Grades PreK-12) 810 Empire Rd., Dickinson, ND 58601 t) 701-483-6092 dcsbusinessoffice@gmail.com www.trinitycatholicschools.com Rev. Grant Dvorak, Chap.; Rev. Christian Smith, Dean; Joshua Kralicek, Prin.; Jolyn Tessier, Prin.; Marya Skaare, Pres.; Sr. Rosemarie Dvorak, Librn.; Rachel Ebach, Librn.; Stds.: 705; Pr. Tchrs.: 2; Sr. Tchrs.: 2; Lay Tchrs.: 49

MINOT

Bishop Ryan Catholic School - (PAR) (Grades PreK-12) 316 11th Ave., N.W., Minot, ND 58703-2260 t) 701-838-3355 president@brhs.com; bnush@brhs.com www.bishopryan.com Rev. Brandon Wolf, Dean; Rev. Gregory Crane, Chap.; Tanya Steckler, Prin.; Rev. Jadyn E. Nelson, Pres.; Stds.: 351; Pr. Tchrs.: 3; Lay Tchrs.: 42

HIGH SCHOOLS

STATE OF NORTH DAKOTA

DICKINSON

Trinity High School - (PAR) (Grades 7-12) 810 Empire Rd., Dickinson, ND 58601 t) 701-483-6081 dcsbusinessoffice@gmail.com www.trinityhighschool.com Marya Skaare, Pres.; Rev. Christian Smith, Dean; Rev. Grant Dvorak, Chap.; Rachel Ebach, Librn.; Stds.: 230; Pr. Tchrs.: 1; Sr. Tchrs.: 1; Lay Tchrs.: 23

INSTITUTIONS LOCATED IN DIOCESE

COLLEGES & UNIVERSITIES [COL]

BISMARCK

University of Mary - 7500 University Dr., Bismarck, ND 58504-9652 t) 701-255-7500 enroll@umary.edu www.umary.edu Rev. Msgr. James P. Shea, Pres.; Rev. Jarad Wolf, Chap.; Rev. Dominic Bouck, Chap.; Diane Fladeland, Vice Pres. Academic Affairs; Stds.: 3,800; Lay Tchrs.: 200; Pr. Tchrs.: 2

CONVENTS, MONASTERIES, AND RESIDENCES FOR WOMEN [CON]

BISMARCK

Annunciation Monastery - 7520 University Dr., Bismarck, ND 58504-9619 t) 701-255-1520 sjzander@annunciationmonastery.org www.annunciationmonastery.org Motherhouse and Novitiate of the Benedictine Sisters of the Annunciation, B.M.V. Rev. Anthony Baker, O.S.B., Chap.; Sr. Nicole Kunze, O.S.B., Prioress; Srs.: 32

St. Mary Sisters - 315 W. Ave. A, Bismarck, ND 58501; Mailing: PO Box 2576, Bismarck, ND 58502-2576 t) 701-557-7837 vocations@stmarysisters.org www.stmarysisters.org Sr. Mary Joseph Campbell, OP, Prioress; Srs.: 4

DICKINSON

Sacred Heart Monastery - 2441 10th Ave. W., Dickinson, ND 58601 t) 701-456-1900 prioress@sacredheartmonastery.com www.sacredheartmonastery.com Motherhouse of the Sisters of the Order of St. Benedict. Sr. Paula Larson, Prioress; Srs.: 15

MANDAN

Servants of the Children of Light - 307 2nd Ave., N.E., Mandan, ND 58554 c) 701-955-3393 srchiaratherese@servantsofthechildrenoflight.org servantsofthechildrenoflight.org Public Association of the Christian Faithful for Women Sr. Chiara Therese Jacobson, Prioress; Srs.: 1

ENDOWMENTS / FOUNDATIONS / TRUSTS [EFT]

BISMARCK

Catholic Foundation of Western North Dakota - 520 N. Washington St, Bismarck, ND 58501; Mailing: P.O. Box 1175, Bismarck, ND 58502 t) (701) 222-3035 www.cfwnd.org Steve Wangler, Pres.;

The Parish Expansion Fund of the Diocese of Bismarck - 520 N. Washington St., Bismarck, ND 58501; Mailing: P.O. Box 1137, Bismarck, ND 58502 t) (701) 222-3035 Most Rev. David D. Kagan, Pres.; Rev. Msgr. Gene E. Lindemann, Vice. Pres.; Dale Eberle, Secy.; Laura J. Huber, Treas.;

DICKINSON

PIA Tegler Benedictine Foundation - 2441 10th Ave. W., Dickinson, ND 58601 t) 701-456-1900 busoffice@sacredheartmonastery.com www.sacredheartmonastery.com Sr. Michael Emond, Pres.;

Sacred Heart Benedictine Foundation - 2441 10th Ave. W., Dickinson, ND 58601 t) 701-456-1900 busoffice@sacredheartmonastery.com www.sacredheartmonastery.com Sr. Paula Larson, Pres.;

WILLISTON

Mercy Medical Foundation - 1301 15th Ave. W., Williston, ND 58801 t) 701-774-7466 thewillistonfoundation@catholichealth.net; brittny.mayo@commonspirit.org www.chistalexiushealth.org Andrew J. Santos III, SVP, Mission Integration;

HOSPITALS / HEALTH SERVICES [HOS]

BISMARCK

St. Alexius Medical Center - 900 E. Broadway, Bismarck, ND 58506-5510; Mailing: P.O. Box 5510, Bismarck, ND 58506 t) 701-530-7000 missionintegrationmidwest@commonspirit.org www.chistalexiushealth.org Sisters of St. Benedict. Reed E. Reyman, Pres.; Andrew J Santos III, SVP, Mission Integration; Bed Capacity: 287; Asstd. Annu.: 125,000; Staff: 1,350

DICKINSON

St. Joseph's Hospital and Health Center - 2500 Fairway St., Dickinson, ND 58601 t) (701) 456-4000 missionintegrationmidwest@commonspirit.org chistalexiushealth.org Carol Enderle, Pres.; Andrew J Santos III, SVP, Mission Integration; Bed Capacity: 25; Asstd. Annu.: 84,042; Staff: 329

GARRISON

Garrison Memorial Hospital (CHI St. Alexius Health Garrison) - 407 3rd Ave., S.E., Garrison, ND 58540-7235 t) 701-463-2275 missionintegrationmidwest@commonspirit.org chistalexiushealth.org Reed E. Reyman, Pres.; Andrew J Santos III, SVP, Mission Integration; Bed Capacity: 48; Asstd. Annu.: 9,133; Staff: 94

WILLISTON

Mercy Medical Center - Affiliate of Catholic Health Initiatives - 1301 15th Ave. W., Williston, ND 58801 t) 701-774-7400 missionintegrationmidwest@commonspirit.org www.chistalexiushealth.org/williston Andrew J Santos III, SVP, Mission Integration; Bed Capacity: 25; Asstd. Annu.: 108,218; Staff: 380

MISCELLANEOUS [MIS]

BISMARCK

Bismarck Diocese - 520 N. Washington St., Bismarck, ND 58501; Mailing: P.O. Box 1575, Bismarck, ND 58502 t) (701) 222-3035 www.bismarckdiocese.com Dale Eberle, Chancellor;

DICKINSON

Benedictine Sponsorship Board - 2441 10th Ave. W., Dickinson, ND 58601 t) 701-456-1900 prioress@sacredheartmonastery.com www.sacredheartmonastery.com Sr. Paula Larson, Pres.;

Cursillo of the Bismarck Diocese - ; Mailing: P.O. Box 263, Dickinson, ND 58601 c) 701-290-0499 kosteleckyfarm@ndsupernet.com Daryl Kostelecky, Dir.;

HEBRON

St. Clement Oratory of Haymarsh - 6787 County Rd. 140, Hebron, ND 58638; Mailing: 520 N. Washington St., Bismarck, ND 58502-1137 t) 701-425-0794 bnaslund@bismarckdiocese.com bismarckdiocese.com/oratory Served from Diocese of Bismarck. Dcn. Brent Naslund, Admin.;

MANDAN

Bismarck Guild - 4907 S. Bay Dr., S.E., Mandan, ND 58554 t) 701-220-2625 doctormercy@icloud.com bismarckdiocese.com/physiciansguild Rev. Msgr. Thomas J. Richter, Chap.;

World Apostolate of Fatima - 802 Division St., N.E., Mandan, ND 58554 t) 701-400-0233 doughelbing@gmail.com Dcn. Douglas Helbing, Pres.;

PORCUPINE

Oratory of St. James, Porcupine - ; Mailing: P.O. Box 394, Fort Yates, ND 58538-0394 t) (701) 854-3473 www.catholicindianmission.com Served from Ft. Yates. Rev. Chad Gion, Pst.; Rev. Jolly George, Par. Vicar; Bro. George Maufort, S.D.S.; Sandy Gallagher, Bus. Mgr.;

RICHARDTON

Sacred Heart Mission - 418 3rd Ave. W., Richardton, ND 58652-7100 t) 701-974-3315 odo@assumptionabbey.com Rev. Odo Muggli, O.S.B., Secy.;

SELFRIDGE

Oratory of St. Philomena, Selfridge - Rural Rte., Selfridge, ND 58568; Mailing: P.O. Box 394, Fort Yates, ND 58538-0394 t) (701) 854-3473 www.catholicindianmission.com Served from Ft. Yates. Rev. Chad Gion, Pst.; Rev. Jolly George, Par. Vicar; Bro. George Maufort, S.D.S.; Sandy Gallagher, Bus. Mgr.;

SOLEN

Oratory of Sacred Heart, Solen - 206 Rice St., Solen, ND 58570; Mailing: P.O. Box 394, Fort Yates, ND 58538-0394 t) (701) 854-3473 www.catholicindianmission.com Served from Ft. Yates. Rev. Chad Gion, Pst.; Rev. Jolly George, Par. Vicar; Bro. George Maufort, S.D.S.; Sandy Gallagher, Bus. Mgr.;

MONASTERIES AND RESIDENCES FOR PRIESTS AND BROTHERS [MON]

RICHARDTON

Assumption Abbey - 418 3rd Ave. W., Richardton, ND 58652; Mailing: P.O. Box A, Richardton, ND 58652 t) 701-974-3315 monks@assumptionabbey.com www.assumptionabbey.com Rt. Rev. Daniel Maloney, O.S.B., Abbot; Rev. Manuel Cely, O.S.B., Prior; Bro. Michael Taffe, O.S.B., Prior; Bro. Jacob Darren Deiss, Subprior; Rev. Gonzalo Blanco, O.S.B., Subprior; Rev. Basil Atwell, O.S.B., Pst.; Rev. Thomas Wordekemper, O.S.B., Pst.; Rev. Hugo L. Blotsky, O.S.B., Assoc. Pst.; Rev. Benedict Fischer, O.S.B., Prof.; Rev. Anthony Baker, O.S.B., Chap.; Rev. James Kilzer, O.S.B., Bus.

Mgr.; Rev. Odo Muggli, O.S.B., Bus. Mgr.; Bro. Alban Petesch, O.S.B., Dir.; Rev. Nicolas Cano, O.S.B., In Res.; Rev. Valerian Odermann, O.S.B., In Res.; Rev. Julian Nix, O.S.B., In Res.; Rev. Boniface Muggli, O.S.B., In Res.; Brs.: 26; Priests: 16

NURSING / REHABILITATION / CONVALESCENCE / ELDERLY CARE [NUR]

BISMARCK

Benedictine Living Communities - Bismarck, Inc. - 4580 Coleman St., Bismarck, ND 58503 t) 701-751-4224 kurran.opp@benedictineliving.org www.benedictineliving.org/bismarck-nd/ Kurran C. Opp, Exec. Dir.; Asstd. Annu.: 350; Staff: 226

Emmaus Place - 1020 N. 26th St., Bismarck, ND 58501; Mailing: PO Box 1137, Bismarck, ND 58502-1137 t) 701-258-2618 glindemann@bismarckdiocese.com Priests retirement home. Rev. Al Bitz; Rev. William Callery; Rev. Paul Cervinski; Rev. Leonard A. Eckroth; Rev. Jerome G. Kautzman; Rev. Marvin J. Klemmer; Asstd. Annu.: 6; Staff: 5

***Marillac Manor, an affiliate of Good Samaritan Society and Sanford Health.** - 1016 N. 28th St., Bismarck, ND 58501 t) 701-323-1871 agreer@good-sam.com good-sam.com Marillac Manor is an Independent Senior Living Community with religious and social opportunities Angela Greer, Dir.; Asstd. Annu.: 90; Staff: 5

***St. Vincent's, A Prospera Community** - 1021 N. 26 St., Bismarck, ND 58501-3199 t) 701-323-1999 prioress@sacredheartmonastery.com http:\\www.good-sam.com Kaylene Kritlinger, Admin.; Asstd. Annu.: 200; Staff: 180

DICKINSON

Benedictine Living Communities, Inc. - 851 Fourth Ave. E., Dickinson, ND 58601 t) 701-456-7242 jon.frantsvog@benedictineliving.org www.benedictineliving.org/dickinson-nd/ Operated by Benedictine Living Communities, Inc. Jon Frantsvog, Exec. Dir.; Asstd. Annu.: 350; Staff: 133

GARRISON

Benedictine Living Communities, Inc. (Benedictine Living Community | Garrison) - 609 4th Ave., N.E., Garrison, ND 58540 t) 701-463-2226 scott.foss@benedictineliving.org www.benedictineliving.org/garrison-nd/ Scott Foss, Exec. Dir.; Asstd. Annu.: 70; Staff: 59

SPECIAL CARE FACILITIES [SPF]

DICKINSON

Benedictine Living Communities, Inc. (Benedict Court) - 830 2nd Ave. E., Dickinson, ND 58601 t) 701-456-7242 jon.frantsvog@benedictineliving.org www.benedictineliving.org/dickinson-nd/ Jon Frantsvog, Exec. Dir.; Bed Capacity: 26; Asstd. Annu.: 100; Staff: 30

SENTINEL BUTTE

Home On The Range - 16351 I-94, Sentinel Butte, ND 58654-9500 t) 701-872-3745 lauraf@hotrnd.com www.hotrnd.com Qualified Residential Treatment Program for youth ages 12-19 Rev. Daniel J. Berg, Chap.; Laura Feldmann, Exec.; Bed Capacity: 36; Asstd. Annu.: 97; Staff: 90

An asterisk (*) denotes an organization that has established tax-exempt status directly with the IRS and is not covered by the USCCB Group Ruling.

Diocese of Boise

(Dioecesis Xylopolitana)

MOST REVEREND PETER F. CHRISTENSEN

Bishop of Boise; ordained May 25, 1985; appointed Bishop of Superior June 28, 2007; consecrated September 14, 2007; installed September 23, 2007; appointed Bishop of Boise November 4, 2014; installed December 17, 2014. Chancery Office, 1501 Federal Way, Boise, ID 83705.

Chancery Office: 1501 Federal Way, Ste. 400, Boise, ID 83705. T: 208-342-1311; F: 208-342-0224. mraper@rcdb.org

ESTABLISHED AS A VICARIATE-APOSTOLIC MARCH 3, 1868.

Square Miles 83,557.

Erected a Diocese by His Holiness Pope Leo XIII, August 26, 1893

Comprises the State of Idaho, with a Total Population of 1,840,000

Legal Title: "Roman Catholic Diocese of Boise".

For legal titles of parishes and diocesan institutions, consult the Chancery Office.

STATISTICAL OVERVIEW

Personnel
Bishop....1
Priests: Diocesan Active in Diocese....54
Priests: Diocesan Active Outside Diocese....4
Priests: Retired, Sick or Absent....26
Number of Diocesan Priests....84
Religious Priests in Diocese....25
Total Priests in your Diocese....109
Ordinations:
Transitional Deacons....2
Permanent Deacons in Diocese....99
Total Brothers....4
Total Sisters....45

Parishes
Parishes....50
With Resident Pastor:
Resident Diocesan Priests....44
Resident Religious Priests....4
Without Resident Pastor:
Administered by Priests....2

Professional Ministry Personnel:
Lay Ministers....31

Welfare
Catholic Hospitals....4
Total Assisted....206,229
Health Care Centers....4
Total Assisted....183,377

Educational
Students from This Diocese....15
Total Seminarians....15
High Schools, Diocesan and Parish....2
Total Students....971
Elementary Schools, Diocesan and Parish....14
Total Students....3,086
Catechesis / Religious Education:
High School Students....1,863
Elementary Students....4,237
Total Students under Catholic Instruction....10,172

Teachers in Diocese:
Priests....1
Lay Teachers....276

Vital Statistics
Receptions into the Church:
Infant Baptism Totals....1,855
Minor Baptism Totals....300
Adult Baptism Totals....173
Received into Full Communion....279
First Communions....1,771
Confirmations....1,300
Marriages:
Catholic....323
Interfaith....61
Total Marriages....384
Deaths....946
Total Catholic Population....202,301
Total Population....1,939,033

LEADERSHIP

Executive Administrative Assistant to Bishop/Vicar General - Marisela Baca;
Vicar General - Rev. Caleb Vogel, Vicar;
Chancery Office - t) 208-342-1311 Mark L. Raper, Chancellor (mraper@rcdb.org);
Director of Diocesan Projects - Christian Welp (cwelp@rcdb.org);
Office of Pastoral Ministries - Dcn. Robert Barros-Bailey;
Notaries - Mark L. Raper (mraper@rcdb.org); Michelle Smith;
Diocesan Tribunal - t) 208-344-1344
Adjutant Judicial Vicar -
Director - Mark L. Raper;
Ecclesiastical Notaries - Rev. Chase R. Hasenoehrl; Mark L. Raper; Colleen Cunningham;
Judicial Vicar - Rev. Joseph F. McDonald III;
Promoter of Justice - Mark L. Raper;
Judges - Rev. Gerald Funke; Mark L. Raper (mraper@rcdb.org); Rev. Francisco H. Godinez;
Defenders of the Bond - Rev. Msgr. Andrew Schumacher; Mark L. Raper (mraper@rcdb.org);
College of Consultors - Rev. Henry Carmona; Rev. Camilo Garcia; Very Rev. John R. Worster;
Deans - Rev. Henry Carmona, Eastern Deanery; Very Rev. John R. Worster, West Central Deanery; Rev. Robert P. Cook, Northern Deanery (rcook@sacredheartboise.org);
Presbyteral Council - Rev. Julio Vicente; Rev. Henry Carmona; Rev. Camilo Garcia;
Priest Personnel Commission - Rev. Camilo Garcia; Rev. Mariusz Majewski (fathermariusz@gmail.com); Rev. Joseph F. McDonald III;
Finance Council - Most Rev. Peter F. Christensen; Rev. Caleb Vogel, Ex Officio; Tom Zabala;
Building Commission - Nick Guho; Tom Zabala; Mark Gier;
Priest Retirement Committee - Rev. Caleb Vogel, Ex Officio; Rev. Paul H. Wander; Rev. John R. Worster;

OFFICES AND DIRECTORS

Bureau of Information - Idaho Catholic Register - Dcn. Eugene Fadness, Editor;
Campus Ministry - t) 208-343-2128 Andrew Furphy, Coord. Campus Min.;
Catholic Campaign for Human Development - Mark L. Raper (mraper@rcdb.org);
Catholic Charities of Idaho, Inc. - Douglas Alles, Exec.; Most Rev. Peter F. Christensen;
Catholic Communications Center - Dcn. Eugene Fadness, Dir.;
Catholic Daughters of the Americas - Rev. Mariusz Majewski, Chap. (fathermariusz@gmail.com); Louise Bluhm, State Regent (lrbluhm1998@roadrunner.com);
Catholic Hospitals - Dcn. Robert Barros-Bailey;
Catholic Liturgical Commission - t) 208-342-1311 Letitia Thornton, Chair (tthornton@rcdb.org); Jake Ineck; Larry Harrison;
Catholic Relief Services - Mark L. Raper (mraper@rcdb.org);
Catholic Schools - Dr. Sarah Quilici, Supt.;
Catholic Scouts - t) 208-238-5037 David L. Davis, Chair; Rev. Roger LaChance, Chap. (fr.lachancercdb@gmail.com);
Censor Librorum - t) 208-746-3362 Rev. Msgr. Andrew Schumacher;
Children, Youth and Adult Protection Director - t) 208-350-7560 Mark L. Raper (mraper@rcdb.org);
Cursillo Movement - Hoang Tan, Admin.; Steven Murray, Region XII Lay Dir. (smurray7880@gmail.com); Rev. Jose T. Ramirez, Spiritual Dir. (Spanish);
Development/Stewardship Office - t) 208-342-1311 Charles Lawrence, Dir.; Margaret Hampton (mhampton@rcdb.org);
Director of Office of Worship - Letitia Thornton, Dir. (tthornton@rcdb.org);
Director of Religious Education and Catechetical Leadership - Jackie Hopper (jhopper@rcdb.org);
Director of the Permanent Diaconate - Dcn. Robert Barros-Bailey, Dir.;
Director of Youth and Young Adult Evangelization - Dcn. Salvador Carranza, Dir. (scarranza@rcdb.org); Cathy Wheaton, Admin. Asst.;
Finance Officer - Charles Lawrence;
Human Resources - Charles Lawrence; Mark L. Raper (mraper@rcdb.org); Dr. Sarah Quilici;
Idaho Catholic Foundation - Most Rev. Peter F. Christensen, Pres.; Micheal Treinan;
Idaho Council of Catholic Women - Pierrette Harris, Pres. (pierrettemadhare62@gmail.com); Rev. Eladio Vieyra, Moderator;
Knights of Columbus - Rev. Benjamin R. Uhlenkott, Chap.; Roy Bartholomay, Contact;
National Board Member - John Dahl;
Newspaper - Most Rev. Peter F. Christensen, Publisher; Dcn. Eugene Fadness, Editor; Ann Bixby, Advertising/Business/Circulation;
Priest Retirement Plan -
Propagation of the Faith - Mark L. Raper (mraper@rcdb.org);
Respect Life/Prison Ministry Coordinator - Dcn. Robert Barros-Bailey;
St. Vincent de Paul Society - Jack Dahl, Pres.;
Vocations - Rev. Nathan Dail, Dir.; Charles Lawrence, Admin. Coord.; Cheri McCormack, Admin. Asst.;

PARISHES, MISSIONS, AND CLERGY

STATE OF IDAHO

AMERICAN FALLS

Presentation of the Lord - 376 Roosevelt St., American Falls, ID 83211; Mailing: P.O. Box 117, American Falls, ID 83211 t) 208-226-5217 im4jcru@gmail.com www.presentationofthelord.org Rev. Gabriel Morales, Admin.; Victoria Rodriguez, DRE; Debra Annen, Bus. Mgr.; CRP Stds.: 215
St. John - 1501 W Sheeptrail Rd., Pingree, ID 83262
St. Mary - t) (208) 226-5217
Blessed Sacrament - 667 S. 4th W., Aberdeen, ID 83210 t) 208-220-0868 im4jmjru@gmail.com

BLACKFOOT

St. Bernard's - 583 W. Sexton St., Blackfoot, ID 83221 t) 208-785-1935 stbernardsblackfoot.org Rev. Jose de Jesus Gonzalez, Pst.; Dcn. Jeff Powers; Julie Lopez, DRE; CRP Stds.: 46
Blessed Kateri Tekakwitha - Sheepskin Rd., Fort Hall, ID 83203 t) (208) 785-1935 www.stbernardsblackfoot.org

BOISE

Cathedral of St. John the Evangelist - 807 N. 8th St., Boise, ID 83702; Mailing: 707 N. 8th St., Boise, ID 83702 t) 208-342-3511 danielg@boisecathedral.org boisecathedral.org Rev. Mariusz Majewski, Rector; Rev. Aleksander Dembowski, Par. Vicar; Dcn. William Burns; Dcn. Mark Geraty; Dcn. Thomas Mannschreck; Dcn. Derrick O'Neill; Dcn. Daniel Gamboa, Admin.; Monica Gamboa, DRE; CRP Stds.: 132
St. Joseph's School - (Grades K-8) 825 W. Fort St., Boise, ID 83702 t) 208-342-4909 www.stjoes.com Randy McCormick, Prin.; Amanda Kuznia, Vice Prin.; Stds.: 380; Lay Tchrs.: 21
St. Mark's - 7960 W. Northview, Boise, ID 83704 t) 208-375-6651 office@stmarksboise.org www.stmarksboise.org Rev. Paul O'Donnell, Pst.; Rev. Adrian Leszko, Par. Vicar; Dcn. Don Blythe; Dcn. Clyde Brinegar; Dcn. Mike Lowe; Dcn. Terry Nelson; Dcn. Chris Privon; Dcn. Joseph Rodriguez; Ginger Mortensen, DRE; CRP Stds.: 233
St. Mark's Catholic School - (Grades PreK-8) 7503 W. Northview, Boise, ID 83704 t) 208-375-6654 dgordon@stmarksschoolboise.com www.stmarksboise.com Donna Gordon, Prin.; Beth Rosania, Librn.; Stds.: 353; Lay Tchrs.: 22
St. Mary's - 2612 W. State St., Boise, ID 83702 t) 208-344-2597 www.stmarysboise.org Rev. John R. Worster, Pst.; Rev. Jesus Camacho, Assoc. Pst.; Dcn. Imanol Betikoetxea; Dcn. John Carpenter; Dcn. Eugene Fadness; Monica Pittman, Bus. Mgr.; CRP Stds.: 75
St. Mary's School - (Grades K-8) 2620 W. State St., Boise, ID 83702 t) 208-342-7476 amcapanella@stmarys-boise.org; bolmes@stmarys-boise.org www.stmarys-boise.org Brian Olmes, Prin.; Amanda Campanella, Bus. Mgr.; Stds.: 140; Lay Tchrs.: 15
Our Lady of the Rosary - 1500 E. Wright, Boise, ID 83706 t) 208-343-9041 olrboise.org Rev. Dat Vu, Pst.; Dcn. Louis Aaron; Dcn. Peter John Cuppage; Dcn. Jim Pasker; Dcn. Mike Servatius; Tina Punnoose, DRE; Teresa DeVino, Spiritual Adv./Care Srvcs.; Noelle Atha, Youth Min.; CRP Stds.: 185
St. Joseph's - 200 E. Wallula St., Idaho City, ID 83706
St. Paul's Student Center - 1915 University Dr., Boise, ID 83706 t) 208-367-1110 www.broncocatholic.org Rev. Nathan Dail, Chap.;
Risen Christ Catholic Community - 11511 W. Lake Hazel Rd., Boise, ID 83709 t) 208-362-6584; 208-362-6584 x107 (CRP) office@risenchristboise.org www.risenchristboise.org Rev. Benjamin R. Uhlenkott; Dcn. Michael Eisenbeiss; Dcn. Ted Vermaas; Audrey Weiss, Parish Life Coord.; Jennifer Hutchings, DRE; Melissa Guerra, Dir.; CRP Stds.: 76
Sacred Heart - 811 S. Latah St., Boise, ID 83705-0127 t) 208-344-8311 office@sacredheartboise.org www.sacredheartboise.org Rev. Roger Fernando, Pst.; Rev. Costance Swai, ALCP, Par. Vicar; Dcn. Rick Bonney; Dcn. Jude Gary; Dcn. Daniel Vawser; Linda Graefe, Admin.; Leigha Zeiszler, Youth Min.; Deborah Fischer, DRE; Janet Rollinger, Bus. Mgr.; CRP Stds.: 49
Sacred Heart School - (Grades PreK-8) 3901 Cassia St., Boise, ID 83705 t) 208-344-9738 jloffer@sacredheartboise.com www.sacredheartboise.com Sara Cox, Prin.; Stds.: 215; Lay Tchrs.: 10

BONNERS FERRY

St. Ann's - 6712 El Paso, Bonners Ferry, ID 83805 t) 208-267-3339; 208-267-2852 (CRP) stannbonnersferry@gmail.com stannsbonnersferry.org Rev. Antony Chinnabathini, Admin.; CRP Stds.: 16

BUHL

Immaculate Conception - 1631 Poplar St., Buhl, ID 83316; Mailing: P.O. Box 626, Buhl, ID 83316 t) 208-543-5136 icbuhlchurch@gmail.com www.icbuhl.org/ Rev. Jorge E. Garcia, Pst.; Dcn. James McCaughey; Dcn. John Plank; Yolanda Hernandez, DRE; CRP Stds.: 67
St. Catherine's - 406 N. State St., Hagerman, ID 83332 t) 208-837-6592 immconchurch@qwestoffice.net

BURLEY

St. Therese Little Flower - 1601 Oakley Ave., Burley, ID 83318 t) 208-678-5453 masfut421@gmail.com; litflowerch@pmt.org www.catholicburley.com Rev. Eladio Vieyra, Pst.; Melissa Santana, DRE; Brenda Sanchez, Bus. Mgr.; CRP Stds.: 290

CALDWELL

Our Lady of the Valley - 1122 W. Linden St., Caldwell, ID 83605 t) 208-459-3653 x3001 churchoffice@olvcaldwell.org www.olvcaldwell.org/ Rev. Jose T. Ramirez, Pst.; Rev. German Ruis Rebollo, Par. Vicar; Dcn. Humberto Almeida; Dcn. Toby Green; Dcn. Kerry Harris; CRP Stds.: 425

COEUR D'ALENE

St. Pius X - 625 E. Haycraft, Coeur d'Alene, ID 83815 t) 208-765-5108 info@stpiuscda.org www.stpiuscda.org Rev. Leonard MacMillan, Pst.; Dcn. Chris Stewart, Pst. Assoc.; CRP Stds.: 106

St. Thomas the Apostle - 919 E. Indiana Ave., Coeur d'Alene, ID 83814 t) 208-664-9259 secretary@stthomascda.org stthomascda.org Rev. Remigius Ihim, Pst.; CRP Stds.: 80

St. Thomas Parish Center - 406 N. 10th St., Coeur d'Alene, ID 83814 t) 208-664-4327 businessmanager@stthomascda.org

COTTONWOOD

St. Mary's - 503 Garrett St., Cottonwood, ID 83522; Mailing: PO Box 425, Cottonwood, ID 83522-0425 t) 208-962-3214 smrectory@triparishchurches.com triparishchurches.com Rev. Paul H. Wander, Pst.; Dcn. Ryan Uhlenkott; Dcn. Eric Wassmuth; Heather Uhlenkott, DRE; Debbie Chicane, Youth Min.; CRP Stds.: 209

Holy Cross - 1131 Keuterville Rd., Keuterville, ID 83522

COUNCIL

St. Jude Station - 2034-2060 US- 95, Council, ID 83612 t) (208) 549-0088 stagnes@catholicweiser.org See St. Agnes, Weiser for details. Rev. Gerald J. Funke;

DESMET

Sacred Heart - 127 Byrnes Ave., DeSmet, ID 83824; Mailing: Box 306, DeSmet, ID 83824 t) 208-274-5871 ladeauxc@yahoo.com; nmvietri@hotmail.com Rev. Peter Byrne, SJ; Dcn. Nick Vietri; Cecelia Curtis-Cook, DRE; CRP Stds.: 120

Our Lady of Perpetual Help - 1173 East St., Plummer, ID 83851; Mailing: PO Box 325, Plummer, ID 83851 churchlaydee@hotmail.com

St. Michael's - W. 9284 I St., Worley, ID 83876; Mailing: 6706 W Brigantine Dr., Worley, ID 83876 t) 208-686-1023 amoslynn13@yahoo.com

EMMETT

Sacred Heart - 211 E. First St., Emmett, ID 83617 t) 208-365-4320 www.sacredheartemmett.com Rev. Oscar Jaramillo, Pst.; Dcn. Chris Roeper; Dcn. Alan Shaber; CRP Stds.: 167

St. Jude - 1056 Banks Lowman Rd., Garden Valley, ID 83622 shc@qestoffice.net Rev. Oscar Jarmillo, Pst.;

FERDINAND

Assumption - 460 Maple St., Ferdinand, ID 83526; Mailing: P.O. Box 425, Cottonwood, ID 83522-0425 t) 208-962-3214 smrectory@triparishchurches.com www.triparishchurches.com Rev. Paul H. Wander, Pst.; Dcn. Ryan Uhlenkott; Dcn. Eric Wassmuth; Heather Uhlenkott, DRE; Debbie Chicane, Youth Min.; CRP Stds.: 209

FRUITLAND

Corpus Christi Catholic Church - 900 N.W. 7th St., Fruitland, ID 83619 t) 208-452-5778 www.cccatholic.org Rev. Francisco H. Godinez, Pst.; Gabrielle Baines, DRE; CRP Stds.: 102

GARDEN VALLEY

St. Jude's - 1056 Banks Lowman Rd., Garden Valley, ID 83622; Mailing: 211 E. 1st St., Emmett, ID 83617 t) 208-365-4320 shc@qwestoffice.net See Sacred Heart, Emmett for details. Rev. Oscar Jaramillo, Pst.;

GENESEE

St. Mary's Station - 138 N. Jackson St., Genesee, ID 83832 t) 208-882-4813 See Contact Info for St. Mary's Parish in Moscow. See St. Augustine's, Moscow for details. Rev. Joseph F. McDonald III, Pst.; CRP Stds.: 20

GLENNS FERRY

Our Lady of Limerick Station - 21 W. Arthur, Glenns Ferry, ID 83623; Mailing: P.O. Box 310, Mountain Home, ID 83647 t) (208) 587-4132 siphosam@icloud.com Rev. Sipho Mathabela, Pst.;

GOODING

St. Elizabeth's - 1515 California St., Gooding, ID 83330; Mailing: Box 147, Gooding, ID 83330-0147 t) 208-934-5634 Rev. Carlos Rosero, Pst.; Denise Ervin, DRE; Cecilia Leija, DRE; Dcn. Javier Leija; CRP Stds.: 48

St. Anthony's - 585 2nd Ave. E., Wendell, ID 83355; Mailing: P.O. Box 811, Wendell, ID 83355 www.stelizabethgooding.com Diana Mers-Kelly, Bus. Mgr.;

GRANGEVILLE

SS. Peter and Paul - 625 Lake St., Grangeville, ID 83530 t) 208-983-0403 stspeterandpaulparish.org/ Rev. Anthony Obgonna Amadi, Pst.; Catherine Calovich, DRE; CRP Stds.: 81

SS. Peter and Paul School - (Grades PreK-8) 330 S. B St., Grangeville, ID 83530 t) 208-983-2182 rmahoney@myspps.org www.myspps.org Rhett Mahoney, Prin.; Stds.: 79; Lay Tchrs.: 7

Holy Trinity - 506 Willow St., Nezperce, ID 83543; Mailing: P.O Box 65, Nez Perce, ID 83543 t) (208) 937-1095

Sacred Heart - 285 River St., White Bird, ID 83554; Mailing: 625 Lake St., Grangeville, ID 83530 office@stpeterandpaulparish.org

GREENCREEK

St. Anthony's - 1070 Greencreek Rd., Greencreek, ID 83533; Mailing: P.O. Box 425, Cottonwood, ID 83522-0425 t) 208-962-3214 smrectory@triparishchurches.com www.triparishchurches.com Rev. Paul H. Wander, Pst.; Dcn. Ryan Uhlenkott; Dcn. Eric Wassmuth; Heather Uhlenkott, DRE; Debbie Chicane, Youth Min.; CRP Stds.: 209

HAGERMAN

St. Catherine's - 466 N. State St., Hagerman, ID 83332 t) 208-837-6592; (208) 543-5136 icbuhlchurch@gmail.com www.icbuhl.org/ See Immaculate Conception, Buhl for details. Rev. Camilo Garcia, Pst.;

HAILEY

St. Charles Borromeo - 313 1st. Ave. S., Hailey, ID 83333; Mailing: PO Box 789, Hailey, ID 83333 t) 208-788-3024 stcharleshailey@gmail.com www.stcharleshailey.org Rev. Ronald Wekerle, Pst.; Dcn. Luis Ruiz; CRP Stds.: 147

Immaculate Conception - 201 Camas St. W., Fairfield, ID 83333

IDAHO FALLS

St. John Paul II Parish - 145 E. 9th St., Idaho Falls, ID 83404 t) 208-522-4366 parish.office@ifcatholics.net ifcatholics.net Rev. Francisco Q. Flores, Pst.; Rev. John Gathungu, Par. Vicar; Rev. Mark Uhlenkott, Par. Vicar; Dcn. Jason Batalden; Dcn. Tom Middleton; Dcn. Alvaro Ponce; Dcn. Wence Rodriquez; CRP Stds.: 624

Holy Rosary Bi-Parish Catholic School - (Grades PreSchool-6) 161 9th St., Idaho Falls, ID 83404 t) 208-522-7781 hrsoffice@holyrosaryschoolif.org www.holyrosaryschoolif.org Carina VanPelt, Prin.; Stds.: 156; Lay Tchrs.: 7

St. Anthony's - 657 N. 2872 Rd. E., Roberts, ID 83444; Mailing: 145 E. 9th St., Idaho Falls, ID 83404

St. Ann's - 1084 Hwy. 33, Mud Lake, ID 83450; Mailing: 145 E. 9th St., Idaho Falls, ID 83404

JEROME

St. Jerome's - 216 2nd Ave. E., Jerome, ID 83338; Mailing: Box 169, Jerome, ID 83338 t) 208-324-8794 stjeromecoordinator@gmail.com www.stjeromeid.org/ Rev. Adrian Vazquez, Pst.; Dcn. John Baumbach;

KAMIAH

St. Catherine of Siena - 407 7th St., Kamiah, ID 83536-0685; Mailing: P O Box 685, Kamiah, ID 83536 t) 208-935-2130 saintcatherines.weebly.com Rev. Bruno Mbamobi, SMMM, Admin.; Jeanie Stettler, DRE; CRP Stds.: 19

KELLOGG

St. Rita's - 27 Kellogg Ave., Kellogg, ID 83837-2626 t) 208-784-7361 Rev. Jerome Montez, O.S.B., Sacr. Min.; Dcn. Tom Kilbourne;

LEWISTON

All Saints Catholic Parish - 3330 14th St., Lewiston, ID 83501 t) 208-743-1012 www.allsaintslewiston.org Rev. Michael A. St. Marie, Pst.; Rev. Joshua Falce, Par. Vicar; Dcn. Christopher Davies; Dcn. Matt Johnston; Dcn. George Ivory; CRP Stds.: 113

All Saints Catholic School - (Grades PreK-8) 3326 14th St., Lewiston, ID 83501 t) 208-743-4411 dhammrich@ascs-pk6.org www.ascs-pk6.org Denise Hammrich, Prin.; Stds.: 243; Lay Tchrs.: 11

MCCALL

Our Lady of the Lake - 501 Cross Rd., McCall, ID 83638; Mailing: PO Box 821, McCall, ID 83638 t) 208-634-5474 Rev. Bradley Neely, Pst.; Dcn. Floyd Loomis; Dcn. Derek Williamson;

St. Katharine Drexel, Cascade - 101 Vista Point Bvld., Cascade, ID 83611 ollidaho.org

St. Jerome's - 318 S. B St., Riggins, ID 83549 ollidaho.org

MELBA

St. Joseph's Chapel - 504 Randolph Ave, Melba, ID 83641; Mailing: 1515 8th St. S., Nampa, ID 83651 t) 208-466-7031 mdeleon@stpaulsnampa.org Rev. Justin Brady, Pst.; CRP Stds.: 68

MERIDIAN

Holy Apostles - 6300 N. Meridian Rd., Meridian, ID 83646; Mailing: PO Box 708, Meridian, ID 83680 t) 208-888-1182 llawrence@holyapostles.net www.holyapostlesmeridian.net Rev. Vitalis Onyeama, SMMM, Pst.; Rev. Emmanuel Chinedu, Par. Vicar; Dcn. Bill Bieker; Dcn. Thomas Blazek; Dcn. Malherbe Desert; Dcn. Ralph Flager; Dcn. Gerald D. Pera; Dcn. Steve Rayburn; Dcn. Bernard Rekiere; Dcn. David Shackley; Dcn. Ed Spano; Jennifer Severance, DRE; Mary Wax, RCIA Coord.; Sandra Carranza, Pst. Assoc.; Kathy Rayburn, Pst. Assoc.; Amy Urian, Youth Min.; Jake Ineck, Music Min.; CRP Stds.: 483

Holy Apostles Columbarium - 6300 N Meridian Rd, Meridian, ID 83646 t) (208) 888-1182 x403 holyapostlesmeridian.net

St. Ignatius Catholic School - (Grades PreK-8) 6180 N. Meridian Rd., Meridian, ID 83646 t) 208-888-4759 akane@stignatiusmeridian.org www.stignatiusmeridian.org Andi Kane, Prin.; Troy Partin, Vice Prin.; Carolyn Brandenburg, Bus. Mgr.; Brad Childers, Librn.; Stds.: 472; Lay Tchrs.: 25

MOSCOW

St. Augustine's - 628 Deakin Ave., Moscow, ID 83843; Mailing: P.O. Box 3457, Moscow, ID 83843 t) 208-882-4613 www.vandalcatholic.com (Catholic Center) Rev. Chase R. Hasenoehrl, Pst.; Dcn. Verne Geidl; Dcn. Dennis Thomas; David Klement, Music Min.; CRP Stds.: 35

St. Mary's - 725 Spruce St., Potlatch, ID 83855 vandalcatholic@outlook.com

St. Mary's - 618 E. First St., Moscow, ID 83843; Mailing: PO Box 9106, Moscow, ID 83843 t) 208-882-4813 stmarysparishmoscow.org/ Rev. Joseph F. McDonald III, Pst.; Dcn. George Canney; CRP Stds.: 20

St. Mary's School - (Grades PreSchool-8) 412 N. Monroe, Moscow, ID 83843 t) 208-882-2121 office@stmarysmoscow.com; sizzo@stmarysmoscow.com www.stmarysmoscow.com Sandy Izzo, Prin.; Stds.: 107; Lay Tchrs.: 10

St. Mary's - 154 N. Jackson St., Genesee, ID 83832 t) (208) 882-4813

MOUNTAIN HOME

Our Lady of Good Counsel - 342 E. Jackson St., Mountain Home, ID 83647; Mailing: P.O. Box 310, Mountain Home, ID 83647 t) 208-587-3046 Rev. Hippolytus Ezenwa, SMMM, Pst.; CRP Stds.: 60

NAMPA

St. Paul's - 510 W. Roosevelt Ave., Nampa, ID 83686; Mailing: 1515 8th St. S., Nampa, ID 83651 t) 208-466-7031 camador@stpaulsnampa.org; mdeleon@stpaulsnampa.org www.nampacatholic.church Rev. Justin Brady, Pst.; Rev. Robert Mendez; Rev. Boniface Osuafor; Dcn. Jose Luis Granados; Dcn. Francisco Amaral; Dcn. Charles Corbalis; Dcn. Brian Flowers; CRP Stds.: 394

St. Paul's School - (Grades PreSchool-8) 1515 8th St. S., Nampa, ID 83651 t) 208-467-3601 www.stpaulsidaho.org Stephany Herrera, Prin.; Stds.: 148; Scholastics: 8; Lay Tchrs.: 12

St. Joseph - 504 Randolph St., Melba, ID 83641

Our Lady of Tears - 1515 8th St. So, Nampa, ID

83686 Mari de Leon, Bus. Mgr.;

Our Lady Queen of Heaven - 1515 8th St. So, Nampa, ID 83686 Mari de Leon, Bus. Mgr.;

Queen of Heaven Chapel - 8102 Oreana Loop Rd., Nampa, ID 83650; Mailing: 1515 8th St. S., Nampa, ID 83651 t) 208-466-7031 mdeleon@stpaulsnampa.org See St. Paul's, Nampa for details. Rev. Justin Brady, Pst.;

NEZPERCE

Holy Trinity - 503 Willow St., Nezperce, ID 83543; Mailing: PO Box 65, Nezperce, ID 83543 t) 208-937-1095 See SS. Peter and Paul, Grangeville for details. Rev. Anthony Obgonna Amadi, Admin.; CRP Stds.: 26

OROFINO

St. Theresa of the Little Flower - 237 C St., Orofino, ID 83544; Mailing: Box 1169, Orofino, ID 83544 t) 208-476-5121 Rev. Bruno Mbamobi, SMMM, Admin.;

Our Lady of Woodland - 101 Woodland Ave., Pierce, ID 83546; Mailing: PO Box 1169, Orofino, ID 83544 www.st-theresacatholicchurch.org

POCATELLO

Holy Spirit Catholic Community - 524 N. 7th Ave., Pocatello, ID 83201 t) 208-232-1196 holyspirit@hscc.org www.hscc.org Rev. Henry Carmona, Pst.; Rev. Emil Parafiniuk, Par. Vicar; Dcn. Scott Pearhill; CRP Stds.: 72

St. John's Catholic Student Center - 920 E. Lovejoy St., I.S.U., Pocatello, ID 83209-0001; Mailing: Box 8129, Pocatello, ID 83209-0001 t) 208-233-0880 director@bengalcatholics.com David O'Neil, Campus Min.;

St. Anthony of Padua Chapel - 504 N. 7th Ave., Pocatello, ID 83201 www.holyspirit@hscc.org

St. Joseph Chapel - 439 N. Hayes St., Pocatello, ID 83204

POST FALLS

St. George's - 2004 N. Lucas St., Post Falls, ID 83854; Mailing: P O Box 10, Post Falls, ID 83877 t) 208-773-4715 x20 pfstgeorge@frontier.com www.stgeorgesidaho.com Rev. Sleeva Raju Madanu, Pst.; Rev. Arogyaiah Madanu, Par. Vicar; Dcn. Michael J. Pentony; Dcn. Erik Schirmer; CRP Stds.: 47

St. Stanislaus - 812 W. 2nd St., Rathdrum, ID 83877 Rev. Sleeva Raju Madanu, Pst.;

St. Joseph - State Hwy. 41, Spirit Lake, ID 83877; Mailing: PO Box 10, Post Falls, ID 83877 Rev. Sleeva Raju Madanu, Pst.;

St. Joan of Arc - 4772 Poleline Ave., Post Falls, ID 83854 t) 208-660-6036 secretary@stjoanarc.com www.stjoanarc.com Latin Mass Rev. Dennis M. Gordon, F.S.S.P., Pst.; Rev. Joseph Terra, Chap.; Rev. Nicholas Eichman, FSSP, Pst. Assoc.; Rev. Michael Flick, Pst. Assoc.; CRP Stds.: 330

POTLATCH

St. Mary Station - 725 Spruce St., Potlatch, ID 83855 t) 208-882-4613 See St. Augustine's, Moscow for details. Rev. Chase R. Hasenoehrl, Pst.; Rev. Thomas Louchs, Assoc. Pst.; CRP Stds.: 10

PRIEST RIVER

St. Catherine's - 393 Summit Blvd., Priest River, ID 83856; Mailing: P.O. Box 445, Priest River, ID 83856 t) 208-448-2127 stcatherineparish445@gmail.com Rev. Reginald Nwauzor, Pst.; CRP Stds.: 5

St. Blanche - 27832 Hwy. 57, Nordman, ID 83858; Mailing: P.O. Box 412, Nordman, ID 83858

RUPERT

St. Nicholas - 802 F St., Rupert, ID 83350-0115; Mailing: P.O. Box 115, Rupert, ID 83350 t) 208-436-3781 x101 stnich@pmt.org saintnicholascc.org Rev. Camilo Garcia, Pst.; Dcn. Paul Henscheid; Dcn. Jose Medina; CRP Stds.: 258

St. Nicholas School - (Grades PreSchool-6) 806 F. St., Rupert, ID 83350; Mailing: P.O. Box 26, Rupert, ID 83350 t) 208-436-6320 secretary@stnicholasrupert.org www.stnicholasrupert.org Colleen Johnson, Prin.; Natalie VanTassell, Librn.; Stds.: 154; Scholastics: 2; Lay Tchrs.: 6

SALMON

St. Charles - 505 Hope Ave., Salmon, ID 83467 t) 208-756-2432 stcharles@custertel.net; stcharlesfinancial@custertel.net www.catholicsalmon.com Rev. John Andrew Mosier, Pst.; Faith Ryan, DRE; Rev. John Gathungu, Par. Vicar; CRP Stds.: 13

St. Ann - 342 Lost River Ave., Arco, ID 83213; Mailing: PO Box 1181, Salmon, ID 83467 t) (208) 756-2432 www.charlessalmon.com

St. Louise - 1285 Pleasant Ave., Challis, ID 83226; Mailing: P.O. Box 572, Challis, ID 83226 Dcn. Dennis Rotondo;

St. Barbara - 505 Park St., Mackay, ID 83251; Mailing: PO Box 1181, Salmon, ID 83467 stcharles!@custertel.net

St. Joseph - 3rd St. & Galena, Salmon, ID 83467; Mailing: PO Box 550, Salmon, ID 83467 t) (208) 756-2432

SANDPOINT

St. Joseph's - 601 S. Lincoln Ave., Sandpoint, ID 83864-0279; Mailing: PO Box 279, Sandpoint, ID 83864 t) 208-263-3720 geraldine@st-joseph-church.net st-joseph-church.net Rev. Robert P. Cook, Pst.; CRP Stds.: 83

Sacred Heart - 125 W. 5th Ave., Clark Fork, ID 83811 t) 208-263-9720 pastor@st-joseph-church.net Rev. Robert P. Cook;

SHOSHONE

St. Peter's - 215 W. B St., Shoshone, ID 83352; Mailing: PO Box 336, Shoshone, ID 83352 t) 208-934-5634 Rev. Carlos Rosero, Pst.; Dcn. Javier Leija; CRP Stds.: 16

SODA SPRINGS

Good Shepherd Catholic Community - 99 W. Center St., Soda Springs, ID 83276 t) 208-547-3200 www.goodshepherdidaho.com Rev. Joseph V Lustig, Admin.; Dcn. David McCarthy; CRP Stds.: 35

Blessed Sacrament - 270 N. 8th St., Montpelier, ID 83254; Mailing: 99 W. Center St., Soda Springs, ID 83276 goodshepherdidaho.com

Soda Springs, St. Mary's - t) (208) 547-3200 goodshepherdidaho.com

St. Peter's - 302 E. Oneida St., Preston, ID 83263; Mailing: 99 W. Center St., Soda Springs, ID 83276 goodshepherdidaho.com

Our Lady of Lourdes - 132 S. First St. W., Lava Hot Springs, ID 83246; Mailing: 99 W. Center St., Soda Springs, ID 83276 gooshepherdidaho@gmail.com goodshepherdidaho.com

St. Paul's - 233 Samaria Ln., Malad, ID 83252; Mailing: 99 W. Center St., Soda Springs, ID 83276 t) (208) 547-3200 goodshepherdidaho.com

ST. ANTHONY

Mary Immaculate - 328 W. 1st N., St. Anthony, ID 83445; Mailing: P.O. Box 527, St. Anthony, ID 83445 t) 208-624-7459 idahocatholic@yahoo.com www.uppervalleycatholic.com/ Rev. John Kucera, Pst.; CRP Stds.: 41

St. Patrick's - 38 S. 3rd St. W., Rexburg, ID 83440; Mailing: PO Box 527, St. Anthony, ID 83445 www.uppervalleycatholic.com

Good Shepherd - 2559 S. Hwy. 33, Driggs, ID 83422

Chapel of the Pines - 4100 S. Big Springs Loop Rd., Island Park, ID 83429

ST. MARIES

St. Mary Immaculate - 921 W. Jefferson Ave., St. Maries, ID 83861; Mailing: P.O. Box 335, St. Maries, ID 83861 t) 208-245-2977 Rev. Jerome Montez, O.S.B., Sacramental Min.; Dcn. Tom Kilbourne; CRP Stds.: 2

Our Lady of Perpetual Help - 100 Frederick Ave., Harrison, ID 83833 t) 208-539-4130 saintmaries@gmail.com

SUN VALLEY

Our Lady of the Snows - 206 Sun Valley Rd., Sun Valley, ID 83353; Mailing: PO Box 1650, Sun Valley, ID 83353 t) 208-622-3432 svcatholic.org Rev. Ronald Wekerle, Pst.; Richard Kulleck, Pst. Assoc.; Dcn. Robert Barros-Bailey; CRP Stds.: 29

TWIN FALLS

St. Edward the Confessor - 161 6th Ave. E, Twin Falls, ID 83301; Mailing: 212 7th Ave. E, Twin Falls, ID 83301-6321 t) 208-733-3907; 208-733-3907 x108 (CRP) rosasj@twinfallscatholic.org twinfallscatholic.org Rev. Julio Vicente, Pst.; Rev. Pawel Pawliszko, Par. Vicar; Juana Rosas, DRE; Rhonda Eldredge, Bus. Mgr.; CRP Stds.: 200

St. Edward the Confessor School - (Grades PreSchool-8) 139 Sixth Ave. E., Twin Falls, ID 83301-6316 t) 208-734-3872 hild-angela@sainteddie.org www.sainteddie.org Angela Hild, Prin.; Stds.: 181; Lay Tchrs.: 12

WALLACE

St. Alphonsus - 214 Pine St., Wallace, ID 83873 t) 208-752-3551 Rev. Jerome Montez, O.S.B., Sacramental Min.; Dcn. Tom Kilbourne; CRP Stds.: 4

St. Michael's - 3rd & Park St., Mullan, ID 83846 t) 208-539-4130 jeromelmontez@gmail.com

WEISER

St. Agnes - 214 E. Liberty, Weiser, ID 83672; Mailing: P.O. Box 87, Weiser, ID 83672 t) 208-549-0088 catholicweiser.org Rev. Gerald J. Funke, Pst.; Dcn. Ignacio Cornejo; CRP Stds.: 105

Holy Rosary - 205 S. 1st St., Cambridge, ID 83610; Mailing: P.O. Box 335, Cambridge, ID 83610-0335 t) (208) 549-0088; (208) 257-3783 Cecelia Sachtjen, Contact;

St. Jude the Apostle - 2054 Hwy. 95 N., Council, ID 83612 t) (208) 549-0088; (208) 866-6866

WENDELL

St. Anthony's - 585 2nd Ave. E., Wendell, ID 83355; Mailing: PO Box 811, Wendell, ID 83355 t) 208-934-5634 See St. Elizabeth's, Gooding for details. Rev. Carlos Rosero; Dcn. Javier Leija; CRP Stds.: 13

SCHOOLS: PRESCHOOL THRU HIGH SCHOOL

SCHOOLS

STATE OF IDAHO

COEUR D'ALENE

Holy Family Catholic School of Coeur d'Alene - (PAR) (Grades PreSchool-8) 3005 W. Kathleen Ave., Coeur d'Alene, ID 83815 t) 208-765-4327 sstyren@hfcs-cda.org; office@hfcs-cda.org www.hfcs-cda.org Susan Styren, Prin.; Beth Franz, Librn.; Stds.: 253; Lay Tchrs.: 12

HIGH SCHOOLS

STATE OF IDAHO

BOISE

Bishop Kelly High School - (PAR) (Grades 9-12) 7009 Franklin Rd., Boise, ID 83709-0922 t) 208-375-6010 mcaldwell@bk.org; rberhan@bk.org www.bk.org Mike Caldwell, Prin.; Cheryl Hutchinson, Vice Prin.; Dr. Sarah Quilici, Vice Prin.; William Avey, Pres.; Laura Ward, Librn.; Stds.: 929; Pr. Tchrs.: 1; Lay Tchrs.: 68

INSTITUTIONS LOCATED IN DIOCESE

CAMPUS MINISTRY / NEWMAN CENTERS [CAM]

BOISE

Boise State University, St. Paul's Catholic Center - 1915

University Dr., Boise, ID 83706 t) 208-343-2128 operations@broncocatholic.org www.broncocatholic.org Rev. Nathan Dail, Chap.; Andrew John Furphy, Admin.;

CALDWELL

The College of Idaho - 1122 W. Linden St., Caldwell, ID 83605 t) 208-459-3653 churchoffice@olvcaldwell.org Rev. Jose T. Ramirez;

COEUR D'ALENE

North Idaho College - St. Pius X, 625 Haycraft Ave., Coeur d'Alene, ID 83815 t) 208-765-5108 triple.eff@gmail.com Rev. Francisco Q. Flores, Pst.;

LEWISTON

Lewis Clark State College - All Saints Catholic Community, 3330 14th St., Lewiston, ID 83501 t) 208-743-1012 frneely@allsaintslewiston.org Rev. Bradley Neely;

MOSCOW

St. Augustine's Catholic Center - 628 Deakin Ave., Moscow, ID 83843-1911; Mailing: P.O. Box 3457, Moscow, ID 83843-1911 t) 208-882-4613 vandalcatholic@gmail.com vandalcatholic.com (Serving University of Idaho) Rev. Chase R. Hasenoehrl, Pst.; Dcn. Verne Geidl; Dcn. Dennis Thomas; Nicole Koepl, Campus Min.; David Klement, Dir. Music Ministry; Eric Meyer, Exec. Dir. of Mission; Heather Meyer, Dir. Oper.;

POCATELLO

Idaho State University, St. John's Catholic Student Center - 917 E. Lovejoy St., Pocatello, ID 83201; Mailing: 921 S. 8th St., Box 8129, Pocatello, ID 83209 t) 208-233-0880 director@bengalcatholics.com www.bengalcatholics.com Bengal Catholics David O'Neill, Campus Min.;

TWIN FALLS

College of Southern Idaho - 630 Falls Ave., Twin Falls, ID 83301-6321; Mailing: 212 7th Ave. E., Twin Falls, ID 83301-6321 t) 208-733-3907 Attended by St. Edward the Confessor, Twin Falls. Rev. Julio Vicente, Pst.; Rev. Pawel Pawliszko, Par. Vicar;

CATHOLIC CHARITIES [CCH]

BOISE

Catholic Charities of Idaho, Inc. - 7201 W. Franklin Rd., Boise, ID 83709; Mailing: P.O. Box 190123, Boise, ID 83719 t) 208-345-6031 dalles@ccidaho.org www.ccidaho.org Most Rev. Peter F. Christensen, Pres.; Douglas Alles, Exec.; Asstd. Annu.: 2,678; Staff: 21

CONVENTS, MONASTERIES, AND RESIDENCES FOR WOMEN [CON]

COTTONWOOD

Monastery of St. Gertrude, Motherhouse and Novitiate - 465 Keuterville Rd., Cottonwood, ID 83522-5183 t) 208-962-3224 monastery@stgertrudes.org www.stgertrudes.org Motherhouse and Novitiate for the Benedictine Sisters of Idaho. Idaho Corporation of Benedictine Sisters. Rev. Meinrad Schallberger, O.S.B., Chap.; Sr. Mary Marge Goeckner, O.S.B., Subprior; Sr. Mary Forman, O.S.B., Prioress; Srs.: 31

MESA

Marymount Hermitage, Inc., Hermit Sisters of Mary - 2150 Hermitage Ln., Mesa, ID 83643-5005 t) 208-256-4354 sisterbeverly@marymount-hermitage.org www.marymount-hermitage.org Rev. William McCann; Sr. Mary Beverly Greger, H.S.M., Supr.; Srs.: 1

POST FALLS

Monastery of Jesus, Mary and Joseph - 18772 W. Riverview Dr., Post Falls, ID 83854 c) 402-310-7212 Rev. Dennis M. Gordon, F.S.S.P., Pst.; Srs.: 13

HOSPITALS / HEALTH SERVICES [HOS]

BOISE

Saint Alphonsus Health System, Inc. - 1055 N. Curtis Rd., Boise, ID 83706 t) 208-367-2000 odette.bolano@saintalphonsus.org www.saintalphonsus.org Odette Bolano, Pres.; Staff: 633

Saint Alphonsus Regional Medical Center, Inc. (Saint Alphonsus Diversified Care, Inc.) - 1055 N. Curtis Rd., Boise, ID 83706-1370 t) 208-367-2121 www.saintalphonsus.org David McFadyen, Pres.; Bed Capacity: 362; Asstd. Annu.: 601,967; Staff: 1,842

COTTONWOOD

St. Mary's Hospital - 701 Lewiston St., Cottonwood, ID 83522; Mailing: P.O. Box 137, Cottonwood, ID 83522 t) 208-962-3251 lbonner@kh.org Sponsored by Sisters of St. Benedict, Duluth, MN through Essentia Health. Rev. Meinrad Schallberger, O.S.B., Chap.; Sr. Barbara A. Bielenberg, O.S.B., Dir.; Lenne Bonner, Pres.; Steve Frei, COO; Bed Capacity: 25; Asstd. Annu.: 26,461; Staff: 227

LEWISTON

SJRMC, Inc. - 415 6th St., Lewiston, ID 83501; Mailing: 4600 Edmundson Rd., St. Louis, MO 63134 t) 314-733-8000 www.ascension.org Craig Cordola, Exec. Vice Pres. & COO; Thomas VanOsdol, Exec. Vice Pres. & Chief Mission Integration Officer;

NAMPA

Saint Alphonsus Medical Center - Nampa, Inc. - 4300 E. Flamingo Ave., Nampa, ID 83686 t) 208-205-0055 Travis Leach, Pres.; Bed Capacity: 106; Asstd. Annu.: 179,541; Staff: 728

MISCELLANEOUS [MIS]

BOISE

Risen in Christ Prison Re-Entry Conference - 7960 W. Northview St., Boise, ID 83704; Mailing: 5256 W. Fairview Ave., Boise, ID 83706 t) 208-331-8409; (208) 344-5403 www.svdpid.org Ralph May, Exec. Dir.;

***Society of St. Vincent de Paul - Southwest Idaho District Council** - 3217 W. Overland Rd., Boise, ID 83705 t) 208-344-5403 john.dahl@svdpid.org svdpid.org John Dahl, Pres.; Ralph May, Exec.; Diana Tetreault, Bus. Mgr.;

***Society of St. Vincent de Paul, Holy Apostles Conference** - 6300A N. Meridian Rd., Meridian, ID 83646; Mailing: 3217 W. Overland Rd., Boise, ID 83705 t) 208-888-1182 www.svdpid.org Cathy Hagdone, Pres.;

***Society of St. Vincent de Paul, Our Lady of Good Counsel Conference** - 342 E. Jackson St., Mountain Home, ID 83647; Mailing: 3217 W. Overland Rd., Boise, ID 83705 t) 208-331-2208 www.svdpid.org Elisa Knox, Pres.;

***Society of St. Vincent de Paul, Our Lady of Guadalupe Conference** - 1515 8th St., S., Nampa, ID 83651; Mailing: 3217 W. Overland Rd., Boise, ID 83705 t) 208-466-3400 www.svdpid.org Maureen Coon, Pres.;

***Society of St. Vincent de Paul, Our Lady of the Valley Conference** - 1122 W. Linden St., Caldwell, ID 83605; Mailing: 3217 W. Overland Rd., Boise, ID 83705 t) 208-331-8409 www.svdpid.org Marilyn Evans, Pres.;

***St. Vincent de Paul Society, Our Lady of the Rosary Conference** - 1500 E. Wright St., Boise, ID 83706-5358; Mailing: 3217 W. Overland Rd., Boise, ID 83705 t) 208-331-2208 www.svdpid.org Brian Krueger, Pres.;

***St. Vincent de Paul Society, St. Mark's Conference** - 7960 Northview, Boise, ID 83704; Mailing: 3217 W. Overland Rd., Boise, ID 83705 t) 208-331-2208 www.svdpid.org Mary Kaineg, Pres.;

***St. Vincent de Paul Society, Risen Christ Conference** - 11511 Lake Hazel Rd., Boise, ID 83709; Mailing: 3217 W. Overland Rd., Boise, ID 83705 t) (208) 362-6584 www.svdpid.org Vicki Laidlaw, Pres.; Cathy Yoder, Pres.;

***St. Vincent de Paul Society, Sacred Heart Conference** - 811 S. Latah St., Boise, ID 83705; Mailing: 3217 W. Overland Rd., Boise, ID 83705 t) 208-331-8409 www.svdpid.org Sue Robinson, Pres.;

***St. Vincent de Paul Society, St. John's Conference** - 775 N. 8th St., Boise, ID 83702; Mailing: 3217 W. Overland Rd., Boise, ID 83705 t) 208-331-2208 www.svdpid.org Kathy Dahl, Pres.;

***St. Vincent de Paul Society, Thrift Stores** - 6464 W. State St., Boise, ID 83703; Mailing: 3217 W. Overland Rd., Boise, ID 83705 t) 208-853-4921 www.svdpid.org Vicky Rowell, Dir.;

COEUR D'ALENE

***St. Vincent de Paul Salvage Bureau, St. Thomas Conference** - 201 E. Harrison Ave., Coeur d'Alene, ID 83814 t) 208-664-3095 jeff@stvincentdepaulcda.org Mike Kennedy, Pres.; Jeff Conroy, Exec.;

COTTONWOOD

Spirit Center - 465 Keuterville Rd., Cottonwood, ID 83522-5183 t) 208-962-2000 spirit-center@stgertrudes.org www.stgertrudes.org Tim Oberholzer, Dir.;

EAGLE

Mercy Properties II, Inc. - 540 N. Eagle Rd., Eagle, ID 83616; Mailing: 1600 Broadway, Ste. 2000, Denver, CO 80202 t) 303-830-3300 Joe Rosenblum, Secy.;

LEWISTON

***Lewis and Clark District Council of St. Vincent de Paul** - 818 11th St., Lewiston, ID 83501 t) 208-798-9574 theresa@mcwessels.org Theresa Wessels, Pres.;

MOUNTAIN HOME

St. Mary's A.F.B. - 366 FW/HC, 420 Gunfighter Ave., Mountain Home, ID 83648 t) 208-828-6987 kelly.gray.3.ctr@us.af.mil www.libertychapelcatholic.weebly.com (Archdiocese for the Military Services) Rev. Mario Rosario, Pst.;

MONASTERIES AND RESIDENCES FOR PRIESTS AND BROTHERS [MON]

BOISE

Monastery of Our Lady of Ephesus (Nazareth Retreat Center) - 4450 N. Five Mile Rd., Boise, ID 83713-2709 t) 208-453-6252 dominiquefaure@hotmail.com Dcn. Germain Steve, Admin.; Brs.: 7; Priests: 2

JEROME

Monastery of the Ascension - 541 E. 100 S., Jerome, ID 83338 t) 208-324-2377 x256 monbusoffice@gmail.com; boniface@idahomonks.org www.idahomonks.org The Benedictine Monks of Idaho, Inc. Rev. Boniface Lautz, O.S.B., Prior; Rev. Kenneth C. Hein, O.S.B.; Rev. Ezekiel Lotz, O.S.B.; Rev. Jerome Montez, O.S.B.; Rev. Meinrad Schallberger, O.S.B.; Bro. Selby Coffman, O.S.B.; Bro. Sylvester Sonnen, O.S.B.; Bro. Tobiah Urrutia, O.S.B.; Rev. Hugh Feiss, O.S.B., Subprior; Brs.: 3; Priests: 6

LEMHI

Hermitage of St. Joseph - 111 1st St., Lemhi, ID 83465; Mailing: P.O. Box 37, Lemhi, ID 83465 t) (208) 350-7560 Hermits of Mt. Carmel. Bro. Henry Soto, Treas.;

An asterisk (*) denotes an organization that has established tax-exempt status directly with the IRS and is not covered by the USCCB Group Ruling.

Archdiocese of Boston

(Archidioecesis Bostoniensis)

HIS EMINENCE SEAN PATRICK CARDINAL O'MALLEY, O.F.M.CAP.

Archbishop of Boston; ordained priest August 29, 1970; ordained Coadjutor Bishop of St. Thomas in the Virgin Islands August 2, 1984; succeeded to the See, October 16, 1985; Named sixth Bishop of Fall River June 16, 1992; installed August 10, 1992; Named fourth Bishop of Palm Beach September 3, 2002; installed October 19, 2002; Named ninth Bishop and sixth Metropolitan Archbishop of Boston July 1, 2003; installed July 30, 2003; Named Cardinal Priest with the title of Santa Maria della Vittoria, in the consistory of March 24, 2006. Office: 66 Brooks Dr., Braintree, MA 02184-3839. T: 617-782-2544; F: 617-779-3820. Res.: Cathedral of the Holy Cross, 75 Union Park St., Boston, MA 02118. T: 617-542-5682; F: 617-542-5926.

Chancery Office: 66 Brooks Dr., Braintree, MA 02184-3839. T: 617-254-0100; F: 617-779-4571. www.bostoncatholic.org

Square Miles 2,465.

Created a Diocese April 8, 1808; Made Metropolitan Archdiocese February 12, 1875. Comprises the Counties of Essex, Middlesex, Norfolk, Suffolk and Plymouth (the towns of Marion, Mattapoisett and Wareham excepted) in the Commonwealth of Massachusetts.

For legal titles of parishes and archdiocesan agencies and institutions, consult the Chancery Office.

Most Reverend Robert Francis Hennessey
Titular Bishop of Tigias, Auxiliary Bishop of Boston, Vicar General and Regional Bishop-Merrimack; ordained priest May 20, 1978; ordained Bishop December 12, 2006. Office & Res.: 110 Lincoln Ave., Haverhill, MA 01830-6739. T: 978-399-0000; merrimackregion@rcab.org.

Most Reverend Peter John Uglietto
Titular Bishop of Thubursicum, Auxiliary Bishop of Boston, Vicar General; ordained priest May 21, 1977; ordained Bishop September 14, 2011. Res.: Saint Denis Rectory, 157 Washington St., Westwood, MA 02090-1336; T: 781-326-5858.

Most Reverend Robert Phili Reed
Titular Bishop of Sufar, Auxiliary Bishop of Boston, Vicar General and Regional Bishop-West; ordained priest July 6, 1985; ordained Bishop August 24, 2016. Office: 34 Chestnut St., Watertown, MA 02471-9196. T: 508-647-0296; F: 617-923-3490; westregion@rcab.org. Saint Patrick Rectory, 34 Chestnut St., Watertown, MA 02472. T: 617-926-9680; F: 617-926-3715.

Most Reverend Mark O'Connell
Titular Bishop of Gigthi, Auxiliary Bishop of Boston, Vicar General and Moderator of the Curia; ordained priest June 16, 1990; ordained Bishop August 24, 2016. Office: 66 Brooks Dr., Braintree, MA 02184-3839. T: 617-746-5619; F: 617-779-5920; vicar_general@rcab.org. Res.: Our Lady Queen of Peace Rectory, 8 Hawthorn Rd., Braintree, MA 02184.

STATISTICAL OVERVIEW

Personnel
Cardinals....1
Auxiliary Bishops....4
Retired Bishops....2
Abbots....1
Retired Abbots....1
Priests: Diocesan Active in Diocese....263
Priests: Diocesan Active Outside Diocese....26
Priests: Retired, Sick or Absent....245
Number of Diocesan Priests....534
Religious Priests in Diocese....335
Total Priests in your Diocese....869
Extern Priests in Diocese....106
Ordinations:
Diocesan Priests....7
Permanent Deacons....9
Permanent Deacons in Diocese....298
Total Brothers....89
Total Sisters....945

Parishes
Parishes....253
With Resident Pastor:
Resident Diocesan Priests....243
Resident Religious Priests....10
Pastoral Centers....17
New Parishes Created....2
Closed Parishes....5
Professional Ministry Personnel:
Sisters....7
Lay Ministers....61

Welfare
Health Care Centers....3
Total Assisted....7,511
Homes for the Aged....15
Total Assisted....2,832
Residential Care of Children....1
Total Assisted....921
Day Care Centers....11
Total Assisted....1,110
Specialized Homes....21
Total Assisted....1,722
Special Centers for Social Services....43
Total Assisted....20,600
Other Institutions....3
Total Assisted....35,410

Educational
Seminaries, Diocesan....3
Students from This Diocese....59
Students from Other Dioceses....52
Diocesan Students in Other Seminaries....1
Seminaries, Religious....1
Students, Religious....33
Total Seminarians....93
Colleges and Universities....4
Total Students....23,264
High Schools, Diocesan and Parish....1
Total Students....433
High Schools, Private....27
Total Students....11,228
Elementary Schools, Diocesan and Parish....57
Total Students....16,994
Elementary Schools, Private....9
Total Students....1,701
Non-residential Schools for the Disabled....2
Total Students....142
Catechesis/Religious Education:
High School Students....28,606
Elementary Students....79,395
Total Students under Catholic Instruction....161,856
Teachers in Diocese:
Priests....11
Brothers....19
Sisters....57
Lay Teachers....2,871

Vital Statistics
Receptions into the Church:
Infant Baptism Totals....7,757
Minor Baptism Totals....3,433
Adult Baptism Totals....655
Received into Full Communion....243
First Communions....8,916
Confirmations....8,005
Marriages:
Catholic....1,423
Interfaith....285
Total Marriages....1,708
Deaths....12,582
Total Catholic Population....1,794,260
Total Population....4,496,207

LEADERSHIP

Administration and Financial Services - t) 617-254-0100 John E. Straub, Chancellor (j_straub@rcab.org);

Cemeteries - t) 781-322-6300 Robert Visconti, Dir.;

Finance and Technology - t) 617-746-5878 Maureen Donnelly-Creedon, Dir.;

General Counsel - t) 617-746-5672; 617-746-5672 Francis O'Connor;

Human Resources - t) 617-746-5829 James DiFrancesco, Dir.;

Parish Services - t) 617-746-5685 Denise McKinnon-Biernat;

Planning Office for Urban Affairs - t) 617-350-8885 Lisa Alberghini, Dir.;

Risk Management - t) 617-746-5740 Joseph F. McEnness, Dir.;

Vicars General - Most Rev. John A. Dooher; Most Rev. Robert F. Hennessey (merrimackregion@rcab.org); Most Rev. Arthur L. Kennedy;

Regional Bishops and Vicars -

Regional Office Central - t) 617-666-2087 Rev. George P. Evans, Pst.; Rev. Richard W. Fitzgerald, Admin.; Very Rev. Robert E. Casey, Pst.;

Regional Office Merrimack - t) 978-399-0000 Rev. Sean M. Maher, Admin.; Rev. Brian E. Mahoney, Pst.; Most Rev. Robert F. Hennessey;

Regional Office North - t) 978-531-1013 Rev. Paul E. Ritt, Pastor, Our Lady of the Assumption and Pastor, Saint Maria Goretti, Lynnfield; Rev. John E. Sheridan, Pastor, Saint Mary of the Assumption, Revere and Pastor, Our Lady of Grace, Chelsea; Most Rev. Mark O'Connell;

Regional Office South - t) 617-746-5670 Rev. Thomas F. Nestor, Pst.; Rev. William B. Palardy, Pst.; Very Rev. Robert L. Connors, Vicar;

Regional Office West - t) 508-647-0296 Very Rev. Frank J. Silva, Pst.; Very Rev. Bryan K. Parrish, Pst.; Most Rev. Robert P. Reed;

Communications and Public Affairs - t) 617-746-5775 Terrence C. Donilon, Secy. (tdonilon@rcab.org);

Pontifical Mission Societies -

Pontifical Association of the Holy Childhood -

Pontifical Society for the Propagation of the Faith -

Pontifical Society of Saint Peter the Apostle - t) 617-779-3865 officestaff@propfaithatboston.org Rev. Gerald J. Osterman, Dir.;

Vicar General and Moderator of the Curia - t) 617-746-5619 Most Rev. Mark O'Connell (northregion@rcab.org);

Archives - t) 617-746-5797 Thomas Lester, Archivist;

Assistant to the Vicar General and Moderator of the Curia for Canonical Affairs - t) 617-746-5650 Bro. James M. Peterson, O.F.M.Cap.;

Special Assistant to the Vicar General and Assistant Vicar for Administration - t) 617-746-5618 Very Rev. William P. Joy;

Massachusetts Catholic Conference - t) 617-746-5630 James F. Driscoll, Exec.;

OFFICES AND DIRECTORS

Archdiocesan Cemeteries -

The Catholic Cemetery Association of the Archdiocese of Boston, Inc. - t) 781-322-6300 www.ccemetery.org

Professional Standards and Oversight - t) 617-782-2544 Mark Dunderdale;

Background Screening - t) 617-746-5840 Lisa Cutulle, Dir.;

Delegate for Investigations - t) 617-746-5639 Jay Crowley, Delegate;

Pastoral Support and Outreach - Vivian Soper, Dir.;

ADVISORY BOARDS, COMMISSIONS, COMMITTEES, AND COUNCILS

College of Consultors - Most Rev. John A. Dooher; Most Rev. Robert F. Hennessey (merrimackregion@rcab.org); Most Rev. Arthur L. Kennedy;

Finance Council - Most Rev. Mark O'Connell (northregion@rcab.org); His Eminence Sean Cardinal O'Malley, O.F.M.Cap., Pres.; John H. McCarthy, Vice Chair;

Health Benefit Trust, Life and Long-Term Disability Insurance Trust, Transition Assistance - Most Rev. Mark O'Connell (northregion@rcab.org); His Eminence Sean P. Cardinal O'Malley, O.F.M.Cap.; John E. Straub (j_straub@rcab.org);

Archdiocese of Boston Pension Plan - Most Rev. Mark O'Connell; His Eminence Sean P. O'Malley, O.F.M.Cap.; John E. Straub;

Attorney for the Trust -

Audit Committee - George E. Massaro, Chair; Rev. Joseph K. Raeke; Paul Hanley;

Investment Advisory Committee - Robert J. Morrissey; Dcn. Charles I. Clough, Chair; Gerald R. Curtis;

Massachusetts Catholic Self Insurance Group, Inc. - John E. Straub, Pres.; Maureen Creedon, Treas.; Rev. James M. DiPerri, Clerk;

Pastoral Building Committee - John E. Straub; Very Rev. Bryan K. Parrish; Rev. Paul R. Soper;

CATHOLIC CHARITIES

Catholic Charitable Bureau of the Archdiocese of Boston, Inc. - t) 617-482-5440 Deborah Kincade Rambo, Pres. (info@ccab.org);

Catholic Charities North - Virginia A. Doocy, Dir.;

Asian Center - t) 781-593-2312

Catholic Charities North at Gloucester - t) 978-283-3055

Catholic Charities North at Lynn - t) 781-593-2312

Catholic Charities North at Salem - t) 978-740-6923

Healthy Families North Shore - t) 781-593-4515

Catholic Charities Senior Management - t) 617-254-0100 Jennifer Mendelsohn, CFO; Kenneth P. Binder, Vice Pres. Devel.; Larry Mayes, Vice Pres. Progs.;

Catholic Charities South - t) 508-587-0815 Beth Chambers, Dir.;

Nursing Assistant Home Health Aide Training Program -

Refugee and Immigration Services - t) 617-464-8100 Marjean A. Perhot, Dir.;

Thrifty Pilgrim Thrift Shop - t) 508-746-6133

Catholic Charities West - t) 508-478-9632 Beth Chambers, Dir.;

Behavioral Health - Family Counseling & Guidance Center - Deborah Kincade Rambo, Dir.;

Brockton Clinic - t) 508-587-0815

Child Care - t) 617-524-9595 Mary Ann Anthony, Dir.;

Child Care Sites: -

Cambridge/Somerville/Malden - t) 617-623-8555 Richard Murphy, Dir.; Sharon Richardson-O'Connell, Dir.;

Caritas Saint Mary Women and Children's Center - t) 617-436-8600 Judith Beckler, Pres.;

Laboure Child Care Center - t) 617-464-8500 Peggy Kelly, Dir.; Kim Murray, Asst. Dir.;

Lynn Child Care - t) 781-598-2759 Janet MacDougall, Dir.; Beverly Prifti, Dir.; Judy Comer, Asst. Dir.;

Malden Early Education & Learning Program - t) 781-397-1556 Diana Makhlouf, Dir.;

Malden High Teen Parent Child Care - t) 781-397-6055 Diana Makhlouf, Dir.; Ginny Cohan, Asst. Dir.;

Nazareth Child Care Center - t) 617-522-4040 Pamela J. Penton, Dir.;

North Cambridge Children's Center - t) 617-876-0503 Cindy Green, Dir.;

Peabody Child Care - t) 978-532-6860 Charles Johnson, Dir.; Beverly Prifti, Dir.; Nadine Lada, Dir.;

Yawkey Konbit-Kreyol Center for Early Education & Care - t) 617-506-6900

Community Interpreter Services - t) 617-451-7979 cis_request@ccab.org

Danvers Clinic - t) 978-774-6820

Driver Alcohol Education - t) 508-587-0815

Immigration Legal Services - t) 617-451-7979

Refugee Employment Services - t) 617-451-7979

Refugee Resettlement - t) 617-451-7979

Greater Boston Catholic Charities - t) 617-506-6600 Beth Chambers, Dir.;

Brigid's Crossing - t) 978-454-0081

Genesis II - t) 617-332-9905

Greater Boston Catholic Charities at Somerville - t) 617-625-1920

Laboure Center - t) 617-268-9670 Sr. Maryadele Robinson, D.C., Dir.;

Nazareth Residence for Mothers and Children - t) 617-541-0100

Robert McBride House - t) 617-236-8319

Saint Ambrose Family Shelter - t) 617-288-7675

St. Patrick's Shelter for Homeless Women - t) 617-628-3015

Seton Manor - t) 617-277-7133

Sunset Point Camp - t) 781-925-0710

Teen Center at Saint Peter's - t) 617-282-3614

Haitian Multi-Service Center (Vacant) -

Merrimack Valley Catholic Charities - Virginia Doocey, Dir.;

Food Pantry of Merrimack Valley - t) 978-454-9946

Haverhill Area Healthy Families - t) 978-521-6265

Lowell Food Pantry - t) 978-454-9946

Merrimack Valley Catholic Charities at Lowell - t) 978-452-1421

Merrimack Valley Young Parents Program - t) 978-459-2387

Open Hand Food Pantry - t) 978-372-2828

Metro Boston -

El Centro del Cardenal - t) 617-542-9292 Deborah Kincade Rambo, Dir.; Robert Hibbard, Dir.; Edward Castro, Dir.;

CLERGY AND RELIGIOUS SERVICES

Clergy Personnel Board - Most Rev. Mark O'Connell (northregion@rcab.org); Rev. Richard W. Fitzgerald; Rev. Thomas F. Nestor (frnestor.stpaul@gmail.com);

Delegate for Pastoral Care for Senior Priests - t) 617-723-3976 Very Rev. Robert L. Connors (rlconnors@rcab.org);

Delegate for Religious - t) 617-746-5637 Sr. Germana Santos, F.S.P., Secy. (sr_marian_batho@rcab.org);

Episcopal Vicar for Clergy - Very Rev. William P. Joy, Vicar (reverendwilliam_joy@rcab.org);

Pastoral Support of Priests - Rev. Robert J. Deehan, Delegate (rdeehan@holyfamilyduxbury.org); Rev. Thomas F. Nestor, Delegate (frnestor.stpaul@gmail.com);

Priests' Recovery Program - Rev. Brian M. Clary, Dir. (revbmc@gmail.com); Rev. Guy F. Sciacca, Dir (sciacca.sje@parishmail.com);

Regina Cleri - t) 617-523-1861 Stephen J. Gust, Dir.;

Secretary for Ministerial Personnel - Rev. Robert M. Blaney, Secy. (frrobert_blaney@rcab.org); Dcn. Christopher Z. Connelly, Dir. (connel_c@rcab.org); Sean Hickey, Asst. Dir. (shickey@rcab.org);

Secular Institutes -

Caritas Christi - t) 508-875-7990 Anne M. Ryan, Secy.;

Lay Dominicans - t) 617-472-4446 Raymond A. DiBona, O.P., Dir.;

Oblate Missionaries of Mary Immaculate - t) 603-362-9960 Pauline Labbe, Dir.;

Secular Augustinians - t) 978-685-1111 Rev. Gary N. McCloskey, O.S.A.;

Secular Carmelites - t) 978-462-1057 Loretta L. Gallagher, O.D.C.S.;

Secular Franciscans - t) 781-344-7719 Jacquelyn D. Walsh, Regl. Min.;

Society of Saint James the Apostle - t) 617-742-4715 Rev. David M. Costello (Ireland), Dir.;

Vicar for Clergy - t) 617-746-5928 Very Rev. William P. Joy (reverendwilliam_joy@rcab.org);

Vocations Office - Rev. Eric F. Cadin, Dir. (ecadin@rcab.org); Rev. Carlos D. Suarez, Asst. Dir. (csuarez@rcab.org); Rev. Michael Zimmerman, Dir. (m_zimmerman@rcab.org);

COMMUNICATIONS

Boston Catholic Directory - t) 617-779-3790 Rev. Robert M. O'Grady (rmogrady@pilotcatholicnews.com);
Catholic Media - t) 617-923-0220 Most Rev. Robert P. Reed, Secy. (westregion@rcab.org); Rick Mosley, Dir. (rmosley@catholictv.org);
Boston Catholic Directory - t) 617-779-3790 rmogrady@pilotcatholicnews.com; directory@pilotcatholicnews.com www.bostoncatholicdirectory.com Rev. Robert M. O'Grady;
CatholicTV Network - Most Rev. Robert P. Reed, Pres.; Jay Fadden, Exec. Vice Pres. & Gen. Mgr.;
The Pilot - Antonio M. Enrique, Editor; Gregory L. Tracy, Mng. Editor;
Pilot Bulletins - t) 617-779-3771 Paul Blanchette, Dir.;
Pilot Media Group - Antonio M. Enrique, Pres.; Most Rev. Robert P. Reed;
Pilot Printing - t) 617-779-3774 Mike Strong, Dir.;
Radio Apostolate (Vacant) -
Pauline Center for Media Studies - t) 617-522-8911 Sr. Mary Sophie Stewart, F.S.P., Dir.;
The Pilot - t) 617-779-3781 Antonio M. Enrique, Editor (aenrique@pilotcatholicnews.com);
Radio - t) 617-923-0220 Most Rev. Robert P. Reed, Dir. (reed@catholictv.org);

CONSULTATIVE BODIES

Archdiocesan Pastoral Council - t) 617-254-0100 His Eminence Sean Cardinal O'Malley, O.F.M.Cap., Pres.; Rev. John J. Ahern; Rev. Gerald A. Souza;
Presbyteral Council -
Appointed Members - Rev. Msgr. William P. Fay; Very Rev. Robert L. Connors; Very Rev. William P. Joy;
Elected Members -
Central Region - Rev. Carlos F. Flor; Rev. John J. Ahern; Rev. Joseph M. White;
Merrimack Region - Rev. Jeremy P. St. Martin; Rev. Christopher L. Lowe; Rev. Kevin J. Deeley;
North Region - Rev. Michael J. Doyle; Rev. David C. Lewis; Rev. Paul K. Hurley;
Senior Priests - Rev. Msgr. Peter V. Conley; Rev. Gerald J. Osterman; Rev. William G. Williams;
South Region - Rev. Matthew M. Williams; Rev. Sean M. Connor; Rev. Jason R. Giombetti;
West Region - Rev. James M. Mahoney; Rev. Michael L. Nolan; Rev. Eric F. Cadin;
Ex Officio Members - Most Rev. John A. Dooher; Most Rev. Robert F. Hennessey; Most Rev. Arthur L. Kennedy;
Religious Members - Rev. John P. Bolduc, S.M.; Rev. William M. Brown, O.M.V.; Rev. Thomas Conway, O.F.M.;

DEVELOPMENT

Boston Catholic Development Services - t) 617-254-0100 Joanne Brown, Gift Processing; Sandra Dowd, Dir.; Kate Doyle, Special Projects Mgr.;
Institutional Advancement - Kathleen F. Driscoll, Secy. (kdriscoll@rcab.org); Lynn Morris, Exec. Asst. & Graphic Designer; Mary Doorley, Vice Pres. Devel.;

EDUCATION

Education - Kathy Mears, Supt.;
Catholic Schools Office - t) 617-779-3601 www.catholicschoolsboston.org Thomas W. Carroll, Supt.;
Associate Superintendent for School Finance & Operations - Martha Hultzman, Asst. Supt.;
Associate Superintendent of Academics & Instruction - Gina Mathews, Supt.;
Associate Superintendent of Catholic Identity - Colleen Donohoe;
Associate Superintendent of Data, Analysis & Technology - John Ribeiro, Supt.;
Associate Superintendent of Government Programs and Grants - Mary Goslin, Asst. Supt.;
Chief of Staff - Stephanie Whelan;
Director of School Communications - Meghan Stellman, Dir.;
Director of School Improvement Planning - Jaime Gaudet, Dir.;
Director of Special Projects - Rebecca Ubiparipovic, Dir.;
Enrollment Specialist - Mariana Fontoura;
Operations Associate - Alexis Parry;
Notre Dame Education Center - t) 617-268-1912 Sr. Joyce Khoury, S.N.D., Dir.;
Notre Dame Education Center - t) 978-682-6441 Sr. Eileen T. Burns, S.N.D., Exec.;
Special Needs -
Braintree Cardinal Cushing Centers, Inc. - t) 781-848-6250 Ron Shepherd, Prin.;
Hanover Cardinal Cushing Centers, Inc. - t) 781-826-6371 Roberta Pulaski, Dir.;

FAMILY LIFE

Respect Life Education Office - t) 617-746-5684 Colleen Donohue, Asst. Dir.;

FINANCE

Catholic Community Fund - Board of Trustees - t) 617-254-0100 Sheila C. Cavanaugh, Corp. Communications Consultant, Belmont; Kevin P. Martin;
Officers - His Eminence Sean P. O'Malley, O.F.M.Cap., Chair; Kathleen F. Driscoll, Pres.; John E. Straub, Treas.;

ORGANIZATIONS

Cor Unum Meal Center - t) 978-688-8900 Diane Jarvis, Dir. (corunummealcenter@comcast.net);
Holy Name Societies - t) 617-325-5905 Robert Quagan (rquagan@comcast.net);
Labor Guild - t) 781-340-7887 laborguild@aol.com www.laborguild.com Allyson Every, Exec.;
L'Arche Irenicon, Inc. - t) 978-374-6928 Swanna Champlin, Exec.;
League of Catholic Women - t) 781-843-6616 Mary Sullivan, Pres.;
Legion of Mary - t) 617-542-5682 James Kjellander, Pres.;
Notre Dame Mission Center - t) 978-682-6441 Sr. Ruth Duffy, S.N.D., Dir.;
Pauline Books and Media - t) 781-326-5385 Sr. Mary Martha Moss, F.S.P., Dir.;
Private Associations of Christ's Faithful -
Foyer of Charity - t) 781-545-1080 fb@foyerofcharity.org www.foyerofcharity.org
Marian Community - t) 508-533-5377 www.mariancommunity.org
Public Association of Christ's Faithful -
Association of Saint Francis De Sales - t) 781-934-7228 Catherine Cullen, Dir.;
Brotherhood of Hope - t) 617-623-9592 Bro. J. Rahl Bunsa, Gen. Supr.;
Franciscans of the Primitive Observance (Vacant) -
Society of Saint Vincent de Paul - t) 781-344-3100 Edward J. Resnick, Exec.; Robert V. Travers Jr., Pres. (execdir@svdpboston.com);
Specialized Catholic Organizations -
Ancient Order of Hibernians - t) 617-924-9765 Richard J. Thompson, Pres.;
Ancient Order of Hibernians - Ladies Auxiliary - Vacant - www.laoh.massboard.org
Archdiocesan Union of Holy Name Societies - t) 508-584-2019 Joseph Lapointe;
Casa Monte Cassino - t) 617-227-1613 casamontecassino@earthlink.net www.casamontecassino.org
Catholic Alumni Club - t) 617-261-9600 Thomas Litrenta, Pres.;
Catholic Association of Foresters - t) 781-848-8221 John F. Anderson, Treas.;
Catholic Daughters of the Americas - t) 617-782-4782 Patricia McShane, Regent;
Catholic Lawyers Guild - t) 617-244-4300 Michael K. Gillis, Pres.;
Daughters of Isabella - t) 508-993-5085 Theresa Lewis, Regent;
Emmaus Ministry for Grieving Parents - t) 800-919-9332 Diane Monaghan;
Equestrian Order of the Holy Sepulchre of Jerusalem - t) 508-752-3311 Gerard J. Foley;
Guild of the Infant Savior - t) 978-683-9846 Sharon Deehan, Pres.;
Healing and Restoration Ministry - t) 617-442-2008 Rev. Robert Lennon, C.Ss.R.;
International Order of the Alhambra - t) 781-396-1979 Cornelius M. Murphy, Secy.;
Knights of Columbus - t) 781-551-0628 state.office@masskofc.org www.massachusettsstatekofc.org
Knights of Peter Claver - t) 617-552-1298 Meyer Chambers, Grand Knight;
Magnificat Joy of Boston - t) 781-344-6616 Louise Scipione, Coord.;
Nocturnal Adoration Society - t) 617-698-6321 George J. Hallett, Pres.;
Pax Christi USA - t) 781-944-0330 Rev. William T. Kremmell, Advisor;
Pieta - t) 508-384-6663 Barbara Waters, Coord.;
Pro Maria Committee - t) 978-649-1813 Irene Tremblay, Dir.;
Pro Parvulis - Beverly C. Baker, Treas.;
Serra Boston - t) 978-462-1057 Brian Gallagher; Loretta Gallagher, Leaders;
Seton Club - t) 781-233-2497 Joseph Weller, Pres.;
Simon of Cyrene Society - t) 617-268-8393 Sr. Margaret Youngclaus, S.N.D., Dir.;
Women Affirming Life - t) 617-254-2277 Frances X. Hogan, Pres.;
World Apostolate of Fatima - t) 508-378-7431 Lynn Kenn, Pres.;

PASTORAL SERVICES

African-American Ministry of Cultural Diversity - t) 617-746-5794 Lorna DesRoses (ldesroses@rcab.org);
Airport Chaplaincy - t) 617-567-2800 Rev. Christopher O'Connor;
Black Catholic Choir - t) 617-448-4578 Meyer Chambers (meyer.chambers.1@bc.edu);
Campus Ministry - t) 617-746-5856 www.bostoncatholic.org Rev. Eric F. Cadin, Dir. (ecadin@rcab.org);
Babson College - t) 781-239-5623 www.babson.edu
Bentley University - t) 781-891-2754 www.bentley.edu Angela Howard McParland, Contact;
Boston College - t) 617-552-3475 ministry@bc.edu www.bc.edu Rev. Anthony Penna, Contact;
Boston University - t) 617-353-3632 www.bu.edu/catholic Rev. David J. Barnes, Contact;
Bridgewater State University - t) 508-531-1346 aezeani@bridgew.edu Amber Ezeani, Contact;
Curry College - t) 617-333-2289 www.curry.edu
Emerson College - t) 617-783-3924 www.emerson.edu Kristelle Angelli, Contact;
Emmanuel College - t) 617-735-9780 www.emmanuel.edu Rev. John P. Spencer, S.J., Contact;
Framingham State University - t) 508-626-4610 www.frc.mass.edu Kristelle Angelli, Contact;
Harvard University - t) 617-868-6585 www.harvardcatholicchaplaincy.org Rev. William T. Kelly, Contact;
Laboure College - t) 617-296-8300 www.labourecollege.org
Massachusetts Institute of Technology - t) 617-253-2981 Rev. Daniel P. Moloney, Contact;
Merrimack College - t) 978-837-5450 www.merrimack.edu Rev. Raymond F. Dlugos, O.S.A., Contact;
Northeastern University - t) 617-373-8964 www.nucatholics.neu.edu Bro. Jason Zink, B.H., Contact;
Regis College - t) 781-768-7063 www.regiscollege.edu

Rev. Paul E. Kilroy, Contact;
Salem State University -
Suffolk University -
Tufts University - t) 781-391-7272 www.tufts.edu Lynn Cooper, Contact;
University of Massachusetts-Boston - t) 617-287-5839 www.umb.edu Rev. Paul D. Helfrich, B.H., Contact;
University of Massachusetts-Lowell - t) 978-934-5032 www.uml.edu Dcn. Michael M. Mott, Contact;
Cape Verdean - Antonio Pina; John Barros;
Charismatic Renewal - t) 781-333-5308 Alvaro Soares, Dir.;
Chrism - Celia Sirois, Coord.;
Congolese - t) 617-746-5794
Courage - t) 617-779-4302 courageboston@gmail.com
Ecumenical and Interreligious Affairs - t) 617-746-5749 Most Rev. Arthur L. Kennedy;
EnCourage (Vacant) -
Eritrean - t) 508-583-1121 Rev. Abayneh Gebremichael;
Ethiopian - t) 508-583-1121 Rev. Abayneh Gebremichael;
Ghanaian - t) 617-323-6458 Patrick Sossou;
Haitian - t) 617-298-0080
Health Care Ministry - t) 617-746-5843 Dcn. James F. Greer, Dir.;
Hispanic Apostolate - t) 617-746-5816 Rev. Francisco J. Anzoategui Peiro; Fernando Fernandez-Arellano, Coord. Prog.;
Jewish Relations - t) 978-922-0113 Rev. David C. Michael, Dir.;
Kenyan - t) 978-985-3685 Dan Kurema;
Marriage Ministry - t) 617-746-5801
Nigerian - t) 617-445-8915 Rev. Jude Thaddeus Osunkwo (Nigeria);
Office of Black Catholics - Lorna DesRoses (ldesroses@rcab.org); Gail Mattulina (gail_mattulina@rcab.org);
Office of the Deaf Apostolate - t) 617-746-5815 www.deafcatholic.org
American Sign -
Danvers - t) 978-774-0445
Middleborough - t) 508-947-0444
Newton - t) 617-969-2248
Coordinator of the Deaf Senior Wellness Program - t) 617-746-5817 Elizabeth Whittacker;
Director - Rev. Shawn P. Carey;
Interpreter Coordinator/Staff Interpreter -
Outreach and Cultural Diversity - Rev. Michael C. Harrington, Dir. (mharrington@rcab.org); Robert Kavanaugh, Office Coord.; Lorna DesRoses, Dir. (ldesroses@rcab.org);
Pastoral Centers -
Centro Bom Samaritano - t) 508-628-3721 centrobomsamaritano@hotmail.com
Centro Comunitario Scalabrini - t) 617-387-0822
Chinese Pastoral Center - t) 617-482-2949 Sr. Madeline Gallagher, M.H.S.H.;
Irish Pastoral Center - t) 617-265-5300 Kathleen Rohan, Admin.; Rev. John M. McCarthy (Ireland), Chap.;
Other Pastoral Centers -
Don Guanella Center - t) 617-889-0179
Our Lady's Guild House - t) 617-536-3000 Connie Pagan, Admin.;
Salesian Boys and Girls Club - t) 617-667-6626
Saint Anthony of Padua Social Action - t) 617-783-2121
Prison Ministry - t) 617-746-5843 Dcn. James F. Greer, Dir.;
Secretariat for Evangelization and Discipleship - Rev. Paul R. Soper, Secy. (paul_soper@rcab.org); Michael Lavigne, Secy. (mlavigne@rcab.org);
Office of Divine Worship - t) 617-779-3640
Office of Lifelong Faith Formation and Parish Support - Michael Lavigne, Dir.; Rev. Matthew M. Williams, Dir.; Patrick Krisak, Dir.;
Office of Outreach and Cultural Diversity - t) 617-746-5939 Rev. Michael C. Harrington, Dir.;
Office of Pastoral Planning - t) 617-746-5865 Rev. Paul R. Soper, Dir.;
Office of Spiritual Life - t) 617-779-3640
Operations Assistant - t) 617-779-3644 Ann M. Cussen;
Ugandan - t) 617-548-9678 Lennie Kafeero;

SOCIAL SERVICES

Community Service Centers and Divisions -
Life Resources - t) 781-849-7751 Lynne Marie Bielecki, Pres.;
Pregnancy Help - Mary B. Girard, Dir.;
Metro-West - t) 508-651-0753 help@pregnancyhelpboston.org www.pregnancyhelpboston.org
Social Services -
Catholic Relief Services - t) 617-746-5733 Rev. J. Bryan Hehir;
Labor Guild - t) 781-340-7887 Allyson Every, Exec.;
L'Arche Irenicon, Inc. - t) 978-374-6928 Swanna Champlin, Exec.;
Life Resources - t) 781-849-7751 Lynne Marie Bielecki, Pres.;
Pregnancy Help - Mary B. Girard, Dir.;
Metro-West - t) 508-651-0753 help@pregnancyhelpboston.org www.pregnancyhelpboston.org
Pro-Life Office - t) 508-651-1900 Marianne P. Luthin, Dir.;
Project Rachel - t) 508-651-3100 Marianne P. Luthin, Dir.;
Related Services -
Cor Unum Meal Center - t) 978-688-8900 Diane Jarvis, Dir.;
The Listening Place - t) 781-592-7396 Rev. Alfonse Ferreira, O.F.M., Dir.;
Project Hope - t) 617-442-1880 Sr. Margaret Leonard, L.S.A., Exec.;
Respect Life Education Office - t) 617-746-5684 Colleen Donohue, Asst. Dir.;
Saint Ann's Home, Inc. - t) 978-685-5276 Denis Grandbois, Pres.;
Social Services and Health Care - Rev. J. Bryan Hehir (bryan-hehir@harvard.edu);

SPIRITUAL LIFE

Cursillo - t) 617-779-3640 MaryAnn McLaughlin, Dir. (maryann_mclaughlin@rcab.org);
Marian Devotions (Vacant) -

TRIBUNAL

Archdiocesan Judges - Rev. Msgr. Michael S. Foster; Rev. W. Chris Palladino; Sr. Margaret L. Sullivan, C.S.J.;
Court Advocate/Petitioner - Rev. Wlodzimierz Sobolewski, C.R.; Julianne Shanklin;
Court Advocate/Respondent - Rev. Andreas R. Davison; Rev. Stephen R. Leblanc; Rev. Marcelino D. D'Arthenay;
Defenders of the Bond - Sr. Mary Lou Walsh, S.N.D.; Rev. Cesar Jaramillo; Sr. Margaret L. Sullivan, C.S.J.;
Notaries - Morayma Thompson; AnnMarie Lascuola-Helmar;
Promoter of Justice ad casum - Rev. W. Chris Palladino;
Staff - Morayma Thompson; AnnMarie Lascuola-Helmar;
Ecclesiastical Court of the Archdiocese of Boston - t) 617-746-5900
Judicial Vicar - Rev. Msgr. Robert W. Oliver, B.H.;

COMMONWEALTH OF MASSACHUSETTS

PARISHES, MISSIONS, AND CLERGY

ABINGTON

St. Bridget - 455 Plymouth St., Abington, MA 02351-1889 t) 781-878-0900 sbparishsecretary@comcast.net www.loccc.org Rev. Adrian A. Milik, Pst.; Dcn. James V. McLaughlin; Dcn. Joseph T. Nickley; Dcn. Paul Breadmore;
St. Bridget School - t) 617-878-8482 sbsoffice@stbridgetschool.us www.stbridgetschool.us Matthew Collins, Prin.;

ACTON

St. Elizabeth of Hungary - 89 Arlington St., Acton, MA 01720-2503 t) 978-263-4305 avcatholic.org Rev. Jeffrey S. Archer, Pst.; CRP Stds.: 200
St. Isidore - 89 Arlington St., Acton, MA 01720-2503 t) 978-263-4305; 978-897-9790 (CRP) janice@applevalleycatholic.org www.stisidorestow.org Rev. Jeffrey S. Archer, Pst.; Dcn. Charles A. Cornell; Shelia Bauer, DRE;

AMESBURY

Holy Family - 2 School St., Amesbury, MA 01913; Mailing: 11 Sparhawk St., Amesbury, MA 01913 t) 978-388-0330; 978-388-3477 (CRP) administrativeassistant@livingwatercatholic.org livingwatercatholic.org Rev. Ronald L. St. Pierre, Pst.; Dcn. Charles A. Hall;
Star of the Sea - 9 Sparhawk St., Amesbury, MA 01913 t) 978-465-3334 administrativeassistant@livingwatercatholic.org livingwatercatholic.org Rev. Ronald L. St. Pierre, Pst.; Dcn. Charles A. Hall; Kyle Gregg, DRE;

ANDOVER

St. Augustine - 43 Essex St., Andover, MA 01810-3748 t) 978-475-0050 info@staugustineparish.org staugustineparish.org Rev. Peter G. Gori, O.S.A., Pst.; Rev. Arthur D. Johnson, O.S.A., Assoc. Pst.; Rev. John F. Dello Russo, O.S.A., Vicar; Dcn. Michael F. Curren; Dcn. Louis J. Piazza; Bridget Rao, DRE;
St. Augustine School - 26 Central St., Andover, MA 01810 t) 978-475-2414 info@staugustineschoolandover.org www.staugustineandover.org Mark Daley, Prin.;
St. Joseph's - 20 High Vale Ln., Ballardville, MA 01810
Sisters of Notre Dame - 47 Essex St., Andover, MA 01810 t) 978-475-0087
St. Robert Bellarmine - 198 Haggetts Pond Rd., Andover, MA 01810-4218 t) 978-683-8922 Rev. Richard T. Conway, Pst.; Amanda Roberts, DRE;

ARLINGTON

Saint Agnes - 32 Medford St., Arlington, MA 02474-3197; Mailing: 51 Medford St., Arlington, MA 02474 t) 781-648-0220 info@cparl.org; smorin@cparl.org www.cparl.org Part of the Catholic Parishes of Arlington Collaborative. Rev. Marc J. Bishop, Pst.; Rev. Alwin Chinnappan, Par. Vicar; Rev. Charles E. Bourke, In Res.; Roger Mansen, Music Min.; Dcn. Peter Bujwid; Meredith Smith, DRE; Bill Healey, Bus. Mgr.; CRP Stds.: 287
St. Agnes School - (Grades PreK-8) 39 Medford St., Arlington, MA 02474 t) 781-643-9031 ssullivan@saintagnesschool.us www.achssas.org Susan Sullivan, Assoc. Prin., PreK-Grade 5; Stds.: 339; Lay Tchrs.: 20
Arlington Catholic High School - (Grades 9-12) 16 Medford St., Arlington, MA 02474 t) 781-646-7770 mainoffice@achs.net www.achssas.org John Graceffa, Prin.; Steve Barrett, Assoc. Prin. Oper. & Mgmt., 6-12; Nathaniel Naughton, Assoc. Prin., Academics, 6-12; Stds.: 375; Lay Tchrs.: 33
St. Camillus - 1175 Concord Tpke., Arlington, MA 02476-7262; Mailing: 51 Medford St., Arlington, MA 02474 t) 781-648-0220 info@cparl.org; smorin@cparl.org www.cparl.org Part of the Catholic Parishes of Arlington Collaborative. Faith Formation program in run together with St. Agnes Parish. Rev. Marc J. Bishop, Pst.; Rev. Alwin Chinnappan, Par. Vicar; Dcn. Peter Bujwid; Rev. Paul E. Kilroy, In Res.;

Roger Mansen, Music Min.; Maredith Smith, DRE; Fabiola Aguilera, Office & Communications Mgr.; Scott Morin, Dir. Evangelization; Mary Wessel, Coord., Communications & Media; Bill Healey, Bus. Mgr.; James Judge, Facilities Mgr.; Charlene Camara, Admin. Asst.; CRP Stds.: 287

ASHLAND

St. Cecilia - 54 Esty St., Ashland, MA 01721-2126 t) 508-881-1107; 508-881-6107 (CRP) business@saintceciliaparish.org www.saintceciliaparish.org Rev. Richard P. Cornell, Pst.; Heather Petruney, DRE; Janet Wilkinson, DRE;

AVON

St. Michael - 87 N. Main St., Avon, MA 02322-1286 t) 508-586-4065 (CRP); 508-586-7210 stmichaelsavon@comcast.net Rev. Thomas C. Boudreau, Pst.; Rev. John E. Kelly, Assoc. Pst.; Elaine Flanagan, DRE;

AYER

St. Mary - 31 Shirley St., Ayer, MA 01432-1219 t) 978-772-2414; 978-772-0727 (CRP) parishoffice@nashobacatholic.org; business@nashobacatholic.org www.nashobacatholic.org Rev. Edmond M. Derosier, Pst.; Marianne Cooper, DRE;

BEDFORD

St. Michael - 90 Concord Rd., Bedford, MA 01730 t) 781-275-6324 (CRP); 781-275-6318 Rev. Msgr. William F. Cuddy, Admin.; Patricia Marks, DRE;

BELLINGHAM

St. Blaise - 1158 S. Main St., Bellingham, MA 02019-1597 t) 508-966-1258 Rev. Albert M. Faretra, Pst.; Dcn. Richard J. Brennan; Beth Grenier, DRE;

St. Brendan - 384 Hartford Ave., Bellingham, MA 02019-1217 t) 508-966-9802 Rev. David J. Mullen, Pst.; Dcn. David R. Ghioni; Gladys Griffin, DRE;

BELMONT

St. Joseph - 130 Common St., Belmont, MA 02478-2418 t) 617-484-0279 info@newroadscatholic.org www.newroadscatholic.org Rev. Thomas A. Mahoney, Pst.; Rev. Austin H. Fleming, Par. Vicar;

St. Luke - 132 Lexington St., Belmont, MA 02478-1239; Mailing: 130 Common St., Belmont, MA 02478 t) 617-484-1996 info@newroadscatholic.org Rev. Thomas A. Mahoney, Pst.;

BEVERLY

St. John the Evangelist - 111 New Balch St., Beverly, MA 01915; Mailing: 253 Cabot St., Beverly, MA 01915 Rev. David C. Michael, Pst.; Dcn. Michael C. Joens; Dr. Margaret McKinnon, DRE;

The Saints Academy - (Grades PreK-8) t) 978-922-0048 info@saintsacademy.org saintsacademy.org Daniel Bouchard, Prin.;

St. Margaret - 672 Hale St., Beverly, MA 01915-2119; Mailing: 552 Cabot St., Beverly, MA 01915 t) 978-927-0069 Rev. David C. Michael, Pst.; Rev. Guy F. Sciacca, Par. Vicar; Rev. James P. Wargovich, Par. Vicar; Dcn. Michael C. Joens;

St. Mary Star of the Sea - 251 Cabot St., Beverly, MA 01915-4597; Mailing: 552 Cabot St., Beverly, MA 01915 t) 978-922-0113 Rev. David C. Michael, Pst.; Rev. Guy F. Sciacca, Par. Vicar; Rev. James P. Wargovich, Par. Vicar; Dcn. Michael C. Joens;

St. Mary Star of the Sea School - 13 Chapman St., Beverly, MA 01915 t) 978-927-3259 Sr. Catherine Fleming, S.N.D., Prin.;

St. Mary - 15 Chapman St., Beverly, MA 01915-4597

BILLERICA

St. Andrew - 45 Talbot Ave., Billerica, MA 01862-1414; Mailing: 1 Grace Ave., Billerica, MA 01821 t) 978-667-9024 (CRP); 978-663-3624 heather.murphy.ccb@gmail.com Rev. Paul J. Aveni, Pst.; Dcn. Phillip T. DiBello; Rev. Theophilus Okpara, In Res.;

St. Mary - 796 Boston Rd., Billerica, MA 01821 Rev. Paul J. Aveni, Pst.; Dcn. Phillip T. DiBello; Dcn. Allan R. Shanahan;

Saint Matthew the Evangelist Parish - 466 Boston Rd., Billerica, MA 01821; Mailing: One Grace Ave., Billerica, MA 01821 t) 978-663-8816 admin@billericacatholic.org www.billericacatholic.org Rev. Paul J. Aveni, Pst.; Rev. Theophilus Okpara, In Res.; Rev. Romain Rurangirwa, In Res.; Dcn. Phillip T. DiBello;

St. Theresa of Lisieux - 466 Boston Rd., Billerica, MA 01821-2504; Mailing: 1 Grace Ave., Billerica, MA 01821 t) 978-663-8816 admin@billericacatholic.org www.billericacatholic.org Rev. Paul J. Aveni, Pst.; Dcn. Phillip T. DiBello;

BOSTON

Cathedral of the Holy Cross - 1400 Washington St., Boston, MA 02118-2141; Mailing: 75 Union Park St., Boston, MA 02118 t) 617-542-5682 cathedral2@rcab.org holycrossboston.com Rev. Msgr. Kevin J. O'Leary, Admin.; Rev. Marcelino D. D'Arthenay, Par. Vicar; Dcn. Luciano Herrera; Dcn. Ricardo M. Mesa; Rev. Robert T. Kickham, In Res.; His Eminence Sean P. O'Malley, O.F.M.Cap., In Res.;

Mission Helpers of Sacred Heart - 286 Shumwut Ave., Boston, MA 02118 t) 617-542-1143

St. Ambrose - 246 Adams St., Boston, MA 02122 t) 617-265-5302 stambroseparish@comcast.net Rev. Linh T. Nguyen, Pst.; Rev. Marcos Enrique, Par. Vicar; Rev. Thomas F. Bouton, In Res.; Rev. Richard C. Conway, In Res.;

St. Angela Merici - 1548 Blue Hill Ave., Boston, MA 02126 t) 617-298-0080 stangelamattapan@gmail.com www.agmcatholic.org Rev. Jean Gustave Miracle (Haiti), Assoc. Pst.; Rev. Thomas Rossi, Assoc. Pst.;

Saint John Paul II Academy - Mattapan Square Campus - 120 Babson St., Dorchester, MA 02126 t) 617-265-0019 louann.melino@popejp2catholicacademy.org www.popejp2catholicacademy.org Kathleen Aldridge, Prin.;

St. Ann - 243 Neponset Ave., Boston, MA 02122-3239 agenovesedff@gmail.com Rev. W. Chris Palladino, Pst.;

Convent - 241 Neponset Ave., Dorchester, MA 02122 t) 617-288-1202

St. Anne - 90 W. Milton St., Boston, MA 02136 t) 857-342-9500 achavez@bluehillscollaborative.org bluehillscollaborative.org Rev. Joseph M. Mazzone, Pst.; Rev. Charles Madi-Okin, Assoc. Pst.;

Convent - 85 W. Milton St., Readville, MA 02136 t) 617-361-8224

St. Anthony of Padua - 43 Holton St., Boston, MA 02134-1397 t) 617-782-0775 Rev. Robert J. Carr, Admin.; Rev. Francisco C. Martins Silva (Brazil), Assoc. Pst.;

St. Brendan - 589 Gallivan Blvd., Boston, MA 02124-5321 t) 617-436-0310; 617-825-8622 (CRP) saintbrendanparish02124@gmail.com saintbrendanparish.org Rev. W. Chris Palladino, Pst.;

St. Brendan School - 29 Rita Rd., Dorchester, MA 02124-5321 t) 617-282-3388 office@stmartindorchester.org www.stbrendanschool.org Maura Burke, Prin.;

St. Brigid of Kildare - 845 E. Broadway, Boston, MA 02127-2302; Mailing: 841 E. Broadway, Boston, MA 02127-2302 t) 617-268-2122 gateofheavenstbrigid@gmail.com www.gateofheavenstbrigid.org Very Rev. Robert E. Casey, Pst.; Rev. Christopher J. Boyle, Par. Vicar;

South Boston Catholic Academy - (Grades PreK-6) 866 E. Broadway, South Boston, MA 02127 t) 617-268-2326 j.brown@sbcatholicacademy.org www.sbcatholicacademy.org Dr. Helenann Civian, Prin.;

St. Cecilia - 18 Belvidere St., Boston, MA 02115-3132 t) 617-536-4548 info@stceciliaboston.org www.stceciliaboston.org Rev. John J. Unni, Pst.; Mark Donohoe, Pst. Assoc.; Scott MacDonald, DRE; Colleen Melaugh, Bus. Mgr.; Robert Duff, Music Min.; CRP Stds.: 150

Congregation of Saint Athanasius - 767 W. Roxbury Pkwy., Boston, MA 02132-2121 Rev. Richard S. Bradford, Admin.;

St. Francis de Sales - 313 Bunker Hill St., Boston, MA 02129-1826 t) 617-242-0147 stfran303@aol.com www.stfrancisdesalescharlestown.com Rev. Daniel J. Mahoney, Pst.;

Gate of Heaven - 615 E. 4th St., Boston, MA 02127-2302; Mailing: 841 E. Broadway, Boston, MA 02127-2302 t) 617-268-3344 gateofheavenstbrigid@gmail.com www.gateofheavenstbrigid.org Very Rev. Robert E. Casey, Pst.; Rev. Christopher J. Boyle, Par. Vicar; Ellen McDonough, DRE;

South Boston Catholic Academy - (Grades PreK-6) 866 E. Broadway, Boston, MA 02127 t) 617-268-2326 h.civian@sbcatholicacademy.org www.sbcatholicacademy.org Dr. Helenann Civian, Prin.;

St. Gregory - 2215 Dorchester Ave., Boston, MA 02124-5607; Mailing: 2223 Dorchester Ave., Dorchester, MA 02124 t) 617-298-2460 stgregoryparish@gmail.com www.stgregoryparish.com Rev. John J. Ahern, Pst.; Rev. Brian McMahon, In Res.; Jean Pierre, DRE;

Holy Family - 24 Hartford St., Boston, MA 02122; Mailing: St. Peter Parish, 278 Bowdoin St., Dorchester, MA 02122 t) 617-265-1132; 617-567-6509 (CRP) stpeterparishdorchester@gmail.com dorchestercatholic.org Rev. John A. Currie, Pst.;

Holy Name - 1689 Centre St., Boston, MA 02132-1292 t) 617-325-4865 contact.hnp@holynameparish.com holynameparish.com Rev. George P. Evans, Pst.; Rev. Denis N. Nakkeeran, Assoc. Pst.; Rev. Brian M. Flatley, In Res.; Rev. Martin J. McNulty, In Res.; Rev. Oscar J. Pratt, In Res.; James Flanagan, DRE; Dcn. Timothy F. Donohue;

Holy Name School - 535 W. Roxbury Pkwy., West Roxbury, MA 02132-1292 t) 617-325-9338 contact.hnps@holynameparish.com holynameparishschool.org

St. James the Greater - 125 Harrison Ave., Boston, MA 02111 t) 617-542-8498 info@bcccstjames.org www.bcccstjames.org Rev. Joseph Zhang, AA, Admin.; Dcn. Francis Sung; Susan Ho, DRE;

St. John Chrysostom - 4750 Washington St., Boston, MA 02132 t) 617-323-4410; 617-323-4411 carolobrien@stjohnchrysostom02132.org www.stjohnchrysostom02132.org Rev. John J. Connolly, Pst.; Rev. Charles J. Higgins, Par. Vicar;

St. Joseph - 68 William Cardinal O'Connell Way, Boston, MA 02114-2709 t) 617-523-4342 office@stjosephboston.com www.stjosephboston.com Rev. Joseph M. White, Admin.;

St. Joseph-St. Lazarus - 59 Ashley St., Boston, MA 02128 t) 617-569-0406 Rev. Miroslaw Kowalczyk, F.D.P., Pst.; Rev. Eucinei DeSouza, F.D.P., Assoc. Pst.; Marianne Cincinnato, DRE;

St. Katharine Drexel - 517 Blue Hill Ave., Boston, MA 02120; Mailing: 175 Ruggles St., Roxbury, MA 02120 t) 617-445-8915 Rev. Oscar J. Pratt, Admin.;

St. Leonard of Port Maurice - 320 Hanover St., Boston, MA 02113-1913 t) 617-523-2110 admin@saintleonardchurchboston.org www.saintleonardchurchboston.org Rev. Michael DellaPenna, O.F.M., Pst.;

St. John - 9 Moon St., Boston, MA 02113 t) 617-227-3143 ccassidy@sjsne.com www.sjsne.com Claire Cassidy, Prin.;

St. Mark - 1725 Dorchester Ave., Boston, MA 02124 t) 617-825-2852 judy.stmarks@comcast.net stmark-stambrose.org Rev. Linh T. Nguyen, Pst.; Rev. Marcos Enrique, Par. Vicar; Dcn. Marcio O. Fonseca;

Saint Martin de Porres Parish - 251 Neponset Ave., Boston, MA 02122 Rev. W. Chris Palladino, Pst.;

St. Mary - St. Catherine of Siena - 55 Warren St., Boston, MA 02129; Mailing: 46 Winthrop St., Charlestown, MA 02129 t) 617-242-4664 office@stmarystcatherine.org www.stmarystcatherine.org Rev. James J. Ronan, Pst.; Rev. Jerome F. Gillespie, In Res.;

St. Mary of the Angels - 97 South St., Boston, MA 02130 t) 617-524-0913 Rev. Carlos F. Flor, Pst.; Rev. Andrea Povero, Par. Vicar; Dcn. Jesus M. Ortiz; Dcn. Jose Perez-Rodriguez; Luz Dary Pelaez, DRE;

St. Matthew - 33 Stanton St., Boston, MA 02124-3716
Saint Monica Parish - 331 Old Colony Ave., Boston, MA 02127
Most Holy Redeemer - 72 Maverick St., Boston, MA 02128-1924; Mailing: 65 London St., East Boston, MA 02128-1924 t) 617-567-3227 info@mhrboston.org www.mostholyredeemerboston.org Member Central Catholic School of East Boston. Rev. Thomas S. Domurat, Pst.; Rev. Joel Americo Santos, Assoc. Pst.; Dcn. Francis W. McHugh; Dcn. Pedro LaTorre; Angelina Monge, DRE;
Most Precious Blood - 25 Maple St., Boston, MA 02136-2755; Mailing: 20 Como Rd., Hyde Park, MA 02136 t) 617-364-9500 achavez@bluehillscollaborative.org bluehillscollaborative.org Rev. Joseph M. Mazzone, Pst.; Rev. Charles Madi-Okin, Assoc. Pst.;
Our Lady of Czestochowa - 655 Dorchester Ave., Boston, MA 02127 t) 617-268-4355 parish@ourladyofczestochowa.com Rev. Jerzy Zebrowski, O.F.M.Conv., Pst.;
Our Lady of Lourdes - 14 Montebello Rd., Boston, MA 02130 t) 617-524-0240 stthsaq@comcast.net catholicjproxbury.com Rev. Carlos F. Flor, Pst.; Rev. Andrea Povero, Par. Vicar; Dcn. Jesus M. Ortiz; Dcn. Jose Perez-Rodriguez; Jose Gonzalez, DRE;
Our Lady of Mount Carmel Parish - 1540 Blue Hill Ave., Boston, MA 02126 t) 617-298-0080 Rev. Garcia Breneville (Haiti), Admin.;
Our Lady of Perpetual Help - 1545 Tremont St., Boston, MA 02120-2909 t) 617-445-2600 Rev. Joseph Tizio, C.Ss.R., Pst.; Rev. John Furey, C.Ss.R., Assoc. Pst.; Rev. Charles Hergenroeder, C.Ss.R., Assoc. Pst.; Rev. Anthony Michalik, C.Ss.R., Assoc. Pst.; Rev. Pierre Desruisseaux, C.Ss.R., Par. Vicar; Joseph Finn, DRE; Rev. Robert Lennon, C.Ss.R., In Res.; Rev. John Devin, C.Ss.R., In Res.;
Our Lady of Perpetual Help Mission Grammar School - (Grades PreSchool-6) 94 St. Alphonsus St., Roxbury, MA 02120 t) 617-442-2660 adutson@missiongrammar.org www.missiongrammar.org Aliece Dutson, Pres.; Caroline Sliney, Prin.;
Our Lady of the Assumption - 404 Sumner St., Boston, MA 02128 t) 617-567-1223 www.olaeastboston.com/ Member East Boston Central Catholic School Consortium. Rev. Ignatius Mushauko (Zambia), Admin.;
St. Patrick - 400 Dudley St., Boston, MA 02119-2706; Mailing: 10 Magazine St., Roxbury, MA 02119 t) 617-445-7645 stpeterparishdorchester@gmail.com dorchestercatholic.org Rev. John A. Currie, Pst.;
St. Peter - 311 Bowdoin St., Boston, MA 02122; Mailing: 278 Bowdoin St., Boston, MA 02122 t) 617-265-1132 stpeterparishdorchester@gmail.com www.dorchestercatholic.org Rev. John A. Currie, Pst.;
St. Peter - 75 Flaherty Way, Boston, MA 02127-2006 t) 617-268-8100 smcleod@sbscatholic.org www.sbscatholic.org Rev. Peter F. DeFazio, Pst.; Rev. Gerald J. Osterman, In Res.; Dcn. Alejandro Iraola; Dcn. Paul M. Kline;
Sacred Heart - 45 Brooks St., Boston, MA 02128-3063; Mailing: 303 Paris St., East Boston, MA 02128 t) 617-567-5776; 617-567-6509 (CRP) sacredhearteb@gmail.com www.sacredhearteb.org Rev. Luis Miguel Hernandez, FSCB, Chap.; Rev. Paolo Cumin, F.S.C.B., Admin.; Sharon A. Rozzi, DRE; Rev. Michele Benetti, FSCB, Prof.; Rev. Luca Brancolini, F.S.C.B., Prof.;
East Boston Central Catholic School Consortium - 69 London St., East Boston, MA 02128 t) 617-567-7456 dgutierrez@ebccs.org www.ebccs.org Robert Casaletto, Prin.;
Sacred Heart - 169 Cummins Hwy., Boston, MA 02131-3739 t) 617-325-3322 sacredheartparish@sh-roslindale.org www.sh-roslindale.org Rev. Brian M. Clary, Pst.; Rev. Succes Jeanty, Vicar; Rev. Elias A. Ojomah (Nigeria), In Res.; Rev. Eugene P. Sullivan, In Res.;
Sacred Heart School - 1035 Canterbury St., Roslindale, MA 02131 t) 617-323-2500 www.sacredheart-boston.org/ Monica Haldiman, Prin.;
St. Stephen - 24 Clark St., Boston, MA 02109-9923 t) 617-523-1230 info@socstjames.com Rev. David M. Costello (Ireland), Admin.; Rev. Patrick J. Universal, In Res.;
Saint Teresa of Calcutta Parish - 800 Columbia Rd., Boston, MA 02125 t) 617-436-2190 bmtdorchester@gmail.com stteresaofcalcuttadorchester.org Rev. John J. Ronaghan, Admin.; Dcn. Paul F. Carroll;
St. Theresa of Avila - 2078 Centre St., Boston, MA 02132-3416; Mailing: 10 St. Theresa Ave., West Roxbury, MA 02132 t) 617-325-1300 sttoffice24@gmail.com; eklein001@gmail.com www.sttheresaparishboston.com Rev. John J. Connolly, Pst.; Rev. Charles J. Higgins, Par. Vicar; Dcn. Brian K. Kean; Ellen K Murphy, DRE; Sr. M. Julie Seguin, scsm, DRE;
St. Theresa of Avila School - (Grades PreK-6) 40 St. Theresa Ave., West Roxbury, MA 02132 t) 617-323-1050 news@sttheresaschoolboston.com www.sttheresaschoolboston.com Gretchen Hawley, Prin.;
St. Thomas Aquinas - 97 South St., Boston, MA 02130 t) 617-524-0240 www.catholicjproxbury.com Collaborative of Parishes of Jamaica Plain & Roxbury Rev. Carlos F. Flor, Pst.; Rev. Andrea Povero, Par. Vicar; Dcn. Jose Perez-Rodriguez; Dcn. Jesus M. Ortiz; Jose Gonzalez, DRE;

BRAINTREE

St. Clare - 856 Washington St., Braintree, MA 02184-8299 t) 781-848-1332 Rev. Paul T. Clifford, Pst.; Rev. Valanarasu Newton-Williamraj, Par. Vicar; Dcn. Joseph E. MacDonald;
St. Francis of Assisi - 856 Washington St., Braintree, MA 02184-6464 t) 781-843-1332 parish@sfab.org Rev. Paul T. Clifford, Pst.; Rev. Valanarasu Newton-Williamraj, Par. Vicar; Dcn. Joseph E. MacDonald;
St. Francis of Assisi School - 850 Washington St., Braintree, MA 02184 t) 781-848-0842 vdebenedictis@sfab.org Brian Cote, Prin.;
St. Thomas More - 7 Hawthorn Rd., Braintree, MA 02184-1402; Mailing: 55 Commercial St., Weymouth, MA 02188 t) 781-337-6333 secretary@shstm.org www.shstm.org Rev. Sean M. Connor, Pst.; Dcn. Bashan Goppee;

BRIDGEWATER

St. Thomas Aquinas - 103 Center St., Bridgewater, MA 02324-1397 t) 508-697-3652 (CRP); 508-697-9528 stthomasaquinas@comcast.net stthomasaquinas.com Rev. William D. Devine, Pst.; Rev. Steven Restrepo, Par. Vicar; Dcn. Leo J. Donoghue;

BRIGHTON

St. Columbkille - 321 Market St., Brighton, MA 02135-2126 t) 617-782-5774 office@brightoncatholic.org www.brightoncatholic.org Rev. Richard W. Fitzgerald, Admin.; Rev. Christopher W. Bae, Assoc. Pst.; Rev. Nathaniel A. Sanders, Par. Vicar; Jose Roberto Mendez, DRE;
St. Columbkille School - (Grades PreK-8) 25 Arlington St., Brighton, MA 02135-2199 t) 617-254-3110 info@stcps.org www.stcps.org Jennifer Kowieski, Prin.; Rachel Rumely, Vice Prin.;

BROCKTON

Christ the King - 54 Lyman St., Brockton, MA 02302-2461; Mailing: 439 West St., Brockton, MA 02301 t) (508) 586-1575 receptionist@brocktoncatholic.org brocktoncatholic.org Very Rev. Matthew J. Westcott, Pst.; Rev. Joseph LaRose, S.M.M., Par. Vicar; Dcn. Philip H. LaFond; Dcn. Robert Balzarini; Marcia Walkama, DRE;
St. Edith Stein - 71 E. Main St., Brockton, MA 02301-2461; Mailing: 439 West St., Brockton, MA 02301 t) 508-588-7032 (CRP); 508-586-6491 receptionist@brocktoncatholic.org brocktoncatholiccatholic.org Very Rev. Matthew J. Westcott, Pst.; Rev. Joseph LaRose, S.M.M., Par. Vicar; Dcn. Philip H. LaFond; Dcn. Robert Balzarini; Dcn. Timothy A. Booker; Marcia Walkama, DRE;
Our Lady of Lourdes - 439 West St., Brockton, MA 02301-4803 t) 508-586-4715 our.lourdes@comcast.net brocktoncatholiccatholic.org Very Rev. Matthew J. Westcott, Pst.; Rev. Joseph LaRose, S.M.M., Par. Vicar; Dcn. Philip H. LaFond; Dcn. Robert Balzarini;
St. Patrick - 335 Main St., Brockton, MA 02301-5396 t) 617-533-0061 office@stpatrickbrockton.com Rev. Przemyslaw Kasprzak, Admin.; Rev. Benito Moreno, Par. Vicar;

BROOKLINE

St. Mary of the Assumption - 3 Linden Pl., Brookline, MA 02445-7311 t) 617-734-0444 info@stmarybrookline.com www.stmarybrookline.com Rev. Jonathan M. Gaspar, Pst.; Rev. Robert A. LeBlanc, Par. Vicar; Sarah Leyden, DRE;
St. Mary of the Assumption School - 67 Harvard St., Brookline, MA 02445 t) 617-566-7184 info@stmarys-brookline.org www.stmarys-brookline.org Dr. Christine Nadjarian, Prin.;

BURLINGTON

St. Malachy - 99 Bedford St., Burlington, MA 01803 t) 781-272-5111 Rev. John M. Capuci, Pst.; Susan Hurton, DRE; Anna Molettieri, DRE; Donald P. Nealon, DRE;
St. Margaret of Antioch - 109 Winn St., Burlington, MA 01803 t) 781-272-3111; 781-935-7373 (CRP) stmargaretparish2@verizon.net www.stmargaretburlington.org Very Rev. Frank J. Silva, Pst.; Rev. Jiwon Yoon, Assoc. Pst.; Dcn. Richard F. Bilotta; Mary Murgo, DRE;
Saint Veronica Parish - 109 Winn St., Burlington, MA 01803 t) 781-272-3111 stveronicama@gmail.com Rev. James M. Mahoney, Pst.;

CAMBRIDGE

St. Anthony of Padua - 400 Cardinal Medeiros Ave., Cambridge, MA 02141-1411 t) 617-547-5593 info@saintanthonyparish.com Rev. Michael C. Harrington, Admin.; Rev. Edinardo DeOliveira, Par. Vicar; Elizabeth Carreiro, DRE;
St. Francis of Assisi - 325 Cambridge St., Cambridge, MA 02141 t) 617-547-5593 saintfranciscambridge@gmail.com Rev. Michael C. Harrington, Admin.; Rev. Edinardo DeOliveira, Par. Vicar;
St. John the Evangelist - 2270 Massachusetts Ave., Cambridge, MA 02140-1837 t) 617-547-4880 info@stjohncambridge.org www.stjohncambridge.org Rev. Joseph T. MacCarthy, Admin.; Maureen Megnia, DRE;
St. Mary of the Annunciation - 135 Norfolk St., Cambridge, MA 02139 t) 617-547-0120; 617-547-0145 (CRP) saintmarycambridge@gmail.com www.stmaryoftheannunciation.com Rev. Michael C. Harrington, Pst.; Rev. Daniel Zinger, Par. Vicar; Dcn. Antonio Perez;
St. Paul - Bow & Arrow Sts., Cambridge, MA 02138-6097; Mailing: 29 Mt. Auburn St., Cambridge, MA 02138 t) 617-491-8400 info@stpaulparish.org; ktucker@stpaulparish.org www.stpaulparish.org Rev. William T. Kelly, Pst.; Rev. Patrick J. Fiorillo, Par. Vicar; Rev. George S. Salzmann, O.S.F.S., Chap.; Dcn. Thomas L. O'Donnell; Kristin Tucker, DRE;
St. Paul's Choir School - (Grades 3-8) 29 Mt. Auburn St., Cambridge, MA 02138 t) 617-868-8658 admin@saintpaulschoirschool.us www.saintpaulschoirschool.us/ Dr. Thomas Haferd, Headmaster;
St. Peter - 100 Concord Ave., Cambridge, MA 02138-2297 t) 617-547-4235 office@saintpetercambridge.org saintpetercambridge.org Rev. Leonard F. O'Malley, Pst.; Dcn. John Czajkowski; Robert Flaherty, DRE; CRP Stds.: 75
St. Peter School - 96 Concord Ave., Cambridge, MA 02138 t) 617-547-0101 admin@saint-peter-school.org www.saint-peter-school.org Dr. Evan Kristiansen,

Head of School;

Sacred Heart - 47 Sixth St., Cambridge, MA 02141-1594 t) 617-547-0399 sacredheartofj@msn.com Rev. Joseph L. Curran, Admin.;

CANTON

Saint Oscar Romero Parish - 700 Washington St., Canton, MA 02021 t) 781-828-0090 welcome@cantoncatholic.org Rev. Thomas S. Rafferty, Pst.;

St. John the Evangelist School - 696 Washington St., Canton, MA 02021-3036 t) 781-828-2130 chris.flieger@sjscanton.org www.sjscanton.org Chris Flieger, Prin.;

CARLISLE

St. Irene - 181 East St., Carlisle, MA 01741-1104 t) 978-369-3940 stirene@comcast.net www.cc-catholic.org Very Rev. Frank J. Silva, Pst.; Rev. Nicholas H. Stano, Par. Vicar; Sr. Dcn. Dean C. Bulpett;

CARVER

Our Lady of Lourdes - Merged Jul 2022 Parish records for all closed, merged & suppressed parishes are located at the Office of the Archives, 66 Brooks Dr., Braintree, MA 02184-3839.

CHELMSFORD

St. John the Evangelist - 115 Middlesex St., Chelmsford, MA 01863-2030 t) 978-251-4310 (CRP); 978-251-8571 churches@chelmsfordcatholic.org Rev. Brian E. Mahoney, Pst.; Rev. Fernando E. Ayala Rosales, Par. Vicar; Courtney Callanan, DRE;

St. Mary - 25 North Rd., Chelmsford, MA 01824-2767 Rev. Brian E. Mahoney, Pst.; Rev. Fernando E. Ayala Rosales, Par. Vicar; Heather Hannaway, DRE;

CHELSEA

St. Rose of Lima - 601 Broadway, Chelsea, MA 02150-2998 t) 617-889-2774 strosechelsea@hotmail.com Rev. Hilario S. Sanez (Poland), Admin.; Rev. Reynaldo Jose Escobar Altamirano (Switzerland), Assoc. Pst.; Dcn. Luis F. Rivera; Marie Horgan, DRE; Danha Nguyen, DRE; Sor Ynocencia, DRE;

St. Rose of Lima School - 580 Broadway, Chelsea, MA 02150-2998 t) 617-884-2626 maryannebabs@hotmail.com www.strosechelsea.com Michele Butler, Prin.;

St. Stanislaus - 171 Chestnut St., Chelsea, MA 02150 t) 617-889-0261 stanislaus61@comcast.net Rev. Andrew T. Grelak, Pst.;

CHESTNUT HILL

St. Ignatius Loyola - 28 Commonwealth Ave., Chestnut Hill, MA 02467 t) 617-552-6100 ignatius@bc.edu www.stignatiuschestnuthill.org Rev. James D. Erps, S.J., Pst.; Rev. Gerald F. Finnegan, S.J., Assoc. Pst.; Andrea Miller, DRE; Katherine Maher, Pst. Min./Coord.; CRP Stds.: 209

COHASSET

St. Anthony of Padua - 2 Summer St., Cohasset, MA 02025; Mailing: 10 Summer St., Cohasset, MA 02025 t) 781-383-0219; 781-383-0630 (CRP) info@christbythesea.net www.saintanthonycohasset.org Rev. Scott A. Euvrard, Pst.; Rev. William P. Sexton, Par. Vicar; Dcn. Paul S. Rooney; CRP Stds.: 609

CONCORD

Holy Family - 12 Monument Sq., Concord, MA 01742; Mailing: PO Box 220, Concord, MA 01742 t) 978-369-7442 info@cc-catholic.org www.cc-catholic.org Very Rev. Frank J. Silva, Pst.; Rev. Nicholas H. Stano, Par. Vicar; Dcn. Gregory J. Burch; Dcn. Charles I. Clough; Jim Barkovic, Music Min.; Mark Callahan, Youth Min.; Maria Rosen, DRE; Paul DeMasi, Bus. Mgr.;

DANVERS

St. Mary of the Annunciation - 24 Conant St., Danvers, MA 01923-2968 t) 978-774-0340 stmarydanvers@comcast.net www.stmarydanvers.org Rev. Michael J. Doyle, Pst.; Dcn. John Koza; CRP Stds.: 193

St. Mary of the Annunciation School - 14 Otis St., Danvers, MA 01923 t) 978-774-0307 sdaigle@stmaryschooldanvers.org www.stmaryschooldanvers.org Stephen Daigle, Prin.;

St. Richard of Chichester - 90 Forest St., Danvers, MA 01923-1806 t) 978-774-7575 stricharddanvers@gmail.com Rev. Bruce G. Flannagan, Pst.; Doreen Verda, DRE;

St. Mary of the Annunciation School - 14 Otis St., Danvers, MA 01923-1806 t) 978-774-0307 sdaigle@stmaryschooldanvers.org www.stmaryschooldanvers.org Stephen Daigle, Prin.;

DEDHAM

St. Mary - 430 High St., Dedham, MA 02026-2892 t) 781-326-0550; 781-329-5488 (CRP) secretary@stmarysdedham.com www.stmarysdedham.com Rev. Wayne L. Belschner, Admin.; Rev. Huan D. Ngo, Par. Vicar; Dcn. Kelley B. McCormick; Rev. Eric F. Cadin, In Res.; Most Rev. Arthur L. Kennedy, In Res.;

St. Susanna - 262 Needham St., Dedham, MA 02026-7009 t) 781-329-9575 saintsusanna@hotmail.com Rev. Stephen S. Josoma, Pst.;

DOVER

Most Precious Blood - 30 Centre St., Dover, MA 02030-0812 t) 508-785-0305; 508-785-9909 (CRP) mpbdover@mpb-stp.org www.mpb-stp.org Rev. Robert James Blaney, Pst.; Ann Carroll, DRE; Regina O'Connor, DRE;

DRACUT

St. Francis of Assisi - 115 Wheeler Rd., Dracut, MA 01826; Mailing: P.O. Box 609, Dracut, MA 01826 t) 978-453-4460 (CRP); 978-452-6611 info@saintfrancis.net www.saintfrancis.net Rev. Kevin M. Sepe, Admin.; Dcn. John C. Hunt; Dcn. Michael P. Tompkins; Jessica Keefe, DRE;

Ste. Marguerite d'Youville - 1340 Lakeview Ave., Dracut, MA 01826-3499 t) 978-957-0322 Rev. Richard F. Clancy, Pst.; Rev. Khahn T. Dao, Assoc. Pst.; Dcn. Everett F. Penney; Karen Desrosiers, DRE;

St. Louis de France - 77 Boisvert St., Lowell, MA 01850 t) 978-458-7594 drltrouville@saintlouisschool.org www.saintlouisschool.org Linda Trouville, Prin.;

Convent - 85 Boisvert St., Lowell, MA 01850 t) 978-454-5742

DUXBURY

Holy Family - 601 Tremont St., Duxbury, MA 02332-4450 t) 781-934-6839 (CRP); 781-934-5055 Rev. Robert J. Deehan, Pst.; Dcn. Arthur J. Keefe; Dcn. Donald Larose;

EAST BRIDGEWATER

St. John the Evangelist - 210 Central St., East Bridgewater, MA 02333-1998 t) 508-378-1521 (CRP); 508-378-4207 Rev. Paul L. Ring, Pst.; Dcn. Christopher Z. Connelly; Nancy Goggin, DRE;

EVERETT

St. Anthony of Padua - 46 Oakes St., Everett, MA 02149; Mailing: 38 Oakes St., Everett, MA 02149 t) 617-387-0310 www.saintanthonyeverett.org/ Rev. Adriano Tezone, Pst.; Rev. Khiet Dang Cao, CS, Vicar; Doris Lopez, DRE; Adam Mendonca, DRE; Eliane Mendonca, DRE;

St. Anthony of Padua School - 54 Oakes St., Everett, MA 02149 t) 617-389-2448 stanthonyeverett@comcast.net www.saseverett.com Kim Palladino, Prin.;

Immaculate Conception - 487 Broadway, Everett, MA 02149-3603; Mailing: 489 Broadway, Everett, MA 02149 t) 617-389-5660 pastor.iceverett@gmail.com www.iceverett.org Rev. Joseph Chacha Marwa, SMA (Tanzania), Admin.; Rev. Gustavo Buccilli, Vicar; Holly Garcia, DRE; William Wallace, Bus. Mgr.;

FOXBOROUGH

St. Mary - 58 Carpenter St., Foxborough, MA 02035; Mailing: 83 Central St., Foxboro, MA 02035 t) 508-543-7726; 508-543-4577 (CRP) hrosenberger@stmarysfoxboro.org www.stmarysfoxboro.org Rev. Kevin T. Hickey, Pst.; Rev. Bertrand L. Proulx, Par. Vicar; Catherine Briggs, DRE;

FRAMINGHAM

St. Bridget - 830 Worcester Rd., Framingham, MA 01702-2902 t) 508-875-5959 administrator@stbridgetparish.org www.stbridgetparish.org Rev. Mark J. DeAngelis, Admin.;

St. Bridget School - (Grades PreK-8) 832 Worcester Rd., Framingham, MA 01702 t) 508-875-0181 mmartucci@sbsframingham.org www.sbsframingham.org/ Marilena Martucci, Prin.;

St. George - 74 School St., Framingham, MA 01701 t) 508-877-5130 Rev. John M. Rowan, Pst.; Paula Dolliver, DRE;

St. Stephen - 221 Concord St., Framingham, MA 01702 t) 508-875-4788 Rev. Francisco J. Anzoategui Peiro, Admin.; Rev. Gabino Oliva Macias (Mexico), Assoc. Pst.; Dcn. Alfredo Nieves; Dcn. Carlos Turcios; Dcn. Wilfredo Dilan Estrada; Rev. Andrew T. Grelak, In Res.; James J. Drummey, DRE; Maria Nieves, DRE;

St. Tarcisius - 562 Waverly St., Framingham, MA 01702-6925 t) 508-875-8623 sttarcisiuspar.bm@gmail.com www.sttarcisiusparish.org Very Rev. Marcio Toniazzo, C.S., Admin.; Rev. German A. Vargas Acevedo, C.S., Assoc. Pst.; Sr. Dcn. Manoel B. DeSousa; Dcn. Clayton Moreira;

FRANKLIN

St. Mary - One Church Sq., Franklin, MA 02038-1896 t) 508-528-0020 parishpublishing@stmarysfranklin.org stmarysfranklin.org Rev. Brian F. Manning, Pst.; Rev. John L. Sullivan, Assoc. Pst.; Rev. Frank Campo, In Res.; Dcn. Guy C. St. Sauveur; Leo Racine, Pst. Assoc.; Karen Ackles, DRE; Patricia Murphy, Bus. Mgr.;

GEORGETOWN

St. Mary - 94 Andover St., Georgetown, MA 01833 t) (978) 352-2024 rectory@stmarysgr.com saintmaryparish.org/ Rev. Michael O'Hara, O.M.I., Pst.; Rev. Harry Winter, O.M.I., Assoc. Pst.; Jeanne Soucy, DRE; Maureen Cannon, Bus. Mgr.;

GLOUCESTER

Holy Family - St. Ann, 74 Pleasant St., Gloucester, MA 01930 t) 978-281-4820 office@ccgronline.com www.ccgronline.com Rev. James M. Achadinha, Pst.; CRP Stds.: 125

Our Lady of Good Voyage - 144 Prospect St., Gloucester, MA 01930-3714 t) 978-283-1490 office@ccgronline.com www.ccgronline.com Rev. James M. Achadinha, Pst.; CRP Stds.: 125

HALIFAX

Holy Apostles Parish - 575 Monponsett St., Halifax, MA 02338 t) 781-293-7971 frmikehobson@holyapostlescatholic.com Rev. Michael A. Hobson, Pst.; Dcn. Marc Gervais; Dcn. James C. Theriault; Matthew Chick, DRE;

HAMILTON

St. Paul - 50 Union St., Hamilton, MA 01982 t) 978-468-3617 (CRP); 978-468-2337 Rev. J. Michael Lawlor, Pst.;

HANOVER

Our Lady of the Angels Parish - 392 Hanover St, Hanover, MA 02339 t) 781-826-4303 info@ourladyoftheangels.com ourladyoftheangels.com Rev. Christopher J. Hickey, Pst.; Rev. Joseph S. McCarthy, Par. Vicar; Rev. William F. Salmon, In Res.; Dcn. John P. Murray; Dcn. James Thompson; Dcn. Richard Ashburn; Ellen McDonough, Pst. Assoc.; Timothy Habeeb, Youth Min.; Maura Dowling, CRE; Karen Gill, CRE; CRP Stds.: 1,700

HAVERHILL

All Saints - 120 Bellevue Ave., Haverhill, MA 01832-4798 t) (978) 372-7721 info@allsaintshaverhill.org Rev. Christopher W. Wallace, Pst.; Rev. Marcos Tullio Pena Portillo, Assoc. Pst.; Dcn. Peter A. Richardson;

St. Joseph - 56 Oak Ter., Haverhill, MA 01832 t) 978-521-4256 sjshavcarolsimone@comcast.net www.sjshav.com Carol J. Simone, Prin.;

St. Joseph's Early Childhood Ed. Center - 100 Bellevue Ave., Haverhill, MA 01832 t) 978-372-0111

St. James - 185 Winter St., Haverhill, MA 01830-4920 t) 978-372-8537 stjamesandstjohnofficeparish@gmail.com www.stjamesandjohnhaverhill.org Rev. Anthony V. Le, Pst.; Dcn. Jose N. Agudelo; Joelle Mather, DRE;

St. John the Baptist - 114 Lincoln Ave., Haverhill, MA 01830 Rev. Anthony V. Le, Pst.; Most Rev. Robert F. Hennessey, In Res.;

Sacred Hearts - 165 S. Main St., Haverhill, MA 01835 t) 978-373-1281 hroche@sacredheartsparish.com www.sacredheartsparish.com Rev. John W. Delaney, Pst.; Rev. Daniel P. McCoy, Assoc. Pst.; Rev. Richard M. O'Brien, In Res.; Dcn. Eric T. Peabody;

St. Bridget School - 31 S. Chestnut St., Haverhill, MA 01835 t) 978-372-5451 jridgely@sacredheartsbradford.org www.sacredheartsbradford.org James J. Grocki Jr., Prin.;

HINGHAM

St. Paul - 147 North St., Hingham, MA 02043-3995 t) 781-749-5568 (CRP); 781-749-0587 www.hinghamcatholic.org Rev. Thomas F. Nestor, Pst.; Rev. Michael J. McNamara, Par. Vicar; Rev. Matthew Norwood, Par. Vicar; Dcn. Philip Anderson; Dcn. Joseph P. Harrington; Dcn. Matthew Porter; Salvatore Bartolotti, Music Min.; Elizabeth Reardon, Pst. Assoc.; Susan Troy, Pst. Min./Coord.; Alyssa Gendreau, Youth Min.; Linda Resca, Bus. Mgr.;

St. Paul School - (Grades PreSchool-8) 18 Fearing Rd., Hingham, MA 02043 t) 781-749-2407 lfasano@spshingham.org www.stpaulschoolhingham.com Lisa Fasano, Prin.;

Resurrection of Our Lord and Savior Jesus Christ - 1057 Main St., Hingham, MA 02043-3995 t) 781-749-3577 www.hinghamcatholic.org Rev. Thomas F. Nestor, Pst.; Rev. Michael J. McNamara, Par. Vicar; Rev. Matthew Norwood, Par. Vicar; Dcn. Philip Anderson; Dcn. Joseph P. Harrington; Dcn. Matthew Porter; Elizabeth Reardon, Pst. Assoc.; Alyssa Gendreau, Youth Min.; Terri Dasco, Faith Formation;

HOLBROOK

St. Joseph - 153 S. Franklin St., Holbrook, MA 02343 t) 781-767-0536 (CRP); 781-767-0605 www.stjosephholbrook.org Rev. Thomas C. Boudreau, Pst.; Rev. John E. Kelly, Par. Vicar; Donna Martyniak, DRE;

HOLLISTON

St. Mary - 8 Church St., Holliston, MA 01746 t) 508-429-4427; 508-429-6076 (CRP) st.marys1870@gmail.com www.stmarysholliston.com Rev. Mark J. Coiro, Pst.; Dcn. John D. Barry; Dcn. Ronald A. Dowding; Fran Crespi, DRE;

HOPKINTON

St. John the Evangelist - 20 Church St., Hopkinton, MA 01748-1836 t) 508-435-3313 x208 (CRP); 508-435-3313 stjohnhopkinton.com Rev. Richard E. Cannon, Pst.; Dcn. Anthony C. Sicuso; Deborah Lysik, DRE; Ken Lysik, DRE; Mary Pawela, DRE;

HUDSON

St. Michael - 23 Manning St., Hudson, MA 01749-2315 t) 978-562-2552; 978-562-7174 (CRP) parish@stmikes.org www.stmikes.org Dcn. Jared R. Auclair; Rev. Laurence M. Tocci, Admin.; Paula O'Brien, DRE;

HULL

St. Mary of the Assumption - 204 Samoset Ave., Hull, MA 02045-0565; Mailing: 10 Summer St., Cohasset, MA 02025 t) 781-383-0219 info@christbythesea.net stmaryhull.com Rev. Scott A. Euvrard, Pst.; Rev. William Sexton, Par. Vicar; CRP Stds.: 104

IPSWICH

Our Lady of Hope - One Pineswamp Rd., Ipswich, MA 01938-2922 t) 978-356-3944 rectory@ipswichcatholics.org www.ipswichcatholics.org Rev. Thomas E. Keyes, Pst.; Rev. John G. Kiley, In Res.; Elisa St. Clair, DRE; Gabriela Twaalfhoven, CRE;

KINGSTON

St. Joseph Parish - 272 Main St., Kingston, MA 02364-1922 t) 781-585-6679 office@stsmaryjoseph.org www.stsmaryjoseph.org Rev. John J. Graham, Pst.; Rev. Antonio dos Santos, C.S.S., Par. Vicar; Dcn. Paul J. Key; Dcn. Kevin J. Winn; CRP Stds.: 265

LAWRENCE

St. Mary of the Assumption - 300 Haverhill St., Lawrence, MA 01840 t) 978-685-1111; 978-685-1112; 978-685-1113 parishoffice@stmarylawrence.org stmaryassumption-lawrence.org Rev. Israel J. Rodriguez, Admin.; Rev. Leonardo C. Moreira, Assoc. Pst.; Dcn. Jesus Castillo; Dcn. Alvaro Arsenio Frias; Dcn. Cristino Ynfante; Rev. Ignacio de Jesus Berrio Guitierrez, In Res.; Rev. Francis X. Mawn, In Res.; Randall Cote, Music Min.; Miguel Queliz, Music Min.; Claudia Chase, Bus. Mgr.; Ana Cardenas, DRE;

St. Patrick - 114 S. Broadway, Lawrence, MA 01843-1427 t) 978-683-9416 saintpatrickparish@comcast.net www.saintpatrickparish.com Rev. Paul B. O'Brien, Pst.; Rev. Alonso Macias Zakoda, Assoc. Pst.; Dcn. George C. Escotto; Dcn. Julio Sanchez; Hosffman Ospino, Pst. Min./Coord.; Guadalupe Ospino, Pst. Min./Coord.; Diane Jarvis, DRE;

LEXINGTON

St. Brigid - 1981 Massachusetts Ave., Lexington, MA 02421-4812; Mailing: 2001 Massachusetts Ave., Lexington, MA 02421 t) 781-862-0335 shepherd@lexingtoncatholic.org www.lexingtoncatholic.org Rev. James G. Burke, Pst.; Rev. Paul S. Sughrue, In Res.; Fran Anderson, DRE;

Sacred Heart - 16 Follen Rd., Lexington, MA 02421-4812 t) 781-862-4646; 781-861-8385 x19 (CRP) shepherd@lexingtoncatholic.org www.lexingtoncatholic.org Rev. James G. Burke, Pst.; Fran Anderson, DRE;

LOWELL

St. Anthony of Padua - 893 Central St., Lowell, MA 01852-3407 t) 978-452-1506 Rev. Nicholas A. Sannella, Pst.; Rev. Kenneth Healey, S.M., Assoc. Pst.; Dcn. Carlos A. DeSousa; Georgina Leal, DRE;

Holy Family - 75 Chamberlain St., Lowell, MA 01852-5006 t) 978-453-2134 holyfamilylowell@gmail.com Rev. Nicholas A. Sannella, Pst.; Rev. Donald G. Lozier, O.M.I., In Res.; Dcn. Alvaro J. Soares; W. Gerald Dockett, DRE;

Holy Trinity - 350 High St., Lowell, MA 01852-2760 t) 978-452-2564 www.holytrinitylowell.org Rev. Nicholas A. Sannella, Pst.; Rev. Kenneth Healey, S.M., Assoc. Pst.; Dcn. Stephen M. Papik;

Immaculate Conception - 144 E. Merrimack St., Lowell, MA 01852 t) 978-458-1474 iclowell@yahoo.com www.iclowell.org Rev. Nicholas A. Sannella, Pst.; Rev. Kenneth Healey, S.M., Assoc. Pst.; Dcn. Stephen M. Papik; Rev. Raju D. Muringayil, O.Praem, In Res.; Claire Couillard, DRE;

Immaculate Conception School - 218 E. Merrimack St., Lowell, MA 01852 t) 978-454-5339 icslowell@hotmail.com www.icslowell.com Catherine Fiorino, Prin.;

St. Margaret of Scotland - 384 Stevens St., Lowell, MA 01851; Mailing: 374 Stevens St., Lowell, MA 01851 t) 978-454-5143; 978-459-4481 (CRP) parish@stmargaretlowell.org www.stmargaretlowell.org Rev. Brian E. Mahoney, Pst.; Rev. Fernando E. Ayala Rosales, Assoc. Pst.; Rev. Joseph A. Ferme; Sr. Dcn. Barry V. Lloyd;

St. Michael - 543 Bridge St., Lowell, MA 01850-2098 t) 978-459-0713; 978-458-1617 (CRP) saintmichaels@comcast.net www.saint-michael.com Rev. Christopher L. Lowe, Admin.; Jean Haumann, DRE; Nicole Walsh, DRE;

St. Michael School - 21 Sixth St., Lowell, MA 01850 t) 978-453-9511 sms@saint-michael.com school.saint-michael.com/ Anne Gallagher, Prin.;

St. Patrick - 282 Suffolk St., Lowell, MA 01854-4297 t) 978-459-0561 stpatricklowell@comcast.net www.stpatricklowell.org Rev. William Acevedo, Pst.; Rev. Joseph Almeida, Par. Vicar; Evelyn Rosales, DRE; Lina Arenas, Bus. Mgr.;

St. Rita - 158 Mammoth Rd., Lowell, MA 01854-2619 t) 978-957-0322 Rev. Richard F. Clancy, Pst.; Rev. Khahn T. Dao, Assoc. Pst.; Karen Desrosiers, DRE;

Sainte Jeanne d'Arc - 68 Dracut St., Lowell, MA 01854 t) 978-453-4114 mwilliams@sjdarc.org www.sjdarc.org Mollie Williams, Prin.;

LYNN

Holy Family - 21 Bessom St., Lynn, MA 01902 t) 781-599-7200; 781-596-2390 (CRP) Rev. Godfrey Musabe, Assoc. Pst.; Dcn. William M. Jackson; Andrew Genovese, DRE;

St. Joseph - 115 Union St., Lynn, MA 01902-2905; Mailing: 29 Green St., Lynn, MA 01902 t) 781-599-7040 office@saintjosephlynn.org www.saintjosephlynn.org Rev. Israel J. Rodriguez, Admin.; Rev. Wellington Oliveira, Par. Vicar;

Convent - 43 Green St., Lynn, MA 01902

St. Mary - 8 S. Common St., Lynn, MA 01902-4489 t) 781-598-4907 Rev. Brian L. Flynn, Pst.; Rev. Brian O'Hanlon, Assoc. Pst.; Dcn. Richard P. Field Jr.;

St. Mary High School - 35 Tremont St., Lynn, MA 01902 t) 781-595-7885 cdimaiti@smhlynn.org www.smhlynn.org Grace Cotter Regan, Headmaster;

Saint Mary of the Sacred Heart Parish - 571 Boston St., Lynn, MA 01905 t) 781-598-4907 Rev. Brian L. Flynn, Pst.; Rev. Brian O'Hanlon, Assoc. Pst.; Dcn. Richard P. Field Jr.; Rev. Francis J. Cloherty, In Res.; Christopher Carmody, DRE;

St. Pius Fifth - 215 Maple St., Lynn, MA 01904-2799 t) 781-581-3503 Rev. Godfrey Musabe, Assoc. Pst.; Dcn. William M. Jackson; Dcn. James T. Hinkle; Rev. John E. MacInnis, In Res.; Andrew Genovese, DRE;

St. Pius Fifth School - 28 Bowler St., Lynn, MA 01904 t) 781-593-8292 info@stpiusvschool.org www.stpiusvschool.org Mary Beth Noe, Prin.;

Sacred Heart - 579 Boston St., Lynn, MA 01905-2160 t) 781-593-8047; 781-592-1963 (CRP) admin@lynncatholic.org www.lynncatholic.org Rev. Brian L. Flynn, Pst.; Rev. Brian O'Hanlon, Assoc. Pst.; Sr. Dcn. John W. Hardy; Dcn. Richard P. Field Jr.; Rev. Francis J. Cloherty, In Res.;

Sacred Heart School - 581 Boston St., Lynn, MA 01905-2160 t) 781-592-7581 alejandra.almas@stmaryslynn.com www.sacredheartschoollynn.org John F. Dolan, Head of School;

LYNNFIELD

Ave Maria Parish - 758 Salem St., Lynnfield, MA 01940; Mailing: 17 Grove St., Lynnfield, MA 01940 t) (781) 598-4313 lcc@ola-smg.org www.avemarialynnfield.org/ Rev. Paul E. Ritt, Pst.; Rev. Anthony V. Luongo, Par. Vicar; Dcn. Thomas L. O'Shea;

Our Lady of the Assumption School - (Grades PreK-8) 40 Grove St, Lynnfield, MA 01940 t) 781-599-4422 cdonovan@ola.school www.ola.school/ Cynthia Donovan, Prin.;

MALDEN

Immaculate Conception - 600 Pleasant St., Malden, MA 02148-5313 t) 781-324-4941; 781-324-5518 (CRP) info@icmalden.com icmalden.org/ Rev. Albert L. Capone, Admin.; Rev. Francis E. Sullivan, Assoc. Pst.; Rev. James J. Barry, In Res.; Rev. William D. Coughlin, In Res.; Rev. James E. Sangu, In Res.; Erin Keith, DRE;

St. Joseph - 770 Salem St., Malden, MA 02148 t) 781-324-0402; 781-324-2444 (CRP) stjosephs2@comcast.net www.stjosephparishmalden.com Rev. William J. Minigan, Pst.; Buffy Walsh, DRE;

Sacred Hearts - 315 Main St., Malden, MA 02148-7414; Mailing: 297 Main St., Malden, MA 02148 t) 781-324-0728 receptionist@sacredheartsparish.org www.sacredheartsparish.org Rev. Kevin P. Leaver, Par. Vicar; Rev. Alejandro Lopez Cardinale, Admin.; Susan Evans, DRE;

Cheverus Catholic School - (Grades PreSchool-8) 30 Irving St., Malden, MA 02148 t) 781-324-6584 jeff.lane@cheverusschool.com www.cheverusschool.com Jeff Lane, Prin.;

MANCHESTER BY THE SEA

Visitation Parish - 62 School St., Manchester by the Sea, MA 01944 t) 978-526-1263 shsjparishmail@comcast.net Rev. Paul G. Flammia, Pst.; Anakin Fleming, DRE;

MARBLEHEAD

Our Lady, Star of the Sea - 85 Atlantic Ave., Marblehead, MA 01945 t) 781-631-8340 (CRP); 781-631-0086 Rev. Msgr. Timothy J. Moran, Pst.; Dcn. John E. Whipple; Mary J. Pagliarulo, DRE;

MARLBOROUGH

Immaculate Conception - 11 Prospect St., Marlborough, MA 01752; Mailing: 9 Washington Ct., Marlborough, MA 01752 t) 508-485-0016; 508-481-7535 (CRP) parish@icmarlboro.org www.icmarlboro.org Rev. Steven Clemence, Pst.; Rev. Kevin P. Pleitez, Assoc. Pst.; Dcn. Elcio Ferreira dos Santos; Dcn. Charles R. Rossignol; Margie Saez, DRE;

St. Matthias - 409 Hemenway St., Marlborough, MA 01752 t) 508-460-9255; 508-460-9256 admin@stmattpar.org www.stmattpar.org Rev. Francis P. O'Brien, Pst.; Dcn. Paul G. Coletti; Sr. Dcn. Douglas P. Peltak; Pst. Assoc.; Sr. Dcn. Russell W. Morey; Theresa Salafia, DRE; Peter Brockmann, Music Min.; CRP Stds.: 68

MARSHFIELD

St. Ann by the Sea - 587 Ocean St., Marshfield, MA 02050 t) 781-834-4953; 781-834-8223 (CRP) office@stanns.net www.stanns.net Rev. John F. Carmichael, Pst.; Catherine Rein, DRE;

St. Christine - 1295 Main St., Marshfield, MA 02050-2029 t) 781-837-0088 Rev. Mario Guarino, Admin.;

St. Theresa's - t) 781-834-6003

Our Lady of the Assumption - 40 Canal St., Marshfield, MA 02050 t) 781-837-3662 (CRP); 781-834-6252 info@olamarshfield.org www.olamarshfield.org Rev. Mark G. Derrane, Admin.; Dcn. John A. Hulme;

MEDFIELD

St. Edward the Confessor - 133 Spring St., Medfield, MA 02052-2513 t) 508-359-2633 stedadmin@ejcatholic.org www.ejcatholic.org Rev. Stephen P. Zukas, Pst.; Rev. Gregory G. Vozzo, Assoc. Pst.; Dcn. Frederick B. Horgan; CRP Stds.: 568

MEDFORD

St. Clement - 71 Warner St., Medford, MA 02155 t) 781-396-3322 (CRP); 781-396-3922; 781-396-3112 secretarystclement@outlook.com Phong Q Pham, Admin.; Dcn. Vuong V. Nguyen;

Mary, Queen of Peace Parish - 118 High St., Medford, MA 02155 t) 781-396-0423 medfordcatholic@gmail.com www.medfordcollaborative.org Rev. Paul V. Sullivan, Pst.; Rev. Peter H. Shen (China), Par. Vicar; Rev. John T. Swencki, In Res.; Doreen Breen, DRE;

St. Joseph School - 132 High St., Medford, MA 02155 t) 781-396-3636 acampbell@sjsmedford.com sjsmedford.com/ Robert G. Chevrier, Prin.;

St. Raphael - 512 High St., Medford, MA 02155 t) 781-488-5444; 781-483-1139 (CRP) www.saintraphaelparish.org Rev. Paul F. Coughlin, Pst.; Dcn. Mark E. Rumley; Ginny McCabe, DRE; CRP Stds.: 299

St. Raphael School - 516 High St., Medford, MA 02155 t) 781-483-3373 dguarino@straphaelparishschool.org www.straphaelparishschool.org Diane Guarino, Prin.;

MEDWAY

St. Joseph - 151 Village St., Medway, MA 02053 t) 508-533-6500; 508-533-7771 (CRP) Rev. Linus Mendis (Sri Lanka), Admin.;

MELROSE

Incarnation of Our Lord and Savior Jesus Christ - 429 Upham St., Melrose, MA 02176 t) 781-662-8844 i.rectory@comcast.net www.incarnationmelrose.org Rev. Stephen J. Madden, Admin.; Rev. Michael D. Ssenfuma, Assoc. Pst.; Dcn. Robert F. Breen; Ann Lahiff, DRE;

St. Mary of the Annunciation - 4 Herbert St., Melrose, MA 02176-3827; Mailing: 46 Myrtle St., Melrose, MA 02176 t) 781-665-0152 dianemacedo@comcast.net www.stmarysmelrose.org Rev. Shawn W. Allen, Pst.;

St. Mary of the Annunciation School - 4 Myrtle St., Melrose, MA 02176 t) 781-665-5037 info@stmaryschoolmelrose.org www.stmaryschoolmelrose.org Christopher J. Beza, Prin.;

MERRIMAC

Holy Redeemer - Nativity, 4 Green St., Merrimac, MA 01985 t) 978-346-8604 holyredeemer@verizon.net www.hriccatholic.org Rev. Timothy A. Harrison, Pst.; Dcn. Paul A. Dow; Dcn. John Moranski; Aaron Giard, DRE;

METHUEN

St. Lucy - 254 Merrimack St., Methuen, MA 01844 t) 978-686-3311; 978-794-0383 (CRP) methuencatholic@gmail.com www.methuencatholic.org Rev. Darin V. Colarusso, Pst.; Rev. Joseph J. D'Onofrio, Assoc. Pst.; Dcn. John Kobrenski;

St. Monica - 212 Lawrence St., Methuen, MA 01844-3852; Mailing: 254 Merrimack, Methuen, MA 01844 t) 978-683-1193; 978-686-9573 (CRP) methuencatholic@gmail.com www.methuencatholic.org Rev. Darin V. Colarusso, Pst.; Rev. Joseph J. D'Onofrio, Par. Vicar; Dcn. John B. Pierce; Wendy Adams, DRE; Laurene Costello, DRE; Claire Tebeau, DRE;

St. Monica School - t) 978-686-1801 smsoffice@methuencatholic.org www.saintmonicaschoolmethuen.org/ Donna Henderson, Prin.;

Convent - t) 978-682-2448

Our Lady of Good Counsel - 22 Plymouth St., Methuen, MA 01844-4299 t) 978-686-3985 Very Rev. Christopher J. Casey, Pst.; Mark Houle, DRE;

MIDDLEBOROUGH

Saint Isidore Parish - 340 Center St., Middleborough, MA 02346 t) 508-947-0444 hollyclark@cranberrycatholic.org Rev. Jude Thaddeus Osunkwo (Nigeria), Pst.; Dcn. Alan Amaral; Michelle Sylvia, DRE;

MIDDLETON

St. Agnes - 24 Boston St., Middleton, MA 01949-2199; Mailing: 22 Boston St., Middleton, MA 01949 t) 978-774-1958 info@agnesandrose.org; akostak@agnesandrose.org agnesandrose.org Rev. Daniel F. Hennessey, Pst.; Amy Kostak, DRE;

MILLIS

St. Thomas the Apostle - 82 Exchange St., Millis, MA 02054-1273 t) 508-376-2621 saintthomasapostle@verizon.net www.stthomastheapostlemillis.org Rev. Sinisa Ubiparipovic, Pst.;

MILTON

St. Agatha - 432 Adams St., Milton, MA 02186-4399 t) 617-698-2439 Rev. William B. Palardy, Pst.; Rev. Thomas J. Stanton, Assoc. Pst.; Dcn. Daniel F. Sullivan; Dcn. Kevin P. Martin; Rev. Patrick J. McLaughlin, In Res.; Beth Peterson, DRE;

St. Agatha School - 440 Adams St., Milton, MA 02186 t) 617-696-3548 ncarr@stagathaparish.org stagatha.org/ Nancy Carr, Prin.;

St. Elizabeth - Merged Jul 2022 Parish records for all closed, merged & suppressed parishes are located at the Office of the Archives, 66 Brooks Dr., Braintree, MA 02184-3839.

St. Mary of the Hills - Merged Jul 2022 Parish records for all closed, merged & suppressed parishes are located at the Office of the Archives, 66 Brooks Dr., Braintree, MA 02184-3839.

Our Lady of the Visitation Parish - 29 St. Mary's Rd., Milton, MA 02186 t) (617) 696-6688 www.visitationmilton.org Rev. Eric M. Bennett, Pst.; Rev. Andreas R. Davison, Par. Vicar;

St. Pius Tenth - 101 Wolcott Rd., Milton, MA 02136 t) 857-342-9500 achavez@bluehillscollaborative.org bluehillscollaborative.org Rev. Joseph M. Mazzone, Pst.; Rev. Charles Madi-Okin, Assoc. Pst.; Sheila Farley, DRE;

NAHANT

St. Thomas Aquinas - 248 Nahant Rd., Nahant, MA 01908-1340 t) (781) 595-7942 (CRP); (781) 581-0023 Rev. James T. Kelly, Admin.; Dcn. Andrew J. Acampora; Kellie Frary, DRE;

NATICK

St. Linus - 119 Hartford St., Natick, MA 01760 t) 508-653-6005 (CRP); 508-653-1093 Rev. George C. Hines, Pst.; Rev. Michael A. Alfano, Assoc. Pst.; Rev. Leroy E. Owens, In Res.; Caitlin D'Alessio, DRE; Jennifer McKiernan, DRE;

St. Patrick - 46 E. Central St., Natick, MA 01760 t) 508-653-1093 natickcatholics@gmail.com natickcatholic.org Rev. George C. Hines, Pst.; Rev. Michael A. Alfano, Assoc. Pst.;

NEEDHAM

St. Bartholomew - 1180 Greendale Ave., Needham, MA 02492-4706 t) 781-444-3434 www.stbartholomew-needham.org Rev. J. Thomas Gignac, Admin.; Rev. John F. Arens, In Res.;

St. Joseph - 1360 Highland Ave., Needham, MA 02492-2694 t) 781-444-0245 www.saintjosephparihneedham.com Very Rev. Bryan K. Parrish, Pst.; Rev. Joseph Kim, Assoc. Pst.; Dcn. Robert P. Horne; Christina Danko, DRE; Michael Lescault, DRE;

Saint Joseph - 90 Pickering St., Needham, MA 02492 t) (781) 444-2571 lsolomon@saintjoes.com www.saintjoes.com/elementary.cfm Elementary School Lauren Solomon, Prin.;

Monsignor James J. Haddad Middle School - 110 May St., Needham, MA 02492 t) 781-449-0133 jbelliveau@saintjoes.com www.saintjoes.com James J. MacDonald, Prin.;

NEWBURYPORT

Immaculate Conception - 42 Green St., Newburyport, MA 01950-2502 t) 978-462-2724 Rev. Timothy A. Harrison, Pst.; Dcn. Paul A. Dow; Dcn. John Moranski; Rev. William H. McLaughlin, In Res.; Rev. Charles R. Stanley, In Res.; Rev. George E. Morin, In Res.; Aaron Giard, DRE;

Immaculate Conception - 1 Washington St., Newburyport, MA 01950 t) 978-465-7780 schoolinfo@icsnewburyport.com www.icsnewburyport.com Joan F. Sullivan, Prin.;

St. James -

NEWTON

Saint Antoine Daveluy - 41 Ash St., Newton, MA 02466 t) 617-558-2711 office.kccb@gmail.com www.stdaveluychurch.org Rev. Dominic K. Jung, C.PP.S., Admin.; Dcn. Cheonil Kim; Dcn. Francis Suh;

Corpus Christi - St. Bernard - 1523 Washington St., Newton, MA 02465 t) 617-244-0608 info@ccsbparish.org; mmarchand@ccsbparish.org www.ccsbparish.org Rev. Daniel C. O'Connell, Pst.; Sr. Jeanette Gaudett, mfic, Pst. Assoc.; Brian Sousa, DRE;

Mary Immaculate of Lourdes - 270 Elliot St., Newton, MA 02464 t) 617-244-0558 Rev. Charles J. Higgins, Pst.; Rev. Stephen R. Leblanc, Assoc. Pst.; Jean Johnson, DRE;

Our Lady Help of Christians - 573 Washington St., Newton, MA 02458-1494 t) 617-527-7560 www.sholnewton.org Rev. Daniel J. Riley, Pst.; Dcn. William B. Koffel; Anne Marie David, Music Min.; Kate A Neal, Pst. Assoc.; Kristina Preman, DRE; Michael Bliss, Bus. Mgr.;

Sacred Heart - 1317 Centre St., Newton, MA 02459-2466; Mailing: 1321 Centre St., Newton, MA 02459 t) 617-969-2248 sacredheart@sholnewton.org www.sholnewton.org Rev. Daniel J. Riley, Pst.; Dcn. William B. Koffel; Erica Johnson, Music Min.; Nick Frega, Pst. Assoc.; Kate A Neal, Pst. Assoc.; Kristina Preman, DRE; Michael Bliss, Bus. Mgr.;

NORFOLK

St. Jude - 86 Main St., Norfolk, MA 02056; Mailing: PO Box 305, Norfolk, MA 02056 t) 508-528-1470 (CRP); 508-528-0170 stjudeadmin@ejcatholic.org www.ejcatholic.org Rev. Stephen P. Zukas, Pst.; Rev.

Gregory G. Vozzo, Par. Vicar; Dcn. Frederick B. Horgan; Rev. Robert Rivard, F.M.S.I., In Res.; Mary Sheedy, Liturgy Dir.; CRP Stds.: 320

NORTH ANDOVER

St. Michael - 196 Main St., North Andover, MA 01845-2598 t) 978-682-9484 (CRP); 978-686-4050 st-michael@comcast.net Rev. Kevin J. Deeley, Pst.; Rev. Joseph Hubbard, Par. Vicar; Rev. Jiwon Yoon, Par. Vicar; Dcn. Vincent J. Gatto; Dcn. Daniel Sheridan; Maryann Marinelli, DRE; Mary Alice Rock, DRE;

St. Michael School - 80 Maple Ave., North Andover, MA 01845 t) 978-686-1862 info@saintmichael.com www.saintmichael.com Susan Gosselin, Prin.;

NORTH READING

St. Theresa of Lisieux - 63 Winter St., North Reading, MA 01864-2282 t) 978-664-2962 info@sttheresanreading.org sttheresarose.org Most Rev. Mark O'Connell, Pst.; Rev. Augustin A. Anda Gomez, Par. Vicar; Dcn. Tam V. Tran;

NORWOOD

St. Catherine of Siena - 547 Washington St., Norwood, MA 02062-0547 t) 781-762-6080 parish@stcatherinenorwood.org www.stcatherinenorwood.org Rev. Stephen S. Donohoe, Pst.; Rev. Maxwell U. Chukwudiebere, Par. Vicar; Dcn. Francis R. Tremblay; Leah Ramsdell, DRE;

St. Catherine of Siena School - 249 Nahatan St., Norwood, MA 02062 t) 781-769-5354 principal@scsnorwood.org www.scsnorwood.com Beth Tanner, Prin.;

St. Timothy - 650 Nichols St., Norwood, MA 02062-1099 t) (781) 769-2522; (781) 762-4868 sttim.net Rev. Gerard Petringa, Pst.; Rev. John J. Grimes, Admin.; Joanne Curry, DRE;

PEABODY

St. Adelaide - 17 Bow St., Peabody, MA 01960-3427 t) 978-535-1985; 978-535-5376 (CRP) parish@saintadelaide.org www.saintadelaide.com Rev. David C. Lewis; Rev. Raymond Van De Moortell; Angela Federico, DRE;

St. Ann - 140 Lynn St., Peabody, MA 01960-6432 t) 978-531-1480; 978-531-5791 (CRP) pastor@saintannpeabody.com www.catholic-church.org/st-ann-peabody Rev. David C. Lewis, Pst.; Rev. Raymond Van De Moortell, Assoc. Pst.; Donna G. Zinna, DRE;

St. John the Baptist - 17 Chestnut St., Peabody, MA 01960-5429 t) 978-532-1586 (CRP); 978-531-0002 joconnor@peabodycatholic.org Rev. Derek J. Borek, Pst.; Rev. Kevin P. Leaver, Assoc. Pst.; Rev. Paul G. McManus, Assoc. Pst.; Karen E. Hinton, DRE;

St. John the Baptist School - 19 Chestnut St., Peabody, MA 01960-5429 t) 978-531-0444 info@stjohns-peabody.com Valerie Shippen, Prin.;

Our Lady of Fatima - 50 Walsh Ave., Peabody, MA 01960-1910 t) 978-532-0272 ourladyoffatima@verizon.net www.ourladyoffatimapeabody.org Rev. Christopher Gomes, Pst.;

St. Thomas the Apostle - 3 Margin St., Peabody, MA 01960 t) 978-531-0224 dalves@peabodycatholic.org www.stthomaspeabody.org Rev. Derek J. Borek, Pst.; Rev. Kevin P. Leaver, Assoc. Pst.; Rev. Paul G. McManus, Assoc. Pst.; Lisa Ann Trainor, DRE;

PEPPERELL

Our Lady of Grace - 28 Tarbell St., Pepperell, MA 01463 t) 978-433-5737 pastor@stjs.page www.stjs.page Rev. Sean M. Maher, Pst.; Rev. Kwang H. Lee, Assoc. Pst.; David Flournoy, DRE;

PLAINVILLE

St. Martha - 219 South St., Plainville, MA 02762 t) 508-699-8543 stmarthaoffice@pwc.church www.saintmarthaschurch.org Very Rev. Joseph F. Mozer Jr., Pst.; Rev. Lambert K. Nieme, Assoc. Pst.; Dcn. Joseph R. Flocco;

PLYMOUTH

St. Bonaventure - 803 State Rd., Plymouth, MA 02360 t) 508-224-3636 stbonoffice1@verizon.net www.stbonaventureplymouth.org Rev. Kenneth C. Overbeck, Pst.; Sheilah Burleigh Segatore, CRE;

St. Catherine's Chapel - 95 White Horse Rd., White Horse Beach, MA 02381

Saint Kateri Tekakwitha - Merged Jul 2022 Parish records for all closed, merged & suppressed parishes are located at the Office of the Archives, 66 Brooks Dr., Braintree, MA 02184-3839.

St. Mary - 313 Court St., Plymouth, MA 02360-4336 t) 508-746-0426 office@stsmaryjoseph.org www.stsmaryjoseph.org Rev. John J. Graham, Pst.; Rev. Antonio dos Santos, C.S.S., Par. Vicar; Dcn. Paul J. Key; Sr. Dcn. Eugene V. Stenstrom; Dcn. Kevin J. Winn; CRP Stds.: 90

Mary, Queen of Martyrs Parish - 10 Memorial Dr., Plymouth, MA 02360 t) (508) 746-0663 www.maryqueenofmartyrs.org Rev. Joseph K. Raeke, Pst.; Rev. Michael S. Rora, Par. Vicar;

St. Peter - Merged Jul 2022 Parish records for all closed, merged & suppressed parishes are located at the Office of the Archives, 66 Brooks Dr., Braintree, MA 02184-3839.

QUINCY

Divine Mercy Parish - 386 Hancock St., Quincy, MA 02171 t) 617-328-8666 office@divinemercyquincy.org www.divinemercyquincy.org Rev. Louis R. Palmieri, Pst.; Rev. Stanley Rousseau (Haiti), Par. Vicar; CRP Stds.: 331

Holy Trinity - 227 Sea St., Quincy, MA 02169 t) 617-479-9200 holytrinityquincyma@gmail.com holytrinityquincy.com Our Lady of Good Counsel Church Most Blessed Sacrament Church Rev. Martin G. Dzengeleski, Pst.; Dr. Flynn Fernandes, DRE;

St. John the Baptist - 21 Gay St., Quincy, MA 02169-6602 t) 617-773-1021 stjohns@stjohnsquincy.org www.stjohnsquincy.org Rev. Matthew M. Williams, Pst.; Rev. Joseph Kwadwo O. Boafo, CSSp, Assoc. Pst.; Dcn. Timothy A. Booker; Rev. Jonathan P. DeFelice, O.S.B., In Res.; Rev. Thomas A. DiLorenzo, In Res.; Rev. Sebastian Varghese, CMI, In Res.; Rev. Arthur F. Wright, In Res.; Francesca Alberti, DRE;

Quincy Catholic Academy - 370 Hancock St., Quincy, MA 02171 t) 617-328-3830 info@quincycatholicacademy.org www.quincycatholicacademy.org Paul Kelly, Prin.;

St. Joseph - 556 Washington St., Quincy, MA 02169-7216 t) 617-472-6321 stjoesquincy@comcast.net www.stjosephsquincy.org Rev. Matthew M. Williams, Pst.; Rev. Joseph Kwadwo O. Boafo, CSSp, Assoc. Pst.; Dcn. Timothy A. Booker;

RANDOLPH

St. Bernadette - 1020 N. Main St., Randolph, MA 02368 t) 781-963-1327 office@stbernadette.us www.stbernadette.us/ Masses in English and Vietnamese Rev. Charles S. Pham, CRM, Admin.; Dcn. Thomas P. Burke; Huyen Ngo, DRE;

St. Mary - 211 N. Main St., Randolph, MA 02368 t) 781-961-5009 (CRP); 781-963-4141 stmary@stmaryrandolph.org Rev. Philip E. McGaugh, Pst.; Patricia O'Connor, DRE;

READING

St. Agnes - Merged Mar 2023 Parish records for all closed, merged & suppressed parishes are located at the Office of the Archives, 66 Brooks Dr., Braintree, MA 02184-3839.

St. Athanasius - Merged Mar 2023 Parish records for all closed, merged & suppressed parishes are located at the Office of the Archives, 66 Brooks Dr., Braintree, MA 02184-3839.

Christ the King Parish - 186 Woburn St., Reading, MA 01867 t) (781) 944-0490 contact@readingcatholic.org readingcatholic.org Very Rev. Stephen B. Rock, Pst.; Dcn. William K. Reidy; Dcn. Neil J. Sumner;

REVERE

St. Anthony of Padua - 250 Revere St., Revere, MA 02151-4618 t) 781-289-1234 stanthonys@stapr.org Rev. Karunaya Xavier Arulraj, Admin.; Rev. Maria Antony H. Washington (India), Assoc. Pst.; Donna Felzani, DRE;

Blessed Mother of the Morning Star Parish - 670 Washington Ave., Revere, MA 02154 t) 781-284-5252 jsheridan@morningstarcatholic.org www.morningstarcatholic.org Rev. Ronald D. Coyne;

Immaculate Conception - 119 Beach St., Revere, MA 02151 t) 781-289-0735; 781-289-8126 (CRP) parishoffice@icrevere.org www.icrevere.com Rev. Wellington Oliveira, Pst.; Rev. Eric J. Velasquez, Assoc. Pst.; Gail Hagstrom, DRE;

Immaculate Conception School - 127 Winthrop Ave., Revere, MA 02151 t) (781) 284-9230 jfelice@icrevere.org icrevere.org/school Donis Tracy, Prin.;

ROCKLAND

Holy Family Parish - 403 Union St., Rockland, MA 02370-1799 t) 781-871-1244 (CRP); 781-878-0160 (Rectory) holyfamilyrockland@yahoo.com; holyfamilyreligiouseducation@yahoo.com holyfamilyrockland.org Rev. James F. Hickey, Pst.; Rev. James O'Driscoll, Par. Vicar; Elizabeth Davis, DRE;

SALEM

St. Anne - 292 Jefferson Ave., Salem, MA 01970-2895; Mailing: 290 Jefferson Ave, Salem, MA 01970 t) 978-744-1930 info@stannesalem.org www.stannesalem.org Rev. Maurice Agbaw-Ebai, Admin.;

Immaculate Conception - 30 Union St., Salem, MA 01970-3709 Rev. Daniel J. Riley, Pst.; Rev. Paul G. McManus, Assoc. Pst.; Rev. Francis E. Sullivan, Assoc. Pst.; Rev. Lawrence J. Rondeau, In Res.; Dcn. Pablo Morel; Dcn. Jesus M. Pena; Margo Morin, Pst. Assoc.;

St. James - 161 Federal St., Salem, MA 01970-3297 t) 978-744-2230 Rev. Daniel J. Riley, Pst.; Rev. Francis E. Sullivan, Assoc. Pst.; Rev. Gregory G. Vozzo, Assoc. Pst.; Rev. Lawrence J. Rondeau, In Res.; Sr. Dcn. Norman P. LaPointe; Dcn. Jesus M. Pena; Margo Morin, Pst. Assoc.; Diane Santos, DRE;

Mary, Queen of the Apostles Parish - 30 Union St., Salem, MA 01970 t) 978-745-9060 info@mqoa.org www.salemcatholiccommunity.org Rev. Robert W. Murray, Pst.; Dcn. Pablo Morel; Dcn. Jesus M. Pena; Steven Antonio, DRE;

SAUGUS

Blessed Sacrament - 14 Summer St., Saugus, MA 01906-2139 operations@sauguscatholics.org sauguscatholics.org Rev. Jason M. Makos, Pst.; Sr. Dcn. Francis M. Gaffney; Dcn. Jorge A. Patino;

St. Margaret - 431 Lincoln Ave., Saugus, MA 01906-3917 t) 781-233-1040 operations@sauguscatholics.org Rev. Jason M. Makos, Pst.; Sr. Dcn. Francis M. Gaffney; Dcn. Jorge A. Patino; Carol Nadeau, DRE;

SCITUATE

St. Mary of the Nativity - One Kent St., Scituate, MA 02066-4215 t) 781-545-3335 ndecoste@stmaryscituate.org Rev. Matthew J. Conley; Rev. Anthony M. Cusack; Dcn. Martin W. Henry;

SHARON

Our Lady of Sorrows - 59 Cottage St., Sharon, MA 02067-2132 t) 781-784-5091 (CRP); 781-784-2265 parish@olossharon.org Rev. Francis J. Daly, Pst.;

SHERBORN

St. Theresa of Lisieux - 35 S. Main St., Sherborn, MA 02030 t) 508-653-6253 www.mpb-stp.org Rev. Robert M. Blaney, Pst.;

SHIRLEY

St. Anthony of Padua - 14 Phoenix St., Shirley, MA 01464; Mailing: 31 Shirley St., Ayer, MA 01432 t) 978-772-2414; 978-772-0727 (CRP) faithformation@nashobacatholic.org; parishoffice@nashobacatholic.org www.nashobacatholic.org Rev. Edmond M. Derosier, Pst.; Dcn. Michael J. Markham; Marianne Cooper, Faith Formation Coord.;

SOMERVILLE

St. Ann - 399 Medford St., Somerville, MA 02143 t) 617-625-1904 parish@stannsomerville.org www.stannsomerville.org Rev. Brian J. McHugh, Pst.; Rev. David P. Callahan, Assoc. Pst.; Rev. Richard G.

Curran, Assoc. Pst.; Dcn. Joseph Breyere Guerrier;
St. Anthony of Padua - 12 Properzi Way, Somerville, MA 02143-3226 t) 617-625-4530 stanthonysomer@aol.com Brazilian Community Rev. Lino Garcia Ayala, CS, Admin.; Dcn. Pedro P. Rodrigues;
St. Benedict - 21 Hathorn St., Somerville, MA 02145-3235; Mailing: 25 Arlington St., Somerville, MA 02145 t) 617-625-0029; 617-825-4333 (CRP) stbenedictps25@gmail.com; pastor@stbenedictps.org www.stbenedictps.org Rev. Alejandro Lopez Cardinale, Pst.; Dcn. Jose B. Torres; Daisy Gomez, DRE; CRP Stds.: 120
St. Catherine of Genoa - 185 Summer St., Somerville, MA 02143-2501 t) 617-666-2087 parishsec@stcgenoa.com www.stcatherinesomerville.com Rev. Brian J. McHugh, Pst.; Rev. David P. Callahan, Assoc. Pst.; Rev. Richard G. Curran, Assoc. Pst.; Dcn. Joseph Breyere Guerrier;
St. Joseph - 262 Washington St., Somerville, MA 02143-3313 t) 617-666-4140 stjoe1869@verizon.net www.somervillecatholic.org Rev. Brian J. McHugh, Pst.; Rev. David P. Callahan, Assoc. Pst.; Rev. Richard G. Curran, Assoc. Pst.; Dcn. Joseph Breyere Guerrier;
Saints Louis and Zelie Martin Parish - 179 Summer St., Somerville, MA 02143 t) 617-666-2087 secretary@stsmartinparish.org www.stsmartinparish.org Rev. Brian J. McHugh, Pst.; Rev. David P. Callahan, Par. Vicar; Dcn. Joseph Breyere Guerrier; Adam Dupre, DRE; Peter Regan, Bus. Mgr.;

St. Theresa of the Child Jesus School - (Grades PreK-8) 192 Summer St., Somerville, MA 02143-2501 t) 617-666-9116 kdonohue@sttheresaschoolsomerville.com www.sttheresaschoolsomerville.com Kevin Donohue, Prin.;

STONEHAM

St. Patrick - 71 Central St., Stoneham, MA 02180 t) 781-438-0960; 781-438-1093 (CRP) stpatstone@aol.com www.stpatrickstoneham.org/ Rev. Mario J. Orrigo, Pst.; Rev. Joseph F Keville, Par. Vicar; Dcn. Francis B. Dello Russo; Dcn. Anthony J Foti; Dcn. Charles Hanafin; CRP Stds.: 607

St. Patrick School - (Grades PreSchool-8) 20 Pleasant St., Stoneham, MA 02180 t) 781-438-2593 office@stpatrickschoolstoneham.org www.stpatrickschoolstoneham.org/index.html Dr. Laurie Sullivan, Prin.; Stds.: 271; Scholastics: 12; Lay Tchrs.: 18

STOUGHTON

Immaculate Conception - 122 Canton St., Stoughton, MA 02072-2204 t) 781-344-2073; 781-341-0611 (CRP) info@stoughtoncatholic.org stoughtoncatholic.org Rev. Carlos D. Suarez, Pst.; Rev. Ishmael Ixon Chateau, Assoc. Pst.; Rev. Jose E. Marques (Brazil), Assoc. Pst.; Dcn. David Giangiordano; Dcn. Patrick E. Guerrini; Mary Ann Caldwell, DRE;
St. James - 560 Page St., Stoughton, MA 02072 t) 781-297-7582 (CRP); 781-344-9121 info@stoughtoncatholic.org Rev. Carlos D. Suarez, Pst.; Rev. Ishmael Ixon Chateau, Assoc. Pst.; Rev. Jose E. Marques (Brazil), Assoc. Pst.; Dcn. David Giangiordano; Dcn. Patrick E. Guerrini; Mary Ann Caldwell, DRE;

SUDBURY

Ascension of Our Lord and Savior Jesus Christ Parish - 160 Concord Rd., Sudbury, MA 01776 t) 978-443-2647 info@theascensionparish.com Rev. Gerald A. Souza, Pst.; Dcn. John W. Pepi; Diane Schafer, Pst. Assoc.; Jared A. Cowell, Bus. Mgr.; CRP Stds.: 353

SWAMPSCOTT

St. John the Evangelist - 174 Humphrey St., Swampscott, MA 01907-2512 t) 781-593-2544; 781-599-4711 (CRP) stjohnsswampscott@gmail.com www.stjohnsswampscott.org Rev. James T. Kelly, Admin.; Dcn. Andrew J. Acampora; Maureen McDonnell, DRE;

TEWKSBURY

St. William - 1351 Main St., Tewksbury, MA 01876-2039 t) 978-851-7331 stwilliams.office@gmail.com www.stwilliamparish.org Rev. Quilin Bouzi, O.M.I., Pst.; Rev. George Roy, O.M.I., Par. Vicar; Dcn. Thomas M. Walsh; Elizabeth Quigley, DRE;

TOPSFIELD

St. Rose of Lima - 12 Park St., Topsfield, MA 01983-0458; Mailing: 22 Boston St, Middleton, MA 01949 t) 978-887-5505; 978-887-5505 x104 (CRP) info@agnesandrose.org; akostak@agnesandrose.org agnesandrose.org Rev. Daniel F. Hennessey, Pst.; Amy Kostak, DRE;

TOWNSEND

St. John the Evangelist - One School St., Townsend, MA 01469 t) 978-597-2297 (CRP); 978-597-2291 pastor@stjs.page stjs.page Rev. Sean M. Maher, Pst.; Rev. Kwang H. Lee, Assoc. Pst.; David Flournoy, DRE;

TYNGSBOROUGH

St. Mary Magdalen - 93 Lakeview Ave., Tyngsborough, MA 01879 t) 978-957-0322 saintmarymagdalen@verizon.net www.stmarymagdalenparish.com Rev. Richard F. Clancy, Pst.; Rev. Khahn T. Dao, Assoc. Pst.; Dcn. David A. Brooks;

WAKEFIELD

St. Florence - 47 Butler Ave., Wakefield, MA 01880-5199 t) 781-245-2711 stflorence@verizon.net www.stflorence.org Rev. Thomas J. Reilly, Admin.; Dcn. Joseph Cooley;
St. Joseph - 173 Albion St., Wakefield, MA 01880-3224 t) 781-245-5770 office@stjosephwakefield.org stjosephwakefield.org Rev. Ronald A. Barker, Pst.; Dcn. Arthur F. Rogers Jr.; Maureen Miller, Bus. Mgr.; Anne Grant, Music Dir.; Sharon Keith, Faith Formation;

St. Joseph School - (Grades PreK-8) 15 Gould St., Wakefield, MA 01880-2700 t) 781-245-2081 aflynn@stjosephschoolwakefield.org www.stjosephschoolwakefield.org Joseph M. Sullivan, Prin.;

Most Blessed Sacrament - 11 Grove St., Wakefield, MA 01880-4222 t) 781-245-4669 (CRP); 781-245-2080 mbsparish1@aol.com www.mbsparishwakefield.com Rev. Stephen J. Madden, Pst.; Rev. Michael D. Ssenfuma, Assoc. Pst.; Dcn. Robert F. Breen;

WALPOLE

Blessed Sacrament - 10 Diamond St., Walpole, MA 02081 t) 508-668-4700 www.matt13catholic.org Rev. George C. Hines, Pst.; Dcn. Alan J. Doty; Dcn. Reynold G. Spadoni;

Blessed Sacrament School - 808 East St., Walpole, MA 02081 t) 508-668-2336 skukstis@blessedsacrament.org school.blessedsacrament.org Sheila Kukstis, Interim Prin.;

Convent - 808 East St., Walpole, MA 02081 t) 508-668-6693

St. Mary - 176 Washington St., Walpole, MA 02032-0131 t) (508) 668-4974 office@stmarywalpole.com Rev. Jean P. Aubin, Pst.; Rev. John J. Healy, Par. Vicar; Dcn. Alan J. Doty; Dcn. Reynold G. Spadoni; Dcn. James S. Hyatt;

WALTHAM

St. Jude - 147-R Main St., Waltham, MA 02453-6622 t) 781-891-5718 (CRP); 781-893-3100 ccroatti@stjudewaltham.org Rev. Jeremy P. St. Martin, Pst.; Rev. Shawn P. Carey;
St. Mary - 133 School St., Waltham, MA 02451-4599 t) 781-891-1730 office@stmarywaltham.org www.stmarywaltham.org Rev. Michael L. Nolan, Pst.; Rev. Fernando J. Vivas, Par. Vicar; Rev. Joseph D. Nguyen, Par. Vicar; Rev. Jude Kaggwa, In Res.; Rev. John Bosco Lugonja, In Res.;
Our Lady, Comforter of the Afflicted - 920-R Trapelo Rd., Waltham, MA 02452 t) 781-894-3481 x2 parish@olca.org www.olca.org Rev. James M. DiPerri, Pst.; Rev. Francis Pham, Par. Vicar;

Our Lady's Academy - 920 Trapelo Rd., Waltham, MA 02452 t) 781-899-0353 office@ourladysacademy.org www.ourladysacademy.org Chandra Minor, Prin.;

Sacred Heart - 311 River St., Waltham, MA 02453 t) 781-899-0469; 781-893-8461 (CRP) sacredheartwaltham@gmail.com sacredheart311.com Rev. William M. Kennedy, Admin.;

WATERTOWN

St. Patrick - 770 Mt. Auburn St., Watertown, MA 02472 t) 617-926-9680; 617-926-3441 (CRP) office@watertowncatholic.com www.stpatswatertown.org Most Rev. Robert Reed, Pst.; Very Rev. Timothy E. Kearney, Admin.; Rev. Michael B. Medas, In Res.; Dcn. John H. Beagan;
Sacred Heart - 770 Mt. Auburn St., Watertown, MA 02472-1567; Mailing: 26R Chestnut St., Watertown, MA 02472 t) 617-926-9680 office@watertowncatholic.com stpatswatertown.org Most Rev. Robert Reed, Pst.; Very Rev. Timothy E. Kearney, Admin.; Rev. Charles E. Salamone, In Res.; Rev. Michael Zimmerman, In Res.;

WAYLAND

St. Ann - 124 Cochituate Rd., Wayland, MA 01778-2610 Rev. James J. Laughlin, Pst.; Sr. Roberta Rzeznik, S.N.D., Pst. Assoc.; Jane Asber, DRE;
Good Shepherd Parish - St. Ann Church, 134 Cochiate Rd., Wayland, MA 01778; Mailing: St. Zepherin Church, 99 Main St., Wayland, MA 01778 t) 508-650-3545 parish@goodshepherdwayland.org www.goodshepherdwayland.org Rev. David M. O'Leary, Pst.; Dcn. Geoffrey W. Higgins; Rev. Austin H. Fleming, In Res.; Rev. Joseph M. Hennessey, In Res.;
St. Zepherin - 124 Cochituate Rd., Wayland, MA 01778-2610 Rev. James J. Laughlin, Pst.;

WELLESLEY

St. John the Evangelist - 9 Glen Rd., Wellesley, MA 02481-1600 t) 781-235-0045 stjohnwellesley@stjohnwellesley.org sjspwellesley.org Rev. James J. Laughlin, Pst.; Rev. J. Bryan Hehir, In Res.; CRP Stds.: 345

St. John the Evangelist School - 9 Ledyard St., Wellesley, MA 02481 t) 781-235-0300 smahoney@saintjohnschool.net www.saintjohnschool.net Siobhan Mahoney, Prin.; Stds.: 221; Lay Tchrs.: 24

St. Paul - 502 Washington St., Wellesley, MA 02482-5907 t) 781-235-1060 office@stpaulwellesley.com www.stpaulwellesley.com Rev. James J. Laughlin, Pst.; CRP Stds.: 256

WEST BRIDGEWATER

St. Ann - 103 N. Main St., West Bridgewater, MA 02379-0427 t) 508-586-4880 stanns@comcast.net www.stannswb.com Rev. Paul L. Ring, Pst.; Dcn. Christopher Z. Connelly;

WESTFORD

Blessed Trinity Parish - 107 N. Main St., Westford, MA 01886 t) 978-320-4220

WESTON

St. Julia - 374 Boston Post Rd., Weston, MA 02493-1581 t) 781-899-2611 stjulia@stjulia.org Rev. Mark A. Mahoney, Pst.; Dcn. Rafeal Brown;

St. Joseph - 142 Lincoln Rd., Lincoln, MA 01773

WESTWOOD

St. Denis - 157 Washington St., Westwood, MA 02090-1336 t) 781-326-5858 Rev. Robert M. Blaney; Rev. Paul Soper; Dcn. Stephen A. May; Most Rev. Peter J. Uglietto, In Res.;
St. Margaret Mary - 845 High St., Westwood, MA 02090 t) 781-326-1071 info@saintmmparish.org saintmmparish.org Rev. Robert M. Blaney, Pst.; Rev. Paul Soper, Pst.; Karlene Duffy, DRE;

WEYMOUTH

St. Albert the Great - 1130 Washington St., Weymouth, MA 02189; Mailing: 234 Pleasant St., South Weymouth, MA 02190 t) 781-337-2171 sfxprsh@gmail.com sagsfx.org Rev. Kenneth V. Cannon, S.X., Pst.; Dcn. Joseph A. Canova;
St. Francis Xavier - 234 Pleasant St., Weymouth, MA

02190 t) 781-337-2171; 781-331-6294 (CRP) sfxprsh@gmail.com; sfxfamilyfaith@gmail.com sagsfx.org Rev. Kenneth V. Cannon, S.X., Pst.; Dcn. Joseph A. Canova; Barbara Spink, DRE; CRP Stds.: 173

St. Francis Xavier School - (Grades 5-8) t) 781-335-6868 dianewalsh@sfxschoolwey.org www.sfxschoolwey.org/ Robert Murphy, Prin.;

Immaculate Conception - 720 Broad St., Weymouth, MA 02189; Mailing: 1203 Commercial St., Weymouth, MA 02189 t) 781-337-0380 office@catholicweymouth.org www.catholicweymouth.org Rev. Huy H. Nguyen, Pst.; Dcn. Timothy J. Maher; Zach Moris, DRE; CRP Stds.: 135

St. Jerome - 632 Bridge St., Weymouth, MA 02191; Mailing: 1203 Commercial St., Weymouth, MA 02189 t) 781-335-2038; 781-337-0380 (Office) office@catholicweymouth.org www.catholicweymouth.org Rev. Huy H. Nguyen, Pst.; Dcn. Timothy J. Maher;

Sacred Heart - 55 Commercial St., Weymouth, MA 02184 t) 781-337-6333 secretary@shstm.org www.shstm.org Rev. Sean M. Connor, Pst.; Dcn. Bashan Goppee;

Sacred Heart School - 75 Commercial St., Weymouth, MA 02188-2604 t) 781-335-6010 admin@sacredheartschoolweymouth.org www.sacredheartschoolweymouth.org Shannon Mazza, Vice Prin.;

WHITMAN

Holy Ghost - School St., Whitman, MA 02382; Mailing: 455 Pylmouth St., Abington, MA 02351-1879 t) 781-447-4421; 781-447-3135 (CRP) sbparishsecretary@comcast.net www.loccc.org Rev. Adrian A. Milik, Pst.; Dcn. James V. McLaughlin; Dcn. Joseph T. Nickley; Dcn. Paul Breadmore;

WILMINGTON

St. Dorothy - Closed Mar 2022 Parish records for all closed, merged & suppressed parishes are located at the Office of the Archives, 66 Brooks Dr., Braintree, MA 02184-3839

Parish of the Transfiguration - 11 Harnden St., Wilmington, MA 01887-3519 t) 978-658-4665 parishsecretary@parishofthetransfiguration.org Rev. Walter A. Carreiro, Pst.; Dcn. Joseph M. Fagan Jr.; Deb Casey, DRE;

St. Thomas of Villanova - Closed Mar 2022 Parish records for all closed, merged & suppressed parishes are located at the Office of the Archives, 66 Brooks Dr., Braintree, MA 02184-3839

WINCHESTER

St. Eulalia - 38 Ridge St., Winchester, MA 01890-3633 t) 781-729-8220 office@sainteulalia.org sainteulalia.org Rev. John S. Chen (China), Admin.; Stephanie Rogers, DRE;

St. Mary - 158 Washington St., Winchester, MA 01890 t) 781-729-1965 (CRP); 781-729-0055 stmaryssecretary@comcast.net Rev. Paul K. Hurley, Admin.; Rev. Augustin Vondou, Assoc. Pst.; Colleen DeBruyckere, DRE;

St. Mary School - 162 Washington St., Winchester, MA 01890-2173 t) 781-729-5515 nriley@stmaryswinchester.org www.stmaryswinchester.org Nancy Riley, Prin.;

WINTHROP

Saint Michael the Archangel Parish - 320 Winthrop St., Winthrop, MA 02152 t) 617-846-7400 info@stjohnswinthrop.org Rev. Christopher K. O'Connor, Pst.; Rev. Patrick F. O'Connor, Par. Vicar; Dcn. Vincent J. Leo;

WOBURN

St. Anthony of Padua - 138 Cambridge Rd., Woburn, MA 01801-1855 t) 781-933-4130 office@woburncatholic.org Rev. Edmund U. Ugwoegbu, Assoc. Pst.; Dcn. Edward S. Giordano; Dcn. William E. Kerns; Christopher Hatton, DRE;

St. Barbara - 138 Cambridge Rd., Woburn, MA 01801-4772 t) 781-935-0529 (CRP); 781-933-4130 office@woburncatholic.org Rev. Edmund U. Ugwoegbu, Assoc. Pst.; Dcn. Edward S. Giordano; Dcn. William E. Kerns; Rev. Paulinus Emeka Nweke, In Res.; Rev. Timothy J. Shea, In Res.; Christopher Hatton, DRE;

St. Charles Borromeo - 280 Main St., Woburn, MA 01801-3294 t) 280-933-0300 office@sccwoburn.com Rev. John M. Capuci, Pst.; Rev. Raphael C. Pinto, Assoc. Pst.; Rev. Gilbert U. Ezeugwu, In Res.; Rev. Paul Mukasa, In Res.; Joanne Campbell, DRE;

St. Charles Borromeo School - 8 Myrtle St., Woburn, MA 01801 t) 781-935-4635 www.saintcharleswoburn.com Donna Cargill, Prin.;

WRENTHAM

St. Mary - 130 South St., Wrentham, MA 02093-0326 t) 508-384-3373; 508-384-7922 (CRP) stmaryoffice@pwc.church www.pwc.church Very Rev. Joseph F. Mozer Jr., Pst.; Rev. Lambert K. Nieme, Assoc. Pst.; Dcn. Joseph R. Flocco; Dcn. James T. Kearney;

SCHOOLS: PRESCHOOL THRU HIGH SCHOOL

SCHOOLS

COMMONWEALTH OF MASSACHUSETTS

BOSTON

St. Columbkille School, Inc. (Saint Columbkille Partnership School) - (PRV) (Grades PreK-8) 25 Arlington St., Boston, MA 02135 t) 617-254-3110 info@stcps.org www.stcps.org Jennifer Kowieski, Prin.; Rachel Rumely, Vice Prin.; Stds.: 400; Sr. Tchrs.: 1; Lay Tchrs.: 35

Saint John Paul II Catholic Academy Inc. - 2200 Dorchester Ave., Boston, MA 02124 t) 617-265-0019 kbrandley@sjp2ca.org www.sjp2ca.org/ Kate Brandley, Dir.;

Columbia Campus - 790 Columbia Rd., Dorchester, MA 02125 t) (617) 265-0019 csheridan@sjp2ca.org Claire Barton Sheridan, Prin.;

Lower Mills Campus - 2214 Dorchester Ave., Dorchester, MA 02124 t) (617) 265-0019 Lisa Warshafsky, Prin.;

Neponset Campus - 239 Neponset Ave., Dorchester, MA 02122 t) (216) 265-0019 Erin Chouinard, Prin.;

BRAINTREE

Cardinal Cushing Centers (St. Coletta's and Cardinal Cushing Schools of MA, Inc.) - (PRV) 85 Washington St., Braintree, MA 02184 t) 617-848-6250 mmarkowitz@cushingcenters.org www.coletta.org Day School for multiple handicapped, developmentally delayed children, ages 4-22 years. Michelle Markowitz, Pres.;

BROCKTON

Trinity Catholic Academy, Inc. - (PRV) 37 Erie Ave., Brockton, MA 02302 t) (508) 583-6225 karsenault@tcabrockton.com tcabrockton.org Michael A. Green, Dir.; Kristin Blanchette, Prin.; Theresa Ballard, Librn.; Jane Clifford, Librn.;

DANVERS

St. Mary of the Annunciation School - (DIO) 14 Otis St., Danvers, MA 01923 t) 978-774-0307 sdaigle@stmaryschooldanvers.org stmaryschooldanvers.org/ Stephen Daigle, Prin.;

DORCHESTER

Mother Caroline Academy for Girls, Inc. - (PRV) 515 Blue Hill Ave., Dorchester, MA 02121 t) 617-427-1177 info@mcaec.org www.mcaec.org Annmarie Quezada, Headmaster;

HANOVER

Cardinal Cushing Centers, Inc. - (PRV) (Grades 1-12) 405 Washington St., Hanover, MA 02339 t) 781-826-6371 info@cushingcenters.org www.cushingcenters.org Michelle Markowitz, CEO; Stds.: 115; Lay Tchrs.: 22

JAMAICA PLAIN

Nativity Preparatory School (Nativity Boston, Inc.) - (PRV) (Grades 4-8) 39 Lamartine St., Jamaica Plain, MA 02130 t) 857-728-0031 bmaher@nativityboston.org www.nativityboston.org A Jesuit Middle School. Brian P. Maher, Pres.; Gadisa Goso, Prin.;

KINGSTON

Sacred Heart School System, Inc. - (PRV) (Grades PreK-6) 329 Bishops Hwy., Kingston, MA 02364 t) 781-585-2114 admissions@sacredheartkingston.com www.sacredheartkingston.com Sr. Lydia Steele, C.D.P., Prin.; Stds.: 150; Sr. Tchrs.: 2; Lay Tchrs.: 8

LAWRENCE

Blessed Stephen Bellesini, O.S.A. Academy, Inc. - (PRV) (Grades 5-8) 94 Bradford St., Lawrence, MA 01840-1003 t) 978-989-0004 office@bellesiniacademy.org www.bellesiniacademy.org Julie DiFilippo, Headmaster; Stds.: 120; Lay Tchrs.: 10

Lawrence Catholic Academy of Lawrence, Massachusetts, Inc. - (PRV) (Grades PreK-8) 101 Parker St., Lawrence, MA 01843 t) 978-683-5822 mkelly@lawrencecatholicacademy.org www.lawrencecatholicacademy.net Rev. Paul B. O'Brien, Trustee; Mary Kelly, Prin.;

LOWELL

Ste. Jeanne d'Arc - (DIO) (Grades PreK-8) 68 Dracut St., Lowell, MA 01854 t) 978-453-4114 mwilliams@sjdarc.org www.sjdarc.org Mollie Williams, Prin.;

St. Patrick School and Education Center, Inc. - 311 Adams St., Lowell, MA 01854

NEWTON

Jackson School Elementary - (PRV) (Grades K-6) 200 Jackson Rd., Newton, MA 02458-1428 t) 617-969-1537 info@jacksonschool.org www.jacksonschool.org Stephen Duffy, Prin.;

Jackson Walnut Park Educational Collaborative, Inc. - (PAR) (Grades PreSchool-6) 47 Walnut Park St., Newton, MA 02458 t) 617-686-0105; 617-969-9208 www.jacksonschool.org Sr. Mary Anne Doyle, Dir.; Stds.: 287; Lay Tchrs.: 42

Mount Alvernia Academy - (PRV) 20 Manet Rd., Newton, MA 02467 t) 617-527-7540 mferrucci@maa.school www.maa.school Mary Ferrucci, Prin.;

Convent - Missionary Franciscan Sisters of the Immaculate Conception.

QUINCY

Quincy Catholic Academy of Quincy, Massachusetts, Inc. - 370 Hancock St., Quincy, MA 02171 t) 617-328-3830 info@quincycatholicacademy.org Paul Kelly, Prin.;

TYNGSBOROUGH

Academy of Notre Dame at Tyngsboro - (PRV) (Grades PreK-12) 180 Middlesex Rd., Tyngsborough, MA 01879 t) 978-649-7611 vpacifico@ndatyngsboro.org www.ndatyngsboro.org Vittoria Pacifico, Pres.;

HIGH SCHOOLS

COMMONWEALTH OF MASSACHUSETTS

BOSTON

Boston College High School - (PRV) 150 Morrissey Blvd., Boston, MA 02125 t) 617-436-3900 bconleysj@bchigh.edu; dmcmanus@bchigh.edu www.bchigh.edu/ Rev. Joseph J. Bruce, S.J.; Rev. Jon D. Fuller, S.J.; Bro. Donald J. Murray, S.J.; Rev. John A. Predmone, S.J.; Rev. Martin G. Shaughnessy, S.J.; Stephen Hughes, Prin.; Rev. Brian J. Conley, S.J., Supr.; Grace Cotter Regan, Pres.;

Cathedral High School, Inc. - (PRV) 74 Union Park St., Boston, MA 02118 t) 617-542-2325 admissions@cathedralhighschool.net www.cathedralhighschool.net Nampeera Lugira, Prin.; Dan Carmody, Headmaster; Paul Chisholm, Chair; Michael Kieloch, Dir., Communs.;

Catholic Memorial School - (PRV) (Grades 7-12) 235 Baker St., Boston, MA 02132-4395 t) 617-469-8000

www.catholicmemorial.org (Boys) Thomas Beatty, Prin.; Peter F. Folan, Pres.;
Cristo Rey Boston High School Corporate Work Study Program, Inc. - 100 Savin Hill Ave., Boston, MA 02125 t) 617-825-2580 jthielman@cristoreyboston.org Jeff Thielman, Contact;
Cristo Rey Boston High School, Inc. - 100 Savin Hill Ave., Boston, MA 02125 t) 617-825-2580 jmacdonald@cristoreyboston.org Beth Degnan, Prin.; James J. MacDonald, Pres.;
Saint Joseph Preparatory High School - (PRV) 617 Cambridge St., Boston, MA 02134-2460 t) 617-254-8383 (Office); 617-783-4747 (Guidance) www.saintjosephprep.org Sponsored by Sisters of St. Joseph of Boston. Eugene Ward, Prin.; Stds.: 206; Lay Tchrs.: 14

BRAINTREE

Archbishop Williams High School, Inc. - (PRV) 80 Independence Ave., Braintree, MA 02184 t) 781-843-3636 mvolonnino@awhs.org www.awhs.org Michael Volonnino, Prin.; Dennis M. Duggan, Pres.; Joanna Sands, Librn.;

BROCKTON

Cardinal Spellman High School, Inc. - (PRV) 738 Court St., Brockton, MA 02302 t) 508-583-6875 cshs@spellman.com www.spellman.com Dorothy Lynch, Prin.; Daniel J. Hodes, Pres.; Diane McDonough, Librn.;

CAMBRIDGE

Matignon High School, Inc. - (PRV) 1 Matignon Rd., Cambridge, MA 02140 t) 617-876-1212 www.matignon-hs.org College Preparatory. Patricia D'Angelo, Prin.; Joseph DiSarcina, Prin.; Thomas F. Galligani, Headmaster;

DANVERS

St. John's Preparatory School - (PRV) (Grades 6-12) 72 Spring St., Danvers, MA 01923 t) 978-774-1050 ehardiman@stjohnsprep.org; bligh@stjohnsprep.org www.stjohnsprep.org Day Students. (Boys) Keith Crowley, Prin.; Edward Hardiman, Headmaster;

DEDHAM

Ursuline Academy - (PRV) (Grades 7-12) 85 Lowder St., Dedham, MA 02026-4299 t) 781-326-6161 klevesque@ursulineacademy.net www.ursulineacademy.net (Girls) Sponsored by Ursuline Sisters of the Central Province, St. Louis, MO. Kate Levesque, Head of School; Stds.: 365; Lay Tchrs.: 32

HINGHAM

Notre Dame Academy - (PRV) 1073 Main St., Hingham, MA 02043 t) 781-749-5930 akenneally@ndahingham.com www.ndahingham.com Annemarie Kenneally, Pres.;

LAWRENCE

Central Catholic High School of Lawrence, Inc. - (PRV) (Grades 9-12) 300 Hampshire St., Lawrence, MA 01841 t) 978-682-0260 dkeller@centralcatholic.net; csullivan@centralcatholic.net www.centralcatholic.net Conducted by the Marist Brothers of the Schools, USA Province Doreen A. Keller, Prin.; Christopher F. Sullivan, Pres.; Stds.: 1,206; Bro. Tchrs.: 2; Lay Tchrs.: 75

LOWELL

Lowell Catholic High School, Inc. - (PRV) 530 Stevens St., Lowell, MA 01851 t) 978-452-1794 ed2000@tiac.net Edward J. Quinn, Prin.;

MALDEN

Malden Catholic High School - (PRV) 99 Crystal St., Malden, MA 02148 t) 781-322-3098 thornburgj@maldencatholic.org www.maldencatholic.org Rose Maria Redman, Prin.;

METHUEN

Notre Dame Cristo Rey High School - (PRV) 203 Lawrence St., Methuen, MA 01844 t) 978-689-8222 www.ndcrhs.org/ (Co-Ed) Anthony Zavagnin, Prin.; Sr. Maryalyce Gilfeather, S.N.D.deN., Pres.;

MILTON

Fontbonne Academy - (PRV) 930 Brook Rd., Milton, MA 02186 t) 617-696-3241 www.fontbonneacademy.org Maura Spignesi, Prin.; Florence Lathrop, Librn.; Stds.: 243; Lay Tchrs.: 19

NEEDHAM

St. Sebastian's School, Inc. - (PRV) (Grades 7-12) 1191 Greendale Ave., Needham, MA 02492 t) 781-247-0163 david_riedell@stsebs.org www.stsebs.org Rev. John F. Arens; Rev. John U. Paris; William L. Burke III, Headmaster;

NEWTON

Country Day School of the Sacred Heart (Boston Academy of the Sacred Heart) - (PRV) (Grades 5-12) 785 Centre St., Newton, MA 02458 t) 617-244-4246 elevine@newtonsh.org www.newtoncountryday.org Sr. Barbara Rogers, R.S.C.J.; Stds.: 370; Sr. Tchrs.: 1; Lay Tchrs.: 80
Mount Alvernia High School - (PRV) (Grades 7-12) 790 Centre St., Newton, MA 02458 t) 617-964-4766 (Convent); 617-969-2260 (School) mahsinfo@mountalverniahs.org mountalverniahs.org Erin DiGuardia, Dir.; Meredith O'Brien, Librn.;

PEABODY

Bishop Fenwick High School, Inc. - (PRV) 99 Margin St., Peabody, MA 01960 t) 978-587-8300 btz@fenwick.org www.fenwick.org Diane Smith, Librn.;

READING

Austin Preparatory School - (PRV) (Grades 6-12) 101 Willow St., Reading, MA 01867 t) 781-944-4900 jhickey@austinprep.org www.austinprep.org Augustinian Secondary School Rev. Patrick S. Armano, Chap.; James Hickey, Headmaster;

TYNGSBOROUGH

Academy of Notre Dame - (PRV) 180 Middlesex Rd., Tyngsborough, MA 01879 t) 978-649-7611 vpacifico@ndatyngsboro.org www.ndatyngsboro.org Dr. Vittoria Pacifico, Pres.;

WESTWOOD

Xaverian Brothers High School - (PRV) 800 Clapboardtree St., Westwood, MA 02090 t) 781-326-6392 admin@xbhs.com www.xbhs.com Jacob Conca, Prin.; Domenic Lalli, Prin.;

ASSOCIATIONS [ASN]

BEVERLY

The Catholic Cemetery Association of the Archdiocese of Boston, Inc. - 100 Cummings Ctr., Ste. 421F, Beverly, MA 01915 t) 781-322-6300 cemetery_contactus@rcab.org www.ccemetery.org Robert Visconti, Exec.; David W. Smith, Secy.;

BRAINTREE

***KOLBE Association, Inc.** - 66 Brooks Dr., Braintree, MA 02184-3839 t) 617-746-5425 rev.michael.medas@sjs.edu His Eminence Sean Cardinal O'Malley, O.F.M.Cap.; Rev. Michael B. Medas, Exec.;

CAMPUS MINISTRY / NEWMAN CENTERS [CAM]

BOSTON

The Catholic Center at Boston University - 211 Bay State Rd., Boston, MA 02215 t) 617-353-3632 catholic@bu.edu www.bu.edu/catholic Rev. Clifton M. Thuma, Chap.; Bro. Parker Jordan, B.H., Campus Min.;
Emmanuel College Campus Ministry - 400 The Fenway, Emmanuel College, Boston, MA 02115 t) 617-735-9703 mission@emmanuel.edu

BRIDGEWATER

Bridgewater State College Catholic Center - 122 Park Ave., Bridgewater, MA 02325 t) 508-531-1346 mnolan@bridgew.edu www.bridgew.edu/depts/cathcntr/ Rev. Michael L. Nolan, Campus Min.;

CAMBRIDGE

Harvard Catholic Center - 29 Mount Auburn St., Cambridge, MA 02138 t) (617) 868-6585 info@harvardcatholic.org www.harvardcatholic.org Rev. William T. Kelly, Chap.; Rev. Patrick J. Fiorillo, Chap.; Rev. George S. Salzmann, O.S.F.S., Chap.; Douglas Zack, Dir.; Douglas Lee, CFO;

INSTITUTIONS LOCATED IN DIOCESE

Massachusetts Institute of Technology - Tech Catholic Community - 40 Massachusetts Ave., W11-012, Cambridge, MA 02139 t) 617-253-2981 catholic@mit.edu www.mitcatholic.org Rev. Michael B. Medas, Dir.;

CHESTNUT HILL

Boston College Campus Ministry - McElroy 233, Chestnut Hill, MA 02467; Mailing: 140 Commonwealth Ave., Chestnut Hill, MA 02467 t) 617-552-3475 ministry@bc.edu www.bc.edu/ministry

DORCHESTER

University of Massachusetts at Boston Campus Ministry - Harbor Campus, Dorchester, MA 02125 t) 617-287-5839 paul.helfrich@umb.edu

FRAMINGHAM

Framingham State College Campus Ministry - 100 State St., Framingham, MA 01701 t) 508-626-4610 kangeli@framingham.edu Kristelle Angelli, Chap.;

LOWELL

UMass, Lowell Catholic Campus Ministry - University Crossing 380, 220 Pawtucket St., Lowell, MA 01854 t) 978-934-5032 catholic_center@uml.edu; bernadine_kensinger@uml.edu www.uml.edu Bernadine Kensinger, Campus Min.;

MEDFORD

Tufts Interfaith Center Tufts University Catholic Chaplaincy - 58 Winthrop St., Medford, MA 02155-5300 t) 617-627-3427 lynn.cooper@tufts.edu www.tufts.edu/chaplaincy Lynn Cooper, Chap.;

NORTH ANDOVER

Merrimack College Campus Ministry Center - 315 Turnpike St., North Andover, MA 01845 t) 978-837-5450 campusmin@merrimack.edu www.merrimack.edu Hugh Hinton, Pst. Min./Coord.; Rev. Raymond F. Dlugos, O.S.A., Dir.;

SALEM

Salem State College, Catholic Campus Ministry - 352 Lafayette St., Salem, MA 01970 t) 978-542-6074 gmckeon@salemstate.edu

WALTHAM

Bentley University Spiritual Life Center - 175 Forest St., Waltham, MA 02452-4705 t) 781-891-2435 mdilorenzo@bentley.edu www.bentley.edu Maria DiLorenzo, Dir.;
Brandeis University Catholic Chaplaincy - Mail stop 205, Waltham, MA 02454-9110; Mailing: P.O. Box 549110, Waltham, MA 02454-9110 t) 781-736-3574 cuenin@brandeis.edu Rev. Walter H. Cuenin;

WELLESLEY

Babson College Campus Ministry - 9 Glen Rd., Wellesley, MA 02181
Wellesley College - Office of Religious and Spiritual Life - t) 781-283-2688 ncorcora@wellesley.edu

WESTON

Regis College Office of Campus Ministry - 235 Wellesley St., Weston, MA 02493 t) 781-768-7027; 781-768-7028; 781-768-7029 ministry@regiscollege.edu www.regiscollege.edu Rev. Paul E. Kilroy, Chap.; Sr. Elizabeth Conway, C.S.J., Dir.;

CATHOLIC CHARITIES [CCH]

BOSTON

Catholic Charitable Bureau of the Archdiocese of Boston, Inc. - 51 Sleeper St., Boston, MA 02210 t) 617-482-5440 info@ccab.org www.ccab.org Social Service Agency Deborah Kincade Rambo, Pres.;
Chinese Catholic Pastoral Center - 78 Tyler St., Boston, MA 02111-1831 t) 617-482-2949
El Centro Del Cardenal/Catholic Charities - 76 Union Park St., Boston, MA 02118 t) 617-542-9292 Elisabeth Zweig-Snippe, Contact;

Little Sisters of the Assumption, Family Health Service, Inc. - 550 Dudley St., Boston, MA 02119 t) 617-442-1880 mleonard@prohope.org www.prohope.org (Project Hope), multi-service agency to move families beyond homelessness and poverty.
Yawky Center for Early Ed & Care Catholic Charities - 185 Columbia Rd., Boston, MA 02121 t) 617-506-6930 esther_garcia@ccab.org www.ccab.org Community Based Agency of the Catholic Charitable Bureau of the Archdiocese of Boston, Inc., Day Care.
BRAINTREE
Archdiocesan Central High Schools, Inc. - 66 Brooks Dr., Braintree, MA 02184-3839 t) 617-779-3601 His Eminence Sean Cardinal O'Malley, O.F.M.Cap.; Thomas Carroll, Supt.;

CEMETERIES [CEM]

ARLINGTON
St. Paul -
BEVERLY
St. Mary -
CAMBRIDGE
North Cambridge Catholic -
CHARLESTOWN
St. Francis de Sales -
CHELMSFORD
St. Joseph Cemetery, Inc. - 96 Riverneck Rd., Chelmsford, MA 01824-2942 t) 978-458-4851 clare.cemetery@gmail.com stjc1894.com Rev. Charles Breault, O.M.I., Dir.; Clare Taddeo, Dir.;
HAVERHILL
St. James, St. Joseph & St. Patrick -
LOWELL
St. Patrick -
LYNN
St. Mary, St. Joseph & St. Jean Baptiste -
MALDEN
Holy Cross & St. Mary -
MARBLEHEAD
Star of the Sea -
SALEM
St. Mary -
SAXONVILLE
St. George -
STONEHAM
St. Patrick -
WALTHAM
Calvary -
WATERTOWN
Mount Auburn & St. Patrick -
WOBURN
Calvary -

COLLEGES & UNIVERSITIES [COL]

BOSTON
Emmanuel College - 400 The Fenway, Boston, MA 02115 t) 617-735-9715 president@emmanuel.edu www.emmanuel.edu Rev. Terrence Devino, S.J., Chap.; Sr. Janet Eisner, S.N.D., Pres.;
CHESTNUT HILL
***Boston College** - 140 Commonwealth Ave., Chestnut Hill, MA 02467 t) 617-552-8000 kevin.shea@bc.edu www.bc.edu (Coed) Rev. William P. Leahy, S.J., Pres.; Thomas Wall, Librn.; David Quigley, Provost;
Carroll Graduate School of Management - t) 617-552-8420 Andrew C. Boynton, Dean;
Carroll School of Management - t) 617-552-8420 Andrew C. Boynton, Dean;
Connell Graduate School of Nursing - t) 617-552-4250 Susan Gennaro, Dean;
Connell School of Nursing - t) 617-552-4250 Susan Gennaro, Dean;
Graduate School of Social Work - t) 617-552-4020 Gautam Yadama, Dean;
Graduate School of the Morrissey College of Arts and Sciences - t) 617-552-3268 Rev. Gregory Kalscheur, S.J., Dean;
Lynch Graduate School of Education - t) 617-552-4200 Stanton Wortham, Dean;
Lynch School of Education - t) 617-552-4200 Stanton Wortham, Dean;
Morrissey College of Arts and Sciences - t) 617-552-2393
School of Law - t) 617-552-4340 Vincent Rougeau, Dean;
The School of Theology and Ministry - t) 617-552-6501 Rev. Thomas D. Stegman, S.J., Dean; Esther Griswold, Librn.;
Woods College of Advancing Studies - t) 617-552-3900 Rev. James P. Burns, I.V.D., Dean;
NORTH ANDOVER
Merrimack College - 315 Turnpike St., North Andover, MA 01845-5800 t) 978-837-5000 dlugosr@merrimack.edu www.merrimack.edu Rev. Raymond F. Dlugos, O.S.A., Dir.; Rev. Bryan Kerns, O.S.A.; Rev. Daniel Madden, O.S.A.; Christopher F. Hopey, Pres.; Allison Gill, Dean;
WESTON
Regis College - 235 Wellesley St., Weston, MA 02493-1571 t) 781-768-7000 admission@regiscollege.edu www.regiscollege.edu Antoinette Hays, Pres.; Stds.: 3,322; Lay Tchrs.: 144; Sr. Tchrs.: 1

CONVENTS, MONASTERIES, AND RESIDENCES FOR WOMEN [CON]

ANDOVER
Monastery of St. Clare - 445 River Rd., Andover, MA 01810-4213 t) 978-683-7599 tmlacroix@comcast.net poorclarenunsandover.wordpress.com/ Sr. Therese Marie Lacroix, O.S.C., Abbess;
BELMONT
Franciscan Missionary Sisters for Africa - 38 Wiley Rd., Belmont, MA 02478 c) 617-415-6944 marymfisher9@gmail.com www.fmsa.net (USA Headquarters) Srs.: 3
BOSTON
Carmelite Convent of Boston - 61 Mt. Pleasant Ave., Boston, MA 02119 t) 617-442-1411 carmelitesofboston@gmail.com www.carmelitesofboston.org Cloistered., Discalced Carmelite Nuns - O.C.D. Sr. Bernadette Therese Huang, O.C.D., Prioress; Srs.: 8
Daughters of St. Paul Inc. - 50 St. Paul's Ave., Boston, MA 02130-3491 t) 617-522-8911 usaprov@paulinemedia.com www.pauline.org Sr. Donald Maria Lynch, FSP, Prov.; Srs.: 76
Pauline Book & Media Center - 885 Providence Hwy., Dedham, MA 02026 t) 781-326-5385
Franciscan Missionaries of Mary - 284 Foster St., Boston, MA 02135 t) 617-787-1505 nkloanfmm@yahoo.com
Franciscan Monastery of St. Clare, The - 920 Centre St., Boston, MA 02130 t) 617-524-1760 bostonpoorclares@yahoo.com www.poorclarenunsboston.org Solemn Vows. Rt. Rev. Clare Frances McAvoy Sr., osc, Abbess; Srs.: 10
Franciscan Sisters of the Atonement - 651 Adams St., Boston, MA 02122 t) 617-378-1723
Little Sisters of the Assumption Convent - 65 Magnolia St., Boston, MA 02125 t) 617-652-2206 aallain@littlesisters.org www.littlesisters.org Sr. Annette Allain, Prov.;
Motherhouse of the Sisters of St. Joseph of Boston - 637 Cambridge St., Boston, MA 02135 t) 617-783-9090 bostoncsj@csjboston.org www.csjboston.org Sr. Leila Hogan, C.S.J., Pres.; Srs.: 174
Sister Disciples of the Divine Master - Convent and Eucharistic Center, 43 West St., Boston, MA 02111 t) 482-682-0978; 482-423-2629 sddmboston@aol.com www.pddm.us Sr. M. Josephine Fallon, Supr.;
Sisters of the Good Shepherd - 35 Tyndale St., Boston, MA 02131 t) 617-469-2492 smhrgs@verizon.net
BROCKTON
Our Lady of Sorrows Convent - 261 Thatcher St., Brockton, MA 02302-3997 t) 508-588-5070 smjv@cjcbrockton.org www.cjcbrockton.org
CAMBRIDGE
Sancta Maria Convent - 799 Concord Ave., Cambridge, MA 02138 t) 617-868-2200 x2950 (Convent); 617-868-2200 x2100 (Office)
CHELSEA
Don Guanella Center, Inc., Daughters of St. Mary of Providence - 37 Nichols St., Chelsea, MA 02150 t) 617-889-0179 dgcenter.chelsea2@verizon.net www.donguanellacenter.com Emergency residential & respite for developmentally disabled women (ages 18 & older).
DANVERS
Discalced Carmelite Monastery - 15 Mt. Carmel Rd., Danvers, MA 01923-3796 t) 978-774-3008 contact@danverscarmel.com
DEDHAM
Ursuline Provincialate - 65 Lowder St., Dedham, MA 02026-4200; Mailing: 353 S. Sappington Rd., Kirkwood, MO 63122 t) 314-821-6884 adele@osucentral.org Sr. Elisa Ryan, OSU; Srs.: 9
EVERETT
Sisters of Notre Dame de Namur - 351 Broadway, Everett, MA 02149-3425 t) 617-387-2500 eileen.burns@sndden.org Sr. Barbara Barry, S.N.D.deN., Prov.; Sr. Eileen T. Burns, S.N.D., Prov.; Sr. Mary M. Farren, S.N.D.deN., Prov.;
FRAMINGHAM
Religious of Christian Education, Inc. - 933 Central St., Framingham, MA 01701; Mailing: 310 George Washington Hwy., Ste. 300, Smithfield, RI 02904 t) 508-309-7747 Sr. Martha Brigham, R.C.E., Contact;
IPSWICH
Sisters of Notre Dame de Namur - 30 Jeffreys Neck Rd., Ipswich, MA 01938-1308 t) 978-380-1372 mary.farren@sndden.org www.sndden.org Sr. Barbara Barry, S.N.D.deN., Prov.; Sr. Eileen T. Burns, S.N.D., Prov.; Sr. Mary M. Farren, S.N.D.deN., Prov.;
Sisters of Notre Dame de Namur Generalate Office - 30 Jeffrey's Neck Rd., Ipswich, MA 01938 t) 978-356-2159 connell@sndden.org www.sndden.org Sr. Lorraine Connell, S.N.D.deN., Treas.;
Casa Generalizia di Suore di Nostra Signora di Namur - (Generalate)
The Sisters of Notre Dame de Namur Generalate - lorraine.connell@sndden.org
Sisters of Notre Dame de Namur United States East-West Province, Inc. - 30 Jeffreys Neck Rd., Ipswich, MA 01938 t) 978-380-1372 mary.farren@sndden.org sndden.eastwest.org/ Sr. Barbara Barry, S.N.D.deN., Prov.; Sr. Eileen T. Burns, S.N.D., Prov.; Sr. Mary M. Farren, S.N.D.deN., Prov.;
KINGSTON
Congregation of the Sisters of Divine Providence - Providence House, 363 Bishops Hwy., Kingston, MA 02364 t) 781-585-7707 mbisbey@cdpsisters.org Mary McCulla, Dir.; Srs.: 15
LAKEVILLE
The Congregation of the Sisters of Our Lady of Mercy - 55 Loon Pond Rd., Lakeville, MA 02122 t) 617-288-1202 mercy@sisterfaustina.org www.sisterfaustina.org/ Sr. Caterina Esselen, ISMM, Supr.;
Sisters of Our Lady of Mercy, Inc. - 55 Loon Pond Rd., Lakeville, MA 02347 t) 617-288-1202 www.sisterfaustina.org/ Sr. Caterina Esselen, ISMM, Dir.; Srs.: 8
LEXINGTON
Congregation of Armenian Catholic Sisters of Immaculate Conception, Inc. - 6 Eliot Rd., Lexington, MA 02421 t) 781-863-5962
Grey Nuns Area Offices - 10 Pelham Rd., Ste. 1000, Lexington, MA 02421-8499 t) 781-674-7401 srjeanneepoor@verizon.net www.sgm.qc.ca Headquarters (U.S.A. Area) of the Sisters of Charity of Montreal. "Grey Nuns". Sr. Jeanne Poor, S.G.M., Prov.; Srs.: 10
LOWELL
St. Joseph Provincial House - 245 University Ave., Lowell, MA 01854-2426; Mailing: 977 Varnum Ave., Lowell, MA 01854 t) 978-458-6632 pmalo3043@gmail.com

www.soeursdelachariteottawa.com Sr. Prescille Malo, S.C.O., Prov.; Sr. Pauline Leblanc, S.C.O., Archivist;

MARLBORO

St. Chretienne Regional Offices - 197 Pleasant St., Marlboro, MA 01752 t) 508-384-8066 ssch@tiac.net sistersofstchretienne.org

Sisters of St. Chretienne - 720 Boston Post Rd. E., Marlboro, MA 01752; Mailing: 929 Upper Union St., Franklin, MA 02038 t) 508-384-8066 ssch@tiac.net www.sistersofstchretienne.org House of Retired Religious Sr. Lisette Michaud, SSCh, Rel. Ord. Ldr.; Srs.: 24

MARLBOROUGH

Assumption Residence of the Sisters of the Assumption of the Blessed Virgin - 720 Boston Post Rd. E., Marlborough, MA 01752 t) (508) 856-9383 www.sasv.ca Sr. Lorraine Normand, S.A.S.V., Treas.; Sr. Muriel Lemoine, S.A.S.V., Congregational Leader; Srs.: 10

Sisters of St. Anne, Provincialate - 720 Boston Post Rd. E., Marlborough, MA 01752 t) 508-485-3791 sydargy@hotmail.com sistersofstanne.org Headquarters of American Province. Sr. Yvette Dargy, S.S.A., Prov.;

Community of the Sisters of Saint Anne -

St. Anne Convent - 720 Boston Post Rd. E., Marlborough, MA 01752 t) 508-485-3791

Sisters of the Assumption of the Blessed Virgin, USA, Inc. - 720 Boston Post Rd. E, Marlborough, MA 01752 t) (978) 935-3419 newdawnsasv@yahoo.com Sr. Judith Curley, SASV, Regl. Support Coord.; Sr. Sandra Dupre, SASV, Regl. Support Coord.;

Sisters of the Good Shepherd - 406 Hemenway St., Marlborough, MA 01752 t) 508-485-8610 Sr. Elish McPartland, R.G.S., Contact;

MATTAPAN

Sisters of the Eucharistic Heart of Jesus - 59 Richmere Rd., Mattapan, MA 02126 t) 617-296-0167 ehjsistersboston1@verizon.net; conyewuche@yahoo.com www.ehjsrsboston.org

METHUEN

Sisters of the Presentation of Mary - 209 Lawrence St., Methuen, MA 01844 t) 978-687-1369 pmprov.us@gmail.com; pmtreasurer209@gmail.com www.presentationofmary-usa.org Sr. Helene Cote, P.M., Prov.; Sr. Annette Laliberte, P.M., Treas.; Srs.: 3

MILTON

Holy Union Sisters - 444 Centre St., Milton, MA 02186-0006; Mailing: P.O. Box 410, Milton, MA 02186-0006 t) 617-696-8765 www.holyunionsisters.org Sr. Joan Guertin, Contact;

NEWTON

Immaculate Conception Provincialate - 790 Centre St., Newton, MA 02458-2530 t) 617-527-1004 mfic@mficusa.org www.mficusa.org Sr. Jeanette Gaudet, MFIC, Prov.; Srs.: 56

Mt. Alvernia Convent - 790 Centre St., Newton, MA 02458-2530 t) 617-969-4766 mfic@mficusa.org www.mficusa.org Srs.: 56

SOMERVILLE

Medical Missionaries of Mary, Inc. - 179 Highland Ave., Somerville, MA 02143-1515 t) 617-666-3223 mmmboston20@gmail.com; mdommm2014@gmail.com www.mmmworldwide.org Srs.: 21

WALTHAM

Marist Missionary Sisters - 349 Grove St., Waltham, MA 02453-6018 t) 781-893-0149 admin@maristsmsm.org www.maristmissionarysmsm.org Sr. Helen Muller, S.M.S.M., Prov.; Srs.: 67

Local Community - 21 Beech St., Belmont, MA 02478-1299 t) 617-489-3587 slfoustsmsm@yahoo.com

Local Community - 4 Craig St., Framingham, MA 01701-7664 t) 508-877-7371

Local Community - 357 Grove St., Waltham, MA 02453-6018 t) 781-899-3839

Provincial Offices - 349 Grove St., Waltham, MA 02453-6018 t) (781) 893-0149

Residence for Senior Sisters - 62 Newton St., Waltham, MA 02453-6058 t) 781-893-3960

WATERTOWN

Rosary Manor - One Rosary Dr., Watertown, MA 02472 t) 617-924-1717 hmccarthy435@gmail.com

WELLESLEY

Marillac Residence, Inc. - 125 Oakland St., Wellesley, MA 02481-5338 t) 781-997-1110 jbreen@schalifax.org www.marillacresidence.org Sr. Judith Breen, S.C., Admin.;

Mount St. Vincent Retirement Community - 125 Oakland St., Wellesley, MA 02481-5338 t) 781-997-1165 pangevine@schalifax.org www.schalifax.com Patricia Angevine, Coord., Care & Community Life;

Sisters of Charity (Halifax) Corporate Mission, Inc. - 125 Oakland St., Wellesley, MA 02481 t) 781-997-1357 bostreasurer@schalifax.org www.schalifax.ca

Sisters of Charity Supporting Corporation - 125 Oakland St., Wellesley, MA 02481-5338 t) 781-997-1126 mafoster@schalifax.org

WOLLASTON

Sisters of Charity (Halifax) - 50 Elm Ave., Wollaston, MA 02170; Mailing: 125 Oakland St., Wellesley, MA 02481 t) 781-997-1126 mafoster@schalifax.org www.schalifax.ca (Boston Office) Sr. Mary Anne Foster, Treas.;

WRENTHAM

Mount St. Mary's Abbey - 300 Arnold St., Wrentham, MA 02093 t) 508-528-1282 sisters@msmabbey.org www.msmabbey.org Mother Sofia M. Millican, O.C.S.O., Abbess; Srs.: 38

ENDOWMENTS / FOUNDATIONS / TRUSTS [EFT]

BOSTON

Daughters of St. Paul Community Foundation, Inc. - 50 St. Paul's Ave., Boston, MA 02130 t) 617-522-8911 treasurer@paulinemedia.com Sr. Edward Marie Smith, Treas.;

Daughters of St. Paul Religious Trust - 50 St. Paul's Ave., Boston, MA 02130 t) 617-522-8911 treasurer@paulinemedia.com

Lanteri Charitable Trust - 1105 Boylston St., Boston, MA 02215-3660 t) 617-536-4141 wbrown@omvusa.org Rev. James Walther, O.M.V., Pres.; Rev. William M. Brown, O.M.V.;

Senior Religious Trust Fund of Marist Fathers of Boston - 13 Isabella St., Boston, MA 02116 t) 617-426-4448 denise.damico@maristsociety.org Rev. Walter L. Gaudreau, S.M., Trustee;

BRAINTREE

The Catholic Health Foundation of Greater Boston, Inc. - 66 Brooks Dr., Braintree, MA 02184 t) 617-746-5693 lisa_lipsett@rcab.org Patricia Kelleher Bartram, Pres.;

Clergy Assistance Trust - 66 Brooks Dr., Braintree, MA 02184-3839 t) (617) 746-5725

Massachusetts Catholic Self-Insurance Group, Inc. - 66 Brooks Dr., Braintree, MA 02184-3839 t) 617-746-5740 joseph_mcenness@rcab.org Rev. Charles J. Higgins; Joseph F. McEnness, Admin.; James P. McDonough, Pres.; John E. Straub, Treas.;

IPSWICH

Blin Charitable Trust - 30 Jeffrey's Neck Rd., Ipswich, MA 01938 t) 978-380-1372 mary.farren@sndden.org www.sndden.org Sr. Mary M. Farren, S.N.D.deN., Contact;

JAMAICA PLAIN

Daughters of St. Paul Defined Pension Plan & Trust - 50 St. Paul's Ave., Jamaica Plain, MA 02130 t) 617-522-8911 treasurer@paulinemedia.com

LOWELL

D'Youville Senior Care Foundation, Inc. - 981 Varnum Ave., Lowell, MA 01854 t) 978-569-1000 nprendergast@dyouville.org www.dyouville.org Naomi M. Prendergast, CEO;

Saints Memorial Medical Center Foundation - ; Mailing: P.O. Box 367, Lowell, MA 01853-0367 t) 978-934-8334 fund.kec@tmmc.org www.saints-memorial.org D. Harold Sullivan, Chair; Thom Clark, Pres.; Kevin E. Coughlin, Vice Pres.;

METHUEN

Caritas Holy Family Hospital Foundation, Inc. - 70 East St., Methuen, MA 01844-4597 t) 978-687-0151 nmallen@cchcs.org www.holyfamilyhosp.org Noreen V. Mallen, Exec.;

NEEDHAM

St. Joseph Parish School Fund, Inc., Needham - 1382 Highland Ave., Needham, MA 02492 t) 781-444-0245 John Brennan, Treas.;

SCITUATE

Mass Times Trust - 91 Surfside Rd., Scituate, MA 02066

WALTHAM

***Marist Missionary Sisters Senior Religious Trust** - 349 Grove St., Waltham, MA 02453 t) 781-893-0149 admin@maristsmsm.org www.maristmissionarysmsm.org Sr. Shirley Foust, Admin.;

HOSPITALS / HEALTH SERVICES [HOS]

BRIGHTON

Franciscan Hospital for Children (Franciscan Children's) - 30 Warren St., Brighton, MA 02135 t) 617-254-3800 fch@fhfc.org; jcollen@franciscanchildrens.org www.franciscanchildrens.org

CAMBRIDGE

***Youville Hospital & Rehabilitation Center, Inc. (Covenant Health Systems, Tewksbury, MA)** - 1575 Cambridge St., Cambridge, MA 02138-4398 t) 617-876-4344 leaheyd@youville.org www.youville.org

MISCELLANEOUS [MIS]

ARLINGTON

Fidelity House - 25 Medford St., Arlington, MA 02474-3105 t) 781-648-2005 fidelityhouse@fidelityhouse.net www.fidelityhouse.org Community center sponsored by the Saint Agnes Parish Edward F. Woods, Dir.;

BOSTON

St. Anthony Shrine - 100 Arch St., Boston, MA 02110-1100 t) 617-542-6440; 646-473-0265 mharlan@hnp.org www.stanthonyshrine.org Rev. Thomas Conway, O.F.M., Exec.; Bro. Anthony Joseph LoGalbo, O.F.M., Vicar; Rev. Frank Sevola, Guardian; Bro. John Maganzini, O.F.M., Spiritual Dir.; Bro. Paul R. Bourque, O.F. M., In Res.; Bro. Christopher Coccia, O.F.M., In Res.; Rev. Brian Cullinane, O.F.M., In Res.; Bro. Gregory Day, O.F.M., In Res.; Rev. Richard C. Flaherty, O.F.M., In Res.; Bro. John Gill, OFM, In Res.; Rev. Hugh Hines, O.F.M., In Res.; Bro. John Jaskowiak, O.F.M., In Res.; Jeffrey Vaughn Jordan, OFM, In Res.; Rev. Cidouane Joseph, OFM (Haiti), In Res.; Rev. Emeric Meier, O.F.M., In Res.; Bro. Daniel Murray, O.F.M., In Res.; Rev. Charles John O'Connor, OFM, In Res.; Bro. Paul O'Keeffe, In Res.; Rev. Gene Pistacchio, O.F.M., In Res.; Rev. Joe Quinn, O.F.M., In Res.; Bro. Paul Santoro, OFM, In Res.; Rev. Raymond C. Selker II, O.F.M., In Res.;

Boston Inter-Community Ministries, Inc. - 637 Cambridge St., Boston, MA 02135 t) 617-921-2087 maureen.doherty@csjboston.org Sr. Maureen Doherty, C.S.J., Contact;

***Catholic Investment Services Inc.** - 200 State St., 14th Fl., Boston, MA 02109

The Catholic Lawyers Guild of the Archdiocese of Boston, Inc. - One Lewis Wharf, Boston, MA 02110 t) 617-722-8175 Hon. Joseph R. Nolan, Pres.;

Chapel of Our Lady of Lourdes - 698 Beacon St., Boston, MA 02215 t) 617-536-2761 denise.damico@maristsociety.org Rev. Philip Parent, Dir.;

Marist Fathers Residence - t) 617-262-2271 Rev. Andrew Albert, S.M.; Rev. Francis Grispino, S.M.;

Chapel of the Holy Spirit - 5 Park St., Boston, MA 02108-4802 t) 617-742-4460 info@paulistcenter.org www.paulistcenter.org Rev. Charles Cunniff, CSP, Par. Vicar; Normand Gouin, Liturgy Dir.; Rev. Michael B. McGarry, C.S.P., Dir.;

St. Clement Archdiocesan Eucharistic Shrine - 1105 Boylston St., Boston, MA 02215-3604 t) 617-266-5999

stclement@omvusa.org www.stclementshrine.org Rev. Peter W. Grover, O.M.V., Admin.; Rev. James Walther, O.M.V., Prov.; Rev. Sean Morris, O.M.V., Dir. Seminary; Rev. John Luong, O.M.V., Vocations Dir.; Bro. Luigi Falbo, In Res.; Rev. Victor Nwabueze, O.M.V., In Res.; Rev. Isaac Abu, O.M.V., In Res.; Rev. Robert Lowrey, O.M.V., In Res.; Bro. Joseph O'Connor, O.M.V., In Res.;

Corporation for the Sponsored Ministries of the Sisters of St. Joseph of Boston - 637 Cambridge St., Boston, MA 02135-2800 t) 617-746-1607 maryanne.doyle@csjboston.org www.csjsponsorship.org Sr. Mary Anne Doyle, Exec.;

St. Francis Chapel - 800 Boylston St., #1001, Boston, MA 02199-8001 t) 617-437-7117 stfrancis@omvusa.org www.stfrancischapel.org Rev. James Doran, O.M.V., Dir.; Rev. Isaac Abu, O.M.V., In Res.; Rev. Michael Warren, O.M.V., In Res.;

Lourdes Bureau - 698 Beacon St., Boston, MA 02215 t) 617-536-2761 denise.damico@maristsociety.org Official Representatives in America for the Shrine of Lourdes, France. Rev. Philip Parent, Dir.;

Madonna Queen of the Universe - 150 Orient Ave., Boston, MA 02128-1006 t) 617-569-8792 madonna_orione@hotmail.com

St. Mary's Center for Women and Children - 90 Cushing Ave., Boston, MA 02125 t) 617-436-8600 dhoutmeyers@stmaryscenterma.org www.stmaryscenterma.org Programs for women & children who are homeless or living in poverty. Deirdre Houtmeyers, Pres.;

Medaille Corporation - 637 Cambridge St., Boston, MA 02135 t) 617-783-9090 bostoncsj@csjboston.org www.csjboston.org Sr. Leila Hogan, C.S.J., Pres.;

Most Holy Name of Jesus Federation of Poor Clare Monasteries in the Eastern Region of the United States - Monastery of Saint Clare, 920 Centre St., Boston, MA 02130 t) 617-524-1760 clarefrancesosc@aol.com Sr. Clare Frances McAvoy, O.S.C., Contact;

Our Lady of the Airways Chapel - First Fl., Tower Bldg., Logan International Airport, Boston, MA 02128 t) 617-846-7400 info@stjohnswinthrop.org Rev. Christopher K. O'Connor, Admin.; Rev. William T. Schmidt, Par. Vicar; Dcn. Vincent J. Leo;

PACE - Parents Alliance for Catholic Education - 14 Beacon St., Ste. 506, Boston, MA 02108 t) 617-723-9890 fkalisz@paceorg.net www.paceorg.net Frederick M. Kalisz Jr., Exec.;

Paulist Center - 5 Park St., Boston, MA 02108 t) 617-742-4460 info@paulistcenter.org www.paulistcenter.org Rev. Charles Cunniff, CSP, Pst. Assoc.; Rev. Michael B. McGarry, C.S.P., Dir.; Normand Gouin, Liturgy Dir.;

Sancta Maria House, Inc. - 11 Waltham St., Boston, MA 02118-2162 t) 617-423-4366

Vox Clara Committee, Inc. - 127 Lake St., Boston, MA 02135 t) 617-254-2610 tempio@aol.com

***Women Affirming Life, Inc.** - ; Mailing: P.O. Box 35532, Boston, MA 02135 t) 617-254-2277 mail@affirmlife.com www.affirmlife.com Frances X. Hogan, Pres.;

BRAINTREE

Chancery Office - 66 Brooks Dr., Braintree, MA 02184-3839 t) 617-254-0100 www.rcab.org Also see Miscellaneous Section for additional listings.

Archdiocese of Boston Clergy Retirement/Disability Trust -

Benefit Trust for Non-Incardinated Priests -

Cardinal Cushing General Hospital Foundation, Brockton -

The Cardinal Medeiros Trust -

Caritas Holy Family Hospital Foundation, Inc. -

The Carney Hospital Foundation, Inc. - 2100 Dorchester Ave., Boston, MA 02124 t) 617-296-1788 (Formerly The New Caritas Christi Hospital, Inc.) J. Barry Driscoll, Pres.; Daniel J. McDevitt, Secy.; William F. Henderson, Exec.; Paul J. Kingston, Vice Pres.;

The Catholic Community Fund of the Archdiocese of Boston, Inc. - t) 617-746-5621 lisa_lipsett@rcab.org Patricia Kelleher Bartram, Pres.;

***Catholic Schools Foundation, Inc.** - (Formerly St. Anthony's Scholarship Fund, Inc.).

St. Charles Borromeo Educational Foundation, Inc. -

Clergy Benefit Trust -

Clergy Fund Society -

Clergy Medical-Hospitalization Trust -

St. Elizabeth's Hospital Foundation, Inc. - 159 Washington St., Brighton, MA 02135

Family Counseling Endowment Fund, Inc. - 141 Tremont St., Boston, MA 02111 t) 617-482-4355

Marist Capital Trust Fund - Sisters of the Society of Mary, Inc., 349 Grove St., Waltham, MA 02154 t) (781) 893-0149 admin@maristsmsm.org Sr. Shirley Foust, Treas.;

St. Mary's High School Foundation, Inc. - 35 Tremont St., Lynn, MA 01902 t) 781-595-7885 Grace Cotter Regan, Contact;

Metropolitan Boston Dialysis Center, Inc. - 736 Cambridge St., Brighton, MA 02135

Mission Promotion - 349 Grove St., Waltham, MA 02453 t) 781-893-0149 admin@maristsmsm.org Sr. Joyce Edelmann, Secy.;

Roman Catholic Archdiocese of Boston Common Investment Fund - t) 617-746-5680

Roman Catholic Archdiocese of Boston Fixed Income Investment Fund - t) 617-746-5680

Roman Catholic Archdiocese of Boston Health Benefit Trust - t) 617-746-5680 James M. Walsh, Admin.;

Roman Catholic Archdiocese of Boston Insurance Trust - t) 617-746-5640 Benefit Office. James M. Walsh, Admin.;

Roman Catholic Archdiocese of Boston Long Term Disability Trust - t) 617-746-5640 James M. Walsh, Admin.;

Roman Catholic Archdiocese of Boston Pension Trust - t) 617-746-5640 Benefit Office. James M. Walsh, Admin.;

Sacred Heart Trust Fund - c/o Society of Jesus, Trustee, 761 Harrison Ave., Boston, MA 02118 t) 617-536-5604

The Catholic Cemetery Association Perpetual Care Trust -

Equestrian Order of the Holy Sepulchre of Jerusalem - c/o Rev. Jonathan Gaspar, Pastoral Ctr., 66 Brooks Dr., Braintree, MA 02184-3839

Northeastern Lieutenancy -

Fides Insurance Group, Inc. - 66 Brooks Dr., Braintree, MA 02184

The Fund for Catholic Schools, Inc. - 66 Brooks Dr., Braintree, MA 02184 t) 617-262-5600 campaignforcatholicschools@rcab.org campaignforcatholicschools.org Mary Flynn Myers, Pres.; James Walsh, Exec.;

Pontifical Mission Societies in the Archdiocese of Boston (The Propagation of the Faith of Boston, Inc.) - 66 Brooks Dr., Braintree, MA 02184-3839 t) 617-542-1776 info@propfaithboston.org www.propfaithboston.org The Society for the Propagation of the Faith, The Missionary Childhood Association, The Society of Saint Peter Apostle & The Missionary Union Maureen Crowley Heil, Dir.; Rev. Gerald J. Osterman, Dir.;

St. Vincent Pallotti Center for Apostolic Development of Boston, Inc. - 66 Brooks Dr., Braintree, MA 02184-3839 t) 617-783-3924 volservice@aol.com www.pallotticenterboston.org

BRIGHTON

The Literacy Connection - 637 Cambridge St., Brighton, MA 02135 t) 617-746-2100 patricia.andrews@csjboston.org Sr. Patricia Andrews, C.S.J., Dir.;

Washington Province Discalced Carmelite Secular Order, Inc. - 166 Foster St., Brighton, MA 02135 t) 617-851-8584 ocdsmainoffice@gmail.com www.ocdswashprov.org Loretta Gallagher, OCDS, Admin.;

BROCKTON

Chapel of Our Savior-Catholic Pastoral and Information Center - 475 Westgate Dr., Brockton, MA 02301-1819 t) 508-583-8357 jerrydigiralamo@gmail.com Bro. Thomas Banacki, S.A., Dir.;

Chapel of Our Saviour - 475 Westgate Dr., Brockton, MA 02301-1819 t) 508-583-8357 lherrera@atonementfriars.org chapelofoursaviorbrockton.org Bro. Thomas Banacki, S.A.;

CAMBRIDGE

Prelature of the Holy Cross and Opus Dei - 25 Follen St., Cambridge, MA 02138 t) 617-354-3204 www.opusdei.org Rev. David J. Cavanagh;

***The Youville House, Inc.** - 1575 Cambridge St., Cambridge, MA 02138-4398 t) 617-876-4344 leaheyd@youville.org www.youville.org Member of Youville Lifecare, Inc. Elizabeth Walsh, Chap.; T. Richard Quigley, Pres.; Patricia Kennedy, Dir.; Marsha V. Whelan, Vice Pres. Mission Integration;

CHESTNUT HILL

Domus Jerusalem, Inc. - 774 Boylston St., Chestnut Hill, MA 02467

EVERETT

Notre Dame Mission Volunteer Corporation - 351 Broadway, Everett, MA 02149 t) (781) 435-0922 c) 617-694-5747 obrien@sndden.org www.sndden.org Sr. Eileen T. Burns, S.N.D., Pres.; Sr. Catherine O'Brien, Contact;

FRAMINGHAM

Bethany Health Care Center, Inc. - 97 Bethany Rd., Framingham, MA 01702-7237 t) 508-872-6750 jacquelyn.mccarthy@csjboston.org www.bethanyhealthcare.org Skilled Nursing Facility and Residential Living Sr. Jacquelyn McCarthy, C.S.J., CEO;

***Bethany Hill Place, Inc.** - 89 Bethany Rd., Framingham, MA 01702 t) 508-875-1117 tappert@bethanyhillschool.org Educational housing for low-income people. Sponsored by the Sisters of St. Joseph of Boston. Sr. Mary Anne Doyle, Exec.;

Bethany Home Care, Inc. - 97 Bethany Rd., Framingham, MA 01702 t) 508-872-6750 Sr. Jacquelyn McCarthy, C.S.J., CEO;

HANOVER

League of Catholic Women of the Archdiocese of Boston - 392 Hanover St., Hanover, MA 02339 t) 781-826-4303 John F. O'Donoghue Jr., Pres.;

HOLLISTON

Our Lady of Fatima Shrine - 101 Summer St., Holliston, MA 01746-2207 t) 508-429-2144 holliston@xaverianmissionaries.org; frrocco@xaverianmissionaries.org www.xaverianmissionaries.org Rev. Rocco N. Puopolo, S.X., Rector; Rev. Carl Chudy, sx, Pst. Assoc.; Rev. Adolph J. Menendez, S.X., Pst. Assoc.; Rev. Francis Signorelli, S.X., Pst. Assoc.; Bro. Pietro Rossini, In Res.;

IPSWICH

Cuvilly Arts and Earth Center, Inc. - 10 Jeffrey Neck Rd., Ipswich, MA 01938 t) 978-356-4288 cuvilly@verizon.net cuvilly.org Sr. Patricia Rolinger, S.N.D.deN., Exec.;

LAWRENCE

M.I. Management, Inc. - 172 Lawrence St., Lawrence, MA 01841 t) 978-685-6321 gerard_foley@mihcs.com www.mihcs.com Management company for all Mary Immaculate Facilities. Sponsored by Covenant Health, Inc., Tewksbury, MA. Gerard J. Foley, Pres.;

Notre Dame Education Center-Lawrence - 354 Merrimack St., Ste. 210, Lawrence, MA 01843 t) 978-682-6441 executivedirector@ndeclawrence.com Alisa Povenmire, Dir.;

LEXINGTON

Youville Place, Inc. - 10 Pelham Rd., Lexington, MA 02421-8408; Mailing: 100 Ames Pond Dr., Ste. 102, Tewksbury, MA 01876 t) 781-861-3535; 978-654-6363 nicolebreslin@youvillehouse.org youvilleassistedliving.org Assisted Living Residence. Sponsored by Covenant Health, Inc., Tewksbury, MA. Joanne R. Scianna, Exec.;

LOWELL

St. Joseph the Worker Shrine - 37 Lee St., Lowell, MA 01852-1103 t) 978-458-6346 info@stjosephshrine.org www.stjosephshrine.org Rev. Michael J. Amesse, O.M.I., Pst.; Rev. Stephen Conserva, OMI, Assoc. Pst.; Rev. Eugene Tremblay, O.M.I., Assoc. Pst.; Rev. Ronald J. Meyer, OMI;

Andre Garin Residence - 27 Kirk St., Lowell, MA 01852-1103 t) 978-937-9594 andregarinresidence@yahoo.com

Saints Medical Center Inc. - One Hospital Dr., Lowell, MA 01852 t) 978-458-1411 sguimond@saintsmedicalcenter.com www.saintsmedicalcenter.com Stephen Guimond, CEO;

METHUEN

Caritas Holy Family Hospital Men's Guild - 70 East St., Methuen, MA 01844-4597 t) 978-687-0156 x2362 www.holyfamilyhosp.org Lester Schindel, Pres.;

Caritas Valley Regional Health System, Inc. - 70 East St., Methuen, MA 01844-4597 t) 978-687-0151 www.holyfamilyhosp.org

Caritas Holy Family Hospital Auxiliary - t) 978-687-0156 x2301

Caritas Holy Family Hospital Foundation, Inc. - t) 978-687-0156 x2104

Caritas Holy Family Hospital Men's Guild - t) 978-687-0156 x2362

Caritas Holy Family Hospital, Inc. -

Caritas Valley Regional Medical Services Corporation -

Caritas Valley Regional Support Services, Inc. -

Caritas Valley Regional Ventures, Inc. -

Greater Lawrence Mental Health Center, Inc. -

Notre Dame High School Corporate Internship Program, Inc. - 203 Lawrence St., Methuen, MA 01844 t) 978-689-8222 mgilfeather@ndcrhs.org Sr. Maryalyce Gilfeather, S.N.D.deN., Pres.;

MILTON

The Guild of St. Luke of the Archdiocese of Boston, Inc. - 26 Houston Ave., Milton, MA 02186 t) 617-698-1748 jjohnb1946@aol.com Prior entities date back to1911. Dr. John Barravecchio, Pres.; Dr. David Ramsey, Vice. Pres.;

NEEDHAM

St. Sebastian's School Fund, Inc. - 1191 Greendale Ave., Needham, MA 02492 t) 781-449-5200 david_riedell@stsebs.org David Riedell, Dir., Fin & Opers.;

NEWTON

Catholic Purchasing Services, Inc. - 580 Washington St., Newton, MA 02458 t) 617-965-4343 jmorrissey@catholicpurchasing.org catholicpurchasing.org Joseph V. Morrissey, Pres.;

PEABODY

St. Theresa Carmelite Chapel - 210 Andover St., Peabody, MA 01960; Mailing: 30 Diane Rd., Peabody, MA 01960 t) 347-283-0631 jilsoncmi@gmail.com www.carmelitepeabody.com Rev. Jilson George, CMI, Dir.;

QUINCY

The Good Shepherd: Maria Droste Services (Maria Droste Counseling Services, Inc.) - 1354 Hancock St., Ste. 209, Quincy, MA 02169 t) 617-471-5686 info@mariadrostecounseling.com mariadrostecounseling.com Sr. Elish McPartland, R.G.S., Prov. Asst.;

ROXBURY

Franciscan Sisters of the Immaculate Conception, Inc. - 1 Magazine St., Roxbury, MA 02118 t) 617-445-6178

STOUGHTON

Society of St. Vincent DePaul, Central Office - 18 Canton St., Stoughton, MA 02072 t) 781-344-3100 ejresnick@svdpboston.org svdpboston.org Edward J. Resnick, Exec.;

TEWKSBURY

Covenant Health, Inc. - 100 Ames Pond, Ste. 102, Tewksbury, MA 01876 t) 978-654-6363 info@covenanthealth.net www.covenanthealth.net Sponsored organizations in Massachusetts, Maine, New Hampshire, Pennsylvania, Rhode Island, & Vermont. David R. Lincoln, Pres.;

***Youville Lifecare, Inc.** - 100 Ames Pond Dr., Ste. 102, Tewksbury, MA 01876 t) 978-654-6363

WATERTOWN

iCatholicMedia, Inc. - 34 Chestnut St., Watertown, MA 02472

MONASTERIES AND RESIDENCES FOR PRIESTS AND BROTHERS [MON]

BOSTON

Augustinians of the Assumption, Inc. - 330 Market St., Boston, MA 02135 t) 617-783-0400 info@assumption.us www.assumption.us Rev. Dennis Gallagher, A.A., Prov.; Rev. Simon Waweru Njuguna, Supr.; Rev. Peter Precourt, A.A., Vicar; Rev. Alex Castro, A.A., Treas.; Rev. Ai Nguyen Chi, AA, Prov. Asst.; Rev. Barry Bercier, A.A., Prof.; Bro. Blair Paulus Nuyda, A.A., Dir.; Rev. Roland Guilmain, A.A., Mem.; Rev. Gerard Messier, A.A., Mem.; Bro. Hugo Fernando Morales Ballesteros, AA, Mem.; Rev. Gary Perron, A.A., Serving Abroad; Brs.: 12; Priests: 39

Assumption Guild - t) 617-783-0495 info@masscardsaa.com masscardsaa.com

Brotherhood of Hope - 785 Parker St., Boston, MA 02120 t) 617-286-2566 bohinfo@brohope.net www.brotherhoodofhope.org Rev. Paul D. Helfrich, B.H., In Res.; Brs.: 5; Priests: 1

Carmelite Monastery - 166 Foster St., Boston, MA 02135-3902 t) 617-787-5056 mdevelisocd@gmail.com Rev. Mark-Joseph DeVelis, O.C.D., Prior; Rev. Paul Fohlin, O.C.D., Subprior; Rev. Leonard Copeland, O.C.D., Treas.; Rev. David Joseph Centner, O.C.D.; Rev. Terrence Dougherty, O.C.D.; Bro. Augustine Wharf, O.C.D.;

St. Christopher Friary - 18 N. Bennet St., Boston, MA 02113 t) 617-742-4190 stchristopherfriary@gmail.com Rev. Robert J. Caprio, O.F.M.; Most Rev. Maurice Muldoon, O.F.M.; Bro. James T. Welch, O.F.M.;

Loyola House - 300 Newbury St., Boston, MA 02115-2801 t) 617-755-1625 jshaughnessy@jesuits.org jesuitseast.org Rev. James M. Shaughnessy, S.J., Supr.; Rev. Richard A. Deshaies, S.J., Admin.; Rev. Peter W. Gyves; Rev. John P. Spencer, S.J.;

Marist Fathers Lourdes Residence - 698 Beacon St., Boston, MA 02215 t) 617-262-2271 denise.damico@maristsociety.org Rev. Philip Parent, Supr.; Rev. Andrew Albert, S.M., In Res.; Rev. Francis Grispino, S.M., In Res.; Priests: 3

Missionary Society of St. Paul the Apostle in Massachusetts - 5 Park St., Boston, MA 02108 t) 617-742-4460 info@paulistcenter.org www.paulistcenter.org Rev. Charles Cunniff, CSP, Supr.; Rev. Michael B. McGarry, C.S.P., Dir.; Rev. John Geaney, CSP; Rev. Charles A. Martin, C.S.P.; Rev. Robert S. Rivers, C.S.P.; Rev. Thomas Ryan;

The Salesian Community - 635 Bennington St., Boston, MA 02128; Mailing: 150 Byron St., East Boston, MA 02128 t) 617-569-6551; 617-567-6626 www.salesiansociety.org Rev. John Joseph Janko, SDB, Dir.; Brs.: 1; Priests: 4

San Lorenzo Friary - 15 Montebello Rd., Boston, MA 02130-2352 t) 617-983-1919 tarrazaw@gmail.com www.capuchin.org (The Province of St. Mary of the Capuchin Order, White Plains, New York) Rev. William Hector Tarraza, Supr.; Rev. Basil Joseph, O.F.M. Cap., In Res.; Rev. D. Scott Surrency, O.F.M. Cap., In Res.; Bro. Anthony Zuba, Mem.;

The Society of St. James the Apostle, Inc. - 24 Clark St., Boston, MA 02109 t) 617-742-4715 director2012@socstjames.com socstjames.com To recruit Diocesan Priest volunteers for South America. Rev. David M. Costello (Ireland), Dir.;

The Order of Friars Minor Province of the Most Holy Name - 100 Arch St., Boston, MA 02110-1102 t) 646-473-0265 mharlan@hnp.org Brs.: 47; Priests: 184

BRIGHTON

Saint Peter Faber Jesuit Community - 188 Foster St., Brighton, MA 02135 t) 617-779-4200 assist.offmgr@faberjc.org Rev. Michael G. Boughton, S.J., Rector; Bro. Darin Mayer, S.J., Treas.; Brs.: 1; Priests: 31

Alberto Hurtado House - 194 Foster St., Boston, MA 02135 t) (617) 779-4285 Rev. Sudzer Charelus, Student, Boston College School of Theology & Ministry; Rev. Jaime Espiniella Garcia, Student, Boston College School of Theology & Ministry; Rev. Chryostom Exaltacion, S.J., Student, Boston College School of Theology & Ministry; Rev. Pascal Loua, Student, Boston College School of Theology & Ministry; Rev. Piotr Stanowski, S.J., Student, Boston College School of Theology & Ministry; Rev. Kenneth J. Hughes, S.J., Staff, Faber Jesuit Community;

Edmund Campion House - 192-A Foster St., Brighton, MA 02135-4620 t) 617-779-4239 Rev. John Baldovin, S.J., Faculty, Boston College School of Theology & Ministry; Rev. Jean Damascene Bavugayabo, Student, Boston College School of Theology & Ministry; Rev. Juan Salazar, Student, Boston College School of Theology & Ministry; Rev. Michal Zalewski, Student, Boston College School of Theology & Ministry;

Francis Xavier House - 190-B Foster St., Brighton, MA 02135-4620 t) 617-779-4219 Rev. Michael McCarthy, Dean, Boston College School of Theology & Ministry; Rev. Rene Shema, Student, Boston College School of Theology & Ministry; Rev. Samuel Afonso, Student, Boston College School of Theology & Ministry; Rev. Brian Dunkle, S.J., Faculty, Boston College School of Theology & Ministry; Rev. Woo-jung Stephen Kim, Student, Boston College School of Theology & Ministry; Rev. Tony Huu Khanh Nguyen, S.J., Student, Boston College School of Theology & Ministry;

Isaac Jogues House - 196-A Foster St., Brighton, MA 02135-4620 t) 617-779-4288 Rev. Vicente Chong, Faculty, Boston College School of Theology & Ministry; Rev. Borja Miro Madariaga, Student, Boston College School of Theology & Ministry; Rev. Andre Brouillette, Faculty, Boston College School of Theology & Ministry; Rev. Javier Fernando Jimenez Mocobono, Student, Boston College School of Theology & Ministry; Rev. Jonathan Marin, Student, Boston College School of Theology & Ministry;

Miguel Pro House - 192-B Foster St., Brighton, MA 02135-4620 t) 617-779-4287 Rev. Andres Gonzalez, Student, Boston College School of Theology & Ministry; Rev. Felix Barutwanayo, Student, Boston College School of Theology & Ministry; Rev. Amedee Fanomezantsoa Rarivoson, Student, Boston College School of Theology & Ministry; Rev. Paul Harman, S.J., Staff, Faber Jesuit Community; Bro. Darin Mayer, S.J., Minister, Faber Jesuit Community; Rev. Hyun-jhik Kim, Student, Boston College School of Theology & Ministry;

Noel Chabanel House - 196-B Foster St., Brighton, MA 02135-4620 t) 617-779-4269 Rev. Richard J. Clifford, S.J., Faculty, Boston College School of Theology & Ministry; Rev. Raneesh Jose, Student, Boston College School of Theology & Ministry; Rev. Matthew Monnig, S.J., Faculty, Boston College School of Theology & Ministry; Rev. Jose Rafael Garrido, Student, Boston College School of Theology & Ministry;

Walter Ciszek House - 190-A Foster St., Brighton, MA 02135-4620 t) 617-779-4286 Rev. Jean Amegble, S.J., Student, Boston College School of Theology & Ministry; Rev. Jean Bosco Niyokwizera, Student, Boston College School of Theology & Ministry; Rev. Vaclav Novotny, S.J., Student, Boston College School of Theology & Ministry; Rev. Bart Geger, Faculty, Boston College School of Theology & Ministry; Rev. Thomas D. Stegman, S.J., Faculty, Boston College School of Theology & Ministry;

Priests of the Assumption, Inc. - 330 Market St., Brighton, MA 02135 t) 617-783-0400 info@assumption.us www.assumption.us Rev. Dennis

Gallagher, A.A., Chair;

BROCKTON

Chapel of Our Savior - 475 Westgate Dr., Brockton, MA 02301-1819 t) 508-583-8357 Bro. Thomas Banacki, S.A., Other;

CHESTNUT HILL

The Jesuit Community at Boston College - 140 Commonwealth Ave., St. Mary's Hall, Chestnut Hill, MA 02467 t) 617-552-8111 opeil@bc.edu www.bc.edu Rev. William P. Leahy, S.J., Pres.; Rev. Cyril Opeil, S.J., Supr. & Assoc. Prof.; Rev. Richard Blake, S.J., Community Admin., Minister; Rev. Giovanni Pietro Basile, Prof.; Rev. Casey C. Beaumier, S.J., Vice Pres. & Univ. Secy., Dir., Institute for Advanced Jesuit Studies; Rev. James W. Bernauer, S.J., Prof. Emeritus; Rev. Erick Berrelleza, Dean; Rev. John Butler, S.J., Vice Pres., Mission & Ministry; Rev. Michael F. Davidson, S.J., Dir., Bowman AHANA & Intercultural Center; Rev. Jean Baptiste Diatta, Graduate Student; Rev. Harvey D. Egan, S.J., Prof. Emeritus; Rev. Frederick Enman, S.J., Adjunct Chap., Law School; Rev. James D. Erps, S.J., Mission & Ministry; Rev. M. Antoni Ucerler, Dir., Ricci Institute; Rev. Gerald F. Finnegan, S.J., Asst. Pastor, St. Ignatius Church; Rev. Charles R. Gallagher, S.J., Prof.; Rev. Robert Gerlich, Institute for Advanced Jesuit Studies; Rev. Daniel Gustafson, S.J., Graduate Student; Rev. Francis R. Herrmann, S.J., Prof. Emeritus, Treas., Jesuit Community; Rev. Kenneth Himes, O.F.M., Prof.; Rev. Joseph (You Guo) Jiang, SJ (China), Prof.; Rev. Gregory Kalscheur, S.J., Dean; Rev. James Keenan, S.J., Vice Provost, global engagement, Dir., Jesuit Institute, Prof.; Rev. Michael Magree, Prof.; Rev. Mark S. Massa, S.J., Prof., Dir., Boisi Center for Religion & American Public Life; Rev. Brett McLaughlin, Graduate Student; Rev. Paul McNellis, S.J., Prof.; Rev. John C. Monahan, S.J., Campus Min.; Rev. Gustavo Morello, S.J. (Argentina), Prof.; Rev. Thomas Murphy, Prof.; Rev. Ponsiano Ngondwe, Graduate Student; Rev. Alejandro Olayo-Mendez, Prof.; Rev. Claude Pavur, S.J., Institute for Advanced Jesuit Studies; Rev. John Piderit, Visiting Fellow, Lynch School of Education & Human Development; Rev. Oliver P. Rafferty, S.J., Prof.; Rev. Juan Rivera, Graduate Student; Rev. Richard Ross, S.J., Prof.; Rev. Henry Shea, Prof.; Rev. John R. Siberski, S.J., Clinician, Ministry for Priest Prog.; Rev. Walter J. Smith, S.J., Prof., St. John XXIII Seminary & Boston College STM; Rev. Ronald K. Tacelli, S.J., Prof.; Rev. Robert Van Alstyne, Graduate Student; Rev. Andrea Vicini, S.J., Prof.; Rev. Joseph Weiss, S.J., Prof.; Rev. William Woody, S.J., Graduate Student; Brs.: 1; Priests: 53

COHASSET

Bellarmine House - 150 Howard Gleason Rd., Cohasset, MA 02025 t) 781-383-0723 (Summer Res. for Jesuits of New England Prov.). Rev. Donald A. MacMillan, S.J., Admin.;

DEDHAM

Society of African Missions - 337 Common St., Dedham, MA 02026-4030; Mailing: P.O. Box 47, Dedham, MA 02026-4030 t) 781-326-3288; 781-326-4670 dedhamhouse@smafathers.org www.smafathers.org Rev. Brendan Darcy, SMA, Supr.; Rev. Richard A Mwisheni, SMA (Kenya), Councilor; Rev. Ulick Bourke, SMA, In Res.; Priests: 3

DUXBURY

Society of the Divine Word - 121 Parks St., Duxbury, MA 02331-0614; Mailing: P.O. Box M, Duxbury, MA 02331-0614 t) 781-585-2460 miramarma@aol.com www.miramarretreat.org

HINGHAM

Glastonbury Abbey - 16 Hull St., Hingham, MA 02043 t) 781-749-2155 office@glastonburyabbey.org www.glastonburyabbey.org Benedictine Monastery. Rev. Thomas J. O'Connor, Abbot; Bro. Daniel F. Walters, O.S.B., Prior; Rev. Timothy J. Joyce; Rev. Nicholas J. Morcone, O.S.B.; Bro. James Crowley, O.S.B.; Bro. David K. Coakley, O.S.B.; Bro. Joseph Prostrollo, OSB; Brs.: 5; Priests: 4

HOLLISTON

Xaverian Missionaries - 101 Summer St., Holliston, MA 01746 t) 508-429-2144 holliston@xaverianmissionaries.org; frrocco@xaverianmissionaries.org www.xaverianmissionaries.org Rev. Rocco N. Puopolo, S.X., Rector; Rev. Carl Chudy, sx, Pst. Assoc.; Rev. Adolph J. Menendez, S.X., Pst. Assoc.; Rev. Francis Signorelli, S.X., Pst. Assoc.; Bro. Pietro Rossini, Mem.; Brs.: 1; Priests: 4

JAMAICA PLAIN

St. Francis of Assisi Friary - 46 Brookside Ave., Jamaica Plain, MA 02130-2370 t) 617-522-6469 www.capuchin.org (The Province of St. Mary of the Capuchin Order, White Plains, NY) Bro. James M. Peterson, O.F.M. Cap., Supr.; Rev. Marvin Bearis, O.F.M. Cap., In Res.; Bro. Paul Fesefeldt, O.F.M.Cap., In Res.;

LAWRENCE

Franciscans of Primitive Observance - Saint Joseph Friary, 10 Highgate St., Lawrence, MA 01841 t) 978-376-4109 fposervant@live.com Rev. Peter F. Giroux, F.P.O., Supr.; Bro. Juan Diego Aguilera, F.P.O.; Rev. Andrew M. Beauregard, F.P.O.; Bro. Pio Anthony Butti, F.P.O.; Rev. Sean Patrick Hurley, F.P.O.; Rev. Joseph Paul Medio, F.P.O.; Bro. James Magdalen Wartman, F.P.O.;

Marist Brothers - 26 Leeds Ter., Lawrence, MA 01843 t) 978-686-7411 Bro. Jerry Dowsky, F.M.S.; Bro. James Halliday, F.M.S.; Bro. John Kachinsky, F.M.S.;

Marist Brothers Residence - 12 Sheridan St., Lawrence, MA 01841 t) 978-682-1163 Bro. Ernest Beland, F.M.S.; Bro. Rene D. Roy, F.M.S., Dir.;

LOWELL

Andre Garin Residence - 27 Kirk St., Lowell, MA 01852-1004 t) 202-269-6706 treasurer@omiusa.org Rev. James Chambers, O.M.I., Treas.; Priests: 1

Andre Garin Retirement Residence - t) 978-937-9594 andregarinresidence@yahoo.com

Missionary Oblates of Mary Immaculate Northern Province - 60 Wyman St., Lowell, MA 01852-2841; Mailing: 486 Chandler St., Tewksbury, MA 01876-2849 t) 978-458-9912 srichards@omiusa.org www.omiusa.org Rev. John F. Hanley, O.M.I., Supr.; Rev. Louis Studer, O.M.I., Prov.; Rev. Charles Breault, O.M.I., Admin.; Rev. Ronald J. Meyer, OMI, Par. Vicar; Rev. Norman Comtois, O.M.I., Spiritual Adv./Care Srvcs.; Rev. Wilfred Harvey, O.M.I., Spiritual Adv./Care Srvcs.; Rev. William Sheehan, O.M.I., Spiritual Adv./Care Srvcs.; Rev. George Brown, O.M.I., Mem.; Bro. Richard Cote, O.M.I., Dir.; Brs.: 2; Priests: 4

St. Eugene House (Residence) - 285 Andover St., Lowell, MA 01852-1438 t) 978-441-0649 Bro. Craig Bonham, O.M.I.;

Oblate Foreign Mission Office, Northeast - 60 Wyman St., Lowell, MA 01852; Mailing: P.O. Box 9088, Lowell, MA 01853-9088 t) 978-337-4287 oblateforeignmissions@omiusa.org

LYNN

Franciscan Community (Province of Immaculate Conception) - 38 Michigan Ave., Lynn, MA 01902 t) 617-592-7396 Rev. Alfonse Ferreira, O.F.M.;

The Listening Place (Counseling Center) - 36 Michigan Ave., Lynn, MA 01902 t) 781-592-7396

MEDFORD

Priestly Fraternity of the Missionaries of St. Charles Borromeo, Inc. - 71 Warner St., Medford, MA 02155 t) 781-396-3922 secretarystclement@outlook.com www.saintclementcatholicparish.org Phong Q Pham, Admin.;

MILTON

Oblate Residence (St. Joseph House) - 65 Fr. Carney Dr., Milton, MA 02186-4206 t) 617-698-6785 retreats@omvusa.org www.omvusa.org Rev. William M. Brown, O.M.V., In Res.; Rev. John Ferrara, O.M.V., In Res.; Rev. Peter P. Gojuk, O.M.V., In Res.; Rev. Craig MacMahon, O.M.V., In Res.; Rev. William Neubecker, O.M.V., In Res.; Rev. Jeremy Paulin, In Res.; Rev. Michael Warren, O.M.V., In Res.; Rev. James Doran, O.M.V., In Res.; Priests: 8

SPRINGFIELD

Stigmatine Fathers & Brothers Provincial House - 123 William St., Springfield, MA 01105 t) 413-734-5433 rsw7713@aol.com www.stigmatines.com

TEWKSBURY

Oblate World/Missionary Association of Mary Immaculate - 486 Chandler St., Tewksbury, MA 01876-0680 t) 978-858-0434 oblateworld@omires.com Rev. John F. Hanley, O.M.I., Supr.; Brs.: 1; Priests: 2

WESTON

Campion Center, Inc. - 319 Concord Rd., Weston, MA 02493 t) 781-788-6800 gcollins@campioncenter.org www.campioncenter.org Rev. Alfred J. Hicks; Rev. Robert Vereecke; Rev. Kevin R. White; Rev. George E. Collins, Supr.; Rev. James M. Bowler; Rev. Thomas Denny; Rev. Joseph P. Duffy, S.J.; Rev. Theodore A. Dziak; Rev. Gary M. Gurtler, S.J.; Rev. Charles J. Healey, S.J.; Rev. John W. Howard, S.J.; Rev. Paul C. Kenney, S.J.; Rev. Robert Levens; Rev. Carsten Martensen; Rev. Joseph V. Owens, S.J.; Rev. James F. Walsh, S.J.; Rev. Terrence W. Curry, S.J.; Priests: 17

Campion Health & Wellness, Inc. - 319 Concord Rd., Weston, MA 02493-1398 t) 781-788-6800 Rev. Charles Allen, SJ; Rev. Joseph A. Appleyard, S.J.; Rev. Stephen J. Bonian, S.J.; Rev. Robert Braunreuther; Rev. Joseph F. Burke, S.J.; Rev. Henry J. Cain, S.J.; Bro. Calvin A. Clarke, S.J.; Rev. Walter J. Conlan, S.J.; Rev. Robert J. Daly, S.J.; Bro. James Thomas Dennehy; Rev. William Joseph Eagan, S.J.; Rev. Robert Farrell, S.J.; Rev. Joseph Fitzpatrick; Rev. David H. Gill, S.J.; Rev. James Aloysius Gillon, S.J.; Rev. Richard P. Guerrera, SJ; Rev. Edward Ifkovits; Rev. John Keegan, SJ; Rev. Arthur R. Madigan, S.J.; Rev. Bruce Maivelett; Rev. Frederic A. Maples, S.J.; Rev. Gerard McLaughlin, S.J.; Bro. James J. Moran, S.J.; Bro. Donald J. Murray, S.J.; Bro. Edward L. Niziolek, S.J.; Rev. James C. O'Brien, S.J.; Rev. Francis O'Connor; Rev. William O'Malley; Rev. John Paris, S.J.; Rev. Frank J. Parker, S.J.; Rev. Ernest F. Passero, S.J.; Rev. Walter R. Pelletier, S.J.; Rev. Robert Phillips, SJ; Rev. John P. Reboli, S.J.; Rev. William C. Russell, S.J.; Rev. Francis J. Ryan, S.J.; Rev. Lawrence David Ryan, S.J.; Rev. Patrick J. Ryan, S.J.; Rev. Stephen J. Sanford, S.J.; Rev. Martin G. Shaughnessy, S.J.; Rev. Thomas J. Sheehan, S.J.; Rev. Simon E. Smith, S.J.; Rev. John P. Spencer, S.J.; Rev. Richard J. Stanley, S.J.; Rev. Thomas D. Stegman, S.J.; Rev. Charles Sullivan; Rev. John E. Surette, S.J.; Rev. Edward Vodoklys, SJ; Rev. John Joseph Walsh, S.J.; Rev. George Williams, SJ; Rev. George P. Winchester, S.J.; Rev. Alfred O. Winshman, S.J.; Brs.: 5; Priests: 47

The Society of Jesus of New England - 319 Concord Rd., Weston, MA 02493; Mailing: P.O. Box 456, Weston, MA 02493 t) 617-607-2800 ueasocius@jesuits.org www.jesuitseast.org See the USA East Province of the Society of Jesus in the Archdiocese of New York. Rev. Richard McGowan, S.J., Treas.;

NURSING / REHABILITATION / CONVALESCENCE / ELDERLY CARE [NUR]

BOSTON

Saint Anthony Residence - 100 Arch St., Boston, MA 02110-1102; Mailing: 103 Arch St., Boston, ME 02110 t) 646-473-0265 dwilson@hnp.org (For Retired Franciscan Friars.)

Regina Cleri Residence - 60 William Cardinal O'Connell Way, Boston, MA 02114 t) 617-523-1861 sgust@reginacleri.org Residence for Retired Archdiocesan Priests. Stephen J. Gust, Dir.;

BROCKTON

St. Joseph Manor Health Care Inc. - 215 Thatcher St., Brockton, MA 02302; Mailing: 100 Ames Pond Dr., Ste. 102, Tewksbury, MA 01876 t) 508-583-5834; 978-654-6363 jkeane@sjmbrockton.org www.sjmbrockton.org Sponsored by Covenant Health Inc., Tewksbury, MA. James Keane, CEO;

Mater Dei Adult Day Health Center - t) 508-583-8313

CAMBRIDGE

Sancta Maria Nursing Facility - 799 Concord Ave.,

Cambridge, MA 02138 t) 617-868-2200 ngilbert@sanctamaria.org An affiliate of Covenant Health, Inc., Tewksbury, MA. Sr. Mary Banach, D.M., Pst. Min./Coord.;

EAST BOSTON

Don Orione Nursing Home - 111 Orient Ave., East Boston, MA 02128-1006 t) 617-569-2100 rgovoni@donorionehome.org Rev. Gino Marchesani, F.D.P., Chap.; Rev. Miroslaw Kowalczyk, F.D.P.;

FRAMINGHAM

Carmel Terrace - 933 Central St., Framingham, MA 01701 t) 508-788-8000 ecollins@carmelterrace.org www.carmelterrace.org Emily Collins, Admin.;

St. Patrick Manor, Inc. - 863 Central St., Framingham, MA 01701 t) 508-879-8000 ewoolf@stpatricksmanor.org www.stpatricksmanor.org The Carmelite System Elisabeth Woolf, Admin.; Asstd. Annu.: 787; Staff: 242

IPSWICH

St. Julie Billiart Residential Care Center, Inc. - 30 Jeffreys Neck Rd., Ipswich, MA 01938 t) 978-380-1475 anna.bussing@sndden.org Anna Bussing, Admin.;

LAWRENCE

***M.I. Adult Day Health Center, Inc.** - 189 Maple St., Lawrence, MA 01841; Mailing: 100 Ames Pond Dr., Ste. 102, Tewksbury, MA 01876 t) 978-682-6321 jeanne_leydon@mihcs.com www.mihcs.com Adult day health care. Sponsored by Covenant Health Inc., Tewksbury, MA. Jeanne Leydon, Pres.;

M.I. Residential Community II, Inc. - 191 Maple St., Lawrence, MA 01841 t) 978-685-6321 gerard_foley@mihcs.com www.mihcs.com Independent & assisted living for elderly and handicapped. Sponsored by Covenant Health, Inc., Tewksbury, MA. Gerard J. Foley, Pres.;

M.I. Residential Community III, Inc. - 193 Maple St., Lawrence, MA 01841 t) 978-682-7575 gerard_foley@mihcs.com www.mihcs.com Independent living for elderly. Sponsored by Covenant Health, Inc., Tewksbury, MA. Gerard J. Foley, Pres.;

M.I. Residential Community, Inc. - 189 Maple St., Lawrence, MA 01841; Mailing: 100 Ames Pond Dr., Ste. 102, Tewksbury, MA 01876 t) 978-685-6321; 978-654-6363 jeanne_leydon@mihcs.com www.mihcs.com Marguerite's House Assisted Living Facility. Sponsored by Covenant Health, Inc., Tewksbury, MA. Jeanne Leydon, Pres.;

***M.I. Transportation, Inc.** - 189 Maple St., Lawrence, MA 01841; Mailing: 100 Ames Pond Dr., Ste. 102, Tewksbury, MA 01876 t) 978-682-7575; 978-654-6363 jeanne_leydon@mihcs.com www.mihcs.com Sponsored by Covenant Health, Inc., Tewksbury, MA. Jeanne Leydon, Pres.;

Mary Immaculate Nursing Restorative Center - 172 Lawrence St., Lawrence, MA 01841; Mailing: 100 Ames Pond Dr., Ste. 102, Tewksbury, MA 01876 t) 978-685-6321; 978-654-6363 jeanne_leydon@mihcs.com www.mihcs.com Multi-level Skilled Nursing Facility; Unit of Mary Immaculate Health Care Services. Sponsored by Covenant Health, Inc., Tewksbury, MA. Jeanne Leydon, Pres.;

LOWELL

D'Youville Senior Care, Inc. - 981 Varnum Ave., Lowell, MA 01854 t) (978) 569-1000 mferrick@dyouville.org www.dyouville.org The Carmelite System Mike Ferrick, Admin.; Asstd. Annu.: 651; Staff: 200

D'Youville Life and Wellness Community, Inc. - 981 Varnum Ave., Lowell, MA 01854 t) 978-569-1000 nprendergast@dyouville.org; mferrick@dyouville.org www.dyouville.org The Carmelite System Mike Ferrick, Admin.; Naomi M. Prendergast, CEO; Asstd. Annu.: 1,609; Staff: 388

MARLBOROUGH

Marie Esther Health Center, Inc. - 720 Boston Post Rd. E., Marlborough, MA 01752 t) 508-485-3791; 508-460-1951 ecaron@sistersofsaintanne.org

SOMERVILLE

Jeanne Jugan Pavilion - 190 Highland Ave., Somerville, MA 02143 t) 718-464-1800 provincialbklyn@littlesistersofthepoor.org www.littlesistersofthepoorboston.org Sr. Alice Marie Jones, L.S.P., Prov.;

Jeanne Jugan Residence - 186 Highland Ave., Somerville, MA 02143 t) 718-464-1800 provincialbklyn@littlesistersofthepoor.org www.littlesistersofthepoor.org Sr. Alice Marie Jones, L.S.P., Prov.;

SOUTH BOSTON

Marian Manor - 130 Dorchester St., South Boston, MA 02127 t) 617-268-3333 mbrown@marianmanor.org; kanderson@marianmanor.org www.marianmanor.org The Carmelite System Kahoney Anderson, Admin.; Asstd. Annu.: 638; Staff: 136

TEWKSBURY

Immaculate Heart of Mary Residence - 486 Chandler St., Tewksbury, MA 01876-2899 t) 978-851-7258 mbutler@omiusa.org Rev. John F. Hanley, O.M.I., Supr.; Rev. Charles Hurkes, O.M.I.; Rev. Robert Lacasse, O.M.I.; Rev. Daniel Nassaney, O.M.I.; Rev. John J. Hogan, O.M.I., Attached: St. Williams Parish; Rev. William O'Donnell, O.M.I., Attached: St. William's Parish; Rev. Charles Beausoleil, O.M.I.; Rev. Lucien Bouchard, O.M.I.; Rev. Francis Demers, O.M.I.; Rev. Donald G. Lozier, O.M.I.; Bro. Jean Emmanuel Meloncourt, OMI; Bro. Augustin Cote, O.M.I.; Bro. Charles Gilbert, O.M.I.; Bro. Richard Cote, O.M.I.; Asstd. Annu.: 35; Staff: 34

WALTHAM

CHS of Waltham - 66 Newton St., Waltham, MA 02453-6063 t) 781-893-0240 cfenn@maristhill.org www.maristhill.org Sponsored by Covenant Health, Inc., Tewksbury, MA. Carolyn Fenn, Pres.;

WELLESLEY

Elizabeth Seton Residence, Inc. - 125 Oakland St., Wellesley, MA 02481 t) 781-997-1100 info@schalifax.org www.elizabethseton.org Skilled Nursing & Rehab Facility. Lori A. Ferrante, Admin.;

PRESCHOOLS / CHILDCARE CENTERS [PRE]

BOSTON

Salesian Boys & Girls Club - 150 Byron St., Boston, MA 02128 t) 617-567-6626 sbgclub@juno.com www.salesianclub.com (Central Unit)

Orient Heights Unit -

GROTON

Country Day School of the Holy Union - 14 Main St., Groton, MA 01450 t) 978-448-5646 cdsgroton@yahoo.com www.cdsgroton.org

JAMAICA PLAIN

Nazareth Child Care Center - 19 St. Joseph St., Jamaica Plain, MA 02130 t) 617-522-4040 pam-penton@ccab.org Pamela J. Penton, Dir.;

NEWTON

Walnut Park Montessori School - 47 Walnut Park, Newton, MA 02458 t) 617-969-9208 office@walnutparkmontessori.org www.walnutparkmontessori.org Stephanie Marcucci, Prin.;

PEABODY

Holy Childhood Nursery & Kindergarten - 5 Wheatland St., Peabody, MA 01960 t) 978-531-4733 carmelite@verizon.net www.carmelitepreschool.com Stds.: 51

RETREAT HOUSES / RENEWAL CENTERS [RTR]

DUXBURY

Miramar Retreat Center - 121 Parks St., Duxbury, MA 02331-0614; Mailing: P.O. Box M, Duxbury, MA 02331-0614 t) 781-585-2460 miramarma@aol.com www.miramarretreat.org

GLOUCESTER

Eastern Point Retreat House - Gonzaga, 37 Niles Pond Rd., Gloucester, MA 01930 t) 978-283-0013 office@easternpoint.org www.easternpoint.org Rev. Richard J. Stanley, S.J.;

WALTHAM

Espousal Retreat House and Conference Center - 554 Lexington St., Waltham, MA 02452 t) 781-209-3120 espousaladmin@gmail.com www.espousal.org

WESTON

Campion Center Conference & Renewal - 319 Concord Rd., Weston, MA 02493-1398 t) (781) 788-4708 abliss@campioncenter.org www.campioncenter.org Temporarily closed. Rev. George E. Collins;

SEMINARIES [SEM]

BOSTON

Oblate Provincialate - 2 Ipswich St., Boston, MA 02215-3607 t) 617-536-4141 office@omvusa.org www.omvusa.org Rev. James Walther, O.M.V., Prov.; Stds.: 8; Lay Tchrs.: 1; Pr. Tchrs.: 2

Our Lady of Grace Seminary - 1105 Boylston St., Boston, MA 02215-3604 t) 617-266-5999 tcarzon@omvusa.org www.omvusa.org Rev. Peter W. Grover, O.M.V., Supr.; Rev. John Luong, O.M.V., Dir.;

BRIGHTON

Saint John's Seminary - 127 Lake St., Brighton, MA 02135 t) 617-254-2610 contact@sjs.edu www.sjs.edu Rev. Stephen E. Salocks, Rector; Rev. Thomas Macdonald, Vice Rector; Paul Metilly, Dean; Rev. Ryan Connors, Dean of Men; Rev. David Barnes, Dir. Spiritual Formation; Rev. Richard W. Fitzgerald, Dir. Pastoral Formation; Rev. Michael MacInnis, Dir. Human Formation; Rev. Peter L. Stamm, Dir. Sacred Liturgy; Stds.: 67; Lay Tchrs.: 4; Pr. Tchrs.: 8

School of Theology - Dr. Anthony Coleman, Dir.;

CHESTNUT HILL

Redemptoris Mater Archdiocesan Missionary Seminary - 774 Boylston St., Chestnut Hill, MA 02467-2501 t) 617-879-9813; 617-879-9814 rmsboston@gmail.com www.rmsboston.org Very Rev. Antonio F. Medeiros, Rector; Rev. Lukasz M. Wisniewski, Vice. Pres.; Rev. Francesco Palombi (Italy), Spiritual Adv./Care Srvcs.; Stds.: 24; Pr. Tchrs.: 3

FRAMINGHAM

Sylva Maria - 567 Salem End Rd., Framingham, MA 01702-5599 t) 508-879-6711 sonskevin@gmail.com www.sonsofmary.com.ph House and Novitiate of the Sons of Mary, Health of the Sick. Rev. John Coss, F.M.S.I.; Rev. Robert Rivard, F.M.S.I.; Bro. Kevin Courtney, F.M.S.I.;

NEWTON

The Ecclesiastical Faculty at Boston College - 140 Commonwealth Ave., Newton, MA 02467 t) 617-552-6501 stm@bc.edu www.bc.edu/stm Rev. Mark S. Massa, S.J., Dean; Rev. William P. Leahy, S.J., Pres.; Esther Griswold, Librn.;

WESTON

Pope Saint John XXIII National Seminary - 558 South Ave., Weston, MA 02493 t) 781-899-5500 seminary@psjs.edu www.psjs.edu A Major National Seminary open to men over thirty studying for the diocesan and religious priesthood. Rev. Paul E. Miceli; Rev. Msgr. James Mongelluzzo; Rev. William F. Murphy; Rev. Brian R. Kiely, Rector; Anthony W. Keaty, Dean; Rev. Stephen J. Linehan, Dean; Barbara Mullen-Neem, Librn.; Rev. I. Michael Bellafiore, S.J., Faculty; Rev. Msgr. Peter V. Conley, Faculty; Rev. Vincent E. Daily, Faculty; Rev. Msgr. William P. Fay, Faculty; Rev. Joseph M. Zwosta, Faculty;

SHRINES [SHR]

LAWRENCE

Holy Rosary Shrine - 28 Union St., Lawrence, MA 01840

SALEM

Saint John Paul II Shrine of Divine Mercy - 28 Saint Peter St., Salem, MA 01970 t) 978-744-1278 dmacedo@jpiidivinemercyshrine.org Rev. Robert Bedzinski, S.Ch., Admin.;

SPECIAL CARE FACILITIES [SPF]

BOSTON

St. Helena House - 89 Union Park St., Boston, MA 02118 t) 617-426-2922 Seniors, low income & disabled persons.

Nazareth Residence for Mothers and Children - 91 Regent St., Boston, MA 02119 t) 617-541-0100 nazareth_residence@ccab.org Home for homeless mothers and children who are HIV positive. Mirta Rodriguez, Dir.;

Our Lady's Guild House - Residence for Women - 20 Charlesgate W., Boston, MA 02215 t) 617-536-3000 Constance Pagan, Admin.;

CAMBRIDGE

***Youville House, Inc.** - 1573 Cambridge St., Cambridge, MA 02138-4398 t) 617-491-1234 info@youvilleassistedliving.org www.youvilleassistedliving.org Assisted living residence. Sponsored by Covenant Health, Inc., Tewksbury, MA. Nicole Breslih, CEO;

METHUEN

St. Ann's Home Special Needs School - 100 A. Haverhill St., Methuen, MA 01844 t) 978-682-5276 dgrandbois@st.annshome.org www.st.annshome.org Ungraded special needs school for emotionally disturbed and behaviorally disordered children. Denis Grandbois, Exec.;

St. Ann's Home, Inc. - 100A Haverhill St., Methuen, MA 01844 t) 978-682-5276 jcronin@st.annshome.org www.st.annshome.org Meghan E Morin, Admin.; Joe Cronin, CEO; Marybeth Gilmore, Bus. Mgr.;

Residential Treatment Center - t) 978-692-5276

An asterisk (*) denotes an organization that has established tax-exempt status directly with the IRS and is not covered by the USCCB Group Ruling.

Diocese of Bridgeport

(Dioecesis Bridgeportensis)

MOST REVEREND FRANK J. CAGGIANO

Bishop of Bridgeport; ordained May 16, 1987; appointed Titular Bishop of Inis Cathaig June 6, 2006; episcopal ordination August 22, 2006; appointed Bishop of Bridgeport July 31, 2013; installed Sept. 19, 2013.

Chancery: The Catholic Center, 238 Jewett Ave., Bridgeport, CT 06606-2892. T: 203-416-1400; F: 203-371-8323. www.bridgeportdiocese.org

ESTABLISHED AUGUST 6, 1953.

Square Miles 633.

Corporate Title: The Bridgeport Roman Catholic Diocesan Corporation.

Comprises all of Fairfield County in the State of Connecticut.

For legal titles of parishes and diocesan institutions, consult the Chancery at The Catholic Center.

STATISTICAL OVERVIEW

Personnel

Bishop	1
Priests: Diocesan Active in Diocese	102
Priests: Diocesan Active Outside Diocese	13
Priests: Retired, Sick or Absent	67
Number of Diocesan Priests	182
Religious Priests in Diocese	10
Total Priests in your Diocese	192
Extern Priests in Diocese	19
Ordinations:	
Diocesan Priests	2
Transitional Deacons	6
Permanent Deacons	5
Permanent Deacons in Diocese	88
Total Sisters	176

Parishes

Parishes	75
With Resident Pastor:	
Resident Diocesan Priests	65
Resident Religious Priests	2
Without Resident Pastor:	
Administered by Priests	4
Pastoral Centers	1
Closed Parishes	2
Professional Ministry Personnel:	
Sisters	176

Welfare

Homes for the Aged	2
Total Assisted	550
Day Care Centers	1
Total Assisted	250
Special Centers for Social Services	11
Total Assisted	13,400

Educational

Seminaries, Diocesan	1
Students from This Diocese	11
Students from Other Dioceses	3
Diocesan Students in Other Seminaries	15
Total Seminarians	26
Colleges and Universities	2
Total Students	16,740
High Schools, Diocesan and Parish	5
Total Students	2,026
High Schools, Private	2
Total Students	1,096
Elementary Schools, Diocesan and Parish	21
Total Students	5,134
Elementary Schools, Private	4
Total Students	647
Non-residential Schools for the Disabled	1
Total Students	18
Catechesis/Religious Education:	
High School Students	1,150
Elementary Students	12,762
Total Students under Catholic Instruction	39,599
Teachers in Diocese:	
Priests	3
Brothers	1
Sisters	8
Lay Teachers	793

Vital Statistics

Receptions into the Church:	
Infant Baptism Totals	2,762
Minor Baptism Totals	171
Adult Baptism Totals	126
Received into Full Communion	303
First Communions	2,842
Confirmations	3,198
Marriages:	
Catholic	485
Interfaith	81
Total Marriages	566
Deaths	2,655
Total Catholic Population	337,969
Total Population	957,419

LEADERSHIP

Office of the Bishop - t) 203-416-1352 Debra Charles, Exec. Admin. Asst. to Bishop (dcharles@diobpt.org); Patricia R. Hansen, Donor Rels. Dir. (phansen@diobpt.org);

Vicar General - t) 203-416-1636 Rev. Msgr. Robert M. Kinnally (MsgrKinnally@diobpt.org); Astrid Alvarez, Contact (astrid.alvarez@diobpt.org);

Chancellor and Secretary of the Curia - t) 203-416-1636 Dcn. Patrick Toole, Chancellor (dntoole@diobpt.org); Astrid Alvarez, Contact (astrid.alvarez@diobpt.org);

Vice-Chancellor - Dcn. William A. Santulli;

Archives -

Vicar for Clergy and Religious - t) 203-416-1633 Rev. Francis T. Hoffmann, Vicar for Clergy; Susan Baldwin, Admin. Asst. (sbaldwin@diobpt.org);

Judicial Vicar - Very Rev. Arthur C. Mollenhauer, Judicial Vicar; Giglia Hernandez, Admin. Asst.;

Episcopal Vicar for Filipino Catholics - Rev. Cyrus Bartolome (frcyrus@assumptionwestport.org);

Episcopal Vicar for African Americans - Rev. Reginald D. Norman, Vicar;

Episcopal Vicar for Brazilians - Rev. Leonel S. Medeiros (frmedeiros@diobpt.org);

Episcopal Vicar for Ecumenical and Interreligious Affairs - Rev. Samuel V. Scott;

Episcopal Vicar for Haitians - Rev. Guy Dormevil (frdormevil@diobpt.org);

Episcopal Vicar for Hispanics -

Episcopal Vicar for Liturgy and Worship - Rev. Peter F. Lenox, Vicar;

Episcopal Vicar for Vietnamese Catholics - Rev. Augustine Nguyen;

Episcopal Vicar for Senior Priests - Rev. Msgr. William J. Scheyd;

ADMINISTRATION

Diocesan Legal Services - t) (203) 862-7824 www.daypitney.com R. Scott Beach, Esq.;

Legal Office - t) (203) 416-1385 Anne O. McCrory, Chief Legal & Real Estate Officer (amccrory@diobpt.org); Sharon Colihan, Paralegal (Sharon.Colihan@diobpt.org); Debra Tietjen, Exec. Asst./Paralegal (dtietjen@diobpt.org);

Chief Financial Officer - t) 203-416-1615 Michael Hanlon, CFO (mhanlon@diobpt.org);

Real Estate and Facilities Management - t) 203-416-1512 Andrew Schulz;

OFFICES AND DIRECTORS

Catholic Lawyers - t) 203-374-2590 Rev. Msgr. J. James Cuneo, Spiritual Adv./Care Srvcs.; Leopold DeFusco, Coord., St. Thomas More Society of Fairfield County;

Diocesan Director of Vocations - t) (203) 416-1625 bridgeportpriest.org/ Rev. Christopher J. Ford;

Insurance Office - t) 203-371-8471 www.catholicmutual.org Dominick Del Corso, Mgr. Claims & Risk, Catholic Mutual Group;

Office of Safe Environment/Victim Assistance - Erin Neil, Dir., Safe Environments & Victim Assistance Coord. (eneil@diobpt.org); Mayte Figueroa-Camilo, VIRTUS Training & Devel. Specialist (mayte.figueroa-camilo@diobpt.org); Diane Scott, Safe Environment Prog. Asst.;

Pontifical Missions Office/Propagation of the Faith of the Diocese of Bridgeport - Dcn. David Flynn, Dir.;

CANONICAL SERVICES

Diocesan Censor Librorum - Rev. Msgr. Donald A. Guglielmi; Rev. Msgr. Christopher J. Walsh;

Ecclesiastical Notary - Debra Charles (dcharles@diobpt.org); Giglia Hernandez;

CATHOLIC CHARITIES

Catholic Charities of Fairfield County, Inc. - t) 203-416-1370 www.ccfairfield.org Angela Piscitello, COO (apiscitello@ccfc-ct.org); Mary Beth Petersen, Human Resources (mpetersen@ccfc-ct.org); Michael Donoghue, Exec. Dir.;

CLERGY AND RELIGIOUS SERVICES

Council of Deans - Most Rev. Frank J. Caggiano, Presider; Rev. Msgr. Robert M. Kinnally, Vicar General (MsgrKinnally@diobpt.org); Rev. Jose Abelardo Vasquez, Deanery A: Queen of Peace;

Diaconal Vocation Advisory and Admission Board - Most Rev. Frank J. Caggiano, Presider; Rev. Francis T. Hoffmann (frhoffman@hotmail.com); Dcn. Gerald M. Lambert;

Diaconate Office - t) 203-416-1323 Dcn. Gerald M. Lambert, Dir., Diaconate & Coord., Diaconate Formation; Laurie Furey, Admin. Asst. (l.furey@diobpt.org);

Coordinator of Diaconate Continuing Formation - Dcn. John DiTaranto;

Diocesan Director of Seminarian Formation - t) (203) 416-1627 bridgeportpriest.org/seminarians/ Rev. Joseph A. Marcello, Dir.; Marianne E Stook, Admin (Marianne.Stook@diobpt.org);

Redemptorist Mater Seminary at the St. Monica Pastoral Center - t) 203-322-5331 Rev. Zbigniew Kukielka, Rector; Rev. Jakov Vidor, Vice Rector;

Vocation Advisory & Admission Board - Rev. John Connaughton; Rev. Jeffrey W. Couture; Rev. Samuel S. Kachuba;

COMMUNICATIONS

Communications - www.bridgeportdiocese.com Brian D. Wallace, Dir. (bdwallace@diobpt.org);

Official Newspaper Fairfield County Catholic - t) 203-416-1464 Most Rev. Frank J. Caggiano, Publisher; Brian D. Wallace, Editor (bdwallace@diobpt.org);

COMMUNITY SERVICES

Diocesan Catholic Committee on Scouting - Rev. Msgr. Robert M. Kinnally (MsgrKinnally@diobpt.org); Astrid Alvarez (astrid.alvarez@diobpt.org);

CONSULTATIVE BODIES

Building and Sacred Arts Commission - Andrew Schulz; Anne O. McCrory (amccrory@diobpt.org); Rev. Peter F. Lenox;

College of Consultors - Rev. Msgr. Robert M. Kinnally, Vicar General (MsgrKinnally@diobpt.org); Rev. John Connaughton; Rev. Corey V. Piccinino;

Connecticut Catholic Conference - t) 203-524-7882 Christopher C. Healy (chealy@ctcatholic.org);

Diaconal Council - Most Rev. Frank J. Caggiano; Rev. Francis T. Hoffmann (frhoffman@hotmail.com); Dcn. Gerald M. Lambert;

Finance Council - Most Rev. Frank J. Caggiano, Presider; Rev. Msgr. Robert M. Kinnally (MsgrKinnally@diobpt.org); Michael Hanlon (mhanlon@diobpt.org);

Presbyteral Council - Most Rev. Frank J. Caggiano, Presider; Rev. Msgr. Robert M. Kinnally, Vicar General (MsgrKinnally@diobpt.org); Rev. Francis T. Hoffmann, Vicar for Clergy;

EDUCATION

Bridgeport Diocesan Schools Corporation - t) 203-416-1375 Dr. Steven Cheeseman, Supt.; Stacie L. Stueber, Deputy Supt. (sstueber@diobpt.org); Sharon Luciano, Exec. Asst.;

Catholic Schools - t) (203) 416-1638 Dr. Steven Cheeseman, Supt.; Stacie L. Stueber, Deputy Supt. (sstueber@diobpt.org); Sharon Luciano, Exec. Asst.;

Ministry for People With Developmental Disabilities - St. Catherine Center for Special Needs, Inc. - t) 203-540-5381 x2010 Helen Burland, Exec. Dir.;

EVANGELIZATION

Vicar for Evangelization - t) 203-748-9029 Rev. Peter J. Towsley, Vicar (frtowsley@diobpt.org);

FACILITIES

Catherine Dennis Keefe Queen of the Clergy Residence - t) 203-358-9906 pleydon@diobpt.org Patrick Leydon, Oper. Property Mgr.;

FINANCE

Office of Finance - Michael Hanlon, CFO (mhanlon@diobpt.org); Arlene Perricone, Controller;

HUMAN RESOURCES

Office of Human Resources - t) 203-416-1419 Tracy Casey, Chief Human Resources Officer (tracy.casey@diobpt.org);

PASTORAL SERVICES

Ministry for Deaf and Hearing Impaired - t) 203-377-4863 Rev. Nicholas S. Pavia (frpavia@diobpt.org);

Respect Life/Project Rachel - t) 203-416-1445 Maureen Ciardiello, Coord. (mciardiello@diobpt.org);

The Institute for Catholic Formation - t) 203-416-1657 formationreimagined.org/ Dr. Patrick Donovan, Exec. Dir. (pdonovan@diobpt.org); Dcn. John DiTaranto, Asst. Dir.; Carmela Williams, Office Admin. (Carmela.Williams@diobpt.org);

STEWARDSHIP

Office of Development - Joseph Gallagher, Chief Devel. Officer (jgallagher@diobpt.org); Robert O'Brien, Senior Dir. Devel., Planned Giving & Major Gifts (ROBrien@diobpt.org); Pamela Rittman, Dir., Devel. & Annual Bishop's Appeal (prittman@diobpt.org);

TRIBUNAL

Tribunal - t) 203-416-1424 www.dob-tribunal.com/ Very Rev. Arthur C. Mollenhauer, Judicial Vicar; Giglia Hernandez, Admin. Asst.;

Judicial Vicar - t) (203) 416-1424 Very Rev. Arthur C. Mollenhauer, Judicial Vicar;

Judges - Rev. Luis Antonio Alicea; Rev. William M. Quinlan (frquinlan@diobpt.org);

Promoter of Justice for Contentious and Penal Cases - Rev. William M. Quinlan (frquinlan@diobpt.org);

Defender of the Bond and Promoter Justice for Matrimonial Cases - Rev. Michael A. Boccaccio (frboccaccio@diobpt.org); Rev. Albert Peter Marcello III;

Ecclesiastical Notary - Debra Charles, Exec. Admin. Asst. to Bishop (dcharles@diobpt.org); Giglia Hernandez, Admin. Asst.;

MISCELLANEOUS / OTHER OFFICES

Cemeteries - t) 203-416-1494 Dean Gestal, Dir. (dean.gestal@diobpt.org);

Notaries - Debra Tietjen (dtietjen@diobpt.org); Sharon Colihan (Sharon.Colihan@diobpt.org);

PARISHES, MISSIONS, AND CLERGY

STATE OF CONNECTICUT

BETHEL

St. Mary's Church Corporation Bethel Connecticut - 26 Dodgingtown Rd., Bethel, CT 06801 t) 203-744-5777 stmaryoffice@comcast.net stmarybethel.org Rev. Corey V. Piccinino, Pst.; Rev. Harry Prieto, Par. Vicar; Dcn. John DeRoin; Dcn. Eric Keener;

Convent - t) 203-743-6985

BRIDGEPORT

The Cathedral Parish - 170 Thompson St., Bridgeport, CT 06604 t) 203-368-6777 office@thecathedralparish.org www.thecathedralparish.org Very Rev. Arthur C. Mollenhauer, Pst.; Rev. John J. Inserra, Par. Vicar; Dcn. Joseph Huong;

The Saint Andrew Roman Catholic Church Corporation - 435 Anton St., Bridgeport, CT 06606 t) 203-374-6171 standrewparish@optimum.net www.standrewchurch.org Rev. Milan Dimic, Pst.; Roland Blier; Rev. Hyginus Ndubueze Agu, In Res.; Rev. Msgr. Matthew Bernelli, In Res.;

St. Ann Roman Catholic Church Corporation - 481 Brewster St., Bridgeport, CT 06605 t) 203-368-1607 reled@stannblackrock.com; office@stannblackrock.com www.stannblackrock.com/ Rev. Ian Jeremiah, Pst.; Dcn. John Piatak; CRP Stds.: 112

The Church of St. Michael, Archangel Bridgeport - 310 Pulaski St., Bridgeport, CT 06608 t) 203-334-1822 franciscansbridgeport@gmail.com www.stmichaelbridgeport.com Rev. Norbert M. Siwinski, O.F.M.Conv., Pst.; Rev. Stefan Morawski, O.F.M.Conv., Par. Vicar;

The Church of the Blessed Sacrament of Bridgeport - 275 Union Ave., Bridgeport, CT 06607 t) 203-333-1202 pastor@blessedsacramentbpt.org www.blessedsacramentbpt.org/ Rev. Joseph J. Karcsinski, Pst.; Karen Soares-Robinson, DRE;

The St. George's Lithuanian Roman Catholic Church - 443 Park Ave., Bridgeport, CT 06604 t) 203-335-1797 secretary@stgeorgebpt.org Rev. Andris Alexis Moronta, Pst.;

St. Mary's Roman Catholic Church Corporation, Inc. (Bridgeport) - 540 Pembroke St., Bridgeport, CT 06608; Mailing: 25 Sherman St., Bridgeport, CT 06608 t) 203-334-8811 office@stmarychurchbridgeport.org stmarychurchbridgeport.org Rev. Rolando Torres, Pst.; Dcn. Reynaldo Olavarria; Luz Cordero, DRE;

Our Lady of Fatima Inc. - 429 Huntington Rd., Bridgeport, CT 06608 t) 203-333-7575 olfchurch.bridgeport@gmail.com www.olf-bridgeport.org Rev. Rogerio Perri, Pst.; Rev. Philip Lahn Phan, In Res.;

St. Peter's R.C. Church of Bridgeport - 695 Colorado Ave., Bridgeport, CT 06605 t) 203-366-5611 Rev. Jhon Gomez, Pst.; Dcn. Luis Torres; Sr. Anna Rodriguez, M.S.S., DRE;

The Roman Catholic Church of St. Charles - 391 Ogden St., Bridgeport, CT 06608 t) 203-333-3557 office@stcharlesbridgeport.org Rev. Jose Abelardo Vasquez, Pst.; Rev. Ivanildo Celestino dos Santos (Brazil), Par. Vicar; Rev. Churchill Penn, Par. Vicar; Mercedes Rojas, DRE;

The Slovak Roman Catholic Church of Saints Cyril and Methodius - 79 Church St., Bridgeport, CT 06608 t) 203-333-7003 stscyrilandmethodius@institute-christ-king.org Rev. Andrew Todd, Pst.;

BROOKFIELD

St. Joseph's Church Brookfield - 163 Whisconier Rd., Brookfield, CT 06804 t) 203-775-1035 parishsec@stjosephbrookfield.com www.stjosephbrookfield.com Rev. George F. O'Neill, Pst.; Dcn. Louis Howe; Dcn. Jeffrey Font; Dcn. Peter J. Kuhn; Dcn. William J. Shaughnessy;

St. Marguerite Bourgeoys - 138 Candlewood Lake Rd., Brookfield, CT 06804 t) 203-775-5117 frjordan@diobpt.org stmarguerite.org Rev. Shawn William Jordan, Pst.; Dcn. Vincent Pia; CRP Stds.: 271

DANBURY

The Church of the Sacred Heart of Jesus, Danbury - 46 Stone St., Danbury, CT 06810 t) 203-748-9029 office@sacredheartdanbury.org www.sacredheartdanbury.org Rev. Norman J. Guilbert, Pst.; Rev. Raymond M. Scherba, Par. Vicar; Rev. Jean-Rony Philippe, In Res.; Marie Fitzgerald, Bus. Mgr.; John Swingler, Music Min.; Debbie McDonald, DRE;

Saint Gregory the Great Roman Catholic Church Corporation - 85 Great Plain Rd., Danbury, CT 06811 t) 203-743-5168 (CRP); 203-797-0222 Rev. Michael L. Dunn, Pst.; Dcn. William D. Murphy; Mary Ann Hauser, DRE; CRP Stds.: 72

Immaculate Heart of Mary, Roman Catholic Church Corporation - 149 Deer Hill Ave., Danbury, CT 06811 t) 203-797-1821 frdasilva@diobpt.org Rev. Marcio Antonio Bueno da Silva (Brazil), Par. Admin.; Dcn. Jose Rodrigues Cabral; Helena Andrade, DRE;

The St. Joseph's Church, Danbury - 8 Robinson Ave., Danbury, CT 06810-5517 t) 203-778-1920 (CRP); 203-748-8177 Rev. Samuel V. Scott, Pst.; Dcn. Richard P. Kovacs;

Our Lady of Aparecida Corporation - 61 Liberty St., Danbury, CT 06810 t) 203-743-2707 Rev. Leonel S. Medeiros, Admin.;

Our Lady of Guadalupe Roman Catholic Church Corporation - 29 Golden Hill Rd., Danbury, CT 06811-4629 t) 203-826-1120 (CRP); 203-826-0585 (CRP) guadalupedanbury@gmail.com Rev. Elio Sosa, I.V.E., Pst.; Rev. Pedro A. Sosa, Par. Vicar; Dcn. Rafael Regus; Esmeralda Abreu, DRE;

St. Peter's Corporate Society - 104 Main St., Danbury, CT 06810 t) 203-743-1048 (CRP); 203-743-2707 office@stpeterdanb.org; spreligioused@stpeterdanb.org www.stpeterdanb.org Rev. Gregg D. Mecca, Pst.; Rev. Leonel S. Medeiros, Assoc. Pst.; Rev. Frank Eldridge, Par. Vicar; Rev. David J. Riley, In Res.; Barbara Siano, DRE; CRP Stds.: 333

DARIEN

St. John's R.C. Church Corporation - 1986 Post Rd., Darien, CT 06820 t) 203-655-1145 religiousedsj@optonline.net; stjohnb@optonline.net stjohndarien.org Rev. William M. Quinlan, Pst.;

The Saint Thomas More Roman Catholic Church Corporation - 384 Middlesex Rd., Darien, CT 06820 t) 203-655-3077 re@stmdarienct.org Rev. Paul G. Murphy, Pst.; Rev. Sunil Pereira, I.M.S., Par. Vicar; Maria Oliveira, Dir.; Michael Brelsford, Youth Min.; Mary Ellen O'Connor, DRE;

EASTON

Notre Dame of Easton Roman Catholic Church Corporation - 655 Morehouse Rd., Easton, CT 06612; Mailing: 640 Morehouse Rd., Easton, CT 06612 t) (203) 268-5838 churchladies@optonline.net notredameofeaston.com Rev. Michael P. Lyons, Pst.; Dcn. Gerald F. Sabol; Patricia Steccato, DRE;

FAIRFIELD

The Church of Our Lady of the Assumption - 545 Stratfield Rd., Fairfield, CT 06825 t) 203-367-1108 (CRP); 203-333-9065 our.lady.assumption@snet.net; assumptionfairfield@gmail.com Rev. Peter A. Cipriani, Pst.; Rev. Michael Flynn, In Res.; Rev. Marcel St. Jean, In Res.; Dcn. Raymond J. Chervenak; Dcn. Robert W. McLaughlin; Frank Macari, DRE;

Parish Center - 591 Stratfield Rd., Fairfield, CT 06825

The Church of Saint Anthony - 149 S. Pine Creek Rd., Fairfield, CT 06824 t) 203-259-0358 office@stanthonyffld.org www.stanthonyffld.org Eleanor W. Sauers, Parish Life Coord.; Dcn. Thomas F. Curran; CRP Stds.: 125

The Holy Cross Church Corporation of Bridgeport - 750 Tahmore Dr., Fairfield, CT 06825-2519 t) 203-372-4595 holy_cross_church@sbcglobal.net; holycrossccd750@gmail.com holycrosschurchfairfield.com Rev. Alfred F. Pecaric, Pst.; Jackie Azarian, DRE; Lory Moomjian, DRE; CRP Stds.: 16

Holy Family and St. Emery Parish Corporation - 700 Old Stratfield Rd., Fairfield, CT 06825; Mailing: 70 Laurel St., Fairfield, CT 06825 t) 203-336-1835 office@holyfamilyrc.org stemerys.com Rev. Sean Kulacz, Pst.; Dcn. Joseph Gagne; Dcn. Joseph DeBiase;

St. Pius X Corporation - 834 Brookside Dr., Fairfield, CT 06824 t) 203-255-6134 secretary@st-pius.org www.st-pius.org Rev. Samuel S. Kachuba, Pst.; Rev. Colin Blatchford, In Res.; Rev. Eric Silva, In Res.; Michael Lantowski, Music Min.; Emily Rauser, Youth Min.; Shari Garcia, DRE; Kim Leon, Bus. Mgr.;

St. Thomas Church Fairfield Connecticut - 1719 Post Rd., Fairfield, CT 06824 t) 203-255-1984 (CCD Office); 203-255-1097 (Parish Office) stthoaqccd@aol.com; stthoaq@aol.com www.stthomasfairfield.com/ Rev. Victor T. Martin, Pst.; Rev. Lawrence A. Larson, In Res.; Rev. Christopher J. Perrella, In Res.; Rev. Christopher J. Samele, In Res.; Dcn. Daniel Ianniello; Mary Jane Edwards, Pst. Assoc.; Jacqueline Herbert, DRE; CRP Stds.: 310

GREENWICH

St. Marys Rom. C. Church Greenwich Connecticut - 178 Greenwich Ave., Greenwich, CT 06830 t) 203-869-9393 saintmre@gmail.com; stmarygrn@gmail.com stmarygreenwich.org Rev. Michael K. Jones, Pst.; Sharon O'Dea-Debold, DRE; CRP Stds.: 130

The Saint Michael Roman Catholic Church Corporation - 469 North St., Greenwich, CT 06830 t) 203-869-5421 reledstmmichael@gmail.com; stmichaelsttim@optonline.net Rev. Richard D. Murphy, Pst.; Loren Procaccini, DRE;

St. Timothy's - 1034 North St., Greenwich, CT 06831

St. Paul's Church of Glenville Connecticut - 84 Sherwood Ave., Greenwich, CT 06831 t) 203-531-4265 (CRP); 203-531-8741 office@stpaulgreenwich.org www.stpaulgreenwich.org Rev. Leszek P. Szymaszek, Pst.; Rosie Pennella, DRE;

The St. Roch's Church Corporation of Greenwich - 10 St. Roch Ave., Greenwich, CT 06830 frmcintosh@strochchurch.com Rev. Carl McIntosh, Pst.; Rev. Nicholas S. Pavia, In Res.;

Sacred Heart Church of East Port Chester, Connecticut - 95A Henry St., Greenwich, CT 06830; Mailing: 38 God St., Greenwich, CT 06830 t) 203-531-8730 reledsh@optimum.net sacredheartgreenwich.org Rev. Mark D'Silva, Pst.;

MONROE

The St. Jude Roman Catholic Church Corporation - 707 Monroe Tpke., Monroe, CT 06468 t) 203-261-6404 religious.education@stjuderc.com; parish.office@stjuderc.com Rev. Joseph Gill, Pst.; Dcn. David Flynn; Dcn. John Tuccio;

NEW CANAAN

St. Aloysius Church Corporation of Connecticut - 40 Maple St., New Canaan, CT 06840 t) (203) 652-1150; (203) 966-0020 office@starcc.com www.starcc.com Rev. Msgr. Robert M. Kinnally, Pst.; Rev. David W. Franklin, Par. Vicar; Rev. David Roman, Par. Vicar; Dcn. William A. Santulli;

NEW FAIRFIELD

St. Edward the Confessor - 21 Brush Hill Rd., New Fairfield, CT 06812 t) 203-746-2200 parishoffice@saintedwardchurch.org saintedwardchurch.org Rev. Robert L Wolfe, Pst.; Rev. Timothy Iannacone, Par. Vicar; Dcn. Patrick Shevlin; Kathryn LaRegina, DRE;

Holy Trinity - 15 Rte. 37 Ctr., Sherman, CT 06784 t) (860) 354-1414

NEWTOWN

St. Rose's Church Newtown - 46 Church Hill Rd., Newtown, CT 06470 t) 203-802-4791 (CRP); 203-426-1014 dre@strosechurch.com; parishsecretary@strosechurch.com Rev. Msgr. Robert E. Weiss, Pst.; Rev. Karol J. Ksiazek, Par. Vicar; Rev. Tomasz Przybyl, SVD (Poland), Par. Vicar; Dcn. Norman Roos; Dcn. Richard Scinto; Cate Gosselin, DRE;

NORWALK

Saint Jerome's Roman Catholic Church Corporation - 23 Half Mile Rd., Norwalk, CT 06851 t) 203-847-5649 office@stjeromenorwalk.org www.stjeromenorwalk.org/ Rev. Rojin Karickal, Pst.; Rev. David W. Blanchfield, In Res.;

St. Joseph and St. Ladislaus Parish Corporation - 85 S. Main St., Norwalk, CT 06854 t) 203-354-8869 office@stj-stl.org stj-stl.org Rev. Edicson Orozco, Pst.; Dcn. Rock Desances;

Convent - 14 Chestnut St., Norwalk, CT 06854

St. Mary's Church, Norwalk - 669 West Ave., Norwalk, CT 06850 t) 203-866-7429 (CRP); 203-866-5546 x102 Rev. Frederick John Ringley Jr., Pst.; Dcn. Stephan A. Genovese;

Saint Matthew's Roman Catholic Church Corporation - 216 Scribner Ave., Norwalk, CT 06854 t) 203-838-3788 x101 stmattparish@hotmail.com; stmattreled@gmail.com www.stmatthewnorwalk.org/ Rev. Jeffrey W. Couture, Pst.; Rev. Jose Ignacio A. Ortigas, Par. Vicar; Rev. Paul Sankar, In Res.; CRP Stds.: 219

St. Philip Roman Catholic Church Corporation - 1 Father Conlon Pl., Norwalk, CT 06851-3821; Mailing: 25 France St., Norwalk, CT 06851-3817 t) 203-847-4549 (CRP) faithformation@stphilipnorwalk.org; info@stphilipnorwalk.org www.stphilipnorwalk.org Rev. Sudhir D'Souza, Pst.; Rev. Michael A. Boccaccio, Temp. Residence; CRP Stds.: 100

St. Thomas the Apostle Roman Catholic Church Corporation - 203 East Ave., Norwalk, CT 06855 t) 203-866-3141 (Rectory Office); 203-866-1189 (CRP) stthomasreledoffice@gmail.com; stthomasnorwalk@optonline.net stthomasnorwalk.org Rev. Miroslaw Stachurski, Pst.; Rev. Ralph Segura, Par. Vicar; Mary Vladimirov, DRE; CRP Stds.: 107

REDDING RIDGE

Sacred Heart and Saint Patrick Parish Corporation - 169 Black Rock Tpke., Redding Ridge, CT 06876 t) 203-938-2253 frtwalsh@diobpt.org Rev. Terrence P. Walsh, Pst.;

RIDGEFIELD

The Saint Elizabeth Seton Roman Catholic Church Corporation - 520 Ridgebury Rd., Ridgefield, CT 06877 t) 203-438-9707 (CRP); 203-438-7292 stsetonparish@comcast.net sesparish.org/ Rev. Joseph A. Prince, In Res.; Cornelia Hurwitz, DRE;

St. Mary's Corporation - 55 Catoonah St., Ridgefield, CT 06877 t) 203-438-6538; 203-438-7335 (CRP) jbrown@smcr.org; ldanner@smcr.org smcr.org Rev. Msgr. Kevin T. Royal, Pst.; Rev. Colin Lomnitzer, Par. Vicar; Rev. Justin Raj, I.M.S. (India), Par. Vicar; Laura Danner, Pst. Assoc.; Dcn. George Kain; Dcn. Richard Lawlor; Dcn. Robert A. Salvestrini;

RIVERSIDE

St. Catherine of Siena and St. Agnes Parish Corporation - 4 Riverside Ave., Riverside, CT 06878 t) 203-637-6331 rectory@stc-sta.org www.stc-sta.org Rev. William F. Platt, Pst.; Rev. Miguel Bernal Rodriguez (Spain), Coord., Hispanic Ministry Greenwich; Rev. Christopher Johnson, O.C.D., In Res.; Dcn. Renato Berzolla; Dcn. Robert Henrey; Dcn. Eduardo Rodrigues;

SHELTON

The St. Joseph's Church of Shelton - 50 Fairmont Pl., Shelton, CT 06484 t) 203-924-8611; 203-924-9677 (CRP) rectory@sjcshelton.org; reled@sjcshelton.org www.sjcshelton.org Rev. Michael F. Dogali, Pst.; Nicholas Stampone, DRE; Dcn. Bradford Smythe; CRP Stds.: 202

Saint Lawrence Corporation - 505 Shelton Ave., Shelton, CT 06484 t) 203-929-5355 stwannabee@aol.com; stlawrpar1@aol.com www.stlawrenceshelton.org Rev. Ciprian Bejan, Pst.; Rev. Krzysztof Kuczynski, Par. Vicar; Dcn. Anthony Cassaneto; Dcn. Frank J. Masso; Dcn. Joseph Klimaszewski; Karen O'Keefe, CRE; CRP Stds.: 353

The Saint Margaret Mary Roman Catholic Church Corporation - 50 Donovan Ln., Shelton, CT 06484 t) 203-924-4929; 203-924-2679 (CRP) stmamar380@yahoo.com stmmshelton.org Rev. Joseph Cervero, Pst.; Dcn. Jeffrey J. Kingsley; Heather Moura, DRE;

SHERMAN

The Holy Trinity Roman Catholic Church Corp. - Merged Jul 2023 Holy Trinity Parish merged with Saint Edward the Confessor Parish through an extinctive union.

STAMFORD

The Saint Bridget Roman Catholic Church Corporation - 278 Strawberry Hill Ave., Stamford, CT 06902 t) 203-357-8157 (CRP); 203-324-2910 parish.office@stbridgetofireland.com; religious.ed@stbridgetofireland.com www.stbridgetofireland.com Rev. James Bates, Pst.; Magdalene Jeffers, DRE; Dcn. Ernest Jeffers; CRP Stds.: 122

St. Cecilia-St. Gabriel Parish Corporation - 1184 Newfield Ave., Stamford, CT 06905-1496 t) 203-322-1562 office@stcecilia-stgabriel.org stcecilia-stgabriel.org/ Rev. John Connaughton, Pst.; Rev. Mariusz Olbrys, Par. Vicar;

The Church of the Holy Name of Jesus - 325 Washington Blvd., Stamford, CT 06902; Mailing: 4 Pulaski St., Stamford, CT 06902 t) 203-323-4546 (CRP); 203-323-4967 info@holynamestamford.org Rev. Pawel M. Hrebenko, Pst.; Rev. Jakub Rachwalski (Poland), Par. Vicar; Malgorzata Berestka Popiolek, DRE; CRP Stds.: 151

The Church of the Sacred Heart Corporation, Stamford - 37 Schuyler Ave., Stamford, CT 06902 t) 203-324-9544 sacredparish@optonline.net stamfordsacredheart.org Rev. Alfonso Picone, Pst.; Rev. Martin P. deMayo, Par. Vicar; Michele Sabia, DRE; CRP Stds.: 144

The Saint Clement's Church Corporation - 535 Fairfield Ave., Stamford, CT 06902 t) 203-348-1233 (CRP); 203-348-4206 stclementre@optonline.net; stclement@optonline.net Rev. Carlos Rodrigues, Pst.; Louise Cronin, DRE;

The Holy Spirit Roman Catholic Church Corporation - 403 Scofieldtown Rd., Stamford, CT 06903-4009 t) 203-322-3722 holyspiritparish@aol.com Rev. Luke P. Suarez, Pst.;

St. John's Catholic Church, Stamford, Connecticut - 279 Atlantic St., Stamford, CT 06901 t) 203-324-1553 religioused@saintjohnsstamford.com; office@stjohnbasilica.org Rev. Cyprian P. LaPastina, Pst.; Rev. Msgr. Stephen M. Di Giovanni, In Res.;

Saint Leo Roman Catholic Church Corporation - 24 Roxbury Rd., Stamford, CT 06902 t) 203-348-0052 Rev. James D. Grosso, Pst.; Rev. Anh Ngoc Quoc Vu, Par. Vicar; Eileen Towne, DRE;

Saint Mary Parish Corporation of Stamford - 566 Elm St., Stamford, CT 06902 t) 203-324-7321 stmarystamford@yahoo.com www.stmarystfd.org Rev. Gustavo A. Falla, Pst.; Rev. Rolando Arias Galvis, Par. Vicar; Rosner Rosas, CRE; CRP Stds.: 280

The Saint Maurice Roman Catholic Church Corporation - 358 Glenbrook Rd., Stamford, CT 06906-2198 t) 203-324-3434; 203-324-3434 x707 (CRP) skluun@smcglenbrook.org; parishoffice@smcglenbrook.org Rev. James Bates, Pst.; Sandra Kluun, DRE;

Notre Dame du Perpetuel Secours Corporation - 894 Newfield Ave., Stamford, CT 06905 t) 203-838-4171 frdormevil@diobpt.org Rev. Guy Dormevil, Par. Vicar;

Our Lady, Star of the Sea Corporation - 1200 Shippan Ave., Stamford, CT 06902 t) 203-324-4634 olssdre@yahoo.com ourladystaroftheseastamford.org Rev. Peter K. Smolik, Pst.; Dee Fumega, DRE;

Convent - 1216 Shippan Ave., Stamford, CT 06902

STRATFORD

The Church of the Holy Name of Jesus, Stratford - 1950 Barnum Ave., Stratford, CT 06614 t) 203-378-7407 (CRP); 203-375-5815 www.hnojchurch.org Rev. Albert G. Pinciaro, Pst.; Sr. Madonna Figura, S.S.C.M., DRE;

Convent - 2 Mary Ave, Stratford, CT 06614

St. James R.C. Church Corporation - 2110 Main St., Stratford, CT 06615 t) 203-375-5887 jkoletar.stjamesparish@gmail.com www.stjamesstratford.com Rev. Peter J. Adamski, Pst.; Dcn. Joseph Koletar;

St. Mark Roman Catholic Church - 500 Wigwam Ln., Stratford, CT 06614 t) 203-377-0444 prnettleton@yahoo.com; pmollica@stmarkstfd.org Rev. Birendra Soreng (India), Pst.; Rev. Russell Augustine, Par. Vicar; Dcn. Andrew Dzujna; Dcn. F. Paul Kurmay; Dcn. T. Emmet Murray; Patricia Nettleton, DRE; Joan Hurley, Bus. Mgr.; CRP Stds.: 160

Our Lady of Grace Parish - 497 Second Hill Ln., Stratford, CT 06614-2595 t) 203-375-6133 (CRP); 203-377-0928 msgrryan@olgstratford.com www.olgstratford.com/ Rev. Msgr. Martin P. Ryan, Pst.; CRP Stds.: 43

Parish Center - 345 Second Hill Ln., Stratford, CT 06614-2595

Our Lady of Peace Roman Catholic Church Corporation - 651 Stratford Rd., Stratford, CT 06615; Mailing: 10 Ivy St., Stratford, CT 06615 t) 203-378-3053 (CRP); 203-377-4863 x10 (Office) ourlady@sbcglobal.net ourladyofpeacestratfordct.weconnect.com Rev. Peter J. Towsley, Pst.; Dcn. Thomas Fekete;

TRUMBULL

Saint Catherine of Siena Corporation - 220 Shelton Rd., Trumbull, CT 06611 t) 203-377-3133 jamespanullo@stcatherinetrumbull.com Rev. Joseph A. Marcello, Pst.; Dcn. Patrick Toole, RCIA Coord.; James Joseph Panullo, Dir.;

Christ the King Roman Catholic Church Corporation - 4700 Madison Ave., Trumbull, CT 06611 t) 203-268-8695 (Office); 203-261-2583 (CRP) office@christthekingtrumbull.org christthekingtrumbull.org Rev. Richard J. Gemza, Pst.; CRP Stds.: 92

St. Stephen's Roman Catholic Church Corporation - 6948 Main St., Trumbull, CT 06611-1340 t) 203-268-6860 (CRP); 203-268-6217 faithformation@ststephentc.org; ststephen@ststephentc.org ststephentc.org Rev. Henry J. Hoffman, Pst.; Dcn. John DiTaranto; Dcn. Donald J. Ross; Janet Wrabel, DRE;

The St. Theresa's Roman Catholic Church Corporation - 5301 Main St., Trumbull, CT 06611 t) 203-261-4706 (CRP); 203-261-3676 cre@sttheresatrumbull.org; parish@sttheresatrumbull.org www.sttheresatrumbull.org Rev. Brian P. Gannon, Pst.; Rev. Flavian Bejan, Par. Vicar; Rev. David C. Leopold, In Res.; Rev. Claudiu Gabriel Neculaesi (Romania), In Res.; Dcn. Gerald M. Lambert; Joanne Durkin, DRE;

WESTON

St. Francis of Assisi - 35 Norfield Rd., Weston, CT 06883 t) 203-227-1341 office@stfrancisweston.org stfrancisweston.org/ Rev. Augustine Nguyen, Pst.; Dcn. Stephen Hodson;

WESTPORT

Church of Assumption, Westport, Connecticut - 98 Riverside Ave., Westport, CT 06880 t) 203-226-5448 (CRP); 203-227-5161 mhankey@assumptionwestport.org; frcyrus@assumptionwestport.org www.assumptionwestport.org Rev. Cyrus Bartolome, Pst.; Rev. Seungyoung Yi (South Korea), Par. Vicar; Michelle Hankey, Bus. Mgr.; Rev. Francis T. Hoffmann, In Res.; Dcn. James Meehan; Cathy Romano, DRE; Michele Harding, Youth Min.; Frank Matto, Music Min.;

Saint Luke's Roman Catholic Church Corporation - 49 N. Turkey Hill Rd., Westport, CT 06880; Mailing: 84 Long Lots Rd., Westport, CT 06880 t) 203-227-7245 x10; 203-226-0729 x11 (CRP); 203-222-0478 x25 (Outreach Ministries); 203-222-0205 x31 (Youth Ministry) stluke-reo@optonline.net; stluke@optonline.net saintlukewestport.org Rev. Udayakumar Xavariapitchai, Pst.; Dcn. Lance C. Fredricks; Dcn. Brian J. Kelly; Dcn. Christopher Greer; Deb Toner, Youth Min.; Jacqueline Frusciante, DRE;

WILTON

Our Lady of Fatima Roman Catholic Church Corporation of Wilton - 229 Danbury Rd., Wilton, CT 06897 t) 203-762-9080 (CRP); 203-762-3928 olfreled@gmail.com; secretary@olfwilton.org www.olfwilton.org Rev. Reginald D. Norman, Pst.; Rev. Philip Lahn Phan, Par. Vicar; Dcn. Anthony Conti; Kathleen Rooney, DRE;

SCHOOLS: PRESCHOOL THRU HIGH SCHOOL

SCHOOLS

STATE OF CONNECTICUT

BETHEL

St. Mary School Bethel Inc - (DIO) (Grades PreK-8) 24 Dodgingtown Rd., Bethel, CT 06801 t) 203-744-2922 ssmith@stmarybethelct.org www.stmarybethel.org Scott Smith, Prin.; Stds.: 190; Lay Tchrs.: 12

BRIDGEPORT

Bridgeport Diocesan Schools Corporation - 238 Jewett Ave, Bridgeport, CT 06606 t) 203-416-1380 schools@diobpt.org Dr. Steven Cheeseman, Supt.;

Catholic Academy of Bridgeport, Inc. - (DIO) (Grades PreK-8) 63 Pequonnock St, Bridgeport, CT 06604 t) 203-362-2990 apohlen@catholicacademybridgeport.org www.catholicacademybridgeport.org Angela Pohlen, Dir.; Stds.: 910; Sr. Tchrs.: 1; Lay Tchrs.: 62

St. Andrew Academy - (Grades PreK-8) 395 Anton St, Bridgeport, CT 06606 t) 203-373-1552 gholmes@diobpt.org standrew.catholicacademybridgeport.org Gene Holmes, Prin.; Stds.: 254; Lay Tchrs.: 14

St. Ann Academy - (Grades PreK-8) 521 Brewster St., Bridgeport, CT 06605-3409 t) 203-334-5856 pgriffin@catholicacademybridgeport.org Patricia Griffin, Prin.; Stds.: 227; Lay Tchrs.: 14

St. Augustine Academy - (Grades PreK-8) 63 Pequonnock St., Bridgeport, CT 06604 t) 203-366-6500 ahurtt@catholicacademybridgeport.org Dr. Allison Hurtt, Prin.; Stds.: 190; Lay Tchrs.: 19

St. Raphael Academy - (Grades PreK-8) 324 Frank St., Bridgeport, CT 06604 t) 203-333-6818 edoyle@catholicacademybridgeport.org catholicacademybridgeport.org Sr. Elizabeth Doyle, ASCJ, Prin.; Stds.: 239; Sr. Tchrs.: 1; Lay Tchrs.: 15

DANBURY

St. Gregory the Great School Inc. - (DIO) (Grades PreK-8) 85 Great Plain Rd., Danbury, CT 06811 t) 203-748-1217 info@sgtgs.org saintgregoryschool.org Suzanne Curra, Prin.; Stds.: 284; Lay Tchrs.: 14

St. Joseph School Danbury Inc. - (DIO) (Grades PreK-8) 370 Main St., Danbury, CT 06810 t) 203-748-6615 sjsoffice@sjsdanbury.org www.sjsdanbury.org Dr. Louis Howe, Prin.; Stds.: 266; Lay Tchrs.: 16

Saint Peter School Inc. - (DIO) (Grades PreK-8) 98 Main St., Danbury, CT 06810 t) 203-748-2895 info@spsdanbury.org www.stpeterschooldanbury.org Mary Lou Torre, Prin.; Stds.: 223; Lay Tchrs.: 16

FAIRFIELD

Assumption Catholic School Inc. - (DIO) (Grades PreK-8) 605 Stratfield Rd., Fairfield, CT 06825 t) 203-334-6271 principal@oloaffld.org www.assumptionfairfield.org Stacy Clements, Prin.; Stds.: 170; Lay Tchrs.: 13

St. Catherine Academy - (DIO) (Grades K-12) 760 Tahmore Dr., Fairfield, CT 06825 t) 203-540-5381 eric.spencer@diobpt.org; hburland@diobpt.org www.stcatherineacademy.org Special Needs School Eric Spencer, Prin.; Helen Burland, Dir.; Stds.: 18; Sr. Tchrs.: 3; Lay Tchrs.: 2

St. Thomas Aquinas Catholic School Inc - (DIO) (Grades PreK-8) 1719 Post Rd., Fairfield, CT 06824 t) 203-255-0556 info@stasonline.net www.stasonline.net Dr. Patrick Higgins, Prin.; Stds.: 337; Lay Tchrs.: 23

GREENWICH

Greenwich Catholic School, Inc. - (DIO) (Grades PreK-8) 471 North St., Greenwich, CT 06830 t) 203-869-4000 rsteck@gcsct.org www.gcsct.org Rebecca Steck, Prin.; Stds.: 346; Lay Tchrs.: 33

Sacred Heart Greenwich - (PRV) (Grades K-12) 1177 King St., Greenwich, CT 06831 t) 203-531-6500 admissionsoffice@cshct.org www.shgreenwich.org Day school for girls. Coed early childhood education Prog. Convent of the Sacred Heart Katie Cullinane, Admin.; Jessica McGibbon, Admin.; John Zwack, Admin.; Michael Baber, Pres.; Stds.: 606; Lay Tchrs.: 115

NEWTOWN

St. Rose of Lima School Inc. - (DIO) (Grades PreK-8) 40 Church Hill Rd., Newtown, CT 06470 t) 203-426-5102 bgjoka@diobpt.org www.stroseschool.com Bardhyl Gjoka, Prin.; Stds.: 259; Lay Tchrs.: 18

NORWALK

All Saints Catholic School Inc - (DIO) (Grades PreK-8) 139 W. Rocks Rd., Norwalk, CT 06851 t) 203-847-3881 ldunn@diobpt.org; svirgadamo@diobpt.org www.allsaintsnorwalk.com Steven Virgadamo, Pres.; Linda Dunn, Prin.; Stds.: 397; Lay Tchrs.: 30

***Anchor Academy, Inc.** - (PRV) ; Mailing: P.O. Box 774, Norwalk, CT 06852

RIDGEFIELD

St. Mary School Ridgefield Inc. - (DIO) (Grades PreK-8) 183 High Ridge Ave., Ridgefield, CT 06877 t) 203-438-7288 ambrosior@smsridgefield.org www.smsridgefield.org Rachel Ambrosio, Prin.; Stds.: 266; Lay Tchrs.: 28

SHELTON

Holy Trinity Catholic Academy, Inc. - (DIO) (Grades PreK-8) 503 Shelton Ave., Shelton, CT 06484 t) 203-929-4422 llanni@holytrinitycatholicacademy.org www.holytrinitycatholicacademy.org Lisa Lanni, Prin.; Stds.: 166; Lay Tchrs.: 12

STAMFORD

St. Aloysius School Inc. - (DIO) (Grades K-8) 403 Scofieldtown Rd., Stamford, CT 06903 t) 203-966-0786 afielding@sasncct.org sasncct.org Adam Fielding, Prin.; Stds.: 83; Lay Tchrs.: 10

Cardinal Kung Academy Inc. - (DIO) (Grades 7-12) 948 Newfield Ave., Stamford, CT 06905 t) 203-329-8296 cardinalkungacademy@gmail.com cardinalkungacademy.org Dr. Alexander Miller, Prin.; Stds.: 107; Lay Tchrs.: 2

The Catholic Academy of Stamford, Inc. - (DIO) (Grades PreK-8) 1186 Newfield Ave., Stamford, CT 06905 t) 203-322-6505; 203-322-7383 www.catholicacademystamford.org/ Patricia Brady, Prin.; Stds.: 308; Lay Tchrs.: 21

***Mater Salvatoris College Preparatory School, Inc.** - (PRV) 914 Newfield Ave., Stamford, CT 06905

STRATFORD

St. James School Inc. - (DIO) (Grades PreK-8) 50 Harvey Pl., Stratford, CT 06615 t) 203-375-5994 chris.robertson@sjssct.org www.stjamesstratford.org Christopher Robertson, Prin.; Stds.: 228; Lay Tchrs.: 13

St. Mark School Inc. - (DIO) (Grades PreK-8) 500 Wigwam Ln., Stratford, CT 06614 t) 203-375-4291 contactus@stmarkschool.org www.stmarkschool.org Melissa Warner, Prin.; Stds.: 234; Lay Tchrs.: 17

TRUMBULL

St. Catherine of Siena School Inc. - (DIO) (Grades PreK-8) 190 Shelton Rd., Trumbull, CT 06611 t) 203-375-1947 info@scsstrumbull.org www.stcatherinesienatrumbull.org Patrice Kopas, Prin.; Stds.: 237; Lay Tchrs.: 16

St. Theresa School Inc. - (DIO) (Grades PreK-8) 55 Rosemond Ter., Trumbull, CT 06611 t) 203-268-3236 info@stesonline.org www.sttheresaschooltrumbull.org Barbara Logsdail, Prin.; Stds.: 230; Lay Tchrs.: 12

WILTON

Our Lady of Fatima Catholic Academy Inc. - (DIO) (Grades PreK-8) 225 Danbury Rd., Wilton, CT 06897 t) 203-762-8100 mafleming99@olfcatholic.org www.olfacademy.org Mary Ann Fleming, Prin.;

HIGH SCHOOLS

STATE OF CONNECTICUT

BRIDGEPORT

Kolbe Cathedral Catholic High School, Inc. - (DIO) (Grades 9-12) 33 Calhoun Pl., Bridgeport, CT 06604 t) 203-335-2554 cfigluizzi@kolbecaths.org www.kolbecaths.org Camille Figluizzi, Prin.; Stds.: 300; Sr. Tchrs.: 1; Lay Tchrs.: 22

DANBURY

Immaculate High School, Inc. - (DIO) (Grades 9-12) 73 Southern Blvd., Danbury, CT 06810 t) 203-744-1510 info@immaculatehs.org immaculatehs.org Wendy Neil, Prin.; Mary R. Maloney, Pres.; Stds.: 385; Lay Tchrs.: 38

FAIRFIELD

Fairfield College Preparatory School - (PRV) (Grades 9-12) 1073 N. Benson Rd., Fairfield, CT 06824 t) 203-254-4200 tdee@fairfieldprep.org www.fairfieldprep.org (Boys) Timothy Dee, Prin.; Christian J. Cashman, Pres.; Stds.: 799; Lay Tchrs.: 54

Notre Dame Catholic High School, Inc. - (DIO) (Grades 9-12) 220 Jefferson St., Fairfield, CT 06825 t) 203-372-6521 ccipriano@notredame.org www.notredame.org Christopher Cipriano, Prin.; Stds.: 484; Pr. Tchrs.: 1; Lay Tchrs.: 38

TRUMBULL

St. Joseph's High School, Inc. - (DIO) (Grades 9-12) 2320 Huntington Tpke., Trumbull, CT 06611 t) 203-378-9378 ndibuono@sjcadets.org www.sjcadets.org Nancy DiBuono, Prin.; David Klein, Pres.; Stds.: 748; Pr. Tchrs.: 2; Lay Tchrs.: 66

CAMPUS MINISTRY / NEWMAN CENTERS [CAM]

DANBURY

Newman Center at Western CT State University - 7 Eighth Ave., Danbury, CT 06810 t) 203-744-5846 mhossan@wcsu.edu

FAIRFIELD

Fairfield University - 1073 N. Benson Rd., Fairfield, CT 06824-5195 t) 203-254-4190 (Fairfield) Rev. Keith Maczkiewicz, S.J., Dir.; Marc Alibrandi, Campus Min.; Katie Byrnes, Campus Min.; Dcn. Thomas F. Curran, RCIA Coord.; Valerie Kisselback, Campus Min.; Kevin Molloy, Campus Min.;

CATHOLIC CHARITIES [CCH]

INSTITUTIONS LOCATED IN DIOCESE

BRIDGEPORT

Catholic Charities - Catholic Center, 238 Jewett Ave., Bridgeport, CT 06606-2892 t) (203) 416-1370 mdonoghue@ccfc-ct.org www.ccfairfield.org Michael Donoghue, Exec. Dir.; Angela Piscitello, COO; Mary Beth Petersen, Vice Pres., Human Resources;

Behavioral Health Counseling, Danbury - 405 Main St., Danbury, CT 06810 t) (203) 743-4412 (Clinic Appts) ccoretto@ccfc-ct.org Charles Coretto, Dir.;

Behavioral Health Counseling, Norwalk - 120 East Ave., Norwalk, CT 06851 t) (203) 750-9711 (Clinic Appts) hely@ccfc-ct.org Heather Ely, Dir.;

Catholic Campaign for Human Development - 238 Jewett Ave., Bridgeport, CT 06606

Catholic Charities, Danbury - 405 Main St., Ste. 503, Danbury, CT 06810 t) (203) 748-0848 ccoretto@ccfc-ct.org Charles Coretto, Dir.;

Catholic Charities, Norwalk - 120 East Ave., Norwalk, CT 06851 t) (203) 794-0819 hely@ccfc-ct.org; mpalacios@ccfc-ct.org Heather Ely, Dir.; Maria Palacios, Immigration Svcs. Dir., Norwalk;

Community Advocacy Program - 120 East Ave., Norwalk, CT 06851 t) (203) 339-2191 kpaz@ccfc-ct.org Kristine Paz, Community Resource Dir.;

Family Directions - 238 Jewett Ave., Bridgeport, CT 06606-2892 t) 203-416-1336 azajac@ccfc-ct.org Adoptions and Home Studies. Amy Zajac, Dir.;

Family Loan Program, Stamford/Norwalk - 120 East Ave., Norwalk, CT 06851 t) (203) 767-4854 dbarston@ccfc-ct.org Diane Barston, Dir.;

Homeless Outreach Team - 405 Main St., Danbury, CT 06810 t) (203) 743-4412 plipp@ccfc-ct.org Paul Lipp, Dir.;

Housing Services - 238 Jewett Ave., Bridgeport, CT

06606-2892 t) 203-416-1317 dhill@ccfc-ct.org Dina Hill, Dir.;

Immigration Services - 238 Jewett Ave., Bridgeport, CT 06606 t) 203-416-1313 aarevalo@ccfc-ct.org Alex Arevalo, Dir., Bridgeport; Maria Palacios, Dir., Norwalk;

Morning Glory Breakfast Program - 11 Spring St., Danbury, CT 06810 t) (203) 349-2848 tespinal@ccfc-ct.org Tamara Espinal, Dir.;

New Covenant Center - 174 Richmond Hill Ave., Stamford, CT 06904 t) 203-964-8228 jgutman@ccfc-ct.org John Gutman, Dir.;

NEW HEIGHTS - 66 West St., Danbury, CT 06810 t) 203-794-0819 jumansky@ccfc-ct.org Jeff Umansky, Dir.;

Room to Grow School Readiness - 208 East Ave., Norwalk, CT 06850 t) 203-855-0637 nowens@ccfc-ct.org Nancy Owens, Dir.;

Senior Nutrition Program - 30 Myano Ln., Ste. 12, Stamford, CT 06902 t) 203-324-6175 mneuberger@ccfc-ct.org

SNAP Outreach and Engagement - 120 East Ave., Norwalk, CT 06851 t) (203) 585-7288 pblanco@ccfc-ct.org

Thomas Merton Center - 43 Madison Ave., Bridgeport, CT 06604 t) 203-367-9036 bcolson@ccfc-ct.org; skuczo@ccfc-ct.org Food Cafe and Eat Smart Food Pantry Bill Colson, Dir.; Sabine Kuczo, Oper. Mgr.;

Victims of a Crime Art Counselor - 24 Grassy Plains St., Bethel, CT 06801 t) (475) 228-7257 Sarah Meyerdiercks, Case Mgr.;

Ways to Work Family Loan Program - 405 Main St., Ste. 503, Danbury, CT 06810 t) 203-743-4412 csilliman@ccfc-ct.org Silliman Carolyn, Dir.;

CEMETERIES [CEM]

BRIDGEPORT

Fairfield County Catholic Cemeteries of the Diocese of Bridgeport LLC - 238 Jewett Ave., Bridgeport, CT 06606 t) (203) 742-1450 funerals@ctcemeteries.org

DANBURY

St. Peter's - 71 Lake Ave. Ext., Danbury, CT 06810 t) 203-743-9626 dean.gestal@ctcemeteries.org Dean Gestal, Exec. Dir.;

DARIEN

St. John's - 25 Camp Ave., Darien, CT 06820 t) 203-322-0455 dean.gestal@ctcemeteries.org Dean Gestal, Exec. Dir.;

GREENWICH

St. Mary's - 399 North St., Greenwich, CT 06830 t) 203-869-7026 dean.gestal@ctcemeteries.org Dean Gestal, Exec. Dir.;

Putnam - 35 Parsonage Rd., Greenwich, CT 06830; Mailing: 399 North Ave., Greenwich, CT 06830 t) 203-869-4828 dean.gestal@ctcemeteries.org Dean Gestal, Exec. Dir.;

NEWTOWN

Resurrection - 208 S. Main St., Newtown, CT 06470; Mailing: c/o Gate of Heaven Cemetery, 1056 Daniels Farm Rd., Trumbull, CT 06611 t) 203-268-5574 dean.gestal@ctcemeteries.org Dean Gestal, Exec. Dir.;

NORWALK

St. John's & St. Mary's - 223 Richards Ave., Norwalk, CT 06850 t) 203-838-4271 dean.gestal@ctcemeteries.org Dean Gestal, Exec. Dir.;

STAMFORD

Queen of Peace - 124 Rock Rimmon Rd., Stamford, CT 06903; Mailing: c/o St. John Cemetery, 25 Camp Ave., Darien, CT 06820 t) 203-322-0455 dean.gestal@diobpt.org Dean Gestal, Exec. Dir.;

STRATFORD

St. Michael's - 2205 Stratford Ave., Stratford, CT 06615 t) 203-378-0404 dean.gestal@ctcemeteries.org Dean Gestal, Exec. Dir.;

TRUMBULL

Gate of Heaven - 1056 Daniels Farms Rd., Trumbull, CT 06611 t) 203-416-1400 dean.gestal@ctcemetries.org Dean Gestal, Exec. Dir.;

WESTPORT

Assumption Green Farms - Greens Farms Rd., Westport, CT 06880; Mailing: c/o St. John Cemetery, 223 Richards Ave., Norwalk, CT 06850

COLLEGES & UNIVERSITIES [COL]

FAIRFIELD

***Fairfield University** - 1073 N. Benson Rd., Fairfield, CT 06824 t) 203-254-4000 www.fairfield.edu (Coed) Mark Nemec, Pres.;

***Sacred Heart University** - 5151 Park Ave., Fairfield, CT 06825-1000 t) 203-371-7901 www.sacredheart.edu John Petillo, Pres.;

St. Vincent's College - 2800 Main St., Bridgeport, CT 06606 t) 203-576-5578

CONVENTS, MONASTERIES, AND RESIDENCES FOR WOMEN [CON]

BRIDGEPORT

Convent of Mary Immaculate, Missionary Sisters of the Blessed Sacrament and Mary Immaculate. - 1111 Wordin Ave., Bridgeport, CT 06605 t) 203-334-5681 januariab@gmail.com Prov. Headquarters. Assisting the Apostolate to Spanish-Speaking People. Sr. Januaria Beleno, Prioress;

Daughters of Charity of the Most Precious Blood Convent - 1482 North Ave., Bridgeport, CT 06604 t) 203-334-7000 www.dcmpb.org Sr. Sheeba Thomas, Supr.;

Institute Servants of the Lord and the Virgin of Matara - 153 Linden Ave., Bridgeport, CT 06604-5730 t) 203-330-8409 c.damaris@servidoras.org www.servidoras.org Sr. Maria in Inatzin Moreno, S.S.V.M., Supr.;

Lovers of the Holy Cross of Govap Bridgeport - 50 Pequonnock St., Bridgeport, CT 06604 t) 203-331-1745 maryvanvu.mtg@gmail.com Sr. Mary Van Vu, L.H.C., Supr.;

Missionaries of Charity - 599 Beechwood Ave., Bridgeport, CT 06604 t) 203-336-5626 Sr. M. Regis Devasia, M.C., Contact;

DARIEN

Convent of St. Birgitta - 4 Rukenhage Rd., Darien, CT 06820 t) 203-655-1068 conventsb@optonline.net www.birgittines-us.com Lilly Sebastian, Contact;

FAIRFIELD

Provincial House, Congregation De Notre Dame, Blessed Sacrament Province, Inc. - Sacred Heart University, 3135 Easton Tpke., Fairfield, CT 06825 t) 203-365-4309 pells@cnd-m.org; sdwan@cnd-m.org Sr. Mary Anne Foley, CND, Rel. Ord. Ldr.; Srs.: 87

MONROE

Dominican Sisters of Our Lady of the Springs of Bridgeport - 124 Bug Hill Rd., Monroe, CT 06468 t) 203-880-4455 Sr. Mary Elizabeth Donoghue, O.P., Prioress;

Sisters of the Holy Family of Nazareth, C.S.F.N. - 1430 Monroe Tpke., Monroe, CT 06468 t) 203-268-6540 dancenyc9@aol.com www.nazarethcsfn.org Sr. Marita Ruppe, CSFN, Supr.; Srs.: 17

NORWALK

Regional House of Sisters of St. Thomas of Villanova - 76 W. Rocks Rd., Norwalk, CT 06851 t) 203-847-2885 sstv_usa@sbcglobal.net www.congregation-stv.org Mother Marie-Therese Lebret, SSTV, Supr.; Sr. Marie-Lucie Monast, SSTV, Vice. Pres.;

STAMFORD

The Bernardine Sisters of the Third Order of St. Francis of Stamford, CT, Inc. Heart of Mary Convent - 163 Sky Meadow Dr., Stamford, CT 06903-3400 t) 203-322-5920 clarechabot8@gmail.com See Schools Section for related schools. Bernardine Franciscan Sisters Sr. Clare Chabot, OSF, Local Minister; Srs.: 3

Villa Maria Education Center, Inc. - 161 Sky Meadow Dr., Stamford, CT 06903 t) 203-322-5886 x100 wdehaven@villamariaschool.org; ebrody@villamariaschool.org www.villamariaschool.org School for children with learning disabilities (Grades K-9). William De Haven, Head of School; Stds.: 52; Lay Tchrs.: 25

Franciscan Sisters of the Immaculate Heart of Mary - 1216 Shippan Ave., Stamford, CT 06902-7425 t) 203-569-0310 fihmstamford@yahoo.com Sr. Balakumari Tiromala Reddy, F.I.H.M., Supr.;

Our Lady of Grace Convent - 635 Glenbrook Rd., Stamford, CT 06906 t) 203-348-5531 sgesuina@aol.com littleworkerposc@aol.com Motherhouse and Novitiate of Little Workers of Sacred Hearts. Sr. Gesuina Gencarelli, P.O.S.C., Supr.;

Sisters of Life, Villa Maria Guadalupe - 159 Skymeadow Dr., Stamford, CT 06903 t) 203-329-1492 vmg@sistersoflife.org Sr. Bernadette Therese Swan, S.V., Supr.; Srs.: 9

Sisters of the Company of the Savior - 914 Newfield Ave., Stamford, CT 06905 t) 203-368-1875 c) 203-997-5421 stamford@ciasalvador.org www.ciasalvador.org Sr. Maria Alguacil, C.S., Supr.; Srs.: 106

Villa Divino Amore Convent, Little Workers of the Sacred Hearts of Jesus & Mary - 117 Hope St., Stamford, CT 06906 t) 203-324-2449 sisterenrica@aol.com Sr. Enrica Capalbo, P.O.S.C., Supr.;

WILTON

Lourdes Health Care Center, Inc. - 345 Belden Hill Rd., Wilton, CT 06897-3898 t) 203-762-3318 adm@lourdeswilton.org Sr. Charmaine Krohe, S.S.N.D., Prov.;

School Sisters of Notre Dame - 345 Belden Hill Rd., Wilton, CT 06897 t) 203-762-3318 ckrohe@amssnd.org www.ssnd.org Sr. Charmaine Krohe, S.S.N.D., Prov.;

ENDOWMENTS / FOUNDATIONS / TRUSTS [EFT]

BRIDGEPORT

The Diocesan Cemetery Care Fund, Inc. - 238 Jewett Ave., Bridgeport, CT 06606 t) 203-416-1491

Fairfield Foundation of the Diocese of Bridgeport, Inc. - 238 Jewett Ave., Bridgeport, CT 06606-2892 t) 203-372-4301

Foundations in Charity Inc. - 238 Jewett Ave., Bridgeport, CT 06606

Foundations in Education Inc. - 238 Jewett Ave., Bridgeport, CT 06606 t) 203-416-1472

Foundations in Faith Inc. - 238 Jewett Ave., Bridgeport, CT 06606

Inner-City Foundation For Charity & Education - 238 Jewett Ave., Bridgeport, CT 06606-2892 t) 203-416-1363 innercity.foundation@snet.net www.innercityfoundation.org Karen Barry Schwarz, Exec.;

St. Vincent's Development Corporation - 2800 Main St., Bridgeport, CT 06606 t) 203-576-6000 william.hoey@hhchealth.org www.stvincents.org Tracy Church, CEO;

St. Vincent's Medical Center Foundation - 2800 Main St., Bridgeport, CT 06606; Mailing: 4600 Edmundson Rd., St. Louis, MO 63134 t) 314-733-8000 craig.cordola@ascension.org Craig Cordola, Exec.;

We Stand With Christ Inc. - 238 Jewett Ave., Bridgeport, CT 06606

STAMFORD

***The Christopher Mueller Foundation for Polyphony & Chant** - 566 Elm St., Stamford, CT 06902

HOSPITALS / HEALTH SERVICES [HOS]

BRIDGEPORT

St. Vincent's Health Services Corporation - 2800 Main St., Bridgeport, CT 06606; Mailing: 4600 Edmundson Rd., St. Louis, MO 63134 t) 475-210-5455 william.hoey@hhchealth.org www.stvincents.org William Jennings, Pres.;

St. Vincent's Medical Center (Ascension Healthcare St. Louis, MO) - 2800 Main St., Bridgeport, CT 06606; Mailing: 4600 Edmundson Rd., St. Louis, MO 63146 t) 314-733-8000 www.ascension.org Craig Cordola, Exec. Vice Pres. & COO; Thomas VanOsdol, Exec. Vice Pres. & Chief Mission Integration Officer;

STAMFORD

St. Camillus Health Center - 494 Elm St., Stamford, CT 06902 t) 203-325-0200 www.stcamillushealth.org Rev. Matthew R. Mauriello, Chap.;

MISCELLANEOUS [MIS]

BRIDGEPORT

St. Ambrose Corporation - 238 Jewett Ave., Bridgeport, CT 06606

Cardinal Shehan Center, Inc. - 1494 Main St., Bridgeport, CT 06604 t) 203-336-4468 lgibbons@shehancenter.org shehancenter.org

Caroline House, Inc. - 574 Stillman St., Bridgeport, CT 06608 t) 203-334-0640 info@thecarolinehouse.org thecarolinehouse.org Lucy Freeman, Exec.; Christine Matthews Paine, Dir.;

Saint Charles Brazilian Children - 238 Jewett Ave., Bridgeport, CT 06606 t) 203-405-1385 josephbi@charter.net Rev. Thomas P. Thorne, Contact;

Holy Rosary, LLC - 238 Jewett Ave., Bridgeport, CT 06606

Marian Work Study Corporation - 33 Calhoun Pl., Bridgeport, CT 06604

***McGivney Community Center, Inc.** - 338 Stillman St., Bridgeport, CT 06608; Mailing: P.O. Box 5220, Bridgeport, CT 06610-0220 t) 203-333-2789 lgibbons@mcgivney.org www.mcgivney.org Lorraine Gibbons, Exec. Dir.;

St. Raphael, LLC - 238 Jewett Ave., Bridgeport, CT 06606

The Seton Collaborative Corporation - 238 Jewett Ave., Bridgeport, CT 06606

DANBURY

Magnificat Bridgeport Diocese CT, Inc. - 6 W. Pine Dr., Danbury, CT 06811-4316 t) 203-744-1856 magnificatbpt@sbcglobal.net www.triumphantheart.org (Triumphant Heart of Mary Immaculate)

FAIRFIELD

St. Catherine Center for Special Needs Inc. - 760 Tahmore Dr., Fairfield, CT 06825 t) 203-540-5381 hburland@diobpt.org; lgrozier@stcatherineacademy.org www.stcatherinecenter.org Helen Burland, Dir.;

GREENWICH

Clemons Productions, Inc. - ; Mailing: P.O. Box 7466, Greenwich, CT 06836 t) 203-316-9394 clemons10@aol.com www.spirituality.org (In association with That's The Spirit Productions, Inc.)

Radio Program: Thoughts for the Week - Spirituality For Today -

***Walking with Purpose, Inc.** - 15 E. Putnam Ave., Greenwich, CT 06830

NEW CANAAN

MyCatholicDoctor Foundation Inc. - 711 Silvermine Rd., New Canaan, CT 06840 t) 314-435-6105 kathleen@mycatholicdoctor.com www.mycatholicdoctor.com Making Catholic Healthcare accessible through telehealth and other means Kathleen Berchelmann, Contact;

Our Lady's Pilgrimage Inc. - 492 Cheese Spring Rd., New Canaan, CT 06840 t) 203-822-3377 info@ourladyspilgrimage.org www.ourladyspilgrimage.org Elizabeth Tamarkin, Contact;

NORWALK

Malta House, Inc. - 139 W. Rocks Rd., Norwalk, CT 06851 t) 203-857-0088 cdougherty@maltahouse.org www.maltahouse.org Carrie Dougherty, Exec. Dir.;

RIDGEFIELD

Veritas Catholic Network Inc. - 55 Catoonah St., Ridgefield, CT 06877; Mailing: P.O. Box 861, Georgetown, CT 06877 t) 475-215-5547 syl@veritascatholic.com www.veritascatholic.com Steve Lee, Contact;

RIVERSIDE

The Mother Teresa of Calcutta Center - ; Mailing: P.O. Box 455, Riverside, CT 06878 t) 203-637-7578 tleogallagher@aol.com

STAMFORD

Haitian American Catholic Center - 93 Hope St., Stamford, CT 06906 t) 203-406-0343 Rev. Jean-Rony Philippe;

***Hard as Nails Ministries, Inc.** - 894 Newfield Ave., Stamford, CT 06905 t) (888) 498-2255 (Ask for Justin Fatica) www.amazingnation.org Private Association of the Faithful Justin Fatica, Exec. Dir.;

***Religious Institute Company of the Savior USA Inc.** - 914 Newfield Ave., Stamford, CT 06905 t) 203-368-1875 c) 203-997-5421 stamford@ciasalvador.org; mater.usa@ciasalvador.org Sr. Maria Alguacil, C.S., Pres.;

TRUMBULL

Courage International, Inc. - 6450 Main St., Trumbull, CT 06611 t) 203-803-1564 office@couragerc.org www.couragerc.org Rev. Philip G. Bochanski, Exec. Dir.; Rev. Colin Blatchford;

MONASTERIES AND RESIDENCES FOR PRIESTS AND BROTHERS [MON]

BRIDGEPORT

Instituto Verbo Encarnado - 443 Park Ave., Bridgeport, CT 06604-5493 t) 203-335-1797 st_george_church@sbcglobal.net

FAIRFIELD

The Fairfield Jesuit Community-Fairfield University - 1073 N. Benson Rd., Fairfield, CT 06824-5195 t) (203) 259-7805 jmulreany@fairfield.edu Rev. John P. Mulreany, Supr.; Rev. Denis G. Donoghue, S.J., Dir., Murphy Center For Ignatian Spirituality; Rev. Thomas J. Fitzpatrick, S.J., Spiritual Dir.; Rev. Gregory N.P. Konz, S.J., Prof.; Rev. Ronald V. Perry, Chap.; Rev. Gerald R. Blaszcak, S.J., Special Asst., Pres. & Alumni Chap.; Rev. Michael J. Doody, S.J., Special Asst., Dean of Students; Rev. Brian G. Konzman, Vice Pres. Instl. Plng. & Research, Fairfield Prep; Rev. Keith A. Maczkiewicz, Dir. Campus Min.; Univ. Chap.; Rev. John P. Murray, S.J., Spiritual Dir.; Prof. of Relg. Studies; Rev. Kevin F. O'Brien, Dean & Exec. Dir. Bellarmine Campus, Fairfield Univ.; Rev. Paul K. Rourke, S.J., Vice Pres., Mission & Min.; Rev. John D. Savard, Special Asst., Dean of School of Educ.; Asst. Dir. Murphy Ctr.; Rev. Joseph J. Schad, S.J., Hospital Chap.; Bro. Jonathan J. Stott, Prof.; Brs.: 1; Priests: 14

STAMFORD

The Catherine Dennis Keefe Queen of the Clergy Retired Priests' Residence - 274 Strawberry Hill Ave., Stamford, CT 06902 t) 203-358-9906 pleydon@diobpt.org Rev. Michael J. Bachman; Rev. James E. Breen; Rev. Msgr. Laurence R. Bronkiewicz; Rev. William G. Carey; Rev. Msgr. Robert J. Crofut; Rev. Msgr. J. Peter Cullen; Rev. Gerard Frantz Desruisseaux; Rev. Msgr. Alan F. Detscher; Rev. Gilbert P. D'Souza; Rev. Martin S. Igoe; Rev. John Paul Long; Rev. Guido G. Montanaro; Rev. Michael C. Palmer; Rev. Msgr. Joseph W. Pekar; Rev. Robert J. Post; Rev. Bruce Roby; Rev. Msgr. John B. Sabia; Rev. Msgr. William J. Scheyd; Rev. Bose Raja Selvaraj; Rev. Msgr. Edward R. Surwilo; Rev. Donald A. Turlick; Rev. James Vattakunnel; Rev. Msgr. Aniceto Villamide;

NURSING / REHABILITATION / CONVALESCENCE / ELDERLY CARE [NUR]

BETHEL

Augustana Homes Inc./Augustana Homes Bethel Congregate (Bishop Curtis Homes - Congregate) - 101 Simeon Rd., Bethel, CT 06801 t) 203-790-9744 caroline.robinson@diobpt.org www.augustanacongregate.org Caroline Robinson, Property Mgr.; Patricia Neves, Asst. Property Mgr.; Asstd. Annu.: 44; Staff: 3

NORWALK

Notre Dame Convalescent Home, Inc. (Notre Dame Health & Rehabilitation Center) - 76 W. Rocks Rd., Norwalk, CT 06851 t) 203-847-5893 srmlmonast@ndhrehab.org; sstv_usa@sbcglobal.net www.ndhrehab.org Own and operated by the Sisters of Saint Thomas of Villanova. Mother Marie-Therese Lebret, SSTV, Supr.; Asstd. Annu.: 60; Staff: 56

TRUMBULL

Carmel Ridge - 6454 Main St., Trumbull, CT 06611 t) 203-261-2229 jennifer.lawler@diobpt.org

Teresian Towers - 6454 Main St., Trumbull, CT 06611 t) 203-261-2229 jennifer.lawler@diobpt.org

PRESCHOOLS / CHILDCARE CENTERS [PRE]

BRIDGEPORT

Daughters of Charity of the Most Precious Blood Day Nursery - 1490 North Ave., Bridgeport, CT 06604 t) 203-334-7000 daughtersofcharity@yahoo.com Sr. Rosamma Joseph Sr., Dir.;

STAMFORD

Our Lady of Grace Preschool & Kindergarten - 635 Glenbrook Rd., Stamford, CT 06906 t) 203-348-5531 sgesuina@aol.com; littleworkerposc@aol.com ourladyofgraceschool.net Owned and operated by the Little Workers of the Sacred Hearts - a pontifical congregation. Sr. Gesuina Gencarelli, P.O.S.C., Supr.;

RETREAT HOUSES / RENEWAL CENTERS [RTR]

BRIDGEPORT

Queen of Saints, The Catholic Center - 238 Jewett Ave., Bridgeport, CT 06606 t) 203-416-1403 Retreat Facility

The Urban Center of St. Charles Parish - 1279 E. Main St., Bridgeport, CT 06608 t) 203-333-2147

St. Charles Outreach Program -

DANBURY

Seton Neumann Religious Education Center (Retreat Center) - 71 Southern Blvd., Danbury, CT 06810

DARIEN

Convent of St. Birgitta - 4 Runkenhage Rd., Darien, CT 06820 t) 203-655-1068 conventsb@optonline.net www.birgittines-us.com Sr. M. Eunice Kulangrathottyil, O.SS.S., Supr.;

MONROE

Marian Heights Convent - 1428 Monroe Tpke., Monroe, CT 06468 t) 203-268-6540 www.nazarethcsfn.org Sisters of the Holy Family of Nazareth

STAMFORD

Villa Maria Guadalupe, Sisters of Life - 159 Sky Meadow Dr., Stamford, CT 06903 t) 203-329-1492 retreatregistrations@sistersoflife.org sistersoflife.org Owned by Knights of Columbus, operated by Sisters of Life Sr. Bernadette Therese Swan, S.V., Supr.;

SEMINARIES [SEM]

STAMFORD

Redemptorist Mater Diocesan Missionary Seminary Diocese of Bridgeport Inc. - 894 Newfield Ave., Stamford, CT 06905 t) 203-588-1785 seminary@rmbridgeport.org www.rmbridgeport.org Rev. Zbigniew Kukielka, Rector;

SHRINES [SHR]

BRIDGEPORT

Shrine of Saint Margaret - 2523 Park Ave., Bridgeport, CT 06604 t) 203-333-9627 saintmargaretshrine@gmail.com stmargaretshrine.org Rev. Peter F. Lenox, Rector; Dcn. Donald P. Foust, Admin.;

SPECIAL CARE FACILITIES [SPF]

TRUMBULL

St. Vincent's Special Needs Center, Inc. - 95 Merritt Blvd., Trumbull, CT 06611 t) 203-375-6400 tracy.church@hhchealth.org www.stvincentsspecialneed.org Tracy Church, CEO;

Diocese of Brooklyn

(Dioecesis Bruklyniensis)

MOST REVEREND ROBERT J. BRENNAN

Eighth Bishop of Brooklyn; ordained May 27, 1989; appointed Titular Bishop of Erdonia and Auxiliary Bishop of Rockville Centre June 8, 2012; consecrated July 25, 2012; appointed Bishop of Columbus January 31, 2019; installed March 29, 2019; appointed Bishop of Brooklyn September 29, 2021; installed November 30, 2021. Office: 310 Prospect Park West, Brooklyn, NY 11215.

Chancery Office: 310 Prospect Park W., Brooklyn, NY 11215. T: 718-399-5990; F: 718-399-5934. curia@diobrook.org

ESTABLISHED JULY 29, 1853.

Square Miles 179.

Comprises Kings and Queens Counties in the State of New York.

Legal Title: The Roman Catholic Diocese of Brooklyn, New York.

For legal titles of parishes and diocesan institutions, consult the Chancery Office.

MOST REVEREND WITOLD MROZIEWSKI, D.D.
Auxiliary Bishop of Brooklyn; ordained June 29, 1991; appointed Auxiliary Bishop of Brooklyn and Titular Bishop of Walla Walla May 19, 2015; installed July 20, 2015. Office: 310 Prospect Park West, Brooklyn, NY 11215. Res.: Holy Cross, 61-21 56 Rd., Maspeth, NY 11378.

MOST REVEREND JAMES MASSA, D.D., V.E.
Auxiliary Bishop of Brooklyn; ordained October 25, 1986; appointed Auxiliary Bishop of Brooklyn and Titular Bishop of Bardstown May 19, 2015; installed July 20, 2015. Office: 201 Seminary Ave., Yonkers, NY 10704.

MOST REVEREND NEIL E. TIEDEMANN, C.P.
Auxiliary Bishop of Brooklyn; ordained May 16, 1975; appointed Bishop of Mandeville, Jamaica May 20, 2008; installed August 6, 2008; appointed Titular Bishop of Cova and Auxiliary Bishop of Brooklyn April 29, 2016. Mailing Address: St. Matthias, 58-15 Catalpa Ave., Ridgewood, NY 11385.

STATISTICAL OVERVIEW

Personnel

Bishop	1
Auxiliary Bishops	3
Retired Bishops	4
Priests: Diocesan Active in Diocese	233
Priests: Diocesan Active Outside Diocese	21
Priests: Retired, Sick or Absent	181
Number of Diocesan Priests	435
Religious Priests in Diocese	147
Total Priests in your Diocese	582
Extern Priests in Diocese	70
Ordinations:	
Diocesan Priests	3
Permanent Deacons in Diocese	208
Total Brothers	73
Total Sisters	539

Parishes

Parishes	176
With Resident Pastor:	
Resident Diocesan Priests	145
Resident Religious Priests	21
Without Resident Pastor:	
Administered by Priests	10
Missions	1

Professional Ministry Personnel:	
Brothers	11
Sisters	178
Lay Ministers	43

Welfare

Homes for the Aged	2
Total Assisted	525
Day Care Centers	15
Total Assisted	2,147
Specialized Homes	7
Total Assisted	16,237
Special Centers for Social Services	25
Total Assisted	497,862

Educational

Seminaries, Diocesan	1
Students from This Diocese	8
Students from Other Dioceses	16
Diocesan Students in Other Seminaries	34
Total Seminarians	42
Colleges and Universities	3
Total Students	23,371
High Schools, Diocesan and Parish	3
Total Students	860
High Schools, Private	12
Total Students	10,251
Elementary Schools, Diocesan and Parish	69
Total Students	18,731
Catechesis/Religious Education:	
High School Students	3,010
Elementary Students	21,419
Total Students under Catholic Instruction	77,684
Teachers in Diocese:	
Lay Teachers	1,604

Vital Statistics

Receptions into the Church:	
Infant Baptism Totals	9,768
Minor Baptism Totals	518
Adult Baptism Totals	375
Received into Full Communion	263
First Communions	6,149
Confirmations	7,188
Marriages:	
Catholic	1,553
Interfaith	132
Total Marriages	1,685
Deaths	6,964
Total Catholic Population	1,319,663
Total Population	4,972,195

LEADERSHIP

Bishop Emeritus - Most Rev. Nicholas A. DiMarzio, Bishop Emeritus;
Bishop of Brooklyn - t) (718) 399-5970 Most Rev. Robert J Brennan, Bishop;
Vicar General - t) 718-399-5995 Rev. Msgr. Joseph R. Grimaldi;
Diocesan Bishop - Most Rev. Robert J Brennan;
Moderator of the Curia - Very Rev. Patrick J. Keating;
Auxiliary Bishops of Brooklyn - Most Rev. James Massa; Most Rev. Witold Mroziewski; Most Rev. Neil E. Tiedemann, C.P.;
Retired Auxiliary Bishop of Brooklyn - Most Rev. Nicholas A. DiMarzio, Bishop Emeritus; Most Rev. Raymond F. Chappetto; Most Rev. Octavio Cisneros;
Vicar for Financial Administration/Econome - t) 718-965-7300 x1060 Very Rev. Patrick J. Keating, Vicar;
Episcopal Vicars-Territorial - t) (718) 965-7300 x1071 (Queens); (718) 965-7300 x1072 (Brooklyn); (718) 399-5959 (Main Office) queensvicariate@diobrook.org; brooklynvicariate@diobrook.org Most Rev. Witold Mroziewski, Episcopal Vicar for Queens; Most Rev. Neil E. Tiedemann, C.P., Episcopal Vicar for Brooklyn;
Vicar for West Indian, Caribbean, and American Black Catholics - Most Rev. Neil E. Tiedemann, C.P., Vicar;
Vicar for Canonical Affairs - Rev. Msgr. Steven J. Aguggia, Vicar; Rev. Robert V. Mucci, Assoc. Vicar;
Secretariat for Development - t) 718-965-7300 Rev. Msgr. Jamie J. Gigantiello, Vicar;
Human Resources Office - t) 718-965-7300 Diana Veloza, Chief Human Resources Officer;
Spiritual Director of the Cathedral Preparatory Seminary - t) (718) 592-6800 cbethge@cathedrdalprep.org www.cathedralprep.org/ Rev. Christopher J. Bethge, Spiritual Formator;
Vicar for Clergy, Consecrated Life and Apostolic Organizations - t) 718-399-5995 Rev. Msgr. Sean G. Ogle;
Special Assistant to Vicar for Clergy - t) 718-326-2185 Rev. Msgr. Edward P. Doran;
Vicar for Catholic Schools - t) 718-965-7300 Rev. Msgr. David L. Cassato;
Protection of Children and Young People, Office for the - t) (718) 281-9670 Maryellen Quinn, Dir.;
Victim Assistance Ministry, Office of - t) 718-623-5236 Elizabeth Harris, Coord.;
Safe Environment, Office of - t) (718) 281-9670 Maryellen Quinn, Coord.;
Vicar for Hispanic Concerns - t) 718-281-9677 Most Rev. Octavio Cisneros;
Vicar for Human Services - t) 718-722-6000 Rev. Msgr. Alfred P. LoPinto, Vicar; Very Rev. Patrick J. Keating, Assoc. Vicar;
Vicar for Migrant and Ethnic Apostolates - t) 718-894-1387 wmroziewski@diobrook.org Most Rev. Witold Mroziewski, Vicar;
Vicar for Ecumenical and Interreligious Affairs - c) (415) 238-7427 mlynch@diobrook.org Very Rev. Michael J. Lynch;
Finance Officer - Very Rev. Patrick J. Keating, Econome (Diocesan Finance Officer); John J. Borgia, Treas.; Martin J. McManus, Comptroller;
General Counsel - t) 718-965-7300 Very Rev. Patrick J. Keating;
Parish Services Corp. - t) 718-965-7300 Rev. Msgr. David L. Cassato, Pres.; John J. Borgia, Vice Pres.; Martin J. McManus, Treas.;
Peter Turner Insurance Co. - John J. Borgia, Exec.; Martin J. McManus, Treas.; Brian T. Cosgrove, Secy.;
Rocklyn Asset Corp. - Coleen A. Ceriello, Exec.; Robert N. Dadona, Dir.; Greg Roach, Dir.;
Chancery Office - t) 718-399-5990 Rev. Msgr. Steven J. Aguggia, Chancellor; Rev. Robert V. Mucci, Vice Chancellor; Rev. Peter J. Purpura, Vice Chancellor;
Assistant to the Bishop - t) 718-399-5970 Dcn. Jaime Varela;
Censors of Books - Rev. John P. Cush; Rev. Msgr. John J. Strynkowski; Rev. Michael J. S. Bruno;
Diocesan Archivist - t) 718-965-7300 Joseph W. Coen;
Tribunal - t) 718-229-8131
Defenders of the Marriage Bond - Rev. Msgr. William M. Hoppe; Rev. Msgr. Joseph C. Mulqueen; Rev. Msgr. Robert J. Sarno;
Diocesan Judges - Rev. Msgr. Jonas Achacoso; Rev. Msgr. Steven J. Aguggia; Very Rev. Francis Kwame Asagba;
Officialis-Judicial Vicar - Very Rev. Francis Kwame Asagba;
Promoters of Justice - Most Rev. Witold Mroziewski; Rev. Msgr. William M. Hoppe;
Attorneys and Counselors at Canon Law - Rev. Msgr. Anthony Hernandez; Rev. Msgr. Steven J. Aguggia; Rev. Msgr. Jonas Achacoso;
Auditor - Dcn. Marco V. Lopez;
Notaries - Aida Jorge; Lizbeth Ugarte; Nora Ugarte;
Religious, Episcopal Delegate for - t) 718-399-5951 Sr. Maryann Seton Lopiccolo, S.C.;
Cemeteries - t) (718) 894-4888 mjr@ccbklyn.org; en@ccbklyn.org www.ccbklyn.org Rev. Msgr. Michael J. Reid, CEO; Edward DuPre, CFO; Elaine Nicodemo, COO;
Education, Offices -
Mediation and Arbitration, Board of - Rev. Msgr. Steven J. Aguggia, Exec. Sec.;
Office of Priestly Life & Ministry - t) 718-886-0201 jfonti@diobrook.org Rev. Joseph G. Fonti, Dir.;
Ministerial Development Program - t) 718-886-0201 Rev. Joseph G. Fonti;
Newspaper "The Tablet" - t) 718-499-9705 Jim DelCioppo, Editor;
Office for Clergy Personnel - t) 718-399-5941 Dcn. Julio C. Barreneche;
Assignment Board - Most Rev. Robert J Brennan; Most Rev. Witold Mroziewski; Most Rev. Neil E. Tiedemann, C.P.;
Pontifical Mission Societies - t) 718-965-7300 tahern@diobrook.org Rev. Thomas W. Ahern, Dir.;
Retirement Board (Priests) - Rev. Msgr. Sean G. Ogle;
Vocations, Office of - t) 718-827-2454 vocations@diobrook.org; cbethge@cathedralprep.org Rev. Christopher J. Bethge;

CONSULTATIVE BODIES

Diocesan Budget Committee - Very Rev. Patrick J. Keating; John J. Borgia; Martin J. McManus;
Diocesan College of Consultors - Most Rev. Robert J Brennan; Rev. Msgr. Joseph R. Grimaldi; Very Rev. Patrick J. Keating, Exec. Sec.;
Diocesan Diaconal Council - Most Rev. Robert J Brennan; Dcn. John R. Sucich; Dcn. Christopher A. Wagner;
Diocesan Finance Council - Most Rev. Robert J Brennan; Rev. Msgr. Joseph R. Grimaldi; Very Rev. Patrick J. Keating, Econome;
Diocesan Pastoral Council - t) (718) 281-9544 jgibino@diobrook.org Most Rev. Robert J Brennan, Pres.; Very Rev. Joseph R. Gibino, Co-Chair; Sr. Maryann Seton Lopiccolo, S.C., Co-Chair;
Presbyteral Council - Most Rev. Robert J Brennan; Rev. Msgr. Joseph R. Grimaldi; Very Rev. Patrick J. Keating;

ORGANIZATIONS

Apostleship of Prayer -
Charismatic Groups, Catholic -
Charismatic Renewal (English-speaking) of the Diocese of Brooklyn - t) (917) 913-4104 Josephine Cachia, Dir.;
Renouveau Charismatique of the Diocese of Brooklyn - t) 718-469-5900 Rev. Msgr. Joseph P. Malagreca, Dir.;
Renovacion Carismatica of the Diocese of Brooklyn - t) 718-469-5900 Rev. Msgr. Joseph P. Malagreca, Dir.;
Confraternity of the Guard of Honor and Confraternity of the Holy Hour (Vacant) -
Confraternity of the Precious Blood - t) 718-436-1120 www.confraternitypb.org Rev. Thomas Doyle, Dir.; Dale Swenson, Mgr.;
Courage Ministry - Rev. Msgr. Thomas G. Caserta;
Guilds -
Accountant Guild - Nicole Steinweiss, Pres.; Very Rev. Patrick J. Keating, Moderator;
Catholic Cemetery Guild - Rev. Msgr. Michael J. Reid, Moderator;
Lawyers - Rev. Msgr. Steven J. Aguggia, Chap.; Very Rev. Patrick J. Keating, Chap.;
Physicians (Vacant) -
Teachers (Vacant) -
Holy Name Society (Vacant) -
Legion of Mary - t) 718-429-2333 Rev. Rodnev Lapommeray, Dir.; Dcn. Emmanuel Coty Jr., Spiritual Adv./Care Srvcs.;
Marriage Encounter - John Torio; Toni Torio;
National Council of Catholic Women - Rev. Jeffry T. Dillon; Maribeth Stewart, Pres.;
Nocturnal Adoration Society - Rev. John Maduri;
St. John's Priests Relief Society - t) (718) 347-3707 gregory2022@aol.com Rev. Edward M. Kachurka, Pres.; Rev. Josephjude C. Gannon, Treas.; Rev. Christopher J. Bethge, Recording Secy.;

PASTORAL SERVICES

Alcoholism Committee - Rev. Thomas M. Haggerty;
Art and Architecture Commission - t) 718-281-9612 acox@diobrook.org Rev. Alonzo Q. Cox, Exec. Secy.;
Catholic Charities - t) 718-722-6000 Very Rev. Patrick J. Keating, Deputy CEO, CFO; Rev. Msgr. Alfred P. LoPinto, CEO;
Catholic Migration and Refugee Office -
Catholic Migration Services, Inc. - t) 718-236-3000 Magdalena Barbosa, Dir.;
Chaplains and Uniformed Services, Official - Rev. Robert J. Romano, Chap.; Rev. Msgr. David L. Cassato, Chap.; Rev. Joseph M. Hoffman;
CYO (Catholic Youth Organization) - t) 718-281-9548 Keith Goldberg, Dir.;
Diaconate Formation Office - Dcn. Jorge Arturo Gonzalez, Dir. (jagonzalez@diobrook.org);
Diocesan Food Service - James Austin, Dir.;
Diocesan Liturgy Office - t) 718-281-9612 acox@diobrook.org; cdost@diobrook.org Rev. Alonzo Q. Cox; Christine Dost, Admin. Asst.;
Diocesan Real Estate Board and Building Commission - Rev. Msgr. Richard J. Ahlemeyer; Rev. Msgr. Edward P. Doran; Rev. William F. Krlis, Chair;
Ecumenical and Interreligious Affairs, Diocesan Commission for - Very Rev. Michael J. Lynch, Vicar;
Catholic Hindu/Buddhist Dialogue (Vacant) - mlynch@diobrook.org Very Rev. Michael Lynch, Contact;
Catholic Muslim Dialogue - mlynch@diobrook.org Very Rev. Michael Lynch, Chair; Rev. Msgr. Guy A. Massie, Contact;
Committee for Catholic-Jewish Relations - Rev. Msgr. Guy A. Massie;
Committee for Catholic-Protestant Relations - Rev. Msgr. John J. Strynkowski, Contact; Rev. John P. Cush, Contact;
Committee for Eastern Orthodox-Catholic Relations - Rev. Msgr. Steven J. Aguggia, Chair; Rev. Msgr. Thomas C. Machalski Jr., Contact;
Home School Association (Vacant) -
Liturgical Commission - t) (718) 281-9612 acox@diobrook.org; cdost@diobrook.org Rev. Alonzo Q. Cox, Exec. Secy.; Very Rev. Joseph R. Gibino; Rev. Msgr. Sean G. Ogle;
Music Commission - t) 718-281-9612 Rev. Alonzo Q. Cox, Exec. Secy.; Steven Vaughn, Dir.; Michael Fontana, Chair;
Office of Music Ministry - t) 718-281-9612
Pastoral Communications, Office of - t) 718-499-9705 Rev. Msgr. Sean G. Ogle;
Pilgrimage Office - t) 718-965-7313 pilgrimage@diobrook.org Very Rev. Joseph R. Gibino, Dir.;

Prison Ministries Office -

Hospital and Healthcare Chaplaincy Program -

Secretariat for Evangelization and Catechesis - t) 718-281-9544 cgeorgi@diobrook.org Rev. Joseph R. Gibino, Vicar (jgibino@diobrook.org);

Director of Adult Faith Formation and the Catechumenate - t) 718-965-7300 x2440 jroa@diobrook.org Joann Roa, Dir.;

Director of Children's Faith Formation and Catechesis - t) 718-965-7300 x5558 nelias@diobrook.org Nelsa I. Elias, Dir.;

Director of Marriage, Family and Respect Life Education - t) 718-965-7300 x5541 crada@diobrook.org Christian S. Rada, Dir.;

PARISHES, MISSIONS, AND CLERGY

STATE OF NEW YORK

ASTORIA

St. Francis of Assisi - 21-17 45 St., Astoria, NY 11105 t) 718-278-0259 (CRP); 718-728-7801 rjmpastor@sfaacademy.org Rev. Msgr. Ralph J. Maresca, Pst.; Rev. Peter Nguyen, C.S.J.B., Par. Vicar; Dcn. Saviour Hili; Dcn. Giovanni Messina; Dcn. Thomas J. Quinn; Dcn. Nicolino Scarlatto; Dcn. John R. Sucich; Sr. Francesca Mumbua Simon, DRE; CRP Stds.: 97

Immaculate Conception - 21-47 29th St., Astoria, NY 11105 t) 718-956-4494 (CRP); 718-728-1613 pastor@immacastoria.org www.immacastoria.org Rev. Msgr. Fernando A. Ferrarese, Pst.; Rev. Liju Augustine, C.M.I., Par. Vicar; Rev. James A. Hughes, Par. Vicar; Rev. William A. McLaughlin, Par. Vicar; Dcn. Francisco J. Hernandez; Dcn. Elkin D. Tamayo; Rev. Msgr. Vincent F. Fullam, In Res.; CRP Stds.: 115

Convent - 21-60 31st St., Long Island City, NY 11105

St. Joseph - 43-19 30th Ave., Astoria, NY 11103 t) 718-545-7338 (CRP); 718-278-1611 sjreled@gmail.com; rectory@stjosephlic.org Rev. Vincent G. Chirichella, Pst.; Rev. Alessandro Linardi, Par. Vicar; Rev. Jean Gerard LaGuerre, In Res.; Rev. William C. Farrugia, In Res.; Rev. Edward A. Cassar, In Res.; Dcn. Raul Ruiz; Silvia Rivera, DRE; CRP Stds.: 177

BAYSIDE

St. Josaphat - 34-32 210th St., Bayside, NY 11361 t) 718-229-1663 stjosaphats@aol.com stjosaphat-queens.org Rev. Stephen A. Saffron, Admin.; Rev. Martin R. Kull, Sr. Active Priest;

Our Lady of the Blessed Sacrament - 34-24 203rd St., Bayside, NY 11361 t) 718-225-6179 (CRP); 718-229-5929 frbob@olbs-queens.org; religioused@olbs-queens.org olbs-queens.org Rev. Robert J. Whelan, Pst.; Dcn. Ernesto A. Avallone; Dcn. William Molloy; Rev. Brian Carney, In Res.; Rev. Nathaniel Ajuluchukwu, In Res.; CRP Stds.: 135

St. Robert Bellarmine - 56-15 213th St., Bayside, NY 11364 t) 718-225-3181 (CRP); 718-229-6465 srb@nyc.rr.com Rev. Gabriel Lee, Pst.; Rev. Pil-koo Hwang, Par. Vicar; Rev. Godofredo Felicitas (Philippines), Par. Vicar; Rev. Msgr. Martin T. Geraghty; Dcn. Michael J. Brainerd; Sr. Colette Moon, DRE; CRP Stds.: 175

Sacred Heart of Jesus - 215-35 38th Ave., Bayside, NY 11361 t) 718-631-1307 (CRP); 718-428-2200 pastorsacredheartbayside@gmail.com Rev. Msgr. Thomas C. Machalski Jr., Pst.; Rev. Kieran Udeze, Par. Vicar; Dcn. John F. DeBiase; Georgette Lyons, DRE; CRP Stds.: 122

BELLE HARBOR

St. Francis de Sales - 129-16 Rockaway Beach Blvd., Belle Harbor, NY 11694 t) 718-945-6911 (CRP); 718-634-6464 101061@diobrook.org Rev. William F. Sweeney, Pst.; Rev. James K. Cunningham, Pst. Assoc.; Dcn. Armand C. D'Accordo; Dcn. Vincent M. LaGamba; Anne Marie Greene, DRE; CRP Stds.: 444

BELLEROSE

St. Gregory the Great - 242-20 88th Ave., Bellerose, NY 11426 t) 718-347-0525 (CRP); 718-347-3707 stgregoffice@aol.com Rev. Edward M. Kachurka, Pst.; Rev. Johnson Nedungadan, C.M. (India), Pst. Assoc.; Dcn. Arthur Cutter; Dcn. Robert J. Zeuner; Alison Morisi, DRE; CRP Stds.: 113

Convent - 88-19 Cross Island Pkwy., Bellerose, NY 11426

BROOKLYN

The Cathedral-Basilica of St. James - 250 Cathedral Pl., Brooklyn, NY 11201 t) 718-852-4002 Rev. Bryan D. Patterson, Rector; Dcn. Ronald Rizzuto, Bus. Mgr.;

Co-Cathedral of Saint Joseph – Saint Teresa of Avila - 856 Pacific St., Brooklyn, NY 11238 t) 718-638-1071 info@stjosephs-brooklyn.org Rev. Christopher R. Heanue, Rector; Rev. Israel Perez, Admin.; Rev. Pascal Louis, Par. Vicar; Most Rev. Nicholas DiMarzio, In Res.; Rev. Msgr. Sean G. Ogle, In Res.; Dcn. Manuel H. Quintana; Jessica A. Figueroa, DRE; CRP Stds.: 85

St. Agatha's - 702 48th St., Brooklyn, NY 11220 t) 718-436-1080 rectory@stagatha-brooklyn.org stagatha-brooklyn.org Rev. Lianjiang Peter Bai, Admin.; Rev. Rodnev Lapommeray, Admin.; Gizeth Vecchio, DRE; CRP Stds.: 203

All Saints – Our Lady of the Rosary of Pompeii - 115 Throop Ave., Brooklyn, NY 11206-4415 t) 718-388-1951 allsaints11206@gmail.com Rev. Vincenzo Cardilicchia, Pst.; Rev. Romulo Marin, Par. Vicar; CRP Stds.: 140

Our Lady of Montserrat Chapel - 134 Vernon Ave., Brooklyn, NY 11206-4415

St. Andrew the Apostle - 6713 Ridge Blvd., Brooklyn, NY 11220 t) 718-836-4679 (CRP); 718-680-1010 standrewrc@gmail.com Ann Smyth, DRE; CRP Stds.: 151

St. Anselm - 356 82nd St., Brooklyn, NY 11209 t) 718-238-2900 stanselmrectory@aol.com www.stanselmbayridge.org Rev. Msgr. John W. Maloney, Pst.; Bro. Robert E. Duffy, O.S.F., RCIA Coord.; Dcn. Thomas G. Davis; Rev. Anthony Alimnonu, Par. Vicar; Rev. Msgr. Michael J. Phillips, Pastor Emer.; CRP Stds.: 75

St. Anthony-St. Alphonsus - 862 Manhattan Ave., Brooklyn, NY 11222 t) 718-383-6935 (CRP); 718-383-3339 ant862@aol.com Rev. George Kurian, CMI (india), Par. Vicar; Sebastian T Augustine, CMI, Admin.; Eugenia Calderon, DRE;

Holy Family - 21 Nassau Ave., Brooklyn, NY 11222 (Worship Site)

Assumption of the Blessed Virgin Mary - 64 Middagh St., Brooklyn, NY 11201 t) 718-625-1161 rectory@assumptionparishbrooklyn.org assumptionparishbrooklyn.org Rev. Michael J. Callaghan, C.O., Pst.; Rev. Mark Paul Amatrucola, C.O., Par. Vicar; Rev. Anthony Andreassi, C.O., Par. Vicar; Rev. Mark J. Lane, C.O., In Res.; Bro. James Simon, C.O., In Res.; Rev. Dennis M. Corrado, C.O.; CRP Stds.: 37

Saint Athanasius - Saint Dominic - 2154 61st St., Brooklyn, NY 11204 t) 718-331-8811 (CRP); 718-236-0124 stathanasiusny@hotmail.com stathanasius-stdominic-brooklyn.org Italian Language Mass and ministry Very Rev. Michael Lynch, Pst.; Rev. Ronald M. D'Antonio, Par. Vicar; Rev. Edwin A Ortiz, Par. Vicar; Rev. Martin Restreppo, Par. Vicar; Dcn. Anthony Mammoliti; Dcn. William V. Kelly; Dcn. Jaime A. Cobham; Maria Luna, DRE; CRP Stds.: 456

Convent - 2201 62nd St., Brooklyn, NY 11204 t) 718-236-2680

St. Augustine - 116 Sixth Ave., Brooklyn, NY 11217 t) 718-783-3132 staugustinerc@verizon.net Rev. John Gribowich, Pst.; Dcn. Dean Dobbins; CRP Stds.: 80

St. Barbara - 138 Bleecker St., Brooklyn, NY 11221 t) 718-453-1406 (CRP); 718-458-3660 101022@diobrook.org Rev. Joseph M. Hoffman, Pst.; Marcos Mota, DRE; CRP Stds.: 265

St. Bernadette - 8201 13th Ave., Brooklyn, NY 11228 t) 718-232-7733 (CRP); 718-837-3400 aquin79@aol.com Rev. Msgr. Thomas G. Caserta, Pst.; Rev. Juan Luxama, Par. Vicar; Dcn. Anthony P. Martucci; Dcn. Frank DeMichele; CRP Stds.: 47

St. Bernard of Clairvaux - 2055 E. 69th St., Brooklyn, NY 11234 t) 718-444-4674 (CRP); 718-763-5533 sbchurchbrooklyn@aol.com Rev. Msgr. Joseph R. Grimaldi, Pst.; Rev. Michael G. Tedone, Par. Vicar; Dcn. Frank J. D'Accordo; Dcn. Christopher A. Wagner; Melissa Wagner, DRE; CRP Stds.: 170

Blessed Sacrament - Saint Sylvester - 198 Euclid Ave., Brooklyn, NY 11208 t) 718-277-3231 (CRP); 718-827-1200 receptionbsbk@gmail.com Rev. Luis F. Laverde, Pst.; Rev. Juan Angel Pichardo, Par. Vicar; Rev. Jorge Mario Vallejo, Par. Vicar; Rev. Felino Reyes, Par. Vicar; Dcn. Rafael Cabrera; Dcn. Carlos R. Pichardo; Sr. Maria Amador, P.C.M., DRE;

St. Boniface - 109 Willoughby St., Brooklyn, NY 11201 t) 718-875-2096 101034@diobrook.org Rev. Mark J. Lane, C.O., Pst.; Christina Matone, DRE; CRP Stds.: 51

St. Brendan - 1525 E. 12th St., Brooklyn, NY 11230 t) 718-377-6932 (CRP); 718-339-2828 stbrendanbklyn@aol.com Rev. Peter D. Gillen, Pst.; Rev. Schned Bruno, Par. Vicar; Dcn. Robert J. Cosgrove; Dcn. Francisco Gonzalez; Carmina DeLaRosa, DRE; CRP Stds.: 112

Convent - 1526 E. 13th St., Brooklyn, NY 11230 t) 718-998-2032

St. Brigid - 409 Linden St., Brooklyn, NY 11237 t) 718-821-6401 (CRP); 718-821-1690 stbrigidinfo@gmail.com Rev. Carlos C Velasquez, Pst.; Rev. Joseph F. Dutan, Par. Vicar; Rev. Msgr. James J. Kelly; Soraida Puente, DRE; CRP Stds.: 610

St. Brigid School - 438 Grove St. E., Brooklyn, NY 11237 t) 718-821-1477

St. Catharine of Alexandria - 1119 41st St., Brooklyn, NY 11218 t) 718-436-2471 (CRP); 718-436-5917 jorellana@diobrook.org Rev. Jose Orellana, Admin.; Rev. Dariusz Strzelecki, Par. Vicar; Dcn. Dean Dobbins, Bus. Mgr.; CRP Stds.: 224

St. Catherine of Genoa - 520 Linden Blvd., Brooklyn, NY 11203 t) 718-282-7162 stcatherineofgenoa@hotmail.com stcatherinegenoabrooklyn.com/ Rev. Raphael Munday Kukana, Pst.; Rev. Peter Justice Mawusi, Par. Vicar; CRP Stds.: 28

St. Charles Borromeo - 21 Sidney Pl., Brooklyn, NY 11201 t) 718-625-1177 rectory@stcharlesbklyn.org Rev. William G. Smith, Pst.; Rev. John Gribowich, In Res.; Rev. Msgr. Alfred P. LoPinto, In Res.; Maureen Pond, DRE; CRP Stds.: 73

St. Columba - 2245 Kimball St., Brooklyn, NY 11234 t) 718-253-8840 (CRP); 718-338-6265 stcolumbac@aol.com Rev. Timothy J. Lambert, Pst.; Dcn. Frederick V. Ritchie, DRE; Dcn. Lawrence E. Coyle, RCIA Coord.; CRP Stds.: 45

SS. Cyril and Methodius - 150 Dupont St., Brooklyn, NY 11222 t) 718-389-4424 parish@cyrilandmethodius.org Rev. Eugeniusz Kotlinski, C.M., Pst.; Rev. Slawomir Szucki, C.M., Assoc. Pst.; Rev. Jan Szylar; Rev. Joseph Wisniewski, C.M.; CRP Stds.: 201

Divine Mercy Roman Catholic Church - 219 Conselyea St., Brooklyn, NY 11211 t) 718-389-2546 (CRP); 718-387-0256 fathertom@dmbk.org Rev. Thomas F. Vassalotti, Pst.; Rev. Pedro Angucho, Par. Vicar; Rev. Cristiano Pinheiro Bede; Dcn. Carlos Valderrama; CRP Stds.: 30

Convent - 312 De Voe St., Brooklyn, NY 11211 Rev. Rafael J. Perez, Par. Vicar;

St. Edmund - 2460 Ocean Ave., Brooklyn, NY 11229-3509 t) 718-743-8107 (CRP); 718-743-0102 Rev. Lukasz Trocha, Pst.; Rev. Michael J. S. Bruno, In Res.; Dcn. Ronald Rizzuto; Debra Perillo, DRE; CRP Stds.: 34

St. Edmund School - (Grades PreSchool-8) 1902 Ave. T, Brooklyn, NY 11229 t) 718-648-9229 x1 saintedmundelem@gmail.com www.stedmundelem.org Andrea D'Emic, Prin.; Stds.: 165; Lay Tchrs.: 12

Denis Maloney Institute/St. Edmund Preparatory High School - 2474 Ocean Ave., Brooklyn, NY 11229 t) 718-743-6100 jlorenzetti@stedmundprep.org www.stedmundprep.org John Lorenzetti, Prin.; Allison McGinnis, Prin.; Kevin Raphael, Prin.; Johanna Motta, Librn.;

St. Ephrem - 929 Bay Ridge Pkwy., Brooklyn, NY 11228 t) 718-745-7486 (CRP); 718-833-1010 stephremrectory@aol.com; 101053@diobrook.org Rev. Robert B. Adamo, Pst.; Rev. Msgr. Theophilus Joseph, Par. Vicar; Rev. Anthony S. Chanan, Par. Vicar; Sr. Mary Ann Ambrose, C.S.J., DRE; Dcn. Anthony Stucchio; Dcn. Kevin McLaughlin; CRP Stds.: 133

St. Ephrem Catholic Academy - (Grades PreK-8) 924 74th St., Brooklyn, NY 11228 t) 718-833-1440 aestevez@stephremacademy.org www.stephremacademy.org Andy Estevez, Prin.; Stds.: 251; Lay Tchrs.: 17

Convent - 935 Bay Ridge Pkwy., Brooklyn, NY 11228 t) 718-833-1555 Rev. Robert B. Adamo, Pst.;

St. Finbar - 138 Bay 20th St., Brooklyn, NY 11214 t) 718-837-3935 (CRP); 718-236-3312 Rev. Jose A. Henriquez, Admin.; Rev. Harold Bernard, Par. Vicar; Dcn. Hector S. Blanco; Dcn. John E. Hull, In Res.; Wanda Marty, DRE; CRP Stds.: 154

Convent - 131 Bay 19 St., Brooklyn, NY 11214 t) 718-259-4439

St. Fortunata - 2609 Linden Blvd., Brooklyn, NY 11208 t) 718-647-2632 stfortunatachurch@netzero.net Rev. Jose F. Herrera, Pst.; Dcn. Osborne Miranda; Dcn. Okafor C. Uzoigwe; Sr. Norieta Tusi, DRE; CRP Stds.: 92

St. Frances Cabrini - 1562 86th. St., Brooklyn, NY 11228 t) 718-232-4228 (CRP); 718-236-9165 sfcabrini1963@gmail.com Rev. Vincent F. Miceli, Pst.; Cynthia Alfonso, DRE; CRP Stds.: 39

St. Frances de Chantal - 1273 58th St., Brooklyn, NY 11219 t) 718-436-6407 stfrancesrectory@gmail.com www.francesdechantal.org Rev. Lukasz Dutkiewicz, Pst.; Rev. Anthony Zemula, S.A.C., Par. Vicar; CRP Stds.: 110

St. Francis of Assisi-St. Blaise - 319 Maple St., Brooklyn, NY 11225 t) 718-778-1302 (CRP); 718-756-2015 sfa-stb@optonline.net Rev. Msgr. Paul W. Jervis, Pst.; Rev. Gerald Dumont, Par. Vicar; Dcn. Wilner Pierre-Louis; Rev. Jean-Pierre Ruiz, In Res.; CRP Stds.: 70

St. Francis Xavier - 225 Sixth Ave., Brooklyn, NY 11215 t) 718-857-2903 (CRP); 718-638-1880 hacreled@aol.com; franxrc@gmail.com Rev. Frank C. Tumino, Pst.; CRP Stds.: 80

Good Shepherd - 1950 Batchelder St., Brooklyn, NY 11229 t) 718-998-2800 gsrcc@aol.com www.goodshepherdbrooklyn.org Rev. Thomas Doyle, Pst.; Rev. James E. Devlin, Pastor Emer.; Rev. Peter J. Penton, Par. Vicar; Dcn. James J. Giorgio; CRP Stds.: 164

Guardian Angel - 2978 Ocean Pkwy., Brooklyn, NY 11235 t) 718-266-1561 guardianangelc2978@gmail.com Rev. Sergiy Emanuel, Admin.; Dcn. Manuel Zelaya;

Holy Cross - 2530 Church Ave., Brooklyn, NY 11226 t) 718-941-5066 (CRP); 718-469-5900 msgrjoe@aol.com holycrossrcchurch.org Rev. Msgr. Joseph P. Malagreca, Pst.; Rev. Saint Martin Estiverne, Par. Vicar; Dcn. Francis C. Cuffie; Wendy Rutherford, DRE; CRP Stds.: 190

Holy Family - Saint Laurence - 9719 Flatlands Ave., Brooklyn, NY 11236 t) 718-257-8016 (Faith Formation Office); 718-257-4423 (Holy Family Worship Site); 718-649-0545 (St.Laurence Worship Site) hfamilyr@aol.com; st.laurence1020@gmail.com holyfamilystlaurence-brooklyn.org/ Very Rev. Edward R. P. Kane, Pst.; Rev. Yvon-Hector Aurelien, Par. Vicar; Rev. Szymon A Galazyn, Par. Vicar; Dcn. Jean J. Rameau; Brendan Egonu, DRE; Lori Ramos Johnson, DRE; CRP Stds.: 100

Holy Family-Saint Thomas Aquinas - 249 Ninth St., Brooklyn, NY 11215 t) 718-768-9471 mmatthias@diobrook.org holyfamily-stthomas-brooklyn.org Rev. Rafael J. Perez, Admin.; Rev. Francis Fayez, In Res.; Rev. Jesus Cuadros; Sr. Doryne M. Bermoy, F.L.P., DRE; CRP Stds.: 117

Holy Family Church - 205 14th St., Brooklyn, NY 11215 (Worship Site)

Holy Innocents - 279 E. 17th St., Brooklyn, NY 11226 t) 718-469-9500 holyinnocentsrcbklyn@yahoo.com Rev. Lucon Rigaud, Pst.; Rev. Alfredo Garcia-Hernandez, Par. Vicar; Rev. Michel Pierre Louis, Par. Vicar; Dcn. Ronald Y. Agnant, RCIA Coord.; Nancy Gerard, DRE; CRP Stds.: 142

Holy Name - 245 Prospect Park W., Brooklyn, NY 11215 t) 718-768-7629 (CRP); 718-768-3071 lawrencedryan@gmail.com Rev. Lawrence D. Ryan, Pst.; Rev. Emmanuel Conduah (Ghana), In Res.; Dcn. Gerard J. Devine; Dcn. Michael A. Saez; Kathryn Sisto, DRE; CRP Stds.: 94

Holy Spirit - 1712 45th St., Brooklyn, NY 11204 t) 718-436-5565 101084@diobrook.org Rev. Jose E. Lopez, Admin.; Martha Castro, DRE; CRP Stds.: 27

Convent - 1679 47th St., Brooklyn, NY 11204

Immaculate Heart of Mary - 2805 Ft. Hamilton Pkwy., Brooklyn, NY 11218 t) 718-854-7326 (CRP); 718-871-1310 frgill@ihmbrooklyn.org Rev. Ilyas Gill, O.F.M. (Pakistan), Pst.; Rev. John P. Cush, In Res.; Rev. Francis Obu-Mends, C.S.Sp., In Res.; Dcn. John Cantirino; Dcn. Antonio J. Gonzalez; Dcn. James D. Noble; CRP Stds.: 99

St. Jerome - 2900 Newkirk Ave., Brooklyn, NY 11226 t) 718-462-0223 stjeromechurch@hotmail.com Rev. Jean Yvon Pierre, Pst.; Rev. Jean-Augustin Francois, Par. Vicar; Dcn. Carlos H. Culajay; CRP Stds.: 70

Convent - 455 E. 29th St., Brooklyn, NY 11226 t) 718-856-3323

St. John the Baptist - 333 Hart St., Brooklyn, NY 11206 t) 718-455-6864 101253@diobrook.org Rev. Astor Rodriguez, C.M., Pst.; Rev. Blas S. Lemos, Par. Vicar; Rev. Stephen Cantwell, Par. Vicar; Eugenia Ortiz, DRE; CRP Stds.: 90

Our Lady of Good Counsel - 915 Putnam Ave., Brooklyn, NY 11221 (Worship Site)

Saint John the Evangelist-Saint Rocco Roman Catholic Church - 250 21st St., Brooklyn, NY 11215 t) 718-768-3751 johnevangelist@verizon.net Rev. Kevin P. Cavalluzzi, Pst.; Rev. Terrence Curry, In Res.; Awilda Rosado, DRE; CRP Stds.: 61

St. Rocco - 216 27th St., Brooklyn, NY 11232 t) 718-768-9798 strcchurch@aol.com www.saintroccochurch.com (Worship Site)

St. Joseph Patron of the Universal Church - 185 Suydam St., Brooklyn, NY 11221 t) 718-386-0175 c) 929-254-9246 st.josephpatronchurch@gmail.com (Scalabrini Fathers) Rev. Juan Lopez, Admin.; Rev. Petrus Pitol, C.S., Par. Vicar; CRP Stds.: 407

St. Jude Shrine Church - 1677 Canarsie Rd., Brooklyn, NY 11236 t) 718-241-4030 (CRP); 718-763-6300 uncjed@optimum.net Rev. Msgr. John E. Delendick, Pst.; Rev. Dominic Peprah (Ghana), Pst. Assoc.; Helen Teifer, DRE; CRP Stds.: 65

Saint Mark – Saint Margaret Mary - 2609 E. 19th St., Brooklyn, NY 11235 t) 718-891-3100; 718-769-6311 (CRP) stmarkbrooklyn@gmail.com Rev. Robert V. Mucci, Pst.; Rev. Michael Panicali, Par. Vicar; Dcn. Paul P. Morin; Joann Pino, DRE; CRP Stds.: 32

Saint Martin de Porres - 583 Throop Ave., Brooklyn, NY 11216 t) 718-574-5772 info@smdpp.org Rev. Alonzo Q. Cox, Pst.; Rev. Franklin Ezeorah, Par. Vicar; Dcn. Leroy P. Branch; Dcn. Rachid Murad; Michelle Jospeh, DRE; CRP Stds.: 25

Our Lady of Victory - (Worship Site)

Holy Rosary - 172 Bainbridge St., Brooklyn, NY 11233 (Worship Site)

St. Peter Claver - 29 Peter Claver Pl., Brooklyn, NY 11238 (Worship Site)

Missionaries of Charity - 262 Macon St., Brooklyn, NY 11216

Daughters of Divine Love -

St. Martin of Tours-Our Lady of Lourdes - 1288 Hancock St., Brooklyn, NY 11221 t) 718-443-8484 jruiz@diobrook.org Rev. Juan Ruiz, Pst.; Rev. Lazaro Nunez-Renteria, Par. Vicar; Rev. Pedro N. Ossa; Dcn. Alberto Cruz; Dcn. Philip Rodriguez; Evelyn Melendez, DRE; CRP Stds.: 302

Our Lady of Lourdes Chapel - 89 Furman Ave., Brooklyn, NY 11207

St. Mary Mother of Jesus - 2326 84th St., Brooklyn, NY 11214 t) 718-449-8263 (CRP); 718-372-4000 smmj2326@optimum.net Rev. Msgr. Andrew J. Vaccari, Pst.; Rev. Richard E. Long, In Res.; Dcn. Bryan J. Amore; Elizabeth Lopez, DRE; CRP Stds.: 130

Mary, Mother of the Church - 749 Linwood St., Brooklyn, NY 11208 t) 718-649-0450 (CRP); 718-257-0612 marymotherofthechurch749@yahoo.com Rev. Edward J. Mason, Pst.; Rev. Stephen P. Lynch; Dcn. Rafael Marte; CRP Stds.: 81

St. John Cantius - 479 New Jersey Ave., Brooklyn, NY 11207 t) 718-342-2679 jcantius@aol.com (Worship Site)

Mary of Nazareth - 41 Adelphi St., Brooklyn, NY 11205 t) 718-625-5115 101264@diobrook.org Rev. Henry Torres, Admin.; CRP Stds.: 85

Sacred Heart - (Worship Site)

St. Michael the Archangel & St. Edward - 108 St. Edward's St., Brooklyn, NY 11205 (Worship Site)

Mary Queen of Heaven - 1395 E. 56th St., Brooklyn, NY 11234 t) 718-763-2590 (CRP); 718-763-2330 mqhchurch@aol.com Rev. Thomas F. Leach, Pst.; Rev. Ikenna Okagbue, Par. Vicar; Dcn. Jean Baptiste Boursiquot; CRP Stds.: 51

Sisters of St. Dominic - 1304 E. 57th St., Brooklyn, NY 11234 t) 718-891-7451

St. Mary Star of the Sea - 467 Court St., Brooklyn, NY 11231 t) 718-625-2270 smss1851@aol.com Rev. Christopher T Cashman, Pst.; CRP Stds.: 5

St. Matthew - 1123 Eastern Pkwy., Brooklyn, NY 11213 t) 718-774-6747 fblack@diobrook.org Rev. Francis A. Black, Pst.; Rev. Paul Agbodza; Rev. Pierre Andre Pierre; Rev. Ralph Theodat; Rev. Thaddeus Abraham (India), In Res.; Dcn. Nickie Colon; Gloria Gonzaga, DRE; CRP Stds.: 80

Our Lady of Charity - 1669 Dean St., Brooklyn, NY 11213 (Worship Site)

St. Gregory the Great - 224 Brooklyn Ave., Brooklyn, NY 11213 (Worship Site)

St. Michael - Saint Malachy - 225 Jerome St., Brooklyn, NY 11207; Mailing: 284 Warwick St., Brooklyn, NY 11207 t) 718-647-1818 stmichael284@yahoo.com www.parishstmichaelstmalachy.org/ Rev. Brendan Buckley, OFM, Cap., Pst.; Rev. Gerard Mulvey, O.F.M.Cap., Par. Vicar; Dcn. Jorge Arturo Gonzalez, Pst. Assoc.; Dcn. Carlos Garcia; Vanessa Garcia, DRE; CRP Stds.: 110

St. Michael - 352 42nd St., Brooklyn, NY 11232 t) 718-768-6065 Rev. Fulgencio Gutierrez, Pst.; Rev. Carlos M. Goris, Par. Vicar; CRP Stds.: 324

Most Holy Trinity - Saint Mary - 138 Montrose Ave., Brooklyn, NY 11206 t) 718-486-6276 (CRP); 718-384-0215 mhtbrooklyn@yahoo.com Rev. Rapael Zwolenkiewicz, Pst.; Rev. Nader Ata, OFM, Conv., Par. Vicar; Rev. Tomasz Ryba, OFM, Conv, Par. Vicar; Rev. Russell Governale, O.F.M.Conv., In Res.; CRP Stds.: 85

Most Precious Blood – Ss. Simon and Jude - 70 Bay 47th St., Brooklyn, NY 11214 t) 718-375-9600; 718-372-8022 rectoryssj@gmail.com; rectoryssj@gmail.com Rev. John Maduri, Pst.; Rev. Sijo Muthanattu George, Par. Vicar; Rev. David Ihenacho, Par. Vicar; Rev. Jean Odny Pierre, Par. Vicar; Rev. Joseph Pierre, Par. Vicar; Dcn. Andrew T. Mastrangelo, Bus. Mgr.; CRP Stds.: 127

Our Lady Help of Christians - 1315 E. 28th St., Brooklyn, NY 11210 t) 718-377-6932 (CRP); 718-338-5242 olhcbrooklyn@gmail.com Rev. Dwayne D. Davis, Admin.; Rev. Josh Hugo, Par. Vicar; Rev. Ralph J. Caputo, In Res.; Bro. James Smith, C.F.X., In

Res.; CRP Stds.: 21

Our Lady of Angels - 7320 Fourth Ave., Brooklyn, NY 11209 t) 718-748-6553 (CRP); 718-836-7200 ola.bayridge@verizon.net Rev. Kevin P. Abels, Pst.; Rev. Arputham Arulsamy, Par. Vicar; Rev. Mark Simmons, Par. Vicar; Rev. Kenneth J. Calder; Rev. Archmandrite Hector Castano, In Res.; CRP Stds.: 276

Our Lady of Consolation - 184 Metropolitan Ave., Brooklyn, NY 11211 t) 718-388-1942 olc11249@gmail.com Rev. Wieslaw P. Strzadala, Pst.; Rev. Andrzej Wasko, S.D.S., Par. Vicar; CRP Stds.: 8

Our Lady of Czestochowa-St. Casimir - 183 25th St., Brooklyn, NY 11232 t) 718-768-5724 olcpny@gmail.com www.olcbrooklyn.org/ Rev. Janusz Dymek, Pst.; Rev. Cezariusz W. Jastrzebski, Par. Vicar; CRP Stds.: 71

Our Lady of Grace - 430 Avenue W, Brooklyn, NY 11223 t) 718-375-0404 (CRP); 718-627-2020 ourladyofgrace7@gmail.com Rev. Gaetano J. Sbordone, Pst.; Rev. Roy Jacob, Par. Vicar; Rev. Nodius Tancial, Par. Vicar; Rev. Edward A. Cassar, In Res.; Rev. Dominick F. Cutrone, In Res.; CRP Stds.: 73

Our Lady of Guadalupe - 7201 Fifteenth Ave., Brooklyn, NY 11228 t) 718-331-4003 (CRP); 718-236-8300 101154@diobrook.org Rev. Msgr. Robert J. Romano, Pst.; Rev. Anthony F. Raso, Par. Vicar; CRP Stds.: 93

Our Lady of Miracles - 757 E. 86th St., Brooklyn, NY 11236 t) 718-649-1006 (CRP); 718-257-2400 ourladyofmiraclesbk@gmail.com ourladyofmiracles-brooklyn.org Rev. Jean Delva, Pst.; Rev. Hugues Berrette, Par. Vicar;

Our Lady of Mount Carmel - Annunciation of the Blessed Virgin Mary - 275 N. Eighth St., Brooklyn, NY 11211 t) (718) 384-0223 Rev. Msgr. Jamie J. Gigantiello, Pst.; Rev. Archmandrite Michele Vricella, Par. Vicar; Rev. Msgr. David L. Cassato; Dcn. Michael Chiricella; Dcn. Philip Franco; Rosemarie Walsh, DRE; CRP Stds.: 86

The Mount Carmel Early Childhood Center - 10 Withers St., Brooklyn, NY 11211 t) (917) 993-1330 info@themountcarmelecc.org; mlorenzen@themountcarmelecc.org www.themountcarmelecc.org Maura Lorenzen, Exec. Dir.; Theresa Feinberg, Educ. Dir.;

Our Lady of Peace - 522 Carroll St., Brooklyn, NY 11215 t) 718-624-5122 oruiz@diobrook.org ourladyofpeace-brooklyn.org/ Rev. Orlando Ruiz, OFM, Pst.; Rev. Octavio Salinas, O.F.M., Par. Vicar; Lillian Flores, DRE; CRP Stds.: 43

Hermanas Franciscanas de la Immaculada - 209 First St., Brooklyn, NY 11215 t) 929-295-0642 hfic1983olp@aol.com

Our Lady of Perpetual Help Basilica - 526-59th St., Brooklyn, NY 11220 t) 718-439-4795 (CRP); 718-492-9200 jwgilmouressr@gmail.com www.olphbkny.org Rev. James Gilmour, C.Ss.R., Pst.; Rev. Joseph Hung Ducq Tran, C.Ss.R., Pst. Assoc.; Rev. Michael Cunningham, C.Ss.R., Assoc. Pst.; Rev. Karl Esker, C.Ss.R., Assoc. Pst.; Rev. Francis Skelly, C.Ss.R., Assoc. Pst.; Rev. Norman S. Bennett, C.Ss.R., Pst. Assoc.; Rev. James Cascione, C.Ss.R., Pst. Assoc.; Rev. Clement Krug, C.Ss.R., Pst. Assoc.; Rev. Kangqiang Lu, Pst. Assoc.; Rev. John Murray, Pst. Assoc.; Rev. Ruskin Piedra, C.Ss.R., Pst. Assoc.; Dcn. Jesus Soto; Rev. Charles Hergenroeder, In Res.; Maritza Mejia, DRE; CRP Stds.: 556

Immigration Services - 545 60th St., Brooklyn, NY 11220 t) 718-439-8160

Our Lady of Refuge - 2020 Foster Ave., Brooklyn, NY 11210 t) 718-434-2090 olrefuge@aol.com Rev. Lucon Rigaud, Pst.; Rev. Michel Pierre Louis, Par. Vicar; CRP Stds.: 136

Our Lady of Solace - 2866 W. 17th St., Brooklyn, NY 11224 t) 718-266-1612 rec@olsbrooklyn.com; olsshiju@olsbrowland.com Rev. Javier Flores Chirino, Pst.; Rev. Rowland Onuegbu, Par. Vicar; CRP Stds.: 38

Our Lady of the Presentation-Our Lady of Mercy Roman Catholic Church - 1677 St. Marks Ave., Brooklyn, NY 11233 t) 718-345-2604 olmchurch@verizon.net Rev. Vincent B. Sullivan, S.J., Admin.; Rev. John Fagan, Par. Vicar; Dcn. Victorino P. Elijio; Dcn. Jaime Varela; Sr. Melba Vasques, DRE; CRP Stds.: 75

Our Lady of Mercy - 680 Mother Gaston Blvd., Brooklyn, NY 11212 (Worship Site)

St. Patrick - 9511 Fourth Ave., Brooklyn, NY 11209 t) 718-238-2600 parish@stpatrickbayridge.org Rev. Brian P. Dowd, Pst.; Rev. Gerard J. Sauer; Rev. Michael Falce, Par. Vicar; Rev. Peter Poonoly, Par. Vicar; Rev. Jun Hee Lee, In Res.; Rev. James W. King; CRP Stds.: 118

Blessed Sacrament Chapel - 418 95th St., Brooklyn, NY 11209 (Worship Site)

Saint Paul and Saint Agnes Roman Catholic Church - 433 Sackett St., Brooklyn, NY 11231 t) 718-625-1717 stpaulstagnes@gmail.com stpaulstagnes.wordpress.org Rev. Paul Anel, Admin.; Rev. Alexandre Morard, In Res.; CRP Stds.: 43

St. Agnes - (Worship Site)

St. Paul - 234 Congress St., Brooklyn, NY 11201 (Worship Site)

SS. Peter and Paul - 71 S. Third St., Brooklyn, NY 11211 t) 718-387-1041 (CRP); 718-388-9576 saintspeterandpaul@gmail.com Rev. Jason N. Espinal, Admin.; Rev. Carlos J. Borgos, Par. Vicar; Sr. Maria Wspomozycielka, DRE; CRP Stds.: 107

Epiphany - 96 S. 9th St., Brooklyn, NY 11211 (Worship Site)

Queen of All Saints - 300 Vanderbilt Ave., Brooklyn, NY 11205 t) 718-638-7625 qasrccoffice@gmail.com Rev. Joseph A. Ceriello, Pst.; Theresa Uy, DRE; CRP Stds.: 47

Resurrection - 2331 Gerritsen Ave., Brooklyn, NY 11229 t) 718-891-0888 (CRP); 718-743-7234 101200@diobrook.org Margaret Foti, DRE; Rev. William A. With, Pst.; Rev. Michael C. Gribbon, Par. Vicar; CRP Stds.: 158

Resurrection Catholic Coptic Church - 328 14th St., Brooklyn, NY 11215 t) (718) 499-6946 francisfayz@yahoo.fr; francis@francisfayez.org www.francisfayez.com Rev. Francis Fayez Abaskhron, Pst.;

St. Rita - 275 Shepherd Ave., Brooklyn, NY 11208 t) 718-647-4910 parishstrita@brooklyn.com Rev. William Chacon, Pst.; Rev. Francisco J. Ares, In Res.; Rev. Robert P. Vitaglione, In Res.; Dcn. Fabio Parra; Dcn. Juan M. Carattini; Yazmin Martinez, DRE; CRP Stds.: 115

St. Rosalia-Regina Pacis - 1230 65th St., Brooklyn, NY 11219 t) 718-236-0909 reginarectory@aol.com Rev. Sebastian T. Andro, Pst.; Rev. Sheng Jiao Lin, C.M., Par. Vicar; Rev. Thomas F. Brosnan, Par. Vicar; Rev. Msgr. Ronald T. Marino, Pastor Emer.; Sr. Clara Wang, Pst. Assoc.; Dcn. John J. Dolan; CRP Stds.: 166

Regina Center, Inc. - 1258 65th St., Brooklyn, NY 11219 t) 718-232-4340

Basilica of Regina Pacis -

St. Rose of Lima - 269 Parkville Ave., Brooklyn, NY 11230 t) 718-434-8040 Rev. Grzegorz Stasiak (Poland), Pst.; Rev. Jon O. Ukaegbu, Par. Vicar; Diana Castillo, DRE; CRP Stds.: 110

Sisters of St. Joseph - 250 Newkirk Ave., Brooklyn, NY 11230 t) 718-859-5722

Sacred Hearts of Jesus and Mary and St. Stephen - 108 Carroll St., Brooklyn, NY 11231 t) 718-596-0880 (CRP); 718-596-7750 mgm099@gmail.com Rev. Msgr. Guy A. Massie, Pst.; Rev. Cletus Forson, Par. Vicar; Rev. A. Nagozi, In Res.; Dcn. Edwin A. Rivera; Michele Twomey, DRE;

St. Saviour - 611 Eighth Ave., Brooklyn, NY 11215 t) 718-768-4055 stsaviourchurch@aol.com Rev. Frank W. Spacek, Pst.; Rev. Kevin P. Cavalluzzi, In Res.; Rev. Daniel S. Murphy; Dcn. Paul Norman; Sr. Mary Walsh Sr., Pst. Assoc.; CRP Stds.: 80

St. Saviour High School - 588 Sixth St., Brooklyn, NY 11215 t) 718-768-4406 mckeown.p@stsaviour.org Sr. Valeria Belanger, S.S.N.D., Prin.;

Convent - 590 6th St., Brooklyn, NY 11215

St. Stanislaus Kostka - 607 Humboldt St., Brooklyn, NY 11222 t) 718-388-0170 skc11222@aol.com www.ststanskostka.org Rev. Grzegorz M. Markulak, C.M. (Poland), Pst.; Rev. Slawomir Szucki, C.M., Par. Vicar; Rev. Joseph Szpilski, C.M., In Res.; Krzysztof Gospodarzec, DRE; CRP Stds.: 208

St. Therese of Lisieux - 1281 Troy Ave., Brooklyn, NY 11203 t) 718-451-1671 (CRP); 718-451-1500 stthereselis@gmail.com (The Little Flower) Rev. Anselmus Mawusi, Admin.; Rev. Bony Monastere, Par. Vicar;

St. Thomas Aquinas - 1550 Hendrickson St., Brooklyn, NY 11234 t) 718-253-4404 x31 (CRP); 718-253-4404 stainfo@stthomasaquinasbrooklyn.com Rev. Dwayne D. Davis, Pst.; Rev. Kieran Udeze, Par. Vicar; Rev. Alexander Olszewski, Par. Vicar; Mary Odenat, DRE; CRP Stds.: 70

Transfiguration - 263 Marcy Ave., Brooklyn, NY 11211 t) 718-388-8773 101231@diobrook.org Rev. Msgr. Anthony Hernandez, Pst.; Rev. Jeremias E Castillo Liranzo, Admin.; Dcn. Israel Rosario; Dcn. Jose M. Tavarez; Desiree Rodriguez, DRE; CRP Stds.: 100

Southside Mission for Social Services - 280 Marcy Ave., Brooklyn, NY 11211 t) 718-388-3784 John Mulhern, Dir.;

St. Vincent Ferrer - 1603 Brooklyn Ave., Brooklyn, NY 11210-3495 t) 718-859-9009 info@saintvincentferrer.org Rev. Antonious Peter Gopaul, Pst.; Margaret Bambara, DRE; CRP Stds.: 54

Visitation of the Blessed Virgin Mary - 98 Richards St., Brooklyn, NY 11231 t) 718-624-1572 visitationbvmredhook@gmail.com; segnykjb@hotmail.com www.visitationbvm-brooklyn.org Rev. Claudio Antecini, Pst.; Rev. Johannes S.A.G. Siegert, Par. Vicar; Rev. Eamon G. Murray; Rev. Sauro Sbarbati; Sr. Frauke Tinat, Pst. Assoc.; CRP Stds.: 50

CAMBRIA HEIGHTS

Sacred Heart - 115-58 222nd St., Cambria Heights, NY 11411 t) 718-528-0577 rectory@sacredheartny.com Rev. Hilaire Belizaire, Pst.; Dcn. Francois G. Cajoux; Dcn. Paul C. Dorsinville; CRP Stds.: 46

COLLEGE POINT

St. Fidelis - 123-06 14th Ave., College Point, NY 11356 t) 718-539-1249 (CRP); 718-445-6164 stfidelischurch01@gmail.com Rev. John Francis, Pst.; Rev. Vito Jumao-As Jr., Par. Vicar; Dcn. Daniel P. Donnelly; Faria Sookdeo, DRE; CRP Stds.: 180

St. Fidelis Mother and Child Residence - t) 718-353-4749

CORONA

St. Leo - 104-05 49th Ave., Corona, NY 11368 t) 718-699-8565 (CRP); 718-592-7569 saintleo@earthlink.net Rev. Carlos A. Agudelo, Pst.; Rev. Jose Diaz, Par. Vicar; Rev. Diego Villegas, Par. Vicar; Rev. Pablo Ruani; Dcn. Rodrigo A. Mendez; Omar Cortez, DRE; CRP Stds.: 616

Our Lady of Mount Carmel - 103-56 52nd Ave., Corona, NY 11368

Our Lady of Sorrows - 104-11 37th Ave., Corona, NY 11368 t) 718-651-5682 (CRP); 718-424-7554 olsccd@aol.com; rectory@olschurch-corona.org Rev. Manuel de Jesus Rodriguez, Pst.; Rev. Gabriel Agudelo Perdomo, Par. Vicar; Rev. Osmin Vargas, Par. Vicar; Rev. Jean Odny Pierre; Dcn. Daniel Diaz; Dcn. Jose F. Tineo; CRP Stds.: 1,370

St. Paul the Apostle - 98-16 55 Ave., Corona, NY 11368 t) 718-271-1100 stpaulcorona@verizon.net Rev. Carlos Quijano, S.J., Admin.; Dcn. Fernando Orozco; CRP Stds.: 55

DOUGLASTON

St. Anastasia - 45-11 245th St., Douglaston, NY 11362; Mailing: 45-14 245th St., Douglaston, NY 11362 t) 718-631-4454 (Office); 718-225-5191 (CRP) info@sta.nyc; dff@sta.nyc www.sta.nyc Rev. David J. Dettmer, Pst.; Rev. Anthony M. Rucando, In Res.; Rev. Msgr. George J. Ryan, In Res.; Rev. Msgr. Anthony F. Sherman, In Res.; Dcn. Joseph C. Chu; Rose Louise Ruesing, DRE; CRP Stds.: 131

EAST ELMHURST

St. Gabriel - 26-26 98th St., East Elmhurst, NY 11369

t) 718-639-0474 stgabriel26@verizon.net Rev. Nicholas Apollonio, Admin.; Rev. Dragan Pusic, Par. Vicar; Rev. Robert J. Sadlack, Par. Vicar; CRP Stds.: 382

ELMHURST

St. Adalbert - 52-29 83rd St., Elmhurst, NY 11373 t) 718-565-8227 (CRP); 718-639-0212 101001@diobrook.org Rev. Miroslaw Podymniak, O.F.M.Conv. (Poland), Pst.; Rev. Ericson De la Pena, Par. Vicar; Rev. Szymanski Lucjan, Par. Vicar; Dcn. Thomas J. Page; Rev. Herman Czaster, O.F.M.Conv., In Res.; CRP Stds.: 125

Ascension - 86-13 55th Ave., Elmhurst, NY 11373 t) 718-335-2626 ascensionrcchurch@gmail.com Rev. Anacleto Asebias, Admin.; Rev. Kyrian C. Echekwu, Par. Vicar; CRP Stds.: 147

St. Bartholomew - 43-22 Ithaca St., Elmhurst, NY 11373 t) 718-898-0096 (CRP); 718-424-5400 stbartselmhurst@gmail.com Rev. Richard J. Beuther, Pst.; Rev. Cesar Pena, Par. Vicar; Rev. Jose Diaz, Par. Vicar; Sr. Lucy Mendez, DRE; CRP Stds.: 982

Our Lady of China Chapel - 54-09 92nd St., Elmhurst, NY 11373; Mailing: 54-17 90th St., Elmhurst, NY 11373 t) 718-699-1929 brotherli@hotmail.com St. John Vianney, Flushing Bro. Peter Li, C.S.J.B.;

Ming Yuan Chinese School - 54-17 90th St., Elmhurst, NY 11373 t) 718-271-3944; 718-439-3656 brotherli2000@yahoo.com Stds.: 745; Bro. Tchrs.: 1; Pr. Tchrs.: 2; Sr. Tchrs.: 1; Scholastics: 1; Lay Tchrs.: 1

FAR ROCKAWAY

St. Mary Star of the Sea and St. Gertrude - 1920 New Haven Ave., Far Rockaway, NY 11691 t) 718-327-1133 101268@diobrook.org Rev. Francis T. Shannon, Pst.; Rev. David P. Bertolotti, Par. Vicar; Rev. Dawit T. Moroda, In Res.; Rev. Pablo Ruani; Dcn. Rene Hernandez; Dcn. Adalberto Montero; Dcn. Michael C. Moss; CRP Stds.: 264

St. Gertrude - 336 Beach 38th St., Far Rockaway, NY 11691 (Worship Site)

FLORAL PARK

Our Lady of the Snows - 258-15 80th Ave., Floral Park, NY 11004 t) 718-347-3511 (CRP); 718-347-6070 rel.ed@olsnows.org; church@olsnows.org Rev. Kevin F. McBrien, Pst.; Rev. Peter Okajima, Par. Vicar; Dcn. Matthew J. Oellinger; Dcn. Steven J. Borheck; Dcn. John Warren; Dcn. Kevin F. Hughes; Rev. Msgr. John J. Gildea, In Res.; CRP Stds.: 175

FLUSHING

St. Andrew Avellino - 35-60 158th St., Flushing, NY 11358 t) 718-445-7012 (CRP); 718-359-0417 revjholcomb@standrewavellinorcchurch.org Rev. Gregory M. V. McIlhenney, Admin.; Rev. Romel P. Penafiel, Par. Vicar; Dcn. Michael B. Fogarty; Maria Tortorella, DRE; Sr. Aileen Halleran, S.C., RCIA Coord.;

Holy Family - 175-20 74th Ave., Flushing, NY 11366-1529 t) 718-591-6438 (CRP); 718-969-2448 holyfamilyflushing@gmail.com Rev. Sean Suckiel, Pst.; Rev. Ralph Edel, Priest; Rev. Casper J. Furnari, Retired; Dcn. Eugene J. Cassidy; Barbara Makolin, DRE; CRP Stds.: 71

Convent - 175-11 75 Ave., Flushing, NY 11366

St. John Vianney - 140-10 34th Ave., Flushing, NY 11354 t) 718-961-5092 (CRP); 718-762-7920 stjv@msn.com Rev. Vincent Nguyen, C.S.J.B., Pst.; Rev. Victor Cao, C.S.J.B., Par. Vicar; Shin Hawy Chang, DRE; Sr. Monica Gan, C.S.T., Pst. Assoc.; Dcn. Daniel A. Garcia; Rev. Tiancang (Joseph) Zheng, Par. Vicar; Dcn. Stanley Tam;

St. Kevin - 45-21 194 St., Flushing, NY 11358 t) 718-357-5317 (CRP); 718-357-8888 stkevin194@gmail.com Rev. Robert Mema, Pst.; Rev. Jerome T. Jecewicz, In Res.; Rev. Jeffry T. Dillon; Dcn. Julio C. Barreneche; Rosaria Surace, DRE; CRP Stds.: 86

Mary's Nativity-Saint Ann Roman Catholic Church - 46-02 Parsons Blvd., Flushing, NY 11355 t) 718-359-5961 (CRP); 718-359-5996 marynatstannoff@aol.com; 101278@diobrook.org www.marynatstann.org Rev. Edward M. Kachurka, Pst.; Rev. Louis J. DeGaetano, Par. Vicar; Rev. Peter Ma, Par. Vicar; Rev. Jed Sumampong, C.P., Par. Vicar; Rev. Enel Almeus, C.S.Sp.; Rev. George A. Pfundstein; Rev. Anthony F. Rosado, In Res.; CRP Stds.: 35

St. Ann - 142-30 58th Ave., Flushing, NY 11355-5314 t) 718-886-3890 (Worship Site)

St. Mel - 26-15 154th St., Flushing, NY 11354 t) 718-461-9840 (CRP); 718-886-0201 101133@diobrook.org Rev. Joseph G. Fonti, Pst.; Rev. Msgr. Kevin B. Noone; Rev. Italo Barozzi; Dcn. Joseph A. Freda; Paula Migliore, DRE; CRP Stds.: 131

St. Michael - 136-76 41st Ave., Flushing, NY 11355 t) 718-961-0312 (CRP); 718-961-0295 stmichael1833@aol.com Rev. Vincentius T. Do, Admin.; Rev. Jaime Hernandez, Par. Vicar; Rev. Yanjun Zhang, Par. Vicar; Rev. Kanh Ha; Dcn. Daniel R. Rodriguez; Gizeth Vecchio, DRE; CRP Stds.: 77

St. Michael School - 136-58 41st Ave., Flushing, NY 11355 t) 718-961-0246 rogonesms@aol.com Maureen Rogone, Prin.;

St. Paul Chong Ha-Sang Roman Catholic Chapel - 32-15 Parsons Blvd., Flushing, NY 11354 t) 718-321-7676 akim@diobrook.org stpaulqueens.org Rev. Andrew M. Kim, Pst.; Rev. Heebong Nam, Par. Vicar; Rev. Hyosick John Park, Par. Vicar; Rev. Joseph R. Veneroso, M.M., DRE; Dcn. Paul M. Chin; Dcn. John Im; CRP Stds.: 166

Olivetan Benedictine Sisters -

Queen of Peace - 141-36 77th Ave., Flushing, NY 11367 t) 718-380-5031 queenofpeacerectory@outlook.com Rev. Msgr. Michael J. Hardiman, Pst.; Rev. Michael Ugbor, Par. Vicar; Rev. James L. Tighe, In Res.; Dcn. Gregory Bizzoco Jr.; Lisa Mehlrose, DRE; CRP Stds.: 33

Convent - t) 718-380-4293

FOREST HILLS

Our Lady of Mercy - 70-01 Kessel St., Forest Hills, NY 11375 t) 718-261-6285 (CRP); 718-268-6143 office@mercyhills.org Rev. Frank L. Schwarz, Pst.; Rev. Msgr. John A. McGuirl, In Res.; Dcn. Dean Dobbins; CRP Stds.: 55

Our Lady Queen of Martyrs - 110-06 Queens Blvd., Forest Hills, NY 11375 t) 718-263-0907 (CRP); 718-268-6251 olqmreled@verizon.net; rectoryolqm@aol.com Most Rev. Paul R. Sanchez, Pst.; Rev. Francis J. Passenant, Admin.; Rev. Antonin Kocurek, Par. Vicar; Rev. Msgr. Joseph L. Cunningham, In Res.; Dcn. Thomas E. Jorge, DRE; Dcn. Gregory Kandra; CRP Stds.: 102

GLENDALE

St. Pancras - 72-22 68th St., Glendale, NY 11385 t) 718-479-0590 (CRP); 718-821-2323 101180@diobrook.org Rev. Msgr. Steven J. Aguggia, Pst.; Rev. Wladyslaw Z. Kubrak, Par. Vicar; CRP Stds.: 120

Convent - 72-25 68th St., Glendale, NY 11385

Sacred Heart of Jesus Church - 83-17 78th Ave., Glendale, NY 11385 t) 718-821-6434 sacredheartglendale@verizon.net www.sacredheartrccglendale.org Rev. Fred Marano, Pst.; Rev. Msgr. Richard E. Marchese, In Res.; Rev. John J. Fullum, In Res.; Dcn. Peter Stamm; Theresia Stalzer, DRE; CRP Stds.: 267

HOLLIS

St. Gerard Majella - 188-16 91st Ave., Hollis, NY 11423-2520 t) 718-468-1166 x22 (CRP); 718-468-6565 saintgerardm@gmail.com stgerardshrine.org Rev. Josephjude C. Gannon, Pst.; Rev. Killick Pierrilus, Par. Vicar; Rev. Joseph Tharackal, In Res.; Dcn. Franklin G. Munoz; Carmen Macchio, DRE; CRP Stds.: 64

HOWARD BEACH

St. Helen - 157-10 83rd St., Howard Beach, NY 11414 t) 718-835-6216 (CRP); 718-738-1616 sthelenhbny@aol.com Rev. Francis A. Colamaria, Pst.; Rev. Stephen M. Giulietti, Par. Vicar; Rev. Michael Panicali, Par. Vicar; Rev. Joseph M. Zwosta, Par. Vicar; Dcn. Richard E. Elrose; Dcn. Andrew T. Mastrangelo; Haiffa Vizoso, DRE; CRP Stds.: 517

Our Lady of Grace - 100-05 159th Ave., Howard Beach, NY 11414 t) 718-835-2165 (CRP); 718-843-6218 olghowardbeach@nyc.rr.com Rev. Marc E. Swartvagher, Pst.; Rev. Msgr. Robert J. Sarno, In Res.; Dcn. Alexander Breviario; Dcn. Antonio Gordon; CRP Stds.: 168

JACKSON HEIGHTS

Blessed Sacrament - 34-43 93rd St., Jackson Heights, NY 11372 t) 718-639-6159 (CRP); 718-639-3888 blessacjh@aol.com www.blessedsacramentjacksonheightsny.com Rev. Gabriel Toro-Rivas, Pst.; Rev. Saint Charles Borno, Par. Vicar; Rev. Juan Angel Pichardo, Par. Vicar; Rev. Alexander Pinacue, Par. Vicar; Rev. Richard Hoare, In Res.; Dcn. Alfredo Rendon; CRP Stds.: 643

Convent - 93-11 35th Ave., Jackson Heights, NY 11372 t) 718-639-1545

St. Joan of Arc - 82-00 35th Ave., Jackson Heights, NY 11372 t) 718-478-5593 (CRP); 718-429-2333 sjareled@netzero.com; joanofarcqueens@aol.com Rev. Msgr. William M. Hoppe, Pst.; Rev. Johnson Chanassery, O.C.D., Par. Vicar; Rev. Paul Osei-Fosu, Par. Vicar; Rev. Alexander Pinacue, Par. Vicar; Rev. Stephen Valdazo; Rev. Msgr. Edward V. Wetterer; Dcn. Paulo A. Salazar; Sr. Maryann McHugh, C.S.J., Pst. Assoc.; Lizbeth Pimentel-Maya, DRE; CRP Stds.: 365

St. Joan of Arc School - (Grades PreK-8) 35-27 82nd St., Jackson Heights, NY 11372 t) 718-639-9020 amosejczuk@diobrook.org www.sjaschoolny.com Agnes Mosejczuk, Prin.; Stds.: 205; Lay Tchrs.: 24

Our Lady of Fatima - 25-02 80th St., Jackson Heights, NY 11370; Mailing: 25-38 80th St., Jackson Heights, NY 11370 t) 718-457-3457 (CRP); 718-899-2801 olfatima11370@msn.com Rev. Darrell Da Costa, Pst.; Rev. Ricardo Perez, Par. Vicar; Rev. James Fedigan, In Res.; Rev. Patrick J. Frawley, In Res.; Rev. Gabriel A. Ahiarakwem, In Res.; Dcn. Marco V. Lopez; Dcn. Fabio Parra; Sr. Patricia Reills, DRE; CRP Stds.: 195

Convent - 25-56 80th St., Jackson Heights, NY 11370 t) 718-747-3457

JAMAICA

St. Bonaventure-St. Benedict the Moor RC Church - 171-17 110th Ave., Jamaica, NY 11434 t) 718-526-4018 xdxn94c@hotmail.com Very Rev. Francis Kwame Asagba, Pst.; Sr. Mary Ann Afiakwah, DRE; CRP Stds.: 24

Immaculate Conception - 86-45 Edgerton Blvd., Jamaica, NY 11432 t) 718-291-3080 (CRP); 718-739-0880 Rev. William Murphy, C.P., Pst.; Rev. Rogie Castellano, C.P., Pst. Assoc.; Rev. Lionel Pacheco, C.P., Pst. Assoc.; Dcn. Daniel R. Rodriguez; CRP Stds.: 128

St. Joseph - 108-43 Sutphin Blvd., Jamaica, NY 11435-5445 t) 718-739-4781 stjjamaica@gmail.com Rev. Krystian J. Piasta, O.F.M., Pst.; CRP Stds.: 58

St. Nicholas of Tolentine - 150-75 Goethals Ave., Jamaica, NY 11432 t) 718-591-6536 (CRP); 718-969-3226 jfs777@aol.com Rev. Jovito B. Carongay Jr., Pst.; Rev. Noel Abao Daduya, CMI, Par. Vicar; Rev. Thomas Joseph, Par. Vicar; Rev. Abraham P. Mathew, In Res.; Dcn. Thomas E. Jorge; Sr. Alice Michael, DRE;

Our Lady of the Skies Chapel - JFK International Airport, Terminal 4, Ste. 461-037, Jamaica, NY 11430 t) 718-656-5348 jfkchapel.org Rev. Krystian J. Piasta, O.F.M., Admin.; Dcn. Vincent A. Lino;

Chapel - JFK International Airport, Terminal 4, Jamaica, NY 11430 www.jfkchapel.org

St. Pius V - 106-12 Liverpool St., Jamaica, NY 11435 t) 718-739-3731 stpiusvqueens@gmail.com Rev. Felix Sanchez, Pst.; Dcn. Alfredo Castellanos; CRP Stds.: 65

Presentation of the Blessed Virgin Mary - 88-19 Parsons Blvd., Jamaica, NY 11432 t) 718-739-0241 pbvmsec@msn.com Rev. Victor M. Bolanos, Pst.; Rev. Angel Medrano-Matos, Par. Vicar; Dcn. John Solarte; Rev. John E. Vesey, In Res.; Evelin Herrera, DRE; CRP Stds.: 181

Youth Ministry Office - 88-13 Parsons Blvd., Jamaica, NY 11432 t) 718-739-2003

LONG ISLAND CITY

St. Mary - 10-08 49th Ave., Long Island City, NY 11101 t) 718-786-0705 stmarylic@yahoo.com Rev. Christopher J. Turczany, Admin.; CRP Stds.: 172

Most Precious Blood - 32-23 36th St., Long Island City, NY 11106 t) 718-721-9850 (CRP); 718-278-3337 mpb1922@yahoo.com Rev. Vedran Kirincic, Pst.; Rev. Sasa Ilijic, Par. Vicar; Rev. William F. Krlis; Dcn. Hector E. Rodriguez; CRP Stds.: 225

Convent - 32-16 36th St., Long Island City, NY 11106 t) 718-278-4706

Our Lady of Mount Carmel - 23-25 Newtown Ave., Long Island City, NY 11102 t) 718-278-1881 (CRP); 718-278-1834 church@mountcarmelastoria.org Rev. Msgr. Cuong M. Pham, Pst.; Rev. Michael J. McHugh, Par. Vicar; Rev. Hung Sy Tran, Par. Vicar; Rev. Jean Gerard LaGuerre; Rev. Edmund P. Brady, In Res.; Rev. John P. Harrington, In Res.; Rev. Josephtan Pham, In Res.; CRP Stds.: 191

St. Margaret Mary - 9-18 27th Ave., Long Island City, NY 11102 (Worship Site)

St. Patrick - 39-38 29th St., Long Island City, NY 11101 t) 718-706-0565 (CRP); 718-729-6060 stpatlic@yahoo.com Rev. Robert M. Powers, Pst.; Dcn. Carlos A. Trochez; Rev. Charles F. Gilley, I.V.Dei., In Res.; Rev. Frederick Cintron; CRP Stds.: 54

Queen of Angels - 44-04 Skillman Ave., Long Island City, NY 11104 t) 718-937-5174 (CRP); 718-392-0011 pastor@queenofangelssnyc.org Rev. Ambiorix Osorio, Pst.; Rev. Nestor A. Martinez, Par. Vicar; Rev. Paulus Rahmat, In Res.; CRP Stds.: 64

St. Raphael - 35-20 Greenpoint Ave., Long Island City, NY 11101 t) 718-729-8957 straphaelrectory@yahoo.com Rev. Paul Y. Kim, Admin.; Rev. William A. McLaughlin, Par. Vicar;

St. Rita - 36-25 11th St., Long Island City, NY 11106 t) 718-361-1884 jcsnyc2@hotmail.com Rev. Jose Carlos Da Silva, Pst.; Rev. Adriano H. Restrepo, Par. Vicar; Dcn. Fernando E. Luces; Helen Foster, DRE; CRP Stds.: 128

MASPETH

Holy Cross - 61-21 56th Rd., Maspeth, NY 11378-2498 t) 718-894-1387 hc6121@aol.com www.holycross-queens.org Most Rev. Witold Mroziewski, Pst.; Rev. Andrzej Salwowski, Admin.; Rev. Daniel K. Rajski, Par. Vicar; Jolanta Neubauer, DRE; CRP Stds.: 225

Parish of Transfiguration – Saint Stanislaus Kostka - 57-15 61st St., Maspeth, NY 11378-2713 t) 718-326-2185 ststanislauskostka@catholicweb.com Rev. Msgr. Joseph P. Calise, Pst.; Rev. Joseph F. Wilson, Par. Vicar; Rev. Msgr. Edward P. Doran; Dcn. Andrzej Lewandowski; Dcn. Edward F. O'Connell; CRP Stds.: 105

St. Stanislaus Kostka Catholic Academy of Queens - (Grades PreSchool-8) 61-17 Grand Ave., Maspeth, NY 11378 t) 718-326-1585 cmangone@ststanscaqn.org www.ststansschool.org Catherine Mangone, Prin.; Sr. Rose Torma, C.S.J., Prin.; Stds.: 332; Lay Tchrs.: 19

MIDDLE VILLAGE

St. Margaret - 66-05 79th Pl., Middle Village, NY 11379 t) 718-381-4048 (CRP); 718-326-1911 stmargaretmv@gmail.com Rev. Robert J. Armato, Pst.; Rev. Joseph Palackal, C.M.I. (India), Par. Vicar; Rev. Msgr. Robert J. Thelen, Par. Vicar; Rev. Michael Udoh, In Res.; Sr. Bridget M. Olwell, O.S.U., Pst. Assoc.; Karen Gonzales, DRE; CRP Stds.: 164

Our Lady of Hope - 61-27 71st St., Middle Village, NY 11379 t) 718-335-8394 (CRP); 718-429-5438 olhrectory1@yahoo.com; macarrano@juno.com www.ourladyofhopeparish.org Rev. Peter J. Purpura, Pst.; Dcn. Robert F. Lavanco; Dcn. Paul Norman; Rev. Emil Parafiniuk, In Res.; CRP Stds.: 208

OAKLAND GARDENS

American Martyrs - 79-43 Bell Blvd., Oakland Gardens, NY 11364 t) 718-464-6411 (CRP); 718-464-4582 americanmartyrs@aol.com amparish.org Rev. Peter J. Rayder, Pst.; Rev. Mark C. Bristol; Dcn. Stanley J. Galazin; CRP Stds.: 127

OZONE PARK

St. Elizabeth - 94-20 85th St., Ozone Park, NY 11416-1237 t) 718-296-4900 stelizabeth94office@gmail.com Rev. Andrzej Wojciech Klocek, Admin.; Rev. Luis Eduardo Garces, Par. Vicar; Rev. Jude Zimoha, Par. Vicar; Rev. Msgr. Paul Kodjo, Part Time; Wilfredo Gonzalez, DRE; CRP Stds.: 105

St. Mary Gate of Heaven - 101-25 104th St., Ozone Park, NY 11416 t) 718-849-9329 (CRP); 718-847-5957 Rev. Baltazar Sanchez Alonzo, Admin.; Rev. James J. Krische, Par. Vicar; Dcn. Ramon Cruz; Dcn. Richard J. Gilligan; Dcn. Bill Velasquez; Ann Farrell, DRE; CRP Stds.: 149

Nativity of the Blessed Virgin Mary-Saint Stanislaus Bishop and Martyr Roman Catholic Church - 101-41 91st St., Ozone Park, NY 11416 t) 718-845-1524 (CRP); 718-845-3691 nativityststans@verizon.net Rev. John Tino, Pst.; Rev. Slawomir Sobiech, Par. Vicar; Dcn. Edward J. Guster Jr.; Rev. Ryszard Koper (Poland), Par. Vicar; Rev. Killick Pierrilus, Par. Vicar; CRP Stds.: 94

St. Stanislaus, Bishop & Martyr - 88-10 102nd Ave., Ozone Park, NY 11416 (Worship Site)

QUEENS VILLAGE

Incarnation - 89-43 Francis Lewis Blvd., Queens Village, NY 11427 t) 718-465-8534 101095@diobrook.org Rev. Reynolds Basilious, O.C.D., Par. Vicar; Rev. Killick Pierrilus; Dcn. Francois Innocent; Dcn. Franklin G. Munoz; CRP Stds.: 37

SS. Joachim and Anne - 218-26 105 Ave., Queens Village, NY 11429 t) 718-465-0124 njean-francois@diobrook.org ssjachurch.org Very Rev. Nixon Jean-Francois, Pst.; Rev. Lamartine Petit, Par. Vicar; Dcn. Nery R. Escobar; Dcn. Emmanuel Coty Jr.; Peggy Savasta, DRE; CRP Stds.: 87

SS. Joachim and Anne School - (Grades PreSchool-8) 218-19 105th Ave., Queens Village, NY 11429 t) 718-465-2230 lfreebes@diobrook.org ssjaschool.org Linda Freebes, Prin.; Stds.: 295; Lay Tchrs.: 17

Our Lady of Lourdes - 92-96 220th St., Queens Village, NY 11428 t) 718-740-4090 (CRP); 718-479-5111 pa411@diobrook.org; ollreligioused@hotmail.com www.ourladyoflourdesqvny.org Rev. Patrick H. Longalong, Pst.; Rev. Msgr. Robert J. Pawson, Pastor Emer.; Rev. Robert Ambalathingal, O.C.D., In Res.; Dcn. Ricardo Moreno; Dcn. Walter C. Zimmermann; CRP Stds.: 114

REGO PARK

Our Lady of the Angelus - Merged Jan 2023 Merged with Resurrection-Ascension, Rego Park to form Resurrection Ascension – Our Lady of the Angelus Roman Catholic Church, Rego Park.

Resurrection Ascension - Our Lady of the Angelus Roman Catholic Church - 61-11 85th St., Rego Park, NY 11374 t) (718) 424-5212; (718) 533-7898 (CRP) rachsch@aol.com Rev. Thomas G. Pettei, Pst.; Rev. Richard W. Conlon, Par. Vicar; Rev. Msgr. Denis M. Herron, In Res.; CRP Stds.: 89

Our Lady of the Angelus - 63-63 98th St., Rego Park, NY 11374 (Worship Site)

RICHMOND HILL

Holy Child Jesus - 111-11 86th Ave., Richmond Hill, NY 11418 t) 718-805-5771 (CRP); 718-847-1860 hcjchurch@aol.com Rev. Israel Perez, Admin.; Rev. Carlos J. Borgos, Par. Vicar; Rev. John Paul Obiaeri, Par. Vicar; Rev. Jorge Mario Vallejo, Par. Vicar; Most Rev. Octavio Cisneros, In Res.; Dcn. Raul S. Elias; Dcn. Dean T. Tully; Mayra Alvarez, DRE; CRP Stds.: 362

Our Lady of the Cenacle - 136-06 87th Ave., Richmond Hill, NY 11418 t) 718-291-2540 olcqueens@gmail.com www.ourladyofthecenacle-queens.org Very Rev. Michael Lynch, Pst.; Dcn. Jose Mauricio Rosales; Dcn. Eduardo Sencion; Rev. Andre F. St. Preux Dabel, In Res.; CRP Stds.: 82

RIDGEWOOD

St. Aloysius - 382 Onderdonk Ave., Ridgewood, NY 11385 t) 718-417-6327 (CRP); 718-821-0231 gpsac@nyc.rr.com Rev. George Poltorak, S.A.C., Pst.; Rev. Mariusz Piatkowski, Par. Vicar; CRP Stds.: 188

St. Matthias - 58-15 Catalpa Ave., Ridgewood, NY 11385 t) 718-386-1077 (CRP); 718-821-6447 101132@diobrook.org Most Rev. Neil E. Tiedemann, C.P., Pst.; Rev. Dariusz Piotr Blicharz, Admin.; Rev. Robinson Olivares, Par. Vicar;

Our Lady of the Miraculous Medal - 62-81 60th Pl., Ridgewood, NY 11385 t) 718-456-3275 (CRP); 718-366-3360 olmm11385@aol.com Rev. Anthony J. Sansone, Pst.; Rev. Valdemaras Lisovski (Lithuania), Par. Vicar; Rev. Jaroslaw Szeraszèwicz, Par. Vicar; CRP Stds.: 100

ROCKAWAY BEACH

St. Rose of Lima - 130 Beach 84th St., Rockaway Beach, NY 11693 t) 718-945-4850 (CRP); 718-634-7394 job616@aol.com; saintrosepastor@gmail.com Rev. James Rodriguez, Pst.; Dcn. Juan M. Carattini; Dcn. Gilberto Laboy; Bridget Murphy, DRE; CRP Stds.: 103

ROCKAWAY PARK

Saint Camillus-Saint Virgilius - 99-15 Rockaway Beach Blvd., Rockaway Park, NY 11694 t) 718-634-8229 camillusrc@aol.com; pastor@stcstv.com www.stcstv.com Rev. Msgr. Richard J. Ahlemeyer, Pst.; Rev. Daniel K. Rajski, Par. Vicar; CRP Stds.: 144

St. Virgilius Church - 16 Noel Rd., Broad Channel, NY 11693 Rev. Thomas Basquel, C.S.Sp., Par. Vicar;

ROCKAWAY POINT

Blessed Trinity Roman Catholic Church - 204-25 Rockaway Point Blvd., Rockaway Point, NY 11697 t) 718-634-6357 blessedtrin@aol.com www.btparish.org Rev. Michael L. Gelfant, Pst.; Rev. Jeremy A.J. Canna, Par. Vicar; Rev. Msgr. Ronald Newland, In Res.; Dcn. Thomas J. Murphy; CRP Stds.: 185

St. Thomas More-St. Edmund - (Worship Site)

St. Genevieve - 6 Beach 178th St., Rockaway Point, NY 11697 (Worship Site)

ROSEDALE

St. Clare - 137-35 Brookville Blvd., Rosedale, NY 11422 t) 718-527-6153 (CRP); 718-341-1018 stclareqns@aol.com Rev. Daniel O. Kingsley, Admin.; Rev. John Nimako, Par. Vicar; Dcn. Christopher E. Barber; Dcn. Richard L. Hurst; Lorena DeFilippis, DRE; CRP Stds.: 94

St. Pius X - 148-10 249th St., Rosedale, NY 11422 t) 718-525-9099 stpiusxrestore@aol.com Rev. Jean-Miguel Auguste, Pst.; Marilyne Jean, DRE; CRP Stds.: 31

SOUTH OZONE PARK

St. Clement Pope - 141-11 123rd Ave., South Ozone Park, NY 11436 t) 718-641-1915 (CRP); 718-529-0273 st.clementpope@gmail.com Rev. Christogonus Iwunze, SDV, Admin.; Rev. Eric Ugochukwu, SDV, Par. Vicar; Rev. Michael Onyekwere, SDV; Rev. Vincent Odoemenam, SDV; Dcn. Nathaniel J. Smith; CRP Stds.: 21

Our Lady of Perpetual Help - 111-50 115th St., South Ozone Park, NY 11420 t) 718-641-6165 (CRP); 718-843-1212 olphchurchqns@hotmail.com Rev. Thomas W. Ahern, Pst.; Dcn. Jorge L. Alvarado; Rev. Donald M. Berran, In Res.; Rev. John Garkowski, In Res.; Rev. Lewis H. Maynard, In Res.; CRP Stds.: 72

Saint Teresa of Avila-Saint Anthony of Padua - 109-26 130th St., South Ozone Park, NY 11420 t) 718-641-5710 (CRP); 718-529-3587 101279@diobrook.org Rev. Hugh Burns, O.P., Admin.; Dcn. Patrick M. Flanagan; Dcn. Louis J. Panico; Dcn. Jose A. Lizama; Mark Kruse, DRE; CRP Stds.: 53

St. Anthony of Padua - 127-17 135th Ave, South Ozone Park, NY 11421 (Worship Site)

SOUTH RICHMOND HILL

St. Benedict Joseph Labre - 94-40 118th St., South Richmond Hill, NY 11419 t) 718-849-0246 (CRP); 718-849-4048 tbenedictjoseph@gmail.com Rev. Israel Perez, Pst.;

SPRINGFIELD GARDENS

Christ the King - 145-39 Farmers Blvd., Springfield Gardens, NY 11434 t) 718-528-6010 mdoylectk@verizon.net; christthekingsg@aol.com christthekingsg.org Rev. Gordon P. Kusi (Ghana), Pst.;

Rev. Mark T. Cregan; Dcn. Lamont A. Blake; Robbin Johnson, DRE; CRP Stds.: 63

St. Mary Magdalene - 218-12 136th Ave., Springfield Gardens, NY 11413 t) 718-949-4311 101126@diobrook.org Rev. Gordon P. Kusi (Ghana), Admin.; Rev. Cosmas Nzeabalu (Nigeria), Par. Vicar; Dcn. Ernest F. Hart; Dcn. Lee C. Williams; CRP Stds.: 56

ST. ALBANS

Our Lady of Light Roman Catholic Church - 112-43 198th St., St. Albans, NY 11412 t) 718-528-1220 101269@diobrook.org Rev. Bartholomew Mrosso, M.Afr., Pst.; Rev. Erick Baldaresa, Par. Vicar; Dcn. Albert Saldana; Dcn. Luis C. Taylor; Dcn. Fernando E. Luces, DRE; CRP Stds.: 20

St. Pascal Baylon - (Worship Site)

St. Catherine of Sienna - 118-22 Riverton St., St. Albans, NY 11412 (Worship Site)

WHITESTONE

Holy Trinity - 14-51 143rd St., Whitestone, NY 11357 t) 718-746-7730 holytrinityfaithformation@verizon.net; holytrinityrcchurch@verizon.net Very Rev. Joseph R. Gibino, Pst.; Rev. Vincent M. Daly; Dcn. Vincent A. Lino; Dcn. John P. Kramer; CRP Stds.: 120

St. Luke - 16-34 Clintonville St., Whitestone, NY 11357 t) 718-746-3409 (CRP); 718-746-8102 stlukewhitestone@aol.com Rev. John J. Costello, Pst.; Most Rev. Raymond F. Chappetto, In Res.; Rev. Dinh Chin Nguyen, Par. Vicar; Sr. Theresa Agliardi, Pst. Assoc.; Sr. Katherine Burke, C.S.J., DRE; Dcn. John P. Kramer; CRP Stds.: 273

St. Luke School - (Grades PreSchool-8) 16-01 150th Pl., Whitestone, NY 11357 t) 718-746-3833 jbrunswick@slswhitestone.org www.slswhitestone.org Jan Brunswick, Prin.; Stds.: 417; Lay Tchrs.: 24

WOODHAVEN

St. Thomas Apostle - 87-19 88th Ave., Woodhaven, NY 11421 t) 718-441-8409 (CRP); 718-847-1353 stthomasapostlewdhvn@verizon.net Rev. Francisco J. Walker, Admin.; Dcn. Jose A. Contreras;

WOODSIDE

Blessed Virgin Mary, Help of Christians - 70-31 48th Ave., Woodside, NY 11377 t) 718-672-4784 (CRP); 718-672-4848 bvmwoodside11377@aol.com stmarysofwinfield.com Rev. Christopher M. O'Connor, Pst.; Dcn. Leopoldo R. Montes; CRP Stds.: 226

Corpus Christi - 31-30 61st St., Woodside, NY 11377 t) 718-278-8114 dre@ccwoodsideny.org; ccparish@ccwoodsideny.org Rev. Msgr. Jonas Achacoso, Pst.; Rev. Mintu Rozario, Par. Vicar; Rev. John O'Neill, Par. Vicar; Rev. John Mendonca, In Res.; Dcn. Juan J. Zhagnay; Augusto F. Lucero, DRE; CRP Stds.: 144

St. Sebastian - 39-63 57th St., Woodside, NY 11377 t) 718-899-3341 (CRP); 718-429-4442 pwest@diobrook.org Rev. Patrick J. West, Pst.; Rev. Ambiorix Osorio, Par. Vicar; Rev. Elvin L. Torres, Par. Vicar; Dcn. Stephen T. Damato; Rebecca Newman, DRE;

St. Teresa - 50-20 45th St., Woodside, NY 11377 t) 718-937-4819 (CRP); 718-784-2123 101224@diobrook.org Rev. Msgr. Steven A. Ferrari, Pst.; Rev. Msgr. Otto L. Garcia, Par. Vicar; Rev. Gary H. Sommermeyer; Dcn. Roberto Abundo; Dcn. Martin D. Soraire; CRP Stds.: 217

SCHOOLS: PRESCHOOL THRU HIGH SCHOOL

SCHOOLS

STATE OF NEW YORK

ASTORIA

St. Francis of Assisi Catholic Academy in Astoria - (PAR) (Grades PreSchool-8) 21-18 46th St., Astoria, NY 11105 t) 718-726-9405 info@sfaacademy.org www.sfaacademy.org Anne Stefano, Prin.; Stds.: 289; Lay Tchrs.: 15

Immaculate Conception Catholic Academy in Astoria - (PAR) (Grades PreK-8) 21-63 29th St., Astoria, NY 11105 t) 718-728-1969 principalbrjr@iccaastoria.org www.iccaastoria.org Bro. Joseph Rocco, S.C., Prin.; Stds.: 200; Lay Tchrs.: 13

BAYSIDE

Our Lady of the Blessed Sacrament Catholic Academy - (PAR) (Grades PreSchool-8) 34-45 202nd St., Bayside, NY 11361 t) 718-229-4434 jkane@olbsacademy.org olbsacademy.org Joan Kane, Prin.; Stds.: 303; Lay Tchrs.: 22

Sacred Heart Catholic Academy of Bayside (Sacred Heart School) - (PAR) (Grades PreK-8) 216-01 38th Ave., Bayside, NY 11361 t) 718-631-4804 aconlan@sacredheartbayside.org www.sacredheartbayside.org Alexandra Conlan, Prin.; Stds.: 223; Lay Tchrs.: 25

BELLE HARBOR

St. Francis De Sales Catholic Academy - 219 Beach 129th St., Belle Harbor, NY 11694 t) 718-634-2775 admin@stfrancisschoolbh.net Christopher Scharbach, Prin.; Stds.: 636; Lay Tchrs.: 30

BROOKLYN

St. Athanasius Catholic Academy - (PAR) (Grades N-8) 6120 Bay Pkwy., Brooklyn, NY 11204 t) 718-236-4791 dcompetello@diobrook.org Diane Competello, Prin.; Stds.: 347; Lay Tchrs.: 17

Bay Ridge Catholic Academy - (DIO) (Grades PreK-8) 365 83rd St., Brooklyn, NY 11209 t) 718-745-7643 gwilliams@diobrook.org bayridgecatholic.org Gary M. Williams, Prin.; Stds.: 371; Lay Tchrs.: 27

St. Bernadette Catholic Academy - (PAR) (Grades PreK-8) 1313 83rd St., Brooklyn, NY 11228 t) 718-236-1560 principal@stbernbk.org www.stbernbk.org Sr. Joan DiRienzo, M.P.F., Prin.; Stds.: 366; Sr. Tchrs.: 3; Lay Tchrs.: 22

St. Bernard Catholic Academy - (PAR) (Grades PreSchool-8) 2030 E. 69th St., Brooklyn, NY 11234 t) 718-241-6040 tflanagan@diobrook.org www.stbernardcatholicacademy.org Tracy Flanagan, Prin.; Stds.: 321; Lay Tchrs.: 14

Blessed Sacrament Catholic Academy - (PAR) (Grades PreK-8) 187 Euclid Ave., Brooklyn, NY 11208 t) 718-235-4863 mcelmer@diobrook.org blessedsacramentca.org Marylou Celmer, Prin.; Stds.: 187; Lay Tchrs.: 11

St. Brigid Catholic Academy - (Grades PreK-8) 438 Grove St., Brooklyn, NY 11237 t) 718-821-1477 msoria@sb-sfc.org Maria Soria, Prin.; Stds.: 191; Lay Tchrs.: 13

***Brooklyn Jesuit Prep** - (PRV) (Grades 5-8) 925 E. 37th St., Brooklyn, NY 11210 t) 718-638-5884 principal@brooklynjesuit.org www.brooklynjesuit.org Russell Quinones, Prin.; Rev. Mario M. Powell, S.J., Pres.; Stds.: 78; Scholastics: 1; Pr. Tchrs.: 1; Lay Tchrs.: 9

Catherine Laboure Special Education Program - 744 E. 87th St., Brooklyn, NY 11236 t) 718-449-1857 catherinelaboure1965@gmail.com www.laboureschool.org Program for mentally challenged students and learning disabled students ages 5-21. Mary Nafash, Prin.;

Saint Catherine of Genoa-Saint Therese of Lisieux Catholic Academy - (DIO) (Grades PreK-8) 4410 Ave. D, Brooklyn, NY 11203 t) 718-629-9330 office@scgstl.org Darlene Gonzalez-Morris, Prin.; Stds.: 155; Lay Tchrs.: 11

St. Frances Cabrini Catholic Academy - 181 Suydam St., Brooklyn, NY 11221 t) 718-386-9277 principal@sfc-ca.net; info@sfc-ca.net Allison Murphy, Prin.;

St. Francis de Sales School for the Deaf in Brooklyn - (PRV) (Grades PreK-8) 260 Eastern Pkwy., Brooklyn, NY 11225 t) 718-636-4573 school@sfdesales.org www.sfdesales.org State-Supported 4201 school for children with deafness. Jodi Falk, Dir.; Jennifer White, Bus. Mgr.; Stds.: 53; Lay Tchrs.: 11

St. Francis of Assisi Catholic Academy - (PAR) (Grades PreSchool-8) 400 Lincoln Rd., Brooklyn, NY 11225 t) 718-778-3700 office@sfabrooklyn.org sfabrooklyn.org Lorraine Pierre, Prin.; Sr. Barbara Yander, Admin.; Stds.: 229; Sr. Tchrs.: 1; Lay Tchrs.: 13

Good Shepherd Catholic Academy - (PAR) (Grades PreSchool-8) 1943 Brown St., Brooklyn, NY 11229 t) 718-339-2745 jobrien@gscabk.org www.gscabk.org John O'Brien, Prin.; Stds.: 429; Lay Tchrs.: 19

St. Gregory the Great Catholic Academy - 2520 Church Ave., Brooklyn, NY 11226 t) 718-774-3330; 718-282-2770 sgg991@yahoo.com Rudolph Cyrus-Charles, Prin.; Arlene Stewart, Librn.;

Holy Angels Catholic Academy - (PAR) (Grades PreK-8) 337 74th St., Brooklyn, NY 11209 t) 718-238-5045 holyangelsoffice@aol.com www.holyangelsbayridge.org Russell Berry, Prin.;

St. Joseph the Worker Catholic Academy - (PAR) (Grades PreK-8) 241 Prospect Park W., Brooklyn, NY 11215 t) 718-768-7629 sgermann@sjwca.org www.sjwca.org Stephanie-Ann Germann, Prin.; Stds.: 270; Lay Tchrs.: 21

St. Mark Catholic Academy (St. Mark School) - (PAR) (Grades PreK-8) 2602 E. 19th St., Brooklyn, NY 11235 t) (718) 332-9304 mwilson@smsonthebay.com www.smcaonthebay.org Mark Francis Wilson, Prin.; Lisa Rizzo, Vice Prin.; Stds.: 354; Lay Tchrs.: 18

Mary Queen of Heaven Catholic Academy - (PAR) (Grades PreK-8) 1326 E. 57 St., Brooklyn, NY 11234 t) 718-763-2360 mqhsec@optonline.net Mary Lillian Bellone, Prin.;

Midwood Catholic Academy - (PAR) (Grades PreSchool-8) 1501 Hendrickson St., Brooklyn, NY 11234 t) 718-377-1800 ntriguero@diobrook.org www.midwoodcatholicacademy.org Elementary School Stds.: 238; Lay Tchrs.: 12

Our Lady of Grace Catholic Academy - (PAR) (Grades PreK-8) 385 Ave. W, Brooklyn, NY 11223 t) 718-375-2081 principal@olgbk.org Kelly Wolf, Prin.; Stds.: 198; Lay Tchrs.: 11

Our Lady of Guadalupe Catholic Academy - (PAR) (Grades PreK-8) 1514 72nd St., Brooklyn, NY 11228 t) 718-236-5587 olgacademy.net Muriel Wilkinson, Prin.;

Our Lady of Perpetual Help Catholic Academy - (PAR) (Grades PreK-8) 5902 6th Ave., Brooklyn, NY 11220 t) 718-439-8067 mtyndall@olphcab.org olphcab.org Margaret Elizabeth Tyndall, Prin.; Stds.: 160; Scholastics: 160; Lay Tchrs.: 13

Our Lady of Trust Catholic Academy - (PRV) (Grades PreK-8) 1696 Canarsie Rd., Brooklyn, NY 11236 t) 718-241-6633 oltcasocialmedia@gmail.com www.ourladyoftrustca.org Muriel Wilkinson, Prin.; Stds.: 180; Lay Tchrs.: 11

Saint Patrick Catholic Academy - (PRV) (Grades PreK-8) 401 97th St., Brooklyn, NY 11209 t) 718-833-0124 administration@stpatrickca.org www.stpatrickca.org Kathleen Curatolo, Prin.; Stds.: 240; Lay Tchrs.: 11

Saint Peter Catholic Academy - (PRV) 8401 23rd Ave., Brooklyn, NY 11214 t) 718-372-0025 dalfeo@stpeteracademy-brooklyn.org Danielle Alfeo, Prin.; Stds.: 253; Scholastics: 18

Queen of the Rosary Catholic Academy - 11 Catherine St., Brooklyn, NY 11211 t) 718-388-7992 queenoftherosaryacademy@gmail.com James Daino, Prin.;

The Ryken Educational Center - (PRV) (Grades 9-12) 7100 Shore Rd., Brooklyn, NY 11209 t) 718-759-5758 cbisciello@xaverian.org; dgambino@xaverian.org www.xaverian.org Robert Alesi, Exec. Dir.; Christian Bisciello, Dir.; Stds.: 72; Lay Tchrs.: 23

Salve Regina Catholic Academy - (Grades PreK-8) 237 Jerome St., Brooklyn, NY 11207 t) 718-277-9000; 718-277-6766 mdonato@srca.org www.srca.org Michelle Donato, Prin.; Stds.: 204; Lay Tchrs.: 13

St. Saviour Catholic Academy - (DIO) (Grades PreSchool-8) 701 Eighth Ave., Brooklyn, NY 11215 t) 718-768-8000 swalsh@sscaparkslope.org; ssgro@sscaparkslope.org www.saintsaviourcatholic.org Sophia Sgro, Admin.; Susan McCabe-Walsh, Prin.; Stds.: 326; Sr. Tchrs.: 1; Lay Tchrs.: 39

St. Stanislaus Kostka Catholic Academy - (PAR) (Grades PreK-8) 12 Newell St., Brooklyn, NY 11222 t) (929) 205-1240 igreen@ststansacademy.org www.ststansacademy.org Dr. Ivan Green, Prin.; Stds.: 233; Lay Tchrs.: 14

Visitation Academy - (PRV) (Grades PreSchool-8) 8902 Ridge Blvd., Brooklyn, NY 11209 t) 718-680-9452 www.visitationacademy.net Jean Bernieri, Prin.; Sr. Susan Marie Kasprzak, V.H.M., Supr.; Stds.: 93; Lay Tchrs.: 16

CAMBRIA HEIGHTS

Sacred Heart Catholic Academy - (PAR) (Grades PreK-8) 115-50 221st St., Cambria Heights, NY 11411 t) 718-527-0123 sacredheartch@gmail.com; shcaoffice@gmail.com shcach.org Yvonne-Therese Russell Smith, Prin.; Stds.: 239; Lay Tchrs.: 11

CORONA

St. Leo Catholic Academy (St. Leo School) - (PAR) (Grades PreK-8) 104-19 49th Ave., Corona, NY 11368 t) 718-592-7050 office@stleocatholicacademy.org www.stleocatholicacademy.org Theresa Picciano, Prin.; Stds.: 243; Lay Tchrs.: 14

Our Lady of Sorrows Catholic Academy - (PAR) (Grades PreK-8) 35-34 105th St., Corona, NY 11368 t) 718-426-5517 info@olscorona.org www.olscorona.org (Co-ed) Francis Serpico, Prin.; Stds.: 320; Lay Tchrs.: 15

DOUGLASTON

Divine Wisdom Catholic Academy - (DIO) (Grades PreK-8) 45-11 245th St., Douglaston, NY 11362 t) 718-631-3153 mbonici@dwcaonline.org; lkeppel@dwcaonline.org dwcaonline.org Miriam Bonici, Prin.; Linda Keppel, Assoc. Prin.; Sylvia Roccia, Assoc. Prin.; Stds.: 354; Lay Tchrs.: 32

ELMHURST

Saint Adalbert Catholic Academy - (DIO) (Grades PreK-8) 52-17 83rd St., Elmhurst, NY 11373 t) 718-424-2376 tmorris@diobrook.org www.saintadalbertca.org Thomas Morris, Prin.; Stds.: 237; Scholastics: 20; Sr. Tchrs.: 2; Lay Tchrs.: 18

St. Bartholomew Catholic Academy - (PAR) (Grades K-8) 44-15 Judge St., Elmhurst, NY 11373 t) 718-446-7575 sbca11373@gmail.com www.stbartholomewca.org Lisandro Pena, Prin.; Stds.: 158; Lay Tchrs.: 9

FLORAL PARK

Our Lady of the Snows Catholic Academy - (PAR) -8) 79-33 258th St., Floral Park, NY 11004 t) 718-343-1346 office@olscafp.org olscafp.org Joseph Venticinque, Prin.; Stds.: 400; Lay Tchrs.: 25

FLUSHING

St. Andrew Avellino Catholic Academy - (PAR) (Grades PreSchool-8) 35-50 158th St., Flushing, NY 11358 t) 718-359-7887 saintandrewavellino@hotmail.com standrewavellinoca.com Debora A. Hanna, Prin.; Stds.: 226; Scholastics: 1; Lay Tchrs.: 13

Holy Family Catholic Academy - (PAR) (Grades PreSchool-8) 74-15 175th St., Flushing, NY 11366 t) 718-969-2124 office@holyfamilyca-freshmeadows.org holyfamilyca-freshmeadows.org Anne Kelly, Prin.; Stds.: 170; Lay Tchrs.: 14

Saint Kevin Catholic Academy - (PAR) (Grades PreK-8) 45-50 195th St., Flushing, NY 11358 t) 718-357-2110 stkevinschool@yahoo.com stkevinca.org Allison Murphy, Prin.; Stds.: 368; Lay Tchrs.: 30

Saint Mel Catholic Academy - (Grades PreK-5) 154-24 26th Ave., Flushing, NY 11354 t) 718-539-8211 abarron@stmelsacademy.org; dvanarsdale@stmelsacademy.org www.stmelsacademy.org Amy Barron, Prin.; Stds.: 203; Lay Tchrs.: 16

St. Michael Catholic Academy - (PAR) (Grades K-8) 136-58 41st Ave., Flushing, NY 11355 t) 718-961-0284; 718-961-0246 www.stmichaelsca.org Philip Heide, Prin.; Stds.: 282; Pr. Tchrs.: 4; Sr. Tchrs.: 5; Lay Tchrs.: 30

FOREST HILLS

Our Lady of Mercy Catholic Academy - 70-25 Kessel St., Forest Hills, NY 11375 t) 718-793-2086 principal@mercyhills.org; dmccann@olmercyca.com Dana McCann, Prin.; Stds.: 320; Lay Tchrs.: 25

Our Lady Queen of Martyrs Catholic Academy - (PAR) (Grades PreK-8) 72-55 Austin St., Forest Hills, NY 11375 t) 718-263-2622 info@olqmca.org www.olqmca.com Anne Zuschlag, Prin.; Stds.: 334; Lay Tchrs.: 17

FRESH MEADOWS

St. Francis Preparatory School - (PRV) (Grades 9-12) 6100 Francis Lewis Blvd., Fresh Meadows, NY 11365 t) 718-423-8810 lconway@stfrancisprep.org; pmclaughlin@stfrancisprep.org www.sfponline.org (Coed) Rev. Ralph Edel, Chap.; Patrick McLaughlin, Prin.; Bro. Leonard Conway, O.S.F., Pres.; Stds.: 2,400; Pr. Tchrs.: 1; Bro. Tchrs.: 2; Sr. Tchrs.: 1; Lay Tchrs.: 125

GLENDALE

Sacred Heart Catholic Academy of Glendale - (PAR) (Grades PreK-8) 84-05 78th Ave., Glendale, NY 11385 t) 718-456-6636 mcallaghan@sacredheartglendale.org; secretary@sacredheartglendale.org sacredheartglendale.org Michael Callaghan, Prin.; Stds.: 294; Lay Tchrs.: 16

HOWARD BEACH

Ave Maria Catholic Academy - (PAR) (Grades N-8) 158-20 101st St., Howard Beach, NY 11414 t) 718-848-7440 mmcmanus@olgcahb.org www.olgcahb.org Marybeth McManus, Prin.;

St. Helen Catholic Academy - (PAR) (Grades PreSchool-8) 83-09 157th Ave., Howard Beach, NY 11414 t) 718-835-4155 info@sthelencatholicacademy.org www.sthelencatholicacademy.org Stds.: 444; Lay Tchrs.: 18

JAMAICA

Immaculate Conception Catholic Academy - (PAR) (Grades PreK-8) 179-14 Dalny Rd., Jamaica, NY 11432 t) 718-739-5933 drcruz@iccajamaica.org www.iccajamaica.org Dr. Cristina Cruz, Prin.; Stds.: 245; Scholastics: 245; Lay Tchrs.: 12

St. Nicholas of Tolentine Catholic Academy - (PAR) (Grades PreSchool-8) 80-22 Parsons Blvd., Jamaica, NY 11432 t) 718-380-1900 office@sntschoolny.org sntschoolny.org Gregory Pirraglia, Prin.; Stds.: 300; Lay Tchrs.: 19

JAMAICA ESTATES

The Mary Louis Academy (College Preparatory) - (PRV) 176-21 Wexford Ter., Jamaica Estates, NY 11432 t) 718-297-2120 principal@tmla.org www.tmla.org (Girls) Ann O'Hagan-Cordes, Prin.; Marie Whelan, Librn.; Stds.: 550; Scholastics: 73; Sr. Tchrs.: 2; Lay Tchrs.: 51

LONG ISLAND CITY

St. Joseph Catholic Academy - (Grades PreK-8) 2846 44th St., Long Island City, NY 11103 t) 718-728-0724 info@sjcalic.org www.sjcalic.org Luke Nawrocki, Prin.; Lucy Alaimo, Early Childhood Dir.; Stds.: 382; Lay Tchrs.: 20

MIDDLE VILLAGE

Saint Margaret Catholic Academy - (PAR) (Grades PreK-8) 66-10 80th St., Middle Village, NY 11379 t) 718-326-0922 principal@stmargaretschoolmv.org Sharon Swift, Prin.; Stds.: 258; Lay Tchrs.: 12

Our Lady of Hope Catholic Academy - (PAR) (Grades PreK-8) 61-21 71st St., Middle Village, NY 11379 t) 718-458-3535 olhoff@olhca.org; olhprin@olhca.org www.olhca.org Giuseppe F. Campailla, Prin.; Stds.: 516; Lay Tchrs.: 30

OZONE PARK

Divine Mercy Catholic Academy - (PRV) (Grades PreK-8) 101-60 92nd St., Ozone Park, NY 11416 t) 718-845-3074 x3 m.lods@dmcacademy.com www.divinemercyca.org Elementary Campus N-8. Sr. Francis Marie Wystepek, C.S.F.N., Prin.; Stds.: 240; Lay Tchrs.: 15

St. Elizabeth Catholic Academy - (Grades PreK-8) 9401 85th St., Ozone Park, NY 11416 t) 718-641-6990 info@stelizabethca.org Jeanne Shannon, Prin.; Stds.: 310; Lay Tchrs.: 16

St. Mary Gate of Heaven Catholic Academy - (PAR) (Grades PreK-8) 104-06 101st Ave., Ozone Park, NY 11416 t) 718-846-0689 pheide@smgh.org www.smgh.org Philip Heide, Prin.;

QUEENS

Our Lady of Fatima Catholic Academy - (PAR) (Grades PreSchool-8) 25-38 80th St., Queens, NY 11370 t) 718-429-7031 olfcainfo@ourladyoffatimaschool.org olfcaqueens.org Margaret Rogers, Prin.; Stds.: 252; Lay Tchrs.: 15

QUEENS VILLAGE

Incarnation Catholic Academy - (PAR) (Grades PreK-8) 89-15 Francis Lewis Blvd., Queens Village, NY 11427 t) 718-465-5066 principal@incarnationqv.org www.incarnationqv.org Mary Lillian Bellone, Prin.; Lay Tchrs.: 12

REGO PARK

Our Lady of the Angelus Catholic Academy - (Grades N-8) 98-05 63rd Dr., Rego Park, NY 11374 t) 718-896-7220 olarcschool@aol.com www.ourladyoftheangelus.com Giuseppe F. Campailla, Prin.;

Resurrection Ascension Catholic Academy - (PAR) (Grades PreSchool-8) 85-25 61st Rd., Rego Park, NY 11374 t) 718-426-4963 raschool443@aol.com; office@raschool.net racatholicacademy.org Joann Heppt, Prin.; Stds.: 275; Lay Tchrs.: 17

RICHMOND HILL

Holy Child Jesus Catholic Academy - (PAR) (Grades PreK-8) 111-02 86th Ave., Richmond Hill, NY 11418 t) 718-849-3988 pwinters@hcjcany.org www.hcjcany.org Patricia Winters, Prin.; Stds.: 375; Lay Tchrs.: 23

RIDGEWOOD

St. Matthias Catholic Academy (St. Matthias School) - (PAR) (Grades PreK-8) 58-25 Catalpa Ave., Ridgewood, NY 11385 t) 718-381-8003 principal@stmatthiasschool.org www.stmatthiasca.org Neil Gerig, Prin.; Stds.: 196; Lay Tchrs.: 10

Notre Dame Catholic Academy of Ridgewood - (Grades PreK-8) 62-22 61st St., Ridgewood, NY 11385 t) 718-821-2221 ww.notredame-ca.org Judith Munno, Prin.; Stds.: 273; Lay Tchrs.: 14

ROCKAWAY BEACH

Saint Rose of Lima Catholic Academy - (PAR) (Grades PreK-8) 154 Beach 84th St., Rockaway Beach, NY 11693 t) 718-474-7079 stroseacademyrb@gmail.com stroseoflimacatholicacademy.org Satti Marchan, Prin.; Stds.: 205; Sr. Tchrs.: 1; Lay Tchrs.: 12

ROSEDALE

Saint Clare Catholic Academy - 137-25 Brookville Blvd., Rosedale, NY 11422 t) 718-528-7174 mbasile@diobrook.org; scca@stclarecatholicacademy.org stclarecatholicacademy.org Mary Rafferty-Basile, Prin.; Stds.: 236; Lay Tchrs.: 9

SOUTH OZONE PARK

Our Lady of Perpetual Help Catholic Academy - (PAR) (Grades PreSchool-8) 111-10 115 St., South Ozone Park, NY 11420; Mailing: 111-50 115th St., South Ozone Park, NY 11420 t) 718-843-4184 fdeluca@diobrook.org olphca.org Frances DeLuca, Prin.; Stds.: 350; Scholastics: 40; Lay Tchrs.: 40

VALLEY STREAM

Martin de Porres School for Exceptional Children, Inc. - (PRV) 50 Rose Ave., Valley Stream, NY 11580 t) 516-758-7501 kreismiller@mdp.org www.mdp.org Specialized day elementary & high school and group residence for emotionally challenged youth ages 6-21. Joseph Trainor, Exec. Dir.; Stds.: 240; Lay Tchrs.: 140

Martin de Porres Elementary School - 621 Elmont Rd., Bldg. A, Elmont, NY 11003 t) 516-616-0671 jgalassi@mdp.org John Galassi, Prin.; Stds.: 147; Lay Tchrs.: 71

Casa de La Salle - 101-25 104th St., Ozone Park, NY 11416 t) 718-850-0191 lbailey@mdp.org Day & residential school for emotionally challenged youth. Lennox Bailey, Dir.; Stds.: 70; Lay Tchrs.: 61

WHITESTONE

Holy Trinity Catholic Academy - (PAR) (Grades PreK-8) 14-45 143rd St., Whitestone, NY 11357 t) 718-746-1479 bkavanagh@htcawhitestone.org Barbara Kavanagh, Prin.;

WOODHAVEN

St. Thomas the Apostle Catholic Academy - (PAR) (Grades PreK-8) 87-49 87th St., Woodhaven, NY 11421 t) 718-847-3904 tpiro@diobrook.org www.sta-catholicacademy.org Thomas R. Piro, Prin.; Stds.: 171; Lay Tchrs.: 12

WOODSIDE

St. Sebastian Catholic Academy - (PAR) (Grades PreSchool-8) 39-76 58th St., Woodside, NY 11377 t) 718-429-1982 staff@stsebastianacademy.org www.stsebastianacademy.org Michelle Picarello, Prin.; Stds.: 364; Lay Tchrs.: 25

HIGH SCHOOLS

STATE OF NEW YORK

ASTORIA

St. John's Preparatory School - (PRV) 21-21 Crescent St., Astoria, NY 11105-3398 t) 718-721-7200 nmartinez@stjohnsprepschool.org www.stjohnsprepschool.org (Coed) Rev. Liju Augustine, Chap.; Nuala Martinez, Pres.; Valerie Bove, Librn.; Stds.: 621; Pr. Tchrs.: 1; Lay Tchrs.: 40

BRIARWOOD

Archbishop Molloy High School - (PAR) (Grades 9-12) 83-53 Manton St., Briarwood, NY 11435 t) 718-441-2100 president@molloyhs.org www.molloyhs.org (Coed) Darius Penikas, Prin.; Richard A. Karsten, Pres.; Stds.: 1,525; Scholastics: 20; Bro. Tchrs.: 5; Lay Tchrs.: 77

BROOKLYN

Bishop Loughlin Memorial High School - (PRV) (Grades 9-12) 357 Clermont Ave., Brooklyn, NY 11238 t) 718-857-2700 dcronin@blmhs.org; dharris@blmhs.org www.loughlin.org (Coed) Bro. Dennis Cronin, F.S.C., Pres.; Edward A. Bolan, Prin.; Cecilia Gottsegen, Asst. Prin., Academics; Luis Montes, Dean; Elisa Randall, Dean; Stds.: 616; Bro. Tchrs.: 1; Lay Tchrs.: 49

Cristo Rey Brooklyn High School - 710 E. 37th St., Brooklyn, NY 11203 t) 718-455-3555 icharles@cristoreybrooklyn.org; bhenson@cristoreybrooklyn.org www.cristoreybrooklyn.org Deanna Philippe, Prin.; Ryan Scheb, Vice Prin.; Paul Scariano, Chair; William Henson, Pres.; Stds.: 297; Lay Tchrs.: 20

Denis Maloney Institute/St. Edmund Preparatory High School - (PAR) (Grades 9-12) 2474 Ocean Ave., Brooklyn, NY 11229 t) 718-743-6100 amcginnis@stedmundprep.org www.stedmundprep.org (Coed) Allison McGinnis, Prin.; Dorothea Breen, Vice Prin.; Peggy McEvoy, Vice Prin.; Suzanne Lemmon, Librn.; Brian Wagner, Vice Prin.; Stds.: 562; Pr. Tchrs.: 2; Lay Tchrs.: 40

Fontbonne Hall Academy - (PRV) (Grades 9-12) 9901 Shore Rd., Brooklyn, NY 11209 t) 718-748-2244 herron@fontbonne.org www.fontbonne.org (Girls) Fred Herron, Prin.; Emma Crean, Asst. Prin.; Stds.: 296; Lay Tchrs.: 29

Nazareth Regional High School - (PRV) 475 E. 57th St., Brooklyn, NY 11203 t) 718-763-1100 x223 rdire@nazarethrhs.org www.nazarethrhs.org (Coed) Robert DiRe, Prin.; Ron Kelley, Asst. Prin., Student Life; Sandy Michel, Asst. Prin., Enrollment; Nancy Roberts, Asst. Prin., Academics; Natalia Rodriguez, Dir. Opers.; Stds.: 350; Lay Tchrs.: 18

St. Saviour High School - (PAR) (Grades 9-12) 588 6th St., Brooklyn, NY 11215 t) 718-768-4406 timpone.c@stsaviour.org; maurer.j@stsaviour.org www.stsaviour.org (Girls) Carolann Timpone, Prin.; Jennifer Maurer, Asst. Prin.; Sharon Keller, Campus Min.; Stds.: 200; Lay Tchrs.: 16

Xaverian - (PRV) (Grades 6-12) 7100 Shore Rd., Brooklyn, NY 11209 t) 718-836-7100 ralesi@xaverian.org; plouisa@xaverian.org www.xaverian.org (Co-ed) Robert Alesi, Pres.; Daniel Sharib, Prin.; Eileen Long Chelales, Dir.; Stds.: 1,588; Lay Tchrs.: 158

EAST ELMHURST

Monsignor McClancy Memorial High School - 71-06 31st Ave., East Elmhurst, NY 11370 t) 718-898-3800 nmelito@msgrmcclancy.info; jcastrataro@msgrmcclancy.info www.msgrmcclancy.org (Coed) Jim Castrataro, Prin.; Nicole Alexis-Kane, Librn.;

FLUSHING

Holy Cross High School - (PRV) 26-20 Francis Lewis Blvd., Flushing, NY 11358 t) 718-886-7250 info@holycrosshs.org www.holycrosshs.org (Co-ed) Edward Burns, Prin.; Mark Mongelluzzo, Pres.; Stds.: 721; Lay Tchrs.: 47

MIDDLE VILLAGE

Christ the King High School - (PRV) 68-02 Metropolitan Ave., Middle Village, NY 11379 t) 718-366-7400 www.ctkny.org (Coed) Rev. Frank W. Spacek, Chap.; Geri Martinez, Prin.; Michael W. Michel, Pres.; Sr. Elizabeth Graham, C.S.J., Campus Min.;

INSTITUTIONS LOCATED IN DIOCESE

ASSOCIATIONS [ASN]

BROOKLYN

The Roman Catholic Pontifical Lay Association Memores Domini - 218 76th St., Brooklyn, NY 11209 t) 917-498-6066 asala218@gmail.com Angela Sala, Treas.;

Men's House - 218 76th St., Brooklyn, NY 11209 c) (917) 498-6066

Women's House - 10 Kraft Ave., Bronxville, NY 10708 t) 914-395-0019 paolafracmessa@yahoo.com

CAMPUS MINISTRY / NEWMAN CENTERS [CAM]

BROOKLYN

Campus Ministers and Ministry Centers (Newman Apostolate, Inc.) - 310 Prospect Park W., Brooklyn, NY 11215 t) 718-965-7300 x5224 mcuria@diobrook.org Rev. Richard Bretone; Rev. Kevin P. Cavalluzzi; Rev. Brian Jordan, O.S.F.; Rev. Richard E. Long; Rev. Anthony F. Rosado; Rev. Michael G. Tedone; Most Rev. James Massa, Vicar; Rev. Grzegorz Dziedzic, Campus Min.;

CATHOLIC CHARITIES [CCH]

BROOKLYN

Catholic Charities, Diocese of Brooklyn - Central Office, 191 Joralemon St., Brooklyn, NY 11201 t) 718-722-6000 www.ccbq.org Thomas Kevin Murtha, Chair; Rev. Msgr. Alfred P. LoPinto, CEO; Very Rev. Patrick J. Keating, Deputy CEO & CFO; Emmie Glynn Ryan, Chief of Staff & Gen. Counsel; Asstd. Annu.: 252,237; Staff: 1,254

Advocate for Persons with Disabilities Services - Richard Slizeski, SVP;

Bereavement Services - Richard Slizeski, SVP;

Community Service - Richard Slizeski, SVP;

Office of Mission - Richard Slizeski, SVP;

Office of Planning & Evaluation - Jim Norcott, SVP;

Vincentian Outreach - Richard Slizeski, SVP;

Catholic Charities Neighborhood Services, Inc. - 191 Joralemon St., Brooklyn, NY 11201 t) 718-722-6000 info@ccbq.org www.ccbq.org Rev. Msgr. Alfred P. LoPinto, CEO; Santos Rodriguez, Chair; Very Rev. Patrick J. Keating, Deputy CEO & CFO; Emmie Glynn Ryan, Chief of Staff & Gen. Counsel; Patricia Bowles, Sr. Vice Pres. & Chief Prog. Of., Integrated Health & Wellness; Gladys Rodriguez, Sr. Vice Pres. & Chief Prog. Officer, Family & Community Svcs.; Asstd. Annu.: 66,716; Staff: 1,040

Catholic Migration Services, Inc. - 191 Joralemon St., 4th Fl., Brooklyn, NY 11201 t) 718-236-3000 pkeating@catholicmigration.org www.catholicmigration.org Very Rev. Patrick J. Keating, CEO;

Catholic Migration Services, Inc. - 191 Joralemon St., 4th Fl., Brooklyn, NY 11201 t) 718-236-3000 pkeating@catholicmigration.org www.catholicmigration.org Very Rev. Patrick J. Keating, CEO; David Colodny, Dir.;

Catholic Immigrant Ministries of Brooklyn and Queens - 191 Joralemon St., Brooklyn, NY 11201

Catholic Migration & Refugee Office - Apostolate Coordinators.

African American Ministry - t) 718-574-5772 Rev. Alonzo Q. Cox;

Arabic Speaking Ministry - t) 718-768-9471 Rev. Francis Fayez Abaskhron;

Brazilian Ministry - t) 718-361-1884 Rev. Jose Carlos Da Silva;

Chinese Ministry-Brooklyn - t) 718-436-1080 Rev. Vincentius T. Do;

Chinese Ministry-Queens - t) 718-961-0714 Rev. Antonius Ho, C.S.J.B. (Taiwan);

Croatian Ministry - t) 718-278-3337 Rev. Vedran Kirincic;

Czech/Slovak Ministry - t) 718-268-6251 Rev. Antonin Kocurek;

Filipino Ministry - t) 718-634-6464 Rev. Patrick H. Longalong;

Ghanaian Ministry - t) 718-282-7162 Rev. Charles Akoto Oduro (Ghana);

Haitian Ministry - t) 718-622-6500 Rev. Saint Charles Borno;

Indian Latin Rite Ministry - t) 718-479-5111 Rev. Robert Ambalathingal, O.C.D.;

Indonesian Ministry - t) 718-897-4444 Rev. Robert Mirsel, S.V.D.;

Irish Ministry - t) 718-392-0011; 718-392-0012; 718-472-2625 Rev. Brian P. Dowd;

Italian Ministry - t) 718-236-0124 Rev. Msgr. David L. Cassato;

Korean Ministry - t) 718-229-6465 Rev. Sun Joong Kwon;

Lithuanian Ministry - t) 718-326-2236 Rev. Vytautas Volertas;

Mexican Ministry - t) 718-821-1690

Nigerian Ministry - t) 718-949-4311 Rev. Cosmas Nzeabalu (Nigeria);

Pakistani Ministry - t) 718-871-1310 Rev. Ilyas Gill, O.F.M. (Pakistan);

Polish Ministry - t) 718-268-6143 Rev. Grzegorz Stasiak (Poland);

Russian Speaking/Ukrainian Ministry - t) 718-891-3100 Rev. Sergiy Emanuel;

Vietnamese Ministry - t) 718-278-1834 Rev. Peter H. Nguyen;

West Indian Ministry - t) 718-774-6747 Rev. Francis A. Black;

Queens Office - 47-01 Queens Blvd., Ste. 203, Sunnyside, NY 11104 t) 347-472-3500

Resources, Inc. -

CCNS - Early Childhood Services - 191 Joralemon St., Brooklyn, NY 11201 t) 718-722-6000 info@ccbq.org Gladys Rodriguez, Sr. Vice Pres. & Chief Prog. Officer; Desiree A Jackson-Fryson, Vice. Pres.; Asstd. Annu.: 1,700

Caritas Training Center - 38-11 27th St., Long Island City, NY 11101 t) 718-937-7640 Desiree Jackson-Fryson, Vice Pres., Early Childhood Svcs.;

Charles F. Murphy Early Childhood Development Center - 2856 W. 15th St., Brooklyn, NY 11224

t) (929) 268-3317

Colin Newell Early Childhood Development Center - 107-65 Merrick Blvd., Jamaica, NY 11433 t) 718-523-1888

St. Malachy Early Childhood Development Center - 220 Hendricks St., Brooklyn, NY 11207 t) 718-647-0966

Msgr. Andrew Landi Early Childhood Development Center - 21-20 35th Ave., Long Island City, NY 11106 t) (718) 806-1598

Parkside Early Childhood Development Center - 525 Parkside Ave., Brooklyn, NY 11226 t) 929-210-9200

Sunset Park Early Childhood Development Center - 5902 6th Ave., Brooklyn, NY 11220 t) 718-768-1012; 718-768-1607

Therese Cervini Annex Early Child Development Center - 35-33 104th St., Corona, NY 11368 t) 718-478-2274; 718-478-2784

Therese Cervini Family Child Care - 35-33 104th St., Corona, NY 11368 t) 718-334-0806; 718-334-0807

Thomas A. DeStefano Early Childhood Development Center - 300 Vernon Ave., Brooklyn, NY 11206 t) 718-443-2900

Vincent J. Caristo Family Child Care - 525 Parkside Ave., Brooklyn, NY 11226 t) 718-788-3035; 718-788-3036

CCNS - Family Stabilization Services - 191 Joralemon St., Brooklyn, NY 11201 t) 718-722-6000 info@ccbq.org www.ccbq.org Mary Hurson, Vice. Pres.; Asstd. Annu.: 16,750; Staff: 210

CCNS Homebase Mott Avenue Annex - 1847 Mott Ave., 1st Fl., Far Rockaway, NY 11691 t) 718-647-1000 Gladys Rodriguez, Sr. Vice Pres. & Chief Prog. Of.;

CCNS Immigrant Services ESOL-Civics - 42-71 65th Pl., Woodside, NY 11377 t) 718-726-9790 allmina.berisha@ccbq.org; laura.dotterer@ccbq.org Gladys Rodriguez, Sr. Vice Pres. & Chief Prog. Of.;

CCNS Immigrant Services ESOL-Civics - 191 Joralemon St., 2nd Fl., Brooklyn, NY 11201 t) 718-722-6009 allmina.berisha@ccbq.org Gladys Rodriguez, Sr. Vice Pres. & Chief Prog. Of.;

CCNS Livonia Avenue Homebase - 560 Livonia Ave., Brooklyn, NY 11207 t) 718-408-7181 Gladys Rodriguez, Sr. Vice Pres. & Chief Prog. Of.;

COMPASS @ PS 50 - 143-26 101st Ave., Jamaica, NY 11435 t) 347-228-7802 Gladys Rodriguez, Sr. Vice Pres. & Chief Prog. Of.;

COMPASS @ PS 106 - 1328 Putnam Ave., Brooklyn, NY 11221 t) 718-628-1905 x1055 Gladys Rodriguez, Sr. Vice Pres. & Chief Prog. Of.;

Healthy Families Bushwick @ PS 106 - 1328 Putnam Ave., Brooklyn, NY 11221 t) 718-628-1905 allmina.berisha@ccbq.org; elaine.ortiz@ccbq.org Gladys Rodriguez, Sr. Vice Pres. & Chief Prog. Of.;

Homebase Homelessness Prevention I - 161-10 Jamaica Ave., 5th Fl., Jamaica, NY 11432 t) 718-674-1000 Gladys Rodriguez, Sr. Vice Pres. & Chief Prog. Of.;

Homebase Homelessness Prevention II - 3060 Fulton St., Brooklyn, NY 11208 t) 929-234-3036 Gladys Rodriguez, Sr. Vice Pres. & Chief Prog. Of.;

Homebase Homelessness Prevention III - 1900A Ralph Ave., Brooklyn, NY 11234 t) (718) 514-8034 Gladys Rodriguez, Sr. Vice Pres. & Chief Prog. Of.;

Queens Mobility Mentoring Program - 161-10 Jamaica Ave., Fl. 4, Jamaica, NY 11432 t) 718-526-5151 Gladys Rodriguez, Sr. Vice Pres. & Chief Prog. Of.;

Jamaica WIC Program - 161-10 Jamaica Ave., 3rd Fl., Ste. 306, Jamaica, NY 11432 t) 718-657-2580 leoniza.nazareno@ccbq.org; mhurson@ccbq.org Gladys Rodriguez, Sr. Vice Pres. & Chief Prog. Of.;

Moving Forward - 191 Joralmeon St., 9th Fl., Brooklyn, NY 11201 t) (718) 722-6112 omar.carrilloperez@ccbq.org; allmina.berisha@ccbq.org Gladys Rodriguez, Sr. Vice Pres. & Chief Prog. Of.;

NYCALI/Adult Literacy Initiative - 42-71 65th Pl., Woodside, NY 11377 t) 718-726-9790 x3010 laura.dotterer@ccbq.org; allmina.berisha@ccbq.org Gladys Rodriguez, Sr. Vice Pres. & Chief Prog. Of.;

Ocean Bay Community Services - 57-10 Beach Channel Dr., Arverne, NY 11692 c) (347) 585-7734 Gladys Rodriguez, Sr. Vice Pres. & Chief Prog. Of.;

Pathway Home - Queens Transition Team - 91-14 Merrick Blvd., 6th Floor, Jamaica, NY 11432 t) (718) 408-7178 Patricia Bowles, Sr. Vice Pres. & Chief Prog. Of.;

Refugee Resettlement Program - 191 Joralemon St., 2nd Fl., Brooklyn, NY 11201 t) 718-722-6009 allmina.berisha@ccbq.org Gladys Rodriguez, Sr. Vice Pres. & Chief Prog. Of.;

Riverdale Osborne Community Services - 440 Watkins Ave., Brooklyn, NY 11212 info@ccbq.org Gladys Rodriguez, Sr. Vice Pres. & Chief Prog. Of.;

Summer Youth Employment (SYEP) - 191 Joralemon St., 2nd Fl., Brooklyn, NY 11201 t) 718-722-6216 lisa.semper@ccbq.org; allmina.berisha@ccbq.org Gladys Rodriguez, Sr. Vice Pres. & Chief Prog. Of.;

Woodside WIC Programs - 42-71 65th Pl., Woodside, NY 11377 t) 718-715-7001 info@ccbq.org Gladys Rodriguez, Sr. Vice Pres. & Chief Prog. Of.;

Work, Learn and Grow Employment Program - 191 Joralmeon St., 9th Fl., Brooklyn, NY 11201 t) 718-722-6216 Gladys Rodriguez, Sr. Vice Pres. & Chief Prog. Of.;

CCNS - Integrated Health and Wellness - 191 Joralemon St., 14th Fl., Brooklyn, NY 11201 t) 718-722-6062 ewageman@ccbq.org Desiree M. Arduini, Vice. Pres.; Martin Sussman, Vice. Pres.; Ellen Wagman, Dir., Opers; Asstd. Annu.: 39,440; Staff: 220

Home & Community Based Services (HCBS-BHS) - 1623 Flatbush Ave., Lower Level, Brooklyn, NY 11210 c) 347-517-3107 info@ccbq.org Residential an Community Habilitation. Patricia Bowles, Sr. Vice Pres. & Chief Prog. Of.;

CCNS - Senior Services - 191 Joralemon St., Brooklyn, NY 11201 t) 718-722-6095 samira.alieva@ccbq.org Samira Alieva, Vice. Pres.;

The Bay Older Adult Center - 3643 Nostrand Ave., Brooklyn, NY 11229 t) 718-648-2053 info@ccbq.org Gladys Rodriguez, Sr. Vice Pres. & Chief Prog. Of.;

Bayside Older Adult Center and Bayside Older Adult Center Transportation Program - 221-15 Horace Harding Expwy., Bayside, NY 11364 t) 718-225-1144 info@ccbq.org www.ccbq.orq Gladys Rodriguez, Sr. Vice Pres. & Chief Prog. Of.;

Benson Ridge Older Adult Center - 6823 5th Ave., 3rd Fl., Brooklyn, NY 11220 t) 718-680-3530 info@ccbq.org Gladys Rodriguez, Sr. Vice Pres. & Chief Prog. Of.;

Catherine Sheridan Older Adult Center - 35-24 83rd St., Jackson Heights, NY 11372 t) 718-458-4600 infor@ccbq.org Gladys Rodriguez, Sr. Vice Pres. & Chief Prog. Of.;

CCNS Depression & Substance Abuse Screening & Assistance Program - 6823 Fifth Ave., 2nd Fl., Brooklyn, NY 11220 t) 718-514-8035 info@ccbq.org Gladys Rodriguez, Sr. Vice Pres. & Chief Prog. Of.;

CCNS NE Queens Home Delivered Meals Program - 91-34 182nd Pl., 2nd Fl., Jamaica, NY 11423 t) 718-357-4903 info@ccbq.org Gladys Rodriguez, Sr. Vice Pres. & Chief Prog. Of.;

CCNS Social Adult Day Alzheimer's Program - 190-04 119th Ave., St. Albans, NY 11412 t) 718-358-3541 info@ccbq.org Gladys Rodriguez, Sr. Vice Pres. & Chief Prog. Of.;

CCNS SW Queens Home Delivered Meals Program - 103-02 101st Ave., Ozone Park, NY 11416 t) 718-847-2168 info@ccbq.org Gladys Rodriguez, Sr. Vice Pres. & Chief Prog. Of.;

CCNS Western Queens Home Delivered Meal Program - 89-18 Astoria Blvd., East Elmhurst, NY 11369 t) 718-806-1080 info@ccbq.org Gladys Rodriguez, Sr. Vice Pres. & Chief Prog. Of.;

St. Charles Jubilee Older Adult Center - 55 Pierrepont St., Brooklyn, NY 11201 t) 718-855-0326 info@ccbq.org Gladys Rodriguez, Sr. Vice Pres. & Chief Prog. Of.;

Della Monica-Steinway Older Adult Center - 23-11 31st Rd., Astoria, NY 11106 t) 718-626-1500 info@ccbq.org Gladys Rodriguez, Sr. Vice Pres. & Chief Prog. Of.;

Glenwood Senior Center - 5701 Ave. H, Brooklyn, NY 11234 t) 718-241-7711 info@ccbq.org Gladys Rodriguez, Sr. Vice Pres. & Chief Prog. Of.;

Hillcrest Older Adult Center - 91-34 182nd Pl., 2nd Fl., Jamaica, NY 11423 t) 718-297-7171 info@ccbq.org Gladys Rodriguez, Sr. Vice Pres. & Chief Prog. Of.;

Howard Beach Older Adult Center - 155-55 Cross Bay Blvd., Howard Beach, NY 11414 t) 718-738-8100 info@ccbq.org Gladys Rodriguez, Sr. Vice Pres. & Chief Prog. Of.;

The Lodge Older Adult Center - 7711 18th Ave., Brooklyn, NY 11214 t) 718-621-1081 info@ccbq.org Gladys Rodriguez, Sr. Vice Pres. & Chief Prog. Of.;

St. Louis Older Adult Center - 230 Kingston Ave., Brooklyn, NY 11213 t) 718-771-7945 info@ccbq.org Gladys Rodriguez, Sr. Vice Pres. & Chief Prog. Of.;

Narrows Older Adult Center - 930 53rd St., Brooklyn, NY 11219 t) 718-232-3211 info@ccbq.org Gladys Rodriguez, Sr. Vice Pres. & Chief Prog. Of.;

Northside Older Adult Center - 179 N. 6th St., Brooklyn, NY 11211 t) 718-387-2316 info@ccbq.org Gladys Rodriguez, Sr. Vice Pres. & Chief Prog. Of.;

Ozone Park Older Adult Center - 103-02 101st Ave., Ozone Park, NY 11416 t) 718-847-2100 info@ccbq.org Gladys Rodriguez, Sr. Vice Pres. & Chief Prog. Of.;

Pete McGuinness Older Adult Center - 715 Leonard St., Brooklyn, NY 11222 t) 718-383-1940 info@ccbq.org Gladys Rodriguez, Sr. Vice Pres. & Chief Prog. Of.;

Riverway Older Adult Center - 230 Riverdale Ave., Brooklyn, NY 11212 t) 718-942-5345 info@ccbq.org Gladys Rodriguez, Sr. Vice Pres. & Chief Prog. Of.;

Seaside Older Adult Center - 320 Beach 94th St., Rockaway Beach, NY 11693 t) 347-926-4119 info@ccbq.org Gladys Rodriguez, Sr. Vice Pres. & Chief Prog. Of.;

Sheepshead Bay Supportive Services (NORC) - 3677 Nostrand Ave. #3A, Brooklyn, NY 11229 t) 718-769-3579 info@ccbq.org Gladys Rodriguez, Sr. Vice Pres. & Chief Prog. Of.;

South Brooklyn Alzheimer's Adult Care Program - 5701 Ave. H, Brooklyn, NY 11234 t) 718-241-7711; 718-241-1936 info@ccbq.org Gladys Rodriguez, Sr. Vice Pres. & Chief Prog. Of.;

Southwest Queens Older Adult Center - 183-16 Jamaica Ave., 2nd Fl., Jamaica, NY 11423 t) 718-217-0126 info@ccbq.org Gladys Rodriguez, Sr. Vice Pres. & Chief Prog. Of.;

Woodhaven-Richmond Hill Older Adult Center - 89-02 91st St., Woodhaven, NY 11421 t) 718-847-9200 info@ccbq.org Gladys Rodriguez, Sr. Vice Pres. & Chief Prog. Of.;

Flowers With Care, Diocese of Brooklyn, Inc. - 191 Joralemon St., Brooklyn, NY 11201 t) 718-722-6000

Housing Development and Management Services - 191 Joralemon St., Brooklyn, NY 11201 t) 718-722-6000 info@ccbq.org Tim McManus, SVP; George Stathoudakis, SVP; Rev. Msgr. Alfred P. LoPinto, CEO; Asstd. Annu.: 3,557; Staff: 153

161-01 89th Avenue Corp. - 191 Joralemon St., Brooklyn, NY 11201 t) (718) 722-6000 www.ccbq.org Emmie Glynn Ryan, Secy.;

Pierrepont Housing Development Fund Corporation - 191 Joralemon St., Brooklyn, NY 11201 t) (718) 722-6000 www.ccbq.org

Bellerose Senior Housing Development Fund Corp., Inc. - 238-11 Hillside Ave., Bellerose, NY 11426; Mailing: 191 Joralemon St., Brooklyn, NY 11201 www.ccbq.org

Bethlehem Community HDFC Inc. - 191 Joralemon St., Brooklyn, NY 11201 t) (718) 722-6000 www.ccbq.org Emmie Glynn Ryan;

Bishop Boardman Senior HDFC - 191 Joralemon St.,

Brooklyn, NY 11201 t) (718) 722-6000 www.ccbq.org
Bishop Francis J. Mugavero Senior HDFC - 191 Joralemon St., Brooklyn, NY 11201 t) (718) 722-6000 www.ccbq.org
St. Brendan Senior Housing Development Fund Corporation - 1215 Ave. O, Brooklyn, NY 11230; Mailing: 191 Joralemon St., Brooklyn, NY 11201 t) (718) 722-6000
Caring Communities Associates HDFC, Inc. - 191 Joralemon St., Brooklyn, NY 11201 t) (718) 722-6000
Casa Betsaida HDFC - 191 Joralemon St., Brooklyn, NY 11201 t) (718) 722-6000 Emmie Glynn Ryan, Secy.;
Casa Betsaida Housing Development Fund Corp. - 191 Joralemon St., Brooklyn, NY 11201 t) (718) 722-6000 www.ccbq.org
Catherine Sheridan HDFC, Inc. - 191 Joralemon St., Brooklyn, NY 11201 t) (718) 722-6000 www.ccbq.org
Catholic Charities Progress of Peoples Development Corporation - 191 Joralemon St., Brooklyn, NY 11201 t) (718) 722-6000 www.ccbq.org Rev. Msgr. Alfred P. LoPinto, CEO;
The David Minkin Residence Housing Development Fund Corporation, Inc. - 5313 9th Ave., Brooklyn, NY 11220; Mailing: 191 Joralemon St., Brooklyn, NY 11201 t) (718) 722-6000
Emmaus of the Diocese of Brooklyn, Inc. - 191 Joralemon St., Brooklyn, NY 11201 t) (718) 722-6000 Emmie Glynn Ryan, Secy.;
Families Together HDFC, Inc. - 191 Joralemon St., Brooklyn, NY 11201 t) (718) 722-6000
55 Pierrepont Housing Development Fund Corporation - 191 Joralemon St., Brooklyn, NY 11201 www.ccbq.org
Holy Spirit Senior Housing Development Fund Corporation - 191 Joralemon St., Brooklyn, NY 11201 t) (718) 722-6000 www.ccbq.org
Howard Beach Housing Development Fund Corporation - 191 Joralemon St., Brooklyn, NY 11201 t) (718) 722-6000
St. Lucy/St. Patrick Housing Development Fund Corporation - 918 Kent Ave., Brooklyn, NY 11205; Mailing: 191 Joralemon St., Brooklyn, NY 11201 t) (718) 722-6000
Mary Immaculate HDFC, Inc. - 191 Joralemon St., Brooklyn, NY 11201 t) (718) 722-6000 Emmie Glynn Ryan, Secy.;
Mary Immaculate, Inc. - 191 Joralemon St., Brooklyn, NY 11201 t) (718) 722-6000 Emmie Glynn Ryan, Secy.;
Mary Star of the Sea Senior HFDC - 191 Joralemon St., Brooklyn, NY 11201 t) (718) 722-6000
Msgr. Edward T. Burke Senior Housing Development Fund Corporation - 720 E. 8th St., Brooklyn, NY 11230 t) (718) 722-6000
Msgr. John P. O'Brien Senior Housing Development Fund Corporation - 4112 Fort Hamilton Pkwy., Brooklyn, NY 11220; Mailing: 191 Joralemon St., Brooklyn, NY 11201 t) (718) 722-6000
Msgr. Joseph F. Stedman Residence Housing Development Fund Corporation - 930 53rd St., Brooklyn, NY 11219; Mailing: 191 Joralemon St., Brooklyn, NY 11201 t) (718) 722-6000
Msgr. Thomas Campbell Senior Housing Development Corporation - 25-63 22nd St., Long Island City, NY 11102; Mailing: 191 Joralemon St., Brooklyn, NY 11201 t) (718) 722-6000
Mount Carmel Senior HDFC - 745 Saint John's Pl., Brooklyn, NY 11216; Mailing: 191 Joralemon St., Brooklyn, NY 11201 t) (718) 722-6000
O.L. Loreto Family Housing Development Fund Corporation - 191 Joralemon St., Brooklyn, NY 11201 t) (718) 722-6000
101-105 South Eighth Street Apartments Housing Development Fund Corporation - 191 Joralemon St., Brooklyn, NY 11201 t) (718) 722-6000 www.ccbq.org
176 South Eighth Street Apartments Housing Development Fund Corporation - 191 Joralemon St., Brooklyn, NY 11201 t) (718) 722-6000 www.ccbq.org
Our Lady of Fatima Apartments Housing Development Fund Corporation, Inc. - 78-01 30th Ave., East Elmhurst, NY 11370; Mailing: 191 Joralemon St., Brooklyn, NY 11201 t) (718) 722-6000
St. Paul the Apostle Senior Housing Development Fund Corporation - 55-06 99th St., Corona, NY 11368; Mailing: 191 Joralemon St., Brooklyn, NY 11201 t) (718) 722-6000
Pierrepont HDFC - 191 Joralemon St., Brooklyn, NY 11201 t) (718) 722-6000
Pierrepont House for the Elderly, Inc. - 191 Joralemon St., Brooklyn, NY 11201 t) (718) 722-6000
St. Pius V Senior Housing Development Fund Corporation - 105-20 Liverpool St., Jamaica, NY 11435; Mailing: 191 Joralemon St., Brooklyn, NY 11201 t) (718) 722-6000
Pope John Paul II Senior Housing Development Fund Corporation - 255 Ovington Ave., Brooklyn, NY 11220; Mailing: 191 Joralemon St., Brooklyn, NY 11201 t) (718) 722-6000
Progress of Peoples Management Corporation - 191 Joralemon St., Brooklyn, NY 11201 t) (718) 722-6000 Rev. Msgr. Alfred P. LoPinto, CEO;
Queens Rehab Corp. - 191 Joralemon St., Brooklyn, NY 11201 t) (718) 722-6000 Emmie Glynn Ryan, Secy.;
Residential & Community Habilitation - 91-14 Merrick Blvd., 6th Fl., Jamaica, NY 11432 t) (718) 262-8190 Patricia Bowles, Sr. Vice Pres. & Chief Prog. Officer;
72 Lewis Avenue Apartments Housing Development Fund Corporation - 80 Lewis Ave., Brooklyn, NY 11206; Mailing: 191 Joralemon St., Brooklyn, NY 11201 t) (718) 722-6000 www.ccbq.org
Sr. Lucian Senior HDFC - 415 Bleecker St., Brooklyn, NY 11237; Mailing: 191 Joralemon St., Brooklyn, NY 11201 t) (718) 722-6000
Sunset Park Housing Development Fund Corporation, Inc. - 4301 8th Ave., Brooklyn, NY 11232; Mailing: 191 Joralemon St., Brooklyn, NY 11201 t) (718) 722-6000
St. Teresa of Avila Senior HDFC - 549-555 St. Johns Pl., Brooklyn, NY 11238; Mailing: 191 Joralemon St., Brooklyn, NY 11201 t) (718) 722-6000

Integrated Health and Wellness - Care Coordination & Case Management - 191 Joralemon St. - 14th Fl., Brooklyn, NY 11201 t) 718-722-6062; 718-722-6222; 718-722-6146 ewageman@ccbq.org www.ccbq.org Desiree Barberio, Vice. Pres.;
Behavioral Health Care Coordination - DOHMH - 1623 Flatbush Ave., Lower Level, Brooklyn, NY 11210 t) 718-398-0153 info@ccbq.org Patricia Bowles, Sr. Vice Pres. & Chief Prog. Office;
Children's Care Coordination - HH - 91-14 Merrick Blvd., 6th Fl., Jamaica, NY 11432 t) 718-408-7178 joseph.mcardle@ccbq.org Joseph McArdle, Dir.;
Justice for Juveniles - 191 Joralemon St., Brooklyn, NY 11201 t) 718-408-6268 info@ccbq.org Patricia Bowles, Sr. Vice Pres. & Chief Prog. Office;

Integrated Health and Wellness - Clinic Recovery & Rehabilitative Services - 191 Joralemon St., 14th Fl., Brooklyn, NY 11201 t) 718-722-6065 claudia.salazar@ccbq.org Claudia Salazar, Vice. Pres.;
Brooklyn Mobile Crisis Team - 1623 Flatbush Ave., Lower Level, Brooklyn, NY 11210 t) 718-514-8031
Call Center - 191 Joralemon St., 7th Fl., Brooklyn, NY 11201 t) 718-722-6001 info@ccbq.org Patricia Bowles, Sr. Vice Pres. & Chief Prog. Of.;
Catholic Charities Behavioral Health Center - Corona Clinic - 94-14 37th Ave., Jackson Heights, NY 11372 t) 718-779-1600 info@ccbq.org Patricia Bowles, Sr. Vice Pres. & Chief Prog. Of.;
Catholic Charities Behavioral Health Center - Jamaica Clinic - 161-10 Jamaica Ave., 2nd Fl., Jamaica, NY 11432 t) 718-704-5488 info@ccbq.org Patricia Bowles, Sr. Vice Pres. & Chief Prog. Of.;
Catholic Charities Behavioral Health Center - PROS - 91-14 37th Ave., Jackson Heights, NY 11372 t) 718-779-1831 info@ccbq.org Patricia Bowles, Sr. Vice Pres. & Chief Prog. Of.;
Catholic Charities Behavioral Health Center - Rockaway Clinic - 18-47 Mott Ave., Far Rockaway, NY 11691 t) 718-337-6800 info@ccbq.org Patricia Bowles, Sr. Vice Pres. & Chief Prog. Of.;
Catholic Charities Behavioral Health Center - Rockaway PROS - 18-47 Mott Ave., Far Rockaway, NY 11691 t) 718-337-6850 info@ccbq.org Patricia Bowles, Sr. Vice Pres. & Chief Prog. Of.;
Flatbush Addiction Treatment Center - 1623 Flatbush Ave., Lower Level, Brooklyn, NY 11210 t) 718-951-9009 megan.kleinman@ccbq.org Patricia Bowles, Sr. Vice Pres. & Chief Prog. Of.;
Flatbush Behavioral Health Clinic - 1623 Flatbush Ave., 1st Fl., Brooklyn, NY 11234 t) 718-377-5755 ccbq.org Patricia Bowles, Sr. Vice Pres. & Chief Prog. Of.;
Glendale Mental Health Clinic - 67-29 Myrtle Ave., 2nd Fl., Glendale, NY 11385 t) 718-456-7001 info@ccbq.org Patricia Bowles, Sr. Vice Pres. & Chief Prog. Of.;
The Open Door Club - 2037 Utica Ave., 2nd Fl., Brooklyn, NY 11234 t) 718-377-7757 info@ccbq.org Patricia Bowles, Sr. Vice Pres. & Chief Prog. Of.;
Peer Advocacy - 2037 Utica Ave., 2nd Floor, Brooklyn, NY 11234 t) 718-377-7757 info@ccbq.org Patricia Bowles, Sr. Vice Pres. & Chief Prog. Of.;
World of Work - Brooklyn - 2037 Utica Ave., 2nd Fl., Brooklyn, NY 11234 t) 718-758-9497 info@ccbq.org Patricia Bowles, Sr. Vice Pres. & Chief Prog. Of.;

Integrated Health and Wellness - Housing - 191 Joralemon St., 14th Floor, Brooklyn, NY 11201 t) 718-262-8190 ginnie.juarez@ccbq.org Martin Sussman, Vice. Pres.;
Brooklyn Community Living Program - 2037 Utica Ave., 2nd Floor, Brooklyn, NY 11234 t) 718-253-1366 ccbq.org Patricia Bowles, Sr. Vice Pres. & Chief Prog. Of.;
Brooklyn Supported Housing Programs I (HCRA, BSHIV, & BSHV) - 2037 Utica Ave., 2nd Floor, Brooklyn, NY 11234 t) 718-253-1366 Patricia Bowles, Sr. Vice Pres. & Chief Prog. Of.;
Casa Betsaida - Congregate and Apartment Programs - 267 Hewes St., Brooklyn, NY 11211 t) 718-218-7890 info@ccbq.org Patricia Bowles, Sr. Vice Pres. & Chief Prog. Of.;
Central Brooklyn Supported Housing - 2037 Utica Ave., 2nd Fl., Brooklyn, NY 11234 t) 718-253-1366 Patricia Bowles, Sr. Vice Pres. & Chief Prog. Of.;
Circle of Hope I & II - 1623 Flatbush Ave., Lower Level, Brooklyn, NY 11210 t) 718-338-4716 Patricia Bowles, Sr. Vice Pres. & Chief Prog. Of.;
Jamaica Community Living - 91-14 Merrick Blvd., Jamaica, NY 11432 t) 718-262-8109 info@ccbq.org Ginnie Juarez, Admin.;
Queens Community Living Program - 35-24 83rd St., Jackson Heights, NY 11372 t) 718-639-0700 info@ccbq.org Patricia Bowles, Sr. Vice Pres. & Chief Prog. Of.;
Queens Supported Housing Programs (I, II, III & IV) - 35-24 83rd St., Jackson Heights, NY 11372 t) 718-639-0700 info@ccbq.org Patricia Bowles, Sr. Vice Pres. & Chief Prog. Of.;
Supported SRO at Caring Communities - Most Holy Trinity SRO - 157 Graham Ave., Brooklyn, NY 11206 t) 718-963-3956 info@ccbq.org Patricia Bowles, Sr. Vice Pres. & Chief Prog. Of.;
Supported SRO at Caring Communities - Our Lady of Good Counsel SRO - 800-826 Madison St., Brooklyn, NY 11221 t) 718-452-3600 info@ccbq.org Patricia Bowles, Sr. Vice Pres. & Chief Prog. Of.;
Supported SRO at Caring Communities - St. Joseph's SRO - 683 Dean St., Brooklyn, NY 11238 t) 718-857-2266 info@ccbq.org Patricia Bowles, Sr. Vice Pres. & Chief Prog. Of.;
Supported SRO at Mercy Gardens - 249 Classon Ave., Brooklyn, NY 11205 t) 718-399-8141 info@ccbq.org Patricia Bowles, Sr. Vice Pres. & Chief Prog. Of.;

GLENDALE

Catholic Kolping Society of Brooklyn (Katholischer

Gesellen Verein) - 65-04 Myrtle Ave., Glendale, NY 11385 t) 718-456-7727; 917-862-0637 kolpingbrooklyn@gmail.com; mrwilliamangelo@aol.com www.kolping.org/brooklyn/ Rev. Christopher R. Heanue, Moderator; William A. Conte, Pres.; Jessica Meyer, Vice Pres.; Patricia Gerage, Treas.;

MIDDLE VILLAGE

Catholic Youth Organization - 66-25 79th Pl., Middle Village, NY 11379 t) 718-281-9549

CEMETERIES [CEM]

BROOKLYN

Trinity - t) 718-894-4888 Most Holy Trinity Parish, Brooklyn.

FAR ROCKAWAY

St. Mary Star of the Sea Cemetery - 1920 New Haven Ave., Far Rockaway, NY 11691 t) 718-894-4888 mreid@diobrook.org Rev. Msgr. Michael J. Reid, Vicar;

MIDDLE VILLAGE

Saint John's Cemetery - 80-01 Metropolitan Ave., Middle Village, NY 11379 t) 718-894-4888 en@ccbklyn.org; mjr@ccbklyn.org www.ccbklyn.org Operating: St. John's Cemetery (Middle Village); Holy Cross Cemetery (Brooklyn); Mount St. Mary Cemetery (Flushing); St. Charles/Resurrection Cemetery Rev. Msgr. Michael J. Reid, CEO; Edward DuPre, Exec.; Celeste Lanci, Exec.; Anthony Nicodemo, Exec.; Christopher Tuohy, Exec.; Randy Van Yahres, Exec.; Elaine Nicodemo, Dir.;

COLLEGES & UNIVERSITIES [COL]

BROOKLYN

***St. Francis College** - 179 Livingston St., Brooklyn, NY 11201 t) 718-522-2300 president@sfc.edu; aliscott@sfc.edu www.sfc.edu Miguel Martinez-Saenz, Pres.; Stds.: 2,662; Bro. Tchrs.: 3; Lay Tchrs.: 103; Pr. Tchrs.: 1

***St. Joseph's University, New York** - 245 Clinton Ave., Brooklyn, NY 11205 t) 718-940-5300 alist@sjny.edu; hbarry@sjny.edu www.sjny.edu Under supervision of Board of Trustees. Dr. Donald Boomgaarden, Pres.; Dr. Heather Barry, Provost; John Roth, CFO; Michelle Papajohn, CIO; Dr. Phillip Dehne, Exec. Dean; Dr. Elizabeth Pollicino Murphy, Exec. Dir., Libraries; Rory Shaffer-Walsh, Vice Pres., Institutional Advancement; Stds.: 1,046; Lay Tchrs.: 60

Branch Campus - 155 W. Roe Blvd., Patchogue, NY 11772 t) 631-687-5100 Dr. Eileen Jahn, Exec. Dean; Stds.: 3,302; Lay Tchrs.: 99; Sr. Tchrs.: 1

QUEENS

St. John's University - 8000 Utopia Pkwy., Queens, NY 11439 t) 718-990-6161 www.stjohns.edu Sponsored by the Vincentian Priests and Brothers Eastern Province of the Congregation of the Mission. Rev. Brian J Shanley, O.P., Pres.; Dr. Simon Geir Moller, Provost & VP for Academic Affairs; Joseph E. Oliva, VP for Admin., Sec. & Gen Counsel; Dr. Rachel Pereira, Vice Pres., Equity & Inclusion; Rev. Aidan R Rooney, C.M., Exec. Vice Pres., Mission; Dr. Christian Vaupel, Vice Pres., Advancement & University Rels.; Sharon Hewitt Watkins, Vice Pres., Business Affairs, CFO & Treas.; Sarah Jean Kelly, Vice Pres., Student Success & Retention Strategy; Nunziatina A Manuli, Vice Pres. & Chief of Staff to Pres.; Stds.: 19,663; Lay Tchrs.: 615; Pr. Tchrs.: 4

CONVENTS, MONASTERIES, AND RESIDENCES FOR WOMEN [CON]

ASTORIA

Provincialate of the Sisters of the Good Shepherd - 25-30 21st Ave., Astoria, NY 11105 t) 718-278-1155 office@nygoodshepherd.org (New York/Toronto Province) Sr. Maureen McGowan, R.G.S., Prov.; Srs.: 45

BROOKLYN

The Congregation of the Daughters of Mary, Brooklyn - 332 E. 32nd St., Brooklyn, NY 11226 t) 718-856-3323 Sr. Juvenia Joseph, Supr.;

Discalced Carmelite Nuns - 361 Highland Blvd., Brooklyn, NY 11207 t) 718-235-0422 carmelofbrooklyn@gmail.com www.brooklyncarmel.org Mother Ana Maria, O.C.D., Prioress; Srs.: 10

Franciscan Sisters of the Poor - Congregational Office, 133 Remsen St., Brooklyn, NY 11201 t) 718-643-1945 sfp@franciscansisters.org www.franciscansisters.org

Hermanas Franciscanas De La Inmaculada Concepcion - 209 1st St., Brooklyn, NY 11215 t) 718-624-6720 Sr. Irex Mejia, HFIC, Supr.;

Missionaries of Charity, Contemplative/Our Lady of Lourdes Convent - 34 Aberdeen St., Brooklyn, NY 11207 t) 718-443-2868 Sr. Margaret Mary Arias, M.C., Contact;

The Sisters Adorers of the Precious Blood - 5400 Fort Hamilton Pkwy., Brooklyn, NY 11219-4037 t) 718-438-6371 Rev. Evans Julce, Chap.; Srs.: 1

Confraternity of the Precious Blood - 5300 Ft. Hamilton Ave., Brooklyn, NY 11219-4035 t) 718-436-1120 Rev. Thomas V. Doyle;

Sisters of Mercy of the Americas, Mid-Atlantic Community - 273 Willoughby Ave., Brooklyn, NY 11205-1487 t) 718-622-5750 Sr. Patricia McDermott, RSM, Pres.; Srs.: 579

Sisters of the Good Shepherd - 348 Ninth St., Brooklyn, NY 11215 t) 718-499-9212 Srs.: 2

Sisters of the Visitation of Brooklyn, NY - 8902 Ridge Blvd., Brooklyn, NY 11209 t) 718-745-5151 vamonastery@aol.com www.brooklynvisitationmonastery.org Sr. Susan Marie Kasprzak, V.H.M., Supr.; Srs.: 13

ELMHURST

Preachers of Christ and Mary - 8734 Whitney Ave., Elmhurst, NY 11373 t) 718-205-5494 Sr. Maria Amador, P.C.M., Supr.;

FLUSHING

Congregation of Sisters of St. Joseph of St. Marc - 46-19-195th St., Flushing, NY 11358 c) 425-301-3414 sjsmny11@yahoo.com Sr. Roseena jacob Cheruvathoor, Supr.; Srs.: 4

The Congregation of the Sisters of Jesus the Savior - 35 50 158th St., Flushing, NY 11358 t) 718-581-6636 Sr. Mary Fidelis Ezemaduka, S.J.S., Contact;

GLENDALE

Convent of the Sisters of Mary Reparatrix - 7225 68th St., Glendale, NY 11385 t) 718-456-4242 www.smr.org Srs.: 2

JAMAICA

Ursuline Sisters of Tildonk - 81-15 Utopia Pkwy., Jamaica, NY 11432-1308 t) 718-591-0681 jcallahan@tildonkursuline.org; mazzara@tildonkursuline.org www.tildonkursuline.org Sr. Joanne Callahan, O.S.U., Prov.;

JAMAICA ESTATES

The Federation of the Congregations of Sisters of Saint Joseph of the United States of America - 86-44 Edgerton Blvd., Jamaica Estates, NY 11432 t) 314-925-7662 info@cssjfed.org cssjfed.org Sr. Patricia Johnson, C.S.J., Exec.;

QUEENS VILLAGE

St. Ann's Novitiate, Little Sisters of the Poor - 110-39 Springfield Blvd., Queens Village, NY 11429; Mailing: P.O. Box 280356, Queens Village, NY 11429 t) 718-464-4920 nvmothersuperior@littlesistersofthepoor.org www.littlesistersofthepoor.org Sr. Michele Mary Mucher, Supr.; Srs.: 4

Little Sisters of the Poor (Province of Brooklyn) - Provincial Res., 110-30 221st St., Queens Village, NY 11429 t) 718-464-1800 provincialbklyn@littlesistersofthepoor.org www.littlesistersofthepoor.org Sr. Alice Marie Jones, L.S.P., Prov.; Srs.: 82

ROCKAWAY PARK

Stella Maris Convent, Sisters of St. Joseph - 140 Beach 112th St., Rockaway Park, NY 11694-2497 t) 718-634-1886

SOUTH OZONE PARK

Daughters of Mary Mother of Mercy - 109-26 130th St., South Ozone Park, NY 11420 t) 718-843-1364; 646-578-9102 Sr. Bernadette DeLourdes, Supr.;

ENDOWMENTS / FOUNDATIONS / TRUSTS [EFT]

BAYSIDE

Ozanam Geriatric Foundation - 42-41 201 St., Bayside, NY 11361 t) 718-971-2020 jcraymond@ozanamhall.org www.ozanamhall.org Sr. M. Joseph Catherine Raymond, O.Carm., CEO;

BRIARWOOD

Archbishop Molloy High School Charitable Trust - 85-53 Manton St., Briarwood, NY 11435 t) 718-441-2100 dpenikas@molloyhs.org; president@molloyhs.org Darius Penikas, Prin.;

BROOKLYN

Catholic Foundation for Brooklyn & Queens - 243 Prospect Park W., FL 3, Brooklyn, NY 11215 t) 718-965-7375 info@cfbq.org www.catholicfoundationbq.org Rev. Msgr. Jamie J. Gigantiello, Vicar;

Compostela Corporation of the Roman Catholic Diocese of Brooklyn, New York - 310 Prospect Park W., Brooklyn, NY 11215 t) 718-965-7300 mreid@diobrook.org Rev. Msgr. Michael J. Reid, Vicar;

St. Elizabeth Ann Seton Charitable Trust - 310 Prospect Park W., Brooklyn, NY 11215 t) 718-965-7300 mreid@diobrook.org Rev. Msgr. Michael J. Reid, Vicar;

St. Francis de Sales School for the Deaf Development Fund - 260 Eastern Pkwy., Brooklyn, NY 11225 t) 718-636-4573 school@sfdesales.org Maria Bartolillo, Dir.; Jennifer White, Bus. Mgr.;

Franciscan Brothers Charitable Trust - 135 Remsen St., Brooklyn, NY 11201 t) 718-858-8217 c) 718-288-8789 generalate@gmail.com; bclally@gmail.com Richard T. Arkwright, Contact;

Franciscan Sisters of the Poor Charitable Trust - 133 Remsen St., Brooklyn, NY 11201 t) 718-643-1945 sfp@franciscansisters.org www.franciscansisters.org

Good Shepherd Charitable Trust - 310 Prospect Park W., Brooklyn, NY 11215 t) 718-965-7300 mreid@diobrook.org Rev. Msgr. Michael J. Reid, Vicar;

St. John Vianney Fund Charitable Trust - 310 Prospect Park W., Brooklyn, NY 11215 t) 718-965-7300 mreid@diobrook.org Rev. Msgr. Michael J. Reid, Vicar;

Mercy Home Foundation - 273 Willoughby Ave., Brooklyn, NY 11205 t) 718-832-1075 Sr. Linda Esposito, Contact;

Parish Assistance Charitable Trust Fund - 310 Prospect Park W., Brooklyn, NY 11215 t) 718-965-7300 mreid@diobrook.org Rev. Msgr. Michael J. Reid, Vicar;

The Roman Catholic Diocese of Brooklyn, New York Group Medical Insurance Trust - 310 Prospect Park W., Brooklyn, NY 11215 t) 718-965-7300 mreid@diobrook.org Rev. Msgr. Michael J. Reid, Vicar;

Saint Vincent DePaul Charitable Trust - 310 Prospect Park W., Brooklyn, NY 11215 t) 718-965-7300 mreid@diobrook.org Rev. Msgr. Michael J. Reid, Vicar;

EAST ELMHURST

The Cor Jesu Foundation, Inc. - 72-02 31st Ave., East Elmhurst, NY 11370 t) 718-397-9343 Nicholas C Melito, Pres.;

FOREST HILLS

The Benoit Trust (Congregation of the Marist Brothers) - 70-20 Juno St., Forest Hills, NY 11375 t) 718-480-1306 brdano@hotmail.com Bro. Richard Carey, F.M.S.; Bro. Benedict Lo Balbo, F.M.S.; Bro. Hank Sammon, F.M.S.;

The Gregoire Trust - 70-20 Juno St., Forest Hills, NY 11375 t) 718-480-1608 maristbrothersus@aol.com Bro.

Richard Carey, F.M.S.; Bro. Benedict Lo Balbo, F.M.S.; Bro. Hank Sammon, F.M.S.;
Lewiston Mission Trust - 70-20 Juno St., Forest Hills, NY 11375 Bro. Yvon Bedard, F.M.S.; Bro. Benedict Lo Balbo, F.M.S.; Bro. Edward J. O'Neill, F.M.S.;

JAMAICA ESTATES

The Paulist Foundation, Inc. - 86-11 Midland Pkwy., Jamaica Estates, NY 11432; Mailing: 415 W. 59 St., New York, NY 10019 t) 212-757-8072 admingenoffice@paulist.org Rev. John Geaney, CSP, Secy.;
Paulist Mission Trust - 86-11 Midland Pkwy., Jamaica Estates, NY 11432; Mailing: 415 W. 59 St., New York, NY 10019 t) 212-757-8072 admingenoffice@paulist.org Rev. John J. Foley, C.S.P.;

MISCELLANEOUS [MIS]

ASTORIA

Good Shepherd Volunteers - 25-30 21st Ave., Astoria, NY 11105 t) 718-943-7489 gsv@gsvolunteers.org www.goodshepherdvolunteers.org Diane Conroy, Dir.;
HandCrafting Justice, Inc. - 25-30 21st Ave., Astoria, NY 11105 t) 718-278-1155 mmcgowanrgs@gmail.com www.handcraftingjustice.org Sr. Maureen McGowan, R.G.S., Dir.;

BROOKLYN

Aid to the Church in Need, Inc. - 725 Leonard St., 3rd Fl., Brooklyn, NY 11222-0384 t) 718-609-0939 info@churchinneed.org www.churchinneed.org Edward Clancy, Secy.;
The Cathedral Club of Brooklyn - ; Mailing: P.O. Box 315, Brooklyn, NY 11209-0315 t) 718-809-2440 www.cathedralclubbrooklyn.org
***Catholic Federation of Social Service Agencies of Brooklyn and Queens** - 191 Joralemon St., Brooklyn, NY 11201 t) 718-722-6000 info@ccbq.org Dawn Saffayeh, Pres.;
***Federation of Oases of Koinonia John the Baptist** - 98 Richards St., Brooklyn, NY 11231 c) 917-515-4225; (347) 533-1515 segnykjb@hotmail.com www.visitationbvm-brooklyn.org Rev. Claudio Antecini, Pst.; Sr. Frauke Tinat, Prioress; Rev. Johannes S.A.G. Siegert, DRE; Rev. Sauro Sbarbati, In Res.; Rev. Eamon G. Murray, In Res.;
Franciscan Sisters of the Poor Communities, Inc. - 133 Remsen St., Brooklyn, NY 11201 t) 718-643-1945 Congregation sponsors: Franciscan Ministries, Inc.
Con-solatio - 26 Olive St., Brooklyn, NY 11211 t) 718-522-2121 info@con-solatio.org www.con-solatio.org Cecile Fourmeaux, Pres.;
***HeartShare Human Services of New York, Roman Catholic Diocese of Brooklyn** - 12 MetroTech Ctr., 29th Fl., Brooklyn, NY 11201 t) 718-422-4200 william.guarinello@heartshare.org; dawn.saffayeh@heartshare.org William R. Guarinello, CEO; Dawn Saffayeh, CEO;
St. John's Bread & Life Program, Inc. - 795 Lexington Ave., Brooklyn, NY 11221 t) 718-574-0058 www.breadandlife.org One of the largest emergency food programs in New York City also providing wrap around social services. Sr. Caroline Tweedy, R.S.M., Exec. Dir.;
St. Joseph Studio Workshop, Inc. - 55 33rd St., Unit A302, Brooklyn, NY 11232
Laudato Si Corporation - 191 Joralemon Ave., Brooklyn, NY 11201 t) (718) 722-6000 Jeanne M Diulio, Secy.;
Mercy Medical Mission (Sisters of Mercy Mid-Atlantic Community) - 273 Willoughby Ave., Brooklyn, NY 11205
National Center of the Haitian Apostolate - 332 E. 32nd St., Brooklyn, NY 11226 t) 718-856-3323 snaa.org Rev. Jean Yvon Pierre, Exec.;
Office of Faith Formation - 310 Prospect Park W., 4th Fl., Brooklyn, NY 11215 t) 718-281-9544 jgibino@diobrook.org; cgeorgi@diobrook.org www.dioceseofbrooklyn.org Very Rev. Joseph R. Gibino, Vicar; Rev. James Kuroly, Dir.; Nelsa I. Elias, Dir.; Christian S. Rada, Dir.; Joann Roa, Dir.; Lucia Morales, Assoc. Dir.;
Office of the Superintendent of Schools - 310 Prospect Park W., Brooklyn, NY 11215 t) 718-965-7300 tchadztko@diobrook.org www.dioceseofbrooklyn.org/catholic-ed Kelly Gonzalez, Admin.; Thomas Chadzutko, Supt.; Bro. Ralph Darmento, F.S.C., Supt.; Roxanna De Pena-Elder, Supt.; Elizabeth Frangella, Supt.; Janet E. Heed, Supt.; Michael A. LaForgia, Supt.; Barbara McArdle, Supt.; Joan McMaster, Supt.; Diane Phelan, Supt.; Maria Viesta, Supt.; Yinet Liriano, Exec.;
Diocese of Brooklyn Education Offices - 310 Prospect Park West, Brooklyn, NY 11215 t) (718) 965-7300 x9501 Legal Titles & Corporations: Department of Education, Diocese of Brooklyn; Program for the Development of Human Potential; Henry M. Hauld HS Assoc.
Rocklyn Asset Corporation - 243 Prospect Park W., Brooklyn, NY 11215 t) 718-965-7300 Coleen A Ceriello, Exec.;
Rocklyn Ecclesiastical Corporation - 243 Prospect Park W., Brooklyn, NY 11215 t) 718-965-7300 cceriello@rocklynasset.org Coleen A Ceriello, Exec.;
Rosary For Life, Inc. - 3309 Ave. P, Brooklyn, NY 11234-3411 t) 718-377-6920 Wyn Powers, Pres.;
Society of the Immaculate Conception of Brooklyn - 310 Prospect Park W., Brooklyn, NY 11215 t) 718-965-7326 jnagle@diobrook.org (Missionary Society)

DIX HILLS

Madonna Heights Services - 151 Burr Ln., Dix Hills, NY 11746; Mailing: P.O. Box 8020, Dix Hills, NY 11746 t) 516-643-8800

DOUGLASTON

Immaculate Conception Center - 7200 Douglaston Pkwy., Douglaston, NY 11362-1997 t) 718-281-9526 sgalazin@diobrook.org Dcn. Stanley J. Galazin, Dir.;

FLUSHING

The Institute of the Apostolic Oblates/Pro Sanctity - 45-30 195th St., Flushing, NY 11358 t) 718-649-0324 agnesrus44@gmail.com www.prosanctity.org
Pro Sanctity Movement - 45-30 195th St., Flushing, NY 11358 t) 718-649-0324 prosanctitynewyork@verizon.net www.nyprosanctity.org Rev. Msgr. Steven J. Aguggia, Spiritual Adv./Care Srvcs.;

GLENDALE

National Italian Apostolate Conference - 72-22 68th St, Glendale, NY 11385 t) 718-649-0324 saguggia@diobrook.org Rev. Msgr. Steven J. Aguggia, Dir.;

HOLLIS HILLS

Glencara, Inc. - 86-05 218th St., Hollis Hills, NY 11427 t) 718-454-9804 seanfoley@verizon.net Eileen Trainor, R.S.M., Pres.; Michael G. Leavy, Vice Pres.; Regina Williams, R.S.M., Secy.; Kathleen O'Malley, Treas.;

JACKSON HEIGHTS

Asociacion Misioneros Contemplativos Laicos - 3543 84th St., Apt. 308, Jackson Heights, NY 11372 t) 718-592-5458 (Lay Association of Contemplative Missionaries) Ana Luisa Ortega, Treas.;
***Eternal Flame of Hope Ministries, Inc.** - c/o Rev. Richard J. Bretone, 74-18 Ditmars Blvd., Jackson Heights, NY 11370 t) 718-274-4919; 718-636-3584 Rev. Richard J. Bretone, Dir.;

JAMAICA

St. Paul's Benevolent, Educational and Missionary Institute, Inc. (Congregation of the Passion - St. Paul of the Cross Province) - 86-45 Edgerton Blvd., Jamaica, NY 11432 t) 929-419-7500 provincialstpaul@cpprov.org www.thepassionists.org Rev. James O'Shea, C.P., Prov.; Rev. James Price, C.P., 1st Consultor; Rev. Salvatore Enzo Del Brocco, C.P., 2nd Consulter; Rev. William Murphy, C.P., 3rd Consultor; Rev. Anibal Rodriguez, C.P., 4th Consultor; Rev. David Monaco, C.P., Treas.; Daniel Flynn, Dir., Healthcare & Social Svcs.; Gregory Hampson, CFO;

JAMAICA ESTATES

Thomas Berry Place, Inc. - 8645 Edgerton Blvd., Jamaica Estates, NY 11432

LONG ISLAND CITY

World Compassion Link - ; Mailing: P.O. Box 4279, Long Island City, NY 11104-9808 t) 718-672-4848 omearanoel@gmail.com; tbasquez@aol.com worldcompassionlink.org Rev. Thomas Basquel, C.S.Sp., Pres.; Rev. Noel P. O'Meara, C.S.Sp., Vice Pres.;

OZONE PARK

Ferrini Welfare League - 101-41 91 St., Ozone Park, NY 11416 t) 718-845-0539

REGO PARK

Lifeway Network, Inc. - 85-10 61st Rd., Rego Park, NY 11374 t) 718-779-8075 contact@lifewaynetwork.org www.lifewaynetwork.org Sr. Rosamond Blanchet, RSHM, Corp. Mem; Sr. Kathleen Kull, SCH, Corp. Mem.; Sr. Maureen McGowan, R.G.S., Corp. Mem.; Sr. Mary Ellen O'Boyle, SCNY, Corp. Mem.;

RIDGEWOOD

Friends of RADIO MARIA, Inc. - 70-05 Fresh Pond Rd., Ridgewood, NY 11385 t) 718-417-0550 info.nyi@radiomaria.us nyi.radiomaria.us Rev. Walter Tonelotto, C.S., Dir.;

WOODHAVEN

School Sisters of Notre Dame Educational Center - 87-04 88th Ave., Woodhaven, NY 11421 t) 718-738-0588 ssndec@aol.com ssndecwomens.com Sr. Catherine Feeney, S.S.N.D., Exec.;

MONASTERIES AND RESIDENCES FOR PRIESTS AND BROTHERS [MON]

BROOKLYN

Brothers of the Christian Schools - 1214-1216 Beverley Rd., Brooklyn, NY 11218 t) 718-857-4311 Bro. David Carroll, F.S.C., Dir.; Bro. Gerard Conforti, F.S.C., Treas.; Bro. John Bassett, F.S.C.; Bro. Peter Bonventre, F.S.C.; Bro. Ralph Darmento, F.S.C.; Bro. Robert Wickman, F.S.C.;
Carmelites of Mary Immaculate, Inc. - 862 Manhattan Ave., Brooklyn, NY 11222 t) 718-383-3339 cmiusa@hotmail.com www.cmiusa.org Rev. George Kurian, CMI (india), Par. Vicar; Sebastian T Augustine, CMI, Supr.; Priests: 95
Carroll Street Jesuit Community - 1101 Carroll St., Brooklyn, NY 11225 Rev. Thomas G. Benz, S.J.; Rev. William P. Cain, S.J.; Rev. Kenneth J. Gavin, S.J.; Rev. Mario M. Powell, S.J.; Rev. Ralph Rivera, S.J.; Rev. Vincent B. Sullivan, S.J.; Bro. Joseph P. Hoover, S.J.; John J. Braithwaite, S.J., Seminarian;
St. Francis Monastery-Generalate Offices of Franciscan Brothers (Franciscan Brothers of Brooklyn) - 135 Remsen St., Brooklyn, NY 11201-4212 t) 718-858-8217 generalate@gmail.com www.franciscanbrothers.org Bro. Gabriel O'Brien, OSF, Supr.; Bro. Joshua Di Mauro, O.S.F., Secy.; Bro. Philip Herte, Treas.; Bro. Richard Contino, OSF, Mem.; Bro. David Migliorino, O.S.F., Mem.; Bro. Damian Novello, O.S.F., Mem.;
St. Michael Friary - 282 Warwick St., Brooklyn, NY 11207 t) 718-827-6990 buckleybp@gmail.com; bpbuckley@yahoo.com Rev. Richard Mattox, OFM Cap., Vicar; Rev. Gerard Mulvey, O.F.M.Cap., Chap.; Friar Brendan Patrick Buckley, OFM Cap., Supr.;
Oratory of Saint Philip Neri, Congregation Pontifical Rite - 64 Middagh St., Brooklyn, NY 11201-1342 t) 718-875-2096 aandreassi@brooklynoratory.org brooklyn-oratory.org Rev. Anthony Andreassi, C.O., Supr.; Rev. Mark Paul Amatrucola, C.O.; Rev. Michael J. Callaghan, C.O.; Rev. Dennis M. Corrado, C.O.; Rev. Mark J. Lane, C.O.; Bro. James Simon, C.O., Vicar;
Our Lady of Good Counsel - 915 Putnam Ave., Brooklyn, NY 11221 t) 718-455-6864 Rev. Joseph V. Cummins, C.M.; Rev. Emmet J. Nolan, C.M., Pst.; Most Rev. Alfonso Cabezas Aristizabal, C.M., In Res.;
Redemptorist Fathers of New York, Inc.-Baltimore Province - 7509 Shore Rd., Brooklyn, NY 11209; Mailing: 3112 7th St., N.E., Washington, DC 20017 t) 202-529-4410 secprovince@redemptorists.net www.redemptorists.net Rev. Gerard J. Knapp, C.Ss.R., Vicar; Rev. Paul J. Borowski, C.Ss.R., Prov.; Rev. Philip Dabney, C.Ss.R., Parish Mission Preacher; Rev. James Wallace, C.Ss.R., Mission Team; Rev. Charles Wherley Jr., C.Ss.R., Communication/Media Contact North

America Conference of Redemptorists; Peter Linh Ba Quoc Nguyen, C.Ss.R., Vocation Dir.; Rev. Henry E. Sattler, C.Ss.R., Secy./Treas.; Rev. Francis Gargani, C.Ss.R., In Res.; Denis Sweeney, C.Ss.R., Vocation Dir.;

DOUGLASTON

Bishop Mugavero Residence - 7200 Douglaston Pkwy., Douglaston, NY 11362 t) 718-229-8001 x411 moellinger@rcdob.org Dcn. Matthew J. Oellinger; Rev. Hugh A. Byrne, In Res.; Rev. Msgr. Michael J. Cantley, In Res.; Rev. Coleman J. Costello, In Res.; Rev. George R. Cowan, In Res.; Rev. Msgr. George T. Deas, In Res.; Rev. Joseph W. Denzer, In Res.; Rev. James T. Devine, In Res.; Rev. James Diffley, In Res.; Rev. Daniel G. Keohane, In Res.; Rev. Msgr. John F. Keppler, In Res.; Rev. Eugene McGovern, In Res.; Rev. James J. Reynolds, In Res.; Rev. Raymond F. Schmidt, In Res.; Rev. Msgr. James F. Spengler, In Res.; Rev. Romano A. Zanon, In Res.;

ELMHURST

Congregation of St. John the Baptist of China - 54-17 90th St., Elmhurst, NY 11373 t) 718-271-3944 brotherli2000@yahoo.com Rev. Vincent Nguyen, C.S.J.B., Pst.; Rev. Victor Cao, C.S.J.B.; Rev. Tiancang (Joseph) Zheng; Bro. Peter Li, C.S.J.B., Prov.; Brs.: 2; Priests: 3

Our Lady of China Chapel - 54-09 92nd St., Elmhurst, NY 11373 t) 718-699-1929 olcny@msn.com Sr. Monica Gan, C.S.T., Admin.;

FOREST HILLS

Marist Brothers of the Schools, Inc. - Champagnat Res., 70-20 Juno St., Forest Hills, NY 11375 t) 718-480-1306 maristbrothersus@aol.com www.maristbr.com

JAMAICA

Immaculate Conception Monastery - 86-45 Edgerton Blvd., Jamaica, NY 11432 t) 718-739-6502 contact@thepassionists.org www.thepassionists.org Rev. Michael Greene, C.P., Dir.; Rev. James O'Shea, C.P., Prov.; Rev. James Price, C.P., Provincial Consultor; Rev. Evans Barasa Fwamba, C.P., Chap.; Rev. Gilbert Otieno Omolo, C.P., Chap.; Rev. William Murphy, C.P., Rector; Rev. Vincent Youngberg, C.P.; Rev. Kenan Peters, C.P.; Rev. John Powers, C.P.; Rev. Patrick Geinzer, C.P., Mem.; Rev. Earl Keating, C.P., Mem.; Rev. Edwin Moran, C.P., Mem.; Rev. Lionel Pacheco, C.P., Mem.; Rev. Paul Wierichs, C.P., Mem.; Rev. Jerome Bracken, C.P., Prof.; Rev. James Barry, C.P., Mem.; Rev. Alberto Cabrera, C.P., Mem.; Rev. Rogie Castellano, C.P., Mem.; Rev. Paul Chenot, C.P., Mem.; Rev. Christopher Cleary, C.P., Mem.; Rev. Theophane Cooney, C.P., Mem.; Rev. Victor Hoagland, C.P., Mem.; Rev. Paul Vaeth, C.P., In Res.; Rev. Joseph F. Jones, C.Ss.R., In Res.; Rev. Thomas P. Brislin, C.P., In Res.; Bro. Michael Stomber, C.P., Mem.; Bro. Robert McKenna, C.P., Mem.; Bro. August Parlavechio, C.P.; Dcn. Luis Daniel Guivas-Gerena, Mem.; Brs.: 3; Priests: 25

Reverend John B. Murray, C.M. House - 8000 Utopia Pkwy., Jamaica, NY 11439 t) 718-990-6161 duongt@stjohns.edu Rev. Peter J. Albano, C.M., Campus Ministry - Staten Island Campus; Most Rev. Alfonso Cabezas, C.M., In Res.; Rev. Michael J. Cummins, C.M., Admin.; Rev. Patrick S. Flanagan, C.M., Prof.; Rev. Patrick J. Griffin, C.M., Exec.; Rev. Donald J. Harrington, C.M.; Rev. Tri Minh Duong, C.M., Supr.; Rev. John Holliday, Campus Min.; Rev. Kevin G. Creagh, C.M., Exec.; Rev. Richard Rock, Campus Min.; Rev. Bernard M. Tracey, C.M., Exec.; Rev. Joseph P. Foley, C.M., Res.; Rev. Gervais Kamwa Kouam (Cameroon), Grad Student - Visiting International Priest; Rev. Phuc (Joseph) Cu Hong, CM, Grad Student - Visiting International Priest; Rev. Aneesh Mathew, CM, Grad Student - Visiting International Priest; Priests: 16

OZONE PARK

Montfort Missionaries Provincialate (Missionaries of the Company of Mary; Montfort Missionaries; Montfort Publications; Montfort Spiritual Association) - 101-18 104th St., Ozone Park, NY 11416; Mailing: 26 S. Saxon Ave., Bay Shore, NY 11706 t) (631) 666-7500 montfort.secretariat@gmail.com montfortusa.org Rev. Matthew J. Considine, S.M.M.; Brs.: 1; Priests: 1

QUEENS VILLAGE

DePaul Residence - 80-14 217th St., Queens Village, NY 11427 t) 718-766-7344 Rev. Michael J. Cummins, C.M.; Rev. Richard J. Devine, C.M.; Rev. Joseph P. Foley, C.M.;

ROCKAWAY PARK

Franciscan Missionary Brothers of North America New York - 99-07 Rockaway Beach Blvd., Rockaway Park, NY 11694 t) 718-634-6476 cmsfny@gmail.com www.cmsfglobal.com Bro. Karimalayil Joseph Joseph, C.M.S.F., Supr.; Brs.: 8

Franciscan Missionary Brothers of North America, NY - 99-07 Rockaway Beach Blvd., Rockaway Park, NY 11694 t) 718-634-6476 sffriary@gmail.com Bro. Joseph Karimalayil, C.M.S.F., Pres.;

SPRINGFIELD GARDENS

Martin De Porres Brothers Community - 136-01 219th St., Springfield Gardens, NY 11413 t) 347-882-8761 rrbfsc@nyc.rr.com; rrbfsc@gmail.com mdpgh.org Bro. Kevin Finn, F.S.C., Dir.; Bro. Raymond R. Blixt, F.S.C., Prof.; Bro. Philip Rofrano, F.S.C., Mem.; Bro. Peter Iorlano, F.S.C., In Res.;

NURSING / REHABILITATION / CONVALESCENCE / ELDERLY CARE [NUR]

BAYSIDE

Ozanam Hall of Queens Nursing Home, Inc. (Carmelite Sisters for the Aged and Infirm and the Diocese of Brooklyn) - 42-41 201st St., Bayside, NY 11361 t) 718-423-2000 jcraymond@ozanamhall.org; atagle@ozanamhall.org www.ozanamhall.org Post-Acute Care Sr. Phillip Ann Bowden, O 'Carm., Admin.; Asstd. Annu.: 1,359; Staff: 362

BROOKLYN

SS. Joachim & Anne Residence, Inc. (Saints Joachim + Anne Nursing and Rehabilitation Center) - 2720 Surf Ave., Brooklyn, NY 11224 t) 718-714-4800 info@ccbq.org ssjoachim.org Skilled nursing facility for short-term rehabilitation and long-term care. Steven Smyth, Admin.; Asstd. Annu.: 1,743; Staff: 170

QUEENS VILLAGE

The Home for the Aged of the Little Sisters of the Poor (Queen of Peace Residence) - 110-30 221st St., Queens Village, NY 11429 t) 718-464-1800 qpmothersuperior@littlesistersofthepoor.org littlesistersofthepoor.org Sr. Joseph Caroline Beutler, L.S.P., Pres.; Asstd. Annu.: 70; Staff: 95

PRESCHOOLS / CHILDCARE CENTERS [PRE]

BROOKLYN

St. Francis Home for Young Men - 132 Eagle St., Brooklyn, NY 11222 t) 718-349-1157 info@stfrancishousebriiklyn.com www.sfhbrooklyn.com Joseph Campo, Dir.;

Little Flower Children and Family Services of New York - 630 Flushing Ave., 3rd Fl., Brooklyn, NY 11206-5026; Mailing: 2450 N. Wading River Rd., Wading River, NY 11792-1402 t) 718-526-9150; (631) 929-6200 info@lfchild.org www.littleflowerny.org Sr. Ellen Zak, CSFN, Local Supr.; Corinne Hammons, Pres. & CEO; Matthew Bredes, CFO;

St. Vincent's Services, Inc. (HeartShare St. Vincent's Services) - 66 Boerum Pl., Brooklyn, NY 11201 t) 718-522-3700 dawn.saffayeh@heartshare.org www.hsvsnyc.org (Formerly St. Vincent's Home for Boys and St. Vincent's Hall, Inc.) Dawn Saffayeh, Exec. Dir.;

GARDEN CITY

SCO Family of Services - 1415 Kellum Pl., Ste. 140, Garden City, NY 11530 t) 516-671-1253; 718-895-2555 klittle@sco.org www.sco.org Helps vulnerable New Yorkers. Keith Little, Pres. & CEO;

ROCKAWAY PARK

St. John's Residence for Boys, Inc. - 150 Beach 110th St., Rockaway Park, NY 11694 t) 718-945-2800 info@stjohnsresidence.org www.stjohnsresidence.org Corinne Hammons, CEO; Matthew Bredes, CFO; Jennifer Horsley, Exec. Dir.;

RETREAT HOUSES / RENEWAL CENTERS [RTR]

BROOKLYN

Jesus of Nazareth Diocesan Retreat Center - 475 E. 57th St., 4th Fl., Brooklyn, NY 11203 t) 347-710-0010 Dcn. Carlos Garcia, Dir.;

SEMINARIES [SEM]

DOUGLASTON

Cathedral Seminary House of Formation - 7200 Douglaston Pkwy., Douglaston, NY 11362 t) 718-631-4600 x2146 ssanto@diobrook.org; info@cathedralseminary.org cathedralseminary.org Rev. Joseph T. Holcomb, Rector; Susan Santo, Registrar; Corey Murray, Librn.; Rev. James W. King, Dir., Spiritual Formation; Rev. Raymond Roden, Spiritual Dir.; Bro. Owen Sadlier, Formation Advisor/Coord., MACPS Prog.; Stds.: 24; Bro. Tchrs.: 1; Pr. Tchrs.: 2

ELMHURST

Cathedral Preparatory School and Seminary - 56-25 92nd St., Elmhurst, NY 11373 t) 718-592-6800 jkuroly@cathedralprep.org www.cathedralprep.org Rev. James A. Kuroly, Rector; Stds.: 139; Lay Tchrs.: 13; Pr. Tchrs.: 2

SHRINES [SHR]

BROOKLYN

Regina Pacis Votive Shrine - 1230 65th St., Brooklyn, NY 11219 t) 718-236-0909 rosalia1230@aol.com For personnel see St. Rosalia.

SPECIAL CARE FACILITIES [SPF]

BROOKLYN

Anthonian Hall, Inc. - 191 Joralemon St., Brooklyn, NY 11201 t) 718-722-6000 info@ccbq.org www.ccbq.org Emmie Glynn Ryan, Secy.;

Care at Home for the Diocese of Brooklyn, Inc. - 168 Seventh St., Brooklyn, NY 11215 t) 718-832-0550 info@cahny.com Broughan Gorey, Pres.; Asstd. Annu.: 222; Staff: 150

Casa Betsaida-Home for people with AIDS - 267 Hewes St., Brooklyn, NY 11211 t) 718-218-7890 jose.morales@ccbq.org Rev. Msgr. Anthony Hernandez, Chair;

Catholic Guild for the Blind, Inc. - 191 Joralemon St., Brooklyn, NY 11201 t) 718-722-6000 info@ccbq.org Emmie Glynn Ryan, Secy.;

Family Home Care Services of Brooklyn and Queens, Inc. - 168th Seventh Ave., Brooklyn, NY 11215 t) 718-832-0550 info@fhcsny.com Broughan Gorey, Pres.; Asstd. Annu.: 554; Staff: 900

Saints Joachim and Anne Nursing and Rehabilitation Center - 2720 Surf Ave., Brooklyn, NY 11224 t) 718-714-4800 info@ccbq.org Steven Smyth, Admin.; Rev. Msgr. Alfred P. LoPinto, CEO; Bed Capacity: 200; Asstd. Annu.: 488; Staff: 180

Mary's Hall, Inc. - 191 Joralemon St., Brooklyn, NY 11201 t) 718-722-6000 info@ccbq.org Emmie Glynn Ryan, Secy.;

Mercy Home for Children - 273 Willoughby Ave., Brooklyn, NY 11205 t) 718-832-1075 info@mercyhomeny.org www.mercyhomeny.org Under the sponsorship of the Sisters of Mercy. Janice Aris, Exec. Dir.; Bed Capacity: 116; Asstd. Annu.: 108; Staff: 258

MercyFirst - 241 37th St., Suite 6A, Brooklyn, NY 11232 t) 718-232-1500 www.mercyfirst.org Foster care, Residential, Family Support, Immigrant Services, Integrated Health Care. Under the sponsorship of the Sisters of Mercy. Renee Skolaski, CEO; Bed Capacity: 409; Asstd. Annu.: 3,000; Staff: 436

Pierrepont Charitable Fund, Inc. - 191 Joralemon St., Brooklyn, NY 11201 t) 718-722-6000 ccbq.org Emmie Glynn Ryan, Secy.;

Providence House, Inc. - 703 Lexington Ave., Brooklyn,

NY 11221 t) 718-455-0197 info@providencehouse.org www.providencehouse.org Danielle Minelli Pagnotta, Exec.; Bed Capacity: 362; Asstd. Annu.: 618; Staff: 80

Bishop Joseph M. Sullivan Residence - 329 Lincoln Rd., Brooklyn, NY 11225; Mailing: 703 Lexington Ave., Brooklyn, NY 11221 t) 929-210-8480 Danielle Minelli Pagnotta, Dir.;

D'Addario Residence - 275 Kosciuszko St., Brooklyn, NY 11221; Mailing: 703 Lexington Ave., Brooklyn, NY 11221 t) 929-210-9355 Danielle Minelli Pagnotta, Dir.;

Providence House 2 - 388 Prospect Ave., Brooklyn, NY 11215; Mailing: 703 Lexington Ave., Brooklyn, NY 11221 t) 718-369-9140 Danielle Minelli Pagnotta, Dir.;

Providence House 4 - 89 Sickles Ave., New Rochelle, NY 10801; Mailing: 703 Lexington Ave., Brooklyn, NY 11221 t) 914-632-4177 Danielle Minelli Pagnotta, Dir.;

Providence House 5 - 396 Lincoln Rd., Brooklyn, NY 11225; Mailing: 703 Lexington Ave., Brooklyn, NY 11221 t) 718-778-1310 Danielle Minelli Pagnotta, Dir.;

Providence House 7 - 701 Lexington Ave., Brooklyn, NY 11221; Mailing: 703 Lexington Ave., Brooklyn, NY 11221 t) 718-574-6847 Danielle Minelli Pagnotta, Dir.;

LONG ISLAND CITY

Hour Children - 36-11 12th St., Long Island City, NY 11106 t) 718-433-4724 sistertesa@hourchildren.org www.hourchildren.org Sr. Teresa Fitzgerald, C.S.J., Exec.;

An asterisk (*) denotes an organization that has established tax-exempt status directly with the IRS and is not covered by the USCCB Group Ruling.

Diocese of Brownsville

(Dioecesis Brownsvillensis)

MOST REVEREND DANIEL E. FLORES, S.T.D.

Bishop of Brownsville; ordained January 30, 1988; appointed Auxiliary Bishop of Detroit and Titular Bishop of Cozyla October 28, 2006; consecrated November 29, 2006; appointed Bishop of Brownsville December 9, 2009; installed February 2, 2010. Mailing Address: P.O. Box 2279, Brownsville, TX 78522-2279.

Chancery: 1910 University Blvd., P.O. Box 2279, Brownsville, TX 78522-2279. T: 956-542-2501; F: 956-542-6751.
www.cdob.org
cdob@cdob.org

ESTABLISHED JULY 10, 1965.

Square Miles 4,296.

Comprises the four Counties of Cameron, Hidalgo, Starr and Willacy in the State of Texas.

For legal titles of parishes and diocesan institutions, consult the Chancery.

Most Reverend Mario A. Aviles, C.O.
Auxiliary Bishop of Brownsville; ordained July 21, 1998; appointed Auxiliary Bishop of Brownsville and Titular Bishop of Cataquas December 4, 2017; consecrated February 22, 2018. Mailing Address: 700 N. Virgen de San Juan Blvd., San Juan, TX 78589.

STATISTICAL OVERVIEW

Personnel
Bishop....1
Auxiliary Bishops....1
Priests: Diocesan Active in Diocese....69
Priests: Diocesan Active Outside Diocese....4
Priests: Retired, Sick or Absent....13
Number of Diocesan Priests....86
Religious Priests in Diocese....23
Total Priests in your Diocese....109
Extern Priests in Diocese....3
Ordinations:
Diocesan Priests....1
Transitional Deacons....1
Permanent Deacons in Diocese....100
Total Brothers....8
Total Sisters....62

Parishes
Parishes....72
With Resident Pastor:
Resident Diocesan Priests....56
Resident Religious Priests....12
Without Resident Pastor:
Administered by Priests....3
Completely vacant....1
Missions....44
Pastoral Centers....2
Professional Ministry Personnel:
Sisters....3
Lay Ministers....32

Welfare
Homes for the Aged....2
Total Assisted....130
Day Care Centers....4
Total Assisted....58
Special Centers for Social Services....6
Total Assisted....311,966
Other Institutions....1
Total Assisted....6,075

Educational
Diocesan Students in Other Seminaries....9
Students, Religious....2
Total Seminarians....11
High Schools, Private....3
Total Students....503
Elementary Schools, Diocesan and Parish....6
Total Students....1,108
Elementary Schools, Private....3
Total Students....327
Catechesis / Religious Education:
High School Students....4,269
Elementary Students....8,562
Total Students under Catholic Instruction....14,780
Teachers in Diocese:
Brothers....1
Sisters....1
Lay Teachers....181

Vital Statistics
Receptions into the Church:
Infant Baptism Totals....3,818
Minor Baptism Totals....342
Adult Baptism Totals....117
Received into Full Communion....107
First Communions....2,628
Confirmations....2,240
Marriages:
Catholic....764
Interfaith....64
Total Marriages....828
Deaths....3,134
Total Catholic Population....1,181,287
Total Population....1,389,750

LEADERSHIP

Office of the Bishop - t) 956-550-1530 Most Rev. Daniel E. Flores (bishopflores@cdob.org);
Office of the Auxiliary Bishop - t) 956-784-5010 Most Rev. Mario A. Aviles, C.O. (bishopaviles@cdob.org);
Vicar General - t) 956-784-5010 Most Rev. Mario A. Aviles, C.O. (bishopaviles@cdob.org);
Moderator of the Curia - t) (956) 784-5010 Most Rev. Mario A. Aviles, C.O., Moderator (bishopaviles@cdob.org); Rev. Andres E. Gutierrez, Asst. Moderator (agutierrez@cdob.org); Rev. Luis Fernando Sanchez, Asst. Moderator (lsanchez@cdob.org);
Office of the Chancellor - t) 956-542-2501 Rev. Andres E. Gutierrez, Chancellor (agutierrez@cdob.org); Rev. Leonel Rodriguez, Vice Chancellor (ldrodriguez@cdob.org);
Deans/Deaneries - Rev. Aglayde Rafael Vega, Dean - Brownsville Deanery (rvega@cdob.org); Rev. Robert Charlton, SS.CC., Dean - Harlingen Deanery (rcharlton@cdob.org); Rev. Msgr. Gustavo Barrera, Dean - McAllen-Edinburg Deanery (gbarrera@cdob.org);
Judicial Department and Diocesan Tribunal - t) 956-784-5070 Rev. Ariel Oliver Angel, Judicial Vicar; Rev. Luis Fernando Sanchez, Adjutant Judicial Vicar (lsanchez@cdob.org); Annita M. Gonzalez, Ecclesiastical Notary & Advocate Facilitator (agonzalez@cdob.org);
Vicar for Priests - t) 956-542-2501 Rev. Msgr. Heberto M. Diaz Jr. (hdiaz@cdob.org);
Vicar for Religious - t) 956-702-4088 Sr. Norma Pimentel, M.J., Assoc.;
Episcopal Vicars - Rev. Alfonso M. Guevara, Apostolic Movements & Pastoral Initiatives (aguevara@cdob.org); Rev. Luis Fernando Sanchez, Canonical Affairs (lsanchez@cdob.org);
Diocesan Attorney - t) 956-541-4914 David Garza;
Diocesan Relations - t) 956-781-5323 Brenda Nettles Riojas, Dir./Editor (briojas@cdob.org);

OFFICES AND DIRECTORS

Campaign for Human Development - t) 956-702-4088 Sr. Norma Pimentel, M.J., Diocesan Coord.;
Catholic Relief Services - t) (956) 787-8571 Ofelia de los Santos, Diocesan Coord. (odelossantos@cdob.org);
Catholic Schools Office - t) 956-787-8571 Sr. Cynthia A. Mello, S.S.D., Supt. (cmello@cdob.org); Sr. Colleen Matarese, S.S.D., Dir. Special Prog.;
Family Life Office - t) 956-784-5012 Lydia Pesina, Dir. (lpesina@cdob.org);
Fiscal Office - t) 956-542-2501 Jack Graham, Comptroller (jgraham@cdob.org);
Health Care Ministries - t) 956-784-5018 Yolanda Carrillo, Dir. (ycarrillo@cdob.org);
Human Resources Office - t) 956-542-2501 x345 Genoveva Trevino, Dir. (gtrevino@cdob.org);
Information Technology - t) 956-542-2501 x340 Alberto Zavala, Dir. (azavala@cdob.org);
Insurance and Priest Pensions - t) 956-542-2501 x349 Maria C. Hernandez, Admin. (mhernandez@cdob.org);
Jail Ministry - t) 956-550-1541 Dcn. Roman Ramos, Dir. (rramos@cdob.org);
Office of Deliverance Ministry - t) 956-784-5079 Dcn. Reynaldo I. Flores, Dir. (rflores@cdob.org);
Office of Evangelization & Catechesis - t) 956-784-5013 Luis Espinoza, Dir. (lespinoza@cdob.org);
Office of Liturgy and Worship - t) 956-542-2501
 Masters of Ceremonies - Lower Valley - Rev. Derlis R. Garcia, MC - Harlingen & Weslaco Deanery;
 Master Of Ceremonies - Upper Valley - Rev. Gregory T. Labus, MC - McAllen-Edinburg & Pharr Deanery; Rev. Joaquin Zermeno, MC - Mission & Rio Grande City Deanery;
Office of Permanent Deacons - t) 956-784-5060 Rev. Fernando Gonzalez, Dir. (fgonzalez@cdob.org);
Parish Accounting Services - t) 956-542-2501 x337 Ruben Olivares, Dept. Supvr. (rolivares@cdob.org);
Pro-Life Office - t) (956) 784-5035 prolife@cdob.org Rev. Derlis R. Garcia, Dir. (dgarcia@cdob.org); Norma Montalvo, Assoc. Dir. (nmontalvo@cdob.org);
Real Estate & Facilities Management - t) 956-781-5323 Clint Brown, Dir. (cbrown@cdob.org);
Safety Awareness Program - t) 956-784-5066 c) 956-457-0010 Margarita (Margie) Garcia, Victim Asst. Coord. (Margie.Garcia@cdob.org);
San Juan Diego Lay Ministry Institute - t) 956-784-5059 Dcn. Luis Zuniga, Dir. (lzuniga@cdob.org);
Stewardship & Grants Office - t) 956-787-8571 x462 Ofelia de los Santos, Dir. (odelossantos@cdob.org);
Strategy & Development Office - t) 956-784-5093 Miguel Santos, Dir. (msantos@cdob.org);
Vocations and Seminarians Office - t) 956-784-5060 Rev. Leonel Rodriguez, Dir. (ldrodriguez@cdob.org);

ADVISORY BOARDS, COMMISSIONS, COMMITTEES, AND COUNCILS

College of Consultors - Most Rev. Daniel E. Flores (bishopflores@cdob.org); Most Rev. Mario A. Aviles, C.O., Mem. (bishopaviles@cdob.org); Rev. Msgr. Gustavo Barrera, Mem. (gbarrera@cdob.org);
Diocesan Finance Council - Most Rev. Daniel E. Flores (bishopflores@cdob.org); Jack Graham, Comptroller (jgraham@cdob.org); Most Rev. Mario A. Aviles, C.O., Mem. (bishopaviles@cdob.org);
Presbyteral Council - Rev. Robert Charlton, SS.CC., Chair (rcharlton@cdob.org); Rev. Ignacio Tapia, Secy. (itapia@cdob.org); Rev. Jose E. Losoya, C.O., Vice-Chmn. (jlosoya@cdob.org);
Priests' Assignment Board - Rev. Leonel Rodriguez, Brownsville Deanery (ldrodriguez@cdob.org); Rev. Rodolfo Franco, Harlingen Deanery; Rev. Gregory T. Labus, McAllen-Edinburg Deanery (glabus@cdob.org);

PARISHES, MISSIONS, AND CLERGY

STATE OF TEXAS

ALAMO

Resurrection - 312 N. 9th St., Alamo, TX 78516 t) 956-787-2963 resurrection@cdob.org (Formerly St. Joseph/Our Lady of Fatima) Rev. Jose Rene Angel, Pst.; CRP Stds.: 276

ALTON

San Martin de Porres - 621 W. Main Ave., Alton, TX 78573 t) 956-585-8001 smdpalton@cdob.org sanmartindeporresalton.org Rev. Arturo Castillo, Pst.; Dcn. Antonio M. Arteaga; Dcn. Armandin Villarreal; CRP Stds.: 401
 Capilla Santa Cecilia - 15905 Cantu Rd., Edinburg, TX 78541 (Monte Cristo)

BROWNSVILLE

Immaculate Conception Cathedral - 1218 E. Jefferson St., Brownsville, TX 78520 t) 956-546-3178 ic-brw@cdob.org Rev. Nicholas J. Harding, O.M.I., Rector; Rev. Edgar R. Garcia, O.M.I., In Res.; Dcn. Roberto Cano; Dcn. Luis Zuniga; CRP Stds.: 99
 St. Thomas - 155 E. Jefferson St., Brownsville, TX 78520
 Sacred Heart - 602 E. Elizabeth St., Brownsville, TX 78520
Christ the King - 2255 Southmost Rd., Brownsville, TX 78521 t) 956-546-1982 christ-the-king@cdob.org; pcl-ckbrw@cdob.org Rev. Ricardo Chavez, Parish Admin.; Dcn. Jose Angel Bernal; CRP Stds.: 86
 San Juan Diego de Guadalupe - 4180 S. Browne Ave., Brownsville, TX 78521 (Valle Escondido)
Church of the Good Shepherd - 2645 Tulipan St., Brownsville, TX 78521 t) 956-542-5142 good-shepherd@cdob.org Rev. Aglayde Rafael Vega, Pst.; Dcn. Sergio Garcia; Dcn. Roman Ramos; CRP Stds.: 211
St. Eugene de Mazenod - 5409 Austin Rd., Brownsville, TX 78521 t) 956-831-9923 st-eugene-de-mazenod@cdob.org steugenedemazenodparish.org Rev. Kevin A. Collins, O.M.I., Pst.; Rev. Paul F. Hughes, O.M.I., In Res.; Dcn. Francisco J. Garza; Dcn. Jesus G. Hernandez; CRP Stds.: 176
Holy Family - 2308 E. Tyler, Brownsville, TX 78520; Mailing: 2405 E. Tyler, Brownsville, TX 78520 t) 956-546-6975 holy-family-brw@cdob.org holyfamilybrw.org Rev. Joshua A. Carlos, Parish Admin.; Dcn. Julio Ibarra; Dcn. Josue Ramirez; Dcn. Miguel A. Ramirez; CRP Stds.: 174
St. Joseph - 555 W. St. Francis St., Brownsville, TX 78520 t) 956-542-2709 saint-joseph-brw@cdob.org www.stjoseph-church.org Rev. Oscar O. Siordia, Pst.; Rev. Eusebio Martinez, In Res.; Dcn. Mario S. Rodriguez; CRP Stds.: 146
St. Luke - 2800 Rockwell Dr., Brownsville, TX 78521 t) 956-541-1480 saint-luke@cdob.org www.stlukecc.org Rev. Fernando Gonzalez, Pst.; Dcn. Cruz Carlos; Dcn. Javier A. Garcia; CRP Stds.: 131
Mary, Mother of the Church - 1914 Barnard Rd., Brownsville, TX 78520 t) 956-546-3800 saint-mary-brw@cdob.org Rev. Msgr. Heberto M. Diaz Jr., Pst.; Rev. Caleb J. De La Rosa, Par. Vicar; Dcn. Juan Pablo Navarro; CRP Stds.: 156
 St. Mary Catholic School - (Grades PreK-6) 1300 Los Ebanos Blvd., Brownsville, TX 78520 t) 956-546-1805 agomez@cdobcs.org www.stmarys-cs.org Ana E. Gomez, Prin.;
 Little Saints Learning Center - 1300 Los Ebanos Blvd., Brownsville, TX 78520 t) 956-546-1805 agomez@cdobcs.org (18 mths to 3 yrs) Ana E. Gomez, Prin.;
Our Lady of Good Counsel - 1055 Military Rd., Brownsville, TX 78520 t) 956-541-8341 lady-of-good-counsel@cdob.org Rev. Rene Gaytan, Parish Admin.; Dcn. Guadalupe Garcia; CRP Stds.: 175
Our Lady of Guadalupe - 1200 E. Lincoln St., Brownsville, TX 78521; Mailing: P.O. Box 4900, Brownsville, TX 78523 t) 956-542-4823 olg-brownsville@cdob.org Rev. Francisco Acosta, Pst.; CRP Stds.: 118
The Parish of the Lord of Divine Mercy - 650 E. Alton Gloor Blvd., Brownsville, TX 78526 t) (956) 544-2112 thelordofdivinemercy@cdob.org divinemercybrownsville.org Rev. Leonel Rodriguez, Pst.; Rev. Robert Moreno Jr., Par. Vicar; Dcn. Noe Longoria; CRP Stds.: 139
San Felipe de Jesus - 2215 Rancho Viejo Ave., Brownsville, TX 78526-8093; Mailing: 2218 Carlos Ave., Brownsville, TX 78526-8093 t) 956-982-2007 san-felipe-de-jesus@cdob.org Rev. Manuel Alfredo Razo, Pst.; Rev. Louis R. Hotop, S.J., Par. Vicar; Rev. Brian A. Strassburger, S.J., Par. Vicar; CRP Stds.: 132
San Pedro Quasi Parish - 7602 Old Military Rd., Brownsville, TX 78520; Mailing: P.O. Box 1658, Olmito, TX 78575 t) 956-542-2596 san-pedro@cdob.org Rev. Joel R. Flores, Parish Admin.; CRP Stds.: 95

DONNA

St. Joseph - 306 South D. Salinas Blvd., Donna, TX 78537 t) 956-464-3331 secretary-sjdonna@cdob.org www.stjosephdonna.com Rev. Franciscus Asisi Eka Yuantoro, M.S.F., Pst.; Dcn. Felipe Almendarez; Dcn. Hugo De la Cruz; CRP Stds.: 262
 Christ the King - 1910 Hutch, Donna, TX 78537 (Colonia Nueva)

EDCOUCH

St. Theresa of the Infant Jesus - 200 P. Salazar St., Edcouch, TX 78538; Mailing: P.O. Box 307, Edcouch, TX 78538 t) 956-262-1347 infant-jesus@cdob.org stij-olg.com Rev. Patrick K. Seitz, Pst.; Rev. Michael Gnanaraj, Par. Vicar; Dcn. Florencio Trevino; CRP Stds.: 206
 Our Lady of Guadalupe - 200 N. Laurel Ave., La Villa, TX 78562 (La Villa)

EDINBURG

Holy Family - 1302 E. Champion St., Edinburg, TX 78539-4864 t) 956-383-5472 holy-family-edinburg@cdob.org Rev. Thomas Luczak, O.F.M., Pst.; Rev. Terrence Gorski, O.F.M., Par. Vicar; Dcn. Ruben Lopez; CRP Stds.: 262

Immaculate Conception - 28212 FM 2058, Edinburg, TX 78541 t) 956-842-3663 ic-mccook@cdob.org Rev. Juan Manuel Salazar, Pst.; CRP Stds.: 33

St. Anne - 36856 N. Expressway 281, Edinburg, TX 78542; Mailing: P.O. Box 134, Linn, TX 78563 (San Manuel)

St. Joseph - 114 W. Fay St., Edinburg, TX 78539 t) 956-383-3728 stjoseph-edinburg@cdob.org stjosephedinburgtx.org Rev. Gregory T. Labus, Pst.; Dcn. Silvestre J. Garcia; CRP Stds.: 118

St. Joseph School - (Grades PreSchool-8) 119 W. Fay St., Edinburg, TX 78539 t) 956-383-3957 akarpinski@cdobcs.org www.st-joseph-catholic-school.com Angelina Karpinski, Prin.;

St. Joseph the Worker - 8310 Highland Ave., Edinburg, TX 78542 t) 956-383-5880 sjwsancarlos@cdob.org Rev. Jose Garza, Pst.; CRP Stds.: 393

St. Frances Xavier Cabrini - Hargill - 29665 N. Couch St., Hargill, TX 78549

St. Theresa - 205 Jefferson Ave., Edinburg, TX 78542 (Faysville)

Sacred Heart - 215 N. 16th Ave., Edinburg, TX 78541 t) 956-383-3253 sh-edinburg@cdob.org www.sacredheartedinburg.org Rev. Manoj Kumar Nayak, SS.CC., Pst.; Rev. William S. Gural, SS.CC., Par. Vicar; Rev. Ajit Baliar-Singh, SS.CC., Par. Vicar; Dcn. Jose Peralez III; Dcn. Raul Rangel; CRP Stds.: 491

Capilla de San Jose - 4101 Flores St., Edinburg, TX 78541 (Lull)

ELSA

Sacred Heart - 1100 N. Broadway, Elsa, TX 78543; Mailing: P.O. Box 6, Elsa, TX 78543 t) 956-262-1406 sacred-heart-elsa@cdob.org Rev. Cesar Uriel Partida, Pst.; Dcn. David C. Carreon; Dcn. Gerardo J. Rosa; CRP Stds.: 190

Christ the King - 123 W. Valdez Rd., Monte Alto, TX 78538 (Monte Alto)

Holy Cross Catechetical Center - 422 E. Mile 15 North, Weslaco, TX 78599 (Mile 15)

HARLINGEN

St. Anthony - 1015 E. Van Buren Ave., Harlingen, TX 78550; Mailing: 209 S. 10th St., Harlingen, TX 78550 t) 956-428-6111 sa-harlingen@cdob.org Rev. Alejandro F. Flores, Pst.; Dcn. Paulo Escobar; Dcn. Genaro Garza III, Diaconal Internship Svc.; CRP Stds.: 319

St. Anthony School - (Grades PreK-6) 1015 E. Harrison Ave., Harlingen, TX 78550 t) 956-423-2486 kstapleton@cdobcs.org www.saintanthonyeagles.com Mindy Escobar, Prin.; Eva Cuellar, Librn.;

Immaculate Heart of Mary - 412 South C St., Harlingen, TX 78550 t) 956-423-0855 ihom@cdob.org www.ihmc-hgn.org Rev. Msgr. Luis Javier Garcia, Pst.; Rev. George A. Gonzalez, In Res.; Rev. Ernesto Magallon, In Res.; CRP Stds.: 16

Our Lady of the Assumption - 1313 W. Buchanan St., Harlingen, TX 78550 t) 956-423-4670 ola-harlingen@cdob.org Rev. Ruben Delgado, Pst.; CRP Stds.: 291

San Felipe - 1706 Rangerville Rd., Harlingen, TX 78550 (Rangerville Rd)

Queen of Peace - 1509 New Combes Hwy., Harlingen, TX 78550 t) 956-423-6341 queen-of-peace@cdob.org www.qphrl.org Rev. Robert Charlton, SS.CC., Pst.; Rev. Deacon Paulo Lui Voreqe, SS.CC., Transitional Dcn/Pastoral Assoc.; Dcn. Jose G. Aguilera; Dcn. Benigno Palacios; Dcn. Juan R. Zamora; CRP Stds.: 140

HIDALGO

Sacred Heart - 208 E. Camelia Ave., Hidalgo, TX 78557; Mailing: P.O. Box 579, Hidalgo, TX 78557 t) 956-843-2463 sacredhearthid@cdob.org Rev. Juan Pablo Davalos, Pst.; CRP Stds.: 98

LA FERIA

St. Francis Xavier - 500 S. Canal St., La Feria, TX 78559; Mailing: P.O. Box 116, La Feria, TX 78559 t) 956-797-2666 st-francis-xavier@cdob.org www.stfrancisxavierlaferia.org Rev. Rodolfo Franco, Pst.; Dcn. Jose G. Gonzalez; CRP Stds.: 130

LA GRULLA

Holy Family - 107 W. Private Lazaro Solis St., La Grulla, TX 78548; Mailing: P.O. Box 67, La Grulla, TX 78548 t) 956-487-3365 bkpr-hfgrulla@cdob.com Dcn. Benito Saenz Jr.; CRP Stds.: 130

Cristo Rey - FM 2360 & Eugenio St., La Victoria, TX 78582 (La Victoria)

Our Lady of the Peace - 6689 FM 1430, La Casita, TX 78582 (La Casita-Garciasville)

LA JOYA

Our Lady, Queen of Angels - 916 S. Leo Ave., La Joya, TX 78560 t) 956-585-5223 olqangels@cdob.org Rev. Joaquin Zermeno, Pst.; CRP Stds.: 96

St. Mary Magdalene - 7100 W. Military Rd., Mission, TX 78572 (Abram-Perezville)

St. Anthony - 1102 S. Main St., Penitas, TX 78576 (Penitas)

San Jose - 41838 Old Military Rd., Havana, TX 78560 (Havana)

LOS FRESNOS

St. Cecilia - 606 W. Ocean Blvd., Los Fresnos, TX 78566 t) 956-233-5619 saint-cecilia@cdob.org Rev. Msgr. Pedro Briseno, Pst.; CRP Stds.: 181

LYFORD

Prince of Peace - 8413 Park Ave., Lyford, TX 78569; Mailing: P.O. Box 460, Lyford, TX 78569 t) 956-347-3580 prince-of-peace@cdob.org Rev. Derlis R. Garcia, Parish Admin.; CRP Stds.: 110

Santa Monica - FM 1018 & 1420, Santa Monica, TX 78569 (Santa Monica)

St. Martin of Tours - 345 N. Martin Cavazos Dr., Sebastian, TX 78569 (Sebastian)

MCALLEN

Holy Spirit - 2201 Martin Ave., McAllen, TX 78504 t) 956-631-5295 receptionist-hsmcallen@cdob.org www.holyspiritmcallen.org Rev. Andres E. Gutierrez, Pst.; Rev. Ernest Ukwueze, Par. Vicar; Dcn. Henry N. Camacopa; Dcn. Reynaldo I. Flores; Dcn. Richard A. Longoria; Dcn. Luis A. Trevino; CRP Stds.: 646

St. Joseph the Worker - 900 S. 23rd St., McAllen, TX 78501; Mailing: 2315 Ithaca St., McAllen, TX 78501 t) 956-682-1351 sjwmcallen@cdob.org Rev. Edouard Atangana, Pst.; Dcn. Felix Felix; CRP Stds.: 136

Saint Juan Diego Cuauhtlatoatzin - 3413 Helena Ave., McAllen, TX 78503; Mailing: 3408 Idela Ave., McAllen, TX 78503 t) 956-682-5155 sjdmcallen@cdob.org www.sjdmcallen.com Rev. Marco Antonio Reynoso, Pst.; Dcn. Jose Javier Garcia; Dcn. Jose G. Vargas; CRP Stds.: 89

Our Lady of Perpetual Help - 2209 Kendlewood Ave., McAllen, TX 78501 t) 956-682-4238 olph-mcallen@cdob.org Rev. Martin De La Cruz, Pst.; Dcn. Santos Chapa; CRP Stds.: 192

Our Lady of Sorrows - 1108 W. Hackberry Ave., McAllen, TX 78501-4304 t) 956-686-0251 ols@cdob.org www.oladyofsorrows.org Rev. Msgr. Gustavo Barrera, Pst.; Rev. Joe Luis Hernandez, Par. Vicar; Rev. Mishael J. Koday, In Res.; Dcn. Juan Gonzalez; Dcn. Crawford A. Higgins; Dcn. Raymond L. Thomas Jr.; CRP Stds.: 530

Our Lady of Sorrows School - (Grades PreK-8) 1100 Gumwood Ave., McAllen, TX 78501 t) 956-686-3651 imartinez@cdobcs.org www.olsschool.org Israel Martinez Jr., Prin.;

Sacred Heart - 306 S. 15th St., McAllen, TX 78501; Mailing: P.O. Box 370, McAllen, TX 78505 t) 956-686-7711 sacred-heart-mcallen@cdob.org www.sacredheartchurch-mcallen.org Rev. Juan Rogelio Gutierrez, Pst.; Dcn. Carlos C. Aguilar; Dcn. George Terrazas; CRP Stds.: 156

MERCEDES

Our Lady of Mercy - 322 S. Vermont Ave., Mercedes, TX 78570; Mailing: P.O. Box 805, Mercedes, TX 78570 t) 956-565-1141 olm@cdob.org www.olmmercedes.org Rev. Jean Olivier M. Sambu, Pst.; CRP Stds.: 140

Sacred Heart Church - 920 Anacuitas, Mercedes, TX 78570 t) 956-565-0271 sacred-heart-mercedes@cdob.org www.sacredheartmercedes.org Rev. Felix A. Cazares, Take Care of Sacramental Needs; Dcn. Gilberto Guardiola Jr.; Dcn. Jose A. Torres; CRP Stds.: 187

MISSION

Our Lady of Guadalupe - 620 Dunlap St., Mission, TX 78572; Mailing: P.O. Box 1047, Mission, TX 78572 t) 956-585-2623 olgmission@cdob.org Rev. Roy Lee Snipes, O.M.I., Pst.; Dcn. Guillermo Bill Castaneda Jr.;

La Lomita - (Chapel)

Our Lady of St. John of the Fields - 1052 Washington St., Mission, TX 78572 t) 956-585-2325 olsjfchurch@cdob.org Rev. Francisco Castillo, Pst.; CRP Stds.: 155

Our Lady of the Holy Rosary - 923 Matamoros St., Mission, TX 78572 t) 956-581-2193 olhrchurch@cdob.org www.olhrmission.org Rev. Genaro Henriquez, Pst.; Dcn. Israel Sagredo; CRP Stds.: 55

St. Paul - 1119 Francisco Ave., Mission, TX 78572 t) 956-585-2701 sp-mission@cdob.org Rev. Isaac Emeka Erondu, Pst.; Dcn. Robert Ledesma; CRP Stds.: 52

San Cristobal Magallanes & Companions - 4501 Santa Engracia, Mission, TX 78572 t) 956-580-4551 scmcmission@cdob.org Rev. Ignacio Tapia, Pst.; CRP Stds.: 286

Our Lady of Lourdes - 2 1/2 Miles S. Conway, Mission, TX 78572 (Madero)

Our Lady of Fatima - 6634 El Camino Real, Mission, TX 78572 (Granjeno)

OLMITO

Our Heavenly Father Parish - 9178 Tomas Cortez Jr. St., Olmito, TX 78575; Mailing: P.O. Box 249, Olmito, TX 78575 t) 956-350-5190 ohf@cdob.org Rev. Juan Pablo Robles, Pst.; Dcn. Augusto Chapa Jr.; CRP Stds.: 108

PENITAS

Saint Anne - 17109 Coconut Palm Dr., Penitas, TX 78576 t) 956-583-9888 sa-penitas@cdob.org www.saintannecatholicchurch.org Rev. Benedicto Lagarde Jr., M.J., Pst.; Rev. Melchor N. Villero, M.J., Par. Vicar; Dcn. Jorge I. Hinojosa; CRP Stds.: 96

Nuestra Senora de Guadalupe - 465 E. Expwy. 83, Sullivan City, TX 78595 t) 956-790-0242 (Sullivan City)

St. Michael the Archangel - Casimiro Ortega St., Los Ebanos, TX 78565 (Los Ebanos)

St. Juan Diego - 7460 Western Rd., Mission, TX 78572 (Colonia El Flaco)

PHARR

St. Anne, Mother of Mary - 801 E. Juarez, Pharr, TX 78577 t) 956-787-8122 stannepharr@cdob.org Rev. Paul Roman, Parish Admin.; CRP Stds.: 63

St. Jude Thaddeus - 505 S. Ironwood, Pharr, TX 78577; Mailing: P.O. Box 1688, Pharr, TX 78577 t) 956-781-2489 sjtadeo@cdob.org www.stjudethaddeus.net Rev. Jose E. Losoya, C.O., Pst.; Very Rev. Leo Francis Daniels, C.O., Par. Vicar; Rev. Jose Juan Ortiz, C.O., Par. Vicar; CRP Stds.: 54

Oratory Academy of St. Philip Neri - (Grades PreK-8) t) 956-781-3056 idiaz@oratoryschools.org www.oratoryschools.org Izkra Diaz, Prin.;

Oratory - Athenaeum for University Preparation - (Grades 9-12) t) 956-781-3056 www.oratoryschools.org Izkra Diaz, Prin.;

St. Margaret Mary - 122 W. Hawk Ave., Pharr, TX 78577 t) 956-787-8563 saint-margaret-mary@cdob.org Rev. Raymond Nwachukwu, Pst.; CRP Stds.: 94

Mother Cabrini Parish - 8001 S. Cage Blvd., Pharr, TX 78577 t) 956-787-3554 st-frances-cabrini@cdob.org Rev. Miguel Angel Ortega, Pst.; Rev. Eduardo Gomez, In Res.; Dcn. Gerardo Garza; CRP Stds.: 297

PORT ISABEL

Our Lady Star of the Sea - 705 S. Longoria St., Port Isabel, TX 78578 t) 956-943-1297 olss@cdob.org www.olsstx.org Rev. Jesus Guadalupe Garza, Pst.; CRP Stds.: 189

Laguna Heights Chapel - 131 Garfield St., Laguna Heights, TX 78578

PROGRESO

Holy Spirit - 210 Watts Ave., Progreso, TX 78579; Mailing: P.O. Box 216, Progreso, TX 78579 t) 956-565-6856 hsprogreso@cdob.org Rev. Amador Garza, Parish Admin.; CRP Stds.: 113

St. Margaret Ann - Military Hwy. 281, Santa Maria, TX 78592 (Santa Maria)

Cristo Rey - Military Hwy. 281, Bluetown, TX 78586 (Bluetown)

RAYMONDVILLE

St. Anthony - 464 S. First St., Raymondville, TX 78580 t) 956-690-4078 jheredia@cdob.org; st-anthony-raymondville@cdob.org Rev. Juan Victor Heredia, Pst.;

Our Lady of Guadalupe - 693 N. Third St., Raymondville, TX 78580 t) 956-689-2408 olg-raymondville@cdob.org Rev. Emmanuel Kwofie (Ghana), Pst.; CRP Stds.: 111

St. Patrick - 1 Mile S. of 186 on Hwy. 1015, Lasara, TX 78561 (Lasara)

St. Anne, Mother of Mary - 1st St. & Paloma St., San Perlita, TX 78590 (San Perlita)

RIO GRANDE CITY

Immaculate Conception - 101 E. Third St., Rio Grande City, TX 78582; Mailing: P.O. Box 1, Rio Grande City, TX 78582 t) 956-487-2317 ic-rgc@cdob.org Rev. Eduardo Ortega, Pst.; Rev. Alejandro Garcia, In Res.; CRP Stds.: 171

Immaculate Conception School - (Grades PreK-8) 305 N. Britton Ave., Rio Grande City, TX 78582 t) 956-487-2558 g.alvarado@cdobcs.org www.icsrio.org Maria Guadalupe Alvarado, Prin.;

Sacred Heart - 169 W. Old Hwy. 83, Rio Grande City, TX 78582 (Los Garcias)

St. Paul the Apostle - 5752 E. Hwy. 83, Rio Grande City, TX 78582; Mailing: P.O. Box 269, Garciasville, TX 78547 t) 956-488-8349 san-pablo-rgc@cdob.org Rev. Alejandro Garcia, Admin.; Dcn. Rosvel Pruneda; CRP Stds.: 33

RIO HONDO

St. Helen - 228 Huisache, Rio Hondo, TX 78583; Mailing: P.O. Box 451, Rio Hondo, TX 78583 t) 956-748-2327 saint-helen@cdob.org Rev. Salvador Ramirez, Parish Admin.; CRP Stds.: 109

St. Vincent de Paul - 2513 E. Brown Tract Rd., Lozano, TX 78568 (Lozano)

ROMA

Our Lady of Refuge - 4 St. Eugene de Mazenod Ave., Roma, TX 78584; Mailing: P.O. Box 156, Roma, TX 78584 t) 956-849-1455 olr-roma@cdob.org Rev. Paul Wilhelm, O.M.I., Parish Admin.; Dcn. Amando Pena Jr.; Dcn. Jose Humberto Rios; CRP Stds.: 311

Holy Trinity - 4 Miles S. FM 2098, Falcon Heights, TX 78545 t) 956-437-9238 (Falcon Heights)

St. Joseph - Iglesia St., Salineño, TX 78585 t) 956-353-8397 (Salineño)

Holy Family - 202 S. Francesca Ave., Los Saenz, TX 78584 t) 956-849-1127 (Los Saenz)

Lamb of God - Church St., Fronton, TX 78584 t) 956-849-2199 (Fronton)

Sacred Heart - 4987 Old Escobares Hwy. 83, Roma, TX 78584; Mailing: P.O. Box 1180, Roma, TX 78584 t) 956-849-1741 sh-escobares@cdob.org Rev. Miguel A. Fernandez Ceja (Mexico), Parish Admin.; Dcn. Rosvel Pruneda; Dcn. Miguel Villarreal; CRP Stds.: 231

Santa Rosa de Lima - 4195 Old Hwy. 83, Rio Grande City, TX 78582 (La Rosita)

Our Lady of Guadalupe - 1155 N. FM 649 (13 Miles N. of Roma), El Sauz, TX 78582 (El Sauz)

SAN BENITO

St. Benedict - 351 S. Bowie, San Benito, TX 78586; Mailing: P.O. Box 1780, San Benito, TX 78586 t) 956-626-1260; 956-626-1265 stbenedict@cdob.org Rev. Leonel Rodriguez, Temp. Parish Admin.; Dcn. Manuel Sanchez; Dcn. Catarino Villanueva III; CRP Stds.: 151

St. Ignatius of Loyola Parish - 24380 W. U.S. Hwy. 281, San Benito, TX 78586 t) 956-399-2022 saint-ignatius@cdob.org Rev. Gerardo Sanchez, M.C.M., Pst.; Rev. Hugo D. Sanchez, M.C.M., Par. Vicar; Dcn. Arturo Escobedo; Dcn. Juan Carlos Jasso; CRP Stds.: 146

Our Lady of Lourdes - 22091 Farmer Ave., San Benito, TX 78586 (La Paloma)

Sacred Heart of Jesus - 1419 W. U.S. Hwy. 281, Los Indios, TX 78567 (Las Rucias)

Our Lady, Queen of the Universe - 1425 N. Sam Houston, San Benito, TX 78586; Mailing: 121 Garrison Dr., San Benito, TX 78586 t) 956-399-2865 ourladyqueenchurch@cdob.org Rev. Francois Tsanga, S.C.J., Admin.; CRP Stds.: 60

St. Joseph - 1001 W. Hwy. 77, San Benito, TX 78586

St. Theresa - 1300 Combes St., San Benito, TX 78586 t) 956-399-3247 sainttheresasb@cdob.org Rev. Jose M. Villalon Jr., Pst.; CRP Stds.: 148

SAN ISIDRO

St. Isidore - 5160 FM 1017, San Isidro, TX 78588; Mailing: P.O. Box 60, San Isidro, TX 78588 t) 956-481-3392 sanisidro@cdob.org Rev. Juan Manuel Salazar, Pst.; CRP Stds.: 36

SAN JUAN

Basilica of Our Lady of San Juan del Valle-National Shrine - 400 N. Virgen de San Juan Blvd., San Juan, TX 78589; Mailing: P.O. Box 747, San Juan, TX 78589 t) 956-787-0033 jgomez@cdob.org; info@olsjbasilica.org www.olsjbasilica.org Rev. Jorge A. Gomez, Rector; Rev. Ariel Oliver Angel, Asst. to Rector; Rev. Mario A. Castro, Asst. to Rector; Rev. Samuel Arizpe, Assit with Confessions; Dcn. Francisco R. Flores;

St. John the Baptist - 216 W. First St., San Juan, TX 78589 t) 956-783-1196 sjbsanjuan@cdob.org sjtbchurch.myplaceofworship.org Rev. Alfonso M. Guevara, Pst.; Rev. Oscar Ortega-Mancha, Par. Vicar; Dcn. Agapito L. Cantu; Dcn. Eduardo Reyna; CRP Stds.: 542

Immaculate Conception - 901 Church St., San Juan, TX 78589 (Lopezville)

SANTA ROSA

St. Mary - 101 San Antonio Ave., Santa Rosa, TX 78593; Mailing: P.O. Box 365, Santa Rosa, TX 78593 t) 956-636-1211 st-mary-santa-rosa@cdob.org Rev. Daniel Herve Oyama (Cameroon), Admin.; Dcn. Gerardo Aguilar; CRP Stds.: 50

WESLACO

St. Joan of Arc - 109 S. Illinois Ave., Weslaco, TX 78596 t) 956-968-3670 saint-joan-of-arc@cdob.org Rev. Francisco J. Solis, Pst.; Dcn. Jesus E. Aguayo; Dcn. Alberto J. Aldana; CRP Stds.: 299

St. Pius X - 600 S. Oklahoma Ave., Weslaco, TX 78596 t) 956-968-7471 saint-pius-x@cdob.org www.facebook.com//spx600 Rev. Luis Fernando Sanchez, Pst.; Dcn. Sergio Gonzalez; Dcn. Juan Carlos Ortiz Jr.; CRP Stds.: 450

San Martin de Porres - 901 N. Texas Blvd., Weslaco, TX 78596 t) 956-968-2691 san-martin-weslaco@cdob.org Rev. Esteban Hernandez, Pst.; Rev. Pedro Hernandez, Par. Vicar; Rev. Felix A. Cazares, In Res.; Dcn. Juan Manuel Delgado; Dcn. Leon Diaz; Dcn. Oscar Garcia; Dcn. Jose G. Garza; Dcn. Lorenzo Soto; CRP Stds.: 364

San Martin de Porres School - (Grades PreSchool-2) 905 N. Texas Blvd., Weslaco, TX 78596 t) 956-973-8642 rortega@cdobcs.org sites.google.com/cdobcs.org/smdpcs/home?pli=1 Reyna Ortega, Prin.;

St. Jude Chapel - Mile 13 1/2 North and Mile 4 West, Weslaco, TX 78599

Nuestra Senora de Guadalupe - 1909 Corpus Christi Dr., Weslaco, TX 78599 (Expressway Heights)

SCHOOLS: PRESCHOOL THRU HIGH SCHOOL

SCHOOLS

STATE OF TEXAS

BROWNSVILLE

Guadalupe Regional Middle School (Guadalupe Educational Center, Inc) - (PRV) (Grades 6-8) 1214 E. Lincoln St., Brownsville, TX 78521 t) 956-504-5568 vmiller@guadalupeprep.org www.guadalupeprep.org Guadalupe Regional Middle School is an All-Scholarship middle school providing a quality Catholic education to boys and girls. Dr. Virginia Miller, Prin.; Stds.: 48; Bro. Tchrs.: 1; Lay Tchrs.: 7

Incarnate Word Academy - (PRV) (Grades PreSchool-8) 244 Resaca Blvd., Brownsville, TX 78520 t) 956-546-4486 edwardcamarillo@iw-academy.org www.iw-academy.org (Convent Academy of the Incarnate Word) Michael Camarillo, Prin.; Edward Camarillo, Pres.; Stds.: 158; Sr. Tchrs.: 1; Lay Tchrs.: 15

St. Mary Catholic School - (PAR) (Grades PreK-6) 1300 Los Ebanos Blvd., Brownsville, TX 78520 t) 956-546-1805 agomez@cdobcs.org stmarys-cs.org Ana E. Gomez, Prin.; Stds.: 431; Lay Tchrs.: 31

EDINBURG

St. Joseph School - (PAR) (Grades PreK-8) 119 W. Fay St., Edinburg, TX 78539 t) 956-383-3957 akarpinski@cdodcs.org www.st-joseph-catholic-school.com Angelina Karpinski, Prin.; Stds.: 106; Lay Tchrs.: 8

HARLINGEN

St. Anthony School - (PAR) (Grades PreK-6) 1015 E. Harrison Ave., Harlingen, TX 78550 t) 956-423-2486 mescobar@cdobcs.org www.saintanthonyeagles.com Mindy Escobar, Prin.; Eva Cuellar, Librn.; Stds.: 67; Lay Tchrs.: 15

MCALLEN

Our Lady of Sorrows School - (PAR) (Grades PreK-8) 1100 Gumwood Ave., McAllen, TX 78501 t) 956-686-3651 imartinez@cdobcs.org www.olsschool.org Israel Martinez Jr., Prin.; Stds.: 422; Lay Tchrs.: 31

PHARR

Oratory Academy of St. Philip Neri - (PRV) (Grades PreK-8) 505 S. Ironwood, Pharr, TX 78577 t) 956-781-3056 www.oratoryschools.org Izkra Diaz, Prin.; Rev. Jose E. Losoya, C.O., Vice Prin.; Very Rev. Leo Francis Daniels, C.O., Headmaster; Rev. Jose Juan Ortiz, C.O., Librn.; Stds.: 131; Lay Tchrs.: 13

RIO GRANDE CITY

Immaculate Conception School - (PAR) (Grades PreK-8) 305 N. Britton Ave., Rio Grande City, TX 78582 t) 956-487-2558 www.icsrio.org Maria Guadalupe Alvarado, Prin.; Stds.: 52; Lay Tchrs.: 6

WESLACO

San Martin de Porres School - (PAR) (Grades PreSchool-2) 905 N. Texas Blvd., Weslaco, TX 78596 t) 956-973-8642 rortega@cdobcs.org www.sanmartindpschool.org Reyna Ortega, Prin.; Timothy J. Martinez, Librn.; Stds.: 30; Lay Tchrs.: 1

HIGH SCHOOLS

STATE OF TEXAS

BROWNSVILLE

Saint Joseph Academy - (PRV) (Grades 7-12) 101 St. Joseph Dr., Brownsville, TX 78520 t) 956-542-3581 president@sja.us www.sja.us Marist Brothers, United States Michael Motyl, Pres.; Melissa Valadez, Prin.; Stds.: 436; Lay Tchrs.: 43

MISSION

***San Juan Diego Catholic Regional High School (Juan Diego Academy)** - (PRV) (Grades 9-12) 5208 S. FM 494, Mission, TX 78572; Mailing: P.O. Box 3888, Mission, TX 78573 t) 956-583-2752 kcarroll@juandiegoacademy.org www.juandiegoacademy.org Dr. Kathleen Carroll, Prin.; Stds.: 67; Lay Tchrs.: 7

PHARR

Oratory Athenaeum for University Preparation - (PRV)

(Grades 9-12) 505 S. Ironwood, Pharr, TX 78577 t) 956-781-3056 www.oratoryschools.org Izkra Diaz, Prin.; Rev. Jose E. Losoya, C.O., Vice Prin.; Very Rev. Leo Francis Daniels, C.O., Headmaster; Rev. Jose Juan Ortiz, C.O., Librn.;

INSTITUTIONS LOCATED IN DIOCESE

CAMPUS MINISTRY / NEWMAN CENTERS [CAM]

SAN JUAN

Ministry with Young People - 700 N. Virgen de San Juan Blvd., San Juan, TX 78589 t) 956-784-5036 myp@cdob.org www.cdob.org/myp Raul Cabrera, Dir.; Rev. Joel R. Flores, Chap.;

Newman Center - Edinburg - 1615 W. Kuhn St., Edinburg, TX 78541 t) 956-383-0133 newmanedinburg@cdob.org www.cdob.org/newmancenter Rev. Manoj Kumar Nayak, SS.CC., Chap.;

CATHOLIC CHARITIES [CCH]

BROWNSVILLE

Catholic Charities of the Rio Grande Valley Brownsville Office - 955 W. Price Rd., Brownsville, TX 78520; Mailing: P.O. Box 1306, San Juan, TX 78589 t) 956-541-0220 npimentel@cdob.org www.catholiccharitiesrgv.org Sr. Norma Pimentel, M.J., Exec. Dir.; Asstd. Annu.: 93,000; Staff: 10

SAN JUAN

Catholic Charities of the Rio Grande Valley San Juan Main Office - 700 N. Virgen de San Juan Blvd., San Juan, TX 78589; Mailing: P.O. Box 1306, San Juan, TX 78589 t) 956-702-4088 npimentel@cdob.org www.catholiccharitiesrgv.org Most Rev. Mario A. Aviles, C.O., Bd. Dir.; Most Rev. Daniel E. Flores, Exec. Bd.; Rev. Msgr. Heberto M. Diaz Jr., Exec. Bd.; Sr. Norma Pimentel, M.J., Exec. Dir. & Ex-Officio; Asstd. Annu.: 191,221; Staff: 13

CONVENTS, MONASTERIES, AND RESIDENCES FOR WOMEN [CON]

ALAMO

***Saint Joseph and Saint Rita Monastery of the Capuchin Poor Clare Nuns** - 725 E. Bowie Ave., Alamo, TX 78516; Mailing: P.O. Box 1099, Alamo, TX 78516 t) 956-781-1044 sclaresalamotx@gmail.com capuchinnunsalamotx.org Sr. Beatriz Ayala, O.S.C. Cap., Contact; Srs.: 3

BROWNSVILLE

Dominican Sisters of Charity of the Presentation - 934 W. St. Charles St., Brownsville, TX 78520 c) (956) 525-5131 dominican20sisters@gmail.com www.domipresen.com/index.php/es/ Sr. Anabertha Ortega, O.P., Supr.; Srs.: 4

Missionaries of Jesus - 1501 W. Adams, Brownsville, TX 78520 t) 956-455-1484 www.missionariesofjesus.org Sr. Arminda Rangel, M.J., Contact; Srs.: 2

Sisters of the Incarnate Word and Blessed Sacrament (Convent Academy of the Incarnate Word) - 200 Resaca Blvd, Brownsville, TX 78520-7436 t) 956-546-1685 smigonzalez@iwbscc.org www.iwbscc.org Sr. Irma Gonzalez, I.W.B.S., Contact; Srs.: 3

PENITAS

Missionary Sisters of the Immaculate Heart of Mary - 18110 Queen Palm Dr., Penitas, TX 78576; Mailing: P.O Box 1017, Penitas, TX 78576 c) 956-257-4308 fatima.santiago6@gmail.com Sr. Fatima Santiago, I.C.M., Contact; Srs.: 4

Proyecto Desarrollo Humano Ministry - t) (956) 257-4308

PROGRESO

Institute of the Sisters of St. Dorothy S.S.D. - 219 W. Palm, Progreso, TX 78579; Mailing: P.O. Box 147, Progreso, TX 78579 t) 956-565-9430 cmello@cdob.org Sr. Cynthia A. Mello, S.S.D., Supr.; Srs.: 4

RIO GRANDE CITY

Benedictine Sisters of the Good Shepherd - 705 Monastery Ln., Rio Grande City, TX 78582 t) 956-486-2680 sanbenito@granderiver.net Sr. Nancy Boushey, O.S.B., Contact; Srs.: 3

SAN JUAN

Missionaries of Jesus - 700 N. Oblate Dr., San Juan, TX 78589 t) 956-455-1484 www.missionariesofjesus.org Sr. Norma Pimentel, M.J., Supr.; Srs.: 1

ENDOWMENTS / FOUNDATIONS / TRUSTS [EFT]

BROWNSVILLE

Catholic Foundation of the Rio Grande Valley - 1910 University Blvd., Brownsville, TX 78520-4998 t) 956-542-2501 hdiaz@cdob.org Most Rev. Mario A. Aviles, C.O., Bd. Vice Chmn.; Rev. Msgr. Heberto M. Diaz Jr., Bd. Secy.; Jack Graham, Exec. Bd. & Comptroller;

The Guadalupe Regional Middle School Endowment - 1214 Lincoln St., Brownsville, TX 78521 t) 956-504-5568 vmiller@guadalupeprep.org Apolonio Borrego, Bd. Dir.; Dr. Virginia Miller, Prin.;

The St. Joseph Academy Endowment - 101 Saint Joseph Dr., Brownsville, TX 78520-7308 t) 956-542-3581 president@sja.us Luis De La Garza, Chair; Michael Motyl, Pres. (Ex-Officio);

Love Builds Hope Foundation - 1910 University Blvd., Brownsville, TX 78520 t) 956-542-2501 jgraham@cdob.org Jack Graham, Sec. & Treas.;

MERCEDES

La Merced Charitable Trust - 413 S. Virginia, Mercedes, TX 78570; Mailing: c/o Diocese of Brownsville, P.O. Box 2279, Brownsville, TX 78522-2279 t) 956-542-2501 dgarza@garzaandgarza.com Most Rev. Daniel E. Flores, Exec. Bd.; Most Rev. Mario A. Aviles, C.O., Trustee; Rev. Eduardo Ortega, Trustee; Daniel Galvan, Trustee;

MISSION

El Rosario Charitable Trust - 119 Retama Ave., Mission, TX 78572; Mailing: c/o Diocese of Brownsville, P.O. Box 2279, Brownsville, TX 78522-2279 t) 956-542-2501 dgarza@garzaandgarza.com Most Rev. Daniel E. Flores, Exec. Bd.; Most Rev. Mario A. Aviles, C.O., Trustee; Rev. Eduardo Ortega, Trustee; Daniel Galvan, Trustee;

MISCELLANEOUS [MIS]

ALAMO

ARISE Adelante - 1417 S. Tower Rd., Alamo, TX 78516; Mailing: P.O. Box 778, Alamo, TX 78516 t) 956-783-6959 arisergv@gmail.com www.arisesotex.org Lourdes Flores, Pres.;

ARISE ADELANTE (Hargill) - 29222 FM 493, Hargill, TX 78549 t) (956) 543-6755 arisehargill@gmail.com

ARISE ADELANTE (Las Milpas) - 125 E. Denny Dr., Pharr, TX 78577 t) 956-783-9293 ariselasmilpas@gmail.com

ARISE ADELANTE (Muniz) - 3917 Jam Sq., Edinburg, TX 78542 t) 956-782-4041 arisemuniz@gmail.com

ARISE ADELANTE (South Tower) - 212 W. San Bernardino, Alamo, TX 78516 t) 956-783-8517 arisesouthtower@gmail.com

BROWNSVILLE

***Bishop Enrique San Pedro Ozanam Center, Inc.** - 656 N. Minnesota Ave., Brownsville, TX 78521 t) 956-831-6331 victor@ozanamcenter.org Victor Maldonado, Exec. Dir.;

Movimiento Familiar Cristiano: Federacion Brownsville - 1844 W. San Marcelo Blvd., Brownsville, TX 78526 t) 956-221-1180; 956-551-4874 aantoniomtz@hotmail.com; cchayomtz@hotmail.com mfcc-brownsville.weebly.com/ Antonio Martinez, Pres.; Rosario Martinez, Pres.; Rev. Oscar O. Siordia, Spiritual Dir.;

***Plaza Amistad** - ; Mailing: P.O. Box 2025, Brownsville, TX 78522-2025 t) 956-542-2501 jgraham@cdob.org Jack Graham, Fiscal Mgr.;

***Proyecto Juan Diego, Inc.** - 3910 Paredes Line Rd, Brownsville, TX 78526 t) 956-542-2488 lidiana.ramirez@proyecto-jd.org www.proyecto-jd.org Lidiana Ramirez, Exec. Dir.;

Villa Maria Language Institute - 224 Resaca Blvd., Brownsville, TX 78520-7436 t) 956-546-7196 edwardcamarillo@iw-academy.org www.villamarialg.com Edward Camarillo, Pres.; Fidencio Balli, Dir.;

EDINBURG

***Shalom Media USA Inc.** - 211 E. Wisconsin Rd., Edinburg, TX 78539 t) 215-366-3031 info@shalomworld.org www.shalomworld.org Santo Thomas, CEO;

MCALLEN

Natural Family Planning - 1510 N. 10th St., Ste. C, McAllen, TX 78501 t) 956-534-4895 lydia.mendez@cdob.org simplenatural.org Lydia Mendez, Dir.;

PHARR

Movimiento Familiar Cristiano Federacion Edinburg - 119 Falcon Ave., Pharr, TX 78577 t) 956-460-0555; 956-566-9598 arnoldo.varela01@gmail.com Arnoldo Varela, Pres.; Ines Varela, Pres.; Dcn. Antonio M. Arteaga, Spiritual Dir.;

SAN BENITO

***La Posada Providencia** - 30094 Marydale Rd., San Benito, TX 78586 t) 956-399-3826 cdplaposada@lppshelter.org www.lppshelter.org A non-profit emergency shelter for indigent immigrants and asylum seekers. Statistics: Total Assisted Annually: 2,391 Cindy Johnson, Interim Exec. Dir.;

SAN JUAN

Catholic Engaged Encounter - 700 N. Virgen de San Juan Blvd., San Juan, TX 78589 t) 956-784-5012 lpesina@cdob.org Lydia Pesina, Dir.; Robert Garza, Lead Coord. Couple; Susan Garza, Lead Coord. Couple; Rev. Jose M. Villalon Jr., Spiritual Dir.;

Diocese of Brownsville Immigration Services - 700 N. Virgen de San Juan Blvd., San Juan, TX 78589 t) 956-784-5057 odelossantos@cdob.org Ofelia de los Santos, Dir.;

The Basilica of Our Lady of San Juan del Valle-National Shrine - 400 N. Virgen de San Juan Blvd., San Juan, TX 78589; Mailing: P.O. Box 747, San Juan, TX 78589 t) 956-787-0033 info@olsjbasilica.org www.olsjbasilica.org Rev. Jorge A. Gomez, Rector;

Religious Gift Shop - t) (956) 787-0033 x309 Elma Calvillo, Dir.;

WESLACO

Movimiento Familiar Cristiano: Federacion Weslaco (Weslaco/Donna/Mercedes) - 3813 Sabatini Dr., Weslaco, TX 78599 t) 956-272-5013; 956-272-4800 ludytono1088@gmail.com Jose Antonio Quezada, Pres.; Ludivina Quezada, Pres.;

MONASTERIES AND RESIDENCES FOR PRIESTS AND BROTHERS [MON]

BROWNSVILLE

Edmund Rice Christian Brothers North America Congregation of Christian Brothers - 1200 E. Lincoln St., Apt. B, Brownsville, TX 78521; Mailing: 1214 Lincoln St., Brownsville, TX 78521 t) (914) 278-0434 Bro. William Joyce, C.F.C., Contact; Brs.: 3

LOS FRESNOS

The Marist Brothers - 32995 Henderson Rd., Los Fresnos, TX 78566 t) 845-380-8347 mikebill@hotmail.com Bro. Michael Williams, F.M.S., Dir.; Bro. Francis Garza, F.M.S., Mem.; Bro. Albert Phillipp, F.M.S., Mem.; Brs.: 3

PHARR

Pharr Oratory of St. Philip Neri of Pontifical Right - 11317 S. Jackson Rd., Pharr, TX 78577; Mailing: P.O.

Box 1698, Pharr, TX 78577 t) 956-843-8217 jlosoya@pharroratory.com Very Rev. Leo Francis Daniels, C.O., Provost; Rev. Jose E. Losoya, C.O., Vicar; Rev. Jose Juan Ortiz, C.O., Secy.; Priests: 3

NURSING / REHABILITATION / CONVALESCENCE / ELDERLY CARE [NUR]

SAN JUAN

St. John Vianney Retirement Home - 100 N. Virgen de San Juan Blvd., San Juan, TX 78589; Mailing: P.O. Box 747, San Juan, TX 78589 t) 956-782-7918 Rev. Jorge A. Gomez, Contact; Asstd. Annu.: 5; Staff: 2

San Juan Nursing Home, Inc. - 300 N. Nebraska Ave., San Juan, TX 78589 t) 956-787-1771 eloisa.fernandez@cdob.org sjnhrgv.org Most Rev. Daniel E. Flores, Exec. Bd.; Rev. Alfonso M. Guevara, Bishop's Liaison; Eloisa Fernandez, Admin.; Asstd. Annu.: 125; Staff: 101

PRESCHOOLS / CHILDCARE CENTERS [PRE]

BROWNSVILLE

Little Saints Learning Center - 1300 Los Ebanos Blvd., Brownsville, TX 78520 t) 956-546-1805 agomez@cdobcs.org (Parochial Daycare) Ana E. Gomez, Prin.; Stds.: 31; Lay Tchrs.: 2

EDINBURG

Little Lambs Learning Center - 119 W. Fay St., Edinburg, TX 78539 t) 956-383-3957 akarpinski@cdobcs.org (Parochial Daycare) Angelina Karpinski, Prin.; Stds.: 6; Lay Tchrs.: 1

WESLACO

Little Lions Learning Center - 905 N. Texas Blvd., Weslaco, TX 78596 t) 956-973-8642 rortega@cdobcs.org (Parochial Daycare) Reyna Ortega, Prin.; Stds.: 11; Lay Tchrs.: 1

RETREAT HOUSES / RENEWAL CENTERS [RTR]

SAN JUAN

St. Eugene de Mazenod Christian Renewal Center - 400 N. Virgin de San Juan Blvd., San Juan, TX 78589; Mailing: P.O. Box 747, San Juan, TX 78589 t) 956-787-0033 aibarra@cdob.org Alma Ibarra, Dir.;

An asterisk (*) denotes an organization that has established tax-exempt status directly with the IRS and is not covered by the USCCB Group Ruling.

Diocese of Buffalo

(Dioecesis Buffalensis)

MOST REVEREND MICHAEL WILLIAM FISHER

Bishop of Buffalo; ordained June 23, 1990; appointed Auxiliary Bishop of Washington and Titular Bishop of Truentum June 8, 2018; ordained to the episcopate June 29, 2018; appointed Bishop of Buffalo December 1, 2020; installed January 15, 2021.

Chancery Office: 795 Main St., Buffalo, NY 14203. T: 716-847-5500; F: 716-847-5557.
www.buffalodiocese.org
dob@buffalodiocese.org

ESTABLISHED APRIL 23, 1847

Square Miles 6,357.

Incorporated under the laws of the State of New York October 30th, 1897. Re-incorporated by special act passed April 5, 1951, Chapter 568 of the laws of 1951.

Corporate Title: The Diocese of Buffalo, N.Y.

Comprises the Counties of Erie, Niagara, Genesee, Orleans, Chautauqua, Wyoming, Cattaraugus and Allegany in the State of New York.

For legal titles of parishes and diocesan institutions, consult the Chancery Office.

STATISTICAL OVERVIEW

Personnel	
Bishop	1
Retired Bishops	2
Priests: Diocesan Active in Diocese	122
Priests: Diocesan Active Outside Diocese	2
Priests: Retired, Sick or Absent	130
Number of Diocesan Priests	254
Religious Priests in Diocese	76
Total Priests in your Diocese	330
Extern Priests in Diocese	14
Ordinations:	
Diocesan Priests	2
Transitional Deacons	2
Permanent Deacons	3
Permanent Deacons in Diocese	137
Total Brothers	21
Total Sisters	506
Parishes	
Parishes	160
With Resident Pastor:	
Resident Diocesan Priests	108
Resident Religious Priests	11
Without Resident Pastor:	
Administered by Priests	39
Administered by Deacons	1
Administered by Religious Women	1
Missions	2
Pastoral Centers	2
Professional Ministry Personnel:	
Brothers	1
Sisters	9
Lay Ministers	71
Welfare	
Catholic Hospitals	4
Total Assisted	1,013,535
Health Care Centers	1
Total Assisted	925
Homes for the Aged	7
Total Assisted	2,388
Day Care Centers	4
Total Assisted	2,182
Specialized Homes	3
Total Assisted	729
Special Centers for Social Services	9
Total Assisted	291,307
Residential Care of Disabled	2
Total Assisted	106
Other Institutions	1
Total Assisted	17,267
Educational	
Diocesan Students in Other Seminaries	9
Seminaries, Religious	1
Students, Religious	1
Total Seminarians	10
Colleges and Universities	7
Total Students	14,408
High Schools, Private	13
Total Students	3,903
Elementary Schools, Diocesan and Parish	37
Total Students	7,120
Elementary Schools, Private	5
Total Students	627
Non-residential Schools for the Disabled	3
Total Students	715
Catechesis / Religious Education:	
High School Students	2,784
Elementary Students	7,817
Total Students under Catholic Instruction	37,384
Teachers in Diocese:	
Priests	8
Brothers	2
Sisters	12
Lay Teachers	1,634
Vital Statistics	
Receptions into the Church:	
Infant Baptism Totals	2,209
Minor Baptism Totals	104
Adult Baptism Totals	59
Received into Full Communion	70
First Communions	2,095
Confirmations	2,140
Marriages:	
Catholic	581
Interfaith	175
Total Marriages	756
Deaths	5,172
Total Catholic Population	557,600
Total Population	1,561,100

LEADERSHIP

The Diocese of Buffalo, N.Y. - Most Rev. Michael W. Fisher, Pres.; Rev. Peter J. Karalus, Vice. Pres.; Sr. Regina Murphy, S.S.M.N., Secy.;
Vicar General - pbaez@buffalodiocese.org Rev. Peter J. Karalus;
Chancellor - rmurphy@buffalodiocese.org Sr. Regina Murphy, S.S.M.N.;
Chief Operating Officer - mjablonski@buffalodiocese.org Richard C. Suchan;
Vicar for Clergy - mpassafiume@buffalodiocese.org Rev. Jerome E. Kopec;
Vicar for Renewal & Development - bzielenieski@buffalodiocese.org Rev. Bryan J. Zielenieski, Vicar;
Delegate for Priestly Life and Care - wszczesny@buffalodiocese.org Rev. Walter J. Szczesny, Bishop's Delegate;
Delegate for Religious - jthompson@buffalodiocese.org Sr. Jean Thompson, O.S.F.;
Diocesan Tribunal - tribunal@buffalodiocese.org Rev. Msgr. Salvatore Manganello, Judicial Vicar;
Promoter of Justice - Rev. Elie G. Kairouz; Rev. Jerome E. Kopec;
Liaison for Retired Priests - t) 716-440-5090 Rev. Charles E. Slisz;
Vicariates: - t) 716-847-5560 Rev. Peter J. Karalus, Vicar General;
Vicars Forane - Rev. Sean E. DiMaria, Southern Erie; Rev. James W. Hartwell, Southern Tier East; Rev. Gregory P. Jakubowicz, O.F.M., Campus Ministry;

OFFICES AND DIRECTORS

Advancement Office - t) 716-847-8369 ngugino@buffalodiocese.org Nancy J Gugino, Exec. Dir.;
Apostleship of the Sea - t) 716-884-0053 Rev. Joseph D. Porpiglia, Dir.;
Archives - archives1@buffalodiocese.org Sr. Jean Thompson, O.S.F., Archivist;
Bishop's Committee for Christian Home and Family - Cheryl M. Calire, Moderator;
Bishop's Representative for Health Care - t) 716-835-8905 Rev. Msgr. Robert E. Zapfel;
Boy Scouts - Rev. Leon J. Biernat, Chap.; James S. Smyczynski, Chair; Dcn. Daniel U. Golinski;
Buildings and Properties - charrower@buffalodiocese.org Michael J. Sullivan, Dir.;
Care for Creation Commission - sgoodremote@fssj.org Sr. Sharon Marie Goodremote, F.S.S.J., Chair;
Catholic Education - mtepley@buffalodiocese.org Dr. Timothy Uhl, Supt.; Kari Buchinger, Deputy Supt.; Christian Riso, Asst. Supt.;
Catholic Medical Association - dukester0@yahoo.com Rev. Richard E. Zajac, Moderator;
Censors--Board of Diocesan Censors of Books and Vigilance for the Faith - Rev. Msgr. Robert E. Zapfel; Rev. Peter J. Drilling;
Charismatic Renewal Program - Rev. Richard S. DiGiulio, Dir.;
Chautauqua Catholic Community, Chautauqua Institution - Rev. Todd M. Remick, Spiritual Dir. & Diocesan Liaison;
Communications/Public Relations - comm@buffalodiocese.org Gregory Tucker, Dir.; Joseph Martone, Mgr.;
Computer Services - pmateja@buffalodiocese.org Paul Mateja, Dir.;
Council of Catholic Men -
Courage/Encourage - deaconhynes@gmail.com Dcn. William J. Hynes, Dir.;
Cursillo Movement - t) 716-515-8725 Dcn. Michael D. Quinn, Dir.; Donald Appenheimer, Dir.;
Deaf Ministry - buffalocatholicdeaf@gmail.com Sr. Conchetta Lopresti, O.S.F., Dir.;
Diocesan Social Worker - aszakacs@buffalodiocese.org Anthony Szakacs;
Ecumenism - t) 716-834-6688 Rev. Francis X. Mazur, Diocesan Liaison; Rev. David R. Glassmire, Delegate to the Network of Rel. Communities;
Faith Formation - lbenzer@buffalodiocese.org Lisa Benzer, Dir.;
Finance Office - mcumming@buffalodiocese.org Ellen Musialowski, CFO; Julie Heftka, Controller;
Holy Name Society - David Grzybek, Exec.; Rev. Paul P. Sabo, Moderator;
Hospital Chaplains - t) 716-859-5600 Rev. Richard H. Augustyn, Dir. Pastoral Care, Buffalo Gen. Hosp.;
Human Resources - jhoffman@buffalodiocese.org Jennifer Hoffman; Lindsay Gibson;
Insurance Services - jscholl@buffalodiocese.org John Scholl, Dir.;
Internal Audit - audit@buffalodiocese.org Beth Pericozzi, Chief Auditor;
Liturgical Commission - t) 716-847-5545 Rev. Sean Paul Fleming, Dir.;
Migrant Ministry - t) 585-343-5800 Rev. Ivan R. Trujillo, Resurrection Parish, Batavia;
Office of Cultural Diversity - ymontanez@buffalodiocese.org Cheryl M. Calire, Dir.;
Office of Worship - ymontanez@buffalodiocese.org Rev. Sean Paul Fleming, Dir.;
Permanent Diaconate - tchriswell@buffalodiocese.org Dcn. Timothy E. Chriswell, Dir.;
Pro-Life/Pastoral Ministries - mescalante@buffalodiocese.org Cheryl M. Calire, Dir.;
Propagation of the Faith - t) 716-847-8773 Rev. Justus Ndyamukama (Tanzania);
Public Policy Committee - jmartone@buffalodiocese.org Joseph Martone, Contact;
Purchasing (Diocesan) - dpd@buffalodiocese.org Shelley Pacillo, Dir.;
Renewal and Development Office - renewal@buffalodiocese.org Rev. Bryan J. Zielenieski, Episcopal Vicar for Renewal & Devel.;
Renewal Mission, Evangelization, and Lay Formation - tmusco@buffalodiocese.org Rev. Bryan J. Zielenieski, Dir.;
Research and Planning - ttaberski@buffalodiocese.org Sr. Regina Murphy, S.S.M.N., Dir.;
Safe Environment - dblowey@buffalodiocese.org Donald R. Blowey Jr., Dir.;
Victim Assistance Coordinator - t) 716-895-3010 jacqueline.joy@ccwny.org Jacqueline Joy, Contact;
Vocation Office and Director of Seminarians - vocations@buffalodiocese.org Rev. David D Baker, Dir.;

CONSULTATIVE BODIES

College of Consultors - t) 716-847-5560 pbaez@buffalodiocese.org Rev. Peter J. Karalus, Vicar General; Rev. Jerome E. Kopec, Vicar for Clergy; Rev. Msgr. David G. LiPuma (dlipuma@olvbasilica.org);
Diocesan Pastoral Council - Joseph Conti, Chair;
Finance Council - t) 716-847-5560 pbaez@buffalodiocese.org James J. Beardi, Chair; Rev. Peter J. Karalus; Karen L. Howard;
Presbyteral Council - t) 716-847-5560 pbaez@buffalodiocese.org Rev. Thomas R. Slon, S.J., Chair; Rev. Daniel J. Fawls, Vice Chair; Rev. Michael LaMarca, Secy.;
Priest Personnel Board - mpassafiume@buffalodiocese.org Rev. Joseph S. Rogliano, Coord.;

PARISHES, MISSIONS, AND CLERGY

STATE OF NEW YORK

AKRON

St. Teresa of Avila - 5771 Buell St., Akron, NY 14001; Mailing: P.O. Box 168, Akron, NY 14001 t) 716-542-9717 (CRP); 716-542-9103 stteresasofakron@verizon.net www.stteresasofakron.com Rev. Arthur E. Mattulke, Pst.; Sr. Mary Ruth Warejko, C.S.S.F., DRE; CRP Stds.: 65

ALBION

Holy Family - 106 S. Main St., Albion, NY 14411 t) 585-589-4243 holyfamilyalbion@rochester.rr.com www.holyfamilyalbion.com Rev. Richard A. Csizmar, Pst.; Dcn. James L. Collichio; Nancy J. Sedita, DRE; CRP Stds.: 54

ALDEN

St. John the Baptist - 2021 Sandridge Rd., Alden, NY 14004 t) 716-937-6959 frdanserbicki@gmail.com www.stjohnalden.com Rev. Daniel J. Serbicki, Pst.; Rev. Patryk Sobczyk, Par. Vicar; Dcn. Peter J. Donnelly; Dcn. Marc R. Leaderstorf; CRP Stds.: 70
St. John the Baptist School - (Grades PreK-8) 2028 Sandridge Rd., Alden, NY 14004 t) 716-937-9483 school.office@stjohnsalden.com www.stjohnsalden.com Jonna Johnson, Prin.; Janyce Phelps, Librn.;

ALFRED

SS. Brendan and Jude - Lower College Dr., Alfred, NY 14802; Mailing: 17 Maple Ave., Wellsville, NY 14895 t) 585-593-4834 kater@iccwlsv.com (Linked with Immaculate Conception, Wellsville, Blessed Sacrament, Andover, St. Mary, Bolivar, and Holy Family of Jesus, Mary & Joseph, Belmont) Rev. James W. Hartwell, Pst.; Rev. Robert Agbo, Par. Vicar; CRP Stds.: 2
St. Jude -

ALLEGANY

St. Bonaventure - 95 E. Main St., Allegany, NY 14706 t) 716-373-1330 sbreligioused@yahoo.com; stbonaschurch@yahoo.com stbonas.weconnect.com Rev. Michael Reyes, OFM, Par. Admin.; Holly Keenan, DRE; CRP Stds.: 75

AMHERST

St. Leo the Great - 885 Sweet Home Rd., Amherst, NY 14226 t) 716-835-8905 office@stleothegreatamherst.com stleothegreatamherst.com Linked with St Benedict Parish, Eggertsville Rev. Msgr. Robert E. Zapfel, Pst.; David Ehrke, Bus. Mgr.;

ANDOVER

Blessed Sacrament - 24 Elm St., Andover, NY 14806; Mailing: 17 Maple Ave., Wellsville, NY 14895 t) 585-593-4834 kater@iccwlsv.com www.icc-ics.com (Linked with SS. Brendan & Jude Parish, Alfred/ Almond, Immaculate Conception, Wellsville, Holy Family of Jesus, Mary and Joseph, Belmont, and St. Mary Rev. James W. Hartwell, Pst.; Rev. Robert Agbo, Par. Vicar; CRP Stds.: 2

ANGOLA

Most Precious Blood - 22 Prospect St., Angola, NY 14006 t) 716-549-0420 rectory14006@gmail.com www.mpbangola.org Rev. Timothy J. Koester, Pst.;

ARCADE

St. Mary - 417 Main St., Arcade, NY 14009-1195 t) 585-492-5330 www.saintmaryarcade.org Parish with two sites: St. Mary, Arcade; St. Mary, East Arcade. Rev. Joseph A. Gullo, Pst.;

ATTICA

SS. Joachim & Anne - 50 East Ave., Attica, NY 14011 t) 585-591-1228 office@ssjoachimanne.org; religioused@ssjoachimanne.org ssjoachimanne.org (Parish with two sites: Attica & Varysburg) Rev. George Devanapalle (India), Pst.; Marlene Lamparelli, DRE; CRP Stds.: 40

BARKER

Our Lady of the Lake - 1726 Quaker Rd., Barker, NY 14012 t) 716-795-3331; 585-590-1791 (CRP) ourladyofthelakeparish@gmail.com Parish with two sites: Barker and Lyndonville, and linked with Holy Trinity, Medina Rev. Bernard U. Nowak, Pst.; Rev. Stephen P. Soares, Par. Vicar;

BATAVIA

Ascension Roman Catholic Church Society of Batavia, New York - 19 Sumner St., Batavia, NY 14020-3634 t) 585-343-1796 office@ascensionrcc.com; bizmgr@ascensionrcc.com www.ascensionrcc.weconnect.com Rev. David R. Glassmire, Pst.; Dcn. Walter T. Szczesny; CRP Stds.: 32

Resurrection - 303 E. Main St., Batavia, NY 14020 t) 585-343-5800 lauriemcmullen60@yahoo.com www.resurrectionbatavia.com Rev. Ivan R. Trujillo, Pst.; Rev. Robert E. Waters, Par. Vicar; Dcn. Henry E. Moscicki, DRE; CRP Stds.: 8

BELFAST

St. Patrick's Roman Catholic Church Society of Belfast, New York - 7 Merton Ave., Belfast, NY 14711; Mailing: c/o Tri-Parish Office, PO Box 198, Fillmore, NY 14735 t) 585-209-4042 nwalleganycatholic@gmail.com stpatsbelfastfillmore.org (Linked with St. Patrick, Fillmore, and Our Lady of the Angels, Cuba) Rev. F. Patrick Melfi, Admin.; Ann Guilford, DRE; CRP Stds.: 21

St. Mark - 9103 School St., Rushford, NY 14777; Mailing: PO Box 198,, Fillmore, NY 14735-0198 frdmancuso@gmail.org

BELMONT

Holy Family of Jesus, Mary & Joseph - 5 Milton St., Belmont, NY 14813; Mailing: 17 Maple Ave., Wellsville, NY 14895 t) 585-593-4834 kater@iccwlsv.com www.icc-ics.com (Linked with St. Mary, Bolivar, Blessed Sacrament in Andover, SS Brendan & Jude in Alfred-Almond and Immaculate Conception in Wellsville) Rev. James W. Hartwell, Pst.; Rev. Robert Agbo, Par. Vicar; CRP Stds.: 3

St. Joseph - Cottage Bridge Rd., Scio, NY 14880

BEMUS POINT

St. Mary of Lourdes (St. Mary's of Mayville and Our Lady of Lourdes of Bemus Point) - 41 Main St., Bemus Point, NY 14712; Mailing: PO Box 500, Bemus Point, NY 14712 t) 716-386-2400 office@smolbp.org www.stmaryoflourdesrcparish.org (Parish with two sites: Bemus Point & Mayville) Rev. David E. Tourville, Admin.; CRP Stds.: 60

BERGEN

St. Brigid - 18 Gibson St., Bergen, NY 14416; Mailing: 44 Lake St., LeRoy, NY 14482 t) 585-768-6543 youthminister@ourladyofmercyleroy.org; bookkeeper@ourladyofmercyleroy.org (Linked with Our Lady of Mercy, LeRoy), Sacramental records at 44 Lake St., LeRoy Rev. Kenneth Breen, OdeM, Par. Vicar; Denise B. Spadaccia, DRE; CRP Stds.: 9

BLASDELL

Our Mother of Good Counsel - 3688 S. Park Ave., Blasdell, NY 14219 t) 716-822-2630 omgcrectory@aol.com www.omgcbny.com Rev. Robert J. Orlowski, Pst.; Dcn. Michael T. Dulak;

BOLIVAR

St. Mary - 111 Wellsville St., Bolivar, NY 14715; Mailing: 17 Maple Ave., Wellsville, NY 14895 t) 585-593-4834 kater@iccwlsv.com www.icc-ics.com (Linked with Holy Family of Jesus, Mary & Joseph, Belmont, SS Brendan & Jude in Alfred Almond, Blessed Sacrament in Andover and Immaculate Conception Rev. James W. Hartwell, Pst.; Rev. Robert Agbo, Par. Vicar;

BOSTON

St. John the Baptist - 6895 Boston Cross Rd., Boston, NY 14025-9601 t) 716-941-3549 reled@stjohnrcchurch.org; rectory@stjohnrcchurch.org stjohnrcchurch.org Rev. Gerard Skrzynski, Pst.; Dianne Franz, DRE; CRP Stds.: 64

St. Mary - 8175 E. Eden Rd., East Eden, NY 14057

BOWMANSVILLE

Sacred Heart of Jesus Roman Catholic Church Society of Bowmansville NY - 5337 Genesee St., Bowmansville, NY 14026-1098 t) 716-683-2375 sheartshrine@gmail.com www.sacredheartshrine.org Rev. Lukasz Kopala, Pst.;

BUFFALO

St. Joseph Cathedral - 50 Franklin St., Buffalo, NY 14202 t) 716-854-5855 www.buffalocathedral.org/ Rev. Sean Paul Fleming, Rector; Dcn. Stephen R. Schumer; Most Rev. Michael William Fisher, In Res.;

All Saints - 127 Chadduck Ave., Buffalo, NY 14207-1531 t) 716-875-8183 nbvm@aol.com; allsaintsbuffalo@yahoo.com allsaintsbuffalo@yahoo.com Rev. Angelo M. Chimera, In Res.; CRP Stds.: 8

St. Anthony of Padua - 160 Court St., Buffalo, NY 14202 t) 716-854-2563 www.stanthonyofpadua-buffalo.org Rev. Michael P. Zuffoletto, Pst.; Rev. Justus Ndyamukama (Tanzania), In Res.;

Assumption - 435 Amherst St., Buffalo, NY 14207 t) 716-875-7626 assumption14207@gmail.com assumptionbuffalo.org Rev. David I. Richards, Pst.; Rev. Christopher Emminger, Par. Vicar; Genevieve Rak, DRE; CRP Stds.: 15

St. Bernard - 414 S. Ogden, Buffalo, NY 14206 t) 716-822-8856 stbernardsch@gmail.com olcbernard.com (Linked with Our Lady of Czestochowa, Cheektowaga) Rev. Czeslaw M. Krysa, Admin.;

Blessed Sacrament - 1035 Delaware Ave., Buffalo, NY 14209-1605 t) 716-884-0053 pastor@blessedsacramentbuffalo.org Rev. Joseph D. Porpiglia, Pst.; Rev. Peter J. Karalus, In Res.; Maureen Meyers, DRE;

Blessed Trinity - 317 Leroy Ave., Buffalo, NY 14214 t) 716-833-0301 blessedtrinitychurch@gmail.com blessedtrinitybuffalo.org Rev. Robert L. Gebhard Jr., Admin.; Patricia Dyer, Pst. Assoc.;

St. Casimir Church - 160 Cable St., Buffalo, NY 14206 t) 716-824-9589 ckrysa@buffalodiocese.org Rev. Czeslaw M. Krysa, Rector;

SS. Columba-Brigid - 75 Hickory St., Buffalo, NY 14204 t) 716-852-3331 sscolumbabrigid@gmail.com sscolumbabrigid.org (Responsible for St. Ann Church site, Broadway & Emslie Sts., Buffalo) Rev. William J. Weiksnar, O.F.M., Pst.; CRP Stds.: 5

Coronation of the Blessed Virgin Mary - 348 DeWitt St., Buffalo, NY 14213; Mailing: 18 Greenwood Pl., Buffalo, NY 14213 t) 716-882-2650 c) 978-729-0822 (Fr. Pham); 716-863-4800 (Dcn Hodson) Rev. Tuan Pham, OMI (Canada), Chap.; CRP Stds.: 27

Corpus Christi - 199 Clark St., Buffalo, NY 14212-1407 t) 716-896-1050 office@corpuschristibuffalo.org Rev. Mariusz Dymek, O.S.P.P.E., Pst.; Rev. Marek Kreis, OSPPE, Par. Vicar;

Holy Cross - 345 Seventh St., Buffalo, NY 14201 t) 716-847-6930 rectory@holycrossbuffalo.com Rev. Felix Nyambe, OMI (Zambia), Admin.; Rev. James Loiacono, O.M.I., Par. Vicar; Dcn. Miguel Santos;

Holy Spirit - 91 Dakota Ave., Buffalo, NY 14216 t) 716-875-8102 holyspirit.northbuffalo@verizon.net www.holyspiritchurchbuffalo.com (Linked with St. Margaret) Rev. David I. Richards, Pst.; Rev. Christopher Emminger, Par. Vicar; Sr. Katherine Marie Bogner, S.S.M.N., Pst. Assoc.; Karen Adamski, DRE; CRP Stds.: 28

St. John Kanty - 101 Swinburne St., Buffalo, NY 14212 t) 716-893-0412 stjohnkantybflo@gmail.com Linked with St. John Gualbert Parish Rev. James M. Monaco, Par. Admin.; Barbara Myskiewicz, DRE;

St. Adalbert - 212 Stanislaus St., Buffalo, NY 14212

St. John the Baptist - 1085 Englewood Ave., Buffalo, NY 14223-1982 t) 716-873-1122 saintjohnsrec@gmail.com stjohnskenmore.org Rev. Michael J. Parker, Pst.; CRP Stds.: 132

St. John the Baptist School - (Grades PreK-8) t) 716-877-6401 jbainbridge@stjohnskenmore.com www.stjohnskenmore.com Stds.: 360; Lay Tchrs.: 29

St. Joseph-University - 3269 Main St., Buffalo, NY 14214 t) 716-833-0298 ledwon@buffalo.edu www.stjosephbuffalo.org Rev. Jacob C. Ledwon, Pst.; Dcn. Paul C. Emerson; Dcn. Thaddeus V. Pijacki; Rev. Gregory P. Jakubowicz, O.F.M., Campus Min.; Patricia Bubar Spear, Pst. Assoc.; Diane M. Brennan, DRE; Lynn Cercone, Bus. Mgr.; CRP Stds.: 277

St. Joseph-University School - (Grades PreK-8) 3275 Main St., Buffalo, NY 14214 t) 716-835-7395 school@stjosephbuffalo.org M. Anne Wojick, Prin.; Mark Mattle, Dir.;

St. Katharine Drexel - 118 Schiller St., Buffalo, NY 14206 t) 716-895-6813 skdbuffalo118@gmail.com Rev. James M. Monaco, Pst.;

St. Lawrence - 1520 E. Delavan Ave., Buffalo, NY 14215 t) 716-892-2471 stlawrencebuffalo@gmail.com Rev. Christopher Okoli (Nigeria), Admin.; Dcn. Paul F. Weisenburger; Patricia Dyer, DRE;

St. Louis - 35 Edward St., Buffalo, NY 14202 t) 716-852-6040 churchoffice@stlouisrcchurch.org www.stlouisrcchurch.org Rev. Msgr. Salvatore Manganello, Pst.; Ashlee Campbell, DRE; CRP Stds.: 28

St. Margaret - 1395 Hertel Ave., Buffalo, NY 14216 t) 716-876-5318 www.stmargaretbuffalo.com (Linked with Holy Spirit) Rev. David I. Richards, Pst.; Sr. Karen Marie Voltz, Pst. Assoc.; Karen Adamski, DRE; CRP Stds.: 7

St. Mark - 401 Woodward Ave., Buffalo, NY 14214 t) 716-836-1600 stmarkbuffalo.com (Linked with St. Rose of Lima) Rev. David I. Richards, Pst.; Rev. Christopher Emminger, Par. Vicar; Sara Kane, DRE; CRP Stds.: 83

St. Mark School - (Grades K-8) 399 Woodward Ave., Buffalo, NY 14214 t) 716-836-1191 rclemens@saintmarkschool.com Christopher Gardon, Prin.;

St. Martin de Porres - 555 Northampton St., Buffalo, NY 14208 t) 716-883-7729 Rev. Joseph S. Rogliano, Admin.; Dcn. Ronald Walker;

St. Martin of Tours - 1140 Abbott Rd., Buffalo, NY 14220 t) 716-823-7077 info@stmartinbuffalo.com www.stmartinbuffalo.com (Linked with St. Thomas Aquinas) Rev. William J. Quinlivan, Pst.;

St. Michael - 651 Washington St., Buffalo, NY 14203 t) 716-854-6726 stmichaelchurchbuffalo@gmail.com stmichaelbuffalo.org Rev. Benjamin Fiore, S.J., Pst.; Rev. Frederick G. Betti, S.J., Assoc. Pst.; Rev. Raymond Sweitzer, SJ, Assoc. Pst.; Rev. James Lee Dugan, S.J., Assoc. Pst.; Rev. Kenneth Hezel, S.J., Assoc. Pst.; Rev. Richard J. Zanoni, S.J., Assoc. Pst.;

Our Lady of Charity - 260 Okell St., Buffalo, NY 14220 t) 716-822-5962 office@olcp.org Parish with two sites: St. Ambrose and Holy Family Rev. William J. Quinlivan, Pst.; Rev. Alphonse Arulanandu (India), Par. Vicar; Elaine Williams, Bus. Mgr.;

Our Lady of Czestochowa - 23 Willowlawn Pkwy., Buffalo, NY 14206 t) 716-822-5590 olccktg@gmail.com (Linked with St. Bernard, Buffalo) Rev. Peter Napierkowski, Admin.;

Our Lady of Hope - 18 Greenwood Pl., Buffalo, NY 14213 t) 716-885-2469 olhbflo@gmail.com www.ourladyofhopewny.org Rev. Felix Nyambe, OMI (Zambia), Admin.; Rev. Tuan Pham, OMI (Canada), Par. Vicar; Ronald Thaler, Pst. Assoc.; Jeffry Sturmer, DRE;

Our Lady of Perpetual Help - 115 O'Connell Ave., Buffalo, NY 14204 t) 716-852-2671 olphpets@gmail.com Rev. Paul D. Seil, Pst.;

St. Rose of Lima - 500 Parker Ave., Buffalo, NY 14216 t) 716-834-6688 rose@saintrosebuffalo.org (Linked with St. Mark) Rev. Francis X. Mazur, In Res.; CRP Stds.: 10

St. Stanislaus - 123 Townsend St., Buffalo, NY 14212 t) 716-854-5510 www.ststansbuffalo.com Rev. Mariusz Dymek, O.S.P.P.E., Admin.; Rev. Marek Kreis, OSPPE, Par. Vicar;

St. Teresa - 1974 Seneca St., Buffalo, NY 14210 t) 716-822-0608 teresa14210@yahoo.com; st.teresa.bookkeeper@gmail.com www.stteresabuffalo.com Rev. William J. Quinlivan, Pst.; Dcn. Robert A. Dobmeier; Cheryl McNerney, DRE; CRP Stds.: 40

St. Thomas Aquinas - 450 Abbott Rd., Buffalo, NY 14220-1796 t) 716-822-1250 www.stthomasbuffalo.com (Linked with St. Martin of Tours) Rev. William J. Quinlivan, Pst.; Rev. Gregory J. Dobson, In Res.;

CANASERAGA

St. Mary - 6 North St., Canaseraga, NY 14822; Mailing:

PO Box 189, Canaseraga, NY 14822 t) 607-545-8601 c) 585-245-2356 therectory@stny.rr.com; stmaryscanaseraga@gmail.com stmaryscanaseraga.org Rev. John J. Cullen, Pst.; Fran Button, DRE;

CATTARAUGUS

St. Mary - 36 Washington St., Cattaraugus, NY 14719 t) 716-257-9351 stmcoord@stjoesgowanda.com www.stmaryscatt.org (Linked with St. Joseph, Gowanda) Rev. Innocent Diala (Nigeria), Pst.; CRP Stds.: 4

CHEEKTOWAGA

St. Aloysius Gonzaga - 157 Cleveland Dr., Cheektowaga, NY 14215 t) 716-833-1715 stalschurch@aol.com Rev. Msgr. Peter J. Popadick, Pst.;

Convent - 130 Highview Rd., Cheektowaga, NY 14215

Infant of Prague - 921 Cleveland Dr., Cheektowaga, NY 14225 t) 716-634-3660 www.iopparish.com Rev. Thomas M. Mahoney, Admin.; Rev. Jerome E. Kopec, In Res.; Dcn. Brian C. Walkowiak;

St. John Gualbert - 83 Gualbert Ave., Cheektowaga, NY 14211 t) 716-892-5746 sjgc@roadrunner.com Linked with St John Kanty Parish Rev. Paul Ladda (Tanzania), Par. Admin.;

St. Josaphat - 20 Peoria Ave., Cheektowaga, NY 14206-2695 t) 716-893-1086 sjrectory@roadrunner.com stjosaphat.com Rev. Jozef W. Dudzik, Admin.; Rev. Marcin Porada (Poland), Par. Vicar;

Our Lady Help of Christians - 4125 Union Rd., Cheektowaga, NY 14225 t) (716) 276-9288 olhc.chapel@gmail.com www.ourladyhelpofchristians.org (National Historic Site) Rev. Jozef W. Dudzik, Pst.; Rev. Marcin Porada (Poland), Par. Vicar;

St. Philip the Apostle - 950 Losson Rd., Cheektowaga, NY 14227 t) 716-668-8370 loaves@spaparish.org spaparish.org Rev. Msgr. Richard W. Siepka, Pst.; CRP Stds.: 189

Queen of Martyrs - 180 George Urban Blvd., Cheektowaga, NY 14225-3095 t) 716-892-1746 (Rectory); 716-895-2162 (CRP) queenofmartyrs180@gmail.com; qmre121@verizon.net www.queenofmartyrsbuffalo.com Rev. Louis S. Klein, Pst.; Michael Sacilowski, DRE; CRP Stds.: 44

Resurrection - 130 Como Park Blvd., Cheektowaga, NY 14227 t) 716-683-8785 (CRP); 716-683-3712 rescheek@yahoo.com Rev. Jozef W. Dudzik, Admin.; Rev. Marcin Porada (Poland), Par. Vicar; Dcn. Robert W. Badaszewski; Dcn. Thaddeus P. May;

CLARENCE

Our Lady of Peace - 10950 Main St., Clarence, NY 14031 t) 716-759-8554 office@olpclarence.org olpclarence.org Rev. Walter J. Szczesny, Pst.; CRP Stds.: 161

ĊLYMER

Christ Our Hope - 1762 French Creek Mina Rd., Clymer, NY 14724-9660 t) 716-355-8891 christourhopeparish@gmail.com (Parish with two sites: French Creek & Sherman) Rev. Romulo Montero (Philippines), Admin.; Dcn. David Armstrong; CRP Stds.: 20

CORFU

St. Maximilian Kolbe Parish - 18 W. Main St., Corfu, NY 14036 t) 585-599-4833 Parish with two sites: Corfu; East Pembroke; linked with Alden Rev. Daniel J. Serbicki, Pst.; CRP Stds.: 65

CUBA

Our Lady of the Angels Roman Catholic Church Society of Cuba, New York - 48 South St., Cuba, NY 14727; Mailing: c/o Tri-Parish Office, PO Box 198, Fillmore, NY 14735 t) 585-209-4042 nwalleganycatholic@gmail.com stpatsbelfastfillmore.org (Linked with St. Patrick, Belfast & St. Patrick, Fillmore) Rev. F. Patrick Melfi, Admin.; Susan Scott, DRE; CRP Stds.: 12

DARIEN CENTER

Immaculate Heart of Mary - 10675 Allegany Rd., Darien Center, NY 14040-9701 t) 585-547-3547 (Parish with two sites: Darien Center & Bennington Center) Rev. Joseph A. Fiore, Pst.; CRP Stds.: 26

DEPEW

Blessed Mother Teresa of Calcutta (dba Saint Mother Teresa of Calcutta) - 496 Terrace Blvd., Depew, NY 14043 t) 716-683-2746 stjamesdepew496@yahoo.com Rev. Msgr. Richard W. Siepka, Pst.; Rev. Aaron F. Kulczyk, Par. Vicar;

Felician Nuns - 55 Westfield Ave., Depew, NY 14043

St. Martha - 10 French Rd., Depew, NY 14043-2129 t) 716-684-6342 (Rectory); 716-685-2544 (School); 716-685-2546 (Faith Formation) info@stmarthadepew.org www.stmarthadepew.org Rev. Bartholomew W. Lipiec, Pst.; Jessica Szpylman, DRE; Dcn. James J. Trzaska; CRP Stds.: 80

Our Lady of the Blessed Sacrament - (Grades PreK-3) 20 French Rd., Depew, NY 14043 nkindred@school.olbsdepew.org www.school.olbsdepew.org Nancy Kindred, Prin.; Stds.: 74; Lay Tchrs.: 8

DUNKIRK

Blessed Mary Angela Parish - 295 Lake Shore Dr. E., Dunkirk, NY 14048 t) 716-366-2307 Rev. Jan Trela (Poland), Pst.; Sr. M. Rachel Mikolajczak, C.S.S.F., Pst. Assoc.;

St. Elizabeth Ann Seton - 328 Washington Ave., Dunkirk, NY 14048 t) 716-366-1750 (CRP); 716-366-1752 www.seasdunkirkny.org Rev. Mark J. Noonan, Admin.; CRP Stds.: 40

Holy Trinity - 1032 Central Ave., Dunkirk, NY 14048 t) 716-366-2306 allarewelcome@holytrinitydunkirk.com holytrinitydunkirk.com Rev. Robert J Owczarczak, Admin.; CRP Stds.: 85

EAST AURORA

Immaculate Conception - 520 Oakwood Ave., East Aurora, NY 14052 t) 716-655-0067 (CRP); 716-652-6400 immaculateconceptionea@icchurchea.org Rev. Robert W. Wardenski, Pst.;

Immaculate Conception School - (Grades K-8) 510 Oakwood Ave., East Aurora, NY 14052 t) 716-652-5855 es39@buffalodiocese.org Scott Kapperman, Prin.; Suzanne Gerard, Librn.;

EDEN

Immaculate Conception - 8791 S. Main St., Eden, NY 14057 t) 716-992-3933 religiousedicc@gmail.com; icceden@gmail.com www.icchsc.org (Linked with Holy Spirit, North Collins) Rev. Piotr F. Zaczynski, Admin.; Michelle Walsh, DRE; CRP Stds.: 73

EGGERTSVILLE

St. Benedict - 1317 Eggert Rd., Eggertsville, NY 14226 t) 716-836-6444 (CRP); 716-834-1041 saintbenedicts.com/ Linked with St. Leo the Great Rev. Msgr. Robert E. Zapfel, Pst.; CRP Stds.: 43

St. Benedict School - (Grades PreK-8) 3980 Main St., Amherst, NY 14226 t) 716-835-2518 mbagwell@saintbenedicts.com www.stbenschool.org Mary Alice Bagwell, Prin.; Stds.: 400; Scholastics: 32

ELLICOTTVILLE

Holy Name of Mary RC Church Society Ellicottville NY - 20 Jefferson St., Ellicottville, NY 14731; Mailing: PO Box 543, Ellicottville, NY 14731 t) 716-699-2592 hnameofmary@roadrunner.com www.maryellicottville.org Family member with Franklinville and Salamanca Catholic communities. Rev. F. Patrick Melfi, Pst.;

St. Pacificus - Chapel Hill Rd., Humphrey, NY 14778

ELMA

Church of the Annunciation - 7580 Clinton St., Elma, NY 14059 t) 716-683-5254 parishoffice.annunciation@gmail.com annunciation.cc/ Rev. Eugene P. Ulrich, Pst.; Dcn. Dennis W. Kapsiak; Dcn. Joseph P. Mercurio; Dcn. James J. Jaworski, Pst. Assoc.; Dcn. David E. Clabeaux; Deborah A. Keenan, Pst. Min./Coord.; Melissa Weisenburg, DRE; CRP Stds.: 133

St. Gabriel - 5271 Clinton St., Elma, NY 14059-7617 t) 716-668-4017 stgabriel@stgabeschurch.com www.stgabeschurch.com Rev. Walter P. Grabowski, Pst.; Dcn. Gregory Moran; Emma Dus, DRE; CRP Stds.: 542

FALCONER

Our Lady of Loreto - 309 W. Everett St., Falconer, NY 14733 t) 716-665-3764 (CRP); 716-665-4253 releddir@gmail.com; rectoryoll@gmail.com (Linked with St. Patrick, Randolph) Marilyn Wozneak, DRE; CRP Stds.: 8

FARNHAM

St. Anthony's - 417 Commercial St., Farnham, NY 14061; Mailing: P.O. Box A9, Farnham, NY 14061 t) 716-549-2867 (CRP); 716-549-1159 stanthonyfarnham@aol.com www.stanthonysfarnham.org Rev. James W. Fliss, Pst.; Keith Dash, Youth Min.; Kathleen Brachmann, DRE; CRP Stds.: 60

FILLMORE

St. Patrick's Roman Catholic Church Society of Fillmore, New York - 109 W. Main St., Fillmore, NY 14735-0198; Mailing: c/o Tri-Parish Office, PO Box 198, Fillmore, NY 14737 t) (585) 209-4042 nwalleganycatholic@gmail.com stpatsbelfastfillmore.org (Linked with St. Patrick, Belfast and Our Lady of the Angels, Cuba) Rev. F. Patrick Melfi, Admin.; Jennifer Austin, DRE; CRP Stds.: 26

FRANKLINVILLE

St. Philomena's Roman Catholic Church Society of Franklinville, NY - 26 N. Plymouth Ave., Franklinville, NY 14737 t) 716-676-3629 office@spvm14737.org www.tcsfh.org Family member with Ellicottville and Salamanca Catholic communities. Rev. F. Patrick Melfi, Pst.;

FREDONIA

St. Anthony - 66 Cushing St., Fredonia, NY 14063 t) 716-679-4096 padua@netsync.net (Linked with St. Joseph, Fredonia) Rev. Joseph Walter, Pst.; Joanne Catalano, DRE; CRP Stds.: 20

St. Joseph - 145 E. Main St., Fredonia, NY 14063 t) 716-672-2647 (CRP); 716-679-4116 jbradley@stjosephfredonia.org; stjosephfredonia@yahoo.com (Linked with St. Anthony, Fredonia) Rev. Joseph Walter, Pst.; Dcn. Matthew A. Hens; Dcn. Michael C. Lemieux;

GETZVILLE

St. Pius X - 1700 N. French Rd., Getzville, NY 14068-1427 t) 716-688-9143; 716-688-5417 (CRP) office@stpiusxgetzville.org; pam@stpiusxgetzville.org www.stpiusxgetzville.org Rev. Robert A. Wozniak, Admin.; Pam Rankin, CRE; CRP Stds.: 116

GOWANDA

St. Josephs Roman Catholic Church Society Inc. - 26 Erie Ave., Gowanda, NY 14070 t) 716-532-5100 reled@stjoesgowanda.com; rectory@stjoesgowanda.com (Linked with St. Mary, Cattaraugus) Rev. Innocent Diala (Nigeria), Pst.; Dcn. Walter Samick; Wilma Parry, DRE; CRP Stds.: 44

GRAND ISLAND

St. Stephen - 2100 Baseline Rd., Grand Island, NY 14072 t) 716-773-7647 ststephenswny@ststephensgi.com Rev. Raymond G. Corbin, Pst.; Dcn. Thomas L. Sutton; Dcn. Frank S. Kedzielawa; Rebecca Cambria, CRE; Karen Sweet, Bus. Mgr.; CRP Stds.: 400

St. Stephen School - (Grades PreK-8) 2080 Baseline Rd., Grand Island, NY 14072 school@ststephensgi.org www.ststephensgi.org Lynn Ortiz, Prin.;

HAMBURG

St. Francis of Assisi - S-4263 St. Francis Dr., Hamburg, NY 14075; Mailing: P.O. Box 182, Athol Springs, NY 14010 t) 716-627-2710 (CRP); 716-627-6649 sfareled@gmail.com; sfaoffice@verizon.net www.stfrancischurch.us Rev. Ross M. Syracuse, O.F.M.Conv., Pst.; Elizabeth Woods, DRE; Mark Godios, Bus. Mgr.; CRP Stds.: 60

St. Mary of the Lake - 4737 Lake Shore Rd., Hamburg, NY 14075 t) 716-627-3123 secretary@smolparish.org; businessmanager@smolparish.org www.smolparish.org Rev. Edward F. Jost, Admin.; Dcn. William J. Walkowiak; Julia Dressler, Pst. Assoc.; Adrienne Codd, Bus. Mgr.; Carrie Ford, Musical Dir.; Helene Friend,

Co-Dir., Faith Formation; William Lake Nistor, Co-Dir., Faith Formation; CRP Stds.: 97

SS. Peter and Paul - 66 E. Main St., Hamburg, NY 14075 t) 716-649-0231 x1 (CRP); 716-649-2765 www.sspphamburg.org Rev. Darrell G. Duffy, Pst.; Dcn. Robert T. Ciezki; Dcn. Dennis P. Conroy; Dcn. Carlton M. Koester; Jennifer Golinski, DRE; CRP Stds.: 248

SS. Peter and Paul School - (Grades PreK-8) 68 E. Main St., Hamburg, NY 14075 t) 716-649-7030 principal@sspphamburg.org sspphamburg.org/our-school/ Sr. Marilyn Ann Dudek, C.S.S.F., Prin.; Stds.: 161; Lay Tchrs.: 16

HOLLAND

St. Joseph - 46 N. Main St., Holland, NY 14080-9509 t) 716-655-2841 (CRP); 716-534-9434 stjholland@roadrunner.com www.stjhollandfaith.org/ Rev. Benjamin Mariasoosai (India), Admin.;

HOLLEY

St. Mary - 13 S. Main St., Holley, NY 14470-1107 t) 585-638-6718 jnau@stmarystmark.org www.stmarystmark.org Linked with St. Mark, Kendall. Rev. John J. Arogyasami, I.M.S., Admin.; Jackie Nau, Pst. Assoc.; CRP Stds.: 16

JAMESTOWN

Holy Apostles - 508 Cherry St., Jamestown, NY 14701 t) 716-484-8958 (CRP); 716-664-5703 dwoleen@gmail.com; sspp@netsync.net A two-site parish also linked with St. James Parish in Jamestown Rev. Todd M. Remick, Admin.; Dianne Woleen, DRE;

St. James - 27 Allen St., Jamestown, NY 14701 t) 716-664-4237 (CRP); 716-487-0125 faithform@windstream.net; stjamesparish@wny.twcbc.com St James Parish is linked with Holy Apostles Parish Rev. Todd M. Remick, Admin.; Dcn. Michael Lennon; Lisa Snyder, DRE;

Our Lady of Victory - 6 Institute St., Frewsburg, NY 14738

KENDALL

St. Mark - 16789 Kenmore Rd., Kendall, NY 14476; Mailing: 13 S. Main St., Holley, NY 14470-1107 t) 585-638-6718 jnau@stmarystmark.org stmarystmark.org Linked with St. Mary, Holley. Rev. John J. Arogyasami, I.M.S., Admin.; Jackie Nau, Pst. Assoc.; CRP Stds.: 5

KENMORE

St. Andrew - 1525 Sheridan Dr., Kenmore, NY 14217 t) 716-873-6716 bulletinstandrew@gmail.com www.standrewsrcchurch.org Rev. Matthew J. Zirnheld, Pst.; Rev. Patrick T. O'Keefe, In Res.; Dcn. Michael J. Ficorilli;

St. Andrew School - (Grades PreK-8) 1545 Sheridan Dr., Kenmore, NY 14217 t) 716-877-0422 pamela.giannantonio@standrewscds.net; office@standrewscds.net www.standrewscds.net Pamela Giannantonio, Prin.;

St. Andrew Kim - 9 O'Hara Rd., Tonawanda, NY 14150 t) 716-243-2430 Pamela Giannantonio, Prin.; Rev. Msgr. Robert E. Zapfel, Admin.;

St. Paul - 33 Victoria Blvd., Kenmore, NY 14217 t) 716-875-2730 St. Paul Parish is linked with Blessed Sacrament Parish, Tonawanda Rev. Martin Gallagher, Admin.; Rev. Peter Ekanem, Par. Vicar;

LACKAWANNA

St. Anthony - 306 Ingham Ave., Lackawanna, NY 14218 t) 716-827-8384 (CRP); 716-823-0782 pastanthony@verizon.net Rev. Msgr. David G. LiPuma, Admin.; Rev. Msgr. David M. Gallivan, Sacr. Min.; Rev. Henry A. Orszulak, Sacr. Min.; Dcn. Michael D. Quinn;

Our Lady of Bistrica - 1619 Abbott Rd., Lackawanna, NY 14218 t) 716-822-0818 rectoryourladyofbistrica@gmail.com www.ourladyofbistrica.org Rev. Christopher Coric, O.F.M.Conv. (Croatia), Pst.;

Our Lady of Victory National Shrine and Basilica - 767 Ridge Rd., Lackawanna, NY 14218 t) 716-828-9444 religioused@olvbasilica.org; olvrectory@olvbasilica.org www.olvbasilica.org Rev. Msgr. David G. LiPuma, Pst.; Rev. Robert Contarin, Par. Vicar; Rev. Romulus Rosolowski, O.F.M.Conv., Par. Vicar; Rev. Msgr. Paul J.E. Burkard, In Res.; Dcn. Mark Bialkowski; Dcn. Michael V. Comerford Jr.; Carmel Zomeri, DRE; CRP Stds.: 116

Our Lady of Victory National Shrine School - (Grades PreK-8) 2760 S. Park Ave., Lackawanna, NY 14218 t) 716-828-9434 elementary@olvbasilica.org www.ourladyofvictoryelementary.org Mary Doyle-Szlosek, Prin.; Stds.: 99; Lay Tchrs.: 13

Queen of Angels - 144 Warsaw St., Lackawanna, NY 14218 t) 716-826-0880 Rev. Robert J. Orlowski, Admin.; Rev. John F. Kasprzak, Sacr. Min.; Dcn. David R. Velasquez;

LAKE VIEW

Saint John Paul II - 2052 Lakeview Rd., Lake View, NY 14085 t) 716-627-2910; 716-627-9397 parish@jp2parish.org www.jp2parish.org Rev. Sean E. DiMaria, Pst.; Dcn. Joseph Gray; Dcn. Neal M. Linnan; Molik Jonathan, Pst. Assoc.; Barbara Manley, DRE; CRP Stds.: 224

LAKEWOOD

Sacred Heart - 380 E. Fairmount Ave., Lakewood, NY 14750-2197 t) 716-763-2815 sacredheartlkwd@yahoo.com (Parish with two sites: Lakewood & Panama) Rev. Piotr F. Zaczynski, Pst.; Dineen Muniz, DRE;

LANCASTER

St. Mary of the Assumption - 1 St. Mary's Hill, Lancaster, NY 14086-2094 t) 716-683-6445 www.stmarysonthehill.com Rev. Msgr. Richard W. Siepka, Pst.; Dcn. John A. Owczarczak; CRP Stds.: 115

St. Mary of the Assumption School - (Grades PreK-8) 2 St. Mary's Hill, Lancaster, NY 14086 t) 716-683-2112 x121 kwitowskik@smeschool.com; jezuitn@smeschool.com www.smeschool.com Kim Kwitowski, Prin.;

Our Lady of Pompeii - 158 Laverack Ave., Lancaster, NY 14086; Mailing: 129 Laverack Ave., Lancaster, NY 14086 t) 716-683-6522 ourladyofpompeii@olpparish.com www.olpparish.com Rev. Msgr. Richard W. Siepka, Pst.; Rev. Aaron F. Kulczyk, Par. Vicar; Rev. Thomas Roman, In Res.; Dcn. David C. Rotterman;

LE ROY

Our Lady of Mercy - 44 Lake St., Le Roy, NY 14482 t) 585-768-6543 youthminister@ourladyofmercyleroy.org www.ourladyofmercyleroy.org (Linked with St. Brigid Parish, Bergen) Dcn. David C. Ehrhart; CRP Stds.: 109

LEWISTON

St. Peter - 620 Center St., Lewiston, NY 14092 t) 716-754-2812 (CRP); 716-754-4118 redirector@stpeterlewiston.org; secretary@stpeterlewiston.org www.stpeterlewiston.org (Parish with two sites: Lewiston and Youngstown) Rev. Cole T. Webster, Admin.; Dianne Wysocki, DRE; CRP Stds.: 161

St. Peter School - (Grades PreK-8) 140 N. 6th St., Lewiston, NY 14092 t) 716-754-4470 mingham@stpeterrc.org www.stpeterrc.org Marlene DiNardo, Prin.; Stds.: 191; Lay Tchrs.: 21

St. Bernard Church - 218 Hinman St., Youngstown, NY 14174; Mailing: 620 Center St., Lewiston, NY 14092 (Worship Site) Rev. Thomas M. Mahoney, Admin.;

LOCKPORT

All Saints Roman Catholic Parish of Lockport, New York - 76 Church St., Lockport, NY 14094 t) 716-433-3707 x401 faithformation@allsaintslockport.org allsaintslockport.org Rev. Daniel E. Ogbeifun, Pst.; Caryn Shanahan, DRE;

St. Joseph - 391 Market St., Lockport, NY 14094; Mailing: 76 Church St., Lockport, NY 14094

St. John the Baptist Roman Catholic Congregation - 168 Chestnut St., Lockport, NY 14094 t) 716-514-9405 (CRP); 716-433-8118 frwaite@stjohnslockport.com; clewandowski@stjohnslockport.com www.stjohnslockport.com Rev. Steven A. Jekielek, Moderator; Rev. Andrew R. Lauricella; Rev. Daniel E. Ogbeifun; Rev. Joseph C. Dumphrey, O.S.F.S.;

MEDINA

Holy Trinity - 211 Eagle St., Medina, NY 14103 t) 585-798-5399 (CRP); 585-798-0112 holytrinitymedina@hotmail.com (Parish with two sites: Medina & Middleport) Rev. Bernard U. Nowak, Pst.; Barbara Daluisio, DRE;

NEWFANE

St. Brendan on the Lake - 3455 Ewings Rd., Newfane, NY 14108-0087; Mailing: P.O. Box 87, Newfane, NY 14108-0087 t) 716-778-9822 stbrendanonthelakeoffice@gmail.com (Parish with two sites: Newfane & Wilson) Rev. Andrew R. Lauricella, Admin.; Meg Thompson, DRE; CRP Stds.: 50

St. Charles Borromeo - 5972 Main St., Olcott, NY 14126

NIAGARA FALLS

Divine Mercy - 2437 Niagara St., Niagara Falls, NY 14303; Mailing: 335 24th St, Niagara Falls, NY 14303 t) 716-284-6641 dmoffice@divinemercynf.org www.divinemercynf.org (Linked with St. Mary of the Cataract, Niagara Falls) Rev. Jacek P. Mazur, Pst.; Dcn. David P. Slish;

Holy Family of Jesus, Mary and Joseph - 1413 Pine Ave., Niagara Falls, NY 14301 t) 716-282-1379 info@holyfamilyrcchurch.org (Parish with two sites) Rev. Duane R. Klizek, Pst.; Rev. Stewart M. Lindsay, O.S.F.S., Senior Parochial Vicar;

St. John de La Salle - 8477 Buffalo Ave., Niagara Falls, NY 14304 t) 716-283-5140 (CRP); 716-283-2238 x301 Rev. James W. Kirkpatrick Jr., Admin.;

St. Mary of the Cataract - 237 Fourth St., Niagara Falls, NY 14303 t) 716-282-0059 stmarysniagara@gmail.com www.stmarysnf.net (Linked with Divine Mercy, Niagara Falls) Rev. Jacek P. Mazur, Pst.;

St. Raphael - 3840 Macklem Ave., Niagara Falls, NY 14305 t) 716-282-5583 srpreledmg@gmail.com; st.raphaelrcparish@gmail.com Rev. Ivan Skenderovic, Pst.; Maria Gleason, DRE; CRP Stds.: 49

St. Vincent de Paul (St.Leo/Prince of Peace) - 1055 Military Rd., Niagara Falls, NY 14304; Mailing: 1040 Cayuga Dr, Niagara Falls, NY 14304-2512 t) 716-297-5010 (CRP); 716-283-2715 x200 r.s.hughson@roadrunner.com; rsfh5172@gmail.com svdparish.org Rev. Robert S. Hughson, Pst.; Rev. Mario Racho, Par. Vicar; Sr. Joanne Suranni, C.S.S.F., DRE; CRP Stds.: 242

Prince of Peace -

St. Leo - 2748 Military Rd., Niagara Falls, NY 14304 t) 716-283-5010 x200

NORTH COLLINS

Epiphany of Our Lord - 10893 Sisson Hwy. (Langford), North Collins, NY 14111 t) 716-337-2686 epiphanyparish@gmail.com www.epiphanyofourlordrc.com Rev. Mitch Byeck, Pst.; Dcn. Roy P. Dibb; CRP Stds.: 71

Holy Spirit - 2017 Halley Rd., North Collins, NY 14111 t) 716-337-3701 icceden@gmail.com www.icchsc.org (Linked with Immaculate Conception, Eden) Rev. Piotr F. Zaczynski, Admin.;

NORTH TONAWANDA

Good Shepherd - 5442 Tonawanda Creek Rd., North Tonawanda, NY 14120-9699 t) 716-625-8594 www.goodshepherdpendleton-campus.org/ Parish with two sites: Pendleton; Clarence. Rev. Daniel A. Young, Pst.; Dcn. Stephen M. Gajewski; Sr. Grace C. Dike, S.C.G.R., DRE; CRP Stds.: 78

St. Jude the Apostle Roman Catholic Parish of North Tonawanda, New York - 800 Niagara Falls Blvd., North Tonawanda, NY 14120 t) 716-694-4540 (CRP); 716-694-0540 stjudesfaith@gmail.com; stjudetheapostle@roadrunner.com www.stjudetheapostleparish.org Rev. James W. Kirkpatrick Jr., Pst.; Dcn. Daniel E. Brick; Dcn. John E. Steiner Jr.; Lynda Mostowy, DRE; CRP Stds.: 166

Our Lady of Czestochowa - 57 Center Ave., North Tonawanda, NY 14120 t) 716-693-3822 www.nt-olc.org Rev. Gary J. Szczepankiewicz, Pst.; CRP Stds.: 81

OAKFIELD

St. Padre Pio - 56 Maple Ave., Oakfield, NY 14125 t) 585-948-5344 Rev. Thaddeus Nicholas Bocianowski, Pst.; Dcn. Paul C. Kulczyk; CRP Stds.: 43

Elba Site - 65 S. Main St., Elba, NY 14058-0185

OLEAN

Basilica of St. Mary of the Angels - 119 W. Henley St., Olean, NY 14760; Mailing: 202 S. Union St., Olean, NY 14760 t) 716-372-4841 sregina@smaolean.org; frjohn@smaolean.org www.smaolean.org Rev. John W. Adams, Rector; Rev. Peter Bassey, Par. Vicar; Sr. Regina G. Aman, DRE; CRP Stds.: 70

Oratory of the Sacred Heart -

St. John - 933 N. Union St., Olean, NY 14760; Mailing: 931 N Union St, Olean, NY 14760 t) 716-372-6633 (CRP); 716-372-5313 office@sjteolean.org www.sjteolean.org Rev. John W. Adams, Admin.; Rev. Peter Bassey; CRP Stds.: 51

ORCHARD PARK

St. Bernadette - 5930 S. Abbott Rd., Orchard Park, NY 14127-4516 t) 716-648-1720 (CRP); 716-649-3090 faithformation@saintbophy.org; office@saintbopny.org Rev. Joseph D. Wolf, Admin.; Sharon Urbaniak, DRE; Dcn. Edward R. Howard; CRP Stds.: 300

St. John Vianney - 2950 Southwestern Blvd., Orchard Park, NY 14127 t) 716-674-9133 (Office) parishoffice@sjvop.org www.saintjohnvianney.com Rev. Mark O. Itua (Nigeria), Pst.; CRP Stds.: 230

St. John Vianney School - (Grades PreK-8) t) 716-674-9232 sjvschool@sjvop.org www.sjvop.org Carolyn Kraus, Prin.;

Nativity of Our Lord - 43 Argyle Pl., Orchard Park, NY 14127 t) 716-662-2169 (CRP); 716-662-9339 smcdonough@nativityschool.net; mpotzler@nativityschool.net www.nativityofourlordop.com Rev. James D. Ciupek, Pst.; Rev. Michael Johnson, Par. Vicar; Dcn. Gary P. Andelora; Mary Barone, DRE;

Nativity of Our Lord School - (Grades PreK-8) 4414 S. Buffalo St., Orchard Park, NY 14127 t) 716-662-7572 cgardon@nativityschool.net Christopher Gardon, Prin.; Nancy McNulty, Librn.;

Our Lady of the Sacred Heart - 3148 Abbott Rd., Orchard Park, NY 14127 t) 716-824-8209 (CRP); 716-824-2935 rectory@olshop.org www.olshop.org Rev. Adolph M. Kowalczyk, Pst.; Dcn. Timothy J. Coughlin; Lynn Lipczynski, DRE;

PAVILION

Mary Immaculate - 11095 Saint Mary St., Pavilion, NY 14525; Mailing: 16 North St., Warsaw, NY 14569 t) (585) 786-2400 errccbusiness@gmail.com www.errcc.org Mary Immaculate is a family of Parishes with St. Michael's and St. Isidore's. Mary Immaculate is a two site Parish in Pavilion and East Bethany Rev. Michael LaMarca, Pst.; Rev. Denning Achidi, Par. Vicar; Dcn. Mark D. Kehl; CRP Stds.: 46

PERRY

St. Isidore - 8 Park St., Perry, NY 14530; Mailing: 16 North St., Warsaw, NY 14569 t) 585-786-2400 errccbusiness@gmail.com; errccoffice@gmail.com www.errcc.org Family of Parishes with St. Michael's and Mary Immaculate. St. Isidore's is a two site Parish in Perry and Silver Springs. Rev. Michael LaMarca, Pst.; Rev. Denning Achidi, Par. Vicar; Dcn. Mark D. Kehl;

RANDOLPH

St. Patrick - 189 Main St., Randolph, NY 14772 t) 716-358-2991 saintpatricksrcc@gmail.com (Linked with Our Lady of Loreto, Falconer) Rev. Donald R Watkins Jr., Admin.; CRP Stds.: 17

RANSOMVILLE

Immaculate Conception - 4671 Townline Rd., Rte. 429, Ransomville, NY 14131-9740 t) 716-731-4822 office@icransomville.org www.icransomville.org Rev. James W. Kirkpatrick Jr., Admin.;

SALAMANCA

Our Lady of Peace - 274 Broad St, Salamanca, NY 14779 t) 716-945-4966 www.olpsal.org Rev. Dennis J. Mancuso, Pst.; Rev. Moses Ikuelogbon, Assoc. Pst.; Dcn. Michael L. Anderson;

SANBORN

Holy Family - 5180 Chew Rd., Sanborn, NY 14132; Mailing: PO Box 167, Youngstown, NY 14174-0167 c) 716-523-9114 pmccrsp@fatimashrine.com (Tuscarora Native Americans) Rev. Peter M. Calabrese, C.R.S.P., Pst.; CRP Stds.: 8

SARDINIA

St. Jude Roman Catholic Church Society of Sardinia, New York - 12820 Genesee Rd., Sardinia, NY 14134-0267; Mailing: P.O. Box 267, Sardinia, NY 14134-0267 t) 716-496-7535 Rev. Alfons M. Osiander, Pst.;

SILVER CREEK

Our Lady of Mt. Carmel - 165 Central Ave., Silver Creek, NY 14136 t) 716-934-2233 olomc14136@gmail.com (Parish with two sites: Silver Creek & Forestville) Rev. Daniel F. Fiebelkorn, Pst.; CRP Stds.: 40

SLOAN

St. Andrew - 34 Francis Ave., Sloan, NY 14212 t) 716-892-0425 saintandrewsloan@roadrunner.com www.standrewsloan.org Rev. Thomas M. Mahoney, Admin.; Rev. James C. O'Connor, Sacr. Min.; James Hill, DRE;

SNYDER

Christ the King - 30 Lamarck Dr., Snyder, NY 14226 t) 716-839-1430 rectoryoffice@ctksnyder.com; plitwin@buffalodiocese.org www.ctksnyder.org Rev. Msgr. Paul A. Litwin, Pst.; CRP Stds.: 117

Christ the King School - (Grades PreK-8) 2 Lamarck Dr., Snyder, NY 14226 t) 716-839-0473 Samuel T. Zalacca, Prin.;

SPRINGBROOK

St. Vincent de Paul Roman Catholic Church - 6441 Seneca St., Springbrook, NY 14140; Mailing: P.O. Box 290, Springbrook, NY 14140 t) 716-652-7242 (CRP); 716-652-3972 (Office) stvincentccd@gmail.com; svdparish@gmail.com svdpspringbrook.com Rev. Karl E. Loeb, Pst.; Julie Cappello, DRE; CRP Stds.: 106

SPRINGVILLE

St. Aloysius - 190 Franklin St., Springville, NY 14141-1199 t) 716-592-2701 staloy@roadrunner.com www.staloy.com (Linked with St. John the Baptist, West Valley) Rev. Daniel J. Fawls, Pst.; Dcn. Jeffrey D. Forster; CRP Stds.: 35

Sisters of St. Francis - 71 W. Main St., Springville, NY 14141

STRYKERSVILLE

St. John Neumann - 3854 Main St., Strykersville, NY 14145-0009; Mailing: P.O. Box 9, Strykersville, NY 14145-0009 t) 585-457-3222 stjohnneumannparish@gmail.com (Parish with two sites: Strykersville & Sheldon) Rev. Johnson Machado (India), Pst.; CRP Stds.: 26

SWORMVILLE

St. Mary - 6919 Transit Rd., Swormville, NY 14051 t) 716-688-9380 familyfaith@stmaryswormville.org; rectory@stmaryswormville.org stmaryswormville.org Rev. Bryan J. Zielenieski, Pst.; Rev. Ryan E Keating, Par. Vicar; Rev. Luke P. Uebler, Par. Vicar; Dcn. Richard R. Stachura Jr.; CRP Stds.: 525

St. Mary School - (Grades PreK-8) t) 716-689-8424 principal@stmaryschoolswormville.org; office@stmaryschoolswormville.org Tristan D'Angelo, Prin.;

TONAWANDA

St. Amelia's Roman Catholic Church Society of the Town of Tonawanda, N.Y. - 210 St. Amelia Dr., Tonawanda, NY 14150 t) 716-833-8647 (CRP); 716-836-0011 stameliareled@yahoo.com; rectoryoffice@stamelia.com stamelia.com/ Rev. Sebastian C. Pierro, Pst.; Rev. Charles Johnson, Par. Vicar; Elaine Volker, DRE; Dcn. Kenneth R. Monaco; CRP Stds.: 236

St. Amelia School - (Grades PreK-8) 2999 Eggert Rd., Tonawanda, NY 14150 t) 716-836-2230 office@stameliaschool.org www.stameliaschool.org Kathryn A. McIntyre, Prin.;

St. Andrew Kim - 9 O'Hara Rd., Tonawanda, NY 14150 t) 716-693-1600 inyongpark521@gmail.com www.bukoca.org Mission for Korean Catholics. Rev. Msgr. Robert E. Zapfel, Admin.;

Blessed Sacrament - 263 Claremont Ave., Tonawanda, NY 14223 t) 716-834-4282 bsctonawanda@gmail.com bsacramentchurch.com/ Rev. Martin Gallagher, Pst.; Rev. Peter Ekanem, Par. Vicar; Sr. M. Lucette Kinecki, C.S.S.F., Pst. Assoc.;

St. Christopher - 2660 Niagara Falls Blvd., Tonawanda, NY 14150-1499 t) 716-694-4310 (CRP); 716-692-2660 reled@saintchris.org; rectory@saintchris.org www.saintchris.org Rev. Michael K. Brown, Pst.; Marie Sajda, DRE; Dcn. Thomas R. Healey; Dcn. David P. McDermott; CRP Stds.: 375

St. Christopher School - (Grades PreK-8) t) 716-693-5604 school@saintchris.org Denise Cronyn, Prin.;

St. Francis of Assisi - 73 Adam St., Tonawanda, NY 14150 t) 716-693-1150 faithformation@stfrancistonawanda.org Rev. Jay W. McGinnis, Admin.; Dcn. Paul H. Bork; Jennifer Burton, DRE; CRP Stds.: 55

St. Timothy - 565 E. Park Dr., Tonawanda, NY 14150 t) 716-875-9430 dre@sttimsparish.org; office@sainttimothyparish.org www.sainttimothyparish.org Rev. Dennis F. Fronckowiak, Pst.; CRP Stds.: 70

WARSAW

St. Michael's R.C. Church Society - 171 N. Main St., Warsaw, NY 14569; Mailing: 16 North St., Warsaw, NY 14569 t) 585-786-2400 errccbusiness@gmail.com; errccoffice@gmail.com www.errcc.org A Family of Parishes with St. Isidore Parish Community and Mary Immaculate Parish. Rev. Michael LaMarca, Pst.; Rev. Denning Achidi, Par. Vicar; Dcn. Mark D. Kehl; CRP Stds.: 56

WELLSVILLE

Immaculate Conception - 36 Maple Ave., Wellsville, NY 14895; Mailing: 17 Maple Ave., Wellsville, NY 14895 t) 585-593-4834 kater@iccwlsv.com www.icc-ics.com Linked to St. Mary (Bolivar); Blessed Sacrament (Andover); SS Brendan & Jude (Alfred-Almond) & Holy Family of Jesus, Mary & Joseph (Belmont) Rev. James W. Hartwell, Pst.; Rev. Robert Agbo, Par. Vicar; CRP Stds.: 56

WEST FALLS

St. George - 74 Old Glenwood Rd., West Falls, NY 14170-9704 t) 716-652-3153 c) 716-292-4262 stgeorge.wf@gmail.com www.stgeorgercchurch.org Rev. Robert W. Wardenski, Moderator; Rev. Msgr. James E. Wall, Sacr. Min.; Sr. Lori High, S.S.M.N., Admin.; CRP Stds.: 3

WEST SENECA

Fourteen Holy Helpers - 1345 Indian Church Rd., West Seneca, NY 14224 t) 716-674-2374 rectory@14hh.org www.14hh.org Home parish for the Deaf Community of the Diocese of Buffalo Rev. David A. Bellittiere, Pst.; Dcn. Thomas E. Scherr; Sharon Voigt, DRE; CRP Stds.: 43

Saint John XXIII - 1 Arcade St., West Seneca, NY 14224 t) 716-823-1090 www.stjohn23.com Rev. John E. Stanton Jr., Pst.; CRP Stds.: 40

Queen of Heaven - 4220 Seneca St., West Seneca, NY 14224 t) 716-675-3714 (CRP); 716-674-3468 rectory@qofhchurch.org qofhchurch.org Rev. Gregory M. Faulhaber, Pst.; Dcn. Michael Dalessandro; Douglas George, DRE; Dr. Dennis Castillo, DRE; CRP Stds.: 209

Queen of Heaven School - (Grades PreK-8) 839 Mill Rd., West Seneca, NY 14224 t) 716-674-5206 mdamico@qofhschool.org qofhschool.org Mary Damico, Prin.; Stds.: 339; Lay Tchrs.: 25

WEST VALLEY

St. John the Baptist - 5381 Depot St., West Valley, NY 14171-0315; Mailing: P.O. Box 315, West Valley, NY 14171-0315 t) 716-942-6874 (CRP); 716-942-3259 (Linked with St. Aloysius, Springville) Rev. Daniel J. Fawls, Pst.; Elaine Ahles, DRE;

WESTFIELD

St. Dominic - 15 Union St., Westfield, NY 14787-1494

t) 716-326-2816 st.dominicrcc@gmail.com www.stdominicrcc.org (Parish with two sites: Westfield & Brocton) Rev. David E. Tourville, Pst.; Barbara Weingart, CRE; Rev. Sean Duggan, O.S.B., Extra Clergy; CRP Stds.: 19

WILLIAMSVILLE

St. Gregory the Great - 200 St. Gregory Ct., Williamsville, NY 14221 t) 716-688-5678 stgregs.org Rev. Leon J. Biernat, Pst.; Rev. Joseph Tokasz, Par. Vicar; Rev. Daniel R. Ulmer, Par. Vicar; Dcn. Greg Gaulin, Par. Vicar; Dcn. Paul Walter; Dcn. Michael G. Bochiechio; CRP Stds.: 459

St. Gregory the Great School - (Grades PreK-8) 250 St. Gregory Ct., Williamsville, NY 14221 t) 716-688-5323 jgajewski@stgregs.org Patricia Freund, Prin.;

Nativity of the Blessed Virgin Mary - 8500 Main St., Williamsville, NY 14221; Mailing: 4375 Harris Hill Rd, Williamsville, NY 14221 t) 716-632-8838 nativityoffice@nativityharrishill.org www.nativityharrishill.org Rev. Ronald P. Sajdak, Pst.; Dcn. Thomas F. Friedman; Dcn. Carmelo Gaudioso; Dcn. Donald C. Weigel Jr.; CRP Stds.: 380

Nativity of the Blessed Virgin Mary School - (Grades PreK-8) 8550 Main St., Williamsville, NY 14221 t) 716-633-7441 office@nativityofmaryschool.org www.nativityofmaryschool.org Nicole C. Richard, Prin.; Stds.: 207; Lay Tchrs.: 22

Ss. Peter and Paul Roman Catholic Church Society of Williamsville, NY - 5480 Main St., Williamsville, NY 14221; Mailing: 17 Grove St., Williamsville, NY 14221 t) 716-632-2678 (CRP); 716-632-2559 (Office) reled@ssppchurch.com; parishoffice@ssppchurch.com ssppchurch.com Rev. Matt Mieczyslaw Nycz, Pst.; Dcn. Charles D. Esposito; Lynn Baker, Bus. Mgr.; Roberta Spencer, DRE; CRP Stds.: 181

SS. Peter and Paul School - (Grades PreK-8) t) 716-632-6146 mlindner@ssppschool.com ssppschool.com Melissa Lindner, Prin.;

SCHOOLS: PRESCHOOL THRU HIGH SCHOOL

SCHOOLS

STATE OF NEW YORK

BATAVIA

St. Joseph Regional School - (DIO) (Grades PreK-6) 2 Summit St., Batavia, NY 14020 t) 585-343-2459 kgreen@sjsbatavia.org www.sjsbatavia.org/ Karen Green, Prin.; Stds.: 180; Lay Tchrs.: 10

BUFFALO

Catholic Academy of West Buffalo - (DIO) (Grades PreK-8) 1069 Delaware Ave., Buffalo, NY 14209-1605 t) 716-885-6111 cawb.org Christine Traum, Librn.; Stds.: 230; Sr. Tchrs.: 1; Lay Tchrs.: 17

Nardin Academy - (PRV) (Grades PreSchool-8) Cleveland Campus - 135 Cleveland Ave., Buffalo, NY 14222 t) 716-881-6262 (Cleveland Campus); (716) 881-6565 (Montessori Campus) jmonaco@nardin.org; mpadmanabha@nardin.org www.nardin.org (Montessori-Grade 8) Sandra Betters, Pres.; Monica Padmanabha, Prin.; Mary Gjurich, Prin.; Jill Monaco, Prin.; Stds.: 392; Lay Tchrs.: 59

The NativityMiguel Middle School of Buffalo - (PRV) (Grades 5-8) 21 Davison Ave., Buffalo, NY 14215 t) 716-852-6854; 716-836-5188 info@nativitymiguelbuffalo.org; cpitek@nativitymiguelbuffalo.org nativitymiguelbuffalo.org Christopher M Pitek, Pres.; Rev. Edward J. Durkin, S.J., Prin.; Stds.: 56; Pr. Tchrs.: 1; Lay Tchrs.: 8

South Buffalo Catholic School (Notre Dame Academy) - (PRV) (Grades PreK-8) 1125 Abbott Rd., 260 Okell, Buffalo, NY 14220 t) 716-824-0726 www.notredamebuffalo.org Rev. Robert M. Mock, Supr.; Stds.: 472; Lay Tchrs.: 32

DEPEW

Cantalician Center for Learning, Inc. - (PRV) (Grades PreK-12) 2049 George Urban Blvd., Depew, NY 14043 t) 716-901-8700 ahirtzel@cantalician.org www.cantalician.org Integrated services to children and adults with developmental disabilities. Mark Bleasy, Prin.; Julie Davis, Prin.; Anne Spisiak, Exec.; Jason Petko, Dir.;

DUNKIRK

Northern Chautauqua Catholic School - (DIO) (Grades PreK-8) 336 Washington Ave., Dunkirk, NY 14048 t) 716-366-0630 aludwig@nccschool.us; jmarsh@nccschool.us www.nccschool.us Andy Ludwig, Prin.; Rev. Robert J Owczarczak, Canonical Admin.; Stds.: 202; Lay Tchrs.: 15

LAKE VIEW

Southtowns Catholic - (Grades PreK-8) 2052 Lakeview Rd., Lake View, NY 14085 t) 716-627-5011 mbandelian@southtownscatholic.org www.southtownscatholic.org Marc Bandelian, Prin.; Stds.: 187; Lay Tchrs.: 20

LEWISTON

Sacred Heart Villa School - (PRV) (Grades PreK-5) 5269 Lewiston Rd., Lewiston, NY 14092 t) 716-284-8273; 716-285-9257 shvillaschool@gmail.com www.shvilla.org Sr. Grace C. Dike, S.C.G.R., Prin.; Stds.: 43; Sr. Tchrs.: 6

LOCKPORT

DeSales Catholic School - (DIO) (Grades PreK-8) 6914 Chestnut Ridge Rd., Lockport, NY 14094 t) 716-433-6422 rahillk@desalescatholicschool.org www.desalescatholicschool.org Karen Rahill, Prin.; Stds.: 315; Lay Tchrs.: 27

NIAGARA FALLS

Catholic Academy of Niagara Falls - (DIO) (Grades PreK-8) 1055 N. Military Rd., Niagara Falls, NY 14304 t) 716-283-1455 info@catholicacademynf.org catholicacademyofniagarafalls.com Johanna Richards, Prin.; Rev. Robert S. Hughson, Admin.;

OLEAN

Southern Tier Catholic School - (DIO) (Grades PreK-8) 208 N. 24th St., Olean, NY 14760 t) 716-372-8122 principal@walshstcs.org; nicholas.burt@walshstcs.org www.stcswalsh.org Nicholas Burt, Admin.; Beth Ann Owens, Supt.; Stds.: 110; Lay Tchrs.: 15

STELLA NIAGARA

Stella Niagara Education Park - (PRV) (Grades PreK-8) 4421 Lower River Rd., Stella Niagara, NY 14144 t) 716-754-4314 snepoffice@stella-niagara.com Sisters of St. Francis of Penance and Christian Charity Sr. Margaret Sullivan, O.S.F., Prin.;

WELLSVILLE

Immaculate Conception School of Allegany County - (PAR) (Grades PreK-8) 24 Maple Ave., Wellsville, NY 14895 t) 585-593-5840 cdewey@icc-ics.org www.icc-ics.org Caitilin Dewey, Prin.; Rev. James W. Hartwell, Pst. Min./Coord.; Stds.: 46; Lay Tchrs.: 6

HIGH SCHOOLS

STATE OF NEW YORK

AMHERST

Buffalo Academy of the Sacred Heart - (PRV) 3860 Main St., Amherst, NY 14226 t) 716-834-2101 info@sacredheartacademy.org www.sacredheartacademy.org Jennifer Demert, Head of School;

BATAVIA

Notre Dame High School of Batavia - (PRV) 73 Union St., Batavia, NY 14020 t) 585-343-2783 ndhs@ndhsbatavia.com www.ndhsbatavia.com Owned and operated by Notre Dame Board of Trustees. Includes Junior High School. Wade Bianco, Prin.;

BUFFALO

Bishop Timon-St. Jude High School - (PRV) 601 McKinley Pkwy., Buffalo, NY 14220 t) 716-826-3610 newton@bishoptmon.com www.bishoptimon.com Dr. James Preston Newton, Prin.; Stds.: 224; Lay Tchrs.: 17

Canisius High School - (PRV) (Grades 9-12) 1180 Delaware Ave., Buffalo, NY 14209 t) 716-882-0466 gaglione@canisiushigh.org www.canisiushigh.org Thomas Coppola, Prin.; Rev. David S. Ciancimino, S.J., Pres.; Stds.: 574; Pr. Tchrs.: 3; Lay Tchrs.: 42

St. Joseph's Collegiate Institute - (PRV) (Grades 9-12) 845 Kenmore Ave., Buffalo, NY 14223-3195 t) 716-874-4024 cfulco@sjci.com www.sjci.com Brothers of the Christian Schools. (De La Salle Christian Brothers). Rev. James C. Croglio, Chap.; James Spillman, Prin.; Dr. Christopher Fulco, Pres.; Stds.: 620; Bro. Tchrs.: 2; Lay Tchrs.: 48

Mount Mercy Academy - (PRV) (Grades 9-12) 88 Red Jacket Pkwy., Buffalo, NY 14220 t) 716-825-8796 mmelligan@mtmercy.org www.mtmercy.org Michele Melligan, Head Of School; Stds.: 172; Lay Tchrs.: 21

Nardin Academy High School - (PRV) (Grades PreSchool-12) 135 Cleveland Ave., Buffalo, NY 14222 t) 716-881-6262 crobertson@nardin.org www.nardin.org Sandra Betters, Pres.; Colleen Robertson, Prin.;

HAMBURG

St. Francis High School - (PRV) (Grades 9-12) 4129 Lake Shore Rd., Hamburg, NY 14075 t) 716-627-1200 foleym@stfrancishigh.org; zygajj@stfrancishigh.org stfrancishigh.org Franciscan Friars Conventual of Our Lady of the Angels Province. Rev. Matthew Foley, O.F.M., Pres.; Stds.: 425; Pr. Tchrs.: 4; Bro. Tchrs.: 2; Lay Tchrs.: 39

KENMORE

Mount St. Mary Academy - (PRV) (Grades 9-12) 3756 Delaware Ave., Kenmore, NY 14217 t) 716-877-1358 kspillman@msmacademy.org msmacademy.org Owned and operated by the Mount St. Mary Academy Board of Trustees. Katherine M Spillman, Prin.; Stds.: 222; Lay Tchrs.: 26

LANCASTER

St. Mary's High School - (PRV) (Grades 9-12) 142 Laverack Ave., Lancaster, NY 14086 t) 716-683-4824 lancer@smhlancers.org www.smhlancers.org Owned and operated by St. Mary's Board of Trustees. Keith Junik, Dean; Kevin Kelleher, Pres.; Stds.: 470; Lay Tchrs.: 35

OLEAN

Archbishop Walsh High School - (PRV) (Grades 9-12) 208 N. 24th St., Olean, NY 14760-1985 t) 716-372-8122 nicholas.burt@walshstcs.org; principal@walshstcs.org www.stcswalsh.org Dr. Colleen Taggerty, Pres.; Beth Ann Owens, Prin.; Rev. Peter Schneible, O.F.M., Admin.;

TONAWANDA

Cardinal O'Hara High School - (PRV) (Grades 9-12) 39 O'Hara Rd., Tonawanda, NY 14150 t) 716-695-2600 mholzerland@cardinalohara.com www.cardinalohara.com Joleen Dimitroff, Prin.; David Lovering, Vice Prin.;

INSTITUTIONS LOCATED IN DIOCESE

ASSOCIATIONS [ASN]

BUFFALO

Kolping Catholic Young Men's Association of Buffalo, NY - 1145 Cleveland Dr., Willi Evelt, Buffalo, NY 14225 t) 716-632-7360 cbaer40@verizon.net Willi Evelt, Pres.;

LEWISTON

Our Lady of Angels Association - 150 S 4th St., Lewiston, NY 14092; Mailing: P.O. Box 1918, Niagara University, NY 14109-1918 t) 716-754-0035 novena@niagara.edu www.ourladyofangels.net Development Office for the Congregation of the Mission, Eastern Province. Rev. Michael J. Carroll, CM, Dir.;

CAMPUS MINISTRY / NEWMAN CENTERS [CAM]

ALFRED

Alfred University and Alfred State College Campus Ministry - Lower College Dr., Alfred, NY 14802; Mailing: P.O. Box 1154, Alfred, NY 14802 t) 607-587-9411 stjude.alfred@gmail.com Rev. James W. Hartwell, Contact;

AMHERST

State University of New York at Buffalo (North Campus) Newman Center - 495 Skinnersville Rd., Amherst, NY 14228 t) 716-636-7495 ubnewman@gmail.com www.newman.buffalo.edu Rev. Msgr. J. Patrick Keleher, Dir.; Rev. Roy T. Herberger, Sacr. Min.; Dcn. Michael J. Colson; Kathleen Colson, Youth Min.; Joshua Merlo, Bus. Mgr.; Leah Merlo, Campus Min.;

BUFFALO

Canisius College, Campus Ministry Office - Canisius College Campus Ministry OM 207, 2001 Main St., Buffalo, NY 14208 t) 716-888-2420 campmin@canisius.edu www.canisius.edu Spencer Liechty, Campus Min.;

D'Youville College - 320 Porter Ave., Buffalo, NY 14201 t) 716-829-7672 campusministry@dyc.edu Janice Mahle, Dir.;

State University of New York at Buffalo (Main St. South Campus) - St. Joseph University Parish, 3269 Main St., Buffalo, NY 14214 t) 716-833-0298 ledwon@buffalo.edu; frgregj@stjosephbuffalo.org www.ubstjoes.org Rev. Jacob C. Ledwon, Dir.; Rev. Gregory P. Jakubowicz, O.F.M., Campus Min.;

SUNY Buffalo State Newman Center - 1219 Elmwood Ave., Buffalo, NY 14222 t) 716-882-1080 newmancenter@buffalostate.edu www.newmancenterbuffalostate.org Rev. Patrick J. Zengierski, Dir.; Austin Reinhart, Campus Min.;

Trocaire College - 360 Choate Ave., Buffalo, NY 14220 t) 716-826-1200 saundersk@trocaire.edu Kathleen Saunders, Contact;

Villa Maria College of Buffalo - 240 Pine Ridge Rd., Buffalo, NY 14225 t) 716-961-1840 monnind@villa.edu www.villa.edu Dr. Donald Monnin, Vice. Pres.;

HAMBURG

Hilbert College, Campus Ministry Office - 5200 S. Park Ave., Hamburg, NY 14075 t) 716-649-7900 jpapia@hilbert.edu Jeffrey Papia, Dir.;

NIAGARA UNIVERSITY

Niagara University - ; Mailing: P.O. Box 2016, Niagara University, NY 14109 t) 716-286-8400 ministry@niagara.edu www.niagara.edu/ministry Kristina Daloia, Dir.;

ST. BONAVENTURE

St. Bonaventure University - 3261 W. State St., St. Bonaventure, NY 14778; Mailing: P.O. Box AR, St. Bonaventure, NY 14778 t) 716-375-2662 ypeace@sbu.edu Rev. Stephen D Mimnaugh, Chap.; Bro. Joseph A. Kotula, O.F.M.; Bro. Kevin Kriso, O.F.M; Rev. Louis M. McCormick, O.F.M.; Rev. Daniel P. Riley, O.F.M.; Alice Miller Nation, Dir.; Amanda Naujoks, Dir.; Rev. Ross Chamberland, O.F.M., Minister in Res.; Rev. Kyle Haden, O.F.M., Minister in Res.; Rev. Peter Schneible, O.F.M., Minister in Res.; Dr. Paula Scraba, Minister in Res.;

CATHOLIC CHARITIES [CCH]

BUFFALO

The Catholic Charities of the Diocese of Buffalo - 741 Delaware Ave., Buffalo, NY 14209 t) 716-218-1400 www.ccwny.org Provides comprehensive Human Services across the eight counties of Western New York. Clara Moran, Chief Devel. Officer; Asstd. Annu.: 125,657; Staff: 350

Agency Administration -

Appeal Administration and Publicity Offices - clara.moran@ccwny.org; rose.caldwell@ccwny.org Rose Caldwell, Chief Communs. Officer;

The Msgr. Carr Institute - 76 W. Humboldt Pkwy., Buffalo, NY 14214; Mailing: 741 Delaware Ave., Buffalo, NY 14209 t) 716-895-1033; 877-448-4466 megan.lostracco@ccwny.org See separate listing in the Miscellaneous section. Megan Lostracco-Reed, Sr. Dir.;

CEMETERIES [CEM]

KENMORE

Catholic Cemeteries of the Roman Catholic Diocese of Buffalo, Inc. - 4000 Elmwood Ave., Kenmore, NY 14217 t) 716-873-6500 info@buffalocatholiccemeteries.org www.buffalocatholiccemeteries.org Cemeteries: Assumption, Gate of Heaven, Holy Cross, Holy Sepulchre, Mount Olivet, Queen of Heaven, and St. Adalbert on behalf of St. John Kanty Parish Michael Attea, Dir.;

COLLEGES & UNIVERSITIES [COL]

BUFFALO

Canisius College - 2001 Main St., Buffalo, NY 14208-1098 t) 716-888-2100; 716-888-2420 montarol@canisius.edu; hayes28@canisius.edu www.canisius.edu Dr. Steve K. Stoute, Pres.;

***D'Youville College** - 320 Porter Ave., Buffalo, NY 14201 t) 716-829-8000 brayjd@dyc.edu www.dyc.edu D'Youville recently received University status: D'Youville University Lorrie A. Clemo, Pres.;

Trocaire College - 360 Choate Ave., Buffalo, NY 14220 t) 716-827-2423 deebb@trocaire.edu www.trocaire.edu Established by the Sisters of Mercy. Bassam M. Deeb, Pres.; Richard T. Linn, Senior Vice Pres.;

Villa Maria College of Buffalo - 240 Pine Ridge Rd., Buffalo, NY 14225-3999 t) 716-896-0700; 716-961-1869 karpinskim@villa.edu www.villa.edu Matthew Giordano, Pres.; Lucy Waite, Librn.; Stds.: 452; Lay Tchrs.: 25; Sr. Tchrs.: 1

HAMBURG

Hilbert College - 5200 S. Park Ave., Hamburg, NY 14075 t) 716-649-7900 mbrophy@hilbert.edu www.hilbert.edu/ Dr. Michael Brophy, Pres.;

NIAGARA UNIVERSITY

Niagara University - 5795 Lewiston Rd., Niagara University, NY 14109 t) 716-286-8350 president@niagara.edu www.niagara.edu Rev. James J. Maher, C.M., Pres.; Debra A. Colley, Exec.; Timothy Ireland, Vice Pres.; Robert Morreale, CFO; Stds.: 3,858; Lay Tchrs.: 175; Sr. Tchrs.: 1; Scholastics: 176

ST. BONAVENTURE

St. Bonaventure University - 3261 W. State Rd., St. Bonaventure, NY 14778 t) 716-375-2000 sstangle@sbu.edu www.sbu.edu School of Arts and Sciences, School of Educ., School of Business, School of Journalism & Mass Communication; School of Franciscan Studies Dr. Jeff Gingerich, Pres.; Stds.: 2,381

CONVENTS, MONASTERIES, AND RESIDENCES FOR WOMEN [CON]

ALLEGANY

Franciscan Sisters of Allegany, New York, Inc. - 115 E. Main St., Attn: Congregational Sec., Allegany, NY 14706; Mailing: P.O. Box W, St. Bonaventure, NY 14778 t) 716-373-0200 fsa@fsallegany.org; fsa.hr@fsallegany.org www.alleganyfranciscans.org Sr. Margaret Magee, OSF, Congregational Min.; Sr. Melissa Scholl, Assoc. Min.; Srs.: 170

St. Elizabeth Motherhouse - t) (716) 373-0200

BUFFALO

Immaculate Heart of Mary Convent - 600 Doat St., Buffalo, NY 14211 t) 716-892-4141 sjudithmk@feliciansisters.org www.feliciansistersna.org Sr. Judith Marie Kubicki, Prov.; Srs.: 77

Sisters of Mercy of the Americas-New York, Pennsylvania, Pacific West Community, Inc. - 625 Abbott Rd., Buffalo, NY 14220 t) 716-826-5051 dswanson@sistersofmercy.org Sr. Pat Flynn, RSM, Pres.; Srs.: 229

Mercy Center - t) 716-825-5531 dswanson@mercynyppaw.org

Sisters of Social Service of Buffalo - 296 Summit Ave., Buffalo, NY 14214-1936 t) 716-834-0197 agnes.patakisss@gmail.com Sr. Agnes Pataki, S.S.S., Delegate; Srs.: 9

Sisters of St. Mary of Namur - St. Mary Ctr., 241 Lafayette Ave., Buffalo, NY 14213-1453 t) 716-884-8221 ssmneasternregion@gmail.com www.ssmneastern.com/ St. Mary Center Sr. Maureen Quinn, SSMN, Regl. Supr.; Srs.: 59

St. Mary Center - 245 Lafayette Ave., Buffalo, NY 14213

Sisters of St. Mary - 160 Lovering Ave., Buffalo, NY 14216 t) 716-873-9002

Sisters of St. Mary - 3100 Elmwood Ave., Kenmore, NY 14217 t) 716-873-8011 mveronicawhite@yahoo.com

Sisters of St. Mary - 104 Garden St., Lockport, NY 14094 t) 716-433-3966

Sisters of St. Mary - 2484 River Rd., Niagara Falls, NY 14304; Mailing: 241 Lafayette Ave., Buffalo, NY 14213 ssmnprov@verizon.net

CLARENCE

Congregation of the Sisters of St. Joseph Generalate - 4975 Strickler Rd., Ste. A, Admin. Offices, Clarence, NY 14031 t) 716-759-6454 mkloss@buffalossj.org www.buffalossj.org Sr. Patrice A Ryan, SSJ, Pres.; Srs.: 45

Sisters of St. Joseph - 4975 Strickler Rd., Clarence Res., Clarence, NY 14031 t) 716-759-6893 mkloss@buffalossj.org Sr. Patrice A Ryan, SSJ, Pres.; Srs.: 25

HAMBURG

Immaculate Conception Convent - 5229 S. Park Ave., Franciscan Sisters of St. Joseph, Hamburg, NY 14075 t) 716-649-1205 x44708 adminassist@fssj.org www.fssj.org Motherhouse of the Franciscan Sisters of St. Joseph Sr. Marcia Ann Fiutko, FSSJ, Rel. Ord. Ldr.; Srs.: 38

LEWISTON

Sisters of the Sacred Heart of Jesus of Ragusa (SCGR) - 5269 Lewiston Rd., Lewiston, NY 14092 t) 716-284-8273 sshj_vocation@yahoo.com www.shvilla.org Sr. Ana Lourdes Salonga, Supr.; Srs.: 10

SILVER CREEK

Missionary Sisters of St. Columban - 2546 Lake Rd., Silver Creek, NY 14136 t) 716-934-4515 sistercorona@stcolumbanshome.org www.columbansisters.org Sr. Corona Colleary, S.S.C., USA Area Leader;

STELLA NIAGARA

Holy Name Province - Provincial Motherhouse - 4421 Lower River Rd., Stella Niagara, NY 14144-1001 t) (716) 754-4312 jgrabowski@stellaosf.org www.stellaosf.org Sr. Jo-Anne Grabowski, O.S.F., Prov.; Srs.: 76

Buffalo Academy of the Sacred Heart, Inc. - 3860 Main St., Buffalo, NY 14226-3398; Mailing: 4421 Lower River Rd., Stella Niagara, NY 14144 t) 716-834-2101 www.sacredheartacademy.org

Center of Renewal, Inc. - t) 716-754-7376 centerofrenewal@stellaosf.org www.center-of-renewal.org

Francis Center - 335 24th St., Niagara Falls, NY 14303 t) 716-284-2050 msmith@franciscenter.com

The Providence Fund - marygracepolino8@gmail.com

Sisters of St. Francis of Holy Name Province, Inc. - 4421 Lower River Rd., Stella Niagara, NY 14144

The Sisters of St. Francis Retirement Fund - t) 716-876-3426 elizabethb1946@gmail.com

The Stella Niagara Education Park Endowment Foundation - t) 716-754-4314 snepoffice@yahoo.com www.stellaniagara.org

Stella Niagara Education Park, Inc. - 4421Lower River Rd., Stella Niagara, NY 14144 t) 716-754-4314 snepoffice@stella-niagara.com www.stella-niagara.org

ENDOWMENTS / FOUNDATIONS / TRUSTS [EFT]

ALLEGANY

Dr. Lyle F. Renodin Foundation, Inc. (Franciscan Ministries Corporation) - 115 E. Main St., Allegany, NY 14706 t) 716-373-1130 lwhitford@fsallegany.org www.renodinfoundation.org Mike DeRose, Chair; Laura Whitford, Pres.;

BUFFALO

St. Clare Apartments Housing Development Fund Company, Inc. - c/o Delta Development of Western New York, 525 Washington St., Buffalo, NY 14203 t) 716-847-1635 j.longergan@ccwny.org www.deltadevelopmentwny.com Low income housing for the elderly age 62 and over. James Lonergan, Exec.;

50-60 Kosciuszko Street Housing Development Fund Company, Inc. - 525 Washington St., Buffalo, NY 14203 t) 716-847-1635 j.lonergan@ccwny.org www.deltadevelopmentwny.com Special Purpose Housing for the chronically mentally ill. James Lonergan, Exec.;

The Foundation of the Roman Catholic Diocese of Buffalo, NY, Inc. - 795 Main St., Buffalo, NY 14203-1250 t) 716-847-8370 devoffice@buffalodiocese.org www.frcdb.org Nancy J Gugino, Dir.;

La Casa De Los Tainos Housing Development Fund Company, Inc. - 525 Washington St., Buffalo, NY 14203 t) 716-847-1635 j.lonergan@ccwny.org www.deltadevelopmentwny.com Low income housing for the elderly age 62 & over. James Lonergan, Exec.;

Monsignor Adamski Village Housing Development Fund Company, Inc. - 795 Main St., Buffalo, NY 14203 t) 716-847-5571 stimmel@buffalodiocese.org Steven D. Timmel, Treas.;

Monsignor Kirby Apartments Housing Development Fund Company, Inc. - 525 Washington St., Buffalo, NY 14203 t) 716-847-1635 j.lonergan@ccwny.org www.deltadevelopmentwny.com Low income housing for the elderly age 62 and over. James Lonergan, Exec.;

158 Chenango Street Housing Development Fund Company, Inc. (St. John Bosco Apartments) - 525 Washington St., Buffalo, NY 14203 t) 716-847-1635 j.lonergan@ccwny.org www.deltadevelopmentwny.com Low income housing for the elderly age 62 and over. James Lonergan, Exec.;

Sisters Hospital Foundation, Inc. - 2157 Main St, Buffalo, NY 14214; Mailing: 144 Genesee St., 6th Fl. W., Buffalo, NY 14203 t) 716-862-1990 asnyder@chsbuffalo.org www.chsbuffalo.org/fch/sisters Anne E. Snyder, Exec. Dir.;

Timon Towers Housing Development Fund Company, Inc. - 525 Washington St., Buffalo, NY 14203 t) 716-847-1635 j.lonergan@ccwny.org deltadevelopmentwny.com Low income housing for the mobility impaired and elderly. James Lonergan, Exec.;

St. Timothy's Park Villa Housing Development Fund Company, Inc. - 525 Washington St., Buffalo, NY 14203 t) 716-847-1635 j.lonergan@wnycc.org www.deltadevelopmentwny.com Low income housing for the elderly age 62 and over. James Lonergan, Exec.;

Wheatfield Housing Development Fund Company, Inc. - 525 Washington St., Buffalo, NY 14203 t) 716-847-1635 j.lonergan@ccwny.org www.deltadevelopmentwny.com Low income housing for the elderly age 62 and over. James Lonergan, Exec.;

KENMORE

Kenmore Mercy Foundation Inc. - 2950 Elmwood Ave., Kenmore, NY 14217; Mailing: 144 Genesee St., 6th Fl. W., Buffalo, NY 14203 t) 716-447-6204 sjandzin@chsbuffalo.org www.chsbuffalo.org/fch/kenmoremercy Susan Jandzinski, Exec. Dir.;

HOSPITALS / HEALTH SERVICES [HOS]

BUFFALO

Catholic Health System, Inc. - 144 Genesee St., Buffalo, NY 14203 t) 716-862-2400 webmaster@wnychs.org www.chsbuffalo.org Mark A Sullivan, Pres. & CEO; James Garvey, Exec. Vice Pres. & COO; Staff: 8,590

McAuley-Seton Home Care - 144 Genesee St., 2nd Fl., Buffalo, NY 14203; Mailing: 144 Genesee St., 6th Fl. W, Buffalo, NY 14203 t) 716-685-4870 tgleason@chsbuffalo.org Tom Gleason, Sr. Vice Pres. Home & Community Based Care; Dcn. Howard M. Morgan, Exec. Res.; Asstd. Annu.: 17,267; Staff: 303

Mercy Hospital - 565 Abbott Rd., Buffalo, NY 14220; Mailing: 144 Genesee St., 6th Fl. W., Buffalo, NY 14203 t) 716-862-2410 mborysza@chsbuffalo.org Sponsored by the Catholic Health System, Inc. Martin Boryszak, SVP Acute Care & Pres., Mercy Hospital of Buffalo; Jessica Visser, Vice Pres., Patient Care Svcs.; William Vaughan, Vice Pres., Mission Integration; Bed Capacity: 387; Asstd. Annu.: 164,415; Staff: 2,141

Sisters of Charity Hospital of Buffalo, NY - 2157 Main St., Buffalo, NY 14214; Mailing: 144 Genesee St., Legal Svcs., 6th Fl. W., Buffalo, NY 14203 t) 716-862-1000 achang@chsbuffalo.org www.chsbuffalo.org Aaron Chang, Pres.; Esther Sanborn, Vice Pres., Mission Integration; Bed Capacity: 413; Asstd. Annu.: 674,367; Staff: 1,824

St. Joseph Campus - 2605 Harlem Rd., Buffalo, NY 14225; Mailing: 144 Genesee St., Buffalo, NY 14203 t) 716-891-2400 lcamara@chsbuffalo.org

KENMORE

Kenmore Mercy Hospital - 2950 Elmwood Ave., Kenmore, NY 14217; Mailing: 144 Genesee St., 6th Fl. W., Buffalo, NY 14203 t) 716-447-6100 wludwig@chsbuffalo.org Sponsored by the Catholic Health System, Inc. Walter Ludwig, Pres.; Heather Telford, Vice Pres., Patient Care Svcs.; Dennis Mahaney, Exec. Res., Mission Integration; Bed Capacity: 184; Asstd. Annu.: 69,820; Staff: 951

LEWISTON

Mount St. Mary's Hospital of Niagara Falls (Catholic Health System, Inc.) - 5300 Military Rd., Lewiston, NY 14092-1997; Mailing: 144 Genesee St., Legal Svcs., 6th Fl. W., Buffalo, NY 14203 t) 716-297-4800 cjurlaub@chsbuffalo.org www.chsbuffalo.org CJ Urlaub, SVP SPI & Care Delivery NC, Pres., Mount St. Mary's Hospital; Healther Telford, Vice Pres., Patient Care Svcs.; Dennis Mahaney, Exec. Res.; Bed Capacity: 175; Asstd. Annu.: 104,933; Staff: 716

MISCELLANEOUS [MIS]

ALDEN

Magnificat - Gentle Women, Mother of Mercy, Buffalo, Inc. - 493 Four Rod Rd., Alden, NY 14004 t) 716-783-2894 marykay1219@yahoo.com A private association of the Christian faithful Mary Kay Schaub, Coord.;

ALLEGANY

Canticle Farm, Inc. - 115 E. Main St., Allegany, NY 14706 t) 716-373-0200 x3358 office@canticlefarm.org www.canticlefarm.org Shauna Keesler, Chair; Gina Anderson, Pres.;

St. Elizabeth Mission Society, Inc. - 115 E. Main St., Allegany, NY 14706; Mailing: PO Box 86, Allegany, NY 14706 t) 716-373-1130 stelizmission@fsallegany.org; lwhitford@fsallegany.org www.franciscanhope.org Supporting the missionary activities of the Franciscan Sisters of Allegany, NY Mark Ash, Chair; Laura Whitford, Pres.;

ATHOL SPRINGS

Fr. Justin Rosary Hour - 4190 St. Francis Dr., Athol Springs, NY 14010; Mailing: P.O. Box 442, Athol Springs, NY 14010 t) 716-627-3861 rosaryhour@yahoo.com www.rosaryhour.com Prayer and catechetical program

BUFFALO

St. Adalbert's Response to Love Center, Inc. - 130 Kosciuszko St., Buffalo, NY 14212 t) 716-894-7030 rtlcoffice@gmail.com www.responsetolove.org Sr. Mary Johnice Rzadkiewicz, C.S.S.F., Dir.;

Catholic Union Store - 795 Main St., Buffalo, NY 14203 t) 716-847-8707 spacillo@buffalodiocese.org Shelley Pacillo, Contact;

Delta Development of Western New York, Inc. - 525 Washington St., Buffalo, NY 14203 t) 716-847-1635 j.lonergan@ccwny.org James Lonergan, Dir.;

St. Joseph Investment Fund, Inc. - 795 Main St., Buffalo, NY 14203 t) 716-847-5500 pkaralus@buffalodiocese.org Rev. Peter J. Karalus, Pres.;

K M H Homes, INC. - 144 Genesee St., 6th Fl. W., Legal Svcs., Buffalo, NY 14203 t) 716-821-4469 lcamara@chsbuffalo.org A holding company of the Catholic Health System. Walter Ludwig, Pres.; Mark A Sullivan, Secy.;

Ladies of Charity of Buffalo, Inc. - 1122 Broadway, Buffalo, NY 14212 t) 716-895-4001 julie.lulek@ccwny.org locbuffalony.org/ A ministry of service to the needy in the spirit of St. Vincent de Paul and St. Louise de Marillac, and affiliated with Catholic Charities. Julie Lulek, Sr. Dir.;

Monsignor Adamski Village, Inc. - 795 Main St., Buffalo, NY 14203 t) 716-847-5571 cmendolera@buffalodiocese.org Facility for elderly and handicapped persons of low income. Chuck Mendolara, CFO;

The Monsignor Carr Institute - 76 W. Humboldt Pkwy., Buffalo, NY 14214 t) 716-895-1033; 877-448-4466 megan.lostracco@ccwny.org www.ccwny.org Licensed outpatient mental health services for children through adults, substance use treatment and relationship counseling. Megan Lostracco-Reed, Dir.;

Mount St. Mary's Housing Development Fund Company, Inc. - 525 Washington St., Buffalo, NY 14203 t) 716-847-1635 j.lonergan@ccwny.org www.deltadevelopmentwny.com James Lonergan, Exec.;

NyPPaW Fides, Inc. - 625 Abbott Rd., Buffalo, NY 14220 t) 716-826-5051 Sr. Judith Frikker, Pres.;

Oblate Vocation Office, Northeast Area - 18 Greenwood Pl., Buffalo, NY 14213 t) 210-349-1475 vocations@omiusa.org Rev. Victor Manuel Patricio-Silva, OMI;

Our Lady of Victory Community Housing Development Organization, Inc. - 144 Genesee St., Legal Svcs., 6th Fl. W., Buffalo, NY 14203 t) 716-821-4469 lcamara@chsbuffalo.org Tom Gleason, SVP Home & Community Based Care;

Our Lady of Victory Renaissance Corporation - 144 Genesee St., 6th Fl. W., Legal Svcs., Buffalo, NY 14203 t) 716-821-4469 tgleason@chsbuffalo.org Tom Gleason, SVP Home & Community Based Care;

Our Mother of Good Counsel Housing Development Fund Co., Inc. - 525 Washington St., Buffalo, NY 14203 t) 716-847-1635 j.lonergan@ccwny.org www.deltadevelopmentwny.com Housing for mobility impaired & elderly (62 & up) of low income. James Lonergan, Exec.;

Salesian Studios - 152 Plymouth Ave., Buffalo, NY 14201-1214 t) 716-886-6597 tribits@yahoo.com Rev. Thomas Ribits, O.S.F.S., Dir.;

Santa Maria Towers Housing Development Fund Company, Inc. - 525 Washington St., Buffalo, NY 14203 t) 716-847-1635 j.lonergan@ccwny.org www.deltadevelopmentwny.com Housing for mobility impaired & elderly age 62 and older of low income. James Lonergan, Exec.;

Victorious Missionaries - 795 Main St., Buffalo, NY 14203; Mailing: 20 Mayfield Dr., West Seneca, NY 14224 t) 716-657-1784 papadeak@verizon.net A spiritual and social movement for the disabled and chronically ill. Carol A. Buchla, Pres.; Dcn. Dennis W. Kapsiak;

CHEEKTOWAGA

Diocesan Counseling Center for Clergy & Religious - 16 Columbus St., Cheektowaga, NY 14227 t) 716-894-2743 james.croglio@ccwny.org Affiliated with Catholic Charities. Rev. James C. Croglio, Dir.;

CLARENCE

Brothers of Mercy Management Company, Inc. - 4520 Ransom Rd., Clarence, NY 14031 t) 716-759-6985 x200 widmer@brothersofmercy.org Peter Eimer, CEO; Joe Widmer, Exec.;

Brothers of Mercy of Montabaur Apartment Complex

Inc. - 4520 Ransom Rd., Clarence, NY 14031 t) 716-407-5100 peter@brothersofmercy.org www.brothersofmercy.org Peter Eimer, CEO;

DEPEW

Catholic Health System Infusion Pharmacy, Inc. - 6350 Transit Rd., Depew, NY 14043; Mailing: 144 Genesee St., Legal Svcs., 6th Fl. W., Buffalo, NY 14203 t) 716-685-4870 tgleason@chsbuffalo.org A Catholic Health System organization. Thomas Gleason, Exec.;

LACKAWANNA

Our Lady of Victory Homes of Charity (Society for the Protection of Destitute Roman Catholic Children at Buffalo, NY) (d/b/a "Father Baker's") (d/b/a OLV Charities) - 780 Ridge Rd., Lackawanna, NY 14218 t) 716-828-9648 dkersten@homesofcharity.org www.olvcharities.org David Kersten, CEO;

Our Lady of Victory Institutions, Inc. - 780 Ridge Rd., Lackawanna, NY 14218 t) 716-828-9640 dlipuma@ourladyofvictory.org Rev. Msgr. David G. LiPuma, Pst.;

NORTH TONAWANDA

Niagara Homemaker Services, Inc. (Mercy Home Care of Western New York) - 3571 Niagara Falls Blvd., North Tonawanda, NY 14120; Mailing: 144 Genesee St., 6th Fl. W., Buffalo, NY 14203 t) 716-668-3511 tgleason@chsbuffalo.org chsbuffalo.org Tom Gleason, SVP Home & Community Based Care; Dcn. Howard M. Morgan, Exec. Res.;

STELLA NIAGARA

DeSales Resources and Ministries, Inc. (Embraced by God) - 4421 Lower River Rd., Stella Niagara, NY 14144-1001 t) 716-754-4948; 800-782-2270 resources@embracedbygod.org www.embracedbygod.org Joanne Kinney, Admin.; Shelly Yamonaco, Bus. Mgr.;

MONASTERIES AND RESIDENCES FOR PRIESTS AND BROTHERS [MON]

BUFFALO

The Canisius Jesuit Community, Inc. - 2001 Main St., Loyola Hall, Buffalo, NY 14208 t) 716-883-7000 tslon@jesuits.org www.canisius.edu Rev. Thomas R. Slon, S.J., Rector; Rev. David S. Ciancimino, S.J., Pres., Canisius High School; Rev. Charles A. Frederico, S.J., Dir. Campus Ministry, Canisius High School; Rev. Michael P. Corcoran, S.J., Campus Min.; Rev. Edward J. Durkin, S.J., Prin., Nativity Miguel Middle School; Rev. Daniel P. Jamros, S.J., Prof. Emer., Canisius College; Rev. Patrick J. Lynch, S.J., Prof. Emer., Canisius College; Priests: 7

The Discalced Carmelite Nuns of Buffalo - Discalced Carmelite Monastery of the Little Flower of Jesus, 75 Carmel Rd., Buffalo, NY 14214 t) 716-837-6499 carmelofbuffalo74@gmail.com buffalocarmel.org Mother Teresa of Jesus, OCD, Prioress; Srs.: 15

CLARENCE

Brothers of Mercy of Mary Help of Christians, Inc. - 4520 Ransom Rd., Clarence, NY 14031 t) (716) 407-3820 x720 (Phone number change.) kenneth@brothersofmercy.org www.brothersofmercy.org Rev. Thomas Roman, Chap.; Bro. Edward E Lewis, FMMA, Vicar; Bro. Kenneth Thomas, F.M.M.A, Supr.; Brs.: 6

DEPEW

Msgr. Conniff Residence - 68 Cowing St., Depew, NY 14043 t) 716-393-3595 eluterek@buffalodiocese.org Rev. David J. Borowiak; Rev. Thomas J. Wopperer; Rev. Lawrence F. Cobel, In Res.; Rev. Richard S. DiGiulio, In Res.; Rev. Msgr. Frederick D. Leising, In Res.; Rev. John J. Mitka, In Res.; Rev. John J. Sardina, In Res.; Rev. Conrad P. Stachowiak, In Res.; Rev. Msgr. W. Jerome Sullivan, In Res.; Rev. Emil P. Swiatek, In Res.; Brs.: 11; Priests: 11

HAMBURG

St. Francis of Assisi Friary - 4214 St. Francis Dr., Hamburg, NY 14075 t) 716-627-5762 sfhsfriary@gmail.com www.stfrancishigh.org Faculty Residence for St. Francis High School Friar Antonio Moualeu, OFM Conv., Campus Min.; Rev. Bryan B. Hajovsky, O.F.M.Conv., Teacher; Bro. Daniel Geary, O.F.M.Conv., In Res.; Rev. Francis Lombardo, O.F.M.Conv., In Res.; Bro. Timothy Blanchard, OFM Conv., Institutional Advancement; Rev. Mark David Skura, O.F.M.Conv., Teacher; Rev. Matthew Foley, O.F.M., Pres.; Rev. Maximilian Avila, OFM Conv., Supr.; Brs.: 2; Priests: 6

St. Maximilian Kolbe Friary - 4190 St. Francis Dr., Hamburg, NY 14075; Mailing: P.O. Box 182, Athol Springs, NY 14010 t) 716-627-2710 fr.ross@verizon.net Rev. Ross M. Syracuse, O.F.M.Conv., Pst.; Rev. Daniel G. Fink, O.F.M.Conv., Supr.; Rev. Romulus Rosolowski, O.F.M.Conv., Par. Vicar; Rev. Justin Kusibab, O.F.M.Conv., In Res.; Rev. Alexander Cymerman, OFM Conv, In Res.; Priests: 6

Fr. Justin Senior Friars Residence - t) 716-627-5203 fbfincoaltownpa@yahoo.com

LACKAWANNA

Bishop Head Residence - 10 Rosary Ave., Lackawanna, NY 14218 t) 716-824-4644 dgolinski2@buffalodiocese.org Rev. Msgr. James E. Wall; Rev. Larry Milby; Rev. Charles R. Amico, In Res.; Rev. James M. Augustyn, In Res.; Rev. Msgr. James F. Campbell, In Res.; Rev. Peter J. Drilling, In Res.; Rev. Joseph G. Fifagrowicz, In Res.; Rev. David G. Griffin, In Res.; Rev. John S. Kwiecien, In Res.; Rev. Paul M. Nogaro, In Res.; Rev. Harry F. Szczesniak, In Res.; Rev. Msgr. William O. Wangler, In Res.; Rev. Charles J. Zadora, In Res.; Brs.: 14; Priests: 14

LE ROY

Our Lady of Mercy Friary - 44 Lake St., Le Roy, NY 14482-9701 t) 585-768-6543 frbrentwood@ourladyofmercyleroy.org www.orderofmercy.org Rev. Scottston F. Brentwood, OdeM, Pst.; Brs.: 1; Priests: 2

NIAGARA UNIVERSITY

Vincentian Community at Niagara University (Congregation of the Mission of St. Vincent de Paul) - Vincentian Residence, Niagara University, NY 14109-2209; Mailing: PO Box 2209, Niagara University, NY 14109-2209 t) 716-286-8110 Rev. Gregory P. Cozzubbo, CM, Supr.; Rev. James J. Maher, C.M., Pres.; Rev. Joseph G. Hubbert, C.M.; Rev. Vincent J. O'Malley, C.M.; Rev. Gregory J. Semeniuk, CM; Rev. Subhashisa Mandel, CM (India); Bro. Martin J. Schneider, C.M.; Brs.: 1; Priests: 8

NORTH TONAWANDA

Society of the Catholic Apostolate - 3452 Niagara Falls Blvd., North Tonawanda, NY 14120-0563; Mailing: P.O. Box 563, North Tonawanda, NY 14120-0563 t) 716-694-4313 Rev. Severyn J. Koszyk, S.A.C.; Rev. John Posiewala, S.A.C., Rector; Priests: 2

ST. BONAVENTURE

St. Bonaventure Friary - 1 Friary Cir., St. Bonaventure, NY 14778 t) 716-375-2423 Rev. Ross Chamberland, O.F.M., Admin.; Rev. David D. Blake, O.F.M., Prof.; Rev. Michael D. Calabria, O.F.M., Prof.; Rev. David Couturier, O.F.M.Cap., Prof.; Rev. Kyle Haden, O.F.M., Prof.; Rev. Peter Schneible, O.F.M., Prof.; Rev. Xavier John Seubert, OFM, Guardian; Rev. Michael Reyes, OFM, In Res.; Bro. Robert Joseph Lentz, OFM, In Res.; Rev. Dominic V. Monti, O.F.M., Vicar; Brs.: 2; Priests: 9

TONAWANDA

O'Hara Residence - 69 O'Hara Rd., Tonawanda, NY 14150-6227 t) 716-743-0037 ohararetirementhome@buffalodiocese.org Rev. Paul R. Bossi, In Res.; Rev. Msgr. Angelo M. Caligiuri, In Res.; Rev. Msgr. Thomas E. Crane, In Res.; Rev. James F. Hassett, In Res.; Rev. Msgr. James G. Kelly, In Res.; Rev. Msgr. Dino J. Lorenzetti, In Res.; Rev. Msgr. J. Thomas Moran, In Res.; Rev. Msgr. John M. Ryan, In Res.; Rev. Msgr. Joseph J. Sicari, In Res.; Rev. Robert A. Stolinski, In Res.; Rev. Paul L. Varuvel, In Res.; Brs.: 11; Priests: 11

NURSING / REHABILITATION / CONVALESCENCE / ELDERLY CARE [NUR]

CLARENCE

Brothers of Mercy Housing Co., Inc. - 10500 Bergtold Rd., Clarence, NY 14031 t) 716-759-2122 peter@brothersofmercy.org www.brothersofmercy.org Affordable, Independent Senior Housing Peter Eimer, CEO; Asstd. Annu.: 115; Staff: 4

Brothers of Mercy Nursing & Rehabilitation Center - 10570 Bergtold Rd., Clarence, NY 14031 t) 716-759-6985 peter@brothersofmercy.org www.brothersofmercy.org Teresa Dillsworth, Admin.; Peter Eimer, CEO; Asstd. Annu.: 925; Staff: 359

Brothers of Mercy Sacred Heart Home, Inc. - 4526 Ransom Rd., Clarence, NY 14031 t) 716-759-2644 mindee@brothersofmercy.org; peter@brothersofmercy.org www.brothersofmercy.org Mindee McDonald, Admin.; Peter Eimer, CEO; Asstd. Annu.: 110; Staff: 133

KENMORE

McAuley Residence - 1503 Military Rd., Kenmore, NY 14217; Mailing: 144 Genesee St., 6th Fl. W., Buffalo, NY 14203 t) 716-447-6600 jdurno@chsbuffalo.org Residential Health Care Facility, Sponsored by the Catholic Health System, Inc. Dcn. Howard M. Morgan; John Durno, Admin.; Asstd. Annu.: 1,044; Staff: 231

LEWISTON

Our Lady of Peace, Inc. - 5285 Lewiston Rd., Lewiston, NY 14092 t) 314-292-9308 ahscm-mission@ascension.org www.ascensionliving.org/ Ryan Endsley, COO; Asstd. Annu.: 266; Staff: 221

ORCHARD PARK

Father Baker Manor - 6400 Powers Rd., Orchard Park, NY 14127; Mailing: 144 Genesee St., 6th Fl. W., Buffalo, NY 14203 t) 716-667-0001 mwheeler@chsbuffalo.org www.chsbuffalo.org Mark Wheeler, Admin.; Dcn. Howard M. Morgan, Exec. Res.; Asstd. Annu.: 631; Staff: 218

SILVER CREEK

St. Columbans on the Lake, Home for the Aged - 2546 Lake Rd., Silver Creek, NY 14136 t) 716-934-4515 ccolleary@stcolumbanshome.org www.stcolumbanshome.org Sr. Corona Colleary, S.S.C., Admin.; Rev. Vincent McCarthy, S.S.C., In Res.; Asstd. Annu.: 150; Staff: 40

PRESCHOOLS / CHILDCARE CENTERS [PRE]

BUFFALO

German Roman Catholic Orphan Home - 795 Main St., Buffalo, NY 14203 t) 716-847-5534 rmurphy@buffalodiocese.org Inactive.

SALAMANCA

Camp Turner - 9150 Allegany State Park Rte. 3, Salamanca, NY 14779; Mailing: P.O. Box 264, Salamanca, NY 14779 t) 716-354-4555 campturner@gmail.com www.campturner.com Resident Camp and Conference Center operated by the Catholic Diocese of Buffalo. Currently not in operation. John Mann, Dir.;

RETREAT HOUSES / RENEWAL CENTERS [RTR]

WEST CLARKSVILLE

Mount Irenaeus, Franciscan Mountain Retreat & Holy Peace Friary (Order of Friars Minor Holy Name Province) - 3621 Roberts Rd., West Clarksville, NY 14786; Mailing: P.O. Box 100, West Clarksville, NY 14786 t) 585-973-2470 mmarc@sbu.edu www.mountainonline.org Rev. Daniel P. Riley, O.F.M., Animator/Founder; Rev. Louis M. McCormick, O.F.M.; Bro. Joseph A. Kotula, O.F.M., Vicar; Bro. Kevin Kriso, O.F.M, Guardian;

SEMINARIES [SEM]

EAST AURORA

Christ the King Seminary - 711 Knox Rd, East Aurora, NY 14052; Mailing: P.O. Box 607, East Aurora, NY 14052 t) 716-847-5500 rsiepka@cks.edu www.cks.edu Fosters formation/education of priests, permanent deacons, and lay ecclesial ministers at other approved institutions. Rev. Msgr. Richard W. Siepka, Rector;

YOUNGSTOWN

St. Anthony M. Zaccaria Seminary - 981 Swann Rd., Youngstown, NY 14174-0167; Mailing: PO Box 167, Youngstown, NY 14174-0167 t) 716-754-7448 pmccrsp@fatimashrine.com www.fatimashrine.com Rev. Richard M. Delzingaro, C.R.S.P., Chancellor; Rev. Julio M. Ciavaglia, C.R.S.P., Vicar; Rev. Peter M. Calabrese, C.R.S.P., Supr.; Rev. Francesco Papa, CRSP, Formator; Stds.: 1

SHRINES [SHR]

NORTH TONAWANDA

Shrine of the Infant Jesus - 3452 Niagara Falls Blvd., North Tonawanda, NY 14120-0563; Mailing: P.O. Box 563, North Tonawanda, NY 14120-0563 t) 716-694-4313 posiewala@verizon.net Administered by the Pallottine Fathers. Rev. John Posiewala, S.A.C., Supr.; Rev. Severyn J. Koszyk, S.A.C., In Res.;

YOUNGSTOWN

Basilica of the National Shrine of Our Lady of Fatima, Inc. - 1023 Swann Rd., Youngstown, NY 14174-0167; Mailing: PO Box 167, Youngstown, NY 14174 t) 716-754-7489 office@fatimashrine.com www.fatimashrine.com Rev. Richard M. Delzingaro, C.R.S.P.; Rev. Peter M. Calabrese, C.R.S.P., Rector; Rev. Francesco Papa, CRSP, Assoc. Dir.; Rev. Julio M. Ciavaglia, C.R.S.P., Rector Emeritus;

SPECIAL CARE FACILITIES [SPF]

BUFFALO

St. Francis of Buffalo, Inc. - 144 Genesee St., Legal Svcs., 6th Fl. W., Buffalo, NY 14203 t) 716-821-4469 lcamara@chsbuffalo.org Formerly known as St. Francis Hospital. Leonardo Sette-Camara, Exec.; Bed Capacity: 36; Asstd. Annu.: 72; Staff: 20

LACKAWANNA

***Baker Victory Services (OLV Human Services)** - 790 Ridge Rd., Lackawanna, NY 14218 t) 716-828-9500; 888-287-1160 clee@olvhs.org www.olvhumanservices.org Assists children, adults and families through a variety of programs. Rev. Msgr. David G. LiPuma, Pres.; Cindy Lee, CEO;

An asterisk (*) denotes an organization that has established tax-exempt status directly with the IRS and is not covered by the USCCB Group Ruling.

Diocese of Burlington

(Dioecesis Burlingtonensis)

MOST REVEREND CHRISTOPHER JAMES COYNE

Bishop of Burlington; ordained June 7, 1986; appointed Auxiliary Bishop of the Archdiocese of Indianapolis January 14, 2011; ordained and installed as Auxiliary Bishop of Indianapolis March 2, 2011; appointed Apostolic Administrator of Indianapolis September 21, 2011; resigned Apostolic Administrator December 3, 2012; appointed Bishop of Burlington December 22, 2014; installed January 29, 2015.

Chancery Office: 55 Joy Dr., South Burlington, VT 05403. T: 802-658-6110; F: 802-658-0436. www.vermontcatholic.org

ESTABLISHED JULY 29, 1853.

Square Miles 9,135.

Comprises the State of Vermont.

For legal titles of parishes and diocesan institutions, consult the Chancery Office.

STATISTICAL OVERVIEW

Personnel
Bishop....1
Priests: Diocesan Active in Diocese....37
Priests: Diocesan Active Outside Diocese....1
Priests: Retired, Sick or Absent....26
Number of Diocesan Priests....64
Religious Priests in Diocese....30
Total Priests in your Diocese....94
Extern Priests in Diocese....6
Ordinations:
Diocesan Priests....2
Permanent Deacons....7
Permanent Deacons in Diocese....42
Total Brothers....15
Total Sisters....50

Parishes
Parishes....66
With Resident Pastor:
Resident Diocesan Priests....31
Resident Religious Priests....10
Without Resident Pastor:
Administered by Priests....24
Administered by Deacons....1
Completely vacant....2
Missions....20
Pastoral Centers....1
Closed Parishes....7
Professional Ministry Personnel:
Lay Ministers....10

Welfare
Homes for the Aged....4
Total Assisted....133
Special Centers for Social Services....2
Total Assisted....2,356

Educational
Diocesan Students in Other Seminaries....7
Total Seminarians....7
Colleges and Universities....1
Total Students....1,400
High Schools, Diocesan and Parish....3
Total Students....455
Elementary Schools, Diocesan and Parish....10
Total Students....1,099
Elementary Schools, Private....2
Total Students....427
Catechesis/Religious Education:
High School Students....165
Elementary Students....1,258
Total Students under Catholic Instruction....4,811
Teachers in Diocese:
Priests....2
Lay Teachers....316

Vital Statistics
Receptions into the Church:
Infant Baptism Totals....357
Minor Baptism Totals....40
Adult Baptism Totals....32
Received into Full Communion....48
First Communions....372
Confirmations....657
Marriages:
Catholic....128
Interfaith....36
Total Marriages....164
Deaths....1,154
Total Catholic Population....100,000
Total Population....645,570

LEADERSHIP

Chancery Office - t) 802-658-6110
Vicar General, Moderator of the Curia and Chancellor - Rev. Msgr. John J. McDermott, Vicar;
Vicar for Clergy - Rev. Msgr. Peter A. Routhier, Vicar;
Finance Office - t) 802-658-6110 Guy Scheiwiller, Diocesan Finance Officer;
Office of the Tribunal - t) 802-658-6110 Rev. Luke P. Austin, Vicar;
Judicial Vicar - Rev. Luke P. Austin;
Case Director - Susan Wing, Dir.;
Judges - Rev. Daniel J. Jordan; Rev. Luke P. Austin;
Promoter of Justice - Rev. Msgr. John J. McDermott;
Defenders of the Bond - Rev. Roger L. Charbonneau; Rev. Thomas V. Mattison; Rev. Msgr. John J. McDermott;
Advocate - Rev. Msgr. Peter A. Routhier;
Notaries - Rev. Roger L. Charbonneau; Rev. John G. Feltz; Susan Wing;
Diocesan Administrative Board - Rev. Msgr. John J. McDermott; Rev. Msgr. Peter A. Routhier; Robert A. Roy;
Diocesan Consultors - Rev. Msgr. John J. McDermott; Rev. Msgr. Peter A. Routhier; Rev. Yvon J. Royer;
Deans - Rev. Msgr. Bernard W. Bourgeois; Rev. Yvon J. Royer; Rev. Patrick J. Forman;
Canon 1742 Panel of Pastors - Rev. William R. Beaudin; Rev. Charles R. Danielson; Rev. Jerome Mercure;

OFFICES AND DIRECTORS

The Blue Army (World Apostolate of Fatima) -
Building Commission - t) 802-658-6110 Peter Beauregard;
Catholic Campaign for Human Development - t) 802-658-6110
Catholic Committee on Scouting - David Ely, Chair; Norbert Vogel, Treas.;
Catholic Daughters of The Americas - Rev. Patrick J. Forman, Chap.;
Catholic Relief Services - t) 802-658-6110
Censor Librorum - Rev. Lance W. Harlow;
Charismatic Renewal - t) 802-479-9407 Rev. Lance W. Harlow; Dcn. Daniel Pudvah;
Daughters of Isabella -
Development Office - t) 802-658-6110 Ellen Kane, Exec. Dir.;
Diocesan Archives - Rev. Msgr. John J. McDermott; Kathleen Messier, Asst. Archivist;
Diocesan Director of Catholic Cemeteries - t) 802-658-6110 Peter Beauregard;
Diocesan Director of Facilities - t) 802-658-6110 Peter Beauregard;
Diocesan Director of Human Resources - t) 802-658-6110 Mary Foster;
Diocesan Finance Council - Guy Scheiwiller, Finance Officer; Rev. Msgr. John J. McDermott; Rev. Msgr. Peter A. Routhier;
Ecumenical Commission -
House of Discernment - t) 802-862-8403 Rev. Msgr. John J. McDermott;
Knights of Columbus - Rev. Timothy P. Naples;
Liturgical Commission - t) 802-658-6110 Joshua Perry;
Magazine - t) 802-658-6110 Ellen Kane, Editor;
Marriage Encounter, Vermont -
Media Relations - Ellen Kane;
National Shrine of the Immaculate Conception, Washington (Vacant) -
Office of Continuing Education for Clergy - t) 802-524-2585 Rev. Msgr. Peter A. Routhier;
Office of Diocesan Pastoral Planning - Rev. Msgr. John J. McDermott, Dir.;
Office of Pastoral Ministries - Dcn. Phil Lawson, Exec. Dir.;
Office of Permanent Diaconate Ministry - Dcn. Peter Gummere;
Office of Safe Environment Programs - John Pfeifer, Mgr. Prog.;
Priests' Benefit Fund - t) 802-658-6110 Rev. William R. Beaudin, Chair;
Prison Ministry - Dcn. Gerald Scilla;
Propagation of the Faith - Rev. Msgr. Peter A. Routhier;
The Review Board - John Pfeifer; Rev. Msgr. John J. McDermott; George Ashline;
Superintendent of Catholic Schools - t) 802-658-6110 David Young, Supt. (davidyoung@vermontcatholic.org);
Vermont Catholic Charities, Inc. - Mary Beth Pinard, Exec. Dir.;
Vermont Catholic Community Foundation - t) 802-658-6110 x1226 ekane@vermontcatholic.org Ellen Kane, Exec. Dir.;
Vermont Cursillo - Rev. Dwight H. Baker, Spiritual Dir.;
Victim's Assistance Coordinator - Sheila Conroy;
Vocations and Seminarians - t) 802-658-6110 Rev. James C. Dodson, Dir.;

PARISHES, MISSIONS, AND CLERGY

STATE OF VERMONT

BARRE

St. Monica - 79 Summer St., Barre, VT 05641 t) 802-476-4020 (CRP); 802-479-3253 stmonica@vermontcatholic.org Rev. Patrick J. Forman, Pst.; Rev. Robert Murphy, Par. Vicar; Dcn. Daniel Pudvah; CRP Stds.: 37

St. Monica - St. Michael School - (Grades PreSchool-8) t) 802-476-5015 smsmschool.org/ Stds.: 141; Scholastics: 141; Lay Tchrs.: 18

BARTON

Most Holy Trinity - 85 St. Paul Ln., Barton, VT 05822 t) 802-525-3711 mostholytrinity@vermontcatholic.org mostholytrinityparishvt.com/ Parish includes St. Paul, Barton, St. Theresa, Orleans & St. John Vianney, Irasburg. Rev. Curtis Miller, Pst.; CRP Stds.: 12

St. Paul School - (Grades PreK-8) 54 Eastern Ave., Barton, VT 05822 t) 802-525-6578 Joanne Beloin, Prin.;

BELLOWS FALLS

St. Charles - 31 Cherry Hill St., Bellows Falls, VT 05101 t) 802-463-3128 stcharles@vermontcatholic.org stcharles.vermontcatholic.org/ Rev. Agnel Samy, H.G.N., Admin.; Dcn. RJ Dourney; Julie Sines, DRE; CRP Stds.: 3

BENNINGTON

Sacred Heart St. Francis de Sales Parish Charitable Trust - 238 Main St., Bennington, VT 05201 t) 802-442-3141 benncath@comcast.net www.sacredheartsaintfrancis.com Rev. Kevin M. Russeau, C.S.C., Pst.; Rev. Hugh Cleary, C.S.C., Assoc. Pst.; CRP Stds.: 57

The School of Sacred Heart St. Francis de Sales - (Grades PreK-8) 307 School St., Bennington, VT 05201 t) 802-442-2446 estesdb@comcast.net David B. Estes, Prin.; Marcia Hendery, Librn.; Kathy Murphy, Librn.;

BETHEL

Our Lady of the Valley Parish - 221 Church St., Bethel, VT 05032; Mailing: P.O. Box 428, Randolph, VT 05060 t) (802) 728-5251 olv@vermontcatholic.org www.ourladyvt.org Parish includes: St. Anthony, Bethel & St. Elizabeth, Rochester. Rev. Scott A. Gratton, Pst.; Rev. Brandon C. Schneider, Par. Vicar; CRP Stds.: 5

BRADFORD

Our Lady of Perpetual Help - 113 Upper Plain, Bradford, VT 05033 t) 802-222-5268 ourladyofperpetualhelp@vermontcatholic.org uppervalleyparishes.org Rev. Andrzej Bednarowicz, Admin.; Dcn. Christopher Noble; CRP Stds.: 18

St. Francis of Assisi -

St. Eugene -

Our Lady of Light -

BRANDON

Our Lady of Good Help (St. Mary) - 38 Carver St., Brandon, VT 05733 t) 802-247-6351 ourladyofgoodhelp@vermontcatholic.org www.ovcc.vermontcatholic.org Rev. Maurice Moreau, OFM Cap, Pst.; CRP Stds.: 2

BRATTLEBORO

St. Michael - 47 Walnut St., Brattleboro, VT 05301 t) 802-257-5101 stmichael@vermontcatholic.org stmichaelvt.com Rev. Henry P. Furman, Pst.; Rev. Gregory Caldwell, Par. Vicar; CRP Stds.: 17

St. Michael School - (Grades PreK-12) 48 Walnut St., Brattleboro, VT 05301 t) 802-254-6320 lindsayoneil@smsvt.info saintmichaelschoolvt.org Elaine Beam, Prin.; Stds.: 125; Lay Tchrs.: 13

BRISTOL

St. Ambrose - 11 School St., Bristol, VT 05443 t) 802-453-2488 ocdedits@nrpdirect.com Rev. Steven Marchand, Admin.; CRP Stds.: 26

BURLINGTON

Cathedral of St. Joseph - 29 Allen St., Burlington, VT 05401; Mailing: 113 Elmwood Ave., Burlington, VT 05401 t) 802-658-4333 sjvt@comcast.net www.stjosephcathedralvt.org Rev. Msgr. Peter A. Routhier, Rector; CRP Stds.: 10

Christ the King-St. Anthony - 305 Flynn Ave., Burlington, VT 05401 t) 802-862-5784 ctkstaoffice@vermontcatholic.org; mcade@vermontcatholic.org www.christandanthony.com Parish includes Christ the King, Burlington & St. Anthony, Burlington. Rev. Justin J. Baker, Pst.; Meghan Cade, DRE; CRP Stds.: 21

St. Mark's - 1251 North Ave., Burlington, VT 05408 t) 802-864-7686 stmark@vermontcatholic.org www.stmarksvt.com Rev. Dallas T. St. Peter, Pst.; Rev. Timothy Sullivan, In Res.; CRP Stds.: 10

CAMBRIDGE

St. Mary - 312 N. Main St., Cambridge, VT 05444; Mailing: PO Box 129, Cambridge, VT 05444 t) 802-644-5073 stmarys@pshift.com Rev. Richard Calapan, Admin.;

CASTLETON

St. John the Baptist - 45 North Rd., Castleton, VT 05735; Mailing: PO Box 128, Castleton, VT 05735 t) (802) 671-8139 (Parish Office) westernvermontchurches@vermontcatholic.org ourladysevendolors.vermontcatholic.org/ Rev. Steven Scarmozzino, Pst.; CRP Stds.: 2

CHARLOTTE

Our Lady of Mount Carmel - 2894 Spear St., Charlotte, VT 05445; Mailing: P.O. Box 158, Charlotte, VT 05445 t) 802-425-2637 carmel@vermontcatholic.org olmcvt.org Rev. James E. Zuccaro, Pst.; CRP Stds.: 13

COLCHESTER

Holy Cross - 416 Church Rd., Colchester, VT 05446 t) 802-863-3002 parishoffice@holycrossvt.org holycross-olog.vermontcatholic.org Rev. Thomas V. Mattison, Par. Vicar; Dorine Boucher, DRE; CRP Stds.: 22

Our Lady of Grace - 800 Main St., Colchester, VT 05446 t) 802-878-5987 ourladyofgrace@vermontcatholic.org holycross-olog.vermontcatholic.org Rev. Dallas T. St. Peter, Pst.; Rev. Thomas V. Mattison, Par. Vicar; Veronica Hershberger, Pst. Min./Coord.; CRP Stds.: 28

ENOSBURG FALLS

St. John the Baptist - 222 Missisquoi St., Enosburg Falls, VT 05450; Mailing: P.O. Box 563, Enosburg Falls, VT 05450 t) 802-933-4464 stjohnvt@vermontcatholic.org stjohnbaptistvt.com Rev. Daniel J. Jordan, Pst.; Rev. Romanus Igweonu, Par. Vicar; Dcn. George Flower; Karoline Flower, DRE; CRP Stds.: 56

ESSEX JUNCTION

Holy Family-St. Lawrence - 4 Prospect St., Essex Junction, VT 05452 t) 802-878-5331 john.mcmahon@essexcatholic.org; holyfamily2@comcast.net www.essexcatholic@vermontcatholic.org Parish includes Holy Family, Essex Junction & St. Lawrence, Essex Junction. Rev. Charles H. Ranges, S.S.E., Pst.; John McMahon, DRE; CRP Stds.: 40

St. Pius X - 20 Jericho Rd., Essex Junction, VT 05452-2707 t) 802-878-5997 saintpiusx@comcast.net www.essexcatholic@vermontcatholic.org Rev. Charles H. Ranges, S.S.E., Pst.; Dcn. Gerald Scilla; CRP Stds.: 40

FAIR HAVEN

Our Lady of Seven Dolors - 10 Washington St., Fair Haven, VT 05743; Mailing: 45 North Rd., Castleton, VT 05735 t) (802) 671-8139 (Parish Office) westernvermontchurches@vermontcatholic.org ourladysevendolors.vermontcatholic.org/ Rev. Steven Scarmozzino, Pst.; CRP Stds.: 7

FAIRFAX

St. Luke - 17 Huntville Rd., Fairfax, VT 05454-0007; Mailing: P.O. Box 7, Fairfax, VT 05454-0007 t) 802-849-6205 office@stlukevt.org wwwstlukevt.org Rev. Karl A. Hahr, Pst.; CRP Stds.: 50

Ascension -

FAIRFIELD

St. Patrick - 116 Church Rd., Fairfield, VT 05455; Mailing: P.O. Box 18, Fairfield, VT 05455 t) 802-827-3203 stpats@vermontcatholic.org Rev. Jerome Mercure, Pst.; CRP Stds.: 64

St. Anthony-St. George -

HARDWICK

Mary Queen of All Saints Parish - 193 S. Main St., Hardwick, VT 05843; Mailing: PO Box 496, Hardwick, VT 05843 t) 802-472-5544 mqas@vermontcatholic.org; cparchment@vermontcatholic.org www.mqasvt.org Parish includes St. Norbert, Hardwick; St. Michael, Greensboro Bend & Our Lady of Fatima, Craftsbury. Rev. Thomas Aquinas Giragori Chinnappan, HGN, Admin.; Susan Sibley, DRE; CRP Stds.: 8

HINESBURG

St. Jude the Apostle - 10759 Rte. 116, Hinesburg, VT 05461-0069; Mailing: P.O. Box 69, Hinesburg, VT 05461-0069 t) 802-482-2290 stjude@vermontcatholic.org stjudevt.org Rev. James E. Zuccaro, Pst.; Dcn. Patrick Leduc; CRP Stds.: 22

LUDLOW

Annunciation of the Blessed Virgin Mary - 7 Depot St., Ludlow, VT 05149 t) 802-228-3451 abvmludlow@comcast.net churchoftheannunciationludlow.org/ Rev. Thomas L. Mosher, Pst.; Eileen Dunseith, DRE;

MANCHESTER CENTER

Christ Our Savior Parish - 398 Bonnet St., Manchester Center, VT 05255 t) 802-362-1380 x1 christosparish@comcast.net christoursavior.vermontcatholic.org Rev. William R. Beaudin, Pst.; CRP Stds.: 60

MIDDLEBURY

Assumption of the Blessed Virgin Mary - 326 College St., Middlebury, VT 05753; Mailing: 73 Weybridge St., Middlebury, VT 05753 t) 802-388-2943 abvmary@vermontcatholic.org stmary.vermontcatholic.org Rev. Luke P. Austin, Pst.; CRP Stds.: 26

St. Bernadette/St. Genevieve -

MIDDLETOWN SPRINGS

St. Anne - Closed Oct 2022

MILTON

St. Ann - 41 Main St., Milton, VT 05468; Mailing: P.O. Box 1, Milton, VT 05468 t) 802-893-2487; 802-893-3897 (Church Hall) stannmilt@comcast.net; stann.reled@comcast.net stannmilton.com Rev. John G. Feltz, Pst.; Dcn. Paul Garrow; Liza Hope Lovelette, DRE; CRP Stds.: 76

MONTPELIER

St. Augustine - 16 Barre St., Montpelier, VT 05602 t) 802-223-5285 saintaugustineoffice@comcast.net Rev. Julian I. Asucan, Pst.; Dcn. Regis E. Cummings; Dcn. Gesualdo Schneider; CRP Stds.: 36

MORRISVILLE

Most Holy Name of Jesus Parish - 301 Brooklyn St., Morrisville, VT 05661 t) 802-888-3318 mhnj@vermontcatholic.org mostholynamevt.org Parish includes Holy Cross, Morrisville, Hyde Park, Eden, & Johnson. Rev. Jon Schnobrich, Pst.; Rev. Sahaya Paul, Par. Vicar; Mary Elfer, DRE; CRP Stds.: 33

NEWPORT

Mater Dei - 191 Clermont Ter., Newport, VT 05855 t) 802-334-5066 c) 802-323-8585 office@materdeivermont.com; littlewayoflove@gmail.com www.materdeivermont.com Rev. Benny Chittilapilly, SDV, Assoc. Pst.; Rev. Thomas George La Russa, SDV, Assoc. Pst.; Rev. Rijo Johnson, S.D.V., Dean; CRP Stds.: 37

St. Edward's Pre-School - t) 802-873-4570 Theresa Forbes, Dir.;

NORTH BENNINGTON

St. John the Baptist - 3-5 Houghton St., North Bennington, VT 05257; Mailing: PO Box 219, North Bennington, VT 05257-0219 t) 802-447-7504 sjtbcc-vt.org/ Rev. Kevin M. Russeau, C.S.C., Pst.; Rev. Hugh Cleary, C.S.C., Assoc. Pst.; Mary Drew, Youth Min.; Kathy Murphy, DRE; CRP Stds.: 18

NORTHFIELD

St. John the Evangelist - 206 Vine St., Northfield, VT 05663 t) 802-485-8313 saintjohnnorthfield@vermontcatholic.org www.sjsevt.org Rev. Scott A. Gratton, Pst.; CRP Stds.: 4

St. Edward - 76 Beckett St, Williamstown, VT 05679; Mailing: c/o St. John the Evangelist Church, 206 Vine St., Northfield, VT 05663 t) (802) 485-8313

ORWELL

St. Paul - 73 Church Rd., Orwell, VT 05760; Mailing: 45 North Rd., Castleton, VT 05735 t) (802) 671-8139 (Parish Office) ourladysevendolors.vermontcatholic.org/ Rev. Steven Scarmozzino, Pst.; CRP Stds.: 2

PITTSFORD

St. Alphonsus Liguori - 2918 U.S. Rte. 7, Pittsford, VT 05763-9499 t) 802-483-2301 stalphonsus@vermontcatholic.org Rev. Maurice Moreau, OFM Cap, Pst.; Sarah Carrara, DRE; CRP Stds.: 7

POULTNEY

St. Raphael - 21 E. Main St., Poultney, VT 05764-1107; Mailing: 45 North Rd., Castleton, VT 05735 t) (802) 671-8139 (Parish Office) Rev. Steven Scarmozzino, Pst.; CRP Stds.: 4

PROCTOR

St. Dominic - 45 South St., Proctor, VT 05765; Mailing: 45 North Rd., Castleton, VT 05735 t) (802) 671-8139 westernvermontchurches@vermontcatholic.org westrutlandcatholic.org Rev. Steven Scarmozzino, Admin.;

RANDOLPH

Our Lady of the Angels - 43 Hebard Hill Rd., Randolph, VT 05060; Mailing: P.O. Box 428, Randolph, VT 05060 t) 802-728-5251 olv@vermontcatholic.org www.ourladyvt.org Rev. Scott A. Gratton, Pst.; Rev. Brandon C. Schneider, Par. Vicar; CRP Stds.: 5

READSBORO

St. Joachim - 342 Tunnel St., Readsboro, VT 05350; Mailing: P.O. Box 188, Wilmington, VT 05363 t) 802-464-7329 olfwil@vermontcatholic.org ourladyoffatima.vermontcatholic.org Rev. Ilayaraja Amaladass, H.G.N., Admin.; CRP Stds.: 3

St. John Bosco - 818 Main Rd., Stamford, VT 05350 t) (802) 464-7329

RICHFORD

All Saints Parish Charitable Trust - 152 Main St., Richford, VT 05476 t) 802-848-7741 allsaintsrichford@vermontcatholic.org Rev. Daniel J. Jordan, Pst.; Rev. Romanus Igweonu, Assoc. Pst.; Dcn. Armand M. Auclair; CRP Stds.: 8

Our Lady of Lourdes - t) (802) 848-7741

St. Isidore - allsaintsrichford.org

RICHMOND

Our Lady of the Holy Rosary - 64 W. Main St., Richmond, VT 05477; Mailing: P.O. Box 243, Richmond, VT 05477 t) 802-434-2521 olhr@gmavt.net; olhr@vermontcatholic.org olhr-ihm.vermontcatholic.org Jill Danilich, DRE; Dcn. Joshua Devin McDonald; CRP Stds.: 57

RUTLAND

Christ the King - 66 S Main St, Rutland, VT 05701 t) 802-773-6820 rwcatholic@gmail.com rwcatholic.org Rev. Msgr. Bernard W. Bourgeois, Pst.; Sandra Carpenter, DRE; CRP Stds.: 43

Immaculate Heart of Mary - Closed Dec 2022

St. Peter - 134 Convent Ave., Rutland, VT 05701 t) 802-775-1994 stpeterrutland@comcast.net Rev. John Tokaz, O.F.M. Cap, Pst.; CRP Stds.: 28

SHELBURNE

St. Catherine of Siena Parish Charitable Trust - 72 Church St., Shelburne, VT 05482; Mailing: PO Box 70, Shelburne, VT 05482 t) 802-985-2373 stcatherineofsiena@vermontcatholic.org www.shelburnecatholic.org Rev. Dwight H. Baker, Pst.; Dcn. John Magnier; Marie Cookson, DRE; CRP Stds.: 30

SHELDON SPRINGS

St. Anthony - 102 Shawville Rd., Sheldon Springs, VT 05483; Mailing: P.O. Box 563, Enosburg Falls, VT 05450 t) 802-933-4464 stjohnvt@vermontcatholic.org stjohnbaptistvt.com Rev. Daniel J. Jordan, Pst.; Rev. Romanus Igweonu, Par. Vicar; Dcn. George Flower;

St. Mary - 145 Square Rd., Franklin, VT 05457 t) (802) 933-4464 stjohnvt@comcast.net (seasonal)

SOUTH BURLINGTON

St. John Vianney - 160 Hinesburg Rd., South Burlington, VT 05403 t) 802-864-4166 x205 (CRP); 802-864-4166 x201 sjvianneysbvt@aol.com; vparzyck@vermontcatholic.org stjohnvianney.vermontcatholic.org/ Rev. Timothy P. Naples, Pst.; Dcn. William Glinka; Dcn. Anthony Previti; Valerie Parzyck, DRE; CRP Stds.: 37

SOUTH HERO

Our Lady of the Lake - 501 U.S. Rte. 2, South Hero, VT 05486 t) 802-372-4092 (South Hero); 802-796-3481 (Alburgh) ourladyofthelakeparish@vermontcatholic.org www.ourladyofthelake.vermontcatholic.org Rev. Joseph Sanderson, Admin.; CRP Stds.: 9

St. Rose of Lima Church (South Hero, VT) - t) 802-372-3092 Rev. Rogelio Organiza, Admin.;

St. Joseph Mission Church (Grand Isle) - 501 U.S. Rte. 2, South Hero, VT 05486

St. Joseph Church (Isle La Motte) - Rte 129 / Main St, Isle La Motte, VT 05463; Mailing: P.O. Box 49, Alburgh, VT 05440 Rev. Rogelio Organiza, Admin.;

St. Amadeus Church (Alburgh, VT) - 75 N. Main St., Alburgh, VT 05440; Mailing: P.O. Box 49, Alburgh, VT 05440 ourladyofthelakeparish@vermont.catholic.org Rev. Rogelio Organiza, Admin.;

SPRINGFIELD

Holy Family Parish - 10 Pleasant St., Springfield, VT 05156 t) 802-885-3400 holyfamilysvt@vermontcatholic.org stmaryjoseph.com Rev. Rogelio Organiza, Admin.; CRP Stds.: 7

ST. ALBANS

Holy Angels - 246 Lake St., St. Albans, VT 05478 t) 802-524-2585 holyangelstalbans@vermontcatholic.org; holyangelstalbans@msn.com stalbanscatholic@vermontcatholic.org Rev. Christopher Micale, Pst.; CRP Stds.: 22

Immaculate Conception - 45 Fairfield St., St. Albans, VT 05478; Mailing: 246 Lake St., St. Albans, VT 05478 t) 802-524-2585 holyangelstalbans@msn.com; holyangelstalbans@vermontcatholic.org Rev. Christopher Micale, Pst.; CRP Stds.: 21

ST. JOHNSBURY

Corpus Christi Parish - 49 Winter St., St. Johnsbury, VT 05819 t) 802-748-8129 corpuschristi@vermontcatholic.org corpuschristi.vermontcatholic.org Rev. Lance W. Harlow, Pst.; Dcn. Peter Gummere; Dcn. Thomas

Lovett; CRP Stds.: 64

STOWE

Blessed Sacrament - 728 Mountain Rd., Stowe, VT 05672; Mailing: P.O. Box 27, Stowe, VT 05672 t) 802-253-7536 blessedsacrament@vermontcatholic.org bscvt.com/ Rev. Jon Schnobrich, Pst.; Rev. Sahaya Paul, Assoc. Pst.; CRP Stds.: 15

SWANTON

Nativity of the Blessed Virgin Mary-St. Louis - 65 Canada St., Swanton, VT 05488 t) 802-868-4262 nativitybvm-stlouis@comcast.net nativitystlouis.com Parish includes Nativity of the Blessed Virgin Mary, Swanton & St. Louis, Highgate Center. Rev. James C. Dodson, Pst.; Jennifer Ploof, DRE; Gerri S. Cobb, Bus. Mgr.; CRP Stds.: 45

TOWNSHEND

Our Lady of Mercy - 92 Grafton Rd., Townshend, VT 05353; Mailing: P.O. Box 235, Townshend, VT 05353 t) 802-387-5861 ourladyofmercy@vermontcatholic.org ourladyofmercyandthewestrivermissions.com Rev. Agnel Samy, H.G.N., Admin.; Dcn. Richard Anderberg; Dcn. Jerome Driscoll; CRP Stds.: 7

Chapel of the Snows -

Our Lady of the Valley -

TROY

St. Andre Bessette Parish - 130 S. Pleasent St., Troy, VT 05868; Mailing: P.O. Box 109, Troy, VT 05868 t) 802-744-4066 standrebessetteparish@vermontcatholic.org shsvsi.com Dcn. Ward Nolan, Admin.; CRP Stds.: 10

Sacred Heart of Jesus - Theresa McAvinney, CRE;

St. Vincent De Paul - 18 N. Pleasent St., Troy, VT 05868; Mailing: P.O. Box 109, Troy, VT 05868

St. Ignatius Loyola - 151 Hazen Notch Rd., Lowell, VT 05847

UNDERHILL CENTER

St. Thomas - 6 Green St., Underhill Center, VT 05489; Mailing: PO Box 3, Underhill Center, VT 05490-0003 t) 802-899-4632; 802-899-4770 rel.ed@stthomasvt.com stthomasvt.com Rev. Richard Calapan, Admin.; Dcn. Peter Brooks; Laura Lynch Wells, DRE; CRP Stds.: 23

VERGENNES

St. Peter - 85 S. Maple St., Vergennes, VT 05491-0924; Mailing: PO Box 324, Vergennes, VT 05491 t) 802-468-7277 (CRP); 802-877-2367 stpetervt.com Rev. Steven Marchand, Admin.; Emma Goff, DRE; CRP Stds.: 35

WALLINGFORD

St. Patrick - 218 N. Main St, Wallingford, VT 05773; Mailing: 66 S. Main St, Rutland, VT 05701 t) 802-773-6820 rwcatholic@gmail.com rwcatholic.org Rev. Msgr. Bernard W. Bourgeois, Pst.;

WATERBURY

St. Andrew - 109 S. Main St., Waterbury, VT 05676 t) 802-244-7734 rcc.office@vermontcatholic.org www.rccwwm.org/ Rev. Matthew Rensch, Pst.; CRP Stds.: 10

Our Lady of the Snows -

St. Patrick -

WEST RUTLAND

St. Bridget - 28 Church St., West Rutland, VT 05777; Mailing: 45 North Rd., Castleton, VT 05735 t) (802) 671-8139 westernvermontchuches@vermontcatholic.org westrutlandcatholic.org Rev. Steven Scarmozzino, Admin.;

St. Stanislaus Kostka - 11 Barnes St., West Rutland, VT 05777; Mailing: 45 North Rd., Castleton, VT 05735 t) (802) 671-8139 westernvermontchurches@vermontcatholic.org westrutlandcatholic.org Rev. Steven Scarmozzino, Admin.;

WHITE RIVER JUNCTION

St. Anthony - 15 Church St., White River Junction, VT 05001 t) 802-295-2225 x3 administrator@saintanthonychurch.comcastbiz.net; info@saintanthonychurchwrj.org stanthony.vermontcatholic.org Rev. Cyrain G. Cabueñas, Admin.; Dcn. John P. Guarino; Diane Usher, DRE; CRP Stds.: 25

Religious Education Center - 53 Church St., White River Junction, VT 05001 t) (802) 295-2225

WILLISTON

Immaculate Heart of Mary - 7417 Williston Rd., Williston, VT 05495; Mailing: PO Box 1047, Williston, VT 05495 t) 802-878-4513 ihmchurch@vermontcatholic.org immaculateheart.vermontcatholic.org/ Dcn. Joshua Devin McDonald; CRP Stds.: 10

WILMINGTON

Our Lady of Fatima - 96 E. Main St., Wilmington, VT 05363; Mailing: PO Box 188, Wilmington, VT 05363 t) 802-464-7329 olfwil@vermontcatholic.org ourladyoffatimavt.org Rev. Ilayaraja Amaladass, H.G.N., Admin.; CRP Stds.: 9

WINDSOR

St. Francis of Assisi - 30 Union St., Windsor, VT 05089; Mailing: P.O. Box 46, Windsor, VT 05089 t) 802-674-4483 (CRP); 802-674-2157 stfranciswindsor@vermontcatholic.org stfranciswindsor.org Rev. Cyrain Cabuenas, Admin.; Asha Plausteiner, DRE; CRP Stds.: 6

WINOOSKI

St. Francis Xavier - 3 St. Peter St., Winooski, VT 05404 t) 802-655-2290 sfxchurch@vermontcatholic.org Rev. Yvon J. Royer, Pst.; Rev. Msgr. Richard G. Lavalley, Pastor Emer.; CRP Stds.: 29

St. Francis Xavier School - (Grades PreK-8) 5 Saint Peter St., Winooski, VT 05404 t) 802-655-2600 Eric Becker, Prin.; Eileen Barendse, Vice Prin.; Kathleen Finn, Librn.;

St. Vincent de Paul Center - t) 802-655-3006

Extension Program - t) 802-655-4660

WOODSTOCK

Our Lady of the Snows - 7 South St., Woodstock, VT 05091-0397; Mailing: P.O. Box 397, Woodstock, VT 05091-0397 t) 802-457-2322 ourladyofthesnows@comcast.net Rev. Michael E. Augustinowitz, Pst.; Sheila Halnon, DRE; CRP Stds.: 20

Our Lady of the Mountains -

SCHOOLS: PRESCHOOL THRU HIGH SCHOOL

SCHOOLS

STATE OF VERMONT

BARRE

St. Monica - St. Michael School - (PAR) (Grades PreSchool-8) 79 Summer St., Barre, VT 05641 t) 802-476-5015 principal@stmonica-stmichael.org smsmschool.org Rev. Patrick J. Forman, Pst.; Stds.: 141; Lay Tchrs.: 18

BARTON

St. Paul's Catholic School - (PAR) (Grades PreK-8) 54 Eastern Ave., Barton, VT 05822 t) 802-525-6578 jbeloin@stpaulscatholicschool.com stpaulscatholicschool.org Joanne Beloin, Prin.; Stds.: 40; Lay Tchrs.: 8

BENNINGTON

The School of Sacred Heart St. Francis de Sales - (PAR) (Grades PreK-8) 307 School St., Bennington, VT 05201 t) 802-442-2446 tiffany.mckenna@sacredheartbennington.org www.sacredheartbennington.org Tiffany L McKenna, Prin.; Marcia Hendery, Librn.; Stds.: 140; Pr. Tchrs.: 2; Lay Tchrs.: 20

BRATTLEBORO

St. Michael School - (PAR) (Grades PreK-12) 48 Walnut St., Brattleboro, VT 05301 t) 802-254-6320 elainebeam@smsvt.info www.smsvt.org Elaine Beam, Prin.; Stds.: 125; Lay Tchrs.: 13

BURLINGTON

Christ The King - (PAR) (Grades PreSchool-8) 136 Locust St., Burlington, VT 05401 t) 802-862-6696 frontoffice@cksvt.org; osteel@cksvt.org www.cksvt.org Odile Steel, Prin.; Stds.: 195; Lay Tchrs.: 15

Mater Christi School - (PRV) (Grades PreSchool-8) 50 Mansfield Ave., Burlington, VT 05401 t) 802-658-3992 tloescher@materchristischool.net www.mcschool.org Timothy Loescher, Prin.; Stds.: 265; Lay Tchrs.: 31

MORRISVILLE

Bishop John A. Marshall School - (PRV) (Grades PreK-8) 680 Laporte Rd., Morrisville, VT 05661 t) 802-888-4758 cwilson@bjams.org www.bjams.org Carrie Wilson, Prin.; Jennifer Nordenson, Vice Prin.; Stds.: 162; Lay Tchrs.: 15

RUTLAND

Christ the King - (DIO) (Grades PreSchool-8) 60 S. Main St., Rutland, VT 05701 t) 802-773-0500 lmillard@cksrutland.org www.cksrutland.org Lila Millard, Prin.; Stds.: 191; Lay Tchrs.: 13

ST. JOHNSBURY

Good Shepherd School - (DIO) (Grades PreSchool-8) 121 Maple St., St. Johnsbury, VT 05819 t) 802-751-8223 lcartularo@goodshepherdschoolvt.org www.goodshepherdschoolvt.org Lynn Cartularo, Prin.; Stds.: 65; Lay Tchrs.: 8

WINOOSKI

St. Francis Xavier - (PAR) 5 St. Peter St., Winooski, VT 05404 t) 802-655-2600 chill@sfxvt.org www.sfxvt.org Craig Hill, Prin.; Kathleen Finn, Librn.; Stds.: 202; Lay Tchrs.: 20

HIGH SCHOOLS

STATE OF VERMONT

RUTLAND

Mount St. Joseph Academy - (DIO) 127 Convent Ave., Rutland, VT 05701 t) 802-775-0151 malexander@msjvermont.org www.msjvermont.org Michael Alexander, Prin.; Stds.: 76; Lay Tchrs.: 10

SOUTH BURLINGTON

Rice Memorial High School - (DIO) 99 Proctor Ave., South Burlington, VT 05403 t) 802-862-6521 www.rmhsvt.org Andrew Keough, Prin.; Stds.: 373; Lay Tchrs.: 31

INSTITUTIONS LOCATED IN DIOCESE

CAMPUS MINISTRY / NEWMAN CENTERS [CAM]

BURLINGTON

University of Vermont-The Catholic Center at UVM - 390 S. Prospect St., Redstone Campus, Burlington, VT 05401 t) 802-862-8403 catholiccenteruvm@gmail.com www.uvmcatholic.com Rev. Msgr. John J. McDermott, Dir.; Dcn. Robert Begley;

Castleton State College - 10 Washington St., Fair Haven, VT 05743 t) 802-468-5706 mdstjohn@yahoo.com Rev. Antony Pittappilly, S.D.V., Chap.;

Goddard College (Plainfield) - 16 Barre St., Montpelier, VT 05602 t) 802-223-5285 saintaugustineoffice@comcast.net Rev. Michael E. Augustinowitz;

Johnson State College (Johnson) - ; Mailing: P.O. Box 339, Morrisville, VT 05661 t) 802-888-3318 holysaints@comcast.net Attended by Holy Cross, Morrisville Rev. Francis R. Prive, Pst.;

Lyndon State College - 49 Winter St., St. Johnsbury, VT 05819 t) 802-748-8129 stjchurch@charter.net Rev. Curtis Miller, Chap.;

Middlebury College - 326 College St., Middlebury, VT 05753 t) 802-388-2943 stmarys11@comcast.net Rev. Luke P. Austin;

Norwich Newman Apostolate - Norwich University, Northfield, VT 05663; Mailing: 206 Vine St., Northfield, VT 05663 t) 802-485-8313 stjohned@trans-video.net Rev. Scott A. Gratton, Chap.; Rev. Brandon C. Schneider, Chap.; Dcn. Christopher Noble;

Vermont Technical College - Our Lady of the Angels Parish, Randolph, VT 05060 t) 802-728-3227 chancery@vermontcatholic.org Rev. John M. Milanese, Chap.;

CEMETERIES [CEM]

SOUTH BURLINGTON

Resurrection Park Cemetery - 200 Hinesburg Rd., South Burlington, VT 05403; Mailing: 55 Joy Dr., South Burlington, VT 05403 t) 802-862-1530 pbeauregard@vermontcatholic.org Peter Beauregard, Dir.;

COLLEGES & UNIVERSITIES [COL]

COLCHESTER

St. Michael's College - One Winooski Park, Colchester, VT 05439 t) 802-654-2000; 802-654-2476 bcummings@smcvt.edu www.smcvt.edu Lorraine Sterritt, Pres.; Rev. Brian J. Cummings, S.S.E., Dir.; Rev. David J. Theroux, S.S.E., Dir.; Rev. David G. Cray, S.S.E., Trustee; Rev. Marcel R. Rainville, S.S.E., Trustee; Patricia Casey, Trustee; Dawn M. Ellinwood, Vice Pres. Student Affairs; Jerome P. Monachino, Music Min.; Stds.: 1,400; Lay Tchrs.: 114; Pr. Tchrs.: 1

CONVENTS, MONASTERIES, AND RESIDENCES FOR WOMEN [CON]

COLCHESTER

Sisters of Mercy of the Americas-Northeast Community - 365 Mountainview Dr., Colchester, VT 05446 t) 802-863-6835 Sr. Laura Della Santa, R.S.M., Contact; Srs.: 22

LOWELL

The Carmelite Nuns of Vermont, Inc. - 386 Stephenson Rd., Lowell, VT 05847 t) 802-744-2346 sdlgocd@gmail.com carmelitesofvermont.com Srs.: 3

WESTFIELD

Monastery of the Immaculate Heart of Mary - 4103 VT Rte. 100, Westfield, VT 05874 t) 802-744-6525 monastery@ihmwestfield.com www.ihmwestfield.com Mother Benedict McLaughlin, Prioress; Sr. Benedicta Gauthier, OSB, Subprioress; Rev. Lawrence Brown, O.S.B., Chap.; Srs.: 17

WINOOSKI

Missionary Sisters of Our Lady of Africa (M.S.O.L.A.) - 47 W. Spring St., Winooski, VT 05404 t) 802-655-2395 Sr. Arlene Gates, Contact; Srs.: 8

MISCELLANEOUS [MIS]

BURLINGTON

Mercy Connections, Inc. - 255 S. Champlain St., Ste. 8, Burlington, VT 05401 t) 802-846-7062 lfalcone@mercyconnections.org www.mercyconnections.org Lisa Falcone, Exec.;

TEWKSBURY

Fanny Allen Corporation - 100 Ames Pond Rd., Ste. 2, Tewksbury, MA 01876 t) 978-654-6363 joseph_oconnell@covenanthealth.net Sponsored by Covenant Health Systems, Tewksbury, MA. Operates a Community Fund that supports charitable organizations.

Fanny Allen Holdings, Inc. - 100 Ames Pond Rd., Ste. 2, Tewksbury, MA 01876 t) 978-654-6363 josephoconnell@covenanthealth.net Sponsored by Covenant Health Systems, Tewksbury, MA. Ellen Kane, Pres.;

MONASTERIES AND RESIDENCES FOR PRIESTS AND BROTHERS [MON]

ARLINGTON

Carthusian Foundation in America, Inc., Charterhouse of the Transfiguration - 1084 Ave Maria Way, Arlington, VT 05250 t) 802-362-2550 carthusians_in_america@chartreuse.info transfiguration.chartreux.org Carthusian Foundation, Association Fraternelle Romande. Rev. Lorenzo Maria Tolentino de la Rosa Jr., O.Cart. (Philippines), Prior; Rev. Mary Joseph Kim, O.Cart. (Korea), Vicar; Brs.: 11; Priests: 5

Equinox Foundation, LLC - 1A Saint Bruno Dr., Arlington, VT 05250 t) 802-362-1115 info@equinoxmountain.com www.equinoxmountain.com Frank Dyer, Bus. Mgr.;

COLCHESTER

Society of St. Edmund - One Winooski Park, Nicolle Hall, Box 270, Colchester, VT 05439 t) 802-654-3400 sse@sse.org www.sse.org (Edmundite Generalate), Central Offices, Society of Saint Edmund. Rev. David G. Cray, S.S.E., Supr.; Brs.: 3; Priests: 16

Society of St. Edmund - sse.org (Edmundite Community at St. Michael's College) Rev. Marcel R. Rainville, S.S.E., House Supr.;

WESTON

The Benedictine Foundation of the State of Vermont, Inc. - 58 Priory Hill Rd., Weston, VT 05161-6400 t) 802-824-5409 brothers@westonpriory.org www.westonpriory.org Rev. Richard Iaquinto, O.S.B., Prior; Rev. Peter Claude Anctil, O.S.B., Mem.; Rev. Placid Gaunay, O.S.B., Mem.; Rev. John Hammond, O.S.B., Mem.; Rev. Michael Hoveling, O.S.B., Mem.; Rev. Mark Ronald Nicolosi, O.S.B., Mem.; Rev. Daniel Saavedra, O.S.B., Mem.; Brs.: 4; Priests: 7

NURSING / REHABILITATION / CONVALESCENCE / ELDERLY CARE [NUR]

BURLINGTON

St. Joseph Residential Care Home - 243 N. Prospect St., Burlington, VT 05401 t) 802-864-0264 mbelanger@vermontcatholic.org Managed by Vermont Catholic Charities. Mary Belanger, Admin.; Mary Beth Pinard, Dir.; Asstd. Annu.: 38; Staff: 30

DERBY LINE

Michaud Manor Residential Care Home - 47 Herrick Rd., Derby Line, VT 05830 t) 802-873-3152 asteinberg@vermontcatholic.org www.vermontcatholic.org Managed by Vermont Catholic Charities. Anne Steinberg, Admin.; Mary Beth Pinard, Dir.; Asstd. Annu.: 35; Staff: 10

RUTLAND

St. Joseph/Kervick Residence - 131 Convent Ave., Rutland, VT 05701 t) 802-775-5133 Managed by Vermont Catholic Charities. Stacey Bowen, Admin.; Mary Beth Pinard, Dir.; Asstd. Annu.: 35; Staff: 22

Loretto/Kervick Home - 59 Meadow St., Rutland, VT 05701 t) 802-773-8840 Managed by Vermont Catholic Charities. Mary Beth Pinard, Dir.; Asstd. Annu.: 35; Staff: 11

PRESCHOOLS / CHILDCARE CENTERS [PRE]

BRATTLEBORO

Camp Neringa, Inc. - 147 Neringa Rd., Brattleboro, VT 05301 t) 978-582-5592 info@neringa.org www.neringa.org Dana Vainauskiene, Dir.;

SHRINES [SHR]

ISLE LA MOTTE

St. Anne's Shrine - 92 Saint Anne's Rd., Isle La Motte, VT 05463; Mailing: P.O. Box 280, Isle La Motte, VT 05463 t) 802-928-3362 sas@sse.org www.saintannesshrine.org Conducted by Fathers of Society of St. Edmund, Rev. Brian J. Cummings, S.S.E., Dir.;

An asterisk (*) denotes an organization that has established tax-exempt status directly with the IRS and is not covered by the USCCB Group Ruling.

Diocese of Camden

(Dioecesis Camdensis)

MOST REVEREND DENNIS J. SULLIVAN

Bishop of Camden; ordained May 29, 1971; appointed Titular Bishop of Enera and Auxiliary Bishop of New York June 28, 2004; consecrated September 21, 2004; appointed Bishop of Camden January 8, 2013; installed February 12, 2013.

Chancery Office: Camden Diocesan Center, 631 Market St., P.O. Box 708, Camden, NJ 08101. T: 856-756-7900; F: 856-963-2655.

ESTABLISHED DECEMBER 9, 1937.

Square Miles 2,691.

Legal Corporate Title: "The Diocese of Camden, New Jersey."

Comprises six Counties in the State of New Jersey–viz., Atlantic, Camden, Cape May, Cumberland, Gloucester and Salem.

For legal titles of parishes and diocesan institutions, consult the Chancery Office.

STATISTICAL OVERVIEW

Personnel

Bishop	1
Priests: Diocesan Active in Diocese	93
Priests: Diocesan Active Outside Diocese	4
Priests: Diocesan in Foreign Missions	1
Priests: Retired, Sick or Absent	80
Number of Diocesan Priests	178
Religious Priests in Diocese	32
Total Priests in your Diocese	210
Extern Priests in Diocese	10
Ordinations:	
Diocesan Priests	5
Permanent Deacons in Diocese	133
Total Brothers	7
Total Sisters	173

Parishes

Parishes	62
With Resident Pastor:	
Resident Diocesan Priests	54
Resident Religious Priests	4
Without Resident Pastor:	
Administered by Priests	4
Missions	3

Professional Ministry Personnel:	
Brothers	7
Sisters	137
Lay Ministers	32

Welfare

Catholic Hospitals	1
Total Assisted	11,608
Health Care Centers	16
Homes for the Aged	3
Day Care Centers	4
Special Centers for Social Services	8
Total Assisted	22,000
Other Institutions	1

Educational

Diocesan Students in Other Seminaries	8
Total Seminarians	8
High Schools, Diocesan and Parish	5
Total Students	2,450
High Schools, Private	3
Total Students	1,000
Elementary Schools, Diocesan and Parish	24
Total Students	6,316
Non-residential Schools for the Disabled	1
Total Students	141
Catechesis/Religious Education:	
Elementary Students	13,295
Total Students under Catholic Instruction	23,210
Teachers in Diocese:	
Sisters	14
Lay Teachers	734

Vital Statistics

Receptions into the Church:	
Infant Baptism Totals	2,985
Minor Baptism Totals	289
Adult Baptism Totals	128
Received into Full Communion	80
First Communions	2,652
Confirmations	3,001
Marriages:	
Catholic	454
Interfaith	119
Total Marriages	573
Deaths	3,463
Total Catholic Population	311,489
Total Population	1,365,458

LEADERSHIP

Camden Diocesan Center - t) 856-756-7900
Advanced Studies for Priests - t) 856-583-2854 Rev. Nicholas Dudo, Vicar;
Advocate for Priests' Health and Wellness - Rev. Thomas A. Newton;
The Diocese of Camden -
Officers - Most Rev. Dennis Joseph Sullivan; Rev. Robert E. Hughes, Vice. Pres.; Rev. Jason T. Rocks, Secy.;
Diocesan Bishop - t) 856-583-2808 Most Rev. Dennis Joseph Sullivan;
College of Consultors - Rev. Msgr. Peter M. Joyce; Rev. Perry A. Cherubini; Rev. Robert E. Hughes (robert.hughes@camdendiocese.org);
Communications and Community Relations -
Diocesan Newspaper - t) 856-583-6142 Jennifer Mauro, Mng. Editor; Michael J. Walsh, Assoc. Publisher; Cynthia E. Soper, Business Mgr.;
Office of Communications - t) 856-583-6143 Michael J. Walsh, Dir.; Maria D'Antonio, Communications Coord.; John Kalitz, Digital Media Mgr.;
Diocesan Historian - t) (856) 583-2874 Rev. Jason T. Rocks (jason.rocks@camdendiocese.org);
Secretary to the Bishop - t) (856) 583-2875 joshua.nevitt@camdendiocese.org Rev. Joshua Nevitt;
Vicar General/Moderator of the Curia - t) 856-583-2807 Rev. Robert E. Hughes (robert.hughes@camdendiocese.org);
Chancellor - t) 856-583-2874 Rev. Jason T. Rocks (jason.rocks@camdendiocese.org);
Vice Chancellors - Rev. Joshua Nevitt; Rev. Msgr. Dominic J. Bottino (dominic.bottino@camdendiocese.org); Rev. Robert L. Sinatra (robert.sinatra@camdendiocese.org);
Vicar for Clergy - t) 856-583-2854 Rev. Nicholas Dudo;
Censor Librorum - t) 856-583-2874 Rev. Jason T. Rocks (jason.rocks@camdendiocese.org);
Delegate for Men Religious - t) (856) 583-2874
Liaison with Retired Priests - Rev. Msgr. William P. Brennan;
Delegate for Temporalities and Diocesan Finance Officer - t) 856-583-2822 Laura J. Montgomery;
Delegate for Women Religious - t) 856-583-2874 Rev. Jason T. Rocks (jason.rocks@camdendiocese.org);
Office of Child and Youth Protection - t) 856-583-6114 Rod J. Herrera, Dir.;
Office of Pastoral Planning - t) 856-583-2874 Rev. Jason T. Rocks (jason.rocks@camdendiocese.org);
Office of Propagation of the Faith and Diocesan Missions - t) 856-583-2831 Deborah Cutter, Coord.;
Office of Vocations - t) 856-583-2864 adam.cichoski@camdendiocese.org Rev. Adam J. Cichoski, Dir.; Rev. Joshua Nevitt, Assoc. Dir.;
Delegate for Hispanic Ministry - t) 856-583-6181 Andres Arango;
Permanent Diaconate - t) 856-583-2854 Rev. Nicholas Dudo, Dir.;
Vicars Forane -
Deanery 1 - West Camden County - Rev. Piotr Szamocki;
Deanery 2 - East Camden County - Rev. Msgr. Louis A. Marucci;
Deanery 3 - Gloucester & Salem Counties - Rev. E. Joseph Byerley;
Deanery 4 - Atlantic County - Rev. Edward F. Heintzelman;
Deanery 5 - Cape May and Cumberland Counties - Rev. William J. Kelly;

ADVISORY BOARDS, COMMISSIONS, COMMITTEES, AND COUNCILS

Canon 1742 Panel - Rev. James L. Bartoloma; Rev. Raymond P. Gormley; Rev. David A. Grover;
Deacon Council - t) 856-583-2854 nicholas.dudo@camdendiocese.org Dcn. Gerard J. Jablonowski (gerard.jablonowski@camdendiocese.org); Dcn. Joseph G. Rafferty Sr.; Dcn. Charles S. Schiapelli;
Diocesan Finance Council - Rev. Msgr. Roger E. McGrath; Rev. Joseph E. Perrault; Rev. John Callaghan;
Ex Officio Members - Most Rev. Dennis Joseph Sullivan; Rev. Robert E. Hughes; Laura J. Montgomery;
Priests Personnel and Policy Board - Most Rev. Dennis Joseph Sullivan; Rev. Robert E. Hughes (robert.hughes@camdendiocese.org); Rev. Nicholas Dudo;
Vocation Advisory Board - Rev. Thomas J. Barcellona; Rev. Adam J. Cichoski; Rev. Rene L. Canales (charismaticrenewal@camdendiocese.org);

CLERGY AND RELIGIOUS SERVICES

Continuing Education & Spiritual Formation of Priests (CESF) - Most Rev. Dennis Joseph Sullivan; Rev. Robert E. Hughes (robert.hughes@camdendiocese.org); Rev. Nicholas Dudo;
Health Advocate for Retired Priests - t) 856-751-2010 Bobbie Bradley;

DEVELOPMENT

Office of Development - t) 856-583-6134 Andrew Goos, Assoc. Dir.;
Office of Stewardship - t) 856-583-6102 Dcn. Russell O. Davis, Dir.;
Planned Giving - t) (856) 583-6195 Andrew Goos, Assoc. Dir.;
South Jersey Catholic Ministries Appeal - t) (856) 583-6195 Andrew Goos, Assoc. Dir.;
South Jersey Scholarship Fund - t) 856-583-6126 Stacy Napolitano;

EDUCATION

Catholic Schools -
Assistant Superintendent of Schools - t) 856-583-6110 Sr. Rose DiFluri, I.H.M.;
Curriculum & Assessment - t) 856-583-6129 Dr. Robert A. Lockwood;
Enrollment and Outreach - t) 856-583-6108 Marianela Nunez, Dir.;
Marketing and Communication - t) 856-583-6107 Michael Bress;
Superintendent of Schools - t) 856-583-6103 Dr. William A. Watson;
Religious Education - t) (856) 583-2903 Rosalie DelleMonache, Dir.;

FACILITIES

Director, Buildings and Project Management - t) 856-583-2959 Daniel G. Bochanski;
Facilities Management - t) 856-583-2870 Jim Burns, Maintenance;

FINANCE

Assistant Comptroller - t) 856-583-2823 Kevin Drum;
Cemeteries - t) 856-583-2820 Paul Martin (paul.martin@camdendiocese.org);
Diocesan Finance Officer & Bishop's Delegate for Temporalities - t) 856-583-2822 Laura J. Montgomery;
Diocesan Liability Insurance Program - t) 856-583-2871 Bevlyn Donohue;
Diocesan Self-Insurance Plan (DSIP) & Pension Funds - t) 856-583-2822 Laura J. Montgomery;
Director of Financial Services - t) 856-583-2827 John M. Wagner;
Human Resources - t) 856-583-2868 Dina Galeotafiore, Dir.; Candy Newhouse, Health Insurance;
Real Estate - t) 856-579-3040 Kenneth McIlvaine, Consultant;
Victim Assistance Coordinator - t) 800-964-6588 Sylvia Loumeau;

PASTORAL SERVICES

Black Catholic Ministries & Cultural Diversity - t) 856-966-6700 Rev. Vincent G. Guest;
Diocesan Gospel Choir - t) 609-502-7414 Tonya Dorsey, Coord.;
Evangelization - t) 856-583-6181 Andres Arango, Dir.;
Faith and Family Life Formation - t) (856) 583-2908 jose.rodriguez@camdendiocese.org Jose J. Rodriguez Jr., Dir.;
Campus Ministries -
Rowan University - t) 856-881-2554 www.rowan.ccm.com Rev. John A. Rossi, Admin.; Rebekah Hardy, Campus Min.;
Rutgers University - t) (856) 583-2908 Jose J. Rodriguez Jr.;
Stockton University - t) 609-707-1067 www.ccmstockton.com Britany Shields; Rev. Renante Orain, Chap.;
Scouting - t) 856-428-2645 Joseph Brennan;
Youth, Young Adult & Campus Ministries - t) 856-583-2908 Jose J. Rodriguez Jr.;
Lay Ministry Formation - t) 856-583-2903
Racial Justice Commission - t) 856-966-6700 Rev. Vincent G. Guest;
Pastoral Outreach Discipleship and Leadership - c) (215) 620-2755 donna.ottaviano@camdendiocese.org Donna Ottaviano-Britt, Dir.;
Worship and Christian Initiation - t) 856-583-2865 Michael Bedics, Dir.;
Liturgical Art and Architectural Commission - Rev. Robert E. Hughes; Michael Bedics;

PARISH SERVICES

Charismatic Renewal - t) 856-229-1571 Rev. Rene L. Canales, Diocesan Moderator (charismaticrenewal@camdendiocese.org);
Ecumenical and Inter-Religious Affairs - t) 609-522-2709 Rev. Cadmus D. Mazzarella, Dir.; Patricia Sandrow, Coord.;
English Cursillo - t) 609-805-2211 Dcn. Joseph A. Garozzo, Spiritual Adv./Care Srvcs. (deacongarozzo@comcast.net);
Hispanic Charismatic Renewal - t) 954-439-8692 Kathia Arango, Diocesan Coord.;
Hispanic Cursillo - t) 856-692-6003 Dcn. Roberto P. Rodriguez;
Ministry with the Deaf and Persons with Disabilities - t) 856-583-6111 Rev. Hugh J. Bradley, Dir. (hugh.bradley@camdendiocese.org);
Office & Worship Site - t) 856-942-1000
Parish Based Senior Services - t) 856-583-6121 Dcn. Gerard J. Jablonowski (gerard.jablonowski@camdendiocese.org);
Parish Nursing - t) 856-583-6120 Nicole Keefer, Dir. (nicole.keefer@camdendiocese.org);
Stephen Ministry - t) 856-583-9196 Dcn. Gerard J. Jablonowski (gerard.jablonowski@camdendiocese.org);
Vitality Catholic Healthcare Services - t) 856-583-9196 Dcn. Gerard J. Jablonowski, Exec. Dir. (gerard.jablonowski@camdendiocese.org);
Vitality Health Ministries -
Care Coordination and Consultation Health Resource Call Center - t) 856-583-6149 Mimi Schaible, Dir.;
Hospital Chaplaincy - t) 856-583-6130 Dcn. Michael G. Bortnowski, Dir.;

TRIBUNAL

Adjutant Judicial Vicars - Rev. Jason T. Rocks (jason.rocks@camdendiocese.org);
Councils -
Appointed Members - Rev. Thomas J. Barcellona; Rev. Perry A. Cherubini; Rev. Anthony J. Manuppella;
Elected Members -
Deanery Representatives - Rev. Vincent G. Guest; Rev. John P. Picinic; Rev. David Rivera;
Representative for Parochial Vicars and Special Ministries - Rev. Adam J. Cichoski;
Representative for Pastors - Rev. Cadmus D. Mazzarella;
Representative for Retired Priests - Rev. Msgr. Roger E. McGrath;
Ex Officio Members - Rev. Robert E. Hughes; Rev. Nicholas Dudo;
Presbyteral Council - Most Rev. Dennis Joseph Sullivan, Presider; Rev. Robert E. Hughes; Rev.

Nicholas Dudo;
Court Expert - Rod J. Herrera;
Defender of the Bond - Rev. Msgr. Dominic J. Bottino (dominic.bottino@camdendiocese.org);
Diocesan Tribunal - t) 856-583-6162
Ecclesiastical Notary - t) 856-583-6151 Evelyn Rodriguez;
Judges - Rev. Msgr. Peter M. Joyce; Rev. James L. Bartoloma; Rev. David J. Klein;
Judicial Vicar - t) 856-583-6162 Rev. David J. Klein;
Marriage Dispensations and Permissions - t) 856-583-6160 Dcn. Thomas E. Jennings;
Promoter of Justice - Rev. Msgr. Peter M. Joyce;

MISCELLANEOUS / OTHER OFFICES
Information Technology Services - t) 856-342-4111 Ron Pilla, Dir.;

PARISHES, MISSIONS, AND CLERGY

STATE OF NEW JERSEY

ABSECON
Church of Saint Elizabeth Ann Seton, Absecon, N.J. - 591 New Jersey Ave., Absecon, NJ 08201 t) 609-641-1480 info@setonabsecon.org setonabsecon.org Rev. Cosme R. de la Pena, Pst.; Rev. Nilsen Logan, Par. Vicar; Dcn. Richard A. Wigglesworth; CRP Stds.: 173

ATCO
Christ the Redeemer Parish, Atco, N.J. - 318 Carl Hasselhan Dr., Atco, NJ 08004-1997 t) (856) 767-0719 fr.wallace@christtheredeemer.us christtheredeemer.us Rev. Cadmus D. Mazzarella, Pst.; Dcn. Joseph F. Janocha; Dcn. Albert A. LaMonaca Jr.; CRP Stds.: 166
Sacred Heart, Cedar Brook -
St. Anthony, Waterford -
Assumption, Atco -

ATLANTIC CITY
The Parish of Saint Monica - 2651 Atlantic Ave., Atlantic City, NJ 08401-6489 t) 609-340-0116 (CRP); 609-345-1878 Rev. Kevin J. Mohan, Pst.; Rev. John Buckthese Chinnappan, Pst. Assoc.; Rev. Andrew T. Pham, Par. Vicar; Rev. Robert B. Matysik, In Res.; CRP Stds.: 305
The Parish of Saint Monica School - (Grades PreK-8) 15 N. California Ave., Atlantic City, NJ 08401 t) 609-345-0648 Susan J. Tarrant, Prin.;
Sisters of Mercy - 25 N. California Ave., Atlantic City, NJ 08401
Our Lady Star of the Sea -
St. Michael -
St. Monica -
St. Nicholas -

AVALON
St. Brendan the Navigator Parish, Avalon, N.J. - 5012 Dune Dr., Avalon, NJ 08202-1333 t) 609-967-3017 (DRE); 609-967-3746 dre@stbrendanavalon.org; pastor@stbrendanavalon.org www.stbrendanavalon.org Rev. William J. Kelly, Pst.; Rev. James Betz, In Res.; Dcn. Robert Dooley; Eileen Barrett, DRE; CRP Stds.: 45
St. Paul, Stone Harbor -
Maris Stella, Avalon -

BELLMAWR
St. Joachim Parish, Bellmawr, N.J. - 601 W. Browning Rd., Bellmawr, NJ 08031-1840 t) (856) 931-6307 annun.church@comcast.net Rev. Piotr Szamocki, Pst.; Dcn. David W. Murnane; Dcn. Gerard V. DeMuro, Retired Deacon; Suzanne Fronzek, DRE; CRP Stds.: 162
Convent - 424 E. Browning Rd., Bellmawr, NJ 08031 Daughters of Our Lady of the Sacred Heart
Annunciation, Bellmawr - (Worship Site)
Saint Anne, Westville - (Worship Site)

BERLIN
Saint Simon Stock Parish, Berlin, N.J. - 178 W. White Horse Pike, Berlin, NJ 08009-2023 t) 856-767-2563 office@stsimonstock.net www.stsimonstock.net Rev. Michael August De Leon, A.M., Pst.; Rev. Dexter Nebrida, A.M., Campus Min.; Dcn. Robert M. Iuliucci; Dcn. Michael S. Vitarelli; CRP Stds.: 386
O.L. Mt. Carmel, Berlin - (Worship Site)

BLACKWOOD
Our Lady of Hope Parish, Blackwood, N.J. - 701 Little Gloucester Rd., Blackwood, NJ 08012-3311 Rev. Joseph T. Szolack, Pst.; Rev. John W. March, Pst. Assoc.; Rev. John A. DelDuca, In Res.; Dcn. Fernando S. Encarnado; Dcn. Robert P. Foley; Dcn. Tobias C. Haley; Mary Jo Dwyer, DRE;
St. Jude, Blackwood -
St. Agnes, Blackwood -

BRIDGETON
The Parish of the Holy Cross, Bridgeton, N.J. - 46 Central Ave., Bridgeton, NJ 08302-2305 Rev. Matthew Weber, Pst.; Rev. Armando Rodriguez Montoya, Pst. Assoc.; Dcn. Christopher D. Nichols; Dcn. Arnaldo A. Santos;
St. Michael, Cedarville -
Immaculate Conception, Bridgeton -
St. Anthony, Port Norris -
St. Mary, Rosenhayn -
Convent - 64 North St., Bridgeton, NJ 08302 Missionary Daughters of the Most Pure Virgin Mary.
St. Teresa Avila, Bridgeton -

BRIGANTINE
St. Thomas' Catholic Church, Brigantine, N.J. - 331 8th St. S., Brigantine, NJ 08203 t) 609-266-2123 www.stthomasbrigantine.org Rev. Edward J. Maher, Pst.; Dcn. Leonard W. Long, DRE; CRP Stds.: 89

CAMDEN
The Parish of the Cathedral of the Immaculate Conception, Camden, N.J. - 642 Market St., Camden, NJ 08102-1183 t) (856) 964-1580 camdencathedral642@gmail.com www.camdencathedral.com Rev. Adam J. Cichoski, Rector; Rev. Stephen Robbins, Par. Vicar; Dcn. Jose Rene Zayas; CRP Stds.: 85
Holy Name School - 5th & Vine Sts., Camden, NJ 08102 t) 856-365-7930 Patricia Quinter, Prin.;
Our Lady of Mount Carmel and Fatima, Camden - 832 S. 4th St., Camden, NJ 08103
Holy Name, Camden -
Cathedral of the Immaculate Conception, Camden -
St. Joseph Catholic Church, East Camden, N.J. (Pro-Cathedral) - 2907 Federal St., Camden, NJ 08105 t) 856-964-2776 lrodriguez@sjprocathedral.org sjprocathedral.org (Pro-Cathedral) Rev. Jaime E. Hostios, Pst.; Rev. Varghese Srambickal, In Res.; Dcn. Pedro J. Espinal, DRE; Licelot Rodriguez, Bus. Mgr.; CRP Stds.: 285
St. Joseph School - (Grades K-8) t) 856-964-4336 Kyle Oroz, Prin.;
St. Joseph Child Development Center, Inc. - 17 Church St., Camden, NJ 08105 t) (856) 963-9202 children@sjcdcnj.org Gisel Cornish, Dir.;
The Church of Sacred Heart - 1739 Ferry Ave., Camden, NJ 08104 Records for St. George kept at Sacred Heart, Camden. Records for Sts. Peter and Paul kept at the Cathedral of the Immaculate Conception, Camden. Rev. Vincent G. Guest, Pst.; Rev. Msgr. Michael J. Doyle, In Res.; Dcn. Thomas E. Jennings;
The Church of Sacred Heart School - (Grades K-8) Fourth & Jaspers Sts., Camden, NJ 08104 t) 856-963-1341 Janet Williams, Prin.;

CAPE MAY
The Church of Our Lady Star of the Sea, Cape May - 520 Lafayette St., Cape May, NJ 08204 t) 609-884-5312 parish@ladystarofthesea.org Rev. David J. Devlin, O.S.F.S., Pst.; Rev. James T. Dever, O.S.F.S., Par. Vicar; Rev. John J. Dolan, Par. Vicar; CRP Stds.: 30
Cape May Point, St. Agnes - (Summer)
Convent - 516 Lafayette St., Cape May, NJ 08204 Sisters of St. Joseph of Chestnut Hill Sr. Nancy Butler, Pst. Assoc.;

CAPE MAY COURT HOUSE
The Church of Our Lady of the Angels, Cape May Court House, N.J. - 35 E. Mechanic St., Cape May Court House, NJ 08210 t) 609-465-5432 wendy@ourladyoftheangels.net; fathertom@ourladyoftheangels.net ourladyoftheangels.net Rev. Thomas J. Barcellona, Pst.; Dcn. Peter R. Davidson; Dana Imperato, CRE; CRP Stds.: 90

CARNEY'S POINT
Saint Gabriel the Archangel Parish, Carneys Point, N.J. - 369 Georgetown Rd., Carney's Point, NJ 08069-2598 Rev. Charles J. Colozzi, Pst.; Rev. Robert J. D'Imperio, Par. Vicar;
St. James, Pennsgrove -
St. Mary, Salem -
Queen of the Apostles, Pennsville -
Corpus Christi, Carneys Point -

CHERRY HILL
The Catholic Community of Christ Our Light, Cherry Hill, N.J. - 402 Kings Hwy. N., Cherry Hill, NJ 08034 Rev. John P. Picinic, Pst.; Rev. Ernest E. Amadi, Par. Vicar; Rev. Joseph P. Capella, S.A.C., In Res.; Dcn. Frank A. Baratta; Dcn. Joseph F. Seaman;
Saint Peter Celestine, Cherry Hill -
Resurrection Catholic School - (Grades PreK-8) t) 856-667-3034 Molly Webb, Prin.; Noel Becker, Librn.;
Convent - Sisters of St. Joseph
Holy Eucharist Parish, Cherry Hill, N.J. - 344 Kresson Rd., Cherry Hill, NJ 08034 t) 856-428-9207 (CRP); 856-429-1330 parishoffice@holyeucharistcherryhill.org Rev. Jason T. Rocks, Pst.; Rev. Michael J. Coffey, In Res.; Dcn. Michael G. Bortnowski; Dcn. Robert W. Hamilton; CRP Stds.: 267
St. Pius X, Cherry Hill -
Holy Rosary, Cherry Hill -
St. Mary's R.C. Church, Delaware Township, N.J. - 2001 Springdale Rd., Cherry Hill, NJ 08003 t) (856) 424-1454 (Rectory/Office); (856) 424-2679 (Relg. Educ.); (856) 424-0955 (Youth Min.) stmarycherryhill@gmail.com; stmaryreligiouseducation@verizon.net www.stmarycherryhill.org Rev. Paul A. Olszewski, Pst.; Dcn. Robert F. Scarpa; Rev. Msgr. Dominic J. Bottino, In Res.; Patricia L. Galie, DRE; Stanley Thompson III, Youth Min.; James Rabic, Music Min.; Lisa Caso, Coord., Evangelization & Spirituality; CRP Stds.: 200
Korean Catholic Mission (St. Yun Yi Il Korean Mission) - t) 856-912-1355 dyfranciskim@gmail.com www.chkcc.org/ Rev. James L. Bartoloma, Admin.; Rev. Francis Kim, Chap.;
The Church of St. Thomas More, Cherry Hill, New Jersey - 1439 Springdale Rd., Cherry Hill, NJ 08003 t) 856-424-3212 sthomasmore@comcast.net stthomasmorenj.org/ Rev. Edward F. Namiotka, Pst.; CRP Stds.: 63

CLAYTON
Parish of St. Michael the Archangel, Franklinville, N.J. - 49 W. North St., Clayton, NJ 08312-1114 t) (856) 881-9155 psma.rectory@gmail.com psma-nj.com Rev. Lawrence E. Polansky, Pst.; CRP Stds.: 56
St. Michael the Archangel School - (Grades PreK-8) 51 W. North St., Clayton, NJ 08312 t) 856-881-0067 office@smrsonline.com Ronald Ferraro, Prin.; Stds.: 184; Lay Tchrs.: 12
Nativity - 2677 Delsea Dr., Franklinville, NJ 08322; Mailing: 49 W. North St., Clayton, NJ 08312 www.psma-nj.com
St. Catherine of Siena, Clayton - 700 N. Delsea Dr., Clayton, NJ 08312 www.psma-nj.com

COLLINGS LAKES
Church of Our Lady of the Lakes, Collings Lakes, N.J. - 19 Malaga Rd., Collings Lakes, NJ 08094 t) 609-561-8313 Rev. Michael J. Goyette, Pst.; CRP Stds.: 31

COLLINGSWOOD
Most Precious Blood Parish, Collingswood, N.J. - 445

White Horse Pike, Collingswood, NJ 08107-1996 t) (856) 854-0364 mpbparish@yahoo.com Rev. Joseph An Nguyen, Pst.; Rev. Raymond Son Thai Tran, Par. Vicar;

St. Teresa of Calcutta Parish - 809 Park Ave., Collingswood, NJ 08108-3147 t) 856-858-0298 cvenafra@stteresaofcalcuttanj.org www.stteresaofcalcuttanj.org Rev. Yvans Jazon, Pst.; Rev. Hugh J. Bradley, Par. Vicar; Dcn. Leo M. Howitz; CRP Stds.: 301

Holy Saviour, Westmont -

St. John, Collingswood -

EGG HARBOR TOWNSHIP

The Church of Saint Katharine Drexel, McKee City, New Jersey - 6077 W. Jersey Ave., Egg Harbor Township, NJ 08234; Mailing: 6075 - 6077 W. Jersey Ave., Egg Harbor Township, NJ 08234 t) 609-645-7313 office@skd-parish.org www.skd-parish.org Rev. Joselito C. Ramos, A.M. (Philippines), Pst.; Rev. Renante Orain, In Res.; CRP Stds.: 283

GALLOWAY

Our Lady of Perpetual Help - 146 S. Pitney Rd., Galloway, NJ 08205 t) 609-652-0008 x208 Rev. Gerard C. Marable, Pst.; Dcn. Francis A. Cerullo;

Assumption Regional Catholic School - t) 608-652-7134 Mary Ellen Schurtz, Prin.;

The Church of the Assumption, Galloway -

St. Nicholas' Church, Egg Harbor City -

GIBBSBORO

St. Andrew the Apostle R.C. Church, Gibbsboro, N.J. - 27 Kresson-Gibbsboro Rd., Gibbsboro, NJ 08026; Mailing: 27 Kresson, Gibbsboro, NJ 08026-1208 t) (856) 784-3878 churchofsaintandrews.org/ Rev. Msgr. Louis A. Marucci, Pst.; Rev. Victorino B. Coronado, Par. Vicar; Dcn. Aaron G. Smith; CRP Stds.: 225

GIBBSTOWN

St. Clare of Assisi Parish, Gibbstown, N.J. - 313 Memorial Ave., Gibbstown, NJ 08027; Mailing: 140 Broad St., Swedesboro, NJ 08085 t) 856-467-5426 (CRP); 856-467-0037 (Office) faithformation@stclarenj.org; info@stclarenj.org stclarenj.org Rev. Edward M. Kennedy, Pst.; Rev. Grace Manano, Par. Vicar; Dcn. Joseph A. Garozzo; Dcn. Gerard J. Jablonowski; Verna Mullen, DRE;

Convent - 320 Memorial Ave., Gibbstown, NJ 08027 Sr. Maria DiRosa, Contact;

GLASSBORO

St. Bridget's Catholic Church, Glassboro, N.J. (St. Bridget University Parish) - 125 Church St., Glassboro, NJ 08028; Mailing: 127 Church St., Glassboro, NJ 08028 t) 856-881-2753 parishoffice@stbridgetup.org www.stbridgetup.org (University Parish) Rev. John A. Rossi, Pst.; Dcn. Samuel Soto; CRP Stds.: 14

Mary, Mother of Mercy Parish, Glassboro, N.J. - 500 Greentree Rd., Glassboro, NJ 08028 t) 856-881-0909 parishoffice@mary-mom.com www.mary-mom.com Rev. Allain B. Caparas, Pst.; Rev. Joseph J. Adamson, In Res.; Rev. Msgr. James R. Tracy, In Res.; Dcn. Kevin L. Laughlin; Dcn. John J. Luko Jr.; Dcn. Anthony J. Petillo; Shannon Cassidy, DRE; Meryl Cerana, Pst. Assoc.; CRP Stds.: 200

Our Lady of Lourdes, Glassboro - (Worship Site)

Our Lady Queen of Peace, Pitman - 161 Pitman Ave., Pitman, NJ 08071 (Worship Site)

GLOUCESTER

St. Mary's Church, Gloucester - 426 Monmouth St., Gloucester, NJ 08030 t) 856-456-0913 (CRP); 856-456-0052 Rev. Msgr. William A. Hodge, Pst.; Dcn. Kevin C. Heil; Rev. David J. Klein, In Res.;

HADDON HEIGHTS

Church of St. Rose, Haddon Heights, N.J. - 300 Kings Hwy., Haddon Heights, NJ 08035-1397 t) 856-547-0564 parishsecretary@strosenj.com www.strosenj.com Rev. David A. Grover, Pst.; Rev. Francis Kim, Par. Vicar; Rev. Allen B. Lovell, Par. Vicar; Dcn. Joseph G. Rafferty Sr.; Dcn. William M. Slaven; CRP Stds.: 194

Church of St. Rose School - (Grades K-8) t) 856-546-6166 principal@strosenj.com William Stonis, Prin.; Marguerite Crowell, Librn.;

HADDONFIELD

Church of Christ the King, Haddonfield, N.J. - 200 Windsor Ave., Haddonfield, NJ 08033 t) (856) 429-1600 parishoffice@ctkhaddonfield.org ctkhaddonfield.org Rev. Jon P. Thomas, Pst.; Dcn. Michael F. Scott; Rev. Francis Oranefo, In Res.; CRP Stds.: 551

St. Joseph the Worker Parish, Haddon Township, N.J. - 901 Hopkins Rd. Ste. A, Haddonfield, NJ 08033-3099 t) 856-240-7813 (CRP); 856-858-1313 sjwadmin@comcast.net www.stjosephtheworker.net Rev. Mark Matthias, Pst.; Dcn. Peter J. Powell; Anita D'Imperio, DRE;

St. Vincent Pallotti, Haddon Township - (Worship Site)

St. Aloysius, Oaklyn - (Worship Site)

HAMMONTON

Saint Mary of Mount Carmel Parish, Hammonton, N.J. - 226 French St., Hammonton, NJ 08037 t) 609-704-5945 rel.ed@comcast.net; parishoffice@smmcp.net www.smmcp.net Rev. David Rivera, Pst.; Rev. Cesar A Rebolledo, Par. Vicar; Lori Scott Divetta, DRE; CRP Stds.: 505

Convent - 285 Rt 206, Hammonton, NJ 08037; Mailing: 226 French St, Hammonton, NJ 08037

St. Anthony, Hammonton -

St. Joseph, Hammonton -

LINDENWOLD

Our Lady of Guadalupe Parish, Lindenwold, N.J. - 135 N. White Horse Pike, Lindenwold, NJ 08021 t) (856) 627-2222 www.guadalupeshrinenj.org Rev. Rene L. Canales, Pst.; Rev. Ernest E. Amadi, Par. Vicar; Rev. Steven V. Pinzon, Par. Vicar; Dcn. Omar M. Aguilar; CRP Stds.: 344

John Paul II Regional School - (Grades PreK-8) 55 Warwick Rd., Stratford, NJ 08084 t) 856-783-3088 www.jp2rs.org Helen Persing, Prin.; Stds.: 229; Scholastics: 229; Lay Tchrs.: 14

St. Lawrence, Lindenwold -

St. Luke, Stratford -

LINWOOD

The Church of Our Lady of Sorrows, Linwood, N.J. - 724 Maple, Linwood, NJ 08221 t) 609-927-0121 Rev. Paul D. Harte, Pst.; Dcn. Joseph W. Lonergan; Melissa Stuchel, DRE;

MANTUA

R.C. Church of the Incarnation, Township of Mantua, New Jersey - 240 Main St., Mantua, NJ 08051 t) 856-468-7566 phouwen@incarnation-church.org Rev. Raymond P. Gormley, Pst.; Rev. Steven J. Bertonazzi, Par. Vicar; Dcn. Philip J. Curran; Dcn. Thomas F. O'Brien; Dcn. J. Peter Traum; CRP Stds.: 654

MARGATE CITY

Holy Trinity Parish, Margate, N.J. - 11 N. Kenyon Ave., Margate City, NJ 08402-1593 t) (609) 822-7105 holytrinitydownbeach.org Rev. Pawel Kryszkiewicz, Pst.; Rev. Christopher T. Bakey, Par. Vicar; Bernadette Southard, CRE; CRP Stds.: 148

Epiphany, Longport -

St. James, Ventnor -

St. Joseph Convent - 14 N. Jerome Ave., Margate City, NJ 08402

Blessed Sacrament, Margate -

MARMORA

The Parish of St. Maximilian Kolbe, Marmora, N.J. - 200 Tuckahoe Rd., Marmora, NJ 08223 t) (609) 390-0664 www.saintmaxkolbe.com Rev. Msgr. Peter M. Joyce, Pst.; Rev. Jose Ainikkal, C.M.I., In Res.; Dcn. Lawrence Schnepp; Agnes Bross, DRE; CRP Stds.: 303

MAYS LANDING

St. Vincent de Paul Parish, Mays Landing, N.J. - 5021 Harding Hwy., Mays Landing, NJ 08330-1707 t) (609) 625-2124 stvincentdepaulmayslanding@verizon.net Rev. Edward F. Heintzelman, Pst.; Dcn. Richard S. Maxwell; CRP Stds.: 91

St. Vincent de Paul, Mays Landing -

St. Vincent de Paul Parish, Mays Landing, N.J. School - (Grades PreK-8) 5809 Main St., Mays Landing, NJ 08330 t) 609-625-1565 Linda Pirolli, Prin.;

MERCHANTVILLE

St. Peter's Catholic Church, Merchantville, N.J. - 43 W. Maple Ave., Merchantville, NJ 08109 t) (856) 663-1373 Rev. Timothy E. Byerley, Pst.; Rev. Wilson Kidangan Paulose, Par. Vicar; CRP Stds.: 56

St. Peter School - (Grades PreK-8) 51 W. Maple Ave., Merchantville, NJ 08109 t) (856) 665-5879 www.stpeterschool.org Kathy O'Callaghan, Prin.; Stds.: 235; Lay Tchrs.: 35

MILLVILLE

The Parish of All Saints, Millville, N.J. - 621 Dock St., Millville, NJ 08332 t) (856) 825-0021 allsaintsnj.org Rev. Peter M. Idler, Pst.; Dcn. Severno S. Nasuti Jr.; Dcn. Russell O. Davis;

MULLICA HILL

Catholic Community of the Holy Spirit, Mullica Hill, N.J. - 17 Earlington Ave., Mullica Hill, NJ 08062-9418 t) 856-478-2294 office@holyspiritweb.org; rfanelli@holyspiritweb.org www.holyspiritweb.org Rev. Michael J. Field, Pst.; Rev. Joseph C. Pham, Par. Vicar; Dcn. Robert M. Fanelli; Dcn. Joseph H. Webb; Sr. Denise C. Ware, SFCC, DRE; CRP Stds.: 500

St. Joseph, Woodstown -

St. Ann, Elmer -

Holy Name of Jesus, Mullica Hill -

NEWFIELD

Our Lady of the Blessed Sacrament, Newfield, N.J. - 104 Catawba Ave., Newfield, NJ 08344-9512 t) 856-213-6259 www.olbsparishnj.com Rev. Ariel Hernandez, Pst.; Dcn. Anthony M. Jadick; Dcn. Charles S. Schiapelli; CRP Stds.: 206

Saint Rose of Lima, Newfield - t) (856) 213-6259 (Worship Site)

St. Mary, Malaga - 253 Dutch Mill Rd., Malaga, NJ 08328 t) (856) 213-6259 (Worship Site)

Our Lady of Victories, Landisville - 202 N.W. Blvd., Landisville, NJ 08326 t) (856) 213-6259 (Worship Site)

Saint Michael, Minotola - 504 S. West Blvd., Minotola, NJ 08341 t) (856) 213-6259 (Worship Site)

Villa Rossello - 1009 Main Rd., Newfield, NJ 08344

St. Padre Pio Shrine - 401 N. Harding Hwy., Landisville, NJ 08326; Mailing: Box 203, Landisville, NJ 08326

St. Barbara Chapel - 2334 E. Oak Rd., Vineland, NJ 08361

NORTH CAPE MAY

The Parish of Saint John Neumann, North Cape May, N.J. - 680 Town Bank Rd., North Cape May, NJ 08204-4413 t) 609-886-7640 Rev. Ernest R. Soprano, Pst.; Rev. Robert J. Fritz, In Res.; Sr. Kathleen Nuckols, I.H.M., DRE;

St. John of God, North Cape May - t) (609) 884-1656 x304 www.parishofstjohnneumann.org Rev. James H. King, Admin.;

St. Raymond, Villas - 800 Bayshore Rd., Villas, NJ 08251; Mailing: 680 Town Bank Rd., N. Cape May, NJ 08204 t) (609) 884-1656 x304 www.parishofstjohnneumann.org Rev. James H. King, Admin.;

Convent - 25 E. Ocean Ave., Villas, NJ 08251

NORTHFIELD

St. Gianna Beretta Molla Parish, Northfield, N.J. - 1421 New Rd., Northfield, NJ 08225-1103 t) 609-484-0249 Rev. Anthony J. Manuppella, Pst.; Rev. Sunny Matthew, In Res.; Rev. Alvaro Diaz;

Church: St. Bernadette, Northfield -

OCEAN CITY

Saint Damien Parish, Ocean City, N.J. - 1337 Asbury Ave., Ocean City, NJ 08226 t) 609-399-0648; 609-399-2643 (CRP) stdamienparish@comcast.net www.stdamienparish.com Rev. Thomas A. Newton, Pst.; Rev. Stephen Robbins;

Saint Augustine, Ocean City - 13th St & Wesley Ave., Ocean City, NJ 08226 (Worship Site)

Our Lady of Good Counsel, Ocean City - 40th St. & Asbury Ave., Ocean City, NJ 08226 (Worship Site)

St. Frances Cabrini, Ocean City - 2nd St. & Atlantic Ave., Ocean City, NJ 08226 (Worship Site)

PENNSAUKEN

Mary, Queen of All Saints, Pennsauken, N.J. - 4824 Camden Ave., Pennsauken, NJ 08110-1921 t) 856-662-2721 Rev. Edward M. Friel, Pst.; Dcn. Pedro J. Espinal; CRP Stds.: 75

Little Angels Child Care Center - 48th St. & Camden Ave., Pennsauken, NJ 08110

St. Cecilia School - (Grades K-8) 4851 Camden Ave., Pennsauken, NJ 08110 t) 856-662-0149 stceciliaschool@yahoo.com Sr. Alicia Perna, S.S.J., Prin.; Denise Carpenter, Librn.;

Saint Cecilia, Pennsauken -

Saint Veronica, Delair -

St. Stephen's R.C. Church, Pennsauken Township, N.J. - 6306 Browning Rd., Pennsauken, NJ 08109 t) 856-662-9338 www.ststephenspennsauken.com Rev. Jose Manjakunnel, Admin.;

RUNNEMEDE

Holy Child Parish, Runnemede, N.J. - 13 E. Evesham Rd., Runnemede, NJ 08078-1700 t) 856-939-1681 holychildparish@comcast.com Rev. Joseph F. Ganiel, Pst.; Rev. Antony Savari Muthu, Assoc. Pst.; Dcn. Leonard P. Carlucci; Dcn. David J. Harkins;

Convent - 18 Ardmore Ave., Runnemede, NJ 08078 Sisters, Servants of the Immaculate Heart of Mary

St. Maria Goretti, Runnemede -

St. Teresa, Runnemede -

SEA ISLE CITY

St. Joseph's Catholic Church, Sea Isle City, N.J. - 126 44th St., Sea Isle City, NJ 08243 t) 609-263-2087 (CRP); 609-263-8696 bookkeeper@stjosephsic.org Rev. Perry A. Cherubini, Pst.; Dcn. Joseph A. Murphy;

SEWELL

Church of the Holy Family, Washington Township - 226 Hurffville Rd., Sewell, NJ 08080 t) 856-228-2215 office@churchoftheholyfamily.org Rev. James L. Bartoloma, Pst.; Rev. Thanh Q. Pham, Par. Vicar; Dcn. Dean P. Johnson; Dcn. Joseph A. Kain Sr.;

SICKLERVILLE

The Church of St. Charles Borromeo, Washington Township, N.J. - 176 Stagecoach Rd., Sicklerville, NJ 08081 t) (856) 629-0411 churchofscb.org/ Rev. Michael J. Matveenko, Pst.; Dcn. Charles R. Dillin; Dcn. Lawrence S. Farmer; Dcn. Michael Kubiak; Mary Ann Exler, DRE; CRP Stds.: 852

SOMERS POINT

St. Joseph's Church, Somers Point, N.J. - 606 Shore Rd., Somers Point, NJ 08244 t) 609-927-3568 parish@stjosephsomerspoint.org www.stjosephsomerspoint.org Rev. Jaromir Michalak, Pst.; Rev. Carlo Santa Teresa, Par. Vicar; Dcn. Robert W. Hamilton; CRP Stds.: 215

St. Joseph Regional School - (Grades PreK-8) t) 609-927-2228 Regionalized with Our Lady of Sorrows Parish, Linwood; Saint Damien, Ocean City. Ted Pugliese, Prin.; Jan Hutton, Librn.;

TURNERSVILLE

The Church of Saints Peter and Paul, Washington Township, Gloucester County, N.J. - 362 Ganttown Rd., Turnersville, NJ 08012; Mailing: P.O. Box 1022, Turnersville, NJ 08012 t) 856-589-3366 office@churchofstspeterandpaul.org www.churchofstspeterandpaul.org Rev. Stephen J. Rapposelli, Pst.; Rev. Tomy O. Thomas, Par. Vicar; Dcn. Frank J. Campisi; Dcn. Anthony R. Cioe; CRP Stds.: 238

VINELAND

Christ the Good Shepherd Parish, Vineland, N.J. - 1655 Magnolia Rd., Vineland, NJ 08361-6598 t) (856) 691-9077 christthegoodshepherd1655@gmail.com christtheshepherdvineland.org/ Rev. Amadito Flores, Pst.; Rev. Anthony Infanti, Par. Vicar; Rev. John D. Wasilewski, Par. Vicar; Felicita Navarro, DRE; CRP Stds.: 116

The Church of Saint Isidore the Farmer, Vineland - christtheshepherdvineland.org/

The Catholic Church of the Sacred Heart, Vineland - 1010 E. Landis Avenue, Vineland, NJ 08360 christtheshepherdvineland.org

Bishop Schad Regional School - (Grades PreSchool-8) 922 E. Landis Ave., Vineland, NJ 08360 t) 856-691-4490 mmcfarland@bsrschool.org www.bsrschool.org Grammar School Sr. Rosa Maria Ojeda, M.D.P.V.M., Prin.; Stds.: 186; Lay Tchrs.: 10

Divine Mercy, Vineland, N.J. - 23 W. Chestnut Ave., Vineland, NJ 08360-5303 t) 856-691-9181 Rev. Joel Arciga Camarillo, Pst.;

Daughters of Mercy - t) 856-691-8129

Pope John Paul II Retreat Center - t) 856-691-2299

St. Francis of Assisi, Vineland -

Immaculate Heart of Mary, Vineland -

St. Padre Pio Parish, Vineland, N.J. - 736 S. Union Rd., Vineland, NJ 08361-6810 t) 856-691-9721 Rev. Robert L. Sinatra, Pst.; Rev. Dimitri Demesmin, Par. Vicar; Dcn. Robert Sampson;

St. Mary School - (Grades PreK-8) 735 Union Rd., Vineland, NJ 08360 t) 856-692-8537 mainoffice@smrschool.org www.smrschool.org Steven Hogan, Prin.; Raymond Yansick, Librn.;

Convent - 741 W. Union Rd., Vineland, NJ 08360

WILDWOOD

Notre Dame de la Mer Parish, Wildwood, N.J. - 1500 Central Ave., Ste. 100, Wildwood, NJ 08260 t) 609-522-2709 dsexton@notredamedelamer.org; mvey@notredamedelamer.org www.notredamedelamer.org Rev. Cadmus D. Mazzarella, Pst.; Rev. César Pirateque Serrano, Par. Vicar; CRP Stds.: 273

Assumption of the Blessed Virgin Mary, Wildwood Crest -

St. Ann, Wildwood -

WILLIAMSTOWN

Our Lady of Peace Parish, Monroe Township, N.J. - 32 Carroll Ave., Williamstown, NJ 08094-1713 t) 856-629-6142 olopp@olopp.org olopp.org Rev. Sanjai Devis, V.C., Pst.; Rev. Shajii Muttathottil, Par. Vicar; Rev. Naveen Borlakunta, In Res.; Dcn. James J. Hallman; Dcn. John J. Kacy; Dcn. Michael McDonaugh; CRP Stds.: 424

Our Lady of Peace Parish, Monroe Township, N.J. School - (Grades K-8) 32A Carroll Ave., Williamstown, NJ 08094 t) 856-629-6190 Patricia Mancuso, Prin.;

Church: Saint Mary, Williamstown -

WOODBURY

Holy Angels Parish, Woodbury, N.J. - 81 Cooper St., Woodbury, NJ 08096-4618 t) 856-845-0123 mail@holyangelsnj.org www.holyangelsnj.org Rev. E. Joseph Byerley, Pst.; Rev. Peter Gallagher, Par. Vicar; Rev. Nicholas Dudo, In Res.; Dcn. Michael A. D'Ariano; Dcn. Vincent Latini; Dcn. Samuel J. Spoto; CRP Stds.: 165

St. Matthew, National Park -

St. Patrick, Woodbury -

WOODBURY HEIGHTS

Infant Jesus Parish, Woodbury Heights, N.J. - 334 Beech Ave., Woodbury Heights, NJ 08097-1317 t) 856-848-0047 theinfantjesusparish@comcast.net www.theinfantjesusparish.org Rev. Joseph Luong Pham, Pst.; Rev. Alfred Mungujakisa, Pst. Assoc.; Dcn. Frank Dunleavy; Dcn. Joseph Farro;

St. Margaret - 845 Third St., Woodbury Hts., NJ 08097; Mailing: 334 Beech Ave., Woodbury Heights, NJ 08097

St. John Vianney - 2901 Good Intent Rd., Deptford, NJ 08096; Mailing: 334 Beech Ave., Woodbury Heights, NJ 08097

Convent - 745 Third St., Woodbury Heights, NJ 08097 t) 856-848-6049 Sr. Dianna Higgins, F.M.I.J., Supr.;

SCHOOLS: PRESCHOOL THRU HIGH SCHOOL

SCHOOLS

STATE OF NEW JERSEY

BERLIN

Our Lady of Mt. Carmel Regional School - (PAR) (Grades PreK-8) One Cedar Ave., Berlin, NJ 08009 t) 856-767-1751 olm@hotmail.com www.olmc-school.org Serving St. Simon Stock, Berlin; St. Andrew, Gibbsboro; Mater Ecclesiae, Bellmawr. Alice Malloy, Prin.;

BLACKWOOD

Our Lady of Hope Regional School - (PAR) (Grades PreK-8) 420 S. Black Horse Pike, Blackwood, NJ 08012 t) 856-227-4442 administration@olohschool.org www.ourladyofhopecatholicschool.org Serving Our Lady of Hope, Blackwood; SS. Peter & Paul, St. Charles Borromeo, & Holy Family, Washington Township. John T. Cafagna, Prin.; Sr. Paula Marie Randow, O.S.F., Prin.; Margie Rocco, Librn.;

CAPE MAY COURT HOUSE

The Bishop James T. McHugh Regional School, Inc. - (PAR) (Grades PreK-8) 2221 Rte. 9 N, Cape May Court House, NJ 08210 t) 609-624-1900 info@bishopmchugh.com www.bishopmchugh.com/ Alicia Farren, Prin.; Sr. Thomas Marie Rakus, Librn.; Stds.: 162; Lay Tchrs.: 11

COLLINGSWOOD

Good Shepherd Regional School - (PAR) (Grades PreK-8) 100 Lees Ave., Collingswood, NJ 08108 t) 856-858-1562 rbonnette@goodshepherdcollingswood.org www.goodshepherdcollingswood.org Serving Saint Teresa of Calcutta Parish, Collingswood; Most Precious Blood Parish, W. Collingswood; St. Joseph the Worker Parish, Haddon Township. Raymond A. Bonnette III, Prin.;

GALLOWAY

Assumption Regional School - (PAR) (Grades PreK-8) 146 S. Pitney Rd., Galloway, NJ 08205 t) 609-652-7134 jdollinger@arcsgalloway.org www.arcsgalloway.org Serving St. Elizabeth Ann Seton, Absecon; Our Lady of Perpetual Help, Galloway; St. Thomas, Brigantine. B. Joan Dollinger, Prin.;

GIBBSTOWN

Guardian Angels Regional School - (PAR) (Grades PreK-8) 150 S. School St., Gibbstown, NJ 08027 t) 856-423-9440 garsadvancement@gars-online.com Sr. Jerilyn Einstein, F.M.I.J., Prin.; Stds.: 220; Sr. Tchrs.: 1; Lay Tchrs.: 11

Gibbstown Campus - (Grades PreK-8) 150 S. School St., Gibbstown, NJ 08027 t) (856) 423-9440 Sr. Jerilyn Einstein, FMIJ, Prin.; Stds.: 220; Sr. Tchrs.: 1; Lay Tchrs.: 11

Paulsboro Campus - (Grades PreK-8) 717 Beacon Ave., Paulsboro, NJ 08066 t) 856-423-9401 Sr. Jerilyn Einstein, FMIJ, Prin.; Stds.: 220; Sr. Tchrs.: 1; Lay Tchrs.: 11

HADDONFIELD

Christ the King Regional School - (PAR) (Grades PreK-8) 164 Hopkins Ave., Haddonfield, NJ 08033 t) 856-429-2084 ahartman@ckrs.org www.ckrs.org Serving Christ the King, Haddonfield; Holy Eucharist, Cherry Hill. Anne Hartman, Prin.; Suzanne Urbach, Librn.;

RUNNEMEDE

St. Teresa Regional School - (PAR) (Grades PreK-8) 27 E. Evesham Rd., Runnemede, NJ 08078 t) 856-939-0333 principal@stteresaschool.org www.stteresaschool.org Sr. Nancy Kindelan, I.H.M., Prin.; Stds.: 148; Lay Tchrs.: 11

Convent - 18 Ardmore Ave., Runnemede, NJ 08078 t) 856-939-5508

VINELAND

Bishop Schad Regional School - (PAR) (Grades PreK-8) 922 E. Landis Ave., Vineland, NJ 08360 t) 856-691-4490 mainofc@bsrschool.org www.bsrschool.us Serving Christ the Good Shepherd; Divine Mercy; Holy Cross. Sr. Rosa Maria Ojeda, M.D.P.V.M., Prin.;

St. Mary's Regional School - (PAR) (Grades PreK-8) 735 Union Rd., Vineland, NJ 08360 t) 856-692-8537 mainoffice@smrschool.org www.smrschool.org Serving St. Padre Pio, East Vineland; All Saints, Millville; Our Lady of the Blessed Sacrament, Newfield. Steven P. Hogan, Prin.;

WESTVILLE GROVE

Archbishop Damiano School - (PRV) (Grades PreK-12) 1145 Delsea Dr., Bldg. B, Westville Grove, NJ 08093 t) 856-848-4700 financeoffice@sjogcs.org www.sjogcs.org Michele McCloskey, Exec.;

WOODBURY HEIGHTS

St. Margaret Regional School - (PAR) (Grades PreK-8) 773 Third St., Woodbury Heights, NJ 08097-1304 t) 856-845-5200 principal@stmargarets-rs.org www.stmargarets-rs.org Serving Infant Jesus Parish, Woodbury Heights; Incarnation, Mantua. Sr. Michele DeGregorio, F.M.I.J., Prin.; Stds.: 489; Lay Tchrs.: 20

HIGH SCHOOLS

STATE OF NEW JERSEY

ABSECON

Holy Spirit High School, Absecon, N.J. - (DIO) 500 S. New Rd., Absecon, NJ 08201 t) 609-646-3000 holyspirithighschool@yahoo.com www.holyspirithighschool.com Susan W. Dennen, Prin.; Rev. Perry A. Cherubini, Pres.; Joann Malecki, Librn.;

CHERRY HILL

Camden Catholic High School, Cherry Hill, N.J. - (DIO) (Grades 9-12) 300 Cuthbert Rd., Cherry Hill, NJ 08002 t) 856-663-2247 anne.buroojy@camdencatholic.org www.camdencatholic.org Mary Whipkey, Pres.; Heather Crisci, Prin.; Stds.: 652; Sr. Tchrs.: 1; Lay Tchrs.: 45

GLOUCESTER

Gloucester Catholic High School, Inc. - (PAR) (Grades 7-12) 333 Ridgeway St., Gloucester, NJ 08030 t) 856-456-4400 info@gchsrams.org www.gchsrams.org Thomas Iacovone Jr., Prin.; Stds.: 300; Lay Tchrs.: 22

HADDONFIELD

Paul VI High School, Haddon Township, N.J. - (DIO) (Grades 9-12) 901 Hopkins Rd., Ste. B, Haddonfield, NJ 08033 t) 856-858-4900 mchambers@pvihs.org; pgianfortune@pvihs.org pvihs.org Rev. Dexter Nebrida, A.M., Campus Min.; Philip Gianfortune, Prin.; Michael Chambers, Pres.; Michelle Anastasia, Librn.; Stds.: 980; Pr. Tchrs.: 1; Sr. Tchrs.: 1; Lay Tchrs.: 66

NEWFIELD

Our Lady of Mercy Academy - (PRV) (Grades 9-12) 1001 Main Rd., Newfield, NJ 08344 t) 856-697-2008 mrs.coyle@olmanj.org www.olmanj.org Daughters of Our Lady of Mercy. Sr. M. Ambrogina Aldeni, Prov.; Brooke A. Coyle, Prin.; Stds.: 221; Sr. Tchrs.: 1; Lay Tchrs.: 21

NORTH WILDWOOD

Wildwood Catholic High School - (PAR) 1500 Central Ave., #200, North Wildwood, NJ 08260 t) 609-522-7257 j.cray@wildwoodcatholic.org wildwoodcatholic.org Joseph Cray, Prin.; Rev. Cadmus D. Mazzarella, Pres.;

PENNSAUKEN

Bishop Eustace Prep School - (PRV) (Grades 9-12) 5552 Rte. 70, Pennsauken, NJ 08109-4798 t) 856-662-2160 x651 brotherjim@eustace.org www.eustace.org Society of the Catholic Apostolate, Province of the Immaculate Conception. Bro. James Beamesderfer, S.A.C., Supr.; Dr. P. Mark Ebner, Prin.; Rev. Jean Baptiste Mvukiyehe, S.A.C. (Rwanda), Chap.; Rev. Robert Nolan, S.A.C., In Res.; Dr. Jacqueline Coccia, CEO; Denise Avellino, Librn.; Stds.: 339; Lay Tchrs.: 36

RICHLAND

St. Augustine Preparatory School - (PRV) (Grades 8-12) 611 Cedar Ave., Richland, NJ 08350-0279 t) 856-697-2600 fr.curry@hermits.com www.hermits.com Order of St. Augustine, Province of St. Thomas of Villanova. Rev. Francis X. Devlin, O.S.A., Prior; Rev. Robert Murray, O.S.A., Pres.; Rev. Anthony Burrascano, O.S.A., Campus Min.; Bro. David Graber, M.SS.CC., Campus Min.; Rev. Stephen Curry, O.S.A., Treas.; Bro. Robert Thornton, O.S.A., Counselor;

INSTITUTIONS LOCATED IN DIOCESE

CAMPUS MINISTRY / NEWMAN CENTERS [CAM]

CAMDEN

Rutgers University - c/o 642 Market St., Camden, NJ 08102 t) 856-963-1285 camdencm@camdendiocese.org Rev. Krzysztof Wtorek, Chap.;

GLASSBORO

Rowan University - 1 Redmond Ave., Glassboro, NJ 08028; Mailing: 127 Church St., Glassboro, NJ 08028 t) 856-881-2554 youthministerkari@gmail.com www.rowanccm.com Rev. John A. Rossi, Pst.;

POMONA

Richard Stockton University - 235 Pomona Rd., Pomona, NJ 08240 t) 609-707-1067 www.ccmstockton.com Rev. James H. King, Chap.; Lois Dark, Dir.;

CATHOLIC CHARITIES [CCH]

CAMDEN

Catholic Charities, Diocese of Camden, Inc. - 1845 Haddon Ave., Camden, NJ 08103 t) 856-342-4100 kevin.hickey@camdendiocese.org www.catholiccharitiescamden.org Kevin H. Hickey, Exec.; Asstd. Annu.: 22,290; Staff: 51

Catholic Charities - Atlantic County - 9 N. Georgia Ave., Atlantic City, NJ 08401 t) 609-345-3448

Catholic Charities - Camden County - catholiccharitiescamden.org

Catholic Charities - Cape May County - Village Shoppes, 1304 Rte. 47 S., Rio Grande, NJ 08242 t) 609-886-2662

Catholic Charities - Cumberland County - 810 Montrose St., Vineland, NJ 08360 t) 856-691-1841

Catholic Charities - Salem County - 114 State St., Penns Grove, NJ 08069 t) 856-299-1296

Catholic Charities - Gloucester County - 1200 N. Delsea Dr., Ste. One, Westville, NJ 08093 t) 856-845-9200 catholiccharitiescamden.org

Counseling Center - Camden - t) 866-682-2166 sylvia.loumeau@camdendiocese.org catholiccharitiescamden.org Sylvia Loumeau, Dir.;

Guadalupe Family Services Inc. - 509 State St., Camden, NJ 08102 t) 856-365-8081 Sr. Helen Cole, S.S.J., Dir.;

CEMETERIES [CEM]

BELLMAWR

St. Mary's Cemetery & Mausoleum - t) 856-931-1570

BERLIN

Gate of Heaven Cemetery - t) 856-767-3354

BRIDGETON

St. Mary's Cemetery - t) 856-455-2323 (Holy Cross)

CAMDEN

Camden Diocesan Center - Cemeteries - 631 Market St., Camden, NJ Marianne Linka, Dir.;

CEDARBROOK

Sacred Heart Cemetery - t) 856-767-0719 (Christ the Redeemer, Atco)

CHERRY HILL

Calvary Cemetery & Mausoleum - t) 856-663-3345

CHEWS LANDING

St. Joseph's Cemetery and Mausoleum - t) 856-228-7588 (St. Joseph, Camden)

CLERMONT

Resurrection Cemetery - t) 609-624-1284

COLD SPRINGS

St. Mary's Cemetery & Mausoleum - t) 609-624-1284

DOROTHY

St. Bernard Cemetery - t) 609-625-2123 (Holy Cross Cemetery, Rte. 40, Mays Landing)

EAST VINELAND

St. Mary's Cemetery - t) 856-691-7526 (Padre Pio)

Our Lady of Pompeii Cemetery - t) 856-691-7526 (Padre Pio)

GLASSBORO

St. Bridget's Cemetery - 125 Church St., Glassboro, NJ 08028 t) 856-881-2753 parishoffice@stbridgeup.org (St. Bridget Church) Rev. John A. Rossi, Pst.;

GOSHEN

St. Elizabeth's Cemetery - t) 609-624-1284

HAMMONTON

Holy Sepulchre Cemetery - t) 609-704-5945 (St. Mary of Mt. Carmel)

LANDISVILLE

Our Lady of Victories Cemetery - t) 856-691-1290

MAYS LANDING

Holy Cross Cemetery & Mausoleum - Rte. 40, Mays Landing, NJ 08330 t) 609-625-2123

MILLVILLE

Holy Cross Cemetery - t) 856-825-0021 (All Saints, Millville)

MULLICA HILL

Holy Name Cemetery - t) 856-478-2294 (Catholic Community of the Holy Spirit)

NEWFIELD

All Saints Cemetery and Mausoleum - t) 856-697-1098

PLEASANT MILLS

Our Lady of the Assumption Cemetery - Closed, (Call Holy Cross Cemetery, Mays Landing)

ROSENHAYN

St. Mary's Cemetery - t) 856-455-2323 (Holy Cross, Bridgeton)

SALEM

St. Mary's Cemetery - t) 856-299-3833 (St. Gabriel Church, Carneys Point)

SWEDESBORO

St. Joseph's Cemetery - t) 856-767-3354

VINELAND

Sacred Heart Cemetery & Mausoleum - t) 856-691-1290

WILLIAMSTOWN

St. Mary's Cemetery - t) 856-767-3354

WOODBINE

St. Casimir's Cemetery - t) 609-624-1284

WOODSTOWN

St. Joseph's Cemetery - t) 856-478-2294 (Catholic Community of the Holy Spirit, Mullica Hill)

CONVENTS, MONASTERIES, AND RESIDENCES FOR WOMEN [CON]

ATLANTIC CITY

St. John's Retreat House - 128 S. Dover Ave., Atlantic City, NJ 08401 t) 609-317-4399

CHERRY HILL

Franciscan Missionary Sisters of the Infant Jesus, Inc. - 1215 Kresson Rd., Cherry Hill, NJ 08003 t) 856-428-8834 fmijusdel@yahoo.com Sr. Jerilyn Einstein, F.M.I.J., Supr.; Srs.: 10

Little Servant Sisters of the Immaculate Conception - 1000 Cropwell Rd., Cherry Hill, NJ 08003 t) 856-424-1962 s.dorotab@gmail.com www.lsic.us Provincialate and Novitiate. Rev. Zbigniew Majcher, S.D.B., Chap.; Mother Dorota Baranowska, L.S.I.C., Prov.;

ELMER

The Sisters of Mary Immaculate of Nyeri, Inc. - 400 State St., Elmer, NJ 08318 t) 856-358-4030 smisep1999@yahoo.com Sr. Anne Mugo, S.M.I., Pres.;

NEWFIELD

Daughters of Our Lady of Mercy - 1009 Main Rd., Newfield, NJ 08344 t) 856-697-2983 daughtersofmercy@gmail.com www.olmanj.org/daughtersofmercyhome/ Provincial House and Novitiate of Daughters of Our Lady of Mercy. Sr. M. Ambrogina Aldeni, Prov.;

PLEASANTVILLE
Hospitaler Sisters of Mercy Novitiate - 915 S. Main St., Pleasantville, NJ 08232 t) 609-677-1407; 609-645-9300 hospitaler@comcast.net; villaraffaella@msn.com www.hospitalersistersofmercy.org Sr. Marykutty Karuvelil, Supr.; Srs.: 12
Hospitaler Sisters of Mercy Convent -
SEA ISLE CITY
The Sisters of St. Francis of Philadelphia - 55th & Landis Ave., Sea Isle City, NJ 08243 t) 610-558-7676 emoore@osfphila.org www.osfphila.org Sr. Eleanor Moore, Admin.;
SOMERS POINT
Sisters of St. Joseph of Chestnut Hill - 580 Shore Rd., Somers Point, NJ 08244
STONE HARBOR
Villa Maria by the Sea - 11101 First Ave., Stone Harbor, NJ 08247 t) 609-368-3621; 609-368-5290 Summer retreat house for Sisters Servants of the Immaculate Heart of Mary. (Immaculata, PA)
VENTNOR
The Benedictine Sisters of Elizabeth, NJ - 114 S. Troy Ave., Ventnor, NJ 08406 t) 609-823-9843
Holy Family, Seaside Convent - 110 S. Dorset Ave., Ventnor, NJ 08406; Mailing: 497 Western Hwy., Blauvelt, NY 10913 t) 845-359-5600; 609-822-5127 mconnolly@opblauvelt.org Sr. Michaela Connolly, Prioress;

ENDOWMENTS / FOUNDATIONS / TRUSTS [EFT]

CAMDEN
Diocese of Camden Healthcare Foundation, Inc. - 631 Market St., Camden, NJ 08102
Diocese of Camden Trusts, Inc. - 631 Market St., Camden, NJ 08102 t) 856-583-2831 Martin F. McKernan Jr., Contact;
Francis, Elizabeth and Edward Roger Welsh Scholarship Trust - 631 Market St., Camden, NJ 08102 t) 856-583-2831 Laura Montgomery, Contact;
The Sharkey Family Charitable Trust - 631 Market St., Camden, NJ 08102 t) 856-583-2802 Rev. James L. Bartoloma, Chancellor;

HOSPITALS / HEALTH SERVICES [HOS]

CAMDEN
Virtua Our Lady of Lourdes Hospital, Inc. - 1600 Haddon Ave., Camden, NJ 08103 t) 856-757-3500 rhansel@virtua.org www.virtua.org Mark Nessel, Pres.;
Our Lady of Lourdes School of Nursing - t) 856-757-3730 hensleyp@lourdesnet.org www.lourdesnursingschool.org Reginald Blaber, Pres.;

MISCELLANEOUS [MIS]

BERLIN
Mater Ecclesiae Mission - 261 Cross Keys Rd., Berlin, NJ 08009-9431 t) 856-753-3408 rector@materecclesiae.org www.materecclesiae.org Rev. Glenn R. Hartman; Rev. Robert C. Pasley, Rector;
CAMDEN
***Camden Center for Law and Social Justice, Inc.** - 509 State St., Camden, NJ 08102 t) 856-583-2950 jdecristofaro@cclsj.org; info@cclsj.org Jeffrey S. DeCristofaro, Dir.;
Camden Center for Law and Social Justice, Inc. Immigration Services & Legal Assistance to the Poor - 126 N. Broadway, Camden, NJ 08103 t) 856-966-8896; 609-348-2111
Catholic Business Network of South Jersey, Inc. - 631 Market St., Camden, NJ 08102
Catholic Partnership Schools, Camden, N.J., Inc. - 2824 River Rd., Camden, NJ 08105; Mailing: PO Box 42, Pennsauken, NJ 08110 t) (856) 966-6791 www.catholicpartnershipschools.org/ Jameka Walker, Exec. Dir.;
DeSales Service Works Inc. - 642 Market St., Camden, NJ 08102; Mailing: 2200 Kentmere Pkwy., Wilmington, DE 19806 t) 215-582-1666 ghoffman@oblates.org Rev. Michael J. McCue, O.S.F.S., Dir.;
The Diocesan Housing Services Corporation of The Diocese of Camden, Incorporated - 1845 Haddon Ave., Camden, NJ 08103 t) 856-342-4125 katherine.boyer@camdendiocese.org James M. Reynolds, Exec.; Katherine Boyer, Dir.;
CAPE MAY
Soul Mates for Jesus, Inc. - 1027 Virginia Ave., Cape May, NJ 08204 t) 609-884-7176
CHERRY HILL
Benedict's Place, Inc. - 206 St. Mary's Dr., Cherry Hill, NJ 08003 t) 856-874-0183 housingservices@camdendiocese.org Katherine Boyer, Dir.;
EGG HARBOR TOWNSHIP
Holy Redeemer Home Care - 6550 Delilah Rd., Ste. 501, Egg Harbor Township, NJ 08234 t) 609-761-0300; 800-788-3029 A subsidiary of Holy Redeemer Health System, Inc.
Atlantic County Office -
Holy Redeemer Home Care - 1801 Rte. 9 N., Cape May Court House, NJ 08210 t) 609-465-2082; 800-745-4693 www.holyredeemer.com A subsidiary of the Holy Redeemer, C.S.R., A Medicare Certified Home Health Agency serving patients in their own homes. Terry Giannetti, Exec. Vice Pres.;
HADDON HEIGHTS
***Collegium Center for Faith and Culture** - 301 White Horse Pike, Haddon Heights, NJ 08035 t) 856-534-0400 brenda@thecollegiumcenter.org Rev. Timothy E. Byerley, Dir.; Brenda Quinn, Dir.;
HAINESPORT
Domicilium Corporation (Davenport Village) - 301 Davenport Ave., Hainesport, NJ 08036 t) 609-702-0138 housingservices@camdendiocese.org Katherine Boyer, Dir.;
LANDISVILLE
Padre Pio Shrine, Buena Borough, N.J., Inc. - 401 N. Harding Hwy., Landisville, NJ 08326-0203; Mailing: Box 203, Landisville, NJ 08326-0203
NORTH CAPE MAY
Christ Child Society, Cape May County Chapter - 680 Town Bank Rd., North Cape May, NJ 08204; Mailing: P. O. Box 882, North Cape May, NJ 08204 t) 609-602-7682 ccscapemay@gmail.com christchildcmc.com Dorothy Bauer, Treas.;
PENNSAUKEN
Stonegate at St. Stephen, Inc. - 5101 Stonegate Dr., Ste. 100, Pennsauken, NJ 08109 t) 856-486-7877 housingservices@camdendiocese.org Katherine Boyer, Dir.;
PLEASANTVILLE
Village at St. Peter's Inc. - 25 W. Black Horse Pike, Pleasantville, NJ 08232 t) 609-382-4181 housingservices@camdendiocese.org Katherine Boyer, Dir.;
WEST DEPTFORD
Shepherd's Farm Senior Housing, Inc. - 981 Grove Rd., West Deptford, NJ 08086 t) 856-848-4913
WESTVILLE GROVE
St. John of God Community Services, Inc. - 1145 Delsea Dr., Bldg. A, Westville Grove, NJ 08093 t) 856-848-4700 x1142 sjogfinanceoffice@sjogcs.org www.sjogcs.org Bro. Thomas Osorio, O.H., Exec.;

MONASTERIES AND RESIDENCES FOR PRIESTS AND BROTHERS [MON]

CHERRY HILL
Sacred Heart Residence for Priests, Inc. - 200 St. Mary's Dr., Cherry Hill, NJ 08003 t) 856-751-2010
Sacred Heart North - 250 St. Mary's Dr., Cherry Hill, NJ 08003 t) 856-424-1741
LINWOOD
Villa Pieta. Missionaries of the Sacred Hearts of Jesus & Mary - 2249 Shore Rd., Linwood, NJ 08221; Mailing: P.O. Box 189, Linwood, NJ 08221 t) 609-927-5600 mssccusa@aol.com missionofsacredhearts.org Rev. Frederick Clement, M.SS.CC., Rector; Rev. John Perdue, M.SS.CC., Rector; Rev. Damian Anumba; Bro. David Graber, M.SS.CC.;
MARGATE
Franciscan Friary - 118 S. Mansfield Ave., Margate, NJ 08402-2516 margate1@comcast.net Holy Name Province.
OCEAN CITY
Augustinian Friars - St. Rita of Cascia Cottage, 823 5th St., Ocean City, NJ 08226 t) 609-398-1299 Rev. Joseph S. Mostardi, O.S.A.;
Ocean Rest Summer School and Retreat House - 3041 Central Ave., Ocean City, NJ 08226; Mailing: 444-A Rte. 35 S., Eatontown, NJ 07724 t) 732-380-7926; 609-840-6045 juliano@fscdena.org Brothers of Christian Schools Retreat House. Bro. Joseph Juliano, F.S.C., Dir.;
PLEASANTVILLE
Villa Raffaella - 917 S. Main St., Pleasantville, NJ 08232 t) 609-645-9300
WESTVILLE GROVE
Hospitaller Order of St. John of God - 1145 Delsea Dr., Westville Grove, NJ 08093 t) 856-848-4700 x1142 tosorio@sjogcs.org; judy@sjog-na.org www.sjog-na.org Bro. Thomas Osorio, O.H., Prior; Brs.: 3

NURSING / REHABILITATION / CONVALESCENCE / ELDERLY CARE [NUR]

CAPE MAY
Victorian Towers, Inc. - 608 Washington St., Cape May, NJ 08204 t) 609-884-5883 housingservices@camdendiocese.org Katherine Boyer, Dir.;
CHERRY HILL
Village Apartments of Cherry Hill, NJ, Inc. - 350 Mt. Carmel Ct., Cherry Hill, NJ 08003 t) 856-424-7913 villageapartments@camdendiocese.org Katherine Boyer, Dir.;
NORTH CAPE MAY
Haven House at St. John of God, Inc. - 676 Townbank Rd., North Cape May, NJ 08204 t) 609-884-4548 housingservices@camdendiocese.org Katherine Boyer, Dir.;
PLEASANTVILLE
Villa Raffaella Assisted Living - 917 S. Main St., Pleasantville, NJ 08232 t) 609-645-9300 villaraffaella@msn.com www.villaraffaella.com Senior Assisted Living Community, Hospitaler Sisters of Mercy. Sr. Elizabeth Rani Gnanapragasam, Admin.; Asstd. Annu.: 60; Staff: 36

PRESCHOOLS / CHILDCARE CENTERS [PRE]

CAMDEN
St. Joseph Child Development Center, Inc. - 17 Church St., Camden, NJ 08105 t) 856-963-9202 stjosephcdc@yahoo.com Jim Steinitz, Admin.; Margaret Klein, Dir.;
CHERRY HILL
Blessed Edmund Early Childhood Education Center - 1000 Cropwell Rd., Cherry Hill, NJ 08003 t) 856-424-3063 blessededmund@verizon.net Sr. Zofia Szczepek, LSIC, Prin.;

RETREAT HOUSES / RENEWAL CENTERS [RTR]

CAPE MAY POINT
Marianist Family Retreat Center - 417 Yale Ave., Cape May Point, NJ 08212-0488; Mailing: Box 488, Cape May Point, NJ 08212-0488 t) 609-884-3829 mfrc@capemaymarianists.org www.capemaymarianists.org Rev. David McGuigan, SM, Chap.; Anthony Fucci, Dir.; Bro. Stan Zubek, S.M.;
SEA ISLE CITY
Saint Joseph by-the-Sea - 18 47th St., Sea Isle City, NJ 08243 t) (215) 248-7205 Sisters of Saint Joseph of Chestnut Hill, Philadelphia Sr. Maureen G. Erdlen, SSJ, Rel. Ord. Ldr.;

VINELAND
Pope John Paul II Retreat Center - 414 S. 8th St., Vineland, NJ 08360 t) 856-691-2299 sccpjiirc@aol.com
Margarita Moran, Dir.;

An asterisk (*) denotes an organization that has established tax-exempt status directly with the IRS and is not covered by the USCCB Group Ruling.

Diocese of Charleston

(Dioecesis Carolopolitana)

MOST REVEREND JACQUES FABRE-JEUNE, C.S.

Bishop of Charleston; ordained October 10, 1986; appointed Bishop of Charleston February 22, 2022; consecrated and installed May 13, 2022. Office: 901 Orange Grove Rd., Charleston, SC 29407.

Chancery Office: 901 Orange Grove Rd., Charleston, SC 29407. T: 843-261-0420; F: 843-804-9408.
charlestondiocese.org
jamie@charlestondiocese.org

ESTABLISHED JULY 11, 1820.

Square Miles 31,189.

Comprises the State of South Carolina.

For legal titles of parishes and diocesan institutions, consult the Chancery Office.

STATISTICAL OVERVIEW

Personnel

Bishop	1
Retired Bishops	1
Retired Abbots	1
Priests: Diocesan Active in Diocese	75
Priests: Diocesan Active Outside Diocese	5
Priests: Retired, Sick or Absent	23
Number of Diocesan Priests	103
Religious Priests in Diocese	48
Total Priests in your Diocese	151
Extern Priests in Diocese	25
Ordinations:	
Diocesan Priests	1
Transitional Deacons	1
Permanent Deacons	15
Permanent Deacons in Diocese	165
Total Brothers	13
Total Sisters	96

Parishes

Parishes	94
With Resident Pastor:	
Resident Diocesan Priests	70
Resident Religious Priests	23
Without Resident Pastor:	
Administered by Priests	1
Missions	21
Professional Ministry Personnel:	
Brothers	1
Sisters	16
Lay Ministers	216

Welfare

Catholic Hospitals	2
Total Assisted	281,219
Homes for the Aged	1
Total Assisted	30
Specialized Homes	1
Total Assisted	175
Special Centers for Social Services	14
Total Assisted	36,906

Educational

Diocesan Students in Other Seminaries	17
Total Seminarians	17
High Schools, Diocesan and Parish	5
Total Students	1,718
High Schools, Private	1
Total Students	659
Elementary Schools, Diocesan and Parish	27
Total Students	5,146
Catechesis / Religious Education:	
High School Students	2,313
Elementary Students	9,280
Total Students under Catholic Instruction	19,133
Teachers in Diocese:	
Priests	5
Sisters	11
Lay Teachers	748

Vital Statistics

Receptions into the Church:	
Infant Baptism Totals	2,430
Minor Baptism Totals	287
Adult Baptism Totals	232
Received into Full Communion	364
First Communions	2,292
Confirmations	2,261
Marriages:	
Catholic	472
Interfaith	198
Total Marriages	670
Deaths	1,446
Total Catholic Population	205,947
Total Population	5,282,634

OFFICES AND DIRECTORS

Archives & Records Management, Office of - t) (843) 410-1720 Brian P. Fahey, Archivist (bfahey@charlestondiocese.org); Melissa J. Mabry, Assoc. Archivist (mmabry@charlestondiocese.org); Charles Wujcik, Archives Asst. (cwujcik@charlestondiocese.org);

Bishop, Office of the - t) 843-225-7349 Most Rev. Jacques Fabre-Jeune, C.S., Bishop; Joan Smith, Exec. Admin. Asst. (jsmith@charlestondiocese.org);

Bishop's Residence - Donald Glover, Mgr. (dglover@charlestondiocese.org);

Cemeteries - t) 843-795-2111 Karmin Meade, Dir. (kmeade@charlestondiocese.org); Laurie Bowdoin-Burns, Cemetery Counselor (lburns@charlestondiocese.org); Charlotte Moore, Admin. Asst. (charlottem@charlestondiocese.org);

Ceremonies, Diocesan Master of -

Chancellor, Office of the - t) (843) 225-7493 Sr. Sandra Makowski, S.S.M.N., Chancellor (smakowski@charlestondiocese.org);

Child & Youth Protection - t) (800) 921-8122 Kristin Eyre, Dir., Victim Assistance Coord. (keyre@charlestondiocese.org); Kiya Felder, Admin. Asst. (kfelder@charlestondiocese.org); Bailey Janowski, Admin. Asst. (bjanowski@charlestondiocese.org);

Continuing Education for Priests - t) 864-582-0674 Rev. David R. Whitman, Dir. (dwhitman@charlestondiocese.org);

Diaconate, Office of - Dcn. John Tempesco, Dir. (jtempesco@charlestondiocese.org); Dcn. Reginald A.T. Armstrong, Dir., Formation (rarmstrong@charlestondiocese.org); Bobbi Wagner, Admin. Asst. (bwagner@charlestondiocese.org);

Divine Worship & Sacraments, Vicar for -

Ecumenical & Interreligious Affairs - t) 843-819-7991 Sr. Pamela Smith, SS.C.M., Dir. (psmith@charlestondiocese.org);

General Counsel and Real Estate, Office of - Elaine H. Fowler, Gen. Counsel & Dir. Real Estate (efowler@charlestondiocese.org); Katelyn S. Davis, Exec. Asst. (kdavis@charlestondiocese.org);

Hermits, Director of - Rev. Michael J. Oenbrink, Dir. (moenbrink@charlestondiocese.org);

Hispanic Ministry, Office of - Rev. Teofilo Trujillo, Vicar (ttrujillo@charlestondiocese.org); Gustavo Valdez, Dir. (gvaldez@charlestondiocese.org); Sr. Guadalupe Flores, O.L.V.M., Hispanic Adult Faith Formation Coord. (gflores@charlestondiocese.org);

Migrant Farmworkers Ministry - Rev. Vincent Henry Finnerty, CM, Hispanic Outreach Priest; Sr. Migdalia Flores, D.C., Migrant Farmworkers Ministry Coord.; Sr. Consuelo Tovar, D.C., Migrant Farmworkers Ministry Coord.;

Information Technology, Office of - t) 864-278-0202 support@unginc.com

Insurance - Eric H. Meister, Risk/Claims Mgr. (emeister@catholicmutual.org); Elizabeth Tarditi, Senior Svc. Office Asst. (etarditi@catholicmutual.org);

Marian Programs - t) 843-355-3527 Rev. Stanley Smolenski, S.P.M.A., Dir. (olscshrine@gmail.com);

Missionary Childhood Association - t) 843-696-9095 propagation@charlestondiocese.org www.propfaithcharlestonsc.com/ Rev. Msgr. Edward D. Lofton, Dir. (elofton@charlestondiocese.org); Helena Moniz, Assoc. Dir.;

Planning and Operations, Office of - Kelly Bruce, Dir. (kbruce@charlestondiocese.org); Jamie K. Zbyrowski, Supvr. (jamie@charlestondiocese.org); David Pfrommer, Project Mgr. (dpfrommer@charlestondiocese.org);

Priest Personnel, Office of - Rev. Msgr. Ronald R. Cellini, Vicar for Priests; Dcn. Jeffrey P. Mevissen, Priest Personnel Coord. (jmevissen@charlestondiocese.org);

Propagation of the Faith - t) 843-696-9095 propagation@charlestondiocese.org www.propfaithcharlestonsc.com/ Rev. Msgr. Edward D. Lofton, Dir. (elofton@charlestondiocese.org); Helena Moniz, Assoc. Dir.;

Religious, Vicar for - Sr. Sandra Makowski, S.S.M.N., Vicar (smakowski@charlestondiocese.org);

Retired Priests, Vicar for - t) (843) 795-3821 Rev. S. Thomas Kingsley, Vicar (skingsley@charlestondiocese.org);

Social Ministry, Office of - t) 843-225-7938 Lydia Doyle, Interim Secy., Social Ministries & Exec. Dir. Catholic Charities (ldoyle@charlestondiocese.org); Kathy Schmugge, Senior Dir. Social Ministries; Mollie Kay, Coord. (mkay@charlestondiocese.org);

Campaign for Human Development - ldoyle@charlestondiocese.org Lydia Doyle;

Family Life, Office of - t) (803) 547-5063 kschmugge@charlestondiocese.org Rev. David D. Nerbun, Vicar; Kathy Schmugge, Dir.; Christy Brown, Respect Life, Project Rachel Coord.;

Intercultural Ministries, Office of -

Asian and Pacific Islander Ministry -

Black Catholic Ministry, Office of - t) (864) 331-2633 kathleen@charlestondiocese.org Rev. Michael C. Okere (Nigeria), Vicar for Black Catholics; Kathleen Merritt, Dir.; Michael Gourdin, Assoc. Dir.;

Vietnamese Ministry - t) (864) 395-0202 dphan@charlestondiocese.org Rev. David Q. Phan, O.F.M.;

International Ministries - gcuervo@charlestondiocese.org Dcn. Gabriel Cuervo, Dir.;

Seafarer Ministries - t) (843) 822-3572 prosenblum@charlestondiocese.org Dcn. Paul M. Rosenblum, Dir.;

Vicar General, Office of the - Rev. Msgr. D. Anthony Droze, Vicar Gen. (vicargeneraldroze@charlestondiocese.org); Rev. Msgr. Richard D. Harris, Vicar Gen. (vicargeneralharris@charlestondiocese.org); Cynde Stacey, Exec. Asst. (cstacey@charlestondiocese.org);

Victim Assistance Coordinator - t) 843-856-0748; 800-921-8122 (Toll Free) Kristin Eyre (keyre@charlestondiocese.org);

Vocations, Office of - Rev. Msgr. Richard D. Harris, Vicar (vicargeneralharris@charlestondiocese.org); Rev. Rhett Butler Williams, Dir. (rwilliams@charlestondiocese.org); Jean-Marie Jump, Coord. (jmjump@charlestondiocese.org);

ADVISORY BOARDS, COMMISSIONS, COMMITTEES, AND COUNCILS

Academy of Life - Rev. Scott Francis Binet, Chair (sbinet@charlestondiocese.org); Kathy Schmugge, Vice Chm.; Rev. John Antonydas Gaspar (jgaspar@charlestondiocese.org);

Accounting and Finance Committee - Terence J. Conway, Chair; Larry Earl; Jack Gallagher;

Building & Renovation Advisory Committee - Rev. Msgr. Richard D. Harris, Chair (vicargeneralharris@charlestondiocese.org); John Barker (jbarker@charlestondiocese.org); Terri Brisson (tbrisson@charlestondiocese.org);

Catechetical Advisors, Diocesan Board of - Dr. Michael Martocchio, Dir. (mmartocchio@charlestondiocese.org); Maureen Arneman, Myrtle Beach Deanery Rep.; Maria Barontini, Greenville Deanery Rep.;

College of Consultors - Rev. Msgr. Richard D. Harris, Vicar General (vicargeneralharris@charlestondiocese.org); Rev. Msgr. D. Anthony Droze, Vicar General (vicargeneraldroze@charlestondiocese.org); Very Rev. C. Thomas Miles, Judicial Vicar (tmiles@charlestondiocese.org);

Curia - Most Rev. Jacques Fabre-Jeune, C.S., Bishop; Rev. Msgr. Richard D. Harris, Vicar Gen. (vicargeneralharris@charlestondiocese.org); Rev. Msgr. D. Anthony Droze, Moderator (vicargeneraldroze@charlestondiocese.org);

Diaconate Board - Dcn. John Tempesco, Chair (jtempesco@charlestondiocese.org); Rev. Msgr. Ronald R. Cellini; Very Rev. Gregory B. Wilson;

Finance Council - Terence J. Conway; Scott Cracraft; Joseph J. Keenan;

Investment Committee - Scott Cracraft, Chair; John Barker, CFO (jbarker@charlestondiocese.org); Georgia French;

Official Catholic Directory Committee - John Barker (jbarker@charlestondiocese.org); Kelly Bruce (kbruce@charlestondiocese.org); Elaine H. Fowler (efowler@charlestondiocese.org);

Presbyteral Council -

Deans - Rev. Msgr. Ronald R. Cellini, Beaufort Dean; Very Rev. Raymond J. Carlo, Charleston Dean; Very Rev. Edward W. Fitzgerald, Myrtle Beach Dean;

Deanery Representatives - Rev. Emmanuel O. Andinam, Aiken Deanery; Rev. Patrick O. Eyinla, Charleston Deanery; Rev. Rafael Boshra Ghattas, Beaufort Deanery;

At Large Representative -

Ex-Officio Members - Rev. Msgr. Richard D. Harris, Moderator; Rev. Msgr. D. Anthony Droze; Very Rev. C. Thomas Miles;

Recorders - Jean-Marie Jump; Daniel Wagner;

Priest Personnel Board - Rev. Msgr. Ronald R. Cellini, Chair; Most Rev. Jacques Fabre-Jeune, C.S.; Rev. Msgr. Richard D. Harris (vicargeneralharris@charlestondiocese.org);

Priest Retirement Committee - John Barker, Chair (jbarker@charlestondiocese.org); Most Rev. Jacques Fabre-Jeune, C.S.; Rev. Msgr. Richard D. Harris (vicargeneralharris@charlestondiocese.org);

Scouting, Diocese of Charleston Catholic Committee on - t) (803) 414-7181 gfaller56@gmail.com www.docccs.org/home Rev. Andrew Jaroslav Fryml, Chap. (afryml@charlestondiocese.org); George Faller, Chair;

Seminary Admissions Board - Rev. Rhett Butler Williams, Chair (rwilliams@charlestondiocese.org); Most Rev. Jacques Fabre-Jeune, C.S.; Rev. Msgr. Richard D. Harris (vicargeneralharris@charlestondiocese.org);

COMMUNICATIONS

Communications and Public Affairs, Secretariat of - t) (843) 261-0535 Michael F. Acquilano, Secy. (macquilano@charlestondiocese.org);

The Catholic Miscellany - themiscellany.org Anne E. Clark, Senior Publications Specialist;

Communications, Office Of - Juanita Bustamante, Video Ministry Producer; Anne E. Clark, Sr. Publications Specialist; Lauren Elfrink, Digital Content Specialist;

South Carolina Catholic Conference - Michael F. Acquilano, Dir.; Caroline Funk, Legislative Affairs Specialist;

DEANERIES

Deans -

Aiken Deanery - t) 803-649-4777 gwilson@charlestondiocese.org Very Rev. Gregory B. Wilson, Dean;

Beaufort Deanery - t) 843-261-0540 rcellini@charlestondiocese.org Rev. Msgr. Ronald R. Cellini, Dean;

Charleston Deanery - t) 843-873-0631 rcarlo@charlestondiocese.org Very Rev. Raymond J. Carlo, Dean;

Columbia Deanery - t) 803-779-0036 glinsky@charlestondiocese.org Rev. Canon Gary S. Linsky, Dean;

Greenville Deanery - t) 864-271-8422 jsnewman@charlestondiocese.org Very Rev. Jay Scott Newman, Dean;

Myrtle Beach Deanery - t) 843-651-3737 efitzgerald@charlestondiocese.org Very Rev. Edward W. Fitzgerald, Dean;

Rock Hill Deanery - t) 803-548-7282 frefosco@charlestondiocese.org Very Rev. Fabio Refosco, C.O., Dean;

EDUCATION

Education, Secretariat for - t) (843) 261-0496 William Ryan, Secy. Educ. & Supt. Catholic Schools (wryan@charlestondiocese.org); Shaileen Riginos, Assoc. Supt., Accreditation & Strategic Planning (sriginos@charlestondiocese.org); Kimberly Hopkins, Coord. (khopkins@charlestondiocese.org);

EVANGELIZATION

Evangelization, Secretariat for - t) (843) 261-0503 Dr. Michael Martocchio (mmartocchio@charlestondiocese.org);

Catechesis and Christian Initiation - Dr. Michael Martocchio, Secy. Evangelization; Cathy Roche, Coord.;

Youth, Young Adult, and Campus Ministry - t) (843) 261-0443 jwhite@charlestondiocese.org Dcn. Jerry White, Dir.; Dr. Ryan Altenbach, Assoc. Dir.; Mary Corder, Coord.;

FINANCE

Finance, Office of - t) (843) 261-0468 John Barker, CFO (jbarker@charlestondiocese.org); Kelsey Shooter, Exec. Admin. Asst. to CFO (kshooter@charlestondiocese.org);

Financial Services - Terri Brisson, Dir.; Christine Brothers, Controller; David Amatangelo, Mgr., Parish Accounting Svcs.;

HUMAN RESOURCES

Human Resources, Office of - t) (843) 261-0422 Elizabeth Isch, Dir. (eisch@charlestondiocese.org); Matt Campbell, Mgr. (mcampbell@charlestondiocese.org); Shelby Vincent, Supvr. (svincent@charlestondiocese.org);

ORGANIZATIONS

Courage South Carolina Chapter - t) (803) 432-6131 couragerc.org/ Rev. John M. Zimmerman, Chap. (jzimmerman@charlestondiocese.org);

STEWARDSHIP

Stewardship & Mission Advancement, Office of - t) (843) 261-0435 Carrie Mummert, Dir. (cmummert@charlestondiocese.org); Brian Alberts, Assoc. Dir. (balberts@charlestondiocese.org); Ruthie Major, Mission Advancement Coord. (rmajor@charlestondiocese.org);

TRIBUNAL

Tribunal, Office of the - t) 843-261-0450 tribunal@charlestondiocese.org

Judicial Vicar - Very Rev. C. Thomas Miles;

Moderator of the Tribunal - Valerie Maxineau;

Tribunal Judges - Rev. Msgr. Charles H. Rowland; Very Rev. Jay Scott Newman; Rev. H. Gregory West;

Defender of the Bond - Very Rev. Edward W. Fitzgerald;

Promoter of Justice - Very Rev. Edward W. Fitzgerald;

Auditor - Katharine Giglio;

Procurators/Advocates - Dcn. Thomas Baranoski; Dcn. David Wagner; Meg Walter;

Ecclesiastical Notary - Katharine Giglio; Charles Wujcik;

Archival Records Technician - Charles Wujcik;

Court Expert - Lee Hartnett;

PARISHES, MISSIONS, AND CLERGY

STATE OF SOUTH CAROLINA

ABBEVILLE

Sacred Heart - 206 N. Main St., Abbeville, SC 29620; Mailing: P.O. Box 812, Abbeville, SC 29620 t) 864-366-5150 gmayer@charlestondiocese.org sacredheartabbeville.com Rev. Jacob P. Joseph, C.M.I., Pst.;

AIKEN

St. Gerard - 640 Edrie St., N.E., Aiken, SC 29801 t) 803-649-3203 msolenberger@charlestondiocese.org stgerardaiken.org Rev. Emmanuel O. Andinam, Admin.;

St. Mary Help of Christians - 203 Park Ave., S.E., Aiken, SC 29801 t) 803-649-4777 pwray@charlestondiocese.org www.stmarys-aiken.org Very Rev. Gregory B. Wilson, Pst.; Rev. Orlando Serrano Ardila, MXY/IMEY, Par. Vicar; Rev. Msgr. William J. Gomes, In Res.; Dcn. Alejandro Leguizamon; Dcn. Al Matousek; Dcn. Robert A. Pierce; Dcn. Stephen Platte; CRP Stds.: 128

St. Mary Help of Christians Catholic School - (Grades K-8) 118 York St. S.E., Aiken, SC 29801 t) 803-649-2071 lwebster@charlestondiocese.org www.stmaryschoolaiken.com Laura Webster, Prin.; Stds.: 224; Lay Tchrs.: 28

ALLENDALE

St. Mary Mission - 3457 Bluff Rd., Allendale, SC 29810; Mailing: c/o St. Andrew, 110 Madison St., Barnwell, SC 29812 t) 803-450-5116 kvargo@charlestondiocese.org Mission of St. Andrew in Barnwell. Rev. Prasad Antony, M.S.S.C.C., Admin.; Rev. A. John DeBritto, M.S.S.C.C., Par. Vicar; CRP Stds.: 12

ANDERSON

St. Joseph - 1200 Cornelia Rd., Anderson, SC 29621; Mailing: 1303 McLees Rd., Anderson, SC 29621 t) 864-225-5341 dthompson@charlestondiocese.org www.sjccs.net Rev. Philip S. Gillespie, Pst.; Rev. David A. Runnion, In Res.; Dcn. Salvatore Cancello; Dcn. Thomas Chet Johns; Dcn. James L. West; CRP Stds.: 44

St. Joseph Catholic School - (Grades PreK-7) t) 864-760-1619 hgiuliani@charlestondiocese.org sjccs.net/school/ Haymee Giuliani, Prin.; Stds.: 101; Lay Tchrs.: 10

St. Mary of the Angels - 1821 White St., Anderson, SC 29624 t) 864-226-8621 officesma@charlestondiocese.org www.sma43.org Rev. Jairo A. Calderon, Admin.; CRP Stds.: 48

BARNWELL

St. Andrew - 110 Madison St., Barnwell, SC 29812 t) 803-450-5116 kvargo@charlestondiocese.org Rev. Prasad Antony, M.S.S.C.C., Admin.; Rev. A. John DeBritto, M.S.S.C.C., Par. Vicar; CRP Stds.: 21

BATESBURG-LEESVILLE

St. John of the Cross - 320 W. Columbia Ave., Batesburg-Leesville, SC 29006; Mailing: P.O. Box 2279, Batesburg-Leesville, SC 29070 t) 803-532-1208 sjc@charlestondiocese.org Rev. Jose Rodolfo Lache-Avila (Colombia), Admin.; CRP Stds.: 100

BEAUFORT

St. Peter - 70 Lady's Island Dr., Beaufort, SC 29907 t) 843-522-9555 asudomerski@charlestondiocese.org www.stpetersbeaufort.org Rev. Andrew Trapp, Pst.; Rev. Agustin Torm, In Res.; Dcn. Michael A. Beeler; Dcn. Daniel Carrera; Dcn. Eugene Kelenski; Sr. Margarita del Carmen Morales Galdamez, D.J.B.P., Hispanic Coord.; CRP Stds.: 117

St. Peter Catholic School - (Grades PreK-6) t) 843-522-2163 afeltner@charlestondiocese.org saintpeters.school Ann Feltner, Prin.; Sr. Agnes Marie Winter, SS.C.M., Office Asst.; Stds.: 160; Sr. Tchrs.: 1; Lay Tchrs.: 16

BENNETTSVILLE

St. Denis - 100 Tyson Ave., Bennettsville, SC 29512; Mailing: c/o St. Peter, 602 Market St., Cheraw, SC 29520 t) 843-537-7351 ntria@charlestondiocese.org Mission of St. Peter in Cheraw. Rev. Noel Tria (Philippines), Pst.;

BLUFFTON

St. Gregory the Great - 31 Saint Gregory Dr., Bluffton, SC 29909 t) 843-815-3100 ctrott@charlestondiocese.org www.sgg.cc Rev. Msgr. Ronald R. Cellini, Pst.; Rev. Saleh Diego, Par. Vicar; Rev. Rafael Boshra Ghattas, Par. Vicar; Rev. Pedro Gomez Barajas, MXY/IMEY, Par. Vicar; Rev. Luis E. Serrano Carrero, Weekly Assistance; Dcn. Dennis Burkett, Marriage & Annulment Coord.; Dcn. Michael Carter; Dcn. John Crapanzano; Dcn. James Graham; Dcn. Brent Heathcott; Dcn. Edward Melton; Dcn. Barry O'Brien; Dcn. Michael Smigelski; CRP Stds.: 485

St. Andrew - 220 Pinckney Colony Rd., Bluffton, SC 29909

St. Gregory the Great Catholic School - (Grades PreK-6) 38 Saint Gregory Dr., Bluffton, SC 29909 t) 843-815-9988 ekelley@charlestondiocese.org www.sggcs.org Elizabeth Kelley, Prin.; Stds.: 187; Lay Tchrs.: 16

BLYTHEWOOD

Transfiguration - 306 N. Pines Rd., Blythewood, SC 29016; Mailing: 9720 Wilson Blvd, Blythewood, SC 29016 t) 803-735-0512 vshealy@charlestondiocese.org www.transfigurationsc.org Rev. Msgr. James L. LeBlanc, Pst.; Dcn. David Shinn; Dcn. John Tempesco; CRP Stds.: 90

BONNEAU

Our Lady of Peace Mission - 224 Murray's Ferry Rd., Bonneau, SC 29431; Mailing: 1404 Old Hwy. 52 S., c/o St. Philip Benizi, Moncks Corner, SC 29461 t) 843-761-3777 kgotz@charlestondiocese.org www.spbcc.org Mission of St. Philip Benizi in Moncks Corner Rev. Allam Marreddy (India), Pst.; Dcn. Jerome P. Remkiewicz; CRP Stds.: 3

CAMDEN

Our Lady of Perpetual Help - 1709 Lyttleton St., Camden, SC 29020 t) 803-432-6131 nromaniello@charlestondiocese.org ourlady-camden.org Rev. John M. Zimmerman, Pst.; Dcn. Stephen Goodman; CRP Stds.: 147

CHAPIN

Our Lady of the Lake - 195 Amicks Ferry Rd., Chapin, SC 29036 t) 803-345-3962 donnie.jameson@charlestondiocese.org www.ollchapin.org Rev. Dennis B. Willey, Pst.; Dcn. James Atkinson; Dcn. James Chin; Dcn. Malcolm Skipper; Dcn. John Stetar; Dcn. Gregory Weigold; CRP Stds.: 266

CHARLESTON

Cathedral of St. John the Baptist - 120 Broad St., Charleston, SC 29401 t) 843-724-8395 sstewart@charlestondiocese.org charlestoncathedral.com Rev. Msgr. D. Anthony Droze, Admin. Pro-tem; Dcn. Thomas Baranoski; Dcn. James Letendre; Dcn. Charles Olimpio; CRP Stds.: 61

Blessed Sacrament - 5 St. Teresa Dr., Charleston, SC 29407 t) 843-556-0801 lroberson@charlestondiocese.org www.blsac.org Rev. Arnulfo Jara Galvez (Colombia), Pst.; Rev. Derrick Sneyd, Par. Vicar; Dcn. Kurt Herbst; Dcn. Joseph Keating; Dcn. James R. Moore; Dcn. Jerry White; Sr. Colie Stokes, SSMN, Director of RCIA; CRP Stds.: 152

Blessed Sacrament School - (Grades PreK-8) 7 St. Teresa Dr., Charleston, SC 29407 t) 843-766-2128 corinnek@charlestondiocese.org www.scbss.org Corinne King, Prin.; Stds.: 274; Lay Tchrs.: 22

Church of the Nativity - 1061 Folly Rd., Charleston, SC 29412 t) 843-795-3821 cmiller@charlestondiocese.org nativitycharleston.org Rev. S. Thomas Kingsley, Pst.; CRP Stds.: 92

Nativity School - (Grades PreK-8) 1125 Pittsford Cir., Charleston, SC 29412 t) 843-795-3975 pdukes@charlestondiocese.org www.nativity-school.com Patricia Dukes, Prin.; Stds.: 104; Lay Tchrs.: 16

St. Joseph - 1695 Wallenberg Blvd., Charleston, SC 29407 t) 843-556-4611 cpucino@charlestondiocese.org www.saintjosephchas.com Rev. Patrick O. Eyinla, Pst.; Dcn. David Wagner; CRP Stds.: 89

St. Mary of the Annunciation - 95 Hasell St., Charleston, SC 29401; Mailing: 89 Hasell St., Charleston, SC 29401 t) 843-722-7696 rachterhof@charlestondiocese.org sma.church Rev. Msgr. D. Anthony Droze, Pst.; Rev.

Patrick Allen, Part-time Parochial Vicar; Dcn. Paul M. Rosenblum; CRP Stds.: 65

St. Patrick - 134 St. Phillip St., Charleston, SC 29403; Mailing: P.O. Box 20726, Charleston, SC 29413 t) 843-723-6066 bbuford@charlestondiocese.org www.stpatrickcharleston.org Rev. Robert F. Higgins, Admin.; Dcn. John Breeden; Dcn. Markus Damwerth; CRP Stds.: 28

Sacred Heart - 888 King St., Charleston, SC 29403 t) 843-722-7018 aprince@charlestondiocese.org www.sacredheartcharleston.org Rev. James Renaurd West, Pst.; Dcn. Jeffrey DeFrehn; Dcn. Gary Ludlam; CRP Stds.: 14

Charleston Catholic School - (Grades PreK-8) 888-A King St., Charleston, SC 29403 t) 843-577-4495 fmckay@charlestondiocese.org www.charlestoncatholic.com Fred S. McKay Jr., Prin.; Stds.: 180; Lay Tchrs.: 18

CHERAW

St. Peter - 602 Market St., Cheraw, SC 29520 t) 843-537-7351 ntria@charlestondiocese.org Rev. Noel Tria (Philippines), Pst.; Dcn. Gustavo Salazar; CRP Stds.: 8

CHESTER

St. Joseph - 110 W. End St., Chester, SC 29706; Mailing: P.O. Box 869, Chester, SC 29706 t) 803-377-4695 jrodgers@charlestondiocese.org josephchester.org Rev. Agustin Guzman, C.O., Pst.;

CLEMSON

St. Andrew - 209 Sloan St., Clemson, SC 29631; Mailing: PO Box 112, Clemson, SC 29633 t) 864-654-1757 saclemson@charlestondiocese.org saclemson.org Rev. Daniel McLellan, O.F.M., Pst.; Rev. Robert J. Menard, O.F.M., In Res.; Dcn. Richard Campana Sr.; Dcn. John Leininger; Dcn. Gordon Snyder; Dcn. Anthony Wagner; CRP Stds.: 113

COLUMBIA

St. John Neumann - 100 Polo Rd., Columbia, SC 29223; Mailing: 721 Polo Rd., Columbia, SC 29223 t) 803-788-0811 info@sjnchurch.com www.stjohnneumannsc.com Rev. C. Alexander McDonald, Pst.; Dcn. Ronald J. Anderson; Dcn. Enrique Bautista; CRP Stds.: 200

St. John Neumann Catholic School - (Grades PreK-6) 721 Polo Rd., Columbia, SC 29223 t) 803-788-1367 rpoles@charlestondiocese.org www.sjncatholic.com Ronald Poles, Prin.; Stds.: 302; Lay Tchrs.: 28

St. Joseph - 3600 Devine St., Columbia, SC 29205; Mailing: 3512 Devine St., Columbia, SC 29205 t) 803-254-7646 info@stjosephcolumbia.org www.stjosephcolumbia.org Rev. Msgr. Richard D. Harris, Pst.; Rev. William C. Frei, Par. Vicar; Sr. Mary Cecile Swanton, C.S.J.B., Dir., Spiritual Devel.; CRP Stds.: 96

St. Joseph Catholic School - (Grades PreK-6) 3700 Devine St., Columbia, SC 29205 t) 803-254-6736 dyarnall@charlestondiocese.org www.stjosdevine.com Donavan Yarnall, Prin.; Stds.: 259; Pr. Tchrs.: 1; Lay Tchrs.: 27

Saint Martin de Porres - 2229 Hampton St., Columbia, SC 29204 t) 803-254-6862 stmartincolumbia@charlestondiocese.org www.stmartincolumbia.org Rev. Michael C. Okere (Nigeria), Pst.; Dcn. Leland Cave; Dcn. Leonard P. Chambliss Jr.; CRP Stds.: 32

St. Martin de Porres Catholic School - (Grades PreK-5) 2225 Hampton St., Columbia, SC 29204 t) 803-254-5477 dgilliard@charlestondiocese.org www.saintmartindeporres.org Delores Gilliard, Prin.; Sr. Vitalina Chimavi, C.S.J.B., Teacher; Stds.: 53; Sr. Tchrs.: 1; Lay Tchrs.: 13

Our Lady of the Hills - 120 Marydale Ln., Columbia, SC 29210 t) 803-772-7400 oloh@charlestondiocese.org www.ourladyofthehillssc.org Rev. Peter E. Sousa, C.Ss.R., Pst.; Rev. Blas Caseres, C.Ss.R., Par. Vicar; Rev. George Rosario, C.Ss.R., In Res.; Dcn. Stephen Burdick; Dcn. Gerard Couture; Dcn. Mark Gray; Dcn. Dennis N. Jones; Dcn. Charles LaRosa Jr.; Dcn. Thomas Souza; Dcn. Jason Werny; Dcn. James Vinson Williams; Sr. Christina Murphy, S.N.D.deN., Pst. Assoc.; CRP Stds.: 272

Minor Basilica of St. Peter - 1529 Assembly St., Columbia, SC 29201; Mailing: P.O. Box 1896, Columbia, SC 29202 t) 803-779-0036 cnowak@charlestondiocese.org; bhaas@charlestondiocese.org www.visitstpeters.org Rev. Canon Gary S. Linsky, Rector; Rev. Gustavo Corredor, PT Par. Vicar; Dcn. Brian Durocher; Dcn. David Thompson; CRP Stds.: 159

St. Peter's Catholic School - (Grades PreK-6) 1035 Hampton St., Columbia, SC 29201 t) 803-252-8285 awall@charlestondiocese.org stpeterscatholicschool.org Aubrey Wall, Prin.; Stds.: 133; Sr. Tchrs.: 1; Lay Tchrs.: 13

St. Thomas More - 1610 Greene St., Columbia, SC 29201 t) 803-799-5870 pamela.scott@charlestondiocese.org stthomasmoreusc.org Rev. Rhett Butler Williams, Pst.; Dcn. Stephen Brown; CRP Stds.: 21

CONWAY

St. James the Younger - 1071 Academy Dr., Conway, SC 29526 t) 843-347-5168 stjames@charlestondiocese.org stjamesconway.org Rev. Oscar Borda Rojas, Pst.; Dcn. Tim Papa; CRP Stds.: 208

DANIEL ISLAND

St. Clare of Assisi - 225 Seven Farms Dr., Ste. 100, Daniel Island, SC 29492 t) 843-471-2121 rvatalaro@charlestondiocese.org clare.church Rev. H. Gregory West, Pst.; Dcn. Gregory W. Sams; CRP Stds.: 335

DARLINGTON

St. Joseph the Worker Mission - 1308 N. Main St., Darlington, SC 29532; Mailing: c/o St. Mary, the Virgin Mother, 363 N. 5th St., Hartsville, SC 29550 t) 843-332-7773 dkavanagh@charlestondiocese.org www.stmaryhartsville.org Mission of St. Mary, the Virgin Mother in Hartsville Rev. Daniel R. Papineau, Pst.;

DILLON

St. Louis - 610 Hwy. 301 N., Dillon, SC 29536; Mailing: 610 A Hwy. 301 N., Dillon, SC 29536 t) 843-627-3311 slcdillon@charlestondiocese.org Rev. Cirilo Bailon Martinez, Admin.; CRP Stds.: 45

EASLEY

St. Luke Mission - 4408 Hwy. 86, Easley, SC 29642 t) 864-855-9039 ekyle@charlestondiocese.org holycrossstluke.org Mission of Holy Cross in Pickens. Rev. James N. Dubrouillet, Pst.; CRP Stds.: 74

EDGEFIELD

St. Mary of the Immaculate Conception - 302 Jeter St., Edgefield, SC 29824 t) 803-637-6248 stmaryscc@charlestondiocese.org www.stmaryedgefieldsc.org Rev. Emeka Emmanuel Ekwelum, M.S.S.C.C., Admin.; Rev. Kentigern Ariríguzo, M.S.S.C.C., Par. Vicar; Rev. Anthony Swamy, M.S.S.C.C., Par. Vicar; Dcn. Larry Deschaine; CRP Stds.: 3

EDISTO ISLAND

Sts. Frederick & Stephen Mission - 554 Hwy. 174, Edisto Island, SC 29438; Mailing: P.O. Box 602, Edisto Island, SC 29438 t) 843-631-1459 edistocatholic@charlestondiocese.org www.edistocatholic.com Mission of St. Mary on Yonges Island. Rev. Jesuprathap Narichetti (India), Pst.;

FLORENCE

St. Ann - 113 S. Kemp St., Florence, SC 29506 t) 843-661-5012 blewis@charlestondiocese.org stannecatholicparish.com Rev. JohnBosco Duraisamy (India), Pst.; Rev. Sylvere Baloza, C.I.C.M., Par. Vicar; Dcn. Robert L. Cox III; Dcn. David Kahn Sr.; CRP Stds.: 41

St. Anthony - 2536 W. Hoffmeyer Rd., Florence, SC 29501; Mailing: PO Box 5327, Florence, SC 29502 t) 843-662-5674 afoyle@charlestondiocese.org www.saintanthony.com Rev. JohnBosco Duraisamy (India), Pst.; Rev. Sylvere Baloza, C.I.C.M., Par. Vicar; Dcn. Reginald A.T. Armstrong; Dcn. Bruce Fortnum; Dcn. Michael Woodall; CRP Stds.: 91

St. Anthony Catholic School - (Grades PreK-8) t) 843-662-1910 kgalemmo@charlestondiocese.org www.saintanthonycatholic.com Kristine Galemmo, Prin.; Stds.: 124; Lay Tchrs.: 13

FOLLY BEACH

Our Lady of Good Counsel - 56 Center St., Folly Beach, SC 29439; Mailing: P.O. Box 1257, Folly Beach, SC 29439 t) 843-588-2336 ndeneane@charlestondiocese.org olgc-follybeach.org/ Rev. Henry N. Kulah (Ghana), Pst.; CRP Stds.: 50

FORT MILL

St. Philip Neri - 292 Munn Rd., Fort Mill, SC 29715 t) 803-548-7282 lcurry@charlestondiocese.org www.saintphilipneri.org Very Rev. Fabio Refosco, C.O., Pst.; Dcn. David Bartholomew; Dcn. Jon E. Dwyer; Dcn. George Johnston; Dcn. Steven Rhodes; CRP Stds.: 750

GAFFNEY

Sacred Heart - 407 Grace St., Gaffney, SC 29340; Mailing: 205 Sams St., Gaffney, SC 29340 t) 864-489-9453 rrodriguez@charlestondiocese.org www.sacredheartgaffney.org/ Rev. Bruce Barnett, Admin.; CRP Stds.: 154

GEORGETOWN

St. Mary, Our Lady of Ransom - 317 Broad St., Georgetown, SC 29440 t) 843-546-7416 stmarygeorgetown@charlestondiocese.org www.stmaryourladyofransom.org Rev. James F. Touzeau, Admin.; Dcn. Michael Brescia; CRP Stds.: 104

GLOVERVILLE

Our Lady of the Valley - 2429 Augusta Rd., Gloverville, SC 29828; Mailing: P.O. Box 419, Gloverville, SC 29828 t) 803-593-2241 bthouin@charlestondiocese.org Rev. Emeka Emmanuel Ekwelum, M.S.S.C.C., Admin.; Rev. Kentigern Ariríguzo, M.S.S.C.C., Par. Vicar; Rev. Anthony Swamy, M.S.S.C.C., Par. Vicar; CRP Stds.: 5

GOOSE CREEK

St. Francis Caracciolo Mission - 510 St. James Ave., Goose Creek, SC 29445 t) 843-572-1270 canebaycc@charlestondiocese.org Rev. Noly Berjuega, C.R.M., Pst.; Rev. Binil Jose Attappattu, C.R.M., Par. Vicar; Rev. Sebastian Thomas, C.R.M., Par. Vicar; Dcn. Joseph Donovan;

Immaculate Conception - 510 St. James Ave., Goose Creek, SC 29445 t) 843-572-1270 cfaretra@charlestondiocese.org www.icgc510.org Rev. Noly Berjuega, C.R.M., Pst.; Rev. Binil Jose Attappattu, C.R.M., Par. Vicar; Rev. Sebastian Thomas, C.R.M., Par. Vicar; Rev. Frank Palmieri, C.R.M., In Res.; Dcn. Pelagio Caoile; Dcn. Jose Mayen; Dcn. Daniel McNerny; Dcn. John Murphy; Dcn. Lawrence Roberts; CRP Stds.: 218

GREAT FALLS

St. Michael Mission - 310 Chester Ave., Great Falls, SC 29055; Mailing: c/o St. Catherine of Siena, 720 W. Meeting St., Lancaster, SC 29720 t) 803-283-3362 stcstm@charlestondiocese.org stcatherinecatholic.org/ Mission of St. Catherine of Siena, Lancaster Rev. Javier Heredia, Admin.;

GREENVILLE

St. Anthony of Padua - 307 Gower St., Greenville, SC 29611 t) 864-233-7717 mcorner@charlestondiocese.org www.newstanthony.com Rev. Wilbroad Mwape, Pst.; Dcn. Phil Allen; Dcn. Anthony J. Cassandra; Dcn. Dexter Gourdin; Dcn. Steven Olson; Dcn. Winston C. Wright; CRP Stds.: 95

St. Anthony of Padua Catholic School - (Grades PreK-5) 311 Gower St., Greenville, SC 29611 t) 864-271-0167 stanthonygreenvillesc.org Mamie Boyd, Interim Prin.; Stds.: 147; Sr. Tchrs.: 1; Lay Tchrs.: 22

St. Mary - 111 Hampton Ave., Greenville, SC 29601 t) 864-271-8422 pperkins@charlestondiocese.org www.smcgvl.org Very Rev. Jay Scott Newman, Pst.; Rev. Jose Orlando Cheverria Jimenez (Colombia), Par. Vicar; Rev. Jonathan C. Duncan, Par. Vicar; Dcn. Diego Ferro; Dcn. Alex Garvey; Dcn. John Heuser; Dcn. Joseph Sanfilippo Jr.; Dcn. George Tierney; Dcn.

Thomas Whalen; CRP Stds.: 126

St. Mary's Catholic School - (Grades PreK-8) 101 Hampton Ave., Greenville, SC 29601 t) 864-271-3870 szimmerman@charlestondiocese.org smsgvl.org Steven Zimmerman, Prin.; Stds.: 321; Sr. Tchrs.: 3; Lay Tchrs.: 18

Our Lady of the Rosary - 3710 Augusta Rd., Greenville, SC 29605 t) 864-422-1648 mmahan@charlestondiocese.org www.olrgreenville.com Rev. Dwight Longenecker, Pst.; Rev. Richard Ballard, Par. Vicar; Dcn. Michael Bannio; Dcn. Jerry Schiffer; CRP Stds.: 67

Our Lady of the Rosary Catholic School - (Grades PreK-12) 2 James Dr., Greenville, SC 29605 t) 864-277-5350 tcurtin@charlestondiocese.org olrschool.net Thomas Curtain, Prin.; Stds.: 257; Lay Tchrs.: 18

San Sebastian Mission - 2300 Old Buncombe Rd., Greenville, SC 29609 t) 864-534-1063 wrivera@charlestondiocese.org www.sansebastiancatholicchurch.org Mission of St. Mary in Greenville. Very Rev. Jay Scott Newman, Pst.; Rev. Jose Orlando Cheverria Jimenez (Colombia), Sacramental Responsibilities & In Res.; CRP Stds.: 304

GREENWOOD

Our Lady of Lourdes - 915 Mathis Rd., Greenwood, SC 29646 t) 864-223-8410 wlordemann@charlestondiocese.org www.olol.org Rev. Francisco Javier Onate-Vargas, Pst.; Dcn. Joseph P. Biviano; Dcn. Matthew Houle; CRP Stds.: 160

GREER

Blessed Trinity - 901 River Rd., Greer, SC 29651 t) 864-879-4225; 864-655-5140 jlawrence@charlestondiocese.org; jcruzrodriguez@charlestondiocese.org www.blessedtrinitysc.org Rev. Jose Gabriel Cruz Rodriguez, Pst.; Dcn. Samuel Aguilar; CRP Stds.: 116

Our Lady of La Vang - 2020 Gibbs Shoals Rd., Greer, SC 29650 t) 864-395-0202 dphan@charlestondiocese.org www.olvnsc.org Rev. David Q. Phan, O.F.M., Admin.; CRP Stds.: 78

HAMPTON

St. Mary Mission - 703 5th St. E., Hampton, SC 29924 t) 843-726-3606 stanthonyridgeland@charlestondiocese.org Mission of St. Anthony in Ridgeland. Rev. Luis E. Serrano Carrero, Admin.;

HANAHAN

Divine Redeemer - 1106 Fort Dr., Hanahan, SC 29410 t) 843-553-0340 msabback@charlestondiocese.org www.divineredeemerchurch.org Rev. Raynier Q. Dabu, C.R.S. (Philippines), Admin.; Dcn. Jim Baker; Dcn. Douglas Erickson; Dcn. Andre J.P. Guillet; CRP Stds.: 117

Divine Redeemer Catholic School - (Grades PreK-8) 1104 Fort Dr., Hanahan, SC 29410 t) 843-553-1521 emartyn@charlestondiocese.org www.drcs.co/ Elizabeth Martyn, Prin.; Stds.: 144; Lay Tchrs.: 15

HARDEEVILLE

St. Anthony Mission - 23049 Whyte Hardee Blvd., Hardeeville, SC 29927; Mailing: 21 Main St., Hardeeville, SC 29927 t) 843-784-2943 stanthonyhardeeville@charlestondiocese.org www.saintanthonymission.com/ Rev. Msgr. Ronald R. Cellini, Admin. Pro-Tem; Dcn. Brian Laws; Dcn. John Lee; Sr. Candelaria Garcia Alvarez, D.J.B.P., Hispanic Ministries Coord.; CRP Stds.: 65

HARTSVILLE

St. Mary the Virgin Mother - 363 N. 5th St., Hartsville, SC 29550 t) 843-332-7773 dkavanagh@charlestondiocese.org www.stmaryhartsville.org Rev. Daniel R. Papineau, Pst.; CRP Stds.: 54

HILTON HEAD ISLAND

St. Francis By the Sea - 45 Beach City Rd., Hilton Head Island, SC 29926 t) 843-681-6350 djenks@charlestondiocese.org www.stfrancishhi.org Rev. Michael J. Oenbrink, Pst.; Rev. Christopher Brenden Loester, Par. Vicar; Rev. Jose P. Quilcate, Par. Vicar; Rev. Maximino E. Tria Jr., Par. Vicar; Dcn. Gerard Hand; Dcn. Joseph J. Nazzaro; Dcn. David Ritter; Dcn. Patrick Sheehan; CRP Stds.: 116

St. Francis Catholic School - (Grades PreK-8) t) 843-681-6501 andrea.smith@charlestondiocese.org www.sfcshhi.com Andrea Smith, Prin.; Stds.: 215; Lay Tchrs.: 24

St. Francis Thrift Shop - 6 Southwood Park Dr., Hilton Head Island, SC 29926 t) 843-689-6563 stfrancisthrifthhi@gmail.com stfrancisthriftshophhi.org Hal Wieland, Dir.;

Holy Family - 24 Pope Ave, Hilton Head Island, SC 29928 t) 843-785-2895 rdewolfe@charlestondiocese.org www.holyfamilyhhi.org Rev. Ronald J. Farrell, Pst.; Rev. Jose P. Quilcate, Par. Vicar; Dcn. John DeWolfe; CRP Stds.: 148

JOANNA

St. Boniface - 401 N. Main St., Joanna, SC 29351 t) 864-923-0780 stbonifacejoanna@charlestondiocese.org Rev. Jose Hugo Ruiz-Marentes, Pst.; CRP Stds.: 17

JOHNS ISLAND

Holy Spirit - 3871 Betsy Kerrison Pkwy., Johns Island, SC 29455 t) 843-768-0357 mlubic@charlestondiocese.org holyspiritsc.org/ Rev. Msgr. Charles H. Rowland, Pst.; Rev. John Antonydas Gaspar, Par. Vicar; Dcn. Mario Cardenas; Dcn. John Hardy; Dcn. Joseph Stocker; CRP Stds.: 43

JOHNSONVILLE

St. Patrick Mission - 110 Church St., Johnsonville, SC 29555; Mailing: c/o St. Philip, the Apostle, P.O. Box 399, Lake City, SC 29560 t) 843-394-8343 rthomy@charlestondiocese.org Mission of St. Philip, the Apostle in Lake City Rev. Artur Przywara, Pst.;

KINGSTREE

St. Ann - 107 Hirsch St., Kingstree, SC 29556; Mailing: P.O. Box 529, Kingstree, SC 29556 t) 843-355-5234 ftaylor@charlestondiocese.org Rev. Artur Przywara, Pst.; Dcn. Harold Jackson;

LAKE CITY

St. Philip the Apostle - 120 Westover St., Lake City, SC 29560; Mailing: PO Box 399, Lake City, SC 29560 t) 843-394-8343 rthomy@charlestondiocese.org Rev. Artur Przywara, Pst.; Dcn. Harold Jackson; Dcn. Asuncion Valadez; CRP Stds.: 10

LAKE WYLIE

All Saints Parish - 530 Hwy. 274, Lake Wylie, SC 29710 t) 803-831-9095 falley@charlestondiocese.org allsaintslakewylie.com Rev. John P. Giuliani, C.O., Pst.; Rev. Edward P. McDevitt, C.O., Par. Vicar; Dcn. Andrew Fatovic; Dcn. John Hall; CRP Stds.: 271

LANCASTER

St. Catherine of Siena - 720 W. Meeting St., Lancaster, SC 29720 t) 803-283-3362 stcstm@charlestondiocese.org www.stcatherinecatholic.org Rev. Javier Heredia, Admin.; CRP Stds.: 56

Our Lady of Grace - 7095 Waxhaw Hwy., Lancaster, SC 29720 t) 803-283-4969 rkubic@charlestondiocese.org www.gracewepray.org Rev. Jeffrey F. Kirby, Pst.; Dcn. Robert Donofrio; Dcn. Thomas Heath; Dcn. Richard Olson; CRP Stds.: 84

LAURENS

Holy Spirit Mission - 1040 W. Main St., Laurens, SC 29360 t) 864-984-2880 hslaurens@charlestondiocese.org holyspiritlaurens.org Mission of St. Boniface in Joanna Rev. Jose Hugo Ruiz-Marentes, Pst.; CRP Stds.: 51

LEXINGTON

Corpus Christi - 2350 Augusta Hwy., Lexington, SC 29072 t) 803-359-4391 gramis@charlestondiocese.org www.corpuschristisc.org Rev. Joseph V. Romanoski, Pst.; Rev. Gustavo Corredor, Part-time Parochial Vicar; Rev. Adam Michael Koncik, C.Ss.R., In Res.; Dcn. Jack L. Crocker; Dcn. Richard Gundlach; Dcn. Dave Kepler; Dcn. Coleman T. Parks; CRP Stds.: 325

LORIS

Church of the Resurrection - 204 Heritage Rd., Loris, SC 29569 t) 843-756-6168 jorourke@charlestondiocese.org Mission of Our Lady, Star of the Sea in North Myrtle Beach Rev. Raymond Joseph Leonard, Pst.; Rev. Cosmus Mutie Wambua, Par. Vicar; Dcn. James Collins; CRP Stds.: 22

MANNING

St. Mary, Our Lady of Hope - 2529 Raccoon Rd., Manning, SC 29102; Mailing: 12 N. Cantey St., Summerton, SC 29148 t) 803-485-2925 stmaryourladyofhope@charlestondiocese.org myoloh.org Rev. Anthony Benjamine (India), Pst.; Dcn. Charles Michael Walsh; CRP Stds.: 11

MARION

Church of the Infant Jesus - 4534 N. Hwy 501 Business, Marion, SC 29571 t) 843-433-8239 ijmmarion@charlestondiocese.org Mission of St. Louis in Dillon Rev. Cirilo Bailon Martinez, Admin.; Dcn. Donald DeNitto; CRP Stds.: 2

MCCORMICK

Good Shepherd - 1401 Greenwood Hwy., McCormick, SC 29835; Mailing: P.O. Box 1468, McCormick, SC 29835 t) 864-852-4722 linda.williford@charlestondiocese.org goodshepherdmccormick.com Rev. Jacob P. Joseph, C.M.I., Pst.;

MONCKS CORNER

St. Philip Benizi - 1404 Old Hwy. 52 S., Moncks Corner, SC 29461 t) 843-761-3777 kgotz@charlestondiocese.org www.spbcc.org Rev. Allam Marreddy (India), Pst.; Dcn. Mike Heidkamp; Dcn. Jerome P. Remkiewicz; CRP Stds.: 15

MOUNT PLEASANT

St. Benedict - 950 Darrell Creek Tr., Mount Pleasant, SC 29466 t) 843-216-0039 stbenedict@charlestondiocese.org www.stbenedictparish.org Rev. Mark S. Good, Pst.; Dcn. Stan Aviles; Dcn. Ed Long; CRP Stds.: 325

Christ Our King - 1149 Russell Dr., Mount Pleasant, SC 29464 t) 843-884-5587 dfisher@charlestondiocese.org www.christourking.org Rev. Robert A. Spencer, Pst.; Rev. Libin Augustine, C.M.I., Par. Vicar; Dcn. Robert Boackle; Dcn. Kevin Campbell; Dcn. Brian Justice; Dcn. Joseph Mauriello; Dcn. Jonathan Santilli; Rev. Andrew Jaroslav Fryml, PT Par. Vicar; CRP Stds.: 95

Christ Our King Stella Maris School - (Grades PreK-8) 1183 Russell Dr., Mount Pleasant, SC 29464 t) 843-884-4721 ssplendido@charlestondiocese.org www.coksm.org Susan Splendido, Prin.; John Byrnes, Pres.; Stds.: 649; Lay Tchrs.: 48

MURPHY VILLAGE

St. Edward - 1370 Edgefield Rd., Murphy Village, SC 29860; Mailing: P.O. Box 6340, North Augusta, SC 29861 t) 803-279-1837 tcarroll@charlestondiocese.org www.stedwardchurchna.org Rev. Cherian Thalakulam, C.M.I. (India), Pst.; CRP Stds.: 229

MURRELLS INLET

St. Michael - 542 Cypress Ave., Murrells Inlet, SC 29576 t) 843-651-3737 vyorzinski@charlestondiocese.org www.saintmichaelsc.net Very Rev. Edward W. Fitzgerald, Pst.; Rev. Christopher Beyuo, Par. Vicar; Dcn. Manny Acosta; Dcn. Robert T. Davis; Dcn. Donald C. Efken; Dcn. Jeffery Pierfy; Dcn. Robert Starr; Dcn. John Tomasicchio; CRP Stds.: 247

St. Michael Catholic School - (Grades PreK-6) t) 843-651-6795 jbaynes@charlestondiocese.org saintmichaelsc.com Jason Baynes, Prin.; Stds.: 102; Lay Tchrs.: 16

MYRTLE BEACH

St. Andrew - 37th Ave. N. & Hwy. 17 (Kings Hwy.), Myrtle Beach, SC 29577; Mailing: 3501 N. Kings Hwy., Ste. 102, Myrtle Beach, SC 29577 t) 843-448-5930 standrewmb@charlestondiocese.org standrewcatholicchurch.org Rev. Roger James Morgan, Pst.; Rev. Emerson Rodriguez-Delgado, O.F.M., Par. Vicar; Dcn. Robert Buzz Barlow; Dcn. Scott Bowen; Dcn. George Ferland; Dcn. Fred LaPiana; Dcn. Scott Alan Ross; Dcn. Anthony Russo; CRP Stds.: 177

St. Andrew Catholic School - (Grades K-8) 3601 N. Kings Hwy., Myrtle Beach, SC 29577 t) 843-448-6062 dwilfong@charlestondiocese.org www.standrewschoolmb.org Debbie Wilfong, Prin.; Stds.: 205; Lay Tchrs.: 21

NEWBERRY

St. Mark - 928 Boundary St., Newberry, SC 29108 t) 803-276-6446 stmarknewberry@charlestondiocese.org www.stmarkcathchurch.org Rev. Jose Hugo Ruiz-Marentes, Pst.; Dcn. Al De Lachica; Dcn. Gerald Loignon Jr.; CRP Stds.: 77

NORTH AUGUSTA

Our Lady of Peace - 139 Way of Peace, North Augusta, SC 29841 t) 803-279-0315 olpnorthaugusta@charlestondiocese.org olpchurchna.org Rev. Richard Charles Wilson, Pst.; Dcn. Robert Hookness; Sr. Eugenia Mayela Ortega, H.C.J.S., Hispanic Ministries; CRP Stds.: 124

Our Lady of Peace School - (Grades PreK-8) 137 Way of Peace, North Augusta, SC 29841 t) 803-279-8396 x100 shickey@charlestondiocese.org olpschool.us Stephen Hickey, Prin.; Stds.: 172; Pr. Tchrs.: 1; Lay Tchrs.: 19

NORTH CHARLESTON

St. John - 3921 St. John's Ave., North Charleston, SC 29405 t) 843-744-6201 jvalenzuela@charlestondiocese.org www.saintjohncatholicsc.org Rev. John F. Valenzuela, C.R.S., Admin.; CRP Stds.: 8

St. John Catholic School - (Grades PreK-8) t) 843-744-3901 kdurand@charlestondiocese.org stjohncatholic.wixsite.com/mysite Karen Durand, Prin.; Stds.: 54; Lay Tchrs.: 8

St. Thomas the Apostle - 6650 Dorchester Rd., North Charleston, SC 29418 t) 843-801-7691 grios@charlestondiocese.org www.stthomascatholicchurch.org Rev. Manuel Morales Lobo, CRS (Philippines), Admin.; Dcn. Jeffrey P. Mevissen; CRP Stds.: 68

NORTH MYRTLE BEACH

Our Lady Star of the Sea - 1100 8th Ave. N., North Myrtle Beach, SC 29582 t) 843-249-2356 lbritzke@charlestondiocese.org olssnmb.com Rev. Raymond Joseph Leonard, Pst.; Rev. David Michael, Par. Vicar; Rev. Cosmus Mutie Wambua, Par. Vicar; Rev. Msgr. Karl A. Chimiak, In Res.; Rev. James M. Crowley, In Res.; Dcn. Richard Flenke; Dcn. Robert Jones; Dcn. Andrew Stoshak; CRP Stds.: 150

Holy Trinity Catholic School - (Grades PreK-5) t) 843-390-4108 kluzzo@charlestondiocese.org www.htcatholicschoolmyrtlebeach.com Karen Luzzo, Prin.; Stds.: 90; Lay Tchrs.: 21

ORANGEBURG

Holy Trinity - 2202 Riverbank Dr., Orangeburg, SC 29118 t) 803-534-8177 pantony@charlestondiocese.org www.holytrinitysc.org Rev. Prasad Antony, M.S.S.C.C., Admin.; Rev. A. John DeBritto, M.S.S.C.C., Par. Vicar; Dcn. David Hanson; Dcn. Gary Janelle; Dcn. Darren Jump; CRP Stds.: 116

PAGELAND

St. Ernest - 510 Evans Mill Rd., Pageland, SC 29728; Mailing: 602 Market St., c/o St. Peter, Cheraw, SC 29520 t) 843-537-7351 ntria@charlestondiocese.org Mission of St. Peter in Cheraw. Rev. Noel Tria (Philippines), Pst.; CRP Stds.: 25

PAWLEYS ISLAND

Precious Blood of Christ - 1633 Waverly Rd., Pawleys Island, SC 29585 t) 843-237-3428 esullivan@charlestondiocese.org www.pbocchurch.com Rev. Paul D. MacNeil, Pst.; Dcn. Michael Appel; Dcn. Timothy Joseph; Dcn. Stephen Olenchok; CRP Stds.: 79

PICKENS

Holy Cross - 558 Hampton Ave., Pickens, SC 29671 t) 864-878-0574 avillano@charlestondiocese.org holycrossstluke.org Rev. James N. Dubrouillet, Pst.; Dcn. John Villano; CRP Stds.: 17

RIDGELAND

St. Anthony - 10128 S. Jacob Smart Blvd., Ridgeland, SC 29936; Mailing: P.O. Box 548, Ridgeland, SC 29936 t) 843-726-3606 stanthonyridgeland@charlestondiocese.org stanthonyridgeland.org Rev. Luis E. Serrano Carrero, Admin.; Sr. Candelaria Garcia Alvarez, D.J.B.P., DRE; CRP Stds.: 31

ROCK HILL

St. Anne - 1694 Bird St., Rock Hill, SC 29730 t) 803-329-2662 john.hall@charlestondiocese.org www.saintanne.com Rev. Joseph Francis Pearce, C.O., Pst.; Rev. Quang D. Pham, C.O., Par. Vicar; Bro. John F. Kummer, C.O., Pst. Assoc.; Dcn. Ted Clement; Dcn. Andrew DaSilva; Dcn. John Hall, Bus. Mgr.; Dcn. James P. Hyland; Dcn. Angel Juarez-Reyes; Dcn. Oliver R. Moore; CRP Stds.: 250

St. Anne Catholic School - (Grades PreK-12) 1698 Bird St., Rock Hill, SC 29730 t) 803-324-4814 jpeter@charlestondiocese.org www.stanneschool.com Rev. Joseph Francis Pearce, C.O., Headmaster; Very Rev. Fabio Refosco, C.O., Chap.; Julie Peter, Interim Prin.; Stds.: 306; Pr. Tchrs.: 2; Sr. Tchrs.: 1; Lay Tchrs.: 40

St. Mary - 902 Crawford Rd., Rock Hill, SC 29730; Mailing: P.O. Box 11982, Rock Hill, SC 29731 t) 803-329-1008 stmaryrh@charlestondiocese.org stmarysrh.org Rev. Agustin Guzman, C.O., Pst.; Dcn. Terrence Chisolm; Dcn. Marcene Emmett; Dcn. Walter W. Hollis; CRP Stds.: 38

SAINT HELENA ISLAND

Holy Cross Mission - 83 Seaside Rd., Saint Helena Island, SC 29920; Mailing: c/o St. Peter, 70 Lady's Island Dr., Beaufort, SC 29907 t) 843-522-9555 asudomerski@charlestondiocese.org www.stpetersbeaufort.org Mission of St. Peter in Beaufort. Rev. Andrew Trapp, Pst.

SANTEE

St. Ann - 2205 State Park Rd., Santee, SC 29142; Mailing: P.O. Box 250, Santee, SC 29142 t) 803-854-5075 srolland@charlestondiocese.org www.stannsantee.org Rev. Anthony Benjamine (India), Pst.; Dcn. David Kahn Sr.; CRP Stds.: 6

SENECA

St. Paul the Apostle - 170 Bountyland Rd., Seneca, SC 29672 t) 864-882-8551 phecht@charlestondiocese.org www.saintpaulseneca.org Rev. William S. Hearne, Pst.; Dcn. Tim Baker; Dcn. Harvey Becker; Dcn. Randy Sexton; CRP Stds.: 111

SIMPSONVILLE

St. Elizabeth Ann Seton - 8 Gillin Dr., Simpsonville, SC 29680; Mailing: P.O. Box 672, Mauldin, SC 29662-0672 t) 864-263-3445 sstrickland@charlestondiocese.org www.seas-church.org Very Rev. C. Thomas Miles, Pst.; Rev. Patrick E. Cooper, In Res.; Dcn. William Hudson; Sr. Amelia Marie Cueva, C.S.JB., DRE; CRP Stds.: 31

St. Mary Magdalene - 2252 Woodruff Rd., Simpsonville, SC 29681 t) 864-288-4884 nchavez@charlestondiocese.org www.smmcc.org Rev. Teofilo Trujillo, Pst.; Rev. Raynald Nacino, Par. Vicar; Rev. Robert Falabella, C.H.S., In Res.; Dcn. Norberto Chavez, Director of Business Administration; Dcn. Joseph Ciavardini; Dcn. Ivan O. Hawk; Dcn. Roger Schonewald; CRP Stds.: 847

SPARTANBURG

Jesus, Our Risen Savior - 2575 Reidville Rd., Spartanburg, SC 29301 t) 864-576-1164 sdobbins@charlestondiocese.org www.jorscc.org Rev. Liam Reza Panganiban, C.R.M., Pst.; Rev. Rafael Padron-Hernandez, C.R.M., Par. Vicar; Rev. Godefroid M. Paluku, C.R.M., Par. Vicar; Dcn. Robert M. Sturm; CRP Stds.: 172

St. Paul the Apostle - 290 E. Main St., Spartanburg, SC 29302; Mailing: 161 N. Dean St., Spartanburg, SC 29302 t) 864-582-0674 rgilliam@charlestondiocese.org www.stpaultheapostlespartanburg.org Rev. David R. Whitman, Pst.; Dcn. Peter Brown; Dcn. Robert L. Mahaffey Jr.; Dcn. George Wilson; CRP Stds.: 132

St. Paul the Apostle Catholic School - (Grades PreK-5) 152 Alabama St., Spartanburg, SC 29302 t) 864-582-6645 lmitro@charlestondiocese.org stpaulschoolsc.com Lauri Mitro, Prin.; Stds.: 48; Lay Tchrs.: 7

SPRINGFIELD

St. Theresa Mission - 155 Railroad Ave., Springfield, SC 29146; Mailing: 2202 Riverbank Dr., c/o Holy Trinity, Orangeburg, SC 29118 t) 803-534-8177 pantony@charlestondiocese.org holytrinitysc.org/ Mission of Holy Trinity in Orangeburg. Rev. Prasad Antony, M.S.S.C.C., Admin.; Rev. A. John DeBritto, M.S.S.C.C., Par. Vicar; CRP Stds.: 5

SULLIVAN'S ISLAND

Stella Maris - 1204 Middle St., Sullivan's Island, SC 29482; Mailing: P.O. Box 280, Sullivan's Island, SC 29482 t) 843-883-3108 jvaughan@charlestondiocese.org stellamarischurch.org Rev. Msgr. Lawrence B. McInerny, Pst.; Rev. Timothy D. Tebalt, Par. Vicar; Dcn. Jason Vaughan, Pst. Assoc.; Dcn. Matthew Story; CRP Stds.: 114

SUMMERTON

St. Mary Mission - 12 N. Cantey St., Summerton, SC 29148 t) 803-485-2925 erossoni@charlestondiocese.org Mission of St. Mary, Our Lady of Hope in Manning. Rev. Anthony Benjamine (India), Pst.;

SUMMERVILLE

St. John the Beloved - 28 Sumter Ave., Summerville, SC 29483 t) 843-873-0631 sjboffice@charlestondiocese.org www.sjbsummerville.org Very Rev. Raymond J. Carlo, Pst.; Dcn. Joseph Dennis; Dcn. Charleston Eick; Dcn. Ronald A. Kolonich; Dcn. Gregory W. Sams, Accountant; Dcn. James Walter; CRP Stds.: 191

St. Theresa the Little Flower - 11001 Dorchester Ave., Summerville, SC 29485 t) 843-875-5002 stlf@charlestondiocese.org sttheresachurch.com Rev. Michael Cellars, Pst.; Dcn. Kenneth Chandlee; Dcn. Michael Regan; CRP Stds.: 152

SUMTER

St. Anne and St. Jude - 216 E. Liberty St., Sumter, SC 29150 t) 803-773-3524 tcouture@charlestondiocese.org www.sasjrcc.org (Formerly St. Anne) Rev. Giovannie B. Nunez, C.R.M., Pst.; Rev. German J. Coquilla Jr., C.R.M., Par. Vicar; Rev. Ronie R. Lorcha, C.R.M., Par. Vicar; CRP Stds.: 100

Holy Angels Academy - (Grades K-6) 11 S. Magnolia St., Sumter, SC 29150 t) 803-775-3632 kdoyle@charlestondiocese.org www.sasjcs.com Kristi Doyle, Prin.;

St. Anne and St. Jude - 611 W. Oakland Ave., Sumter, SC 29151; Mailing: 216 E. Liberty St., Sumter, SC 29150 t) 803-773-9244 tcouture@charlestondiocese.org www.sasjrcc.org (Formerly St. Jude) Rev. Giovannie B. Nunez, C.R.M., Pst.; Dcn. Greg Tavarez;

TAYLORS

Prince of Peace - 1209 Brushy Creek Rd., Taylors, SC 29687 t) 864-268-4352 mrauch@charlestondiocese.org www.princeofpeacetaylors.net Rev. Christopher Smith, Pst.; Rev. Richard B. Tomlinson, Par. Vicar; Dcn. Nestor Acosta; Dcn. Michael Cavin; Dcn. Robert Smith; Dcn. Gus Suarez; Dcn. Mark Thompson; Dcn. Michael Thompson; CRP Stds.: 182

Prince of Peace Catholic School - (Grades PreK-8) t) 864-331-2145 tlopez@charlestondiocese.org www.popcatholicschool.org Steven Cunningham, Prin.; Stds.: 179; Lay Tchrs.: 15

UNION

St. Augustine - 103 E. South St., Union, SC 29379; Mailing: 205 Sams St., c/o Sacred Heart, Gaffney, SC 29340 t) 864-489-9453 rrodriguez@charlestondiocese.org www.sacredheartgaffney.org/st-augustine-parish Rev. Bruce Barnett, Admin.; Dcn. William Bower;

WALHALLA

St. Francis of Assisi - 103 W. Mauldin St., Walhalla, SC 29691; Mailing: 170 Bountyland Rd., c/o St. Paul the Apostle, Seneca, SC 29672 t) 864-882-8551 phecht@charlestondiocese.org www.saintpaulseneca.org Mission of St. Paul the Apostle in Seneca. Rev. William S. Hearne, Pst.;

WALTERBORO

St. Anthony - 925 S. Jefferies Blvd., Walterboro, SC 29488 t) 843-549-5230 mmccollum@charlestondiocese.org Rev. Msgr. Thomas X. Hofmann, Pst.; Dcn. Carlos Marin; CRP Stds.: 35

St. James the Greater - 3087 Ritter Rd., Walterboro, SC 29488; Mailing: 925 S. Jefferies Blvd., c/o St. Anthony,

Walterboro, SC 29488 t) 843-549-5230 mmccollum@charlestondiocese.org Mission of St. Anthony in Walterboro Rev. Msgr. Thomas X. Hofmann, Pst.; CRP Stds.: 7

WARD

St. William - 1199 Ridge Spring Hwy., Ward, SC 29166 t) 864-445-7215 wrodgers@charlestondiocese.org stwilliamsward.org Rev. Vincent Henry Finnerty, CM, Pst.; CRP Stds.: 25

WINNSBORO

St. Theresa - 162 Hwy. 321 Bypass N., Winnsboro, SC 29180; Mailing: P.O. Box 1004, Winnsboro, SC 29180 t) 803-635-2541 ann.smith@charlestondiocese.org sttheresascc.org/ Rev. Msgr. James L. LeBlanc, Pst.;

YONGES ISLAND

St. Mary - 4255 State Hwy. 165, Yonges Island, SC 29449 t) 843-889-8549 stmarys165@charlestondiocese.org stmarysyongesisland.org Rev. Jesuprathap Narichetti (India), Pst.; CRP Stds.: 15

YORK

Divine Saviour - 232 Herndon Ave., York, SC 29745; Mailing: P.O. Box 341, York, SC 29745 t) 803-684-3431 tlebanno@charlestondiocese.org www.divine-saviour.org/ Rev. Adilso Coelho, C.O., Pst.; Dcn. James Ball; Dcn. Henry Bernal; Dcn. Henry de Mena; Dcn. Scott Hart; Dcn. Edward Kelly; CRP Stds.: 67

SCHOOLS: PRESCHOOL THRU HIGH SCHOOL

SCHOOLS

STATE OF SOUTH CAROLINA

SUMMERVILLE

Summerville Catholic School - (PAR) (Grades PreK-8) 226 Black Oak Blvd., Summerville, SC 29485 t) 843-873-9310 jtisdale@charlestondiocese.org summervillecatholic.org Charlie Tisdale, Prin.; Stds.: 230; Lay Tchrs.: 16

HIGH SCHOOLS

STATE OF SOUTH CAROLINA

CHARLESTON

Bishop England High School - (DIO) (Grades 9-12) 363 Seven Farms Dr., Charleston, SC 29492 t) 843-849-9599 maryanne.b.tucker@charlestondiocese.org www.behs.com Patrick Finneran, Pres.; Mary Anne Tucker, Prin.; Rev. Andrew Jaroslav Fryml, Chap.; Rev. James Renaurd West, Teacher; Stds.: 729; Pr. Tchrs.: 1; Lay Tchrs.: 60

COLUMBIA

Cardinal Newman School - (DIO) (Grades 7-12) 2945 Alpine Rd., Columbia, SC 29223 t) 803-782-2814 kelly.burke@charlestondiocese.org www.cnhs.org Rev. William C. Frei, Chap.; Kelly Burke, Prin.; Stds.: 506; Lay Tchrs.: 48

GREENVILLE

***St. Joseph's Catholic School** - (PRV) (Grades 6-12) 100 St. Joseph's Dr., Greenville, SC 29607 t) 864-234-9009 kkiser@sjcatholicschool.org; llawrence@sjcatholicschool.org www.sjcatholicschool.org Rev. Jonathan C. Duncan, Chap.; Keith F. Kiser, Headmaster; Sr. Lucita Bacat, C.S.J.B., Teacher; Stds.: 659; Sr. Tchrs.: 1; Lay Tchrs.: 56

MYRTLE BEACH

St. Elizabeth Ann Seton Catholic School - (DIO) (Grades 6-12) 1300 Carolina Forest Blvd., Myrtle Beach, SC 29579 t) 843-903-1400 kblake@charlestondiocese.org setoncatholicsc.org/ Rev. Paul D. MacNeil, Chap.; Kelly Blake, Prin.; Stds.: 77; Sr. Tchrs.: 1; Lay Tchrs.: 15

RIDGELAND

John Paul II Catholic School - (DIO) (Grades 6-12) 4211 N. Okatie Hwy., Ridgeland, SC 29936 t) 843-645-3838 hrembold@charlestondiocese.org www.johnpaul2school.org Rev. Rafael Boshra Ghattas, Chap.; John McCarthy, Pres.; Heather Rembold, Prin.; Dcn. Brent Heathcott, Teacher; Stds.: 332; Sr. Tchrs.: 2; Lay Tchrs.: 30

INSTITUTIONS LOCATED IN DIOCESE

CAMPUS MINISTRY / NEWMAN CENTERS [CAM]

CHARLESTON

Catholic Campus Ministry at the College of Charleston and Medical University of South Carolina - 34 Wentworth St., Charleston, SC 29401; Mailing: 901 Orange Grove Rd., Charleston, SC 29407 c) 843-697-0854 tgregory@charlestondiocese.org www.cofccsa.org/ Rev. Andrew Jaroslav Fryml; Thomas Gregory, Campus Min.;

The Citadel, Catholic Campus Ministry - 171 Moultrie St., Charleston, SC 29409; Mailing: The Citadel M.S.C. 58, Charleston, SC 29409-0058 t) 843-670-4664 tlicari@charlestondiocese.org www.citadel.edu/root/catholic Rev. James Renaurd West, Chap.; Tony Licari, Campus Min.;

Columbia College - 901 Orange Grove Rd., Charleston, SC 29407 t) 843-261-0443 mcorder@charlestondiocese.org

CLEMSON

Clemson University, Southern Wesleyan University, and TriCounty Technical College - 209 Sloan St., St. Andrew Catholic Student Center, Clemson, SC 29631; Mailing: P.O. Box 112, Clemson, SC 29633 t) 864-654-7804 csa@clemson.edu www.clemsoncatholic.org Catholic Campus Ministry for Clemson University; St. Andrew Catholic Student Association Rev. Daniel McLellan, O.F.M., Campus Min.; Stephanie Manasa, Assoc. Campus Min.;

CLINTON

Presbyterian College - 503 S. Adair St., Clinton, SC 29325 t) (864) 833-8465 (Office Phone) gbriguente@presby.edu Dr. Giovanni Briguente, Advisor;

COLUMBIA

Allen University and Benedict College - 2229 Hampton St., c/o St. Martin de Porres Parish, Columbia, SC 29204 t) 803-254-6862 lgharrison@me.com L. Harrison, Advisor;

University of South Carolina - 1610 Greene St., Newman Club, St. Thomas More, Columbia, SC 29201 t) 803-638-8795 kelly@stthomasmoreusc.org stthomasmoreusc.org Rev. Rhett Butler Williams, Chap.; Kelly Guilbeau, Campus Min.;

CONWAY

Coastal Carolina University - 396 W. Cox Ferry Rd., Conway, SC 29526 t) 843-290-4106 coastalcatholics@gmail.com coastalcatholics.org/ Theodore Lmbardi, Campus Min.; Dcn. Jim Hinnerschitz;

FLORENCE

Francis Marion University - 4822 E. Palmetto St., Florence, SC 29506 t) 843-661-1806 cmasters@frmarion.edu Christine Masters, Faculty Advisor;

GREENVILLE

Furman University Campus Ministry - 307 Gower St., c/o St. Anthony of Padua, Greenville, SC 29611 t) 864-294-2318 brian.goess@furman.edu; jduncan@charlestondiocese.org Rev. Jonathan C. Duncan, Chap.; Brian Goess, Faculty Advisor;

GREENWOOD

Lander University Catholic Ministry - 320 Stanley Ave., Greenwood, SC 29649; Mailing: 101 Marble Ct., Greenwood, SC 29649 t) (843) 261-0443 mcorder@charlestondiocese.org

ORANGEBURG

South Carolina State University, Claflin University, and Orangeburg Calhoun Technical College - 2202 Riverbank Dr., c/o Holy Trinity Parish, Orangeburg, SC 29118 t) 803-655-5137 gljanelle@gmail.com Dcn. Gary Janelle, Advisor;

ROCK HILL

Winthrop University - c/o The Oratory, Rock Hill, SC 29731; Mailing: P.O. Box 11586, Rock Hill, SC 29731 t) 980-729-6360 winthropnewman@yahoo.com; aguzman@charlestondiocese.org winthropnewman.wixsite.com/newman Rev. Agustin Guzman, C.O., Chap.; Courtney Hull, Campus Min.;

SPARTANBURG

Converse College - 544 D N. Church St., Spartanburg, SC 29303 t) 843-697-0133 mscheske@charlestondiocese.org Michael Scheske, Campus Min.;

Spartanburg Regional Campus Ministry - 544 D N. Church St., Spartanburg, SC 29303 t) 843-697-0133 mscheske@charlestondiocese.org Michael Scheske, Campus Min.;

University of South Carolina - Upstate - 800 University Way, Catholic Student Assoc., Spartanburg, SC 29303 t) 864-503-5826 malexander@uscupstate.edu uscupstate.edu Myles Alexander, Advisor;

Wofford College - 544 D N. Church St., Spartanburg, SC 29303 t) 843-697-0133 mscheske@charlestondiocese.org Michael Scheske, Campus Min.; David Alvis, Advisor;

CATHOLIC CHARITIES [CCH]

CHARLESTON

Catholic Charities of South Carolina - 901 Orange Grove Rd., Charleston, SC 29407 t) 843-531-5542 ccharities@charlestondiocese.org www.charitiessc.org Michele Corkum, Dir., Field Oper.; Lydia Doyle, Interim Sec., Social Ministries & Exec. Dir., Catholic Charities; Asstd. Annu.: 36,906; Staff: 27

Coastal Regional Office - 1662 Ingram Rd., Charleston, SC 29407; Mailing: 901 Orange Grove Rd., Charleston, SC 29407 t) 843-531-5570 rmaldonado@charlestondiocese.org charitiessc.org/coastal Rocio Maldonado, Site Admin.;

Columbia Regional Office - 809 Calhoun St., Columbia, SC 29201 t) 803-726-7764 tmaybay@charlestondiocese.org charitiessc.org/midlands Teresa Maybay, Site Admin.; Sr. Angelita Vazzano, S.S. J.B, Client Advocate;

Georgetown Outreach Services Office - 1905 Front St., Georgetown, SC 29440 t) 843-546-1470 cgeathers@charlestondiocese.org charitiessc.org/georgetown Crystal Geathers, Site Admin.;

Gloverville Regional Office - 2443 Augusta Rd., Gloverville, SC 29828 t) 803-593-2634 joely@charlestondiocese.org charitiessc.org/gloverville Joely Leguizamon, Site Admin.;

Immigration Services - Berea Office - 2300 Old Buncombe Rd., Greenville, SC 29609 t) (864) 365-0047 bsuarez@charlestondiocese.org charitiessc.org/immigration-legal-services Vanessa Garcia, Assoc. Dir., Immigration Svcs.;

Immigration Services - Charleston Office - 1662 Ingram Rd., Charleston, SC 29407 t) 843-388-0089 chaire@charlestondiocese.org charitiessc.org/immigration-legal-services Andrea Penafiel, BIA Accredited Rep.; Claudia Haire, Admin. Asst.;

Immigration Services - Greenville Office - 204 Douthit St., Ste. A1, Greenville, SC 29601 t) (864) 331-2619 vgarcia@charlestondiocese.org charitiessc.org/immigration-legal-services Vanessa Garcia, Immigration Attorney;

Immigration Services - Hilton Head Office - 1000 Main St., Ste. 200D, Hilton Head Island, SC 29926 t) 843-785-2200 mchoy@charlestondiocese.org charitiessc.org/immigration-legal-services Mily Choy, BIA Accredited Rep.;

Immigration Services - Rock Hill Office - 524 Charlotte Ave., Rock Hill, SC 29730 t) 803-327-7144 rturner@charlestondiocese.org charitiessc.org/immigration-legal-services Rakia Turner, Immigration Attorney;
Lowcountry Regional Office - 19869 Whyte Hardee Blvd., Hardeeville, SC 29927 t) 843-208-2276 x1 mbassick@charlestondiocese.org charitiessc.org/lowcountry Sr. Mary Frances Bassick, D.C., Site Admin.;
Pee Dee Regional Office - 2294 Technology Blvd., Conway, SC 29526 t) 843-438-3083 cgeathers@charlestondiocese.org charitiessc.org/pee-dee Crystal Geathers, Site Admin.;
Office of Prison Ministry - 1427 Pickens St., Columbia, SC 29201; Mailing: P.O. Box 112, Clemson, SC 29633 t) (803) 602-0397 jleininger@charlestondiocese.org Rev. Adam Michael Koncik, C.Ss.R., Chap.; Dcn. John Leininger, Coord., Prison Ministry;
Restorative Justice - 809 Calhoun St., Columbia, SC 29201 t) (803) 726-7769 nikkigrimball@charlestondiocese.org charitiessc.org/restorative-justice Nikki Grimball, Prog. Specialist;
Upstate Regional Office - 2300 Old Buncombe Rd., Greenville, SC 29609 t) (864) 331-2629 jthrall@charlestondiocese.org charitiessc.org/upstate Jessica Thrall, Site Admin.;

CEMETERIES [CEM]

CHARLESTON
Holy Cross - 604 Ft. Johnson Rd., Charleston, SC 29412 t) 843-795-2111 kmeade@charlestondiocese.org Karmin Meade, Dir.;
St. John Cemetery - 200 Coming St., Charleston, SC 29402; Mailing: 604 Ft. Johnson Rd., c/o Holy Cross Cemetery, Charleston, SC 29412 t) 843-795-2111 kmeade@charlestondiocese.org Karmin Meade, Dir.;
St. Lawrence Cemetery - 60 Huguenin Ave., Charleston, SC 29403; Mailing: 604 Ft. Johnson Rd., c/o Holy Cross Cemetery, Charleston, SC 29412 t) 843-795-2111 kmeade@charlestondiocese.org Karmin Meade, Dir.;
NORTH CHARLESTON
St. Peter Cemetery - 2726 Spruill Ave., North Charleston, SC 29405; Mailing: 604 Ft. Johnson Rd., c/o Holy Cross Cemetery, Charleston, SC 29412 t) 843-795-2111 kmeade@charlestondiocese.org Karmin Meade, Dir.;

CONVENTS, MONASTERIES, AND RESIDENCES FOR WOMEN [CON]

CHARLESTON
Sisters of Charity of Our Lady of Mercy, Inc. - 1061 Folly Rd., Charleston, SC 29412; Mailing: P.O. Box 12410, Charleston, SC 29422 t) 843-795-6083 went1050@aol.com sistersofcharityolm.org Sr. Mary Joseph Ritter, O.L.M., Gen. Supr.; Sr. Carol Wentworth, O.L.M., Gen. Treas.; Srs.: 12
TRAVELERS REST
Franciscan Monastery of St. Clare, Franciscan Poor Clare Nuns. - 37 McCauley Rd., Travelers Rest, SC 29690 t) 864-834-8015 info@poorclaresc.com www.poorclaresc.com Sr. Nancy Shively, O.S.C., Abbess; Srs.: 15

ENDOWMENTS / FOUNDATIONS / TRUSTS [EFT]

CHARLESTON
The Barry Charitable Trust - 1061 Folly Rd., Charleston, SC 29412; Mailing: P.O. Box 12410, Charleston, SC 29422 t) (843) 795-6083 went1050@aol.com Dennis Atwood, Trustee; Danny Croghan, Trustee; Sarah Jones Cuskley, Trustee; Sr. Hertha Longo, C.S.A., Trustee; Sr. Carol Wentworth, O.L.M., Trustee;
Catholic Community Foundation of South Carolina - 901 Orange Grove Rd., Charleston, SC 29407 t) (843) 261-0470 jbarker@charlestondiocese.org John Barker, Treas.;
COLUMBIA
Sisters of Charity Foundation of South Carolina - 2711 Middleburg Dr., Ste. 115, Columbia, SC 29204-2413 t) 803-254-0230 scfsc@sistersofcharitysc.com www.sistersofcharitysc.com Donna Waites, Pres.;

HOSPITALS / HEALTH SERVICES [HOS]

CHARLESTON
***Bon Secours St. Francis Xavier Hospital** - 2095 Henry Tecklenburg Dr., Charleston, SC 29414 t) 843-402-1001 bonnie.paterniti@rsfh.com www.rsfh.com Sponsored by Bon Secours Ministries. Jeffrey DiLisi, Pres.; Adriana Day, CFO; Bed Capacity: 190; Asstd. Annu.: 154,385; Staff: 1,254
GREENVILLE
Bon Secours St. Francis Health System, Inc. - 1 St. Francis Dr., Greenville, SC 29601 t) 864-255-1000 irene_holcombe@bshsi.org; sdschitter@mercy.com www.bonsecours.com/ Matthew T. Caldwell, Pres.; Dcn. Alex Garvey, Senior VP of Mission;
St. Francis Hospital, Inc. - Bed Capacity: 375; Asstd. Annu.: 126,834; Staff: 1,953

MISCELLANEOUS [MIS]

CAMDEN
***Children of Mary Religion Camp** - 1841 Lockhart Rd., Camden, SC 29020; Mailing: P.O. Box 2111, Camden, SC 29020 t) 704-853-9534 childrenofmarycamp@gmail.com childrenofmarycamp.com Shaun Barry, Pres.;
CHARLESTON
SACS Enterprises, LLC - 901 Orange Grove Rd., Charleston, SC 29407 t) 843-261-0470 jbarker@charlestondiocese.org John Barker, Contact;
St. Thomas Aquinas Scholarship Funding Organization - 901 Orange Grove Rd., Charleston, SC 29407 t) 843-261-0470 jbarker@charlestondiocese.org John Barker, Contact;
COLUMBIA
***Family Honor, Inc.** - 1226 Pickens St., Ste. 101, Columbia, SC 29201; Mailing: P.O. Box 1414, Columbia, SC 29202 t) 803-929-0858 famhonor@aol.com www.familyhonor.org Mission: Provide a Catholic framework on the truth and meaning of sexuality, love, and family. Rev. Philip S. Gillespie, Chap.; Brenda Cerkez, Exec. Dir.;
Healthy Learners - 2711 Middleburg Dr., Ste. 304, Columbia, SC 29204 t) (803) 454-0350 asplittgerber@healthylearners.com www.healthylearners.com Healthy Learners works collaboratively with communities, schools, healthcare providers & families to remove health barriers. Pre K-8th. Amy Splittgerber, Dir.;
JOHNS ISLAND
Our Lady of Mercy Community Outreach Services, Inc. - 1684 Brownswood Rd., Johns Island, SC 29455; Mailing: P.O. Box 607, Johns Island, SC 29457 t) 843-559-4109 info@olmoutreach.org www.olmoutreach.org Sponsored by Sisters of Charity of Our Lady of Mercy. Ryan Vrba, Dir. Prog.; Asstd. Annu.: 5,500; Staff: 22
KINGSTREE
Felician Center, Inc. - 908 Thorne Ave., Kingstree, SC 29556 t) 843-354-9415 stann@ftc-i.net www.feliciancentersc.org Compassionate ministry, education, health services and Christ-like loving care. Sr. Mary Johnna Ciezobka, C.S.S.F., Pres. & Outreach Coord.; Sr. Susanne Dziedzic, C.S.S.F., Dir.;
Convent -
SIMPSONVILLE
Magnificat-Greenville, SC Chapter - 304 Hearthwood Ln., Simpsonville, SC 29681 t) 864-967-7463 irvinglucille@gmail.com Lucille Irving, Coord.;
***Society of St. Vincent de Paul** - 700 Farming Creek Dr., Simpsonville, SC 29680 t) 864-979-8429 bergassoc@aol.com Thomas Berg, Diocesan Council Pres.; Dorothy Clinton, Coastal District Council Pres.; Rob Cunningham, Midlands District Council Pres.; Bill Luke, Piedmont District Council Pres.;
ST. HELENA ISLAND
St. Francis Center - 85 Mattis Dr., St. Helena Island, SC 29920; Mailing: P.O. Box 682, St. Helena Island, SC 29920 t) 843-838-3924 canice.adams@gmail.com; marcinesscm@hotmail.com Sisters of Saints Cyril and Methodius, Danville, PA Sr. Canice Adams, SS.C.M., Co-Dir.; Sr. Marcine Klocko, SS.C.M., Co-Dir.; Srs.: 3

MONASTERIES AND RESIDENCES FOR PRIESTS AND BROTHERS [MON]

MONCKS CORNER
Mepkin Abbey - 1098 Mepkin Abbey Rd., Moncks Corner, SC 29461-4796 t) 843-761-8509 fr.kevinocso@gmail.com www.mepkinabbey.org/ (Trappist Monks) Order of Cistercians of the Strict Observance Rev. Joseph Tedesco, O.C.S.O., Supr. ad Nutum; Rev. Stanislaus Gumula, O.C.S.O., Retired Abbot; Rev. Kevin V. Walsh, O.C.S.O, Prior, Novice Dir., Vocation Dir.; Rev. Guerric Frederick A. Heckel, O.C.S.O., Guestmaster; Rev. Gerard-Jonas Palmares, O.C.S.O.; Bro. John Corrigan, O.C.S.O., Cellarer; Bro. Juan Fahrner, O.C.S.O.; Bro. Paul Gosselin, O.C.S.O.; Bro. Vincent Rohaley, O.C.S.O.; Bro. Richard Bradley, O.C.S.O., Novice; Bro. Ambrose Porter, O.C.S.O., Novice; Bro. Kyle Berceau, O.C.S.O., Postulant; Bro. Steven Webster, O.C.S.O., Postulant; Rev. Jack Mattimore, S.J., Transfer; Brs.: 8; Priests: 6
ROCK HILL
Oratory of St. Philip Neri, Congregation of the Oratory of Pontifical Rite - 434 Charlotte Ave., Rock Hill, SC 29730; Mailing: P.O. Box 11586, Rock Hill, SC 29731-1586 t) 803-327-2097 rhoratory@comporium.net rockhilloratory.org/ Very Rev. Fabio Refosco, C.O., Provost; Rev. Quang D. Pham, C.O., Par. Vicar; Rev. Adilso Coelho, C.O.; Rev. John P. Giuliani, C.O.; Rev. Agustin Guzman, C.O.; Rev. Edward P. McDevitt, C.O.; Rev. Joseph Francis Pearce, C.O.; Bro. Joseph Guyon, C.O., Vicar; Bro. John F. Kummer, C.O., Deputy; Bro. Charles Andrew Tupta, C.O., Seminarian; Bro. Johnni do Bonfim Silva, C.O., Seminarian; Bro. Kevin D. O'Connor, C.O., Seminarian; Brs.: 5; Priests: 7

NURSING / REHABILITATION / CONVALESCENCE / ELDERLY CARE [NUR]

CHARLESTON
Carter-May Home Assisted Living & St. Joseph Residence for Retired Priests - 1660 Ingram Rd., Charleston, SC 29407 t) 843-556-8314 janine@charlestondiocese.org charitiessc.org/carter-may-home Janine N. Bauder, Admin.; Rev. Patrick O. Eyinla, Sac. Responsibilities; Asstd. Annu.: 30; Staff: 27

SHRINES [SHR]

KINGSTREE
Shrine of Our Lady of South Carolina-Our Lady of Joyful Hope - 330 E. Main St., Kingstree, SC 29556; Mailing: 300 Ashton Ave., Kingstree, SC 29556 t) 843-355-3527 olscshrine@gmail.com Administered by the Diocese of Charleston Rev. Stanley Smolenski, S.P.M.A., Dir.;

SPECIAL CARE FACILITIES [SPF]

CHARLESTON
St. Clare's Home - 901 Orange Grove Rd., Charleston, SC 29407; Mailing: 1754 Woodruff Rd., #170, Greenville, SC 29607 t) (864) 275-5505 stclareshome@charlestondiocese.org www.stclareshomesc.org/ Maternity home Valerie Baronkin, Exec. Dir.; Sr. Theresa Adeboye, SSMA, Prog. Mgr.; Sr. Stella Mary Okogie, SSMA, Residential Supvr.; Bed Capacity: 8; Asstd. Annu.: 175; Staff: 4

An asterisk (*) denotes an organization that has established tax-exempt status directly with the IRS and is not covered by the USCCB Group Ruling.

Diocese of Charlotte

(Dioecesis Carolinana)

MOST REVEREND PETER J. JUGIS, J.C.D.

Bishop of Charlotte; ordained June 12, 1983; appointed Bishop of Charlotte August 1, 2003; episcopal ordination October 24, 2003.

Chancery: 1123 S. Church St., Charlotte, NC 28203. T: 704-370-6299; F: 704-370-3379.
www.CharlotteDiocese.org
chancery@rcdio.org

ERECTED JANUARY 12, 1972

Square Miles 20,470.

Comprises the Counties of Alexander, Alleghany, Anson, Ashe, Avery, Buncombe, Burke, Cabarrus, Caldwell, Catawba, Cherokee, Clay, Cleveland, Davidson, Davie, Forsyth, Gaston, Graham, Guilford, Haywood, Henderson, Iredell, Jackson, Lincoln, Macon, Madison, McDowell, Mecklenburg, Mitchell, Montgomery, Polk, Randolph, Richmond, Rockingham, Rowan, Rutherford, Stanly, Stokes, Surry, Swain, Transylvania, Union, Watauga, Wilkes, Yadkin and Yancey in the State of North Carolina.

For legal titles of parishes and diocesan institutions, consult the Chancery.

STATISTICAL OVERVIEW

Personnel
Bishop....1
Abbots....1
Priests: Diocesan Active in Diocese....99
Priests: Diocesan Active Outside Diocese....2
Priests: Retired, Sick or Absent....36
Number of Diocesan Priests....137
Religious Priests in Diocese....27
Total Priests in your Diocese....164
Extern Priests in Diocese....16
Ordinations:
Diocesan Priests....2
Transitional Deacons....3
Permanent Deacons in Diocese....141
Total Brothers....12
Total Sisters....82

Parishes
Parishes....76
With Resident Pastor:
Resident Diocesan Priests....67
Resident Religious Priests....9
Missions....18
Pastoral Centers....2
New Parishes Created....1
Professional Ministry Personnel:
Brothers....2
Sisters....10
Lay Ministers....117

Welfare
Health Care Centers....8
Total Assisted....70,188
Homes for the Aged....1
Total Assisted....448
Specialized Homes....6
Total Assisted....1,200
Special Centers for Social Services....8
Total Assisted....18,762

Educational
Seminaries, Diocesan....1
Students from This Diocese....21
Diocesan Students in Other Seminaries....28
Total Seminarians....49
Colleges and Universities....1
Total Students....1,459
High Schools, Diocesan and Parish....3
Total Students....2,059
High Schools, Private....1
Total Students....33
Elementary Schools, Diocesan and Parish....16
Total Students....5,876
Catechesis/Religious Education:
High School Students....2,635
Elementary Students....15,555
Total Students under Catholic Instruction....27,666
Teachers in Diocese:
Priests....1
Sisters....1
Lay Teachers....544

Vital Statistics
Receptions into the Church:
Infant Baptism Totals....2,222
Minor Baptism Totals....2,806
Adult Baptism Totals....316
Received into Full Communion....479
First Communions....3,520
Confirmations....4,092
Marriages:
Catholic....699
Interfaith....200
Total Marriages....899
Deaths....1,294
Total Catholic Population....546,370
Total Population....5,505,666

LEADERSHIP

Office of the Bishop - t) 704-370-3327 bishopsoffice@rcdoc.org Most Rev. Peter J. Jugis;
Vicar General, Chancellor and Moderator of the Curia - t) 704-370-6299; 704-370-3326 chancery@rcdoc.org Very Rev. Msgr. Patrick J. Winslow;
Catechetical Formation - t) 704-370-3210 Rev. Roger K. Arnsparger, Vicar;
Campus & Young Adult Ministry - t) 704-370-3212 Mary Wright, Dir.;
Catechetical and Faith Formation - t) 704-370-3246 Rev. Roger K. Arnsparger, Dir.; Chris Beal, Prog. Dir.;
Youth Ministry - t) 704-370-3211 Paul Kotlowski;
Catholic Charities - t) 704-370-3228 Gerard A. Carter, Exec.;
Campaign for Human Development - t) 704-370-3283 Joseph Purello, Dir.;
Social Concerns and Advocacy - t) 704-370-3225 Joseph Purello, Dir.;
Catholic Education - t) 704-370-3271 Very Rev. Timothy S. Reid, Vicar for Education for Catholic Schools; Gregory Monroe, Supt.;
Mecklenburg Area Catholic Schools - t) 704-370-3265 discovermacs.org Sissie Kilby, Dir.;
Chancellor - Bryan T. Somerville, Asst. Chancellor;
Archives - t) 704-370-3215 Dcn. Matthew Hanes, Asst. Archivist;
Chief Financial Officer / Chief Administrative Officer - t) 704-370-3405 Matthew P. Ferrante, CFO/CAO;
Controller - t) 704-370-3312 Mason T. Beaumont;
Diocesan Properties - t) 704-370-3311 Anthony J. Morlando, Dir.;
Planning and Research - t) 704-370-3328 George K. Cobb, Dir.;
Risk and Insurance - t) 704-370-3321 Ronald J. Lordo, Mgr.;
Technology Services - t) 704-370-3388 helpdesk@rcdoc.org Scott Long, Dir.;
Communications - t) 704-370-3336 Liz Chandler, Dir.;
Newspaper: "Catholic News Herald" - Patricia L. Guilfoyle, Editor;
Development - t) 704-370-3302; 704-370-3301 James K. Kelley, Dir.; David Walsh, Assoc. Dir.;
Diocesan Attorney - t) 704-370-3346 Joe Dodge;
Hispanic Ministry - t) 704-370-3274 Very Rev. Julio C. Dominguez, Vicar; Sr. Joan Pearson, S.S.J., Admin. Asst.;
Human Resources - Molly V. Beckert, Dir.;
Victim Assistance Coordinator - t) 336-714-3202 David W. Harold;
Judicial Vicar - t) 704-370-3293 Very Rev. John T. Putnam, Judicial Vicar; Lisa D. Sarvis, Head of Tribunal Office; Debbie M. Wright, Case Processor;
Office of Divine Worship - t) 704-334-2283 Very Rev. Christopher A. Roux, Rector;
Office of Family Life - Rev. Peter Ascik, Dir.;
Marriage Preparation - Alecia Acquaviva, Dir.;
Natural Family Planning - Batrice Adcock, Dir.;
Respect Life Ministry - Alecia Acquaviva, Dir.;
Other Departments and Agencies -
African-American Ministry - t) 704-370-6299 Rosheene Adams;
Airport Ministry Program - t) 704-370-3344 Dcn. Patrick J. Devine; Dcn. George A. Szalony;
Boy Scouts - Dcn. Martin Ricart III;
Prison Ministry - t) 704-370-3344 Dcn. James H. Witulski, Dir.;
Propagation of the Faith - Rev. J. Patrick Cahill;
Permanent Diaconate - t) 704-370-3344 john.kopfle@rcdoc.org Dcn. John Kopfle, Dir.;
Vocations - t) 704-370-3353 vocationsmail@rcdoc.org Very Rev. Christopher M. Gober, Dir.; Rev. Jason K. Barone, Promoter of Vocations;

CONSULTATIVE BODIES

Diocesan Consultors - Very Rev. Msgr. Patrick J. Winslow, Contact;
Presbyteral Council - Rev. Benjamin A. Roberts, Chair; Rev. Christian Cook, Vice-Chmn.; Very Rev. John T. Putnam, Treas.;

PARISHES, MISSIONS, AND CLERGY

STATE OF NORTH CAROLINA

ALBEMARLE

Our Lady of the Annunciation - 416 N. Second St., Albemarle, NC 28001 t) 704-982-2910 olaalbemarle@rcdoc.org; church@annunciationalbemarle.com annunciationcatholicalbemarle.com Rev. Peter L. Fitzgibbons, Pst.; Michelle Pantore, DRE; CRP Stds.: 56

ANDREWS

Holy Redeemer - 214 Aquone Rd., Andrews, NC 28901-9776 t) 828-321-4463 holyredeemerandrews@rcdoc.org; gdbyers@rcdoc.org charlottediocese.org Rev. George D. Byers, C.P.M., Pst.; Jeanne Burns, DRE;
Prince of Peace - 704 Talluah Rd., Rte. 129 S., Robbinsville, NC 28771; Mailing: c/o Holy Redeemer, 214 Aquone Rd., Andrews, NC 28901 t) 828-689-3719 charlottediocese.org Rev. James M. Byer, Pst.;

ARDEN

St. Barnabas - 109 Crescent Hill Dr., Arden, NC 28704; Mailing: P.O. Box 39, Arden, NC 28704 t) 828-684-6098 stbarnabasarden@rcdoc.org; info@saintbarnabasarden.org www.saintbarnabasarden.org/ Very Rev. Adrian Porras, Pst.; Dcn. Frank Moyer; Dcn. Charles Moss; Simeon Willis, DRE;

ASHEBORO

St. Joseph - 512 W. Wainman Ave., Asheboro, NC 27203-5342 t) 336-629-0221 stjosephasheboro@rcdoc.org; stjoe@triad.rr.com www.stjoenc.org/ Rev. Philip Kollithanath, Pst.; Dawn Harris, DRE; Maria Pincus, Youth Min.;

ASHEVILLE

Basilica of St. Lawrence - 97 Haywood St., Asheville, NC 28801; Mailing: PO Box 1850, Asheville, NC 28802 t) 828-252-6042 basilicacomm@gmail.com saintlawrencebasilica.org Rev. Roger K. Arnsparger, Pst.; Rev. Nohe Torres, Par. Vicar; Dcn. Philip B. Miles; Barclay Roberts, Pst. Assoc.; Andrew Davis, Music Min.;
St. Eugene - 72 Culvern St., Asheville, NC 28804 t) 828-254-5193 churcheugene@steugene.org; steugeneasheville@rcdoc.org www.steugene.org Rev. J. Patrick Cahill, Pst.; Dcn. Michael Zboyovski Sr.; Tracy Jedd, DRE; Dcn. John Langlois; CRP Stds.: 261

BELMONT

Queen of the Apostles - 503 N. Main St., Belmont, NC 28012 t) 704-825-9600 x26 (CRP); 704-825-9600 officeofthepastor@queenoftheapostles.org www.queenoftheapostles.org Rev. Paul Buchanan, Pst.; Dcn. John Panzica; Dcn. William H. Wilson; Chrissy Glisson, Music Min.; Jeanne LaFrancis, Pst. Assoc.; Debbie Seeger, DRE; CRP Stds.: 250

BISCOE

Our Lady of the Americas - 298 Farmers Market Rd., Biscoe, NC 27209; Mailing: P.O. Box 519, Candor, NC 27229 t) 910-974-3051 olabiscoe@rcdoc.org; ourlady298@embarqmail.com www.ourladycandor.org/ Rev. Ricardo Sanchez, Pst.; Dcn. Charles Hindbaugh; Penny McGrath, Music Min.; Jorge Chavez, DRE; Eduardo Sanchez, Accountant; Nicolasa Salgado, Youth Min.;

BOONE

St. Elizabeth - 259 Pilgrims Way, Boone, NC 28607 t) 828-264-8338 stelizabethboone@gmail.com www.saintecc.org Rev. Brendan Buckler, Pst.; Vanessa Carson, DRE;
Church of the Epiphany - 163 Galax Ln., Blowing Rock, NC 28605; Mailing: 259 Pilgrims Way, Boone, NC 28607 t) (828) 264-8338

BOONVILLE

Divine Redeemer (Divino Redentor) - 209 Lon Ave., Boonville, NC 27011; Mailing: P.O. Box 370, Boonville, NC 27011 t) 336-367-7067 divineredeemercc@gmail.com divineredeemercc@gmail.com Rev. Jean-Pierre Swamunu Lhoposo, Pst.; Dcn. Michael Langsdorf; CRP Stds.: 450

BREVARD

Sacred Heart - 150 Brian Berg Ln., Brevard, NC 28712 t) 828-883-9572 shcc@sacredheartnc.org; jenni@sacredheartnc.org sacredheartcatholicchurchbrevardnc.org Rev. Shawn O'Neal, Pst.; Dcn. Patrick Crosby; Dcn. James Frederick; Jenni Pogue, Youth Min.; Patricia Poche, DRE & Bus. Mgr.;
St. Jude - 3011 U.S. Hwy. 64 E., Sapphire, NC 28774 t) 828-743-5717 stjudesapphirevalley@rcdoc.org; stjudeofsv@gmail.com www.stjudeofsapphirevalley.org Rev. Jason K. Barone, Par. Admin.;

BRYSON CITY

St. Joseph - 316 Main St., Bryson City, NC 28713; Mailing: PO Box 727, Bryson City, NC 28713 t) 828-488-6766 stjosephbrysoncity@rcdoc.org stjosephbryson.org Rev. Peter J. Shaw, Pst.; Dcn. William S. Shaw;
Our Lady of Guadalupe - 82 Lambert Branch Rd., Cherokee, NC 28719 t) 828-497-9755

CANDLER

St. Joan of Arc - 768 Ashbury Rd., Candler, NC 28715 t) 828-670-0051 stjoanofarc@rcdoc.org; stjoanofarc3640@bellsouth.net stjoanofarccandler.org Rev. Dean Cesa, Pst.; Tim Kelley, DRE;

CHARLOTTE

St. Patrick Cathedral - 1621 Dilworth Rd. E., Charlotte, NC 28203 t) 704-334-2283 info@stpatricks.org; stpatrickcharlotte@rcdoc.org www.stpatricks.org Very Rev. Christopher A. Roux, Rector; Rev. Ernest Nebangongnjoh, Par. Vicar; Dcn. Paul Bruck; Dcn. Brian P. McNulty; Dcn. Carlos A. Medina Sr.;
St. Ann Catholic Church - 3635 Park Rd., Charlotte, NC 28209 t) 704-523-4641 stanncharlotte@rcdoc.org www.stanncharlotte.org Very Rev. Timothy S. Reid, Pst.; Rev. Brandon H. Jones, Par. Vicar; Dcn. Thomas D. Sanctis; Dcn. Peter Tonon; Virginia Blatchford, DRE; CRP Stds.: 124
St. Gabriel - 3016 Providence Rd., Charlotte, NC 28211 t) 704-364-5431 aalbritton@stgabrielchurch.org; stgabrielcharlotte@rcdoc.org stgabrielchurch.org/ Rev. Richard Frank Sutter, Pst.; Rev. Mike Mitchell I, Par. Vicar; Dcn. Michael F. Goad; Dcn. Lawrence P. O'Toole; Dcn. Chris Vigliotta; Dcn. Bernard Wenning Jr.; Dr. David B. Glascow, DRE; Adrian Quintero, Youth Min.;
St. John Lee (Korean) - 7109 Robinson Church Rd., Charlotte, NC 28215 t) 704-531-8417 stjohnleecharlotte@gmail.com www.charlottekoreancatholic.org Rev. Jong Un Lim, Pst.;
St. John Neumann - 8451 Idlewild Rd., Charlotte, NC 28227 t) 704-536-6520 office@4sjnc.org; stjohnneumanncharlotte@rcdoc.org www.4sjnc.org/ Very Rev. John Francis Starczewski, Pst.; Dcn. James Gorman; Rev. Peter T. Pham, In Res.; Dcn. Mark Diener; CRP Stds.: 582
St. Joseph Church - 4929 Sandy Porter Rd., Charlotte, NC 28273 t) 704-504-0907 stjosephcharlotte@rcdoc.org; giaoxuthanhgiusecharlotte@gmail.com www.giaoxuthanhgiuse.net/ Rev. Tri Vinh Truong, Pst.; Dcn. Quang Nguyen; Duc Quang Le, DRE;

St. Matthew - 8015 Ballantyne Commons Pkwy., Charlotte, NC 28277; Mailing: P.O. Box 49349, Charlotte, NC 28277-0077 t) 704-543-7677 office@stmatthewcatholic.org stmatthewcatholic.org/ Rev. John Allen, Admin.; Rev. Binoy P. Davis, Par. Vicar; Rev. Juan Miguel Sanchez, Par. Vicar; Rev. Jonathan Torres, Par. Vicar; Dcn. Daren S. Bitter; Dcn. William G. Griffin; Dcn. James Hamrlik; Dcn. Paul H. Herman; Dcn. Gary J. Schrieber; Dcn. Jack G. Staub; Dcn. Lon Phillips; Dcn. Joseph Becker; Diane M. Kiradjieff, DRE;

Our Lady of Consolation - 2301 Statesville Ave., Charlotte, NC 28206-1400; Mailing: 1235 Badger Ct., Charlotte, NC 28206 t) 704-375-4339 olccharlotte@rcdoc.org www.ourladyofconsolation.org/ Rev. Basile Sede, Pst.; Dcn. Eduardo Bernal; Denise Duliepre, Youth Min.; Angela Peterson, DRE;

St. Helen - 341 Dallas-Spencer Mountain Rd., Gastonia, NC 28056; Mailing: 1235 Badger Ct, Charlotte, NC 28206 olccharlotte@charlottediocese.org charlottediocese.org/parishes/st-helen/ Dcn. Guy Piche; Barbara Gardin, DRE;

Our Lady of Guadalupe Church - 6212 Tuckaseegee Rd., Charlotte, NC 28214 t) 704-391-3732 olgcharlotte@rcdoc.org; nsguadalupe@bellsouth.net parroquiansguadalupe.com/ Rev. Leo Tiburcio, CM, Pst.; Rev. Hugo Medelin, CM, Par. Vicar; Maria A. Rodriguez, DRE; Juan Cajero, Youth Min.;

Our Lady of the Assumption - 4207 Shamrock Dr., Charlotte, NC 28215 t) 704-535-9965 ourlady11@bellsouth.net; olacharlotte@rcdoc.org www.ourladyoftheassumptioncharlotte.org/ Rev. Philip J. Scarcella, Pst.; Dcn. Peter Duca; Dcn. Luis Flores; Dcn. Stephen Fohn; Dcn. David S. Reiser; Dcn. Kevin Williams; Karen R. Posadas, DRE;

St. Peter - 507 S. Tryon St., Charlotte, NC 28202 t) 704-332-2901 office@stpeterscatholic.org; stpetercharlotte@rcdoc.org www.stpetercatholic.org Rev. Timothy J. Stephens, SJ, Pst.; Rev. John Michalowski, S.J., Par. Vicar; Dcn. James E. Bozik; Dcn. Clarke Cochran; Carmen San Juan, DRE; CRP Stds.: 266

St. Thomas Aquinas - 1400 Suther Rd., Charlotte, NC 28213 t) (704) 549-1607; (704) 549-5160 (CRP) church@stacharlotte.com www.stacharlotte.com/ Rev. Matthew P. Codd, Pst.; Rev. Raymond Ekosse, Par. Vicar; Rev. Innocent Amasiorah (Nigeria), Campus Min.; Dcn. Joseph A. Diaz; Dcn. Martin Ricart III; Dcn. James H. Witulski; Sr. Regina Ladoing, OP, DRE; Sr. Jessica Jurado, OP, Youth Min.;

Convent - t) 704-549-1607 Sr. Zeny Mofada, OP, Local Supr.;

St. Vincent de Paul - 6828 Old Reid Rd., Charlotte, NC 28210 t) 704-554-7088 stvincentcharlotte@rcdoc.org stvincentdepaulchurch.com/ Rev. Joshua A. Voitus, Pst.; Rev. Francis Olalekan Raji, MSP, Par. Vicar; Dcn. Herbert Quintanilla; Dcn. John Kopfle; Dcn. Ruben A. Tamayo; Riley Provost, DRE;

CONCORD

St. James - 139 Manor Ave., S.W., Concord, NC 28025 t) 704-720-0600 bonniew@saintjamescatholic.org; communication@saintjamescatholic.org www.saintjamescatholic.org/ Rev. Jerome L. Chavarria, C.Ss.R., Pst.; Rev. Charles Donovan, C.Ss.R., Assoc. Pst.; Rev. Fabio Marin Morales, C.Ss.R., Par. Vicar; Rev. Glenn Parker, Pst. Assoc.; Kayla D'Allura, DRE; Dcn. Todd Labonte; CRP Stds.: 477

DENVER

Holy Spirit - 537 N.NC 16 Business, Denver, NC 28037-9235 t) 704-483-6448 holyspiritdenver@rcdoc.org www.holyspiritnc.org/ Rev. Carmen Malacari, Pst.; Dcn. Webster James; Dcn. Matthew Reilly Jr.; Faye Anne Nye, DRE; Laura Cameron Rowe, Youth Min.;

EDEN

St. Joseph of the Hills - 316 Boone Rd., Eden, NC 27288 t) 336-623-2661 stjosephofthehills.eden@yahoo.com; stjosepheden@rcdoc.org Rev. Pragasam Mariasoosai, Pst.; Dcn. Gerald Potkay; Elizabeth Berteotti, DRE;

FOREST CITY

Immaculate Conception - 1024 W. Main St., Forest City, NC 28043 t) 828-245-4017 sgdate@rcdoc.org; immconcepforestcity@rcdoc.org www.immaculateconceptionforestcity.org Very Rev. Herbert T. Burke, Pst.; Dcn. David Faunce; Dcn. David V. Puscas; Dcn. Andrew Cilone, DRE;

FRANKLIN

St. Francis of Assisi - 299 Maple St., Franklin, NC 28734 t) 828-524-2289 stfrancis299@gmail.com; stfrancisfranklin@rcdoc.org www.stfrancisassisifranklin.org Rev. Tien H. Duong, Pst.; Dcn. David Ramsey; Kristen Ann Fox, DRE;

Our Lady of the Mountains - 315 N. 5th St., Highlands, NC 28741 t) 828-526-2418 olmountainshighlands@rcdoc.org olmhighlands.com Rev. Jason K. Barone, Parochial Admin.;

GASTONIA

St. Michael - 708 St. Michael's Ln., Gastonia, NC 28052 t) 704-867-6212 stmichaelgastonia@rcdoc.org stmccg.org Rev. Lucas C. Rossi, Pst.; Dcn. Timothy Mueller; Dcn. John P. Weisenhorn; Rev. James A. Ebright, In Res.; Dcn. William Melton Jr.; Rev. Jose Juya, In Res.; Shane Page, DRE; Matt Tortorich, Youth Min.;

St. Michael School - (Grades PreK-8) 704 St. Michael's Ln., Gastonia, NC 28052; Mailing: 708 St. Michael's Ln., Gastonia, NC 28052 t) 704-865-4382 school@stmichaelsgastonia.org www.stmichaelcs.com Michelle Vollman, Prin.;

GREENSBORO

St. Benedict - 109 W. Smith St., Greensboro, NC 27401 t) 336-272-0303 stbenedictgreensboro@rcdoc.org www.stbenedictgreensboro.net Rev. James Duc H. Duong, Pst.; Lynne McGrath, DRE;

St. Mary - 1414 Gorrell St., Greensboro, NC 27401 t) 336-272-8650 stmarygreensboro@rcdoc.org; info@stmarysgreensboro.org stmarysgreensboro.org Rev. John P. Timlin, CM, Pst.; Rev. Joseph Nguyen, CM, Par. Vicar; Rev. Erik Sanchez, CM, Par. Vicar; Dcn. Pierre M. K'Briuh; Dcn. Vincent Shaw Jr.; Dallana Janet Hernandez de Aguilera, DRE; Eze Ike, Youth Min.;

Our Lady of Grace - 2203 W. Market St., Greensboro, NC 27403 t) 336-274-6520 olggreensboro@rcdoc.org; olgchurch@olgchurch.org www.olgchurch.org (Ethel Clay Price Memorial) Rev. Casey A. Coleman, Pst.; Rev. Joseph Wasswa, Par. Vicar; Dcn. Carlos Mejias; Dcn. Timothy Rohan; Dcn. Jim Toner; Dcn. Jack Yarbrough; Amanda Mast, DRE;

Our Lady of Grace School - (Grades K-8) 201 S. Chapman St., Greensboro, NC 27403; Mailing: 2203 W. Market St., Greensboro, NC 27403 t) 336-275-1522 olgschool@olg.org www.olgsch.org Catherine Rusch, Prin.;

St. Paul the Apostle - 2741 Horsepen Creek Rd., Greensboro, NC 27410 t) 336-294-4696 stpaulgreensboro@rcdoc.org www.stpaulcc.org Rev. Joseph W. Mack, Pst.; Dcn. Larry Lisk; Dcn. Michael J. Martini; Mary L. Smith, DRE; Susan Rabold, Youth Min.;

St. Peter Yu - 4112 Romaine St., Greensboro, NC 27407 t) 336-292-6424 stpeteryu@gmail.com Rev. HyoSuk Lee, Pst.;

St. Pius the Tenth - 2210 N. Elm St., Greensboro, NC 27408; Mailing: P.O. Box 13588, Greensboro, NC 27415-3588 t) 336-272-4681 spxmail@stpiusxnc.com; stpiusgreensboro@rcdoc.org www.stpiusxnc.com/ Rev. Msgr. Anthony J. Marcaccio, Pst.; Dcn. Robert E. Morris; Dcn. Richard Pinto; Albert Abram, Pst. Assoc.; Lindsay M. Sartorio, DRE; Matthew Lopina, Youth Min.; CRP Stds.: 299

St. Pius the Tenth School - (Grades K-8) 2200 N. Elm St., Greensboro, NC 27408 t) 336-273-9865 www.spxschool.com/ Christopher Kloesz, Prin.;

HAMLET

St. James - 1018 W. Hamlet Ave., Hamlet, NC 28345; Mailing: PO Box 1208, Hamlet, NC 28345-1208 t) 910-582-0207 stjameshamlet@rcdoc.org www.stjameshamlet.com Rev. Fidel C. Melo, Pst.; Cecilia Wilson, DRE;

Sacred Heart - 205 Rutherford St., Wadesboro, NC 28710; Mailing: P.O. Box 1208, Hamlet, NC 28345-1208

HENDERSONVILLE

Immaculate Conception - 208 7th Ave. W., Hendersonville, NC 28791; Mailing: 611 N. Church St., Hendersonville, NC 28792-3623 t) 828-693-6901 churchoffice@icwnc.com; immconcephendersonville@rcdoc.org www.immaculateconceptionchurch.com/ Rev. W. Christian Cook, Pst.; Dcn. Mark D. Nash;

Immaculata - (Grades PreK-8) 711 Buncombe St., Hendersonville, NC 28791-3609 t) 828-693-3277 lstott@immac.org www.immac.org Margaret Beale, Prin.;

HICKORY

St. Aloysius - 921 Second St., N.E., Hickory, NC 28601 t) 828-327-2341 staloysiushickory@rcdoc.org; info@staloysiushickory.org www.staloysiushickory.org Rev. Lawrence M. LoMonaco, Pst.; Dcn. Ronald R. Caplette; Dcn. C. William Schreiber; Dcn. Francisco Pina; Isabel Romero, DRE; Jennifer Soto, Youth Min.;

HIGH POINT

Christ the King - 1505 E. Martin Luther King, Jr. Dr., High Point, NC 27260-5455 t) 336-883-0244 christthekinghp@gmail.com www.christthekinghp.org Rev. Joseph Long Dinh, Pst.; Dcn. Emmanuel O. Ukattah; Daphne McAdoo, DRE;

Immaculate Heart of Mary - 4145 Johnson St., High Point, NC 27265 t) 336-884-5352 (CRP); 336-869-7739 information@ihmchurch.org; fformation@ihmchurch.org www.ihmchurch.org Rev. Peter Leonard, O.S.F.S., Pst.; Rev. Baiju Paul Puthussery, O.S.F.S., Par. Vicar; Rev. Thomas P. Norris, O.S.F.S., In Res.; Dcn. John A. Clarke; Dcn. Francis Skinner; Dcn. Walter Haarsgaard, DRE;

Immaculate Heart of Mary School - (Grades PreK-8) t) (336) 887-2613 info@ihm-school.com www.ihm-school.com Dr. Maryann Leonard, Prin.; Jane Pirkl, Bus. Mgr.;

HUNTERSVILLE

St. Mark - 14740 Stumptown Rd., Huntersville, NC 28078 t) 704-948-1306 (CRP); 704-948-0231 scott.bruno@stmarknc.org; stmarkhuntersville@charlottediocese.org www.stmarknc.org Very Rev. John T. Putnam, Pst.; Rev. Mechesideck Yumo, Par. Vicar; Rev. Michael Carlson, Par. Vicar; Rev. Aaron Huber, Par. Vicar; Dcn. Thomas Martin; Dcn. Richard McCarron; Dcn. Thomas E. McGahey; Dcn. Thomas McMahon; Dcn. Robert T. Murphy; Dcn. Louis A. Pais; Dcn. Ronald D. Sherwood; Dcn. Ramon Tapia; CRP Stds.: 909

JEFFERSON

St. Francis of Assisi - 167 St. Francis Pl., Jefferson, NC 28640; Mailing: PO Box 634, Jefferson, NC 28640 t) 336-246-9151 stfrancis@skybest.com; stfrancisjefferson@rcdoc.org stfrancisofassisi-jefferson.org Rev. A. Cory Catron, Pst.; Dcn. Lee T. Levenson; Joanne Kuszaj, DRE; Jim Kuszaj, Youth Min.;

St. Frances of Rome - 29 Highland Dr., Sparta, NC 28675; Mailing: P.O. Box 367, Sparta, NC 28675 t) 336-372-8846 charlottediocese.org Rev. James A. Stuhrenberg, Pst.; Debbie Whittle, DRE;

KANNAPOLIS

St. Joseph Church - 108 Saint Joseph St., Kannapolis, NC 28083-6346 t) 704-932-4607 stjosephchurch@ctc.net; stjosephkannapolis@rcdoc.org www.saintjosephcatholic.org Rev. Fabio De Jesus Marin Morales, C.Ss.R., Pst.; Dcn. Bernardino Velez; Dcn. Chris Vigliotta; Kelly Whitley, DRE; Christine DePascale, Bus. Mgr.;

KERNERSVILLE

Holy Cross - 616 S. Cherry St., Kernersville, NC 27284 t) 336-996-5109 holycrosskernersville@rcdoc.org www.holycrossnc.com Rev. Noah C. Carter, Pst.; Rev. Jacob A. Mlaker, Par. Vicar; Dcn. Marcos Mejias; CRP

Stds.: 325

Child Developmental Center - t) 336-996-5144 Cathie Reel, Dir.;

LENOIR

St. Francis of Assisi - 328-B Woodsway Ln., N.W., Lenoir, NC 28645-4356 t) 828-754-5281 stfrancislenior@rcdoc.org; stfrancislenoir@charter.net www.stfrancislenoir.com/ Very Rev. Stephen M. Hoyt, Pst.; Dcn. A. Stephen Pickett; Kim Ann Clarke, DRE; Gerardo Cruz Nava, Youth Min.;

LEXINGTON

Our Lady of the Rosary - 619 S. Main St., Lexington, NC 27292-3238 t) 336-248-2463 parish@olr-nc.org; olrosarylexington@rcdoc.org olr-nc.org/ Rev. Sebastian Umouyo, MSP, Pst.; Maria Segura, DRE;

LINCOLNTON

St. Dorothy - 148 St. Dorothy Ln., Lincolnton, NC 28092-9801 t) 704-735-5575 office@stdorothys.com; saintdorothys@gmail.com www.stdorothys.com Rev. David P. Miller, Pst.; Margaret Barrett, DRE; CRP Stds.: 170

MAGGIE VALLEY

St. Margaret of Scotland - 37 Murphy Dr., Maggie Valley, NC 28751-1359; Mailing: P.O. Box 1359, Maggie Valley, NC 28751 t) 828-926-0106 stmargaretmv@bellsouth.net; stmargaretmaggievalley@rcdoc.org www.stmargaretofscotlandmv.org/ Rev. W. Becket Soule, OP, Pst.;

MARS HILL

St. Andrew the Apostle - 149 Brook St., Mars Hill, NC 28754-1406; Mailing: P.O. Box 1406, Mars Hill, NC 28754 t) 828-689-3719 standrewmarshill@rcdoc.org www.standrew-sacredheart.org Rev. Frederick H. Werth, Pst.;

Sacred Heart - 20 Summit St., Burnsville, NC 28714 t) (828) 689-3719

MINT HILL

St. Luke - 13700 Lawyers Rd., Mint Hill, NC 28227 t) 704-545-1224 stlukeminthill@rcdoc.org; info@stlukechurch.net www.stlukechurch.net/ Rev. Paul Gary, Pst.; Dcn. Jeffrey S. Evers; Dcn. Rafael J. Torres; Kathy McKinney, DRE; Katy De'Ath, Youth Min.;

MOCKSVILLE

St. Francis of Assisi - 862 Yadkinville Rd., Mocksville, NC 27028; Mailing: 838 Mr. Henry Rd., Mocksville, NC 27028 t) 336-751-2973 sfamox862@gmail.com; stfrancismocksville@rcdoc.org sfamox.org Rev. Eric Kowalski, Pst.; Renee Hoke, DRE; David Taylor, Bus. Mgr.;

MONROE

Our Lady of Lourdes - 725 Deese St., Monroe, NC 28112 t) 704-289-2773 lourdes@ollmonroe.org www.ourladymonroe.org Rev. Benjamin A. Roberts, Pst.; Dcn. Guillermo Anzola; Dcn. Roland R. Geoffroy; Dcn. Sidney Huff; Dcn. Margarito Franco Torres; Dcn. William D. Powers, DRE;

MOORESVILLE

St. Therese - 217 Brawley School Rd., Mooresville, NC 28117 t) 704-664-3992; 704-664-7762 (CRP) office@sainttherese.net; sttheresemooresville@rcdoc.org www.sainttherese.net Rev. Mark S. Lawlor, Pst.; Rev. Bernard Oleru, MSP, Par. Vicar; Dcn. Myles Decker; Dcn. Joseph R. Santen; Dcn. John E. Sims; Carmen San Juan, DRE; Dcn. Joseph Smith;

MORGANTON

St. Charles Borromeo - 728 W. Union St., Morganton, NC 28655 t) 828-437-3108 scbchurch417@gmail.com; stcharlesmorganton@rcdoc.org www.saintcharlesborromeo.org/ Rev. Kenneth L. Whittington, Pst.; Dcn. Edward A. Konarski; Dcn. John Martino; Dcn. Miguel P. Sebastian; Gail Watson, DRE;

Our Lady of the Angels - 258 N. Garden St., Marion, NC 28752 t) 828-559-0678 olotachurch@gmail.com; olamarion@rcdoc.org charlottediocese.org Enrique Montiel, DRE; Rev. Carl E. Kaltreider, Par. Admin.;

MT. AIRY

Holy Angels - 1208 N. Main St., Mt. Airy, NC 27030-3640 t) 336-786-8315 holyangelsmtairy@gmail.com; holyangelsmountairy@rcdoc.org www.mountairycatholicsha.com/ Rev. Peter Nouck, Pst.; Dcn. Wayne J. Nacey; Stella Neal, DRE;

MURPHY

St. William - 765 Andrews Rd., Murphy, NC 28906; Mailing: PO Box 546, Murphy, NC 28906 t) 828-837-2000 stwilliammurphy@rcdoc.org; stwilli@frontier.com st-william.net/ Rev. H. Alejandro Ayala, Pst.; Dcn. Carl Hubbell; Dr. Ruth Charlesworth, DRE;

Immaculate Heart of Mary - 1433 Hwy. 64 W., Hayesville, NC 28904 t) 828-389-3758 ihmhayesville@rcdoc.org; willi@frontier.com www.ihmhayesville.org

NEWTON

St. Joseph - 720 W. 13th St., Newton, NC 28658-3899 t) 828-464-9207 stjoseph78@bellsouth.net; stjosephnewton@rcdoc.org www.stjosephrcc.org/ Rev. James M. Collins, Pst.; Dcn. Scott D. Gilfillan; Kara Antonio, DRE;

NORTH WILKESBORO

St. John Baptist de LaSalle - 275 C.C. Wright School Rd., North Wilkesboro, NC 28659 t) 336-838-5562 info@stjohnnc.org; stjohnnwilkesboro@rcdoc.org stjosephrcc.org Rev. John D. Hanic, Pst.; Dcn. Harold Markle; Sr. Janice McQuade, S.S.J., Pst. Assoc.; Felix Fernando Salazar, DRE;

St. Stephen - 101 Hawthorne Rd., Elkin, NC 28621; Mailing: c/o St. John Baptist de la Salle, 275 CC Wright School Rd., North Wilkesboro, NC 28659 t) 336-835-3007 connect@ststephennc.org; ststephenelkin@rcdoc.org www.ststephennc.org

REIDSVILLE

Holy Infant - 1042 Freeway Dr., Reidsville, NC 27320; Mailing: P.O. Box 1197, Reidsville, NC 27320-1197 t) 336-342-1448 holyinfant.reidsville@gmail.com; holyinfantreidsville@rcdoc.org holyinfantrnc.org Rev. Frank J. Seabo, Pst.; Victoria Meraz, DRE; CRP Stds.: 134

SALISBURY

Sacred Heart - 375 Lumen Christi Ln., Salisbury, NC 28147 t) 704-633-0591 sburges@shcatholic.org; sacredheartsalisbury@rcdoc.org www.salisburycatholic.org Rev. John J. Eckert, Pst.; Dcn. James Mazur; John Baughman, DRE;

Sacred Heart School - (Grades K-8) 385 Lumen Christi Ln., Salisbury, NC 28147 t) 704-633-2841 ebrinkley@salisburycatholicschool.org www.salisburycatholicschool.org/ Erin Brinkley, Prin.; Lynn Frank, Librn.;

SHELBY

St. Mary Help of Christians - 818 McGowan Rd., Shelby, NC 28150 t) 704-487-7697 stmaryshelby@rcdoc.org www.saintmaryshelby.org Rev. Peter Ascik, Pst.; Dcn. James P. Trombley; Eloisa Amaya, Youth Min.;

Christ the King - 714 Stone St., Kings Mountain, NC 28086; Mailing: 818 McGowan Rd., Shelby, NC 28150

SPRUCE PINE

St. Lucien - 695 Summit Ave., Spruce Pine, NC 28777-0688; Mailing: P.O. Box 688, Spruce Pine, NC 28777 t) 828-765-2224 stbernadettelinville@rcdoc.org Rev. Christopher A. Bond, Pst.; Olga Aguayo, DRE;

St. Bernadette - 2085 State Hwy. 105, Linville, NC 28646; Mailing: P.O. Box 1252, Linville, NC 28646 t) 828-898-6900 www.stbernadettelinville.org Bobbie Havron, DRE;

STATESVILLE

St. Philip the Apostle - 525 Camden Dr., Statesville, NC 28687; Mailing: P.O. Box 882, Statesville, NC 28687-0882 t) 704-872-2579 stphilipapostle@bellsouth.net; stphillipstatesville@rcdoc.org stphilipapostle.com Rev. Thomas Kessler, Pst.; Edgar Noveron, DRE;

Holy Trinity - 1039 NC Hwy. 90 W., Taylorsville, NC 28681 t) 828-632-8009 holytrinitytaylorsville@rcdoc.org www.holytrinitycatholicnc.org Rev. Jose Camilo Cardenas-Bonilla, Par. Admin.; Paula Matheson, DRE;

SWANNANOA

St. Margaret Mary - 102 Andrews Pl., Swannanoa, NC 28778 t) 828-686-8833 stmmc@charter.net; stmargaretswannanoa@rcdoc.org saintmmc.com Rev. Brian Becker, Pst.; Dcn. Ralph R. Eckoff; Dcn. Dan Hoffert; Sarah Kramer, DRE;

SYLVA

St. Mary - 22 Bartlett St., Sylva, NC 28779 t) 828-586-9496 stmarysylva@rcdoc.org; smmgoffice@stmarymotherofgod.com stmarymotherofgod.com/ Rev. Paul Asoh, Pst.; Dcn. Matthew Newsome; Dcn. John Szarek; Lucia Castillo, DRE;

THOMASVILLE

Our Lady of the Highways - 943 Ball Park Rd., Thomasville, NC 27360 t) 336-475-2667 olhighwaysthomasville@rcdoc.org; olhsecretary@gmail.com www.ourladyofthehighwayscatholicchurch.com/ Rev. Gabriel Carvajal-Salazar, Pst.; Dcn. Martin Sheehan; Dcn. Wayne Adams; Kathy Laskis, DRE;

TRYON

St. John the Baptist - 180 Laurel Ave., Tryon, NC 28782 t) 828-895-9574 stjohnchurch@windstream.net; stjohntryon@rcdoc.org stjohntryon.com Rev. Jason M. Christian, Pst.; Dcn. John J. Riehl; Theresa Finch, DRE;

WAYNESVILLE

St. John the Evangelist - 234 Church St., Waynesville, NC 28786 t) 828-456-6707 stjohnwaynesville@gmail.com; stjohnwaynesville@rcdoc.org stjohnrcc.com Rev. Paul McNulty, Pst.; Nicki Conroy, DRE; Jessica Martin, Youth Min.;

Immaculate Conception - 42 Newfound Rd., Canton, NC 28716; Mailing: 234 Church St., Waynesville, NC 28786

WINSTON-SALEM

St. Benedict the Moor - 1625 E. Twelfth St., Winston-Salem, NC 27101 t) 336-725-9200 stbenedictwinstonsalem@rcdoc.org; sbcchmsd@gmail.com saintbenedictthemoor.org/ Rev. Henry Tutuwan, Pst.;

Good Shepherd - 105 Good Shepherd Dr., King, NC 27021; Mailing: 108 E. 12th St., Winston-Salem, NC 27101 t) 336-985-8695 goodshepherdking@rcdoc.org; goodshepherd-king@hotmail.com www.goodshepherdking.org/ Dcn. David Boissey Sr.; Dcn. Carl Brown;

Holy Family - 4820 Kinnamon Rd., Winston-Salem, NC 27103; Mailing: PO Box 130, Clemmons, NC 27012 t) 336-778-0600; 336-766-0600 x214 (CRP) holyfamilyclemmons@rcdoc.org; office@holyfamilyclemmons.com holyfamilyclemmons.com Rev. James A. Stuhrenberg, Pst.; Rev. James Kueh Kang, Par. Vicar; Dcn. John Harrison; Dcn. Stephen Fohn; Peggy Schumacher, DRE; Jenn Barlow, Youth Min.; CRP Stds.: 503

St. Leo the Great - 335 Springdale Ave., Winston-Salem, NC 27104 t) 336-724-0561 stleowinstonsalem@rcdoc.org; info@stleocatholic.org www.stleocatholic.org/ Very Rev. Christopher M. Gober, Pst.; Rev. Felix Nkafu, Par. Vicar; Rev. Britt A. Taylor, Par. Vicar; Dcn. Ralph D'Agostino; Dcn. Robert DeSautels; Lauren Garner, DRE;

St. Leo the Great School - (Grades PreK-8) 333 Springdale Ave., Winston-Salem, NC 27104 t) 336-748-8252 www.stleocatholic.com Gary Callus, Prin.; Alexandra Randall, Librn.;

Convent - 1975 Georgia Ave., Winston-Salem, NC 27104 t) 336-723-3639

Our Lady of Mercy - 1730 Link Rd., Winston-Salem, NC 27103-4626 t) 336-722-7001 www.ourladyofmercync.org Rev. David R. McCanless, Pst.; Rev. Alfonso Gamez, Par. Vicar; Dcn. Ramon

Ediberto Tejada; Sr. Kathleen Ganiel, O.S.F., DRE; Dcn. Serge Bernatchez; Dcn. Joseph N. Schumacher;

Our Lady of Mercy School - (Grades K-8) t) 336-722-7204 grogers@ourladyofmercyschool.org www.ourladyofmercyschool.org Sr. Geri Rogers, SSJ, Prin.;

Convent - 2141 New Castle Dr., Winston-Salem, NC 27103 t) 336-774-3956

Our Lady of Fatima - 211 W. 3rd St., Winston-Salem, NC 27101; Mailing: 1730 Link Rd., Winston-Salem, NC 27104 olfwinstonsalem@charlottediocese.org Rev. Carl S. Zdancewicz, O.F.M.Conv., Pst.;

SCHOOLS: PRESCHOOL THRU HIGH SCHOOL

SCHOOLS

STATE OF NORTH CAROLINA

ASHEVILLE

Asheville Catholic School - (PAR) (Grades PreK-8) 12 Culvern St., Asheville, NC 28804 t) 828-252-7896 info@ashevillecatholic.org www.ashevillecatholic.org Michael Miller, Prin.; Shonra McManus, Librn.;

CHARLOTTE

Mecklenburg Area Catholic Schools (M.A.C.S.) - (DIO) (Grades PreK-12) 1123 S. Church St., Charlotte, NC 28203 t) 704-370-3265 discovermacs.org Catholic School System of nine Schools. Dr. Gregory P. Monroe, Supt.; Crystal W. Koury, Asst. Supt.;

Charlotte Catholic High School (Bishop Hafey Memorial) - (Grades PreK-12) 7702 Pineville Matthews Rd., Charlotte, NC 28226 t) 704-543-1127 www.charlottecatholic.org/ Randy Belk, Dean; Kurt Telford, Prin.; Terri Taylor, Librn.;

Holy Trinity Catholic Middle School - (Grades PreK-12) 3100 Park Rd., Charlotte, NC 28209 t) 704-527-7822 www.htcms.org Rev. Joseph Matlak, Chap.; Kevin Parks, Prin.; Elizabeth Wise, Librn.;

St. Matthew School - (Grades PreK-12) 8015 Ballantyne Commons Pkwy., Charlotte, NC 28277 t) 704-544-2070 stmatthewschool@stmatthewschool.net www.stmattwildcats.com Kevin O'Herron, Prin.;

Our Lady of the Assumption School - (Grades PreK-12) 4225 Shamrock Dr., Charlotte, NC 28215 t) 704-531-0067 olafrontdesk@olaschool.net www.olacatholic.org Tyler Kulp, Prin.;

St. Ann School - (Grades PreK-12) 600 Hillside Ave., Charlotte, NC 28209 t) 704-525-4938 cwhargett@stannschool.net www.stanncatholic.org/ Michelle Kuhn, Prin.;

St. Gabriel School - (Grades PreK-12) 3028 Providence Rd., Charlotte, NC 28211 t) 704-366-2409 mmtew@stgabrielschool.net www.stgabrielcatholicschool.org Michelle Snoke, Prin.; Ellen Chase, Librn.;

St. Patrick School - (Grades PreK-12) 1125 Buchanan St., Charlotte, NC 28203 t) 704-333-3174 www.saintpatrickschool.org Amy Tobergte, Prin.; Julie Laney, Librn.;

St. Mark School - (Grades PreK-12) 14750 Stumptown Rd., Huntersville, NC 28078 t) 704-766-5000 frontdesk@stmarkcatholic.net stmarkcatholicschool.net Julie Thornley, Prin.; Lisa Rox, Librn.;

Christ the King Catholic High School - (Grades PreK-12) 2011 Crusader Way, Huntersville, NC 28078 t) 704-799-4400 ctkfrontdesk@ctkchs.org www.ctkchs.org Carl Semmler, Prin.;

HIGH SCHOOLS

STATE OF NORTH CAROLINA

KERNERSVILLE

Bishop McGuinness Catholic High School - (DIO) 1725 NC Hwy. 66 S., Kernersville, NC 27284 t) 336-564-1010 jrashford@bmhs.us www.bmhs.us Dr. Jared M. Rashford, Prin.; Leslie Redmon, Librn.;

INSTITUTIONS LOCATED IN DIOCESE

CAMPUS MINISTRY / NEWMAN CENTERS [CAM]

CHARLOTTE

Diocesan Office of Campus Ministry - 1123 S. Church St., Charlotte, NC 28203 t) 704-370-3243 campusministry@rcdoc.org www.charlottediocese.org Mary Wright, Dir.; Darien Clark, Asst. Dir.; Ann Kilkelly, Devel. Dir.;

Appalachian State University - Catholic Campus Ministry Center, 232 Faculty St., Boone, NC 28607 t) 828-264-7087 appstatecatholic@gmail.com sites.google.com/site/appstateccm/ Erin Kotlowski, Campus Min.;

Davidson College - Alvarez Student Union Ste. 405, Chaplain's Office, Davidson, NC 28035; Mailing: Campus Box 7196, Davidson, NC 28035 t) 704-894-2423 scsalvato@davidson.edu www.davidsonccm.com Scott Salvato, Campus Min.;

High Point University - 1 University Pkwy., Hayworth Memorial Chapel, High Point, NC 27262; Mailing: P.O. Box 6515, High Point, NC 27262 t) 704-996-7620 mnnjoh@rcdoc.org hpucatholic.com/ Rev. Moses Nikume Njoh (Cameroon), Campus Min.;

NC Agricultural and Technical State University - Thea House, 131 N. Dudley St., Greensboro, NC 27401 t) 336-907-3543 theahouse.org Rev. Marcel Amadi (Nigeria), Campus Min.;

University of North Carolina-Asheville/Mars Hill College - 138 Sevier St., Asheville, NC 28804; Mailing: P.O. Box 8067, Asheville, NC 28814 t) 828-226-3809 ashevilleccm@gmail.com ashevilleccm.com David Mayeux, Campus Min.;

University of North Carolina-Charlotte - 1400 Suther Rd., Catholic Campus Ministry Center, Charlotte, NC 28213 t) 347-445-1334 ccmuncc@gmail.com charlotteccm.org/ Rev. Innocent Amasiorah (Nigeria), Campus Min.;

University of North Carolina-Greensboro - Catholic Campus Ministry, 500 Stirling St, Greensboro, NC 27402 t) 336-334-5130 hello@greensborocatholic.com greensborocatholic.com Gregg Cecconi, Campus Min.;

Wake Forest University - Catholic Lounge, Collins Residence Hall, Winston-Salem, NC 27109; Mailing: P.O. Box 7204, Reynolda Station, Winston-Salem, NC 27109 t) 336-758-5018 orrej@wfu.edu; amadimc@wfu.edu wakeforestcatholic.com/ Rev. Marcel Amadi (Nigeria), Sacr. Min.; Liz Orr, Coord., Catholic Life;

Western Carolina University - 197 Forest Hills Rd., Cullowhee, NC 28723; Mailing: PO Box 2766, Cullowhee, NC 28723 t) 828-293-9374 ccm@wcucatholic.org wcucatholic.org/ Dcn. Matthew Newsome, Campus Min.;

CATHOLIC CHARITIES [CCH]

CHARLOTTE

Catholic Charities Diocese of Charlotte - 1123 S. Church St., Charlotte, NC 28203 t) 800-227-7261 ccdoc@rcdoc.org www.ccdoc.org Gerard A. Carter, Exec.;

Catholic Charities-Charlotte Regional Office - t) 704-370-3262 Sandy Buck, Dir.;

Catholic Charities-Murphy Office - 27 Hatchett St., Murphy, NC 28906 t) 828-835-3535 nwmcfaddin@rcdoc.org

Catholic Charities-Piedmont Triad Office - 1612 E. 14th St., Winston-Salem, NC 27105 t) 336-727-0705 Becky DuBois, Dir.;

Catholic Charities-Refugee Resettlement Office - t) 704-370-3262 gacarter@rcdoc.org Sandy Buck, Dir.;

Catholic Charities-Western Regional Office - 50 Orange St., Asheville, NC 28801 t) 828-255-0146 clrhodes@rcdoc.org Mark Nash, Dir.;

Social Concerns and Advocacy - t) 704-370-3225 jtpurello@charlottediocese.org Joseph Purello, Dir.;

COLLEGES & UNIVERSITIES [COL]

BELMONT

***Belmont Abbey College** - 100 Belmont-Mount Holly Rd., Belmont, NC 28012-1802 t) 704-461-6700 contollersoffice@bac.edu belmontabbeycollege.edu (Coed) Liberal Arts Senior College. Rt. Rev. Placid D. Solari, O.S.B., Chancellor; William Thierfelder, Pres.; Allan Mark, Exec.; Donald Beagle, Dir.; David Williams, Vice-Provost; Margot Rhoads, Registrar;

Belmont Abbey College Campus Ministry - t) 704-461-5094 wesleynelson@bac.edu belmontabbeycollege.edu Patrick Ford, Dir.;

Sacred Heart College - 101 Mercy Dr., Belmont, NC 28012-4805 t) 704-829-5100 College ceased academic operation, effective August 1987. Corporation intact. Sisters of Mercy Sr. Rosalind Picot, R.S.M., Pres.;

CONVENTS, MONASTERIES, AND RESIDENCES FOR WOMEN [CON]

ARCHDALE

Congregation of the Sisters of Charity of St. Vincent De Paul - St. Vincent Convent, 1225 Elon Pl., Archdale, NC 27263 t) 336-687-7005 Sr. M. Vinaya, SCV, Supr.;

BELMONT

Sisters of Mercy of the Americas, South Central Community, Inc. - Sacred Heart Convent, 500 Sacred Heart Cir., Belmont, NC 28012 t) 704-829-5100 ljordan@sistersofmercy.org Sr. Lillian Jordan, Admin.; Srs.: 33

Sisters of Mercy of the Americas, South Central Community, Inc. - 101 Mercy Dr., Belmont, NC 28012-2898 t) 704-829-5260 Sr. Pat Flynn, RSM, Pres.; Srs.: 324

CHARLOTTE

Missionaries of Charity - 1625 Glenn St., Charlotte, NC 28205; Mailing: 335 E. 145th St., Bronx, NY 10451 t) 704-531-2943 Convent and Gift of Mary home for expectant mothers Sr. Maria Christy, MC, Supr.; Sr. M. Jonathan MC, Regl. Supr.; Srs.: 5

HIGH POINT

Poor Servants of the Mother of God Inc. - 1315 Greensboro Rd., High Point, NC 27260 t) 336-454-3014 sisterlucy@pennybyrn.org www.smgsisters.com Sr. Lucy Hennessy, S.M.G., Mission Leader;

MOORESBORO

St. Joseph Adoration Monastery - Timber Dr., Mooresboro, NC 28114; Mailing: 3222 County Rd. 548, Hanceville, AL 35077 t) 205-795-5739 www.stjosephmonastery.com Merged with Our Lady of the Angels Monastery in Hanceville, Alabama Mother Mary Paschal, PCPA, Contact;

VALE

Maryvale Motherhouse - 2522 June Bug Rd., Vale, NC 28168 t) 704-276-2626 mvsrs1961@hughes.net www.maryvalesisters.com Parish ministry, day-care center, spiritual/retreat center. Sr. Mary Louis, CLHC, Supr.;

WINSTON-SALEM

Sisters of St. Joseph of Chestnut Hill, PA - 1975 Georgia Ave., Winston-Salem, NC 27104 t) 336-727-3778 srann@bmhs.us Sr. Ann Thomas, Contact;

ENDOWMENTS / FOUNDATIONS / TRUSTS [EFT]

ASHEVILLE

Catherine McAuley Mercy Foundation, Inc. - 1201

Patton Ave., Ste. 200, Asheville, NC 28806; Mailing: P.O. Box 16367, Asheville, NC 28816 t) 828-281-2598 sharon@mercyurgentcare.org www.mercyurgentcare.org Rachel Sossoman, CEO;

BELMONT

Holy Angels Foundation, Inc. - 6600 Wilkinson Blvd., Belmont, NC 28012; Mailing: P.O. Box 710, Belmont, NC 28012-0710 t) 704-825-4161 hainfo@holyangelsnc.org www.holyangelsnc.org/ Kerri C. Massey, Pres.;

Sisters of Mercy of North Carolina Legacy - 100 McAuley Cir., Belmont, NC 28012; Mailing: P.O. Box 987, Belmont, NC 28012 t) 704-366-0087 cheryl@sistersofmercyfoundation.org; pwilliams@mercysc.org www.somncfdn.org Sr. Debbie Kern, RSM, Chair; Cheryl Brownd, Exec.; Sr. Paulette Williams, R.S.M., Vice Pres.;

CHARLOTTE

Foundation of the Roman Catholic Diocese of Charlotte - 1123 S. Church St., Charlotte, NC 28203 t) 704-370-3396; 704-370-3301

HOSPITALS / HEALTH SERVICES [HOS]

ASHEVILLE

Sisters of Mercy Urgent Care, Inc. dba Mercy Urgent Care - 1201 Patton Ave., Asheville, NC 28806-0367; Mailing: P.O. Box 16367, Asheville, NC 28816 t) 828-210-2121 sharon@mercyurgentcare.org mercyurgentcare.org/ Rachel Sossoman, CEO; Asstd. Annu.: 70,188; Staff: 112

MISCELLANEOUS [MIS]

BELMONT

***Catherine's House** - 141 Mercy Dr., Belmont, NC 28012; Mailing: P.O. Box 1633, Belmont, NC 28012 t) 704-825-9599 cherylfabino@catherineshouseinc.org; kathygauger@catherineshouseinc.org www.catherineshouseinc.org Transitional housing for women and women with children who are homeless. Kathy E Gauger, Pres.;

Holy Angels, Inc. - 6600 Wilkinson Blvd., Belmont, NC 28012; Mailing: P.O. Box 710, Belmont, NC 28012-0710 t) 704-825-4161 hainfo@holyangelsnc.org Kerri C. Massey, Pres.;

Holy Angels, Inc. Camp Hope - 120 River Run Rd., Belmont, NC 28012 t) (704) 825-4161 reginam@holyangelsnc.org Recreational opportunities for individuals with developmental disabilities.

Holy Angels, Inc. Carrabaun - t) (704) 825-4161 holyangelsnc.org Adult group home.

Holy Angels, Inc. Cherub Cafe - 23 N. Main St., Belmont, NC 28012 t) 704-825-0414 (Age 18+), Job coaching, work options.

Holy Angels, Inc. Gary Home - t) (704) 825-4161 www.holyangelsnc.org Adult group home.

Holy Angels, Inc. Great Adventures Social Club - t) (704) 825-4161 info@holyangelsnc.org www.holyangelsnc.org Adults with Intellectual Development Disabilities.

Holy Angels, Inc. Lakewood - t) (804) 825-4161 www.holyangelsnc.org Adult group home.

Holy Angels, Inc. Morrow Center - 6600 Wilkinson Blvd., Belmont, NC 28012 t) (704) 825-4161 www.holyangelsnc.org (Children newborn-20)

Holy Angels, Inc. South Point - t) (704) 825-4161 www.holyangelsnc.org Adult group home.

House of Mercy, Inc. - 100 McAuley Cir., Belmont, NC 28012; Mailing: P.O. Box 808, Belmont, NC 28012 t) 704-825-4711 office@thehouseofmercy.org www.thehouseofmercy.org Provides housing and supportive services for people living with HIV or AIDS in an 11 county region. Latoya M Gardner, CEO;

Mercy Community Housing North Carolina (MCHNC) - 6531 Wilkinson Blvd., Belmont, NC 28012 t) (303) 830-3300 www.mercyhousing.org Paula Grant, Vice Pres.;

Mercy Housing, South East, Inc. - 6531 Wilkinson Blvd., Belmont, NC 28012; Mailing: 1600 Broadway, Ste. 2000, Denver, CO 80202 t) 303-830-3300 dbendell1958@gmail.com; jrosenblum@mercyhousing.org www.mercyhousing.org Purpose: provide housing and supportive services to low income, special needs populations and seniors. James Alexander, Pres.;

Mercy Place Belmont - 6531 Wilkinson Blvd., Belmont, NC 28012; Mailing: 1600 Broadway, Ste. 2000, Denver, CO 80202 t) 303-830-3300 Provides housing and support services for very low-income seniors. James Alexander, Pres.;

Sisters of Mercy of the Americas, South Central Community, Inc. - Mercy Administration Center, 101 Mercy Dr., Belmont, NC 28012-2898 t) 704-829-5260 Sr. Pat Flynn, RSM, Pres.;

South Central FIDES, Inc. - 101 Mercy Dr., Belmont, NC 28012 t) 704-829-5260 Sr. Anne Marie Miller, RSM, Pres.;

Veterum Sapientia Institute - 5088 Abbington Way, Belmont, NC 28012 t) (828) 468-8099 info@veterumsapientia.org veterumsapientia.org/ Forms clerics, religious, and laity in the Latin and Greek languages in support of the evangelizing mission of the Church. Christopher Dale Owens, CEO;

CHARLOTTE

***Carolina Family Coalition** - 1235 East Blvd., Ste. 144, Charlotte, NC 28203 t) (704) 313-8414

Cathedral Publishing - 1123 S. Church St., Charlotte, NC 28203

Catholic Diocese of Charlotte Advancement Corporation - c/o Finance Department, 1123 S. Church St., Charlotte, NC 28203 t) 704-370-3405 charlottediocese.org Mason T. Beaumont, Controller; Matthew P. Ferrante, CFO;

Catholic Diocese of Charlotte Housing Corp. - 1123 S. Church St., Charlotte, NC 28203 t) 704-370-3248 cdchc@charlottediocese.org charlottediocese.org/housing/ Develops housing facilities and services for seniors and individuals with special needs. Very Rev. Msgr. Patrick J. Winslow, Pres.; Gerard C. Carter, Vice Pres.; William G. Weldon, Treas.; Adriel Cardenas, Dir.;

Charlotte Catholic Women's Group - 1123 S. Church St., Charlotte, NC 28203 t) 704-370-3210 rkarnsparger@charlottediocese.org www.charlottecatholicwomensgroup.org Rev. Roger K. Arnsparger, Chap.; Connie Hudack, Pres.;

Diocesan Hispanic Ministry - 1123 S. Church St., Charlotte, NC 28203 t) 704-370-6299 jcdominguez@rcdoc.org; jwpearson@rcdoc.org Very Rev. Julio C. Dominguez, Vicar; Dcn. Enedino S. Aquino, Greensboro Vicariate Coord.; Aleksandra Banasik, Boone Vicariate Coord.; Dcn. Eduardo Bernal, Charlotte Vicariate Coord.; Ibis Centeno, Salisbury Vicariate Coord.; Dcn. Sigfrido A. Della Valle, Smoky Mountain Vicariate Coord.; Juan Antonio Garcia, Asheville Vicariate Coord.; Dcn. Dario Garcia, Hickory Vicariate Coord.; Rev. Jose Juya, Gastonia Vicariate Coord.; Sergio Lopez, Winston-Salem Vicariate Coord.;

DL Catholic, Inc. - 1123 S. Church St., c/o Finance Department, Charlotte, NC 28203 t) 704-370-3396 charlottediocese.org Matthew P. Ferrante, CFO; Mason T. Beaumont, Controller;

***MiraVia (Room at the Inn, Inc.)** - 3737 Weona Ave., Charlotte, NC 28209; Mailing: PO Box 11499, Charlotte, NC 28220-1400 t) 704-525-4673 debbiecapen@miravia.org www.miravia.org Long-term maternity and aftercare services for single, pregnant women, with their babies. Debbie Capen, Exec.;

GASTONIA

Daughters of the Virgin Mother, Inc. - 1112 S. Belvedere Ave., Gastonia, NC 28054

***Seton Media House, Inc.** - 1520 S. York St., Gastonia, NC 28053; Mailing: PO Box 269, Gastonia, NC 28053 setonhouse@aol.com www.setonmediahouse.org Purpose: Distribution of printed materials reflective of Catholic teaching to Catholic schools and religious educ. programs at no cost to students. Richard G. Hoefling, Pres.;

GREENSBORO

Franciscan Center - 233 N. Greene St., Greensboro, NC 27401 t) 336-273-2554 franciscancenter233@gmail.com www.catholicgiftshoponline.com Rev. Louis Canino, O.F.M., Dir.; Rev. David Hyman, O.F.M.;

Room At The Inn, Inc. - 734 Park Ave., Greensboro, NC 27405; Mailing: P.O. Box 13936, Greensboro, NC 27415 t) 336-996-3788 roomattheinn@triad.rr.com www.roominn.org O. Albert Hodges, Pres.;

Society of St. Vincent De Paul - 109 W. Smith St., Greensboro, NC 27401 t) 336-272-0336; 336-210-3745 Financial assistance, furniture and appliances.

HICKORY

Catholic Conference Center - 1551 Trinity Ln., Hickory, NC 28602-9247 t) 828-327-7441 info@catholicconference.org www.catholicconference.org Dcn. Scott D. Gilfillan, Dir.;

MOORESVILLE

***Be Not Afraid, Inc.** - 134 Yellow Birch Loop, Mooresville, NC 28117 t) 704-651-9255 sandy.buck@benotafraid.net www.benotafraid.net Comprehensive support for parents carrying to term following a prenatal diagnosis, and Catholic service development and mentoring. Sandy Buck, Dir.; Tracy Winsor, Dir.;

SALISBURY

Cursillos in Christianity - 218 W. Thomas St., Salisbury, NC 28144

MONASTERIES AND RESIDENCES FOR PRIESTS AND BROTHERS [MON]

BELMONT

Belmont Abbey (Southern Benedictine Society of North Carolina, Inc.) - 100 Belmont-Mount Holly Rd., Belmont, NC 28012-1802 t) 704-461-6675 belmontabbey.org Rt. Rev. Placid D. Solari, O.S.B., Abbot; Rev. Christopher A. Kirchgessner, O.S.B., Prior; Bro. Tobiah Abbott, O.S.B.; Rev. David G. Brown, O.S.B.; Rev. Elias Correa-Torres, O.S.B.; Bro. Anselm Cundiff, O.S.B.; Rev. Francis P. Forster, O.S.B.; Bro. Edward Mancuso, O.S.B.; Bro. James Raber, O.S.B.; Bro. George Rumley, O.S.B.; Bro. Paul Shanley, O.S.B.; Bro. Emmanuel Slobodzian, O.S.B.; Bro. Anthony Swofford, O.S.B.; Bro. Bede McKeon, Archivist; Bro. Leo Young, Mem.; Brs.: 12; Priests: 5

CHARLOTTE

St. Peter Jesuit Community - 939 Ideal Way, Charlotte, NC 28203; Mailing: 507 S. Tryon St., St. Peter Catholic Church, Charlotte, NC 28202 t) 704-332-2901 tstephens@jesuits.org Rev. John Michalowski, S.J., In Res.; Rev. Timothy J. Stephens, SJ, In Res.; Priests: 2

STONEVILLE

Franciscan Friary - 477 Grogan Rd., Stoneville, NC 27048 t) 336-573-3751 info@stfrancissprings.com Rev. David Hyman, O.F.M.; Rev. Louis Canino, O.F.M., Dir.;

NURSING / REHABILITATION / CONVALESCENCE / ELDERLY CARE [NUR]

HIGH POINT

Maryfield Nursing Home - 1315 Greensboro Rd., High Point, NC 27260 t) 336-821-4000 sisterlucy@pennybyrn.org www.pennybyrnliving.org Maryfield, Inc. DBA Pennybyrn Sr. Lucy Hennessy, S.M.G., Chair; Asstd. Annu.: 448; Staff: 450

Pennybyrn at Maryfield - info@pennybyrn.org Dcn. David E. King, Chap.;

RETREAT HOUSES / RENEWAL CENTERS [RTR]

HAMPTONVILLE

Well of Mercy Inc. - 181 Mercy Ln., Hamptonville, NC 27020 t) 704-539-5449 mercy@wellofmercy.org www.wellofmercy.org Individual and Group Retreats. Sandra Hunter O'Brien, Dir.;

MAGGIE VALLEY

Living Waters Catholic Reflection Center - 103 Living

Waters Ln., Maggie Valley, NC 28751 t) 828-926-3833 livingwaters@catholicretreat.org www.catholicretreat.org Retreats, days of recollection & continuing education. Dcn. William S. Shaw, Dir.;

STONEVILLE

***St. Francis Springs Prayer Center** - 477 Grogan Rd., Stoneville, NC 27048 t) 336-573-3751 info@stfrancissprings.com www.stfrancis.today Rev. David Hyman, O.F.M., Chap.; Steve Swayne, Dir.;

SEMINARIES [SEM]

MOUNT HOLLY

St. Joseph College Seminary, Inc. - 22 Actus Ave., Mount Holly, NC 28120 t) 704-370-3402 mraphael@stjcs.org; mkauth@stjcs.org Rev. Matthew K. Kauth, Rector;

SPECIAL CARE FACILITIES [SPF]

BELMONT

***Holy Angels Services, Inc.** - 6600 Wilkinson Blvd., Belmont, NC 28012; Mailing: P.O. Box 710, Belmont, NC 28012 t) 704-825-4161 hainfo@holyangelsnc.org www.holyangelsnc.org Residential and developmental programs and services for children and adults with IDD and delicate medical conditions. Kerri C. Massey, Pres.; Bed Capacity: 48; Asstd. Annu.: 48; Staff: 144

McAuley Residence IID Group Homes -

Diocese of Cheyenne

(Dioecesis Cheyennensis)

MOST REVEREND STEVEN R. BIEGLER, D.D., S.T.L.

Bishop of Cheyenne; ordained July 9, 1993; appointed Bishop of Cheyenne March 16, 2017; installed June 5, 2017. Office: 2121 Capitol Ave., Cheyenne, WY 82001.

Chancery Office: 2121 Capitol Ave., P.O. Box 1468, Cheyenne, WY 82003-1468. T: 307-638-1530; F: 307-637-7936.

www.dcwy.org

dmcintyre@dcwy.org

ESTABLISHED AUGUST 2, 1887.

Square Miles 97,548.

Comprises the State of Wyoming and Yellowstone National Park.

For legal titles of parishes and diocesan institutions, consult the Chancery Office.

STATISTICAL OVERVIEW

Personnel

Bishop....1
Retired Bishops....1
Priests: Diocesan Active in Diocese....37
Priests: Diocesan Active Outside Diocese....3
Priests: Retired, Sick or Absent....17
Number of Diocesan Priests....57
Religious Priests in Diocese....2
Total Priests in your Diocese....59
Extern Priests in Diocese....4

Ordinations:
Diocesan Priests....1
Permanent Deacons in Diocese....40
Total Sisters....6

Parishes

Parishes....36

With Resident Pastor:
Resident Diocesan Priests....29

Without Resident Pastor:
Administered by Priests....7

Missions....33
Closed Parishes....2

Professional Ministry Personnel:
Lay Ministers....58

Welfare

Homes for the Aged....2
Total Assisted....124
Residential Care of Children....1
Total Assisted....107
Other Institutions....1
Total Assisted....50

Educational

Diocesan Students in Other Seminaries....8
Total Seminarians....8
Elementary Schools, Diocesan and Parish....6
Total Students....794

Catechesis/Religious Education:
High School Students....646
Elementary Students....2,155
Total Students under Catholic Instruction....3,603

Teachers in Diocese:
Lay Teachers....95

Vital Statistics

Receptions into the Church:
Infant Baptism Totals....430
Minor Baptism Totals....59
Adult Baptism Totals....64
Received into Full Communion....66
First Communions....661
Confirmations....622

Marriages:
Catholic....81
Interfaith....41
Total Marriages....122
Deaths....587
Total Catholic Population....48,393
Total Population....584,309

LEADERSHIP

Vicar General - t) 307-638-1530 Very Rev. Carl J. Gallinger;
Chancellor - t) 307-638-1530 Jean M. Chrostoski, Chancellor;
Director of Parish Services - Tammy Skala, Exec. Dir. (tskala@dcwy.org);
Judicial Vicar - Rev. Thomas E. Cronkleton Jr.;
Tribunal Office - t) 307-638-1530; 866-790-0014 Rev. Thomas E. Cronkleton Jr.; Sarah Lauhead, Dir. (slauhead@dcwy.org); Pamela Miller (pmiller@dcwy.org);
Ecclesiastical Notary - Dorene McIntyre;
Judicial Vicar - Rev. Thomas E. Cronkleton Jr.;
Tribunal Case Instructor - Pamela Miller;
Chief Financial Officer - dplacke@dcwy.org Dan Placke;

ADVISORY BOARDS, COMMISSIONS, COMMITTEES, AND COUNCILS

Finance Council - Aaron Courtney, Chair; Dave Balling; Very Rev. Carl Gallinger;
Building Commission - Herbert W. Stoughton, Chair; Bill Fehringer; Dan Placke;

CLERGY AND RELIGIOUS SERVICES

Office of Worship - t) 307-745-5461 Very Rev. Robert Spaulding, Dir. (rspaulding@dcwy.org);
Ongoing Formation of Clergy - cjacobson@dcwy.org Very Rev. Clifford Jacobson;
Deacon Personnel - kcarroll@dcwy.org Dcn. Kim Carroll;
Vicar for Priests - akoeune@dcwy.org Rev. August Koeune;

COMMUNICATIONS

Director of Communications - t) 307-638-1530 Diana Marie Waggener, Exec. Dir.;
Legislative Liaison and Catholic Social Teaching - t) 307-638-1530 Dcn. Michael Leman;
"Wyoming Catholic Register" and Social Media - t) 307-638-1530 dwaggener@dcwy.org Diana Marie Waggener, Exec. Dir.;

CONSULTATIVE BODIES

College of Consultors - Rev. Thomas E. Cronkleton Jr.; Very Rev. Carl Gallinger; Very Rev. Robert Spaulding (rspaulding@dcwy.org);
Diocesan Review Board - t) 307-638-1530 x105 Tim Jurkowski, Chair; Jean M. Chrostoski, Chancellor; Toni Williams;
Diocese of Cheyenne, Board of Directors - Most Rev. Steven Biegler; Very Rev. Carl Gallinger; Connie Janney;
Pastor Consultors - Rev. Augustine Carrillo; Very Rev. Clifford Jacobson; Rev. Ray Rodriguez;
Presbyteral Council - Very Rev. Carl J. Gallinger, Chair; Rev. Thomas E. Cronkleton Jr.; Rev. Brian J. Hess;
Vicars Forane - Very Rev. James Heiser, Sheridan Deanery; Very Rev. William Hill, Rock Springs Deanery; Very Rev. Cliff Jacobson, Casper Deanery;

FAITH FORMATION

Vocation Office - t) (307) 439-4368 bhess@dcwy.org Rev. Brian J. Hess, Dir.; Rita Tystad, Secy.;
Formation of Permanent Deacons - jsandrini@dcwy.org Dcn. Joseph Sandrini, Dir.;
Office of Pastoral Formation - t) 307-638-1530 Theresa Meuer, Assoc. Dir.; Dcn. Benny Yupanqui, Assoc. Dir.;

SOCIAL SERVICES

Catholic Charities of Wyoming - Genevieve Mougey, Exec. Dir.;
Respect Life Catholic Pro-Life Ministry - t) 307-638-1530 Dcn. Michael Leman; Maria Ward;

STEWARDSHIP

Propagation of the Faith - mmartinson@dcwy.org Dcn. Michael Martinson;
Tithing Committee - Dcn. Doug Vlchek, Chair; Dcn. Joseph Bush; Dorene McIntyre;

MISCELLANEOUS / OTHER OFFICES

Victim Assistance Coordinator - t) 307-638-1530 x105 jchrostoski@dcwy.org Teresa Klatka;

PARISHES, MISSIONS, AND CLERGY

STATE OF WYOMING

BUFFALO

St. John the Baptist - 532 N. Lobban, Buffalo, WY 82834 t) 307-278-0193 (CRP); 307-684-7268 www.sjbc-buffalo.com Very Rev. James Heiser, Pst.; Dcn. Jay Garland; Carol Gagliano, DRE; CRP Stds.: 102
St. Mary - 1601 Clear Creek Ave., Clearmont, WY 82834 t) (307) 684-7268 (Mission of St. John the B)
St. Hubert - 1080 Sussex Dr., Kaycee, WY 82834 t) (307) 684-7268 (Mission of St. John the B)

CASPER

St. Anthony of Padua - 644 S. Center St., Casper, WY 82601; Mailing: 604 S. Center St., Casper, WY 82601 t) 307-266-2666 religious.ed@stanthonyscasper.org; frrayrod27@gmail.com stanthonyscasper.org Rev. Raymond P. Rodriguez, Pst.; Rev. Philip J Vaske, Chap.; Clareesa King, Liturgy Dir.; Sheila Wiggins, DRE; LaVonne Carlson, Bus. Mgr.; CRP Stds.: 78
St. Anthony Tri-Parish School - (Grades PreK-8) 1145 W. 20th St., Casper, WY 82604 sascasper.com Stds.: 229; Lay Tchrs.: 21
Our Lady of Fatima - 1401 CY Ave., Casper, WY 82604 t) 307-265-5586 church@fatimaincasper.org www.fatimaincasper.org Rev. Clark Lenz, Pst.; CRP Stds.: 68
St. Patrick's Catholic Church of Casper - 400 Country Club Rd., Casper, WY 82609; Mailing: P.O. Box 51010, Casper, WY 82605-1010 t) 307-235-5535 andrea@stpatricks-casper.com; trina@stpatricks-casper.com www.stpatricks-casper.com Very Rev. Cliff Jacobson, Pst.; Andrea Hodges, DRE; CRP Stds.: 189

CHEYENNE

St. Mary's Cathedral - 2107 Capitol Ave., Cheyenne, WY 82001; Mailing: P.O. Box 1268, Cheyenne, WY 82003-1268 t) 307-635-9261 stewardship@stmarycathedral.com www.stmarycathedral.com Rev. Thomas E. Cronkleton Jr., Pst.; Rev. Randall J. Oswald, Assoc. Pst.; Rev. Seth Hostetler, Assoc. Pst.; Rev. August Koeune, Pastor Emer.; Dcn. Steve Cox; Dcn. Stanley Piasecki; Karen Stolz, DRE; Damion Aldana, Youth Min.; CRP Stds.: 217
St. Mary's Cathedral School - (Grades PreK-6) 2200 O'Neil Ave., Cheyenne, WY 82001 t) 307-638-9268 jennifer.bridges@stmaryswyo.org stmaryswyo.org Jennifer Bridges, Prin.; Stds.: 152; Scholastics: 6; Lay Tchrs.: 12
Church of the Holy Trinity - 1836 Hot Springs Ave., Cheyenne, WY 82001-5337 t) 307-632-5872 www.holytrinitycheyenne.org Very Rev. Carl J. Gallinger, Pst.; Rev. Linh Vu, Par. Vicar; Dcn. Michael Leman; Dcn. David Zelenka; CRP Stds.: 84
St. Joseph's - 603 House Ave., Cheyenne, WY 82007; Mailing: P.O. Box 1141, Cheyenne, WY 82003-1141 t) 307-634-4625 ecabrera@dcwy.org; agregorio@sjdcwy.org www.stjosephscheyenne.org Rev. Emilio Cabrera, Assoc. Pst.; Dcn. Thomas Niemann; CRP Stds.: 181

CODY

St. Anthony - 1333 Monument St., Cody, WY 82414-3406 t) 307-587-2567 (CRP); 307-587-3388 apadua@stanthonycody.org; info@stanthonycody.org www.stanthonycody.org Rev. Charles Heston Joseph, Pst.; Dcn. Tom Caudle; Dcn. Gerald Boydston; Dcn. Joseph Bush; Dcn. Richard Moser; Kellie Edwards, DRE; CRP Stds.: 71
St. Therese - 1406 State, Meeteetse, WY 82433 t) (307) 587-3388
Our Lady of the Valley - 35 Rd. 1 AFW, Clark, WY 82435 t) (307) 587-3388

DIAMONDVILLE

St. Patrick's - 65 McGovern Ave., Diamondville, WY 83116; Mailing: Box 311, Kemmerer, WY 83101-0311 t) 307-877-4573 Rev. David Erickson, Pst.; CRP Stds.: 35
LaBarge Community - 373 N. Wildcat, LaBarge, WY 83123; Mailing: P.O. Box 311, Kemmerer, WY 83101 t) (307) 877-4573

DOUGLAS

St. James - 311 S. 5th St., Douglas, WY 82633-1500; Mailing: P.O. Box 1500, Douglas, WY 82633 t) 307-358-2338 stjames@stjamesdouglas.com; faithformation@stjamesdouglas.com www.stjamesdouglas.org Rev. Lucas K. Simango (Zambia), Pst.; Jenny Halquist, DRE; Mary Kay Lenzen, Bus. Mgr.; CRP Stds.: 70
Our Lady of Lourdes - 423 A. St., Glendo, WY 82213 t) (307) 358-2338

EVANSTON

St. Mary Magdalen - 849 Center St., Evanston, WY 82930; Mailing: Box 163, Evanston, WY 82931-0163 t) 307-789-2189 office@stmmagdalen.com; reled@stmmagdalen.com www.stmmagdalen.com Rev. Augustine Carrillo, Pst.; CRP Stds.: 54
St. Helen - 37117 I-80 Business Loop, Fort Bridger, WY 82933; Mailing: PO Box 183, Fort Bridger, WY 82933 t) (307) 782-6190 stmarymagdalen813@gmail.com

GILLETTE

St. Matthew's - 900 Butler Spaeth Rd., Gillette, WY 82716 t) 307-682-3319 c.pasek@stmatthewswy.org www.stmatthewswy.weconnect.com Rev. Steven Titus, Pst.; Rev. Bryce Lungren, Assoc. Pst.; William Heili, DRE; Dcn. Kim Carroll; CRP Stds.: 255
Blessed Sacrament - 624 Wright Blvd., Wright, WY 82732; Mailing: 1000 Butler Spaeth Rd., Gillette, WY 82716 t) (307) 682-3319
St. Matthews Church - 206 Hunter, Hulett, WY 82720 t) (307) 682-3319
St. Patrick - 2116 N. Belle Fourche, Moorecroft, WY 82721 t) (307) 682-3319
John Paul II Catholic School - 1000 Butler Spaeth Rd., Gillette, WY 82716 t) (307) 686-4114 stjohnpauliicatholicschool.com Vanessa Gemar, Prin.; Stds.: 185; Lay Tchrs.: 15

GLENROCK

St. Louis Catholic Church - 601 S. 5th St., Glenrock, WY 82637-0027; Mailing: PO Box 27, Glenrock, WY 82637 t) 307-436-9529 church@stlouisglenrock.org Rev. Lucas K. Simango (Zambia), Pst.; Dcn. Kevin Halvorsen; CRP Stds.: 20

GREEN RIVER

Immaculate Conception - 900 Hitching Post Dr., Green River, WY 82935 t) 307-875-2184; 307-875-2441 iccgrwy@dcwy.com gricc.net/ Rev. Denis D'Souza, Pst.; Dcn. Wes Nash; Kimberly Chavez, Youth Min.; Desiree Gomez, CRE; CRP Stds.: 55

GREYBULL

Church of the Sacred Heart - 544 5th Ave. N., Greybull, WY 82426-0231; Mailing: P.O. Box 231, Greybull, WY 82426-0231 t) 307-765-2438 sacredheartgreybull@gmail.com sacredheartgreybull.com Rev. Glen Szczechowski, Pst.; CRP Stds.: 27

GUERNSEY

St. Anthony's - 397 W. Whalen St., Guernsey, WY 82214-0430; Mailing: PO Box 430, Guernsey, WY 82214-0430 t) 307-836-2586; 307-534-5002 (CRP) strose.torrington@gmail.com Rev. Raymond B. Moss, Pst.; Rev. Daniel Kostelc, Assoc. Pst.; Sarah Seyfang, DRE; CRP Stds.: 8

JACKSON

Our Lady of the Mountains - 201 S. Jackson St., Jackson,

WY 83001-0992; Mailing: P O Box 992, Jackson, WY 83001 t) 307-733-2516 lizzetolm@gmail.com www.olmcatholic.org Rev. Demetrio Penascoza (Philippines), Pst.; Rev. Philip Vanderlin, O.S.B., Assoc. Pst.; Dcn. Richard Harden; Dcn. Matthew Ostdiek; Dcn. Doug Vlchek; Dcn. Philip Wanek; CRP Stds.: 165

Holy Family - ; Mailing: P.O. Box 1036, Thayne, WY 83127 t) (307) 883-3429 hfccofficemanager@gmail.com holyfamilywy.org

The Chapel of the Sacred Heart - Teton Park Rd., Jackson, WY 83001 t) (307) 733-2516 (Grand Teton National Park)

LANDER

Holy Rosary - 163 Leedy Rd., Lander, WY 82520-1047; Mailing: PO Box 1047, Lander, WY 82520 t) 307-332-4952 rstong@holyrosarylander.org holyrosarylander.org Rev. Jason Marco, Pst.; Dcn. Rich Miller; Sarah Susanka, DRE; Eliner Shields, Bus. Mgr.; CRP Stds.: 101

Church of the Ascension - Ohio St., Hudson, WY 82515 t) (307) 332-4952

LARAMIE

St. Laurence O'Toole - 319 E. Grand Ave., Laramie, WY 82070-1045; Mailing: 617 S. Fourth St., Laramie, WY 82070 t) 307-745-3115 office@stlaurenceotoole.org www.stlaurenceotoole.org Rev. Jaimon Dominic (India); CRP Stds.: 75

St. Paul's Newman Center - 1800 E. Grand Ave., Laramie, WY 82070-4316 t) 307-745-5461 newman@newmancenter.org www.newmancenter.org Very Rev. Robert Spaulding, Pst.; Lillie Rodgers, Pst. Min./Coord.; CRP Stds.: 40

LOVELL

St. Joseph's - 1141 Shoshone Ave., Lovell, WY 82431-0185; Mailing: P.O. Box 185, Lovell, WY 82431-0185 t) 307-548-2282 stjosephlovell@gmail.com www.stjosephlovell.com Rev. Glen Szczechowski, Pst.; CRP Stds.: 14

LUSK

St. Leo's - 900 W. Fifth St., Lusk, WY 82225-0959; Mailing: PO Box 959, Lusk, WY 82225-0959 t) 307-334-2702 Rev. Raymond B. Moss, Pst.; Rev. Daniel Kostelc, Assoc. Pst.; CRP Stds.: 12

NEWCASTLE

Church of Corpus Christi - 19 W. Winthrop, Newcastle, WY 82701 t) 307-746-4219 jabernathy@wyocatholic.org newcastlecorpuschristi.org Dcn. Kenneth Pitlick; Dcn. Joseph Sandrini; Rev. Brian J. Hess, Pst.; CRP Stds.: 71

St. Paul - 805 E. Oak St., Sundance, WY 82729; Mailing: P.O. Box 28, Sundance, WY 82729 t) (307) 746-4219 wyocatholic.org Jane Abernathy, Secy.;

St. Anthony - 610 Juniper St., Upton, WY 82730; Mailing: P.O. Box 177, Upton, WY 82730 t) (307) 746-4219 wyocatholic.org Jane Abernathy, Secy.;

PINE BLUFFS

St. Paul's - 501 E. 4th St., Pine Bluffs, WY 82082-0097; Mailing: PO Box 97, Pine Bluffs, WY 82082-0097 t) 307-245-3761 stpaul@stpaulpinebluffs.org stpaulpinebluffs.org Rev. Kevin A. Koch, Pst.; Ann Gebauer, DRE; CRP Stds.: 45

St. Joseph - 2898 WY-215, Albin, WY 82050 Very Rev. Carl J. Gallinger;

St. Peter - 316 4th St., Carpenter, WY 82054 Very Rev. Carl J. Gallinger;

PINEDALE

Our Lady of Peace - 112 S. Sublette, Pinedale, WY 82941-0070; Mailing: P.O. Box 70, Pinedale, WY 82941-0070 t) 307-367-2359 Rev. Peter James Mwaura, Pst.; CRP Stds.: 50

St. Anne - 411 Piney Dr., Big Piney, WY 83113 t) (307) 637-2359

POWELL

St. Barbara - 115 E. Third St., Powell, WY 82435-0818; Mailing: P.O. Box 818, Powell, WY 82435 t) 307-754-2480 stbarb@tctwest.net; stbarbs.religiousedu@gmail.com Rev. James Schumacher, Pst.; Dcn. Steven Penwell; Leslie Cannon, Admin.; Katherine Stensing, DRE; CRP Stds.: 91

RAWLINS

St. Joseph's - 219 W. Pine St., Rawlins, WY 82301-0068; Mailing: P.O. Box 68, Rawlins, WY 82301 t) 307-324-4631 www.stjosephsrawlins.org Rev. Florante Marcelo, Pst.; CRP Stds.: 59

Our Lady of the Sage - Hwy. 70 and 2nd St., Baggs, WY 82321 t) (307) 324-4621

RIVERTON

St. Margaret's - 618 Fremont Ave., Riverton, WY 82501 t) 307-856-3757; 307-850-8164 (CRP) Very Rev. Louis M. Shea, Pst.; CRP Stds.: 58

St. Margaret's School - (Grades PreK-5) 220 N. 7th E., Riverton, WY 82501 t) 307-856-5922 stmarg@wyoming.com stmargaretriverton.com/school/ Meagan Mosbrucker, Prin.; Stds.: 73; Lay Tchrs.: 7

St. Joseph - 211 Wyoming St., Shoshoni, WY 82649 t) 307-876-2760

Our Lady of the Woods - 4 S. Riverton St., Dubois, WY 82513; Mailing: P.O. Box 1134, Dubois, WY 82513 t) 307-455-2533

St. Edward - 11350 US Hwy. 26, Kinnear, WY 82516 t) 307-856-5502

ROCK SPRINGS

Holy Spirit Catholic Community - 116 Broadway, Rock Springs, WY 82901 t) 307-362-2611 hsccwyo.org/ Very Rev. William Hill, Pst.; Dcn. Luis Enrique Hernandez Vivas; Dcn. Bill Hill; CRP Stds.: 147

St. Christopher - 3650 Hwy. 91, Eden, WY 82926 t) (307) 362-2611 Rev. Emilio Cabrera (Colombia), Assoc. Pst.;

Holy Spirit Catholic School - (Grades PreK-6) 210 A St., Rock Springs, WY 82901 t) 307-362-6077 hscsoffice@wyoming.com www.rshscs.com/ Dr. Angie Spann, Prin.; Stds.: 90; Lay Tchrs.: 9

St. Vivian - County Hwy. 371, Superior, WY 82945 t) (307) 362-2611

SARATOGA

Church of St. Ann - 218 W. Spring Ave., Saratoga, WY 82331; Mailing: P.O. Box 667, Saratoga, WY 82331 t) 307-326-5461 stann@dcwy.org Rev. August Koeune, Par. Admin.; Cathy Lynch, DRE; CRP Stds.: 41

St. Joseph - 3 Heather Dr., Hanna, WY 82327 t) (307) 326-5461

SHERIDAN

Holy Name - 260 E. Loucks, Sheridan, WY 82801; Mailing: 9 S. Connor, Sheridan, WY 82801 t) 307-672-2848 dchoong@holynamesheridan.org; faith@holynamesheridan.org www.holynamesheridan.org Rev. Glenn Whewell, Pst.; Dcn. John Bigelow; Dcn. Gregory Marino; Doreen Choong, Admin.; Monique Barron, DRE; CRP Stds.: 100

Holy Name School - (Grades PreK-5) 121 S. Connor, Sheridan, WY 82801 t) 307-672-2021 m.legler@hncswy.org www.hncswy.org Mary Legler, Prin.; Stds.: 65; Lay Tchrs.: 7

Our Lady of the Pines - 34 Wagon Box Rd., Story, WY 82842 t) (307) 672-2848

St. Edmund - 310 Historic Hwy. 14, Ranchester, WY 82839; Mailing: PO Box 217, Ranchester, WY 82839 c) (307) 760-6113 stedmundsranchester@outlook.com holynamesheridan.org/stedmunds Katelynn Doherty, Secy.;

ST. STEPHENS

St. Stephen's - 33 St. Stephens Rd., St. Stephens, WY 82524; Mailing: Box 250, St. Stephens, WY 82524 t) 307-856-7806 melissa.brown@saintstephensmission.com www.saintstephensmission.com Indian Mission for the Shoshone and Arapaho Indians. St. Stephen's Indian Mission, Inc. Rev. Andrew Duncan, Pst.; Sr. Teresa Frawley, O.S.F., Pst. Assoc.; Sr. Monica Suhayda, C.S.J., Pst. Assoc.; Patti McMahon, DRE; CRP Stds.: 31

St. Joseph - 468 Ethete Rd., Ethete, WY 82520; Mailing: Box 8358, Ethete, WY 82520 t) (307) 856-5937

Blessed Sacrament - #9 Black Coal Dr., For Washake, WY 82514 t) (307) 856-5937

THERMOPOLIS

St. Francis - 808 Arapahoe, Thermopolis, WY 82443-0272; Mailing: PO Box 272, Thermopolis, WY 82443 t) 307-864-2458 stmarym@rtconnect.net stfrancisthermopolis.com/ Rev. Robert Rodgers, Pst.; Sharon Cordingly, DRE; CRP Stds.: 28

TORRINGTON

St. Rose - 605 E. 22nd Ave., Torrington, WY 82240 t) 307-532-5556; 307-532-3177; 307-532-3155 www.strosetorrington.org Rev. Raymond B. Moss, Pst.; Rev. Daniel Kostelc, Par. Vicar; Megan Griggs, DRE; CRP Stds.: 100

WHEATLAND

St. Patrick's - 1009 Ninth St., Wheatland, WY 82201 t) 307-322-2070 stpatrick1009@gmail.com www.stpatricks-wheatland.com Rev. Hiep X. Nguyen (Vietnam), Pst.; Dcn. Terry Archbold; Dcn. Steve Lucas; Dcn. Chuck Ruwart; CRP Stds.: 60

Mary Queen of Heaven - 401 5th St., Chugwater, WY 82201 t) (307) 322-2070 Rev. Hiep Nguyen;

WORLAND

St. Mary Magdalen - 1099 Charles Ave., Worland, WY 82401-0901 t) 307-347-2820; 307-347-6441 (Office) stmarym@rtconnect.net www.worlandcatholic.com Rev. Robert Rodgers, Pst.; Dcn. Michael Martinson; CRP Stds.: 78

INSTITUTIONS LOCATED IN DIOCESE

CAMPUS MINISTRY / NEWMAN CENTERS [CAM]

CASPER

St. Francis Newman Center - 1732 S. Elm St., Casper, WY 82601; Mailing: 604 S. Center, Casper, WY 82601 t) 307-266-2666 finance@stanthonyscasper.org Rev. Ray Rodriguez, Pst.;

LARAMIE

St. Paul's Newman Center, University Catholic Community (University of Wyoming) - 1800 E. Grand Ave., Laramie, WY 82070-4316 t) 307-745-5461 newman@newmancenter.org www.newmancenter.org Very Rev. Robert Spaulding, Pst.; Lillie Rodgers, Pst. Min./Coord.;

POWELL

John Henry Newman Center, Northwest College - 674 N. Absaroka St., Powell, WY 82435; Mailing: P.O. Box 818, Powell, WY 82435 t) 307-754-9220 nwcnewmancenter@gmail.com Attended by St. Barbara, Powell. Eliza Higgins, Campus Min.;

CATHOLIC CHARITIES [CCH]

CHEYENNE

Catholic Charities of Wyoming, Inc. - 2121 Capitol Ave., Cheyenne, WY 82001; Mailing: P.O. Box 907, Cheyenne, WY 82003-0907 c) (307) 631-4206 gmougey@ccwy.org charitieswyoming.org/ Most Rev. Steven Biegler, Pres.; Genevieve Mougey, Exec. Dir.; Very Rev. Carl Gallinger, Vice Pres.; Asstd. Annu.: 500; Staff: 1

CEMETERIES [CEM]

CHEYENNE

Olivet Cemetery - 100 W. 21st St., Cheyenne, WY 82003-1268; Mailing: P.O. Box 1268, Cheyenne, WY 82003-1268 t) 307-635-9261 tcronkleton@dcwy.org www.stmarycathedral.com Rev. Thomas Cronkleton Jr., Pst.;

COLLEGES & UNIVERSITIES [COL]

LANDER

***Wyoming Catholic College** - 306 Main St., Lander, WY

82520 t) 307-332-2930 info@wyomingcatholic.edu www.wyomingcatholic.edu Rev. David Anderson, Chap.; Rev. Godfrey Okwunka (Nigeria), Chap.; Glenn Arbery, Pres.; Stds.: 189; Lay Tchrs.: 17

ENDOWMENTS / FOUNDATIONS / TRUSTS [EFT]

CASPER

St. Anthony Tri-Parish Catholic School Foundation - 1145 W. 20th St., Casper, WY 82604 t) 307-337-1361 foundation@sascasper.com www.stanthonyschoolfoundation.org Rev. Raymond P. Rodriguez, Pst.; Robert Cerkovnik, Pres.;

Knights of Columbus Charitable Trust for Seminarian Education and Priests' Retirement - 4572 New Market Cir., Casper, WY 82609 t) 307-262-8976 info@wyomingkc.org Ronald Morris, Dir.;

CHEYENNE

Holy Trinity Youth Education Trust - 1836 Hot Springs Ave., Cheyenne, WY 82001-5337 t) 307-632-5872 tcronkleton@holytrinitycheyenne.org Very Rev. Carl Gallinger, Trustee; Maria Henschel, Trustee; Tiffany Hopkins, Trustee; Randi Losalu, Trustee;

St. Mary's School Foundation - 100 W. 21st St., Cheyenne, WY 82001-3651; Mailing: P.O. Box 1268, Cheyenne, WY 82003-1268 t) 307-635-9261 tcronkleton@dcwy.org www.stmarysschoolfoundation.org Rev. Thomas E. Cronkleton Jr., Pres.; Kenneth Dugas, Vice. Pres.; Catherine W. Stoughton, Secy.; Connie K. Janney, Treas.;

The Wyoming Catholic Ministries Foundation - 2121 Capitol Ave, Cheyenne, WY 82001; Mailing: P.O. Box 227, Cheyenne, WY 82003 t) 307-631-4084 info@wycmf.org www.wycmf.org Gay Woodhouse, Pres.; Tom Botts, Vice. Pres.; Peg Louiselle, Exec. Dir.; Erica Turk, Admin.; Rita Meyer, Secy.; Dr. Joseph Russo, Treas.; Most Rev. Steven Biegler, Mem.; Donna Kinskey, Mem.; Jeff Marsh, Mem.; Rev. Gary J. Ruzicka, Mem.;

ROCK SPRINGS

Rock Springs Catholic School Foundation - 2712 Affirmed Dr., Rock Springs, WY 82901 t) 307-362-2611 Very Rev. William Hill, Pst.; Dr. Angie Spann, Prin.;

ST. STEPHENS

St. Stephens Indian Mission Foundation - 33 St. Stephens Rd., St. Stephens, WY 82524; Mailing: P.O. Box 278, St. Stephens, WY 82524-0278 t) 307-856-6797 ssimf@wyoming.com Ronald Mamot, Dir.;

MISCELLANEOUS [MIS]

CASPER

St. Vincent De Paul Thrift Store - 301 E. H St., Casper, WY 82601 t) 307-237-2607 camilleeliz@hotmail.com

CHEYENNE

Mall at St. Vincent DePaul - 100 W. 21st St., Cheyenne, WY 82001; Mailing: P.O. Box 1268, Cheyenne, WY 82001 t) 307-514-0365 jsantos@stmarycathedral.com stmarycathedral.com/parish-community Josephine Santos, Admin.;

MONASTERIES AND RESIDENCES FOR PRIESTS AND BROTHERS [MON]

MEETEETSE

Monks of the Most Blessed Virgin Mary of Mt. Carmel (Carmelite Monks) - 1079 Meeteetse Creek Rd., Meeteetse, WY 82433; Mailing: PO Box 2747, Cody, WY 82414 t) 307-645-3310 carmelite.inquiries@gmail.com www.carmelitemonks.org Carmelite Monks Rev. Joseph Marie of Jesus Gibbons, M.Carm., Postulant Master/ Dir.; Rev. Daniel Mary Schneider, M.Carm., Prior/ Pres./Dir.; Rev. Nicholas Maroney, Secy./Dir.; Rev. Michael Mary of the Trinity Wright, M.Carm., Subprior/Vocations Dir./Dir.; Brs.: 23; Priests: 4

NURSING / REHABILITATION / CONVALESCENCE / ELDERLY CARE [NUR]

CASPER

St. Anthony Manor - 211 E. Sixth St., Casper, WY 82601 t) 307-237-0843 tfunch@archhousing.com; mpena@archhousing.com Tonja Funch, Admin.; Asstd. Annu.: 64; Staff: 5

CHEYENNE

Holy Trinity Manor - 2516 E. 18th St., Cheyenne, WY 82001 t) 307-778-8850 holytrinitymanor@archdiocesanhousing.org; dschmidt@archhousing.com Daniel Schmidt, Property Mgr.; Asstd. Annu.: 60; Staff: 2

PRESCHOOLS / CHILDCARE CENTERS [PRE]

TORRINGTON

St. Joseph's Children's Home - 1419 Main St., Torrington, WY 82240-3340; Mailing: PO Box 1117, Torrington, WY 82240-1117 t) 307-532-4197 rmeyer@stjoseph-wy.org www.stjoseph-wy.org A Psychiatric Residential Treatment Facility (PRTF) serving severely emotionally disturbed youth ages 6-17. Paula Krotz, Prin.; Ronda Meyer, Dir.; Stds.: 107; Lay Tchrs.: 7

An asterisk (*) denotes an organization that has established tax-exempt status directly with the IRS and is not covered by the USCCB Group Ruling.

Archdiocese of Chicago

(Archidioecesis Chicagiensis)

HIS EMINENCE BLASE CARDINAL CUPICH

Archbishop of Chicago; ordained August 16, 1975; appointed Bishop of Rapid City July 7, 1998; ordained and installed September 21, 1998; appointed Bishop of Spokane June 30, 2010; installed September 3, 2010; appointed Archbishop of Chicago September 11, 2014; installed November 18, 2014; created Cardinal Priest November 19, 2016.

Archbishop Quigley Center & Cardinal Meyer Center: P.O. Box 1979, Chicago, IL 60690-1979. T: 312-534-8200
www.archchicago.org

ESTABLISHED NOVEMBER 28, 1843; CREATED 1880.

Square Miles 1,411.

Comprises the Counties of Cook and Lake in the State of Illinois.

Legal Title: The Catholic Bishop of Chicago, a Corporation Sole. For legal titles of institutions, consult The Pastoral Center.

Most Reverend Joseph N. Perry
Auxiliary Bishop of Chicago; ordained May 24, 1975; appointed Auxiliary Bishop of Chicago and Titular Bishop of Lead May 5, 1998; consecrated June 29, 1998 Mailing Address: 3525 S. Lake Park Ave., Chicago, IL 60653. T: 312-534-8376; F: 312-534-5317.

Most Reverend Robert G. Casey
Auxiliary Bishop of Chicago; ordained May 21, 1994; appointed Auxiliary Bishop of Chicago and Titular Bishop of Thuburbo Maius July 3, 2018; Episcopal ordination September 17, 2018. Mailing Address: 835 N. Rush St., Chicago, 60611. T: 312-534-8271; F: 312-534-6379.

Most Reverend Andrew P. Wypych
Auxiliary Bishop of Chicago; ordained April 29, 1979; appointed Auxiliary Bishop of Chicago and Titular Bishop of Naraggara June 13, 2011; Episcopal ordination August 10, 2011. Mailing Address: 2330 W. 118th St., Chicago, IL 60643. T: 773-779-8440; F: 773-779-8469.

Most Reverend Kevin M. Birmingham
Auxiliary Bishop of Chicago; ordained May 24, 1997; appointed Auxiliary Bishop of Chicago and Titular Bishop of Dolia September 11, 2020; Episcopal ordination November 13, 2020. Mailing Address: 1400 S. Austin Blvd., Cicero, IL 60804. T: 312-534-8087; F: 312-534-3856.

Most Reverend Robert Lombardo
Auxiliary Bishop of Chicago; ordained May 12, 1990; appointed Auxiliary Bishop of Chicago and Titular Bishop of Munaziana September 11, 2020; Episcopal ordination November 13, 2020. Mailing Address: 528 N. Ada St., Chicago, IL 60642. T: 312-534-8399; F: 312-243-4970.

Most Reverend Mark A. Bartosic
Auxiliary Bishop of Chicago; ordained May 21, 1994; appointed Auxiliary Bishop of Chicago and Titular Bishop of Naratcata July 3, 2018; Episcopal ordination September 17, 2018. Mailing Address: 1641 W. Diversey Pkwy., Chicago, IL 60614. T: 773-388-8670; F: 773-388-8672.

Most Reverend Jeffrey S. Grob
Auxiliary Bishop of Chicago; ordained May 23, 1992; appointed Auxiliary Bishop of Chicago and Titular Bishop of Abora September 11, 2020; Episcopal ordination November 13, 2020. Mailing Address: Building 101P, 1000 E. Maple Ave., Mundelein, IL 60060. T: 847-970-4964.

STATISTICAL OVERVIEW

Personnel
Cardinals....1
Auxiliary Bishops....7
Retired Bishops....5
Priests: Diocesan Active in Diocese....419
Priests: Diocesan Active Outside Diocese....28
Priests: Retired, Sick or Absent....235
Number of Diocesan Priests....682
Religious Priests in Diocese....432
Total Priests in your Diocese....1,114
Extern Priests in Diocese....94
Ordinations:
Diocesan Priests....2
Religious Priests....3
Transitional Deacons....5
Permanent Deacons....20
Permanent Deacons in Diocese....627
Total Brothers....149
Total Sisters....1,068

Parishes
Parishes....221
With Resident Pastor:
Resident Diocesan Priests....181
Resident Religious Priests....33
Without Resident Pastor:
Administered by Priests....7
Missions....14
Pastoral Centers....5
New Parishes Created....21
Closed Parishes....46
Professional Ministry Personnel:
Brothers....1
Sisters....35
Lay Ministers....211

Welfare
Catholic Hospitals....16
Total Assisted....2,021,000
Health Care Centers....1
Total Assisted....11,200
Homes for the Aged....44
Total Assisted....6,100
Residential Care of Children....2
Total Assisted....510
Day Care Centers....8
Total Assisted....1,800
Specialized Homes....2
Total Assisted....203
Special Centers for Social Services....100
Total Assisted....371,870
Residential Care of Disabled....6
Total Assisted....1,220
Other Institutions....11
Total Assisted....2,412

Educational
Seminaries, Diocesan....1
Students from This Diocese....27
Students from Other Dioceses....105
Diocesan Students in Other Seminaries....7
Seminaries, Religious....1
Students, Religious....108
Total Seminarians....142
Colleges and Universities....5
Total Students....45,000
High Schools, Diocesan and Parish....3
Total Students....489
High Schools, Private....27
Total Students....18,894
Elementary Schools, Diocesan and Parish....152
Total Students....42,791
Elementary Schools, Private....8
Total Students....2,530
Non-residential Schools for the Disabled....2
Total Students....100
Catechesis/Religious Education:
High School Students....3,600
Elementary Students....39,000
Total Students under Catholic Instruction....152,546
Teachers in Diocese:
Priests....30
Scholastics....3
Brothers....13
Sisters....28
Lay Teachers....4,000

Vital Statistics
Receptions into the Church:
Infant Baptism Totals....19,770
Adult Baptism Totals....1,200
Received into Full Communion....920
First Communions....14,750
Confirmations....15,000
Marriages:
Catholic....3,100
Interfaith....535
Total Marriages....3,635
Deaths....11,700
Total Catholic Population....2,093,000
Total Population....5,980,000

LEADERSHIP

Vicar General - Most Rev. Robert G. Casey;
Episcopal Vicars -
Vicariate I - Most Rev. Jeffrey S. Grob;
Vicariate II - Most Rev. Mark A. Bartosic;
Vicariate III - Most Rev. Robert Lombardo, C.F.R.;
Vicariate IV - Most Rev. Kevin Birmingham;
Vicariate V - Most Rev. Andrew P. Wypych;
Vicariate VI - Most Rev. Joseph N. Perry;
Deans -
Deanery I-A - Rev. Jerome J. Jacob;
Deanery I-B - Rev. Timothy J. O'Malley;
Deanery I-C - Rev. Michael A. Nacius;
Deanery I-D - Rev. Timothy J. Fairman;
Deanery I-E - Rev. Christopher Ciomek;
Deanery I-F - Rev. Esequiel Sanchez;
Deanery II-A - Rev. Wayne F. Watts, Dean;
Deanery II-B - Rev. Phi H. Nguyen;
Deanery II-C - Rev. Manuel Dorantes, Dean;
Deanery II-D - Rev. Lawrence M. Lisowski;
Deanery II-E - Rev. Ronald N. Kalas;
Deanery II-F - Rev. James Wallace;
Deanery III-A - Rev. John R. Waiss;
Deanery III-B - Rev. John R. Waiss;
Deanery III-C - Rev. Thomas E. Cima;
Deanery III-D - Rev. Lawrence R. Dowling;
Deanery III-E - Rev. Donald J. Nevins;
Deanery IV-A - Rev. Thomas P. May;
Deanery IV-B - Rev. Stanislaw Kuca;
Deanery IV-C - Rev. Waldemar Latkowski, CSSR, Dean;
Deanery IV-D - Rev. Paul D. Cao;
Deanery IV-E - Rev. Carl Morello;
Deanery V-A - Rev. Jose Antonio Murcia Abellan;
Deanery V-B - Rev. Wojciech Kwiecien;
Deanery V-C - Rev. James A. Mezydlo;
Deanery V-D - Rev. Dennis A. Ziomek;
Deanery V-E - Rev. William T. Corcoran;
Deanery VI-A - Rev. David A. Jones;
Deanery VI-B - Rev. Thomas G. Belanger;
Deanery VI-C - Rev. Walter Yepes;
Deanery VI-D - Rev. Ralph H. Zwirn;
College of Consultors - Rev. Kenneth A. Budzikowski; Rev. Hernan Cuevas-Contreras; Rev. Msgr. Patrick J. Pollard;
Presbyteral Council - Rev. Matthew O'Donnell, Chair; Rev. James A. Heneghan; Rev. Maciej D. Galle;
Finance Council - Michael O'Grady; Edward J. Wehmer; Most Rev. Robert G. Casey;
Pastoral Council - Bernita Ferdinand, Chair; John McNichols, Vice Chair;
Women's Committee - Mary Brennan, Chair; Tanya Woods, Vice Chair;

OFFICES AND DIRECTORS

Office of the Archbishop - Rev. Robert M. Fedek, Admin. Secy. to Archbishop;
Mundelein Seminary/University of St. Mary of the Lake - Rev. John F. Kartje, Rector;
Archdiocesan Vocations - t) 312-534-8298 vocations@archchicago.org www.chicagopriest.com Rev. Timothy F. Monahan, Dir.;
Vocation Office/Spirituality Year - Rev. Timothy F. Monahan, Dir.;
Office of Catholic Schools - Greg Richmond, Supt.; Matthew Walter, COO;
Canonical Affairs - t) 312-534-8205 Very Rev. Daniel Andree, C.Ss.R., Vicar (dandree@archchicago.org); Rev. Francis Q. Kub (fkub@archchicago.org); Suzette Cash, Secy. (scash@archchicago.org);
Chancellor - t) 312-534-8283 Dcn. David J. Keene, Chancellor (dkeene@archchicago.org);
Archives and Records - t) 312-534-4400 Meg Hall, Archivist;
Vicar General - t) 312-534-8271 Rev. Robert G. Casey;
Vicar for the Personal and Professional Development of Priests - t) 312-642-1837 Rev. Kenneth C. Simpson;
Diocesan Priests' Placement Board - t) 312-534-5276 Rev. John S. Siemianowski, Exec. Sec.;
Archbishop's Delegate for Extern and International Priests - t) 312-534-5276 Rev. John S. Siemianowski;
Vicar for Priests - t) 312-534-7051 Rev. Kurt D. Boras; Rev. Michael P. Knotek;
Vicar for the Diaconate Community - t) 708-366-8900 Dcn. James E. Norman, Vicar; Dcn. David Brencic, Assoc. Dir. Diaconate; Dcn. Fred Ortiz, Assoc. Dir. Diaconate;
Religious, Office for - Sr. Joan McGlinchey, M.S.C., Dir.; Sr. Lovina Pammit, O.S.F., Coord. Rel. Vocation Ministries; Sr. Mary Ann Penner, I.H.M., Coord. Retirement for Rel.;
Vicar for Senior Priests - Rev. Charles T. Rubey, Vicar; Rev. Ronald N. Kalas;
Office for Protection of Children and Youth - t) 312-534-5319 Nelly Bonilla, Interim Dir.;
Assistance Ministry - t) 312-534-8267 Tom Tharayil, Dir.;
Child Abuse Investigations and Review - t) 312-534-5205 Nelly Bonilla, Dir.;
Safe Environment - t) 312-534-5238 Myra Flores, Coord.;
Ecumenical and Interreligious Affairs, Office for - t) 312-534-3867 Daniel Olsen, Dir.;
Health/Hospital Affairs - t) 312-534-8339 Rev. William P. Grogan, Archbishop's Delegate for Hospitals;
Bio Ethics Commission - t) 312-534-8339 Rev. William P. Grogan, Chair;
Chaplaincies/Chaplain Affairs - t) 312-534-8271 Most Rev. Robert G. Casey;
Chicago Airports Catholic Chaplaincy - t) 773-686-2636 Rev. Michael G. Zaniolo, Chap. (ordchapel@aol.com);
Fire Department Chaplain - t) 312-738-9246 Rev. John P. McNalis, Chap.;
Police Department Chaplain - Rev. Daniel J. Brandt, Dir.;

FINANCE

Chief Operating Officer - t) 312-534-8218 Betsy Bohlen, Dir.;
Chief of Parish and School Ops. - t) 312-534-8357 Dcn. Gerald M. Keenan;
Capital Assets - t) 312-534-8394 Eric Wollan, Dir.;
Facilities and Construction - Celine Coath, Dir.;
Communications and Public Relations - t) 312-534-8289 Paula Waters, Chief Communications Officer;
Chicago Catholic - t) 312-534-7577 Joyce Duriga, Editor;
Hispanic Communications - t) 312-534-7880 Alejandro Castillo, Dir.;
Chicago Catolico - Alejandro Castillo, Gen. Mgr.;
New World Publications - t) 312-534-7110 Grant Gallicho, Dir.;
Office of Radio & Television - t) 312-534-8277 Vince Gerasole, Dir.;
Financial Services - t) 312-534-8293 Paul Mannino, CFO;
Controller's Operations - t) 312-534-5266 Christine Duszynski, Controller;
Parish Operations - Dcn. Gerald M. Keenan, Chief of Parish/School Ops;
Information Technology - John Dicello, Dir.; Gang Chen, Mgr. Applications Svcs.;
Insurance and Risk Management - t) 312-534-8295 Cheryl Curtis, Mgr.;
St. Benedict's Technology Consortium - www.sbtcsupport.org Scott Bell, Dir.;
Catholic Cemeteries - t) 708-449-6100 Rev. Lawrence J. Sullivan, Dir.;
Legal Services and Policy Development - t) 312-534-8303 James Geoly, Gen. Counsel;
Personnel Services - t) 312-534-8349 Timothy Dee, Chief Admin. Officer;
Department of Stewardship and Development - t) 312-534-5271 Brendan Keating, Chief Devel. Officer;
Development Services/Annual Catholic Appeal - t) 312-534-7944 Barbara Shea Collins, Dir.;
Joseph and Mary Retreat House - t) 847-566-6060 Rev. Msgr. John F. Canary, Dir.;
Food Service Professionals, Archdiocese - t) 773-385-5100 www.fspro.com Bradley Black, Dir.;

PARISH SERVICES

Department of Parish Vitality and Mission - t) 312-534-8039 Tim Weiske, Dir.;
Office for the Evangelization and Missionary Discipleship - Elizabeth White, Dir.;
Office of Lifelong Formation - t) 312-534-3317 Kevin Foy, Dir.;
Marriage and Family Ministries - t) 312-534-8351
Catechetical Ministry - t) 312-534-8053
Certification and Ongoing Faith Formation - t) 312-534-8606
Youth and Young Adult Ministries - t) 312-534-8600
Office of Young Adult Engagement - t) 312-534-5354 Juan Pablo Padilla;
Special Religious Development (SPRED) - t) 312-842-1039 Sr. Mary Therese Harrington, S.H.; Sr. Susanne Gallagher, S.P.;
Divine Worship and Sacraments, Office for - t) 312-534-5153 Todd Williamson, Dir.; Wendy Barton Silhavy, Dir.;
Office of Human Dignity and Solidarity - t) 312-534-8057 Dr. Angela Swain, Dir.;
Catholic Campaign for Human Development/Parish Sharing - t) 312-534-5333 Danielle Bodette, Coord.;
Immigration Ministries - Elena Segura, Senior Coord.; Miguel Salazar, Senior Coord.;
Catholic Relief Services and Justice Education - Dr. Angela Swain, Dir.;
Respect Life/Pro-Life Office - t) 312-534-5355 Dawn Fitzpatrick, Dir.;
Project Rachel - t) 312-337-1962; 800-456-4673 (Toll Free)
Chastity Education Initiative - t) 312-534-5355
Jail Ministry/Kolbe House - t) 773-247-0070 MaryClare Birmingham;
Domestic Violence Outreach - t) 312-226-6161 x224 Rev. Charles W. Dahm, O.P.;
Amate House/Young Adult Volunteer Program - t) 773-376-2445 Jeannie A. Balanda, Exec.;
Global Missions Office - t) 312-534-3317 Dr. Megan Mio, Dir. (missions@archchicago.org);
The Society for the Propagation of the Faith, Missionary Childhood Association - t) 312-534-3322 Dr. Megan Mio, Dir. (missions@archchicago.org);
Ethnic Initiatives -
Asian Catholic Initiative - St. Henry - Rev. Phi H. Nguyen;
Black Catholic Initiative - t) 312-534-5397
Consejo Hispano - t) 773-523-3917 Rev. Ismael Sandoval;
Ministry to Polonia - t) 312-787-8040 Rev. Marek Maciej Smolka;
Native American Initiative - t) 773-588-6484 Rev. Stephen F. Kanonik, (St. Benedict);
Ethnic Apostolates -
Haitian Catholic Apostolate - t) 773-721-6365
Indochinese Catholic Center - t) 773-784-1932
Archdiocesan Council of Catholic Women (ACCW) - t) 312-534-8325 Joan Billingham, Pres.;
Liturgy Training Publications (LTP) - t) 773-579-4900 Deanna Keefe, Dir.;
Strategic Planning and Implementation - t) 312-534-8125
Renew My Church - t) 312-534-5010

SOCIAL SERVICES

Department of Human Services - t) 312-655-7460 Sally Blount, Dir.;
Catholic Charities of Chicago - t) 800-244-0505; 312-655-7000 (Central Intake) Sally Blount, Pres.;
Catholic Office of the Deaf - Rev. Joseph A. Mulcrone, Dir.; Margaret Swatek, DRE (cathdeafch@archchicago.org);
Mercy Home for Boys and Girls - t) 312-738-9240 Rev. Scott Donahue, Pres.;

TRIBUNAL

Metropolitan Tribunal - t) 312-534-8280 tribunal@archchicago.org Sr. Christine M. Kub, O.P., Secy.; Ellen Sochacki, Head Notary;
Judicial Vicar - t) 312-534-8205 Very Rev. Daniel Andree, C.Ss.R. (dandree@archchicago.org);
Adjutant Judicial Vicars - Very Rev. Krzysztof Swierczynski; Rev. John P. Lucas;
Promoter of Justice - Rev. Msgr. Patrick R. Lagges;
Judges - Rev. John M. Griffiths; Sr. Stefania Galka, M.Ch.R.; Rev. Robeth O. Molina Torres;
Defenders of the Bond - Rev. William H. Woestman, O.M.I.; Jesus Cabrera; Very Rev. Grzegorz Podwysocki;
Delegate of the Archbishop for Privilege Cases - Rev. Joseph C. Mol;
Auditors - R. Douglas Bond; Luis Flores Vega; Sr. Barbara Kosinska, M.Ch.R.;
Advocates - Rev. Arthur Anderson, O.F.M.; Luis Flores Vega; Elizabeth Kabacinski;

MISCELLANEOUS / OTHER OFFICES

Catholic Conference of Illinois - t) 312-368-1066 Robert F. Gilligan;

PARISHES, MISSIONS, AND CLERGY

STATE OF ILLINOIS

ALSIP

St. Terrence - Merged Jul 2022 Merged with Incarnation Parish to form Incarnation and St. Terrence Parish.

ARGO

Blessed Martyrs of Chimbote Parish - 6101 S. 75th Ave., Argo, IL 60501 t) 708-458-0246 (CRP); 708-458-8772 (CRP); 708-458-0007 stblase@archchicago.org Rev. Wojciech Kwiecien, Pst.; Dcn. Ignacio Alvarez; Dcn. Jesus Chavez;

ARLINGTON HEIGHTS

St. Edna - 2525 N. Arlington Heights Rd., Arlington Heights, IL 60004 t) 847-398-3362 stedna@archchicago.org www.stedna.org/ Rev. Darrio L. Boscutti, Pst.; Rev. Tomy Abraham, Assoc. Pst.; Dcn. James Pauwels; Dcn. Joseph Yannotta; CRP Stds.: 212

St. James - 820 N. Arlington Heights Rd., Arlington Heights, IL 60004 t) 224-345-7200 stjames-arlington@archchicago.org www.stjamesah.org/ Rev. Edward S. Pelrine, Pst.; Rev. Pawel Barwikowski, Assoc. Pst.; Rev. Ryan McMillin, Assoc. Pst.; Rev. William J. Zavaski, Pastor Emer.; Dcn. Samuel J. Resch; Dcn. James R. Bannon; Dcn. John R Burnett; Dcn. Matthew Hahn; Dcn. Pierce Sheehan; CRP Stds.: 617

St. James School - (Grades PreK-8) t) 224-345-7145 secretaries@stjamesschoolah.org Michael Kendrick, Prin.; Stds.: 546

Mision San Juan Diego - 2323 N. Wilke Rd., Arlington Heights, IL 60004 t) 847-590-9332 juandiego-mission@archchicago.org www.misionsanjuandiego.org/ Rev. John W. Dearhammer, Pst.; Dcn. Jose C. Quiroz; Dcn. Hector Soto; Dcn. Luis Zaragoza;

Our Lady of the Wayside - 432 W. Park St., Arlington Heights, IL 60005 t) 847-398-5011 (CRP); 847-253-5353 ol-wayside@archchicago.org olwparish.org/ Rev. Wojciech A. Marat, Pst.; Rev. Gilbert Mashurano, Assoc. Pst.; Rev. Daniel J. Brady, Sr. Priest; Dcn. Gerald Brennan; Dcn. Thomas Corcoran; Dcn. Donald R. Grossnickle; Dcn. Peter Letourneau; Dcn. Paul Onischuk; CRP Stds.: 240

Our Lady of the Wayside School - -8) 432 S. Mitchell Ave., Arlington Heights, IL 60005 t) 847-253-0050 dwood@olwschool.org David W. Wood, Prin.; Stds.: 390

BARRINGTON

St. Anne - 120 N. Ela St., Barrington, IL 60010 t) 847-382-5300 stanne-ela@archchicago.org stannebarrington.org/ Rev. Bernard J. Pietrzak, Pst.; Rev. Rodolfo Gaytan Ramirez, Assoc. Pst.; Rev. Balajoji Thanugundla, Assoc. Pst.; Dcn. Robert Powers; Dcn. Thomas Westerkamp; CRP Stds.: 415

St. Anne School - 319 E. Franklin St., Barrington, IL 60010 t) 847-381-0311 dkapka@stannschoolbarrington.org www.stanneschoolbarrington.org/ Dawn M. Kapka, Prin.; Stds.: 249; Scholastics: 249

BARTLETT

St. Peter Damian - 109 S. Crest Ave., Bartlett, IL 60103 t) 630-830-2295 (CRP); 630-837-5411 stpeter-damian@archchicago.org Rev. Christopher Ciomek, Pst.; Dcn. David Sattler; Dcn. Mariusz J. Kosla; CRP Stds.: 265

BERWYN

St. Mary of Celle - Merged Jul 2022 Merged with St. Frances of Rome to form St. Mary Frances of the Five Wounds.

St. Odilo - 2244 East Ave., Berwyn, IL 60402 t) 708-484-2161 stodilo@archchicago.org Rev. Bartholomew J. Juncer, Pst.; Rev. Salvador Den Hallegado, Assoc. Pst.; Dcn. Jesus Casas; Dcn. Alfonso Salgado; CRP Stds.: 97

St. Odilo School - (Grades PreK-8) 6617 W. 23rd St., Berwyn, IL 60402 t) 708-484-0755 donegan@saintodilo.org William Donegan, Prin.; Stds.: 183

Poor Souls -

St. Pius X and St. Leonard Parish - 3318 S. Clarence Ave., Berwyn, IL 60402 t) 708-795-5919 (CRP); 708-484-0015 stleonard@archchicago.org www.stleonard.org/ Rev. Robert Krueger, Pst.; Rev. Alex G. Ojachor, Assoc. Pst.; Dcn. Jose Cisneros; CRP Stds.: 136

St. Leonard School - -8) 3322 S. Clarence Ave., Berwyn, IL 60402 t) 708-749-3666 www.stleonardschool.org/ Scott S Decaluwe, Prin.; Stds.: 206

BLUE ISLAND

St. Donatus - 1939 Union St., Blue Island, IL 60406 t) 708-385-2890 stdonatus@archchicago.org www.stdonatuschurch.org/ Rev. Diego Cadavid, Pst.; Dcn. Tomas Herrera; CRP Stds.: 281

St. Mary Magdalene Parish - 2339 York St., Blue Island, IL 60406 t) 708-385-8510 stbenedict-york@archchicago.org Rev. Msgr. Dennis J. Lyle, Pst.; Dcn. William J. Hynes; Dcn. Juan Limon; Dcn. Lawrence Palmer; Dcn. Roberto Reyes; Dcn. Abundio Valadez; Ernesto Vargas, DRE; CRP Stds.: 130

St. Walter-St. Benedict School - -8) 2324 New St., Blue Island, IL 60406 t) 708-385-2016 stbenbengals@hotmail.com Emily Hanlon, Prin.; Stds.: 260

BRIDGEVIEW

St. Fabian - 8300 S. Thomas Ave., Bridgeview, IL 60455 t) 773-599-1110 stfabian@archchicago.org saint-fabian.org/ Rev. Grzegorz Warmuz, Pst.; Dcn. Kevin O'Donnell; Dcn. Joseph Stalcup Sr.; Dcn. Ronald Zielinski; CRP Stds.: 161

BROOKFIELD

Czech Mission of Saints Cyril and Methodius - 9415 Rochester Ave., Brookfield, IL 60513 t) 708-656-7472 sscyril-methodius-mission@archchicago.org Rev. Dusan Hladik, Dir.;

Holy Guardian Angels - 4008 Prairie Ave., Brookfield, IL 60513 t) 708-485-2900 parishoffice@hgaparish.org www.hgaparish.com/ Rev. Brian Kean, Pst.; Rev. Rodrigo Pena Jimenez, Assoc. Pst.; Dcn. David Brencic; Dcn. Thomas Carlson; CRP Stds.: 211

Youth Ministry - 1144 Harrison Ave., La Grange Park, IL 60526 t) 708-352-7388

BUFFALO GROVE

St. Mary - 10 N. Buffalo Grove Rd., Buffalo Grove, IL 60089 t) 847-537-9423 (CRP); 847-541-1450 stmary-buffalogrove@archchicago.org www.stmarybg.org/ Rev. Daniel R. Whiteside, Pst.; Rev. Denis Carneiro, Assoc. Pst.; Rev. Richard E. Sztorc, Pastor Emer.; Dcn. Daniel T. Georgen; Dcn. Eugene Kukla;

St. Mary School - (Grades PreK-8) 50 N. Buffalo Grove Rd., Buffalo Grove, IL 60089 t) 847-459-6270 school@stmarybg.org John D Fuja, Prin.; Stds.: 250

BURBANK

St. Albert the Great - 5555 W. State Rd., Burbank, IL 60459 t) 708-636-0406 (CRP); 708-423-0321 stalbert@archchicago.org www.stalbertgreat.com/ Rev. Mariusz J. Nawalaniec (Poland), Pst.; Rev. Siarhei Anhur, SCH, Assoc. Pst.; Rev. Bernardo Lozano, Assoc. Pst.; Rev. Joseph C. Mol, Assoc. Pst.; Dcn. Irvin Bryce; Dcn. Raymundo Diaz De Leon; Dcn. Raul Duque;

St. Albert the Great School - -8) 5535 W. State Rd., Burbank, IL 60459 t) 708-424-7757 jmclawhorn@satgschool.org Jodi McLawhorn, Prin.; Stds.: 223

CALUMET CITY

Jesus, Shepherd of Souls - 768 Lincoln Ave., Calumet City, IL 60409 t) 708-862-4165 jesusshepherdodsouls@archchicago.org jesusshepherdofsouls.com/ Rev. Luis Valerio Romero, Pst.; Rev. Leonard A. Dubi, Pastor Emer.; Dcn. Thomas Knetl; Dcn. Jose O. Oporto; Dcn. Dan Ragonese; Dcn. Philip R Wroblewski;

CHICAGO

Holy Name Cathedral - 730 N. Wabash Ave., Chicago, IL 60611 t) 312-787-8040 holyname-cathedral@archchicago.org holynamecathedral.org/ Rev. Gregory Sakowicz, Rector; Rev. Don Einars Cambe, Assoc. Pst.; Rev. Andrew W Matijevic, Assoc. Pst.; Rev. Ton Thai Nguyen, Assoc. Pst.; Dcn. Michael McCloskey; Dcn. Dennis R. Robak; Dcn. Stanley Strom; Dcn. Daniel G. Welter; Rev. Louis J. Cameli, In Res.; Rev. Ramil E. Fajardo, In Res.; Rev. William J. Moriarity, In Res.; CRP Stds.: 72

Archbishop's Residence - 1555 N. State Pkwy., Chicago, IL 60610

Oblate Sisters of Jesus the Priest -

Bishop Quarter House - 750 N. Wabash, Chicago, IL 60611 t) 312-640-1065

St. Agatha - Merged Jul 2022 Merged with St. Martin de Porres to form St. Agatha and St. Martin de Porres Parish.

St. Agatha and St. Martin De Porres Parish - 5112 W. Washington Blvd., Chicago, IL 60644 t) 773-287-0206 stmartin@archchicago.org www.stmartindeporresparish.com/ Rev. Lawrence R. Dowling, Pst.; Rev. Thadeo E. Mgimba, Assoc. Pst.; Dcn. William Pouncy; Christine Riley, DRE; CRP Stds.: 17

St. Agnes of Bohemia - 2651 S. Central Park Ave., Chicago, IL 60623 t) 773-277-5446 (CRP); 773-522-0142 stagnes-central@archchicago.org stagnesofbohemia.org/ Rev. Donald J. Nevins, Pst.; Rev. Misabet Garcia Gil, Assoc. Pst.; Rev. Juan C. Bautista Camargo, Assoc. Pst.; Dcn. Juan Carlos Bautista; Dcn. Angel Favila;

St. Agnes of Bohemia School - -8) 2643 S. Central Park Ave., Chicago, IL 60623 t) 773-522-0143 btaylor@school.stagnesofbohemia.org Clair E Zaffaroni, Prin.; Stds.: 310

Misioneras de San Pio X - 2658 S. Central Park Ave., Chicago, IL 60623 t) 773-762-3229 Sr. Blanca Fuentes Rascon, Contact;

St. Aloysius - Closed Jan 2022

St. Alphonsus - 1429 W. Wellington Ave., Chicago, IL 60657 t) 773-525-0709 stalphonsus-wellington@archchicago.org www.stalphonsuschicago.org/ Rev. Steven Bauer, Pst.; Rev. Patrick Gorman, Assoc. Pst.; Dcn. Guido Pozo; CRP Stds.: 88

Alphonsus Academy and Center for the Arts - -8) t) 773-348-4629 Gerit McAllister, Prin.; Stds.: 528

St. Andrew - 3546 N. Paulina St., Chicago, IL 60657 t) 773-525-3016 standrew@archchicago.org standrew.org/ Rev. Sergio Romo, Pst.; Rev. Silvanus S

Kidaha, Assoc. Pst.; Dcn. Mark J. Purdome; Dcn. Eric Sorensen; Rev. Arlin J. Louis, O.M.I., In Res.; David Heimann, Pst. Assoc.; CRP Stds.: 129

St. Andrew School - (Grades K-8) 1710 W. Addison, Chicago, IL 60613 t) 773-248-2500 gosaintandrew.com/ Sarah E Casavechia, Prin.; Stds.: 423

St. Anthony of Padua - 11533 S. Prairie Ave., Chicago, IL 60628 t) 773-468-1200 stanthony-prairie@archchicago.org Rev. Mark J. Krylowicz, Pst.; CRP Stds.: 57

Assumption of the Blessed Virgin Mary - 323 W. Illinois St., Chicago, IL 60654-7812 t) 312-644-0036 assumption-illinois@archchicago.org Rev. Joseph Chamblain, O.S.M., Pst.; Rev. Michael Doyle, O.S.M., Sr. Priest; Rev. Timothy Kremen, OSM, In Res.; Rev. John M. Pawlikowski, O.S.M., In Res.; Dcn. Kevin T. Zajdel;

St. Barnabas - 10134 S. Longwood Dr., Chicago, IL 60643 t) 773-445-3450 (CRP); 773-779-1166 stbarnabas@archchicago.org www.stbarnabasparish.org/ Rev. James J. Donovan Jr., Pst.; Rev. Raymond J. Tillrock, Pastor Emer.; Dcn. William R. Flamm; Dcn. Christopher J. Parker; Dcn. Andrew Neu; Kitty T. Ryan, Pst. Assoc.; CRP Stds.: 64

St. Barnabas School - -8) 10121 S. Longwood Dr., Chicago, IL 60643 t) 773-445-7711 jstack@stbarnabasparish.org www.stbarnabasparish.school/ Jonathan W Stack, Prin.; Stds.: 531

St. Basil/Visitation - 843 W. Garfield Blvd., Chicago, IL 60621 t) 773-846-3570 stbasil@archchicago.org www.stbasilvisitation.org/ Rev. Norman H. Moran-Rosero, Admin.; Dcn. Candelario Rodriguez; CRP Stds.: 27

Visitation School - -8) 900 W. Garfield Blvd., Chicago, IL 60609 t) 733-373-5200 elem.visitation@archchicago.org www.visitationschoolchicago.net/ Jennifer Markoff, Prin.; Stds.: 136

St. Bede the Venerable and St. Denis Parish - 8200 S. Kostner Ave., Chicago, IL 60652 t) 773-884-2038 (CRP); 773-884-2000 stbede-venerable@archchicago.org Rev. Carlos A. Aranciba Bermudez, Pst.; Rev. Scott Haynes, S.J.C., Assoc. Pst.; Dcn. Vincente Haro; Dcn. Ramiro Serna; Dcn. Guillermo Y. Tejeda;

St. Bede the Venerable School - -8) 4440 W. 83rd St., Chicago, IL 60652 t) 773-884-2020 sstewart@stbedechicago.org Sherry Stewart, Prin.; Stds.: 212

St. Benedict - 2215 W. Irving Park Rd., Chicago, IL 60618 t) 773-588-6484 stbenedict-irvingpark@archchicago.org parish.stbenedict.com/ Rev. Stephen F. Kanonik, Pst.; Rev. Thomas G. Refermat, Assoc. Pst.; Rev. Robert W. Beaven, Pastor Emer.; Dcn. David Reyes; Elaine Lindia, Pst. Assoc.; CRP Stds.: 579

St. Benedict Preparatory Schools - -8) 3920 N. Leavitt St., Chicago, IL 60618 t) 773-463-6797 sbps.stbenedict.com Rachael Bernhardt, Prin.; Stds.: 697

St. Benedict the African - 340 W. 66th St., Chicago, IL 60621 t) 773-873-4464 stbenedict-66th@archchicago.org benedicttheafrican.org/ Rev. David A. Jones, Pst.;

Academy of St. Benedict the African - -8) 6020 S. Laflin, Chicago, IL 60636 t) 773-776-3316 info@academystbenedict.org www.academystbenedict.org/ Jennifer Farrand, Prin.; Stds.: 222

Blessed Alojzije Stepinac Croatian Mission - 6346 N. Ridge, Chicago, IL 60660 t) 773-262-0535 blessedaloysius-mission@archchicago.org (Independent Mission) Rev. Drazan Boras, OFM, Dir.; Dcn. Ivan M. Mikan;

Blessed Carlo Acutis Parish - 2226 N. Hoyne Ave., Chicago, IL 60647 t) 773-486-1660 sthedwig@archchicago.org Rev. Tomasz Wojciechowski, C.R., Pst.; Rev. Patrick M. Marshall, Assoc. Pst.; Dcn. Guillermo Mendizabal; Dcn. Rodolfo Urquiza; Dcn. Daniel Cabrera; Dcn. Kevin M. Kucik; Rev. Eugene Szarek, C.R., In Res.; CRP Stds.: 84

St. John Berchmans School - (Grades PreSchool-8) 2511 W. Logan Blvd., Chicago, IL 60647 t) 773-486-1334 info@stjohnberchmans.org Margaret A. Roketenetz, Prin.; Stds.: 247

Blessed Maria Gabriella Parish - 2248 W. Washington Blvd., Chicago, IL 60612 t) 312-733-1068 stmalachy@archchicago.org Rev. Matthew Eyerman, Pst.; Dcn. David Castaneda; Rev. Vinicio Jiminez, Assoc. Pst.; CRP Stds.: 87

St. Malachy + Precious Blood School - (Grades PreK-8) 2252 W. Washington Blvd., Chicago, IL 60612 t) 312-733-2252 b.miller@stmalachychicago.com Vikki Stokes, Prin.; Stds.: 208

Blessed Sacrament - 3528 S. Hermitage Ave., Chicago, IL 60609-1217 t) 773-523-3917 blessedsacrament@archchicago.org www.bspchicago.org/ Rev. Ismael Sandoval, Pst.; Dcn. Francisco Medina; Dcn. Juan M. Rosales; CRP Stds.: 54

SS. Bruno and Richard Parish - 5030 S. Kostner Ave., Chicago, IL 60632 t) 773-585-1221 strichard@archchicago.org Rev. Andrzej A. Bartos, Pst.; Dcn. Edward Sajdak; Dcn. Salvatore Villa; Rev. Andrzej Juszczec, Assoc. Pst.; Dcn. Lawrence J. Chyba;

St. Richard School - -8) 5025 S. Kenneth Ave., Chicago, IL 60632 t) 773-582-8083 mnapier@strichard.net Michelle Augustyn-Napier, Prin.;

St. Bruno School - -8) 4839 S. Harding Ave., Chicago, IL 60632 t) 773-847-0697 office@stbruno.com Carla Sever, Prin.;

St. Cajetan - 2445 W. 112th St., Chicago, IL 60655 t) 773-474-7800 stcajetan@archchicago.org www.cajetan.org/ Rev. Kenneth A. Budzikowski, Pst.; Dcn. Joseph J. Roccasalva; Rev. William A. Burke, Pastor Emer.; CRP Stds.: 59

St. Cajetan School - -8) 2447 W. 112th St., Chicago, IL 60655 t) 773-233-8844 info@cajetan.org Michelle Nitsche, Prin.; Stds.: 417

Christ the King - 9235 S. Hamilton Ave., Chicago, IL 60643-6360 t) 773-238-4877 christtheking@archchicago.org www.ckchicago.org/ Rev. Lawrence J. Sullivan, Pst.; Dcn. Alfred Antonsen; Rev. Msgr. Michael J. Adams, Senior Priest; CRP Stds.: 319

Christ the King School - -8) 9240 S. Hoyne Ave., Chicago, IL 60643-6303 t) 773-779-3329 info@ck-school.org Ann Marie Riordan, Prin.; Stds.: 382

St. Christina - 11005 S. Homan Ave., Chicago, IL 60655 t) 773-779-7181 stchristina@archchicago.org stchristinaparish.org/ Rev. Thomas P. Conde, Pst.; Rev. Wayne A. Svida, Assoc. Pst.; Dcn. Alfredo Adolfo; Dcn. John Mutnansky; Dcn. Stanley Rakauskas; CRP Stds.: 399

St. Christina School - -8) 3333 W. 110th St., Chicago, IL 60655 t) 773-445-2969 schooloffice@stchristina.org Carrie A Spano, Prin.; Stds.: 475

St. Clement - 642 W. Deming Pl., Chicago, IL 60614 t) 773-281-0371 x14 (CRP); 773-281-0371 stclement@archchicago.org www.clement.org/ Rev. Przemyslaw Wojcik, Pst.; Rev. Matthew Litak, Assoc. Pst.; CRP Stds.: 108

St. Clement School - -8) 2524 N. Orchard St., Chicago, IL 60614 t) 773-348-8212 info@stclementschool.org Kristen E. Fink, Prin.; Stds.: 466

SS. Constance and Robert Bellarmine Parish - 4646 N. Austin Ave., Chicago, IL 60630-3157 t) 773-286-0956 (CRP); 773-777-2666 strobert@archchicago.org Rev. Robert J. Lojek, Pst.; Rev. Brendan Guilfoil, Assoc. Pst.; Rev. Franciszek Florczyk, Assoc. Pst.; Dcn. James Schiltz; Dcn. William J. Frere; Sr. Dcn. Rudolf Kotleba;

St. Robert Bellarmine School - (Grades PreK-8) 6036 W. Eastwood Ave., Chicago, IL 60630 t) 773-725-5133 cmijal@srb-chicago.org Catherine L Tenzillo, Prin.; Stds.: 256

St. Constance School - -8) 5841 W. Strong St., Chicago, IL 60630 t) 773-283-2311 office@stconstanceschool.org Eva M. Panczyk, Prin.; Stds.: 116

Cristo Rey Parish - 2524 S. Keeler Ave., Chicago, IL 60623 t) 773-521-1112 epiphany@archchicago.org Rev. Sergio Rivas Tamayo, Pst.; Rev. Rene Mena Beltran, Assoc. Pst.; Rev. Daniel Long, Assoc. Pst.; CRP Stds.: 280

Epiphany School - 4223 W. 25th St., Chicago, IL 60623 t) 773-762-1542 martinez@epiphanychicago.org Scott J. Ernst, Prin.; Stds.: 246

St. Daniel the Prophet - 5300 S. Natoma Ave., Chicago, IL 60638 t) 773-229-8794 (CRP); 773-586-1223 stdaniel@archchicago.org church.stdan.net/ Rev. Rafal Stecz, Pst.; Rev. Piotr Samborski, Assoc. Pst.; Dcn. Adam Danielewicz; Dcn. Robert Montelongo; CRP Stds.: 128

St. Daniel the Prophet School - (Grades PreK-8) 5337 S. Natoma, Chicago, IL 60638 t) 773-586-1225 principal@stdan.net Cynthia A. Zabilka, Prin.; Stds.: 588

St. Edward - 4350 W. Sunnyside Ave., Chicago, IL 60630-4147 t) 773-545-6496 stedward@archchicago.org www.stedwardchurch.com/ Rev. Dominic Clemente Jr., Pst.; Rev. Dominic Vinh Van Ha, Assoc. Pst.; Dcn. Michael McManus; Rev. James P. McIlhone, In Res.; Rev. Joseph C. Taylor, In Res.; CRP Stds.: 107

St. Edward School - -8) 4343 W. Sunnyside Ave., Chicago, IL 60630-4146 t) 773-736-9133 office@stedwardschool.com Sara Lasica, Prin.; Stds.: 283

St. Faustina Kowalska - 5252 S. Austin Ave., Chicago, IL 60638 t) 773-767-2411 stfaustina@archchicago.org Rev. Thaddeus Dzieszko, Pst.; Dcn. Romuald Morowczynski; CRP Stds.: 105

St. Jane de Chantal School - 5201 S. McVicker Ave., Chicago, IL 60638 t) 773-767-1130 school@stjanedechantal.com Nancy A. Andrasco, Prin.;

St. Ferdinand - 5900 W. Barry Ave., Chicago, IL 60634 t) 773-622-5900 x366 (CRP); 773-622-5900 stferdinand@archchicago.org www.stferdinandchurch.com/ Rev. Piotr Gnoinski, Pst.; Rev. Mariusz P. Stefanowski, Assoc. Pst.; Rev. Lukasz Pyka, Assoc. Pst.; CRP Stds.: 65

St. Ferdinand School - (Grades PreK-8) 3131 N. Mason Ave., Chicago, IL 60634 t) 773-622-3022 school@saintferdinand.org Erin Folino, Prin.; Stds.: 181

Convent - 5936 W. Barry Ave., Chicago, IL 60634

Christ Our Light Parish - 13145 S. Houston Ave., Chicago, IL 60633 t) 773-646-4877 stflorian@archchicago.org www.colparish.org/ Rev. David J. Simonetti, Pst.; Rev. Kilian J. Knittel, Pastor Emer.;

St. Francis Borgia - 8033 W. Addison St., Chicago, IL 60634 t) 773-625-1705 (CRP); 773-625-1118 stfrancis-borgia@archchicago.org borgiachicago.org Rev. Marek Maciej Smolka, Pst.; Rev. Marcin D. Szczypula, Assoc. Pst.; Rev. Joseph A. Mulcrone, In Res.; Dcn. Ireneusz Mocarski; CRP Stds.: 118

St. Francis Borgia School - (Grades PreK-8) 3535 N. Panama Ave., Chicago, IL 60634 t) 773-589-1000 sbetzolt@sfborgia.org Susan L. Betzolt, Prin.; Stds.: 159

Convent - 3521 N. Panama St., Chicago, IL 60634

St. Francis of Assisi - 813 W. Roosevelt Rd., Chicago, IL 60608 t) 312-226-7575 stfrancisassisi-roosevelt@archchicago.org www.sfachicago.org/ Rev. Walter D. Mallo, I.V.E., Pst.; Rev. Alejandro A Garcia Ortiz, IVE, Assoc. Pst.; CRP Stds.: 166

St. Gall - 5511 S. Sawyer Ave., Chicago, IL 60629 t) 773-737-3113 stgall@archchicago.org stgall.org/ Rev. Matthew E. Foley, Pst.; Rev. Ricardo Castillo, Assoc. Pst.; Rev. Francis Q. Kub, Pastor Emer.; Dcn. Alfredo

Alviar; Dcn. Miguel Arellano; Dcn. John Bumbul; Dcn. Albert Herrera; CRP Stds.: 601

St. Gall School - -8) 5515 S. Sawyer Ave., Chicago, IL 60629 t) 773-737-3454 info@stgallschool.com Thomas F Houlihan, Prin.; Stds.: 207

St. Simon the Apostle - 5157 S. California Ave., Chicago, IL 60632

St. Gertrude - 1420 W. Granville Ave., Chicago, IL 60660 t) 773-764-3621 stgertrude-granville@archchicago.org stgertrudechicago.org/ Rev. Richard J. Prendergast, Pst.; Rev. Michael A. Gabriel, Assoc. Pst.; Dcn. Rogelio Soto; Rev. Michael Bradley, In Res.; Rev. William P. Grogan, In Res.; Rev. Pius C Nwiyi, In Res.; Arthur Blumberg, Pst. Assoc.; Kevin Chears, Pst. Assoc.; CRP Stds.: 82

St. Pio of Pietrelcino Parish - 5600 N. Fairfield Ave., Chicago, IL 60659 t) 773-561-3474 sthilary@archchicago.org Rev. Aloysius Funtila, Pst.; Rev. Juan Carlos Arrieta Correa, Assoc. Pst.; Rev. Jo Andre B. Beltran, Pst. Assoc.; Dcn. Raymund C Torralba; Rev. Roger J. Caplis, Pastor Emer.; Rev. Robert G. Darow, Pastor Emer.; Rev. Thomas A. Libera, In Res.; CRP Stds.: 106

St. Hilary School - (Grades PreK-8) 5614 N. Fairfield Ave., Chicago, IL 60659 t) 773-561-5885 donovan@sthilarychicago.org Kathleen M. Donovan, Prin.; Stds.: 141

Our Lady of the Holy Family - 1335 W. Harrison St., Chicago, IL 60607-3318 t) 312-243-7400 olhfparish@archchicago.org www.olhfchi.org/ Rev. Peter B. McQuinn, Pst.; Rev. A. Paul Reicher, Pastor Emer.; Rev. Michael P. Knotek, In Res.; Dcn. Andrew L. Sorce;

Children of Peace School - 1900 W. Taylor St., Chicago, IL 60612 t) 312-243-8186 info@childrenofpeaceschool.org www.childrenofpeacechicago.org/ Lydia Nantwi, Prin.; Stds.: 117

Holy Trinity School for the Deaf - (Grades PreK-8) 1900 W. Taylor St., Chicago, IL 60612 t) 312-243-0785 ktarello@childrenofpeaceschool.org Kathy Tarello, Dir.;

Holy Trinity Mission - 1118 N. Noble St., Chicago, IL 60642 t) 773-489-4140 holytrinity-mission@archchicago.org trojcowo.com/ Rev. Andrzej Totzke, S.Ch., Pst.; Rev. Piotr Janas, SCH, Assoc. Pst.; Rev. Mariusz Lis, Assoc. Pst.;

St. Hyacinth Basilica - 3636 W. Wolfram St., Chicago, IL 60618 t) 773-342-3636 sthyacinth@archchicago.org www.sthyacinthbasilica.org/ Rev. Stanislaw Jankowski, C.R., Pst.; Rev. Steven Bartczyszyn, C.R., Assoc. Pst.; Rev. Anthony Dziorek, C.R., Assoc. Pst.; Rev. Stanislaw Lasota, C.R. (Poland), Assoc. Pst.; Dcn. Frank Girjatowicz; CRP Stds.: 139

Immaculate Conception - 7211 W. Talcott Ave., Chicago, IL 60631 t) 773-775-0545 x216 (CRP); 773-775-3833 ic-talcott@archchicago.org www.icchicago.org/ Rev. Matthew Heinrich, Pst.; Dcn. Michael A. Bednarz; Dcn. Richard H. Moritz; Sr. Dcn. Ronald Gronek; CRP Stds.: 429

Immaculate Conception School - (Grades PreK-9) 7263 W. Talcott Ave., Chicago, IL 60631 info@iccowboys.net Susan Canzoneri, Prin.; Stds.: 538

Immaculate Conception and Five Holy Martyrs - 2745 W. 44th St., Chicago, IL 60632-1999 t) 773-523-1402 icfhmchicago@gmail.com immaculateconception-fiveholymartyrs.org/ Rev. Miguel Venegas, Pst.; Rev. Sebastian Zebrowski, Assoc. Pst.; CRP Stds.: 420

Pope John Paul II School, Five Holy Martyrs Campus - (Grades PreK-8) 4325 S. Richmond St., Chicago, IL 60632 t) 773-523-6161 principal@pjpiischool.org Philip Cahill, Prin.; Stds.: 140

Immaculate Conception and St. Michael - 2944 E. 88th St., Chicago, IL 60617 t) 773-768-2100 ic-88th@archchicago.org www.icparishexc.org/ Rev. Pius Eusebius Kokose, C.S.Sp. (Ghana), Pst.; Rev. Armando Morales Martinez, Assoc. Pst.; Dcn. Abraham Chavez; Dcn. Jose M. Sandoval; CRP Stds.: 116

Immaculate Conception of the Blessed Virgin Mary School - 8739 S. Exchange, Chicago, IL 60617 t) 773-375-4674 principal@immaculateconceptionsouth.org Sr. Claudia Carrillo, Prin.; Stds.: 169

Immaculate Conception and St. Joseph - 1107 N. Orleans St., Chicago, IL 60610 t) 312-787-7174 info@icsjparish.org www.icsjparish.org Rev. Lawrence M. Lisowski, Pst.; Dcn. Neil Rogers; Kim Rak, DRE; CRP Stds.: 80

Immaculate Conception St. Joseph School - -8) 1431 N. Park, Chicago, IL 60610 t) 312-944-0304 ksullivan@icsjschool.org Catherine Sullivan, Prin.; Stds.: 384

St. James - 2907 S. Wabash Ave., Chicago, IL 60616 t) 312-842-1919 stjames-wabash@archchicago.org www.stjameswabash.org/ Rev. John S. Edmunds, S.T., Pst.; Dcn. Alfred Coleman II; CRP Stds.: 10

St. James Food Pantry -

St. James - 5730 W. Fullerton Ave., Chicago, IL 60639 t) 773-237-1474 stjames-fullerton@archchicago.org Rev. Richard Alejunas, S.D.B, Admin.; Rev. Krzysztof Cepil, Assoc. Pst.; Dcn. Orlando Perez; CRP Stds.: 444

Convent - 2441 N. Menard Ave., Chicago, IL 60639

St. Jerome - 1709 W. Lunt Ave., Chicago, IL 60626 t) 773-262-3170 stjerome-lunt@archchicago.org www.sjerome.org/ Rev. Noel Beltran Reyes, Pst.; Rev. Joel R Ricafranca, Assoc. Pst.; Dcn. Fritz Jean-Pierre; Dcn. Francisco Marin; Dcn. Eliseo Ramos; CRP Stds.: 103

Jesus, Bread of Life Parish - 2915 W. Palmer St., Chicago, IL 60647 t) 773-772-9082 (CRP); 773-235-3646 stsylvester@archchicago.org Rev. Samson Ngatia Mukundi, Pst.; Dcn. Benjamin Diaz; Dcn. Fred Ortiz; Dcn. Miguel A. Santillan; Dcn. Ernesto Robles; CRP Stds.: 242

St. Sylvester School - (Grades PreK-8) 3027 W. Palmer Blvd., Chicago, IL 60647 t) 773-772-5222 doyle@stsylvesterschool.org Allyn Doyle, Prin.; Stds.: 206

Our Lady of Grace School - 2446 N. Ridgeway Ave., Chicago, IL 60647 t) 773-342-0170 ritarangeop@yahoo.com Kaitlin D Reichart, Prin.; Stds.: 148

St. John Bosco - 2250 N. McVicker Ave., Chicago, IL 60639 t) 773-622-4620 stjohn-bosco@archchicago.org www.sjbchicago.org/ Rev. Richard Alejunas, S.D.B, Pst.; Rev. Krzysztof Cepil, Assoc. Pst.; Rev. Gregory Fishel, S.D.B., Assoc. Pst.; Rev. Andrzej Papiez, SDB, Assoc. Pst.; Rev. Juan Pablo Rubio, SDB, Assoc. Pst.; Rev. David Sajdak, SDB, Assoc. Pst.; Dcn. Simon P Anguiano; Dcn. Victor M. Moreno; CRP Stds.: 444

St. John Cantius - 825 N. Carpenter St., Chicago, IL 60642 t) 312-243-7373 stjohn-cantius@archchicago.org www.cantius.org/ Rev. Joshua Caswell, S.J.C., Pst.; Rev. Joseph Brom, S.J.C., Assoc. Pst.; Rev. Nathan Ford, S.J.C., Assoc. Pst.; Rev. Dennis Kolinski, S.J.C., Assoc. Pst.; Rev. Trenton Rauck, SJC, Assoc. Pst.; Rev. Anthony Rice, S.J.C., Assoc. Pst.; Rev. Matthew Schuster, S.J.C., Assoc. Pst.; Rev. Scott Thelander, S.J.C., Assoc. Pst.; Rev. Albert Tremari, S.J.C., Assoc. Pst.; Rev. David Yallaly, S.J.C., Assoc. Pst.; Dcn. Tomas Mackevicius; Judith Keefe, DRE; CRP Stds.: 204

St. John de la Salle - Merged Jul 2022 Merged with Holy Name of Mary and SS. Peter and Paul to form Our Lady of Kibeho Parish.

St. John Fisher - 10234 S. Washtenaw Ave., Chicago, IL 60655 t) 773-238-1851 (CRP); 773-445-6565 stjohn-fisher@archchicago.org www.stjohnfisherparish.net/ Rev. Kenneth A. Budzikowski, Pst.; Rev. Martin T. Marren, Assoc. Pst.; Dcn. Robert O. Carroll Jr.; Dcn. Clayton Kort; Dcn. Raymond Reilly; Dcn. Thomas Siska; Elena Chermak, DRE; CRP Stds.: 73

St. John Fisher School - -8) 10200 S. Washtenaw Ave., Chicago, IL 60655 t) 773-445-4737 jmcgrath@sjfschool.net Maura Nash, Prin.; Stds.: 558

St. Josaphat - 2311 N. Southport Ave., Chicago, IL 60614 t) 773-327-8955 stjosaphat@archchicago.org www.stjosaphatparish.org/ Rev. Francis M. Bitterman, Pst.; Dcn. Patrick S. Casey; CRP Stds.: 30

St. Josaphat School - -8) 2245 N. Southport Ave., Chicago, IL 60614 t) 773-549-0909 nmullens@stjosaphat.net Nel Mullens, Prin.; Stds.: 367

St. Josephine Bakhita Parish - 2132 E. 72nd St., Chicago, IL 60649 t) 773-768-0105 ol-peace@archchicago.org www.stbakhitachicago.org/ Rev. Thomas G. Belanger, Pst.; Dcn. Rameau Buissereth; Rev. Peter E. Muojekwu, In Res.; CRP Stds.: 2

St. Philip Neri School - -8) 2110 E. 72nd St., Chicago, IL 60649 t) 773-288-1138 lsanders@spnschoolchicago.org Diane T Asberry, Prin.; Stds.: 92

St. Philip Neri -

St. Juliana - 7200 N. Osceola Ave., Chicago, IL 60631 t) 773-631-4127 stjuliana@archchicago.org www.stjuliana.org/ Rev. John S. Siemianowski, Pst.; Rev. Prasad Akula, Assoc. Pst.; Rev. Elliott Richard Dees, Assoc. Pst.; Dcn. Edward Dolan; Dcn. Thomas J. Dombai; Dcn. Robert E. Ryan Sr.; Rev. Roger J. Caplis, In Res.; CRP Stds.: 231

St. Juliana School - -8) 7400 W. Touhy, Chicago, IL 60631 t) 773-631-2256 mmarshall@stjuliana.org Catherine Scotkovsky, Prin.; Stds.: 523

St. Katharine Drexel - 9015 S. Harper Ave., Chicago, IL 60619 t) 773-374-2345 stkatharinedrexelchgo@gmail.com Rev. Paul de Porres Whittington, O.P., Pst.; Rev. Herbert C Hayek, OP, Assoc. Pst.; Dcn. Roscoe B. Dixon Jr.; Dcn. Herbert Johnson; CRP Stds.: 12

St. Ailbe School - -8) 9037 S. Harper Ave., Chicago, IL 60619 t) 773-734-1386 Shauntae Davis, Prin.; Stds.: 136

St. Kilian - Merged Jul 2022 Merged with St. Margaret of Scotland to form SS. Martha, Mary, and Lazarus Parish.

St. Ladislaus - 5345 W. Roscoe St., Chicago, IL 60641 t) 773-545-5809 (CRP); 773-725-2300 stladislaus@archchicago.org Rev. Tomasz Ludwicki, SCH, Pst.; Rev. Jozef K Siedlarz, SCH, Assoc. Pst.; Rev. Jan F. Kaplan, Pastor Emer.;

Convent - 5330 W. Henderson St., Chicago, IL 60641

Holy Child Jesus - 2324 W. Chase Ave., Chicago, IL 60645 t) 773-764-0615 webadmin@hcjp.org hcjp.org/ Rev. Phi H. Nguyen, Pst.; Rev. Arthur Bautista, Assoc. Pst.; Rev. Harold B. Murphy, Pastor Emer.; Dcn. Neba Ambe; Dcn. Duc Van Nguyen; Dcn. David V. Pham; Dcn. Joseph T. Than;

St. Jerome (Croatian) - 2823 S. Princeton Ave., Chicago, IL 60616 t) 312-842-1871 stjeromecroatian@gmail.com stjeromecroatian.org/splash/ Rev. Ivica Majstorovic, O.F.M., Pst.; Rev. Antonio Musa, O.F.M., Assoc. Pst.; CRP Stds.: 41

St. Jerome School - 2801 S. Princeton Ave., Chicago, IL 60616 t) 312-842-7668 j.segvich@stjeromeschool.net Mary T Hyland, Prin.; Stds.: 129

SS. Martha, Mary, and Lazarus Parish - 9830 S. Vincennes Ave., Chicago, IL 60643 t) 773-779-5151 stmargaretofscotland@archchicago.org www.smosparish.com/ Rev. Donald Eruaga, M.S.P., Pst.; Dcn. Leroy Gill Jr.;

St. Margaret of Scotland School - -8) 9833 S. Throop St., Chicago, IL 60643 t) 773-238-1088 sdavis@smoschicago.org Shauntae Davis, Prin.; Stds.: 209

St. Ethelreda - (Grades PreK-8) 8734 S. Paulina St., Chicago, IL 60620 t) 773-238-1757 welcome@stethelreda.org Denise Spells, Prin.; Stds.: 222

Mary, Mother of God - 1220 W. Catalpa Ave., Chicago, IL 60640 t) 773-561-5343 office@saintita.org www.motherofgodchicago.org/ Rev. Robert Cook, O.F.M.Conv., Pst.; Rev. Thomas A. Fetz, O.F.C.V., Assoc. Pst.; Dcn. Ubaldo Munoz; Dcn. Juan Ramirez; Dcn. Antonio Rodriguez; Dcn. Paul Spalla; Dcn.

Ronald Stricker; CRP Stds.: 86

St. Thomas of Canterbury School - -8) 5525 N. Magnolia, Chicago, IL 60640 t) 773-271-8655 cboyd@stmary-stthomas.org Christine M. Boyd, Prin.; Stds.: 186

St. Mary of Perpetual Help, All Saints and St. Anthony - 1039 W. 32nd St., Chicago, IL 60608 t) 773-927-6646 stmaryph@aol.com Rev. Thomas G. Aschenbrener, Pst.; Dcn. Jake L. Vercimak;

St. Mary of the Angels - 1850 N. Hermitage Ave., Chicago, IL 60622 t) 773-278-2644 stmary-angels@archchicago.org www.sma-church.org/ Rev. John R. Waiss, Pst.; Rev. Hilary F. Mahaney, Assoc. Pst.; Dcn. Glenn Tylutki; Rev. Roderrick Esclanda, In Res.;

St. Mary of the Angels School - -8) 1810 N. Hermitage Ave., Chicago, IL 60622 t) 773-486-0119 bdolack@sma-school.org Elizabeth M. Dolack, Prin.; Stds.: 260

St. Mary of the Lake and Our Lady of Lourdes Parish - 4200 N. Sheridan Rd., Chicago, IL 60613 t) 773-472-3711 stmary-lake@archchicago.org Rev. Manuel Dorantes, Pst.; Rev. Elvio Baldeon Lope, Assoc. Pst.; Rev. Donald C. Woznicki, Assoc. Pst.; Rev. Daniel J. Collins, Senior Priest; CRP Stds.: 100

St. Mary of the Lake School - -8) 1026 W. Buena Ave., Chicago, IL 60613 t) 773-281-0018 cboyd@stmary-stthomas.org Christine M. Boyd, Prin.; Stds.: 160

St. Mary of the Woods - 7033 N. Moselle Ave., Chicago, IL 60646 t) 773-763-0206 stmary-woods@archchicago.org www.smow.org/ Rev. Richard Jakubik, Pst.; Rev. Jesudas Gudime, Assoc. Pst.;

St. Mary of the Woods School - -8) 6959 N. Hiawatha Ave., Chicago, IL 60646 t) 773-763-7577 myamoah@smow.org Amanda Parker, Prin.; Stds.: 378

Mary, Mother of Mercy - 7114 S. Hamlin Ave., Chicago, IL 60629 t) 773-582-4662 queen-universe@archchicago.org www.mmmparish.org/ Rev. Jose Antonio Murcia Abellan, Pst.; Rev. John F. Villa-Holguin, Assoc. Pst.; Dcn. Ruben Aguilar; Dcn. Juan Valadez;

Queen of the Universe School - -8) 7130 S. Hamlin Ave., Chicago, IL 60629 t) 773-582-4266 mporod@qofu.org Linda M Kelly, Prin.; Stds.: 188

St. Mary, Star of the Sea - 6435 S. Kilbourn Ave., Chicago, IL 60629 t) 773-767-7078 (CRP); 773-767-1246 stmary-sea@archchicago.org www.smsschurch.org/ Rev. Roger A. Corrales-Diaz, Pst.; Rev. Erasto Nyoni, Assoc. Pst.; Dcn. Angelo Cordoba; Therese A. Navarro, DRE; CRP Stds.: 179

St. Mary Star of the Sea School - -8) 6424 S. Kenneth Ave., Chicago, IL 60629 t) 773-767-6160 cusauskas@stmarystaroftheseaschool.org Candice M. Usauskas, Prin.; Stds.: 198

St. Michael in Old Town - 1633 N. Cleveland Ave., Chicago, IL 60614 t) 312-642-2498 information@st-mikes.org www.st-mikes.org Rev. Lawrence E. Sanders, C.Ss.R., Pst.; Rev. Edward Vella, C.Ss.R., Assoc. Pst.; Rev. Ramon Dompke, C.Ss.R., In Res.; Rev. J. Robert Fenili, C.Ss.R., In Res.; Rev. James Keena, C.Ss.R., In Res.; CRP Stds.: 21

St. Monica and St. Rosalie Parish - 5136 N. Nottingham Ave., Chicago, IL 60656 t) 773-631-7810 (CRP); 773-763-1661 stmonica@archchicago.org stmonica.us/ Rev. Grzegorz Lorens, Pst.; Rev. Thomas J. Campana, Assoc. Pst.; Rev. Tomasz P. Wilk, O.S.P.P.E., Assoc. Pst.; Rev. Grzegorz Wojcik, Assoc. Pst.; Rev. William M. Holbrook, In Res.; Dcn. Patrick Brenner; Dcn. Edward Podgorski; CRP Stds.: 118

St. Monica Academy - -8) 5115 N. Mont Clare Ave., Chicago, IL 60656 t) 773-631-7880 rcoleman@stmonicachicago.com Nancy Zver, Prin.; Stds.: 256

St. Moses the Black Parish - 331 E. 71st St., Chicago, IL 60619 t) 773-224-1022 stcolumbanus@archchicago.org Rev. Matthew O'Donnell, Pst.; Dcn. Wallace Harris;

Augustus Tolton Catholic Academy - (Grades PreK-8) 7120 S. Calumet, Chicago, IL 60619 t) 773-224-3811 dsmith@toltonacademy.org (Ministry of St. Dorothy and St. Columbanus) Andrew J Jahnke, Prin.; Stds.: 128

Mother of the Americas Parish - 2434 S. California Ave., Chicago, IL 60608 t) 773-247-6644 assumption-california@archchicago.org Rev. Thomas Boharic, Pst.; Rev. Martin Marulanda, Assoc. Pst.; Dcn. Manuel Salgado; CRP Stds.: 210

Convent - 2831 W. 24th St. Blvd., Chicago, IL 60623

Our Lady of Tepeyac School - -8) 2235 S. Albany, Chicago, IL 60623 t) 773-522-0024 pkrielaart@ourladyoftepeyac.org www.tepeyacelementary.org Patricia Y. Krielaart, Prin.; Stds.: 180

Our Lady of Tepeyac High School - 2228 S. Whipple St., Chicago, IL 60623 t) 773-522-0023 info@ourladyoftepeyac.org www.ourladyoftepeyac.org Rebecca Noonan, Prin.; Stds.: 153

St. Mother Teresa of Calcutta - 2859 S. Throop St., Chicago, IL 60608 t) 312-842-7979 stmotherteresaparish@archchicago.org www.stmotherteresaparish.org/ Rev. Li F. Dong Ping, Pst.; Rev. John P. Cuff, M.M., In Res.; CRP Stds.: 20

St. Therese Catholic Chinese Church School - -8) 247 W. 23rd St., Chicago, IL 60616 t) 312-326-2837 principal@sttheresechicago.org Lisa D. Oi, Prin.; Stds.: 350

Nativity of Our Lord and St. Gabriel Parish - 653 W. 37th St., Chicago, IL 60609 t) 773-927-6263 nativitygabrieloffice@nativitystgabriel.org www.nativitystgabriel.org/ Rev. James F. Hurlbert, Pst.; Dcn. Erik Zeimys; Dcn. Robert F. Morris II; CRP Stds.: 75

St. Gabriel School - (Grades PreSchool-8) 4500 S. Wallace St., Chicago, IL 60609 t) 773-268-6636 info@stgabrielchicago.com Daniel M Flaherty, Prin.; Stds.: 177

Nativity of the Blessed Virgin Mary - 6812 S. Washtenaw Ave., Chicago, IL 60629 t) 773-776-4600 nativity-bvm@archchicago.org Rev. Jaunius Kelpsas (Lithuania), Pst.; Rev. Gediminas Kersys, Assoc. Pst.;

Convent - 6804 S. Washtenaw Ave., Chicago, IL 60629

St. Nicholas of Tolentine - 3721 W. 62nd St., Chicago, IL 60629 t) 773-284-2635 (CRP); 773-735-1121 stnicholas-tolentine@archchicago.org Rev. Miguel Flores, Admin.; Dcn. Ernesto Robles; CRP Stds.: 206

St. Nicholas of Tolentine School - -8) 3741 W. 62nd St., Chicago, IL 60629 t) 773-735-0772 mmenden@stnicksschool.com Mariagnes Menden, Prin.; Stds.: 417

Old St. Mary - 1500 S. Michigan, Chicago, IL 60605 t) 312-922-3444 oldstmarys@archchicago.org oldstmarys.com/ Rev. Bradford C. Schoeberle, CSP, Pst.; Rev. Patrick D. Johnson, C.S.P., Assoc. Pst.; Rev. Stuart Wilson Smith, CSP, Assoc. Pst.; CRP Stds.: 57

Old St. Mary School - (Grades PreK-8) 1474 S. Michigan Ave., Chicago, IL 60605 t) 312-386-1560 jmartin@osmschool.com www.osmschool.com April Greer, Prin.; Stds.: 503

Old St. Patrick's - 700 W. Adams St., Chicago, IL 60661 t) 312-648-1021 oldstpatricks@archchicago.org www.oldstpats.org/ Rev. Patrick E. McGrath, S.J., Pst.; Rev. Michael R Simone, SJ, Assoc. Pst.; CRP Stds.: 463

Shrine of Our Lady of Pompeii - t) 312-421-3757 Rev. Richard Fragomeni, Rector;

St. Oscar Romero Parish - 4821 S. Hermitage Ave., Chicago, IL 60609 t) 773-254-2366 stjoseph-hermitage@archchicago.org Rev. Jose Carmen Mandez Izquierdo, Pst.; Rev. Sergio Mena-Mena, Assoc. Pst.; Dcn. Jose Gonzalez; Dcn. Javier Pineda;

Our Lady of Africa Parish - 615 E. Oakwood Blvd., Chicago, IL 60653 t) 773-624-5375 holyangels@archchicago.org Rev. Robert Kelly, S.V.D., Pst.; Rev. Francis Rayappan, Assoc. Pst.; Dcn. Michael Foggie; Dcn. Ivan Lazcano; Dcn. Mervin O. Johnson; Dcn. Bruce McElrath; CRP Stds.: 37

Holy Angels School - (Grades PreK-8) 750 E. 40th St., Chicago, IL 60653 t) 772-624-0727 sstalling@holyangelschicago.org Maria M Brown, Prin.; Stds.: 175

Our Lady of Fatima and St. Pancratius - 4025 S. Sacramento Ave., Chicago, IL 60632 t) 773-523-5666 ol-fatima@archchicago.org www.fatimapancratius.org/ Rev. Nestor Saenz (Peru), Pst.; Dcn. Jose Negrete; CRP Stds.: 194

Shrine of St. Anne -

Our Lady of Guadalupe - 3200 E. 91st, Chicago, IL 60617 t) 773-768-0793 olgfrontoffice@gmail.com shrineofstjude.org Rev. Hector M. Navalo, C.M.F., Pst.; Rev. Anthony Duy Luong, CMF, Assoc. Pst.; Rev. Steve Niskanon, C.M.F., Assoc. Pst.; Dcn. Jose M. Estrada; Dcn. Ramon Jimenez; Dcn. Raul Nunez; CRP Stds.: 350

Our Lady of Guadalupe School - -8) 9050 S. Burley, Chicago, IL 60617 t) 773-768-0999 bhall@olgschicago.org Hall L. Bonnie, Prin.; Stds.: 160

National Shrine of St. Jude - ; Mailing: 205 W. Monroe St., 7th Fl., Chicago, IL 60606 t) 312-236-7782 www.shrineofstjude.org (Claretian Missionaries) Rev. Stephen Niskanen, CMF, Admin.;

Our Lady of Kibeho Parish - 11159 S. Loomis St., Chicago, IL 60643 t) 773-238-6800 holyname-mary@archchicago.org hnm.archchicago.org/ Rev. Robert J. Gilbert, Pst.; Dcn. James G. Maslanka;

Sacred Heart - 11652 S. Church St., Chicago, IL 60643

St. John de la Salle Catholic Academy - -8) 10212 S. Vernon Ave., Chicago, IL 60628 t) 773-785-2331 ssantellano@johndls.org Sally Santellano, Prin.; Stds.: 132

Our Lady of Mercy - 4432 N. Troy St., Chicago, IL 60625 t) 773-588-1637 (CRP); 773-588-2620 ol-mercy@archchicago.org olm.church/ Rev. Joseph P. Tito, Admin.; Rev. Lorenzo Gamboa Cadena, Assoc. Pst.; Rev. Pedro Campos, Assoc. Pst.; Rev. Bolivar G. Molina-Ramirez, Assoc. Pst.; Dcn. Ramiro B. Carrion; Dcn. Juan C Diaz-Maravilla; Dcn. Aurelio Garcia; Dcn. Juan Gonzalez; Dcn. Robert Janega; Dcn. Efrain Lopez; Dcn. Allan G. Origenes; Dcn. Francisco Rivera; Dcn. Uriol Rodriguez; CRP Stds.: 424

Our Lady of Mount Carmel - 708 W. Belmont, Chicago, IL 60657 t) 872-260-4100 parishoffice@ourlmc.org ourlmc.org/ Rev. Patrick J. Lee, Pst.; Dcn. Richard Johnson; Dcn. Thomas Lambert; Razia S. Khokhar, DRE; CRP Stds.: 32

Our Lady of Mount Carmel School - -8) 720 W. Belmont Ave., Chicago, IL 60657 t) 773-525-8779 staszcuk@olmca.org Shane P. Staszcuk, Prin.; Stds.: 252

Our Lady of Nazareth Parish - 11128 S. Ave. G, Chicago, IL 60617-6925 t) 773-221-1040 stfrancisdesales-ewing@archchicago.org Rev. Walter Yepes, Pst.; CRP Stds.: 147

Annunciata School - -8) 3750 E. 112th St., Chicago, IL 60617 t) 773-375-5711 erenasannunciatags@gmail.com Sr. Claudia Carrillo, Prin.; Stds.: 152

Our Lady of Pompeii - 1224 W. Lexington St., Chicago, IL 60607-4111 t) 312-421-3757 ol-pompeii-shrine@archchicago.org See Old St. Patrick, Shrine of Our Lady of Pompeii Rev. Richard Fragomeni, Rector;

Our Lady of Sorrows, Basilica of - 3121 W. Jackson Blvd., Chicago, IL 60612 t) 773-638-0159 ol-sorrows@archchicago.org ols-chicago.org/ Rev. Christopher M. Krymski, O.S.M., Pst.; Dcn. James E. Norman; CRP Stds.: 4

National Shrine of St. Peregrine - t) 773-638-5800

Our Lady of the Rosary Parish - 3935 N. Melvina Ave., Chicago, IL 60634 t) 773-725-7641 x22 (CRP); 773-725-7641 stpascal@archchicago.org Rev. Michael W. O'Connell, Pst.; Rev. Mariusz P. Stefanowski, Assoc. Pst.; Rev. James A. Heneghan, Assoc. Pst.; Rev. Michael J. Shanahan, In Res.; Rev. Abraham M. Jacob,

In Res.; Dcn. Michael Ahern; Dcn. Eugene L. Kummerer; Dcn. Jamie Rios; Dcn. Charles T. Shallcross; Dcn. Victor M. Uruchima; CRP Stds.: 310

Ciezadlo Center - 3954 N. Meade Ave., Chicago, IL 60634

Pope Francis Global Academy - -8) 6143 W. Irving Park Rd., Chicago, IL 60634 t) 773-763-7080 torourke@pfgacademy.org (Regional School) Eli Argamaso, Prin.; Stds.: 187

St. Bartholomew School - -8) 4941 W. Patterson Ave., Chicago, IL 60641 t) 773-282-9373 krebhancsuk@stbartholomew.net Nilma Osieki, Prin.; Stds.: 156

Our Lady of the Snows - 4858 S. Leamington Ave., Chicago, IL 60638 t) 773-582-4904 (CRP); 773-582-2266 ol-snows@archchicago.org www.ourladyofthesnowsparish.org/ Rev. Juan Luis Andrade-Limon, Pst.; CRP Stds.: 310

Our Lady of the Snows School - -8) 4810 S. Leamington Ave., Chicago, IL 60638 t) 773-735-4810 Christina Mikus, Prin.; Stds.: 157

Our Lady of Unity Parish - 2315 W. Augusta Blvd., Chicago, IL 60622 t) 773-235-3575 sthelen@archchicago.org Rev. Claudio Diaz Jr., Pst.; Rev. Agustin Garcia Candanosa, Assoc. Pst.; Dcn. Ramon Arroyo; Dcn. William Smyser; Dcn. Adolfo Lopez, CRE; Dcn. Antonio Navarro; CRP Stds.: 57

St. Helen School - (Grades PreK-8) 2347 W. Augusta Blvd., Chicago, IL 60622 t) 773-486-1055 info@sthelenchicago.org Dana M Vance, Prin.; Stds.: 292

Our Lady, Mother of the Church - Merged Jul 2022 Merged with St. Eugene and Divine Savior to form Queen of Peace Parish.

St. Paul - 2127 W. 22nd Pl., Chicago, IL 60608 t) 773-847-6100 stpaul-22nd@archchicago.org Rev. Michael P. Enright, Pst.; Dcn. Rodrigo Silva; CRP Stds.: 84

St. Ann School - 2211 W. 18th Pl., Chicago, IL 60608-1807 t) 312-829-4153 Mary M. Corrigan, Prin.; Stds.: 180

SS. Peter and Paul - Merged Jul 2022 Merged with St. John De La Salle and Holy Name of Mary to form Our Lady of Kibeho Parish.

St. Peter's - 110 W. Madison St., Chicago, IL 60602 t) 312-372-5111 stpeter-madison@archchicago.org Rev. Michael Fowler, OFM, Pst.;

St. Pius V - 1919 S. Ashland Ave., Chicago, IL 60608 t) 312-226-6161 stpiusv@archchicago.org Rev. Thomas P. Lynch, O.P., Pst.; Rev. Donald Goergen, OP, In Res.; Rev. Brian G. Bricker, O.P., Assoc. Pst.; Rev. Mark Paraday, O.P., In Res.; Rev. Charles W. Dahm, O.P., In Res.; CRP Stds.: 102

St. Pius V School - -8) t) 312-226-1590 nnasko@saintpiusv.org Melissa Talaber, Prin.; Stds.: 137

Shrine of St. Jude Thaddeus - t) 312-226-0020 www.shrineofsaintjude.com

St. Priscilla - 6949 W. Addison St., Chicago, IL 60634 t) 773-685-3785 (CRP); 773-545-8840 stpriscilla@archchicago.org Rev. Maciej D. Galle, Pst.; Rev. Daniel K. Kusa, Assoc. Pst.; CRP Stds.: 79

St. Procopius - 1641 S. Allport St., Chicago, IL 60608 t) 312-226-7887 Rev. Adan Sandoval Duron, Pst.; Rev. Deogratias Mbonyumugenzi, Assoc. Pst.; CRP Stds.: 137

St. Procopius School - -8) 1625 S. Allport St., Chicago, IL 60608 t) 312-421-5135 griselda.ferguson@stprocopiusschool.org Dr. Robert M Bassett, Prin.; Stds.: 175

Queen of All Saints Basilica - 6280 N. Sauganash Ave., Chicago, IL 60646 t) 773-736-6060 queen-saints@archchicago.org www.qasparish.org/ Rev. Simon F. Braganza, Pst.; Rev. Msgr. Wayne F. Prist, Pastor Emer.; Rev. Edward D. Grace, In Res.; CRP Stds.: 261

Queen of All Saints Basilica School - -8) 6230 N. Lemont Ave., Chicago, IL 60646 t) 773-736-0567 www.qasschool.org/ Emily Carlson, Prin.; Stds.: 575

Queen of Apostles Parish - 4412 N. Western Ave., Chicago, IL 60625 t) 773-539-7510 parish@queenofangelschicago.org Rev. Msgr. James T. Kaczorowski, Pst.; Dcn. Dennis Ramos;

St. Matthias School - -8) 4910 N. Claremont Ave., Chicago, IL 60625 t) 773-784-0999 sheila.klich@stmatthiasschool.org Kathleen A. Carden, Prin.; Stds.: 313

Queen of Angels School - -8) 4520 N. Western Ave., Chicago, IL 60625 t) 773-769-4211 jkelly@queenofangelschicago.org Rana J Brizgys, Prin.; Stds.: 338

Queen of Peace Parish - 7958 W. Foster Ave., Chicago, IL 60656-1651 t) 773-775-6659 steugene@archchicago.org st-eugene.org/ Rev. Richard Yanos, Pst.; Rev. Jacek A. Dada, Assoc. Pst.; Rev. James J. O'Brien, M.A., Pastor Emer.; CRP Stds.: 90

St. Eugene School - (Grades PreK-8) 7930 W. Foster Ave., Chicago, IL 60656-1651 t) 773-763-2235 school@st-eugene.org Margaret Kinel, Prin.;

St. Rita of Cascia - 6243 S. Fairfield Ave., Chicago, IL 60629 t) 773-434-9600 strita@archchicago.org Rev. Homero Sanchez Gomez, O.S.F., Pst.; Rev. Samuel L. Joutras, O.S.A., Assoc. Pst.; Dcn. David D. Andrade; Dcn. Oscar Gonzalez; Dcn. Miguel A. Martinez; CRP Stds.: 311

St. Clare of Montefalco - 5443 S. Washtenaw Ave., Chicago, IL 60632

St. Sabina - 1210 W. 78th Pl., Chicago, IL 60620 t) 773-483-4300 stsabina@archchicago.org Rev. Thulani D. Magwaza, Pst.; Dcn. Leonard M. Richardson; Kimberly Lymore, DRE; CRP Stds.: 9

St. Sabina Academy - -8) 7801 S. Throop St., Chicago, IL 60620 t) 773-483-5000 office@stsabinaacademy.org Janice Wells, Prin.; Stds.: 145

Sacred Heart - 2864 E. 96th St., Chicago, IL 60617 t) 773-768-1423 sacredheart-croatian@archchicago.org www.sacredheartcroatian.org/ Rev. Stephen Bedenikovic, O.F.M., Pst.; Rev. Dragan Bolcic, OFM, Assoc. Pst.; CRP Stds.: 139

Sacred Heart School - -8) 2906 E. 96th St., Chicago, IL 60617 t) 773-773-3728 www.shschool96.org/ Kathleen M. Tomaszewski, Prin.; Stds.: 152

Sacred Heart Mission of Holy Name of Mary - 11652 S. Church St., Chicago, IL 60643 t) 773-233-3955 sacredheart-mission@archchicago.org Rev. Robert J. Gilbert, Rector;

San Jose Luis Sanchez del Rio - 3647 W. North Ave., Chicago, IL 60647 t) 773-722-9401 sanjoselitooffice@gmail.com www.sanjosesanchezdelrio.org/ Rev. Jose Maria Garcia-Maldonado, Pst.; Rev. Marco Antonio Franco Luna, Assoc. Pst.; Dcn. Jorge Garcia; Dcn. Felipe Gonzalez; Dcn. Floro Hita; Dcn. Francisco Ramos; Dcn. Milton Rodriguez; Dcn. Cornelio Tecruceno; CRP Stds.: 336

Maternity of the Blessed Virgin Mary School - -8) 1537 N. Lawndale Ave., Chicago, IL 60651 t) 773-227-1140 cmolina@maternitybvmchicago.com Christine Molina, Prin.; Stds.: 158

St. Stanislaus Kostka - 1351 W. Evergreen Ave., Chicago, IL 60622 t) 773-278-2470 ststanislaus-evergreen@archchicago.org Rev. Anthony Bus, C.R., Pst.; Dcn. Nicolas Flores; Dcn. Jorge Salinas;

St. Stanislaus Kostka School - -8) 1255 N. Noble St., Chicago, IL 60622 t) 773-278-4560 principal@ststanschicago.org Robert F Vickman, Prin.; Stds.: 171

SS. Genevieve and Stanislaus Bishop and Martyr - 5352 W. Belden Ave., Chicago, IL 60639 t) 773-237-5800 ssgsbm@archchicago.org www.genstan.org/ Rev. Diego Cadavid, Pst.; Rev. Yorman A. Beltran Arias, Assoc. Pst.; Rev. Edgar Rodriguez, Assoc. Pst.; Dcn. Antonio Delgado; Dcn. Gustavo Rebolledo Rebolledo; Dcn. Faustino Villasenor; CRP Stds.: 442

St. Genevieve School - -8) 4854 W. Montana St., Chicago, IL 60639 t) 773-237-7131 aparker@stgschool.org www.stgschool.org/ Amanda Parker, Prin.; Stds.: 224

St. Stephen, King of Hungary Mission - 2015 W. Augusta Blvd., Chicago, IL 60622 t) 773-486-1896 ststephen-augusta@archchicago.org Rev. Edward J. Cronin, Admin.;

St. Teresa of Avila - 1930 N. Kenmore, Chicago, IL 60614-4139 t) 773-528-6650 stteresa@archchicago.org teresa.church/ Rev. Frank J. Latzko, Pst.;

St. Elizabeth of the Trinity - 6020 W. Ardmore Ave., Chicago, IL 60646 t) 773-763-8828 office@stelizabethtrinity.org stelizabethtrinity.org/ Rev. Michael Grisolano, Pst.; Rev. Christopher Landfried, Assoc. Pst.; Rev. Lukas O. Ouda, Assoc. Pst.; Rev. Daniel P. McCarthy, Pastor Emer.; Rev. Edwin D. Pacocha, Pastor Emer.; Rev. Gerald E. Rogala, Pastor Emer.; Dcn. Jose Adan-Bernabe; Dcn. Gregory M. Bzdon; Dcn. John Rottman; Dcn. Steven J. Wagner; Rev. John M. Griffiths, In Res.; Rev. Ronald P. Stake, In Res.; CRP Stds.: 126

St. Elizabeth of the Trinity - -8) 6040 W. Ardmore Ave., Chicago, IL 60646 t) 773-763-3380 k.collins@stelizabethtrinityschool.org stelizabethtrinityschool.org/ Kristine A. Hillmann, Prin.; Stds.: 209

St. Thomas Apostle - 5472 S. Kimbark Ave., Chicago, IL 60615 t) 773-324-2626 stthomas-apostle@archchicago.org stapostleparish.org/ Rev. Michael Trail, Pst.; Rev. Aliaksandr Audziayuk, Assoc. Pst.; Dcn. Kurt E. Davis; Dcn. Thomas Murphy; CRP Stds.: 215

St. Thomas Apostle School - -8) 5467 S. Woodlawn Ave., Chicago, IL 60615 t) 773-667-1142 tgallo@stapostleschool.com Kenneth Koll, Prin.; Stds.: 369

St. Thomas More Mission - 2825 W. 81st St., Chicago, IL 60652 t) 773-436-4444 stthomas-more@archchicago.org Rev. Msgr. Richard M. Zborowski, Pst.; Rev. Scott Haynes, S.J.C., Assoc. Pst.; Dcn. George Borha;

St. Turibius - 5646 S. Karlov Ave., Chicago, IL 60629 t) 773-581-2730 stturibius@archchicago.org turibius.org/ Rev. William E. Lego, O.S.A., Pst.; Rev. John J. Dowling, O.S.A., Assoc. Pst.; Dcn. Carlos Alvarado; Dcn. Thomas Christensen; Sr. Mary Beth Bromer, DRE; CRP Stds.: 184

Two Holy Martyrs Parish - 6135 S. Austin Ave., Chicago, IL 60638 t) 773-767-1523 info@twoholymartyrs.org www.twoholymartyrs.org/ Rev. Robert Regan, Pst.; Rev. Matthew Ross Compton, Assoc. Pst.; Rev. Peter P. Paurazas, Pastor Emer.; Dcn. Thomas Hyde; CRP Stds.: 189

St. Symphorosa and Seven Sons School - -8) 6125 S. Austin Ave., Chicago, IL 60638 t) 773-585-6888 kberry@stsymphorosaschool.org Kathleen M. Berry, Prin.; Stds.: 231

SS. Viator and Wenceslaus Parish - 4170 W. Addison St., Chicago, IL 60641 t) 773-286-4040 stviator@archchicago.org Rev. Benjamin Lupercio, Pst.; Rev. Martin D. Ibarra, Assoc. Pst.; Dcn. William Burns; Dcn. Victor Flores; Dcn. Mario Hernandez; CRP Stds.: 132

St. Viator School - -8) 4140 W. Addison St., Chicago, IL 60641 t) 773-545-2173 principal@stviatorchicago.org Lisa Rieger, Prin.; Stds.: 278

St. Vincent de Paul - 1010 W. Webster Ave., Chicago, IL 60614 t) 773-544-5217 stvincent-depaul@archchicago.org stvdep.org/ Rev. Joseph S Williams, Pst.;

St. William - 2600 N. Sayre Ave., Chicago, IL 60707 t) 773-637-6565 stwilliam@archchicago.org www.saintwilliamparish.org/ Rev. Ryszard Gron, Pst.; Dcn. Leonel Segura; Dcn. Edward Simola; CRP Stds.: 60

St. William School - -8) 2559 N. Sayre Ave., Chicago, IL 60707 t) 773-637-5130 msegvich@stwilliamschool.org Jennifer M Frazzini, Prin.; Stds.: 161

CHICAGO HEIGHTS

SS. Paul, Agnes, and Kieran Parish - 724 W. 195th St., Chicago Heights, IL 60411 t) 708-754-0484 (CRP);

708-755-0074 stkieran@archchicago.org Rev. Gary M. Graf, Pst.; Rev. Juan C. Gavancho, Assoc. Pst.; Dcn. Martin Horta; Dcn. Manuel A. Ruiz; Dcn. David Dutko; Dcn. Emil Vasek; CRP Stds.: 68

St. Agnes School - (Grades PreK-8) 1501 Chicago Rd., Chicago Heights, IL 60411 t) 708-709-2333 admin@saintagnes.us Matthew T. Lungaro, Prin.; Stds.: 199

CICERO

St. Anthony of Padua - 1510 S. 49th Ct., Cicero, IL 60804 t) 708-652-0231 stanthony-49th@archchicago.org Rev. Sergio Solis, Pst.; Dcn. Manuel Orozco; Rev. Alejandro Garrido, In Res.;

St. Anthony Center -

St. Mary Frances of the Five Wounds - 1428 S. 59th Ct., Cicero, IL 60804 t) 708-656-8632 (CRP); 708-652-2140 stfrances-rome@archchicago.org www.sfr-church.org/ Rev. Radoslaw Jaszczuk, CSSR, Pst.; Dcn. Jesus Blanco; Dcn. Hans P. Goeckner; Dcn. Benjamin Villalobos; CRP Stds.: 25

St. Frances of Rome School - -8) 1401 S. Austin Blvd., Cicero, IL 60804 t) 708-652-2277 office@sfr-school.org www.sfr-school.org Phillip Jackson, Prin.; Stds.: 194

Mary, Queen of Heaven - Merged Jul 2022 Merged with Our Lady of the Mount-Cicero to form Our Lady, the Mystical Rose Parish.

Our Lady of Charity - Merged Jul 2022 Merged with St. Mary of Czestochowa to form Our Lady of Czestochowa and Charity Parish.

Our Lady of Czestochowa and Charity Parish - 3010 S. 48th Ct., Cicero, IL 60804 t) 708-652-0948 stmary-czestochowa@archchicago.org stmczcicero.com/ Rev. Waldemar Latkowski, CSSR, Pst.; Rev. Marian Furca, C.Ss.R., Assoc. Pst.; Dcn. Maximino Montalvo; CRP Stds.: 104

Our Lady of Charity School - -8) 3620 57th Ct., Cicero, IL 60804 t) 708-652-0262 office@olc-school.org www.olc-school.org Dr. Frank Zarate Jr., Prin.; Stds.: 229

Our Lady, the Mystical Rose Parish - 2414 S. 61st Ave., Cicero, IL 60804 t) 708-652-2791 ol-mount@archchicago.org ourladyofthemountparish.org/ Most Rev. Kevin M. Birmingham, Admin.; Rev. Sergio De la Torre Carrillo, Assoc. Pst.; Rev. Jesus Romero-Galan, Assoc. Pst.; Dcn. Benito Gallegos; Dcn. Jesus J. Garcia; Dcn. Martin Encisco;

COUNTRY CLUB HILLS

St. Emeric - Merged Jul 2022 Merged with St. Joseph and St. Anne to form St. John Neumann.

CRESTWOOD

Incarnation and St. Terrence Parish - 5757 W. 127th St., Crestwood, IL 60418-2402 t) 708-388-4004 (CRP); 708-597-3180 incarnation@archchicago.org incparish.com Rev. Arkadiusz Falana, Pst.; Rev. Pawel Komperda, Assoc. Pst.; Dcn. James Langwell; Kathryn L. McNicholas, DRE; CRP Stds.: 215

DEERFIELD

Holy Cross - 724 Elder Ln., Deerfield, IL 60015 t) 847-945-0430 holycross-elder@archchicago.org holycrossparish.net/ Rev. Richard J. LoBianco, Pst.; Rev. James F. Blazek, Assoc. Pst.; Dcn. Jeremy N. Carter; Dcn. Kevin Garvey; Rev. Kenneth J. Fischer, In Res.; CRP Stds.: 146

DES PLAINES

St. Mary - Merged Jul 2022 Merged with St. Stephen Protomartyr to form Mary, Mother of Martyrs.

Mary, Mother of Martyrs - 1880 Ash St., Des Plaines, IL 60018 t) 847-824-2026; 847-297-3844 (CRP) ststephen@sbcglobal.net www.ststephen-desplaines.org Rev. Manuel Arcila, Pst.; Rev. Gerald K. O'Reilly, Assoc. Pst.; Dcn. Jose Figueroa; Dcn. James J. O'Leary; Dcn. William H. Warmouth; Dcn. Conrad Wojnar; CRP Stds.: 140

St. Paul Chong Hasang - 725 Dursey Ln., Des Plaines, IL 60016 t) 847-699-6334 stpaul-mission@archchicago.org Rev. Esequiel Sanchez, Admin.;

St. Zachary - 567 W. Algonquin Rd., Des Plaines, IL 60016 t) 847-956-1175 (CRP); 847-956-7020 stzachary@archchicago.org www.saintzachary.org/ Rev. Piotr Rapcia, Pst.; Dcn. David Brezinski; Dcn. John J. Smith; Rev. Lawrence F. Springer, In Res.; CRP Stds.: 138

St. Zachary School - -8) t) 847-437-4022 principal@saintzachary.org Darlene Potenza, Prin.; Stds.: 131

ELK GROVE VILLAGE

Our Lady of the Blessed Sacrament - 680 Elk Grove Blvd., Elk Grove Village, IL 60007 t) 847-593-8938 (CRP); 847-437-0403 olbscares@archchicago.org www.qotr.org/ Rev. Dan Ignatius Folwaczny, Pst.; Rev. Loius M. Mboe, Assoc. Pst.; Dcn. Jerrold S. Szostak; CRP Stds.: 189

Queen of the Rosary School - -8) 690 Elk Grove Blvd., Elk Grove Village, IL 60007 t) 847-437-3322 kmcginn@qrcougars.org Kathleen McGinn, Prin.; Stds.: 254

ELMWOOD PARK

St. Mother Theodore Guerin - 3020 N. 76th Ct., Elmwood Park, IL 60707 t) 708-453-2555 stguerinparish.org/ Rev. Paul D. Cao, Pst.; Rev. Moises Navarro, Assoc. Pst.; Dcn. Michael DeLarco; Dcn. Rolando J. Merced; Dcn. Miguel A. Negron; Rev. Kenneth D. Ekekwe, In Res.; Most Rev. Jeffrey S. Grob, In Res.; Rev. Filbert Ngwila, In Res.; CRP Stds.: 147

St. Celestine School - -8) 3017 N. 77th Ave., Elmwood Park, IL 60707 t) 708-453-8234 jjrocchi@stcelestineschool.org Sheila Klich, Prin.; Stds.: 387

EVANSTON

St. Joan of Arc - Merged Jul 2022 Merged with St. Athanasius to form St. John Newman.

St. John Newman - 1615 Lincoln St., Evanston, IL 60201 t) 847-328-1430 stathanasius@archchicago.org www.saintasparish.org/ Rev. Kenneth Anderson, Pst.; Rev. Paul G. Stemn, Assoc. Pst.; Margaret Waldron, DRE; CRP Stds.: 108

St. Athanasius School - -8) 2510 Ashland Ave., Evanston, IL 60201 t) 847-864-2650 jberg@saintas.net Kelly M Foyle, Prin.; Stds.: 272

St. John XXIII - 806 Ridge Ave., Evanston, IL 60202 t) 847-864-1185 stnicholas@archchicago.org Rev. Koudjo K Lokpo, MCCJ, Pst.; Rev. Jose Manuel Sanchez Ortiz, MCCJ, Assoc. Pst.; Dcn. Ramon Navarro; Dcn. Jaime Rojas; CRP Stds.: 230

Pope John XXIII - 1120 Washington, Evanston, IL 60202 t) 847-475-5678 gail.hulse@popejohn23.org Dr. Molly Cinnamon, Prin.; Stds.: 244

St. Mary - Merged Jul 2022 Merged with St. Nicholas to form St. John XXIII.

Syro-Malankara Catholic Mission of the Archdiocese of Chicago - 1208 Ashland St., Evanston, IL 60202 t) 847-332-1794

St. Mary's Malankara Catholic Church - Rev. Babu Madathilpambil-Thomas, Dir.; Rev. Joseph Kandathikudy, In Res.;

EVERGREEN PARK

St. Bernadette - Merged Jul 2022 Merged with Queen of Martyrs to form Queen of Martyrs and St. Bernadette Parish.

Most Holy Redeemer - 9525 S. Lawndale Ave., Evergreen Park, IL 60805 t) 708-346-8185 (CRP); 708-425-5354 holyredeemer@archchicago.org www.mostholyredeemer.org/ Rev. James M. Hyland, Pst.; Rev. Paul Guzman, Assoc. Pst.; Dcn. Mark Phelan; Rev. Albert R. Adamich, Senior Priest;

Most Holy Redeemer School - -8) 9536 S. Millard Ave., Evergreen Park, IL 60805 t) 708-422-8280 nharmening@mhrschool.com Nancy A. Harmening, Prin.; Stds.: 326

Queen of Martyrs and St. Bernadette Parish - 10233 S. Central Park Ave., Evergreen Park, IL 60805-3799 t) 708-422-1647 (CRP); 708-428-8110 queen-martyrs@archchicago.org www.qmstbparish.org Rev. Benedykt M. Pazdan, Pst.; Rev. Richie Ortiz, Assoc. Pst.; Dcn. Robert J. Landuyt; Rev. Mathieu Mboudou Abina, In Res.; CRP Stds.: 129

Queen of Martyrs School - -8) 3550 W. 103rd St., Chicago, IL 60655 t) 708-422-1540 www.qmschool.com/ Michael B Johnson, Prin.; Stds.: 241

FLOSSMOOR

St. Veronica - 1131 Douglas Ave., Flossmoor, IL 60422 t) 708-799-5400 infantjesus@archchicago.org www.ijpparish.org/ Rev. Krzysztof Paluch, Pst.; Rev. Ronald L. Kondziolka, Assoc. Pst.; CRP Stds.: 72

Infant Jesus of Prague School - -8) 1101 Douglas Ave., Flossmoor, IL 60422 t) 708-799-5200 pdull@ijpschool.org Charlotte Kelly, Prin.; Stds.: 226

FRANKLIN PARK

St. Gertrude - 9613 Schiller Blvd., Franklin Park, IL 60131 t) 847-455-1100 stgertrude-schiller@archchicago.org www.gertrudeonline.com/ Rev. Eryk Czarnecki (Poland), Pst.; Rev. Krzysztof T. Pankanin (Poland), Assoc. Pst.; Rev. Alfred P. Corbo, Pastor Emer.; Dcn. Robert Murphy; CRP Stds.: 146

GLENVIEW

St. Catherine Laboure - 3535 Thornwood Ave., Glenview, IL 60026 t) 847-729-1414 stcatherine-laboure@archchicago.org www.sclparish.org/ Rev. Isaac Lara, Pst.; Sr. Dcn. Raymond Gavin; Dcn. Michael Bretz; Dcn. Rodrigo A. Ranola; CRP Stds.: 117

St. Catherine Laboure School - -8) 3425 Thornwood Ave., Glenview, IL 60026 t) 847-724-2240 administrator@sclschool-glenview.org Jodi Reuter, Prin.; Stds.: 184

Our Lady of Perpetual Help - 1775 Grove St., Glenview, IL 60025 t) 847-998-5289 (CRP); 847-729-1525 ol-help@archchicago.org www.olphglenview.org/ Rev. Jeremiah M. Boland, Pst.; Rev. Larry Basbas, Assoc. Pst.; Rev. Patrick Kizza, Assoc. Pst.; Rev. Thomas E. Hickey, Pastor Emer.; Dcn. Weiland Christopher; Dcn. David J. Kalina; Dcn. James Revord; Rev. James L. Barrett, In Res.; CRP Stds.: 483

Our Lady of Perpetual Help School - -8) 1123 Church St., Glenview, IL 60025 t) 847-724-6990 amills@olph-il.org Amy Mills, Prin.; Stds.: 797

GRAYSLAKE

St. Gilbert - 301 E. Belvidere Rd., Grayslake, IL 60030 t) 847-223-3071 (CRP); 847-223-4731 stgilbert@archchicago.org www.stgilbert.org/ Rev. John P. Chrzan, Pst.; Rev. Pawel Adamus, Assoc. Pst.; Rev. Eugene J. Nowak, Pastor Emer.; Dcn. Alan Biegel; Dcn. Brian R. Fisher; Dcn. Richard J. Globis; Dcn. Mark Plaiss; Sr. Donna Schmitt, O.S.F., DRE; CRP Stds.: 288

St. Gilbert School - -8) 231 E. Belvidere Rd., Grayslake, IL 60030 t) 847-223-8600 school.office@stgilbertschool.org Kristine A Buckley, Prin.;

GURNEE

St. Paul the Apostle - 6401 Gages Lake Rd., Gurnee, IL 60031 t) 847-816-8677 (CRP); 847-918-0600 stpaul-apostle@archchicago.org Rev. Krzysztof D. Ciaston, Pst.; Rev. Joseph C. Curtis, Assoc. Pst.; Dcn. Andrew J. Baker; Dcn. Brent E. Bertke; Dcn. Robert Birck; Dcn. Michael Penich Jr.; Dcn. Roderick Reyes; Dcn. Ivan Siap; CRP Stds.: 426

HANOVER PARK

St. Ansgar - 2040 Laurel Ave., Hanover Park, IL 60133 t) 630-837-5553 stansgar@archchicago.org stansgar.weebly.com/ Rev. Eduardo Garcia-Ferrer, Pst.; Rev. Mario H. Pelayo Corona, Assoc. Pst.; Dcn. Alberto Contreras; Dcn. Pedro Benitez; CRP Stds.: 239

HARVEY

Lord of Mercy Parish - 15746 Union Ave., Harvey, IL 60426 t) 708-333-0184 stjohn-baptist@archchicago.org Rev. Gary M. Graf, Admin.; Dcn. Thomas R. Carvlin;

HARWOOD HEIGHTS-NORRIDGE

St. Rosalie - Merged Jul 2022 Merged with St. Monica to form St. Monica and St. Rosalie Parish.

HAZEL CREST

St. Anne - Merged Jul 2022 Merged with St. Joseph and St. Emeric to form St. John Neumann.

HICKORY HILLS

St. Patricia - 9050 S. 86th Ave., Hickory Hills, IL 60457 t) 708-599-1221 (CRP); 708-598-5222 stpatricia@archchicago.org Rev. Michael G. Meany, Pst.; Rev. Christopher Kituli, Assoc. Pst.; Dcn. Charles Keegan; Dcn. Norbert Weitendorf; CRP Stds.: 211

St. Patricia School - (Grades PreK-8) 9000 S. 86th Ave., Hickory Hills, IL 60457 t) 708-598-8200 jnowinski@stpatriciaparish.com Erick R Passarelli, Prin.; Stds.: 195

HIGHLAND PARK

Christ Our Hope Parish - 770 Deerfield Rd., Highland Park, IL 60035 t) 847-433-2224 (CRP); 847-433-0130 ic-greenbay@archchicago.org www.icparish.org/ Rev. Hernan Cuevas-Contreras, Pst.; Dcn. Louis Vignocchi; Dcn. Luis R. Lara; Mary Nelson, Pst. Assoc.; CRP Stds.: 100

HIGHWOOD

St. James - Merged Jul 2022 Merged with Immaculate Conception, Highland Park to form Christ Our Hope Parish.

HILLSIDE

Queen of All Nations - 4940 Washington St., Hillside, IL 60162 t) 708-449-8430; 708-449-1558 (CRP) stdomitilla@archchicago.org www.stdomitilla.org/ Rev. Julio Lam, Pst.; Dcn. Victor Chairez; Dcn. Sergio Lopez; CRP Stds.: 138

HOFFMAN ESTATES

St. Hubert - 729 Grand Canyon St., Hoffman Estates, IL 60169 t) 847-855-7703 (CRP); 847-885-7700 sthubert@archchicago.org sainthubert.org/ Rev. Michael G. Scherschel, Pst.; Dcn. Steven Baldasti; Dcn. Lawrence J. Smith; Dcn. Allen Tatara; Michael Keenan, DRE; CRP Stds.: 336

St. Hubert School - -8) 255 Flagstaff Ln., Hoffman Estates, IL 60169 t) 847-885-7702 office@sthubertschool.org Julie L. Martin, Prin.; Stds.: 198

HOMEWOOD

St. John Neumann - 17951 Dixie Hwy., Homewood, IL 60430 t) 708-798-6311 (CRP); 708-798-0622 stjoseph-dixie@archchicago.org www.posjhomewood.org/ Rev. Edmond Aristil, C.S.Sp., Pst.; Rev. Ralph H. Zwirn, Assoc. Pst.; Dcn. Gary Miarka; Dcn. George Maddock; CRP Stds.: 86

INDIAN CREEK

St. Mary of Vernon - 236 U.S. Hwy. 45, Indian Creek, IL 60061 t) 847-362-0653 (CRP); 847-362-1005 stmary-vernon@archchicago.org maryofvernon.org/ Rev. Ignatius I. Anaele, Pst.; Rev. Przemyslaw Tomczyk, Assoc. Pst.; Dcn. John Glenn; Dcn. Daniel Moore; Dcn. Gerald Nora; Dcn. Philip Pagnotta Jr.; Dcn. James Wogan; Dcn. Mark R. Zwolski; CRP Stds.: 284

INGLESIDE

Our Lady of the Lakes - 36455 N. Wilson Rd., Ingleside, IL 60041 t) 847-587-2301 (CRP); 847-587-2251 stbedemail@stbedechurch.org Rev. George Koeune, Pst.; Rev. Michael Grzesik, Assoc. Pst.; Dcn. David Bresemann; Dcn. Lawrence Spohr; Dcn. Gregory Zeifert; Mark Buckley, DRE;

St. Bede School - -8) 36399 N. Wilson Rd., Ingleside, IL 60041 t) 847-587-5541 pstrang@stbedeschool.com David Wieters, Prin.; Stds.: 211

St. Peter - 557 W. Lake St., Antioch, IL 60002

St. Bede - parishoffice@ollonline.org ourladyofthelakesparish.org

INVERNESS

Holy Family - 2515 W. Palatine Rd., Inverness, IL 60067 t) 847-359-0042 holyfamily-palatine@archchicago.org www.holyfamilyparish.org/ Rev. Terence M. Keehan, Pst.; Rev. Medard P. Laz, Pastor Emer.; Dcn. Dennis G. Brown; Marsha Adamczyk, Pst. Assoc.; CRP Stds.: 441

Holy Family Catholic Academy - -8) t) 847-907-3452 info@holyfamilycatholicacademy.net Catherine A. O'Brien, Prin.; Stds.: 428

LA GRANGE

St. Cletus - 600 W. 55th St., La Grange, IL 60525 t) 708-352-2383 (CRP); 708-352-6209 stcletus@archchicago.org stcletusparish.com/ Rev. Elmer Romero, Pst.; Rev. Michael Novick, Assoc. Pst.; Dcn. Ramon Cazales; CRP Stds.: 380

St. Cletus School - -8) 700 W. 55th St., La Grange, IL 60525 t) 708-352-4820 Gregory Porod, Prin.; Stds.: 327

St. Francis Xavier - 124 N. Spring Ave., La Grange, IL 60525 t) 708-352-4555 (CRP); 708-352-0168 stfrancisxavier-spring@archchicago.org www.sfxlg.org/ Rev. William Tkachuk, Pst.; Rev. Richard Milek, Assoc. Pst.; Dcn. Andrew Allison; Dcn. Philip Gianatasio; CRP Stds.: 531

St. Francis Xavier School - -8) 145 N. Waiola Ave., La Grange, IL 60525 t) 708-352-2175 sfxmain@sfxlg.org Sharon Garcia, Prin.; Stds.: 448

LAKE FOREST

St. Mary - 175 E. Illinois Rd., Lake Forest, IL 60045 t) 847-234-0090 (CRP); 847-234-0205 stmary-illinois@archchicago.org www.churchofstmary.org/ Rev. Michael A. Nacius, Pst.; Rev. Radley Alcantara, Assoc. Pst.; Dcn. John Herrmann; Dcn. Robert J. Thomas; Loretta Nugent, Pst. Assoc.; CRP Stds.: 290

St. Mary School - -8) 185 E. Illinois Rd., Lake Forest, IL 60045 t) 847-234-0371 Julie Brua, Prin.; Stds.: 417

St. Patrick - 991 S. Waukegan Rd., Lake Forest, IL 60045 t) 847-234-2179 (CRP); 847-234-1401 stpatrick-waukegan@archchicago.org Rev. Msgr. Robert J. Dempsey, Pst.; Dcn. Frank DeFrank; Dcn. Raymond C. Loman; CRP Stds.: 180

LAKE VILLA

Prince of Peace - 135 S. Milwaukee Ave., Lake Villa, IL 60046 t) 847-356-5850 (CRP); 847-356-7915 princeofpeace@archchicago.org www.princeofpeacelv.org/ Rev. Gerald G. Walsh, Pst.; Rev. John G. Hetland, Assoc. Pst.; Dcn. James Even; Dcn. Timothy Leonard; Dcn. James R. Minor; Dcn. John R. Ruskin; Dcn. Christopher Savage; Dcn. Mark M. Weiss; CRP Stds.: 154

Prince of Peace School - -8) t) 847-356-6111 Erica J Whitmore, Prin.; Stds.: 256

LAKE ZURICH

St. Francis de Sales - 135 S. Buesching Rd., Lake Zurich, IL 60047 t) 847-726-4850 (CRP); 847-438-6622 stfrancisdesales-main@archchicago.org www.stfrancislzparish.org/ Rev. James E. Merold, Admin.; Dcn. Robert Arvidson; Dcn. George Flaherty; CRP Stds.: 515

St. Francis de Sales School - -8) 11 S. Buesching Rd., Lake Zurich, IL 60047 t) 847-438-7921 schoolinfo@stfrancislz.org Mary C Keller, Prin.; Stds.: 324

LANSING

All Souls Parish - 3010 Ridge Rd., Lansing, IL 60438 t) 708-895-5970 (CRP); 708-895-6700 stann-ridge@archchicago.org www.allsoulscatholicparish.org/ Rev. Mark Kalema, Pst.; Rev. Joseph Kaye, In Res.; CRP Stds.: 141

Convent - 21903 Orion St., Sauk Village, IL 60411

LEMONT

St. Alphonsus and St. Patrick Parish - 210 E. Logan, Lemont, IL 60439 t) 630-257-2371 (CRP); 630-257-2414 stalphonsus-logan@archchicago.org www.st-als.org/ Rev. Brian Ardagh, Pst.; Rev. Collins Kisaka Nyache, Assoc. Pst.; Rev. Richard J. Shannon, Pastor Emer.; Dcn. Timothy F. Callahan; Dcn. William Lubben; Dcn. Terrance McGuire; Dcn. Michael P. O'Neill; Dcn. Lawrence A. Oskielunas; Dcn. Daniel Rittenhouse; Dcn. Joseph Winblad; Kevin Cody, DRE; CRP Stds.: 255

St. Alphonsus-St. Patrick Consolidated - (Grades K-8) 20 W. 145 Davey Rd., Lemont, IL 60439 t) 630-783-2220 schooloffice@stals-stpats.org www.stals-stpats.org/ Michelle Augustyn-Napier, Prin.; Stds.: 219

Blessed Jurgis Matulaitis Mission - 14915-127th St., Unit 101, Lemont, IL 60439 t) 630-257-5613 blessedjurgis-mission@archchicago.org Rev. Vaidas Lukosevicius, S.J., Dir.;

SS. Cyril and Methodius - 608 Sobieski St., Lemont, IL 60439 t) 630-257-9314 (CRP); 630-257-2776 sscm@archchicago.org www.stcyril.org/ Rev. Waldemar Stawiarski, Pst.; Rev. Thomas R. Koys, Assoc. Pst.; CRP Stds.: 366

SS. Cyril and Methodius School - -8) 607 Sobieski St., Lemont, IL 60439 t) 630-257-6488 shirleyt@stcyril.org Shirley A. Tkachuk, Prin.; Stds.: 217

St. James at Sag Bridge Mission - 10600 S. Archer Ave., Lemont, IL 60439-9344 t) 630-257-7000 stjames-archer@archchicago.org Rev. Waldemar Stawiarski, Dir.;

Slovenian Catholic Mission - 14246 Main St., Lemont, IL 60439-0608; Mailing: P.O. Box 608, Lemont, IL 60439-0608 t) 630-257-2068 Rev. Metod Ogorevc, O.F.M., Pst.; Dcn. John Vidmar;

LIBERTYVILLE

St. Joseph - 121 E. Maple Ave., Libertyville, IL 60048 t) 847-362-2073 stjoseph-maple@archchicago.org www.stjoseph-libertyville.org/ Rev. John Trout, S.P.S., Pst.; Rev. Martin Luboyera, Assoc. Pst.; Rev. Jesus Torres-Fuentes, Assoc. Pst.; Rev. John E. Hennessey, Pastor Emer.; Dcn. Daniel E. Coughlin; Dcn. George Kashmar; Dcn. Dennis Mudd Sr.; David Retseck, Pst. Assoc.; CRP Stds.: 595

St. Joseph School - -8) 221 Park Pl., Libertyville, IL 60048 t) 847-362-0730 aphoenix@sjslibertyville.org Elizabeth A Hein, Prin.; Stds.: 402

MATTESON

St. Lawrence O'Toole - Merged Jul 2022 Merged with Infant Jesus of Prague and St. Irenaeus to form St. Veronica Parish.

MELROSE PARK

St. Charles Borromeo - 1637 N. 37th Ave., Melrose Park, IL 60160 t) 708-343-7646 stcharles@archchicago.org www.scbparish.com/ Rev. Jesus Ramirez Cerda, C.S., Pst.; Rev. Van S Nguyen, CS, Assoc. Pst.; Dcn. Freddy Palacios;

Our Lady of Mount Carmel - 1101 N. 23rd Ave., Melrose Park, IL 60160 t) 708-344-4140 ol-mtcarmel-23rd@archchicago.org olmcparish.org/ Rev. Leandro Fossa, CS, Pst.; Rev. Adriano Barbiero, Assoc. Pst.; Dcn. John P. Battisto; Rev. Colon Jackson, In Res.; Modesta Martinez, DRE; CRP Stds.: 355

Shrine of Our Lady of Mt. Carmel -

Sacred Heart and St. Eulalia - 819 N. 16th Ave., Melrose Park, IL 60160 t) 708-344-0757 parish@shsparish.org shsparish.org/ Rev. Francisco I. Ortega Munoz, Pst.; Rev. Tomasz Wajdzik, Assoc. Pst.; Rev. Erwin J. Friedl, Pastor Emer.; Dcn. Michael K. Barnish; Dcn. Giulio Camerini; Dcn. Gabriel Nevarez; Dcn. Eduardo Rodriguez; Dcn. Dwight Sullivan; CRP Stds.: 91

Sacred Heart School - 815 N. 16th Ave., Melrose Park, IL 60160 t) 708-681-0240 school@shsmelrosepark.com Barbara J. Ciconte, Prin.;

Convent - 1503 W. Rice St., Melrose Park, IL 60160

MIDLOTHIAN

St. Augustine Parish - 4130 W. 147th St., Midlothian, IL 60445 t) 708-388-4040 (CRP); 708-388-8190 stchristopher@archchicago.org www.stchrisparish.net/ Rev. Robinson Ortiz, Pst.; CRP Stds.: 124

St. Christopher School - -8) 14611 S. Keeler Ave., Midlothian, IL 60445 t) 708-385-8776 info@stchrisschool.org Nicole M Tzoumas, Prin.; Stds.: 243

MT. PROSPECT

St. Cecilia - 700 S. Meier Rd., Mt. Prospect, IL 60056 t) 847-437-6310 (CRP); 847-437-6208 stcecilia@archchicago.org stceciliamtprospect.com/ Rev. Oswaldo Guillen, S.D.B. (Venezuela), Pst.; Rev. Daniel J. Brady, Pastor Emer.; Dcn. Leonardo Pena; Dcn. Valdemar Silva; CRP Stds.: 115

St. Emily - 1400 E. Central Rd., #101, Mt. Prospect, IL 60056 t) 847-299-5865 (CRP); 847-824-5049 stemily@archchicago.org www.stemily.org/ Rev. James Presta, Pst.; Rev. Henry D Lyon, Assoc. Pst.; Dcn. Pavel Jurkulak; Dcn. David J. Schuster; Rev. John W. Roller, In Res.; Gail Goleas, Pst. Assoc.; Sr. M. Danielle Jacob, Pst. Assoc.; CRP Stds.: 268

St. Emily School - -8) 1400 E. Central Rd., Mt.

Prospect, IL 60056 t) 847-296-3490 schoolinfo@stemily.org Karen Booth, Prin.; Stds.: 259

St. Raymond de Penafort - 301 S. I Oka St., Mt. Prospect, IL 60056 t) 847-253-8600 x150 (CRP); 847-253-8600 straymond@archchicago.org Rev. W. Scott Hebden, Pst.; Rev. Rodlin Rodrigue, Assoc. Pst.; Dcn. David Babczak; Dcn. John Lorbach; CRP Stds.: 311

St. Raymond de Penafort School - -8) 300 S. Elmhurst Ave., Mt. Prospect, IL 60056 t) 847-253-8555 maryeileen.ward@st-raymond.org Mary Eileen Ward, Prin.;

St. Thomas Becket - 1321 Burning Bush Ln., Mt. Prospect, IL 60056 t) 847-296-9051 (CRP); 847-827-9220 stthomas-becket@archchicago.org www.stthomasbecketmp.org/ Rev. Krzysztof A. Kulig, Pst.; Rev. John W. Roller, Pastor Emer.;

MUNDELEIN

Santa Maria Del Popolo - 116 N. Lake St., Mundelein, IL 60060 t) 847-990-6865 (CRP); 847-949-8300 samtamariadelpopolo@archchicago.org www.santamariadelpopolomundelein.com/ Rev. Miguel Angel Martinez, Pst.; Rev. Christopher Landfried, Assoc. Pst.; Rev. James W. Kinn, Pastor Emer.; Sr. Dcn. David D. Auld; Dcn. Raphael Romani; Dcn. Felipe Vasquez; CRP Stds.: 292

Convent - 133 N. Lincoln Ave., Mundelein, IL 60060 t) 847-566-7343

St. Mary of the Annunciation - 22333 W. Erhart Rd., Mundelein, IL 60060 t) 847-223-0010 stmary-erhart@archchicago.org stmaryfc.org/ Rev. Jerome J. Jacob, Pst.; Rev. Daniel F. Costello, Assoc. Pst.; Dcn. Miguel Alandy; Dcn. Gary L. Kupsak; Dcn. Robert A. Poletto; Dcn. Alan Sedivy; CRP Stds.: 135

Frassati Catholic Academy-Mundelein Campus - (Grades PreK-5) 22277 W. Erhart Rd., Mundelein, IL 60060 t) 847-223-4021 tkleckner@frassaticatholicacademy.org Member of Catholic Consortium of Lake County. Tammy A. Kleckner, Prin.; Stds.: 241

Our Lady of Siluva Lithuanian Mission - 116 N. Lake St., Mundelein, IL 60060; Mailing: 6812 S. Washtenaw, Chicago, IL 60629 t) 773-776-4600 Rev. Jaunius Kelpsas (Lithuania), Dir.;

NILES

All Saints Parish - 8149 Golf Rd., Niles, IL 60714 t) 847-966-1180 (CRP); 847-967-1060 stisaac@archchicago.org Rev. Thomas F. Baldonieri, Pst.; Rev. Anthony B Castello, SFX, Assoc. Pst.; Rev. Carlos P. Pereira, S.F.X., Assoc. Pst.; Dcn. Leke Brisku; Dcn. Paul Stanton; Dcn. Joseph Tony R. Valdez; Delores Stanton, DRE;

The Shrine of All Saints -

St. John Brebeuf - 8307 N. Harlem Ave., Niles, IL 60714 t) 847-966-3269 (CRP); 847-966-8145 stjohn-brebeuf@archchicago.org www.sjbrebeuf.org/ Rev. Zdzislaw J. Torba, Pst.; Rev. Slawomir Kurc, Assoc. Pst.; Rev. Robert S. Banzin, Pastor Emer.; Dcn. Andrew J. Beierwaltes; Dcn. Lawrence Skaja; Dcn. Krzysztof Slowikowski; CRP Stds.: 166

St. John Brebeuf School - -8) 8301 Harlem Ave., Niles, IL 60714 t) 847-966-3266 office@sjbschool.org Mary Maloney, Prin.; Stds.: 244

Our Lady of Ransom - 8624 W. Normal, Niles, IL 60714 t) 847-696-2994 (CRP); 847-823-2550 ol-ransom@archchicago.org Rev. Matthew Bozovsky, Pst.; Rev. Alejandro Jesus Marca Mansilla, O.C.D., Assoc. Pst.; Rev. John S. Szmyd, Assoc. Pst.; Dcn. Francisco Foti; Dcn. Keith F. Strohm; CRP Stds.: 72

NORRIDGE

Divine Savior - Merged Jul 2022 Merged with St. Edward and OL Mother of the Church to form Queen of Peace Parish.

NORTHBROOK

St. Norbert and Our Lady of the Brook Parish - 1809 Walters Ave., Northbrook, IL 60062 t) 847-272-3086 (CRP); 847-272-7090 parishoffice@northbrookcatholic.church Rev. Christopher M. Gustafson, Pst.; Rev. Ismael Garcia, Assoc. Pst.; Rev. Laurence J. Dunn, In Res.; Sr. Dcn. Peery Duderstadt; Dcn. James Fruge; CRP Stds.: 335

St. Norbert School - -8) 1817 Walters Ave., Northbrook, IL 60062 t) 847-272-0051 glawler@stnorbertschool.org Margaret L Hoody, Prin.; Stds.: 174

NORTHLAKE

St. John Vianney, Cure of Ars - 46 N. Wolf Rd., Northlake, IL 60164 t) 708-562-1466 x120 (CRP); 708-562-0500 stjohn-vianney@archchicago.org sjv-parish.org/ Rev. Luke E. Winkelmann, Pst.; Rev. Hugo Morales, Assoc. Pst.; Rev. Phillip T. Owen, Assoc. Pst.; Dcn. Thomas G. Imbordino; Dcn. James M. Sinacore;

St. John Vianney, Cure of Ars School - -8) 27 N. Lavergne Ave., Northlake, IL 60164 info@sjvsonline.org Heidi Reith, Prin.; Stds.: 209

OAK FOREST

St. Damian - 5250 W. 155th St., Oak Forest, IL 60452 t) 708-687-1370 stdamian@archchicago.org www.stdamianchurch.org/ Rev. Joseph T. Noonan, Pst.; Rev. Michael Olson, Assoc. Pst.; Dcn. Thomas Hipelius; Dcn. Richard Korepanow; Dcn. Thomas J. Ruzevich; Dcn. William Stearns; Mary Jo Landuyt, DRE; CRP Stds.: 190

St. Damian School - -8) 5300 W. 155th St., Oak Forest, IL 60452 t) 708-687-4230 www.stdamianschool.org/ Jennifer Jermano Miller, Prin.; Stds.: 334

OAK LAWN

St. Catherine of Alexandria - 4100 W. 107th St., Oak Lawn, IL 60453 t) 708-425-5747 (CRP); 708-425-2850 stcatherine-107th@archchicago.org www.parish.scaoaklawn.org/ Rev. Dennis A. Ziomek, Pst.; Rev. Fred Pesek Jr., Assoc. Pst.; CRP Stds.: 76

St. Catherine of Alexandria School - -8) 10621 S. Kedvale Ave., Oak Lawn, IL 60453 t) 708-425-5547 www.scaoaklawn.org/ Kristine A. Owens, Prin.; Stds.: 490

St. Gerald - 9310 S. 55th Ct., Oak Lawn, IL 60453 t) 708-423-0458 (CRP); 708-422-0234 stgerald@archchicago.org stgerald.com/ Rev. Robert M. Pajor, Pst.; Rev. Stanley Stuglik, Assoc. Pst.; Rev. William Browne (Jamaica), In Res.; CRP Stds.: 441

St. Gerald School - -8) 9320 S. 55th Ct., Oak Lawn, IL 60453 t) 708-422-0121 school@stgerald.com Thesesa Fiscella, Prin.; Stds.: 310

Our Lady at St. Germaine - 9711 S. Kolin Ave., Oak Lawn, IL 60453 t) 708-636-5060 ourladystgermaine@archchicago.org www.ourladyatstgermaine.org/ Rev. Thomas S. Cabala, Pst.; Rev. George Velloorattil, Assoc. Pst.; Dcn. Joseph Gonzalez; Dcn. John L. Malone; Dcn. Frank Mamolella; CRP Stds.: 134

St. Germaine School - -8) 9735 S. Kolin Ave., Oak Lawn, IL 60453 t) 708-425-6063 mrkreedy@stgol.org Philip J O'Rourke, Prin.; Stds.: 191

Our Lady of the Ridge and St. Linus Parish - 10300 S. Lawler Ave., Oak Lawn, IL 60453 t) 708-636-4373 (CRP); 708-422-2400 stlinus@archchicago.org Rev. Mark J. Walter, Pst.; Rev. Ryan Brady, Assoc. Pst.; Rev. Gene F. Smith, Senior Priest; Dcn. Edwin Hill; Dcn. John Orzechowski; Cheryl A. Antos, DRE; CRP Stds.: 216

St. Linus School - -8) 10400 S. Lawler Ave., Oak Lawn, IL 60453 t) 708-425-1656 mhayes@stlinusschool.org Margaret Hayes, Prin.; Stds.: 360

OAK PARK

Ascension and St. Edmund Parish - 808 S. East Ave., Oak Park, IL 60304 t) 708-848-3099 (CRP); 708-848-2703 ascension-east@archchicago.org www.ascensionoakpark.com/ Rev. Joseph Anthony Pillai, C.Ss.R., Pst.; Mary Meek, Pst. Assoc.; Rev. John P. Lucas, In Res.; CRP Stds.: 245

Ascension School - -8) 601 Van Buren, Oak Park, IL 60304 t) 708-386-7282 school@ascensionoakpark.com Maureen O'Neill Nielsen, Prin.; Stds.: 376

St. Catherine of Siena-St. Lucy - Merged Jul 2022 Merged with St. Giles to form St. Catherine of Siena-St. Lucy and St. Giles Parish.

St. Catherine of Siena-St. Lucy and St. Giles Parish - 1025 Columbian Ave., Oak Park, IL 60302 t) 708-383-4185 (CRP); 708-383-3430 stgiles@archchicago.org www.stgilesparish.org/ Rev. Carl Morello, Pst.; Rev. Edward P. Salmon, Sr. Priest; Dcn. John A. Henricks; Dcn. John Walters;

St. Catherine of Siena-St. Lucy School - -8) 27 Washington Blvd., Oak Park, IL 60302 t) 708-386-5286 info@catherinelucy.org www.catherinelucy.org/ Sharon Leamy, Prin.; Stds.: 175

St. Giles School - -8) 1034 Linden Ave., Oak Park, IL 60302 t) 708-383-6279 office@stgilesschool.org Meg Bigane, Prin.; Stds.: 355

St. Edmund - Merged Jul 2022 Merged with Ascension to form Ascension and St. Edmund Parish.

OLD MILL CREEK

St. Raphael the Archangel - 40000 N. U.S. Hwy. 45, Old Mill Creek, IL 60046 t) 847-395-3474 rectory@straphaelcatholic.org www.straphaelcatholic.org Rev. Matthew Kowalski, O.S.B., Pst.; Dcn. Gregory Webster; CRP Stds.: 111

ORLAND HILLS

St. Elizabeth Seton - 9300 W. 167th St., Orland Hills, IL 60477 t) 708-403-0101 stelizabeth-seton@archchicago.org steseton.com/ Rev. William T. Corcoran, Pst.; Rev. Kevin McCray, Assoc. Pst.; Rev. John Zurek, Assoc. Pst.; Rev. William T. O'Mara, Pastor Emer.; Dcn. Francis Gildea; Dcn. John F. Sobol; Dcn. Robert J. Velcich; CRP Stds.: 216

Cardinal Joseph Bernardin - -8) 9250 W. 167th St., Orland Hills, IL 60477 t) 708-403-6525 info@cjbschool.org Inter-Parish School serving St. Elizabeth Seton, St. Francis of Assisi, St. Julie Billiart and St. Stephen, Deacon and Martyr. Kelly Bourrell, Prin.; Stds.: 469

ORLAND PARK

St. Francis of Assisi - 15050 S. Wolf Rd., Orland Park, IL 60467 t) 708-460-0042 stfrancisassisi-wolf@archchicago.org www.sfaorland.org/ Rev. Artur J. Sowa, Pst.; Rev. Gael Gensler, O.S.F., Assoc. Pst.; Rev. Jason J. Suero, Assoc. Pst.; Rev. Edward F. Upton, Pastor Emer.; Dcn. John Donahue; Dcn. Michael E. Kiley; Dcn. Timothy J. McCormick; Dcn. Michael J. Pindelski; Dcn. Brian K. Whiteford; Mary Kay Burberry, DRE; CRP Stds.: 539

St. Michael - 14310 Highland Ave., Orland Park, IL 60462 t) 708-349-0903 stmichael-highland@archchicago.org saintmike.com/ Rev. Frank A. Kurucz, Pst.; Rev. Geofrey Andama, Assoc. Pst.; Rev. Daniel Villalobos, Assoc. Pst.; Rev. Edward McLaughlin, Pastor Emer.; Dcn. Tony Cocco; Dcn. Colin J. Huie; Dcn. James Janicek; Dcn. Michael McDonough; Dcn. Abel B. Trujillo; Patricia A. Chuchla, Pst. Assoc.; Sr. Marietta Umlor, C.S.C., Pst. Assoc.; CRP Stds.: 332

St. Michael School - -8) 14355 Highland Ave., Orland Park, IL 60462 t) 708-349-0068 psmith@saintmike.org Paul W. Smith, Prin.; Stds.: 536

Our Lady of the Woods - 10731 W. 131st St., Orland Park, IL 60462 t) 708-361-9435 (CRP); 708-361-4754 ol-woods@archchicago.org ourladyofthewoods.org/ Rev. Michael G. Foley, Pst.; Rev. Robert Marchwiany, Assoc. Pst.; Rev. William J. Finnegan, Pastor Emer.; Dcn. John Macarol; Dcn. Douglas Szarzynski; Rev. Edward M. Mikolajczyk, In Res.; Most Rev. John R. Gorman, Senior Priest; CRP Stds.: 488

PALATINE

St. Theresa - 455 N. Benton, Palatine, IL 60067 t) 847-358-2846 (CRP); 847-358-7760 sttheresa@archchicago.org sttheresachurch.org/ Rev. Timothy J. Fairman, Pst.; Rev. Thomas Bishop, Assoc. Pst.; Rev. Matthew Jamesson, Assoc. Pst.; Rev. Michael J. Wanda, Assoc. Pst.; Dcn. James Devine; Dcn. Andrew D. Kim; Dcn. Richard Pizzato; Dcn. Louis

Riccio; Dcn. Lawrence R. Schumacher; Dcn. Gregory Vogt; Elizabeth Vogt, DRE; CRP Stds.: 221

Pauline Center/Ministry Center -

St. Theresa School - -8) 445 N. Benton, Palatine, IL 60067 t) 847-359-1820 mkeenley@sttheresaschool.com Mary Kay J. Keenley, Prin.; Stds.: 415

St. Thomas of Villanova - 1201 E. Anderson Dr., Palatine, IL 60074 t) 847-358-2386 (CRP); 847-358-6999 stthomas-villanova@archicago.org www.stov.org/ Rev. Krzysztof Janczak, Pst.; Rev. Marcin Zasada, Assoc. Pst.; Rev. Raymond A. Yadron, Pastor Emer.; Dcn. John Breit; Dcn. Mark Duffey; Dcn. Thomas Dunne; Dcn. William T. Karstenson; Dcn. Leonard Marturano; Dcn. Derek K. Oliver; CRP Stds.: 215

St. Thomas of Villanova School - -8) 1141 E. Anderson Dr., Palatine, IL 60074 t) 847-358-2110 stvprincipal@stvschool.org Matthew Martino, Prin.; Stds.: 198

PALOS HEIGHTS

St. Alexander - 7025 W. 126th St., Palos Heights, IL 60463 t) 708-448-6624 (CRP); 708-448-4861 stalexander@archchicago.org stalexanderpalos.org/ Rev. Martin E. Michniewicz, Pst.; Rev. Colm B Mitchell, Assoc. Pst.; Rev. William J. Vollmer, Assoc. Pst.; Dcn. Michael Ciciura; Dcn. James Horton; Dcn. Francis J Pendergast III; CRP Stds.: 162

St. Alexander School - -8) 126th St. at 71st Ave., Palos Heights, IL 60463 t) 708-448-0408 info@stalexanderschool.com stalexanderschool.com/ Sharon M. O'Toole, Prin.; Stds.: 253

PALOS HILLS

Sacred Heart - 8245 W. 111th St., Palos Hills, IL 60465 t) 708-974-3900 (CRP); 708-974-3336 sacredheart-111th@archchicago.org sacredheartpalos.org/ Rev. Jacek Wrona (Poland), Pst.; Rev. Jaroslaw Maciejewski, Assoc. Pst.; Dcn. Dominic Andriacchi; Dcn. Thomas J. Rzendzian; CRP Stds.: 255

PARK FOREST

St. Irenaeus - Merged Jul 2022 Merged with Infant Jesus of Prague and St. Lawrence O'Toole to form St. Veronica Parish.

PARK RIDGE

Mary, Seat of Wisdom - 920 Granville Ave., Park Ridge, IL 60068 t) 847-825-8763 (CRP); 847-825-3153 mary-wisdom@archchicago.org www.mswparish.org/ Rev. Derek Ho, Pst.; Rev. Ronald N. Kalas, Pastor Emer.; Dcn. Kevin Blindauer; Dcn. Edward J. Schipp; CRP Stds.: 294

Mary, Seat of Wisdom School - (Grades PreK-8) 1352 S. Cumberland, Park Ridge, IL 60068 t) 847-825-2500 jdue@mswschool.org Julie T. Due, Prin.; Stds.: 571

St. Paul of the Cross - 320 S. Washington St., Park Ridge, IL 60068 t) 847-825-7605 stpaul-cross@archchicago.org Rev. James Wallace, Pst.; Rev. Nicholas Cavallari, Assoc. Pst.; Dcn. Robert T. Bulger; Dcn. Andrew P. Cameron; Anna Mae Parkhill, DRE; CRP Stds.: 952

St. Paul of the Cross School - -8) 140 S. Northwest Hwy., Park Ridge, IL 60068 t) 847-825-6366 nagnew@spc-school.net Dr. Erika Mickelburgh, Prin.; Stds.: 698

POSEN

St. Stanislaus Bishop and Martyr - Merged Jul 2022 Merged with St. Christopher to form St. Augustine Parish.

PROSPECT HEIGHTS

St. Alphonsus Liguori - 411 N. Wheeling Rd., Prospect Heights, IL 60070 t) 847-255-9490 (CRP); 847-255-7452 stalphonsus-liguori@archchicago.org www.saintalphonsus.com/ Rev. Joseph N. Le, Pst.; Dcn. Stephen Stecker; Dcn. Calvin Blickle Jr.; Rev. John W. Hurley, In Res.; CRP Stds.: 148

St. Alphonsus Liguori School - -8) t) 847-255-5538 info@saintalphonsus.com www.saintalphonsusschool.com/ Peter F Trumblay, Prin.; Stds.: 155

RIVER FOREST

St. Luke and St. Bernardine Parish - 528 Lathrop Ave., River Forest, IL 60305-1835 t) 708-771-5959 (CRP); 708-771-8250 stluke@archchicago.org Rev. Stanislaw Kuca, Pst.; Rev. Edward R. Fialkowski, Assoc. Pst.; Rev. Leroy A. Wickowski, Senior Priest; Very Rev. Krzysztof Swierczynski, In Res.; Dcn. John Baier; Dcn. Terrance Norton; Dcn. Robert Slobig; Dcn. Lendell Richardson; CRP Stds.: 434

St. Luke School - -8) 519 Ashland Ave., River Forest, IL 60305-1824 t) 708-366-8587 twesley@stlukeparish.org Andrew Dimarco, Prin.; Stds.: 294

St. Vincent Ferrer - 1530 Jackson Ave., River Forest, IL 60305 t) 708-366-7090 stvincent-ferrer@archchicago.org Rev. Richard L Barranger, OP, Pst.; Rev. John J. Meany, OP, Assoc. Pst.; Rev. Christopher Saliga, Assoc. Pst.; Dcn. John Gaughan; Rev. Peter J. Hereley, O.P., In Res.; Rev. John J. O'Malley, O.P., In Res.; CRP Stds.: 67

St. Vincent Ferrer School - -8) 1515 Lathrop Ave., River Forest, IL 60305 t) 708-771-5905 jglimco@svfschool.org Maureen R Aspell, Prin.; Stds.: 259

RIVERSIDE

St. Paul VI - 126 Herrick Rd., Riverside, IL 60546 t) 708-447-6812 (CRP); 708-447-1020 stmary-herrick@archchicago.org Rev. Thomas P. May, Pst.; Rev. Matthew Nemchausky, Assoc. Pst.; Rev. Robert J. Burnell, Pastor Emer.; Dcn. Randy Belice; Dcn. Robert Boharic; Dcn. Peter A. Brown; Dcn. Ronald Pilarski; CRP Stds.: 324

St. Mary School - -8) 97 Herrick Rd., Riverside, IL 60546 t) 708-442-5747 principal@stmaryriverside.org Nicole Nolazco, Prin.; Stds.: 337

Mother of Mothers - 2431 S. 10th Ave., North Riverside, IL 60546

ROLLING MEADOWS

St. Colette - 3900 S. Meadow Dr., Rolling Meadows, IL 60008 t) 847-394-8100 stcolette@archchicago.org www.stcolette.org/ Rev. Augustine Mahonge, Pst.; Dcn. Moyossola J. Boussari; Dcn. Raul Trejo; CRP Stds.: 92

ROSEMONT

Our Lady of Hope Mission - 9711 W. Devon Ave., Rosemont, IL 60018 t) 847-825-4673 ol-hope@archchicago.org Rev. Wojciech Jan Oleksy, Pst.; Dcn. James J. Ernst;

ROUND LAKE

St. Joseph - 114 N. Lincoln Ave., Round Lake, IL 60073 t) 847-546-3554 (CRP); 847-546-3610 stjoseph-lincoln@archchicago.org www.stjosephchurchrl.com/ Rev. Michael L. Zoufal, Pst.; Dcn. Rajan M. Fernando; Dcn. Joel Ruiz; CRP Stds.: 505

SCHAUMBURG

Church of the Holy Spirit - 1451 W. Bode Rd., Schaumburg, IL 60194 t) 847-882-7580 holyspirit@archchicago.org www.churchoftheholyspirit.org/ Rev. Jeremy Thomas, Pst.; Rev. George J. Kane, Pastor Emer.; Dcn. Wayne Beyer; Dcn. Xavier Carrera; Dcn. Mario Contreras; Dcn. Raymond Doud; Dcn. Michael Enger; Sr. Marianne Supan, O.P., Pst. Assoc.; CRP Stds.: 377

St. Marcelline - 822 Springinsguth Rd., Schaumburg, IL 60193 t) 847-524-4429 stmarcelline@archchicago.org stmarcelline.com/ Rev. Antoni Bury, Pst.; Dcn. Michael Filipucci; Dcn. Thomas LaMantia; Dcn. Howard P. Lanctot; Dcn. Donald R. Maiers; Dcn. Paul Migala; CRP Stds.: 138

St. Matthew - 1001 E. Schaumburg Rd., Schaumburg, IL 60194 t) 847-891-1220 stmatthew@archchicago.org www.stmatthewparish.org/ Rev. Joseph Glab, C.R., Pst.; Milissa Bartold, Pst. Assoc.; CRP Stds.: 169

SCHILLER PARK

Holy Virgin Martyrs: St. Beatrice and St. Maria Goretti Parish - 4157 Atlantic Ave., Schiller Park, IL 60176 t) 847-678-0138 stbeatrice@archchicago.org www.hvmparish.org/ Rev. Robert Schultz, Pst.; CRP Stds.: 140

St. Maria Goretti - 3929 N. Wehrman Ave., Schiller Park, IL 60176

SKOKIE

SS. Peter and Lambert Parish - 8116 Niles Center Rd., Skokie, IL 60077 t) 847-679-1202 (CRP); 847-673-1492 stpeter-nilescenter@archchicago.org Rev. Henry C. Kricek, Pst.; Rev. Paul O. Adaja, Assoc. Pst.; Rev. John B. Atoyebi, Assoc. Pst.; Rev. Mariano Rondael, Assoc. Pst.; Rev. Edward D. Grace, Pastor Emer.; Sr. Kathleen Maloney, O.S.B., DRE; CRP Stds.: 175

SOUTH HOLLAND

Christ Our Savior - 880 E. 154th St., South Holland, IL 60473 t) 708-225-1180 (CRP); 708-333-3550 christoursavior@archchicago.org www.christoursaviorparish.org Rev. Gosbert Rwezahura, Pst.; Dcn. James Renwick; Dcn. Melvin Stasinski; CRP Stds.: 38

STICKNEY

St. Pius X - Merged Jul 2022 Merged with St. Leonard to form St. Pius X and St. Leonard Parish.

STREAMWOOD

St. John the Evangelist - 502 S. Park Blvd., Streamwood, IL 60107 t) 630-837-1060 (CRP); 630-837-6500 stjohn-evangelist@archchicago.org Rev. Grzegorz P. Gorczyca, Pst.; Rev. Nathaniel Payne, Assoc. Pst.; Rev. William J. Moriarity, Pastor Emer.; Dcn. Michael S. Benoit; Dcn. Timothy W Davidson; Dcn. Joseph L. Esposito; Dcn. James Furey; Dcn. Joseph P. McCain; Dcn. Jozef S. Mika; Dcn. Robert Pasdiora; Dcn. Lawrence Rybicki; CRP Stds.: 171

St. John the Evangelist School - -8) 513 Parkside Cir., Streamwood, IL 60107 school@mystjohns.org Elizabeth C Wennerstrom, Prin.; Stds.: 222

TINLEY PARK

St. George - 6707 W. 175th St., Tinley Park, IL 60477 t) 708-532-2243 stgeorge-175th@archchicago.org stgeorge60477.org/ Rev. Paul G. Seaman, Pst.; Rev. Puslecki Tomasz, Assoc. Pst.; Dcn. Gregory Bartos; Dcn. Timothy Keating; Dcn. Joseph Panek; Dcn. Thomas Schutzius; Dcn. Jerry T. Souta; CRP Stds.: 109

St. George School - -8) 6700 W. 176th St., Tinley Park, IL 60477 t) 708-532-2626 info@stgeorgeschool.org Charlotte A. Pratl, Prin.; Stds.: 198

Saint Julie Billiart - 7399 W. 159th St., Tinley Park, IL 60477 t) 708-429-1044 (CRP); 708-429-6767 stjulie@archchicago.org stjulie.org/ Rev. Tirso S. Villaverde Jr., Pst.; Rev. Roy Belocura, Assoc. Pst.; Dcn. John T. Benz; Dcn. Edward Pluchar; Dcn. Richard Miska; CRP Stds.: 256

St. Stephen, Deacon and Martyr - 17500 S. 84th Ave., Tinley Park, IL 60487 t) 708-342-2400 ststephen-84th@archchicago.org Rev. Michael Wyrzykowski, Pst.; Rev. Robert Stuglik, Assoc. Pst.; Dcn. Charles McFarland; Dcn. Robert Conlin; Dcn. William Engler; Dcn. Peter Van Merkestyn; CRP Stds.: 656

VOLO

St. Peter - 27551 Volo Village Rd., Volo, IL 60073 t) 815-385-5496 stpeter-volovillage@archchicago.org Rev. Nathan Caswell, S.J.C., Pst.; Rev. Brendan Gibson, S.J.C., Assoc. Pst.; Rev. Robin Kwan, S.J.C., Assoc. Pst.; CRP Stds.: 100

WADSWORTH

St. Brigid - 15000 Wadsworth Rd., Wadsworth, IL 60083 t) 847-236-9131 (CRP); 847-244-4161 stpatrick-wadsworth@archchicago.org Rev. Wojciech Jan Oleksy, Pst.; Dcn. Joseph Casey; Dcn. William Gibbons; Dcn. Marcelino Hernandez; Dcn. Richard Holevoet; Dcn. Joseph Krame; Dcn. Louis Abboud; Dcn. Michael Mercure; CRP Stds.: 88

St. Patrick School - -8) 15020 Wadsworth Rd., Wadsworth, IL 60083 t) 847-623-8446 mvitulli@stpatrickwadsworth.org Mary A. Vitulli, Prin.; Stds.: 387

Our Lady of Humility School - -8) 10601 Wadsworth Rd., Zion-Beach Park, IL 60099 t) 847-746-3722 pbrowne@olhschool.org Mary A. Vitulli, Prin.; Stds.: 209

WAUCONDA

Transfiguration - 316 W. Mill St., Wauconda, IL 60084 t) 847-526-6400 (CRP); 847-526-2400 transfiguration-mill@archchicago.org Rev. Juan Pablo Avila-Ibarra, Pst.; Rev. Javier Garcia Vasquez, Assoc. Pst.; Dcn. Christopher C. Fisher; Dcn. Jose Mancilla-Martinez; Dcn. Israel Santiago; CRP Stds.: 187

Frassati Catholic Academy - (Grades 6-8) t) 847-487-5600 tkleckner@frassaticatholicacademy.org Ministry of St. Mary of the Assumption; Santa Maria del Popolo, Mundelein., Member of Catholic Consortium of Lake County. Tammy A. Kleckner, Prin.; Stds.: 241

WAUKEGAN

Little Flower Parish - 2600 Sunset Ave., Waukegan, IL 60087 t) 847-623-2875 stdismas@archchicago.org www.littleflowerwaukegan.com/ Rev. Xamie M. Reyes, Pst.; Rev. Flavio V. Gonzalez, Assoc. Pst.; Rev. Giovanny A Navarro Sanchez, Assoc. Pst.; Rev. John M. Ryan, Pastor Emer.; Dcn. Genaro Mendez; Dcn. Bruce Peters; Dcn. Victor Ruiz; Dcn. Anthony Sacramento; CRP Stds.: 162

St. Anastasia School - -8) 629 Glen Flora Ave., Waukegan, IL 60085 t) 847-623-8320 www.stanastasiaschool.org/ Robin E McAfee, Prin.; Stds.: 198

Most Blessed Trinity - 450 Keller Ave., Waukegan, IL 60085-5030 t) 847-623-2655 blessedtrinity@archchicago.org mostblessedtrinityparish.org/ Rev. Timothy J. O'Malley, Pst.; Rev. Armand Ramirez Ruiz, Assoc. Pst.; Rev. Felipe Vaglienty, Assoc. Pst.; Dcn. Pablo Albarran; Dcn. John A. Haderlein; Dcn. Salvador Martinez; Dcn. Gary Munda; Dcn. Fredy Munoz; Dcn. Jorge Soto; CRP Stds.: 440

Most Blessed Trinity Academy - -8) 510 Grand Ave., Waukegan, IL 60085 t) 847-623-4110 lsaccaro@mostblessedtrinityacademy.org Dr. Lynne Saccaro, Prin.; Stds.: 187

WESTCHESTER

Mary, Mother of Divine Grace - 2550 S. Mayfair Ave., Westchester, IL 60154 t) 708-562-3364; 708-562-3422 (CRP) marymotherofdivinegraceparish@archchicago.org marymotherofdivinegrace.org/ Rev. Neil E. Fackler, Pst.; Dcn. James R. Sponder; CRP Stds.: 137

Divine Providence School - 2500 S. Mayfair Ave., Westchester, IL 60154 t) 708-562-2258 Lynn M. Letourneau, Prin.; Stds.: 209

WESTERN SPRINGS

St. John of the Cross - 5005 Wolf Rd., Western Springs, IL 60558 t) 708-246-4404 stjohn-cross@archchicago.org www.stjohnofthecross.org/ Rev. Marc W. Reszel, Pst.; Rev. Walter J Takuski, Assoc. Pst.; Dcn. John E. Schopp IV; Dcn. Richard Voytas; Janet Caschetta, DRE; CRP Stds.: 570

St. John of the Cross School - -8) 705 51st St., Western Springs, IL 60558 t) 708-246-4454 gorman@sjc.pvt.k12.il.us Mary C Kennedy, Prin.; Stds.: 636

WHEELING

St. Joseph the Worker - 181 W. Dundee Rd., Wheeling, IL 60090 t) 847-537-4182 (CRP); 847-537-2740 stjoseph-worker@archchicago.org stjosephworker.com/ Rev. Marcin Karwot, SVD, Pst.; Rev. Jesus Mata Martinez, S.V.D., Assoc. Pst.; Rev. Messan K Tettekpoe, SVD, Assoc. Pst.; Dcn. Martin Carrillo; CRP Stds.: 189

Polska Parafialna Szkola Im. Juliusza Slowackiego, NFP - www.juliuszlowacki.com

WILLOW SPRINGS

Our Lady, Mother of the Church Polish Mission - 116 Hilton St., Willow Springs, IL 60480; Mailing: Box 334, Argo, IL 60501 t) 708-467-0436 cistercianmission@gmail.com www.cystersichicago.net/ Rev. Michael Blicharski, O.Cist., Mission Dir.; Rev. Marek S Wlodarczyk, Assoc. Pst.;

Shrine of Saint John Paul II -

WILMETTE

SS. Joseph and Francis Xavier - 1747 Lake Ave., Wilmette, IL 60091 t) 847-251-0771 officesjfx@ssjfx.org ssjfx.org Rev. Wayne F. Watts, Pst.; Rev. Robert S. Ryan, Assoc. Pst.; Dcn. Robert Kerls; Dcn. Charles C. Robey; Dcn. Derald Shinkle; CRP Stds.: 505

St. Francis Xavier School - -8) 808 Linden Ave., Wilmette, IL 60091-2714 t) 847-256-0644 colleenbarrett@sfx-school.org Christine Elliot, Prin.; Stds.: 663

WINNETKA

Divine Mercy - 1077 Tower Rd., Winnetka, IL 60093 t) 847-446-0856 dmns.information@divinemercynorthshore.org www.divinemercynorthshore.org/ Rev. Steven M. Lanza, Pst.; Dcn. Gerald M. Keenan; Dcn. Michael McNulty; Dcn. Robert Puhala; Rev. Daniel J. Cassidy, In Res.; CRP Stds.: 253

Sacred Heart School - -8) 1095 Gage St., Winnetka, IL 60093 t) 847-446-0005 kfink@shwschool.org Margaret M Webb, Prin.; Stds.: 213

SS. Faith, Hope and Charity - 191 Linden St., Winnetka, IL 60093 t) 847-446-1828 (CRP); 847-446-7646 ssfhc@archchicago.org www.faithhope.org/ Rev. Martin E. O'Donovan, Pst.; Rev. Thomas Philip, Assoc. Pst.; Dcn. Michael Cavanaugh; Dcn. John J. Murray; Rev. William J. Flaherty, Senior Priest; CRP Stds.: 367

SS. Faith, Hope and Charity School - -8) 180 Ridge Ave., Winnetka, IL 60093 t) 847-446-0031 office@faithhopeschool.org Dr. Thomas Meagher, Prin.; Stds.: 258

ZION-BEACH PARK

Our Lady of Humility - Merged Jul 2022 Merged with St. Patrick-Wadsworth to form St. Brigid.

SCHOOLS: PRESCHOOL THRU HIGH SCHOOL

SCHOOLS

STATE OF ILLINOIS

CHICAGO

St. Angela School - (Grades PreSchool-8) 1332 N. Massasoit Ave., Chicago, IL 60651-1108 t) 773-626-2655 kwittenberg@saintangela.org www.saintangela.org William Schooler, Prin.; Stds.: 197

Bridgeport Catholic Academy - (PAR) (Grades PreK-8) 3700 S. Lowe, Chicago, IL 60609 t) 773-376-6223 ckoster@bcachicago.org www.bcachicago.org Serving the following parishes: All Saints-St. Anthony and Nativity of Our Lord. Caroline Koster, Prin.;

Chicago Jesuit Academy - (PRV) (Grades 3-8) 5058 W. Jackson Blvd., Chicago, IL 60644-4324 t) 773-638-6103 info@cjacademy.org www.cjacademy.org Full-scholarship, college prep, Catholic, Jesuit middle school serving students from historically disinvested-from Chicago West Side communities Thomas Beckley, Prin.; Kelly Tyson, Headmaster; Matthew Lynch, Pres.; Stds.: 185; Lay Tchrs.: 44

The Frances Xavier Warde School - (Grades PreSchool-8) 120 S. Des Plaines St., Chicago, IL 60661-3515 t) 312-466-0700 community@fxw.org www.fxw.org Courtney Britton, Prin.; Lauren Fitchett, Prin.; Stds.: 883; Lay Tchrs.: 110

Northside Catholic Academy - (PAR) (Grades PreK-8) 6216 N. Glenwood Ave., Chicago, IL 60660 t) 773-743-6277 chuzenis@ncaweb.org www.northsidecatholic.org Christine Huzenis, Prin.;

Middle School Campus - 7318 N Oakley, Chicago, IL 60645 t) 773-271-2008 northsidecatholic.org Serving the following parishes: St. Gertrude; St. Margaret Mary; St. Ignatius; St. Henry; St. Jerome; St. Gregory.

Sacred Heart Schools (Academy of the Sacred Heart for Girls, Hardey Prep. for Boys) - (PRV) (Grades PreK-8) 6250 N. Sheridan Rd., Chicago, IL 60660-1730 t) 773-262-4446 www.shschicago.org Religious of the Sacred Heart. Meg Steele, Headmaster; Elizabeth Coleman, Prin.; Karen Uselmann, Prin.; Dan Gargano, Prin.; Stds.: 606; Lay Tchrs.: 61

San Miguel Febres Cordero School, Inc. (San Miguel School and Community Center) - (PRV) (Grades 6-8) 1954 W. 48th St. 4th Fl., Chicago, IL 60609 t) 773-890-0233; 773-890-1481 www.sanmiguelchicago.org Operated by DeLaSalle Christian Brothers. Catholic Middle School and Community Center for at risk youth; graduate support through high school. Bro. Mark Snodgrass, Prin.; Jeffrey Smart, Pres.;

DES PLAINES

***Willows Academy** - 1015 Rose Ave., Des Plaines, IL 60016 t) 847-824-6900 Jeanne Petros, Dir.;

EVANSTON

***The Academy of St. Joan of Arc** - 9245 N. Lawndale, Evanston, IL 60203 t) 847-972-1003 contactus@theacademysja.org www.theacademysja.org Kristina L. Heidkamp-Reyes, Prin.;

LAKE FOREST

***East Lake Academy** - (PRV) (Grades PreK-8) 13911 W. Laurel Dr., Lake Forest, IL 60045 t) 847-247-0035 rechavez@eastlakeacademy.org www.eastlakeacademy.org Rosario Echavez, Prin.; Stds.: 145; Lay Tchrs.: 16

LEMONT

Everest Academy of Lemont, Inc. - (PRV) (Grades PreK-8) 11550 Bell Rd., Lemont, IL 60439 t) 630-243-1995 everestadmin@everestlemont.com www.everestadvantage.org Candy Hamilton, Prin.; Rev. Michael Vanderbeek, LC, Chap.; Stds.: 192; Lay Tchrs.: 18

HIGH SCHOOLS

STATE OF ILLINOIS

ARLINGTON HEIGHTS

St. Viator High School - (PRV) (Grades 9-12) 1213 E. Oakton St., Arlington Heights, IL 60004 t) 847-392-4050; 224-625-1216 dlydon@saintviator.com; cabrahamian@saintviator.com www.saintviator.com Clerics of St. Viator Rev. Daniel J. Lydon, C.S.V., Pres.; Rev. Charles G. Bolser, C.S.V., Chap.; Jonathon P. Baffico, Prin.; Stds.: 777; Scholastics: 1; Pr. Tchrs.: 1; Bro. Tchrs.: 2; Lay Tchrs.: 58

BURBANK

St. Laurence High School, Inc. - (PRV) 5556 W. 77th St., Burbank, IL 60459 t) 708-458-6900 mhermanek@stlaurence.com www.stlaurence.com Congregation of Christian Brothers. Kristy Kane, Prin.; Joseph Martinez, Pres.; Stds.: 986; Sr. Tchrs.: 1; Lay Tchrs.: 70

CHICAGO

Brother Rice High School - (PRV) (Grades 9-12) 10001 S. Pulaski Rd., Chicago, IL 60655-3356 t) 773-429-4300 mdonahue@brrice.org www.brotherrice.org Congregation of Christian Brothers & Edmund Rice Brothers. Robert Alberts, Prin.; Mark Donahue, Pres.;

Christ the King Jesuit College Preparatory School - (PRV) (Grades 9-12) 5088 W. Jackson Blvd., Chicago, IL 60644 t) 773-261-7505 cmartin@ctkjesuit.org www.ctkjesuit.org Participant in the Cristo Rey Work/Study Program, Inc. Katie Olson, Prin.; Clement V. Martin, Pres.; Stds.: 370; Lay Tchrs.: 24

Cristo Rey Jesuit High School, Inc. - (PRV) 1852 W. 22nd Pl., Chicago, IL 60608 t) 773-890-6800 info@cristorey.net www.cristorey.net Mayra Gradilla, Prin.; Antonio Ortiz, Pres.; Stds.: 543; Scholastics: 1; Sr. Tchrs.: 1; Lay Tchrs.: 25

Cristo Rey Work/Study Program, Inc. - lsellers@cristorey.net Lillie Sellers, Dir.;

De La Salle Institute, Brothers of the Christian Schools - (PRV) 3434 S. Michigan Ave., Chicago, IL 60616 t) 312-842-7355 webmaster@dls.org www.dls.org Anne Marie Tirpak, Pres.; Thomas Schergen, Prin.; Stds.: 771; Lay Tchrs.: 54

DePaul College Prep - (PRV) (Grades 9-12) 3333 N.

Rockwell St., Chicago, IL 60618 t) 773-539-3600 lpilcher@depaulprep.org; mdempsey@depaulprep.org www.depaulprep.org Dr. Megan Stanton-Anderson, Prin.; Joseph Voss, Vice Prin.; Maria Hill, Vice Prin.; Mary Dempsey, Pres.; Lisa Pilcher, CFO; Stds.: 1,081; Lay Tchrs.: 94

St. Francis de Sales High School - (PRV) 10155 S. Ewing Ave., Chicago, IL 60617 t) 773-731-7272 info@sfdshs.org www.sfdshs.org John Kimec, Prin.;

***Hales Franciscan High School, Inc.** - (PRV) 4930 Cottage Grove Ave., Chicago, IL 60615 t) 773-285-8400 Friar Johnpaul Cafiero, O.F.M.; Rev. David Rodriguez, O.F.M.; Nichole M. Jackson, Prin.;

Hales Services, Inc. - Rev. Edouard Kalubi, O.de.M.;

Holy Trinity High School - (PRV) 1443 W. Division St., Chicago, IL 60642 t) 773-278-4212 mlynch@holytrinity-hs.org www.holytrinity-hs.org Brothers of Holy Cross. Marianne Lynch, Prin.; Timothy Bopp, Pres.;

St. Ignatius College Prep - (PRV) (Grades 9-12) 1076 W. Roosevelt Rd., Chicago, IL 60608-1594 t) 312-421-5900 john.chandler@ignatius.org www.ignatius.org John. J. Chandler, Pres.; Stds.: 1,515; Scholastics: 1; Pr. Tchrs.: 4; Sr. Tchrs.: 4; Lay Tchrs.: 106

St. Ignatius Jesuit Community - (PRV) 1025 W. Taylor St., Chicago, IL 60607 t) 312-829-2297 Rev. Patrick E. McGrath, S.J., Pst.; Rev. Christopher J Manahan, S.J., Prov. Asst.; Rev. Patrick Mugisho, S.J. (Democratic Republic of Congo), Development; Rev. William Blazek, SJ, Chap.; Rev. Aaron Bohr, SJ, Teacher; Rev. Patrick Alexis Fairbanks, S.J., Supr.; Rev. Paul Kalenzi, S.J., Devel. Intern; Rev. Mark Luedtke, S.J., Pst. Min./Coord.; Rev. Vaidas Lukosevicius, S.J., Pst. Min./Coord.; Rev. Jeremiah Lynch, SJ, Chap.; Rev. Joshua Peters, SJ, Teacher; Rev. Brian Taber, Teacher; Bro. Matthew Galway Wooters, S.J., Vocations Promoter; Stds.: 1,550; Pr. Tchrs.: 5; Sr. Tchrs.: 4; Lay Tchrs.: 106

Josephinum Academy (Josephinum, Inc.) - (PRV) (Grades 9-12) 1501 N. Oakley Blvd., Chicago, IL 60622 t) 773-276-1261 lourdes.weber@josephinum.org www.josephinum.org Lourdes Weber, Prin.; Susan McGowan, Librn.;

Leo High School - (PRV) 7901 S. Sangamon, Chicago, IL 60620 t) 773-224-9600 admin@leohighschool.org www.leohighschool.org Shaka Rawls, Prin.; Dan McGrath, Pres.;

Marist High School - (PRV) 4200 W. 115th St., Chicago, IL 60655-4306 t) 773-881-5300 laurencell.karen@marist.net www.marist.net Larry N. Tucker, Prin.; Bro. Patrick McNamara, F.M.S., Pres.; Kristen Rademacher, Librn.;

Marist Brothers -

Mother McAuley Liberal Arts High School - (PRV) 3737 W. 99th St., Chicago, IL 60655 t) 773-881-6500 charrington@mothermcauley.org; kbaal@mothermcauley.org www.mothermcauley.org Sisters of Mercy Kathryn Baal, Prin.; Carey Harrington, Pres.; Stds.: 821; Sr. Tchrs.: 1; Lay Tchrs.: 61

Mount Carmel High School - (PRV) 6410 S. Dante Ave., Chicago, IL 60637 t) 773-324-1020 bconroy@mchs.org www.mchs.org Carmelites. Scott Tabernacki, Prin.; Brendan Conroy, Pres.;

St. Patrick High School, Brothers of the Christian Schools - (PRV) 5900 W. Belmont Ave., Chicago, IL 60634 t) 773-282-8844 www.stpatrick.org Jonathon P. Baffico, Prin.; Joseph Schmidt, Pres.; Rachele R. Esola, Librn.;

Resurrection College Prep High School - (PRV) 7500 W. Talcott Ave., Chicago, IL 60631 t) 773-775-6616 www.reshs.org Christian Brothers of the Midwest, Inc. Dr. Richard Piwowarski, Prin.; Dr. Daniel Zepp, Pres.; Maura Collins, Bus. Mgr.;

St. Rita of Cascia High School Corporation - (PRV) 7740 S. Western Ave., Chicago, IL 60620 t) 773-925-6600 strita@stritahs.com www.stritahs.com Brendan Conroy, Prin.; Ernest J. Mrozek, Pres.; Robyn Kurnat, Librn.;

St. Rita of Cascia High School Foundation - mgallagher@stritahs.com

St. Rita of Cascia High School Facilities, Inc. -

CHICAGO HEIGHTS

Marian Catholic High School - (PRV) 700 Ashland Ave., Chicago Heights, IL 60411 t) 708-755-7565 mchsinfo@marianchs.com www.marianchs.com Dominican Sisters (Springfield, IL). Steve Tortorello, Prin.; Vince Krydynski, Pres.;

LA GRANGE PARK

Nazareth Academy - (PRV) (Grades 9-12) 1209 W. Ogden Ave., La Grange Park, IL 60526 t) 708-354-0061 dtracy@nazarethacademy.com www.nazarethacademy.com Congregation of St. Joseph. Therese Hawkins, Prin.; Deborah Tracy, Pres.; Stds.: 764; Lay Tchrs.: 47

LAKE FOREST

Woodlands Academy of the Sacred Heart - (PRV) 760 E. Westleigh Rd., Lake Forest, IL 60045-3298 t) 847-234-4300 info@woodlandsacademy.org www.woodlandsacademy.org Madonna L. Edmunds, Prin.; Ellen Hines, Librn.;

MUNDELEIN

Carmel Catholic High School - (PRV) (Grades 9-12) One Carmel Pkwy., Mundelein, IL 60060 t) 847-566-3000 (name)@carmelhs.org www.carmelhs.org Bradley Bonham, Pres.; Jason Huther, Prin.; Ric Elert, Chair; Eric Franklin, Librn.; Stds.: 1,074; Pr. Tchrs.: 1; Lay Tchrs.: 67

NILES

Notre Dame College Prep. - (PRV) (Grades 9-12) 7655 Dempster St., Niles, IL 60714 t) 847-965-2900 hr@nddons.org www.nddons.org (Boys) Daniel Tully, Prin.; Shay Boyle, Pres.; Kevin Burke, Exec.; Karyn Kozyra, CFO; Stds.: 760; Lay Tchrs.: 50

OAK PARK

Fenwick High School - (PRV) (Grades 9-12) 505 Washington Blvd., Oak Park, IL 60302 t) 708-386-0127 jwilson@fenwickfriars.com www.fenwickfriars.com Dominican Order. Peter Groom, Prin.; Rev. Richard A. Peddicord, O.P., Pres.; Nancy M. Bufalino, Exec.; Christopher Ritten, Exec.; Bro. Joseph Trout, Teacher; Judy Tichacek, Librn.; Rev. Christopher Johnson, OP, Teacher; Rev. Matthew Strabala, OP, Teacher;

RIVER FOREST

Trinity High School - (PRV) (Grades 9-12) 7574 W. Division St., River Forest, IL 60305 t) 708-771-8383 lcurley@trinityhs.org; agallie@trinityhs.org www.trinityhs.org Dominican Sisters (Sinsinawa, WI). Amy Gallie, Prin.; Laura Curley, Pres.; Stds.: 350; Lay Tchrs.: 48

WAUKEGAN

Cristo Rey St. Martin College Prep - (PRV) (Grades 9-12) 3106 Bevidere Rd., Waukegan, IL 60085 t) 224-215-9400 pkendall@cr-sm.org www.cr-sm.org Michael Odiotti, Prin.; G. Preston Kendall, Pres.; Pierre Edmonds, Dean; Jim Dippold, Campus Min.; Stds.: 403; Lay Tchrs.: 29

CRSM Work Study, Inc. - (Grades 9-12) t) 847-244-6895 Michelle Mehlis, Dir. of Corporate work Study;

WESTCHESTER

St. Joseph High School - (PRV) 10900 W. Cermak Rd., Westchester, IL 60154-4299 t) 708-562-4433 ronald.hoover@stjoeshs.org stjoeshs.org De La Salle Christian Brothers. Ronald Hoover, Prin.; Bro. Thomas Harding, F.S.C., Pres.;

WILMETTE

Loyola Academy - (PRV) 1100 Laramie Ave., Wilmette, IL 60091-1021 t) 847-256-1100 pmcgrath@loy.org; tmetzler@loy.org www.goramblers.org Dr. Alexandra Cruz, Dean; Charles Heintz, Prin.; Rev. Patrick E. McGrath, S.J., Pres.; Dennis Stonequist, Vice. Pres.; Brian Hake, CFO;

Regina Dominican High School - (PRV) (Grades 9-12) 701 Locust Rd., Wilmette, IL 60091 t) 847-256-7660 www.rdpanthers.org (Catholic School for Women) Sisters of St. Dominic (Adrian, MI). Kathleen Porreca, Prin.; Elizabeth Schuster, Pres.; Stds.: 225; Lay Tchrs.: 28

ASSOCIATIONS [ASN]

CHICAGO

***Anthonian Association of the Friends of St. Anthony of Padua, Inc.** - 6107 N. Kenmore Ave., Ste. 5, Chicago, IL 60660 t) (812) 923-6356 www.stanthonyusa.com We are dedicated to the transforming power of St Anthony's message of hope and Christ's love. We spread the Gospel and help those less fortunate. Maria Hart, Contact;

Illinois Catholic Health Association - 65 E. Wacker Pl., Ste. 1620, Chicago, IL 60601 t) 312-368-0011 pcacchione@il-cha.org www.il-cha.org Patrick J. Cacchione, Exec.;

Jesuit Seminary Association - 1010 N. Hooker St., Chicago, IL 60642 t) 773-975-6363; 773-975-6888 umisocius@jesuits.org www.jesuitsmidwest.org Rev. Timothy R. Lannon, S.J., Treas.;

***Saint John Paul II Eucharistic Adoration Association, Inc.** - 230 W. Monroe St., Ste. 2540, Chicago, IL 60606 t) 312-444-1784 information@pjp2ea.org www.pjp2ea.org Stephen Hegarty, Pres.; Charles Smith, Treas.;

***Presence Legacy Association** - 208 S. LaSalle St., Ste. 814, c/o CT Corporation System, Chicago, IL 60604;

INSTITUTIONS LOCATED IN DIOCESE

Mailing: 151 N. Franklin St., Ste. 2500, c/o Connie Mayer, Hinshaw & Culbertson LLP, Chicago, IL 60606 t) 312-704-3578 fka Presence Health Network; Presence Legacy Association dba Presence Health Connie Mayer, Asst. Secy.;

CHICAGO HEIGHTS

Dominican Association of Secondary Schools, Inc. - 700 S. Ashland Ave., Chicago Heights, IL 60411 t) 708-755-7565 www.dominicanschools.org Sr. Kathleen Anne Tait, O.P., Contact;

EVANSTON

Solidarity Lay Association - 1577 Florence Ave., Evanston, IL 60201 t) 847-224-1712 solidbridge@gmail.com www.sla-als.org A med/surgical mission organization that sponsors Solidarity Bridge, Puente de Solidaridad and Solidarity Medical Equipping. Dr. Juan L. Hinojosa, Pres.;

FOREST PARK

***Association of U.S. Catholic Priests** - 1038 Ferdinand, Forest Park, IL 60130 t) (708) 771-4000 auscp.org/ Rev. Stephen P. Newton, C.S.C., Exec. Dir.;

CATHOLIC CHARITIES [CCH]

CHICAGO

Austin Peoples Action Center - 5125 W. Chicago Ave., Chicago, IL 60651 t) 773-378-8760

Bronzeville Service Center - 2907 S. Wabash Ave., Chicago, IL 60616 t) 312-326-5020 eirizarr@catholiccharities.net Eliu Irizarry, Dir.;

Catholic Charities of the Archdiocese of Chicago-Archdiocesan Offices - 721 N. LaSalle St., Chicago, IL 60654 t) 312-655-7000 sallyblount@catholiccharities.net catholiccharities.net Sally Blount, Pres. & CEO; Rev. Charles T. Rubey; Rev. Wayne F. Watts; Steve Podder, Dir.; Elida Hernandez, CFO; Maria Simon, Gen. Counsel;

Accolade Adult Day Care - 112 S. Humphrey, Oak Park, IL 60302-2704 t) 708-445-1300

Ada S. Niles Adult Day Care - 6717 S. Elizabeth, Chicago, IL 60639 t) 773-488-5400 abailey@catholiccharities.net Angela Bailey, Assoc. VP;

Ada S. Niles Senior Center and Adult Day Care Services - 653 W. 63rd St., Chicago, IL 60621 t) 312-745-3307 abailey@catholiccharities.net

Administration - Child Care Centers - 721 N. LaSalle St., Chicago, IL 60654 t) 708-303-3650 c) (312)

636-5398 drodrigu@catholiccharities.net Diane Rodriguez, Dir.;
Adoption Preservation and Respite Services - 2313 W. Roosevelt Rd. 2nd Flr., Chicago, IL 60608 t) 312-655-8357 lmolina@catholiccharities.net
Ailbe Assisted Housing Corporation - 721 N. LaSalle St., Chicago, IL 60654
St. Ailbe Faith Apartments - 1244 E. 93rd St., Chicago, IL 60619 t) 773-721-0903 lwells@catholiccharities.net Linda Wells, Property Mgr.;
St. Ailbe Hope Apartments - 9101-9103 S. Harper, Chicago, IL 60619 t) 773-721-0903 lwells@catholiccharities.net Linda Wells, Property Mgr.;
St. Ailbe Love Apartments - 9240 S. Kimbark Ave., Chicago, IL 60619 t) 773-721-0903 lwells@catholiccharities.net Linda Wells, Property Mgr.;
Ailbe Senior Housing Corporation - 721 N. LaSalle St., Chicago, IL 60654
All Saints Residence - 11701 S. State St., Chicago, IL 60628 t) 773-995-9000 ajackson@catholiccharities.net
All Saints Senior Housing, NFP - 721 N. LaSalle St., Chicago, IL 60654
Antioch/Lake Villa Home Delivered Meal Distribution and Congregate Site - 1625 Deep Lake Rd., Lake Villa, IL 60046 t) 847-838-6415 mbibat@catholiccharities.net Mary Ann Bibat, Pres.;
Archdiocesan AIDS Ministry Office - 1800 N. Hermitage Ave., Chicago, IL 60622 t) 312-948-6500 pdrott@catholiccharities.net Patricia Drott, Dir.;
Arts of Living Institute - 2601 W. Marquette Rd., Chicago, IL 60629 t) 312-382-2566 cupton@catholiccharities.net Constance Upton, Prog. Dir.;
Augustus Tolton Peace Center - 5645 W. Lake St., Chicago, IL 60644 jmancuso@catholiccharities.net John M Mancuso, Staff;
Bernardin Manor - 1700 Memorial Dr., Calumet City, IL 60409 t) 708-832-1700 kejackson@catholiccharities.net Kevin Jackson, Property Mgr.;
Bernardin Senior Housing Corporation - 721 N. LaSalle St., Chicago, IL 60654
Bishop Edwin M. Conway Residence - 1900 N. Karlov Ave., Chicago, IL 60639 t) 773-252-9941 gsaldana@catholiccharities.net Gabriela Saldana, Dir.;
Bishop Goedert Residence - 53 Tripp Ave., Bldg. 53, Hines, IL 60141 t) 708-273-6600 sgonzale@catholiccharities.net Sonya Gonzalez, Property Mgr.;
Bishop T.J. Lyne Residence for Retired Priests - 12230 S. Will-Cook Rd., Palos Park, IL 60464-7332 t) 630-257-2291 rmaguran@catholiccharities.net Roberta Magurany, Admin.;
St. Blase Child Development Center - 7438 W. 61st Pl., Summit, IL 60501 t) 708-496-1193 cmccall@catholiccharities.net Carolyn McCall, Dir.;
St. Blase Service Center - 7438 W. 61st St., Summit, IL 60501 t) (708) 563-2407 eirizarr@catholiccharities.net Eliu Irizarry, Dir.;
Board Relations - 721 N. LaSalle St., Chicago, IL 60654 t) (312) 948-6895 msimon@catholiccharities.net
Brendan Senior Housing Corporation - 721 N. LaSalle St., Chicago, IL 60654
Bridge Subsidy Program - 2601 W. Marquette Rd., Chicago, IL 60629 t) 312-948-6503 lsanchez@catholiccharities.net Leticia Sanchez, Dir.;
Calumet Park Service Center - 12420 S. Ada St., Calumet Park, IL 60827 t) (708) 597-7088 Eliu Irizarry, Dir.;
Catholic Charities Housing Development Corporation - t) 312-655-7490 housingmanagement@catholiccharities.net
Chicago Services - t) 312-655-7700 kmulvaney@catholiccharities.net Kate Mulvaney, Dir.;
Child, Youth, and Families - 721 N. LaSalle St., Chicago, IL 60654 t) (312) 655-8570 Laura Rios, Vice. Pres.;
Communications - 721 N. LaSalle St., Chicago, IL 60654 c) (312) 622-2640 pzepeda@catholiccharities.net Phil Zepeda, VP Communications;
Community Counseling and Addiction Services - 1800 N. Hermitage Ave., Chicago, IL 60622 t) 312-655-7725 pdavis@catholiccharities.net Pamela Davis, Dir.;
Community Based Violence Intervention and Prevention Program - 5645 W. Lake St., Chicago, IL 60644
Cortland Manor Development Corporation - 721 N. LaSalle St., Chicago, IL 60654
Development - 721 N. LaSalle St., Chicago, IL 60654 t) (312) 948-6865 mdaigler@catholiccharities.net Michael Daigler, VP of Principal Giving;
Donald W. Kent Residence - 100 S. Wolf Rd., Northlake, IL 60164 t) 708-409-4710 ycastro@catholiccharities.net Yadira Castro, Property Mgr.;
Family Stabilization Services - t) 312-655-7500 stillmon@catholiccharities.net Sharon Tillmon, Dir.;
Facilities Operations - t) 312-655-7920 spodder@catholiccharities.net
Finance - 721 N. LaSalle St., Chicago, IL 60654 t) (312) 948-6520 bseaman@catholiccharities.net Beth Seaman, VP Finance;
Frances Manor - 1270 E. Golf Rd., Des Plaines, IL 60016 t) 847-390-1270 gfucik@catholiccharities.net Gegg Fucik, Property Mgr.;
Frances Senior Housing Corporation - 721 N. LaSalle St., Chicago, IL 60654
Goedert Senior Housing Corporation - 721 N. LaSalle St., Chicago, IL 60654
Government Relations - 721 N. LaSalle St., Chicago, IL 60654 t) 312-655-7020 bosullivan@catholiccharities.net Brendan O'Sullivan, Dir.;
Grayslake Senior Center and Congregate Site - 50 Library Ln., Grayslake, IL 60030 t) 847-543-1041 mbibat@catholiccharities.net Mary Ann Bibat, Pres.;
Hayes Manor - 1211 W. Marquette Rd., Chicago, IL 60636 t) 773-873-7400 Beverly Howard, Property Mgr.;
Hayes Senior Housing Corporation - 721 N. LaSalle St., Chicago, IL 60654
Holy Family Villa - 12220 S. Will-Cook Rd., Palos Park, IL 60464-7332 t) (312) 655-7460 sblount@catholiccharities.net www.holyfamilyvilla.net
Homelessness Prevention Call Center - 1800 N. Hermitage St., Chicago, IL 60622 t) 312-698-5080 wavila@catholiccharities.net Wendy Avila, Dir.;
House of the Good Shepherd of Chicago - ; Mailing: P.O. Box 13453, Chicago, IL 60613 jkielty@catholiccharities.net Sr. Jean Kielty, Dir.;
Housing Development - 721 N. LaSalle St., Chicago, IL 60654 t) (312) 948-6820 jcunnea@catholiccharities.net James Cunnea, Vice Pres.;
Housing Services - 721 N. LaSalle St., Chicago, IL 60654 t) (312) 655-7490 trodriguez@catholiccharities.net; ehiggins@catholiccharities.net Eileen Higgins, Vice. Pres.; Roberta Magurany, Assoc. Vice Pres.; Millicent Ntiamoah, Assoc. Vice Pres.; Antwaun Smith, Assoc. Vice Pres.;
Human Resources - 721 N. LaSalle St., Chicago, IL 60654 t) (312) 655-7130 eomalley@catholiccharities.net Erica O'Malley, Senior VP;
Immediate and Basic Needs - 721 N. LaSalle St., Chicago, IL 60654 t) (312) 655-7151 Peggy Arizzi, Vice. Pres.; Bob Haennicke, Assoc. Vice Pres.; Maureen Murphy, Assoc. Vice Pres.;
Immigration & Naturalization Services - 205 W. Monroe St., Chicago, IL 60606 t) 312-427-7078 ngavilan@catholiccharities.net Nancy Gavilanes, Dir.;
Intact Family Services - 1800 N. Hermitage Ave., Chicago, IL 60622 t) 312-382-2505 mhenderson@catholiccharities.net Mary J. Henderson, Dir.;
Jadonal E. Ford Center for Adolescent Parenting - 11255 S. Michigan Ave., Chicago, IL 60628 t) 312-236-5384 vwalker@catholiccharities.net Velma Brown-Walker, Dir.;
St. Joseph Apartments - 2601 W. Marquette Rd., Chicago, IL 60629 t) 312-655-7235 mntiamoa@catholiccharities.net Millicent Ntiamoah, Assoc. Vice Pres.;
Joseph Cardinal Bernardin Center for Lake County Services - 671 S. Lewis Ave., Waukegan, IL 60085 t) 847-782-4000 Lisa Roti, Reg. Svcs. Dir.;
Josephine P. Argento Senior Center - 1700 N. Memorial Dr., Calumet City, IL 60409 t) 708-832-1208 rboyd@catholiccharities.net
Keenager News - 721 N. LaSalle St., Chicago, IL 60654 t) 312-655-7425 kbredemann@catholiccharities.net Katie Bredemann, Communications Mgr.;
Kelvyn Park Senior Center Satellite - 2715 N. Cicero Ave., Chicago, IL 60639 t) 312-744-3350 mbibat@catholiccharities.net Martha Lavaire, Contact;
Lake County Family Self-Sufficiency - 671 S. Lewis, Waukegan, IL 60085 t) 847-782-4100 nguzman@catholiccharities.net Nelly Guzman, Prog. Supvr.;
Lake County HIV/AIDS Case Management - 671 S. Lewis, Waukegan, IL 60085 t) 847-782-4100 astyx@catholiccharities.net Ashley Styx, Dir.;
Lake County Housing Case Management - 671 S. Lewis, Waukegan, IL 60085 t) 847-782-4000 ddrinka@catholiccharities.net
Lake County Nutrition Program Sites (Congregate and Home Delivered Meals) - 671 S. Lewis Ave., Waukegan, IL 60085 t) 847-782-4268 bmeyer@catholiccharities.net Brenda Meyer, Dir.;
Lake County Senior Case Management Services - 116 N. Lincoln, Round Lake, IL 60073 t) 847-546-5733 mharris@catholiccharities.net Marla Harris, Dir.;
Lawrence Manor - 21425 Southwick Dr., Matteson, IL 60443 t) 708-481-1200 erinconeno@catholiccharities.net Emilio Rinconeno, Property Mgr.;
Lawrence Senior Housing Corporation - 721 N. LaSalle St., Chicago, IL 60654
Legal and Compliance Services - 721 N. LaSalle St., Chicago, IL 60654 t) (312) 948-6895 msimon@catholiccharities.net
Legal Assistance - t) (312) 655-7240 snavarro@catholiccharities.net Sylvia Navarro, Intake Specialist;
St. Leo Assisted Housing, NFP - 721 N. LaSalle St., Chicago, IL 60654
St. Leo Development Association - 721 N. LaSalle St., Chicago, IL 60654
LOSS (Loving Outreach to Survivors of Suicide) - t) 312-655-7283 dmajor@catholiccharities.net Deborah Major, Dir.;
Madonna Campus Child Development Center - 1114 W. Grace, Chicago, IL 60613 t) 773-935-3434 marivera@catholiccharities.net Marianet Rivera, Site Dir;
Madonna House - 1114 W. Grace St., Chicago, IL 60613 t) 773-327-1605
St. Mary of Celle - 1428 S. Wesley Ave., Berwyn, IL 60402 t) 708-303-3650 snewsome@catholiccharities.net Stephanie Newsome, Site Dir.;
Pregnancy, Parenting, and Adoption Services - 1800 N. Hermitage Ave., Chicago, IL 60622 t) 312-655-7086 kherrera@catholiccharities.net Kathryn Herrera

Herrrera, Prog. Dir.;
Matthew Manor - 271 N. Albany Ave., Chicago, IL 60612 t) 773-533-0001 mrios@catholiccharities.net Margarita Rios, Property Mgr.;
Matthew Senior Housing Corporation - 721 N. LaSalle St., Chicago, IL 60654
McHenry County Nutrition Services - 3519 N. Richmond Rd., Johnsburg, IL 60051 t) 815-385-8260 bmeyer@catholiccharities.net Brenda Meyer, Dir.;
New Hope Apartments - 2601 W. Marquette Rd., Chicago, IL 60629 t) 312-655-7235 slove@catholiccharities.net Sharon Love, Dir.;
North Center Senior Housing, NFP - 721 N. LaSalle St., Chicago, IL 60654
North Suburban Services - 1717 Rand Rd., Des Plaines, IL 60016 t) 847-376-2100 akelly@catholiccharities.net Adriana Kelly, Reg. Svcs. Dir;
Northeast/Northwest Chicago Case Management Services - 3125 N. Knox, Chicago, IL 60641 t) 773-583-9224 gcleggs@catholiccharities.net Gina Cleggs, Senior VP;
Northlake Senior Housing, NFP - 721 N. LaSalle St., Chicago, IL 60654
Northwest Suburban Senior Services - 1801 W. Central, Arlington Heights, IL 60005 t) 847-253-5500 cgunders@catholiccharities.net Cynthia Gunderson, Deputy Dir.;
Northwest Suburban Services - 1717 Rand Rd., Des Plaines, IL 60016 t) 847-376-2100 mwaters@catholiccharities.net Rose Marie Lesniak-Mendez, Reg. Svcs. Dir;
Ozanam Village - 251 N. Albany Ave., Chicago, IL 60612 t) 773-533-0001 mrios@catholiccharities.net
Palos Park Senior Housing, NFP - 721 N. LaSalle St., Chicago, IL 60654
Park Place Home Delivered Meal Distribution and Congregate Site - 414 S. Lewis Ave., Waukegan, IL 60085 t) 847-662-0085
Performance Quality Improvement and Data Analysis - 721 N. LaSalle St., Chicago, IL 60654 t) (312) 655-7126 asweeney@catholiccharities.net Anne Sweeney, Dir.;
St. Peter Claver Courts - 14115 S. Claire Blvd., Robbins, IL 60472 t) 708-389-1570 bwhitby@catholiccharities.net Barbara Whitby, Property Mgr.;
St. Peter Claver Senior Housing Corporation - 721 N. LaSalle St., Chicago, IL 60654
Pope John Paul II Residence - 7741 S. Emerald Ave., Chicago, IL 60620 t) 773-651-9950 csteen@catholiccharities.net
Porta Coeli Residence - 2260 E. 99th St., Chicago, IL 60617 t) 773-374-2470 kmcfern@catholiccharities.net Karroll McFern, Property Mgr.;
Porta Coeli Senior Housing, NFP - 721 N. LaSalle St., Chicago, IL 60654
Refugee Resettlement Program - 4837 N. Kenmore Ave., Chicago, IL 60640 t) 312-655-7856 ekulovic@catholiccharities.net Elmida Kulovic, Dir.;
Roseland Manor - 11717 S. State St., Chicago, IL 60628 t) 773-995-9000 ajackson@catholiccharities.net Andiera Jackson, Property Mgr.;
Roseland Senior Housing Corporation - 721 N. LaSalle St., Chicago, IL 60654
Round Lake Home Delivered Meals Distribution Site - 116 N. Lincoln, Round Lake, IL 60073 t) 847-740-6714 mbibat@catholiccharities.net Mary Ann Bibat, Pres.;
St. Sabina Elders Village - 1222 W. 79th St., Chicago, IL 60620 t) 773-994-7850 lmyles@catholiccharities.net Linda Myles, Property Mgr.;
Sabina Senior Housing Corporation - 721 N. LaSalle St., Chicago, IL 60654
St. Ailbe Adult Day Care - 9249 S. Avalon, Chicago, IL 60619 t) 773-721-0177 ltennent@catholiccharities.net LaDonna Tennet, Dir.;
St. Francis of Assisi Residence - 12218 S. Will-Cook Rd., Palos Park, IL 60464 t) 630-343-1880 acole@catholiccharities.net Aneisha Cole, Property Mgr.;
St. Josephs Carondelet Child Center - 721 N. LaSalle St., Chicago, IL 60654 t) (312) 948-6895 msimon@catholiccharities.net
Senior Aides Employment Program - 2601 W. Marquette Rd., Chicago, IL 60629 t) 773-349-8035 sjohnigan@catholiccharities.net Stephanie Johnigan, Dir.;
Senior Food and Nutrition Program (SNFP) - 1965 W. Pershing Rd., Chicago, IL 60609 t) 773-523-5758 eirizarr@catholiccharities.net Eliu Irizarry, Dir.;
Senior Food and Nutrition Program (SNFP) Warehouse - 1965 W. Pershing Rd., Chicago, IL 60609 t) (312) 951-9370 mheroldt@catholiccharities.net Michael Heroldt, Dir.;
Senior Services - 721 N. LaSalle St., Chicago, IL 60654 t) (312) 948-7412 Mary Ann Bibat, Vice. Pres.; Meisha Lyons, Vice. Pres.; Angela Taylor, Assoc. Vice Pres.;
Seniors Farmers Market Nutrition Program (SFMNP) - 416 E. 43rd St., Chicago, IL 60653 t) 773-924-7043 yjames@catholiccharities.net Yolanda James, Contact;
Sisters of St. Casimir Center - 2601 W. Marquette Rd., Chicago, IL 60629 t) 312-655-7920
SNFP Outreach - Yolanda James, Contact;
South Suburban Senior Services - 15300 S. Lexington, Harvey, IL 60426 t) 708-596-2222 umcintosh@catholiccharities.net Umekia McIntosh, Deputy Dir.;
South Suburban Services - 12732 Wood St., Calumet Park, IL 60827 t) 708-333-8379 cltorres@catholiccharities.net Christopher Torres, Dir.;
Southwest Suburban Services - 12731 S. Wood St., Blue Island, IL 60827 t) 708-586-1355 cltorres@catholiccharities.net Christopher Torres, Reg. Svcs. Dir.;
Special Supplemental Food & Nutrition Programs-Senior Programs - t) 773-729-3912 mheroldt@catholiccharities.net Congregate Meals; Home Delivered Meals; Summer Food Program; Child Adult Care Food Program (CACFP); Safe Haven Michael Heroldt, Dir.;
St. Brendan Apartments - 6718 S. Racine Ave., Chicago, IL 60636 t) 773-846-8600 bhoward@catholiccharities.net Beverly Howard, Property Mgr.;
St. Leo Residence for Veterans - 7750 S. Emerald Ave., Chicago, IL 60620 t) 773-651-9950 csteen@catholiccharities.net
Supportive Services for Veterans Families - 2601 W. Marquette Rd., Chicago, IL 60629 t) 312-948-6898 maugustave@catholiccharities.net Magalie Augustave, Dir.;
The Peace Corner, Inc. - 5022 W. Madison St., Chicago, IL 60644 t) 773-924-7043 gcleggs@catholiccharities.net Gina Cleggs, VP;
Tolton Manor - 6345 S. Stewart Ave., Chicago, IL 60621 t) 773-783-7800 ajackson@catholiccharities.net
Tolton Senior Housing Corporation - 721 N. LaSalle St., Chicago, IL 60654
Veterans Employment Program - 2601 W. Marquette Rd., Chicago, IL 60629 t) 773-808-2958 maugustave@catholiccharities.net Magalie Augustave, Mgr.;
St. Vincent de Paul Residence - 4040 N. Oakley Ave., Chicago, IL 60618 t) 773-539-2660
St. Vincent De Paul Residence North Center Senior Satellite - 4040 N. Oakley St., Chicago, IL 60618 t) (773) 539-2660 gfucik@catholiccharities.net Gegg Fucik, Property Mgr.;
West Suburban Services - 1400 S. Austin Blvd., Cicero, IL 60804 t) 708-329-4022 ezepeda@catholiccharities.net Michael Waters, Reg. Svcs. Dir.;
Women, Infants and Children (WIC) Food and Nutrition Centers Program - 6202 S. Halsted, Chicago, IL 60621 t) (773) 729-3915 sdickson@catholiccharities.net Shivonnia Dickson, Dir.;
WIC Food Center #4501 - 2907 S. Wabash Ave., Chicago, IL 60616
WIC Food Center #4502 - 416 E. 43rd St., Chicago, IL 60653
WIC Food Center #4504 - 6202 S. Halsted St., Chicago, IL 60621
WIC Food Center #4505 - 5332 S. Western Ave., Chicago, IL 60609
WIC Food Center #4506 - 2310 W. Roosevelt Rd., Chicago, IL 60608
WIC Food Center #4507 - 3110 W. Armitage Ave., Chicago, IL 60647
WIC Food Center #4508 - 5125 W. Chicago Ave., Chicago, IL 60651
WIC Food Center #4509 - 1734 W. Chicago Ave., Chicago, IL 60622
WIC Food Center #4510 - 1643 W. Cermak Rd., Chicago, IL 60608
WIC Food Center #4511 - 3932 W. Madison Ave., Chicago, IL 60624
WIC Food Center #4512 - 1802 E. 71st St., Chicago, IL 60649
WIC Food Center #4513 - 4620 W. Diversey Ave., Chicago, IL 60639
WIC Food Center #4514 - 11255 S. Michigan Ave., Chicago, IL 60628
WIC Food Center #4515 - 2400 S. Kedzie Ave., Chicago, IL 60623
WIC Food Center #4516 - 8959 S. Commercial Ave., Chicago, IL 60617
WIC Food Center #4517 - 1106 W. 79th St., Chicago, IL 60620
Youth Counseling Department - 2310 W. Roosevelt Rd., 2nd Fl., Chicago, IL 60608 t) 312-655-7489 hrivera@catholiccharities.net Hector Rivera, Dept. Dir.;
CHA Family Works - Regional Family Works Office, 4802 N. Broadway, Ste. 205, Chicago, IL 60640 t) 773-409-4754 mlucas@catholiccharities.net Melissa Lucas, Dir.;
Englewood Service Center - 6202 S. Halsted, Chicago, IL 60621 t) 773-488-6800 eirizarr@catholiccharities.net Eliu Irizarry, Dir.;
EPIC Program - 6202 S. Halsted St., Chicago, IL 60621 t) 312-655-7330 gcleggs@catholiccharities.net Gina Cleggs, Assoc. Vice Pres.;
Korean Self-Help Center - 4934 N. Pulaski Rd., Chicago, IL 60630 t) 773-545-8348
Logan Square Service Center - 3110 W. Armitage Ave., Chicago, IL 60647 t) 773-395-4207
Lunch-N-More Catering and Food Service Enterprise; Painting Enterprise; Veterans Independent Painting - 6202 S. Halsted St., Chicago, IL 60621 t) 312-655-7330 gcleggs@catholiccharities.net Gina Cleggs, Assoc. Vice Pres.;
One Summer Chicago Plus Program - 6202 S. Halsted St., Chicago, IL 60621 t) 312-655-7330 Gina Cleggs, Assoc. Vice Pres.;
Pilsen Service Center - 1643 W. Cermak Rd., Chicago, IL 60608 t) 773-523-0409
Southeast Service Center - 8959 S. Commercial Ave., Chicago, IL 60617 t) 773-978-6235
Summer Youth Employment Program - 6202 S. Halsted St., Chicago, IL 60621 t) 312-655-7330 gcleggs@catholiccharities.net Gina Cleggs, Assoc. Vice Pres.;
Translation and Interpretation Network (TIN) - 721 N. La Salle St., 7th Fl., Chicago, IL 60654 t) 312-655-7483 mmoiron@catholiccharities.net Michael Moiron, Dir.;

CEMETERIES [CEM]

CALUMET CITY

Holy Cross -

CRESTWOOD
St. Benedict -
DES PLAINES
All Saints -
EVANSTON
Calvary -
EVERGREEN PARK
St. Mary -
FOX LAKE
St. Bede -
FREMONT CENTER
St. Mary -
GLENWOOD
Assumption -
HIGHLAND PARK
St. Mary -
HILLSIDE
Central Office - 1400 S. Wolf Rd., Hillside, IL 60162-2197 t) 708-449-6100 www.cathcemchgo.org Theodore Ratajczyk, Exec. Dir.; Rev. Lawrence J. Sullivan, Archdiocesan Dir.;
St. Boniface -
St. Casimir -
St. Henry -
Mt. Olivet -
Mt. Carmel -
Our Lady of Sorrows -
Queen of Heaven -
JUSTICE
Resurrection -
LAKE FOREST
St. Mary -
LEMONT
St. Alphonsus -
SS. Cyril & Methodius -
St. James, Sag Bridge -
St. Patrick -
LIBERTYVILLE
Ascension -
NILES
St. Adalbert -
Maryhill -
NORTHBROOK
Sacred Heart -
OAK FOREST
St. Gabriel -
ORLAND PARK
St. Michael -
PALATINE
St. Michael the Archangel -
PARK FOREST
St. Anne -
RIVER GROVE
St. Joseph -
ROSENCRANS
St. Patrick -
ROUND LAKE
St. Joseph -
SAUK VILLAGE
St. James -
SKOKIE
St. Peter -
STEGER
Calvary -
VOLO
St. Peter -
WAUCONDA
Transfiguration -
WAUKEGAN
St. Mary -
WEST LAKE FOREST
St. Patrick -
WILMETTE
St. Joseph -
WORTH
Holy Sepulchre -

COLLEGES & UNIVERSITIES [COL]

CHICAGO
De Paul University - One E. Jackson Blvd., Attn: Office of the General Counsel, Chicago, IL 60604 t) 312-362-8000; 312-362-8865 mdevona@depaul.edu www.depaul.edu Campuses: Downtown, Lincoln Park. Sponsored by the Congregation of the Mission (Vincentian Fathers and Brothers). Robert Manuel, Pres.; Rev. Dennis H. Holtschneider, C.M., Chancellor; Kathryn Stieber, Secy.; Brian Sullivan, Treas.; Rev. Guillermo Campuzano, CM, Vice Pres. Mission and Ministry; Stds.: 20,917; Bro. Tchrs.: 1; Lay Tchrs.: 862; Pr. Tchrs.: 2; Sr. Tchrs.: 1
College of Communication - 14 E. Jackson Blvd., Ste. 1800, Chicago, IL 60604
College of Computing and Digital Media - 243 S. Wabash Ave., Chicago, IL 60604-2302 t) 312-362-8381 David Miller, Dean;
College of Education - 2320 N. Kenmore Ave., Chicago, IL 60614 t) 773-325-7740 Paul Zionts, Dean;
College of Law - 931 Lewis Center, 25 E. Jackson Blvd., Chicago, IL 60604 t) 312-362-8701 Jennifer Rosato Perea, Dean;
College of Liberal Arts and Sciences - 990 W. Fullerton Ave., Ste. 4200, Chicago, IL 60614 t) 773-325-7310 Guillermo Vasquez de Velasco, Dean;
College of Science and Health - 1110 W. Belden Ave., Chicago, IL 60614 t) 773-325-8300 Dorothy Kozlowski, Interim Dean;
Kellstadt Graduate School of Business Driehaus College of Business - 7103 DePaul Center, One E. Jackson Blvd., Chicago, IL 60604 t) 312-362-6783 Misty Johanson, Dean;
School of Music - 200 Music Bldg., 804 W. Belden, Chicago, IL 60614 t) 773-325-7260 Ronald Caltabiano, Dean;
The Theatre School - 2135 N. Kenmore Ave., Chicago, IL 60614 t) 773-325-7917 John Culbert, Dean;
Jesuit Community at Loyola University Chicago - 6324 N. Kenmore, Chicago, IL 60660 t) 773-508-2196 lujc.minister@gmail.com; dgodleski@luc.edu The Jesuit Community Corporation at Loyola University Rev. Mark P. Scalese, S.J., Supr.; Rev. David A. Godleski, S.J., Minister/Treas.; Rev. Mark G. Henninger, S.J., Chap.; Rev. T. Jerome Overbeck, S.J., Chap.; Rev. Tuan Le, S.J., Chap.; Rev. Tho Vu, SJ, Campus Min.; Rev. Thomas W. Neitzke, S.J., Dean; Rev. Thomas Krettek, S.J., Dean; Rev. James S. Prehn, S.J., Vice. Pres.; Rev. Glen Chun, S.J., Prov. Asst.; Rev. Charles Rodrigues, S.J., Prov. Asst.; Rev. Richard Patrick Salmi, S.J., Rector; Rev. Gail G. Bohr, S.J., Mission & Identity Dir.; Rev. Daniel F. Hartnett, S.J., Pst. Min./Coord.; Rev. John J. O'Callaghan, S.J., Pst. Min./Coord.; Rev. Paul J. Faulstich, S.J., Pastoral Ministry; Rev. William E. Creed, S.J., Pst. Min./Coord.; Rev. Peter J. Bernardi, S.J., Scholar/Pastoral and Sacramental Ministry; Rev. Paul Shelton, S.J., Vocation Dir.; Rev. Michael Simone, S.J., Assoc. Pst.; Rev. Peter W. Breslin, S.J., Prof.; Rev. Jayme Stayer, S.J., Prof.; Rev. David G. DeMarco, S.J., Prof.; Rev. John F. Costello, S.J., Prof.; Rev. Matthew Dunch, S.J., Prof.; Rev. Patrick Gilger, Prof.; Rev. D. Scott Hendrickson, S.J., Prof.; Rev. Jose A. Mesa, S.J., Prof.; Rev. Stephen Schloesser, S.J., Prof.; Rev. Stephen F. Mitten, S.J., Prof.; Rev. James G. Murphy, S.J., Prof.; Michael Pederson, S.J., Prof.; Bro. Mark Mackey, S.J., Adjunct faculty; Rev. John M. McManamon, S.J., Researcher & Writer; Rev. Mitchell C. Pacwa, S.J., Television Ministry; Rev. Choobe Maambo, S.J., Graduate Student; Rev. Gonzalo Benavides Mesones, S.J., Graduate Student; Rev. Raj Kumar, S.J. (India), Graduate Student; Rev. Max A. Landman, SJ, Graduate Student; Rev. Ternan Monteiro, S.J., Graduate Student; Rev. Emmanuel Patton, Graduate Student; Rev. Augustine Pushparaj, S.J., Graduate Student; Rev. Samir Talati, S.J., Graduate Student; Bro. Miguel Ceron Becerra, S.J., Graduate Student; Luis Delgado del Valle, S.J., Graduate Student; Stds.: 16,899; Bro. Tchrs.: 1; Lay Tchrs.: 887; Pr. Tchrs.: 20; Scholastics: 1
***Loyola University of Chicago, Illinois** - 1032 W. Sheridan Rd., Chicago, IL 60660 t) 773-274-3000 www.luc.edu Susan Sher, Chair; Mark C. Reed, Pres.; Stds.: 16,899; Bro. Tchrs.: 1; Pr. Tchrs.: 19; Scholastics: 887
Arrupe College - 820 N. Michigan Ave., Chicago, IL 60611 t) 800-262-2373 arrupeadmission@luc.edu www.luc.edu/arrupe Rev. Tom Nietzke, S.J., Dean; Stds.: 358; Bro. Tchrs.: 1; Pr. Tchrs.: 1; Scholastics: 22
The College of Arts and Sciences - 1032 W. Sheridan Rd, Chicago, IL 60626 t) 773-508-3500 casloyola@luc.edu www.luc.edu/cas Peter Schraeder, Dean; Stds.: 7,016; Pr. Tchrs.: 8; Scholastics: 397
The Graduate School - 6439 N Sheridan Rd, Chicago, IL 60626 t) 773-508-3396 admissions@luc.edu www.luc.edu/gradschool Emily Barman, Dean; Stds.: 1,042
Loyola University Stritch School of Medicine - 2160 S. First Ave., Maywood, IL 60153 t) 708-216-3229 ssom-admissions@luc.edu www.ssom.luc.edu Sam Marzo, Dean; Stds.: 686; Pr. Tchrs.: 2; Scholastics: 112
President's Office - 820 N. Michigan Ave., Chicago, IL 60611 t) 312-915-6400 president@luc.edu Margaret Callahan, Provost; Rev. James S. Prehn, S.J., Vice Pres. & Chief of Staff; Rev. Thomas Chillikulam, S.J., Campus Min.; Rev. D. Scott Hendrickson, S.J., Assoc. Provost, Global Community Engagement; Rev. Mark G. Henninger, S.J., Chap.; Rev. Tuan Le, S.J., Chap.;
The Quinlan School of Business - 820 N. Michigan Ave., Chicago, IL 60611 t) 312-915-6113 quinlanubus@luc.edu www.luc.edu/quinlan/ Behnam Michael, Dean; Stds.: 2,511; Scholastics: 78
School of Communication - 820 N. Michigan Ave., Chicago, IL 60611 t) 312-915-6548 www.luc.edu/soc Elizabeth Coffman, Interim Dean; Stds.: 661; Scholastics: 30
School of Continuing & Professional Studies - 820 N. Michigan Ave., Chicago, IL 60611 t) 312-915-8900 www.luc.edu/adult-education Jeanne Widen, Interim Dean; Stds.: 234; Scholastics: 8
The School of Education - 820 N. Michigan Ave., Chicago, IL 60611 t) 312-915-6800 schleduc@luc.edu www.luc.edu/education Malik Henfield, Dean; Stds.: 785; Pr. Tchrs.: 1; Scholastics: 36
The School of Law - 25 E. Pearson St., Chicago, IL 60611 t) (312) 915-7120 www.luc.edu/law Michele Alexandre, Dean; Stds.: 1,228; Pr. Tchrs.: 2; Scholastics: 52
The School of Nursing - 2160 S. First Ave., Maywood, IL 60153 t) (708) 216-9101 schoolofnursing@luc.edu www.luc.edu/nursing Lorna Finnegan, Dean; Stds.: 1,305; Scholastics: 69
School of Social Work - 1 E. Pearson St., Chicago, IL 60611; Mailing: 820 N. Michigan Ave., Chicago, IL 60611 t) 312-915-7005 gpem@luc.edu www.luc.edu/socialwork/ Marley James, Interim Dean; Stds.: 694; Scholastics: 28
Mundelein College - 6525 N. Sheridan Rd., Chicago, IL 60626; Mailing: 820 N. Michigan Ave., Ste. 750, Chicago, IL 60611 t) 312-915-6239; 773-508-3029 pcostas@luc.edu www.luc.edu Wayne Magdziarz, Pres. & Chmn., Bd. of Trustees; Janet W. Sisler, Vice Pres. & Treas.; Pamela G. Costas, Secy.;
***Resurrection University** - 1431 N. Claremont Ave., Chicago, IL 60622
Saint Xavier University - 3700 W. 103rd St., Chicago, IL 60655-3105 t) 773-298-3000 (Info Desk); 773-341-5734 (Mission & Heritage) missionandheritage@sxu.edu www.sxu.edu Sponsorship: Institute of the Sisters of Mercy of the Americas. Dr. Jenny DeVivo, Admin.; Dr. Laurie M. Joyner, Pres.; Stds.: 3,523; Lay Tchrs.: 131
College of Arts and Sciences - t) 773-298-3090 (Dean); 773-298-3207 (Assoc. Dean) rylaarsdam@sxu.edu; coutts@sxu.edu www.sxu.edu/academics/cas/index.aspx Dr. Greg Coutts, Admin.; Dr. Robin

Rylaarsdam, Dean;
Graham School of Management - t) 773-298-3601 rosenbaum@sxu.edu www.sxu.edu/academics/gsm/index.aspx Dr. Mark Rosenbaum, Dean;
School of Nursing and Health Sciences - t) 773-298-3700 ggeorge@sxu.edu www.sxu.edu/academics/sonhs/index.aspx Dr. Gwendoyln George, Dean;

RIVER FOREST

Dominican University (Formerly Rosary College) - 7900 W. Division St., River Forest, IL 60305 t) 708-366-2490 president@dom.edu www.dom.edu Dominican University, Dominican Sisters of Sinsinawa, WI. Sr. Antoinette Harris, Prioress; Dr. Glena G Temple, Pres.; Sara Acosta, VP University Advancement; Genaro Balcazar, VP Enrollment Mgmt.; Dr. Barrington Price, VP Student Success and Engagement; Mark Titzer, VP Finance; Stds.: 3,196; Lay Tchrs.: 139
Brennan School of Business - t) 708-524-6828 Dr. Roberto Curci, Dean;
Rosary College of Arts and Sciences at Dominican University - t) 708-524-6816 Chad Rohman, Interim Dean;

CONVENTS, MONASTERIES, AND RESIDENCES FOR WOMEN [CON]

ARLINGTON HEIGHTS

Missionaries of the Sacred Heart of Jesus and Our Lady of Guadalupe M.S.C.Gpe. - 1212 E. Euclid Ave., Arlington Heights, IL 60004 t) 847-255-5616

BARTLETT

Immaculata Congregational Home - 801 W. Bartlett Rd., Bartlett, IL 60103-4401 t) 630-837-4061 ssj801@sbcglobal.net

BLUE ISLAND

Mother of Sorrows Convent - 13811 S. Western Ave., Blue Island, IL 60406-4172 srloustu@yahoo.com Mantellate Sisters Servants of Mary Sr. Marianne Talian, O.S.M., Supr.;

CHICAGO

Adrian Dominican Sisters, Dominican Midwest Mission Chapter - 10024 S. Central Park Ave., Chicago, IL 60655-3132 t) 773-253-3827 kklingen@adriandominicans.org www.adriandominicans.org Sr. Kathleen Klingen, O.P., Prioress;
Benedictine Sisters of Chicago - St. Scholastica Monastery, 7430 N. Ridge Blvd., Chicago, IL 60645 t) 773-764-2413 prioress@osbchicago.org www.osbchicago.org Sr. Judith Murphy, O.S.B., Prioress; Sr. Virginia Jung, O.S.B., Archivist; Srs.: 24
Congregation of the Albertine Sisters - 1550 N. Astor, Chicago, IL 60610 t) 312-642-5838 dpekala@archchicago.org Sr. Theodosia Lichosyt, Supr.; Sr. Domicela Pekala, Contact;
Convent - 4117 S. Michigan, Chicago, IL 60653
Daughters of St. Mary of Providence - Provincialate: 4200 N. Austin Ave., Chicago, IL 60634-1615 t) 773-205-1313 icp.provincial@dsmpic.org; sr.rita@dsmpic.org www.dsmpic.org Sr. Rita Butler, Prov.; Srs.: 56
Providence Soup Kitchen - 1350 W. Evergreen Ave., Chicago, IL 60642
Daughters of St. Paul - 172 N. Michigan, Chicago, IL 60601 t) 312-346-4902 (Convent); 312-346-4228 (Center) chicago@pauline.org www.pauline.org Sr. Majorina Zamatta, F.S.P., Supr.;
St. Elizabeth Convent - 1356 N. Claremont Ave., Chicago, IL 60622 www.poorhandmaids.org Poor Handmaids of Jesus Christ. Sr. Bonnie Boilini, P.H.J.C., Contact;
Little Sisters of Jesus - 1529 S. Sawyer St., Chicago, IL 60623 t) 773-277-5061 littlesrs.chg@juno.com www.rc.net/org/littlesisters
Little Sisters of the Poor of Chicago, Inc. - 2325 N. Lakewood Ave., Chicago, IL 60614 t) 773-935-9600 mschicago@littlesistersofthepoor.org www.littlesistersofthepoorchicago.org Sr. Julie Horseman, Supr.;
Mary Ward Center - 3215 E. 91st St., Chicago, IL 60617 Housing for Institute of the Blessed Virgin Mary (Loretto Sisters).
Missionaries of Charity - 2325 W. 24th Pl., Chicago, IL 60608 t) 773-847-8771 Convent with maternity home Sr. M. Jonathan, M.C., Regl. Supr.; Sr. Salvinette M.C., Supr.; Srs.: 7
Missionary Sisters of Christ the King - 4910 N. Menard Ave., Chicago, IL 60630 t) 773-481-1831 annablauciak@gmail.com; katarzynazar17@gmail.com Sr. Katarzyna Zaremba, M.Ch.R., Supr.; Sr. Anna Blauciak, M.Ch.R., Secy.; Sr. Malgorzata Tomalka, Treas.; Srs.: 206
Missionary Sisters of Christ the King - 5936 W. Barry Ave., Chicago, IL 60634-5130 t) 773-889-7979 Sr. Dorota Domin, M.Ch.R., Supr.;
Missionary Sisters of Christ the King - 3651 W. George St., Chicago, IL 60618 t) 773-395-3520 Sr. Iwona Boronska, M.Ch.R., Supr.;
Missionary Sisters of Christ the King - 5555 W. State St., Burbank, IL 60459 t) 708-458-8556 Sr. Weronika Ilnicka, M.Ch.R., Supr.;
Missionary Sisters of Christ the King - 1118 N. Noble St., Chicago, IL 60622 t) 773-489-0714 Sr. Gertruda Szymanska, M.Ch.R., Supr.;
Missionary Sisters of Christ the King - 2441 N. Menard Ave., Chicago, IL 60639-2334 t) 773-637-9187 Sr. Stefania Galka, M.Ch.R., Supr.;
Missionary Sisters of the Sacred Heart - 434 W. Deming Pl., Chicago, IL 60614 t) 773-883-7302 joaquiac@comcast.net Sr. Joaquina Costa, M.S.C., Treas.; Srs.: 3
Missionary Sisters of the Sacred Heart of Jesus - Holy Spirit Region - 434 W. Deming Pl., Chicago, IL 60614 t) 773-388-7329 joaquiac@comcast.net; joaquiac@gmail.com Sr. Joaquina Costa, M.S.C., Treas.; Srs.: 16
Mother of Good Counsel Convent - 3800 W. Peterson Ave., Chicago, IL 60659-3116 t) 773-463-3020 sjudithmk@feliciansisters.org www.feliciansistersna.org Felician Sisters: Mother of Good Counsel Convent; Our Lady of the Angels Convent; Archives; (*) Felician Services, Inc. The Felician Sisters of the Un Sr. Judith Marie Kubicki, Prov.; Srs.: 86
Felician Volunteers in Mission, Inc. -
North American Province of the Congregation of Our Lady of the Cenacle, Inc. - 3800 W. Peterson Ave., Chicago, IL 60659-3116 t) 773-528-6300 cenacleprovincialate@usa.net www.cenaclesisters.org Sr. Pamela J. Falkowski, r.c., Prov.; Srs.: 38
Cenacle Sisters -
***Oblate Sisters of Jesus the Priest** - 730 N. Wabash Ave., Chicago, IL 60611 t) 312-840-7498 Sr. Landy C Tun Pinto, Supr.;
School Sisters of Notre Dame - 2148 W. Foster Ave., Chicago, IL 60625 t) 773-561-7290 ckrohe@amssnd.org www.ssnd.org Sr. Charmaine Krohe, Prov.;
Sisters of Mercy of the Americas West Midwest Community, Inc. - 10024 S. Central Park Ave., Chicago, IL 60655-3132 t) 773-779-6011 www.sistersofmercy.org Sr. Susan M. Sanders, R.S.M., Vice. Pres.; Srs.: 417
Sisters of Our Lady of LaSalette - 4220 N. Sheridan Rd., Chicago, IL 60613 t) 773-248-4047 marijosnds@starpower.com; sr_emie@yahoo.com Sr. Emelita S. Sobrepena, S.N.D.S., Supr.;
Sisters of St. Casimir, Motherhouse and Novitiate - 2601 W. Marquette Rd., Chicago, IL 60629-1817 t) 773-776-1324 mzalot@ssc2601.com www.sistersofstcasimir.org Sr. Immacula Wendt, Supr.; Srs.: 30
Sisters of St. Casimir Trust - imac@ssc2601.com
Sisters of the Good Shepherd - 1114 W. Grace St., Chicago, IL 60613 t) 773-935-3434 Sr. Lakshmie Napagoda, Contact;
Sisters of the Holy Cross - 7422 N. Harlem, Chicago, IL 60631-4409 t) 574-284-5660 Sr. Kathleen Moroney, C.S.C., Treas.;
Sisters of the Holy Cross - 16130 Pine Dr., Tinley Park, IL 60477 t) 708-403-5134
Sisters of the Resurrection Provincial House and Novitiate - 7260 W. Peterson Ave., E-216, Chicago, IL 60631 c) 773-620-3492 srdonna01@gmail.com Sisters of the Resurrection, Congregation of the Sisters of the Resurrection, Chicago Province. Sr. Donna Marie Wolowicki, C.R., Prov.; Srs.: 21
Society of Helpers - 2226 W. Pratt Blvd., Chicago, IL 60645 t) 773-405-9884 jeankielty@yahoo.com helpers.org Sr. Rayo Cuaya-Castillo, SH, Prov.; Sr. Alicia Gutierrez, SH, Prov.; Sr. Jean Kielty, Prov.;
Society of Helpers - 2043 N. Humboldt Blvd., 2nd Fl., Chicago, IL 60647 t) 773-342-8832
Society of Helpers - 4541 S. Wood, Chicago, IL 60609 t) 773-807-8561
Society of Helpers - 2258 S. Marshall Blvd., Chicago, IL 60623 t) 773-522-9160
Society of Helpers - 2043 N. Humboldt Blvd., 1st Fl., Chicago, IL 60647
Society of Helpers - 2648 Pershing Rd., Chicago, IL 60632 t) 872-444-5315
Society of Helpers - 2226 W. Pratt Blvd., Chicago, IL 60645 t) 773-405-9884 jeankielty@yahoo.com www.helpers.org Sr. Alicia Gutierrez, SH, Prov.; Sr. Rayo Cuaya-Castillo, SH, Prov. Asst.; Sr. Jean Kielty, Prov. Asst.; Srs.: 16

DES PLAINES

Monastery of Discalced Carmelites - 949 N. River Rd., Des Plaines, IL 60016 t) 847-298-4241 Attended by priests of the Archdiocese. Mother Marie Benedicta of the Cross; Srs.: 19
Sisters of the Living Word - 950 Lee St., Ste. 200, Des Plaines, IL 60016 t) 847-577-5972 slw@slw.org www.slw.org Srs.: 43

EVERGREEN PARK

Little Company of Mary Sisters - USA - 2800 W. 95th St., Evergreen Park, IL 60805 t) (708) 229-5490 lguest@lcmh.org www.lcmsistersusa.org American Province of Little Company of Mary Sisters Charitable Trust. Srs.: 10

HOFFMAN ESTATES

Poor Handmaids of Jesus Christ, Annunciation Convent - 1480 Ashley Rd., Hoffman Estates, IL 60169-4818 www.poorhandmaids.org Sr. Patricia Kolas, Contact;

JUSTICE

Dominican Sisters Immaculate Conception Province - 9000 W. 81st St., Justice, IL 60458 t) 708-458-3040 rosaryhill@sbcglobal.net www.sistersop.org Sr. Helena Cempa Sr., O.P., Prov.;

LA GRANGE PARK

Congregation of St. Joseph - 1515 W. Ogden Ave., La Grange Park, IL 60526 t) 708-354-9200 pwarbritton@csjoseph.org csjoseph.org Sr. Chris March, Contact; Srs.: 44

LAKE VILLA

Handmaids of the Precious Blood - 724 Petite Lake Rd., Lake Villa, IL 60046-9619 t) 423-241-7065 Mother Mother Marietta, H.P.B., Prioress;

LEMONT

Franciscan Sisters of Chicago, General Administration Building - 11500 Theresa Dr., Lemont, IL 60439-2727 t) 630-243-3600 www.chicagofranciscans.org Sr. M. Bernadette Bajuscik, O.S.F., General Minister; Srs.: 17
Mount Assisi Convent, School Sisters of St. Francis of Christ the King - 13900 Main St., Lemont, IL 60439-9736 t) 630-257-7495 lemontfranciscans1909@gmail.com lemontfranciscans.org Sr. Therese Ann Quigney, Prov.; Srs.: 24
Our Lady of the Angels Retreat Ministries - 13820 Main St., Lemont, IL 60439
Our Lady of Victory Convent - 11400 Theresa Dr., Lemont, IL 60439-2728 t) 630-243-3600 www.chicagofranciscans.org General Motherhouse of the Franciscan Sisters of Chicago. Sr. M. Bernadette Bajuscik, O.S.F., General Minister; Srs.: 17

MELROSE PARK

Missionary Sisters of St. Charles Borromeo (Scalabrinians) - 1414 N. 37th Ave., Melrose Park, IL 60160 t) 708-343-2162 provincial.mscs.olf@gmail.com;

secretarymscsolf@gmail.com www.scalabriniane.org Provincialate and Bishop Scalabrini Community. Sr. Luiza Dal Moro, Prov.; Sr. Catherine Petalcurin, Secy.; Sr. Marissonia Daltoe, Treas.;

NORTHFIELD

Missionary Sisters Servants of the Holy Spirit - 319 Waukegan Rd., Northfield, IL 60093-2719; Mailing: P.O. Box 6026, Techny, IL 60082 t) 847-441-0126 provinceleader@ssps-us.org www.ssps-usa.org/ Sr. Dorota Maria Piechaczek Sr., Prov.; Srs.: 52

Arnold Janssen Foundation -

Helena Stollenwerk Foundation -

NORTHLAKE

Daughters of Divine Love Congregation - 133 N. Prater Ave., Northlake, IL 60164 t) 708-223-0262 ddloveus@aol.com A Pontifical Religious Institute. Sr. Mary Agbakoba, S.R.M.O., Supr.; Srs.: 1,028

OAK FOREST

Missionary Sisters of St. Benedict of Illinois, Inc. - 5900 W. 147th St., Oak Forest, IL 60452 t) 708-535-9623 missionarysis@sbcglobal.net Sr. Assumpta Wrobel, Supr.;

PALOS HEIGHTS

Religious Hospitallers of St. Joseph - 12251 S. 80th Ave., Palos Heights, IL 60463; Mailing: P.O. Box 82, Palos Heights, IL 60463 t) 708-448-9278 adoyle9657@aol.com

PALOS PARK

Poor Clare Monastery of the Immaculate Conception of Illinois - 12210 S. Will Cook Rd., Palos Park, IL 60464-7332 t) 708-361-1810 www.chicagopoorclares.org Sr. M. Teresita, P.C.C., Abbess;

STICKNEY

Franciscan Missionaries of Mary - 4311 S. Grove Ave., Stickney, IL 60402 t) 708-317-5075 bcfmm29@gmail.com www.fmmusa.org

WESTERN SPRINGS

Loretto Convent - 5103 Carolina, Western Springs, IL 60558 Housing for Institute of the Blessed Virgin Mary (Loretta Sisters)

WILMETTE

Maria Immaculata Convent-The SCC Center - 2041 Elmwood Ave., Wilmette, IL 60091-1431 t) 847-920-9341 srmaryann@sccwilmette.org www.sccwilmette.org The Society of the Sisters of Christian Charity, Corporation of Mallinckrodt College of the North Shore Sr. Juliana Miska, Supr.; Srs.: 5

Sacred Heart Convent - 2221 Elmwood Ave., Wilmette, IL 60091-1435 t) 847-251-3770 srjanice@sccwilmette.org www.sccwilmette.org A home for aged and infirm Sisters of Christian Charity. Motherhouse in Wilmette, Illinois. Sr. Janice Boyer, S.C.C., Supr.;

ENDOWMENTS / FOUNDATIONS / TRUSTS [EFT]

ARLINGTON HEIGHTS

***Foundation For Children In Need** - 725 N. Pine Ave., Arlington Heights, IL 60004; Mailing: P.O. Box 1247, Arlington Heights, IL 60006-1247 t) 847-670-1145 tomchitta@hotmail.com www.fcn-usa.org FCN is a Catholic lay organization established to reach out to the neediest in the rural villages of India. Tom Chitta, Dir.;

CHICAGO

Amate House Foundation - 3600 S. Seeley Ave., Chicago, IL 60609-1148 t) 773-376-2445 info@amatehouse.org; jbalanda@amatehouse.org amatehouse.org Jeannie Balanda, Dir.;

***Bethany Trust Fund** - Brown Brothers Harriman Trust Company, N.A., 150 S. Wacker Dr., Ste. 3250, Chicago, IL 60606 t) 312-781-7140

Catholic Education Scholarship Trust - 50 S. LaSalle St., Chicago, IL 60603

Catholic Kolping Society of America-National Endowment Fund - 5826 N. Elston Ave., Chicago, IL 60646-5544 t) 877-659-7237 patfarkas@optonline.net www.kolping.org Funds for National Kolping Lisa Brinkmann, Pres.;

Charitable Trust of the Order of Friar Servants of Mary, United States of America Province, Inc. - 3121 W. Jackson Blvd., Chicago, IL 60612-2729 t) 773-533-0360 arnaldosanchez@servitesusa.org www.servite.org Bro. Arnaldo Sanchez, OSM, Treas.;

***DeSales Charitable Trust** - Brown Brothers Harriman Trust Company, N.A., 150 S. Wacker Dr., Ste. 3250, Chicago, IL 60606 t) 312-781-7140

Haddon 3601 Trust - 3601 N. California Ave., Chicago, IL 60618 t) 773-320-5782 Bro. William Hallas, C.R., Contact;

***Hermitage Charitable Trust** - Brown Brothers Harriman Trust Company, N.A., 150 S. Wacker Dr., Ste. 3250, Chicago, IL 60606 t) 312-781-7140

Janski Trust - 3601 N. California Ave., Chicago, IL 60618 t) 773-320-5782 Bro. William Hallas, C.R., Contact;

***Fr. John Kolkman Foundation** - 2844 W. Sherwin Ave., Upper Room, Chicago, IL 60654 t) 309-270-2887 fjk@jkolkman.org jkolkman.org Increasing public awareness, early detection, and prevention and management of sickle cell disease Dcn. Michael Neba, Exec.;

John McKniff Peruvian Formation Charitable Trust - 5401 S. Cornell Ave., Chicago, IL 60615

LaSalle Pastoral Foundation - 111 S. Wacker Dr., Chicago, IL 60606 t) 312-443-1823

Le Royer Foundation - 326 W. 64th St., Chicago, IL 60621 t) 773-962-4073

***Misericordia Foundation** - 6300 N. Ridge, Chicago, IL 60660 t) (773) 273-4160 Lois Gates, Exec. Dir.;

***Mughamba Scholarship Foundation** - 120 LaSalle St., Ste. 3800, Chicago, IL 60602 Rev. Kombo L. Peshu, Pres.;

National Fund for Catholic Religious Vocations (NFCRV) - 5401 S. Cornell Ave., Ste. 207, Chicago, IL 60615 c) (312) 318-0180 ploftus@nfcrv.org www.nfcrv.org Promotes Catholic religious vocations by providing education debt grants to members of the NRVC for candidates entering their communities. Philip R. Loftus, Exec. Dir.;

Oblates for International Pastoral (Oblate International Pastoral Investment Trust) - 161 N. Clark St., Ste. 4700, Chicago, IL 60601 t) 410-433-2279 c) 210-421-3426; 202-491-4031 rwhitley@oiptrust.org; avandyke@oiptrust.org www.oiptrust.org Rev. Rufus J. Whitley, O.M.I., Pres./Bd. Mem.; Rev. Seamus P. Finn, O.M.I., Chief of Faith Consistent Investing; Rev. James P. Brobst, O.M.I., Trustee; Rev. Raymond Cook, O.M.I., Trustee; Rev. James Chambers, O.M.I., Trustee/ Bd. Mem.; Rev. Marc Dessureault, O.M.I., Trustee/ CEO/Bd. Chair; Rev. Charles Rensburg, OMI, Bd. Mem.; Anne Van Dyke, COO;

Ray Ryan Formation Charitable Trust - 5401 S. Cornell Ave., Chicago, IL 60615

Semenenko Trust - 3601 N. California Ave., Chicago, IL 60618 t) 773-320-5782 Bro. William Hallas, C.R., Contact;

St. Thomas Aquinas Priory - 1910 S. Ashland Ave., Chicago, IL 60608-2904 t) 312-243-0011 office@opcentral.org (STAF) (St. Albert the Great Prov.) Rev. James V. Marchionda, O.P., Prov.;

ELK GROVE VILLAGE

BLFR Foundation, LLC - 600 Alexian Way, Elk Grove Village, IL 60007 t) 847-264-8704 Bro. Daniel McCormick, C.F.A., CEO;

EVERGREEN PARK

American Province of Little Company of Mary Sisters Charitable Trust - 9350 S. California, Evergreen Park, IL 60805 t) 708-422-0130 swalsh@lcmh.org www.lcmsisters.org

LAKE FOREST

Barat Education Foundation - ; Mailing: P.O. Box 457, Lake Forest, IL 60045 t) 847-501-1726 alumni@thebaratfoundation.org www.thebaratfoundation.org Maureen Ryan, Exec.;

LEMONT

Franciscan Community Benefit Services (Madonna Foundation) - 11500 Theresa Dr., Lemont, IL 60439 t) 331-318-5200 egarbrecht@franciscanministries.org www.franciscanministries.org Focused on ministry of Franciscan Sisters of Chicago & increasing access to Catholic education. Sponsored by the Franciscan Sisters of Chicago. Regina Umanskiy, Pres. & CEO; Elizabeth Garbrecht, Dir. Madonna Foundation;

St. Joseph Property Trust - 11500 Theresa Dr., Lemont, IL 60439 t) 630-243-3554 jduckett@chicagofranciscans.com

Mother Theresa Care & Mission Trust - 11500 Theresa Dr., Lemont, IL 60439 t) (630) 243-3557 jduckett@chicagofranciscans.com Sr. Francis Clare Radke, Trustee;

MUNDELEIN

Civitas Dei Foundation - 1000 E. Maple Ave., Mundelein, IL 60060 t) 847-837-4516 Rev. Michael J. K. Fuller;

Foundation for Adult Catechetical Teaching Aids - 22333 W. Erhart Rd., Mundelein, IL 60060 t) 847-223-0010 foundationacta@gmail.com www.actafoundation.org Rev. Lawrence R. Dowling, Pres.;

OLYMPIA FIELDS

***Franciscan Health Foundation - South Suburban Chicago** - 20201 S. Crawford Ave., Olympia Fields, IL 60461 t) 708-852-2430 sscfoundation@franciscanalliance.org www.franciscanhealthfoundation.org Laurie Crosby, Dir.;

TECHNY

Blessed Arnold Religious Charitable Trust - 1985 Waukegan Rd., Techny, IL 60082-6067; Mailing: P.O. Box 6067, Techny, IL 60082-6067 t) 847-272-2700 www.divineword.org Society of the Divine Word. Bro. Mathew Zemel, S.V.D., Chair; Rev. Nhan Tran, S.V.D., Treas.;

Divine Word Missionaries, Inc. - 1835 Waukegan Rd., Techny, IL 60082-6099; Mailing: Box 6099, Techny, IL 60082-6099 t) 847-272-7600 director@svdmissions.org www.svdmissions.org Rev. Dennis Callan, S.V.D., Supr.; David Gallagher, Treas.; Bro. Daniel Holman, S.V.D., Dir.;

Divine Word Techny Community Corporation - 1901 Waukegan Rd., Techny, IL 60082; Mailing: P.O. Box 6067, Techny, IL 60082 t) 847-272-2700 provincial@uscsvd.org www.divineword.org Rev. James W. Miller, Pres.; Rev. Dennis Callan, S.V.D., Vice. Pres.; Rev. Quang Duc Dinh, S.V.D., Vice. Pres.; Rev. Nhan Tran, S.V.D., Secy. Treas.; Rev. Janusz Horowski, Asst. Secry. Treas.; Rev. Matheus Ro, S.V.D., Asst. Secy. Treas.; Bro. Mathew Zemel, S.V.D., Asst. Secy. Treas.;

WESTERN SPRINGS

***Society of Friends of the John Paul II Foundation** - 116 Hilton St., Western Springs, IL 60480 t) 630-308-2609 fjp2chicago@gmail.com Elizabeth Ceisel-Mikowska, Contact;

HOSPITALS / HEALTH SERVICES [HOS]

BERWYN

***Gottlieb Community Health Services Corporation** - 3249 Oak Park Ave., Berwyn, IL 60402 t) 708-783-9100 macnealhospital.org

BLUE ISLAND

St. Francis Hospital and Health Center - 12935 S. Gregory St., Blue Island, IL 60406

BROADVIEW

***Presence Behavioral Health** - 1820 S. 25th Ave., Broadview, IL 60155 t) 708-681-2324 john.halstead1@ascension.org www.ascension.org Sponsored by Ascension Health Ministries (Ascension Sponsor), a public juridic person. ProCare Centers; Employee Resource Center Polly Davenport, COO; John Halstead, Chief Mission Integration Officer; Asstd. Annu.: 11,246; Staff: 157

CHICAGO

Saint Anthony Hospital (Saint Anthony Health Ministries) - 2875 W. 19th St., Chicago, IL 60623 t) 773-484-1000 Rev. Cajetan Ebuziem (Nigeria); Rev. Benedict Ezeoke (Nigeria); Sr. Benigna Morais, M.S.C., Chap.; Peter V. Fazio Jr., Chair; Guy A. Medaglia, CEO;

St. Bernard Hospital & Health Care Center - 326 W. 64th St., Chicago, IL 60621 t) 773-962-3900 cholland@stbh.org stbh.org St. Bernard Hospital, Religious Hospitallers of St. Joseph/Catholic Health International. Charles Holland, Pres.;

Holy Cross Hospital - 2701 W. 68th St., Chicago, IL 60629 t) 773-884-9000 www.holycrosshospital.org Affiliated with Sinai Health System. Holy Cross Hospital, Sisters of St. Casimir of Chicago. Sr. Laura Parker, S.P., Dir.; Karen Teitelbaum, Pres. & CEO;

Presence Care Transformation Corporation - 200 S. Wacker, 11th Fl., Chicago, IL 60606; Mailing: 2601 Navistar Dr., Legal, Lisle, IL 60532 t) 312-308-3200 john.halstead1@ascension.org www.ascension.org Sponsored by Ascension Health Ministries (Ascension Sponsor), a public juridic person Polly Davenport, COO; John Halstead, Chief Mission Integration Officer; Staff: 64

Presence Resurrection Medical Center (Presence Chicago Hospitals Network) - 7435 Talcott Ave., Chicago, IL 60631 t) 773-774-8000 john.halstead1@ascension.org www.ascension.org Sponsored by Ascension Health Ministries (Ascension Sponsor), a public juridic person. DBA Ascension Resurrection. John Halstead, Chief Mission Integration Officer; Polly Davenport, COO; Bed Capacity: 320; Asstd. Annu.: 51,572; Staff: 1,249

Presence Saint Joseph Hospital Chicago (Presence Chicago Hospitals Network) - 2900 N. Lake Shore Dr., Chicago, IL 60657 t) 773-665-3000 john.halstead1@ascension.org www.ascension.org Sponsored by Ascension Health Ministries (Ascension Sponsor), a public juridic person. DBA Ascension Saint Joseph - Chicago. Polly Davenport, COO; John Halstead, Chief Mission Integration Officer; Bed Capacity: 319; Asstd. Annu.: 32,788; Staff: 907

Presence Saints Mary and Elizabeth Medical Center (Presence Chicago Hospitals Network) - 2233 W. Division, Chicago, IL 60622 t) 312-770-2000 john.halstead1@ascension.org ascension.org Sponsored by Ascension Health Ministries (Ascension Sponsor), a public juridic person. DBA Ascension Saint Elizabeth. John Halstead, Chief Mission Integration Officer; Polly Davenport, COO; Bed Capacity: 446; Asstd. Annu.: 62,286; Staff: 1,278

DES PLAINES

Presence Holy Family Medical Center (Presence Chicago Hospitals Network) - 100 N. River Rd., Des Plaines, IL 60016 t) 847-297-1800 john.halstead1@ascension.org www.ascension.org Sponsored by Ascension Health Ministries (Ascension Sponsor), a juridic person. DBA Ascension Holy Family. Polly Davenport, COO; John Halstead, Chief Mission Integration Officer; Bed Capacity: 172; Asstd. Annu.: 2,016; Staff: 414

ELK GROVE VILLAGE

Alexian Brothers Medical Center - 800 Biesterfield Rd., Elk Grove Village, IL 60007-3392; Mailing: 200 S. Wacker, Legal, Chicago, IL 60606 t) 847-437-5500 john.halstead1@ascension.org www.ascension.org Sponsor: Ascension Health Ministries. DBA Asc Alexian Bros., Asc Alexian Bros. Rehab. Hosp., Asc Alexian Bros. Hspc, Asc @ Home IL Polly Davenport, COO; John Halstead, Chief Mission Integration Officer; Bed Capacity: 376; Asstd. Annu.: 138,960; Staff: 1,764

EVANSTON

Presence Saint Francis Hospital (Presence Chicago Hospitals Network) - 355 Ridge Ave., Evanston, IL 60202 t) 847-316-4500 john.halstead1@ascension.org www.ascension.org Sponsored by Ascension Health Ministries (Ascension Sponsor), a public juridic person. DBA Ascension Saint Francis. Polly Davenport, COO; John Halstead, Chief Mission Integration Officer; Bed Capacity: 191; Asstd. Annu.: 42,270; Staff: 699

EVERGREEN PARK

OSF Little Company of Mary Medical Center (The Little Company of Mary Hospital and Health Care Centers) - 2800 W. 95th St., Evergreen Park, IL 60805 t) 708-422-6200 robert.brandfass@osfhealthcare.org www.osfhealthcare.org Rev. James R. Gallagher, Chap.; Sr. Christa Henrich, Chap.; Sr. Sharon Ann Walsh, L.C.M., Chair; Kathleen Kinsella, Pres.; Dcn. Richard Warfield; Bed Capacity: 298; Asstd. Annu.: 350,570; Staff: 2,045

Burbank Office Building - 4901 W. 79th St., Burbank, IL 60459; Mailing: 2800 W. 95th St., Evergreen Park, IL 60805 t) 708-422-0300 bmeller@lcmh.org Dennis Reilly, Secy.;

Mary Potter Pavilion - 2850 W. 95th St., Evergreen Park, IL 60805 t) 708-229-5785 bmeller@lcmh.org Dennis Reilly, Secy.;

Oak Lawn Care Station - 5660 W. 95th St., Oak Lawn, IL 60453; Mailing: 2800 W. 95th St., Evergreen Park, IL 60805 t) 708-499-2273 bmeller@lcmh.org Dennis Reilly, Secy.;

Palos Office Center - 12450 S. Harlem, Palos Heights, IL 60463 t) 708-448-1207 bmeller@lcmh.org Dennis Reilly, Secy.;

HOFFMAN ESTATES

Alexian Brothers Behavioral Health Hospital - 1650 Moon Lake Blvd., Hoffman Estates, IL 60169; Mailing: 2601 Navistar Dr., Legal, Lisle, IL 60532 t) 847-882-1600 john.halstead1@ascension.org www.ascension.org Sponsored by Ascension Health Ministries (Ascension Sponsor), a public juridic person. DBA Ascension Alexian Brothers Behavioral Health Hospital Polly Davenport, COO; John Halstead, Chief Mission Integration Officer; Bed Capacity: 141; Asstd. Annu.: 211,544; Staff: 600

Alexian Brothers Hospital Network - 200 S. Wacker Dr., Chicago, IL 60606; Mailing: 2601 Navistar Dr., Lisle, IL 60606 t) 224-273-2334 ascension.org

St. Alexius Medical Center - 1555 Barrington Rd., Hoffman Estates, IL 60169; Mailing: 2601 Navistar Dr., Legal, Lisle, IL 60532 t) 847-843-2000 john.halstead1@ascension.org www.ascension.org Sponsored by Ascension Health Ministries (Ascension Sponsor), a public juridic person. DBA Ascension Saint Alexius. Polly Davenport, COO; John Halstead, Chief Mission Integration Officer; Bed Capacity: 318; Asstd. Annu.: 110,482; Staff: 1,335

MAYWOOD

***Loyola University Medical Center (Foster G. McGaw Hospital)** - 2160 S. First Ave., Maywood, IL 60153 t) 708-216-7766; 708-216-3229 ssom-admissions@luc.edu loyolamedicine.org Shawn Vincent, CEO; Richard Freeman, Chief Clinical Officer, Loyola Medicine; Tad Gomez, Pres.;

MELROSE PARK

***Gottlieb Memorial Hospital** - 701 W. North Ave., Melrose Park, IL 60160 t) 708-681-3200 gottliebhospital.org

OLYMPIA FIELDS

Franciscan Health Olympia Fields (Franciscan Alliance, Inc.) - 20201 S. Crawford Ave., Olympia Fields, IL 60461 t) 708-747-4000 www.franciscanhealth.org Raymond Grady, Pres.; Sr. M. Ruth Luthman, O.S.F., Vice Pres. Mission Integration; Rev. Philip E. Cyscon, Chap.; Rev. Ted Ostrowski, Chap.; Bed Capacity: 214; Asstd. Annu.: 409,567; Staff: 1,707

MISCELLANEOUS [MIS]

ARLINGTON HEIGHTS

***Alexian Brothers Center for Mental Health** - 3436 N. Kennicott Ave., Arlington Heights, IL 60004; Mailing: 2601 Navistar Dr., Legal, Lisle, IL 60532 t) 847-952-7460 john.halstead1@ascension.org www.ascension.org Sponsored by Ascension Health Ministries (Ascension Sponsor), a public juridic person. DBA Ascension Illinois Center for Mental Health Polly Davenport, COO; John Halstead, Chief Mission Integration Officer;

CRI, Inc. - 1212 E. Euclid Ave., Arlington Heights, IL 60004 t) 708-997-9746 cristoreynetwork.org William Kunkel, Contact;

BERWYN

Focolare Movement - 7018 W. 34th St., Berwyn, IL 60402 t) 708-484-9771 wfoc.chicago@focolare.us www.focolare.us A Gospel-based ecclesial movement for spiritual & social renewal.It's spirituality of unity has become a lifestyle for people of all ages & background Juliana Hyun, Dir.; Gary Brandl, Dir.;

Focolare Movement, Men's Branch (Illinois) (Work of Mary) - t) (708) 484-9771 A Gospel-based ecclesial movement for spiritual & social renewal.It's spirituality of unity has become a lifestyle for people of all ages & background

Focolare Movement, Women's Branch (Illinois) (Work of Mary) - t) (708) 484-9771 A Gospel-based ecclesial movement for spiritual & social renewal.It's spirituality of unity has become a lifestyle for people of all ages & background

BLUE ISLAND

***Society of St. Vincent de Paul Archdiocese of Chicago** - 12731 S. Wood St., Blue Island, IL 60406 t) (773) 779-6700 Harry Ohde, Volunteer Pres/CEO;

BURBANK

Westcourt Corporation - 5550 W. 87th St., Burbank, IL 60459 t) 773-429-4343 bropathayes@gmail.com Bro. Patrick Hayes, C.F.C.;

CHICAGO

***Aid for Women, Inc.** - 8 S. Michigan Ave., Ste. 1418, Chicago, IL 60603-3311 t) 312-621-1107 sbarrett@aidforwomen.org www.helpaidforwomen.org Maintains five pregnancy care centers and two maternity homes for pregnant woman. Susan Barrett, Exec.;

Alexian Brothers Bonaventure House (Alexian Brothers Housing and Health Alliance; Alexian Brothers Bonaventure House dba AMITA Health Housing & Health Alliance) - 825 W. Wellington Ave., Chicago, IL 60657 t) 773-327-9921 john.halstead1@ascension.org www.ascension.org Housing & supportive services for otherwise homeless persons w/ HIV/AIDS. Sponsor:Ascension Health Ministries.dba Ascension Illinois Bonaventure House Polly Davenport, COO; John Halstead, Chief Mission Integration Officer;

Alexian Brothers Bettendorf Place, LLC - 8425 S. Saginaw Ave., Chicago, IL 60617 t) 773-359-4902 dba Ascension Illinois Bettendorf Place

Alexian Brothers Community Services - 200 S. Wacker Dr., Chicago, IL 60606; Mailing: 2601 Navistar Dr., Lisle, IL 60532 t) 314-292-9308 ahscm-mission@ascension.org www.ascensionliving.org/ Ryan Endsley, COO;

Alexian Brothers Health System (Alexian Brothers Foundation) - 200 S. Wacker Dr., Chicago, IL 60606; Mailing: 2601 Navistar Dr., Legal, Lisle, IL 60532 t) 224-273-2334 john.halstead1@ascension.org www.ascension.org Sponsor: Ascension Health Ministries. DBA Ascension Medical Group Illinois, DBA Alexian Brothers Foundation, DBA Ascension Illinois Foundation Polly Davenport, COO; John Halstead, Chief Mission Integration Officer;

Alexian Brothers Senior Ministries (Ascension Health Senior Care) - 200 S. Wacker Dr., Chicago, IL 60606; Mailing: 2601 Navistar Dr., Lisle, IL 60532 t) 314-292-9308 ahscm-mission@ascension.org www.ascensionliving.org/ Ryan Endsley, COO;

The Aquin Guild - 3525 S. Lake Park Ave., Chicago, IL 60653-1402 t) 312-534-3700 Rev. John W. Clemens, Dir.;

Aquinas Literacy Center (ESL) - 1751 W. 35th St., Chicago, IL 60609 t) 773-927-0512 info@aquinasliteracycenter.org www.aquinasliteracycenter.org Alison Altmeyer, Admin.;

St. Bernard Health Network - 326 W. 64th St., Chicago, IL 60621

St. Bernard Housing Development Corp. - 326 W. 64th St., Chicago, IL 60621 t) 773-962-4165 www.stbh.org A subsidy of St. Bernard Hospital, Chicago. Diahann Sinclair, Exec.;

***Bethany House of Hospitality** - 5121 S. University Ave., Chicago, IL 60615; Mailing: 7430 N. Ridge Blvd., Chicago, IL 60645 t) 630-855-5909 kmulcahy@bethanyhouseofhospitality.com bethanyhouseofhospitality.com/ Housing & support services to young immigrant women. Sr. Kathlyn

Mulcahy, OP, Exec. Dir.;
***Big Shoulders Fund** - 212 W. Van Buren St., Ste. 900, Chicago, IL 60607 t) 312-751-8337 www.bigshouldersfund.org Provides support to the Catholic Schools in the neediest areas of inner-city Chicago. Joshua Hale, CEO;
St. Bonaventure Oratory - 1641 W. Diversey Pkwy., Chicago, IL 60614 t) 773-281-6588 stbonaventure@archchicago.org Rev. Przemyslaw Wojcik, Admin.;
***Brother David Darst Center for Justice and Peace, Spirituality and Education** - 6336 S Kilbourn Ave, Chicago, IL 60629 t) 312-225-3099 director@darstcenter.org www.darstcenter.org Keith Donovan, Exec.;
***Brothers and Sisters of Love** - c/o St. James Church, 2907 S. Wabash, Chicago, IL 60616 t) 312-842-1919 x208 brjim@brothersandsistersoflove.com brothersandsistersoflove.com Bro. Jim Fogarty, Exec.;
Campus Ministries - 835 N. Rush St., Chicago, IL 60611 t) 312-534-8271

Northwestern University, Sheil Center - 2110 N. Sheridan Rd., Evanston, IL 60201 t) 847-328-4648 Rev. Kevin J. Feeney, Dir.;
University of Chicago Calvert House - 5735 S. University Ave., Chicago, IL 60637 t) 773-288-2311 calvert.uchicago@gmail.com www.uofccatholic.com Rev. Andrew Wawrzyn, Chap.;
University of Illinois at Chicago - St. John Paul II Newman Center - 700 S. Morgan St., Chicago, IL 60607-3429 t) 312-226-1880 www.jp2newman.com Rev. Connor Coyle Danstrom, Chap.; Rebecca Siar, Campus Min.;

***Canons Regular of Saint John Cantius** - 825 N. Carpenter St., Chicago, IL 60642-5499 t) 312-243-7373 pastor@cantius.org www.canons-regular.org Rev. Joshua Caswell, S.J.C.; Rev. Nathan Caswell, S.J.C.; Rev. Nathan Ford, S.J.C.; Rev. Brendan Gibson, S.J.C.; Rev. Scott Haynes, S.J.C.; Rev. James Isaacson, S.J.C.; Rev. Dennis Kolinski, S.J.C.; Rev. Robin Kwan, S.J.C.; Rev. Kevin Mann, S.J.C.; Rev. C. Frank Phillips, C.R.; Rev. Trenton Rauck, SJC; Rev. Anthony Rice, S.J.C.; Rev. Matthew Schuster, S.J.C.; Rev. Scott Thelander, S.J.C.; Rev. Albert Tremari, S.J.C.; Rev. David Yallaly, S.J.C.;
The Catholic Church Extension Society of the United States of America - 150 S. Wacker Dr., 20th Fl., Chicago, IL 60606-4200 t) 312-236-7240 info@catholicextension.org www.catholicextension.org His Eminence Blase J. Cupich, Chancellor; Rev. John J. Wall, Pres.;
The Catholic Education Institute - 6537 N. Ashland - Unit 1N, Chicago, IL 60626-4929 t) 312-515-3152 wpmgrogan@gmail.com www.catholicexcellence.org Rev. William P. Grogan, Pres.;
***The Catholic Kolping Society of Chicago** - 5826 N. Elston, Chicago, IL 60646 t) 773-792-2190 chicagokolping@aol.com Community Center Rev. Michael G. Scherschel;
Catholic League for Religious Assistance to Poland - 2330 W. 118th St., Chicago, IL 60643 t) 312-534-5050 awypych@archchicago.org Most Rev. Andrew P. Wypych, Exec.; Rev. Idzi Stacherczak;
Center for the Study of Religious Life - 5401 S. Cornell Ave., Chicago, IL 60615-5698 t) 773-752-2720 csrl@religious-life.org www.religious-life.org Sponsored by the Conference of Major Superiors of Men, the Leadership Conference of Women Religious and Catholic Theological Union at Chicago. Sr. Mary Charlotte Chandler, R.S.C.J., Dir.;
***Central American Martyrs Center (Su Casa Catholic Worker Community)** - 5045 S. Laflin, Chicago, IL 60609 t) 773-376-9263 sucasacw@gmail.com www.sucasacw.org Bro. Denis Murphy, F.S.C.;
Chicago Airports Catholic Chaplaincy - Terminal 2 - Mezzanine Level, 10000 W. O'Hare, Chicago, IL 60666-0353; Mailing: PO Box 66353, Chicago, IL 60666-0353 t) 773-686-2636 ordchapel@aol.com www.airportchapels.org Rev. Michael G. Zaniolo, Chap.; Susan Schneider, Bus. Mgr.;
Claretian Associates, Inc. - 3039 E. 91st St., Chicago, IL 60617 t) 773-734-9181 angelah@claretianassociates.org; ellist@claretianassociates.org www.claretianassociates.org Organization to provide affordable housing and encourage neighborhood improvement in South Chicago. Angela Hurlock, Exec.; Tevonne Ellis, Dir., Progs.;
Collaborative Dominican Novitiate - 4950 S. Ellis Ave., Chicago, IL 60615-2708 t) 517-270-9293 lreaume@adriandominicans.org Sr. Lorraine Reaume, O.P., Contact;
***Communicators for Women Religious (CWR)** - 5401 S. Cornell Ave., Chicago, IL 60615 nschaefer@c4wr.org www.c4wr.org Nicholas Schaefer, Exec.;
***Cristo Rey Network** - 11 E. Adams St., Ste. 800, Chicago, IL 60603 t) 312-784-7200 egoettl@cristoreynetwork.org; bmorris@cristoreynetwork.org www.cristoreynetwork.org Supports 38 Catholic, career focused, college preparatory high schools. Elizabeth Goettl, CEO;
***Felician Services, Inc.** - 3800 W. Peterson Ave., FSI, Chicago, IL 60659-3116 t) 773-463-3806 connect@felicianservices.org www.felicianservices.org/ Sr. Geralyn Marie Mroczkowski, CSSF, CEO;
Franciscan Friars Retirement Corporation - 6107 Kenmore Ave., Chicago, IL 60660-2797 t) 773-274-7681 dmk9271@gmail.com Very Rev. Paul Joseph Langevin, O.F.M. Conv., Prov.;
***Franciscan Works** - 4870 N. Marmora, Chicago, IL 60630; Mailing: P.O. Box 56007, Chicago, IL 60656 t) 773-809-4008 joan@franciscanworks.org www.franciscanworks.org Serving Liberia Mission Incorporated, Blacktom Town, Montserrado County, Liberia, West Africa. Breaking the cycle of poverty Joseph Sehnert, Exec.;
Franciscans of the Eucharist of Chicago - 3808 W. Iowa St., Chicago, IL 60651 t) 773-486-8431 fevocations@gmail.com www.franciscansoftheeucharistofchicago.org Serving the poor, evangelization and teaching, retreat work and Eucharistic Adoration. Most Rev. Robert Lombardo, C.F.R., Pres.;
Freres des Ecoles Chretiennes - c/o Locke Lord LLP, 111 S. Wacker Dr., Chicago, IL 60606 t) 312-443-1823 mrenetzky@lockelord.com Kenneth Payne, Pres.;
General Assistance, Inc. - 3335 N. Whipple St., Chicago, IL 60618-5717; Mailing: 4328 Westminster Pl., Saint Louis, MO 63108-2624 c) (512) 565-7491 teresa.george@doc.org Support organization for the Daughters of Charity; aka Daughters of Charity International Project Services Sr. Teresa George, DC, Contact;
Holy Cross Educators of Illinois, Inc. - 1443 W. Division St., Chicago, IL 60622 t) 574-631-2908 Bro. Ken Haders, C.S.C., Prov.;
Holy Family Church, Inc. - 1010 N. Hooker St., Chicago, IL 60642 t) 773-975-6363; 773-975-6888 umisocius@jesuits.org Rev. Glen Chun, S.J., Contact;
The Holy Spirit Life Learning Center - 2020 W. Morse Ave., Unit 1S, Chicago, IL 60645 t) 773-764-3000 hsllc.mission@gmail.com www.ssps-usa.org/hsllc-rgp-w.html Improving learning skills & developing self-confidence. Sr. Rosa Da Costa Menezes, SSpS, Dir.;
***Home to Enhance African Life, Inc.** - 807 N. Wabash Ave., Apt. 2W, Chicago, IL 60611-6058; Mailing: PO Box 10523, Chicago, IL 60610-0523 t) 312-952-4855 nick@healnigeria.org www.healnigeria.org Nicola Costello, Pres.;
Hopebound Ministries, Inc. - 3800 W. Peterson Ave., Chicago, IL 60659 t) 773-463-3806 mrparrillo@felicianservices.org Sr. Mary Clarette Stryzewski, C.S.S.F., Pres.;
Ignatian Spirituality Project - 205 W. Monroe St., Ste. 317, Chicago, IL 60606 t) 312-226-9184 info@ispretreats.org; catherine@ispretreats.org www.ispretreats.org Retreats & spiritual reflections for individuals recovering from homelessness & addiction. Christine Curran, Exec.;
Ignatius Productions, Inc. - 1010 N. Hooker St., Chicago, IL 60642 t) 773-975-6363 umisocius@jesuits.org www.fathermitchpacwa.org Rev. Timothy R. Lannon, S.J., Treas.;
The Illinois Patrons of the Arts in the Vatican Museums - 835 N. Rush St., Chicago, IL 60611 t) 312-534-5351; 312-534-5391 illinoispatrons@gmail.com www.vaticanpatronschicago.org His Eminence Blase J. Cupich, Chair; Anne Shea, Pres.;
Intercommunity Housing Corporation - c/o Law Offices of Edward T. Joyce & Associates, 135 S. LaSalle St., Ste. 2200, Chicago, IL 60603 t) 312-641-2600 ejoyce@joycelaw.com Promotes the development and establishment of affordable residential retirement housing for religious, clergy and laity. David E. Myles, Pres.; Edward T. Joyce, Secy.;
Italian Catholic Federation - 2825 W. 81st St., Chicago, IL 60652 t) 773-436-4444 info@icf.org www.icf.org Rev. Charles V. Fanelli, Chap.;
Jan Beyzym Society, Inc. - 4105 N. Avers Ave., Chicago, IL 60618 t) 773-588-7476 agendajomu@gmail.com www.jezuici.us Polish Jesuits Foreign Missions. Rev. Jozef Polak, S.J., Pres.; Rev. Jerzy Brzoska, S.I., Secy.; Rev. Marek Janowski, S.J., Treas.; Rev. Tomasz Szymczyk, S.J., Dir.; Bro. Adam Poreba, Dir.;
Jesuit International Missions, Inc. - 1010 N. Hooker St., Chicago, IL 60642 t) 773-975-6363; 773-975-6888 umitreasurer@jesuits.org; umisocius@jesuits.org Rev. Glen Chun, S.J.; Rev. Timothy R. Lannon, S.J., Treas.;
The Jesuit Partnership - 1010 N. Hooker St., Chicago, IL 60642 t) 773-975-6888 umisocius@jesuits.org Rev. Thomas A. Lawler, S.J., Pres.; Rev. Glen Chun, S.J., Secy.; Rev. Timothy R. Lannon, S.J., Treas.;
St. Jude League - 205 W. Monroe St., 9th Fl., Chicago, IL 60606 t) 312-236-7782 brummelm@claretians.org www.claretiansusa.org Rev. Mark J. Brummel, C.M.F., Dir.; John Blais, Exec. Dir.; Brs.: 8; Priests: 75
Kolbe House - 2434 S. California Ave., Chicago, IL 60608 t) 773-247-0070 info@kolbehouseministry.org Catholic jail ministry. MaryClare Birmingham, Exec. Dir.; Dcn. Pablo A. Perez, Assoc. Dir.;
Loyola Press - 8770 W. Bryn Mawr Ave., Ste. 1125, Chicago, IL 60631 t) 773-281-1818 cicciarelli@loyolapress.com www.loyolapress.com Joeylln Cicciarelli, Pres.;
Lumen Christi Institute - 1220 E. 58th St., Chicago, IL 60637-1507 t) 773-955-5887 info@lumenchristi.org www.lumenchristi.org Michael Thomas Le Chevallier, Exec.;
Maria Kaupas Center - 2740 W. 68th St., Chicago, IL 60629 t) 773-925-8686 info@mariakaupascenter.org www.mariakaupascenter.org Sr. Margaret Zalot, S.S.C., Contact; Melinda Rueden, Interim;
Marist Volunteer Program - 4200 W. 115th St., Chicago, IL 60655-4306 t) 773-881-5343 maristvolunteerprogram@yahoo.com Bro. Hugh Turley, F.M.S., Contact;
Medical Missionaries of Mary - 4425 W. 63rd St., Ste. 100, Chicago, IL 60629-5565; Mailing: 3410 W. 60th Pl., Chicago, IL 60629-3602 t) 773-735-3712 mdommm2014@gmail.com www.mmmworldwide.org Sr. Joanne Bierl, M.M.M., Dir.;
Midtown Residence - 1825 N. Wood St., Chicago, IL 60622 t) 773-292-5450; 773-292-0660 coordinatorchicago@gmail.com www.opusdei.org Prelature of the Holy Cross and Opus Dei Rev. Charles M. Ferrer; Rev. Hilary F. Mahaney; Rev. Deogracias Rosales; Rev. John R. Waiss;
Mother Cabrini League - 434 W. Deming Pl., Chicago, IL 60614 t) 773-388-7329 mothercabrinileague@gmail.com Sr. Joaquina Costa, M.S.C., Dir.;
***The National Center for the Laity** - 3422 W. 59th Pl., Chicago, IL 60629; Mailing: P.O. Box 291102, Chicago, IL 60629 t) 773-776-9036 wdroel@cs.com www.catholiclabor.org/ncl.htm Lauren Sukul, Pres.;
National Organization for Continuing Education of Roman Catholic Clergy, Inc. - 333 N. Michigan Ave. Ste

1205, Chicago, IL 60601; Mailing: Assn. for the Ongoing Formation of Priests, P.O. Box 5977, Timonium, MD 21094 t) 410-978-3676 office@aofpriests.org www.aofpriests.org Promotes and supports ongoing formation for priests and presbyterates. Rev. John M. McCrone, Pres.; Patricia LeNoir, Admin.;

National Religious Vocation Conference (NRVC) - 5480 S. Cornell Ave., Ste. 110/111, Chicago, IL 60615; Mailing: 5416 S. Cornell Ave., Chicago, IL 60615 t) 773-363-5454 nrvc@nrvc.net www.nrvc.net Member organization that provides professional development, research, resources, etc. to vocation directors of Catholic religious institutes. Sr. Deborah Marie Borneman, SS.C.M., Dir., Mission Integration;

Network for Mercy Education - 10024 S. Central Park Ave., Chicago, IL 60655 t) 708-295-6614 cravenrsm@gmail.com Sr. Corinne Raven, R.S.M., Dir.;

New World Publications - 835 N. Rush St., Chicago, IL 60611 t) 312-534-7777 mail@catholicnewworld.com www.catholicnewworld.com Publishers of Catholic New World, Chicago Catolico, and the Archdiocesan Directory. Grant Gallicho, Dir.; Joyce Duriga, Editor;

Northview University Center - 7225 N. Greenview Ave., Chicago, IL 60626 t) 773-465-3468 www.opusdei.org Prelature of the Holy Cross and Opus Dei Rev. Juan R. Velez;

***NPH USA** - 134 N. LaSalle St., Ste. 500, Chicago, IL 60602 t) 312-386-7499 info@nphusa.org www.nphusa.org Improving the lives of orphaned, abandoned & disadvantaged children. Casey Guevara-Lehker, Exec.;

Office for Mission Advancement - 1910 S. Ashland Ave., Chicago, IL 60608-2904 t) 312-226-0020 office@opcentral.org www.opcentral.org Dominicans: Province of St. Albert the Great. Robert Dixon, Dir.;

Order of Friar Servants of Mary United States of America Province, Inc. - 3121 W. Jackson Blvd., Chicago, IL 60612-2729 t) 773-533-0360 arnaldosanchez@servitesusa.org www.servite.org Rev. Eugene M. Smith, O.S.M., Prov.; Bro. Arnaldo Sanchez, OSM, Treas.;

Our Lady of the Angels Mission Center - 3808 W. Iowa St., Chicago, IL 60651 t) 773-486-8431 olamission@gmail.com www.missionola.com Catholic outreach on Chicago's west side. Most Rev. Robert Lombardo, C.F.R., Dir.;

The Peace Corner, Incorporated - ; Mailing: P.O. Box 440113, Chicago, IL 60644 t) 773-261-5330 thepeacecorner@yahoo.com www.thepeacecorner.org A ministry of the Comboni Missionaries of the Heart of Jesus, Inc., Youth center. Angel Gutierrez, Vice Pres.;

Precious Blood Ministry of Reconciliation - 5114 S. Elizabeth St., Chicago, IL 60609-0379; Mailing: P.O. Box 09379, Chicago, IL 60609-0379 t) 773-952-6643 dkelly@pbmr.org www.pbmr.org A ministry of the Cincinnati and Kansas City provinces of the Missionaries of the Precious Blood that responds to violence and conflict. Rev. Dennis Kinderman, C.PP.S.; Rev. David A. Kelly, C.PP.S., Exec.;

Precious Blood Spirituality Institute - 845 E. Drexel Sq., Chicago, IL 60615 t) (773) 451-6710 office@pbspiritualityinstitute.org www.pbspiritualityinstitute.org/ Promotes the spirituality of the Precious Blood. Vicky Otto, Exec. Dir.; Sr. Maria Hughes, ASC, Bd. Chair; Kevin Considine, Dir.;

Prelature of the Holy Cross and Opus Dei - 5800 N. Keating Ave., Chicago, IL 60646 t) 773-283-5800 coordinatorchicago@gmail.com www.opusdei.org Office of the Vicar for Central United States Rev. Leo Agustina; Rev. Frank J. Hoffman; Rev. Peter V. Armenio, Vicar;

Presence Chicago Hospitals Network - 200 S. Wacker Dr., 12th Fl., Chicago, IL 60606 t) 312-308-3221 john.halstead1@ascension.org www.ascension.org Sponsored by Ascension Health Ministries (Ascension Sponsor), a public juridic person Polly Davenport, COO; John Halstead, Chief Mission Integration Officer;

Presence Healthcare Services - 100 N. River Rd., Des Plaines, IL 60016 t) 773-774-8000

Presence Senior Services - Chicagoland - t) (314) 292-9308 Ryan Endsley, COO; Kenneth (Bob) Smoot, CMIO;

Radio Maryja - 6965 W. Belmont Ave., Chicago, IL 60634 t) 773-385-8472 admin@radiomaryjachicago.org www.radiomaryjachicago.org Redemptorist religious radio.

Redemptorist Apostolic Works - 1633 N. Cleveland Ave., c/o The Redemptorists/Denver Province, Chicago, IL 60614 t) 312-248-8894 Rev. Gregory May, C.Ss.R., Treas.;

S.F.V., Inc. - 1645 W. LeMoyne St., Chicago, IL 60622 t) 773-278-6724 Sponsor corporation of St. Francis Village (a retirement village) in Crowley, TX. Rev. Kurt Hartrich, O.F.M., Pres.;

St. Joseph Services, Inc. - 4123 W. Grand Ave., Chicago, IL 60651 t) 773-278-0484 gpreston@stjosephservices.org www.stjosephservices.org Supports the mission of the Daughters of Charity to serve persons in poverty. Guadalupe Preston, Exec. Dir.;

***Second Sense** - 65 E. Wacker Pl., Ste. 1010, Chicago, IL 60601 t) 312-236-8569 www.second-sense.org Provides devotional services David J. Tabak, Exec.;

Serra International - 70 E. Lake St., Ste. 1210, Chicago, IL 60601 t) 312-419-7411; 800-488-4008 serra@serra.org www.serra.org John W. Woodward, Exec.;

USA Council of Serra International - t) 312-201-6549; 888-777-6681 (toll free) serraus@serraus.org www.serraus.org E.V. Verbeke, Exec.;

Servite Secular Order, Inc. - 3121 W. Jackson Blvd., Chicago, IL 60612 t) 773-533-0360 x212 arnaldosanchez@servitesusa.org www.secularservites.org Rev. Dennis Kriz, O.S.M., National Asst.;

***Society of Jesus Worldwide** - 1010 N. Hooker St., Chicago, IL 60642 t) 773-975-6363; 773-975-6888 umisocius@jesuits.org Rev. Timothy R. Lannon, S.J., Treas.; Rev. Glen Chun, S.J., Contact;

St. Anthony Hospital - 2875 W. 19th St., Chicago, IL 60623 t) 773-484-4300 www.saintanthonyhospital.org Sponsored by Ascension Health and the Missionary Sisters of the Sacred Heart of Jesus to operate St. Anthony Hospital.

Saint Anthony Health Affiliates -

***Taller de Jose** - 2831 W. 24th Blvd., Chicago, IL 60623 t) 773-523-8320 info@tallerdejose.org www.tallerdejose.org Connects individuals to health, legal, and social services. Member of the Congregation of St. Joseph Mission Network. Anna Mayer, Exec.;

The Society for the Propagation of the Faith - 3525 S. Lake Park Ave., Chicago, IL 60653-1402 t) 312-534-3322 missions@archchicago.org www.wearemissionary.org Dr. Megan Mio, Dir.;

United Stand/United Stand Family Center - 3731 W. 62nd St., Chicago, IL 60629 t) 773-585-4499 united-stand@comcast.net united-stand.org Education, Prevention, Problem Identification, Consultation, and Intervention with Children and Families. Sr. Kim Mis, C.S.S.F., Exec.;

USA Midwest Province of the Society of Jesus, Inc. - 1010 N. Hooker St., Ste. 200, USA Midwest Jesuits, Chicago, IL 60642 t) 773-975-6363 umisocius@jesuits.org www.jesuitsmidwest.org Rev. Karl J Kiser, S.J., Prov.; Rev. Glen Chun, S.J., Prov. Asst.; Rev. Christopher J Manahan, S.J., Prov. Asst.; Rev. Daniel McDonald, Prov. Asst.; Rev. Charles Rodrigues, S.J., Prov. Asst.; Rev. Timothy R. Lannon, S.J., Treas.; Bro. John L. Moriconi, S.J., Secy.;

Clark Street Jesuit Residence Community - 357 W. Dickens Ave., Chicago, IL 60614; Mailing: 1010 N. Hooker St., Chicago, IL 60642 t) 773-975-6888 Rev. Lawrence Biondi, S.J.; Rev. Albert J. Di Ulio, S.J.; Rev. Stephen T. Krupa, S.J., Prof.;

Detroit Province of the Society of Jesus - Provincial Office - 1010 N. Hooker St., Chicago, IL 60642 t) (773) 975-6888 Rev. Timothy Lannon, S.J., Treas.;

USA Midwest Province of the Society of Jesus Aged and Infirmed Trust - 1010 N. Hooker St., Ste. 200: USA Midwest Jesuits, Chicago, IL 60642 t) 773-975-6870; (773) 975-6888 www.jesuitsmidwest.org/

USA Midwest Province of the Society of Jesus Apostolic Works Trust - 1010 N. Hooker St., Ste. 200: USA Midwest Jesuits, Chicago, IL 60642 t) 773-975-6888

USA Midwest Province of the Society of Jesus Formation Trust - 1010 N. Hooker St., Ste. 200: USA Midwest Jesuits, Chicago, IL 60642 t) 773-975-6888

USA Midwest Province of the Society of Jesus Foundation Trust - 1010 N. Hooker St., Ste. 200: USA Midwest Jesuits, Chicago, IL 60642 t) 773-975-6888

USA Midwest Province of the Society of Jesus St. Ignatius Trust - 1010 N. Hooker St., Ste. 200: USA Midwest Jesuits, Chicago, IL 60642 t) 773-975-6888

Zaccheus House - 12242 S. Parnell Ave., Chicago, IL 60628 t) 773-568-7822 zacchaeushouse@archchicago.org www.zacchaeushouse.org A ministry of Deacons offering hospitality and life skills education to men in transition to stability in their lives. Most Rev. Joseph N. Perry, Pres.;

CHICAGO HEIGHTS

San Rocco Oratory - 315 E. 22nd St., Chicago Heights, IL 60411; Mailing: 16565 S. State, South Holland, IL 60473 t) 708-331-5485 sanrocco-oratory@archchicago.org www.srocco.org Rev. Michael J. Gilligan, Rector;

CICERO

Musica Pacis - 2438 S. 61st Ct., Office of the President, Cicero, IL 60804 t) 312-285-6609 president@musicapacis.org www.musicapacis.org Rev. Scott Haynes, S.J.C., Pres.;

DES PLAINES

***Dalit Solidarity** - 557 Dulles Rd., Des Plaines, IL 60016 c) (708) 612-4248 dalitsolidarity@gmail.com dalitsolidarity.org/ Rev. Benjamin Chinnappan, Pres. & Exec. Dir.;

Shrine of Our Lady of Guadalupe - 1170 N. River Rd., Des Plaines, IL 60016 t) 847-294-1806 info@santuarioguadalupe.com www.solg.org Rev. Esequiel Sanchez, Rector;

Sisters of the Holy Family of Nazareth - U.S.A., Inc. - 310 N. River Rd., Des Plaines, IL 60016 t) 847-298-6760 info@nazarethcsfn.org info@nazarethcsfn.org Sr. Kathleen Maciej, C.S.F.N., Chair;

Sisters of the Holy Family of Nazareth, Holy Family Province - 310 N. River Rd., Des Plaines, IL 60016 t) 847-298-6760 info@nazarethesfn.org; secretary@nazarethcsfn.org www.nazarethcsfn.org Sr. Kathleen Maciej, C.S.F.N., Chair; Srs.: 187

ELK GROVE VILLAGE

Alexian Brothers Communities and Ministries - 600 Alexian Way, Elk Grove Village, IL 60007 t) 847-264-8704 www.alexianbrothers.org Congregation of Alexian Brothers, Immaculate Conception Province. Bro. Daniel McCormick, C.F.A., Prov.;

St. Alexius Outreach Ministries, Inc. - www.alexianbrothers.org/ Bro. Steve Fogt, C.F.A., Pres.; Bro. Richard Lowe, C.F.A., Vice. Pres.; Bro. Thomas Klein, C.F.A., Exec. Dir., Treas./Secy.;

EVANSTON

***Solidarity Bridge, Inc.** - 1703 Darrow Ave., #1, Evanston, IL 60201 t) 847-328-7748 info@solidaritybridge.org www.solidaritybridge.org International mission opportunities Ann Rhomberg, Dir.;

GLENVIEW

***Coalition in Support of Ecclesia Dei, Ltd.** - ; Mailing: P.O. Box 2071, Glenview, IL 60025-6071 t) 847-724-7151 ecclesiadei@sbcglobal.net www.ecclesiadei.org Assists priests, seminarians and laity in the implementation of Pope Benedict XVI's Summorum Pontificum Mary M. Kraychy, Pres.;

GURNEE

***Aid for Women of Northern Lake County** - 4606 W. Old

Grand Ave., Unit 4, Gurnee, IL 60031 t) 847-249-2700 www.aidforwomenlakecounty.org Pregnancy help.
Assisi Homes of Gurnee, Inc. - 3495 W. Grand Ave., Gurnee, IL 60031 t) 847-336-4428; 303-830-3300 mrankin@mercyhousing.org www.mercyhousing.org Melissa Clayton, Contact;
***Caritas For Children, Inc.** - 6615 Grand Ave., Ste. B-PMB 105, Gurnee, IL 60031-4591 t) (414) 406-2300; (414) 323-5000 cthoar@caritas.us www.caritas.us A private juridic person in the Archdiocese of Chicago, Promotes and supports inter-country adoptions from Poland Christopher T. Hoar, OFS, Contact;

HILLSIDE

Priests' Retirement and Mutual Aid Assn. of the Archdiocese of Chicago - 1400 S. Wolf Rd., Bldg. 3, Fl. 2, Hillside, IL 60162 t) (708) 449-8026 Kevin J. Marzalik, Exec. Dir.;

LA GRANGE PARK

***Joyful Again** - 543 N. Dover Ave., La Grange Park, IL 60526-9465; Mailing: P.O. Box 1365, La Grange Park, IL 60526-9465 t) 708-354-7211 joyfulagain7211@gmail.com www.joyfulagain.org Support program for widowed men and women. Rev. Medard P. Laz, Exec.; Charlotte Hrubes, Dir.;
The Well Spirituality Center - 1515 W. Ogden Ave., La Grange Park, IL 60526 t) 708-482-5048; 708-482-5039 thewell@csjoseph.org www.csjthewell.org Bridget Sperduto, Exec.;

LAKE FOREST

***New Ethos** - 825 S. Waukegan Rd. A8 #225, Lake Forest, IL 60045 t) 312-208-8777 newethosfilm@gmail.com www.new-ethos.org Collaborates with the Entertainment Industry. Rev. Donald C. Woznicki, Exec.;

LEMONT

Franciscan Communities, Inc. (Addolorata Villa; Franciscan Village; Marian Village; Mount Alverna Village; St. Joseph Village of Chicago; The Village at Victory Lakes) - 11500 Theresa Dr., Lemont, IL 60439 t) 331-318-5200 rumanskiy@franciscanministries.org www.franciscanministries.org A senior living and healthcare ministry sponsored by Franciscan Sisters of Chicago serving over 1500 residents. Regina Umanskiy, Pres. & CEO; Karen Larson, COO; Daniel Noonan, CFO;
***Franciscan Ministries Sponsored by the Franciscan Sisters of Chicago** - 11500 Theresa Dr., Lemont, IL 60439 t) 331-318-5200 rumanskiy@franciscanministries.org www.franciscanministries.org Franciscan Sisters of Chicago Service Corporation d/b/a Franciscan Ministries Sponsored by the Franciscan Sisters of Chicago. Senior living ministry. Regina Umanskiy, Pres. & CEO; Karen Larson, COO; Daniel Noonan, CFO; Dawn Mayer, Chief Mission Integration & Pastoral Care Officer;

LINCOLNSHIRE

***Relevant Radio, Inc.** - 680 Barclay Blvd., Lincolnshire, IL 60069 t) 877-291-0123 info@relevantradio.com relevantradio.com Catholic radio/media network Rev. Francis J. Hoffman, CEO; Margaret Kleinschmidt, Sr. Exec. Admin.;

MELROSE PARK

***Dominican Literacy Center (ESL)** - 1503 Rice St., Melrose Park, IL 60160 t) 708-338-0659 judithcurran@yahoo.com

MUNDELEIN

***Institute on Religious Life** - 1000 E. Maple Ave., Bldg. 201P, Mundelein, IL 60060; Mailing: P.O. Box 7500, Libertyville, IL 60048-7500 t) 847-573-8975 irlstaff@religiouslife.com www.religiouslife.com Jeffrey Karls, Exec.; Rev. Thomas Nelson, O.Praem., Dir.;

NORTHLAKE

Ascension Living Casa Scalabrini Village (Presence Senior Services - Chicagoland) - 420 N. Wolf Rd., Northlake, IL 60164 t) 314-292-9308 ahscm-mission@ascension.org www.ascensionliving.org/ Ryan Endsley, COO;

PALATINE

***Friends of St. Thomas of Villanova School** - ; Mailing: P.O. Box 2627, Palatine, IL 60078 t) 847-383-6480 friends@fostovs.org www.fostovs.org

RIVER FOREST

***Dominican Volunteers USA** - 533 Ashland Ave., River Forest, IL 60305 t) 312-226-0919 info@dvusa.org www.dvusa.org Full-time volunteer opportunities for lay people. Megan Rupp, Exec.;
Equestrian Order of the Holy Sepulchre of Jerusalem - 7575 Lake St. #2A, River Forest, IL 60305 t) 708-771-6886 dr.tort@comcast.net www.eohsjnorthcentral.org North Central Lieutenancy Max Douglas Brown, Lieutenant of Honor, Registered Agent;

SOUTH HOLLAND

***American Catholic Press** - 16565 S. State St., South Holland, IL 60473 t) 708-331-5485 acp@acpress.org www.americancatholicpress.org Makes available resources on liturgy and liturgical music Rev. Michael J. Gilligan, Exec.;

TECHNY

Techny Land Corporation, NFP - 1985 Waukegan Rd., Techny, IL 60082; Mailing: P.O. Box 6038, Techny, IL 60082 t) 847-272-2700 x1670 mzemel@uscsvd.org Rev. Nhan Tran, S.V.D.; Bro. Mathew Zemel, S.V.D., Pres.;
Techny Land Investments - 1985 Waukegan Rd., Techny, IL 60082; Mailing: P.O.Box 6038, Techny, IL 60082 t) 847-272-2700 theusro@uscsvd.org Rev. Matheus Ro, S.V.D., Pres.; Bro. Mathew Zemel, S.V.D., Treas.;

WAUKEGAN

Alexian Brothers The Harbor - 826 North Ave., Waukegan, IL 60085; Mailing: 825 W. Wellington Ave., Chicago, IL 60657 t) 847-782-8015 john.halstead1@ascension.org www.ascension.org Legal Title: Alexian Brothers Bonaventure House. Housing/ supportive services for otherwise homeless persons w/ HIV/AIDS. Ascension Illinois The Harbor Polly Davenport, COO; John Halstead, Chief Mission Integration Officer;

WILMETTE

Loyola Recreational Facility Corp. - 1100 Laramie Ave., Wilmette, IL 60091-1021 t) 847-256-1100 pmcgrath@loy.org; tmetzler@loy.org www.goramblers.org Rev. Patrick E. McGrath, S.J.;
Miles Jesu - 142 Millbrook Ln., Wilmette, IL 60091 t) 773-372-3474 administration@milesjesu.com www.milesjesu.org Maire Duggan, M.J., Admin.;

MONASTERIES AND RESIDENCES FOR PRIESTS AND BROTHERS [MON]

ARLINGTON HEIGHTS

Viatorian Province Center-Clerics of St. Viator - 1212 E. Euclid Ave., Arlington Heights, IL 60004-5747 t) 847-398-1354 www.viatorians.com Rev. Charles G. Bolser, C.S.V., Viatorian Province Center - Clerics of St. Viator, Arlington Heights, IL; Rev. Daniel R. Belanger, C.S.V., Serving Elsewhere in the U.S.A. - Diocese of Joliet, IL; Rev. Corey D. Brost, C.S.V., Serving Elsewhere in the Archdiocese of Chicago, IL; Rev. Daniel R. Hall, C.S.V., Serving Elsewhere in the Archdiocese of Chicago, IL; Bro. Diego F Carvajal, CSV, Serving Abroad - Archdiocese of Bogota; Rev. Alejandro Adame, C.S.V., Serving Abroad - Archdiocese of Bogota, Colombia; Bro. Edwin Barreto, Serving Abroad - Archdiocese of Bogota, Colombia; Rev. Carlos Luis Claro, C.S.V., Serving Abroad - Archdiocese of Bogota, Colombia; Rev. Fredy Contreras, C.S.V., Serving Abroad - Archdiocese of Tunja, Colombia; Bro. Michael T. Gosch, C.S.V., Serving Elsewhere in the Archdiocese of Chicago, IL; Bro. Patrick T. Drohan, C.S.V., Serving Elsewhere in the U.S.A. - Diocese of Rockford, IL; Rev. Mark R. Francis, C.S.V., Prov.; Rev. Richard A. Rinn, C.S.V., Prov. Asst.; Rev. Robert M. Egan, C.S.V., International Superior General, Diocese of Las Vegas; Most Rev. Christopher J. Glancy, C.S.V., Serving Elsewhere in the Archdiocese of Chicago, IL; Rev. Daniel T. Nolan, C.S.V., Viatorian Province Center, Clerics of St. Viator, Arlington Heights, IL; Bro. E. Jhobany Orduz, C.S.V., Serving Elsewhere in the Archdiocese of Chicago, IL; Rev. John M. Palmer, C.S.V., Viatorian Province Center, Clerics of St. Viator, Arlington Heights, IL; Rev. Frank Encisco, C.S.V., Serving Abroad - Archdiocese of Bogota, Colombia; Rev. Donald J. Fitzsimmons, C.S.V., Viatorian Province Center - Clerics of St. Viator, Arlington Heights, IL; Bro. Carlos Ernesto Florez, C.S.V., Serving Elsewhere in the U.S.A. - Diocese of Las Vegas, NV; Rev. William F. Haesaert, C.S.V., Serving Elsewhere in the U.S.A. - Diocese of Las Vegas, NV; Rev. Pedro E. Herrera, C.S.V., Serving Abroad - Archdiocese of Tunja, Colombia; Rev. C. Gregory Jones, C.S.V., Serving Elsewhere in the U.S.A. - Diocese of Tucson, AZ; Rev. Lawrence D. Lentz, C.S.V., Serving Elsewhere in the U.S.A. - Diocese of Las Vegas, NV; Bro. James E. Lewnard, C.S.V., Viatorian Province Center - Clerics of St. Viator, Arlington Heights, IL; Rev. Thomas E. Long, C.S.V., Serving Elsewhere in the Archdiocese of Chicago, IL; Rev. Gustavo C. Lopez, C.S.V., Serving Abroad - Archdiocese of Bogota, Colombia; Rev. Luis E. Lopez, C.S.V., Serving Abroad - Archdiocese of Bogota, Colombia; Bro. Parmenio Medina, Serving Abroad - Archdiocese of Bogota, Colombia; Rev. Daniel J. Mirabelli, C.S.V., Serving Elsewhere in the U.S.A. - Diocese of Peoria, IL; Rev. Jose Felipe Montes, C.S.V., Serving Abroad - Archdiocese of Bogota, Colombia; Rev. Jason P. Nesbit, C.S.V., Serving Elsewhere in the U.S.A. - Diocese of Joliet, IL; Bro. Luis O. Pedroza, CSV, Serving Abroad - Archdiocese of Bogota, Colombia; Bro. John J. Dodd, C.S.V., Viatorian Province Center - Clerics of St. Viator, Arlington Heights, IL; Rev. John N. Peeters, C.S.V., Serving Elsewhere in the U.S.A. - Diocese of Joliet, IL; Rev. Arnold E. Perham, C.S.V., Viatorian Province Center - Clerics of St. Viator, Arlington Heights, IL; Rev. Richard J. Pighini, C.S.V., Serving Elsewhere in the U.S.A. - Diocese of Joliet, IL; Rev. John A. Pisors, C.S.V., Serving Abroad - Archdiocese of Tunja, Colombia; Bro. Juan Ramirez, Serving Abroad - Archdiocese of Tunja, Colombia; Rev. Edwin J. Ruiz, C.S.V., Serving Abroad - Archdiocese of Bogota, Colombia; Rev. Fredy L. Santos, C.S.V., Serving Abroad - Archdiocese of Bogota, Colombia; Rev. Erwin M. Savela, C.S.V., Serving Elsewhere in the U.S.A. - Diocese of San Bernardino, CA; Rev. Edgar Suarez, C.S.V., Serving Abroad - Archdiocese of Bogota, Colombia; Bro. Juan Carlos Ubaque, C.S.V., Serving Abroad - Archdiocese of Tunja, Colombia; Rev. John E. Van Wiel, C.S.V., Viatorian Province Center - Clerics of St. Viator, Arlington Heights, IL; Rev. Albeyro Vanegas, C.S.V., Serving Abroad - Archdiocese of Bogota, Colombia; Rev. Thomas R. von Behren, C.S.V., Serving Elsewhere in the U.S.A. - Diocese of Las Vegas, NV; Rev. Donald R. Wehnert, C.S.V., Serving Elsewhere in the U.S.A. - Diocese of Joliet, IL; Bro. John Avellaneda, Serving Abroad - Archdiocese of Tunja; Bro. John R. Eustice, C.S.V., Serving Elsewhere in the USA - Diocese of Joliet, IL; Bro. Peter N. Lamick, C.S.U., Serving elsewhere in the Archdiocese of Chicago; Rev. Daniel J. Lydon, C.S.V., Serving Elsewhere in the Archdiocese of Chicago; Rev. Moises L. Mesh, C.S.V., Servincg Elsewhere in the USA - Diocese of Joliet; Rev. Patrick W. Render, C.S.V., Serving Elsewhere in the USA - Diocese of Joliet; Bro. Michael A. Rice, C.S.V., Viatorian Province Center-Clerics of St. Viator, Arlington Heights, IL; Bro. Rob Robertson, C.S.V., Serving Elsewhere in the Archdiocese of Chicago; Rev. Alan M. Syslo, C.S.V., Viatorian Province Center-Clerics of St. Viator, Arlington Heights, IL; Brs.: 17; Priests: 40

BLUE ISLAND

Marist Brothers - 12212 Irving Ave., Blue Island, IL 60406 t) 708-385-1488 brown.gerry@yahoo.com Bro. Gerard Brown, F.M.S.; Bro. Christopher Shannon;
Rogationists of the Heart of Jesus - St. Matthew Province - 1939 Union St., Blue Island, IL 60406 t) (708) 385-2890 www.rcj.ph/ Rev. Orville Cajigal, R.C.J., Prov.;

BURBANK

Congregation of Christian Brothers (Christian Brothers of Ireland, Inc.) - 5550 W. 87th St., Burbank, IL 60459-2914 t) 773-429-4353 bropathayes@gmail.com Bro. Patrick Hayes, C.F.C., Secy.; Bro. Patrick T. Varilla, C.F.C., In Res.; Thomas Mahoney, CFC, In Res.; Paul Messick, CFC, In Res.; Brs.: 4

Callan Community - 5120 S. Kimbark, Chicago, IL 60615 karlwalczak@gmail.com Bro. Daniel Casey, CFC, In Res.; Bro. Thomas J. Collins, C.F.C., In Res.; Bro. Charles Fitzsimmons, CFC, In Res.; Bro. Karl Walczak, CFC, In Res.;

CHICAGO

Assumption Priory - 323 W. Illinois St., Chicago, IL 60654 t) 312-644-0036 pastor@assumption-chgo.org www.assumption-chgo.org Rev. Lawrence Michael Doyle, O.S.M., In Res.; Rev. Michael M. Guimon, O.S.M., In Res.; Rev. Joseph Chamblain, O.S.M., In Res.; Rev. John M. Fontana, O.S.M., In Res.; Rev. John M. Pawlikowski, O.S.M., In Res.; Bro. Arnaldo Sanchez, OSM, In Res.; Brs.: 1; Priests: 5

St. Augustine Friary - 5413 S. Cornell Ave., Chicago, IL 60615-5603 t) 773-358-6500 ttaylor11406@gmail.com Rev. James G. Thompson, O.S.A., Prior; Rev. Joseph Mostardi, Dir.; Bro. Thomas Taylor, O.S.A., Treas.;

The Augustinians-Provincialate - Augustinian Province Offices, 10161 S. Longwood Dr., Chicago, IL 60643 t) 872-265-1100 secretary@midwestaugustinians.org www.midwestaugustinians.org Very Rev. Anthony B. Pizzo, O.S.A., Prov.; Bro. Nicholas Mullarkey, OSA, Secy.; Rev. James R Halstead, OSA, Treas.; Patrick Griffin, Bus. Mgr.; Brs.: 13; Priests: 57

Chicago Province of the Society of Jesus - 1010 N. Hooker St., Ste. 200: USA Midwest Jesuits, Chicago, IL 60642 t) 773-975-6363; 773-975-6888 umisocius@jesuits.org www.jesuitsmidwest.org Rev. Karl J Kiser, S.J., Prov.; Rev. Glen Chun, S.J., Prov. Asst.;

St. Clare Friary - 3407 S. Archer Ave., Chicago, IL 60608-6817 t) 773-890-1238 jscher56@gmail.com www.capuchinfranciscans.org Rev. Michael J Groark, OFM Cap., Dir.; Rev. Roach Gaspar, O.F.M.Cap., Dir.; Rev. Edward Foley, O.F.M.Cap., Vice Postulator, Blessed Solanus Casey; Rev. John Scherer, OFM Cap., Pst. Min./Coord.; Rev. Gerald Pehler, In Res.; Rev. Begashaw Teklemariam, O.F.M. Cap., In Res.; Bro. Alin Antonysamy, O.F.M. Cap., In Res.; Bro. McLean Bennett, In Res.; Bro. Jaico George, In Res.; Bro. Baudry Metangmo, OFM Cap., In Res.; Bro. Shebin Philip, In Res.; Bro. Jose Vera, OFM Cap., In Res.; Bro. Anthony Yousif, In Res.; Brs.: 34; Priests: 84

Claretian Missionaries U.S.A.-Canada Province, Inc. - 205 W. Monroe St., 7th Fl., Chicago, IL 60606 t) 312-544-8220 petersg@claretians.org www.claretiansusa.org Rev. Rosendo Urrabazo, C.M.F., Prov.; Rev. Marco J. Cardenas, C.M.F., Dir., Radio Claret America; Rev. Fernando Ferrera, C.M.F., Prov. Consultor; Rev. Paul Keller, C.M.F., Prov. Consultor & Secy.; Rev. Thomas McGann, C.M.F., Prov. Econome; Rev. Jose Sanchez, C.M.F., Prov. Consultor; Rev. Manuel Villalobos, C.M.F., Dir., Claretian Biblical Animation Team; Brs.: 8; Priests: 75

Claret Center, Inc. - 5536 S. Everett Ave., Chicago, IL 60637 t) 773-643-6259 office@claretcenter.org www.claretcenter.org Resources for Counseling and Spiritual Direction

Claret House (Formation Residence) - 5540 S. Everett St., Chicago, IL 60637 t) 773-493-8119 beauplancmf@gmail.com; rubistoncmf@gmail.com Rev. Beauplan Derilus, CMF, Supr.; Rev. Eddie De Leon, CMF, Prof.; Rev. Sahaya Rubiston Peter, C.M.F., Vocations Dir.; Rev. Francisco Javier Reyes, C.M.F., Asst. Prefect, Formation;

Claretian Missionaries Charitable Property Trust - 205 W. Monroe St., 7th Fl., Chicago, IL 60606 t) (312) 544-8220 Gail Peters, Admin.;

Claretian Missionaries Community Support Trust - 400 N. Euclid Ave., Oak Park, IL 60302 t) 708-848-2076

Claretian Missionaries Continuing Care Trust - 205 W. Monroe St., 7th Fl., Chicago, IL 60606 t) (312) 544-8220 Gail Peters, Admin.;

Claretian Missionaries Endowment Trust - t) 312-544-8132

Claretian Missionaries Service Corporation - 205 W. Monroe St., 7th Fl., Chicago, IL 60606 t) (312) 544-8195 chambers@claretians.org Susan Chambers, Human Resources Mgr.;

Claretian Volunteers and Lay Missionaries - 205 W. Monroe St., Chicago, IL 60606 t) 312-544-8135 vocationofficeassistant@claretians.org www.claretianvolunteers.org

Claretians, Inc. - 205 W. Monroe, Chicago, IL 60606 www.claretians.org

Provincial Residence - 400 N. Euclid Ave., Oak Park, IL 60302 t) 708-848-2076 mcgannt@claretians.org Most Rev. Placido Rodriguez, CMF; Rev. Mark J. Brummel, C.M.F., In Res.; Bro. Gustavo Hernandez, CMF, In Res.; Bro. Daniel Magner, C.M.F., In Res.; Bro. Richard Wilga, C.M.F., In Res.;

Columban Fathers Theologate - 5103 S. Ellis Ave., Chicago, IL 60615 t) 773-955-0660 Rev. Leo Distor, S.S.C., Rector; Rev. Timothy Mulroy, S.S.C., Rector;

Conventual Franciscans of St. Bonaventure Province - 6107 N. Kenmore Ave., Chicago, IL 60660 t) 773-274-7681 dmk9271@gmail.com Very Rev. Paul Joseph Langevin, O.F.M. Conv., Prov.; Brs.: 12; Priests: 19

Saint Bonaventure Friary - t) 773-764-8811 Rev. Anthony Lajato, O.F.M.Conv.; Bro. Joseph Graff; Bro. Joseph Schenk, O.F.M.Conv., Secy.; Rev. Robert Cook, O.F.M.Conv., Pst.;

Croatian Franciscan Custody of the Holy Family - 4848 S. Ellis Ave., Chicago, IL 60615 t) 773-536-0552 chicagoofm@gmail.com www.crofranciscans.com Rev. Marko Puljic-Vlahic, OFM; Brs.: 3; Priests: 23

St. Anthony's Friary - t) 773-373-3463 Rev. Josip N. Galic, O.F.M.; Rev. Ljubo Krasic, O.F.M.; Rev. Zvonimir Kutlesa, O.F.M.; Rev. Philip Pavich, O.F.M.;

Croatian Franciscan Fathers - 6346 N. Ridge, Chicago, IL 60660 t) 773-262-0535 bastepinacchicago@sbcglobal.net Rev. Paul Maslach, O.F.M.;

Crosier Community of Chicago - 5401 S. Cornell Ave., Chicago, IL 60615 t) 773-684-6975 Rev. Thomas Enneking, O.S.C.; Bro. David Donnay, O.S.C.;

DePaul Vincentian Residence - 2233 N. Kenmore Ave., Chicago, IL 60614-3594 c) 573-513-0138 jwill168@depaul.edu Congregation of the Mission, Society of Priests. Rev. Joseph S Williams, Supr.; Rev. Robert R. Rohrich, C.M.; Rev. Stanislav Bindas, C.M., Chap.; Rev. William R Piletic, Chap.; Rev. Daniel P. Borlik, C.M., Campus Min.; Rev. John E. Rybolt, C.M., Vincentian Scholar; Rev. Guillermo Campuzano, CM, Vice Pres., Mission & Ministry; Rev. Hugh F O'Donnell, CM, Dir., Formation; Rev. David Windsor, CM, Dir., Counseling Svcs.; Rev. Edouard Ayirwanda, C.M., In Res.; Rev. Yohanes Fery, In Res.; Rev. Ranjan Kumar Lima, In Res.; Rev. Jose Francisco Orozco Ortigosa, C.M., In Res.; Greg Hallam, Treas.; Priests: 15

Dominicans (Provincial Office) - 1910 S. Ashland Ave., Chicago, IL 60608-2904 t) 312-243-0011 office@opcentral.org www.opcentral.org Dominicans, Province of St. Albert the Great, U.S.A. (Central Dominican Province) Rev. James V. Marchionda, O.P., Prov.; Rev. Andrew-Carl Wisdom, O.P., Vicar, Office for Mission Advancement; Rev. Donald Goergen, OP, Vicar Prov., Socius; Rev. Samuel P. Hakeem, OP, Vocation Dir.; Rev. John J. Meany, OP, Vicar Prov., Prior;

The Bolivian Trust of the Dominicans - Dominican Shrine of St. Jude Thaddeus - t) 312-226-0020 Promotes, supports & develops the apostolate of preaching and healing in the Province of St. Albert the Great. Rev. Michail Ford, O.P., Dir.;

St. Dominic's Mission Society of the Dominican Fathers of the Province of St. Albert the Great - t) 312-242-0011 Organized to seek funds for the support of the foreign missionary work of the Dominican Fathers of the Province. Rev. Gerald Stookey, OP, Dir.;

St. Jude Legacy Fund - Rev. Kevin Neihoff, Treas.;

The New Priory Press - newprioryppress@opcentral.org www.newpriorypress.com Patrick Hieronymus Baikauskas, OP, Dir.;

Office for Mission Advancement of the Dominicans, Province of St. Albert the Great, U.S.A. - This Office coordinates the activities of the Shrine of St. Jude Thaddeus, the Society for Vocational Support and St. Dominic Mission Society. Robert Dixon, Exec. Dir.;

St. Pius V Priory - 1909 S. Ashland Ave., Chicago, IL 60608-2904 t) 312-226-0074 stpiusv@gmail.com Rev. Thomas P. Lynch, O.P., Pst.; Rev. Brian G. Bricker, O.P., Par. Vicar; Rev. Jon Alexander, OP, In Res.; Bro. Terrence George Bullock, OP, In Res.; Rev. Joachim Culotta, OP, In Res.; Rev. David Delich, O.P., In Res.; Rev. Francis X. Dyer, O.P., In Res.; Rev. Michael Augustine Garcia, OP, In Res.; Rev. Peter J. Hereley, O.P., In Res.; Rev. Thomas M. Jackson, O.P., In Res.; Rev. Albert G. Judy, O.P., In Res.; Rev. Walter T. O'Connell, O.P., In Res.; Rev. John J. O'Malley, O.P., In Res.; Rev. Mark Paraday, O.P., In Res.; Rev. Patrick R. Rearden, O.P., In Res.; Rev. Edward H. Riley, O.P., In Res.; Rev. Michael B. Ruthenberg, O.P., In Res.; Rev. Gabriel J. Torretta, O.P., In Res.; Rev. John Vincent Blake, O.P., Assigned but Living Elsewhere; Rev. Gerard B. Cleator, O.P., Assigned but Living Elsewhere; Rev. Charles W. Dahm, O.P., Assigned but Living Elsewhere; Rev. Rapael A. Fabish, O.P., Assigned but Living Elsewhere; Rev. Kevin R. Fane, O.P., Assigned but Living Elsewhere; Rev. Michail Ford, O.P., Dir, Shrine of St. Jude Thaddeus; Rev. Daniel W. Morrissey, O.P., Assigned but Living Elsewhere; Bro. John Paul Peterson, OP, Social Worker; Rev. Benedict T. Viviano, O.P., Assigned but Living Elsewhere; Rev. Brian G. Walker, O.P., Itinerant Preacher;

Society for Vocational Support of St. Albert the Great Province, an Illinois Not-for-Profit Corporation - t) 312-226-0020 To educate poor boys for the priesthood.

Federation of Augustinians of North America - 5413 S. Cornell Ave., Chicago, IL 60615-5664 c) 510-499-9304 director@fanaosa.org www.fanaosa.org Very Rev. Gary Sanders, O.S.A., Prior; Rev. Kevin C. Mullins, OSA, Exec.; Rev. Kevin C. Mullins, O.S.A., Secy.; Very Rev. Rob Hagen, OSA, Mem.; Very Rev. Anthony B. Pizzo, O.S.A., Mem.; Brs.: 20; Priests: 215

Franciscan House of Studies - 6107 N. Kenmore Ave., Chicago, IL 60660 t) 773-764-8811 dmk9271@gmail.com A Formation House of Conventual Franciscan Friars.

Holy Evangelists Friary - 4513 N. Ashland Blvd., Chicago, IL 60651-5401 t) 773-878-3723 friarjpc@gmail.com Order of Friars Minor. Friar Johnpaul Cafiero, O.F.M.; Rev. Robert Pawell; Rev. Eulogio Roselada, O.F.M.;

Holy Name Friary - 3800 W. Peterson Ave., Assumption BVM Province, Chicago, IL 60659-3116 t) 708-209-6889 Rev. Camillus Janas, O.F.M., Assoc. Pst.; Rev. Lawrence Janowski, O.F.M., Chap.; Rev. Bernard Kennedy, O.F.M., Dir.;

Holy Spirit Friary, Order of Friars Minor - 5225 S. Greenwood Ave., Chicago, IL 60615-4335 t) 773-753-1920 Rev. Gilberto Cavazos-Gonzales, O.F.M.; Rev. Albert Haase, O.F.M.; Rev. Phil D. Hogan, O.F.M.; Rev. Gilbert Ostdiek, O.F.M.; Rev. Charles E. Payne, O.F.M.; Bro. Charles Reid, O.F.M.; Rev. David Rodriguez, O.F.M.;

Institute of Christ the King Sovereign Priest - 6415 S. Woodlawn Ave., Chicago, IL 60637-3817 t) 773-363-7409 info@institute-christ-king.org www.institute-christ-king.org Rev. Msgr. R. Michael Schmitz, Vicar Gen.; Rev. Canon Matthew L. Talarico, Prov.; Rev. Canon Luke Zignego, Rector; Rev. Canon

David Le, Secy.; Rev. Canon James Hoogerwerf, In Res.; Brs.: 7; Priests: 27

Shrine of Christ the King Sovereign Priest - 6401 S. Woodlawn Ave., Chicago, IL 60637; Mailing: 6415 S. Woodlawn Ave., Chicago, IL 60637 t) (773) 363-7821 shrine@institute-christ-king.org Rev. Canon David Le, In Res.;

St. John Stone Friary - 1165 E. 54th Pl., Chicago, IL 60615-5109 t) 773-684-6510 www.midwestaugustinians.org Rev. Karl A. Gersbach, O.S.A., Prior; Rev. Michael J. O'Connor, O.S.A.; Rev. James J. Sheridan; Rev. John Szura, O.S.A.; Rev. Reinhard J. Sternemann, O.S.A., Treas.; Bro. Fred R. Kaiser, O.S.A., Subprior; Bro. David W. Adelsbach, O.S.A.; Bro. John Patrick Currier, O.S.A.;

St. Joseph Interprovincial Post-Novitiate Formation House - 5495 S. Hyde Park Blvd., Chicago, IL 60615 t) 301-509-6412 jrozanskyofm@gmail.com (A Franciscan House of the Sacred Heart Province) Rev. Joseph Rozansky;

Korean Catholic Center - 4115 N. Kedvale, Chicago, IL 60641 t) 773-283-3979 Rev. John Smith, S.S.C., Dir.;

La Salette Theologate - 4541 S. Greenwood Ave., Chicago, IL 60653 t) 678-258-5661

Lithuanian American Jesuits (Jesuit Fathers of Della Strada Inc.) - 2345 W. 56th St., Chicago, IL 60636; Mailing: 1116 Amber Dr., Lemont, IL 60439 t) 630-257-5570 baniulisa@gmail.com www.jezuitai.lt (Della Strada Residence and Lithuanian Youth Center) Rev. Algis Baniulis, S.J., Pres.;

Baltic Jesuits Advancement Project - 1380 Castlewood Dr., Lemont, IL 60439-6732 t) 630-243-6234 lithjesuit@hotmail.com Rev. Antanas Grazulis, S.J., Secy.;

Blessed Jurgis Matulaitis Mission - 14911 E. 127th St., Lemont, IL 60439 t) 630-257-5613 matulaitismission@gmail.com www.matulaitismission.com

Lithuanian Youth Center Inc. - 5620 S. Claremont Ave., Chicago, IL 60636 t) 773-778-7500

Marist Brothers - Monastery Community, 4200 W. 115th St., Chicago, IL 60655 t) 773-881-6380 moran.kevin@marist.net www.marist.net Bro. Paul Forgues; Bro. Richard Grenier; Bro. Julian Roy; Bro. Christopher Shannon;

Marist Brothers - 10114 S. Leavitt, St. Ann Residence, Chicago, IL 60643 t) 773-239-4116 Bro. Brendan Brennan; Bro. Henry Hammer; Bro. Stephen Synan; Bro. Hugh Turley, F.M.S.; Bro. Vito Aresto, Dir.;

Maryknoll Fathers & Brothers (Catholic Foreign Mission Society of America, Inc.) - 5128 S. Hyde Park Blvd., Chicago, IL 60615-4217 t) 773-288-3143 chicago@maryknoll.org maryknollsociety.org Rev. Russell J. Feldmeier, M.M., Rector; Bro. Mark Gruenke, M.M., Mem.; Rev. John P. Cuff, M.M., Mem.; Brs.: 1; Priests: 2

Monastery of the Holy Cross - 3111 S. Aberdeen St., Chicago, IL 60608-6503 t) 773-927-7424 edward@chicagomonk.org www.chicagomonk.org Benedictine Monks (Subiaco Cassinese Congregation). Rev. Peter Funk, O.S.B., Prior; Rev. Brendan D. Creeden, O.S.B., Novice Master; Rev. Edward J. Glanzmann, O.S.B., Porter; Guests; Bro. Gabriel Sumeral, O.S.B., Sacristan; Web Master; Bro. Timothy Ferrell, O.S.B., Asst. Cellarer; Bro. Augustine Jusas, O.S.B., Property Mngmt.; Bro. Ignatius Isaac, O.S.B., Librn.; Bro. Joseph Woudenberg, O.S.B., Gift Shop Mgr.; Grounds;

Order of Friar Servants of Mary (Servites) United States of America Province, Inc. - 3121 W. Jackson Blvd., Servite Provincial Center, Chicago, IL 60612-2729 t) 773-533-0360 x212 arnaldosanchez@servitesusa.org www.servite.org Rev. Eugene M. Smith, O.S.M., Prov.; Rev. Donald M. Siple, O.S.M., Asst. Prov.; Rev. Joseph Chamblain, O.S.M., Prov. Councilor; Rev. Joseph M Cheah, OSM, Prov. Councilor; Bro. Arnaldo Sanchez, OSM, Treas.; Rev. Paul M. Gins, O.S.M., Archivist; Eddie Murphy, Vocation Dir.; Brs.: 7; Priests: 43

Monastery of Our Lady of Sorrows - t) 773-638-5800 chriskrymski@aol.com Rev. Eugene M. Smith, O.S.M., In Res.; Rev. Timothy Kremen, OSM, In Res.; Rev. Luke M Stano, O.S.M., In Res.; Rev. Conrad M. Borntrager, O.S.M., In Res.; Bro. Michael M. Callary, O.S.M., In Res.; Rev. Frank M. Falco, O.S.M., In Res.; Bro. Robert M. Fandel, O.S.M., In Res.; Rev. Christopher M. Krymski, O.S.M., In Res.;

National Shrine of St. Peregrine, O.S.M. - t) 773-638-5800 x19 chriskrymski@aol.com Rev. Christopher M. Krymski, O.S.M., Dir.; Rev. John Fontana, Dir.;

Servants of Mary (Servite) Development Office - 1439 S. Harlem Ave., Berwyn, IL 60402 t) 708-795-8885 jamesfoerster@servitesusa.org James Foerster, Dir.;

Passionist Community of St. Vincent Strambi - 5417 S. Cornell Ave., Chicago, IL 60615 t) 773-324-2704 dcolhour@passionist.org Rev. Tu-Jin Paul Kim, C.P., Pst.; Rev. David Colhour, C.P., Supr.; Rev. Arthur Carrillo, C.P., Mem.; Rev. Francis X. Keenan, C.P., Resident, Presence St. Benedict Nursing/Rehab Center; Bro. Cristian Joel Martinez Montalvo, C.P., Student; Jonathan Ramos, Student; Rev. Robin Ryan, C.P., CTU Faculty; Rev. Alfredo Ocampo, C.P., Formation Dir., Asst. Supr.; Rev. Donald Webber, C.P., Dir., Office of Mission Effectiveness; Brs.: 1; Priests: 7

St. Patrick's Missionary Society - 8422 W. Windsor Ave., Chicago, IL 60656-4252 t) 773-887-4741 spsil@spms.org spms.org Rev. Michael Madigan, S.P.S.; Rev. Michael Moore, S.P.S.;

St. Patrick's Fathers Guilds and Associates -

St. Peter's Friary - 110 W. Madison St., Chicago, IL 60602-4196 t) 312-372-5111 www.stpetersloop.org Order of Friars Minor. Rev. Arthur Anderson, O.F.M.; Rev. William Burton, O.F.M.; Rev. Kenneth Capalbo, O.F.M.; Rev. Wenceslaus Church; Rev. Mario DiCicco, O.F.M.; Rev. Thomas Ess, O.F.M.; Bro. Leo Geurts, O.F.M.; Rev. Juan Carlos Ruiz Guerrero, O.F.M; Bro. Dot Hoang, O.F.M.; Rev. James A. Hoffman, O.F.M.; Rev. Robert Hutmacher, O.F.M.; Rev. James Hwang, O.F.M.; Rev. Robert Karris, O.F.M.; Bro. Joseph Middleton, O.F.M.; Rev. George Musial, O.F.M.; Rev. Michael Perry, O.F.M.; Rev. Glenn Phillips, O.F.M.; Rev. Elric Sampson, O.F.M.; Bro. Raymond Shuhert, O.F.M.; Rev. Peter Minh Van Dau, O.F.M.; Rev. Kurt Hartrich, O.F.M., Pst.; Rev. Edward Shea, O.F.M., Vicar; Bro. William Lanning, O.F.M., Bus. Mgr.; Bro. Herbert Rempe, O.F.M., Bus. Mgr.; Bro. Clarence Klingert, O.F.M., Dir.; Bro. Thomas Krull, O.F.M., Dir.; Bro. William Schulte, O.F.M., Librn.;

Premonstratensian Fathers and Brothers (Norbertines) - 4841 S. Woodlawn Ave., Chicago, IL 60615 t) 773-548-8020 www.norbertines.org Holy Spirit House of Studies Rev. Jay J. Fostner, O. Praem., Supr.; Bro. Patricio Chacon, O. Praem., In Res.; Bro. Lucas Myers, O. Praem., In Res.; Bro. Jacob Sircy, O. Praem., In Res.; Bro. Charles Burris, O. Praem., In Res.; Brs.: 4; Priests: 1

Provincial Office of the Congregation of the Resurrection - 3601 N. California Ave., Chicago, IL 60618-4602 t) 773-463-7506 whallascr@gmail.com; businessoffice.usa.cr@gmail.com www.resurrectionists.com Rev. Steven Bartczyszyn, C.R., Prov.;

The Redemptorist Fathers of Chicago - 1633 N. Cleveland Ave., Chicago, IL 60614 t) 312-642-2498 Rev. Kevin Zubel, C.Ss.R., Prov. Supr.; Very Rev. Daniel Andree, C.Ss.R., Judicial Vicar; Rev. Lawrence E. Sanders, C.Ss.R., Pst.; Rev. Edward Vella, C.Ss.R., Assoc. Pst.; Rev. Aaron Meszaros, C.Ss.R., Vicar; Rev. Anthony Phuc Nguyen, C.Ss.R., Consultor; Rev. Joseph Dorcey, C.Ss.R., Missionary, Suriname; Rev. J. Robert Fenili, C.Ss.R., In Res.; Rev. James Keena, C.Ss.R., In Res.; Rev. Gregory May, C.Ss.R., In Res.; Rev. John Phelps, C.Ss.R., In Res.; Rev. John Steingraeber, C.Ss.R., In Res.; Rev. Ramon Dompke, C.Ss.R., In Res.; Priests: 13

The Redemptorists/Denver Province - 1633 N. Cleveland Ave., Chicago, IL 60614 t) 312-248-8894 admin@redemptorists-denver.org www.redemptoristsdenver.org Rev. Kevin Zubel, C.Ss.R., Prov. Supr.; Rev. Aaron Meszaros, C.Ss.R., Vicar; Rev. Anthony Phuc Nguyen, C.Ss.R., Consultor; Rev. Gregory May, C.Ss.R., Treas.; Rev. John Steingraeber, C.Ss.R., Asst. Treas.; Rev. Joseph Dorcey, C.Ss.R., Serving Elsewhere; Rev. Theodore Dorcey, C.Ss.R., Serving Elsewhere; Rev. Scott Katzenberger, C.Ss.R., Serving Elsewhere; Bro. Laurence Lujan, C.Ss.R., Serving Elsewhere; His Eminence Joseph Tobin, C.Ss.R., Serving Elsewhere; Brs.: 23; Priests: 111

St. Rita Monastery - 7740 S. Western Ave., Chicago, IL 60620-5867 t) 773-476-3879 (See High Schools, Private) Rev. Bernard Danber, O.S.A., Prior; Rev. Bernard C. Scianna, O.S.A., Prov.; Rev. Alfred M. Burke, O.S.A.; Rev. Stephen M. Curry, O.S.A.; Rev. Edwin J. Dodge, O.S.A.; Rev. Thomas R. McCarthy, O.S.A.; Rev. John P. Tasto, O.S.A.; Rev. Gerald J. Van Overbeek, O.S.A.; Bro. Joe Ruiz, O.S.A.; Bro. Lawrence Sparacino, O.S.A.;

Sacred Heart Mission House (The Polish Messenger of The Sacred Heart, Inc.) - 4105 N. Avers Ave., Chicago, IL 60618 t) 773-588-7476 www.jezuici.org Rev. Jozef Polak, S.J., Supr.; Rev. Marek Janowski, S.J., Mem.; Rev. Jerzy Brzoska, S.I., Mem.; Rev. Tomasz Szymczyk, S.J., Mem.; Bro. Adam Poreba; Brs.: 1; Priests: 4

Jan Beyzym Society, Inc. - (Polish Jesuit Foreign Missions)

Jesuit Millennium Center - 5835 W. Irving Park Rd., Chicago, IL 60634 t) 773-777-7000 www.jezvici.org

Sant'Angelo Community at St. Cyril Priory - 6401 S. Harper Ave., Chicago, IL 60637 t) 773-324-0020 baguilar@carmelnet.org www.mchs.org Rev. Benjamin Aguilar, O.Carm., Prior; Bro. Neil Conlisk; Rev. Leopold Glueckert; Rev. Carl J. Markelz, O.Carm.; Rev. Tony Mazurkiewicz, O.Carm.; Rev. Enrique Varela;

Scalabrini House of Theology - 5121 S. University Ave., Chicago, IL 60615 t) 773-684-5230; 773-684-1706 scalajmr@hotmail.com Rev. Mauro Lazzarato, C.S.; Rev. Jesus Reyes, C.S., Rector; Rev. Gino Dalpiaz, C.S., Dir.;

Vincentian Community, Congregation of the Mission, Western Province - 2210-12 N. Racine Ave., Chicago, IL 60614 c) 312-217-1187 gkelly@depaul.edu Rev. Richard B. Benson, C.M.; Rev. Robert D. Lucas, C.M., Chap.; Rev. Gerard P. Kelly, C.M., Supr.; Bro. Mark Elder, C.M., Faculty; Rev. Christopher S. Robinson, C.M., Faculty; Rev. Edward R. Udovic, C.M., Archivist; Rev. J. Patrick Murphy, C.M., Emeritus Prof.;

Wisconsin Province of the Society of Jesus - 1010 N. Hooker St., Chicago, IL 60642 t) (773) 975-6888 Rev. Glen Chun, S.J., Socius;

COUNTRYSIDE

St. Gratian Friary, Franciscan Friars - 5536 S. Edgewood Ln., Countryside, IL 60525-3426 t) 708-482-4546 stgratian@aol.com Rev. Dennis Koopman, O.F.M., Vicar; Rev. Charles Faso, O.F.M.; Rev. James Walton, O.F.M.; Bro. Clarence Klingert, O.F.M.; Bro. Leon Beranek, O.F.M.;

ELK GROVE VILLAGE

Congregation of Alexian Brothers Immaculate Conception Province, Inc. - 600 Alexian Way, Elk Grove Village, IL 60007 t) 847-264-8704 www.alexianbrothers.org Bro. Daniel McCormick, C.F.A., Prov.; Bro. Richard Lowe, C.F.A., Prov. Asst.; Bro. Thomas Klein, C.F.A., Secy.; Bro. Steve Fogt, C.F.A., Treas.; Bro. Warren Longo, C.F.A., Dir.; Brs.: 27

Brothers of St. Alexius Health and Welfare Fund, Inc. - t) 847-264-8700

EVANSTON

Canisius House Jesuit Community - 201 Dempster St., Evanston, IL 60201-4704 t) (847) 563-8380 canisiushouse201@gmail.com Rev. Stanislaw Czarnecki, S.J., Supr.; Rev. Gregory J. Ostdiek, S.J., Pres.; Alexander DeWitt, SJ, Campus Min.; Rev. Thomas W. Florek, S.J., Dir.; Rev. Ted Munz, S.J., Dir.; Priests: 4

HICKORY HILLS

Legion of Christ - 8601 W. 89th St., Hickory Hills, IL 60457 t) 773-372-5142 chicago@legionaries.org Rev.

Michael Mitchell, L.C., Supr.; Rev. John Brender, L.C.; Rev. Michael Moriarty, L.C.; Rev. Joshua West, L.C.; Rev. Bruce Wren, L.C.; Dcn. Peter Krezelec, L.C.; Dcn. Brett Taira, L.C.;

LA GRANGE PARK

Comboni Missionaries - 1615 E. 31st St., La Grange Park, IL 60526-1377 t) 708-354-1999 chicago@combonimissionaries.org www.combonimissionaries.org/ Rev. Jean Philippe Lokpo, MCCJ, Mem.; Rev. Jose Manuel Sanchez Ortiz, MCCJ, Mem.; Rev. Godwin Kwame Kornu, MCCJ, Mem.; Rev. Jerome - Nerio Missay Soku, MCCJ, Student at Loyola U for Masters Pastoral Counseling; Priests: 4

LEMONT

The Slovene Franciscan Fathers, Order of Friars Minor, Commissariat of the Holy Cross - 14246 Main St., Lemont, IL 60439; Mailing: P.O. Box 608, Lemont, IL 60439 t) 630-257-2494 metodofm@gmail.com lemont-svs.org Rev. Krizolog Cimerman, O.F.M., Pst.; Rev. Bernard Karmanocky, O.F.M., Pst.; Rev. Metod Ogorevc, O.F.M., Pres.; Priests: 3

***Slovenian Catholic Center** - 14252 Main St., Lemont, IL 60439; Mailing: P.O. Box 634, Lemont, IL 60439 t) 630-243-0670 jvidmar@archchicago.org www.slovenian-center.org Dcn. John Vidmar;

LIBERTYVILLE

Marytown, Our Lady of Fatima Friary - 1600 W. Park Ave., Libertyville, IL 60048-2593 t) 847-367-7800 broaug510@aol.com; mail@kolbeshrine.org www.kolbeshrine.org Rev. Hans Flonder, O.F.M.Conv., Dir.; Bro. Augustine Kelly, O.F.M.Conv.;

Conventual Franciscan Friars of Marytown - National Shrine of St. Maximilian Kolbe -

MATTESON

Austin Friary - 5245 Stoneridge Ct., Matteson, IL 60443-2269 t) 708-747-2732 Rev. Terry A. Deffenbaugh, O.S.A., Prior; Rev. Michael J. O'Connor, O.S.A., Dir.; Rev. Edward Andrews, O.S.A.; Bro. David W. Adelsbach, O.S.A.;

NILES

Society of the Missionaries of St. Francis Xavier - 8149 W. Golf Rd., Niles, IL 60714 t) (847) 967-1060 Rev. Carlos Paulo Pereira, sfx (India); Priests: 2

OAK PARK

Dominican Community of St. Martin de Porres - 204 S. Humphrey, Oak Park, IL 60302 martindeporressyndic@gmail.com www.domcentral.org Rev. Brendan A. Curran, O.P., Supr.; Rev. Alfred A. Lopez, OP, Itinerant Preacher; Rev. Herbert C Hayek, OP, In Res.; Rev. Michael A. Winkels, O.P., In Res.; Scott Edward Steinkerchner, OP, Webmaster / Theologian - Interfaith Dialogue; Priests: 5

Missionaries of Saint Charles - 546 N. East Ave., Provincial Residence, Oak Park, IL 60302 t) 708-386-4430 sjbprovince@comcast.net www.scalabrinians.org Rev. Miguel Alvarez-Galindo, Prov.;

Scalabrini Development Office - t) 708-848-1616

Scalabrinians Community Formation Corporation, Oak Park -

Scalabrinians Community Support Corporation, Oak Park -

PARK RIDGE

Passionist Provincial Office (The Congregation of the Passion, Holy Cross Province) - 660 Busse Hwy., Park Ridge, IL 60068 t) 847-518-8844 x2301 moonsjoe@yahoo.com www.passionist.org Rev. Joseph Moons, C.P., Prov.; Rev. David Colhour, C.P., Asst. Prov.; Rev. Alfredo Ocampo, C.P., Consultor; Rev. Philip Paxton, C.P., Consultor; Rev. James Strommer, C.P., Consultor; Brs.: 7; Priests: 31

Holy Cross Province Development Office - t) (847) 518-8844 x2303 keith@cppo.org passionist.org Keith Zekind, Exec. Dir.;

Passionist Archives - t) (847) 518-8844 x2301 Sr. Loretta Ciesielski, SSJ-TOSF, Archivist;

Passionist Missions, Inc. - t) (847) 518-8844 x2301 Sr. Loretta Ciesielski, SSJ-TOSF, Dir.;

Province Finance Office - t) (847) 518-8844 x2303 keith@cppo.org Rev. John Schork, C.P., Treas.; Susan Arvanitis, Controller; Keith Zekind, Dir. Finance;

TECHNY

Divine Word Residence - 1901 Waukegan Rd., Techny, IL 60082-6000; Mailing: P.O. Box 6000, Techny, IL 60082-6000 t) 847-412-1100 svdrector@technydwr.org; provincial@uscsvd.org www.divineword.org (Formerly Divine Word Seminary-St. Mary's Mission House). Divine Word Techny Community Corporation. Rev. Quang Duc Dinh, S.V.D., Prov.; Rev. Walter Miller, S.V.D., Rector; Rev. Stephan Brown, S.V.D.; Rev. Kenneth Hamilton, S.V.D.; Rev. Michael Hutchins, S.V.D.; Most Rev. Michael Blume, SVD, In Res.; Rev. Jesus Briones, SVD, In Res.; Rev. Thomas A Krosnicki, SVD, In Res.; Rev. Francis Rayappan, In Res.; Rev. James Braband, S.V.D., In Res.; Rev. Joseph Bugner, S.V.D., In Res.; Rev. Dennis Callan, S.V.D., In Res.; Rev. Francis Drzaic, S.V.D., In Res.; Rev. Robert Fisher, In Res.; Rev. Dennis Flynn, SVD, In Res.; Rev. Lucien Gaudreault, S.V.D., In Res.; Rev. Thomas Griffith Sr., SVD, In Res.; Rev. William Halvey, S.V.D., In Res.; Rev. Raymond Hannah, S.V.D., In Res.; Rev. James Heiar, In Res.; Rev. Raymond Hober, S.V.D., In Res.; Rev. Janusz Horowski, In Res.; Rev. Ronald Lange, S.V.D., In Res.; Rev. Matheus Ro, S.V.D., Treas.; Rev. Timothy Lenchak, S.V.D., In Res.; Rev. Raymond Lennon, S.V.D., In Res.; Rev. Joseph Logue, S.V.D., In Res.; Rev. Robert Mertes, S.V.D., In Res.; Rev. Elmer Nadicksbernd, SVD, In Res.; Rev. Tan Viet Nguyen, S.V.D., In Res.; Rev. Gerard O'Doherty, S.V.D., In Res.; Rev. William Seifert, S.V.D., In Res.; Rev. Derek Simons, S.V.D., In Res.; Rev. David Streit, S.V.D., In Res.; Rev. Gerard Theis, S.V.D., In Res.; Rev. Nhan Tran, S.V.D., In Res.; Rev. Thomas Umbras, SVD, In Res.; Bro. Larry Camilleri, In Res.; Bro. Matt Connors, In Res.; Bro. Raymond Albers, S.V.D., In Res.; Bro. Joachim Brignac, S.V.D., In Res.; Bro. George Haegele, S.V.D., In Res.; Bro. Kenneth Valois, S.V.D., In Res.; Bro. Daniel Holman, S.V.D., In Res.; Bro. James Zabransky, SVD, In Res.; Bro. Mathew Zemel, S.V.D., In Res.; Brs.: 8; Priests: 37

Society of the Divine Word, Provincial Headquarters-Chicago Prov. - 1985 Waukegan Rd., Techny, IL 60082-6038; Mailing: P.O. Box 6038, Techny, IL 60082-6038 t) 847-272-2700 provincial@uscsvd.org www.divineword.org (Province of Saint Joseph Freinademetz, S.V.D.) Rev. Quang Duc Dinh, S.V.D., Prov.; Rev. Matheus Ro, S.V.D., Treas.; Brs.: 23; Priests: 147

Blessed Arnold Charitable Trust - ; Mailing: P.O. Box 6067, Techny, IL 60082-6067 treasurer@uscsvd.org

Divine Word Funds, Inc. - 1985 Waukegan Rd., Techny, IL 60082-6038; Mailing: P.O. Box 6067, Techny, IL 60082-6067 treasurer@uscsvd.org www.annuitysvd.org

Divine Word Novitiate - 1945 Waukegan Rd., Techny, IL 60082-6000; Mailing: P.O. Box 6000, Techny, IL 60082-6000 t) 847-412-1444 Rev. Timothy Lenchak, S.V.D., Dir.; Bro. Mathew Zemel, S.V.D., Dir.;

DWTCRE Charitable Trust - 1901 Waukegan Rd., Techny, IL 60082; Mailing: P.O. Box 6067, Techny, IL 60082 dgarbaciak@uscsvd.org

S.V.D. Funds, Inc. - ; Mailing: P.O. Box 6067, Techny, IL 60082-6067 treasurer@uscsvd.org www.annuitysvd.org

Vocation Office - 102 Jacoby Dr., S.W., Epworth, IL 52045; Mailing: P.O. Box 380, Epworth, IL 52045-0380 t) 800-553-3321 svdvocations@dwci.edu www.svdvocations.org Len Uhal, Dir.;

WILLOW SPRINGS

Cistercian Fathers, Our Lady Mother of the Church Polish Mission - 116 Hilton St., Willow Springs, IL 60480-1697 t) 708-467-0436 cistercianmission@gmail.com Cistercian Priory dependant monastery of the Abbey in Szczyrzyc, Poland (Polish Congregation) est. 1982. Rev. Konrad Ciechanowski, O.Cist., Assoc. Pst.; Rev. Michael Blicharski, O.Cist., Dir.;

NURSING / REHABILITATION / CONVALESCENCE / ELDERLY CARE [NUR]

CHICAGO

Ascension Living Resurrection Village Life Center (Presence Senior Services - Chicagoland) - 7370 W. Talcott Ave., Chicago, IL 60631 t) 314-292-9308 ahscm-mission@ascension.org www.ascensionliving.org/ Ryan Endsley, COO; Asstd. Annu.: 512; Staff: 93

Catholic Home Care - 721 N. LaSalle St., Chicago, IL 60654 t) 312-655-8368 cbrooks@catholiccharities.net Home health agency, Medicare certified, JCAHO accredited, providing health care to individuals in their homes in Cook and Lake Counties. Carla Turner-Brooks, Dir.;

Catholic Home Care Home Services - 721 N. LaSalle St., Chicago, IL 60610 t) 312-655-7415 cbrooks@catholiccharities.net Home health agency, private duty, JCAHO accredited Carla Turner-Brooks, Dir.;

Cortland Manor Retirement Home - 1900 N. Karlov, Chicago, IL 60639 t) 773-235-3670 gsaldana@catholiccharities.net Catholic Charities Housing Development Corporation. Gabriela Saldana, Dir.;

Franciscan Communities, Inc. (St. Joseph Village of Chicago) - 4021 W. Belmont Ave., Chicago, IL 60641; Mailing: 11500 Theresa Dr., Lemont, IL 60439 t) 773-328-5500 mshaw@franciscancommunities.org; blozano@franciscancommunities.org www.franciscanministries.org A senior living and healthcare services ministry sponsored by the Franciscan Sisters of Chicago. Marcus Shaw, Exec. Dir.; Bridget Lozano, Mission & Pastoral Care Dir.; Staff: 81

Jugan Terrace - 2300 N. Racine Ave., Chicago, IL 60614 t) 773-935-9600 mschicago@littlesistersofthepoor.org www.littlesistersofthepoorchicago.org Little Sisters of the Poor of Chicago, Inc. Sr. Julie Horseman, Pres.;

Little Sisters of the Poor Center for the Aging (Little Sisters of the Poor of Chicago, Inc.) - 2325 N. Lakewood Ave., Chicago, IL 60614 t) 773-935-9600 mschicago@littlesistersofthepoor.org www.littlesistersofthepoorchicago.org Independent living and skilled care facility. Sr. Julie Horseman, Pres.;

Mercy Circle - 3659 W. 99th St., Chicago, IL 60655 t) 773-253-3600 www.mercycircle.org Independent living apartments, licensed assisted living apartments, licensed skilled nursing units. Sponsored by Sisters of Mercy of the Americas West Frances Lachowicz, Exec.;

Ascension Living Resurrection Village (Presence Chicago Hospitals Network) - 7262 W. Peterson Ave., Chicago, IL 60631 t) 314-292-9308 ahscm-mission@ascension.org www.ascensionliving.org/ Ryan Endsley, COO; Asstd. Annu.: 519; Staff: 40

DES PLAINES

Ascension Living Nazarethville Place (Presence Senior Services - Chicagoland) - 300 N. River Rd., Des Plaines, IL 60016 t) 314-292-9308 ahscm-mission@ascension.org www.ascensionliving.org/ Ryan Endsley, COO; Asstd. Annu.: 102; Staff: 60

***Presence Home Care Chicagoland** - 2380 E. Dempster St., Des Plaines, IL 60016 t) 847-493-4800 john.halstead1@ascension.org www.ascension.org Sponsored by Ascension Health Ministries (Ascension Sponsor), a public juridic person Polly Davenport, COO; John Halstead, CMIO; Asstd. Annu.: 65,501; Staff: 115

EVANSTON

Saint Francis Nursing and Rehabilitation Center - 500 Ashbury Ave., Evanston, IL 60202 t) 847-316-3320 www.seniors.reshealth.org A division of Resurrection Senior Services, Comprehensive nursing, rehabilitation and social services. Lauren Ivory, Chap.; Michael Kaplan, Admin.; Sandra Bruce, Pres.; Leszek Baczkura, Coord. Spiritual Svcs.;

JUSTICE

Rosary Hill Home - 9000 W. 81st St., Justice, IL 60458 t) 708-458-3040 rosaryhill@sbcglobal.net www.sistersop.org Operated by the Dominican Sisters Immaculate Conception Province Sr. M. Natalie, O.P., Admin.; Asstd. Annu.: 60; Staff: 48

LA GRANGE PARK

Ascension Living Bethlehem Woods Village (Presence Senior Services - Chicagoland) - 1571 W. Ogden Ave., La Grange Park, IL 60526 t) 314-292-9308 ahscm-mission@ascension.org www.ascensionliving.org Ryan Endsley, COO; Asstd. Annu.: 243; Staff: 43

LaGrange Park Center, Inc. - 1515 W. Ogden Ave., La Grange Park, IL 60526 t) 708-354-9573 rmolitor@csjinitiatives.org csjoseph.org Provides housing to the aged, infirm, and disabled. Congregation of the Sisters of St. Joseph. Ron Molitor, Admin.; Asstd. Annu.: 26; Staff: 35

LEMONT

Alvernia Manor Senior Living - 13950 Main St., Lemont, IL 60439 t) 630-257-7721 info@alverniamanor.org www.alverniamanor.org Sponsored by The School Sisters of St. Francis of Christ the King. Sr. Cynthia Drozd, O.S.F., Admin.;

Franciscan Communities, Inc. (Franciscan Village) - 1270 Village Dr., Lemont, IL 60439; Mailing: 11500 Theresa Dr., Lemont, IL 60439 t) 630-243-3500 vzaprzal@franciscancommunities.org www.franciscanministries.org Continuing Care Retirement Community. A senior living and healthcare services ministry sponsored by the Franciscan Sisters of Chicago. Nicole Prom, Exec. Dir.; Rev. Robert D. Lucas, C.M., Chap.; Vincent Zaprzal, Dir., Mission Integration; Asstd. Annu.: 360; Staff: 220

LINDENHURST

Franciscan Communities, Inc. (The Village at Victory Lakes) - 1075 E. Victory Dr., Lindenhurst, IL 60046; Mailing: 11500 Theresa Dr., Lemont, IL 60439 t) 847-356-4600 mmcdonough@franciscancommunities.org www.franciscanministries.org Continuing Care Retirement Community. Senior living & healthcare services ministry sponsored by the Franciscan Sisters of Chicago Calvin Isaacson, Exec. Dir.; Mary McDonough, Dir., Mission Integration & Pastoral Care; Asstd. Annu.: 95; Staff: 217

NILES

Ascension Living Saint Benedict Village (Presence Senior Services - Chicagoland) - 6930 W. Touhy Ave., Niles, IL 60714 t) 314-292-9308 ahscm-mission@ascension.org www.ascensionliving.org/ Ryan Endsley, COO; Asstd. Annu.: 347; Staff: 77

NORTHLAKE

Ascension Living Casa Scalabrini Village (Presence Senior Services - Chicagoland) - 480 N. Wolf Rd., Northlake, IL 60164-1667 t) 314-292-9308 ahscm-mission@ascension.org www.ascensionliving.org/ Ryan Endsley, COO; Asstd. Annu.: 539; Staff: 293

Ascension Living Casa Scalabrini Village (Ascension Senior Services-Chicagoland; Casa San Carlo Retirement Community) - 420 N. Wolf Rd., Northlake, IL 60164 t) 708-562-4300 eliana.mejia@ascension.org www.ascension.org Sponsored by Ascension Health Ministries. Rev. Daniel R. Steiner, Chap.; Eliana Mejia, Admin.; Asstd. Annu.: 212

PALATINE

St. Joseph's Home for the Elderly (Little Sisters of the Poor of Palatine, Inc.) - 80 W. Northwest Hwy., Palatine, IL 60067 t) 847-358-5700 mspalatine@littlesistersofthepoor.org littlesistersofthepoorpalatine.org Sr. Mercy Stella Andrades, lsp, Supr.; Asstd. Annu.: 93; Staff: 105

PALOS PARK

Holy Family Villa - 12220 S. Will-Cook Rd., Palos Park, IL 60464 t) 630-257-2291 hfv12375@aol.com Catholic Charities, Archdiocese of Chicago. Roberta Magurany, Admin.;

PARK RIDGE

Ascension Living Resurrection Place (Presence Senior Services - Chicagoland) - 1001 N. Greenwood Ave., Park Ridge, IL 60068 t) 314-292-9308 ahscm-mission@ascension.org www.ascensionliving.org/ Ryan Endsley, COO; Asstd. Annu.: 393; Staff: 95

WHEELING

***Addolorata Villa (Franciscan Communities, Inc.)** - 555 McHenry Rd., Wheeling, IL 60090-3899; Mailing: 11500 Theresa Dr., Lemont, IL 60439 t) 847-537-2900 jwenghofer@franciscancommunities.org www.franciscanministries.org Continuing Care Retirement Community. Senior Living & Healthcare Services Ministry Sponsored by the Franciscan Sisters of Chicago. Dawn Cohn, Exec. Dir.; Maureen Tokar, Admin.; Jolilorlyn Wenghofer, Pst. Min./Coord.; Asstd. Annu.: 100; Staff: 187

PRESCHOOLS / CHILDCARE CENTERS [PRE]

BARTLETT

Bartlett Learning Center - 801 Carillon Dr., Bartlett, IL 60103 t) 630-289-4221 Operates Bartlett Learning Center Day School Program and the Cupertino Home, Warrenville, IL. Day School program serves developmentally delayed. Michael Meis, Prin.; Moisette McNerney, Librn.;

CHICAGO

Marillac St. Vincent Family Services, Inc. - 2145 N. Halsted St., Chicago, IL 60614; Mailing: PO Box 14699, Chicago, IL 60614 t) 312-943-6776 info@marillacstvincent.org www.marillacstvincent.org Programs: Early Childhood Ed (Birth-5); after school (5-13); pregnant/parenting teens; food pantry; home visiting (seniors); workforce development Maureen Hallagan, COO; Michael Condron, Chair; Stds.: 400; Lay Tchrs.: 85

Marillac Social Center - 212 S. Francisco, Chicago, IL 60612

St. Vincent de Paul Center - 2145 N. Halstead St., Chicago, IL 60614

Marillac St. Vincent Ministries, Inc. - 2145 N. Halsted St., Chicago, IL 60614; Mailing: P.O. Box 14699, Chicago, IL 60614 t) 312-943-6776 info@marillacstvincent.org Supports Marillac St. Vincent Family Services Maureen Hallagan, COO; Michael Condron, Chair;

Mission of Our Lady of Mercy-Mercy Home for Boys and Girls - 1140 W. Jackson Blvd., Chicago, IL 60607 t) 312-738-7560 info@mercyhome.org www.mercyhome.org Rev. L. Scott Donahue, Pres.; Alban Fisher, Vice. Pres.; Tom Gilardi, Vice. Pres.; Liz Kuhn Tomka, Vice. Pres.; Steve Snyder, Vice. Pres.; Joseph Wronka, Vice. Pres.; Cheryl Murphy, CFO;

OAK FOREST

Guardian Angel Day Care Center, Inc. - 5900 W. 147th St., Oak Forest, IL 60452 t) 708-535-9623 Sr. Bonaventure Barbara Balicka, OSB, Pres.;

RETREAT HOUSES / RENEWAL CENTERS [RTR]

BARRINGTON

Bellarmine Jesuit Retreat House, Inc. - 420 W. County Line Rd., Barrington, IL 60010 t) 847-381-1261 info@jesuitretreat.org www.jesuitretreat.org Erin Maiorca, Exec. Dir.; Rev. Tom Krettek, Supr./Retreat Dir.; Rev. James P. Gschwend, S.J., Retreat Dir.; Rev. Richard H. McGurn, S.J., Retreat Dir.; Rev. Roc O'Connor, S.J., Retreat Dir.; Rev. J. Michael Sparough, S.J., Retreat Dir.;

CHICAGO

Monastery of the Holy Cross/Ascension Guest House - 3111 S. Aberdeen St., Chicago, IL 60608 t) 773-927-7424; 888-539-4261 (toll free) fatheredwardglanzmann@gmail.com www.chicagomonk.org Rev. Edward J. Glanzmann, O.S.B.;

DES PLAINES

Cabrini Retreat Center - 9430 Golf Rd., Des Plaines, IL 60016; Mailing: 222 E. 19th St., Ste. 5B, New York, NY 10003 t) 847-297-6530 inquiries@msshnyc.org (Formerly St. Frances Cabrini Retreat House), Retreats for youth, laity, religious and immigrants. Sr. Diane Olmstead, Prov.;

LEMONT

St. Mary's Retreat House - 14230 Main St., Lemont, IL 60439; Mailing: P.O. Box 608, Lemont, IL 60439 t) 630-257-5102; 630-257-2494 baragasmrh@gmail.com www.baragasmrh.com/ Rev. Metod Ogorevc, O.F.M., Dir.;

MUNDELEIN

Joseph and Mary Retreat House - 1300 Stritch Dr., Mundelein, IL 60060-0455; Mailing: PO Box 455, Mundelein, IL 60060 t) 847-566-6060 info@josepkandmaryretreat.org www.josephandmaryretreat.org Serves the clergy, Catholic laity and ministers of Chicago and Region VII. Rev. Msgr. John Canary, Dir.; Jennifer Cummings, Bus. Mgr.;

TECHNY

Techny Towers Retreat and Conference Center - 2001 Waukegan Rd., Techny, IL 60082-0176; Mailing: P.O. Box 176, Techny, IL 60082-0176 t) 847-272-1100; 847-790-8087 chaplain@technytowers.org www.technytowers.org A full-service conference facility used by parish groups, religious communities, nonprofit organizations and schools. Rev. Dennis Callan, S.V.D., Admin.;

SEMINARIES [SEM]

CHICAGO

Catholic Theological Union - 5416 S. Cornell Ave., Chicago, IL 60615 t) 773-371-5400 www.ctu.edu Major Seminary. Rev. Edward Foley, O.F.M.Cap., Dir.; Rev. Robin Ryan, CP, Dir.; Rev. Roger P. Schroeder, S.V.D., Vice. Pres.; Rev. Richard Fragomeni; Rev. vanThanh Nguyen, S.V.D.; Rev. Stephen B. Bevans, S.V.D., Prof.; Rev. Mark R. Francis, C.S.V., Prof.; Rev. Anthony Gittins, C.S.Sp., Prof.; Rev. Gilbert Ostdiek, O.F.M., Prof.; Rev. John M. Pawlikowski, O.S.M., Prof.; Rev. Antonio Sison, C.P.P.S., Prof.;

Divine Word Theologate - 5342 S. University, Chicago, IL 60615-5106 t) 773-288-7923 (Res.); 847-412-1651 www.divineword.org Rev. Mark Edward Weber, S.V.D., Rector; Rev. Roger P. Schroeder, S.V.D., Vice Rector; Rev. vanThanh Nguyen, S.V.D.; Rev. Stephen B. Bevans, S.V.D.; Bro. Rodney Bowers, S.V.D., Brother's Formation Dir.; Rev. Bang Cong Nguyen, S.V.D., Formation Dir.; Stds.: 32

MUNDELEIN

University of Saint Mary of the Lake/Mundelein Seminary - 1000 E. Maple Ave., Mundelein, IL 60060-1174 t) 847-566-6401 jkartje@usml.edu www.usml.edu Rev. John F. Kartje, Rector; Rev. Emery de Gaal, Prof.; Rev. Marek J. Duran, Prof.; Rev. Dennis Kasule, Prof.; Rev. Ronald T. Kunkel, Prof.; Rev. Anthony Muraya, Prof.; Rev. August J. Belauskas, Prof. Emeritus; Rev. Patrick M. Boyle, S.J., Prof. Emeritus; Rev. Thomas Byrne, Coord., Chicago Seminarians; Rev. Joseph Henchey, C.S.S., Adjunct Spiritual Dir.; Rev. Lawrence R. Hennessey, Prof. Emeritus; Rev. John G. Lodge, Prof. Emeritus; Rev. Brendan P. Lupton, Pres., Pontifical Faculty of Theology; Dcn. Pat Quagliana, Asst. Dean of Formation; Formation Advisor; Rev. Carlos Rodriguez, Coord., Counseling Svcs; Rev. Elmer Romero, Formation Advisor, Coord. Hispanic Min; Rev. Robert Schoenstene, Prof. Emeritus; Rev. Daniel S. Siwek, Prof. Emeritus; Rev. Dennis Spies, S.T.L., Formation Advisor; Coord. Pre-Theo; Rev. Raymond J. Webb, Prof. Emeritus; Rev. Bradley Angelo Zamora, USML Dir., Worship; Rev. David Mowry, Instructor; Rev. Edward S. Pelrine, Vice Rector; Rev. Paul Maina Waithaka, Dean of Formation; Rev. Martin Zielinski, Assoc. Professor; Dcn. Robert Puhala, Dir., Diaconal Studies;

Conference Center - t) 847-837-4505 Michelle Perez, Front Office Manager;

Feehan Memorial Library -

Institute for Diaconal Studies - t) 847-837-4563 Katarzyna Kasiarz, Assoc.;

Institute for Pastoral Leadership - t) 847-837-4550 Bob Alexander, Assoc.; Dr. Catherine S. Sims, Assoc.;

Instituto De Liderazgo Pastoral (Hispanic Programs

for Lay Ministry and Permanent Diaconate) - t) 847-837-4556 Nelly Lorenzo, Dir.; Rev. Geraldo Carcar, Dir., Spiritual Formation;

The Liturgical Institute - t) 847-837-4542 www.liturgicalinstitute.org Kevin Thornton, Publications Mgr.;

SHRINES [SHR]

CHICAGO

National Shrine of St. Frances Xavier Cabrini, Inc. - 2520 N. Lakeview Ave., Chicago, IL 60614 t) 773-360-5115 admin@cabrinishrinechicago.com www.cabrinishrinechicago.com Rev. Ramil E. Fajardo, Rector;

SPECIAL CARE FACILITIES [SPF]

CHICAGO

Catholic Office of the Deaf - 3525 S. Lake Park Ave., Chicago, IL 60653-1402 t) 312-534-7899 (Voice); 312-751-8368 (TDD) cathdeafch@archchicago.org www.deafchurchchicago.org Rev. Joseph A. Mulcrone, Dir.;

***Claver House of Renewal, Inc.** - 8514 S. Avalon St., Chicago, IL 60619 t) 773-731-3294 Food pantry, soup kitchen, home-bound senior citizen care, after-school youth recreational programs; mentoring; tutoring and scholarship assistance. Edward Chatman, Pres.;

Franciscan Outreach - 1645 W. LeMoyne St., Chicago, IL 60622 t) 773-278-6724 www.franoutreach.org Diana Faust, O.F.S., Exec.;

House of the Good Shepherd, Catholic Charities of the Archdiocese of Chicago. - ; Mailing: P.O. Box 13453, Chicago, IL 60613 t) 773-935-3434 Shelter for abused women with children.

St. Mary of Providence - 4200 N. Austin Ave., Chicago, IL 60634 t) 773-545-8300 sr.charleen@smopchicago.org; srjanetdsmp@gmail.com www.smopchicago.org Developmental training and residential care of developmentally disabled adults. Rev. Thomas A. Mulcrone, Chap.; Sr. Janet Kosman, DSMP, Admin.; Sr. Rita Butler, Pres.; Sr. Charleen M Badiola, DSMP, Dir.; Bed Capacity: 96; Asstd. Annu.: 120; Staff: 160

Misericordia Home (Misericordia Foundation) - 6300 N. Ridge, Chicago, IL 60660-1017 t) 773-973-6300 frjack@misericordia.com www.misericordia.com Children and adults with developmental disabilities. Rev. John J. Clair, Pres.; Sr. Rosemary Connelly, R.S.M., Exec.;

***Port Ministries** - 5013 S. Hermitage Ave., Chicago, IL 60609 t) 773-778-5955 info@theportministries.org www.theportministries.org A Franciscan outreach to the poor and homeless; mobile soup kitchen, GED, ESL, family svcs., neighborhood gym and free clinic.

Villa Guadalupe Senior Services Corporation - 3201 E. 91st St., Chicago, IL 60617 t) 773-734-9181 angelah@claretianassociates.org www.claretianassociates.org Organization to provide affordable housing and related services for Senior Citizens in South Chicago. Angela Hurlock, Exec.; Rev. Mark J. Brummel, C.M.F., Dir.;

DES PLAINES

Maryville Academy - 1150 N. River Rd., Des Plaines, IL 60016 t) 847-294-1999 www.maryvilleacademy.org Sr. Catherine M. Ryan, O.S.F., Exec.;

Casa Esperanza - 951 W. Barlett Rd., Bartlett, IL 60103 t) 847-294-2815 mccannm@maryvilleacademy.org Jose Sanchez-Argueta, Dir.;

Casa Imani - t) 630-736-7488 gastons@maryvilleacadmey.org Sabrina Gaston, Dir.;

Casa Imani Program - 951 W. Bartlett Rd., Bartlett, IL 60103 t) 630-736-7450 Evelyn Smith, Dir.;

Casa Salama Program - 951 W. Bartlett Rd., Bartlett, IL 60103 t) 630-736-7450 Sabrina Gaston, Dir.;

Children's HealthCare Center - 4015 N. Oak Park Ave., Chicago, IL 60634 t) 773-205-3600 Shawn Pickett, Dir.;

Crisis Nursery - 4015 N. Oak Park Ave., Chicago, IL 60634 t) 773-205-3600 Amy Kendal-Lynch, Dir.;

CYO (Catholic Youth Organization) Program - 1658 W. Grand Ave., Chicago, IL 60622 t) 312-491-3500 Kimberly Williams, Dir.;

St. Dominic Savio Program - t) 847-390-3056 kajcicl@maryvilleacademy.org Liliana Kajcic, Dir.;

Family Engagement Program - 1658 W. Grand Ave., Chicago, IL 60622 t) 312-491-3500 ryanc@maryvilleacademy.org Nina Aliprandi, Dir.;

Maryville Behavioral Health Hospital - 555 Wilson Ln., Des Plaines, IL 60016 t) 847-768-5430 Joseph Novak, CEO;

Maryville CYO - 1658 W. Grand Ave., Chicago, IL 60622 t) 312-491-3500

Maryville Family Behavioral Health Clinic - 1455 Golf Rd., Ste. 105, Des Plaines, IL 60016

Maryville Jen School - t) 847-390-3020

Maryville Madden Shelter - 1658 W. Grand Ave., Chicago, IL 60622 t) 312-491-3500 LaTanya Carter, Dir.;

Maryville Saint George Program - t) 847-294-2815 Sabrina Gaston, Dir.;

Maryville Stephen Sexton Training Institute - t) 847-294-1970 heydenc@maryvilleacademy.org Cheryl M. Heyden, Dir.;

St. Monica Program - 1658 W. Grand Ave, Chicago, IL 60622 t) 312-491-3514 jacksond2@maryvilleacademy.org Donita Jackson, Dir.;

San Francisco Program - t) 847-294-2815 mccannm@maryvilleacademy.org Mary Sanchez, Dir.;

Supervised Visitation Program - ryanc@maryvilleacademy.org Nina Aliprandi, Dir.;

Viator House of Hospitality - 1150 N. River Rd., 100/150 Halpin Bldg., Des Plaines, IL 60016 www.viatorhouseofhospitality.com Rev. Corey D. Brost, C.S.V., Dir.; Bro. Michael T. Gosch, C.S.V., Dir.;

FOREST PARK

***L'Arche Chicago** - 7313 Madison St., Forest Park, IL 60130 t) 708-660-1600 hello@larchechicago.org www.larchechicago.org People with intellectual disabilities live together with their staff members in homes of faith. Michael Altena, Dir.; Bed Capacity: 11; Asstd. Annu.: 11; Staff: 35

LAKE ZURICH

Mt. St. Joseph Home - 24955 N. Hwy. 12, Lake Zurich, IL 60047 t) 847-438-5050 msjlz@aol.com mtstjosephhome.com Intermediate Care Facility for Developmentally Disabled. Operated by the Daughters of St. Mary of Providence. Sr. Charleen M Badiola, DSMP, Dir.;

OAK PARK

Daughters of the Heart of Mary (Ephpheta Center) - 140 N. Euclid Ave., #401, Oak Park, IL 60302-1684 t) 708-386-0190 anitadhm@att.net www.dhm.org Sr. Marilyn Smith, D.H.M., Supr.;

RIVER FOREST

Big Sisters - ; Mailing: P.O. Box 5728, River Forest, IL 60305 t) 708-488-8893 Caroline Brogan, Pres.;

TINLEY PARK

St. Coletta's of Illinois, Inc. - 18350 Crossing Dr., Tinley Park, IL 60487 t) 708-342-5200 mconerty@stcil.org; askafgaard@stcil.org www.stcil.org Sponsored by the Sisters of St. Francis of Assisi. Residential care, education, job training/placement for developmentally disabled children & adults. Annette Skafgaard, Dir.; Bed Capacity: 140; Asstd. Annu.: 300; Staff: 207

St. Coletta's of Illinois Foundation - t) (708) 342-5200 askargaard@stcil.org www.stcolettasofil.org Affiliate.

Kennedy Vocational Job Training Center, Tinley Park -

Lt. Joseph P. Kennedy Jr. School, Tinley Park - c/o St. Coletta's of Illinois, Inc., 18350 Crossing Dr., Tinley Park, IL 60487

An asterisk (*) denotes an organization that has established tax-exempt status directly with the IRS and is not covered by the USCCB Group Ruling.

Archdiocese of Cincinnati

(Archidioecesis Cincinnatensis)

MOST REVEREND DENNIS M. SCHNURR, D.D., J.C.D.

Archbishop of Cincinnati; ordained July 20, 1974; appointed Bishop of Duluth January 18, 2001; ordained April 2, 2001; appointed Coadjutor Archbishop of Cincinnati October 17, 2008; installed December 7, 2008; Succeeded to the See December 21, 2009. Office: 100 E. Eighth St., Cincinnati, OH 45202-2129.

Archdiocesan Offices: 100 E. Eighth St., Cincinnati, OH 45202-2129. T: 513-421-3131; F: 513-421-6225.
www.catholicaoc.org

Square Miles 8,543.

Erected Diocese June 19, 1821; Archdiocese July 19, 1850.

Comprises that part of the State of Ohio lying south of 40 degrees, 41 minutes, being the 19 Counties south of the northern line of Mercer, Auglaize, and Logan, all west of the eastern line of Logan, Champaign, Clark, Greene, Clinton, Highland and Adams Counties.

For legal titles of parishes and archdiocesan institutions, consult the Chancery Office.

STATISTICAL OVERVIEW

Personnel	
Archbishops	1
Retired Bishops	1
Priests: Diocesan Active in Diocese	135
Priests: Diocesan Active Outside Diocese	1
Priests: Retired, Sick or Absent	92
Number of Diocesan Priests	228
Religious Priests in Diocese	169
Total Priests in your Diocese	397
Extern Priests in Diocese	15
Ordinations:	
Diocesan Priests	7
Transitional Deacons	7
Permanent Deacons	14
Permanent Deacons in Diocese	222
Total Brothers	101
Total Sisters	531
Parishes	
Parishes	209
With Resident Pastor:	
Resident Diocesan Priests	42
Resident Religious Priests	14
Without Resident Pastor:	
Administered by Priests	153
Professional Ministry Personnel:	
Brothers	23
Sisters	40
Lay Ministers	440
Welfare	
Catholic Hospitals	7
Total Assisted	801,968
Homes for the Aged	7
Total Assisted	2,353
Special Centers for Social Services	6
Total Assisted	40,118
Other Institutions	1
Total Assisted	3,800
Educational	
Seminaries, Diocesan	1
Students from This Diocese	40
Students from Other Dioceses	43
Diocesan Students in Other Seminaries	6
Total Seminarians	46
Colleges and Universities	4
Total Students	20,367
High Schools, Diocesan and Parish	12
Total Students	5,698
High Schools, Private	11
Total Students	6,144
Elementary Schools, Diocesan and Parish	82
Total Students	25,368
Elementary Schools, Private	7
Total Students	2,540
Non-residential Schools for the Disabled	1
Total Students	48
Catechesis/Religious Education:	
High School Students	1,386
Elementary Students	8,119
Total Students under Catholic Instruction	69,716
Teachers in Diocese:	
Priests	9
Brothers	9
Sisters	18
Lay Teachers	2,798
Vital Statistics	
Receptions into the Church:	
Infant Baptism Totals	4,610
Minor Baptism Totals	324
Adult Baptism Totals	232
Received into Full Communion	445
First Communions	5,157
Confirmations	4,873
Marriages:	
Catholic	1,032
Interfaith	258
Total Marriages	1,290
Deaths	3,935
Total Catholic Population	435,362
Total Population	3,091,874

LEADERSHIP
Archbishop - Most Rev. Dennis M. Schnurr;
Vicar General - Rev. Steve J. Angi;

ADMINISTRATION
Director - t) 513-263-3342 Rev. Jason A. Williams;
Archives - t) 513-263-3387 Michelle Smith;
Chancellor - t) 513-263-3342 chancellor@catholicaoc.org Rev. Jason A. Williams, Chancellor & Masters of Ceremonies;
Coordinator of Ministry to Survivors of Abuse - t) 513-263-6623; 800-686-2724 x6623 Teresa Maley (tmaley@catholicaoc.org);
Office for Consecrated Life - t) 513-263-6683 Maria Reinagel, Dir.;
Permanent Diaconate Office - t) 513-263-6641 Dcn. Mark J. Machuga, Dir.;
Safe Environment Office - t) 513-263-3347 Bill Mitchell, Dir.;
Tribunal-Archdiocese of Cincinnati - t) 513-421-3131
Adjutant Judicial Vicar - Rev. Steve J. Angi;
Assessors - Ami R. Quinn; Kelly M. Terry;
Defenders of the Bond - Rev. Dennis J. Caylor; Dcn. Richard D. Hobbs; Sr. Victoria Vondenberger, R.S.M.;
Director - Kelly M. Terry;
Judges - Rev. Christopher R. Armstrong; Rev. David J. Endres; Dcn. Richard D. Hobbs;
Judicial Vicar - Rev. Barry M. Windholtz;
Notaries - Candy L. Engelke; Lynn M. Hericks; Christy Thornberg;
Promoter of Justice - Sr. Victoria Vondenberger, R.S.M.;

OFFICES AND DIRECTORS
Office of the Archbishop - t) 513-263-6612 Linda J. Heidi, Exec. Sec. to the Archbishop;
Priests' Personnel Director - Rev. David J. Endres, Dir.; Rev. David A. Sunberg, Asst. Dir.;
Vocations Office - Rev. Daniel J. Schmitmeyer, Dir.;

COMMUNICATIONS
Director - t) 513-263-6626 Michael A. Schafer;
Media Relations - t) 513-263-6618 Jennifer Schack;
"The Catholic Telegraph" Magazine - t) 513-263-6634 Most Rev. Dennis M. Schnurr, Publisher; Jessica Rinaudo, Editor;

COMMUNITY SERVICES
Director - Anthony C. Stieritz (tstieritz@ccswoh.org);
Archdiocesan Department of Life, Human Dignity and Charity - Anthony C. Stieritz, Dir. (tstieritz@ccswoh.org);
Catholic Charities of Southwestern Ohio - t) 513-241-7745 www.ccswoh.org Anthony C. Stieritz, CEO (tstieritz@ccswoh.org);
Su Casa Hispanic Center - Giovanna Alvarez, Dir.;
Catholic Social Action - t) 513-263-6690 Andrew Musgrave, Dir. (amusgrave@catholicaoc.org); Sara Seligmann, Regl. Dir. (sseligmann@catholicaoc.org);
Catholic Rural Life - Sr. Christine Pratt, O.S.U.;
Catholic Social Services of Miami Valley - t) 937-223-7217 Laura Roesch, CEO (roeschl@cssmv.org);
Persons With Disabilities - t) 513-263-6674 Bob Wurzelbacher, Dir. (bwurzelbacher@catholicaoc.org); Lisa Averion, Assoc. Dir. (laverion@catholicaoc.org);
Respect Life Ministries - t) 513-263-6674 Bob Wurzelbacher, Dir. (bwurzelbacher@catholicaoc.org);

EDUCATION
Director - Susan M. Gibbons;
School Office - t) 513-263-3447 Susan M. Gibbons, Supt.;

EVANGELIZATION
Director - t) 513-263-6626 Michael A. Schafer;
The Center for the New Evangelization - t) 513-263-6673 Sean Ater, Dir.;
College & Young Adult Evangelization - t) 513-263-3391 Wayne Topp, Dir.;
Hispanic Evangelization - t) 513-263-6647 Samuel Vasquez, Dir.;
Marriage & Family Evangelization - t) 513-263-6648 Adriana Vasquez, Dir.;
Youth Evangelization & Discipleship - t) (513) 263-6685 Christen Aquino, Dir.;

FINANCE
Chief Financial Officer - t) 513-263-6607 Thomas P. Jennings;
Assistant Controller - Mary Ann Beiter; Jenny Hansen;
Controller - t) 513-263-3350 Thomas L. Twilling;
Director of Benefits and Risk Management - t) (513) 263-3354 Bill Maly;
Senior Auditor - t) 513-263-3349 Dave Abele;
Cemeteries - t) 513-489-0300 Thomas Jordan, Dir.;
Office of Property Management and Real Estate - t) 513-263-6602 Joseph H. Mangan, Dir.;

HUMAN RESOURCES
Director - t) 513-263-6611 Robert J. Reid;
HR Consultant - t) 513-263-3341 Margaret H. Paul;
HR Generalist I - t) 513-263-3360 Karen A. Brannon;
Administrative Assistant - t) 513-263-3362 humanresources@catholicaoc.org Gloria Ann Castleman;

PASTORAL SERVICES
Director - t) 513-263-6653 Very Rev. Jan Kevin Schmidt;
African American Pastoral Ministries - t) 513-263-6640 Dcn. Royce E. Winters, Dir.;
Health and Hospital Ministries - t) (513) 503-3445 Rev. Ronald Combs, Dir.;
Incarceration Ministries - t) 513-263-6652 Martin Arlinghaus, Dir.;
Mission and Pontifical Mission Societies - t) 513-263-6680 Dr. Mike Gable, Dir.;
Center for Parish Vitality - t) (513) 263-6692 vitality@catholicaoc.org Jeremy Helmes, Dir.;
Divine Worship and Sacraments - t) (513) 263-6609 Jeremy Helmes, Dir.; Matthew Geerlings, Archdiocesan Music Dir.;
Parish Leadership Formation - Jeremy Helmes, Dir.;
Pastoral Planning - t) (513) 263-3363 Dcn. Michael E. Lippman, Dir.;
Strategic Planning - t) 513-263-6687 Rob Brock, Dir.;

STEWARDSHIP
Department of Stewardship - t) 513-263-3381 David W. Kissell, Dir.;
Development Communications - t) 513-263-6639 Carl Brown, Mgr.;
Development Operations - t) 513-263-6672 Matthew Reinkemeyer, Dir.;
Donor Relations - t) 513-263-3469 Toni Alexander, Coord.;

PARISHES, MISSIONS, AND CLERGY

STATE OF OHIO

AMELIA
St. Bernadette - 1479 Locust Lake Rd., Amelia, OH 45102-1798 t) 513-753-5566 pastor@stbameliaparish.org; admin@stbameliaparish.org www.stbameliaparish.org Rev. Timothy W. Ralston, Pst.; CRP Stds.: 34
St. Bernadette School - (Grades K-8) 1453 Locust Lake Rd., Amelia, OH 45102-1703 t) 513-753-4744 lingram@stbernadetteamelia.org; jell@stbernadetteamelia.org www.stbameliaschool.org Lizann Ingram, Prin.;

ANNA
Sacred Heart of Jesus - 9377 State Rte. 119 W., Anna, OH 45302-9520 t) 937-394-3823 Rev. Jarred Kohn, Pst.; Rev. Aaron Hess, Par. Vicar; Rev. Andrew M Reckers, Par. Vicar; Rev. Stephen J. Mondiek, Par. Vicar; Dcn. Paul Luthman; CRP Stds.: 479

BATAVIA
Holy Trinity - 140 N. 6th St., Batavia, OH 45103; Mailing: P. O. Box 85, 210 N. Broadway, Owensville, OH 45160 t) 513-732-2218 (CRP); 513-732-2218 www.cccatholics.org Rev. Thomas H. McCarthy, Pst.; CRP Stds.: 5

BEAVERCREEK
St. Luke - 1440 N. Fairfield Rd., Beavercreek, OH 45432 t) 937-426-1733 saintluke@saintlukeparish.org; tpeters@saintlukeparish.org www.saintlukeparish.org Dcn. Richard D. Simpson; CRP Stds.: 167
St. Luke School - (Grades PreK-8) t) 937-426-8551 dsutton@stlsbeavercreek.org; tburgos@stlsbeavercreek.org www.saintlukeparishschool.org Leslie Vondrell, Prin.; Stds.: 351; Lay Tchrs.: 24
Queen of Apostles - 4435 E. Patterson Rd., Beavercreek, OH 45430-1033 t) 937-429-0510 qacohio@sbcglobal.net www.qac-ohio.org Rev. Thomas A. Schroer, S.M., Pst.; Dcn. Greg Cecere, Pst. Assoc.; Amie Terri Herbert, DRE; CRP Stds.: 11

BELLEFONTAINE
St. Patrick - 320 E. Patterson Ave., Bellefontaine, OH 43311; Mailing: 316 E. Patterson Ave., Bellefontaine, OH 43311 t) 937-592-1656 ashleyroberts.dre@gmail.com www.catholicbellefontaine.org Rev. Shawn R. Landenwitch, Pst.; Rev. Jacob Lindle, Vicar; Ashley F. Roberts, DRE; CRP Stds.: 50

BETHEL
St. Mary - 3398 State Rte. 125, Bethel, OH 45106 t) 513-734-4041 c) 513-460-4509 sccr.parish@outlook.com; sccr.deaconjerry@outlook.com sccrohio.org (Part of the SE-6 Family of Parishes) Rev. Timothy W. Ralston, Pst.; Rev. Thomas E. Dorn, Par. Vicar; Rev. William C. Wagner, Par. Vicar; Rev. David J. Endres, Pst. Assoc.; Dcn. Jerry Etienne; Nancy Shula, DRE; CRP Stds.: 30

BOTKINS
Immaculate Conception - 116 N. Mill St., Botkins, OH 45306; Mailing: 309 Perry St, Wapakoneta, OH 45895 t) 419-738-2115 office@petersburgparishes.org www.petersburgparishes.org Rev. Sean M. Wilson, Pst.; Rev. Michael A Willig, Par. Vicar; Dcn. Terrell Coleman; CRP Stds.: 247
St. Lawrence - 16053 Botkins Rd., (Rhine), Botkins, OH 45306; Mailing: 309 Perry St, Wapakoneta, OH 45895 t) 419-738-2115 office@petersburgparishes.org www.petersburgparishes.org Rev. Sean M. Wilson, Pst.; Rev. Michael A Willig, Par. Vicar; Dcn. Terrell Coleman; CRP Stds.: 80

BRADFORD
Immaculate Conception - 200 Clay St., Bradford, OH 45308; Mailing: 14 E. Wood St., Versailles, OH 45380 t) 937-526-4945 www.bfvcatholic.org/ Rev. Ned J. Brown, Pst.; Rev. Matthew S. Feist, Par. Vicar; Rev. Stephen P. Jones, Par. Vicar; Rev. James Reutter, Par. Vicar;

BURTKETTSVILLE
St. Bernard - 71 W. Main St., Burtkettsville, OH 45310; Mailing: 272 E. Main St., PO Box 350, St. Henry, OH 45883 t) 419-678-4118 office@sthenrycluster.com www.sthenrycluster.com (St. Henry Cluster) Rev. Andrew Hess, Pst.; Rev. Louis Jacquemin, Par. Vicar; Dcn. Randy Balster; Dcn. Jerry Buschur; Dcn. Gregg Elking; Bro. Nicholas Renner, C.PP.S; CRP Stds.: 132

CAMDEN
St. Mary - 7721 N. Main St., Camden, OH 45311; Mailing: 407 E. Main St., Eaton, OH 45320 t) 937-456-3395 preblecountycatholics.org Rev. David A. Doseck, Pst.; Rev. Thomas L. Bolte, Vicar;

CARTHAGENA

St. Aloysius - 6036 State Rte. 274, Carthagena, OH 45822; Mailing: P. O. Box 350, St. Henry, OH 45883 t) 419-678-4118 office@sthenrycluster.com www.sthenrycluster.com (St. Henry Cluster) Rev. Andrew Hess, Pst.; Rev. Louis Jacquemin, Par. Vicar; Bro. Nicholas Renner, C.PP.S; Dcn. Randy Balster; Dcn. Jerome L. Buschur; Dcn. Gregg Elking;

CELINA

Immaculate Conception of the Blessed Virgin Mary - 229 W. Anthony St., Celina, OH 45822-1608 t) 419-586-6648 vatervonfunf@gmail.com www.celina-ic.org Rev. John W. Tonkin, Pst.; Rev. Robert K. Muhlenkamp, Par. Vicar; CRP Stds.: 200

Immaculate Conception of the Blessed Virgin Mary School - (Grades PreK-6) 200 W. Wayne St., Celina, OH 45822-1469 t) 419-586-2379 polly.muhlenkamp@icschool-celina.org icschool-celina.org Pauline Muhlenkamp, Prin.; Stds.: 164; Lay Tchrs.: 13

St. Sebastian - 3280 State Rte. 716A, Celina, OH 45822; Mailing: 7428 State Rte. 119, Maria Stein, OH 45860 t) 419-925-4775 www.marioncatholiccommunity.org (Marion Catholic Community) - NW8 Rev. Kenneth Schnipke, C.PP.S., Pst.; Rev. Mark Hoying, C.PP.S., Par. Vicar; Rev. Kenneth Alt, Par. Vicar; Rev. Matthew Jozefiak, C.PP.S., Par. Vicar; Dcn. Bradley M. Feltz; Dcn. Roger L. Klosterman; Dcn. Gregory Bornhorst; Dcn. Steven Broering; Dcn. Kenneth Wuebker; Judy Forsthoefel, DRE; Sue Roeckner, Bus. Mgr.; Sharon Kremer, Parish Life Coord.; CRP Stds.: 76

CENTERVILLE

St. Francis of Assisi - 6245 Wilmington Pike, Centerville, OH 45459 t) 937-433-1013 bulletin@sfacc.org; info@sfacc.org www.sfacc.org Rev. Brian W. Phelps, Pst.; Dcn. Roger E. Duffy; Dcn. Robert C. Zinck Jr.; Dcn. Chris Rauch, Bus. Mgr.; CRP Stds.: 156

Incarnation - 55 Williamsburg Ln., Centerville, OH 45459 t) 937-433-3377 (CRP); 937-433-1188 incarnation-parish.com/ Rev. Brian W. Phelps, Pst.; Rev. Ignatius Madanu, Assoc. Pst.; Dcn. Roger E. Duffy; Dcn. Robert Zinck; Kevin Samblanet, Liturgy Dir.; Debbie Field, Parish Life Coord.; Daniel Dunn, Youth Min.; Molli Glowacki, DRE; CRP Stds.: 265

Incarnation School - (Grades PreK-8) 45 Williamsburg Ln., Centerville, OH 45459 t) 937-433-1051 info@incarnation-school.com www.incarnation-school.com Leah Coghlan, Prin.; Stds.: 927; Lay Tchrs.: 51

CHICKASAW

Most Precious Blood - 35 S. Maple St., Chickasaw, OH 45826; Mailing: 7428 State Rte. 119, Maria Stein, OH 45860 t) 419-925-4775 www.marioncatholiccommunity.org (Marion Catholic Community) - NW8 Rev. Kenneth Schnipke, C.PP.S., Pst.; Rev. Mark Hoying, C.PP.S., Par. Vicar; Rev. Kenneth Alt, Par. Vicar; Rev. Matthew Jozefiak, C.PP.S., Par. Vicar; Dcn. Gregory Bornhorst; Dcn. Roger L. Klosterman; Dcn. Bradley M. Feltz; Dcn. Kenneth Wuebker; Dcn. Steven Broering; Missy Moeller, DRE; Sue Roeckner, Bus. Mgr.; Sharon Kremer, Parish Life Coord.; CRP Stds.: 151

CINCINNATI

The Cathedral Basilica of St. Peter in Chains - 325 W. Eighth St., Cincinnati, OH 45202 t) 513-421-5354 office@cathedralaoc.org www.cathedralaoc.org Very Rev. Jan Kevin Schmidt, Rector; Rev. Raymond E. Larger, Par. Vicar; Dcn. Edward B. Bayliss, Bus. Mgr.; Dcn. Michael A. Trimpe; Dcn. Larry H. Day; Matthew Geerlings, Liturgy Dir.; Blake Callahan, Music Min.; Rev. Kevin Scalf, CPPS, In Res.;

All Saints - 8939 Montgomery Rd., Cincinnati, OH 45236 t) 513-792-4600 www.allsaints.cc Rev. Daniel P. Hunt, Pst.; Rev. J. Thomas Wray, Par. Vicar; Dcn. Robert J. Leever, Pst. Assoc.; Dcn. Brian Caperton Sr., Pst. Assoc.; Dcn. Amado Lim; Brendan Hemmerle, Music Min.; Emalee Ridgway, CRE; CRP Stds.: 235

All Saints School - (Grades K-8) t) 513-792-4732 khartman@allsaints.cc Kevan Hartman, Prin.;

St. Aloysius Gonzaga - 4366 Bridgetown Rd., Cincinnati, OH 45211 t) 513-574-4840 jfightmaster@saintmartin.org Rev. Matthew Robben, Pst.; CRP Stds.: 50

St. Aloysius Gonzaga School - (Grades K-8) 4390 Bridgetown Rd., Cincinnati, OH 45211 saintaloysius5@gmail.com Jason Fightmaster, Prin.;

St. Aloysius-on-the-Ohio - 6218 Portage St., Cincinnati, OH 45233 t) 513-941-3445 kathywandstrat@gmail.com www.stalsontheohio.org Rev. Benedict D. O'Cinnsealaigh, Pst.;

St. Ann - 2900 W. Galbraith Rd., Cincinnati, OH 45239 t) 513-521-8440 www.saintannparish.org Rev. James M. Wedig, Pst.; Rev. Bryan T. Reif, Par. Vicar; Rev. Reynaldo S. Taylor, Par. Vicar; Dcn. Douglas P. Moore; Dcn. John M. Quattrone; CRP Stds.: 42

Annunciation of the Blessed Virgin Mary - 3547 Clifton Ave., Cincinnati, OH 45220 t) 513-381-6400 frethan@uptowncatholic.org; sarahrose@uptowncatholic.org www.uptowncatholic.org (Part of the Uptown Catholic Family of Parishes) Rev. Ethan M. Moore, Pst.; Rev. Christopher Komoroski, Par. Vicar; CRP Stds.: 7

Annunciation of the Blessed Virgin Mary School - (Grades K-4) 3545 Clifton Ave., Cincinnati, OH 45220 t) 513-221-1230 www.school.annunciationbvmparish.org Meg Harzog, Prin.; Stds.: 24; Lay Tchrs.: 4

St. Anthony Church - 6104 Desmond St., Cincinnati, OH 45227; Mailing: c/o St. Cecilia Church, 3105 Madison Ave., Cincinnati, OH 45209 t) (513) 321-1207 (St. Mary Hyde Park) admin@stanthonychurch.net www.stanthonychurch.net/ Rev. James P. Weber, Pst.; Rev. Kenneth E. Schartz, Par. Vicar; Rev. Anthony Marcelli, Par. Vicar; Cody Egner, DRE; Shannon Benvenuti, Bus. Mgr.;

St. Antoninus - 1500 Linneman Rd., Cincinnati, OH 45238 t) 513-922-2500 x2031 (CRP); 513-922-5400 x1 www.saintantoninus.org Rev. Matthew J. Robben, Pst.; Rev. Anthony M. Dattilo, Par. Vicar; Rev. Terence J. Hamilton, Par. Vicar; Rev. James S. Romanello, Par. Vicar; Dcn. Robert J. Schroeder, Pst. Assoc.; Jeff Rinear, Bus. Mgr.; CRP Stds.: 4

St. Antoninus School - (Grades K-8) 5425 Julmar Dr., Cincinnati, OH 45238 kahny@saintantoninus.org Shelly Kahny, Prin.; Stds.: 373; Lay Tchrs.: 21

St. Bartholomew - 9375 Winton Rd., Cincinnati, OH 45231 t) 513-522-3680 kathy.rothschild@esbarts.org estbarts.org Rev. Andrew J. Umberg, Pst.; Rev. Ronald C. Haft, Par. Vicar; Rev. George Jacquemin, Par. Vicar; Julie Zinser, CRE; Dcn. Gerald A. Flamm; Dcn. Conrad C. Kolis; Milt Goedde, Music Min.; Sandy Hornbach, Pst. Assoc.; Kathleen Rothschild, Bus. Mgr.; CRP Stds.: 20

St. Bernard - 735 Derby Ave., Cincinnati, OH 45232; Mailing: 740 Circle Ave., Cincinnati, OH 45232 t) 513-541-3732 www.stbernardcincy.org Rev. Andrew J. Umberg, Pst.; Sr. Marjorie Niemer, OSF, Admin.;

St. Bernard - 7130 Harrison Rd., Cincinnati, OH 45247 t) 513-353-4207 stbernardtc.church Rev. James M. Wedig, Pst.; Rev. Bryan T. Reif, Par. Vicar; Rev. Roberto Carolos Becerra Reyes (Mexico), Par. Vicar; Rev. Reynaldo S. Taylor, Par. Vicar; CRP Stds.: 11

St. Bernard School - (Grades K-8) 7115 Springdale Rd., Cincinnati, OH 45247 t) 513-353-4224 laib@stbernardtc.org www.stbernardtc.church Courtney Brown, Prin.; Stds.: 152; Lay Tchrs.: 12

St. Boniface - 1750 Chase Ave., Cincinnati, OH 45223 t) 513-541-1563 parish@stbonifaceschool.net www.stbonifacecincinnati.com Rev. Rodolpho Coaquira, MCCJ (Peru), Pst.; Dcn. Jerry Yetter; Jenni Lindgren, Bus. Mgr.; CRP Stds.: 179

St. Boniface School - (Grades K-8) 4305 Pitts Ave., Cincinnati, OH 45223 t) 513-541-5122 school@stbonifaceschool.net www.stbonifaceschool.net Serving the parishes of St. Boniface, St. Leo and Mother of Christ, Cincinnati. Paul Ebert, Prin.; Stds.: 213; Sr. Tchrs.: 1; Lay Tchrs.: 12

St. Catharine of Siena - 2848 Fischer Pl., Cincinnati, OH 45211 t) 513-661-0651 condren_p@stcatharinesiena.org www.stcathos.org Rev. Anthony M. Dattilo, Vicar; Therese Bower Hibdon, Pastoral Min.;

St. Catharine of Siena School - (Grades PreK-8) 3324 Wunder Ave., Cincinnati, OH 45211 t) 513-481-7683 metz_j@stcatharinesiena.org Jerry Metz, Prin.;

St. Cecilia - 3105 Madison Rd., Cincinnati, OH 45209 t) 513-871-5757 x202 www.stceciliacincinnati.org Rev. James P. Weber, Pst.; Rev. Kenneth E. Schartz, Par. Vicar; Rev. Anthony Marcelli, Par. Vicar; Dcn. Nathan Beiersdorfer; Cody Egner, DRE; Shannon Benvenuti, Bus. Mgr.; CRP Stds.: 138

St. Cecilia School - (Grades PreK-8) 4115 Taylor Ave., Cincinnati, OH 45209 t) 513-533-6060 www.school.stceciliacincinnati.org Michael Goedde, Prin.;

Church of the Assumption - 7711 Joseph St., Cincinnati, OH 45231 t) 513-521-7274 Rev. Andrew J. Umberg; Dcn. Robert A. Staab Jr.; CRP Stds.: 21

Church of the Resurrection - Bond Hill - 1619 California Ave., Cincinnati, OH 45237 t) 513-242-0400 office@resurrectioncinci.org; deacon@resurrectioncinci.org www.resurrectioncinci.org Rev. Patrick L. Sloneker, Pst.; Rev. Jerome J. Gardner, Par. Vicar; Rev. David A. Lemkuhl, Par. Vicar; Dcn. Royce E. Winters, Admin.; CRP Stds.: 36

St. Clare - 1443 Cedar Ave., Cincinnati, OH 45224 t) 513-541-2100 office@saintclareparish.org www.saintclareparish.org Rev. Andrew J. Umberg, Pst.; Rev. Ronald C. Haft, Par. Vicar; Rev. George Jacquemin, Par. Vicar; Rev. Robert J. Hater, In Res.; CRP Stds.: 15

St. Clement - 4536 Vine St., Cincinnati, OH 45217 t) 513-641-3176 office@stclementcincinnati.org stclementcincinnati.org Rev. John Stein, O. F. M., Pst.; Dcn. John P. Gerke; Dcn. David Harcourt; Colleen Gerke, DRE;

St. Clement School - (Grades PreK-8) 4534 Vine St., Cincinnati, OH 45217 t) 513-641-2137 www.stcschool.org

Corpus Christi - 2014 Springdale Rd., Cincinnati, OH 45231 t) 513-825-0618 info@corpuschristicommunity.org www.corpuschristicommunity.org Rev. Peter T. St. George, Pst.; Rev. Mark J. Burger, Par. Vicar; Rev. Don J. West, Par. Vicar; Dcn. John Corson; Dcn. Larry H. Day; Tyler Castrucci, Pst. Assoc.; Chelsea Doering, Pst. Assoc.; William Marshall, Pst. Assoc.; Kelsey Koverman, Youth Min.; CRP Stds.: 72

St. Dominic - 4551 Delhi Pike, Cincinnati, OH 45238 t) 513-471-7741 kbrandstetter@stdominicdelhi.org www.stdominicdelhi.org Rev. Benedict O'Cinnsealaigh, Pst.; Rev. Chris Lack, Assoc. Pst.; Rev. James J. Walsh, Pastor Emer.; Dcn. Mark A. Bardonaro, Admin.; Karen Brandstetter, DRE; CRP Stds.: 59

St. Dominic School - (Grades PreK-8) 371 Pedretti Ave., Cincinnati, OH 45238 t) 513-251-1276 jobrien@stdominicdelhi.org Jennifer O'Brien, Prin.; Stds.: 390; Lay Tchrs.: 24

St. Francis de Sales - 1600 Madison Rd., Cincinnati, OH 45206 t) 513-961-1945 info@stfrancisds.com www.stfrancisds.com Rev. Michael Francis Nartker, S.M., Pst.; Bro. Paul Hoffman, S.M., Pst. Assoc.;

St. Francis de Sales School - (Grades PreK-8) 1602 Madison Rd., Cincinnati, OH 45206 t) 513-961-1953 browarsky_j@desalescincy.org www.desalescincy.org Joanne Browarsky, Prin.; Stds.: 229; Bro. Tchrs.: 1; Lay Tchrs.: 22

St. Francis Seraph - 1615 Vine St., Cincinnati, OH 45202 c) 513-535-2719 jcox@sfsparish.org www.sfsparish.org Rev. Alan Hirt, OFM, Pst.; Bro. Timothy Sucher, O.F.M., Pst. Assoc.; CRP Stds.: 2

St. Francis Seraph School - (Grades K-8) 14 E. Liberty St., Cincinnati, OH 45202 t) 513-721-7778 hmabry@sfsschool.com www.stfrancisseraphschool.org Halsey Mabry, Prin.; Cindy George, Librn.;

St. Francis Xavier Church - 611 Sycamore St., Cincinnati, OH 45202 t) 513-721-4045 business@stxchurch.org www.stxchurch.org Rev. Paul A. Lickteig, Pst.; Rev. James C. Ackerman, SJ, Pst. Assoc.; Rev. Jacob Boddicker, SJ, Pst. Assoc.; CRP Stds.: 18

St. Gabriel - 48 W. Sharon Ave., Cincinnati, OH 45246 t) 513-771-4700 Rev. Edward M. Burns, Pst.; Rev. W. Michael Hay, Par. Vicar; Kris Koch, DRE; CRP Stds.: 48

St. Gertrude - 6543 Miami Ave., Cincinnati, OH 45243 t) 513-561-5954; 513-561-8369 (Evangelization) parishoffice@stgertrude.org www.stgertrude.org Rev. John Paul Walker, O.P., Pst.; Rev. Joachim Kenney, O.P., Par. Vicar; Rev. John Mark Solitario, O.P., Par. Vicar; Rev. John Langlois, O.P., Prior; Rev. Michael Mary Dosch, O.P., Novice Master; Rev. Joseph Alobaidi, O.P., In Res.; Rev. John Corbett, O.P., In Res.; Rev. Darren Pierre, O.P., In Res.; Don Regan, Bus. Mgr.; Walter Plummer, Youth Formation Coord.; Laura Potter, High School Ministry Coord.; Michelle Duchensky, Communications Coord.; Mary Beth Thiemann, Catechesis of the Good Shepherd Coord.; CRP Stds.: 308

St. Gertrude School - (Grades K-8) t) 513-561-8020 office@stgertrudesch.org www.stgertrudesch.org Sr. Maria Christi Greve, O.P., Prin.; Stds.: 316; Sr. Tchrs.: 4; Lay Tchrs.: 21

The Community of the Good Shepherd - 8815 E. Kemper Rd., Cincinnati, OH 45249 t) 513-489-8815 www.good-shepherd.org Most Rev. Joseph R. Binzer, Pst.; Rev. Jack W. Wehman, Par. Vicar; Dcn. Richard W. Gallenstein; Dcn. James Jones; Dcn. Stephen P. Lindner, Dir., Liturgical Min.; Dcn. Max Schellman; Dcn. Mark Westendorf, Coord., Outreach Min.; Teri Cunningham, Bus. Mgr.; Grace Curtis, Youth Min.; Doug Schmutte, Music Min.; Emily Weierman, RCIA Coord.; Sr. Elaine Winter, S.N.D., DRE; CRP Stds.: 425

Guardian Angels - 6531 Beechmont Ave., Cincinnati, OH 45230 t) 513-624-3146 (CRP); 513-231-7440 Rev. Steve J. Angi, Pst.; Rev. Thomas M. King, Par. Vicar; Dcn. Peter J. Caccavari; Dcn. Paul W. Feie; Dcn. Robert Fey; George Stegeman, Music Min.; Kay Froehlich, DRE; Bradley Barnes, Youth Min.; CRP Stds.: 76

Guardian Angels School - (Grades PreK-8) 6539 Beechmont Ave., Cincinnati, OH 45230 t) 513-624-3141 cstoops@gaschool.org www.gaschool.org Corey Stoops, Prin.;

St. Jerome - 131 Rhode Ave., Cincinnati, OH 45230; Mailing: 5858 Kellogg Ave, Cincinnati, OH 45230 t) 513-231-7042 admin@st-jerome-cinci.org

Holy Cross-Immaculata - 30 Guido St., Cincinnati, OH 45202 t) 513-721-6544 parishoffice@hciparish.org hciparish.org Rev. Adam D. Puntel, Pst.;

Holy Family - 814 Hawthorne Ave., Cincinnati, OH 45205; Mailing: 3006 W. 8th St., Cincinnati, OH 45205 t) 513-921-7527 office@holyfamilycincinnati.org; mmurray@holyfamilycincinnati.org www.holyfamilycincinnati.org Rev. Rodolfo Coaquira Hilaje, M.CCJ., Pst.; CRP Stds.: 60

Holy Family School - 3001 Price Ave., Cincinnati, OH 45205 t) 513-921-8483 kputhoff@theholyfamilyschool.org holyfamilycincinnati.org Katie Puthoff, Prin.; Stds.: 225; Scholastics: 21; Lay Tchrs.: 10

San Antonio da Padova - 1950 Queen City Ave., Cincinnati, OH 45214

Holy Name - 2422 Auburn Ave,, Cincinnati, OH 45219 t) (513) 381-6400 www.uptowncatholic.org Rev. Ethan M. Moore, Pst.; CRP Stds.: 6

Holy Trinity Church - 2420 Drex Ave., Cincinnati, OH 45212 t) 513-366-4400 holytrinitynorwood@gmail.com Rev. Patrick L. Sloneker, Pst.; Rev. Jerome J. Gardner, Par. Vicar; Rev. David A. Lemkuhl, Par. Vicar;

St. Ignatius of Loyola - 5222 N. Bend Rd., Cincinnati, OH 45247 t) 513-661-6565 www.sainti.org Rev. Thomas M. Mannebach, Pst.; Rev. Christian Cone Lombarte, Par. Vicar; Dcn. Michael C. Erb; Dcn. Anthony Gagliarducci; Dcn. Timothy M. Helmick; Dcn. John Homoelle; Patty Stretch, Music Min.; Emily Branscum, Youth Min.; Elaine Kroger, DRE; Richard Berning, Bus. Mgr.; CRP Stds.: 374

St. Ignatius of Loyola School - (Grades PreK-8) t) 513-389-3242 office@saintischool.org www.saintischool.org Kevin Vance, Prin.; Stds.: 1,155; Lay Tchrs.: 64

Immaculate Heart of Mary - 7820 Beechmont Ave., Cincinnati, OH 45255 t) 513-388-4093 (CRP); 513-388-4466 formation@ihom.org; parish@ihom.org www.ihom.org Rev. Steve J. Angi, Pst.; Rev. Alex Biryomumeisho, Par. Vicar; Rev. Thomas Ebong (Uganda), Par. Vicar; Rev. Thomas M. King, Par. Vicar; Dcn. Edward B. Bayliss; Dcn. Graham B. Galloway; Dcn. Michael J. Cassani; Dcn. J. Russell Feldkamp; Dcn. Mark U. Johnson; Dcn. William Mullaney; Dcn. David Shaffer; Dcn. David Shea; David Auxier, Music Min.; Donna Wenstrup, DRE; Joan Cardone, Bus. Mgr.; CRP Stds.: 271

Immaculate Heart of Mary School - (Grades PreK-8) 7800 Beechmont Ave., Cincinnati, OH 45255 t) 513-388-4086 school@ihom.org www.ihomschool.org Krista Devine, Prin.; Stds.: 562; Lay Tchrs.: 6

St. James the Greater - 3565 Hubble Rd., Cincinnati, OH 45247 t) 513-741-5300 info@stjameswhiteoak.com www.stjameswhiteoak.com Rev. James M. Wedig, Pst.; Rev. Bryan T. Reif, Par. Vicar; Rev. Reynaldo S. Taylor, Par. Vicar; Dcn. Tim A. Crooker, Pst. Assoc.; CRP Stds.: 10

St. James the Greater School - (Grades K-8) 6111 Cheviot Rd., Cincinnati, OH 45247 t) 513-741-5333 infosjs@stjameswo.org www.stjameswo.org Christina Riggins, Prin.; Stds.: 603; Lay Tchrs.: 38

St. John Fisher - 3227 Church St., Cincinnati, OH 45244 t) 513-561-9431 sjfchurch.org Rev. Steve J. Angi, Pst.; Rev. Alex Biryomumeisho, Assoc. Pst.; Dcn. Thomas M. Gaier; CRP Stds.: 50

St. John Neumann - 12191 Mill Rd., Cincinnati, OH 45240 t) 513-742-0953 (CRP); 513-742-0953 x10 www.sjnews.org Rev. Peter T. St. George, Pst.; Rev. Mark J. Burger, Vicar; Rev. Don J. West, Vicar; CRP Stds.: 24

St. John the Baptist - 5361 Dry Ridge Rd., Cincinnati, OH 45252 t) 513-385-8010 www.stjohnsdr.org Rev. Peter T. St. George, Pst.; Rev. Mark J. Burger, Vicar; Rev. Don J. West, Vicar; CRP Stds.: 60

St. John the Evangelist - 7121 Plainfield Rd., Cincinnati, OH 45236; Mailing: 4136 Myrtle, Cincinnati, OH 45236 t) 513-791-9004 business@blr.church stjohndp.org Rev. Patrick L. Sloneker, Pst.; Rev. Jerome J. Gardner, Vicar; Rev. David A. Lemkuhl, Vicar; Dcn. Jerome Cain; CRP Stds.: 60

St. Joseph - 745 Ezzard Charles Dr., Cincinnati, OH 45203 t) 513-381-4526 church@stjosephcincinnati.org www.stjosephcincinnati.org Rev. Rodolfo Coaquira Hilaje, M.CCJ., Pst.; Dcn. Dennis Edwards; Shon Hubble, Music Min.; Mary Roberson, Bus. Mgr.;

St. Jude the Apostle - 5924 Bridgetown Rd., Cincinnati, OH 45248 t) 513-574-1230 x30 (CRP); 513-574-1230 ken.schultz@stjudebridgetown.org Rev. Donald E. Siciliano; CRP Stds.: 50

St. Jude the Apostle School - (Grades K-8) 5940 Bridgetown Rd., Cincinnati, OH 45248 t) 513-598-2100 hornsby.m@stjudebulldogs.org Louis Eichhold, Prin.; Stds.: 503; Lay Tchrs.: 30

St. Lawrence - 3680 Warsaw Ave., Cincinnati, OH 45205 t) 513-921-0328 www.stlawrenceparish.org Rev. Mark T. Watkins, Pst.; Sr. Helen Julia Hahn, Pst. Min./Coord.;

St. Lawrence School - (Grades PreK-8) 1020 Carson Ave., Cincinnati, OH 45205 t) 513-921-4996 school@stlawrenceparish.org www.stlawrenceparish.org/school.htm Richard A. Klus, Prin.;

St. Leo the Great - 2573 St. Leo Pl., Cincinnati, OH 45225-1960 t) 513-921-1044 info@saint-leo.org www.saint-leo.org Rev. Rodolfo Coaquira Hilaje, M.CCJ., Pst.; Jennifer Lindgren, Bus. Mgr.; CRP Stds.: 45

St. Margaret - St. John Parish - 4100 Watterson St., Cincinnati, OH 45227 t) 513-271-0856 marymathers@fuse.net www.smsjparish.com Rev. James P. Weber, Pst.; Rev. Anthony Marcelli, Assoc. Pst.; Cody Egner, Dir.;

St. Margaret Mary - 1830 W. Galbraith Rd., Cincinnati, OH 45239 t) 513-521-7387 Rev. James M. Wedig, Pst.; Wilma McGlasson, DRE; CRP Stds.: 10

St. Martin of Tours - 3720 St. Martin Pl., Cincinnati, OH 45211 t) 513-661-2000 hellosmot1911@gmail.com www.saintmartin.org Rev. Terence J. Hamilton, Par. Vicar; CRP Stds.: 210

St. Martin of Tours School - (Grades K-8) 3729 Harding Ave., Cincinnati, OH 45211 t) 513-661-7609 jfightmaster@saintmartin.org saintmartin.org/school Jason Fightmaster, Prin.;

St. Mary - 2853 Erie Ave., Cincinnati, OH 45208 t) 513-321-1207 cbrigger@smshp.com www.smchp.com/ Rev. James P. Weber, Pst.; Rev. Kenneth E. Schartz, Par. Vicar; Rev. Anthony Marcelli, Par. Vicar; Dcn. John A. Schuler; Cody Egner, CRE; Katie Barton, Music Min.; Shannon Benvenuti, Bus. Mgr.; CRP Stds.: 64

St. Mary School - (Grades K-8) 2845 Erie Ave., Cincinnati, OH 45208 t) 513-321-0703 lkoslovsky@smshp.com www.smshp.com Jennifer Reker Murphy, Prin.;

St. Matthias - 1050 W. Kemper Rd., Cincinnati, OH 45240 t) 513-851-1930 info@wintonwyomingpr.org www.wintonwyomingpr.org Part of the Winton Wyoming Pastoral Region Rev. Alexander C. McCullough, Pst.; Rev. Jeffrey Stegbauer, Par. Vicar; David Crowe, Bus. Mgr.;

St. Michael - 11144 Spinner Ave., Cincinnati, OH 45241 t) 513-563-6377 (CRP); 513-563-6377 www.saintmichaelchurch.net Rev. Edward M. Burns, Pst.; Rev. W. Michael Hay, Par. Vicar; Brian Bisig, Liturgy Dir.; Tom Giordano, Pst. Assoc.; Scott Hungler, Bus. Mgr.; CRP Stds.: 54

St. Michael School - (Grades K-8) 11136 Oak St., Cincinnati, OH 45241 t) 513-554-3555 cmurphy@stmichaelsharonville.org www.stmichaelsharonville.org Carolyn Murphy, Prin.; Stds.: 368; Lay Tchrs.: 27

St. Monica-St. George Parish Newman Center - 328 W. McMillan St., Cincinnati, OH 45219 t) 513-381-6400 frethan@uptowncatholic.org; office@uptowncatholic.org (Part of the Uptown Catholic Family of Parishes) Rev. Ethan M. Moore, Pst.; Rev. Christopher Komoroski, Assoc. Pst.; CRP Stds.: 197

Mother of Christ - 5301 Winneste Ave., Cincinnati, OH 45232 t) 513-541-3732 mniemer@oldenburgosf.com motherofchristcincy.com/ Rev. Andrew J. Umberg, Pst.; Sr. Marjorie Niemer, OSF, Admin.;

Nativity of Our Lord - 5935 Pandora Ave., Cincinnati, OH 45213-2017 t) 513-531-3164 www.nativity-cincinnati.org Rev. Patrick L. Sloneker, Pst.; Rev. Jerome J. Gardner, Vicar; Rev. David A. Lemkuhl, Vicar; Sr. Janet Schneider, C.D.P., DRE; CRP Stds.: 45

Nativity of Our Lord School - (Grades K-8) 5936 Ridge Ave., Cincinnati, OH 45213-1699 t) 513-458-6767 Lisa McCoy, Prin.;

Old St. Mary - 123 E. 13th St., Cincinnati, OH 45202 t) 513-721-2988 secretary@oldstmarys.org www.oldstmarys.org Very Rev. Jon-Paul Bevak, C.O., Pst.; Rev. Adrian J. Hilton, C.O., Par. Vicar; Rev. Henry Hoffmann, C.O., Par. Vicar; CRP Stds.: 200

Our Lady of Lourdes - 3426 Lumardo Ave., Cincinnati, OH 45238; Mailing: 3450 Lumardo Ave., Cincinnati, OH 45238 t) (513) 922-0715 (Parish Office); (513) 347-2646 (DRE) kkrimm@lourdes.org; parish@lourdes.org www.lourdes.org Rev. Matthew J. Robben, Pst.; Rev. James S. Romanello, Par. Vicar; Kristina Krimm, DRE; Leslie Erin Dwyer, Pst. Assoc.; Dcn. Mark J. Madden; Dcn. Thomas E. Westerfield; CRP Stds.: 20

Our Lady of Lourdes School - (Grades K-8) 5835 Glenway Ave., Cincinnati, OH 45238 t) 513-347-2660 hbessler@lourdes.org Heather Bessler, Prin.; Stds.: 234; Lay Tchrs.: 16

Our Lady of the Rosary - 17 Farragut Rd., Cincinnati, OH 45218 t) 513-825-8626 info@wintonwyomingpr.org www.wintonwyomingpr.org Part of Winton Wyoming Pastoral Region Rev. Alexander C. McCullough, Pst.; Rev. Jeffrey Stegbauer, Par. Vicar; Dcn. Walter A. Hucke Jr.; Dcn. Matthew R. Skinner; Dcn. Steven A. Ryan; David Crowe, Bus. Mgr.; Jose Martinez, DRE; CRP Stds.: 53

Our Lady of the Visitation - 3172 South Rd., Cincinnati, OH 45248 t) 513-922-2056 olvisitation@olvisitation.org olvisitation.org/ Rev. Donald E. Siciliano, Pst.; Rev. Martin E. Bachman, Vicar; Rev. Gerard P. Hiland, Vicar; Dcn. Marc Alexander; Stephanie Audette, DRE; Michael Bissonnette, Pst. Assoc.; Leslee House, Bus. Mgr.; Ken Meymann, Pst. Min./Coord.; CRP Stds.: 68

Our Lady of the Visitation School - (Grades PreSchool-8) 3180 South Rd., Cincinnati, OH 45248 t) 513-347-2222 haug@olvisitation.org olvisitation.org Holly Aug, Prin.; Stds.: 775; Lay Tchrs.: 34

Our Lady of Victory - 810 Neeb Rd., Cincinnati, OH 45233 t) 513-922-4460 www.olvdehi.org Rev. Benedict D. O'Cinnsealaigh, Pst.; Dcn. Charles Jenkins; Dcn. Mark J. Machuga;

Our Lady of Victory School - (Grades PreSchool-8) t) 513-347-2072 matthewsa@olv-school.org school.olv.org Amy Borgman, Prin.; Stds.: 478; Lay Tchrs.: 32

Our Lord, Christ the King - 3223 Linwood Ave., Cincinnati, OH 45226 t) 513-321-4121 www.olctk.org Rev. Adam D. Puntel, Pst.; Rev. Eric P. Roush, Par. Vicar; Dcn. Donald Gloeckler; CRP Stds.: 85

Cardinal Pacelli - (Grades PreSchool-8) 927 Ellison, Cincinnati, OH 45226 t) 513-321-1048 cento_t@cardinalpacelli.org cardinalpacelli.org Terri Cento, Prin.;

Resurrection of Our Lord - 1750 First Ave., Cincinnati, OH 45205-1018 t) 513-471-2700 resurrectionpricehill.org Rev. Robert L. Keller, Pst.;

St. Robert Bellarmine - 3800 Victory Pkwy., Cincinnati, OH 45207-2211 t) 513-745-3398 office@bellarminechapel.org www.bellarminechapel.org Rev. Eric M. Sundrup, S.J., Pst.; Rev. Ed Schmidt, Assoc. Pst.; Richard Becker, Music Min.; Roberta Whitely, Music Min.; Mary Stutler, Bus. Mgr.; Jane Myers, Dir., Parish Life;

St. Rose of Lima - 2501 Riverside Dr., Cincinnati, OH 45202 t) 513-871-1162 office@strosecincinnati.org strosecincinnati.org Rev. Adam D. Puntel; CRP Stds.: 20

Sacred Heart - 2733 Massachusetts Ave., Cincinnati, OH 45225 t) 513-541-4654 www.sacredheartcincinnati.com Very Rev. Jon-Paul Bevak, C.O., Pst.; Rev. Adrian J. Hilton, C.O., Par. Vicar; Rev. Henry Hoffmann, C.O., Par. Vicar; CRP Stds.: 50

St. Saviour - 4136 Myrtle Ave., Cincinnati, OH 45236 t) 513-791-9004 info@stsaviourparish.org stsaviourparish.org Rev. Patrick L. Sloneker, Pst.; Rev. Jerome J. Gardner, Vicar; Rev. David A. Lemkuhl, Vicar; Dcn. Jerome Cain; CRP Stds.: 60

St. Simon the Apostle - 825 Pontius Rd., Cincinnati, OH 45233 t) 513-941-3656 mbschumacher@fuse.net; kathywandstrat@gmail.com www.stsimonparish.org Rev. Michael L. Cordier, Pst. Assoc.; Mary Beth Schumacher, DRE; CRP Stds.: 60

St. Stephen - 3804 Eastern Ave., Cincinnati, OH 45226; Mailing: 320 Donham Ave., Cincinnati, OH 45226 t) 513-871-3373 parish@saintstephen.church www.saintstephen.church Rev. Edward P. Smith, Pst.; Rev. J. Thomas Fitzsimmons, In Res.; Rev. Benjamin Asibvo Kusi, In Res.; Beth Worland, Admin.; CRP Stds.: 17

St. Teresa of Avila - 1175 Overlook Ave., Cincinnati, OH 45238 t) 513-921-9200 mwilliams@stteresa-avila.org; office@stteresa-avila.org www.stteresa-avila.org Rev. Zachary Cecil, Pst.; Rev. K. Scott Morgan, Par. Vicar; Dcn. David P. Steinwert; Maria Williams, DRE; CRP Stds.: 15

St. Teresa of Avila School - (Grades K-8) 1194 Rulison Ave., Cincinnati, OH 45238 t) 513-471-4530 ostertag_j@stteresa.net www.stteresa.net Jennifer Ostertag, Prin.; Chris Artmayer, Librn.;

St. Therese Little Flower - 5560 Kirby Ave., Cincinnati, OH 45239 t) 513-541-5560 www.littleflower-church.org Rev. Rodolfo Coaquira Hilaje, M.CCJ., Pst.; Kathy Parsons, Music Min.; Greg Niehaus, DRE; Kelsey Schneider, Bus. Mgr.;

St. Thomas More - 800 Ohio Pike, Cincinnati, OH 45245-2219 t) 513-752-2080 bready@sttm.org; sttm@sttm.org sttm.org Rev. Timothy W. Ralston, Pst.; Rev. Thomas E. Dorn, Par. Vicar; Rev. William C. Wagner, Par. Vicar; Dcn. Michael T. Thomas, Pst. Assoc.; Dcn. Robert L. Brazier, CRE; Dcn. Frederick J. Haas; Becky Ready, DRE; CRP Stds.: 29

St. Thomas More School - (Grades K-8) 788 Ohio Pike, Cincinnati, OH 45245-2156 t) 513-753-2540 x122 principal@sttm.org www.sttmschool.org Candace Hurley, Prin.; Stds.: 213; Lay Tchrs.: 12

St. Veronica - 4473 Mt. Carmel-Tobasco Rd., Cincinnati, OH 45244 t) 513-528-1622 www.stveronica.org Rev. P. Del Staigers, Pst.; Rev. Benson Lotiang'a Lokidiryo, Par. Vicar; Rev. Jeffrey M. Kemper, Par. Vicar; Dcn. R. Daniel Murphy; Rev. Patrick H. Crone, Sacr. Min.; Lori Anne Fothergill, DRE; CRP Stds.: 73

St. Veronica School - (Grades PreK-8) 4475 Mt. Carmel-Tobasco Rd., Cincinnati, OH 45244 t) 513-528-0442 school@stveronica.org; sharon.bresler@stveronica.org www.school.stveronica.org Sharon Bresler, Prin.; Sherry Dumford, Prin.; Stds.: 316; Lay Tchrs.: 24

St. Vincent de Paul - 4026 River Rd., Cincinnati, OH 45204 t) 513-451-5714 svdpcin@hotmail.com www.svdpcin.org Rev. Benedict D. O'Cinnsealaigh, Pst.; Rev. Donald R. Rettig, Pastor Emer.;

St. Vincent Ferrer - 7754 Montgomery Rd., Cincinnati, OH 45236 t) 513-791-9030 parishoffice@svfchurch.org www.svfchurch.org Rev. Daniel P. Hunt, Pst.; Rev. J. Thomas Wray, Par. Vicar; Dcn. Brian Caperton Sr., Pst. Assoc.; CRP Stds.: 42

St. Vincent Ferrer School - (Grades PreK-8) t) 513-791-6320 dunkley_m@svf-school.org www.svf-school.org Mikki Dunkley, Prin.; Stds.: 149; Lay Tchrs.: 11

St. Vivian - 7600 Winton Rd., Cincinnati, OH 45224 t) 513-728-4331; 513-728-4339 (CRP) rectory@stvivian.org; julie.zinser@stvivian.org stvivian.org Rev. Andrew J. Umberg, Pst.; Rev. Ronald C. Haft, Par. Vicar; Rev. George Jacquemin, Par. Vicar; Julie Borgerding, Music Min.; Sandy Hornbach, Pst. Assoc.; Dcn. Larry Maag; Julie Zinser, DRE; Kathleen Rothschild, Bus. Mgr.; CRP Stds.: 84

St. Vivian School - (Grades PreK-8) 885 Denier Pl., Cincinnati, OH 45224 t) 513-522-6858 jane.brack@stvivian.org mystvivian.org Jane Brack, Prin.; Cathy Bennett, Librn.;

St. William - 4108 W. Eighth St., Cincinnati, OH 45205; Mailing: 4125 St. William Ave, Cincinnati, OH 45205 t) 513-921-0247 info@saintwilliam.com saintwilliam.com/ Rev. Zachary Cecil, Pst.; Rev. K. Scott Morgan, Par. Vicar; Dcn. George Bruce; CRP Stds.: 170

St. William School - (Grades PreK-8) 4125 St. William Ave., Cincinnati, OH 45205 t) 513-471-2989 jschmitz@saintwilliam.com; contact@saintwilliam.com www.saintwilliam.com John Schmitz, Prin.; Stds.: 253; Lay Tchrs.: 20

COLDWATER

Holy Trinity - 120 E. Main St., Coldwater, OH 45828; Mailing: P.O. Box 107, Coldwater, OH 45828 t) 419-678-4802 cbettinger@coldwatercluster.org www.coldwatercluster.org (Coldwater Cluster) Rev. Alexander T. Witt, Pst.; Rev. Ethan Hoying, Par. Vicar; Rev. Michael Kapolka, Par. Vicar; Rev. Joseph Kumar Pasala (India), Par. Vicar; Charmaine Bettinger, DRE; CRP Stds.: 686

St. Mary - 3821 Philothea Rd., Coldwater, OH 45828; Mailing: P.O. Box 107, Coldwater, OH 45828 t) 419-678-4802 (Coldwater Cluster) Rev. Alexander T. Witt, Pst.; Rev. Ethan Hoying, Par. Vicar; Rev. Michael Kapolka, Par. Vicar; Rev. Joseph Kumar Pasala (India), Par. Vicar; Pam Wehrkamp, DRE; CRP Stds.: 85

COVINGTON

St. Teresa of the Infant Jesus - 6925 W. U.S. Rte. 36, Covington, OH 45318 t) 937-473-2970 www.stteresacovington.org Rev. Eric A. Bowman, Pst.; Rev. James S. Duell, Par. Vicar; Rev. Matthew K. Lee, Par. Vicar; Rev. Steven L. Shoup, Par. Vicar;

CRANBERRY

St. Francis - 1509 Cranberry Rd., Cranberry, OH 45883; Mailing: PO Box 350, St Henry, OH 45883 t) 419-678-4118 office@sthenrycluster.com www.sthenrycluster.com (St. Henry Cluster) Rev. Andrew Hess, Pst.; Rev. Louis Jacquemin, Par. Vicar; Dcn. Randy Balster; Dcn. Jerome L. Buschur; Dcn. Gregg Elking; Bro. Nicholas Renner, C.PP.S;

DAYTON

St. Anthony of Padua - 830 Bowen St., Dayton, OH 45410 t) 937-253-9132 x120 satishjoseph@icparishdayton.org Rev. Satish Antony Joseph, Pst.; CRP Stds.: 2

St. Anthony of Padua School - (Grades K-8) 1824 St. Charles Ave., Dayton, OH 45410 t) 937-253-6251 acampion@stanthonydayton.org school.stanthonydayton.org Alana Campion, Prin.; Stds.: 187; Scholastics: 5; Lay Tchrs.: 8

St. Benedict the Moor - 519 Liscum Dr., Dayton, OH 45417 t) 937-268-6697 unitedinhope.org Rev. Francis Tandoh, C.S.Sp., Pst.; CRP Stds.: 15

St. Benedict the Moor School - -5) 138 Gramont Ave., Dayton, OH 45417 t) 937-268-6391 janice1us@aol.com Marianne Pitts, Prin.;

Emmanuel - 149 Franklin St., Dayton, OH 45402 t) 937-228-2013 www.emmanuelcatholic.com Rev. Angelo Anthony, C.PP.S., Pst.; Rev. Seraphine Lesiriam, Assoc. Pst.; Bro. Matt Schaefer, DRE; Michelle Carner, Liturgy & Music Dir.; CRP Stds.: 58

St. Helen - 5000 Burkhardt Dr., Dayton, OH 45431; Mailing: 605 Granville Pl., Dayton, OH 45431 t) 937-254-6233; 937-256-8815 (CRP) office@sthelenparish.org www.sthelenparish.org Rev. Satish Antony Joseph, Pst.; Dcn. Susano Mascorro; Dcn. Ralph O'Bleness; Mary Heider, Pst. Assoc.; Mel McWilliams, Bus. Mgr.; Deb Danner, DRE; Dcn. John Danner; CRP Stds.: 51

St. Helen School - (Grades PreK-8) 5086 Burkhardt Rd., Riverside, OH 45431 t) 937-256-1761 cwalters@sainthelenschool.org www.sainthelenschool.org Christine Buschur, Prin.;

St. Henry - 6696 Springboro Rd., Dayton, OH 45449 t) 937-434-9231 akunka@sthenryparish.com www.sthenryparish.com Rev. Martin E. Fox, Pst.; Rev. David G. Howard, Par. Vicar; Rev. James J. Manning, Par. Vicar; Rev. Jerome R. Bishop, Par. Vicar; CRP Stds.: 81

Holy Angels - 211 L St., Dayton, OH 45409; Mailing: 1322 Brown St., Dayton, OH 45409 t) 937-229-5909 hasadayton.org Rev. Satish Antony Joseph, Pst.; Rev. Uriel Santos Garcia, Par. Vicar; Rev. Leonard C. Wenke, Par. Vicar; CRP Stds.: 35

Holy Angels School - (Grades PreK-8) 223 L St., Dayton, OH 45409 t) 937-229-5959 www.hasadayton.org Alana Campion, Prin.; Stds.: 228; Lay Tchrs.: 9

Holy Cross - 1924 Leo St., Dayton, OH 45404; Mailing: 6161 Chambersburg Rd., Huber Heights, OH 45424 t) 937-233-1503 jbarbour@saintpeterparish.org Rev. Kyle E. Schnippel, Pst.; Rev. W. Robert Hale IV, Par. Vicar; Rev. Ambrose Dobrozsi, Par. Vicar; Joy Blaul, Pst. Assoc.;

Holy Family - 140 S. Findlay St., Dayton, OH 45403 t) 937-938-6098 pastor@daytonlatinmass.org www.daytonlatinmass.org Rev. George Gabet, F.S.S.P.,

Pst.; Rev. Carlos Casavantes Jr., FSSP, Par. Vicar; CRP Stds.: 51

Holy Trinity - 272 Bainbridge St., Dayton, OH 45402 t) 937-228-1223 busmgr.holytrinity@gmail.com holytrinitydayton.org Rev. Angelo Anthony, C.PP.S., Pst.; Lynda K Middleton, Pst. Assoc.; Krista Schupbach, Music Min.; Judith L. Trick, Bus. Mgr.; CRP Stds.: 20

St. Joseph - 411 E. Second St., Dayton, OH 45402 t) 937-228-9272 www.stjosephdayton.org/ Rev. Angelo Anthony, C.PP.S., Pst.; Rev. Seraphine Lesiriam, Assoc. Pst.;

St. Mary - 310 Allen St., Dayton, OH 45410-1818 t) 937-256-5633 stmaryparish@stmarydayton.org www.stmarydayton.org Rev. Satish Antony Joseph, Pst.; Rev. Uriel Santos Garcia, Par. Vicar; Rev. Leonard C. Wenke, Par. Vicar; CRP Stds.: 65

Our Lady of Grace Parish - 220 W. Siebenthaler Ave., Dayton, OH 45405 t) 937-274-2107 www.ourladyofgracedayton.org Rev. Francis Tandoh, C.S.Sp., Pst.; Rev. Benoit Mukamba, C.S.Sp., Par. Vicar;

Corpus Christi Church - 527 Forest Ave., Dayton, OH 45405 (Worship Site)

Our Lady of Mercy Church - 533 Odlin Ave., Dayton, OH 45405 (Worship Site)

Our Lady of the Immaculate Conception - 2300 S. Smithville Rd., Dayton, OH 45420 t) 937-252-9919 office@icparishdayton.org; debbauer@icparishdayton.org www.icparishdayton.org Rev. Satish Antony Joseph, Pst.; Rev. Leonard C. Wenke, Par. Vicar; Rev. Uriel Santos Garcia, Par. Vicar; Dcn. Michael Montgomery, O.F.M.; CRP Stds.: 84

Our Lady of the Immaculate Conception School - (Grades PreK-8) 2268 S. Smithville Rd., Dayton, OH 45420 t) 937-253-8831 jwalling@icsdayton.org www.icsdayton.org Christine Buschur, Prin.; Stds.: 409; Lay Tchrs.: 21

Our Lady of the Rosary - 22 Notre Dame Ave., Dayton, OH 45404; Mailing: 6161 Chambersburg Rd., Huber Heights, OH 45424 t) 937-228-8802 jbarbour@saintpeterparish.org daytonxii.org Rev. Kyle E. Schnippel, Pst.; Rev. W. Robert Hale IV, Par. Vicar; Rev. Ambrose Dobrozsi, Par. Vicar; Joy Blaul, Pst. Assoc.;

Our Lady of the Rosary School - (Grades K-8) 40 Notre Dame Ave., Dayton, OH 45404 t) 937-222-7231 school@olrdayton.com Jacki Loffer, Prin.; Stds.: 216; Bro. Tchrs.: 1; Lay Tchrs.: 14

Precious Blood - 4961 Salem Ave., Dayton, OH 45416 t) 937-276-5954 jhurr@preciousbloodchurch.org www.northwestdaytoncatholic.org Rev. Anthony Fortman, C.PP.S., Pst.; Dcn. Michael F. Prier; Dcn. Andrew R. Rammel; Narisa Lao, Liturgy Dir.; Erica Rudemiller, Youth Min.; Dcn. Dale DeBrosse, DRE; Curtis Kneblik, DRE; Joseph Hurr, Bus. Mgr.; CRP Stds.: 150

Mother Maria Anna Brunner School - (Grades PreK-8) 4870 Denlinger Rd., Dayton, OH 45426 t) 937-277-2291 rjohnson@brunnercatholicschool.org www.brunnercatholicschool.org Robin Johnson, Prin.;

Queen of Martyrs - 4134 Cedar Ridge Rd., Dayton, OH 45414; Mailing: 4144 Cedar Ridge Rd., Dayton, OH 45414 t) 937-277-2092 mphillips@qmdayton.org www.qmdayton.org Rev. Francis Tandoh, C.S.Sp., Pst.; Rev. Benoit Mukamba, CSSp, Par. Vicar; Dcn. Skip Royer; CRP Stds.: 12

St. Rita - 5401 N. Main St., Dayton, OH 45415 t) 937-278-5815 www.northwestdaytoncatholic.org Rev. Anthony Fortman, C.PP.S., Pst.; Narisa Lao, Music Min.; Dcn. James C. Olinger; Matt Ruttle, Pst. Assoc.; Curtis Kneblic, DRE; Joseph Hurr, Bus. Mgr.;

EATON

Visitation of the Blessed Virgin Mary - 407 E. Main St., Eaton, OH 45320 t) 937-456-3395 preblecountycatholics.org Rev. David A. Doseck, Pst.; Rev. Thomas L. Bolte, Vicar; Renee Piekutowski, CRE; CRP Stds.: 70

ENGLEWOOD

St. Paul - 1000 W. Wenger Rd., Englewood, OH 45322 t) 937-836-7535 office@stpaulenglewood.org northwestdaytoncatholic.org/ Rev. Anthony Fortman, C.PP.S., Pst.; Dcn. Dale J. De Brosse; Dcn. Michael F. Prier; Dcn. Andrew R. Rammel; Dcn. Brian K. Seibert; Dcn. Joseph Subler; Curtis Kneblik, Adult Faith Formation; Erica Rudemiller, Children's Faith Formation / Youth Ministry; Narisa Lao, Dir. Music & Liturgy; CRP Stds.: 165

FAIRBORN

Mary Help of Christians - 954 N. Maple Ave., Fairborn, OH 45324-5498 t) 937-878-8353 parishoffice@mhcparish.org www.mhcparish.org Rev. Jason Edward Bedel, Pst.; Rev. Ambrose Dobrozsi, Par. Vicar; Dcn. Max Roadruck; CRP Stds.: 38

FAIRFIELD

Sacred Heart of Jesus - 400 Nilles Rd., Fairfield, OH 45014 t) 513-858-4213 (CRP); 513-858-4210 www.sacredheart-fairfield.org Rev. Larry R. Tharp, Pst.; CRP Stds.: 50

Sacred Heart of Jesus School - (Grades K-8) t) 513-858-4215 jstclair@shjs.org www.shjs.org Joseph Nagle, Prin.;

FAYETTEVILLE

St. Angela Merici - 130 Stone Alley, Fayetteville, OH 45118; Mailing: P.O. Box 279, Fayetteville, OH 45118 t) 513-875-5020 www.ohiocatholic.org Rev. Frank G. Amberger, Pst.; Rev. Andrew P. Cordonnier, Par. Vicar; CRP Stds.: 119

St. Patrick Chapel -

St. Martin Chapel -

FORT LORAMIE

St. Michael - 33 Elm St., Fort Loramie, OH 45845; Mailing: P.O. Box 7, Fort Loramie, OH 45845 t) 937-295-2179 (CRP); 937-295-2891 (Office) georges@nflregion.org www.nflregion.org/ Rev. Jarred Kohn, Pst.; Dcn. Paul L. Timmerman; Rose Meyer, Pst. Assoc.; Wendy Gerstner, DRE; Melissa Hoying, DRE; Sholtis George, Bus. Mgr.; Amy Noykos, Liturgy Dir.; CRP Stds.: 580

SS. Peter and Paul - 6788 State Rte. 66, Fort Loramie, OH 45845; Mailing: P.O. Box 199, Fort Loramie, OH 45845 t) 937-295-2891 Lisa Monnin, DRE; CRP Stds.: 35

FORT RECOVERY

St. Anthony - 471 St. Anthony Rd., Fort Recovery, OH 45846; Mailing: P.O. Box 107, Coldwater, OH 45828 t) 419-678-4802 cmuhlenkamp@coldwatercluster.org coldwatercluster.org (Coldwater Cluster) Rev. Alexander T. Witt, Pst.; Rev. Ethan Hoying, Par. Vicar; Rev. Michael Kapolka, Par. Vicar; Rev. Joseph Kumar Pasala (India), Par. Vicar; Cindy Muhlenkamp, DRE; CRP Stds.: 62

St. Joseph - 1689 St. Joe Rd., Fort Recovery, OH 45846; Mailing: 403 Sharpsburg Rd., Fort Recovey, OH 45846 t) 419-375-4153 www.fortrecoverycatholics.org (Fort Recovery Cluster) Rev. Alexander T. Witt, Pst.; Rev. Michael Kapolka, Par. Vicar; CRP Stds.: 52

Mary Help of Christians - 403 Sharpsburg Rd., Fort Recovery, OH 45846 t) 419-375-4153 mhc@fortrecoverycatholics.org www.fortrecoverycatholics.org (Fort Recovery Cluster) Rev. Alexander T. Witt, Pst.; Rev. Ethan Hoying, Par. Vicar; Rev. Joseph Kumar Pasala (India), Par. Vicar; Rev. Michael Kapolka, Par. Vicar; CRP Stds.: 402

St. Paul - 517 Meiring Rd, Fort Recovery, OH 45846; Mailing: 403 Sharpsburg Rd, Fort Recovery, OH 45846 t) 419-375-4153 www.fortrecoverycatholics.org (Fort Recovery Cluster) Rev. Alexander T. Witt, Pst.; Rev. Ethan Hoying, Par. Vicar; Rev. Joseph Kumar Pasala (India), Par. Vicar; Rev. Michael Kapolka, Par. Vicar; CRP Stds.: 169

St. Peter Catholic Church - 403 Sharpsburg Rd., Fort Recovery, OH 45846 t) 419-375-4153 fortrecoverycatholics.org (Fort Recovery Cluster) Rev. Alexander T. Witt, Pst.; Rev. Michael Kapolka, Par. Vicar; CRP Stds.: 144

GEORGETOWN

St. George - 509 E. State St., Georgetown, OH 45121; Mailing: 16 N. Fourth St., Ripley, OH 45167 t) 937-392-1116 www.ohiocatholic.org Rev. Frank G. Amberger, Pst.; Joan St. Clair, DRE; Susan Caproni, Bus. Mgr.; Dcn. Ronald S. Dvorachek; CRP Stds.: 17

St. Mary - 6647 Van Buren St., Georgetown, OH 45121; Mailing: 16 N. Fourth St., Ripley, OH 45167 t) 937-392-1116 www.ohiocatholic.org Rev. Frank G. Amberger, Pst.; Dcn. Ronald S. Dvorachek; Marilyn Fryer, Pst. Assoc.; Linda Mulvaney, DRE; CRP Stds.: 34

GERMANTOWN

St. Augustine - 6939 Weaver Rd., Germantown, OH 45327; Mailing: 6891 Weaver Rd, Germantown, OH 45327 t) 937-855-2289 www.catholicsmart.com Rev. Francis Tandoh, C.S.Sp., Pst.; Dcn. Kenneth R. Stewart, RCIA Coord.;

GREENFIELD

St. Benignus - 204 S. Second St., Greenfield, OH 45123; Mailing: P.O. Box 399, Greenfield, OH 45123 t) 937-981-2785 stbenignus@gmail.com www.stbenignus.com Rev. Michael A. Paraniuk, Pst.; Rev. Mark Bredestege, Par. Vicar; Paula Miller, Bus. Mgr.; CRP Stds.: 28

GREENVILLE

St. Mary - 233 W. 3rd St., Greenville, OH 45331 t) 937-548-1616 barb@stmgv.org www.stmarysgreenville.org Rev. Ned J. Brown, Pst.; Rev. Matthew S. Feist, Par. Vicar; Rev. Stephen P. Jones, Par. Vicar; Rev. James Reutter, Par. Vicar; Dcn. Thomas H. Graber; Monica Masso-Rivetti, DRE; CRP Stds.: 86

St. Mary School - (Grades PreK-8) 238 W. 3rd St., Greenville, OH 45331 t) 937-548-2345 ahadden@smsgvl.com Tim Wiedenmann, Prin.; Stds.: 75; Lay Tchrs.: 5

HAMILTON

St. Aloysius - 3350 Chapel Rd., Hamilton, OH 45013; Mailing: P.O. Box 95, Shandon, OH 45063-0095 t) 513-738-1014 x301 (CRP) www.stalshandon.org Rev. Richard W. Walling, Pst.; Rev. Jeffrey P. Silver, Par. Vicar; Rev. Edward Hoffmann, Par. Vicar; Dcn. Bill Brunsman; CRP Stds.: 192

St. Ann - 3028 Pleasant Ave., Hamilton, OH 45015 t) 513-863-4963 (CRP); 513-863-4983 businessmgr@saintanncc.com; bookkeeper@saintanncc.com www.saintanncc.com Rev. Larry R. Tharp, Pst.; CRP Stds.: 5

St. Ann School - (Grades PreK-8) 3064 Pleasant Ave., Hamilton, OH 45015 t) 513-863-0604 info@saintanncs.com www.saintanncs.com Sarah Bitzer, Prin.;

St. Joseph - 171 Washington St., Hamilton, OH 45011 t) 513-863-1424 Rev. Richard W. Walling, Pst.; Rev. James H. Elsbernd, Sacr. Min.; Rev. Edward J. Hoffman, Par. Vicar;

St. Joseph School - (Grades K-8) 925 Second St., Hamilton, OH 45011 t) 513-863-8758 tstenger@sjcshamilton.org www.sjcshamilton.org J. William Hicks, Prin.;

St. Julie Billiart - 224 Dayton St., Hamilton, OH 45011-1634 t) 513-863-1040 dbokeno@stjulie.net www.hamiltoncatholic.org Rev. Richard W. Walling, Pst.; Rev. Edward J. Hoffman, Par. Vicar; Mary Pat Austing, DRE; Elizabeth Moran, Bus. Mgr.; Jonathan Alexander, Music Min.; CRP Stds.: 234

St. Peter in Chains - 382 Liberty Ave., Hamilton, OH 45013 t) 513-863-3938 harth@stpeterinchains.org stpeterinchains.org Rev. Richard W. Walling, Pst.; Rev. Edward J. Hoffman, Par. Vicar; Dcn. Jeff Merrell; Elizabeth Moran, Bus. Mgr.; CRP Stds.: 3

St. Peter in Chains School - (Grades PreK-8) 451 Ridgelawn Ave., Hamilton, OH 45013 t) 513-863-0685 schooloffice@stpeterinchains.org Michael Collins, Prin.;

Queen of Peace - 2550 Millville Ave., Hamilton, OH 45013 t) 513-863-4344 parishoffice@qpchurch.org www.queeofpeacechurch.net Rev. Richard W. Walling,

Pst.; Rev. Edward Hoffmann, Par. Vicar; Rev. Jeffrey P. Silver, Par. Vicar; Dcn. Michael E. Mignery; CRP Stds.: 65

Queen of Peace School - (Grades PreK-8) t) 513-863-8705 queenofpeacehamilton.org Tina Conners, Prin.;

HARRISON

St. John the Baptist - 10010 Carolina Trace, Harrison, OH 45030; Mailing: 509 Harrison Ave., Harrison, OH 45030 t) 513-367-9086; 513-367-9086 x221 (CRP) pruwe@stjb.net; aland@stjb.net www.stjb.net Rev. Paul A. Ruwe, Pst.; Rev. William J. Dorrmann, Assoc. Pst.; Rev. Edward J. Shine, Assoc. Pst.; Jonathan Schaefer, DRE; CRP Stds.: 145

St. John the Baptist School - (Grades PreSchool-8) 508 Park Ave., Harrison, OH 45030 t) 513-367-6826 herrmann_n@sjbharrison.org sjbharrison.org Nicole Herrmann, Prin.; Stds.: 244; Lay Tchrs.: 14

HILLSBORO

St. Mary Catholic Church - 212 S. High St., Hillsboro, OH 45133-1445 t) 937-393-1742 stmarycre119@gmail.com saintmaryhillsboro.org Rev. Michael A. Paraniuk, Pst.; Rev. Mark Bredestege, Par. Vicar; Michelle Vanzant-Salyer, DRE; CRP Stds.: 33

St. Mary School - (Grades PreSchool-5) 119 E. Walnut St., Hillsboro, OH 45133 t) 937-840-9932 stmaryprincipal@cinci.rr.com www.stmaryofhillsboro.com Amanda J Hunter, Prin.;

HUBER HEIGHTS

St. Peter - 6161 Chambersburg Rd., Huber Heights, OH 45424 t) 937-233-1503; 937-237-3516 (CRP) jbarbour@saintpeterparish.org; jblaul@saintpeterparish.org daytonxii.org Rev. Kyle E. Schnippel, Pst.; Rev. W. Robert Hale IV, Par. Vicar; Rev. Andrew Smith, Par. Vicar; Dcn. Leo N. Cordonnier; Dcn. Robert W. Gutendorf; Dcn. David M. McCray; Dcn. Norbert Nagy; Dcn. Daniel J. Wade; Rev. Joseph Kindel, In Res.; Joy Blaul, Pst. Assoc.; Maria Aknin, Bus. Mgr.; Kelly Collier, Bus. Mgr.; CRP Stds.: 162

St. Peter School - (Grades PreK-8) 6185 Chambersburg Rd., Huber Heights, OH 45424 t) 937-233-8710 kmoorman@saintpeterparish.org daytonxii.org/saint-peter-school Kathy Moorman, Admin.; Kellie Kadel, Prin.; Kellie Jobe, Registrar; Veronica Konokotin, Dir.; Stds.: 410; Lay Tchrs.: 22

JAMESTOWN

St. Augustine - 44 E. Washington St., Jamestown, OH 45335; Mailing: P. O. Box 189, Jamestown, OH 45335 t) 937-675-2601 Rev. Jason Edward Bedel, Pst.; Della Weidel, DRE; CRP Stds.: 22

KETTERING

St. Albert the Great - 3033 Far Hills Ave., Kettering, OH 45429 t) 937-298-2402 (CRP); 937-293-1191 (Rectory office) kgaston@stalbertthegreat.net www.stalbertthegreat.net Rev. Edward T. Pratt, Pst.; Dcn. Jeffrey D. Hall Sr.; Rev. Thomas A. Nevels, Pst. Assoc.; Rev. Daniel J Meyer, In Res.; Dcn. Dick Strominger; Dcn. David E. Zink; Rev. Chibueze Asiegbulem (Nigeria), Pst. Assoc.; Tom Hutchinson, Bus. Mgr.; CRP Stds.: 208

St. Albert the Great School - (Grades PreSchool-8) 104 W. Dorothy Ln., Kettering, OH 45429 t) 937-293-9452 sgabert@stag-school.org Sherry Gabert, Prin.;

Ascension - 2025 Woodman Dr., Kettering, OH 45420 t) 937-253-5171; 937-254-5411; 937-254-0622 epratt@ascensionkettering.org; cmagness@ascensionkettering.org www.ascensionkettering.org Rev. Edward T. Pratt, Pst.; Joseph Ollier, Parish Life Coord.; Cathy Magness, Pst. Assoc.; Jeanne Fairbanks, Youth Min.; Tara Schumacher, CRE; Ann Gross, Bus. Mgr.; Sharon Christy, Pst. Min./Coord.; CRP Stds.: 170

Ascension School - (Grades K-8) 2001 Woodman Dr., Kettering, OH 45420 sdigiorgio@ascensionkettering.org school.ascensionkettering.org Susan Digiorgio, Prin.; Matthew Himes, Librn.; Stds.: 204; Lay Tchrs.: 22

St. Charles Borromeo - 4500 Ackerman Blvd, Kettering, OH 45429 t) 937-434-6081 stcharles-kettering.org Rev. Edward T. Pratt, Pst.; Rev. Chibueze Asiegbulem (Nigeria), Par. Vicar; Rev. Thomas A. Nevels, Par. Vicar; Dcn. Franklin Jesse Fanning; Chris Kreger, Pst. Assoc.; Christian Cosas, Music Min.; Sarah Archuleta, DRE; Erin Fanning, CRE; Kelly Summers, Youth Min.; Steve Morris, Bus. Mgr.; CRP Stds.: 145

St. Charles Borromeo School - (Grades PreK-8) 4600 Ackerman Blvd., Dayton, OH 45429 t) 937-434-4933 office@stcharleskettering.org stcharles-kettering.org/school David Bogle, Prin.; Margaret Brown, Librn.; Stds.: 504; Lay Tchrs.: 38

LEBANON

St. Francis de Sales - 20 Desales Ave., Lebanon, OH 45036 t) 513-932-2601 parishoffice@stfrancisdesales-lebanon.org www.stfrancisdesales-lebanon.org Rev. Craig Best, Pst.; Rev. Robert J. Farrell, Par. Vicar; Dcn. Jay Rettig; Carl Whittenburg, Dir.; Joan Emma Roenfanz, Bus. Mgr.; Philip Ehling, DRE; CRP Stds.: 183

St. Francis de Sales Parish School - (Grades K-8) t) 513-932-6501 stfrancisdesales-lebanon.org Sarah Bitzer, Prin.; Stds.: 156; Lay Tchrs.: 9

LIBERTY TOWNSHIP

St. Maximilian Kolbe - 5720 Hamilton-Mason Rd., Liberty Township, OH 45011 t) 513-777-4322 www.saint-max.org Rev. James J. Riehle, Pst.; Dcn. John Paul Back; Dcn. Michael W. Hinger; Dcn. Michael E. Lippman; CRP Stds.: 360

LOVELAND

St. Columban - 894 Oakland Rd., Loveland, OH 45140 t) 513-683-0105 cnagy@stcolumban.org www.stcolumban.org Rev. Christopher J. Worland, Pst.; Rev. Lawrence R. Tensi, Par. Vicar; Rev. Edward P. Smith, Par. Vicar; Dcn. Greg Doud; Dcn. Thomas Jabs; Dcn. James Miller; Dcn. Jim Verhoff; Scott Mussari, DRE; Terri Kerley, CRE; Mary Beth Meyer, Pst. Assoc.; Mary Bellman, Music Min.; Patrick Lesher, Bus. Mgr.; CRP Stds.: 332

St. Columban School - (Grades PreK-8) 896 Oakland Rd., Loveland, OH 45140 t) 513-683-7903 dmuchmore@saintcolumbanschool.org www.saintcolumbanschool.org Donna Muchmore, Prin.;

St. Margaret of York - 9499 Columbia Rd., Loveland, OH 45140-1560 t) 513-697-3100 receptionist@smoy.org smoy.org/ Rev. Christopher J. Worland, Pst.; Rev. Edward P. Smith, Par. Vicar; Rev. Lawrence R. Tensi, Par. Vicar; Rev. Maria Raju Pasala, Par. Vicar; Dcn. Jeffrey M. Perkins; Dcn. Paul H. Blessing; Dcn. Mike Huffman; Dcn. Mike Muse; CRP Stds.: 212

St. Margaret of York School - (Grades K-8) 9495 Columbia Rd., Loveland, OH 45140-1560 t) (513) 697-3100 info@smoyschool.com www.smoyschool.com Kristin Penley, Prin.; Stds.: 526; Lay Tchrs.: 32

MARIA STEIN

St. John the Baptist - 8533 State Rte. 119, Maria Stein, OH 45860; Mailing: 7428 State Rte. 119, Maria Stein, OH 45860 t) 419-925-4775 cwibbenmeyer@marioncatholiccommunity.org www.marioncatholiccommunity.org (Marion Catholic Community) Rev. Kenneth Schnipke, C.PP.S., Pst.; Rev. Mark Hoying, C.PP.S., Par. Vicar; Rev. Kenneth Alt, Par. Vicar; Rev. Matthew Jozefiak, C.PP.S., Par. Vicar; Dcn. Roger L. Klosterman; Dcn. Kenneth Wuebker; Dcn. Gregory Bornhorst; Dcn. Bradley M. Feltz; Dcn. Steven Broering; Chris Wibbenmeyer, DRE; Sharon Kremer, Parish Life Coord.; CRP Stds.: 302

Nativity of the Blessed Virgin Mary - 6524 State Rte. 119, Maria Stein, OH 45860; Mailing: 7428 State Rte. 119, Maria Stein, OH 45860 t) 419-925-4775 dtkka@reagan.com marioncatholiccommunity.org (Marion Catholic Community) Rev. Kenneth Schnipke, C.PP.S., Pst.; Rev. Mark Hoying, C.PP.S., Par. Vicar; Rev. Kenneth Alt, Par. Vicar; Rev. Matthew Jozefiak, C.PP.S., Par. Vicar; Dcn. Gregory Bornhorst; Dcn. Bradley M. Feltz; Dcn. Roger L. Klosterman; Dcn. Kenneth Wuebker; Dcn. Steven Broering; Tess Mescher, DRE; Sue Fortkamp, Bus. Mgr.; Sharon Kremer, Parish Life Coord.; CRP Stds.: 100

St. Rose - 7428 State Rte. 119, Maria Stein, OH 45860 t) 419-925-4775 marioncatholiccommunity.org (Marion Catholic Community)-NW8 Rev. Mark Hoying, C.PP.S., Pst.; Rev. Kenneth Schnipke, C.PP.S., Pst.; Rev. Kenneth Alt, Par. Vicar; Rev. Matthew Jozefiak, C.PP.S., Par. Vicar; Dcn. Gregory Bornhorst; Dcn. Bradley M. Feltz; Dcn. Roger L. Klosterman; Dcn. Kenneth Wuebker; Dcn. Steven Broering; Carla Hartings, DRE; Sue Fortkamp, Bus. Mgr.; Sharon Kremer, Parish Life Coord.; CRP Stds.: 74

MASON

St. Susanna - 616 Reading Rd., Mason, OH 45040 t) 513-398-3821 www.stsusanna.org Rev. Barry J. Stechschulte, Pst.; Rev. Elias Mwesigye, Par. Vicar; Dcn. Louis F. Wong; Dcn. Patrick A. Palumbo; Robert Keever, Bus. Mgr.; CRP Stds.: 600

St. Susanna School - (Grades K-8) 500 Reading Rd., Mason, OH 45040 albrinckd@stsusanna.org Dan Albrinck, Prin.;

MECHANICSBURG

St. Michael Church - 40 Walnut St., Mechanicsburg, OH 43044; Mailing: 231 Washington Ave., C/O St. Mary Church, Urbana, OH 43078 t) 937-653-1375 www.champaigncatholics.org Rev. Shawn R. Landenwitch, Pst.; Rev. Jacob Lindle, Par. Vicar; Amy Brinker, Bus. Mgr.;

MIAMISBURG

Our Lady of Good Hope - 6 S. Third St., Miamisburg, OH 45342 t) 937-866-1432 info@olghchurch.com olghchurch.com Rev. Martin E. Fox, Pst.; Rev. Jerome R. Bishop, Par. Vicar; Rev. David G. Howard, Par. Vicar; Rev. James J. Manning, Par. Vicar; Dcn. Terry Martin; CRP Stds.: 49

MIDDLETOWN

Holy Family - 201 Clark St., Middletown, OH 45042 t) 513-422-0602 www.holyfamilymiddletown.com Rev. Paul L. Gebhardt, Pst.; Rev. John R. Civille, Par. Vicar; Dcn. John T. Lyons; CRP Stds.: 100

MILFORD

St. Andrew - 552 Main St., Milford, OH 45150 t) 513-831-3353 religioused@standrew-milford.org www.standrew-milford.org Rev. P. Del Staigers, Pst.; Rev. Jeffrey M. Kemper, Par. Vicar; Rev. Benson Lotiang'a Lokidiryo, Par. Vicar; Dcn. Timothy Schutte; Kathy Bitzer, DRE; CRP Stds.: 200

St. Andrew-St. Elizabeth Seton - (Grades PreK-8) 5900 Buckwheat Rd., Milford, OH 45150 t) (513) 575-0093 www.saseasschool.org Consolidated school with St. Elizabeth Ann Seton Parish

St. Elizabeth Ann Seton - 5900 Buckwheat Rd., Milford, OH 45150; Mailing: 5890 Buckwheat Rd., Milford, OH 45150 t) 513-575-0119 www.setonmilford.org Rev. P. Del Staigers, Pst.; Rev. Jeffrey M. Kemper, Par. Vicar; Rev. Benson Lotiang'a Lokidiryo, Par. Vicar; Dcn. Steve R. Brown; CRP Stds.: 85

St. Elizabeth Ann Seton School (St. Andrew-St. Elizabeth Ann Seton Catholic School (SASEAS) - (Grades PreK-5) t) 513-575-0093 griecon@saseas.org www.saseasschool.org

Preschool - t) 513-575-9900 www.setonpreschool.org Aimee Limberg, Dir.;

MINSTER

St. Augustine - 48 N. Hanover St., Minster, OH 45865; Mailing: P O Box 93, Minster, OH 45865 t) 419-628-2614 (Office); 419-628-3434 (PSR) www.staugie.com Rev. Kenneth Schnipke, C.PP.S.; Rev. Kenneth Alt; Rev. Mark Hoying, C.PP.S.; Rev. Matthew Jozefiak, C.PP.S.; Dcn. Roger L. Klosterman; Dcn. Kenneth Wuebker; CRP Stds.: 682

St. Joseph - 02441 SR 364, Minster, OH 45865 t) 419-628-2614; 419-628-3434 (CRP) info@staugie.com Clustered with St. Augustine, Minster. Rev. Kenneth Schnipke, C.PP.S.;

MONROE

Our Lady of Sorrows - 330 Lebanon St., Monroe, OH

45050 t) 513-539-8061 olos@cinci.rr.com www.olosmonroe.com Rev. Paul L. Gebhardt, Pst.; Rev. John R. Civille, Par. Vicar; Rev. Stephen Lattner, O.S.B., Par. Vicar; Dcn. Jack Schaefer; Karen Redmond, Pst. Assoc.; Joe Whatley, Dir., Music; Christine Baumgardner, DRE; CRP Stds.: 45

MONTEZUMA

Our Lady of Guadalupe - 6701 State Rte. 219, Montezuma, OH 45866; Mailing: P.O. Box 69, Montezuma, OH 45866 t) 419-268-2312 ourladyofg.org/ Rev. John W. Tonkin, Pst.; Ruth Wynk, DRE; CRP Stds.: 77

MORROW

St. Philip the Apostle - 944 E. US 22 & 3, Morrow, OH 45152-9690 t) 513-899-3601 parishoffice@stphilipmorrow.org Rev. Craig Best; Rev. Robert J. Farrell, Par. Vicar; Dcn. Paul F. Leibold; Dcn. John O'Maley; Dcn. James H. Woeste; CRP Stds.: 83

MT. ORAB

St. Michael - 220 S. High St., Mt. Orab, OH 45154; Mailing: P.O. Box 279, 130 Stone Alley, Fayetteville, OH 45118 t) 513-875-5020 x2 www.ohiocatholic.org Rev. Frank G. Amberger, Pst.; Rev. Andrew P. Cordonnier, Par. Vicar; Regina Pritchard, DRE; CRP Stds.: 25

NEW BREMEN

Holy Redeemer - 120 S. Eastmoor Dr., New Bremen, OH 45869; Mailing: P.O. Box 67, New Bremen, OH 45869 t) 419-629-2543 holyredeemer@nktelco.net hrcatholic.org Rev. Ken Schnipke, C.PP.S., Pst.; Rev. Kenneth Alt, Par. Vicar; Rev. Mark Hoying, C.PP.S., Par. Vicar; Rev. Matthew Jozefiak, C.PP.S., Par. Vicar; Dcn. Gregory Bornhorst; Dcn. Bradley M. Feltz; CRP Stds.: 402

NEW CARLISLE

Sacred Heart - 209 W. Lake Ave., New Carlisle, OH 45344; Mailing: 476 N. Scott St., New Carlisle, OH 45344 t) 937-845-3121 office@sacredheartnc.net sacredheartnc.net Bilingual, Bicultural Parish (Anglo & Hispanic) in the Archdiocese of Cincinnati Rev. Jason Edward Bedel, Pst.; Rev. Ambrose Dobrozsi, Par. Vicar; Kristen Kosey, Music Min.; Richard Kraus, Bus. Mgr.; CRP Stds.: 83

NEW PARIS

St. John the Evangelist - 400 N. Spring St., New Paris, OH 45347; Mailing: 407 E. Main St., Eaton, OH 45320 t) 937-456-3395 preblecountycatholics.org Rev. David A. Doseck, Pst.; Rev. Thomas L. Bolte, Vicar;

NEW RICHMOND

St. Peter - 1192 Bethel-New Richmond Rd., New Richmond, OH 45157 t) 513-553-3267 c) 513-335-7886 sccr.parish@outlook.com; sccr.dre@outlook.com sccrohio.org (Part of the SE-6 Family of Parishes) Rev. Timothy W. Ralston, Pst.; Rev. Thomas E. Dorn, Par. Vicar; Rev. William C. Wagner, Par. Vicar; Rev. David J. Endres, Pst. Assoc.; Dcn. Ronald L. Stang; CRP Stds.: 22

NORTH BEND

St. Joseph - 25 E. Harrison Ave., North Bend, OH 45052 t) 513-941-3661 (CRP); 513-941-3661 x10 stjoseph@stjosephnorthbend.com; bscholl@stjosephnorthbend.com www.stjosephnorthbend.com Rev. Donald E. Siciliano, Pst.; BethAnn Scholl, DRE; CRP Stds.: 120

NORTH LEWISBURG

Immaculate Conception - 164 W. Elm St., North Lewisburg, OH 43060; Mailing: C/O St. Mary, 231 Washington Ave., Urbana, OH 43078 t) 937-653-1375 www.champaigncatholics.org Rev. Shawn R. Landenwitch, Pst.; Rev. Jacob Lindle, Par. Vicar; Amy Brinker, Bus. Mgr.;

NORTH STAR

St. Louis - 15 Star Rd., North Star, OH 45350; Mailing: 128 Church St., PO Box 9, Osgood, OH 45351 t) 419-582-2531 Rev. Ned J. Brown, Pst.; Rev. Matthew S. Feist, Par. Vicar; Rev. Stephen P. Jones, Par. Vicar; Rev. James Reutter, Par. Vicar; Linda Wehrkamp, DRE; CRP Stds.: 229

OSGOOD

St. Nicholas - 128 Church St., Osgood, OH 45351; Mailing: P.O. Box 9, Osgood, OH 45351 t) 419-582-2531 Rev. Ned J. Brown, Pst.; Rev. Matthew S. Feist, Par. Vicar; Rev. Stephen P. Jones, Par. Vicar; Rev. James Reutter, Par. Vicar; Amy Schoen, DRE; CRP Stds.: 200

OWENSVILLE

St. Louis - 210 N. Broadway, Owensville, OH 45160; Mailing: P.O. Box 85, Owensville, OH 45160 t) 513-732-2218 www.cccatholics.org Rev. Thomas H. McCarthy, Pst.; CRP Stds.: 24

St. Louis School - (Grades PreK-8) 250 N. Broadway, Owensville, OH 45160 t) 513-732-0636 leu.betsy@stlouischool.org stlparish.org Elizabeth Leu, Prin.; Stds.: 132; Lay Tchrs.: 11

St. Philomena - 5240 Stonelick Williams Corner Rd., Owensville, OH 45160; Mailing: P. O. Box 85, 210 N. Broadway, Owensville, OH 45160 t) 513-732-2218 gstamm@cccatholics.org www.cccatholics.org Rev. Thomas H. McCarthy; CRP Stds.: 1

OXFORD

St. Mary Church - 111 E. High St., Oxford, OH 45056 t) 513-523-2153 info@stmox.org stmox.org (Miami Univ. OH) Rev. David A. Doseck, Pst.; Rev. Thomas L. Bolte, Par. Vicar; Rev. Jacob Willig, Chap.; Pam Burk, Bus. Mgr.; CRP Stds.: 75

PEEBLES

St. Mary Queen of Heaven - 205 Wendell Ave., Peebles, OH 45660; Mailing: 612 E. Mulberry St., West Union, OH 45693 t) 937-544-2757 secretary@holytrinity-ac.org holytrinity-ac.org (Vicariate) Rev. Michael A. Paraniuk, Pst.; Rev. Mark Bredestege, Par. Vicar;

PIQUA

St. Boniface - 310 S. Downing St., Piqua, OH 45356 t) 937-773-1656; (937) 773-2665 stboniface@piquaparishes.org; diane@piquaparishes.org www.piquaparishes.org Rev. Eric A. Bowman, Pst.; Rev. James S. Duell, Par. Vicar; Rev. Matthew K. Lee, Par. Vicar; Rev. Steven L. Shoup, Par. Vicar; Diane Mengos, DRE; CRP Stds.: 37

St. Mary - 528 Broadway St., Piqua, OH 45356 t) 937-773-1327 stmary@piquaparishes.org piquaparishes.org Rev. Eric A. Bowman; CRP Stds.: 39

READING

Our Lady of the Valley Parish - 1109 Church St., Reading, OH 45215; Mailing: 330 W. Vine St., Reading, OH 45215 t) 513-554-1010 office@catholicolv.org catholicolv.org/ Rev. Alexander C. McCullough, Pst.; Rev. Jeffrey Stegbauer, Par. Vicar; Dcn. Charles W. Roemer; Beth Pettigrew, Pst. Assoc.; Angie Touvelle, Bus. Mgr.; Ryan Leep, Dir. of Music & Worship; CRP Stds.: 27

Our Lady of the Sacred Heart - 177 Siebenthaler Ave., Reading, OH 45215

Sts. Peter and Paul Church - 330 Vine St., Reading, OH 45215

RIPLEY

St. Michael - 16 N. Fourth St., Ripley, OH 45167 t) 937-392-1116 www.ohiocatholic.org Rev. Frank G. Amberger, Pst.; Dcn. Ronald S. Dvorachek; Joan St. Clair, DRE; Susan Caproni, Bus. Mgr.; CRP Stds.: 4

St. Michael School - (Grades PreK-8) 300 Market St., Ripley, OH 45167 t) 937-392-4202 andy.arn@stmichaelripley.com www.stmichaelcatholicschool.com Andrew Arn, Prin.; Stds.: 123

ROCKFORD

St. Teresa - 4227 State Rte. 707, Rockford, OH 45882; Mailing: P.O. Box 445, Rockford, OH 45882-0445 t) 419-363-2633 stteresachurch@bright.net; crestteresa@bright.net www.stteresa-rockford.org Rev. John W. Tonkin, Pst.; Rev. Robert K. Muhlenkamp, Par. Vicar; Dcn. Charlie Salway; CRP Stds.: 83

RUSSELLS POINT

St. Mary of the Woods - 464 Madison Ave., Russells Point, OH 43348; Mailing: P.O. Box 329, Russells Point, OH 43348-0329 t) 937-843-3127 office@saintmaryofthewoods.com www.saintmaryofthewoods.com Rev. Shawn R. Landenwitch, Pst.; Rev. Jacob Lindle, Par. Vicar; CRP Stds.: 31

RUSSIA

St. Remy - 108 E. Main St., Russia, OH 45363 t) 937-526-3437 www.stremychurch.com Rev. Ned J. Brown, Pst.; Rev. Matthew S. Feist, Par. Vicar; Rev. Stephen P. Jones, Par. Vicar; Rev. James Reutter, Par. Vicar; CRP Stds.: 370

SIDNEY

Holy Angels - 119 E. Water St., Sidney, OH 45365 t) 937-498-2307 hareligioused@hotmail.com; info@holyangelssidney.com www.holyangelssidney.com Rev. Jarred Kohn, Pst.; Rev. Stephen J. Mondiek, Par. Vicar; Rev. Aaron Hess, Par. Vicar; Rev. Andrew M Reckers, Par. Vicar; Dcn. Philip Myers; CRP Stds.: 104

Holy Angels School - (Grades K-8) 120 E. Water St., Sidney, OH 45365-3199 t) 937-492-9293 bspicer@holyangelscatholic.com; mjbaker@holyangelscatholic.com www.holyangelscatholic.com Beth Spicer, Prin.;

SOUTH CHARLESTON

St. Charles Borromeo - 31 S. Chillicothe St., South Charleston, OH 45368-0806; Mailing: 225 E. High St., Springfield, OH 45505 t) 937-323-7523 psbso1860@gmail.com Rev. John D. MacQuarrie, Pst.; Rev. Elijah R. Puthoff, Par. Vicar;

SPRINGBORO

St. Mary of the Assumption - 9579 Yankee Rd., Springboro, OH 45066 t) 937-557-1711; 937-557-1711 x102 (CRP) jand@stmaryassumption.church; cathyw@stmaryassumption.church www.stmaryassumption.church (Part of the NE-9 Family of Parishes) Rev. Martin E. Fox, Pst.; Rev. Jerome R. Bishop, Par. Vicar; Rev. David G. Howard, Par. Vicar; Rev. James J. Manning, Par. Vicar; Dcn. Stephen Bermick III; Dcn. Richard D. Hobbs; Dcn. Victor O'Basuyi; Dcn. Tom Platfoot; CRP Stds.: 174

SPRINGFIELD

St. Bernard - 910 Lagonda Ave., Springfield, OH 45503 t) 937-324-2870 (CRP); 937-322-5243 stbernard-springfield.org Rev. John D. MacQuarrie, Pst.; Trish Evans, DRE; Rev. Elijah R. Puthoff, Par. Vicar; CRP Stds.: 17

St. Joseph - 801 Kenton St., Springfield, OH 45505; Mailing: 225 E. High St., Springfield, OH 45505 t) 937-323-7523 pmckean44@gmail.com josephraphael.org Rev. John D. MacQuarrie, Pst.; Rev. Elijah R. Puthoff, Par. Vicar;

St. Raphael - 225 E. High St., Springfield, OH 45505 t) 937-323-7523 (CRP); 937-323-7523 psbso1860@gmail.com; frputhoff@gmail.com josephraphael.org Rev. John D. MacQuarrie, Pst.; Rev. Elijah R. Puthoff, Par. Vicar;

St. Teresa of the Child Jesus - 1827 N. Limestone St., Springfield, OH 45503 t) 937-342-8861 www.stteresaspgfldoh.org/ Rev. John D. MacQuarrie, Pst.; Rev. Elijah R. Puthoff, Par. Vicar; Rev. Lawrence Gearhart, In Res.; Lucianne Lilienthal, DRE; CRP Stds.: 65

ST. HENRY

St. Henry - 272 E. Main St., St. Henry, OH 45883; Mailing: Box 350, St. Henry, OH 45883 t) 419-678-4118 office@sthenrycluster.com www.sthenrycluster.com (St. Henry Cluster) Rev. Andrew Hess, Pst.; Rev. Louis Jacquemin, Par. Vicar; Dcn. Gregg Elking; Bro. Nicholas Renner, C.PP.S., Brother; Dcn. Randy Balster; Dcn. Jerry Buschur; CRP Stds.: 716

ST. MARYS

Holy Rosary - 511 E. Spring St., St. Marys, OH 45885 t) 419-394-5050 mielkecrew@yahoo.com www.holyrosarychurch.us Rev. John W. Tonkin, Pst.; Rev. Robert K. Muhlenkamp, Par. Vicar; Dcn. Martin J. Brown; Nan Mielke, DRE; CRP Stds.: 179

Holy Rosary School - (Grades PreK-8) 128 S. Pine St., Saint Marys, OH 45885 t) 419-394-5291 lkrugh@holyrosaryschool.us www.holyrosaryschool.us Stds.: 127; Lay Tchrs.: 9

St. Patrick - 6959 Glynwood Rd, St. Marys, OH 45885;

Mailing: 511 E Spring St, Saint Marys, OH 45885 t) 419-394-5050 Rev. John W. Tonkin, Pst.; Rev. Robert K. Muhlenkamp, Par. Vicar; Sara Ott, DRE; Shannon Schwartz, DRE; CRP Stds.: 36

ST. PARIS

Sacred Heart (St. Paris) - 121 E. Walnut St., St. Paris, OH 43072; Mailing: 231 Washington Ave., c/o St. Mary Church, Urbana, OH 43078 t) 937-653-1375 www.champaigncatholics.org Rev. Shawn R. Landenwitch, Pst.; Rev. Jacob Lindle, Par. Vicar; Amy Brinker, Bus. Mgr.;

TIPP CITY

St. John the Baptist - 753 S. Hyatt St., Tipp City, OH 45371-1255 t) 937-667-3419 (CRP); 937-667-3419 vhammermeister@stjohntippcity.org; nshearer@stjohntippcity.org www.stjohntippcity.org Rev. Kyle E. Schnippel, Pst.; Rev. W. Robert Hale IV, Par. Vicar; Rev. Andrew Smith, Par. Vicar; Norm Shearer, Admin.; Dcn. Charles O. Wright; CRP Stds.: 184

TRENTON

Holy Name - 222 Hamilton Ave., Trenton, OH 45067 t) 513-988-9348 (CRP); 513-988-6335 www.holynameofjesuscatholicchurch.org Rev. Paul L. Gebhardt, Pst.; Rev. John R. Civille, Par. Vicar; Rev. Stephen Lattner, O.S.B., Par. Vicar; Dcn. Lawrence D. Gronas; Dcn. William E. Schaefer; CRP Stds.: 20

TROY

St. Patrick - 409 E. Main St., Troy, OH 45373 t) 937-335-2833 aschmidt@stpattroy.org; sanderson@stpattroy.org www.stpattroy.org Rev. Eric A. Bowman, Pst.; Rev. James S. Duell, Vicar; Rev. Matthew K. Lee, Vicar; Rev. Steven L. Shoup, Vicar; Dcn. John Carlin; CRP Stds.: 145

St. Patrick School - (Grades PreK-8) 420 E. Water St., Troy, OH 45373 t) 937-339-3705 ccathcart@stpattroy.org www.stpattroyschool.org Cyndi Cathcart, Prin.;

URBANA

St. Mary - 228 Washington Ave., Urbana, OH 43078; Mailing: 231 Washington Ave., Urbana, OH 43078 t) 937-653-1375 www.champaigncatholics.org Rev. Shawn R. Landenwitch, Pst.; Rev. Jacob Lindle, Par. Vicar; Dan Shinton, DRE; Amy Brinker, Bus. Mgr.; CRP Stds.: 85

VANDALIA

St. Christopher - 435 E. National Rd., Vandalia, OH 45377 t) 937-898-3542 x105 (CRP); 937-898-3542 esas@scpchurch.org; christophervandalia@scpchurch.org www.scpchurch.org Rev. Kyle Schnipple, Pst.; Rev. W. Robert Hale IV, Par. Vicar; Rev. Andrew Smith, Par. Vicar; Dcn. Charles O. Wright; Elise Sas, DRE; CRP Stds.: 172

St. Christopher School - (Grades K-8) 405 E. National Rd., Vandalia, OH 45377 t) 937-898-5104 toloughlin@scpschool.org scpschool.org Timothy O'Loughlin, Prin.;

VERSAILLES

St. Denis - 14 E. Wood St., Versailles, OH 45380 t) 937-526-4945 ccd@bfvcatholic.org www.bfvcatholic.org/ Rev. Ned J. Brown, Pst.; Rev. Matthew S. Feist, Par. Vicar; Rev. Stephen P. Jones, Par. Vicar; Rev. James Reutter, Par. Vicar; Julie Meyer, DRE; CRP Stds.: 338

Holy Family - 11255 State Rte. 185, Versailles, OH 45380; Mailing: 14 E. Wood St., Versailles, OH 45380-1440 t) 937-526-4945 www.bfvcatholic.org Rev. Ned J. Brown, Pst.; Rev. Matthew S. Feist, Par. Vicar; Rev. Stephen P. Jones, Par. Vicar; Rev. James Reutter, Par. Vicar; Julie Meyer, DRE;

WAPAKONETA

St. John - 11319 Van Buren St., (Fryburg), Wapakoneta, OH 45895-8467; Mailing: 309 Perry St., Wapakoneta, OH 45895-2118 t) 419-738-2115 office@petersburgparishes.org www.petersburgparishes.org Rev. Sean M. Wilson, Pst.; Rev. Michael A Willig, Par. Vicar; Dcn. Nicholas Jurosic; CRP Stds.: 63

St. Joseph - 101 W. Pearl St., Wapakoneta, OH 45895; Mailing: 309 Perry St., Wapakoneta, OH 45895-2197 t) 419-738-2115 office@petersburgparishes.org www.petersburgparishes.org Rev. Sean M. Wilson, Pst.; Rev. Michael A Willig, Par. Vicar; Dcn. Richard L. Westbay; Dcn. Jeffrey A. Little; CRP Stds.: 243

WAYNESVILLE

St. Augustine - 5715 Lytle Rd., Waynesville, OH 45068 t) 513-897-0545 amuth@staugustinewaynesville.com; jcain@staugustinewaynesville.com Rev. Bernard J. Weldishofer, Pst.; Ann Muth, DRE; CRP Stds.: 68

WENDELIN

St. Wendelin - 2980 Ft. Recovery-Minster Rd., Wendelin, OH 45883; Mailing: PO Box 350, St. Henry, OH 45883 t) 419-678-4118 office@sthenrycluster.com www.sthenrycluster.com (St. Henry Cluster) Rev. Andrew Hess, Pst.; Rev. Louis Jacquemin, Par. Vicar; Dcn. Randy Balster; Dcn. Jerome L. Buschur; Dcn. Gregg Elking; Bro. Nicholas Renner, C.PP.S;

WEST CHESTER

St. John the Evangelist - 9080 Cincinnati-Dayton Rd., West Chester, OH 45069 t) 513-777-6433 info@stjohnwc.org www.stjohnwc.org Rev. Edward M. Burns, Pst.; Rev. W. Michael Hay, Par. Vicar; Dcn. James A. Merritt; Dcn. Richard J. Reder; CRP Stds.: 172

WEST MILTON

Transfiguration - 972 S. Miami St., West Milton, OH 45383 t) 937-698-4520 www.transfigurationcatholicchurch.org/ Rev. Eric A. Bowman, Pst.; Rev. James S. Duell, Vicar; Rev. Matthew K. Lee, Vicar; Rev. Steven L. Shoup, Vicar; CRP Stds.: 50

WEST UNION

Holy Trinity - 612 E. Mulberry St., West Union, OH 45693 t) 937-544-2757 religious.ed@holytrinity-ac.org; secretary@holytrinity-ac.org holytrinity-ac.org Rev. Michael A. Paraniuk, Pst.; Rev. Mark Bredestege, Vicar; CRP Stds.: 42

WILLIAMSBURG

St. Ann - 370 S. Fifth St., Williamsburg, OH 45176; Mailing: P. O. Box 85, 210 N. Broadway, Owensville, OH 45160 t) 513-732-2218 www.cccatholics.org Rev. Thomas H. McCarthy, Pst.;

WILMINGTON

St. Columbkille - 73 N. Mulberry St., Wilmington, OH 45177-2277 t) 937-382-1596 (CRP); 937-382-2236 www.stcolumbkille.org Rev. Bernard J. Weldishofer, Pst.; Dcn. Robert G. Baker; Debbie Valley, DRE; CRP Stds.: 109

WYOMING

St. James of the Valley - 411 Springfield Pk., Wyoming, OH 45215 t) 513-948-1218 info@wintonwyomingpr.org www.wintonwyomingpr.org Part of the Winton Wyoming Pastoral Region Rev. Alexander C. McCullough, Pst.; Rev. Jeffrey Stegbauer, Par. Vicar; Dcn. Walter A. Hucke Jr.; David Crowe, Bus. Mgr.; Jose Martinez, DRE; CRP Stds.: 60

XENIA

St. Brigid - 312 Fairground Rd., Xenia, OH 45385; Mailing: 258 Purcell Dr., Xenia, OH 45385 t) 937-372-3193 awagner@stbrigidxenia.org www.stbrigidxenia.org Rev. Jason Edward Bedel, Pst.; Dcn. Mark A. Danis; Dcn. Dennis Kall; CRP Stds.: 37

St. Brigid School - (Grades PreK-8) t) 937-372-3222 tadkins@stbrigidxenia.org Terry Adkins, Prin.; Stds.: 207; Lay Tchrs.: 10

YELLOW SPRINGS

St. Paul - 308 Phillips St., Yellow Springs, OH 45387 t) 937-372-3191 office@stpaulyellowsprings.org; finance@stpaulyellowsprings.org www.stpaulyellowsprings.org Rev. Jason Edward Bedel, Pst.;

SCHOOLS: PRESCHOOL THRU HIGH SCHOOL

SCHOOLS

STATE OF OHIO

CINCINNATI

Corryville Catholic Elementary School - (DIO) (Grades PreK-8) 108 Calhoun St., Cincinnati, OH 45219 t) 513-281-4856 lclements@corryvillecatholic.org www.corryvillecatholic.org Lauren Clements, Prin.; Stds.: 202; Lay Tchrs.: 15

St. Gabriel Consolidated School - (PAR) (Grades K-8) 18 W. Sharon Ave., Cincinnati, OH 45246 t) 513-771-5220 s.wendt@stgabeschool.org; info@stgabeschool.org www.stgabeschool.org Kerry Shelton, Prin.; Stds.: 280; Lay Tchrs.: 16

***The Good Shepherd Catholic Montessori School (Queen of Angels Montessori)** - (PRV) (Grades PreK-8) 4460 Berwick St., Cincinnati, OH 45227 t) 513-271-4171 gscm@gscmontessori.org www.gscmontessori.org Anne Marie Vega, Prin.; Stds.: 212; Lay Tchrs.: 18

John Paul II Catholic School (St. Bartholomew Consolidated School) - (PAR) (Grades PreK-8) 9375 Winton Rd., Cincinnati, OH 45231 t) 513-521-0860 nroach@jpiics.org www.jpiics.org Leanora Roach, Prin.; Linda Arnold, Librn.; Stds.: 415; Lay Tchrs.: 25

St. John the Baptist Catholic School - (PAR) (Grades PreK-8) 5375 Dry Ridge Rd., Cincinnati, OH 45252 t) 513-385-7970 cdreyer@stjohnsdrschool.org; cweinheimer@stjohnsdrschool.org www.stjohnsdrschool.org Pastoral area school serving St. John the Baptist, St. John Neumann and Corpus Christi parishes. Courtney Weinheimer, Prin.; Stds.: 381; Lay Tchrs.: 27

St. Joseph Catholic School - (PAR) (Grades PreK-8) 737 Ezzard Charles Dr., Cincinnati, OH 45203 t) 513-381-2126 info@saintjoeschool.org Ashley Toney, Prin.; Sean O'Brien, Bus. Mgr.; Stds.: 160; Lay Tchrs.: 15

Our Lady of Grace - (PAR) (Grades K-8) 2940 W. Galbraith Rd., Cincinnati, OH 45239 t) 513-931-3070 mkirk@olgcs.org; mdesmier@olgcs.org olgcs.org/ Mandy Kirk, Prin.; Mike Desmier, Bus. Mgr.; Stds.: 400; Lay Tchrs.: 26

St. Rita School for the Deaf - (PAR) (Grades PreK-12) 1720 Glendale-Milford Rd., Cincinnati, OH 45215 t) 513-771-7600 afrith@srsdeaf.org; mhavens@srsdeaf.org www.srsdeaf.org Day school for deaf and hard of hearing, and hearing children with special communication needs. Natalie Marsh, Prin.; Angela Frith, Pres.; Ken Raupach, CFO/COO; Stds.: 86; Lay Tchrs.: 29

The Summit Country Day School - (PRV) (Grades PreK-12) 2161 Grandin Rd., Cincinnati, OH 45208-3300 t) 513-871-4700 schiess_k@summitcds.org www.summitcds.org Affiliated with the Sisters of Notre Dame de Namur Kelley Schiess, Headmaster; Lauren Guip, Dir.; Mike Johnson, Dir.; Stds.: 1,092; Pr. Tchrs.: 1; Lay Tchrs.: 124

St. Ursula Villa - (PRV) (Grades PreK-8) 3660 Vineyard Pl., Cincinnati, OH 45226 t) 513-871-7218 j.sedler@stursulavilla.org www.stursulavilla.org Jody Sedler, Pres.; Stds.: 436; Lay Tchrs.: 33

Xavier Jesuit Academy - (PRV) (Grades 3-8) 201 E. Fifth St., Ste. 2010, PNC Center, Cincinnati, OH 45247 c) (513) 427-5480 nwendt@jesuits.org www.xavierja.org Rev. Nathan Wendt, S.J., Pres.;

HAMILTON

St. Joseph Consolidated School - (PAR) (Grades PreK-8) 925 S. Second St., Hamilton, OH 45011 t) 513-863-8758 info@sjcshamilton.org www.sjcshamilton.org Serving the parishes of St. Aloysius, Shandon and St. Joseph, Hamilton. J. William Hicks, Prin.; Stds.: 253; Lay Tchrs.: 14

LIBERTY TOWNSHIP

Mother Teresa Catholic Elementary School - (PRV) (Grades K-8) 7197 Mother Teresa Ln., Liberty

Township, OH 45044-9426 t) 513-779-6585 abriggs@mtces.org; mmeyer@mtces.org www.mtces.org Denise Harvey, Prin.; Michelle Hinton, Asst. Prin.; Stds.: 612; Lay Tchrs.: 40

MASON

***Royalmont Academy** - (PRV) (Grades PreK-12) 200 Northcrest Dr., Mason, OH 45040 t) 513-754-0555 jater@royalmont.org www.royalmontacademy.org Member of Regnum Christi Education Joshua Ater, Headmaster; Rev. Jesus Salinas, LC (Mexico), Chap.; Stds.: 170; Scholastics: 1; Pr. Tchrs.: 1; Lay Tchrs.: 25

MIAMISBURG

Bishop Leibold School - (DIO) (Grades PreK-8) 24 S. Third St., Miamisburg, OH 45342 t) 937-866-3021; 937-434-9343 twallace@bishopleibold.org; help@bishopleibold.org www.bishopleibold.org Theodore Wallace, Prin.; Stds.: 325; Lay Tchrs.: 32

West Campus - (Grades PreK-8) Julie Wehner, Sec. (West Campus);

East Campus - (Grades PreK-8) 6666 Springboro Pike, Dayton, OH 45449 Kathy Stonecash, Librn.;

MIDDLETOWN

St. John XXIII Catholic School - (PAR) (Grades PreK-8) 3806 Manchester Rd., Middletown, OH 45042 t) 513-424-1196 info@stjohn23school.org; pfairbanks@stjohn23school.org stjohn23school.org Serving the parishes of Holy Family, Middletown; St. Mary, Franklin; Holy Name, Trenton; Our Lady of Sorrows, Monroe. Dawn Pickerill, Prin.; Stds.: 453; Lay Tchrs.: 25

PIQUA

Piqua Catholic School - (PAR) (Grades PreK-8) 503 W. North St., Piqua, OH 45356 t) 937-773-1564 (K-8 Bldg.); 937-773-3876 (Preschool) zimmermanb@piquacatholic.org www.piquacatholic.org Serving the parishes of St. Boniface and St. Mary. Bradley Zimmerman, Prin.; Rachel Thornsberry, Librn.; Stds.: 171; Lay Tchrs.: 13

SPRINGFIELD

Catholic Central School - (DIO) (Grades PreK-8) 1200 E. High St., Springfield, OH 45505-1124 t) 937-325-9204 www.ccirish.org Kathy Anderson, Prin.; Michael Raiff, Pres.; Stds.: 324; Lay Tchrs.: 23

HIGH SCHOOLS

STATE OF OHIO

CINCINNATI

DePaul Cristo Rey High School - (PRV) (Grades 9-12) 3440 Central Pkwy., Cincinnati, OH 45225 t) 513-861-0600 siobhan.taylor@dpcr.net www.depaulcristorey.org Sponsored by Sisters of Charity of Cincinnati Siobhan Taylor, Pres.; James Schurrer, Prin.; Randy Koehler, Bus. Mgr.; Stds.: 300; Lay Tchrs.: 26

Elder High School - (PAR) (Grades 9-12) 3900 Vincent Ave., Cincinnati, OH 45205-1699 t) 513-921-3744 ruffingkd@elderhs.net www.elderhs.org Kurt Ruffing, Prin.; Stds.: 770; Lay Tchrs.: 62

La Salle High School - (PAR) (Grades 9-12) 3091 N. Bend Rd., Cincinnati, OH 45239-7696 t) 513-741-3000 azernich@lasallehs.net www.lasallehs.net/ Aaron Marshall, Prin.; Stds.: 522; Lay Tchrs.: 32

Archbishop McNicholas High School - (PAR) (Grades 9-12) 6536 Beechmont Ave., Cincinnati, OH 45230 t) 513-231-3500 www.mcnhs.org Dr. Denver Stanfield, Pres.; David Mueller, Prin.; Rev. Kevin Scalf, CPPS, Chap.; Jeffry Hutchinson-Smyth, Campus Min.; Stds.: 521; Pr. Tchrs.: 1; Lay Tchrs.: 52

Mercy McAuley High School - 6000 Oakwood Ave., Cincinnati, OH 45224 t) 513-681-1800 www.mercymcauley.org Denise Krueger, Pres.; Connie Kampschmidt, Prin.; Stds.: 373; Lay Tchrs.: 21

Moeller High School - (DIO) (Grades 9-12) 9001 Montgomery Rd., Cincinnati, OH 45242-7780 t) 513-791-1680 nbeiersdorfer@moeller.org www.moeller.org Carl Kremer, Prin.; Marshall Hyzdu, Pres.; Dcn. Nathan Beiersdorfer, CFO; Stds.: 890; Lay Tchrs.: 67

Mount Notre Dame High School - (PAR) 711 E. Columbia Ave., Cincinnati, OH 45215 t) 513-821-3044 mnd@mndhs.org www.mndhs.org Karen Day, Prin.; Judy Gerwe, Pres.; Stds.: 688; Sr. Tchrs.: 2; Lay Tchrs.: 50

Purcell Marian High School - (PAR) (Grades 9-12) 2935 Hackberry St., Cincinnati, OH 45206 t) 513-751-1230 ldamico@purcellmarian.org; info@purcellmarian.org www.purcellmarian.org (East Walnut Hills) Andrew Farfsing, Prin.; Stds.: 370; Sr. Tchrs.: 1; Lay Tchrs.: 39

Roger Bacon High School - (PAR) (Grades 9-12) 4320 Vine St., Cincinnati, OH 45217 t) 513-641-1300 tburke@rogerbacon.org; sschad@rogerbacon.org www.rogerbacon.org The Province of St. John the Baptist of the Order of Friars Minor Steve Schad, Prin.; Thomas Burke, Pres.; Rev. Mark J. Hudak, O.F.M., Technology Dir.; Rev. Roger Lopez, O.F.M., Outreach Dir.;

Seton High School - (PRV) (Grades 9-12) 3901 Glenway Ave., Cincinnati, OH 45205 t) 513-471-2600 whitek@setoncincinnati.org www.setoncincinnati.org (Price Hill) Karen White, Prin.; Shelly Anderson, Vice Prin.; Kathy Ciarla, Pres.; Stds.: 679; Lay Tchrs.: 52

The Summit Country Day School - (PRV) (Grades 9-12) 2161 Grandin Rd., Cincinnati, OH 45208-3300 t) 513-871-4700 wilson_r@summitcds.org www.summitcds.org Affiliated through the Sisters of Notre Dame de Namur Kelly Cronin, Dir.;

St. Ursula Academy - (PRV) (Grades 9-12) 1339 E. McMillan St., Cincinnati, OH 45206 t) 513-961-3410 lkramer@saintursula.org www.saintursula.org Dr. Mari Thomas, Prin.; Lelia Kramer, Pres.; Stds.: 632; Lay Tchrs.: 58

Ursuline Academy of Cincinnati - (PRV) (Grades 9-12) 5535 Pfeiffer Rd., Cincinnati, OH 45242 t) 513-791-5791 jhallahan@ursulineacademy.org www.ursulineacademy.org Senior High School. Ursuline Sisters of Brown Co. Saint Martin, OH. Jill Hallahan, Prin.; Amy Hensley, Prin.; Kerrie Katsetos, Prin.; Ramona Payne, Pres.; Corey Holthaus, Librn.;

St. Xavier High School - (PRV) (Grades 9-12) 600 W. North Bend Rd., Cincinnati, OH 45224 t) 513-761-7600 bschulte@stxavier.org www.stxavier.org Boys. Timothy Reilly, Pres.; Daniel J Lynch, Prin.; Jason Ahlers, Admin.; Brian Schaeper, Admin.; Jennifer Ziebol, Admin.; Stds.: 1,355; Pr. Tchrs.: 3; Lay Tchrs.: 114

DAYTON

Archbishop Carroll High School - (DIO) (Grades 9-12) 4524 Linden Ave., Dayton, OH 45432 t) 937-253-8188 msableski@carrollhs.org; mmonell@carrollhs.org www.carrollhs.org Matthew T. Sableski, Prin.; Stds.: 698; Lay Tchrs.: 57

Chaminade Julienne Catholic High School - (PAR) 505 S. Ludlow St., Dayton, OH 45402 t) 937-461-3740 gmueller@cjeagles.org www.cjeagles.org Conducted by the Society of Mary (Marianists) and Sisters of Notre Dame de Namur. Dan Meixner, Pres.; Stephen Fuchs, Prin.; Greg Mueller, Prin.; Patrick Rizer, Vice Prin.; John Marshall, Admin.; Kelli Kinnear, Dir.; Stds.: 701; Lay Tchrs.: 58

FRANKLIN

Bishop Fenwick High School - (PAR) (Grades 9-12) 4855 State Rte. 122, Franklin, OH 45005 t) 513-423-0723 bcollison@fenwickfalcons.org; bstier@fenwickfalcons.org www.fenwickfalcons.org Blane Collison, Prin.;

HAMILTON

Stephen T. Badin High School - (PAR) (Grades 9-12) 571 New London Rd., Hamilton, OH 45013 t) 513-863-3993 bpendergest@badinhs.org badinhs.org Brian Pendergest, Pres.; Stds.: 644; Lay Tchrs.: 53

KETTERING

Archbishop Alter High School - (PAR) (Grades 9-12) 940 E. David Rd., Kettering, OH 45429 t) 937-434-4434 info@alterhs.org www.alterhs.org Lourdes Lambert, Prin.; Theresa Metter, Librn.;

SIDNEY

Lehman Catholic High School - (DIO) (Grades 9-12) 2400 St. Mary's Ave., Sidney, OH 45365 t) 937-498-1161 v.gaier@lehmancatholic.com www.lehmancatholic.com Veronica Gaier, Prin.; Stds.: 168; Lay Tchrs.: 17

SPRINGFIELD

Catholic Central School - (PAR) (Grades 9-12) 1200 E. High St., Springfield, OH 45505-1124 t) 937-325-9204 www.ccirish.org Kathy Anderson, Prin.; Michael Raiff, Pres.; Stds.: 140; Lay Tchrs.: 10

INSTITUTIONS LOCATED IN DIOCESE

ASSOCIATIONS [ASN]

CINCINNATI

Cincinnati Catholic Women's Association - 958 Marion Ave., Cincinnati, OH 45229 t) 513-961-3566 teddie@fuse.net cincinnaticatholicwomen.org Susan Dorward, Pres.; Teddie Curry, Treas.;

The Comboni Lay Missionaries Association - 1318 Nagel Rd., Cincinnati, OH 45255-3120 t) 513-474-4997 info@laymission-comboni.org www.laymission-comboni.org Mark Banga, Mem.; Dr. Caren Gaines, Mem.; Spencer McSorley, Mem.; Marco Tavanti, Mem.; Don Twoomey, Mem.;

CAMPUS MINISTRY / NEWMAN CENTERS [CAM]

CINCINNATI

University of Cincinnati Newman Center - 328 W. McMillan St., Cincinnati, OH 45219-1224 t) 513-381-6400 campusministry@catholicbearcat.com www.catholicbearcat.com Rev. Ethan M. Moore, Pst.; Rev. Christopher Komoroski, Vicar;

Xavier University Dorothy Day Center for Faith & Justice - 3800 Victory Pkwy., Cincinnati, OH 45207-2141; Mailing: 3815 Saint Francis Xavier Way, Rm. 310, Gallagher Student Ctr., Cincinnati, OH 45207 t) 513-745-3567 minning@xavier.edu www.xavier.edu/cfj Rev. Dan Larkin Jr.; Rev. Albert J. Bischoff, S.J., Campus Min.;

DAYTON

Sinclair Community College Campus Ministry - 444 W. Third St., Dayton, OH 45402 t) 937-512-2481 larry.lindstrom@sinclair.edu www.sinclair.edu/campus-ministry/ Wayne Topp, Dir.;

University of Dayton Campus Ministry - 300 College Park, Dayton, OH 45469-0408 t) 937-229-3339 campusministry@udayton.edu www.udayton.edu/ministry Rev. Robert Jones, S.M., Chap.; Crystal Sullivan, Dir.;

FAIRBORN

Catholic Campus Ministry - 3650 Colonel Glenn Hwy., Fairborn, OH 45324-2096 t) 937-426-1836 joan.lapore@wright.edu www.raidercatholics.com Rev. Timothy Fahey, Dir.; Nic Kovatch, Campus Min.; Joan LaPore, Admin.; Denise Jasek, Music Min.;

OXFORD

Miami University Catholic Campus Ministry - 15 S. Poplar St., Oxford, OH 45056 t) 513-273-0044 willigj@miamioh.edu catholicredhawk.com Rev. Jacob Edward Willig, Chap.;

WILMINGTON

Wilmington College Campus Ministry - 73 N. Mulberry St., Wilmington, OH 45177 t) 937-382-2236 www.stcolumbkille.org Pastoral care available through St. Columbkille Parish. Rev. Bernard J. Weldishofer, Pst.;

CATHOLIC CHARITIES [CCH]

CINCINNATI

Healthy Moms & Babes, Inc. - 2270 Banning Rd., Ste. 200, Cincinnati, OH 45239 t) 513-591-5600 tcruise@healthymomsandbabes.org www.healthymomsandbabes.org Sr. Patricia Cruise, S.C., Pres.; Asstd. Annu.: 3,800; Staff: 22

CEMETERIES [CEM]

CINCINNATI

Catholic Calvary Cemetery Association - 1721 Duck Creek Rd., Cincinnati, OH 45207 t) 513-704-6261 jayccc576@gmail.com; larry.ungerer@juno.com Ronald Hibbard, Supt.;

Gate of Heaven Cemetery - 11000 Montgomery Rd., Cincinnati, OH 45249 t) 513-489-0300 tjordan@gateofheaven.org www.gateofheaven.org Thomas Jordan, Dir.;

St. John - 4423 Vine St., Cincinnati, OH 45217; Mailing: 3819 W. 8th St., Cincinnati, OH 45205 t) 513-557-2306; 513-242-4191 jerry@cccsohio.org www.cccsohio.org Operated by Cincinnati Catholic Cemetery Society Jerome Auer, Pres.; Stephen E. Bittner, Trustee;

St. Joseph - 3819 W. 8th St., Cincinnati, OH 45205 t) 513-557-2306 (Admin. Office); 513-921-3050 (Office) jerry@cccsohio.org www.cccsohio.org Operated by Cincinnati Catholic Cemetery Society Jerome Auer, Pres.; Stephen E. Bittner, Trustee;

St. Joseph New Cemetery Association - 4500 Foley Rd., Cincinnati, OH 45238 t) 513-251-3110 rwinter@stjoenew.com www.stjoenew.com Robert Winter, Gen. Mgr.;

St. Mary - 701 E. Ross Ave., Cincinnati, OH 45217; Mailing: 3819 W. 8th St., Cincinnati, OH 45205 t) 513-242-4191 (Office); 513-557-2306 x319 (Admin. Office) jerry@cccsohio.org www.cccsohio.org part of Cincinnati Catholic Cemetery Society Jerome Auer, Pres.; Stephen E. Bittner, Trustee;

DAYTON

The Calvary Cemetery Association - 1625 Calvary Dr., Dayton, OH 45409 t) 937-293-1221 scottw@ccadayton.org calvarycemeterydayton.org/ Rick Meade, Exec.; Scott Wright, Exec.;

SPRINGFIELD

Calvary - 3155 E. Possum Rd., Springfield, OH 45502 t) 937-323-7474 tjordan@gateofheaven.org Thomas Jordan, Dir.; James P. Matthews, Supt.;

COLLEGES & UNIVERSITIES [COL]

CINCINNATI

Mount St. Joseph University - 5701 Delhi Rd., Cincinnati, OH 45233-1670 t) 513-244-4200; 800-654-9314 info@msj.edu www.msj.edu Coed. Chartered by the State of Ohio. Janet Cox, Dean; Rev. John Amankwah, Prof.; Dr. H. James Williams, Pres.; Jeff Briggs, Exec.; Sr. Karen Elliott, C.PP.S., Dir.; Scott Lloyd, Librn.; Dr. Diana Davis, Provost; Stds.: 2,027; Lay Tchrs.: 119; Pr. Tchrs.: 1

Xavier University - 3800 Victory Pkwy., Cincinnati, OH 45207 t) 513-745-3501 balloum@xavier.edu; sampsonn@xavier.edu www.xavier.edu Dr. Colleen M Hanycz, Pres.; Rev. Eric M. Sundrup, S.J., Pst.; Stds.: 6,129; Lay Tchrs.: 409; Pr. Tchrs.: 2; Sr. Tchrs.: 1

DAYTON

The University of Dayton - 300 College Park Ave., Dayton, OH 45469-1638 t) 937-229-1000 www.udayton.edu (Coed) Society of Mary (Marianists). Rev. James Fitz, S.M., Rector; Rev. Joseph F. Kozar, S.M., Asst. Rector; Eric Spina, Pres.; Paul H. Benson, Provost; Rev. Charles J. Stander, S.M.; Rev. Bakpenam Sebastien Abalodo, S.M.; Rev. Bertrand A. Buby, S.M.; Rev. Theodore K. Cassidy, S.M.; Bro. Magdaleno Ceballos, SM; Bro. Raymond L. Fitz, S.M.; Rev. Paul Fitzpatrick, SM; Bro. Thomas Giardino, S.M.; Bro. John Habjan, S.M.; Bro. Robert H. Hughes, S.M.; Bro. Thomas Oldenski; Bro. Ronald Overman, S.M.; Bro. Thomas J. Pieper, S.M.; Rev. Johan G. Roten, S.M.; Rev. James A. Russell, S.M.; Bro. Thomas Wendorf, S.M.; Stds.: 11,770; Bro. Tchrs.: 5; Pr. Tchrs.: 5; Sr. Tchrs.: 2; Scholastics: 1

Institute for Pastoral Initiatives - 1700 S. Patterson Blvd, Dayton, OH 45469-7013; Mailing: 300 College Park, Dayton, OH 45469-7013 t) 937-229-3126 azukowski1@udayton.edu udayton.edu/artssciences/ctr/ipi/index.php Sr. Angela Ann Zukowski, M.H.S.H., Dir.;

The Marian Library/International Marian Research Institute (IMRI) - t) 937-229-4214 scahalan1@udayton.edu Rev. Thomas A. Thompson, S.M.; Kathleen M. Webb, Dean; Sarah Cahalan, Dir.;

CONVENTS, MONASTERIES, AND RESIDENCES FOR WOMEN [CON]

CINCINNATI

Franciscan Monastery of St. Clare (Poor Clares) - 1505 Miles Rd., Cincinnati, OH 45231-2427 t) 513-825-7177 poorclareprayers@gmail.com www.poorclarescincinnati.org Sr. Anna Marie Covely, OSC, Abbess; Srs.: 10

Franciscan Sisters of the Poor - 60 Compton Rd., Cincinnati, OH 45215 t) 513-761-9040 x101 office@franciscansistersofthepoor.org www.franciscansistersofthepoor.org Sr. Ann Cecile Albers, S.F.P., Community Min.; Sr. Marilyn Trowbridge, S.F.P., Congregational Councilor; Srs.: 28

Provincial House, Health Center of Sisters of Notre Dame de Namur - 699 E. Columbia Ave., Cincinnati, OH 45215 t) 513-821-7448 www.sndohio.org Sr. Kathleen Harmon, SNDdeN, Prov.; Sr. Evelyn Fitzke, SNDdeN, Moderator; Sr. Teresita Weind, SNDdeN, Moderator; Sarah Ferrari, Admin.; Srs.: 63

Ursulines of Cincinnati - 1339 E. McMillan St., Cincinnati, OH 45206-2164 t) 513-961-3410 x146 sisters@ursulinesofcincinnati.org cincinnatiursuline.org Ursuline Sisters. Srs.: 4

DAYTON

Sisters of the Precious Blood Generalate - 4000 Denlinger Rd., Dayton, OH 45426 t) 937-837-3302 ehess@cppsadmin.org www.preciousbloodsistersdayton.org Sr. Edna Hess, Pres.; Sr. Patricia Kremer, Vice. Pres.; Sr. Margo Young, Secy.; Sr. Linda Pleiman, C.PP.S., Treas.; Sarah Aisenbrey, Archivist; Srs.: 81

Sisters of the Precious Blood, Salem Heights Convent - 4960 Salem Ave., Dayton, OH 45416-1797 t) 937-278-0871 smccormick@cppsdayton.org www.preciousbloodsistersdayton.org Sr. Edna Hess, Pres.; Srs.: 42

MOUNT SAINT JOSEPH

Sisters of Charity of Cincinnati, Ohio - 5900 Delhi Rd., Mount Saint Joseph, OH 45051 t) 513-347-5201 pat.hayden@srcharitycinti.org www.srcharitycinti.org Sr. Patricia Hayden Sr., Pres.; Srs.: 204

ST. MARTIN

Ursulines of Brown County (Ursuline Order, Congregation of Paris) - 20860 State Rte. 251, St. Martin, OH 45118 t) 513-875-2020 x27 phoman@tds.net www.ursulinesofbc.org Sr. Patricia Homan, Rel. Ord. Ldr.; Srs.: 17

ENDOWMENTS / FOUNDATIONS / TRUSTS [EFT]

CINCINNATI

The Angela Foundation for Ursuline Education - 7659 Montgomery Rd., Ste. 2, Cincinnati, OH 45236 t) 513-221-5500 jwimberg@ursuline-education.com Judith Wimberg, Exec.;

***Catholic Community Foundation for the Archdiocese of Cincinnati, Inc.** - 100 E. 8th St., Cincinnati, OH 45202 t) 513-263-6615 dkissell@catholicaoc.org www.1faith1hope1love.org David W. Kissell, Dir.;

***The Catholic Social Workers National Association Foundation** - ; Mailing: P.O. Box 498531, Cincinnati, OH 45249 t) 317-416-8285 ksn1956.kn@gmail.com www.cswna.org Kathleen Neher, Pres.;

Cincinnati Catholic Group Trust - 100 E. Eighth St., Cincinnati, OH 45202 t) (513) 263-3479; (513) 681-1800 (Denise Krueger) Denise Krueger, Trustee;

Community Support Charitable Trust for the Province of St. John the Baptist of the Order of Friars Minor - 1615 Vine St., Cincinnati, OH 45202 t) 513-721-4700 sjbcfo@franciscan.org franciscan.org Rev. Kenan Freson, O.F.M.; Rev. Jeremy Harrington, O.F.M.; Bro. Vincent Delorenzo, O.F.M.; David P. O'Brien, Admin.;

Friars Club Foundation, Inc. - 4300 Vine St, Cincinnati, OH 45217 t) 513-721-4700; (513) 488-8777 (main office) c) (513) 381-5432 (Annie Timmons) atimmons@friarsclubinc.org www.friarsclubinc.org Larry R Vignola, Trustee; John O'Connor, Finance Chair & Trustee;

Good Samaritan Hospital Foundation of Cincinnati, Inc. - 375 Dixmyth Ave., Cincinnati, OH 45220-2489 t) 513-862-3786 mary_rafferty@trihealth.com www.gshfoundation.com Mary L. Rafferty, Contact;

Roger Bacon High School Endowment - 4320 Vine St., Cincinnati, OH 45217 t) 513-641-1300 mengel@rogerbacon.org www.rogerbacon.org Steve Schad, Prin.; Thomas Burke, Pres.; Michael Engel, Treas.;

Sisters of Notre Dame De Namur, Ohio Province, Charitable Trust - 701 E. Columbia Ave., Cincinnati, OH 45215-3999 t) 513-761-7636 www.sndohio.org Sr. Kathleen Harmon, SNDdeN, Prov.;

The Summit Country Day School Foundation - 2161 Grandin Rd., Cincinnati, OH 45208 t) 513-871-4700 lottman_b@summitcds.org summitcds.org Tom Theobald, Chair; Rick Grzymajlo, Pres.;

Ursulines of Cincinnati, Ohio Charitable Trust - 1339 E. McMillan St., Cincinnati, OH 45206-2164 t) 513-961-3410 x146 sisters@ursulinesofcincinnati.org Carol Beyersdorfer, Chair;

DAYTON

Community Support Charitable Trust - 431 E. Second St., Dayton, OH 45402 t) 937-228-9263 provtreas@cpps-preciousblood.org Bro. Joseph J. Fisher, C.PP.S., Admin.; Rev. Angelo Anthony, C.PP.S., Trustee; Rev. Matthew Jozefiak, C.PP.S., Trustee; Rev. William Nordenbrock, C.PP.S., Trustee; Cynthia Hill, Trustee; John York, Trustee;

MOUNT SAINT JOSEPH

SC Ministry Foundation, Inc. - 5900 Delhi Rd., Mount Saint Joseph, OH 45051 t) 513-347-1122 diane.geiser@srcharitycinti.org www.srcharitycinti.org/ministries/empowerment/ Sr. Patricia Hayden Sr., Pres.;

Sisters of Charity of Cincinnati-Charitable Trust - 5900 Delhi Rd., Mount Saint Joseph, OH 45051 t) 513-347-5201 pat.hayden@srcharitycinti.org www.srcharitycinti.org Fund to primarily support older and infirm members of the congregation. Sr. Patricia Hayden Sr., Pres.;

HOSPITALS / HEALTH SERVICES [HOS]

CINCINNATI

The Good Samaritan Hospital of Cincinnati, Ohio - 375 Dixmyth Ave., Cincinnati, OH 45220 t) 513-862-1400; 513-862-1771 frank_nation@trihealth.com www.trihealth.com Catholic Health Initiatives (CHI) / CommonSpirit Health Mark Clement, CEO; Kelvin Hanger, Pres.; Frank Nation, Vice. Pres.; Austin M. Schafer, Mission Leader/Mgr. for Pastoral Care; Bed Capacity: 562; Asstd. Annu.: 455,000; Staff: 3,700

Good Samaritan College of Nursing and Health Science - t) 513-862-2631 admissions@email.gscollege.edu www.gscollege.edu Judy Kronenberger, Pres.; Stds.: 441; Lay Tchrs.: 55

SPRINGFIELD

Community Mercy Health Partners (Mercy Health Springfield) - 100 Medical Center Dr., Springfield, OH 45504 t) 937-523-1000 www.mercy.com Adam Groshans, Pres.;

Mercy McAuley Center - 906 Scioto St., Urbana, OH 43078 t) 937-653-5432 Jamie J. Houseman, Exec.;

Mercy Memorial Hospital - 904 Scioto St., Urbana, OH 43078 t) 937-484-6112 Jamie J. Houseman, CEO; Bed Capacity: 35; Asstd. Annu.: 14,390; Staff: 154

Oakwood Village - 1500 Villa Rd., Springfield, OH 45503 t) 937-390-9000 www.oakwoodvillage.com Jamie J. Houseman, Exec.;

Springfield Regional Medical Center - 100 Medical Center Dr., Springfield, OH 45504 t) (937) 523-1000 Bed Capacity: 262; Asstd. Annu.: 77,018; Staff: 1,364

MISCELLANEOUS [MIS]

CELINA

***St. Marys Deanery Center** - 2860 U.S. Rte. 127, Celina, OH 45822 t) 419-925-5022 director@stmarysdeanery.com www.stmarysdeanery.com/ Rev. Richard W. Walling, Dean; Tom Kueterman, Dir.;

The Society of the Precious Blood Senior Housing Corporation - 2860 U.S. Rte. 127, Celina, OH 45822 t) 419-925-4516 tdisalvo1971@gmail.com www.stcharlesseniorliving.org Teresa DiSalvo, Dir.;

CENTERVILLE

St. Leonard Faith Community - 8100 Clyo Rd., Centerville, OH 45458 t) 937-435-3626 slfc.office@gmail.com; slfc.pa01@gmail.com www.stleonardfaithcommunity.org Rev. Lawrence E. Mick, Chap.;

CINCINNATI

St. Andrew Kim Korean Catholic Community - 3171 Struble Rd., Cincinnati, OH 45251 c) 513-800-7124 kcincy@gmail.com www.cincykoreancatholic.org/ Rev. Dong-Hyuk Jeon, Admin.; Jung Ja Lee, Pres.;

Bon Secours Mercy Health, Inc. - 1701 Mercy Health Pl., Cincinnati, OH 45237 t) 513-952-5000 www.bsmhealth.org healthcare system John M. Starcher, CEO; Katherine Vestal, Chair;

Bon Secours Mercy Health Medical Group LLC - 1701 Mercy Health Pl., Cincinnati, OH 45237 t) (513) 952-5000 Staci Lucius, Pres.;

Health Select Services LLC - t) (513) 952-5000 Wael Haidar, Pres.;

Mercy Franciscan Senior Health and Housing LLC - 1701 Mercy Health Pl., Cincinnati, OH 45237

Mercy Franciscan Social Ministries LLC - 1701 Mercy Health Pl., Cincinnati, OH 45237

Mercy Health Cincinnati LLC - 1701 Mercy Health Pl., Cincinnati, OH 45237 t) (513) 952-5000 www.e-mercy.com Donald Kline, Pres.; Asstd. Annu.: 1,082,483; Staff: 127

Mercy Health Select LLC - t) (513) 952-5000

Mercy Health-Anderson Hospital LLC - 7500 State Rd., Cincinnati, OH 45255; Mailing: 1701 Mercy Health Pl., Cincinnati, OH 45237 t) 513-624-4500; 513-952-4747 www.e-mercy.com Kenneth James, Pres.; Bed Capacity: 286; Asstd. Annu.: 52,995; Staff: 1,063

Mercy Health-Clermont Hospital LLC - 3000 Hospital Dr., Batavia, OH 45103; Mailing: 1701 Mercy Health Pl., Cincinnati, OH 45237 t) 513-732-8200; 513-952-4747 www.e-mercy.com Shane w. Knisley, Pres.; Bed Capacity: 165; Asstd. Annu.: 52,188; Staff: 708

Mercy Health-Fairfield Hospital LLC - 3000 Mack Rd., Fairfield, OH 45014; Mailing: 1701 Mercy Health Pl., Cincinnati, OH 45237 t) 513-870-7000; 513-952-4747 www.e-mercy.com Justin Krueger, Pres.; Bed Capacity: 226; Asstd. Annu.: 59,600; Staff: 1,246

Mercy Health-Kings Mills Hospital LLC - 1701 Mercy Health Pl., Cincinnati, OH 45237

Mercy Health-West Hospital LLC - 3300 Mercy Health Blvd., Cincinnati, OH 45211; Mailing: 1701 Mercy Health Pl., Cincinnati, OH 45237 t) 513-853-5000; 513-952-4747 www.e-mercy.com Michael Kramer, Pres.; Bed Capacity: 239; Asstd. Annu.: 90,777; Staff: 1,263

***CISE (Catholic Inner-city Schools Education)** - 100 E. Eighth St., Cincinnati, OH 45202 t) 513-263-3471 cise@cisekids.org www.cisekids.org Phil McHugh, Dir.;

***CISE - SGO** - 100 E. Eighth St., Cincinnati, OH 45202 t) (513) 263-3471 cise@cisekids.org cisekids.org/ Phil McHugh, Pres.;

Claver Jesuit Ministry - 5301 Winneste Ave., Cincinnati, OH 45232-1132 t) 513-319-3865 clavmin@gmail.com www.claverjesuit.org Rev. Joseph D. Folzenlogen, S.J., Dir.;

The Comboni Missionaries Auxiliary, Inc. - 1318 Nagel Rd., Cincinnati, OH 45255-3120 t) 513-474-4997 info@combonimissionaries.org www.combonimissionaries.org Stacey Potts, Pres.; Rev. Louis Gasparini, M.C.C.J.; Heather Kaufman, Vice. Pres.; Barb Bohmer, Secy.; Maria Lanzot, Treas.;

De Paul Cristo Rey Work Study Program Corporation - 1133 Clifton Hills Ave., Cincinnati, OH 45220 t) 513-861-0600 siobhan.taylor@dpcr.net www.discoverdepaul.org Sponsored by Sisters of Charity of Cincinnati Sr. Jeanne Bessette, O.S.F., Pres.; Abby Held, Dir.;

St. Dymphna Ministry - 1101 Summit Rd., Cincinnati, OH 45237 t) 513-961-4422

***St. Francis Seraph Ministries** - 1615 Republic St., Cincinnati, OH 45202 t) 513-549-0542 team@sfsministries.org; aanderson@sfsministries.org www.sfsministries.org Christine M Schuermann, CEO; Annise Anderson, Bus. Mgr.; Lawrence Austing, Finance Mgr.;

Franciscan Central Purchasing - St. Clement Friary, 4536 Vine St., Cincinnati, OH 45217 t) 513-641-2257 frankjasper@franciscan.org Rev. Frank Jasper, O.F.M., Dir.;

Franciscan Media, LLC - 28 W. Liberty St., Cincinnati, OH 45202 t) 513-241-5615 info@franciscanmedia.org www.franciscanmedia.org Rev. Daniel Kroger, O.F.M.; Kelly McCracken, Pres.;

***Franciscan Ministries, Inc.** - 110 Compton Rd., Cincinnati, OH 45215 t) 513-761-1697 info@franciscanministriesinc.org www.franciscanministriesinc.org Sr. Marilyn Trowbridge, S.F.P., Chair;

Franciscan Missionary Union - 1615 Vine St., Cincinnati, OH 45202 t) 513-721-4700 x3222 sjbcfo@franciscan.org www.franciscan.org Rev. John Bok, O.F.M., Pres.; Bro. Louis Zant, O.F.M., Vice. Pres.; Bro. Gene Mayer, O.F.M., Secy.; David O'Brien, Treas.; Bro. Thomas Gerchak, O.F.M., Trustee;

Franciscans Network - 1605 Main St., Cincinnati, OH 45202 t) 513-739-3969 jquigleyofm@gmail.com; dlaake@me.com www.franciscansnetwork.org Rev. Murray L. Bodo, O.F.M.; Rev. John Quigley, O.F.M.;

St. Joseph Housing Corporation - 10722 Wyscarver Rd., Cincinnati, OH 45241 t) 513-563-2520 jneidhard@stjosephhome.org Janet Stegman Neidhard, Treas.;

Marian Center of Cincinnati - 5862 Harvey Cir., Cincinnati, OH 45233 t) 513-922-1250 Lois A. Hater, Secy.; Robert E. Hater, Dir.;

***Mercy Neighborhood Ministries, Inc.** - 1602 Madison Rd., Cincinnati, OH 45206 t) 513-751-2500 skathman@mnministries.org www.mercyneighborhoodministries.org Suzanne M. Kathman, Exec.;

Ministers of Service - 745 Ezzard Charles, Cincinnati, OH 45203 t) 513-381-0630 church3824@cs.com Provides training in urban ministry, primarily but not exclusively for African American laypersons. Jack D. McWilliams, Dir.;

National Fraternity of the Secular Franciscan Order, U.S.A. - 1615 Vine St., Cincinnati, OH 45202 t) 636-734-9979 jansfo@yahoo.com www.secularfranciscansusa.org Jan Parker, Pres.;

New Jerusalem Community - 745 Derby Ave., Cincinnati, OH 45232 t) 513-541-4748 njcommunity@juno.com Paul Moore, Pres.;

Ohio Lux Mundi - 100 E. Eighth St., Cincinnati, OH 45202 t) 513-421-3131 Tom Jennings, Treas.;

***Pregnancy Center West, Inc.** - 2859 Boudinot Ave., Ste. 320, Cincinnati, OH 45238 t) 513-244-5700 pcwest@fuse.net; lorrie@pc-west.org www.pc-west.org Non-profit pregnancy resource center whose mission is to get those experiencing a crisis pregnancy to choose life. Lorrie McNickle, Exec.;

***Presentation Ministries, Inc.** - 3230 McHenry Ave., Cincinnati, OH 45211 t) 513-662-5378 orders@presentationministries.com www.presentationministries.com Catholic faith formation via publications, podcasts, and retreats Jerry Cappel, Head Dir.; Mark Hennessey, Dir.; Paul Weckenbrock, Dir.; David Willig, Dir.;

***Ruah Woods** - 6675 Wesselman Rd., Cincinnati, OH 45248 t) 513-407-8672 mreckers@ruahwoods.org www.ruahwoods.org Tony Maas, Chair; Michael Grasinski, Pres.; Andrew Sodergren, Exec.;

***Serenelli Project, Inc.** - 8345 Curzon Ave., Cincinnati, OH 45216; Mailing: P.O. Box 15170, Cincinnati, OH 45215 t) (440) 364-4813 c) (513) 240-3466 www.serenelliproject.org A monastic community for prison re-entry Martin Arlinghaus, Contact;

***Society of Saint Philip Neri, Inc. (The Cincinnati Oratory)** - 123 E. 13th St., Cincinnati, OH 45202 t) 513-721-2988 provost@cincinnatioratory.com www.cincinnatioratory.com Rev. Adrian J. Hilton, C.O., Vicar; Rev. Henry Hoffmann, C.O., Mem.; Very Rev. Jon-Paul Bevak, C.O., Provost;

The Company of St. Ursula - USA - 3021 Fairfield Ave, Apt. B-7, Cincinnati, OH 45206 t) 513-961-0667 csu@fuse.net companyofstursula.org/ Secular institute of Catholic women Mary-Cabrini Durkin, Pres.;

Ursuline Education Network - 7659 Montgomery Rd., Ste. 2, Cincinnati, OH 45236 t) 513-221-5300 jwimberg@ursuline-education.com www.ursuline-education.com UEN is a service to all Ursuline Schools. Judith Wimberg, Exec.;

Vietnamese Catholic Community of Our Lady of Lavang - 314 Township Ave., Cincinnati, OH 45216 t) 513-242-2933 lavangcinti@gmail.com Rev. Chau Pham, S.V.D., Chap.;

St. Xavier Church Property Corporation - 611 Sycamore St., Cincinnati, OH 45202 t) 513-721-4045 office@stxchurch.org; pastor@stxchurch.org www.stxchurch.org Rev. Paul A. Lickteig, SJ, Pres.; Rev. Timothy Lannon, S.J., Treas.; Rev. Walter C. Deye, S.J., Rector;

DAYTON

Catholic Social Services of the Miami Valley - 922 W. Riverview Ave., Dayton, OH 45402 t) (937) 223-7217 roeschl@cssmv.org Laura Roesch, CEO;

Catholic Vietnamese Community of Dayton - 217 W. Fourth St., Dayton, OH 45402 t) 937-224-3904 sacredheartdayton@yahoo.com Rev. Basil Toan Quang Doan, CRM, Chap.;

***Change and Be Changed, Inc.** - 4400 Shakertown Rd., Dayton, OH 45430; Mailing: P.O. Box 221, Xenia, OH 45385 c) 937-657-7474 thomas.hangartner@wright.edu; ehangart@gmail.com changeandbechanged.com/ Rev. Thomas A. Schroer, S.M., Pst.;

Marianist Lay Community of North America (MLC-NA) - Alumni Hall, Room 225, University of Dayton, Dayton, OH 45469-0323; Mailing: P.O. Box 19444, Cincinnati, OH 45219 c) 513-324-9530 rob.brodrick@mlc-na.org www.mlcna.org Dr. Rob Brodrick, Dir.;

One More Soul - 1846 N. Main St., Dayton, OH 45405 t) 937-952-2688; 937-279-5433 (Office) news@onemoresoul.com onemoresoul.com A Catholic lay apostolate promoting the blessing of children and raising awareness of the harm of contraception. Dcn. Russell O. Baldwin, Bd. Mem.;

FAIRBORN

National Diaconate Institute for Continuing Education, Inc. - 330 Chatham Dr., Fairborn, OH 45324 t) 937-879-5332 maxroadruck2@ameritech.net www.ndice.org Max J. Roadruck Jr., Pres.;

FAIRFIELD

Glenmary Home Missioners Charity, Inc. - 4119 Glenmary Trace, Fairfield, OH 45014 t) 513-874-8900 ccarpenter@glenmary.org Rev. Dominic R. Duggins, Pres.;

HARRISON

St. Mark's Chaplaincy for the Extraordinary Form - ; Mailing: P.O. Box 1, Harrison, OH 45030 Ashley Paver, Pres.;

MARIA STEIN

Maria Stein Shrine of the Holy Relics - 2291 St. Johns Rd., Maria Stein, OH 45860; Mailing: PO Box 128, Maria Stein, OH 45860 t) 419-925-4532 www.mariasteinshrine.org Donald C. Rosenbeck, Pres.;

MOUNT SAINT JOSEPH

Archivists for Congregations of Women Religious - 5900

Delhi Rd., Mount Saint Joseph, OH 45051 t) 513-347-4080 archivistsacwr@gmail.com www.archivistsacwr.org Assists lay & religious archivists in the management, interpretation, & preservation of the history of Catholic women religious in the US & abroad. Veronica Buchanan, Secy.;

NORWOOD

***The Couple to Couple League International** - 5440 Moeller Ave, Ste. 149, Norwood, OH 45212 t) 513-471-2000 ccli@ccli.org www.ccli.org Katie Zulanas, Exec.;

SPRINGFIELD

***Go To Galilee** - 101 S. Fountain Ave., Springfield, OH 45502

ST. MARTIN

The Chatfield Edge - 20918 State Rte. 251, St. Martin, OH 45118 t) 513-875-3344 robert.elmore@chatfield.edu www.chatfieldedge.org Robert P. Elmore, Pres.;

XENIA

Catholic Cursillo of Cincinnati - 1700 Sutts Tr., Xenia, OH 45385; Mailing: P.O. Box 317655, Cincinnati, OH 45321 t) 937-773-2700 c) 937-469-7012 communications@cincinnati-cursillo.org; blake.rinderle@yahoo.com www.cincinnati-cursillo.org Retreat/weekend experience Blake Rinderle, Dir.;

MONASTERIES AND RESIDENCES FOR PRIESTS AND BROTHERS [MON]

CELINA

St. Charles - 2860 U.S. Rte. 127, Celina, OH 45822 t) 419-925-4516 hrmanager@cpps-preciousblood.org Rev. Joseph Brown, C.PP.S.; Bro. Paul Chase; Rev. James Dugal, C.PP.S.; Rev. Linus Evers, C.PP.S.; Rev. Juan Gonzalez, C.PP.S.; Rev. Thomas Hemm, C.PP.S.; Rev. Joseph Hinders, C.PP.S.; Rev. David Hoying; Rev. John Hoying, C.PP.S.; Rev. William Hoyng, C.PP.S.; Rev. Edgar Jutte, C.PP.S.; Rev. James McCabe, C.PP.S.; Bro. Charles McCafferty; Rev. William Miller, C.PP.S.; Rev. Charles Mullen, C.PP.S.; Rev. Alfred Naseman, C.PP.S.; Rev. Fred Nietfeld; Rev. Edward Oen; Rev. Patrick Patterson, C.PP.S.; Bro. Nick Renner; Rev. Louis Schmit, C.PP.S.; Rev. Kenneth J. Schroeder, C.PP.S.; Rev. Donald J. Thieman, C.PP.S.; Rev. Paul W. Wohlwend, C.PP.S.; Rev. Thomas Brenberger, C.PP.S., Vicar; Rev. Anthony Batt, In Res.; Rev. David L. Zink, In Res.; Bro. Timothy Cahill, C.PP.S., Mem.; Rev. James Franck, C.PP.S., Mem.; Bro. Timothy Hemm, C.PP.S., Mem.; Rev. Andrew O'Reilly, C.PP.S., Mem.; Bro. Jerome Schulte, C.PP.S., Mem.; Bro. Jerome A Schwieterman, Mem.; Rev. Jerome P. Stack, C.PP.S., Mem.; Bro. Theophane Woodall, C.PP.S., Mem.; Rev. John Butler, Resident;

CINCINNATI

Brothers of the Poor of St. Francis - 7831 Ayerdayl Ln., Cincinnati, OH 45255; Mailing: P.O.Box 30359, Cincinnati, OH 45230 t) 513-924-0111 hibrothers@fuse.net Bro. Edward Kesler, C.F.P., Supr.; Brs.: 12

Cincinnati Jesuit Community - 3844 Victory Pkwy., Cincinnati, OH 45207 t) 513-745-3858 Members of the Jesuit Community (Society of Jesus, S.J.). Rev. Albert Fritsch, S.J., Pst.; Rev. Paul A. Lickteig, SJ, Pst.; Rev. Eric M. Sundrup, S.J., Pst.; Rev. Albert J. Bischoff, S.J.; Rev. Richard W. Bollman, S.J.; Rev. Walter C. Deye, S.J., Rector; Rev. Michael J. Graham, S.J., In Res.; Rev. Robert E. Hurd, S.J.; Rev. Thomas P. Kennealy, S.J.; Rev. John J. LaRocca, S.J.; Rev. Christopher A. Mapunda, S.J., Graduate Student; Rev. James M. McCann; Rev. Kenneth R. Overberg, S.J., Chap.; Rev. Robert J. Ross, S.J.; Rev. Edward W. Schmidt, S.J.; Rev. Walter Bado, S.J., In Res.; Rev. Nathan Wendt, S.J., Admin.; Matthew R Zurcher, S.J., Campus Min.;

St. Clare Friary - 5831 Saranac Ave., Cincinnati, OH 45224 t) 513-541-0488 Rev. Patrick McCloskey, O.F.M., Supr.; Rev. David Kohut, O.F.M., Chap.; Bro. Christopher Meyer, O.F.M., Vicar;

St. Clement Friary - 4536 Vine St., Cincinnati, OH 45217 t) 513-641-2257 frankjasper@franciscan.org St. John the Baptist Province. Residence for Retired Friars, Pastor of St. Clement Parish and other Friars. Rev. Frank Jasper, O.F.M., Supr.; Rev. John Stein, OFM, Pst.; Rev. Bruce Hausfeld; Rev. Bryant Hausfeld; Rev. John Bok, O.F.M.; Rev. Damian Cesanek, O.F.M.; Rev. John Paul Flajole, O.F.M.; Rev. Fred Link, O.F.M.; Rev. Ric Schneider, OFM; Rev. Thomas Speier I, O.F.M.; Bro. Kenneth Beetz, O.F.M.; Bro. Norbert Bertram, O.F.M.; Bro. Michael Charron, O.F.M.; Bro. David Crank, O.F.M.; Bro. Kevin Duckson, O.F.M.; Bro. Thomas Gerchak, O.F.M.; Bro. Marcel Groth, O.F.M.; Brs.: 7; Priests: 10

Comboni Missionaries (Verona Fathers)-Comboni Mission Center - 1318 Nagel Rd., Cincinnati, OH 45255-3120 t) 513-474-4997 info@combonimissionaries.org www.combonimissionaries.org Houses Comboni Missionaries of the Heart of Jesus, Inc., The Offices of the Province of North America, including the Office of the Provincial. Rev. Joseph Bragotti, M.C.C.J.; Rev. Kenneth Gerth, M.C.C.J.; Rev. Rudolfo Coaquira Hilage, M.C.C.J.; Rev. Paul J. Ewers, MCCJ; Rev. Louis Gasparini, M.C.C.J., Supr.; Rev. Ruffino Ezama, M.C.C.J., Prov.; Rev. David Paul Baltz, MCCJ; Rev. John M. Converset, M.C.C.J.; Rev. Thomas Michael Vermiglio, MCCJ; Priests: 9

De Sales Crossings Marianist Community - 1600 Madison Rd., Cincinnati, OH 45206-1815 t) 513-961-1945; 513-961-2257 bobdzubinski@yahoo.com Bro. Robert S. Dzubinski, S.M., Dir.; Bro. Robert P. Donovan, S.M.; Bro. William I. Grundish, S.M.; Bro. Edward Longbottom; Bro. Robert A. Politi, S.M.; Brs.: 8; Priests: 1

Marianist Community - 9025 Montgomery Rd., Cincinnati, OH 45242-7711 Bro. Robert Flaherty, Dir.; Bro. Ronald Luksic; Rev. Lawrence Schoettelkotte;

St. Francis Seraph Friary - 1615 Vine St., Cincinnati, OH 45202-6400 t) 513-721-4700 sjbsec@franciscan.com www.franciscan.org Provincial Headquarters of the Province of St. John the Baptist of the Order of Friars Minor. Rev. Mark Soehner, O.F.M., Prov.; Rev. William Farris, O.F.M., Vicar; Rev. Daniel J. Anderson, O.F.M., Secy.; Rev. James M. Bok, O.F.M.; Rev. John Bok, O.F.M., Dir.; Rev. Robert Bruno, O.F.M., Chap.; Bro. John Carey, O.F.M.; Sr. Eileen Connelly, OSU, Dir.; Rev. Matthias Crehan, O.F.M., Parochial Substitute; Rev. Larry Dunham, O.F.M.; Rev. Arthur Espelage, O.F.M.; Rev. Harold Geers, O.F.M.; Bro. Thomas Gerchak, O.F.M.; Rev. Blane Grein, O.F.M.; Rev. Bert Heise, O.F.M.; Rev. Alan Hirt, Pst.; Bro. Timothy Lamb, O.F.M.; Rev. Max Langenderfer, O.F.M.; Bro. Dominic Lococo, O.F.M.; Bro. Brian Maloney, O.F.M., In Res.; Rev. Patrick McCloskey, O.F.M., Dir.; Bro. Scott Obrecht, O.F.M.; David O'Brien, CFO; Bro. Giovanni Ried, O.F.M.; Rev. Ricardo Russo, O.F.M.; Rev. Thomas Speier I, O.F.M.; Bro. Bill Spond, O.F.M.; Bro. Timothy Sucher, O.F.M., Pst. Assoc.; Rev. Francis S. Tebbe, O.F.M., Dir.; Rev. Manuel Viera, O.F.M.; Brs.: 19; Priests: 9

Brother Juniper Friary - 4344 Sullivan Ave., Cincinnati, OH 45217-1747 c) (513) 678-6535 Bro. John Boissy, OFM; Bro. Chris Cahill, O.F.M.; Rev. Mark J. Hudak, O.F.M.; Rev. Roger Lopez, O.F.M.;

St. Gertrude Priory - 7630 Shawnee Run Rd., Cincinnati, OH 45243 t) 513-561-5954 john.langlois@opeast.org www.stgertrude.org Rev. John Paul Walker, O.P., Pst.; Rev. John Langlois, O.P., Prior; Rev. Joachim Kenney, O.P., Par. Vicar; Rev. John Mark Solitario, O.P., Par. Vicar; Rev. Michael Mary Dosch, O.P., Novice Master; Rev. Joseph Alobaidi, O.P., In Res.; Rev. John Corbett, O.P., In Res.; Rev. Darren Pierre, O.P., In Res.; Brs.: 12; Priests: 8

Jesuit Community at St. Xavier High School - 7361 View Pl., Cincinnati, OH 45224 t) 513-761-5522 tbaum@jesuits.org Rev. Terrence Baum, SJ, Admin.; Rev. Jacob Boddicker, SJ, Par. Vicar; Rev. James Ackerman, Assoc. Pst.; Rev. Robert J. Thesing, S.J., Sacr. Min.; Rev. Thomas C Manahan, S.J., Prof.; Rev. Richard Millbourn, S.J., Prof.; Rev. David E. Watson, SJ, Retreat Ministry; Rev. Paul Macke, Spiritual Dir.; Priests: 8

St. John the Baptist Friary - 10722 Wyscarver Rd., Cincinnati, OH 45241-3083 t) 513-769-1613 Bro. Gene Mayer, O.F.M., Supr.; Rev. John Joseph Gonchar, OFM, In Res.; Rev. Joseph Ricchini, O.F.M., In Res.; Rev. Maynard Tetreault, O.F.M., In Res.; Bro. Josef Anderlohr, O.F.M., In Res.; Bro. Gabriel Balassone, O.F.M., In Res.; Bro. Louis Lamping, O.F.M., In Res.; Brs.: 4; Priests: 3

Pleasant Street Friary - 1723 Pleasant St., Cincinnati, OH 45202-6413 c) 513-313-1439 jquigleyofm@gmail.com Friar Alan C Hirt, OFM, Pst.; Rev. Mark Soehner, O.F.M., Prov.; Rev. Murray L. Bodo, O.F.M.; Rev. John Quigley, O.F.M.; Priests: 4

DAYTON

Society of the Precious Blood, Cincinnati Province, Inc. - 431 E. Second St., Dayton, OH 45402-1764 t) 937-228-9263 treasurer@cpps-preciousblood.org www.cpps-preciousblood.org Rev. William Nordenbrock, C.PP.S., Contact;

Society of the Precious Blood, United States Province, Inc. - 431 E. Second St., Dayton, OH 45402 t) (312) 639-4320 cpps-preciousblood.org Rev. Jeffrey Kirch, C.PP.S., Prov.; Rev. Jeffrey Kirch, C.PP.S., Prov.; Rev. Joseph Nassal, C.PP.S., Vice Prov.; Rev. Joseph Nassal, C.PP.S., Vice Prov.; Rev. William Nordenbrock, C.PP.S., Secy./Treas.; Rev. Stephen Dos Santos, C.PP.S., Vocation Dir./Mem.; Rev. Benjamin Berinti, C.PP.S., Counselor; Rev. Ron Will, C.PP.S., Counselor; Bro. Daryl Charron, C.PP.S., Counselor; Rev. Joseph Bathke, C.PP.S., Mem.; Rev. Dennis Chriszt, C.PP.S., Mem.; Rev. Joseph F. Deardorff, C.PP.S., Mem.; Rev. William Delaney, C.PP.S., Mem.; Rev. Barry J. Fischer, C.PP.S., Mem.; Rev. Richard Friebel, C.PP.S., Mem.; Rev. Larry J. Hemmelgarn, C.PP.S., Mem.; Rev. William Hubmann, C.PP.S., Mem.; Rev. Fred Licciardi, C.PP.S., Mem.; Rev. Jack McClure, C.PP.S., Mem.; Rev. John Mencsik, C.PP.S., Mem.; Rev. LeRoy Moreeuw, C.PP.S., Mem.; Rev. Kenneth Pleiman, C.PP.S., Mem.; Rev. Dennis Schaab, C.PP.S., Mem.; Rev. William Stang, C.PP.S., Mem.; Rev. Jerome Steinbrunner, C.PP.S., Mem.; Rev. Daniel Torson, Mem.; Rev. Joseph Uecker, C.PP.S., Mem.; Rev. Thomas Welk, C.PP.S., Mem.; Rev. Clarence Williams, C.PP.S., Mem.; Bro. Juan Acuna Gonzalez, C.PP.S., Mem.; Bro. Benjamin Basile, C.PP.S., Mem.; Bro. James Ballmann, C.PP.S., Mem.; Bro. Brian Boyle, C.PP.S., Mem.; Bro. Joseph J. Fisher, C.PP.S., Mem.; Bro. Robert Reuter, Mem.; Bro. Jerome A Schwieterman, Mem.; Brs.: 18; Priests: 100

FAIRFIELD

Headquarters of Glenmary Home Missioners (The Home Missioners of America) - 4119 Glenmary Trace, Fairfield, OH 45246-5618; Mailing: Glenmary Home Missioners, P.O. Box 465618, Cincinnati, OH 45246-5618 t) 513-874-8900 ccarpenter@glenmary.org; ddorsey@glenmary.org www.glenmary.org Rev. Daniel Dorsey, Pres.; Bro. Larry Johnson, Vice. Pres.; Rev. R. Aaron Wessman, Vice. Pres.; Charlotte T. Carpenter, Treas.; Rev. Don Tranel, Pst.; Rev. Bruce C. Brylinski, Dir.; Bro. Dennis Craig, Senior Member; Rev. Robert Dalton, Senior Member; Bro. Craig Digmann, Outreach Ministry - Catholic Presence Ministry, Hartsville, TN; Rev. Dominic R. Duggins, House Dir., Senior Member; Rev. David Glockner, Senior Member; Rev. Chet Artysiewicz, Mem.; Rev. Ed Gorny, Senior Member; Rev. Robert Hare, Senior Member; Bro. David Henley, Vocation Dir.; Bro. Jack Henn, Senior Member; Rev. Dennis Holly, Senior Member; Bro. Curt Kedley, Senior Member residing in Windsor, NC; Rev. Thomas Kirkendoll, Co-Dir., Novitiate; Bro. Levis Kuwa, Nursing Missionary in Blakely, GA; Rev. Fid Levri, Senior Member in Reed, KY; Bro. Jason Muhlenkamp, Outreach Ministry in Blakely, GA; Rev. Steve Pawelk, Co-Dir., Novitiate; Rev. Francois Pellissier, G.H.M., Outreach Ministry; Rev. Gerald Peterson, Senior Member; Rev. Frank Ruff, Senior member; Rev. Les Schmidt, GHM, Regional Worker/Senior Member

-Maynardsville TN; Bro. Thomas Sheehy, Outreach Ministry - Erwin, TN; Bro. Virgil Siefker, Outreach Ministry - Windsor, NC; Bro. Joe Steen, Outreach Ministry-Maynardsville, TN; Rev. Wil Steinbacher, Senior Member; Bro. Ken Woods, Senior Member in Kingsport, TN; Brs.: 12; Priests: 29

NURSING / REHABILITATION / CONVALESCENCE / ELDERLY CARE [NUR]

CENTERVILLE

***St. Leonard** - 8100 Clyo Rd., Centerville, OH 45458 t) 937-433-0480 matthew.walters900@commonspirit.org www.homeishere.org An operating unit of CHI Living Communities, which is a subsidiary of CommonSpirit Health Bob Jackson, Chap.; Mary Houston, Mission Integration; Asstd. Annu.: 1,251; Staff: 342

CINCINNATI

Archbishop Leibold Home for the Aged - 476 Riddle Rd., Cincinnati, OH 45220-2493 c) (513) 706-5039 x153 mscincinnati@littlesistersofthepoor.org www.littlesistersofthepoorcincinnati.org Little Sisters of the Poor-Cincinnati Mother Marie Edward lsp, Supr.; Asstd. Annu.: 100; Staff: 104

St. Margaret Hall - 1960 Madison Rd., Cincinnati, OH 45206-1896 t) 513-751-5880 kharris@stmargarethall.org www.stmargarethall.com Carmelite Sisters for the Aged and Infirm and the Diocese of Cincinnati Robert Burns, Admin.; Asstd. Annu.: 249; Staff: 112

Bayley Senior Care - 990 Bayley Dr., Cincinnati, OH 45233 t) 513-347-5500 tina.mersmann@bayleylife.org www.bayleylife.org Adrienne Walsh, Pres.; Asstd. Annu.: 656; Staff: 360

RETREAT HOUSES / RENEWAL CENTERS [RTR]

CINCINNATI

***Our Lady of the Holy Spirit Center** - 5440 Moeller Ave., Cincinnati, OH 45212 t) 513-351-9800 info@olhsc.org www.olhsc.org Daniel Green, Dir.;

DAYTON

Bergamo Center for Lifelong Learning - 4400 Shakertown Rd., Dayton, OH 45430-1075 t) 937-426-2363 info@bergamocenter.org www.bergamocenter.org Brent Devitt, Exec. Dir.;

MILFORD

Jesuit Spiritual Center at Milford - 5361 S. Milford Rd., Milford, OH 45150-9746 t) 513-248-3500 poat@jesuitspiritualcenter.com www.jesuitspiritualcenter.com Stephen Poat, Exec.;

SEMINARIES [SEM]

CINCINNATI

The Athenaeum of Ohio - 6616 Beechmont Ave., Cincinnati, OH 45230 t) 513-231-2223 ath@athenaeum.edu www.athenaeum.edu Incorporated March 24, 1928 by the State of Ohio and presently has two divisions: Mount St. Mary's Seminary of the West and The School of Theology. Most Rev. Dennis M. Schnurr, Chancellor; Rev. Anthony R. Brausch, President & Rector; Rev. David J. Endres, Dean; Rev. Ryan Thomas Ruiz, Dean; Stds.: 182; Lay Tchrs.: 9; Pr. Tchrs.: 9

The St. Gregory Seminary Trust -

Mount St. Mary's School of Theology - 6616 Beechmont Ave., Cincinnati, OH 45230 t) 513-231-1200

Dominican Novitiate - 7630 Shawnee Run Rd., Cincinnati, OH 45243 t) 513-527-3972 novicemaster@stgertrude.org www.op-stjoseph.org Rev. Michael Mary Dosch, O.P., Contact; Stds.: 12

Mount St. Mary's Seminary of the West - 6616 Beechmont Ave., Cincinnati, OH 45230 t) 513-231-2223 ath@athenaeum.edu www.athenaeum.edu Rev. Anthony R. Brausch, Pres./Rector; Rev. Christopher M. Geiger, Vice Rector & Dir. Formation; Rev. David J. Endres, Dean; Rev. Ryan Ruiz, S.L.D., Dean; Rev. Daniel K. Hess, Dean; Rev. Christopher R. Armstrong, Dir.; Rev. Eric M. Wood, Dir.; Rev. David A. Sunberg, Dir.; Rev. Andrew Moss, Instructor in Canon Law; Rev. Timothy P. Schehr, Emeritus Professor of Biblical Studies; Rev. Daniel J. Schmitmeyer, In Res.; Connie Song, M.L.S., Librn.; Ken Birck, Dir.; Jeff Royer, Registrar; Melissa McCarthy, Senior Accountant / Financial Reporting; Stds.: 85; Lay Tchrs.: 9; Pr. Tchrs.: 9

DAYTON

Marianist Community - 100 Chambers St., Dayton, OH 45409-2817 t) 937-627-8998 Rev. Charles J. Stander, S.M., Chap.; Rev. Robert Jones, S.M., Dir.; Bro. Magdaleno Ceballos, SM; Bro. Justin Quiroz; Bro. Mawaba Jean-Chrysostome Tagba; Bro. Tchamie Thierry Kadja, S.M.; Bro. Robert H. Hughes, S.M.; Brs.: 5; Priests: 2

Marianist Community - Meyer Hall, 4435 E. Patterson Rd., Dayton, OH 45430-1033 t) 937-426-7852 kosmowskia1@udayton.edu Bro. Andrew J. Kosmowski, S.M., Dir.; Bro. J. Mitchell Schweickart, S.M.; Bro. Jeffrey Sullivan, S.M.;

Marianist Community - 312 Stonemill Rd., Dayton, OH 45409-2543 t) 937-627-1553 tgiardino@sm-usa.org Bro. Thomas Giardino, S.M., Dir.; Rev. Bertrand A. Buby, S.M.; Rev. Theodore K. Cassidy, S.M.; Bro. Raymond Fitz, S.M.; Bro. Paul Kagece Ndungu;

Marianist Community - 121 Sawmill Rd., Dayton, OH 45409-2524 c) (937) 545-9878 Bro. Alex J. Tuss, S.M., Dir.; Bro. Philip Aaron, S.M.; Bro. Will Halloway;

Marianist Community - Alumni Hall, 300 College Park, Dayton, OH 45469-0300 t) 937-229-3556 Bro. Ronald Overman, S.M., Dir.; Rev. Sebastien Abalodo, SM; Bro. James Brown, S.M.; Rev. J. Eugene Contadino, SM; Rev. Paul Fitzpatrick, SM; Bro. Louis Fournier, S.M.; Bro. John Habjan, S.M.; Rev. Joseph F. Kozar, S.M.; Bro. M. Gary Marcinowski, S.M.; Rev. Johan G. Roten, S.M.; Rev. James A. Russell, S.M.;

Marianist Community - 301 Kiefaber St., Dayton, OH 45409-2537 t) 937-627-8091 Bro. Thomas J. Pieper, S.M., Dir.; Rev. James F. Fitz, S.M., Vice Pres., Mission & Rector; Bro. Kouame Wolfgang Adela;

Marianist Community - 9636 Lakeshore Dr., E., Huntsville, OH 43324-9520 t) 937-842-4902 joe.kamis1946@gmail.com Bro. Joseph Kamis, SM; Rev. Sylverius Kerketta, SM (India); Bro. Roy McLoughlin; Bro. William Schlosser, S.M.; Bro. Donald Smith, S.M.;

Marianist Community, Novitiate - 4435 E. Patterson Rd., Dayton, OH 45430-1033 t) 937-426-5721 dbautista@sm-usa.org Bro. Dennis Bautista, SM, Dir.; Rev. Timothy Eden, SM, Mem.; Bro. Thomas Redmond, Mem.; Bro. Thomas Wendorf, S.M., Mem.;

Marianist Environmental Education Center - 4435 E. Patterson Rd., Dayton, OH 45430-1095 t) 937-429-3582 meec@udayton.edu Sr. Leanne Jablonski, FMI, Dir.;

Marianist Mission - 4435 E. Patterson Rd., Dayton, OH 45434-1033; Mailing: P.O. Box 340998, Dayton, OH 45434-0998 t) 937-222-4641; 800-348-4732 linda.hayes@marianistmission.org Linda Hayes, Dir.;

Marianist Network for the Arts - 4400 Shakertown Rd., Dayton, OH 45430-1075 t) 937-320-5405 www.dayton-gallery-saintjohn.org Rev. Michael F. Nartker, S.M.; Bro. A. Joseph Barrish, S.M.; Bro. John Lemker, S.M.; Bro. Donald Smith, S.M.; Bro. Louis Fournier, S.M.;

North American Center for Marianist Studies - 4435 E. Patterson Rd., Dayton, OH 45430-1083 t) 937-429-2521 George Lisjak, Dir.;

Siena Woods Marianist Community - 6105 N. Main St., Dayton, OH 45415-3110 c) 314-497-3437 cjohnson@sm-usa.org Bro. Charles Johnson, S.M., Dir.; Rev. Lawrence Schoettelkotte; Rev. Albert Koch, SM; Rev. Thomas A. Schroer, S.M.; Rev. Thomas A. Thompson, S.M.; Bro. Kenneth Thompson, S.M.; Bro. A. Joseph Barrish, S.M.; Bro. David Betz, SM; Bro. Paul Bredestege; Bro. Paul Jablinski, S.M.; Bro. Nicholas Rufo, S.M.; Bro. Donald Neff, SM; Bro. John Lemker, S.M.; Bro. Charles Gausling, S.M.;

SHRINES [SHR]

CINCINNATI

St. Anthony Shrine - 5000 Colerain Ave., Cincinnati, OH 45223-1213 t) 513-541-2146 vincedel@franciscan.org Bro. Vincent Delorenzo, O.F.M., Supr.; Rev. William Farris, O.F.M., Vicar; Bro. Jerome Beetz, O.F.M., In Res.; Rev. Thomas Richstatter, O.F.M., In Res.; Rev. Daniel Kroger, O.F.M., CEO; Bro. Dominic Lococo, O.F.M., In Res.; Bro. Brian Maloney, O.F.M., In Res.; Rev. Kenan Freson, O.F.M., In Res.;

SPECIAL CARE FACILITIES [SPF]

CINCINNATI

Friars Club - 4300 Vine St., Cincinnati, OH 45217 t) 513-488-8777 info@friarsclubinc.org www.friarsclubinc.org Annie Timmons, Pres.; Asstd. Annu.: 1,000; Staff: 6

An asterisk (*) denotes an organization that has established tax-exempt status directly with the IRS and is not covered by the USCCB Group Ruling.

Diocese of Cleveland

(Dioecesis Clevelandensis)

MOST REVEREND EDWARD C. MALESIC, J.C.L.

Bishop of Cleveland. Ordained a priest May 30, 1987; appointed Bishop of Greensburg April 24, 2015; installed and consecrated July 13, 2015; appointed Bishop of Cleveland July 16, 2020; installed September 14, 2020. Office: 1404 E. Ninth St., Cleveland, OH 44114.

Cathedral Square Plaza: 1404 E. Ninth St., Cleveland, OH 44114. T: 216-696-6525; T: 800-869-6525 (Ohio only); F: 216-621-7332.
www.dioceseofcleveland.org
info@dioceseofcleveland.org

ESTABLISHED APRIL 23, 1847.

Square Miles 3,414.

Comprises, since July 22, 1943, eight counties in the north-central part of the State of Ohio, namely Ashland, Cuyahoga, Geauga, Lake, Lorain, Medina, Summit and Wayne Counties.

For legal titles of parishes and diocesan institutions, consult the Chancery Office.

Most Reverend Michael G. Woost, S.T.L.
Auxiliary Bishop. Ordained a priest June 9, 1984; appointed Titular Bishop of Sertei and Auxiliary Bishop of the Diocese of Cleveland May 9, 2022; consecrated August 4, 2022. Mailing address: 1404 East Ninth Street, Cleveland, OH 44114. T: 216-696-6525, ext. 3630.

STATISTICAL OVERVIEW

Personnel
Bishop ... 1
Auxiliary Bishops ... 1
Retired Bishops ... 1
Abbots ... 1
Retired Abbots ... 1
Priests: Diocesan Active in Diocese ... 203
Priests: Diocesan Active Outside Diocese ... 4
Priests: Diocesan in Foreign Missions ... 2
Priests: Retired, Sick or Absent ... 111
Number of Diocesan Priests ... 320
Religious Priests in Diocese ... 77
Total Priests in your Diocese ... 397
Extern Priests in Diocese ... 16
Ordinations:
Diocesan Priests ... 3
Transitional Deacons ... 4
Permanent Deacons ... 2
Permanent Deacons in Diocese ... 196
Total Brothers ... 13
Total Sisters ... 665

Parishes
Parishes ... 185
With Resident Pastor:
Resident Diocesan Priests ... 138
Resident Religious Priests ... 16
Without Resident Pastor:
Administered by Priests ... 26
Administered by Deacons ... 2
Administered by Religious Women ... 1
Administered by Lay People ... 2
Missions ... 1
Pastoral Centers ... 1

Welfare
Catholic Hospitals ... 4
Total Assisted ... 329,537
Health Care Centers ... 1
Total Assisted ... 715
Homes for the Aged ... 2
Total Assisted ... 662
Residential Care of Children ... 1
Total Assisted ... 92
Day Care Centers ... 5
Total Assisted ... 3,705
Specialized Homes ... 4
Total Assisted ... 968
Special Centers for Social Services ... 16
Total Assisted ... 139,264
Residential Care of Disabled ... 1
Total Assisted ... 92
Other Institutions ... 5
Total Assisted ... 33,879

Educational
Seminaries, Diocesan ... 2
Students from This Diocese ... 48
Students from Other Dioceses ... 12
Students, Religious ... 2
Total Seminarians ... 50
Colleges and Universities ... 3
Total Students ... 5,396
High Schools, Diocesan and Parish ... 5
Total Students ... 2,368
High Schools, Private ... 15
Total Students ... 9,408
Elementary Schools, Diocesan and Parish ... 78
Total Students ... 24,599
Elementary Schools, Private ... 9
Total Students ... 2,101
Non-residential Schools for the Disabled ... 3
Total Students ... 332
Catechesis/Religious Education:
High School Students ... 1,688
Elementary Students ... 16,097
Total Students under Catholic Instruction ... 62,039
Teachers in Diocese:
Priests ... 31
Scholastics ... 1
Brothers ... 9
Sisters ... 40
Lay Teachers ... 3,051

Vital Statistics
Receptions into the Church:
Infant Baptism Totals ... 4,160
Minor Baptism Totals ... 292
Adult Baptism Totals ... 220
Received into Full Communion ... 707
First Communions ... 4,705
Confirmations ... 4,750
Marriages:
Catholic ... 1,028
Interfaith ... 340
Total Marriages ... 1,368
Deaths ... 6,852
Total Catholic Population ... 604,089
Total Population ... 2,782,321

LEADERSHIP

Office of the Bishop - t) 216-696-6525 x2030 Lisa Leondarides, Exec. Asst.;
Vicar General and Moderator of the Curia - t) 216-696-6525 x3800 Rev. Donald P. Oleksiak;
Vicar General - t) 216-696-6525 x4000 Rev. Gary D. Yanus;
Secretary and Vicar for Clergy and Religious - t) 216-696-6525 x2440 Rev. Daniel F. Schlegel;
Vicar for Evangelization - t) 216-696-6525 x2540 Rev. Damian J. Ference;

ADMINISTRATION

Chancellor - t) 216-696-6525 x2080 Vincent Gardiner;
Archives - t) 216-696-6525 x1270 Emily R Ahlin, Archivist;
Sacramental records - www.dioceseofcleveland.org Kathy C Tempestelli, Registrar;
Finance Office - t) 216-696-6525 x5960 financeoffice@dioceseofcleveland.org James P. Gulick, Finance Officer;
Benefit Plans: Health Benefits, Group Life, and Pension - t) (216) 696-6525 x8760 Donna B. Speagle, Dir.;
Diocesan Insurance Office - John C. Easton, Dir.; Kathleen Pierce;
Human Resources Office - t) (216) 696-6525 x3930 Mary Ann Blakeley, Exec. Dir.;
Workers' Compensation - John C. Easton, Dir.; Kathleen Pierce;
Legal Office - t) 216-696-6525 x1072 legaloffice@dioceseofcleveland.org Kevin T. Burke, Gen. Counsel; Brian Heskamp, Assoc. Gen. Counsel; Kelly Spring, Assoc. Gen. Counsel;

OFFICES AND DIRECTORS

Office for Worship - t) 216-696-6525 x3630 Most Rev. Michael G. Woost, Interim Dir.;
Mission Office, Society for the Propagation of the Faith - t) 216-696-6525 x4240 Rev. R. Stephen Vellenga, Dir.;

ADVISORY BOARDS, COMMISSIONS, COMMITTEES, AND COUNCILS

College of Consultors - Rev. Donald P. Oleksiak; Rev. Lawrence Jurcak; Rev. Edward T. Estok;
Presbyteral Council - Rev. Vincent J. Hawk; Rev. William A. Thaden; Rev. Martin Dober;
Diocesan Finance Council - Michael Meehan, Chair; Jill Branthoover; Donald Dailey;
Diocesan Pastoral Council - Mary Murphy, Chair; James Lepi, Vice Chair;

CANONICAL SERVICES

Secretariat for Canonical Services - t) 216-696-6525 x4000 Rev. Gary D. Yanus, Secy. & Vicar;
Matrimonial Dispensations, Permissions and Nihil Obstat - Lee Ann Calvert, Contact;
Lawyers' Guild of the Catholic Diocese of Cleveland - Rev. Gary D. Yanus;

CLERGY AND RELIGIOUS SERVICES

Secretariat for Clergy and Religious - t) 216-696-6525 x2440 Rev. Daniel F. Schlegel, Secy. & Vicar;
Delegate for Senior Priests - Rev. John C. Chlebo, Delegate;
Delegate for Senior Deacons - Dcn. Edmund A. Gardias;
Delegate for Religious - t) 216-696-6525 x2920 Sr. Mary Alice Mrema, CBNK, Dir.;
Continuing Education and Formation of Ministers - t) 440-943-7474 Rev. Thomas M. Dragga, Dir.;
Vocation Office - t) 440-943-7660 Rev. Eric S. Garris, Dir.;
Avilas of the Diocese of Cleveland - t) 440-442-7538 Marlyn Tunnell, Pres.;
Permanent Diaconate Formation Office - t) 440-943-7652 Dcn. George P. Malec, Dir.;
Clergy Pension Plan: Retirement Committee - Rev. Michael J. Troha, Chair (stignatiusparish@aol.com); Rev. Gary D. Yanus, Correspondence Secy.;

COMMUNICATIONS

Office of Communications - t) 216-696-6525 x3290 Nancy Fishburn, Exec. Dir. (nfishburn@dioceseofcleveland.org);

EDUCATION

Secretariat for Education - t) 216-696-6525 x1022 folinn@dioceseofcleveland.org Dr. Frank O'Linn, Secy. Educ. & Supt. Schools;
Assistant Superintendent - Elementary Schools - sbiggs@dioceseofcleveland.org Susan Biggs;
Assistant Superintendent - Elementary Schools - mdietz@dioceseofcleveland.org Monica Dietz;
Associate Superintendent, Secondary Schools - t) 216-696-6525 x4980 Michael Zelenka;
Associate Superintendent - tarnone@dioceseofcleveland.org Tracey Arnone;
Catholic Education Endowment Trust - cwilliams@dioceseofcleveland.org Cindy Williams;
Curriculum - jmiroglotta@dioceseofcleveland.org Jennifer Miroglotta, Coord.;
Educational Technology - dbruno@dioceseofcleveland.org Dolores Bruno;
Enrollment Management Coordinator - dhummon@dioceseofcleveland.org Dene Hummon;
Finance/School Controller - dbeckstrom@dioceseofcleveland.org Dennis Beckstrom;
Government Programs - pouzts@dioceseofcleveland.org Pam Ouzts, Dir.;
Mandated Services - pouzts@dioceseofcleveland.org Pamela Ouzts, Coord.;
Nutrition Services/Summer Food Program - emorel@dioceseofcleveland.org Edward Morel, Dir.;
Special Education - bettertogether@dioceseofcleveland.org
Special Projects/Voucher Programs - pouzts@dioceseofcleveland.org Pamela Ouzts, Coord.;
Teacher Personnel Services - mhokanson@dioceseofcleveland.org Melissa Hokanson, Dir.;
Technology - tmcbride@dioceseofcleveland.org Thomas McBride, Dir.;
Tuition Assistance - t) 216-696-6525 x1032

FAITH FORMATION

Secretariat for Catechetical Formation - t) 216-696-6525 x3220 Gregory Coogan (gcoogan@dioceseofcleveland.org);
Catechetical Formation Consultants -
Central - t) 216-696-6525 x3380 lmcbride@dioceseofcleveland.org Laura McBride;
West and Hispanic Parishes - t) 216-696-6525 x1028 hrodriguez@dioceseofcleveland.org Hortensia Rodriguez;
South - t) 216-696-6525 x8910 dsmithberger@dioceseofcleveland.org Denise Smithberger;
Newman Campus Catholic Ministry - t) 216-696-6525 x3226 jpiotrkowski@dioceseofcleveland.org Dr. Joann Rymarczyk-Piotrkowski, Dir.;
University of Akron - t) 330-208-0703 jszarwark@dioceseofcleveland.org John Szarwark;
Ashland University - t) 419-289-5481 nediger@dioceseofcleveland.org Nate Ediger;
Baldwin Wallace University - t) (216) 696-6525 x3226 Dr. Joann Rymarczyk-Piotrkowski, Interim;
Case Western Reserve University - t) 216-800-8653 sperry@dioceseofcleveland.org Steve Perry;
Cleveland State University - t) (216) 696-6525 x3226 jalto@dioceseofcleveland.org Joseph Alto;
College of Wooster & Oberlin College - t) 330-263-2262 ahoy@dioceseofcleveland.org A.J. Hoy;

PARISH SERVICES

Secretariat for Parish Life and Special Ministries - t) (216) 696-6525 x2540 dference@dioceseofcleveland.org Rev. Damian J. Ference, Secy. & Vicar for Evangelization;
Assistant Secretary - t) 216-696-6525 x2550 lsaenz@dioceseofcleveland.org Lynette Saenz;
Diocesan Interfaith Commission - t) 216-696-6525 x5110 Rev. Joseph T. Hilinski, Delegate;
Office for Human Life - t) 216-696-6525 x2335 Mary Von Carlowitz, Dir.;
Office of Lay Ecclesial Ministry - t) 440-943-7672 Michelle Nowak, Dir.;
Office of Black Catholic Ministries - t) (216) 696-6525 x3020 Sr. Jane Nesmith, S.B.S., Dir.;
Office for the Protection of Children and Youth - t) 216-696-6525 x1157 Sharon Minson, Dir.;
Office of Hispanic Ministry - t) 216-696-6525 x4300 Misael Mayorga, Dir.;
Office of Marriage and Family Ministry - t) 216-696-6525 x2322 Teresa Yohman, Dir.;
Office of Missionary Discipleship - t) 216-696-6525 x2552 Christy Cabaniss;
Office of Young Adult Ministry - t) 216-696-6525 x2331 Michael Hayes, Dir.;
Office of Youth Ministry - t) 216-696-6525 x2334 Francine Costantini, Dir.;
Apostleship of the Sea Chaplain for the Diocese of Cleveland (Port Chaplain) - Rev. Walter H. Jenne, Chap.;
Ethnic Ministries - t) 216-696-6525 x2550 Lynette Saenz;
Korean Catholic Apostolate (see Saint Andrew Kim Pastoral Center) -
Philippine-American Ministry - t) 216-771-6666 Rev. Joselito delos Reyes;
Vietnamese-American Ministry - t) 216-961-2713 x2540 Rev. Hilary Khanh Hai Nguyen, C.R.M.;

TRIBUNAL

Tribunal - t) 216-696-6525 x4000 Rev. Gary D. Yanus, Judicial Vicar;
Adjunct Judicial Vicars - Rev. Richard Bona; Rev. Charles F. Strebler;
Judges - Vincent Gardiner; Lynette Tait;
Defenders of the Bond - Rev. Timothy J. Roth; Rev. A. Jonathan Zingales; Rev. Joseph A. Bacevice;
Promoters of Justice - Rev. Richard Bona; Rev. A. Jonathan Zingales;
Staff Advocate (DC art. 133) - Rev. Adam A. Zajac;
Auditors - Kristen L. Craig; Mollie Kulig; Jill M. Latkovich;
Ecclesiastical Notaries & Notaries Public - Lee Ann Calvert; Amanda L. Hockenberry; Anita Tokarcik;

PARISHES, MISSIONS, AND CLERGY

STATE OF OHIO

AKRON

St. Anthony of Padua - 83 Mosser Pl., Akron, OH 44310-3184 t) 330-762-7277; 330-762-7278 www.stanthony-akron.com Rev. Edward A. Burba, Pst.; Terri Bullock, DRE; CRP Stds.: 13
St. Anthony of Padua School - (Grades K-8) 80 E. York St., Akron, OH 44310 t) 330-253-6918 sch_stanthonyakron@dioceseofcleveland.org Kathleen Wolf, Prin.;
Convent - 93 Mosser Pl., Akron, OH 44310
St. Bernard Parish - 44 University Ave., Akron, OH 44308-1609 t) 330-253-5161 communications@stbernardstmary.org Rev. Christopher J. Zerucha, Pst.; Dcn. Ramon DiMascio; Rev. Frank Basa, In Res.;
Blessed Trinity - 300 E. Tallmadge Ave., Akron, OH 44310-2399 t) 330-376-5144

blessedtrinityakron@dioceseofcleveland.org www.blessedtrinityakron.org Rev. Joseph A. Warner, Pst.; Dcn. John J. Hirnikl; Terri Bullock, DRE; CRP Stds.: 11

St. Francis de Sales - 4019 Manchester Rd., Akron, OH 44319-2193 t) 330-644-2225 parishoffice@stfparish.com www.stfparish.com Rev. Jeremy D. Merzweiler, Pst.; Rev. David Verbsky, Par. Vicar; Dcn. Raymond S. Herrick; Dcn. Richard C. Butz; CRP Stds.: 145

St. Francis de Sales School - (Grades PreK-8) 4009 Manchester Rd., Akron, OH 44319 t) 330-644-0638 mrskdougherty@stfparishschool.org stfparishschool.org Kathryn Dougherty, Prin.;

Immaculate Conception - 2101 17th St. S.W., Akron, OH 44314 t) 330-753-8429 ickenmore@yahoo.com www.ickenmore.org Melissa Keegan, Parish Life Coord.; Rev. Samuel R. Ciccolini, In Res.;

St. John the Baptist - 1044 Brown St., Akron, OH 44301-1596; Mailing: 87 Broad St., Akron, OH 44305 t) 330-535-4502 visitationofmary@dioceseofcleveland.org Rev. Dismas Byarugaba, A.J., Admin.; Edward Coia, Bus. Mgr.; Raymond Schmidt, Music Min.;

St. Mary - 750 S. Main St., Akron, OH 44311; Mailing: 44 University Ave., Akron, OH 44308 t) 330-253-5161 info@stbernardstmary.org Rev. Christopher J. Zerucha, Pst.; Dcn. Ramon DiMascio;

St. Mary School - (Grades K-8) 44 University Ave., Akron, OH 44308-1609; Mailing: 750 S. Main St., Akron, OH 44311 t) 330-253-1233 pnugent@stmaryakron.com Patricia Nugent, Prin.;

St. Matthew - 2603 Benton Ave., Akron, OH 44312-1694 t) 330-733-9944 gmichael@stmatthewparish.net stmatthewparish.net Rev. G. Michael Williamson, Pst.; CRP Stds.: 89

Nativity of the Lord Jesus - 2425 Myersville Rd., Akron, OH 44312-4951 t) 330-699-5086; 330-699-5086 x1016 (CRP) father@nativityofthelord.org; nativitydre@nativityofthelord.org www.nativityofthelord.org Rev. Zachary M. Kawalec, Pst.; CRP Stds.: 42

St. Paul - 1580 Brown St., Akron, OH 44301-2798; Mailing: 433 Mission Dr., Akron, OH 44301 t) 330-724-1263 www.stpaulparishakron.org Rev. Matthew E. Pfeiffer, Pst.; Dcn. John Amedeo; Jeanne Bearer, Bus. Mgr.;

St. Sebastian - 476 Mull Ave., Akron, OH 44320-1299 t) 330-836-2233 johnsonj@stsebastian.org; church@stsebastian.org www.stsebastian.org Rev. John A. Valencheck, Pst.; Rev. Jozef A. Bozek (Poland), Par. Vicar; Keith Johnson, DRE; CRP Stds.: 61

St. Sebastian School - 500 Mull Ave., Akron, OH 44320 t) 330-836-9107 sch_stsebastian@dioceseofcleveland.org Anthony Rohr, Prin.;

St. Vincent de Paul Parish - 164 W. Market St., Akron, OH 44303-2373 t) 330-535-3135 support@stvincentchurch.com www.stvincentchurch.com Rev. Norman K. Douglas, Pst.; Rev. David J. Halaiko, In Res.; Rita Kingsbury, Dir., Faith Formation; CRP Stds.: 27

St. Vincent de Paul Parish School - (Grades PreK-8) 17 S. Maple St., Akron, OH 44303 t) 330-762-5912 Diane Salamon, Prin.;

Visitation of Mary - 87 Broad St., Akron, OH 44305 t) 330-535-4141 visitationofmary@dioceseofcleveland.org www.visitationofmary.org Rev. Dismas Byarugaba, A.J., Admin.; Rev. Bernard Kyara, A.J., In Res.; Rev. Odemary Bahati Kisaka, AJ, In Res.; Dcn. Scott T. Proper; David Jordan, Music Min.; Edward Coia, Bus. Mgr.; Diana Herhold, Pastoral Min.;

AMHERST

St. Joseph - 200 St. Joseph Dr., Amherst, OH 44001-1663 t) 440-988-2848 parishoffice@stjosephamherst.com stjosephamherst.com Rev. Timothy J. O'Connor, Pst.; Sharon Angell, Bus. Mgr.; Kailey Baca, Dir., Youth Activities; Christina Dupre, Worship & Liturgy Coord.; Angela Ann Eads, Prin. Parish School of Rel.; CRP Stds.: 118

St. Joseph School - (Grades PreK-8) 175 St. Joseph Dr., Amherst, OH 44001 t) 440-988-4244 sch_stjosephamherst@dioceseofcleveland.org www.sjsamherst.org Amy Makruski, Prin.; Stds.: 197; Lay Tchrs.: 14

Convent - 151 St. Joseph Dr., Amherst, OH 44001 t) (440) 988-2848 (Parish Office)

ASHLAND

St. Edward - 501 Cottage St., Ashland, OH 44805-2167 t) 419-289-7224 Rev. Rodney A. Kreidler, Pst.; CRP Stds.: 35

St. Edward School - (Grades PreSchool-8) 433 Cottage St., Ashland, OH 44805 t) 419-289-7456 principal@stedwardashland.org; school@stedwardashland.org www.stedwardashland.org Suellen Valentine, Prin.;

AVON

Holy Trinity - 33601 Detroit Rd., Avon, OH 44011-1999 t) 440-937-5363 office@holytrinityavon.com holytrinityavon.com/ Rev. Vincent J. Hawk, Pst.; CRP Stds.: 340

Holy Trinity School - (Grades PreK-8) 2610 Nagel Rd., Avon, OH 44011 t) 440-937-6420 michael.modzeleski@htsavon.org Kim Kuchta, Prin.; Michael Modzeleski, Prin.;

St. Mary of the Immaculate Conception - 2640 Stoney Ridge Rd., Avon, OH 44011-1899 t) 440-934-4212 parish@stmaryavon.org www.stmaryavon.org Rev. C. Thomas Cleaton, Pst.; Dcn. Daniel J. Hancock; CRP Stds.: 210

St. Mary of the Immaculate Conception School (St. Mary - Avon) - (Grades PreK-8) 2680 Stoney Ridge Rd., Avon, OH 44011-1899 t) 440-934-6246 cschager@stmayravon.org Bart Chatfield, Prin.;

AVON LAKE

Holy Spirit - 410 Lear Rd., Avon Lake, OH 44012-2004 t) 440-933-3777 hsp@hspal.org www.hspal.org Rev. Charles F. Strebler, Pst.; Rev. Daniel R. Fickes, In Res.; Dcn. Robert K. Walling; Michael Schmiesing, Pastoral Asst.; Nathan Hetrick, Music Min.; Dr. William Christopher Hoag, DRE; CRP Stds.: 164

St. Joseph - 32929 Lake Rd., Avon Lake, OH 44012-1497 t) 440-933-3152 office@stjosephavonlake.org www.stjosephavonlake.org/ Rev. Ronald Wearsch, Pst.; Dcn. Keith A. Jenkins; Rozann Swanson, DRE; CRP Stds.: 325

St. Joseph School - 32946 Electric Blvd., Avon Lake, OH 44012 t) 440-933-6233 principal@stjosephavonlake.org John Stipek, Prin.;

BARBERTON

St. Augustine - 204 Sixth St., N.W., Barberton, OH 44203-2198 t) 330-745-0011 www.staugustinebarberton.org Rev. David J. Majikas, Pst.; CRP Stds.: 49

St. Augustine School - 195 Seventh St., N.W., Barberton, OH 44203 t) 330-753-6435 sch_staugustine@dioceseofcleveland.org www.staugschool.net Elaine Faessel, Prin.;

BAY VILLAGE

St. Raphael - 525 Dover Center Rd., Bay Village, OH 44140-2366 t) 440-871-1100 Rev. Timothy W. Gareau, Pst.; Rev. James T. Winings, Par. Vicar; Dcn. Larry D. Gregg; Terri Telepak, Pst. Assoc.; CRP Stds.: 406

St. Raphael School - t) 440-871-6760 amiller@saintraphaelparish.com Ann Miller, Prin.;

BEDFORD

St. Mary - 340 Union St., Bedford, OH 44146-4594 t) 440-359-8205 www.saintmarybedford.org Rev. Joseph G. Seebauer, Pst.;

Our Lady of Hope - 400 Center Rd., Bedford, OH 44146-2296 t) 400-232-8166 ourladyofhopebedford.org Rev. Joseph G. Seebauer, Pst.;

BEREA

St. Adalbert - 66 Adalbert St., Berea, OH 44017-1799 t) 440-234-6830 saintadalbertparish.org Rev. Charles Butkowski, Pst.; Dcn. Edmund A. Gardias; CRP Stds.: 36

St. Mary - 250 Kraft, Berea, OH 44017 t) 440-243-3877 information@stmaryberea.org stmaryberea.org Rev. John P. Singler, Pst.; Rev. Thomas E. Stock, Par. Vicar; Dcn. Thomas A. Cully; Rev. Robert J. Cole, In Res.; CRP Stds.: 82

St. Mary School - (Grades PreK-8) 265 Baker St., Berea, OH 44017-1515 t) 440-243-4555 info@smsberea.org Andrew Carner, Prin.;

BRECKSVILLE

St. Basil the Great - 8700 Brecksville Rd., Brecksville, OH 44141-1999 t) 440-526-3520 (CRP); 440-526-1686 www.basilthegreat.org Rev. Ryan J. Mann, Pst.; Dcn. Dave Pecot; Gregory Paparizos, Music Min.; Stephanie Baka, Dir., Music Ministry; Tommy Dome, Dir. Evangelization; Erin Prokop, Dir. Youth Ministry; Terri Shawhan, Pastoral Asst.; Robin Youngs, Parish Life Activities Coord.; Andrea Wasinski, DRE; CRP Stds.: 581

BROADVIEW HEIGHTS

Assumption - 9183 Broadview Rd., Broadview Heights, OH 44147-2596 t) 440-526-1177 www.coabvm.org Rev. Justin Dyrwal, O.S.B., Pst.; Rev. Louis Michael Carey, O.S.B., Assoc. Pst.; Dcn. David A. Streeter; Mary Zabrecky, DRE; CRP Stds.: 90

Assumption School (St. Albert the Great at Assumption Academy) - (Grades PreK-8) t) 440-526-4877 sch_assumption@dioceseofcleveland.org Richard Kaliszewski, Prin.;

BROOK PARK

Mary, Queen of the Apostles Parish - 6455 Engle Rd., Brook Park, OH 44142 t) (216) 433-1440 mqabrookpark@gmail.com mqabrookpark.org Rev. James R. Stenger, Pst.; Rev. Robert J. Reidy, Par. Vicar; Dcn. Thomas P. Bizon; Patricia Solon, DRE; CRP Stds.: 57

BROOKLYN

St. Thomas More - 4170 N. Amber Dr., Brooklyn, OH 44144-1399 t) 216-749-0414 psr@stmparish.net; rectory@stmparish.net stmparish.net Rev. Michael J Feldtz, Admin.; Terri Sozio, DRE; CRP Stds.: 18

St. Thomas More School - 4180 N. Amber Dr., Brooklyn, OH 44144 t) 216-749-1660 jfrancis@stmschool.com Jennifer Francis, Prin.;

BRUNSWICK

St. Ambrose - 929 Pearl Rd., Brunswick, OH 44212-2597 t) 330-460-7300 jmajka@stambrose.us; bstec@stambrose.us stambrose.us/ Rev. Robert G. Stec, Pst.; Rev. Andrew J. Hoover, Par. Vicar; Dcn. Matthew Harley; Dcn. Frank Weglicki; Dcn. Thomas J. Sheridan; Janet Majka, DRE; CRP Stds.: 680

St. Ambrose School - (Grades PreSchool-8) 923 Pearl Rd., Brunswick, OH 44212 t) 330-460-7301 lcinadr@staschool.us www.saintambroseschool.us Lisa Cinadr, Prin.;

St. Colette - 330 W. 130th St., Brunswick, OH 44212-2309 t) 330-273-5500 cmpizon@gmail.com stcolettecatholicchurch.com Rev. William R. Krizner, Pst.; Rev. Thomas G. Montavon, Pastor Emer.; Lisa Radey, Pst. Assoc.; Larry Pizon, DRE; Chris Pizon, DRE; CRP Stds.: 291

CHAGRIN FALLS

Holy Angels - 18205 Chillicothe Rd., Chagrin Falls, OH 44023-4879 t) 440-708-0808 (CRP); 440-708-0000 office@holyangelschurch.com; cathy@holyangelschurch.com www.holyangelschurch.com Rev. G. Max Cole, Pst.; Rev. George Smiga, Par. Vicar; Dcn. Gerard Ziemkiewicz; CRP Stds.: 488

St. Joan of Arc - 496 E. Washington St., Chagrin Falls, OH 44022-2999 t) 440-247-3606 (CRP); 440-247-7183 officeoffaithformation@stjoanofarc.org stjoanofarcchurch.org Rev. Gary J. Malin, Pst.; Rev. John R. Olsavsky, Pastor Emer.; Dcn. Jeffrey Dunlop; Dcn. Dennis A. Guritza; Mary Vincenti, Pst. Min./Coord.; Amanda Haberman, DRE; CRP Stds.: 210

St. Joan of Arc School - 498 E. Washington St., Chagrin Falls, OH 44022-2998 t) 440-247-6530 sdibacco@stjoanofarc.org Shelley DiBacco, Prin.;

CHARDON

St. Mary - 401 North St., Chardon, OH 44024 t) 440-285-7051 stmarychardon.org/ Rev. Scott D Goodfellow, Admin.; Dcn. Lawrence Boehnlein; Dcn. Thomas J. Peshek; CRP Stds.: 278

St. Mary School - t) 440-286-3590 mpetelin@stmarychardon.org Julie Fedak, Prin.;

CHESTERLAND

St. Anselm - 12969 Chillicothe Rd., Chesterland, OH 44026-3115 t) 440-729-9575 nmarra@ursulinesisters.org; office@stanselm.org www.stanselm.org Rev. Christopher A. Cox, Admin.; Dcn. Robert Kovach; Sr. Denise Marie Vlna, O.S.U., Pst. Assoc.; Sr. Noel Marra, DRE; Sr. Mary Ellen Brinovec, O.S.U., RCIA Coord.; CRP Stds.: 229

St. Anselm School - (Grades PreK-8) 13013 Chillicothe Rd., Chesterland, OH 44026 t) 440-729-7806 office@stanselmschool.org stanselmschool.org Adam Cottos, Prin.; Stds.: 215; Scholastics: 15; Lay Tchrs.: 14

Convent - 13055 Chillicothe Rd., Chesterland, OH 44026 t) (440) 729-9575

CLEVELAND

Cathedral of St. John the Evangelist - 1007 Superior Ave. E., Cleveland, OH 44114-2582 t) 216-771-6666 stjohns@dioceseofcleveland.org saintjohncathedral.com Rev. Sean P. Ralph, Rector; Rev. Joselito delos Reyes, Par. Vicar; Rev. Eric S. Garris, In Res.; Rev. Donald P. Oleksiak, In Res.; Rev. Daniel F. Schlegel, In Res.; Carolyn Apperson-Hansen, DRE; CRP Stds.: 17

St. Adalbert - 2347 E. 83rd St., Cleveland, OH 44104 t) 216-881-7647; 216-881-6250 garychmura@stadalbertschool.net stadalbertschool.net Rev. Gary D. Chmura, Pst.;

Saint Adalbert Catholic School - (Grades PreK-8) 2345 E. 83rd St., Cleveland, OH 44104 jdsmith@stadalbertschool.net www.stadalbertschool.net James Smith, Prin.;

St. Agnes - Our Lady of Fatima - 6800 Lexington Ave., Cleveland, OH 44103-3297 t) 216-391-1655 pastor@saolf.org; agnesfatimaclev@dioceseofcleveland.org www.saolf.org Rev. James Watson, OFM Cap, Pst.; Rev. David Domanski, OFM Cap, Par. Vicar; Dcn. Hardin M. Martin; CRP Stds.: 30

St. Aloysius - St. Agatha - 10932 St. Clair Ave., Cleveland, OH 44108-1939 t) 216-451-3262 mjraymon@yahoo.com Rev. Anthony Simone, Par. Vicar; Sr. Mary Jean Raymond, Parish Life Coord.; CRP Stds.: 10

St. Aloysius - St. Agatha School - (Grades PreK-8) 640 Lakeview Rd., Cleveland, OH 44108 t) 216-451-2050 sch_stagathastal@dioceseofcleveland.org staloysiuscleveland.com K Frank Jones, Prin.; Mary Ann Okey, Vice Prin.; Stds.: 276; Lay Tchrs.: 15

St. Andrew Kim Pastoral Center - 2310 W. 14th St., Cleveland, OH 44113-3613 t) 216-861-4630 Rev. Seonghoon Cheong, Pst.; Dcn. Charles C. Shin; CRP Stds.: 33

St. Augustine - 2486 W. 14th St., Cleveland, OH 44113-4449 t) 216-781-5530 staugch@earthlink.net www.staugustinecleveland.org Rev. William O'Donnell, C.PP.S, Admin.; Rev. Benjamin P. Jimenez, S.J., Par. Vicar; Dcn. Christopher DePenti; Dcn. David Mayer; Robert Duda, Pst. Min./Coord.; CRP Stds.: 24

St. Barbara - 1505 Denison Ave., Cleveland, OH 44109-2890 t) 216-661-1191 st.barbara@att.net Rev. Joseph Hilinski, Pst.;

Blessed Trinity Parish - 14040 Puritas Ave., Cleveland, OH 44135-2822 t) 216-671-5890 office@blessedtrinitycleveland.org www.blessedtrinitycleveland.org Rev. Douglas H. Koesel, Pst.; Dcn. Richard C. Beercheck; Kathleen Corbett, Pst. Assoc.; CRP Stds.: 21

St. Boniface - 3545 W. 54th St., Cleveland, OH 44102-5798 t) 216-961-2713 c) (216) 269-3353 (Parish Secy.) Rev. Hilary Khanh Nguyen, Pst.; Katherine Stary, DRE; CRP Stds.: 20

St. Casimir - 8223 Sowinski Ave., Cleveland, OH 44103-2298 t) 216-341-9091 pastorkaz@hotmail.com st.casimir.com Polish Rev. Eric S. Orzech, Pst.;

St. Casimir - 18022 Neff Rd., Cleveland, OH 44119-2644 t) 216-481-3157 www.saintcasimirparish.org Rev. Joseph A. Bacevice, Pst.;

St. Colman - 2027 W. 65th St., Cleveland, OH 44102-4394 t) 216-651-0550 Rev. Caroli Borromeo Shao, A.J., Pst.; Sr. Audrey Koch, C.S.J., Pst. Assoc.; Rev. Benjamin Koka, A.J., Par. Vicar; CRP Stds.: 19

Convent - 2007 W. 65th St., Cleveland, OH 44102

St. Elizabeth of Hungary - 9016 Buckeye Rd., Cleveland, OH 44104-0175 t) 216-231-0325 www.stelizabethcleveland.org/ Rev. Richard Bona, Pst.;

St. Emeric - 1860 W. 22nd St., Cleveland, OH 44113-3185 t) 216-965-0061 stemeric.com/ Rev. Richard Bona, Pst.;

Holy Name - 8328 Broadway Ave., S.E., Cleveland, OH 44105-3931 t) 216-271-4242 www.holynamecleveland.org Rev. Msgr. Richard C. Antall, Pst.;

Holy Name School - (Grades K-8) t) 216-341-0084 jones@holyname-elementary.org Lorenzo Jones, Prin.;

Holy Redeemer - 15712 Kipling Ave., Cleveland, OH 44110-3104 t) 216-531-3313 holyredeemerparish@gmail.com www.holyredeemer-cleveland.weconnect.com Rev. Martin F. Polito, Pst.; Dayna White, DRE; Joel Pantano, Bus. Mgr.; CRP Stds.: 12

Holy Rosary - 12021 Mayfield Rd., Cleveland, OH 44106-1996 t) 216-421-2995 www.holy-rosary.org Rev. Joseph Previte, Pst.; Dcn. Bruce J. Battista; Lorenzo Salvagni, Music Min.; Laura Bastulli-Parran, Pst. Assoc.; Tammy Moore, Pst. Assoc.; CRP Stds.: 38

St. Ignatius of Antioch - 10205 Lorain Ave., Cleveland, OH 44111-5435 t) 216-251-0300 ignatiusofantioch@dioceseofcleveland.org sioa.weconnect.com/ Rev. Kevin E. Estabrook, Pst.; CRP Stds.: 3

St. Ignatius of Antioch School - t) 216-671-0535 sch_stignatiuses@dioceseofcleveland.org Margaret Ricksecker, Prin.;

Immaculate Conception - 4129 Superior Ave., Cleveland, OH 44103-1179 t) 216-431-5900 Rev. Frank G. Godic, Pst.; Rev. John J. Hayes, In Res.;

Immaculate Heart of Mary - 6700 Lansing Ave., Cleveland, OH 44105-3797 t) 216-341-2734; 216-341-2735 www.immaculateheartchurch.org Rev. Ralph Hudak, Pst.; Rev. Andrzej Panek, Assoc. Pst.; CRP Stds.: 12

Convent - 6804 Lansing Ave., Cleveland, OH 44105

St. Jerome - 15000 Lake Shore Blvd., Cleveland, OH 44110-1298 t) 216-481-8200 jeromeclev@dioceseofcleveland.org www.stjeromecleveland.org Rev. Joseph J. Fortuna, Admin.; Rev. Anthony Simone, Par. Vicar; Dcn. Peter Travalik; Marguerite DiPenti, DRE; Cathy Brown, Bus. Mgr.; CRP Stds.: 9

St. Jerome School - 15100 Lake Shore Blvd., Cleveland, OH 44110 t) 216-486-3587 sch_stjerome@dioceseofcleveland.org Susan Coan, Prin.;

St. John Cantius - 906 College Ave., S.W., Cleveland, OH 44113-4494 t) 216-781-9095 froach@stjohncantiuschurch.org www.stjohncantiuschurch.org Rev. James Roach, Pst.; Joseph Sutowski, Music Min.; CRP Stds.: 12

St. John Nepomucene - 3785 Independence Rd., Cleveland, OH 44105-3357 t) 216-641-8444; 216-641-8445 fatherjasany@st-john-nepomucene.org; sjnsyody@st-john-nepomucene.org st-john-nepomucene.org Rev. Robert J. Jasany, Pst.; CRP Stds.: 5

St. Leo the Great - 4940 Broadview Rd., Cleveland, OH 44109-5799 t) 216-661-1006 info@leothegreat.org; ncapone@leothetgreat.org leothegreat.org Rev. James P. Schmitz, Pst.; Joan Berigan, Pst. Min./Coord.; Joann Deranek, DRE; CRP Stds.: 23

St. Leo the Great School - 4900 Broadview Rd., Cleveland, OH 44109 t) 216-661-2120 dburns@leothegreat.org Denise Burns, Prin.;

St. Malachi - 2459 Washington Ave., Cleveland, OH 44113-2380 t) 216-861-5343 rectory@stmalachi.org; jeanette.s@stmalachi.org www.stmalachi.org Rev. Michael K. Gurnick, Admin.; Stephanie Pritts, DRE; CRP Stds.: 3

St. Mark - 15800 Montrose Ave., Cleveland, OH 44111 t) 216-226-7577 jpuckett@stmarkcleveland.com stmarkcleveland.com Rev. Adam A. Zajac, Pst.; Dcn. David J. Lundeen, Bus. Mgr.; CRP Stds.: 42

St. Mark School - 15724 Montrose Ave., Cleveland, OH 44111 t) 216-521-4115 cocita@stmarkwestpark.com

St. Mary - 15519 Holmes Ave., Cleveland, OH 44110-2497 t) 216-761-7740 www.stmaryscollinwood.com Rev. John M. Kumse, Pst.; Dcn. David S. Kushner; CRP Stds.: 33

Mary Queen of Peace - 4423 Pearl Rd., Cleveland, OH 44109-4266 t) 216-749-2323 info@maryqop.org www.maryqop.org Rev. Douglas T. Brown, Pst.; CRP Stds.: 18

Mary Queen of Peace Elementary School - (Grades PreSchool-8) 4419 Pearl Rd., Cleveland, OH 44109-4268 t) 216-741-3685 jessica.robertson@maryqueenofpeaceschool.com maryqueenofpeaceschool.com/ Jessica Robertson, Prin.; Nicholas Blazek, Vice Prin.; Stds.: 302; Lay Tchrs.: 22

St. Mel - 14436 Triskett Rd., Cleveland, OH 44111-2263 t) 216-941-4313 www.stmel.net Rev. Adam A. Zajac, Pst.; Rev. Gary D. Yanus, In Res.; CRP Stds.: 3

St. Michael the Archangel - 3114 Scranton Rd., Cleveland, OH 44109-1632 t) 216-621-3847 info@smacleveland.net www.smacleveland.net Rev. Mark R. Riley, Pst.; Rev. James H. McCreight, Pastor Emer.; Rev. Dennis R. O'Grady, Pastor Emer.; Dcn. Gonzalo Lopez; Dcn. Francisco A. Miranda; Sr. Juana Mendez, Pst. Min./Coord.; Marlene Rios, DRE; Robert Dillon, Music Min.; CRP Stds.: 43

Our Lady of Angels - 3644 Rocky River Dr., Cleveland, OH 44111-3998 t) 216-252-2332 eme@olangels.org www.olangels.org Dcn. Mark Yantek;

Our Lady of Angels Parish - (Grades PreK-8) t) 216-251-6841 kkrupar@olangels.org Kathy Krupar, Prin.;

Our Lady of Lourdes - 3395 E. 53rd St., Cleveland, OH 44127-1692 t) 216-641-2829 olol@ourladyoflourdes-cle.com ourladyoflourdes-cle.com Rev. Joseph H. Callahan, Pst.; Michael Irizarry, Music Min.; Mayumi Naramura, Music Min.; Sr. Charlotte Hobelman, SND, Pst. Min./Coord.; Sr. Charlotte Hocevar, Pst. Min./Coord.; Eileen M. Murray, Bus. Mgr.; CRP Stds.: 54

Convent - 3401 E. 53rd St., Cleveland, OH 44127

Our Lady of Mount Carmel - 6928 Detroit Ave., Cleveland, OH 44102-3093 t) 216-651-5043 olmc.cleveland@gmail.com www.olmcchurchcleveland.org/ CRP Stds.: 185

Our Lady of Mount Carmel School - (Grades K-8) 1355 W. 70th St., Cleveland, OH 44102 t) 216-281-7146 sch_olmtcarmelclev@dioceseofcleveland.org Danielle Blansette, Prin.; Gina Feijoo, Vice Prin.; Michael Shumate, Bus. Mgr.; Stds.: 187; Sr. Tchrs.: 3; Lay Tchrs.: 9

Convent - t) 216-281-9304

Our Lady of Peace - 12601 Shaker Blvd., Cleveland, OH 44120-1498; Mailing: 12503 Buckingham Ave., Cleveland, OH 44120 t) 216-421-4211 jlpekoc@yahoo.com; office@olpchurch.com www.olpchurch.com Rev. Gary Chmura, Pst.; Rev. Andrew Morkunas, In Res.; Jean Pekoc, DRE; CRP Stds.: 47

St. Patrick - 3602 Bridge Ave., Cleveland, OH 44113-3314 t) 216-631-6872 www.stpatrickbridge.org/ Rev. Michael K. Gurnick, Pst.; Rev. Mark L. Hollis, In Res.; Dcn. William Merriman; CRP Stds.: 38

St. Patrick - 4427 Rocky River Dr., Cleveland, OH 44135-2551 t) 216-251-1200 stpatrickparishwp@gmail.com www.stpatrickwp.org Rev. John M. Pfeifer, Pst.; Rev. Clyde K. Foster, Par. Vicar; CRP Stds.: 8

St. Paul - 1369 E. 40th St., Cleveland, OH 44103-1194 t) 216-431-1895 Rev. Zvonko Blasko, Pst.; CRP Stds.: 26

St. Peter - 1533 E. 17th St., Cleveland, OH 44114-2999 t) 216-344-2999 Rev. Philip Bernier, O.F.M. Cap., Admin.;

St. Rocco - 3205 Fulton Rd., Cleveland, OH 44109-1495 t) 216-961-8331 x7008 jchia@saintroccocleveland.com; mbuhaley@saintroccocleveland.com saintroccocleveland.com Rev. James Mayer, O.de.M., Pst.; Rev. Gene Costa, Par. Vicar; Rev. Paschal Rosca, O.de.M., In Res.; Bro. Matthew Levis, Pst. Assoc.; Rev. James Chia, Chap.; CRP Stds.: 5

St. Rocco School - t) 216-961-8557 sch_strocco@dioceseofcleveland.org Renee Cerny, Prin.; Stds.: 137; Lay Tchrs.: 12

Sagrada Familia - 7719 Detroit Ave., Cleveland, OH 44102-2811 t) 216-631-2888 rreidy@dioceseofcleveland.org Rev. Francisco Honorato Garnica, CSJ, Pst.; Dcn. Victor R. Colon; Dcn. Ignacio Miranda; Dcn. Frederick Simon; Dcn. Epifanio Torres; Marylin Caraballo, DRE; CRP Stds.: 50

St. Stanislaus - 3649 E. 65th St., Cleveland, OH 44105-1293 t) 216-341-9091; 216-341-9092 Rev. Eric S. Orzech, Pst.; Dan Kane, Bus. Mgr.; David Krakowski, Dir.;

St. Stanislaus School - 6615 Forman Ave., Cleveland, OH 44105 t) 216-883-3307 martind@ststanislaus.us Deborah Martin, Prin.;

St. Stephen - 1930 W. 54th St., Cleveland, OH 44102-3206 t) 216-631-5633 ststephendh@gmail.com www.ststephencleveland.org Rev. Caroli Borromeo Shao, A.J., Pst.; Rev. Benjamin Koka, A.J., Assoc. Pst.;

Convent - 1891 W. 57th St., Cleveland, OH 44102 t) 216-631-0754

St. Vincent de Paul - 13400 Lorain Ave., Cleveland, OH 44111-3470 t) 216-252-2626 church@svdpcleveland.org www.svdpcleveland.org Rev. John M. Pfeifer, Pst.; Rev. Clyde Foster, Par. Vicar; Dcn. Kenneth J. Hill; David Jaronowski, Bus. Mgr.;

St. Vitus - 6019 Lausche Ave., Cleveland, OH 44103-1455 t) 216-361-1444 frjcretar@gmail.com www.saintvitus.org Personal parish. Rev. John C. Retar, Pst.; Rev. A. Jonathan Zingales, In Res.; Rev. Cirilo A. Nacorda, In Res.; Sr. Mary Avsec, S.N.D., Pst. Assoc.; CRP Stds.: 28

St. Wendelin Parish - 2281 Columbus Rd., Cleveland, OH 44113-4230 t) 216-696-1926 office@stwendelincleveland.org stwendelincleveland.org Rev. Robert J. Kropac, Pst.; Gerald Arnold, Bus. Mgr.; CRP Stds.: 12

CLEVELAND HEIGHTS

Communion of Saints Parish - 2175 Coventry Rd., Cleveland Heights, OH 44118 t) 216-321-0024 office@communionofsaintsparish.org www.communionofsaintsparish.org Two worship sites, St. Ann Church in Cleveland Heights, OH and St. Philomena Church in E. Cleveland, OH Rev. John P. McNulty, Pst.; Joseph Alto, DRE; Lynette Krych, Pst. Min./Coord.; Meg Matuska, Music Min.; CRP Stds.: 44

Communion of Saints Parish School - 2160 Stillman Rd., Cleveland Heights, OH 44118 t) 216-932-4177 gwhiteley@olleuclid.org Loretta Pilla, Prin.;

Worship Site of Communion of Saints Parish at St. Philomena Church - 13824 Euclid Ave., East Cleveland, OH 44112

COLUMBIA STATION

St. Elizabeth Ann Seton - 25801 Royalton Rd., Columbia Station, OH 44028-0968; Mailing: P O Box 968, Columbia Station, OH 44028-0968 t) 440-236-5095 st.elizabethannseton@yahoo.com www.seascolumbiastation.org Rev. Edward T. Holland, Pst.; CRP Stds.: 20

CONCORD TWP.

St. Gabriel - 9925 Johnnycake Ridge Rd., Concord Twp., OH 44060-6294 t) 440-352-8282 phaumesser@st-gabriel.org www.st-gabriel.org Rev. Frederick F. Pausche, Pst.; Rev. David Stavarz, Par. Vicar; Rev. Edward J. Janoch, Par. Vicar; Dcn. Ronald Adkins; Dcn. Daniel P. Clavin; Dcn. Robert H. Grgic; Samantha Coffman, Campus Min.; Kevin Donahue, Music Min.; Maureen Dowd, Pst. Assoc.; Linda Hlebak, Bus. Mgr.; Regina Skrtic, DRE; CRP Stds.: 343

St. Gabriel School - (Grades PreK-8) 9935 Johnnycake Ridge Rd., Concord Twp., OH 44060 t) 440-352-6169 sgsoffice@st-gabrielschool.org www.st-gabrielschool.org Robert M. Kumazec III, Prin.; Leah Myers, Vice Prin.; Stds.: 567; Lay Tchrs.: 30

Convent - 9918 Johnnycake Ridge Rd., Concord Twp., OH 44060

COPLEY

Guardian Angels - 1686 Cleveland-Massillon Rd., Copley, OH 44321-1976 t) 330-666-1373 office@copleyangels.org www.copleyangels.org Rev. Christopher H. Weber, Pst.; CRP Stds.: 71

CUYAHOGA FALLS

St. Eugene - 1821 Munroe Falls Ave., Cuyahoga Falls, OH 44221-3699 t) 330-923-5244 sainteugene.org Rev. Peter Colletti, Pst.; CRP Stds.: 52

Immaculate Heart of Mary - 1905 Portage Tr., Cuyahoga Falls, OH 44223-1792 t) 330-929-8361 jbowling@ihmcfo.org www.ihmcfo.org Rev. James E. Singler, Pst.; Dcn. Gregory Hoefler; Dcn. William J. Yoho Jr.; Rev. Ralph W. Thomas, In Res.; Jeff Mills, Liturgy Dir.; Jeff Andrea, Music Min.; Kira Andrea, Music Min.; Amy Incorvati-Aloisi, Pst. Min./Coord.; Liam Eitman, DRE; CRP Stds.: 91

Immaculate Heart of Mary School - (Grades PreK-8) 2859 Lillis Dr., Cuyahoga Falls, OH 44223 t) 330-923-1220 kfriess@ihmgradeschool.org www.ihmgradeschool.org Kathleen Friess, Prin.; Stds.: 275; Lay Tchrs.: 19

St. Joseph - 1761 Second St., Cuyahoga Falls, OH 44221-3999; Mailing: 215 Falls Ave., Cuyahoga Falls, OH 44221 t) 330-928-2173 Rev. Jared P. Orndorff, Pst.; Dcn. Kent L. Davis; Rev. David J. McCarthy, In Res.; CRP Stds.: 18

St. Joseph School - 1909 Third St., Cuyahoga Falls, OH 44221-3894 t) 330-928-2151 stjoe@saintjoe.org www.saintjoe.org Carrie DePasquale, Prin.;

DOYLESTOWN

SS. Peter and Paul - 161 W. Clinton St., Doylestown, OH 44230-1297 t) 330-658-2145 njohns@stsppc.org www.stspeterpauldoy.weconnect.com Rev. Peter Morris, Admin.; Dcn. Dale A. Youngblood; Rev. David J. McCarthy, Pastor Emer.; CRP Stds.: 56

SS. Peter and Paul School - 169 W. Clinton St., Doylestown, OH 44230 t) 330-658-2804 sch_peternpauldoy@dioceseofcleveland.org Jennifer Rauber, Prin.; Stds.: 70; Lay Tchrs.: 6

EASTLAKE

St. Justin Martyr - 35781 Stevens Blvd., Eastlake, OH 44095-5095 t) 440-946-1177; 440-946-3287 (CRP); 440-946-1178 charles@stjustin.net; sjmoffice@stjustin.net www.stjustin.net Rev. Kevin M. Liebhardt, Pst.; Dcn. Timothy J. Shell; Beth Rossetti, Pst. Assoc.; Charles Hunt, DRE; CRP Stds.: 53

ELYRIA

St. Agnes - 611 Lake Ave., Elyria, OH 44035-3541 t) 440-322-5622 saintagnes@oh.rr.com www.saintagneselyria.church Rev. Charles T. Diedrick, Admin.; Dcn. Bruce H. Tennant; CRP Stds.: 7

St. Jude - 590 Poplar St., Elyria, OH 44035-3999 t) 440-366-5711 sjwebmaster@saintjudeparish.org saintjudeparish.org Rev. Joseph Scalco, CSJ, Pst.; Rev. Richard A. Gonser, In Res.; Rev. Frank P. Kosem, Pastor Emer.; Dcn. Patrick J. Humphrey; CRP Stds.: 52

St. Jude School - (Grades PreK-8) 594 Poplar St., Elyria, OH 44035 t) 440-366-1681 mhibler@stjudejaguars.org www.stjudejaguars.org Molly Hibler, Prin.;

St. Mary - 320 Middle Ave., Elyria, OH 44035 t) 440-322-3054 (CRP); 440-323-5539; 440-323-5530 office@stmaryelyria.com www.stmaryelyria.org Rev. Charles T. Diedrick, Pst.; Dcn. Edward R. Dillon; Dcn. Frank A. Humphrey III; CRP Stds.: 49

St. Mary School - 237 Fourth St., Elyria, OH 44035 t) 440-322-2808 surig@smselyria.org Sharon Urig, Prin.;

St. Vincent de Paul - 41295 N. Ridge Rd., Elyria, OH 44035-1098 t) 440-324-4212 jackiesvdp@gmail.com www.svdpelyria.com Rev. Neil Walters, Admin.; Dcn. Edgar Gonzalez; CRP Stds.: 34

EUCLID

St. John of the Cross - 140 Richmond Rd., Euclid, OH 44143-1299 t) 216-289-0770 info@sjceuclid.com www.sjceuclid.com Rev. John D. Betters, Pst.; Dcn. Thomas Shetina; Rev. Gerald J. Bednar, In Res.; Rev. John F. Loya, In Res.; CRP Stds.: 9

Our Lady of the Lake Parish - 19951 Lake Shore Blvd., Euclid, OH 44119 t) 216-486-0850 joe@olleuclid.org olleuclid.org Rev. Joseph J. Fortuna, Pst.; Dr. Deborah Scopacasa, DRE; CRP Stds.: 13

Our Lady of the Lake Elementary School - 175 E. 200th St., Euclid, OH 44119 t) 216-481-6824 rkingsbury@olleuclid.org Rita Kingsbury, Prin.;

SS. Robert & William - 367 E. 260th St., Euclid, OH 44132-1495 t) 216-731-1515 info@srweuclid.cc www.srweuclid.cc Rev. John D. Betters, Pst.; Rev. Thomas Kowatch, Assoc. Pst.; Renee Barber, Pst. Assoc.; CRP Stds.: 62

SS. Robert & William - 351 E. 260 St., Euclid, OH 44132 t) 216-731-3060 mcosgriff@srwschool.cc www.srwschool.cc Margaret Cosgriff, Prin.; Martha Dodd, Prin.;

FAIRLAWN

St. Hilary - 2750 W. Market St., Fairlawn, OH 44333-4236 t) 330-867-1055 lcamerato@sthilarychurch.org www.sthilarychurch.org Rev. Steven K. Brunovsky, Pst.; Rev. Cameron D. Popik, Par. Vicar; CRP Stds.: 224

St. Hilary School - 645 Moorfield Rd., Fairlawn, OH 44333 t) 330-867-8720 tarnone@st-hilary.com Jennifer Woodman, Prin.;

FAIRPORT HARBOR

St. Anthony of Padua - 316 Fifth St., Fairport Harbor, OH 44077-5696 t) 440-354-4525 steve@stafh.org; gmalec@stafh.org www.stafh.org Rev. Frederick F. Pausche, Moderator; Dcn. George P. Malec, Parish Life Coord.; Dcn. John T. Wenzel; Steve Biro, Youth Min.; CRP Stds.: 56

FAIRVIEW PARK

St. Angela Merici - 20970 Lorain Rd., Fairview Park, OH 44126-2023 t) 440-333-2133 dre@samparish.org; secretary@samparish.org www.samparish.org Rev. Michael J. Lanning, Pst.; Rev. Donald Dunson, Par. Vicar; Dcn. Erick Lupson; Caitlin Smith, Pst. Min./Coord.; Kathleen A. Lynch, DRE; Dcn. James L. Agrippe, Sr. Deacon, Retired; CRP Stds.: 150

St. Angela Merici School - 20830 Lorain Rd., Fairview Park, OH 44126 t) 440-333-2126 sch_stangela@dioceseofcleveland.org Elizabeth Andrachik, Prin.; Lisa Whelan, Prin.; Stds.: 390; Lay Tchrs.: 23

GARFIELD HEIGHTS

Holy Spirit Parish - 4341 E. 131st St., Garfield Heights, OH 44105-5563 t) 216-581-0981 pastor@holyspiritcleveland.org; office@holyspiritcleveland.org www.holyspiritcleveland.org Rev. David Nestler, Pst.; CRP Stds.: 34

St. Monica - 13623 Rockside Rd., Garfield Heights, OH 44125-5197 t) 216-662-8685 sshepka@saintmonicachurch.net www.saintmonicachurch.net Rev. John J. Mullee, Pst.; Rev. Theodore Marszal, Par. Vicar; Rev. Thomas G. Montavon, In Res.; Dcn. Stan Drozell; CRP Stds.: 7

SS. Peter and Paul - 4750 Turney Rd., Garfield Heights, OH 44125-1448 t) 216-429-1515 gkoenig@peterandpaulcleveland.com Rev. John J.

Schneider, Pst.; CRP Stds.: 10
St. Therese - 5276 E. 105th St., Garfield Heights, OH 44125-2698 t) 216-581-2852 www.sttheresegarfield.org Rev. John J. Schneider, Pst.; Dcn. Robert J. Bugaj; Frank Kozuch, Music Min.; Nancy Heineke, DRE; CRP Stds.: 9

GATES MILLS

St. Francis of Assisi - 6850 Mayfield Rd., Gates Mills, OH 44040-9635 t) 440-461-0066 info@stfrancisgm.org www.stfrancisgm.org Rev. Stephen A. Flynn, Pst.; Rev. Peter T. Kovacina, Par. Vicar; Rev. Andrzej Knapik, Chap.; Margaret Zetzer, DRE; CRP Stds.: 200

St. Francis of Assisi School - (Grades PreK-8) t) 440-442-7450 sherman@sfaschoolgm.org www.sfaschoolgm.org Susan Herman, Prin.;

GRAFTON

Our Lady Queen of Peace Parish - 708 Erie St., Grafton, OH 44044 t) 440-926-2364 info@olqpgrafton.org; frjohn@olqpgrafton.org www.olqpgrafton.org Rev. John P. Seabold, Pst.; Elizabeth Miketo, DRE; CRP Stds.: 112

HIGHLAND HEIGHTS

St. Paschal Baylon - 5384 Wilson Mills Rd., Highland Heights, OH 44143-3023 t) 440-442-3410 www.saintpaschal.com Very Rev. John Thomas Joseph Lane Sr., S.S.S., Pst.; Rev. Michael J Arkins, SSS, Par. Vicar; Rev. Juancho Choy Ramos, Par. Vicar; Roberta Modica, Music Min.; George Peko, DRE; Michelle Mazza, Bus. Mgr.; CRP Stds.: 200

St. Paschal Baylon School - 5360 Wilson Mills Rd., Highland Heights, OH 44143 t) 440-442-6766 cjansky@saintpaschal.com Carol Jansky, Prin.;

HINCKLEY

Our Lady of Grace - 1088 Ridge Rd., Hinckley, OH 44233-9602 t) 330-278-4121 psr@olghinckley.org; office@olghinckley.org www.olghinckley.org Rev. William A. Smith, Pst.; Dcn. Bruce E. Dobbins Jr.; Lori Geyer, Music Min.; Marc Weagraff, Music Min.; Bridget Kovalik, DRE; CRP Stds.: 103

HUDSON

St. Mary - 340 N. Main St., Hudson, OH 44236-4720 t) 330-653-8118 frjurcak@stmaryhudson.cc; jstraub@stmaryhudson.cc www.stmaryhudson.cc Rev. Lawrence Jurcak, Pst.; Rev. Scott Swinerton, Par. Vicar; Dcn. Carl H. Winterich; CRP Stds.: 564

INDEPENDENCE

St. Michael - 6912 Chestnut Rd., Independence, OH 44131-3399 t) 216-524-4212 (Dir., Music, DRE); 216-524-1394; 216-524-1395 rectory@stmichaelchurchindependence.org stmichaelchurchindependence.org Rev. Matthew Jordan, Admin.; CRP Stds.: 140

St. Michael School - 6906 Chestnut Rd., Independence, OH 44131 t) 216-524-6405 sch_stmichael@dioceseofcleveland.org Margaret Campisi, Prin.;

KIRTLAND

Divine Word - 8100 Eagle Rd., Kirtland, OH 44094-9714 t) 440-256-1412; 440-256-1413 dwoost@dioceseofcleveland.org; dgermano@divinewordkirtland.org www.divinewordkirtland.org Rev. David G. Woost, Pst.; Dcn. John Grazia; Shari Allwood, Bus. Mgr.; Debbie Lokar, Pst. Assoc.; Mary Pat Frey, Pst. Assoc.; Rebecca Harper, Music Min.; Gina Rensi, DRE; CRP Stds.: 241

LAKEWOOD

St. Clement - 2022 Lincoln Ave., Lakewood, OH 44107-6099 t) 216-226-5116 Rev. Joseph G. Workman, Pst.; Dcn. Daniel L. Bryan; Rev. Deogratias M. Ruwaainenyi, In Res.; CRP Stds.: 29
St. James - 17400 Northwood Ave., Lakewood, OH 44107 t) 216-712-6755 Rev. Joseph G. Workman, Pst.; CRP Stds.: 20
St. Luke - 1212 Bunts Rd., Lakewood, OH 44107-2699 t) 216-521-0184 www.stlukelakewood.org Rev. Kevin P. Elbert, Pst.; Dcn. John D. Henderson; Lawrence Wallace, Music Min.; Joe Costello, Youth Min.; Max Hall, DRE; CRP Stds.: 93
Transfiguration - 12608 Madison Ave., Lakewood, OH 44107 t) 216-521-7288; 216-521-9091 transfiguration@ohiocoxmail.com Rev. Theodore Haag, O.F.M., Pst.;

LITCHFIELD

Our Lady Help of Christians Parish - 9608 Norwalk Rd., Litchfield, OH 44253-9598 t) 330-722-1180 office@olhc-parish.com www.olhc-parish.com Rev. Edward F. Suszynski Jr., Pst.; Rev. Curtis L. Kondik, Par. Vicar; Dcn. Michael F. Jervis Sr.; Sandra J. Lynn, Pst. Assoc.; CRP Stds.: 63

Our Lady Help of Christians in Litchfield - (Worship Site)
Our Lady Help of Christians in Nova - 240 State Rte. 511, Nova, OH 44859 (Worship Site)
Our Lady Help of Christians in Seville - 60 High St., Seville, OH 44273 (Worship Site)
Our Lady Help of Christians in Lodi - 8240 Buffham Rd., Lodi, OH 44254 (Worship Site)

LORAIN

St. Anthony of Padua - 1305 E. Erie Ave., Lorain, OH 44052-2226; Mailing: PO Box 2199, Sheffield Lake, OH 44054-0199 t) 440-288-0106; 440-288-0107 info@stanthonylorain.com www.stanthonylorain.org Rev. Edward J. Smith, Pst.; Dcn. Paul R. Heise; CRP Stds.: 15

St. Anthony of Padua School - (Grades PreK-8) 1339 E. Erie Ave., Lorain, OH 44052-2226 t) 440-288-2155; 440-288-2156 stanthonylorain.org Julio Alarcon, Prin.;

St. Frances Xavier Cabrini Parish (St. John the Baptist, St. Vitus, Saints Cyril and Methodius) - 2143 Homewood Dr., Lorain, OH 44055-2799 t) 440-277-7266; 440-324-4212 (CRP) skowalczk@saintfrancesxcabrini.org www.saintfrancesxcabrini.org Rev. Neil Walters, Admin.; CRP Stds.: 15
St. Mary - 309 Seventh St., Lorain, OH 44052-1879 t) 440-245-5283 lorainstmarychurch.org Rev. Daniel O. Divis, Pst.; CRP Stds.: 10
Nativity of the Blessed Virgin Mary - 1454 Lexington Ave., Lorain, OH 44052; Mailing: 418 W. 15th St., Lorain, OH 44052 t) 440-244-9090; 440-245-6251 natbvm@outlook.com nativitybvmlorain.org Rev. Craig M. Hovanec, Admin.; CRP Stds.: 23
St. Peter - 3655 Oberlin Ave., Lorain, OH 44053-2759 t) 440-282-9103 www.stpeterlorain.org Rev. Craig M. Hovanec, Pst.; Dcn. Jay R. Ogan; CRP Stds.: 47

St. Peter School - 3601 Oberlin Ave., Lorain, OH 44053 t) 440-282-9909 sch_stpeterlorain@dioceseofcleveland.org Rebecca Brown, Prin.;
Convent - 3651 Oberlin Ave., Lorain, OH 44053

Sacred Heart Chapel - 4301 Pearl Ave., Lorain, OH 44055-3311 t) 440-277-7231 sacredheartchapellorain@gmail.com sacredheartchapel.org Rev. William A. Thaden, Pst.; Sr. Catherine McConnell, H.M., Pst. Assoc.; CRP Stds.: 52

LOUDONVILLE

St. Peter - 220 E. Butler St., Loudonville, OH 44842-1235 t) 419-994-4396 linda@loudonvillecatholic.org; kkuruc@loudonvillecatholic.org www.loudonvillecatholic.org Kenneth Kuruc, Parish Life Coord.; CRP Stds.: 15

LYNDHURST

St. Clare - 5659 Mayfield Rd., Lyndhurst, OH 44124-2981 t) 440-449-4242 x101; 440-449-4242 x119 (CRP) parishsecretary14@att.net; lmascia.stclare@att.net www.saintclare.net Rev. Stanley J. Klasinski, Pst.; Rev. Joseph R. Brankatelli, Par. Vicar; Lori Mascia, Pst. Assoc.; CRP Stds.: 70

Corpus Christi Academy - (Grades PreK-8) 5655 Mayfield Rd., Lyndhurst, OH 44124 t) (440) 449-4244 x102 principal@corpuschristiacad.org www.corpuschristiacad.org Matthew Tabar, Prin.; Stds.: 220; Lay Tchrs.: 18

MACEDONIA

Our Lady of Guadalupe - 9080 Shepard Rd., Macedonia, OH 44056 t) 330-468-2194 secretary@olg.cc www.olg.cc Rev. Kevin C. Shemuga, Pst.; Dcn. David Govern; Nancy Freibott, Pst. Assoc.; CRP Stds.: 84

MADISON

Immaculate Conception - 2846 Hubbard Rd., Madison, OH 44057-2934 t) 440-428-5164; 440-428-1083 (CRP) office@iccmadison.com; pcl_immaculatemad@dioceseofcleveland.org www.iccmadison.com Rev. Sean J. Donnelly, Pst.; Dcn. Thomas G. Hupertz; Dcn. Richard F. Kuhlman; Dcn. Kenneth C. Meade; CRP Stds.: 87

MAPLE HEIGHTS

St. Martin of Tours - 14600 Turney Rd., Maple Heights, OH 44137-4788 t) 216-475-4300 rlbugaj-smt44137@sbcglobal.net Rev. Luigi C. Miola, Pst.; CRP Stds.: 41

MEDINA

St. Francis Xavier - 606 E. Washington St., Medina, OH 44256-2183 t) 330-725-4968 francismedina@dioceseofcleveland.org sfxmedina.com/parish Rev. Anthony F. Sejba, Pst.; Rev. Curtis L. Kondik, Par. Vicar; Rev. John Mulhollan; Dcn. Bob Cavanaugh; Dcn. Paul Kipfstuhl; Summer Kish, DRE; CRP Stds.: 336

St. Francis Xavier School - 612 E. Washington St., Medina, OH 44256 t) 330-725-3345 bseislove@sfxmedina.org Danene Beal, Prin.;

Holy Martyrs - 3100 Old Weymouth Rd., Medina, OH 44256-9207 t) 330-722-6633 churchoffice@holymartyrs.net www.holymartyrs.net Rev. Stephen J. Dohner, Pst.; Janet Payton, Pst. Assoc.; Darrell McQuate, Youth Min.; Brandon Woods, Youth Min.; Diane Bruce, DRE; CRP Stds.: 242

MENTOR

St. Bede the Venerable - 9114 Lake Shore Blvd., Mentor, OH 44060-1697 t) 440-257-5544; 440-257-6988 www.stbedementor.org Rev. Timothy J. Plavac, Pst.; Dcn. John Burke Jr., Pst. Assoc.; Dcn. Kenneth Knight, Pst. Assoc.; Laura Ruque, DRE; Mark Rus, Bus. Mgr.; Cynthia Cole, Coordinator of Parish Ministries; CRP Stds.: 125
St. John Vianney - 7575 Bellflower Rd., Mentor, OH 44060-3948 t) 440-255-0600 frjohns@sjvmentor.org sjvmentor.org Rev. Thomas W. Johns, Pst.; Rev. Martin Dober, Par. Vicar; Rev. Alexander Clark, Par. Vicar; Dcn. Gregory A. Leisure; James Hickey, Pst. Assoc.; Katie Cooper, Music Min.; Mandy Hart, DRE; Lydia Donatelli, RCIA Coord.; CRP Stds.: 396
St. Mary of the Assumption - 8560 Mentor Ave., Mentor, OH 44060-5853 t) 440-255-3404 angela.collins@stmarysmentor.org www.stmarysmentor.org Rev. Thomas G. Elsasser, Pst.; Angela Collins, DRE; CRP Stds.: 219

St. Mary of the Assumption School - (Grades PreK-8) 8540 Mentor Ave., Mentor, OH 44060 t) 440-255-9781 principal@stmarysmentor.org www.stmarymentorschool.org Mary Benns, Prin.;

MIDDLEBURG HEIGHTS

St. Bartholomew - 14865 E. Bagley Rd., Middleburg Heights, OH 44130-5502 t) 440-842-5400 ldechant@dioceseofcleveland.org stbartsweconnect.com Rev. Leo Ambrose Dechant, CSJ, Pst.; CRP Stds.: 74

Academy of St. Bartholomew - 14875 E. Bagley Rd., Middleburg Heights, OH 44130-5502 t) 440-845-6660 sch_stbartholomew@dioceseofcleveland.org Chrystal Manos, Prin.;

MIDDLEFIELD

St. Lucy - 16280 E. High St., Middlefield, OH 44062; Mailing: P O Box 709, Parkman, OH 44080 t) 440-548-3812 www.edwardlucy.com Rev. Jacob Bearer, Admin.; CRP Stds.: 31

NEWBURY

St. Helen - 12060 Kinsman Rd., Newbury, OH 44065-9678 t) 440-564-5805 mflauto@sthelen.com; secretary@sthelen.com www.sthelen.com Rev. James G. McPhillips, Pst.; Dcn. Lawrence Somrack; CRP Stds.: 185

St. Helen School - t) 440-564-7125 srmargaret@sthelen.com Sr. Margaret Hartman,

S.N.D., Prin.;

NORTH OLMSTED

St. Brendan - 4242 Brendan Ln., North Olmsted, OH 44070-2999 t) (440) 777-7222; (440) 777-3702 (Religious Ed Office); (440) 777-8433 (School) stbrendanreo@yahoo.com; stbrendannolmsted@yahoo.com www.stbrendannortholmsted.org Rev. Thomas G. Woost, Pst.; Dcn. Robert D. Herron; Mary Oldja, DRE; CRP Stds.: 102

St. Brendan School - jonacila@stbrendannorthholmsted.org Julie Onacila, Prin.;

St. Clarence - 30106 Lorain Rd., North Olmsted, OH 44070-3986 t) 440-734-2414 popremcak@st-clarence.org www.st-clarence.org Rev. Neil P. Kookoothe, Pst.; Dcn. Neal J. Novak; Grace Kincaid Murphy, DRE; CRP Stds.: 159

Youth Ministry House - 30072 Lorain Rd., North Olmsted, OH 44070 t) 440-665-6615

St. Richard - 26855 Lorain Rd., North Olmsted, OH 44070-3260 t) 440-779-7529 (CRP); 440-777-5050 psrdirector@st-richard.org; richardnolmsted@dioceseofcleveland.org www.st-richard.org Rev. Thomas G. Woost, Admin.; Maureen Coughlin, Pst. Assoc.; Rev. Damian Ezeani, In Res.; Rev. Gregory Neuzil, In Res.; CRP Stds.: 33

NORTH RIDGEVILLE

St. Julie Billiart - 5545 Opal Dr., North Ridgeville, OH 44039-2025 t) 440-324-1978 Rev. Robert J. Franco, Admin.; CRP Stds.: 72

St. Peter - 35777 Center Ridge Rd., North Ridgeville, OH 44039-3097 t) 440-327-2201 groh@stpeternr.org www.stpeternr.org Rev. Robert J. Franco, Pst.; Dcn. Donald M. Jankowski; Sr. Sean Groh, S.N.D., DRE; CRP Stds.: 234

St. Peter School - 35749 Center Ridge Rd., North Ridgeville, OH 44039 t) 440-327-3212 rogerbrooks@stpeterschoolnr.org Roger Brooks, Prin.;

NORTH ROYALTON

St. Albert the Great - 6667 Wallings Rd., North Royalton, OH 44133-3067 t) 440-237-6760 Rev. Edward T. Estok, Pst.; Rev. Michael Petkosek, Par. Vicar; Rev. Joshua F. Trefney, Par. Vicar; Sr. Kathryn Mary O'Brien, O.S.U., DRE; CRP Stds.: 282

St. Albert the Great School - t) 440-237-1032 schooloffice@saint-albert.org www.saint-albert.org Edward A. Vittardi, Prin.;

NORTHFIELD

St. Barnabas - 9451 Brandywine Rd., Northfield, OH 44067-2484 t) 330-467-7959 stbarnabasfamily.org/ Rev. Ralph E. Wiatrowski, Pst.; Rev. James J. Kulway, Admin.; CRP Stds.: 277

St. Barnabas School - (Grades PreK-8) 9200 Olde Eight Rd., Northfield, OH 44067 t) 330-467-7921 sch_stbarnabas@dioceseofcleveland.org Erin Faetanini, Prin.;

NORTON

St. Andrew the Apostle - 4022 Johnson Rd., Norton, OH 44203-5931 t) 330-825-8264 (CRP); 330-825-2617 (Rectory) frlthomas@standrewnorton.com Rev. Louis H. Thomas, Pst.; Dcn. Gregory A. Wunderle; Rev. James G. Maloney, Pastor Emer.; CRP Stds.: 15

Prince of Peace - 1263 Shannon Ave., Norton, OH 44203-6792 t) 330-825-9543 ppeacechurch@princeofpeaceparish.org www.princeofpeaceparish.org Rev. Robert H. Jackson, Pst.; Dcn. Robert A. Youngblood; CRP Stds.: 150

OBERLIN

Sacred Heart of Jesus Catholic Church - 410 W. Lorain St., Oberlin, OH 44074-1002 t) 440-707-6707 secretary@shoj.cc shoj.cc Rev. David R. Trask, Pst.; CRP Stds.: 57

OLMSTED FALLS

St. Mary of the Falls - 25615 Bagley Rd., Olmsted Falls, OH 44138-1915 t) 440-235-2808 (CRP); 440-235-2222 (Main) smofparish@gmail.com www.stmaryofthefalls.org Rev. Ryan J. Cubera, Pst.; Dcn. Richard Mueller, Bus. Mgr.; CRP Stds.: 334

St. Mary of the Falls School - (Grades PreK-8) 8262 Columbia Rd., Olmsted Falls, OH 44138-2242 t) 440-235-4580 sch_stmaryfalls@dioceseofcleveland.org; annemarie.rajnicek@stmaryofthefallsschool.com www.stmaryofthefallsschool.com Annemarie Aquaviva Rajnicek, Prin.;

ORRVILLE

St. Agnes - E. Oak St. & Lake St., Orrville, OH 44667-2414; Mailing: 541 Spring St., Orrville, OH 44667 t) 330-682-3606; 330-682-2611 stagnesorrv@embarqmail.com; agnesorrville@dioceseofcleveland.org Rev. Ronald J. Turek, Admin.; CRP Stds.: 40

PAINESVILLE

St. Mary - 242 N. State St., Painesville, OH 44077-4095 t) 440-354-6200 Rev. R. Stephen Vellenga, Pst.; Rev. Alexander C. Spenik, Par. Vicar; CRP Stds.: 296

PARKMAN

St. Edward - 16150 Center St., Parkman, OH 44080-0709; Mailing: P.O. Box 709, Parkman, OH 44080 t) 440-548-3812 www.edwardlucy.com Rev. Jacob Bearer, Admin.; CRP Stds.: 25

St. Lucy - 16280 E. High St., Middlefield, OH 44062; Mailing: P O Box 709, Parkman, OH 44080

PARMA

St. Anthony of Padua - 6750 State Rd., Parma, OH 44134-4518 t) 440-842-2666 office@stanthonypaduaparma.org; frdale@stanthonypaduaparma.org www.stanthonypaduaparma.org Rev. Dale W. Staysniak, Pst.; Rev. Daniel Samide, Par. Vicar; Dcn. Gerard Blanda; CRP Stds.: 92

St. Anthony of Padua School - 6800 State Rd., Parma, OH 44134-4632 t) 440-845-3444 pklimkewicz@stanthonypaduaschool.org Patrick Klimkewicz, Prin.;

Convent - 6834 State Rd., Parma, OH 44134

St. Bridget of Kildare - 5620 Hauserman Rd., Parma, OH 44130-1698 t) 440-886-4434 www.stbridgetparma.com/ Rev. Robert W. Wisniewski, Pst.; Rev. Lawrence J. Bayer, Pastor Emer.; Steven Malec, Bus. Mgr.; Dcn. James J. Armstrong; Dana Steimle, DRE; CRP Stds.: 37

St. Charles Borromeo - 5891 Ridge Rd., Parma, OH 44129-3642 t) 440-884-3030 www.stcharlesonline.org Rev. John T. Carlin, Pst.; Rev. Joshua Cochrac, Assoc. Pst.; Rev. Kevin Fox, Par. Vicar; Dcn. Daniel M. Galla; Dcn. John A. Talerico; Brian Pelcin, Pst. Assoc.; Cynthia Zalek, Pst. Assoc.; Paula Leigh, DRE; Thomas Holzheimer, Bus. Mgr. & Music Min.; CRP Stds.: 73

St. Charles Borromeo School - 7107 Wilber Ave., Parma, OH 44129-3445 t) 440-886-5546 sch_stcharlesbor@dioceseofcleveland.org Eileen Updegrove, Prin.;

St. Columbkille Parish - 6740 Broadview Rd., Parma, OH 44134-4898 t) 216-524-1987; 216-524-1988; 216-524-4816 x43 (CRP) stcolumbkilleparish@gmail.com; schmura@stcolumbkilleparish.org www.stcolumbkilleparish.org Rev. Anthony J. Suso, Pst.; Rev. Joseph P. Robinson, Par. Vicar; Rev. Patrick A. Spicer, Par. Vicar; Dcn. Paul C. Kutolowski; Shari Chmura, DRE; CRP Stds.: 106

St. Columbkille School - rcernystcolumbkille@ohiocoxmail.com Renee Cerny, Prin.;

St. Francis de Sales - 3434 George Ave., Parma, OH 44134-2904 t) 440-884-2319 church_sfds@sbcglobal.net stfrancisdesales-church.org Rev. Mark J. Peyton, Pst.; Rev. John G. Crawford, In Res.; CRP Stds.: 21

Holy Family - 7367 York Rd., Parma, OH 44130-5162 t) 440-842-5533; 440-842-5533 x347 (DRE); (440) 842-5533 x327 (PSR Principal) amihaloew@holyfamparma.org; sryvonne@holyfamparma.org www.holyfamparma.org Rev. Richard A. Evans, Pst.; Rev. Joseph R. Spolny, Par. Vicar; Rev. Kenneth F. Wallace, Senior Parochial Vicar/Part-time; Dcn. Joseph P. Litke; Sr. Yvonne Spenoso, DRE; Dara Hoffman, CRE; CRP Stds.: 38

Holy Family School - (Grades K-8) t) 440-842-7785 office@holyfamilyschoolparma.org www.holyfamilyschoolparma.org Tom Brownfield, Prin.; Stds.: 237; Lay Tchrs.: 9

St. Matthias - 1200 W. Sprague Rd., Parma, OH 44134-6801 t) 440-888-8220 matthiasparma@dioceseofcleveland.org www.stmatthiaschurch.org Rev. Michael J. Denk, Admin.; Dcn. Thomas A. Litwinowicz; Joseph Mikolajczyk, Pst. Min./Coord.; CRP Stds.: 20

PARMA HEIGHTS

St. John Bosco - 6480 Pearl Rd., Parma Heights, OH 44130-2997 t) 440-886-3500 sjbinfo@sjbparmaheights.org www.sjbparmaheights.org Rev. Matthew J. Byrne, Pst.; Dcn. Roger Polefko, Pst. Min./Coord.; Norman Cotone, Music Min.; Christine Kall, DRE; CRP Stds.: 75

PENINSULA

Mother of Sorrows - 6034 S. Locust St., Peninsula, OH 44264-9726 t) (330) 657-2631 motherofsorrowspeninsula.org Rev. Allen F. Corrigan, Admin.; CRP Stds.: 68

PERRY

St. Cyprian - 4223 Middle Ridge Rd., Perry, OH 44081-9794 t) 440-259-2344 www.stcypriansparish.com Rev. Jerzy Kusy, Pst.; Dcn. James F. Daley Jr.; CRP Stds.: 140

RICHFIELD

St. Victor - 3435 Everett Rd., Richfield, OH 44286-0461 t) 330-659-6591 www.saintvictorparish.org Rev. Allen F. Corrigan, Pst.; Darlene Bednarz, Pst. Min./Coord.; CRP Stds.: 126

RITTMAN

St. Anne - 139 S. First St., Rittman, OH 44270-1492; Mailing: 161 W Clinton St, Doylestown, OH 44230 t) (330) 658-2145 Rev. Peter Morris, Admin.;

ROCKY RIVER

St. Christopher - 20141 Detroit Rd., Rocky River, OH 44116-2420 t) 440-331-6226 (CRP); 440-331-4255 stchrisreo@stchrisparish.com stchrisparish.com Rev. John C. Chlebo, Pst.; Rev. Timothy M. Daw, Par. Vicar; Rev. Anthony J. Marshall, S.S.S., Par. Vicar; Dcn. Dennis A. Conrad; Gayle Cilimburg, Pst. Assoc.; Logan Feldkamp, Pst. Assoc.; Sharon Armstrong, DRE; CRP Stds.: 326

St. Christopher School - (Grades K-8) 1610 Lakeview Ave., Rocky River, OH 44116-2409 t) 440-331-3075 stchrisschool@scsrr.org www.scsrr.org Scott Raiff, Prin.;

SHAKER HEIGHTS

St. Dominic - 3450 Norwood Rd., Shaker Heights, OH 44122-4967 t) 216-991-1444 lwoconish@stdominicchurch.net; kmcdevitt@stdominicchurch.net www.stdominicchurch.net/ Rev. Thomas G. Fanta, Pst.; Gerald Bowers, Pst. Assoc.; Liz Woconish, DRE; CRP Stds.: 265

St. Dominic School - 3455 Norwood Rd., Shaker Heights, OH 44122-4901 t) 216-561-4400 info@stdominicschool.net www.stdominicschool.net Susan Biggs, Prin.;

SHEFFIELD LAKE

St. Thomas the Apostle - 521 Harris Rd., Sheffield Lake, OH 44054-1409 t) 440-949-7744 Rev. Stephen L. Shields, Pst.; CRP Stds.: 5

SHEFFIELD VILLAGE

St. Teresa of Avila - 1878 Abbe Rd., Sheffield Village, OH 44054-2322 t) 440-934-4227 church@stteresaparish.com www.stteresaparish.com Rev. Edward J. Smith, Pst.;

SOLON

Resurrection of Our Lord - 32001 Cannon Rd., Solon, OH 44139-1699 t) 440-248-0980 Rev. Thomas M. Dragga, Pst.; Sr. Susan Javorek, SND, Pst. Assoc.; Julie Parrotta, DRE; Matthew D. Nadalin, Music Min.; CRP Stds.: 177

St. Rita - 32820 Baldwin Rd., Solon, OH 44139-4098

t) 440-248-1350 www.stritaparish.com Rev. Thomas J. Behrend, Admin.; Rev. Edward J. Janoch, Par. Vicar; Dcn. Mark D. Janezic; Christine Cola, DRE; Roger Greene, Bus. Mgr.; Albert E. Leko, Pst. Assoc.; CRP Stds.: 375

St. Rita School - 33200 Baldwin Rd., Solon, OH 44139 dgrgic@stritaschool.com Deborah Grgic, Prin.;

SOUTH AMHERST

Nativity of Blessed Virgin Mary - 333 S. Lake St., South Amherst, OH 44001-2013 t) 440-986-7011 toconnor@dioceseofcleveland.org Rev. Timothy J. O'Connor, Pst.;

SOUTH EUCLID

Sacred Heart of Jesus Parish - 1545 S. Green Rd., South Euclid, OH 44121-4085 t) 216-382-7601 office@sacredheartofjesusparish.org sacredheartofjesusparish.org Rev. Dave R. Ireland, Pst.; Rev. Thomas J. Winkel, In Res.; Dcn. David N. Chordas; CRP Stds.: 14

Corpus Christi Academy - 5655 Mayfield Rd., Lyndhurst, OH 44121 t) 440-449-4242 principal@corpuschristiacad.org Matthew Tabar, Prin.;

STOW

Holy Family - 3450 Sycamore Dr., Stow, OH 44224-3999 t) 330-688-6412 mccandless@holyfamilystow.org www.holyfamilystow.org Rev. Michael P. McCandless, Pst.; Rev. Andrew J. Gonzalez, Assoc. Pst.; Rev. Paul J. Rosing, Pastor Emer.; Dcn. John D. Green; Sandy Michaels, Music Min.; Barbie Byrne, Parish Life Coord.; Abby Gresser, DRE; Amy Rich, Bus. Mgr.; CRP Stds.: 129

Holy Family School - 3163 Kent Rd., Stow, OH 44224 t) 330-688-3816 sfournier@holyfamilyschoolstow.org Heather Hawk-Frank, Prin.;

STRONGSVILLE

St. John Neumann - 16271 Pearl Rd., Strongsville, OH 44136-6095 t) 440-238-1770 Rev. Barry T. Gearing, Pst.; Dcn. Kenneth J. Piechowski; Dcn. Keith A. Walcutt; CRP Stds.: 305

St. Joseph - 12700 Pearl Rd., Strongsville, OH 44136-3484 t) 440-238-5555 www.sjohio.org Rev. Joseph R. Mamich, Pst.; Rev. Kevin J. Klonowski, Par. Vicar; Dcn. Robert Lester; CRP Stds.: 188

SS. Joseph and John Interparochial - 12580 Pearl Rd., Strongsville, OH 44136-3422 t) 440-238-4877 dthomas@sjjschool.com Darlene Thomas, Prin.;

TALLMADGE

Our Lady of Victory - 73 North Ave., Tallmadge, OH 44278-1996 t) 330-633-3637 mmatusz@ourladyofvictory.net; jpasko@ourladyofvictory.net www.ourladyofvictory.net Rev. Michael A. Matusz, Pst.; Linda Herold, Pst. Min./Coord.; Joanne Pasko, DRE; CRP Stds.: 126

THOMPSON

St. Patrick - 16550 Rock Creek Rd., Thompson, OH 44086-8753 t) 440-298-1327 office@stpatrickthompson.org www.stpatrickthompson.org Rev. Scott D. Goodfellow, Pst.; Dcn. Phillip P. Kraynik; Dcn. Robert F. Schwartz; CRP Stds.: 48

TWINSBURG

SS. Cosmas and Damian - 10419 Ravenna Rd., Twinsburg, OH 44087-1726 t) 330-405-8141 www.catholictwinsburg.org Rev. Michael J. Stalla, Pst.; Dcn. Edward J. Chernick; Keri Knowles, Pst. Assoc.; Joni Smith, Pst. Assoc.; CRP Stds.: 167

UNIONTOWN

Queen of Heaven - 1800 Steese Rd., Uniontown, OH 44685-9555 t) 330-896-2345 office@qofh.church www.queenofheavenparish.org Rev. David R. Durkee, Pst.; Rev. Robert E. Pahler, Pastor Emer.; Rev. James R. Semonin, In Res.; CRP Stds.: 369

UNIVERSITY HEIGHTS

Gesu - 2470 Miramar Blvd., University Heights, OH 44118-3896 t) 216-932-0617 gesucleveland@churchofthegesu.org churchofthegesu.org Rev. Lukas Laniauskas, SJ, Pst.; Rev. Michael A. Vincent, S.J., Assoc. Pst.; Dcn. James K. O'Donnell; Rev. Gregory Hyde, SJ, In Res.; Sr. Kathleen Flannery, O.S.U., Pst. Assoc.; Marcia Leous, DRE; Mary O'Neill, DRE; CRP Stds.: 74

Gesu School - 2450 Miramar Blvd., University Heights, OH 44118 t) 216-932-0620 rkazel@gesu.com gesu.com Regan Kazel, Prin.;

Convent - 4070 Meadowbrook Blvd., University Heights, OH 44118; Mailing: 2470 Miramar Blvd., University Heights, OH 44118

VALLEY CITY

St. Martin of Tours - 1800 Station Rd., Valley City, OH 44280-9522 t) 330-483-3808 www.stmartinvc.org Rev. Daniel J. Reed, Pst.; Dcn. William H. Perkins; Colene Conley, Pst. Assoc.; Sarah Sidor, CRE; Rosie Strack, Bus. Mgr.; CRP Stds.: 116

WADSWORTH

Sacred Heart of Jesus - 260 Broad St., Wadsworth, OH 44281-2113 t) 330-336-3049 church@shofjesus.com shofjesus.com Rev. Joseph L. Labak, Pst.; Rev. Patrick R. Schultz, Par. Vicar; Dcn. Roger N. Klaas; Dcn. Richard Michney; Annette Bernard, Parish Life Coord.; CRP Stds.: 429

Sacred Heart of Jesus School - 110 Humbolt Ave., Wadsworth, OH 44281 t) 330-334-6272 sah_badams@tccsa.net; sch_sacredheart@dioceseofcleveland.org www.sacredheartexcellence.org William Adams, Prin.;

WELLINGTON

St. Patrick - 512 N. Main St., Wellington, OH 44090-1198 t) 440-647-4375 stpatrick.cc Rev. David R. Trask, Pst.; Dcn. Dino Paoletta; CRP Stds.: 39

WEST SALEM

St. Stephen - 44 Britton St., West Salem, OH 44287-9318 t) 419-853-4946 info@ststephen.ws www.ststephen.ws Dcn. Peter J. Foradori, Parish Life Coord.; CRP Stds.: 20

WESTLAKE

St. Bernadette - 2256 Clague Rd., Westlake, OH 44145-4328 t) 440-734-1300 emorris@stbern.net saintbernadetteparish.org Rev. Philip G. Racco, Pst.; Rev. Joseph Menkhaus Jr., Par. Vicar; Dcn. Mark A. Cunningham; Sr. Donna Marie Bradesca, OSU, Dir., Faith Formation; CRP Stds.: 87

St. Bernadette School - 2300 Clague Rd., Westlake, OH 44145 t) 440-734-7717 office@stbern.net Maureen Goodwin, Prin.;

St. Ladislas - 2345 Bassett Rd., Westlake, OH 44145-2999 t) 440-835-2300 www.stlads.org Rev. Donald E. Snyder, Pst.; Dcn. Dennis A. Conrad; Sr. Mary Joan, O.S.U., Music Min.; Sr. Johnica D'amico, Pst. Assoc.; Robert Hertl, Pst. Assoc.; Mike McClain, Pst. Assoc.; Sr. Marilyn Zgonc, Pst. Assoc.; CRP Stds.: 138

WICKLIFFE

Our Lady of Mount Carmel - 29850 Euclid Ave., Wickliffe, OH 44092; Mailing: 1730 Mt. Carmel Dr., Wickliffe, OH 44092 t) 440-585-0700 iccpastor44094@gmail.com; frjodonnell@olmcwickliffe.org www.olmcwickliffe.org Rev. Michael J. Troha, Admin.; Rev. Joseph P. O'Donnell, Par. Vicar; Rev. Gregory F. Schaut, In Res.; Rev. Gregory J. Olszewski, In Res.; Rev. David G. Baugh, In Res.; Raquel A. Nelson, DRE; Mary D. Brown, Bus. Mgr.; CRP Stds.: 39

WILLOUGHBY

Immaculate Conception Parish - 37940 Euclid Ave., Willoughby, OH 44094-5899 t) 440-942-4500 www.immaculate.net Rev. Michael James Troha, Pst.; Rev. Dennis McNeil, Par. Vicar; Michael Kelley, Music Min.; Sr. Josephine Rasoamampionona, DRE; Elayne Kramer, Bus. Mgr.; CRP Stds.: 101

WILLOUGHBY HILLS

St. Noel - 35200 Chardon Rd., Willoughby Hills, OH 44094-9193 t) 440-946-0887 stnoel.org Rev. Terrence M. Grachanin, Pst.; Dcn. David T. Nethery; Michele Baetzold, DRE; CRP Stds.: 46

WILLOWICK

St. Mary Magdalene - 32114 Vine St., Willowick, OH 44095-3581 t) 440-943-2133 smmwillowick.org Rev. Steven H. Breck, Pst.; Dcn. Carl Toomey; CRP Stds.: 77

WOOSTER

St. Mary of the Immaculate Conception - 527 Beall Ave., Wooster, OH 44691-0109 t) 330-264-8824; 330-264-5838 (CRP) stmarywoosteroffice@gmail.com; jviator.stmarywooster@gmail.com stmarywooster.org Rev. Stephen P. Moran, Pst.; Rev. Richard Samide, Par. Vicar; Dcn. Robert Zerrer; Camille Horvath, Pst. Assoc.; Rachel Teague, Youth Min.; Sarah Nussbaum, DRE; CRP Stds.: 75

St. Mary of the Immaculate Conception School - (Grades PreK-8) 515 Beall Ave., Wooster, OH 44691 t) 330-262-8671 stm_lmarvin@tccsa.net www.stmwoo.org Laura Marvin, Prin.;

SCHOOLS: PRESCHOOL THRU HIGH SCHOOL

SCHOOLS

STATE OF OHIO

AKRON

Julie Billiart School of St. Sebastian Parish, Akron - (PRV) (Grades K-8) 380 Mineola Ave., Akron, OH 44320; Mailing: 4982 Clubside Rd., Lyndhurst, OH 44124 t) 234-206-0941; 216-381-1191 ldavis@jbschool.org; ssweigert@jbschool.org www.juliebilliartschool.org Children with special learning needs Jason Wojnicz, Prin.; Stds.: 115; Lay Tchrs.: 31

Our Lady of the Elms School - (PAR) (Grades PreK-12) 1375 W. Exchange St., Akron, OH 44313-7108 t) 330-867-0880 (High School); 330-752-2506 (High School) kkelly@theelms.org www.theelms.org Kevin Michael Kelly, Dean; Deborah Farquhar Jones, Pres.; Stds.: 281; Lay Tchrs.: 35

CHARDON

Notre Dame Elementary School - (PRV) (Grades PreK-8) 13000 Auburn Rd., Chardon, OH 44024 t) 440-279-1127 www.ndes.org Dr. Jacqueline Hoynes, Prin.; Dr. Michael Bates, Pres.; Stds.: 388; Sr. Tchrs.: 2; Lay Tchrs.: 24

Notre Dame PreSchool - (Grades PreK-8) ndes.org Stds.: 38; Lay Tchrs.: 2

CLEVELAND

Archbishop James P. Lyke Elementary School - (PAR) (Grades K-8) 18230 Harvard Ave., Cleveland, OH 44128 t) 216-991-9644 sch_lykeelementary@dioceseofcleveland.org www.archbishoplykeschool.org Nancy Lynch, Prin.; Stds.: 216; Scholastics: 1; Lay Tchrs.: 10

St. Francis School - (DIO) (Grades PreK-8) 7206 Myron Ave., Cleveland, OH 44103 t) 216-361-4858 admin@stfranciscleveland.org; gracec@stfranciscleveland.org www.stfranciscleveland.com Carrie Grace, Prin.; Stds.: 247; Lay Tchrs.: 13

Metro Catholic School - (DIO) (Grades PreK-8) 3555 West 54, Cleveland, OH 44102 t) 216-281-4044 x332 www.metrocatholic.org Bob Finkovich, Dir.; Stds.: 433; Sr. Tchrs.: 2; Lay Tchrs.: 27

St. Stephen Bldg. (Grade 5-8) - (Grades PreK-8) 1910 W. 54th St., Cleveland, OH 44102 malinea@metrocatholic.net Robert Finkovich, Admin.;

St. Michael Bldg. (Grades 2-4) - (Grades PreK-8) 1910 W. 54th St., Cleveland, OH 44102 metro@leeca.org Sr. Karen Bohan, O.S.U., Dir.;

St. Boniface Bldg. (PreK-1) - (Grades PreK-8)

t) 216-631-5733 Angela Weinrich, Dir.; Jeanna Forhan, Librn.;

St. Thomas Aquinas School - (DIO) (Grades K-8) 9101 Superior Ave., Cleveland, OH 44106 t) 216-421-4668 sch_stthomasaquinas@dioceseofcleveland.org Rachael Dengler, Prin.; Tricia Matune, Bus. Mgr.; Stds.: 221

GARFIELD HEIGHTS

St. Benedict Catholic School - (DIO) (Grades PreK-8) 13633 Rockside Rd., Garfield Heights, OH 44125 t) 216-662-9380 loriti@stbenedictohio.com www.stbenedictohio.org Lisa Oriti, Prin.; Rev. Luigi C. Miola, Pres.; Rev. Thomas A. Haren, Treas.; Stds.: 405; Scholastics: 25; Lay Tchrs.: 25

St. Benedict Early Learning Center - (Grades PreK-8) 14600 Turney Rd., Maple Heights, OH 44137 t) 216-475-3633

HUDSON

Seton Catholic School - (PRV) (Grades PreK-8) 6923 Stow Rd., Hudson, OH 44236 t) 330-342-4200 fritzp@setoncatholicschool.org www.setoncatholicschool.org Karen Alestock, Prin.; Annie Deemer, Prin.; Michael Hudec, Chair; Bibiana Seislove, Campus Min.; Stds.: 463; Lay Tchrs.: 30

LAKEWOOD

Lakewood Catholic Academy - (PAR) (Grades PreSchool-8) 14808 Lake Ave., Lakewood, OH 44107 t) 216-521-0559 info@lcasaints.com www.lakewoodcatholicacademy.com Brenna Warrell, Prin.; Brian Sinchak, Pres.; Stds.: 450; Lay Tchrs.: 33

LYNDHURST

Corpus Christi Academy - (Grades PreK-8) 5655 Mayfield Rd., Lyndhurst, OH 44124 t) 440-449-4244 office@corpuschristiacad.org www.corpuschristiacad.org Matthew Tabar, Prin.; Stds.: 215; Lay Tchrs.: 18

Julie Billiart School - 4982 Clubside Rd., Lyndhurst, OH 44124-2596 t) 216-381-1191 ldavis@jbschool.org; ssweigert@jbschool.org www.juliebilliartschool.org Children with special learning needs. Lannie Davis-Frecker, Pres.; Stds.: 130; Sr. Tchrs.: 1; Lay Tchrs.: 37

PARMA HEIGHTS

Incarnate Word Academy - (PAR) (Grades PreK-8) 6620 Pearl Rd., Parma Heights, OH 44130 t) 440-842-6818 mwisnor@incarnatewordacademy.org; scongelio@incarnatewordacademy.org incarnatewordacademy.org Steffany Congelio, Prin.; Michael Wisnor, Pres.; Stds.: 348; Lay Tchrs.: 26

WESTLAKE

Julie Billiart School, Westlake - 3600 Crocker Rd., Westlake, OH 44145 t) 440-471-4150 ldavis@jbschool.org; ssweigert@jbschool.org Samantha Evers, Prin.; Stds.: 84; Sr. Tchrs.: 1; Lay Tchrs.: 29

WICKLIFFE

All Saints of St. John Vianney School - (DIO) (Grades PreK-8) 28702 Euclid Ave., Wickliffe, OH 44092 t) 216-943-1395 info@allsaintssjv.com www.allsaintssjv.org Katy Rankin, Prin.; Paula Kirchner, Librn.; Stds.: 287; Lay Tchrs.: 18

Mater Dei Academy - (DIO) (Grades PreSchool-8) 29840 Euclid Ave., Wickliffe, OH 44092 t) 440-585-0800 info@materdeiacademy.us www.materdeiacademy.us Joanie Klemens, Prin.; Rev. Gregory J. Olszewski, Admin.; Stds.: 243; Sr. Tchrs.: 1; Lay Tchrs.: 24

HIGH SCHOOLS

STATE OF OHIO

AKRON

Archbishop Hoban High School - (PRV) (Grades 9-12) One Holy Cross Blvd., Akron, OH 44306 t) 330-773-6658 dimauroc@hoban.org www.hoban.org (Coed). Brothers of Holy Cross T. Kirk Griffith, Prin.; Christopher A DiMauro, Pres.; Stds.: 805; Bro. Tchrs.: 1; Lay Tchrs.: 57

St. Vincent-St. Mary High School - (PRV) (Grades 9-12) 15 N. Maple St., Akron, OH 44303 t) 330-253-9113 webmaster@stvm.com www.stvm.com Kimberlee Gorr, Prin.; Leo Hyland, Pres.; Amie Hale, Dean; Kelly Widders, Dean; Julianne Goshe, Campus Min.; Stds.: 661; Lay Tchrs.: 53

CHARDON

Notre Dame-Cathedral Latin School - (PRV) (Grades 9-12) 13000 Auburn Rd., Chardon, OH 44024 t) 440-286-6226 joseph.waler@ndcl.org www.ndcl.org Christopher Poulos, Prin.; Denice Teeples, Prin.; Joseph A. Waler, Prin.; Dr. Michael Bates, Pres.; Stds.: 706; Sr. Tchrs.: 2; Lay Tchrs.: 58

CLEVELAND

Benedictine High School - (PRV) (Grades 9-12) 2900 Martin Luther King Dr., Cleveland, OH 44104-4898 t) 216-421-2080 cbhs@cbhs.edu www.cbhs.edu Rt. Rev. Gary Hoover, O.S.B., Chancellor; Ryan Ryzner, Pres.; Christopher Lorber, Dir.; Terri Wysocki, Bus. Mgr.; Rev. Michael Brunovsky, O.S.B., Prof.; Rev. Bede Kotlinski, O.S.B., Prof.; Rev. Finbar Ramsak, O.S.B, Prof.; Rev. Anselm Zupka, O.S.B., Prof.; Stds.: 285; Pr. Tchrs.: 5; Lay Tchrs.: 19

Cleveland Central Catholic High School - (DIO) 6550 Baxter Ave., Cleveland, OH 44105 t) 216-441-4700 allisonmarie@ccc-hs.org; jsimon@ccc-hs.org www.centralcatholichs.org Sr. Allison Marie Gusdanovic, S.N.D., Prin.; John R Simon, Pres.; Stds.: 426; Bro. Tchrs.: 1; Lay Tchrs.: 34

St. Ignatius High School - (PRV) (Grades 6-12) 1911 W. 30th St., Cleveland, OH 44113 t) 216-651-0222 pwalcutt@ignatius.edu www.ignatius.edu Rev. Daniel Reim, Supr.; Rev. Raymond P. Guiao, S.J., Pres.; Stds.: 1,411; Pr. Tchrs.: 4; Lay Tchrs.: 113

Saint Joseph Academy - (PRV) (Grades 9-12) 3470 Rocky River Dr., Cleveland, OH 44111 t) 216-251-6788 info@sja1890.org www.sja1890.org Jeff Sutliff, Prin.; Kathryn Purcell, Pres.; Stds.: 685; Lay Tchrs.: 59

***St. Martin de Porres High School** - (PRV) (Grades 9-12) 6202 St. Clair Ave., Cleveland, OH 44103 t) 216-881-1689 www.saintmartincleveland.org Adam Trifiro, Prin.; Charles Napoli, Pres.; Stds.: 400; Lay Tchrs.: 35

Villa Angela-St. Joseph High School - (DIO) (Grades 9-12) 18491 Lakeshore Blvd., Cleveland, OH 44119 t) 216-481-8414 ljones@vasj.com; tcarone@vasj.com www.vasj.com Lorenzo Jones, Prin.; Thomas M. Carone, Pres.; Stds.: 452; Lay Tchrs.: 33

CLEVELAND HEIGHTS

Beaumont School - (PRV) (Grades 9-12) 3301 N. Park Blvd., Cleveland Heights, OH 44118 t) 216-321-2954 advancement@beaumontschool.org www.beaumontschool.org Ursuline Sisters. Ann Hoelzel, Prin.; Wendy Hoke, Pres.; Lisa Andreani, CFO; Stds.: 300; Sr. Tchrs.: 1; Lay Tchrs.: 33

CUYAHOGA FALLS

Walsh Jesuit High School - (PRV) 4550 Wyoga Lake Rd., Cuyahoga Falls, OH 44224 t) 330-929-4205; 800-686-4694 (Cleveland) info@walshjesuit.org www.walshjesuit.org Sean Lynch, Prin.; Rev. Donald J. Petkash, S.J., Supr.; Karl Ertle, Pres.; Rev. Kenneth A. Styles, S.J., Pst. Min./Coord.; Stds.: 984; Pr. Tchrs.: 2; Lay Tchrs.: 77

ELYRIA

Elyria Catholic High School - (DIO) (Grades 9-12) 725 Gulf Rd., Elyria, OH 44035 t) 440-365-1821 www.elyriacatholic.com (Coed) Suzanne Lester, Prin.; Annie Heidersbach, Pres.; Stds.: 474; Lay Tchrs.: 33

GARFIELD HEIGHTS

Trinity High School - (PRV) 12425 Granger Rd., Garfield Heights, OH 44125 t) 216-581-1644 billsvoboda@ths.org; meadowsl@ths.org www.ths.org Sisters of St. Joseph of the Third Order of St. Francis. Laurie Lynn Meadows, Dir.; William Svoboda, Prin.; Stds.: 338; Lay Tchrs.: 31

GATES MILLS

Gilmour Academy - (PRV) (Grades PreK-12) 34001 Cedar Rd., Gates Mills, OH 44040-9356 t) 440-473-8000 admission@gilmour.org; kennyk@gilmour.org www.gilmour.org Day and Resident College Preparatory School. Congregation of Holy Cross. Kathleen C. Kenny, Headmaster; Fred G. Botek, Chair; Whitney Daly, Pst. Min./Coord.; Rev. John Blazek, C.S.C., Campus Min.; Stds.: 750; Pr. Tchrs.: 1; Lay Tchrs.: 72

LAKEWOOD

St. Edward High School - (PRV) (Grades 9-12) 13500 Detroit Ave., Lakewood, OH 44107 t) 216-221-3776 kcmkenna@sehs.net www.sehs.net (Boys) KC McKenna, Pres.; Matthew Stepnowski, Prin.; Stds.: 905; Lay Tchrs.: 61

MENTOR

Lake Catholic High - (DIO) (Grades 9-12) 6733 Reynolds Rd., Mentor, OH 44060 t) 440-578-1020 info@lakecatholic.org www.lakecatholic.org Thomas McKrill, Prin.; Mark Crowley, Pres.; Stds.: 440; Lay Tchrs.: 31

PARMA

Padua Franciscan High School - (PRV) (Grades 9-12) 6740 State Rd., Parma, OH 44134 t) 440-845-2444 padua@paduafranciscan.com www.paduafranciscan.com David G. Stec, Pres.; Robert DiRocco, Prin.; Elizabeth Oles Smith, Vice Prin.; Sarah Jesse, Campus Min.; Alexandra Frech, Librn.; Stds.: 725; Pr. Tchrs.: 1; Lay Tchrs.: 57

PARMA HEIGHTS

Holy Name High School - (DIO) (Grades 9-12) 6000 Queens Hwy., Parma Heights, OH 44130 t) 440-886-0300 shelbreyblanc@holynamehs.com; lcsank@holynamehs.com www.holynamehs.com (Coed) Shelbrey Blanc, Pres.; Karen Carter, Prin.; Sr. Paula Greggila, Librn.; Stds.: 568; Sr. Tchrs.: 1; Lay Tchrs.: 40

ROCKY RIVER

Magnificat High School - (PRV) (Grades 9-12) 20770 Hilliard Blvd., Rocky River, OH 44116 t) 440-331-1572 tmessmore@maghs.org www.magnificaths.org (Girls) Moira Clark, Pres.; Stds.: 705; Lay Tchrs.: 66

INSTITUTIONS LOCATED IN DIOCESE

CATHOLIC CHARITIES [CCH]

CLEVELAND

Catholic Charities Corporation - 7911 Detroit Ave., Cleveland, OH 44102 t) 216-334-2900 pgareau@ccdocle.org www.ccdocle.org Patrick Gareau, Pres.; Fredy Robles, Exec.; James Graham, CFO; Lisa Black, Gen. Counsel; Andrea Harris, Chief Admin. Officer;

Bishop William M. Cosgrove Center - 1736 Superior Ave., Cleveland, OH 44114 t) 216-781-8262 info@ccdocle.org Eric Milkie, Dir.;

Camp Christopher - 1930 N. Hametown Rd., Akron, OH 44333 t) 330-256-5140 campchristopher@ccdocle.org; tflannery@ccdocle.org Tess Flannery, Dir.;

Catholic Charities Annual Appeal - 1404 E. Ninth St., Cleveland, OH 44114 t) 216-696-6525 x1910 sgozur@catholiccommunity.org Sarah Gozur, Dir.;

Catholic Charities Community Services of Ashland County - 34 W. Second St., Ste. 18, Ashland, OH 44805-2000 t) 419-289-1903 svillegas@ccdocle.org Sheryl Villegas, Dir.;

Catholic Charities Community Services of Geauga County - 602 South St., Ste. D1, Chardon, OH 44024 t) 800-242-9755 mbertman@ccdocle.org Michelle Bertman, Dir.;

Catholic Charities Community Services of Lake County - 8 N. State St., Ste. 455, Painesville, OH 44077-3954 t) 440-946-7264 ecurriemanring@ccdocle.org Emily Currie-Manring, Dir.;

Catholic Charities Community Services of Lorain County - 628 Poplar St., Elyria, OH 44035 t) 440-366-1106 x20 c) 216-310-9592 ambundy@ccdocle.org Amber Bundy, Dir.;

Catholic Charities Community Services of Medina

County - 4210 N. Jefferson, Ste. A, Medina, OH 44256 t) 330-723-9615 makipfstuhl@ccdocle.org Michelle Kipfstuhl, Dir.;
Catholic Charities Community Services of Summit County - 812 Biruta St., Akron, OH 44307-1104 t) 330-762-2961 contactus@ccdocle.org; tflannery@ccdocle.org www.ccsummitcounty.org Tess Flannery, Dir.;
Catholic Charities Community Services of Wayne County - 521 Beall Ave., Wooster, OH 44691-3523 t) 330-262-7836 svillegas@ccdocle.org Sheryl Villegas, Dir.;
Catholic Charities Mission and Specialized Ministries - t) 216-334-2958 Dobie Moser, Dir.;
Catholic Charities Services and Ministries to Persons with Disabilities Office - t) 216-334-2962 mjscott@ccdocle.org Marilyn Scott, Contact;
Catholic Charities Treatment, Prevention and Recovery Services - t) 216-334-2977 wskline@ccdocle.org Part of the health & human services delivery system of the Diocese. Spencer Kline, Dir.;
Catholic Commission of Cuyahoga County - 7911 Detroit Ave., Cleveland, OH 44102 t) 216-939-3843 kabon@ccdocle.org Kelly Bon, Dir.;
Catholic Commission of Lake/Geauga Counties - 28700 Euclid Ave., Wickliffe, OH 44092 t) 216-939-3843 www.ccdocle.org/dsao Kelly Bon, Dir.;
Catholic Commission of Lorain County - 628 Poplar St., Lorain, OH 44052 t) 440-366-1106 www.ccdocle.org/dsao Shawn Witmer, Dir.;
Catholic Commission of Summit County - 795 Russell Ave., Akron, OH 44307 t) 330-535-2787 www.ccdocle.org/dsao Jeff Campbell, Dir.;
Catholic Commission of Wayne, Ashland and Medina Counties - 4210 N. Jefferson St., Suite A, Medina, OH 44256 t) 330-723-9615 x11; 330-703-7979 pjkipfstuhl@ccdocle.org Paul Kipfstuhl, Dir.;
Catholic Relief Services and the Catholic Campaign for Human Development - 28700 Euclid Ave., Wickliffe, OH 44092 t) 216-939-3843 Kelly Bon, Dir.;
The Covenant - 1515 W. 29th St., Cleveland, OH 44113 t) 216-574-9000 wskline@ccdocle.org Youth & family mental health & chemical dependency counseling. Spencer Kline, Dir.;
CYO Office - t) 216-334-1261 dxmoser@ccdocle.org Dobie Moser, Dir.;
Diocesan Social Action Office - 7911 Detroit Ave., Cleveland, OH 44102 t) 216-939-3843 kabon@ccdocle.org Kelly Bon, Dir.;
Emergency Assistance Services - t) 216-334-2924 mkmcguan@ccdocle.org Emergency assistance, hunger network, parish partnerships. Meghan McGuan, Dir.;
Employment & Training Services - 2265 Columbus Rd., St. Wendelin's Campus, Cleveland, OH 44113 t) (216) 391-4415 awinfield@ccdocle.org Autumn Winfield, Dir.;
Family Centers & Early Learning Programs - 7911 Detroit Ave., Cleveland, OH 44102 t) 216-334-2936 jhinkelman@ccdocle.org Joan Hinkelman, Dir.;
Fatima Family Center - 6600 Lexington Ave., Cleveland, OH 44103 t) 216-391-0505 ljray@ccdocle.org LaJean Ray, Dir.;
Head Start - 7911 Detroit Ave., Cleveland, OH 44102 t) 216-334-2942 Linda Schettler, Dir.;
Hispanic Senior Center - 7800 Detroit Ave., Cleveland, OH 44102 t) 216-939-3714 rrjohnson@ccdocle.org Ramonita Rodriguez-Johnson, Dir.;
La Providencia Family Center - 1515 W. 29th St., Cleveland, OH 44113 t) 216-624-4312 rrjohnson@ccdocle.org Ramonita Rodriguez-Johnson, Dir.;
St. Martin de Porres Family Center - 1264 E. 123rd St., Cleveland, OH 44108-4042 t) 216-268-3909 mmckenzie@ccdocle.org Karnese McKenzie, Dir.;
Matt Talbot for Men - 6753 State Rd., Parma, OH 44134 t) 440-345-3020 jtulli@ccdocle.org Jennifer Tulli, Dir.;
Matt Talbot for Women - 6753 State, Parma, OH 44134 t) (440) 843-5505 jktulli@ccdocle.org Jennifer Tulli, Dir.;
Migration & Refugee Services - 7800 Detroit Ave., Cleveland, OH 44102 t) (216) 939-3840 hrosenberger@ccdocle.org Heath Rosenberger, Dir.;
Pastoral Care Services - 1404 E. Ninth St., 6th Fl., Cleveland, OH 44114 t) 216-696-6525 x2440 dschlegel@dioceseofcleveland.org Rev. Daniel F. Schlegel, Dir.;
St. Phillip Neri Family Center - 799 E. 82nd St., Cleveland, OH 44103 t) 216-391-4415 awinfield@ccdocle.org Autumn Winfield, Dir.;
Regional Services - 7911 Detroit Ave., Cleveland, OH 44102 t) (216) 319-0620 cathier@ccdocle.org Catherine Thier, Dir.;

Catholic Charities Housing Corporation (CCHC) - 1404 E. Ninth St., Cleveland, OH 44114 t) 216-696-6525 x1501 Bill Brady, Dir.;
St. Malachi Center, Inc. - 2416 Superior Viaduct, Cleveland, OH 44113 t) 216-771-3036 shauna@malachicenter.org www.malachicenter.org Shauna Sanders, Dir.; Asstd. Annu.: 1,200; Staff: 12
Malachi House, Inc. - 2810 Clinton Ave., Cleveland, OH 44113 t) 216-621-8831 jhilow@malachihouse.org; vrains@malachihouse.org www.malachihouse.org Unskilled, family-like care to the dying poor without cost. Judy Ghazoul Hilow, Dir.; Asstd. Annu.: 110; Staff: 25
Office of Hispanic Ministry - Diocese of Cleveland, 1404 E. 9th St., Cleveland, OH 44114 t) 216-696-6525 x4300 mmayorga@dioceseofcleveland.org www.dioceseofcleveland.org/hispanicministry Misael Mayorga, Dir.; Staff: 2
Hispanic Parishes: Iglesia La Sagrada Familia - 7719 Detroit Ave., Cleveland, OH 44102 t) 216-631-6817 sagrada1997rob@yahoo.com Rev. Robert J. Reidy;
St. Mary's - Painesville - 242 N. State St., Painesville, OH 44077 t) 440-354-4381 Rev. R. Stephen Vellenga;
St. Michael - 3114 Scranton Rd., Cleveland, OH 44109 t) 216-621-3847 smarcangel.wixsite.com/44109 Rev. Mark R. Riley, Pst.; Rev. Dennis R. O'Grady, Pastor Emer.;
Our Lady of Lourdes - 3395 E. 53rd St., Cleveland, OH 44127 t) 216-641-2829 ourladyoflourdescle@yahoo.com www.ourladyoflourdes-cle.org Rev. Joseph H. Callahan;
Parishes with Ministry to Spanish Speaking: St. Bernard - 44 University Ave., Akron, OH 44308 t) 330-253-5161 djreed@stbernardstmary.org Rev. Daniel J. Reed;
Sacred Heart Chapel - 4301 Pearl Ave., Lorain, OH 44055 t) 440-277-7231; 440-277-7232 sacredheartchapellorain@gmail.com Rev. William A. Thaden, Admin.;
St. Mary of the Immaculate Conception - 527 Beall Ave., Wooster, OH 44691; Mailing: P.O. Box 109, Wooster, OH 44691 t) 330-264-8824; 330-264-8822 stmarywoost@embarqmail.com Rev. Stephen P. Moran, Pst.; Judith Caraballo-Arzuaga, Dir.;

LORAIN

St. Elizabeth Center - 2726 Caroline Ave., Lorain, OH 44055 t) 440-242-0056 lwricehead@ccdocle.org Barbara Hammond, Dir.;

PARMA

Parkview - 5210 Loya Pkwy., Parma, OH 44134 t) 440-885-2429 leschettler@ccdocle.org Linda Schettler, Contact;

CEMETERIES [CEM]

CHARDON

All Souls Cemetery - 10366 Chardon Rd., Chardon, OH 44024; Mailing: P.O. Box 605310, Cleveland, OH 44105 t) 216-641-7575 alah@clecem.org www.clecem.org Andrej N. Lah, Dir.;

CLEVELAND

The Catholic Cemeteries Association of the Diocese of Cleveland - 10000 Miles Ave., Cleveland, OH 44105 t) 216-641-7575 alah@clevelandcatholiccemeteries.org Andrej N. Lah, Dir.;
Callistian Guild - alah@clecem.org
Assumption of Mary Cemetery - 14900 Brookpark Rd., Cleveland, OH 44135; Mailing: P.O. Box 605310, Cleveland, OH 44105 t) 216-641-7575 x3 alah@clecem.org www.clecem.org Andrej N. Lah, CEO;
All Saints Cemetery - 480 W. Highland Rd., Northfield, OH 44067; Mailing: P.O. Box 605310, Cleveland, OH 44105 Andrej N. Lah, Dir.;
Calvary Cemetery - 555 N. Ridge Rd. W., Lorain, OH 44053; Mailing: P.O. Box 605310, Cleveland, OH 44105 t) (216) 641-7575 Andrej N. Lah, Dir.;
Calvary Cemetery - 10000 Miles Ave., Cleveland, OH 44105; Mailing: P.O. Box 605310, Cleveland, OH 44105 t) (216) 641-7575 Andrej N. Lah, Dir.;
Elmhurst Park Cemetery - 32787 Detroit Rd., Avon, OH 44011; Mailing: P.O. Box 605310, Cleveland, OH 44105 t) (216) 641-7575 (Non-Sectarian)
Holy Cross Cemetery - 14609 Brookpark Rd., Brook Park, OH 44142; Mailing: 10000 Miles Ave., Cleveland, OH 44105 t) (216) 641-7575
Holy Cross Cemetery - 100 E. Waterloo Rd., Akron, OH 44319; Mailing: P.O. Box 605310, Cleveland, OH 44105 t) (216) 641-7575
Holy Trinity Cemetery - 2886 Jaycox Rd., Avon, OH 44011; Mailing: P.O. Box 605310, Cleveland, OH 44105 t) (216) 641-7575 Andrej N. Lah, Dir.;
Holy Trinity Cemetery - 33843 Detroit Rd., Avon, OH 44011; Mailing: P.O. Box 605310, Cleveland, OH 44105 t) (216) 641-7575
St. John Cemetery - 7000 Woodland Ave., Cleveland, OH 44104; Mailing: P.O. Box 605310, Cleveland, OH 44105 t) (216) 641-7575 Andrej N. Lah, Dir.;
St. Joseph Cemetery - 7916 Woodland Ave, Cleveland, OH 44104; Mailing: P.O. Box 605310, Cleveland, OH 44105 t) (216) 641-7575 Andrej N. Lah, Dir.;
St. Joseph Cemetery - 32789 Detroit Rd., Avon, OH 44011; Mailing: P.O. Box 605310, Cleveland, OH 44105 t) (216) 641-7575 Andrej N. Lah, Dir.;
St. Mary Cemetery - 2677 W. 41st St., Cleveland, OH 44113; Mailing: P.O. Box 605310, Cleveland, OH 44105 t) (216) 641-7575
St. Mary Cemetery - 4720 E. 71st St., Cuyahoga Heights, OH 44125; Mailing: P.O. Box 605310, Cleveland, OH 44105 t) (216) 641-7575
St. Mary Cemetery - 7284 Lake Ave., Elyria, OH 44035; Mailing: P.O. Box 605310, Cleveland, OH 44105 t) (216) 641-7575 Andrej N. Lah, Dir.;
St. Mary of the Falls Cemetery - 1260 W. Bagley Rd., Berea, OH 44017; Mailing: P.O. Box 605310, Cleveland, OH 44105 t) (216) 641-7575 Andrej N. Lah, Dir.;
Resurrection Cemetery - 6303 Center Rd., Valley City, OH 44280; Mailing: P.O. Box 605310, Cleveland, OH 44105 t) (216) 641-7575 Andrej N. Lah, Dir.;

EUCLID

St. Paul Cemetery - 1231 Chardon Rd., Euclid, OH 44117; Mailing: P.O. Box 605310, Cleveland, OH 44105 t) 216-641-7575 alah@clecem.org www.clecem.org Andrej N. Lah, Dir.;

COLLEGES & UNIVERSITIES [COL]

PEPPER PIKE

Ursuline College - 2550 Lander Rd., Pepper Pike, OH 44124 t) 440-449-4200 helen.jones-toms@ursuline.edu; marketing@ursuline.edu www.ursuline.edu Sr. Christine De Vinne, OSU, Pres.; Deanne Hurley, Vice Pres. Student Affairs; Richard Konisiewicz, Vice. Pres. Inst. Advancement; Stds.: 950; Lay Tchrs.: 64

SOUTH EUCLID

Notre Dame College - 4545 College Rd., South Euclid, OH 44121 t) (216) 373-6469 pr@ndc.edu www.notredamecollege.edu Ted Steiner, Campus Min.; Stds.: 1,524; Lay Tchrs.: 57

UNIVERSITY HEIGHTS

John Carroll Jesuit Community - 2520 Miramar Blvd.,

University Heights, OH 44118-3821 t) 216-397-1886 jesuits@jcu.edu www.jcu.edu Rev. Lukas Laniauskas, SJ, Pst.; Rev. Gregory Hyde, S.J., Assoc. Pst.; Rev. Michael A. Vincent, S.J., Assoc. Pst.; Rev. Bernard F. McAniff, S.J., Chap.; Rev. Thomas Joseph Pipp, Rector; Rev. James Bretzke, S.J., Prof.; Rev. Donald Serva, S.J., Prof.; Andrew Cera, S.J., Teacher; Rev. Atakelt Hailu, S.J., In Res.; Pr. Tchrs.: 8; Scholastics: 1

***John Carroll University** - 1 John Carroll Blvd., University Heights, OH 44118 t) 216-397-1886; 216-397-1590 (Legal Affairs Office) jkrukones@jcu.edu www.jcu.edu Alan Miciak, Pres.; Rebecca Drenovsky, Dean, Graduate Studies; Elad Granot, Dean, Boler College of Business; Bonnie Gunzenhauser, Dean, College of Arts & Sciences; Steven Herbert, Provost & Academic Vice Pres.; Edward J. Peck, Vice Pres., Univ. Mission & Identity; Naomi Sigg, Vice Pres., Diversity, Equity, Inclusion, & Belonging; Ryan Daly, Vice Pres., Univ. Advancement; Sherri Crahen, Vice Pres., Student Affairs; Ray Brown, Interim Vice Pres., Enrollment Mgmt.; Jennifer Rick, Asst. Vice Pres., Human Resources; Michael Scanlan, Asst. Vice Pres., Mktg. & Comm.; Jeremiah Swetel, Asst. Vice Pres., Facilities & Auxiliary Svcs.; Michelle Morgan, Senior Dir., Athletics; Colleen Treml, Gen. Counsel & Corp. Secy.; Paul Hulseman, Special Asst. to Pres.; Stds.: 2,922; Bro. Tchrs.: 1; Lay Tchrs.: 144; Pr. Tchrs.: 3

CONVENTS, MONASTERIES, AND RESIDENCES FOR WOMEN [CON]

AKRON

Dominican Sisters of Peace - 1230 W. Market St., Our Lady of the Elms Convent, Akron, OH 44313-7108; Mailing: 1375 W. Exchange St., Akron, OH 44313-7619 t) 330-836-4908 barbara.ebner@oppeace.org www.oppeace.org Srs.: 21

CHARDON

Provincial House of the Sisters of Notre Dame, Juniorate, Novitiate - 13000 Auburn Rd., Notre Dame Educ. Ctr., Chardon, OH 44024 t) 440-286-7101 mgorman@sndusa.org www.sndusa.org Sr. M. Patricia Teckman, Admin.; Srs.: 231

CLEVELAND

Carmel of the Holy Family - 2541 Arlington Rd., Cleveland, OH 44118-4009 t) 216-321-6568 barb.carmel@gmail.com; clevelandcarmelites@gmail.com Discalced Carmelite Nuns. Sr. Barbara Losh, O.C.D., Supr.; Srs.: 7

Congregation of the Sisters of St. Joseph, Inc. - 3430 Rocky River Dr., Cleveland Ctr., Cleveland, OH 44111-2997 t) 216-252-0440 pwarbritton@csjoseph.org www.csjoseph.org Sponsored ministries: St. Joseph Academy, River's Edge Sr. Patricia Warbritton, Treas.; Srs.: 356

Monastery of the Poor Clares - 3501 Rocky River Dr., Cleveland, OH 44111-2998 t) 216-941-2820 clare.cleveland@mail.com www.pcc-cle.org Mother Mary Dolores Warner, PCC, Supr.; Srs.: 13

Motherhouse and Novitiate of the Sisters of the Holy Spirit - 10102 Granger Rd., Cleveland, OH 44125; Mailing: 1404 E. Ninth St., c/o Diocese of Cleveland, Office of the Chancellor, Cleveland, OH 44114 t) 216-696-6525 x2070 vgardiner@dioceseofcleveland.org Vincent Gardiner, Chancellor;

Poor Clares of Perpetual Adoration - 4108 Euclid Ave., Cleveland, OH 44103 t) 216-361-0783 angelspcpa@sbcglobal.net thepoorclares.com Mother Mary James, P.C.P.A., Supr.; Srs.: 19

Sisters of St. Joseph of St. Mark - 21800 Chardon Rd., Cleveland, OH 44117-2199 t) 216-531-7426 sister_raphael@msjorg.net www.mountstjoseph.net Mother M. Raphael Gregg, SJSM, Supr.; Srs.: 2

Ursuline Sisters of Cleveland (The Ursuline Academy of Cleveland) - 6085 Parkland Blvd., Suite 175, Cleveland, OH 44124 t) 440-229-5618 rwelsh@ursulinesisters.org www.ursulinesisters.org Sr. Ritamary Welsh, Pres.; Srs.: 117

EUCLID

Provincial House of Sisters of the Most Holy Trinity - 21281 Chardon Rd., Euclid, OH 44117 t) 216-481-8232 spaolofourdeseuclid@yahoo.com www.srstrinity.com Attended from Center for Pastoral Leadership. Sr. Phyllis Ann Lavalle, Supr.; Srs.: 15

PARMA HEIGHTS

Sisters of the Incarnate Word and Blessed Sacrament - 6618 Pearl Rd., Parma Heights, OH 44130-3808 t) 440-886-6440 x401 mtaylor.incarnatewordorder@gmail.com Sr. Margaret Taylor, S.I.W., Congregational Leader; Srs.: 14

RICHFIELD

The Sisters of Charity of St. Augustine - 5232 Broadview Rd., Richfield, OH 44286-9608 t) 330-659-5100 jak@srsofcharity.org www.srsofcharity.org Sr. Judith Ann Karam, C.S.A., Congregational Leader; Srs.: 23

Regina Health Center - t) 330-659-4161

ENDOWMENTS / FOUNDATIONS / TRUSTS [EFT]

AKRON

The Daughters of Divine Charity, St. Mary Province, Charitable Trust - 39 N. Portage Path, Akron, OH 44303-1183 t) 330-867-4960 sistermartingreen@gmail.com Sr. M. Martin Green, F.D.C., Contact;

CHARDON

The Sisters of Notre Dame Charitable Trust - 13000 Auburn Rd., Chardon, OH 44024 t) 440-286-7101 mgorman@sndusa.org www.sndchardon.org Sr. Margaret Mary Gorman, S.N.D., Chair;

CLEVELAND

Congregation of the Sisters of St. Joseph Charitable Trust - 3430 Rocky River Dr., Cleveland, OH 44111-2997 t) 216-252-0440 pwarbritton@csjoseph.org Sr. Marguerite O'Brien, Chair;

St. John Cathedral Endowment Trust - 1007 Superior Ave. E., Cleveland, OH 44114-2582 t) 216-771-6666 www.saintjohncathedral.com Rev. Sean P. Ralph, Pst.; Rev. Joselito delos Reyes, Par. Vicar;

Saint Joseph Academy Scholarship Granting Organization - 3470 Rocky River Dr., Cleveland, OH 44111-2997

Poor Clares Perpetual Adoration Foundation of Cleveland, Ohio - 4108 Euclid Ave., Cleveland, OH 44103; Mailing: 134 Western Ave, Akron, OH 44313 t) 330-996-4090 barbara@pcpafnd.org www.pcpafnd.org Sharon Deitrick, Pres.;

Scholarship Granting Organization of the Catholic Community Foundation - 1404 E. 9th St., Cleveland, OH 44114 t) (216) 696-6525 x5750 Patrick J. Grace, Pres.;

Sisters of Charity Foundation of Cleveland - 2475 E. 22nd St., 4th Fl., Cleveland, OH 44115 t) 216-357-4460 www.socfcleveland.org Susanna H. Krey, Pres.;

The Thomas C. and Sandra S. Sullivan Foundation - 1404 E. 9th St., 8th Fl., Cleveland, OH 44114 t) 216-696-6525 x4080 lpavia@catholiccommunity.org www.catholiccommunity.org Patrick J. Grace, Exec.;

Villa Angela-St. Joseph High School Education Endowment Trust - 18491 Lakeshore Blvd., Cleveland, OH 44119 t) 216-481-8414 tcarone@vasj.com www.vasj.com Lorenzo Jones, Prin.; Thomas M. Carone, Pres.;

St. Vincent Charity Development Foundation - 2351 E. 22nd St., Cleveland, OH 44115 t) 216-696-8401 foundation@stvincentcharity.com; mcotleur@sistersofcharityhealth.org stvincentcharity.com Mark A Cotleur, Contact;

CUYAHOGA FALLS

HMH Foundation - 2251 Front St., Ste. 210, Cuyahoga Falls, OH 44221 t) 234-525-6400 fberry@hmhousing.org www.hmhousing.org Fred Berry, Pres.;

Walsh Jesuit High School Foundation - 4550 Wyoga Lake Rd., Cuyahoga Falls, OH 44224 t) 330-929-4205 mitchellc@walshjesuit.org Colleen Joyce, Chair; Richard P Bedell, Treas.; Christopher Scala, Mem.; Charles Abraham, Mem.;

FAIRLAWN

St. Hilary Parish Foundation - 2750 W. Market St., Fairlawn, OH 44333 c) 330-608-4787 d.sarkis@sthilaryfoundation.org www.sthilaryfoundation.org Stephen L. Strayer, Pres.; Diane Sarkis, Dir.;

MEDINA

Friends of the Poor Clares Foundation - 3701 Hunting Run Rd., Medina, OH 44256 t) 216-903-9080 John Grillo, Pres.;

NORTHFIELD

***The Fit from Faith Foundation** - 9451 Brandywine Rd., Northfield, OH 44067; Mailing: PO Box 670129, Northfield, OH 44067 t) (440) 561-0291 lindsay@fitfromfaith.com Addresses child hunger & provides health & wellness education for Catholics in impoverished areas. Lindsay Fullerman, Pres.;

PARMA HEIGHTS

Incarnate Word Academy Student and Faculty Advancement Endowment (IWA Endowment) - 6620 Pearl Rd., Parma Heights, OH 44130 t) 440-842-6818 mwisnor@incarnatewordacademy.org www.incarnatewordacademy.com Steffany Congelio, Prin.; Michael Wisnor, Pres.;

SHAKER HEIGHTS

St. Dominic Endowment Fund - 3450 Norwood Rd., Shaker Heights, OH 44122 t) 216-991-1444 tfanta@dioceseofcleveland.org www.stdominicchurch.net Rev. Thomas G. Fanta, Pres.;

WELLINGTON

St. Patrick Endowment Trust - 512 N. Main St., Wellington, OH 44090 t) 440-647-4375 secretary@stpatrick.cc Rev. David R. Trask, Pst.;

WOOSTER

St. Mary of the Immaculate Conception Elementary Day School Endowment Trust - 527 Beall Ave., Wooster, OH 44691; Mailing: P.O. Box 109, Wooster, OH 44691 t) 330-264-8824 stmarywoosteroffice@gmail.com stmarywooster.org Darcy Pajak, Contact;

HOSPITALS / HEALTH SERVICES [HOS]

CLEVELAND

St. Vincent Charity Medical Center dba St. Vincent Charity Community Health Center - 2351 E. 22nd St., Cleveland, OH 44115 t) 216-861-6200 jean.mey@stvincentcharity.com stvincentcharity.com Outpatient ambulatory care. Dr. Adnan Tahir, Pres.; Asstd. Annu.: 152,890; Staff: 150

GARFIELD HEIGHTS

Marymount Hospital, Inc. - 12300 McCracken Rd., Garfield Heights, OH 44125 t) 216-587-8080 napierd@ccf.org www.marymount.org Rev. Dennis Mrosso, A.J.; Janet Elaine McDonald, Chap.; Rev. Jeremy Pfeister, FGBC, Chap.; Dr. Daniel Napierkowski, Pres.; Mary Tracy, Dir.; Bed Capacity: 269; Asstd. Annu.: 97,236; Staff: 1,271

LORAIN

Mercy Health - Regional Medical Center, LLC - 3700 Kolbe Rd., Lorain, OH 44053 t) 440-960-4000 Gilbert Palmer, Pres.; Catherine Bartek-Woskobnick, Admin.; Bed Capacity: 245; Asstd. Annu.: 63,425; Staff: 1,102

OBERLIN

Mercy Health - Allen Hospital, LLC - 200 W. Lorain St., Oberlin, OH 44074; Mailing: 3700 Kolbe Rd., Lorain, OH 44053 t) 440-776-7000 Carrie Jankowski, Pres.; Catherine Bartek-Woskobnick, Admin.; Bed Capacity: 22; Asstd. Annu.: 15,986; Staff: 161

MISCELLANEOUS [MIS]

AKRON

***Crown Point Ecology Center** - 3220 Ira Rd., Akron, OH 44333; Mailing: P.O. Box 484, Bath, OH 44210 t) 330-668-8992 admin@crownpointecology.org www.crownpointecology.org Kevin Gross, Exec. Dir.;

First Friday Club of Greater Akron - 795 Russell Ave., Akron, OH 44307 t) 330-535-7668 ffcofga@gmail.com www.firstfridayclubofgreaterakron.org Mike Herhold, Pres.;

Leonora Hall Residence - 39 N. Portage Path, Akron, OH 44303 t) 330-867-1752 sistermartingreen@gmail.com Home for Women. Sr. M. Martin Green, F.D.C., Admin.; Srs.: 1

CHARDON

Christ Child Society-Geauga Chapter - ; Mailing: P.O. Box 1133, Chardon, OH 44024 t) (440) 286-1534 Gail M Hufgard, Pres.;

Notre Dame Schools - 13000 Auburn Rd., Chardon, OH 44024 t) 440-286-6226 Dr. Michael Bates, Pres.;

Notre Dame Schools Scholarship Granting Organization - 13000 Auburn Rd., Chardon, OH 44024 t) (440) 279-1079

Notre Dame Village - 13000 Auburn Rd., Chardon, OH 44024 t) 440-279-9400 mgorman@sndusa.org Sr. Margaret Mary Gorman, S.N.D., Contact;

SND National Ministry Corp. - 13000 Auburn Rd., Chardon, OH 44024 t) 440-286-7101 mgorman@sndusa.org Sr. Margaret Mary Gorman, S.N.D., Prov. Supr.;

SND Operations Corp. - 13000 Auburn Rd., Chardon, OH 44024 t) 440-286-7101 mgorman@sndusa.org Sisters of Notre Dame Sr. Margaret Mary Gorman, S.N.D., Prov. Supr.;

CLEVELAND

***St. Augustine Services Corporation** - 7801 Detroit Ave., Cleveland, OH 44102 t) 216-634-7400 rmeserini@st-aug.org Rick Meserini, Pres.;

Catholic Community Connection - 2475 E. 22nd St., 5th Fl., Cleveland, OH 44115 t) (216) 377-4358 Marian R. Rubin, Pres.;

Catholic Community Foundation - 1404 E. 9th St., Cleveland, OH 44144 t) 216-696-6525 www.catholiccommunity.org Patrick J. Grace, Exec.;

***Christ Child Society of Cleveland** - 7901 Detroit Ave., Ste. 300, Cleveland, OH 44102 t) 216-939-3859 christchildcleveland@yahoo.com www.christchildsocietycleveland.org Paula Conrad, Pres.;

Community of Little Brothers and Sisters of the Eucharist, Inc. - 3675 W. 165th St., Cleveland, OH 44111 c) 216-926-1956 littlesismaggie@gmail.com; 1abbajim@gmail.com Sr. Maggie Walsh, Dir.; Rev. James P. O'Donnell, Mem.;

Congregation of the Sisters of St. Joseph Ministries, Inc. (CSJ Ministries) - 3430 Rocky River Rd., Cleveland, OH 44111-2997; Mailing: CSJ Ministries, 1515 W. Ogden Ave., La Grange Park, IL 60526 t) (708) 354-9200 Theresa Denton, Exec. Dir.;

CSJ Initiatives, Inc. - 3430 Rocky River Dr., Cleveland, OH 44111; Mailing: 3450 N. Rock Rd., Ste. 605, Wichita, KS 67226 t) 316-364-3356 kdavis@csjinitiatives.org www.csjinitiatives.org Consulting for religious communities care of aged and properties and management services Denise Gannon, CEO;

Diocese of Cleveland Facilities Services Corp. - 1404 E. 9th St., Cleveland, OH 44114 t) 216-696-6525 www.dioceseofcleveland.org Bill Brady, Dir.; Staff: 12

***First Friday Club of Cleveland, Inc.** - ; Mailing: P.O. Box 141066, Cleveland, OH 44114 t) (216) 696-6525 x1101 Patrick McCarthy, Pres.;

St. Ignatius High School Scholarship Granting Organization - 1911 W. 30th St., Cleveland, OH 44113 t) (216) 651-0222 www.ignatius.edu/wildcat-fund Rev. Raymond P. Guiao, S.J.;

St. John Hospital - 2475 E. 22nd St., Cleveland, OH 44115 t) 216-696-5560 www.sistersofcharityhealth.org St. John Hospital Corporate Office Janice Murphy, Pres.;

Joseph House of Cleveland, Inc. - 6108 St. Clair Ave., Cleveland, OH 44103 t) 440-256-1412; 216-431-7200 josephhouseofcleveland.org Housing and clothing bank for refugees. Rev. Zvonko Blasko, Dir.; Rev. Frank G. Godic, Dir.; Rev. John C. Retar, Dir.; Rev. David G. Woost, Dir.;

L'Arche, Cleveland - 11811 Shaker Blvd., Ste. 116, Cleveland, OH 44120; Mailing: P.O. Box 20450, Cleveland, OH 44120 t) 216-721-2614 office@larchecleveland.org www.larchecleveland.org An ecumenical community providing homes for adults with developmental disabilities. Jennifer O'Malia, Dir.;

Ninth Street CDC - 1404 E. Ninth St., Ste. 701, Cleveland, OH 44114-1722 t) 216-696-6525 x4360 kburke@dioceseofcleveland.org James Gulick, Pres.;

Sisters of Charity of St. Augustine Health System - 2475 E. 22nd St., Cleveland, OH 44115 t) 216-696-5560 www.sistersofcharityhealth.org Serves as Member of St. Vincent Charity Community HC, Fdns, & Health Care Corps. sponsored by SOC Health System Ministries, a PJP of pontifical right. Janice Murphy, Pres.;

Sisters of St. Joseph - 3430 Rocky River Dr., Cleveland, OH 44111-2997 t) 216-252-0440 pwarbritton@csjoseph.org Mary Zavoda, Contact;

***Society of St. Vincent de Paul, Diocesan Council** - 1404 E. 9th St., 3rd Fl., Cleveland, OH 44114 t) 216-696-6525 info@svdpcle.org www.svdpcle.org Provides basic needs emergency assistance to people struggling with poverty through volunteers at member parishes. Ed Leszynski, Pres.; Gary Allen Sole, CEO;

***The Community of Jesus, The Living Mercy** - 3675 W. 165th St., Cleveland, OH 44111; Mailing: P.O. Box 694, Berea, OH 44017 t) 800-482-4100; 440-570-1087 bethesdahouse@aol.com; reachout@bethesdahouseofmercy.org bethesdahouseofmercy.org Healing support for post-abortive women and men Rachel Benda, Dir.;

St. Vincent Charity Health Campus, Inc. - 2475 E. 22nd St., Cleveland, OH 44115 t) (216) 875-4609

***St. Vitus Development Corporation** - 6019 Lausche Ave., Cleveland, OH 44103 t) 216-361-1444 skuhar@hotmail.com; frjcretar@gmail.com www.saintvitus.org Independent Senior Living Rev. John C. Retar, Pres.; Stane Kuhar, Secy.; Joseph V. Hocevar, Treas.; Rev. Joseph P. Boznar, Pastor Emer.;

Women Religious Archives Collaborative - 2475 E. 22nd St., 4th Fl., Cleveland, OH 44115 t) (216) 287-5176

CLEVELAND HEIGHTS

Beaumont School Scholarship Granting Organization - 3301 N. Park Blvd., Cleveland Heights, OH 44118 t) (216) 321-2954 Wendy Hoke, Pres.;

CLINTON

Faith and Light U.S.A., Inc. - 700 Killinger Rd., Loyola Retreat House, Inc., Clinton, OH 44216-9653; Mailing: 6152 State St., Louisville, OH 44641 t) 330-666-6816; 314-556-2222 beckihaller@aol.com; kirtbromley@yahoo.com Elizabeth R. Haller, Treas.;

CUYAHOGA FALLS

Christ Child Society of Akron - 2115 Lindbergh Ave., Cuyahoga Falls, OH 44223; Mailing: PO Box 13411, Akron, OH 44334-8811 t) 330-922-3700 treasurer@christchildsocietyakron.org; president@christchildsocietyakron.org christchildsocietyakron.org Rita Burkley, Pres.; Nancy Parks, Treas.;

Humility of Mary Housing, Inc. - 2251 Front St., Ste. 210, Cuyahoga Falls, OH 44221 t) 234-525-6400 fberry@hmhousing.org www.hmhousing.org Affordable housing and housing related services Fred Berry, Pres.;

HM Housing Development Corporation - 1561 E. 30th St., Lorain, OH 44055 t) 330-384-2144

H.M. Life Opportunity Services - t) 330-384-2144

Walsh Jesuit High School Scholarship Granting Organization - 4550 Wyoga Lake Rd., Cuyahoga Falls, OH 44224 t) (330) 929-4205 x166

ELYRIA

First Friday Forum of Lorain County - 320 Middle Ave., Elyria, OH 44035 t) 440-244-0643 ffflorain@gmail.com Jack Giovannazzo, Chair;

GARFIELD HEIGHTS

Jennings Manor Housing Corporation - 10204 Granger Rd., Garfield Heights, OH 44125 t) 216-581-2900 welcome@jenningsohio.org www.jenningsohio.org 61 unit apartment building - HUD 202 Supportive Housing for Older Adults. Allison Q. Salopeck, Pres.;

Marymount Health Care Systems - 5200 Marymount Village Dr., Garfield Heights, OH 44125 t) 216-587-8627 c) 216-469-9179 jmyers@ccf.org Provides comprehensive health and human services in response to the needs of the local community by owning, leasing and operating health care. Dr. Daniel Napierkowski, Pres.;

MHCS Real Estate Holding Company - 12300 McCracken Rd., Garfield Heights, OH 44125-2975 t) 216-587-8627 c) 212-469-9179 jmyers@ccf.org Dr. Daniel Napierkowski, Pres.;

Village Property Holding Company, LLC - 5200 Marymount Village Dr., Garfield Heights, OH 44125 t) 216-332-1100 jmyers@ccf.org Jeffry Myers, CEO;

LAKEWOOD

SEHS Scholarship Granting Organization - 13500 Detroit Ave., Lakewood, OH 44107 t) (216) 221-3776

LORAIN

Mercy Health - Lorain, LLC - 3700 Kolbe Rd., Lorain, OH 44053 t) 440-960-3295 John Luellen, Pres.; Catherine Bartek-Woskobnick, Admin.;

LYNDHURST

Julie Billiart Network - 4982 Clubside Rd., Lyndhurst, OH 44124 t) 216-381-1191 ssweigert@jbschool.org www.juliebilliartschool.org Alaine Davis, Contact;

MENTOR

Christ Child Society of the Western Reserve - 9324 Mentor Ave. - Unit 1, Mentor, OH 44060 t) 440-350-9836 karenmunson11@gmail.com www.christchildwesternreserve.org Bobbie McArthur, Pres.;

PARMA

Society of St. Joseph the Worker - 7033 State Rd., Parma, OH 44134-4952 t) 440-888-4872 bsjw@msn.com www.bsjw.org Brothers of St. Joseph the Worker Bro. Lawrence R. Verbiar, Dir.;

RICHFIELD

Society of Our Lady of the Way/ Madonna della Strada - 5232 Broadview Rd., Richfield, OH 44286 t) 216-381-5502 matslow@aol.com www.saecimds.com Secular Institute for Single Women.

ROCKY RIVER

Magnificat Scholarship Granting Organization - 20770 Hilliard Blvd., Rocky River, OH 44116 t) (440) 331-1572 x230

SOLON

***Retrouvaille of Cleveland, Inc.** - 5470 N. Woods Ln., Solon, OH 44139 t) 216-509-0301 shelly@peet-martinko.com retrouvailleofcleveland.catholicweb.com Rev. Ryan J. Mann, Chap.;

WICKLIFFE

Center for Pastoral Leadership Services, Inc. - 28700 Euclid Ave., Wickliffe, OH 44092-2585 t) 440-943-7600 pguban@dioceseofcleveland.org Rev. Mark Latcovich, CEO; Philip J. Guban, Treas.;

COAR Peace Mission, Inc. - 28700 Euclid Ave., Wickliffe, OH 44092 t) (216) 269-1710 info@coarpeacemission.org coarpeacemission.org/ Development and outreach office for the COAR Children's Village in the Archdiocese of San Salvador, El Salvador Mary Katherine Stevenson, CEO; Susan E. Barnish, Progs. Dir.;

COAR Children's Village - Comunidad Oscar Arnulfo Romero-COAR: residential foster care & preK-12 school for vulnerable children in Zaragoza, El Salvador, Central America.

***Parents of Priests of the Diocese of Cleveland, Inc.** - 28700 Euclid Ave., Wickliffe, OH 44092 t) 330-668-9068 trentalouis@gmail.com Louis Trenta, Pres.;

MONASTERIES AND RESIDENCES FOR PRIESTS AND BROTHERS [MON]

AVON

Congregation of St. Joseph - 4076 Case Rd., Avon, OH 44011 t) 440-934-6270 frjscalco@gmail.com www.murialdo.org Fathers and Brothers of St. Joseph Rev. Joseph Scalco, CSJ, Dir.; Brs.: 1; Priests: 3

BROOKLYN

St. Anthony of Padua Friary - 4185 Brookway Ln., Brooklyn, OH 44144 t) 314-409-1111 allanofm@me.com Rev. Theodore Haag, O.F.M., Pst.; Rev. Marc Sheckells I, OFM, Prof.; Rev. Johnpaul

Cafiero, OFM, Spiritual Adv./Care Srvcs.; Rev. Charles Hart, O.F.M.; Rev. Allan DaCorte, O.F.M.; Bro. Gary Jeriha, OFM, Music Min.; Brs.: 1; Priests: 5

CLEVELAND

Benedictine Order of Cleveland (St. Andrew Abbey) - 10510 Buckeye Rd., Cleveland, OH 44104-3725 t) 216-721-5300 business@standrewabbey.org; proc@standrewabbey.org www.standrewabbey.org Rt. Rev. Gary Hoover, O.S.B., Abbot; Bro. Peter Ancell, OSB, Prior; Rev. Michael Brunovsky, O.S.B., Subprior; Rev. Conrad Wald Wald, OSB, Bus. Mgr.; Rev. Bede Kotlinski, O.S.B., Mem.; Rev. Anselm Zupka, O.S.B., Mem.; Most Rev. Roger W. Gries, O.S.B., Bishop; Brs.: 7; Priests: 16

Assumption Church - 9183 Broadview Rd., Broadview Heights, OH 44147 t) 440-526-1177 finbar@cbhs.edu Rev. Finbar Ramsak, O.S.B, Contact;

Mercedarians (Fathers of Our Lady of Mercy, Inc. / Order of the B.V.M. of Mercy / Mercedarian Friars USA) - 6928 Detroit Ave., Cleveland, OH 44102-3093 t) 216-651-5043 (Mt. Carmel); 216-961-8331 (St. Rocco) c) 215-435-2300 vicar@orderofmercy.org; economo@orderofmercy.org orderofmercy.org Rev. Gene Costa, Par. Vicar; Rev. James Chia; Rev. James Mayer, O.de.M.; Rev. Paschal Rosca, O.de.M.; Priests: 4

St. Paul Friary - 4120 Euclid Ave., Cleveland, OH 44103 t) 216-431-8854 stpaulshrine@sbcglobal.net www.saintpaulshrine.com Rev. Philip Bernier, O.F.M. Cap., Pst.; Rev. W. Nestler, O.F.M. Cap., Pst.; Rev. David Domanski, OFM Cap., Par. Vicar; Rev. Anthony Essien, Teacher; Priests: 5

HIGHLAND HEIGHTS

Congregation of the Blessed Sacrament Provincial House - 5384 Wilson Mills Rd., Highland Heights, OH 44143-3092 t) 440-442-6311 susandwork@blessedsacrament.com www.blessedsacrament.com Province of St. Ann. Fathers of the Blessed Sacrament. Very Rev. John Thomas Joseph Lane Sr., S.S.S., Prov.; Brs.: 7; Priests: 17

NURSING / REHABILITATION / CONVALESCENCE / ELDERLY CARE [NUR]

AKRON

Francesca Residence - 39 N. Portage Path, Akron, OH 44303 t) 330-867-6334 sistermartingreen@gmail.com Sr. M. Martin Green, F.D.C., Admin.; Asstd. Annu.: 16; Staff: 8

BEDFORD

Light of Hearts Villa, Inc. - 283 Union St., Bedford, OH 44146 t) 440-232-1991 www.lightofheartsvilla.org Devoted to providing premier senior residential living and community outreach services Breanne Cavileer, Dir.; Asstd. Annu.: 63; Staff: 45

CLEVELAND

St. Augustine Manor (St. Augustine Health Ministries) - 7801 Detroit Ave., Cleveland, OH 44102 t) 216-634-7400 info@st-aug.org; advancement@st-aug.org www.staugministries.org Affiliated with Catholic Charities. Mark McGrievy, Chair; Rick Meserini, Pres.; Asstd. Annu.: 1,680; Staff: 516

St. Augustine Child Enrichment Center -

St. Augustine Health Campus Skilled Nursing Facility -

St. Augustine Towers Assisted Living Residencies - 7821 Lake Ave., Cleveland, OH 44102 t) 216-634-7444 Brigid Nolan, Dir.;

Holy Family Home Health Care & Hospice - 6707 State Rd, Parma, OH 44134 t) 440-888-7722 kgraham@holyfamilyhome.com; info@holyfamilyhome.com www.holyfamilyhome.com Residential hospice facility. Kristin Graham, Dir.;

CSJ Rocky River, Inc. - 3440 Rocky River Dr., Cleveland, OH 44111-2997 t) 216-252-0440 ftayor@csjinitiatives.org www.csjinitiatives.org Assisted living facility. Frank Taylor, Admin.; Asstd. Annu.: 30; Staff: 61

Mount St. Joseph - 21800 Chardon Rd., Cleveland, OH 44117 t) 216-531-7426 sister-raphael@msjorg.net www.mountstjoseph.net Conducted by Sisters of St. Joseph of St. Mark - Mount St. Joseph. Mother M. Raphael Gregg, SJSM, Admin.; Asstd. Annu.: 148; Staff: 120

FAIRLAWN

The Village at St. Edward - 3131 Smith Rd., Fairlawn, OH 44333 t) 330-666-1183 danielle.maur@vased.org www.vased.org Rev. David A. Novak, Chap.; John P. Stoner, Pres.; Asstd. Annu.: 400; Staff: 232

The Village of St. Edward (St. Edward Home) - t) 330-668-2828 www.vsecommunities.org

GARFIELD HEIGHTS

Jennings Center for Older Adults - 10204 Granger Rd., Garfield Heights, OH 44125 t) 216-581-2900 welcome@jenningsohio.org www.jenningsohio.org Continuing care retirement community for older adults. Allison Q. Salopeck, Pres.; Asstd. Annu.: 1,300; Staff: 403

St. Agnes Terrace Apartments - 10300 Granger Rd., Garfield Heights, OH 44125 t) (216) 581-2900 Independent Housing

Eva L. Bruening Adult Day Center - 10204 Granger Rd., Garfield Heights, OH 44125 t) (216) 581-2900

Holy Spirit Ridge at Jennings - 10102 Granger Rd., Garfield Heights, OH 44125

Holy Spirit Villas - 10204 Granger Rd., Garfield Heights, OH 44125 t) (216) 581-2900 Independent Housing

Jennings Assisted Living - 10210 Granger Rd., Garfield Heights, OH 44125 t) (216) 581-2900

Jennings at Brecksville - 8736 Brecksville Rd., Brecksville, OH 44141 t) (216) 581-2900

Jennings Hall Skilled Nursing Facility - 10204 Granger Rd., Garfield Heights, OH 44125 t) (216) 581-2900 Skilled Nursing Facility

Jennings Manor Housing Corporation - 10200 Granger Rd., Garfield Heights, OH 44125 t) (216) 581-2900 Apartment Building for HUD Section 202 Supportive Housing for the Elderly

Jennings Operating, LLC - 10204 Granger Rd., Garfield Heights, OH 44125 t) (216) 581-2900

Jennings Real Estate, LLC - 10204 Granger Rd., Garfield Heights, OH 44125 t) (216) 581-2900

The Learning Circle Child Day Care Center - 10204 Granger Rd., Garfield Heights, OH 44125 t) (216) 581-2900

St. Rita Apartments - 10614 Granger Rd., Garfield Heights, OH 44125 t) (216) 581-2900 Apartments for adults 55+

Village at Marymount - 5200 Marymount Village Dr., Garfield Heights, OH 44125 t) 216-332-1100 jmyers@ccf.org www.villageatmarymount.org Comprehensive health care services Jeffry Myers, Pres.; Sr. Mary Alice Jarosz, S.S.F.-T.O.S.F., Dir.; Asstd. Annu.: 996; Staff: 296

PARMA

Franciscan Communities, Inc. (Mount Alverna Village) - 6765 State Rd., Parma, OH 44134; Mailing: 11500 Theresa Dr., Lemont, IL 60439 t) 440-843-7800 pwelsh@franciscancommunities.org www.franciscanministries.org Continuing Care Retirement Community. A senior living and healthcare services ministry sponsored by the Franciscan Sisters of Chicago. Patrick M. Welsh, Exec. Dir.; Sr. Angela Nikwobazeirwe, Chap.; Joseph McCartney, Dir., Mission Integration/Pastoral Care; Asstd. Annu.: 128; Staff: 307

RICHFIELD

Regina Health Center - 5232 Broadview Rd., Richfield, OH 44286-9608 t) 330-659-4161 myantek@reginahealthcenter.org www.reginahealthcenter.org Sponsored by Sisters of Charity of St. Augustine. Dcn. Mark Yantek, Exec.; Asstd. Annu.: 148; Staff: 167

PRESCHOOLS / CHILDCARE CENTERS [PRE]

GARFIELD HEIGHTS

Marymount Child Care Center - 12215 Granger Rd., Garfield Heights, OH 44125 t) (216) 365-3341 marymountcare@aol.com Michelle C. Kreiger, Dir.; Stds.: 85; Lay Tchrs.: 16

LAKEWOOD

Lakewood Catholic Academy Early Childhood Program - 14808 Lake Ave., Lakewood, OH 44107 t) 216-521-4352 jberardinelli@lcasaints.com; bwarrell@lcasaints.com lakewoodcatholicacademy.com Jennifer Berardinelli, Vice. Pres.; Stds.: 200; Lay Tchrs.: 16

RETREAT HOUSES / RENEWAL CENTERS [RTR]

AVON

St. Leonard Youth Retreat Center (Fathers of St. Joseph, Inc.) - 4076 Case Rd., Avon, OH 44011 t) 440-934-6270 stleonardyrc@gmail.com www.stleonardyrc.com For youth and young adults Rev. Leo Ambrose Dechant, CSJ, Dir.;

CLINTON

Loyola Retreat House, Inc. - 700 Killinger Rd., Clinton, OH 44216 t) 330-896-2315 office@loyolaretreathouse.com www.loyolaretreathouse.com Katy Karg, Exec.;

PARMA

Jesuit Retreat House - 5629 State Rd., Parma, OH 44134 t) 440-884-9300 info@jesuitretreatcenter.org; bhobbs@jesuitretreatcenter.org www.jesuitretreatcenter.org William Hobbs, Dir.;

SEMINARIES [SEM]

WICKLIFFE

Borromeo Seminary - 28700 Euclid Ave., Wickliffe, OH 44092-2585 t) 440-943-7600 mal@dioceseofcleveland.org www.borromeoseminary.org Rev. Mark Latcovich, Pres.; Rev. John Paul Kuzma, OFM Cap., Mem.; Rev. Patrick S. Anderson, Dir.; Rev. William G. Bouhall, Dir.; Rev. Damian J. Ference, Dir.; Rev. Michael Joyce, O.F.M.Cap., Dir.; Alan K. Rome, Librn.; Stds.: 20; Lay Tchrs.: 2; Pr. Tchrs.: 3; Sr. Tchrs.: 1

Saint Mary Seminary and Graduate School of Theology - 28700 Euclid Ave., Wickliffe, OH 44092-2585 t) 440-943-7600 mal@dioceseofcleveland.org stmarysem.edu (Our Lady of the Lake) Sr. Mary McCormick, O.S.U., Dean; Most Rev. Michael G. Woost, Prof.; Rev. Patrick Manning, Prof.; Rev. Mark S. Ott, Prof.; Rev. George Smiga, Prof.; Rev. Christopher J. Trenta, Prof.; Rev. Mark Latcovich, Pres.; Rev. Joseph M. Koopman, Vice. Pres.; Rev. G. David Bline, Dir.; Rev. Andrew B. Turner, Dir.; Alan K. Rome, Librn.; Stds.: 124; Lay Tchrs.: 2; Pr. Tchrs.: 10; Sr. Tchrs.: 3

SHRINES [SHR]

CLEVELAND

The Conversion of St. Paul Shrine - 4120 Euclid Ave., Cleveland, OH 44103; Mailing: 4108 Euclid Ave., Cleveland, OH 44103 t) 216-361-0783 srcarmelpcpa@gmail.com www.thepoorclares.com Mother Mary James, P.C.P.A., Abbess;

EUCLID

Our Lady of Lourdes Shrine - 21281 Chardon Rd., Euclid, OH 44117 t) 216-481-8232 www.srstrinity.com Euclid, (U.S. Rtes. 20 & 6). Administered by the Sisters of the Most Holy Trinity. Sr. Phyllis Ann Lavalle, Supr.;

GARFIELD HEIGHTS

Our Lady of Czestochowa Shrine - 12215 Granger Rd., Garfield Heights, OH 44125 t) 216-518-2101 Administered by the Sisters of St. Joseph Third Order of St. Francis (S.S.J.-T.O.S.F.) Cindy Matteson, CEO;

PARMA HEIGHTS

Queen of the Holy Rosary Shrine - 6618 Pearl Rd., Parma Heights, OH 44130-3808 t) 440-886-6440 x401 mtaylor.incarnatewordorder@gmail.com www.incarnatewordorder.org Administered by the Sisters of the Incarnate Word and Blessed Sacrament

(S.I.W.) Sr. Margaret Taylor, S.I.W., Supr.;

SPECIAL CARE FACILITIES [SPF]

CLEVELAND

Rose Mary, The Johanna Grasselli Rehabilitation and Education Center - 2346 W. 14th St., Cleveland, OH 44113 t) 216-481-4823 contact@rose-marycenter.com rmcle.org Gina Kerman, Contact; Bed Capacity: 76; Asstd. Annu.: 150; Staff: 250

NORTHFIELD

St. Barnabas Villa, Inc. - 9234 Olde Eight Rd., Northfield, OH 44067 t) 330-467-3758 A shared living facility for 11 people over 60 years of age. Natalie Priest, Dir.;

WELLINGTON

***St. Patrick Manor, Inc. c/o Humility of Mary Housing, Inc.** - 120 Maple St., Wellington, OH 44090; Mailing: 2251 Front St., Ste. 210, Cuyahoga Falls, OH 44221 t) 440-647-0406 fberry@hmhousing.org www.hmhousing.org Senior Housing Apartments Kimberlie Taylor, Property Mgr.; Bed Capacity: 49; Asstd. Annu.: 56; Staff: 3

An asterisk (*) denotes an organization that has established tax-exempt status directly with the IRS and is not covered by the USCCB Group Ruling.

Diocese of Colorado Springs

MOST REVEREND JAMES R. GOLKA

Bishop of Colorado Springs; ordained June 3, 1994; appointed Bishop of Colorado Springs April 30, 2021; ordained June 29, 2021; succeeded to the See June 29, 2021.

Diocesan Offices: 228 N. Cascade Ave., Colorado Springs, CO 80903-1498. T: 719-636-2345; F: 719-636-1216.

ESTABLISHED AND CREATED A DIOCESE JANUARY 30, 1984.

Square Miles 15,493.

Comprising the Counties of Chaffee, Cheyenne, Douglas, Elbert, El Paso, Kit Carson, Lake, Lincoln, Park and Teller.

For legal titles of parishes and diocesan institutions, consult the Diocesan Offices.

STATISTICAL OVERVIEW

Personnel
Bishop....1
Retired Bishops....1
Priests: Diocesan Active in Diocese....37
Priests: Diocesan Active Outside Diocese....3
Priests: Retired, Sick or Absent....10
Number of Diocesan Priests....50
Religious Priests in Diocese....23
Total Priests in your Diocese....73
Extern Priests in Diocese....8
Ordinations:
Diocesan Priests....2
Transitional Deacons....1
Permanent Deacons in Diocese....87
Total Brothers....2
Total Sisters....60

Parishes
Parishes....39
With Resident Pastor:
Resident Diocesan Priests....25
Resident Religious Priests....3
Without Resident Pastor:
Administered by Priests....11
Pastoral Centers....4
Professional Ministry Personnel:
Brothers....2
Sisters....60

Welfare
Catholic Hospitals....2
Total Assisted....195,719
Health Care Centers....2
Total Assisted....318
Homes for the Aged....2
Total Assisted....113
Day Care Centers....2
Total Assisted....100
Special Centers for Social Services....3
Total Assisted....12,137

Educational
Diocesan Students in Other Seminaries....12
Students, Religious....10
Total Seminarians....22
High Schools, Private....2
Total Students....200
Elementary Schools, Diocesan and Parish....6
Total Students....937
Catechesis/Religious Education:
High School Students....728
Elementary Students....4,175
Total Students under Catholic Instruction....6,062
Teachers in Diocese:
Priests....1
Sisters....2
Lay Teachers....145

Vital Statistics
Receptions into the Church:
Infant Baptism Totals....777
Minor Baptism Totals....78
Adult Baptism Totals....172
Received into Full Communion....122
First Communions....857
Confirmations....796
Marriages:
Catholic....152
Interfaith....54
Total Marriages....206
Deaths....545
Total Catholic Population....194,953
Total Population....1,218,457

LEADERSHIP

Diocesan Offices - t) 719-636-2345
Chancellor - dflinn@diocs.org Dcn. Douglas Flinn; Donna Hessel, Vice Chancellor (dhessel@diocs.org);
Ecclesiastical Notary - mmagalong@diocs.org Donna Hessel; Maria Magalong; Jocelyn Olipane;
Bishop - Most Rev. James R Golka;
Vicar General - Rev. Msgr. Robert E. Jaeger;
Vicar for Clergy - Rev. Gregory Golyzniak;
Vicar for Religious - Rev. John Toepfer, O.F.M.Cap. (fjtoepfer@olgcos.org);
Vice Chancellor - gfagan@diocs.org Donna Hessel (dhessel@diocs.org);
Presbyteral Council - Rev. Msgr. Robert E. Jaeger; Rev. Gregory Golyzniak; Rev. Gregory W. Bierbaum;
College of Consultors - Rev. Msgr. Robert E. Jaeger; Rev. George V. Fagan; Rev. Nathaniel Hinds;
Deaneries - Rev. Gregory W. Bierbaum, Vicar; Rev. Carlos Gallardo, Vicar; Rev. Gregory Golyzniak, Vicar;
Eastern Deanery - Rev. Carlos Gallardo, Vicar;
Metro-North Deanery (Colorado Springs) - Rev. Gregory Golyzniak, Vicar;
Metro-South Deanery (Colorado Springs) - Rev. Msgr. Robert E. Jaeger;
Northern Deanery - Rev. Gregory W. Bierbaum, Vicar;
Western Deanery - Rev. James Williams, Vicar;

OFFICES AND DIRECTORS

Office of the Bishop -
Bishop - Most Rev. James R Golka;
Vicar General - Rev. Msgr. Robert E. Jaeger;
Chancellor and General Counsel - dflinn@diocs.org Dcn. Douglas M. Flinn;
Executive Assistant to the Bishop - egriffith@diocs.org Esperanza A. Griffith, Dir.;
Diocesan Special Projects - mthomas@diocs.org Mary Theresa Thomas, Dir.;
Diocesan Senior Staff -
Vicar General - Rev. Msgr. Robert E. Jaeger;
Finance Officer - wpaton@diocs.org Wayne Paton, CFO;
Chancellor and General Counsel - dflinn@diocs.org Dcn. Douglas M. Flinn;
President and CEO of Catholic Charities of Central Colorado - abarton@ccharitiescc.org Andy Barton;
Superintendent of Catholic Schools - swhalen@diocs.org Sheila Whalen;
Stewardship & Development - jcrane@diocs.org Jamie Crane, Dir.;
Hispanic Ministry - jcervantes@diocs.org Javier Cervantes, Dir.;
Diocesan Offices and Ministries -
Catholic Charismatic Renewal Services - t) 719-597-4249 deaconchuck@holyapostlescc.org Dcn. Charles Matzker, Liaison;
Priests Continuing Formation Committee - Rev. Francisco Quezada, Assoc. Dir.; Rev. Michael Holmquist, Assoc. Dir.;
Human Resources Specialist - mhatch@diocs.org Mark Hatch;
Information Technology - gshuck@diocs.org Gary Schuck, Dir.;
Webmaster & Social Media - abekurs@diocs.org Andrea Bekurs, Content Coord.;
Traumatic Brain Injury Ministry - lamontglen@mac.com Dcn. Patrick Jones, Coord.;
Victim Assistance Coordinator - aschott@diocs.org Angella Schott;
Vocations - vocations@diocs.org Rev. Kyle Ingels; Rev. James Baron;
Young Adult and Consecrated Women - lgonzalez@diocs.org Sr. Linda Gonzalez, Dir.;
Editor of The Colorado Catholic Herald & Communications Director - vambuul@coloradocatholicherald.com Veronica Ambuul, Editor;
College Campus Ministry - kingels@diocs.org Rev. Kyle Ingels, Dir.;
Finance Office - wpaton@diocs.org Wayne Paton, Dir.;
Accounting - Jose Rodriguez, Dir.;
Benefits - jhutchinson@diocs.org Janet Hutchinson, Coord.;
Pontifical Missions and Propagation of the Faith - egriffith@diocs.org Esperanza A. Griffith, Dir.;
Office of Catholic Schools - swhalen@diocs.org Sheila Whalen, Supt.;

ADVISORY BOARDS, COMMISSIONS, COMMITTEES, AND COUNCILS

Colorado Springs Council of Black Catholics - t) 719-822-7861 ayoung@diocs.org Aisha Young, Pres.;
Buildings and Properties Committee - Rev. Msgr. Robert E. Jaeger; Dcn. Douglas M. Flinn; John Gatto (jgatto@crestonedevelopment.com);

CONSULTATIVE BODIES

Diocesan Pastoral Council -
Diocesan Finance Council - Don Billings; Jason P. Homec; Rev. Msgr. Robert E. Jaeger;

PASTORAL SERVICES

Pastoral Services & Permanent Diaconate Life and Ministry - dillingworth@diocs.org Dcn. David Illingworth, Dir.;
Care Facility Ministry - dtomich@diocs.org Dcn. Daniel Tomich;
Catechesis, Evangelization, and Youth Ministry - gniemerg@diocs.org Gary Niemerg, Dir.;
Child and Youth Protection - tdickinson@diocs.org Dcn. Thomas Dickinson, Dir.;
Jail Ministry - cdonnelly@diocs.org Dcn. Clifford Donnelly;
Permanent Diaconate Formation - cdonnelly@diocs.org Dcn. Clifford Donnelly, Dir.;
Respect Life Apostolate - jbailey@diocs.org Julie Bailey, Dir.;

TRIBUNAL

Diocesan Tribunal - Rev. Jaimes Ponce; Allessandro Fanella; Silvia Pavone (spavone@diocs.org);
Judicial Vicar - jponce@diocs.org Rev. Jaimes Ponce, Vicar;
Assessor - Dcn. Robert Elliott; Jocelyn Olipane;
Defender of the Bond - Rev. George V. Fagan; Most Rev. Richard C. Hanifen; Silvia Pavone;
Advocates - Dcn. Andrew Berry; Dcn. Richard Bowles; Dcn. Matthew Brend;

PARISHES, MISSIONS, AND CLERGY

STATE OF COLORADO

BAILEY

St. Mary of the Rockies - 224 Buggy Whip Rd., Bailey, CO 80421-8319; Mailing: P.O. Box 319, Bailey, CO 80421-8319 t) 303-838-2375 stmaryrockies@gmail.com www.stmaryrockies.org Rev. Bogdan Siewiera (Poland), Pst.; CRP Stds.: 3

BUENA VISTA

St. Rose of Lima - 118 S. Gunnison Ave., Buena Vista, CO 81211; Mailing: P.O. Box 458, Buena Vista, CO 81211-0458 t) 719-395-8424 c) 561-301-0325 (CRE); 720-878-5509 chris_williams07@comcast.net; office@strosebuenavista.org strosebuenavista.org Rev. Stephen J. Parlet, Pst.; Dcn. Russell Barrows; Patricia Barrows, Bus. Mgr.; Christopher Williams, CRE; CRP Stds.: 23

St. Joseph - 455 Castello Ave, Fairplay, CO 80440; Mailing: PO Box 458, Buena Vista, CO 81211-0458 stjoesfairplay.weebly.com/ Val White, Contact;

BURLINGTON

St. Catherine of Siena - 450 3rd St., Burlington, CO 80807; Mailing: P.O. Box 38, Burlington, CO 80807 t) 719-346-7156 nohnmacht@stcharlesborromeocos.org www.stcatherineofsienacos.org Rev. Carlos Gallardo Morales, Pst.; Dcn. Norbert Ohnmacht; CRP Stds.: 88

CALHAN

St. Michael's - 574 8th St., Calhan, CO 80808; Mailing: Box 199, Calhan, CO 80808 t) 719-347-2290 Rev. Michael Goodyear, Pst.; CRP Stds.: 13

CASTLE ROCK

St. Francis of Assisi - 2746 Fifth St., Castle Rock, CO 80104 t) 303-688-3025; 720-215-4522 mkochivar@stfranciscr.org; acihak@stfranciscr.org www.stfranciscr.org Rev. Mark Zacker, Pst.; Rev. Homero Cardozo Vargas, Par. Vicar; Dcn. Edward DeMattee; Dustin Duncan; Vicki Arndt, DRE; Tod Masters, DRE; Maribel Talafuse, DRE; CRP Stds.: 616

CHEYENNE WELLS

Sacred Heart - 105 W. 5th N., Cheyenne Wells, CO 80810; Mailing: P.O. Box 819, Cheyenne Wells, CO 80810 t) 719-767-5272 www.cheyennecountycatholicco.org/ Rev. ViJay Bonagiri, Pst.; CRP Stds.: 23

St. Augustine - 301 Church St., Kit Karson, CO 80825 t) (719) 767-5272

COLORADO SPRINGS

St. Mary's Cathedral - 22 W. Kiowa St., Colorado Springs, CO 80903 t) 719-473-4633 staff@stmaryscathedral.org; mtantanella@stmaryscathedral.org www.stmaryscathedral.org Rev. David Ramsey Price, Rector; Rev. Ricardo Rosales, L.C., Par. Vicar; Dcn. Mark Griffith; Dcn. Frank Ricotta Jr.; Dcn. John Riley; Margie Tantanella, DRE; CRP Stds.: 140

St. Andrew Kim Parish - 4515 E. Pikes Peak Ave., Colorado Springs, CO 80916 t) 719-638-0100 sakcolorado@yahoo.com Rev. Dongyoung Augustine Kim, Pst.; CRP Stds.: 13

Corpus Christi - 2318 N. Cascade Ave., Colorado Springs, CO 80907 t) 719-633-1457 x15 (CRP); 719-633-1457 parish@corpuschristicos.org corpuschristicos.org Rev. Brian A Roeseler, Pst.; CRP Stds.: 70

Corpus Christi Catholic School - (Grades PreK-8) 2410 N. Cascade Ave., Colorado Springs, CO 80907 t) 719-634-6294 Bill Carroll, Prin.; Stds.: 193; Lay Tchrs.: 12

Divine Redeemer - 927 N. Logan Ave., Colorado Springs, CO 80909; Mailing: 926 Farragut Ave., Colorado Springs, CO 80909 t) 719-234-0342 (CRP); 719-633-5559 (Parish Office) dcooper@divineredeemer.net; divineredeemerparish@gmail.com www.divineredeemer.net Rev. Jason Keas, Pst.; Rev. Joseph Dygert, In Res.; Rev. Donald Billiard, OFM, In Res.; Dcn. Larry Rossow; Dcn. Rob Rysavy; Dcn. Dave Sekel; Dcn. Ed Wilmes; DeAnna Cooper, DRE; CRP Stds.: 194

Divine Redeemer School - (Grades PreK-8) 901 N. Logan, Colorado Springs, CO 80909 t) 719-471-7771 ksmith@divineredeemer.net; jdamerell@divineredeemer.net www.divineredeemer.net/school Kari Smith, Prin.; Stds.: 169; Lay Tchrs.: 15

St. Francis of Assisi - 2650 Parish View, Colorado Springs, CO 80919 t) 719-599-5031 parish@stfranciscs.org stfranciscs.org Rev. Erin Kochivar, Pst.; Dcn. James Bachta; Dcn. Rick Bauer; Dcn. Andy Berry; Terrie Hernandez, DRE; Jennifer Lehrman, DRE; CRP Stds.: 156

St. Gabriel the Archangel - 8755 Scarborough, Colorado Springs, CO 80920 t) 719-528-8407 office@saintgabriel.net www.saintgabriel.net Rev. Kirk Slattery, Pst.; Dcn. David Geislinger; Dcn. Andre Mason; Dcn. Mike McGrady, DRE; Marc Lanning, Bus. Mgr.; CRP Stds.: 319

Holy Apostles - 4925 N. Carefree Cir., Colorado Springs, CO 80917 t) 719-597-4249 office@holyapostlescc.org www.holyapostlescc.org Rev. Tomasz Jamka, Pst.; Rev.

Matthew Kane, Par. Vicar; Dcn. Rick Athey; Dcn. Kevin Barkocy; Dcn. Charles Matzker; Dcn. Patrick O'Connor; Dcn. David Thompson; CRP Stds.: 160

Preschool - t) 719-591-1566 hapreschool@holyapostlescc.org www.ucsdcs.org/holyapostles McKenna Anderson, Dir.;

Holy Trinity - 3122 Poinsetta Dr., Colorado Springs, CO 80907 t) 719-633-2132 holytrinitycatholicparish@comcast.net; htparishoffice@holytrinitycos.org Rev. David Gregory Boroff, Pst.; Dcn. Andrew Dunnam; Dcn. Peter McCann; CRP Stds.: 11

St. Joseph's - 1830 S. Corona Ave., Colorado Springs, CO 80905 t) 719-632-9903 greg@stjosephcos.org www.stjosephcos.org Rev. August Stewart, Pst.; Dcn. Michael Bowen; Dcn. Russell Estey; Dcn. Albert E. Kimminau; Dcn. John Selig; Gregory Morgan, Pst. Assoc.; Brandon Allen, DRE; CRP Stds.: 73

Our Lady of Guadalupe - 2715 E. Pikes Peak, Colorado Springs, CO 80909 t) 719-633-7204 office@olgcos.org olgcos.org Rev. John Toepfer, O.F.M.Cap., Pst.; Dcn. Juan Moreno; Ricardo Sanchez, DRE; CRP Stds.: 395

Our Lady of the Pines-Black Forest - 11020 Teachout Rd., Colorado Springs, CO 80908 t) 719-495-2351 office@ourladyofthepines.org; evangelization@ourladyofthepines.org ourladyofthepines.org Rev. Andrzej Szczesnowicz, Pst.; Dcn. Gene Eastham; Dcn. Joseph Forgue; Dcn. Charles W. Specht; Dcn. Bill Bollwerk; CRP Stds.: 387

St. Patrick - 6455 Brook Park Dr., Colorado Springs, CO 80918 t) 719-598-3595 stpatscs@stpatscs.org; mhkasper@stpatscs.org www.stpatscs.org Rev. Francisco Quezada, Pst.; Dcn. James Bachta; Dcn. Richard Brown; Dcn. Matthias J. Kasper; Dcn. Donbosco Le; Dcn. Steven Prebeck; Martha Kasper, DRE; CRP Stds.: 161

Saint Paul - 9 El Pomar Rd., Colorado Springs, CO 80906 t) 719-219-2704 (CRP); 719-471-9700 stpaul@stpaulcos.org Rev. Msgr. Robert E. Jaeger, Pst.; Dcn. Richard J. Bowles; Dcn. Gregory Papineau; Evenly Cedrun, DRE; CRP Stds.: 195

St. Paul Catholic School - (Grades PreK-8) 1601 Mesa Ave., Colorado Springs, CO 80906; Mailing: 9 El Pomar Rd., Colorado Springs, CO 80906 t) 719-632-1846 cbench@stpaulcos.org Jim Welte, Prin.; Stds.: 168; Lay Tchrs.: 17

Sacred Heart - 2030 W. Colorado Ave., Colorado Springs, CO 80904; Mailing: 2021 W. Pikes Peak Ave., Colorado Springs, CO 80904 t) 719-633-8711; 719-633-8711 x105 (CRP) office@sacredheartcos.org; formationdirector@sacredheartcos.org www.sacredheartcos.org Rev. Jarrod Waugh, csc, Pst.; Rev. Randall C Rentner, Assoc. Pst.; CRP Stds.: 104

Our Lady of Perpetual Help - 218 Ruxton Ave., Manitou Springs, CO 80829 t) (719) 633-8711

Holy Rosary - 4435 Holiday Tr., Cascade, CO 80809 t) (719) 633-8711

The Vietnamese Holy Martyrs Parish - 1133 N. Wahsatch Ave., Colorado Springs, CO 80903 t) 719-351-1845 lm.vuminh@gmail.com Rev. Joseph P. Minh Vu, Pst.; CRP Stds.: 41

FALCON

St. Benedict Catholic Church - 12130 Falcon Hwy., Falcon, CO 80831 t) 719-495-1426 stbeninfo@qwestoffice.net stbenedictfalcon.org Rev. Michael Goodyear, Pst.; Dcn. Gordon Brenner; Dcn. John Hancock; Dcn. Paul Mahefky; Harriet Bauer, DRE; CRP Stds.: 68

HIGHLANDS RANCH

St. Mark Catholic Church - 9905 Foothills Canyon Blvd., Highlands Ranch, CO 80129 t) 720-348-9700 karols@stmarkhr.org; kathyn@stmarkhr.org www.stmarkhr.org Rev. Gregory W. Bierbaum, Pst.; Rev. Wlliam Dwayer, Assoc. Pst.; Dcn. Robert Seydel; Dcn. Dustin Duncan; Karol Seydel, DRE; CRP Stds.: 251

KIOWA

Our Lady of the Visitation - 34201 County Rd. 33, Kiowa, CO 80117; Mailing: P.O. Box 1689, Elizabeth, CO 80107 t) 303-646-4964 olvoffice@olv.cc www.ourladyofthevisitation.org Rev. Michael Holmquist, Pst.; CRP Stds.: 66

LEADVILLE

Holy Family Parish - 609 Poplar St., Leadville, CO 80461 t) 719-486-1382 himtnchurch@hotmail.com holyfamilyleadville Rev. Rafael Torres-Rico, Pst.; CRP Stds.: 14

LIMON

Our Lady of Victory - 425 H Ave., Limon, CO 80828; Mailing: P.O. Box 790, Limon, CO 80828 t) 719-775-9382 tjamka@diocs.org www.diocs.org/parishes/our-lady-of-victory Rev. Tomasz Jamka, Pst.; CRP Stds.: 71

St. Anthony of Padua - 133 Fifth St., Hugo, CO 80821 t) (719) 775-9382 Rev. James J. Klein, Pst.;

St. Mary - t) (719) 775-9382 Rev. James J. Klein, Pst.;

LITTLETON

Pax Christi Catholic Church - 5761 McArthur Ranch Rd., Littleton, CO 80124 t) 303-799-1036 supportstaff@paxchristi.org www.paxchristi.org Rev. Andrzej Szczesnowicz, Pst.; Ginger Gieser, DRE; Lisa Walker, Bus. Mgr.; CRP Stds.: 290

MONUMENT

St. Peter - 55 Jefferson St., Monument, CO 80132 t) 719-481-3511 april.charlton@petertherock.org; claire.ramos@petertherock.org www.petertherock.org Rev. Gregory Golyzniak, Pst.; Dcn. G. Scott Bowen; Dcn. Thomas Dickinson; Dcn. Douglas Flinn; Dcn. Thomas Tenpenny; Claire Ramos, DRE; CRP Stds.: 167

St. Peter School - (Grades PreK-8) 124 First St., Monument, CO 80132 t) 719-481-1855 www.petertherockschool.org Debbie Brook, Prin.; Stds.: 175; Lay Tchrs.: 16

PARKER

Ave Maria - 9056 E. Parker Rd., Parker, CO 80138-7209 t) 303-841-3750 avemariacatholicparish.org Rev. Nathaniel Hinds, Pst.; Rev. Timothy O'Connell, Par. Vicar; Rev. Mathew Suresh, Par. Vicar; Dcn. Gregory Archunde; Dcn. Paul Ruff; CRP Stds.: 371

Ave Maria School - (Grades PreK-8) t) 720-842-5000 Stds.: 459; Lay Tchrs.: 27

SALIDA

St. Joseph - 320 E. 5th St., Salida, CO 81201; Mailing: P.O. Box 847, Salida, CO 81201 t) 719-539-6419 stjosephsalida@q.com www.stjosephsalida.org Rev. Jim M. Williams, Pst.; Angels Flora, DRE; CRP Stds.: 40

SECURITY

St. Dominic - 5354 S. Hwy. 85/87, Security, CO 80911 t) 719-392-7653 stdominic@stdominiconline.org www.stdominiconline.org Rev. John David Stearns, Pst.; Dcn. John J Doherty; Dcn. Jerry Ray McMinn; Dcn. Douglas Marsh; Dcn. Daniel Tomich; Dr. Eliana Murphy-Elllis, Music Min.; Amanda Pettiette, DRE; Paul Lara, Bus. Mgr.; CRP Stds.: 204

Immaculate Conception Parish - 626 Aspen Dr., Security, CO 80911; Mailing: P.O. Box 5211, Colorado Springs, CO 80931-5211 t) 719-382-0121 sanctealphonse@gmail.com Rev. James J. Gordon, F.S.S.P., Pst.; CRP Stds.: 95

STRATTON

St. Charles Borromeo - 513 Colorado Ave., Stratton, CO 80836; Mailing: P.O. Box 266, Stratton, CO 80836 t) 719-348-5336 nohnmacht@stcharlesborromeocos.org www.stcharlesborromeocos.org Dcn. Norbert Ohnmacht; Rev. Carlos Gallardo Morales, Pst.; CRP Stds.: 31

WOODLAND PARK

Our Lady of the Woods Catholic Parish - 220 S. West St., Woodland Park, CO 80866-5590; Mailing: P.O. Box 5590, Woodland Park, CO 80866-5590 t) 719-687-9345 tellercatholic@gmail.com www.tellercatholic.org Rev. Marek Krol, Pst.; Dcn. David Illingworth; Dcn. Mark Thuli; CRP Stds.: 40

SCHOOLS: PRESCHOOL THRU HIGH SCHOOL

SCHOOLS

STATE OF COLORADO

LITTLETON

St. Katharine Drexel Catholic School - 5761 McArthur Ranch Rd., Littleton, CO 80124 t) 720-214-0691 mlupher@paxchristi.org Mandi Lupher, Dir.; Stds.: 50; Lay Tchrs.: 5

HIGH SCHOOLS

STATE OF COLORADO

COLORADO SPRINGS

***St. Mary's High School** - (PRV) (Grades 9-12) 2501 E. Yampa, Colorado Springs, CO 80909 t) 719-635-7540 jtrechter@smhscs.org www.smpirates.org Robyn Cross, Prin.; Dcn. Rob Rysavy, Pres.; Joe Trechter, Dir.; Stds.: 200; Pr. Tchrs.: 1; Lay Tchrs.: 18

INSTITUTIONS LOCATED IN DIOCESE

CATHOLIC CHARITIES [CCH]

COLORADO SPRINGS

Catholic Charities of Central Colorado, Inc. (Catholic Charities of Colorado Springs) - 228 N. Cascade Ave., Colorado Springs, CO 80903 t) 719-636-2345 info@ccharitiescc.org www.ccharitiescc.org Andy Barton, CEO; Asstd. Annu.: 12,003; Staff: 68

CONVENTS, MONASTERIES, AND RESIDENCES FOR WOMEN [CON]

COLORADO SPRINGS

***Benet Hill Monastery of Colorado Springs, CO, Inc.** - 3190 Benet Ln., Colorado Springs, CO 80921-1509 t) 719-633-0655 info@benethillmonastery.org www.benethillmonastery.org Benedictine Sisters. Sr. Marie Therese Summers, OSB, Prioress; Sr. Margaret Meaney, Archivist; Srs.: 23

Sisters of St. Francis of Perpetual Adoration - 7665 Assisi Hts., Colorado Springs, CO 80919-3837 t) 719-598-5486 www.stfrancis.org Provincial House. Sisters of St. Francis of Perpetual Adoration, Province of St. Joseph (The Sisters of St. Francis of Colorado Springs). Sr. Marietta Spenner, O.S.F., Prov.; Srs.: 29

ENDOWMENTS / FOUNDATIONS / TRUSTS [EFT]

COLORADO SPRINGS

The Catholic Foundation of the Diocese of Colorado Springs, Inc. - 228 N. Cascade Ave., Colorado Springs, CO 80903 t) 719-636-2345 jcrane@diocs.org www.diocs.org Jamie Crane, Dir.;

Fostering Hope Foundation - 111 S. Tejon St., Ste. 112, Colorado Springs, CO 80903; Mailing: 655 N. 79th St., Wauwatosa, WI 53213 t) 719-634-8588 c) 719-200-5293; (414) 915-9026 (Angela Carron) brian@fosteringhopefoundation.org; angela.carron@fosteringhopefoundation.org www.fosteringhopefoundation.org Supportive services for foster families and emancipated foster youth Angela Carron, CEO;

The Franciscan Foundation of Colorado Springs - 7665 Assisi Hts., Colorado Springs, CO 80919-3836 t) 719-598-5163 Sr. Marietta Spenner, O.S.F., Pres.;

***St. Mary's Catholic Education Foundation** - 2501 E.

Yampa St., Colorado Springs, CO 80909 t) 719-635-7540 jtrechter@smhscs.org Joe Trechter, Exec.;

HOSPITALS / HEALTH SERVICES [HOS]

COLORADO SPRINGS

Penrose-St. Francis Health Services - 2222 N. Nevada, Colorado Springs, CO 80907; Mailing: 9100 E. Mineral Cir,, Centennial, CO 80112 t) 719-776-5007 patrickgaughan@centura.org www.centura.org An operating unit of Catholic Health Initiatives Colorado (an affiliate of CommonSpirit Health formerly known as Catholic Health Initiatives) Bed Capacity: 617; Asstd. Annu.: 198,245; Staff: 3,100

St. Francis Medical Center - 6001 E. Woodmen Rd., Colorado, CO 80923; Mailing: 9100 E. Mineral Cir., Centennial, CO 80112 t) 719-571-1000; 303-673-8104 An operating unit of Catholic Health Initiatives Colorado (an affiliate of Catholic Health Initiatives) Rev. Patrick Sharp;

Penrose Hospital - 2222 N. Nevada Ave., Colorado Springs, CO 80907; Mailing: 9100 E. Mineral Cir., Centennial, CO 80112 t) 719-776-5000 An operating unit of Catholic Health Initiatives Colorado (an affiliate of Catholic Health Initiatives) Theresa Gregoire, Chap.; Rev. Stephen Akujobi, Sacramental Min.; Rev. Dan Ayers, Sacramental Min.;

MISCELLANEOUS [MIS]

COLORADO SPRINGS

Catholic Center at the Citadel - 750 Citadel Dr. E., Ste. 3056, Colorado Springs, CO 80909 t) 719-573-7364 olacsguardian@gmail.com capuchins.org/the-catholic-center/ Rev. William Kraus, O.F.M. Cap., Dir.; Rev. Brandon Berg, Mem.; Rev. Gene Emrisek, O.F.M.Cap., Mem.; Rev. Amlesom Gaim Gawed, O.F.M. Cap., Mem.; Rev. Frank X. Grinko, O.F.M. Cap., Mem.;

Colorado Springs Cursillo Movement - 228 N. Cascade Ave., Colorado Springs, CO 80903 t) 719-205-0163

Inferno - 228 N. Cascade Ave., Colorado Springs, CO 80903 t) (719) 373-1122 mission@infernomen.com www.infernomen.com Luke Vercollone, Exec. Dir.;

***Partners in Housing, Inc.** - 455 Gold Pass Hts., Colorado Springs, CO 80906 t) 719-473-8890 www.partnersinhousing.org Mary Stegner, Exec.;

***St. Thomas Aquinas Society** - 228 N. Cascade Ave., Colorado Springs, CO 80903; Mailing: P.O. Box 62908, Colorado Springs, CO 80962-2908 t) 719-448-0020 contact@stthomasaquinassociety.org www.stthomasaquinassociety.org Therese Lorentz, Dir.;

***Villa Santa Maria, Inc.** - 405 E. St. Elmo Ave., Colorado Springs, CO 80905 t) 719-632-7444 mvancel@archdiocesesanhousing.org www.archhousing.com Kathy Vannerson, Dir.;

***The Villas in Southgate** - 405 E. St. Elmo Ave., Colorado Springs, CO 80905 t) 719-632-7444 mvancel@archdiocesanhousing.org www.archhousing.com Part of Archdiocesan Housing (an affiliate of Catholic Charities). Kathy Vannerson, Dir.;

Women Partnering - 961 E. Colorado Ave., Colorado Springs, CO 80903 t) 719-577-9404 womenpart@gmail.com; jentaylorwp@gmail.com stfrancis.org Sr. Jeannette Kneifel, O.S.F., Pres.;

PARKER

Ave Maria Catholic School Corporation - 9056 E. Parker Rd., Parker, CO 80138 t) 720-842-5400 bskoog@avemariacatholicparish.org school.avemariacatholicparish.org Beatrice Skoog, Prin.;

WOODLAND PARK

Magnificat - Pikes Peak Region, Colorado Chapter - 647 Lovell Gulch Rd, Woodland Park, CO 80863 t) (505) 850-9944 magnificatofpikespeak@gmail.com Heather Davis, Dir.;

MONASTERIES AND RESIDENCES FOR PRIESTS AND BROTHERS [MON]

CASCADE

Holy Cross Novitiate (Congregation of Holy Cross, United States Province) - 7872 W. Hwy. 24, Cascade, CO 80809; Mailing: P.O. Box 749, Cascade, CO 80809-0749 t) 719-684-9277 jcooper@holycrossusa.org; tgiumenta@holycrossusa.org Rev. Jeffrey Cooper, C.S.C., Novice Master; Bro. Thomas Giumenta, C.S.C., Asst. Novice Master; Brs.: 1; Priests: 1

COLORADO SPRINGS

Our Lady of the Angels Friary - 8095 Walker Rd., Colorado Springs, CO 80908 t) 719-495-2228 olacsguardian@gmail.com Rev. William Kraus, O.F.M. Cap., Supr.; Rev. Cyrus Gallagher, O.F.M.Cap., Vicar; Friar David Gottschalk, O.F.M.Cap., Mem.; Friar Matthew Gross, O.F.M.Cap., Mem.; Friar Julian Haas, Mem.; Friar Felix Shinsky, O.F.M.Cap., Mem.; Brs.: 1; Priests: 5

Solanus Casey Friary - 5 University Dr., Colorado Springs, CO 80910 t) 719-632-7584 frank.grinko@capuchins.org Rev. Frank X. Grinko, O.F.M. Cap., Supr.; Rev. Amlesom Gaim Gawed, O.F.M. Cap., Vicar; Rev. John Toepfer, O.F.M.Cap., Bursar; Rev. Gene Emrisek, O.F.M.Cap., In Res.; Bro. Luke Jordan, O.F.M.Cap., In Res.; Bro. Joseph Mary Quinlan, Fraternal Min.; Brs.: 2; Priests: 4

SEDALIA

Sacred Heart Jesuit Community - 4801 N. Hwy. 67, Sedalia, CO 80135; Mailing: P.O. Box 185, Sedalia, CO 80135-0185 t) 303-688-4198 reservations@sacredheartretreat.org www.sacredheartretreat.org Rev. Hanh D. Pham, S.J., Supr.; Rev. Vincent E. Hovley, S.J., Dir.; Rev. Edward Kinerk, S.J., Dir.; Rev. Paul B. Patin, S.J., Dir.; Priests: 4

NURSING / REHABILITATION / CONVALESCENCE / ELDERLY CARE [NUR]

COLORADO SPRINGS

***St. Francis Nursing Center (Sisters of St. Francis of Perpetual Adoration)** - 7550 Assisi Hts., Colorado Springs, CO 80919 t) 719-598-1336 stfrancis.org/mt-st-francis-nursing-center/ Gerald Wintz, Chap.; Almaz Berhe, Admin.; Michael Maschka, Exec.; Asstd. Annu.: 213; Staff: 121

RETREAT HOUSES / RENEWAL CENTERS [RTR]

COLORADO SPRINGS

***Benet Hill Retreat Center** - 3190 Benet Ln., Colorado Springs, CO 80921-1509 t) 719-633-0655 info@benethillmonastery.org www.benethillmonastery.org Sr. Marie Therese Summers, OSB, Prioress;

Franciscan Retreat Center, Inc. - 7740 Deer Hill Grove, Colorado Springs, CO 80919-3836 t) 719-955-7025 frc@stfrancis.org www.franciscanretreatcenter.org Terri Gray, Dir.;

SEDALIA

Sacred Heart Jesuit Retreat House - 4801 N. Hwy. 67, Sedalia, CO 80135-0185; Mailing: P.O. Box 185, Sedalia, CO 80135-0185 t) 303-688-4198 www.sacredheartretreat.org Rev. Kevin L. Cullen, S.J., Spiritual Adv./Care Srvcs.; Rev. Tom Cwik, S.J., Spiritual Dir.; Rev. Edward Kinerk, S.J., Spiritual Dir.; Sr. Eileen Currie, M.S.C., Spiritual Dir.;

SPECIAL CARE FACILITIES [SPF]

COLORADO SPRINGS

Franciscan Community Counseling, Inc. - 7665 Assisi Hts., Colorado Springs, CO 80919 t) (719) 955-7009 danielle@stfrancis.org www.franciscancommunitycounseling.org Danielle Tagliaferro, Exec. Dir.; Asstd. Annu.: 450; Staff: 6

Namaste Alzheimer Center - 2 Penrose Blvd., Colorado Springs, CO 80906 t) 719-442-4240 lanesha.johnson@commonspirit.org www.homeishere.org An operating unit of CHI Living Communities, which is a subsidiary of CommonSpirit Health LaNesha Johnson, Admin.; Julie Britsch, Mission Integration/Spiritual Care; Bed Capacity: 64; Asstd. Annu.: 98; Staff: 82

An asterisk (*) denotes an organization that has established tax-exempt status directly with the IRS and is not covered by the USCCB Group Ruling.

Diocese of Columbus

(Dioecesis Columbensis)

MOST REVEREND EARL K. FERNANDES

Bishop of Columbus; ordained May 18, 2022; appointed as the 13th Bishop of Columbus on April 2, 2022; episcopal ordination and installation May 31, 2022.

Chancery Office: 198 E. Broad St., Columbus, OH 43215. T: 614-224-2251; F: 614-224-6306.

www.columbuscatholic.org

ESTABLISHED 1868.

Square Miles 11,310.

Comprises the following 23 Counties in the State of Ohio: Hardin, Marion, Morrow, Knox, Holmes, Tuscarawas, Union, Delaware, Licking, Coshocton, Madison, Franklin, Muskingum, Fayette, Pickaway, Fairfield, Perry, Ross, Hocking, Pike, Jackson, Vinton and Scioto.

For legal titles of parishes and diocesan institutions, consult the Chancery Office.

STATISTICAL OVERVIEW

Personnel

Bishop	1
Retired Bishops	2
Priests: Diocesan Active in Diocese	83
Priests: Diocesan Active Outside Diocese	4
Priests: Retired, Sick or Absent	39
Number of Diocesan Priests	126
Religious Priests in Diocese	42
Total Priests in your Diocese	168
Extern Priests in Diocese	14
Permanent Deacons in Diocese	117

Parishes

Parishes	103
With Resident Pastor:	
Resident Diocesan Priests	65
Resident Religious Priests	10
Without Resident Pastor:	
Administered by Priests	28
Missions	2
Pastoral Centers	1
Professional Ministry Personnel:	
Brothers	2
Sisters	226
Lay Ministers	99

Welfare

Catholic Hospitals	6
Total Assisted	384,649
Health Care Centers	2
Total Assisted	326
Homes for the Aged	17
Total Assisted	1738
Residential Care of Children	2
Total Assisted	101
Day Care Centers	2
Total Assisted	68
Special Centers for Social Services	15
Total Assisted	259,326

Educational

Seminaries, Diocesan	1
Students from This Diocese	20
Students from Other Dioceses	38
Diocesan Students in Other Seminaries	4
Total Seminarians	24
Colleges and Universities	2
Total Students	2,042
High Schools, Diocesan and Parish	10
Total Students	4,245
High Schools, Private	1
Total Students	429
Elementary Schools, Diocesan and Parish	41
Total Students	10,616
Catechesis/Religious Education:	
High School Students	2,430
Elementary Students	6,568
Total Students under Catholic Instruction	26,354
Teachers in Diocese:	
Priests	6
Brothers	7
Sisters	24
Lay Teachers	1,296

Vital Statistics

Receptions into the Church:	
Infant Baptism Totals	1,563
Minor Baptism Totals	992
Adult Baptism Totals	222
Received into Full Communion	222
First Communions	2,487
Confirmations	2,623
Marriages:	
Catholic	351
Interfaith	179
Total Marriages	530
Deaths	1,552
Total Catholic Population	344,881
Total Population	2,794,439

LEADERSHIP

Vicar General - t) (614) 224-2251 Rev. Msgr. Stephan J. Moloney;
Chancery Office - t) 614-224-2251 chomailbox@columbuscatholic.org Dcn. Thomas M. Berg Jr., Chancellor;
Vicar for Clergy - t) 614-224-2251 Rev. William P. Hahn;
Chief Operating Officer - t) 614-221-4640 Matthew Schlater;
Chief Financial Officer - t) 614-224-1221 John Mackessy;

OFFICES AND DIRECTORS

Catholic Center - t) 614-228-2453 Michael Pirik, Dir. Oper.;
Catholic Record Society - t) 614-241-2571 Michael Finn, Dir.; Donald Schlegel, Secy.;
Cemeteries - t) 614-491-2751 Richard Finn, Dir. (rfinn@columbuscatholic.org); Dcn. Jeffrey D. Fortkamp, Assoc. Dir.;
Central Purchasing Service - t) 614-262-0010 orders@columbuscatholic.org Joshua Springer, Dir.;
Communications - t) 614-241-2555 Jason Mays, Dir.; Andrew Zuk, Assoc. Dir.;
Diocesan Council of Catholic Women - t) 614-228-8601 Annette Roth, Pres.;
Evangelization - t) 614-221-4641 Rev. Adam A. Streitenberger, Sr. Dir.;
University and Young Adult Ministry - Rev. Adam A. Streitenberger, Dir.; Patrick McNulty, Assoc. Dir.;
Parish Missionary Disciple Formation - Liz Christy, Coord.;
Diocesan Scouting Program - Dcn. Christopher J. Reis, Chap.;
Finance - t) 614-224-1221 John Mackessy, CFO; Ingrid Sotak, Controller;
General Counsel - t) 614-241-2525 Angel Fox;
Hispanic Ministry - t) 614-221-7992 latinos@columbuscatholic.org Rev. David A. Schalk, Vicar; Lisset Mendoza, Mgr.;
Human Resources - t) 614-241-2537 Anne Streitenberger, Assoc. Dir.;
Information Technology - t) 614-221-1182 John Mackessy, Dir.;
Insurance - t) 614-224-1221 Teresa DePassio; Rhonda Frissora;
Marriage and Family Life - t) 614-241-2560 flomailbox@columbuscatholic.org Liz Christy, Assoc. Dir.;
Missions - t) 614-228-8603 Sr. Zephrina Mary Gracykutty, FIH, Dir.;
Pontifical Mission Societies -
Divine Worship - t) (614) 241-2528 divineworship@columbuscatholic.org Rev. Paul Jerome Keller, OP, Dir.;
Permanent Diaconate - t) 614-241-2545 Dcn. Frank A. Iannarino, Dir.; Dcn. Stephen A. Petrill, Assoc. Dir.;
Real Estate and Facilities - t) 614-228-2457 Andy Johanni, Sr. Dir.; Robert Sisson, Dir.;
Safe Environment - t) 614-241-2568 Regina E. Quinn, Dir.;
Victim Assistance Coordinator - t) 866-448-0217 (Toll Free) helpisavailable@columbuscatholic.org; llewis@columbuscatholic.org Laura Lewis;
The Catholic Times, Inc. - t) 614-224-5195 Doug Bean, Editor;
Tribunal - t) 614-241-2500 Rev. Robert J. Kitsmiller, Judicial Vicar; Dcn. John R. Crerand, Moderator;
Defenders of the Bond - Rev. Hilary C. Ike (Nigeria); Daniel M. Shakal;
Diocesan Judges - Rev. Msgr. John K. Cody; Rev. Msgr. John G. Johnson; Dcn. John R. Crerand;
Tribunal Auditors/Notaries - Mary Beth Krecsmar; Sue Ulmer; Karen Kitchell;
Tribunal Psychologists - Timothy M. Luis;
Vicariate Support - t) (614) 221-4640 Wendy Piper, Dir.;
Vocations - t) 614-221-5565 Rev. William P. Hahn, Dir.; Rev. Brian O'Connor, Assoc. Dir.;

CATHOLIC CHARITIES

Catholic Charities - t) (614) 241-2540 Mark H. Huddy, Dir.;
J.O.I.N. (Joint Organization for Inner-City Needs) - t) (614) 241-2530 Lisa Keita, Dir.;
Saint Francis Evangelization Center - t) (740) 596-5820 Lisa Keita, Dir.;
Social Concerns - t) (614) 241-2540 Jerry Freewalt, Dir.; Erin Cordle, Assoc. Dir.;
Catholic Campaign for Human Development - Erin Cordle;
Respect Life - Jerry Freewalt;
Rural Life Apostolates - Jerry Freewalt;

CONSULTATIVE BODIES

College of Consultors - Rev. Msgr. Stephan J. Moloney; Rev. William P. Hahn; Rev. Michael R. Hartge;
Council for Religious - t) 614-224-2251 Rev. Stash Dailey, Vicar for Rel.; Sr. Maureen Anne Shepard, Pres.; Sr. John Paul Maher, Secy.;
Diocesan Board of Review for the Protection of Children - t) (866) 448-0217 llewis@columbuscatholic.org Laura Lewis;
Diocesan Finance Council - John Mackessy, CFO; Ingrid Sotak, Secy.;
Presbyteral Council - Rev. Msgr. Stephan J. Moloney; Rev. William P. Hahn; Rev. Leo L. Connolly;
Priests Personnel Board - Rev. William P. Hahn;

EDUCATION

Office of Catholic Schools - t) 614-221-5829 Dr. Adam J. Dufault, Supt.;
Diocesan Recreation Association - t) 614-241-2580 Marty Raines, Dir.;

MISCELLANEOUS / OTHER OFFICES

Diocesan Charities Membership Corporation - Mark H. Huddy, Trustee & Sec.;

PARISHES, MISSIONS, AND CLERGY

STATE OF OHIO

ADA

Our Lady of Lourdes - 222 E. Highland Ave., Ada, OH 45810 t) 419-634-2626 office@lourdesada.org lourdesada.org Rev. Edward Shikina, Pst.; Rev. Jeffrey E. Tigyer, Par. Vicar; Dcn. Nicholas Klear; CRP Stds.: 43

BOLIVAR

Church of the Holy Trinity - 1835 Dover Zoar Rd., N.E., Bolivar, OH 44612 t) 330-874-4716 bulletin@holytrinityzoar.net www.holytrinityzoar.net Rev. James H. Hatfield III, Pst.; Rev. Tomas Carvajal y Basto, Par. Vicar; Dcn. Lyn Houze;

BREMEN

St. Mary - 602 Marietta St., Bremen, OH 43107 t) 740-862-8839 (CRP); 740-569-7738 Rev. Tyron J. Tomson, Pst.;

BUCKEYE LAKE

Our Lady of Mt. Carmel - 5133 Walnut Rd., S.E., Buckeye Lake, OH 43008-7788; Mailing: PO Box 45, Buckeye Lake, OH 43008-0045 t) 740-928-3266; 740-928-3264 (CRP) office@olmcbuckeyelake.org www.olmcbuckeyelake.org Rev. William A. Hritsko, Pst.; Dcn. Richard B. Busic, Pst. Assoc.;

CANAL WINCHESTER

St. John XXIII (Pope John XXIII) - 5170 Winchester Southern Rd., N.W., Canal Winchester, OH 43110 t) 614-920-1563 office@sjxxiiiparish.org www.sjxxiiiparish.org Rev. Brian O'Connor, Pst.; Marcella Travis, DRE; Heather Messmer-Frame, Bus. Mgr.; CRP Stds.: 92

CARDINGTON

Sacred Hearts - 4680 U.S. Hwy. 42, Cardington, OH 43315 t) 419-946-3611; 740-341-5681 www.sacredheartschurch.org Rev. Thomas J. Buffer, Pst.; Rev. Seth M. Keller, Par. Vicar; CRP Stds.: 12

CHILLICOTHE

St. Mary - 61 S. Paint St., Chillicothe, OH 45601 t) 740-772-2061 www.stmarychillicothe.com Rev. Timothy M. Hayes, Pst.; Rev. Process Milton Kiocha, A.J., Par. Vicar;
Bishop Flaget Elementary - (Grades PreSchool-8) 570 Parsons Ave., Chillicothe, OH 45601 t) 740-774-2970 lcorcora@cdeducation.org www.bishopflaget.org Laura Corcoran, Prin.;

St. Peter - 118 Church St., Chillicothe, OH 45601; Mailing: 285 W. Water St., Chillicothe, OH 45601 t) 740-774-1407 yec@stpeterchillicothe.com www.stpeterchillicothe.com Rev. Timothy M. Hayes, Pst.; Rev. Process Milton Kiocha, A.J., Par. Vicar; Dcn. Reed T. Hauser;

CIRCLEVILLE

St. Joseph - 134 W. Mound St., Circleville, OH 43113; Mailing: P.O. Box 40, Circleville, OH 43113 t) 740-477-2549 www.saintjosephcircleville.com Rev. Theodore F. Machnik, Pst.; Vanessa Butterbaugh, DRE; CRP Stds.: 85

COLUMBUS

St. Joseph Cathedral - 212 E. Broad St., Columbus, OH 43215 t) 614-224-1295 x2101 jneal@saintjosephcathedral.org; magriesti@saintjosephcathedral.org www.saintjosephcathedral.org Rev. Eugene Joseph, Par. Vicar; Rev. Elias Udeh, C.S.Sp. (Nigeria), Par. Vicar; Rev. Robert J. Kitsmiller, Rector;

St. Agatha - 1860 Northam Rd., Columbus, OH 43221 t) 614-488-4975 (CRP); 614-488-6149 www.st-agatha.org Rev. Mark S. Summers, Pst.; Dcn. Maurice N. Milne III;
St. Agatha School - (Grades K-8) 1880 Northam Rd., Columbus, OH 43221 t) 614-488-9000 lalshara@cdeducation.org www.saintagathaschool.org Luna Alsharaiha, Prin.;

St. Agnes - 2364 W. Mound St., Columbus, OH 43204-2903; Mailing: 473 S. Roys Ave., Columbus, OH 43204 t) 614-276-5413 stagnescolumbus.com Rev. Eduardo Velazquez, M.S.P., Admin.;

St. Aloysius - 2165 W. Broad St., Columbus, OH 43204-2903; Mailing: 473 S. Roys Ave., Columbus, OH 43204 t) 614-276-6587 www.staloysiuscolumbus.org Rev. Slawomir Siok, SAC (Poland), Admin.;

St. Andrew - 1899 McCoy Rd., Columbus, OH 43220 t) 614-451-2855 (CRP); 614-451-4290 anaporano@standrewparish.cc www.standrewparish.cc Rev. Msgr. Stephan J. Moloney, Pst.; Rev. William J. Ferguson, Par. Vicar; Dcn. Thomas M. Berg Jr.; Dcn. Daniel Dowler;
St. Andrew School - (Grades PreSchool-8) 4081 Reed Rd., Columbus, OH 43220 t) 614-451-1626 jwichtma@cdeducation.org www.standrewschool.com Joel Wichtman, Prin.;

St. Andrew Kim Taegon Korean Catholic Community - 720 Hamlet St., Columbus, OH 43215 c) 614-208-3649 office@kcolumbus.org www.kcolumbus.org Rev. Dukwoo Antonio Kim, Pst.;

Saint Anthony - 1300 Urban Dr., Columbus, OH 43229 t) 614-885-4857; 614-888-8190 (CRP) st.anthony@sbcglobal.net stanthonycolumbus.org Rev. Thomas G. Petry, Pst.; Dcn. Craig Smith; CRP Stds.: 30
Saint Anthony School - (Grades K-8) t) 614-888-4268 ciaconis@cdeducation.org Chris Iaconis, Prin.;

Sts. Augustine and Gabriel - 1567 Loretta Ave., Ste. 111, Columbus, OH 43211-1677 t) 614-268-3123 www.staugustinegabriel.com Rev. Joseph N. Bay, Pst.; Dcn. Jason Minh Nguyen;

St. Catharine - 500 S. Gould Rd., Columbus, OH 43209 t) 614-231-4509 info@stcatharine.com www.stcatharine.com Rev. Matthew B. Morris, Pst.;

Dcn. Christopher J. Reis; Rev. William Thomas Kessler, In Res.;

St. Catharine School - (Grades PreSchool-8) 2865 Fair Ave., Columbus, OH 43209 t) 614-235-1396 info@stcathschool.com stcatharineschool.com/ Mark Watts, Prin.;

St. Cecilia - 434 Norton Rd., Columbus, OH 43228 t) 614-878-0133 (CRP); 614-878-5353 www.saintceciliachurch.org Rev. Nicola Ventura, Pst.; Rev. Kyle Tennant, Par. Vicar; Dcn. John R. Malone Jr.; Dcn. Mark O'Loughlin;

St. Cecilia School - (Grades K-8) 440 Norton Rd., Columbus, OH 43228 t) 614-878-3555 jbeattie@cdeducation.org

Christ the King - 2777 E. Livingston Ave., Columbus, OH 43209 t) 614-237-0401 christthekingcolumbus@gmail.com christthekingcolumbus.com Rev. David A. Schalk, Pst.; Rev. Michael R. Fulton, Par. Vicar;

All Saints Academy - (Grades PreSchool-8) 2855 E. Livingston Ave., Columbus, OH 43209 t) 614-231-3391 lmiller@cdeducation.org asacatholic.org St. Thomas, St. Phillip & Christ the King. Laura Miller, Prin.;

St. Christopher - 1420 Grandview Ave., Columbus, OH 43212 t) 614-754-8888 saintchristophercc.com Rev. Wojciech Stachura, SAC, Pst.;

Trinity - (Grades PreSchool-8) 1440 Grandview Ave., Columbus, OH 43212 t) 614-488-7650 kmoehrma@cdeducation.org trinity.education.org

Columbus Vietnamese Catholic Community - 1567 Loretta Ave., Ste. 111, Columbus, OH 43211-1677 t) 614-268-3123 duson07@yahoo.com www.staugustinegabriel.com Rev. Joseph N. Bay, Chap.;

Community of Holy Rosary and St. John - 648 S. Ohio Ave., Columbus, OH 43205 t) 614-252-5926 www.hrsj.org Rev. Ramon Macoy Owera, Admin.;

Corpus Christi - 1111 Stewart Ave., Columbus, OH 43206; Mailing: 277 Reeb Ave., Columbus, OH 43207 t) 614-443-2828 parishccslcolumbus@gmail.com www.ccslcolumbus.org/ Rev. Vincent T. Nguyen, Pst.;

St. Dominic - 453 N. 20th St., Columbus, OH 43203; Mailing: 648 S. Ohio Avenue, Columbus, OH 43205 t) 614-252-5926 www.stdominic-church.org Rev. Ramon Macoy Owera, Admin.;

St. Elizabeth - 6077 Sharon Woods Blvd., Columbus, OH 43229 t) 614-891-0150 stelizabethreled@sbcglobal.net www.stelizabethchurch.org Rev. Antony Chooravady Varghese, C.F.I.C., Admin.; Rev. Jesse Chi Chick, C.F.I.C., Asst. Admin.; Rev. Sudhakar Reddy Thirumalareddy, C.F.I.C., Asst. Admin.; Dcn. Dean W. Racine; Dave Gruber, DRE;

St. Francis of Assisi - 386 Buttles Ave., Columbus, OH 43215 t) 614-299-5781 www.sfacolumbus.org Rev. Fritzner Valcin (Haiti), Admin.;

Holy Cross - 204 S. Fifth St., Columbus, OH 43215 t) 614-224-3416 www.holycrosscolumbus.com Rev. Michael C. Gentry, Pst.;

Holy Family - 584 W. Broad St., Columbus, OH 43215-2710 t) 614-221-4323 www.holyfamilycolumbus.org Mercedarian House of Studies Rev. Michael Donovan, O.de.M., Pst.; Dcn. W. Earl McCurry; Rev. Joseph Eddy, O.de.M., In Res.; Rev. Daniel Bowen, O. de M., In Res.;

Holy Name of Jesus - 154 E. Patterson Ave., Columbus, OH 43202 t) 614-262-0390 office@holynamercc.org www.holynamercc.com Rev. Antonio Carvalho, Pst.;

Holy Spirit - 4383 E. Broad St., Columbus, OH 43213 t) 614-861-1521 www.holyspiritcolumbus.org Rev. William L. Arnold, Pst.; Dcn. George A. Zimmermann Jr.; Mark Butler, DRE;

Holy Spirit School - (Grades K-8) 4382 Duchene Ln., Columbus, OH 43213 t) 614-861-0475 Amy Chessler, Prin.;

Immaculate Conception - 414 E. North Broadway St., Columbus, OH 43214 t) 614-267-9241 www.iccols.org/ Rev. Matthew N. Hoover, Pst.; Dcn. Christopher Campbell;

Immaculate Conception School - (Grades K-8) 366 E. North Broadway, Columbus, OH 43214 t) 614-267-6579 cokent@cdeducation.org www.iccols.org Colleen Kent, Prin.;

St. James the Less - 1652 Oakland Park Ave., Columbus, OH 43224 t) 614-262-1179 office@stjames-cpps.org www.stjames-cpps.org Rev. Antonio Baus, C.PP.S., Pst.; Rev. Santiago (Jim) Gaynor, Par. Vicar; Bro. Tom Bohman, C.PP.S., Pst. Assoc.;

St. James the Less School - (Grades K-8) 1628 Oakland Park Ave., Columbus, OH 43224 t) 614-268-3311 scecchetti@cdeducation.org www.saintjamestheless.com Samary Cecchetti, Prin.;

St. John the Baptist - 720 Hamlet St., Columbus, OH 43215-1534; Mailing: 168 E. Lincoln St., Columbus, OH 43215 t) 614-294-5319 www.sjbitaliana.com Rev. Andrzej Kozminski, SAC, Admin.;

St. Ladislas - 277 Reeb Ave., Columbus, OH 43207-1978 t) 614-443-2828 parishccslcolumbus@gmail.com www.ccslcolumbus.org Rev. Vincent T. Nguyen, Pst.;

St. Margaret of Cortona - 1600 Hague Ave., Columbus, OH 43204-1606 t) 614-274-1922 (CRP); 614-279-1690 stmargaretcol@yahoo.com; aboyd@cdeducation.org www.stmargaretcolumbus.org Rev. Jeffrey J. Rimelspach, Pst.; Dcn. Andrew W. Naporano; Dcn. Thomas J. Rowlands; CRP Stds.: 118

St. Mary - 684 S. 3rd St., Columbus, OH 43206 t) 614-445-9668 www.stmarygv.org Rev. Vincent T. Nguyen, Pst.; Dcn. Roger Minner;

St. Mary Magdalene - 473 S. Roys Ave., Columbus, OH 43204 t) 614-274-1121 www.saintsalivecolumbus.com Rev. Slawomir Siok, SAC (Poland), Admin.;

St. Mary Magdalene School - (Grades PreSchool-8) 2940 Parkside Rd., Columbus, OH 43204 t) 614-279-9935 rfumi@cdeducation.org Mark Watts, Prin.;

St. Matthias - 1582 Ferris Rd., Columbus, OH 43224 t) 614-267-3406 www.stmatthiascolumbus.com Rev. Anthony Davis, Pst.;

St. Matthias School - (Grades K-8) 1566 Ferris Rd., Columbus, OH 43224 t) 614-268-3030 dkinley@cdeducation.org

Our Lady of Peace - 20 E. Dominion Blvd., Columbus, OH 43214 t) 614-263-8824 dmahler@olp-parish.org www.olp-parish.org Rev. Sean Dooley, Pst.; Dcn. Jeffrey D. Fortkamp; CRP Stds.: 131

Our Lady of Peace School - (Grades K-8) 40 E. Dominion Blvd., Columbus, OH 43214 t) 614-267-4535 olp@cdeducation.org www.olpcolumbus.org James Silcott, Prin.;

Our Lady of the Miraculous Medal - 5225 Refugee Rd., Columbus, OH 43232 t) 614-868-1414 (CRP); 614-861-1242 www.churchofourladycolumbus.org Rev. James Coleman, Pst.; Dcn. Stephen A. Venturini, Pst. Assoc.;

Our Lady of Victory - 1559 Roxbury Rd., Columbus, OH 43212 t) 614-488-2428; 614-486-7678 (CRP) office@ourladyofvictory.cc www.ourladyofvictory.cc Rev. William A. Metzger, Pst.; Dcn. Rob Joseph; Krista Joseph, DRE; Diana Matthews, Bus. Mgr.; CRP Stds.: 203

St. Patrick - 280 N. Grant Ave., Columbus, OH 43215 t) 614-224-9522 office@stpatrickcolumbus.org www.stpatrickcolumbus.org Rev. Stephen Alcott, O.P., Pst.; Rev. Albert Connor Dempsey, O.P., Par. Vicar; Rev. Paul Marich, O.P., Par. Vicar; Rev. Paul Jerome Keller, O.P., Diocesan Dir., Liturgy & Par. Vicar; Rev. Thomas Blau, O.P., Diocesan Mission Preacher; Rev. Stephen-Dominic Hayes, O.P., Prior; Rev. Peter Fegan, O.P., Prof., Pontifical College Josephinum; Rev. Bernard Mulcahy, O.P., Prof., Pontifical College Josephinum;

Saint Margaret Shrine - t) 614-240-5915 director@littlemargaret.org www.littlemargaret.org/guild.html Mary Leathley, Secy.;

St. Peter - 6899 Smoky Row Rd., Columbus, OH 43235-1998 t) 614-889-1407 (CRP); 614-889-2221 stpetercolumbus@gmail.com www.stpetercolumbus.com Rev. Christopher Tuttle, Pst.;

St. Philip the Apostle - 1555 Elaine Rd., Columbus, OH 43227; Mailing: 1573 Elaine Rd., Columbus, OH 43227 t) 614-237-1671 www.stphilipcolumbus.org Rev. William L. Arnold, Pst.;

Sacred Heart - 893 Hamlet St., Columbus, OH 43201; Mailing: 168 E. Lincoln St., Columbus, OH 43215 t) 614-299-4191 www.sacredheartchurchcolumbus.org Rev. Andrzej Kozminski, SAC, Admin.;

Santa Cruz Parish - 143 E. Patterson Ave., Columbus, OH 43202 t) 614-784-9732 Rev. Antonio Carvalho, Pst.; Celia Palma, DRE;

Saint Stephen the Martyr - 4131 Clime Rd., Columbus, OH 43228 t) 614-272-5206 x105 (CRP); 614-272-5206 ststephenmartyr.org Rev. Efrain Villalobos, MSP (Mexico), Admin.; CRP Stds.: 300

St. Thomas the Apostle - 767 N. Cassady Ave., Columbus, OH 43219 t) 614-252-0976 adeleon@saintthomasapostle.com www.jmjcolumbus.org Rev. David A. Schalk, Pst.; Rev. Michael R. Fulton, Vicar; Dcn. Thomas D. Phillips; CRP Stds.: 40

St. Timothy - 1088 Thomas Ln., Columbus, OH 43220 t) 614-451-2671 c) 614-371-4618 www.sttimchurch.org/ Rev. David A. Poliafico, Pst.; Dcn. Victor Nduaguba; Dcn. Marion E. Smithberger;

St. Timothy School - (Grades K-8) 1070 Thomas Ln., Columbus, OH 43220 t) 614-451-0739 gmoshold@cdeducation.org www.sttimschool.org George Mosholder, Prin.;

CORNING

St. Bernard - 425 Adams St., Corning, OH 43730; Mailing: 309 N. Main St., New Lexington, OH 43764-1204 t) 740-342-1348 strosepcc.org Rev. Todd Lehigh, Pst.; Dcn. Edward Christ; Dcn. Mark R. Weiner;

COSHOCTON

Sacred Heart - 805 Main St., Coshocton, OH 43812 t) 740-622-8817 www.sacredheartcoshocton.org Rev. Thomas Gardner, Pst.; Dcn. Douglas Mould, DRE;

Sacred Heart School - (Grades PreK-6) 39 Burt Ave., Coshocton, OH 43812 t) 740-622-3728 mkobel@cdeducation.org

CROOKSVILLE

Church of the Atonement - 320 Winter St., Crooksville, OH 43731; Mailing: 309 N. Main St., New Lexington, OH 43764-1204 t) 740-342-1348 www.strosepcc.org Rev. Todd Lehigh, Pst.; Dcn. Edward Christ; Dcn. Mark R. Weiner;

DANVILLE

St. Luke - 307 S. Market St., Danville, OH 43014; Mailing: P.O. Box P, Danville, OH 43014 t) 740-599-6362 www.stlukedanvilleoh.org Rev. Mark J. Hammond, Pst.; Rev. Paul Joseph Brandimarti, Par. Vicar; Dcn. Timothy J. Birie;

St. Luke Community Center - 7 W. Rambo, Danville, OH 43014 t) 740-507-1731

DELAWARE

St. Mary - 82 E. William St., Delaware, OH 43015 t) 740-369-8228 (CRP); 740-363-4641 twhite@delawarestmary.org www.delawarestmary.org Rev. Brett Garland, Pst.; Dcn. Feliz F. Azzola; Dcn. Todd M. Tucky; Rev. Max Kenneth Acosta (Australia), Par. Vicar;

St. Mary School - (Grades PreK-8) 66 E. William St., Delaware, OH 43015 t) 740-362-8961 gstull@cdeducation.org www.stmarydelaware.org Gina Stull, Prin.;

DENNISON

Immaculate Conception - 206 N. First St., Dennison, OH 44621 t) 740-922-3533 icdennison@sbcglobal.net icdennison.com Rev. Jeffrey J. Coning, Pst.;

Immaculate Conception School - (Grades PreSchool-6) 100 Sherman St., Dennison, OH 44621 t) 740-922-3539 mritzert@cdeducation.org Matthew Ritzert, Prin.;

DOVER

St. Joseph - 613 N. Tuscarawas Ave., Dover, OH 44622

t) 330-364-6661 stjosephdover.org Rev. James H. Hatfield III, Pst.;

Tuscarawas Central Catholic Elementary - (Grades PreK-6) 600 N. Tuscarawas Ave., Dover, OH 44622 t) 330-343-9134 mritzert@cdeducation.org Matthew Ritzert, Prin.;

DRESDEN

St. Ann - 405 Chestnut St., Dresden, OH 43821; Mailing: Box 107, Dresden, OH 43821 t) 740-754-2221 Rev. Ryan M. Schmit, Pst.; Dcn. David Lozowski; CRP Stds.: 27

St. Mary - stannstmary.org

DUBLIN

St. Brigid of Kildare - 7179 Avery Rd., Dublin, OH 43017; Mailing: P.O. Box 3130, Dublin, OH 43016-0062 t) 614-761-1176 (CRP); 614-761-3734 www.stbrigidofkildare.org Rev. Msgr. Joseph M. Hendricks, Pst.; Rev. Timothy Lynch, Par. Vicar; Dcn. Stephen A. Petrill; Dcn. Frank A. Iannarino; Dcn. Paul J. Zemanek; Dcn. Donald Poirier; CRP Stds.: 622

St. Brigid of Kildare School - (Grades PreSchool-8) 7175 Avery Rd., Dublin, OH 43017 t) 614-718-5825 koreilly@cdeducation.org Kathleen O'Reilly, Prin.;

GAHANNA

St. Matthew the Apostle Catholic Church & School - 807 Havens Corners Rd., Gahanna, OH 43230 t) 614-471-0212 (Main Office); 614-532-0620 (Family Life Office) aallwein@stmatthew.net; mdougherty@stmatthew.net www.stmatthew.net Rev. Theodore K. Sill, Pst.; Rev. Stephen F. Carmody, O.P., Par. Vicar; Dcn. Joseph C. Meyer; Dcn. Christopher Walsh; CRP Stds.: 224

St. Matthew School - (Grades PreK-8) 795 Havens Corners Rd., Gahanna, OH 43230 t) 614-471-4930 smaloy@cdeducation.org www.cdstmatthew.org/ John Rathburn, Prin.;

GRANVILLE

St. Edward the Confessor - 785 Newark-Granville Rd., Granville, OH 43023-1450 t) 740-587-4160 (CRP); 740-587-3254 church@saintedwards.org; reled@saintedwards.org www.saintedwards.org Rev. Msgr. Paul P. Enke, Pst.; Dcn. John C. Barbour;

GROVE CITY

Our Lady of Perpetual Help - 3730 Broadway, Grove City, OH 43123 t) 614-875-9345 (CRP); 614-875-3322 (Church) www.ourladyofperpetualhelp.net Rev. Joseph T. Yokum, Pst.; Rev. Michael B. Watson, Par. Vicar; Dcn. Michael T. Kopczewski;

Our Lady of Perpetual Help School - (Grades PreK-8) 3752 Broadway, Grove City, OH 43123 t) (614) 875-6779 jfreeman@cdeducation.org

GROVEPORT

St. Mary - 5684 Groveport Rd., Groveport, OH 43125 t) 614-497-1437 (CRP); 614-497-1324 secretary@groveportstmary.org groveportstmary.org Rev. Hilary C. Ike (Nigeria), Admin.;

HEATH

St. Leonard - 57 Dorsey Mill Rd., Heath, OH 43056 t) 740-522-5270 parish@stleonard-heath.com www.stleonard-heath.com Rev. William A. Hritsko, Pst.; Dcn. Larry Wilson;

HILLIARD

St. Brendan - 4475 Dublin Rd., Hilliard, OH 43026 t) 614-876-9533 (CRP); 614-876-1272 www.stbrendans.net Rev. Robert Penhallurick, Pst.; Rev. Frank Brown, Par. Vicar; Dcn. James Morris; Dcn. Douglas A. Saunders; Dcn. Douglas Yglesias;

St. Brendan School - (Grades K-8) t) 614-876-6132 wgruber@cdeducation.org William T. Gruber, Prin.;

JACKSON

Holy Trinity - 215 Columbia St., Jackson, OH 45640; Mailing: 227 S. New York Ave., Wellston, OH 45692 t) 740-384-2359 office@jacksonvintoncatholic.org www.jacsonvintoncatholic.org Rev. Thomas Herge, Pst.;

JOHNSTOWN

Church of the Ascension - 555 S. Main St., Johnstown, OH 43031-1231 t) 740-967-7871; 740-967-1338 (CRP) office@johnstownascension.org www.johnstownascension.org Rev. Stephen Smith, Pst.; Dcn. Byron Phillips; Kelly Pertee, DRE; CRP Stds.: 87

JUNCTION CITY

St. Patrick - 1170 State Rte. 668 S., Junction City, OH 43748; Mailing: 309 N. Main St., New Lexington, OH 43764-1204 t) 740-342-1348 strosepcc.org Rev. Todd Lehigh, Pst.; Dcn. Edward Christ; Dcn. Mark R. Weiner;

KENTON

Immaculate Conception - 215 E. North St., Kenton, OH 43326; Mailing: 222 E. North St., Kenton, OH 43326-1523 t) 419-675-1162 icckenton.org Rev. Edward Shikina, Pst.; Dcn. Nicholas Klear; Dcn. J. Michael Hood; CRP Stds.: 24

LANCASTER

The Basilica of St. Mary of the Assumption - 132 S. High St., Lancaster, OH 43130 t) 740-653-0997 www.stmarylancaster.org Named a minor Basilica by Pope Francis on July 7, 2022. Rev. Craig R. Eilerman, Rector; Rev. James L. Colopy, Assoc. Pst.; Dcn. Frank K. Sullivan; CRP Stds.: 60

St. Mary School - (Grades PreSchool-8) 309 E. Chestnut St., Lancaster, OH 43130 t) 740-654-1632 kelrich@cdeducation.org www.saintmarylancaster.org Kayla Walton, Prin.;

St. Bernadette - 1343 Wheeling Rd., Lancaster, OH 43130-8701 t) 740-654-1893 www.stbernadetteparish.net Rev. Tyron J. Tomson, Pst.; Dcn. Jeffrey P. Carpenter; Dcn. Mark A. Scarpitti;

St. Bernadette School - (Grades PreSchool-5) 1325 Wheeling Rd., Lancaster, OH 43130 t) 740-654-3137 stbernlan@cdeducation.org www.stbernadetteschool.com

St. Mark - 324 Gay St., Lancaster, OH 43130 t) 740-653-1229 Rev. Peter M. Gideon, Pst.; Dcn. Jeffrey Hurdley;

LOGAN

St. John - 351 N. Market St., Logan, OH 43138 t) 740-385-2549 info@stjohnlogan.com stjohnlogan.com Rev. Stephen L. Krile, Pst.; Dcn. Donald Robers;

St. John School - (Grades PreSchool-6) 321 N. Market St., Logan, OH 43138 t) 740-385-2767 bhuffman@cdeducation.org stjohnlogan.org

LONDON

St. Patrick - 61 S. Union St., London, OH 43140 t) 740-852-0942 anna@stpatricklondon.org www.stpatricklondon.org Rev. Patrick A. Toner, Admin.; Dcn. Daniel W. Hann;

St. Patrick School - (Grades PreSchool-8) 226 Elm St., London, OH 43140 t) 740-852-0161 dadamczak1@cdeducation.org Deb Adamczak, Prin.;

MARION

St. Mary - 251 N. Main St., Marion, OH 43302 t) 740-382-2262 (CRP); 740-382-2118 www.marionstmary.org Rev. Thomas J. Buffer, Pst.; Rev. Seth M. Keller, Par. Vicar; CRP Stds.: 127

St. Mary School - (Grades PreSchool-8) 274 N. Prospect St., Marion, OH 44302 t) 740-382-1607 school@marionstmary.org

MARYSVILLE

Our Lady of Lourdes - 1033 W. Fifth St., Marysville, OH 43040 t) 937-644-6020; 937-644-6030 olol.marysville@rrohio.com; kkavanagh.olol@rrohio.com www.olol.cc Rev. Kevin J. Kavanagh, Pst.; Dcn. David Bezusko; Dcn. Charles Knight; Dcn. John Westover;

MILLERSBURG

St. Peter - 379 S. Crawford St., Millersburg, OH 44654-1463 t) 330-674-1671 holmescatholic.net Rev. Thomas Gardner, Pst.;

SS. Peter and Paul - 139 Main St., Glenmont, OH 44628 t) (330) 674-1671

MT. VERNON

St. Vincent de Paul - 303 E. High St., Mt. Vernon, OH 43050 t) 740-392-4711 www.stvincentmountvernon.org Rev. Mark J. Hammond, Pst.; Rev. Paul Joseph Brandimarti, Par. Vicar; Dcn. Timothy J. Birie;

St. Vincent de Paul School - (Grades PreSchool-8) 206 E. Chestnut St., Mt. Vernon, OH 43050 t) 740-393-3611 mdowns@cdeducation.org

NEW ALBANY

Church of the Resurrection - 6300 E. Dublin-Granville Rd., New Albany, OH 43054 t) 614-855-1400 slarson@cotrna.org; pkehres@cotrna.org www.cotrna.org Rev. Denis S. Kigozi, Pst.;

NEW LEXINGTON

St. Rose of Lima - 309 N. Main St., New Lexington, OH 43764 t) 740-342-1348 strosepcc.org Rev. Todd Lehigh, Pst.; Dcn. Edward Christ; Dcn. Mark R. Weiner; CRP Stds.: 31

NEW PHILADELPHIA

Sacred Heart - 139 3rd St., N.E., New Philadelphia, OH 44663-3900 t) 330-343-6876 www.sacredheartnewphila.org Rev. Jeffrey J. Coning, Pst.; Dcn. Ronald E. Onslow;

NEWARK

Church of the Blessed Sacrament - 378 E. Main St., Newark, OH 43055; Mailing: 394 E. Main St., Newark, OH 43055 t) 740-345-4290 office@blsac.net; deacon394@outlook.com www.blessedsacramentnewark.com Rev. Anthony P. Lonzo, Pst.; Dcn. Patrick Wilson; Rev. Mark V. Ghiloni, In Res.; CRP Stds.: 59

Church of the Blessed Sacrament School - (Grades K-8) 394 E. Main St., Newark, OH 43055 t) 740-345-4125 jcaton@cdeducation.org blsacschool.net Josh Caton, Prin.;

St. Francis de Sales - 40 Granville St., Newark, OH 43055 t) 740-345-9874 info@stfrancisparish.net www.stfrancisparish.net Rev. David Sizemore, Pst.; Dcn. Steven DeMers; Dcn. Eric Wright;

St. Francis de Sales School - (Grades PreK-8) t) 740-345-4049 smummey@cdeducation.org www.stfrancisparish.net/school/home Sally Mummey, Prin.; Dr. Kelly Cahill Roberts, Vice Prin.;

NEWCOMERSTOWN

St. Francis de Sales - 440 River St., Newcomerstown, OH 43832 t) 740-498-7368 Rev. Thomas Gardner, Moderator; Dcn. Frank A. Duda;

PICKERINGTON

Seton Parish - 600 Hill Rd. N., Pickerington, OH 43147-9201 t) 614-833-0485 (CRP); 614-833-0482 www.setonparish.com Rev. Leo L. Connolly, Pst.; Rev. Stephen Ondrey, Par. Vicar; Dcn. Charles G. Waybright, Pst. Min./Coord.;

PLAIN CITY

Saint Joseph Catholic Church - 670 W. Main St., Plain City, OH 43064 t) 614-873-8850 office@stjosephpc.org www.stjosephpc.org Rev. Joseph J. Trapp II, Pst.;

PORTSMOUTH

Holy Redeemer - 1325 Gallia St., Portsmouth, OH 45662; Mailing: 514 Market St., Portsmouth, OH 45662 t) 740-354-4551 www.sciotocatholic.org Rev. Brian Beal, Pst.; Rev. Patrick Watikha, AJ, Par. Vicar; Dcn. Terrance A. Acox; Dcn. James M. Sturgeon; Dcn. Christopher Veracalli;

Notre Dame Elementary - (Grades PreK-6) 1401 Gallia St., Portsmouth, OH 45662 t) 740-353-2354 jmcmackin@cdecucation.org www.notredameschools.com Serving all 7 parishes in Scioto County. Michelle Ashley, Prin.;

St. Mary - 514 Market St., Portsmouth, OH 45662 t) 740-354-4551 www.sciotocatholic.org Rev. Brian Beal, Pst.; Rev. Patrick Watikha, AJ, Par. Vicar; Dcn. Terrance A. Acox; Dcn. James M. Sturgeon; Dcn. Christopher Varacalli;

Holy Trinity - 9493 Carey's Run, Pond Creek, OH 45663; Mailing: 514 Market St., Portsmouth, OH 45662 t) 740-858-4600

POWELL

St. Joan of Arc - 10700 Liberty Rd. S., Powell, OH 43065-9303 t) 614-761-0905 contactus@stjoanofarcpowell.org www.stjoanofarcpowell.org Rev. James P. Black, Pst.; Dcn. James Elchert; Dcn. Stephen A. Petrill; Rev. Eugene Joseph, Par. Vicar;

REYNOLDSBURG

St. Pius X - 1051 Waggoner Rd., Reynoldsburg, OH

43068 t) 614-864-3505 (CRP); 614-866-2859 stpiusx@spxreynoldsburg.com www.spxreynoldsburg.com Rev. David J. Young, Pst.; Dcn. James W. Kelly; Dcn. John Vellani;

St. Pius X School - (Grades PreSchool-8) 1061 Waggoner Rd., Reynoldsburg, OH 43068 t) 614-866-6050 dasmith@cdeducation.org www.coeducation.org/schools/px/index.html

SOMERSET

Holy Trinity - 228 S. Columbus St., Somerset, OH 43783; Mailing: P.O. Box 190, Somerset, OH 43783 t) 740-743-1317; 740-743-1855 (CRP) Rev. Andre-Joseph LaCasse, O.P., Pst.;

Holy Trinity School - (Grades PreK-8) 225 S. Columbus St., Somerset, OH 43783 t) 740-743-1324 holytrinitypacers.com William Noll, Prin.;

St. Joseph - 5757 State Rte. 383, Somerset, OH 43783; Mailing: P.O. Box 190, Somerset, OH 43783 t) 740-743-1855 (CRP); 740-743-1317 Rev. Andre-Joseph LaCasse, O.P., Pst.; Dcn. Eugene C. Dawson;

SUGAR GROVE

St. Joseph - 308 N. Elm St., Sugar Grove, OH 43155-0209; Mailing: P.O. Box 209, Sugar Grove, OH 43155-0209 t) 740-746-8302 Rev. Peter M. Gideon, Admin.;

SUNBURY

St. John Neumann - 9633 E. State Rte. 37, Sunbury, OH 43074 t) 740-965-1358 www.saintjohnsunbury.org Rev. Daniel J. Dury, Pst.; Dcn. Carl A. Calcara Jr.;

WASHINGTON COURT HOUSE

St. Colman - 219 S. North St., Washington Court House, OH 43160 t) 740-335-5005 (CRP); 740-335-5000 www.stcolmanwch.org Rev. Cyrus M. Haddad, Pst.;

WAVERLY

St. Mary, Queen of the Missions - 407 S. Market St., Waverly, OH 45690 t) 740-947-2436 stmary_qm@frontier.com www.stmarywaverly.com Rev. Timothy M. Hayes, Pst.; Rev. Process Milton Kiocha, A.J., Par. Vicar; Dcn. Reed T. Hauser;

WELLSTON

SS. Peter and Paul - 227 S. New York Ave., Wellston, OH 45692 t) 740-384-2359 office@jacksonvintoncatholic.org www.jacksonvintoncatholic.org Rev. Thomas Herge, Pst.;

SS. Peter and Paul School - (Grades PreSchool-8) 229 S. New York Ave., Wellston, OH 45692 t) 740-384-6354 kfulton@cdeducation.org

WEST JEFFERSON

SS. Simon and Jude - 9350 High Free Pike, West Jefferson, OH 43162-9704 t) 614-879-8562 kjones@stsimonjude.org; dwaynemcnew702@yahoo.com stsimonjude.org Rev. Dwayne A. McNew, Pst.; Dcn. Joseph A. Knapke;

WESTERVILLE

St. Paul the Apostle - 313 N. State St., Westerville, OH 43082 t) 614-882-5045 (CRP); 614-882-2109 www.stpaulcatholicchurch.org Rev. Jonathan F. Wilson, Pst.; Rev. Daniel Olvera, Par. Vicar; Dcn. Joseph W. Ciaciura; Dcn. Mickey B. Hawkins; Dcn. Ken Johanning; Rev. David E. Gwinner, In Res.;

St. Paul the Apostle School - (Grades K-8) 61 Moss Rd., Westerville, OH 43082 t) 614-882-2710 sstreitenberger@cdeducation.org Susan Streitenberger, Prin.;

WHEELERSBURG

St. Peter - 2167 Lick Run Lyra Rd., Wheelersburg, OH 45694; Mailing: 514 Market St., Portsmouth, OH 45662 t) 740-345-4551 www.sciotocatholic.org Rev. Brian Beal, Pst.; Rev. Patrick Watikha, AJ, Par. Vicar; Dcn. Terrance A. Acox; Dcn. James M. Sturgeon; Dcn. Christopher Veracalli;

WORTHINGTON

St. Michael - 5750 N. High St., Worthington, OH 43085 t) 614-888-5384 (CRP); 614-885-7814 www.saintmichael-cd.org Rev. Anthony A. Dinovo Jr., Pst.; Dcn. John R. Crerand; Dcn. William F. Demidovich Jr.; Rev. Emmanuel Adu Addai, Pst. Min./Coord.;

St. Michael School - (Grades PreSchool-8) 64 E. Selby Blvd., Worthington, OH 43085-3986 t) 614-885-3149 srjp@cdeducation.org www.cdeducation.org/schools/mi Sr. John Paul Maher, Prin.;

ZALESKI

St. Sylvester - 119 N. Second St., Zaleski, OH 45698-0264; Mailing: 227 S. New York Ave., Wellston, OH 45692 t) 740-384-2359 office@jacksonvintoncatholic.org www.jacksonvintoncatholic.org Rev. Thomas Herge, Pst.; Rev. David E. Young, In Res.;

ZANESVILLE

St. Nicholas - 925 E. Main St., Zanesville, OH 43701; Mailing: 955 E. Main St., Zanesville, OH 43701 t) 740-453-0597 dginikos@stnickparish.org www.stnickparish.org Rev. Martin J. Ralko, Pst.; Dcn. Burdette N. (Pete) Peterson Jr.; CRP Stds.: 56

Bishop Fenwick School - (Grades PreSchool-8) 1030 E. Main St., Zanesville, OH 43701 t) 740-453-2637 ksagan@cdeducation.org Kelly Sagan, Prin.;

St. Thomas Aquinas - 144 N. Fifth St., Zanesville, OH 43701 t) 740-453-3301; 740-453-3301 (CRP) parish@saintthomaszanesville.org www.saintthomaszanesville.org Rev. Jan C. Sullivan, Pst.;

Bishop Fenwick Early Childhood Center - (Grades PreSchool-PreK) 139 N. Fifth St., Zanesville, OH 43701 t) 740-454-9731 bschiele@cdeducation.org Kelly Sagan, Exec. Dir.;

SCHOOLS: PRESCHOOL THRU HIGH SCHOOL

SCHOOLS

STATE OF OHIO

COLUMBUS

St. Joseph Montessori School - (PAR) 933 Hamlet St., Columbus, OH 43201-3595 t) 614-291-8601 sjmsoffice@cdeducation.org; bhuth@cdeducation.org www.sjms.net Brenda Huth, Dir.;

St. Mary School, Inc. - (DIO) (Grades PreSchool-8) 700 S. Third St., Columbus, OH 43206 t) 614-444-8994 gstull@stmaryschoolgv.org www.stmaryschoolgv.com Gina Stull, Prin.;

HIGH SCHOOLS

STATE OF OHIO

COLUMBUS

Bishop Hartley High School - (DIO) (Grades 9-12) 1285 Zettler Rd., Columbus, OH 43227 t) 614-237-5421 hartley@cdeducation.org www.bishop-hartley.org Christopher Kowalski, Prin.;

Bishop Ready High School - (DIO) 707 Salisbury Rd., Columbus, OH 43204 t) 614-276-5263 mbrickne@cdeducation.org www.brhs.org Matthew Brickner, Prin.; Rocco Fumi, Dean;

Bishop Watterson High School - (DIO) 99 E. Cooke Rd., Columbus, OH 43214 t) 614-268-8671 ccampbel@cdeducation.org www.cd.education.org/schools/bw Rev. Paul A. Noble, Chap.; Dcn. Christopher Campbell, Prin.; Ryan P. Schwieterman, Vice Prin.;

St. Francis de Sales High School - (DIO) 4212 Karl Rd., Columbus, OH 43224 t) 614-267-7808 dgarrick@cdeducation.org sfdstallions.org Dan Garrick, Prin.;

The Preparatory School of Saint Charles Borromeo - (DIO) 2010 E. Broad St., Columbus, OH 43209 t) 614-252-6714 jlower@scprep.org www.stcharlesprep.org James Lower, Prin.;

LANCASTER

William V. Fisher Catholic High School - (DIO) (Grades 9-12) 1803 Granville Pike, Lancaster, OH 43130 t) 740-654-1231 dburley@cdeducation.org fishercatholic.org Rev. Tyron J. Tomson, Campus Min.; Stds.: 138; Lay Tchrs.: 12

NEW PHILADELPHIA

Tuscarawas Central Catholic Junior/Senior High School - (DIO) (Grades 7-12) 777 Third St., N.E., New Philadelphia, OH 44663 t) 330-343-3302 jcalvo@cdeducation.org www.tccsaints.com Jennifer Calvo, Prin.;

NEWARK

Newark Catholic High School - (DIO) 1 Green Wave Dr., Newark, OH 43055 t) 740-344-3594 thawk@newarkcatholic.org www.newarkcatholic.org/ Thomas Pickering, Prin.;

PORTSMOUTH

Notre Dame High School - (DIO) (Grades 7-12) 2220 Sunrise Ave., Portsmouth, OH 45662 t) 740-353-2354 twalker@cdeducation.org (Junior/Senior High School) J. McKenzie III, Prin.;

ZANESVILLE

Bishop Rosecrans High School - (DIO) 1040 E. Main St., Zanesville, OH 43701 t) 740-452-7504 ksagan@cdeducation.org www.rosecrans.cdeducation.org Kelly Sagan, Dir.;

INSTITUTIONS LOCATED IN DIOCESE

ASSOCIATIONS [ASN]

HILLIARD

***Catholic Medical Association of Central Ohio** - 4475 Dublin Rd., Hilliard, OH 43026 t) 614-806-2222 jp2cmacolumbus@gmail.com www.cmacbus.com Marian K. Schuda, Secy.;

CAMPUS MINISTRY / NEWMAN CENTERS [CAM]

COLUMBUS

St. Thomas More Newman Center at The Ohio State University - 64 W. Lane Ave., Columbus, OH 43201 t) 614-291-4674 mailbox@buckeyecatholic.com www.buckeyecatholic.com Rev. Adam A. Streitenberger, Exec. Dir.;

CEMETERIES [CEM]

COLUMBUS

Mount Calvary - 581 Mt. Calvary Ave., Columbus, OH 43223-2217; Mailing: 6440 S. High St., Lockbourne, OH 43137-9208 t) 614-491-2751 ccocsj@columbuscatholic.org catholiccemeteriesofcolumbus.org Richard Finn, Dir.;

LEWIS CENTER

Resurrection Cemetery - 9571 N. High St., Lewis Center, OH 43035-9413; Mailing: 6440 S. High St., Lockbourne, OH 43137-9208 t) 614-888-1805 ccocres@columbuscatholic.org catholiccemeteriesofcolumbus.org Richard Finn, Dir.;

LOCKBOURNE

St. Joseph - 6440 S. High St., Lockbourne, OH 43137-9208 t) 614-491-2751 ccocsj@columbuscatholic.org catholiccemeteriesofcolumbus.org Richard Finn, Dir.;

PATASKALA

Holy Cross Cemetery - 11539 National Rd., S.W., Pataskala, OH 43062-8304; Mailing: 6440 S. High St., Lockbourne, OH 43137-9208 t) 740-927-4442 ccochc@columbuscatholic.org catholiccemeteriesofcolumbus.org Richard Finn, Dir.;

COLLEGES & UNIVERSITIES [COL]

COLUMBUS

Ohio Dominican University - 1216 Sunbury Rd., Columbus, OH 43219 t) 614-251-4500 admissions@ohiodominican.edu www.ohiodominican.edu Dominican Sisters of Peace

Connie Gallaher, Pres.; Manuel Martinez, Vice. Pres.; Rev. Daniel J. Millisor, Chap.; Stds.: 1,276

CONVENTS, MONASTERIES, AND RESIDENCES FOR WOMEN [CON]

COLUMBUS

Dominican Sisters of Peace, Inc. - 2320 Airport Dr., Columbus, OH 43219-2098 t) 614-416-1900 sister.peace@oppeace.org www.oppeace.org Sr. Patricia Twohill, O.P., Prioress; Srs.: 350

Dominican Sisters of Peace Columbus Motherhouse - t) 614-416-1092

Franciscan Sisters of the Immaculate Heart Convent - 60 E. Dominion Blvd., Columbus, OH 43214

Mother Angeline McCrory Manor Convent - 5199 E. Broad St., Columbus, OH 43213 t) 614-751-5700 Carmelite Sisters for the Aged and Infirm. Sr. Robert McCrory Mullen, O.Carm; Srs.: 5

GROVE CITY

Daughters of Mary Mother of Mercy Convent - 5242 Lilac Ave., Grove City, OH 43123 t) 267-237-5614 laboure_okoroafor@yahoo.com Sr. Laboure Okoroafor, DMMM, Prioress; Srs.: 1

ENDOWMENTS / FOUNDATIONS / TRUSTS [EFT]

COLUMBUS

***The Foundation of the Catholic Diocese of Columbus (The Catholic Foundation)** - 257 E. Broad St., Columbus, OH 43215 t) 614-443-8893 lbrown@catholic-foundation.org www.catholic-foundation.org Loren P. Brown, Pres.;

LANCASTER

***St. Mary of the Assumption Foundation** - 132 S. High St., Lancaster, OH 43130 t) 740-653-0997 info@stmarylancaster.org Rev. Craig R. Eilerman, Contact;

***William V. Fisher Catholic High School Endowment Fund** - 1803 Granville Pike, Lancaster, OH 43130 t) 740-654-1231 dburley@cdeducation.org fishercatholic.org Kevin Crabtree, Chair;

NEW PHILADELPHIA

Tuscarawas Central Catholic High School Endowment Fund - 777 Third St., N.E., New Philadelphia, OH 44663 t) 330-343-3302 jcalvo@cdeducation.org Jennifer Calvo, Prin.;

NEWARK

***Newark Catholic High School Foundation** - One Green Wave Dr., Newark, OH 43055 t) 740-344-5671 nbourne@newarkcatholic.org Thomas Pickering, Contact;

ZANESVILLE

Bishop Rosecrans High School Foundation - 1040 E. Main St., Zanesville, OH 43701 t) 740-452-7504 ksagan@cdeducation.org www.rosecrans.cdeducation.org Kelly Sagan, Dir.;

St. Nicholas Foundation - 955 E. Main St., Zanesville, OH 43701 t) 740-453-0597 tomcstnick@rrohio.com www.stnickparish.org Rev. Martin J. Ralko, Pres.;

HOSPITALS / HEALTH SERVICES [HOS]

COLUMBUS

Mohun Health Care Center - 2340 Airport Dr., Columbus, OH 43219 t) 614-416-6132 aqueener@mohun.org Rev. Elias Curtis Henritzy, OP, Chap.;

Mount Carmel Health System (Mount Carmel East Hospital, Mount Carmel St Anns Hospital, Mount Carmel New Albany Surgical Hospital, Mount Carmel Grove City, Mount Carmel Fitness and Health, Mount Carmel West Hospital) - 6150 E. Broad St., Columbus, OH 43213-1574 t) 614-546-4533 communitybenefit@mchs.com mountcarmelhealth.com Lorraine Lutton, CEO;

Mount Carmel College of Nursing - 127 S. Davis Ave., Columbus, OH 43222 t) 614-234-5800 mccnbusinessoffice@mccn.edu; admissions@mccn.edu www.mccn.edu Dr. Kathleen Williamson, Pres.; Stds.: 746

Mount Carmel Health System Foundation - t) 614-546-4500 givetomc@mchs.com www.mountcarmelfoundation.org

DENNISON

Trinity Hospital Twin City, an Affiliate of Catholic Health - 819 N. First St., Dennison, OH 44621 t) 740-922-2800 mrainsberger@trinitytwincity.org Rev. Thomas Gardner, Spiritual Adv./Care Srvcs.;

ZANESVILLE

***Genesis HealthCare System** - 2951 Maple Ave., Zanesville, OH 43701 t) 740-454-5000 sfuller@genesishcs.org; dwood@genesishcs.org genesishcs.org Sr. Bernadette Selinsky, Chap.; Bed Capacity: 321; Asstd. Annu.: 544,369; Staff: 3,314

Genesis Hospital - t) 740-454-4633 mperry@genesishc.org Bed Capacity: 321

MISCELLANEOUS [MIS]

CENTERBURG

***Catholic Youth Summer Camp, Inc. (Damascus)** - 7550 Ramey Rd., Centerburg, OH 43011 t) 740-480-1288 info@damascus.net; registration@cysc.com damascus.net A missionary apostolate providing formation, worship, retreats, conferences, and Catholic youth summer camp for middle school and high school students Dan DeMatte, Exec.; Aaron Richards, Exec.;

COLUMBUS

Catholic Social Services, Inc. - 197 E. Gay St., Columbus, OH 43215 t) 614-221-5891 www.colscss.org Rachel Lustig, Pres.; Nicholas Borchers, COO;

The Christ Child Society of Columbus, Inc. - ; Mailing: P.O. Box 340091, Columbus, OH 43234-0091 t) 614-436-5518 columbus@christchildsociety.org www.christchildsociety.org Michele Bianconi, Pres.;

Diocesan Charities Membership Corporation - 198 E. Broad St., Columbus, OH 43215 t) 614-224-2251 chomailbox@columbuscatholic.org Rev. Msgr. Joseph M. Hendricks, Contact;

Diocesan Education Corporation - 197 E. Gay St., Columbus, OH 43215 t) 614-221-5829 officeofcatholicschools@columbuscatholic.org Dr. Adam J. Dufault, Contact;

Diocesan Retirement Community Corp. - 198 E. Broad St., Columbus, OH 43215 t) 614-224-2251 chomailbox@columbuscatholic.org Rev. Msgr. Joseph M. Hendricks, Pres.;

Haitian Catholic Coalition of Ohio - 1582 Ferris Rd., Columbus, OH 43224 t) 614-778-0459 frval2@yahoo.com Rev. Fritzner Valcin (Haiti);

St. Leo the Great Oratory (Institute of Christ the King Sovereign Priest, Inc.) - 221 Hanford St., Columbus, OH 43206 t) 614-443-7685 stleo@icksp.org institute-christ-king.org/columbus-home Rev. Canon David Silvey, I.C., Rector;

Mother Angeline McCrory Manor, Inc. - 5199 E. Broad St., Columbus, OH 43213 t) 614-751-5700 srann@carmeliteseniorliving.org; jfawley@carmeliteseniorliving.org www.carmeliteseniorliving.org The Carmelite System Jenna Fawley, Admin.; Sr. Ann Brown, O.Carm., CEO;

***Museum of Catholic Art and History** - 257 E. Broad St., Columbus, OH 43215; Mailing: P.O. Box 164234, Columbus, OH 43216 t) 614-618-4030 kenneyshawn@yahoo.com; info@catholicmuseum.org www.catholicmuseum.org Shawn Kenney, Dir.;

The Nigerian Catholic Community in Columbus, Ohio, Inc. - 1582 Ferris Rd., c/o St. Matthias Church, Columbus, OH 43224 c) 614-507-3744 nigeriancatholiccolumbus@gmail.com www.nigeriancatholiccolumbus.org Rev. Hilary C. Ike (Nigeria), Chap.;

Shrine of Blessed Margaret of Castello - 280 N. Grant Ave., Columbus, OH 43215 t) 614-240-5915 director@littlemargaret.org www.littlemargaret.org Shrine dedicated to promoting the sanctity of life, and the cause of canonization of Blessed Margaret of Castello, O.P. Rev. Stephen Alcott, O.P., Dir.;

St. Stephen's Community House - 1500 E. 17th Ave., Columbus, OH 43219 t) 614-294-6347 jpegues@saintstephensch.org www.saintstephensch.org Marilyn Mehaffie, Admin.;

St. Vincent Family Center - 1490 E. Main St., Columbus, OH 43205 t) 614-252-0731 Susan Lewis Kaylor, Pres.;

PLAIN CITY

***Villas at St. Therese Plain City Assisted Living** - 7025 Club Park Dr., Plain City, OH 43064; Mailing: P.O. Box 3130, Dublin, OH 43016 t) 614-761-3734 jhendricks@stbrigidofkildare.org Rev. Msgr. Joseph M. Hendricks, Contact;

***The Villas at St. Therese Plain City Independent Living** - 7079 Club Park Dr., Plain City, OH 43064; Mailing: PO Box 3130, Dublin, OH 43016 t) 614-761-3734 jhendricks@stbrigidofkildare.org Rev. Msgr. Joseph M. Hendricks, Contact;

UPPER ARLINGTON

Columbus Catholic Women's Conference - 2280 W. Henderson Rd., #205, Upper Arlington, OH 43220 t) 614-398-2292 info@columbuscatholicwomen.com www.columbuscatholicwomen.com Michele Faehnle, Chair;

WORTHINGTON

Catholic Men's Ministry - 7080 Westview Dr., Worthington, OH 43085 t) 614-505-6605 mail@catholicmensministry.com catholicmensministry.com Chuck Wilson, Dir.;

NURSING / REHABILITATION / CONVALESCENCE / ELDERLY CARE [NUR]

COLUMBUS

Seton South Columbus, Inc. - 155 Highview Blvd., Columbus, OH 43207 t) 614-492-9944 coneal@borror.com Connie O'Neal, Admin.;

Seton Square, Inc. - 1776 Drew Ave., Columbus, OH 43235 t) 614-451-1995 fhinklin@borror.com J. D. Dowell, Bus. Mgr.;

Seton Square, West - 3999 Clime Rd., Columbus, OH 43228 t) 614-274-8550 vthomas@borror.com

The Villas at St. Therese, Inc. (The Carmelite System) - 25 Noe Bixby Rd., Columbus, OH 43213 t) 614-864-3576 srann@carmeliteseniorliving.org; kharris@carmeliteseniorliving.org www.carmeliteseniorliving.org/ Sr. Ann Brown, O.Carm., CEO;

COSHOCTON

Seton Coshocton, Inc. - 377 Clow Ln., Coshocton, OH 43812 t) 740-622-7664 rconkle@borror.com

DOVER

Seton Development, Inc. - 501 S. James St., Dover, OH 44622 t) 330-343-3611 thoover@borror.com Rev. Msgr. Joseph M. Hendricks, Chair;

Seton Square Dover, II, Inc. - 139 Filmore Ave., Dover, OH 44622 t) 330-343-3611 thoover@borror.com J. D. Dowell, Bus. Mgr.;

KENTON

Seton Kenton, Inc. - 699 Morningside Dr., Kenton, OH 43326 t) 419-673-7202 kmelton@borror.com Karen Melton, Admin.;

LANCASTER

Seton Lancaster, Inc. - 232 Gay St., Lancaster, OH 43130 t) 740-681-1403 drose@borror.com J. D. Dowell, Bus. Mgr.;

LONDON

Seton London, Inc. - 350 Cambridge Dr., London, OH 43140 t) 740-852-4233 vthomas@borror.com J. D. Dowell, Bus. Mgr.;

MARION

Seton Square Marion, Inc. - 255 Richland Rd., Marion, OH 43302 t) 740-389-4746 dreyneke@borror.com J. D. Dowell, Bus. Mgr.;

REYNOLDSBURG

Seton Square East, Inc. - 1235 Briarcliff Rd., Reynoldsburg, OH 43068 t) 614-861-4860 jclipner@borror.com J. D. Dowell, Bus. Mgr.;

WASHINGTON COURT HOUSE

Seton Washington Court House - 400 N. Glenn Ave., Washington Court House, OH 43160 t) 740-335-2292 khoty@borror.com J. D. Dowell, Bus. Mgr.;

WELLSTON

Seton Square Wellston, Inc. - 570 W. First St., Wellston, OH 45692 t) 740-384-6174 npetersen@borror.com Nyla Petersen, Admin.;

ZANESVILLE

Seton Housing, Inc. - 516 Sheridan St., Zanesville, OH 43701 t) 740-453-4422 kmendenhall@borror.com Kellie Mendenhall, Admin.;

PRESCHOOLS / CHILDCARE CENTERS [PRE]

COLUMBUS

St. John Paul II Early Childhood Education Center - 957 E. Broad St., Columbus, OH 43205 t) 614-372-5656 stjohnpaul2preschool@gmail.com stjohnpaul2preschool.com Early education, including Catechesis of the Good Shepherd. Sr. Bozena Tyborowska, Dir.; Stds.: 40

Our Lady of Bethlehem School and Childcare (Our Lady of Bethlehem Schools, Inc.) - 4567 Olentangy River Rd., Columbus, OH 43214 t) 614-459-8285 lharrington@cdeducation.org; jyanko@cdeducation.org www.ourladyofbethlehem.org Lori Dulin, Prin.;

SEMINARIES [SEM]

COLUMBUS

Pontifical College Josephinum - 7625 N. High St., Columbus, OH 43235-1498 t) 614-885-5585 bcheek@pcj.edu www.pcj.edu Most Rev. Christophe Pierre, Chancellor; Most Rev. Earl Kenneth Fernandes, Vice Chancellor; Rev. Steven P. Beseau, Rector; Rev. Brett A. Brannen, Prof.; Rev. Kenneth D. Brighenti; Most Rev. Frederick F. Campbell, Prof.; Rev. Dylan James, Prof.; Rev. Msgr. John G. Johnson, Prof.; Rev. Ervens Mengelle, I.V.E., Dean; Rev. William Thomas Kessler, Prof.; Rev. Victor Antonio Moratin, CPM, Prof.; Rev. Marek Kasperczuk, Prof.; Rev. Bernard Mulcahy, O.P., Assoc. Prof.; Rev. David A. Schalk, Prof.; Stds.: 59; Lay Tchrs.: 10; Pr. Tchrs.: 10

An asterisk (*) denotes an organization that has established tax-exempt status directly with the IRS and is not covered by the USCCB Group Ruling.

Diocese of Corpus Christi

(Dioecesis Corporis Christi)

MOST REVEREND WM. MICHAEL MULVEY, S.T.L., D.D.

Eighth Bishop of Corpus Christi; ordained June 29, 1975; appointed Bishop of Corpus Christi January 18, 2010; ordained March 25, 2010. Mailing Address: P.O. Box 2620, Corpus Christi, TX 78403-2620. Res.: 6301 Kostoryz Rd., Corpus Christi, TX 78415.

The Chancery Office: 555 N. Carancahua, Ste. 750, Corpus Christi, TX 78401. Mailing Address: P.O. Box 2620, Corpus Christi, TX 78403-2620. T: 361-882-6191; F: 361-882-1018.

www.diocesecc.org
chancery@diocesecc.org

Square Miles 10,951.

Erected a Vicariate Apostolic in 1874; elevated to a Diocese March 23, 1912.

The territory embraced by the Diocese of Corpus Christi comprises the Counties of Aransas, Bee, Brooks, Duval, Jim Wells, Kleberg, Kenedy, Live Oak, Nueces, Refugio, San Patricio, and parts of McMullen in the State of Texas.

For legal titles of parishes and diocesan institutions, consult the Chancery Office.

STATISTICAL OVERVIEW

Personnel

Bishop	1
Retired Bishops	2
Priests: Diocesan Active in Diocese	62
Priests: Diocesan Active Outside Diocese	3
Priests: Retired, Sick or Absent	29
Number of Diocesan Priests	94
Religious Priests in Diocese	31
Total Priests in your Diocese	125
Extern Priests in Diocese	5
Ordinations:	
Diocesan Priests	2
Transitional Deacons	2
Permanent Deacons in Diocese	100
Total Brothers	4
Total Sisters	231

Parishes

Parishes	69
With Resident Pastor:	
Resident Diocesan Priests	57
Resident Religious Priests	6
Without Resident Pastor:	
Administered by Priests	6
Missions	29

Professional Ministry Personnel:	
Lay Ministers	82

Welfare

Catholic Hospitals	6
Total Assisted	368,265
Health Care Centers	7
Total Assisted	33,030
Homes for the Aged	1
Total Assisted	53
Day Care Centers	1
Total Assisted	4
Special Centers for Social Services	1
Total Assisted	55,980

Educational

Diocesan Students in Other Seminaries	6
Students, Religious	1
Total Seminarians	7
High Schools, Diocesan and Parish	1
Total Students	180
High Schools, Private	1
Total Students	175
Elementary Schools, Diocesan and Parish	9
Total Students	1,343
Elementary Schools, Private	2
Total Students	317
Catechesis/Religious Education:	
High School Students	1,929
Elementary Students	3,645
Total Students under Catholic Instruction	7,596
Teachers in Diocese:	
Priests	1
Sisters	6
Lay Teachers	197

Vital Statistics

Receptions into the Church:	
Infant Baptism Totals	895
Minor Baptism Totals	118
Adult Baptism Totals	105
Received into Full Communion	116
First Communions	1,008
Confirmations	829
Marriages:	
Catholic	271
Interfaith	40
Total Marriages	311
Deaths	1,421
Total Catholic Population	208,633
Total Population	585,266

LEADERSHIP

Diocesan Curia -

Office of the Bishop - t) 361-882-6191 Most Rev. Wm. Michael Mulvey; Very Rev. James G. Stembler, Vicar; Very Rev. Richard A. Libby, Chancellor;

Bishops Emeriti - Most Rev. Edmond Carmody; Most Rev. Rene H. Gracida;

Consultative Bodies -

Council of Religious - Sr. Mary Claire Strasser, SOLT;

Vicars Forane - Very Rev. Darryl J. D'Souza, Corpus Christi Northside Deanery; Very Rev. Paul A. Hesse, Corpus Christi Southside Deanery (phesse@stpiusxcc.org); Very Rev. Andrew Sensenig, OMI, Kingsville Deanery (andyomi@gmail.com);

College of Consultors - Rev. Pedro T. Elizardo Jr.; Very Rev. Richard Gonzales; Very Rev. Richard A. Libby;

Diaconate Formation Screening Committee - Very Rev. Raju Thottankara (India); Elva Mantz, Recording Sec.; Dcn. Michael Mantz, Dir.;

Finance Council - Most Rev. Wm. Michael Mulvey; Misty Smith, CFO; Dr. Osbert Blow (osbert.blow@christushealth.org);

Building Commission - Most Rev. Wm. Michael Mulvey; Marc Cervantes, Gen. Counsel; Dcn. Michael Mantz;

Presbyteral Council - Very Rev. Raju Thottankara (India), Vicar for Clergy / Moderator of the Curia; Very Rev. Richard A. Libby, Chancellor; Very Rev. Darryl J. D'Souza;

Tribunal - Rev. Msgr. Thomas P. Feeney, Vicar;

- **Defender of the Bond -** Rev. Angel Montano;
- **Instructor (Vacant) -**
- **Judges -** Rev. Msgr. Thomas P. Feeney; Rev. Joseph Lopez; Rev. Msgr. Michael Howell;
- **Notary-Secretary -** Belinda Harris;
- **Promoter of Justice -**

ADMINISTRATION

The Chancery Office - t) 361-882-6191 chancery@diocesecc.org

- **Archives -** Patricia Roeser, Records Admin.;
- **Bishops Emeriti -** Most Rev. Edmond Carmody; Most Rev. Rene H. Gracida;
- **Catholic Cemeteries -** Jill Hundley;
- **Catholic Schools Office -** Dr. Rosemary J. Henry, Supt.;
- **Chancellor -** Very Rev. Richard A. Libby, Chancellor;
- **Consecrated Life & Women Vocations -** Sr. Mary Claire Strasser, SOLT, Dir.;

Controller - Misty Smith, Controller;

Executive Administrative Assistant to the Bishop - Cecilia Fuentes;

Fiscal Officer - Misty Smith, CFO;

General Counsel - Marc Cervantes;

Information Technology Services - Dcn. Lee Alvarado;

Judicial Vicar - Rev. Msgr. Thomas P. Feeney;

Ministry & Life Enrichment for Persons with Disabilities -

Office for Child and Youth Protection (OCYP) - Stephanie Bonilla, Dir.;

Office of Communications and Evangelization - Katia Uriarte, Dir.;

Office of Divine Worship - Rev. Pedro T. Elizardo Jr., Dir.;

Office of Multicultural and Social Ministry - Jaime Reyna, Dir.;

Office of Pastoral Parish Services - Dcn. Santos R. Jones III, Dir.; Jaime Reyna, Dir.;

Office of the Bishop - Most Rev. Wm. Michael Mulvey;

Office of the Permanent Diaconate - Dcn. Michael Mantz, Dir.;

Propagation of the Faith Office - Rev. Raynaldo Yrlas Jr.;

Real Property Office - Dcn. Michael Mantz;

Risk Services - t) (361) 882-6191 Dcn. Mark Arnold, Risk Mgr.; Hilda Garza-Martinez, Risk Service Specialist;

Senior Administrative Assistant to the Chancellor - Margie Rivera;

Senior Administrative Assistant to Vicar General - Olivia Rodriguez;

The South Texas Catholic - Most Rev. Wm. Michael Mulvey, Publisher;

Theological Advisor to the Bishop -

Vicar for Clergy - Very Rev. Raju Thottankara (India);

Vicar General - Very Rev. James G. Stembler;

Victim Assistance Coordinator - Kristi Skrobarczyk;

Vocations Director & Seminary Formation - Bob Cummings, Dir.;

Web Development Office -

ORGANIZATIONS

Alhambra - Ed Rotter, Grand Commander; Terese Peterson, Grand Sultana (teresepeterson@hotmail.com);

Campus Ministries - Jesus Zambrana, Campus Min. Newman Catholic Student Center Beeville; Angela Castellano, Campus Min. Texas A&M Kingsville; Amy Barragree, Campus Min. for Texas A&M in Corpus Christi and Del Mar College;

The Catholic Charismatic Renewal Movement - t) 361-438-0935 Jay Dillashaw;

Catholic Charities - t) 361-884-0651 Dr. Michele Johnston, Exec. Dir.;

Catholic Daughters of the Americas - Erica Lozano, Dist. 16 & Dist. 41, Corpus Christi; Bertie Almendarez, Dist. 36, Corpus Christi; Delma Cantu, Dist. 47, Odem;

Cursillo Movement - Maria Castillo, Pres.;

- **English Cursillo -** t) 361-563-8562 Maria Castillo;
- **Spanish Cursillo -** t) 361-877-5048 Manuel Rangel, Dir.;

Diocesan Council of Catholic Women - Diana Zavala, Pres.; Very Rev. James G. Stembler, Spiritual Adv./Care Srvcs.;

Diocesan Telecommunications Corporation - t) 361-289-6437 Dcn. Mark Cazalas, Exec. VP/General Manager (mcazalas@goccn.org);

Diocese of Corpus Christi Deposit and Loan Fund, Inc. - t) 361-882-6191

Diocese of Corpus Christi Perpetual Benefit Endowment Fund, Inc. -

Disaster Response Program - t) 361-884-0651 x245 Angie Garcia, Dir.;

Emergency Aid - Elma Ortiz, Mgr.;

Family Counseling - Gloria Garcia, Mgr.;

La Fazenda de Esperanza - Most Rev. Wm. Michael Mulvey; Marc Cervantes;

Housing Counseling - Sr. Rency Moonjely, S.A.B.S., Oper. Supvr.;

Immigration Services - Juanita Cardiel, DOJ, Accredited Rep.;

Knights of Columbus - t) 361-215-8487 Mikell West;

Legion of Mary - t) 361-877-1598 Delma Torres, Pres.; Dcn. Solomon T. Willis III, Dir.;

Marriage Encounter - Rob Johnson; Cris Johnson (georob6316@sbcglobal.net);

Radio Stations - KLUX FM HD - t) 361-289-2487 Dcn. Mark Cazalas, Exec. Vice Pres. & Gen. Mgr. (mcazalas@goccn.org);

Serra International - t) 361-947-1346 Ron Alonzo, Pres.;

PARISHES, MISSIONS, AND CLERGY

STATE OF TEXAS

AGUA DULCE

St. Frances of Rome - 410 Simmons St., Agua Dulce, TX 78330; Mailing: P.O. Box 598, Agua Dulce, TX 78330 t) 361-998-2216 stfrancescc@yahoo.com Rev. John Chavarria, Admin.;

ALICE

St. Elizabeth of Hungary - 603 E. 5th St., Alice, TX 78332 t) 361-664-7719 (CRP); 361-664-6481 st.elizabeth1918@gmail.com stelizabethofhungaryalice.org Rev. Dennis P. Zerr, Pst.; Dcn. Bobby Bourlon Sr.; Dcn. James A. Carlisle; Dcn. Ernesto Gutierrez; CRP Stds.: 78

St. Joseph - 801 S. Reynolds St., Alice, TX 78332 t) 361-664-7551; 361-664-2397 info@sjcatholicchurch.org www.sjcatholicchurch.org Rev. Chris Becerra, Pst.; Dcn. Julian M. Ortiz Sr.; Dcn. John L. Pierce; Michelle Ortiz, DRE; CRP Stds.: 120

- **Perpetual Eucharistic Adoration -**

Our Lady of Guadalupe - 1300 Guerra St., Alice, TX 78332; Mailing: 1318 Guerra St., P.O. Box 411, Alice, TX 78333 t) 361-664-0437 (CRP); 361-664-2953; (361) 664-2957 olgalice@yahoo.com olgalice.org Rev. Biju Joseph Thoompunkal, Pst.; Dcn. Emede Gonzalez; CRP Stds.: 122

- **Santo Nino De Atocha -** 918 CR 122 (Tecolote), Alice, TX 78333; Mailing: P.O. Box 411, Alice, TX 78333 pastor@olgalice.org

ARANSAS PASS

St. Mary, Star of the Sea - 342 S. Rife St., Aransas Pass, TX 78336 t) 361-758-2662 office@stmaryss.org; dre@stmaryss.org www.stmaryss.org Rev. Emilio Jimenez, Pst.; CRP Stds.: 50

BANQUETE

Saint Michael the Archangel - 4317 Fourth St., Banquete, TX 78339; Mailing: P.O. Box 9, Banquete, TX 78339 t) 361-387-8371 saintmichaelbanquete@outlook.com Rev. John Chavarria, Pst.; Dcn. Pilar M. Gonzalez; CRP Stds.: 80

BEEVILLE

St. James - 605 S. Alta Vista, Beeville, TX 78102 t) 361-358-4825 stjamesbeeville@yahoo.com stjamesbeeville.org Rev. Jacob John Valayath, Pst.; CRP Stds.: 37

St. Joseph - 609 E. Gramman St., Beeville, TX 78102 t) 361-358-3239 office@stjosephbeeville.org stjosephbeeville.org Very Rev. Richard Gonzales, Pst.; Dcn. Luis Trevino; Dcn. Santos R. Jones III, Pst. Assoc.; Linda Mae Gomez, Youth Min.; Victor Gomez, Youth Min.; Debra Olivares, DRE; CRP Stds.: 114

Our Lady of Victory - 707 North Ave. E., Beeville, TX 78102 t) 361-358-0088; 361-542-9409 (CRP) churcholv@yahoo.com; lalyarteaga@yahoo.com www.olvbeeville.org Rev. Lukose Thirunelliparambil (India), Pst.; Dcn. Rogelio Rosenbaum; Laly Arteaga, DRE; CRP Stds.: 129

- **Sacred Heart Mission - Pettus -** 104 N. Bee St., Pettus, TX 78146; Mailing: 707 N. Ave. E, Beeville, TX 78102

BEN BOLT

St. Peter Mission - 221 Salazar Ave., Ben Bolt, TX 78342; Mailing: P.O. Box 678, Ben Bolt, TX 78342 t) (361) 664-7551 benboltcatholicparish@gmail.com sjcatholicchurch.org/st-peter-catholic-mission Rev. Chris Becerra, Admin.;

BENAVIDES

Santa Rosa de Lima - 203 Santa Rosa de Lima St., Benavides, TX 78341; Mailing: P.O. Box W, Benavides, TX 78341-0923 t) 361-256-3427 benavideschurch@yahoo.com Rev. P. George Thomas, Pst.; Beatriz Canas, DRE; CRP Stds.: 25

- **St. Joseph -**
- **Sacred Heart -**

BISHOP

St. James - 603 W. 3rd St., Bishop, TX 78343 t) 361-584-3250 stjameschurch603@yahoo.com Rev. Lukose Thirunelliparambil, Pst.; CRP Stds.: 75

- **St. James -** 310 W. Ave. B, Driscoll, TX 78351

CORPUS CHRISTI

Saint Andrew By the Sea Parish - 14238 Encantada Ave., Corpus Christi, TX 78418-6432 t) 361-949-7193 (CRP) standrewcc@standrewcctx.org www.standrewcctx.org Rev. Hanh Van Pham, Pst.; Cheryl Hooper, DRE; CRP Stds.: 72

St. Anselm Anglican Use Community - 15849 Grenadine Dr., Corpus Christi, TX 78413 t) 361-961-4999 (Suffragan to: Our Lady of Guadalupe Chapel, NAS, Corpus Christi) Rev. John Vidal, Pst.;

Corpus Christi Cathedral - 505 N. Upper Broadway, Corpus Christi, TX 78401 t) 361-883-4213 info@cccathedral.com; religioused@ccathedral.com www.cccathedral.com Rev. Pedro T. Elizardo Jr., Rector; Dcn. Michael Mantz; Dcn. Adelfino Palacios Jr.; Dcn. Amando Leal; CRP Stds.: 120

Emmanuel - (Crypt)

Blessed Sacrament -

Christ the King - 3423 Rojo, Corpus Christi, TX 78415 t) 361-883-2821 churchoffice@ctk-cc.org www.ctk-cc.org Rev. William K. Bakyil, S.O.L.T. (Ghana), Pst.; Dcn. Manuel Marroquin; Sr. Maria Caritas, DRE; CRP Stds.: 78

Convent -

SS. Cyril and Methodius - 3210 S. Padre Island Dr., Corpus Christi, TX 78415 t) 361-853-7371 kmjgarcia@sscmc.org; sscyrilandmethodius@sscmc.org sscmc.org/ Rev. James Vasquez, Pst.; Dcn. Alberto Galvan III; Dcn. Fernando Perez; Kiki Garcia, DRE; CRP Stds.: 136

Saint Helena of the True Cross of Jesus - 7634 Wooldridge Rd, Corpus Christi, TX 78414 t) 361-994-8783 x22 (CRP); 361-994-8783 sthelenasecretary@gmail.com sthelenacc.com Very Rev. Richard A. Libby, Pst.; Dcn. Richard Longoria; Irene Pena, Supt.; Catalina Longoria, DRE; CRP Stds.: 23

Holy Cross - 1109 N. Staples St., Corpus Christi, TX 78401 t) 361-888-4012 hcrosstx@gmail.com www.holycrosscc.net Rev. Roy Kalayil (India), Pst.; CRP Stds.: 12

Holy Family Church - 3157 MacArthur St., Corpus Christi, TX 78416; Mailing: 2509 Nogales St., Corpus Christi, TX 78416 t) 361-882-3245 x13 (CRP); 361-882-3245 melissa@holyfamilycc.net; church@holyfamilycc.net www.holyfamilycc.net Very Rev. Darryl J. D'Souza, Pst.; Rev. Gerardo M Ponce (Mexico), Par. Vicar; Dcn. Lee Alvarado; Jesusa Melissa Riojas, Parish Life Coord.; CRP Stds.: 128

Saint John the Baptist - 7522 Everhart Rd., Corpus Christi, TX 78413 t) 361-991-4400 churchoffice@sjbcctx.org www.sjbcctx.org Rev. Rodolfo D. Vasquez, Pst.; Dcn. Julio Dimas; Dcn. Jesse Lee Hinojosa;

St. Joseph - 710 S. 19th St., Corpus Christi, TX 78465-5196; Mailing: P.O. Box 5196, Corpus Christi, TX 78465 t) 361-882-7912; 361-882-7912 (CRP) stjoseph@stx.rr.com; stjosephcctx@gmail.com stjosephcorpuschristi.com Rev. Rogel Rosalinas, S.O.L.T., Pst.; Dcn. Juan Carlos Ayala; Dcn. Reynaldo Rojas; CRP Stds.: 52

Most Precious Blood - 3502 Saratoga Blvd., Corpus Christi, TX 78415 t) 361-854-3800 mpb@mpbchurch.org www.mpbchurch.org Rev. Joseph Lopez, Pst.; Rev. Ramiro Regalado, Par. Vicar; Rev. Peter G. Martinez, In Res.; Dcn. Frank N. Newchurch; Dcn. Ken Bockholt; Dcn. David Castillo; Dcn. Mark Cazalas; CRP Stds.: 414

Nuestra Senora de San Juan de Los Lagos, Madre de la Iglesia - 1755 Frio St., Corpus Christi, TX 78417; Mailing: 1723 Frio St., Corpus Christi, TX 78417 t) 361-852-0249 sanjuanlagos3@yahoo.com Rev. Juan Fernando Gamez (Colombia), Pst.; Dcn. Marco Anes; CRP Stds.: 99

Our Lady of Guadalupe - 540 Hiawatha St., Corpus Christi, TX 78405 t) 361-882-1951 olgcctx@gmail.com olgcctx.com/ Rev. Salvatore James Farfaglia, Pst.; Dcn. Armando Botello; CRP Stds.: 24

Our Lady of Mount Carmel - 1080 S. Clarkwood Rd., Corpus Christi, TX 78406 t) 361-241-2004 Rev. Gabriel P. Coelho, Pst.;

Our Lady of the Rosary - ourladyofrosary@stx.rr.com

St. Vivian - 3516 FM 665 W., Robstown, TX 78380

Our Lady of Perpetual Help - 5830 Williams Dr., Corpus Christi, TX 78412 t) 361-991-7891 olphoffice@olphcctx.org www.olphcctx.org Rev. Frank X. Martinez, Pst.; Dcn. Fred Castillo; Dcn. Arnold Marcha; Dcn. Rodolfo R. Martinez; Dcn. Armando Sanchez; CRP Stds.: 165

Our Lady of Pilar - 1101 Bloomington St., Corpus Christi, TX 78416 t) 361-852-6327 ourladyofpilarcc@gmail.com Rev. Jose Naul Ordonez, Pst.; CRP Stds.: 230

Our Lady of the Rosary - 1123 Main Dr., Corpus Christi, TX 78409 t) 361-241-2004 ourladyoftherosary@stx.rr.com www.ourladyofherosarycc.com Rev. Gabriel P. Coelho, Pst.; CRP Stds.: 2

Our Lady of Mt. Carmel Mission -

St. Vivian Mission -

Our Lady Star of the Sea - 3110 E. Causeway Blvd., Corpus Christi, TX 78402 t) 361-883-4507 olss.church@gmail.com www.olsscc.org/ Rev. Roy Kalayil (India), Admin.; CRP Stds.: 8

St. Patrick Church - 3350 S. Alameda St., Corpus Christi, TX 78411 t) 361-855-7391 (CRP); 361-855-7567 (CRP) religioused@stpatrickchurchcc.org; stpatchurch.cctx@gmail.com www.stpatrickchurchcc.org Very Rev. Msgr. Roger R. Smith, Pst.; Dcn. Hector Salinas; Marian Rose Swetish, DRE; Dcn. Eleazar (Larry) Rodriguez; Rev. Jaison Mathew, HGN, Par. Vicar; CRP Stds.: 106

St. Paul the Apostle - 2233 Waldron Rd., Corpus Christi, TX 78418 t) 361-937-6908 (CRP); 361-937-3864; 361-937-5875 office@stpaultheapostlecc.com stpaultheapostlecc.com Rev. Joseph T. Nguyen, Admin.; Dcn. Francisco Rodriguez Jr., Pst. Assoc.; Dcn. Gary Wayne Robinson, DRE; CRP Stds.: 115

St. Peter, Prince of Apostles - 3901 Violet Rd., Corpus Christi, TX 78410-2924 t) 361-241-3249 www.stpeterprince.net Very Rev. Raju Thottankara (India), Pst.; CRP Stds.: 268

St. Mary - 4849 Cynthia, Corpus Christi, TX 78410 t) (361) 241-3249 Rev. Msgr. Seamus McGowan;

St. Philip the Apostle - 3513 Cimarron Rd., Corpus Christi, TX 78414 t) (361) 991-8786 (CRP); 361-991-5146 info@stphilipcc.com www.stphilipcc.com Rev. John Xaviour, Pst.; Dcn. Billy Quintanilla, Bus. Mgr.; Dcn. Bob Allen; Dcn. Narciso Ortiz, Parish Life Coord.; Dcn. Daniel P. Shaunessey, RCIA Coord.; CRP Stds.: 295

St. Pius X - 5620 Gollihar Rd., Corpus Christi, TX 78412 t) 361-993-4053 phesse@stpiusxcc.org; parishoffice@stpiusxcc.org www.stpiusxcc.org Very Rev. Paul A. Hesse, Pst.; Rev. Carlos Tomas De La Rosa, Par. Vicar; Dcn. Salvador Alvarado; Dcn. Loni Lugo; Elizabeth Hinojosa, Prin.; CRP Stds.: 134

Sacred Heart - 1322 Comanche St., Corpus Christi, TX 78415 t) 361-883-6082 sacredheart1322@gmail.com sacredheartcorpus.org Rev. Pedro T. Elizardo Jr., Pst.; Dcn. Feliz Muniz; Nelda Ibarra, DRE; CRP Stds.: 4

Navarro Place -

St. Theresa - 1302 Lantana St., Corpus Christi, TX 78407 t) 361-289-2238 (CRP); 361-289-2759 secretary@sainttheresacc.org Rev. Ryszard Koziol, Pst.; Dcn. Stephen Nolte; Josie Martinez, DRE; CRP Stds.: 27

St. Thomas More Parish - 2045 18th St., Corpus Christi, TX 78404-3862 t) 361-888-9308 smccutchon@gmail.com; lisagodinez322@gmail.com www.stthomasmorecc.org Rev. Peter G. Martinez, Pst.; Sandra McCutchon, DRE; Lisa Godinez, Youth Min.; Erin Morales, RCIA Coord.; CRP Stds.: 47

EDROY

Our Lady of Guadalupe Mission - 18012 County Rd. 1598, Edroy, TX 78352; Mailing: P.O. Box 127, Edroy, TX 78352 t) 361-368-9156 sacredheartodem@yahoo.com See Sacred Heart of Jesus Parish, Odem. Rev. Isaias Estepa (Colombia), Pst.;

FALFURRIAS

Sacred Heart - 310 S. Caldwell St., Falfurrias, TX 78355 t) 361-325-3455 shcfal@outlook.com Rev. Pradeep Joseph Puthen; Dcn. Ricardo E. Costley; Joan Bostwick, DRE; CRP Stds.: 143

St. Ann - c/o Sacred Heart Parish, Encino, TX 78355

FREER

St. Mary - 1500 Duval St., Freer, TX 78357; Mailing: PO Drawer B, Freer, TX 78357 t) (361) 394-6832 stmarysparishfreer@yahoo.com Rev. Francis Sebastian, M.S.T., Admin.; Dcn. Eluterio Bitoni; Dcn. Pedro R. Trevino Jr.; CRP Stds.: 95

GEORGE WEST

St. George Catholic Church - 304 Crockett St., George West, TX 78022; Mailing: PO Box 580, George West, TX 78022 t) 361-447-2893 stgeorge_west@yahoo.com st-george-parish.org Rev. Romeo Salinas, Pst.; Deborah Brown, DRE; Kristina Gebhard, DRE; Virginia Crawford, Bus. Mgr.; CRP Stds.: 79

St. Joseph - County Rd. 799, Gussetville, TX 78022 t) (361) 447-2983 stgeoge_west@yahoo.com

GREGORY

Immaculate Conception - 107 Church St., Gregory, TX 78359; Mailing: P.O. Box 108, Gregory, TX 78359-0108 t) 361-643-4505 www.iccgregory.org Rev. Andrew Hejdak (Poland), Pst.; CRP Stds.: 164

INGLESIDE

Our Lady of the Assumption - 2414 Main, Ingleside, TX 78362 t) 361-776-2446 rmorin78362@gmail.com oloaingleside.org Rev. Patrick G. Higgins (Ireland), Admin.; CRP Stds.: 120

KINGSVILLE

St. Gertrude - 1120 S. 8th St., Kingsville, TX 78363 t) 361-592-7351 stgckingsville@gmail.com Rev. Bob Dunn, Pst.; Dcn. John R. Joiner; Dcn. Richard B. Morin; Dcn. Edwin N. Rowley; Dcn. Ruben Soliz; CRP Stds.: 176

St. Joseph - 1400 Brookshire, Kingsville, TX 78364-1602; Mailing: P.O. Box 1602, Kingsville, TX 78364-1602 t) 361-592-5689 stjosephkingsv@sbcglobal.net Rev. Paulson Panakal (India), Pst.; Dcn. Ricardo Gonzalez; Dcn. Richard B. Morin; Sylvia Molina, DRE;

St. Martin - 715 N. Eighth St., Kingsville, TX 78363 t) 361-592-4602 stmartincatholic@sbcglobal.net stmartinkingsville.org Rev. L. Alfredo Villarreal, Pst.; Rev. Eric G. Chapa, Par. Vicar; Dcn. Danny L. Herrera; Dcn. Michael L. Seymour; Maria Isabel Guzman, DRE; CRP Stds.: 200

Convent - 919 N. Ninth St., Kingsville, TX 78363

Christ the King -

Our Lady of Good Counsel - 1102 E. Kleberg Ave., Kingsville, TX 78363 t) 361-592-3489 ourladykingsville.org Rev. Paulson Panakal (India), Pst.;

MATHIS

St. Pius X Mission - Sandia - 217 W. San Patricio Ave., c/o Sacred Heart, Mathis, TX 78368 t) 361-547-9181; 361-249-0087 (CRP) sacredheartchurchmathis@gmail.com; noelbrel@gmail.com Rev. Peter Thenan (India), Pst.; Dcn. Walter Noel Breland, DRE;

Sacred Heart - 217 W. San Patricio Ave., Mathis, TX 78368-2259 t) 361-547-9181 sacredheartchurchmathis@gmail.com Rev. Peter Thenan (India), Pst.; Dcn. Mark Christoph; Dcn. Antonio S. Lara; CRP Stds.: 160

ODEM

Sacred Heart - 401 W. Willis St., Odem, TX 78370; Mailing: PO Box 276, Odem, TX 78370 t) 361-368-2746 c) 361-368-9156 sacredheartodem@yahoo.com Rev. Isaias Estepa (Colombia), Admin.; Dcn. Robert Flores;

Our Lady of Guadalupe Mission -

ORANGE GROVE

St. John of the Cross - 200 S. Metz St., Orange Grove, TX 78372-0329; Mailing: P.O. Box 329, Orange Grove, TX 78372-0329 t) 361-384-2795 saintjohn0003@aol.com; pastororangegrovetx@gmail.com www.st-johnog.org Rev. Patrick K. Donohoe, Pst.; Dcn. Armando Cavada; Dcn. Jim N Culpepper; Terrie Silva, DRE; CRP Stds.: 180

St. Francis of Assisi Mission - 303 County Rd. 185, Sandia, TX 78383 t) 361-547-2442

stfrancisassisilagarto@gmail.com

PETTUS

Sacred Heart Mission - 104 N. Bee Ave., Pettus, TX 78102; Mailing: 707 North Ave. E., c/o Our Lady of Victory, Beeville, TX 78102 t) 361-358-0088 Suffragan to Our Lady of Victory, Beeville. Rev. Lukose Thirunelliparamabil (India), Pst.;

PORT ARANSAS

St. Joseph - 422 Lantana Dr., Port Aransas, TX 78373; Mailing: P.O. Box 1546, Port Aransas, TX 78373 t) 361-749-5825; 361-749-5509 stjosephportaransastx@gmail.com www.stjosephportaransas.com Rev. George Johnson Vallamattam, Pst.; CRP Stds.: 20

PORTLAND

Our Lady of Mount Carmel - 1008 Austin St., Portland, TX 78374 t) 361-643-3548 (CRP); 361-643-7533 parish@olmcportland.com olmcportland.com Rev. Piotr A. Koziel, Pst.; Dcn. Robert Rosales; CRP Stds.: 363

PREMONT

St. Theresa of the Infant Jesus - 235 S.W. 4th St., Premont, TX 78375-0569; Mailing: P.O. Box 569, Premont, TX 78375-0569 t) (361) 348-2202; (361) 348-4142 sttheresaij@gmail.com Rev. Sanish Mathew, HGN, Pst.; Dcn. Ruben Maldonado; Dcn. Ramiro Davila, Sacr. Min.; CRP Stds.: 121

Immaculate Conception -

Our Lady of Guadalupe -

REFUGIO

St. James the Apostle - 202 E. Santiago St., Refugio, TX 78377 t) 361-526-4454 agomez.stjamesccd@yahoo.com Rev. Bill Marquis, Pst.; CRP Stds.: 73

St. Catherine Mission - Hwy. 2441, Blanconia, TX 78377

Our Lady of Refuge - 1008 S. Alamo St., Refugio, TX 78377 t) 361-526-2083 Rev. Bill Marquis, Pst.; CRP Stds.: 42

RIVIERA

Our Lady of Consolation - 204 Palm Ave., Riviera, TX 78379 t) 361-297-5255 ourlady@rivnet.com ourladyatriviera.tripod.com/ Rev. Andy Sensenig, OMI, Pst.; Dcn. Michael Valenzuela; CRP Stds.: 60

Our Lady of Guadalupe - 111 S. Second St., Riviera, TX 78379 t) (361) 297-5255 ourladyatriviera.tripod.com Very Rev. Andrew Sensenig, OMI, Pst.;

Sacred Heart - W. County Rd. 2160, Ricardo, TX 78363 ourladyatriviera.tripod.com

ROBSTOWN

St. Anthony - 204 Dunne St., Robstown, TX 78380-0792; Mailing: P.O. Box 792, Robstown, TX 78380 t) 361-387-2774 stanthonyparish@gmail.com stanthonyrobstown.org Rev. Gerard J. Sheehan, S.O.L.T., Pst.; Rev. John M. Patterson II, S.O.L.T., Par. Vicar; Rev. Richard Klepac, Par. Vicar; Dcn. Emilio Flores; Dcn. Homer Martinez; CRP Stds.: 75

St. Mary - 911 Garcia St., Robstown, TX 78380

St. John Nepomucene - 603 N. First St., Robstown, TX 78380 t) 361-933-1200 st.johns.robstown@gmail.com www.stjohnnrtx.org/ Rev. Mark Wheelan, S.O.L.T., Pst.; Diana Ochoa, DRE; CRP Stds.: 35

St. Thomas the Apostle - 16602 FM 624, Robstown, TX 78380 t) 361-387-1312; 361-387-7842 aramos@christon624.com; stthomastheapostle@christon624.com www.christon624.com Rev. Philip Panackal (India), Pst.; CRP Stds.: 169

St. Patrick Mission - 20742 Magnolia St., Mathis, TX 78368 t) (361) 387-1312

ROCKPORT

St. Peter's Parish - 2761 FM1781, Rockport, TX 78382; Mailing: P.O. Box 1060, Rockport, TX 78382 t) 361-729-3008 stpeterparishoffice@stpeterfultonmo.org Rev. Tung T. Tran, Admin.;

Sacred Heart - 209 N. Church St., Rockport, TX 78382 t) 361-729-8283 (CRP); 361-729-9203; 361-729-2174 reled@rockport.twcbc.com; shrockport@rockport.twcbc.com www.shcrockport.org Rev. Raynaldo Yrlas Jr., Pst.; Dcn. Daniel Joseph Boehm; Dcn. Ronald Janota; Gloria J. Scott, DRE; CRP Stds.: 135

Convent - t) 361-729-5311

SAN DIEGO

St. Francis de Paula - 401 S. Victoria St., San Diego, TX 78384 t) (361) 279-3596 stfrancisdepaulachurch@yahoo.com stfrancisdepaulachurch.church Rev. James Farfaglia, Pst.; CRP Stds.: 157

St. Joseph - 2688 FM 735, Palito Blanco, TX 78384

SAN PATRICIO

Saint Patrick Mission - 20742 Magnolia St., San Patricio, TX 78368; Mailing: 16602 FM 624, c/o St. Thomas the Apostle, Robstown, TX 78380 t) 361-387-1312; 361-387-7842; 361-244-2138 (CRP) stthomastheapostle@christon624.com; aramos@christon624.com www.christon624.com Rev. Philip Panackal (India), Pst.; Michele Hoelscher, DRE;

SARITA

Our Lady of Guadalupe - 140 S. Main St., Sarita, TX 78385; Mailing: P.O. Box 6, Sarita, TX 78385 t) 361-294-5350 asensenig@omiusa.org; olgsaritatx@gmail.com Very Rev. Andrew Sensenig, OMI, Pst.; CRP Stds.: 3

SINTON

Our Lady of Guadalupe - 725 Sodville Ave., Sinton, TX 78387 t) 361-364-2210; 361-364-4007 (CRP) office@olgsinton.org olgsinton.org Rev. Glen F. Mullan, Pst.; CRP Stds.: 167

Sacred Heart - 906 E. Sinton St., Sinton, TX 78387-0266; Mailing: P.O. Box 266, Sinton, TX 78387 t) 361-364-1768 office@shcsinton.org www.shcsinton.org Rev. Yul Ibay, Pst.; Dcn. Solomon T. Willis III; Mary Connors, DRE; CRP Stds.: 221

St. Paul - CR 798 Hwy. 181, Sinton, TX 78387-0266 t) (361) 364-1768

SKIDMORE

Immaculate Conception - 300 First St., Skidmore, TX 78389; Mailing: P.O. Box 189, Skidmore, TX 78389 t) 361-287-3256 iccskidmore@yahoo.com iccskidmore.com Rev. Richard Gutierrez, Pst.; CRP Stds.: 24

St. Francis Xavier - Frio St., Tynan, TX 78384

TAFT

Holy Family - 702 McIntyre Ave, Taft, TX 78390; Mailing: P.O. Box 173, Taft, TX 78390-0173 t) 361-528-3132 holyfamilytaft@cableone.net Rev. John McKenzie, Pst.;

Immaculate Conception - 120 E. Escobedo St., Taft, TX 78390; Mailing: P.O. Box 868, Taft, TX 78390 t) 361-528-2626 immaculate.conception.taft@gmail.com Rev. John McKenzie, Pst.;

THREE RIVERS

Sacred Heart - 303 E. Alexander St., Three Rivers, TX 78071-0729; Mailing: P.O. Box 729, Three Rivers, TX 78071-0729 t) 361-786-3398 sh.threerivers@diocesecc.org www.shthreerivers.org Rev. Ryszard Zielinski (Poland), Pst.; CRP Stds.: 16

Our Lady of Guadalupe -

TIVOLI

Our Lady of Guadalupe - 501B William St., P.O. Drawer I, Tivoli, TX 77990 t) 361-237-3634 tivoliclerk@gmail.com Rev. Ponnuswamy R. Victor, Pst.; CRP Stds.: 12

St. Anthony of Padua -

St. Dennis -

VIOLET

St. Anthony - 3894 County Rd. 61, Violet, TX 78380 t) 361-387-4434 stanthonyviolet@yahoo.com Rev. Tomasz Kozub (Poland), Pst.;

WOODSBORO

St. Therese, The Little Flower - 315 Pugh St., Woodsboro, TX 78393; Mailing: P.O. Box 1076, Woodsboro, TX 78393 t) (361) 441-2040 sttherese1076@gmail.com Rev. Bill Marquis, Pst.; CRP Stds.: 52

St. Mary -

SCHOOLS: PRESCHOOL THRU HIGH SCHOOL

SCHOOLS

STATE OF TEXAS

ALICE

St. Elizabeth School - (PAR) (Grades PreSchool-6) 615 E. Fifth, Alice, TX 78332 t) 361-664-6271 mtorres@sesalice.org; vvavrusa@sesalice.org sesalice.org Valerie Vavrusa, Prin.; Stds.: 151; Lay Tchrs.: 9

CORPUS CHRISTI

Bishop Garriga Middle Preparatory School - (DIO) (Grades 6-8) 3114 Saratoga Blvd., Corpus Christi, TX 78415 t) 361-851-0853 mderocher@bgmps.org www.bgmps.org Norma Castaneda, Prin.; Rev. Peter G. Martinez, Pres.; Stds.: 143; Sr. Tchrs.: 1; Lay Tchrs.: 8

SS. Cyril and Methodius School - (PAR) (Grades PreK-5) 5002 Kostoryz Rd., Corpus Christi, TX 78415 t) 361-853-9392 lsamaniego@sscmcschool.org www.sscmc.org Lilly Samaniego, Prin.; Carol Sanchez, Librn.; Stds.: 120; Lay Tchrs.: 10

Incarnate Word Academy Elementary Level - (PRV) (Grades PreK-5) 450 Chamberlain St., Corpus Christi, TX 78404 t) 361-883-0857 iwaccel@iwacc.org www.iwacc.org Pamela Carrillo, Prin.; Sammie Grunwald, Pres.; Stds.: 206; Sr. Tchrs.: 1; Lay Tchrs.: 27

Incarnate Word Academy Middle School - (PRV) (Grades 6-8) 2917 Austin St., Corpus Christi, TX 78404 t) 361-883-0857 x113 iwaccml@iwacc.org www.iwacc.org Marci Levings, Prin.; Sammie Grunwald, Pres.; LaQuita Hilzinger, Librn.; Stds.: 114; Sr. Tchrs.: 2; Lay Tchrs.: 14

Most Precious Blood School - (PAR) (Grades PreK-5) 3502 Saratoga Blvd., Corpus Christi, TX 78415 t) 361-852-4800 nelda.bazan@mpbcs.net www.mpbcs.net Nelda Bazan, Prin.; Stds.: 132; Lay Tchrs.: 10

Our Lady of Perpetual Help Academy - (PAR) (Grades PreK-8) 5814 Williams Dr., Corpus Christi, TX 78412 t) 361-991-3305; 361-992-5951 osalazar@olphacademycc.org www.olphacademycc.org Orlando Salazar, Prin.; Stds.: 142; Lay Tchrs.: 9

St. Patrick School - (PAR) (Grades PreK-6) 3340 S. Alameda St., Corpus Christi, TX 78411 t) 361-852-1211 eburton@stpatrickschoolcc.org; rbaysinger@stpatrickschoolcc.org www.stpatrickschoolcc.org Evelyn Burton, Prin.; Veronica L Baysinger, Bus. Mgr.; Stds.: 247; Lay Tchrs.: 24

St. Pius X Catholic School - (PAR) (Grades PreK-6) 737 St. Pius Dr., Corpus Christi, TX 78412 t) 361-992-1343 www.stpiusxschoolcc.org Bryan Krnavek, Prin.; Stds.: 146; Lay Tchrs.: 12

ROBSTOWN

St. Anthony School - (PAR) (Grades PreK-8) 203 Dunne Ave., Robstown, TX 78380 t) 361-387-3814 anthonyschoolsaint@yahoo.ca www.stanthonysaints.org Norma Castaneda, Dean; Anna Gonzalez, Prin.; Stds.: 131; Lay Tchrs.: 10

ROCKPORT

Sacred Heart School - (PAR) (Grades PreK-5) 213 S. Church St., Rockport, TX 78382 t) 361-729-2672 shskbarnes@shsrockport.org www.shsrockport.org Katherine K. Barnes, Prin.; Randall E. Barnes, Librn.; Stds.: 116; Lay Tchrs.: 9

HIGH SCHOOLS

STATE OF TEXAS

CORPUS CHRISTI

Incarnate Word Academy High School - (PRV) (Grades 9-12) 2910 S. Alameda, Corpus Christi, TX 78404 t) 361-883-0857 retas@iwacc.org www.iwacc.org Jose Torres, Prin.; Sammie Grunwald, Pres.; LaQuita Hilzinger, Librn.; Ashley Cartwright, Campus Min.; Stds.: 175; Sr. Tchrs.: 1; Lay Tchrs.: 25

St. John Paul II High School - (DIO) 3036 Saratoga Blvd., Corpus Christi, TX 78415 t) 361-855-5744 frmartinez@jpiihighschool.org www.jpiihighschool.org Rev. Peter G. Martinez, Pres.; Stds.: 175; Pr. Tchrs.: 1; Sr. Tchrs.: 1; Lay Tchrs.: 13

INSTITUTIONS LOCATED IN DIOCESE

CONVENTS, MONASTERIES, AND RESIDENCES FOR WOMEN [CON]

CORPUS CHRISTI

Blessed Sacrament Chapel - 4105 Ocean Dr., Corpus Christi, TX 78411-1223 t) 361-852-6212 blessedsacramentconvent4105@gmail.com www.mountgraceconvent.org Sister-Servants of the Holy Spirit of Perpetual Adoration, "Pink Sisters" Sr. Mary Angelica, Supr.; Srs.: 6

Dominicas de Santo Tomas de Aquino (DSTA) - 12217 Hearn Rd., Corpus Christi, TX 78410 t) 361-242-8829 Sr. Maria P. Vega, Supr.; Srs.: 3

Incarnate Word Convent - 5201 Lipes Blvd., Corpus Christi, TX 78413 t) 361-882-5413 sawagner@iwbscc.org; smigonzalez@iwbscc.org www.iwbscc.org Convent Academy of the Incarnate Word, Sisters of the Incarnate Word and Blessed Sacrament Sr. Joann Saenz, IWBS, Contact; Sara Phillips, Treas.; Srs.: 29

Incarnate Word Ranch - Bluntzer - 5201 Lipes Blvd, Corpus Christi, TX 78413 t) 361-882-5413; 361-877-1232 smasnapka@gmail.com; smigonzalez@iwbscc.org Sr. Annette Wagner, I.W.B.S., Supr.; Srs.: 2

Missionaries of Christ's Charity - 6333 N. Washam, Corpus Christi, TX 78414 t) 361-815-4974 ttbheip@yahoo.com Sr. Mary Ann Hiep Truong, Supr.; Srs.: 6

Mount Tabor Convent - 12940 Leopard St., Corpus Christi, TX 78410 t) 361-241-1955 mounttabormjmj@gmail.com Central Regional House of the Missionary Sisters of Jesus, Mary, and Joseph. Sr. Milagros Tormo, M.J.M.J., Supr.; Srs.: 7

The Ark Assessment Center & Emergency Shelter for Youth - 12960 Leopard St., Corpus Christi, TX 78410 t) 361-241-6566

Pax Christi Institute - 4601 Calallen Dr., Corpus Christi, TX 78410 t) 361-241-2833 paxchristisisters@gmail.com www.paxchristisisterscc.org Mother Maria Elva Reyes, P.C.I., Supr.; Srs.: 10

Religious Missionaries of St. Dominic, Inc. - 2237 Waldron Rd., Corpus Christi, TX 78418 t) 361-937-5978 Sr. Rosario Reyes, Prioress; Srs.: 7

Sisters of Adoration of Blessed Sacrament - 454 Haroldson Dr., Corpus Christi, TX 78412 t) 361-288-7353 Sr. Elizabeth Pathiparambil, Supr.; Srs.: 17

Sisters of Adoration of the Blessed Sacrament - 5313 Grayford Pl., Corpus Christi, TX 78413 t) 361-884-7136 c) 361-558-1073 sabs2000@sbcglobal.net; elizabethsabs@gmail.com sabscongregation.org Sr. Elizabeth Pathiparambil, Supr.; Srs.: 4

Sisters of Adoration of the Blessed Sacrament, SABS - 222 Ocean View, Corpus Christi, TX 78411 t) 361-854-2820 srrosepaul@yahoo.co.uk Sr. Rose Paul Madassery, S.A.B.S., Contact; Srs.: 14

Sisters of the Incarnate Word - 3002 Austin St., Corpus Christi, TX 78404-2413 c) (361) 688-5360 sawagner@iwbscc.org iwbscc.org Incarnate Word Residence Sr. Annette Wagner, I.W.B.S., Contact; Srs.: 2

Sisters of the Society of Our Lady of the Most Holy Trinity - 1200 Lantana St., Corpus Christi, TX 78407 t) 361-654-0054 generalsisterservant@solt.net www.solt.net Sr. Megan Mary Thibodeau, S.O.L.T., Supr.; Srs.: 110

KINGSVILLE

Missionary Daughters of the Most Pure Virgin Mary - 919 N. Ninth St., Kingsville, TX 78363 t) 361-595-1087 aduba@hotmail.com Sr. Agueda Durazo, M.D.P.V.M., Supr.; Srs.: 6

ROCKPORT

Schoenstatt Sisters of Mary - 134 Front St., Rockport, TX 78382-7800 t) 361-729-2019 schoenstattlamartx@corpus.twcbc.com Secular Institute of the Schoenstatt Sisters of Mary Sr. M. Jacinta Brunner, Supr.; Srs.: 8

SARITA

Oblate La Parra Center - 500 La Parra Ranch Rd, Sarita, TX 78385; Mailing: PO Box 9, Sarita, TX 78385-0009 t) 361-294-5369 admin@lebhshomea.org www.lebhshomea.org Rev. James Chambers, O.M.I., Treas.; Srs.: 1

ENDOWMENTS / FOUNDATIONS / TRUSTS [EFT]

CORPUS CHRISTI

Incarnate Word Academy Foundation - 5201 Lipes Blvd., Corpus Christi, TX 78413 t) 361-882-5413 sawagner@iwbscc.org; dtamez@iwbscc.org www.iwacc.org Sr. Annette Wagner, I.W.B.S., Pres.;

HOSPITALS / HEALTH SERVICES [HOS]

ALICE

CHRISTUS Spohn Hospital Alice - 2500 E. Main St., Alice, TX 78404; Mailing: 5920 Saratoga Blvd., Ste. 540, Corpus Christi, TX 78414 t) (361) 985-5577 g.saenz@christushealth.org www.christusspohn.org Sisters of Charity of the Incarnate Word (San Antonio, TX). Dcn. Ernesto Gutierrez, Chap.; Dcn. Richard B. Morin, Pres.; Bed Capacity: 54; Asstd. Annu.: 43,769; Staff: 203

BEEVILLE

CHRISTUS Spohn Hospital Beeville - 1500 E. Houston Hwy., Beeville, TX 78102; Mailing: 5920 Saratoga Blvd., Ste. 540, Corpus Christi, TX 78414 t) (361) 985-5577 g.saenz@christushealth.org www.christusspohn.org Sisters of Charity of the Incarnate Word (San Antonio, TX). Rev. Jacob John Valayath, Chap.; Michael Perez, Pres.; Bed Capacity: 49; Asstd. Annu.: 35,434; Staff: 158

CHRISTUS Spohn Medical Clinic - 1602 E. Houston Hwy., Ste.A, Beeville, TX 78102; Mailing: 5920 Saratoga Blvd., Ste. 540, Corpus Christi, TX 78414 t) 361-358-6249 g.saenz@christushealth.org www.christusspohn.org Sisters of Charity of the Incarnate Word (San Antonio, TX). Irma Serna, Bus. Mgr.; Asstd. Annu.: 1,801; Staff: 3

CORPUS CHRISTI

CHRISTUS Spohn Family Health Center - Padre Island - 14202 S. Padre Island Dr., Corpus Christi, TX 78418; Mailing: 5920 Saratoga Blvd., Ste. 540, Corpus Christi, TX 78414 t) (361) 985-5577 humberto.ramos@christushealth.org; g.saenz@christushealth.org Sisters of Charity of the Incarnate Word (San Antonio, TX).

CHRISTUS Spohn Family Health Center - Westside - 4617 Greenwood Dr., Corpus Christi, TX 78416; Mailing: 5920 Saratoga Blvd., Ste. 540, Corpus Christi, TX 78414 t) 361-857-2872 Sisters of Charity of the Incarnate Word (San Antonio, TX). Sylvia Salazar, Bus. Mgr.; Asstd. Annu.: 8,408; Staff: 9

CHRISTUS Spohn Health System Corporation - 5920 Saratoga Blvd., Ste. 540, Corpus Christi, TX 78414 t) (361) 985-5577 g.saenz@christushealth.org Sisters of Charity of the Incarnate Word (San Antonio, TX). Dominic Dominguez, CEO; Stephen Kazanjian, Vice Pres., Mission Integration; Bed Capacity: 710; Asstd. Annu.: 368,265; Staff: 2,954

CHRISTUS Spohn Hospital Corpus Christi - Memorial - 2606 Hospital Blvd., Corpus Christi, TX 78405; Mailing: 5920 Saratoga Blvd., Ste. 540, Corpus Christi, TX 78414 t) (361) 985-5577 g.saenz@christushealth.org Sisters of Charity of the Incarnate Word (San Antonio, TX). Dominic Dominguez, Exec.; Asstd. Annu.: 35,704; Staff: 94

CHRISTUS Spohn Hospital Corpus Christi - Shoreline - 600 Elizabeth St., Corpus Christi, TX 78404; Mailing: 5920 Saratoga Blvd., Ste. 540, Corpus Christi, TX 78414 t) (361) 985-5577 g.saenz@christushealth.org; craig.desmond@christushealth.org Sisters of Charity of the Incarnate Word (San Antonio, TX). Craig Desmond, Pres.; Rev. E. Julian Cabrera, Chap.; Rev. Silas Onuoha, Chap.; Rev. Mathias Arularasu, Chap.; Sr. Mary (Mary Immaculate of the Eucharist) Rinaldi, Chap.; Martha Garza, Chap.; Nancy Cook, Chap.; Bed Capacity: 406; Asstd. Annu.: 138,480; Staff: 1,693

CHRISTUS Spohn Hospital Corpus Christi - South - 5950 Saratoga Blvd., Corpus Christi, TX 78414; Mailing: 5920 Saratoga Blvd., Ste. 540, Corpus Christi, TX 78414 t) (361) 985-5577 g.saenz@christushealth.org; lanell.scott@christushealth.org Sisters of Charity of the Incarnate Word (San Antonio, TX). Rev. Thomas Kizito Nwachukwu, Chap.; Sr. Pauline Obasi, Chap.; LaNell Scott, Pres.; Bed Capacity: 151; Asstd. Annu.: 70,335; Staff: 611

CHRISTUS Spohn Medical Group Family Medicine Academic Center - Central - 2601 Hospital Blvd., Ste. 117 & 112, Corpus Christi, TX 78405 t) 361-902-4789 Sisters of Charity of the Incarnate Word (San Antonio, TX). Dr. Yvonne Hinojosa, Dir.;

CHRISTUS Spohn Memorial - Specialty Clinic - 2606 Hospital Blvd., Corpus Christi, TX 78405; Mailing: 5920 Saratoga Blvd., Ste. 540, Corpus Christi, TX 78414 t) 361-902-4765 humberto.ramos@christushealth.org; g.saenz@christushealth.org Sisters of Charity of the Incarnate Word (San Antonio, TX). Dominic Dominguez, CEO; Asstd. Annu.: 3,993; Staff: 5

Dr. Hector P. Garcia Memorial Family Health Center-Memorial Quick Care - 2606 Hospital Blvd., Corpus Christi, TX 78405; Mailing: 5920 Saratoga Blvd, Suite 540, Corpus Christi, TX 78414 t) (361) 902-6102 g.saenz@christushealth.org Sisters of Charity of the Incarnate Word (San Antonio, TX). Mary Spicak, Bus. Mgr.; Humberto Ramos, Dir.; Asstd. Annu.: 11,947; Staff: 15

FREER

CHRISTUS Spohn - Freer Clinic - 111 E. Riley St., Freer, TX 78357; Mailing: 5920 Saratoga Blvd., Ste. 540, Corpus Christi, TX 78414 t) 361-394-7311 g.saenz@christushealth.org www.christusspohn.org Sisters of Charity of the Incarnate Word (San Antonio, TX). Margot Rios, Dir.; Asstd. Annu.: 2,866; Staff: 4

KINGSVILLE

CHRISTUS Spohn Hospital Kleberg - 1311 General Cavazos Blvd., Kingsville, TX 78363; Mailing: 5920 Saratoga Blvd., Ste. 540, Corpus Christi, TX 78414 t) (361) 985-5577 g.saenz@christushealth.org www.christusspohn.org Sponsorship: Sisters of Charity of the Incarnate Word (San Antonio, TX). Dcn. Ernesto Gutierrez, Chap.; Dcn. Richard B. Morin, Pres.; Bed Capacity: 50; Asstd. Annu.: 44,543; Staff: 195

ROBSTOWN

CHRISTUS Spohn Family Health Center - Robstown - 1038 Texas Yes Blvd., Robstown, TX 78380; Mailing: 5920 Saratoga Blvd., Ste. 540, Corpus Christi, TX 78414 t) (361) 861-9001 Sisters of Charity of the Incarnate Word (San Antonio, TX). Carla Cavazos, Bus. Mgr.; Asstd. Annu.: 4,075; Staff: 5

MISCELLANEOUS [MIS]

CORPUS CHRISTI

The Cathedral Concert Series - 505 N. Upper Broadway,

Corpus Christi, TX 78401; Mailing: P.O. Box 2620, Corpus Christi, TX 78403 t) 361-882-6191 www.ccseries.org Rev. Pedro T. Elizardo Jr., Rector;
Journey to Damascus, Inc. - 555 N. Carancahua, Ste. 750, Corpus Christi, TX 78401 t) (361) 882-6191 x692 www.journeytodamascus.org Rev. Joseph Lopez;
***La Fazenda de Esperanza** - 555 N. Carancahua, Ste. 750, Corpus Christi, TX 78401
Mother Teresa Shelter, Inc. - 513 Sam Rankin, Corpus Christi, TX 78401 t) 361-883-7372 mteresashelter@diocesecc.org motherteresashelter.org A day shelter used as a homeless gathering facility; providing bath, laundry, limited eating facilities and counseling services. Dr. Michele Johnston, Exec. Dir.;
Natural Family Planning Outreach - ; Mailing: P.O. Box 2620, Corpus Christi, TX 78403 t) 361-882-6191 sjones@diocesecc.org Dcn. Santos R. Jones III;
Secular Institute of the Schoenstatt Fathers - 4343 Gaines St., Corpus Christi, TX 78412-2541 t) 361-992-9841 frgerold@hotmail.com

KINGSVILLE

St. Thomas Aquinas Newman Center and Chapel (Texas A&M University Kingsville) - 1457 Retama, Kingsville, TX 78363; Mailing: 1120 S. 8th St., Kingsville, TX 78363 t) 361-221-1103 kingsvillenewman@gmail.com newmankingsville.com Rev. Eric G. Chapa; Rev. Alfredo Villarreal;

LAMAR

Stella Maris Chapel - 222 Hagey Dr., Lamar, TX 78382; Mailing: P.O. Box 1980, Fulton, TX 78358 t) 361-790-5277 Very Rev. Raynaldo Yrlas Jr.;

MONASTERIES AND RESIDENCES FOR PRIESTS AND BROTHERS [MON]

BENAVIDES

Catholic Solitudes - 11053 Hwy. 16 N., Benavides, TX 78341; Mailing: P.O. Box 748, Hebbronville, TX 78361 t) 361-527-4636 catholic.solitudes@gmail.com Rev. Patrick Meaney; Priests: 1

CORPUS CHRISTI

Society of Our Lady of the Most Holy Trinity - 1200 Lantana St., Corpus Christi, TX 78407 t) 361-654-0054 generalpriestservant@solt.net; generalprocurator@solt.net www.solt.net Rev. Peter Marsalek, S.O.L.T., Supr.; Rev. Jerry Drolshagen, S.O.L.T., Prov.; Rev. John Gaffney, S.O.L.T., Treas.; Rev. Brady Williams, S.O.L.T., Secy.; Rev. William K. Bakyil, S.O.L.T. (Ghana), Pst.; Rev. Rogel Rosalinas, S.O.L.T., Pst.; Rev. Gerard J. Sheehan, S.O.L.T., Pst.; Rev. Mark Wheelan, S.O.L.T., Pst.; Rev. Michael Edward Crump, S.O.L.T., Assoc. Pst.; Rev. John M. Patterson II, S.O.L.T., Assoc. Pst.; Rev. Juan Villagomez, SOLT, Assoc. Pst.; Rev. Samuel Medley, S.O.L.T., Dir.; Rev. Zachary of the Mother of God Shallow, SOLT, Vocations; Rev. James R. Kelleher, S.O.L.T.; Rev. Scott Braathen, SOLT; Rev. Paul Ming Dou, SOLT, In Res.; Rev. Robert Shaldone, In Res.; Rev. Dominic Zimmermann, S.O.L.T., In Res.; Bro. Martin McGough; Bro. Peter McArdle, SOLT; Bro. Nicholas Anderson Coombs, Youth Min.; Bro. John DeMay, SOLT, In Res.; Dcn. Bernard Vessa; Brs.: 3; Priests: 20

NURSING / REHABILITATION / CONVALESCENCE / ELDERLY CARE [NUR]

CORPUS CHRISTI

Villa Maria, Inc. - 3146 Saratoga Blvd., Corpus Christi, TX 78415 t) 361-857-6171 villamaria@corpus.twcbc.com Apartment complex for senior adults. Patricia Cantu, Exec.; Staff: 4

PRESCHOOLS / CHILDCARE CENTERS [PRE]

CORPUS CHRISTI

Our Lady of the Rosary Learning Center - 2237 Waldron Rd., Corpus Christi, TX 78418 t) 361-939-9847 olrcs.org Sr. Fe Laguitao Gamotin, O.P., Dir.; Stds.: 25

ROBSTOWN

St. Joseph's Dream - 3660 Jack Dr., Robstown, TX 78380 t) 361-387-9598 paxsolt@aol.com

RETREAT HOUSES / RENEWAL CENTERS [RTR]

CORPUS CHRISTI

Our Lady of Corpus Christi Retreat Center - 1200 Lantana St., Bldg. C, Corpus Christi, TX 78407 t) 361-289-9095 x321 info@ourladyofcc.org Rev. Samuel Medley, S.O.L.T.;
Pax Christi Liturgical Retreat Center - 4601 Calallen Dr., Corpus Christi, TX 78410-4940 t) 361-241-5479 director@paxchristisisterscc.org www.paxchristisisterscc.org

ROBSTOWN

Fannie Bluntzer Nason Renewal Center, Inc. - 5528 FM 3088, Robstown, TX 78380; Mailing: 5201 Lipes Blvd., Corpus Christi, TX 78413 t) 361-888-7537 (Bus. Office); 361-816-6567 (Event Booking) sawagner@iwbscc.org; aclark@bluntzerspiritcenter.org www.bluntzerspiritcenter.org/ Amy Clark, Assoc. Dir.; Ricardo Guzman, Treas.;

SARITA

Oblate La Parra Center - 500 La Parra Ranch Rd., Sarita, TX 78385; Mailing: PO Box 9, Sarita, TX 78385-0009 t) 361-294-5369 oblatelaparra@omiusa.org www.lebhshomea.org Rev. Roger Bergkamp, O.M.I., In Res.; Rev. James Chambers, O.M.I., In Res.; Rev. Robert Leising, O.M.I., In Res.; Very Rev. Andrew Sensenig, OMI, In Res.; Rev. James Taggart, O.M.I., In Res.; Rev. David Ullrich, O.M.I., In Res.;

An asterisk (*) denotes an organization that has established tax-exempt status directly with the IRS and is not covered by the USCCB Group Ruling.

Diocese of Covington

(Dioecesis Covingtonensis)

MOST REVEREND JOHN C. IFFERT

Bishop of Covington; ordained June 7, 1997; appointed Bishop of Covington July 13, 2021; consecrated and installed September 30, 2021. Mailing Address: 1125 Madison Ave., Covington, KY 41011-3115. T: 859-392-1512; F: 859-392-1508.

1125 Madison Ave., KY 41011-3115. T: 859-392-1500; F: 859-392-1589.
www.covdio.org
porecchio@covdio.org

ESTABLISHED JULY 29, 1853.

Square Miles 3,359.

Comprises 14 Counties of the Commonwealth of Kentucky in the north and east of the Commonwealth, including Bracken, Boone, Campbell, Carroll, Fleming, Gallatin, Grant, Harrison, Kenton, Lewis, Mason, Owen, Pendleton and Robertson Counties.

For legal titles of parishes and diocesan institutions, consult the Chancery Office.

STATISTICAL OVERVIEW

Personnel

Bishop	1
Retired Bishops	1
Priests: Diocesan Active in Diocese	51
Priests: Diocesan Active Outside Diocese	3
Priests: Retired, Sick or Absent	28
Number of Diocesan Priests	82
Religious Priests in Diocese	7
Total Priests in your Diocese	89
Extern Priests in Diocese	7
Ordinations:	
Diocesan Priests	1
Transitional Deacons	1
Permanent Deacons	4
Permanent Deacons in Diocese	43
Total Brothers	2
Total Sisters	187

Parishes

Parishes	48
With Resident Pastor:	
Resident Diocesan Priests	43
Resident Religious Priests	2
Without Resident Pastor:	
Administered by Priests	2
Administered by Religious Women	1
Missions	5
Pastoral Centers	1
Professional Ministry Personnel:	
Brothers	5
Sisters	10
Lay Ministers	39

Welfare

Catholic Hospitals	5
Total Assisted	1,132,116
Health Care Centers	1
Total Assisted	3,304
Homes for the Aged	3
Total Assisted	1,192
Residential Care of Children	1
Total Assisted	800
Day Care Centers	1
Total Assisted	34
Special Centers for Social Services	9
Total Assisted	149,527
Other Institutions	1
Total Assisted	2,154

Educational

Diocesan Students in Other Seminaries	6
Total Seminarians	6
Colleges and Universities	1
Total Students	2,269
High Schools, Diocesan and Parish	7
Total Students	2,034
High Schools, Private	2
Total Students	749
Elementary Schools, Diocesan and Parish	29
Total Students	6,049
Elementary Schools, Private	2
Total Students	275
Catechesis/Religious Education:	
High School Students	126
Elementary Students	1,828
Total Students under Catholic Instruction	13,336
Teachers in Diocese:	
Priests	5
Sisters	5
Lay Teachers	854

Vital Statistics

Receptions into the Church:	
Infant Baptism Totals	631
Minor Baptism Totals	314
Adult Baptism Totals	118
Received into Full Communion	46
First Communions	1,062
Confirmations	1,203
Marriages:	
Catholic	194
Interfaith	75
Total Marriages	269
Deaths	776
Total Catholic Population	90,886
Total Population	543,038

LEADERSHIP

Office of the Bishop - t) 859-392-1500 x1512 porecchio@covdio.org Most Rev. John Curtis Iffert; Rev. Jordan M. Hainsey; Pam Orecchio, Secy.;

Office of the Vicar General - rbarnes@covdio.org Very Rev. Mark A. Keene, Vicar;

Deans - Very Rev. Ryan L. Maher, Covington; Rev. Msgr. Gerald L. Reinersman, Campbell County; Very Rev. Baiju Kidaagen, V.C., Dean;

ADMINISTRATION

Chief Operating Officer - porecchio@covdio.org Dcn. James A. Fortner, COO;

Office of the Chancellor - jschroeder@covdio.org Jamie N. Schroeder, Chancellor; Rev. Jordan M. Hainsey;

Finance Office - dhenson@covdio.org Dale Henson, CFO;

OFFICES AND DIRECTORS

Archives - storres@covdio.org Sarah Torres, Archivist;

Buildings and Property - klinkugel@covdio.org Don Knochelmann, Dir.;

Cemeteries - Brian Harvey, Dir.;

Catechesis and Evangelization - ltaylor@covdio.org David Cooley, Dir.; Isaak A. Isaak, Dir.;

Family Ministry -

Religious Education -

Youth and Young Adult Ministry -

Catholic Charities - t) 859-581-8974 Alan B. Pickett, Dir.;

Catholic Schools - asmorey@covdio.org Kendra McGuire, Supt.;

Alliance for Catholic Urban Education (A.C.U.E.) - bruehlmann@covdio.org Beth Ruehlmann;

Communication - lkeener@covdio.org Laura Keener, Dir.;

Ecumenism - Rev. Msgr. William F. Cleves, Dir.;

Hispanic Ministry -

Newspaper "Messenger" - lkeener@covdio.org Laura Keener, Editor;

Office of Priestly Vocations - sbarnes@covdio.org Rev. A. Conor Kunath, Dir.;

Permanent Deacon Formation - sbarnes@covdio.org Rev. Msgr. William B. Neuhaus, Dir.;

Pro Life - froch@covdio.org Faye Roch, Dir.;

Safe Environment - jfeinauer@covdio.org Julie Feinauer, Dir.;

Victim Assistance Coordinator - t) 859-392-1515 Julie Feinauer;

Stewardship and Mission Services - mmurray@covdio.org Michael Murray, Dir.;

Worship - sbarnes@covdio.org Very Rev. Daniel L. Schomaker, Dir.;

ADVISORY BOARDS, COMMISSIONS, COMMITTEES, AND COUNCILS

Diocesan Consultors - Very Rev. Ryan L. Stenger; Rev. Msgr. Roger P. Cooney; Rev. Matthew A. Cushing;

Continuing Education of Priests - Rev. Msgr. Gerald L. Reinersman, Contact;

Deanery Pastoral Council - Very Rev. Mark A. Keene, Contact;

Diocesan Board of Education - Kendra McGuire, Contact;

Disabilities Committee - Stephen Koplyay, Chair;

Due Process Board of Administrative Review - Stephen Koplyay, Contact;

Presbyteral Council - Very Rev. Mark A. Keene, Contact;

Priests' Retirement Fund Committee - Very Rev. Mark A. Keene, Chair;

CLERGY AND RELIGIOUS SERVICES

Liaison for Retired Priests - Rev. Msgr. Daniel J. Vogelpohl;

Ministry Development Program for Deacons - Rev. Msgr. William B. Neuhaus;

Priest Personnel - Very Rev. Mark A. Keene, Contact;

Vicar for Religious - Sr. Marla Monahan, S.N.D.;

PASTORAL SERVICES

Campus Ministry -

Northern Kentucky University Newman Club - deaconb@nku.edu Rev. Lawrence A. Schaeper, Chap.; Dcn. Brian R. Cox, Campus Min.;

Thomas More University Campus Ministry - t) 859-344-3683 andrew.cole@thomasmore.edu Rev. Msgr. Gerald E. Twaddell, Chap.; Andrew Cole, Campus Min.;

Catholic Scouting - dcooley@covdio.org David Cooley, Contact;

Deaf Ministry - t) 859-291-2288

SPIRITUAL LIFE

Charismatic Renewal (Mustard Seed Community) - t) 859-341-5932 Carol Hodge, Contact;

Covington Youth Retreat Committee - dcooley@covdio.org David Cooley, Contact;

Cursillo Movement - Vince Lonnemann, Dir.;

Legion of Mary -

Serra Club for Vocations of Diocese of Covington - Michael Murray, Pres.; Rev. A. Conor Kunath, Chap.;

TRIBUNAL

Diocesan Tribunal - mstallmeyer@covdio.org Very Rev. Ryan L. Stenger, Vicar; Sr. Margaret Stallmeyer, C.D.P., Dir.; Karen A. Guidugli, Case Promoter & Notary;

Defenders of the Bond - Rev. Gregory E. Osburg; Rev. Msgr. John R. Schulte; Rev. Msgr. Gerald E. Twaddell;

Judges - Sr. Margaret Stallmeyer, C.D.P.; Rev. Michael D. Barth; Rev. Barry M. Windholtz;

Promoter of Justice - Rev. Msgr. William B. Neuhaus;

PARISHES, MISSIONS, AND CLERGY

COMMONWEALTH OF KENTUCKY

ALEXANDRIA

St. Mary of the Assumption - 8246 E. Main St., Alexandria, KY 41001 t) 859-635-4188 stmaryalex@fuse.net; joseph.gallenstein@saintmaryparish.com saintmaryparish.com Rev. Joseph A. Gallenstein, Pst.; Rev. Edward J. Brodnick, Par. Vicar; Dcn. Timothy A. Britt; Jennifer Ledonne, DRE; CRP Stds.: 101

St. Mary of the Assumption School - (Grades PreSchool-8) 9 S. Jefferson St., Alexandria, KY 41001-1394 t) 859-635-9539 jennifer.geiman@saintmaryparish.com Jennifer Geiman, Prin.; Stds.: 562; Lay Tchrs.: 28

AUGUSTA

St. Augustine - 215 E. Fourth St., Augusta, KY 41002-1117; Mailing: 203 E. 4th St., Augusta, KY 41002 t) 606-756-3229 jshelton@covdio.org www.saintaugustine-augusta.org Rev. Joey Shelton, Pst.; Dcn. Frank Estill; CRP Stds.: 21

BELLEVUE

Divine Mercy - 318 Division St., Bellevue, KY 41073-1104 t) 859-261-6172 divinemercyoffice@gmail.com dmsbcatholic.com Rev. Martin John Pitstick, Pst.; CRP Stds.: 6

BROOKSVILLE

St. James - 122 Garrett Ave., Brooksville, KY 41004-0027 t) 606-735-2271 c) 606-217-1947 jshelton@covdio.org; sally.kalb@outlook.com Rev. Joey Shelton, Pst.; Sally Kalb, DRE; CRP Stds.: 32

BURLINGTON

Immaculate Heart of Mary - 5876 Veterans Way, Burlington, KY 41005-8824 t) 859-689-5010; 859-689-4303; 859-689-5010 x225 (DRE) rickpegwells@yahoo.com; srarmella@ihm-ky.org ihm-ky.org Rev. Msgr. Dominic K. Fosu, Pst.; Dcn. Gregory L. Meier, Pst. Assoc.; Dcn. Richard S. Malsi; Sr. Armella Pietrowski, C.D.P., DRE; John Doubrava, Bus. Mgr.; CRP Stds.: 170

Immaculate Heart of Mary School - (Grades PreK-8) kthorburn@ihmkyschool.org www.ihmkyschool.org Theresa Guard, Prin.; Kristin Harper, Vice Prin.; Stds.: 363; Lay Tchrs.: 27

CALIFORNIA

Sts. Peter and Paul - 2162 California Crossroads, California, KY 41007-9713 t) 859-635-2924; (859) 215-0004; 859-635-4382 (CRP) lstenkencdp@yahoo.com; parishoffice@stspp.com www.parish.stspp.com Rev. Jacob Varghese, V.C., Pst.; Sr. Lynn Stenken, C.D.P., DRE; CRP Stds.: 16

Sts. Peter and Paul School - (Grades PreK-8) 2160 California Crossroads, California, KY 41007 t) (859) 635-4382 office@stspp.com www.stspp.com Michelle Humphreys, Prin.; Stds.: 93; Lay Tchrs.: 9

Immaculate Conception - 174 Stepstone Church Rd., Butler, KY 41006; Mailing: 2162 California Crossroads, Sts. Peter & Paul Church, California, KY 41007 t) (859) 635-2924 (no phone on site.) frjacobv@gmail.com

CAMP SPRINGS

St. Joseph - 6833 Four Mile Rd., Camp Springs, KY 41059-9746 t) 859-635-2491 parishoffice@stjosephcampsprings.org www.stjosephcampsprings.org Very Rev. Ryan L. Stenger, Pst.;

St. Joseph School - (Grades PreK- t) (859) 635-2491 Stds.: 60; Lay Tchrs.: 3

CARROLLTON

St. John the Evangelist - 503 Fifth St., Carrollton, KY 41008-1203 t) 502-732-5776 dwrightsr@hotmail.com www.stjohncarrollton.org Rev. Thomas F. Picchioni, Pst.; Dcn. Michael J. Keller; Don Wright, Bus. Mgr.; CRP Stds.: 129

Transfiguration - 260 Inverness Rd., Perry Park, KY 40363 t) (502) 732-5776

COLD SPRING

St. Joseph - 4011 Alexandria Pk., Cold Spring, KY 41076-1895 t) 859-441-1604 stjosephcoldspring.com Rev. Msgr. Gerald L. Reinersman, Pst.; Rev. Matthias M. Wamala, Par. Vicar; Dcn. Stephen J. Bennett III; CRP Stds.: 57

St. Joseph School - (Grades PreK-8) t) 859-441-2025 eurlage@stjoeschool.net www.stjosephcoldspring.com Emily T Urlage, Prin.; Stds.: 446; Lay Tchrs.: 24

COVINGTON

Cathedral, Basilica of the Assumption (St. Mary's Cathedral) - 1130 Madison Ave., Covington, KY 41011-3116; Mailing: 1101 Madison Ave., Covington, KY 41011-3116 t) 859-431-2060 tbrundage@covcathedral.com www.covcathedral.com Very Rev. Ryan L. Maher, Rector; Sr. Barbara Woeste, O.S.B., DRE; Dcn. Gerald R. Franzen;

St. Augustine - 1839 Euclid Ave., Covington, KY 41014-1162; Mailing: 413 W. 19th St., Covington, KY 41014 t) 859-431-3943 dschomaker@covdio.org www.staugustines.net Very Rev. Daniel L. Schomaker, Pst.;

St. Augustine School - (Grades K-8) 1840 Jefferson Ave., Covington, KY 41014-1165 t) 859-261-5564 knienaber@staugustines.net Kathleen Nienaber, Prin.; Stds.: 103; Lay Tchrs.: 9

St. Augustine Outreach Center - 2523 Todd Ct., Covington, KY 41011 t) 859-491-4584 Dcn. John D. Leardon;

St. Benedict - 338 E. 17th St., Covington, KY 41014-1315 t) 859-431-5607 stbenedict@zoomtown.com stbenedictcovington.com Rev. Gregory J. Bach, Pst.; Dcn. Phillip J. Racine;

Church of Our Savior - 246 E. 10th St., Covington, KY 41011-3026 t) 859-491-5872 jbucher@fuse.net Sr. Janet Marie Bucher, C.D.P., Parish Life Collaborator;

Holy Cross - 3612 Church St., Covington, KY

41015-1431 t) 859-431-0636 secretary@holycrosscov.org holycrosscov.org Rev. Michael C. Hennigen, Pst.; Rev. A.J. Gedney, Par. Vicar; Rev. Thomas C. Barnes, Pastor Emer.; Dcn. Eric Ritchie; David Arnold, Pst. Assoc.; Sr. Helen Charles Wilke, C.D.P., Pst. Assoc.; Jackie Dabbelt, Bus. Mgr.; Tony Wagner, Music Min.; CRP Stds.: 160

Holy Cross School - (Grades K-8) 3615 Church St., Covington, KY 41015 t) 859-581-6599 main@holycrosselem.com www.holycrosselem.com Lisa Timmerding, Prin.; Stds.: 160; Lay Tchrs.: 11

St. John - 627 Pike St., Covington, KY 41011-2148 t) 859-431-5314 lindagob88@gmail.com lindagob88@gmail.com Rev. G. Michael Greer, Pst.; Dcn. Steven I. Durkee; Linda O'Bryan, Bus. Mgr.;

St. Ann - 1274 Parkway, Covington, KY 41011-1060 t) 859-261-9548 fr.mick@gmail.com

Mother of God - 119 W. 6th St., Covington, KY 41011-1409 t) 859-291-2288 www.mother-of-god.org Rev. Michael E. Comer, Pst.;

CRESCENT SPRINGS

St. Joseph - 2470 Lorraine Ct., Crescent Springs, KY 41017-1406 t) 859-341-6609 apappas@stjosephcsky.org; salcini@stjosephcsky.org www.stjosephcrescent.com Rev. Eric M. Boelscher, Pst.; Dcn. Hudson L. Henry; Tina Klare, DRE; Andrea Pappas, Bus. Mgr.; CRP Stds.: 59

St. Joseph School - (Grades PreK-8) 2474 Lorraine Ct., Crescent Springs, KY 41017 t) 859-578-2742 szeck@sjscrescent.org; aborchers@sjscrescent.org www.sjscrescent.com Sally Zeck, Prin.; Stds.: 399; Lay Tchrs.: 21

CYNTHIANA

St. Edward - 107 N. Walnut St., Cynthiana, KY 41031-1225 t) 859-234-5444 churchoffice@stedwardky.org; nkannai@stedwardky.org stedwardky.org Rev. Niby Kannai, Pst.; CRP Stds.: 18

St. Edward School - (Grades PreSchool-5) t) 859-234-2731 schooloffice@stedwardky.org; ssowder@stedwardky.org Stds.: 37; Lay Tchrs.: 6

DAYTON

St. Bernard - 401 Berry St., Dayton, KY 41074-1139 t) 859-261-8506 saintbernardoffice@gmail.com dmsbcatholic.com/ Rev. Martin John Pitstick, Pst.;

EDGEWOOD

St. Pius X - 348 Dudley Rd., Edgewood, KY 41017-2609 t) 859-341-4900 jcasson@staff.stpiusx.com; jtallarigo@staff.stpiusx.com parish.stpiusx.com Very Rev. Baiju Kidaagen, V.C., Pst.; Rev. Joseph Rielage, Par. Vicar; Dcn. James S. Fedor; Jennifer Casson, Bus. Mgr.; Joanna Tallarigo, DRE; CRP Stds.: 39

St. Pius X School - (Grades K-8) jlonnemann@teachers.stpiusx.com school.stpiusx.com/ Jill Lonnemann, Prin.; Stds.: 724; Lay Tchrs.: 39

ELSMERE

St. Henry - 3813 Dixie Hwy., Elsmere, KY 41018-1809 t) 859-727-2035 x301; 859-727-2035 x313 (CRP) mbraun@sthenrynky.com sthenrychurch.net Rev. Joshua L. Lange, Pst.; Rev. Aby Thampi, C.M.I., Par. Vicar; Dcn. Michael T. Lyman; Jacqueline Boemker, CRE; Simeon Skilling, Music Min.; CRP Stds.: 35

St. Henry School - (Grades PreK-8) 3825 Dixie Hwy., Elsmere, KY 41018-1809 t) 859-342-2551 clageman@sthenrynky.com www.sthenryschool.net Dennis Wolff, Prin.; Stds.: 351; Lay Tchrs.: 20

ERLANGER

St. Barbara - 4042 Turkeyfoot Rd., Erlanger, KY 41018-2921 t) 859-371-3100 jkoop@stbarbaraky.org; stb@stbarbaraky.org www.stbarbaraky.org/ Rev. John J. Sterling, Pst.; Dcn. Bernard J. Kaiser; Dcn. Charles J. Melville; Jackie Koop, CRE; CRP Stds.: 124

Mary, Queen of Heaven - 1150 Donaldson Rd., Erlanger, KY 41018-1048 t) 859-525-6909 kkahmann@mqhparish.com; lkleisinger@mqhparish.com Rev. Kevin James Kahmann, Pst.; Rev. James P. Schaeper, In Res.; Dcn. Lawrence L. Kleisinger, DRE; Dcn. Richard J. Dames, Sacr. Min.; CRP Stds.: 24

Mary, Queen of Heaven School - (Grades K-8) 1130 Donaldson Rd., Erlanger, KY 41018 t) 859-371-8100 Meg Piatt, Prin.; Stds.: 176; Lay Tchrs.: 14

FALMOUTH

St. Francis Xavier - 202 W. Second St., Falmouth, KY 41040-1118 t) 859-654-8241 stxoffice@gmail.com; stxpastor@gmail.com www.stxfalmouth.com Rev. Britton Hennessey, Pst.; CRP Stds.: 21

FLEMINGSBURG

St. Charles Borromeo - 211 Mt. Carmel Ave., Flemingsburg, KY 41041-1315 t) 606-849-9415 c) 859-630-0158 stcharlesandstrose@gmail.com; pdevous@covdio.org Rev. Phillip W. DeVous, Pst.; CRP Stds.: 13

FLORENCE

Cristo Rey - 25 Cavalier Blvd., Florence, KY 41042-1684 t) 859-538-1175; 859-538-1176 cristorey195@gmail.com www.micristorey.com Rev. Allan R. Frederick, Pst.; Dcn. Antonio L. Escamilla; CRP Stds.: 149

St. Paul - 7301 Dixie Hwy., Florence, KY 41042-2126; Mailing: P.O. Box 366, Florence, KY 41022-0366 t) 859-371-8051; 859-371-8051 x222 (CRP) stpaul@stpaulnky.org; jwahba@stpaulnky.org www.stpaulnky.org Rev. Jason M. Bertke, Pst.; Rev. Eric L. Andriot, Par. Vicar; Dcn. Scott A. Folz; Dcn. Thomas E. Kathman; Dcn. Nicholas J. Schwartz; CRP Stds.: 41

St. Paul School - (Grades PreK-8) 7303 Dixie Hwy, Florence, KY 41042 t) 859-647-4070 stpaul1@stpaulnky.org stpaulnky.org/school/ Joanne Nesmith, Prin.; Stds.: 278; Lay Tchrs.: 19

FORT MITCHELL

Blessed Sacrament - 2409 Dixie Hwy., Fort Mitchell, KY 41017-2993 t) 859-331-4302 x10; 859-331-4302 x22 (CRP) rthomas@bscky.org; parish@bscky.org bscky.org Rev. Damian J. Hils, Pst.; Rev. Augustine Kingsford Aidoo, Par. Vicar; Dcn. James J. Bayne; Dcn. James A. Fortner; Rosanne Thomas, DRE; CRP Stds.: 121

Blessed Sacrament School - (Grades K-8) 2407 Dixie Hwy., Fort Mitchell, KY 41017 t) 859-331-3062 bssoffice@bssky.org www.bssky.org Stds.: 461; Lay Tchrs.: 38

FORT THOMAS

St. Catherine of Siena - 1803 N. Ft. Thomas Ave., Fort Thomas, KY 41075-1170 t) 859-441-1352; 859-441-1352 x21 (CRP) church@stcatherineofsiena.org; jdkimes@stcatherineofsiena.org www.stcatherineofsiena.org Rev. Stephen M. Bankemper, Pst.; Dcn. Brian R. Cox; Dcn. Barry J. Henry; John David Kimes, CRE; CRP Stds.: 96

St. Catherine of Siena School - (Grades K-8) 23 Rossford Ave., Fort Thomas, KY 41075-1170 t) 859-572-2680 klorenz@stcatherineofsiena.org Michael Jacks, Prin.; Stds.: 122; Lay Tchrs.: 10

St. Thomas - 26 E. Villa Pl., Fort Thomas, KY 41075-2223 t) 859-441-1282 rkelsch@stthomasnky.org www.stthomasnky.org Rev. V. Ross Kelsch, Pst.; Rev. Raymond N. Enzweiler, In Res.; Dcn. Charles J. Hardebeck; George Garrett Everett, DRE; CRP Stds.: 120

St. Thomas School - (Grades PreK-8) 428 S. Fort Thomas Ave., Fort Thomas, KY 41075 t) 859-572-4641 khuser@sttschool.org saintthomasschool.org Kimberly Marie Huser, Prin.; Stds.: 210; Lay Tchrs.: 20

FORT WRIGHT

St. Agnes - 1680 Dixie Hwy., Fort Wright, KY 41011-2779 t) 859-431-1802; 859-431-1803 (CRP) parishoffice@saintagnes.com www.saintagnes.com Very Rev. Mark A. Keene, Pst.; Rev. Trinity Knight, Assoc. Pst.; Dcn. Robert A. Stoeckle; Dcn. Gary R. Scott; Dcn. Adam D. Feinauer; Anita Dunn, DRE; CRP Stds.: 39

St. Agnes School - (Grades K-8) 1322 Sleepy Hollow Rd., c/o St. Agnes Parish, Fort Wright, KY 41011-2779 t) 859-261-0543 saintagnes@saintagnes.com Erin Redleski, Prin.; Stds.: 387; Lay Tchrs.: 30

INDEPENDENCE

St. Cecilia - 5313 Madison Pike, Independence, KY 41051-8611 t) 859-363-4311 www.saintceciliaky.org Rev. Harry A. Settle Jr., Pst.; CRP Stds.: 49

St. Cecilia School - (Grades PreK-8) t) 859-363-4314 jkathman@stcindependence.org; rjent@stcindependence.org www.stceciliaky.org Jeanetta Kathman, Prin.; Stds.: 421; Lay Tchrs.: 24

LUDLOW

Sts. Boniface and James - 304 Oak St., Ludlow, KY 41016-1417 t) 859-261-5340 stbonjames@fuse.net www.bonifaceandjames.org Rev. Lawrence A. Schaeper, Pst.; CRP Stds.: 9

MAY'S LICK

St. Rose of Lima - 5011 Raymond Rd., May's Lick, KY 41055; Mailing: 211 Mt. Carmel Ave., Flemingsburg, KY 41041 t) 606-849-9415 c) 859-630-0158 pdevous@covdio.org Rev. Phillip W. DeVous, Pst.; CRP Stds.: 5

MAYSVILLE

St. Patrick - 110 E. Third St., Maysville, KY 41056-0248 t) 606-564-9015 lwilson@stpatschool.com Very Rev. Andrew L. Young, Pst.; Rev. Michael A. Black, Par. Vicar; CRP Stds.: 20

St. James - Kentucky Rd. 435, Minerva, KY 41062; Mailing: 110 E. 3rd Street, Maysville, KY 41056-0248 t) (606) 564-9015

St. Patrick School - (Grades PreK-8) 318 Limestone St., Maysville, KY 41056-0248 t) 606-564-5949 rnoll@stpatschool.com; alittle@stpatschool.com www.stpatschool.com Dr. Rachel Noll, Prin.; Stds.: 138; Lay Tchrs.: 10

MELBOURNE

St. Philip - 5746 Mary Ingles Hwy., Melbourne, KY 41059-9766 t) 859-441-8949 recphilip@stphilipky.org www.stphilipky.org/ Rev. Robert A. Rottgers, Pst.; Dcn. Peter J. (Pete) Freeman; Dcn. Thomas J. Murrin;

St. Philip School - (Grades K-8) t) 859-441-3423 www.stphilipky.org Jennifer Twehues, Prin.; Stds.: 78; Lay Tchrs.: 6

MORNING VIEW

St. Matthew - 13782 Decoursey Pk., Morning View, KY 41063 t) 859-356-6530 Rev. Jacob E. Straub, Pst.; Roseanne Rawe, DRE; CRP Stds.: 12

NEWPORT

Holy Spirit - 825 Washington Ave., Newport, KY 41071-1999 t) 859-431-2533 office@holyspiritnky.org www.holyspiritnky.org Rev. Msgr. William F. Cleves, Pst.; Dcn. Dave Profitt; Dcn. Joseph A. Wiedeman; Seth Cutter, Music Min.; R. Alex Bramel, Bus. Mgr.;

Holy Spirit Child Development Center - 840 Washington Ave., Newport, KY 41071-1946 t) 859-888-0777 childcare@holyspiritnky.org Michelle Mabrey, Dir.;

PARK HILLS

Our Lady of Lourdes Parish - 1101 Amsterdam Rd., Park Hills, KY 41011 t) 859-291-1854 info@ourladyoflourdes.info www.ourladyoflourdes.info Rev. Shannon M. Collins, M.S.J.B., Pst.; Rev. Sean P. Kopczynski, M.S.J.B., Par. Vicar;

Oratory of the Holy Family - 2750 Beaver Rd., Union, KY 41091 t) (859) 291-1854

SOUTHGATE

St. Therese of the Infant Jesus - 11 Temple Pl., Southgate, KY 41071-3133 t) 859-441-1654 parishoffice@sainttherese.ws sainttherese.ws Rev. Michael Grady, Pst.; Dcn. Joseph E. McGraw; Dcn. William R. Theis; CRP Stds.: 25

St. Therese of the Infant Jesus School - (Grades PreSchool-8) 2516 Alexandria Pike, Southgate, KY 41071 t) 859-441-0449 boruskek@sainttherese.ws Katie Boruske, Prin.; Ellen Lonneman, Librn.; Stds.: 153; Lay Tchrs.: 15

TAYLOR MILL

St. Anthony - 485 Grand Ave., Taylor Mill, KY 41015-0219 t) 859-431-1773; 859-431-5987 stanthonychurch@stanth.org saintanthonytaylormill.org Rev. Ivan Kalamuzi (Uganda), Pst.; CRP Stds.: 12

St. Anthony School - (Grades K-8) t) (859) 431-5987 (FAX 859 431-5972) school@stanth.org www.saintanthonytaylormill.org/school Veronica Schweitzer, Prin.; Stds.: 68; Lay Tchrs.: 4

St. Patrick - 3285 Mills Rd., Taylor Mill, KY 41015-2480 t) 859-356-5151 parishoffice@stpat.church stpat.church/ Rev. Jeffrey D. Von Lehmen, Pst.; Mallory Hamilton, DRE; CRP Stds.: 129

St. Patrick Primary School TM - (Grades PreSchool-2) t) 859-344-7040 nunnelleyp@stpat.church stpat.school/ Pamela Nunnelley, Prin.; Stds.: 52; Lay Tchrs.: 5

UNION

St. Timothy - 10272 U.S. Hwy. 42, Union, KY 41091-0120; Mailing: P.O. Box 120, Union, KY 41091-0120 t) 859-384-5100 (CRP); 859-384-1100 clense@saint-timothy.org; lprofitt@saint-timothy.org www.saint-timothy.org/ Rev. Richard G. Bolte, Pst.; Rev. Samuel Kwadwo Owusu, Par. Vicar; Dcn. Thomas L. Nolan; Dcn. Steven E. Alley; Dcn. Dave Philbrick; Dcn. Kevin Cranley; Deb Geers, DRE; CRP Stds.: 387

St. Timothy Catholic School - (Grades K-8) 10268 U.S. Hwy. 42, Union, KY 41091 t) (859) 384-5100 dgeers@saint-timothy.org saint-timothy-school.org/ Stds.: 251; Lay Tchrs.: 31

VANCEBURG

Holy Redeemer - 239 KY 59, Vanceburg, KY 41179; Mailing: P.O. Box 8, Vanceburg, KY 41179-0008 t) 606-796-3052; 606-796-2830 (CRP) ttolle@windstream.net; tericantor@aol.com Very Rev. Andrew L. Young, Par. Admin.; CRP Stds.: 7

WALTON

All Saints - 1 Beatrice Ave., Walton, KY 41094-1029 t) 859-485-4476 allsaintswalton.com Rev. Matthew A. Cushing, Pst.; Dcn. Paul V. Yancey; CRP Stds.: 35

WARSAW

St. Joseph - 602 Main Cross, Warsaw, KY 41095-0495; Mailing: P.O. Box 495, Warsaw, KY 41095-0495 t) 859-567-2425; 859-334-2079 (Emergency Number) mbarth@covdio.org; parishpriest@sjseky.org www.sjseky.org Rev. Michael D. Barth, Pst.; Rev. David B. Gamm, In Res.; CRP Stds.: 42

St. Edward - 1335 Hwy. 22 E., R.R. 4, Owenton, KY 40359-9003; Mailing: P.O. Box 495, Warsaw, KY 41095-0495 t) (859) 567-2425

WILDER

St. John the Baptist - 1307 John's Hill Rd., Wilder, KY 41076-9129 t) 859-781-2117 stjohnwilder@gmail.com Rev. Gregory E. Osburg, Pst.;

WILLIAMSTOWN

St. William - 6 Church St., Williamstown, KY 41097-9454 t) 859-824-5381 bclift@saint-william.org; sroland@saint-william.org saint-william.org Rev. Benton M. Clift Sr., Pst.; CRP Stds.: 36

St. John's - 834 Center Ridge Rd. (Hwy. 3184), De Mossville, KY 41033 t) (859) 824-5381

SCHOOLS: PRESCHOOL THRU HIGH SCHOOL

SCHOOLS

COMMONWEALTH OF KENTUCKY

BELLEVUE

Holy Trinity Elementary School - (PAR) (Grades PreK-8) 235 Division St., Bellevue, KY 41073-1101 t) 859-291-6937 principal@holytrinity-school.org; htinfo@holytrinity-school.org holytrinity-school.org Michele Carle-Bosch, Prin.; Stds.: 101; Lay Tchrs.: 10

COVINGTON

Holy Family Catholic School - (PAR) (Grades K-8) 338 E. 16th St., Covington, KY 41014-1398 t) 859-581-0290 evieth@holyfamilycovington.org; ctabor@holyfamilycovington.org www.holyfamilycovington.org Parochial Beth Vieth, Prin.; Stds.: 57; Lay Tchrs.: 5

Prince of Peace School - (PAR) (Grades PreK-8) 625 W. Pike St., Covington, KY 41011; Mailing: 627 W. Pike St., Covington, KY 41011 t) 859-431-5153 kmiddendorf@popcov.com; crice@popcov.com www.popcov.com Montessori Pre Primary (Age 3-6) Christina M Rice, Prin.; Stds.: 51; Lay Tchrs.: 5

FORT MITCHELL

Guardian Angel (Beechwood Independent Schools) - (Grades 1-8) 75 Orphanage Rd., Fort Mitchell, KY 41017-0007; Mailing: P.O. Box 17007, Fort Mitchell, KY 41017-0007 t) 859-331-2040 School for the Emotional Behavioral Disabled. Nikki Benson, Dir.; Stds.: 30; Lay Tchrs.: 4

VILLA HILLS

Villa Madonna Academy - (PRV) (Grades K-6) 2500 Amsterdam Rd., Villa Hills, KY 41017-3798 t) 859-331-6333 sbosley@villamadonna.net; pmcqueen@villamadonna.net www.villamadonna.org Pamela McQueen, Exec. Dir.; Soshana Bosley, Prin.; Stds.: 236; Lay Tchrs.: 22

WALTON

Saint Joseph Academy, Inc. - (PRV) (Grades PreK-8) 48 Needmore St., Walton, KY 41094-1028 t) 859-485-6444 principal@sjawalton.com www.sjawalton.com Sr. Patricia Jean Cushing, SJW, Prin.; Stds.: 97; Lay Tchrs.: 8

HIGH SCHOOLS

COMMONWEALTH OF KENTUCKY

ALEXANDRIA

Bishop Brossart High School - (DIO) (Grades 9-12) 4 Grove St., Alexandria, KY 41001-1295 t) 859-635-2108 info@bishopbrossart.org www.bishopbrossart.org Rev. Edward J. Brodnick, Chap.; Chris Holtz, Prin.; Rev. Msgr. Gerald L. Reinersman, Admin.; Stds.: 304; Lay Tchrs.: 26

COVINGTON

Covington Latin School - (DIO) (Grades 7-12) 21 E. 11th St., Covington, KY 41011-3196 t) 859-291-7044 headmaster@covingtonlatin.org; leighann.divine@covingtonlatin.org www.covingtonlatin.org Very Rev. Ryan L. Maher, Admin.; Rev. Michael Grady, Chap.; Dr. John Kennedy, Headmaster; Matt Krebs, Dean; Stds.: 202; Pr. Tchrs.: 1; Sr. Tchrs.: 1; Lay Tchrs.: 13

Holy Cross High School - (DIO) (Grades 9-12) 3617 Church St., Covington, KY 41015-1498 t) 859-431-1335 mike.holtz@hchscov.com; shelley.crowley@hchscov.com hchscov.com Rev. Thomas P. Robbins, Chap.; Rev. Jeffrey D. Von Lehmen, Chap.; Michael Holtz, Prin.; Stds.: 321; Scholastics: 1; Pr. Tchrs.: 2; Sr. Tchrs.: 1; Lay Tchrs.: 32

ERLANGER

St. Henry District High School - (DIO) (Grades 9-12) 3755 Scheben Dr., Erlanger, KY 41018-3597 t) 859-525-0255 gbrannen@shdhs.org www.shdhs.org Rev. Kevin James Kahmann, Admin.; Rev. Jason M. Bertke, Chap.; Grant Brannen, Prin.; Stds.: 456; Lay Tchrs.: 43

MAYSVILLE

St. Patrick High School - (DIO) (Grades 9-12) 318 Limestone St., Maysville, KY 41056-1248 t) 606-564-5949 alittle@stpatschool.com Rev. Michael A. Black, Chap.; Very Rev. Andrew L. Young, Admin.; Dr. Rachel Noll, Prin.; Stds.: 66; Pr. Tchrs.: 1; Lay Tchrs.: 7

NEWPORT

Newport Central Catholic High School - (DIO) (Grades 9-12) 13 Carothers Rd., Newport, KY 41071-2497 t) 859-292-0001 mdaley@ncchs.com www.ncchs.com Kenny Collopy, Prin.; Rev. Michael E. Comer, Admin.; Stefanie Piegols, Admin.; Stds.: 210; Pr. Tchrs.: 1; Lay Tchrs.: 19

PARK HILLS

Covington Catholic High School - (DIO) (Grades 9-12) 1600 Dixie Hwy., Park Hills, KY 41011-2797 t) 859-491-2247 browe@covcath.org www.covcath.org Boys. Rev. Michael C. Hennigen, Chap.; Very Rev. Mark A. Keene, Admin.; Robert J. Rowe, Prin.; Matthew Hansman, Asst. Prin.; Anthony Zechella, Asst. Prin.; Stds.: 472; Lay Tchrs.: 40

Notre Dame Academy, Inc. - (PRV) (Grades 9-12) 1699 Hilton Dr., Park Hills, KY 41011-2796 t) 859-261-4300 vonhandorfj@ndapandas.org; ginneym@ndapandas.org www.ndapandas.org Sisters of Notre Dame. Jack Von Handorf, Prin.; Stds.: 500; Sr. Tchrs.: 1; Lay Tchrs.: 40

VILLA HILLS

Villa Madonna Academy High School/Junior High - (PRV) (Grades 7-12) 2500 Amsterdam Rd., Villa Hills, KY 41017-3798 t) 859-331-6333 pmcqueen@villamadonna.net www.villamadonna.net Very Rev. Baiju Kidaagen, V.C., Chap.; Pamela McQueen, Pres.; Stds.: 251; Lay Tchrs.: 26

INSTITUTIONS LOCATED IN DIOCESE

CAMPUS MINISTRY / NEWMAN CENTERS [CAM]

HIGHLAND HEIGHTS

Catholic Newman Club - Northern Kentucky University - 19 Clearview Dr., Highland Heights, KY 41076-1449 c) (859) 663-1822 deaconb@nku.edu nkunewmancenter.org Dcn. Brian R. Cox, Campus Min.;

CATHOLIC CHARITIES [CCH]

COVINGTON

Catholic Charities of the Diocese of Covington, Inc. - 3629 Church St., Covington, KY 41015-1499 t) 859-581-8974 apickett@covingtoncharities.org; vbauerle@covingtoncharities.org www.covingtoncharities.org Alan B. Pickett, Exec. Dir.; Asstd. Annu.: 7,000; Staff: 24

Notre Dame Urban Education Center, Inc. - 14 E. 8th St., Covington, KY 41011 t) 859-261-4487 smtherese@nduec.org www.nduec.org Sr. Maria Therese Schappert, S.N.D., Dir.; Asstd. Annu.: 125; Staff: 8

Parish Kitchen - 1561 Madison Ave., Covington, KY 41011-2362; Mailing: P.O. Box 1234, Covington, KY 41012-1234 t) 859-581-7745 apickett@covingtoncharities.org covingtoncharities.org Alan B. Pickett, Exec. Dir.; Asstd. Annu.: 43,388; Staff: 6

ERLANGER

***Society of St. Vincent de Paul, Council of Northern Kentucky** - 2655 Crescent Springs Rd., Erlanger, KY 41017 t) 859-446-7723; 859-446-7727 karen.zengel@svdpnky.org; lou.settle@svdpnky.org www.svdpnky.org Karen Zengel, Exec.; Asstd. Annu.: 42,000; Staff: 95

CEMETERIES [CEM]

COLD SPRING

St. Joseph - 4011 Alexandria Pike, Cold Spring, KY 41076; Mailing: 1125 Madison Ave., Diocese of Covington, Covington, KY 41011-3115 t) (859) 414-2567 klinkugel@covdio.org covdio.org/buildings-properties-2/cemeteries/ Brian Harvey, Dir.;

FORT MITCHELL

St. John - 1 St. John Rd., Fort Mitchell, KY 41017 t) (859) 414-2380 klinkugel@covdio.org covdio.org/buildings-properties-2/cemeteries/ Brian Harvey, Dir.;

St. Mary - 2201 Dixie Hwy., Fort Mitchell, KY 41017-2905 t) (859) 414-2204 klinkugel@covdio.org covdio.org/buildings-properties-2/cemeteries/ Brian Harvey, Dir.;

FORT THOMAS

St. Stephen - 1523 Alexandria Pk., Fort Thomas, KY 41075-2592 t) (859) 414-2567 klinkugel@covdio.org covdio.org/buildings-properties-2/cemeteries/ Brian Harvey, Dir.;

WILDER

St. Joseph - 1307 Johns Hill Rd., Wilder, KY 41076; Mailing: 1125 Madison Ave., Diocese of Covington, Covington, KY 41011-3115 t) (859) 414-2380 klinkugel@covdio.org covdio.org/buildings-properties-2/cemeteries/ Brian Harvey, Dir.;

COLLEGES & UNIVERSITIES [COL]

CRESTVIEW HILLS

Thomas More University - 333 Thomas More Pkwy., Crestview Hills, KY 41017 t) 859-341-5800 admissions@thomasmore.edu www.thomasmore.edu (Coed) Rev. Msgr. Gerald E. Twaddell, Chap.; Dr. Joseph L Chillo, Pres.; Rev. Raymond N. Enzweiler, Prof.; Andrew Cole, Campus Min.; Stds.: 2,269; Lay Tchrs.: 77; Pr. Tchrs.: 2; Sr. Tchrs.: 1

CONVENTS, MONASTERIES, AND RESIDENCES FOR WOMEN [CON]

COVINGTON

The Franciscan Daughters of Mary (F.D.M.) - 336 E. 16th St., Covington, KY 41014; Mailing: P.O. Box 122070, Covington, KY 41012-2070 t) 859-491-3899 c) 859-512-0333 www.fdofmary.org (Public Association of the Faithful) Mother Seraphina Marie Quinlan, F.D.M., Supr.; Sr. Clare Marie Borchard, F.D.M., Vicar; Srs.: 7

***Rose Garden Center for Hope and Healing** - 2020 Madison Ave., Covington, KY 41012; Mailing: P.O. Box 122038, Covington, KY 41012 t) (859) 261-0323 rosegardenmission@gmail.com www.fdofmary.org/center-for-hope-and-healing.php

Rose Garden Home Mission - 2040 Madison Ave., Covington, KY 41012; Mailing: P.O. Box 122070, Covington, KY 41012-2070 t) (859) 491-7673 rosegardenmission@gmail.com www.fdofmary.org/rose-garden-home-mission.php

Sisters of Notre Dame of Covington, Kentucky - 1601 Dixie Hwy., Covington, KY 41011-2701 t) 859-291-2040 shemmer@sndusa.org Juniorate, Novitiate (1924) Sr. Margaret M Gorman Sr., Prov.; Srs.: 74

St. Walburg Monastery (Villa Madonna Academy, Benedictine Sisters) - 2500 Amsterdam Rd., Covington, KY 41017-5316 t) 859-331-6324 www.stwalburg.org Sr. Aileen Bankemper, O.S.B., Prioress; Srs.: 29

ERLANGER

Monastery of the Sacred Passion - 1151 Donaldson Hwy., Erlanger, KY 41018-1000 t) 859-371-8568 sister.marycatherine@outlook.com www.erlangerpassionists.org Passionist Nuns. Rev. Msgr. Gerald E. Twaddell, Chap.; Srs.: 6

MELBOURNE

St. Anne Province Center (Provincial House and Novitiate of the Sisters of Divine Providence of Kentucky) - 5300 St. Anne Dr., Melbourne, KY 41059-9603 t) 859-441-0700 info@cdpkentucky.org www.cdpkentucky.org Sr. Barbara Rohe, CDP, Prov.; Srs.: 72

Congregation of Divine Providence of Melbourne KY Inc. - 5300 St. Anne Dr., Melbourne, KY 41059-9601 t) 859-441-0700 brohe@cdpkentucky.org www.cdpkentucky.org Sr. Barbara Rohe, CDP, Prov.; Srs.: 72

Holy Family Home - 5300 St. Anne Dr., Melbourne, KY 41059-9604 t) 859-781-0712 cschumacher@cdpkentucky.org Sr. Carleen Schumacher, C.D.P., Admin.; Srs.: 32

WALTON

St. William Convent - 1 St. Joseph Ln., Walton, KY 41094-1026 t) 859-485-4256 motherchristinasjw@gmail.com Sisters of St. Joseph the Worker Mother Christina Murray, S.J.W., Supr.; Srs.: 4

HOSPITALS / HEALTH SERVICES [HOS]

COVINGTON

St. Elizabeth, Covington (St. Elizabeth Medical Center, Inc.) - 1500 James Simpson Jr. Way, Covington, KY 41011-0800 t) 859-301-2000 www.stelizabeth.com An Ambulatory Care Center. Rev. Robert J. Henderson, Chap.; Garren Colvin, Pres.; Dave Johnson, Vice. Pres.; Gary Blank, Exec.; Asstd. Annu.: 73,165; Staff: 144

EDGEWOOD

St. Elizabeth, Edgewood (Saint Elizabeth Medical Center, Inc.) - 1 Medical Village Dr., Edgewood, KY 41017-3441 t) 859-301-2000 dave.johnson@stelizabeth.com www.stelizabeth.com Hospital of St. Elizabeth Healthcare Rev. Robert J. Henderson, Chap.; Garren Colvin, Pres.; Dave Johnson, Vice. Pres.; Gary Blank, Exec. Vice Pres. & COO; Bed Capacity: 578; Asstd. Annu.: 780,829; Staff: 4,453

FLORENCE

St. Elizabeth, Florence (Saint Elizabeth Medical Center, Inc.) - 4900 Houston Rd., Florence, KY 41042-4824 t) 859-212-5200 dave.johnson@stelizabeth.com www.stelizabeth.com Hospital of St. Elizabeth Healthcare Rev. Robert J. Henderson, Chap.; Garren Colvin, Pres.; Dave Johnson, Vice. Pres.; Bruno Giacomuzzi, Admin.; Gary Blank, Exec.; Bed Capacity: 188; Asstd. Annu.: 145,501; Staff: 1,178

FORT THOMAS

St. Elizabeth, Fort Thomas (Saint Elizabeth Medical Center, Inc.) - 85 N. Grand Ave., Fort Thomas, KY 41075-1793 t) 859-301-2000 dave.johnson@stelizabeth.com www.stelizabeth.com Hospital of St. Elizabeth Healthcare Rev. Robert J. Henderson, Chap.; Garren Colvin, Pres.; Dave Johnson, Vice. Pres.; John Mitchell, Admin.; Gary Blank, Exec.; Bed Capacity: 178; Asstd. Annu.: 88,162; Staff: 821

WILLIAMSTOWN

St. Elizabeth, Grant County (Saint Elizabeth Medical Center, Inc.) - 238 Barnes Rd., Williamstown, KY 41097-9482 t) 859-824-8240 rosanne.nields@stelizabeth.com www.stelizabeth.com Critical Access Hospital of St. Elizabeth Healthcare Rev. Robert J. Henderson, Chap.; Garren Colvin, Pres.; Dave Johnson, Vice. Pres.; Bruno Giacomuzzi, Admin.; Gary Blank, Exec.; Bed Capacity: 25; Asstd. Annu.: 44,459; Staff: 135

MISCELLANEOUS [MIS]

COVINGTON

Shrine of St. Ann - 1274 Parkway Ave, Covington, KY 41011-1060 t) 859-261-9548 fr.mick@gmail.com www.stjohnstanncovington.com Attached to St. Ann Mission. Rev. G. Michael Greer, Pst.;

Sisters of Notre Dame International, Inc. - 1601 Dixie Hwy., Covington, KY 41011 t) 859-291-2040 x102 mmeadows@sndusa.org Sr. Mary Ann Culpert, Supr.;

NEWPORT

***Faith Community Pharmacy, Inc.** - 601 Washington Ave., Ste. 100, Newport, KY 41071 t) (859) 426-7837 info@faithcommunitypharmacy.org www.faithcommunitypharmacy.org Provides 100% free prescription medications for chronic diseases. Aaron Broomall, Dir.;

SOUTHGATE

Shrine of the Little Flower - St. Therese Parish, 11 Temple Pl, Southgate, KY 41071-3133 t) 859-441-1654 parishoffice@sainttherese.ws www.sainttherese.ws Attached to St. Therese Church. Rev. Michael Grady, Pst.;

NURSING / REHABILITATION / CONVALESCENCE / ELDERLY CARE [NUR]

COVINGTON

St. Charles Care Center, Inc. (Charlie's Club, St. Charles Community, St. Charles Lodge, St. Charles Village, St. Charles Homestead, St. Charles at Home, Senior Resource Center) - 600 Farrell Dr., Covington, KY 41011-5126 t) 859-331-3224 lbender@stcharlescommunity.org www.stcharlescommunity.org Adult Day Health Program, In and Outpatient Therapy Department, Private Duty Nursing, In Home Care, Personal Care, Housing and Community Outreach. Nicole Smith, Admin.; Asstd. Annu.: 673; Staff: 91

FORT THOMAS

Carmel Manor - 100 Carmel Manor Rd., Fort Thomas, KY 41075-2395 t) 859-781-5111 leahmksmith@carmelitesystem.org carmelmanor.com Carmelite Sisters for the Aged and Infirm and the Diocese of Covington Leah Marie Killian-Smith, Admin.; Asstd. Annu.: 212; Staff: 84

VILLA HILLS

Madonna Manor - 2344 Amsterdam Rd., Villa Hills, KY 41017-3712 t) 859-426-6400 dcorrou@chilivingcomm.org www.homeishere.org An operating unit of CHI Living Communities, which is a subsidiary of CommonSpirit Health Denise Corrou, Exec. Dir.; Rev. John J. Riesenberg, Chap.; Asstd. Annu.: 307; Staff: 118

PRESCHOOLS / CHILDCARE CENTERS [PRE]

PARK HILLS

Julie Learning Center, Inc. - 1601 Dixie Hwy., Park Hills, KY 41011 t) 859-392-8231 directorjlc2014@gmail.com Children ages 4-6. Mary Hedger, Dir.; Stds.: 18; Lay Tchrs.: 8

VILLA HILLS

Villa Madonna Montessori - 2402 Amsterdam Rd., Villa Hills, KY 41017-5316 t) 859-341-5145 villamadonnamontessori@gmail.com villamadonnamontessori.org Stacey R. Brosky, Admin.; Stds.: 50; Lay Tchrs.: 6

SPECIAL CARE FACILITIES [SPF]

FORT MITCHELL

Diocesan Catholic Children's Home (DCCH Center for Children and Families) - 75 Orphanage Rd., Fort Mitchell, KY 41017-2730; Mailing: P.O. Box 17007, Fort Mitchell, KY 41017-2730 t) 859-331-2040 bwilson@dcchcenter.org www.dcchcenter.org Nikki Benson, Prin.; Robert J. Wilson, Exec. Dir.; Stds.: 30; Lay Tchrs.: 4; Bed Capacity: 32; Asstd. Annu.: 800; Staff: 100

An asterisk (*) denotes an organization that has established tax-exempt status directly with the IRS and is not covered by the USCCB Group Ruling.

Diocese of Crookston

(Dioecesis Crookstoniensis)

MOST REVEREND ANDREW H. COZZENS, S.T.D., D.D.

Bishop of Crookston; ordained May 31, 1997; Episcopal ordination December 9, 2013; appointed eighth Bishop of Crookston December 6, 2021. Chancery Office: 620 Summit Ave. N., Crookston, MN 56716. T: 218-281-4533.

Chancery Office: 620 Summit Ave. N., P.O. Box 610, Crookston, MN 56716. T: 218-281-4533; F: 218-281-5991.
www.crookston.org
bishopcozzens@crookston.org

ESTABLISHED BY HIS HOLINESS PIUS X, DECEMBER 31, 1909.

Square Miles 17,210.

Comprises the Counties of Becker, Beltrami, Clay, Clearwater, Hubbard, Kittson, Lake of the Woods, Marshall, Mahnomen, Norman, Pennington, Polk, Red Lake and Roseau in the State of Minnesota.

Patroness of the Diocese: The Immaculate Conception.

Legal Title: Diocese of Crookston.

For legal titles of parishes and diocesan institutions, consult the Chancery Office.

STATISTICAL OVERVIEW

Personnel

Bishop	1
Retired Bishops	2
Priests: Diocesan Active in Diocese	28
Priests: Diocesan Active Outside Diocese	1
Priests: Diocesan in Foreign Missions	1
Priests: Retired, Sick or Absent	11
Number of Diocesan Priests	41
Religious Priests in Diocese	4
Total Priests in your Diocese	45
Extern Priests in Diocese	5
Ordinations:	
Transitional Deacons	1
Permanent Deacons	4
Permanent Deacons in Diocese	29
Total Sisters	27

Parishes

Parishes	66
With Resident Pastor:	
Resident Diocesan Priests	28
Resident Religious Priests	2
Without Resident Pastor:	
Administered by Priests	36
Professional Ministry Personnel:	
Sisters	27
Lay Ministers	168

Welfare

Catholic Hospitals	3
Total Assisted	7,047
Homes for the Aged	3
Total Assisted	297

Educational

Diocesan Students in Other Seminaries	6
Total Seminarians	6
High Schools, Diocesan and Parish	1
Total Students	200
Elementary Schools, Diocesan and Parish	8
Total Students	1,196
Catechesis/Religious Education:	
High School Students	1,025
Elementary Students	1,510
Total Students under Catholic Instruction	3,937
Teachers in Diocese:	
Lay Teachers	110

Vital Statistics

Receptions into the Church:	
Infant Baptism Totals	262
Minor Baptism Totals	26
Adult Baptism Totals	14
Received into Full Communion	39
First Communions	335
Confirmations	213
Marriages:	
Catholic	44
Interfaith	40
Total Marriages	84
Deaths	371
Total Catholic Population	27,395
Total Population	269,335

LEADERSHIP
Vicar General & Moderator of the Curia - Most Rev. Andrew H Cozzens, Moderator (cozzensa@crookston.org); Rev. Msgr. Timothy H. McGee, Vicar (tmcgee@crookston.org);
Chancery Office - t) 218-281-4533 Most Rev. Andrew H Cozzens (cozzensa@crookston.org); Rev. Msgr. Timothy H. McGee, Vicar (tmcgee@crookston.org); Janelle Gergen, Chancellor;
Chancellor - t) 218-281-4533 Janelle Gergen;
Information Officer - t) 218-281-4533 tmcgee@crookston.org Rev. Msgr. Timothy H. McGee (tmcgee@crookston.org);
Finance Officer - t) 218-281-4533 x417 cryan@crookston.org Chad Ryan;
Diocesan Tribunal - Rev. Joseph Richards (tribunal@crookston.com);
Defenders of the Bond - Rev. Virgil Helmin;
Judicial Vicar - Rev. Joseph Richards;
Notaries - Janelle Gergen; Carol Gwin; Rev. Adam A. Hamness;
Psychological Consultant - Geraldine Cariveau;

OFFICES AND DIRECTORS
Office of Administration - Chad Ryan; Sharon Dufault (sdufault@crookston.org); Terri Johnson;
Adoption Referral/Post Adoption Search - t) 218-281-4533 x416 Carol Gwin, Contact;
Benefits Committee of the Priests Pension Plan - Rev. Larry Delaney; Rev. Vincent Miller; Rev. George E. Noel;
Boy Scouts - t) 218-745-5423 Don Votava; Rev. Thomas Friedl;
Catholic Campaign for Human Development - t) 218-281-4533 x439 Robert Noel (bnoel@crookston.org);
Catholic Charities - Robert Noel, Dir. (bnoel@crookston.org);
Catholic Relief Services - t) 218-281-4533 x439 Robert Noel, Dir. (bnoel@crookston.org);
Office of Catholic Schools - t) 218-236-5066 LaCosta Potter (lpotter@crookston.org);
Commission on Building and Planning - Mary Dahl, Chair; Don Schoff; Curt Block;
Commission on Liturgy, Sacred Music and Art - Jeff Wiegrefe; Mary Dahl, Chair; Daniel Ewens;
Office of Communications - communications@crookston.org www.crookston.org/offices/communications Janelle Gergen, Dir.;
Cursillo - t) 701-866-5706 Bobbi Mercil (cbmercil@gmail.com);
Deans - Rev. Antony Fernando, Dean; Rev. Augie Gothman, Dean; Rev. Xavier Ilango, Dean;
Diaconate Office - t) 218-281-4533 x425 Dcn. Mark Krejci (mkrejci@crookston.org);
Diocesan Board of Conciliation and Arbitration - t) 218-281-4533 x419
Diocesan Consultors - Rev. Xavier Ilango; Rev. Vincent Miller; Rev. John Kleinwachter;
Finance Council - Most Rev. Andrew H Cozzens (cozzensa@crookston.org); Rev. Msgr. Timothy H. McGee (tmcgee@crookston.org); Janelle Gergen;
Office of Formation in Discipleship - Dcn. Mark Krejci, Dir. (mkrejci@crookston.org); Robert Noel (bnoel@crookston.org); Cassandra Johnson;
Holy Childhood Association - Rev. Msgr. Timothy H. McGee (tmcgee@crookston.org);
Ministerial Review Board - Judith Meyer, Chair; Rev. Vincent Miller; Jennifer Messelt;
Newspaper, "Our Northland Diocese" - t) 218-281-4533 x425 Janelle Gergen, Editor;
Office of Worship - Mary Dahl, Dir.;
Priests' Council - Most Rev. Andrew H Cozzens (cozzensa@crookston.org); Rev. Msgr. Timothy H. McGee (tmcgee@crookston.org); Rev. Vincent Miller, Chair;
Priests' Personnel Board - Most Rev. Andrew H Cozzens (cozzensa@crookston.org); Rev. Msgr. Timothy H. McGee (tmcgee@crookston.org); Rev. Vincent Miller;
Propagation of the Faith - t) 218-281-4533 x439 Rev. Msgr. Timothy H. McGee (tmcgee@crookston.org);
Office of Safe Environment & Ministerial Standards - t) 218-281-4224 Jim Remer, Dir.; Renee Tate (rtate@crookston.org);
Office of Stewardship & Development - Reathel Giannonatti, Dir. (rgiannonatti@crooskton.org);
Victim Assistance Coordinator - t) 218-281-7895 Cindy Hulst (chulst@crookston.org);
Office of Vocations - c) 218-230-4814 mschmitz@crookston.org Rev. Matthew Schmitz, Dir.;

PARISHES, MISSIONS, AND CLERGY

STATE OF MINNESOTA
ADA
St. Joseph's - 405 E. Thorpe Ave., Ada, MN 56510 t) 218-784-4131 sjchurchlady@yahoo.com; fatherpat14@gmail.com Rev. Patrick Sullivan, Pst.; Teresa Steen, Parish Life Coord.; CRP Stds.: 38
Holy Family -
St. William -
ANGUS
Holy Trinity Catholic (Tabor) - 37639 140th St., N.W., Angus, MN 56762-8929; Mailing: 200 3rd St., N.W., Sacred Heart, East Grand Forks, MN 56721 t) 218-773-0877 mletexier@sacredheartegf.net; shanson@sacredheartegf.net Served by Sacred Heart, East Grand Forks. Rev. Msgr. Michael H. Foltz, Pst.; Rev. Matthew Schmitz, Assoc. Pst.; Rev. James Khembo (Malawi), Assoc. Pst.; Dcn. Mark LeTexier;
ARGYLE
St. Rose of Lima - 501 W. 3rd St., Argyle, MN 56713; Mailing: PO Box 277, Argyle, MN 56713 t) 218-437-6341 Served by St. Stephen, Stephen, Assumption Church, Florian MN Rev. Luis Segundo Buitron, Pst.; Dawn Hoeper, DRE; CRP Stds.: 53
BADGER
St. Mary's (Badger) - 504 N. Main St., Badger, MN 56714; Mailing: 403 Main Ave. N., Roseau, MN 56751 t) 218-463-2441 shcroseau@centurylink.com; frjohn@centurylink.net Served by Sacred Heart, Roseau. Rev. John Kleinwachter, Pst.;
BAGLEY
St. Joseph - 16 Red Lake Ave., Bagley, MN 56621; Mailing: P.O. Box 67, Bagley, MN 56621 t) 218-694-6416 frjohnstmstj@gmail.com www.stjosephsbagley.org Served by St. Mary, Fosston. Rev. John Melkies Suvakeen, Pst.; CRP Stds.: 40
BARNESVILLE
Assumption - 307 Front St. N., Barnesville, MN 56514; Mailing: 112 4th Ave. N.W., P.O. Box 339, Barnesville, MN 56514 t) 218-354-7320 assumption@bvillemn.net assumptioncatholicchurchbarnesville.com Rev. Todd Arends, Pst.; Phyllis Peppel, DRE; CRP Stds.: 101
St. Cecilia -
BAUDETTE
St. Joseph (Williams) - 104 1st St. SW, Baudette, MN 56623; Mailing: P.O. Box 33, Warroad, MN 56763 t) 218-634-2689 ourlady@mncable.net; jim@lukenbill.net Served by Sacred Heart, Baudette. Dcn. James Lukenbill, Pst. Assoc.;
Sacred Heart - 104 1st St., S.W., Baudette, MN 56623; Mailing: P.O. Box 738, Baudette, MN 56623 t) 218-634-2689 (CRP); 218-386-1178 ourlady@mncable.net sacredheartbaudette.org Served by St. Mary's, Warroad. Rev. Andrew Obel, Pst.; Dcn. James Lukenbill;
St. Joseph - 400 Park Ave., Williams, MN 56686
BEMIDJI
St. Philip's - 702 Beltrami Ave., N.W., Bemidji, MN 56601-3046 t) 218-441-4944 (CRP); 218-444-4262 rector@stphilipsbemidji.org; tjohnson@stphilipsbemidji.org stphilipsbemidji.org Rev. William DeCrans, Pst.; Rev. Christon Muhero, Assoc. Pst.; Rev. Michael Arey, Assoc. Pst.; Dcn. Kermit Erickson; Dcn. Robb Naylor; Kris Jensen, DRE; CRP Stds.: 165
St. Philip's School - (Grades PreK-8) t) 218-444-4938 sglen1@stphilipsbemidji.org; jnorgaard1@stphilipsbemidji.org Jana Norgaard, Prin.; Stds.: 378; Lay Tchrs.: 28
St. Charles - 2500 Scenic Hwy., N.E., Pennington, MN 56663; Mailing: 702 Beltrami Ave., N.W., Bemidji, MN 56601
BLACKDUCK
St. Ann's (Blackduck) - 388 1st St. E., Blackduck, MN 56650; Mailing: P.O. Box 187, Kelliher, MN 56650 t) 218-647-8300 stpatrick@catholicexchange.com Served by St. Patrick's, Kelliher. Rev. Joseph Kennady, Pst.; Ginger Kaiser, DRE;
CALLAWAY
Assumption - 206 Dakota St., Callaway, MN 56521; Mailing: P.O. Box 67, Callaway, MN 56521 t) 218-375-3571; 218-334-4221 shfre@loretel.net; ahamness@crookston.org Served by Sacred Heart, Frazee Rev. Adam A. Hamness, Pst.;
CROOKSTON
Cathedral of the Immaculate Conception - 702 Summit Ave., Crookston, MN 56716-2736 t) 218-281-1735 hbach@crookstoncathedral.com; arobertson@crookstoncathedral.com www.crookstoncathedral.com Rev. Msgr. David Baumgartner, Rector; Dcn. Daniel Hannig; Dcn. Dennis Bivens; Mary Dahl, Liturgy Dir.; Hope Bach, Youth Min.; CRP Stds.: 86
The Cathedral School - (Grades PreK-6) t) 218-281-1835 swebster@crookstoncathedral.com; cschool@crookstoncathedral.com www.mycathedral.school Stephanie Webster, Prin.; Stds.: 76; Lay Tchrs.: 8
St. Peter's Church - 25823 185th Ave., S.W., Crookston, MN 56716-2736; Mailing: 702 Summit Ave., Crookston, MN 56716
St. Peter's (Gentilly) - 25723-185th Ave., S.W., Crookston, MN 56716; Mailing: 702 Summit Ave., Crookston, MN 56651 t) 218-281-1735; 218-281-1688 (CRP) dmbivens@crookstoncathedral.com; arobertson@crookstoncathedral.com Served by Cathedral of the Immaculate Conception, Crookston. Rev. Msgr. David Baumgartner, Rector; Dcn. Dennis Bivens; Hope Bach, DRE;
DETROIT LAKES
Holy Rosary - 1043 Lake Ave., Detroit Lakes, MN 56501-3499 t) 218-847-1393 parish@holyrosarycc.org www.holyrosarycc.org Rev. Charles Joseph Huck, Pst.; Dcn. Gary Hager; Mary A. Hager, Admin.; Abby Jasken, CRE; Kathy A. Olson, DRE; CRP Stds.: 316
Holy Rosary School - (Grades PreK-8) frchuck@holyrosarycc.org Rev. Chuck Huck, Supt.; Cathy A Larson, Prin.;
St. Mary of the Lakes - 20996 County Hwy. 20, Detroit Lakes, MN 56501 t) 218-439-3937 stmaryofthelakes@loretel.net stmaryofthelakes.cc Rev. Bob J. LaPlante, Pst.; Sue Livermore, DRE;
St. Francis Xavier - t) 218-238-6639 sfxchurch@loretel.net
DILWORTH
St. Elizabeth - 207 Main St. N., Dilworth, MN 56529-0307; Mailing: PO Box 307, Dilworth, MN 56529 t) 218-287-2705 karen@stlizdilworth.org; kaylie@stlizdilworth.org www.stlizdilworth.org Rev. August Gothman, Pst.; Kaylie Hanson, DRE; CRP Stds.: 82
St. Andrew - agothman@crookston.org
EAST GRAND FORKS
Sacred Heart - 200 Third St., N.W., East Grand Forks, MN 56721-1806 t) 218-773-0877 mfoltz@sacredheartegf.net www.sacredheartegf.net Rev.

Msgr. Michael H. Foltz, Pst.; Rev. James Khembo (Malawi), Pst. Assoc.; Rev. Matthew Schmitz, Assoc. Pst.; Dcn. Mark LeTexier; Dcn. Steve Thomas; CRP Stds.: 139

Sacred Heart School - (Grades PreK-12) t) 218-773-0230 (HS); 218-773-1579 (Elem) cadolphson@sacredheartegf.net Nevin Lubarski, Prin.; Carl Adolphson, Pres.; Stds.: 526; Lay Tchrs.: 35

St. Francis - 302 Park Ave, Fisher, MN 56721; Mailing: 200 Third St., N.W., East Grand Forks, MN 56721-1806 sthomas@sacredheartegf.net

Holy Trinity - 130 St. N.W., Angus, MN 56762; Mailing: 200 Third St. NW, East Grand Forks, MN 56721-1806 mletexier@sacredheartegf.net

EUCLID

St. Mary (Euclid) - 13439 U.S. Hwy. 75, S.W., Euclid, MN 56717; Mailing: 208 N. 7th St., Warrren, MN 56762 t) 218-745-4511 donnag@invisimax.com; xavier.ilango@gmail.com Served by Sts. Peter & Paul, Warren. Rev. Xavier Ilango, Pst.;

FERTILE

St. Joseph - 10480 438th St. S.W., Fertile, MN 56540 t) 218-945-6649 stjoesfertile@gvtel.com www.stjosephsfertile.com Rev. Larry Delaney, Pst.; CRP Stds.: 24

FISHER

St. Francis of Assisi - 302 Park Ave., Fisher, MN 56723; Mailing: 200 Third St., N.W., East Grand Forks, MN 56721-1806 t) 218-773-0877 sthomas@sacredheartegf.net Served by Sacred Heart, East Grand Forks. Rev. Msgr. Michael H. Foltz, Pst.; Rev. Joshy Mathew, Assoc. Pst.; Rev. Matthew Schmitz, Assoc. Pst.; Dcn. Steve Thomas;

FOSSTON

St. Mary's - 725 6th St., N.E., Fosston, MN 56542 t) 218-435-6484 frjohnstmstj@gmail.com stmarysfosston.org Rev. John Melkies Suvakeen, Pst.; Linda Hand, Bus. Mgr.; CRP Stds.: 35

FRAZEE

Sacred Heart - 202 W. Maple Ave., Frazee, MN 56544 t) 218-334-4221 shfre@loretel.net; christined.shfre@arvig.net frazeesacredheart.org Rev. Msgr. David Baumgartner, Pst.; Christine Dornbush, DRE;

Assumption - 206 Dakota St., Callaway, MN 56521 t) 218-334-4226 frdavid.shfre@arvig.net

GEORGETOWN

St. John - 308 Probstfield St., Georgetown, MN 56546; Mailing: 601 15th Ave. N., St. Francis de Sales Parish, Moorhead, MN 56560 t) 218-233-3934; 218-233-4780 jherm@feltontel.net; fatherraul@gmail.com Served by St. Francis de Sales, Moorhead. Rev. Raul Perez-Cobo, Pst.;

GOODRIDGE

St. Anne (Goodridge) - 202 Osmund Ave., Goodridge, MN 56725; Mailing: PO Box 126, c/o St. Francis Xavier Church, Oklee, MN 56742 t) 218-378-4529 parishstaff@oggcatholic.org www.oggcatholic.org Served by St. Francis Xavier, Oklee. Rev. Bryan Kujawa, Admin.;

GREENBUSH

Blessed Sacrament - 342 4th St. S., Greenbush, MN 56726; Mailing: PO Box A, Greenbush, MN 56726 t) 218-782-2467; 218-556-6090 (CRP) blessedsacrament@wiktel.com; jessicafoss14@gmail.com bscgreenbush.com Rev. George E. Noel, Pst.; Jess Foss, DRE; CRP Stds.: 41

St. Joseph -

St. Edward - 119 Harding St. S, Karlstad, MN 56732

GRYGLA

St. Clement (Grygla) - 130 N. Marshall Ave., Grygla, MN 56727; Mailing: c/o St. Francis Xavier Church, P.O. Box 126, Oklee, MN 56742 t) 218-796-5844 parishstaff@oggcatholic.org www.oggcatholic.org Served by St. Francis Xavier, Oklee. Rev. Bryan Kujawa, Admin.; CRP Stds.: 10

HALLOCK

Holy Rosary - 170 5th St. S., Hallock, MN 56728; Mailing: P.O. Box 596, Hallock, MN 56728 t) 218-843-2323 stpatrickshallock@gmail.com; jmathew@crookston.org Served by St. Patrick, Hallock. Rev. Joshy Mathew, Admin.;

Saint Patrick's Catholic Parish - 170 5th St. S., Hallock, MN 56728-0596; Mailing: P.O. Box 596, Hallock, MN 56728-0596 t) 218-843-2323 stpatrickshallock@gmail.com; jmathew@crookston.org saintpatrickhallock.com Rev. Joshy Mathew, Admin.; CRP Stds.: 31

Holy Rosary - 3843 290th Ave, Lancaster, MN 56735 t) (218) 843-2323 www.saintpatrickhallock.com/

HALSTAD

Holy Family (Halstad) - 307 5th St. E., Halstad, MN 56548; Mailing: 405 E. Thorpe Ave., Ada, MN 56510 t) 218-784-4131 stjoseph@loretel.net nccatholicchurch.com Served by St. Joseph, Ada. Rev. Patrick Sullivan, Pst.; Teresa Steen, DRE;

HAWLEY

St. Andrew - 1418 Main St., Hawley, MN 56549-0129; Mailing: PO Box 129, Hawley, MN 56549 t) 218-483-4264 parish@standrewshawley.org www.standrewshawley.org Served by St. Elizabeth, Dilworth. Rev. Augie Gothman, Pst.; Dcn. Tom Jirik; CRP Stds.: 140

KARLSTAD

St. Edward the Confessor (Karlstad) - 119 Harding St. S., Karlstad, MN 56732; Mailing: P.O. Box A, Greenbush, MN 56726 t) 218-782-2467 blessedsacrament@wiktel.com bscgreenbush.com Served by Blessed Sacrament, Greenbush. Rev. George E. Noel, Pst.; CRP Stds.: 23

KELLIHER

St. Patrick - 131 5th St., N.E., Kelliher, MN 56650; Mailing: P. O. Box 187, Kelliher, MN 56650 t) 218-647-8300 jkennady@crookston.org; knbcatholic@gmail.com triparish.org Rev. Joseph Kennady, Pst.; Natalie Nistler, DRE;

St. Ann - 388 First St., N.E., Blackduck, MN 56630 t) (218) 647-8300 www.triparish.org Marie Kovar, DRE;

St. John - 27867 Irvine Ave., N.E., Nebish, MN 56667 t) (218) 647-8300 www.triparish.org Ashley Wavrin, DRE;

LAKE PARK

St. Francis Xavier's - 2066 Second St., Lake Park, MN 56554 t) 218-239-6639; 218-238-6639 (CRP) sfxchurch@loretel.net Served by St. Mary of the Lakes, Detroit Lakes. Rev. Bob J. LaPlante, Pst.;

LAPORTE

St. Theodore of Tarsus (Laporte) - 580 County Rd. 39, Laporte, MN 56461; Mailing: P.O. Box 378, 205 Main St. W., Nevis, MN 56467 t) 218-652-4005 c) 218-308-7887 parishofficenevis@gmail.com; olpfaithform@gmail.com www.nevislaportecatholics.org Served by Our Lady of the Pines Church, Nevis Rev. Antony Fernando, Pst.; Ardis Johnson, Pst. Assoc.; CRP Stds.: 9

MAHNOMEN

St. Joseph Parish (Beaulieu) - 120 W. Jefferson Ave., Mahnomen, MN 56557 t) 218-935-2503 stmikes@arvig.net; dsuper@stmichaelmahnomen.org Served by St. Michael, Mahnomen. Rev. David J. Super, Pst.; Peggy Darco, DRE; Jolynn Pribula, DRE;

St. Michael's Parish - 120 W. Jefferson Ave., Mahnomen, MN 56557 t) 218-935-2503 stmikes@arvig.net; dsuper@stmichaelmahnomen.org www.stmichaelmahnomen.org Rev. David J. Super, Pst.; Dcn. Timothy Pribula; Peggy Darco, DRE; Theresa Zettel, DRE; CRP Stds.: 77

St. Michael's Parish School - (Grades PreK-6) t) 218-935-5222 schalich@stmichaelmahnomen.org stmichaelmahnomenschool.weebly.com/ Sarah Chalich, Prin.;

St. Joseph Church - 2312 222nd Ave., Mahnomen, MN 56557 t) (218) 935-2503 stmichaelmahnomen.org

MENTOR

St. Lawrence - 16180 336th St., S.E., Mentor, MN 56736; Mailing: P.O. Box 51, Mentor, MN 56736 t) 218-637-8178 stlawrence@gvtel.com www.stlawrencementor.org Rev. Larry Delaney, Pst.; Amy Kolden, DRE; Anita Revier, DRE; CRP Stds.: 34

MIDDLE RIVER

St. Joseph, Husband of Mary (Middle River) - 535 N 1st St., Middle River, MN 56737; Mailing: P.O. Box A, Greenbush, MN 56726 t) 218-782-2467 blessedsacrament@wiktel.com bscgreenbush.com Served by Blessed Sacrament, Greenbush. Rev. George E. Noel, Pst.; CRP Stds.: 5

MOORHEAD

St. Francis de Sales - 601 15th Ave. N., Moorhead, MN 56560 t) 218-233-4780 info@stfrancismhd.org www.stfrancismhd.org Rev. Maschio Mascarenghas (India), Pst.; Devan Hirning, DRE; CRP Stds.: 70

St. John the Baptist - t) (218) 233-4780

St. Joseph's - 218 10th St. S., Moorhead, MN 56560 t) 218-236-5066 khaugrud@stjoesmhd.com; mhundcerna@stjoesmhd.com www.stjoesmhd.com Rev. Vincent Miller, Pst.; Rev. Nate Brunn, Pst. Assoc.; Dcn. Courtney Abel; Dcn. Paul Erickson; Dcn. Mark Krejci; Dcn. Allen Kukert; Dcn. Robert Thom; Jeff Wiegrefe, Liturgy Dir.; Kate Hendrickx, DRE; Melissa Hund-Cerna, DRE; CRP Stds.: 305

St. Joseph's School - (Grades PreK-8) 1005 2nd Ave. S., Moorhead, MN 56560 t) 218-233-0553; 218-233-0556 saints@stjoesmhdschool.com www.stjoesmhdschool.com Laurie Johnson, Prin.; Katie WIse, Dir.; Stds.: 216; Pr. Tchrs.: 2; Lay Tchrs.: 9

NAYTAHWAUSH

St. Anne - 202 County Rd. 4, Naytahwaush, MN 56566; Mailing: 1112-3rd St., Waubun, MN 56589 t) 218-473-2101 1112sta@arvig.net whiteearthcatholiccommunity.com (Naytahwaush). Served by St. Ann's, Waubun. Rev. John Cox, O.M.I., Pst.;

NEBISH

St. John (Nebish) - 27867 Irvine Ave., N.E., Nebish, MN 56667; Mailing: P. O. Box 187, Kelliher, MN 56650 t) 218-647-8300 frjohn@triparish.org; stpatrick@catholicexchange.com Served by St. Patrick, Kelliher. Rev. Joseph Kennady, Pst.;

NEVIS

Our Lady of the Pines - 205 Main St., W., Nevis, MN 56467; Mailing: P.O. Box 378, Nevis, MN 56467 t) 218-652-4005 (Office); 218-652-2785 (Rectory) c) 218-308-7887 (Office) parishofficenevis@gmail.com; ccnevis@gmail.com www.nevislaportecatholics.org Rev. Antony Fernando, Pst.; Ardis Johnson, Pst. Assoc.; CRP Stds.: 49

St. Theodore of Tarsus Church - 580 County Rd. 39, Laporte, MN 56461; Mailing: 205 Main St., PO Box 378, Nevis, MN 56467

OGEMA

Most Holy Redeemer - 106 Ontario St., Ogema, MN 56569-0057; Mailing: P.O. Box 57, Ogema, MN 56569-0057 t) 218-983-3261; 218-473-2101 (CRP) owep@tvutel.com; 1113sta@arvig.net www.whiteearthcatholiccommunity.com Rev. Benny Lipalata, O.M.I., Par. Vicar; Rev. Gregory R Gallagher, O.M.I., Pst.; Janet Lhotka, DRE; CRP Stds.: 31

St. Benedict - nassaney@omiusa.org Rev. Daniel Nassaney, O.M.I., Pst.;

St. Theodore - nassaney@omiusa.org Rev. Daniel Nassaney, O.M.I., Pst.;

OKLEE

St. Francis Xavier's (Oklee) - 301 Governor St., Oklee, MN 56742; Mailing: PO Box 126, Oklee, MN 56742 t) 218-796-5844 parishstaff@oggcatholic.org; bkujawa@crookston.org www.oggcatholic.org Rev. Bryan Kujawa, Admin.;

St. Anne - 202 Osmund Ave., Goodridge, MN 56725

St. Clement - 130 N. Marshall Ave., Grygla, MN 56727

OSLO

St. Joseph - 515 Main St., Oslo, MN 56744; Mailing: 208 N. 7th St., Sts. Peter & Paul Parish, Warren, MN 56762 t) 218-695-2641 stjosephoslo1@gmail.com Served by SS.

Peter and Paul, Warren. Rev. Xavier Ilango, Pst.;

PARK RAPIDS

St. Mary's (Two Inlets) - 55744 County Hwy. 44, Park Rapids, MN 56470; Mailing: 305 W. 5th St., P.O. Box 353, Park Rapids, MN 56470 t) 218-732-5142 (CRP); 218-732-4046 sm2inlets@stpeterpr.org; office@stpeterpr.org www.stmarys-twoinlets-churchandgrotto.com Served by St. Peter, Park Rapids. Rev. Joseph Richards, Pst.; Dcn. John Zinniel; Annette Haas, DRE; CRP Stds.: 13

St. Peter the Apostle - 305 W. 5th St., Park Rapids, MN 56470; Mailing: P.O. Box 353, Park Rapids, MN 56470-0353 t) 218-732-5142 office@stpeterpr.org; jrichards@crookston.org www.stpeterpr.org Rev. Joseph Richards, Pst.; Dcn. John Zinniel; Annette Haas, DRE; CRP Stds.: 150

St. Mary - 55744 County Hwy 44, Park Rapids, MN 56470 t) 218-732-4046 sm2inlets@stpeterpr.org stmarys-twoinlets-churchandgrotto.com Two Inlets, Becker Co., MN.

PENNINGTON

St. Charles Catholic Church of Pennington - Scenic Hwy. 39, Pennington, MN 56663; Mailing: 702 Beltrami Ave., N.W., Bemidji, MN 56601-3046 t) 218-444-4262 tjohnson1@stphilipsbemidji.org Served by St. Philip's, Bemidji. Rev. William DeCrans, Pst.; Rev. Michael Arey, Assoc. Pst.; Rev. Christon Muhero;

PONSFORD

St. Theodore of Ponsford - 48500 Co. Hwy. 124, Ponsford, MN 56575; Mailing: P.O. Box 57, Ogema, MN 56569-0057 t) 218-983-3261 owep@tvutel.com whiteearthcatholiccommunity.com Served by Most Holy Redeemer, Ogema. Rev. Gregory R Gallagher, O.M.I., Pst.; Rev. Benny Lipalata, O.M.I., Par. Vicar;

RED LAKE

St. Mary's Mission Church - ; Mailing: Hwy #1 P.O. Box 189, Red Lake, MN 56671-0189 t) 218-679-3615; 218-679-3614 jchristianson@crookston.org Rev. John Christianson, Pst.;

St. Mary's Mission Church School - (Grades PreK-6) ; Mailing: P.O. Box 189, Red Lake, MN 56671-0189 t) 218-679-3388

Sacred Heart - t) 218-678-3614

RED LAKE FALLS

St. Joseph - 112 Edward Ave., Red Lake Falls, MN 56750-0400; Mailing: P.O. Box 400, Red Lake Falls, MN 56750-0400 t) 218-253-2188 deb@go2joseph.org; frschreiner@go2joseph.org go2joseph.org Rev. Robert Schreiner, Pst.; CRP Stds.: 118

St. Joseph -

St. Joseph (Church of Brooks) - ; Mailing: P.O. Box 400, Red Lake Falls, MN 56750-0400 t) 218-253-2188 frschreiner@go2joseph.org Served by St. Joseph's, Red Lake Falls. Rev. Robert Schreiner, Pst.;

ROSEAU

St. Philip (Falun) - 403 Main Ave. N., Roseau, MN 56751 t) 218-463-2441 shcroseau@centurylink.net; frjohn@centurylink.net Served by Sacred Heart, Roseau. Rev. John Kleinwachter, Pst.; Tracy Borowicz, DRE;

Sacred Heart - 403 Main Ave. N., Roseau, MN 56751 t) 213-463-2441; 218-242-4053 (CRP) shcroseau@centurylink.net; frjohnk@centurylink.net roseaucatholic.org Rev. John Kleinwachter, Pst.; Tracy Borowicz, DRE;

St. Mary's - t) 218-463-2441

St. Philip - t) 218-463-2441

SABIN

St. Cecilia (Sabin) - 20 Halloway Ave. S., Sabin, MN 56580; Mailing: PO Box 52, Sabin, MN 56580 t) 218-354-7320 assumption@bvillemn.net stceciliascatholicchurch.org/ Served by Assumption, Barnesville. Rev. Todd Arends, Pst.; CRP Stds.: 13

STEPHEN

St. Stephen's - 515 5th St., Stephen, MN 56757; Mailing: PO Box 507, Stephen, MN 56757 t) 218-478-2231 ststephens@wiktel.com Rev. Luis Segundo Buitron, Pst.; CRP Stds.: 29

Assumption Church of Florian - 26932 - 390th St., N.W., Strandquist, MN 56758 t) 218-478-3578 assumptionchurch@wiktel.com

St. Rose of Lima - 501 W. Third St., Argyle, MN 56713; Mailing: PO Box 277, Argyle, MN 56713 t) 218-437-6341 stroser@wiktel.com

STRANDQUIST

Assumption - Church of Florian - 26932 390th St., N.W., Strandquist, MN 56758 t) 218-478-3578 assumptionchurch@wiktel.com www.wiktel.net/assumption Served by St. Stephen, Stephen. Rev. Luis Segundo Buitron, Pst.; CRP Stds.: 29

THIEF RIVER FALLS

St. Bernards - 105 Knight Ave. N., Thief River Falls, MN 56701 t) 218-681-3571 margaret.rasmussen@stbernardstrf.com; laura.brickson@stbernardstrf.com www.stbernardscc.org/ Rev. Richard D. Lambert, Pst.; Misty Mehrkens, Youth Min.; Margaret Rasmussen, DRE;

St. Bernards School - (Grades PreK-6) t) 218-681-1539 Laura Brickson, Prin.;

TWIN VALLEY

St. William (Twin Valley) - 500 Lincoln Ave., N.W., Twin Valley, MN 56584; Mailing: 405 E. Thorpe Ave., Ada, MN 56510 t) 218-784-4131 stjoseph@loretel.net nccatholicchurch.com Served by St. Joseph, Ada. Rev. Patrick Sullivan, Pst.; Dcn. Nick Revier;

WARREN

SS. Peter and Paul - 208 N. Seventh St., Warren, MN 56762 t) 218-745-4511 donnag@invisimax.com; peterandpaul@invisimax.com Rev. Xavier Ilango, Pst.; CRP Stds.: 93

St. Joseph - Oslo - ; Mailing: P.O. Box 97, Oslo, MN 56744 t) 218-695-2641 stjoseph@wiktel.com

St. Mary - Rev. Emmanuel Sylvester, Pst.;

WARROAD

St. Mary's - 511 Cedar Ave., N.W., Warroad, MN 56763; Mailing: PO Box 33, Warroad, MN 56763 t) 218-386-1178 aobel@crookston.org; stmarys2@mncable.net stmaryswarroad.org Rev. Andrew Obel, Pst.; Dcn. James Lukenbill; CRP Stds.: 100

WAUBUN

St. Ann - 1112 3rd St., Waubun, MN 56589-9402 t) 218-473-2101 1112sta@arvig.net; jcoxomi@mindspring.com whiteearthcatholiccommunity.com Rev. John Cox, O.M.I., Pst.; Rev. Benny Lipalata, O.M.I., Assoc. Pst.; Janet Lhotka, DRE; CRP Stds.: 112

St. Anne - 204 County Rd. #4, Naytahwaush, MN 56566

St. Frances Cabrini - 39719 County Hwy. 35, Big Elbow Lake, MN 56589; Mailing: 1112 3rd St., Waubun, MN 56589

St. Frances Cabrini (Big Elbow Lake) - 39719 County Hwy. 35, Waubun, MN 56589; Mailing: 1112 3rd St., Waubun, MN 56589 t) 218-473-2101 1112sta@arvig.net whiteearthcatholiccommunity.com Served by St. Ann, Waubun. Rev. John Cox, O.M.I., Pst.;

WHITE EARTH

St. Benedict (White Earth) - 36352 Co Hwy 21, White Earth, MN 56569; Mailing: P.O. Box 57, Ogema, MN 56569-0057 t) 218-983-3261; 218-473-2101 (CRP) owep@tvutel.com; 1112sta@arvig.net whiteearthcatholiccommunity.com Served by Most Holy Redeemer, Ogema. Rev. Gregory R Gallagher, O.M.I., Pst.; Rev. Benny Lipalata, O.M.I., Par. Vicar; Janet Lhotka, DRE; CRP Stds.: 14

WILTON

Sacred Heart (Wilton) - 135 3rd St., N.W., Wilton, MN 56619; Mailing: P.O. Box 189, Red Lake, MN 56671 t) 218-751-8446 jchristianson@crookston.org Served by St. Mary's Mission, Red Lake. Rev. John Christianson, Pst.;

INSTITUTIONS LOCATED IN DIOCESE

CAMPUS MINISTRY / NEWMAN CENTERS [CAM]

BEMIDJI

Holy Spirit Newman Center - 702 Beltrami Ave., N.W., Bemidji, MN 56601-2607 t) 218-444-4262 ncenter@paulbunyan.net; frmichael1@stphilipsbemidji.org www.newmancenterbsu.org Rev. Michael Arey, Assoc. Pst.;

MOORHEAD

St. Thomas Aquinas Newman Center - 218 S. 10th St., Moorhead, MN 56560 t) 218-236-5066 x114 nate.brunn@stjoesmhd.com Rev. Nate Brunn, Par. Vicar;

CONVENTS, MONASTERIES, AND RESIDENCES FOR WOMEN [CON]

CROOKSTON

Mount St. Benedict Monastery - 620 Summit Ave., Crookston, MN 56716-2713 t) 218-281-3441 crxbenedictines@gmail.com www.msb.net Motherhouse of the Order of the Sisters of St. Benedict of Pontifical Jurisdiction-The Federation of St. Gertrude. Sr. Jane Becker, Admin.; Sr. Kathleen McGeary, O.S.B., Subprior; Srs.: 26

ENDOWMENTS / FOUNDATIONS / TRUSTS [EFT]

CROOKSTON

***The Diocese of Crookston Catholic Community Foundation** - 1200 Memorial Dr., Crookston, MN 56716 t) 218-281-4533 ccf@crookston.org www.crookston.org/ccf Reathel Giannonatti, Dir.;

***Mount Saint Benedict Foundation** - 620 Summit Ave., Crookston, MN 56716-2799 t) 218-281-3441 crxbenedictines@gmail.com www.msb.net Sr. Jane Becker, Admin.; Heidi Whiting, Dir.;

HOSPITALS / HEALTH SERVICES [HOS]

BAUDETTE

CHI LakeWood Health - 600 Main Ave. S., Baudette, MN 56623 t) 218-634-2120 missionintegrationmidwest@commonspirit.org www.lakewoodhealthcenter.org Affiliate of Catholic Health Initiatives. Jeffry Stampohar, Pres.; Andrew J Santos III, SVP, Mission Integration; Bed Capacity: 15; Asstd. Annu.: 126; Staff: 146

CHI Lakewood Health Care Center - andrew.santos@commonspirit.org Affiliate of Catholic Health Initiatives. Andrew J. Santos III, SVP, Mission Integration; Ben Koppelman, Admin.; Bed Capacity: 15; Asstd. Annu.: 126; Staff: 146

DETROIT LAKES

***Essentia Health St. Mary's** - 1027 Washington Ave., Detroit Lakes, MN 56501 t) 218-847-5611 linda.wainright@essentiahealth.org www.essentiahealth.org Kurt Jacobson, Chap.; Linda Wainright, Chap.; Tanner Goodrich, Vice. Pres.; Bed Capacity: 36; Asstd. Annu.: 5,977; Staff: 850

PARK RAPIDS

St. Joseph Area Health Services - 600 Pleasant Ave., Park Rapids, MN 56470 t) 218-732-3311 benkoppelman@catholichealth.net; missionintegrationmidwest@commonspirit.org chisjh.org Affiliate of Catholic Health Initiatives. Ben Koppelman, Pres.; Andrew J Santos III, SVP, Mission Integration; Bed Capacity: 25; Asstd. Annu.: 944; Staff: 267

MISCELLANEOUS [MIS]

CROOKSTON

Newman Outreach - 702 Summit Ave., Crookston, MN 56716 t) 218-281-1735 hbach@crookstoncathedral.com Hope Bach, Dir.;

NURSING / REHABILITATION / CONVALESCENCE / ELDERLY CARE [NUR]

ADA

Bridges Care Center (Benedictine Living Community|Ada) - 201 9th St. W., Ste. 2, Ada, MN 56510 t) 218-784-5500 morgan.hviding@benedictineliving.org www.benedictineliving.org/ada-mn/ Subs. of Benedictine Health System. Sponsored by the Benedictine Sisters Benevolent Association, Duluth. Morgan Hviding, Exec. Dir.; Asstd. Annu.: 67; Staff: 89

CROOKSTON

Villa St. Vincent (Benedictine Living Community|Crookston) - 516 Walsh St., Crookston, MN 56716 t) 218-281-3424 lindsey.erdman@benedictineliving.org www.benedictineliving.org/crookston-mn/ Lindsey Erdman, Exec. Dir.; Asstd. Annu.: 230; Staff: 214

DETROIT LAKES

St. Mary's Nursing Center - 1027 Washington Ave., Detroit Lakes, MN 56501 t) 218-844-0776 tthompson@trustedcareforlife.com Christy Brinkman, Admin.;

An asterisk (*) denotes an organization that has established tax-exempt status directly with the IRS and is not covered by the USCCB Group Ruling.

Diocese of Dallas

(Dioecesis Dallasensis)

MOST REVEREND EDWARD J. BURNS

Bishop of Dallas; ordained June 25, 1983; appointed Bishop of Juneau January 19, 2009; ordained March 3, 2009; installed April 2, 2009; appointed Bishop of Dallas December 13, 2016; installed February 9, 2017.

Diocesan Pastoral Center: 3725 Blackburn St., P.O. Box 190507, Dallas, TX 75219. T: 214-379-2800; F: 214-443-3827. www.cathdal.org

ESTABLISHED DIOCESE OF DALLAS ON JULY 15, 1890.

Square Miles 7,523.

Redesignated Diocese of Dallas-Fort Worth on October 20, 1953. Redesignated Diocese of Dallas on August 27, 1969.

Comprises the following nine Counties in the State of Texas: Collin, Dallas, Ellis, Fannin, Grayson, Hunt, Kaufman, Navarro and Rockwall.

Legal Corporate Title: Roman Catholic Diocese of Dallas.

For legal titles of parishes and diocesan institutions, consult the Diocesan Pastoral Center.

Most Reverend J. Gregory Kelly

Auxiliary Bishop of Dallas; ordained May 15, 1982; appointed Auxiliary Bishop of Dallas and Titular Bishop of Jamestown December 16, 2015; ordained February 11, 2016.

STATISTICAL OVERVIEW

Personnel
Bishop....1
Auxiliary Bishops....1
Abbots....1
Priests: Diocesan Active in Diocese....86
Priests: Diocesan Active Outside Diocese....1
Priests: Retired, Sick or Absent....34
Number of Diocesan Priests....121
Religious Priests in Diocese....93
Total Priests in your Diocese....214
Extern Priests in Diocese....32
Ordinations:
Diocesan Priests....6
Religious Priests....2
Transitional Deacons....8
Permanent Deacons....17
Permanent Deacons in Diocese....181
Total Brothers....21
Total Sisters....100

Parishes
Parishes....69
With Resident Pastor:
Resident Diocesan Priests....37
Resident Religious Priests....13
Without Resident Pastor:
Administered by Priests....17
Administered by Deacons....2
Missions....5

Pastoral Centers....4
Professional Ministry Personnel:
Brothers....2
Sisters....16
Lay Ministers....926

Welfare
Homes for the Aged....4
Total Assisted....491
Other Institutions....88
Total Assisted....128,346

Educational
Seminaries, Diocesan....2
Students from This Diocese....27
Students from Other Dioceses....38
Diocesan Students in Other Seminaries....26
Seminaries, Religious....1
Students, Religious....6
Total Seminarians....59
Colleges and Universities....1
Total Students....2,328
High Schools, Diocesan and Parish....3
Total Students....2,145
High Schools, Private....5
Total Students....2,898
Elementary Schools, Diocesan and Parish....26
Total Students....6,571
Elementary Schools, Private....2
Total Students....272
Non-residential Schools for the Disabled....1
Total Students....142
Catechesis/Religious Education:
High School Students....8,747
Elementary Students....25,716
Total Students under Catholic Instruction....48,878
Teachers in Diocese:
Priests....23
Brothers....2
Sisters....16
Lay Teachers....1,543

Vital Statistics
Receptions into the Church:
Infant Baptism Totals....10,532
Adult Baptism Totals....607
Received into Full Communion....337
First Communions....6,610
Confirmations....7,271
Marriages:
Catholic....1,443
Interfaith....290
Total Marriages....1,733
Deaths....2,094
Total Catholic Population....1,379,188
Total Population....4,505,229

ADMINISTRATION

Diocesan Pastoral Center - t) 214-379-2800 www.cathdal.org

Vicar General and Moderator of the Curia - Most Rev. Gregory Kelly;

Chancellor - t) 214-379-2819 chancellor@cathdal.org Gregory Caridi;

Judicial Vicar - Rev. Msgr. John P. Bell, J.C.L.;

Deans -

Central - Very Rev. John Libone;

Eastern - Very Rev. Sean Martin;

North Central - Very Rev. Edwin Leonard IV;

Northeast - Very Rev. J. Eduardo Gonzalez;

Northern - Very Rev. Michael D. Forge;

Southeast - Very Rev. Jimwell Goyo;

Southwest - Very Rev. Eugene Okoli;

Vicar for Clergy - t) 214-379-2821 Most Rev. Gregory Kelly; Rev. Arthur Unachukwu, Assoc. Dir.;

College of Consultors - Rev. Joshua Whitfield, Pres.; Very Rev. John Libone, Vice. Pres.;

Ex-Officio Members - Most Rev. Gregory Kelly; Rev. Arthur Unachukwu;

Presbyteral Council - Rev. Joshua Whitfield, Pres.; Very Rev. John Libone, Vice. Pres.;

Ex-Officio Members - t) (214) 379-2821 Most Rev. Gregory Kelly; Rev. Arthur Unachukwu;

Priest Personnel Board - Rev. Arthur Unachukwu; Rev. Michael Guadagnoli;

Priest Ongoing Formation Board - Very Rev. Michael D. Forge, Chair; Very Rev. Edwin Leonard IV; Rev. Michal Markiewicz;

Bishop's Delegate to the Religious - t) 214-379-2897 tkhirallah@cathdal.org Sr. Theresa Khirallah, S.S.N.D.;

Liaison for Statistical Data - t) 214-379-2853 Rita Gracia;

Diocesan Tribunal - t) 214-379-2840 Nwazi Nyirenda, Dir. (nnyirenda@cathdal.org);

Auditors - Elvia Ramirez;

Defensor Vinculi - John P. Gargan;

Diocesan Judges - Anne Kirby; Diane L. Barr; Lynda Robitaille;

Moderator of the Tribunal Office - Mary Margaret Hernandez;

Notaries - Maria Longoria Chavez;

Censor Librorum - Gregory Caridi, Chancellor;

OFFICES AND DIRECTORS

I. Office of the Clergy - t) 214-379-2821 Most Rev. Gregory.Kelly; Rev. Arthur Unachukwu, Assoc. Dir.;

Diaconal Ministry and Formation - t) (214) 379-2861 Rev. Emmett Hall, Dir.; Dcn. David Banowsky, Assoc. Dir.; Dcn. Vince Vaillancourt, Assoc. Dir.;

Vocations - t) 214-379-2880 Rev. Zachary Webb, Dir.; Rev. Paul Bechter, Dir.;

II. Office of the Chancellor - t) 214-379-2819 Gregory Caridi;

Archives - t) 214-379-2870

Media Relations - t) 214-379-2876 kkiser@cathdal.org Katy Kiser, Dir.;

Safe Environment Office - t) 214-379-2853 Rita Gracia, Assoc. Dir.;

Victim Assistance Coordinator - t) 214-379-2812 Barbara Landregan;

III. Chief of Staff - t) (214) 379-2800 Laura Tornaquindici;

Human Resources - t) (214) 379-2800

IV. Office of the Chief Operating Officer - t) 214-379-2844 William Keffler;

Bishop's Delegate for Ecumenism and Legislative Advocacy - t) 214-319-2854 Lynn Rossol;

Construction and Real Estate - t) (214) 379-3162

Security - t) 214-379-2811 Gilberto Garza, Dir.;

V. Office of Catholic Schools - t) (214) 379-3166 Dr. Veronica Alonzo, Assoc. Supt.;

VI. Office of the Chief Financial Officer - t) 214-379-2805 Cecilia Colbert;

Controller - t) 214-379-2814 Rachel Geoffray;

Financial Services - t) 214-379-2814 Barry Hanner, Dir.;

IT/Network - t) 214-379-2804 Ben Geeding, Dir.;

Parish Finance - Ronny Rusli, Dir.;

Risk Management / Purchasing / Claims - t) 214-379-3161 Cindy Herndon, Dir.;

Saint Raphael Retreat Center - t) 214-943-6585 Bertha De Bastiani, Dir.;

School Finance - t) 214-379-2828 Mark Lawrence, Dir.;

VII. Office of Development - t) (214) 379-3178 Kelly Halaszyn, Dir.;

VIII. The Texas Catholic and La Revista Catolica - t) 214-379-2888 www.texascatholic.com Most Rev. Edward J. Burns, Publisher; Michael Gresham, Editor (mgresham@cathdal.org); Constanza Morales, Editor;

IX. Catholic Charities of Dallas - t) 866-223-7500 Dave Woodyard, Pres.;

X. Office of Ministries and Senior Director of Ministries - t) 214-379-2896 Peter Ductram, Dir.;

Catholic Social Ministries - t) 214-379-2883 Dcn. Charles Stump Jr., Dir.;

Communications - t) (214) 379-2890 kkiser@cathdal.org Katy Kiser, Dir.;

Cultural Diversity - t) 214-379-2875 jcmoreno@cathdal.org Juan Carlos Moreno, Dir.;

Evangelization, Catechesis and Family Life - t) (214) 379-2875 jcmoreno@cathdal.org Juan Carlos Moreno, Dir.;

Worship - t) 214-379-2872 JeanneMarie Miles, Dir.;

Youth and Young Adult and Campus Ministries - t) 214-379-2867 Joshua Salinas, Dir.;

ADVISORY BOARDS, COMMISSIONS, COMMITTEES, AND COUNCILS

Finance Council - Most Rev. Edward J. Burns; Most Rev. Gregory Kelly; William Keffler;

Building Commission - William Keffler, COO; Cecilia Colbert, CFO;

PARISHES, MISSIONS, AND CLERGY

STATE OF TEXAS

ALLEN

St. Jude Catholic Parish - 1515 N. Greenville Ave., Allen, TX 75002 t) 972-727-1177 shawthorne@stjudeparish.com www.stjudeparish.com Rev. Andrew V. Semler, Pst.; Rev. Ricardo Reyes-Mata, Par. Vicar; Rev. Simeon Nwankwo, Pst. Assoc.; Dcn. John Boyle; Dcn. Ronald Fejeran; Dcn. Robert Holladay; Dcn. Al Karcher; Dcn. Craig Malone; Dcn. Kenneth Steponaitis; Julie Buchanan, DRE; CRP Stds.: 1,380

Our Lady of Angels Catholic Parish - 1914 Ridgeview Dr., Allen, TX 75013 t) 469-467-9669 pchisolm@ourladyofangels.com; fsantos@ourladyofangels.com www.ourladyofangels.com Rev. Msgr. John P. Bell, J.C.L., Pst.; Dcn. Coy Pierce; Rosemary Crocker, Pst. Assoc.; Fernando Santos, Bus. Mgr.; CRP Stds.: 420

BONHAM

St. Elizabeth Catholic Parish - Bonham - 916 Maple St., Bonham, TX 75418 t) 903-583-7734 info@se-bonham.com Rev. Delfin Condori, I.V.E., Admin.; CRP Stds.: 81

CARROLLTON

Sacred Heart of Jesus Christ Catholic Parish - 2121 N. Denton Dr., Carrollton, TX 75006 t) 972-446-3461; 469-289-7922 (CRP) info@thanhtamdallas.org; dominicppham@gmail.com thanhtamdallas.org Rev. Dominic Phuc Pham, C.Ss.R., Pst.; Trung Tran, DRE; CRP Stds.: 295

COMMERCE

St. Joseph Catholic Parish - Commerce - 2207 Monroe St., Commerce, TX 75428; Mailing: P.O. Box 832, Commerce, TX 75429 t) 903-886-7135; 903-246-3426 admasst.stj@gmail.com; frmarcus.stj@gmail.com www.stjoetx.org Rev. Marcus Chidozie, Pst.; Dcn. Joe Webber; CRP Stds.: 65

COPPELL

St. Ann Catholic Parish - Coppell - 180 Samuel Blvd., Coppell, TX 75019 t) 972-393-5544 parishoffice3@stannparish.org www.stannparish.org Very Rev. Edwin Leonard IV, Pst.; Rev. Ramiro Alvarez, Pst. Assoc.; Rev. Samuel Martinez, Pst. Assoc.; Dcn. Ron Blanton; Dcn. Eduardo Barajas; Dcn. Kory Killgo; Dcn. Pete Markwald; CRP Stds.: 1,691

CORSICANA

Immaculate Conception Catholic Parish - Corsicana - 3000 Hwy. 22 W., Corsicana, TX 75110; Mailing: P.O. Box 798, Corsicana, TX 75151 t) 903-874-4473; 903-847-4473 (CRP) jmarin@iccorsicana.org www.iccorsicana.org Rev. Juan Carlos Marin, Pst.; Dcn. Lewis J. Palos; Ana Rosas, DRE; CRP Stds.: 274

James L. Collins Catholic School - (Grades PreK-8) t) 903-872-1751 jpicha@cathdal.org James Picha, Bus. Mgr.; Stds.: 121; Lay Tchrs.: 16

DALLAS

Cathedral Santuario de Guadalupe - 2215 Ross Ave., Dallas, TX 75201 t) 214-871-1362 info@cathedralguadalupe.org; jminter@cathedralguadalupe.org www.cathedralguadalupe.org Rev. Jesus Belmontes, Rector; Rev. Mark Garrett, Par. Vicar; Dcn. Chris Volkmer; Dcn. Roberto Alvarez; Imelda Ramirez, DRE; CRP Stds.: 456

All Saints Catholic Parish - 5231 Meadowcreek, Dallas, TX 75248 t) 972-661-9282 pmuscat@allsaintsdallas.org www.allsaintsdallas.org Rev. Jovita Okoli, Pst.; Rev. Garrett Bockman, Par. Vicar; Rev. Paul Nguyen, C.Ss.R., Par. Vicar; Dcn. Robert Rayner; Dcn. Mark Venincasa; Dcn. Michael Bolesta; Dcn. Denis Simon; CRP Stds.: 530

All Saints Catholic School - (Grades PreK-8) 7777 Osage Plaza Pkwy., Dallas, TX 75252 t) 214-217-3300 www.allsaintsdallas.org/school Shana Druffner, Prin.; Colin Campbell, Pres.; Stds.: 320; Lay Tchrs.: 25

St. Anthony Catholic Parish - Dallas - 3788 Myrtle St., Dallas, TX 75215; Mailing: 2711 Romine Ave., Dallas, TX 75215 t) 214-428-6926 c) 469-556-9920 deacondenis@gmail.com holycrosscatholicdallas.org Rev. Arthur Unachukwu, Pst.; Dcn. Denis D. Corbin, Admin.; CRP Stds.: 4

St. Augustine Catholic Parish - 1054 N. St. Augustine Dr., Dallas, TX 75217 t) 214-398-1583; 214-391-6796 (CRP) churchoffice@stadallas.com stadallas.net Rev. Luca Simbula, Pst.; Rev. Herbert Sebastian Martinez, Par. Vicar; Dcn. Jorge Castillo; CRP Stds.: 496

St. Bernard of Clairvaux Catholic Parish - 1404 Old Gate Ln., Dallas, TX 75218; Mailing: 1423 San Saba Dr., Dallas, TX 75218 t) 214-321-0454; 214-321-0454 x202 (CRP) nzuniga@sbdallas.org; stbernard@sbdallas.org www.stbernards.us Rev. Luis Prado, I.V.E., Pst.; Rev. Andy Kmetz, IVE, Vicar; Elizabeth Torres, DRE; CRP Stds.: 333

St. Bernard of Clairvaux Catholic School - (Grades PreK-8) 1420 Old Gate Ln., Dallas, TX 75218 t) 214-321-2897 lsenecal@sbdallas.org stbernardccs.org/ Laurie Senecal, Prin.; Sally Walsh, Librn.; Stds.: 151; Sr. Tchrs.: 2; Lay Tchrs.: 11

Blessed Sacrament Catholic Parish - 231 N. Marsalis Ave., Dallas, TX 75203 t) 214-948-6535 lmartinez@bsdallas.org Very Rev. Jimwell Goyo, Pst.; Rev. Benito Tamez, Par. Vicar; Dcn. Jose L. Hernandez; Dcn. Christopher Paulsen; Francisco Manzo, RCIA Coord.; CRP Stds.: 107

St. Cecilia Catholic Parish - 1845 W. Davis St., Dallas, TX 75208; Mailing: 1809 W. Davis St., Dallas, TX 75208 t) 214-941-5821 info@stceciliadallas.org; dre@stceciliadallas.org stceciliadallas.org Rev. Cruz Calderon, Pst.; Rev. Ignacio Olvera, Par. Vicar; Dcn. Andres Larraza; Dcn. Gonzalo Porras; CRP Stds.: 721

St. Cecilia Catholic School - (Grades PreK-8) 635

Marycliff Rd., Dallas, TX 75208 t) 214-948-8628 ltorrez@stcecilia1935.org Lydia Torrez, Prin.; Guadalupe Moreno, Librn.; Stds.: 140; Lay Tchrs.: 15

Christ the King Catholic Parish - 8017 Preston Rd., Dallas, TX 75225 t) 214-365-1200 lninesling@ctkdallas.org www.ctkdallas.org Rev. Anthony F. Lackland, Pst.; Rev. Ryan Hiaeshutter, Par. Vicar; CRP Stds.: 414

Christ the King Catholic School - (Grades PreK-8) 4100 Colgate Ave., Dallas, TX 75225 t) 214-365-1234 posullivan@cks.org www.cks.org/ Patrick O'Sullivan, Prin.; Stds.: 474; Lay Tchrs.: 50

St. Elizabeth of Hungary Catholic Parish - 4015 S. Hampton Rd., Dallas, TX 75224 t) 214-331-4328 ghudgins@stelizabethdallas.org; miorivera@aol.com Rev. Uche Aladi, Par. Vicar; Rev. Emmett Hall, Admin.; Dcn. Paul Williams; Elizabeth Seidemann, DRE; CRP Stds.: 109

St. Elizabeth of Hungary Catholic School - (Grades PreK-8) 4019 S. Hampton Rd., Dallas, TX 75224 t) 214-331-5139 stelizabethpastor@gmail.com saintspride.com Jennifer Borth, Prin.; Monica Connelly, Librn.; Stds.: 184; Lay Tchrs.: 20

Holy Cross Catholic Parish - 5004 Bonnie View Rd., Dallas, TX 75241; Mailing: 4910 Bonnie View Rd., Dallas, TX 75241 frarthur@holycrosscathdal.org; deacondenis@holycrosscathdal.org www.holycrosscatholicdallas.org Rev. Arthur Unachukwu, Pst.; Rev. Elmer Herrera Guzman, Par. Vicar; Dcn. Salvador Pina; Paula Martinez, DRE; Dcn. Randy Nease; CRP Stds.: 552

Holy Trinity Catholic Parish - 3811 Oak Lawn Ave., Dallas, TX 75219; Mailing: 3826 Gilbert Ave., Dallas, TX 75219 t) 214-526-8555 general@htccd.org; ecooper@htccd.org www.htccd.org Rev. Milton Ryan, C.M., Pst.; Dcn. Roberto Loera; CRP Stds.: 120

Holy Trinity Catholic School - (Grades PreK-8) 3815 Oak Lawn Ave., Dallas, TX 75219 t) 214-526-5113 mdavis@htcsdallas.org; ccrutcher@htcsdallas.org www.htcsdallas.org Marion Davis, Prin.; Nina Little, Librn.; Stds.: 135; Lay Tchrs.: 19

St. James Catholic Church - 1002 E. Saner Ave., Dallas, TX 75216; Mailing: P.O. Box 763338, Dallas, TX 75376 t) 214-371-9209; (214) 371-9256 faithformation@stjamescath.org; secretary@stjamescath.org www.stjamescath.org Rev. Mauricio Sosa, M.N.M., Pst.; Rev. Dario Clara Giron, M.N.M. (Mexico), Par. Vicar; Dcn. Vincent F. Jimenez; Dcn. Filemon Villegas; Juan Calixto, DRE; Eduardo Rendon, Bus. Mgr.; Jenny Elizabeth Villegas Toledo, Contact; CRP Stds.: 567

St. Jude Chapel - 1521 Main St., Dallas, TX 75201 t) (214) 742-2508 info@stjudechapel.org stjudechapel.org Rev. Stephen W. Bierschenk, Chap.; Augustine Jalomo, Bus. Mgr.;

Mary Immaculate Catholic Parish - 2800 Valwood Pkwy., Dallas, TX 75234 t) 972-243-7104 aliciag@maryimmaculatechurch.org www.maryimmaculatechurch.org Rev. Alfonse Nazzaro, Pst.; Rev. Jean-Lou Marrel Franck Agbowai, Par. Vicar; Rev. Aristeo Berrum, Par. Vicar; Dcn. William Mejia; Dcn. Dennis Duffin; Dcn. David Dusse; CRP Stds.: 718

Mary Immaculate Catholic School - (Grades K-8) 14032 Dennis Ln., Dallas, TX 75234 t) 972-243-7105 srmaryanne@mischool.org Sr. Mary Anne Zuberbueler, O.P., Prin.; Stds.: 385; Sr. Tchrs.: 3; Lay Tchrs.: 27

St. Mary of Carmel Catholic Parish - 2900 Vilbig Rd., Dallas, TX 75212 t) 214-747-1433 secsmc@gmail.com smcparishdallas.org/ Rev. Jenaro de la Cruz, OCD, Pst.; Rev. James A. Curiel, OCD, Par. Vicar; CRP Stds.: 210

St. Monica Catholic Parish - 9933 Midway Rd., Dallas, TX 75220 t) 214-358-1453 info@stmonicachurch.org www.stmonicachurch.org Rev. Michael Guadagnoli, Pst.; Rev. Elijiah Thomson, Par. Vicar; Dcn. Abel Cortes; Dcn. Peter Raad; Dcn. Daryl Avery; CRP Stds.: 397

St. Monica Catholic School - (Grades PreK-8) 4140 Walnut Hill Ln., Dallas, TX 75229 t) 214-351-5688 atrudell@stmonicaschool.org www.stmonicaschool.org Stds.: 744; Lay Tchrs.: 56

Nuestra Senora del Pilar - 4455 W. Illinois Ave., Dallas, TX 75211 t) 214-467-9116 info@nspdallas.org www.nuestrasenoradelpilar.com Rev. Branimir Pavelin, Par. Vicar; Roshan Fernandes, Admin.; CRP Stds.: 568

Our Lady of Lourdes Catholic Parish - 5605 Bernal Dr., Dallas, TX 75212 t) 214-637-6673; 214-678-0487 (CRP) lourdesdallas@tx.rr.com www.lourdesdallas.org/ Friar Pedro Romero, OFM Cap., Pst.; Friar Angel Rios, OFM. Cap, Assoc. Pst.; Dcn. Greg Burciaga; CRP Stds.: 205

Our Lady of Perpetual Help Catholic Parish - 7617 Cortland Ave, Dallas, TX 75235 t) 214-352-6012 olph@olphdallas.org www.olphdallas.org Rev. Giuseppe Spoto, Par. Admin.; Dcn. Jose Ocaña; Rev. Msgr. Milam Joseph, Pastor Emer.; Rev. Rafael M. Ramirez, S.S.D., In Res.; CRP Stds.: 300

Our Lady of Perpetual Help Catholic School - (Grades PreK-8) 7625 Cortland Ave., Dallas, TX 75235 t) 214-351-3396 info@olphdallas.org Maria Searle, Prin.; Stds.: 161; Sr. Tchrs.: 3; Lay Tchrs.: 14

Daughters of the Sacred Heart - 7617 Cortland Ave., Dallas, TX 75235 t) 214-351-4338 molkdsh@gmail.com Sr. Molly Kurin, Supr.;

Quasi-Parish of Our Lady of San Juan De Los Lagos - St. Theresa - 2601 Singleton Blvd., Dallas, TX 75212 t) 214-631-9627; 214-688-0942 (CRP) susanna.ramirez@gpisd.org; hsalinas78132@hotmail.com www.olsanjuandallas.org Dcn. Hugo A. Salinas, Admin.; Susanna Ramirez, DRE; CRP Stds.: 91

St. Patrick Catholic Parish - Dallas - 9643 Ferndale Rd., Dallas, TX 75238 t) 214-348-7380 office@spccdallas.org www.spccdallas.org Rev. Charles Githinji, Pst.; Rev. Adam Musielak, Par. Vicar; Dcn. David Banowsky; Dcn. Doug Breckenridge; Dcn. Timothy J. Vineyard; Rev. Josef Vollmer-Konig, In Res.; CRP Stds.: 477

St. Patrick Catholic School - (Grades PreK-8) 9635 Ferndale Rd., Dallas, TX 75238 t) 214-348-8070 jhendry@spsdallas.org www.stpatrickschool.org Julie Hendry, Prin.; Stds.: 438; Lay Tchrs.: 32

St. Peter the Apostle Catholic Parish - 2907 Woodall Rodgers Fwy., Dallas, TX 75204 t) 214-855-1384 saintpeter@stpeterdal.com www.stpeterdal.com Rev. Jacek Wesolowski, SChr, Pst.; Marcella Savala-Hamilton, DRE; Linda M Dugo, Bus. Mgr.; CRP Stds.: 26

St. Peter Vietnamese Catholic Parish - 10123 Garland Rd., Dallas, TX 75218 t) 214-321-9493 mjpcm@sbcglobal.net Rev. Pham M. Joseph, C.M., Pst.; Rev. Minh J. Pham, C.M., Pst.; CRP Stds.: 60

St. Philip the Apostle Catholic Parish - 8131 Military Pkwy., Dallas, TX 75227 t) 214-388-5464 clazo@stphilipcatholicchurch.org www.stphilipcatholicchurch.org Very Rev. J. Eduardo Gonzalez, Pst.; Dcn. Asuncion Gloria; Sr. Carmen Lazo, S.S.N.D., DRE; CRP Stds.: 74

St. Pius X Catholic Parish - 3030 Gus Thomasson Rd., Dallas, TX 75228 t) 972-279-6155 cpierotti@spxdallas.org www.spxdallas.org Rev. Salvador Guzman, Pst.; Rev. Paul Mallam, Par. Vicar; Dcn. Francis Huynh; Dcn. Victor Manuel Medrano; Dcn. Victor Carpio; CRP Stds.: 515

St. Pius X Catholic School - (Grades PreK-8) t) 972-279-2339 tscott@spxdallas.org Margaret White, Admin.; Stephanie Garza, Prin.; Stds.: 182; Lay Tchrs.: 20

St. Rita Catholic Parish - 12521 Inwood Rd., Dallas, TX 75244 t) 972-934-8388 sbrockett@stritaparish.net www.stritaparish.net Rev. Joshua Whitfield, Admin.; Rev. Michael Baynham, Par. Vicar; Dcn. Bill Fobes; Dcn. Chris Knight; Dcn. Robert McDermott; Dcn. Charles T. Sylvester; Paul Vetter; CRP Stds.: 450

St. Rita Catholic School - (Grades PreK-8) 12525 Inwood Rd., Dallas, TX 75244 t) 972-239-3203 mwixted@strita.net www.strita.net Michael Wixted, Prin.; Emmy Robison, Vice Prin.; Sonbol Mannas, Registrar; Stds.: 780; Lay Tchrs.: 52

San Juan Diego Catholic Parish - 10919 Royal Haven Ln., Dallas, TX 75229 t) 214-271-4691 lfrausto@sanjuandiegodallas.org www.sanjuandiegodallas.org Rev. Daniel Rendon, Admin.; Rev. Juan R. Torres, Par. Vicar; Lupita Frausto, DRE; Maria Martinez, DRE; CRP Stds.: 1,567

Santa Clara of Assisi Catholic Parish - 321 Calumet Ave., Dallas, TX 75211; Mailing: P.O. Box 210 888, Dallas, TX 75211 t) 214-337-3936 info@santaclararcc.org santaclaracatholicchurch.org/ Rev. Paolo Capra, Pst.; Rev. Artemio Patino, Pst. Assoc.; Dcn. Felicito Laguna; CRP Stds.: 640

Santa Clara of Assisi Catholic Academy - (Grades PreK-8) t) 214-333-9423 kmartinez@santaclaraacademy.org Alejandra Gonzalez, Admin.; Kristy Martinez, Prin.; Stds.: 203; Lay Tchrs.: 14

St. Edward Catholic Parish - 4001 Elm St., Dallas, TX 75226; Mailing: 4014 Simpson St., Dallas, TX 75246 t) 214-823-1291; 214-887-1484 (CRP) mpicazorendon@stedwardparish.org; cservin@stedwardparish.org www.stedwardparish.org Rev. Antonio Liberman-Ormaza, Vicar; Rev. Edison Vela, Par. Admin.; Dcn. Rafael Andrade; Dcn. Ricardo Riojas; CRP Stds.: 312

St. Thomas Aquinas Catholic Parish - 6306 Kenwood Ave., Dallas, TX 75214 t) 214-821-3360; 469-930-5532 (CRP) campise@stadallas.org; antosh@stadallas.org www.stthomasaquinas.org Very Rev. John Libone, Pst.; Dcn. Anthony J. Campise; Dcn. Kenneth Reisor; Brandon Barker, DRE; Rev. Luke Turner, OSB, Par. Vicar; CRP Stds.: 365

St. Thomas Aquinas Catholic School - Upper School - (Grades 3-8) 3741 Abrams Rd., Dallas, TX 75214 t) 214-826-0566 jwatts@staschool.org Jenn Watts, Prin.; Patrick Magee, Pres.; Stds.: 529; Lay Tchrs.: 34

St. Thomas Aquinas Catholic School - Lower School - (Grades PreK-2) 6255 E. Mockingbird, Dallas, TX 75214 t) 469-341-0911 lroberts@staschool.org Lauren Roberts, Prin.; Patrick Magee, Pres.; Stds.: 334; Lay Tchrs.: 34

DENISON

St. Patrick Catholic Parish - Denison - 314 N. Rusk Ave., Denison, TX 75020 t) 903-463-3275 parishoffice@saintpats.net www.saintpats.net Rev. Stephen J. Mocio, Pst.; Kelly Chaffin, DRE; Lisa Linnebur, Bus. Mgr.; CRP Stds.: 71

DUNCANVILLE

Holy Spirit Catholic Parish - 1111 W. Danieldale Rd., Duncanville, TX 75137-3719 t) 972-298-4971 leonardozapata@holyspiritcc.org holyspiritcatholic.com Very Rev. Eugene Okoli, Pst.; Rev. Esteban D. Antes, Par. Vicar; Dcn. Al Evans; Dcn. Gene Freeman; Dcn. Charles Ruelas; Dcn. Paul Wood; Deborah Pearson, DRE; CRP Stds.: 500

ENNIS

St. John Nepomucene Catholic Parish - 401 E. Lampasas St., Ennis, TX 75119 t) 972-875-2834 joannag@stjohncc.net; marial@stjohncc.net stjohncc.net Rev. John Dick, Pst.; Rev. Agustin Fuertes, Par. Vicar; Dcn. Don Campbell; Dcn. Don Griffith; Kaleb Trojacek, Youth Min.; Karim Sullivan, DRE; CRP Stds.: 538

FERRIS

Corpus Christi Catholic Parish - 111 N. Wood St., Ferris, TX 75125 t) 972-544-2161 corpuschristiferris@yahoo.com; financeofficecccc@yahoo.com corpuschristiferris.org Rev. Manuel Sabando, Admin.; Dcn. Jose Muniz; CRP Stds.: 112

FORNEY

St. Martin of Tours Catholic Parish - 9470 CR 213, Forney, TX 75126 t) 972-564-9114 office@stmartinforney.org; faithformation@stmartinforney.org www.stmartinforney.org Rev. Patrick Olaleye, Par. Admin.; Dcn. Robert J. Catalano; Dorothy Morgan,

DRE; CRP Stds.: 255

FRISCO

St. Francis of Assisi Catholic Parish - Frisco - 8000 Eldorado Pkwy., Frisco, TX 75033 t) 972-712-2645 office@stfoafrisco.org www.stfoafrisco.org Rev. Rodolfo Garcia, Pst.; Rev. Robert Brawanski, Par. Vicar; Rev. Joseph C. Lee, Par. Vicar; Rev. Bartholomew Onyeka Nwafor (Nigeria), Par. Vicar; Dcn. Martin Armendariz; Dcn. Alex Barbieri; Dcn. John R. Costello; Dcn. Francisco Gomez; Dcn. Gregg Kahrs; Dcn. Saul Vazquez; Dcn. Henry Wiechman; CRP Stds.: 1,361

GARLAND

Good Shepherd Catholic Parish - 1304 Main St., Garland, TX 75040; Mailing: 1224 Main St., Garland, TX 75040 t) 972-276-8587 info@gschurch.org www.gschurch.org Rev. Israel Gonzalez, Pst.; Rev. Jose Luis Esparza, F.N., Par. Vicar; Rev. Javier D Ramirez, FN (Mexico), Par. Vicar; Dcn. Jim Harris; Dcn. Jose E. Lopez; Dcn. Oscar Morales; Patricia Rodriguez, DRE; CRP Stds.: 1,237

Good Shepherd Catholic School - (Grades PreSchool-8) 214 S. Garland Ave., Garland, TX 75040 t) 972-272-6533 grichardsonbassett@gscschool.org www.gscschool.org Gail R. Bassett, Prin.; Stds.: 212; Lay Tchrs.: 15

St. Michael the Archangel Catholic Parish - Garland - 950 Trails Pkwy., Garland, TX 75043 t) 972-279-6581 x101 parishoffice@stmichaelgarland.org www.stmichaelgarland.org Rev. Joseph A. Mehan Jr., Pst.; Rev. Martin Mwangi, Par. Vicar; Dcn. Andrew Pena; Sherri Williams, DRE; CRP Stds.: 255

Mother of Perpetual Help Catholic Parish - 2121 W. Apollo Rd., Garland, TX 75044 t) 972-414-7073 dmhcggarland@gmail.com dmhcg.org Rev. Paul Hai Nguyen, C.Ss.R., Pst.; CRP Stds.: 665

GRAND PRAIRIE

Immaculate Conception Catholic Parish - Grand Prairie - 610 N.E. 17th St., Grand Prairie, TX 75050 t) 972-262-5137; 972-264-8385 (CRP) fhawkins@icgrandprairie.org; tadames@icgrandprairie.org icgrandprairie.org/ Rev. Joseph Son Van Nguyen, Pst.; Rev. Luis Fermin Sierra, Par. Vicar; Dcn. David Maida; Teresa Adames, DRE; CRP Stds.: 306

Immaculate Conception Catholic School - (Grades PreK-8) 400 N.E. 17th St., Grand Prairie, TX 75050 t) 972-264-8777 lsantos@icgrandprairie.org school.icgrandprairie.org Linda Santos, Prin.; Stds.: 129; Sr. Tchrs.: 1; Lay Tchrs.: 10

St. Joseph Vietnamese Parish - 1902 S. Beltline Rd., Grand Prairie, TX 75051 t) 972-237-1700 f_bui@dallascatholic.org Rev. Francis Quyet Bui, S.D.D., Pst.; CRP Stds.: 289

St. Michael the Archangel Catholic Parish - Grand Prairie - 2910 Corn Valley Rd., Grand Prairie, TX 75052 t) 972-262-0552; 972-262-6590 (CRP) mary@stmichaelgptx.org; anabel@stmichaelgptx.org www.stmichaelgptx.org Rev. Marco Rangel, Pst.; Dcn. Boy Arocha; Dcn. J. Robert Miller; Dcn. Pete Rodriguez; CRP Stds.: 600

GREENVILLE

St. William Catholic Parish - 4300 Stuart St., Greenville, TX 75401 t) 903-450-1177 office@stwilliamconfessor.org www.saintwilliamtheconfessor.org Rev. Robert Williams, Pst.; Dcn. Marco Antonio Cruz; Dcn. James Starr;

IRVING

St. Andrew Kim Catholic Parish - 2111 Camino Lago, Irving, TX 75039 t) 972-620-9150 c) 469-835-5923 office@dallaskoreancatholic.org; helenmko@gmail.com www.dallaskoreancatholic.org Rev. Nam Gil Andrew Kim, Pst.; Dcn. John Lee; John S. Lee, DRE; CRP Stds.: 113

Church of the Incarnation - 1845 E. Northgate Dr., Irving, TX 75062 t) 972-721-5375 udcampmin@udallas.edu udallas.edu/church Church on the University of Dallas Campus. Rev. Joseph Paul Albin, O.P., Rector;

Holy Family of Nazareth Catholic Parish - 2323 Cheyenne St., Irving, TX 75062; Mailing: 2330 Cheyenne St., Irving, TX 75062 t) 972-252-5521 info@holyfamilychurch.net www.holyfamilychurch.net Rev. Jacob Dankasa, Pst.; Rev. Joshua Mavelil (India), Par. Vicar; Dcn. James Glynn Baird; Dcn. George Chou; Dcn. Larry Harmon; Dcn. Ron Morgan; Rose Blake; Bus. Mgr.; Christie McGee, DRE; Michelangelo Serapio, Youth Min.; CRP Stds.: 337

Holy Family Catholic Academy - (Grades PreK-8) t) 972-255-0205 admin@hfca-irving.org www.hfca-irving.org Kathryn Carruth, Prin.; Stds.: 140; Sr. Tchrs.: 1; Lay Tchrs.: 14

St. Luke Catholic Parish - 1015 Schulze Dr., Irving, TX 75060 t) 972-259-3222; 972-259-1832 (CRP) mary.osullivan@stlukeirving.org www.stlukeirving.org Rev. Ernesto Esqueda Sanchez, Pst.; Rev. Hap Tran, C.S. (Vietnam), Par. Vicar; Rev. Richard Bezzegato, C.S., Par. Vicar; Bro. Raul Ochoa Encinas, C.S., DRE; Dcn. Jose Trevino; Dcn. Patrick Lamers; Dcn. Daniel D. Segovia; Sr. Irene Dinh, CMR, DRE; Antonia Morales, CRE; CRP Stds.: 1,181

Mater Dei Personal Parish - 2030 E. Hwy. 356, Irving, TX 75060 t) 972-438-7600; 972-793-0484 (CRP) info@materdeiparish.com www.materdeiparish.com Rev. Peter Bauknecht, Pst.; Rev. Michael Cunningham, Par. Vicar; Rev. Brian McDonnell, Par. Vicar; Rev. David Ramirez, Par. Vicar; Rev. James Buckley, In Res.; CRP Stds.: 24

ITALY

Epiphany Catholic Parish - 434 S. Ward, Italy, TX 76651; Mailing: 401 E. Lampasas St., Ennis, TX 75119 t) 972-875-2834 marial@stjohncc.net; joannag@stjohncc.net Rev. John Dick, Pst.; Rev. Agustin Fuertes, Par. Vicar; Karim Sullivan, DRE; CRP Stds.: 51

KAUFMAN

St. Ann Catholic Parish - Kaufman - 806 N. Washington St., Kaufman, TX 75142 t) 972-962-3247 jmb4church@mycvc.net; pclsapkau@mycvc.net Rev. Henry Erazo, Pst.; Dcn. Michael Friske; Alma Sipriano, DRE; CRP Stds.: 288

LANCASTER

St. Francis of Assisi Catholic Parish - Lancaster - 1537 Rogers Ave., Lancaster, TX 75134 t) 972-227-4124; 972-227-0770 (CRP) stfranparoff@att.net; business.office@stfrancislancaster.org www.stfrancislancaster.org Rev. Joseph Hoa Duc Trinh; Dcn. Sergio Carranza; Dcn. Ben Rodriguez; Dcn. Lawrence Seidemann; CRP Stds.: 323

MCKINNEY

St. Gabriel the Archangel Catholic Parish - 110 St. Gabriel Way, McKinney, TX 75071 t) 972-542-7170 generalmailbox@stgabriel.org www.stgabriel.org Rev. Donald Zeiler, Pst.; Dcn. David Rekieta; Dcn. Shawn French; Dcn. Barry Schliesmann; Rev. Cristian Casado (Spain), Par. Vicar; Dcn. John Rapier; CRP Stds.: 887

St. Michael Catholic Parish - McKinney - 652 Redbud Blvd., McKinney, TX 75069; Mailing: 411 Paula Rd., McKinney, TX 75069 t) 972-542-4667 stmichael@stmichaelmckinney.org www.stmichaelmckinney.org Rev. Jet Garcia, Pst.; Rev. Desmond Ndikum, Par. Vicar; Rev. Peter Chinnappan, Par. Vicar; Dcn. Sidney Little; Dcn. George Polcer; Dcn. Luis Feliciano; Dcn. Andrew Tanner; Dcn. Anthony Trippi; Dcn. Jose Vazquez; CRP Stds.: 516

MESQUITE

Divine Mercy of Our Lord Catholic Parish - 1585 E. Cartwright Rd., Mesquite, TX 75149 t) 972-591-5294; 972-591-5294 x228 (CRP) carmen@divinemercytx.org; faithformation@divinemercytx.org Very Rev. Wilmer de Jesus Daza, Pst.; Rev. Gil Mediana, Vicar; Dcn. Ismael Reyes; CRP Stds.: 139

PLANO

St. Elizabeth Ann Seton Catholic Parish - 2700 W. Spring Creek Pkwy., Plano, TX 75023; Mailing: 2701 Piedra Dr., Plano, TX 75023 t) 972-596-5505 bbaumann@eseton.org; sozowski@eseton.org www.setonparish.org Very Rev. Bruce Bradley, Pst.; Rev. Sinu Puthenpurackal Joseph, Par. Vicar; Rev. Tuan Lee, Par. Vicar; Dcn. Michael Seibold; Dcn. Vince Vaillancourt; Dcn. Norm Smith; Dcn. Paul Viramontes; Bruce Baumann, DRE; CRP Stds.: 514

St. Mark the Evangelist Catholic Parish - 1105 W. 15th St., Plano, TX 75075 t) 972-423-5600 vfonseca@stmarkplano.org www.stmarkplano.org Very Rev. Jason Cargo, Pst.; Rev. Jack W. Hopka, Par. Vicar; Rev. Michael Likoudis, Par. Vicar; Rev. Ricardo Regalado, Par. Vicar; Dcn. Dominic T. Hoang; Dcn. Luis Garzon; Dcn. Juan Jorge Hernandez; Dcn. Gabriel Hernandez; Dcn. Luis Boy; Dcn. Fred Rotchford; CRP Stds.: 926

St. Mark Catholic School - (Grades PreK-8) 1201 Alma Dr., Plano, TX 75075 t) 972-578-0610 patricia.opon@stmcs.net www.stmcs.net Patricia Opon, Prin.; Stds.: 456; Lay Tchrs.: 60

Prince of Peace Catholic Parish - 5100 W. Plano Pkwy., Plano, TX 75093 t) 972-380-2100 mcmarinoni@popplano.org www.popplano.org Very Rev. Michael D. Forge, Pst.; Rev. Lucas Moreira de Sales, Par. Vicar; Dcn. Joe Coleman; Dcn. John Gorman; Dcn. Scott Johnson; Dcn. John O'Leary; CRP Stds.: 254

Prince of Peace Catholic School - (Grades PreK-8) t) 972-380-5505 mjones@popschool.net Mary Catherine Marinoni, Contact; Stds.: 763; Lay Tchrs.: 84

Sacred Heart of Jesus Catholic Parish - Plano - 4201 14th St., Plano, TX 75074 t) 972-516-8500 communication@chinese-catholic.org www.chinese-catholic.org Rev. Vincent Lin Yu Ming, Pst.; CRP Stds.: 29

QUINLAN

Our Lady of Fatima Catholic Parish - 1579 E. Quinlan Pkwy., Quinlan, TX 75474; Mailing: 4300 Stuart St., Greenville, TX 75401 t) 903-450-1177 office@stwilliamconfessor.org Rev. Robert Williams, Pst.;

RICHARDSON

St. Joseph Catholic Parish - Richardson - 600 S. Jupiter Rd., Richardson, TX 75081 t) 972-231-2951; 972-690-5588 (CRP) receptionist@stjosephcc.net www.josephcatholic.org Rev. Stephen Ingram, Par. Admin.; Rev. Felipe Vives, Par. Vicar; Rev. Joseph Nedumankuzhiyil, In Res.; Dcn. Randall L. Engel; Dcn. Michael Hastings; Dcn. Richard Nelson; Dcn. Hector Rodriguez; CRP Stds.: 609

St. Joseph Catholic School - (Grades K-8) t) 972-692-4594 fthompson@stjosephccschool.net Fran Thompson, Prin.; Stds.: 223; Lay Tchrs.: 24

St. Paul the Apostle Catholic Parish - 720 S. Floyd Rd., Richardson, TX 75080; Mailing: 900 St. Paul Dr., Richardson, TX 75080 t) 972-235-6105 (Office); 972-235-2598 (CRP) linda@saintpaulchurch.org; rbuchanan@saintpaulchurch.org www.saintpaulchurch.org Rev. John Szatkowski, Pst.; Rev. Ruben Ortiz-Montelongo, Par. Vicar; Dcn. Bob Bonomi; Ryan Buchanan, Pst. Min./Coord.; CRP Stds.: 293

St. Paul the Apostle Catholic School - (Grades PreK-8) t) 972-235-3263 c.demakas@spsdfw.org Courtney DeMakas, Prin.; Stds.: 120; Lay Tchrs.: 12

ROCKWALL

Our Lady of the Lake Catholic Parish - 1305 Damascus Rd., Rockwall, TX 75087 t) 972-961-9384 (CRP); 972-771-6671; 972-961-9373 pcl@ourladyrockwall.org; receptionist@ourladyrockwall.org www.ourladyrockwall.org Rev. Sean Charles Martin, Pst.; Rev. Antonio Hernandez, Par. Vicar; Dcn. Charles Stump Jr.; Dcn. Steve Marcoe; Dcn. Randy Wilson; Dcn. Oscar Miranda; Sara Campbell, DRE; CRP Stds.: 786

ROWLETT

Sacred Heart Catholic Parish - 3905 Hickox Rd., Rowlett, TX 75089 t) 972-475-4405 x5 (Parish Office) c) (214) 444-1195 (Emergency Last Rites) parishoffice@sacredheartrowlett.org www.sacredheartrowlett.org Rev. Inigo Lopez, Par. Admin.; Rev. Robinson Agbadugo, Par. Vicar; Dcn. Jack Hopkins; Dcn. Leo Cortinas III; Dcn. Ruben Vargas; Dcn. Kenneth Melston; Nancy Hampton, DRE; CRP Stds.: 224

SHERMAN

St. Mary Catholic Parish - 727 S. Travis, Sherman, TX 75090 t) 903-893-5148 ndobbs@stmarych.org; dpurcell@stmarych.org www.stmarych.org Rev. Martin Castañeda, Pst.; Rev. Merlito Abiog, Par. Vicar; Dcn. Jim Adlof; Dcn. Chris Schraeder; Dcn. Albert Miller; Dawn Purcell, DRE; CRP Stds.: 320

St. Mary Catholic School - (Grades PreK-8) 713 Travis St., Sherman, TX 75090 t) 903-893-2127 dledbetter@stmarys-sch.org www.stmarys-sch.org Dr. Danny Ledbetter, Prin.; Stds.: 167; Lay Tchrs.: 12

TERRELL

St. John the Apostle Catholic Parish - 702 N. Frances St., Terrell, TX 75160 t) 972-563-3643; 972-524-8610 (CRP) chsectr701@sbcglobal.net; michellegobert@sbcglobal.net Rev. James P. Orosco, Pst.; Michelle Gobert, DRE; CRP Stds.: 362

VAN ALSTYNE

Holy Family Catholic Parish - 919 Spence Rd., Van Alstyne, TX 75495; Mailing: PO Box 482, Van Alstyne, TX 75495 t) 903-482-6322 office@holyfamily-vanalstyne.org www.holyfamily-vanalstyne.org Rev. Jet Garcia, Pst.; Rev. Desmond Ndikum, Par. Vicar; Rev. Peter Chinnappan, Par. Vicar; Dcn. Patrick Hayes; CRP Stds.: 173

WAXAHACHIE

St. Joseph Catholic Parish - Waxahachie - 609 Kaufman St., Waxahachie, TX 75165 t) 972-938-1953 receptionist@stjosephwaxahachie.com; formation@stjosephwaxahachie.com www.saintjosephwaxahachie.com Rev. James Yamauchi, Pst.; Dcn. John Waedekin; CRP Stds.: 521

St. Joseph Catholic School - (Grades 9-12) 506 E. Marvin St., Waxahachie, TX 75165 t) 972-937-0956 www.stjosephwaxahachie.com Autumn Helland, Prin.; Penny Walden, Librn.; Stds.: 182; Lay Tchrs.: 17

WHITESBORO

St. Francis of Assisi Catholic Parish - Whitesboro - 807 N. Union, Whitesboro, TX 76273; Mailing: 727 S Travis St, Sherman, TX 75090 t) 903-893-5148 ndobbs@stmarych.org; dpurcell@stmarych.org stfachurch.org/ Rev. Merlito Abiog, Par. Vicar; Dawn Purcell, DRE; CRP Stds.: 86

WYLIE

St. Anthony Catholic Parish - Wylie - 404 N. Ballard Ave., Wylie, TX 75098 t) 972-442-2765 frtony@saint-anthony.com; debbie@saint-anthony.com Rev. Anthony M. Densmore, Pst.; Rev. Francisco Orozco, O.C.D., Par. Vicar; Dcn. Greg Hawley; Dcn. Federico Marquez; CRP Stds.: 500

SCHOOLS: PRESCHOOL THRU HIGH SCHOOL

SCHOOLS

STATE OF TEXAS

DALLAS

St. Mary of Carmel School, Inc. - (PAR) (Grades PreK-8) 1716 Singleton Blvd., Dallas, TX 75212 t) 214-748-2934 rita.deleon@smcschool.org smcschool.org/ Kaetlyn Aguilar, Prin.; Stds.: 165; Lay Tchrs.: 17

Mount Carmel Center - 4600 W. Davis St., Dallas, TX 75211-3498 t) 214-331-6224 admin@mountcarmelcenter.org; executivedirector@carmelitefriarsocd.com www.mountcarmelcenter.org Adult Center for Catholic Spirituality. (Discalced Carmelite Fathers Dallas, Inc.) Friar John Suenram, OCD, Dir.; Friar Marion Bui, OCD, Mem.; Rev. James A. Curiel, OCD, Mem.; Pr. Tchrs.: 3

***Mount St. Michael Catholic School** - (PRV) (Grades PreK-8) 4500 W. Davis St., Dallas, TX 75211; Mailing: P.O. Box 225159, Dallas, TX 75222-5159 t) 214-337-0244 info@msmcatholic.org www.msmcatholic.org Melissa Castro, Prin.; Stds.: 126; Lay Tchrs.: 10

Notre Dame of Dallas Schools, Inc. - (PRV) (Grades 1-12) 2018 Allen St., Dallas, TX 75204 t) 214-720-3911 cobrien@notredameschool.org www.notredameschool.org Day School: for children with developmental disabilities, ages 6-15. & Vocational Center. Dr. Caroline O'Brien, Pres.; Carmen Fernandez, Prin.; Stds.: 162; Lay Tchrs.: 35

St. Philip & St. Augustine Catholic Academy, Inc. - (Grades PreK-8) 8151 Military Pkwy., Dallas, TX 75227 t) 214-381-4973 sshirley@spsacatholic.org spsacatholic.org Dianne Brungardt, Prin.; Stds.: 288; Lay Tchrs.: 41

HIGH SCHOOLS

STATE OF TEXAS

DALLAS

Bishop Dunne Catholic School, Inc. - (DIO) (Grades 6-12) 3900 Rugged Dr., Dallas, TX 75224 t) 214-339-6561 mmarchiony@bdcs.org; kperry@bdcs.org www.bdcs.org (Coed) Kathryn Perry, Admin.; Mary Beth Marchiony, Pres.; Melanie Gibson, Librn.; Stds.: 416; Lay Tchrs.: 35

Bishop Lynch High School, Inc. - (DIO) 9750 Ferguson Rd., Dallas, TX 75228 t) 214-324-3607 jennifer.adamcik@bishoplynch.org www.bishoplynch.org Chad Riley, Prin.; Christopher Rebuck, Pres.; Alison Bednarczyk, Librn.; Stds.: 1,008; Lay Tchrs.: 69

***Cristo Rey Dallas High School, Inc.** - (PRV) (Grades 9-12) 9701 San Leon, Dallas, TX 75217 t) 469-844-7956 sgarza@cristoreydallas.org cristoreydallas.org Sylvia Garza, Academic Mgr./Registrar; Stds.: 425; Lay Tchrs.: 36

Jesuit College Preparatory School - (PRV) (Grades 9-12) 12345 Inwood Rd., Dallas, TX 75244 t) 972-387-8700 mearsing@jesuitcp.org; connect@jesuitcp.org www.jesuitdallas.org (Boys) Society of Jesus. Michael A. Earsing, Pres.; Thomas Garrison, Prin.; Stds.: 1,141; Lay Tchrs.: 139

Ursuline Academy of Dallas, Inc. - (PRV) 4900 Walnut Hill Ln., Dallas, TX 75229-6599 t) 469-232-1800 gkane@ursulinedallas.org www.ursulinedallas.org (Girls) Elizabeth Smith, Dean; Andrea Shurley, Prin.; Gretchen Z. Kane, Pres.; Jim Koehler, Bus. Mgr.; Stds.: 878; Lay Tchrs.: 112

IRVING

C Preparatory (Cistercian Preparatory School) - (PRV) (Grades 5-12) 3660 Cistercian Rd., Irving, TX 75039 t) 469-499-5400 fr-paul@cistercian.org Rev. Paul McCormick, O.Cist., Headmaster; Stds.: 356; Pr. Tchrs.: 12; Lay Tchrs.: 38

The Highlands School - (PRV) (Grades PreK-12) 1451 E. Northgate Dr., Irving, TX 75062 t) 972-554-1980 info@thehighlandsschool.org www.thehighlandsschool.org Veronica Moreno, Exec. Dir.; Stds.: 352; Lay Tchrs.: 30

PLANO

John Paul II High School, Inc. - 900 Coit Rd., Plano, TX 75075 t) 972-867-0005 brianmcpheeters@johnpauliihs.org; doreenhewes@johnpauliihs.org www.johnpauliihs.org Dr. Marlene Hammerle, Prin.; Robert Gharis, Dir.; Stds.: 700; Sr. Tchrs.: 1; Lay Tchrs.: 60

CAMPUS MINISTRY / NEWMAN CENTERS [CAM]

DALLAS

Catholic Campus Ministry at Southern Methodist University - 3057 University Blvd., Neuhoff Catholic Student Ctr., Dallas, TX 75205 t) 214-987-0044 smucatholic@smu.edu smucatholic.org Rev. Wade Bass, Chap.;

IRVING

University of Dallas - Campus Ministry - 1845 E. Northgate Dr., Irving, TX 75062 t) 972-721-5375 tbarba@udallas.edu www.udallas.edu

RICHARDSON

Catholic Center on Campbell - 2105 Waterview Pkwy., Richardson, TX 75080; Mailing: P.O. Box 190507, Dallas, TX 75219 t) 214-862-4831 bhanner@cathdal.org Rev. Tymoteusz Ksiazkiewicz, Chap.; Dcn. Timothy M. Bray, Campus Min.; Dcn. Kevin Lovett, Campus Min.;

University Catholic Center at UT Dallas - 2105 Waterview Pkwy, Richardson, TX 75080; Mailing: P.O. Box 190507, Dallas, TX 75219 t) 214-862-4831 joleary@cathdal.org Rev. Tymoteusz Ksiazkiewicz, Chap.;

INSTITUTIONS LOCATED IN DIOCESE

CATHOLIC CHARITIES [CCH]

DALLAS

Catholic Charities Dallas Children's Services - 1421 W. Mockingbird, Dallas, TX 75247 t) 866-223-7500 dwoodyard@ccdallas.org www.ccdallas.org David Woodyard, CEO; Asstd. Annu.: 241; Staff: 37

Catholic Charities of Dallas, Inc. - 1421 W. Mockingbird Ln., Dallas, TX 75247 t) 866-223-7500 info@ccdallas.org www.ccdallas.org David Woodyard, Pres.; Asstd. Annu.: 123,346; Staff: 303

Education Services - t) (214) 701-0358 aschaller@ccdallas.org Ana Schaller, Dir.;

Family Stability Services - t) (214) 389-1435 tandrews@ccdallas.org Maria Rivera, Contact;

Homeless, Housing & Disaster - t) (866) 223-7500 kjanes@ccdallas.org Kaylee Janes, Dir.;

Immigration and Legal Services - 1421 W. Mockingbird Ln., Dallas, TX 75247 t) 214-634-7182 dwoodyard@ccdallas.org www.ccdallas.org David Woodyard, CEO; Asstd. Annu.: 21,351; Staff: 46

Refugee Services - 1421 W. Mockingbird Ln., Dallas, TX 75247 t) 866-223-7500 dwoodyard@ccdallas.org www.ccdallas.org/need-help/refugee-services/ David Woodyard, CEO; Asstd. Annu.: 2,165; Staff: 43

CEMETERIES [CEM]

ALLEN

St. Jude Parish Columbarium - 1515 N. Greenville Ave., Allen, TX 75002 t) 972-727-1177 shawthorne@stjudeparish.com Rev. Andrew V. Semler, Pst.;

CORSICANA

Calvary Catholic Cemetery - 2100 Block of W. 2nd Ave., c/o Immaculate Conception Parish, Corsicana, TX 75110; Mailing: P.O. Box 798, Corsicana, TX 75151 t) 903-874-4473 mhensley@iccorsicana.org Rev. Marco Rangel, Pst.;

DALLAS

Calvary Hill Cemetery - 3235 Lombardy Ln., Dallas, TX 75220; Mailing: P.O. Box 190507, Dallas, TX 75219 t) 214-357-5754; 214-379-2803 bhanner@cathdal.org www.calvaryhillcemetery.com A corporation that owns and operates Diocesan cemeteries. Barry Hanner, Dir.;

Old Calvary Hill - 2500 N. Hall St., Dallas, TX 75201; Mailing: 3725 Blackburn St., P.O. Box 190507, Dallas, TX 75219 t) 214-357-5754; 214-379-2803 bhanner@cathdal.org Barry Hanner, Dir.;

DENISON

St. Patrick Parish-Calvary Cemetery - 314 N. Rusk Ave.,

Denison, TX 75020 t) 903-463-3275 parishoffice@saintpats.net Rev. Stephen J. Mocio, Pst.;

DESOTO

Holy Redeemer Cemetery - 1500 S. Westmoreland, Desoto, TX 75115; Mailing: 3725 Blackburn St., P.O. Box 190507, Dallas, TX 75219 t) 214-357-5754 bhanner@cathdal.org www.holyredeemerdesoto.com Barry Hanner, Dir.;

ENNIS

St. Joseph Cemetery - 401 E. Lampasas, Ennis, TX 75119 t) 972-878-2834 bhanner@cathdal.org Barry Hanner, Contact;

FARMERS BRANCH

Mary Immaculate Church - Columbarium - 2800 Valwood Pkwy., Farmers Branch, TX 75234 t) 972-243-7104 marisaw@maryimmaculatechurch.org Rev. Alfonse Nazzaro, Pst.;

GARLAND

Mother of Perpetual Help Church - Columbarium - 2121 W. Apollo Rd., Garland, TX 75044 t) 972-414-7073 dmhcggarland@gmail.com Rev. Paul Hai Nguyen, C.Ss.R., Pst.;

PLANO

St. Elizabeth Ann Seton Parish Columbarium - 2700 W. Spring Creek Pkwy., Plano, TX 75023; Mailing: 2701 Piedra Dr., Plano, TX 75023 t) 972-596-5505 cchristenson@eseton.org www.setonparish.org Very Rev. Bruce Bradley, Pst.;

St. Mark the Evangelist Parish - Columbarium - 1201 Alma Dr., Plano, TX 75075 t) 972-423-5600 vfonseca@stmarkplano.org stmarkplano.org Very Rev. Jason Cargo, Pst.; Michael Zeleski, Bus. Mgr.;

Prince of Peace Church - Columbarium - 5100 Plano Pkwy., Plano, TX 75093 t) 972-380-2100 mcmarinoni@popplano.org Mary Catherine Marinoni, Contact;

ROWLETT

Sacred Heart Cemetery - 3900 Rowlett Rd., Rowlett, TX 75088; Mailing: 3725 Blackburn St., P.O. Box 190507, Dallas, TX 75219 t) 214-357-5754; 214-379-2803 bhanner@cathdal.org Barry Hanner, Dir.;

SHERMAN

St. Mary Parish-St. Mary Cemetery - 727 S. Travis St., Sherman, TX 75090 t) 903-893-5148 ndobbs@stmarych.org www.stmarych.org Rev. Merlito Abiog, Par. Vicar;

WYLIE

St. Paul Cemetery - 404 N. Ballard Ave., Wylie, TX 75098 t) 972-442-2765 debbie@saint-anthony.com Rev. Anthony M. Densmore, Pst.;

COLLEGES & UNIVERSITIES [COL]

IRVING

University of Dallas - 1845 E. Northgate, Office of the General Counsel, Irving, TX 75062 t) (972) 721-5363 hlachenauer@udallas.edu www.udallas.edu Dr. Jonathan J Sanford, Pres.; Rev. Joseph Paul Albin, O.P., Chap.; Rev. Paul Bechter, Assoc. Chap.; Stds.: 2,328; Lay Tchrs.: 127; Pr. Tchrs.: 5; Sr. Tchrs.: 3

CONVENTS, MONASTERIES, AND RESIDENCES FOR WOMEN [CON]

DALLAS

Carmelite Nuns of Dallas - 600 Flowers Ave., Dallas, TX 75211 t) 214-330-7440 dallascarmelites@yahoo.com Mother Juanita Marie Horan, O.C.D., Prioress; Srs.: 16

Daughters of the Sacred Heart - 7621 Cortland Ave., Dallas, TX 75235 t) 214-351-4338 Sr. Mercy Mary, Supr.; Srs.: 4

Missionaries of Charity - 2704 Harlandale Ave., Dallas, TX 75216 t) 214-374-3351 Convent and Our Lady of Guadalupe home for expectant mothers Sr. M. Flora MC, Supr.; Sr. M. Jonathan, MC, Regl. Supr.; Srs.: 4

School Sisters of Notre Dame - 1421 W. Mockingbird Ln., Dallas, TX 75247; Mailing: P.O. Box 227275, Dallas, TX 75222 t) 214-330-9152 jdaigle@ssndcp.org www.ssnd.org Srs.: 9

Sisters of Our Lady of Charity of the Good Shepherd - Dallas Inc. - 4500 W. Davis St., Dallas, TX 75211; Mailing: 620 Roswell Rd., S.W., P.O. Box 340, Carrollton, OH 44615 t) 214-331-1754 peacedovegl@hotmail.com Sr. Cruz Celia Gomez, RGS, Supr.; Sr. Yolanda Martinez, O.L.C., Subprior; Srs.: 5

Ursuline Sisters of Dallas - 4900 Walnut Hill Ln., Dallas, TX 75229 t) 214-799-2454 www.osucentral.org Sr. Lois Castillon, OSU, Prioress; Srs.: 6

GRAND PRAIRIE

Sisters of the Holy Family of Nazareth - 1814 Egyptian Way, Grand Prairie, TX 75050 t) 972-641-4496 smariettao@yahoo.com nazarethcsfn.org/ (Holy Family Province) Sr. Marrietta Osinska, C.S.F.N., Contact; Srs.: 14

IRVING

Congregation of Mary, Queen-American Region (CMR) - 723 Sunset Dr., Irving, TX 75061 t) 469-417-0123 cmrvocation@yahoo.com www.trinhvuong.org Sr. Eileen Nguyen, Chap.; Srs.: 4

ENDOWMENTS / FOUNDATIONS / TRUSTS [EFT]

ALLEN

St. Jude Parish Building Trust - 1515 N. Greenville Ave., Allen, TX 75002 t) 972-727-1177 shawthorne@stjudeparish.com www.stjudeparish.com Rev. Andrew V. Semler, Pst.;

Our Lady of Angels Building Trust - 1914 Ridgeview Dr., Allen, TX 75013 t) 469-467-9669 fsantos@ourladyofangels.com www.ourladyofangels.com Fernando Santos, Bus. Mgr.;

DALLAS

Bishop Dunne Catholic School Building and Endowment Fund - 3900 Rugged Dr., Dallas, TX 75224 t) 214-339-6561 rsuarez@bdcs.org www.bdcs.org Mary Beth Marchiony, Pres.;

Bishop Lynch High School Building and Endowment Trust - 9750 Ferguson Rd., Dallas, TX 75228 t) 214-324-3607 chris.rebuck@bishoplynch.org; jaynie.poff@bishoplynch.org www.bishoplynch.org Christopher Rebuck, Pres.; Jaynie Poff, Treas.;

Bishop Lynch High School Education and Endowment Trust - 9750 Ferguson Rd., Dallas, TX 75228 t) 214-324-3607 jayne.poff@bishoplynch.org Jaynie Poff, CFO;

Carmelite Nuns Foundation - 600 Flowers Ave., Dallas, TX 75211 t) 214-330-7440 dallascarmelites@yahoo.com Mother Juanita Marie Horan, O.C.D., Prioress;

Catholic Charities Endowment Trust - 1421 W. Mockingbird Ln., Dallas, TX 75247 t) 866-223-7500 dwoodyard@ccdallas.org www.ccdallas.org David Woodyard, Pres.;

Catholic Charities of Dallas (Collins Estate/St. Joseph Orphanage) Trust - 3725 Blackburn St., Dallas, TX 75219; Mailing: P.O. Box 190507, Dallas, TX 75219 t) 214-379-2803 bhanner@cathdal.org Barry Hanner, Dir.;

Dallas Diocesan Education Endowment Trust - 3725 Blackburn St., Dallas, TX 75219; Mailing: P.O. Box 190507, Dallas, TX 75219 t) 214-379-2800 bhanner@cathdal.org Barry Hanner, Dir.;

Diocesan Seminary Burse Endowment Fund Trust - 3725 Blackburn St., Dallas, TX 75219; Mailing: P.O. Box 190507, Dallas, TX 75219 t) 214-379-2803 bhanner@cathdal.org Trust Fund for education of seminarians for Diocese of Dallas. Barry Hanner, Dir.;

James L. Collins Catholic School Education Trust - 3725 Blackburn St., Dallas, TX 75219; Mailing: P.O. Box 190507, Dallas, TX 75219 t) 214-379-2803 bhanner@cathdal.org Barry Hanner, Dir.;

***Jesuit College Preparatory School of Dallas Foundation, Inc.** - 12345 Inwood Rd., Dallas, TX 75244 t) 972-387-8700 BJ Antes, Contact;

St. Mary of Carmel Building Trust - 2900 Vilbig Rd., Dallas, TX 75212 t) 214-747-1433 secsmc@gmail.com Rev. Jenaro de la Cruz, OCD, Pst.;

Our Faith - Our Future Trust - 3725 Blackburn St., Dallas, TX 75219; Mailing: P.O. Box 190507, Dallas, TX 75219 t) 214-379-2803 bhanner@cathdal.org Barry Hanner, Dir.;

Santa Clara School Endowment Fund Trust - 3725 Blackburn St., Dallas, TX 75219; Mailing: P.O. Box 190507, Dallas, TX 75219 t) 214-379-2803 bhanner@cathdal.org Barry Hanner, Dir.;

Ursuline Academy of Dallas Foundation, Inc. - 4900 Walnut Hill Ln., Dallas, TX 75229 t) 469-232-3580 jkohler@ursulinedallas.org www.ursulinedallas.org Gretchen Z. Kane, Pres.; Jim Kohler, Exec.;

IRVING

CHRISTUS Health Foundation - 919 Hidden Ridge, Irving, TX 75038-3813 t) 469-282-2649 nancy.rodill@christushealth.org; josee.field@christushealth.org Gabriela Saenz, Exec.;

Cistercian Abbey Foundation - 3550 Cistercian Rd., Irving, TX 75039 t) 972-438-2044 fr-peter@cistercian.org Rt. Rev. Peter Verhalen, O.Cist., Contact;

Cistercian Prep Foundation - 3550 Cistercian Rd., Irving, TX 75039 t) 972-438-2044 fr-peter@cistercian.org Rt. Rev. Peter Verhalen, O.Cist., Contact;

Holy Trinity Seminary Scholarship Trust - 3131 Vince Hagan Dr., Irving, TX 75062; Mailing: P.O.Box 190507, Dallas, TX 75219 t) 214-379-2800 bhanner@cathdal.org Barry Hanner, Contact;

PLANO

John Paul II High School Building and Endowment Fund - 900 Coit Rd., Plano, TX 75075 t) 469-229-5206; 972-867-0005 doreenhewes@johnpauliihs.org www.johnpauliihs.org Robert Gharis, Contact;

3701 Cardinals, LLC - t) (972) 867-0005 bobgharis@johnpauliihs.org Robert Gharis, Admin.;

RICHARDSON

St. Paul Parish Endowment Trust Fund - 900 St. Paul Dr., Richardson, TX 75080 t) 972-235-6105 mercedes@saintpaulchurch.org Rev. John Szatkowski, Pst.; Kathy Kelley, Bus. Mgr.;

HOSPITALS / HEALTH SERVICES [HOS]

IRVING

CHRISTUS Health - 919 Hidden Ridge, Mission Dept., Irving, TX 75038-3813 t) 469-282-3504 deidra.hill-webb@christushealth.org; karen.oliver@christushealth.org www.christushealth.org Ernie W. Sadau, Pres.; Marty Margetts, Exec.; Bed Capacity: 6,965; Asstd. Annu.: 6,300,000; Staff: 48,000

CHRISTUS Health Liability Retention Trust - t) 469-282-2000 www.christushealth.org/

CHRISTUS St. Joseph Village - 1201 E. Sandy Lake Rd., Coppell, TX 75019 t) 972-304-0300 mitchell.george@christushealth.org Senior Residential Care Mitchell D. George, Dir.;

MISCELLANEOUS [MIS]

ADDISON

The Catholic Pro-Life Community, Inc. - 14675 Midway Rd., #121, Addison, TX 75001 t) (972) 267-5433 cplc@prolifedallas.org www.prolifedallas.org Geralyn Kaminsky, CEO;

ALLEN

OLACP-RC - 1914 Ridgeview Dr., Allen, TX 75013; Mailing: P.O. Box 190507, Dallas, TX 75219 t) 214-379-2805 Cecilia Colbert, Contact;

SJCP-RC - 1515 N. Greenville Ave., Allen, TX 75002; Mailing: P.O. Box 190507, Dallas, TX 75219-4404 t) 214-379-2800 Cecilia Colbert, Contact;

BONHAM

SECPB-RC - 916 Maple St., Bonham, TX 75418; Mailing: P.O. Box 190507, Dallas, TX 75219-4404 t) 214-379-2800 Cecilia Colbert, Contact;

CARROLLTON

SHJCCP-RC - 2121 N. Denton Dr., Carrollton, TX 75006; Mailing: P.O. Box 190507, Dallas, TX 75219 t) 214-379-2800 Cecilia Colbert, Contact;

COMMERCE

SJCPC-RC - 2207 Monroe, Commerce, TX 75428; Mailing: P.O. Box 190507, Dallas, TX 75219 t) 214-379-2800 Cecilia Colbert, Contact;

COPPELL

SACPC-RC - 180 Samuel Blvd., Coppell, TX 75019; Mailing: P.O. Box 190507, Dallas, TX 75219-4404 t) (214) 379-2800 Cecilia Colbert, Contact;

CORSICANA

ICCPC-RC - 3000 W. Hwy. 22, Corsicana, TX 75110; Mailing: P.O. Box 190507, Dallas, TX 75219 t) (214) 379-2800 Cecilia Colbert, Contact;

DALLAS

Archangels Academy Foundation - 3725 Blackburn St., Dallas, TX 75219 t) 214-379-2800 Barry Hanner, Dir.;

ASCP-RC - 5231 Meadowcreek Ln., Dallas, TX 75248; Mailing: P.O. Box 190507, Dallas, TX 75219 t) 214-379-2800 Cecilia Colbert, CEO;

BSCP-RC - 231 N. Marsalis Ave., Dallas, TX 75203; Mailing: P.O. Box 190507, Dallas, TX 75219 t) 214-379-2800 ccolbert@cathdal.org Cecilia Colbert, CEO;

***Catholic Charismatic Services of Dallas Texas, Inc. (Culture of Life Network) (Christian Community of God's Delight)** - 4500 W. Davis, Dallas, TX 75211; Mailing: P.O. Box 225008, Dallas, TX 75222 t) 214-333-2337 info@godsdelight.org www.godsdelight.org Charismatic Covenant Community David Peterman Jr., Pres.;

Catholic Community Appeal, Inc. (Bishop's Annual Appeal for Catholic Ministries) - 3725 Blackburn St., Dallas, TX 75219; Mailing: P.O. Box 190507, Dallas, TX 75219 t) 214-379-2803 bhanner@cathdal.org www.cathdal.org Barry Hanner, Dir.;

Catholic Community Educational Services of Dallas, Inc. - 3725 Blackburn St., Dallas, TX 75219-4404; Mailing: P.O. Box 190507, Dallas, TX 75219-4404 t) 214-379-2873 bhanner@cathdal.org Barry Hanner, Dir.;

***Catholic Crisis Pregnancy Centers of Dallas, Texas (Birth Choice of Dallas)** - 8610 Greenville Ave., Ste. 200, Dallas, TX 75243 t) 214-631-2402 info@birthchoicedallas.org www.birthchoicedallas.org Aaron Fowler, Dir.;

Catholic Physicians Guild of Dallas - 11220 Shelterwood Ln., Dallas, TX 75229 t) 214-750-9153 cathmeddallas@gmail.com; jeffrey.thompson@cathmeddallas.org www.cathmeddallas.org Dcn. Charles Stump Jr., Chap.; Dr. Jeffrey R. Thompson, Pres.;

CCD-PM Corporation - 1421 W. Mockingbird Ln., Dallas, TX 75243 t) 866-223-7500 dwoodyard@ccdallas.org David Woodyard, CEO;

CCD-RC - 1421 W. Mockingbird Ln., Dallas, TX 75247 t) 214-520-6590 dwoodyard@ccdallas.org www.ccdallas.org David Woodyard, Pres. & CEO;

CCM-RC - 3057 University Blvd, Dallas, TX 75205; Mailing: P.O. Box 190507, Dallas, TX 75219 t) 214-379-2805 Cecilia Colbert, CEO;

CCM2-RC - 3725 Blackburn St., Dallas, TX 75219; Mailing: P.O. Box 190507, Dallas, TX 75219 t) 214-379-2800 ccolbert@cathdal.org Cecilia Colbert, Contact;

CKCP-RC - 8017 Preston Rd., Dallas, TX 75225; Mailing: P.O. Box 190507, Dallas, TX 75219 t) (214) 379-2800 Cecilia Colbert, CEO;

Commission on Ecumenism - 3725 Blackburn St., Dallas, TX 75219-4404; Mailing: P.O. Box 190507, Dallas, TX 75219-4404 t) 214-528-2240 lrossol@cathdal.org; a_lackland@dallascatholic.org Lynn Rossol, Contact;

CSG-RC - 2215 Ross Ave., Dallas, TX 75201; Mailing: P.O. Box 190507, Dallas, TX 75219 t) 214-379-2805 Cecilia Colbert, Contact;

Dallas Vocation Guild - 7238 Lane Park Dr., Dallas, TX 75225 t) 214-739-2586 Rosalyn Huff, Contact;

HCCP-RC - 2926 Ledbetter Dr., Dallas, TX 75216; Mailing: P.O. Box 190507, Dallas, TX 75219 t) 214-379-2805 Cecilia Colbert, CFO;

HTCP-RC - 3826 Gilbert St., Dallas, TX 75219; Mailing: P.O. Box 190507, Dallas, TX 75219 t) 214-379-2805 Cecilia Colbert, Contact;

St. Joseph Residence, Inc. - 330 W. Pembroke, Dallas, TX 75208-6532 t) 214-948-3597 richard@stjr.org; ron@stjr.org stjr.org For elderly. Conducted by Daughters of the Sacred Heart of Jesus (Bethlemitas). Sr. Carolina Botero, Admin.;

Ladies of Charity of Dallas - 8448 Walnut Hill Ln., Dallas, TX 75359-0666; Mailing: P.O. Box 595666, Dallas, TX 75359-0666 t) 214-821-5775 mmgriggs@swbell.net Mary Griggs, Pres.;

NSPCP-RC - 4455 W. Illinois Ave., Dallas, TX 75211; Mailing: P.O. Box 190507, Dallas, TX 75219 t) 214-379-2805 Cecilia Colbert, Contact;

OLLCP-RC - 5605 Bernal Dr., Dallas, TX 75212; Mailing: P.O. Box 190507, Dallas, TX 75219 t) 214-379-2805 Cecilia Colbert, Contact;

OLPHCP-RC - 7617 Cortland Ave., Dallas, TX 75235; Mailing: P.O. Box 190507, Dallas, TX 75219 t) 214-379-2805 Cecilia Colbert, Contact;

OLSJLSTCP-RC - 2601 Singleton Blvd., Dallas, TX 75212; Mailing: P.O. Box 190507, Dallas, TX 75219-4404 t) 214-379-2805 Cecilia Colbert, Contact;

RCDD-RC - 3725 Blackburn St., Dallas, TX 75219; Mailing: P.O. Box 190507, Dallas, TX 75219-4404 t) 214-379-2800 Barry Hanner, Contact;

SACP-RC - 1054 N. St. Augustine Dr., Dallas, TX 75217; Mailing: P.O. Box 190507, P.O. Box 190507, Dallas, TX 75219-4404 t) 214-379-2800 Cecilia Colbert, Contact;

SACPD-RC - 2711 Romaine Ave., Dallas, TX 75215; Mailing: P.O. Box 190507, Dallas, TX 75219 t) 214-379-2800 Cecilia Colbert, Contact;

SBCCP-RC - 1404 Old Gate Ln., Dallas, TX 75218; Mailing: P.O. Box 190507, Dallas, TX 75219-4404 t) 214-379-2800 Cecilia Colbert, Contact;

SCCP-RC - 1809 W. Davis St., Dallas, TX 75208; Mailing: P.O. Box 190507, Dallas, TX 75219-4404 t) 214-379-2800 Cecilia Colbert, Contact;

SCOACP-RC - 321 Calumet St., Dallas, TX 75211; Mailing: P.O. Box 190507, Dallas, TX 75219-4404 t) 214-379-2800 Cecilia Colbert, Contact;

SECP-RC - 4001 Elm St., Dallas, TX 75226; Mailing: P.O. Box 190507, Dallas, TX 75219-4404 t) 214-379-2800 Cecilia Colbert, Contact;

SEHCP-RC - 4015 S. Hampton Rd., Dallas, TX 75224; Mailing: P.O. Box 190507, Dallas, TX 75219-4404 t) 214-379-2800 Cecilia Colbert, Contact;

SJAMCP-RC - 1002 E. Saner Ave., Dallas, TX 75216; Mailing: P.O. Box 190507, Dallas, TX 75219-4404 t) 214-379-2800 Cecilia Colbert, Contact;

SJC-RC - 1521 Main St., Dallas, TX 75201; Mailing: P.O. Box 190507, Dallas, TX 75219 t) 214-379-2800 Cecilia Colbert, Contact;

SJDCP-RC - 10919 Royal Haven Ln., Dallas, TX 75229; Mailing: P.O. Box 190507, Dallas, TX 75219-4404 t) 214-379-2800 Cecilia Colbert, Contact;

SJRI-RC - 330 Pembroke, Dallas, TX 75208; Mailing: P.O. Box 190507, Dallas, TX 75219-4404 t) 214-379-2805 ccolbert@cathdal.org Cecilia Colbert, CEO;

SMCCP-RC - 2900 Vilbig Rd., Dallas, TX 75212; Mailing: P.O. Box 190507, Dallas, TX 75219 t) 214-379-2800 Cecilia Colbert, Contact;

SMOCP-RC - 9933 Midway Rd., Dallas, TX 75220; Mailing: P.O. Box 190507, Dallas, TX 75219 t) 214-379-2800 Cecilia Colbert, Contact;

***Society of St. Vincent de Paul Diocesan Council of Dallas, Inc. (Society of St. Vincent de Paul North Texas)** - 3826 Gilbert Ave., Dallas, TX 75219 t) 214-520-0650 operations@svdpdallas.org svdpdallas.org/ Joanne Baird, Dir.;

***Society of St. Vincent de Paul Charitable Pharmacy of North Texas, Inc.** - 5750 Pineland Dr., Ste. 280, Pineland Medical Office Bldg., Dallas, TX 75231; Mailing: 3826 Gilbert Ave., Dallas, TX 75219 t) 469-232-9902 pharmacyops@svdpdallas.org Luis Gonzalez, CEO; Carlos Irula, Contact;

***Society of St. Vincent de Paul Community Outreach of North Texas, Inc. (St. Vincent Center)** - 1120 Randlett St., St. Vincent Ctr., Lancaster, TX 75146; Mailing: 3826 Gilbert Ave., Dallas, TX 75219-4404 t) (214) 520-0650 Luis Gonzalez, CEO;

***Society of St. Vincent de Paul Thrift Store of Dallas** - 3052 W. Northwest Hwy., Dallas, TX 75220 t) 214-373-7837 info@svdpthrift.org Alex Lopez, Dir.;

SPCPDA-RC - 9643 Fendale Rd., Dallas, TX 75238; Mailing: P.O. Box 190507, Dallas, TX 75219-4404 t) 214-379-2800 Cecilia Colbert, Contact;

SPEACP-RC - 2907 Woodall Rodgers Fwy., Dallas, TX 75204; Mailing: P.O. Box 190507, Dallas, TX 75219 t) 214-379-2800 Cecilia Colbert, Contact;

SPHACP-RC - 8131 Military Pkwy., Dallas, TX 75227; Mailing: P.O. Box 190507, Dallas, TX 75219-4404 t) 214-379-2800 Cecilia Colbert, Contact;

SPVCP-RC - 10123 Garland Rd., Dallas, TX 75218; Mailing: P.O. Box 190507, Dallas, TX 75219-4404 t) 214-379-2800 Cecilia Colbert, Contact;

SPXCP-RC - 3030 Gus Thomasson Rd., Dallas, TX 75228; Mailing: P.O. Box 190507, Dallas, TX 75219 t) 214-379-2800 Cecilia Colbert, Contact;

SRCP-RC - 12521 Inwood Rd., Dallas, TX 75244; Mailing: P.O. Box 190507, Dallas, TX 75219-4404 t) 214-379-2800 Cecilia Colbert, Contact;

STACP-RC - 6306 Kenwood Ave., Dallas, TX 75214; Mailing: P.O. Box 190507, Dallas, TX 75219-4404 t) 214-379-2800 Cecilia Colbert, Contact;

STACP-RC Commercial - 6306 Kenwood Ave., Dallas, TX 75214; Mailing: P.O. Box 190507, Dallas, TX 75219 t) 214-379-2805 ccolbert@cathdal.org Cecilia Colbert, CFO;

Texas Catholic Publishing Company - 3725 Blackburn St., Dallas, TX 75219; Mailing: P.O. Box 190507, Dallas, TX 75219 t) 214-379-2803 bhanner@cathdal.org www.texascatholic.com Barry Hanner, Dir.;

***Young Catholic Professionals** - 6060 N. Central Expwy., Ste. 500, Dallas, TX 75206 t) 832-306-1919 national@youngcatholicprofessionals.org www.youngcatholicprofessionals.org Peter Blute, Contact;

DENISON

SPCPDE-RC - 314 N. Rusk Ave., Denison, TX 75020; Mailing: P.O. Box 190507, Dallas, TX 75219-4404 t) 214-379-2800 Cecilia Colbert, Contact;

DUNCANVILLE

HSCP-RC - 1111 W. Danieldale Rd., Duncanville, TX 75137; Mailing: P.O. Box 190507, Dallas, TX 75219 t) 214-379-2805 Cecilia Colbert, CFO;

ENNIS

SJNCP-RC - 401 E. Lampasas, Ennis, TX 75119; Mailing: P.O. Box 190507, Dallas, TX 75219 t) 214-379-2800 Cecilia Colbert, Contact;

FARMERS BRANCH

MICP-RC - 2800 Valwood Pkwy., Farmers Branch, TX 75234; Mailing: P.O. Box 190507, Dallas, TX 75219 c) 214-379-2805 Cecilia Colbert, Contact;

FERRIS

CCCP-RC - 111 N. Wood St., Ferris, TX 75125; Mailing: P.O. Box 190507, Dallas, TX 75219 t) 214-379-2800 ccolbert@cathdal.org Cecilia Colbert, CEO;

FORNEY

SMTCP-RC - 9470 CR 213, Forney, TX 75126; Mailing: P.O. Box 190507, Dallas, TX 75219 t) 214-379-2800 Cecilia Colbert, Contact;

FRISCO

SFACPF-RC - 8000 Eldorado Pkwy., Frisco, TX 75033; Mailing: P.O. Box 190507, Dallas, TX 75219-4404 t) 214-379-2800 Cecilia Colbert, Contact;

GARLAND

GSCP-RC - 1224 Main St., Garland, TX 75040; Mailing: P.O. Box 190507, Dallas, TX 75219 t) 214-379-2805 Cecilia Colbert, CEO;

MPHCP-RC - 2121 W. Apollo Rd., Garland, TX 75044; Mailing: P.O. Box 190507, Dallas, TX 75219 t) 214-379-2805 Cecilia Colbert, Contact;

***New Evangelization of America** - 5002 Sandestin Ct., Garland, TX 75044 c) 307-757-5454 neamail@msn.com; marylwilsonwy@msn.com deospace.com Gracie Stanford, Secy.; Mary Wilson, Treas.;

SMACPG-RC - 950 Trails Pkwy., Garland, TX 75043; Mailing: P.O. Box 190507, Dallas, TX 75219

t) 214-379-2800 Cecilia Colbert, Contact;

GRAND PRAIRIE

ICCPGP-RC - 610 N.E. 17th St., Grand Prairie, TX 75050; Mailing: P.O. Box 190507, Dallas, TX 75219 t) 214-379-2800 Cecilia Colbert, Contact;

SJVCP-RC - 1902 S. Beltline Rd., Grand Prairie, TX 75051; Mailing: P.O. Box 190507, Dallas, TX 75219 t) 214-379-2800 Cecilia Colbert, Contact;

SMACPGP-RC - 2910 Corn Valley Rd., Grand Prairie, TX 75052; Mailing: P.O. Box 190507, Dallas, TX 75219-4404 t) 214-379-2800 Cecilia Colbert, Contact;

GREENVILLE

SWCP-RC - 4300 Stuart St., Greenville, TX 75401; Mailing: P.O. Box 190507, Dallas, TX 75219 t) 214-379-2800 Cecilia Colbert, Contact;

HONEY GROVE

***DJM Ministries, Inc.** - 310 County Rd. 2801, Honey Grove, TX 75446-3612 t) 903-378-2324 djmi@djmfamily.org www.disciplesofjesusandmary.org Louise Lahola, Contact;

One America International, Inc. - 2236 CR 2415, Honey Grove, TX 75446 c) 214-335-5290 mary.matasso@catholicmediainternational.org catholicmediainternational.org Thomas Matasso, Pres.;

IRVING

CREC - 3550 Cistercian Rd., Irving, TX 75039 t) 972-438-2044 fr-peter@cistercian.org Rt. Rev. Peter Verhalen, O.Cist., Contact;

***Disaster Services Corporation - Society of St. Vincent de Paul USA** - 320 Decker Dr., Ste. 100, Irving, TX 75062 t) 202-380-9664 ldisco@svdpdisaster.org www.svdpdisaster.org Elizabeth Disco-Shearer, CEO;

***Explore Your Faith** - 400 E. Royal Ln., Ste. 290, Irving, TX 75039-3602 t) 972-725-9306 c) 469-417-9797 info@exploreyourfaith.org www.exploreyourfaith.org Maria Bocalandro, Pres.;

HFNCP-RC - 2330 Cheyenne St., Irving, TX 75062; Mailing: P.O. Box 190507, Dallas, TX 75219 t) 214-379-2805 Cecilia Colbert, CEO;

MDPP-RC - 2030 E. Hwy. 356, Irving, TX 75060; Mailing: P.O. Box 190507, Dallas, TX 75219-4404 t) 214-379-2805 Cecilia Colbert, Contact;

Opus Dei - 3610 Wingren, Irving, TX 75062 t) 972-650-0064 wingrencenter@gmail.com www.opusdei.org Prelature of the Holy Cross and Opus Dei Rev. John E. Solarski; Rev. Joseph Thomas;

SAKCP-RC - 2111 Camino Lago, Irving, TX 75039; Mailing: P.O. Box 190507, Dallas, TX 75219-4404 t) 214-379-2800 Cecilia Colbert, Contact;

SLCP-RC - 202 S. MacArthur Blvd., Irving, TX 75060; Mailing: P.O. Box 190507, Dallas, TX 75219-4404 t) 214-379-2800 Cecilia Colbert, Contact;

***Theology of the Body Evangelization Team, Inc. (TOBET)** - 948 Blaylock Cir., Irving, TX 75061 t) 972-849-6543 mashour@tobet.org; egudde@tobet.org tobet.org Monica Ann Ashour, Pres.;

St. Thomas More Society of Diocese of Dallas, Texas - 408 Guadalajara Circle, Irving, TX 75062; Mailing: P.O. Box 913, Colleyville, TX 76034 c) 214-490-0058 president@stmsdallas.org; info@stmsdallas.org www.stmsdallas.org Bennett Rawicki, Pres.;

ITALY

ECP-RC - 434 S. Ward St., Italy, TX 76651; Mailing: P.O. Box 190507, Dallas, TX 75219-4404 t) 214-379-2805 Cecilia Colbert, CEO;

KAUFMAN

Domus Dei Clerical Society of Apostolic Life - 7650 FM 1388, Kaufman, TX 75142 c) 504-544-2400 domusdeiusa@gmail.com www.nhachua.org Rev. Dieu Van Tran, SDD, Supr.; Bro. Paul An Tran, SDD, Mem.; Rev. Paul Thien Vu, SD, Mem.; Dcn. Thanh Duc Vu, Mem.; Rev. Minh Van Nguyen, SDD, Mem.; Rev. Francis Quyet Bui, S.D.D., Mem.;

SACPK-RC - 806 N. Washington St., Kaufman, TX 75142; Mailing: P.O. Box 190507, Dallas, TX 75219-4404 t) 214-379-2800 Cecilia Colbert, Contact;

LANCASTER

SFACPL-RC - 1537 Rogers Ave., Lancaster, TX 75134; Mailing: P.O. Box 190507, Dallas, TX 75219 t) 214-379-2800 Cecilia Colbert, Contact;

MCKINNEY

SGACP-RC - 110 St. Gabriel Way, McKinney, TX 75071; Mailing: P.O. Box 190507, Dallas, TX 75219 t) 214-379-2800 Cecilia Colbert, Contact;

SMCPMK-RC - 411 Paula Rd., McKinney, TX 75069; Mailing: P.O. Box 190507, Dallas, TX 75219-4404 t) 214-379-2800 Cecilia Colbert, Contact;

MESQUITE

DMOLCP-RC - 1585 E. Cartwright Rd., Mesquite, TX 75149; Mailing: P.O. Box 190507, Dallas, TX 75219 t) 214-379-2805 ccolbert@cathdal.org Cecilia Colbert, CEO;

MURPHY

***Vera Aqua Vera Vita** - 406 Sagebrush Trl., Murphy, TX 75094 c) 469-577-9465 jniemeier@veraaquaveravita.org veraaquaveravita.org/ Jacob Niemeier, Contact;

PLANO

Dallas Diocesan Council of Catholic Women - 3409 Premier Dr., Apt. 417, Plano, TX 75023 c) (817) 995-2928 (Mary Clare Cieslewicz's) nccw.org Sr. Theresa Khirallah, S.S.N.D., Spiritual Adv./Care Srvcs.;

PPCP-RC - 5100 Plano Pkwy. W., Plano, TX 75093; Mailing: P.O. Box 190507, Dallas, TX 75219 t) 214-379-2805 Cecilia Colbert, Contact;

SEASCP-RC - 2700 W. Spring Creek Pkwy., Plano, TX 75023; Mailing: P.O. Box 190507, Dallas, TX 75219 t) 214-379-2800 Cecilia Colbert, Contact;

SHJCPP-RC - 4201 E. 14th St., Plano, TX 75074; Mailing: P.O. Box 190507, Dallas, TX 75219-4404 t) 214-379-2800 Cecilia Colbert, Contact;

SMECP-RC - 1105 W. 15th St., Plano, TX 75075; Mailing: P.O. Box 190507, Dallas, TX 75219 t) 214-379-2800 Cecilia Colbert, Contact;

QUINLAN

OLFCP-RC - 4300 Stuart St., Quinlan, TX 75401; Mailing: P.O. Box 190507, Dallas, TX 75219-4404 t) 214-379-2805 Cecilia Colbert, Contact;

RICHARDSON

St. Joseph Church - Columbarium - 600 S. Jupiter Rd., Richardson, TX 75081 t) 972-231-2951 lsmith@stjosephcc.net Loretta Smith, Contact;

SJCPR-RC - 600 S. Jupiter Rd., Richardson, TX 75081; Mailing: P.O. Box 190507, Dallas, TX 75219 t) 214-379-2800 Cecilia Colbert, Contact;

SPAACP-RC - 900 St. Paul Dr., Richardson, TX 75080; Mailing: P.O. Box 190507, Dallas, TX 75219-4404 t) 214-379-2800 Cecilia Colbert, Contact;

ROCKWALL

OLLACP-RC - 1305 Damascus Rd., Rockwall, TX 75087; Mailing: P.O. Box 190507, Dallas, TX 75219 t) 214-379-2805 Cecilia Colbert, Contact;

ROWLETT

SHCP-RC - 3905 Hickox Rd., Rowlett, TX 75089; Mailing: P.O. Box 190507, Dallas, TX 75219-4404 t) 214-379-2800 Cecilia Colbert, Contact;

SHERMAN

SMCP-RC - 727 S. Travis St., Sherman, TX 75090; Mailing: P.O. Box 190507, Dallas, TX 75219 t) 214-379-2800 Cecilia Colbert, Contact;

TERRELL

SJACP-RC - 702 N. Frances St., Terrell, TX 75160; Mailing: P.O. Box 190507, Dallas, TX 75219-4404 t) 214-379-2800 Cecilia Colbert, Contact;

VAN ALSTYNE

HFCP-RC - 919 Spence Rd., Van Alstyne, TX 75495; Mailing: P.O. Box 190507, Dallas, TX 75219 t) 214-379-2805 Cecilia Colbert, CEO;

WAXAHACHIE

SJCPW-RC - 609 Kaufman St., Waxahachie, TX 75165; Mailing: P.O. Box 190507, Dallas, TX 75219 t) 214-379-2800 Cecilia Colbert, Contact;

WHITESBORO

SFACPW-RC - 807 N. Union St., Whitesboro, TX 75090; Mailing: P.O. Box 190507, Dallas, TX 75219-4404 t) 214-379-2800 Cecilia Colbert, Contact;

WYLIE

SACPW-RC - 404 N. Ballard St., Wylie, TX 75098; Mailing: P.O. Box 190507, Dallas, TX 75219 t) 214-379-2800 Cecilia Colbert, Contact;

MONASTERIES AND RESIDENCES FOR PRIESTS AND BROTHERS [MON]

DALLAS

St. Aloysius Gonzaga Jesuit Community - 5024 Sugar Mill Rd., Dallas, TX 75244 t) 314-574-9585 wsidney@jesuits.org Rev. Carlos D. Esparza, S.J., Graduate Student; Rev. Roy M Joseph, S.J., Retreat Dir.; Rev. Dong (Derek) P Vo, S.J., Retreat Dir.; Priests: 5

Capuchin Franciscan Friars, Custody Mexico - Texas - 2911 Lapsley St., Dallas, TX 75212 t) 214-377-7643 beto080@gmail.com Friar Pedro Romero, OFM Cap., Pst.; Friar Angel Rios, OFM. Cap, Vicar; Rev. Juan Alejandro Ortiz, OFM Cap., Spiritual Adv./Care Srvcs.; Priests: 4

Congregation of the Mission, Western Province - 3826 Gilbert Ave., Dallas, TX 75219 t) 214-526-0234 cmsouth@sbcglobal.net www.vincentian.org Rev. F. Patrick Hanser, C.M.; Rev. Minh J. Pham, C.M., Pst.; Rev. Milton Ryan, C.M., Pst.; Rev. Derek C Swanson, C.M., Par. Vicar; Priests: 4

St. John Neumann Formation House - 3912 S. Ledbetter Dr., Dallas, TX 75236 t) 972-296-6735 haidinh1@juno.com www.dccthaingoai.com Vietnamese Redemptorist Mission Rev. Thach Nguyen, Supr.; Rev. Joseph Le, Vicar; Rev. Viet Nguyen, Chap.; Rev. Dominic Hai Dinh, C.Ss.R., Dir.; Brs.: 6; Priests: 4

Mt. Carmel Center (Discalced Carmelite Fathers of Dallas, Inc.) - 4600 W. Davis St., Dallas, TX 75211 t) 214-331-6224 admin@mountcarmelcenter.org; executivedirector@carmelitefriarsocd.com www.mountcarmelcenter.org Friar John Suenram, OCD, Supr.; Friar Marion Bui, OCD, Mem.; Rev. James A. Curiel, OCD, Mem.; Rev. Jenaro de la Cruz, OCD, In Res.; Priests: 4

IRVING

Dominican Priory of St. Albert the Great and Novitiate - 3150 Vince Hagan St., Irving, TX 75062-4701 t) 972-438-1626 pnpowellop@gmail.com opdallas.com Rev. Philip Neri Powell, OP, Prior; Rev. Francis Orozco, O.P., Novice Master; Rev. Joseph Paul Albin, O.P., Campus Min.; Rev. Jude Siciliano, O.P.; Bro. Joseph Thomas Henriquez; Bro. Thomas Peter Hicks; Bro. Moses Owens; Rev. Brian Pierce, O.P.; Bro. Anthony Price; Bro. Bede Raymond Saucer; Brs.: 5; Priests: 7

Our Lady of the Rosary of Pompeii Dominican Laity Chapter - c) 817-312-5421 nateeter@yahoo.com Natasha Childress, Contact;

Legionaries of Christ - 3813 Cabeza de Vaca Cir., Irving, TX 75062 t) 214-529-3324 foduill@legionaries.org rcdallas.com/ L.C. Pastoral Services Rev. Fergal O'Duill, L.C., Supr.; Rev. Ben O'Loughlin, LC, Dir.; Rev. Jared Loehr, LC, Chap.; Rev. Michael Picard, L.C., Chap.; Rev. Owens Kearns, L.C., Chap.; Rev. Ryan Richardson, LC, Chap.; Rev. Gregory Usselmann, LC, Chap.; Rev. Timothy Wysocki, LC, Chap.; Priests: 8

Our Lady of Dallas Cistercian Abbey - 3550 Cistercian Rd., Irving, TX 75039 t) 972-438-2044 fr-peter@cistercian.org www.cistercian.org Rt. Rev. Peter Verhalen, O.Cist., Abbot; Rev. Paul McCormick, O.Cist., Prior; Rev. Thomas Esposito, O.Cist., Subprior; Rev. John Bayer, O.Cist.; Rev. Anthony Bigney, O.Cist.; Rev. Lawrence Brophy, O.Cist.; Rev. Stephen Gregg, O.Cist.; Rev. Francis Gruber, O.Cist.; Rev. Augustine Hoelke, O.Cist.; Rev. Philip Neri Lastimosa, O.Cist.; Rev. James Lehrberger, O.Cist.; Rev. Julius Leloczky, O.Cist.; Rev. Robert Maguire, O.Cist.; Rev. Bernard Marton, O.Cist.; Rev. Ignatius Peacher, O.Cist.; Rev. Mark Ripperger, O.Cist.; Rev. Ambrose Strong, O.Cist.; Rev. Joseph Van House, O.Cist.; Rev. Gregory Schweers, O.Cist.; Rev. Rafael Schaner, O.Cist.; Rev. Matthew Hegemann, O.Cist., In Res.; Bro. Barnabas Robertson, O. Cist; Bro. Daniel Miller, In Res.; Bro. Ephram Malone, In Res.; Dcn. Christopher Kalan, O. Cist., In Res.; Brs.: 4; Priests: 22

KERENS

***Benedictine Monastery of Thien Tam** - 13055 S.E. County Rd. 4271, Kerens, TX 75144 t) 903-396-3201 www.thientamosb.org Rev. Paulavang Vuong, O.S.B., Subprior; Brs.: 5; Priests: 7

SEMINARIES [SEM]

DALLAS

The Redemptoris Mater House of Formation (Redemptoris Mater Seminary) - 419 N. Cockrell Hill Rd., Dallas, TX 75211; Mailing: P.O. Box 211669, Dallas, TX 75211 t) 214-467-2255 www.rmdallas.org Rev. Fernando Carranza, Rector; Rev. Alan Paul McDonald, Vice Rector; Rev. Michal Markiewicz, Spiritual Dir.; Rev. Daniel Rendon, Adjunct Spiritual Dir.; Stds.: 27; Pr. Tchrs.: 4

IRVING

Holy Trinity Seminary - 3131 Vince Hagan Dr., Irving, TX 75062 t) 972-438-2212 vanyama@holytrinityseminary.org; kwilwert@holytrinityseminary.org www.holytrinityseminary.org Diocesan College and Pre-Theology Seminary. Very Rev. Vincent C. Anyama, Rector; Rev. Eugene Azorji, Spiritual Adv./Care Srvcs.; Rev. Russell Mower, Dir.; Rev. Zachary Webb, Dir.; Rev. Kevin Wilwert, Dir.; Sarah Penuela, Dir.; Dr. Matthew Walz, Dir.; Stds.: 45; Lay Tchrs.: 2; Pr. Tchrs.: 5

An asterisk (*) denotes an organization that has established tax-exempt status directly with the IRS and is not covered by the USCCB Group Ruling.

Diocese of Davenport

(Dioecesis Davenportensis)

MOST REVEREND THOMAS R. ZINKULA, JD, JCL

Bishop of Davenport; ordained May 26, 1990; appointed Bishop of Davenport April 19, 2017; ordained and installed June 22, 2017.

Chancery: 780 W. Central Park Ave., Davenport, IA 52804-1901. T: 563-324-1911; F: 563-324-5842.
www.davenportdiocese.org
communication@davenportdiocese.org

ERECTED MAY 8, 1881.

Square Miles 11,438.

Comprises that part of the State of Iowa bounded on the east by the Mississippi River; on the west by the western boundaries of the counties of Jasper, Marion, Monroe and Appanoose; on the south by the State of Missouri; on the north by the northern boundaries of the Counties of Jasper, Poweshiek, Iowa, Johnson, Cedar and Clinton.

For legal titles of diocesan institutions, consult the Chancery.

STATISTICAL OVERVIEW

Personnel

Bishop.....1
Retired Bishops.....2
Priests: Diocesan Active in Diocese.....48
Priests: Diocesan Active Outside Diocese.....2
Priests: Retired, Sick or Absent.....46
Number of Diocesan Priests.....96
Religious Priests in Diocese.....3
Total Priests in your Diocese.....99
Extern Priests in Diocese.....12
Ordinations:
Diocesan Priests.....2
Transitional Deacons.....2
Permanent Deacons.....7
Permanent Deacons in Diocese.....58
Total Brothers.....2
Total Sisters.....85

Parishes

Parishes.....74
With Resident Pastor:
Resident Diocesan Priests.....39
Resident Religious Priests.....3
Without Resident Pastor:
Administered by Priests.....30
Administered by Deacons.....2
Professional Ministry Personnel:
Lay Ministers.....78

Welfare

Catholic Hospitals.....3
Total Assisted.....606,429
Homes for the Aged.....2
Total Assisted.....1,196
Special Centers for Social Services.....6
Total Assisted.....79,873

Educational

Diocesan Students in Other Seminaries.....5
Total Seminarians.....5
Colleges and Universities.....1
Total Students.....2,748
High Schools, Diocesan and Parish.....5
Total Students.....892
Elementary Schools, Diocesan and Parish.....13
Total Students.....3,699
Catechesis / Religious Education:
High School Students.....1,658
Elementary Students.....4,029
Total Students under Catholic Instruction.....13,031
Teachers in Diocese:
Priests.....1
Lay Teachers.....475

Vital Statistics

Receptions into the Church:
Infant Baptism Totals.....909
Minor Baptism Totals.....53
Adult Baptism Totals.....40
Received into Full Communion.....71
First Communions.....1,025
Confirmations.....1,004
Marriages:
Catholic.....141
Interfaith.....97
Total Marriages.....238
Deaths.....967
Total Catholic Population.....85,437
Total Population.....787,159

LEADERSHIP
Vicar General - Rev. Thomas J. Hennen;
Chancellor / Chief of Staff - Dcn. David Montgomery;
Executive Secretary - Emily Pries;
Vice-Chancellor - Rev. Paul J. Appel;
Tribunal -
Judicial Vicar - Rev. Paul J. Appel, Vice Chancellor;
Adjutant Judicial Vicar - Rev. Nicholas O. Akindele (Nigeria);
Judge - Rev. Rudolph T. Juarez;
Defenders of the Bond - Rev. John P. Gallagher; Rev. Francis Mensah (Ghana); Rev. William E. Reynolds;
Promoter of Justice - Rev. Joseph M. Wolf;
Delegate for the Bishop in Matrimonial Matters - Rev. Christopher R. Young;
Consultors - Most Rev. Thomas R. Zinkula;
Deans - Rev. Thomas J. Hennen, Contact;
Diocesan Corporate Board - Most Rev. Thomas R. Zinkula;
Finance Officer - Thomas Tallman, CFO;
Finance Council - Most Rev. Thomas R. Zinkula;
Vicar for Hispanics - Rev. Rudolph T. Juarez, Vicar;

OFFICES AND DIRECTORS
Catholic Campaign for Human Development - Dcn. Kent Ferris, Dir.;
Catholic Charities - Dcn. Kent Ferris, Dir.;
Catholic Relief Services - Dcn. Kent Ferris, Dir.;
Communication - Dcn. David Montgomery, Chancellor;
Deacon Formation - Dcn. Francis L. Agnoli, Dir.;
Diaconate - Dcn. Jeffrey C. Schuetzle;
Evangelization - Patrick Schmadeke, Dir.;
Faith Formation - Trevor Pullinger, Dir.;
Finance - Thomas Tallman, CFO;
Human Resources & Risk Management - Tiara Hatfield, Dir.;
Liturgy - Dcn. Francis L. Agnoli, Dir.;
Multicultural Ministry - Miguel Moreno, Dir.;
Parish Planning - Dan Ebener, Dir.;
Propagation of the Faith - Dcn. Kent Ferris, Dir.;
Schools - Lynne Devaney, Supt.;
Social Action - Dcn. Kent Ferris, Dir.;
Immigration Program - Gricelda Garnica, Contact; Karina Garnica, Contact;
Stewardship - Jennifer Praet, Dir.;
Technology - Robert Butterworth, Dir.;
Victim Assistance - t) 563-349-5002 vac@diodav.org Alicia Owens, Contact;
Vocations - Rev. Jacob M. Greiner, Dir.;

ADVISORY BOARDS, COMMISSIONS, COMMITTEES, AND COUNCILS
Presbyteral Council - Most Rev. Thomas R. Zinkula;
Pastoral Council - Most Rev. Thomas R. Zinkula;

MISCELLANEOUS / OTHER OFFICES
The Catholic Messenger (Newspaper) - t) 563-323-9959 messenger@davenportdiocese.org www.catholicmessenger.net/ Barb Arland-Fye, Editor;

PARISHES, MISSIONS, AND CLERGY

STATE OF IOWA

ALBIA
St. Mary Church of Albia, Iowa - 730 Benton Ave. W., Albia, IA 52531; Mailing: P.O. Box 365, Albia, IA 52531 t) 641-932-5130; 641-932-5589 (CRP) scrallalbia@iowatelecom.net; albiastmary@diodav.org stmarysalbia.org Rev. Mark V. Yates, C.PP.S., Pst.; Sharon Crall, DRE; CRP Stds.: 78
St. Patrick Church of Georgetown, Iowa - Hwy. 34 W., Albia, IA 52531; Mailing: P.O. Box 183, Albia, IA 52531 t) 641-932-5589 georgetownstpat@diodav.org; scrallalbia@iowatelecom.net www.stmarysalbia.org Rev. Mark V. Yates, C.PP.S., Pst.; Sharon Crall, Pst. Assoc.; CRP Stds.: 17

BETTENDORF
St. John Vianney Church of Bettendorf, Iowa - 4097 18th St., Bettendorf, IA 52722-2120 t) 563-332-7910 bettsjv@diodav.org; re@sjvbett.org www.sjvbett.org Rev. Richard A. Adam, Pst.; Dcn. Daryl G. Fortin; Dcn. Charles A. Metzger, Sacr. Min.; Dcn. John R. Weber, Sacr. Min.; Jeanne Moran, DRE; CRP Stds.: 657
St. John Vianney Church of Bettendorf School - (Grades PreK- t) 563-332-5308 preschool@sjvbett.org Karen Emard, Dir.; Stds.: 35
Our Lady of Lourdes Church of Bettendorf, Iowa - 1506 Brown St., Bettendorf, IA 52722; Mailing: 1414 Mississippi Blvd., Bettendorf, IA 52722-4915 t) 563-359-0345 bettlourdesdre@diodav.org; bettlourdes@diodav.org www.lourdescatholic.org Rev. Jason K. Crossen, Pst.; Rev. Ben G. Snyder, Par. Vicar; Dcn. Patrick L Murphy; Dcn. Charles A. Metzger; Dcn. John R. Weber; Morgan T Davis, CRE; CRP Stds.: 101
Our Lady of Lourdes Church of Bettendorf, Iowa School (Lourdes Catholic School) - (Grades PreK-8) 1453 Mississippi Blvd., Bettendorf, IA 52722 t) 563-359-3466 Michael Hughes, Prin.; Stds.: 300; Lay Tchrs.: 22

BLOOMFIELD
St. Mary Magdalen Church of Bloomfield, Iowa - 108 Weaver Rd., Bloomfield, IA 52537; Mailing: 222 N. Ward St., Ottumwa, IA 52501 t) 641-682-4212; 641-980-8808 (CRP) bloomstmarymag@diodav.org; angela.hunter@operint.com Rev. Patrick J. Hilgendorf, Pst.; CRP Stds.: 9

BLUE GRASS
St. Andrew Church of Blue Grass, Iowa - 333 W. Lotte St., Blue Grass, IA 52726 t) 563-381-1363 bluegrassstandrew@diodav.org; bluegrassstandrewdre@diodav.org www.standrewbluegrass.org Rev. Thomas J. Hennen, Moderator; Rev. Robert L. Grant, Sacr. Min.; Phyllis Avesing, DRE; Dcn. Steven E. Barton, Parish Life Coord.; CRP Stds.: 45

BROOKLYN
St. Patrick Church of Brooklyn, Iowa - 215 Jackson St., Brooklyn, IA 52211; Mailing: P.O. Box 512, Brooklyn, IA 52211 t) 319-647-2294 (Office phone); 319-647-2220 (Pastor Rectory) brooklynstpat@diodav.org; brooklynstpatdre@diodav.org stpatrick-stbridget.org Rev. Scott G. Lemaster, Pst.; Rachel Corbett, DRE; CRP Stds.: 52

BUFFALO
St. Peter Church of Buffalo, Iowa - 406 4th St., Buffalo, IA 52728; Mailing: P.O. Box 488, Buffalo, IA 52728 t) (563) 333-6151 buffalostpeter@diodav.org Rev. Ross M. Epping, Pst.; Dcn. Larry F. Dankert; Nancy Stalder, DRE; CRP Stds.: 36

CAMANCHE
Church of the Visitation of Camanche, Iowa - 1028 Middle Rd., Camanche, IA 52730-1032 t) 563-259-1188 camanchevisitation@diodav.org Rev. Apo T. Mpanda, Pst.; Dcn. Matthew J. Levy; Brandon Mennenoh, DRE; CRP Stds.: 38

CENTERVILLE
St. Mary Church of Centerville, Iowa - 828 S. 18th St., Centerville, IA 52544 t) 641-437-1984 centervillestmary@diodav.org stmaryscenterville.org Rev. Timothy Armbruster, C.PP.S., Pst.; Meho Clark, DRE; Chira McKee, DRE; CRP Stds.: 44

CHARLOTTE
Assumption and St. Patrick Church of Charlotte, Iowa - 147 Broadway St., Charlotte, IA 52731; Mailing: PO Box 293, Delmar, IA 52037 t) 563-674-4240 delmarstpatrickcluster@diodav.org Rev. Robert J. Cloos, Pst.; Katie Johnson, DRE; CRP Stds.: 33

CLINTON
Jesus Christ, Prince of Peace Roman Catholic Church of Clinton, Iowa - 1105 LaMetta Wynn Dr., Clinton, IA 52732 t) 563-242-3311 www.jcpop.org Rev. Paul J. Appel, Pst.; Rev. John D. Lamansky, Par. Vicar; Dcn. Jeffrey C. Schuetzle; Annette Lyons, Pst. Assoc.; Dcn. Andrew Hardigan; Brenda Bertram, DRE; David Schnier, Bus. Mgr.; CRP Stds.: 60
Jesus Christ, Prince of Peace Roman Catholic Church of Clinton, Iowa School (Prince of Peace Catholic Education System) - (Grades PreK-12) 312 S. 4th St., Clinton, IA 52732 t) 563-242-1663 joseph.brown@staff.prince.pvt.k12.ia.us www.prince.pvt.k12.ia.us Joe Brown, Prin.; Stds.: 190; Lay Tchrs.: 17

COLFAX
Immaculate Conception Church of Colfax, Iowa - 305 E. Howard, Colfax, IA 50054-1025 t) 515-674-3711 colfaximmconc@diodav.org www.immaculateconceptioncolfax.org Rev. Ronald E. Hodges, Pst.; Dcn. Joseph F. Dvorak; CRP Stds.: 27

COLUMBUS JUNCTION
St. Joseph Church of Columbus Junction, Iowa - 815 Second St., Columbus Junction, IA 52738 t) 319-728-8210; 319-627-2229 coljctstjoseph@diodav.org www.saintjosephcj.webs.com Rev. Guillermo Trevino Jr., Pst.; Catalina Valdez, DRE; CRP Stds.: 70

CORALVILLE
St. Thomas More Church of Coralville, Iowa - 3000 12th Ave., Coralville, IA 52241 t) 319-337-2173; 319-337-4231 (CRP) coralstmdre@diodav.org; crlvlsttmore@diodav.org www.stmparishfamily.com Rev. Charles A. Adam, Pst.; Dcn. Steven A. George; Dcn. David L. Krob, Sacr. Min.; Shannon Duffy, DRE; CRP Stds.: 527

DAVENPORT
Sacred Heart Cathedral of Davenport, Iowa - 422 E. 10th St., Davenport, IA 52803-5499 t) 563-324-3257 davsacredheart@diodav.org www.shcdavenport.org Rev. Thomas J. Hennen, Pst.; Dcn. Daniel L. Huber, Pst. Assoc.; Dcn. John E. Jacobsen; CRP Stds.: 26
St. Alphonsus Church of Davenport, Iowa - 2618 Boies Ave., Davenport, IA 52802 t) 563-322-0987 davstaldre@diodav.org; davstalfin@diodav.org stalphonsusdav.org Rev. Nicholas O. Akindele (Nigeria), Pst.; Mary Ann Hagemann, DRE; CRP Stds.: 25
St. Anthony Church of Davenport, Iowa - 417 N. Main St., Davenport, IA 52801 t) 563-322-3303 davstanthonydre@diodav.org; davstanthony@diodav.org www.stanthonysdavenportiowa.org Rev. Rudolph T. Juarez, Pst.; John Cooper, Pst. Assoc.; Kay Steele, DRE; Kim Nofsker, Music Min.; CRP Stds.: 172
Holy Family Church of Davenport, Iowa - 1923 N. Fillmore St., Davenport, IA 52804; Mailing: 1315 W. Pleasant St., Davenport, IA 52804 t) 563-322-0901 davholyfamily@diodav.org holyfamilydavenport.com Rev. Nicholas O. Akindele (Nigeria), Pst.; Rev. Christopher R. Young, Par. Vicar; Diane Lannan, DRE; CRP Stds.: 48
Holy Family Teddy Bear Club - 1341 W. Pleasant St., Davenport, IA 52804 t) 563-322-6648 www.teddybearclubholyfamily.com (Pre-school & daycare program) Cassandra Collum, Dir.;
Our Lady of Victory Church of Davenport, Iowa - 4105 N. Division St., Davenport, IA 52806 t) 563-391-4245; 563-391-8384 (CRP) davolv@diodav.org; davolvcre@diodav.org www.olvjfk.com Rev. Jacob M. Greiner, Pst.; Rev. Andrew Rauenbuehler, Par. Vicar; Dcn. Francis L. Agnoli; Dcn. Albert G. Boboth; Dcn. Marcel G. Mosse; Dcn. John J. Wagner; Kaye Meyers, DRE; CRP Stds.: 85
John F. Kennedy Catholic School - (Grades PreK-8) 1627 W. 42nd St., Davenport, IA 52806 t) 563-391-3030 chad.steimle@olvjfkmail.com olvjfk.com Chad Steimle, Prin.; Stds.: 329; Lay Tchrs.: 25
St. Paul the Apostle Church of Davenport, Iowa - 916 E. Rusholme St., Davenport, IA 52803 t) 563-322-7994 davstpauldre@diodav.org; davstpaul@diodav.org

www.stpaulcatholicparish.org Rev. Bruce A. DeRammelaere, Pst.; Dcn. Ryan Burchett; Dcn. Robert W. Shaw; Madeline Dudziak, DRE; CRP Stds.: 116

St. Paul the Apostle Church of Davenport, Iowa School - (Grades PreK-8) 1007 E. Rusholme St., Davenport, IA 52803 t) 563-322-2923 julie.delaney@st-paul.pvt.k12.ia.us Julie Delaney, Prin.; Stds.: 423; Lay Tchrs.: 31

DELMAR

St. Patrick Church of Delmar, Iowa - 405 Delmar Ave., Delmar, IA 52037; Mailing: PO Box 293, Delmar, IA 52037 t) 563-674-4240 delmarstpatrickcluster@diodav.org Rev. Robert J. Cloos, Pst.;

DEWITT

St. Joseph Church of DeWitt, Iowa - 417 Sixth Ave., DeWitt, IA 52742 t) 563-659-3514 dewittstjoseph@diodav.org; sjyouth@gmtel.net stjoseph-dewitt.weconnect.com Rev. Stephen C. Page, Pst.; Dcn. Mark A. Comer; Sr. Janet Heiar, S.S.N.D., Pst. Assoc.; Jasmin Tone, DRE; CRP Stds.: 105

St. Joseph Church of DeWitt School, Iowa - (Grades PreK-8) t) 563-659-3812 sharon.roling@st-joseph-dwt.pvt.k12.ia.us www.st-joseph-dwt.pvt.k12.ia.us Sharon Roling, Prin.; Stds.: 182; Lay Tchrs.: 14

EAST PLEASANT PLAIN

Ss. Joseph and Cabrini Catholic Church - 1174 Reed Ave., East Pleasant Plain, IA 52540; Mailing: P.O. Box 37, Brighton, IA 52540-0037 t) 319-694-3672 richlandssjosephcabrini@diodav.org; mcsjrich@windstream.net Rev. Robert A. Lathrop, Admin.; Rev. Damian Ilokaba (Nigeria), Sacr. Min.;

FAIRFIELD

St. Mary's Church of Fairfield, Iowa - 3100 W. Madison Ave., Fairfield, IA 52556-2466 t) 641-472-3179 www.fairfieldstmary.org Rev. Nicholas J. Adam, Pst.; Jean Dorothy, DRE; CRP Stds.: 92

FARMINGTON

St. Boniface Church of Farmington, Iowa - 609 Washington St., Farmington, IA 52626; Mailing: P.O. Box 247, Farmington, IA 52626 t) 319-837-6808 westpointstmary@diodav.org; westpointstmarydre@diodav.org Rev. Daniel R. Dorau, Pst.; Dcn. Michael G. Linnenbrink; Dixie Booten, DRE; CRP Stds.: 13

FORT MADISON

Holy Family Parish of Fort Madison, Iowa - 1111 Ave. E, Fort Madison, IA 52627 t) 319-372-2127 fortmadholyfamilydre@diodav.org; fortmadholyfamily@diodav.org holyfamilyfm.com Rev. Joseph P. V. Phung, Pst.; Rev. John J. Stack, Par. Vicar; Dcn. Robert R. Gengengbacher; Dcn. Ronald K. Stein; CRP Stds.: 52

GRAND MOUND

SS. Philip and James Church of Grand Mound, Iowa - 606 Fulton St., Grand Mound, IA 52751; Mailing: P.O. Box 7, Grand Mound, IA 52751-0007 t) 563-847-2271 grandmssphilipjames@diodav.org Rev. Stephen C. Page, Pst.; Maureen Schrader, DRE; CRP Stds.: 58

GRINNELL

St. Mary Church of Grinnell, Iowa - 1002 Broad St., Grinnell, IA 50112; Mailing: P.O. Box 623, Grinnell, IA 50112 t) 641-236-7486 grinnellstmarydre@diodav.org; grinnellstmary@diodav.org www.stmarygrinnell.com/ Rev. Scott Foley, Pst.; Dcn. John S. Osborne; Angelinia Willard, DRE; CRP Stds.: 60

HILLS

St. Joseph Church of Hills, Iowa - 209 Brady St., Hills, IA 52235; Mailing: P.O. Box 187, Hills, IA 52235-0187 t) 319-679-2271 hillsstjoseph@diodav.org stsmaryandjoseph.com Rev. Hai D. Dinh, Pst.; Carol Kaalberg, Pst. Min./Coord.; Nancy Waldschmidt, DRE; CRP Stds.: 1

HOUGHTON

St. John Church of Houghton, Iowa - 105 Main St., Houghton, IA 52631; Mailing: 205 Denning, P O Box 100, Houghton, IA 52631 t) 319-469-2001; 319-837-6808 (CRP) westpointstmarydre@diodav.org stjj.weconnect.com Rev. Daniel R. Dorau, Pst.; Dcn. Michael G. Linnenbrink; Dixie Booten, DRE; Joan Holtkamp, Bus. Mgr.; CRP Stds.: 9

IOWA CITY

St. Mary Church of Iowa City, Iowa - 228 E. Jefferson St., Iowa City, IA 52245; Mailing: 302 E. Jefferson St., Iowa City, IA 52245 t) 319-337-4314; 319-351-7638 (CRP) icstmary@diodav.org www.icstmary.org Rev. Stephen J. Witt, Pst.; Rev. Symphorien O. Lopoke (Democratic Republic of Congo), Par. Vicar; Dcn. Joseph B. Welter; Sr. Mary Agnes Giblin, B.V.M., Pst. Assoc.; Carolyn Brandt, DRE; CRP Stds.: 89

St. Patrick Church of Iowa City, Iowa - 4330 St. Patrick Dr., Iowa City, IA 52240 t) 319-337-2856; 319-351-7638 (CRP) icstpat@diodav.org; office@stpatsic.com www.stpatsic.com Rev. Joseph M. Sia, Pst.; Dcn. Angel Hernandez; CRP Stds.: 71

St. Wenceslaus Church of Iowa City, Iowa - 630 E. Davenport St., Iowa City, IA 52245; Mailing: 618 E. Davenport St., Iowa City, IA 52245 t) 319-337-4957; 319-351-7638 (CRP) icstwenc@diodav.org; carolyn.brandt@regina.org stwenc-ic.com Rev. Gary L. Beckman, Pst.; Dcn. Christopher L. Kabat; Carolyn Brandt, DRE; CRP Stds.: 78

KEOKUK

Church of All Saints of Keokuk, Iowa - 310 S. Ninth St., Keokuk, IA 52632 t) 319-524-8334 keokukallsaints@diodav.org www.allsaintskeokuk.org Rev. David L. Brownfield, Pst.; CRP Stds.: 18

Keokuk Catholic Schools, Inc. - (Grades PreK-5) 2981 Plank Rd., Keokuk, IA 52632-2399 t) 319-524-5450 shari.bozorgzad@keokukcatholic.org www.keokukcatholicschools.org Shari Bozorgzad, Prin.; Stds.: 78; Lay Tchrs.: 7

KEOTA

Holy Trinity Church of Keota/Harper, Iowa - 109 N. Lincoln St., Keota, IA 52248-9757 t) 641-636-3883 keotaholytrinity@diodav.org; shannon.greiner@sigourneyschools.com Rev. Robert A. Lathrop, Pst.; Shannon Greiner, DRE; CRP Stds.: 75

KNOXVILLE

St. Anthony Church of Knoxville, Iowa - 1201 Woodland Dr., Knoxville, IA 50138; Mailing: 1202 Woodland Dr., Knoxville, IA 50138 t) 641-828-7050 knoxvillestanthony@diodav.org; knoxvillestanthonydre@diodav.org www.stanthonyknoxville.com Rev. Dennis L. Hoffman, Pst.; Dcn. Thomas A. Hardie; CRP Stds.: 14

LECLAIRE

Our Lady of the River Church of Le Claire-Princeton, Iowa - 28200 226th St., LeClaire, IA 52753; Mailing: P.O. Box 32, LeClaire, IA 52753 t) 563-289-5736 www.olotr.org Rev. Apo T. Mpanda, Pst.; Dcn. Matthew J. Levy; Roberta Pegorick, DRE; CRP Stds.: 83

LONE TREE

St. Mary Church of Lone Tree, Iowa - 216 W. Jayne St., Lone Tree, IA 52755; Mailing: P. O. Box 187, Hills, IA 52235-0187 t) 319-679-2271 lonetreestmary@diodav.org stsmaryandjoseph.com Rev. Hai D. Dinh, Pst.; Carol Kaalberg, Pst. Min./Coord.; Nancy Waldschmidt, DRE; CRP Stds.: 11

LONG GROVE

St. Ann Church of Long Grove, Iowa - 16550 290th St., Long Grove, IA 52756 t) 563-285-4596 longrovestann@diodav.org; jkloft@stannslonggrove.org www.stannslonggrove.org Rev. Joseph M. Wolf, Pst.; Joyce Kloft, DRE; CRP Stds.: 230

LOST NATION

Our Lady of the Holy Rosary Catholic Church of Lost Nation, Iowa - 903 Main St., Lost Nation, IA 52254; Mailing: P.O. Box 127, Lost Nation, IA 52254-0127 t) 563-678-2200; (563) 674-4240 lostnationholyrosary@diodav.org; delmarstpatrickcluster@diodav.org Rev. Robert J. Cloos, Pst.; Kristin Bowman, DRE; CRP Stds.: 15

LOVILIA

St. Peter Church of Lovilia, Iowa - 601 W. 6th St., Lovilia, IA 50150; Mailing: P.O. Box 8, Lovilia, IA 50150 t) 641-946-8298; 641-932-5589 (CRP) loviliastpeter@diodav.org Rev. Mark V. Yates, C.PP.S., Pst.; Sharon Crall, DRE; CRP Stds.: 2

MARENGO

St. Patrick Church of Marengo, Iowa - 957 Western Ave., Marengo, IA 52301; Mailing: P.O. Box 183, Marengo, IA 52301 t) 319-642-5438; 319-560-8476 (CRP) marengostpat@diodav.org; angela.carney@mercer.com Rev. David F. Wilkening, Pst.; Angie Carney, DRE; CRP Stds.: 34

MECHANICSVILLE

St. Mary Church of Mechanicsville, Iowa - 302 W. Reeder St., Mechanicsville, IA 52306; Mailing: P. O. Box 309, Tipton, IA 52772 t) 563-886-2506 www.stmarystipton.net Rev. Richard U. Okumu, Pst.; Lori Crock, DRE; CRP Stds.: 16

MELCHER

Sacred Heart Church of Melcher, Iowa - 204 S.W. D St., Melcher, IA 50163; Mailing: P.O. Box 277, Melcher Dallas, IA 50163 t) 641-947-4981 melchersacredheart@diodav.org; sacredheartmd@iowatelecom.net Rev. Dennis L. Hoffman, Pst.; Dcn. Thomas A. Hardie; Shari Schneider, DRE; CRP Stds.: 41

MELROSE

St. Patrick Church of Melrose, Iowa - 200 Trinity Ave., Melrose, IA 52569 t) 641-732-3531 melrosestpat@diodav.org; melrosestpatdre@diodav.org Rev. Timothy Armbruster, C.PP.S., Pst.; Dcn. Edwin D. Kamerick; Jane Kamerick, DRE; CRP Stds.: 24

MONTROSE

St. Joseph Church of Montrose, Iowa - 508 Cedar St., Montrose, IA 52639; Mailing: 1111 Avenue E, Fort Madison, IA 52627 t) (319) 372-2127 fortmadholyfamilyfin@diodav.org Rev. Joseph P. V. Phung, Pst.;

MOUNT PLEASANT

St. Alphonsus Church of Mt. Pleasant, Iowa - 607 S. Jackson St., Mount Pleasant, IA 52641-2696 t) 319-385-8410 mtpleasantstal@diodav.org www.mtpalphonsus.org Rev. Paul E. Connolly, Pst.; Kelley Tansey, DRE; CRP Stds.: 70

MUSCATINE

SS. Mary and Mathias Church of Muscatine, Iowa - 215 W. Eighth St., Muscatine, IA 52761 t) 563-263-1416; 563-263-3848 (CRP) muscssmarymathias@diodav.org; srcheryl@marymathias.org marymathias.org Rev. Christopher Weber, Pst.; Rev. Khoa Le (Vietnam), Par. Vicar; Dcn. Dennis H. McDonald; Sr. Mary Cheryl Demmer, P.B.V.M., DRE; CRP Stds.: 272

Saints Mary and Mathias Catholic School - (Grades PreK-8) 2407 Cedar St., Muscatine, IA 52761-2696 t) 563-263-3264 ben.nietzel@muscatinesaints.org www.muscatinesaints.org Benjamin Nietzel, Prin.; Stds.: 324; Lay Tchrs.: 17

NEWTON

Sacred Heart Church of Newton, Iowa - 1115 S. Eighth Ave. E., Newton, IA 50208; Mailing: P.O. Box 1478, Newton, IA 50208-1478 t) 641-792-2050; 641-792-4625 newtonsacredheart@diodav.org; shlifelongff@gmail.com shcnewton.org Rev. Anthony J. Herold, Pst.; Luke Gregory, DRE; CRP Stds.: 106

NICHOLS

St. Mary Church of Nichols, Iowa - 201 Short St., Nichols, IA 52766; Mailing: P. O. Box 187, Hills, IA 52235-0187 t) 319-679-2271 nicholsstmary@diodav.org stsmaryandjoseph.com Rev. Hai D. Dinh, Pst.; Carol Kaalberg, Pst. Min./Coord.; Nancy Waldschmidt, DRE; CRP Stds.: 2

NORTH ENGLISH

St. Joseph Church of North English, Iowa - 221 N. Knollridge St., North English, IA 52316; Mailing: P.O. Box 219, North English, IA 52316 t) 319-664-3325 northenglishstjoseph@diodav.org; northenglishstjosephdre@diodav.org Rev. David F. Wilkening, Pst.; Georgia Gent, DRE; Amanda Westphal, DRE; CRP Stds.: 45

OSKALOOSA

St. Mary Church of Oskaloosa, Iowa - 315 1st Ave. E.,

Oskaloosa, IA 52577-2823; Mailing: 301 High Ave. E., Oskaloosa, IA 52577 t) 641-673-0659; 641-673-6680 oskystmarydre@diodav.org; oskystmary@diodav.org stmarysosky.com Rev. Troy A. Richmond, Pst.; Dcn. Donald L. Efinger; Dcn. Lowell W. Van Wyk; Thomas Leah, DRE; CRP Stds.: 81

OTTUMWA

Church of St. Mary of the Visitation - 216 N. Court St., Ottumwa, IA 52501-2586 t) 641-682-4559 ottstmary@diodav.org www.stmaryottumwa.org/ Rev. James G. Betzen, C.PP.S., Pst.; Rev. Dale E Mallory, Par. Vicar; Dcn. James J. Vonderhaar; Anna De La Torre, DRE; CRP Stds.: 128

St. Patrick Church of Ottumwa, Iowa - 222 N. Ward St., Ottumwa, IA 52501 t) 641-682-4212; 641-682-0320 (CRP) ottstpat@diodav.org; ottstpatdre@diodav.org www.stpatrickottumwa.com Rev. Patrick J. Hilgendorf, Pst.; Gail Bates, DRE; CRP Stds.: 36

OXFORD

St. Mary Church of Oxford, Iowa - 215 Summit St., Oxford, IA 52322; Mailing: P.O. Box 80, Oxford, IA 52322-0080 t) 319-828-4180; 319-668-9532 (CRP) oxfordstmary@diodav.org; oxfordstmarydre@diodav.org sites.google.com/site/stmaryoxford/ Rev. Francis Mensah (Ghana), Pst.; Dcn. David Montgomery; Dcn. Joseph T. Rohret; Dorene Francis, DRE; CRP Stds.: 94

St. Peter Church of Cosgrove, Iowa - 4022 Cosgrove Rd., S.W., Oxford, IA 52322 t) 319-545-2077 cosgrovestpeter@diodav.org; cosgrovestpeterdre@diodav.org www.stpetercosgrove.weebly.com Rev. Francis Mensah (Ghana), Pst.; Dcn. David Montgomery; Dcn. Joseph T. Rohret; Jennifer Ness, DRE; CRP Stds.: 27

PELLA

St. Mary Church of Pella, Iowa - 726 218th Pl., Pella, IA 50219-7500 t) 641-628-3078 pellastmary@diodav.org; pellastmarydre@diodav.org www.stmarypella.org Rev. Troy A. Richmond, Pst.; Dcn. Donald L. Efinger; Dcn. Lowell W. Van Wyk; Paulina Loaiza, DRE; CRP Stds.: 226

PETERSVILLE

Immaculate Conception Church of Petersville, Iowa - 2885 145th St., Petersville, IA 52731; Mailing: PO Box 293, Delmar, IA 52037 t) 563-674-4240 delmarstpatrickcluster@diodav.org Rev. Robert J. Cloos, Pst.;

PRESTON

Ss. Mary and Joseph Church of Sugar Creek, Iowa - 3218 110th St, Preston, IA 52069; Mailing: PO Box 293, Delmar, IA 52037 t) 563-674-4240 delmarstpatrickcluster@diodav.org Rev. Robert J. Cloos, Pst.; Katie Johnson, DRE; CRP Stds.: 9

RIVERSIDE

Holy Family Church of Riverside, Iowa - 360 N. Washburn St., Riverside, IA 52327; Mailing: P.O. Box C, Riverside, IA 52327 t) 319-648-2331 riversideholyfamily@diodav.org; rfiagle79@gmail.com holyfamilyrrw.org Rev. William D. Roush, Pst.; Dcn. Derick K. Cranston, Pst. Assoc.; CRP Stds.: 135

SIGOURNEY

St. Mary Church of Sigourney, Iowa - 415 E. Pleasant Valley St., Sigourney, IA 52591 t) 641-622-3426; 641-622-3698 (CRP) sigourneystmary@diodav.org; sigourneystmarydre@diodav.org Rev. Robert A. Lathrop, Pst.; Dcn. James L. Striegel; Deb Fritz, DRE; CRP Stds.: 34

SOLON

St. Mary Church of Solon, Iowa - 1749 Racine Ave., N.E., Solon, IA 52333-9638 t) 319-624-2228 solonstmary@diodav.org; solonstmarydre@diodav.org www.solonstmary.org Rev. Charles J. Fladung, Pst.; Dcn. Mitchell A. Holte; Dcn. David L. Krob; Jeri Bollwitt, DRE; CRP Stds.: 232

SPERRY

St. Mary Church of Dodgeville, Iowa - 13204 Dodgeville Rd., Sperry, IA 52650; Mailing: 502 W. Mt. Pleasant St., West Burlington, IA 52655 t) 319-752-8771; 319-752-6733 (CRP) dodgevillestmary@diodav.org; dodgevillestmarydre@diodav.org www.dmcountycatholic.org Rev. Martin G. Goetz, Pst.; Rev. James Flattery, Par. Vicar; Dcn. Andrew Reif; Cindy Pfeiff, DRE; CRP Stds.: 60

ST. PAUL

St. James Church of St. Paul, Iowa - 2044 Locust St., St. Paul, IA 52657; Mailing: 205 Denning, P O Box 100, Houghton, IA 52631-0100 t) 319-469-2001; 319-837-6808 (CRP) westpointstmarydre@diodav.org stjj.weconnect.com Rev. Daniel R. Dorau, Pst.; Dcn. Michael G. Linnenbrink; Dixie Booten, DRE; Joan Holtkamp, Bus. Mgr.; CRP Stds.: 11

TIPTON

St. Mary Church of Tipton, Iowa - 208 Meridian St., Tipton, IA 52772; Mailing: P.O. Box 309, Tipton, IA 52772-0309 t) 563-886-2506; 319-321-0715 (CRP) tiptonstmary@diodav.org; stmarymaryb@gmail.com www.stmarystipton.net Rev. Richard U. Okumu, Pst.; Mary Barnum, DRE; CRP Stds.: 64

VICTOR

St. Bridget Church of Victor, Iowa - 104 Third St., Victor, IA 52347 t) 319-647-2220; 319-647-2294 victorstbridget@diodav.org; victorstbridgetdre@diodav.org www.stpatrick-stbridget.org Rev. Scott G. Lemaster, Pst.; Evan VanOtegham, DRE; CRP Stds.: 40

WASHINGTON

St. James Church of Washington, Iowa - 602 W. 2nd St., Washington, IA 52353-1994 t) 319-653-4504 washstjames@diodav.org; washstjamesdre@diodav.org www.stjameswashington.org Rev. Bernard E. Weir, Pst.; Lori Fritz, DRE; CRP Stds.: 162

St. James Church of Washington School, Iowa - (Grades PreK-5) t) 319-653-3631 rclarahan@sjknights.org www.sjknights.org Rebecca Clarahan, Prin.; Stds.: 111; Lay Tchrs.: 7

WEST BRANCH

St. Bernadette Church of West Branch, Iowa - 507 E. Orange, West Branch, IA 52358-0103; Mailing: PO Box 103, West Branch, IA 52358 t) 319-643-2095 westbranchstbern@diodav.org; westbranchstberndre@diodav.org wbstbernadette.wordpress.com/ Rev. Gary L. Beckman, Pst.; CRP Stds.: 28

WEST BURLINGTON

Divine Mercy Parish of Burlington-West Burlington - 502 W. Mt. Pleasant St., West Burlington, IA 52655 t) 319-752-8690 (CRP); 319-752-6733; 319-752-8771 burldivinedre@diodav.org; burldivinem@diodav.org www.dmcountrycatholic.org Rev. Martin G. Goetz, Pst.; Rev. James Flattery, Par. Vicar; Dcn. Gary Johnson; CRP Stds.: 63

WEST LIBERTY

St. Joseph Church of West Liberty, Iowa - 107 W. Sixth St., West Liberty, IA 52776-1246 t) 319-627-2229 westlibstjoseph@diodav.org www.stjosephwestliberty.org Rev. Guillermo Trevino Jr., Pst.; Aaron Campbell, DRE; Hannah Campbell, DRE; CRP Stds.: 125

WEST POINT

St. Mary Church of West Point, Iowa - 119 4th St., West Point, IA 52656; Mailing: P.O. Box 68, West Point, IA 52656 t) 319-837-6808 westpointstmarydre@diodav.org; westpointstmary@diodav.org www.westpointstmary.org Rev. Daniel R. Dorau, Pst.; Dcn. Michael G. Linnenbrink; Dixie Booten, DRE; CRP Stds.: 10

WILLIAMSBURG

St. Mary Church of Williamsburg, Iowa - 102 E. Penn St., Williamsburg, IA 52361; Mailing: P.O. Box 119, Williamsburg, IA 52361 t) 319-668-1397; 319-668-2757 (CRP) williamsburgstmary@diodav.org; williamsburgstmarydre@diodav.org saintmarywburgia.com/ Rev. David F. Wilkening, Pst.; Trilby Owens, DRE; CRP Stds.: 114

WILTON

St. Mary Church of Wilton, Iowa - 701 E. 3rd St., Wilton, IA 52778 t) 563-732-2271 c) (563) 320-2462 (PLC) wiltonstmary@diodav.org; freemand@diodav.org www.stmarywilton.org Rev. Robert L. Grant, Sacr. Min.; Dcn. Dan E. Freeman, Parish Life Coord.; CRP Stds.: 80

SCHOOLS: PRESCHOOL THRU HIGH SCHOOL

SCHOOLS

STATE OF IOWA

BURLINGTON

Notre Dame Elementary School - (PAR) (Grades PreSchool-5) 700 S. Roosevelt Ave., Burlington, IA 52601-1602 t) 319-752-3776; 319-754-4417 bill.maupin@bnotredame.org; deb.trine@bnotredame.org www.burlingtonnotredame.com Bill Maupin, Prin.; Stds.: 155; Lay Tchrs.: 12

DAVENPORT

All Saints Catholic School (Scott County Catholic Education Services) - (PAR) (Grades PreK-8) 1926 N. Marquette St., Davenport, IA 52804-2199 t) 563-324-3205 kapplegate@saints.pvt.k12.ia.us ascsdav.org Kerry Applegate, Prin.; Stds.: 413; Lay Tchrs.: 27

Scott County Catholic Schools - 1020 W. Central Park Ave., Davenport, IA 52804-1899 t) (563) 326-5313 andy.craig@assumptionhigh.org www.assumptionhigh.org Andrew Craig, Pres.;

IOWA CITY

The Regina Inter-Parish Catholic Education Center - (PAR) (Grades PreK-12) 2140 Rochester Ave., Iowa City, IA 52245 t) 319-337-2580; 319-351-7638 (CRP) michelle.winders@regina.org; carolyn.brandt@regina.org regina.org Glenn Plummer, Admin.; Celeste Vincent, Admin.; Stds.: 910; Lay Tchrs.: 66

Regina Junior Senior High School - (Grades PreK-12) 2150 Rochester Ave., Iowa City, IA 52245 t) 319-338-5436 glenn.plummer@regina.org Vanessa Kelley, Vice Prin.; Stds.: 364; Lay Tchrs.: 33

Regina Elementary School - (Grades PreK-12) 2120 Rochester Ave., Iowa City, IA 52245-3527 t) 319-337-5739 celeste.vincent@regina.org Vanessa Kelley, Vice Prin.; Stds.: 473; Lay Tchrs.: 33

Regina Preschool-Daycare - t) 319-337-6198

Regina Special Events Office - t) (319) 358-2455 Shane Schemmel, Dir.;

OTTUMWA

Seton Catholic School - (PAR) (Grades PreK-5) 117 E. 4th St., Ottumwa, IA 52501-2992 t) 641-682-8826 james.wessling@oseton.com; fara.rullman@oseton.com www.oseton.com James A. Wessling, Prin.; Stds.: 96; Lay Tchrs.: 7

HIGH SCHOOLS

STATE OF IOWA

BURLINGTON

Notre Dame Middle School - High School - (PAR) (Grades 6-12) 702 S. Roosevelt Ave., Burlington, IA 52601-1602 t) 319-754-8431 bill.maupin@bnotredame.org www.burlingtonnotredame.org Bill Maupin, Prin.; Stds.: 220; Lay Tchrs.: 19

DAVENPORT

Assumption High School - (PAR) (Grades 9-12) 1020 W. Central Park Ave., Davenport, IA 52804-1899 t) 563-326-5313 andy.craig@assumptionhigh.org www.assumptionhigh.org Bridget Murphy, Prin.; Andrew Craig, Pres.; Stds.: 429; Lay Tchrs.: 25

FORT MADISON

Holy Trinity Jr./Sr. High School (Holy Trinity Catholic

Schools, Inc.) - (PAR) (Grades 7-12) 2600 Avenue A, Fort Madison, IA 52627; Mailing: 413 Avenue C, West Point, IA 52656 t) 319-372-2486; 319-837-6131 x4 (Bus. Office) nicole.holtkamp@holytrinityschools.org; craig.huebner@holytrinityschools.org www.holytrinityschools.org Craig Huebner, Prin.; Stds.: 103; Lay Tchrs.: 14

INSTITUTIONS LOCATED IN DIOCESE

CAMPUS MINISTRY / NEWMAN CENTERS [CAM]

IOWA CITY

Newman Catholic Student Center - 104 E. Jefferson St., Iowa City, IA 52245 t) 319-337-3106 info@newman-ic.org www.newman-ic.org Rev. Jeffry Belger, Dir.;

CATHOLIC CHARITIES [CCH]

DAVENPORT

St. Vincent's Home - 780 W. Central Park Ave., Davenport, IA 52804-1901 t) 563-324-1911 ferris@davenportdiocese.org www.davenportdiocese.org Dcn. Kent Ferris, Contact; Asstd. Annu.: 12; Staff: 2

COLLEGES & UNIVERSITIES [COL]

DAVENPORT

***St. Ambrose University** - 518 W. Locust St., Davenport, IA 52803-2898 t) 563-333-6000; 563-333-6213 raapkimberlyd@sau.edu www.sau.edu Dr. Amy C. Novak, Pres.; Paul Koch, Provost & Vice Pres., Academic & Student Affairs; Michael Poster, Vice Pres. Finance; Le Shane Saddler, Vice. Pres.; Dr. Toby Arquette, Vice. Pres.; Anne Gannway, Vice. Pres.; Rev. Ross M. Epping, Chap.; Rev. Robert L. Grant, Prof.; Stds.: 2,748; Lay Tchrs.: 179; Pr. Tchrs.: 1

CONVENTS, MONASTERIES, AND RESIDENCES FOR WOMEN [CON]

CLINTON

The Canticle - 841 13th Ave. N., Clinton, IA 52732-5162 t) 563-242-7903 jcebula@clintonfranciscans.com www.clintonfranciscans.com Residence of the Sisters of St. Francis, Clinton, Iowa. Sr. Janice I. Cebula, O.S.F., Contact; Srs.: 26

Carmel of the Queen of Heaven Discalced Carmelite Nuns - 841 13th Ave. N., Clinton, IA 52732-5115 t) 563-285-8387 carmelitesistersqh@gmail.com Sr. JonFe De Torres, Local Supr.; Srs.: 5

Sisters of St. Francis, Clinton, Iowa - 843 13th Ave. N., Clinton, IA 52732-5115 t) 563-242-7611 jcebula@clintonfranciscans.com www.clintonfranciscans.com Sr. Janice I. Cebula, O.S.F., Pres.; Srs.: 43

DAVENPORT

Franciscan Sisters of Christ the Divine Teacher - 2605 Boies Ave., Davenport, IA 52802 t) 563-323-1502 www.divineteacher.org Mother Susan Rueve, O.S.F., Supr.; Srs.: 2

Humility of Mary Center - Motherhouse of the Congregation of the Humility of Mary - 820 W. Central Park Ave., Davenport, IA 52804-1900 t) 563-323-9466 sisters@chmiowa.org chmiowa.org Sr. Johanna Rickl, Pres.; Srs.: 53

Our Lady of the Prairie Retreat - 2664 145th Ave., Wheatland, IA 52777 t) (563) 374-1092 olpretreat@chmiowa.org www.chmiowa.org Marie Thompson, Dir.;

ENDOWMENTS / FOUNDATIONS / TRUSTS [EFT]

BETTENDORF

Catholic Endowment of Bettendorf, Iowa, Inc. - 1414 Mississippi Blvd, Bettendorf, IA 52722; Mailing: PO Box 4, Bettendorf, IA 52722 t) 309-314-1998 bboeye@melfosterco.com catholicendowmentofbettendorf.org

BURLINGTON

***Burlington Notre Dame Foundation** - 700 S. Roosevelt Ave., Burlington, IA 52601 t) 319-754-8431 x385 jon.billups@bnotredame.org; christine.horne@bnotredame.org burlingtonnotredame.com Provides financial support for Burlington Notre Dame Schools Jon D Billups, Dir.;

CENTERVILLE

St. Mary's Foundation of Centerville - 828 S. 18th St., Centerville, IA 52544 t) 641-437-1984 centervillestmary@diodav.org Rev. Timothy Armbruster, C.PP.S., Pst.;

CLINTON

Sisters of St. Francis, Clinton, Iowa, Charitable Trust - 843 13th Ave. N., Clinton, IA 52732 t) 563-242-7611 jcebula@clintonfranciscans.com www.clintonfranciscans.com Sr. Janice I. Cebula, O.S.F., Pres.;

CORALVILLE

St. Thomas More New Season Charitable Trust - 3000 12th Ave., Coralville, IA 52241 t) 319-337-2173 coralstm@diodav.org www.stmparishfamily.com Rev. Charles A. Adam, Contact;

DAVENPORT

***Assumption Foundation for K-12 Schools** - 1020 W. Central Park Ave., Davenport, IA 52804 t) 563-326-5313 andy.craig@assumptionhigh.org www.assumptionhigh.org/ Andrew Craig, Pres.;

***Catholic Foundation for the Diocese of Davenport** - 780 W. Central Park Ave., Davenport, IA 52804-1901 t) 563-324-1911 praet@davenportdiocese.org www.davenportdiocese.org Jennifer Praet, Exec. Dir.;

Congregation of the Humility of Mary Charitable Trust - 820 W. Central Park Ave., Davenport, IA 52804-1900 t) 563-323-9466 sisters@chmiowa.org www.chmiowa.org Sr. Johanna Rickl, Pres.;

St. Paul the Apostle Foundation - 916 E. Rusholme St., Davenport, IA 52803 t) 563-322-7994 davstpaul@diodav.org Rev. Bruce A. DeRammelaere, Pst.;

***Sacred Heart Cathedral Foundation, Inc.** - 422 E. 10th St., Davenport, IA 52803 t) 563-324-3257 davsacredheartfin@diodav.org www.shcdavenport.org Rev. Thomas J. Hennen, Pres.;

IOWA CITY

***Mercy Hospital Foundation** - 500 E. Market St., Iowa City, IA 52245-2689 t) 319-339-3657 michelle.marks@mercyic.org; lisa.steigleder@mercyic.org www.mercyiowacity.org/mercyfoundation Lisa Steigleder, Pres.;

***Regina Foundation** - 2140 Rochester Ave., Iowa City, IA 52245 t) 319-354-5866 foundation@regina.org www.regina.org/foundation Kecia Boysen, Dir.;

HOSPITALS / HEALTH SERVICES [HOS]

CENTERVILLE

***MercyOne Centerville Medical Center** - 1 St. Joseph's Dr., Centerville, IA 52544 t) 641-437-4111 www.mercyone.org/centerville Owned by Trinity Health Systems Nicole Clapp, Pres.; Bed Capacity: 25; Asstd. Annu.: 131,831; Staff: 287

CLINTON

***MercyOne Clinton Medical Center** - 1410 N. Fourth St., Clinton, IA 52732 t) 563-244-5609 x5609 sprengem@mercyhealth.com A subsidiary of Trinity-Health, Inc. Amy Berentes, Admin.; Bed Capacity: 163; Asstd. Annu.: 37,600; Staff: 945

IOWA CITY

***Mercy Hospital** - 500 E. Market St., Iowa City, IA 52245 t) 319-339-0300 mike.trachta@mercyic.org www.mercyiowacity.org Mike Trachta, CEO; Bed Capacity: 194; Asstd. Annu.: 436,998; Staff: 1,226

MISCELLANEOUS [MIS]

BETTENDORF

***School Tuition Organization of Southeast Iowa** - 5247 Pinecreek Ln., Bettendorf, IA 52722 t) 563-391-1845 steve.roling@roling.tax stoseiowa.org Steven M. Roling, Dir.;

BURLINGTON

***St. Vincent De Paul Society, St. John the Baptist Church Conference** - 700 Division St., Ste. 1, Burlington, IA 52601 t) 319-752-9332 burldivinemfin@diodav.org Larry Christ, Dir.;

CORALVILLE

***John Paul II Medical Research Institute** - 2500 Crosspark Rd., Ste. W230, Coralville, IA 52241 t) 319-665-3001; 319-887-2873 jay.kamath@jp2mri.org jp2mri.org Jay Kamath, Dir.;

DAVENPORT

Ambrose Ventures - 518 W. Locust St., Davenport, IA 52803-2898 t) (563) 333-6000 postermichaelc@sau.edu www.sau.edu Michael Poster, Vice. Pres.;

***Cafe on Vine** - 932 W. 6th St., Davenport, IA 52802; Mailing: P.O. Box 3375, Davenport, IA 52808 t) 563-324-4472 cafeonvine2@aol.com www.cafeonvine.com Free meal site for those experiencing homelessness and food insecurity. Waunita Sullivan, Dir.;

***Catholic Service Board** - 230 W. 35th St., Davenport, IA 52806 t) 563-323-1923 (Cinderella Cellar shop) www.kahlhomedav.com Rose Hoenig, Contact;

***Eagles' Wings Incorporated** - 5816 Telegraph Rd., Davenport, IA 52804 t) 563-324-7263 marcia@eagleswings.ws www.eagleswings.ws House of Prayer/Counseling/Spiritual Renewal Center Marcia Moore, Dir.;

***Holy Land Military Rosary, Inc.** - 780 W. Central Park Ave., Davenport, IA 52804 c) 563-321-0124 kneemillerw@diodav.org holylandmilitaryrosary.org Mission to promote the Military Rosary Rev. William C. Kneemiller, Dir.;

The Priests' Aid Society, Inc. - 780 W. Central Park Ave., Davenport, IA 52804-1901 t) (563) 324-1911 Most Rev. Thomas R. Zinkula, Contact;

***Project Renewal of Davenport, Inc.** - 906 W. Fifth St., Davenport, IA 52802-3403 t) 563-324-0800 projectrenewal@revealed.net www.projectrenewal.net Ann Schwickerath, Exec. Dir.; Carl Callaway, Site Supvr.;

Roman Catholic Ministries of Iowa City, Iowa - 780 W. Central Park Ave., Davenport, IA 52804 t) 563-324-1911 Rev. Thomas J. Hennen, Contact;

***Scott County Catholic Education Services, Inc. (All Saints Catholic School)** - 1926 Marquette St., Davenport, IA 52804 t) 563-324-3205 kapplegate@saints.pvt.k12.ia.us www.ascsdav.org dba All Saints Catholic School Kerry Applegate, Prin.;

***Spirit, Inc.** - 2214 Harrison St., Davenport, IA 52803 t) 563-324-1776 c) 563-323-5499; 563-340-1269 pdroe61@gmail.com High School aged Youth Group/ Singing Group Paul Roe, Pres.; Timothy Heinrichs, Vice Pres./Treas.; Diane Roe, Secy.;

***St. Thomas Aquinas Guild of the Quad Cities** - 2939 E. 44th Ct., Davenport, IA 52807 t) 563-343-6647 stthomasaquinasguild@gmail.com www.stthomasaquinasguildqc.com Dr. Tim Millea, Contact;

***Vietnamese Catholic Community of Our Lady of Mong Trieu** - 422 E. 10th St., Davenport, IA 52803 t) 563-324-3257 davsacredheartfin@diodav.org Rev. Thomas J. Hennen, Pst.;

KNOXVILLE

St. Joseph's Church of Bauer, Iowa - 1202 Woodland Dr., Knoxville, IA 50138-1013 t) (641) 828-7050 Rev. Dennis L. Hoffman, Admin.;

MONASTERIES AND RESIDENCES FOR PRIESTS AND BROTHERS [MON]

DAVENPORT

St. Vincent Center - 780 W. Central Park Ave.,

Davenport, IA 52804-1901 t) 563-324-1911 montgomery@davenportdiocese.org Rev. Thomas R. Doyle, In Res.; Rev. John P. Gallagher, In Res.; Rev. Msgr. John M. Hyland, In Res.; Rev. Adrian Kaimukirwa (Tanzania), In Res.; Rev. William C. Kneemiller, In Res.; Rev. Michael J. Spiekermeier, In Res.; Rev. John E. Stecher, In Res.; Rev. Thomas F. Stratman, In Res.; Most Rev. Thomas R. Zinkula, In Res.; Priests: 9

WEVER

Brothers of the Poor of Saint Francis - 3405 190th St., Wever, IA 52658 t) 319-372-9543 Bro. Mark Gastel; Brs.: 2

NURSING / REHABILITATION / CONVALESCENCE / ELDERLY CARE [NUR]

CLINTON

***The Alverno Health Care Facility, Trinity Health** - 849 13th Ave. N., Clinton, IA 52732 t) 563-242-1521 alvernoinfo@mercyhealth.com www.thealverno.com Elizabeth Waneta Heard, Chap.; Letha Dolph, Admin.; Asstd. Annu.: 400; Staff: 120

DAVENPORT

***Kahl Home for the Aged and Infirm** - 6701 Jersey Ridge Rd., Davenport, IA 52807 t) 563-324-1621 leahmksmith@carmelitesystem.org; khufsey@kahlhomedav.com kahlhomedav.com The Carmelite System Kimberly Hufsey, Admin.; Asstd. Annu.: 796; Staff: 161

SPECIAL CARE FACILITIES [SPF]

CLINTON

***MercyOne Clinton Home Care and Hospice** - 638 S. Bluff, Clinton, IA 52732 t) 563-244-3766 timothy.shinbori@trinity-health.org; lisa.mason-hagen@mercyhealth.com www.mercyone.org Timothy T. Shinbori, Exec.; Asstd. Annu.: 200; Staff: 39

An asterisk (*) denotes an organization that has established tax-exempt status directly with the IRS and is not covered by the USCCB Group Ruling.

Archdiocese of Denver

(Archidioecesis Denveriensis)

MOST REVEREND SAMUEL J. AQUILA

Archbishop of Denver; ordained June 5, 1976; appointed Coadjutor Bishop of Fargo June 12, 2001; ordained August 24, 2001; Succeeded to the See March 18, 2002; appointed Archbishop of Denver May 29, 2012; installed July 18, 2012. Pastoral Center: 1300 S. Steele St., Denver, CO 80210.

Pastoral Center: 1300 S. Steele St., Denver, CO 80210.
T: 303-722-4687
www.archden.org

ESTABLISHED A VICARIATE-APOSTOLIC IN 1868.

Square Miles 40,154.

Erected a Diocese August 16, 1887; created an Archdiocese November 15, 1941.

Comprises the northern part of the State of Colorado, including the 25 Counties of Adams, Arapahoe, Boulder, Broomfield, Clear Creek, Denver, Eagle, Garfield, Gilpin, Grand, Jackson, Jefferson, Larimer, Logan, Moffat, Morgan, Phillips, Pitkin, Rio Blanco, Routt, Sedgwick, Summit, Washington, Weld and Yuma.

MOST REVEREND JORGE H. RODRIGUEZ
Auxiliary Bishop of Denver; ordained December 24, 1987; appointed Titular Bishop of Azura and Auxiliary Bishop of Denver August 25, 2016; installed November 4, 2016. Pastoral Center: 1300 S. Steele St., Denver, CO 80210.

STATISTICAL OVERVIEW

Personnel	
Retired Cardinals	1
Archbishops	1
Auxiliary Bishops	1
Priests: Diocesan Active in Diocese	151
Priests: Diocesan Active Outside Diocese	6
Priests: Diocesan in Foreign Missions	1
Priests: Retired, Sick or Absent	60
Number of Diocesan Priests	218
Religious Priests in Diocese	95
Total Priests in your Diocese	313
Extern Priests in Diocese	42
Ordinations:	
Diocesan Priests	8
Transitional Deacons	2
Permanent Deacons in Diocese	195
Total Brothers	25
Total Sisters	148

Parishes	
Parishes	124
With Resident Pastor:	
Resident Diocesan Priests	102
Resident Religious Priests	16
Without Resident Pastor:	
Administered by Priests	5
Completely vacant	1
Missions	19

Welfare	
Catholic Hospitals	4
Total Assisted	530,111
Health Care Centers	6
Total Assisted	22,616
Homes for the Aged	3
Total Assisted	272
Day Care Centers	6
Total Assisted	354
Specialized Homes	2
Total Assisted	1,395
Special Centers for Social Services	31
Total Assisted	85,641
Residential Care of Disabled	2
Total Assisted	8
Other Institutions	28
Total Assisted	4,629

Educational	
Seminaries, Diocesan	2
Students from This Diocese	48
Students from Other Dioceses	65
Diocesan Students in Other Seminaries	1
Seminaries, Religious	7
Total Seminarians	49
Colleges and Universities	2
Total Students	9,548
High Schools, Diocesan and Parish	2
Total Students	918
High Schools, Private	7
Total Students	3,251
Elementary Schools, Diocesan and Parish	33
Total Students	7,089
Elementary Schools, Private	2
Total Students	587
Catechesis / Religious Education:	
High School Students	1,378
Elementary Students	8,729
Total Students under Catholic Instruction	31,549
Teachers in Diocese:	
Priests	15
Brothers	3
Sisters	17
Lay Teachers	1,127

Vital Statistics	
Receptions into the Church:	
Infant Baptism Totals	5,433
Minor Baptism Totals	378
Adult Baptism Totals	279
Received into Full Communion	368
First Communions	5,412
Confirmations	6,610
Marriages:	
Catholic	948
Interfaith	246
Total Marriages	1,194
Deaths	2,611
Total Catholic Population	598,964
Total Population	3,807,037

LEADERSHIP

The Pastoral Center - t) 303-722-4687
Archbishop of Denver - Most Rev. Samuel J. Aquila;
Auxiliary Bishop of Denver -
Vicar General - Very Rev. R. Michael Dollins;
Vicar for Clergy - Very Rev. Angel Perez-Lopez;
Chancellor - David Uebbing;
Chief Operating Officer - Keith Parsons;
Chief Financial Officer - Brenda Cannella;
Chief Mission Officer - Scott Elmer;
Superintendent of Catholic Schools - Elias Moo;

OFFICES AND DIRECTORS

Curia and Ministry Offices -
Archbishop's Office - t) 303-722-4687 Rev. Thomas Scherer, Secy. to Archbishop; Christina Buches, Office Oper. Mgr.;
Archives - t) 303-722-4687 Karyl Klein, Archivist;
Black Catholics - t) 303-722-4687 Kateri Joda Williams, Dir.;
Catholic Schools - t) 303-722-4687 Elias Moo, Supt.; Barbara Anglada, Spec. Prog. Dir. & Asst. to Supt.;
Colorado Catholic Conference - t) 303-894-8808 ccc@cocatholicconference.org www.cocatholicconference.org Brittany Vessely, Exec. Dir.;
Consecrated Life - t) 303-722-4687 Sr. Sharon Ford, R.S.M., Dir.;
Diaconate - t) 303-722-4687 Dcn. Ernest Martinez, Dir.; Amy Vigil, Coord.;
Episcopal Support and Holy Trinity Center - t) 303-722-4687 Sandra Miley, Mgr.;
Evangelization and Family Life Ministries - t) 303-722-4687 Andrew McGown, Exec. Dir.; Alejandra Bravo, Dir.; Sandra Morales, Assoc. Dir.;
Hispanic Ministry - t) 303-722-4687 (Hispanic Evangelization); 303-295-9470 (Centro San Juan Diego) Alfonso Lara, Dir., Centro San Juan Diego;
Liturgy - t) 303-722-4687 Hung Pham, Dir.;
Marketing and Communications - t) 303-722-4687 Kevin Greaney, Exec. Dir.;
Minor and At-Risk Adult Protection - t) 303-722-4687 Christi Sullivan, Dir.;
Mission Advancement - t) 303-722-4687 Paul Dudzic, Chief Devel. Officer;
Office of the Vicar for Clergy - t) 303-722-4687 Dcn. Timothy Hathaway, Oper. Mgr.;
Pastoral Outreach - t) 303-722-4687 Mike Baird, Dir.; Robbyn Celestin, Oper. Mgr.;
Priestly Vocations - t) 303-722-4687 Rev. Jason Wallace, Dir.;

Finance, Administration and Planning -
Accounting - t) 303-722-4687 Rhiannon Baldivia, Dir.;
Cemeteries and Mortuary - t) 303-425-9511 Gary Schaaf, Exec. Dir.;
Construction and Planning - t) 303-722-4687 Mike Wisneski, Dir.;
Facilities Management - t) 303-722-4687 Michael McKee, Dir.;
Human Resources - t) 303-722-4687 Keegan O'Rourke, Dir.;
Information Systems - t) 303-722-4687 Jason Whitehouse, Dir.;
Insurance and Risk Management - t) 303-722-4687 Brenda Cannella, Dir.;
Internal Audit - t) 303-722-4687 John Vunovich, Dir.;
Legal Department - t) 303-722-4687
Parish Finance - t) 303-722-4687 Michele Buice, Dir.;
Real Estate - t) 303-722-4687 Patrick Brady, Dir.;
Treasury - t) 303-722-4687 Mick Bleyle, Dir.;

DEANERIES

Boulder - Very Rev. Michael Carvill, F.S.C.B.;
Central East Denver - Very Rev. Samuel Morehead;
Central West Denver - Very Rev. Joseph McLagan;
East Denver - Very Rev. David Bluejacket;
Eastern Plains - Very Rev. Michael Bodzioch;
Fort Collins - Very Rev. Simon Kalonga, Dean;
Greeley - Very Rev. Angel Perez-Brown, Dean;
Northeast Denver - Very Rev. James S. Spahn;
Northwest Denver - Very Rev. Christopher A. Renner;
Southeast Denver - Very Rev. John L. Hilton, Dean;
Southwest Denver - Very Rev. Matthew Book;
West Denver - Very Rev. Joseph Tran, Dean;
Western Slope - Very Rev. Peter Wojda, Dean;

TRIBUNAL

Metropolitan Tribunal and Office of Canonical Affairs - t) (303) 894-8994
Judicial Vicar - Rev. Giovanni Capucci;
Metropolitan Judges - Carlos Venegas; Anthony St. Louis-Sanchez; Steven Hancock;
Promoter of Justice - Rev. Vincent Phung;
Defenders of the Bond - Sr. Francisca Igweilo, O.P.; Rev. Vincent Phung; Shannon C. Fossett;
Judicial Auditors - Soraya Gonzalez; Peter Waymel;
Ecclesiastical Notaries - D. Jacques; Lucinda Marques;
Tribunal Chancellor - Anthony St. Louis-Sanchez;
Coordinator of Second Instance - Soraya Gonzalez;

PARISHES, MISSIONS, AND CLERGY

STATE OF COLORADO

AKRON

St. Joseph Catholic Parish in Akron - 551 W. 6th St., Akron, CO 80720 t) 970-345-6996 office@stjosephsakron.org Rev. Marek Ciesla, S.Chr., Pst.;

ARVADA

St. Joan of Arc Catholic Parish in Arvada - 12735 W. 58th Ave., Arvada, CO 80002 t) 303-420-1232 father.goebel@archden.org www.stjoanarvada.org Rev. Nathan Goebel, Pst.; Dcn. Matt Archer; Dcn. Joseph Gerber; Dcn. Rex Pilger;

Shrine of St. Anne Catholic Parish in Arvada - 7555 Grant Pl., Arvada, CO 80002 t) 303-420-1280 mseifert@shrineofstanne.org www.shrineofstanne.org Rev. Sean J. McGrath, Pst.; Dcn. Glenn Allison; Dcn. Ron Beck;

Shrine of St. Anne Catholic School - (Grades K-8) 7320 Grant Pl., Arvada, CO 80002 t) 303-422-1800 info@stannescatholic.org www.stannescatholic.com Theresa Donahue, Prin.;

Spirit of Christ Catholic Parish in Arvada - 7400 W. 80th Ave., Arvada, CO 80003 t) 303-422-9173 staff@spiritofchrist.org www.spiritofchrist.org Very Rev. Christopher A. Renner, Pst.; Dcn. Charles Hahn; Dcn. Anthony John Misiti; Dcn. Joe Nowak;

ASPEN

St. Mary Catholic Parish in Aspen - 533 E. Main St., Aspen, CO 81611 t) 970-925-7339 admin@stmaryaspen.org stmaryaspen.org/ Rev. Darrick Leier, Pst.;

AULT

St. Mary in Ault - 267 E. 4th St., Ault, CO 80610; Mailing: 1250 7th St., Windsor, CO 80550 t) 970-686-5084 father.pedersen@archden.org; office@ourladyofthevalley.net www.stmarysault.com Administered by Our Lady of the Valley, Windsor. Very Rev. Gregg Pedersen, Pst.;

AURORA

St. Lawrence Korean Catholic Parish in Aurora - 4310 S. Pitkin St., Aurora, CO 80015-1974 t) 303-617-7400 father.kim@archden.org; lawrencenewsletter@gmail.com stlawrencekcc.org Rev. Raphael JeongHun Kim, Pst.;

St. Michael the Archangel Catholic Parish in Aurora - 19099 E. Floyd Ave., Aurora, CO 80013 t) 303-690-6797 stmtac@stmichael-aurora.org www.stmichael-aurora.org Very Rev. Terrence Kissell, Pst.; Rev. Felipe Colombo, Par. Vicar; Dcn. Christopher Pomrening; Dcn. Greg Perzinski;

St. Pius X Catholic Parish in Aurora - 13670 E. 13th Pl., Aurora, CO 80011 t) 303-364-7435 father.aguera@archden.org; akemi@stpiusxparish.org www.stpiusxparish.org Rev. Jorge Aguera, D.C.J.M. (Spain), Pst.;

St. Pius X Catholic School - (Grades PreK-8) 13680 E. 14th Pl., Aurora, CO 80011 t) 303-364-6515 emichalczyk@stpiusxschool.net stpiusxschool.net Karen Shannahan, Prin.;

Queen of Peace Catholic Parish in Aurora - 13120 E. Kentucky Ave., Aurora, CO 80012 t) 303-364-1056 father.medina@archden.org www.queenofpeace.net Rev. Felix Medina-Algaba, Pst.;

St. Therese Catholic Parish in Aurora - 1243 Kingston St., Aurora, CO 80010 t) 303-344-0132 sbeat@comcast.net www.theresecatholic.com Rev. Hector Chiapa-Villarreal, Pst.; Rev. Jose Saenz, Par. Vicar; Rev. Denis Mandamuna, In Res.; Steve Vaughan, Prin.; Sandy Beatty, Bus. Mgr.; Dora Alfaro, DRE;

St. Therese Catholic School - (Grades PreK-8) 1200 Kenton St., Aurora, CO 80010 t) 303-364-7494 admin@sttheresesschool.com www.sttheresesschool.com

BASALT

St. Vincent Catholic Parish in Basalt - 250 Midland Ave., Basalt, CO 81621; Mailing: 397 White Hill Rd., Carbondale, CO 81623 t) 970-704-0820 office@stvincentstmary.com; education@stvincentstmary.com www.stvincentstmary.com Rev. Salvador Sanchez, Pst.;

BOULDER

St. Martin de Porres Catholic Parish in Boulder - 3300 Table Mesa Dr., Boulder, CO 80305 t) 303-499-7744 father.dellinger@archden.org; businessoffice@smdpchurch.org www.smdpchurch.org Rev. Jonathan Dellinger, Pst.;

Sacred Heart of Jesus Catholic Parish in Boulder - 1318 Mapleton Ave., Boulder, CO 80304; Mailing: 2312 14th St., Boulder, CO 80304 t) 303-442-6158 shjboulder.org Rev. Mark S. Kovacik, Pst.; Rev. Tomislav Tomic, Par. Vicar; Dcn. Chris Byrne; Dcn. David Luksch;

Sacred Heart of Jesus Catholic School - (Grades PreK-8) 1317 Mapleton Ave., Boulder, CO 80304 t) 303-447-2362 www.school.shjboulder.org Marie Dunn, Prin.;

St. Rita in Nederland - 326 CO-119, Nederland, CO 80466; Mailing: P. O. Box 901, Nederland, CO 80466 t) 303-258-3060; (303) 442-6158 x116

Sacred Heart of Mary Catholic Parish in Boulder - 6739 S. Boulder Rd., Boulder, CO 80303 t) 303-494-7572 admin@sacredheartofmary.com www.sacredheartofmary.org Rev. Jonathan Dellinger, Pst.; Rev. Emmanuel Osigwe, Par. Vicar;

St. Thomas Aquinas University Catholic Parish in Boulder - 898 14th St., Boulder, CO 80302; Mailing: 904 14th St., Boulder, CO 80302 t) 303-443-8383 father.mussett@archden.org; gabriella@thomascenter.org www.thomascenter.org University of Colorado, Campus Ministry. Rev. Peter Mussett, Pst.; Gabriella Reyes-Diaz, Bus. Mgr.;

St. Thomas Aquinas Catholic Center - 1520 Euclid Ave., Boulder, CO 80302 father.mussett@thomascenter.org

BRECKENRIDGE

St. Mary Catholic Parish in Breckenridge - 109 S. French St., Breckenridge, CO 80424; Mailing: P.O. Box 23109, Silverthorne, CO 80498 t) 970-668-0250 eraine@summitcatholic.org www.summitcatholic.org Administered at Our Lady of Peace Silverthorne Mission. Rev. Boguslaw Rebacz, Par. Vicar; Dcn. James Doyle; Dcn. Charles Lamar; Dcn. Daniel Cook;

Our Lady of Peace Silverthorne - 89 Smith Ranch Rd., Silverthorne, CO 80498; Mailing: PO Box 23109, Silverthorne, CO 80498 parishoffice@summitcatholic.org Rev. Stephen A. Siebert, Pst.;

BRIGHTON

St. Augustine Catholic Parish in Brighton - 178 S. 6th Ave., Brighton, CO 80601 t) 303-659-1410 staugustine.main@gmail.com www.staugustinebrighton.org Rev. Jose Anibal Chicas, Pst.; Rev. Jose Saenz, Par. Vicar; Dcn. Louis Arambula;

BROOMFIELD

Nativity of Our Lord Catholic Parish in Broomfield - 900 W. Midway Blvd., Broomfield, CO 80020 t) 303-469-5171 m.carvill@nool.us www.nool.us Very Rev. Michael Carvill, F.S.C.B., Pst.; Rev. Emanuele Fadini, Assoc. Pst.; Rev. Matteo Invernizzi, FSCB, Assoc. Pst.; Rev. Accursio Ciaccio, F.S.C.B., Par. Vicar; John Roderick, FSCB, Pst. Assoc.;

Nativity: Faith and Reason - (Grades PreK-8) t) 303-466-4177 Sebastian Calvino, Prin.;

BRUSH

St. Mary Catholic Parish in Brush - 340 Stanford St., Brush, CO 80723 t) 970-842-2216 father.ciesla@archden.org www.stmarybrush.org Administered by St. Joseph, Akron. Rev. Marek Ciesla, S.Chr., Pst.;

St. John in Stoneham - 41629 Granite Ave., Stoneham, CO 80754; Mailing: 340 Standford St., Brush, CO 80723 pastor@stmarybrush.org

BYERS

Our Lady of the Plains Catholic Parish in Byers - 193 W. Bijou Ave., Byers, CO 80103; Mailing: 186 N. McDonnell St., Byers, CO 80103 t) 303-822-5880 ourladyoftheplains@gmail.com; ourladyoftheplains.secretary@gmail.com www.ourladyoftheplains.org Very Rev. Jeffrey Wilborn; Dcn. John Doubrava;

CARBONDALE

St. Mary of the Crown Catholic Parish in Carbondale - 397 White Hill Rd., Carbondale, CO 81623 t) 970-704-0820 father.sanchez@archden.org; office@stvincentstmary.com www.stvincentstmary.com Administered by St. Vincent, Basalt. Rev. Salvador Sanchez, Pst.;

CENTENNIAL

St. Thomas More Catholic Parish in Centennial - 8035 S. Quebec St., Centennial, CO 80112 t) 303-770-1155; 303-770-0531 (CRP) johnc@stthomasmore.org; stm@stthomasmore.org www.stthomasmore.org Very Rev. Randy Michael Dollins, Pst.; Rev. Matthew Hartley, Par. Vicar; Rev. Christopher Marbury, Par. Vicar; Rev. Rohan Miranda, O.C.D., Par. Vicar; Rev. Ivan Monteiro, O.C.D., Par. Vicar; Dcn. George Brown; Dcn. Robert Cropp; Dcn. Timothy Hathaway; Dcn. George C. Morin Jr.; Dcn. Alan Rastrelli; Dcn. Steven Stemper; Dcn. Tim Walsh; John Cox, DRE; Steven Bush, Dir.;

St. Thomas More Catholic School - (Grades PreK-8) 7071 E. Otero Ave., Centennial, CO 80112 t) 303-770-0441 dianeb@stthomasmore.org www.stmcatholic.org Gretchen DeWolfe, Prin.;

CENTRAL CITY

St. Mary Assumption in Central City - 135 Pine St., Central City, CO 80427; Mailing: 1632 Colorado Blvd., P.O. Box 848, Idaho Springs, CO 80452 t) 303-567-4662 www.godrushcatholic.org Administered by St. Paul, Idaho Springs. Rev. John Green, Pst.;

COMMERCE CITY

Our Lady Mother of the Church Catholic Parish in Commerce City - 6690 E. 72nd Ave., Commerce City, CO 80022 t) 303-289-6489 msgr.santos@archden.org; olmcparish@gmail.com www.parisholmc.org Rev. Msgr. Jorge de los Santos, Pst.;

CONIFER

Our Lady of the Pines Catholic Parish in Conifer - 9444 Eagle Cliff Rd., Conifer, CO 80433 t) 303-838-0338 office@olpconifer.org www.olpconifer.org

St. Elizabeth in Buffalo Creek - Rev. Timothy Gaines;

CRAIG

St. Michael Catholic Parish in Craig - 678 School St., Craig, CO 81625 t) 970-824-5330 nwtriparish@gmail.com nwtriparish.com Rev. Gerardo Puga, Pst.; Rev. John Francis Croghan, Par. Vicar;

DENVER

Cathedral Basilica of the Immaculate Conception Catholic Parish in Denver - 1530 Logan St., Denver, CO 80203; Mailing: 1535 Logan St., Denver, CO 80203 t) 303-831-7010 cbic2016@denvercathedral.org www.denvercathedral.org Very Rev. Samuel Morehead, Pst.; Rev. Michael Rapp, Par. Vicar; Dcn. Robert Rinne; Dcn. William Martinez;

St. Elizabeth of Hungary Catholic Church - 1060 St. Francis Way, Denver, CO 80204 t) 303-534-4014 saintelizabeth@qwestoffice.net

All Saints Catholic Parish in Denver - 2559 S. Federal Blvd, Denver, CO 80219; Mailing: 2560 S. Grove St., Denver, CO 80219 t) 303-922-3758 msgr.nguyenp@archden.org Rev. Msgr. Peter Quang Nguyen, Pst.; Dcn. Charles W. Parker Jr.;

Annunciation Catholic Parish in Denver - 3601 Humboldt St., Denver, CO 80205; Mailing: 1408 E. 36th Ave., Denver, CO 80205 t) 303-296-1024 father.polifka@archden.org; pastor@lukeone26.org annunciationdenver.org Rev. Charles J. Polifka, O.F.M.Cap., Pst.;

Annunciation Catholic School - (Grades K-8) 3536 Lafayette St., Denver, CO 80205 t) 303-295-2515 info@annunciationk8.org www.annunciationk8.org Deborah Roberts, Prin.;

Twin Parishes Food Bank - 3663 Humboldt St., Denver, CO 80205 t) 303-294-0684 tpfoodbankdirector@gmail.com Kevin Holwerda-Hommes, Dir.;

St. Anthony of Padua Catholic Parish in Denver - 3801 W. Ohio Ave., Denver, CO 80219 t) 303-935-2431 www.stanthonysdenver.org Rev. Arturo Chagala, Pst.; Rev. Miljenko Pavkovic, Vicar; Dcn. Paul M. Zajac; Rev. Peter Urban, In Res.;

Assumption of the Blessed Virgin Mary Catholic Parish in Denver - 2361 E. 78th Ave., Denver, CO 80229 t) 303-288-2442; 303-288-2442 x132 (CRP) mmatthew@assumptiondenver.org; pklopfenstein@assumptiondenver.org www.assumptiondenver.org Rev. Nicholas Larkin IV, Pst.; Megan Matthew, DRE;

Assumption of the Blessed Virgin Mary Catholic School - (Grades PreK-8) 2341 E. 78th Ave., Denver, CO 80229 t) 303-288-2159 dellis@assumptiondenver.org Dana Ellis, Prin.; Stds.: 136; Lay Tchrs.: 13

Blessed Sacrament Catholic Parish in Denver - 4900 Montview Blvd., Denver, CO 80207; Mailing: 1912 Eudora St., Denver, CO 80220 t) 303-355-7361 www.blessedsacrament.net Rev. John Ludanha;

Blessed Sacrament Catholic School - (Grades PreK-8) 1958 Elm St., Denver, CO 80220 t) 303-377-8835 b.urban@bscs-denver.net www.bscs-denver.net Brooke Urban, Prin.;

St. Cajetan Catholic Parish in Denver - 299 S. Raleigh St., Denver, CO 80219; Mailing: 4325 W. Alameda Ave., Denver, CO 80219 t) 303-922-6306 officemanager@stcajetanparish.com stcajetan.denverparish.com/ Rev. Israel Perez Lopez, Par. Vicar;

St. Catherine of Siena Catholic Parish in Denver - 4200 Federal Blvd., Denver, CO 80211 t) 303-455-9090 stcatherineofsiena@comcast.net www.saintcatherine.us Rev. Luc-Marie Vaillant, C.B., Pst.; Rev. Nilson Leal de Sa, C.B., Par. Vicar;

Christ the King Catholic Parish in Denver - 830 Elm St., Denver, CO 80220-4313 t) 303-388-1643 churchoffice@christthekingdenver.org www.christthekingdenver.org Rev. Rocco Porter, Pst.;

Christ the King Catholic School - (Grades PreK-8) 860 Elm St., Denver, CO 80220 t) 303-321-2123 hdignan@ckrcs.org www.ckrcs.org Kili Hady, Prin.;

Church of the Ascension Catholic Parish in Denver - 14050 Maxwell Pl., Denver, CO 80239 t) 303-373-4950 ascensionchurch71@gmail.com www.acpden.com Rev. Daniel J. Norick, Pst.; Rev. Juan Adrian Hernandez-Dominguez, Par. Vicar; Rev. Alvaro Panqueva, Par. Vicar; Dcn. Ruben Estrada;

Cure d'Ars Catholic Parish in Denver - 3201 Dahlia St., Denver, CO 80207; Mailing: 4701 Martin Luther King Blvd., Denver, CO 80207-1862 t) 303-322-1119 curedarschurchoffice@gmail.com curedars.org Rev. Joseph Cao, Pst.; Dcn. Clarence G. McDavid;

St. Dominic Parish - 2905 Federal Blvd., Denver, CO 80211; Mailing: 3005 W. 29th Ave., Denver, CO 80211 t) 303-455-3613 info@stdominicdenver.org www.stdominicdenver.org Rev. Luke Christopher Barder, O.P., Pst.; Dcn. Antonio Guerrero; Rev. Robert Barry, O.P., In Res.; Rev. Robert Kelly, O.P., In Res.; Rev. Louis S. Morrone, O.P., In Res.; Rev. David F. Wright, O.P., In Res.;

St. Francis de Sales Catholic Parish in Denver - 300 S. Sherman St., Denver, CO 80209; Mailing: 301 S. Grant St., Denver, CO 80209 t) 303-744-7211 Rev. Francesco Basso, Pst.;

Saint Gianna Beretta Molla Catholic Parish - 6890 Argonne St., Unit B, Denver, CO 80249 t) 303-968-0533 father.wunsch@archden.org; stgiannadenver@gmail.com stgiannadenver.org Rev. Jason F. Wunsch, Pst.;

Good Shepherd Catholic Parish in Denver - 2626 E. Seventh Ave. Pkwy., Denver, CO 80206-3809 t) 303-322-7706 parishinfo@goodshepherddenver.org www.goodshepherdchurchdenver.org Rev. James E. Fox, Pst.; Mark Leonard;

Good Shepherd Catholic School - (Grades PreK-8) 620 Elizabeth St., Denver, CO 80206 t) 303-321-6231 mark.strawbridge@goodshepherddenver.org www.goodshepherddenver.org Mark Strawbridge, Prin.;

Guardian Angels Catholic Parish in Denver - 1843 W. 52nd Ave., Denver, CO 80221 t) 303-433-8361 gangelsdenver@gmail.com guardianangelschurchdenver.org Rev. Daniel Zimmerschied, Pst.;

Guardian Angels Catholic School - (Grades PreK-8) t) (303) 480-9005 Mary Gold, Prin.;

Holy Family Catholic Parish in Denver - 4380 Utica St., Denver, CO 80212; Mailing: 4377 Utica St., Denver, CO 80212 t) 303-455-1664 office@holyfamilydenver.com Rev. Patrick Dolan, Pst.;

Holy Ghost Catholic Parish in Denver - 1900 California St., Denver, CO 80202 t) 303-292-1556 father.uhl@archden.org; holyghostden@gmail.com www.holyghostchurch.org Rev. Paul Nguyen, O.M.V., Pst.; Rev. Andrew Huhtanan, O.M.V., Par. Vicar; Rev. Rafael Solorio, O.M.V., Par. Vicar; Rev. Gregory Cleveland, O.M.V., Weekend Asst; Rev. John Paul Klein, O.M.V., Weekend Asst;

Holy Rosary Catholic Parish in Denver - 4688 Pearl St., Denver, CO 80216-2731 t) 303-297-1962 info@holyrosarydenver.org; secretary@holyrosarydenver.org holyrosarydenver.org

St. Ignatius Loyola Catholic Parish in Denver - 2301 York St., Denver, CO 80205; Mailing: 2309 Gaylord St., Denver, CO 80205 t) 303-322-8042 parish@loyoladenver.org www.loyoladenver.org Rev. Dirk Dunfee, S.J., Pst.; Rev. Patrick T Quinn, S.J., Par. Vicar;

St. James Catholic Parish in Denver - 1311 Oneida St., Denver, CO 80220; Mailing: 1314 Newport St., Denver, CO 80220 t) 303-322-7449 father.garciaj@archden.org www.stjamesdenver.org Rev. Jose de Jesus Garcia, Pst.;

St. James Catholic School - (Grades PreK-8) 1250 Newport St., Denver, CO 80220 t) 303-333-8275 school.office@stjamesdenver.org www.stjamesdenver.org/school Carol Hovell-Genth, Prin.;

St. Joseph Catholic Parish in Denver - 600 Galapago St., Denver, CO 80204; Mailing: 623 Fox St., Denver, CO 80204 t) 303-534-4408 edlin.alvarado@stjosephdenver.org; mary.jacob@stjosephdenver.org www.stjosephdenver.org Most Rev. Jorge H. Rodriguez Novelo, Pst.;

St. Joseph Polish Catholic Parish in Denver - 517 E. 46th Ave., Denver, CO 80216 t) 303-296-3217

st.josephpolish@gmail.com stjosephpolish.org Rev. Stanislaw Michalek, Pst.;

St. Mary Magdalene Catholic Parish in Denver - 2771 Zenobia St., Denver, CO 80212 t) 303-455-1968 stmarymagdalenedenver@gmail.com saintmarymagdenver.org/ Rev. Luke Christopher Barder, O.P., Pst.;

Most Precious Blood Catholic Parish in Denver - 2200 S. Harrison St., Denver, CO 80210; Mailing: 3959 E. Iliff Ave., Denver, CO 80210 t) 303-756-3083 father.ciucci@archden.org www.mpbdenver.org Rev. Daniel Ciucci, Pst.; Rev. Micah Flores, Par. Vicar;

Most Precious Blood Catholic School - (Grades K-8) 3959 E. Iliff, Denver, CO 80210 t) 303-757-1279 swyatt@mpbdenver.org school.mpbdenver.org Colleen McManamon, Prin.;

Early Learning Center of Most Precious Blood - (Grades PreSchool-PreK) 2225 S. Colorado Blvd., Denver, CO 80222 t) 303-756-4252 Kellie Peterson, Dir.;

Mother of God Catholic Parish in Denver - 475 Logan St., Denver, CO 80203 t) 303-744-1715 businessmanager@motherofgoddenver.com www.motherofgoddenver.com Rev. Vincent Phung, Pst.;

Notre Dame Catholic Parish in Denver - 2190 S. Sheridan Blvd., Denver, CO 80219; Mailing: 5100 W. Evans Ave., Denver, CO 80219 t) 303-935-3900 pastor@denvernotredame.org www.denvernotredame.org Rev. Msgr. Edward Buelt, Pst.; Rev. John Therese Creus, Par. Vicar; Dcn. Kevin Leiner; Dcn. Ernest Martinez;

Notre Dame Catholic School - (Grades PreK-8) 2165 S. Zenobia St., Denver, CO 80219 t) 303-935-3549 gcaudle@notredamedenver.org www.notredamedenver.org Greg Caudle, Prin.;

Our Lady of Grace Catholic Parish in Denver - 2645 E. 48th Ave., Denver, CO 80216 t) 303-297-3440 father.zermeno-martin@archden.org; ourladyofgrace@msn.com Rev. Felix Zermeno-Martin, Pst.;

Our Lady of Guadalupe Catholic Parish in Denver - 1209 W. 36th Ave., Denver, CO 80211 t) 303-477-1402; 303-477-8113 father.hernandez@archden.org www.ologdenver.org Rev. Benito A. Hernandez, C.R., Pst.;

Our Lady of Lourdes Catholic Parish in Denver - 2298 S. Logan St., Denver, CO 80210; Mailing: 2200 S. Logan St., Denver, CO 80210 t) 303-722-6861 admin@lourdesdenver.org www.lourdesdenver.org Rev. Brian Larkin, Pst.; Rev. Sean Conroy, Par. Vicar; Rev. Witold Kaczmarzyk, Par. Vicar;

Our Lady of Lourdes Catholic School - (Grades PreK-8) 2256 S. Logan St., Denver, CO 80210 t) 303-722-7525 office@lourdesclassical.org lourdesclassical.org Rosemary Vander Weele, Prin.;

Our Lady of Mount Carmel Catholic Parish in Denver - 3549 Navajo St., Denver, CO 80211-3040 t) 303-455-0447 father.guentner@archden.org; cpeccia@mtcarmel7.com ourladymountcarmel.com Rev. Hugh M. Guentner, O.S.M., Pst.; Rev. Mark Franceschini, O.S.M., In Res.;

Presentation of Our Lady Catholic Parish in Denver - 695 Julian St., Denver, CO 80204; Mailing: 665 Irving St., Denver, CO 80204 t) 303-534-4882 father.poehlmann@archden.org www.presentationdenver.org Rev. Edward J. Poehlmann, Pst.;

Risen Christ Catholic Parish in Denver - 3060 S. Monaco Pkwy., Denver, CO 80222 t) 303-758-8826 father.bailey@archden.org www.risenchristchurch.org Rev. Scott Bailey, Pst.;

St. Rose of Lima Catholic Parish in Denver - 355 S. Navajo St., Denver, CO 80223; Mailing: 1320 W. Nevada Pl., Denver, CO 80223 t) 303-778-7673 father.frias@archden.org www.srldenver.org Rev. Martin Frias-Guardado, Pst.; Dcn. Don Tracy;

St. Rose of Lima Catholic School - (Grades PreK-8) 1345 W. Dakota Ave., Denver, CO 80223 t) 303-733-5806 strosedenver@gmail.com srldenver.org/school Tricia Cárdenas, Prin.;

Sacred Heart Catholic Parish in Denver - 2760 Larimer St., Denver, CO 80205 t) 303-294-9830 maria@sacredheartdenver.org Rev. Eric D. Zegeer, Par. Admin.;

St. Vincent De Paul Catholic Parish in Denver - 2375 E. Arizona Ave., Denver, CO 80210 t) 303-744-6119 info@saintvincents.org www.saintvincents.org Very Rev. John L. Hilton, Pst.;

St. Vincent De Paul Catholic School - (Grades PreK-8) 1164 S. Josephine St., Denver, CO 80210 t) 303-777-3812 info@svdpk8.com www.svdpk8.com Sr. Marie Isaac Staub, Prin.;

EDWARDS

St. Clare of Assisi Catholic Parish in Edwards - 31622 U.S. Hwy. 6, Edwards, CO 81632; Mailing: P.O. Box 1390, Edwards, CO 81632 t) 970-926-2821 father.quera@archden.org stclareparish.com Rev. Jose Maria Quera (Spain), Pst.; Rev. John Robert Mrozek II, Par. Vicar; Rev. Jose de Jesus Murillo Ferro, Par. Vicar; Rev. Shannon Thurman, Par. Vicar;

St. Mary in Eagle - 215 Capitol St., Eagle, CO 81631

St. Clare of Assisi Catholic School - (Grades K-8) 31622 US Hwy. 6, Edwards, CO 81632 t) 970-926-8980 admin@stclareparish.com www.stclarecatholicschool.com Sr. Regina Marie Connor, RSM, Prin.;

ENGLEWOOD

All Souls Catholic Parish in Englewood - 4950 S. Logan St., Englewood, CO 80113-6847 t) 303-789-0007; 303-789-0007 x2702 (CRP) allsouls@allsoulscatholic.org allsoulscatholic.org Rev. Richard Nakvasil, Pst.; Rev. Francis Therese Krautter, CSJ, Par. Vicar; Dcn. Kelvin R. Brath; Dcn. Martin A. Wager; Rev. Nathan Cromly, C.S.J., In Res.; Rev. John Therese, CSJ, In Res.; Joseph Ignowski, Youth Min.; Johnna Alyse Heasley, DRE; Dani Ayers, Bus. Mgr.;

All Souls Catholic School - (Grades K-8) 4951 S. Pennsylvania St., Englewood, CO 80113 t) 303-789-2155 Tracy Alarcon, Prin.; Sue Troxel, Vice Prin.;

All Souls Early Learning Center - 4951 S. Pennsylvania St., Englewood, CO 80113 t) 303-783-9099 Bridget Cunningham, Dir.;

Holy Name Catholic Parish in Englewood - 3290 W. Milan Ave., Englewood, CO 80110 t) 303-781-6093 business@holynamedenver.org www.holynamedenver.org Rev. Daniel Cardo, S.C.V., Pst.;

St. Louis-King of France Catholic Parish in Englewood - 3310 S. Sherman St., Englewood, CO 80113 t) 303-761-3940 jan@lourdesdenver.org; receptionist@stlouiscatholicparish.org www.stlouiscatholicparish.org Rev. Brian Larkin, Pst.; Rev. Sean Conroy, Par. Vicar; Rev. Witold Kaczmarzyk, Par. Vicar;

ERIE

St. Scholastica Catholic Parish in Erie - 615 Main St., Erie, CO 80516; Mailing: P.O. Box 402, Erie, CO 80516 t) 303-828-4221 parishoffice@stscholasticaerie.org www.stscholasticaerie.org Rev. Robert L. Wedow, Pst.;

ESTES PARK

Our Lady of the Mountains Catholic Parish in Estes Park - 920 Big Thompson Ave., Estes Park, CO 80517 t) 970-586-8111 info@olmestes.org www.olmestes.org Rev. Faustinus Anyamele, Pst.; Dcn. Stan Rymes;

EVERGREEN

Christ the King Catholic Parish in Evergreen - 4291 Evergreen Pkwy., Evergreen, CO 80439-7723 t) 303-674-3155 ctkevergreen.com Rev. James R. Fox, Pst.; Dcn. Robert Hoffman;

FORT COLLINS

St. Elizabeth Ann Seton Catholic Parish in Ft. Collins - 5450 S. Lemay Ave., Fort Collins, CO 80525 t) 970-226-1303 father.toledo@archden.org www.seas-parish.org Rev. Joseph Toledo, Pst.; Dcn. Donald Weiss; Dcn. Richard Antinora; Dcn. Vernon Dobelmann; Dcn. Robert Lanciotti;

Holy Family Catholic Parish in Ft. Collins - 328 N. Whitcomb St., Fort Collins, CO 80521; Mailing: 326 N. Whitcomb St., Fort Collins, CO 80521 t) 970-482-6599 holyfamily.ftcollins@comcast.net Very Rev. Simon Kalonga, Admin.; Rev. Jean-Marie Mwenze, Par. Vicar;

St. John XXIII Catholic Parish in Ft. Collins - 1220 University Ave., Fort Collins, CO 80521 t) 970-484-3356 sandy@john23.com www.saintjohn.church Rev. Joseph LaJoie, Pst.;

St. Joseph Catholic Parish in Ft. Collins - 300 W. Mountain Ave., Fort Collins, CO 80521; Mailing: 101 N. Howes St., Fort Collins, CO 80521 t) 970-482-4148 jlcoleman@stjosephfc.org; frsimon@stjosephfc.org www.stjosephfc.org Very Rev. Simon Kalonga, Pst.; Rev. Joseph A. Hartmann, Par. Vicar; Dcn. Greg Reynolds; Dcn. Jerome Kraft;

St. Joseph Catholic School - (Grades PreK-8) 127 N. Howes St., Fort Collins, CO 80521 t) 970-484-1171 dklein@gosaintjoseph.org Nick Blanco, Prin.;

FORT LUPTON

St. William Catholic Parish in Ft. Lupton - 1025 Fulton Ave., Fort Lupton, CO 80621 t) 303-857-6642 accounting@saintwilliamchurch.org www.saintwilliamchurch.org Rev. Grzegorz Wojcik, Pst.; Dcn. Pedro Reyes;

Our Lady of Grace in Wattenburg - 1956 Grace Ave., Ft. Lupton, CO 80621; Mailing: 1025 Fulton Ave., Ft. Lupton, CO 80621 secretary@saintwilliamchurch.org

FORT MORGAN

St. Helena Catholic Parish in Ft. Morgan - 917 W. 7th Ave., Fort Morgan, CO 80701 t) 970-867-2885 father.vigil@archden.org; infor@sthelenachurch.org www.sthelenachurch.org Rev. Erik Vigil Reyes, Pst.;

St. Francis of Assisi in Weldona - 801 Warren St, Weldona, CO 80653

Our Lady of Lourdes in Wiggins -

FOXFIELD

Our Lady of Loreto Catholic Parish in Foxfield - 18000 E. Arapahoe Rd., Foxfield, CO 80016 t) 303-766-3800 father.bluejacket@archden.org; mail@ourladyofloreto.org www.ourladyofloreto.org Very Rev. David Bluejacket, Pst.; Rev. Ireneusz Kuźmicki, Par. Vicar; Dcn. Michael Magee; Dcn. Richard Miller; Dcn. Christopher Tranchetti; Dcn. Wayne Lauer; Dcn. Carl Redman;

Our Lady of Loreto Catholic School - (Grades PreK-8) t) 303-951-8330 sadm@ourladyofloreto.org www.ololcatholicschool.org Kate Hatch, Prin.; Deanne Martinez, Vice Prin.;

FREDERICK

St. Theresa Catholic Parish in Frederick - 5503 Bella Rosa Pkwy., Frederick, CO 80504 t) 303-833-2966 father.florez@archden.org www.sttheresafred.org Rev. Hernan Florez Albarracin, Pst.;

GLENWOOD SPRINGS

St. Stephen Catholic Parish in Glenwood Springs - 1885 Blake Ave., Glenwood Springs, CO 81601 t) 970-945-6673 ststephen1885@sopris.net www.ststephen1885.org Very Rev. Elbert Chilson, Pst.; Rev. Anthony Maxwell Davis, Par. Vicar;

St. Stephen Catholic School - (Grades PreK-8) 414 S. Hyland Park Dr., Glenwood Springs, CO 81601 t) 970-945-7746 goliver@sscs414.org www.scsglenwood.org Glenda Oliver, Prin.;

GOLDEN

St. Joseph Catholic Parish in Golden - 969 Ulysses St., Golden, CO 80401 t) 303-279-4464 info@stjoegold.org Very Rev. Joseph Tran, Pst.; Dcn. Edward Clements; Dcn. Dennis J. Langdon;

GRAND LAKE

St. Anne Catholic Parish in Grand Lake - 360 Hancock St., Grand Lake, CO 80447; Mailing: P.O. Box 2029, Granby, CO 80446 t) 970-887-0032 admin@grandcatholic.com www.grandcatholic.com Very Rev. Peter Wojda, Pst.; Rev. Mathias Bayiha, Assoc. Pst.;

Our Lady of the Snow in Granby - 300 N. 11th St., 300 N. 11th St., Granby, CO 80446; Mailing: P. O. Box

2029, Granby, CO 80446
St. Bernard Montjoux in Fraser - 275 E. Rendezvous Rd, Fraser, CO 80442

GREELEY

St. Mary Catholic Parish in Greeley - 2222 23rd Ave., Greeley, CO 80634 t) 970-352-1724 socorro.garcia@stmarygreeley.org; stmarysecretary@stmarygreeley.org www.stmarygreeley.org Rev. Wojciech Gierasimczyk, Pst.; Rev. Crispin Kibambe Kya Bela Mema, Par. Vicar; Dcn. Frederick L. Torrez; Alfie Rael, DRE; Susan Benke, Bus. Mgr.;
St. Mary Catholic School - (Grades PreK-8) 2351 22nd Ave., Greeley, CO 80631 t) 970-353-8100 principal@stmarycs.net www.stmarycs.net Stacey Chavez, Prin.;
Our Lady of Peace Catholic Parish in Greeley - 220 14th Ave., Greeley, CO 80631; Mailing: 1311 Third St., Greeley, CO 80631 t) 970-353-1747 pastor@ourladyofpeacegreeley.org; olpgreeley@gmail.com ourladyofpeacegreeley.org/
St. Peter Catholic Parish in Greeley - 915 12th St., Greeley, CO 80631 t) 970-352-1060 cheryl@stpetergreeley.org www.stpetergreeley.org Rev. Tomasz Strzebonski, Pst.;

HOLYOKE

Catholic Parish of Saint Patrick in Holyoke - 541 S. Interocean Ave., Holyoke, CO 80734; Mailing: 519 S. Interocean Ave., Holyoke, CO 80734 t) 970-854-2762 c) 720-339-1472 patrickpeterctk@gmail.com; jerryrohr@gmail.com catholicsoftheplains.org Rev. Jerry Rohr, Pst.;
Christ the King in Haxtun - 306 N. Iris Ave., Haxtun, CO 80731
St. Peter the Apostle in Fleming - 40027 CR 18, Fleming, CO 80728 t) 970-265-2792

IDAHO SPRINGS

St. Paul Catholic Parish in Idaho Springs - 1632 Colorado Blvd., Idaho Springs, CO 80452; Mailing: P.O. Box 848, Idaho Springs, CO 80452 t) 303-567-4662 info@godrushcatholic.org www.godrushcatholic.org Rev. John Green, Pst.;
Our Lady of Lourdes in Georgetown - 902 Taos St., Georgetown, CO 80444

ILIFF

St. Catherine in Iliff - 111 S. Fifth St., Iliff, CO 80736; Mailing: 326 S. 3rd St., Sterling, CO 80751 t) 970-522-6422 pastor@saintanthonyssterling.org www.saintanthonyssterling.org Administered by St. Anthony, Sterling. Very Rev. Michael Bodzioch, Pst.;

JOHNSTOWN

St. John the Baptist Catholic Parish in Johnstown - 1000 Country Acres Dr., Johnstown, CO 80534 t) 970-587-2879 contactus@sjbjohnstown.org www.sjbjohnstown.org Very Rev. Angel Perez-Brown, Pst.;

JULESBURG

St. Anthony of Padua Catholic Parish in Julesburg - 606 W. 3rd St., Julesburg, CO 80737 t) 970-474-2655 father.nsubuga@archden.org Rev. Herman Joseph Nsuguba JJuuko, Admin.;
St. Peter in Crook - 612 E. 3rd Ave., Crook, CO 80726; Mailing: 606 W. 3rd St., Julesburg, CO 80737

KREMMLING

St. Peter Catholic Parish in Kremmling - 106 S. 5th St., Kremmling, CO 80459; Mailing: P.O. Box 2029, Granby, CO 80446 t) 970-887-0032 x5 admin@grandcatholic.com www.grandcatholic.com Administered by St. Anne, Grand Lake. Very Rev. Peter Wojda, Pst.; Rev. Mathias Bayiha, Assoc. Pst.;

LAFAYETTE

Immaculate Conception Catholic Parish in Lafayette - 715 Cabrini Dr., Lafayette, CO 80026-2676 t) 303-665-5103 father.galvin@archden.org; jenifer@lafayettecatholic.org www.lafayettecatholic.org Rev. Shaun Galvin, Pst.; Rev. Jaime Valdez Vargas (Mexico), Par. Vicar;

LAKEWOOD

St. Bernadette Catholic Parish in Lakewood - 7240 W. 12th Ave., Lakewood, CO 80214 t) 303-233-1523 connect@stbernadettelakewood.org www.stbernadettelakewood.org Very Rev. Joseph McLagan, Pst.;
St. Bernadette Catholic School - (Grades PreK-8) 1100 Upham St., Lakewood, CO 80214 t) 303-237-0401 office@stbcs.net Avery Coats, Prin.;
Christ on the Mountain Catholic Parish in Lakewood - 13922 W. Utah Ave., Lakewood, CO 80228-4110 t) 303-988-2222 frdavid@christonthemountain.org www.christonthemountain.net Rev. David Allen, Pst.; Dcn. Michael Fletcher;
St. Jude Catholic Parish in Lakewood - 9405 W. Florida Ave., Lakewood, CO 80232-5111 t) 303-988-6435 mail@saintjudelakewood.org www.saintjudelakewood.org Rev. Jason M. Thuerauf, Pst.; Dcn. Michael L. Bunch; Dcn. Joseph Hensley; Dcn. John Volk;
Our Lady of Fatima Catholic Parish in Lakewood - 1985 Miller St., Lakewood, CO 80215 t) 303-233-6236 frhenri@fatimalakewood.org; secretary@fatimalakewood.org fatimalakewood.com Very Rev. Henri Tshibambe, Pst.; Dcn. Michael Daly; Carl Zarlengo, Bus. Mgr.;
Our Lady of Fatima Catholic School - (Grades PreK-8) 10530 W. 20th Ave., Denver, CO 80215 t) 303-233-2500 ltaylor@olfcs.com; czarlengo@fatimalakewood.com www.olfcs.com Lisa Taylor, Prin.;

LITTLETON

St. Frances Cabrini Catholic Parish in Littleton - 6673 W. Chatfield Ave., Littleton, CO 80128 t) 303-979-7688 dfantz@sfcparish.org www.sfcparish.org Rev. John Paul Leyba, Pst.; Rev. Jeevan D'Almeda, O.C.D., Assoc. Pst.; Dcn. Brian J. Kerby; Rev. Ronald Sequeira, Pst. Assoc.; Dcn. Marc Nestorick; Dcn. Chet Ubowski;
Light of the World Roman Catholic Parish in Littleton - 10316 W. Bowles Ave., Littleton, CO 80127 t) 303-973-3969 jennifer@lotw.org www.lotw.org Very Rev. Matthew Book, Pst.; Rev. Isidore Orjikwe, Par. Vicar; Dcn. Joseph H. Donohoe; Dcn. Rick Montagne; Dcn. Jesse Taitano; Dcn. Mark Wolbach;
St. Mary Catholic Parish in Littleton - 6853 S. Prince St., Littleton, CO 80120 t) 303-798-8506 kathy.reuter@stmarylittleton.org stmarylittleton.org Rev. Jose Noriega, D.C.J.M., Pst.; Rev. Javier Nieva, D.C.J.M. (Spain), Par. Vicar; Rev. Javier O'Connor, DCJM, Par. Vicar; Dcn. Greg Frank; Dcn. Timothy M. Kilbarger; Dcn. Michael Seback;
St. Mary Catholic School - (Grades PreK-8) 6833 S. Prince St., Littleton, CO 80120 t) 303-798-2375 kboscia@stmarylittleton.com www.littletoncatholicschool.com Rev. Jamie de Cendra, D.C.J.M. (Spain), Prin.;
Our Lady of Mount Carmel Catholic Parish in Littleton - 5612 S. Hickory St., Littleton, CO 80120 t) 303-703-8538 secretary@olmcfssp.org olmcfssp.org Rev. Matthew John McCarthy, FSSP, Pst.; Rev. Daniel Nolan, Assoc. Pst.;

LONGMONT

St. Francis of Assisi Catholic Parish in Longmont - 3791 Pike Rd., Longmont, CO 80503 t) 303-772-6322 www.sfassisi.org Rev. James H. Crisman, Pst.;
St. John the Baptist Catholic Parish in Longmont - 323 Collyer St., Longmont, CO 80501 t) 303-776-0737 info@johnthebaptist.org www.johnthebaptist.org Rev. John Stapleton, Par. Vicar; Dcn. Mike Berens; Dcn. Jose Rodriguez;
St. John the Baptist Catholic School - (Grades PreK-8) 350 Emery St., Longmont, CO 80501 t) 303-776-8760 schooloffice@johnthebaptist.org school.johnthebaptist.org Kemmery Hill, Prin.;

LOUISVILLE

St. Louis Catholic Parish in Louisville - 902 Grant Ave., Louisville, CO 80027 t) 303-666-6401 parishoffice@stlp.org www.stlp.org Rev. Timothy Hjelstrom, Pst.; Dcn. Daniel McConville;
St. Louis Catholic School - (Grades PreK-8) 925 Grant Ave., Louisville, CO 80027 t) 303-666-6220 lwelty@stlp.org school.stlp.org Amy Licata, Prin.;

LOVELAND

St. John the Evangelist Catholic Parish in Loveland - 1730 W. 12th St., Loveland, CO 80537 t) 970-635-5800 info@saintjohns.net www.saintjohns.us Rev. Shannon Thurman, Pst.; Rev. Gustavo Adolfo Becerra Mendez (Mexico), Par. Vicar; Dcn. August Cordova; Dcn. Pat Travis; Dcn. Dennis Wallisch;
St. John the Evangelist Catholic School - (Grades PreK-8) t) 970-635-5830 saintjohnsschool@saintjohns.net www.school.saintjohns.net Julie Rossi, Prin.;

MEAD

Guardian Angels Catholic Parish in Mead - 109 S. Third St., Mead, CO 80542; Mailing: P.O. Box 444, Mead, CO 80542 t) 970-535-0721 father.cattany@meadangels.org; info@meadangels.org www.meadangels.org Rev. Ronald Cattany, Pst.;

MEEKER

Holy Family in Meeker - 889 Park Ave., Meeker, CO 81641; Mailing: P.O. Box 866, Meeker, CO 81641 t) 970-878-3300 nwtriparish@gmail.com nwtriparish.com Administered by St. Michael, Craig. Rev. Gerardo Puga, Pst.; Rev. John Francis Croghan, Par. Vicar;

MINTURN

St. Patrick Catholic Parish in Minturn - 476 Pine St., Minturn, CO 81645; Mailing: P.O. Box 219, Minturn, CO 81645-0219 t) 970-926-2821 father.quera@archden.org www.saintpatrickminturn.com Administered by St. Clare of Assisi, Edwards. Rev. Jose Maria Quera (Spain), Pst.;

NORTHGLENN

Immaculate Heart of Mary Catholic Parish in Northglenn - 11385 Grant Dr., Northglenn, CO 80233 t) 303-452-2041 deacontaylor@ihmco.org; information@ihmco.org www.ihmco.org Rev. Ernest Bayer, Pst.; Rev. Andrew Kemberling, Par. Vicar; Rev. Miljenko Pavkovic, Par. Vicar; Dcn. Jerome Durnford; Dcn. Taylor Elder; Dcn. Paul Louderman;

PEETZ

Sacred Heart in Peetz - 621 Logan St., Peetz, CO 80747; Mailing: 326 S. 3rd St., Sterling, CO 80751 t) 970-522-6422 pastor@saintanthonyssterling.org www.saintanthonyssterling.org Administered by St. Anthony, Sterling. Very Rev. Michael Bodzioch, Pst.;

PLATTEVILLE

St. Nicholas Catholic Parish in Platteville - 514 Marion Ave., Platteville, CO 80651; Mailing: 520 Marion Ave., P.O. Box 576, Platteville, CO 80651 t) 970-785-2143 stnicholasplatteville72@gmail.com www.stnicholasplatteville.org Rev. Angel Perez Brown, Pst.; Rev. Tomasz Surma, Par. Vicar;

RANGELY

St. Ignatius of Antioch in Rangely - 109 S. Stanolind Ave., Rangely, CO 81648; Mailing: 678 School St., Craig, CO 81625 t) 970-824-5330 nwtriparish@gmail.com nwtriparish.com Administered by St. Michael, Craig. Rev. Gerardo Puga, Pst.; Rev. John Francis Croghan, Par. Vicar;

RIFLE

St. Mary Catholic Parish in Rifle - 761 Birch Ave., Rifle, CO 81650; Mailing: P.O. Box 191, Rifle, CO 81650 t) 970-625-5125 father.garciag@archden.org www.stmaryrifle.com Rev. Gerardo Garcia Jimenez (Mexico), Pst.;
Sacred Heart in Silt - 230 N. 6th St., Silt, CO 81652; Mailing: 761 Birch Ave., PO Box 191, Rifle, CO 81650 t) (970) 625-5125 fr.garcia@stmaryrifle.com Rev. Gerardo Garcia-Jimenez, Pst.;

ROGGEN

Sacred Heart Catholic Parish in Roggen - 38044 Weld County Rd. 16, Roggen, CO 80652 t) 303-849-5313 sacredheart@rtebb.net www.thesacredheartchurch.org Rev. Peter Dinh, Pst.;
Holy Family in Keenesburg - 100 Ash St., Keenesburg, CO 80643; Mailing: 38044 Weld County Rd. 16, Roggen, CO 80652

STEAMBOAT SPRINGS

Holy Name Catholic Parish in Steamboat Springs - 524 Oak St., Steamboat Springs, CO 80487; Mailing: PO Box 774198, Steamboat Springs, CO 80477-4198 t) 970-879-0671 holyname@catholicsteamboat.org www.catholicsteamboat.org Rev. Gregory Cioch, Pst.; Rev. Miguel Angel Soubrier, Par. Vicar;

St. Martin in Oak Creek - 400 S. Sharp Ave., Oak Creek, CO 80467; Mailing: P. O. Box 774198, Steamboat Springs, CO 80477-4198

STERLING

St. Anthony Catholic Parish in Sterling - 333 S. 3rd St., Sterling, CO 80751; Mailing: 326 S. 3rd St., Sterling, CO 80751 t) 970-522-6422 pastor@saintanthonyssterling.org www.saintanthonyssterling.org Very Rev. Michael Bodzioch, Pst.;

THORNTON

Holy Cross Catholic Parish in Thornton - 9371 Wigham St., Thornton, CO 80229 t) 303-289-2258 father.castro@archden.org; holy.cross@comcast.net www.holycrossthornton.com Rev. Warli de Araujo Castro, Pst.; Rev. Juan Manuel Madrid Maureira, Par. Vicar;

Saint John Paul II Catholic Parish in Thornton - 3951 Cottonwood Lakes Blvd., Thornton, CO 80241; Mailing: 11385 Grant Dr., c/o Immaculate Heart of Mary Catholic Parish, Northglenn, CO 80233 t) 303-452-2041 father.spahn@archden.org; deacontaylor@stjohnpaul2.org stjohnpaul2.org Dcn. Milinazzo Richard;

WALDEN

St. Ignatius Catholic Parish in Walden - 448 LaFever St., Walden, CO 80430; Mailing: P.O. Box 2029, Granby, CO 80446 t) 970-887-0032 x5 admin@grandcatholic.com www.grandcatholic.com Administered by St. Anne, Grand Lake. Very Rev. Peter Wojda, Pst.; Rev. Mathias Bayiha, Assoc. Pst.;

WESTMINSTER

Holy Trinity Catholic Parish in Westminster - 7595 N. Federal Blvd., Westminster, CO 80030 t) 303-428-3594 parishoffice@htcatholic.org www.htcatholic.org Rev. Carlos Wilson Bello-Ayala, Pst.; Rev. Juan Manuel Bonilla, Vicar;

Our Lady of Visitation in Denver - 2531 W. 65th Pl., Denver, CO 80221; Mailing: 7595 N. Federal Blvd, Westminster, CO 80030

St. Mark Catholic Parish in Westminster - 3141 W. 96th Ave., Westminster, CO 80031 t) 303-466-8720 father.baird@archden.org www.saintmarkcc.org Rev. James Baird, Pst.;

WHEAT RIDGE

Sts. Peter & Paul Catholic Parish in Wheat Ridge - 3900 Pierce St., Wheat Ridge, CO 80033 t) 303-424-3706 info@peterandpaulcatholic.org; adminassistant@peterandpaulcatholic.org www.peterandpaulcatholic.org Rev. James K. Goggins, Pst.; Msgr. Emile Martin Dibongue (Cameroon), Par. Vicar; Rev. Darrell Schaffer, In Res.; Dcn. Scott Ditch; Dcn. Mark Kinnare;

Sts. Peter & Paul Catholic School - (Grades PreK-8) 3920 Pierce St., Wheat Ridge, CO 80033 t) (303) 424-0402 mgosage@sppscatholic.com www.sppscatholic.com Sr. Faustia Deppe, O.C.D., Prin.;

Queen of Vietnamese Martyrs Catholic Parish in Wheat Ridge - 4655 Harlan St., Wheat Ridge, CO 80033 t) 303-431-0382 father.caimyloc@archden.org Rev. Bonaventure Cai My Loc, C.M.C., Pst.;

WINDSOR

Our Lady of the Valley Catholic Parish in Windsor - 1250 7th St., Windsor, CO 80550 t) 970-686-5084 office@ourladyofthevalley.net www.ourladyofthevalley.net Very Rev. Gregg Pedersen, Pst.; Rev. Christian Mast, Par. Vicar; Dcn. Andrew Sanchez;

WRAY

St. Andrew the Apostle Catholic Parish in Wray - 412 Dexter St., Wraý, CO 80758 t) 970-332-5858 standrewapostlewray@gmail.com Rev. Felicien Mbala, Pst.;

YUMA

St. John the Evangelist Catholic Parish in Yuma - 508 S. Ash St., Yuma, CO 80759 t) 970-848-5973 father.mbala@archden.org; mbalafe@gmail.com www.yumacountycatholic.org Rev. Felicien Mbala, Pst.;

SCHOOLS: PRESCHOOL THRU HIGH SCHOOL

SCHOOLS

STATE OF COLORADO

DENVER

Escuela De Guadalupe - (PRV) (Grades PreK-8) 660 Julian St., Denver, CO 80204 t) 303-964-8456 natalie_hopper@escuelaguadalupe.org; michelle@escuelaguadalupe.org www.escuelaguadalupe.org Mariella Robledo, Prin.; Michelle Galuszka, Pres.; Stds.: 209; Lay Tchrs.: 11

***Sophia Montessori Academy** - (PRV) (Grades PreK-12) 2626 E. Louisiana Ave., Denver, CO 80210 t) 303-927-6550 info@sophiamontessori.com www.sophiamontessori.com Pauline Meert, Dir.; Stds.: 35; Lay Tchrs.: 4

ENGLEWOOD

St. Mary's Academy Lower School - (PRV) (Grades PreK-5) 4545 S. University Blvd., Englewood, CO 80113 t) 303-762-8300 ksmith@smanet.org; inatarajan@smanet.org stmarys.academy Sisters of Loretto at the Foot of the Cross. Karen Smith, Prin.; Missy Ochoa, Librn.; Stds.: 230; Lay Tchrs.: 31

St. Mary's Academy Middle School - (PRV) (Grades 6-8) 4545 S. University Blvd., Englewood, CO 80113 t) 303-762-8300 lscott@smanet.org; inatarajan@smanet.org stmarys.academy Sisters of Loretto at the Foot of the Cross Andy Aldrich, Prin.; Iswari Natarajan, Vice. Pres.; Jennifer Colmenero, Librn.; Stds.: 191; Lay Tchrs.: 22

THORNTON

Frassati Catholic Academy - (DIO) (Grades PreK-8) 3951 Cottonwood Lakes Blvd., Thornton, CO 80241 t) 303-451-9607 sylvia.prusinowska@gofrassati.org; eileen.michalczyk@gofrassati.org gofrassati.org Rev. Juan Manuel Madrid Maureira, Chap.; Eileen Michalczyk, Exec. Dir.; Stds.: 365; Lay Tchrs.: 24

WESTMINSTER

Bl. Miguel Pro Catholic Academy, Inc. - (DIO) (Grades PreK-8) 3050 W. 76th Ave., Westminster, CO 80030 t) 303-427-5632 ann.zeches@miguelpro.org www.miguelpro.org Dr. Ann Zeches, Prin.; Stds.: 135; Lay Tchrs.: 13

HIGH SCHOOLS

STATE OF COLORADO

AURORA

***Regis Jesuit High School Corporation** - (PRV) (Grades 9-12) 6300 S. Lewiston Way, Aurora, CO 80016 t) 303-269-8000 communications@regisjesuit.com www.regisjesuit.com Jesuit high school offering single-gender instruction to young men & women on the same campus Jimmy Tricco, Prin.; David Card, Pres.; Stds.: 1,714; Pr. Tchrs.: 3; Lay Tchrs.: 114

BROOMFIELD

Holy Family High School - (DIO) 5195 W. 144th Ave., Broomfield, CO 80023 t) 303-410-1411 matt.hauptly@holyfamilyhs.com www.holyfamilyhs.com Matthew Hauptly, Prin.; Dana St. John, Librn.;

CENTENNIAL

Chesterton Academy of Our Lady of Victory, Inc. - (PRV) (Grades 9-12) 6495 S. Colorado Blvd., Centennial, CO 80121; Mailing: P.O. Box 2062, Centennial, CO 80161 t) (720) 953-8187 office@ourladyofvictorydenver.com ourladyofvictorydenver.com Jeremie Solak, Headmaster; David Holman, Chair; Stds.: 71; Lay Tchrs.: 9

DENVER

Arrupe Jesuit High School - (PRV) 4343 Utica St., Denver, CO 80212 t) 303-455-7449 dhug@arrupejesuit.com www.arrupejesuit.com Rev. John R. Nugent, S.J., Prin.; Michael O'Hagan, Pres.; Stds.: 417; Scholastics: 1; Pr. Tchrs.: 2; Lay Tchrs.: 25

Bishop Machebeuf High School - (DIO) (Grades 9-12) 458 Uinta Way, Denver, CO 80230-6934 t) 303-344-0082 kweyandt@machebeuf.org; president@machebeuf.org www.machebeuf.org Erich Hoffer, Pres.; Rev. Julio C. Amezcua-Martin, Chap.; Stds.: 175; Bro. Tchrs.: 2; Sr. Tchrs.: 2; Lay Tchrs.: 17

Central Denver Classical High School (St. John Paul the Great Catholic High School) - 2330 S Sherman St., Denver, CO 80210 t) (720) 881-0395 x301 www.jpthegreatdenver.org/ Bob Gross, Treas.; Stds.: 24; Lay Tchrs.: 4

J K Mullen High School - (PRV) (Grades 9-12) 3601 S. Lowell Blvd., Denver, CO 80236 t) 303-761-1764 info@mullenhigh.com; james.uvalle@mullenhigh.com www.mullenhigh.com Coed High School. The Christian Brothers of Mullen High School, Brothers of the Christian Schools Dr. Raul Cardenas Jr., Pres.; Jeff Howard, Prin.; Stds.: 735; Scholastics: 119; Pr. Tchrs.: 1; Lay Tchrs.: 66

ENGLEWOOD

St. Mary's Academy High School - (PRV) (Grades 9-12) 4545 S. University Blvd., Englewood, CO 80113 t) 303-762-8300 inatarajan@smanet.org; kferguson@smanet.org stmarys.academy Sisters of Loretto at the Foot of the Cross. Iswari Natarajan, Prin.; Kristin Ferguson, Librn.; Stds.: 256; Lay Tchrs.: 28

WINDSOR

St. John Paul II High School - (Grades 9-12) 1250 7th St., Windsor, CO 80550 t) (970) 281-5269 info@jpiihs.com jpiihs.com/ Blaise Hockel, Headmaster; Stds.: 36; Lay Tchrs.: 6

INSTITUTIONS LOCATED IN DIOCESE

ASSOCIATIONS [ASN]

DENVER

The Catholic Community of the Beatitudes - 2924 W. 43rd Ave., Denver, CO 80211 t) 720-855-9412 beatitudes.usa@yahoo.com denver.beatitudes.org/ Ecclesial Family of Consecrated Life. Rev. Nilson Leal de Sa, C.B., Supr.;

Companions of Christ - 1050 Pennsylvania St., Denver, CO 80203 t) 720-933-4185 denver.companions@gmail.com www.denvercompanionsofchrist.org Very Rev. Matthew Book;

KEENESBURG

Societas Matris Dolorosissimae - 3510 County Rd. 55, Keenesburg, CO 80643; Mailing: P.O. Box 311, Keenesburg, CO 80643 t) 970-370-7933 info@dolorans.org dolorans.org Rev. Chad Ripperger, Moderator;

CAMPUS MINISTRY / NEWMAN CENTERS [CAM]

GENESEE

***Fellowship of Catholic University Students (FOCUS)** - 603 Park Point Dr., Genesee, CO 80401; Mailing: P.O. Box 17408, Denver, CO 80217 t) 303-962-5750 info@focus.org www.focus.org Craig Miller, Pres.;

CATHOLIC CHARITIES [CCH]

DENVER

Archdiocesan Housing, Inc. - 6240 Smith Rd., Denver, CO 80216 t) 303-830-0215 jraddatz@archhousing.com www.archhousing.com Maria Rightmyer, Exec.; Justin Raddatz, Exec.; Asstd. Annu.: 3,082; Staff: 73

Archdiocesan Family Housing, Inc. - c/o 6240 Smith Rd., Denver, CO 80216 t) (303) 922-1442

Cathedral Plaza Inc. - c/o 6240 Smith Rd., Denver, CO 80216 t) (303) 837-1424 www.archdiocesanhousing.org

Colorado Affordable Catholic Housing Corp. - c/o 6240 Smith Rd., Denver, CO 80216 t) (303) 830-0215 www.archdiocesanhousing.org Affordable housing financing services.

Golden Spike, Inc. - c/o 6240 Smith Rd., Denver, CO 80216 t) (303) 922-6606 www.archdiocesanhousing.org Senior & disabled housing apts.

Higgins Plaza, Inc. - c/o 6240 Smith Rd., Denver, CO 80216 t) (303) 320-4990 www.archdiocesanhousing.org Affordable housing.

Holy Cross Village, Inc. - c/o 6240 Smith Rd., Denver, CO 80216 t) (970) 524-0125 www.archdiocesanhousing.org Affordable housing.

Holy Family Plaza, Inc. - c/o 6240 Smith Rd., Denver, CO 80216 t) (303) 455-4433 www.archdiocesanhousing.org Affordable housing.

Housing Management Services, Inc. - c/o 6240 Smith Rd., Denver, CO 80216 t) (303) 830-0215 www.archdiocesanhousing.org Affordable housing.

Immaculata Plaza, Inc. - c/o 6240 Smith Rd., Denver, CO 80216 t) (303) 830-0215 www.archdiocesanhousing.org

Machebeuf Apartments, Inc. - c/o 6240 Smith Rd., Denver, CO 80216 t) (970) 945-9792 www.archdiocesanhousing.org Afforable housing.

Madonna Plaza, Inc. - c/o 6240 Smith Rd., Denver, CO 80216 www.archdiocesanhousing.org Affordable housing.

Marian Plaza, Inc. - c/o 6240 Smith Rd., Denver, CO 80216 t) (303) 837-1818 www.archdiocesanhousing.org

St. Martin Plaza, Inc. - c/o 6240 Smith Rd., Denver, CO 80216 t) (303) 297-1414 www.archdiocesanhousing.org Affordable housing.

Prairie Rose Plaza - c/o 6240 Smith Rd., Denver, CO 80216 t) (303) 289-3430 www.archdiocesanhousing.org Affordable housing.

Villa Sierra Madre, Inc. - c/o 6240 Smith Rd., Denver, CO 80216 t) (970) 262-2354 www.archdiocesanhousing.org Affordable housing.

Villas de Santa Lucia, Inc. - c/o 6240 Smith Rd., Denver, CO 80216 t) (970) 963-8061 www.archdiocesanhousing.org Affordable housing.

Catholic Charities and Community Services of the Archdiocese of Denver, Inc. - 6240 Smith Rd., Denver, CO 80216 t) 303-742-0828 info@ccdenver.org www.ccdenver.org Shelters for the Homeless, Emergency Assistance Services, Individual & Family Counseling Services, Pregnancy Counseling, Senior Services, Early Educ. Darren Walsh, CEO; Asstd. Annu.: 80,592; Staff: 557

Catholic Charities Early Childhood Education - 6240 Smith Rd., Denver, CO 80216 rbieker@ccdenver.org Rick Bieker, Dir.;

Catholic Charities Family Services - 6240 Smith Rd., Denver, CO 80216 jmcintosh@ccdenver.org Respect Life, Adoption, Adult Services, Kinship, Homebased Counseling Jan McIntosh, Exec.;

Catholic Charities Farm Labor Housing Corporation - 6240 Smith Rd., Denver, CO 80216 t) 970-378-1171 pvottiero@ccdenver.org Philip Vottiero, Exec.;

Catholic Charities Guadalupe Shelter for Homeless - 1442 N. 11th Ave., Greeley, CO 80631; Mailing: 6240 Smith Rd., Denver, CO 80216 t) 970-353-6433 jsarr@ccdenver.org Emergency Assistance, Senior Services, Case Management, Immigration Services. Mike Sinnett, Exec.;

Catholic Charities Immigration Services - c/o 6240 Smith Rd., Denver, CO 80216 apalmaroberts@ccdenver.org Jan McIntosh, Exec.;

Catholic Charities Larimer Regional Office - 460 Linden Center Dr., Fort Collins, CO 80524; Mailing: 6240 Smith Rd., Denver, CO 80216 t) 970-484-5010 The Mission Shelter for Homeless, Emergency Assistance, Senior Services, Immigration Services. Mike Sinnett, Exec.;

Catholic Charities Marisol Family - 6240 Smith Rd., Denver, CO 80216 kwebster@ccdenver.org Provides for basic material needs of families. Jan McIntosh, Exec.;

Catholic Charities Marisol Health - 6240 Smith Rd., Denver, CO 80216 t) 303-731-6130 slugo@ccdenver.org Full range of women's & family health svcs. Jan McIntosh, Exec.;

Catholic Charities Marisol Home - c/o 6240 Smith Rd., Denver, CO 80216 t) 720-799-9400 msinnett@ccdenver.org Homeless Shelter Mike Sinnett, Exec.;

Catholic Charities Mulroy Senior Center - 3550 W. 13th Ave., Denver, CO 80204; Mailing: 6240 Smith Rd., Denver, CO 80216 t) 303-892-1540 jmcintosh@ccdenver.org Morgan Rossow, Contact;

Catholic Charities Plaza Del Milagro - 2500 1st Ave., Greeley, CO 80631; Mailing: 6240 Smith Rd., Denver, CO 80216 t) 970-346-2888 wwolberg@ccdenver.org Migrant & Seasonal Housing. Wayne Wolberg, Exec.;

Catholic Charities Plaza Del Sol - 2501 Ash Ave., #36, Greeley, CO 80631; Mailing: 6240 Smith Rd., Denver, CO 80216 t) 970-378-1171 wwolberg@ccdenver.org Migrant & Seasonal Housing. Wayne Wolberg, Exec.;

Catholic Charities Samaritan House - 2301 Lawrence St., Denver, CO 80205; Mailing: 6240 Smith Rd., Denver, CO 80216 t) 303-294-0241 msinnett@ccdenver.org Homeless Shelter Mike Sinnett, Exec.;

Catholic Charities Western Slope Office - 1004 Grand Ave., Glenwood Springs, CO 81601; Mailing: 6240 Smith Rd., Denver, CO 80216 t) 970-384-2060 mmcdonough@ccdenver.org Community Integration Services, Emergency Assistance, Transitional Housing. Mike Sinnett, Exec.;

Little Flower Center - 11149 E. 14th Ave., Aurora, CO 80010 t) 303-360-6986 littleflower@ccdenver.org www.ccdenver.org/the-little-flower Mike Sinnett, Exec.;

St. Raphael Counseling - 750 W. Hampden Ave., Ste. 415, Englewood, CO 80112 t) 720-377-1359 Jim Langley, Dir.;

CEMETERIES [CEM]

AURORA

St. Simeon Cemetery Association - 22001 E. State Hwy. 30, Aurora, CO 80018 t) 303-502-9179 gary.schaaf@archden.org cfcscolorado.org Gary Schaaf, Dir.;

WHEAT RIDGE

Archdiocese of Denver Mortuary at Mount Olivet, Inc. - 12801 W. 44th Ave., Wheat Ridge, CO 80033 t) 303-425-9511 gary.schaaf@archden.org Gary Schaaf, Dir.;

The Mount Olivet Cemetery Association - 12801 W. 44th Ave., Wheat Ridge, CO 80033 t) 303-425-9511 Gary Schaaf, Dir.;

COLLEGES & UNIVERSITIES [COL]

DENVER

Regis University - 3333 Regis Blvd., Denver, CO 80221-1099 t) (303) 458-4190 president@regis.edu www.regis.edu A university conducted under the auspices of the Society of Jesus. Rev. Kevin F. Burke, SJ, Vice. Pres.; Stds.: 4,668; Lay Tchrs.: 300; Pr. Tchrs.: 2; Sr. Tchrs.: 1

GREENWOOD VILLAGE

***Augustine Institute, Inc.** - 6160 S. Syracuse Way, Ste. 310, Greenwood Village, CO 80111 t) 303-937-4420 info@augustineinstitute.org www.augustineinstitute.org Tim Gray, Pres.;

CONVENTS, MONASTERIES, AND RESIDENCES FOR WOMEN [CON]

DENVER

***Marian Community of Reconciliation (Fraternas)** - 1060 St. Francis Way, Denver, CO 80204 t) 303-629-0500 denver@fraternas.org Sr. Luciane Urban, Supr.; Srs.: 6

Missionaries of Charity - 633 Fox St., Denver, CO 80204 t) 303-860-8040 Provides shelter for homeless women (8 Beds). Srs.: 4

Sisters of St. Francis of Penance and Christian Charity (Sisters of St. Francis, Denver, Colorado) - 5314 Columbine Rd., Denver, CO 80221-1277 t) 303-458-6270 sueaf@franciscanway.org www.franciscanway.org Sr. Susan Artone-Fricke, OSF, Prov.; Srs.: 18

Casa Chiara - 5312-5326 Columbine Rd., Denver, CO 80221 t) (303) 458-6270

LITTLETON

Carmel of the Holy Spirit - 6138 S. Gallup St., Littleton, CO 80120-2702 t) 303-798-4176 The Discalced Carmelite Nuns of Colorado, Discalced Carmelites (O.C.D.). Mother Mary of Jesus Doran, O.C.D., Prioress;

VIRGINIA DALE

Abbey of St. Walburga, Inc. - 1029 Benedictine Way, Virginia Dale, CO 80536-7633 t) 970-472-0612 abbey@walburga.org www.walburga.org Rev. Mother Maria-Michael Newe, O.S.B., Abbess; Srs.: 19

HOSPITALS / HEALTH SERVICES [HOS]

DENVER

Saint Joseph Hospital - 1375 E. 19th Ave., Denver, CO 80218 t) 303-812-2000 sjhcommunications@sclhealth.org www.saintjosephdenver.org Rev. Gabriel Okafor, Chap.; Jameson Smith, CEO; Bed Capacity: 400; Asstd. Annu.: 285,183; Staff: 2,400

FRISCO

St. Anthony Summit Hospital - 340 Peak One Dr., Frisco, CO 80443; Mailing: 9100 E. Mineral Cir., Centennial, CO 80112 t) (303) 673-8970 patrickgaughan@centura.org An operating unit of Catholic Health Initiatives Colorado (an affiliate of CommonSpirit Health formerly known as Catholic Health Initiatives). Lee Boyles, CEO; Bed Capacity: 35; Asstd. Annu.: 44,852; Staff: 272

LAKEWOOD

St. Anthony Hospital - 11600 W. 2nd Pl., Lakewood, CO 80112; Mailing: 9100 E. Mineral Cir., Centennial, CO 80112 t) 720-321-0000 patrickgaughan@centura.org An operating unit of Catholic Health Initiatives Colorado (an affiliate of CommonSpirit Health formerly known as Catholic Health Initiatives). Kevin Jenkins, CEO; Bed Capacity: 238; Asstd. Annu.: 140,781; Staff: 1,575

WESTMINSTER

St. Anthony Hospice - 2551 W. 84th Ave., Westminster, CO 80031; Mailing: 9100 E. Mineral Cir., Centennial, CO 80112 t) (303) 673-8970 An operating unit of Catholic Health Initiatives Colorado (an Affiliate of CommonSpirit Health formerly known as Catholic Health Initiatives). Asstd. Annu.: 70; Staff: 3

St. Anthony North Hospital - 14300 Orchard Pkwy., Westminster, CO 80023; Mailing: 9100 E. Mineral Cir., Centennial, CO 80112 t) (303) 673-8970 patrickgaughan@centura.org An operating unit of Catholic Health Initiatives Colorado (an affiliate of CommonSpirit Health formerly known as Catholic Health Initiatives). Constance Schmidt, CEO; Bed Capacity: 121; Asstd. Annu.: 83,461; Staff: 780

MISCELLANEOUS [MIS]

ALLENSPARK

Camp St. Malo Visitor and Heritage Center - 10758 Hwy. 7, Allenspark, CO 80510; Mailing: 1300 S. Steele

St., Denver, CO 80210 t) 303-747-2786 kyle.mills@campstmalo.org; bernadette.buches@campstmalo.org campstmalo.org/ Kyle Mills, Dir.;

AURORA

***4 Others Africa** - 8217 S. Winnepeg Cir., Aurora, CO 80016 t) (303) 845-0595 Susan Bosold, Pres.;

BOULDER

Sacred Heart School Foundation - 2312 14th St., Boulder, CO 80304; Mailing: 2242 Juniper Ct., Boulder, CO 80304 t) 303-444-3478 c) 720-471-5409 timeileen@msn.com shjsf.org James Mullen, Contact;

BROOMFIELD

SCL Health Foundation - 500 Eldorado Blvd., Ste. 4300, Broomfield, CO 80021 t) 303-813-5000; 303-812-6460 megan.mahncke@imail.org; cindy.p.cooper@imail.org Megan Mahncke, Pres.;

Sisters of Charity of Leavenworth Health System, Inc. (SCL Health) - 500 Eldorado Blvd., Ste. 4300, Broomfield, CO 80021 t) 303-813-5190 peaks_ocd-contact@imail.org sclhealth.org Mark Korth, Pres.;

CENTENNIAL

Catholic Health Initiatives Colorado - 9100 E. Mineral Cir., Centennial, CO 80112 t) 303-290-6500 patrickgaughan@centura.org An affiliate of CommonSpirit Health formerly known as Catholic Health Initiatives Peter Banko, CEO;

DENVER

The Archdiocese of Denver Cemeteries Perpetual Care Trust - 1300 S. Steele St., Denver, CO 80210 t) 303-722-4687 Keith A. Parsons, Admin.;

The Archdiocese of Denver Irrevocable Revolving Fund Trust - 1300 S. Steele St., Denver, CO 80210 t) 303-722-4687 Keith A. Parsons, Admin.;

The Archdiocese of Denver Management Corporation - 1300 S. Steele St., Denver, CO 80210 t) 303-722-4687 Keith A. Parsons, Pres.;

The Archdiocese of Denver Risk Management Property/ Casualty Insurance Trust - 1300 S. Steele St., Denver, CO 80210 t) 303-722-4687 Brenda Cannella, Dir.;

The Archdiocese of Denver Welfare Benefits Trust - 1300 S. Steele St., Denver, CO 80210 t) 303-722-4687 Keith A. Parsons, Admin.;

Arrupe Corporate Work Study Program - 4343 Utica St., Denver, CO 80212 t) 303-455-7449 x237 ccookinham@arrupejesuit.com www.arrupejesuit.com Chad Cookinham, Dir.;

Ask a Bishop/Project Finding Calcutta - 4570 Julian St., Denver, CO 80211; Mailing: 4482 County Rd. 2208, Greenville, TX 75402 c) 402-202-3762 anand@askabishop.com www.projectfindingcalcutta.com Teaching Videos by Catholic bishops, Service Projects at Local Parishes and Mission Trips to India Anand Bheemarasetti, Exec. Dir.;

Project Finding Calcutta - Quenching the thirst of Christ Jesus, by mobilizing Catholic volunteers to do the Corporal Works of Mercy in their own cities every month.

***Capuchin Province of Mid-America Mission Fund** - 3613 Wyandot St., Denver, CO 80211 t) 303-477-5436 Bro. Augustine Rohde, O.F.M. Cap., Secy.; Bro. Mark Schenk, O.F.M.Cap., Contact;

Catholic Health Initiatives Colorado Foundation - 2525 S. Downing St., Mason Hall, 3rd Fl., Denver, CO 80210; Mailing: 9100 E. Mineral Cir., Centennial, CO 80112 t) (303) 673-8970 patrickgaughan@centura.org Patrick Gaughan, Contact;

Penrose-St. Francis Health Foundation - An affiliate division of Catholic Health Initiatives Colorado Foundation.

Christ Child Society of Denver - 2754 E. Amherst Ave., Denver, CO 80210; Mailing: P.O. Box 100869, Denver, CO 80250-0869 t) 303-995-6467 denverchristchild@gmail.com Elizabeth Haskell, Secy.;

***Christ in the City** - 3401 N. Pecos St., Denver, CO 80211 t) 303-952-9743 info@christinthecity.org www.christinthecity.org Linda Weigand, Contact;

***Christian Life Movement, Inc.** - 1060 Saint Francis Way, Denver, CO 80204 t) 303-629-5100 denverclm@clmusa.org www.clmusa.org Carlos Keen, Pres.;

***Clare Gardens, Inc.** - 2626 Osceola St., Denver, CO 80212; Mailing: 1600 Broadway, Ste. 2000, Denver, CO 80202 t) 303-830-3300 www.mercyhousing.org Affordable housing Melissa Clayton, Pres.;

***Colorado Vincentian Volunteers** - 1732 Pearl St., Denver, CO 80203 t) 303-863-8141 cvv@covivo.org www.covivo.org Amanda Orta, Dir.;

***Creatio, Inc.** - 623 Fox St, Denver, CO 80204 t) 720-441-2927 info@creatio.org www.creatio.org Bro. Christopher Raymond Lanciotti, Contact;

Emmaus Catholic Hospice (formal corporate name: Dominican Home Health Agency, Inc. - 5290 E. Yale Cir., Ste. 100, Denver, CO 80222 t) 303-322-1413 accounting@emmauscatholichospice.org www.emmauscatholichospice.org In home Catholic hospice care John Kelly, Chair; Jean Finegan, Exec.; Leeanne K Super, C.P.A., CFO; Asstd. Annu.: 6; Staff: 6

***Francis Heights, Inc.** - 2626 Osceola St., Denver, CO 80212; Mailing: 1600 Broadway, Ste. 2000, Denver, CO 80202 t) 303-830-3300 Affordable Housing. Melissa Clayton, Pres.;

Saint John Paul II Center for the New Evangelization - 1300 S. Steele St., Denver, CO 80210 t) 303-722-4687 Michael P. McKee, Pres.;

***Saint Joseph Hospital Foundation** - 1375 E. 19th Ave., Denver, CO 80218 t) (303) 812-6437 Leslie McKay, Dir.;

Mercy Housing Management Group, Inc. - 1600 Broadway, Ste. 2000, Denver, CO 80202 t) 303-830-3300 Cheryll O'Bryan, Pres.;

***Mercy Housing, Inc.** - 1600 Broadway, Ste. 2000, Denver, CO 80202 t) 303-830-3300 www.mercyhousing.org Affordable Housing Properties. Dee Walsh, Vice. Pres.;

***Miguel Pro Mission** - 3801 W. Ohio Ave., St. Anthony of Padua Catholic Parish, Denver, CO 80219; Mailing: PO Box 150480, Denver, CO 80215-0480 t) 720-394-4476 www.miguelpromission.com Rev. Peter Urban, Pres.;

The Sacred Heart of Jesus Housing Foundation - c/o 1300 S. Steele St., Denver, CO 80210 t) (303) 722-4687 Keith A. Parsons, Contact;

Seeds of Hope Charitable Trust - 1300 S. Steele St., Denver, CO 80210 t) 303-715-3127 info@seedsofhopedenver.org www.seedsofhopedenver.org Tricia Sullivan, Exec. Dir.;

Seeds of Hope of Northern Colorado, Inc. - 1300 S. Steele St., Denver, CO 80210 t) 303-715-3127 info@seedsofhopedenver.org www.seedsofhopedenver.org Tricia Sullivan, Exec. Dir.;

Special Religious Education-Pastoral Care of Developmentally Disabled Persons - 3101 W. Hillside Pl., Denver, CO 80219 t) 303-934-1999 smcbridge@comcast.net; vsaykally@comcast.net archden.org/eflm/family/#spirit Religious education of intellectually disabled children and adults (a ministry of the Archdiocese of Denver) Rev. Roland P. Freeman, Dir.;

ENGLEWOOD

Association for Catholic Formation and Leadership, Inc. - 3290 W. Milan Ave., Englewood, CO 80110 t) 303-902-4233 bermudez@tilmastrategies.com www.institutotepeyac.com Alejandro Bermudez, Exec.;

***Association for the Promotion of Apostolate, Inc.** - 3290 W. Milan Ave., Englewood, CO 80110 t) 303-547-5132 eregal@gmail.com Eduardo Regal, Exec.;

Bella Natural Women's Care (Bella Health + Wellness) - 180 E. Hampden Ave., Ste. 100, Englewood, CO 80113 t) 303-789-4968 info@bellawellness.org Dede Chism, CEO;

***Catholic Sports** - 4775 S. Pearl St., Englewood, CO 80113; Mailing: P.O. Box 102584, Denver, CO 80250 t) 720-924-6333 info@catholicsports.net catholicsport.net Build Authentic (new evangelization) Community through Recreational Sports -- Formerly "Catholic Young Adult Sports (CYAS)" Paul Spotts, Pres.;

CHI National Home Care - 198 Inverness Dr. W., Englewood, CO 80112 t) 303-383-2795 pam.koerner@commonspirit.org www.catholichealthinit.org Pam Koerner, Contact;

CHI National Services - 198 Inverness Dr. W., Englewood, CO 80112 t) 303-383-2795 pam.koerner@commonspirit.org www.catholichealthinit.org Pam Koerner, Contact;

CommonSpirit Health - 198 Inverness Dr. W., Englewood, CO 80112 t) 303-383-2795 pam.koerner@commonspirit.org www.catholichealthinit.org Wright Lassiter III, CEO; Lloyd Dean, CEO;

***Saint John Institute** - 4775 S. Pearl St., Englewood, CO 80113 t) (303) 876-7695 lisa.odenbeck@saintjohninstitute.org; father.nathan@saintjohninstitute.org www.saintjohninstitute.org Catholic-infused leadership formation within families, workplaces, and communities. Rev. Nathan Cromly, C.S.J., Pres.;

ESTES PARK

***Our Lady of Tenderness, Poustinia** - 1190 Soul Shine Rd., Estes Park, CO 80517; Mailing: P.O. Box 4311, Estes Park, CO 80517 t) (970) 577-1383 c) 303-877-0728 oltadmin@oltpoustinia.org Poustinia - a Catholic Center Ilene Gleason, Dir.; Rev. Robert L. Wedow, Dir.;

GREELEY

***Catholic Psychotherapy Association, Inc.** - 7251 W. 20th St, M-2, Greeley, CO 80634; Mailing: 511 E John Carpenter Fwy, Irving, TX 75062 c) 913-426-2948; 904-420-0536; (972) 559-0083 admin@catholicpsychotherapy.org www.catholicpsychotherapy.org Matthew Moleski, Exec. Dir.; Mary Hanys, Opers. Mgr.;

St. Mary's Catholic Education Foundation Greeley - 2222 23rd Ave., Greeley, CO 80634 t) 970-352-1724 susan.benke@stmarygreeley.org Susan Benke, Treas.;

GREENWOOD VILLAGE

***The Catholic Foundation for the Roman Catholic Church in Northern Colorado** - 6160 S. Syracuse Way, Ste. 111, Greenwood Village, CO 80111 t) 303-468-9885 info@thecatholicfoundation.com www.thecatholicfoundation.com Dcn. Steven Stemper, Pres.;

***Endow** - 6160 S. Syracuse Way, Ste. 150, Greenwood Village, CO 80111 t) 720-382-5242 info@endowgroups.org; annette.bergeon@endowgroups.org endowgroups.org Endow calls women together to study the important documents of the church. Through Endow groups, women discover their dignity and mission in life. Annette J Bergeon, CEO;

***Real Life Catholic** - 6160 S. Syracuse Way, Ste. 100, Greenwood Village, CO 80111 t) 330-732-5228 info@reallifecatholic.com www.reallifecatholic.com Chris Stefanick, Pres.;

***The Vine Foundation (The Amazing Parish)** - 6160 S. Syracuse Way, Ste. 220, Greenwood Village, CO 80111 t) 303-481-4320 team@amazingparish.org www.amazingparish.org Matt Rudolph, Dir.;

LAKEWOOD

St. Anthony Health Foundation - 11600 W. 2nd Pl., Lakewood, CO 80228; Mailing: 9100 E. Mineral Cir., Centennial, CO 80112 t) (303) 673-8970 An operating unit of Catholic Health Initiatives Colorado Foundation.

LITTLETON

***Andrew Ministries** - 7128 S. Lafayette Way, Littleton, CO 80122 t) 303-909-2736 everett@andrew-ministries.com andrew-ministries.com Everett Fritz, Exec.;

Family of Nazareth, Inc. - 7189 S. Kline St., Littleton, CO 80127 t) 303-949-1764 stevewaymel@gmail.com Steven Waymel, Pres.;

***Highlight Catholic Ministries (Frassati Sports & Adventure, Badano Sports)** - 5490 W. Geddes Ave.,

Littleton, CO 80128; Mailing: P.O. Box 10, Littleton, CO 80160 t) 720-593-1903 admin@frassatisports.org highlightcatholic.org Ryan O'Connor, Pres.;

***In Ipso, Inc.** - 8818 W. Glasgow Pl., Littleton, CO 80128 t) 720-934-1353 dana@in-ipso.org; peter@in-ipso.org www.in-ipso.org Spiritual Formation institute for laity, deaconate and pre-seminary programs offering also spiritual direction and silent retreats. Peter Stur, Pres.;

Magnificat-Denver, CO Chapter, Inc. - 5418 S. Iris St., Littleton, CO 80123 t) 303-884-3902 magnificatofdenver@gmail.com

LOUISVILLE

Camp Wojtyla, Inc. - 114 S Fillmore Ave, Louisville, CO 80027; Mailing: P.O. Box 116, Erie, CO 80516 t) 970-405-9858 eferril@camp-w.com www.camp-w.com Annie Powell, Exec. Dir.;

WESTMINSTER

***Clare of Assisi Homes - Westminster, Inc.** - 2451 W. 82 Pl., Westminster, CO 80031-4099; Mailing: 1600 Broadway, Ste. 2000, c/o Mercy Housing, Denver, CO 80202 t) 303-830-3300 jrosenblum@mercyhousing.org www.mercyhousing.org Affordable housing Melissa Clayton, Pres.;

***Villa Maria, Inc.** - 2461 W. 82nd Pl., Westminster, CO 80031-4099; Mailing: 1600 Broadway, Ste. 2000, Denver, CO 80202 t) 303-830-3300 www.mercyhousing.org Affordable housing. Melissa Clayton, Pres.;

WHEAT RIDGE

Little Sisters of the Poor, Home for the Aged, Denver, Colorado - 4175 Harlan St., Ste. 120, Wheat Ridge, CO 80033; Mailing: P.O. Box 1027, Arvada, CO 80001 t) 303-433-7221 c) (847) 732-1013 chicagocp@littlesistersofthepoor.org www.littlesistersofthepoordenver.org Sr. Mary Sylvia Karl, l.s.p., Pres.;

MONASTERIES AND RESIDENCES FOR PRIESTS AND BROTHERS [MON]

BROOMFIELD

Priestly Fraternity of St. Charles Borromeo (F.S.C.B.) - 900 W. Midway Blvd., Broomfield, CO 80020 t) 508-369-2197 m.carvill@gmail.com www.fraternityofsaintcharles.org Very Rev. Michael Carvill, F.S.C.B.; Rev. Accursio Ciaccio, F.S.C.B.;

CENTENNIAL

Regis High Jesuit Community - 16810 E Caley Ave, Centennial, CO 80016 c) (337) 308-2673 jgoeke@jesuits.org (Society of Jesus, United States Central and Southern Province) Rev. John Craig, S.J., Chap.; Rev. Thomas Rochford, S.J., Chap.; Rev. James Goeke, S.J., Supr.; Rev. Eric Ramirez, S.J., Dir.; Priests: 4

DENVER

Capuchin Province of Mid-America, Inc. (Capuchin Province of St. Conrad) - 3613 Wyandot St., Denver, CO 80211-2950 t) 303-477-5436 contact@capuchins.org www.capuchins.org Order of Friars Minor Capuchin, Province of St. Conrad Rev. William Kraus, O.F.M. Cap., Vicar; Rev. Sojan Parapilly, O.F.M.Cap., Treas.; Bro. Mark Schenk, O.F.M.Cap., Prov.; Rev. Blaine Burkey, O.F.M.Cap., Archivist; Brs.: 18; Priests: 38

St. Anthony of Padua Friary - 3805 W. Walsh Pl., Denver, CO 80219-3241 t) 303-936-6242 Bro. Charbel Allen, O.F.M.Cap., In Res.; Rev. Restom Amine, O.F.M.Cap. (Eritrea), In Res.; Bro. Gregory Armstrong, O.F.M.Cap., In Res.; Dcn. Vincent Mary Carrasco, O.F.M.Cap., In Res.; Bro. Kriston Mary Gloria, O.F.M.Cap., In Res.; Bro. Brian Nwaokolo, O.F.M.Cap., In Res.; Rev. Sales Pathrose, O.F.M.Cap. (India), In Res.; Bro. Antonio Villafranca, O.F.M.Cap., In Res.; Rev. Vittorio Bora, O.F.M. Cap., In Res.; Rev. Christopher Gama, O.F.M.Cap., In Res.; Bro. Jude Quinto, O.F.M.Cap., In Res.;

St. Francis of Assisi Friary - 3553 Wyandot St., Denver, CO 80211-2948 t) 303-477-5542 sojan.parapilly@capuchins.org (Order of Friars Minor Capuchin) Rev. David Songy, O.F.M.Cap., In Res.; Rev. Michael Suchnicki, O.F.M.Cap., In Res.; Rev. Joseph Mary Elder, O.F.M.Cap., In Res.; Rev. Simeon Gallagher, O.F.M. Cap., In Res.; Rev. John Lager, O.F.M. Cap., In Res.; Bro. Augustine Rohde, O.F.M. Cap., In Res.;

San Antonio Friary - 3554 Humboldt St., Denver, CO 80205-3940 t) (303) 477-5436 Order of Friars Minor Capuchin Rev. Charles J. Polifka, O.F.M.Cap., Pst.; Rev. Jason Moore, OFM Cap., Chap.; Rev. Keith Windsor, O.F.M.Cap. (Great Britain), In Res.; Rev. Job Arakkamparambil, O.F.M. Cap., In Res.; Bro. Anthony Monahan, O.F.M.Cap., In Res.;

Dominican Friars, St. Dominic Priory, Denver, Inc. - 2901 Grove St., Denver, CO 80211-3749 t) 303-455-3614 l.morrone@opcentral.org St. Dominic Priory & Dominican Novitiate; Province of St. Albert the Great. Rev. Louis S. Morrone, O.P., Prior; Rev. Luke Christopher Barder, O.P., Subprior; Rev. Patrick Tobin, OP, Par. Vicar; Bro. John Steilberg, OOP, In Res.; Rev. Robert Barry, O.P., In Res.; Rev. Robert Kelly, O.P., In Res.; Rev. David F. Wright, O.P., In Res.; Brs.: 1; Priests: 7

Monastery of Our Lady of Light (Capuchin Poor Clares) - 3325 Pecos, Denver, CO 80211 t) 303-458-6339 www.capuchinpoorclaresdenver.org Capuchin Poor Clares of Denver, Colorado Sr. Maria de Cristo Palafox, Abbess; Srs.: 8; Brs.: 8

Regis Jesuit Community (The Jesuits at Regis University) - Regis University Jesuit Community M-12, 3333 Regis Blvd., Denver, CO 80221-1154 t) 303-964-5500 regisjesuitcommunity@gmail.com; jesuitrector@regis.edu US Central and Southern Province. Rev. Thomas B. Curran, S.J., Supr.; Rev. Marcus C Fryer, SJ, Supr.; Rev. Eustace Sequeira, S.J., Sacr. Min.; Rev. Jason E Brauninger, S.J., Prof.; Marco A Machado, S.J., Prof.; Rev. John R. Nugent, S.J., Prin.; Rev. Fernando Alvarez-Lara, SJ, Prof.; Rev. Kevin F. Burke, SJ, Vice. Pres.; Rev. Kevin B. Dyer, S.J.; Rev. Joseph Tuoc Nguyen, S.J.; Rev. Hung T. Pham, S.J.; Rev. Michael Wegenka, S.J.; Priests: 11

Servants of Christ Jesus - 4022 S. Olive St., Denver, CO 80237 t) 720-458-3038 servants@scjesus.org www.scjesus.org Rev. John Ignatius, SCJ, Supr.;

Society of Jesus - St. Ignatius Loyola Jesuit Community - 2309 Gaylord St., Denver, CO 80205-5627 t) 303-322-8042 parish@loyoladenver.org www.loyoladenver.org Rev. Dirk Dunfee, S.J., Pst.; Rev. Patrick T Quinn, S.J., Par. Vicar; Priests: 2

The Theatine Fathers - 1050 S. Birch St., Denver, CO 80246 t) 303-691-6972 www.theatinesusa.com Rev. Antonio Flores-Cota, Prov.;

Xavier Jesuit Center - 3450 W. 53rd, Denver, CO 80221-6568 t) 303-480-3900 xavierguest1552@gmail.com; xjcmanager@gmail.com (Society of Jesus, Central and Southern (UCS)) Rev. Hung T Pham, S.J., Dir.; Priests: 1

LITTLETON

Disciples of the Hearts of Jesus and Mary - 6853 S. Prince St., Littleton, CO 80120 t) 303-798-8506 luisgranados@dcjm.org www.dcjm.org Rev. Jose Noriega, D.C.J.M., Pst.; Rev. Jamie de Cendra, D.C.J.M. (Spain), Par. Vicar; Rev. Javier Nieva, D.C.J.M. (Spain), Par. Vicar; Rev. Javier O'Connor, DCJM, Par. Vicar; Brs.: 3; Priests: 4

SNOWMASS

St. Benedict's Monastery - 1012 Monastery Rd., Snowmass, CO 81654 t) 970-279-4400 retreat@rof.net www.snowmass.org Order of the Cistercians of the Strict Observance (O.C.S.O., Trappists) Rev. Damian Carr, O.C.S.O., Supr.; Rev. Edward Hoffman, O.C.S.O.; Rev. Micah Schonberger, O.C.S.O.; Rev. Charles Albanese, O.C.S.O., Treas.; Brs.: 2; Priests: 4

NURSING / REHABILITATION / CONVALESCENCE / ELDERLY CARE [NUR]

AURORA

St. Anna's Home (Congregation of Sisters of Charity of St. Vincent de Paul, Colorado Chapter Inc.) - 13901 E. Quincy Ave., Aurora, CO 80015 t) 303-627-2986 st.annashome@hotmail.com Assisted Living Residence Sr. Johanna (Hyun Sook) Soh, Dir.; Sr. Ambrosia (Hyeonok) Ham, Finance; Sr. Stephanie (Kwangmi) Lee, Nursing; Asstd. Annu.: 5; Staff: 3

DENVER

Gardens at St. Elizabeth - 2835 W. 32nd Ave., Denver, CO 80211; Mailing: 198 Inverness Dr. W., Englewood, CO 80112 t) 303-383-2795 aram.haroutunian@commonspirit.org www.catholichealthinit.org An operating unit of CHI Living Communities which is a subsidiary of CommonSpirit Health. Aram Haroutunian, Chap.; Asstd. Annu.: 258; Staff: 91

Prophet Elijah House - 1330 S. Steele St., Denver, CO 80210; Mailing: 1300 S. Steele St., Denver, CO 80210 t) 303-715-2461 deacon.wolbach@archden.org Archdiocese of Denver priest retirement facility. Dcn. Mark Wolbach, Dir.; Asstd. Annu.: 10; Staff: 4

RETREAT HOUSES / RENEWAL CENTERS [RTR]

ESTES PARK

Annunciation Heights - 7400 Hwy. 7, Estes Park, CO 80517; Mailing: c/o 1300 S. Steele St., Denver, CO 80210 t) 970-586-5689 kyle.mills@annunciationheights.org; jerry.bellendir@annunciationheights.org annunciationheights.org/ Kyle Mills, Dir.;

LITTLETON

***Jesus Our Hope Hermitage** - 10519 S. Deer Creek Rd., Littleton, CO 80127 t) 303-697-7539 jesusourhoperetreat@gmail.com www.jesus-our-hope.org Dcn. Robert Alan Hoffman, Chair; Sr. Magdalit Bolduc, Contact;

PINE

Emmaus Catholic Retreat and Conference Center - 13034 U.S. Hwy. 285, Pine, CO 80470; Mailing: c/o 1300 S. Steele St., Denver, CO 80210 t) (303) 747-2786 Keith A. Parsons, Pres.;

SEMINARIES [SEM]

DENVER

Saint John Vianney Theological Seminary - 1300 S. Steele St., Denver, CO 80210 t) 303-282-3427 father.leonard@archden.org; infosjv@archden.org sjvdenver.edu Rev. Daniel Leonard, Rector; Rev. John Nepil, Rector; Dr. Alphonso Pinto, Dean; Rev. Daniel Barron, Dir.; Rev. Braden Wagner, Dir.; Dcn. Timothy Unger, Dir.; Stds.: 120; Lay Tchrs.: 8; Pr. Tchrs.: 7

St. Francis School of Theology for Deacons - t) 303-715-3236 deacons.info@archden.org

Saint John Vianney Theological Seminary Lay Division - t) 303-715-3195 laydivision@archden.org sjvlaydivision.org/ Daniel Campbell, Dir.;

Redemptoris Mater House of Formation - 3434 E. Arizona Ave., Denver, CO 80210 t) 303-733-2220 father.clemence@archden.org www.rmsdenver.org Rev. William Clemence, Rector; Rev. Giovanni Capucci, Vice Rector; Rev. Emilio Franchomme, Spiritual Dir. & Prefect of Studies; Stds.: 29

SHRINES [SHR]

GOLDEN

Mother Cabrini Shrine, Inc. - 20189 Cabrini Blvd., Golden, CO 80401 t) 303-526-0758 jefflewis@mothercabrinishrine.org www.mothercabrinishrine.org Missionary Sisters of the Sacred Heart Jeff Lewis, Admin.;

SPECIAL CARE FACILITIES [SPF]

DENVER

The Bridge Community, Inc. - 3101 W. Hillside Pl., Denver, CO 80219 t) 303-935-4740 vsaykally@comcast.net Veronica Saykally, Contact; Bed Capacity: 8; Asstd. Annu.: 5; Staff: 10

Mount St. Vincent Home, Inc. - 4159 Lowell Blvd., Denver, CO 80211 t) 303-458-7220 caitlin.pride@imail.org www.msvhome.org Jenessa Williams, Exec. Dir.; Stds.: 76; Lay Tchrs.: 31; Asstd. Annu.: 212; Staff: 80

Sacred Heart House of Denver - 2844 Lawrence St., Denver, CO 80205 t) 303-296-6686 jlmdenver45@gmail.com sacredhearthouse.com Housing and services for single mothers with children and single women experiencing homelessness. Janet L. Morris, Exec. Dir.; Bed Capacity: 21; Asstd. Annu.: 1,288; Staff: 4

An asterisk (*) denotes an organization that has established tax-exempt status directly with the IRS and is not covered by the USCCB Group Ruling.

Diocese of Des Moines

(Dioecesis Desmoinensis)

MOST REVEREND WILLIAM M. JOENSEN, PH.D.

Bishop of Des Moines; ordained June 24, 1989; appointed Bishop of Des Moines July 18, 2019; installed September 27, 2019. Pastoral Center, 601 Grand Ave., Des Moines, IA 50309.

Chancery: 601 Grand Ave., Des Moines, IA 50309. T: 515-243-7653; F: 515-237-5070.
www.dmdiocese.org
communications@dmdiocese.org

ERECTED BY POPE ST. PIUS X, AUGUST 12, 1911.

Square Miles 12,446.

Comprises that part of the State of Iowa which is bounded on the east by the eastern boundaries of the Counties of Polk, Warren, Lucas and Wayne; on the south by the State of Missouri; on the west by the Missouri River; and on the north by the northern boundaries of the Counties of Harrison, Shelby, Audubon, Guthrie, Dallas and Polk.

Patrons of the Diocese: I. Blessed Virgin Mary Queen; II. Pope Saint Pius X. Diocese solemnly consecrated to the Immaculate Heart of Mary on May 16, 1948.

Legal Title: "The Roman Catholic Diocese of Des Moines."

For legal titles of parishes and diocesan institutions, consult the Chancery Office.

STATISTICAL OVERVIEW

Personnel	
Bishop	1
Retired Bishops	2
Priests: Diocesan Active in Diocese	44
Priests: Diocesan Active Outside Diocese	4
Priests: Retired, Sick or Absent	42
Number of Diocesan Priests	90
Religious Priests in Diocese	5
Total Priests in your Diocese	95
Extern Priests in Diocese	23
Ordinations:	
Diocesan Priests	3
Transitional Deacons	1
Permanent Deacons in Diocese	102
Total Brothers	2
Total Sisters	42
Parishes	
Parishes	80
With Resident Pastor:	
Resident Diocesan Priests	63
Resident Religious Priests	8
Without Resident Pastor:	
Administered by Priests	8
Administered by Deacons	1
Professional Ministry Personnel:	
Sisters	43
Lay Ministers	77
Welfare	
Catholic Hospitals	4
Total Assisted	1,812,817
Health Care Centers	1
Total Assisted	494
Residential Care of Children	1
Total Assisted	2,500
Special Centers for Social Services	7
Total Assisted	18,896
Educational	
Diocesan Students in Other Seminaries	15
Total Seminarians	15
Colleges and Universities	1
Total Students	911
High Schools, Diocesan and Parish	2
Total Students	1,615
Elementary Schools, Diocesan and Parish	15
Total Students	6,166
Catechesis/Religious Education:	
High School Students	2,945
Elementary Students	6,255
Total Students under Catholic Instruction	17,907
Teachers in Diocese:	
Priests	2
Sisters	1
Lay Teachers	503
Vital Statistics	
Receptions into the Church:	
Infant Baptism Totals	1,343
Minor Baptism Totals	130
Adult Baptism Totals	73
Received into Full Communion	132
First Communions	1,550
Confirmations	1,261
Marriages:	
Catholic	242
Interfaith	81
Total Marriages	323
Deaths	739
Total Catholic Population	107,898
Total Population	944,646

LEADERSHIP

Vicar General - t) 515-237-5039 mamadeo@dmdiocese.org Rev. Michael A. Amadeo;

Chancery - t) 515-243-7653 www.dmdiocese.org/

Chancellor's Office - t) 515-237-5061; 515-237-5056 Jason Kurth, Chancellor; Adam Storey, Vice Chancellor;

Executive Assistant to the Bishop - t) 515-237-5039 ahemmingsen@dmdiocese.org Angie Hemmingsen;

Finance Officer - t) (515) 237-5030 blarson@dmdiocese.org Robert Larson, Dir.;

Vicar for Finance - t) 515-556-9057 Rev. Msgr. Edward Hurley, Vicar; Rev. Joseph Pins, Vicar;

Diocesan Consultors - Rev. Michael A. Amadeo, Vicar Gen.; Rev. Joseph Pins, Vicar of Fin.; Rev. David Fleming, Mem. (dfleming@dmdiocese.org);

Diocesan Corporation Board - Most Rev. William Joensen (wjoensen@dmdiocese.org); Rev. Michael Amadeo; Jason Kurth;

OFFICES AND DIRECTORS

Administrative Services - t) 515-237-5048 Sr. Jude Fitzpatrick, C.H.M., Dir.; Norm Bormann, Property Mgmt. Dir. (nbormann@dmdiocese.org);

Archives - lwingert@dmdiocese.org Lynn Wingert;

Campus Ministry - t) 515-271-1929 office2@stcatherinedrake.org

Communications, Office of - t) 515-237-5057 communications@dmdiocese.org Anne Marie Cox, Dir.;

Continuing Education for Clergy - t) 712-323-2916 frtomcc@gmail.com Rev. Protas Okwalo, S.J., Chair (fr.okwalo@stcatherinedrake.org); Rev. Raphael Assamah, Mem. (rassamah@dmdiocese.org); Rev. Thomas V. Dooley, Mem. (tdooley@dmdiocese.org);

Diaconate Formation - t) 515-237-5037 Dcn. Matthew Halbach, Dir. (dcnmatt@saintluketheevangelist.org);

Diaconate (Permanent) - t) 515-237-5014 Dcn. James Houston, Dir. (houstonjj4u@gmail.com);

Faith Journey - t) 515-237-5006 John Huynh, Dir.;

Finance Office - blarson@dmdiocese.org Robert Larson, Dir.; Laura Hofstrand, Controller (lhofstrand@dmdiocese.org); Jane Gaffney, Internal Controls (jagaffney@dmdiocese.org);

Hispanic Ministry - mmoriel@dmdiocese.org Mayra Moriel de Banuelos, Coord.;

Human Resources - evaldez@dmdiocese.org Eileen Valdez, Dir.;

Newspaper - t) 515-237-5057 Anne Marie Cox, Editor;

Office for Worship (Liturgy, Music, Art and Architecture) - t) 515-237-5046 (Des Moines Office); 712-243-4721 (Atlantic Office) worship@dmdiocese.org Rev. Trevor Chicoine, Dir. (tchicoine@dmdiocese.org);

Office of Evangelization and Catechesis - t) 515-237-5026 John Gaffney, Dir.; Patty Origer, Persons With Disabilities Coord. (poriger@dmdiocese.org);

Office of Marriage Ministry - t) 515-237-5056 Adam Storey, Dir.;

Priests' Pension Fund Society - Rev. Msgr. Edward Hurley; Rev. Msgr. Stephen L. Orr (sorr@dmdiocese.org); Rev. Michael Amadeo;

Propagation of the Faith - t) 515-237-5048 jfitzpatrick@dmdiocese.org Sr. Jude Fitzpatrick, C.H.M.;

St. Vincent de Paul Society - t) 515-288-7411 Rev. John Bertogli, Spiritual Adv./Care Srvcs. (jbertogli@dmdiocese.org);

Schools - t) 515-237-5040 Donna Bishop, Supt.; Denise Mulcahy, Dir. (dmulcahy@dmdiocese.org); Nicole Castillo Waller, Dir. (nwaller@dmdiocese.org);

Stewardship Office - t) 515-237-5079 Maureen Kenney, Dir.;

Tribunal - t) 515-237-5004 Cathy Gearhart, Coord.;

Advocates - Rev. John P. Ludwig; Rev. John Dorton; Dcn. Dennis Luft;

Coordinator of Tribunal - Cathy Gearhart;

Defenders of the Bond - Rev. Lawrence R. Hoffmann; Rev. David J. Polich; Rev. Daniel F. Krettek;

Judges - Rev. Christopher Pisut; Rev. Christopher Hartshorn; Rev. Msgr. Stephen L. Orr;

Judicial Vicar - t) 515-237-5031 cpisut@dmdiocese.org Rev. Christopher Pisut, Judicial Vicar; Rev. Adam Westphal, Assoc. Judicial Vicar & Canonical Advisor;

Notary - Cathy Gearhart;

Victim Assistance Coordinator - t) 515-286-2015 sam.porter@polkcountyiowa.gov Sam Porter (advocate@dmdiocese.org);

Vocations Center / Seminarians - t) 515-237-5014 vocations@dmdiocese.org Rev. Ross Parker, Dir. (rparker@dmdiocese.org); Cathy Jordan, Coord. (cjordan@dmdiocese.org);

Youth Ministry/Young Adult Ministry, Office of - t) 515-237-5098 Justin White, Dir.;

PARISHES, MISSIONS, AND CLERGY

STATE OF IOWA

ADAIR

St. John - 501 Adair St., Adair, IA 50002; Mailing: c/o All Saints, 216 All Saints Dr., P.O. Box 605, Stuart, IA 50250 t) 515-523-1943 allsaintsoffice@gmail.com adairstjohn.org/ Rev. Antony Mathew, Pst.; CRP Stds.: 24

ADEL

St. John - 24043 302nd Pl., Adel, IA 50003-0185; Mailing: P O Box 185, Adel, IA 50003-0185 t) 515-993-4482; 515-993-4590 (CRP) office@stjohnsadel.org; re@stjohnsadel.org www.stjohnsadel.org Rev. Remigius C. Okere, C.S.Sp., Pst.; Stephanie Howard, DRE; Erin Merschman, Youth Min.; Michael Cooper, Music Min.; Angela Oberreuter, Bus. Mgr.; CRP Stds.: 251

AFTON

St. Edward - 104 W. Union St., Afton, IA 50830; Mailing: 406 W. Clark St., Creston, IA 50801 t) 641-782-5278 www.uccat.org Attended by Holy Spirit Parish from Creston. Rev. Patrick K. Amedeka, Assoc. Pst.; Lindsay Thelen, DRE; Michelle Moore, Bus. Mgr.; CRP Stds.: 33

ALTOONA

SS. John and Paul - 1401 1st Ave. S., Altoona, IA 50009 t) 515-967-3796 ssjohnpaul@ssjohnpaul.org www.ssjohnpaul.org Rev. Mark McGeary, Pst.; Dcn. Steve McGee; Maxine McEnany, Bus. Mgr.; Patty Hormann, Dir. of Music; Jenni Lihs, DRE; Maria Haas, Youth Min.; Kristina Frank, Youth Min.; CRP Stds.: 230

ANITA

St. Mary - 302 Chestnut St, Anita, IA 50020; Mailing: 600 Locust St, Atlantic, IA 50022 t) 712-243-4721 officemanager@sspeterpaulandmary.org www.peterpaulandmary.org Rev. Trevor Chicoine, Pst.; Kristi Wernimont, Bus. Mgr.;

ANKENY

St. Luke the Evangelist Catholic Church - 1102 N.W. Weigel Dr., Ankeny, IA 50023 t) 515-964-1278 www.slte.org Rev. Kenneth Halbur, Pst.; Rev. James Downey, Assoc. Pst.; Dcn. Fred Cornwell; Dcn. Matthew Halbach; Dcn. Fred Pins; Dcn. Don Shannon; David Reising, DRE; CRP Stds.: 353

St. Luke the Evangelist School - (Grades K-8) 2110 N.W. Weigel Dr., Ankeny, IA 50023 t) 515-985-7074 misty.hade@slte-school.org; kendra.smith@slte-school.org www.saintluketheevangelistschool.org Misty Hade, Prin.; Stds.: 302; Lay Tchrs.: 20

Our Lady's Immaculate Heart - 510 E. First St., Ankeny, IA 50021 t) 515-964-3038; 515-964-3545 (CRP) olih@olih.org www.olih.org/ Rev. Michael Amadeo, Pst.; Rev. Nicholas Smith, Par. Vicar; Dcn. Jeffrey Boehlert; Dcn. Gregory Kolbinger; Dcn. Steven Udelhofen; Erin Stoltenberg, Liturgy Dir.; Randy Henderson, Youth Min.; Tom Primmer, DRE; Becky J. Robovsky, Bus. Mgr.; CRP Stds.: 826

Our Lady's Immaculate Heart Charitable Foundation -

ATLANTIC

SS. Peter and Paul - 106 W. 6th St., Atlantic, IA 50022; Mailing: 600 Locust St., Atlantic, IA 50022 t) 712-243-4721 officemanager@sspeterpaulandmary.org; faithformation@sspeterpaulandmary.org www.sspeterpaulandmary.org Rev. Trevor Chicoine, Pst.; Kristi Wernimont, Bus. Mgr.; Julie Williamson, DRE; CRP Stds.: 130

AUDUBON

St. Patrick - 116 E. Division St., Audubon, IA 50025 t) 712-563-2283 spht@iowatelecom.net www.stpatrickholytrinity.org Rev. David Nkrumah, Pst.; April Brand, DRE; Linda Blomme, Bus. Mgr.; CRP Stds.: 90

AVOCA

St. Mary, Mediatrix of All Graces - 109 N. Maple St., Avoca, IA 51521-0038; Mailing: P.O. Box 38, Avoca, IA 51521-0038 t) 712-343-6948; 712-343-6951 smpavoca@walnutel.net stmarysavoca.wordpress.com Rev. Seth Nana Kwame Owusu, Pst.; Kathryn Denning, DRE; Stephanie Geraghty, DRE; Pamela Paulson, Liturgy Coord.; CRP Stds.: 54

BAYARD

St. Patrick - 214 Prairie St., Bayard, IA 50029; Mailing: 603 Main St., Guthrie Center, IA 50115 t) 641-747-3843 stcstmstp@netins.net www.st-mary-patrick-cecilia.com Rev. Raymond Higgins, Pst.; CRP Stds.: 20

BEDFORD

Sacred Heart - 707 Main St., Bedford, IA 50833; Mailing: 300 E. Lincoln St., Clarinda, IA 51632 t) 712-542-2030 www.dmdiocese.org/mass.htm St. Clare, Clarinda. Rev. Sylvester Okoh, Pst.; CRP Stds.: 8

CARLISLE

St. Elizabeth Seton - 2566 Scotch Ridge Rd., Carlisle, IA 50047; Mailing: P. O. Box 35, Carlisle, IA 50047 t) 515-989-0659 www.stelizabethcarlisle.com Rev. George Komo, Admin.; Jen Dowler, Pres.; Chris Schneider, Treas.; Sarah Clayton, DRE; Molly Lauer, Bus. Mgr.; CRP Stds.: 124

CHARITON

Sacred Heart - 407 N. Main, Chariton, IA 50049 t) 681-774-4978; 641-344-3100 (CRP) pontieradams@aol.com; shch@iowatelecom.net Mary Chapman, Bus. Mgr.; Sheila Adams, DRE; CRP Stds.: 45

CLARINDA

St. Clare - 300 E. Lincoln Blvd., Clarinda, IA 51632 t) 712-542-2030 Rev. Sylvester Okoh, Pst.; Mark Baldwin, DRE; Emily Akers, DRE; CRP Stds.: 5

CORNING

St. Patrick - 504 Grove Ave., Corning, IA 50841 t) 515-322-3363 pat_corning@yahoo.com www.stpatrickcorning.com Rev. Emmanuel Bassey, Par. Admin.; Jamie Hogan, Liturgy Dir.; CRP Stds.: 33

CORYDON

St. Francis - 213 W. Jackson St., Corydon, IA 50060; Mailing: c/o 407 N. Main St., Chariton, IA 50019 t) 641-774-4978; 712-328-7272 (CRP) shch@iowatelecom.net www.dmdiocese.org/mass.htm Chariton of the South Central Catholic Ministry Team. Rev. Samuel Danso, Pst.; Sheila Adams, DRE; Mary Chapman, Bus. Mgr.;

COUNCIL BLUFFS

Corpus Christi - 3304 4th Ave., Council Bluffs, IA 51501 t) 712-323-1163 (CRP); 712-323-2916; 712-323-4716 (Hispanic Min.) officemanager@corpuschristiia.com www.corpuschristiparishiowa.org/ Rev. Ross Parker, Admin.; Rev. Jacob Epstein, Assoc. Pst.; Dcn. Darwin Kruse; Dcn. Bob McClellan; Dcn. Monty Montagne; CRP Stds.: 163

Our Lady, Queen of Apostles - (Worship Site)

Holy Family - 2217 Ave. B, Council Bluffs, IA 51501 (Worship Site)

Our Lady of Carter Lake - 3501 N. 9th St., Carter Lake, IA 51510 (Worship Site)

St. Patrick - 4 Valley View Dr., Council Bluffs, IA 51503 t) 712-323-1484 faith.formation@stpatrickcb.org; secretary@stpatrickcb.org www.dmdiocese.org/mass.htm Rev. James Ahenkora, Pst.; Rev. Maxwell Carson, Pst. Assoc.; Dcn. Charles Hannan; Dcn. James Mason; Dcn. Emmet Tinley; Dcn. John Pfenning, RCIA Coord.; Jill Faust, DRE; CRP Stds.: 204

Saint Patrick Church of Council Bluffs Iowa Foundation -

St. Peter - One Bluff St., Council Bluffs, IA 51503 t) 712-322-8889 ckottas@aol.com; jeanthomas@cox.net www.dmdiocese.org/mass.htm Rev. Charles Kottas, Pst.; Dcn. Pat Snook; Dcn. Stephen Rallis; Jean Thomas, Bus. Mgr.; Heather Olson, DRE; CRP Stds.: 130

St. Francis Worship Center - 238 6th St., Council Bluffs, IA 51501 t) (712) 322-8889; (712) 322-8889

CRESTON

Holy Spirit Church of Creston - 107 W. Howard St., Creston, IA 50801; Mailing: 406 W. Clark St., Creston, IA 50801 t) 641-782-5278 bhudson@iowatelecom.net; pamedeka@dmdiocese.org www.uccat.org Rev. Patrick K. Amedeka, Assoc. Pst.; Barb Hudson, DRE; Michelle Moore, Bus. Mgr.; CRP Stds.: 64

St. Malachy School - (Grades PreK-8) 403 W. Clark St., Creston, IA 50801 t) 641-782-7125 crestonstmalachy.org/ Jennifer Simmons, Prin.; Stds.: 163; Lay Tchrs.: 13

St. Malachy School Foundation - 406 W. Clark St., Creston, IA 50801 t) (641) 782-5278

CUMBERLAND

St. Timothy - 69488 Wichita Rd., Cumberland, IA 50843; Mailing: 600 Locust St., Atlantic, IA 50022 t) 712-243-4721 olgsttim@sspeterpaulandmary.org Rev. Michael Berner, Pst.; Charlotte Schroeder, Bus. Mgr.;

CUMMING

St. Patrick Catholic Church, Irish Settlement - 3396 155th St., Cumming, IA 50061; Mailing: 1026 N. 8th Ave., Winterset, IA 50273 t) 515-462-1083; 515-462-5701 office@saintjosephchurch.net www.dmdiocese.org Rev. Thomas V. Dooley, Pst.; Dcn. Eric Pugh; Dcn. Sam Sullivan; Mike Drysdale, Bus. Mgr.; CRP Stds.: 28

DEFIANCE

St. Peter - 501 Fifth St., Defiance, IA 51527; Mailing: P.O. Box 127, Defiance, IA 51527 t) 712-748-3501 stpeters@netins.net; drestpeters@fmctc.com www.dmdiocese.org/mass.htm Served from Earling. Rev. Andrew Windschitl, Pst.; Mary Gross, DRE; Diane Mulligan, Liturgy Coord.; Nancy Schaben, Bus. Mgr.; CRP Stds.: 22

DES MOINES

St. Ambrose Cathedral - 607 High St., Des Moines, IA 50309 t) 515-288-7411 nmccarthy@saintambrosecathedral.org saintambrosecathedral.org Rev. Nipin Scaria (India), Rector; Rev. Ambrose Ladu Daniel, Assoc. Pst.; Dcn. Francis Chan; Dcn. James Obradovich; Dcn. Chris Rohwer; Dcn. Ly Pao Yang; Vern S. Rash, RCIA Coord.; CRP Stds.: 132

All Saints - 650 N.E. 52nd Ave., Des Moines, IA 50313 t) 515-265-5001; 515-265-5001 x201 (CRP) info@dmallsaints.org; office@dmallsaints.org www.dmallsaints.org Rev. Robert Harris, Pst.; Dcn. Mark Burdt; Janice Carpenter, Treas.; Rosa Villar-Cordova Scott, Music Min.; Jamie Clyde, DRE; Mary Treanor, Bus. Mgr.; CRP Stds.: 41

Nick R. and Carole P. Zagar Endowment Scholarship Fund - treanor840@msn.com

St. Anthony's - 15 Indianola Rd., Des Moines, IA 50315 t) 515-244-4709; 515-244-1119 (CRP) www.stanthonydsm.org/ Rev. Christopher Reising, Pst.; Rev. Rodrigo Mayorga Landeros, Vicar; Dcn. Juan Bustamante; Dcn. Quang Tong; Marilu Mendez, Director of Hispanic Ministry; Mark Paris, Bus. Mgr.; Daniela Ceballos, Secy.; CRP Stds.: 285

St. Anthony's School - (Grades K-8) 16 Columbus Ave., Des Moines, IA 50315 t) 515-243-1874 saschool@stanthonydsm.org Jennifer Raes, Prin.; Stds.: 308; Lay Tchrs.: 23

St. Augustin's - 545 42nd St., Des Moines, IA 50312 t) 515-255-1175 info@staugustin.org; janis@staugustin.org www.staugustin.org Rev. Christopher Pisut, Pst.; Dcn. Joseph Coan; Dcn. Kurt Heinrich; Dcn. Mike Manno; Dcn. Kevin Heim, RCIA Coord.; Marion Scott, Music Min.; Kurt Phillips, Bus. Mgr.; Mary Hemman, Youth Min.; Janis Falk, DRE; CRP Stds.: 112

St. Augustin's School - (Grades PreK-8) 4320 Grand Ave., Des Moines, IA 50312 t) 515-279-5947 kkautzky@staugustinschool.org; rwatters@staugustinschool.org staugustinschool.org Kristel Spike, Prin.; Stds.: 248; Lay Tchrs.: 23

Basilica of Saint John - 1915 University Ave., Des Moines, IA 50314 t) 515-244-3101; 515-244-3101 x204 (CRP) basilicadm@msn.com; margarets@basilicaofstjohn.org basilicofstjohn.org Rev. Aquinas Nichols, Pst.; Dcn. Luke Tieskoetter; Dcn. Mark Campbell, Youth Min.; Dcn. Steve Tatz; Charles Stastny, Bus. Mgr.; Margaret Stastny, DRE; Gail Johll, Music Min.; CRP Stds.: 131

Basilica of St. John Foundation -

St. Catherine of Siena Catholic Student Center - 1150 28th St., Des Moines, IA 50311-4142 t) 515-650-8646 office@stcatherinedrake.org stcatherinedrake.org (Non-Territorial University Parish) Rev. Emmanuel Offiong, Assoc. Pst.; Dcn. Rick Condon; Erin Smith, Campus Min.; Dave & Sheila Lingwall, Liturgy Dir.; Dennis Hendrickson, Music Min.; Melinda Hendrickson, Music Min.; Laura Carruthers-Green, DRE; Janet Blessum, Bus. Mgr.; CRP Stds.: 22

Christ the King - 5711 S.W. 9th St., Des Moines, IA 50315; Mailing: 820 Porter Ave., Des Moines, IA 50315 t) 515-285-2888 officemanager@christthekingparish.org; jfeeney@christthekingparish.org christthekingparish.org Rev. PJ McManus, Pst.; Rev. Nicholas Stark, Assoc. Pst.; Dcn. Tony Valdez; Jason Feeney, DRE; Karla Garcia, DRE; Dcn. Larry Kehoe, RCIA Coord.; Eren Muniz, Hispanic Ministry; CRP Stds.: 170

Christ the King School - (Grades PreK-8) 701 Wall St., Des Moines, IA 50315 t) 515-285-3349 dthole@cksdesmoines.com cksdesmoines.com/ Daniel Thole, Prin.; Stds.: 218; Lay Tchrs.: 16

Christ the King Foundation -

Christ the King Housing Services -

Church of St. Peter Vietnamese Catholic Community - 618 E. 18th St., Des Moines, IA 50316 t) 515-266-1160 office@stpeterdesmoines.org Rev. Ly Chu, Pst.; Dcn. Gene Jager; Dcn. Paul Tran; Sr. Dieu Tuyet Nguyen, Youth Min.; Kelly Truong, Contact; CRP Stds.: 48

Holy Trinity - 2926 Beaver Ave., Des Moines, IA 50310-4040 t) 515-255-3162; 515-255-3162 x224 (CRP) johnm@holytrinitydm.org; parishoffice@holytrinitydm.org www.holytrinitydm.org Rev. Mark Neal, Pst.; Dcn. James Obradovich; Dcn. Douglas Renze; John Mertes, DRE; Dan Maxcy, Pst. Min./Coord.; Mary Gisler, Bus. Mgr.; CRP Stds.: 177

Holy Trinity School - (Grades PreK-8) t) (515) 255-3162 x116 mmorrison@htschool.org Monica Morrison, Prin.; Stds.: 387; Lay Tchrs.: 31

St. Joseph Catholic Church - 3300 Easton Blvd., Des Moines, IA 50317 t) 515-266-2226; 515-266-2449 (CRP) lstarnold@stjosephcatholicdsm.org; dmuse@stjosephcatholicdsm.org stjosephcatholicdsm.org Rev. Christopher Fontanini, Pst.; Dcn. Marvin Brewer; Dcn. Randy Lynch; Dcn. William Hare, RCIA Coord.; David Ortega, Bus. Mgr. & DRE; CRP Stds.: 145

St. Joseph Catholic School - (Grades PreK-8) 2107 E. 33rd St., Des Moines, IA 50317 t) 515-266-3433 Jodi Halligan, Prin.; Stds.: 194; Lay Tchrs.: 14

St. Joseph School Foundation -

St. Mary of Nazareth - 4600 Meredith Dr., Des Moines, IA 50310 t) 515-276-4042; 515-276-7589 (CRP) stmarys@stmarysdsm.org; melindah@stmarysdsm.org www.stmarysdsm.org Rev. John M. Frost, Pst.; Melinda Headlee, DRE; CRP Stds.: 203

Our Lady of the Americas - 1271 E. 9th St., Des Moines, IA 50316 t) 515-266-6695; 515-266-6695 x200 (CRP) vcalderon@oloadsm.com; frfabian2013@gmail.com oloadsm.com/ Rev. Fabian Moncada, Pst.; Erika Mendez, Youth Min.; CRP Stds.: 223

St. Theresa of the Child Jesus - 1230 Merle Hay Rd., Des Moines, IA 50311-2098 t) 545-279-4654; 515-279-4654 (CRP) teischeid@stsdsm.com www.sainttheresaiowa.org Rev. Raphael Assamah, Pst.; Dcn. David Schmidt, Pst. Assoc.; Barbara Woods, RCIA Coord.; Megan Howes, Youth Min.; Jane Ann Becicka, DRE; CRP Stds.: 140

St. Theresa of the Child Jesus School - (Grades PreK-8) 5810 Carpenter Ave., Des Moines, IA 50311-2026 t) 515-277-0178 gwatznauer@stsdsm.com sainttheresaiowa.org/school/ Gretchen Watznauer, Prin.; Stds.: 250; Lay Tchrs.: 18

St. Theresa of the Child Jesus Foundation - 1230 Merle Hay Rd, Des Moines, IA 50311 t) (515) 279-4654 sainttheresaiowa@gmail.com sainttheresaiowa.org John McMichael, Accountant;

St. Theresa's School Foundation - 1230 Merle Hay Rd, Des Moines, IA 50311 t) (515) 279-4654 sainttheresaiowa@gmail.com John McMichael, Accountant;

DUNLAP

St. Patrick - 509 S. 3rd St., Dunlap, IA 51529 t) 712-643-5808; 712-643-5115 churchspsh@gmail.com stpatrickchurchdunlap.com/ Rev. Joel McNeil, Pst.; Dcn. Marvin Klein; Debbie Gaul-Rusch, Bus. Mgr.; CRP Stds.: 75

EARLING

St. Joseph - 212 2nd St., Earling, IA 51530; Mailing: P.O. Box 225, Earling, IA 51530 t) 712-747-2091; 712-747-2781 (CRP) stjoseph@fmctc.com www.dmdiocese.org/mass.htm Rev. Andrew Windschitl, Pst.; Mary Gross, Bus. Mgr.; Cathy Mary Assman, Bus. Mgr.; CRP Stds.: 49

ELKHART

St. Mary/Holy Cross - 460 N.W. Washington Ave., Elkhart, IA 50073; Mailing: P.O. Box 110, Elkhart, IA 50073 t) 515-367-2685 smhc@saintmaryhc.org www.saintmaryhc.org Rev. Michael Amadeo, Admin.; Dcn. Terry Schleisman; Geneveve Loraditch, DRE; Tracy Miller, DRE; Andrea Fisher, Youth Min.; Melissa Kahler, Youth Min.; Sue Schmidt, Music Min.; Candy Zidon, Bus. Mgr.; CRP Stds.: 229

EXIRA

Holy Trinity - 218 N. Kilworth St., Exira, IA 50076; Mailing: 116 E. Division St., Audubon, IA 50025 t) 712-563-2283 spht@iowatelecom.net www.stpatrickholytrinity.org Rev. David Nkrumah, Pst.; Judy Bintner, Bus. Mgr.; Linda Blomme, Bus. Mgr.; April Brand, DRE; CRP Stds.: 90

GLENWOOD

Our Lady of the Holy Rosary - 24116 Marian Ave., Glenwood, IA 51534-5291 t) 712-527-5211 holyrosarych@msn.com www.holyrosaryglenwood.org Rev. Daniel E. Siepker, Pst.; Theresa Romens, DRE; CRP Stds.: 181

GRAND RIVER

St. Patrick - 460 Wabonsy St., Grand River, IA 50108; Mailing: 222 E. Pearl St., Osceola, IA 50213 t) 641-342-2850 stbernardiowa@gmail.com stbernardiowa.wixsite.com/website Served from St. Bernard, Osceola Rev. Tomson Thomas (India), Par. Admin.; Brenda Hernandez, Bus. Mgr.;

GRANGER

Assumption of the Blessed Virgin Mary - 1906 Sycamore, Granger, IA 50109; Mailing: PO Box 159, Granger, IA 50109 t) 515-999-2239; (515) 999-2211 parish@assumptiongranger.org; cdavidson@assumptiongranger.org www.assumptiongranger.com Rev. Dominic Assim, Pst.;

Dcn. Thomas Schenk Sr., RCIA Coord.; Gretchen Watznauer, Youth Min.; Cathy Davidson, DRE; Anita Meiners-Stahowick, Bus. Mgr.; LuAnn Small, Trustee; Dr. Lori Ancona, Music Dir.; Jeff Dirkx, Trustee; CRP Stds.: 161

GREENFIELD

St. John - 303 N.E. Elm St., Greenfield, IA 50849 t) 641-343-7065; (515) 401-8484 (CRP) stjohnsgreenfieldia@gmail.com stjohns3.wixsite.com/home Rev. Philip Yaw Bempong, Pst.; Michelle C. Carns, Stewardship Ministry Lead; CRP Stds.: 52

GRISWOLD

Our Lady of Grace - 203 Adair St., Griswold, IA 51535; Mailing: 600 Locust St., Atlantic, IA 50022 t) 712-243-4721 olgsttim@sspeterpaulandmary.org www.dmdiocese.org/mass.htm Rev. Michael Berner, Pst.; Charlotte Schroeder, Bus. Mgr.;

GUTHRIE CENTER

St. Mary - 603 Main St., Guthrie Center, IA 50115 t) 641-747-3843 stcstmstp@netins.net www.st-mary-patrick-cecilia.com Rev. Raymond Higgins, Pst.; CRP Stds.: 73

HAMBURG

St. Mary - 1306 Washington St., Hamburg, IA 51640; Mailing: P.O. Box 67, Hamburg, IA 51640 c) 712-382-4316 stmaryshamburg@gmail.com St. Mary, Shenandoah. Monica Bissen, DRE; CRP Stds.: 38

HARLAN

St. Michael - 2001 College Pl., Harlan, IA 51537; Mailing: 1912 18th St., Harlan, IA 51537 t) 712-755-5244; 712-755-5366 (CRP) dre@stmichaelparish.com Rev. Clement Owusu, Pst.; Dcn. James DeBlauw; Rhonda Buck, DRE; John Rosman, Liturgy Coord. & Music Min.; CRP Stds.: 92

St. Michael School - (Grades PreK-5) 2005 College Pl., Harlan, IA 51537 t) 712-755-5634 jerlbach@shelcocath.pvt.k12.ia.us Ann Anderson, Prin.; Joanne Erlbacher, Bus. Mgr.; Stds.: 93; Lay Tchrs.: 6

St. Michael Parish Foundation - 1912 18th St, Harlan, IA 51537 t) (712) 755-5244

IMOGENE

St. Patrick - 304 Third St., Imogene, IA 51645; Mailing: PO Box 375, Shenandoah, IA 51601 c) 712-370-3285 stpatsimogene@gmail.com stpatrickchurchimogeneiowa.weebly.com Rev. Lazarus Kirigia, Pst.; Rita Laughlin, DRE; CRP Stds.: 29

INDIANOLA

St. Thomas Aquinas - 210 S. Wesley St., Indianola, IA 50125 t) 515-961-3026 jsayredre@gmail.com; stthomas50125@gmail.com stthomasindianola.com Rev. Adam Westphal, Pst.; Jo Ann Sayre, DRE; Leasa Garrett, Bus. Mgr.; CRP Stds.: 255

LACONA

Holy Trinity Church of Southeast Warren County - 222 Washington Ave., Lacona, IA 50139; Mailing: 304 N. Washington Ave., Lacona, IA 50139 t) 641-534-4691 www.dmdiocese.org/mass.htm Rev. Eze Venantius Umunnakwe, C.S.Sp., Pst.; Barb Ripperger, Youth Min.; Beverly Schurman, Bus. Mgr.; CRP Stds.: 15

Worship Centers -

St. Mary of the Assumption Church -

St. Augustine -

LENOX

St. Patrick - 600 W. Michigan, Lenox, IA 50851 t) 641-333-2565 stpatl@lenoxia.com www.dmdiocese.org/mass.htm Rev. Emmanuel Bassey, Admin.; Kathy Ecklin, DRE; CRP Stds.: 29

LEON

St. Brendan - 1001 N.W. Church St., Leon, IA 50144 t) 641-446-4789 c) 641-344-9521 southch3@gmail.com; terrijleahy@gmail.com www.dmdiocese.org/mass.htm Rev. Samuel Danso, Pst.; Terri J Leahy, DRE; Marilyn Arndorfer, Bus. Mgr.; Kim Downey, Bus. Mgr.; CRP Stds.: 29

LOGAN

St. Anne - 104 W. 3rd St., Logan, IA 51546; Mailing: 112 W. 3rd St., Logan, IA 51546 t) 712-644-2520 www.dmdiocese.org/mass.htm Rev. Raphael Masabakhwa, Pst.; Dcn. Dennis Lovell; Wilfred Uhing, DRE; Annette Lorenz, Bus. Mgr.; Kathy Lovell, Liturgy Coord.; CRP Stds.: 13

MASSENA

St. Patrick - 503 Main St., Massena, IA 50853; Mailing: P.O. Box 61, Massena, IA 50853 t) 712-779-3397 lantzkyc1@gmail.com; st.patricksmassena@gmail.com www.dmdiocese.org Served from Greenfield. Rev. Philip Yaw Bempong, Pst.; CRP Stds.: 42

MISSOURI VALLEY

St. Patrick - 215 N. Seventh St., Missouri Valley, IA 51555 t) 712-642-2611; 712-642-3155 (CRP) stpatsch@loganet.net movalleycatholics.wordpress.com Rev. Raphael Masabakhwa, Pst.; Dcn. Michael Carney; Carol Poole, DRE; CRP Stds.: 38

MONDAMIN

Holy Family - 97 Mulberry, Mondamin, IA 51557; Mailing: 509 S. 3rd St., Dunlap, IA 51529 t) 712-644-2092 jzahner@windstream.net; churchspsh@gmail.com St. Patrick. Rev. Joel McNeil, Pst.; Dcn. Dennis Lovell; Ruth Zahner, Music Min.; John Davie, Bus. Mgr.; Loene Herman, Liturgy Coord.; CRP Stds.: 1

MT. AYR

St. Joseph - 100 N. Polk St., Mt. Ayr, IA 50854; Mailing: 222 E. Pearl St., Osceola, IA 50213 t) 641-464-2826 stbernardiowa@gmail.com stbernardiowa.wixsite.com/website Served from St. Bernard, Osceola Rev. Tomson Thomas (India), Par. Admin.; Brenda Hernandez, Bus. Mgr.; CRP Stds.: 18

NEOLA

St. Patrick - 311 3rd St., Neola, IA 51559; Mailing: PO Box 127, Neola, IA 51559 t) (712) 485-2750 (Office); (712) 485-2753 (Priest); (712) 485-2754 (DRE) office@stpatricksneola.com; dre@stpatricksneola.com www.stpatricksneola.com Rev. Julius Itamid (Nigeria), Admin.; Dcn. Darrl Scott Brooks; Shannon Nye, DRE; RaeShelle Jensen, Bus. Mgr.; CRP Stds.: 176

Saint Patrick Foundation - stpatricksneola.com

NORWALK

St. John the Apostle Church - 720 Orchard Hills Dr., Norwalk, IA 50211 t) 515-981-4855 apieper@stjohnsnorwalk.org; mhill@stjohnsnorwalk.org www.stjohnsnorwalk.org Rev. Daniel J. Kirby, Pst.; Dcn. Michael Huntsman; Dcn. David Miller; Dcn. Kelly Stone; Rachel Weeks, Youth Min.; Melissa Hill, DRE; Jacque M Mahoney, Bus. Mgr.; CRP Stds.: 284

Shrine of the Assumption, Churchville -

OSCEOLA

St. Bernard - 222 E. Pearl St., Osceola, IA 50213 t) 641-342-2850 stbernardiowa@gmail.com stbernardiowa.wixsite.com/website Rev. Tomson Thomas (India), Par. Admin.; Brenda Hernandez, Bus. Mgr.; CRP Stds.: 15

PANAMA

St. Mary of the Assumption - 200 N. 2nd St., Panama, IA 51562; Mailing: P.O. Box 203, Panama, IA 51562 t) 712-489-2030 smpanama@fmctc.com Barb King, DRE; Lorene Kaufmann, Bus. Mgr.; CRP Stds.: 57

PANORA

St. Cecilia - 220 N. 1st St., Panora, IA 50216; Mailing: 603 Main St., Guthrie Center, IA 50115 t) 641-747-3843 stcstmstp@netins.net www.st-mary-patrick-cecilia.com St. Mary, Guthrie Center. Rev. Raymond Higgins, Pst.; CRP Stds.: 44

PERRY

St. Patrick - 1312 3rd St., Perry, IA 50220 t) 515-465-4387; 515-465-4232 www.stpatsperry.com Rev. Luis Alonso Mejia, Pst.; Barbara Wolter, DRE; Michael Wilson, Bus. Mgr.; CRP Stds.: 116

St. Patrick School - (Grades K-8) 1302 5th St., Perry, IA 50220 t) 515-465-4186 stpatrickschool@stpatricks-perry-ia.org www.stpatricks-perry-ia.org/ Kandice Roethler, Prin.; Stds.: 85; Lay Tchrs.: 9

PORTSMOUTH

St. Mary, Our Lady of Fatima - 412 4th St., Portsmouth, IA 51565; Mailing: P.O. Box 98, Portsmouth, IA 51565 t) 712-743-2625 hankhu@iowatelecom.net www.dmdiocese.org Henrietta Hughes, Bus. Mgr. & DRE; CRP Stds.: 14

RED OAK

St. Mary - 1510 Highland Ave., Red Oak, IA 51566 t) 712-623-2744 stmarysrosecretary@gmail.com www.stmarysredoak.com Rev. Lazarus Kirigia, Pst.; Alan Vonnahme, DRE; Peyton Honeyman, Bus. Mgr.; CRP Stds.: 80

SHENANDOAH

St. Mary - 512 W. Thomas Ave., Shenandoah, IA 51601 t) 712-246-1718 saintmaryoffice.shen@gmail.com www.dmdiocese.org Rev. Tom Thakadipuram, Pst.; Sue Hanna, Music Min.; Kim Leininger, DRE; CRP Stds.: 41

ST. MARYS

Immaculate Conception - 101 St. James St., St. Marys, IA 50241; Mailing: P.O. Box 88, St. Marys, IA 50241 t) (515) 961-3026 joro23@juno.com; immacula@myomnitel.com www.dmdiocese.org Rev. Eze Venantius Umunnakwe, C.S.Sp., Pst.; Michelle Fick, DRE; CRP Stds.: 39

STUART

All Saints - 216 All Saints Dr., Stuart, IA 50250; Mailing: P.O. Box 605, Stuart, IA 50250 t) 515-523-1943 allsaintsoffice@gmail.com; allsaintsff@outlook.com stuartallsaints.org Rev. Antony Mathew, Pst.; Jill Gerling, DRE; CRP Stds.: 62

UNDERWOOD

St. Columbanus - 22720 Weston Ave., Underwood, IA 51576; Mailing: PO Box 127, Neola, IA 51559 t) (712) 485-2750 (Office); (712) 485-2753 (Priest); (712) 485-2754 (DRE) office@stpatricksneola.com; dre@stpatricksneola.com stpatricksneola.com Served from St. Patrick, Neola Rev. Julius Itamid (Nigeria), Admin.; Dcn. Darrl Scott Brooks; Shannon Nye, DRE; RaeShelle Jensen, Bus. Mgr.; CRP Stds.: 14

URBANDALE

St. Pius X - 3663 66th St., Urbandale, IA 50322 t) 515-276-2059; 515-278-5684 (CRP) slyddon@saintpiuschurch.org; cfournier@saintpiuschurch.org www.stpiusxurbandale.org Rev. David Fleming, Pst.; Rev. Bradley Robey, Par. Vicar; Dcn. James Houston; Dcn. Rob Stark; Dcn. Troy Thompson; Cheryl Fournier, DRE; Mary Sue Lone, RCIA Coord.; CRP Stds.: 298

St. Pius X School - (Grades PreK-8) 3601 66th St., Urbandale, IA 50322 t) 515-276-1061 www.stpiusxschool.org Alex Baranosky, Prin.; Stds.: 375; Lay Tchrs.: 29

St. Pius X Parish Foundation -

VILLISCA

St. Joseph - 131 W. High St., Villisca, IA 50864; Mailing: 300 E. Lincoln St., Clarinda, IA 51632 t) 712-542-2030 St. Clare, Clarinda. Rev. Sylvester Okoh, Pst.;

WALNUT

St. Patrick - 718 Antique City Dr., Walnut, IA 51521-0038; Mailing: PO Box 38, Avoca, IA 51521 t) 712-343-6948; 712-343-6951 smpavoca@walnutel.net stmarysavoca.wordpress.com St. Mary, Mediatrix of All Graces, Avoca Rev. Seth Nana Kwame Owusu, Pst.; Kathryn Denning, DRE; Stephanie Geraghty, DRE; Donna Muell, Liturgy Coord.; CRP Stds.: 15

WAUKEE

St. Boniface - 1200 S. Warrior Ln., Waukee, IA 50263-9587 t) 515-987-4597 office@stbonifacechurch.org; mvosika@stbonifacechurch.org stbonifacechurch.org Rev. Chinnappan M. Devaraj, O.F.M., Pst.; Faye Akers, DRE; Catherine Bellis, Bus. Mgr.; Sara Krohnke, Pastoral Care Minster; CRP Stds.: 779

WEST DES MOINES

St. Francis of Assisi - 7075 Ashworth Rd., West Des Moines, IA 50266 t) 515-223-4577; 515-440-1030 (CRP) www.saintfrancischurch.org Rev. Joseph Pins, Pst.; Rev. John Brobbey, Assoc. Pst.; Dcn. Dan Dombrosky; Dcn. Oran Struecker; Dcn. William Richer; Tim Schulte, Bus. Mgr.; Emily Schmid, Music Min.; Vivian Day, RCIA

Coord.; Erica Schieffer, Family Faith Formation Coord.; Claire Sevenich, Youth Min. Coord.; Katie Patrizio, DRE; CRP Stds.: 451

St. Francis of Assisi School - (Grades PreSchool-8) t) 515-457-7167 sfaschool@saintfrancisschool.org www.saintfrancisschool.org Diane Jones, Prin.; Stds.: 753; Lay Tchrs.: 53

Sacred Heart - 1627 Grand Ave., West Des Moines, IA 50265 t) 515-225-6414 www.sacredheartwdm.org/ Rev. Christopher Hartshorn, Pst.; Rev. Litto Thomas, Assoc. Pst.; Dcn. Ed Garza; Leah Mohlman, Music Min.; Kayla Richer, DRE; Jose Batres, DRE; Julie Sokolowski, Youth Min.; Joan Miller, RCIA Coord.; Loralee Chase, Bus. Mgr.; CRP Stds.: 386

Sacred Heart School - (Grades PreK-8) 1601 Grand Ave., West Des Moines, IA 50265 t) 515-223-1284 scott.ehlinger@sacredheartwdm.org sacredheartschoolwdm.org/ Scott Ehlinger, Prin.; Susan Battani, Vice. Pres.; Stds.: 580; Lay Tchrs.: 33

WESTPHALIA

St. Boniface - 305 Duren Strasse, Westphalia, IA 51578; Mailing: P.O. Box 86, Westphalia, IA 51578 t) 712-627-4255 Rev. Michael Antoh (Ghana), Admin.; Lorene Kaufmann, Bus. Mgr.; CRP Stds.: 17

WINTERSET

St. Joseph - 1026 N. 8th Ave., Winterset, IA 50273 t) 515-462-1083; 515-462-5701 office@saintjosephchurch.net www.saintjosephchurch.net Rev. Thomas V. Dooley, Pst.; Dcn. Sam Sullivan; Melody Miller, Music Min.; Mike Drysdale, Bus. Mgr.; CRP Stds.: 66

WOODBINE

Sacred Heart - 33 7th St., Woodbine, IA 51579; Mailing: 509 S. 3rd St., Dunlap, IA 51529 t) 712-643-5115; 712-643-5808 churchspsh@gmail.com stpatrickchurchdunlap.com/ St. Patrick's, Dunlap. Rev. Joel McNeil, Pst.; Mary Kay Eby, Music Min.; CRP Stds.: 88

SCHOOLS: PRESCHOOL THRU HIGH SCHOOL

SCHOOLS

STATE OF IOWA

COUNCIL BLUFFS

Council Bluffs Area Catholic Education Systems, Inc. (Saint Albert Catholic Schools) - (PAR) (Grades PreK-12) 400 Gleason Ave., Council Bluffs, IA 51503 t) 712-329-9000 rohlinga@saintalbertschools.org www.saintalbertschools.org Anne Marie Rohling, Pres.; Stds.: 641; Lay Tchrs.: 48

St. Albert Elementary School - (Grades PreK-12) t) (712) 329-9000 x361 saintalbertschools.org Stds.: 344; Lay Tchrs.: 20

St. Albert Middle & High School - (Grades PreK-12) t) (712) 329-9000 saintalbertschools.org/ Dcn. Vernon Dobelmann, Exec.; Stds.: 297; Lay Tchrs.: 28

DES MOINES

Holy Family School - (PAR) (Grades PreK-8) 1265 E. 9th St., Des Moines, IA 50316 t) 515-262-8025 mpflaherty@hfsdm.org; doriger@hfsdm.org hfsdm.org Participating parishes: Our Lady of the Americas; Basilica of St. John; St. Ambrose Cathedral; All Saints; St. Peter. Martin P. Flaherty, Prin.; Darin Origer, Bus. Mgr.; Traci Rogo, Librn.; Stds.: 251; Lay Tchrs.: 20

HARLAN

Shelby County Catholic School - (PAR) (Grades PreK-5) 2005 College Pl., Harlan, IA 51537 t) 712-755-5634 jerlbach@shelcocath.com; aanderse@shelcocath.com www.shelcocath.pvt.k12.ia.us Ann Andersen, Prin.; Stds.: 93; Lay Tchrs.: 6

WEST DES MOINES

St. Joseph Educational Center - (PAR) 1400 Buffalo Rd., West Des Moines, IA 50265 t) 515-225-1084 tquinlan@sjeciowa.org www.sjeciowa.org Thomas Quinlan, Dir.;

Religious Education - t) 515-222-1084

HIGH SCHOOLS

STATE OF IOWA

COUNCIL BLUFFS

Saint Albert Catholic Schools - (PAR) 400 Gleason Ave., Council Bluffs, IA 51503 t) 712-329-9000 businessoffice@saintalbertschools.org www.saintalbertschools.org Serving all parishes in Council Bluffs; St. Patrick, Missouri Valley; St. Patrick, Neola; Holy Rosary, Glenwood; St. Columbanus, Weston. Anne Marie Rohling, Prin.; Stds.: 641; Lay Tchrs.: 48

WEST DES MOINES

Dowling Catholic High School (Dowling College Inc.) - (PAR) (Grades 9-12) 1400 Buffalo Rd., West Des Moines, IA 50265 t) 515-225-3000 dryan@dowlingcatholic.org www.dowlingcatholic.org Serving all parishes in Des Moines. Dr. Dan Ryan, Pres.; Matt Meedering, Prin.; Rev. Reed Flood, Chap.; Carol Aina, Registrar; Megan Anderson, Librn.; Stds.: 1,318; Pr. Tchrs.: 2; Lay Tchrs.: 97

INSTITUTIONS LOCATED IN DIOCESE

CAMPUS MINISTRY / NEWMAN CENTERS [CAM]

DES MOINES

St. Catherine of Siena Catholic Student Center - 1150 28th St., Des Moines, IA 50311-4142 t) 515-271-4747 office@stcatherinedrake.org stcatherinedrake.org (Drake Newman Community) Rev. Protas Opondo Okwalo, S.J., Pst.; Erin Smith, Campus Min.; Teresa Smith, Secy.;

CEMETERIES [CEM]

COUNCIL BLUFFS

St. Joseph Catholic Cemetery Association - 1 Bluff St., Council Bluffs, IA 51503 t) 712-322-8889 jeanthomas@cox.net Rev. Charles Kottas, Admin.; Jean Thomas, Bus. Mgr.; Adam Thomas, Contact;

COLLEGES & UNIVERSITIES [COL]

DES MOINES

Mercy College of Health Sciences - 928-6th Ave., Des Moines, IA 50309-1239 t) 515-643-3180 ministry@mercydesmoines.org; foundation@mercydesmoines.org www.mchs.edu Sponsored by MercyOne Dr. Adreain M. Henry, Pres.; Thomas Leahy, Vice. Pres.; Matthew Romkey, Vice. Pres.; Bo Bonner, Senior Advisor, Mission Initiatives; Stds.: 911; Lay Tchrs.: 50

ENDOWMENTS / FOUNDATIONS / TRUSTS [EFT]

COUNCIL BLUFFS

St. Albert Educational Foundation - 400 Gleason Ave., Council Bluffs, IA 51503 t) 712-329-9000 x339 faurotc@saintalbertschools.org www.saintalbertschools.org Rev. Charles Kottas, Pst.; Martin Shudak, Chair;

Mercy Hospital Foundation, Council Bluffs, Iowa - 800 Mercy Dr., Council Bluffs, IA 51503 t) 712-328-5000 kathryn.bertolini@alegent.org; missionintegrationmidwest@commonspirit.org Kathy Bertolini, Division Vice Pres. Philanthropy; Andrew J. Santos III, SVP, Mission Integration;

DES MOINES

The Catholic Foundation of Southwest Iowa - 601 Grand Ave., Des Moines, IA 50309 t) 515-237-5044 smcentee@cfswia.org; rseidl@cfswia.org www.cfswia.org Sue McEntee, Exec. Dir.; Teresa Smith, Mktg. Mgr.;

Catholic Pastoral Center Foundation - 601 Grand Ave., Des Moines, IA 50309 t) 515-237-5061 jkurth@dmdiocese.org Jason Kurth, Secy.;

Holy Family School Inner-City Youth Foundation - 1265 E. 9th St., Des Moines, IA 50316; Mailing: P.O. Box 8437, Des Moines, IA 50301 t) 515-262-7466 info@hfcsfoundation.org www.hfcsdm.org Molly West, Admin.;

Mercy Foundation of Des Moines - Affiliate of Catholic Health Initiatives - 411 Laurel St., Ste. 2250, Des Moines, IA 50314 t) 515-247-3248 foundation@mercydesmoines.org foundation.mercydesmoines.org/ Shannon Cofield, Pres.;

HARLAN

Shelby County Catholic Education Foundation - 2005 College Pl., Harlan, IA 51537 t) 712-755-5634 aanderse@shelcocath.pvt.k12.ia.us; jerlbach@shelcocath.pvt.k12.ia.us shelcocath.pvt.k12.ia.us Ann Anderson, Admin.; Rev. John M. Frost, Admin.; Joanne Erlbacher, Bus. Mgr.;

WEST DES MOINES

Dowling-St. Joseph Alumni Association Investment Co. L.L.C. - 1400 Buffalo Rd., West Des Moines, IA 50265 t) 515-225-3000 dryan@dowlingcatholic.org www.dowlingcatholic.org Dr. Dan Ryan, Pres.;

Dowling-St. Joseph Alumni Foundation - 1400 Buffalo Rd., West Des Moines, IA 50265 t) 515-225-3000 dryan@dowlingcatholic.org www.dowlingcatholic.org Dr. Dan Ryan, Pres.;

St. Francis of Assisi Roman Catholic School Foundation - 7075 Ashworth Rd., West Des Moines, IA 50266 t) 515-223-4577 www.saintfrancischurch.org Rev. Joseph Pins, Pst.;

HOSPITALS / HEALTH SERVICES [HOS]

CORNING

Alegent Health Mercy Hospital - 603 Rosary Dr., Corning, IA 50841 t) 641-322-3121 missionintegrationmidwest@commonspirit.org www.chihealth.com Alicia Reed, Pres.; Andrew J. Santos III, SVP, Mission Integration; Kurt Sargent; Andrew Santos; Bed Capacity: 14; Asstd. Annu.: 3,500; Staff: 123

COUNCIL BLUFFS

CHI Health: Mercy Hospital (Alegent Health-Bergan Mercy Health System) - 800 Mercy Dr., Council Bluffs, IA 51503 t) 712-328-5000 missionintegrationmidwest@commonspirit.org www.chihealth.com Ann Schumacher, Pres.; Andrew J. Santos III, SVP, Mission Integration; Andrew Santos; Bed Capacity: 148; Asstd. Annu.: 88,000; Staff: 525

DES MOINES

MercyOne - Des Moines - 1111 Sixth Ave., Des Moines, IA 50314-2611 t) 515-247-3121 lwenman@mercydesmoines.org www.mercyone.org/desmoines.org Trinity Health, Livonia, MI Michael Wegner, Pres.; Laura C Wenman, Vice. Pres.; Rev. Stephen Audu, Spiritual Adv./Care Srvcs.; Bed Capacity: 802; Asstd. Annu.: 1,803,317; Staff: 4,973

Graduate Medical Education -

Iowa Heart Center -

Mercy Children's Hospital & Clinics - t) (515) 247-3222

Mercy Clinics, Inc. - 405 S.W. 5th St., Des Moines, IA 50309 t) 515-643-7378

Mercy College of Health Sciences - 928 6th Ave., Des Moines, IA 50309-1239 t) 515-643-3180 ministry@mercydesmoines.org; bbonner@mercydesmoines.org www.mchs.edu Thomas Leahy, Interim Pres.; Bo Bonner, Senior Advisor;

Mercy Foundation -

Mercy Foundation of Des Moines (Mercy Foundation,

Bishop Drumm Retirement Center, Mercy Hospice-Johnston) -

Mercy Hospice and Home Care -

MISSOURI VALLEY

***Alegent Health Community Hospital of Missouri Valley, IA** - 631 N. 8th St., Missouri Valley, IA 51555 t) 712-642-2784 missionintegrationmidwest@commonspirit.org www.chihealth.com David Jones, Pres.; Andrew J. Santos III, SVP, Mission Integration; Andrew Santos; Bed Capacity: 25; Asstd. Annu.: 6,000; Staff: 110

MISCELLANEOUS [MIS]

DES MOINES

Catholic Council for Social Concern - 601 Grand Ave., Des Moines, IA 50309 t) 515-237-5045; 515-237-5053 bdecker@catholiccharitiesdm.org www.catholiccharitiesdm.org Catholic Charities Barbara Q. Decker, Exec.;

Catholic Tuition Organization, Diocese of Des Moines - 601 Grand Ave., Des Moines, IA 50309 t) 515-237-5010 mareed@dmdiocese.org www.ctoiowa.org Mark Allen Reed Sr., Exec. Dir.;

City Hospital Chaplaincy Service - 921 Sixth Ave. #509, Des Moines, IA 50309 c) (515) 985-8331 eoffiong@dmdiocese.org Serving all non-Catholic hospitals in Des Moines. Rev. Emmanuel Offiong, Chap.;

Iowa Catholic Conference - 530-42nd St., Des Moines, IA 50312-2707 t) 515-243-6256 info@iowacatholicconference.org www.iowacatholicconference.org Thomas Chapman, Exec.;

PANORA

St. Thomas More Center - 6177 Panorama Rd., Panora, IA 50216 t) 515-309-1936 office@stmcenter.com; janderson@stmcenter.com www.stmcenter.com Home of Catholic Youth Camp (Iowa) Rev. Ross Parker, Chap.;

URBANDALE

Emmaus House - 3315 70th St., Urbandale, IA 50322 t) 515-282-4839 director@theemmaushouse.org www.theemmaushouse.org Spiritual Ministry to the Diocese Kevin O'Donnell, Dir.; April Young, Assoc. Dir.;

WEST DES MOINES

***St. Gabriel Communications (Iowa Catholic Radio)** - 1355 50th St., Ste. 500, West Des Moines, IA 50266 t) 515-223-1150 contact@kwky.com; bsweeney@iowacatholicradio.com www,iowacatholicradio.com Brian Sweeney, Bus. Mgr.;

Western Iowa Equestrian Order of the Holy Sepulchre of Jerusalem - 7887 Cody Dr., West Des Moines, IA 50266 c) (515) 554-3213 Charles Schneider, Dir.;

NURSING / REHABILITATION / CONVALESCENCE / ELDERLY CARE [NUR]

JOHNSTON

Bishop Drumm Retirement Center - 5837 Winwood Dr., Johnston, IA 50131-1651 t) 515-270-1100 abraden@chilivingcomm.org www.homeishere.org An operating unit of CHI Living Communities, which is a subsidiary of CommonSpirit Health Rev. Bede Inekwere (Nigeria), Chap.; Adam Braden, Exec.; Asstd. Annu.: 494; Staff: 190

Martina Place Assisted Living Residence - 5815 Winwood Dr., Johnston, IA 50131-1666 t) 515-251-7999 adam.braden@commonspirit.org homeishere.org CHI Living Communities, a business line of CommonSpirit Health Adam Braden, Exec.;

McAuley Terrace Apts. - 5921 Winwood Dr., Johnston, IA 50131-1670 t) 515-270-6640 adam.braden@commonspirit.org homeishere.org Bishop Drumm Retirement Center is part of CHI Living Communities, a business line of CommonSpirit Health Adam Braden, Exec.;

PRESCHOOLS / CHILDCARE CENTERS [PRE]

DES MOINES

Mercy Child Development Center - 1111 Sixth Ave., Des Moines, IA 50314 t) 515-247-3121 lwenman@mercydesmoines.org Diane Engelking, Dir.;

RETREAT HOUSES / RENEWAL CENTERS [RTR]

GRISWOLD

Creighton University Retreat Center - 16493 Contrail Ave., Griswold, IA 51535 t) 712-778-2466 curc@creighton.edu www.creighton.edu/ministry/retreatcenter/ Dr. Kathy Kemler, Dir.;

SPECIAL CARE FACILITIES [SPF]

DES MOINES

House of Mercy - 1409 Clark St., Des Moines, IA 50314-1964 t) 515-643-6500 rpeterson@mercydesmoines.org houseofmercydesmoines.org Substance abuse residential treatment Rebecca Peterson, Dir.; Bed Capacity: 80; Asstd. Annu.: 2,500; Staff: 100

An asterisk (*) denotes an organization that has established tax-exempt status directly with the IRS and is not covered by the USCCB Group Ruling.

Archdiocese of Detroit

(Archidioecesis Detroitensis)

MOST REVEREND ALLEN H. VIGNERON, D.D.

Archbishop of Detroit; ordained July 27, 1975; appointed Auxiliary Bishop of Detroit and Titular Bishop of Sault Ste. Marie June 12, 1996; consecrated July 9, 1996; appointed Coadjutor Bishop of Oakland January 10, 2003; installed February 26, 2003; succeeded to See October 1, 2003; appointed Archbishop of Detroit January 5, 2009; installed January 28, 2009.

Archbishop's Office: 12 State St., Detroit, MI 48226. T: 313-237-5816; F: 313-237-4642.

Square Miles 3,901.

Established March 8, 1833; Created An Archbishopric August 3, 1937.

Comprises the Counties of Lapeer, Macomb, Monroe, Oakland, St. Clair and Wayne.

For legal titles of parishes and archdiocesan institutions, consult the Archbishop's Office.

Most Reverend Paul Fitzpatrick Russell
Auxiliary Bishop of Detroit; ordained June 20, 1987; Appointed Apostolic Nuncio to Turkey and Turkmenistan and Titular Archbishop of Novi March 19, 2016; consecrated June 3, 2016; appointed Apostolic Nuncio to Azerbaijan April 7, 2018; appointed Auxiliary Bishop of Detroit May 23, 2022; installed July 7, 2022. Office: 12 State St., Detroit, MI 48226.

Most Reverend Donald Francis Hanchon
Auxiliary Bishop of Detroit; ordained October 19, 1974; appointed Auxiliary Bishop of Detroit and Titular Bishop of Horreomargum March 22, 2011; consecrated May 5, 2011. Office: 4311 Central Ave., Detroit, MI 48210-2785.

Most Reverend Jose Arturo Cepeda Escobedo
Auxiliary Bishop of Detroit; ordained June 1, 1996; appointed Auxiliary Bishop of Detroit and Titular Bishop of Tagase April 18, 2011; consecrated May 5, 2011. Office: 241 Pearson St., Ferndale, MI 48220-1824.

Most Reverend Robert Joseph Fisher
Auxiliary Bishop of Detroit; ordained June 27, 1992; appointed Titular Bishop of Forum Popilii and Auxiliary Bishop of Detroit November 23, 2016; consecrated January 25, 2017. Office: 23965 23 Mile Rd., Macomb, MI 48042- 4511.

Most Reverend Gerard William Battersby
Auxiliary Bishop of Detroit; ordained May 30, 1998; appointed Titular Bishop of Eguga and Auxiliary Bishop of Detroit November 23, 2016; consecrated January 25, 2017. Office: 12 State St., Detroit, MI 48226.

STATISTICAL OVERVIEW

Personnel
Retired Cardinals....1
Archbishops....1
Auxiliary Bishops....5
Retired Bishops....2
Priests: Diocesan Active in Diocese....211
Priests: Diocesan Active Outside Diocese....6
Priests: Retired, Sick or Absent....100
Number of Diocesan Priests....317
Religious Priests in Diocese....189
Total Priests in your Diocese....506
Extern Priests in Diocese....30
Ordinations:
Transitional Deacons....5
Permanent Deacons....3
Permanent Deacons in Diocese....179
Total Brothers....55
Total Sisters....489

Parishes
Parishes....214
With Resident Pastor:
Resident Diocesan Priests....199
Resident Religious Priests....47
Without Resident Pastor:
Administered by Priests....6
Missions....1
Pastoral Centers....1
Professional Ministry Personnel:
Brothers....20
Sisters....42
Lay Ministers....660

Welfare
Catholic Hospitals....9
Health Care Centers....14
Homes for the Aged....18
Residential Care of Children....3
Day Care Centers....3
Specialized Homes....7
Special Centers for Social Services....15
Other Institutions....11

Educational
Seminaries, Diocesan....2
Students from This Diocese....21
Students from Other Dioceses....64
Diocesan Students in Other Seminaries....3
Seminaries, Religious....2
Students, Religious....19
Total Seminarians....43
Colleges and Universities....3
Total Students....7,973
High Schools, Diocesan and Parish....8
Total Students....2,536
High Schools, Private....15
Total Students....6,598
Elementary Schools, Diocesan and Parish....53
Total Students....16,878
Elementary Schools, Private....4
Total Students....1,155
Catechesis/Religious Education:
High School Students....2,712
Elementary Students....23,377
Total Students under Catholic Instruction....61,272
Teachers in Diocese:
Priests....19
Scholastics....1
Brothers....11
Sisters....18
Lay Teachers....2,649

Vital Statistics
Receptions into the Church:
Infant Baptism Totals....5,339
Minor Baptism Totals....346
Adult Baptism Totals....311
Received into Full Communion....435
First Communions....5,802
Confirmations....5,742
Marriages:
Catholic....1,326
Interfaith....369
Total Marriages....1,695
Deaths....7,263
Total Catholic Population....907,921
Total Population....4,323,432

LEADERSHIP

Moderator of the Curia - Very Rev. Jeffrey Day; Rev. Mario V. Amore, Asst. to Moderator; Brian Mooney, COO;

ADMINISTRATION

General Information and Reference - t) 313-237-5800

Office of the Archbishop - t) 313-237-5816 Rev. David M. Tomaszycki, Priest Sec. to Archbishop;

Archdiocesan Vicars Forane - t) 313-237-5847 chancellor@aod.org Rev. Lee E. Acervo, Blue Water (stedwardparish@hotmail.com); Rev. Joseph J. Gembala, Central Macomb (contact@stmalachychurch.org); Rev. David Bechill, Downriver;

OFFICES AND DIRECTORS

Department of Catholic Schools - t) 313-237-5775 Dcn. Sean Costello, Supt.; May Bluestein, Assoc. Supt.; Jill Haines, Assoc. Supt.;

Health, Athletics and Physical Safety - t) 313-237-5960 Victor Michaels, Admin.; Michael Evoy, Assoc. Admin.;

Department of Communications - t) 313-237-5943 Edmundo Reyes, Dir.; Emily Mentok, Assoc. Dir.; Holly Fournier, Assoc. Dir., Communications;

Office of Printing and Publications - t) 313-237-5967 Bob Pawlak, Dir.;

Public Relations - t) 313-237-4677 Ned McGrath, Dir.;

Department of Development and Mission Advancement - t) 313-596-7400 Jim Thomas, Dir.; Wendy Miller-Bueche, Assoc. Dir.;

Advancement for Catholic Schools - t) 313-596-7423 Kathryn Woodstock, Assoc. Dir.;

Alumni and Events Mgr. - t) 313-596-7424 Emily Berschback;

Annual Giving - t) 313-596-7422 Wendy Miller-Bueche, Assoc. Dir.;

Operations - t) 313-596-7407 Wendy Miller-Bueche, Assoc. Dir.;

Grants Management - t) 313-596-7408 Jessica I. Orzechowski, Mgr.;

Major Gifts - t) 313-596-7409 Marita Cowan, Assoc. Dir.; Kathryn Woodstock, Assoc. Dir.;

Department of Evangelization and Missionary Discipleship - t) 313-596-7140 Dr. Marlon De La Torre, Exec. Dir. (delatorre.marlon@aod.org);

Office for Discipleship Formation - t) 313-237-4683 Dr. Marlon De La Torre, Ministerial Certification - Exec. Dir.; Tom Clark, Children's Faith Formation - Coord.; Katy Frederick, Youth Ministry, Coord. Small Groups & Support;

Office for Family Life - t) 313-237-4683 Nicole Joyce, Marriage Ministry - Natural Family Planning; David P. Grobbel, Marriage Ministry - Specialist; Tara Stenger, Ministry Placement/Evangelization Support Groups - Coord., Family Ministry / Family Support Groups - Coord.;

Office of Cultural Ministry - t) 313-596-7103 Victoria Figueroa, Multi-Cultural Ministries - Coord.; Antonio Guzman, Hispanic Ministries - Coord.; Gros-Louis Chantal, Native American - Coord.;

Office of Engagement - t) 313-237-5908 Rev. Matthew Hood, Campus Ministry - Dir.; Gerardo Butalid, Campus Ministry - Assoc. Dir.; Patrick Howard, Young Adult Ministry - Coord.;

Office of Evangelical Charity - t) 313-237-4683 Carolyn Wilson, Pro-Life - Volunteer Coord.; Rev. Michael Depcik, O.S.F.S., Deaf Ministry - Dir.; Veronica Balcarcel, Deaf Ministry - Coord.;

Office of Sacred Worship - t) 313-237-4697 Sr. Esther Mary Nickel, R.S.M., Dir.; Dr. Horst Buchholz, Dir., Sacred Music;

Department of Finance and Administration - Michael Schoenle, Finance Officer; Brian Mooney, Dir., Oper. Officer; Donald Genotti, Dir. Finance & Controller;

Accounting and Treasury - t) 313-237-5825 Donald Genotti, Controller; Jolanta Kepa, Treas.;

Parish Support Services - Michael Felcyn, Assoc. Dir.;

Department of Process, Data and Technology - t) 313-596-7157 Marco DeCapite, Dir.;

Financial Analysis & Special Projects - t) 313-237-5835 Michael Felcyn, Assoc. Dir. Parish Svcs.;

Office of Real Estate - Donald Genotti, Dir.; Michael Edgar, Assoc. Dir.; Michael McInerney, Assoc. Dir.;

Parish Accounting Services - t) 313-596-7163 Michael Felcyn, Assoc. Dir.;

Sacred Heart Major Seminary and Cathedral Building Administration - John Duncan, Dir.; Dcn. Lazarus Der-Ghazarian, Assoc. Dir.;

Department of Human Resources - t) 313-237-5948 Chantale Stevenson, Dir.;

Human Resources Manager - t) 313-596-7156 Erin Taft; Rev. Msgr. G. Michael Bugarin, Episcopal Vicar, Archbishop's Delegate to the Archdiocesan Review Bd.;

Promoter of Ministerial Standards - t) 313-237-4813 Ina Grant;

Safe Environments - t) 313-596-5826 Anthony Latarski, Coord.;

Senior Employee Relations and Compliance Manager - t) 313-596-7442 Stacey Washington;

Victim Assistance Coordinator and Clergy Discipline - t) 586-601-1221 Anthony Latarski;

Department of Missionary Strategic Plans - Dcn. Michael Houghton, Dir.; Dcn. David P. Casnovsky, Coach; Mary Martin, Coach;

Department of Parish Care and Sustainability - t) 313-237-5978 Lory McGlinnen, Dir.;

Ecumenical/Interfaith Relations - t) 313-237-4678 Rev. Msgr. John C. Kasza, Archbishop's Ecumenical/ Interfaith Advisor; David J. Conrad, Coord.;

Office for Clergy and Consecrated Life - t) 313-596-7155 Rev. Robert R. Spezia, Dir.;

Delegate for Consecrated Life - t) 313-596-7143 Dcn. Aaron Poyer, Delegate;

Immigration Legal Services for Clergy, Consecrated Life and Schools - t) 313-596-7148 Viviana Lande, Immigration Lawyer;

Permanent Diaconate Program - t) 313-596-7142 Dcn. Christopher Beltowski, Assoc. Dir.;

Office of Priestly Vocations - t) 313-237-5875 Rev. Craig Giera, Dir.; Alex Slavsky, Mktg. Events Coord.;

Office of the Chancellor - t) 313-237-5847 Michael R. Trueman, Chancellor; Rev. Timothy J. Wezner, Vice Chancellor;

Archives - t) 313-237-5864 Steven Wejroch, Archivist;

Priests Conference for Polish Affairs of the Archdiocese of Detroit - Rev. Stanley A. Ulman, Pres.;

CANONICAL SERVICES

Marriage Permissions/Dispensations - t) 313-237-5848 dispensations@aod.org Dcn. Phil McCown, Coord. (wadephil@yahoo.com);

CONSULTATIVE BODIES

Archdiocesan Finance Council - Mark VanFaussien, Chair; Michael Schoenle, CFO; Joseph A. Amine;

College of Consultors - Rev. John Bettin; Rev. David Cybulski (frcybulski@saintisaacjogues.com); Rev. Gerald A. McEnhill;

Presbyteral Council - Rev. Msgr. Charles G. Kosanke, Chair (pastor@mostholytrinityministries.org); Rev. Scott A. Thibodeau, Vice-Chmn.; Rev. David Cybulski, Secy. (frcybulski@saintisaacjogues.com);

Unleash the Gospel Archdiocesan Pastoral Council - Most Rev. Gerard W. Battersby; Janet Diaz; Richard S. Genthe;

ORGANIZATIONS

Association of the Holy Childhood - t) 313-237-5807 Rev. Msgr. James A. Moloney;

Catholic Youth Organization - t) 313-963-7172 Michael Shapiro, CEO (mshapiro@cyodetroit.org);

Propagation of the Faith (Missions) - t) 313-237-5807 Rev. Msgr. James A. Moloney;

Saints Mary and Joseph Chapel - t) (734) 414-1104 Janette Villeneuve, Coord.;

TRIBUNAL

The Metropolitan Tribunal - t) 313-237-5865

Adjutant Judicial Vicar - Rev. Robert Hayes Williams;

Advocates - Rev. Msgr. Michael C. LeFevre;

Coordinator of Administrative Support Staff - Lindsay Martinez;

Defenders of Bond - Rev. Michael Loyson; Rev. Norman D. Nawrocki; Patricia Mkrtumian;

Judges - Rev. Thomas E. Urban; Rev. Paul Czarnota; Rev. Salvatore Palazzolo;

Judicial Vicar - Very Rev. Ronald T. Browne;

Notaries - Adam Dwornick; Lindsay Martinez; Barbara Somerton;

PARISHES, MISSIONS, AND CLERGY

STATE OF MICHIGAN

ALLEN PARK

St. Frances Cabrini Allen Park - 9000 Laurence Ave., Allen Park, MI 48101 t) 313-381-5601; 313-928-4727 (CRP) office@cabriniparish.org cabriniparish.org Rev. Timothy P. Birney, Priest in Solidum; CRP Stds.: 175

St. Frances Cabrini Grade School - (Grades 1-8) 15300 Wick Rd., Allen Park, MI 48101 t) 313-928-6610 Kelly Stetz, Prin.; Stds.: 285; Lay Tchrs.: 24

St. Frances Cabrini High School - (Grades 7-12) 15305 Wick Rd., Allen Park, MI 48101 t) 313-388-0110 Stds.: 210; Lay Tchrs.: 26

ALLENTON

St. John the Evangelist Parish Allenton - 883 Capac Rd., Allenton, MI 48002; Mailing: 872 Capac Rd., P.O. Box 10, Allenton, MI 48002 t) (810) 669-1029 (CRP) office@stjohnallenton.com stjohnallenton.com Rev. Michael R. Gawlowski, Priest in Solidum;

ARMADA

St. Mary Mystical Rose Parish Armada - 24040 Armada Ridge Rd., Armada, MI 48005 t) 586-784-5966; 586-784-5966 x107 (CRP) kglowicki@stmarymysticalrose.org www.stmarymysticalrose.org Rev. Philip Ching, Priest in Solidum; Kim Glowicki, DRE; CRP Stds.: 77

AUBURN HILLS

St. John Fisher Chapel University Parish Auburn Hills - 3665 E. Walton Blvd., Auburn Hills, MI 48326 t) 248-373-6457 assist@sjfchapel.org www.sjfchapel.org Rev. James F. Kean, Priest in Solidum; Rev. Steven J. Mateja, Priest in Solidum; Judie McGuire, DRE; Lori Ann Rafferty, Bus. Mgr.; CRP Stds.: 48

Sacred Heart Parish Auburn Hills - 3400 S. Adams Rd., Auburn Hills, MI 48326 t) 248-852-4170 sacredheartauburnhills@gmail.com esacredheart.org Rev. Joseph Grimaldi, Priest in Solidum; CRP Stds.: 20

BELLEVILLE

St. Anthony Parish Belleville - 409 W. Columbia Ave., Belleville, MI 48111 t) 734-697-1211 cweipert@stanthonybelleville.com www.stanthonybelleville.com Rev. Bryan Shackett, Priest in Solidum; Dcn. John Burke;

BERKLEY

Our Lady of La Salette Parish Berkley - 2600 Harvard Rd., Berkley, MI 48072 t) 248-541-3762 office@lasalette-church.org www.lasalette-church.org Rev. Patrick J. Connell, Priest in Solidum; Dcn. Daniel M. Darga, Pst. Assoc.; Dcn. Clement Stankiewicz; CRP Stds.: 16

BEVERLY HILLS

Our Lady Queen of Martyrs Parish Beverly Hills - 32340 Pierce St., Beverly Hills, MI 48025 t) 248-644-8620; 248-647-6068 (CRP) kwolff@olqm-parish.org; mgarlow@olqm-parish.org www.olqm-parish.org Rev.

James A. Smalarz, Priest in Solidum; Dcn. Christopher Beltowski; Mary Garlow, DRE; CRP Stds.: 172

Our Lady Queen of Martyrs School - (Grades PreSchool-8) 32460 Pierce Ave., Beverly Hills, MI 48025 t) 248-642-2616 jgeden@olqm-parish.org www.olqmcatholicschool.org Jill Geden, Prin.; Stds.: 321; Lay Tchrs.: 21

BIRMINGHAM

Holy Name Parish Birmingham - 630 Harmon St., Birmingham, MI 48009 t) 248-646-2244 info@hnchurch.org www.hnchurch.org Rev. Msgr. John P. Zenz, Priest in Solidum; Dcn. Michael J. McKale; Deborah Shinder, Pst. Assoc.; Maureen Apap, DRE; Susan Davis, Bus. Mgr.; Brandon Gauvin, Music Min.; CRP Stds.: 174

Holy Name School - (Grades PreK-8) 680 Harmon St., Birmingham, MI 48009 t) 248-644-2722 dbrzezinski@hnschool.com school.hnchurch.org DeAnn Brzezinski, Prin.; Elizabeth Kozadinos, Vice Prin.; Stds.: 341; Scholastics: 26; Lay Tchrs.: 19

BLOOMFIELD HILLS

St. Hugo of the Hills Parish Bloomfield Hills - 2215 Opdyke Rd., Bloomfield Hills, MI 48304 t) 248-644-5460; 248-283-2213; 248-283-2212 barbara.rund@sthugo.org; patty.sinta@sthugo.org www.sthugo.org Rev. Mark S. Brauer, Priest in Solidum; Rev. Adam Nowak, Priest in Solidum; Dcn. Oscar A. Brown; Dcn. Michael T. Smith; Sr. Barbara Rund, O.P., Pst. Assoc.; CRP Stds.: 170

St. Hugo of the Hills School - (Grades 1-8) 380 E. Hickory Grove, Bloomfield Hills, MI 48304 t) 248-425-1974 kelly.ryan@sthugoschool.org Joseph Vincler, Pres.; Stds.: 649; Lay Tchrs.: 36

St. Owen Parish Bloomfield Hills - 6869 Franklin Rd., Bloomfield Hills, MI 48301 t) 248-626-0840; 248-626-2300 (CRP) parishoffice@stowen.org www.stowen.org Rev. Msgr. Michael C. LeFevre, Priest in Solidum; Kathleen Susalla Rochon, DRE; Mary Mills, Youth Min.; CRP Stds.: 104

St. Regis Parish Bloomfield Hills - 3695 Lincoln Rd., Bloomfield Hills, MI 48301-4055 t) 248-646-2686 www.stregis.org Rev. David A. Buersmeyer, Priest in Solidum; CRP Stds.: 95

St. Regis School - (Grades PreK-8) 3691 Lincoln Rd., Bloomfield Hills, MI 48301-4055; Mailing: 3695 Lincoln Rd., Bloomfield Hills, MI 48301 t) 248-724-3377 businessoffice@stregis.org Katie Brydges, Prin.; Stds.: 478; Lay Tchrs.: 29

CANTON

Saint John Neumann Parish Canton - 44800 Warren Rd., Canton, MI 48187 t) 734-455-5910; 734-455-5986 x114 (Faith Formation) y.corey@sjncanton.org; pballien@sjncanton.org www.sjncanton.org Rev. Paul K. Ballien, Priest in Solidum; Rev. Paulo Dias, Priest in Solidum; Dcn. Patrick Conlen; CRP Stds.: 167

Resurrection Parish Canton - 48755 Warren Rd., Canton, MI 48187-1216 t) 734-451-0444 resoffice@resurrectionparish.net; karen.hogan@resurrectionparish.net www.resurrectionparish.net Rev. Thomas J. Kramer, Priest in Solidum; CRP Stds.: 54

St. Thomas a'Becket Parish Canton - 555 S. Lilley Rd., Canton, MI 48188 t) 734-981-1333 grace.pellerito@abecket.org www.abecket.org Rev. Christopher P. Maus, Priest in Solidum; Dcn. James Ward; CRP Stds.: 370

CAPAC

St. Nicholas Parish Capac - 4331 Capac Rd., Capac, MI 48014; Mailing: Box 129, Capac, MI 48014 t) 810-395-7572 staff@imlaysacredheart.org Rev. Noel Emmanuel Cornelio, Priest in Solidum; CRP Stds.: 24

CARLETON

Divine Grace Parish Carleton - 2996 W. Labo Rd., Carleton, MI 48117 t) 734-654-2500 divinegraceparish@yahoo.com; divinegracedre@gmail.com www.divinegraceparish.com Rev. Michael Allen Woroniewicz, Priest in Solidum; Dcn. Tracy Esper; Tim Bolster, DRE; CRP Stds.: 93

St. Patrick School - (Grades 1-8) 2970 W Labo Rd, Carleton, MI 48117 t) 734-654-2522 saintpatrick@chartermi.net www.stpatscarleton.com/ Carl Lenze, Prin.; Stds.: 110; Lay Tchrs.: 6

CENTER LINE

St. Mary, Our Lady Queen of Families Parish Warren - 25320 Van Dyke, Center Line, MI 48015; Mailing: 8075 Ritter, Center Line, MI 48015 t) 586-757-3306 stccpsrishoffice@gmail.com; smolqf.reled@gmail.com www.ourladyqueenoffamilies.net Rev. Robert A. Bauer, Priest in Solidum; Dcn. Stanley Avery; Donna Van Gheluwe, DRE; CRP Stds.: 35

CLARKSTON

St. Daniel Parish Clarkston - 7010 Valley Park Dr., Clarkston, MI 48346 t) 248-625-4580 jbettin@stdanielclarkston.org; vtoth@stdanielclarkston.org Rev. John Bettin, Priest in Solidum; CRP Stds.: 217

CLAWSON

Guardian Angels Parish Clawson - 581 E. 14 Mile Rd., Clawson, MI 48017 t) 248-588-1222 johndavidk@guartdiana.com; michaelk@guardiana.com www.guardiana.com Rev. Tony Richter, Priest in Solidum; Dcn. Christopher Stark; John David Kuhar, DRE; CRP Stds.: 66

Guardian Angels School - (Grades PreK-8) 521 E. 14 Mile Rd., Clawson, MI 48017 t) 248-588-5545 ortisit@gaschool.com www.gaschool.com Stephen Turk, Prin.; Stds.: 271; Lay Tchrs.: 19

CLINTON TOWNSHIP

St. Louis Parish Clinton Township - 24415 Crocker Blvd., Clinton Township, MI 48036 t) 586-468-8734; 586-468-8734 x104 (CRP) stlouischurchslc@comcast.net www.stlouiscatholiccommunity.com Rev. John Maksym, Priest in Solidum; CRP Stds.: 52

St. Paul of Tarsus Parish Clinton Township - 41300 Romeo Plank Rd., Clinton Township, MI 48038 t) 586-228-1210; 586-228-6651 x4 (CRP) pdeclercq@spotcatholic.org; parish@spotcatholic.org spotcatholic.org Rev. John J. Kiselica, Priest in Solidum; Janice Krygowski, DRE; CRP Stds.: 212

St. Ronald Parish Clinton Township - 17701 15 Mile Rd., Clinton Township, MI 48035-2401 t) 586-792-1190; 586-792-1191; 586-792-1276 parishoffice@stronald.com; lisa.stronald@gmail.com www.stronald.com Rev. William J. Herman, Priest in Solidum; CRP Stds.: 60

San Francesco (Italian) Parish Clinton Township - 22870 S. Nunneley Rd., Clinton Township, MI 48035 t) 586-792-5346 rburrell@comcast.net; giulioschiavi79@gmail.com sanfrancescochurch.org Rev. Dino Vanin, PIME, Priest in Solidum; Ann Burrell, DRE; CRP Stds.: 20

St. Thecla Parish Clinton Township - 20740 Nunneley Rd., Clinton Township, MI 48035-1628 t) 586-791-3930 receptionist@stthecla.com www.stthecla.com Parish & Elementary School Rev. Kevin Roelant, Priest in Solidum; Dcn. Thomas Houle; Dcn. Timothy Maxwell; CRP Stds.: 51

St. Thecla School - 20762 S. Nunneley Rd., Clinton Township, MI 48035 t) 586-791-2170 maloneyd@stthecla.com stthecla.com/school Martha Karwoski, Prin.; Stds.: 267; Lay Tchrs.: 23

DEARBORN

St. Alphonsus - St. Clement Parish Dearborn - 13540 Gould St., Dearborn, MI 48126; Mailing: 7469 Calhoun St., Dearborn, MI 48126 t) 313-581-5218 info@sta-stc.comcastbiz.net Rev. Gregory J. Deters, Priest in Solidum;

St. Barbara Parish Dearborn - 13534 Colson Ave., Dearborn, MI 48126 t) 313-582-8383 saintbarbara@sbcglobal.net www.stbarbaradearborn.org Rev. Zbigniew Grankowski, Priest in Solidum; Michael Peck, DRE; Emily Anne Sherwood, Music Min.; Judith Kadela, Bus. Mgr.; CRP Stds.: 33

Divine Child Parish Dearborn - 1055 N. Silvery Ln., Dearborn, MI 48128 t) 313-277-3110 alicia@divinechild.org www.divinechild.org Rev. Robert J. McCabe, Priest in Solidum; Rev. David Pellican, Priest in Solidum; Rev. John Dudek, Priest in Solidum; Dcn. Robert Calleja; Dawn Dwyer, DRE; CRP Stds.: 43

Divine Child School - (Grades 1-8) 25001 Herbert Weier Dr., Dearborn, MI 48128 t) 313-562-1090 readm@dces.info www.divinechildelementaryschool.org J. Mike Courage, Prin.; Kristy Kubik, Vice Prin.; Stds.: 563; Sr. Tchrs.: 2; Lay Tchrs.: 35

Divine Child High School - 1001 N. Silvery Ln., Dearborn, MI 48128 t) 313-562-1990 ripley@divinechildhighschool.org www.divinechildhighschool.org Anthony Trudel, Prin.; Stds.: 722; Lay Tchrs.: 69

Convent - 1045 N. Silvery Ln., Dearborn, MI 48128 t) 313-561-5455

St. Kateri Tekakwitha Parish Dearborn - 16101 Rotunda Dr., Dearborn, MI 48120 t) 313-336-3227 info@stkateridearborn.org stkateridearborn.org Rev. Terrence D. Kerner, Priest in Solidum; Dcn. Thomas Leonard; Lawrence David Winey, DRE; CRP Stds.: 36

Sacred Heart Parish Dearborn - 22430 W. Michigan Ave., Dearborn, MI 48124; Mailing: 912 S. Military St., Dearborn, MI 48124 t) 313-278-5555 redirector@shparish.org www.shparish.org Rev. Kenneth M. Chase, Priest in Solidum; Julie Wieleba-Milkie, DRE; CRP Stds.: 91

Sacred Heart School - (Grades K-8) 22513 Garrison, Dearborn, MI 48124 t) 313-561-9192 principal@shparish.org Kim Ayrault, Prin.; Stds.: 204; Lay Tchrs.: 11

DEARBORN HEIGHTS

St. Anselm Parish Dearborn Heights - 17650 W. Outer Dr., Dearborn Heights, MI 48127 t) 313-565-4808; 313-561-0512 (CRP) maryann.w@saintanselmparish.org; msgrmoloney@gmail.com www.saintanselmparish.org Rev. Msgr. James A. Moloney, Priest in Solidum; Maryanne Walkuski, DRE; CRP Stds.: 60

St. Anselm School - (Grades PreK-8) 17700 W. Outer Dr., Dearborn Heights, MI 48127 t) 313-563-3430 akraetke@saintanselmschool.org www.saintanselmschool.org Angela Kraetke, Prin.; Stds.: 174; Lay Tchrs.: 11

St. Linus Parish Dearborn Heights - 6466 Evangeline, Dearborn Heights, MI 48127-2086 t) 313-274-4500 frpatrick@stlinusparish.org stlinus.info Rev. Patrick Stoffer, OFM, Conv., Priest in Solidum; Shannon Pryce, DRE; CRP Stds.: 16

St. Linus School - (Grades 1-8) 6466 N. Evangeline, Dearborn Heights, MI 48127 t) 313-274-5320 stlinuscatholicschoolmi@gmail.com www.stlinuscatholicchurch.org/school Cat Poslaiko, Prin.; Stds.: 126; Lay Tchrs.: 9

St. Maria Goretti Parish Dearborn Heights - 20710 Colgate St., Dearborn Heights, MI 48125 t) 313-562-5356 parishoffice@smgoretti.com www.stmariagorettiparish.com Rev. David Lesniak, Priest in Solidum; Dcn. Regis Buckley; Dcn. Lawrence Girard; CRP Stds.: 46

St. Sabina Parish Dearborn Heights - 25605 Ann Arbor Tr., Dearborn Heights, MI 48127 t) 313-561-1977 deaconmatthewwisniewski@gmail.com Rev. James F. Lopez, Priest in Solidum; Dcn. Matthew Wisniewski;

DETROIT

Most Blessed Sacrament Cathedral Parish Detroit - 9844 Woodward Ave., Detroit, MI 48202 t) 313-865-6300 cathedral@aod.org cathedral.aod.org/ Rev. John J. Mech, Rector & Priest in Solidum; Christopher J Jaskowiec, Bus. Mgr.;

St. Aloysius Parish Detroit - 1234 Washington Blvd., Detroit, MI 48226 t) 313-237-5810 amore.mario@aod.org www.staloysiusdetroit.com Rev. Mario V. Amore, Priest in Solidum; CRP Stds.: 2

SS. Andrew and Benedict Parish Detroit - 2400 S. Beatrice St., Detroit, MI 48217 t) 313-381-1184 info@smmssab.com smmssab.com Rev. Timothy P. Birney, Priest in Solidum; Rev. Charles Mmaduekwe, Priest in Solidum; CRP Stds.: 31

Ste. Anne Basilica Parish de Detroit - 1000 Ste. Anne St.,

Detroit, MI 48216 t) 313-496-1701 businessoffice@steannedetroit.org ste-anne.org Rev. Msgr. Charles G. Kosanke, Rector; Rev. Ryan J. Adams, Priest in Solidum; Dcn. Kenneth Fry; Juanita Sanchez, DRE; Anne-Marie Marie Fry, Pst. Assoc.; CRP Stds.: 77

Assumption of the Blessed Virgin Mary (Grotto) Parish Detroit - 13770 Gratiot Ave., Detroit, MI 48205 t) 313-372-0762 parish@assumptiongrotto.com assumptiongrotto.com/ Rev. John Christopher Bustamante, Priest in Solidum; CRP Stds.: 34

St. Augustine and St. Monica Parish Detroit - 4151 Seminole St., Detroit, MI 48214 t) 313-921-4107 office@saintamparish.org saintamparish.org Rev. Msgr. Daniel J. Trapp, Priest in Solidum; Kathleen Williams-Trice, Pst. Min./Coord.; Dcn. Christopher Rabaut;

St. Charles Borromeo Parish Detroit - 1491 Baldwin Ave., Detroit, MI 48214 t) 313-331-0253 stcharlesborremeodetroit@yahoo.com www.stcharlesdetroit.org/ Rev. Msgr. Daniel J. Trapp, Priest in Solidum; CRP Stds.: 25

St. Charles Lwanga Parish Detroit - 10400 Stoepel Ave., Detroit, MI 48204 t) (313) 933-6788 stcharleslwanga@outlook.com saintcharleslwanga.org Rev. Theodore K. Parker, Priest in Solidum; Patricia Dixon, DRE; Angela Thomas-Weldon, Contact; CRP Stds.: 24

Christ the King Parish Detroit - 20800 Grand River, Detroit, MI 48219; Mailing: 16805 Pierson, Detroit, MI 48219 t) 313-532-1211 christking@ameritech.net www.christthekingcatholicdetroit.org Rev. John McKenzie, Priest in Solidum; Dcn. Christian Remus; Dcn. Joseph Urbiel; CRP Stds.: 10

Christ the King School - (Grades 1-8) 16800 Trinity, Detroit, MI 48219 t) 313-532-1213 alund.ctk@gmail.com; schooloffice.ctk@gmail.com Amanda Lund, Prin.;

St. Christine Christian Services - 22261 Fenkell, Detroit, MI 48223 t) 313-535-7272; (313) 543-1527 (Food Pantry); (313) 255-0312 (Soup Kitchen) sccsdetroit.org/ Tracy Clark, Pres.; Leon Tupper, Treas.;

Corpus Christi Parish Detroit - 19800 Pembroke Ave, Detroit, MI 48219-2145 t) 313-537-5770 parishoffice.cc@corpuschristi-detroit.org www.corpuschristi-detroit.org Rev. Patrick Gonyeau, Priest in Solidum; Dcn. Paul Mueller; Dcn. Aaron Poyer; Sr. Therese MacKinnon, D.C., DRE; CRP Stds.: 81

St. Cunegunda Parish Detroit - 5900 St. Lawrence, Detroit, MI 48210 t) 313-843-4717 stcunegunda.detroit@gmail.com Rev. Dennis Walsh, S.O.L.T., Priest in Solidum; Rev. Anthony Blount, S.O.L.T., Priest in Solidum; Rev. Jeremy Davis, S.O.L.T., Priest in Solidum;

St. Elizabeth Parish Detroit - 3138 E. Canfield St., Detroit, MI 48207 t) 313-921-9225 www.stelizabethdetroit.com Rev. Norman P. Thomas, Priest in Solidum; Velma Coleman, DRE; CRP Stds.: 35

St. Francis D'Assisi - St. Hedwig Parish - 3245 Junction St., Detroit, MI 48210-3203 t) (313) 894-5409 stfrancis.sthedwigparish@gmail.com www.stfrancis-sthedwig.com/ Rev. Bernardo Cruz, Priest in Solidum;

St. Gabriel Parish Detroit - 8118 W. Vernor Hwy., Detroit, MI 48209 t) 313-841-0753; 313-841-0753 x400 (CRP) julia@archangel-gabriel.org Rev. Dennis Walsh, SOLT, Priest in Solidum; Rev. Anthony Blount, S.O.L.T., Priest in Solidum; Rev. Jeremy Davis, S.O.L.T., Priest in Solidum; CRP Stds.: 328

Gesu Parish Detroit - 17180 Oak Dr., Detroit, MI 48221 t) 313-862-4400 info@gesudetroit.org gesudetroit.com Rev. Lorn J. Snow, S.J., Priest in Solidum; Rev. Jeffrey R Dorr, S.J., Priest in Solidum; Laura Silveri, DRE; CRP Stds.: 41

Gesu School - (Grades PreK-8) 17139 Oak Dr., Detroit, MI 48221 t) 313-863-4677 friday.m@gesudetroit.org www.gesuschool.udmercy.edu/ Mark Friday, Prin.; Stds.: 235; Lay Tchrs.: 11

Holy Cross (Hungarian) Parish Detroit - 8423 South St., Detroit, MI 48209 t) 313-842-1133 holycross1905@att.net www.holycrosshungarian.com Southwest Detroit Family of Parishes Friar Barnabas G. Kiss, O.F.M., Priest in Solidum; Friar Angelus Ligeti, O.F.M., Priest in Solidum; Emma T. Mahar, DRE; CRP Stds.: 25

Holy Family (Italian) Parish Detroit - 641 Walter P. Chrysler Service Dr., Detroit, MI 48226 t) 313-963-2046 holyfamilypd@gmail.com www.hfdet.org Rev. Paul Ward, Priest in Solidum; CRP Stds.: 1

Holy Redeemer Parish Detroit - 1721 Junction Ave., Detroit, MI 48209 t) 313-842-3450; 313-841-5230 (CRP) hredeemer72@yahoo.com; 1880mhredeemer@gmail.com Rev. Dennis Walsh, S.O.L.T., Priest in Solidum; Rev. Anthony Blount, S.O.L.T., Priest in Solidum; Rev. Jeremy Davis, S.O.L.T., Priest in Solidum; Rev. Mark Wendling, S.O.L.T. (Canada), In Res.; Marcela Solis, DRE; CRP Stds.: 592

Holy Redeemer School - (Grades 1-8) 1711 Junction Ave., Detroit, MI 48209 t) (313) 841-5230 Sr. Kateri Burbee, S.O.L.T., Prin.; Stds.: 214; Sr. Tchrs.: 3; Lay Tchrs.: 13

St. Hyacinth Parish Detroit - 3151 Farnsworth Ave., Detroit, MI 48211 t) 313-922-1507 st.hyacinth@att.net www.sainthyacinth.com Rev. Janusz Iwan, Priest in Solidum;

St. John Paul II Parish Detroit - 5830 Simon K, Detroit, MI 48212 t) 313-305-7394 sjp2parish@gmail.com Former Name: Church of the Transfiguration Rev. Andrew Wesley, Priest in Solidum; Debbie Warren, DRE;

St. Joseph Shrine Parish Detroit (St. Joseph Roman Catholic Church) - 1828 Jay St., Detroit, MI 48207 t) 313-784-9152 sjdetroit@institute-christ-king.org www.stjosephshrined.org/ Rev. Canon Jean-Baptiste Commins, I.C.R.S.S., Rector; Rev. Canon Adrian Sequeira, I.C.R.S.S., Priest in Solidum;

St. Juan Diego Parish Detroit - 7800 Woodmont Ave., Detroit, MI 48228 t) 313-584-7460 serrato.claudia@stjuandiegoparish.com; leszczynski.dottie@stjuandiegoparish.com www.stjuandiegoparish.com/ Rev. Jaime Hinojos, Priest in Solidum; CRP Stds.: 89

St. Jude Parish Detroit - 15889 E. Seven Mile Rd., Detroit, MI 48205 t) 313-527-0380 stjudedetroit@hotmail.com www.stjudedetroit.org Rev. Michael C. Nkachukwu, Pst.; Rev. Tyrone Robinson, Par. Vicar; CRP Stds.: 2

St. Mary of Redford Parish Detroit - 16098 Grand River Ave., Detroit, MI 48227; Mailing: 14601 Mansfield St., Rectory Office, Detroit, MI 48227 t) 313-273-1100 administrator@saintmaryofredford.church saintmaryofredford.church Rev. Athanasius Fornwalt, FHS, Priest in Solidum; CRP Stds.: 15

St. Mary Parish Detroit - 646 Monroe Ave., Detroit, MI 48226 t) 313-961-8711 rectory@oldstmarysdetroit.com www.oldstmarysdetroit.com Rev. Godfrey Mgonja, C.S.Sp., Priest in Solidum; Rev. John Owusu-Achiaw, C.S.Sp., Priest in Solidum; Rev. LeRoy Moreeuw, C.S.Sp., In Res.; CRP Stds.: 6

St. Matthew Parish Detroit - 6021 Whittier Ave., Detroit, MI 48224 t) 313-884-4470 stmatthew27@aol.com stmatthewdetroit.com Rev. Duane R. Novelly, Priest in Solidum;

St. Moses the Black Parish Detroit - 1125 Oakman Blvd., Detroit, MI 48238; Mailing: 9844 Woodward, Detroit, MI 48202 t) 313-868-4308 office@stmosestheblack.org Rev. Marko Djonovic, Priest in Solidum; CRP Stds.: 14

Most Holy Trinity Parish Detroit - 1050 Porter St., Detroit, MI 48226 t) 313-965-4450 businessoffice@mhtdetroit.org mhtdetroit.org Rev. Msgr. Charles G. Kosanke, Priest in Solidum; Rev. Ryan J. Adams, Priest in Solidum; Dcn. Kenneth Fry; Juanita Sanchez, DRE;

Most Holy Trinity School - (Grades K-8) 1229 Labrosse, Detroit, MI 48226 t) 313-961-8855 www.mhtdetroit.org Karina Lepkowski, Prin.; Stds.: 115; Lay Tchrs.: 14

Mother of Divine Mercy Parish Detroit - 4440 Russell St., Detroit, MI 48207 t) 313-831-6659 parishoffice@motherofdivinemercy.org motherofdivinemercy.org Rev. Gregory Tokarski, Priest in Solidum; Dcn. Joseph Lennon; Carol Sniezyk, DRE; CRP Stds.: 10

Nativity of Our Lord Parish Detroit - 5900 McClellan Ave., Detroit, MI 48213 t) 313-922-0033 nativityol@sbcglobal.net nativitydetroit.org Rev. Msgr. Daniel J. Trapp, Priest in Solidum; Joseph Taylor, Pst. Min./Coord.; CRP Stds.: 16

Our Lady of Guadalupe Parish Detroit - 4200 Martin, Detroit, MI 48210-2736 t) 313-841-0783 parish@olgdetroit.com olgdetroit.com Rev. Adalberto Espinoza, Priest in Solidum; CRP Stds.: 150

Our Lady Queen of Heaven - Good Shepherd Parish Detroit - 8200 Rolyat Ave., Detroit, MI 48234 t) 313-891-4553 ladyofgoodshepherd@att.net Rev. Michael C. Nkachukwu, Priest in Solidum; Rev. Tyrone Robinson, Priest in Solidum; Gayle Koyton, DRE; CRP Stds.: 5

SS. Peter and Paul (Jesuit) Parish Detroit - 629 E. Jefferson Ave., Detroit, MI 48226; Mailing: 438 St. Antoine St., Detroit, MI 48226 t) 313-961-8077 office@ssppjesuit.org www.ssppjesuit.org Rev. Gary R. Wright, S.J., Priest in Solidum; Julie Berra, Liturgy Dir.; Lydia Maola, Bus. Mgr.;

SS. Peter and Paul (Westside) Parish Detroit - 7685 Grandville Ave., Detroit, MI 48228 t) 313-846-2222 ssppdetroit.net Rev. Jaroslaw Pilus, Priest in Solidum; Anna Clougherty, Pst. Assoc.;

St. Peter Claver Parish Detroit - 13305 Grove Ave., Detroit, MI 48235 t) 313-342-5292 parishoffice@spcccdetroit.org www.spcccdetroit.org Rev. John Phelps, C.Ss.R., Priest in Solidum; CRP Stds.: 3

Presentation - Our Lady of Victory Parish Detroit - 17305 Ashton Ave., Detroit, MI 48219 t) 313-255-9000 hubertsanders60@icloud.com www.presentationourladyofvictory.org Dcn. Hubert Sanders, Admin.; Wanda Sanders, DRE; Jeanine Murphy, Bus. Mgr.; CRP Stds.: 13

St. Raymond - Our Lady of Good Counsel Parish Detroit - 20103 Joann Ave., Detroit, MI 48205 t) 313-527-0525 infosaintraymond@gmail.com www.straymondolgc.org Rev. Michael C. Nkachukwu, Priest in Solidum; Rev. Tyrone Robinson, Priest in Solidum; Gayle Koyton, DRE; CRP Stds.: 2

Community Outreach - 20055 Joann Ave., Detroit, MI 48205 t) 313-372-0437 Food pantry, community meetings/AA, and thrift store.

Sacred Heart (African American) Parish Detroit - 1000 Eliot St., Detroit, MI 48207 t) 313-831-1356 info@sacredheartdetroit.com; npt@sacredheartdetroit.com sacredheartdetroit.com Rev. Norman P. Thomas, Priest in Solidum; CRP Stds.: 100

St. Scholastica Parish Detroit - 8201 W. Outer Dr., Detroit, MI 48219; Mailing: 17320 Rosemont Rd., Detroit, MI 48219 t) 313-531-0140 stscholastica@gmail.com www.scholastica.church Rev. James Lowe, C.C., Priest in Solidum; CRP Stds.: 7

Convent - 17305 Ashton, Detroit, MI 48219

St. Suzanne - Our Lady Gate of Heaven Parish Detroit - 19321 West Chicago, Detroit, MI 48228; Mailing: 9357 Westwood Ave., Detroit, MI 48228 t) 313-838-6780 ssolgh@sbcglobal.net Rev. John McKenzie, Priest in Solidum;

DRYDEN

St. Cornelius Parish Dryden - 3834 Mill St., Dryden, MI 48428; Mailing: P.O. Box 208, Dryden, MI 48428 t) 810-796-2926; 810-796-4701 (CRP) faithformation-west@fmsaints.com; office@fmsaints.com www.fmsaints.com Rev. Noel Emmanuel Cornelio, Priest in Solidum; Holly Shanefelt, Music Min.; Julie Allison, DRE; CRP Stds.: 116

EASTPOINTE

St. Basil Parish Eastpointe - 22800 Schroeder Ave., Eastpointe, MI 48021; Mailing: 22851 Lexington Ave., Eastpointe, MI 48021 t) 586-777-5610; 586-772-5434 (CRP) stbasileastpoint@comcast.net; stbasilreligioused@comcast.net www.stbasileastpointe.com Rev. Eric Fedewa, Priest in Solidum; Carolyn Mikula, DRE; CRP Stds.: 35

St. Veronica Parish Eastpointe - 21440 Universal Ave., Eastpointe, MI 48021-2998 t) 586-777-0331 Rev. Stanley L. Pachla Jr., Priest in Solidum; Rev. Kulan-Daisamy Arokiasamy (India), In Res.; Carolyn Mikula, DRE; CRP Stds.: 45

ECORSE

St. André Bessette Parish Ecorse - 4250 W. Jefferson Ave., Ecorse, MI 48229-1597 t) 313-383-8514 reled@standreparish.org; office@standreparish.org www.standreparish.org Rev. Cornelius Okeke, Priest in Solidum; Miranda Garcia, DRE; CRP Stds.: 114

EMMETT

Our Lady of Mount Carmel Parish Emmett - 10828 Brandon Rd., Emmett, MI 48022 t) 810-384-1338; 810-384-1338 x41 (CRP) olmcshydre@gmail.com; olmcshyreceptionist@gmail.com www.eastthumbcatholic.org/ Rev. Thomas Kuehnemund, Priest in Solidum; Dcn. William Kolarik; Brenda Krzak, DRE; Deanna White, Youth Min.; CRP Stds.: 74

ERIE

St. Joseph Parish Erie - 2214 Manhattan Ave., Erie, MI 48133 t) 734-848-6125 parish@stjosepherie.com www.stjosepherie.com/ Rev. Mark P. Prill, Priest In Solidum; CRP Stds.: 45

St. Joseph School - (Grades PreSchool-8) 2238 Manhattan St., Erie, MI 48133 t) 734-848-6985 julie.miazgowicz@stjosepherie.com Amy Cousino, Prin.; Stds.: 92; Lay Tchrs.: 10

Convent - Manhattan Ave., Erie, MI 48133

FARMINGTON

St. Gerald Parish Farmington - 21300 Farmington Rd., Farmington, MI 48336 t) 248-477-7470; 248-476-7677 (CRP) marytaylor.sgp@gmail.com; stgeraldsecretary@yahoo.com stgeraldparish.org Rev. Krzysztof Nowak, Priest in Solidum; Mary Taylor, DRE; CRP Stds.: 58

Our Lady of Sorrows Parish Farmington - 23815 Power Rd., Farmington, MI 48336-2461 t) 248-474-5720; 248-474-6480 (CRP) ofd@olsorrows.com; info@olsorrows.com olsorrows.com Rev. Canon Walter J. Ptak, Priest in Solidum; Rev. Derik E. Peterman, Priest in Solidum; Rev. James Livingston, In Res.; Erik Coules, DRE; CRP Stds.: 130

Our Lady of Sorrows School - (Grades PreSchool-8) 24040 Raphael, Farmington, MI 48336-2465 t) 248-476-0977 kambrose@olsorrows.com Kathie Ambrose, Prin.; Stds.: 847; Lay Tchrs.: 39

FARMINGTON HILLS

St. Fabian Parish Farmington Hills - 32200 W. 12 Mile Rd., Farmington Hills, MI 48334 t) 248-553-4610; 248-553-4860 (CRP) ppyrkosz@stfabian.org; kkerwin@stfabian.org stfabian.org Rev. Msgr. Timothy D. Hogan, Priest in Solidum; Rev. Mark Tibai, Priest in Solidum; Peggy Aoun, Pst. Min./Coord.; Kim Kerwin, DRE; Paul Pyrkosz, Bus. Mgr.; CRP Stds.: 229

St. Fabian School - (Grades 1-8) t) 248-553-2750 info@stfabian.org www.stfabian.org/school Courtney Nixon, Prin.; Stds.: 328; Lay Tchrs.: 20

FLAT ROCK

St. Roch Parish Flat Rock - 25022 Gibraltar Rd., Flat Rock, MI 48134 t) 734-782-4471 stroch@strochflatrock.com www.strochflatrock.com Rev. Raymond H. Lewandowski, Priest in Solidum; Cheryl Knapp, DRE; CRP Stds.: 194

GARDEN CITY

St. Thomas the Apostle Parish Garden City - 31530 Beechwood, Garden City, MI 48135-1935 t) 734-427-1533 frlarry@thomastheapostle.org thomastheapostle.org Rev. Lawrence Zurawski, Priest in Solidum; CRP Stds.: 67

GROSSE ILE

Sacred Heart Parish Grosse Ile - 21599 Parke Ln., Grosse Ile, MI 48138 t) 734-676-1378 Rev. Marc A. Gawronski, Priest in Solidum; CRP Stds.: 223

GROSSE POINTE FARMS

St. Paul Parish Grosse Pointe Farms - 157 Lake Shore Rd., Parish Office, Grosse Pointe Farms, MI 48236 t) 313-885-8855 (Office); 313-885-7022 (CRP); 313-884-8761 (Rectory) info@stpaulonthelake.org stpaulonthelake.org Rev. James D. Bilot, Priest in Solidum; Rev. Colin Fricke, Priest in Solidum; Rev. Thomas F. Slowinski, Priest in Solidum; Dcn. William E. Jamieson, Pst. Assoc.; CRP Stds.: 335

St. Paul on the Lake Catholic Church School - (Grades PreK-8) 170 Grosse Pointe Blvd., Grosse Pointe Farms, MI 48236 t) 313-885-3430 office@stpaulonthelake.org; tforsythe@stpaulonthelake.org www.stpaulonthelake.com Tina Forsythe, Prin.; Stds.: 404; Lay Tchrs.: 21

GROSSE POINTE PARK

St. Ambrose Parish Grosse Pointe Park - 15020 Hampton, Grosse Pointe Park, MI 48230 t) 313-822-2814; 313-332-5631 x125 reled.stambrose@comcast.net; stambrose@comcast.net stambrosechurch.net Rev. Timothy R. Pelc, Priest in Solidum; Charles J. Dropiewski, Pst. Assoc.; Kelly Woolums, DRE; CRP Stds.: 145

St. Clare of Montefalco Parish Grosse Pointe Park - 1401 Whittier Rd., Grosse Pointe Park, MI 48230 t) 313-647-5000; 313-647-5056 (CRP); 313-647-5110 (CRP) stclarem.org Rev. Andrzej Kowalczyk, C.S.M.A., Priest in Solidum; Sr. Kathleen Jo Avery, O.S.M., DRE; CRP Stds.: 69

St. Clare of Montefalco School - (Grades PreK-8) 16231 Charlevoix, Grosse Pointe Park, MI 48230 t) 313-647-5100 shensien@aod.org stclareschool.net Sarah Hensien, Prin.; Stds.: 137; Lay Tchrs.: 9

GROSSE POINTE WOODS

Our Lady Star of the Sea Parish Grosse Pointe Woods - 467 Fairford, Grosse Pointe Woods, MI 48236 t) 313-884-5554; 313-884-7407 (CRP) parish@stargp.org www.olsos.org Rev. Msgr. Gary T. Smetanka, Priest in Solidum; CRP Stds.: 82

Our Lady Star of the Sea School - (Grades 1-8) t) 313-884-1070 l.garazsi@stargp.org Meghan Carter-Waid, Prin.; Stds.: 212; Lay Tchrs.: 25

HAMTRAMCK

St. Florian Parish, Hamtramck - 2626 Poland Ave., Hamtramck, MI 48212 t) 313-871-2778 office@stflorianparish.org www.stflorianparish.org Rev. Tomasz Pietrzak, SChr, Priest in Solidum; Bro. Bogdan Barton, S.Chr., Mem.; CRP Stds.: 81

Our Lady Queen of Apostles Parish Hamtramck - 3851 Prescott Ave., Hamtramck, MI 48212-3115 t) 313-891-1520 qofaparish1917@gmail.com Rev. Janusz Iwan, Priest in Solidum; Debbie Warren, DRE; CRP Stds.: 8

HARRISON TOWNSHIP

St. Hubert Parish Harrison Township - 38775 Prentiss St., Harrison Township, MI 48045 t) 586-463-5877 office@sthubertchurch.com www.sthubertchurch.com Rev. Douglas Bignall, Priest in Solidum; CRP Stds.: 109

HAZEL PARK

St. Justin - St. Mary Magdalen Parish Hazel Park - 50 E. Annabelle, Hazel Park, MI 48030 t) 248-542-8060 doris-sjsmm@comcast.net Rev. Robert Hayes Williams, Priest in Solidum; Connie M. Grden, DRE; CRP Stds.: 13

HIGHLAND

Holy Spirit Parish Highland - 3700 Harvey Lake Rd., Highland, MI 48356 t) 248-887-5364; 248-887-1634 (CRP); 248-889-5888 (CRP); 248-887-0027 jillian@holyspirithighland.com www.holyspirithighland.com Rev. Wayne G. Ureel, Priest in Solidum; Dcn. Michael Somervell; Jillian Peck, DRE; CRP Stds.: 80

HOLLY

St. Rita Parish Holly - 302 E. Maple, Holly, MI 48442; Mailing: 309 E. Maple St, Holly, MI 48442 t) 248-634-4841 stritaholly@sbcglobal.net www.stritaholly.org Rev. David J. Blazek, Priest in Solidum; Nicole Hagle, Pst. Assoc.; Kellie Rao, Music Min.; Jennie Marcinkoski, Youth Min.; CRP Stds.: 141

IDA

St. Gabriel Parish Ida - 8295 Van Aiken St., Ida, MI 48140; Mailing: P.O. Box F, Ida, MI 48140 t) 734-529-2097 (CRP); 734-269-3895; 734-529-2160 stgabrieldre@gmail.com; parish@stgabrielida.org Rev. Gerard J. Cupple, Priest in Solidum; Dcn. Michael Hammond; Maryellen Monico, DRE; CRP Stds.: 75

IMLAY CITY

Sacred Heart Parish Imlay City - 700 Maple Vista, Imlay City, MI 48444 t) 810-724-1135 staff@imlaysacredheart.org staff@imlaysacredheart.org Rev. Noel Emmanuel Cornelio, Priest in Solidum; CRP Stds.: 109

IRA TOWNSHIP

Immaculate Conception Parish Ira Township - 9764 Dixie Hwy., Ira Township, MI 48023 t) 586-725-3051; 586-725-1762 (CRP) parish@iccatholic.org; kovalcik@iccatholic.org iccatholic.org Rev. Joseph M. Esper, Priest in Solidum; Dcn. David Ebner; Sr. Dcn. Kenneth Nowicki; Tina Kovalcik, DRE; CRP Stds.: 116

Immaculate Conception School - (Grades 1-8) 7043 Church Rd., Ira Township, MI 48023 t) 586-725-0078 secretary@iccatholic.org www.immaculateconceptionschool.org Lawrence Ricard, Prin.; Stds.: 128; Lay Tchrs.: 11

LAKE ORION

Christ the Redeemer Parish Lake Orion - 2700 Waldon Rd., Lake Orion, MI 48360 t) 248-391-1621 dre@ctredeemer.org; officemgr@ctredeemer.org ctredeemer.org Rev. William J. Promesso, Priest in Solidum; Lisa Brown, DRE; Mari Reyes, Music Min.; CRP Stds.: 400

St. Joseph Parish Lake Orion - 715 N. Lapeer Rd., Lake Orion, MI 48362 t) 248-693-0440; 248-693-9555 (CRP) dforn6@stjoelo.org; iauge3@stjoelo.org Rev. James F. Kean, Priest in Solidum; Rev. Steven J. Mateja, Priest in Solidum; Dcn. John Manera; Dcn. Anthony Maciorowski; Doris Fornasiero, DRE; Leszek Bartkiewicz, Music Min.; CRP Stds.: 531

St. Joseph School - (Grades 1-8) 703 N. Lapeer Rd., Lake Orion, MI 48362 t) 248-693-6215 jzmik9@stjoelo.org school.stjoelo.org Joe Zmilky, Prin.; Stds.: 442; Lay Tchrs.: 30

LAKEPORT

St. Edward on the Lake Parish Lakeport - 6945 Lakeshore Rd., Lakeport, MI 48059 t) 810-385-4340 stedwardparish@hotmail.com stedwardonthelake.org Rev. Lee E. Acervo, Priest in Solidum; Paula McCarthy, DRE; CRP Stds.: 150

St. Edward's on the Lake School - (Grades PreK-5) 6995 Lakeshore Rd., Lakeport, MI 48059 t) 810-385-4461 stedwardschool@hotmail.com stedwardonthelakeschool.org/ Denis Metty Jr., Prin.; Stds.: 100; Sr. Tchrs.: 1; Lay Tchrs.: 7

LAPEER

Immaculate Conception Parish Lapeer - 814 W. Nepessing St., Lapeer, MI 48446 t) 810-664-8594; 810-664-0808 (CRP) office@lapeercatholic.org; kdupont@lapeercatholic.org www.lapeercatholic.org Rev. Brian K. Hurley, Priest in Solidum; CRP Stds.: 86

LINCOLN PARK

Christ the Good Shepherd Parish Lincoln Park - 1540 Riverbank Ave., Lincoln Park, MI 48146 t) 313-928-1324 parish@christgoodsheherd.org www.christgoodshepherd.org Rev. David Bechill, Priest in Solidum; CRP Stds.: 85

John Paul II Classical Catholic School - (Grades PreK-8) 1590 Riverbank St., Lincoln Park, MI 48146 t) 313-386-0633 school@jp2catholic.com jp2catholic.com Stds.: 104; Lay Tchrs.: 8

LIVONIA

St. Aidan Parish Livonia - 17500 Farmington Rd., Livonia, MI 48152 t) 734-425-5950; 734-425-9333 (CRP) bulletin@staidanlivonia.org www.saintaidanlivonia.org Rev. Kevin Thomas, Priest in Solidum; David J. Conrad, DRE; CRP Stds.: 89

St. Colette Parish Livonia - 17600 Newburgh Rd., Livonia, MI 48152-2699 t) 734-464-4433; 734-464-4435 (CRP) religioused@stcolette.net; parishoffice@stcolette.net www.stcolette.net Rev. Gary Michalik, Priest in Solidum; Dcn. Gary Pardo; CRP Stds.: 221

St. Edith Parish Livonia - 15089 Newburgh Rd., Livonia, MI 48154 t) 734-464-1222; 734-464-2020 (CRP) lkramer@stedith.org; parishoffice@stedith.org www.stedith.org St. Edith Church Rev. James McNulty, Priest in Solidum; Dcn. Donald Esler; Linda Kramer, DRE; CRP Stds.: 266

St. Edith School - (Grades PreK-8) t) 734-464-1250 gwojciechowski@stedith.org www.stedithschool.com Lynsey Genarro, Prin.; Stds.: 220; Lay Tchrs.: 11

St. Genevieve - St. Maurice Parish Livonia - 29015 Jamison St., Livonia, MI 48154-4021 t) 734-427-5220 cbiddinger@stgenevieve.org www.stgenevieve-stmaurice.org Rev. Tomasz Wilisowski, C.S.M.A., Priest in Solidum; Phyllis Chudzinski, DRE; Colleen M. Biddinger, Bus. Mgr.; CRP Stds.: 71

St. Michael Parish Livonia - 11441 Hubbard Ave., Livonia, MI 48150 t) 734-261-1455; 734-261-1455 x235 (CRP) parish@livoniastmichael.org; darmstrong@livoniastmichael.org www.livoniastmichael.org Rev. Msgr. William Tindall, Priest in Solidum; Rev. Pathrose Panuvel, Priest in Solidum; CRP Stds.: 65

St. Michael School - (Grades PreK-8) 11311 Hubbard, Livonia, MI 48150 t) 734-421-7360 Kathy Nold, Prin.; Nancy Kuszczak, Prin.; Stds.: 470; Lay Tchrs.: 18

St. Priscilla Parish Livonia - 19120 Purlingbrook St., Livonia, MI 48152 t) 248-476-4700; 248-476-4702 (CRP) rose@saintpriscilla.org; dre@saintpriscilla.org saintpriscilla.org Rev. Joseph Tuskiewiecz, Priest in Solidum; Alyssa Choraszewski, Pst. Assoc.; CRP Stds.: 45

MACOMB

St. Isidore Parish Macomb Township - 18201 Twenty-Three Mile Rd., Macomb, MI 48042 t) 586-286-1700 info@stisidore.church stisidore.church/ Rev. Matthew Ellis, Priest in Solidum; Rev. Ronald Victor, Priest in Solidum; Dcn. Jeff Loeb; Ann DeRey, DRE;

MADISON HEIGHTS

St. Vincent Ferrer Parish Madison Heights - 28353 Herbert St., Madison Heights, MI 48071 t) 248-542-8720 sheryl@stvincentferrer.net www.stvincentferrer.net Rev. John C. Esper, Priest in Solidum; CRP Stds.: 25

MARINE CITY

Our Lady on the River Parish Marine City - 610 S. Water St., Marine City, MI 48039-3601 t) 810-765-3568; 810-765-8300 (CRP) parish@ourladyontheriver.net; religiousedolr@gmail.com www.ourladyontheriver.net Rev. John Dumas, Priest in Solidum; Rev. Louis Charles Lapeyre, Priest in Solidum; Dcn. Michael Oldani; Cassidy Johnson, DRE; CRP Stds.: 107

Holy Cross Catholic School - (Grades PreSchool-8) 618 S. Water St., Marine City, MI 48039 t) 810-765-3591 school@holycrossonline.net www.holycrossonline.net Betsy Davenport, Prin.; Stds.: 131; Lay Tchrs.: 10

MARYSVILLE

St. Christopher Parish Marysville - 1000 Michigan Ave., Marysville, MI 48040 t) 810-364-4100 ssenyk@stchrismi.org www.stchrismi.org Rev. James Fredrick Arwady, Priest in Solidum; CRP Stds.: 119

MELVINDALE

St. Mary Magdalen Parish Melvindale - 19624 Wood St., Melvindale, MI 48122 t) 313-381-8566; 313-381-8566 x104 (CRP) smmparish@comcast.net smmssab.com Rev. Timothy P. Birney, Priest in Solidum; Armando Bravo, DRE; CRP Stds.: 118

MEMPHIS

Holy Family Parish Memphis - 79780 Main St., Memphis, MI 48041 t) 810-392-2056 sfinely@holyfamily-online.org; bquigley@holyfamily-online.org holyfamily-online.org Rev. Philip Ching, Priest in Solidum; Dcn. Alan Gwozdz; Dcn. Richard Kliemann; Susan Finley, DRE; CRP Stds.: 100

MILFORD

St. Mary Parish Milford - 1955 E. Commerce St., Milford, MI 48381 t) 248-685-1482; 248-685-2702 (CRP) faithformation@stmarymilfordmi.org; parishoffice@stmarymilfordmi.org www.stmarymilfordmi.org Rev. Tomy Kattikanayil, M.S.F.S., Priest in Solidum; Colleen Gonzalez, DRE; CRP Stds.: 451

MONROE

St. Anne Parish Monroe - 2420 N. Dixie Hwy., Monroe, MI 48162 t) 734-289-2910 stanneparish.2420@gmail.com; dre@stcharlesnewport.com www.stannemonroe.org/ Rev. Hendrico Rebello, S.A.C., Priest in Solidum; Janice Doederlein, DRE; CRP Stds.: 23

St. John the Baptist Parish Monroe - 511 S. Monroe St., Monroe, MI 48161 t) 734-241-8910 dffmonroe@gmail.com; parishoffice@stjohnmonroe.com www.stjohnmonroe.com Rev. David G. Burgard, Priest in Solidum; Rev. Michael A. Anagbogu, Priest in Solidum; Leslee Smith, DRE; CRP Stds.: 36

St. Mary Parish Monroe - 127 N. Monroe St., Monroe, MI 48162-2686 t) 734-241-1644; 734-241-6097 (CRP) parishoffice@stmarymonroe.org www.stmarymonroe.org Rev. Michael A. Anagbogu, Priest in Solidum; Rev. David G. Burgard, Priest in Solidum; Dcn. Michael Stewart; Leslee Smith, DRE; CRP Stds.: 55

St. Michael Parish Monroe - 502 W. Front St., Monroe, MI 48161 t) 734-241-8645; 734-241-6097 (CRP) parishoffice@stmichaelmonroe.com; faithformation@stmarymonroe.org www.stmichaelmonroe.com Rev. Kishore Battu, SAC, Priest in Solidum; CRP Stds.: 16

MOUNT CLEMENS

St. Peter Parish Mount Clemens - 95 Market St., Mount Clemens, MI 48043; Mailing: 110 New St., Mount Clemens, MI 48043 t) 586-468-4578 information@spmconline.com stpetermtclemens.com Rev. John A. Maksym, Priest in Solidum; Rev. Christopher Muer, Priest in Solidum; Jeanine Walker, DRE; Tori Kearney, Youth Min.; Moira Shaum, Bus. Mgr.; CRP Stds.: 180

St. Mary - (Grades PreSchool-8) 2 Union St., Mount Clemens, MI 48043 t) 586-468-4570 mmiscavish@stmarymtclemens.com www.stmarymtclemens.com Patrick Adams, Prin.; Kathy Faulk, Vice Prin.; Stds.: 470; Lay Tchrs.: 27

NEW BALTIMORE

St. Mary Queen of Creation Parish New Baltimore - 51041 Maria St., New Baltimore, MI 48047; Mailing: 50931 Maria St., New Baltimore, MI 48047 t) 586-725-2441; 586-725-7579 (CRP) www.smqoc.com Rev. Charles White IV, Priest in Solidum; Dcn. Lawrence Paczkowski; CRP Stds.: 265

NEW BOSTON

St. Stephen Parish New Boston - 18858 Huron River Dr., New Boston, MI 48164-9272 t) 734-753-4722 (CRP); 734-753-5268 parishoffice@ststephennewboston.org; dre.ststephen@outlook.com www.ststephennewboston.org Rev. John P. Hedges, Priest in Solidum; Joan M. Gutierrez, DRE; CRP Stds.: 75

St. Stephen School - (Grades 1-8) 18800 Huron River Dr., New Boston, MI 48164-9272 t) 734-753-4175 principal@ststephennb.org www.ststephennb.org Patrick Bevier, Prin.; Stds.: 100; Lay Tchrs.: 7

Convent - t) 734-753-9937

NEWPORT

St. Charles Borromeo Parish Newport - 8109 Swan Creek Rd., Newport, MI 48166; Mailing: 8033 N. Dixie Hwy., Newport, MI 48166 t) 734-586-2531 x1 secretary@stcharlesnewport.com; dre@stcharlesnewport.com stcharlesnewport.org/ Rev. Henry Rebello, S.A.C., Priest in Solidum; Janice Doederlein, DRE; CRP Stds.: 60

St. Charles Borromeo Catholic Academy - (Grades 1-8) 8125 Swan Creek Rd., Newport, MI 48166 t) (734) 586-2531 scs@stcharlesnewport.com Beth Lechy, Prin.; Stds.: 227; Lay Tchrs.: 11

NORTH BRANCH

St. Mary Burnside Parish North Branch - 5622 Summers Rd., North Branch, MI 48461; Mailing: P.O. Box 268, North Branch, MI 48461 t) 810-688-3797 sspeterpaul@northbranchcatholic.com www.sspeterpaulnb.org Rev. Sama Muma, Priest in Solidum; Rev. Richard L. Treml, Priest in Solidum; Dcn. Pete Lynch; CRP Stds.: 21

Sacred Heart Mission Brown City - 7090 Cade Rd., Brown City, MI 48416; Mailing: P.O. Box 208, North Branch, MI 48461 www.northbranchcatholic.com

SS. Peter and Paul Parish North Branch - 6645 Washington St., North Branch, MI 48461; Mailing: P.O. Box 208, North Branch, MI 48461 t) 810-688-3797 sspeterpaul@northbranchcatholic.com www.sspeterpaulnb.org Rev. Sama Muma, Priest in Solidum; Rev. Richard L. Treml, Priest in Solidum; Dcn. Pete Lynch; Dianne Knox, DRE; CRP Stds.: 70

St. Patrick's - 9851 Main St., Clifford, MI 48727

NORTHVILLE

St. Andrew Kim (Korean) Parish Northville - 21177 Halsted Rd., Northville, MI 48167 t) 248-442-9026 email@standrewkimdetroit.org Rev. Seungsoo Oh, Priest in Solidum; CRP Stds.: 156

Our Lady of Victory Parish Northville - 133 Orchard Dr., Northville, MI 48167 t) 248-349-2621 olvoffice@olvnorthville.net olvnorthville.org Rev. Denis B. Theroux, Priest in Solidum; Dcn. Ric Misiak, Pst. Assoc.; Dcn. Fred Billotto; CRP Stds.: 390

Our Lady of Victory School - (Grades 1-8) 132 Orchard Dr., Northville, MI 48167 t) 248-349-3610 kszuba@olvnorthville.net Kate Szuba, Prin.; Emily Wesley, Vice Prin.; Stds.: 500; Lay Tchrs.: 26

NOVI

Holy Family Parish Novi - 24505 Meadowbrook, Novi, MI 48375 t) 248-349-8847; 248-349-8837 (CRP) admin@hfnovi.com; admin@holyfamilynovi.org www.holyfamilynovi.org Rev. Clifford Hennings, OFM, Priest in Solidum; Rev. Robert A. LaCroix, Priest in Solidum; Dcn. Robert Ervin; CRP Stds.: 249

St. James Parish Novi - 46325 Ten Mile Rd., Novi, MI 48374-3007 t) 248-347-7778; 248-347-3434 (CRP) ezaorski@sjnovi.net; parishsecretary@sjnovi.net www.stjamesnovi.org Rev. Edward F. Zaorski, Priest in Solidum; Dcn. Peter Cornell; Dcn. Leo Maciolek; Daniel Hull, Pst. Min./Coord.; Meredith Skowronski, DRE; CRP Stds.: 578

OAK PARK

Our Mother of Perpetual Help Parish Oak Park - 13500 Oak Park Blvd., Oak Park, MI 48237-3630 t) 248-545-2310 natalielacroix@ymail.com; omophparish@gmail.com www.omoph.org Rev. Paul Chateau, Priest in Solidum; Rev. Joy Chakian, In Res.; Natalie LaCroix, DRE; CRP Stds.: 2

ORCHARD LAKE

Our Lady of Refuge Parish Orchard Lake - 3700 Commerce Rd., Orchard Lake, MI 48324; Mailing: 3725 Erie Dr., Orchard Lake, MI 48324-1527 t) 248-682-0920; 248-682-6381 (CRP) cbishop@olorcc.org; re@olorcc.org www.olorcc.org Rev. Ronald Richards, Priest in Solidum; CRP Stds.: 56

Our Lady of Refuge School - (Grades 1-8) 3750 Commerce Rd., Orchard Lake, MI 48324 t) 248-682-3422 drichards@olr-school.net www.olr-school.net Lauri Hoffman, Prin.; Erin Martinez, Vice Prin.; Stds.: 407; Lay Tchrs.: 25

ORTONVILLE

St. Anne Parish Ortonville - 825 S. Ortonville Rd., Ortonville, MI 48462-8641 t) 248-627-3965; 248-627-3965 x131 (CRP) marianne@churchofstanne.org; anne@churchofstanne.org churchofstanne.org Rev. Craig F. Marion, Priest in Solidum; Marianne Boesch, DRE; CRP Stds.: 64

PLYMOUTH

St. Kenneth Parish Plymouth - 14951 N. Haggerty Rd., Plymouth, MI 48170 t) 734-420-0288 recoordinator@stkenneth.org; padretom@stkenneth.org www.stkenneth.org Rev. Thomas A. Belczak, Priest in Solidum; CRP Stds.: 292

Our Lady of Good Counsel Parish Plymouth - 47650 N. Territorial Rd., Plymouth, MI 48170 t) 734-453-0326 oshaughnessys@olgcparish.net; diane.jouppi26@gmail.com Rev. Msgr. Todd J. Lajiness, Priest in Solidum; Rev. Anthony Camilleri, Priest in Solidum; Rev. Zaid Chabaan, Priest in Solidum; Dcn. Vincent Small; Sandy O'Shaughnessy, DRE; CRP Stds.: 253

Our Lady of Good Counsel School - (Grades 1-8) 1151 William St., Plymouth, MI 48170 jouppid@olgcparish.net Leann Sauve, Prin.; Stds.: 457; Lay Tchrs.: 31

PONTIAC

St. Damien of Molokai Parish Pontiac - 120 Lewis St., Pontiac, MI 48342 t) 248-332-0283; 248-332-0284 www.st-damien.org Rev. Jacob A. Van Assche, Priest in Solidum; Rev. Andrew Ryan Mabee, Priest in Solidum; Dcn. Michael Merlo; CRP Stds.: 305

PORT HURON

Holy Trinity Parish Port Huron - 325 32nd St., Port Huron, MI 48060 t) 810-984-2689; 810-985-9609 (CRP) denise@holytrinityph.org; karen@holytrinityph.org holytrinityph.org Rev. Bradley Forintos, Priest in Solidum; Dcn. Dennis Crimmins; Karen Clor, DRE; CRP Stds.: 128

St. Mary Parish Port Huron - 1505 Ballentine St., Port Huron, MI 48060 t) 810-982-7906 stmaryporthuron@gmail.com www.stmaryporthuron.com Rev. Zbigniew Zomerfeld, Priest in Solidum; Dcn. John Fitzmaurice; Mary Shoudy, DRE; CRP Stds.: 57

St. Mary/McCormick Catholic Academy - (Grades PreSchool-8) 1429 Ballentine St., Port Huron, MI 48060 t) (810) 982-7906 x105 office@stmarymccormick.com www.stmarymccormick.com/ Stephanie Weaver, Prin.; Stds.: 154; Lay Tchrs.: 10

RAY TOWNSHIP

St. Francis of Assisi - St. Maximilian Kolbe Parish Ray Township - 62811 New Haven Rd., Ray Township, MI 48096 t) 586-598-3314; 586-598-3314 x302 (CRP) stfrancisnh@comcast.net stfrancis-stmaximilian.com Rev. Christopher Talbot, Priest in Solidum; Dcn. Richard Rhein; Betty Sheehan, DRE; CRP Stds.: 123

REDFORD

St. John XXIII Parish Redford Charter Township - 12100 Beach Daly Rd., Redford, MI 48239 t) 248-800-6081 www.stjohnxxiiiredford.org Rev. Gregory A. Piatt, Priest in Solidum;

Our Lady of Loretto Parish Redford - 25700 W. Six Mile Rd., Redford, MI 48240; Mailing: 17116 Olympia St., Redford, MI 48240 t) 313-534-9000; 313-680-6132 (CRP) mrkohn@aol.com; oll48240@gmail.com www.ourladyoflorettoparish.org Rev. Socorro Fernandes, S.A.C., Priest in Solidum; Sr. Margretta Wojcik, O.S.F., Pst. Min./Coord.; Dcn. Ronald Vader; Donna Kohn, DRE; CRP Stds.: 23

St. Valentine Parish Redford - 14841 Beech Daly Rd., Redford, MI 48239; Mailing: 25881 Dow, Redford, MI 48239 t) 313-532-4394 stvalsparish@stvalentineschool.com Rev. Socorro Fernandes, S.A.C., Priest in Solidum; CRP Stds.: 58

St. Valentine School - (Grades 1-8) 25875 Hope St., Redford, MI 48239 t) 313-533-7149 rdamuth@stvalentineschool.com stvalentineschool.com Rachel Damuth, Prin.; Maureen Kelly, Librn.; Stds.: 160; Lay Tchrs.: 11

RICHMOND

St. Augustine Parish Richmond - 68035 Main St., Richmond, MI 48062 t) 586-727-5215; 586-727-9290 (CRP) staugustinerichmond@comcast.net www.staugustinecatholicparish.org Rev. Philip Ching, Priest in Solidum; Rev. Kishore Raju Beezam, SAC (India), Priest in Solidum; Rev. Raymond E. Arwady, In Res.; Dcn. Alan Gwozdz; Dcn. Richard Kliemann; Susan Finley, DRE; CRP Stds.: 162

St. Augustine School - (Grades PreK-8) 67901 Howard, Richmond, MI 48062 t) 586-727-9365 admin@staugustinecatholicschool.com www.staugustinecatholicschool.com Emily Lenn, Prin.; Stds.: 164; Lay Tchrs.: 10

RIVERVIEW

St. Cyprian Parish Riverview - 13249 Pennsylvania, Riverview, MI 48193 t) 734-283-1366; 734-283-1366 x118 (CRP) ssurcek@stcyprian.com; lhussey@stcyprian.com www.stcyprian.com Rev. Marc A. Gawronski, Priest in Solidum; CRP Stds.: 87

ROCHESTER

St. Andrew Parish Rochester - 1400 Inglewood, Rochester, MI 48307 t) 248-651-7486; 248-651-6571 (CRP) contact@standrewchurch.org www.standrewchurch.org Rev. Brian K. Cokonougher, Priest in Solidum; Rev. Grayson D. Heenan, Priest in Solidum; Dcn. Marc Gemellaro; Dcn. Thomas Sliney; Barbara Pacella, DRE; CRP Stds.: 504

ROCHESTER HILLS

St. Irenaeus Parish Rochester Hills - 771 Old Perch Rd., Rochester Hills, MI 48309 t) 248-651-9595; 248-651-2443 (CRP) www.stirenaeus.org/ Rev. Gerard LeBoeuf, Priest in Solidum; Kathy Freer, DRE; CRP Stds.: 404

St. Rosa-O.C.I.M.A. - ; Mailing: P.O. Box 952, Bloomfield Hills, MI 48303-0952 info@ocimaya.org www.ocimaya.org/orphanagesantaelena.html Patricia Egan-Meyers, DRE;

St. Mary of the Hills, Rochester Hills - 2675 John R Rd., Rochester Hills, MI 48307-4652 t) 248-853-5390; 248-243-0257 (CRP) stmary89@smoth.org; businessmanager@smoth.org www.smoth.org Rev. Stanley A. Ulman, Priest in Solidum; Holly Abolins, DRE; CRP Stds.: 348

St. Paul (Albanian) Parish Rochester Hills - 525 Auburn Rd., Rochester Hills, MI 48307 t) 248-844-2150 www.stpaulalbaniancatholicchurch.org Rev. Frederik Kalaj, Priest in Solidum; Franz Grishaj, DRE; Nikola Gjonaj, Bus. Mgr.; CRP Stds.: 337

ROCKWOOD

St. Mary, Our Lady of the Annunciation Parish Rockwood - 32477 Church St., Rockwood, MI 48173 t) 734-379-9248 ljswayze@yahoo.com; stmaryrockwood@sbcglobal.net www.stmaryannunciation.org Rev. James R. Rafferty, Priest in Solidum; CRP Stds.: 70

ROMEO

St. Clement of Rome Parish Romeo - 343 S. Main St., Romeo, MI 48065 t) 586-752-9611; 586-752-6591 (CRP) Rev. Stephen C. Reckker, Priest in Solidum; Dcn. Kurt Godfryd; CRP Stds.: 324

ROMULUS

St. Aloysius Parish Romulus - 11280 Ozga St., Romulus, MI 48174; Mailing: 37200 Neville St., Romulus, MI 48174 t) 734-941-5056 st_aloysiuschurch@yahoo.com www.staloysiusromulus.org Rev. John Nedumcheril, Priest in Solidum;

ROSEVILLE

Holy Innocents - St. Barnabas Parish Roseville - 16359 Frazho, Roseville, MI 48066; Mailing: 26100 Ridgemont St, Roseville, MI 48066 t) 586-777-7543 hisb@live.com www.hisbparish.us Rev. John Wynnycky, Priest in Solidum; Dcn. Michael Lang Sr.; Maureen Romeo, DRE; CRP Stds.: 20

St. Pio of Pietrelcina Parish Roseville - 18720 E. 13 Mile Rd., Roseville, MI 48066 t) 586-777-9116 stpiosecretary@gmail.com; stpiocservice@gmail.com stpioparish.org Roxanne Gronkiewicz, DRE; Selma Yaldoo, Bus. Mgr.; CRP Stds.: 65

ROYAL OAK

St. Mary Parish Royal Oak - 730 Lafayette Ave. S., Royal Oak, MI 48067 t) 248-547-1818 (parish office); 248-547-1810 (Faith Formation); 247-547-1819 (parish office); (248) 545-2140 (school) dtrudell@st-mary.org; parishoffice@st-mary.org www.stmaryroyaloak.com Rev. Paul M. Snyder, Priest in Solidum; Donna Trudell, DRE; CRP Stds.: 153

St. Mary School - (Grades PreK-8) 628 Lafayette Ave. S., Royal Oak, MI 48067 t) 248-545-2140 gbala@st-mary.org www.stmaryroyaloak.org Gabriela Bala, Prin.; Stds.: 313; Lay Tchrs.: 18

National Shrine of the Little Flower Basilica - 2100 W. 12-Mile Rd., Royal Oak, MI 48073-3973 t) 248-541-4122; 248-541-5133 (CRP) www.shrinechurch.com Rev. Joseph Horn, Rector & Priest in Solidum; Rev. Joseph Lang, Priest in Solidum; Rev. Mark Livingston, Priest in Solidum; Dcn. Dave Casnovsky; Dcn. Hector Anaya-Bustos; Beth Spizarny, DRE; CRP Stds.: 183

National Shrine of the Little Flower Basilica School - (Grades PreSchool-5) 1621 Linwood, Royal Oak, MI 48067 wisniewski@shrineschools.com www.shrineschools.com Joanne Jones, Supt.; Scott Wisniewski, Prin.; Erika Zwolinski, Vice Prin.; Stds.: 532; Lay Tchrs.: 34

National Shrine of the Little Flower Basilica High School - (Grades 6-12) 3500 W. Thirteen Mile Rd., Royal Oak, MI 48073 t) 248-549-2925 jmio@shrineschools.com; kaminsky@shrineschools.com www.shrineschools.com Joanne Jones, Supt.; Dr. Julie Kaminsky, Prin.; James Mio, Prin.; Pamela Olejniczak, Vice Prin.; Stds.: 456; Lay Tchrs.: 41

SHELBY TWP.

St. John Vianney Parish Shelby Township - 54045 Schoenherr Rd., Shelby Twp., MI 48315 t) 586-781-6525 dkennard@sjvshelby.org; parish@sjvshelby.org sjvshelby.org Rev. James Grau, Priest in Solidum; Dcn. Michael Houghton; David Troiano, Music Min.; Carly Fleury, Youth Min.; Jennifer Kowalski, Liturgy Dir.; Lori Ann Rafferty, Bus. Mgr.; CRP Stds.: 822

St. Kieran Parish Shelby Township - 53600 Mound Rd., Shelby Twp., MI 48316 t) 586-781-4901; 586-781-6515 (CRP) jeanee@stkieran.org www.stkieran.org Rev. Joseph Mallia, Priest in Solidum; CRP Stds.: 324

St. Therese of Lisieux Parish Shelby Township - 48115 Schoenherr Rd., Shelby Twp., MI 48315-4225 t) 586-254-4433; 586-254-2944 (CRP) info@stol.church stol.church Rev. Ronald Essman, Priest in Solidum; Rev. Charles D. Fox, Priest in Solidum; Rev. Msgr. John C. Kasza, Priest in Solidum; Rev. Peter Ryan, S.J., Priest in Solidum; Dcn. Gregory Willoughby; CRP Stds.: 284

SOUTH LYON

St. Joseph Parish South Lyon - 830 S. Lafayette St, South Lyon, MI 48178 t) 248-446-8700; 248-446-8700 x115 (CRP) theresa.durant@stjcc.org; office@stjcc.org stjcc.org Rev. Stan Tokarski, Priest in Solidum; Dcn. Chris Booms; Kimberly Donahue, DRE; CRP Stds.: 434

SOUTHFIELD

Church of the Transfiguration Parish Southfield - 25225 Code Rd., Southfield, MI 48033 t) 248-356-8787 scheelerj@transfigsfld.org www.transfigsfld.org Rev. Jeremy Harrington, Priest in Solidum; Rev. Jeffrey Scheeler, O.F.M., Priest in Solidum; Diane Klucka, DRE; CRP Stds.: 27

Divine Providence (Lithuanian) Parish Southfield - 25335 W. 9 Mile Rd., Southfield, MI 48033-3933 t) 248-354-3429 dplithuanianchurch@gmail.com www.divineprovidencechurch.com Rev. Tomas Miliauskas (Lithuania), Priest in Solidum; Vilija Jurgutis, DRE; CRP Stds.: 8

Our Lady of Albanians Parish Southfield - 29350 Lahser Rd., Southfield, MI 48034 t) 248-353-3410 olalbanians@yahoo.com Rev. Nue Gjergji, Priest in Solidum; Gjecka Gjelaj, DRE;

SOUTHGATE

St. Pius X Parish Southgate - 14101 Superior Ave., Southgate, MI 48195 t) 734-285-1100 dsolis@saintpius-x.org; church@saintpius-x.org Rev. Suresh Rajaian, S.A.C., Priest in Solidum; Dcn. Charles Dault; David Nickens, DRE; CRP Stds.: 65

St. Pius X School - (Grades 1-8) 14141 Pearl St., Southgate, MI 48195 t) 734-284-6500 mseward@saintpius-x.org www.saintpiusschool.org Kathleen England, Prin.; Stds.: 300; Lay Tchrs.: 18

ST. CLAIR

St. Mary Parish St. Clair - 415 N. 6th St., St. Clair, MI 48079; Mailing: 800 Orchard St., St. Clair, MI 48079 t) 810-329-2255; 810-329-7801 (CRP); 810-329-4150 www.stmarystclair.com Rev. Michael Christopher Zuelch, Priest in Solidum; Lisa Yamin, DRE; CRP Stds.: 86

ST. CLAIR SHORES

St. Isaac Jogues Parish St. Clair Shores - 21100 Madison, St. Clair Shores, MI 48081 t) 586-778-5100 parishoffice@saintisaacjogues.com www.saintisaacjogues.com Rev. David Cybulski, Priest in Solidum; CRP Stds.: 34

St. Isaac Jogues School - (Grades 1-8) t) 586-771-3525 kmoore@saintisaacjogues.com; principal@saintisaacjogues.com www.stisaacjoguesschool.org Sr. Maria Maria Guadalupe Hallee, Prin.; Stds.: 192; Sr. Tchrs.: 4; Lay Tchrs.: 13

St. Joan of Arc Parish St. Clair Shores - 22412 Overlake, St. Clair Shores, MI 48080 t) 586-777-3670; 586-772-1282 (CRP); 586-777-1342 (Emergency Number) info@sjascs.org www.sjascs.org Rev. Msgr. G. Michael Bugarin, Priest in Solidum; Rev. Andrew Dawson, Priest in Solidum; Dcn. Dominick Pastore; Dcn. Thomas Strasz; Dina Ciaffone, Bus. Mgr.; CRP Stds.: 192

St. Joan of Arc School - (Grades PreK-8) 22415 Overlake St., St. Clair Shores, MI 48080 t) (586) 775-8370 info@stjoan.net www.stjoan.net Amy Patty, Prin.; Charles Kaiser, Vice Prin.; Stds.: 278; Lay Tchrs.: 27

St Lucy Parish, St. Clair Shores - 23401 Jefferson, St. Clair Shores, MI 48080 t) 586-771-8300 parish@stlucychurch.com www.stlucychurch.com Rev. James E. Commyn, Priest in Solidum; CRP Stds.: 12

St. Margaret of Scotland Parish St. Clair Shores - 21201 Thirteen Mile Rd., St. Clair Shores, MI 48082 t) 586-293-2240 (CRP); 586-293-2240 x121 thehighlander@sms-scs.org www.stmargaret-scsmi.org Rev. Ronald DeHondt, Priest in Solidum; Dcn. Val Buyle; Dcn. Ronald Channell; Dcn. Michael P. O'Keefe; CRP Stds.: 63

Our Lady of Hope Parish St. Clair Shores - 28301 Little Mack, St. Clair Shores, MI 48081 t) 586-771-1750; 586-771-1750 x124 (CRP) sgudenau@olohscs.org; ssopfe@olohscs.org www.olohscs.org Rev. James L. Bjorum, Priest in Solidum; Dcn. John Thompson; Susan Gudenau, DRE; CRP Stds.: 121

St. Germaine - (Grades PreK-8) 28250 Rockwood, St. Clair Shores, MI 48081 t) 586-771-0890 jdegrez@stgermaine.org www.stgermaine.org Colleen Macciejewski, Prin.; Stds.: 161; Lay Tchrs.: 14

STERLING HEIGHTS

St. Blase Parish Sterling Heights - 12151 E. 15 Mile Rd., Sterling Heights, MI 48312-5120 t) 586-268-2244 parishstaff@stblase.org www.stblase.org Rev. Randall Phillips, Priest in Solidum; Dcn. Edwin McLeod; Dr. Mary Dumm, Pst. Assoc.; Diann Chase, DRE; Stephen Petrunak, Music Min.; CRP Stds.: 96

SS. Cyril and Methodius (Slovak) Parish Sterling Heights - 41233 Ryan Rd., Sterling Heights, MI 48314 t) 586-726-6911 parishoffice@saintcyrils.church www.saintcyrils.church Rev. Libor Marek, Priest in Solidum; Rev. Juraj Nuota, Priest in Solidum; Dcn. Phil McCown; Carroll Schuller, DRE; Paul Schuller, DRE; CRP Stds.: 180

St. Ephrem Parish Sterling Heights - 38900 Dodge Park Rd, Sterling Heights, MI 48312 t) 586-264-1230; 586-264-2777 (Religious Education) office@stephrems.org; religioused@stephrems.org www.saintephremchurch.org/ Rev. Arokiaselvam Nithiyaselvam, MSFS, Priest in Solidum; CRP Stds.: 41

St. Jane Frances de Chantal Parish Sterling Heights - 38750 Ryan Rd., Sterling Heights, MI 48310 t) 586-977-8080 jgazo@sjfparish.org sjfparish.org Rev. Anthony Sulkowski, Priest in Solidum; CRP Stds.: 42

St. Malachy Parish Sterling Heights - 14115 E. 14 Mile Rd., Sterling Heights, MI 48312-6506 t) 586-264-1220; 586-264-1220 x4 (CRP) contact@stmalachychurch.org; ffs@stmalachychurch.org saintmalachychurch.org Rev. Joseph J. Gembala, Priest in Solidum; CRP Stds.: 141

St. Matthias Parish Sterling Heights - 12311 Nineteen Mile Rd., Sterling Heights, MI 48313 t) 586-731-1300; 586-731-0650 (CRP) parishoffice@stmatthiascatholicchurch.com Rev. Francisco Restrepo, Priest in Solidum; CRP Stds.: 45

St. Michael Parish Sterling Heights - 40501 Hayes Rd., Sterling Heights, MI 48313 t) 586-247-0020; 586-247-0098 (CRP) www.stmichaelcc.org Rev. Artemio Galos, Priest in Solidum; Rev. Michael W. Quaine, Priest in Solidum; Dcn. Franz Hoffer; Claudia Welbes, DRE; CRP Stds.: 218

Our Lady of Czestochowa (Polish) Parish Sterling Heights - 3100 18 Mile Rd., Sterling Heights, MI 48314-3810 t) 586-977-7267 info@parisholc.org www.parisholc.org Rev. Jan Michalski, TChr, Priest in Solidum; Sr. Wioletta Koltun, DRE; CRP Stds.: 235

St. Rene Goupil Parish Sterling Heights - 35955 Ryan Rd., Sterling Heights, MI 48310 t) 586-939-7500 Rev. Steven C. Koehler, Priest in Solidum; Michael Novak, DRE; CRP Stds.: 60

TAYLOR

St. Alfred Parish Taylor - 24175 Baske St., Taylor, MI 48180 t) 313-291-6464 stalfredchurchtaylormi@gmail.com; stalfredreligioused@gmail.com stalfredtaylor.org Rev. Charles K. Altermatt, Priest in Solidum; Dcn. Scott LaForest; Kathleen Operhall, DRE; CRP Stds.: 97

St. Constance Parish Taylor - 21555 Kinyon Rd., Taylor, MI 48180 t) 313-291-4050 stconstancechurch@comcast.net www.stconstance.com Rev. Leo F. Sabourin, Priest in Solidum; Roseanna Rogers, DRE; CRP Stds.: 85

Our Lady of the Angels Parish Taylor - 6442 Pelham Rd., Taylor, MI 48180 t) 313-381-3000 mail@loacc.org loacc.org Rev. Dariusz Strzalkowski, Priest in Solidum; Dcn. William A. Thome;

TEMPERANCE

St. Anthony Parish Temperance - 4605 St. Anthony Rd., Temperance, MI 48182 t) 734-854-1143; 734-854-1160 (CRP) stanthony@bex.net; stanthonytemperancere@gmail.com stanthonytemperance.org Rev. Robert J. Slaton, Priest in Solidum; Virginia Stout, DRE; CRP Stds.: 15

Our Lady of Mount Carmel Parish Temperance - 8330 Lewis Ave., Temperance, MI 48182 t) 734-847-2805; 734-847-1725 x21 (CRP) olmc@bex.net mountcarmeltemperance.org Rev. Don A. LaCuesta, Priest in Solidum; Dcn. Martin Selmek; Tyler O'Brien, DRE; CRP Stds.: 110

TRENTON

St. Joseph Parish Trenton - 2565 Third St., Trenton, MI 48183 t) 734-676-9082 kathy@stjosephtrenton.com www.stjosephtrenton.com Rev. Marc A. Gawronski, Priest in Solidum; Sarah Hogan, DRE; CRP Stds.: 197

St. Joseph School - (Grades 1-1) 2675 Third St., Trenton, MI 48183 t) 734-676-2565 principal@stjosephschooltrenton.com wwww.stjosephschooltrenton.com Teri Thomas, Prin.; Stds.: 223; Lay Tchrs.: 14

St. Timothy Parish Trenton - 2901 Manning Dr., Trenton, MI 48183 t) 734-676-5115 secretary.st.timothy@gmail.com www.sttimothytrenton.org Rev. Marc A. Gawronski, Priest in Solidum;

TROY

St. Anastasia Parish Troy - 4571 John R. Rd., Troy, MI 48085 t) 248-689-8380 lharrison@stanastasia.org; office@stanastasia.org www.stanastasia.org Rev. Steven A. Wertanen, Priest in Solidum; Rev. James Houbeck, Priest in Solidum; Dcn. Tom Caporuscio; CRP Stds.: 339

Christ Our Light Parish Troy - 3077 Glouchester, Troy, MI 48084 t) 248-649-5510; 248-649-5510 x107 (CRP) christourlight@comcast.net; joann.bonahoom@coltroy.org christourlight.weconnect.com/ Rev. Donald L. Demmer, Priest in Solidum; JoAnn Bonahoom, DRE; CRP Stds.: 193

St. Elizabeth Ann Seton Parish Troy - 280 E. Square Lake Rd., Troy, MI 48085 t) 248-879-1310 secretary@saintliz.org www.saintliz.org Rev. Dominic Macioce, Priest in Solidum; Dcn. Charlie Pace; Terri Konwinski, DRE; Ruth Hoppe, Pst. Assoc.; Tim Palmer, Music Min.; Deb Peltier, Bus. Mgr.; CRP Stds.: 70

St. Lucy (Croatian) Parish Troy - 200 E. Wattles Rd., Troy, MI 48085 t) 248-619-9910 st.lucy@outlook.com www.stlucycro.com/ Croatian Mission in Michigan Rev. Tony Richter, Priest in Solidum; Rev. Alberto P. Bondy, Sacr. Min.; Leonardo Ljuljduraj, DRE & Organist; CRP Stds.: 9

St. Thomas More Parish - 4580 Adams Rd., Troy, MI 48098 t) 248-647-2222; 248-647-4680 (CRP) inquiry@stmoffice.com stthomasmoretroy.org Rev. Msgr. Thomas G. Rice, Priest in Solidum; Dcn. Michael Stach, Pst. Assoc.; Dcn. Donald Baross; Josylin Mateus, DRE; Curtis Schuelke, Youth Min.; Robert Leonardi, Bus. Mgr.; CRP Stds.: 99

UTICA

St. Lawrence Parish Utica - 44633 Utica Rd., Utica, MI 48317 t) 586-731-5347; 586-731-5072 (CRP) lrajnicek@stlawrenceparish.com www.stlawrenceparish-utica.com Rev. Roman Pasieczny, Priest in Solidum; Rev. Paul W. Graney, Priest in Solidum; Rev. Alberto P. Bondy, In Res.; Lisa Rajnicek, DRE; CRP Stds.: 250

St. Lawrence School - (Grades PreK-8) 44429 Utica Rd., Utica, MI 48317 t) 586-731-0135 ldimercurio@stlawrenceparish.com Lisa Dimercurio, Prin.; Brian Barker, Asst. Prin.; Stds.: 978; Lay Tchrs.: 34

WALLED LAKE

St. William Parish Walled Lake - 531 Common St., Walled Lake, MI 48390-3417 t) 248-624-1421; 248-624-1371 (CRP) rectory1@stwilliam.com www.stwilliam.com Rev. Michael G. Savickas, Priest in Solidum; Dcn. John Liddle; Dcn. Michael Chesley, RCIA Coord.; Karen Sommers, Pst. Min./Coord.; Drew Labbe, Youth Min.; William Richart, Music Min.; Deborah Diviny, Bus. Mgr.; CRP Stds.: 109

St. William School - (Grades PreSchool-8) 135 O'Flaherty, Walled Lake, MI 48390 t) 248-669-4440 bgabrish@stwilliam-school.com www.stwilliam-school.com Elizabeth Gabrish, Prin.; Stds.: 180; Lay Tchrs.: 11

WARREN

St. Anne Parish Warren - 32000 Mound Rd., Warren, MI 48092 t) 586-264-0713 dhathaway@st-anne.net; rectoryoffice@st-anne.net www.st-anne.net Rev. John D. Kopson, Priest in Solidum; Debbie Hathaway, DRE;

St. Anne School - (Grades PreK-8) 5920 Arden, Warren, MI 48092 t) 586-264-2911 mainoffice@st-anne.net st-anne.net Stds.: 357; Lay Tchrs.: 16

St. Faustina Parish Warren - 14025 Twelve Mile Rd., Warren, MI 48088 t) 586-773-9220 (CRP); 586-772-2720 stfaustina@comcast.net stfaustinawarren.org Rev. Bogdan Milosz, Priest in Solidum; Lynn McKnight, DRE; CRP Stds.: 44

St. Louise de Marillac Parish Warren - 2500 E. Twelve Mile Rd., Warren, MI 48092 t) 586-751-3340 fathera@stldm.org www.stldm.org Rev. Andrew Czarnecki, Priest in Solidum; Dcn. Thomas Avery; CRP Stds.: 30

St. Mark Parish Warren - 4401 Bart Ave., Warren, MI 48091 t) 586-759-3020 parishcenter@stmarkparishwarren.org; abrewer@stmarkparishwarren.org stmarkparishwarren.com Rev. Stanley Obloj, Priest in Solidum; Dcn. Brian Carroll; Amanda Brewer, DRE; CRP Stds.: 45

St. Martin de Porres Parish Warren - 31555 Hoover Rd., Warren, MI 48093 t) 586-264-7515; 586-264-7970 (CRP) parishoffice@smdeporres.com www.smdeporres.com Rev. Nicholas Zukowski, Priest in Solidum; Sandy Acord, DRE; CRP Stds.: 65

Our Lady of Grace (Vietnamese) Parish Warren - 26256 Ryan Rd., Warren, MI 48091 t) 586-755-1313 www.ologwarren.org Rev. Hoang Chi Lam, Priest in Solidum; Dcn. Kevin Tietz, DRE; CRP Stds.: 60

WASHINGTON

Ss. John and Paul Parish Washington Township - 7777 W. 28 Mile Rd., Washington, MI 48094 t) 586-781-9010; 586-781-9488 (Faith Formation) office@ssjohnandpaul.org www.ssjohnandpaul.org Rev. Festus N. Ejimadu, Priest in Solidum; Dcn. Aleks Stanaj; George Efthemiou, Pst. Assoc.; Beth Mersino, DRE; CRP Stds.: 130

WATERFORD

St. Benedict Parish Waterford - 40 S. Lynn Ave., Waterford, MI 48328; Mailing: 80 S. Lynn Ave., Waterford, MI 48328 t) 248-681-1534 gloria.armstrong.stben@gmail.com; stbenz80@gmail.com stbencc.org Rev. James A. Mayworm, Priest in Solidum; Gloria Armstrong, DRE; CRP Stds.: 92

Parish Center - 80 S. Lynn Ave., Waterford, MI 48328

Our Lady of the Lakes Parish Waterford - 5481 Dixie Hwy., Waterford, MI 48329 t) 248-623-0274 parishoffice@ollonline.org ollonline.org Rev. Scott A. Thibodeau, Priest in Solidum; Rev. Robert Voiland, Priest in Solidum; Dcn. Paul Nickels; Jean Hartman, DRE; Artha Horowitz, Pst. Min./Coord.; Michelle M Konarzewski, Pst. Min./Coord.; Martin Zaporski, Music Min.; Maureen Burton, Bus. Mgr.; CRP Stds.: 309

Our Lady of the Lakes School - (Grades PreK-8) 5495 Dixie Hwy., Waterford, MI 48329 t) 248-623-0340 jeanine.kenny@ollonline.org Jeanine Kenny, Prin.; Nichole Campbell, Registrar; Stds.: 286; Lay Tchrs.: 21

Our Lady of the Lakes High School - (Grades 9-12) 5495 Dixie Hwy., Waterford, MI 48329 t) 248-623-0340 jeanine.kenny@ollonline.org Jeanine Kenny, Prin.; Nichole Campbell, Registrar; Stds.: 97; Lay Tchrs.: 15

St. Perpetua Parish Waterford - 134 Airport Rd., Waterford, MI 48327 t) 248-682-6431 stper682@aol.com stperpetuaparish.org Rev. Thomas L. Meagher, Priest in Solidum; Dcn. Robert Gajda; CRP Stds.: 57

WAYNE

St. Mary Parish Wayne - 34530 W. Michigan Ave., Wayne, MI 48184-1748 t) 734-721-8745 parishoffice@stmarywayne.org www.stmarywayne.org Rev. Sean P. Bonner, Priest in Solidum; Dcn. Ralph Luddecke; Paul Zdzieblowski, DRE; CRP Stds.: 90

WEST BLOOMFIELD

Prince of Peace Parish West Bloomfield - 4300 Walnut Lake Rd., West Bloomfield, MI 48323 t) 248-681-9424; 248-681-5070 (CRP) parishsecretary@princeofpeacecatholic.church princeofpeacecatholic.church Rev. Ronald J. Jozwiak, Priest in Solidum; CRP Stds.: 45

WESTLAND

St. Mary, Cause of Our Joy Parish Westland - 8200 N. Wayne Rd., Westland, MI 48185 t) 734-425-4421; 734-425-4421 x217 (CRP) faithformation@stmarycooj.org; office@stmarycooj.org www.stmarycooj.org Rev. Shafique Masih, Priest in Solidum; Sabrina S. Queen, DRE; CRP Stds.: 50

St. Richard Parish Westland - 35851 Cherry Hill, Westland, MI 48186 t) 734-729-2240 frsean-smsrhf@usa.net Rev. Sean P. Bonner, Priest in Solidum;

SS. Simon and Jude Parish Westland - 32500 Palmer Rd., Westland, MI 48186 t) 734-722-1343 pastor@stssimonandjude.com www.stssimonandjude.com Rev. Joseph A. Plawecki, Priest in Solidum; Mary Ann Kocsis, DRE; Margaret Reyez, DRE;

WHITE LAKE

St. Patrick Parish White Lake - 9086 Hutchins Rd., White Lake, MI 48386 t) 248-698-3100 (Parish Office); 248-698-3240 (School Office) kdelorey@stpwl.org; cholling@stpwl.org www.stpatrickwhitelake.org/ Rev. Thomas L. Meagher, Priest in Solidum; Rev. Susaikannua Esack, SAC, Priest in Solidum; CRP Stds.: 150

St. Patrick School - (Grades 1-8) 9040 Hutchins Rd., White Lake, MI 48386 jclark@stpwl.org Jeremy Clark, Prin.; Charles Hoying, Vice Prin.; Bridget Page, Librn.; Stds.: 502; Lay Tchrs.: 24

WOODHAVEN

Our Lady of the Woods Parish Woodhaven - 21892 Gudith Rd., Woodhaven, MI 48183 t) 734-671-5101 frbob@olow.org; rgonzalez@olow.org olow.org Rev. Robert Joseph Johnson, SVD, Priest in Solidum; Claudette Wagner, DRE; CRP Stds.: 107

WYANDOTTE

Our Lady of the Scapular (Our Lady of Mount Carmel and St. Stanislaus Kostka) - 976 Pope John Paul II Ave. (Superior Blvd.), Wyandotte, MI 48192-3496 t) 734-284-9135 frmarkb@aol.com; ourladyofthescapular@wyan.org ourladyofthescapular.org Rev. Mark Borkowski, Priest in Solidum;

St. Vincent Pallotti Parish Wyandotte - 334 Elm St., Wyandotte, MI 48192 t) 734-285-9840 dre@stvpp.org; kristine.m@stvpp.org www.stvpp.org Rev. Brendan McCarrick, S.A.C. (Ireland), Priest in Solidum; Rev. Stephen Muli Mutie, SAC (Kenya), Priest in Solidum; Rev. Suresh Rajaian, S.A.C., Priest in Solidum; Julie Dzanbazoff, DRE; CRP Stds.: 188

YALE

Sacred Heart Parish Yale - 310 N. Main St., Yale, MI 48097-2845 t) 810-387-9800; 810-387-9800 x41 (CRP) olmcshyff@gmail.com; olmcshyreceptionist@gmail.com Rev. Thomas Kuehnemund, Priest in Solidum; Dcn. William Kolarik; Brenda Krzak, DRE; CRP Stds.: 42

SCHOOLS: PRESCHOOL THRU HIGH SCHOOL

SCHOOLS

STATE OF MICHIGAN

BLOOMFIELD HILLS

Academy of the Sacred Heart - (PRV) (Grades PreSchool-12) 1250 Kensington Rd., Bloomfield Hills, MI 48304-3029 t) 248-646-8900 www.ashmi.org Religious of the Sacred Heart Damian Hermann, Prin.; Stds.: 376; Lay Tchrs.: 37

CANTON

All Saints Catholic School - (PAR) (Grades PreSchool-8) 48735 Warren Rd., Canton, MI 48187-1233 t) 734-459-2490 office@allsaintscs.com www.allsaintscs.com Kristen Strausbaugh, Prin.; Gary Yee, Vice Prin.; Stds.: 601; Lay Tchrs.: 29

CLARKSTON

Everest Academy - (PRV) (Grades PreK-12) 5935 Clarkston Rd., Clarkston, MI 48348 t) 248-620-3390 mnalepa@everestacademy.org; ccarter@everestacademy.org www.everestcatholic.org Susan Ender, Prin.; Greg Reichert, Prin.; Brian Kitz, Chair; Julie Werner, Librn.; Stds.: 442; Pr. Tchrs.: 2; Lay Tchrs.: 31

MONROE

Monroe Catholic Elementary Schools - (PAR) (Grades 1-8) 151 N. Monroe St., Monroe, MI 48162 t) 734-241-6335 kubik@monroecatholicschools.com www.mcesmonroe.com Kyle Kubik, Prin.; Stds.: 418; Lay Tchrs.: 27

St. Michael Archangel Campus - (Grades 1-8) 510 W. Front St., Monroe, MI 48161 t) 734-241-3923

St. John the Baptist Campus - (Grades 1-8) 521 S. Monroe St., Monroe, MI 48161 t) 734-241-1670 Stds.: 454; Lay Tchrs.: 26

St. Mary Campus - (Grades 1-8) 151 N. Monroe St., Monroe, MI 48162 t) 734-241-3377

PONTIAC

Notre Dame Preparatory School and Marist Academy - (PRV) (Grades PreSchool-12) 1300 Giddings Rd., Pontiac, MI 48340 t) 248-373-5300 aguest@ndpma.org; ndpma@ndpma.org www.ndpma.org An Independent, Catholic Co-ed School with three divisions sponsored by the Society of Mary, USA Province. Rev. Joseph C. Hindelang, S.M., Prov.; Rev. Leon M. Olszamowski, S.M., Pres.; Rev. James Strasz, S.M., Admin.; Rev. Ronald Nikodem, S.M., Campus Min.; Kim Anderson, Prin.; Diana C. Atkins, Prin.; Brandon Jezdimir, Prin.; Andrew Guest, Headmaster; Bro. Louis Plourde, SM, In Res.; Stds.: 1,046; Pr. Tchrs.: 3; Bro. Tchrs.: 2; Lay Tchrs.: 153

Notre Dame Preparatory - High School - (Grades PreSchool-12) t) (248) 373-5300 x8011 Stds.: 563; Bro. Tchrs.: 1; Lay Tchrs.: 94; Pr. Tchrs.: 3

Notre Dame Marist Academy - Middle Division - (Grades PreSchool-12) t) 248-373-5371 Stds.: 214; Lay Tchrs.: 18

Notre Dame Marist Academy - Lower Division - (Grades PreSchool-12) 1425 Giddings Road, Pontiac, MI 48340 t) 248-373-2573 Stds.: 266; Lay Tchrs.: 29

ROCHESTER HILLS

Holy Family Regional School - South Campus & North Campus - (PAR) (Grades K-8) 2633 John R. Rd., (South Campus), Rochester Hills, MI 48307 t) 248-299-3798; 248-656-1234 myers.jon@holyfam.org www.holyfam.org Jon R. Myers, Prin.; Stds.: 920; Lay Tchrs.: 48

HIGH SCHOOLS

STATE OF MICHIGAN

BLOOMFIELD HILLS

Academy of the Sacred Heart - (PRV) 1250 Kensington Rd., Bloomfield Hills, MI 48304-3029 t) 248-646-8900 www.ashmi.org Religious of the Sacred Heart Damian Hermann, Prin.; Stds.: 74; Lay Tchrs.: 18

Brother Rice High School - (PRV) (Grades 9-12) 7101 Lahser Rd., Bloomfield Hills, MI 48301-4045 t) 248-833-2000 mcnamara@brrice.edu www.brrice.edu Congregation of Christian Brothers. Ed Okuniewski, Prin.; Thomas Reidy, Pres.; Stds.: 525; Bro. Tchrs.: 3; Sr. Tchrs.: 2; Lay Tchrs.: 37

Marian High School for Young Women - (PRV) 7225 Lahser Rd., Bloomfield Hills, MI 48301 t) 248-644-1750 cushmans@marian-hs.org www.marian-hs.org Stacey Cushman, Prin.; Rev. Msgr. John P. Zenz, Chap.; Stds.: 372; Lay Tchrs.: 30

CHESTERFIELD

Austin Catholic High School - (PRV) (Grades 9-12) 25925 23 Mile Rd., Chesterfield, MI 48051 t) 586-200-0143 austin@austincatholichighschool.org www.austincatholichighschool.org Janel M. Coppens, Prin.; Rev. Msgr. John C. Kasza, Chair; Stds.: 114; Lay Tchrs.: 20

DETROIT

Detroit Cristo Rey High School, Inc. - 5679 Vernor Hwy., Detroit, MI 48209 t) 313-843-2747 clynch@detroitcristorey.org; jvalgoi@detroitcristorey.org www.detroitcristorey.org Joellyn Valgoi, Prin.; Christopher Lynch, Pres.; Karla Gudino, Vice Prin.; Stds.: 291; Lay Tchrs.: 23

Detroit Cristo Rey High School Corporate Work Study Program, Inc. - 5679 W. Vernor Hwy, Detroit, MI 48209 t) (313) 843-2747

Loyola High School - (PAR) (Grades 9-12) 15325 Pinehurst, Detroit, MI 48238-1633 t) 313-861-2407 dsmith@loyolahsdetroit.org; loyola@loyolahsdetroit.org www.loyolahsdetroit.org Co-sponsored by the Archdiocese of Detroit and the

Midwest Province of the Society of Jesus Wyatt Jones III, Prin.; David R. Smith, Pres.; Stds.: 156; Lay Tchrs.: 17

Loyola Work Experience Program, Inc. - (Grades 9-12) mluedtke@loyolahsdetroit.org Rev. Mark W. Luedtke, S.J., Pres.; Stds.: 152; Lay Tchrs.: 14

University of Detroit Jesuit High School and Academy - (PRV) (Grades 7-12) 8400 S. Cambridge, Detroit, MI 48221-1699 t) 313-862-5400 christopher.smith@uofdjesuit.org www.uofdjesuit.org Dr. Christopher Smith, Prin.; Bro. James J. Boynton, S.J., Pres.; Rev. Benard Omondi, S.J., In Res.; Rev. Robert A. Ytsen, S.J., In Res.; Rev. Trevor J. Rainwater, S.J., In Res.; Erin Chekal, Librn.; Stds.: 826; Pr. Tchrs.: 3; Bro. Tchrs.: 1; Lay Tchrs.: 79

FARMINGTON HILLS

Mercy High School for Girls - (PRV) (Grades 9-12) 29300 W. Eleven Mile Rd., Farmington Hills, MI 48336 t) 248-476-8020 mhs@mhsmi.org www.mhsmi.org Religious Sisters of Mercy. Patricia Sattler, Prin.; Cheryl Delaney Kreger, Pres.; Stds.: 560; Lay Tchrs.: 47

MADISON HEIGHTS

Bishop Foley Catholic High School - (DIO) (Grades 9-12) 32000 Campbell Rd., Madison Heights, MI 48071 t) 248-585-1210 accavitti@bishopfoley.org; mainoffice@bishopfoley.org www.bishopfoley.org Frank Accavitti III, Prin.; Nona Moore, Bus. Mgr.; Stds.: 289; Pr. Tchrs.: 1; Lay Tchrs.: 26

MARINE CITY

Cardinal Mooney Catholic School - (PAR) (Grades 9-12) 660 S. Water Street, Marine City, MI 48039 t) 810-765-8825 devans@cardinalmooney.org www.cardinalmooney.org Jennifer Stachelski, Interim Prin.; Kathleen Meyers, Exec.; Beth Engel, Bus. Mgr.; Stds.: 162; Lay Tchrs.: 15

MONROE

St. Mary Catholic Central High School - (PAR) (Grades 9-12) 108 W. Elm Ave., Monroe, MI 48162 t) 734-241-7622 advancement@smccmonroe.com www.smccmonroe.com (Coed) Sean Jorgensen, Pres.; Jason Linster, Prin.; Timothy Magg, Campus Min.; Stds.: 347; Lay Tchrs.: 22

NOVI

Detroit Catholic Central High School - (PRV) (Grades 9-12) 27225 Wixom Rd., Novi, MI 48374 t) 248-596-3810 smartin@catholiccentral.net www.catholiccentral.net Congregation of St. Basil Rev. Patrick W. Fulton, C.S.B., Prin.; Rev. Dennis Paul Noelke, CSB, Chap.; Rev. Dennis Kauffman, C.S.B., Dir., School Improvement; Rev. Robert W. Moslosky, C.S.B., Webmaster; Stds.: 933; Scholastics: 1; Lay Tchrs.: 61

ORCHARD LAKE

St. Mary's Preparatory - (PRV) (Grades 9-12) 3535 Commerce Rd., Orchard Lake, MI 48324 t) 248-836-1292 lkosco@stmarysprep.com www.stmarysprep.com Robert Pyles, Headmaster; Candace Castiglione, Dean of Admissions; Stds.: 789; Lay Tchrs.: 44

RIVERVIEW

Gabriel Richard Catholic High School - (PAR) 15325 Pennsylvania Rd., Riverview, MI 48193 t) 734-284-1875 admissions@gabrielrichard.org www.gabrielrichard.org Joseph Whalen, Prin.; Stds.: 242; Lay Tchrs.: 23

WARREN

De La Salle Collegiate - (PRV) 14600 Common Rd., Warren, MI 48088-3387 t) 586-778-2207 agriffin@delasallehs.com www.delasallehs.com High School Brothers of the Christian Schools. Bro. Kenneth Kalinowski, Prin.; Lawrence Rancilio, Pres.; Sheryl Anderson, IT Manager; Stds.: 532; Bro. Tchrs.: 2; Sr. Tchrs.: 2; Lay Tchrs.: 65

Regina High School for Girls - (PRV) (Grades 9-12) 13900 Masonic Blvd., Warren, MI 48088 t) 586-585-0500 adiamond@reginahs.com; mtrederlang@reginahs.com www.reginahs.com Ann E. Diamond, Prin.; Mary Treder Lang, Pres.; Kyle J. Smith, CFO; Stds.: 302; Lay Tchrs.: 26

WIXOM

St. Catherine of Siena Academy - (PRV) (Grades 9-12) 28200 Napier Rd., Wixom, MI 48393 t) 248-946-4848 info@saintcatherineacademy.org www.saintcatherineacademy.org Girls. Judith Hehs, Prin.; Lia Johnston, Pres.; Daniel Bumpus, Dean; Sr. Mary Ann Foggin, Campus Min.; Stds.: 240; Sr. Tchrs.: 1; Lay Tchrs.: 25

INSTITUTIONS LOCATED IN DIOCESE

ASSOCIATIONS [ASN]

BLOOMFIELD HILLS

***Ladies of Charity of St. Vincent de Paul Oakland County Association** - 2215 Opdyke Rd., Bloomfield Hills, MI 48304; Mailing: P.O. Box 602, Bloomfield Hills, MI 48303 t) 248-646-0920 loc@theladiesofcharity.org theladiesofcharity.org/ Leslie Swanson, Pres.;

CAMPUS MINISTRY / NEWMAN CENTERS [CAM]

DEARBORN

Gabriel Richard Student Center - 5001 Evergreen Rd., Dearborn, MI 48128 t) (313) 237-5954 www.detroitcatholiccampusministry.org Rev. Matthew Hood, Chap.; Claire Krakowiak, Engagement Coord.; Anna Picasso, Outreach Coord.;

DETROIT

Detroit Catholic Campus Ministry - 5930 Woodward Ave., Detroit, MI 48202 t) 313-237-5954 detroitcatholiccampusministry.com/ Rev. Matthew Hood, Chap.;

University of Detroit Mercy University Ministry - 4001 W. McNichols Rd., Detroit, MI 48221-3038 t) 313-993-1560 ministry@udmercy.edu www.udmercy.edu/ministry Anita Klueg, Dir.;

McNichols Campus - www.udmercy.edu/life/ministry/ Sr. Erin McDonald, C.S.J., Svc. & Social Justice Min.;

LIVONIA

Madonna University Campus Ministry - 36600 Schoolcraft, Livonia, MI 48150 t) 734-432-5839 jdcox@madonna.edu www.madonna.edu Jesse Cox, Dir.;

CATHOLIC CHARITIES [CCH]

DETROIT

Capuchin Soup Kitchen - 1820 Mt. Elliott, Detroit, MI 48207 t) 313-579-2100 brgary@cskdetroit.org www.cskdetroit.org Rev. Gary Wegner, O.F.M. Cap., Exec.; Bro. Tien Dinh, O.F.M. Cap., Dir.; Asstd. Annu.: 134,700; Staff: 50

Capuchin Services - 6333 Medbury, Detroit, MI 48211; Mailing: 1820 Mt. Elliott St., Detroit, MI 48207 t) 313-925-1730 x3100 tdinh@cskdetroit.org Bro. Robert Roemer, Dir.; Rev. Fred Cabras, O.F.M. Cap., Dir.;

Conner Kitchen - 4390 Conner, Detroit, MI 48215; Mailing: 1820 Mt. Elliott St., Detroit, MI 48207 t) 313-822-8606 tdinh@cskdetroit.org Rev. Robert Wotypka, Dir.;

Jefferson House - 8311 E. Jefferson, Detroit, MI 48214; Mailing: 1820 Mt. Elliott St., Detroit, MI 48207 t) 313-331-8900 tdinh@cskdetroit.org Transitional alcohol-drug residence. Amy Kinner, Dir.;

Meldrum Kitchen - 1264 Meldrum, Detroit, MI 48207; Mailing: 1820 Mt. Elliot St., Detroit, MI 48207 t) (313) 579-2100 x2210 tdinh@cskdetroit.org Alison Costello, Dir.;

On the Rise Bakery - 1780 Mt. Elliot St., Detroit, MI 48207 t) 313-922-8510 tdinh@cskdetroit.org cskdetroit.org/bakery

Manna Community Meal - 1950 Trumbull Ave., Detroit, MI 48216; Mailing: 1050 Porter St., Detroit, MI 48226 c) 313-265-7271; 313-580-7089 mariannearbogast@gmail.com (Soup Kitchen) Rev. Thomas Lumpkin; Asstd. Annu.: 600; Staff: 5

Pope John XXIII Hospitality House - 3977 2nd Ave., Detroit, MI 48201 t) 313-965-4450 Cancer outpatient-residents, Transportation for Area Pediatric Cancer Patients.

Society of St. Vincent de Paul Detroit - 3000 Gratiot Ave., Detroit, MI 48207 t) 313-393-2930 mlfdonovan@svdpdetroit.org www.svdpdetroit.org Mary Lynn Fauda Donovan, CEO; Asstd. Annu.: 97,577; Staff: 100

St. Vincent and Sarah Fisher Center (SVSF Center) - 16800 Trinity, Detroit, MI 48219 t) 313-535-9200 diane.renaud@svsfcenter.org www.svsfcenter.org Free personalized educational programs for low-income, at-risk, children and adults Diane Renaud, Exec. Dir.; Asstd. Annu.: 1,000; Staff: 20

CEMETERIES [CEM]

BROWNSTOWN

Our Lady of Hope - 18303 Allen Rd., Brownstown, MI 48193 t) 734-285-2155 cortese.deanna@aodcemeteries.org; vanhooser.donna@aodcemeteries.org www.cfcsdetroit.org (owned & operated by the Archdiocese of Detroit) Deanna Cortese, Dir.;

CLINTON TOWNSHIP

Resurrection - 18201 Clinton River Rd., Clinton Township, MI 48038 t) 586-286-9020 tburrows@mtelliott.com; mchilcote@mtelliott.com www.mtelliott.com (owned & operated by the Mt. Elliott Cemetery Assoc.) Michael Chilcote, Exec.; Timothy Burrows, Dir.;

DEARBORN HEIGHTS

St. Hedwig Cemetery - 23755 Military, Dearborn Heights, MI 48127 t) 313-562-1900 shcdaz@aol.com (owned & operated by the Conventual Franciscan Friars) David Zielinski, Exec.;

DETROIT

Holy Cross - 8850 Dix Ave., Detroit, MI 48209 t) 734-285-2155 cortese.deanna@aodcemeteries.org (owned by the Archdiocese of Detroit), Cemetery now inactive. All mail and inquiries should be sent to: c/o Our Lady of Hope. Robert Hojnacki, Dir.;

Mt. Elliott - 1701 Mt. Elliott Ave., Detroit, MI 48207; Mailing: 17100 Van Dyke, Detroit, MI 48234 t) 313-567-0048; 313-365-5650 mgracely@mtelliott.com; mchilcote@mtelliott.com www.mtelliott.com (owned & operated by the Mt. Elliott Cemetery Assoc.) Michael Chilcote, Exec.; Mark Gracely, Dir.;

Mt. Olivet - 17100 Van Dyke, Detroit, MI 48234 t) 313-365-5650; 313-365-6460 mgracely@mtelliott.com; mchilcote@mtelliott.com www.mtelliott.com (owned & operated by the Mt. Elliott Cemetery Assoc.) Michael Chilcote, Exec.; Mark Gracely, Dir.;

MONROE

St. Joseph Cemetery - 909 N. Monroe St., Monroe, MI 48162 t) 734-241-1411 cortese.deanna@aodcemeteries.org Robert Hojnacki, Dir.;

ROCHESTER

Guardian Angel - 4701 Rochester Rd., Rochester, MI 48306 t) 800-275-9574; 248-601-2900 wmann@mtelliott.com; mchilcote@mtelliott.com www.mtelliott.com (owned & operated by the Mt. Elliott Cemetery Assoc.) Michael Chilcote, Exec.; Wendy Mann, Dir.;

SOUTHFIELD

Holy Sepulchre - 25800 W. Ten Mile Rd., Southfield, MI 48033 t) 248-350-1900 cortese.deanna@aodcemeteries.org; stark.christopher@aodcemeteries.org www.cfcsdetroit.org (owned & operated by the Archdiocese of Detroit) Robert Hojnacki, Dir.;

WATERFORD

All Saints - 4401 Nelsey Rd., Waterford, MI 48329

t) 248-623-9633 rburns@mtelliott.com; mchilcote@mtelliott.com www.mtelliott.com (owned & operated by the Mt. Elliott Cemetery Assoc.) Russ Burns, Dir.; Michael Chilcote, Exec.;

COLLEGES & UNIVERSITIES [COL]

DETROIT

University of Detroit Mercy - 4001 W. McNichols Rd., Detroit, MI 48221-3038 t) 313-993-1455 president@udmercy.edu www.udmercy.edu Dr. Donald B Taylor, Pres.; Stds.: 5,360; Lay Tchrs.: 326; Pr. Tchrs.: 3; Sr. Tchrs.: 1

LIVONIA

Madonna University - 36600 Schoolcraft Rd., Livonia, MI 48150 t) 734-432-5300 www.madonna.edu A Felician-Sponsored Ministry Ian Day, Pres.; Dr. Deborah Dunn, Provost & Vice Pres. Academic Affairs; Stds.: 2,123; Lay Tchrs.: 96; Pr. Tchrs.: 1; Sr. Tchrs.: 2

Macomb University Center - 44575 Garfield Rd., UC-1, Rm. 120, Clinton Township, MI 48038-1139 t) 586-263-6330 lmcintyre@madonna.edu

SWEEP Center - 5716 Michigan Ave., Detroit, MI 48210 t) 313-965-5334

CONVENTS, MONASTERIES, AND RESIDENCES FOR WOMEN [CON]

ALLEN PARK

Sisters of Mary Reparatrix - 10065 Northway Ave., Allen Park, MI 48101 t) 313-383-3312 kasparek@comcast.net wwwmaryrep.org Sr. Ann Kasparek, S.M.R., Rel. Ord. Ldr.; Sr. Veronica Blake Sr., SMR, Rel. Ord. Ldr.; Srs.: 11

BLOOMFIELD HILLS

Daughters of Divine Charity - Holy Family Province - 39315 Woodward Ave., Bloomfield Hills, MI 48304 t) 248-644-1011; 248-644-8052 madonnahallconvent@gmail.com www.briarbank.com Daughters of Divine Charity of Detroit, Inc. Sr. Mary Carmella Chojnacki, FDC, Supr.; Sr. Mary Coffelt, FDC, Prov.;

CLINTON TOWNSHIP

Monastery of St. Therese of the Child Jesus - 35750 Moravian Dr., Clinton Township, MI 48035-2138 t) 586-790-7255 carmelctwp@sbcglobal.net www.carmelctwp.org Discalced Carmelite Nuns. Mother Mary Elizabeth, Prioress; Srs.: 13

DEARBORN HEIGHTS

Sisters of the Good Shepherd (RGS) - 20651 W. Warren St., Dearborn Heights, MI 48127-2622 t) 313-253-2090 srjanicergs@gmail.com Province of Mid-North America, Sisters of the Good Shepherd of Detroit, Vista Maria Srs.: 1

DETROIT

Missionaries of Charity - 1917 Cabot St., Detroit, MI 48209 t) 313-841-1394 Sr. M. Imeldina MC, Supr.; Sr. M. Jonathan, MC, Regl. Supr.; Srs.: 5

Sisters, Home Visitors of Mary Convent - 121 E. Boston, Detroit, MI 48202 t) 313-869-2160 homevisitors@att.net; brcwolff@wowway.com Sr. Barbara Dakoske, H.V.M., Admin.; Srs.: 22

EASTPOINTE

Marist Sisters, Inc. - 16057 Hauss, Eastpointe, MI 48021 t) 586-772-2577 constance56@comcast.net Sr. Linda Sevcik, S.M., Supr.; Srs.: 6

FARMINGTON HILLS

Bernardine Franciscan Sisters of Michigan - Our Lady of the Rosary Convent, 27405 W. 10 Mile Rd., Farmington Hills, MI 48336-2201 t) 248-476-4111 selenaosf@gmail.com www.bfranciscan.org Bernardine Sisters of the Third Order of St. Francis. Sr. John Ann Proach, osf, Rel. Ord. Ldr.; Srs.: 16

Monastery of the Blessed Sacrament - 29575 Middlebelt Rd., Farmington Hills, MI 48334-2311 t) 248-626-8253 opnunsfh@sbcglobal.net www.opnuns-fh.org Nuns of the Order of Preachers (Cloistered Dominican Nuns, Perpetual Adoration). Rev. David J. Santoro, O.P, Chap.; Sr. Mary Peter, Prioress; Srs.: 25

Sisters of Mercy of the Americas West Midwest Community, Inc. - 29000 Eleven Mile Rd., Farmington Hills, MI 48336 t) 248-476-8000 Sr. Aine O'Connor, RSM, Pres.; Srs.: 417

West Midwest FIDES, Inc. - Sr. Pat Flynn, RSM, Pres.;

LIVONIA

Presentation of the BVM Convent (Provincial House of the Congregation of the Sisters of St. Felix, C.S.S.F., Felician Sisters) - 36800 Schoolcraft Rd., Livonia, MI 48150-1172 t) 734-591-1730 sjudithmk@feliciansisters.org; presentationmi@feliciansisters.org www.feliciansistersna.org Sr. Judith Marie Kubicki, Prov.; Srs.: 54

MONROE

Servants of Jesus - 821 W. Elm Ave., Monroe, MI 48162 t) 734-344-7050 pcooney@ihmsisters.org Sr. Paula Cooney, Supr.; Srs.: 11

Sisters, Servants of the Immaculate Heart of Mary, Leadership Council - 610 W. Elm Ave., Monroe, MI 48162-7909 t) 734-240-9700 mtylinski@ihmsisters.org www.ihmsisters.org Sr. Mary Jane Herb, I.H.M., Pres.; Sr. Marianne Gaynor, Vice. Pres.; Sr. Margaret Chapman, Treas.; Sr. Patricia McCluskey, I.H.M., Mission Councilor; Sr. Ellen Rinke, Mission Councilor; Srs.: 209

Institute for Communal Contemplation and Dialogue - 8531 W. McNichols, Detroit, MI 48221 t) 313-971-3668 circles@engagingimpasse.org engagingimpasse.org Sr. Nancy Sylvester, I.H.M., Exec.;

Maxis Spirituality Center - 17380 Grange Rd., Riverview, MI 48193 t) 734-240-5494 lmoldenhauer@ihmsisters.org Sr. Lynne Moldenhauer, Coord.;

ORTONVILLE

Our Lady of Mt. Thabor Monastery - 1295 Bald Eagle Lake Rd., Ortonville, MI 48462 t) 248-627-4355 mtthabor@aol.com www.mtthabornunsop.com Dominican Nuns of Mt. Thabor. Sr. Mary Joseph, Prioress;

WATERFORD

Dominican Sisters of Peace - 2300 Watkins Lake Rd, Waterford, MI 48328-1439 t) (614) 416-1036 www.oppeace.org Lourdes Convent Sr. Patricia Twohill, OP, Prioress; Srs.: 6

ENDOWMENTS / FOUNDATIONS / TRUSTS [EFT]

BLOOMFIELD HILLS

The Brother Rice Endowment Fund - 7101 Lahser Rd., Bloomfield Hills, MI 48301-4045 t) 248-833-2000 mcnamara@brrice.edu; lengers@brrice.edu www.brrice.edu Mike Tyranski, Pres.;

***The Catholic Foundation of Michigan** - 1145 W. Long Lake Rd., Ste. 201, Bloomfield Hills, MI 48302 t) 248-204-0332 catholicfoundationmichigan.org/ Angela Moloney, Pres.;

DETROIT

Archdiocese of Detroit Endowment Foundation, Inc. - 12 State St., Detroit, MI 48226 t) 313-596-7401 David Kelley, Secy.;

Archdiocese of Detroit Priests' Pension Plan, Inc. - 12 State St., Detroit, MI 48226 t) 313-596-7151 Rev. Robert R. Spezia, Vicar;

Detroit Catholic Parishes and Schools Trust - 12 State St., Detroit, MI 48226 t) (313) 237-5800 Michael Schoenle, Trust Mgr.; Jolanta Kepa, Treas.;

Ste. Anne Restoration Fund - 1000 Ste. Anne St., Detroit, MI 48216 t) 313-496-1701 businessoffice@steannedetroit.org Rev. Msgr. Charles G. Kosanke, Contact;

FARMINGTON HILLS

Divine Mercy Academy Foundation - 27555 Executive Dr., Ste. 165, Farmington Hills, MI 48331 t) 248-347-6800 ddoyle@doylecpa.net Michael Dewan, Pres.; Daniel Doyle, Treas.;

LIVONIA

***Christ Medicus Foundation** - ; Mailing: P.O. Box 530901, Livonia, MI 48153 t) 248-478-5959 info@christmedicus.org christmedicus.org/ Michael J. O'Dea, Exec.;

Felician Sisters of Livonia Foundation - 36800 Schoolcraft, Livonia, MI 48150 t) 734-591-1730 sjudithmk@feliciansisters.org www.feliciansistersna.org Sr. Judith Marie Kubicki, Pres.;

MONROE

Servants of Jesus Charitable Trust - 821 W. Elm Ave., Monroe, MI 48162 t) 734-344-7050 pcooney@ihmsisters.org Sr. Paula Cooney, Supr.;

SSIHM Charitable Trust - 610 W. Elm Ave., Monroe, MI 48162-7909 t) 734-240-9700 mtylinski@ihmsisters.org Sr. Margaret Chapman, Treas.;

ROMEO

***Blessed Virgin Mary Foundation (BVM Foundation)** - 11070 W. Gates St., Romeo, MI 48065; Mailing: 119 Church St., #236, Romeo, MI 48065 t) 586-752-6744 (Exec. Offices); 586-281-4110 b.v.m.foundation.edu@gmail.com Kaitlin Farms; Romeo Hills Academy Brian Palmer, Pres.;

WATERFORD

Lourdes Campus Fund - 2300 Watkins Lake Rd., Waterford, MI 48328 t) 248-674-4732 cburke@lourdes-sc.org www.lourdes-sc.org Sr. Maureen Comer, O.P., CEO;

WIXOM

St. Catherine of Siena Academy Foundation - 28200 Napier Rd., Wixom, MI 48393 t) 248-946-4848 ljohnston@saintcatherineacademy.org Judith Hehs, Prin.; Lia Johnston, Pres.;

HOSPITALS / HEALTH SERVICES [HOS]

BRIGHTON

Ascension Brighton Center for Recovery (Brighton Center for Recovery, Brighton Hospital, Brighton Hospital Foundation, Michigan Alcoholic Rehabilitation Foundation) - 12851 Grand River Rd., Brighton, MI 48116 t) 810-227-1211 paula.caruso@ascension.org healthcare.ascension.org A member of Ascension Michigan Kenneth Berkovitz, CEO; Bed Capacity: 70; Asstd. Annu.: 15,458; Staff: 118

DETROIT

Ascension St. John Hospital (St. John Hospital and Medical Center, St. John Hospital and Medical Center Corporation, St. John Hospital Corporation) - 22101 Moross Rd., Detroit, MI 48236 t) 313-343-4000 paula.caruso@ascension.org healthcare.ascension.org A member of Ascension Michigan Christopher McClead; Bed Capacity: 592; Asstd. Annu.: 976,796; Staff: 4,035

EAST CHINA

Ascension River District Hospital (St. John River District Hospital, River District Hospital) - 4100 River Rd., East China, MI 48054 t) 810-329-7111 paula.caruso@ascension.org healthcare.ascension.org A member of Ascension Michigan Christopher McClead; Bed Capacity: 22; Asstd. Annu.: 72,192; Staff: 220

LIVONIA

Trinity Health Livonia - 36475 W. Five Mile Rd., Livonia, MI 48154 t) 734-655-1646 www.trinity-health.org Rev. Luke Iwuji; Rev. Peter Ben Opara; Bed Capacity: 304; Asstd. Annu.: 270,000; Staff: 2,085

NOVI

Ascension Providence Hospital (Ascension Providence Hospital, Novi Campus) - 47601 Grand River Ave., Novi, MI 48374 t) 248-465-4100 paula.caruso@ascension.org A member of Ascension Michigan - Providence-Providence Park Hospital, Providence Hospital and Medical Centers, Inc., Providence Hospital Brant Russell, Pres.; Bed Capacity: 251; Asstd. Annu.: 427,096; Staff: 1,639

PONTIAC

St. Joseph Mercy Oakland - 44405 Woodward Ave., Pontiac, MI 48341-2985 t) 248-858-3000 www.stjoesoakland.com (A division of Trinity Health-Michigan) Charles Kibirgie, Chap.; Linda Thompson, Chap.; Shannon Striebich, Pres.;

SOUTHFIELD

Ascension Providence Hospital (Providence-Providence

Park Hospital, Providence Hospital and Medical Centers, Inc., Providence Hospital) - 16001 W. Nine Mile Rd., Southfield, MI 48037 t) 248-849-3000 paula.caruso@ascension.org healthcare.ascension.org A member of Ascension Michigan -- Providence-Providence Park Hospital, Providence Hospital and Medical Centers, Inc., Providence Hospital Christopher McClead, CIO; Bed Capacity: 384; Asstd. Annu.: 452,755; Staff: 2,342

WARREN

Ascension Macomb-Oakland Hospital (St. John Macomb-Oakland Hospital, St. John River Macomb-Oakland Hospital, St. John Health System-Detroit-Macomb Campus) - 11800 Twelve Mile Rd., Warren, MI 48093 t) 586-573-5000 paula.caruso@ascension.org healthcare.ascension.org A member of Ascension Michigan. Christopher McClead; Bed Capacity: 511; Asstd. Annu.: 267,676; Staff: 2,642

MISCELLANEOUS [MIS]

BLOOMFIELD HILLS

Clarkston Pastoral Center, Inc. - 2460 Opdyke Rd., Bloomfield Hills, MI 48304 t) (770) 828-4950 fformolo@legionaries.org Rev. Jason Brooks, L.C., Admin.; Rev. Frank Formolo, Secy.;

***Mary's Mantle** - ; Mailing: PO Box 115, Bloomfield Hills, MI 48303 t) 248-376-5338 info@marysmantle.net www.marysmantle.net Katie Montes, Dir.;

Opdyke, Inc. - 2460 Opdyke Rd., Bloomfield Hills, MI 48304 t) (770) 828-4950 fformolo@arcol.org Rev. Frank Formolo, Secy.;

BROWNSTOWN

Magnificat - Detroit, MI Chapter - 24353 Sand Lake Ln., Brownstown, MI 48134 t) 734-771-4151 gramma627@hotmail.com

CANTON

***Trinity Health-Michigan** - 1600 Canton Center Rd., Ste. 300, Canton, MI 48188 t) 734-343-1000 moorej@trinity-health.org www.trinity-health.org Organization owns & operates 6 hospital divisions in Michigan. Robert Casalou, Pres. & CEO;

CLINTON TOWNSHIP

Catholic Charities of Southeast Michigan - 15945 Canal Rd., Clinton Township, MI 48038 t) 855-882-2736 info@ccsem.org; agbyi@ccsem.org www.ccsem.org Paul Propson, CEO;

DEARBORN HEIGHTS

Council of Catholic Women Archdiocese of Detroit - ; Mailing: P.O. Box 10, Dearborn Heights, MI 48127 t) 586-731-6894 sharondege@wowway.com Sharon Di Giovanni, Pres.;

DETROIT

Acts XXIX - Mobilizing for Mission - 1050 Porter St., Detroit, MI 48226 t) 313-315-3320 info@actsxxix.org www.actsxxix.org/ Church renewal and transformation Rev. John Riccardo, Exec.;

All Saints Literacy Center - 3553 W. Vernor Hwy., Ste. D, Detroit, MI 48216 t) 313-297-1399 info@allsaintsliteracy.org www.allsaintsliteracy.org/ Roger Frank, Dir.;

Cabrini Clinic - 1050 Porter St., Detroit, MI 48226 t) 303-965-4450 contactus@cabriniclinic.org www.cabriniclinic.org Rev. Msgr. Charles G. Kosanke, Contact;

Christ Child Society (Christ Child House) - 15751 Joy Rd., Detroit, MI 48228 t) 313-584-6077 christchildsocietydetroit@gmail.com ccsdetroit.org Christ Child Society is a non-profit organization serving children-in-need throughout metropolitan Detroit. Elaina Ryder, Pres.; Rev. Msgr. John P. Zenz, Mem.;

Priest Health Plan - 12 State St., Chancery Bldg., Detroit, MI 48226 t) 313-237-5803 austin.richard@aod.org Dan Oliver, Contact;

St. Dominic Outreach Center - 4826 Lincoln, Detroit, MI 48208 t) 313-831-6070 stdominiccenter@aol.com www.stdominicoutreach.org/ Rev. Mario V. Amore, Admin.;

Dominican Literacy Center - 5555 Conner Ave., Ste. 1414, Detroit, MI 48213 t) 313-267-1000 kwilliams@dlcliteracy.org www.dlcliteracy.org Adult Basic Education, GED preparation, English as a Second Language instruction Kimberly Williams, Dir.;

Gabriel Richard Historical Society - 1000 Ste. Anne St., Detroit, MI 48216 t) 313-496-1701 businessoffice@steannedetroit.org Rev. Msgr. Charles G. Kosanke;

Institute for Communal Contemplation and Dialogue - 8531 W. McNichols, Detroit, MI 48221 t) 313-971-3668 nsylvester@aol.com www.iccdinstitute.org Sr. Nancy Sylvester, I.H.M., Exec.;

Jesuit Volunteer Corps. - 7333 W. Seven Mile Rd., Detroit, MI 48221; Mailing: P.O. Box 21936, Detroit, MI 48221-0936 t) 313-345-3480 jvcmw@jesuitvolunteers.org www.jesuitvolunteers.org DeGarmo Ben, Bus. Mgr.;

Latino Cultural Pastoral Center - 4329 Central, Detroit, MI 48210 Dcn. Raul Feliciano, Contact;

***Mercy Education Project** - 1450 Howard St., Detroit, MI 48216 t) 313-963-5881 mep@mercyed.net; hraubenolt@mercyed.net www.mercyed.net Heidi Marie Raubenolt, Exec.;

Mooney Real Estate Holdings - 12 State St., Detroit, MI 48226 t) 313-393-7574 Christopher Dine, Contact;

***St. Patrick Senior Center, Inc.** - 58 Parsons St., Detroit, MI 48201-2202 t) 313-833-7080 info@stpatsrctr.org www.stpatsrctr.org Senior Center SaTrice Coleman-Betts, Exec.;

***Pope Francis Center** - 438 St. Antoine St., Detroit, MI 48226 t) 313-964-2823 info@popefranciscenter.org www.popefranciscenter.org Homeless warming center Rev. Timothy McCabe, S.J.;

Siena Literacy Center - 16888 Trinity St., Detroit, MI 48219 t) 313-532-8404 jbrown@sienaliteracy.org www.sienaliteracy.org Sr. Janice Brown, OP, Dir.;

SJH Legacy, Inc, - 12 State St., Detroit, MI 48226 t) 313-237-5764 Formerly St. John's Holdings, Inc. Dan Oliver, Contact;

Solanus Casey Center - 1780 Mt. Elliott, Detroit, MI 48207-3596 t) 313-579-2100 srkropp@gmail.com www.solanuscaseycenter.org Rev. Steven R. Kropp, O.F.M.Cap., Dir.; Rev. Raymond Chinnappan, OFM Cap, Assoc. Dir.; Rev. George Kooran, Pst. Min./Coord.; Bro. Richard Merling, O.F.M.Cap., Solanus Heritage Project; Angela Morris, Mgr.;

***St. Suzanne Cody Rouge Community Resource Center** - 19321 W. Chicago, Detroit, MI 48228 t) 313-493-9129 waskosteve@aol.com; stsuzannecrc@gmail.com www.stsuzannecodyrouge.org Steven Wasko, Dir.;

FARMINGTON HILLS

***Cranbrook Hospice Care (St. Joseph Mercy Home Care and Hospice)** - 34505 W. 12 Mile Rd, Ste. 100, Farmington Hills, MI 48331 t) 855-559-7178 erin.denholm@trinity-health.org www.trinityhealthathome.org Erin Denholm, Pres.;

Dominican Center for Religious Development - 29000 W. 11 Mile Rd., Farmington Hills, MI 48336 t) 248-536-3142 director@dominicancenter.org www.dominicancenter.org Rev. Victor Clore; Sr. Adrienne Schaffer, O.P., Dir.;

Living Faith - Fine Arts Apostolate - 36703 Kenmore Dr., Farmington Hills, MI 48335 t) 248-444-1034 kelly@crossandlight.com www.crossandlight.com Kelly Nieto, Pres.;

Mercy Homecare - Oakland - 34505 W. 12 Mile Rd, Ste. 100, Farmington Hills, MI 48331 t) 855-559-7178 erin.denholm@trinity-health.org www.trinityhealthathome.org Erin Denholm, Pres.;

LAKE ORION

Guest House, Inc. - 1601 Joslyn Rd., Lake Orion, MI 48360 t) 248-393-8913 info@guesthouse.org; jhenrich@guesthouse.org www.guesthouse.org State licensed, CARF-accredited residential addiction treatment center for priests, brothers, deacons, seminarians, sisters and women in formation. Jeff Henrich, Pres.;

Guest House - Men's Program - 1720 W. Scipps Rd., Lake Orion, MI 48360; Mailing: 1601 Joslyn Rd., Lake Orion, MI 48360 t) 800-626-6910; 248-393-0186 dbell@guesthouse.org guesthouse.org

Guest House for Women Religious - 1740 W. Scripps Rd., Lake Orion, MI 48360 t) 800-626-6910 dbell@guesthouse.org Residential treatment center for Catholic sisters and women in formation. Sr. Julie Bruss, Outreach to Women Religious;

LEXINGTON

Camp Stapleton - 3753 Lakeshore Rd., Lexington, MI 48450; Mailing: 3000 Gratiot Ave., Detroit, MI 48207 t) (313) 393-2899 (Rental Inquiry); (313) 393-2871 (Other) jhohner@svdpdetroit.org www.svdpdet.org Former SVdP girls summer camp now available as rental property for retreats, sports camps, reunions, and more. Julia Hohner, Dir.;

LIVONIA

Catholic Biblical School of Michigan, Ltd. - 16138 Southampton, Livonia, MI 48154; Mailing: 14200 E. Ten Mile Rd., Warren, MI 48089 t) 313-570-8105 fmorath@msn.com cbsmich.org Dr. Peter S Williamson, Chair; Frederick Lawrence Morath, Pres.;

CHE Trinity, Inc. - 20555 Victor Pkwy., Livonia, MI 48152 t) 734-343-1392 moorej@trinity-health.org Michael Slubowski, Pres.;

Marian Village Corporation (Marywood Nursing Care Center) - 36975 Five Mile Rd., Livonia, MI 48154 t) 734-464-0600 j.mimnaugh@marywoodncc.com www.marywoodnursingcarecenter.org John Mimnaugh, Pres.;

Mercy Services for Aging, Non-profit Housing Corporation - 17410 College Pkwy., Ste. 200, Livonia, MI 48152-2363 t) 248-656-6300 steven.kastner@trinity-health.org www.trinityhealthseniorcommunities.org/ Wholly owned subsidiary of Trinity Continuing Care Services Steven Kastner, Pres.;

Trinity Continuing Care Services - Indiana, Inc. - 20555 Victor Pkwy., Livonia, MI 48152-2363 t) (734) 343-6634 megan.leblanc@trinity-health.org www.trinityhealthseniorcommunities.org/

Trinity Continuing Care Services - Massachusetts - 20555 Victor Pkwy., Livonia, MI 48152 t) 734-343-6634 Janice Hamilton-Crawford, Pres.;

***Trinity Health Corporation** - 20555 Victor Pkwy., Livonia, MI 48152 t) 734-343-1000 moorej@trinity-health.org www.trinity-health.org Michael Slubowski, Pres. & CEO;

Trinity Health PACE - 20555 Victor Pkwy., Livonia, MI 48152-7018 t) 734-343-1000 murraym@trinity-health.org www.trinityhealthpace.org/ Daniel Drake, Pres.;

Trinity Home Health Services - 17410 College Pkwy., Ste. 150, Livonia, MI 48152 t) 877-827-0788 murraym@trinity-health.org www.trinityhomehealth.org Mark McPherson, CEO;

MACOMB

National Alliance of Parishes Restructuring into Communities (NAPRC) - 23375 Spring Creek Dr., Macomb, MI 48042 t) 800-214-9909 naprc.net/ Rev. Arthur R. Baranowski, Dir.;

PLEASANT RIDGE

The Cardinal Club of Detroit - 19 Elm Park Blvd., Pleasant Ridge, MI 48069 c) 248-310-0538 andrew.curoe@outlook.com Andrew Curoe, Contact;

PLYMOUTH

***New Leaven Inc.** - 51275 Northview, Plymouth, MI 48170 t) 313-268-7265 newleavenfinance@gmail.com newleaven.org Dcn. Robert Ervin, Pres.; Francisco Gavrilides, Vice. Pres.; Edward Connolly, Treas.;

PONTIAC

***Terra Sancta Pilgrimages** - 400 South Blvd., W., Pontiac, MI 48341 t) 313-727-9784 abunaalex@yahoo.com mothermarypontiac.org Patricia Giangrande, O.F.S., Dir.; Rev. Alex Kratz, OFM, Dir.;

ROCHESTER

Catholic Kolping Society of America, Detroit Branch, Inc. - 1201 Rock Valley Dr., Rochester, MI 48307 t) 248-650-6275 cjl961@aol.com Matthew Tiza, Pres.; Mary Dolland, Treas.;

SHELBY TWP.

Holy Trinity Apostolate - 53565 Sherwood Ln., Shelby

Twp., MI 48315 t) 586-781-6051 barbaramm@sbcglobal.net Founded by Servant of God, Rev. John A. Hardon, S.J. Barbara Middleton, Pres.;

SOUTH LYON

***Christ Music** - 22510 Clarkshire Dr., South Lyon, MI 48178 t) 717-324-7469 christmusic2002@gmail.com Martin Doman, Pres.;

SOUTHFIELD

***Mother and Unborn Baby Care Inc.** - 24500 Southfield Rd., Southfield, MI 48075; Mailing: P.O. Box 3250, Southfield, MI 48037 t) 248-559-7576 www.maubc.org Michael J. O'Dea, Founder;

STERLING HEIGHTS

***Retrouvaille of Metro Detroit** - 12900 Hall Rd., Ste. 400, Sterling Heights, MI 48313 t) 248-382-8281 Sean House, Contact; Tess House, Contact;

WARREN

St. John Providence (St. John Providence Health System, St. John Health, St. John Health System, St. John Health Corporation, St. Clair Health Corporation, St. Clair Health Services Corporation) - 28000 Dequindre Rd., Warren, MI 48092 t) 586-753-0911 paula.caruso@ascension.org ascension.org A member of Ascension Michigan Kenneth Berkovitz, CEO;

WATERFORD

Dominican Health Care Corporation - 2300 Walkins Lake Rd., Waterford, MI 48328 t) 248-886-5600 cburke@lourdes-sc.org www.lourdes-sc.org Sr. Maureen Comer, O.P., CEO;

WESTLAND

Chinese Catholic Society of Michigan, Inc. - 39375 Joy Rd., Westland, MI 48185 t) 248-855-4517 Francis G. King, Pres.; Thomas McGuire, Dir.;

WYANDOTTE

Detroit Catholic Charismatic Renewal Center - 2322 Ford Ave, Wyandotte, MI 48192-2317 t) 734-282-6244 dccrcenter@aol.com www.dccr.info Arlene Apone, Dir.;

MONASTERIES AND RESIDENCES FOR PRIESTS AND BROTHERS [MON]

BERKLEY

Dun Scotus Friary - 2600 Harvard Rd., Berkley, MI 48072 c) 412-417-8472 michaellenzofm@gmail.com Rev. Michael George Lenz, OFM, Supr.; Rev. Dennet Jung, OFM, Vicar; Bro. Albert Mascia, OFM, Treas.; Bro. Michael Dubec, OFM, In Res.; Bro. Michael Radomski, OFM, In Res.; Brs.: 3; Priests: 2

BLOOMFIELD HILLS

Congregation of Christian Brothers, Mater Dei Community - 7350 Parkstone Ln., Bloomfield Hills, MI 48301 t) 248-258-1186 c) 815-272-7742 bromaccfc@yahoo.com Bro. Arthur M. Arndt, Mem.; Bro. Daniel J. Casey, Mem.; Bro. James McDonald, Mem.; Bro. Daniel Thomas LeJeune, CFC, Contact; Brs.: 4

CLARKSTON

Colombiere Center - 9075 Big Lake Rd., Clarkston, MI 48346-1015 t) 248-625-5611 colombiere@colombiere.com www.colombierejesuits.com Jesuit Health Care Community for the United States Midwest Province Rev. Bradley M. Schaeffer, S.J., Supr.; Rev. R. Gerard Albright, S.J., In Res.; Rev. Dennis Ahern, S.J., In Res.; Rev. James C.L. Arimond, S.J., In Res.; Rev. Carl A. Bonk, S.J., In Res.; Rev. Francis E. Canfield, S.J., In Res.; Rev. Eugene Carmichael, S.J., In Res.; Rev. James J. Creighton, S.J., In Res.; Rev. Dennis T. Dillon, S.J., In Res.; Rev. Denis Dirscherl, In Res.; Rev. Gene Donatelli, S.J., In Res.; Rev. Keith J. Esenther, S.J., In Res.; Rev. John M. Ferone, S.J., In Res.; Rev. John P. Foley, S.J., In Res.; Rev. Joseph D. Folzenlogen, S.J., In Res.; Rev. Dennis T. Glasgow, S.J., In Res.; Rev. John P. Heim, S.J., In Res.; Rev. John L. Kieffer, S.J., In Res.; Rev. George Lane, S.J., In Res.; Rev. John F. Libens, S.J., In Res.; Rev. Daniel P. Liderbach, S.J., In Res.; Bro. John P. Martin, S.J., In Res.; Rev. Jerome K. Odbert, S.J., In Res.; Bro. Michael O'Grady, S.J., In Res.; Rev. Patrick Peppard, In Res.; Rev. Paul Peterson, S.J., In Res.; Rev. Cletus H. Pfab, S.J., In Res.; Bro. Jerome Pryor, S.J., In Res.; Rev. Theodore C. Ross, S.J., In Res.; Rev. John A. Saliba, S.J., In Res.; Rev. L. Harold Sanford, S.J., In Res.; Rev. James W. Schulzi, S.J., In Res.; Rev. Robert T. Sears, S.J., In Res.; Bro. James E. Small, S.J., In Res.; Rev. John M. Staudenmaier, S.J., In Res.; Rev. James A. Stoeger, S.J., In Res.; Rev. James Strzok, S.J., In Res.; Rev. Richard H. Twohig, S.J., In Res.; Rev. Benjamin J. Urmston, S.J., In Res.; Rev. George Von Kaenel, In Res.; Bro. Denis Weber, S.J., In Res.; Rev. Jared Wicks, In Res.; Brs.: 5; Priests: 37

DEARBORN HEIGHTS

All Saints Friary - 23755 Military Rd., Dearborn Heights, MI 48127 t) 313-278-5129 mariebernardolol@hotmail.com www.franciscancommunity.com (This is a subsidiary of St. Bonaventure, Chicago, IL.) Bro. James O'Brien, O.F.M.Conv.; Brs.: 1; Priests: 2

Mariannhill Mission Society - 23715 Ann Arbor Tr., Dearborn Heights, MI 48127-1449 t) 313-561-7140; 313-561-8888; 313-561-2330 cmm-usa@juno.com www.mariannhill.us Leaves Magazine, Congregation of the Missionaries of Mariannhill, Mariannhill Fathers, Mariannhill Missionaries Rev. Raymond Lucasinsky, C.M.M., Supr.; Rev. Thomas Szura, C.M.M., Supr.; Rev. Kevin O'Doherty, C.M.M.; Rev. Thomas Heier, C.M.M., Editor; Bro. James Miller, C.M.M., Bus. Mgr.; Rev. Vergil Heier, C.M.M., In Res.; Rev. Michael Sheehy, C.M.M., In Res.; Brs.: 1; Priests: 6

DETROIT

St. Bonaventure Monastery - 1740 Mt. Elliott Ave., Detroit, MI 48207-3496 t) 313-579-2100 whugo@thecapuchins.org www.thecapuchins.org Province of St. Joseph of the Capuchin Order, Inc. Bro. Nicholas Blattner, OFM Cap., Dir.; Rev. Raymond Chinnappan, OFM Cap, Assoc. Dir.; Rev. Mark Joseph Costello, O.F.M. Cap., Prov.; Rev. William Hugo, Admin.; Rev. George Kooran, Pst. Min./Coord.; Rev. David Preuss, O.F.M.Cap., Pst. Min./Coord.; Rev. Daniel Crosby, OFM Cap., Pst. Assoc.; Rev. Anthony Kote-Witah, Pst. Assoc.; Rev. Steven R. Kropp, O.F.M.Cap., Vicar; Rev. Patrick McSherry, O.F.M.Cap., Rome Assignment; Rev. Daniel J. Fox, O.F.M.Cap., Saginaw Assignment; Rev. Jose Savior, Archivist; Rev. Francis Voris, OFM Cap., Saginaw Assignment; Rev. Gary Wegner, O.F.M. Cap., In Res.; Rev. Albert Sandor, O.F.M.Cap., In Res.; Rev. Art Cooney, In Res.; Rev. Philip Naessens, O.F.M.Cap., In Res.; Rev. James Andres, O.F.M.Cap., In Res.; Rev. Dijan Michael Pattamparambil, In Res.; Rev. Bede Louzon, O.F.M.Cap., In Res.; Rev. James Hast, OFM Cap., In Res.; Rev. Robert Wotypka, In Res.; Bro. Gebreyesus Boyine, OFM Cap., Pst. Min./Coord.; Bro. Igor De Bliquy, Pst. Min./Coord.; Bro. Tien Dinh, O.F.M. Cap., Rel. Ord. Ldr.; Bro. Michael Gaffney, O.F.M.Cap., In Res.; Bro. Larry LaCross, O.F.M.Cap., In Res.; Bro. Richard Merling, O.F.M.Cap., Solanus Casey History; Brs.: 34; Priests: 84

Provincialate - 1820 Mt. Elliott Ave., Detroit, MI 48207-3485 dpiontkowski@thecapuchins.org Rev. Vito Santiago Martinez, O.F.M. Cap., Communications Dir.; Diane Simpkins, Treas.;

Companions of the Cross - Visitation House, 17330 Quincy St., Detroit, MI 48221 t) 866-885-8824 Rev. Rick Jaworski, C.C., Supr.; Brs.: 13; Priests: 6

Institute of Christ the King Sovereign Priest, Inc. - 1828 Jay St., Detroit, MI 48207 t) (313) 784-9152 www.institute-christ-king.org Rev. Msgr. R. Michael Schmitz, Vicar Gen.; Rev. Canon Matthew L. Talarico, Prov.;

Jesuit Community at the University of Detroit Mercy - 4001 W. McNichols Rd., Lansing-Reilly Hall, Detroit, MI 48221-3038 t) 313-993-1625 lrjesuit@gmail.com (Corporate Title: The Jesuit Community Corporation at the University of Detroit). Rev. Gary R. Wright, S.J., Pst.; Rev. Jeffrey R Dorr, S.J., Assoc. Pst.; Rev. Gilbert Sunghera, S.J., Rector; Rev. Donald Vettese, Chap.; Rev. Mark George, S.J., Chap.; Rev. Joel G. Medina, S.J., Chap.; Rev. J. Timothy Hipskind, S.J., Admin.; Rev. Timothy McCabe, S.J., Admin.; Rev. Bernard Owens, S.J., Prof.; Rev. Justin J. Kelly, S.J., Prof.; Rev. Patrick M. Kelly, S.J., Prof.; Rev. Simon J. Hendry, S.J., Prof.; Rev. Stephen F. Hurd, S.J.; Bro. Denis Weber, S.J., Admin.; Bro. Richard D. Hittle, S.J., Editor; Cleophas Owino Odinga, S.J., Scholastic; Brs.: 2; Priests: 14

St. Mary's Friary - 1057 Parker, Detroit, MI 48214-2612 t) 313-821-5883 fcabras05@gmail.com www.thecapuchins.org Rev. Fred Cabras, O.F.M. Cap., Pst. Min./Coord.; Rev. Tom Nguyen, OFM Cap., In Res.; Bro. Tien Dinh, O.F.M. Cap., In Res.; Bro. Rob Roemer, O.F.M.Cap., In Res.; Bro. Joseph Monachino, O.F.M.Cap., In Res.; Brs.: 34; Priests: 84

St. Paul of the Cross Community, Congregation of the Passion - 23335 Schoolcraft, Detroit, MI 48223 t) (313) 531-9563 thepassionistsdetroit@gmail.com A center for the Passionist Fathers & Brothers in mid-western & north central United States. Rev. Patrick Brennan, C.P., Dir.; Rev. Enno H Dango, CP, Supr.; Rev. Alex Steinmiller, CP, Mem.; Rev. Richard Cassidy, In Res.; Rev. John Phelps, C.Ss.R., In Res.; Bro. Raymond Sanchez, C.P., Mem.; Brs.: 1; Priests: 3

PIME Missionaries - 17330 Quincy St., Detroit, MI 48221 t) 313-342-4066 info@pimeusa.org www.pimeusa.org (Pontifical Institute for Foreign Missions) Rev. Kenneth Mazur, PIME, Supr.; Rev. Daniele Criscione, PIME, Mission Center Dir.; Rev. Dennis Koltz, PIME, Treas.; Rev. Marco Brioschi, PIME, Councilor; Rev. Phillip Mayfield, PIME, Councilor & Rector; Rev. George Berendt, PIME, Mem., Delegation; Rev. Bruno Piccolo, PIME, Mem., Delegation; Priests: 10

GROSSE POINTE PARK

Congregation of St. Michael the Archangel - Michaelite Fathers - 1401 Whittier Rd., Grosse Pointe Park, MI 48230 t) 313-647-5030 www.michaelites.ca Rev. Andrzej Kowalczyk, C.S.M.A., Pst.; Rev. Tomasz Wilisowski, C.S.M.A., Admin.; Priests: 2

OXFORD

St. Benedict Monastery - 2711 Drahner Rd, Oxford, MI 48370 t) 248-628-2249 Rev. Damien Gjonaj, O.S.B., Prior; Rev. Gregory David Jones, O.S.B., Subprior; Rev. John Martin Shimkus, O.S.B., Treas.; Rev. Michael R. Green, O.S.B., Mem.; Brs.: 3; Priests: 4

REDFORD

Society of the Catholic Apostolate-Indian Province of the State of Michigan - 17116 Olympia Ave., Redford, MI 48240; Mailing: 1651 Kingsway Ct., Trenton, MI 48183 t) 313-534-9000 socorro313@gmail.com Rev. Hendrico Rebello, SAC, Supr.; Rev. Socorro Fernandes, S.A.C., Secy.; Priests: 25

SOUTH LYON

Miles Christi - 25300 Johns Rd., South Lyon, MI 48178 t) 248-596-9677 infousa@mileschristi.org www.mileschristi.org Rev. Caesar Bertolacci, MC, Supr.; Brs.: 1; Priests: 3

WYANDOTTE

Society of the Catholic Apostolate (Pallottine Fathers) - 3352 Fourth St., Wyandotte, MI 48192 t) 734-285-2966 office@irishpallottines.org; frbrendan@irishpallottins.org www.irishpallottines.org Pallottine Fathers (Irish Province) Rev. Brendan Joseph McCarrick, S.A.C. (Ireland), Pres.; Very Rev. Michael T. O'Sullivan, S.A.C., Treas.; Rev. Emmet O'Hara, S.A.C, Secy.; Rev. James Amasi; Rev. Stephen Muli Mutie, SAC (Kenya); Rev. Matthew Sanka, S.A.C.; Rev. Lawrence Gould, SAC (Ireland), In Res.; Bro. Faustino Paez, S.A.C., In Res.; Brs.: 1; Priests: 7

Pallottine Missionary Center (Irish Province) - 424 Orange St., Wyandotte, MI 48192 t) (734) 282-2966 office@irishpallottins.org Irish Pallottine Fathers. Rev. Brendan McCarrick, S.A.C. (Ireland), Secy.; Rev. John Kelly, S.A.C., Treas.;

NURSING / REHABILITATION / CONVALESCENCE / ELDERLY CARE [NUR]

CLINTON TOWNSHIP

A Friend's House Adult Day Services - 15945 Canal Rd., Clinton Township, MI 48038 t) 586-412-8494 info@ccsem.org www.ccsem.org Daytime care for older adults. Support services for caregiving families. A service of Catholic Services of Southeast Michigan. Hershell Masten, Dir.;

Clinton Villa - 17825 Fifteen Mile Rd., Clinton Township, MI 48035 t) 586-792-0358 kaylsj@trinity-health.org www.trinityhealthseniorcommunities.org Part of St. Joseph Mercy Senior Communities. Sheri Kayl, Admin.;

FARMINGTON HILLS

Marian Oakland - 29250 W. Ten Mile Rd., Farmington Hills, MI 48336 t) 248-474-7204 angela.walton@trinity-health.org www.trinityhealthseniorcommunities.org Part of St. Joseph Mercy Senior Communities. Angela Walton, Admin.;

FORT GRATIOT

Sanctuary at Mercy Village - 4170 24th Ave., Fort Gratiot, MI 48059 t) 810-989-7440 warshekk@trinity-health.org www.trinityhealthseniorcommunities.org (A member of Trinity Senior Living Communities) Kelsey Warshefski, Admin.;

IMLAY CITY

Maple Vista - 600 Maple Vista, Imlay City, MI 48444 t) 810-724-6300 ehrlichr@trinity-health.org www.trinityhealthseniorcommunities.org Part of St. Joseph Mercy Senior Communities.

LIVONIA

Marywood Nursing Care Center - 36975 Five Mile Rd., Livonia, MI 48154 t) 734-464-0600 j.mimnaugh@marywoodncc.com www.marywoodnursingcarecenter.org Skilled Nursing Facility. John Mimnaugh, Admin.; Staff: 200

Senior Clergy Village of Livonia, Inc. - 14461 Levan Rd., Livonia, MI 48154 t) 734-838-0457 info@seniorclergyvillage.org www.seniorclergyvillage.org Karen Richter, Admin.; Sr. Beatrice Marie Plamondon, Dir.; Asstd. Annu.: 20; Staff: 3

Trinity Continuing Care Services - 20555 Victor Pkwy., Livonia, MI 48152-2363 t) (734) 343-6634 murraym@trinity-health.org www.trinityhealthseniorcommunities.org/ Janice Hamilton-Crawford, Pres.; Asstd. Annu.: 6,000; Staff: 2,300

Villa Marie - 15131 Newburgh, Livonia, MI 48154 t) 734-464-9494 sharon.cuddington@trinity-health.org www.trinityhealthseniorcommunities.org Part of St. Joseph Mercy Senior Communities.

MONROE

IHM Senior Living Community, Inc. - 610 W. Elm Ave., Monroe, MI 48162 t) 734-240-8230 info@ihmsisters.org www.ihmslc.org/ Nicole Kennedy, Dir.; Christine Horney, Dir.; Asstd. Annu.: 152; Staff: 114

Marian Place - 408 W. Front St., Monroe, MI 48161 t) 734-241-2414 www.trinityhealthseniorcommunities.org Part of Trinity Health Senior Communities. Asstd. Annu.: 60; Staff: 11

SOUTHGATE

Maryhaven - 11350 Reeck Rd., Southgate, MI 48195 t) 734-287-2111 dewyerm@trinity-health.org www.trinityhealthseniorcommunities.org Part of St. Joseph Mercy Senior Communities. Melissa Dewyer, Admin.;

WATERFORD

Fox Manor, Inc. - 2350 Watkins Lake Rd., Waterford, MI 48328 t) 248-674-9590 racho@lourdes-sc.org www.lourdesseniorcommunity.org Residential facility for independent senior citizens of moderate or limited means. Dominican Sisters of Peace. Richard Acho, CEO; Robin McClintock, Dir.; Asstd. Annu.: 63; Staff: 14

Lourdes Assisted Living Corporation (Joseph T. Mendelson Assisted Living Home) - 2450 Watkins Lake Rd., Waterford, MI 48328 t) 248-886-5100 racho@lourdes-sc.org www.lourdesseniorcommunity.org Residential facility for independent senior citizens requiring assistance with activities of daily living. Richard Acho, CEO; Robin McClintock, Dir.; Asstd. Annu.: 83; Staff: 63

Lourdes Nursing Home (Lourdes Rehabilitation and Healthcare Center) - 2300 Watkins Lake Rd., Waterford, MI 48328 t) 248-886-5600; 248-674-2241 racho@lourdes-sc.org www.lourdesseniorcommunity.org Skilled & basic nursing facility for rehabilitation and 24 hour nursing care. Richard Acho, CEO; Maureen McGee, Admin.; Asstd. Annu.: 191; Staff: 149

PRESCHOOLS / CHILDCARE CENTERS [PRE]

CARSONVILLE

Camp Ozanam - 7303 Walker Rd., Carsonville, MI 48419; Mailing: 3000 Gratiot Ave., Detroit, MI 48207 t) (313) 393-2899 (Rental/Registration); (313) 393-2871 (Other) jhohner@svdpdetroit.org www.svdpdet.org A free week-long Christian camping experience for boys and girls 8-14. Recruitment through Parish Conferences of the Society of St. Vincent de Paul. Julia Hohner, Dir.; Stds.: 243

CLINTON TOWNSHIP

King House-Holy Cross Services - 24455 Crocker Blvd., Clinton Township, MI 48036; Mailing: 1013 N. River Rd., Saginaw, MI 48609 t) 586-463-7130; 989-596-3557 cdevaux@hccsnet.org www.holycrossservices.org (part of HCCS, Diocese of Lansing) Sharon Berkobien, CEO;

DEARBORN HEIGHTS

Vista Maria - 20651 W. Warren Ave., Dearborn Heights, MI 48127 t) 313-271-3050 info@vistamaria.org www.vistamaria.org Residential treatment programs for adolescent girls. Community-based programs, including foster care and after school programs for boys and girls. Angela Aufdemberge, Pres.; Stds.: 100

DETROIT

Holy Cross Services-Bowman House - 17200 Rowe St., Detroit, MI 48205; Mailing: 1013 N. River Rd., Saginaw, MI 48609 t) 313-469-8152; 989-596-3557 cdevaux@hccsnet.org www.holycrossservices.org (part of HCCS, Diocese of Lansing) Sharon Berkobien, CEO;

C.Y.O. Boys Camp - 12 State St., Detroit, MI 48226 t) 313-963-7172 info@cyodetroit.org Michael Shapiro, Exec. Dir.;

C.Y.O. Girls Camp - 12 State St., Detroit, MI 48226 t) 313-963-7172 info@cyodetroit.org www.cyocamps.org Michael Shapiro, Exec. Dir.;

Christ Child House - 15751 Joy Rd., Detroit, MI 48228 t) 313-584-6077 mlessnau@christchildhouse.org www.christchildhouse.org Non-profit residential facility Maria Elaina Lessnau, Exec.; Stds.: 20; Lay Tchrs.: 1

LIVONIA

Felician Sisters Child Care Centers, Inc. (Montessori Center of Our Lady Child Care Center and Montessori School; St. Mary Child Care Center) - 14200 Newburgh Rd., Livonia, MI 48154; Mailing: PO Box 532437, Livonia, MI 48153 t) 734-793-3853 (Gail Jones); 734-793-3852 (Karen Richter) k.richter@feliciansisters.org; g.jones@feliciansisters.org www.fsccc.org Montessori Center of Our Lady Child Care Center and Montessori School; St. Mary Child Care Center and St. Joseph Child Care Center Karen Richter, Pres.; Gail Jones, Dir.; Stds.: 209; Lay Tchrs.: 87

RETREAT HOUSES / RENEWAL CENTERS [RTR]

BLOOMFIELD HILLS

Manresa Jesuit Retreat House - 1390 Quarton Rd., Bloomfield Hills, MI 48304-3554 t) 248-644-4933 office@manresa-sj.org www.manresa-sj.org Rev. Peter J. Fennessy, S.J., Supr.; Rev. Leo P. Cachat, S.J., Dir.; Rev. Francis J. Daly, S.J., Dir.; Rev. Robert Stanley Flack, SJ, Dir.; Rev. Robert J. Scullin, S.J., Dir.; Sr. Linda Sevcik, S.M., Exec. Dir.; Steve Raymond, Assoc. Dir.;

Queen of the Family Retreat Center - 2460 Opdyke Rd., Bloomfield Hills, MI 48304 t) (770) 828-4950 Rev. Jason Brooks, L.C., Pres.;

Visitation North Spirituality Center - 7227 Lahser Rd., Bloomfield Hills, MI 48301 t) 248-433-0950 visitationnorth@ihmsisters.org www.visitationnorth.org Sr. Kathleen Budesky, Dir.;

DETROIT

St. Paul of the Cross Passionist Retreat and Conference Center - 23333 Schoolcraft Rd., Detroit, MI 48223-2499 t) 313-535-9563 info@stpaulretreat.org stpaulretreat.org Conducted by the Passionist Community. Rev. Enno H Dango, CP, Supr.; Rev. Pat Brennan, C.P., Dir.; Faith Offman, Dir.;

MONROE

River House - IHM Spirituality Center - 805 W. Elm Ave., Monroe, MI 48162 t) 734-240-5494 riverhouse@ihmsisters.org www.ihmsisters.org Sponsorship of I.H.M. Congregation. Sr. Julie Vieira, IHM, Dir.; Sr. Judith Bonini, Spiritual Direction; Cristy Smith, Coord.;

WASHINGTON

Capuchin Retreat - 62460 Mt. Vernon Rd., Washington, MI 48094; Mailing: P.O. Box 396, Washington, MI 48094 t) 248-651-4826 info@capretreat.org www.capretreat.org Rev. Vito Santiago Martinez, O.F.M. Cap., Dir.; Rev. Anton y Milton, Pst. Assoc.; Rev. Biju Parakkalayil, Pst. Min./Coord.; Rev. Michael Sullivan, O.F.M.Cap., In Res.; Bro. Bob Malloy, O.F.M.Cap., In Res.;

SEMINARIES [SEM]

DETROIT

Sacred Heart Major Seminary, Inc. - 2701 Chicago Blvd., Detroit, MI 48206 t) 313-883-8500 information@shms.org www.shms.edu Rev. Stephen Burr, Rector; Rev. Charles D. Fox, Vice Rector; Rev. Timothy A. Laboe, Dean; Astrid Caicedo, Dean; Leslie Jones, Registrar; Ann Marie Connolly, Dir.; Jane Jeffrey, Dir.; Kathryn Luberski, Dir.; Jeffrey Mesch, Dir.; Ryan Cahill, Dir.; Stds.: 410; Lay Tchrs.: 16; Pr. Tchrs.: 12

The College of Liberal Arts - t) (313) 883-8500 Rev. Clint W. McDonell, Dir., Undergraduate Seminarians; Stephanie Nofar-Kelly, Dir., Liturgical Music; Rev. Peter Ryan, S.J., Spiritual Dir., Undergraduate Seminarians; Teresa Lubienecki, Librn.;

The Institute for Lay Ministry (ILM) - t) 313-885-8300 Dr. Kevin Clarke, Dean;

The School of Theology - www.shms.edu/ Rev. Stephen Pullis, Dir., Graduate Pastoral Formation; Rev. Pieter vanRooyen, Dir., Graduate Seminarians; Rev. Msgr. Daniel J. Trapp, Graduate Spiritual Dir.; Stds.: 490; Lay Tchrs.: 16; Pr. Tchrs.: 12

ORCHARD LAKE

SS. Cyril and Methodius Seminary - 3535 Commerce Rd., Orchard Lake, MI 48324 t) (248) 836-1273 www.sscms.edu Rev. Bernard Witek, S.D.S., Rector; Rev. Gregory Banazak, Dean & Registrar; Pr. Tchrs.: 2

OXFORD

St. Benedict Monastery, House of Formation - 2711 Drahner Rd., Oxford, MI 48370 t) 248-628-2249 www.benedictinemonks.com Headquarters Novitiate House of Sylvestrine Benedictine Monks in the United States. Rev. Damien Gjonaj, O.S.B., Prior; Rev. Gregory David Jones, O.S.B., Junior Monk Dir.; Rev. John Martin Shimkus, O.S.B., Novice Dir.; Stds.: 1

SHRINES [SHR]

CLINTON TOWNSHIP

Servants of Jesus of The Divine Mercy - 33826 Beaconsfield, Clinton Township, MI 48035 t) 586-777-8591 info@divinemercy.org; jbeltowski@sjdivinemercy.org www.sjdivinemercy.org Catherine M. Lanni, Pres.; Jacqueline Beltowski, Grants Coord.;

SPECIAL CARE FACILITIES [SPF]

EASTPOINTE

St. John's Deaf Center - 16103 Chesterfield Ave.,

Eastpointe, MI 48021 t) 586-439-0146 depcik@oblates.us 26170.sites.ecatholic.com Rev. Michael Depcik, O.S.F.S., Dir.; Veronica Balcarcel, Pst. Min./Coord.; Paul Kuplicki, Bus. Mgr.; Asstd. Annu.: 150; Staff: 3

FRASER

Fraser Villa - 33300 Utica Rd., Fraser, MI 48026 t) 586-293-3300 delaneye@trinity-health.org www.trinityhealthseniorcommunities.org Part of St. Joseph Mercy Senior Communities. Libby Delaney, Exec.;

LIVONIA

***Angela Hospice Home Care, Inc.** - 14100 Newburgh Rd., Livonia, MI 48154-5010 t) 734-464-7810 www.angelahospice.org Marti A Coplai, CEO; Bed Capacity: 32; Asstd. Annu.: 1,768; Staff: 195

ROCHESTER HILLS

Bellbrook - 873 W. Avon Rd., Rochester Hills, MI 48307 t) 248-656-6300 steven.kastner@trinity-health.org www.trinityhealthseniorcommunities.org Part of St. Joseph Mercy Senior Communities. Steven Kastner, Pres.;

WATERFORD

Lourdes Alzheimers Special Care Center (Clausen Manor Memory Care) - 2400 Watkins Lake Rd., Waterford, MI 48328 t) 248-674-4732 racho@lourdes-sc.org; cburke@lourdes-sc.org www.lourdesseniorcommunity.org Richard Acho, CEO; Bed Capacity: 20; Asstd. Annu.: 32; Staff: 20

WHITE LAKE

The Neighborhoods of White Lake - 10770 Elizabeth Lake Rd., White Lake, MI 48386 t) 248-618-4100 steven.kastner@trinity-health.org www.trinityhealthseniorcommunities.org Part of St. Joseph Mercy Senior Communities. Steven Kastner, Pres.;

An asterisk (*) denotes an organization that has established tax-exempt status directly with the IRS and is not covered by the USCCB Group Ruling.

Diocese of Dodge City

(Dioecesis Dodgepolis)

MOST REVEREND JOHN B. BRUNGARDT

Bishop of Dodge City; ordained May 23, 1998; appointed Bishop of Dodge City December 15, 2010; installed February 2, 2011. Office: 910 Central Ave., P.O. Box 137, Dodge City, KS 67801-0137.

Catholic Church Offices: 910 Central Ave., P.O. Box 137, Dodge City, KS 67801-0137. T: 620-227-1500; F: 620-227-1545.

www.dcdiocese.org

dcdiocese@dcdiocese.org

ESTABLISHED MAY 19, 1951.

Square Miles 23,000.

Comprises the following Counties in the State of Kansas: Barton, Stafford, Pratt, Barber, Rush, Ness, Lane, Scott, Wichita, Greeley, Hamilton, Kearny, Finney, Hodgeman, Pawnee, Edwards, Ford, Gray, Haskell, Grant, Stanton, Morton, Stevens, Seward, Meade, Clark, Kiowa and Comanche.

Principal Patron: Our Lady of Guadalupe.

Secondary Patron: St. John the Baptist.

For legal titles of parishes and diocesan institutions, consult the Chancery Office.

STATISTICAL OVERVIEW

Personnel	
Bishop	1
Retired Bishops	2
Priests: Diocesan Active in Diocese	15
Priests: Retired, Sick or Absent	13
Number of Diocesan Priests	28
Religious Priests in Diocese	4
Total Priests in your Diocese	32
Extern Priests in Diocese	7
Ordinations:	
Diocesan Priests	1
Permanent Deacons in Diocese	6
Total Sisters	35
Parishes	
Parishes	47
With Resident Pastor:	
Resident Diocesan Priests	13
Resident Religious Priests	3
Without Resident Pastor:	
Administered by Priests	24
Administered by Lay People	1
Completely vacant	1
Missions	1
Professional Ministry Personnel:	
Sisters	9
Lay Ministers	19
Welfare	
Catholic Hospitals	1
Total Assisted	40,675
Homes for the Aged	1
Total Assisted	63
Special Centers for Social Services	2
Total Assisted	9,235
Educational	
Diocesan Students in Other Seminaries	4
Total Seminarians	4
Elementary Schools, Diocesan and Parish	6
Total Students	683
Catechesis/Religious Education:	
High School Students	850
Elementary Students	2,702
Total Students under Catholic Instruction	4,239
Teachers in Diocese:	
Lay Teachers	54
Vital Statistics	
Receptions into the Church:	
Infant Baptism Totals	646
Minor Baptism Totals	70
Adult Baptism Totals	27
Received into Full Communion	29
First Communions	570
Confirmations	712
Marriages:	
Catholic	95
Interfaith	32
Total Marriages	127
Deaths	432
Total Catholic Population	54,762
Total Population	206,129

LEADERSHIP

Chancery Office and Administration - t) 620-227-1500 dcdiocese@dcdiocese.org www.dcdiocese.org

Vicar General - t) 620-227-1555 vicargeneral@dcdiocese.org Rev. Ted D. Stoecklein, Vicar;

Chancellor - t) 620-227-1527 jgrochowsky@dcdiocese.org Sr. Janice Grochowsky, C.S.J.;

Diocesan Archivist Emeritus - t) 620-227-1556 Timothy F. Wenzl, Archivist;

Finance Officer - t) 620-227-1525 Theresa Tate;

Director of the Curia - t) 620-227-1531 gpaz@dcdiocese.org Georgina Paz;

Seminarians - t) 620-227-1533 Rev. Wesley W. Schawe, Dir.; Rev. Ted D. Stoecklein, Asst. Dir.; Rev. Jacob Schneider, Asst. Dir.;

Executive Secretary to the Bishop - t) 620-227-1530 executivesecretary@dcdiocese.org

Receptionist - t) 620-227-1500 receptionist@dcdiocese.org Monica Del Real, Receptionist;

Safe Environment -

Coordinator - t) 620-227-1531 Georgina Paz, Contact;

Reports of Suspected Abuse Made To - t) 620-285-3219 crbefort@cox.net Charles Befort;

Kansas Department for Children and Families - t) 800-922-5330

Kansas Bureau of Investigation - t) 800-572-7463 clergyabuse@kbi.ks.gov

Assistance Minister - c) (806) 678-5810 tracy@tsimpsoncpc.com Tracy Simpson-Turner, Assistance Min.;

Office of Stewardship - t) 620-227-1537 Eric Haselhorst, Dir.;

Office of Development -

Office of Finance - t) 620-227-1525 Theresa Tate, Dir.;

Tribunal - t) 620-227-1527 jgrochowsky@dcdiocese.org

Defender of the Bond - t) 620-355-6405 Rev. Peter Trong Tran;

Judge - t) (620) 356-1532 Rev. Charles Seiwert;

Judicial Vicar - Rev. John V. Hotze;

Notary - Sr. Janice Grochowsky, C.S.J.;

Promoter of Justice (Vacant) -

OFFICES AND DIRECTORS

Catholic Charities of Southwest Kansas - t) 620-227-1588 www.catholiccharitiesswks.org/ Debbie Snapp, Exec.;

Office of Matrimony, Family Life & Natural Family Planning - t) 620-227-1546 Diana Ramirez, Dir.; Rev. Ted A. Skalsky, Moderator;

Respect Life & Social Justice Activities - t) 620-227-1540 dcyouth@dcdiocese.org Emma Webs, Dir.;

Satellite Offices - t) 620-793-8075 (Sommerset Place); 620-792-1885 (Family Crisis Center--Crisis Line)

Catholic Education and Formation -

Catechist Support - t) 620-227-1537 Eric Haselhorst, Coord. English;

Catholic Elementary Schools - t) 620-227-1513 Trina Delgado, Supt.;

Pastoral Ministry Formation - t) 620-227-1538 Georgina Paz, Coord. (Spanish); Coleen Stein, Coord. (English);

Young Adult Ministry - t) 620-227-1550 gheimerman@dcdiocese.org Gentry Heimerman, Dir.;

Youth Ministry - t) 620-227-1540 dcyouth@dcdiocese.org Emma Webs, Dir.;

Consultative Bodies -

College of Consultors - Rev. Ted D. Stoecklein; Rev. Anselm Eke, MSP (Nigeria); Rev. Ted A. Skalsky;

Deans - Rev. James P. Dieker, Dodge City; Rev. Warren L. Stecklein, Garden City; Rev. Bernard H. Felix, Great Bend;

Diocesan Finance Council - Most Rev. John B. Brungardt, Ex Officio; Rev. Donald E. Bedore; Rev. Ted D. Stoecklein;

Diocesan Review Board - Regis Lopata, Chair; Debbie Schartz-Robinson; Mike Martinez;

Presbyteral Council - Rev. Bernard H. Felix; Most Rev. John B. Brungardt; Rev. Ted A. Skalsky;

Hispanic Ministry - t) 620-227-1555 Rev. Ted D. Stoecklein;

Legal Services -

Diocesan Attorney - t) 620-225-1674 Tamara L. Davis;

Media and Communications -

Diocesan Newspaper - t) 620-227-1519 skregister@dcdiocese.org David Myers, Editor;

Interactive Television Network - t) 620-227-1538 Coleen Stein, Coord.;

Media/Press Liaison - t) 620-227-1555 vicargeneral@dcdiocese.org Rev. Ted D. Stoecklein;

Mission Outreach and Propagation of the Faith - t) (620) 227-1517 Erika Oldham, Coord.;

Priest Continuing Formation Commission - Rev. Terrance W. Klein, Chair; Rev. Wesley W. Schawe (vocations@dcdiocese.org); Rev. John Forkuoh (Ghana) (frjohn47@yahoo.com);

Priest Personnel Council - Rev. Wesley W. Schawe (vocations@dcdiocese.org); Rev. Donald E. Bedore; Rev. James P. Dieker;

Scouting -

Catholic Committee on Scouting - t) (620) 430-2123 davegeist.dcks@gmail.com Dave Geist;

Vietnamese Ministry - t) 620-355-6405 Rev. Peter Trong Tran, Chap.;

PARISHES, MISSIONS, AND CLERGY

STATE OF KANSAS

ASHLAND

St. Joseph Catholic Church of Ashland, Kansas - 512 Cedar St., Ashland, KS 67831-0577; Mailing: P.O. Box 577, Ashland, KS 67831-0577 t) 620-635-2338; 620-200-7258 (CRP) ericawuah2000@yahoo.com Rev. Eric Awuah Gyamfi (Ghana), Pst.; CRP Stds.: 54

BELPRE

St. Bernard Catholic Church of Belpre, Kansas - 203 Hudson St., Belpre, KS 67519; Mailing: 1111 State St., Larned, KS 67550 t) 620-285-2035; 620-348-4725 (CRP) eleenduncan@embarqmail.com Rev. Bernard H. Felix, Pst.; Eleen Duncan, DRE; CRP Stds.: 5

CLAFLIN

Immaculate Conception Catholic Church of Claflin, Kansas - 310 Main St., Claflin, KS 67525; Mailing: P.O. Box 197, Claflin, KS 67525 t) 620-587-3628; 620-587-2339 (Parish Center) khipp@usd112.org; claflinparishoffice@gmail.com www.iccclaflin.com Rev. Terrance W. Klein, Pst.; Keeley Hipp, DRE; CRP Stds.: 37

COLDWATER

Holy Spirit - 200 N. Philadelphia, Coldwater, KS 67029; Mailing: P.O. Box 332, Coldwater, KS 67029 t) 620-582-2106 ericawuah2000@yahoo.com Quasi-parish. Sacramental records can be found at St. Joseph, Ashland. Rev. Eric Awuah Gyamfi (Ghana), Admin.; Kim Alexander, DRE; CRP Stds.: 5

DEERFIELD

Christ the King Catholic Church of Deerfield, Kansas - 812 Main St., Deerfield, KS 67838; Mailing: P.O. Box 455, Deerfield, KS 67838 t) 620-355-6405 petertrong@hotmail.com Rev. Peter Trong Tran, Pst.; CRP Stds.: 25

DIGHTON

St. Theresa Catholic Church of Dighton, Kansas - 322 S. First St., Dighton, KS 67839; Mailing: P.O. Box 787, Dighton, KS 67839-0787 t) 620-397-5357; 620-397-2910 (CRP) gcvonl02@gmail.com Rev. Donald E. Bedore, Par. Admin.; Rene Roberts, DRE; CRP Stds.: 58

DODGE CITY

Cathedral of Our Lady of Guadalupe Catholic Church of Dodge City, Kansas - 3231 N. 14th St., Dodge City, KS 67801; Mailing: P.O. Box 670, Dodge City, KS 67801 t) 620-225-4802; 620-227-3442 info@dodgecitycathedral.com; nalvarez@dodgecitycathedral.com www.dodgecitycathedral.com Rev. Wesley W. Schawe, Pst.; Rev. John Albert Stang, Vicar; Sr. Gregoria Bueno, Pst. Min./Coord.; Sr. Yolanda Maria Figueroa, Pst. Min./Coord.; Sr. Julieta Mondragon, Pst. Min./Coord.; Norma Alvarez, DRE; CRP Stds.: 352

Sacred Heart Cathedral School - (Grades PreK-8) 905 Central Ave., Dodge City, KS 67801 t) 620-227-6532 lynee.habiger@dcshcs.com www.dodgecitycathedral.com/school Lynee Habiger, Prin.; Stds.: 186; Lay Tchrs.: 14

ELKHART

St. Joan of Arc Catholic Church of Elkhart, Kansas - 723 S. Baca Ave., Elkhart, KS 67950-0570; Mailing: P.O. Box 570, Elkhart, KS 67950-0570 t) 620-697-4622; 620-697-4587 (CRP) stlohanlon@hotmail.com Rev. Rudin Din (Philippines), Pst.; Traci O'Hanlon, DRE; CRP Stds.: 45

ELLINWOOD

St. Joseph Catholic Church of Ellinwood, Kansas - 214 N. Main St., Ellinwood, KS 67526 t) 620-564-2534 stjosephellinwood.com/ Rev. Terrance W. Klein, Pst.; Rachel Schneider, DRE; CRP Stds.: 30

St. Joseph Catholic School - (Grades K-8) 111 W. Third, Ellinwood, KS 67526 t) 620-564-2721 cthomas@stjosephellinwood.com Cami Thomas, Prin.; Stds.: 60; Lay Tchrs.: 5

FOWLER

St. Anthony Catholic Church of Fowler, Kansas - 411 Fourth St., Fowler, KS 67844; Mailing: P.O. Box 80, Fowler, KS 67844 t) 690-646-5297 c) 620-575-5520; (620) 338-5072 (Parish Administrator); (620) 338-6253 diekerjames@gmail.com; stanthonyfowler@gmail.com meadecocatholic.com Rev. James P. Dieker, Pst.; Judy Dewell, Pst. Assoc.; Steve Dewell, Pst. Assoc.; Rhonda Milford, CRE; CRP Stds.: 39

GARDEN CITY

St. Dominic Catholic Church of Garden City, Kansas - 615 J C St., Garden City, KS 67846 t) 620-276-2024; 620-276-3500 (CRP) rformation@st-dominic.org st-dominic.org/ Rev. Warren L. Stecklein, Pst.; Sr. Myra Arney, O.P., DRE; Jennifer Mahoney, Youth Min.; CRP Stds.: 138

St. Dominic Catholic School - (Grades 1-6) 617 J. C. St., Garden City, KS 67846 t) 620-276-8981 ldrevnick@st-dominic.org www.st-dominic.org/school/ Trina Delgado, Prin.; Stds.: 118; Lay Tchrs.: 9

St. Mary Catholic Church of Garden City, Kansas - 509 St. John St., Garden City, KS 67846 t) 620-275-4204; 620-276-2716 (CRP) pastor@stmarygc.com stmarygc.com Rev. Jacob Schneider, Pst.; Rev. Louis Trung Dinh Hoang, Par. Vicar; Maria Sanchez, DRE; CRP Stds.: 490

St. Mary Catholic School - (Grades 1-6) 503 St. John St., Garden City, KS 67846 t) 620-276-2241 mmead@gckschools.com Michelle Mead, Prin.; Stds.: 119; Lay Tchrs.: 12

GREAT BEND

Prince of Peace Catholic Church of Great Bend, Kansas - 4100 Broadway, Great Bend, KS 67530; Mailing: P.O. Box 87, 1423 Holland - Res., Great Bend, KS 67530-0087 t) 620-792-1396 secretarypop4100@gmail.com; drepop4100@gmail.com www.greatbendcatholic.com St. Patrick and St. Rose of Lima merged in 2006 to form Prince of Peace Parish. Both worship sites are still active. Rev. Prakash Kola, MSFS (India), Par. Vicar; Luke Blair, Pst. Min./Coord.; Jill Lane, DRE; Rev. Aneesh Parappanattu, MSFS (India), Pst.; CRP Stds.: 153

Holy Family School - (Grades PreK-6) 4200 Broadway, Great Bend, KS 67530 t) 620-793-3265 office@gbholyfamily.org gbholyfamily.eduk12.net Rev. Pascal Klein, Prin.; Stds.: 182; Lay Tchrs.: 10

GREENSBURG

St. Joseph Catholic Church of Greensburg, Kansas - 820 Walnut, Greensburg, KS 67054 t) 620-726-6110 kb82565@gmail.com Kathleen Blair, Parish Life Coord.; Rev. Ted A. Skalsky, Sacr. Min.; CRP Stds.: 19

HANSTON

St. Anthony Catholic Church of Hanston, Kansas - 102 S. Douglas St., Hanston, KS 67849; Mailing: P.O. Box 54, Hanston, KS 67849 t) 620-357-8791; 620-357-5583 (CRP) Rev. John Forkuoh (Ghana), Pst.; Jaimi Burke, DRE; CRP Stds.: 32

HOISINGTON

St. John the Evangelist Catholic Church of Hoisington, Kansas - 122 E. 5th St., Hoisington, KS 67544 t) 620-653-2963; 620-653-2695 stjohnevangelist122@gmail.com; stjohndre544@gmail.com Rev. Anselm Eke, MSP (Nigeria), Pst.; Rose Debes, DRE; CRP Stds.: 80

HUGOTON

St. Helen Catholic Church of Hugoton, Kansas - 1011 S. Jefferson St., Hugoton, KS 67951-2823 t) 620-544-2551 Rev. Rudin Din (Philippines), Pst.; Carrie Baeza, DRE; CRP Stds.: 120

INGALLS

St. Stanislaus Catholic Church of Ingalls, Kansas - 200 N. Rush, Ingalls, KS 67853; Mailing: P.O. Box 175, Ingalls, KS 67853 t) 620-335-5202 pastor@st-dominic.org; emilyfeldt2826@gmail.com ststanislausingalls.com Rev. Warren L. Stecklein, Pst.; Emily Feldt, DRE; CRP Stds.: 57

JETMORE

St. Lawrence Catholic Church of Jetmore, Kansas - 413 Niederacher, Jetmore, KS 67854-0278; Mailing: P.O. Box 278, Jetmore, KS 67854-0278 t) 620-357-8791 kolson0505@gmail.com Rev. John Forkuoh (Ghana), Pst.; Katie Olson, DRE; CRP Stds.: 37

JOHNSON

St. Bernadette Catholic Church of Johnson, Kansas - 105 N. Chestnut St., Johnson, KS 67855; Mailing: 804 N. Colorado St., Ulysses, KS 67880 t) 620-356-1532; 620-492-1454 (CRP) maryqueenofpeaceandstbernadette.org Rev. Charles Seiwert, Pst.; CRP Stds.: 69

KINSLEY

St. Nicholas Catholic Church of Kinsley, Kansas - 706 E. Sixth St., Kinsley, KS 67547; Mailing: P.O. Box 285, Kinsley, KS 67547 t) 620-659-2692; 620-659-2521 stkinsley@hotmail.com; stnick2008@live.com stnicholaskinsley.org Rev. Benjamin F. Green, Pst.; CRP Stds.: 60

KIOWA

St. John the Apostle Catholic Church of Kiowa, Kansas - 920 E. Main St., Kiowa, KS 67070 t) 620-825-4361 barbercountycatholic.org Rev. Emmanuel Kosikumah, Pst.; Lindsey McMoran, DRE; CRP Stds.: 12

LACROSSE

St. Michael Catholic Church of LaCrosse, Kansas - 918 Lincoln St., LaCrosse, KS 67548; Mailing: P.O. Box 309, LaCrosse, KS 67548-0309 t) 785-222-2561; 785-222-3292 (CRP) church@gbta.net rushcountycatholicchurches.com Rev. Stephen Dabanka (Ghana), Pst.; Jill George, DRE; CRP Stds.: 44

LAKIN

St. Anthony of Padua Catholic Church of Lakin, Kansas - 600 Soderberg St., Lakin, KS 67860; Mailing: P.O. Box 983, Lakin, KS 67860 t) 620-355-6405 petertrong@hotmail.com; noels86@hotmail.com Rev. Peter Trong Tran, Pst.; Lisa Gannett, DRE; CRP Stds.: 94

LARNED

Sacred Heart of Jesus Catholic Church of Larned, Kansas - 1111 State St., Larned, KS 67550 t) 620-285-2035 sacredheartlarned.org Rev. Bernard H. Felix, Pst.; CRP Stds.: 76

LEOTI

St. Anthony of Padua Catholic Church of Leoti, Kansas - 600 S. 4th St., Leoti, KS 67861; Mailing: 208 N. 2nd St., Marienthal, KS 67863 t) 620-379-4427 office@wbsnet.org; tshickey@icloud.com www.westernkansascatholic.com Rev. Timothy S. Hickey, Pst.; CRP Stds.: 30

LIBERAL

St. Anthony of Padua Catholic Church of Liberal, Kansas - 1510 N. Calhoun St., Liberal, KS 67901 t) 620-624-4135 frsalas@stanthonyliberalks.com; sap.parish@stanthonyliberalks.com www.stanthonyliberalks.org Rev. Juan Manuel Salas Alanis, Pst.; Rev. Augustine Owusu (Ghana), Par. Vicar; Dcn. Victor Mencos; Dcn. Hector Rios; Dcn. Oscar Rodriguez; Dcn. Ruben Sigala; Veronica Vazquez, DRE; CRP Stds.: 300

LIEBENTHAL

St. Joseph Catholic Church of Liebenthal, Kansas - 202 Main St., Liebenthal, KS 67553 t) 785-222-3292 church@gbta.net Rev. Stephen Dabanka (Ghana), Pst.;

MARIENTHAL

St. Mary Catholic Church of Marienthal, Kansas - 208 N. Second St., Marienthal, KS 67863 t) 620-379-4427 tshickey@icloud.com www.westernkansascatholic.com Rev. Timothy S. Hickey, Pst.; CRP Stds.: 25

MEADE

St. John the Baptist Catholic Church of Meade, Kansas - 412 W. Carthage St., Meade, KS 67864; Mailing: PO Box 1207, Meade, KS 67864 t) 620-873-2003 flavins2004@gmail.com; diekerjames@gmail.com meadecocatholic.org Rev. James P. Dieker, Pst.; Heather Flavin, DRE; CRP Stds.: 27

MEDICINE LODGE

Holy Rosary Catholic Church of Medicine Lodge, Kansas - 300 Curry Ln., Medicine Lodge, KS 67104 t) 620-886-3596 barbercountycatholic.org Rev. Emmanuel Kosikumah, Pst.; Cheri Dohrmann, DRE; CRP Stds.: 26

NESS CITY

Sacred Heart Catholic Church of Ness City, Kansas - 510 S. School St., Ness City, KS 67560 t) 785-798-3530 Rev. Pascal L. Klein, Pst.; CRP Stds.: 36

Sacred Heart School - (Grades 1-8) t) (785) 798-3530 Rev. Pascal Klein, Prin.; Stds.: 18; Lay Tchrs.: 4

ODIN

Holy Family Catholic Church of Odin, Kansas - 1387 N.E. 90th Ave., Odin, KS 67525; Mailing: P.O. Box 197, Claflin, KS 67525 t) 620-587-3628 claflinparishoffice@gmail.com www.holyfamilyodin.com Rev. Terrance W. Klein, Pst.; CRP Stds.: 28

OFFERLE

St. Joseph Catholic Church of Offerle, Kansas - 111 W. 1st Ave., Offerle, KS 67563; Mailing: P.O. Box 285, Kinsley, KS 67547 t) 620-659-2692; 620-659-2521 (CRP) stkinsley@hotmail.com stjosephofferle.org Rev. Benjamin F. Green, Pst.; CRP Stds.: 10

OLMITZ

St. Ann Catholic Church of Olmitz, Kansas - 115 Cleveland St., Olmitz, KS 67564; Mailing: P.O. Box 8, Olmitz, KS 67564 t) 620-653-2963; 620-923-4225 (CRP) stjohnevangelist122@gmail.com; barhl2015@gtba.net Rev. Anselm Eke, MSP (Nigeria), Pst.; Lisa Starr, DRE; CRP Stds.: 36

PLAINS

St. Patrick Catholic Church of Plains, Kansas - 601 Superior St., Plains, KS 67869-0247; Mailing: P.O. Box 247, Plains, KS 67869-0247 t) 620-873-2003 diekerjames@gmail.com meadecocatholic.org Rev. James P. Dieker, Pst.; Minerva Bernabe, DRE; CRP Stds.: 87

PRATT

Sacred Heart Catholic Church of Pratt, Kansas - 338 N. Oak St., Pratt, KS 67124; Mailing: 332 N. Oak St., Pratt, KS 67124 t) 620-672-6352; 620-388-1455 (CRP) tkiley@sacredheartpratt.com; ecrouch@sacredheartpratt.com sacredheartpratt.com/ Rev. Charles Atuah, MSP (Nigeria), Pst.; Tonya Kiley, DRE; CRP Stds.: 98

RANSOM

St. Aloysius Catholic Church of Ransom, Kansas - 107 Vermont Ave., Ransom, KS 67572-0096; Mailing: P.O. Box 96, Ransom, KS 67572-0096 t) 785-731-2497; 785-731-2988 (CRP) Rev. Pascal L. Klein, Pst.; Troyette Lawson, DRE; CRP Stds.: 15

SATANTA

St. Alphonsus Catholic Church of Satanta, Kansas - 603 Tecumseh, Satanta, KS 67870; Mailing: P.O. Box 65, Satanta, KS 67870 t) 620-649-2692 catholic@pld.com; hildamacias32@hotmail.com www.stalphonsusks.org Rev. Juan Manuel Salas Alanis, Pst.; Rev. Augustine Owusu (Ghana), Par. Vicar; Hilda Macias, DRE; CRP Stds.: 70

SCOTT CITY

St. Joseph Catholic Church of Scott City, Kansas - 1006 S. Main St., Scott City, KS 67871; Mailing: PO Box 228, Scott City, KS 67871-0228 t) 620-872-3644 kykaye@hotmail.com; stjosephscparish@outlook.com stjosephscottcity.org/ Rev. Donald E. Bedore, Pst.; Challie Metzger, DRE; Kylie Stoecklein, DRE; CRP Stds.: 171

SHARON

St. Boniface Catholic Church of Sharon, Kansas - 410 N. Main St., Sharon, KS 67138; Mailing: PO Box 118, Sharon, KS 67138-0118 t) 620-294-5526 barbercountycatholic.org Rev. Emmanuel Kosikumah, Pst.; Shelon Schmidt, DRE; CRP Stds.: 22

SPEARVILLE

St. John the Baptist Catholic Church of Spearville, Kansas - 100 S. Main St., Spearville, KS 67876; Mailing: P.O. Box 187, Spearville, KS 67876 t) (620) 385-2202; (620) 385-2212 info@stjohnspearville.com; frjohn47@yahoo.com Rev. John Forkuoh (Ghana), Pst.; Judy Gleason, DRE; CRP Stds.: 97

ST. JOHN

St. John the Apostle Catholic Church of St. John, Kansas - 609 E. Fourth St., St. John, KS 67576; Mailing: P.O. Box 475, St. John, KS 67576 t) 620-549-3847 stjohn-church@hotmail.com; frcharles@sacredheartpratt.com Rev. Charles Atuah, MSP (Nigeria), Pst.; Gayle Davis, DRE; CRP Stds.: 67

SYRACUSE

St. Raphael Catholic Church of Syracuse, Kansas - 506 E. Ave. F, Syracuse, KS 67878-0731; Mailing: P.O. Box 731, Syracuse, KS 67878-0731 t) 620-384-7357 church@straphaelsyracuse.org; locution95@yahoo.com Rev. Peter Trong Tran, Pst.; Logie Asebedo, DRE; CRP Stds.: 48

TIMKEN

Holy Trinity Catholic Church of Timken, Kansas - 103 S. Main St., Timken, KS 67575 t) 785-222-2561; 785-356-2238 (CRP) church@gbta.net Rev. Stephen Dabanka (Ghana), Pst.; Lydia Flax, DRE; CRP Stds.: 8

TRIBUNE

St. Joseph the Worker Catholic Church of Tribune, Kansas - 801 N. Broadway, Tribune, KS 67879; Mailing: P.O. Box 67, Tribune, KS 67879 t) 620-379-4427 office@wbsnet.org; tristashafer@gmail.com www.westernkansascatholic.com Rev. Timothy S. Hickey, Pst.; Trista Shafer, DRE; CRP Stds.: 17

ULYSSES

Mary, Queen of Peace Catholic Church of Ulysses, Kansas - 804 N. Colorado, Ulysses, KS 67880 t) 620-356-1532; 620-356-3994 (CRP) mqopdre@pld.com maryqueenofpeaceandstbernadette.org/ Rev. Charles Seiwert, Pst.; Dcn. Apolonio Rodriguez; Toney Hernandez, DRE; CRP Stds.: 182

WRIGHT

St. Andrew Catholic Church of Wright, Kansas - 10893 St. Andrew Rd., Wright, KS 67882; Mailing: P.O. Box 125, Wright, KS 67882 t) 620-227-3363 regina.lix@gmail.com; vicargeneral@dcdiocese.org saintandrewwright.org Rev. Ted Dean Stoecklein, Pst.; Regina Lix, DRE; CRP Stds.: 32

INSTITUTIONS LOCATED IN DIOCESE

ASSOCIATIONS [ASN]

HUTCHINSON

St. Rose - Dominican Nurses Alumnae Association - 609 W. 24th Ave., Hutchinson, KS 67502 t) 620-793-3679 mkchacon@cox.net Kathleen Chacon, R.N., Treas.;

CONVENTS, MONASTERIES, AND RESIDENCES FOR WOMEN [CON]

GREAT BEND

Dominican Sisters of Peace, Inc. - 3600 Broadway Ave., Great Bend, KS 67530-3692 t) 620-792-1232 ehertel@oppeace.org www.oppeace.org Srs.: 25

ST. JOHN

Congregation of the Sisters of the Third Order of St. Francis of Perpetual Adoration (LaCrosse, WI) - 609 E. 4th St., St. John, KS 67576; Mailing: P.O. Box 475, St. John, KS 67576 t) 620-377-5006 pinstenes@fspa.org Sr. Paulynn Instenes, FSPA, In Res.; Sr. Jean Michael Treba, FSPA, In Res.; Srs.: 2

ENDOWMENTS / FOUNDATIONS / TRUSTS [EFT]

DODGE CITY

Catholic Social Service Endowment Fund - 906 Central Ave., Dodge City, KS 67801 t) 620-227-1562 dsnapp@catholiccharitiesswks.org Deborah Snapp, Admin.;

Dechant Foundation - 107 Layton St., Ste. A, Dodge City, KS 67801; Mailing: P.O. Box 741, Dodge City, KS 67801 t) 620-225-1674 tdavis@tldavispa.com Most Rev. John B. Brungardt;

Sacred Heart Cathedral School Endowment Fund - 3231 N. 14th St., Dodge City, KS 67801; Mailing: P.O. Box 670, Dodge City, KS 67801 t) 620-225-4802 info@dodgecitycathedral.com Rev. Wesley W. Schawe, Pst.;

ELLINWOOD

St. Joseph School Education Endowment Fund - 109 W. Third St., Ellinwood, KS 67526 t) 620-564-2534 church@stjosephellinwood.com Rev. Terrance W. Klein, Pst.;

GARDEN CITY

St. Catherine Hospital Development Foundation - 401 E. Spruce, Garden City, KS 67846 t) 620-272-2376 www.schdf.org

St. Dominic Grade School Endowment Fund - 615 J.C. St., Garden City, KS 67846 t) 620-276-2024 Chris Heiman, Chair;

St. Mary Catholic Education Endowment Fund - 509 St. John St., Garden City, KS 67846 t) 620-275-4204 pastor@stmarygc.com Rev. Jacob Schneider, Pst.;

GREAT BEND

The Holy Family Grade School Education Endowment Fund - 4200 Broadway, Great Bend, KS 67530; Mailing: P O Box 87, Great Bend, KS 67530 t) 620-792-1396 www.greatbendcatholic.com Rev. Aneesh Parappanattu, MSFS (India), Pst.;

LARNED

Sacred Heart Endowment Fund, Inc. - 1111 State St., Larned, KS 67550 t) 620-285-2035 Rev. Bernard H. Felix, Pst.;

LIBERAL

St. Anthony School Endowment Fund - 1510 N. Calhoun St., Liberal, KS 67901 t) 620-624-4135 frsalas@stanthonyliberalks.com Rev. Juan Manuel Salas Alanis, Pst.;

NESS CITY

The Sacred Heart School Endowment Fund - 510 S. School St., Ness City, KS 67560 t) 785-798-3530 shschool@gbta.net Christy Seib, Secy.;

PRATT

The Sacred Heart Endowment, Inc. - 332 N. Oak St., Pratt, KS 67124 t) 620-672-6352 frcharles@sacredheartpratt.com Rev. Charles Atuah, MSP (Nigeria), Pst.;

HOSPITALS / HEALTH SERVICES [HOS]

GARDEN CITY

St. Catherine Hospital - 401 E. Spruce, Garden City, KS 67846-5679 t) 620-272-2222 patrickgaughan@centura.org www.stcatherinehosp.com Affiliated with CommonSpirit Health formerly known as Catholic Health Initiatives. Amanda Vaughan, CFO; Bed Capacity: 97; Asstd. Annu.: 40,675; Staff: 389

MISCELLANEOUS [MIS]

DODGE CITY

Deposit and Loan Fund of the Catholic Diocese of Dodge City - 107 Layton St., Ste. A, Dodge City, KS 67801; Mailing: P.O. Box 863, Dodge City, KS 67801 t) 620-225-1674 tdavis@tldavispa.com Most Rev. John B. Brungardt;

The Diocese of Dodge City Priest Retirement Fund, Inc. - 2210 1st Ave., Dodge City, KS 67801 t) 620-227-6792 rdechant@sbcglobal.net Raymond Dechant, Contact;

Manna House - 1012 First Ave., Dodge City, KS 67801 t) 620-227-6707 jredmanco@hotmail.com Short-term housing and food distribution need. Joel Redman, Dir.; John Askew, Pres.; Zach Schneweis, Treas.;

Newman University - 236 San Jose, #26, Dodge City, KS 67801 t) 620-227-9616 birdj@newmanu.edu www.newmanu.edu Jessica Bird, Dir.;

NURSING / REHABILITATION / CONVALESCENCE / ELDERLY CARE [NUR]

GREAT BEND

Cedar Park Place, Inc. - 3910 Cedar Park Pl., Great Bend, KS 67530-3162 t) 620-793-8115 jmurray@mercyhousing.org Low and Middle Income Housing for Elderly and Disabled. Jana Murray, Admin.; Asstd. Annu.: 63; Staff: 2

RETREAT HOUSES / RENEWAL CENTERS [RTR]

DODGE CITY

Grace That Reigns Society USA - 2002 Fairway Dr., Dodge City, KS 67801 t) 620-338-3334 Offering retreats for clergy, laity or parishes; days of recollection; conferences. Most Rev. Ronald M. Gilmore;

GREAT BEND

Heartland Center for Spirituality - 3600 Broadway, Great Bend, KS 67530-3692 t) 620-792-1232 office@heartlandspirituality.org www.heartlandspirituality.org Retreat Center. Sr. Renee Dreiling, O.P., Dir.;

PAWNEE ROCK

Heartland Farm - 1049 County Rd. 390, Pawnee Rock, KS 67567-7002 t) 620-923-4585 hfarm@gbta.net Organic sustainable agriculture, body massage, retreats. A Ministry of the Dominican Sisters of Peace. Christi Abel, Contact;

An asterisk (*) denotes an organization that has established tax-exempt status directly with the IRS and is not covered by the USCCB Group Ruling.

Archdiocese of Dubuque

(Archidioecesis Dubuquensis)

MOST REVEREND MICHAEL OWEN JACKELS

Archbishop of Dubuque; ordained May 30, 1981; appointed Bishop of Wichita January 28, 2005; ordained April 4, 2005; appointed Archbishop of Dubuque April 8, 2013; installed May 30, 2013.

Chancery-Archdiocesan Pastoral Center: 1229 Mount Loretta Ave., Dubuque, IA 52003. T: 563-556-2580; F: 563-556-5464. www.dbqarch.org

Square Miles 17,403.

Established July 28, 1837; Created an Archdiocese June 15, 1893.

Patrons of the Archdiocese: Primary: St. Raphael, the Archangel; Secondary: St. John Mary Vianney, Cure of Ars.

Corporate Title: The Archdiocese of Dubuque.

Comprises 30 Counties, that part of the State of Iowa north of the Counties of Polk, Jasper, Poweshiek, Iowa, Johnson, Cedar and Clinton and east of the Counties of Kossuth, Humboldt, Webster and Boone.

For legal titles of parishes and archdiocesan institutions, consult the Chancery.

STATISTICAL OVERVIEW

Personnel
Archbishops....1
Retired Archbishops....1
Abbots....1
Retired Abbots....1
Priests: Diocesan Active in Diocese....73
Priests: Diocesan Active Outside Diocese....2
Priests: Retired, Sick or Absent....57
Number of Diocesan Priests....132
Religious Priests in Diocese....26
Total Priests in your Diocese....158
Extern Priests in Diocese....15
Ordinations:
Diocesan Priests....1
Transitional Deacons....2
Permanent Deacons in Diocese....129
Total Brothers....17
Total Sisters....417

Parishes
Parishes....166
With Resident Pastor:
Resident Diocesan Priests....68
Without Resident Pastor:
Administered by Priests....94
Administered by Lay People....3
Pastoral Centers....1

Professional Ministry Personnel:
Brothers....1
Sisters....7
Lay Ministers....487

Welfare
Catholic Hospitals....7
Total Assisted....1,125,901
Health Care Centers....1
Total Assisted....100
Homes for the Aged....4
Total Assisted....370
Special Centers for Social Services....4
Total Assisted....27,518
Other Institutions....1
Total Assisted....15

Educational
Seminaries, Diocesan....1
Students from This Diocese....5
Students from Other Dioceses....7
Diocesan Students in Other Seminaries....10
Seminaries, Religious....1
Students, Religious....105
Total Seminarians....120
Colleges and Universities....3
Total Students....3,839
High Schools, Diocesan and Parish....7
Total Students....1,852
Elementary Schools, Diocesan and Parish....37
Total Students....8,368
Catechesis/Religious Education:
High School Students....2,003
Elementary Students....5,491
Total Students under Catholic Instruction....21,673
Teachers in Diocese:
Priests....1
Lay Teachers....726

Vital Statistics
Receptions into the Church:
Infant Baptism Totals....1,988
Minor Baptism Totals....99
Adult Baptism Totals....51
Received into Full Communion....165
First Communions....2,092
Confirmations....1,929
Marriages:
Catholic....338
Interfaith....170
Total Marriages....508
Deaths....2,100
Total Catholic Population....183,586
Total Population....1,013,157

LEADERSHIP

Archbishop - t) 563-556-2580 x216 dbqcabsec@dbqarch.org Most Rev. Michael Owen Jackels; Sarah Otting, Secy.;
Vicar General - t) 563-556-2580 dbqcvgd@dbqarch.org Rev. Msgr. Thomas E. Toale; Sarah Otting, Secy.;
Chancellor - dbqcco@dbqarch.org Janine Marie Idziak, Chancellor; Sarah Otting, Secy.;
Judicial Vicar - Rev. Paul Attah-Nsiah (Ghana);
Moderator of the Curia - dbqcvgd@dbqarch.org Rev. Msgr. Thomas E. Toale;
Finance Officer - t) 563-556-2580 x222 dbqcfo@dbqarch.org Brian Harris, CFO;
College of Consultors - Rev. Msgr. Daniel J. Knepper; Rev. Neil J. Mantenach; Rev. Msgr. Thomas E. Toale;

ADMINISTRATION

The Archdiocese of Dubuque Corporate Board - Most Rev. Michael Owen Jackels, Pres.; Rev. Msgr. Thomas E. Toale, Vice. Pres.; Brian Harris, Treas.;
Archives - dbqcao@dbqarch.org Jim Betzner, Archivist;
Metropolitan Tribunal - t) 563-556-2580 Rev. Paul Attah-Nsiah (Ghana), Judicial Vicar; Peg Jones, Office Mgr. & Notary;
Defenders of the Bond - Rev. Msgr. James O. Barta; Rev. Msgr. Richard P. Funke; Rev. Donald J. Plamondon;
Promoters of Justice - Dcn. Gerald T. Jorgensen; Rev. Msgr. Richard P. Funke;

OFFICES AND DIRECTORS

Hispanic Ministry - t) 319-364-7121 dbqcffhm@dbqarch.org Ariadne Rodriguez, Dir.;
Pastoral Planning and Leadership Development - dbqcppld@dbqarch.org Kim Hermsen, Dir.;
Permanent Diaconate - dbqcpd@dbqarch.org Dcn. John Stierman, Dir.;
Protection of Children and Young People - dbqcopc@dbqarch.org Lynn Osterhaus;
Victim Assistance Coordinator - t) 563-584-3000 Stephen Frommelt;
Stewardship Development Office - dbqcdevdir@dbqarch.org Jeff Schneider, Dir.; Cassie Bird, Assoc. Dir.;
Vocations/Seminarians - t) 563-580-0027 dbqcvo@dbqarch.org Rev. Mark D. Murphy, Vocations Dir.;
Worship Office - dbqchw@dbqarch.org Rev. Greg E. Bahl, Dir.;

ADVISORY BOARDS, COMMISSIONS, COMMITTEES, AND COUNCILS

Archdiocesan Catholic School Board - Angie Long, Chair; Zoe Houlihan, Secy.; Cathy Walz, Exec. Officer;
Archdiocese of Dubuque Deposit & Loan Fund Board - Most Rev. Michael Owen Jackels, Pres.; Rev. Msgr. Thomas E. Toale, Vice. Pres.; Brian Harris, Treas.;
Archdiocese of Dubuque Education Fund Board - Most Rev. Michael Owen Jackels, Pres.; Rev. Msgr. Thomas E. Toale, Vice. Pres.; Brian Harris, Treas.;
Archdiocese of Dubuque Perpetual Care Fund Board - Most Rev. Michael Owen Jackels, Pres.; Rev. Msgr. Thomas E. Toale, Vice. Pres.; Brian Harris, Treas.;
Archdiocese of Dubuque Seminarian Education Fund Board - Most Rev. Michael Owen Jackels, Pres.; Rev. Msgr. Thomas E. Toale, Vice. Pres.; Brian Harris, Treas.;
Finance Council - Most Rev. Michael Owen Jackels, Chair; Brian Harris, Contact;
Pastoral Council - Most Rev. Michael Owen Jackels, Pres.; Maggie England, Chair; Kim Hermsen, Contact;
Priests' Council - Rev. Kenneth J. Glaser, Chair; Most Rev. Michael Owen Jackels, Pres.;
Priests Pension Plan Board of Trustees - Most Rev. Michael Owen Jackels, Pres.; Rev. Msgr. Thomas E. Toale, Vice. Pres.; Brian Harris, Plan Admin.;
Review Board for the Protection of Minors - Brendan Quann, Chair; Lynn Osterhaus, Staff Contact;
Worship Commission - dbqcwh@dbqarch.org Anastasia Nicklaus, Chair; Rev. Greg E. Bahl, Staff;

COMMUNICATIONS

Communications - Dcn. John Robbins, Dir.; Dan Russo, Content Specialist; Tara Brothers, Graphic Designer;
Information Technology - Jeremy Jones, IT Admin.; Ben Miers, IT Admin.;

EDUCATION

Catholic Schools - dbqsupt@dbqarch.org Cathy Walz, Supt.; Amy Conlon, Assoc. Dir. Educ.; Mindy Hart, Assoc. Dir. Educ.;

FACILITIES

Maintenance - Bob Hancock, Dir.; Jim Foust, Assoc. Dir.;

FAITH FORMATION

Faith Formation - Joanne Pohland, Formation of Children & Family; Kevin Feyen, Youth & Young Adult Ministry; Matthew Selby, Adult Formation & Marriage and Family Life Ministries;

FINANCE

Catholic Cemeteries of the Archdiocese of Dubuque - Ken Funke, Dir.;
Finance Office - Brian Harris, Dir.; Penny Minnihan, Auditor; Kathy Wuertzer, Controller;
Insurance: Property and Liability (Dubuque Archdiocesan Protection Program) - Rich Earles, Claims Risk Mgr., Archdiocesan Ctr.;

HUMAN RESOURCES

Human Resources - dbqchr@dbqarch.org Lynn Osterhaus, Dir.; Jen Hayes, Benefits Specialist;

ORGANIZATIONS

Archdiocesan Council of Catholic Women - t) (641) 752-2410 dbqaccw@dbqarch.org Monica Fulton, Pres.; Rev. Daniel J. Knipper, Spiritual Advisor;
Catholic Committee on Scouting - t) 319-310-7125 Craig Pilcher, Chair; Dcn. Michael Klappholz, Chap.;
PAMAD (Pastoral Associates/Ministers of the Archdiocese of Dubuque) - Brenda Strayer, Pres.;

MISCELLANEOUS / OTHER OFFICES

Campaign for Human Development - Tracy Morrison, Dir.;
Health Care Ethics - Janine Marie Idziak, Consultant;

PARISHES, MISSIONS, AND CLERGY

STATE OF IOWA

ACKLEY

St. Mary's Church of Ackley, Ackley, Iowa - 611 Sherman Ave., Ackley, IA 50601 t) 641-847-2329 dbq097@dbqarch.org www.franklinhardincatholic.org Rev. Kevin R. Earleywine, Pst.;

ALTA VISTA

Saint Bernard's Church, Alta Vista, Iowa - 116 E. Washington St., Alta Vista, IA 50603; Mailing: 203 7th St., Elma, IA 50628 t) 641-393-2520 dbq075@dbqarch.org www.holyrosarycluster.org Very Rev. Jerry F. Kopacek, Pst.;

AMES

St. Cecilia Church, Ames, Iowa - 2900 Hoover Ave., Ames, IA 50010-4498 t) 515-233-3092 dbq003@dbqarch.org www.stceciliaparish.org Rev. Donald J. Czapla, Pst.; Dcn. Charles Bernhard; Dcn. Alan Christy; Dcn. Ron Smith;
St. Cecilia School - (Grades PreSchool-5) t) 515-232-5290 dbqe01@dbqarch.org Ervin Rowlands, Prin.; Stds.: 149; Lay Tchrs.: 12
S.S. Peter and Paul Church, Gilbert, Iowa - 14238 500th Ave., Ames, IA 50014; Mailing: P.O. Box 327, Gilbert, IA 50105 t) (515) 291-2272 dbq218@dbqarch.org www.ssppgilbert.net Rev. Francis Kwame Anane (Ghana), Pst.;
St. Thomas Aquinas Church, Ames, Iowa - 2210 Lincoln Ave., Ames, IA 50014-7184 t) 515-292-3810 dbq004@dbqarch.org www.staparish.net Campus parish at Iowa State University, Ames Rev. Kyle M. Digmann, Pst.; Dcn. Frank Montabon;

ANAMOSA

St. Patrick's Church, Anamosa, Iowa - 217 N. Garnavillo St., Anamosa, IA 52205-1121; Mailing: 215 N Garnavillo St, Anamosa, IA 52205 t) 319-462-2141 dbq005@dbqarch.org www.stpatchurch.com Rev. Sean Smith, Pst.; Dcn. Douglas Bean; Dcn. David U. Sallen;
St. Patrick School - (Grades PreSchool-4) 216 N. Garnavillo St., Anamosa, IA 52205-1122 t) 319-462-2688 dbqe02@dbqarch.org Michael Volk, Prin.; Stds.: 72; Lay Tchrs.: 6

BALLTOWN

St. Francis Church, Balltown, Iowa - 468 Balltown Rd., Balltown, IA 52073; Mailing: 835 Church St., P.O. Box 398, Holy Cross, IA 52053 t) 563-870-4041 dbq104@dbqarch.org www.lasallepastorate.com Rev. Tyler C Raymond, Pst.;

BELLE PLAINE

St. Michael Church, Belle Plaine, Iowa - 1304 Ninth Ave., Belle Plaine, IA 52208; Mailing: 900 Park St., Tama, IA 52339 t) 641-484-3039 dbq197@dbqarch.org www.cofsaints.org Rev. Michael T. McAndrew, Pst.; Dcn. Joseph Behounek; Dcn. Stan Upah;

BELLEVUE

St. Joseph's Church, Bellevue, Iowa - 405 Franklin St., Bellevue, IA 52031 t) 563-872-3234 dbq012@dbqarch.org www.sjandspp.com Rev. G. Robert Gross, Pst.; Rev. David J. Ambrosy, Assoc. Pst.; Dcn. Loras Weber;

BELMOND

St. Francis Church, Belmond, Iowa - 1207 3rd St., N.E., Belmond, IA 50421; Mailing: 608 2nd Ave., N.E., Clarion, IA 50525 t) 515-532-3586 dbq039@dbqarch.org www.holyfamilycluster.org Rev. Jerry W. Blake, Pst.; Dcn. Pedro Garcia; Dcn. Michael Whitters;

BERNARD

St. Patrick Church, Garryowen, Bernard, Iowa - 28914 46th Ave., Bernard, IA 52032; Mailing: 408 3rd Ave., N.W., P.O. Box 699, Cascade, IA 52033-0699 t) 563-852-3524 dbq023@dbqarch.org www.stapastorate.org Very Rev. Mark Osterhaus, Pst.; Dcn. Daniel Kurt; Dcn. Ray Noonan; Dcn. Mark Otting; Dcn. Joe Schockemoehl;
The Sacred Heart Church, Fillmore, Iowa - 19661 Sacred Heart Ln., Bernard, IA 52032; Mailing: 408 Third Ave., N.W., P.O. Box 699, Cascade, IA 52033-0699 t) 563-852-3524 dbq023@dbqarch.org www.stapastorate.org Very Rev. Mark Osterhaus, Pst.; Dcn. Daniel Kurt; Dcn. Ray Noonan; Dcn. Mark Otting; Dcn. Joe Schockemoehl;

BLAIRSTOWN

St. John's Church, Blairstown, Iowa - 105 West St., N.W., Blairstown, IA 52209; Mailing: 405 4th Ave., P.O. Box 250, Van Horne, IA 52346-0250 t) 319-228-8131 dbq150@dbqarch.org www.queenofsaints.com Rev. Craig E. Steimel, Pst.; Dcn. Robert Pailthorpe;

BRITT

St. Patrick Church, Britt, Iowa - 335 1st Ave. S.E., Britt, IA 50423; Mailing: 906 W. O St., Forest City, IA 50436 t) 641-585-4856 dbq088@dbqarch.org www.archangelscc.org Rev. Andrew D. Marr, Pst.; Rev. Benjamin P Valentine, Assoc. Pst.; Dcn. Tom Blomme; Dcn. John Roisen; Dcn. Francisco Vazquez;
St. Wenceslaus Church, Duncan, Iowa - 2343 Navy Ave., Britt, IA 50423; Mailing: 990 W. O St., Forest City, IA 50436 t) 641-585-4856 dbq088@dbqarch.org www.archangelscc.org Rev. Andrew D. Marr, Pst.; Rev. Benjamin P Valentine, Assoc. Pst.; Dcn. Tom Blomme; Dcn. John Roisen; Dcn. Francisco Vazquez;

BUFFALO CENTER

St. Patrick's Church, Buffalo Center, Iowa - 115 5th Ave., N.W., Buffalo Center, IA 50424; Mailing: 906 W. O St., Forest City, IA 50436 t) 641-585-4856 dbq088@dbqarch.org www.archangelscc.org Rev. Andrew D. Marr, Pst.; Rev. Benjamin P Valentine, Assoc. Pst.; Dcn. Tom Blomme; Dcn. John Roisen; Dcn. Francisco Vazquez;

CALMAR

St. Aloysius Church (Calmar, Iowa) - 306 S. Maryville St, Calmar, IA 52132; Mailing: PO Box 819, Calmar, IA 52132-0819 t) 563-562-3045 dbq019@dbqarch.org www.cfosparishes.org Rev. Henry P. Huber, Pst.; Dcn. Dan O'Brien;

CASCADE

St. Matthias Parish, Cascade, Iowa - 410 Third Ave. N.W., Cascade, IA 52033; Mailing: 408 Third Ave., N.W., P.O. Box 699, Cascade, IA 52033 t) 563-852-3524 dbq023@dbqarch.org www.stapastorate.org Very Rev. Mark Osterhaus, Pst.; Dcn. Daniel Kurt; Dcn. Ray Noonan; Dcn. Mark Otting; Dcn. Joe Schockemoehl;

St. Peter's Church, Temple Hill, Cascade, Iowa - 20123 Temple Hill Rd., Cascade, IA 52033; Mailing: 408 Third Ave. N.W., P.O. Box 699, Cascade, IA 52033-0699 t) 563-852-3524 dbq023@dbqarch.org www.stapastorate.org Very Rev. Mark Osterhaus, Pst.; Dcn. Daniel Kurt; Dcn. Ray Noonan; Dcn. Mark Otting; Dcn. Joe Schockemoehl;

CEDAR FALLS

St. Patrick's Church, Cedar Falls, Iowa - 8th & Washington Sts., Cedar Falls, IA 50613; Mailing: 705 Main St., Cedar Falls, IA 50613 t) 319-266-3523 dbq025@dbqarch.org www.saintpatrickcf.org Rev. Ivan R. Nienhaus, Pst.; Dcn. Alan Weber;

St. Patrick School - (Grades PreSchool-8) 615 Washington St., Cedar Falls, IA 50613 t) 319-277-6781 dbqe07@dbqarch.org Jon Wiebers, Prin.; Stds.: 239; Lay Tchrs.: 19

CEDAR RAPIDS

All Saints Church, Cedar Rapids, Iowa - 720 29th St., S.E., Cedar Rapids, IA 52403-3099 t) 319-363-6130 dbq026@dbqarch.org www.allsaintscr.com Rev. John R. Flaherty, Pst.; Dcn. Michael Klappholz; Dcn. Edward Martin;

All Saints School - (Grades PreSchool-5) t) 319-363-4110 Lynn Holverson, Prin.; Stds.: 148; Lay Tchrs.: 9

Immaculate Conception Church, Cedar Rapids, Iowa - 857 3rd St., S.E., Cedar Rapids, IA 52406-1247; Mailing: 1224 5th St., S.E., Cedar Rapids, IA 52401 t) 319-362-7181 dbq027@dbqarch.org www.iccr.church Rev. Dennis C. Conway, Pst.; Rev. Aaron R. Junge, Assoc. Pst.; Dcn. Dave Harris;

St. John XXIII Parish, Cedar Rapids, Iowa - 8100 Roncalli Dr., S.W., Cedar Rapids, IA 52404-9178 t) 319-846-3139 dbq227@dbqarch.org www.stjohn23cr.org Rev. Richmond Dzekoe (Ghana), Pst.; Dcn. R. Joseph Blanck; Dcn. Stanley Scheiding;

St. Jude Church, Cedar Rapids, Iowa - 50 Edgewood Rd. N.W., Cedar Rapids, IA 52405 t) 319-390-3520 dbq028@dbqarch.org www.judes.org Rev. Nicholas B. March, Pst.; Dcn. John Winkel;

St. Ludmila's Church, Cedar Rapids, Iowa - 211 21st Ave. S.W., Cedar Rapids, IA 52404; Mailing: 2107 J St., S.W., Cedar Rapids, IA 52404-3615 t) 319-362-7282 dbq029@dbqarch.org www.stludmila.org Rev. Kenneth J. Glaser, Pst.; Dcn. Paul Jim Berger; Dcn. Mark Sandersfeld;

St. Matthew's Church, Cedar Rapids, Iowa - 2310 First Ave., N.E., Cedar Rapids, IA 52402-4999 t) 319-363-8269 dbq030@dbqarch.org www.stmatthewcr.org Rev. Douglas J. Loecke, Pst.; Dcn. Steven Bauer; Dcn. Richard Wallace;

St. Matthew School - (Grades PreSchool-5) 2244 1st Ave., N.E., Cedar Rapids, IA 52402 t) 319-362-3021 Brianna Richard, Prin.; Stds.: 294; Lay Tchrs.: 16

St. Patrick Church, Cedar Rapids, Iowa - 500 1st Ave., N.W., Cedar Rapids, IA 52405; Mailing: 120 5th St., N.W., Cedar Rapids, IA 52405 t) 319-362-7966 dbq031@dbqarch.org ww.stpatrickscr.org Rev. Dennis W. Miller, Pst.; Dcn. Daniel Hoeger; Dcn. Dan Rouse;

St. Pius the X Church, Cedar Rapids, Iowa - 4949 Council St., N.E., Cedar Rapids, IA 52402-2492 t) 319-393-4445 dbq032@dbqarch.org www.crpiusx.org Rev. Jon M. Seda, Pst.; Dcn. Ron Ridder; Dcn. Scott Zogg;

St. Wenceslaus Church, Cedar Rapids, Iowa - 1224 5th St., S.E., Cedar Rapids, IA 52401 t) 319-362-8061 dbq027@dbqarch.org www.swcr.church Rev. Dennis C. Conway, Pst.; Rev. Aaron R. Junge, Assoc. Pst.; Dcn. Dave Harris;

CENTRAL CITY

St. Stephen's Church, Central City, Iowa - 4700 Valley Farm Rd., Central City, IA 52214-0496; Mailing: P.O. Box 496, Central City, IA 52214-0496 t) 319-438-6625 dbq005@dbqarch.org www.northlinncc.org Rev. Sean Smith, Pst.; Dcn. Douglas Bean; Dcn. David U. Sallen;

CHARLES CITY

The Immaculate Conception Church, Charles City, Iowa - 106 Chapel Ln., Charles City, IA 50616-2810 t) 641-228-1071 dbq035@dbqarch.org www.iccharlescity.com Rev. Thomas Heathershaw, Pst.; Dcn. Michael Ward;

Immaculate Conception School - (Grades PreSchool-6) 1203 Clark St., Charles City, IA 50616 t) 641-228-1225 dbqe14@dbqarch.org Laurie Field, Prin.; Stds.: 191; Lay Tchrs.: 14

CHELSEA

St. Joseph Church, Chelsea, Iowa - 307 Station St., Chelsea, IA 52215; Mailing: 900 Park St., Tama, IA 52339 t) 641-484-3039 dbq197@dbqarch.org www.cofsaints.org Rev. Michael T. McAndrew, Pst.; Dcn. Joseph Behounek; Dcn. Stan Upah;

CLARION

St. John Church, Clarion, Iowa - 608 Second Ave., N.E., Clarion, IA 50525-0026 t) 515-532-3586 dbq039@dbqarch.org www.holyfamilycluster.org Rev. Jerry W. Blake, Pst.; Dcn. Pedro Garcia; Dcn. Michael Whitters;

CLEAR LAKE

St. Patrick Church, Clear Lake, Iowa - 1001 Ninth Ave. S., Clear Lake, IA 50428-2615 t) 641-357-3214 dbq040@dbqarch.org www.stpatrickcommunity.com Rev. Joshua J Link, Pst.; Dcn. Darrel Courrier;

CLERMONT

St. Peter Church, Clermont, Iowa - 608 Larrabee, Clermont, IA 52135; Mailing: P.O. Box 25, Clermont, IA 52135-0025 t) 563-422-3184 dbq195@dbqarch.org www.stjosephtheworkercluster.com Rev. Ralph E. Davis, Pst.; Dcn. Michal Schemmel;

COGGON

St. John's Church, Coggon, Iowa - 211 N. 2nd St., Coggon, IA 52218; Mailing: 4700 Valley Farm Rd., P.O. Box 496, Central City, IA 52214 t) 319-438-6625 dbq005@dbqarch.org www.northlinncc.org Rev. Sean Smith, Pst.; Dcn. Douglas Bean; Dcn. David U. Sallen;

COLESBURG

St. Patrick's Church, Colesburg, Iowa - 708 Delaware St., Colesburg, IA 52035; Mailing: 203 S. Locust, P.O. Box 365, Edgewood, IA 52042-0365 t) 563-928-7200 dbq072@dbqarch.org www.vibrantcatholic.com Rev. John S. Haugen, Pst.; Dcn. Paul Dolan;

COLO

St. Mary Church, Colo, Iowa - 422 4th St., Colo, IA 50056; Mailing: 410 Bailey St., P.O. Box 236, Colo, IA 50056-0236 t) 515-382-2974 (Cluster Office) dbq192@dbqarch.org www.storymarshallcluster.org Rev. Rick D. Dagit, Pst.; Dcn. James Kurtenbach; Dcn. Steven Van Kerckvoorde; Dcn. Mark Wyant;

CRESCO

Notre Dame Church, Cresco, Iowa - 223 2nd Ave. E., Cresco, IA 52136; Mailing: 116 Third St. E., Cresco, IA 52136 t) 563-547-3565 dbq047@dbqarch.org www.notredamecresco.com Rev. Jacob D. Rouse, Pst.;

Notre Dame School - (Grades PreSchool-6) 221 Second Ave. E., Cresco, IA 52136 t) 563-547-4513 dbqe15@dbqarch.org Kathryn Schmitt, Prin.; Stds.: 188; Lay Tchrs.: 12

DECORAH

St. Benedict Church, Decorah, Iowa - 307 W. Main St., Decorah, IA 52101-1778 t) 563-382-9631 dbq049@dbqarch.org www.stbenedictcc.com Rev. Donald A. Hertges, Pst.; Dcn. Nick Francois;

St. Benedict School - (Grades PreSchool-8) 402 Rural Ave., Decorah, IA 52101 t) 563-382-4668 dbqe16@dbqarch.org Stephen Haluska, Prin.; Stds.: 171; Lay Tchrs.: 15

DELHI

St. John Church, Delhi, Iowa - 303 South St., Delhi, IA 52223; Mailing: 307 South St., P.O. Box 187, Delhi, IA 52223-0187 t) 563-922-2251 dbq123@dbqarch.org www.blessedtrinitycluster.org Rev. Gabriel C. Anderson, Pst.;

DORCHESTER

St. Mary's Church, Dorchester, Iowa - 594 Waterloo Creek Dr., Dorchester, IA 52140; Mailing: 109 2nd St., S.W., Waukon, IA 52172 t) 563-568-3671 dbq216@dbqarch.org www.stpatrickwaukon.com Very Rev. John A. Moser, Pst.; Dcn. Jeff Molitor;

DUBUQUE

St. Raphael's Cathedral Church, Dubuque, Iowa - 231 Bluff St., Dubuque, IA 52001-6918 t) 563-582-7646 dbq054@dbqarch.org www.cathedralstpats.org Very Rev. Dennis J. Quint, Pst.; Dcn. Jim Luksetich;

St. Anthony Church (Dubuque, Iowa) - 1880 St. Ambrose St., Dubuque, IA 52001-4196; Mailing: 1870 St. Ambrose St., Dubuque, IA 52001-4196 t) 563-588-0571 dbq060@dbqarch.org www.stanthony-dubuque.org Rev. Steven J. Rosonke, Pst.; Dcn. William Hickson; Dcn. William Mauss; Dcn. Brian Zeman;

St. Catherine Church, St. Catherine, Iowa - 5189 St. Catherine Rd, Dubuque, IA 52003; Mailing: 405 Franklin St., Bellevue, IA 52031 t) 563-872-3234 dbq012@dbqarch.org www.sjandspp.com Rev. G. Robert Gross, Pst.; Rev. David J. Ambrosy, Assoc. Pst.; Dcn. Loras Weber;

The Church of the Nativity, Dubuque, Iowa - 1225 Alta Vista St., Dubuque, IA 52001 t) 563-582-1839 dbq057@dbqarch.org www.nativitydbq.com Rev. Andrew J Upah, Pst.; Dcn. Mike Timmerman; Dcn. Steve Whiteman;

Church of the Resurrection, Dubuque, Iowa - 4300 Asbury Rd., Dubuque, IA 52002 t) 563-556-7511 dbq058@dbqarch.org www.res-dbq.org Very Rev. Phillip G. Gibbs, Pst.; Dcn. Mike Ellis, Pst. Assoc.; Dcn. Gerald T. Jorgensen; Dcn. John Robbins; Dcn. Jim Schmidt;

St. Columbkille Church, Dubuque, Iowa - 1230 Rush St., Dubuque, IA 52003-7598; Mailing: 1240 Rush St., Dubuque, IA 52003-7598 t) 563-583-9117 dbq061@dbqarch.org www.stcolumbkille.net Rev. Thomas J. McDermott, Pst.; Very Rev. David A. Schatz, Pst.; Dcn. William Biver; Dcn. Travis King;

Holy Spirit Church, Dubuque, Iowa - 2215 Windsor Ave., Dubuque, IA 52001 t) 563-583-1709 dbq059@dbqarch.org www.holyspiritdbq.org Rev. Steven M. Garner, Pst.; Dcn. Dave Brinkmoeller; Dcn. David Roth; Dcn. John Stierman; Dcn. James J. Thill;

Holy Trinity Church - 1701 Rhomberg Ave., Dubuque, IA 52001

Sacred Heart Church -

Holy Ghost Church - 2921 Central Ave., Dubuque, IA 52001

St. Joseph's Church, Key West, Iowa - 10270 Key West Dr., Dubuque, IA 52003; Mailing: 10204 Key West Dr., Dubuque, IA 52003 t) 563-582-7392 dbq111@dbqarch.org www.stjosephkeywest.com Rev. Msgr. Thomas E. Toale, Pst.; Rev. Martin Obeng (Ghana), Assoc. Pst.;

St. Joseph the Worker Church of Dubuque, Dubuque, Iowa - 2001 Saint Joseph St., Dubuque, IA 52001; Mailing: 60 S. Algona St., Dubuque, IA 52001-5605 t) 563-588-1433 dbq062@dbqarch.org www.theworker.org Rev. Brian M. Dellaert, Pst.; Dcn. William Biver;

St. Patrick's Church, Dubuque, Iowa - 15th & Iowa Sts., Dubuque, IA 52001; Mailing: 1425 Iowa St., Dubuque,

IA 52001 t) 563-583-9749 dbq054@dbqarch.org www.cathedralstpats.org Very Rev. Dennis J. Quint, Pst.; Dcn. Jim Luksetich;

DUNKERTON

St. Francis Church, Barclay, Iowa - 7830 E. Airline Hwy., Dunkerton, IA 50626-9715; Mailing: 7837 E. Airline Hwy., Dunkerton, IA 50626-9715 t) 319-822-7477 dbq109@dbqarch.org Rev. Benjamin Nkrumah (Ghana), Pst.;

DURANGO

St. Joseph Church, Rickadsville, Iowa - 20249 St. Joseph Dr., Durango, IA 52039; Mailing: 835 Church St., P.O. Box 398, Holy Cross, IA 52053 t) 563-870-4041 dbq104@dbqarch.org www.lasallepastorate.com Rev. Tyler C Raymond, Pst.;

DYERSVILLE

Basilica of St. Francis Xavier, Dyersville, Iowa - 2nd St., S.W. & 1st Ave. W., Dyersville, IA 52040; Mailing: 104 Third St., S.W., Dyersville, IA 52040 t) 563-875-7325 dbq067@dbqarch.org www.spiresoffaith.com Rev. Christopher R. Podhajsky, Pst.; Rev. Philip Agyei (Ghana), Assoc. Pst.; Rev. Gabriel Mensah (Ghana), Assoc. Pst.; Dcn. Keith McCarraher; Dcn. James Steger;

S.S. Peter and Paul Church, Petersburg, Iowa - 1625 300th Ave., Dyersville, IA 52040; Mailing: 104 Third St., S.W., Dyersville, IA 52040 t) 563-875-7325 dbq067@dbqarch.org www.spiresoffaith.com Rev. Christopher R. Podhajsky, Pst.; Rev. Philip Agyei (Ghana), Assoc. Pst.; Rev. Gabriel Mensah (Ghana), Assoc. Pst.; Dcn. Keith McCarraher; Dcn. James Steger;

EAGLE GROVE

The Sacred Heart Church, (Eagle Grove, Iowa) - 204 S. Jackson Ave., Eagle Grove, IA 50533; Mailing: 608 2nd Ave. N.E., Clarion, IA 50525 t) 515-532-3586 dbq039@dbqarch.org www.holyfamilycluster.org Rev. Jerry W. Blake, Pst.; Dcn. Pedro Garcia; Dcn. Michael Whitters;

EARLVILLE

St. Joseph's Church, Earlville, Iowa - 303 Mary St., Earlville, IA 52041; Mailing: 104 Third St., S.W., Dyersville, IA 52040-1969 t) 563-875-7325 dbq067@dbqarch.org www.spiresoffaith.com Rev. Christopher R. Podhajsky, Pst.; Rev. Philip Agyei (Ghana), Assoc. Pst.; Rev. Gabriel Mensah (Ghana), Assoc. Pst.; Dcn. Keith McCarraher; Dcn. James Steger;

EDGEWOOD

St. Mark's Church, Edgewood, Iowa - 203 S. Locust St., Edgewood, IA 52042; Mailing: P.O. Box 365, Edgewood, IA 52042 t) 563-928-7200 dbq072@dbqarch.org www.vibrantcatholic.com Rev. John S. Haugen, Pst.; Dcn. Paul Dolan;

ELDORA

St. Mary's Church, Eldora, Iowa - 614 Washington St, Eldora, IA 50627-1257 t) 641-939-5545 dbq108@dbqarch.org www.franklinhardincatholic.org Rev. Rodney M. Allers, Pst.; Dcn. Robin Claypool;

ELKADER

St. Joseph's Church, Elkader, Iowa - 330 First St., Elkader, IA 52043-0626; Mailing: P.O. Box 626, Elkader, IA 52043-0626 t) 563-245-2548 dbq072@dbqarch.org www.vibrantcatholic.com Rev. John S. Haugen, Pst.; Dcn. Paul Dolan;

ELMA

The Immaculate Conception Church, Elma, Iowa - 207 Seventh St., Elma, IA 50628; Mailing: 203 Seventh St., Elma, IA 50628 t) 641-393-2520 dbq075@dbqarch.org www.holyrosarycluster.org Very Rev. Jerry F. Kopacek, Pst.;

Our Lady of Lourdes Church, Lourdes, Iowa - 14068 175th St., Elma, IA 50628; Mailing: 203 7th St., Elma, IA 50628 t) 641-393-2520 dbq075@dbqarch.org www.holyrosarycluster.org Very Rev. Jerry F. Kopacek, Pst.;

EPWORTH

St. Clement Church, Bankston, Iowa - 24287 New Vienna Rd., Epworth, IA 52045-9732; Mailing: 104 First St., S.E., P.O. Box 286, Epworth, IA 52045-0286 t) 563-876-5540 dbq076@dbqarch.org www.stelizabethpastorate.com Rev. Michael G. Schueller, Pst.; Rev. Scott F. Boone, Sacramental Priest; Dcn. James Koetz; Dcn. Dan O'Connell; Dcn. John Wolfe; Dcn. Nicholas Elliott;

St. John Church, Placid, Epworth, Iowa - 22481 E. Pleasant Grove Rd., Epworth, IA 52045; Mailing: 104 1st St., S.E., P.O. Box 286, Epworth, IA 52045-0286 t) 563-876-5540 dbq076@dbqarch.org www.stelizabethpastorate.com Rev. Michael G. Schueller, Pst.; Rev. Scott F. Boone, Sacramental Priest; Dcn. Nicholas Elliott; Dcn. James Koetz; Dcn. Dan O'Connell; Dcn. John Wolfe;

St. Patrick Church, Epworth, Iowa - 102 First St., S.E., Epworth, IA 52045; Mailing: P.O. Box 286, Epworth, IA 52045-0286 t) 563-876-5540 dbq076@dbqarch.org www.stelizabethpastorate.com Rev. Michael G. Schueller, Pst.; Rev. Scott F. Boone, Sacramental Priest; Dcn. Nicholas Elliott; Dcn. James Koetz; Dcn. Dan O'Connell; Dcn. John Wolfe;

FAIRBANK

Immaculate Conception Church, Fairbank, Iowa - 106 Iowa St., Fairbank, IA 50629; Mailing: P.O. Box 505, Fairbank, IA 50629-0505 t) 319-635-2211 dbq151@dbqarch.org www.icfairbank.weebly.com Rev. Ray E. Atwood, Pst.; Dcn. Jim Patera;

FARLEY

Saint Joseph's Church, Farley, Iowa - 202 2nd Ave., S.E., Farley, IA 52046; Mailing: 104 First St., S.E., P.O. Box 286, Epworth, IA 52045 t) 563-876-5540 dbq076@dbqarch.org www.stelizabethpastorate.com Rev. Michael G. Schueller, Pst.; Rev. Scott F. Boone, Sacramental Priest; Dcn. Nicholas Elliott; Dcn. James Koetz; Dcn. Dan O'Connell; Dcn. John Wolfe;

FAYETTE

St. Francis Church, Fayette, Iowa - 205 Lovers Ln., Fayette, IA 52142; Mailing: P.O. Box 276, Fayette, IA 52142-0276 t) 563-578-8227 dbq195@dbqarch.org www.stjosephtheworkercluster.com Rev. Ralph E. Davis, Pst.; Dcn. Michal Schemmel;

FOREST CITY

St. James Catholic Church, Forest City, Iowa - 906 W. O St., Forest City, IA 50436 t) 641-585-4856 dbq088@dbqarch.org www.archangelscc.org Rev. Andrew D. Marr, Pst.; Rev. Benjamin P Valentine, Assoc. Pst.; Dcn. Tom Blomme; Dcn. John Roisen; Dcn. Francisco Vazquez;

FORT ATKINSON

St. John Church, Fort Atkinson, Iowa - 201 Oak St., Fort Atkinson, IA 52144; Mailing: 110 Commercial Ave., P.O. Box 205, Protivin, IA 52163 t) 563-569-8259 dbq166@dbqarch.org www.christourhopecluster.com Rev. Nicholas R Radloff, Pst.; Dcn. Jim Zajicek;

Our Lady of Seven Dolors Church, Festina, Iowa - 2348 County Rd. B32, Fort Atkinson, IA 52144; Mailing: P.O. Box 819, Calmar, IA 52132-0819 t) 563-562-3045 dbq019@dbqarch.org www.cfoparishes.org Rev. Henry P. Huber, Pst.; Dcn. Dan O'Brien;

GARNAVILLO

St. Joseph Church, Garnavillo, Iowa - 204 W. Oak, Garnavillo, IA 52049; Mailing: PO Box 100, Garnavillo, IA 52049 t) 563-964-2234 dbq096@dbqarch.org www.maryicjoseph.org Rev. Marvin J. Bries, Pst.; Dcn. James Pfaffly;

GARNER

St. Boniface Church, Garner, Iowa - 600 Bush Ave., Garner, IA 50438; Mailing: 906 W. O St., Forest City, IA 50436 t) 641-585-4856 dbq088@dbqarch.org www.archangelscc.org Rev. Andrew D. Marr, Pst.; Rev. Benjamin P Valentine, Assoc. Pst.; Dcn. Tom Blomme; Dcn. John Roisen; Dcn. Francisco Vazquez;

GILBERTVILLE

Immaculate Conception Church, Gilbertville, Iowa - 325 15th Ave., Gilbertville, IA 50634; Mailing: 311 15th Ave., P.O. Box 136, Gilbertville, IA 50634-0136 t) 319-296-1092 dbq092@dbqarch.org www.icsjchurch.com Rev. Noah J. Diehm, Pst.; Dcn. Kevin Hagarty;

GREENE

St. Mary Church, Greene, Iowa - 105 N. Main St., Greene, IA 50636; Mailing: P.O. Box 480, Greene, IA 50636-0480 t) 641-823-4146 dbq094@dbqarch.org www.butlerfloydcatholic.org Rev. Franz Augustin (Haiti), Pst.; Dcn. Matt Miller;

GUTTENBERG

St. Mary Church, Guttenberg, Iowa - 518 S. Second St., Guttenberg, IA 52052; Mailing: 520 S. Second St., P.O. Box 847, Guttenberg, IA 52052-0847 t) 563-252-1247 dbq096@dbqarch.org www.maryicjoseph.org Rev. Marvin J. Bries, Pst.; Dcn. James Pfaffly;

HAMPTON

St. Patricks Church, Hampton, Iowa - 1405 N. Federal, Hampton, IA 50441 t) 641-456-4857 dbq097@dbqarch.org www.franklinhardincatholic.org Rev. Kevin R. Earleywine, Pst.;

HARPERS FERRY

St. Ann-St. Joseph Church, Harpers Ferry, Iowa - 307 W. Orange St., Harpers Ferry, IA 52146; Mailing: 648 Main St., Lansing, IA 52151 t) 563-538-4171 dbq115@dbqarch.org www.holyfamilyofthebluffs.org Rev. Joseph J Sevcik, Pst.;

HIAWATHA

St. Elizabeth Ann Seton Church, Hiawatha, Iowa - 1350 Lyndhurst Dr., Hiawatha, IA 52233 t) 319-393-3778 dbq103@dbqarch.org www.seasp.org Rev. Gary A. Mayer, Pst.; Dcn. Frank Easton; Dcn. Dennis Mulherin; Dcn. Scott Zogg;

HOLY CROSS

Holy Cross Church, Holy Cross, Iowa - 875 Church St., Holy Cross, IA 52053; Mailing: 835 Church St, P.O. Box 398, Holy Cross, IA 52053-0398 t) 563-870-4041 dbq104@dbqarch.org www.lasallepastorate.com Rev. Tyler C Raymond, Pst.;

HOPKINTON

St. Luke's Church, Hopkinton, Iowa - 206 First St., S.E., Hopkinton, IA 52237-0159; Mailing: P.O. Box 159, Hopkinton, IA 52237-0159 t) 563-926-2613 dbq136@dbqarch.org www.sacredheartstluke.com Rev. Paul C. Baldwin, Pst.; Dcn. Ed Goldsmith;

INDEPENDENCE

St. John's Church, Independence, Iowa - 209 Fifth Ave. N.E., Independence, IA 50644-1998 t) 319-334-7191 dbq106@dbqarch.org www.stjohnstpat.org Rev. David M. Beckman, Pst.; Dcn. Tim Post;

St. John School - (Grades PreSchool-8) 314 Third St., NE, Independence, IA 50644 t) 319-334-7173 dbqe35@dbqarch.org Jim Gieryng, Prin.; Stds.: 173; Lay Tchrs.: 10

IONIA

St. Boniface Church (Ionia, Iowa) - 204 E. Prairie, Ionia, IA 50645; Mailing: 313 W. Court St., New Hampton, IA 50659 t) 641-394-2105 dbq141@dbqarch.org www.goodshepherdcluster.com Rev. James Goerend, Pst.; Dcn. Victor J. DeSloover;

IOWA FALLS

St. Mark's Church, Iowa Falls, Iowa - 415 Main St., Iowa Falls, IA 50126-0368; Mailing: P.O. Box 368, Iowa Falls, IA 50126-0368 t) 641-648-9547 dbq108@dbqarch.org www.franklinhardincatholic.org Rev. Rodney M. Allers, Pst.; Dcn. Robin Claypool;

JESUP

St. Athanasius Church, Jesup, Iowa - 623 Stevens St., Jesup, IA 50648; Mailing: 635 Stevens St., P.O. Box 316, Jesup, IA 50648-0316 t) 319-827-6682 dbq109@dbqarch.org www.saintaparish.com Rev. Benjamin Nkrumah (Ghana), Pst.;

St. Athanasius School - (Grades PreSchool-8) 641 Stevens St., Jesup, IA 50648-0288; Mailing: P.O. Box 288, Jesup, IA 50648-0288 t) 319-827-1314 dbqe36@dbqarch.org Jennifer Sornson, Prin.; Stds.: 119; Lay Tchrs.: 11

LA PORTE CITY

Sacred Heart Church (LaPorte City, Iowa) - 1021 Poplar St., La Porte City, IA 50651; Mailing: 1102 Walnut St., Traer, IA 50675 t) 319-478-2222 dbq199@dbqarch.org www.princeofpeacecluster.com Rev. Anthony Boahen Nketiah (Ghana), Pst.;

LAKE MILLS

St. Patrick's Church, Lake Mills, Iowa - 406 S. Grant St., Lake Mills, IA 50450; Mailing: 906 W. O St., Forest City, IA 50436 t) 641-585-4856 dbq088@dbqarch.org www.archangelscc.org Rev. Andrew D. Marr, Pst.; Rev. Benjamin P Valentine, Assoc. Pst.; Dcn. Tom Blomme; Dcn. John Roisen; Dcn. Francisco Vazquez;

LANSING

The Immaculate Conception Church, Lansing, Iowa - 660 Main St., Lansing, IA 52151; Mailing: 648 Main St., Lansing, IA 52151 t) 563-538-4171 dbq115@dbqarch.org www.holyfamilyofthebluffs.org Rev. Joseph J Sevcik;

Immaculate Conception Church, Wexford, Iowa - 1416 Great River Rd., Lansing, IA 52151; Mailing: 648 Main St., Lansing, IA 52151 t) 563-538-4171 dbq115@dbqarch.org www.holyfamilyofthebluffs.org Rev. Joseph J Sevcik, Pst.;

LAWLER

Assumption Church, Little Turkey, Lawler, Iowa - 3303 160th St., Lawler, IA 52154; Mailing: 110 Commercial Ave., P.O. Box 205, Protivin, IA 52163 t) 563-569-8259 dbq166@dbqarch.org www.christourhopecluster.com Rev. Nicholas R Radloff, Pst.; Dcn. Jim Zajicek;

Our Lady of Mt. Carmel Church, Lawler, Iowa - 3030 IA Hwy. 24, Lawler, IA 52154; Mailing: 110 Commercial Ave., P.O. Box 205, Protivin, IA 52163-0205 t) 563-569-8259 dbq166@dbqarch.org www.christourhopecluster.com Rev. Nicholas R Radloff, Pst.; Dcn. Jim Zajicek;

LUXEMBURG

Holy Trinity Church, Luxemburg, Iowa - 103 S. Andres St., Luxemburg, IA 52065; Mailing: 835 Church St., P.O. Box 398, Holy Cross, IA 52053 t) 563-870-4041 dbq104@dbqarch.org www.lasallepastorate.com Rev. Tyler C Raymond, Pst.;

MANCHESTER

St. Mary's Church, Manchester, Iowa - 119 W. Fayette St., Manchester, IA 52057-1596 t) 563-927-4710 dbq123@dbqarch.org www.blessedtrinitycluster.com Rev. Gabriel C. Anderson, Pst.; Dcn. Dave Loecke; Dcn. Roger Luensmann;

St. Mary School - (Grades K-6) 132 W. Butler, Manchester, IA 52057-1502 t) 563-927-3689 dbqe37@dbqarch.org Kelley Harbach, Prin.; Stds.: 238; Lay Tchrs.: 17

MANLY

Sacred Heart Church, Manly, Iowa - 410 N. Broadway, Manly, IA 50456-0160; Mailing: P.O. Box 160, Manly, IA 50456-0160 t) (641) 454-2559 dbq130@dbqarch.org www.sacredheartmanly.org Rev. Neil J. Manternach, Pst.; Rev. Jacob A Dunne, Assoc. Pst.; Dcn. Matthew F. Berry; Dcn. Michael G. Byrne; Dcn. Charles Cooper;

MAQUOKETA

The Sacred Heart Church, Maquoketa, Iowa - 200 S. Vermont St., Maquoketa, IA 52060 t) 563-652-6931 dbq125@dbqarch.org www.shparishmaq.com Rev. Austin J. Wilker, Pst.; Dcn. Greg Michel; Dcn. John Schmidt;

Sacred Heart School - (Grades PreSchool-6) 806 Eddy St., Maquoketa, IA 52060 t) 563-652-3743 dbqe38@dbqarch.org Erik Rockwell, Prin.; Stds.: 156; Lay Tchrs.: 9

MARBLE ROCK

St. Mary Church (Roseville), Marble Rock, Iowa - 2397 Hwy. 14, Marble Rock, IA 50653; Mailing: 105 N. Main, P.O. Box 480, Greene, IA 50636-0480 t) 641-823-4146 dbq094@dbqarch.org www.butlerfloydcatholic.org Rev. Franz Augustin (Haiti), Pst.; Dcn. Matt Miller;

MARION

St. Joseph Church, Marion, Iowa - 1790 14th St., Marion, IA 52302-2267 t) 319-377-4869 dbq126@dbqarch.org www.stjoesmarion.org Very Rev. David H. O'Connor, Pst.; Dcn. Kenneth Bauer; Dcn. Dennis Ternes; Dcn. Jeffrey Volker;

St. Joseph School - (Grades PreSchool-8) 1430 14th St., Marion, IA 52302-2499 t) 319-377-6348 dbqe39@dbqarch.org Casey Kettmann, Prin.; Stds.: 202; Lay Tchrs.: 16

MARSHALLTOWN

St. Francis of Assisi Parish, Marshalltown, Iowa - 107 S. 1st St., Marshalltown, IA 50158 t) 641-752-6278 dbq128@dbqarch.org www.st-francis.net Rev. Alan J. Dietzenbach, Pst.; Rev. Kyle T Tietz, Assoc. Pst.; Dcn. Mark Dolash; Dcn. Jeff Harris; Dcn. Roger Polt; Dcn. Gary Pusillo; Dcn. Tom Renze;

St. Henry Church - 221 W. Olive St., Marshalltown, IA 50158

St. Mary Church - 11 W. Linn St., Marshalltown, IA 50158

MASON CITY

Epiphany Parish, Mason City, Iowa - 300 Fifth St., S.E., Mason City, IA 50401 t) 641-423-5001 dbq130@dbqarch.org www.epiphanyparish.org Rev. Neil J. Manternach, Pst.; Rev. Jacob A Dunne, Pst. Assoc.; Dcn. Matthew F. Berry; Dcn. Michael G. Byrne; Dcn. Charles Cooper;

Holy Family Church - 722 N. Adams Ave., Mason City, IA 50401

St. Joseph Church - 302 Fifth St. S.E., Mason City, IA 50401

MASONVILLE

Immaculate Conception Church, Masonville, Iowa - 606 Bernhart St., Masonville, IA 50654; Mailing: 119 W. Fayette St., Manchester, IA 52057 t) 563-927-4710 dbq123@dbqarch.org www.blessedtrinitycluster.org Rev. Gabriel C. Anderson, Pst.; Dcn. Dave Loecke; Dcn. Roger Luensmann;

MCGREGOR

St. Mary's Church, McGregor, Iowa - 311 7th St., McGregor, IA 52157; Mailing: 405 S. East St., P.O. Box 1521, Monona, IA 52159 t) 563-539-4442 dbq134@dbqarch.org www.trinitycluster.com Rev. Martin P Coolidge, Pst.; Dcn. Patrick J. Malanaphy;

MONONA

St. Patrick's Church, Monona, Iowa - 405 S. East St., Monona, IA 52159-0557; Mailing: P.O. Box 1521, Monona, IA 52159-0557 t) 563-539-4442 dbq134@dbqarch.org www.trinitycluster.com Rev. Martin P Coolidge, Pst.; Dcn. Patrick J. Malanaphy;

MONTICELLO

Sacred Heart Church (Monticello, Iowa) - 302 N. Sycamore St., Monticello, IA 52310; Mailing: 210 E. Third St., Monticello, IA 52310-1535 t) 319-465-5944 dbq136@dbqarch.org www.sacredheartstluke.com Rev. Paul C. Baldwin, Pst.; Dcn. Ed Goldsmith;

Sacred Heart School - (Grades PreSchool-6) 234 N. Sycamore St., Monticello, IA 52310-1515 t) 319-465-4605 dbqe42@dbqarch.org Susan Hucker, Prin.; Stds.: 133; Lay Tchrs.: 8

MOUNT VERNON

St. John's Church, Mt. Vernon, Iowa - 212 7th St., S.E., Mount Vernon, IA 52314 t) 319-895-6246 dbq137@dbqarch.org www.stjohnmv.org Rev. Andrew Awotwe-Mensah (Ghana), Pst.;

NASHUA

St. Michael's Church, Nashua, Iowa - 602 Cedar St., Nashua, IA 50658; Mailing: 612 Cedar St., P.O. Box 308, Nashua, IA 50658-0308 t) 641-435-2070 dbq035@dbqarch.org Rev. Thomas Heathershaw, Pst.; Dcn. Michael Ward;

NEVADA

St. Patrick Church, Nevada, Iowa - 1127 10th St., Nevada, IA 50201; Mailing: 410 Bailey St., PO Box 236, Colo, IA 50056 t) 515-382-2974 dbq192@dbqarch.org www.storymarshallcluster.org Rev. Rick D. Dagit, Pst.; Dcn. James Kurtenbach; Dcn. Steven Van Kerckvoorde; Dcn. Mark Wyant;

NEW ALBIN

St. Joseph Church, New Albin, Iowa - 154 3rd St., N.E., New Albin, IA 52160; Mailing: 648 Main St., Lansing, IA 52151 t) 563-538-4171 dbq115@dbqarch.org www.holyfamilyofthebluffs.org Rev. Joseph J Sevcik, Pst.;

NEW HAMPTON

Holy Family Church, New Hampton, Iowa - 202 N. Broadway, New Hampton, IA 50659; Mailing: 313 W. Court St., New Hampton, IA 50659 t) 641-394-2105 dbq141@dbqarch.org www.goodshepherdcluster.com Rev. James Goerend, Pst.; Dcn. Victor J. DeSloover;

St. Joseph Community School - (Grades PreSchool-8) 216 N. Broadway Ave., New Hampton, IA 50659 t) 641-394-2865 dbqe43@dbqarch.org Michele Nehls, Prin.; Stds.: 125; Lay Tchrs.: 14

NEW VIENNA

St. Boniface Church of New Vienna, New Vienna, Iowa - 7401 Columbus St., New Vienna, IA 52065; Mailing: 104 Third St., S.W., Dyersville, IA 52040 t) 563-875-7325 dbq067@dbqarch.org www.spiresoffaith.com Rev. Christopher R. Podhajsky, Pst.; Rev. Philip Agyei (Ghana), Assoc. Pst.; Rev. Gabriel Mensah (Ghana), Assoc. Pst.; Dcn. Keith McCarraher; Dcn. James Steger;

NEWHALL

St. Paul's Church, Newhall, Iowa - 306 3rd Ave., Newhall, IA 52315; Mailing: 405 Fourth Ave., P.O. Box 250, Van Horne, IA 52346-0250 t) 319-228-8131 dbq150@dbqarch.org www.queenofsaints.com Rev. Craig E. Steimel, Pst.; Dcn. Robert Pailthorpe;

NORTH BUENA VISTA

Immaculate Conception Church, North Buena Vista, Iowa - 218 Main St., North Buena Vista, IA 52066; Mailing: P.O. Box 7, North Buena Vista, IA 52066 t) 563-252-1247 dbq096@dbqarch.org www.maryicjoseph.org Rev. Marvin J. Bries, Pst.; Dcn. James Pfaffly;

NORTH WASHINGTON

Immaculate Conception Church, North Washington, Iowa - 114 N. Wapsi St., North Washington, IA 50659; Mailing: 313 W. Court St., New Hampton, IA 50659 t) 641-394-2105 dbq141@dbqarch.org www.goodshepherdcluster.com Rev. James Goerend, Pst.; Dcn. Victor J. DeSloover;

NORWAY

St. Michael Church, Norway, Iowa - 512 Evergreen St., Norway, IA 52318; Mailing: 405 Fourth Ave., P.O. Box 250, Van Horne, IA 52346-0250 t) 319-228-8131 dbq150@dbqarch.org www.queenofsaints.com Rev. Craig E. Steimel, Pst.; Dcn. Robert Pailthorpe;

OELWEIN

Sacred Heart Church, Oelwein, Iowa - 626 S. Frederick Ave., Oelwein, IA 50662; Mailing: 600 1st Ave. S.W., Oelwein, IA 50662 t) 319-283-3743 dbq151@dbqarch.org www.sacredheartoelwein.com Rev. Ray E. Atwood, Pst.; Dcn. Jim Patera;

OSAGE

St. Peter's Church, New Haven, Iowa - 2985 360th St., Osage, IA 50461; Mailing: 203 7th St., Elma, IA 50628 t) 641-393-2520 dbq075@dbqarch.org www.holyrosarycluster.org Very Rev. Jerry F. Kopacek, Pst.;

Sacred Heart Church (Osage, Iowa) - 1204 State St., Osage, IA 50461; Mailing: 218 S. 12th St., Osage, IA 50461 t) 641-732-4342 dbq152@dbqarch.org www.stisidorecluster.org Rev. Raymond A. Burkle, Pst.;

OSSIAN

St. Francis Church, Ossian, Iowa - 420 E. Main St., Ossian, IA 52161; Mailing: P.O. Box 819, Calmar, IA 52132-0819 t) 563-562-3045 dbq019@dbqarch.org www.cfoparishes.org Rev. Henry P. Huber, Pst.; Dcn. Dan O'Brien;

OXFORD JUNCTION

Sacred Heart Church (Oxford Junction, Iowa) - 309 Church St., Oxford Junction, IA 52323; Mailing: PO Box 98, Oxford Junction, IA 52323 t) (319) 826-2611 dbq137@dbqarch.org www.sacredheartoj.org Rev. Andrew Awotwe-Mensah (Ghana), Pst.;

PEOSTA

Holy Family Church, New Melleray, Peosta, Iowa - 16318 Holy Family Ln., Peosta, IA 52068; Mailing: 10204 Key West Dr., Dubuque, IA 52003 t) 563-582-7392 dbq111@dbqarch.org www.stjosephkeywest.com Rev. Msgr. Thomas E. Toale, Pst.; Rev. Martin Obeng (Ghana), Assoc. Pst.;

St. John the Baptist Church of Peosta, Iowa - 241 Peosta

St., Peosta, IA 52068; Mailing: 104 First St., S.E., P.O. Box 286, Epworth, IA 52045-0286 t) 563-876-5540 dbq076@dbqarch.org www.stelizabethpastorate.com Rev. Michael G. Schueller, Pst.; Rev. Scott F. Boone, Sacramental Priest; Dcn. Nicholas Elliott; Dcn. James Koetz; Dcn. Dan O'Connell; Dcn. John Wolfe;

POSTVILLE

St. Bridget Church (Postville, Iowa) - 135 W. Williams St., Postville, IA 52162; Mailing: 405 S. East St., P.O. Box 1521, Monona, IA 52159-0557 t) 563-539-4442 dbq134@dbqarch.org www.trinitycluster.com Rev. Martin P Coolidge, Pst.; Dcn. Patrick J. Malanaphy;

PRAIRIEBURG

St. Joseph's Church, Prairieburg, Iowa - 300 West Ave., Prairieburg, IA 52219; Mailing: 4700 Valley Farm Rd., P.O. Box 496, Central City, IA 52214-0496 t) 319-438-6625 dbq005@dbqarch.org www.northlinncc.org Rev. Sean Smith, Pst.; Dcn. Douglas Bean; Dcn. David U. Sallen;

PRESTON

St. Joseph's Church, Preston, Iowa - 250 S. Faith St., Preston, IA 52069-0309; Mailing: P.O. Box 309, Preston, IA 52069-0309 t) 563-689-5161 dbq125@dbqarch.org www.stjosephprestonia.com Rev. Austin J. Wilker, Pst.; Dcn. Greg Michel; Dcn. John Schmidt;

PROTIVIN

Holy Trinity Church, Protivin, Iowa - 124 N. Main St., Protivin, IA 52163; Mailing: 110 Commercial Ave., P.O. Box 205, Protivin, IA 52163-0205 t) 563-569-8259 dbq166@dbqarch.org www.christourhopecluster.com Rev. Nicholas R Radloff, Pst.; Dcn. Jim Zajicek;

RAYMOND

St. Joseph's Church, Raymond, Iowa - 313 E. Central St., Raymond, IA 50667; Mailing: 311 15th Ave., P.O. Box 136, Gilbertville, IA 50634 t) 319-296-1092 dbq092@dbqarch.org www.icsjchurch.com Rev. Noah J. Diehm, Pst.; Dcn. Kevin Hagarty;

REINBECK

Holy Family Church, Reinbeck, Iowa - 21275 U Ave., Reinbeck, IA 50669 t) 319-345-2006 dbq169@dbqarch.org www.holyfamilycatholicparish.com Rev. David G. Kucera, Pst.; Dcn. Rick Nilles; Dcn. John Schwennen;

St. Patrick Church - 302 Second St., Parkersburg, IA 50665

St. Gabriel Church - 21275 U Ave, Reinbeck, IA 50669

RICEVILLE

Immaculate Conception Church, Riceville, Iowa - 211 E. Main St., Riceville, IA 50466; Mailing: 203 7th St., Elma, IA 50628 t) 641-393-2520 dbq075@dbqarch.org www.holyrosarycluster.org Very Rev. Jerry F. Kopacek, Pst.;

ROCKFORD

The Holy Name Church, Rockford, Iowa - 507 First Ave. N.W., Rockford, IA 50468 t) 641-823-4146 dbq094@dbqarch.org www.butlerfloydcatholic.org Rev. Franz Augustin (Haiti), Pst.; Dcn. Matt Miller;

ROCKWELL

Sacred Heart Church (Rockwell, Iowa) - 305 Elm St. E., Rockwell, IA 50469; Mailing: P.O. Box 30, Rockwell, IA 50469-0030 t) 641-822-4950 dbq040@dbqarch.org www.sacredheartrockwell.org Rev. Joshua J Link, Pst.;

RYAN

St. Patrick's Church, Ryan, Iowa - 600 Franklin St., Ryan, IA 52330; Mailing: 119 W. Fayette St., Manchester, IA 52057 t) 563-927-4710 dbq123@dbqarch.org www.blessedtrinitycluster.org Rev. Gabriel C. Anderson, Pst.; Dcn. Dave Loecke; Dcn. Roger Luensmann;

SHERRILL

S.S. Peter and Paul Church, Sherrill, Iowa - 5131 Sherrill Rd., Sherrill, IA 52073; Mailing: 835 Church St., P.O. Box 398, Holy Cross, IA 52053-0398 t) 563-870-4041 dbq104@dbqarch.org www.lasallepastorate.com Rev. Tyler C Raymond, Pst.;

SPILLVILLE

St. Wenceslaus Church, Spillville, Iowa - 207 Church St., Spillville, IA 52168; Mailing: P.O. Box 819, Calmar, IA 52132-0819 t) 563-562-3045 dbq019@dbqarch.org www.cfoparishes.org Rev. Henry P. Huber, Pst.; Dcn. Dan O'Brien;

SPRINGBROOK

SS. Peter and Paul Church, Springbrook, Iowa - 107 E. Main St., Springbrook, IA 52075; Mailing: 405 Franklin St., Bellevue, IA 52031 t) 563-872-3234 dbq012@dbqarch.org www.sjandspp.com Rev. G. Robert Gross, Pst.; Rev. David J. Ambrosy, Assoc. Pst.; Dcn. Loras Weber;

SPRINGVILLE

Saint Isidore Church, Springville, Iowa - 603 6th St. S., Springville, IA 52336; Mailing: P.O. Box 318, Springville, IA 52336 t) 319-854-6141 dbq137@dbqarch.org www.stisidorespringville.org Rev. Andrew Awotwe-Mensah (Ghana), Pst.;

ST. DONATUS

St. Donatus Church, St. Donatus, Iowa - 97 1st St. E., St. Donatus, IA 52071; Mailing: 405 Franklin St., Bellevue, IA 52031 t) 563-872-3234 dbq012@dbqarch.org www.sjandspp.com Rev. G. Robert Gross, Pst.; Rev. David J. Ambrosy, Assoc. Pst.; Dcn. Loras Weber;

ST. LUCAS

St. Luke's Church, St. Lucas, Iowa - 215 E. Main, St. Lucas, IA 52166; Mailing: 110 Commercial Ave., P.O. Box 205, Protivin, IA 52163-0205 t) 563-569-8259 dbq166@dbqarch.org www.christourhopecluster.com Rev. Nicholas R Radloff, Pst.; Dcn. Jim Zajicek;

STACYVILLE

Visitation Church, Stacyville, Iowa - 604 N. Broad St., Stacyville, IA 50476; Mailing: 218 S. 12th St., Osage, IA 50461 t) 641-732-4342 dbq152@dbqarch.org www.stisidorecluster.org Rev. Raymond A. Burkle, Pst.;

STATE CENTER

St. Joseph's Church, State Center, Iowa - 610 3rd St., S.W., State Center, IA 50247; Mailing: 410 Bailey St., P.O. Box 236, Colo, IA 50056 t) 641-377-2710 dbq192@dbqarch.org www.storymarshallcluster.org Rev. Rick D. Dagit, Pst.; Dcn. James Kurtenbach; Dcn. Steven Van Kerckvoorde; Dcn. Mark Wyant;

STRAWBERRY POINT

St. Mary Church, Strawberry Point, Iowa - 314 W. Mission St., Strawberry Point, IA 52076-9432 t) (563) 928-7200 dbq072@dbqarch.org www.vibrantcatholic.com Rev. John S. Haugen, Pst.; Dcn. Paul Dolan;

SUMNER

Immaculate Conception Church, Sumner, Iowa - 404 W. First St., Sumner, IA 50674 t) (563) 578-8227 dbq195@dbqarch.org www.stjosephtheworkercluster.com Rev. Ralph E. Davis, Pst.; Dcn. Michal Schemmel;

TAMA

St. Patrick's Church, Tama, Iowa - 900 Park St., Tama, IA 52339 t) 641-484-3039 dbq197@dbqarch.org www.cofsaints.org Rev. Michael T. McAndrew, Pst.; Dcn. Stan Upah; Dcn. Joseph Behounek;

TRAER

St. Paul Church, Traer, Iowa - 1102 Walnut St., Traer, IA 50675-1440 t) 319-478-2222 dbq199@dbqarch.org www.princeofpeacecluster.com Rev. Anthony Boahen Nketiah (Ghana), Pst.;

URBANA

St. Mary's Church, Urbana, Iowa - 402 Ash Ave., Urbana, IA 52345; Mailing: 516 Rowley St., P.O. Box 116, Walker, IA 52352-0116 t) 319-448-4241 dbq203plc@dbqarch.org www.heartofmary.org Rev. Gary A. Mayer, Priest Supvr.; Rev. James P. Brokman, Sacramental Priest; Dcn. Steven Ford; Marcia Reilly, Parish Life Coord.;

VAN HORNE

Immaculate Conception Church, Van Horne, Iowa - 405 Fourth Ave., Van Horne, IA 52346-0250; Mailing: P.O. Box 250, Van Horne, IA 52346-0250 t) 319-228-8131 dbq150@dbqarch.org www.queenofsaints.com Rev. Craig E. Steimel, Pst.; Dcn. Robert Pailthorpe;

VINTON

St. Mary Church, Vinton, Iowa - 2200 Second Ave., Vinton, IA 52349 t) 319-472-3368 dbq203plc@dbqarch.org www.heartofmary.org Rev. Gary A. Mayer, Priest Supvr.; Rev. James P. Brokman, Sacramental Priest; Dcn. Steven Ford; Marcia Reilly, Parish Life Coord.;

VOLGA

Sacred Heart Church (Volga City, Iowa) - 306 White St., Volga, IA 52077; Mailing: 330 First St. S.W., P.O. Box 626, Elkader, IA 52043-0626 t) 563-245-2548 dbq072@dbqarch.org www.vibrantcatholic.com Rev. John S. Haugen, Pst.; Dcn. Paul Dolan;

WALKER

Sacred Heart Church, Walker, Iowa - 518 Rowley St., Walker, IA 52352; Mailing: 516 Rowley St., P.O. Box 116, Walker, IA 52352 t) 319-448-4241 dbq203plc@dbqarch.org www.heartofmary.org Rev. Gary A. Mayer, Priest Supvr.; Rev. James P. Brokman, Sacramental Priest; Dcn. Steven Ford; Marcia Reilly, Parish Life Coord.;

WATERLOO

Blessed Sacrament Church, Waterloo, Iowa - 650 Stephan Ave., Waterloo, IA 50701 t) 319-233-6179 dbq208@dbqarch.org www.blessedsacramentwaterloo.org Rev. Anthony J. Kruse, Pst.; Dcn. Chris Evans;

St. Edward's Church, Waterloo, Iowa - 1423 Kimball Ave., Waterloo, IA 50702 t) 319-233-8060 dbq210@dbqarch.org www.sted.org Very Rev. Scott E. Bullock, Pst.; Dcn. Brad Kneeland; Dcn. Tom Lang; Dcn. Raymond Larsen; Dcn. Richard Lynch;

St. Mary's Church, Eagle Center, Iowa - 1435 E. Eagle Rd., Waterloo, IA 50703; Mailing: 1102 Walnut St., Traer, IA 50675 t) 319-478-2222 dbq199@dbqarch.org www.princeofpeacecluster.com Rev. Anthony Boahen Nketiah (Ghana), Pst.;

Queen of Peace Church, Waterloo, Iowa - 320 Mulberry St., Waterloo, IA 50703 t) 319-226-3655 dbq213@dbqarch.org www.queenofpeaceparish.net Rev. Nils Hernandez, Pst.;

Sacred Heart Church, Waterloo, Iowa - 623 W. Fourth St., Waterloo, IA 50702; Mailing: 627 W. Fourth St., Waterloo, IA 50702 t) 319-234-4996 dbq209@dbqarch.org www.sacredheartwloo.org Rev. Paul Hta I Naw (Myanmar), Pst.; Dcn. Dan Rigel;

WATKINS

St. Patrick Church, Watkins, Iowa - 109 2nd St., Watkins, IA 52354; Mailing: 405 Fourth Ave., P.O. Box 250, Van Horne, IA 52346 t) 319-228-8131 dbq150@dbqarch.org www.queenofsaints.com Rev. Craig E. Steimel, Pst.; Dcn. Robert Pailthorpe;

WAUCOMA

St. Mary Church, Waucoma, Iowa - 218 3rd St., N.W., Waucoma, IA 52171; Mailing: 110 Commercial Ave., P.O. Box 205, Protivin, IA 52163-0205 t) 563-569-8259 dbq166@dbqarch.org www.christourhopecluster.com Rev. Nicholas R Radloff, Pst.; Dcn. Jim Zajicek;

WAUKON

St. Mary's Church, Hanover, Iowa - 2096 Hwy. 76, Waukon, IA 52172; Mailing: 109 Second St., S.W., Waukon, IA 52172 t) 563-568-3671 dbq216@dbqarch.org www.stpatrickwaukon.com Very Rev. John A. Moser, Pst.; Dcn. Jeff Molitor;

St. Patrick's Church, Waukon, Iowa - 101 Second St., S.W., Waukon, IA 52172; Mailing: 109 Second St., S.W., Waukon, IA 52172 t) 563-568-3671 dbq216@dbqarch.org www.stpatrickwaukon.com Very Rev. John A. Moser, Pst.; Dcn. Jeff Molitor;

St. Patrick School - (Grades PreSchool-6) 200 Second St., S.W., Waukon, IA 52172 t) 563-568-2415 dbqe54@dbqarch.org Katherine Fahey, Prin.; Stds.: 225; Lay Tchrs.: 14

WAVERLY

St. Mary's Church, Waverly, Iowa - 2700 Horton Rd., Waverly, IA 50677 t) 319-352-2493 dbq217@dbqarch.org www.stmarysfamily.com Rev. Douglas O. Wathier, Pst.; Dcn. Phil Paladino;

WEBSTER CITY

St. Thomas Aquinas Church, Webster City, Iowa - 1008 Des Moines St., Webster City, IA 50595-2147; Mailing:

1000 Des Moines St, Webster City, IA 50595-2147 t) 515-832-1190 dbq218@dbqarch.org www.stthomaswc.org Rev. Francis Kwame Anane (Ghana), Pst.; Dcn. Daniel Hurt;

St. Thomas Aquinas School - (Grades PreSchool-6) 624 Dubuque St., Webster City, IA 50595-2245 t) 515-832-1346 dbqe55@dbqarch.org Theresa Schleisman, Prin.; Stds.: 110; Lay Tchrs.: 7

WEST UNION

Holy Name Church, West Union, Iowa - 128 N. Walnut St., West Union, IA 52175 t) 563-422-3184 dbq195@dbqarch.org www.stjosephtheworkercluster.com Rev. Ralph E. Davis, Pst.; Dcn. Michal Schemmel;

WILLIAMS

St. Mary Church, Williams, Iowa - 404 4th St., Williams, IA 50271; Mailing: 1000 Des Moines St., Webster City, IA 50595-2147 t) 515-832-1190 dbq218@dbqarch.org www.sthomaswc.org Rev. Francis Kwame Anane (Ghana), Pst.; Dcn. Daniel Hurt;

WINTHROP

St. Patrick Church, Winthrop, Iowa - 535 1st St. S., Winthrop, IA 50682; Mailing: 209 5th Ave., N.E., Independence, IA 50644 t) 319-334-7191 dbq106@dbqarch.org www.stjohnstpat.org Rev. David M. Beckman, Pst.; Dcn. Tim Post;

WORTHINGTON

St. Paul Church, Worthington, Iowa - 301 2nd Ave., S.W., Worthington, IA 52078; Mailing: 104 3rd St., S.W., Dyersville, IA 52040 t) (563) 875-7325 dbq067@dbqarch.org www.spiresoffaith.com Rev. Christopher R. Podhajsky, Pst.; Rev. Philip Agyei (Ghana), Assoc. Pst.; Rev. Gabriel Mensah (Ghana), Assoc. Pst.; Dcn. Keith McCarraher; Dcn. James Steger;

ZEARING

St. Gabriel Church, Zearing, Iowa - 302 N. Center St., Zearing, IA 50278; Mailing: 410 Bailey St., P.O. Box 236, Colo, IA 50056-0236 t) 641-377-2710 dbq192@dbqarch.org www.storymarshallcluster.org Rev. Rick D. Dagit, Pst.; Dcn. James Kurtenbach; Dcn. Steven Van Kerckvoorde; Dcn. Mark Wyant;

ZWINGLE

St. Lawrence Church, Otter Creek, Iowa - 17434 Bellevue-Cascade Rd., Zwingle, IA 52079; Mailing: 200 S. Vermont, Maquoketa, IA 52060 t) 563-652-6931 dbq125@dbqarch.org Rev. Austin J. Wilker, Pst.; Dcn. Greg Michel; Dcn. John Schmidt;

SCHOOLS: PRESCHOOL THRU HIGH SCHOOL

SCHOOLS

STATE OF IOWA

BELLEVUE

Marquette High School, Bellevue, Iowa - (PAR) (Grades PreSchool-12) 502 Franklin St., Bellevue, IA 52031 t) 563-872-3356 (High School); (563) 872-3284 (Elementary) dbqe04@dbqarch.org Parishes Served: St. Joseph, Bellevue; St. Catherine, St. Catherine; St. Donatus, St. Donatus; SS. Peter and Paul, Springbrook. Geoffrey Kaiser, Prin.; Rev. G. Robert Gross, Pst. Min./Coord.; Stds.: 59; Lay Tchrs.: 8

Bellevue Area Consolidated School - (Grades PreSchool-12) 403 Park St., Bellevue, IA 52031 t) 563-872-3284 Parishes Served: St. Joseph, Bellevue; SS. Peter & Paul, Springbrook; St. Donatus, St. Donatus. Stds.: 190; Lay Tchrs.: 12

CALMAR

St. Teresa of Calcutta Faith Formation, Calmar, Iowa - (PAR) 107 E. South St., Calmar, IA 52132; Mailing: P.O. Box 819, Calmar, IA 52132 t) 563-562-3045 dbqrt1@dbqarch.org Serving: St. Aloysius, Calmar; Our Lady of Seven Dolors, Festina; St. Francis de Sales, Ossian; St. Wenceslaus, Spillville Yvette Anderson, Dir.; Rev. Henry P. Huber, Pastoral Coord.; Stds.: 110

CASCADE

Aquin Educational System, Cascade, Iowa - (PAR) (Grades PreSchool-8) 608 Third Ave., N.W., Cascade, IA 52033-0460; Mailing: P.O. Box 460, Cascade, IA 52033-0460 t) 563-852-3331 dbqe06@dbqarch.org Serving: St. Matthias, Cascade; Sacred Heart, Fillmore; St. Patrick, Garryowen; St. Peter, Temple Hill Dcn. Mark Otting, Pastoral Coord.; Stds.: 230; Lay Tchrs.: 21

Little Angels - t) 563-852-7020

Aquin Elementary School - (Grades PreSchool-8) t) (563) 852-3331 Laura Herbers, Prin.; Stds.: 230; Lay Tchrs.: 21

Aquin School of Religion - (Grades PreSchool-8) dbq023ff@dbqarch.org Nicole Casey, DRE; Stds.: 50

CEDAR RAPIDS

LaSalle Catholic, Cedar Rapids, Iowa - (PAR) (Grades PreSchool-8) 3700 First Ave., N.W., Cedar Rapids, IA 52405 t) 319-396-7818 (Elem.); 319-396-7792 (Middle School) dbqe12@dbqarch.org Serving the parishes of: St. John XXIII, St. Jude, St. Ludmila and St. Patrick, Cedar Rapids. Zach Zeckser, Admin.; Rev. Nicholas B. March, Pastoral Coord.; Stds.: 322; Lay Tchrs.: 36

LaSalle Middle School - (Grades PreSchool-8)

LaSalle Elementary - (Grades PreSchool-8) dbqe09@dbqarch.org Heather Williams, Prin.;

St. Pius and St. Elizabeth Ann Seton Schools, Cedar Rapids, Iowa - (Grades PreSchool-5) 4901 Council St., N.E., Cedar Rapids, IA 52402-2402 t) 319-393-4507 dbqe13@dbqarch.org Stephanie Sears, Prin.; Rev. Jon M. Seda, Pastoral Coord.; Stds.: 406; Lay Tchrs.: 23

Regis Middle School, Cedar Rapids, Iowa - (PAR) (Grades 6-8) 735 Prairie Dr., N.E., Cedar Rapids, IA 52402 t) 319-363-1968 dbqm02@dbqarch.org Parishes Served: All Saints, Immaculate Conception, St. Matthew, St. Pius X, and St. Wenceslaus, Cedar Rapids; St. Elizabeth Ann Seton, Hiawatha. Joshua Gredys, Prin.; Rev. John R. Flaherty, Pastoral Coord.; Stds.: 283; Lay Tchrs.: 20

DUBUQUE

Holy Family Catholic Schools, Dubuque, Iowa - (PAR) (Grades PreSchool-12) 2005 Kane St., Dubuque, IA 52001 t) 563-582-5456 dbqmd01@dbqarch.org Serves the parishes of Dubuque and St. Joseph, Key West. Phillip Bormann, Chief Admin.; Very Rev. Dennis J. Quint, Pastoral Coord.; Stds.: 1,896; Lay Tchrs.: 114

Our Lady of Guadalupe School - (Grades PreSchool-12) 2005 Kane St, Dubuque, IA 52001 t) 563-556-2820 dbqe21@dbqarch.org Kathleen Konrardy, Prin.; Stds.: 310; Lay Tchrs.: 18

St. Columbkille School - (Grades PreSchool-12) 1198 Rush St., Dubuque, IA 52003 t) 563-582-3532 dbqe22@dbqarch.org Sr. Catherine Stewart, OP, Prin.; Stds.: 335; Lay Tchrs.: 19

Resurrection School - (Grades PreSchool-12) 4320 Asbury Rd., Dubuque, IA 52002 t) 563-583-9488 dbqe20@dbqarch.org Denise Grant, Prin.; Stds.: 338; Lay Tchrs.: 18

Holy Ghost Daycare Center - (Grades PreSchool-12) 2981 Central Ave., Dubuque, IA 52001 t) 563-556-1511 Anita Valentine, Dir.;

Wahlert High School - (Grades PreSchool-12) 2005 Kane St., Dubuque, IA 52001 t) 563-583-9771 dbqh04@dbqarch.org Parishes Served: The Parishes in Dubuque; Holy Family, New Melleray; St. Joseph's, Key West. Mariah Reeves, Prin.; Rev. Andrew J Upah, Chap.; Stds.: 446; Lay Tchrs.: 30

Mazzuchelli Catholic Middle School - (Grades PreSchool-12) 2005 Kane St, Dubuque, IA 52001 t) 563-582-1198 dbqm03@dbqarch.com Daniel Thole, Prin.; Rev. Andrew J Upah, Chap.; Stds.: 339; Lay Tchrs.: 25

St. Joseph the Worker Early Childcare Center - 2105 Saint Joseph St., Dubuque, IA 52001 t) 563-582-1246 Anita Valentine, Dir.;

Resurrection Daycare Center - (Grades PreSchool-12) 4320 Asbury Rd., Dubuque, IA 52002 t) 563-583-5206 Anita Valentine, Dir.;

DYERSVILLE

St. Francis Xavier School, Dyersville, Iowa - (PAR) (Grades PreK-6) 203 Second St., S.W., Dyersville, IA 52040 t) 563-875-7376 dbqe26@dbqarch.org Serves: St. Francis Xavier, Dyersville; St. Joseph, Earlville; St. Boniface, New Vienna; SS. Peter & Paul, Petersburg; St. Paul, Worthington Peter Smith, Prin.; Rev. Christopher R. Podhajsky, Pastoral Coord.; Stds.: 351; Lay Tchrs.: 24

GILBERTVILLE

Bosco Catholic School System, Gilbertville, Iowa - (PAR) (Grades PreK-12) 405 16th Ave., Gilbertville, IA 50634 t) 319-296-1692 dbqh06@dbqarch.org Rev. Noah J. Diehm, Pastoral Coord.; Stds.: 309; Lay Tchrs.: 30

Don Bosco High School - (Grades PreK-12) 405 16th Ave, Gilbertville, IA 50634 t) (319) 296-1962 Parishes Served: Barclay, Eagle Center, Gilbertville, Jesup, and Raymond Shelby Douglas, Prin.; Stds.: 93; Lay Tchrs.: 12

Immaculate Conception School - (Grades PreK-12) 311 16th Ave., Gilbertville, IA 50634 t) 319-296-1089 dbqe31@dbqarch.org Shelby Douglas, Prin.; Stds.: 216; Lay Tchrs.: 17

St. Joseph School - (Grades PreK-12) 6916 Lafayette Rd., Raymond, IA 50667; Mailing: P.O. Box 158, Raymond, IA 50667 t) 319-233-5980 dbqe31@dbqarch.org Parishes served: Immaculate Conception, Gilbertville; St. Joseph, Raymond. Shelby Douglas, Prin.;

HOLY CROSS

LaSalle Elementary Schools, Holy Cross, Iowa - (PAR) (Grades PreSchool-6) 835 Church St., Holy Cross, IA 52053-0368; Mailing: P.O. Box 368, Holy Cross, IA 52053-0368 t) 563-870-2405 dbqe34@dbqarch.org Serves the following parishes: Balltown, Holy Cross, Luxemburg, Rickardsville, and Sherrill Brenda Lansing, Prin.; Rev. Tyler C Raymond, Pastoral Coord.; Stds.: 70; Lay Tchrs.: 5

MARSHALLTOWN

St. Francis Catholic School, Marshalltown, Iowa - (PAR) (Grades PreSchool-6) 310 Columbus Dr., Marshalltown, IA 50158 t) 641-753-8744 dbqe40@dbqarch.org Terry Eisenbarth, Prin.; Rev. Alan J. Dietzenbach, Pastoral Coord.; Stds.: 216; Lay Tchrs.: 18

MASON CITY

Newman Catholic School System - (PAR) (Grades PreSchool-12) 2445 19th St., S.W., Mason City, IA 50401 t) 641-423-6939 Rev. Neil J. Manternach, Pastoral Coord.; Stds.: 627; Lay Tchrs.: 40

Newman High School - (Grades PreSchool-12) 2445 19th St., S.W., Mason City, IA 50401 t) (641) 423-6939 dbqh07@dbqarch.org Parishes Served: St. Patrick, Clear Lake; Sacred Heart, Manly; Epiphany, Mason City; Sacred Heart, Rockwell. Tony Adams, Prin.; Stds.: 314; Lay Tchrs.: 19

Newman Child Care - 2050 S. McKinley Ave., Mason City, IA 50401 t) 641-423-0168 Kendra Mennen, Dir.;

Newman Elementary School - (Grades PreSchool-12) 2000 S. McKinley Ave., Mason City, IA 50401 t) 641-423-3101 dbqe41@dbqarch.org Vicki Ries, Lead Teacher; Stds.: 313; Lay Tchrs.: 22

NEW HAMPTON

St. John School of Religion, New Hampton, Iowa - (PAR) 823 W. Main St., New Hampton, IA 50659; Mailing: 313 W. Court St., New Hampton, IA 50659 t) 641-394-2404 dbqrt4@dbqarch.org Serves: St. Bernard, Alta Vista; St. Boniface, Ionia; Our Lady of Lourdes, Lourdes; Holy Family, New Hampton; Immaculate Conception, North Washington Jayden Burke, Dir.; Rev. James Goerend, Pastoral Coordinator; Stds.: 88

OSSIAN

St. Teresa of Calcutta School, Calmar, Iowa - (PAR) (Grades PreSchool-8) 414 E. Main St., Ossian, IA 52161 t) 563-532-9353 Serves the parishes of: St. Aloysius, Calmar; Our Lady of Seven Dolors, Festina; St. Francis de Sales, Ossian; and St. Wenceslaus, Spillville Kristin

Kriener, Prin.; Rev. Henry P. Huber, Pastoral Coord.; Stds.: 220; Lay Tchrs.: 16

St. Francis de Sales Center - (Grades PreSchool-8) 414 East Main St, Ossian, IA 52161 t) (563) 532-9353

St. Wenceslaus Center - (Grades PreSchool-8) 207 Church St., Spillville, IA 52168; Mailing: P.O. Box 68, Spillville, IA 52168 t) 563-562-3617

PEOSTA

Seton Catholic Schools, Farley, Iowa - (PAR) (Grades PreK-8) 7597 Burds Rd., Peosta, IA 52068 t) 563-556-5967 dbqe28@dbqarch.org Serves the parishes of: St. Clement, Bankston; St. Patrick, Epworth; St. Joseph, Farley; St. John the Baptist, Peosta; and St. John, Placid Eric Meyer, Prin.; Rev. Michael G. Schueller, Pastoral Coord.; Stds.: 335; Lay Tchrs.: 24

St. Joseph Center - (Grades PreK-8) 210 2nd Ave., S.E., Farley, IA 52046 t) 563-744-3290

Peosta Center - (Grades PreK-8) 7597 Burds Rd., Peosta, IA 52068

PROTIVIN

Trinity Catholic School, Protivin, Iowa - (PAR) (Grades K-6) 116 N. Main St., Protivin, IA 52163 t) 563-569-8556 dbqe47@dbqarch.com Serves: Holy Trinity, Protivin; St. Luke, St. Lucas; St. John, Fort Atkinson. Jerry Brown, Prin.; Rev. Nicholas R Radloff, Pastoral Coord.; Stds.: 49; Lay Tchrs.: 5

WATERLOO

Cedar Valley Catholic Schools, Waterloo, Iowa - (PAR) (Grades PreSchool-12) 3231 W. 9th St., Waterloo, IA 50702 t) 319-232-1422 dbqmw01@dbqarch.org Serving the parishes of Waterloo. Thomas Novotney, Admin.; Very Rev. Scott E. Bullock, Pastoral Coord.; Stds.: 779; Lay Tchrs.: 58

Blessed Sacrament Daycare - (Grades PreSchool-12) 600 Stephan Ave., Waterloo, IA 50701 t) 319-233-7863 Carley Epling, Dir.; Stds.: 109; Lay Tchrs.: 4

St. Edward School - (Grades PreSchool-12) 139 E. Mitchell Ave, Waterloo, IA 50702 t) 319-233-6202 dbqe51@dbqarch.org Serves the parishes of Waterloo. Aaron Becker, Prin.; Stds.: 293; Lay Tchrs.: 21

Columbus High School - (Grades PreSchool-12) 3231 W 9th St, Waterloo, IA 50702 t) 319-233-3358 dbqh08@dbqarch.org Parishes Served: St. Patrick, Cedar Falls; Blessed Sacrament, Queen of Peace, Sacred Heart and St. Edward, Waterloo. Tony Harrington, Prin.; Stds.: 234; Lay Tchrs.: 20

Blessed Maria Assunta Pallotta Middle School - (Grades PreSchool-12) 3225 W. 9th St., Waterloo, IA 50702 t) 319-232-6592 dbqm04@dbqarch.org Parishes served: the parishes of Waterloo. Aaron Becker, Prin.; Stds.: 143; Lay Tchrs.: 13

HIGH SCHOOLS

STATE OF IOWA

CEDAR RAPIDS

Xavier High School, Cedar Rapids, Iowa - (PAR) (Grades 9-12) 6300 42nd St., N.E., Cedar Rapids, IA 52411 t) 319-294-6635 Serving the parishes of Cedar Rapids; St. Elizabeth Ann Seton, Hiawatha; and St. Joseph, Marion Angela Olson, Prin.; Rev. Richmond Dzekoe (Ghana), Chap.; Rev. Gary A. Mayer, Pastoral Coord.; Chris McCarville, Pres.; Stds.: 593; Lay Tchrs.: 40

DYERSVILLE

Beckman Catholic High School, Dyersville, Iowa - (PAR) (Grades 7-12) 1325 Ninth St., S.E., Dyersville, IA 52040 t) 563-875-7188 dbqh05@bdqarch.org Serves: St. Francis Xavier, Dyersville; St. Joseph, Earlville; St. Boniface, New Vienna; Ss. Peter and Paul, Petersburg; and St. Paul, Worthington Marcel Kielkucki, Prin.; Steven Lueck, Asst. Prin.; Rev. Christopher R. Podhajsky, Pastoral Coord.; Stds.: 352; Lay Tchrs.: 26

INSTITUTIONS LOCATED IN DIOCESE

CAMPUS MINISTRY / NEWMAN CENTERS [CAM]

AMES

St. Thomas Aquinas Church, Ames, Iowa - 2210 Lincoln Way, Ames, IA 50014-7184 t) 515-292-3810 dbq004@dbqarch.org www.staparish.net Serves the campus of Iowa State University, Ames. Rev. Kyle M. Digmann, Pst.; Dcn. Frank Montabon; Emily Klaus, Dir., Campus Ministry;

CEDAR FALLS

Catholic Student Center of Cedar Falls, Iowa - 1019 W. 23rd St., Cedar Falls, IA 50613-3550 t) 319-266-9863 dbq303@dbqarch.org www.ststephenuni.org Serves the campus of the University of Northern Iowa, Cedar Falls. Rev. Mark D. Murphy, Chap.; Paul Lee, Dir., Campus Ministry;

CATHOLIC CHARITIES [CCH]

CEDAR RAPIDS

Metro Catholic Outreach - Sister Mary Lawrence Community Center, 420 6th St., S.E., #120, Cedar Rapids, IA 52401 t) 319-739-5490 info@metrocatholicoutreach.org www.metrocatholicoutreach.org Social Justice organization Kate Getty, Exec. Dir.;

DUBUQUE

Catholic Charities of the Archdiocese of Dubuque - 1229 Mt. Loretta Ave., Dubuque, IA 52003 t) 563-588-0558 dbqccced@dbqarch.org www.catholiccharitiesdubuque.org Tracy Morrison, Exec. Dir.; Asstd. Annu.: 15,731

Catholic Charities - Ames Office - 2210 Lincoln Way, Ames, IA 50014; Mailing: 1229 Mount Loretta Ave., Dubuque, IA 52003 t) 515-296-2759 Lisa Turner, Clinical Dir./Counselor; Sarah Thomas, Counselor;

Catholic Charities - Cedar Rapids Office - 420 Sixth St., S.E., Ste. 220, Cedar Rapids, IA 52401; Mailing: 1229 Mount Loretta Ave., Dubuque, IA 52003 t) 319-364-7121 Yer Vang, Dir./Immigration Attorney; Jim Jacobson, Immigration Attorney; Denise Patters, Immigration Attorney; Saadat Ahmadi, Interpreter/Navigator; Gloire Sabwira, Case Mgr.;

Catholic Charities - Decorah Office - 307 W. Main St., Decorah, IA 52101; Mailing: 1229 Mount Loretta Ave., Dubuque, IA 52003 t) (563) 382-1926 Lori Eastwood, Counselor; Holly Reilly, Counselor;

Catholic Charities - Waterloo Office - 1425 Kimball Ave., Waterloo, IA 50702; Mailing: 1229 Mount Loretta Ave., Dubuque, IA 52003 t) 319-272-2080 Miryam Antunez De Mayolo, Immigration Attorney; Megan Stammeyer, PR Dir.; Julianne Klesel, Counselor; Daniel Shafer, Jail & Prison Reentry Coord.;

Catholic Charities - Dubuque - 1229 Mt. Loretta Ave, Dubuque, IA 52003 t) (563) 588-0558 Ry Meyer, Immigration Attorney; Angella Link, Counselor/Post Adoption Search Coord.; Lindsey Hageman, Counselor; Amy Mahoney, Counselor; Todd Ostwinkle, Counselor; Karen Hoeger, Jail & Prison Reentery Coord.; Stacy Sherman, Community Outreach Dir.;

Catholic Charities Housing - 1229 Mt. Loretta Ave., Dubuque, IA 52003 t) 563-556-8476 dbqcchss@dbqarch.org Properties owned: Carter Plaza, Ecumenical Tower & Kennedy Park West; Heartland East (Maquoketa); and Alabar Plaza (Waterloo). Michael DeMoully, Dir.;

Opening Doors - 2100 Asbury Rd., Ste. 8, Dubuque, IA 52001 t) 563-582-7480 cgebhart@openingdoorsdbq.org www.openingdoorsdbq.org Sponsors: Sinsinawa Dominicans, Sisters of the Presentation, Sisters of Charity, B.V.M, Sisters of the Visitation and Dubuque Franciscan Sisters. Carol Gebhart, Exec. Dir.;

Maria House - 1561 Jackson St., Dubuque, IA 52001 t) 563-582-6286

Teresa Shelter - 1111 Bluff St., Dubuque, IA 52001 t) 563-690-0086

Presentation Lantern - Schmid Innovation Center, 900 Jackson St., Ste. LL5-1, Dubuque, IA 52001 t) 563-557-7134 info@thelanterncenter.org www.thelanterncenter.org Education and welcome center for immigrants. Megan Ruiz, Dir.;

CEMETERIES [CEM]

CEDAR RAPIDS

St. John's Cemetery Association, Cedar Rapids, Iowa - 2107 J St., S.W., Cedar Rapids, IA 52404 t) 319-362-8894 Rev. Kenneth J. Glaser, Corp. Secy.;

St. Joseph's Cemetery Association, Clinton Township, Linn County, Iowa - Sisley Grove Rd., Cedar Rapids, IA 52405; Mailing: 50 Edgewood Rd., N.W., Cedar Rapids, IA 52405 t) 319-390-3520 Rev. Nicholas B. March, Corp. Secy.;

Mt. Cavalry Cemetery Association, Cedar Rapids, Iowa - 2310 1st. Ave., Cedar Rapids, IA 52402 t) 319-362-4659 Rev. Douglas J. Loecke, Corp. Secy.;

DUBUQUE

Catholic Cemeteries, Incorporated, of the Archdiocese of Dubuque - 1229 Mt. Loretta Ave., Dubuque, IA 52003 t) 563-556-2580 dbqcopsdir@dbqarch.org Ken Funke, Dir.;

Mount Calvary Cemetery Association - 1111 Davis St., Dubuque, IA 52001 t) 563-583-4329 Rev. Steven M. Garner, Corp. Secy.;

Mount Olivet Cemetery Association - 10556 Military Rd., Dubuque, IA 52003 t) 563-582-7059 Rev. Thomas J. McDermott, Corp. Secy.;

OSAGE

St. Patrick's Cemetery Association, McIntire, Mitchell County, Iowa - Timber Ave, Osage, IA 50461; Mailing: 218 S. 12th St., Osage, IA 50461 t) 641-732-4342 Rev. Raymond A. Burkle, Corp. Secy.;

WATERLOO

Catholic Cemeteries of Waterloo, Waterloo, Iowa - 3912 W. 4th St., Waterloo, IA 50701 t) 319-233-0746 Very Rev. Scott E. Bullock, Contact;

COLLEGES & UNIVERSITIES [COL]

CEDAR RAPIDS

Mount Mercy University - 1330 Elmhurst Dr., N.E., Cedar Rapids, IA 52402-4797 t) 319-363-8213 president@mtmercy.edu www.mtmercy.edu Founded by the Sisters of Mercy Dr. Todd Olson, Pres.; Sr. Linda Bechen, R.S.M., Vice Pres. Mission & Ministry; Dr. Timothy Laurent, Provost & Vice Pres., Academic Affairs; Todd Coleman, Vice Pres., Enrollment & Mktg.; Anne Gillespie, Vice Pres., Bus. & Fin.; Brenda Haefner, Vice Pres., Devel. & Alumni Rels.; Dr. Nate Klein, Vice Pres., Student Success; Stds.: 1,526; Lay Tchrs.: 79

DUBUQUE

Clarke University of Dubuque, Iowa - 1550 Clarke Dr., Dubuque, IA 52001 t) 563-588-6300 presidentsoffice@clarke.edu www.clarke.edu Conducted by the Sisters of Charity, B.V.M. Fletcher M Lamkin, Interim Pres.; Rev. Dustin L. Vu, Chap.; Eden Wales Freedman, Vice Pres., Academic Affairs; Elizabeth McGrath, Vice Pres., Bus. & Fin.; Julie A. Cirks, Vice Pres., Enrollment Mngmt.; Bill Biebuyck, Vice Pres., Institutional Advancement; Kate Zanger, Vice Pres., Student Life; Jody Pfohl, Dir., H.R.; Susanne Leibold, Library Dir.; Stds.: 956; Lay Tchrs.: 76; Sr. Tchrs.: 1

Loras College - 1450 Alta Vista St., Dubuque, IA 52001 t) 563-588-7100 jim.collins@loras.edu www.loras.edu (Accredited by the North Central Assoc. of Colleges and Secondary Schools) Jim Collins, Pres.; Rev. Dustin L. Vu, Chap.; Stds.: 1,357; Lay Tchrs.: 93

CONVENTS, MONASTERIES, AND RESIDENCES FOR WOMEN [CON]

CEDAR RAPIDS

Sisters of Mercy of the Americas West Midwest Community, Inc. Sacred Heart Convent - 1125 Prairie Dr., N.E., Cedar Rapids, IA 52402-4737 t) 319-364-5196 tbkokontis@sistersofmercy.org www.sistersofmercy.org Residence for the Sisters of Mercy of the Americas - West Midwest Community. Sr. Susan Sanders, R.S.M., Vice. Pres.; Srs.: 417

Catherine McAuley Center, Cedar Rapids - 866 4th Ave. SE, Cedar Rapids, IA 52403 t) 319-363-4993 paula@cmc-cr.org

DUBUQUE

Mt. Loretto Convent - 2360 Carter Rd., Dubuque, IA 52001-2997 t) 563-588-2008 www.dbqpbvms.org Motherhouse and Novitiate of the Sisters of the Presentation of the B.V.M. Sr. Carmen Hernandez, P.B.V.M., Pres.; Sr. Rita Menart, P.B.V.M., Vice. Pres.; Rev. Mark A. Ressler, Chap.; Srs.: 80

Mt. St. Francis (Sisters of St. Francis of the Holy Family Charitable Trust) - 3390 Windsor Ave., Dubuque, IA 52001-1326 t) 563-583-9786 info@osfdbq.org www.osfdbq.org Motherhouse and Novitiate of the Sisters of St. Francis of the Holy Family Sr. Kathy Knipper, O.S.F., Pres.; Sr. Pat Clemen, O.S.F., Vice. Pres.; Stacy Francois, Secy.; Srs.: 35

Our Lady of the Mississippi Abbey (Trappistine Nuns, Inc.) - 8400 Abbey Hill Ln., Dubuque, IA 52003 t) 563-582-2595 sisters@olmabbey.org www.mississippiabbey.org Iowa Cistercians of the Strict Observance Mother Rebecca Stramoski, O.C.S.O., Abbess; Srs.: 20

Sisters of Charity of the Blessed Virgin Mary - 1100 Carmel Dr., Dubuque, IA 52003-7991 t) 563-588-2351 www.bvmsisters.org Sr. LaDonna Manternach, B.V.M., Pres.; Sr. Carol Marie Baum, B.V.M., Vice. Pres.; Sr. Kate Hendel, B.V.M., Vice. Pres.; Sr. Katherine Kandefer, B.V.M., Vice. Pres.; Srs.: 221

Sisters of the Visitation - 2360 Carter Rd., Dubuque, IA 52001-2997 t) (563) 588-2008 carmen@dbqpbvms.org Legal Name: Sisters of the Visitation of the Immaculate Heart of Mary, Dubuque, Iowa. Sr. Patricia Clark, S.V.M., Pres.; Srs.: 3

ENDOWMENTS / FOUNDATIONS / TRUSTS [EFT]

CEDAR FALLS

***Sartori Health Care Foundation, Inc. (MercyOne Cedar Falls Foundation)** - 515 College St., Cedar Falls, IA 50613 t) 319-268-3161 joe.surma@mercyhealth.com; tim.huber@mercyhealth.com www.mercyone.org Joe Surma, Dir.;

CEDAR RAPIDS

***Catholic Foundation for the Archdiocese of Dubuque** - 120 5th St., N.W., Cedar Rapids, IA 52405 t) 563-552-0176 cfad@ourcfad.org www.ourcfad.org Michele Brock, Dir.;

Mercy Medical Center, Endowment Foundation, Inc., Cedar Rapids, IA - 701 Tenth St., S.E., Cedar Rapids, IA 52403 t) 319-398-6894; 319-398-6793 jsatterlee@mercycare.org Cheryle Mitvalsky, Chair; Lorrie Erusha, Pres.;

Xavier High School Foundation - 6300 42nd St., N.E., Cedar Rapids, IA 52411; Mailing: P.O. Box 10956, Cedar Rapids, IA 52410 t) 319-378-4571 mharken@xavierfoundation.org Financially supports Xavier High School, Cedar Rapids, Iowa. Mary Harken, Dir.; Very Rev. David H. O'Connor, Pastoral Coord.;

DUBUQUE

Archdiocese of Dubuque Education Fund - 1229 Mt. Loretta Ave., Dubuque, IA 52003-8787 t) 563-556-2580 dbqcfo@dbqarch.org Brian Harris, Contact;

Archdiocese of Dubuque Seminarian Education Fund - 1229 Mt. Loretta Ave., Dubuque, IA 52003-8787 t) 563-556-2580 dbqcfo@dbqarch.org Brian Harris, Contact;

Catholic Charities Foundation (St. Mary's Home) - 1229 Mt. Loretta Ave., Dubuque, IA 52003 t) 563-556-2580 dbqccced@dbqarch.org Supports the work of Catholic Charities of the Archdiocese of Dubuque. Most Rev. Michael Owen Jackels, Pres.; Rev. Msgr. Thomas E. Toale, Vice. Pres.; Tracy Morrison, Exec. Dir.;

Declaration of Trust of the Paul & Janet Auterman Charitable Educational Trust - 4300 Asbury Rd., Dubuque, IA 52002 t) 563-556-7511 dbq058@dbqarch.org; dbq058bm@dbqarch.org Purpose: Fund to assist students attending our local Catholic schools (Pre-K to 12th). Very Rev. Phillip G. Gibbs, Contact;

Hennessy Charitable Trust - 2360 Carter Rd., Dubuque, IA 52001-2997 t) 563-588-2008 joy@dbqpbvms.org www.dbqpbvms.org Virginia Foletta, Chair; Marjorie Healy, Trustee; Elaine Hoye, Trustee; Ann Jackson, Trustee; Sr. Laura Reicks, R.S.M., Trustee;

WATERLOO

MercyOne Waterloo Medical Center Foundation - 3421 W. Ninth St., Waterloo, IA 50702 t) 319-272-7676; 319-272-7302 joe.surma@mercyhealth.com; tim.huber@mercyhealth.com www.mercyone.org Joe Surma, Dir.;

WEBSTER CITY

St. Thomas Aquinas Foundation of Webster City, Iowa - 1000 Des Moines St., Webster City, IA 50595-2147 t) 515-832-1190 dbq218@dbqarch.org www.stthomaswc.org Rev. Francis Kwame Anane (Ghana), Pst.;

HOSPITALS / HEALTH SERVICES [HOS]

CEDAR FALLS

MercyOne Cedar Falls Medical Center (Sartori Memorial Hospital, Inc.) - 515 College St., Cedar Falls, IA 50613 t) 319-268-3000 jack.dusenbery@mercyhealth.com; tim.huber@mercyhealth.com www.mercyone.org Tim Huber, Contact; Bed Capacity: 101; Asstd. Annu.: 43,610; Staff: 164

CEDAR RAPIDS

Mercy Medical Center-Cedar Rapids - 701 Tenth St., S.E., Cedar Rapids, IA 52403 t) 319-398-6894; 319-398-6793 jsatterlee@mercycare.org; kgrady@mercycare.org www.mercycare.org Sponsored by the Institute of the Sisters of Mercy of the Americas. Dr. Timothy Quinn, CEO; Rev. James P. Brokman, Chap.; Tammy Buseman, Chap.; Yvette Jackson, Chap.; Shuji Moriichi, Chap.; Emily Steeples, Chap.; Janet McGrath Satterlee, Dir.; Bed Capacity: 358; Asstd. Annu.: 165,000; Staff: 2,873

Mercycare Service Corporation - 701 10th St. S.E., Cedar Rapids, IA 52403 t) 319-398-6894; 319-398-6793 jsatterlee@mercycare.org; kgrady@mercycare.org (Parent Corp.), Sponsored by the Institute of the Sisters of Mercy of the Americas. Dr. Timothy Quinn, CEO; Bed Capacity: 358; Asstd. Annu.: 165,000; Staff: 2,873

DUBUQUE

MercyOne Dubuque Medical Center - 250 Mercy Dr., Dubuque, IA 52001 t) 563-589-8000 mercydubuque@mercyhealth.com www.mercydubuque.com A member of Mercy Health Network. Legal Name: Mercy Health Services - Iowa, Corp. Kay Takes, Pres.; Deb Fleming, Chap.; Malissa Sue Sprenger, Vice. Pres.; Bed Capacity: 247; Asstd. Annu.: 52,000; Staff: 1,402

DYERSVILLE

MercyOne Dyersville Medical Center - 1111 Third St., S.W., Dyersville, IA 52040 t) 563-875-7101 mercydyersville@mercyhealth.com www.mercydubuque.com A Member of Mercy Health Network. Legal Name: Mercy Health Services - Iowa, Corp. Kay Takes, Pres.; Malissa Sue Sprenger, Vice. Pres.; Bed Capacity: 20; Asstd. Annu.: 4,250; Staff: 100

MASON CITY

MercyOne - North Iowa - 1000 4th St. S.W., Mason City, IA 50401 t) 641-428-7000 questions@mercyhealth.com Rod Schlader, Pres.; Rev. Paul E. Lippstock, Chap.; Bed Capacity: 342; Asstd. Annu.: 565,000; Staff: 2,454

NEW HAMPTON

MercyOne - New Hampton Medical Center - 308 N. Maple Ave., New Hampton, IA 50659 t) 641-394-4121 newhampton@mercyhealth.com www.mercynewhampton.com Legal Name: Mercy Health Services - Iowa, Corp. Aaron Flugum, Pres.; Sr. Victoria Arndorfer, R.S.M., Chap.; Bed Capacity: 18; Asstd. Annu.: 53,195; Staff: 122

OELWEIN

MercyOne Oelwein Medical Center - 201 8th Ave., S.E., Oelwein, IA 50662 t) 319-283-6000 jack.dusenbery@mercyhealth.com; tim.huber@mercyhealth.com www.mercyone.org A member of MercyOne. Legal Name: Mercy Hospital of Franciscan Sisters, Inc. Jack Dusenbery, CEO; Bed Capacity: 64; Asstd. Annu.: 21,530; Staff: 99

WATERLOO

MercyOne Northeast Iowa - 3421 W. Ninth St., Waterloo, IA 50702 t) 319-272-8000 iaadmin@mercyhealth.com; nancy.schaefer@mercyhealth.com www.mercyone.org Legal Name: Wheaton Franciscan Healthcare-Iowa, Inc. Jack Dusenbery, Pres.;

MercyOne Waterloo Medical Center - 3421 W. Ninth St., Waterloo, IA 50702 t) 319-272-8000 jack.dusenbery@mercyhealth.com; tim.huber@mercyhealth.com www.mercyone.org Member of Mercy Health Network. Legal Name: Covenant Medical Center, Inc. Jack Dusenbery, Pres.; Rev. Solomon Farinto (Nigeria), Chap.; Bed Capacity: 346; Asstd. Annu.: 221,316; Staff: 1,057

MISCELLANEOUS [MIS]

CEDAR RAPIDS

St. Vincent de Paul Particular Council of Cedar Rapids, Iowa - 928 7th St., S.E., Cedar Rapids, IA 52401; Mailing: P.O. Box 1093, Cedar Rapids, IA 52406-1093 t) 319-365-5091 store.crsvdp@gmail.com www.crsvdp.org Jacqueline Buchman, Dir.;

DUBUQUE

Archdiocese of Dubuque Alternative Investments Grantor Trust - 1229 Mt. Loretta Ave., Dubuque, IA 52003 t) 563-556-2580 dbqcfo@dbqarch.org Brian Harris, Contact;

Archdiocese of Dubuque Deposit and Loan Fund - 1229 Mt. Loretta Ave., Dubuque, IA 52003-8787 t) 563-556-2580 dbqcfo@dbqarch.org Brian Harris, Contact;

Archdiocese of Dubuque Perpetual Care Fund - 1229 Mt. Loretta Ave., Dubuque, IA 52003-8787 t) 563-556-2580 dbqcfo@dbqarch.org Brian Harris, Contact;

Bureau of Education of the Archdiocese of Dubuque - 1229 Mt. Loretta Ave., Dubuque, IA 52003 t) 563-556-2580 dbqsupt@dbqarch.org Cathy Walz, Supt.;

Metropolitan Office of Catholic Education - 120 5th St., N.W., Cedar Rapids, IA 52405 t) 319-366-2517

Our Faith, Our Children, Our Future, School Tuition Organization - 1229 Mt. Loretta Ave., Dubuque, IA 52003 t) 563-556-2580 dbqcfo@dbqarch.org www.ourfaithsto.org Purpose: provide tuition assistance to students enrolled in accredited non public schools located within the Archdiocese. Jennifer Decker, Bd. Pres.; Steve Kane, Contact; Brian Harris, Treas.;

St. Raphael Priest Fund Society of the Archdiocese of Dubuque - 1229 Mt. Loretta Ave., Dubuque, IA 52003 t) 563-556-2580 dbqcfo@dbqarch.org To assist the Archdiocese of Dubuque in the support and care of its retired, disabled & infirm priests. Most Rev. Michael Owen Jackels, Pres.; Rev. Msgr. Thomas E. Toale, Vice. Pres.; Rev. Steven J. Rosonke, Treas.;

Villa Raphael - 1155 Mt. Loretta Ave., Dubuque, IA 52003 t) 563-588-2049 dbqvilla@dbqarch.org Administered by the Archdiocese of Dubuque and funded by the St. Raphael Priest Fund Society. Patricia Flores, Dir.;

PEOSTA

Cistercian Studies Quarterly, Inc. - 6632 Melleray Cir., New Melleray Abbey, Peosta, IA 52068 t) 563-588-2319 x111 csq@newmelleray.org www.cistercian-studies-quarterly.org Sponsor: Cistercian Order of the Strict Observance of the USA Region. Bro. Paul Andrew Tanner, O.C.S.O., Editor;

MONASTERIES AND RESIDENCES FOR PRIESTS AND BROTHERS [MON]

PEOSTA

New Melleray Abbey, Order of Cistercians of the Strict Observance (Corporation of New Melleray) - 6632 Melleray Cir., Peosta, IA 52068 t) 563-588-2319 frsteve@newmelleray.org www.newmelleray.org Rt. Rev. Brendan J. Freeman, O.C.S.O., Supr.; Rev. David R. Bock, O.C.S.O., Mem.; Bro. Gilbert B. Cardillo, O.C.S.O., Mem.; Bro. Cyprian Griffith, O.C.S.O., Mem.; Bro. Paul Halaburt, O.C.S.O., Mem.; Rev. Cyprian Harrison, O.C.S.O., Mem.; Rev. Ephrem Poppish, O.C.S.O., Prior; Bro. Thomas Imhoff, O.C.S.O., Mem.; Bro. Nicholas Koenig, O.C.S.O., Mem.; Bro. Paul Andrew Tanner, O.C.S.O., Subprior; Rev. Alberic R. Farbolin, O.C.S.O., Mem.; Bro. Joseph Kronebusch, O.C.S.O., Mem.; Bro. Juan Diego Lavado, O.C.S.O., Mem.; Rev. Thomas A. MacMaster, O.C.S.O., Mem.; Rev. Alberic Maisog, O.C.S.O., Mem.; Bro. John O'Driscoll, O.C.S.O., Mem.; Bro. Robert Simon, O.C.S.O., Mem.; Bro. Francis Flaherty, O.C.S.O., Mem.; Bro. Dennis Vavra, O.C.S.O., Mem.; Rev. Stephen Verbest, O.C.S.O., Contact; Brs.: 13; Priests: 8

NURSING / REHABILITATION / CONVALESCENCE / ELDERLY CARE [NUR]

CEDAR RAPIDS

Hallmar-Mercy Medical Center - 701 Tenth St. S.E., Cedar Rapids, IA 52403 t) 319-398-6894; 319-398-6793 jsatterlee@mercycare.org Cedar Rapids Regional, owned and operated by Mercy Medical Center. Institute of the Sisters of Mercy of the Americas. Dr. Timothy Quinn, CEO; Asstd. Annu.: 55; Staff: 53

DUBUQUE

Stonehill Franciscan Services, Inc. - 3485 Windsor Ave., Dubuque, IA 52001-1312 t) 563-557-7180 gbrown@stonehilldbq.com www.stonehilldbq.com Gretchen Brown, Pres.; Kim Budde, Bd. Pres.; Rev. Paul Attah-Nsiah (Ghana), Chap.; Asstd. Annu.: 200; Staff: 400

Stonehill Benevolent Foundation - Sponsored by Sisters of St. Francis of the Holy Family. Paul Kronlage, Bd. Chair;

DYERSVILLE

Ellen Kennedy Living Center - 1177 7th St., S.W., Dyersville, IA 52040 t) 563-875-6323 oakcrest@mercyhealth.com Sponsor: MercyOne Dyersville. Purpose: provide funds to assure persons of limited resources access to programs and services at the Center Kari A. Wittmeyer, Dir.; Asstd. Annu.: 50; Staff: 29

MercyOne Dyersville Medical Center-OakCrest Manor - 1111 Third St., S.W., Dyersville, IA 52040 t) 563-875-7101 mercydyersville@mercyhealth.com www.mercydubuque.com (A Division of Mercy Health Services - Iowa) Kay Takes, Pres.; Malissa Sue Sprenger, Vice. Pres.; Asstd. Annu.: 65; Staff: 40

RETREAT HOUSES / RENEWAL CENTERS [RTR]

DUBUQUE

Shalom Spirituality Center - 1001 Davis St., Dubuque, IA 52001-1306 t) 563-582-3592 info@shalomretreats.org www.shalomretreats.org Sisters of St. Francis of Dubuque, Iowa Sr. Pat Clemen, O.S.F., Contact;

HIAWATHA

Prairiewoods Franciscan Spirituality Center - 120 E. Boyson Rd., Hiawatha, IA 52233-1277 t) 319-395-6700 ecospirit@prairiewoods.org www.prairiewoods.org Prairiewoods (sponsored by Franciscan Sisters of Perpetual Adoration) is a sacred space to explore & nurture a relationship with God, self & creation Leslie Wright, Dir.;

PEOSTA

New Melleray Guest House - 6632 Melleray Cir., Peosta, IA 52068 t) 563-588-2319 guesthouse@newmelleray.org www.newmelleray.org Bro. Paul Andrew Tanner, O.C.S.O., Contact;

SEMINARIES [SEM]

DUBUQUE

Seminary of St. Pius X - 1235 Mt. Loretta Ave., Dubuque, IA 52003 t) 563-556-2580 dbqspx@dbqarch.org Very Rev. David A. Schatz, Rector; Rev. Thomas J. McDermott, Spiritual Dir.; Stds.: 12

EPWORTH

Divine Word College - 102 Jacoby Dr., S.W., Epworth, IA 52045-0380; Mailing: P.O. Box 380, Epworth, IA 52045-0380 t) 563-876-3353 tascheman@dwci.edu www.dwci.edu Society of the Divine Word (S.V.D.). Rev. Thang Hoang, S.V.D., Rector; Rev. Thomas J. Ascheman, S.V.D., Pres.; Rev. John Szukalski, S.V.D., Vice. Pres.; Rev. Long Phi Nguyen, S.V.D., Vice Pres., Formation & Dean, Students; Rev. Raymond Asagdem Akumbilim, SVD, Assoc. Dean, Students; Rev. Stephen Kha Nguyen, S.V.D., Prof.; Rev. Sam Cunningham, S.V.D., Prof.; Rev. Alexander Roedlach, S.V.D., Prof.; Bro. Tony Kreinus, S.V.D., Librn.; Bro. Brian McLauchlin, S.V.D., Instructor; Rev. Akizou Gerard Kamina, S.V.D., Instructor; Rev. Paul Malinit Aquino, S.V.D., Liturgy Dir.; Rev. James Bergin, S.V.D., Spiritual Adv./Care Srvcs.; Rev. Edmundus Yosef Soni De Class, S.V.D., Spiritual Adv./Care Srvcs.; Rev. Xuan Hien Pham, S.V.D., In Res.; Rev. William Shea, S.V.D., In Res.; Bro. Daniel Yunck, S.V.D., In Res.; Rev. Ky Ngoc Dinh, S.V.D., Devel.; Rev. Simon Thoi Hoang, S.V.D., Spiritual Dir. & Instructor; Rev. George Koottappillil, S.V.D., Spiritual Svcs.; Rev. Son Peter Le, S.V.D., Technical Svcs.; Rev. Adam MacDonald, S.V.D., Vocations Min.; Rev. Linh Pham, S.V.D., Devel.; Bro. Vinh Vincent Trinh, S.V.D., Tech Svcs.; Bro. Michael Decker, S.V.D., Spiritual Adv./Care Srvcs.; Bro. Larry Kieffer, S.V.D., In Res.; Rev. Tuan Hoang, S.V.D., Vocation Recruiter; Rev. Joseph McDermott, S.V.D., In Res.; Rev. Thinh Cuong Ngo, SVD, Vocation Recruiter; Rev. Anthony Cong Nguyen, S.V.D., Vocation Recruiter; Stds.: 105; Bro. Tchrs.: 1; Lay Tchrs.: 20; Pr. Tchrs.: 12; Sr. Tchrs.: 2

SPECIAL CARE FACILITIES [SPF]

DUBUQUE

Clare House - 3340 Windsor Ave., Dubuque, IA 52001-1326 t) 563-583-9786 info@osfdbq.org www.osfdbq.org Sisters of St. Francis, Dubuque. Sr. Kathy Knipper, O.S.F., Pres.; Sr. Bertha Bonert, O.S.F., Dir.; Bed Capacity: 76; Asstd. Annu.: 100; Staff: 155

Diocese of Duluth

(Dioecesis Duluthensis)

MOST REVEREND DANIEL J. FELTON

Bishop of Duluth; ordained, June 13, 1981; appointed Bishop of Duluth, April 7, 2021; ordained May 20, 2021.

Pastoral Center: 2830 E. Fourth St., Duluth, MN 55812. T: 218-724-9111; F: 218-724-1056.
www.dioceseduluth.org

ESTABLISHED OCTOBER 3, 1889.

Corporate Title: Diocese of Duluth.

Square Miles 22,354.

Comprises the counties of Aitkin, Carlton, Cass, Cook, Crow Wing, Itasca, Koochiching, Lake, Pine and St. Louis in the State of Minnesota.

For legal titles of parishes and diocesan institutions, consult the Chancery Office.

STATISTICAL OVERVIEW

Personnel
Bishop....1
Priests: Diocesan Active in Diocese....39
Priests: Diocesan Active Outside Diocese....3
Priests: Retired, Sick or Absent....22
Number of Diocesan Priests....64
Religious Priests in Diocese....2
Total Priests in your Diocese....66
Extern Priests in Diocese....5
Ordinations:
Diocesan Priests....2
Transitional Deacons....1
Permanent Deacons....4
Permanent Deacons in Diocese....62
Total Sisters....43

Parishes
Parishes....70
With Resident Pastor:
Resident Diocesan Priests....33
Resident Religious Priests....2
Without Resident Pastor:
Administered by Priests....33
Administered by Deacons....2
Pastoral Centers....1
Professional Ministry Personnel:
Lay Ministers....30

Welfare
Catholic Hospitals....2
Total Assisted....276,149
Homes for the Aged....1
Total Assisted....920

Educational
Diocesan Students in Other Seminaries....11
Total Seminarians....11
Colleges and Universities....1
Total Students....3,512
High Schools, Diocesan and Parish....1
Total Students....12
Elementary Schools, Diocesan and Parish....7
Total Students....1,512
Catechesis/Religious Education:
High School Students....1,587
Elementary Students....1,844
Total Students under Catholic Instruction....8,478
Teachers in Diocese:
Sisters....2
Lay Teachers....294

Vital Statistics
Receptions into the Church:
Infant Baptism Totals....402
Minor Baptism Totals....36
Adult Baptism Totals....12
Received into Full Communion....69
First Communions....430
Confirmations....402
Marriages:
Catholic....104
Interfaith....41
Total Marriages....145
Deaths....632
Total Catholic Population....41,493
Total Population....452,293

LEADERSHIP

Office of Bishop - Most Rev. Daniel J. Felton;
Pastoral Center - t) 218-724-9111 www.dioceseduluth.org
Vicar General - Rev. James B. Bissonette;
Finance Officer - Franz Hoefferle;
Diocesan Corporate Board - Rev. James B. Bissonette; Rev. Steven Laflamme; Catherine VonRuden;
Moderator of the Curia (Vacant) -
Safe Environment - Rev. James B. Bissonette;
Chancellor - Rev. Steven Laflamme;
Judicial Vicar - Rev. Steven Laflamme;
Marriage Tribunal Coordinator - Shawna Hansen;
Defenders of the Bond - Heather Eichholz; Ashley Subler;
Procurator (Vacant) -
Promoter of Justice - Rev. James B. Bissonette;
Notaries - Rose Marie Eichmueller; Shawna Hansen; Michelle Lynn Wright;
College of Consultors - Rev. Steven Langenbrunner, Mem.; Rev. Brandon Moravitz, Mem. (fr.brandon.moravitz@duluthcatholic.org); Rev. Michael Garry, Mem.;
Diocesan Deans - Rev. Michael Garry, Dean; Rev. Joseph A. Sirba, Dean; Rev. Steven Langenbrunner, Dean;
Diocesan Finance Council Chair - Most Rev. Daniel J. Felton;

OFFICES AND DIRECTORS

Archivist (Historical) - Laurie Bisel, Archivist;
Boy Scouts (Vacant) -
Campus Ministry - Rev. Michael Schmitz;
Cemeteries - Rev. James B. Bissonette;
Censor of Books - Rev. Steven Laflamme;
Council of Catholic Women - t) 218-728-3646 Rev. Anthony Wroblewski, Moderator;
Department of Catechesis, RCIA, and Lay Apostolate - Grace Woitalla, Dir.;
Department of Catholic Schools - Wade Mathers, Dir.;
Department of Communications - Dcn. Kyle Eller, Dir.;
Department of Continuing Formation of Clergy - Rev. Steven Laflamme;
Department of Indian Ministry (Vacant) -
Department of Liturgy - Rev. Joel Hastings;
Department of Marriage and Family Life - Betsy Kneepkens, Dir.;
Department of Ministry to Priests - Rev. Anthony Wroblewski, Dir.;
Department of Mission Advancement - Margaret Slawin, Dir.;
Department of Permanent Diaconate - Dcn. Dan Goshey, Dir.;
Department of Protection of Children & Young People - Ernie Stauffenecker, Dir.;
Victim Assistance Coordinators - Esther Reagan; Tab Baumgartner;
Department of Social Apostolate and CHD - Patrice Critchley-Menor, Dir.;
Department of Vocations and Priestly Formation - Rev. Nicholas Nelson, Dir.;
Department of Youth and Young Adult Ministry - Rev. Michael Schmitz, Dir.;
Diocesan Newspaper "The Northern Cross" - Dcn. Kyle Eller, Editor;
Mission Outreach and Propagation of the Faith - Dcn. William Stein;

PARISHES, MISSIONS, AND CLERGY

STATE OF MINNESOTA

AITKIN

St. James - 299 Red Oak Dr., Aitkin, MN 56431 t) 218-927-6581 aitkincatholic.org Rev. Michael Patullo, Pst.; Dcn. Michael Eisenbraun; Dcn. William Stein; Dcn. Michael Barta; CRP Stds.: 89

AURORA

Our Lady of Hope - 16 W. Fifth Ave. N., Aurora, MN 55705 t) 218-229-3210 debbie.servaty@duluthcatholic.org; deidre.westover@duluthcatholic.org Rev. Kristoffer T. McKusky, Pst.; Dcn. Mark Skala; CRP Stds.: 54

BABBITT

St. Pius X - 15 Ash Blvd., Babbitt, MN 55706 t) 218-827-2291 kathy.roethler@duluthcatholic.org Rev. Charles Friebohle, Pst.; Dcn. Don Klick; CRP Stds.: 10

BEROUN

St. Joseph - 19390 Praha Ave., Beroun, MN 55063; Mailing: 555 8th St. SW, Pine City, MN 55063 t) 320-629-2935 stjosephsberoun@gmail.com; vicki.pixley@duluthcatholic.org Rev. Msgr. Aleksander Suchan, Pst.; Dcn. Mark Pulkrabek;

BIGFORK

Our Lady of the Snows - 320 Golf Course Ln., Bigfork, MN 56628; Mailing: PO Box 11, Bigfork, MN 56628 t) 218-743-3255 ourladyofthesnows@duluthcatholic.org www.olschurch.us Rev. Jeremy Bock, Pst.; CRP Stds.: 4

BRAINERD

All Saints - 16898 Carlson Lake Rd., Brainerd, MN 56401; Mailing: 411 N. 10th St., Brainerd, MN 56401-0327 t) 218-822-4040 sfasoffice@duluthcatholic.org www.blccnorth.org Rev. Michael Garry, Pst.; Rev. Matthew Miller, Par. Vicar; Rev. Scott Daniel Padrnos, Par. Vicar; Dcn. Joseph Des Marais; Dcn. Thomas Freece; Dcn. Michael Knuth; CRP Stds.: 59

St. Andrew - 1108 Willow St., Brainerd, MN 56401 t) 218-829-1340 st.andrews@lakescatholic.org www.blccsouth.org Rev. Gabriel Waweru, Pst.; Dcn. Gerald Bock; Dcn. Keith Grow; Dcn. Mike Koecheler; Dcn. John G Kroll; Dcn. Daniel O'Reilly; CRP Stds.: 557

St. Francis - 404 N. 9th St., Brainerd, MN 56401; Mailing: 411 N. 10th St., Brainerd, MN 56401-3027 t) 218-822-4040 djohnson@lakescatholic.org; sfasoffice@duluthcatholic.org www.blccnorth.org Rev. Michael Garry, Pst.; Rev. Matthew Miller, Par. Vicar; Dcn. Ralph Bakeberg; Dcn. Michael Knuth; Dcn. Joseph Des Marais; Dcn. Thomas Freece; Celeste Badger, DRE; Britt Johnson, DRE; Dan Johnson, DRE; Maureen Pickar, Bus. Mgr.; CRP Stds.: 238

St. Francis of the Lakes - (Grades PreK-8) 817 Juniper St., Brainerd, MN 56401 t) 218-829-2344 office@sf-school.org www.stfranciscatholicschool.org Jennifer Nagel, Prin.; Stds.: 239; Lay Tchrs.: 15

St. Thomas - 11395 Pine Beach Peninsula Rd., Brainerd, MN 56401; Mailing: 411 N. 10th St., Brainerd, MN 56401-3027 t) 218-822-4040 sfasoffice@duluthcatholic.org Rev. Michael Garry, Pst.; Rev. Matthew Miller, Par. Vicar; Dcn. Ralph Bakeberg; Dcn. Joseph DesMarais; Dcn. Thomas Freece; Dcn. Michael Knuth;

BUHL

Our Lady of the Sacred Heart - 118 Pennsylvania Ave., Buhl, MN 55713-0027; Mailing: P.O. Box 27, Buhl, MN 55713-0027 t) 218-254-5703 c) 218-421-3365 sjolsh@duluthcatholic.org Rev. Paul Strommer, Admin.; CRP Stds.: 3

CARLTON

St. Francis - 31 County Rd. 1, Carlton, MN 55718; Mailing: 509 Sunrise Dr., Carlton, MN 55718 t) 218-384-4563 stfmjcatholic@gmail.com stfmjcatholic.org Rev. Joel Hastings, Pst.; Dcn. Steven Hedlund; CRP Stds.: 38

CASS LAKE

St. Charles - 308 Central Ave. N., Cass Lake, MN 56633; Mailing: PO Box 98, Deer River, MN 56636 t) 218-335-2359; (218) 246-8582 stmarys@paulbunyan.net stcharleschurch.weconnect.com Rev. Kuriakose Nediakala, M.C.B.S., Admin.; Maria Patten, DRE; CRP Stds.: 15

CHISHOLM

St. Joseph - 113 Fourth St., S.W., Chisholm, MN 55719 t) 218-254-5703; 218-421-3365 sjolsh@duluthcatholic.org www.chisholmbuhlcatholic.org Rev. Paul Strommer, Admin.; CRP Stds.: 58

CLOQUET

Holy Family - 280 Reservation Rd., Cloquet, MN 55720; Mailing: 102 4th St., Cloquet, MN 55720 t) 218-879-6793 queenofpeaceoffice@duluthcatholic.org Rev. Nicholas Nelson, Pst.; Dcn. Jon Skansgaard;

Queen of Peace - 102 4th St., Cloquet, MN 55720 t) 218-879-6793 queenofpeaceoffice@duluthcatholic.org qopparish.com Rev. Nicholas Nelson, Pst.; Dcn. Jon Skansgaard; Bekah Swanson, DRE; CRP Stds.: 76

Queen of Peace School - (Grades PreK-6) t) 218-879-8516 queenofpeaceschool.org/ David Douglas, Prin.; Stds.: 108; Lay Tchrs.: 11

COHASSET

St. Augustine - 601 N.W. 2nd Ave., Cohasset, MN 55721; Mailing: 315 S.W. 21st St., Grand Rapids, MN 55744 t) 218-326-2843 www.itascacatholic.org Rev. Blake Edward Rozier, Pst.; Dcn. Steve Schuler; Dcn. Ron Guertin;

COLERAINE

Mary Immaculate - 10 Corey St., Coleraine, MN 55722; Mailing: P.O. Box 290, Coleraine, MN 55722 t) 218-885-6321 (CRP); 218-885-1126 www.scmicatholic.com Rev. Joseph T. Sobolik, Pst.; Mari Jo Anderson, DRE;

COOK

St. Mary - 124 5th St., S.E., Cook, MN 55723; Mailing: P.O. Box 609, Cook, MN 55723 t) 218-666-5334 stmaryscook@q.com www.stmmhc.com Rev. Beau Braun, Pst.; CRP Stds.: 16

CROMWELL

Immaculate Conception - 5944 Hwy. 210, Cromwell, MN 55726; Mailing: PO Box 378, Floodwood, MN 55736 t) 218-476-2367 churchstlouis@gmail.com nemncatholic.com Rev. Pio Atonio, Pst.;

CROSBY

St. Joseph's Church, Crosby - 617 Poplar St., Crosby, MN 56441 t) 218-546-6559 crosbycatholic@gmail.com cuyunacatholic.org Rev. Elias Gieske, Pst.; Dcn. Dan Goshey; Dcn. Roger Marks; Dcn. Philip Mayer; CRP Stds.: 151

CROSSLAKE

Immaculate Heart Church - 35208 County Rd. 37, Crosslake, MN 56442; Mailing: PO Box 155, Crosslake, MN 56442 t) 218-692-3731 www.crosslakecatholic.com Rev. David Forsman; Dcn. James Kirzeder; Dcn. Barry Olson; CRP Stds.: 72

Our Lady of Snows -

DEER RIVER

St. Joseph - 51061 Wolf Dr., Deer River, MN 56636; Mailing: PO Box 98, Deer River, MN 56636 t) 218-246-8582 stmarys@paulbunyan.net deerrivercatholic.com Rev. Kuriakose Nediakala, M.C.B.S., Admin.;

St. Mary - 15 1st Ave., N.W., Deer River, MN 56636; Mailing: P.O. Box 98, Deer River, MN 56636 t) 218-246-8582 stmarys@paulbunyan.net deerrivercatholic.com Rev. Kuriakose Nediakala, M.C.B.S., Admin.; Liann Bommersbach, DRE; CRP Stds.: 47

DULUTH

Cathedral of Our Lady of the Rosary - 2801 E. 4th St., Duluth, MN 55812 t) 218-728-3646 duluth.cathedral@duluthcatholic.org www.duluthcathedral.com Rev. Trevor Peterson, Par. Vicar; Rev. Anthony Wroblewski, Rector; Dcn. Rodger Brannan; Dcn. James Philbin; CRP Stds.: 107

St. Benedict - 1419 St. Benedict St., Duluth, MN 55811 t) 218-724-4828 faithformation@stbensduluth.org; secretary@stbensduluth.org www.stbensduluth.org Rev. Seth Gogolin, Pst.; Dcn. Kyle Eller; Dcn. John Specht; Dcn. John Weiske; Elizabeth Cyr, Parish Life Coord.;

Sonya Morris, DRE; CRP Stds.: 35

Holy Family - 2430 W. 3rd St., Duluth, MN 55806-1801 t) 218-722-4445 holyfamilyduluth@yahoo.com catholicduluth.org Rev. Anthony John Craig, Pst.; Dcn. Timothy Kittelson; Dcn. John Foucault;

Indian Missions - 2830 E. Fourth St., Duluth, MN 55812 t) 218-724-9111

St. James - 721 N. 57th Ave. W., Duluth, MN 55807 t) 218-624-0125 youth@stjamesduluth.org; slaveau@stjamesduluth.org www.stjamesparishduluth.com/ Rev. Richard Kunst, Pst.; Dcn. Lyle Johnson; CRP Stds.: 53

St. John - 3 W. Chisholm St., Duluth, MN 55803; Mailing: 4230 St. John's Ave., Duluth, MN 55803 t) 218-724-6332 www.saintjohnsduluth.org Rev. Seth Gogolin, Pst.; Dcn. Walt Beier; CRP Stds.: 54

St. Joseph - 151 W. Linden St., Duluth, MN 55811; Mailing: 2410 Morris Thomas Rd., Duluth, MN 55811 t) (218) 481-7161 stjosephduluthheights@gmail.com www.stjosephduluth.com Rev. John C. Petrich, Admin.; CRP Stds.: 12

St. Lawrence - 2410 Morris Thomas Rd., Duluth, MN 55811 t) 218-722-2259 stlawrencechurch@msn.com www.catholicduluth.org Rev. Anthony John Craig; Dcn. John Foucault; Dcn. Timothy Kittelson; Karen Ball, DRE; CRP Stds.: 153

St. Mary Star of the Sea - 325 E. Third St., Duluth, MN 55805 t) 218-722-3078 stmarystarofthesea@duluthcatholic.org www.stmarystaroftheseaduluth.com/ Rev. Anthony Wroblewski, Pst.; Rev. Trevor Peterson, Par. Vicar; Dcn. Rodger Brannan; Dcn. James Philbin; CRP Stds.: 4

St. Michael - 4901 E. Superior St., Duluth, MN 55804 t) 218-525-1902 denise.connolly@duluthcatholic.org; fr.andrew.knop@duluthcatholic.org stmichaelsduluth.org Rev. William C. Graham, Pst.; Rev. Andy Knop, Admin.; CRP Stds.: 37

St. Raphael - 5779 Seville Rd., Duluth, MN 55811 t) 218-729-7537 raphaelchurch@yahoo.com www.straphaelandstrose.com Rev. James B. Bissonette, Pst.; Dcn. Paul Sever; Dcn. Thomas Kubat; Dcn. Carl Provost; Kathy Ellingson, DRE; CRP Stds.: 96

ELY

St. Anthony - 231 E. Camp St., Ely, MN 55731 t) 218-365-4017 stanthonydef@gmail.com; fr.charles.friebohle@duluthcatholic.org www.stanthonysely.org Rev. Charles Friebohle, Pst.; Dcn. Don Klick; CRP Stds.: 34

EMILY

St. Emily - 39922 Lake St., Emily, MN 56447; Mailing: PO Box 25, Emily, MN 56447 t) 218-763-2101 2stemily@gmail.com www.emilycatholic.com Rev. David Forsman, Pst.; Dcn. James Kirzeder; Dcn. Barry Olson;

EVELETH

Resurrection - 301 Adams Ave., Eveleth, MN 55734; Mailing: P.O Box 586, Eveleth, MN 55734 t) 218-744-3277 nicole.nguyen@duluthcatholic.org; mary.hecimovich@duluthcatholic.org Rev. Justin Fish, Pst.; Ashley Judnick, DRE; Janine Lavigne, Homebound Ministry Coord.; CRP Stds.: 75

FLOODWOOD

St. Louis - 105 E. 4th Ave., Floodwood, MN 55736; Mailing: P.O. Box 378, Floodwood, MN 55736 t) 218-476-2367 churchstlouis@gmail.com Rev. Pio Atonio, Pst.; CRP Stds.: 28

FORT RIPLEY

St. Mathias - 4529 County Rd. 121, Fort Ripley, MN 56449; Mailing: 1108 Willow St., Parish Office of St. Andrew's & St. Mathias, Brainerd, MN 56401 t) 218-829-1340 st.andrews@lakescatholic.org www.blccsouth.org Rev. Gabriel Waweru, Pst.; Dcn. Gerald Bock; Dcn. Keith Grow; Dcn. Michael Koecheler; Dcn. Daniel O'Reilly; Dcn. John G Kroll; CRP Stds.: 45

Crow Wing State Park -

GARRISON

Our Lady of Fatima - 27332 Central St., Garrison, MN 56450; Mailing: 617 Poplar St., Crosby, MN 56441 t) 218-546-6559 crosbycatholic@gmail.org cuyunacatholic.org Rev. Elias Gieske, Pst.; Dcn. Roger Marks; Dcn. Dan Goshey; Dcn. Philip Mayer;

GILBERT

St. Joseph - 515 Summit & Louisiana Ave. W., Gilbert, MN 55741; Mailing: Box 586, Eveleth, MN 55734 t) 218-744-3277 nicole.nguyen@duluthcatholic.org; mary.hecimovich@duluthcatholic.org Rev. Justin Fish, Pst.; Ashley Judnick, DRE; Janine Lavigne, Homebound Ministry Coord.; CRP Stds.: 13

GNESEN

St. Joseph - 6110 Church Rd., Gnesen, MN 55803; Mailing: 4901 E. Superior St., Duluth, MN 55804 t) 218-525-1902 Rev. Andrew Knop, OMI, Pst.; CRP Stds.: 13

GRAND MARAIS

St. John - 10 E. 5th St., Grand Marais, MN 55604; Mailing: P.O. Box 549, Grand Marais, MN 55604 t) 218-387-1409 www.stjohns-holyrosary.org Rev. Steven Langenbrunner, Pst.; CRP Stds.: 20

GRAND PORTAGE

Holy Rosary - 43 Upper Rd., Grand Portage, MN 55605; Mailing: PO Box 549, Grand Marais, MN 55604 t) 218-387-1409 www.stjohns-holyrosary.org Rev. Steven Langenbrunner, Pst.; CRP Stds.: 3

GRAND RAPIDS

St. Joseph - 315 S.W. 21st St., Grand Rapids, MN 55744 t) 218-326-2843 www.itascacatholic.org/ Rev. Blake Edward Rozier, Admin.; Dcn. Steve Schuler; Dcn. Ron Guertin; Lisa Neary, DRE; CRP Stds.: 205

St. Joseph School - (Grades PreK-6) t) 218-326-6232 principal@stjosephscatholic.org www.itascacatholic.org Teresa Matetich, Prin.; Stds.: 195; Lay Tchrs.: 8

HACKENSACK

Sacred Heart - 300 First St. N., Hackensack, MN 56452; Mailing: Box 874, Walker, MN 56484 t) 218-547-1054 stagneswalkermn@gmail.com stagnesandsacredheart.com Rev. Timothy John Lange, Pst.;

HIBBING

Blessed Sacrament - 2310 7th Ave. E., Hibbing, MN 55746 t) 218-262-5541 parish@blsachibbing.org www.blessedsacramenthibbing.org Rev. Daniel Weiske, Pst.; Dcn. Grant Toma; Ben Milani, Youth Min.; Deborah Toma, Family Faith Formation; Jennifer Steinbrecher, Sunday School Coord.; CRP Stds.: 110

Assumption Catholic School - (Grades PreSchool-6) t) 218-263-3054 secretary@acshibbing.org www.acshibbing.org David Pritschet, Prin.; Stds.: 156; Lay Tchrs.: 8

Blessed Sacrament Chapel - 12825 Sturgeon Rd., Side Lake, MN 55781; Mailing: 2310 7th Ave. E., Hibbing, MN 55746 t) (218) 262-5541 www.blsachibbing.org

HINCKLEY

St. Patrick - 203 Lawler Ave. S., Hinckley, MN 55037-0490; Mailing: PO Box 490, Hinckley, MN 55037 t) 952-221-1183 (CRP); 320-384-6313 x3 jimmostek@yahoo.com; saintpatricks@scicable.com stpatrick-luke.org Rev. Joseph A. Sirba, Pst.; Dcn. Steve Odegard; Dcn. James Mostek, DRE; CRP Stds.: 59

INTERNATIONAL FALLS

St. Thomas Aquinas - 810 Fifth St., International Falls, MN 56649 t) 218-283-3293 x200 stthomasifalls.org Rev. Thomas Galarneault, Pst.; CRP Stds.: 30

St. Thomas Aquinas School - (Grades PreSchool-4) t) 218-283-3430 www.stthomascatholicschool.com/ Megan Whelchel, Prin.; Stds.: 28; Lay Tchrs.: 3

LITTLEFORK

St. Columban - 1017 4th Ave., Littlefork, MN 56653; Mailing: 810 Fifth St., International Falls, MN 56649 t) 218-283-3293 www.stthomasifalls.org/ Rev. Thomas Galarneault, Pst.; CRP Stds.: 2

LONGVILLE

St. Edward - 4905 MN-84, Longville, MN 56655; Mailing: P.O. Box 38, Longville, MN 56655-0038 t) 218-363-2799 stedwardlongville@yahoo.com stedwardandstpaul.org/ Dcn. Richard Paine, Admin.;

MCGRATH

Our Lady of Fatima - 102 S. Hwy. 65, McGrath, MN 56350; Mailing: 299 Red Oak Dr., Aitkin, MN 56431 t) 218-927-6581 www.mcgregorcatholicchurch.org Rev. Michael Patullo, Pst.; Dcn. Michael Barta;

MCGREGOR

Holy Family - 2 S. Maddy St., McGregor, MN 55760; Mailing: 299 Red Oak Dr., Aitkin, MN 56431 t) 218-927-6581 www.mcgregorcatholicchurch.org Rev. Michael Patullo, Pst.; Dcn. Michael Barta; CRP Stds.: 19

MEADOWLANDS

St. Mary - 9999 Hwy. 133, Meadowlands, MN 55765; Mailing: PO Box 378, Floodwood, MN 55736 t) 218-476-2367 churchstlouis@gmail.com nemncatholic.com Rev. Pio Atonio, Pst.;

MOOSE LAKE

Holy Angels - 60 Hartman Dr., Moose Lake, MN 55767; Mailing: PO Box 487, Moose Lake, MN 55767 t) 218-485-8214 holyangels@duluthcatholic.org www.mooselakecatholiccommunity.com/ Rev. Francis Kabiru, Pst.; CRP Stds.: 85

NASHWAUK

St. Cecilia's - 326 Second St., Nashwauk, MN 55769 t) 218-885-6321 (CRP); 218-885-1126 marijo.andersen@duluthcatholic.org www.scmicatholic.com/ Rev. Joseph T. Sobolik, Pst.; Dcn. Richard Johnston; Mari Jo Anderson, DRE; CRP Stds.: 38

NORTHOME

St. Michael - 12026 Lake St., Northome, MN 56661; Mailing: PO Box 11, c/o Our Lady of the Snows, Bigfork, MN 56628 t) 218-743-3255 Rev. Jeremy Bock, Pst.; CRP Stds.: 11

ORR

Holy Cross - 10696 Shady Grove Ln. S., Orr, MN 55771; Mailing: P.O. Box 609, Cook, MN 55723 t) 218-666-5334 stmaryscook@q.com www.stmmhc.com Rev. Beau Braun, Pst.; CRP Stds.: 10

PEQUOT LAKES

Our Lady of the Lakes - 30918 Rasmussen Rd., Pequot Lakes, MN 56472; Mailing: PO Box 759, Pequot Lakes, MN 56472 t) 218-568-4760 stalicechurch@gmail.com www.ourladylakes.com Rev. Michael Garry, Admin.; Dcn. David Craig; Dcn. Mike Marvin; Dcn. Richard Paine; CRP Stds.: 103

PINE CITY

Immaculate Conception - 555 8th St., S.W., Pine City, MN 55063 t) 320-629-3911 (CRP); 320-629-2935 iccoffice@duluthcatholic.org; vicki.pixley@duluthcatholic.org iccpinecity.org Rev. Msgr. Aleksander Suchan, Pst.; Dcn. Eugene Biever; Dcn. Mark Pulkrabek; CRP Stds.: 111

PROCTOR

St. Rose - 2 Sixth Ave., Proctor, MN 55810; Mailing: 5779 Seville Rd., Duluth, MN 55811 t) 218-624-0007 saintroseproctor@qwestoffice.net www.straphaelandstrose.com Rev. James B. Bissonette, Pst.; Dcn. Thomas Kubat; Dcn. Carl Provost; Dcn. Paul Sever; Suzanne Lott, DRE; CRP Stds.: 26

REMER

St. Paul - 101 3rd Ave., S.E., Remer, MN 56672; Mailing: P.O. Box 38, Longville, MN 56655 t) 218-363-2799 stedwardlongville@yahoo.com Dcn. Richard Paine, Admin.; CRP Stds.: 12

SANDSTONE

St. Luke - 122 Commercial Ave. N., Sandstone, MN 55072; Mailing: P.O. Box 644, Sandstone, MN 55072 t) 320-245-5175 saintlukes@scicable.com stpatrick-luke.org Rev. Joseph A. Sirba, Pst.; Dcn. James W Mostek; Dcn. Steve Odegard; CRP Stds.: 49

SAWYER

SS. Mary & Joseph - 1225 Mission Rd., Sawyer, MN 55780; Mailing: 509 Sunrise Dr., Carlton, MN 55718 t) 218-384-4563 stfmjcatholic@gmail.com stfmjcatholic.org Rev. Joel Hastings, Pst.; Dcn. Bryan Bassa; CRP Stds.: 25

SILVER BAY

St. Mary - 57 Horn Blvd., Silver Bay, MN 55614

t) 218-226-3100 stmarysilverbay@outlook.com stmarysilverbay.org Rev. Steven Laflamme, Pst.; Rev. Michael J. Lyons, In Res.; CRP Stds.: 22

SQUAW LAKE

St. Catherine - 52265 State Hwy. 46, Squaw Lake, MN 56681; Mailing: PO Box 11, c/o Our Lady of the Snows, Bigfork, MN 56628 t) 218-743-3255 Rev. Jeremy Bock, Pst.; CRP Stds.: 7

STURGEON LAKE

St. Isidore - 9010 Main St., Sturgeon Lake, MN 55783; Mailing: 8118 Lake St., Willow River, MN 55795-0097 t) 218-372-3284; 218-485-8214 (CRP) st.mary.church@frontiernet.net; holyangels@duluthcatholic.org wwwmooselakecatholiccommunity.com Rev. Francis Kabiru, Pst.; Teresa Danelski, DRE; Kari Janz, DRE; CRP Stds.: 15

TOWER

St. Martin - 107 N. 3rd St., Tower, MN 55790; Mailing: P.O. Box 757, Tower, MN 55790 t) 218-753-4310 maryann.rot@duluthcatholic.org www.stmmhc.com Rev. Beau Braun, Pst.; CRP Stds.: 7

TWO HARBORS

Holy Spirit - 227 Third St., Two Harbors, MN 55616 t) 218-834-4659 www.holyspirittwoharbors.org Rev. Steven Laflamme, Pst.; Dcn. Timothy Egan; CRP Stds.: 63

VIRGINIA

Holy Spirit - 306 S. Second St., Virginia, MN 55792 t) 218-741-6344 ben.frost@duluthcatholic.org; jessica.haverkamp@duluthcatholic.org www.holyspiritvirginia.com Rev. Brandon Moravitz, Pst.; Dcn. Daniel Schultz; Dcn. Richard Moravitz; CRP Stds.: 59

Marquette Catholic School - (Grades PreK-8) 311 Third St. S., Virginia, MN 55792 t) 218-741-6811 mcsprincipal01@gmail.com www.marquettecatholicschool.com Lisa Kvas, Prin.; Stds.: 204; Lay Tchrs.: 15

WALKER

St. Agnes - 210 Division St., Walker, MN 56484; Mailing: PO Box 874, Walker, MN 56484 t) 218-547-1054 stagneswalkermn@gmail.com stagnesandsacredheart.com Rev. Timothy John Lange, Pst.; Taylor Knight, DRE; CRP Stds.: 80

WILLOW RIVER

St. Mary - 8118 Lake St., Willow River, MN 55795 t) 218-372-3284 (CRP); 218-485-8214 st.mary.church@frontiernet.net; holyangels@duluthcatholic.org mooselakecatholiccommunity.com Rev. Francis Kabiru, Pst.; Teresa Danelski, DRE; Kari Janz, DRE; CRP Stds.: 15

SCHOOLS: PRESCHOOL THRU HIGH SCHOOL

SCHOOLS

STATE OF MINNESOTA

DULUTH

Stella Maris Academy (Duluth Area Catholic Schools, Holy Rosary School, St. James School, St. John's School) - (DIO) (Grades PreK-10) 4321 Allendale Ave., Duluth, MN 55803 t) 218-623-6253 andrew.hilliker@stellamaris.academy www.stellamaris.academy Andrew Dean Hilliker, Pres.; Jesse Murray, Prin.; Julianne Blazevic, Prin.; Michael Mazzio, Bus. Mgr.; Stds.: 580; Lay Tchrs.: 44

Holy Rosary School - (Grades PreK-10) 2802 E. 4th St., Duluth, MN 55812 t) 218-724-8565 jesse.murray@stellamaris.academy Stds.: 280; Lay Tchrs.: 18

St. James Catholic School - (Grades PreK-10) 715 N. 57th Ave., W., Duluth, MN 55807 t) 218-624-1511 julianne.blazevic@stellamaris.academy www.stellamaris.academy/ Stds.: 140; Lay Tchrs.: 13

St. John's School - (Grades PreK-10) 1 W. Chisholm St., Duluth, MN 55803 t) 218-724-9392 jesse.murray@stellamaris.academy Stds.: 150; Lay Tchrs.: 13

Stella Maris Academy Jr. / Sr. High School - (Grades PreK-10) 4321 Allendale Ave., Duluth, MN 55803 t) (218) 724-6201 Chris Lemke, Prin.; Stds.: 12; Sr. Tchrs.: 1; Lay Tchrs.: 3

INSTITUTIONS LOCATED IN DIOCESE

ASSOCIATIONS [ASN]

TWO HARBORS

Saint Raphaels Guild A Chartered Guild of the Catholic Medical Association - 398 Scenic Dr., Two Harbors, MN 55616 c) 218-349-9175 Timothy J. Egan, Pres.;

CAMPUS MINISTRY / NEWMAN CENTERS [CAM]

DULUTH

Newman Catholic Campus Ministry - 421 W. Marie St., Duluth, MN 55811 t) 218-728-3757 heather.serena@duluthcatholic.org www.bulldogcatholic.org Heather Serena, Campus Min.; Rev. Michael Schmitz, Dir.;

CEMETERIES [CEM]

DULUTH

Calvary Cemetery - 4820 Howard Gnesen Rd., Duluth, MN 55803 t) 218-724-3376 tim.sailstad@duluthcatholic.org; calvaryduluth@gmail.com www.calvarycemeteryduluth.com

COLLEGES & UNIVERSITIES [COL]

DULUTH

College of St. Scholastica - 1200 Kenwood Ave., Duluth, MN 55811 t) 218-723-6000; 800-447-5444 www.css.edu Barbara McDonald, Pres.; Sr. Kathleen Del Monte, O.S.B., Assoc. Vice Pres., Mission Integration; Stds.: 3,512; Lay Tchrs.: 187

CONVENTS, MONASTERIES, AND RESIDENCES FOR WOMEN [CON]

DULUTH

Motherhouse and Novitiate of the Sisters of Saint Benedict - St. Scholastica Monastery, 1001 Kenwood Ave., Duluth, MN 55811 t) 218-723-6555 braway@css.edu www.duluthbenedictines.org Sr. Luce Marie Dionne, O.S.B., Archivist; Srs.: 43

ENDOWMENTS / FOUNDATIONS / TRUSTS [EFT]

CLOQUET

Educational Endowment Trust, Queen of Peace Church - 102 4th St., Cloquet, MN 55720 t) 218-879-6793 qopoffice@gmail.com Rev. Nicholas Nelson, Pst.;

DULUTH

Holy Rosary Parish Endowment Fund - 2801 E. Fourth St., Duluth, MN 55812 t) 218-728-3646 business@duluthcathedral.com Rev. Anthony Wroblewski, Rector;

The Human Life and Development Fund of the Diocese of Duluth - 2830 E. Fourth St., Duluth, MN 55812 t) 218-724-9111 franz.hoefferle@duluthcatholic.org Franz Hoefferle, Dir.;

The Seminarian Endowment Fund of the Diocese of Duluth - 2830 E. 4th St., Duluth, MN 55812 t) 218-724-9111 franz.hoefferle@duluthcatholic.org Franz Hoefferle, Secy.;

The Catholic Religious Education Endowment Fund of the Diocese of Duluth - 2830 E. 4th St., Duluth, MN 55812 t) 218-724-9111 franz.hoefferle@duluthcatholic.org Franz Hoefferle, Dir.;

HIBBING

Hibbing Catholic Schools Endowment Fund - 2310 7th Ave. E., Hibbing, MN 55746 t) 218-262-5541 parish@blsachibbing.org Rev. Daniel Weiske, Pst.;

HOSPITALS / HEALTH SERVICES [HOS]

BRAINERD

St. Joseph's Medical Center - 523 N. Third St., Brainerd, MN 56401 t) 218-829-2861; (218) 786-4010 info@essentiahealth.org; bret.reuter@essentiahealth.org www.essentiahealth.org Bret David Reuter, Admin.; Dr. Jon Pryor, Pres.; Bed Capacity: 127; Asstd. Annu.: 68,483; Staff: 868

DULUTH

St. Mary's Medical Center (Essentia Health-St. Mary's Medical Center) - 407 E. Third St., Duluth, MN 55805 t) 218-786-4000; (218) 786-4215 (Chapel/Catholic Priest) tom.foster@essentiahealth.org; bret.reuter@essentiahealth.org www.essentiahealth.org Part of the Essentia Health system Dr. Jon Pryor, Pres.; Rev. Thomas J. Foster, Chap.; Bret David Reuter, Admin.; Bed Capacity: 362; Asstd. Annu.: 131,442; Staff: 1,995

MISCELLANEOUS [MIS]

BEMIDJI

S.W. Deanery Chapter of Magnificat of the Diocese of Duluth - 3625 Waville Rd., N.E., Bemidji, MN 56601 t) 218-675-6180 garoutte@tds.net Mary Rients, Contact;

DEER RIVER

***Our Lady of the Holy Trinity Magnificat Chapter** - 33350 State Hwy. 46, Deer River, MN 56636 t) 218-251-6556 rtnorris7@gmail.com (Sub-chapter of S.W. Deanery Chapter of the Magnificat-Our Lady of the Lakes)

DULUTH

Benedictine Sisters Benevolent Association - 1001 Kenwood Ave., Duluth, MN 55811-2300 t) 218-723-6089 braway@css.edu www.duluthbenedictines.org Sr. Beverly Raway, O.S.B., Pres.;

Benedictine Foundation - 4560 Norway Pines Pl., Hermantown, MN 55811 t) 218-786-2370 laurie.hennen@benedictineliving.org giving.benedictineliving.org/ Benedictine Associated Foundations located in Dioceses of Bismarck, Fargo, New Ulm, St. Paul and Minneapolis, and Winona-Rochester. Laurie Hennen, Pres.; Jerry Carley, CEO;

Benedictine Health Center dba Benedictine Living Community - 935 Kenwood Ave., Duluth, MN 55811 brian.pattock@bhshealth.org www.benedictineliving.org/duluth-mn/ (Sub. of Benedictine Health System) Brian Pattock, Admin.;

Benedictine Health System (Sponsored by Benedictine Sisters Benevolent Association) - 4560 Norway Pines Pl., Hermantown, MN 55811 t) 218-786-2370 jerry.carley@benedictineliving.org www.benedictineliving.org Sponsored facilities include, among others, Benedictine Care Centers, DBA Benedictine Living Community New Brighton (STP) Sr. Joan Marie Stelman, O.S.B., SVP Mission Integration; Jerry Carley, Pres.;

Benedictine Living Communities Inc. - 4560 Norway Pines Pl., Hermantown, MN 55811 t) 218-786-2370 BLC-Garrison, BLC-Dickinson/Benedict Court; (FAR) BLC-Ellendale/Evergreen Place, BLC-LaMoure, BLC-Wahpeton/Siena Court Jerry Carley, CEO;

St. Joseph's Medical Center, Brainerd - 523 N. Third St., Brainerd, MN 56401 t) 218-829-2861 Affiliated with Essentia Health Dr. Kevin Casey, Chief Medical Officer; Bed Capacity: 162; Asstd. Annu.: 80,536; Staff: 1,135

St. Mary's Medical Center - 407 E. Third St., Duluth, MN 55805 t) 218-786-4000 Affiliate: St. Mary's Hospital of Superior, WI Janice Schade, Admin.; Anne Stephen, Chief Medical Officer; Rev. Thomas J. Foster, Chap.; Bed Capacity: 337; Asstd. Annu.: 132,789; Staff: 2,399

Polinsky Medical Rehabilitation Center - 1600 Miller Trunk Hwy., Building C, Duluth, MN 55811 t) 218-786-5360 (Sub. of St. Mary's Medical Center) Joan Jeanetta, Dir.; Asstd. Annu.: 35,300; Staff: 216

PROCTOR

Christ Child Society of Duluth, Inc. - 5566 Halie Rd., Proctor, MN 55810 t) 218-624-4583 kathfors@hotmail.com Rev. Pio Antonio, Spiritual Adv./Care Svcs.;

NURSING / REHABILITATION / CONVALESCENCE / ELDERLY CARE [NUR]

DULUTH

Benedictine Living Community of Duluth (Benedictine Health Center) - 935 Kenwood Ave., Duluth, MN 55811 t) 218-522-8900 brian.pattock@benedictineliving.org www.benedictineliving.org/duluth-mn/ (Subs. of Benedictine Health System) Brian Pattock, Exec. Dir.; Asstd. Annu.: 920; Staff: 387

An asterisk (*) denotes an organization that has established tax-exempt status directly with the IRS and is not covered by the USCCB Group Ruling.

Diocese of El Paso

(Dioecesis Elpasensis)

MOST REVEREND MARK J. SEITZ

Bishop of El Paso; ordained May 17, 1980; appointed Titular Bishop of Cozyla and Auxiliary Bishop of Dallas March 11, 2010; ordained Bishop April 27, 2010; appointed Bishop of El Paso May 6, 2013; installed July 9, 2013. Office: 499 St. Matthews St., El Paso, TX 79907.

Chancery Office: 499 St. Matthews St., El Paso, TX 79907. T: 915-872-8407; F: 915-872-8413. www.elpasodiocese.org

ERECTED MARCH 3, 1914.

Square Miles 26,686.

Comprises in Texas, the Counties of El Paso, Brewster, Culberson, Hudspeth, Jeff Davis, Loving, Presidio, Reeves, Ward and Winkler.

For legal titles of parishes and diocesan institutions, consult the Chancery Office.

STATISTICAL OVERVIEW

Personnel

Bishop....1
Priests: Diocesan Active in Diocese....43
Priests: Retired, Sick or Absent....15
Number of Diocesan Priests....58
Religious Priests in Diocese....48
Total Priests in your Diocese....106
Extern Priests in Diocese....6
Ordinations:
Diocesan Priests....7
Religious Priests....1
Transitional Deacons....6
Permanent Deacons in Diocese....43

Parishes

Parishes....58
With Resident Pastor:
Resident Diocesan Priests....1
Resident Religious Priests....37
Without Resident Pastor:
Administered by Priests....6
Administered by Deacons....1
Administered by Religious Women....1
Missions....13
Pastoral Centers....1

Professional Ministry Personnel:
Brothers....5
Sisters....10
Lay Ministers....149

Welfare

Health Care Centers....1
Total Assisted....1,416
Special Centers for Social Services....1
Total Assisted....35,652

Educational

Seminaries, Diocesan....1
Students from This Diocese....2
Diocesan Students in Other Seminaries....16
Seminaries, Religious....2
Total Seminarians....18
High Schools, Diocesan and Parish....1
Total Students....368
High Schools, Private....3
Total Students....559
Elementary Schools, Diocesan and Parish....6
Total Students....1,193
Elementary Schools, Private....2
Total Students....350

Catechesis / Religious Education:
High School Students....2,933
Elementary Students....3,504
Total Students under Catholic Instruction....8,925
Teachers in Diocese:
Lay Teachers....211

Vital Statistics

Receptions into the Church:
Infant Baptism Totals....1,754
Minor Baptism Totals....191
Adult Baptism Totals....101
Received into Full Communion....344
First Communions....1,590
Confirmations....1,465
Marriages:
Catholic....487
Interfaith....38
Total Marriages....525
Deaths....1,879
Total Catholic Population....715,654
Total Population....963,546

LEADERSHIP

Office of the Bishop - t) 915-872-8419 officeofthebishop@elpasodiocese.org Most Rev. Mark J. Seitz;

Vicar General and Moderator of the Curia - t) 915-872-8407 bflores@elpasodiocese.org Very Rev. Benjamin Flores;

Vicar for Clergy - Rev. Miguel Briseno, O.F.M.Conv.;

Chancellor - t) 915-872-8407 plopez@elpasodiocese.org Patricia López Rueda;

Liaison for Women Religious - t) 915-872-8419

Diocesan Pastoral Center - t) 915-872-8400 chancery0ffice@elpasodiocese.org www.elpasodiocese.org

Diocesan Tribunal - t) 915-872-8402 tribunaloffice@elpasodiocese.org Rev. Anthony C. Celino;

OFFICES AND DIRECTORS

Campaign for Human Development - t) 915-872-8422 mraposo@elpasodiocese.org Marco Raposo, Dir.;

Catholic Campus Ministry - t) (915) 838-0300 Dcn. Carlos Rubio, Dir.;

University of Texas at El Paso - t) (915) 838-0300 Dcn. Carlos E. Rubio;

Catholic Communications Ministry - t) 915-872-8414 Fernando Ceniceros (fceniceros@elpasodioces.org);

Catholic Properties - t) 915-872-8403 properties@catholicpropertiesofelpaso.org Sergio Ornelas, Dir.;

Diocesan Newspaper - Rio Grande Catholic - t) 915-872-8414 Fernando Ceniceros, Editor;

Finance Office - t) 915-872-8404 finance@elpasodiocese.org Greg Watters, Dir.;

Human Resources - t) 915-872-8407 hr@elpasodiocese.org Patricia López Rueda, Dir.;

Missions Office/Propagation of the Faith/Catholic Relief Services - t) 915-872-8407 chancery0ffice@elpasodiocese.org Very Rev. Benjamin Flores;

Mt. Carmel Cemetery - t) 915-860-0606 cemetery@elpasodiocese.org Rudy Rios, Dir.;

Native American (Tigua) Ministry - t) 915-859-9848 Mike Lara;

Office of Education - t) 915-872-8426 officeofeducation@elpasodiocese.org Dr. Lanny Hollis, Supt.;

Office of Marriage and Family Life - t) 915-872-8401 Dcn. Daniel Bejarano, Dir.;

Natural Planning - t) 915-872-8401 Grace Akers;

Office of Safe Environment - t) 915-872-8427 Diana Bulko, Coord.;

Office of Worship - t) 915-872-8400 Rev. Marcus McFadin;

Catholic Counseling - t) 915-872-8424 catholiccounseling@elpasodiocese.org Jose Castrellon, Dir.;

Peace & Justice Office - t) 915-872-8422 justice@elpasodiocese.org Marco Raposo, Dir.;

Permanent Diaconate Office - t) 915-872-8420 Dcn. Jesus A. Cardenas, Dir.;

Religious Formation - t) 915-262-4700 religiousformation@elpasodiocese.org Dr. Veronica Rayas, DRE;

Reverence for Life Ministry - t) 915-872-8401 Grace Akers; Dcn. Daniel Bejarano, Dir.;

Tepeyac Institute - t) 915-872-8420 tepeyacinstitute@elpasodiocese.org Dcn. Jesus A. Cardenas, Dir.;

Victim Assistance Coordinator - t) 915-872-8424 smartinez@elpasodiocese.org Susan Martinez;

Vocations & Seminarians - t) 915-872-8460; 915-872-8403 vocationoffice@elpasodiocese.org Rev. John Telles, Rector; Rev. German Alzate, Dir.;

Diocesan Master of Ceremonies - t) 915-872-8400 Rev. Marcus McFadin, Dir.;

Youth and Young Adult Ministry - t) 915-872-8410 youthministry@elpasodiocese.org Rev. Fabian Marquez, Dir.;

ADVISORY BOARDS, COMMISSIONS, COMMITTEES, AND COUNCILS

College of Consultors - t) 915-872-8419 officeofthebishop@elpasodiocese.org Very Rev. Benjamin Flores; Rev. Miguel Alcuino; Rev. Anthony C. Celino;

Diocesan Building Committee - t) 915-872-8419 Most Rev. Mark J. Seitz; Very Rev. Benjamin Flores; Sergio Ornelas, Dir.;

Diocesan Pastoral Council - t) 915-872-8419 www.elpasodiocese.org Most Rev. Mark J. Seitz; Very Rev. Benjamin Flores; Patricia López Rueda;

Diocesan Review Board - t) 915-872-8419 Jose Castrellon; Susan Martinez; Rev. Joe Molina;

Finance Council - t) 915-872-8419 Most Rev. Mark J. Seitz; Very Rev. Benjamin Flores; Greg Watters, Dir.;

Presbyteral Council - t) 915-872-8419 Most Rev. Mark J. Seitz; Very Rev. Benjamin Flores; Rev. Francisco Hernandez;

Pastoral Response Committee - t) 915-872-8419 Jose Castrellon; Rev. Joe Molina; Michael Bulko;

Priests' Retirement and Disability Plan - t) 915-872-8419 Very Rev. Benjamin Flores; Patricia López Rueda, Chancellor; Rev. Anthony C. Celino;

Vicariates -

Vacariate of St. Luke -

Vicariate of Our Lady of Guadalupe -

Vicariate of St. John -

Vicariate of St. Mark -

Vicariate of St. Matthew -

Vicariate of St. Paul -

Vicariate of St. Peter -

DEVELOPMENT

Office of Foundation and Progress - t) 915-872-8412 Linda Caro, Dir. (lcaro@elpasodiocese.org);

FAITH FORMATION

Office of Vocations - t) 915-872-8460 Rev. John Telles, Rector;

SOCIAL SERVICES

Diocesan Migrant & Refugee Services - t) 915-532-3975 Melissa López, Exec. Dir.; Anna Hey, Exec.;

Hope Border Institute - t) 915-872-8400 x200 Dylan Corbett, Dir.;

TRIBUNAL

Judges - t) 915-872-8402 tribunaloffice@elpasodiocese.org Rev. Anthony C. Celino; Rev. Robert S. Kobe; Rev. James W. Hall;

Defenders of the Bond - t) 915-872-8402 tribunaloffice@elpasodiocese.org Diane Masson, C.S.S.F.; Anne Bryant;

Advocates - t) 915-872-8402 tribunaloffice@elpasodiocese.org Rev. Francisco Hernandez; Rev. Ivan A Montelongo; Rev. Mark N.P. Salas;

Lay Advocates - t) 915-872-8402

Tribunal Ecclesiastical Notary - t) 915-827-8402 tribunaloffice@elpasodiocese.org Elizabeth Najera, Secy. (enajera@elpasodiocese.org);

Peritus (Vacant) - t) 915-872-8402

Promoter of Justice (Vacant) -

PARISHES, MISSIONS, AND CLERGY

STATE OF TEXAS

ALPINE

Our Lady of Peace - 406 S. Sixth, Alpine, TX 79830 t) 432-837-3304 olpalpine@gmail.com olpalpine.wixsite.com/website Rev. Pablo Matta, Pst.; Rev. Victorino Loresca, Par. Vicar; Dcn. Alfonso Coronado; Barbara Tucker, DRE; CRP Stds.: 90

St. Mary's Mission - 203 N.W. 3rd St., Marathon, TX 79842; Mailing: P.O. Box 268, Marathon, TX 79842 t) (432) 837-3304

St. Joseph Mission - 800 N. State St. [Hwy. 171], Ft. Davis, TX 79734; Mailing: 406 S. Sixth St., Alpine, TX 79830 Rev. Edilberto Beto Lopez, Pst.;

CANUTILLO

St. Patrick - 7065 Second St., Canutillo, TX 79835; Mailing: P. O. Box 10, Canutillo, TX 79835 t) 915-877-3997 canutillostpatrick@att.net Rev. Kenneth John Moody, M.M., Pst.; Rev. Hector Chicas, O. P., Admin.; CRP Stds.: 95

Immaculate Heart of Mary - 8300 De Alva Rd., Westway, TX 79835 t) 915-886-3539

CLINT

San Lorenzo - 13021 Center St., Clint, TX 79836; Mailing: P.O. Box 215, Clint, TX 79836 t) 915-851-2255; (915) 851-2216 (CRP) sanlorenzo1914@sbcglobal.net; lorenzolawrence2014@yahoo.com www.sanlorenzocatholicchurch.com Rev. Enrique Omar Soto, M.N.M (Mexico), Pst.; Rev. Martin Alonso Bustos, M.N.M. (Mexico), Par. Vicar; CRP Stds.: 258

EL PASO

St. Patrick Cathedral - 1118 N. Mesa St., El Paso, TX 79902 t) 915-533-4451 stpatrickclerks@yahoo.com; enrocha2111@aol.com saintpatrickcathedral.org Rev. Cong Chi Vo, Vicar; Rev. Marcus McFadin, Rector; Dcn. Ernesto Rodriguez; Dcn. Andres Ruvalcaba; CRP Stds.: 176

St. Patrick Cathedral School - (Grades K-8) 1111 N. Stanton St., El Paso, TX 79902 t) 915-532-4142 ecarreon@stpatrickelpaso.org Elizabeth Carreon, Prin.;

All Saints - 1415 Dakota St., El Paso, TX 79930 t) 915-566-9711 allsaintselptx@aol.com www.allsaintselpaso.org Friar Francsico Javier rodriguez Roman, OFM, Pst.; Paula Favela, DRE; CRP Stds.: 52

Blessed Sacrament - 9025 Diana Dr., El Paso, TX 79904 t) 915-755-7658 www.epblessedsacrament.org Rev. John Paul Madanu (India), Admin.; Dcn. Ignacio M. Bustillos; CRP Stds.: 270

Christ the Savior - 5301 Wadsworth Ave., El Paso, TX 79924 t) 915-821-3766 elpaso.church Rev. Gleen Carpe, Pst.; CRP Stds.: 130

Corpus Christi - 9205 N. Loop Dr., El Paso, TX 79907 t) 915-858-0488 corpuschristifinance@gmail.com www.corpuschristicc.com Rev. Ralph Solis Jr., Pst.; Dcn. Juan M. Alvarez; Dcn. Carlos E. Rubio; CRP Stds.: 405

Cristo Rey Church - 8011 Williamette, El Paso, TX 79907 t) 915-591-0688 cristorey8011@sbcglobal.net Gloria Ibarra, DRE; Dcn. Arturo R. Medina; CRP Stds.: 154

El Buen Pastor Mission - 311 Peyton Rd., El Paso, TX 79928 t) 915-852-4010 elbuencatholic@sbcglobal.net; rguerrra@elpasodiocese.org Dcn. Roberto (Bob) Guerra, Admin.; Rev. Carl Quebedeaux, CMF, Sacr. Min.; Francisca Renteria, DRE; CRP Stds.: 162

La Resurreccion Mission - 1140 Timothy Dr., El Paso, TX 79928

St. Frances Xavier Cabrini Parish - 12200 Vista del Sol, El Paso, TX 79936 t) 915-857-1263 Very Rev. Benjamin Flores, Pst.; Dcn. Dagoberto Gonzalez; Dcn. James T. Szostek; CRP Stds.: 419

St. Francis of Assisi - 5750 A Doniphan, El Paso, TX 79932; Mailing: P. O. Box 220034, El Paso, TX 79913 t) 915-584-7130 mail@stfrancisofelpaso.org www.sanfranciscoelpaso.com Rev. Jose Alfredo Ramirez, O.F.M., Pst.; Rev. Juan Francisco Figueroa Moran, OFM, Par. Vicar; Dcn. Lucio Alfonso Sandoval; CRP Stds.: 320

St. Francis Xavier - 519 S. Latta St., El Paso, TX 79905 t) 915-532-2761 sfxcc519@yahoo.com; prprecourt@gmail.com www.stfrancisxaviercatholicchurch.com Rev. Peter

Precourt, A.A., Pst.; Rev. Marciano Lopez Solis, AA, Assoc. Pst.; Rev. Ronald Sibugan, A.A., Assoc. Pst.;
Guardian Angel - 3021 Frutas Ave., El Paso, TX 79905 t) 915-533-2077 Friar Humberto Flores Cruz, O.A.R., Pst.; Rev. Jesus Martinez-Espronceda, O.A.R., Vicar; Edelmira Gonzalez, Parish Life Coord.; Izak Trejo, Parish Life Coord.; CRP Stds.: 57
Holy Family - 104 Fewel St., El Paso, TX 79902 t) 915-532-8462 holyfamily.elpaso@gmail.com Rev. Marcus McFadin, Rector;
St. Ignatius of Loyola - 408 Park St., El Paso, TX 79901 t) 915-532-9534 sanignaciochurch@gmail.com Rev. Tobias Macias, O.S.M., Pst.; Rev. Jorge M. Palacio, O.S.M., Par. Vicar; Robert Hernandez, DRE; CRP Stds.: 143
Immaculate Conception - 118 N. Campbell St., El Paso, TX 79901-2404 t) 915-533-3427 ic.ecclesia@gmail.com; iscorchado@gmail.com Rev. Kevin O'Neill, F.S.S.P., Pst.; Rev. Joseph Dalimata, FSSP, Par. Vicar;
Saint John Paul II - 518 Gallagher St., El Paso, TX 79915 t) 915-592-5245 saintjohnpaul2churchelpaso@gmail.com Rev. Federico M. Franco, O.S.M., Pst.; Aurelio Melucci;
St. Joseph's - 1315 Travis St., El Paso, TX 79903 t) 915-566-9396 mdsianez@gmail.com; sjosephschurch@aol.com Rev. Fabian Marquez, Pst.; Dolores Sianez, DRE; CRP Stds.: 102
St. Joseph's School - (Grades K-8) 1300 Lamar, El Paso, TX 79903 t) 915-566-1661 stjosephs@aol.com Marcela Hernandez, Prin.;
St. Luke - 930 E. Redd Rd., El Paso, TX 79912 t) 915-585-0255 maryhrndz2@ymail.com; stlukeparish@att.net www.stlukeelpaso.org Rev. Edward C. Carpenter, Pst.; Dcn. John Farley; Rev. Edroud Jean; Dcn. Karl Twichell; Dcn. Carlos Viesca; Mary L. Hernandez, DRE; CRP Stds.: 431
St. Mark - 11700 Pebble Hills Blvd., El Paso, TX 79936 t) 915-300-2800 stmarkcatholic14@gmail.com home.catholicweb.com/stmarkcatholic/ Rev. Jose A. Morales, Pst.; Dcn. Luis Buena; Dcn. Jesus A. Cardenas; Rev. Cesar Garcia, Vicar; CRP Stds.: 1,488
St. Matthew - 400 W. Sunset Rd., El Paso, TX 79922 t) 915-584-3461 stmatthew400@gmail.com stmatthewcatholicchurch.org Rev. Frank Lopez, Pst.; Dcn. Astry Deraly; Dcn. Guillermo Jiron; Dcn. Luis Angel Santos; CRP Stds.: 223
St. Matthew Catholic School - (Grades K-8) t) 915-581-8801 vdelacruz@stmatthewelpaso.org www.stmatthewelpaso.org Veronica De La Cruz, Prin.;
Most Holy Trinity - 10000 Pheasant Rd., El Paso, TX 79924 t) 915-751-6416 mostholytrinity@gmail.com Rev. Antonio De Guzman Jr., Admin.; Rev. Cesar Garcia; Dcn. Martin H Soltero;
Most Holy Trinity School - (Grades K-8) t) 915-751-2566 jhoran@mhtcrusaders.org James Horan, Prin.;
Our Lady of Assumption - 4805 Byron St., El Paso, TX 79930 t) 915-566-4040 rmedina024.rm@gmail.com; pservian68@gmail.com olaep.org Rev. Mark N.P. Salas, Pst.; Dcn. Wade S. Horsch; CRP Stds.: 61
Our Lady of Guadalupe - 2709 Alabama St., El Paso, TX 79930 t) 915-562-4304 ourladyofguadalupeparishelpaso@gmail.com Friar Juan Manuel Heredia Hernandez, OFM, Pst.; CRP Stds.: 125
Our Lady of Mt. Carmel - 131 S. Zaragoza Rd., El Paso, TX 79907 t) 915-859-9848 olmcsecretary@yahoo.com ysletamission.org Rev. Miguel Briseno, O.F.M.Conv., Pst.; Friar Jaroslaw Wysoczanski, OFM Conv., Par. Vicar; Dcn. Hector Melendez; Friar Mario L. Serrano, OFM Conv., Campus Min.; Mike Lara, DRE; Friar Juan Zuniga, OFM Conv., Assoc. Priest; CRP Stds.: 144
Our Lady of Sorrows - 7712 Rosedale St., El Paso, TX 79915 t) 915-433-8694 olsorrows1977@gmail.com Rev. Felipe Maria Mariscal Chavez, O.S.M., Pst.; Rev. Federico M. Franco, O.S.M., Par. Vicar; Friar Mateus Maria Pol, OSM, Par. Vicar; Sr. Enedina Tirres, DRE;
Our Lady of the Light - 4700 Delta Dr., El Paso, TX 79905 t) 915-532-1757 valdiviezcookie@yahoo.com; olol4700@yahoo.com Rev. Wilson Cuevas, Pst.; Rev. Roberto Alvarado, Par. Vicar; Rev. Antonio Lasheras, O.A.R., Par. Vicar; Dcn. Roberto E. Saucedo; Sr. Maria del Rosario Lopez, RCIA Coord.; CRP Stds.: 97
Our Lady of the Valley - 8600 Winchester Rd., El Paso, TX 79907 t) 915-859-7939 olvchurch@elp.rr.com www.olvchurchep.org Dcn. Ray H. Niblett; Dcn. Carlos Rubio; David Perez, DRE; CRP Stds.: 91
St. Paul the Apostle - 7424 Mimosa Ave., El Paso, TX 79915 t) 915-778-5304 Rev. Apolinar Samboni, Pst.; Dcn. Vicente G. Aguirre; CRP Stds.: 101
Sts. Peter and Paul - 673 Old Hueco Tanks Rd., El Paso, TX 79927 t) 915-859-3758 stspeterandpaulccd@gmail.com; stspeterandpaulelp@yahoo.com Rev. Angel M. Maldonado, O.S.M., Pst.; Dcn. Jose Zaragoza; Marisol Anchondo, DRE; CRP Stds.: 407
St. Pius X - 1050 N. Clark Rd., El Paso, TX 79905 t) 915-772-0224 (CRP); 915-772-3226 stpiusxparish@sbcglobal.net; rvargas@elpasostpiusx.org Rev. Edilberto Beto Lopez, Pst.; Rev. Wilbert Colas, Vicar; Dcn. Ricardo Corella; CRP Stds.: 300
St. Pius X School - (Grades PreK-8) 1007 Geronimo, El Paso, TX 79905 t) 915-262-4846 asilva@elpasostpiusx.org Ana Silva, Prin.;
Queen of Peace - 1551 Belvidere, El Paso, TX 79912 t) 915-584-5817 secretary@queenofpeaceparishep.org www.qpelp.com Rev. Allan Oluoch Alaka, Pst.; Dcn. Orlando Sanchez; Dcn. Adolfo Rubio; Elizabeth Mata, DRE; CRP Stds.: 425
St. Raphael - 2301 Zanzibar Rd., El Paso, TX 79925 t) 915-598-3431 straphaelparishep@sbcglobal.net Rev. Anthony C. Celino, Pst.; Rev. Edroud Jean, Par. Vicar; Dcn. Victor Acosta, Pst. Assoc.; Dcn. Daniel Bejarano; Dcn. Alfredo Solano; Guillermo Tajonar, DRE; CRP Stds.: 651
St. Raphael School - (Grades K-8) 2310 Woodside, El Paso, TX 79925 t) 915-598-2241 info@straphaelelpaso.org Graciela Fernandez, Prin.; Maria Farina, Librn.;
Sacred Heart - 602 S. Oregon St., El Paso, TX 79901 t) 915-532-5447; 915-544-4970 (CRP); 915-351-6181 (CRP) reception@sacredheartelpaso.org; accounting@sacredheartelpaso.org www.sacredheartelpaso.org Rev. Rafael Garcia, S.J., Pst.; Rev. Daniel Mora, S.J., Par. Vicar; Rev. Samuel Rosales, S.J., In Res.; Rev. Hung T Nguyen, S.J., DRE; Rev. Michael Gallagher, S.J., Migrant & Refugee Ministry; Efren Loya, CRE; CRP Stds.: 68
San Antonio - 503 Hunter Dr., El Paso, TX 79915 t) 915-598-1457 sanantoniocc@sbcglobal.net www.paduaofelpaso.org Rev. Mariano H. Lopez, Pst.; Dcn. Samuel Bernal; Dcn. Jose M. Gonzalez; Luis Roberto Ortega, DRE; CRP Stds.: 140
San Juan Bautista - 5649 Dailey St., El Paso, TX 79905; Mailing: 1050 N. Clark, El Paso, TX 79905 t) 915-779-1583 Rev. Edilberto Beto Lopez, Pst.; Rev. Charles Michael Rajan, O.C.D., Vicar; Dcn. Ricardo Corella; CRP Stds.: 49
San Juan Diego Parish - 14520 E. Montana Ave., El Paso, TX 79938 t) 915-855-2217; 915-855-2217 x103 (CRP); 915-855-2680 soyuncordel@gmail.com; oijasso23@yahoo.com Rev. Rolando Fonseca, Pst.; Luz Patricia DeLoera, DRE; CRP Stds.: 145
San Isidro Mission - 214 E. Broadway, Dell City, TX 79837
San Judas Tadeo - 4006 Hidden Way, El Paso, TX 79922 t) 915-584-1095 www.santuariosanjudastadeo.com Rev. Miguel Angel Sanchez, Pst.; Rev. Esteban Sescon, Par. Vicar; Dcn. Jose William Arevalo; Dcn. Julio Diaz; Rudy Gonzales, DRE; CRP Stds.: 139
Santa Teresita - 3400 Zapal St., El Paso, TX 79922 Rev. Miguel Angel Sanchez, Admin.;
San Pedro de Jesus Maldonado Mission - 3000 Tim Foster, El Paso, TX 79938 t) 915-271-8060 Rev. German Alzate, Admin.; Dcn. Arturo Araiza; CRP Stds.: 255
Santo Nino De Atocha - 210 S. Clark, El Paso, TX 79905 t) 915-779-3164 Rev. Wilson Cuevas, Pst.; Rev. Antonio Lasheras, O.A.R., Par. Vicar; Dcn. Roberto E. Saucedo; CRP Stds.: 84
St. Stephen, Deacon and Martyr - 1700 George Dieter, El Paso, TX 79936 t) 915-855-1661 receptionist@ststephendeaconandmartyr.org Rev. Joe Molina, Pst.; Rev. Ivan A. Montelongo, Vicar; Dcn. Hector E. Grijalva; Deborah Montoya, DRE; CRP Stds.: 263
Saint Therese of the Little Flower Parish - 171 Polo Inn Rd., El Paso, TX 79915 t) 915-772-1285 littleflowerchurch@outlook.com Rev. Bonilla Alfonso, Pst.; Laura Gonzalez, DRE; CRP Stds.: 40
St. Thomas Aquinas - 10970 Bywood Dr., El Paso, TX 79936 t) 915-592-1313 saintthomasa@sbcglobal.net; sta.records@icloud.com www.stthomas-elpaso.com Rev. Kennon Y. Ducre, Pst.; Dcn. Jose E. Soto; Dcn. Francisco R. Segura; Erika Romero, DRE; CRP Stds.: 133

FABENS

Our Lady of Guadalupe - 127 W. Main, Fabens, TX 79838; Mailing: P. O. Box 356, Fabens, TX 79838 t) 915-764-3942 Rev. Celimo Osorio, Pst.; Dcn. Robert Garcia; Terry Avila, DRE;
San Jose -
Santa Rita - 19235 Cobb St., Tornillo, TX 79853
San Luis -

FORT DAVIS

St. Joseph - 800 N. State St. (Hwy. 171), Fort Davis, TX 79734; Mailing: P.O. Box 787, Fort Davis, TX 79734 t) 432-837-3304 Rev. Pablo Matta, Pst.; Rev. Victorino Loresca, Par. Vicar; Dcn. Alfonso Coronado; CRP Stds.: 10

FORT HANCOCK

Santa Teresa - 1042 N. Knox Ave., Fort Hancock, TX 79839; Mailing: P.O. Box 215, Fort Hancock, TX 79839 t) 915-769-3771 Sr. Silvia Chacon, A.S.C., Pastoral Life Coord.;

HORIZON CITY

Holy Spirit - 14600 Horizon Blvd., Horizon City, TX 79928 t) 915-852-3582; 915-852-3520 (CRP) faithformation@hscc4u.org; office@hscc4u.org www.hscc4u.org Rev. Miguel Perez, Pst.; CRP Stds.: 327

KERMIT

St. Thomas & St. Joseph - 838 Bellaire Rd., Kermit, TX 79745 t) 432-586-3922 Rev. Carles Raj Michael, O.C.D., Admin.; Kathy Barriga, DRE; CRP Stds.: 100

MARFA

St. Mary's - 211W. San Antonio St., Marfa, TX 79843; Mailing: Box 356, Marfa, TX 79843 t) 432-729-4694 church.marfa@gmail.com stmarymarfa.wixsite.com/website Rev. Pablo Matta, Admin.;
Sacred Heart Mission - 217 W. San Antonio, Marfa, TX 79843; Mailing: P. O. Box 356, Marfa, TX 79843 Rev. Pablo Matta, Pst.;

MONAHANS

St. John the Apostle and Evangelist - 5th & S. Ike St., Monahans, TX 79756; Mailing: 502 S. Harry, Monahans, TX 79756 t) 432-943-5114 stjohnmonahans.com Rev. Mount Joseph Duri Raj, S.J., Admin.; Dcn. Ruben J. Gomez; Christine Gomez, DRE; CRP Stds.: 188
St. Gertrude - ; Mailing: P.O. Box 181, Grandfalls, TX 79742 Rev. Allan Oluoch Alaka, Admin.;

PECOS

St. Catherine - 1201 S. Plum, Pecos, TX 79772; Mailing: P. O. Box 686, Pecos, TX 79772 t) 432-445-2309 Rev. Jose Delacruz Longoria, M.N.M., Pst.; Rev. Valentin A. Cota, M.N.M., Par. Vicar;
Christ the King - ; Mailing: P.O. Box 686, Pecos, TX 79772 t) 432-445-2309 wtcc@classic.net Under pastoral care of Santa Rosa, Pecos. Rev. Jose Delacruz Longoria, M.N.M., Pst.; Rev. Valentin Cota, Vicar; Sonia Urias, DRE; Dominga Villegas, Coord.;
Our Lady of Guadalupe - Rte. 1 #3, Balmorhea, TX 79718; Mailing: P. O. Box 686, Pecos, TX 79772 atcc@classicnet.net
Santa Rosa de Lima - 620 E. 4th St., Pecos, TX 79772;

Mailing: P.O. Box 686, Pecos, TX 79772 t) 432-445-2309 Rev. Jose Delacruz Longoria, M.N.M., Pst.; Rev. Valentin A. Cota, M.N.M., Par. Vicar; Dcn. Oscar Marruffo Machuca Sr.; Dcn. Rudy Villegas Sr.; Sonia Urias, DRE; CRP Stds.: 235

Our Lady of Refuge -

St. Emily -

Our Lady of Guadalupe Shrine - t) 432-455-2309

Christ the King -

PRESIDIO

Santa Teresa de Jesus - 1101 W. O'Reilly St., Presidio, TX 79845; Mailing: P.O. Box 2049, Presidio, TX 79845 t) 432-229-3235 santateresachurch.2014@gmail.com Rev. Miguel Alcuino, Pst.; CRP Stds.: 56

Sgdo. Corazon de Jesus -

Our Lady of Peace -

Lajitas Mission -

San Jose -

SAN ELIZARIO

San Elceario - 1556 San Elizario Rd., San Elizario, TX 79849; Mailing: P.O. Box 910, San Elizario, TX 79848 t) 915-851-2333 estheramparansecc@gmail.com; sanelcearioparish@gmail.com Rev. Juan Victor Gamino, M.N.M., Admin.; CRP Stds.: 228

SOCORRO

La Purisima - 328 S. Nevarez St., Socorro, TX 79927 t) 915-859-7718; 915-859-2979; 915-307-4349 (Safe Environ./CRP) lapurisima@earthlink.net Rev. Emanuel Alcazar, Pst.; Dcn. Ignacio J. Torres; Eloy Carmona, DRE; CRP Stds.: 105

San Felipe de Jesus - 401 Passmore, Socorro, TX 79849; Mailing: P.O. Box 291419, El Paso, TX 79929 t) 915-851-3039 sanfelipedejusus401@outlook.com; sanfelipedejesus@outlook.com Rev. Antonio Mena, Pst.; Dcn. Pilar Grijalva Jr.; David Solis, DRE; CRP Stds.: 90

VAN HORN

Our Lady of Fatima - 308 S. Almond St., Van Horn, TX 79855; Mailing: P. O. Box 398, Van Horn, TX 79855 t) 432-283-1058 ourladyoffatimac@gmail.com ourladyoffatimac.wixsite.com/website Rev. Francisco Hernandez, Admin.; Carmen Garibay, DRE; CRP Stds.: 60

Our Lady of Miracles - 556 E. Cavender, Sierra Blanca, TX 79851; Mailing: P.O. Box 398, Van Horn, TX 79855 t) (432) 283-1058

SCHOOLS: PRESCHOOL THRU HIGH SCHOOL

SCHOOLS

STATE OF TEXAS

EL PASO

Father Yermo Schools (Servants of the Sacred Heart of Jesus and of the Poor) - (PRV) (Grades PreK-12) 220 Washington St., El Paso, TX 79905 t) 915-532-6875 a.omana@fatheryermoschools.com fatheryermoschools.com Mother Maria Aurea Garcia, Supr.; Sr. Angelica Omana, SSHP, Pres.; Stds.: 260; Sr. Tchrs.: 4; Lay Tchrs.: 25

HIGH SCHOOLS

STATE OF TEXAS

EL PASO

Cathedral High School, Inc. - (PRV) (Grades 9-12) 1309 N. Stanton St., El Paso, TX 79902 t) 915-532-3238 asanchez@cathedral-elpaso.org cathedral-elpaso.org (Boys) Adolfo Sanchez, Prin.;

Loretto Academy - (PRV) (Grades PreK-12) 1300 Hardaway St., El Paso, TX 79903 t) 915-566-8400 ncobb@loretto.org www.loretto.org Sisters of Loretto at the Foot of the Cross Homero Silva, Prin.; Stds.: 575; Sr. Tchrs.: 2; Lay Tchrs.: 68

INSTITUTIONS LOCATED IN DIOCESE

CAMPUS MINISTRY / NEWMAN CENTERS [CAM]

ALPINE

Sul Ross State University Newman Center - Hwy. 90 East, Alpine, TX 79830; Mailing: PO Box C78, Alpine, TX 79832 c) 432-295-0699 p.alfonso.coronado@hotmail.com Judith Loya, Dir.;

EL PASO

Catholic Campus Ministry at University of Texas at El Paso - 2230 N. Oregon, El Paso, TX 79902 t) 915-838-0300 friarmarioserrano@gmail.com Friar Mario L. Serrano, OFM Conv., Campus Min.;

CEMETERIES [CEM]

EL PASO

Mount Carmel - 401 S. Zaragoza Rd., El Paso, TX 79907; Mailing: P.O Box 17655, El Paso, TX 79917 t) 915-860-0606 rrios@mtcarmelep.org Rudy Rios, Dir.;

CONVENTS, MONASTERIES, AND RESIDENCES FOR WOMEN [CON]

EL PASO

Adorers of the Blood of Christ (A.S.C.) - 199 Pendale Rd., El Paso, TX 79907 t) 915-566-5855 micasa2chante@msn.com Sr. Silvia Chacon, ASC, Parish Life Coord.;

Daughters of Charity of St. Vincent De Paul (D.C.) - 3014 Taylor Ave., El Paso, TX 79930 t) 915-564-5921 doris.clippard@doc.org Sr. Doris Clippard, DC, Contact;

Daughters of Charity of St. Vincent De Paul - 9213 Moye Dr., El Paso, TX 79925 t) 915-401-4272 isabel.fierro@yahoo.com Sr. Isabel Fierro, D.C., Supr.;

Hermanas Contemplativas del Buen Pastor (H.C.B.P.) - 8824 Old County Rd., El Paso, TX 79917; Mailing: P.O. Box 17254, El Paso, TX 79917 t) 915-859-3683 sistertnt@gmail.com (Cloistered) Sr. Ernestina Estrada, Supr.;

Hermanas Dominicas de la Doctrina Cristiana (O.P.) - 634 Hampton Rd., El Paso, TX 79907 t) 915-590-3107 mnc_terrazas79@yahoo.com Sr. Gloria Gil, Supr.; Sr. Celia Gonzalez Trujillo, OP, Supr.; Sr. Sara Cisneros, O.P., Mistress of Postulants; Sr. Maria Guadalupe Garcia, Local Vicar, Convent, Hermans Dominicas; Sr. Monica P. Terrazas, Dir., Novices;

Missionary Sisters of Jesus, Mary & Joseph - 7681 Barton, El Paso, TX 79915 t) 915-533-4451 sistertnt@gmail.com Sr. Julia Doñez, MJMJ, Supr.;

Missionary Sisters of Jesus, Mary & Joseph (M.J.M.J.) - 7681 Barton Dr., El Paso, TX 79915 t) 915-779-6943 sistertnt@gmail.com Sr. Julia Doñez, MJMJ, Supr.;

Servants of the Sacred Heart of Jesus and of the Poor (S.S.H.J.P.) - Father Yermo Convent, 237 Tobin Pl., El Paso, TX 79905 t) 915-777-1385 sryolandaf@gmail.com; sistertnt@gmail.com Sr. Maria Yolanda Fernandez, S.S.H.J.P., Supr.; Srs.: 13

Queen of Peace Convent - 3119 Pera Ave., El Paso, TX 79905 t) 915-533-0590 queenofpeaceconvent@gmail.com Mother Maria de Lourdes Cuesta, SSHJP, Supr.;

Sisters of Loretto at the Foot of the Cross (S.L.) - 1300 Hardaway St., El Paso, TX 79903 t) 915-566-8400 bboesen@loretto.org; sistertnt@gmail.com www.lorettocommunity.org Sr. Mary Beth Buffy Boesen, S.L., Supr.;

Sisters of Our Lady of Charity of the Good Shepherd - El Paso, Inc. - 415 N. Glenwood Dr., El Paso, TX 79905; Mailing: 620 Roswell Rd., S.W., P.O. Box 340, Carrollton, OH 44615 t) 915-772-0737 sistertnt@gmail.com Sr. Martha Hernandez, R.G.S., Coord.;

Sisters of Our Lady of Charity of the Good Shepherd (R.G.S.) - 8824 Old County Rd., El Paso, TX 79907; Mailing: P.O. Box 17635, El Paso, TX 79907 t) 915-858-0692 chiobuenpastor1@aol.com Sr. Maria del Rocio Hernandez, Supr.;

Sisters of Perpetual Adoration (A.P.) - Corpus Christi Monastery, 451 Mockingbird Ln., El Paso, TX 79907 t) 915-591-5662 ccmonast@aol.com; sistertnt@gmail.com (Cloistered) Sr. Maria Gema del Santisimo Sacramento, A.P., Supr.;

Sisters of Perpetual Adoration (Monastery of Perpetual Adoration) - 145 N. Cotton St., El Paso, TX 79901 t) 915-533-5323 mary.guadalupe@att.net www.christthekingmonastery.org Sr. Ma Zoial Flores, Supr.;

ENDOWMENTS / FOUNDATIONS / TRUSTS [EFT]

EL PASO

Catholic Foundation for the Diocese of El Paso - 499 St. Matthews, El Paso, TX 79907 t) 915-872-8412 lcaro@catholicfoundationelpaso.org www.elpasodiocesefoundation.org Linda Caro, CEO;

Diocese of El Paso Charity Trust - 499 St. Matthews St., El Paso, TX 79907 t) 915-872-8400 Greg Watters, Dir.;

Diocese of El Paso Clergy Continuing Education Trust - 499 St. Matthews St., El Paso, TX 79907 t) 915-872-8404 Greg Watters, Dir.;

Diocese of El Paso Education Assistance Fund, Inc. - c/o 499 St. Matthews, El Paso, TX 79907 t) 915-872-8404 Dr. Lanny Keith Hollis, Supt.; Greg Watters, Dir.;

Diocese of El Paso Historic Missions Restoration Trust - 499 St. Matthews St., Bldg. G, El Paso, TX 79907 t) 915-872-8404 gwatters@elpasodiocese.org Greg Watters, Dir.;

Diocese of El Paso Insurance Trust - 499 St. Matthews St. Bldg. D, El Paso, TX 79907 t) 915-872-8404 Greg Watters, Dir.;

Diocese of El Paso Investment Trust - 499 St. Matthews St. Bldg. D, El Paso, TX 79907 t) 915-872-8404 Greg Watters, Dir.;

Diocese of El Paso Seminarian Education Trust - 499 St. Matthews St. Bldg. D, El Paso, TX 79907 t) 915-872-8404 Greg Watters, Dir.;

Mount Carmel Cemetery Perpetual Care Trust - 401 S. Zaragoza, El Paso, TX 79907; Mailing: 499 St. Matthews, El Paso, TX 79907 t) 915-860-0606; 915-872-8404 Greg Watters, Admin.; Rudy Rios, Dir.;

Zaragosa, Texas Catholic Relief Trust - 499 St. Matthews St., El Paso, TX 79907 t) 915-872-8412 Greg Watters, Dir.;

HOSPITALS / HEALTH SERVICES [HOS]

EL PASO

Centro San Vicente - 8061 Alameda, El Paso, TX 79915 t) 915-859-7545; 314-733-8000 christina.paz@sanvicente.org www.sanvicente.org Ascension Health, corporate member. John Tersigni, Chief Mission Integration Officer; Christina Paz, CEO; Asstd. Annu.: 14,275; Staff: 226

MISCELLANEOUS [MIS]

EL PASO

Adoracion Nocturna (Nocturnal Adoration) - 499 St. Matthews, c/o Liaison for Women Religious, El Paso, TX 79907 t) 915-820-8567 marriaga@elpasodiocese.org Jorge Maldonado, Pres.;

Annunciation House - 1003 E. San Antonio, El Paso, TX 79901; Mailing: c/o 499 St. Matthews St., El Paso, TX 79901 t) 915-533-4675 rubengarcia@annunciationhouse.org www.annunciationhouse.org Ruben Garcia, Dir.;

Apostolado de la Cruz (Apostolate of the Cross) - 131 S. Zaragoza Rd., El Paso, TX 79907 t) 915-859-9848 olmcsecretary@yahoo.com Friar Miguel Briseño, OFM, Conv., Pst.;

Casa Vides - 325 Leon St., El Paso, TX 79901 t) 915-533-4675 rubengarcia@annunciationhouse.org (Shelter for displaced families) Ruben Garcia, Dir.;

Catholic Properties of El Paso, Inc. - 499 St. Matthews St., Bldg. B, El Paso, TX 79907 t) 915-872-8406 sornelas@catholicpropertiesofelpaso.org catholicpropertiesofelpaso.org Sergio Ornelas, Exec. Dir.; Edgar Hernandez, IT Mgr./ Office Mgr.;

Christ Child Society, Katherine Haninger Chapter - 10560 Lakewood, El Paso, TX 79925 t) 915-592-3032 Gloria Mendoza, Pres.;

Cursillos de Cristianidad - 499 St. Matthews, Bldg. F - Deacon's Director, El Paso, TX 79907 t) 915-613-6785 aureliomelucci@hotmail.com Dcn. Jesus A. Cardenas, Dir.;

Diocesan Migrant and Refugee Services, Inc. - 2400-A E. Yandell, El Paso, TX 79903 t) 915-532-3975 www.dmrs-ep.org Legal Representation for Immigrants Melissa M. Lopez, Exec. Dir.;

El Paso Villa Maria - 920 S. Oregon, El Paso, TX 79901 t) 915-544-5500 villamaria_elp@sbcglobal.net Isis Portillo, Dir.; Naomi Orona, Case Mgr.;

Franciscans, Secular Order of Franciscans - 131 S. Zaragoza Rd., El Paso, TX 79907 t) 915-859-9848 frbriseno@ysletamission.org Rev. Miguel Briseno, O.F.M.Conv.;

Historic Missions Restoration, Inc. - 499 St. Matthews St., El Paso, TX 79907 t) 915-872-8412 Greg Watters, Dir.;

Legion of Mary - c/o 499 St. Matthews St., El Paso, TX 79907 t) 915-872-8401 dbejarano@elpasodiocese.org Dcn. Daniel Bejarano;

Open Arms Community, Centro Santa Fe - 8210 N. Loop Dr., El Paso, TX 79907 t) 915-595-0589 openarmselpaso@gmail.com openarmscommunity.org Joanne D. Ivey, Dir.;

Our Lady's Youth Center - 501 E. Paisano, El Paso, TX 79901; Mailing: P.O. Box 1371, El Paso, TX 79948 t) 915-533-9122 olyc77@gmail.com Ellen Hogarty, Pres.; Michael Reuter, Vice. Pres.;

World Apostolate of Fatima - 499 St. Matthews St., Bldg. A - Bishop's Office, El Paso, TX 79907 t) 915-872-8419 lily@reedcommunicatios.com; ilopez@elpasodiocese.org Bruce Reed, Chair;

MONASTERIES AND RESIDENCES FOR PRIESTS AND BROTHERS [MON]

EL PASO

Christian Brothers - 1204 N. Mesa, El Paso, TX 79902-4012 t) 915-532-9314 info@cathedral-elpaso.org Bro. Paul-Andre Durham, Youth Min.; Bro. Javier Hansen, FSC, Youth Min.; Bro. Mariano Lopez, FSC, Youth Min.;

SEMINARIES [SEM]

EL PASO

St. Anthony's School of Theology - 4601 Hastings Dr., El Paso, TX 79903 t) 915-566-2261 c) 915-731-2477 st.anthony'sseminary.org Friar Emilio Flores, O.F.M., Rector; Dcn. Jesus Eduardo Cordero Cordero; Dcn. Francisco Javier Dimas Bernal; Rev. Juan Francisco Figueroa Moran, OFM, Prof.; Rev. Jose A. Morales, Prof.; Rev. Alfredo Ramirez, O.F.M., Prof.; Rev. Gerardo Francisco Salgado, O.F.M., Prof.; Stds.: 15; Pr. Tchrs.: 5; Scholastics: 4

St. Charles Seminary - 8330 Park Haven, El Paso, TX 79907 t) 915-872-8460 dstoecklein@elpasodiocese.org; gregalado@elpasodiocese.org Rev. John Telles, Rector; Sr. Darlene Stoecklein, A.S.C., Librn.; Stds.: 3; Pr. Tchrs.: 1; Sr. Tchrs.: 1

Roger Bacon College - 2400 Marr St., El Paso, TX 79903 t) 915-565-2921 www.rogerbaconcollege.org Minor Seminary of the Franciscan Fathers, Province of the Holy Gospel. Friar Flavio Alberto Hernandez, O.F.M., Rector; Friar Framcisco Javier Lopez Camarena, OFM, Prof.; Stds.: 18; Pr. Tchrs.: 5; Scholastics: 18

SPECIAL CARE FACILITIES [SPF]

EL PASO

Catholic Counseling Services, Inc. - 499 St. Matthews St., El Paso, TX 79907 t) 915-872-8424 jcastrellon@elpasodiocese.org; rpiedra@elpasodiocese.org Jose Castrellon, Exec.; Asstd. Annu.: 4,157; Staff: 3

An asterisk (*) denotes an organization that has established tax-exempt status directly with the IRS and is not covered by the USCCB Group Ruling.

Diocese of Erie

(Dioecesis Eriensis)

MOST REVEREND LAWRENCE T. PERSICO, J.C.L.

Bishop of Erie; ordained April 30, 1977; appointed Bishop of Erie July 31, 2012; consecrated October 1, 2012.

Chancery: St. Mark Catholic Center, 429 E. Grandview Blvd., Erie, PA 16504. T: 814-824-1111; F: 814-824-1128.
www.eriercd.org

ESTABLISHED 1853.

Square Miles 10,167.

Comprises the following Counties in Northwestern Pennsylvania: Erie, Crawford, Mercer, Venango, Forest, Clarion, Jefferson, Clearfield, Cameron, Elk, McKean, Potter and Warren.

For legal titles of parishes and diocesan institutions, consult the Chancery.

STATISTICAL OVERVIEW

Personnel

Bishop	1
Priests: Diocesan Active in Diocese	93
Priests: Diocesan Active Outside Diocese	5
Priests: Retired, Sick or Absent	54
Number of Diocesan Priests	152
Religious Priests in Diocese	5
Total Priests in your Diocese	157
Extern Priests in Diocese	9
Ordinations:	
Diocesan Priests	3
Transitional Deacons	2
Permanent Deacons in Diocese	76
Total Sisters	179

Parishes

Parishes	94
With Resident Pastor:	
Resident Diocesan Priests	69
Resident Religious Priests	3
Without Resident Pastor:	
Administered by Priests	22
Missions	26
Professional Ministry Personnel:	
Lay Ministers	20

Welfare

Homes for the Aged	6
Total Assisted	1,747
Day Care Centers	4
Total Assisted	567
Specialized Homes	3
Total Assisted	2,446
Special Centers for Social Services	6
Total Assisted	23,554
Residential Care of Disabled	1
Total Assisted	28
Other Institutions	3
Total Assisted	13,151

Educational

Seminaries, Diocesan	1
Students from This Diocese	3
Students from Other Dioceses	5
Diocesan Students in Other Seminaries	5
Total Seminarians	8
Colleges and Universities	2
Total Students	7,877
High Schools, Diocesan and Parish	5
Total Students	1,121
High Schools, Private	1
Total Students	445
Elementary Schools, Diocesan and Parish	23
Total Students	3,442
Catechesis/Religious Education:	
High School Students	2,174
Elementary Students	2,860
Total Students under Catholic Instruction	17,927
Teachers in Diocese:	
Priests	8
Lay Teachers	810

Vital Statistics

Receptions into the Church:	
Infant Baptism Totals	710
Minor Baptism Totals	28
Adult Baptism Totals	45
Received into Full Communion	47
First Communions	908
Confirmations	921
Marriages:	
Catholic	143
Interfaith	73
Total Marriages	216
Deaths	1,976
Total Catholic Population	194,456
Total Population	810,232

LEADERSHIP

Office of the Bishop - t) 814-824-1120 Roberta Palmisano, Secy.;
Vicar General/Moderator of the Curia - t) 814-824-1130 Rev. Msgr. Edward M. Lohse;
Episcopal Vicars -
Vicar for Clergy - t) 814-824-1144 Very Rev. Nicholas J. Rouch;
Eastern Vicariate - t) 814-371-8556 Rev. Msgr. Richard R. Siefer;
Northern Vicariate - Rev. Msgr. Edward M. Lohse;
Western Vicariate - t) 724-981-5566 Very Rev. V. David Foradori, Vicar;
Chancery - t) 814-824-1130 Rev. Christopher J. Singer, Chancellor; Dcn. G. Frank Hannah, Vice Chancellor;

OFFICES AND DIRECTORS

Archives - Rev. Justin P. Pino, Archivist;
Diocesan Tribunal - t) 814-824-1140
Judicial Vicar - Rev. Marc A. Stockton;
Auditor - Sr. Sylvia Burnett, O.S.B.M.;
Coordinator of the Office of Matrimonial Concerns and Tribunal - Sr. Sylvia Burnett, O.S.B.M.;
Defender of the Bond - Daniela Knepper;
Matrimonial Judges - Rev. Marc A. Stockton; Rev. Daniel R. Hoffman; Dcn. Richard D. Shewman;
Promoter of Justice - Rev. Christopher J. Singer; Rev. Msgr. Daniel E. Magraw, Bishop's Delegate for Dispensation & Permissions;
Secretaries/Notaries - Cindy Mangiaracina; Patricia Wierbinski;
Human Resources - t) 814-824-1189 James Tometsko, Dir.;
Office for Divine Worship - t) 814-824-1271 Rev. Matthew J. Kujawinski, Admin.; Maripat Grant, Coord.;
Office for the Protection of Children and Youth - t) 814-824-1195 Rev. Msgr. Edward M. Lohse, Dir.; Cynthia Zemcik, Coord.; Dr. Gerard Tobin, Victim Assistance Coord.;
Office of Diocesan and International Missions - Indira Suarez, Dir.;

CATHOLIC CHARITIES

Office of Catholic Charities - Erin Tubbs, Exec. Dir.;
Catholic Charities Counseling and Adoption Services - t) 814-456-2091 Dcn. Richard Brogdon, CEO;
Eastern Vicariate - DuBois Office - t) 814-371-4717 Nanci Mattison;
Northern Vicariate - Erie Office - Dcn. Richard Brogdon;
Western Vicariate - Sharon Office - t) 866-852-6875 Dcn. Richard Brogdon;
Good Samaritan Center - t) 814-768-7229 Douglas Bloom, CEO;
Office of Social Justice and Life - Patrice Swick, Dir.;
Prince of Peace Center - t) 724-346-5777 Jennifer Wallace, CEO;
St. Elizabeth Center - t) 814-677-0203 Jessica Struthers, CEO;
***St. Martin Center** - t) 814-452-6113 David Gonzalez, CEO;

CLERGY AND RELIGIOUS SERVICES

Clergy Continuing Formation Committee - t) 814-824-1144 Very Rev. Nicholas J. Rouch, Chair;
Episcopal Delegate for Retired Priests - Rev. Philip M. Oriole;
Office for Religious - t) 814-824-1200 Sr. Nancy Fischer, S.S.J., Dir.;
Permanent Diaconate Program - t) 814-824-1144 Dcn. Thomas McAraw, Dir.;
St. Mark Seminary - t) 814-824-1200 Rev. Scott W. Jabo, Rector; Rev. David M. Renne, Vice Rector (dmrenne@eriercd.org); Rev. Christopher J. Singer, Resident Spiritual Dir.;
Vocation Office - t) 814-824-1200 Rev. Scott W. Jabo, Dir.;

COMMUNICATIONS

Office of Communications - Anne-Marie Welsh, Dir.;
Faith Magazine - t) 814-824-1167 faith@eriercd.org Vince Dragone, Editor;

EDUCATION

Superintendent of Catholic Schools - t) 814-824-1243 James Gallagher;
Assistant Superintendent - t) 814-824-1247 Laura Blake;
Curriculum, Instruction and Assessment - t) 814-824-1248 Lisa Panighetti, Dir.;
Government Programs - t) 814-824-1238 Roberta Bucci, Dir.;

FAITH FORMATION

Executive Director - Dcn. Stephen J. Washek, Exec.;
Faith Formation for Catechesis and Sacraments - t) 814-824-1222 Mary Hickin, Dir.;
Faith Formation for Marriage and Family Life - t) 814-824-1261 Kate Wilson, Dir.;
Chastity Education - t) 814-824-1259 Cathy Dornisch, NFP Coord.; Cassondra Dragone, Coord. for Chastity;
Faith Formation for Parish Support - t) 814-824-1224 Danielle Schoenfeldt, Dir.;
Faith Formation for Young Adult and Youth Ministry - t) 814-824-1219 Jillian Zaczyk, Dir.;

FINANCE

Financial Services Office - t) 814-824-1180 James Hubert, CFO (jahubert@eriercd.org); James L. Bogniak, Controller;
Diocesan Attorney - t) 814-833-2222 John B. Fessler;
Erie Diocesan Cemeteries - t) (814) 838-7724 questions@eriedc.org Korac John Timon, Exec. Dir. (korac@eriedc.org); Rev. Philip M. Oriole, Bishop's Liaison;

SOCIAL SERVICES

Catholic Rural Ministry - Oil City Deanery - t) (814) 677-2032 Sr. Marian Wehler, O.S.B., Dir. (marianwehler@yahoo.com); Sr. Tina Geiger, R.S.M., Dir. (srtinag@gmail.com);

MISCELLANEOUS / OTHER OFFICES

Bishop's Delegate to the Hispanic Apostolate - t) (814) 824-1130 Rev. Christopher J. Singer;
Bread of Life Community - t) 814-452-2982 Rev. Lawrence R. Richards, Moderator;
Cursillo Movement - t) 814-824-1111 Dcn. Thomas McAraw, Spiritual Adv./Care Srvcs.;
Legion of Mary -
Pennsylvania Catholic Conference - t) 814-824-1144 Very Rev. Nicholas J. Rouch, Personal Rep. of the Bishop;
Pennsylvania Conference on Inter-Church Cooperation - Rev. T. Shane Mathew;
Word of Life Charismatic Renewal - t) 814-824-1286 Rev. Johnathan P. Schmolt, Bishop's Liason; Diane Wiler, Office Mgr.;
World Apostolate of Fatima (Blue Army) - t) 814-454-6494 Rev. Jerry S. Priscaro, Chap.;

PARISHES, MISSIONS, AND CLERGY

COMMONWEALTH OF PENNSYLVANIA

ALBION

St. Lawrence the Martyr - 180 E. State St., Albion, PA 16401 t) 814-756-3623 stlawrencealbion@gmail.com www.stlawrencealbion.org Rev. Marc J. Solomon, Pst.; Dcn. Paul McCoy; CRP Stds.: 22
St. Lawrence Catechetical Center - 129 E. Pearl St., Albion, PA 16401 t) 814-756-4840
St. Philip - 25797 State Hwy. 98, Edinboro, PA 16412; Mailing: 180 E. State St., c/o St. Lawrence the Martyr Parish, Albion, PA 16401

BRADFORD

St. Bernard - 98 E. Corydon St., Bradford, PA 16701; Mailing: P.O. Box 2394, Bradford, PA 16701 t) 814-362-6825 sboffice@atlanticbb.net www.stbernardcatholic.org Rev. John B. Jacquel, Pst.; Rev. James G. Gutting, Assoc. Pst.; CRP Stds.: 89
St. Francis of Assisi - 15 St. Francis Dr., Bradford, PA 16701; Mailing: P.O. Box 2394, 95 E. Corydon St., Bradford, PA 16701 t) 814-362-6825 sboffice@atlanticbb.net stbernardcatholic.org Rev. John B. Jacquel, Pst.; Rev. James G. Gutting, Assoc. Pst.; Rev. Raymond C. Gramata, Pastor Emer.;
Our Mother of Perpetual Help - 37 Lafayette Ave, Lewis Run, PA 16738 Rev. Stanley Swacha, Assoc. Pst.;

BROCKWAY

St. Tobias - 1135 Hewitt St., Brockway, PA 15824 t) 814-268-3655 tobias@brockwaytv.com www.sttobias.com Rev. John J. Detisch, Pst.; Tara Starr, DRE; CRP Stds.: 110

BROOKVILLE

Immaculate Conception - 129 Graham Ave., Brookville, PA 15825 t) 814-849-8697 www.icbrookville.com Rev. William M. Laska, Pst.; Penny Rakovan, DRE; CRP Stds.: 66
St. Dominic - Catholic Church Rd., Sigel, PA 15860

CAMBRIDGE SPRINGS

St. Anthony of Padua - 165 Beach Ave., Cambridge Springs, PA 16403; Mailing: P.O. Box 214, Cambridge Springs, PA 16403 t) 814-398-4234 office@stanthonycambridgesprings.org stanthonycambridgesprings.org Rev. Mark A. Nowak, Pst.; CRP Stds.: 16
St. Bernadette - 222 Renner Ln., Saegertown, PA 16433 Josie Osiecki, Contact;

CLARION

Immaculate Conception - 715 E. Main St., Clarion, PA 16214; Mailing: 720 Liberty St., Clarion, PA 16214 t) 814-226-8433; 814-226-8433 x103 (CRP) montysayers@hotmail.com; tdfrederick@comcast.net www.icclarion.org Very Rev. B. LaMounte Sayers, Pst.; Dcn. Joseph Glover; CRP Stds.: 103
Immaculate Conception School - (Grades PreK-6) 729 E. Main St., Clarion, PA 16214 t) (814) 226-8433 lcratty@clarionichawks.net Lori Cratty, Prin.; Stds.: 69; Lay Tchrs.: 7

CLEARFIELD

St. Francis - 211 S. Second St., Clearfield, PA 16830; Mailing: 212 S. Front St., Clearfield, PA 16830 t) 814-765-9671 msgrglynn@atlanticbb.net; jbungo@stfrancisclearfield.org Very Rev. Robert Horgas, Pst.; Rev. Msgr. Henry L. Krebs, Senior Assoc.; Dcn. Robert Wilson; JJ Bungo, DRE; CRP Stds.: 54
St. Francis School - (Grades PreK-8) 230 S. Second St., Clearfield, PA 16830 t) 814-765-2618 sfsoffice@stfrancisclearfield.org Anna Boughner, Prin.; Stds.: 171; Lay Tchrs.: 16

COALPORT

St. Basil the Great - 183 Locust St., Coalport, PA 16627 t) 814-672-3561 stbasiloffice@yahoo.com www.stbasilgreat.org Rev. Zab Amar, Pst.; Annette Smith, CRE; CRP Stds.: 52

CONNEAUT LAKE

Our Lady Queen of the Americas - 155 S. 9th St., Conneaut Lake, PA 16316 t) 814-382-7256 (CRP); 814-382-7252 office@olqachurch.org olqachurch.org Rev. David E. Carter, Pst.; Amanda Sovisky, DRE; CRP Stds.: 40

CONNEAUTVILLE

St. Peter - 501 Washington St., Conneautville, PA 16406; Mailing: 401 S. Mercer St., Linesville, PA 16424 t) 814-683-5313 ss.ppmainffice@gmail.com stspeterphilip.com Very Rev. Christopher M. Hamlett, Pst.;

CORRY

St. Thomas the Apostle - 203 W. Washington St., Corry, PA 16407 t) 814-663-3041 secretary@stparish.org; business@stparish.org www.stthomastheapostle.church

Rev. Matthew J. Strickenberger, Pst.; Dcn. Randy Kondrlik; Melissa Silka, DRE; CRP Stds.: 38

COUDERSPORT

St. Eulalia - 6 E. Maple St., Coudersport, PA 16915 t) 814-274-8646 steulalia@zitomedia.net www.steulalia-stgabriel.org Partnered with St. Gabriel the Archangel Parish and St. Bibiana Parish Rev. Daniel R. Hoffman, Pst.; Rev. Christopher A. Wheeler, Par. Vicar; Rev. Joseph V. Dougherty; CRP Stds.: 65

CURWENSVILLE

St. Timothy - 306 Walnut St., Curwensville, PA 16833 t) 814-236-1845 sttimothychurch@atlanticbb.net Rev. Stephen L. Collins, Pst.; Terri A. Clarkson, DRE;

DU BOIS

St. Catherine of Siena - 123 S. State St., Du Bois, PA 15801; Mailing: 118 S. State St., Du Bois, PA 15801 t) 814-371-8556 www.stcathstmikedubois.org Rev. Msgr. Richard R. Siefer, Pst.; Rev. Benjamin Joseph Daghir, Par. Vicar; Dcn. Daniel F. Satterlee; Mary Jo Yebernetsky, DRE; CRP Stds.: 212

St. Michael - 15 Robinson St., Du Bois, PA 15801; Mailing: 118 S. State St., c/o St. Catherine of Siena Parish, DuBois, PA 15801 t) 814-371-8556 stmichaeldubois@gmail.com www.stcathstmikedubois.org Rev. Msgr. Richard R. Siefer, Pst.; Dcn. Daniel F. Satterlee;

EAST BRADY

St. Eusebius - 301 E. 2nd St., East Brady, PA 16028 t) 724-526-3366 Rev. William M. Kuba, Admin.;

St. Richard - Purity Ave., Rimersburg, PA 16248; Mailing: 301 E. Second St., c/o St. Eusebius Parish, East Brady, PA 16028 Mary Donaldson, Contact;

EDINBORO

Our Lady of the Lake - 128 Sunset Dr., Edinboro, PA 16412 t) 814-734-3113 ololchurch.office@gmail.com ololake.com/ Rev. Mark A. Hoffman, Pst.; Dcn. David Romanowicz; Mary Rose Shinsky, DRE; CRP Stds.: 113

ELDRED

St. Raphael - 16 First St., Eldred, PA 16731; Mailing: P.O. Box 252, Eldred, PA 16731 t) 814-225-4231; 814-697-6900 www.straphaeleldred.org Rev. Thomas E. Brown, Pst.; CRP Stds.: 5

St. Mary - 630 Newell Creek Rd., Eldred, PA 16731

St. Theresa - 111 S. Puritan St., Shinglehouse, PA 16748

EMLENTON

St. Michael - 807 Chestnut St., Emlenton, PA 16373; Mailing: P.O. Box 177, Emlenton, PA 16373 t) 724-867-2422 info@stmichaelrcchurch.org www.stmichaelrcchurch.org Rev. Johnathan P. Schmolt, Admin.; Elisa Cirell, DRE; CRP Stds.: 24

EMPORIUM

St. Mark - 235 E. 4th St., Emporium, PA 15834 t) 814-486-0569 stmarkcatholicemp@gmail.com stmarkemporium.org/ Rev. Paul S. Siebert, Pst.; Jennifer Abriatis, DRE; CRP Stds.: 41

St. James - 7305 3rd St., Driftwood, PA 15832 Kim McFall, Contact;

ERIE

St. Peter Cathedral - 230 W. 10th St., Erie, PA 16501 t) 814-453-6677 info@stpetercathedral.com Very Rev. Michael P. Ferrick, Rector; Dcn. Raymond Sobina; Dcn. Jeffrey Swanson; CRP Stds.: 18

St. Andrew - 1116 W. Seventh St., Erie, PA 16502; Mailing: 816 W. 26th St., c/o Sacred Heart of Jesus Parish, Erie, PA 16508 t) 814-456-6256 triparish.secretary816@gmail.com www.saintandrewerie.org Partnered with Sacred Heart and St. Paul parishes Rev. Mark O'Hern, Pst.; Dcn. Ralph DeCecco; CRP Stds.: 12

Blessed Sacrament - 1626 W. 26th St., Erie, PA 16508 t) 814-454-0171 dfisher@bserie.org www.bsparisherie.org Rev. Phillip Pinczewski, Pst.; Dcn. Kevin Kunik; CRP Stds.: 70

St. Boniface - 9367 Wattsburg Rd., Erie, PA 16509 t) 814-825-4439 x230 (CRP); 814-825-4439 secretary@stbonifaceparisherie.org www.stbonifaceparisherie.org Rev. Marc A. Stockton, Pst.; Dcn. Timothy Good; Jeanne Yaple, DRE; CRP Stds.: 81

St. George - 5145 Peach St., Erie, PA 16509 t) 814-866-0622 bvossler@stgeorgeerie.org; office@stgeorgeerie.org www.stgeorgeerie.org Rev. Brian E. Vossler, Pst.; Rev. Nicholas J. Fratus, Par. Vicar; Dcn. Stephen Washek; Michael Palmer, DRE; CRP Stds.: 120

Holy Rosary - 2701 East Ave., Erie, PA 16504 t) 814-456-4254 parish.secretary@holyrosaryerie.org stjohn-holyrosary-erie.org Partnered with St. John the Baptist Parish, Erie Rev. David Baetzold, Pst.; Dcn. Matthew C. Ochalek; Mary Hickin, DRE; CRP Stds.: 1

Holy Trinity - 2220 Reed St., Erie, PA 16503 t) 814-456-0671 parishoffice@holytrinityrc.org www.holytrinityrc.org Partnered with St. Stanislaus Church, Erie, PA Rev. Jason A. Glover, Pst.; Rev. Msgr. Daniel Magraw, Assoc. Pst.;

St. James - 2635 Buffalo Rd., Erie, PA 16510 t) 814-899-6187 rectory@saintjamesrcc.org www.saintjamesrcc.org Rev. James P. McCormick, Pst.; Dcn. Charles Adamczyk; Rev. Msgr. Casimir A. Bogniak, Sacr. Min.; Rev. Scott W. Jabo, Sacr. Min.; CRP Stds.: 73

St. John the Baptist - 509 E. 26th St., GPS Address, Erie, PA 16504; Mailing: 2701 East Ave., Erie, PA 16504 t) 814-454-2873 secretary@sjberie.org stjohn-holyrosary-erie.org Partnered with Holy Rosary Parish, Erie Rev. David Baetzold; Dcn. Denis Coan; Mary Hickin, DRE; CRP Stds.: 2

St. Joseph - 147 W. 24th St., Erie, PA 16502 t) 814-452-2982 office@stjoesbol.org www.stjoesbol.org Rev. Lawrence R. Richards, Pst.; Dcn. Douglas Konzel; Dcn. Jim DiSimoni, DRE; CRP Stds.: 85

St. Jude the Apostle - 2801 W. 6th St., Erie, PA 16505 t) 814-833-0927 secretary@stjudeapos.org www.stjudeapos.org Rev. Ross R. Miceli, Pst.; Dcn. Richard Brogdon; Rev. T. Shane Mathew, Sacr. Min.; Jesse Spanogle, DRE; CRP Stds.: 150

St. Julia - 638 Roslyn Ave., Erie, PA 16505 t) 814-833-4347 x3 cjulia@roadrunner.com www.stjuliaerie.com Rev. Msgr. Edward M. Lohse; Dcn. Jerome Peterson; Cheryl Ann Morrison, DRE; CRP Stds.: 16

St. Luke - 421 E. 38th St., Erie, PA 16504 t) 814-825-6920 stluke@slserie.org www.stlukeerie.org Very Rev. John P. Malthaner, Pst.; Rev. Walter E. Packard, Senior Assoc.; Dcn. Glenn Kuzma; Dcn. Richard Shewman; CRP Stds.: 131

St. Mark the Evangelist - 695 Smithson Ave., Erie, PA 16511 t) 814-899-3000 office@smmc.church; pmarshall@smmc.church www.stmarkmtcalvary.church Rev. Thomas Trocchio, Pst.; Dcn. Dave Jacquel; Katie Leuschen, Youth Min.; CRP Stds.: 39

Mount Calvary - 2022 E. Lake Rd., Erie, PA 16511; Mailing: 695 Smithson Ave, Erie, PA 16511 t) 814-454-0061; 814-899-3000 office@smmc.church www.stmarkmtcalvary.church Rev. Thomas Trocchio, Pst.; Dcn. Dave Jacquel; Katie Leuschen, Youth Min.; CRP Stds.: 39

Our Lady of Mt. Carmel - 1531 E. Grandview Blvd., Erie, PA 16510 t) 814-825-7313 sberdis@olmc-erie.org www.olmc-erie.org Very Rev. Nicholas J. Rouch, Par. Admin.; Rev. Casimir Wozniak, Weekend Asst.; Dcn. Frank Pregler; Rev. Ian R. McElrath, In Res.; CRP Stds.: 59

Our Lady of Peace - 2401 W. 38th St., Erie, PA 16506 t) 814-833-7701 olp@olp.org olp.org Rev. Richard J. Toohey, Pst.; Rev. David Whiteford, Par. Vicar; Dcn. John Mang; Dcn. Joseph Yochim; Rev. T. Shane Mathew, In Res.; Tammie Mang, DRE; CRP Stds.: 252

Our Mother of Sorrows - 630 Hess Ave., Erie, PA 16503 t) 814-452-4832 gangemi@twc.com www.motherofsorrowerie.org Very Rev. John P. Malthaner, Admin.; Dcn. Jerome Sobrowski; Rev. Jerry S. Priscaro, In Res.;

St. Ann Church - 921 East Ave., Erie, PA 16503; Mailing: 630 Hess Ave., Erie, PA 16503 c) (814) 452-4832

St. Casimir Church - 629 Hess Ave., Erie, PA 16503; Mailing: c/o Our Mother of Sorrows Parish, 913 Fulton St., Erie, PA 16503

Holy Family Church -

St. Patrick - 130 E. 4th St., Erie, PA 16507 t) 814-454-8085 stpats@neo.rr.com www.saintpatrickparisherie.org Rev. Michael J DeMartinis, Pst.; CRP Stds.: 53

St. Paul - 1617 Walnut St., Erie, PA 16502; Mailing: c/o Sacred Heart Parish, 816 W. 26th St., Erie, PA 16508 t) 814-456-6256 triparish.secretary816@gmail.com www.stpaulrcerie.org Partnered with Sacred Heart and Saint Andrew parishes Rev. Mark O'Hern, Pst.; Dcn. Anthony J. Alleruzzo;

Sacred Heart - 816 W. 26th St., Erie, PA 16508 t) 814-456-6256 triparish.secretary816@gmail.com; sacredheart.secretary816@gmail.com sacredhearterie.org Partnered with St. Andrew and St. Paul parishes Rev. Mark O'Hern, Pst.; Rev. Jerome S. Simmons, In Res.;

St. Stanislaus - 516 E. 13th St., Erie, PA 16503 t) 814-452-6606 ststaner@outlook.com www.ststanserie.org Rev. Jason A. Glover, S.T.L., Pst.; Rev. Msgr. Daniel E. Magraw, Senior Assoc.;

St. Hedwig - 521 E. 3rd St., Erie, PA 16507; Mailing: 516 E. 13th St., Erie, PA 16503 Rev. Msgr. Bernard J. Urbaniak, Pst.;

St. Stephen - 1237 W. 21 St., Erie, PA 16502 t) 814-459-0543 csegovia@eriercd.org Rev. Cesar Segovia, Pst.; Dcn. Miguel Alvarez; Dcn. Denis Coan, Admin.;

FAIRVIEW

Holy Cross - 7100 W. Ridge Rd., Fairview, PA 16415; Mailing: P. O. Box 10, Fairview, PA 16415 t) 814-474-2605 www.holycrossfairview.org Rev. Thomas L. Tyler, Pst.; CRP Stds.: 78

FALLS CREEK

St. Bernard - 205 Taylor Ave., Falls Creek, PA 15840; Mailing: P.O. Box 362, Falls Creek, PA 15840 t) 814-371-0428 stbernardrcc@yahoo.com Rev. Msgr. Richard R. Siefer, Pst.; Rev. Benjamin Joseph Daghir, Par. Vicar; Rev. Edward J. Walk, Assoc. Pst.; CRP Stds.: 10

FARRELL

Our Lady of Fatima - 601 Roemer Blvd., Farrell, PA 16121 t) 724-346-3359 olfrectory@yahoo.com sap-olf.org Rev. Matthew J. Ruyechan, Pst.;

FORCE

St. Joseph - 17764 Bennetts Valley Hwy., Force, PA 15841; Mailing: P O Box 124, Force, PA 15841 t) 814-787-4151 x3 Rev. Mark J Mastrian, Pst.; Dcn. Paul Bauman; Mary Stoker, DRE;

FRANKLIN

St. Patrick - 949 Liberty St., Franklin, PA 16323 t) 814-437-5763 church@stpatrickfranklin.org; npowell@stpatrickfranklin.org Rev. James C. Campbell, Pst.; Nicole Powell, DRE; Dcn. Richard O'Polka; CRP Stds.: 66

FRENCHVILLE

St. Mary of the Assumption - 64 St. Mary's Ln., Frenchville, PA 16836; Mailing: P.O. Box 159, Frenchville, PA 16836 t) 814-263-4354 northmoshannoncluster.org Rev. David A. Perry, Pst.; CRP Stds.: 22

SS. Peter & Paul - Grassflat Ave., Frenchville, PA 16836

St. Severin - 6789 Kylertown-Drifting Hwy., Drifting, PA 16834 Jessica Minor, Contact;

FRYBURG

St. Michael - 18765 Rte. 208, Fryburg, PA 16326; Mailing: P.O. Box 9, c/o St. Joseph Parish, Lucinda, PA 16235 t) 814-226-7288 marcia.ochs@stjosephlucinda.com www.stjoseph-stmichaelparishes.org Rev. Michael C. Polinek, Pst.; Elizabeth Beal, DRE; CRP Stds.: 56

Parish Office - 84 Rectory Ln., Lucinda, PA 16235; Mailing: PO Box 9, Lucinda, PA 16235 Rev. Marc J. Solomon, Admin.;

GALETON

St. Bibiana - 111 Germania St., Galeton, PA 16922 t) 814-435-2303 Rev. Daniel R. Hoffman, Pst.;

St. Augustine - 33 Turner St., Austin, PA 16720; Mailing: 111 Germania St., Galeton, PA 16922

Sacred Heart - 263 Main St., Genesee, PA 16923; Mailing: 111 Germania St., c/o St. Bibiana, Galeton, PA 16922 Renee Kratz, Contact;

GIRARD

St. John the Evangelist - 1001 Main St. E., Girard, PA 16417; Mailing: P.O. Box 32, Girard, PA 16417 t) 814-774-4061 (CRP); 814-774-4108 office@stjohngirard.org stjohngirard.org Rev. Scott P. Detisch, Pst.; Jennifer King, DRE; CRP Stds.: 59

GRAMPIAN

St. Bonaventure - 461 Main St., Grampian, PA 16838; Mailing: 306 Walnut St., c/o St. Timothy Parish, Curwensville, PA 16833 t) 814-236-1845 (Partnered Parish Office) stbon@verizon.net Rev. Stephen L. Collins, Pst.; Terri A. Clarkson, DRE; CRP Stds.: 50

GREENVILLE

St. Michael - 85 N. High St., Greenville, PA 16125 t) 724-588-9800 st.michaelchurch@neohio.twcbc.com stmichaelgreenville.com Rev. Brandon M. Kleckner, Pst.; Dcn. Marty Aubel; Dcn. Frank Luciani; Teia Barger, DRE; CRP Stds.: 71

St. Michael School - (Grades PreK-8) 80 N. High St., Greenville, PA 16125 t) 724-588-7050 ezgonc@smike1.org www.saintmichael1.org Emily Zgonc, Prin.; Stds.: 72; Lay Tchrs.: 9

St. Margaret - 701 Denver St., Jamestown, PA 16134; Mailing: 85 N. High St., c/o St. Michael, Greenville, PA 16125 t) (724) 588-9800 Patricia Joyce Meehan, Secy.;

GROVE CITY

Beloved Disciple - 1310 S. Center St. Ext., Grove City, PA 16127 t) 724-748-6700 secretary@beloveddiscipleparish.org Very Rev. V. David Foradori, Pst.; Dcn. Owen Wagner;

GUYS MILLS

St. Hippolyte - 26012 N. Frenchtown Rd., Guys MIlls, PA 16327; Mailing: 25997 State Hwy. 27, Guys Mills, PA 16327 t) 814-789-2022 www.sainthippolytechurch.com Rev. Jeffrey Lucas, Pst.; Joyce Tarr, DRE; CRP Stds.: 69

Our Lady of Lourdes - 251 S. Franklin St., Cochranton, PA 16314; Mailing: 25997 Hwy. 27, c/o St. Hippolyte Parish, Guys Mills, PA 16327 t) 814-425-7550

HARBORCREEK

Our Lady of Mercy - 837 Bartlett Rd., Harborcreek, PA 16421 t) 814-899-5342; 814-899-6132 (CRP) info@ourladyofmercychurch.org www.ourladyofmercychurch.org Rev. Matthew J. Kujawinski, Pst.; Dcn. Paul Barko; Irene Lucas, DRE; CRP Stds.: 87

HERMITAGE

Notre Dame - 2325 Highland Rd., Hermitage, PA 16148 t) 724-981-5566 churchoffice@notredame-pa.org www.notredame-pa.org Very Rev. Richard J. Allen, Pst.; Joe Ranelli, DRE;

HOUTZDALE

Christ the King - 100 Brisbin St., Houtzdale, PA 16651; Mailing: 123 Good St., Houtzdale, PA 16651 t) 814-378-7653 christtheking.office@comcast.net Rev. Joseph R. Czarkowski, Pst.; Dcn. Eugene Miller Jr.; CRP Stds.: 75

JOHNSONBURG

Holy Rosary - 210 Bridge St., Johnsonburg, PA 15845; Mailing: 606 Penn St., Johnsonburg, PA 15845 t) 814-965-2819; 814-965-5528 Rev. David J. Wilson, Pst.; Margaret Griffin, DRE; CRP Stds.: 125

St. Anne - 75 Buchanan St., Wilcox, PA 15870

KANE

St. Callistus - 342 Chase St., Kane, PA 16735 t) 814-837-6694 pastor@stcallistuskane.org www.stcallistuskane.org Rev. William J. O'Brien, Pst.; Michele Smith, DRE; CRP Stds.: 66

KERSEY

St. Boniface - 355 Main St., Kersey, PA 15846 t) (814) 885-4488 church.office@st-boniface.org www.st-boniface.org Rev. Kevin Holland, Pst.; CRP Stds.: 35

LEEPER

St. Mary - 117 Lencer Dr., Leeper, PA 16233 t) 814-744-9919 stmarycrown.com Rev. James P. Power, Pst.; Dcn. Michael J Dittman; Sheila Martz, DRE; CRP Stds.: 43

St. Ann - 101 Hemlock St., Marienville, PA 16239 Rev. Christopher M. Barnes, Pst.;

LINESVILLE

St. Philip the Apostle - 401 S. Mercer St., Linesville, PA 16424 t) 814-683-5313 ss.ppmainoffice@gmail.com stspeterphilip.com Very Rev. Christopher M. Hamlett, Pst.;

LUCINDA

St. Joseph - 84 Rectory Ln., Lucinda, PA 16235; Mailing: PO Box 9, Lucinda, PA 16235 t) 814-226-7288; 814-297-0161 marcia.ochs@stjosephlucinda.com www.stjoseph-stmichaelparishes.org Rev. Michael C. Polinek, Pst.; Judy Wolbert, DRE; CRP Stds.: 49

St. Joseph School - (Grades PreK-6) 72 Rectory Ln., Lucinda, PA 16235; Mailing: P.O. Box 9, Lucinda, PA 16235 t) 814-226-8018 bochs.stjoseph@gmail.com Betsy Ochs, Prin.; Stds.: 56; Lay Tchrs.: 9

MC KEAN

St. Francis Xavier - 8880 Main St., Mc Kean, PA 16426-0317; Mailing: P.O. Box 317, McKean, PA 16426 t) 814-476-7657 office@stfrancisxaviermckean.org www.stfrancisxaviermckean.org Rev. Jason R. Feigh, Pst.; Dcn. Ronald Fronzaglia;

MEADVILLE

The Epiphany of the Lord - 353 Pine St., Meadville, PA 16335 t) 814-336-1112 contact@catholic-meadville.org epiphanymeadville.org/ Rev. Jeffery J. Lucas, Pst.; Rev. Joseph Petrone, Par. Vicar; Dcn. Edward R. Horneman; Dcn. Kenneth Reisenweber; Dcn. Todd Sommers; CRP Stds.: 41

St. Agatha - t) (814) 336-1112

St. Brigid - 383 Arch St., Meadville, PA 16335; Mailing: 353 Pine St., Meadville, PA 16335 t) (814) 336-1112

St. Mary of Grace - 1085 Water St., Meadville, PA 16335; Mailing: 353 Pine St., Meadville, PA 16335 t) (814) 336-1112

Seton School - (Grades PreSchool-8) 385 Pine St., Meadville, PA 16335 t) (814) 336-2320 chess@seton-school.com www.seton-school.com Christine Hess, Prin.; Stds.: 132; Lay Tchrs.: 12

MERCER

Immaculate Heart of Mary - 100 Penn Ave., Mercer, PA 16137 t) 724-662-2999 ihm@zoominternet.net www.ihmcmercer.com/ Rev. Andrew M. Boyd, Pst.; CRP Stds.: 45

St. Hermenegild - 28 Church Rd., Mercer, PA 16137; Mailing: 100 Penn Ave., c/o Immaculate Heart of Mary Parish, Mercer, PA 16137 (Secondary Church)

MORRISDALE

St. Agnes - 65 Deer Creek Rd., Morrisdale, PA 16858; Mailing: 22 St. Agnes Dr., Morrisdale, PA 16858 t) 814-342-2583 Rev. William R. Barron, Pst.; Dcn. Dennis Socash;

SS. Peter & Paul - Sixth St., Hawk Run, PA 16840

NEW BETHLEHEM

St. Charles Church - 201 Washington St., New Bethlehem, PA 16242 t) 814-275-3446 stcharles@dioceseoferie.org dioceseoferie.org/stcharlesbethlehem/ Rev. Samuel Bungo, Pst.; Tina Roy, DRE; CRP Stds.: 30

St. Nicholas - 3028 Shannondale Rd., Mayport, PA 16240; Mailing: 201 Washington St., c/o St. Charles Parish, New Bethlehem, PA 16242 Dan Landers, Contact;

NORTH EAST

St. Gregory Thaumaturgus - 48 S. Pearl St., North East, PA 16428; Mailing: 136 W. Main St., North East, PA 16428 t) 814-725-9691 stgregs@roadrunner.com www.stgregoryparish.info Rev. Thomas M. Brooks, Pst.; Dcn. Richard E. Winschel; Jennifer Humes, DRE; CRP Stds.: 150

St. Gregory Thaumaturgus School - (Grades PreK-8) 140 W. Main St., North East, PA 16428 t) 814-725-4571 npierce@stgregs.net Nancy Pierce, Prin.; Stds.: 65; Lay Tchrs.: 7

OIL CITY

St. Joseph - 35 Pearl Ave., Oil City, PA 16301; Mailing: 210 Reed St., c/o St. Stephen Rectory, Oil City, PA 16301 t) 814-677-3020 office@oilcitycatholic.com Rev. John L. Miller III, Pst.; Rev. Johnathan P. Schmolt, Par. Vicar; CRP Stds.: 87

St. Stephen Church -

OSCEOLA MILLS

Immaculate Conception Parish - 408 Stone St., Osceola Mills, PA 16666; Mailing: 22 St. Agnes Dr., c/o St. Agnes Parish, Morrisdale, PA 16858 t) 814-339-7321 stagnesrcc@gmail.com Rev. William R. Barron, Pst.;

PORT ALLEGANY

St. Gabriel the Archangel - 203 E. Arnold Ave., Port Allegany, PA 16743; Mailing: 6 E. Maple St., Coundersport, PA 16915 t) 814-274-8646 www.steulalia-stgabriel.org Partnered with St. Eulalia Parish Rev. Daniel R. Hoffman, Pst.; Rev. Christopher A. Wheeler, Par. Vicar; Rev. Joseph V. Dougherty, Senior Assoc.;

PUNXSUTAWNEY

SS. Cosmas and Damian - 616 W. Mahoning St., Punxsutawney, PA 15767 t) 814-938-6540 sscdofc@comcast.net www.sscdchurch.com Rev. Msgr. Joseph J. Riccardo, Pst.; CRP Stds.: 63

SS. Cosmas and Damian School - (Grades PreK-6) 205 N. Chestnut St., Punxsutawney, PA 15767 t) 814-938-4224 heather.kunselman@sscdschool.com sscdschool.com Heather Kunselman, Prin.; Stds.: 62; Lay Tchrs.: 6

REYNOLDSVILLE

St. Mary - 607 E. Main St., Reynoldsville, PA 15851 t) 814-653-8586 stmaryschurch2@verizon.net Rev. Msgr. Richard R. Siefer, Pst.; Rev. Benjamin Joseph Daghir, Par. Vicar; Rev. Edward J. Walk, Senior Assoc.; Barb Murray, DRE; CRP Stds.: 48

RIDGWAY

St. Leo Magnus - 111 Depot St., Ridgway, PA 15853 t) 814-772-3135 secretary@stleomagnus.org stleomagnus.org Rev. Justin P. Pino, Pst.; CRP Stds.: 160

SHARON

St. Anthony - 804 Idaho St., Sharon, PA 16146 t) 724-342-7391 themustardseed3@yahoo.com www.sap-olf.org Rev. Matthew J. Ruyechan, Pst.;

St. Joseph - 79 Case Ave., Sharon, PA 16146 t) 724-981-3232 office@stjosephs-sharon.org www.stjosephs-sharon.org Rev. Thomas J. Whitman, Pst.; Sr. Sandy Pedone, H.M., DRE; CRP Stds.: 127

SHARPSVILLE

St. Bartholomew - 311 W. Ridge Ave., Sharpsville, PA 16150 t) 724-962-7130 secretary@saintbartholomews.com www.saintbartholomews.com Very Rev. Richard J. Allen, Pst.; Dcn. G. Frank Hannah; CRP Stds.: 100

SMETHPORT

St. Elizabeth - 307 Franklin St., Smethport, PA 16749 t) 814-887-9254 elizabethsaint17@gmail.com Very Rev. Vincent P. Cieslewicz, Pst.;

St. Joseph - 20 Division St., Mt. Jewett, PA 16740; Mailing: 307 Franklin St., c/o St. Elizabeth of Hungary Parish, Smethport, PA 16749 stelizabethrcc@comcast.net

ST. MARYS

St. Mary - 315 Church St., St. Marys, PA 15857; Mailing: 325 Church St., St. Marys, PA 15857 t) 814-781-1019 smchurch1@windstream.net thesmchurch.com Rev. Thomas More Sikora, O.S.B., Pst.; Dcn. Raymond Ehrensberger; CRP Stds.: 61

Queen of the World - 134 Queens Rd., St. Marys, PA 15857 t) 814-834-4701 qwchurch@qwchurch.com www.qwchurch.com/ Rev. Jeffery J. Noble, Pst.; CRP Stds.: 120

Sacred Heart - 346 Center St., St. Marys, PA 15857;

Mailing: 337 Center St., St. Marys, PA 15857 t) 814-834-7861 sacredheartparish.us Rev. Thomas Curry, OSB, Pst.; Dcn. Andrew Froberg; Dcn. William Gibson; CRP Stds.: 86

STONEBORO

St. Columbkille - 70 Franklin St., Stoneboro, PA 16153; Mailing: P.O. Box 206, Stoneboro, PA 16153 t) 724-376-3393 office@stcolumbkillechurch.org Rev. Robert A. Manning, Pst.;

SYKESVILLE

Assumption of Blessed Virgin Mary - 20 Shaffer St., Sykesville, PA 15865; Mailing: P.O. Box J, Sykesville, PA 15865 t) 814-653-8586; 814-894-2772 abvmchurch20@gmail.com Rev. Msgr. Richard R. Siefer, Pst.; Rev. Benjamin Joseph Daghir, Par. Vicar; Rev. Edward J. Walk, Senior Assoc.; Dcn. Stephen D. Rowan;

TIDIOUTE

St. John - 25 First St., Tidioute, PA 16351 t) 814-484-7747 Rev. Joseph Kalinowski, Pst.; Kimberly Hunt, DRE;

St. Anthony - 112 Bridge St., Tionesta, PA 16353; Mailing: 25 First St., Tidioute, PA 16351 Jane Downey, Contact;

TITUSVILLE

St. Titus - 513 W. Main St., Titusville, PA 16354 t) 814-827-4636 Rev. Christopher M. Barnes, Pst.; Dcn. Kevin Harmon; Kathleen Puleo, DRE; CRP Stds.: 48

Immaculate Conception - 17932 Wright Rd., Centerville, PA 16404; Mailing: 513 W. Main St., c/o Titus Parish, Titusville, PA 16354

St. Walburga - 120 Brook St., Titusville, PA 16354; Mailing: 513 W. Main St., c/o St. Titus Parish, Titusville, PA 16354

UNION CITY

St. Teresa of Avila - 9 Third Ave., Union City, PA 16438; Mailing: 203 W. Washington St., Corry, PA 16407 t) 814-438-3408; (814) 663-3041 business@stparish.org; secretary@stparish.org st-teresa-unioncity.org Rev. Matthew J. Strickenberger, Pst.; Dcn. Randy Kondrlik; Melissa Silka, DRE; CRP Stds.: 48

Our Lady of Fatima - 36198 Lake Rd., Union City, PA 16438; Mailing: 9 Third Ave., c/o St. Teresa Parish, Union City, PA 16438 t) 814-438-2000

WARREN

Holy Redeemer - 11 Russell St., Warren, PA 16365 t) 814-723-4222 hrparishoffice1@atlanticbbn.net; hrpastor@atlanticbbn.net www.holyredeemerwarren.com Rev. Stephen J. Schreiber, Pst.; Dcn. Raymond Wiehagen; Jennifer Wortman, DRE;

St. Anthony - 7222 Rte. 6, Sheffield, PA 16347; Mailing: c/o Holy Redeemer Parish, Warren, PA 16365

St. Joseph - 600 Penna Ave., W., Warren, PA 16365 t) 814-723-2090 office.sjc@westpa.net stjosephwarrenpa.org Rev. Richard C. Tomasone, Pst.; Dcn. Lawrence Tyers;

St. Luke - 420 N. Main St., Youngsville, PA 16371; Mailing: 600 Pennsylvania Ave. W., Warren, PA 16365

WATERFORD

All Saints - 11264 Rte. 97 N., Waterford, PA 16441 t) 814-796-3023 allsaint@allsaintsrcc.org allsaintsrcc.org Rev. Gregory P. Passauer, Pst.; Dcn. Thomas McAraw; Maria Burkley, DRE; CRP Stds.: 77

WEST MIDDLESEX

Good Shepherd - 3613 Sharon Rd., West Middlesex, PA 16159; Mailing: PO Box 226, West Middlesex, PA 16159 t) 724-528-3539 x11 (Pastor); 724-528-3539 (CRP) parishoffice@goodshepherdwm.org www.goodshepherdwm.org Rev. Glenn R. Whitman, Pst.; Lauren DeFelice, DRE; CRP Stds.: 72

SCHOOLS: PRESCHOOL THRU HIGH SCHOOL

SCHOOLS

COMMONWEALTH OF PENNSYLVANIA

DU BOIS

DuBois Area Catholic School System - (DIO) (Grades PreK-12) 200/210 Central Christian Rd., Du Bois, PA 15801; Mailing: 200 Central Christian Rd., P.O. Box 567, DuBois, PA 15801 t) 814-371-3060 gcaruso@duboiscatholic.com www.duboiscatholic.com Rev. Benjamin Joseph Daghir; Gretchen Caruso, Pres.; Stds.: 416; Lay Tchrs.: 37

DuBois Central Catholic High School - (Grades PreK-12) 200 Central Christian Rd., Du Bois, PA 15801; Mailing: P.O. Box 567, Du Bois, PA 15801 t) (814) 371-2570 kmiller@duboiscatholic.com Karrie Miller, Prin.; Theresa Liddle, Vice Prin.; Stds.: 129; Lay Tchrs.: 11

DuBois Central Catholic Middle School - (Grades PreK-12) 200 Central Christian Rd., Du Bois, PA 15801-5706; Mailing: P.O. Box 567, Du Bois, PA 15801-5706 t) (814) 371-2570 kmiller@duboiscatholic.com; tliddle@duboiscatholic.com Karrie Miller, Prin.; Theresa Liddle, Vice Prin.; Stds.: 91; Lay Tchrs.: 8

DuBois Central Catholic Elementary School - (Grades PreK-12) 210 Central Christian Rd., Du Bois, PA 15801-1698; Mailing: P.O. Box 567, Du Bois, PA 15801-1698 t) 814-371-2570 tliddle@duboiscatholic.com Karrie Miller, Prin.; Theresa Liddle, Vice Prin.; Stds.: 195; Lay Tchrs.: 17

ERIE

Erie Catholic School System, Inc. - 1531 E. Grandview Blvd., Ste. 100, Erie, PA 16510 t) 814-806-2423 office@eriecatholic.org www.eriecatholic.org Bridget Philip, Pres.; Stds.: 1,981; Sr. Tchrs.: 1; Lay Tchrs.: 118

Blessed Sacrament School, Erie - 2510 Greengarden Rd., Erie, PA 16502-2112 t) 814-455-1387 whall@eriecatholic.org www.eriecatholic.org/bss/ William Hall, Prin.; Stds.: 216; Sr. Tchrs.: 1; Lay Tchrs.: 13

Our Lady of Peace School - 2401 W. 38th St., Erie, PA 16506 t) 814-838-3548 ssuri@eriecatholic.org www.eriecatholic.org/olp Shivani Suri, Prin.; Stds.: 469; Lay Tchrs.: 27

St. George School - 1612 Bryant St., Erie, PA 16509 t) 814-864-4821 jschroeck@eriecatholic.org www.eriecatholic.org/sgs John Schroeck, Prin.; Stds.: 495; Lay Tchrs.: 28

St. James School - 2602 Buffalo Rd., Erie, PA 16510 t) 814-899-3429 gbrennan@eriecatholic.org www.eriecatholic.org/sja Gina Brennan, Prin.; Stds.: 220; Lay Tchrs.: 13

St. Jude School - 606 Lowell Ave., Erie, PA 16505 t) 814-838-7676 hmorphy@eriecatholic.org www.eriecatholic.org/sju Holly Morphy, Prin.; Stds.: 265; Lay Tchrs.: 16

St. Luke School - 425 E. 38th St., Erie, PA 16504 t) 814-825-7105 dfuller@eriecatholic.org www.eriecatholic.org/sls Donald Fuller, Prin.; Stds.: 316; Lay Tchrs.: 21

Mercyhurst Preparatory School - (PRV) (Grades 9-12) 538 E. Grandview Blvd., Erie, PA 16504 t) 814-824-2210 jhaas@mpslakers.com www.mpslakers.com Joseph Haas, Pres.; Tom Rinke, Prin.; Rev. Ian R. McElrath, Chap.; Stds.: 443; Pr. Tchrs.: 1; Lay Tchrs.: 36

Villa Maria Cathedral Preparatory Catholic School System dba Cathedral Preparatory School and Mother Teresa Academy - (DIO) (Grades K-12) 250 W. 10th St., Erie, PA 16501 t) 814-453-7737 patty.kirik@prep-villa.com www.prep-villa.com Kevin Smith, Pres.; Stds.: 883; Pr. Tchrs.: 3; Lay Tchrs.: 71

Villa Maria Cathedral Preparatory Catholic School System dba Cathedral Preparatory School and Mother Teresa Academy - (Grades K-12) 160 W. 11th St., Erie, PA 16501 t) 814-455-0580 jason.laouceur@mtasaints.com Jason Ladouceur, Prin.; Stds.: 166; Lay Tchrs.: 14

Villa Maria Cathedral Preparatory Catholic School System dba Cathedral Preparatory School and Mother Teresa Academy - (Grades K-12) 250 W. 50th St., Erie, PA 16501 t) (814) 453-7737 x2251 teresa.fratus@cathedralprep.com William Pituch, Vice. Pres.; Stds.: 717; Pr. Tchrs.: 3; Lay Tchrs.: 57

HERMITAGE

Shenango Valley Catholic School System, Inc. - (DIO) (Grades PreK-12) 2120 Shenango Valley Fwy., Hermitage, PA 16148-3011 t) 724-346-5531 jhalicki@kennedycatholicschools.org kennedycatholicschools.org Janet Halicki, Prin.; Kathryn Tiefenthal, Prin.; Stds.: 264; Lay Tchrs.: 27

Saint John Paul II Elementary School - (Grades PreK-12) 2335 Highland Rd., Hermitage, PA 16148-2820 t) 724-342-2205 ktiefenthal@kennedycatholicschools.org Stds.: 134; Lay Tchrs.: 14

Kennedy Catholic Middle School - (Grades PreK-12) 2120 Shenango Valley Fwy., Hermitage, PA 16148-3011 t) (724) 346-5531 Stds.: 40; Lay Tchrs.: 2

Kennedy Catholic High School - (Grades PreK-12) 2120 Shenango Valley Fwy., Hermitage, PA 16148 t) (724) 346-5531 Stds.: 90; Lay Tchrs.: 13

OIL CITY

Venango Region Catholic School - (DIO) (Grades PreSchool-12) 1505 W. First St., Oil City, PA 16301 t) 814-677-3098 katherine.chandley@venangocatholic.org www.venangocatholic.org Katherine Chandley, Prin.; Stds.: 150; Lay Tchrs.: 15

St. Stephen School - (Grades PreSchool-12) 214 Reed St., Oil City, PA 16301; Mailing: 1505 W. 1st St., Oil City, PA 16301 t) 814-677-3035 Stds.: 105; Lay Tchrs.: 8

ST. MARYS

Elk County Catholic School System, Inc. - (DIO) (Grades PreK-12) 600 Maurus St., St. Marys, PA 15857 t) 814-834-7812 macdonalds@eccss.org www.eccss.org Sam MacDonald, Pres.; Stds.: 750; Pr. Tchrs.: 1; Lay Tchrs.: 65

St. Leo Elementary School - (Grades PreK-12) 125 Depot St., Ridgway, PA 15853-1304 t) 814-772-9775 kucenskil@eccss.org Lynne Kucenski, Prin.; Stds.: 108; Lay Tchrs.: 10

Elk County Catholic High School - (Grades PreK-12) 600 Maurus St., St. Marys, PA 15857 t) 814-834-7800 schneiderj@eccss.org John Schneider, Prin.; Dana Gebauer, Librn.; Stds.: 171; Lay Tchrs.: 16

St. Marys Catholic Middle School - (Grades PreK-12) 600 Maurus St., St. Marys, PA 15857 t) 814-834-2665 schneiderj@eccss.org John Schneider, Prin.; Stds.: 120; Lay Tchrs.: 11

St. Marys Catholic Elementary School - (Grades PreK-12) 114 Queens Rd., St. Marys, PA 15857 t) 814-834-4169 slayd@eccss.org Patricia Cotter, Campus Min.; Deborah Slay, Prin.; Stds.: 233; Lay Tchrs.: 16

INSTITUTIONS LOCATED IN DIOCESE

ASSOCIATIONS [ASN]

ERIE

St. Thomas More Society - 429 E. Grandview Blvd., Erie, PA 16514-0397; Mailing: P.O. Box 10397, Erie, PA 16514-0397 t) 814-824-1130 csinger@eriercd.org Rev. Christopher J. Singer, Admin.;

CAMPUS MINISTRY / NEWMAN CENTERS [CAM]

ERIE

Newman Centers and Campus Ministry - 429 E. Grandview Blvd., Erie, PA 16514-0397; Mailing: P.O. Box 10397, Erie, PA 16514-0397 t) 814-824-1210 ffroess@eriercd.org Dcn. Steve Washek, Exec.; Jillian Zaczyk, Dir.;

Allegheny College - 520 N. Main St., Catholic Campus Ministry, Meadville, PA 16335; Mailing: P.O. Box 14, Meadville, PA 16335 t) 814-336-1112 Rev. Jeffrey Lucas, Chap.; Dcn. Edward R. Horneman;

Clarion State University of PA - Venango Campus - 21 State St., St. Stephen Parish, Oil City, PA 16301; Mailing: 210 Reed St., St. Stephen Parish, Oil City, PA 16301 t) 814-677-3020 Rev. John L. Miller III, Pst.;

Clarion University of Pennsylvania - 720 Liberty St., Clarion, PA 16214 t) 814-226-8433 x102 Very Rev. B. LaMounte Sayers, Chap.; Dcn. Joseph Glover;

Gannon University - 109 University Sq., Erie, PA 16541 t) 814-871-7435 Rev. Michael T. Kesicki, Chap.; Brent Heckman, Dir.; Statia Brown, Campus Min.; Emily Muntean, Campus Min.;

Grove City College - 321 N. Broad St., Grove City, PA 16127; Mailing: 1310 S. Center St Grove City, PA 16127 t) 724-748-6700 Very Rev. V. David Foradori, Chap.;

Indiana University of PA - Punxsutawney Campus - 616 W. Mahoning St., Punxsutawney, PA 15767 t) 814-938-6540 Rev. Msgr. Joseph J. Riccardo, Pst.;

Lock Haven University - Clearfield Campus - 211 S. Second St., Clearfield, PA 16830; Mailing: 212 S. Front St., Clearfield, PA 16830 t) 814-765-9671 Very Rev. Robert Horgas, Pst.;

Mercyhurst University - 501 E. 38th St., Erie, PA 16546 t) 814-824-2467 Rev. James Piszker, Chap.; Sr. Natalie Rossi, Campus Min.; Michelle Scully, Campus Min.; Jenell Patton, Assoc. Dir.;

Penn State Erie, The Behrend College - 4701 College Dr., Erie, PA 16563-0906 t) 814-898-6245 Rev. Ian MacElrath, Chap.; Christopher Wilson, Campus Min.;

Penn State University - DuBois Campus - 123 S. State St., DuBois, PA 15801; Mailing: 118 S. State St., DuBois, PA 15801 t) 814-371-8556 Rev. Msgr. Richard Siefer, Pst.;

Penn State University - Shenango Valley Campus - 79 Case Ave., Sharon, PA 16146 t) 724-981-3232 Rev. Thomas J. Whitman, Pst.;

Penn West - 128 Sunset Dr., Edinboro, PA 16412 t) 814-734-3113 x104 Rev. Mark A. Hoffman, Chap.; Nicole House, Campus Min.; Matt Erickson, Campus Min.;

Thiel College - 85 N. High St., St. Michael Parish, Greenville, PA 16125 t) 724-588-9800 Dcn. Marty Aubel; Rev. Brandon M. Kleckner, Chap.;

University of Pittsburgh - Bradford Campus - 95 E. Corydon St., Bradford, PA 16701; Mailing: P.O. Box 2394, Bradford, PA 16701 t) 814-362-6825 Rev. Not Available, Pst.;

University of Pittsburgh - Titusville Campus - 513 W. Main St., St. Titus Parish, Titusville, PA 16354 t) 814-827-4636 Rev. Christopher M. Barnes, Pst.;

CATHOLIC CHARITIES [CCH]

ERIE

Catholic Charities Counseling and Adoption Services, Inc. - 390 W. 10th St., Erie, PA 16502 t) (814) 456-2091 www.cccas.org Dcn. Richard Brogdon, CEO; Asstd. Annu.: 3,330; Staff: 35

Catholic Charities of the Diocese of Erie, Inc. - 429 E. Grandview Blvd., Erie, PA 16504 t) 814-824-1260 info@ccincerie.org ccincerie.org Tina P. Espin, Contact; Staff: 1

CEMETERIES [CEM]

ERIE

Queen of Peace - 6000 Lake Pleasant Rd., Erie, PA 16509; Mailing: 3325 West Lake Rd., Erie, PA 16505 t) 814-838-7724 korac@eriedc.org Korac John Timon, Exec. Dir.;

Trinity, Calvary & Gate of Heaven - 3325 W. Lake Rd., Erie, PA 16505 t) 814-838-7724 korac@eriedc.org www.eriedc.org Korac John Timon, Exec. Dir.;

COLLEGES & UNIVERSITIES [COL]

ERIE

Gannon University - 109 University Sq., Erie, PA 16541 t) 814-871-7000 www.gannon.edu Keith Taylor, Pres.; Walter Iwanenko, Vice. Pres.; Rev. T. Shane Mathew, Assoc. Vice Pres. & Faculty; Rev. Michael T. Kesicki, Chap. & Faculty; Rev. Jason Mitchell, Faculty; Rev. Casimir Wozniak, Faculty; Rev. David M. Renne, Faculty; Rev. Joseph C. Gregorek; Rev. George E. Strohmeyer; Stds.: 5,218; Lay Tchrs.: 241; Pr. Tchrs.: 1

Mercyhurst University - 501 E. 38th St., Erie, PA 16546 t) 814-824-2000 president@mercyhurst.edu www.mercyhurst.edu Rev. James Piszker, Chap.; Dr. Kathleen A. Getz, Pres.; Darcy Jones, Librn.; Stds.: 2,659; Lay Tchrs.: 152

CONVENTS, MONASTERIES, AND RESIDENCES FOR WOMEN [CON]

ERIE

Holy Family Monastery - 510 E. Gore Rd., Erie, PA 16509-3799 t) (814) 824-1269 www.eriercd.org/carmelites/ Carmelite Monastery of Erie Pennsylvania Dcn. G. Frank Hannah, Bus. Mgr.;

Julia House (The Spiritual Family The Work) - 4415 Briggs Ave., Erie, PA 16504 t) 814-520-8559 erie@thework-fso.org www.thework-fso.org Sr. Kathleen Marie Dietz, FSO, Supr.; Srs.: 3

Mount Saint Benedict Monastery - 6101 E. Lake Rd., Erie, PA 16511 t) 814-899-0614 sschmidt@eriebenedictines.org www.eriebenedictines.org Benedictine Sisters of Erie Sr. Diane Rabe, O.S.B., Subprior; Sr. Stephanie Schmidt, O.S.B., Prioress; Srs.: 76

Saint Benedict Community Center - 320 E. 10th St., Erie, PA 16503 t) 814-459-2406 iluv2kayak@earthlink.net Sr. Dianne Sabol, O.S.B., Dir.;

Benedicta Riepp Priory - 3904 Tuttle Ave., Erie, PA 16504 t) 814-825-2767 Sr. Janet Goetz, In Res.; Sr. Mary Jane Vergotz, In Res.;

Benet Priory - 346 E. 10th St., Erie, PA 16503 t) 814-459-5103

Pax Priory - 345 E. 9th St., Erie, PA 16503 t) 814-452-6318

St. Scholastica Priory - 355 E. 9th St., Erie, PA 16503 t) 814-454-4052 sdoubet@mtstbenedict.org Sr. Anne Wambach, O.S.B., Prioress;

St. Walburga Priory - 302 E. 10th St., Erie, PA 16503 t) 814-454-4846 bsisters@neo.rr.com Sr. Theresa Zoky, O.S.B., Contact;

Sisters of Mercy of the Americas - New York, Pennsylvania, Pacific West Community - 444 E. Grandview Blvd., Erie, PA 16504 t) 814-824-2516 www.sistersofmercy.org Msgr. David A. Rubino, Chap.; Sr. Pat Flynn, RSM, Pres.; Srs.: 229

Sisters of Our Lady of Charity of the Good Shepherd - Erie, Inc. - 416 Euclid Ave., Erie, PA 16511 c) 814-392-8554 sseveriana@aol.com rgs.gssweb.org/ Sr. Severiana Morales, R.G.S., Pst. Assoc.; Srs.: 1

Sisters of Saint Joseph of Northwestern Pennsylvania - 5031 W. Ridge Rd., Erie, PA 16506-1249 t) 814-836-4100 catherine.shimek@ssjerie.org www.ssjerie.org Rev. Jerome S. Simmons, Chap.; Sr. Mary Drexler, S.S.J., Pres.; Srs.: 70

ENDOWMENTS / FOUNDATIONS / TRUSTS [EFT]

ERIE

The Catholic Foundation of the Roman Catholic Diocese of Erie, Inc. (Catholic Foundation of Northwest Pennsylvania) - 429 E. Grandview Blvd., Erie, PA 16504; Mailing: PO Box 10397, Erie, PA 16514-0397 t) 814-824-1237 info@cfnwpa.org www.mycatholicfoundation.org Lisa Louis, Exec.;

Sisters of St. Joseph Mission & Ministries Foundation - 5031 W. Ridge Rd., Erie, PA 16506 t) 814-836-4202 almi.clerkin@ssjerie.org www.ssjerie.org Sr. Mary Drexler, S.S.J., Trustee;

Star Foundation - 429 E. Grandview Blvd., Erie, PA 16504; Mailing: P.O. Box 10397, Erie, PA 16514-0397 t) 814-824-1188 ssignorino@eriercd.org Dr. Samuel Signorino, Contact;

MISCELLANEOUS [MIS]

CLEARFIELD

Good Samaritan Center - 11 N. Front St., Clearfield, PA 16830 t) (814) 765-6880 goodsamcentercc@gmail.com ccincerie.org/good-samaritan-center Douglas Bloom, CEO;

ERIE

Alliance for International Monasticism (AIM)-USA Secretariat (AIM-USA) - 345 E. 9th St., Erie, PA 16503-1107 t) 814-453-4724 aim@aim-usa.org; director@aim-usa.org www.aim-usa.org Assists Benedictine & Cistercian monasteries in Africa, Asia, the Caribbean, Eastern Europe and Latin America. Sr. Ann Hoffman, OSB, Exec.;

Bishop Michael J. Murphy Residence for Retired Priests - 400 E. Gore Rd., Erie, PA 16509 t) 814-825-0680 lfeikles@eriercd.org Home for retired diocesan priests. Rev. Christopher J. Singer, Dir.; Very Rev. Nicholas J. Rouch, Dir.;

The Catholic Deposit and Loan Fund of Northwest Pennsylvania - 429 E. Grandview Blvd., Erie, PA 16504; Mailing: P.O. Box 10397, Erie, PA 16514 t) 814-824-1180 jahubert@eriercd.org James Hubert, Secy.;

Emmaus Ministries, Inc. - 345 E. 9th St., Erie, PA 16503 t) 814-459-8349 mkloecker@emmauserie.org www.emmauserie.org Sr. Mary Miller, O.S.B., Dir.;

Inner-City Neighborhood Art House - 201 E. 10th St., Erie, PA 16503 t) 814-455-5508 kstolar@neighborhoodarthouse.org Kelly Stolar, Exec.;

St. James Place Erie - 2622 Buffalo Rd., Erie, PA 16510 t) 814-898-1182 Rev. James P. McCormick, Pst.;

L'Arche Erie - 3745 W. 12th St., Erie, PA 16505 t) 814-452-2065 office@larcheerie.org www.larcheerie.org Rochelle Von Hoff, Exec.;

Mercy Hilltop Center, Inc. - 3715 Pennsylvania Ave, Erie, PA 16504 t) 814-824-2214 dscribner@mercyhilltopcenter.com www.mercyhilltopcenter.com Senior Community Activity Center Dina Scribner, Exec.;

Partnership of Women Religious - 6101 E. Lake Rd., Erie, PA 16511 t) 814-899-0614 sschmidt@eriebenedictines.org Sr. Stephanie Schmidt, O.S.B., Prioress;

Sisters of St. Joseph Neighborhood Network, Inc. - 425 W. 18th St., Erie, PA 16502 t) 814-454-7814 info@ssjnn.org www.ssjnn.org Heather May Caspar, Exec.;

Word of Life Catholic Charismatic Renewal Center - 429 E. Grandview Blvd., Erie, PA 16514-0397 t) 814-824-1285; 814-833-9717 (Bd. Chair) office@wordoflifeccrc.org www.wordoflifeccrc.org Dr. Jaci Sabol, Contact;

FAIRVIEW

Camp Notre Dame Inc. - 400 Eaton Rd., Fairview, PA 16415; Mailing: P.O. Box 74, Fairview, PA 16415 t) 814-474-5001 office@campnotredame.com www.campnotredame.com William Hilbert Jr., Pres.; John Yonko, Exec.;

FARRELL

Prince of Peace Center - 502 Darr Ave., Farrell, PA 16121; Mailing: P.O. Box 89, Farrell, PA 16121 t) (724) 346-5777 princeofpeacecenter.org Jennifer Wallace, CEO;

FRENCHVILLE

Anawim Community of Frenchville - 1031 Germania Rd.,

Frenchville, PA 16836; Mailing: PO Box 35, Frenchville, PA 16836 t) 814-263-4177 c) 814-762-6217 anawimco@gmail.com; ruthann.madera@yahoo.com www.anawimcommunity.org Sr. Ruth Ann Madera, CA, Supr.; Sr. Suzanne D Thibault, CA, Youth Min.;

NURSING / REHABILITATION / CONVALESCENCE / ELDERLY CARE [NUR]

DU BOIS

Christ the King Manor, Inc. - 1100 W. Long Ave., Du Bois, PA 15801 t) 814-371-3180 info@christthekingmanor.org www.ctkmanor.org Rev. Matias M. Quimno, Chap.; Paula Felton-Werner, CEO; Edward Andrulonis, COO; Asstd. Annu.: 715; Staff: 330

ERIE

Saint Mary's Home of Erie - 1781 W. 26th St., Erie, PA 16508 t) 814-836-5300 abonace@stmaryshome.org www.stmaryshome.org Allen Bonace, Pres.; Asstd. Annu.: 559; Staff: 205

Carleton Court - 2710 Carleton Ct., Erie, PA 16506; Mailing: 1781 W. 26th St., Erie, PA 16508-1256 t) 814-452-3681 Apartments (Independent Living) - not part of the CCRC. Not specifically seniors.

The Carriage Homes at Asbury Ridge - 4855 W. Ridge Rd., Erie, PA 16506; Mailing: 1781 W. 26th St., Erie, PA 16508-1256 t) 814-836-4394 eberkstresser@stmaryshome.org Independent Living Homes for Seniors Emma Berkstresser, Dir.;

Saint Mary's at Asbury Ridge - 4855 W. Ridge Rd., Erie, PA 16506 Nursing and Personal Care Home Rev. G. William Fischer, O.S.F.S., Chap.; Mary Venezia, Admin.;

Mercy Terrace Apartments - 430 E. Grandview Blvd., Erie, PA 16504 t) 814-825-6791 mercyterrace@sistersofmercy.org Sponsored by Sisters of Mercy of the Americas. Mary E. Zenner, Exec.; Asstd. Annu.: 73; Staff: 3

HARBORCREEK

***Benetwood Apartments for Persons Elderly and Disabled** - 641 Troupe Rd., Harborcreek, PA 16421-1048 t) 814-899-0088 benetwood@neohio.twcbc.com Benedictine Sisters of Erie. Sr. Patricia Hause, O.S.B., Admin.; Asstd. Annu.: 100; Staff: 9

HERMITAGE

Saint John XXIII Home - 2250 Shenango Fwy., Hermitage, PA 16148 t) 724-981-3200 klhawthorne@john23home.org www.saintjohnxxiiihome.org Kirk L. Hawthorne, Admin.; Asstd. Annu.: 290; Staff: 126

PRESCHOOLS / CHILDCARE CENTERS [PRE]

ERIE

St. Benedict Child Development Center - 345 E. 9th St., Erie, PA 16503 t) 814-454-4514 ckepple@stbenedictctr.com Carrisa Kepple, Dir.; Stds.: 125; Lay Tchrs.: 39

St. Benedict Education Center - 330 E. 10th St., Erie, PA 16503 t) 814-452-4072 x299 nsabol@stben.org www.sbec-erie.org Nancy Sabol, Dir.; Stds.: 337; Lay Tchrs.: 24

Erie East Coast Migrant Program - 345 E. 9th St., Erie, PA 16503 t) 814-454-4514 ckepple@stbenedictctr.com Benedictine Sisters of Erie. Carrisa Kepple, Dir.;

Mercy Center of the Arts - 1531 E. Grandview Blvd., Erie, PA 16510 t) 814-824-2519 mercycenterofthearts@gmail.com www.mercycenterofthearts.com Preschool for 3-6 yrs old. Amanda Elizabeth Boots, Dir.;

RETREAT HOUSES / RENEWAL CENTERS [RTR]

ERIE

Glinodo Center - 6270 E. Lake Rd., Erie, PA 16511 t) 814-899-0614 drabe@eriebenedictines.org www.eriebenedictines.org Benedictine Sisters of Erie. Sr. Diane Rabe, O.S.B., Dir.;

FRENCHVILLE

Young People Who Care Inc. - 1031 Germania Rd., Frenchville, PA 16836; Mailing: PO Box 129, Frenchville, PA 16836 t) 814-263-4177 ypwcmission@gmail.com; bethanyyouthcenter@gmail.com ypwcministries.org Sr. Suzanne D Thibault, CA, Admin.; Sr. Ruth Ann Madera, Dir.;

SEMINARIES [SEM]

ERIE

St. Mark Seminary - 429 E. Grandview Blvd., Erie, PA 16514-0397; Mailing: P.O. Box 10397, Erie, PA 16514-0397 t) 814-824-1200 seminary@eriercd.org www.erievocations.org Rev. Scott W. Jabo, Rector & Dir., Vocations; Rev. David M. Renne, Vice-Rector; Rev. Christopher J. Singer, Resident Spiritual Dir.; Stds.: 9; Pr. Tchrs.: 2

SPECIAL CARE FACILITIES [SPF]

ERIE

Mercy Center for Women - 1039 E. 27th St., Erie, PA 16504 t) 814-455-4577 jhagerty@mcwerie.org www.mcwerie.org Jennie Hagerty, Exec.;

St. Patrick Haven, Inc. - 239 E. 12 St., Erie, PA 16503; Mailing: 5031 W. Ridge Rd., Erie, PA 16506 t) 814-454-7219; 814-836-4153 betsy.wiest@ssjerie.org Sr. Carol Morehouse, Contact; Bed Capacity: 23; Asstd. Annu.: 189; Staff: 4

MEADVILLE

St. James Haven - 779 N. Main St., Meadville, PA 16335; Mailing: P.O. Box 15, Meadville, PA 16335 t) 814-337-6082 samantha.stump@ssjerie.org www.stjameshaven.org Samantha Stump, Exec. Dir.; Bed Capacity: 14; Asstd. Annu.: 205; Staff: 3

An asterisk (*) denotes an organization that has established tax-exempt status directly with the IRS and is not covered by the USCCB Group Ruling.

Diocese of Evansville

(Dioecesis Evansvicensis)

MOST REVEREND JOSEPH M. SIEGEL

Bishop of Evansville; ordained June 4, 1988; appointed Auxiliary Bishop of Joliet October 28, 2009; ordained January 19, 2010; appointed Bishop of Evansville October 18, 2017; installed December 15, 2017. Mailing Address: Catholic Center, 4200 N. Kentucky Ave., P.O. Box 4169, Evansville, IN 47724-0169.

Catholic Center: 4200 N. Kentucky Ave., P.O. Box 4169, Evansville, IN 47724-0169. T: 812-424-5536; F: 812-421-1334.
www.evdio.org

ESTABLISHED NOVEMBER 11, 1944.

Square Miles 5,010.

Comprises twelve Counties in the Southwestern part of Indiana: Daviess, Dubois, Gibson, Greene, Knox, Martin, Pike, Posey, Spencer (except township of Harrison), Sullivan, Vanderburgh, Warrick.

The Diocese of Evansville was established by decree of Pope Pius XII, November 11, 1944, and the See was fixed at Evansville.

For legal titles of parishes and diocesan institutions, consult the Chancery.

STATISTICAL OVERVIEW

Personnel

Bishop	1
Retired Bishops	1
Priests: Diocesan Active in Diocese	37
Priests: Retired, Sick or Absent	32
Number of Diocesan Priests	69
Religious Priests in Diocese	6
Total Priests in your Diocese	75
Extern Priests in Diocese	1
Ordinations:	
Transitional Deacons	1
Permanent Deacons in Diocese	68
Total Sisters	186

Parishes

Parishes	45
With Resident Pastor:	
Resident Diocesan Priests	25
Without Resident Pastor:	
Administered by Priests	18
Administered by Deacons	1
Administered by Lay People	1
Professional Ministry Personnel:	
Sisters	1
Lay Ministers	62

Welfare

Catholic Hospitals	2
Total Assisted	720,043
Homes for the Aged	2
Total Assisted	17
Day Care Centers	1
Total Assisted	177
Special Centers for Social Services	9
Total Assisted	77,505

Educational

Diocesan Students in Other Seminaries	16
Total Seminarians	16
High Schools, Diocesan and Parish	4
Total Students	1,400
Elementary Schools, Diocesan and Parish	22
Total Students	5,233
Catechesis/Religious Education:	
High School Students	1,119
Elementary Students	3,042
Total Students under Catholic Instruction	10,810
Teachers in Diocese:	
Sisters	2
Lay Teachers	522

Vital Statistics

Receptions into the Church:	
Infant Baptism Totals	778
Minor Baptism Totals	87
Adult Baptism Totals	68
Received into Full Communion	62
First Communions	930
Confirmations	897
Marriages:	
Catholic	197
Interfaith	80
Total Marriages	277
Deaths	767
Total Catholic Population	71,025
Total Population	508,709

LEADERSHIP

Catholic Center - t) 812-424-5536
Vicar General - Very Rev. Alex J. Zenthoefer, Vicar;
Chancellor and Chief Operating Officer - Timothy J. McGuire;
Vice Chancellor - Brad Clark;
Secretary to the Bishop - Nancy Oskins;
Diocesan Finance Officer - Dean Happe;
Associate in Finance Office - Karen Cain;
Staff Accountants - Rhonda Weis; Renee Werner;
Office of the Tribunal -
Judicial Vicar - Very Rev. J. Kenneth Walker; Mary Gen Blittschau, Dir.;
Judges - Rev. Stephen P. Lintzenich; Mary Gen Blittschau;
Defender of the Bond - Rev. Jason B. Gries;
Court Psychological Expert - Dcn. Thomas E. Holsworth;
Advocates - Rev. Zachary J. Etienne; Rev. Anthony Ernst;
Ecclesiastical Notaries - Linda Payne; Leigh Anne Costlow;
Archivist - Brad Clark, Vice Chancellor;
College of Consultors - Very Rev. J. Kenneth Walker; Very Rev. Alex J. Zenthoefer; Rev. Jason B. Gries;
Council of Priests - Very Rev. J. Kenneth Walker; Very Rev. Alex J. Zenthoefer; Rev. Paul A. Ferguson;
Clergy Personnel Board - Dcn. David Rice, Dir.; Dcn. Richard Leibundguth; Rev. David H. Nunning;
Deans - Very Rev. John L. Boeglin, East; Very Rev. Godfrey Mullen, O.S.B., South; Very Rev. Edward C. Schnur, West;
Vicar for Retired Priests -
Censor of Books - Mary Gen Blittschau;

OFFICES AND DIRECTORS

Campus Ministry - t) 812-465-7095 Christine Hoehn, Coord.;
Catholic Charities - t) 812-423-5456 Denise Seibert Townsend, Dir.;
Catholic Committees for Boy Scouts and Girl Scouts - t) 812-422-5150 Dcn. Charles Koressel, Chap.;
Catholic Diocese of Evansville, Inc. - Most Rev. Joseph M. Siegel;
Catholic Education Endowment, Inc. (Washington) - t) 812-254-3433 Lynn Williams, Pres.;
Catholic Education Foundation, Inc. (Evansville) - t) 812-402-6700 John Browning, Dir.;
Catholic Education Office - t) 812-424-5536 Daryl Hagan, Supt.; Michelle Priar, Asst. Supt.;
The Catholic Foundation of Southwestern Indiana, Inc. - Todd Brock, Exec.;
Catholic Hospitals, Bishop's Representatives - Mary Gen Blittschau; Rev. Claude T. Burns; Very Rev. J. Kenneth Walker;
Catholic Relief Services - t) 812-423-5456 Denise Seibert Townsend;
Cemeteries - t) 812-424-5536 Rev. Eugene A. Schroeder, Dir.;
Christian Educational Foundation of Vincennes, Inc. - t) 812-882-5889 Debbie Thomas, Pres.;
Communications Office - t) 812-424-5536 Timothy Lilley, Dir.;
Cursillos in Christianity - t) 812-455-7653 Pete Berry, Dir.;
Deaf Ministry - t) 812-490-1000 Rev. Henry Kuykendall;
Diocesan Finance Council - Very Rev. Alex J. Zenthoefer; Gary Beckman; Jeff Bone;
Diocese of Evansville Retirement Trust Agreement and Plan for Priests - t) 812-424-5536
Holy Trinity Endowment Committee - t) 812-482-3076 Brian Eckman, Pres.;
Justice and Peace -
Legion of Mary -
Message, The - Most Rev. Joseph M. Siegel, Publisher; Timothy Lilley, Editor;
Missionary Priests - t) 812-424-5536 Rev. Anthony R. Ernst, Coord.;
Newly Ordained - t) 812-424-5536 Very Rev. Alex J. Zenthoefer, Dir.;
Office of Catechesis - t) 812-424-5536 Joel Padgett, Dir.; Mary Kaye Falcony, Asst. Dir.;
Office of Ecumenism - t) 812-424-5536
Office of Evangelization - t) 812-424-5536
Office of Family and Life - t) 812-424-5536 Eric Girten, Dir.;
Office of Hispanic Ministry - t) 812-424-5536 Bertha Melendres, Dir.;
Office of Stewardship - t) 812-424-5536 Matthew N. Potter, Dir.;
Ongoing Formation for Priests - t) 812-424-5536 Rev. Christopher Lee Droste, Dir.;
Permanent Diaconate Program - Dcn. Thomas Evans, Dir.; Dcn. James King, Asst. Dir.;
Propagation of the Faith and Holy Childhood Association - t) 812-424-5536
Rural Life Conference - t) 812-424-5536 Very Rev. John L. Boeglin, Dir.;
Sarto Retreat House - t) 812-424-5536 Andy Reckelhoff, Dir. Maintenance;
Secretariat for Charismatic Renewal - t) 812-544-2239 John Bennett;
Victim Assistance Coordinator - t) 812-490-9565 (local); 866-200-3004 (long distance) Sylvia Groves;
Vocation Office - t) 812-424-5536 Rev. Tyler R. Tenbarge, Dir.; Rev. Anthony R. Ernst, Assoc. Dir.;
Worship - t) 812-424-5536 Matthew Miller, Dir.;
Youth and Young Adult Ministry - t) 812-424-5536 Steven Dabrowski Jr., Dir.;

PARISHES, MISSIONS, AND CLERGY

STATE OF INDIANA

BICKNELL

St. Philip Neri - 605 W. Fourth St., Bicknell, IN 47512 t) 812-735-4069 Rev. Anthony Ernst, Pst.; Rev. Garrett Braun, Par. Vicar; Dcn. Rey Carandang; Dcn. Paul Vonderwell; Dcn. Cletus Yochum Jr.; Elaine Pepmeier, DRE; CRP Stds.: 27

BLOOMFIELD

Holy Name - 700 Lincoln Dr., Bloomfield, IN 47424 t) 812-847-7821 Rev. Simon Natha, Admin.; CRP Stds.: 13

BOONVILLE

St. Clement - 422 E. Sycamore St., Boonville, IN 47601 t) 812-897-4653 www.stclementparish.weconnect.com Rev. Jack J. Durchholz, Pst.; Dcn. Tom Lambert; Dcn. David Seibert; CRP Stds.: 99

CELESTINE

St. Isidore the Farmer - 6864 E. State Rd. 164, Celestine, IN 47521; Mailing: P.O. Box 1, Celestine, IN 47521 t) 812-634-1875 www.saintisidoreparish.com Rev. John Pfister, Pst.; Dcn. Michael Seibert; Glenda Reckelhoff, DRE; CRP Stds.: 335

CHRISNEY

St. Martin - 58 S. Church St., Chrisney, IN 47611 t) 812-649-4811 www.stmartinchrisney.org Rev. Ronald Kreilein, Pst.; Dcn. Stephen McGinnis; Dcn. Michael Waninger; Carolyn Thorpe, DRE; CRP Stds.: 27

DALE

St. Francis of Assisi - 8 E. Maple St., Dale, IN 47523; Mailing: P.O. Box 684, Dale, IN 47523 t) 812-937-2200 www.saintfrancisofassisi.net Rev. Crispine Adongo, Pst.; Dcn. James Woebkenberg; Stephanie Wollenmann, CRE; CRP Stds.: 226

EVANSVILLE

St. Benedict Cathedral - 1328 Lincoln Ave., Evansville, IN 47714 t) 812-425-3369 www.saintbenedictcathedral.org Very Rev. Alex J. Zenthoefer, Rector; Rev. Eugene R. Schmitt, Par. Vicar; Dcn. David Rice; Sr. Patricia McGuire, O.S.B., Pst. Assoc.;

St. Benedict Cathedral School - (Grades PreK-8) 530 S. Harlan Ave., Evansville, IN 47714 t) 812-425-4596 www.saintbenedictcathedral.org/school Kari Ford, Prin.; Stds.: 279; Lay Tchrs.: 23

All Saints - 704 1st Ave., Evansville, IN 47710-1632 t) 812-423-5209 allsaintsevansville.org Rev. Zachary J. Etienne, Moderator; Sharon Vogler, Parish Life Coord.; CRP Stds.: 23

Annunciation of the Lord - 3010 E. Chandler Ave., Evansville, IN 47714 t) 812-476-3061 www.annunciationevv.org Rev. Benny Alikandayil Chacko, Pst.; Dcn. John McMullen; CRP Stds.: 11

Annunciation of the Lord School - (Grades PreK-8) 3101 Bayard Park Dr., Evansville, IN 47714 t) 812-476-1792; 812-477-9082 www.annunciationangels.org/ David Memmer, Prin.; Matthew Moore, Prin.; Stds.: 388; Lay Tchrs.: 30

St. Boniface - 1626 Glendale Ave, Evansville, IN 47712 t) 812-423-1721 stbonifaceevansville.com Rev. Christopher Lee Droste, Pst.; Dcn. Wayne Hoy; Dcn. Robert Mattingly; Jenny Mayer, DRE; CRP Stds.: 17

Westside Catholic School - (Grades PreK-8) 1620 Glendale Ave, Evansville, IN 47712 t) 812-422-1014 www.westsidecatholic.org Kelsey Meier, Prin.; Stds.: 192; Lay Tchrs.: 18

Corpus Christi - 5528 Hogue Rd., Evansville, IN 47712 t) 812-422-2027 www.corpuschristievansville.org Rev. Tyler Tenbarge, Sacr. Min.; Dcn. Tom Goebel, Parish Life Coord.; Cecilia Reising, CRE; CRP Stds.: 20

Corpus Christi School - (Grades PreK-8) 5530 Hogue Rd, Evansville, IN 47712 t) 812-422-1208 corpuschristischoolevansville.org Martha Craig, Prin.; Stds.: 191; Lay Tchrs.: 14

Good Shepherd - 2301 N. Stockwell, Evansville, IN 47715 t) 812-477-5405 gsparish.org Rev. Zachary J. Etienne, Pst.; Dcn. Dan DeCastra; Sue Kroupa, DRE; CRP Stds.: 19

Good Shepherd School - (Grades PreK-8) t) 812-476-4477 gsparish.org/good-shepherd-catholic-school Kristen Girten, Prin.; Stds.: 427; Lay Tchrs.: 26

Holy Redeemer - 918 W. Mill Rd., Evansville, IN 47710 t) 812-424-8344 www.holyredeemerchurch.org Rev. Jason B. Gries, Pst.; Dcn. Kevin Bach; Dcn. Thomas Cervone; Anne Stofleth-Martin, DRE; CRP Stds.: 14

Holy Redeemer School - (Grades PreK-8) t) 812-422-3688 holyredeemercatholicschool.com Andrea Dickel, Prin.; Stds.: 256; Lay Tchrs.: 15

Holy Rosary - 1301 S. Green River Rd., Evansville, IN 47715 t) 812-477-8923 hrparish.org Rev. Bernard T. Etienne, Pst.; Rev. Martin Estrada, Par. Vicar; Dcn. Christian Borowiecki; Dcn. Jose Garrido; Sr. Mary Mundy, S.P., Pst. Assoc.; Carol Ann Gaddis, DRE; CRP Stds.: 31

Holy Rosary School - (Grades PreK-8) 1303 S. Green River Rd., Evansville, IN 47715 t) 812-477-2271 holyrosaryrams.org Joan Fredrich, Prin.; Stds.: 446; Lay Tchrs.: 25

St. John the Evangelist - 5301 Daylight Dr., Evansville, IN 47725 t) 812-867-3718 www.catholicdaylight.org Rev. Christopher Forler, Pst.; Dcn. Vincent Bernardin; Dcn. Richard Leibundguth; CRP Stds.: 126

St. Joseph - 6202 W. St. Joseph Rd., Evansville, IN 47720 t) 812-963-3273 www.stjoeco.org Rev. Eugene A. Schroeder, Pst.; Jessica Reckelhoff, CRE; CRP Stds.: 9

St. Joseph School - (Grades PreK-8) 6130 W. St. Joseph Rd., Evansville, IN 47720 t) 812-963-3335 stjoeco.org/school Nathan Winstead, Prin.; Stds.: 195; Lay Tchrs.: 11

Sts. Mary & John - 613 Cherry St., Evansville, IN 47713 t) 812-425-1577 stsmaryandjohnparish.org Very Rev. Alex J. Zenthoefer, Pst.; Rev. Eugene R. Schmitt, Assoc. Pst.; Dcn. Thomas Kempf; Dcn. Dennis Russell;

Resurrection - 5301 New Harmony Rd., Evansville, IN

47720 t) 812-963-3121 www.resurrectionevv.com Rev. Jerry Pratt, Admin.; CRP Stds.: 45

Resurrection School - (Grades PreK-8) t) 812-963-6148 resurrectioncatholicschool.org Theresa Berendes, Prin.; Stds.: 399; Lay Tchrs.: 25

St. Wendel - 10542 W. Boonville-New Harmony Rd., Evansville, IN 47720 t) 812-963-3733 www.saintwendelparish.org Very Rev. Edward C. Schnur, Pst.; Dcn. Mark McDonald; Sherie Cooley, DRE;

St. Wendel School - (Grades PreK-8) 4725 St. Wendel Cynthiana Rd., Wadesville, IN 47638 t) 812-963-3958 saintwendelschool.org Hallie Scheu, Prin.; Stds.: 224; Lay Tchrs.: 11

FERDINAND

Christ the King - 341 E. 10th St., Ferdinand, IN 47532; Mailing: P.O. Box 156, Ferdinand, IN 47532 t) 812-367-1212 christthekingdc.org Rev. Anthony Govind, Admin.; Dcn. James King; Debbie Schmitt, DRE; Jack Tuinier, DRE; CRP Stds.: 391

FORT BRANCH

St. Bernard - 5342 E. State Rd. 168, Fort Branch, IN 47648 t) 812-385-2617 www.stbernardsnakerun.org Rev. Christopher Forler, Pst.; Rose Obert, CRE; CRP Stds.: 48

Holy Cross - 305 E. Walnut St., Fort Branch, IN 47648 t) 812-753-3548 www.holycrossparish.info Rev. Gary Edward Kaiser, Pst.; Dcn. Joseph Siewers; Laura Goedde, CRE; CRP Stds.: 115

Holy Cross School - (Grades PreK-5) 202 S. Church St., Fort Branch, IN 47648 t) 812-753-3280 holycrossparish.info/holy-cross-school.html John Hollis, Prin.; Stds.: 139; Lay Tchrs.: 7

HAUBSTADT

St. James - 12300 S. 50 W., Haubstadt, IN 47639 t) 812-867-5175 www.stjameshaubstadt.com Rev. Andrew Thomas, Pst.; Rev. Kenneth Betz, Par. Vicar; Dcn. William Brandle; Dcn. Joseph Siewers; Laura Goedde, CRE; CRP Stds.: 56

St. James School - (Grades PreK-8) 12394 S. 40 W., Haubstadt, IN 47639 t) 812-867-2661 www.stjameshaubstadt.com/ Eric Chamberlain, Prin.; Stds.: 187; Sr. Tchrs.: 1; Lay Tchrs.: 13

SS. Peter and Paul - 211 N. Vine St., Haubstadt, IN 47639 t) 812-768-6457 www.stsppchurch.com Rev. Andrew Thomas, Pst.; Dcn. William Brandle; Dcn. Joseph Siewers; Laura Goedde, CRE; CRP Stds.: 140

SS. Peter and Paul School - (Grades PreK-5) 210 N. Vine St., Haubstadt, IN 47639 t) 812-768-6775 www.stsppchurch.com/school Megan Howington, Prin.; Stds.: 230; Lay Tchrs.: 15

HUNTINGBURG

Visitation of the Blessed Virgin Mary - 313 Washington St., Huntingburg, IN 47542 t) 812-683-2372 www.stmaryshuntingburg.org Rev. Biju Thomas, Admin.; Rev. Homero Rodriguez, Parochial Vicar - Part-Time; Dcn. Thomas E. Holsworth; Rachel Wright, DRE; CRP Stds.: 348

JASPER

Annunciation of the Blessed Virgin Mary - 2829 N. 500 W., Jasper, IN 47546; Mailing: P.O. Box 67, Ireland, IN 47545 t) 812-482-7041 stmary.irelandindiana.com (St. Mary's) Rev. Luke Hassler, Pst.; Martha Schmitt, DRE; CRP Stds.: 367

Holy Family - 950 E. Church Ave., Jasper, IN 47546 t) 812-482-3076 www.holyfamilyjasper.com Rev. Jeffrey W. Read, Pst.; Dcn. Michael Helfter; Dcn. David McDaniel; Joseph Munning IV, DRE; CRP Stds.: 43

St. Joseph - 1029 Kundek St., Jasper, IN 47546 t) 812-482-1805 www.saintjosephjasper.org Rev. John Brosmer, Pst.; Rev. Christian Raab, O.S.B., Assoc. Pst.; Rev. Homero Rodriguez, Assoc. Pst.; Pam Freyberger, DRE; CRP Stds.: 395

Precious Blood - 1385 W. 6th St., Jasper, IN 47546 t) 812-482-4461 www.preciousbloodjasperin.org Rev. Brian S. Emmick, Pst.; Dcn. Gerald Gagne; Dcn. Michael A. Jones; Emily Ketzner, DRE; CRP Stds.: 51

LINTON

St. Peter - 489 E. St., N.E., Linton, IN 47441 t) 812-847-7821 Rev. Simon Natha, Admin.; CRP Stds.: 18

LOOGOOTEE

St. John - 408 Church St., Loogootee, IN 47553 t) 812-295-2225 www.stjohnloogootee.com Rev. J. Kenneth Walker, Pst.; Dcn. William Consley; CRP Stds.: 151

MONTGOMERY

St. Peter - 305 N. 2nd St., Montgomery, IN 47558; Mailing: P.O. Box 10, Montgomery, IN 47558 t) 812-486-3149 stpetermontgomery.org/ Rev. Sudhakar Bhastati, Pst.; CRP Stds.: 108

MOUNT VERNON

St. Matthew - 421 Mulberry St., Mount Vernon, IN 47620 t) 812-838-2535 www.stmatthewparish.us Rev. Ryan P. Hilderbrand, Pst.; Dcn. Thomas Evans; CRP Stds.: 23

St. Matthew School - (Grades PreK-5) 401 Mulberry St., Mt. Vernon, IN 47620 t) 812-838-3621 stmatthewmtvernon.org Christan M Shockley, Prin.; Stds.: 101; Lay Tchrs.: 8

St. Philip - 3500 St. Philip Rd. S., Mount Vernon, IN 47620 t) 812-985-2275 saintphilipchurch.net Rev. Ryan P. Hilderbrand, Pst.; Dcn. Charles Koressel; CRP Stds.: 41

St. Philip School - (Grades PreK-8) 3420 St. Phillips Rd., Mt. Vernon, IN 47620 t) 812-985-2447 stphilipschool.net Kellie Kelsey, Prin.; Stds.: 224; Lay Tchrs.: 14

NEWBURGH

St. John the Baptist - 625 Frame Rd., Newburgh, IN 47630 t) 812-490-1000 sjbnewburgh.org Rev. Claude T. Burns, Pst.; Rev. Srinivasa Malaka (India), Assoc. Pst.; Dcn. Anthony Schapker; Dcn. Joseph Seibert; CRP Stds.: 183

St. John the Baptist School - (Grades PreK-8) 725 Frame Rd., Newburgh, IN 47630 t) 812-490-2000 sjbschoolnewburgh.org Elizabeth Flatt, Prin.; Stds.: 459; Lay Tchrs.: 31

OAKLAND CITY

Blessed Sacrament - 11092 E. Lincoln Hgts. Rd., Oakland City, IN 47660 t) 812-749-4474 Rev. Frank G. Renner, Pst.; Lori Stolz, CRE; CRP Stds.: 6

PETERSBURG

SS. Peter and Paul - 711 Walnut St., Petersburg, IN 47567 t) 812-354-6942 Rev. Frank G. Renner, Pst.; Dcn. Mark Wade; Gary Keepes, CRE; CRP Stds.: 8

POSEYVILLE

St. Francis Xavier - 10 N. St. Francis Ave., Poseyville, IN 47633; Mailing: PO Box 100, Poseyville, IN 47633 t) 812-874-2220 www.saintwendelparish.org Very Rev. Edward C. Schnur, Pst.; Dcn. Mark McDonald; Sherie Cooley, DRE; CRP Stds.: 99

PRINCETON

St. Joseph - 410 S. Race St., Princeton, IN 47670 t) 812-385-2617 stjosephprinceton.org Rev. Gary Edward Kaiser, Pst.; CRP Stds.: 42

St. Joseph School - (Grades PreK-5) 427 S. Stormont St., Princeton, IN 47670 t) 812-385-2228 stjosephprinceton.com Lynde Anquillare, Prin.; Stds.: 147; Lay Tchrs.: 9

ROCKPORT

St. Bernard - 547 Elm St., Rockport, IN 47635 t) 812-649-4811 www.stbernardrockport.org Rev. Ronald Kreilein, Pst.; Dcn. Stephen McGinnis; Dcn. Michael Waninger; Carolyn Thorpe, DRE; CRP Stds.: 42

St. Bernard School - (Grades PreK-8) 207 N. 6th St., Rockport, IN 47635 t) 812-649-2501 stbernardschool.info Ryan Nowak, Prin.; Stds.: 144; Lay Tchrs.: 11

ST. ANTHONY

Divine Mercy - 4444 S. Ohio St., St. Anthony, IN 47575; Mailing: P.O. Box 98, St. Anthony, IN 47575 t) 812-326-2777 www.divinemercyduco.org Rev. Jose Thomas, Admin.; Dcn. Charles Johnson; Janie Kempf, CRE; CRP Stds.: 287

SULLIVAN

St. Joan of Arc - 105 E. Jackson St., Sullivan, IN 47882; Mailing: P.O. Box 506, Sullivan, IN 47882 t) 812-268-4088 www.stmarys-sullivan.com St. Mary, Sullivan. Rev. John Pfister, Admin.; Dcn. Albert Frabutt;

St. Mary - 105 E. Jackson St., Sullivan, IN 47882; Mailing: P.O. Box 506, Sullivan, IN 47882 t) 812-268-4088 www.stmarys-sullivan.com Rev. John Pfister, Admin.; Dcn. Albert Frabutt;

VINCENNES

St. Francis Xavier - 803 Main St., Vincennes, IN 47591 t) 812-882-5638 www.stfrancisxaviervincennes.com Rev. Anthony Ernst, Pst.; Rev. Garrett Braun, Par. Vicar; Dcn. Cletus Yochum Jr.; Dcn. Rey Carandang; Dcn. Paul Vonderwell; CRP Stds.: 92

Flaget Elementary School - (Grades PreK-5) 800 Vigo St., Vincennes, IN 47591 t) (812) 882-5460 www.flagetces.org/home Samantha McClure, Prin.; Stds.: 207; Lay Tchrs.: 11

WASHINGTON

Our Lady of Hope - 315 N.E. Third St., Washington, IN 47501 t) 812-254-2883 www.ccwash.org Rev. Paul A. Ferguson, Pst.; Rev. Juan Ramirez, Par. Vicar; Dcn. Dennis Hilderbrand; Yvonne Evans, Pst. Assoc.; Maria Batz, DRE; CRP Stds.: 71

Our Lady of Hope School - (Grades PreK-4) 310 N.E. Second St., Washington, IN 47501 t) 812-254-3845 wccardinals.org Washington Catholic Interparochial Schools. Kelsi Edwards, Prin.; Stds.: 155; Lay Tchrs.: 7

SCHOOLS: PRESCHOOL THRU HIGH SCHOOL

SCHOOLS

STATE OF INDIANA

JASPER

Holy Trinity School - (Grades PreK-8) 1385 W. 6th St., Jasper, IN 47546 t) 812-482-4461 www.holytrinitysaints.com Jenna Seng, Prin.; Jonathan Temple, Prin.; Stds.: 478; Sr. Tchrs.: 1; Lay Tchrs.: 32

HIGH SCHOOLS

STATE OF INDIANA

EVANSVILLE

Mater Dei High School - (PAR) (Grades 9-12) 1300 Harmony Way, Evansville, IN 47720 t) 812-426-2258 www.materdeiwildcats.com Darin Knight, Prin.; Dcn. Dan Niemeier, Pres.; Rev. Christopher Lee Droste, Priest Delegate; Melba Wilderman, Asst. Prin.; Stds.: 501; Lay Tchrs.: 36

Reitz Memorial High School - (PAR) (Grades 9-12) 1500 Lincoln Ave., Evansville, IN 47714 t) 812-476-4973 www.reitzmemorial.org Aaron Schmitt, Prin.; Christian Mocek, Pres.; Rev. Christopher Forler, Priest-Delegate; Darlene Quinlin, Asst. Prin., Curriculum; Stds.: 589; Lay Tchrs.: 48

VINCENNES

Jean Francois Rivet High School - (PAR) (Grades 6-12) 210 Barnett St., Vincennes, IN 47591 t) 812-882-6215 www.rivethighschool.com Janice Jones, Prin.; Stds.: 170; Lay Tchrs.: 13

WASHINGTON

Washington Catholic Interparochial Schools - (PAR) (Grades 5-12) 201 N.E. Second St., Washington, IN 47501 t) 812-254-2050 www.wccardinals.org Karie Craney, Prin.; Stds.: 140; Lay Tchrs.: 13

INSTITUTIONS LOCATED IN DIOCESE

CAMPUS MINISTRY / NEWMAN CENTERS [CAM]

EVANSVILLE

Newman Center for the University of Evansville - 1901 Lincoln Ave., Evansville, IN 47714 t) 812-477-6446 Sr. Jessica Vitente, S.P., Dir.;

University of Southern Indiana Newman Center - 8600 University Blvd., Evansville, IN 47712 t) 812-465-7095 Jeremy Goebel, Dir.;

OAKLAND CITY

Oakland City College Newman Center - R.R. 1, Oakland City, IN 47660; Mailing: Box 72-A, Oakland City, IN 47660 t) 812-749-4474 Jeremy Goebel, Dir.;

VINCENNES

Vincennes University-Newman Center - 803 Main St., Vincennes, IN 47591 t) 812-882-1762 Jeremy Goebel, Dir.;

CEMETERIES [CEM]

EVANSVILLE

St. Joseph - 2500 Mesker Park Dr., Evansville, IN 47712 t) 812-423-1356 Joe Shake, Contact;

JASPER

Fairview - 1215 Newton St., Jasper, IN 47546 t) 812-634-7525 Brad Popp, Contact;

VINCENNES

Calvary - S. 6th Street Rd., Vincennes, IN 47591; Mailing: P.O. Box 4, Vincennes, IN 47591 t) 812-882-4691 Rev. Anthony Ernst, Contact;

WASHINGTON

St. John - 101 N. Meridian St., Washington, IN 47501 t) 812-698-0301 Ron Murphy, Contact;

CONVENTS, MONASTERIES, AND RESIDENCES FOR WOMEN [CON]

EVANSVILLE

Daughters of Charity of St. Vincent de Paul - Mater Dei Residence - 9400 New Harmony Rd., Evansville, IN 47720 t) 812-963-7517 tom.beck@doc.org www.daughtersofcharity.org Sr. Sheila Carney, Supr.; Srs.: 10

Monastery of St. Clare - Franciscan Monastery of St. Clare, 6825 Nurrenbern Rd., Evansville, IN 47712 t) 812-425-4396 janemdelevin@gmail.com www.poorclareofevansville.com Franciscan Poor Clare Nuns. Sr. Jane Marie DeLand, O.S.C., Abbess; Srs.: 6

Seton Residence - 9200 New Harmony Rd., Evansville, IN 47720-8918; Mailing: 4330 Olive St., Saint Louis, MO 63108 t) 812-963-7600 tom.beck@doc.org Home for the Senior Sisters of the Daughters of Charity of St. Vincent de Paul. Sr. Judith Bright, Supr.; Staff: 137; Srs.: 56

FERDINAND

Sisters of St. Benedict of Ferdinand, IN, Inc., Monastery Immaculate Conception - 802 E. Tenth St., Ferdinand, IN 47532-9239 t) 812-367-1411 sisters@thedome.org www.thedome.org Sisters of St. Benedict. Rev. Jeremy King, O.S.B., Chap.; Sr. Anita Louise Lowe, OSB, Prioress; Srs.: 114

ENDOWMENTS / FOUNDATIONS / TRUSTS [EFT]

EVANSVILLE

Catholic Education Foundation, Inc. - 520 S. Bennighof, Evansville, IN 47714 t) 812-402-6700 x302 John Browning, Interim Dir.;

JASPER

Memorial Hospital Foundation, Inc. - 800 W. 9th St., Jasper, IN 47546 t) 812-996-8428 William A. Rubino, Chair, Bd. Dirs.;

HOSPITALS / HEALTH SERVICES [HOS]

EVANSVILLE

St. Mary's Health, Inc. (St. Vincent Evansville) - 3700 Washington Ave., Evansville, IN 47750 t) 812-485-4000 www.healthcare.ascension.org Jonathan Nalli, CEO; Ann Varner, Exec.; Bed Capacity: 377; Asstd. Annu.: 409,583; Staff: 1,875

JASPER

Memorial Hospital and Health Care Center, Little Company of Mary Hospital of Indiana, Inc. - 800 W. 9th St., Jasper, IN 47546 t) 812-996-2345 x198 dkempf@mhhcc.org www.mhhcc.org Kyle Bennett, Pres.; Bed Capacity: 137; Asstd. Annu.: 310,460; Staff: 1,850

MISCELLANEOUS [MIS]

EVANSVILLE

Evansville Catholic Interparochial High Schools - 4200 N. Kentucky Ave., Evansville, IN 47724; Mailing: P.O. Box 4169, Evansville, IN 47724 t) 812-424-5536 jbrowning@evdio.org John Browning, Contact;

Marian Educational Outreach - 520 S. Bennighof, Evansville, IN 47714 t) 812-402-6700 x312 www.meoforkids.org Emily Schnapf, Dir.;

VINCENNES

Old Cathedral Library & Museum, Inc. - 205 Church St., Vincennes, IN 47591 t) 812-882-7016 evdio.org Rev. Anthony Ernst, Contact;

NURSING / REHABILITATION / CONVALESCENCE / ELDERLY CARE [NUR]

FERDINAND

Hildegard Health Center, Inc. - 802 E. 10th St., Ferdinand, IN 47532-9239 t) 812-367-2022 prioress@thedome.org www.thedome.org Mike Van Hoy, Admin.; Asstd. Annu.: 17; Staff: 25

PRESCHOOLS / CHILDCARE CENTERS [PRE]

EVANSVILLE

St. Vincent Early Learning Center, Inc. - 730 W. Delaware St., Evansville, IN 47710 t) 812-424-4780 kwedding@stvincentelc.org www.stvincentearlylearningcenter.org Krista Wedding, Exec. Dir.; Stds.: 177; Lay Tchrs.: 36

RETREAT HOUSES / RENEWAL CENTERS [RTR]

EVANSVILLE

Sarto Retreat House - 4200 N. Kentucky Ave., Evansville, IN 47724-0169; Mailing: P.O. Box 4169, Evansville, IN 47724-0169 t) 812-424-5536 evdio.org Rob Underwood, Admin.;

FERDINAND

Benedictine Hospitality Center - 802 E. 10th St., Ferdinand, IN 47532-9216 t) 812-367-1411 hospitality@thedome.org www.thedome.org/hospitality Benedictine Hospitality Center Sr. Anita Louise Lowe, OSB, Prioress; Sr. Rose Mary Rexing, Dir.;

An asterisk (*) denotes an organization that has established tax-exempt status directly with the IRS and is not covered by the USCCB Group Ruling.

Diocese of Fairbanks

(VACANT SEE)

Chancery Office: 1316 Peger Rd., Fairbanks, AK 99709. T: 907-374-9500; F: 907-374-9580.
dioceseoffairbanks.org
info@cbna.org

Square Miles 409,849.

Corporate Title: "Catholic Bishop of Northern Alaska."

Established as the Prefecture Apostolic of Alaska, July 27, 1894.

Erected into the Vicariate of Alaska, Dec. 22, 1916; elevated to a Diocese, Aug. 8, 1962.

Comprises the State of Alaska, north of the old Territorial Third Judicial Division whose boundary extended in a northwesterly direction from the Canadian Border along the crest of the Alaska range to Mount McKinley, thence southwesterly to Cape Newenham and west along the 58 parallel north of the Pribilof Islands.

For legal titles of parishes and diocesan institutions, consult the Chancery Office.

Most Reverend Andrew E. Bellosario, C.M.
Apostolic Administrator of Fairbanks and Archbishop of Anchorage-Juneau; ordained June 16, 1984; appointed Bishop of Juneau July 11, 2017; ordained and installed October 10, 2017; appointed Apostolic Administrator of Anchorage June 7, 2018; appointed first Archbishop of Archdiocese of Anchorage-Juneau May 19, 2020; ordained and installed September 17, 2020; appointed Apostolic Administrator of Fairbanks on September 27, 2022.

STATISTICAL OVERVIEW

Personnel

Priests: Diocesan Active in Diocese....4
Priests: Diocesan Active Outside Diocese....1
Priests: Retired, Sick or Absent....4
Number of Diocesan Priests....9
Religious Priests in Diocese....7
Total Priests in your Diocese....16
Extern Priests in Diocese....9
Ordinations:
Diocesan Priests....2
Permanent Deacons....1
Permanent Deacons in Diocese....26
Total Brothers....2
Total Sisters....4

Parishes

Parishes....46
With Resident Pastor:
Resident Diocesan Priests....2
Resident Religious Priests....2
Without Resident Pastor:
Administered by Priests....33
In the care of professed men religious other than Priests or Permanent Deacons....2
Administered by Lay People....7
Missions....4
Professional Ministry Personnel:
Brothers....2
Sisters....3

Welfare

Special Centers for Social Services....1
Total Assisted....25,975

Educational

High Schools, Diocesan and Parish....1
Total Students....165
Elementary Schools, Diocesan and Parish....1
Total Students....186
Catechesis / Religious Education:
High School Students....59
Elementary Students....257
Total Students under Catholic Instruction....667
Teachers in Diocese:
Lay Teachers....47

Vital Statistics

Receptions into the Church:
Infant Baptism Totals....119
Minor Baptism Totals....8
Adult Baptism Totals....15
Received into Full Communion....16
First Communions....90
Confirmations....97
Marriages:
Catholic....20
Interfaith....9
Total Marriages....29
Deaths....194
Total Catholic Population....10,492
Total Population....164,727

LEADERSHIP

Vicar General -

Superior Regular - Rev. Richard P. Magner, S.J., Pastoral Ministry;

Chancery Office - t) 907-374-9500 info@cbna.org

Chancellor - Carolyn Dukes, Chancellor;

Chief Financial Officer - Susan Clifton;

Diocesan Tribunal -

Tribunal Administrator - Rev. Robert Fath;

Judicial Vicar - Rev. Robert Fath, Vicar;

Defender of the Bond - Rev. Scott Garrett;

Promoter of Justice -

Notaries - Carolyn Dukes; Katrina Francesco;

Presbyteral Council - Rev. Alphonsus Afina; Rev. Simon Jingbe (Zimbabwe); Rev. Robert Fath;

Consultors - Rev. Richard P. Magner, S.J.; Rev. Alphonsus Afina; Rev. Simon Jingbe (Zimbabwe);

Diocesan Archivist - David Schienle, Archivist;

Vicar for Clergy and Consecrated Life - Rev. Ross Tozzi;

OFFICES AND DIRECTORS

Alaskan Shepherd Office - c) (907) 799-6240 Misty Mealey, Editor;

Campus Ministry - t) 907-374-9564 Mary Pat Boger;

Catholic Campaign for Human Development - Susan Clifton;

Catholic Relief Services - Susan Clifton;

Catholic Trust of Northern Alaska - Susan Clifton, Exec.;

Construction Committee - Rev. Ross Tozzi; Bill Chrisman; James Walter;

Engaged Encounter - Timothy Woster; Jill Woster;

Finance Advisory Board - Rev. Robert Fath; Jim Haselberger; Robert Hajdukovich;

Hispanic Ministry - Lourdes Bernal, Coord.;

Ministry of Sick, Aged and Imprisoned - t) 907-978-5281 Ann Nickerson, Dir.;

Native Alaskan Ministries Coordinators - Sr. Kathleen Radich, O.S.F.; Bro. Robert J. Ruzicka, O.F.M.;

Office of Child Protection - t) 907-374-9553

Office of Native Permanent Diaconate - Rev. Gregg D. Wood, S.J., Dir.;

Office of Stewardship and Development - t) (907) 374-9536

Schools - t) (907) 313-3291 www.catholic-schools.org Amanda Angaiak, Dir.;

Victim Assistance Coordinator - t) (907) 374-9553

Vocation Director - Rev. Robert Fath;

PARISHES, MISSIONS, AND CLERGY

STATE OF ALASKA

ALAKANUK

St. Ignatius Catholic Church Alakanuk - ; Mailing: P.O. Box 53, Alakanuk, AK 99554 t) (907) 374-9500 Rev. Stanislaw Jaszek; Dcn. Denis Shelden; Mary Ayunerak, Admin.; CRP Stds.: 4

St. Peter Catholic Church Nunam Iqua - t) 907-374-9500

ANIAK

St. Theresa Catholic Church Aniak - ; Mailing: P.O. Box 308, Aniak, AK 99557 t) (907) 675-4448 info@cbna.org Edith Morgan, Acting Parish Admin.;

BARROW

St. Patrick Catholic Church - ; Mailing: P.O. Box 389, Barrow, AK 99723 t) 907-852-3515 barrowstpatrickchurch@gmail.com Peata Tuifua, Admin.;

BETHEL

Immaculate Conception Catholic Church Bethel - ; Mailing: PO Box 429, Bethel, AK 99559 t) (907) 543-2464 www.bethelcatholic.org Rev. Abraham Nemaisa; Rev. Gregg D. Wood, S.J.; Susan Murphy, Admin.;

CHEFORNAK

St. Catherine of Siena Catholic Church Chefornak - ; Mailing: P.O. Box 90, Chefornak, AK 99561 t) 907-374-9500 cyf_st_catherine@yahoo.com Rev. Abraham Nemaisa; Rev. Gregg D. Wood, S.J.; Dcn. Joe Avugiak; Agnes Kairaiuak, Admin.;

CHEVAK

Sacred Heart Catholic Church Chevak - ; Mailing: P.O. Box 249, Chevak, AK 99563 t) 907-858-7826 info@cbna.org Rev. Richard P. Magner, S.J.; Dcn. Peter Boyscout; CRP Stds.: 6

DELTA JUNCTION

Our Lady of Sorrows Catholic Church Delta Junction - 2565 Deborah St., Delta Junction, AK 99737; Mailing: P.O. Box 446, Delta Junction, AK 99737 t) 907-895-5232 olsdelta@wildak.net sites.google.com/view/ourladyofsorrowstest2/ Rev. Dominik Wojcik, Par. Vicar; Rev. Welcome Chipiro, Par. Admin.; CRP Stds.: 24

Mission (St. Francis Xavier Catholic Church Eagle) - t) (907) 895-5232

EMMONAK

Sacred Heart Catholic Church Emmonak - ; Mailing: P.O. Box 69, Emmonak, AK 99581 t) 907-949-1012 info@cbna.org Rev. Stanislaw Jaszek; Dcn. Dominic Hunt; Dcn. Raymond Waska; Dcn. Phillip Yupanik; Patrick Tam, Parish Facilitator; CRP Stds.: 9

FAIRBANKS

Sacred Heart Cathedral Catholic Church Fairbanks - 1300 Peger Rd., Fairbanks, AK 99709 t) 907-474-9032 shcparishoffice@gmail.com www.sacredheartak.org Rev. Ross Tozzi, Rector; Rev. Piotr Oprych, Par. Vicar; Rev. Jaime Abúndiz, IVE, Hispanic Ministry; Rev. Cezary Ejsymont; Dcn. Robert P. Barnard; Dcn. Chuck Bowman; Dcn. Paul Perreault; Mother Mary Way of Salvation, SSVM, CRE; CRP Stds.: 72

Immaculate Conception Catholic Parish Fairbanks - 2 Doyon Pl., Fairbanks, AK 99701 t) 907-452-3533 iccsecretary@cbna.org www.iccfairbanks.org Rev. Gerardus Hauwert, IVE, Pst.; Rev. Jaime Abúndiz, IVE, Par. Vicar; Dcn. Sean Stack; Mother Mary Way of Salvation, SSVM, CRE; CRP Stds.: 9

St. Mark University Catholic Parish Fairbanks - 1316 Peger Rd., Fairbanks, AK 99709; Mailing: P.O. Box 750166, Fairbanks, AK 99775-0166 t) 907-374-9564 stmark@cbna.org stmarksuaf.org Rev. Ross Tozzi, Pst.; Rev. Piotr Oprych, Par. Vicar; Dcn. Warren Lucero; Mary Pat Boger, Parish Admin.; CRP Stds.: 10

Campus Ministry - 1300 Peger Rd, Fairbanks, AK 99709 t) (907) 374-9564

St. Raphael Catholic Church Fairbanks - 1125 Old Steese Hwy. N., Fairbanks, AK 99710; Mailing: P.O. Box 10508, Fairbanks, AK 99710 t) 907-457-6603 straphaelcatholicparish@gmail.com www.straphaelfairbanks.org Rev. Simon Jingbe (Zimbabwe), Par. Admin.; Dcn. George Bowder; CRP Stds.: 30

GALENA

St. John Berchmans Catholic Church Galena - ; Mailing: P.O. Box 131, Galena, AK 99741 t) (907) 888-2266 info@cbna.org Bro. R Justin Huber, O.F.M., Parish Min.; Bro. Robert J. Ruzicka, O.F.M., Parish Admin.; Agnes Sweetsir, Acting Parish Admin.;

HEALY

Holy Mary of Guadalupe Catholic Church Healy - Tri-Valley Subdivision. Carbon Way & Graphite Ln., Healy, AK 99743; Mailing: PO Box 32, Healy, AK 99743 t) (907) 683-2535 holymaryofguadalupe@gmail.com www.hmogcatholic.org (Served out of Fairbanks, Immaculate Conception Church.) Rev. Jaime Abúndiz, IVE;

Mission (Denali National Park Catholic Community) - Denali Park Rd., Denali National Park and Preserve, Denali Park, AK 99755; Mailing: P.O. Box 32, Healy, AK 99743 www.hmogcatholic.com

HOLY CROSS

Holy Family Catholic Church Holy Cross - ; Mailing: PO Box 101, Holy Cross, AK 99602 t) (907) 374-9500 info@cbna.org Connie Werba, Acting Parish Admin.;

HOOPER BAY

Little Flower of Jesus Catholic Church Hooper Bay - ; Mailing: PO Box 9, Hooper Bay, AK 99604 t) 907-758-4620 info@cbna.org Rev. Richard P. Magner, S.J.;

HUSLIA

St. Francis Regis Catholic Church Huslia - ; Mailing: P.O. Box 89, Huslia, AK 99746-0089 t) (907) 374-9500 info@cbna.org Bro. R Justin Huber, O.F.M., Parish Min.;

KALSKAG

Immaculate Conception Catholic Church Kalskag - ; Mailing: PO Box 11, Kalskag, AK 99607 t) (907) 471-2298 info@cbna.org Bonnie Perrson, Acting Parish Admin.; Dwayne Hoffman, Contact;

KALTAG

St. Teresa Catholic Church - ; Mailing: P.O. Box 69, Kaltag, AK 99748 t) 907-534-2218 info@cbna.org Rev. Joseph Hemmer, O.F.M., Pst.;

KOTLIK

St. Joseph Catholic Church Kotlik - ; Mailing: P.O. Box 20228, Kotlik, AK 99620 t) 907-899-4715 info@cbna.org Rev. Stanislaw Jaszek; CRP Stds.: 5

KOTZEBUE

St. Francis Xavier Catholic Church Kotzebue - ; Mailing: P.O. Box 358, Kotzebue, AK 99752 t) 206-661-6077 stfrancisxavier@cbna.org www.walaskacatholic.org Rev. Alphonsus Afina; Rev. Michał Ulaski; Winifred Reeve, Parish Admin.;

KOYUKUK

St. Patrick Catholic Church - ; Mailing: P.O. Box 54010, Koyukuk, AK 99754 t) 907-927-2240 info@cbna.org Rev. Thinh Van Tran, OFM, Par. Admin.; Eliza Jones, Acting Parish Admin.;

MARSHALL

Immaculate Heart of Mary Catholic Church Marshall - ; Mailing: P.O. Box 69, Marshall, AK 99585 t) 907-679-6639 info@cbna.org Rev. Abraham Nemaisa; Rev. Gregg D. Wood, S.J.; Clara Shorty, Parish Admin./Parish Life Coord.;

Our Lady of Guadalupe Catholic Church Russian Mission - ; Mailing: PO Box 56, Russian Mission, AK 99657-0056 t) 907-374-9500 Rev. Jim Falsey; Mae Pitka, Acting Parish Admin.;

MCGRATH

St. Michael Catholic Church McGrath - ; Mailing: P.O. Box 141, McGrath, AK 99627 t) 907-374-9500 info@cbna.org Rev. Jim Falsey, Visiting Priest; Sharon R. Strick, Acting Parish Admin.;

MOUNTAIN VILLAGE

St. Lawrence Catholic Church Mountain Village - ; Mailing: P.O. Box 32205, Mountain Village, AK 99632 t) 907-374-9500 info@cbna.org Rev. Yakubu Aiden; Dcn. Elmer Beans; Karen Peterson, Parish Admin.; CRP Stds.: 23

NENANA

St. Theresa Catholic Church Nenana - 706 N. B St., Nenana, AK 99760; Mailing: P.O. Box 312, Nenana, AK 99760 t) 907-832-5617 rbowman@cbna.org (Served out of Fairbanks, Immaculate Conception Church.) Rev. Jaime Abúndiz, IVE; Ruth Bowman, Acting Parish Admin.; CRP Stds.: 9

NEWTOK

Holy Family Catholic Church Newtok - ; Mailing: PO Box 5569, Newtok, AK 99559 t) (907) 237-2427 info@cbna.org Rev. Abraham Nemaisa; Rev. Gregg D. Wood, S.J.; Dcn. John F. Andy;

NIGHTMUTE

Our Lady of Perpetual Help - ; Mailing: P.O. Box 90035, Nightmute, AK 99690 t) 907-647-6428 nightmutechurch@yahoo.com Rev. Thomas G. Provinsal, S.J.; Dcn. Christopher Tulik; Anna Tom, Acting Parish Admin.;

NOME

St. Ann Catholic Church Teller - c/o St. Joseph Church, Nome, AK 99762; Mailing: P.O. Box 1010, Nome, AK 99762 t) 907-443-5527 stjoseph@cbna.org walaskacatholic.org/ (Served out of Nome) Rev. Alphonsus Afina, Priest; Rev. Michał Ulaski, Priest; Paula Alvanna, Parish Administrator;

St. Joseph Catholic Church Nome - 100 W. King Pl., Nome, AK 99762; Mailing: P.O. Box 1010, Nome, AK 99762 t) 907-443-5527 stjoseph@cbna.org www.walaskacatholic.org Rev. Alphonsus Afina; Rev. Michał Ulaski; CRP Stds.: 2

St. Jude Catholic Church Little Diomede - c/o St. Joseph Church, Nome, AK 99762 t) (907) 443-5527 st.joseph@cbna.org walaskacatholic.org/

NORTH POLE

St. Nicholas Catholic Church North Pole - 707 St. Nicholas Dr., North Pole, AK 99705 t) (907) 488-2595 stnicks@cbna.org www.stnicholasnp.org Rev. Welcome Chipiro, Par. Admin.; Rev. Dominik Wojcik, Par. Vicar; Dcn. Ronald Jones; Nick Shamrell, Youth Min.; Heather Pariera-Kimmerling, DRE; Betsy Jones, Bus. Mgr.; CRP Stds.: 107

NULATO

Our Lady of Snows Catholic Church Nulato - ; Mailing: PO Box 89, Nulato, AK 99765 t) 907-898-2242 info@cbna.org Rev. Thinh Van Tran, OFM, Par. Admin.;

PILOT STATION

St. Charles Spinola Catholic Church Pilot Station - ; Mailing: P.O. Box 5120, Pilot Station, AK 99650 t) 907-549-3231 info@cbna.org Rev. Yakubu Aiden; Regina Mike, Acting Parish Admin.; CRP Stds.: 7

RUBY

St. Peter-in-Chains Catholic Church - ; Mailing: P.O. Box 68207, Ruby, AK 99768 t) 907-468-4413 info@cbna.org Rev. Joseph Hemmer, O.F.M., Pst.;

SCAMMON BAY

Blessed Sacrament Catholic Church Scammon Bay - ; Mailing: PO Box 170, Scammon Bay, AK 99662 t) (907) 558-5230 info@cbna.org Rev. Richard P. Magner, S.J.;

ST. MARYS

Church of the Nativity Catholic Church St. Marys - ; Mailing: PO Box 109, St. Marys, AK 99658 t) (907) 438-2133 info@cbna.org Rev. Yakubu Aiden; CRP Stds.: 4

ST. MICHAEL

St. Michael Catholic Church St. Michael - ; Mailing: P.O. Box 29, St. Michael, AK 99659 t) 907-923-3151 info@cbna.org Rev. Alphonsus Afina; Rev. Michał Ulaski;

STEBBINS

St. Bernard Catholic Church Stebbins - ; Mailing: P.O. Box 71102, Stebbins, AK 99671 t) 907-934-3151 info@cbna.org Rev. Alphonsus Afina; Rev. Michał Ulaski;

TANANA

St. Aloysius Catholic Church - ; Mailing: P.O. Box 77006, Tanana, AK 99777 t) 907-366-7238 info@cbna.org Lois Huntington, Parish Admin.;

TOK

Holy Rosary Catholic Church Tok - ; Mailing: P.O. Box 369, Tok, AK 99780 t) 907-388-8434 hrtok@aptalaska.net Rev. Welcome Chipiro, Par. Admin.; CRP Stds.: 1

TOKSOOK BAY

St. Peter the Fisherman - ; Mailing: P.O. Box 37046, Toksook Bay, AK 99637 t) 907-427-7813 stpeter@gci.net Rev. Thomas G. Provinsal, S.J.; Dcn. Joe Asuluk; Dcn. Henry Simons; Maggie John, Parish Admin. & Parish Life Coord.;

TUNUNAK

St. Joseph Catholic Church Tununak - ; Mailing: P.O. Box 9, Tununak, AK 99681 t) 907-652-6214 tununakchurch@yahoo.com Rev. Thomas G. Provinsal, S.J.;

UNALAKLEET

Church of the Holy Angels Catholic Church Unalakleet - ; Mailing: PO Box 358, Unalakleet, AK 99684 t) (907) 374-9500 info@cbna.org Rev. Alphonsus Afina; Rev. Michał Ulaski; Anne Ivanoff, Acting Parish Admin.;

SCHOOLS: PRESCHOOL THRU HIGH SCHOOL

SCHOOLS

STATE OF ALASKA

FAIRBANKS

Immaculate Conception Grade School - (DIO) (Grades PreK-6) 615 Monroe St., Fairbanks, AK 99701 t) 907-313-3062 info@catholic-schools.org www.catholic-schools.org Kristy Parrish, Prin.; Kerry Halvarson, Librn.; Stds.: 186; Lay Tchrs.: 23

HIGH SCHOOLS

STATE OF ALASKA

FAIRBANKS

Monroe Catholic Junior-Senior High School - (DIO) (Grades 7-12) 615 Monroe St., Fairbanks, AK 99701 t) 907-313-3062 info@catholic-schools.org www.catholic-schools.org Patrick Riggs, Prin.; Kerry Halvarson, Librn.; Stds.: 165; Lay Tchrs.: 24

INSTITUTIONS LOCATED IN DIOCESE

ENDOWMENTS / FOUNDATIONS / TRUSTS [EFT]

FAIRBANKS

Catholic Trust of Northern Alaska - 1316 Peger Rd., Fairbanks, AK 99709 t) (907) 374-9500 Susan Clifton, Exec.;

***Monroe Foundation, Inc.** - 718 Betty St., Fairbanks, AK 99701-3020; Mailing: PO Box 71620, Fairbanks, AK 99707-1620 t) (907) 313-3291 foundation@catholic-schools.org www.catholic-schools.org Amanda Angaiak, Pres.;

MISCELLANEOUS [MIS]

BETHEL

Brother Joe Prince Jesuit Community - ; Mailing: PO Box 3064, Bethel, AK 99559 t) (907) 545-1123 Rev. Richard P. Magner, S.J., Supr.; Rev. Thomas G. Provinsal, S.J.; Rev. Gregg D. Wood, S.J.;

EMMONAK

Native Ministry Training Program - ; Mailing: P.O. Box 36, Emmonak, AK 99581-0036 t) 907-949-6238 nmtp@juno.com Malora (Lala) Hunt, Co-Dir.; Dcn. Dominic Hunt, Co-Dir.;

FAIRBANKS

Bl. Pier Giorgio Frassati House of Discernment - 1316 Peger Rd., Fairbanks, AK 99709 t) 907-374-9500 info@cbna.org Rev. Robert Fath, Dir.;

***Little Flower Ministries** - 1 Church St., Fairbanks, AK 99708; Mailing: P.O. Box 81476, Fairbanks, AK 99708 t) (907) 451-4868 info@kqhe.org kqhe.org Steve Mullins, Pres.;

St. Mary's of the Lake - c/o 1316 Peger Rd., Fairbanks, AK 99709 t) 907-374-9500 info@cbna.org Rev. Welcome Chipiro, Contact;

NOME

***KNOM Radio Mission, Inc.** - 107 W. Third Ave., Nome, AK 99762; Mailing: P.O. Box 190649, Anchorage, AK 99519 t) 907-443-5221 business@knom.org www.knom.org Alaska Radio Mission – KNOM (Former Name) Davis Hovey, Interim Gen. Mgr.;

MONASTERIES AND RESIDENCES FOR PRIESTS AND BROTHERS [MON]

FAIRBANKS

St. Ignatius Residence - 2890 Kobuk Ave., Fairbanks, AK 99709; Mailing: 1316 Peger Rd., Fairbanks, AK 99709 t) 907-374-9500 info@cbna.org Rev. Gerardus Hauwert, IVE, In Res.; Rev. Jaime Abúndiz, IVE, In Res.; Rev. Ross Tozzi, In Res.; Rev. Piotr Oprych, In Res.; Rev. Cezary Ejsymont, In Res.; Priests: 5

An asterisk (*) denotes an organization that has established tax-exempt status directly with the IRS and is not covered by the USCCB Group Ruling.

Diocese of Fall River

(Dioecesis Riverormensis)

MOST REVEREND EDGAR MOREIRA DA CUNHA, S.D.V., D.D.

Bishop of Fall River; ordained March 27, 1982; appointed Titular Bishop of Ucres and Auxiliary Bishop of Newark June 27, 2003; Episcopal ordination September 3, 2003; appointed Bishop of Fall River July 3, 2014; installed September 24, 2014.

Office of Most Rev. Edgar Moreira da Cunha, S.D.V. , D.D., Bishop of Fall River: 47 Underwood St., Fall River, MA 02720-3701. T: 508-675-1311; F: 508-679-9220.

The Chancery: 450 Highland Ave., Fall River, MA 02720-3701. T: 508-675-1311; F: 508-730-2447.
bishopsoffice@dioc-fr.org
chancery@dioc-fr.org
www.fallriverdiocese.org

ESTABLISHED MARCH 12, 1904.

Square Miles 1,194.

Comprises Bristol, Barnstable, Dukes and Nantucket Counties, and the Towns of Marion, Mattapoisett and Wareham in Plymouth County, Massachusetts.

For legal titles of parishes and diocesan institutions, consult the Chancery Office.

STATISTICAL OVERVIEW

Personnel
Bishop....1
Retired Bishops....1
Priests: Diocesan Active in Diocese....58
Priests: Diocesan Active Outside Diocese....5
Priests: Retired, Sick or Absent....72
Number of Diocesan Priests....135
Religious Priests in Diocese....67
Total Priests in your Diocese....202
Extern Priests in Diocese....6
Ordinations:
Diocesan Priests....4
Transitional Deacons....4
Permanent Deacons in Diocese....78
Total Brothers....7
Total Sisters....92

Parishes
Parishes....72
With Resident Pastor:
Resident Diocesan Priests....54
Resident Religious Priests....7
Without Resident Pastor:
Administered by Priests....11
Closed Parishes....2

Professional Ministry Personnel:
Brothers....6
Sisters....17
Lay Ministers....45

Welfare
Homes for the Aged....5
Total Assisted....762
Residential Care of Children....2
Total Assisted....109
Day Care Centers....1
Total Assisted....50
Special Centers for Social Services....16
Total Assisted....35,325
Other Institutions....1
Total Assisted....940

Educational
Diocesan Students in Other Seminaries....7
Total Seminarians....7
Colleges and Universities....1
Total Students....2,579
High Schools, Diocesan and Parish....3
Total Students....893
High Schools, Private....1
Total Students....1,086
Elementary Schools, Diocesan and Parish....15
Total Students....3,326
Catechesis/Religious Education:
High School Students....2,364
Elementary Students....8,167
Total Students under Catholic Instruction....18,422
Teachers in Diocese:
Priests....8
Sisters....4
Lay Teachers....561

Vital Statistics
Receptions into the Church:
Infant Baptism Totals....1,694
Minor Baptism Totals....89
Adult Baptism Totals....31
Received into Full Communion....81
First Communions....1,616
Confirmations....1,855
Marriages:
Catholic....479
Interfaith....82
Total Marriages....561
Deaths....2,971
Total Catholic Population....265,468
Total Population....860,070

LEADERSHIP

Office of the Bishop - t) (508) 675-1311 Most Rev. Edgar Moreira da Cunha, S.D.V., Bishop of Fall River - Diocesan Ordinary (bishopsoffice@dioc-fr.org); Selina Krauzyk, Exec. Asst. (selinak@dioc-fr.org); Jodi Sullivan, Exec. Asst. (jsullivan@dioc-fr.org);

Vicar General - t) (508) 675-1311 Very Rev. David C. Frederici (dcf@dioc-fr.org);

Vicar for Priests - t) 508-993-2351 Very Rev. David A. Pignato (dpignato@dioc-fr.org);

The Chancery - t) 508-675-1311

Chancellor and Chief Financial Officer - t) (508) 675-1311 Kevin R. Kiley, Chancellor/CFO (kkiley@dioc-fr.org);

Diocesan Consultors - Most Rev. Edgar Moreira da Cunha, S.D.V., Bishop (bishopsoffice@dioc-fr.org); Very Rev. David C. Frederici, Vicar General (dcf@dioc-fr.org); Very Rev. David A. Pignato, Vicar for Priests (dpignato@dioc-fr.org);

OFFICES AND DIRECTORS

Apostolate for Persons with Disabilities - t) 508-997-7337 Matthew Dansereau, Dir. (mdansereau@cssdioc.org); Dennis Canulla, Office Mgr. (dennisc@cssdioc.org);

Bereavement Ministry - t) 508-674-4681 x1111 Rose Mary Saraiva, Bereavement & Mental Health Ministry Coord. (rsaraiva@cssdioc.org);

Brazilian Apostolate - Rev. Marcos V. Alexandre-Caldeira (mvacaldeira@gmail.com); Rev. Edivar Ribeiro DaSilva (edivarrs@hotmail.com); Very Rev. Thomas Washburn, Rector (frtom@3fallriver.org);

Catholic Charities of the Diocese of Fall River - t) 508-674-4681 cssdioc.org Susan Mazzarella, CEO (smazzarella@cssdioc.org); Happiness Nosike-Unaka, COO (hunaka@cssdioc.org); Rui Rosa, CFO (rrosa@cssdioc.org);

The Catholic Foundation of Southeastern Massachusetts - t) 508-985-6510 www.catholicfoundationsema.org Miriam Finn Sherman, CEO (msherman@catholicfoundationsema.org); Christina Duggan, Vice Pres. Oper. (cduggan@catholicfoundationsema.org); Shawna Erickson, Dir., Major Gifts & Grants (serickson@catholicfoundationsema.org);

Catholic Schools Office - t) 508-687-7301 info@catholicsa.org www.catholicschoolalliance.org Daniel S. Roy, Supt. Schools (droy@catholicsa.org); Vincent Mancuso, Asst. Supt. (vmancuso@catholicsa.org); Denise M. Peixoto, Asst. Supt. (dpeixoto@catholicsa.org);

Clergy Support - t) 508-492-0995 www.fallriverclergysupport.org Matthew S. Robinson, Dir. (mrobinson@dioc-fr.org);

Diocesan Archives - t) 508-675-1311 Kevin R. Kiley, Chancellor/CFO (kkiley@dioc-fr.org);

Diocesan Department of Pastoral Care for the Sick - t) (774) 265-2708 Dcn. Robert M. Craig, Dir. (rcraig@dioc-fr.org);

Cape Cod Hospital - t) 508-862-5286 Gretchen MacKoul;

Charlton Memorial Hospital - t) 508-679-3131 Rev. Joseph Pasala, Hospital Ministry; Sr. Roberta O'Connell, F.C.J., Hospital Ministry; Dcn. Paul Spearin, Hospital Ministry;

Falmouth Hospital - t) 508-548-5300 Dcn. Bruce J. Baxter, Dir.;

Morton Hospital - t) 508-828-7000 Dcn. Anthony A. Cipriano, Dir.; Dcn. Philip E. Bedard;

St. Anne's Hospital - t) 508-674-5741 x2061 Rev. Leonard Kayondo; Sr. Carole V.M. Mello, O.P.; Sr. Marie Therese Dyer, F.C.J.;

St. Luke's Hospital - t) 508-997-1515 Denise Benjamin, Coord.; Sr. Judith Costa, S.S.D.; Sr. Fatima Simas, S.S.D.;

Spaulding Rehabilitation Hospital of the Cape and Islands - t) 508-833-4000 Kathy Snow;

Sturdy Memorial Hospital - t) 508-236-8560 Rev. Deacon Del Malloy, Dir.; Elizabeth Dodge; Halina Malec;

Tobey Hospital - t) 508-273-4105 Dcn. Paul D. Coughlin;

Diocesan Guild for the Blind - t) 508-674-4681 Susan Mazzarella, Dir. (smazzarella@cssdioc.org);

Diocesan Health Facilities - t) 508-679-8154 www.dhfo.org Joanne M. Roque, CEO (joanner@dhfo.org);

Diocesan Hispanic Ministry - t) (508) 615-1311 x6533 Sr. Paulina Hurtado, O.P., Diocesan Dir. (sr.paulina@dioc-fr.org); Rev. German Correa Agudelo, Par. Admin. (germancorrea72@outlook.com); Rev. Matthew Gill, Pst. (frmggill@olvparish.org);

Diocesan Insurance Department - t) (508) 985-6518 Joseph A. Figlock, Benefits Specialist (jfiglock@dioc-fr.org);

Diocesan Newspaper - t) 508-675-7151 www.anchornews.org David B. Jolivet, Editor (davejolivet@anchornews.org); Wayne R. Powers, Advertising (waynepowers@anchornews.org);

Diocesan Office of Catholic Cemeteries - t) 508-567-1844 fallrivercatholiccemeteries.org David J. Raposa Jr., Dir. (draposa@dioc-fr.org); Robert A Pacific, Mgr. (rpacific@dioc-fr.org);

Diocesan Office of Communications - t) (508) 675-1311 fallriverdiocese.org John E. Kearns Jr., Dir. Communications (jkearns@dioc-fr.org);

Early Education Center - t) 508-455-0145 Donna Paris, Dir. (director@littleflowerelc.org);

Ecumenical and Inter-religious Affairs Office - t) 508-477-7700 Rev. Edward J. Healey, Ecumenical Officer (pastor@christthekingparish.com);

Episcopal Representative for Religious and Associate Director of Vocations - t) (508) 675-1311 Sr. Paulina Hurtado, O.P. (sr.paulina@dioc-fr.org);

Finance Office - t) 508-675-1311 Joseph Harrington, Dir. Finance (jharrington@dioc-fr.org); Jessica Andrews, Accounting Mgr. (jandrews@dioc-fr.org);

The Foundation to Advance Catholic Education (FACE) - t) 508-985-6510 Most Rev. Edgar Moreira da Cunha, S.D.V., Bishop of Fall River (bishopsoffice@dioc-fr.org); Claudine Cloutier, Chair;

Human Resources and Administration - t) (508) 985-6507 Peter J. Powers, Exec. Dir. (ppowers@dioc-fr.org);

Mental Health Ministry - t) (508) 674-4681 x1111 Rose Mary Saraiva, Bereavement & Mental Health Ministry Coord. (rsaraiva@cssdioc.org);

Minister for Priests - t) 508-990-5617 Rev. George C. Bellenoit (fr.georgebellenoit@gmail.com);

Missionary Cooperative Plan - t) 508-995-6168 Rev. Msgr. John J. Oliveira, Dir. (propoffaithnb@verizon.net);

Office for Divine Worship - t) 508-761-8111 odwfr@aol.com Rev. Jon-Paul Gallant, Dir.;

Office of Facilities and Real Estate - t) (508) 675-1311 Paul Brooks, Dir. (pbrooks@dioc-fr.org); Diane Pray, Exec. Asst. (dpray@dioc-fr.org);

Office of Safe Environment - t) (508) 985-6508 Carolyn Shipp, Dir., Safe Environment & Victim Assistance (cshipp@dioc-fr.org); Cathleen Ryan, CORI & Safe Environment Training Coord. (cryan@dioc-fr.org); Michele Figlock, Coord., OSE Compliance & Data (mfiglock@dioc-fr.org);

Office of Strategic and Pastoral Planning - t) (508) 617-5304 www.fallriverplanning.org Laura M. Carrillo, Dir. (lcarrillo@dioc-fr.org); Dcn. Joseph P. Harrington, Assoc. Dir. (jpharrington@dioc-fr.org);

Office of the General Counsel - t) (508) 617-5307 Michael Carroll, Gen. Counsel/Chief Legal Officer (mcarroll@dioc-fr.org); Amy Calise, Exec. Asst. (acalise@dioc-fr.org);

Permanent Diaconate Program - t) 508-990-0341 www.frpermanentdiaconate.com Dcn. Frank R. Lucca, Dir. (deaconfranklucca@frpermanentdiaconate.com);

Portuguese Apostolate - t) (508) 675-1050 Rev. John J. Oliveira, Coord.;

Propagation of the Faith - t) (508) 995-6168 Rev. Msgr. John J. Oliveira, Dir. (propoffaithnb@verizon.net);

St. Vincent De Paul Society - t) 508-699-4185 Stephen Meaney, Pres.;

Secretariat of the New Evangelization - t) (508) 658-9088 www.fallriverfaithformation.org David Carvalho;

Adult and Child Discipleship - t) (508) 658-9089 cpaul@dioc-fr.org Dcn. Chris Paul, Dir.;

Family and Respect Life - t) (508) 669-7966 idelucca@dioc-fr.org; dledoux@dioc-fr.org Irina De Lucca, Dir.; Deborah LeDoux, Coord.;

Parish and Leader Evangelization - t) (508) 658-9088 dcarvalho@dioc-fr.org David Carvalho, Secy., New Evangelization;

Youth Evangelization and CYO - t) (508) 658-2955 orivera@dioc-fr.org Oscar A. Rivera Jr., Dir., Youth Evangelization & CYO; Gregory Parker, New Bedford Area Coord. of CYO; Matt Bednarz, Fall River Area Coord. of CYO;

Secretariat of the New Evangelization - Campus Ministry - t) (508) 999-8872 flucca@umassd.edu Dcn. Frank R. Lucca (deaconfranklucca@frpermanentdiaconate.com);

Bristol Community College - t) (508) 999-8872 www.bcccatholics.com

Cape Cod Community College/Massachusetts Maritime Academy - t) (508) 999-8872

Newman House - t) (774) 202-3047

Stonehill College - t) (508) 565-1487 aszakaly@stonehill.edu www.stonehill.edu/offices-services/campus-ministry Rev. Anthony V. Szakaly, C.S.C., Dir., Campus Ministry;

University of Massachusetts Dartmouth - t) (508) 999-8872 www.umassdcatholics.com

Wheaton College - www.wheatoncatholics.com

St. Vincent's Services - t) (508) 679-8511 www.saintvincentsservices.org Kristen Dutra, CEO (kdutra@saintvincentsservices.org);

Television Apostolate - t) 508-548-0108 Rev. Msgr. Stephen J. Avila, Dir. (frsteve@falmouthcatholic.org);

Vocations - t) (508) 336-5549 Rev. Kevin A. Cook, Dir. (frcook@fallrivervocations.org); Very Rev. John M. Schrader, Assoc. Dir. (frschrader@fallrivervocations.org); Very Rev. David C. Frederici, Liaison to Seminarians (dcf@dioc-fr.org);

ADVISORY BOARDS, COMMISSIONS, COMMITTEES, AND COUNCILS

Catholic Campaign for Human Development and Grants - t) 508-674-4681 Susan Mazzarella (smazzarella@cssdioc.org);

Catholic Scouting - t) 508-992-7505 frdavid@stmarysdartmouth.org Very Rev. David C. Frederici, Chap. (dcf@dioc-fr.org);

Continuing Education and Formation of the Clergy - t) 508-674-9131 Very Rev. Riley J. Williams, Dir. (frwilliams@holynamefr.com);

Diocesan Council of Catholic Women - t) 508-993-3742 Rev. Michael S. Racine, Moderator; Bea Perreira, Pres.;

Diocesan Finance Council - Most Rev. Edgar Moreira da Cunha, S.D.V., Bishop of Fall River, Council Chair (bishopsoffice@dioc-fr.org); Very Rev. David C. Frederici, Vicar Gen. (dcf@dioc-fr.org); Cynthia R. Baptiste;

Diocesan Liaison with Charismatic Groups - t) 508-824-5577 Rev. Edward A. Murphy, Dir. (freamurphy1@verizon.net);

Diocesan Liaison with Portuguese Charismatic Groups - t) 508-675-1050 Rev. Henry S. Arruda;

Diocesan Pastoral Council - t) 508-617-5304 Most Rev. Edgar Moreira da Cunha, S.D.V., Bishop, Council Pres. (bishopsoffice@dioc-fr.org); Michael Murray, Chair;

Legion of Mary - t) (508) 993-4016 Joyce Sylvia, Dir.;

TRIBUNAL

Diocesan Tribunal - t) 508-675-7150 tribunal@dioc-fr.org www.fallrivertribunal.com

Judicial Vicar - Very Rev. Jeffrey Cabral;

Promotor Justitiae - Rev. Gerard A. Hebert; Rev. Jay T. Maddock;

Judges - Rev. Thomas L. Rita; Rev. Jay T. Maddock; Rev. Thomas E. McGlynn;

Defenders of the Bond - Rev. Gerard A. Hebert; Rev. Msgr. Daniel F. Hoye;

Procurator-Advocates - Rev. Dariusz Kalinowski; **Auditors** - Very Rev. David C. Frederici, Vicar Gen.; Rev. Dariusz Kalinowski; Rev. Thomas E. McGlynn, J.C.L.; **Office Manager** - Janet Neubecker;

PARISHES, MISSIONS, AND CLERGY

COMMONWEALTH OF MASSACHUSETTS

ACUSHNET

St. Francis Xavier's - 125 Main St., Acushnet, MA 02743 t) 508-995-7600 office@sfxparish.com www.sfxparish.com/ Rev. Ryan Healy, Pst.; Dcn. David B. Pepin; CRP Stds.: 92

St. Francis Xavier School - (Grades PreK-8) 223 Main St., Acushnet, MA 02743 t) 508-995-4313 info@sfxacushnet.com www.sfxacushnet.com Michelle Russo, Prin.;

ASSONET

St. Bernard's - 32 S. Main St., Assonet, MA 02702; Mailing: P.O. Box 370, Assonet, MA 02702 t) 508-644-2032 (CRP); 508-644-5585 stbernardassonet@rectory.comcastbiz.net www.stbernardassonet.org Rev. Gerard A. Hebert, Pst.; Brian Correia, DRE; Marlene Correia, DRE; Dennis Robinson, Music Min.; CRP Stds.: 250

ATTLEBORO

St. John the Evangelist - One St. John Pl., Attleboro, MA 02703-2249 t) 508-222-1206 office@attleborocatholics.org attleborocatholics.org/ Rev. Craig A. Pregana, Pst.; Rev. Deacon Del Malloy; Dcn. David O. Harum; Margaret Keenan, DRE; CRP Stds.: 431

St. John the Evangelist School - (Grades PreK-8) 13 Hodges St., Attleboro, MA 02703 t) 508-222-5062 mholden@sje-school.com www.sje-school.com Participating Parishes: O.L. Queen of Martyrs, Seekonk; St. Theresa's, South Attleboro; St. Mary's, Mansfield, Norton, Wrentham & North Attleboro; Sac Kellie Kickham, Prin.;

Holy Ghost Church - 71 Linden St., Attleboro, MA 02703 t) (508) 222-1206 (Worship Site)

St. Theresa of the Child Jesus - 18 Baltic St., Attleboro, MA 02703 t) 508-761-5367 (CRP); 508-761-8111 sttcj@aol.com www.sainttheresaattleboro.org Rev. Jon-Paul Gallant, Pst.; Dcn. Wilfred R. Varieur; Nancy Hale, DRE; George Creighton, Music Min.; CRP Stds.: 84

Saint Vincent de Paul Parish - Merged Jan 2022 Merged with St. John the Evangelist Parish, Attleboro. For inquiries of parish records, please contact St. John the Evangelist, Attleboro.

BREWSTER

Our Lady of the Cape - 468 Stony Brook Rd., Brewster, MA 02631-7799; Mailing: P.O. Box 1799, Brewster, MA 02631 t) 508-385-3252 ourladyofthecapebrewster@gmail.com www.ourladyofthecape.org Rev. Paul Mandziuk, M.S., Pst.; Rev. John R. Dolan, M.S., Par. Vicar; Janet Rengucci, DRE; CRP Stds.: 65

Immaculate Conception - 2580 Main St., Rte. 6A, Brewster, MA 02631 t) (508) 385-3252 Rev. William Kaliyadan, M.S., Pst.;

BUZZARDS BAY

St. Margaret - 141 Main St., Buzzards Bay, MA 02532 t) 508-759-7777 office@stmargaretbbay.org; dre@stmargaretbbay.org stmargaretbbay.org Rev. Marek Chmurski, Pst.; Dcn. Ralph J. Guerra; Dcn. George E. Hults; Ernest Joseph Boucher, DRE; CRP Stds.: 32

St. Mary Star of the Sea - 4 Onset Bay Ln., Onset, MA 02558; Mailing: 141 Main St., Buzzards Bay, MA 02532 t) (508) 759-7777 office@stmargaretbbay.com

CENTERVILLE

Our Lady of Victory - 230 S. Main St., Centerville, MA 02632 t) 508-775-5744; 508-775-5744 x119 (CRP) pastor@olvparish.org www.olvparish.org Rev. Gregory A. Mathias, Pst.; Rev. Laurent Valliere, Par. Vicar; Dcn. Theodore E. Lukac; Dcn. Keith Caldwell; Dcn. Richard J. Murphy; William Bussiere, DRE; CRP Stds.: 407

Our Lady of Hope - 1581 Main St., West Barnstable, MA 02668; Mailing: 230 S. Main St., Centerville, MA 02632 t) (508) 775-5744

CHATHAM

Holy Redeemer - 57 Highland Ave., Chatham, MA 02633 t) 508-945-0677 parish@holyredeemerchatham.org www.holyredeemerchatham.org Rev. John M. Sullivan, Pst.; Dcn. Joseph F. Mador; Bethel Norcross, DRE; Howard Whelden, Bus. Mgr.; Cheryl L. Duerr, Music Min.; CRP Stds.: 17

Our Lady of Grace - 60 Meetinghouse Rd. Rte. 137, South Chatham, MA 02659 t) (508) 945-0677

EAST FALMOUTH

St. Joseph, Guardian of the Holy Family - 167 E. Falmouth Hwy., East Falmouth, MA 02536 t) 508-548-0108 office@falmouthcatholic.org falmouthcatholic.org St. Joseph, Guardian of the Holy Family Parish is comprised of three former Parishes in Falmouth: St. Anthony, St. Elizabeth Seton, St. Patrick Rev. Msgr. Stephen J. Avila, Pst.; Rev. Matthew F. Laird, Par. Vicar; Dcn. Peter M. Guresh; Dcn. Paul J. Harney; Dcn. William W. Hays; Dcn. Patrick J. Mahoney; Dcn. John E. Simonis; CRP Stds.: 200

Chapel of St. Joseph - 33 Millfield St., Woods Hole, MA 02543; Mailing: 167 E. Falmouth Hwy., E. Falmouth, MA 02536 t) (508) 548-0108

St. Thomas - 440 Grand Ave., Falmouth, MA 02540; Mailing: 167 E. Falmouth Hwy., E. Falmouth, MA 02536 t) (508) 548-0108

EAST FREETOWN

St. John Neumann - 157 Middleboro Rd., East Freetown, MA 02717; Mailing: P.O.Box 718, East Freetown, MA 02717 t) 508-763-2240 contact@sjnfreetown.org www.sjnfreetown.org Very Rev. John M. Schrader, Pst.; Dcn. Bruce J. Bonneau; CRP Stds.: 288

EAST SANDWICH

Corpus Christi - 324 Quaker Meetinghouse Rd., East Sandwich, MA 02537-1327 t) 508-888-0209 frgharrison@corpuschristiparish.org www.corpuschristiparish.org Rev. George E. Harrison, Pst.; Rev. Andrew Johnson, Par. Vicar; Dcn. Arthur LaChance; Dcn. George E. Hults; Jennifer Cho, DRE; CRP Stds.: 247

EAST TAUNTON

Holy Family - 370 Middleboro Ave., East Taunton, MA 02718; Mailing: P.O. Box 619, East Taunton, MA 02718 t) 508-824-5707; 508-824-3578 (CRP) secretary@holyfamilytaunton.org; dre@holyfamilytaunton.org hfparish.net Rev. Matthew Gill, Pst.; Dcn. John J. Fitzpatrick; Dcn. Kevin Gingras; Shannon Doel, DRE; Kellie-jo Duarte, DRE; CRP Stds.: 129

FAIRHAVEN

St. Joseph's - 74 Spring St., Fairhaven, MA 02719 t) 508-994-9714 secretary@stjosephparish.comcastbiz.net www.stjosephparishfairhaven.weebly.com Rev. Stephen Banjare, SS.CC., Pst.; Dcn. Douglas Medeiros; CRP Stds.: 86

St. Joseph School - (Grades PreK-8) 100 Spring St., Fairhaven, MA 02719 t) 508-996-1983 www.saintjosephschool.org Faith Piazza, Prin.;

St. Mary's - 440 Main St., Fairhaven, MA 02719; Mailing: 41 Harding Rd., Fairhaven, MA 02719-4500 t) 508-992-7300; 508-992-8721 (CRP) stmarysfairhaven@comcast.net; stmarysreligioused@comcast.net www.stmarysfairhaven.org Rev. Jeremy Sabugo, SS.CC., Par. Admin.; Rebecca A. Newall, DRE; CRP Stds.: 92

FALL RIVER

Cathedral of St. Mary of the Assumption - 327 Second St., Fall River, MA 02721 t) 508-673-2833 frtom@3cfallriver.org; athadeu@3cfallriver.org www.3cfallriver.org Very Rev. Thomas Washburn, Rector; Rev. Juan Munoz, Par. Vicar; Dcn. Christopher Paul; Dcn. Alan J. Thadeu, Dir., Collaborative Oper.; Rev. Leonard Kayondo, In Res.; CRP Stds.: 112

St. Anthony of Padua - 48 Sixteenth St., Fall River, MA 02723 t) 508-674-1986 (CRP); 508-673-2402 Rev. Maurice O. Gauvin, Pst.; CRP Stds.: 91

Espirito Santo - 311 Alden St., Fall River, MA 02723 t) 508-672-3352 esfallriver@yahoo.com Rev. Maurice O. Gauvin, Pst.; CRP Stds.: 190

Espirito Santo School - (Grades PreK-8) 143 Everett St., Fall River, MA 02723 t) 508-672-2229 araposo@es.dfrcs.org www.espiritosantoschool.org Andrew J. Raposo, Prin.;

Holy Name - 709 Hanover St., Fall River, MA 02720 t) 508-679-6732; 401-556-9729 (CRP) office@holynamefr.com; faithformation@holynamefr.com www.holynamefr.com Very Rev. Riley J. Williams, Pst.; Dorothy Mahoney-Pacheco, DRE; CRP Stds.: 126

Holy Name School - (Grades PreK-8) 850 Pearce St., Fall River, MA 02720 t) 508-674-9131 dflanagan@hnsfr.org www.hnsfr.org David J. Flanagan, Prin.;

Holy Trinity - 951 Stafford Rd., Fall River, MA 02721 t) 508-672-3200 holytrinityparish@comcast.net www.holytrinityfallriver.com Rev. Robert A. Oliveira, Pst.; CRP Stds.: 75

Holy Trinity School - (Grades PreK-8) 64 Lamphor St., Fall River, MA 02721 t) 508-673-6772 bgagnon@htfr.dfrcs.org Brenda Gagnon, Prin.;

St. Joseph - 1335 N. Main St., Fall River, MA 02720 t) 508-567-3638 (CRP); 508-673-1123 stjosephsfallriver@gmail.com www.stjosephschurchfr.com Rev. Jay Mello, Pst.; Dcn. Paul R. Levesque; Ana Mello, DRE; Lisa Ouellette, DRE; CRP Stds.: 176

St. Michael - 189 Essex St., Fall River, MA 02720 t) 508-567-3638 (Relg. Educ. Prog.); (508) 672-6713 stmichaelsfallriver@gmail.com www.smpfr.org Rev. Jay Mello, Pst.; Dcn. Paul R. Levesque; Shanna Lubold, Dir.; Ana Mello, DRE; Lisa Ouellette, DRE; CRP Stds.: 176

St. Michael School - (Grades PreK-8) 209 Essex St., Fall River, MA 02720 t) 508-678-0266 pleary@smsfr.dfrcs.org Ryan Klein, Prin.;

Parish of the Good Shepherd - 1598 S. Main St., Fall River, MA 02724-2586 t) 508-673-2833 frtomw@gmail.com; athadeu@3cfallriver.org www.3cfallriver.org Very Rev. Thomas Washburn, Pst.; Rev. Juan Munoz, Par. Vicar; Dcn. Alan J. Thadeu, Director of Collaborative Operations; CRP Stds.: 53

Santo Christo - 240 Columbia St., Fall River, MA 02721; Mailing: 185 Canal St., Fall River, MA 02721-1405 t) 508-675-3007 (CRP); 508-676-1184 office@santochristo.com; faithformation@santochristo.com www.santochristo.com Portuguese National Parish Very Rev. Jeffrey Cabral, Pst.; Rev. Dariusz Kalinowski, Par. Vicar; Osvaldo Pacheco, DRE; CRP Stds.: 171

St. Stanislaus - 36 Rockland St., Fall River, MA 02724 t) 508-673-2833 frtomw@gmail.com; athadeu@3cfallriver.org www.3cfallriver.org Very Rev. Thomas Washburn, Admin.; Rev. Juan Munoz, Par. Vicar; CRP Stds.: 39

St. Stanislaus School - (Grades PreK-8) 37 Rockland St., Fall River, MA 02724; Mailing: P.O. Box 300, Fall River, MA 02724 t) 508-674-6771 jwillis@saintstanislaus.com www.saintstanislaus.com Beth Mahoney, Prin.;

HYANNIS

St. Francis Xavier's - 21 Cross St., Hyannis, MA 02601 t) 508-775-0818 stfrancis@sfxhyannis.org www.sfxhyannis.org Rev. Michael J. Fitzpatrick, Pst.;

Rev. Marcos Vinicius Alexandre-Caldeira, Par. Vicar; Dcn. Bruce J. Baxter; Dcn. David R. Boucher; Dcn. Steven M. Minninger; CRP Stds.: 75

Sacred Heart Chapel - 32 Summer St., Yarmouth Port, MA 02675 t) (508) 775-0818

MANSFIELD

St. Mary's - 330 Pratt St., Mansfield, MA 02048-1581 t) 508-339-2981; 508-339-2982 office@stmarymans.org www.stmarymans.org Rev. Michael K. McManus, Pst.; Dcn. Thomas P. Palanza; Patricia Colbert, DRE; CRP Stds.: 710

St. Mary Catholic School - (Grades PreK-8) t) 508-339-4800 info@stmarymansschool.org www.stmarymansschool.org Matthew Bourque, Prin.; Stds.: 245; Lay Tchrs.: 18

MARION

St. Rita's - 121 Front St., Marion, MA 02738; Mailing: PO Box 501, 22 Barstow St., Mattapoisett, MA 02739 t) 508-758-3719 stritamarion@comcast.net; anthonyrita745@gmail.com anthonyandrita.com Rev. Christopher Stanibula, Par. Admin.; CRP Stds.: 37

MASHPEE

Christ the King - 5 Jobs Fishing Rd., Mashpee, MA 02649; Mailing: P.O. Box 1800, Mashpee, MA 02649 t) 508-477-7700; 508-477-7700 x21 (CRP) office@christthekingparish.com; pastor@christthekingparish.com www.christthekingparish.com Rev. Edward J. Healey, Pst.; Dcn. Brendan W. Brides; Dcn. Frank D. Fantasia; Dcn. Robert D. Lemay; Dcn. David E. Pierce; Dcn. Peter Schutzler; Kathleen Laird, DRE; CRP Stds.: 127

MATTAPOISETT

St. Anthony's - 22 Barstow St., Mattapoisett, MA 02739; Mailing: P.O. Box 501, Mattapoisett, MA 02739 t) 508-758-3719; 508-758-3735 (CRP) office@stanthony.comcastbiz.net; faithformation@stanthony.comcastbiz.net www.anthonyandrita.com Rev. Christopher Stanibula, Par. Admin.; Mary Chaplain, DRE; CRP Stds.: 110

NANTUCKET

St. Mary's, Our Lady of the Isle - 3 Federal St., Nantucket, MA 02554-1168; Mailing: P.O. Box 1168, Nantucket, MA 02554-1168 t) 508-228-0100 stmarys@stmarysnantucket.org www.stmarysnantucket.org Rev. John M. Murray, Pst.; Rev. Carlos Patino, Par. Vicar; Susan Woodley, Admin.; Kezia Duarte, Assoc. Dir.; Dr. Greta Feeney, Music Min.; Judy DeBaggis, DRE; CRP Stds.: 221

NEW BEDFORD

St. Anthony of Padua's - 1359 Acushnet Ave., New Bedford, MA 02746 t) 508-993-1691; 774-929-0337 (CRP) office@saintanthonynewbedford.com; sapccd@gmail.com www.saintanthonynewbedford.com Catechesis and Religious Program is collaborated with Immaculate Conception Rev. Mariano O. Varela, I.V.E., Pst.; Rev. Marcelo Da Silva, IVE, Par. Vicar; Dcn. Eduardo M. Borges; CRP Stds.: 127

St. Francis of Assisi - 247 North St., New Bedford, MA 02740 t) 508-992-3184 frmike@whalingcitycatholics.org; nancy@whalingcitycatholics.org whalingcitycatholics.org Rev. Michael S. Racine, Par. Admin.; CRP Stds.: 16

St. Gabriel the Archangel - 343 Tarkiln Hill Rd., New Bedford, MA 02745-2516; Mailing: 106 Illinois St., New Bedford, MA 02745-2516 t) 508-995-3593 co-pastorandmoderator@ccnbn.org; secretary@ccnbn.org ccnbn.org/ Rev. Sudhir Christodas Nayak, SS.CC., Pst.; Rev. John A. Raposo, Pst.; Dcn. Antonio M. Pimentel; CRP Stds.: 178

All Saints Catholic School - 115 Illinois St., New Bedford, MA 02745 smassoud@ascs.dfrcs.org www.ascsnb.org Susan Massoud, Prin.;

Holy Name of the Sacred Heart of Jesus - 121 Mt. Pleasant St., New Bedford, MA 02740 t) 508-996-8654 (CRP); 508-992-3184 holynamesacredheartparish@comcast.net; jackie@whalingcitycatholics.org whalingcitycstholics.org Rev. Michael Scott Racine, Pst.; Dcn. Eugene E. Sasseville; Theodore Machado, DRE; CRP Stds.: 100

St. Lawrence Martyr - 565 County St., New Bedford, MA 02740; Mailing: 110 Summer St., New Bedford, MA 02740 t) 508-992-4251; 774-202-5758 (CRP) office@whalingcitycatholics.org; ted@whalingcitycatholics.org www.whalingcitycatholics.org Whaling city Catholic Collaborative Rev. Michael Scott Racine, Pst.; Dcn. Maurice A. Ouellette; CRP Stds.: 70

Our Lady of Guadalupe Parish at St. James Church - 233 County St., New Bedford, MA 02740-4717 t) 508-992-9408 guadalupenewbedford@gmail.com www.guadalulpenewbedford.com Rev. German Correa Agudelo, Par. Admin.; CRP Stds.: 128

Our Lady of Mt. Carmel - 230 Bonney St., New Bedford, MA 02744 t) 508-984-7097 (CRP); 508-993-4704 olmcnb@comcast.net Rev. Christopher M Peschel, Pst.; Dcn. Paul J. Macedo; Dcn. Abilio Pires; Nancy Morin, DRE; CRP Stds.: 210

Saint Teresa of Calcutta - (Grades PreK-8) 180 Orchard St., New Bedford, MA 02740 t) 508-996-0534 principal@stocschool.org www.stteresaofcalcuttaschool.org Cristina Viveiros-Serra, Prin.;

Our Lady of Perpetual Help - Closed Jan 2022 For inquiries of parish records contact St. Anthony of Padua, New Bedford.

Our Lady of the Assumption - 47 S. 6th St., New Bedford, MA 02740 t) 508-994-7602 oloaoffice@verizon.net Rev. David Lupo, SS.CC., Pst.; Rev. Alphonsus McHugh, SS.CC., In Res.; Maria Grace, DRE;

Our Lady of the Immaculate Conception - 136 Earle St., New Bedford, MA 02746 t) 508-992-9892 i.conception@comcast.net Rev. Mariano O. Varela, I.V.E., Pst.; Rev. Marcelo Da Silva, IVE, Par. Vicar; Dcn. Eduardo M. Borges; Dcn. Albertino F. Pires; Delia Silva, DRE; CRP Stds.: 136

NORTH ATTLEBOROUGH

Transfiguration of the Lord - 14 Park St., North Attleborough, MA 02760 t) 508-695-6161; 508-695-3823 (CRP) stmaryna@noozi.com; transfigurationreled@gmail.com www.saintmaryna.com/ Rev. Michael A. Ciryak, Admin.; Dcn. Joseph E. Regali; Elaine Corvese, DRE; CRP Stds.: 567

St. Mary-Sacred Heart School - (Grades PreK-8) 57 Richards Ave., North Attleboro, MA 02760 t) 508-695-3072 smshna@smshna.dfr.org www.smshna.com Charlotte Lourenco, Prin.;

Sacred Heart - 58 Church St., North Attleboro, MA 02760; Mailing: 14 Park St., North Attleboro, MA 02760 www.saintmaryna.com

St. Mark - 105 Stanley St., Attleboro Falls, MA 02763; Mailing: 14 Park St., North Attleboro, MA 02760 www.saintmaryna.com

St. Mary of the Immaculate Conception - 14 Park Street, North Attleborough, MA 02760 www.saintmaryna.com

NORTH DARTMOUTH

St. Julie Billiart - 494 Slocum Rd., North Dartmouth, MA 02747 t) 508-990-0287 (CRP); 508-993-2351 sng@saintjulies.org www.saintjulies.org Very Rev. David A. Pignato, Pst.; Rev. Gregory K. Quenneville, Par. Vicar; Steven N. Guillotte, Bus. Mgr.; Kathy Kosinski, DRE; Joseph Martino, Youth Min.; CRP Stds.: 232

NORTH DIGHTON

St. Nicholas of Myra Parish - 499 Spring St., North Dighton, MA 02764; Mailing: P.O. Box 564, North Dighton, MA 02764 t) 508-824-6581 (CRP); 508-822-1425 st.nicholasofmyra@comcast.net; stnicholasfaithformation@gmail.com saintnicholasofmyra.org Rev. David C. Deston Jr., Admin.; Rev. Daniel Nunes, Par. Vicar; Maureen Brawley, DRE; CRP Stds.: 198

NORTH EASTON

Immaculate Conception - 193 Main St., North Easton, MA 02356 t) 508-238-3232 (Office); 508-238-3230 (CRP) rectory@icceaston.org; religioused@icceaston.org www.icceaston.org Very Rev. Neil Wack, C.S.C., Pst.; Lynne Stewart, DRE; CRP Stds.: 239

NORTON

St. Mary's - One Power St., Norton, MA 02766-0430 t) 508-285-6642 secretary@stmarysnorton.com www.stmarysnorton.com Very Rev. Timothy P. Reis, Pst.; Dcn. Alan J. Thadeu; Rebecca Molloy, DRE; Elizabeth MacDonald, DRE; Laura Vergow, RCIA Coord.; Judy Burgess, Pst. Assoc.; Anna McReynolds, Music Min.; Jan Meier, Bus. Mgr.; CRP Stds.: 366

OAK BLUFFS

Good Shepherd - 55 School St., Oak Bluffs, MA 02557; Mailing: PO Box 1058, Vineyard Haven, MA 02568 t) 508-693-0342 frfedak@goodshepherdmv.com www.goodshepherdmv.com Rev. Paul C. Fedak, Pst.; Rev. Edivar Ribeiro DaSilva, Par. Vicar; CRP Stds.: 64

Our Lady Star of the Sea - 22 Massasoit Ave., Oak Bluffs, MA 02557 (Worship Site)

St. Elizabeth's Church - 86 Main St., Edgartown, MA 02539 (Worship Site)

St. Augustine's Church - 56 Franklin St., Vineyard Haven, MA 02568 (Worship Site)

ORLEANS

St. Joan of Arc - 61 Canal Rd., Orleans, MA 02653 t) 508-255-0170 rectory@joanarc.org www.joanarc.org Rev. Steven Booth, Admin.; Judy Burt-Walker, DRE; Dcn. Norman McEnaney; CRP Stds.: 45

OSTERVILLE

Our Lady of the Assumption - 76 Wianno Ave., Osterville, MA 02655 t) 508-428-2011 office@assumption-capecod.org www.assumption-capecod.org Rev. Gregory A. Mathias, Pst.; Rev. Laurent Valliere, Par. Vicar; Dcn. Theodore E. Lukac;

POCASSET

St. John the Evangelist - 841 Shore Rd., Pocasset, MA 02559; Mailing: PO Box 1558, Pocasset, MA 02559 t) 508-563-5887 patty@sjeparish.com www.stjohnspocasset.org Rev. Thomas A. Frechette, Pst.; Dcn. John J. Burkly; Deborah Boucher, DRE; John Brennan, Music Min.; CRP Stds.: 115

PROVINCETOWN

St. Peter the Apostle - 11 Prince St., Provincetown, MA 02657 t) 508-487-0095 stpetersptown@aol.com www.stpeters-ptown.org Rev. Philip N. Hamel, Pst.; CRP Stds.: 9

RAYNHAM

St. Ann - 675 N. Main St., Raynham, MA 02767; Mailing: P.O. Box 247, Raynham Center, MA 02768 t) 508-824-9021 (CRP); 508-823-9833 office@stannsraynham.org; religioused@stannsraynham.org www.stannsraynham.org Rev. James M. Fitzpatrick, Pst.; Dcn. Joseph A. McGinley; Dcn. Paul Spearin; Joan Lynn, DRE; CRP Stds.: 449

SEEKONK

Our Lady of Mt. Carmel - 984 Taunton Ave., Seekonk, MA 02771; Mailing: P.O. Box 519, Seekonk, MA 02771 t) 508-336-5549 olmcchurch1@gmail.com olmcseekonk.org Rev. Kevin A. Cook, Pst.; Dcn. Matthew T. Sweeney; Christine Gregorek, DRE; Lori J. Lavigne, DRE; CRP Stds.: 203

Our Lady Queen of Martyrs - 385 Central Ave., Seekonk, MA 02771 t) 508-399-8440; 508-399-7534 (CRP) olqmseekonk@comcast.net www.olqmseekonk.org Rev. Raymond Cambra Jr., Pst.; Rose Parenteau, Pst. Assoc.; Cynthia Gamache, DRE; CRP Stds.: 164

SOMERSET

St. John of God - 1036 Brayton Ave., Somerset, MA 02726; Mailing: 996 Brayton Ave., Somerset, MA 02726 t) 508-678-5513 office@sjogsomerset.org www.sjogsomerset.org Rev. Jason Brilhante, Pst.; Carlos Tavares, DRE; John Lema, Music Min.; Tobias Monte, Music Min.; John Travers, Music Min.; CRP Stds.: 186

St. Patrick's - 306 South St., Somerset, MA 02726-5617; Mailing: 386 Luther Ave., Somerset, MA 02726 t) (508) 675-1073 (CRP); 508-673-7831 sldfo@comcast.net olopsomerset.org Merged with St. Thomas More, Somerset and St. Louis De France, Swansea to form Our Lady of Peace, Somerset, January 1, 2023. Rev. David A. Costa, Pst.; Dcn. Robert M. Craig; Sr. Kathleen Corrigan, S.U.S.C., Pst. Assoc.; Anne Cabral, DRE;

St. Thomas More - 386 Luther Ave., Somerset, MA 02726 t) 508-673-7831; 508-679-1236 (CRP) office@stthomasmoresomerset.org; religiosued@stthomasmoresomerset.org olopsomerset.org Merged with St. Patrick's, Somerset and St. Louis De France, Swansea to form Our Lady of Peace, Somerset, January 1, 2023. Rev. David A. Costa, Pst.; Dcn. Robert M. Craig; Sr. Kathleen Corrigan, S.U.S.C., Pst. Assoc.; Anne Cabral, DRE; CRP Stds.: 325

SOUTH DARTMOUTH

St. Mary's - 789 Dartmouth St., South Dartmouth, MA 02748 t) 508-992-7505 info@stmarysdartmouth.org www.stmarysdartmouth.org Very Rev. David C. Frederici, Pst.; Rev. William O'Donnell, Par. Vicar; Dcn. Frank R. Lucca, Pst. Assoc.; Patricia Charros, Bus. Mgr.; David Arruda, Music Min.; Beni Costa-Reedy, DRE; Gloria Alferes, Dir. Member Care; CRP Stds.: 230

SOUTH EASTON

Holy Cross - 225 Purchase St., South Easton, MA 02375 t) 508-238-2235 info@holycrosseaston.org www.holycrosseaston.org Rev. Bradley J. Metz, C.S.C., Pst.; Dcn. Gary Donahue; Christopher Iannitelli, Music Min.; CRP Stds.: 472

SOUTH YARMOUTH

St. Pius X - 5 Barbara St., South Yarmouth, MA 02664 t) 508-394-0709 (CRP); 508-398-2248 stpiusxreled@comcast.net; stpiusxoffice@comcast.net stpiusxsy.com Rev. John Kelleher, Pst.; Rev. James R. Mattaliano, S.J., Par. Vicar; Dcn. Thomas Bailey; Dcn. C. Michael Hickey; Dcn. Anthony R. Surozenski; Dcn. Richard C. Zeich; CRP Stds.: 120

Our Lady of the Highway - Rte. 28, South Yarmouth, MA 02664 t) (508) 398-2248 Rev. John P. Kelleher, O.S.B., Pst.;

St. Pius Tenth School - (Grades PreK-8) 321 Wood Rd., South Yarmouth, MA 02664 t) 508-398-6112 info@spxschool.org www.spxschool.org Anne Dailey, Prin.;

SWANSEA

St. Dominic's - 1277 Grand Army Hwy., Swansea, MA 02777; Mailing: P.O. Box 205, Swansea, MA 02777 t) 508-675-7206 saintdominicparish@comcast.net www.stdominicswansea.org Rev. Thomas E. Costa, Pst.; Dcn. Gary M. John; Barbara Domingue, Dir., Faith Formation; Debra Fontaine, Faith Formation; Joy Viveiros, Confirmation Coord.;

Saint Francis of Assisi - 270 Ocean Grove Ave., Swansea, MA 02777 t) 508-674-0024 (CRP); 508-673-2808 stfrancisswansea@comcast.net www.stfrancisswansea.com Rev. Thomas Edward Costa Jr., Pst.; Dcn. Gary M. John; Barbara Domingue, Dir., Faith Formation; Debra Fontaine, Faith Formation; Joy Viveiros, Confirmation Coord.; CRP Stds.: 179

St. Louis de France - 56 Buffington St., Swansea, MA 02777; Mailing: 386 Luther Ave., Somerset, MA 02726 t) 508-673-7831 sldfo@comcast.net olopsomerset.org Merged with St. Patrick's, Somerset and St. Thomas More, Somerset to form Our Lady of Peace, Somerset, January 1, 2023. Rev. David A. Costa, Pst.; Sr. Kathleen Corrigan, S.U.S.C., Pst. Assoc.; Dcn. Robert M. Craig; Anne Cabral, DRE;

TAUNTON

Saint Andrew the Apostle Parish - 19 Kilmer Ave., Taunton, MA 02780 t) 508-824-5577 standrewtaunton@comcast.net www.cstaunton.org Rev. Edward A. Murphy, Pst.; Sally Medeiros, DRE; Joseph Sollecito, DRE; CRP Stds.: 121

Annunciation of the Lord - 31 First St., Taunton, MA 02780; Mailing: 282 Somerset Ave., Taunton, MA 02780 t) 508-823-2521 aoltaunton@gmail.com www.annunciationtaunton.com Rev. David C. Deston Jr., Admin.; Rev. Daniel Nunes, Par. Vicar; CRP Stds.: 191

St. Anthony's - 126 School St., Taunton, MA 02780 t) 508-824-6241 (CRP); 508-824-3330 office@sataunton.org cntaunton.org Rev. Fred Babiczuk, Pst.; Dcn. Jose H. Medina; Dcn. Philip E. Bedard; Dcn. Joseph P. Medeiros; CRP Stds.: 250

St. Jude the Apostle Parish - 249 Whittenton St., Taunton, MA 02780 t) 508-824-3333; 508-824-4545 (CRP) office@cntaunton.org cntaunton.com Rev. Fred Babiczuk, Pst.; Dcn. Philip E. Bedard; Dcn. Joseph P. Medeiros; Elizabeth Hoye, DRE;

Chapel of Our Lady of the Holy Rosary - 80 Bay St., Taunton, MA 02780 t) (508) 824-3333

St. Mary's - 14 St. Mary's Square, Taunton, MA 02780 t) 508-822-3048 (CRP); 508-824-3330 smcctaunton@gmail.com www.cntaunton.org Rev. Freddie Babiczuk, Pst.; Dcn. Philip E. Bedard; Dcn. Joseph P. Medeiros; Dcn. Jose H. Medina;

WAREHAM

St. Patrick's - 82 High St., Wareham, MA 02571-0271 t) 508-295-2411 info@stpatrickswareham.org www.stpatrickswareham.org Rev. Antonio da Silva, S.D.V., Pst.; Rev. Patrick Nwachukwu, Par. Vicar; Dcn. David C. Murphy, DRE; CRP Stds.: 180

St. Anthony - Gault Rd., W. Wareham, MA 02576; Mailing: 82 High St., Wareham, MA 02571 t) (508) 295-2411 stpatrickswareham.org

WELLFLEET

Our Lady of Lourdes - 2282 Rt. 6, Wellfleet, MA 02667-1414; Mailing: P.O. Box 1414, Wellfleet, MA 02667-1414 t) 508-349-2222 (CRP); 508-487-0095 olol2282@comcast.net Rev. Philip N. Hamel, Pst.; CRP Stds.: 6

WEST HARWICH

Holy Trinity - 246 Main St. (Rte. 28), West Harwich, MA 02671; Mailing: P. O. Box 428, West Harwich, MA 02671 t) 508-432-4000; 508-432-2898 (CRP) htchurch@comcast.net; holytrinityreled@comcast.net holytrinitycapecod.org Rev. Marc P. Tremblay, Pst.; Dcn. Ralph F. Cox; Dcn. Christian Devos; Dcn. John W. Foley; Barbara-Anne Foley, DRE; Mary Wall, DRE; CRP Stds.: 56

WESTPORT

St. George's - 12 Highland Ave., Westport, MA 02790 t) 508-636-2941 (CRP); 774-319-5579 office@stgeorgecatholics.org www.stgeorgecatholics.org Rev. Paul Bernier, Pst.; Rev. Peter R. Scheffer Jr., Pst.; Joy Viveiros, DRE; CRP Stds.: 71

St. John the Baptist - 945 Main Rd., Westport, MA 02790; Mailing: Box 3328, Westport, MA 02790 t) 508-636-2251 stjb@sprintout.net www.stjohnthebaptistwestport.org Rev. Peter Scheffer, Pst.; Rev. Paul Bernier, Pst.; CRP Stds.: 125

Our Lady of Grace - 569 Sanford Rd., Westport, MA 02790 t) 508-675-5857 (CRP); 508-674-6271 ologwestportma@aol.com ologwestport.com Rev. Peter R. Scheffer Jr., Pst.; Dcn. Timothy E. Flaherty; Jane Callahan, DRE; CRP Stds.: 105

SCHOOLS: PRESCHOOL THRU HIGH SCHOOL

HIGH SCHOOLS

COMMONWEALTH OF MASSACHUSETTS

ATTLEBORO

Bishop Feehan High School - (DIO) (Grades 9-12) 70 Holcott Dr., Attleboro, MA 02703 t) 508-226-6223 webmaster@bfhs.dfrcs.org; lcayer@bishopfeehan.com www.bishopfeehan.com Sean Kane, Prin.; Timothy B. Sullivan, Pres.;

FALL RIVER

Bishop Connolly High School - (DIO) 373 Elsbree St., Fall River, MA 02720 t) 508-676-1071 kstlaurent@bchs.dfrcs.org www.bishopconnolly.com Kathleen St. Laurent, Pres.; Stds.: 150; Lay Tchrs.: 17

HYANNIS

St. John Paul II School - (Grades 5-12) 120 High School Rd., Hyannis, MA 02601 t) 508-862-6336 mvalentino@jpiihyannis.org; bkelley@jpiihyannis.org www.jpiihyannis.org Elizabeth Kelley, Prin.; Mona Lisa Valentino, Prin.;

NORTH DARTMOUTH

Bishop Stang High School - (DIO) 500 Slocum Rd., North Dartmouth, MA 02747-2999 t) 508-996-5602 office@bishopstang.org www.bishopstang.org James Benson, Pres.;

INSTITUTIONS LOCATED IN DIOCESE

CATHOLIC CHARITIES [CCH]

FALL RIVER

Campaign For Human Development Apostolate - 1600 Bay St., Fall River, MA 02724; Mailing: P.O. Box M, S. Sta., Fall River, MA 02724 t) 508-674-4681 smazzarella@cssdioc.org; dberg@cssdioc.org Susan Mazzarella, CEO;

Catholic Social Services of Fall River - 1600 Bay St., Fall River, MA 02724 t) 508-674-4681 smazzarella@cssdioc.org Pamela Benoit, Admin.; Susan Mazzarella, CEO; Happiness Nosike-Unaka, Vice. Pres.; Rui Rosa, Vice. Pres.; Asstd. Annu.: 30,000; Staff: 145

Catholic Social Services of Cape Cod - 261 South St., Hyannis, MA 02601 t) 508-771-6771

Catholic Social Services of New Bedford - 238 Bonney St., New Bedford, MA 02744 t) 508-997-7337

St. Dominic's Apartments, Inc. - 818 Middle St., Fall River, MA 02721; Mailing: 72 Eighth St., New Bedford, MA 02740 t) 508-916-2434 eabdow@cafbh.org; nlawson@cafbh.org Arlene A. McNamee, CEO;

CEMETERIES [CEM]

ATTLEBORO

St. John -

St. Stephen -

ATTLEBORO FALLS

St. Mary - Towne St., Attleboro Falls, MA 02763; Mailing: 14 Park St., North Attleboro, MA 02760 t) 508-695-1173 stmaryna@noozi.com Rev. David A. Costa, Pst.;

EAST FALMOUTH

St. Anthony -

FALL RIVER

St. John -

St. Mary -

New Bedford Catholic Cemeteries - 1540 Stafford Rd., Fall River, MA 02721 t) 508-998-1195 cemetery2@verizon.net

Notre Dame -

St. Patrick -

HYANNIS

St. Francis -

MATTAPOISETT

St. Anthony -

NANTUCKET

St. Mary -

NEW BEDFORD

St. John -

St. Mary -

Sacred Heart -

NORTH ATTLEBORO

St. Mary -

NORTH EASTON

Immaculate Conception - t) (508) 238-3232 Very Rev. Neil Wack, C.S.C., Par. Admin.;

OAK BLUFFS
Sacred Heart -
PROVINCETOWN
St. Peter - 11 Prince St., Provincetown, MA 02657 t) (508) 487-0095 Rev. Philip N. Hamel, Pst.;
SANDWICH
St. Peter -
SOMERSET
St. Patrick - t) (508) 673-7831 Rev. David A. Costa, Pst.;
TAUNTON
St. Francis -
St. James -
St. Joseph -
St. Mary -
TRURO
Sacred Heart -
WAREHAM
St. Patrick -
WELLFLEET
Our Lady of Lourdes - 2282 Rt. 6, Wellfleet, MA 02667 t) (508) 349-2222 Rev. Philip N. Hamel, Pst.;
WEST HARWICH
Holy Trinity -

COLLEGES & UNIVERSITIES [COL]

NORTH EASTON
Holy Cross Fathers Religious - 480 Washington St., North Easton, MA 02356 t) 508-230-8828 nwack@holycrossusa.org holycrossusa.org Very Rev. Neil Wack, C.S.C., Supr.; Rev. Timothy Mouton, C.S.C., Asst. Supr.; Rev. Jeffrey L. Allison, C.S.C., In Res.; Rev. Adam David Patrick Booth, CSC, In Res.; Rev. James W. Chichetto, C.S.C., In Res.; Rev. John F. Denning, C.S.C., In Res.; Rev. James J. Doherty, C.S.C, In Res.; Rev. Marc F. Fallon, C.S.C., In Res.; Rev. Thomas P. Gariepy, C.S.C., In Res.; Rev. Fred Jenga, CSC, In Res.; Rev. Boby John, CSC (India), In Res.; Rev. William H. Kelley, C.S.C., In Res.; Rev. Pinto Paul, C.S.C., In Res.; Rev. George Piggford, C.S.C., In Res.; Rev. Leo Polselli, C.S.C., In Res.; Rev. Wilfred J. Raymond, C.S.C., In Res.; Rev. Robert E Roetzel, CSC, In Res.; Rev. Kevin P. Spicer, C.S.C., In Res.; Rev. Anthony V. Szakaly, C.S.C., In Res.; Bro. James A. Walters, CSC, In Res.; Rev. Stephen S. Wilbricht, C.S.C., In Res.; Stds.: 2,500; Pr. Tchrs.: 7
Stonehill College - 320 Washington St., North Easton, MA 02356 t) 508-565-1301 president@stonehill.edu www.stonehill.edu Rev. James W. Chichetto, C.S.C.; Rev. Thomas P. Gariepy, C.S.C.; Rev. Richard E. Gribble, C.S.C.; Rev. George Piggford, C.S.C.; Rev. Kevin P. Spicer, C.S.C.; Rev. Stephen S. Wilbricht, C.S.C.; Rev. Jeffrey L. Allison, C.S.C., Registrar; Rev. Anthony V. Szakaly, C.S.C., Supr.; Rev. John F. Denning, C.S.C., Pres.;

CONVENTS, MONASTERIES, AND RESIDENCES FOR WOMEN [CON]

DARTMOUTH
Dominican Sisters of Hope - 51 Middle St., Dartmouth, MA 02748 t) 508-996-1305 mtacy@umassd.edu www.ophope.org
DIGHTON
Dominican Sisters of Charity of the Presentation of the Blessed Virgin - 3012 Elm St., Dighton, MA 02715 t) 508-669-5425; 508-669-5023 (Novitiate) domsrs@presentation-op-usa.org www.presentation-op-usa-.org Provincial House-Residence, Residence for Aged Sisters, Novitiate. Sr. Marta Ines Vimala Toro, OP, Supr.;
FAIRHAVEN
Sisters of the Sacred Hearts, Community Headquarters - 35 Huttleston Ave., Fairhaven, MA 02719-3154 t) 508-994-9341 cbouchard@sscc.org Sisters of the Sacred Hearts of Jesus and Mary and of Perpetual Adoration, SS.CC. Sr. Claire Bouchard, SS.CC., Supr.; Srs.: 3
TAUNTON
Villa Fatima - 90 County St., Taunton, MA 02780 t) 508-822-6282 roe23roe@aol.com www.sistersofsaintdorothy.org Sisters of St. Dorothy.

ENDOWMENTS / FOUNDATIONS / TRUSTS [EFT]

FALL RIVER
Foundation to Advance Catholic Education, Inc. - 450 Highland Ave., Fall River, MA 02720; Mailing: P.O. Box 2577, Fall River, MA 02722 t) 508-675-1311 sduxbury@dioc-fr.org www.face-dfr.org Sandi Duxbury, Exec. Dir.;

MISCELLANEOUS [MIS]

FAIRHAVEN
Congregation of the Sacred Hearts - United States Province (Sacred Hearts Fathers; Sacred Hearts Missions) - 73 Adams St., Fairhaven, MA 02719; Mailing: P.O. Box 111, Fairhaven, MA 02719 t) 508-993-2442 usprovincial21@gmail.com www.sscc-usa.org Rev. Lane K. Akiona, Prov.; Rev. Robert Charlton, SS.CC., Vicar; Rev. Richard J. Danyluk, SS.CC., Dir.; Rev. Edward Popish, SS.CC., Dir.; Rev. Stephen Banjare, SS.CC., Dir.; Rev. David Lupo, SS.CC.; Rev. Jeremy Sabugo, SS.CC.;
Damien Residence Retirement Home - t) 508-996-0500 Rev. Kevin (Columban) Crotty, SS.CC., Dir.; Bro. Paul R. Alves, SS.CC., In Res.; Rev. Martin T. Gomes, SS.CC., In Res.; Rev. Michael Kelly, SS.CC., In Res.; Rev. Michael Shanahan, SS.CC., In Res.; Rev. Matthias Shanley, SS.CC., In Res.; Rev. Desmond (Fintan) Sheeran, SS.CC., In Res.; Rev. James E. McDonough, SS.CC., In Res.;
National Center of the Enthronement - 77 Adams St., Fairhaven, MA 02719; Mailing: P.O. Box 111, Fairhaven, MA 02719 t) 508-999-2680 necenter@juno.com Sr. Claire Bouchard, SS.CC., Dir.; Rev. Kevin (Columban) Crotty, SS.CC., Dir.;
FALL RIVER
Assisi Housing Corporation - 1600 Bay St., Fall River, MA 02724; Mailing: 72 Eighth St., New Bedford, MA 02740 t) 508-997-0130 nlawson@cafbh.org Arlene A. McNamee, CEO;
Diocesan Facilities Self-Insurance Group, Inc. - 450 Highland Ave., Fall River, MA 02720; Mailing: P.O. Box 1110, Fall River, MA 02722 t) 508-675-1311 shaunk@dioc-fr.org Rev. John M. Murray;
NEW BEDFORD
Community Action for Better Housing, Inc. - 72 Eighth St., New Bedford, MA 02740 t) 508-997-0130 amcnamee@cafbh.org
The Institute of the Incarnate Word, Inc. - 1359 Acuschnet Ave., New Bedford, MA 02746 t) 508-993-1691 octaviocortez@ive.org www.saintanthonynewbedford.com Rev. Octavio Cortez, I.V.E.;
Missionaries of Charity - 556 County St., New Bedford, MA 02740 t) 508-997-7347 srpaulina.hurtado@yahoo.com Shelter for homeless women. Sr. Benedict Ann, Supr.;
Oscar Romero House, Inc. - 8 Allen St., New Bedford, MA 02740; Mailing: 72 Eighth St., New Bedford, MA 02740 t) 774-202-6971; 508-997-0130 sfyock@cafbh.org; nlawson@cafbh.org Arlene A. McNamee, CEO;
NORTH EASTON
Holy Cross Family Ministries - 518 Washington St., North Easton, MA 02356-1200 t) 508-238-4095 swallace@hcfm.org; amcmenamy@hcfm.org www.hcfm.org Corporate Name: The Family Rosary, Inc., Sponsored by Congregation of Holy Cross (U.S. Province). Rev. Wilfred Raymond, C.S.C., Pres.; Elizabeth Ponce, Exec.; Cynthia Slattery, Exec.; Susan Wallace, Exec.; Rev. David Guffey, C.S.C., Dir.; Rev. Pinto Paul, C.S.C., Dir.;

MONASTERIES AND RESIDENCES FOR PRIESTS AND BROTHERS [MON]

ATTLEBORO
La Salette Missionary Association (Missionaries of La Salette (MA), Inc.) - 947 Park St., Attleboro, MA 02703; Mailing: P.O. Box 2965, Attleboro, MA 02703 t) 508-222-0027 lsmajp@aol.com www.lasalettemissionary.org Rev. Rene J. Butler, M.S., Prov.; Rev. Bernard B. Baris, M.S., Dir.;
La Salette Shrine & Retreat Center - 947 Park St., Attleboro, MA 02703 t) 508-222-5410 lasaletteshrinesecretary@gmail.com www.lasalette-shrine.org Rev. Flavio Gillio, M.S., Contact; Rev. Brian Schloth, M.S., Supr.; Rev. Edward J. Brown, M.S., Dir., La Salette Retreat Center; Rev. Bernard B. Baris, M.S., Dir., La Salette Mission Assoc.; Bro. Paul Boucher, M.S., In Res.; Bro. Lucien Brodeur, M.S., In Res.; Bro. Anthony Casso, In Res.; Rev. Ernest Corriveau, In Res.; Rev. Messias de Nazaret Malanga, In Res.; Rev. Ronald G. Gagne, M.S., In Res.; Bro. Roger Moreau, M.S., In Res.; Rev. John R. Nuelle, M.S., In Res.; Rev. Andre A. Patenaude, M.S., In Res.; Bro. Carlos Ruiz, In Res.; Rev. Rosanno Soriano, In Res.; Bro. Ronald Taylor, M.S., In Res.; Rev. Raymond Vaillancourt, M.S., In Res.; Bro. Donald Wininski, M.S., In Res.; Brs.: 7; Priests: 11
FALL RIVER
Cardinal Medeiros Residence-Retirement Facility for Priests - 375 Elsbree St., Fall River, MA 02720-7211 t) 508-675-1050 lisab@dhfo.org; ejfitzgerald@dhfo.org Lisa Breton, Admin.;
Priests' Hostel - 2402 Highland Ave., Fall River, MA 02720 t) 508-672-1632 ejfitzgerald@dhfo.org Joanne M. Roque, CEO;
NEW BEDFORD
Marian Friary of Our Lady, Queen of the Seraphic Order - 600 Pleasant St., New Bedford, MA 02740-6299 t) 508-996-8274 ffi@marymediatrix.com; fr.maximilian@gmx.com www.marymediatrix.com Rev. Joseph McShane; Friar John M. Risse, F.I.; Friar Cyprian Costello, Supr.; Rev. Alan Bernardine Wharton, F.I.; Rev. Maximilian M. Warnisher, F.I., Secy.; Rev. Andre M. Feain, FI, Priest; Rev. Joachim Mudd, Vicar; Brs.: 2; Priests: 5

NURSING / REHABILITATION / CONVALESCENCE / ELDERLY CARE [NUR]

FAIRHAVEN
Our Lady's Haven of Fairhaven Inc. - 71 Center St., Fairhaven, MA 02719 t) 508-999-4561 madasilva@dhfo.org www.dhfo.org Rev. James E. McDonough, SS.CC., Chap.; Lisa Cadime, Admin.;
FALL RIVER
Catholic Memorial Home Inc. - 2446 Highland Ave., Fall River, MA 02720-4599 t) 508-679-0011 thealy@dhfo.org Rev. Michael J. O'Hearn; Thomas F. Healy, Supr.;
NEW BEDFORD
Sacred Heart Home - 359 Summer St., New Bedford, MA 02740 t) 508-996-6751 jdavis@dhfo.org www.dhfo.org Rev. Alphonsus McHugh, SS.CC., Chap.; Jennifer Davis, Admin.;
NORTH ATTLEBORO
Madonna Manor Inc. - 85 N. Washington St., North Attleboro, MA 02760 t) 508-699-2740 mmurpy@dhfo.org www.dhfo.org Mary-Ellen Murphy, Admin.; Halina Malec, Dir.;
TAUNTON
Bethany House Adult Day Care - 72 Church Green, Taunton, MA 02780 t) 508-822-9200 pworcester@dhfo.org Jessica L. Costa, Admin.;
Marian Manor Inc. - 33 Summer St., Taunton, MA 02780 t) 508-822-4885 jcosta@dhfo.org Rev. Bernard Vanasse, Chap.; Jessica L. Costa, Admin.;

RETREAT HOUSES / RENEWAL CENTERS [RTR]

ATTLEBORO
La Salette Retreat and Conference Center - 947 Park St., Attleboro, MA 02703-0965 t) 508-222-8530; 508-222-5410 office@lasaletteretreatcenter.com; lasaletteshrinedirector@gmail.com www.lasaletteretreatcenter.com Rev. Edward J. Brown, M.S., Dir.; Bro. Donald Wininski, M.S.;

EAST FREETOWN

Cathedral Camp Retreat Center - 167 Middleboro Rd., East Freetown, MA 02717-0428; Mailing: P.O. Box 428, East Freetown, MA 02717-0428 t) 508-763-8874

NORTH EASTON

Holy Cross Retreat House - 490 Washington St., North Easton, MA 02356-1294 t) 508-238-2051 holycrossretreathouse@gmail.com www.retreathouse.org Nancy Smith, Dir.; Theresa Orcutt, Assoc. Dir.; Dcn. Daniel F. Sullivan, Assoc. Dir.; Rev. James J. Doherty, C.S.C, Spiritual Dir.;

SPECIAL CARE FACILITIES [SPF]

FALL RIVER

Saint Vincent's Services, Inc. - 2425 Highland Ave., Fall River, MA 02720 t) 508-679-8511 www.saintvincentsservices.org Residential and Community-Based/Outpatient Behavioral Health services provided for children, adolescents and families. Kristen Dutra, CEO;

HYANNIS

St. Clare's Residence for Women - 949 Pitcher's Way, Hyannis, MA 02601 t) 508-775-5096 Elaine Haley, Contact;

An asterisk (*) denotes an organization that has established tax-exempt status directly with the IRS and is not covered by the USCCB Group Ruling.

Diocese of Fargo

(Dioecesis Fargensis)

MOST REVEREND JOHN T. FOLDA

Bishop of Fargo; ordained May 27, 1989; appointed Bishop of Fargo April 8, 2013; ordained June 19, 2013. Chancery Office: 5201 Bishops Blvd., S., Ste. A, Fargo, ND 58104-7605.

Chancery Office: 5201 Bishops Blvd., S., Ste. A, Fargo, ND 58104-7605. T: 701-356-7900; F: 701-356-7999.
www.fargodiocese.org
news@fargodiocese.org

Square Miles 35,351.

Corporate Title: The Diocese of Fargo. Formerly Diocese of Jamestown.

Established November 12, 1889; Transferred to Fargo, April 6, 1897.

Comprises the Counties of Barnes, Benson, Bottineau east of U.S. Highway 83 and State Highway 256, Cass, Cavalier, Dickey, Eddy, Foster, Grand Forks, Griggs, Kidder, LaMoure, Logan, McHenry, McIntosh, Nelson, Pembina, Pierce, Ramsey, Ransom, Richland, Rolette, Sargent, Sheridan, Steele, Stutsman, Towner, Traill, Walsh and Wells in the State of North Dakota.

For legal titles of parishes and diocesan institutions, consult the Chancery Office.

STATISTICAL OVERVIEW

Personnel

Bishop	1
Priests: Diocesan Active in Diocese	81
Priests: Diocesan Active Outside Diocese	3
Priests: Retired, Sick or Absent	31
Number of Diocesan Priests	115
Religious Priests in Diocese	7
Total Priests in your Diocese	122
Extern Priests in Diocese	3
Ordinations:	
Diocesan Priests	2
Permanent Deacons in Diocese	47
Total Sisters	63

Parishes

Parishes	129
With Resident Pastor:	
Resident Diocesan Priests	63
Resident Religious Priests	3
Without Resident Pastor:	
Administered by Priests	63
Professional Ministry Personnel:	
Sisters	11
Lay Ministers	43

Welfare

Catholic Hospitals	8
Total Assisted	135,804
Homes for the Aged	12
Total Assisted	1,758
Specialized Homes	1
Total Assisted	70
Special Centers for Social Services	3
Total Assisted	16,200
Residential Care of Disabled	1
Total Assisted	250

Educational

Diocesan Students in Other Seminaries	15
Total Seminarians	15
Colleges and Universities	1
Total Students	250
High Schools, Diocesan and Parish	1
Total Students	312
Elementary Schools, Diocesan and Parish	12
Total Students	1,806
Catechesis / Religious Education:	
High School Students	1,172
Elementary Students	4,141
Total Students under Catholic Instruction	7,696
Teachers in Diocese:	
Priests	4
Lay Teachers	258

Vital Statistics

Receptions into the Church:	
Infant Baptism Totals	734
Minor Baptism Totals	47
Adult Baptism Totals	31
Received into Full Communion	106
First Communions	842
Confirmations	876
Marriages:	
Catholic	153
Interfaith	83
Total Marriages	236
Deaths	909
Total Catholic Population	73,697
Total Population	427,525

LEADERSHIP

Chancery Office - t) 701-356-7900
Moderator of the Curia - Rev. Msgr. Joseph P. Goering;
Vicar General - Rev. Msgr. Joseph P. Goering;
Chancellor - Timothy Olson;
Vicar for Clergy - Rev. Msgr. Joseph P. Goering;
Vice Chancellor - Rev. Jayson Miller;
Archivist - Timothy Olson;
Chief Financial Officer - Scott A. Hoselton;
Diocesan Tribunal - t) 701-356-7940
Judicial Vicar - Rev. James Goodwin;
Promotor Justitiae - Rev. Daniel Good;
Defensor Vinculi - Jay Cozemius; Rev. Msgr. Daniel J. Pilon; Raphael Frackiewicz;
Judges - Rev. Jared Kadlec; Rev. James Goodwin; Rev. Jason Asselin;
Auditor - Timothy Olson;
Ecclesiastical Notaries - Timothy Olson, Chancellor; Rev. Msgr. Gregory J. Schlesselmann; Scott A. Hoselton;
Deans - Rev. H. Gerard Braun; Rev. Paul C. Duchschere; Rev. Wenceslaus Katanga;

OFFICES AND DIRECTORS

Corporate Board - Rev. Msgr. Joseph P. Goering; Timothy Olson; Mike St. Onge;
Apostleship of Prayer - Rev. Chad F. Wilhelm, Dir.;
Arbitration & Conciliation Board - Rev. Msgr. Joseph P. Goering; Barb Augdahl;
Catechesis - Mary Hanbury;
Catholic Cemeteries - Scott A. Hoselton;
Catholic Church Deposit & Loan Fund of Eastern North Dakota - Most Rev. John Folda; Rev. Msgr. Joseph P. Goering; Timothy Olson;
Catholic Education and Formation - Rev. Andrew Jasinski, Diocesan D.R.E.;
Catholic Schools - Michael Hagstrom;
Censor Librorum - Timothy Olson;
Communications - Paul Braun;
Continuing Education of Priests - Rev. Kurtis Gunwall;
Diocesan Finance Council - Rev. Msgr. Joseph P. Goering; Timothy Olson; Richard Schlosser;
Director of Stewardship and Development - Steven Schons, Dir.;
Ecumenical Commission (Vacant) -
Evangelization - t) (701) 356-7908 Steve Splonskowski, Dir. (steve.splonskowski@fargodiocese.org);
Healthcare Director - Rev. Dale H. Kinzler, Dir.; Rev. Ross Laframboise;
Hispanic Ministry - Rev. Timothy Schroeder;
Holy Childhood Association - Timothy Olson;
Liaison with Charismatic Movement - Rev. Neil J. Pfeifer;
Liturgy Office - Rev. Jayson Miller;
Marriage & Family Life - Brad Gray; Jennie Korsmo;
The "New Earth" (Diocesan Magazine) - Paul Braun;
North Dakota Catholic Conference - Christopher Dodson;
Pension Plan - Scott A. Hoselton;
Permanent Diaconate - Rev. Msgr. Gregory J. Schlesselmann, Dir.; Rev. Kyle P. Metzger, Sec. Diaconate;
Prison Apostolate - Rev. Paul R. Schuster;
Propagation of the Faith - Timothy Olson;
Respect Life Office - Tim Mosser;
Rural Life - t) 701-465-3780 Rev. Thomas Graner, Dir.;
Technology/Computer Office - Loren Loh;
Vocation Director - Rev. Kyle P. Metzger, Dir.; Rev. Jayson Miller, Assoc. Dir.;
Youth/Young Adults - Brady Borslien;

PARISHES, MISSIONS, AND CLERGY

STATE OF NORTH DAKOTA

ALCIDE

St. Anthony Church of Alcide - 5 miles west on Hwy. #5, Alcide, ND 58316; Mailing: P.O. Box 2000, Belcourt, ND 58316 t) 701-477-5601 sasecretary@utma.com Served from St. Ann, Belcourt. Rev. Michael Slovak, SOLT, Pst.;

ANAMOOSE

St. Francis Xavier Church of Anamoose - 605 1st St. W., Anamoose, ND 58710; Mailing: PO Box 49, Anamoose, ND 58710-0049 t) 701-465-3780 stfx@gondtc.com www.stfxnd.org Also serving Drake & McClusky. Rev. Thomas Graner, Pst.; CRP Stds.: 7

ANETA

Sacred Heart Church of Aneta - 307 1st St. N., Aneta, ND 58212; Mailing: P.O. Box 217, Cooperstown, ND 58425 t) 701-797-2624 stgeorge@mlgc.com Served from Cooperstown. Rev. Dale H. Kinzler, Pst.; CRP Stds.: 2

ARGUSVILLE

St. William's Church of Argusville - 107 Drake Ave., Argusville, ND 58005 t) 701-484-5211 stwilliamscc@live.com www.stwilliamschurch.org/ Served from Hillsboro. Rev. Msgr. Dennis A. Skonseng, Pst.; CRP Stds.: 59

ASHLEY

St. David's Church of Ashley - 601 2nd Ave., N.E., Ashley, ND 58413; Mailing: P.O. Box 293, Wishek, ND 58495 t) 701-423-5494; 701-452-2970 (CRP) wenceslaus.katanga@fargodiocese.org Served from Wishek. Rev. Wenceslaus Katanga, Pst.; CRP Stds.: 8

BALTA

Our Lady of Mt. Carmel Church of Balta - 301 Main St. N., Balta, ND 58313; Mailing: 218 3rd St., S.E., Rugby, ND 58368 t) 701-776-6388 lfparish@gondtc.com Served from Rugby Rev. Franklin Miller, Pst.; Rev. John F. Aerts, Par. Vicar; CRP Stds.: 24

BELCOURT

St. Ann's Church of Belcourt - 1115 Louis Riel Dr., Belcourt, ND 58316; Mailing: P.O. Box 2000, Belcourt, ND 58316 t) 701-477-5601 sasecretary@utma.com stannsmission.org/ Also serving St. Anthony. Rev. Michael Slovak, SOLT, Pst.; Rev. Fred Alexander, S.O.L.T., Par. Vicar; Rev. David Brokke, SOLT, Par. Vicar; Rev. Anthony Hession, Par. Vicar; CRP Stds.: 12

St. Ann - Indian Mission, Belcourt, ND 58316 t) 701-477-5601 Rev. Michael Slovak, SOLT, Pst.;

St. Anthony - Indian Mission, Belcourt, ND 58316; Mailing: P.O. Box 2000, Belcourt, ND 58316-2000 t) 701-477-5601 Served from St. Ann's Belcourt. Rev. Michael Slovak, SOLT, Pst.;

St. Benedict - 3821 BIA Rd. 6, Belcourt, ND 58316; Mailing: PO Box 170, St. John, ND 58369 t) 701-477-3081 Served from Saint John. Rev. Richard Fineo, Pst.;

St. Benedict's Church of Belcourt - 3821 Bureau of Indian Affairs Rd. #6, Belcourt, ND 58316; Mailing: PO Box 170, St. John, ND 58369-0170 t) 701-477-3081 saintjohnthebaptistnd@gmail.com Served from St. John. Rev. Richard Fineo, Pst.; CRP Stds.: 2

BISBEE

Holy Rosary Church of Bisbee - 304 3rd Ave. W., Bisbee, ND 58317 t) 701-246-3449 shrolette@fargodiocese.org Served from Rolette. Rev. Paulraj Thondappa, HGN, Pst.; CRP Stds.: 4

BOTTINEAU

St. Mark's Church of Bottineau - 322 Sinclair St., Bottineau, ND 58318-1024 t) 701-228-3164; 701-228-5164 (Rectory) stsmanda@utma.com www.stmark-standrew.org Also serving Westhope. Rev. Jared Kadlec, Pst.; CRP Stds.: 46

BUCHANAN

St. Margaret Church of Buchanan - 410 Main St., Buchanan, ND 58420; Mailing: 622 1st Ave. S., Jamestown, ND 58401 t) 701-252-0119; 701-252-0478 (CRP) basilica@stjamesbasilica.org; ffsecretary@stjamesbasilica.org Served from Jamestown. Rev. Neil J. Pfeifer, Pst.; Rev. Kevin Lorsung, Par. Vicar; Rev. Joseph Barrett, Par. Vicar; CRP Stds.: 7

BUFFALO

St. Thomas Church of Buffalo - 401 3rd St. N., Buffalo, ND 58011; Mailing: PO Box 340, Casselton, ND 58012 t) 701-347-4609 stleo@casselton.net Served from Casselton. Rev. James Ermer, Pst.; CRP Stds.: 31

CANDO

Sacred Heart Church of Cando - 304 3rd St., Cando, ND 58324; Mailing: PO Box 399, Cando, ND 58324 t) (701) 968-3462 Also serving Leeds. Rev. Daniel Musgrave, Pst.; CRP Stds.: 37

CARRINGTON

Sacred Heart Church of Carrington - 663 1st St. S., Carrington, ND 58421; Mailing: P.O. Box 420, Carrington, ND 58421 t) 701-652-2072 (CRP); 701-652-2519 sacredheart@daktel.com; sacredheartccd@outlook.com www.sacredheartcarrington.org Also serving Sykeston. Rev. Thomas E. Dodge Jr., Pst.; CRP Stds.: 86

CASSELTON

St. Leo's Church of Casselton - 211 Langer Ave. N., Casselton, ND 58012; Mailing: PO Box 340, Casselton, ND 58012 t) 701-347-4609 stleo@casselton.net Also serving Buffalo. Rev. James Ermer, Pst.; CRP Stds.: 181

CAVALIER

St. Brigid of Ireland Church of Cavalier - 107 W. 1st Ave. S., Cavalier, ND 58220; Mailing: P.O. Box 280, Cavalier, ND 58220 t) 701-265-8877 charles.lacroix@fargodiocese.org Also serving Crystal. Rev. Charles LaCroix, Pst.; CRP Stds.: 22

CAYUGA

Sts. Peter & Paul Church of Cayuga - 229 Franklin Ave. W., Cayuga, ND 58013; Mailing: 230 1st St., N.W., Lidgerwood, ND 58053 t) 701-538-4604 stboniface@rrt.net stboniface.net Served from Lidgerwood. Rev. Peter J. Anderl, Pst.; CRP Stds.: 2

COOPERSTOWN

St. George Church of Cooperstown - 804 Foster Ave., N.W., Cooperstown, ND 58425; Mailing: PO Box 217, Cooperstown, ND 58425-0217 t) 701-797-2624 stgeorge@mlgc.com www.stgeorgecooper.org Also serving Aneta, Jessie, Finley. Rev. Dale H. Kinzler, Pst.; Dcn. Wallace Dalman; CRP Stds.: 19

CRYSTAL

St. Patrick's Church of Crystal - 4th & Garfield, Crystal, ND 58222; Mailing: P.O. Box 280, Cavalier, ND 58220 t) 701-265-8877; 701-993-8434 (CRP) charles.lacroix@fargodiocese.org Served from Cavalier. Rev. Charles LaCroix, Pst.; CRP Stds.: 21

DAZEY

St. Mary's Church of Dazey - 1609 115 Ave., S.E., Dazey, ND 58429; Mailing: P.O. Box 9, Wimbledon, ND 58492 t) 701-435-2310 boniface@daktel.com; st.bonifacend@gmail.com Served from Wimbledon. Rev. Sean P. Mulligan, Pst.; CRP Stds.: 9

DEVILS LAKE

St. Joseph Church - 501 4th St., N.E., Devils Lake, ND 58301; Mailing: PO Box 898, Devils Lake, ND 58301 t) 701-662-7558; 701-662-5071 (CRP) stjosephchurch@gondtc.com; stjoesre@gmail.com www.stjosephdlnd.com Rev. Chad F. Wilhelm, Pst.; Rev. Joseph Littlefield, Par. Vicar; CRP Stds.: 130

St. Joseph's Church of Devils Lake School - (Grades PreK-8) 824 10th Ave., N.E., Devils Lake, ND 58301 t) 701-662-5016 michelle.clouse@stjosephschooldl.org www.stjoseph.k12.nd.us Michelle Clouse, Prin.; Stds.: 207; Pr. Tchrs.: 1; Lay Tchrs.: 11

DICKEY

Assumption Church of Dickey - 106 Main St., Dickey, ND 58458; Mailing: PO Box 217, LaMoure, ND 58458 t) 701-883-5987 holyrosery.church@gmail.com www.holyrosarylamoure.com Served from LaMoure. Rev. Gregory Haman, Pst.;

DRAKE

St. Margaret Mary Church of Drake - 605 Main St., Drake, ND 58736; Mailing: PO Box 197, Drake, ND 58736-0197 t) 701-465-3780 www.stfxnd.org Served by Anamoose. Rev. Thomas Graner, Pst.; CRP Stds.: 11

DRAYTON

St. Edward's Church of Drayton - 102 E. Wallace Ave., Drayton, ND 58225; Mailing: P.O. Box 215, Drayton, ND 58225 t) 701-454-6171; 701-771-7944 (CRP) stedward@polarcomm.com Rev. Robert Wapenski, Pst.; CRP Stds.: 6

DUNSEITH

St. Michael the Archangel Dunseith - 112 1st St., N.W., Dunseith, ND 58329; Mailing: P.O. Box 160, Dunseith, ND 58329 t) 701-244-5738 stmichaeldunseith@gmail.com stmichaeldunseith.com Rev. Michael Slovak, SOLT, Pst.; Rev. David Brokke, SOLT, Par. Vicar; CRP Stds.: 27

EDGELEY

Transfiguration Church of Edgeley - 205 Main St., Edgeley, ND 58433; Mailing: PO Box 347, Edgeley,, ND 58433 t) 701-493-2387 transholy@drtel.net Also serving Nortonville. Rev. Jake Miller, Pst.; CRP Stds.: 60

ELLENDALE

St. Helena's Church of Ellendale - 421 N. 2nd St., Ellendale, ND 58436; Mailing: PO Box 796, Ellendale, ND 58436 t) 701-349-3297 patrick.parks@fargodiocese.org Also serving Fullerton. Rev. Patrick Parks, Pst.; CRP Stds.: 38

ENDERLIN

St. Patrick's Church of Enderlin - 302 Bluff St., Enderlin, ND 58027 t) 701-437-2791 stpatrick@mlgc.com www.enderlinfingalsheldon.org Also serving Sheldon and Fingal. Rev. Scott Karnik, Admin.; CRP Stds.: 16

ESMOND

St. Boniface Church of Esmond - 108 Alta Ave. N., Esmond, ND 58332-3202; Mailing: 105 7th Ave. S., Fessenden, ND 58438 t) 701-547-3430 (Fessenden rectory); 701-249-8360 www.feesmacatholic.com Served by St. Augustine's, Fessenden. Formerly St. Agnes Church of Esmond Rev. Steven Wirth, Pst.;

FAIRMOUNT

St. Anthony's Church of Fairmount - 204 2nd St. N., Fairmount, ND 58030; Mailing: PO Box 292, Fairmount, ND 58030 t) 701-474-5518 saintphilip@fargodiocese.org Served from Hankinson. Rev. Msgr. Brian G. Donahue, Pst.;

FARGO

St. Mary's Cathedral of Fargo - 604 Broadway, Fargo, ND 58102; Mailing: 619 7th St. N., Fargo, ND 58102 t) 701-235-4289 cathedral@fargodiocese.org www.cathedralofstmary.com Catholic Cathedral located in downtown Fargo. Rev. Msgr. Joseph P. Goering, Rector; Rev. Riley Riley Durkin, Par. Vicar; Rev. Charles Fischer, In Res.; Dcn. Raymond Desjarlais; Dcn. George Loegering; CRP Stds.: 96

Sts. Anne & Joachim Church of Fargo - 5202 25th St. S., Fargo, ND 58104 t) 701-235-5757 stsaaj@stsaaj.org www.stsaaj.org Rev. Luke D. Meyer, Pst.; Rev. Robert Foertsch, Par. Vicar; Dcn. Patrick Breen; Dcn. Michael Dodge; Dcn. Ben Seitz; Rev. Kyle P. Metzger, In Res.; Rev. William Slattery, In Res.; CRP Stds.: 325

St. Anthony of Padua's Church of Fargo - 710 S. 10th St., Fargo, ND 58103 t) 701-237-6063 deidra@stanthonyfargo.org www.stanthonyfargo.org Rev. H. Gerard Braun, Pst.; Rev. Prabhakar Marneni, Par. Vicar; Dcn. Stuart Longtin; Dcn. Terrence O'Dell Fischer; CRP Stds.: 66

Holy Spirit Church of Fargo - 1420 7th St. N., Fargo, ND 58102 t) 701-232-5900 info@holyspiritfargo.com www.holyspiritfargo.com Rev. Ross Laframboise, Pst.; Rev. Msgr. Gregory J. Schlesselmann, In Res.; Rev. Robert Keller, Par. Vicar; Dcn. Paul Schneider; CRP Stds.: 135

Nativity Church of Fargo - 1825 11th St. S., Fargo, ND 58103 t) 701-232-2414 kathyb@nativitycatholicchurch.net; billg@nativitycatholicchurch.net nativitycatholicchurch.net Rev. William P. Gerlach, Pst.; Rev. Anthony Cruz, HGN, Par. Vicar; CRP Stds.: 77

St. Paul's Newman Church of Fargo - 1141 University Dr. N, Fargo, ND 58102 t) 701-235-0142 frcheney@bisoncatholic.org; re@bisoncatholic.org www.bisoncatholic.org/ Rev. James Cheney, Pst.; Rev. Msgr. Gregory J. Schlesselmann, Dir.; CRP Stds.: 21

FESSENDEN

St. Augustine's Church of Fessenden - 105 7th Ave. S., Fessenden, ND 58438-7404 t) 701-547-3430 www.feesmacatholic.com Also serving St. Boniface Church of Esmond and St. William Church of Maddock. Rev. Steven Wirth, Pst.; CRP Stds.: 10

FINGAL

Holy Trinity Church of Fingal - 419 1st Ave., Fingal, ND 58031; Mailing: 302 Bluff St., Enderlin, ND 58027 t) 701-437-2791 stpatrick@mlgc.com www.enderlinfingalsheldon.org Served by Enderlin. Rev. Scott Karnik, Admin.; CRP Stds.: 11

FINLEY

St. Olaf Church of Finley - 100 Taft St., Finley, ND 58230; Mailing: P.O. Box 217, Cooperstown, ND 58425 t) 701-797-2624 stgeorge@mlgc.com www.stgeorgecooper.org Served from Cooperstown. Rev. Dale H. Kinzler, Pst.; CRP Stds.: 8

FORMAN

St. Mary Church of Forman - 484 4th St., S.W., Forman, ND 58032 t) 701-724-3319 4steeples@drtel.net www.stmarysforman.org/ Served from Oakes. Rev. Timothy Schroeder, Pst.; CRP Stds.: 19

FORT TOTTEN

Christ the King Church of Tokio - 134 2nd St., Fort Totten, ND 58335; Mailing: P.O. Box 299, Fort Totten, ND 58335 t) 701-766-4314 Served from Fort Totten. Rev. Antony Samy, Pst.;

Seven Dolors Indian Mission - 213 Dakotah Rd, Fort Totten, ND 58335; Mailing: Box 299, Fort Totten, ND 58335 t) 701-766-4314 Also serving Crow Hill, Tokio. Rev. Antony Samy, Pst.;

Seven Dolors of Fort Totten - 213 Dakotah Rd., Fort Totten, ND 58335-0299; Mailing: P.O. Box 299, Fort Totten, ND 58335-0299 t) 701-766-4314 antony.samy@fargodiocese.org Also serving Crow Hill, Tokio. Rev. Antony Samy Michael, HGN, Pst.; Dcn. Anthony McDonald; CRP Stds.: 5

FULLERTON

St. Patrick Church of Fullerton - 207 Monroe St. N., Fullerton, ND 58441; Mailing: PO Box 796, Ellendale, ND 58436 t) 701-349-3297 patrick.parks@fargodiocese.org Served from Ellendale. Rev. Patrick Parks, Pst.; CRP Stds.: 10

GENESEO

St. Martin's Church of Geneseo - 413 Main St., Geneseo, ND 58053; Mailing: 230 1st St., N.W., c/o St. Boniface, Lidgerwood, ND 58053 t) 701-538-4604 stboniface@rrt.net stboniface.net Served from Lidgerwood. Rev. Peter J. Anderl, Pst.; CRP Stds.: 23

GRAFTON

St. John the Evangelist's Church of Grafton - 344 15th St. W., Grafton, ND 58237 t) 701-352-1648 mike@stjohnsgrafton.com; kathy@stjohnsgrafton.com stjohnsgrafton.com Also Serving Oakwood. Rev. Jeff Eppler, Pst.; Dcn. Michael Grzadzielewski; CRP Stds.: 150

St. Luke's Church of Veseleyville - 14207 63rd St., N.E., Grafton, ND 58237 t) 701-284-6165 stmarys@polarcomm.com www.saintsml.org Served from Park River. Rev. Bert Miller, Pst.; CRP Stds.: 3

Sacred Heart Church of Oakwood - 344 W. 15th St., Grafton, ND 58237-8860 t) 701-352-1648 kathy@stjohnsgrafton.com Served from Grafton. Rev. Jeff Eppler, Pst.;

GRAND FORKS

Holy Family Church of Grand Forks - 1018 18th Ave. S., Grand Forks, ND 58201-6828 t) 701-746-1454 elizabeth@holyfamilygf.org www.holyfamilygf.org Rev. James Meyer, Pst.; Rev. Petro Ndunguru, Par. Vicar; CRP Stds.: 129

Holy Family Church of Grand Forks School - (Grades PreK-5) 1001 17th Ave. S., Grand Forks, ND 58201-6828 t) 701-775-9886 kmayer@hfsmschool.org www.hfsmschool.org Katie Mayer, Prin.; Stds.: 113; Lay Tchrs.: 6

St. Mary Church of Grand Forks - 216 Belmont Rd., Grand Forks, ND 58201 t) 701-775-9318 stmarysgfnd@yahoo.com stmarysgfnd.com Rev. James Gross, Pst.; CRP Stds.: 82

St. Michael's Church of Grand Forks - 524 5th Ave. N., Grand Forks, ND 58203; Mailing: 418 N. 6th St., Grand Forks, ND 58203 t) 701-772-2624; 701-772-2282 (CRP) www.stmichaelschurchgf.com Rev. Raymond P. Courtright, Pst.; Rev. Jered Grossman, Par. Vicar; Rev. Msgr. Daniel J. Pilon, In Res.; CRP Stds.: 125

St. Michael's Church of Grand Forks School - (Grades PreK-5) 504 5th Ave. N., Grand Forks, ND 58203 t) 701-772-1822 sara.dudley@stmichaelsgf.com stmichaelsgf.com/school Sara Dudley, Prin.; Stds.: 189; Lay Tchrs.: 15

St. Thomas Aquinas Newman Center of Grand Forks - 410 Cambridge St., Grand Forks, ND 58203 t) (701) 402-3806 jessica.kuznia@undcatholic.org www.undcatholic.org Rev. Christopher J. Markman, Pst.;

HANKINSON

St. Philip's Church of Hankinson - 612 S. Main, Hankinson, ND 58041; Mailing: PO Box 419, Hankinson, ND 58041 t) 701-242-7327 saintphilip@fargodiocese.org Rev. Msgr. Brian G. Donahue, Pst.; CRP Stds.: 51

HARVEY

St. Cecilia's Church of Harvey - 413 E. Brewster St., Harvey, ND 58341 t) 701-324-2144; 701-721-7483 (CRP) stcecilia@gondtc.com; aziegler@gondtc.com stceciliaharvey.org Also serving Selz. Rev. Kevin Boucher, Pst.; Dcn. Jeffrey M. Faul; CRP Stds.: 58

HILLSBORO

St. Rose of Lima's Church of Hillsboro - 503 3rd St., S.E., Hillsboro, ND 58045-0459; Mailing: P.O. Box 459, Hillsboro, ND 58045 t) 701-636-4541; 701-636-5981 (CRP) dennis.skonseng@fargodiocese.org Also serves Argusville. Rev. Msgr. Dennis A. Skonseng, Pst.; CRP Stds.: 81

HOPE

St. Agatha's Church of Hope - 604 Steele Ave., Hope, ND 58046; Mailing: 606 5th St., c/o St. Bernard's Church of Oriska, Oriska, ND 58063 t) 701-845-3713 bernard@bektel.com www.stbernards-oriska.org/ Served from Oriska. Rev. Brian Bachmeier, Pst.; CRP Stds.: 12

HORACE

St. Benedict's Church of Wild Rice - 11743 38th St. S., Horace, ND 58047-9512 t) 701-588-4288 office@stbensnd.org www.stbensnd.org Rev. Andrew Jasinski, Pst.; CRP Stds.: 76

HUNTER

St. Agnes Church of Hunter - 102 1st St. E., Hunter, ND 58048; Mailing: 846 5th St., S.E., Mayville, ND 58257 t) 701-788-3234 olpstagnes@midco.net Served by Mayville. Rev. Robert F. Smith Jr., Pst.; CRP Stds.: 22

JAMESTOWN

St. James Basilica of Jamestown - 622 1st Ave. S., Jamestown, ND 58401-4648 t) 701-252-0119; 701-252-0478 (CRP) basilica@stjamesbasilica.org; ffsecretary@stjamesbasilica.org www.stjamesbasilica.org Also Serving Buchanan and Windsor. Rev. Neil J. Pfeifer, Pst.; Rev. Kevin Lorsung, Par. Vicar; Rev. Joseph Barrett, Par. Vicar; Dcn. Thomas Geffre; Dcn. Kirk Ripplinger; Dcn. Kenneth Votava; CRP Stds.: 97

St. John Academy - (Grades PreK-7) 215 5th St., S.E., Jamestown, ND 58401 t) 701-252-3397 jeff.trumbauer@k12.nd.us www.stjamesbasilica.org/stjohn Jeff Trumbauer, Prin.; Stds.: 117; Pr. Tchrs.: 2; Lay Tchrs.: 14

JESSIE

St. Lawrence Church of Jessie - 105 Dewey St., Jessie, ND 58452; Mailing: P.O. Box 217, Cooperstown, ND 58425 t) 701-797-2624 stgeorge@mlgc.com Served from Cooperstown. Rev. Dale H. Kinzler, Pst.; CRP Stds.: 20

KARLSRUHE

Sts. Peter & Paul Church of Karlsruhe - 401 Main St., Karlsruhe, ND 58744 t) 701-338-2663 velvakarls@srt.com stceciliavelvand.org Served from Velva. Rev. Matthew M Kraemer, Pst.; CRP Stds.: 21

KENSAL

St. John's Church of Kensal - 407 Pleasant Ave., Kensal, ND 58455; Mailing: PO Box 9, Wimbledon, ND 58492 t) 701-435-2310 boniface@daktel.com; st.bonifacend@gmail.com Served from Wimbledon. Rev. Sean P. Mulligan, Pst.; CRP Stds.: 3

KINDRED

St. Maurice Church of Kindred - 5313 165th Ave., S.E., Kindred, ND 58051; Mailing: PO Box 272, Kindred, ND 58051 t) 701-428-3094 stmaurice58051@gmail.com www.stmaurices.org Rev. James Goodwin, Pst.; Dcn. Clarence Vetter; CRP Stds.: 72

KNOX

St. Mary's Church of Knox - 129 Morgan St., Knox, ND 58343; Mailing: 218 3rd St., S.E., c/o St. Therese the Little Flower, Rugby, ND 58368-1814 t) 701-776-5327; 701-776-6388 lfparish@gondtc.com Served from Rugby. Rev. Franklin Miller, Pst.; Rev. John F. Aerts, Par. Vicar; CRP Stds.: 16

LA MOURE

Holy Rosary Church of La Moure - 209 1st St., S.E., La Moure, ND 58458; Mailing: PO Box 217, LaMoure, ND 58458 t) 701-883-5987 holyrosery.church@gmail.com www.holyrosarylamoure.org Also serving Dickey and Verona. Rev. Gregory Haman, Pst.; CRP Stds.: 59

LAKOTA

St. Mary's Church of Lakota - 109 East Ave. E., Lakota, ND 58344; Mailing: PO Box 509, Lakota, ND 58344 t) 701-247-2584 smcc@polarcomm.com Also serving Tolna and Michigan. Rev. Steven Meyer, Pst.; CRP Stds.: 19

LANGDON

St. Alphonsus Church of Langdon - 1010 3rd St., Langdon, ND 58249 t) 701-256-5966 saints@utma.com www.stalphonsuslangdon.com/ Also serving Nekoma and Wales. Rev. Kurtis L. Gunwall, Pst.; CRP Stds.: 60

St. Alphonsus Elementary - (Grades PreSchool-8) 209 10th Ave., Langdon, ND 58249 t) (701) 256-2354 stalphonsussaints.com Carrie Hope, Prin.; Stds.: 103; Lay Tchrs.: 8

LANKIN

St. Joseph's Church of Lankin - 506 4th Ave., Lankin, ND 58250; Mailing: PO Box 27, Pisek, ND 58273 t) 701-284-6060 stjohnne@polarcomm.com plb.org Served by Pisek. Rev. Jason Lefor, Pst.; CRP Stds.: 2

Sts. Peter & Paul Church of Bechyne - 11951 County Rd. 19, Lankin, ND 58250; Mailing: P.O. Box 27, Pisek, ND 58273 t) 701-284-6060 stjohnne@polarcomm.com plbnd.org Served from Pisek. Rev. Jason Lefor, Pst.; CRP Stds.: 18

LARIMORE

St. Stephen's Church of Larimore - 311 W. Front St., Larimore, ND 58251; Mailing: P.O. Box 778, Larimore, ND 58251 t) 701-343-2377 ststlarimore@msn.com larimoreststephens.weebly.com Rev. K. S. Kopacz, Pst.; CRP Stds.: 36

LEEDS

St. Vincent de Paul Church of Leeds - Central Ave., Leeds, ND 58346; Mailing: PO Box 399, Cando, ND 58324 t) (701) 968-3462 Served from Cando. Rev. Daniel Musgrave, Pst.; CRP Stds.: 2

LIDGERWOOD

St. Boniface Church of Lidgerwood - 230 1st St., N.W., Lidgerwood, ND 58053 t) 701-538-4604 stboniface@rrt.net; stbonifacedre@rrt.net www.stboniface.net Also serving Geneseo and Cayuga. Rev. Peter J. Anderl, Pst.; CRP Stds.: 50

LISBON

St. Aloysius Church of Lisbon - 701 Oak St., Lisbon, ND 58054 t) 701-683-4620 staloysius@drtel.net www.parishesonline.com Also serving Gwinner. Rev. Scott Sautner, Pst.; CRP Stds.: 68

St. Vincent's Church of Gwinner - 701 Oak St., Lisbon, ND 58054 t) 701-683-4620 staloysius@drtel.net Served from Lisbon. Rev. Scott Sautner, Pst.; CRP Stds.: 6

MADDOCK

St. William Church of Maddock - 204 Roosevelt Ave., Maddock, ND 58348; Mailing: 105 7th Ave. S., Fessenden, ND 58438 t) 701-547-3430 (Fessenden Rectory); 701-438-2668 www.feesmacatholic.com Served from St. Augustine's, Fessenden. Rev. Steven Wirth, Pst.; CRP Stds.: 13

MANTADOR

Sts. Peter & Paul Church of Mantador - 609 Cty. Rd. 25, Mantador, ND 58058; Mailing: PO Box 25, Mantador, ND 58058 t) 701-274-8259 mooretonmantadorcatholic@gmail.com mooretonmantadorcatholic.org Served from Mooreton. Rev. Michael Hickin, Pst.; CRP Stds.: 7

MANVEL

St. Timothy's Church of Manvel - 1207 Oldham Ave., Manvel, ND 58256-4335 t) 701-696-2219 sttimothys@invisimax.com www.stmanvel.org Rev. John Ejike, Pst.; CRP Stds.: 68

MAYVILLE

Our Lady of Peace Church of Mayville - 846 5th St., S.E., Mayville, ND 58257 t) 701-788-3234 olpstagnes@midco.net Also serving Hunter. Rev. Robert F. Smith Jr., Pst.; CRP Stds.: 63

MCCLUSKY

Holy Family Church of McClusky - 409 Ave. B E, McClusky, ND 58463; Mailing: PO Box 49, c/o St. Francis Xavier Catholic Church, Anamoose, ND 58710 t) 701-465-3780 www.stfxnd.org Served from Anamoose. Rev. Thomas Graner, Pst.; CRP Stds.: 2

MCHENRY

Sts. Peter & Paul Church of McHenry - 391 Conn St., McHenry, ND 58464; Mailing: 116 -1st Ave. N., New Rockford, ND 58356-1802 t) 701-947-5325 reese.weber@fargodiocese.org; stjohnsnr@outlook.com www.newrockford.com Served from New Rockford. Rev. Reese Weber, Pst.; CRP Stds.: 12

MEDINA

St. Mary's Church of Medina - 105 3rd Ave., S.E., Medina, ND 58467; Mailing: P.O. Box 87, 220 4th St., S.W., Steele, ND 58482 t) 701-475-2333 stfrancis@bektel.com steeletappenmedina.org Served from Steele. Rev. Peter Sharpe, Pst.; CRP Stds.: 9

MICHIGAN

St. Lawrence O'Toole's Church of Michigan - 214 Broadway N, Michigan, ND 58259; Mailing: PO Box 509, Lakota, ND 58344 t) 701-247-2584 steven.meyer@fargodiocese.org Served from Lakota. Rev. Steven Meyer, Pst.; CRP Stds.: 14

MILNOR

St. Arnold's Church of Milnor - 107 3rd St., Milnor, ND 58060 t) 701-427-9288 starnolds@drtel.net Served from Wyndmere. Rev. Troy K. Simonsen, Pst.; CRP Stds.: 27

MINTO

Sacred Heart Church of Minto - 621 3rd St., Minto, ND 58261; Mailing: PO Box 316, Minto, ND 58261-0316 t) 701-248-3589 sacredheartminto@hotmail.com www.sh-ss.org Also serving Warsaw. Rev. Brian Moen, Pst.; CRP Stds.: 58

MOORETON

St. Anthony's Church of Mooreton - 204 Mooreton Ave. N., Mooreton, ND 58061 t) 701-274-8259 mooretonmantadorcatholic@gmail.com mooretonmantadorcatholic.org Also serving Mantador. Rev. Michael Hickin, Pst.; CRP Stds.: 58

MUNICH

St. Mary Church of Munich - 607 Main, Munich, ND 58352; Mailing: PO Box 159, Munich, ND 58352 t) 701-682-5178 stmarys@utma.com Also serving Starkweather. Rev. Mathew V. Pamplaniyil, Pst.; CRP Stds.: 30

NAPOLEON

St. Philip's Church of Napoleon - 401 Broadway, Napoleon, ND 58561-7013 t) 701-754-2860 c) 701-321-2145 stphilipneri@bektel.com; allebek@bektel.com stphilipnerinapoleon.org Rev. John Fisher Kizito, Pst.; Dcn. Allen Baumgartner; Dcn. Gary Schumacher; CRP Stds.: 132

NECHE

Sts. Nereus & Achilleus Church of Neche - 6th St., Neche, ND 58265; Mailing: P.O. Box 228, Walhalla, ND 58282 t) 701-549-3256 boniface@utma.com Served from Walhalla. Rev. Jason Asselin, Pst.;

NEKOMA

St. Edward Church of Nekoma - 323 Main St., Nekoma, ND 58355; Mailing: 1010 3rd St., Langdon, ND 58249 t) 701-256-5966 saints@utma.com www.stalphonsuslangdon.com Served from Langdon. Rev. Kurtis L. Gunwall, Pst.; CRP Stds.: 3

NEW ROCKFORD

St. John's Church of New Rockford - 116 1st Ave. N., New Rockford, ND 58356 t) 701-947-5325 stjohnsnr@outlook.com www.cityofnewrockford.com Also serving McHenry. Rev. Reese Weber, Pst.; Dcn. Bart Salazar; CRP Stds.: 58

NORTONVILLE

Holy Spirit Church of Nortonville - 201 5th Ave, Nortonville, ND 58454; Mailing: PO Box 348, Edgeley, ND 58433 t) 701-493-2387 transholy@drtel.net Served from Edgeley. Rev. Jake Miller, Pst.; CRP Stds.: 5

OAKES

St. Charles Church of Oakes - 410 Seventh St. N., Oakes, ND 58474 t) 701-742-2418 timothy.schroeder@fargodiocese.org Also serving Forman. Rev. Timothy Schroeder, Pst.; CRP Stds.: 53

OBERON

St. Jerome - Crow Hill - 3971 69th Ave., N.E., Oberon, ND 58335; Mailing: PO Box 299, Fort Totten, ND 58335 t) (701) 766-4314 Served from Fort Totten. Rev. Antony Samy, Pst.;

St. Jerome's Church of Crow Hill - 3971 69th Ave., N.E., Oberon, ND 58357; Mailing: Box 299, Fort Totten, ND 58335 t) 701-766-4314 antony.samy@fargodiocese.org Served from Fort Totten. Rev. Antony Samy, Pst.; CRP Stds.: 1

ORISKA

St. Bernard's Church of Oriska - 606 5th St., Oriska, ND 58063 t) 701-845-3713 bernard@bektel.com www.stbernards-oriska.org/ Also serving Hope and Sanborn. Rev. Brian Bachmeier; Dcn. Jim McAllister;

PARK RIVER

St. Mary Church of Park River - 505 Park St. E., Park River, ND 58270-0110; Mailing: PO Box 110, Park River, ND 58270 t) 701-284-6165 stmarys@polarcomm.com; cherylddre@polarcomm.com www.saintsml.org Also serving Veseleyville. Rev. Bert Miller, Pst.; CRP Stds.: 32

PEMBINA

Assumption Church of Pembina - 143 Hayden St., Pembina, ND 58271 t) 701-825-6266 Served from Drayton. Rev. Robert Wapenski, Pst.; CRP Stds.: 10

PISEK

St. John Nepomucene's Church of Pisek - 167 Newton Ave., Pisek, ND 58273; Mailing: PO Box 27, Pisek, ND 58273 t) 701-284-6060 stjohnne@polarcomm.com; stjohnne@polarcomm.com plbnd.org Also serving Lankin and Bechyne. Rev. Jason Lefor, Pst.; CRP Stds.: 35

REYNOLDS

Our Lady of Perpetual Help Church of Reynolds - 421 Sanborn St, Reynolds, ND 58275-0068; Mailing: PO Box 68, Reynolds, ND 58275-0068 t) 701-847-3096 john.cavanaugh@fargodiocese.org; kristi.unterseher@gmail.com www.olphsj.org Serves St Jude's Church in Thompson. Rev. John Cavanaugh, Pst.; CRP Stds.: 35

ROCK LAKE

Immaculate Heart of Mary Church of Rock Lake - 54 Eller Ave., Rock Lake, ND 58365; Mailing: P.O. Box 788, Rolla, ND 58367 t) 701-477-5277 stjpastor@utma.com; stjhm@utma.com Served from Rolla. Rev. Thaines Arulandu, Pst.; CRP Stds.: 11

ROLETTE

Sacred Heart Church of Rolette - 505 Main St., Rolette, ND 58366; Mailing: PO Box 127, Rolette, ND 58366 t) 701-246-3449 shrolette@fargodiocese.org Also serving Willow City and Bisbee. Rev. Paulraj Thondappa, HGN, Pst.; CRP Stds.: 11

ROLLA

St. Joachim's Church of Rolla - 210 2nd St., N.E., Rolla, ND 58367-0788; Mailing: PO. Box 788, Rolla, ND

58367 t) 701-477-5277 stjpastor@utma.com; stjhm@utma.com Also serving Rock Lake. Rev. Thaines Arulandu, Pst.; CRP Stds.: 55

RUGBY

St. Theresa, Little Flower Church of Rugby - 218 3rd St., S.E., Rugby, ND 58368-1814 t) 701-776-6388; 701-776-5327 lfparish@gondtc.com www.littleflowerrugby.org Also serves Balta and Knox. Rev. Franklin Miller, Pst.; Rev. John F. Aerts, Par. Vicar; Dcn. Arlen Blessum; Dcn. Richard Lagasse; CRP Stds.: 105

St. Theresa, Little Flower Church of Rugby School - (Grades PreK-6) 306 Third Ave., S.E., Rugby, ND 58368 t) 701-776-6258 lfs@gondtc.com www.little-flower.k12.nd.us Kevin Leier, Prin.; Sr. Jean Louise Schafer, O.S.F., Librn.; Stds.: 57; Lay Tchrs.: 4

SANBORN

Sacred Heart Church of Sanborn - 711 4th St., Sanborn, ND 58480; Mailing: 606 5th St., Oriska, ND 58063 t) 701-845-3713 bernard@bektel.com www.stbernards-oriska.org/ Served from Oriska. Rev. Brian Bachmeier, Pst.;

SELZ

St. Anthony Church of Selz - 29 Girard St., Selz, ND 58341 t) 701-324-4059; 701-324-2144 (St. Cecilia, Harvey) stcecilia@gondtc.com Served from Harvey. Rev. Kevin Boucher, Pst.; CRP Stds.: 2

SHELDON

Our Lady of the Scapular Church of Sheldon - 145 Crosswell St., Sheldon, ND 58068; Mailing: 302 Bluff St., Enderlin, ND 58027 t) 701-437-2791 stpatrick@mlgc.com www.enderlinfingalsheldon.org Served from Enderlin. Rev. Scott Karnik, Admin.; CRP Stds.: 15

ST. JOHN

St. John's Church of St. John - 107 Saint Ann St., S.E., St. John, ND 58369; Mailing: P.O. Box 170, St. John, ND 58369 t) 701-477-3081 saintjohnthebaptistnd@gmail.com Also serves St. Benedict, Belcourt. Rev. Richard Fineo, Pst.; CRP Stds.: 38

ST. MICHAEL

St. Michael's Church of St. Michael - 136 St. Michaels Ct., St. Michael, ND 58370; Mailing: P.O. Box 958, Devils Lake, ND 58301 t) 701-766-4151 michaels@gondtc.com; michaelsmission@fargodiocese.org Rev. Paul R. Schuster, Pst.; CRP Stds.: 15

St. Michael's Church of St. Michael - 136 1st St., St. Michael, ND 58370-0042; Mailing: P.O. Box 958, Devils Lake, ND 58301 t) 701-766-4151 paul.schuster@fargodiocese.org Rev. Paul Schuster, Pst.;

STARKWEATHER

Assumption Church of Starkweather - 502 Main St., Starkweather, ND 58377; Mailing: P.O. Box 159, Munich, ND 58352-0159 t) 701-682-5178 mathew.pamplaniyil@fargodiocese.org Served from Munich. Rev. Mathew V. Pamplaniyil, Pst.; Charlotte Nilles Kitsch, DRE; CRP Stds.: 8

STEELE

St. Francis de Sales Church of Steele - 318 2nd St., S.W., Steele, ND 58482; Mailing: PO Box 87, 220 4th St., S.W., Steele, ND 58482 t) 701-475-2333 stfrancis@bektel.com steeletappenmedina.org Also serves Tappen and Medina. Rev. Peter Sharpe, Pst.; CRP Stds.: 45

SYKESTON

St. Elizabeth's Church of Sykeston - 130 Anson Ave., N.E., Sykeston, ND 58486; Mailing: P.O. Box 312, Sykeston, ND 58486 t) 701-984-2266 stelizabeth@daktel.com Served from Carrington. Rev. Thomas E. Dodge Jr., Pst.; CRP Stds.: 12

TAPPEN

St. Paul of Tappen - 218 1st St., N.E., Tappen, ND 58487; Mailing: PO Box 87, 220 4th St., S.W., Steele, ND 58482 t) 701-475-2333 stfrancis@bektel.com steeletappenmedina.org Served from Steele. Rev. Peter Sharpe, Pst.; CRP Stds.: 7

THOMPSON

St. Jude's Church of Thompson - 329 Broadway St., Thompson, ND 58278-0305; Mailing: PO Box 305, Thompson, ND 58278-0305 t) 701-599-2574; 701-847-3096 john.cavanaugh@fargodiocese.org; kims4church@gmail.com www.olphsj.org Served from Our Lady of Perpetual Help, Reynolds ND. Rev. John Cavanaugh, Pst.; Rev. Deacon Jim West; CRP Stds.: 103

TOKIO

Christ the King - Tokio - 134 2nd St., Tokio, ND 58335; Mailing: Box 299, Fort Totten, ND 58335-0299 t) 701-766-4314 Rev. Antony Samy, Pst.;

TOLNA

St. Joseph Church of Tolna - 220 Main St., Tolna, ND 58380; Mailing: PO Box 509, Lakota, ND 58344 t) 701-247-2584 steven.meyer@fargodiocese.org Served from Lakota. Rev. Steven Meyer, Pst.; CRP Stds.: 7

TOWNER

St. Cecilia's Church of Towner - 503 1st St., S.W., Towner, ND 58788; Mailing: PO Box 267, Towner, ND 58788 t) 701-537-5133 stcs@srt.com Rev. Michael Schommer, Pst.; CRP Stds.: 37

VALLEY CITY

St. Catherine's Church of Valley City - 540 Third Ave., N.E., Valley City, ND 58072-2628 t) 701-845-0354; 701-845-1453 (CRP) stcatherinesparishoffice@gmail.com www.stcatherine.k12.nd.us Rev. Paul C. Duchschere, Pst.; Dcn. Arlie Braunberger; Dcn. Edward Didier; Dcn. Raphael Grim; Dcn. Joseph Leitner; Dcn. Thomas Vanorny; CRP Stds.: 58

St. Catherine's Church of Valley City School - (Grades K-6) t) (701) 845-1453 Joshua Gow, Prin.; Stds.: 48; Lay Tchrs.: 13

VELVA

St. Cecilia's Church of Velva - 201 2nd Ave. W., Velva, ND 58790-0496; Mailing: PO Box K, Velva, ND 58790 t) 701-338-2663 velvakarls@srt.com stceciliavelvand.org Also serving Karlsruhe. Rev. Matthew M. Kraemer, Pst.; CRP Stds.: 83

VERONA

St. Raphael's Church of Verona - 205 1st St., Verona, ND 58490; Mailing: PO Box 217, LaMoure, ND 58458 t) 701-883-5987 holyrosery.church@gmail.com www.holyrosarylamoure.org Served from Lamoure. Rev. Gregory Haman, Pst.; CRP Stds.: 1

WAHPETON

St. John's Church of Wahpeton - 115 Second St. N., Wahpeton, ND 58075 t) 701-642-6982 stoffice@rrt.net www.stjohns-wahpeton.org Rev. Dale Lagodinski, Pst.; Rev. Paul Kuhn, Par. Vicar; CRP Stds.: 99

St. John's Church of Wahpeton School - (Grades PreK-6) 212 Dakota Ave., Wahpeton, ND 58075 t) 701-642-6116 www.stjohns-wahpeton.org/school/ Stds.: 131; Lay Tchrs.: 8

WALES

St. Michael's Church of Wales - 221 2nd Ave., Wales, ND 58281; Mailing: 1010 3rd St., Langdon, ND 58249 t) 701-256-5966 saints@utma.com www.stalphonsuslangdon.com Served from Langdon. Rev. Kurtis L. Gunwall, Pst.; CRP Stds.: 1

WALHALLA

St. Boniface Church of Walhalla - 801 Central Ave., Walhalla, ND 58282; Mailing: PO Box 228, Walhalla, ND 58282 t) 701-549-2729; 701-549-2750 (CRP) boniface@utma.com; carignan@utma.com Also serving Neche. Rev. Jason Asselin, Pst.; CRP Stds.: 33

WARSAW

St. Stanislaus Church of Warsaw - 6098 Cty. Rd. 4, Warsaw, ND 58261-0316; Mailing: PO Box 316, Minto, ND 58261-0316 t) 701-248-3589 sacredheartminto@hotmail.com www.sh-ss.org Served from Minto. Rev. Brian Moen, Pst.; CRP Stds.: 43

WEST FARGO

Blessed Sacrament Church of West Fargo - 210 Fifth Ave. W., West Fargo, ND 58078-1747 t) 701-282-3321 www.bscwf.org Rev. Gary Luiten, Pst.; Rev. Thomas Feltman, In Res.; CRP Stds.: 88

Holy Cross Church of West Fargo - 2711 7th St. E., West Fargo, ND 58078 t) 701-282-7217 holycrosscc@holycrosswestfargo.com www.holycrosswestfargo.com Rev. Phillip Ackerman, Pst.; Dcn. Tony Finneman; Rev. Karmalraj Balasamy, Par. Vicar; Rev. Eric Seitz, Par. Vicar; Dcn. James Eggl; CRP Stds.: 508

WESTHOPE

St. Andrew's Church of Westhope - 260 1st Ave. E, Westhope, ND 58793-0365; Mailing: PO Box 365, Westhope, ND 58793-0365 t) 701-245-6171; 701-228-3164 stsmanda@utma.com www.stmark-standrew.org Served from Bottineau. Rev. Jared Kadlec, Pst.; CRP Stds.: 48

WILLOW CITY

Notre Dame de la Victoire Church of Willow City - 215 1st St. N., Willow City, ND 58384; Mailing: PO Box 115, Willow City, ND 58384 t) 701-246-3449 shrolette@fargodiocese.org Served by Rolette. Rev. Paulraj Thondappa, HGN, Pst.;

WIMBLEDON

St. Boniface Church of Wimbledon - 302 1st St. N., Wimbledon, ND 58492; Mailing: PO Box 9, Wimbledon, ND 58492 t) 701-435-2310 boniface@daktel.com; st.bonifacend@gmail.com Also serving Kensal and Dazey. Rev. Sean P. Mulligan, Pst.; CRP Stds.: 28

WINDSOR

St. Mathias Church of Windsor - 207 Washington Ave., Windsor, ND 58424; Mailing: 622 1st Ave. S., Jamestown, ND 58401 t) 701-252-0119; 701-252-0478 (CRP) basilica@stjamesbasilica.org; ffsecretary@stjamesbasilica.org Served from Jamestown. Rev. Neil J. Pfeifer, Pst.; Rev. Kevin Lorsung, Par. Vicar; Rev. Joseph Barrett, Par. Vicar; CRP Stds.: 11

WISHEK

St. Patrick Church of Wishek - 305 7th St. S., Wishek, ND 58495-0293; Mailing: PO Box 293, Wiskek, ND 58495 t) 701-452-2970 wenceslaus.katanga@fargodiocese.org; kaybek@bektel.com Also serving Zeeland and Ashley. Rev. Wenceslaus Katanga, Pst.; CRP Stds.: 32

WYNDMERE

St. John the Baptist Church of Wyndmere - 628 6th St., Wyndmere, ND 58081; Mailing: 630 6th St., Wyndmere, ND 58081 t) 701-439-2200 johnthebaptist.arnolds@gmail.com Also serving St. Arnold in Milnor. Rev. Troy K. Simonsen, Pst.; CRP Stds.: 60

ZEELAND

St. Andrew's Church of Zeeland - 301 1st Ave., S.E., Zeeland, ND 58581; Mailing: PO Box 293, Wishek, ND 58495 t) 701-423-5494 wenceslaus.katanga@fargodiocese.org Served from Wishek. Rev. Wenceslaus Katanga, Pst.; Becky Rohrich, DRE; CRP Stds.: 13

SCHOOLS: PRESCHOOL THRU HIGH SCHOOL

SCHOOLS

STATE OF NORTH DAKOTA

FARGO

St. John Paul II Catholic Schools Network (Blessed John Paul II Catholic Schools, Fargo Catholic Schools Network) - (DIO) (Grades PreK-12) 5600 25th St., S.W., Fargo, ND 58104 t) 701-893-3200 mike.hagstrom@jp2schools.org; mary.b.traynor@jp2schools.org www.jp2schools.org

Rev. William Slattery, Chap.; Rev. Kyle P. Metzger, Prin.; Michael Hagstrom, Pres.; Stds.: 1,153; Lay Tchrs.: 88

Holy Spirit Elementary School - (Grades PreK-12) 1441 8th St. N., Fargo, ND 58102 t) 701-232-4087 jason.kotrba@jp2schools.org Jason Kotrba, Prin.; Stds.: 106; Lay Tchrs.: 13

Nativity Elementary School - (Grades PreK-12) 1825 11th St. S., Fargo, ND 58103 t) 701-232-7461 Christopher Dalton, Prin.; Stds.: 222; Lay Tchrs.: 17

Shanley High School - (Grades PreK-12) 5600 25th St. S., Fargo, ND 58104 t) (701) 893-3220 Mary Beth Traynor, Vice. Pres.; Stds.: 312; Lay Tchrs.: 27; Pr. Tchrs.: 1

Sacred Heart Middle School - (Grades PreK-12) 5600 25th St. S., Fargo, ND 58104 t) (701) 893-3288 leon.knodel@jp2schools.org Leon Knodel, Prin.; Mary Beth Traynor, Vice. Pres.; Stds.: 225; Lay Tchrs.: 15

Trinity Elementary School - (Grades PreK-12) 2811 7th St. E., West Fargo, ND 58078 t) 701-356-0793 Karissa Flieth, Prin.; Stds.: 288; Lay Tchrs.: 19

INSTITUTIONS LOCATED IN DIOCESE

ASSOCIATIONS [ASN]

FARGO

Catholic Chaplains Association - 5201 Bishops Blvd. S., Ste. A, Fargo, ND 58104 t) 701-356-7900 Rev. Andrew Jasinski, Dir.;

GRAND FORKS

Calvary Cemetery Association - 216 Belmont Rd., Grand Forks, ND 58201 t) 701-772-7911 calvarycemeterygfnd@yahoo.com Rev. H. Gerard Braun, Vice Pres.; Darlyne Votava, Secy.;

CAMPUS MINISTRY / NEWMAN CENTERS [CAM]

FARGO

St. Paul's Newman Church of Fargo - 1141 University Dr. N, Fargo, ND 58102 t) 701-235-0142 frcheney@bisoncatholic.org; info@bisoncatholic.org www.bisoncatholic.org Rev. James Cheney, Pst.; Rev. Msgr. Gregory J. Schlesselmann, Spiritual Adv./Care Srvcs.;

GRAND FORKS

St. Thomas Aquinas Newman Church of Grand Forks - 410 Cambridge St., Grand Forks, ND 58203 t) (701) 402-3806 jessica.kuznia@undcatholic.org www.undcatholic.org Rev. Christopher J. Markman, Pst.;

JAMESTOWN

University of Jamestown - 214 4th St., S.E., Jamestown, ND 58401 t) 701-252-0478 youth@stjamesbasilica.org Rev. Neil J. Pfeifer, Pst.;

VALLEY CITY

Valley City State University Newman Center - c/o St. Catherine, 540 3rd Ave., N.E., Valley City, ND 58072 t) 701-845-0354 dennis.skonseng@fargodiocese.org Rev. Paul C. Duchschere;

CATHOLIC CHARITIES [CCH]

FARGO

Catholic Charities North Dakota - Fargo - 5201 Bishops Blvd., Ste. B, Fargo, ND 58104 t) 701-235-4457 info@catholiccharitiesnd.org www.catholiccharitiesnd.org Statewide social service agency providing adoption services, guardianship services, pregnancy services, Adults Adopting Special Kids (AASK). Dianne Nechiporenko, Exec.; Asstd. Annu.: 2,900; Staff: 82

GRAND FORKS

St. Joseph's Social Care and Thrift Store - 620 8th Ave. S., Grand Forks, ND 58201-4816 t) 701-795-8614 mickey@stjosephssocialcaregf.org www.stjosephssocialcaregf.org Mickey Munson, Dir.; Asstd. Annu.: 13,000; Staff: 15

MINTO

Saint Gianna and Pietro Molla Maternity Home - 15605 Cty. Rd. 15, Minto, ND 58261 t) 701-248-3077 sgpmollahome@outlook.com www.sgpmollahome.org Residence for pregnant women and their children. Mary Pat Jahner, Dir.; Rev. Joseph Christensen, F.M.I., Chap.; Asstd. Annu.: 70; Staff: 7

CEMETERIES [CEM]

FARGO

Holy Cross Cemeteries of Fargo - 1502 32nd Ave., N., Fargo, ND 58102 t) 701-237-6671 Bob Reichel, Dir.;

CONVENTS, MONASTERIES, AND RESIDENCES FOR WOMEN [CON]

FARGO

Presentation Center-Sacred Heart Convent - 5300 12 St. S. #110, Fargo, ND 58104 t) 701-237-4857 c) 714-473-7381 srmarilynopbvm@aol.com www.pbvmunion.org Sr. Marilyn Omieczynski, PBVM, Supr.; Srs.: 25

HANKINSON

Franciscan Sisters of Dillingen - 102 6th St., S.E., Hankinson, ND 58041; Mailing: PO Box 447, Hankinson, ND 58041-0447 t) 701-242-7195 dillingenfranciscansusa@rrt.net; ndfrancican@yahoo.com www.ndfranciscans.org Sr. Donna M Welder, OSF, Prov.; Rev. Armond Brooks, Chap.; Srs.: 14

VALLEY CITY

Sisters of Mary of the Presentation - 3150 116A Ave., S.E., Ste. B, Valley City, ND 58072 t) 701-845-2864 suzanne.stahl@smphs.org www.sistersofmaryofthepresentation.org Sr. Suzanne Stahl, Supr.; Rev. Donald A. Leiphon, Chap.; Srs.: 11

WAHPETON

Carmel of Mary - 17765 78th St., S.E., Wahpeton, ND 58075 t) 701-642-2360 carmelwahpeton@gmail.com www.carmelofmary Carmelite Nuns of the Ancient Observance. Rev. Jim Tiu, Chap.; Mother Madonna of the Assumption, O.Carm., Prioress; Srs.: 8

ENDOWMENTS / FOUNDATIONS / TRUSTS [EFT]

FARGO

Catholic Development Foundation - 5201 Bishops Blvd. S., Ste A, Fargo, ND 58104-7605 t) 701-356-7930 steve.schons@fargodiocese.org www.cdfnd.org A nonprofit foundation for religious charitable and educational purposes. Steve Schons, Pres.;

LANGDON

St. Alphonsus School Foundation - 908 3rd St., Langdon, ND 58249 t) 701-256-3717 lyonsh@utma.com Cameron Sillers, Pres.;

HOSPITALS / HEALTH SERVICES [HOS]

BOTTINEAU

SMP Health - St. Andrew's - 316 Ohmer St., Bottineau, ND 58318 t) 701-228-9300 calbertson@stahc.net smphealth.org/standrews Chris Albertson, CEO; Bed Capacity: 25; Asstd. Annu.: 8,978; Staff: 96

CARRINGTON

Carrington Health Center (CHI St. Alexius Health Carrington Medical Center) - 800 N. 4 St., Carrington, ND 58421; Mailing: P.O. Box 461, Carrington, ND 58421 t) 701-652-3141 rebecca.pretzer@commonspirit.org www.carringtonhealthcenter.org Catholic Health Initiatives. Mariann Doeling, Admin.; Bed Capacity: 25; Asstd. Annu.: 20,000; Staff: 120

DEVILS LAKE

CHI St. Alexius Health Devils Lake Hospital (Mercy Hosptial of Devils Lake) - 1031 7th St., N.E., Devils Lake, ND 58301-2798 t) 701-662-2131 missionintegrationmidwest@commonspirit.org www.chistalexiushealth.org Mariann Doeling, Pres.; Andrew J. Santos III, SVP, Mission Integration; Bed Capacity: 25; Asstd. Annu.: 20,531; Staff: 125

FARGO

SMP Health - 1202 Page Dr. S., Fargo, ND 58103 t) 701-237-9290 aaron.alton@smphs.org smphealth.org Aaron K. Alton, CEO; Staff: 20

HARVEY

SMP Health - St. Aloisius - 325 E. Brewster St., Harvey, ND 58341 t) 701-324-4651 asams@staloisius.com smphealth.org/staloisius/ Alfred Sams, CEO; Bed Capacity: 25; Asstd. Annu.: 46,972; Staff: 240

LISBON

Lisbon Area Health Services - 905 Main St., Lisbon, ND 58054; Mailing: P.O. Box 353, Lisbon, ND 58054 t) 701-683-6400 missionintegrationmidwest@commonspirit.org lisbonhospital.com Julie Mallett, Pres.; Andrew J. Santos III, SVP, Mission Integration; Bed Capacity: 25; Asstd. Annu.: 12,076; Staff: 75

OAKES

CHI Oakes Hospital - 1200 N. 7th St., Oakes, ND 58474-2502 t) 701-742-3291 missionintegrationmidwest@commonspirit.org www.oakeshospital.com Rebecca Thompson, Pres.; Andrew J. Santos III, SVP, Mission Integration; Bed Capacity: 20; Asstd. Annu.: 6,726; Staff: 75

ROLLA

SMP Health - St. Kateri - 213 Second Ave., N.E., Rolla, ND 58367-0759; Mailing: P.O. Box 759, Rolla, ND 58367-0759 t) 701-477-3161 chrisalbertson@pmc-rolla.com smphealth.org/stkateri Chris Albertson, CEO; Bed Capacity: 25; Asstd. Annu.: 9,521; Staff: 85

VALLEY CITY

Mercy Hospital of Valley City (CHI Mercy Health) - 570 Chautauqua Blvd., Valley City, ND 58072 t) 701-845-6400 missionintegrationmidwest@commonspirit.org www.mercyhospitalvalleycity.org Catholic Health Initiatives. Darryl Fowler, Pres.; Andrew J. Santos III, SVP, Mission Integration; Bed Capacity: 25; Asstd. Annu.: 11,000; Staff: 52

MISCELLANEOUS [MIS]

BATHGATE

Bethlehem Community - 10194 Garfield St. S., Bathgate, ND 58216 t) 701-265-3717 contact@bethlehembooks.com Lydia Reynolds, Contact;

COOPERSTOWN

Marriage Encounter - 804 Foster Ave., N.W., Cooperstown, ND 58425; Mailing: P.O. Box 217, Cooperstown, ND 58425 t) 701-797-2624 stgeorge@mlgc.com Rev. Dale H. Kinzler;

FARGO

Beginning Experience Apostolate - 5201 Bishops Blvd. S. Ste. A, Fargo, ND 58104-7605 t) 701-282-3321 gary.luiten@fargodiocese.org Rev. Gary Luiten, Dir.;

Cursillo Movement of the Fargo Diocese - 5201 Bishops Blvd. S., Ste. A, Fargo, ND 58104 t) 701-356-7900 www.natl-cursillo.org Rev. Duaine Cote, Chap.;

Fargo Guild of Catholic Physicians - 5201 Bishops Blvd. S., Fargo, ND 58104 t) 701-356-7900 andrew.jasinski@fargodiocese.org Timothy Olson, Chancellor;

Hughes, Inc. - 5300 12th St., S #110, Fargo, ND 58104 t) 701-237-4857 kfennell@pbvmunion.org www.pbvmunion.org Assisting, providing and expanding low-cost housing (in part for senior citizens along with other groups). Sr. Katherine Fennell, P.B.V.M., Treas.;

Newman Living - 1119 University Dr., N., Fargo, ND 58102 t) 701-235-0142 info@bisoncatholic.org Rev. James W. Cheney, Pst.;

Presentation Partners in Housing - 219 7th St., Fargo,

ND 58103 t) 701-235-6861 cheri@fmppih.org www.fmppih.org Cheri Gerken, Dir.;

Sisters of Mary of the Presentation Health Ministry - 1202 Page Dr. S., Fargo, ND 58103 t) 701-237-9290 suzanne.stahl@smphs.org Sr. Suzanne Stahl, Chair;

MINTO

***Third Order Franciscans of Mary Immaculate** - 6098 Cty. Rd. 4, Minto, ND 58261-9455 t) 701-248-3020 fmi@fmifriars.com www.fmifriars.com Rev. Joseph Christensen, F.M.I., Supr.;

NURSING / REHABILITATION / CONVALESCENCE / ELDERLY CARE [NUR]

EDGELEY

Manor St. Joseph - 404 Fourth Ave., Edgeley, ND 58433; Mailing: P.O. Box 305, Edgeley, ND 58433 t) 701-493-2477 stjoseph@drtel.net Tammy Jangula, Admin.; Asstd. Annu.: 20; Staff: 28

ELLENDALE

***Ellendale Evergreen Place, Inc.** - 241 Main St., Ellendale, ND 58436

Prince of Peace Care Center (Benedictine Living Communities, Inc.) - 201 8th St. N., Ellendale, ND 58436 t) 701-349-3312 naomi.grueneich@benedictineliving.org www.benedictineliving.org/ellendale-nd/ Naomi Grueneich, Exec. Dir.; Asstd. Annu.: 71; Staff: 61

ENDERLIN

SMP Health - Maryhill - 110 Hillcrest Dr., Enderlin, ND 58027 t) 701-437-3544 bailyn.walz@smphs.org smphealth.org/maryhill Bailyn Walz, Admin.; Asstd. Annu.: 156; Staff: 76

FARGO

Riverview (CHI Riverview) - 5300 12th St. S., Fargo, ND 58104 t) 701-237-4700 kdew@chilivingcomm.org www.homeishere.org An operating unit of CHI Living Communities, which is a subsidiary of CommonSpirit Health Kari Dew, Admin.; Asstd. Annu.: 173; Staff: 62

SMP Health - St. Catherine North - 1351 Broadway N., Fargo, ND 58102 t) 701-277-7999 matt.ahrndt@smphs.org smphealth.org/stcatherinenorth/ Matthew Ahrndt, Admin.; Asstd. Annu.: 218; Staff: 175

SMP Health - St. Catherine South - 3102 University Dr. S., Fargo, ND 58103 t) 701-293-7750 matt.ahrndt@smphs.org smphealth.org/stcatherinesouth Matthew Ahrndt, Admin.; Asstd. Annu.: 161; Staff: 150

GRAND FORKS

St. Anne's Guest Home - 524 N. 17th St., Grand Forks, ND 58203 t) 701-746-9401 stannesguesthome@gmail.com www.stannesguesthome.org Sr. Rebecca Metzger, O.S.F., Admin.; Asstd. Annu.: 69; Staff: 34

HANKINSON

St. Gerard Community of Care - 613 1st Ave., S.W., Hankinson, ND 58041; Mailing: P.O. Box 448, Hankinson, ND 58041 t) 701-242-7891 jill.foertsch@stgerards.org stgerards.org Jill Foertsch, Admin.; Sr. Mary Louise, O.S.F., Admin.; Asstd. Annu.: 65; Staff: 72

JAMESTOWN

SMP Health - Ave Maria - 501 19th St., N.E., Jamestown, ND 58401 t) 701-252-5660 tonie.lagodinski@smphs.org smphealth.org/avemaria/ Tonie Lagodinski-Stoen, Admin.; Asstd. Annu.: 308; Staff: 160

LAMOURE

Benedictine Living Community | LaMoure - 315 1st St., S.E., LaMoure, ND 58458 t) 701-883-5363 kelsey.peterson@benedictineliving.org www.benedictineliving.org/lamoure-nd/ Kelsey Peterson, Exec. Dir.; Asstd. Annu.: 75; Staff: 56

VALLEY CITY

SMP Health - St. Raphael - 979 N. Central Ave., Valley City, ND 58072 t) 701-845-8222 maren.gemar@smphs.org smphealth.org/straphael Maren Gemar, Admin.; Asstd. Annu.: 192; Staff: 206

WAHPETON

Benedictine Living Community of Wapheton - 1307 N. 7th St., Wahpeton, ND 58075 t) 701-642-6667 jim.cornelius@benedictineliving.org www.blcwahpeton.org Operated by Benedictine Living Communities, Inc. Jim Cornelius, Admin.; Asstd. Annu.: 250; Staff: 120

St. Catherine's Living Center (Benedictine Living Communities, Inc.) - 1307 N. Seventh St., Wahpeton, ND 58075 t) 701-642-6667 jim.cornelius@benedictineliving.org www.benedictineliving.org/wahpeton-nd/ Operated by Benedictine Living Communities, Inc. Jim Cornelius, Admin.; Asstd. Annu.: 250; Staff: 120

RETREAT HOUSES / RENEWAL CENTERS [RTR]

FARGO

Presentation Prayer Center - 5300 12th St., S. #110, Fargo, ND 58104 t) 701-237-4857 presprayerctr@pbvmunion.org Scott Mathern-Jacobson, Dir.;

VALLEY CITY

Maryvale - 3150 116A Ave., S.E., Valley City, ND 58072-9633 t) (701) 845-2864 www.sistersofmaryofthepresentation.org Convent, spiritual retreat center, and the U.S. headquarters of Sisters of Mary of the Presentation. Sr. Suzanne Stahl, Supr.;

SPECIAL CARE FACILITIES [SPF]

FARGO

Villa Nazareth (CHI Friendship, Presentation Sisters (PBVM) and Catholic Health Initiatives) - 801 Page Dr., Fargo, ND 58103 t) 701-235-8217 dorileslie@catholichealth.net; missionintegrationmidwest@commonspirit.org www.chifriendship.com A community-based facility providing an array of residential, vocational, educational, social and clinical services. Dori Leslie, Pres.; Andrew J. Santos III, SVP, Mission Integration; Asstd. Annu.: 300; Staff: 440

An asterisk (*) denotes an organization that has established tax-exempt status directly with the IRS and is not covered by the USCCB Group Ruling.

Diocese of Fort Wayne-South Bend

(Dioecesis Wayne Castrensis-South Bendensis)

MOST REVEREND KEVIN C. RHOADES, D.D., S.T.L., J.C.L.

Bishop of Fort Wayne-South Bend; ordained July 9, 1983; appointed Bishop of Harrisburg October 14, 2004; consecrated December 9, 2004; appointed Bishop of Fort Wayne-South Bend November 14, 2009; installed Bishop of Fort Wayne-South Bend January 13, 2010. Mailing Address: P.O. Box 390, Fort Wayne, IN 46801.

Archbishop Noll Catholic Center: 915 S. Clinton St., P.O. Box 390, Fort Wayne, IN 46801. T: 260-422-4611; F: 260-969-9145.
www.diocesefwsb.org
bishopsoffice@diocesefwsb.org

ESTABLISHED SEPTEMBER 22, 1857.

Square Miles 5,792.

Redesignated Diocese of Fort Wayne-South Bend on July 22, 1960.

Comprises the Counties of Adams, Allen, Dekalb, Elkhart, Huntington, Kosciusko, La Grange, Marshall, Noble, St. Joseph, Steuben, Wabash, Wells, Whitley in the State of Indiana.

For legal titles of parishes and diocesan institutions, consult the Chancery Office.

STATISTICAL OVERVIEW

Personnel
Bishop....1
Priests: Diocesan Active in Diocese....61
Priests: Diocesan Active Outside Diocese....4
Priests: Retired, Sick or Absent....21
Number of Diocesan Priests....86
Religious Priests in Diocese....161
Total Priests in your Diocese....247
Extern Priests in Diocese....25
Ordinations:
Diocesan Priests....3
Religious Priests....3
Transitional Deacons....5
Permanent Deacons in Diocese....29
Total Brothers....54
Total Sisters....286

Parishes
Parishes....81
With Resident Pastor:
Resident Diocesan Priests....62
Resident Religious Priests....18
Without Resident Pastor:
Administered by Priests....1
Pastoral Centers....3
Professional Ministry Personnel:
Sisters....2
Lay Ministers....90

Welfare
Catholic Hospitals....2
Total Assisted....484,000
Health Care Centers....5
Total Assisted....68,833
Homes for the Aged....9
Total Assisted....1,522
Specialized Homes....3
Total Assisted....73
Special Centers for Social Services....9
Total Assisted....192,824
Other Institutions....2
Total Assisted....7,129

Educational
Diocesan Students in Other Seminaries....17
Seminaries, Religious....2
Students, Religious....49
Total Seminarians....66
Colleges and Universities....4
Total Students....15,504
High Schools, Diocesan and Parish....4
Total Students....2,952
Elementary Schools, Diocesan and Parish....39
Total Students....10,323
Catechesis/Religious Education:
High School Students....701
Elementary Students....5,415
Total Students under Catholic Instruction....34,961
Teachers in Diocese:
Sisters....4
Lay Teachers....900

Vital Statistics
Receptions into the Church:
Infant Baptism Totals....1,249
Minor Baptism Totals....683
Adult Baptism Totals....149
Received into Full Communion....173
First Communions....2,081
Confirmations....2,231
Marriages:
Catholic....458
Interfaith....150
Total Marriages....608
Deaths....1,232
Total Catholic Population....147,996
Total Population....2,628,320

LEADERSHIP

Chancery Office - t) 260-422-4611; 574-234-0687 Very Rev. Mark A. Gurtner, Chancellor;
Diocese of Fort Wayne-South Bend, Inc. -
Board of Directors - Most Rev. Kevin C. Rhoades, Pres.; Very Rev. Mark A. Gurtner, Vice. Pres.; Joseph Ryan, Secy.;
Vicar General/Chancellor - t) 260-422-4611 Very Rev. Mark A. Gurtner;
Moderator of the Curia - t) 260-422-4611 Very Rev. Mark A. Gurtner;
Judicial Vicar - t) 260-422-4611 Very Rev. Jacob Runyon;
Assistant to the Bishop in Pastoral Care - t) 260-422-4611 Mary L. Glowaski, Dir.;
Secretary for Administrative Services - Joseph Ryan, Secy.;
Secretary for Communications - t) 260-456-2824 Nicole Hahn, Dir. (Nhahn@diocesefwsb.org);
Secretariat for Pastoral Ministries and Catechesis - t) 574-234-0687 tdelgado@diocesefwsb.org Carl Loesch, Exec. Dir. (cloesch@diocesefwsb.org);
Catechesis - t) 260-422-4611 Jonathan Kaltenbach, Dir.;
Catholic Campaign for Human Development - Shawn Storer, Dir.;
Catholic Relief Services - Shawn Storer, Dir.;
Diocesan Catholic Committee on Scouting - Carl Loesch, Chair; Rev. Nathan Maskal, Chap.;
Ecumenical Ministry - Shawn Storer, Coord.;
Hispanic Ministry - Esther Terry, Dir.;
Marriage and Family Ministry - Lisa Everett, Dir.; Caty Burke, Assoc. Dir.;
Courage/EnCourage - Chaplain Fort Wayne Area - t) 260-482-9411 Rev. William J. Kummer, Chap.;
Courage/EnCourage - Chaplain South Bend Area - t) 574-234-3134 Rev. Matthew Fase, C.S.C., Chap.;
Youth and Young Adult Ministry - John Pratt, Dir.; Jocelyn Alcala, Assoc. Dir.;
Secretary for Stewardship and Development - t) 574-258-6571; 260-422-4611 Jeffery Boetticher, Dir.;
Vicar for Clergy - Very Rev. Matthew M. Coonan, Vicar;
Permanent Diaconate - t) 260-422-4611 Dcn. Stanley LeMieux, Dir.; Very Rev. Matthew M. Coonan;
Vocation Office - Rev. Andrew Budzinski, Dir.;

OFFICES AND DIRECTORS

Black Catholic Ministry - t) 574-707-1231 Dcn. Melvin Tardy, Chair (mtardy@nd.edu);
Budget Committee - Joseph Ryan; Very Rev. Mark A. Gurtner;
Buildings and Improvements Advisory Board - Joseph Ryan; Very Rev. Mark A. Gurtner; Bill Arnold;
Business Administration Office - Joseph Ryan, CFO;
Catholic Cemetery - t) 260-426-2044 cmiller@divinemercyfuneralhome.org Casey Miller, Supt.;
Catholic Schools - t) 260-422-4611 Joseph A. Brettnacher, Supt.;
Catholic Youth Organizations (CYO) - Ava Meyer;
Inter City Catholic League - Tony Violi, Pres.; Rev. Jason Freiburger, Moderator;
Censor Librorum - Rev. Msgr. Michael W. Heintz;
Clergy Retirement Board - Very Rev. Mark A. Gurtner; Very Rev. Matthew M. Coonan; Joseph Ryan;
College of Consultors - Very Rev. Mark A. Gurtner; Very Rev. Jacob Runyon; Very Rev. Matthew M. Coonan;
Communications/Today's Catholic Official Publication - t) 260-456-2824; 260-399-1453 Nicole Hahn, Dir. (Nhahn@diocesefwsb.org);
Continuing Formation of Priests and Deacons - t) 260-422-4611 Very Rev. Matthew M. Coonan;
Diocesan Archives - Janice Cantrell, Archivist;
Diocesan Finance Council - Very Rev. Mark A. Gurtner; Joseph Ryan, CFO; Jacob Benedict;
Diocesan Museum - t) 260-422-0812 Kathy Imler;
Diocesan Purchasing Agency - t) 260-422-4611 Mike Gibson, Mgr. (mgibson@diocesefwsb.org);
Good Shepherd Books & Gifts - t) 260-399-1442 Kara Slocum, Coord.;
Operations Manager - Brian Tusing, Contact (btusing@diocesefwsb.org);
Pontifical Mission Societies - t) 260-396-2552 kayschneider@embarqmail.com Kathleen Schneider, Dir.;
Presbyteral Council - Very Rev. Mark A. Gurtner; Very Rev. Jacob Runyon; Very Rev. Matthew M. Coonan;
Safe Environment/Youth Protection - Joseph Garcia, Coord. (jgarcia@diocesefwsb.org);
Stewardship and Development - t) 574-258-6751; 260-422-4611 Jeffery Boetticher, Dir.;
Today's Catholic Official Publication - t) 260-456-2824 Nicole Hahn, Mgr. (Nhahn@diocesefwsb.org);
Tribunal - t) 260-422-4611 www.diocesefwsb.org Very Rev. Jacob Runyon, Judicial Vicar;
Advocates - Rev. David Violi; Vicki Ferrier;
Auditors - Ellen Becker;
Court of First Instance Judges - Very Rev. Jacob Runyon; Rev. Francis Chukwuma (Nigeria); Rev. Wimal Jayasuria;
Pro-Synodal Judges - Very Rev. Mark A. Gurtner; Rev. Msgr. Michael W. Heintz; Rev. Msgr. Bruce Piechocki;
Promoter of Justice - Rev. Msgr. Bruce Piechocki;
Worship Office - Brian MacMichael, Dir.;
Liturgical Commission - Rev. Msgr. William C. Schooler, Chair; Rev. Brian C. Ching, C.S.C.; David Fagerberg;
Sacred Art and Architecture Committee - Very Rev. Mark A. Gurtner; William Coleman Jr.; Rev. Jacob A. Meyer;

HUMAN RESOURCES

Human Resources - t) 260-422-4611 Laurie Haverty, Dir. (lhaverty@diocesefwsb.org);

PARISHES, MISSIONS, AND CLERGY

STATE OF INDIANA

ALBION

Blessed Sacrament - 2290 N. State Rd. 9, Albion, IN 46701 t) 260-636-2072 blessedsacramentc@gmail.com www.blessedsacramentalbion.org Rev. John Steele, C.S.C., Pst.; Susan Curtis, DRE; CRP Stds.: 37

ANGOLA

St. Anthony of Padua - 700 W. Maumee St., Angola, IN 46703 t) 260-665-2259 office@stanthonyangola.com www.stanthonyangola.com Rev. Osman Guzman Ramos, F.M. (Nicaragua), Pst.; Rev. Jose Raul Marroquin-Monroy, F.M. (Guatemala), Par. Vicar; Cathy Bryan, DRE; Marilee Roederer, Music Min.; Diana Miller, Music Min.; Katie Waltke, Bus. Mgr.; CRP Stds.: 150

AUBURN

Immaculate Conception - 500 E. 7th St., Auburn, IN 46706 t) 260-925-3930 office@iccauburn.com www.iccauburn.com Rev. Mark Enemali, CssP (Nigeria), Pst.; CRP Stds.: 47

AVILLA

St. Mary of the Assumption - 228 N. Main St., Avilla, IN 46710-0700; Mailing: Box 700, Avilla, IN 46710-0700 t) 260-897-3261 stmaryassumption@embarqmail.com bedwards@stmaryavilla.org Rev. David W. Voors, Pst.; CRP Stds.: 14
St. Mary of the Assumption School - (Grades PreK-8) 232 N. Main St., Avilla, IN 46710-0109; Mailing: PO Box 109, Avilla, IN 46710-0109 t) 260-897-3481 aadams@stmaryavilla.org stmaryavilla.org Andrew Adams, Prin.; Stds.: 138; Lay Tchrs.: 11

BLUFFTON

St. Joseph - 1300 N. Main St., Bluffton, IN 46714-1127 t) 260-824-1380 stjosephchurch@adamswells.com stjosephchurchbluffton.org/ Rev. David Violi, Pst.; Michelle Paxton, DRE; CRP Stds.: 99

BREMEN

St. Dominic - 803 W. Bike St., Bremen, IN 46506 t) 574-546-3601 office@stdominic.info; rita.jeffirs@gmail.com stdominiccatholicchurch.yolasite.com Rev. Daniel Niezer, Pst.; Rita Jeffirs, DRE; CRP Stds.: 154

BRISTOL

St. Mary of the Annunciation - 411 W. Vistula St., Bristol, IN 46507; Mailing: P.O. Box 245, Bristol, IN 46507 t) 574-848-4305 (Office); 574-622-0039 (Rectory) annunciationchurch-bristol@hotmail.com www.stmarysbristol.com Rev. Robert Van Kempen, Pst.; Rev. Nji Tegha Afuhwi, Par. Vicar; CRP Stds.: 120

CHURUBUSCO

St. John Bosco - 216 N. Main St., Churubusco, IN 46723 t) 260-693-9578 saintjohn.bosco@gmail.com stjohnboscochurubusco.org Rev. Andrew Curry, Pst.; CRP Stds.: 70

COLUMBIA CITY

St. Catherine of Alexandria - 9989 S. SR 9, Columbia City, IN 46725; Mailing: P.O. Box 250, Roanoke, IN 46783 t) 260-672-2838; 260-396-2552 (CRP) sscatherineandjoseph@comcast.net Rev. Dale A. Bauman, Pst.; Kathleen Schneider, DRE; CRP Stds.: 5
St. Paul of the Cross - 315 S. Line St., Columbia City, IN 46725 t) 260-244-5723 saintpaulchurch@embarqmail.com saintpaulcc.org Rev. Jose Arroyo, Pst.; Jeanne Stefanko, Bus. Mgr.; CRP Stds.: 97

CULVER

St. Mary of the Lake - 124 College Ave., Culver, IN 46511; Mailing: 605 N. Plymouth St., Culver, IN 46511 t) 574-842-3667 (Office); 574-842-2522 (Rectory) bmeininger@stmaryculver.org; dmckee@stmaryculver.org www.stmaryculver.org Rev. William A. Meininger, Pst.; Tamala Slykas, Bus. Mgr.; Donna McKee, DRE; Evan Akers, Music Min.; CRP Stds.: 38

DECATUR

St. Mary of the Assumption - 414 W. Madison St., Decatur, IN 46733 t) 260-724-9159 x126 (Secy); 260-724-9159 x101 (CRP); 260-724-9159 x128 (Bus. Mgr.) madams@sjdecatur.org; frdave@sjdecatur.org www.stmarysdecatur.org Rev. David Ruppert, Pst.; Rev. LeeAllen Fortin, Par. Vicar; Judith Converset, Bus. Mgr.; Stephanie Ortiz-Brite, DRE; CRP Stds.: 250
St. Joseph - (Grades PreK-8) 127 N. Fourth St., Decatur, IN 46733 t) 260-724-2765 school@sjdecatur.org www.stjosephdecatur.org Brian J. Baker, Prin.; Stds.: 250; Lay Tchrs.: 18

ELKHART

St. Thomas the Apostle - 1405 N. Main St., Elkhart, IN 46514 t) 574-264-0491 (CRP); 574-262-1505 bmahaffa@stselkhart.com; frjason@stselkhart.com Rev. Levi UC Nkwocha (Nigeria), Pst.; CRP Stds.: 70
St. Thomas the Apostle School - (Grades PreK-8) 1331 N. Main St., Elkhart, IN 46514 t) 574-264-4855 www.stselkhart.com Christopher Adamo, Prin.; Stds.: 260; Lay Tchrs.: 24
St. Vincent de Paul - 1108 S. Main St., Elkhart, IN 46516 t) 574-293-8071 (CRP); 574-293-8231 r.campanello@svcelkhart.org; h.palmer@svcelkhart.org www.svcelkhart.org Rev. Craig Borchard, Pst.; Rev. Eloy Jimenez (Mexico), Par. Vicar; Rev. Benjamin Landrigan, Par. Vicar; Harry Palmer, DRE; CRP Stds.: 490
St. Vincent de Paul School - (Grades PreK-8) 1114 S. Main St., Elkhart, IN 46516 t) 574-293-8451 t.lundy@svcelkhart.org Tara Lundy, Prin.; Stds.: 190; Lay Tchrs.: 12

FORT WAYNE

Cathedral of the Immaculate Conception - 1122 S.

Clinton St., Fort Wayne, IN 46802 t) 260-424-1485 jrunyon@cathedralfw.org www.cathedralfortwayne.org Very Rev. Jacob Runyon, Pst.; Rev. Peter Dee De (Myanmar), Assoc. Pst.; CRP Stds.: 85

St. Mother Theodore Guerin Chapel - 1139 S. Calhoun St., Fort Wayne, IN 46802; Mailing: 1102 S. Clinton St, Fort Wayne, IN 46802 t) (260) 424-1485

St. Charles Borromeo - 4916 Trier Rd., Fort Wayne, IN 46815 t) 260-482-2186; 260-484-7322 (CRP); 260-484-3392 (school) fathertom@scbfw.org; schooladministration@stcharelsschoolfw.org stcharlesfortwayne.org Rev. Thomas Shoemaker, Pst.; Rev. Daniel Koehl, Assoc. Pst.; Rev. James Kumbakkeel, O.S.B. (India), Assoc. Pst.; Robert Carroll, Bus. Mgr.; Amy Johns, DRE; Cynthia Stults, DRE; Stacey Huneck, Youth Min.; Anna Laisure, Youth Min.; Casey Ryan, RCIA Coord.; Timothy Robison, Liturgy Dir.; Karen Hope, Liturgy Dir.; CRP Stds.: 70

St. Charles Borromeo School - (Grades PreK-8) 4910 Trier Rd., Fort Wayne, IN 46815 schooloffice@stcharlesschoolfw.org; schooladministration@stcharlesschoolfw.org www.stcharlesschoolfw.org Robert Sordelet, Prin.; Kevin Hoersten, Vice Prin.; Sr. Genevieve Raupp, OSF, Vice Prin.; Stds.: 803; Lay Tchrs.: 35

St. Elizabeth Ann Seton - 10700 Aboite Center Rd., Fort Wayne, IN 46804 t) 260-432-0268 parish@seasfw.org www.seasfw.org Rev. Terrence M. Coonan Jr., Pst.; Rev. Stephen Felicichia, Par. Vicar; Rev. Luke Okoye (Nigeria), Par. Vicar; Kim Conte, DRE; CRP Stds.: 295

St. Elizabeth Ann Seton School - (Grades PreK-8) 10650 Aboite Center School Rd., Fort Wayne, IN 46804 t) 260-432-4001 lwidner@seascsfw.org www.seascsfw.org Lois Widner, Prin.; Stds.: 579; Lay Tchrs.: 40

St. Henry - 5711 Saint Henry's Ln., Fort Wayne, IN 46806 t) 260-447-4100 sainthenrys49@gmail.com Very Rev. Matthew M. Coonan, Pst.; Rev. Evaristo R. Olivera, Par. Vicar; Dcn. Huberto Vasquez Osorio; CRP Stds.: 204

St. John the Baptist - 4500 Fairfield Ave., Fort Wayne, IN 46807; Mailing: 4525 Arlington Ave., Fort Wayne, IN 46807 t) 260-744-4393 rnoll@stjohnsfw.org www.saintjohnfortwayne.com Rev. Andrew Budzinski, Pst.; Rev. Paolo Degasperi, Par. Vicar; Ed Fox, DRE; Rhonda Noll, Bus. Mgr.; CRP Stds.: 15

St. John the Baptist School - (Grades PreK-8) t) 260-456-3321 mkeefer@stjohnsfw.org Mary Keefer, Prin.; Stds.: 298; Lay Tchrs.: 18

St. Joseph - 2213 Brooklyn Ave., Fort Wayne, IN 46802 t) 260-432-5113; 260-432-5113 x319 (CRP) aponce@saintjosephfw.org; rteetsel@saintjosephfw.org www.saintjosephcatholicchurchfw.org Rev. Kevin M. Bauman, Pst.; Ken Jehle, Music Min.; Ana Ponce, DRE; CRP Stds.: 118

St. Joseph Catholic School - (Grades PreK-8) 2211 Brooklyn Ave., Fort Wayne, IN 46802 t) 260-432-4000 cjordan@saintjosephfw.org www.saintjosephcatholicfw.org Cristy Jordan, Prin.; Stds.: 160; Lay Tchrs.: 14

St. Joseph - 11337 Old U.S. 27 S., Fort Wayne, IN 46816 t) 260-639-3748 (Office); 260-639-3058 (Rectory) secretary@stjoehc.org www.stjoehc.org Rev. William J. Kummer, Pst.; Michelle Boroff, DRE; Thomas Saul, Music Min.; Michelle Rupright, Bus. Mgr.; CRP Stds.: 5

St. Joseph School - (Grades PreK-8) 11521 Old U.S. 27 S., Fort Wayne, IN 46816 t) 260-639-3580 jskordos@stjoehc.org Jeanine Skordos, Prin.; Lori Price, Bus. Mgr.; Stds.: 172; Lay Tchrs.: 9

St. Jude - 2155 Randallia Dr., Fort Wayne, IN 46805; Mailing: 2130 Pemberton Dr., Fort Wayne, IN 46805 t) 260-484-6609 info@stjudefw.org Rev. Msgr. Robert C. Schulte, Pst.; Rev. Michael Ammer, Par. Vicar; Dcn. Jim Tighe; CRP Stds.: 109

St. Jude School - (Grades PreK-8) 2110 Pemberton Dr., Fort Wayne, IN 46805 t) 260-484-4611 mobergfell@stjudefw.org www.stjudefw.org/school Mike Obergfell, Prin.; Colin Wilkins, Vice Prin.; Stds.: 378; Lay Tchrs.: 24

St. Mary's Catholic Church - 1101 S. Lafayette St., Fort Wayne, IN 46802-3202; Mailing: P.O. Box 11383, Fort Wayne, IN 46857-1383 t) 260-424-8231 stmarysfw@stmarysfw.org www.stmaryfsw.org Rev. Wimal Jayasuriya (Sri Lanka), Pst.; CRP Stds.: 19

Most Precious Blood - 1515 Barthold St., Fort Wayne, IN 46808 t) 260-424-5535 (CRP); 260-424-5535 fadafrancis@preciousblood.org; espringer@preciousblood.org preciousblood.org Rev. Francis Chukwuma (Nigeria), Pst.; CRP Stds.: 23

Most Precious Blood School - (Grades PreK-8) 1529 Barthold St., Fort Wayne, IN 46808 t) 260-424-4832 pbloodschool@preciousblood.org Stanley Liponoga IV, Prin.; Stds.: 192; Lay Tchrs.: 12

Our Lady of Good Hope - 7215 Saint Joe Rd., Fort Wayne, IN 46835 t) 260-485-9615 x107 (CRP); 260-485-9615 (Parish) dre@olghfw.com; info@olghfw.com olghfw.com Very Rev. Mark A. Gurtner, Pst.; Rev. Daniel Whelan, Par. Vicar; Jackie Oberhausen, Pst. Assoc.; David Zehr, Pst. Assoc.; Kelly Ley, DRE; Jeanne Kawiecki, Liturgy & Music Dir.; Kyle Craig, Teen & Young Adult Min.; CRP Stds.: 133

Our Lady School - (Grades PreK-8) t) 260-485-5289 bea.royal@ourladyfortwayne.org ourladyfortwayne.org Beatrice Royal, Prin.; Stds.: 139; Lay Tchrs.: 10

St. Patrick - 2120 S. Harrison St., Fort Wayne, IN 46802 t) 260-744-1450 x116 (CRP); 260-744-1450 st.patrick.f.w@gmail.com; drereligioused@gmail.com saintpatrickfw.com Rev. Dominic Dung Anh Nguyen, SVD, Pst.; Rev. Nam Vu, S.V.D., Assoc. Pst.; CRP Stds.: 143

St. Patrick - 12305 Arcola Rd., Fort Wayne, IN 46818 t) 260-625-4104 (CRP); 260-625-4151 stpatarcola@earthlink.net Rev. Thadeus Balinda (Uganda), Pst.; Roberta Davis, DRE; CRP Stds.: 60

St. Peter - 518 E. Dewald St, Fort Wayne, IN 46803 t) 260-744-2765 hello@saintpetersfortwayne.org www.saintpetersfortwayne.org Rev. Patrick Hake, Pst.; CRP Stds.: 33

Queen of Angels - 1500 W. State Blvd., Fort Wayne, IN 46808 t) 260-482-9411 pastor@queenofangelsfw.org; parishsecretary@queenofangelsfw.org queenofangelsfw.org Rev. Spenser St. Louis, Pst.; Christopher Lushis, Pst. Assoc.; CRP Stds.: 15

Queen of Angels School - (Grades PreK-8) 1600 W. State Blvd., Fort Wayne, IN 46808 t) 260-483-8214 principal@queenofangelsschool.com Dennis Wiegmann, Prin.; Stds.: 163; Lay Tchrs.: 18

Sacred Heart - 4643 Gaywood Dr., Fort Wayne, IN 46806 t) 260-744-2519 office@sacredheartfwin.org sacredheartfw.org Rev. Mark Wojdelski, F.S.S.P., Pst.; Rev. Dominic Savoie, FSSP, Par. Vicar; CRP Stds.: 12

St. Therese - 2304 Lower Huntington Rd., Fort Wayne, IN 46819 t) 260-747-9139 secretary@sttheresefw.org; mcoonan@sttheresefw.org www.sttheresefw.org Very Rev. Matthew M. Coonan, Pst.; Rev. Evaristo R. Olivera, Par. Vicar; Amy Carsten, Admin.; CRP Stds.: 15

St. Therese School - (Grades K-8) 2222 Lower Huntington Rd., Fort Wayne, IN 46819 t) 260-747-2343 rruhl@sttheresefw.org; eoberley@sttheresefw.org Rick Ruhl, Prin.; Stds.: 106; Lay Tchrs.: 14

St. Vincent de Paul - 1502 E. Wallen Rd., Fort Wayne, IN 46825 t) 260-489-3537 x204 (CRP); 260-489-3537 church@saintv.org www.saintv.org Rev. Daniel Scheidt, Pst.; Rev. Brian Isenbarger, Par. Vicar; Rev. Polycarp Fernando, Par. Vicar; Rev. Jose Panamattathil Chandy, Par. Vicar; Thomas Schuerman, Bus. Mgr.; Dorothy Schuerman, Pst. Assoc.; Justin Aquila, Pst. Assoc.; Monica Aquila, Pst. Assoc.; Jessica Hayes, Pst. Assoc.; Debbie Blackburn, DRE; Lindsay Lushis, Youth Min.; Scott Nguyen, Youth Min.; CRP Stds.: 293

St. Vincent de Paul School - (Grades K-8) 1720 E. Wallen Rd., Fort Wayne, IN 46825 school@saintv.org www.school.saintv.org Zachary Coyle, Prin.; Stds.: 765; Lay Tchrs.: 44

FREMONT

St. Paul Chapel - 8780 E. 700 N., Fremont, IN 46737; Mailing: 700 W. Maumee St., Angola, IN 46703 t) 260-665-2259 info@stpaulcatholicchapel.org www.stpaulcatholicchapel.org/ Rev. Osman Guzman Ramos, F.M. (Nicaragua), Pst.; Rev. Jose Raul Marroquin-Monroy, F.M. (Guatemala), Par. Vicar; Katie Waltke, Bus. Mgr.; Therese Shiffler, DRE; CRP Stds.: 35

GARRETT

St. Joseph - 300 W. Houston St., Garrett, IN 46738-1424 t) 260-357-3122 parish@stjosephgarrett.org; sarrazine@stjosephgarrett.org stjosephgarrett.com Rev. James A. Shafer, Pst.; Eileen Sarrazine, Pst. Assoc.; Kathy Guthrie, Bus. Mgr.; CRP Stds.: 24

St. Joseph School - (Grades PreK-5) 301 W. Houston, Garrett, IN 46738 t) 260-357-5137 office@stjosephgarrett.org www.stjosephgarrett.org Kathleen Mulligan, Prin.; Stds.: 109; Lay Tchrs.: 8

GENEVA

St. Mary of the Presentation - 5790 E. 1100 S., Geneva, IN 46740-9132 t) 260-997-6558 chinonye75@gmail.com www.stmarysgeneva.org Rev. Jonathan Agbedo (Nigeria), Pst.;

GOSHEN

St. John the Evangelist - 417 S. Main St., Goshen, IN 46526; Mailing: 117 W. Monroe St., Goshen, IN 46526 t) 574-533-3385 parishoffice@stjohncatholic.com www.stjohncatholic.com Rev. Royce Gregerson, Pst.; Rev. Logan Parrish, Par. Vicar; Dcn. Giovani Munoz; Dcn. Christian Nieves; CRP Stds.: 379

St. John the Evangelist School - (Grades PreK-6) 117 W. Monroe St., Goshen, IN 46526 t) 574-533-9480 schooloffice@stjohncatholic.com Virginia Muñoz, Prin.; Stds.: 152; Lay Tchrs.: 8

GRANGER

St. Pius X - 52553 Fir Rd., Granger, IN 46530 t) 574-272-8462; 574-277-5760 rkiley@stpius.net; parishoffice@stpius.net www.stpius.net Rev. Msgr. William C. Schooler, Pst.; Rev. Augustine Onuoha, Par. Vicar; Robby Kiley, DRE; CRP Stds.: 421

St. Pius X School - (Grades PreK-8) t) 574-272-4935 ksandor@stpius.net Elaine Holmes, Prin.; Stds.: 650; Lay Tchrs.: 36

HUNTINGTON

St. Mary - 903 N. Jefferson St., Huntington, IN 46750 t) 260-356-4398 stmary083@gmail.com; tzehr@huntingtoncatholic.org Rev. Thomas Zehr, Pst.; CRP Stds.: 50

Huntington Catholic School - (Grades PreK-8) 820 Cherry St., Huntington, IN 46750 t) 260-356-1926; 260-356-2320 dboone@huntingtoncatholic.org www.huntingtoncatholic.org Derek Boone, Prin.; Stds.: 168; Lay Tchrs.: 11

SS. Peter and Paul - 860 Cherry St., Huntington, IN 46750 t) 260-356-4798 kjennings@sspeterpaulparish.org; dstuart@sspeterpaulparish.org sspeterpaulparish.org Rev. Anthony Steinacker, Pst.; Drew Stuart, DRE; Susanne Meadows, Music Min.; CRP Stds.: 212

KENDALLVILLE

Immaculate Conception - 301 E. Diamond St., Kendallville, IN 46755; Mailing: 319 E Diamond St, Kendallville, IN 46755 t) 260-347-4045 icckendallville@live.com Rev. John Steele, C.S.C., Pst.; CRP Stds.: 33

LAGRANGE

St. Joseph - 050 N. 100 E., LaGrange, IN 46761 t) 260-585-5891 (CRP); 260-463-3472 stjosephlagrange@gmail.com Rev. Osman Guzman Ramos, F.M. (Nicaragua), Pst.; Rev. Jose Raul Marroquin-Monroy, F.M. (Guatemala), Par. Vicar; CRP Stds.: 107

LAOTTO

Immaculate Conception - 7046 E. 400 S., Laotto, IN 46763; Mailing: 216 N. Main St., Churubusco, IN 46723 t) 260-693-9578 saintjohn.bosco@gmail.com iccege.org Rev. Andrew Curry, Pst.; CRP Stds.: 55

LIGONIER

St. Patrick - 300 Ravine Park Dr., Ligonier, IN 46767-1301 t) 260-894-4946 stpatlig@ligtel.com Rev. Zachary Barry, Pst.; Ricardo Garcia; Dcn. Stanley LeMieux; CRP Stds.: 237

MISHAWAKA

St. Bavo - 502 W. 7th St., Mishawaka, IN 46544 t) 574-255-1437 office@stbavochurch.com www.stbavochurch.com Rev. Peter Pacini, C.S.C., Pst.; Gus Zuehlke, Pst. Min./Coord.; CRP Stds.: 23

Mishawaka Catholic School - (Grades PreSchool-2) 524 W. 8th St., Mishawaka, IN 46544; Mailing: 223 W. Grove St., Mishawaka, IN 46545 t) 574-259-4214 info@mcmish.org; ksalvador@mcmish.org www.mcmish.org Karen Salvador, Prin.; Stds.: 125; Lay Tchrs.: 10

St. Joseph - 225 S. Mill St., Mishawaka, IN 46544; Mailing: 220 W. 4th St, Mishawaka, IN 46544 t) 574-255-6134 parish@stjoemish.com www.stjoemish.com Rev. Christopher R. Lapp, Pst.; Rev. Kenneth Amadi (Nigeria), Par. Vicar; CRP Stds.: 16

Mishawaka Catholic School - (Grades 3-5) 230 S. Spring St., St. Joseph Campus, Mishawaka, IN 46544 t) 574-255-5554 info@mcmish.org www.mcmish.org Karen Salvador, Prin.; Beth Whitfield, Vice Prin.; Stds.: 79; Lay Tchrs.: 18

St. Monica - 222 W. Mishawaka Ave., Mishawaka, IN 46545 t) 574-255-2247 www.stmonicamish.org Rev. Jason Freiburger, Pst.; Victoria Zmirski, Bus. Mgr.; CRP Stds.: 52

Mishawaka Catholic School - (Grades 6-8) 223 W. Grove St., Mishawaka, IN 46545 t) 574-255-0709 ksalvador@mcmish.org; tchristianson@mcmish.org www.mcmish.org Karen Salvador, Prin.; Beth Whitfield, Vice Prin.; Stds.: 307; Lay Tchrs.: 25

Queen of Peace - 4508 Vistula Rd., Mishawaka, IN 46544 t) 574-255-9674 parishoffice@queenofpeace.cc www.queenofpeace.cc Rev. John Eze (Nigeria), Pst.; Rev. Emmanuel Abuh, Par. Vicar; Dcn. Robert Byrne; Preston Harrell, Dir., Sacred Music; Tamara Shackelford, Bus. Mgr.; CRP Stds.: 52

Queen of Peace School - (Grades PreK-8) t) 574-255-0392 school@queenofpeace.cc school.queenofpeace.cc/ Kim Obringer, Prin.; Stds.: 136; Lay Tchrs.: 11

MONROEVILLE

St. Rose of Lima - 207 Mulberry St., Monroeville, IN 46773; Mailing: 209 Mulberry St., PO Box 406, Monroeville, IN 46773 t) 260-623-6439 mikelobo1967@gmail.com; strosemonroeville@outlook.com www.strosedelima.org Rev. Maicaal Lobo (India), Pst.; Karen Marie Castleman, Bus. Mgr.;

St. Rose of Lima - (Grades PreK-8) 401 Monroe St., Monroeville, IN 46773 t) 260-623-3447 srsoffice@strosemonroeville.org www.saintrosemonroeville.org Travis Heckber, Prin.; Stds.: 120; Lay Tchrs.: 7

NEW CARLISLE

St. Stanislaus Kostka - 55756 Tulip Rd., New Carlisle, IN 46552 t) 574-654-3781 dianeststan@embarqmail.com; pastorstan@embarqmail.com ststansnewcarlisle.org Rev. Robert Garrow, Pst.; Diane Oudhuis, Admin.; Kathy Henderson, DRE; Blaise Waldstein, Music Min.; CRP Stds.: 22

NEW HAVEN

St. John the Baptist - 943 Powers St., New Haven, IN 46774 t) 260-493-4553; 260-749-9903; 260-493-4553 x306 (CRP) stjohn111@diocesefwsb.org; kelly.mouch@sjnewhaven.org www.sjnewhaven.org Rev. Nathan Maskal, Pst.; Kelly Mouch, DRE; CRP Stds.: 10

St. John the Baptist School - (Grades PreK-8) 204 S. Rufus St., New Haven, IN 46774 info@sjnewhaven.org Justin Pranger, Vice Prin.; Stds.: 217; Lay Tchrs.: 13

St. Louis - 15535 Lincoln Hwy. E., New Haven, IN 46774 t) 260-749-4525 secretary@stlouisb.org; josie.ball@stlouisb.org www.stlouisb.org Rev. Tyrell J. Alles, O.S.B. (Sri Lanka), Pst.; CRP Stds.: 7

St. Louis School - (Grades PreK-8) 15529 Lincoln Hwy. E., New Haven, IN 46774 t) 260-749-5815 vdiller@stlouisacademy.org www.stlouisacademy.org Vanessa Diller, Prin.; Stds.: 155; Scholastics: 2; Lay Tchrs.: 12

NORTH MANCHESTER

St. Robert Bellarmine - 1203 State Rd., 114 E., North Manchester, IN 46962 t) 260-982-4404 strobertsnm@gmail.com www.strobertsnmanchester.org Rev. Dennis M. Di Benedetto, Pst.; CRP Stds.: 48

NOTRE DAME

Sacred Heart - 104 Sacred Heart Parish Ctr., Notre Dame, IN 46556-5662 t) 574-631-7511 sacheart@nd.edu sacredheartparish.nd.edu Rev. John E. Conley, C.S.C., Pst.; Dcn. William J. Gallagher; CRP Stds.: 28

PIERCETON

St. Francis Xavier - 408 W. Catholic St., Pierceton, IN 46562; Mailing: P.O. Box 376, Pierceton, IN 46562 t) 574-594-5750 sfxpierceton@aol.com www.sfxpierceton.org Rev. Daniel Chukwuleta (Nigeria), Pst.; Sharon DeLong, DRE; CRP Stds.: 16

PLYMOUTH

St. Michael - 612 N. Walnut St., Plymouth, IN 46563 t) 574-936-4935 businessmanager@saintmichaelplymouth.org stmichaelplymouth.org Rev. Fernando M. Jimenez, Pst.; Rev. Keeton Lockwood, Par. Vicar; CRP Stds.: 177

St. Michael School - (Grades K-8) 612 N. Center St., Plymouth, IN 46563 t) 574-936-4329 aweidner@saintmichaelschool.org www.saintmichaelschool.org Amy Weidner, Prin.; Stds.: 177; Lay Tchrs.: 12

ROANOKE

St. Joseph - 641 N. Main St., Roanoke, IN 46783-0250; Mailing: P.O. Box 250, Roanoke, IN 46783 t) 260-672-2838; 260-396-2552 (CRP) kayschneider@embarqmail.com; sscatherineandjoseph@comcast.net Rev. Dale A. Bauman, Pst.; Kathleen Schneider, DRE; CRP Stds.: 38

ROME CITY

St. Gaspar del Bufalo - 10871 N. State Rd. 9, Rome City, IN 46784 t) 260-854-3100 info@stgasparrc.org www.stgasparrc.org Rev. Louis Fowoyo (Nigeria), Pst.; CRP Stds.: 4

SOUTH BEND

Cathedral of Saint Matthew - 1701 Miami St., South Bend, IN 46613 t) 574-289-4535 (CRP); 574-289-5539 info@stmatthewcathedral.org www.stmatthewcathedral.org Rev. Terry Fisher, Rector; Rev. Brian Carpenter, Par. Vicar; Cassandra Horner, Admin.; John Fyrqvist, DRE; Trina Koldyke, Bus. Mgr.; CRP Stds.: 31

Cathedral School of Saint Matthew - (Grades PreK-8) 1015 E. Dayton, South Bend, IN 46613 sistergiannamarie@smcathedral.org stmatthewblazers.org Sr. Gianna Marie Webber, Prin.; Stds.: 297; Sr. Tchrs.: 3; Lay Tchrs.: 25

St. Adalbert - 2505 W. Grace St., South Bend, IN 46619 t) 574-288-5708 stadalbertparish.org/ Rev. Ryan Pietrocarlo, C.S.C., Pst.; Rev. Zachary Rathke, CSC, Assoc. Pst.; Rev. Drew Clary, C.S.C., Par. Vicar; CRP Stds.: 200

St. Adalbert School - (Grades PreK-8) 519 S. Olive St., South Bend, IN 46619 t) 574-288-6645 Joseph Miller, Prin.; Stds.: 231; Bro. Tchrs.: 1; Pr. Tchrs.: 1; Lay Tchrs.: 12

St. Anthony de Padua - 2310 E. Jefferson Blvd., South Bend, IN 46615 t) 574-282-2308 church@stasb.org www.stasb.org/ Rev. Arthur Joseph Ssembajja, Pst.;

St. Anthony de Padua School - (Grades PreK-8) t) 574-233-7169 kbogol@stasb.org www.school.stasb.org Karen Bogol, Prin.; Stds.: 218; Lay Tchrs.: 13

St. Augustine - 1501 W. Washington St., South Bend, IN 46628; Mailing: P.O. Box 3198, South Bend, IN 46619-0198 t) 574-234-7082 leonardcollins@att.net www.saintaugustineparish.org Rev. Leonard J. Collins, C.S.C., Pst.; Dcn. Melvin Tardy; CRP Stds.: 20

St. Casimir - 1308 Dunham St., South Bend, IN 46619; Mailing: 2505 Grace St., South Bend, IN 46619 t) 574-288-5708 www.stcasimirparish.net Rev. Ryan Pietrocarlo, C.S.C., Pst.; Rev. Zachary Rathke, CSC, Assoc. Pst.; Rev. Drew Clary, C.S.C., Par. Vicar;

Christ the King - 52473 Indiana State Rte. 933, South Bend, IN 46637 t) 574-272-3113 christthekingonline.com Rev. Stephen A. Lacroix, C.S.C., Pst.; Rev. Geoffrey Mooney, CSC, Assoc. Pst.; Teresa Oross, DRE; CRP Stds.: 12

Christ the King School - (Grades PreK-8) t) 574-272-3922 shoffman@christthekingonline.org school.christthekingonline.com Stephen Hoffman, Prin.; Stds.: 486; Lay Tchrs.: 29

Corpus Christi - 2822 Corpus Christi Dr., South Bend, IN 46628 t) 574-272-9982 corpuschristi2005@sbcglobal.net www.corpuschristisb.org Rev. Daryl Rybicki, Pst.; Michael Rafinski, DRE; CRP Stds.: 9

Corpus Christi School - (Grades PreK-8) 2817 Corpus Christi Dr., South Bend, IN 46628 t) 574-272-9868 m.willerton@corpuschristisb.org; j.kiley@corpuschristisb.org Mattie Willerton, Prin.; Stds.: 162; Lay Tchrs.: 15

St. Hedwig - 331 S. Scott St., South Bend, IN 46601 t) 574-287-8932 hedwigmemorial@gmail.com sthedwigsb.org Rev. Cyril Fernandes, Pst.; Rev. David Kashangaki, C.S.C., Assoc. Pst.;

Holy Cross - 920 Wilber St., South Bend, IN 46628 t) 574-233-2179 parish@hcpsb.org www.hcpsb.org Rev. James E. Fenstermaker, C.S.C., Pst.; Rev. Thomas K Zurcher, CSC, Pst. Assoc.; Rev. John M. Santone, C.S.C., In Res.; Logan Wishart, DRE; CRP Stds.: 30

Holy Cross School - (Grades PreK-8) 1020 Wilber St., South Bend, IN 46628-2637 t) 574-234-3422 info@holycrosscrusaders.org www.holycrosscrusaders.org Ann Borjas, Prin.; Stds.: 360; Lay Tchrs.: 26

Holy Family - 56405 Mayflower Rd., South Bend, IN 46619-1517 t) 574-282-2317; 574-289-7375 (CRP) hfamily135@diocesefwsb.org; jthornburg@hfssb.org www.holyfamilysouthbend.org Rev. Glenn Kohrman, Pst.; Rev. Sunday Akuh (Nigeria), Assoc. Pst.; CRP Stds.: 45

Holy Family School - (Grades PreK-8) 56407 Mayflower Rd., South Bend, IN 46619-1517 t) (574) 289-7375 bkorpal@hfssb.org Brittany Korpal, Prin.; Stds.: 290; Lay Tchrs.: 30

St. John the Baptist - 3526 St. Johns Way, South Bend, IN 46628 t) 574-233-5414; 574-282-2317 (CRP) johnthebaptistcc@aol.com stjohnsb.com Rev. Glenn Kohrman, Pst.; Rev. Sunday Akuh (Nigeria), Assoc. Pst.;

St. John the Baptist School - (Grades PreK-8) 3616 St. Johns Way, South Bend, IN 46628 t) 574-232-9849 office@stjohnsb.com www.stjohnspartans.com Shannon Jones, Prin.; Stds.: 123; Lay Tchrs.: 10

St. Joseph - 226 N. Hill St., South Bend, IN 46617 t) 574-234-3134 secretary@stjoeparish.com www.stjoeparish.com Rev. Matthew Fase, C.S.C., Pst.; Rev. David W. Smith, CSC, Assoc. Pst.; Sean Driscoll, DRE; CRP Stds.: 270

St. Joseph School - (Grades PreSchool-8) 216 N. Hill St., South Bend, IN 46617 t) 574-234-0451 mgreen@stjosephgradeschool.com www.stjosephgradeschool.com Melissa Green, Prin.; Stds.: 435; Lay Tchrs.: 26

St. Jude Church - 19704 Johnson Rd., South Bend, IN 46614 t) 574-291-0570 office@stjudeparish.net; business@stjudeparish.net www.stjudeparish.net Rev. John Delaney, Pst.; Rev. Gregory Abuya (Nigeria), Par. Vicar; Emily Nufer, Bus. Mgr.; Heather Buison, DRE; CRP Stds.: 43

St. Jude Catholic School - (Grades PreK-8) 19657 Hildebrand St., South Bend, IN 46614 t) 574-291-3820 principal@stjudeschool.net www.stjudeschool.net Ana Maria Lewis, Prin.; Stds.: 200; Lay Tchrs.: 12

Our Lady of Hungary - 829 W. Calvert St., South Bend, IN 46613; Mailing: 731 W. Calvert St., South Bend, IN 46613 t) 574-287-1700; 574-289-3272 rectoryourladyofhungary@gmail.com; olhp@sbcglobal.net www.ourladyofhungary.org Rev. Wilson O. Corzo (Colombia), Pst.; Alan Jaquez, DRE; CRP Stds.: 88

Our Lady of Hungary School - (Grades PreK-8) 735 W. Calvert St., South Bend, IN 46613 olhsec@olhsb.org ourladyofhungary.org/ Kevin Goralczyk, Prin.; Stds.: 154; Lay Tchrs.: 11

St. Patrick - 309 S. Taylor St., South Bend, IN 46601; Mailing: 331 S. Scott St., South Bend, IN 46601 t) 574-287-8932 r.burns.churchoffice@gmail.com www.stpatricksb.org Rev. Cyril Fernandes, Pst.; Rev. David Kashangaki, C.S.C., Assoc. Pst.; Mary Nyers, DRE; Jim Nowinski, Music Min.; CRP Stds.: 3

Sacred Heart of Jesus (Lakeville) - 63568 Old US 31 S., South Bend, IN 46614; Mailing: P.O. Box 2528, South Bend, IN 46680-2528 t) 574-291-3775 sacredheart11@juno.com; faith@stjudeparish.net www.sacredheartlakeville.org Rev. John Delaney, Pst.; Rev. Gregory Abuya (Nigeria), Par. Vicar; Heather Buison, DRE; Emily Nufer, Bus. Mgr.; CRP Stds.: 15

St. Stanislaus Bishop and Martyr - 415 N. Brookfield St., South Bend, IN 46628 t) 574-223-1217 pastor@ststanparish.com www.ststanparish.com Rev. Msgr. John Fritz, F.S.S.P., Pst.; CRP Stds.: 51

St. Therese, Little Flower (Little Flower Catholic Church) - 54191 Ironwood Rd., South Bend, IN 46635 t) 574-272-7070; 574-243-3439 (CRP) bulletin@littleflowerchurch.org; alexis@littleflowerchurch.org littleflowerchurch.org Rev. Julius Okojie (Nigeria), Pst.; Rev. William Ikhianosimhe Orbih (Nigeria), Par. Vicar; Alexis Duffy, DRE; CRP Stds.: 81

SYRACUSE

St. Martin de Porres - 6941 E. Waco Dr., Syracuse, IN 46567-9496 t) 574-457-8176 stmartinchurch@yahoo.com stmartinchurchsyracuse.org Rev. Andrew Nazareth (India), Pst.; Cathy McGonigal, DRE; CRP Stds.: 25

WABASH

St. Bernard - 207 N. Cass St., Wabash, IN 46992 t) 260-563-4750 saintbchurch@gmail.com www.stbwabash.org Rev. Jay Horning, Pst.; CRP Stds.: 10

St. Bernard School - (Grades K-6) 191 N. Cass St., Wabash, IN 46992 t) 260-563-5746 stbernardcatholicschool.org Abigail Stanley, Prin.; Stds.: 50; Lay Tchrs.: 5

WALKERTON

St. Patrick - 807 Tyler St., Walkerton, IN 46574 t) 547-586-7152; 574-586-7152 (CRP) dre@saintpatricks.church; info@saintpatricks.church saintpatricks.church Rev. Donald J. Davison, C.PP.S., Pst.; Barbara Blad, DRE; Anna Chaffee, Music Min.; CRP Stds.: 39

WARSAW

Our Lady of Guadalupe - 225 Gilliam Dr., Warsaw, IN 46581-1136; Mailing: P.O. Box 1136, Warsaw, IN 46581-1136 t) 574-267-5324 olog.warsaw225@gmail.com Rev. Constantino Rocha, Pst.; Dcn. Marco Antonio Castillo; CRP Stds.: 68

Sacred Heart - 125 N. Harrison St., Warsaw, IN 46580 t) 574-267-5842 shc@shcwarsaw.org Rev. Jonathan Norton, Pst.; Laura Gillis, Bus. Mgr.; Susan Armacost, Pst. Min./Coord.; Cathy Smith, DRE; Abigael Black, Liturgy Dir.; Ida List, Youth Min.; CRP Stds.: 220

Sacred Heart School - (Grades PreK-6) 135 N. Harrison, Warsaw, IN 46590 t) 574-267-5874 office@shswarsaw.org www.sacredheart-warsaw.org Mike McClain, Prin.; Stds.: 220; Lay Tchrs.: 10

WATERLOO

St. Michael the Archangel - 1098 County Rd. 39, Waterloo, IN 46793-9779 t) 260-837-7115 secretary@stmichaelwaterloo.com; pastor@stmichaelwaterloo.com stmichaelwaterloo.com Rev. Vincent Rathappillil Joseph, VC, Pst.; Arica Swaygart, DRE; MarySue Kriegel, RCIA Coord.; Jenny Buchs, Youth Min.; CRP Stds.: 78

St. Mary of the Angels - 5965 S. 1025 E., Hudson, IN 46747-9605; Mailing: 1098 County Rd. 39, Waterloo, IN 46793 t) 260-351-3823 stmary.biglong@gmail.com Donna Garman, Bus. Mgr.;

YODER

St. Aloysius - 14623 Bluffton Rd., Yoder, IN 46798-9741 t) 260-622-4491 parish@stalyoder.org stalyoder.org Rev. Msgr. Bruce Piechocki, Pst.; CRP Stds.: 36

St. Aloysius School - (Grades PreK-8) 14607 Bluffton Rd., Yoder, IN 46798-9741 t) 260-622-7151 tvoors@saintaloysiusyoder.info www.saintaloysiusyoder.info/school Carin Freiburger, Prin.; Stds.: 60; Lay Tchrs.: 9

SCHOOLS: PRESCHOOL THRU HIGH SCHOOL

HIGH SCHOOLS

STATE OF INDIANA

FORT WAYNE

Bishop Dwenger High School - (DIO) 1300 E. Washington Center Rd., Fort Wayne, IN 46825 t) 260-496-4700 saints@bishopdwenger.com www.bishopdwenger.com Jason Garrett, Pst. Min./Coord.; Jason Schiffli, Prin.; Susan Schenkel, Bus. Mgr.; Jill Schriner, Librn.; Katie Slee, Dir.; Stds.: 930; Lay Tchrs.: 68

Bishop Luers High School - (DIO) (Grades 9-12) 333 E. Paulding Rd., Fort Wayne, IN 46816 t) 260-456-1261 jhuth@bishopluers.org www.bishopluers.org Kevin Mann, Dean; James Huth, Prin.; Randy Hawkins, Vice Prin.; Stds.: 507; Lay Tchrs.: 37

MISHAWAKA

Marian High School - (DIO) 1311 S. Logan St., Mishawaka, IN 46544 t) 574-259-5257 mhs@marianhs.org www.marianhs.org Mark Kirzeder, Prin.; Mary Dlugosz, Librn.; Stds.: 699; Sr. Tchrs.: 2; Lay Tchrs.: 47

SOUTH BEND

Saint Joseph High School - (DIO) (Grades 9-12) 453 N. Notre Dame Ave., South Bend, IN 46617 t) 574-233-6137 sbdstjoehs@saintjoehigh.com www.saintjoehigh.com Rev. Geoffrey Mooney, CSC, Chap.; Rev. Augustine Onuoha, Chap.; John Kennedy, Prin.; Corey Luczynski, Vice Prin.; Ben Dillon, Vice Prin.; Leslie Brenner, Librn.; Stds.: 819; Lay Tchrs.: 55

INSTITUTIONS LOCATED IN DIOCESE

ASSOCIATIONS [ASN]

NOTRE DAME

American Maritain Association - 430 Geddes Hall, Notre Dame, IN 46556; Mailing: 443 W. Hillsdale St., Inglewood, CA 90302-1123 t) 310-671-4412 jhanink70@gmail.com Jim Hanink, Pres.; Heather Erb, Treas.;

CATHOLIC CHARITIES [CCH]

FORT WAYNE

Catholic Charities of the Diocese of Ft. Wayne-South Bend, Inc. - 915 S. Clinton St., Fort Wayne, IN 46802; Mailing: P.O. Box 10630, Fort Wayne, IN 46853 t) 260-422-5625 ccoffice@ccfwsb.org www.ccfwsb.org Most Rev. Kevin C. Rhoades, Chair; Daniel P. Florin, CEO; Very Rev. Mark A. Gurtner, Mem.; Joseph Ryan, Mem.; Asstd. Annu.: 19,385; Staff: 64

Catholic Charities Auburn Office - 107 W. 5th St., Auburn, IN 46706 t) 260-925-0917 Aaron Roberts, Dir.;

Catholic Charities Fort Wayne Office & Administrative Office - 915 S Clinton St., Fort Wayne, IN 46802; Mailing: P.O. Box 10630, Fort Wayne, IN 46853 t) (260) 422-5625 www.ccfwsb.org/

Catholic Charities South Bend Office - 1817 Miami St., South Bend, IN 46613 t) 574-234-3111 Claire Coleman, Dir.;

CEMETERIES [CEM]

FORT WAYNE

Catholic Cemetery Association of Fort Wayne, Inc. - 3500 Lake Ave., Fort Wayne, IN 46805-5572 t) 260-426-2044 cmiller@divinemercyfuneralhome.com www.catholic-cemetery.org Divine Mercy Funeral Home Casey Miller, Dir.;

Saint Leo Catholic Cemetery - t) (260) 426-2044 cmiller@catholic-cemetery.org

Saint Michael Catholic Cemetery at Pierre Settlement - t) (260) 426-2044 cmiller@catholic-cemetery.org

COLLEGES & UNIVERSITIES [COL]

FORT WAYNE

University of Saint Francis - 2701 Spring St., Fort Wayne, IN 46808-3994 t) 260-399-7700 x6910 ezimmer@sf.edu www.sf.edu Conducted by Sisters of St. Francis of Perpetual Adoration. Rev. Eric A. Zimmer, Pres.; Rev. Dermot Gahan (Ireland), Chap.; Maureen McMahon, Librn.; Stds.: 1,903; Lay Tchrs.: 120; Sr. Tchrs.: 2

NOTRE DAME

Holy Cross College, Holy Cross College, Inc. - 54515 State Rd., 933 N., Notre Dame, IN 46556-0308; Mailing: P.O. Box 308, Notre Dame, IN 46556-0308 t) 574-239-8402 mclark@hcc-nd.edu www.hcc-nd.edu Dr. Marco Clark, Pres.; Monica Markovich, Vice Pres. Finance; Stds.: 415; Lay Tchrs.: 27

Saint Mary's College - 156 LeMans Hall, Notre Dame, IN 46556 t) 574-284-4556 dstrait@saintmarys.edu; jmillar@saintmarys.edu www.saintmarys.edu Women. Sisters of the Holy Cross. Sheila Catherine Conboy, Pres.; Stds.: 1,502; Lay Tchrs.: 142; Sr. Tchrs.: 1

***University of Notre Dame Du Lac** - 304 Main Bldg., Office of Mission Engagement & Church Affairs, Notre Dame, IN 46556 t) (574) 631-5950; (574) 631-1212 (Church Affairs) ahorcher@nd.edu www.nd.edu Rev. Nicholas R. Ayo, C.S.C.; Rev. Thomas E. Blantz, C.S.C.; Rev. Christopher Brennan, CSC; Rev. Richard S. Bullene, C.S.C.; Rev. Joseph H. Carey, C.S.C.; Rev. Gary S. Chamberland, C.S.C.; Rev. Michael E. Connors, C.S.C.; Rev. Joseph V. Corpora, C.S.C.; Rev. William R. Dailey, C.S.C.; Rev. Louis A. DelFra, C.S.C.; Rev. John M. DeRiso, C.S.C.; Rev. Thomas Eckert, CSC; Rev. James A. Bracke, C.S.C., Chap.; Rev. Francis J. Murphy, C.S.C., Chap.; Rev. Timothy L. O'Connor, C.S.C., Chap.; Rev. John I. Jenkins, C.S.C., Pres.; Rev. Austin I. Collins, C.S.C., Vice Pres., Mission Engagement & Church Affairs; Rev. Robert A. Dowd, C.S.C., Vice Pres. & Assoc. Provost; Rev. Daniel G. Groody, C.S.C., Vice Pres. & Assoc. Provost; Rev. Edward A. Malloy, C.S.C., Pres. Emeritus; Rev. Gerard J. Olinger, CSC, Vice Pres. for Student Affairs; Rev. Terrence P. Ehrman, C.S.C.; Rev. James K. Foster, C.S.C.; Rev. Gabriel J. Griggs, CSC; Rev. Kevin G. Grove, C.S.C.; Rev. Ralph L. Haag, C.S.C.; Rev. Gregory P. Haake, C.S.C.; Rev. Stephen J. Kempinger, C.S.C.; Rev. James B. King, CSC; Rev. Stephen Koeth, CSC; Rev. Paul V. Kollman, C.S.C.; Rev. Matthew C. Kuczora, C.S.C.; Rev. Stephen A. Lacroix, C.S.C.; Rev. James M. Lies, C.S.C.; Rev. Robert J. Lisowski, CSC; Rev. Michael C. Mathews, C.S.C.; Rev. Brendan J. McAleer, CSC; Rev. Peter M. McCormick, C.S.C.; Rev. James E. McDonald, C.S.C.; Rev. Aaron Michka, CSC; Rev. Wilson D. Miscamble, C.S.C.; Rev. Stephen P. Newton, C.S.C.; Rev. Martin Lam Nguyen, C.S.C.; Rev. Mark Joseph Pedersen, CSC; Rev. Mark L.

Poorman, C.S.C.; Rev. Christopher Rehagen, C.S.C.; Rev. Peter D. Rocca, C.S.C.; Rev. George A. Rozum, C.S.C.; Rev. Kevin J. Sandberg, C.S.C.; Rev. John M. Santone, C.S.C.; Rev. Eric Schimmel, CSC; Rev. Mark B. Thesing, C.S.C.; Rev. Richard S. Wilkinson, C.S.C.; Rev. Oliver F. Williams, C.S.C.; Rev. Nathan D. Wills, C.S.C.; Rev. Khaled Anatolios; Rev. Yury Avvakumov; Rev. William R. Headley; Rev. Emmanuel Katongole; Rev. John Paul Kimes; Rev. Paulinus I. Odozor, C.S.Sp.; Rev. Robert E. Sullivan, Assoc. Vice Pres., Academic Mission Support; Dcn. Melvin Tardy; Rev. Brian C. Ching, C.S.C., Rector, Basilica of the Sacred Heart; Stds.: 13,139; Lay Tchrs.: 1,503; Pr. Tchrs.: 15; Sr. Tchrs.: 1

CONVENTS, MONASTERIES, AND RESIDENCES FOR WOMEN [CON]

DONALDSON

Convent Ancilla Domini - 9601 Union Rd., Donaldson, IN 46513; Mailing: P.O. Box 1, Donaldson, IN 46513 t) 574-936-9936 www.poorhandmaids.org Provincialate, Poor Handmaids of Jesus Christ (The Ancilla Domini Sisters) Sr. Shirley Bell, PHJC, Prov.; Srs.: 55

Catherine Kasper Home - 20155 9B Rd., Plymouth, IN 46563; Mailing: P.O. Box 1, Donaldson, IN 46513 t) 574-935-1742 cklc.poorhandmaids.org Nursing home for retired sisters & laity.

Catherine Kasper Life Center, Inc. - 9601 Union Rd., Plymouth, IN 46563; Mailing: PO Box 1, Donaldson, IN 46513 t) 574-935-1742 cklc.poorhandmaids.org

***Catherine Kasper Place, Inc.** - 347 W. Berry St., Ste. 101, Fort Wayne, IN 46802 t) 260-969-2001 mdistler@sjchf.org catherinekasperplace.org Meg Distler, Exec.;

Catherine's Cottage - 9601 Union Rd., Plymouth, IN 46563; Mailing: P.O. Box 1, Donaldson, IN 46513 t) 574-935-1703 Sr. Jolise May, P.H.J.C., Contact;

St. Joseph Community Health Foundation - 347 W. Berry St., Fort Wayne, IN 46802 t) 260-969-2001 mdistler@sjchf.org sjchf.org Meg Distler, Dir.;

St. Joseph Medical Center of Fort Wayne, Inc. - 9601 Union Rd., Plymouth, IN 46563; Mailing: 1419 S. Lake Park Ave., Hobart, IN 46342-6635 t) 219-947-8529 John Chandler, Chairperson;

Lindenwood, Retreat & Conference Center - 9601 Union Rd., Plymouth, IN 46563; Mailing: PO Box 1, Donaldson, IN 46513 t) 574-935-1780 lindenwood@poorhandmaids.org www.lindenwood.org Paul Mach, Dir.;

Maria Center - 9601 Union Rd., Plymouth, IN 46563; Mailing: PO Box 1, Donaldson, IN 46513 t) 574-935-1784 jbrinkman@poorhandmaids.org cklc.poorhandmaids.org Senior Apartments (Efficiency and Singles) Jeff Brinkman, Exec. Dir.;

Moontree Community - 9601 Union Rd., Plymouth, IN 46563; Mailing: P.O. Box 1, Donaldson, IN 46513 t) 574-935-1716 mcelmer@poorhandmaids.org www.moontreecomunity.org Matthew Celmer, Dir.;

Poor Handmaids of Jesus Christ Community Support Trust - 9601 Union Rd., Plymouth, IN 46563 t) (574) 936-9936 abrown@poorhandmaids.org poorhandmaids.org Amy Brown, Contact;

***Poor Handmaids of Jesus Christ Foundation, Inc.** - 1419 S. Lake Park Ave., Hobart, IN 46342 t) 219-947-8500 amaynard@poorhandmaids.org Sr. Michele Dvorak, PHJC, Chair; Amanda Maynard, Dir.;

FORT WAYNE

Sisters of St. Joseph of the Third Order of St. Francis Residences S.S.J.-T.O.S.F. - 2222 Abbey Dr., Fort Wayne, IN 46835 c) 260-409-8680 terriduclos@frontier.com Sr. Therese Duclos, Contact; Srs.: 1

HUNTINGTON

Victory Noll - Motherhouse of Our Lady of Victory Missionary Sisters - 1900 W. Park Dr., Door 17, Huntington, IN 46750 t) (260) 200-1738 (Exec. Asst.) victorynoll@olvm.org; jenny@olvm.org www.olvm.org Legal Holding: Victory Noll Sisters Community Support Trust. Sr. Jenny Howard, SP, Pres.; Srs.: 30

MISHAWAKA

St. Francis Provincialate - 1515 W. Dragoon Trl., Mishawaka, IN 46544-4710; Mailing: P.O. Box 766, Mishawaka, IN 46546-0766 t) 574-259-5427 sister.angela@franciscanalliance.org www.ssfpa.org St. Francis Convent and Novitiate of Immaculate Heart of Mary Province. Sisters of St. Francis of Perpetual Adoration, Inc. Sr. M. Angela Mellady, O.S.F., Prov.; Srs.: 97

Our Lady of the Angels Convent - 1515 W. Dragoon Trl., Mishawaka, IN 46544; Mailing: P.O. Box 766, Mishawaka, IN 46546-0766 t) 574-259-5427 sister.angela@franciscanalliance.org www.ssfpa.org Convent for retired and infirm sisters. Rev. Paul Reczek, OFM, Chap.; Sr. M. Madonna Rougeau, O.S.F., Supr.; Srs.: 27

NOTRE DAME

Congregation of the Sisters of the Holy Cross (CSC Consultation Services) - 309 Bertrand Hall, Saint Mary's of the Immaculate Conception, Notre Dame, IN 46556-5000 t) 574-284-5550 www.cscsisters.org Sr. M. Veronique Wiedower, C.S.C., Pres.; Sr. Catherine Osimo, C.S.C., Secy.; Sr. Suzanne Brennan, C.S.C., Rel. Ord. Ldr.; Sr. Esther Adjoa Entsiwah, C.S.C., Rel. Ord. Ldr.; Sr. Pushpa Teresa Gomes, C.S.C., Rel. Ord. Ldr.; Sr. Mary Tiernan, C.S.C., Rel. Ord. Ldr.; Srs.: 357

All Saints Convent - 100 Lourdes Hall-Saint Mary's, Notre Dame, IN 46556-5014 t) 574-284-5660

Andre - East - 100 Andre East-Saint Mary's, Notre Dame, IN 46556-5015 t) 574-284-5644

Andre - West - 100 Andre West-Saint Mary's, Notre Dame, IN 46556-5016 t) 574-284-5645

Saint Ann Convent - 300 Augusta Hall-Saint Mary's, Notre Dame, IN 46556-5002 t) 574-284-5713

Bethany Convent - 100 Bethany Convent, Saint Mary's, Notre Dame, IN 46556-5038 t) 574-284-5674

Saint Claire Convent - 400 Augusta Hall-Saint Mary's, Notre Dame, IN 46556-5002 t) 574-284-5892

The Corporation of Saint Mary's College - 153 Le Mans Hall, Notre Dame, IN 46556-5000 t) (574) 284-4553 jmillar@saintmarys.edu Sponsored Ministry. Sheila Catherine Conboy, Pres.;

Guadalupe Convent - 300 Augusta Hall-Saint Mary's, Notre Dame, IN 46556-5002 t) 574-284-5717

Holy Spirit Convent - 300 Augusta Hall-Saint Mary's, Notre Dame, IN 46556-5002 t) 574-284-5715

House of Shalem - 100 House of Shalem, Saint Mary's, Notre Dame, IN 46556-5025 t) 574-284-5740

Immaculata Convent - 200 Augusta Hall-Saint Mary's, Notre Dame, IN 46556-5002 t) 574-284-5707

International Novitiate at Saint John's - 100 Solitude-Saint Mary's, Notre Dame, IN 46556-5020 t) 574-284-5625

International Novitiate at the Solitude - 100 Saint Mary's, Notre Dame, IN 46556-5020 t) 574-284-5120 Mary's Solitude and Joseph's Solitude

Kateri Convent - 400 Augusta-Hall Saint Mary's, Notre Dame, IN 46556-5002 t) 574-284-5993

Madonna Convent - 400 Augusta Hall-Saint Mary's, Notre Dame, IN 46556-5002 t) 574-284-5890

Marian Convent - 300 Augusta Hall-Saint Mary's, Notre Dame, IN 46556-5002 t) 574-284-5710

Saint Mary Convent - 100 Saint Mary's Convent, Notre Dame, IN 46556-5007 t) 574-284-5688

Moreau Convent - 100 Lourdes Hall-Saint Mary's, Notre Dame, IN 46556-5030 t) 574-284-5663

Nazareth Convent - 200 Augusta Hall-Saint Mary's, Notre Dame, IN 46556-5002 t) 574-284-5822

Rosary Convent - 100 Rosary Convent, Saint Mary's, Notre Dame, IN 46556-5013 t) 574-284-5707

Saint Bridget Convent - 100 Saint Bridget's Convent, Saint Mary's, Notre Dame, IN 46556-5024 t) 574-284-5725

Sisters of the Holy Cross - Saint Mary's of the Immaculate Conception, 309 Bertrand Hall, Notre Dame, IN 46556-5000

Sisters of the Holy Cross - 2121 E. Madison St., South Bend, IN 46617-2517 t) 574-287-6071

Sisters of the Holy Cross - 1023 Portage Ave., South Bend, IN 46616 t) 574-234-3208

Sisters of the Holy Cross - 3827 Denfeld Ave., Kensington, MD 20895

Saint Theresa Convent - 400 Augusta Hall-Saint Mary's, Notre Dame, IN 46556-5002 t) 574-284-5995

Visitation Convent - 200 Augusta Hall-Saint Mary's, Notre Dame, IN 46556-5002 t) 574-284-5820

SOUTH BEND

Handmaids of the Most Holy Trinity Monastery-Hermitage - 23089 Adams Rd., South Bend, IN 46628-9674 t) (574) 272-9425 Srs.: 1

Sarah House - 1213 E. Bronson St., South Bend, IN 46615 t) 574-287-8342 cbach@poorhandmaids.org www.poorhandmaids.org Owned by the Poor Handmaids of Jesus Christ. Sr. Connie Bach, P.H.J.C., Dir.; Srs.: 2

The Sisters of St. Joseph of the Third Order of St. Francis, S.S.J.-T.O.S.F. - 1425 Clayton Dr., South Bend, IN 46614 c) 574-213-4540 sis@chiarahomerespite.org Sr. Gretchen Clark, S.S.J.-T.O.S.F., Contact; Srs.: 1

ENDOWMENTS / FOUNDATIONS / TRUSTS [EFT]

FORT WAYNE

Catholic Community Foundation of Northeast Indiana, Inc. - 9025 Coldwater Rd., Ste. 300, Fort Wayne, IN 46825 t) 260-422-4611 x3348; 260-399-1436 mshade@ccfnei.org; akennerk@ccfnei.org www.ccfnei.org Michael Shade, CEO; Aaron Kennerk, Bus. Mgr.;

Diocese of Fort Wayne-South Bend Investment Trust, Inc. - 915 S. Clinton St., Fort Wayne, IN 46801; Mailing: P.O. Box 390, Fort Wayne, IN 46801 t) 260-422-4611 jryan@diocesefwsb.org Most Rev. Kevin C. Rhoades, Admin.; Joseph Ryan, Contact;

The St. Joseph Community Health Foundation, Inc. - 347 W. Berry St., Ste. 101, Fort Wayne, IN 46802 t) 260-969-2001 mdistler@sjchf.org; mrust@sjchf.org www.sjchf.org Meg Distler, Exec. Dir.; Mark Burkholder, Multimedia Coord.; Marla Rust, Exec. Asst. & Oper. Coord.; Angela Stanley, Vulnerable Populations Prog. Officer; Mary Tyndall, Food & Nutrition Insecurity Prog. Officer & Chief Storyteller;

MISHAWAKA

***Franciscan Heath Foundation, Inc.** - 3510 Park Pl. W., Ste. 200, Mishawaka, IN 46544 t) 574-273-3855 foundation@franciscanalliance.org www.franciscanhealthfoundation.org/ Caitlin A. Leahy, Vice. Pres.;

NEW HAVEN

***The Creighton Model Education Foundation, Inc.** - 146 N. Rufus St., New Haven, IN 46774 c) 260-494-6444 theresa.a.schortgen@frontier.com tcmef.org/ Educates women about their menstrual health using a moral and ethical family planning system. Phil Marlin, Pres.; Dave Morris, Vice. Pres.; Gabriel Renbarger, Secy.; Austin Hamilton, Treas.; Renate Guise, Mktg./Publications; Stephanie Hamilton, Bd. Member; Theresa Schortgen, Bd. Member; Anne Therese Stephens, Bd. Member;

NOTRE DAME

Blessed Basil Moreau Endowment Trust - 54515 State Rd. 933 N., Notre Dame, IN 46556; Mailing: P.O. Box 774, Notre Dame, IN 46556-0774 t) 574-631-3700 aszakaly@holycrossusa.org Rev. Anthony V. Szakaly, C.S.C., Trustee;

Brothers of Holy Cross Life Development Trust - 54515 State Rd. 933 N., Notre Dame, IN 46556; Mailing: P.O. Box 460, Notre Dame, IN 46556 t) 574-631-4000 Bro. William Dygert, C.S.C., Chair; Bro. James Spooner, Trustee; Matthew Shannon, Trustee; Fred G. Botek, Trustee; Bro. Robert Lavelle, C.S.C., Trustee; Bro. James Leik, C.S.C., Trustee; Bro. Lawrence Skitzki, C.S.C., Trustee;

Father Edward Sorin Trust - 54515 State Rd. 933 N., Notre Dame, IN 46556-0774; Mailing: P.O. Box 774, Notre Dame, IN 46556-0774 t) 574-631-3700 bching@holycrossusa.org Rev. Brian C. Ching, C.S.C.,

Trustee;
Holy Cross in East Africa Benefit Trust - 54515 State Rd. 933 N., Notre Dame, IN 46556; Mailing: P.O. Box 774, Notre Dame, IN 46556 t) (574) 631-0488 Kyle Marscola, Controller;
Saint Andre Bessette Continuing Care Trust - 54515 State Rd. 933 N., Notre Dame, IN 46556-0774; Mailing: P.O. Box 774, Notre Dame, IN 46556-0774 t) 574-631-3700 jfoster@holycrossusa.org Rev. James K. Foster, C.S.C., Trustee;
SOUTH BEND
The Foundation of Saint Joseph Health System (The Foundation of Saint Joseph Regional Medical Center, Inc.) - 707 E. Cedar St., Ste. 100, South Bend, IN 46617 t) 574-335-4540 thefoundation@sjrmc.com www.sjmed.com Michelle Peters, Dir.;

HOSPITALS / HEALTH SERVICES [HOS]

MISHAWAKA
Saint Joseph Regional Medical Center - 5215 Holy Cross Pkwy., Mishawaka, IN 46545 t) 574-335-2342 chad.towner@sjrmc.com; karamc@sjrmc.com www.sjmed.com Chad Towner, CEO; Sr. Carole Langhauser, PHJC, Dir.; Bed Capacity: 294; Asstd. Annu.: 400,000; Staff: 2,080
NOTRE DAME
University Health Services - 201 St. Liam Hall, Notre Dame, IN 46556-5693 t) 574-631-7103 aloutze1@nd.edu www.nd.edu/~uhs Rev. James A. Bracke, C.S.C., Chap.; Asstd. Annu.: 30,000; Staff: 25
PLYMOUTH
Saint Joseph Regional Medical Center - Plymouth - 1915 Lake Ave., Plymouth, IN 46563; Mailing: P.O. Box 670, Plymouth, IN 46563 t) 574-948-5000 karamc@sjrmc.com; carole.langhauser@sjrmc.org www.sjmed.com Sr. Carole Langhauser, PHJC, Dir.; Bed Capacity: 58; Asstd. Annu.: 84,500; Staff: 280

MISCELLANEOUS [MIS]

BLUFFTON
St. Paul Evangelization Society, Inc. - 300 S. State Rd. 201, Bluffton, IN 46714-0000 c) 317-727-2901 (Pres.); 812-459-6206 (VP) gwitwer@spesinchrist.org; vbernardin@spesinchrist.org www.spesinchrist.com George Witwer, Pres.; Dcn. Vincent Bernardin, Vice. Pres.;
ELKHART
***The Heritage and Research Center at St. Mary's, Inc.** - 2114 E. Jackson, Elkhart, IN 46516; Mailing: 100 Center Bldg., St. Mary's, Notre Dame, IN 46555-5000 t) 574-284-5625 rkeck@cscsisters.org Sr. Kathleen Moroney, C.S.C., Contact;
FORT WAYNE
Saint Anne Home & Retirement Community - 1900 Randallia Dr., Fort Wayne, IN 46805 t) 260-484-5555 elaine.wilson@sacfw.org sacfw.org Rev. John Overmyer, Chap.; Most Rev. Kevin C. Rhoades, Mem.; Rev. James A. Shafer, Mem.;
Saint Anne at Victory Noll (Saint Anne Home of the Diocese of Fort Wayne-South Bend, Inc.) - 25 Victory Noll Dr., Huntington, IN 46750 t) 260-224-6848 tracy.schultz@sacfw.org www.sacfw.org Rev. Philip DeVolder, Chap.;
Saint Anne Home at Randallia Place (Saint Anne Home of the Diocese of Fort Wayne-South Bend, Inc.) - www.sacfw.org Rev. Adam Schmitt, In Res.;
***The Christ Child Society of Fort Wayne, Inc.** - Archbishop Noll Catholic Center, Fort Wayne, IN 46802; Mailing: P.O. Box 12708, Fort Wayne, IN 46864 t) 260-414-6755 president@christchildfw.org www.christchildfw.org Lori Neumann, Pres.;
Diocesan Museum - 1103 S. Calhoun St., Fort Wayne, IN 46802; Mailing: P.O. Box 390, Fort Wayne, IN 46801 kimler@diocesefwsb.org Kathryn Imler, Dir.;
***Fort Wayne Catholic Radio Group, Inc.** - 4618 E. State Blvd., Ste. 200, Fort Wayne, IN 46815 t) 260-436-9598 info@redeemerradio.com www.redeemerradio.com (Redeemer Radio, 106.3 FM Fort Wayne & 95.7 FM South Bend) Cindy Black, CEO; Michael S Rorick, CFO;
***The Fort Wayne-South Bend Diocesan Division: World Apostolate of Fatima, The Blue Army** - 146 N. Rufus St., Fort Wayne, IN 46774 t) 574-621-0372 president@fatimafwsb.org www.fatimafwsb.org Jerry Horban, Pres.; Rev. Robert Garrow, Spiritual Adv./Care Srvcs.; Rev. Glenn Kohrman, Spiritual Adv./Care Srvcs.;
His Kingdom Builders, Inc. - 521 Windrift Ln., Fort Wayne, IN 46825 c) 260-602-6921 maryjo@buildingthroughhim.com www.buildingthroughhim.com Mary Jo Parrish, Dir.; Lisa Everett, Diocesan Liaison;
***A Mother's Hope, Inc.** - 5322 N. Clinton St., Fort Wayne, IN 46825 t) 260-444-4975 hello@amhfw.org amothershopefw.org Maternity home for pregnant, homeless women Stasia Roth, Dir.;
Scholarship Granting Organization of Northeast Indiana, Inc. - 915 S. Clinton St., Fort Wayne, IN 46801; Mailing: P.O. Box 390, Fort Wayne, IN 46801 t) 260-422-4611 mgurtner@diocesefwsb.org Very Rev. Mark A. Gurtner, Contact;
HUNTINGTON
Our Sunday Visitor, Inc. - 200 Noll Plaza, Huntington, IN 46750 t) 260-356-8400 bthompson@osv.com www.osv.com Most Rev. Kevin C. Rhoades, Chair; Kyle Hamilton, CEO; Linda Teeters, CFO;
MISHAWAKA
Christ Child Society of South Bend - 2366 Miracle Ln., Mishawaka, IN 46545 t) 574-288-6028 info@christchildsb.org www.christchildsb.org Monique Deguara, Pres.; Suzanne Wiwi, Pres.;
Franciscan Alliance, Inc. - 1515 W. Dragoon Trl., Mishawaka, IN 46544; Mailing: P.O. Box 1290, Mishawaka, IN 46546-1290 t) 574-256-3935 sister.lethia@franciscanalliance.org www.franciscanalliance.org Kevin D. Leahy, CEO;
***Hannah's House, Inc.** - 518 W. 4th St., Mishawaka, IN 46544; Mailing: P.O. Box 1413, Mishawaka, IN 46546 t) 574-254-7271 info@hannahshousemichiana.com www.hannahshousemichiana.org Susan Frucci, Dir.;
***Hills Insurance Company, Inc.** - 1515 W. Dragoon Trl., Mishawaka, IN 46544; Mailing: P.O. Box 1290, Mishawaka, IN 46546-1290 t) 574-254-6218 dan.conner@franciscanalliance.org Sr. Jane Marie Klein, O.S.F., Chair;
Saint Joseph PACE, Inc. - 250 E. Day Rd., Mishawaka, IN 46545 t) 574-247-8700 saintjosephpace@trinity-health.org Bobbie Costigan, Dir.;
Saint Joseph Regional Medical Center, Inc. - 5215 Holy Cross Pkwy., Mishawaka, IN 46545 t) 574-335-5000 karamc@sjrmc.com; carole.langhauser@sjrmc.org www.sjmed.com Sr. Carole Langhauser, PHJC, Dir.;
Sisters of St. Francis of Perpetual Adoration, Inc. - 1515 W. Dragoon Trl., Mishawaka, IN 46544-4710; Mailing: P.O. Box 766, Mishawaka, IN 46546-0766 t) 574-259-5427 sister.angela@franciscanalliance.org www.ssfpa.org Sr. M. Angela Mellady, O.S.F., Prov.;
Sisters of St. Francis Charitable Mission Trust - ; Mailing: P.O. Box 766, Mishawaka, IN 46546-0766 t) (574) 259-5427
Sisters of St. Francis of Perpetual Adoration, Inc. Capital Improvements Trust - ; Mailing: P.O. Box 766, Mishawaka, IN 46546-0766 t) (574) 259-5427
Sisters of St. Francis of Perpetual Adoration, Inc., Medical Benefits Trust - ; Mailing: P.O. Box 766, Mishawaka, IN 46546-0766 t) (574) 259-5427
Sisters of St. Francis Retirement Fund - ; Mailing: P.O. Box 766, Mishawaka, IN 46546-0766 t) (574) 259-5427
SSFPA Ministry Corporation - 1515 W. Dragoon Trl., Mishawaka, IN 46544-4710; Mailing: P.O. Box 766, Mishawaka, IN 46546-0766 t) 574-259-5427 sister.angela@franciscanalliance.org www.ssfpa.org Sr. M. Angela Mellady, O.S.F., Prov.;
NOTRE DAME
Ave Maria Press, Inc. - 1865 Moreau Dr., Notre Dame, IN 46556; Mailing: P.O. Box 428, Notre Dame, IN 46556 t) 574-287-2831 avemariapress.1@nd.edu www.avemariapress.com Owned and operated by the Congregation of Holy Cross, United States Province. Karey Circosta, Publisher and CEO;
Holy Cross Foreign Mission Society, Inc. (Holy Cross Mission Center) - 1837 Moreau Dr., Notre Dame, IN 46556; Mailing: P.O. Box 543, Notre Dame, IN 46556-0543 t) 574-631-5477 hcmc@holycrossusa.org hcmc.holycrossusa.org Rev. Thomas Eckert, CSC, Dir.;
The Society of Catholic Scientists - 240D Geddes Hall, Notre Dame, IN 46556; Mailing: 9 N. Wynwyd Dr., Newark, DE 19711 t) 302-453-7433 smpbarr@gmail.com www.catholicscientists.org For fellowship & discussion among Catholic scientists. Stephen Barr, Pres.;
SOUTH BEND
***Ablaze Mission, Inc.** - 336 S. Saint Peter St., South Bend, IN 46617; Mailing: P.O. Box 68, Notre Dame, IN 46556 c) (858) 354-9006 sallen@ablazemission.org ablazemission.org Evangelization of Young Adults (18-30s) Sean Allen, Pres.;
Chiara Home, Inc. - 1425 Clayton Dr., South Bend, IN 46614 t) 574-287-5435 sis@chiarahomerespite.org www.chiarahomerespite.org Respite Care for people with special needs. Sr. Gretchen Clark, S.S.J.-T.O.S.F., Pres.;
Jesuit Community - Henri de Lubac House, 1713 Burdette St., South Bend, IN 46637 t) 574-243-0601 Rev. Jason LaLonde, S.J., Supr.; Rev. Matthew Cortese, S.J., Mem.; Rev. Christopher Grodecki, Mem.; Rev. Andrij Hlabse, Mem.;
Prelature of the Holy Cross and Opus Dei - Windmoor Study Center, 1121 N. Notre Dame Ave., South Bend, IN 46617 t) 574-232-0550 info@windmoor.org www.windmoor.org Rev. Oscar Regojo, Chap.;
***Women's Care Center, Inc.** - 360 N. Notre Dame Ave., South Bend, IN 46617 t) 574-234-0363 annmanion1@hotmail.com; wccinc.business@gmail.com www.supportwcc.org Ann Manion, Pres.;

MONASTERIES AND RESIDENCES FOR PRIESTS AND BROTHERS [MON]

NOTRE DAME
Congregation of Holy Cross-Eastern Province, Inc. - 54515 State Rd. 993 N., Notre Dame, IN 46556-0774; Mailing: P.O. Box 1064, Notre Dame, IN 46556-1064 t) 574-631-3700 ssimmonds@holycrossusa.org Rev. E. William Beauchamp, C.S.C., Treas.;
Congregation of Holy Cross, Midwest Province - 54515 State Rd. 933 N., Notre Dame, IN 46556-0460; Mailing: P.O Box 460, Notre Dame, IN 46556 t) 574-631-4000 khaders@brothersofholycross.com www.brothersofholycross.com Brothers of Holy Cross, Inc. Bro. Kenneth Haders, C.S.C., Prov. Supr.; Bro. Robert Lavelle, C.S.C., Asst. Prov. & Vicar; Bro. Lewis Brazil, C.S.C., Dir., Healthcare & Aging; Bro. Robert Livernois, Prov. Asst.; Bro. James Spooner, Treas.; Bro. John Badu Affum, C.S.C., Councilor; Bro. Christopher Torrijas, C.S.C., Councilor; Bro. James Van Dyke, Councilor; Brs.: 110
Columba Hall - 1 St Mary's Dr. - Columba Hall, Notre Dame, IN 46566; Mailing: PO Box 776, Notre Dame, IN 46556-0776 t) (574) 631-6284 cdreyer@brothersofholycross.com Bro. Douglas Roach, C.S.C., Supr.; Bro. Christopher Dreyer, C.S.C., Asst. Supr.;
Dujarie House, Infirmary - Dujarie House, Holy Cross Village, Notre Dame, IN 46556-0706; Mailing: P.O. Box 706, Notre Dame, IN 46556-0706 t) 574-245-7800 ctorrijas@hcc-nd.edu Bro. Christopher Torrijas, Supr.; Maureen Miller, Chair;
Helen D. Schubert Villa, Assisted Living - 54515 State Rd. 933 N., Holy Cross Village, Notre Dame, IN 46556; Mailing: P.O Box 460, Notre Dame, IN 46556 t) 574-245-7800 ctorrijas@brothersofholycross.com Jack Mueller, Admin.;
Holy Cross Village - 54515 SR 933 N., Notre Dame, IN 46556; Mailing: P.O Box 839, Notre Dame, IN 46556 t) 574-245-7800 www.holycrossvillage.org

Brandon Kastnor, Admin.; Bro. Joseph Fox, Dir.;

Congregation of Holy Cross, Southern Province, Inc. - 54515 State Rd. 933 N, Notre Dame, IN 46556; Mailing: P.O. Box 1064, Notre Dame, IN 46556-1064 t) 574-631-6196 ssimmonds@holycrossusa.org Rev. E. William Beauchamp, C.S.C., Secy.;

Congregation of Holy Cross, United States Province of Priests and Brothers - Province Administration Center, 54515 State Rd. 933 N., Notre Dame, IN 46556; Mailing: P.O. Box 1064, Notre Dame, IN 46556-1064 t) 574-631-6196 ssimmonds@holycrossusa.org www.holycrossusa.org Rev. William M. Lies, C.S.C., Prov.; Rev. Peter A. Jarret, C.S.C., Vicar; Rev. E. William Beauchamp, C.S.C., Treas.; Rev. Christopher A. Kuhn, C.S.C., Archivist; Rev. Genaro P Aguilar, CSC, Mem.; Rev. William G. Blum, C.S.C., Mem.; Rev. James A. Bracke, C.S.C., Mem.; Rev. Leonard J. Collins, C.S.C., Mem.; Rev. James T. Connelly, C.S.C., Mem.; Rev. William Dorwart, C.S.C., Mem.; Rev. Lawrence J. Henry, C.S.C., Mem.; Rev. David Kashangaki, C.S.C., Mem.; Rev. John P. Keefe, C.S.C., Mem.; Rev. Charles W. Kohlerman, C.S.C., Mem.; Rev. John S. Korcsmar, C.S.C., Mem.; Rev. James R. Lackenmier, CSC, Mem.; Rev. Louis A. Manzo, C.S.C., Mem.; Rev. Wilson D. Miscamble, C.S.C., Mem.; Rev. Daniel Ponisciak, C.S.C., Mem.; Rev. David J. Porterfield, C.S.C., Mem.; Rev. Thomas G. Streit, C.S.C., Mem.; Rev. Herbert C. Yost, C.S.C., Mem.; Rev. Francis D. Zagorc, C.S.C., Mem.; Rev. Thomas K Zurcher, CSC, Mem.; Brs.: 13; Priests: 341

Holy Cross House - 1842 Moreau Dr., Notre Dame, IN 46556; Mailing: P.O. Box 1048, Notre Dame, IN 46556-1048 t) 574-631-6337 Rev. Mark B. Thesing, C.S.C., Admin.; Rev. Thomas J. Jones, CSC, Supr.; Rev. Paul F. Doyle, C.S.C., Asst. Supr.; Bro. Joseph J DeAgostino, CSC, Asst. Supr.; Rev. Robert J. Austgen, C.S.C., In Res.; Rev. George C. Bernard, C.S.C., In Res.; Rev. Thomas E. Blantz, C.S.C., In Res.; Rev. Robert J. Brennan, C.S.C., In Res.; Rev. David B. Burrell, C.S.C., In Res.; Rev. Francis T. Cafarelli, C.S.C., In Res.; Bro. Thomas J. Combs, CSC, In Res.; Rev. John Connor, C.S.C., In Res.; Rev. Richard J. Conyers, CSC, In Res.; Rev. James J. Denn, C.S.C., In Res.; Rev. Donald W. Dilg, C.S.C., In Res.; Rev. Thomas Elliott, C.S.C., In Res.; Rev. Jerome C. Esper, C.S.C., In Res.; Rev. Harold W Essling, CSC, In Res.; Rev. David E. Farrell, CSC, In Res.; Rev. James J. Ferguson, C.S.C., In Res.; Rev. Robert Gilmour, CSC, In Res.; Rev. Andrew R. Guljas, C.S.C., In Res.; Rev. Richard C. Hockman, C.S.C., In Res.; Rev. William Hund, C.S.C., In Res.; Rev. Thomas King, C.S.C., In Res.; Rev. Edward C. Krause, C.S.C., In Res.; Rev. Richard Laurick, C.S.C., In Res.; Rev. Charles J. Lavely, C.S.C., In Res.; Rev. Andre E. Leveille, C.S.C., In Res.; Bro. Edward C. Luther, C.S.C, In Res.; Rev. James P. Madden, C.S.C., In Res.; Rev. Thomas F. McNally, C.S.C., In Res.; Bro. James H. Miller, C.S.C., In Res.; Rev. Kenneth M. Molinaro, C.S.C., In Res.; Rev. James Murphy, C.S.C., In Res.; Rev. Edward D. O'Connor, C.S.C., In Res.; Rev. Fred Serraino, C.S.C., In Res.; Rev. Kenneth J. Silvia, CSC, In Res.; Rev. Patrick J. Sullivan, C.S.C., In Res.; Rev. Charles E. Van Winkle, CSC, In Res.; Rev. James N Watzke, CSC, In Res.; Rev. John L. Young, C.S.C., In Res.; Rev. Richard P Zang, CSC, In Res.;

Holy Cross Community, Corby Hall, University of Notre Dame - 124 Corby Hall, Notre Dame, IN 46556-5680 t) 574-631-7325 tfaulkner@holycrossusa.org Rev. Robert A. Dowd, C.S.C., Supr.; Rev. Christopher Rehagen, C.S.C., Asst. Supr.; Rev. Gregory P. Haake, C.S.C., Asst. Supr.; Rev. Joseph H. Carey, C.S.C., Steward; Rev. Nicholas R. Ayo, C.S.C., In Res.; Rev. William Beauchamp, C.S.C., In Res.; Rev. James A. Bracke, C.S.C., In Res.; Rev. Christopher Brennan, CSC, In Res.; Rev. Richard S. Bullene, C.S.C., In Res.; Rev. Gary S. Chamberland, C.S.C., In Res.; Rev. Brian C. Ching, C.S.C., In Res.; Rev. Austin I. Collins, C.S.C., In Res.; Rev. John E. Conley, C.S.C., In Res.; Rev. Michael E. Connors, C.S.C., In Res.; Rev. Joseph V. Corpora, C.S.C., In Res.; Rev. William R. Dailey, C.S.C., In Res.; Rev. Louis A. DelFra, C.S.C., In Res.; Rev. John M. DeRiso, C.S.C., In Res.; Rev. Carl F. Ebey, C.S.C., In Res.; Rev. Thomas Eckert, CSC, In Res.; Rev. Terrence P. Ehrman, C.S.C., In Res.; Rev. Robert Epping, C.S.C., In Res.; Rev. James K. Foster, C.S.C., In Res.; Rev. Gabriel J. Griggs, CSC, In Res.; Rev. Daniel G. Groody, C.S.C., In Res.; Rev. Kevin G. Grove, C.S.C., In Res.; Rev. Ralph L. Haag, C.S.C., In Res.; Rev. John I. Jenkins, C.S.C., In Res.; Rev. Stephen J. Kempinger, C.S.C., In Res.; Rev. James B. King, CSC, In Res.; Rev. Stephen Koeth, CSC, In Res.; Rev. Paul V. Kollman, C.S.C., In Res.; Rev. James M. Lies, C.S.C., In Res.; Rev. Robert J. Lisowski, CSC, In Res.; Bro. Patrick J. Lynch, C.S.C., In Res.; Rev. Edward A. Malloy, C.S.C., In Res.; Rev. Brendan J. McAleer, CSC, In Res.; Rev. Peter M. McCormick, C.S.C., In Res.; Rev. James E. McDonald, C.S.C., In Res.; Rev. Aaron Michka, CSC, In Res.; Rev. Francis J. Murphy, C.S.C., In Res.; Rev. Stephen P. Newton, C.S.C., In Res.; Rev. Martin Lam Nguyen, C.S.C., In Res.; Rev. Timothy L. O'Connor, C.S.C., In Res.; Rev. Gerard J. Olinger, CSC, In Res.; Rev. Mark Joseph Pedersen, CSC, In Res.; Rev. Mark L. Poorman, C.S.C., In Res.; Rev. Karl Romkema, CSC, In Res.; Rev. George A. Rozum, C.S.C., In Res.; Rev. Kevin J. Sandberg, C.S.C., In Res.; Rev. Eric Schimmel, CSC, In Res.; Rev. S. Douglas Smith, C.S.C., In Res.; Bro. Donald Stabrowski, C.S.C., In Res.; Rev. Thomas G. Streit, C.S.C., In Res.; Rev. Michael B. Sullivan, C.S.C., In Res.; Rev. Mark B. Thesing, C.S.C., In Res.; Rev. David T. Tyson, C.S.C., In Res.; Rev. Richard S. Wilkinson, C.S.C., In Res.; Rev. Oliver F. Williams, C.S.C., In Res.; Rev. Nathan D. Wills, C.S.C., In Res.; Brs.: 3; Priests: 60

Priests of Holy Cross, Indiana Province, Inc. - 54515 State Rd. 933 N., Notre Dame, IN 46556-1064; Mailing: P.O. Box 1064, Notre Dame, IN 46556-1064 t) 574-631-6196 ssimmonds@holycrossusa.org Rev. E. William Beauchamp, C.S.C., Secy.;

NURSING / REHABILITATION / CONVALESCENCE / ELDERLY CARE [NUR]

AVILLA

Ascension Living Sacred Heart Village (Presence Life Connections Incorporated) - 515 N. Main St., Avilla, IN 46710-9602 t) 314-292-9308 ahscm-mission@ascension.org www.ascensionliving.org Ryan Endsley, COO; Asstd. Annu.: 65; Staff: 124

LaVerna Terrace Housing Corporation - 517 N. Main St., Avilla, IN 46710 t) 314-292-9308 ahscm-mission@ascension.org www.ascensionliving.org/ Daniel Stricker, Pres.; Asstd. Annu.: 51; Staff: 15

DONALDSON

Catherine Kasper Life Center, Inc. - 9601 Union Rd., Donaldson, IN 46513; Mailing: P.O. Box 1, Donaldson, IN 46513 t) 574-935-1742 cklc.poorhandmaids.org Sponsored by the Poor Handmaids of Jesus Christ. (The Ancilla Domini Sisters, Inc.) Jeff Brinkman, Exec. Dir.; Sr. Shirley Bell, PHJC, Pres. & Bd. Chair; Sr. Carole Langhauser, PHJC, Vice Pres. & Secy.; Donna Sikorski, Treas.; Asstd. Annu.: 218; Staff: 80

NOTRE DAME

Holy Cross Village at Notre Dame - 54515 State Rd. 933 N., Notre Dame, IN 46556; Mailing: P.O. Box 303, Notre Dame, IN 46556-0303 t) 574-245-7800 www.holycrossvillage.com Independent Apartments & Assisted Living. Rev. Timothy L. O'Connor, C.S.C., Chap.; Kathryn Mach, Pst. Min./Coord.; Maureen Miller, Chair; Jack Mueller, Exec.; Asstd. Annu.: 390; Staff: 128

SOUTH BEND

St. Joseph's Tower, Inc. (Trinity Tower) - Trinity Tower, 316 S. Martin Luther King, Jr. Blvd., South Bend, IN 46601 t) 574-335-1900 milltram@trinity-health.org www.trinityhealthseniorcommunities.org Tracy Miller, Admin.; Asstd. Annu.: 86; Staff: 4

RETREAT HOUSES / RENEWAL CENTERS [RTR]

DONALDSON

Lindenwood Retreat & Conference Center - The Center at Donaldson, 9601 Union Rd., Donaldson, IN 46513-0001; Mailing: P.O. Box 1, Donaldson, IN 46513-0001 t) 574-935-1780 lindenwood@poorhandmaids.org www.lindenwood.org Overnight facilities for 100 people, conference rooms for 250, Handicapped accessibility. Paul Mach, Dir.;

SOUTH BEND

Forever Learning Institute, Inc. - 54191 Ironwood Rd., South Bend, IN 46635 t) 574-282-1901 director@foreverlearninginstitute.org www.foreverlearninginstitute.org To improve the quality and dignity of senior adult life Eve Finnessy, Dir.;

SEMINARIES [SEM]

NOTRE DAME

Moreau Seminary - 1837 Moreau Dr., Notre Dame, IN 46556; Mailing: P.O. Box 668, Notre Dame, IN 46556 t) (574) 631-5571 morsem@holycrossusa.org Rev. Jim Gallagher, C.S.C., Supr./Rector; Rev. Thomas C. Bertone, C.S.C., Asst. Supr.; Rev. Michael C. Mathews, C.S.C., Postulant Dir.; Rev. Donald G. Fetters, C.S.C., Formation Staff; Bro. Chester Freel, C.S.C., Formation Staff; Rev. Eric Schimmel, CSC, Formation Staff; Bro. Donald Stabrowski, C.S.C., Formation Staff; Rev. Karl Romkema, CSC, Old College Dir.; Rev. Peter D. Rocca, C.S.C., Dir., Liturgy; Rev. Michael Shami, Guest Res.; Rev. Matthew Gummess, OCarm., Guest Res.; Rev. Matthew C. Kuczora, C.S.C., In Res.; Rev. Charles McCoy, C.S.C., In Res.; Rev. Robert H. Moss, C.S.C., In Res.; Rev. Stephen Pepper, In Res.; Rev. Paschal Sarker, CSC, In Res.; Bro. J. Rodney Struble, C.S.C., In Res.; Stds.: 41

Old College - 200 Old College, University of Notre Dame, Notre Dame, IN 46556; Mailing: P.O. Box 638, Notre Dame, IN 46556-0638 t) 574-631-0778 kromkema@holycrossusa.org www.holycrossusa.org Rev. Karl Romkema, CSC, Dir.; Edward J Dolphin, CSC, Asst. Dir.; Bro. Donald Stabrowski, C.S.C., Procurator; Stds.: 9

Diocese of Fort Worth

(Dioecesis Arcis-Vorthensis)

MOST REVEREND MICHAEL F. OLSON, S.T.D.

Bishop of Fort Worth; ordained June 3, 1994; appointed Bishop of Fort Worth November 19, 2013; installed fourth Bishop of the Diocese of Fort Worth January 29, 2014.

The Catholic Center: 800 West Loop 820 S., Fort Worth, TX 76108. T: 817-560-3300; F: 817-244-8839.
www.fwdioc.org

ESTABLISHED AUGUST 09, 1969.

Square Miles 23,950.

Comprises the following twenty-eight Counties in the State of Texas: Archer, Baylor, Bosque, Clay, Comanche, Cooke, Denton, Eastland, Erath, Foard, Hardeman, Hill, Hood, Jack, Johnson, Knox, Montague, Palo Pinto, Parker, Shackleford, Stephens, Somervell, Tarrant, Throckmorton, Wichita, Wilbarger, Wise and Young.

For legal titles of parishes and diocesan institutions, consult the Chancery.

STATISTICAL OVERVIEW

Personnel
Bishop....1
Priests: Diocesan Active in Diocese....41
Priests: Retired, Sick or Absent....26
Number of Diocesan Priests....67
Religious Priests in Diocese....58
Total Priests in your Diocese....125
Extern Priests in Diocese....10
Ordinations:
Transitional Deacons....3
Permanent Deacons....13
Permanent Deacons in Diocese....117
Total Sisters....48

Parishes
Parishes....92
With Resident Pastor:
Resident Diocesan Priests....40
Resident Religious Priests....48
Without Resident Pastor:
Administered by Priests....1
New Parishes Created....1
Professional Ministry Personnel:
Sisters....10
Lay Ministers....238

Welfare
Homes for the Aged....1
Total Assisted....560
Special Centers for Social Services....4
Total Assisted....13,840

Educational
Diocesan Students in Other Seminaries....24
Total Seminarians....24
High Schools, Diocesan and Parish....3
Total Students....778
Elementary Schools, Diocesan and Parish....15
Total Students....2,893
Catechesis / Religious Education:
High School Students....6,363
Elementary Students....13,136
Total Students under Catholic Instruction....23,194
Teachers in Diocese:
Sisters....10
Lay Teachers....309

Vital Statistics
Receptions into the Church:
Infant Baptism Totals....4,399
Minor Baptism Totals....300
Adult Baptism Totals....213
Received into Full Communion....636
First Communions....4,136
Confirmations....3,432
Marriages:
Catholic....782
Interfaith....159
Total Marriages....941
Deaths....1,333
Total Catholic Population....1,200,000
Total Population....4,103,476

LEADERSHIP

Vicar General - Very Rev. Jonathan Wallis;
Chancellor/Moderator of the Curia - Rev. Msgr. E. James Hart;
Deans -
Arlington Deanery - Very Rev. Daniel P. Kelley;
East Central Deanery - Very Rev. John Robert Skeldon;
North Deanery - Very Rev. Stephen Hauck;
Northeast Deanery - Very Rev. Raymond McDaniel;
Northwest Deanery - Very Rev. Alexander Ambrose, H.G.N.;
South Deanery - Very Rev. Fernando Preciado;
Southwest Deanery -
West Central Deanery - Very Rev. Hoa Nguyen;
College of Consultors - Very Rev. Jonathan Wallis; Rev. Msgr. E. James Hart; Very Rev. Hoa Nguyen;
Presbyteral Council - Very Rev. Jonathan Wallis; Rev. Msgr. E. James Hart; Very Rev. Raymond McDaniel;

ADVISORY BOARDS, COMMISSIONS, COMMITTEES, AND COUNCILS

Diocesan Building Commission - Rev. Msgr. E. James Hart; Stephen Becht; Donald L. Wagner;
Diocesan Finance Council - Most Rev. Michael F. Olson, Chair; Rev. Msgr. E. James Hart; Donald L. Wagner;
Diocesan Pastoral Finance Committee - Rev. Msgr. E. James Hart, Chair; Donald L. Wagner; Kevin O'Brien;
Employee Benefits Advisory Committee - Rev. Msgr. E. James Hart; Donald L. Wagner; Rev. Jonathan Michael Demma;
Employee Pension Plan, Board of Trustees - Rev. Msgr. E. James Hart; Gary R. Patton, Secy.; Donald L. Wagner;
Priests' Pension Plan Board of Trustees - Rev. Msgr. E. James Hart; Very Rev. Jonathan Wallis; Donald L. Wagner;

MISCELLANEOUS / OTHER OFFICES

Campaign for Human Development (Vacant) -
Catholic Schools Department - Brinton Smith, Supt.; Melissa Kasmeier, Associate Supt.;
School Nurses Consultant - Lindsay Karant;
Catholic Women, Council of - Rev. Msgr. E. James Hart;
Chancery -
Administrative Associate - Josie Castillo;
Executive Assistant to the Bishop & the Vicar General - Ashley Hance;
Executive Assistant to the Chan./Mod. of the Curia & General Counsel - Maria Soto;
Manager of Chancery Events - Anna Mudd;
Chaplaincy Department - Dcn. Don Warner;
Communications Department - Pat Svacina, Dir.;
Communications - Pat Svacina, Dir.;
Communications/News Magazine - Juan Guajardo, Editor; Susan Moses, Assoc. Editor;
Communications/Social Media Specialist - Annette Mendoza-Smith;
Communications/Web Site Services - Chris Kastner, Coord.; Ambil Palatty, Asst. Coord.;
Conduct Review Board - Rev. Msgr. E. James Hart; Sandra Schrader-Farry, Dir.;
Deacons - Dcn. Don Warner, Dir.;
Deaf Ministry - Connie Martin;
Delegate for Women Religious - Sr. Diana Rodriguez, H.C.G.;
Diocesan Mission Council - Rev. Brijil Lawrence, S.A.C., Chair; Colleen Cargile; Bob Eilenfeldt;
Diocesan Office of Pontifical Missions - Rev. Brijil Lawrence, S.A.C., Dir.;
Evangelization and Catechesis Department - Jason Whitehead, Dir.;
Adult Catechesis - Jason Whitehead, Dir.;
Faith Formation/Children's Catechesis/RCIA - Jason Whitehead, Dir.;
Hispanic Ministry - Dcn. Rigoberto Leyva, Dir.;
Marriage and Family Life - Chris Vaughan, Dir.;
Natural Family Planning - Brenda Reyes De Lara, Coord.;
Respect Life - Theresa Schauf;
St. Francis De Sales Institute; St. Junipero Serra Institute - Jason Whitehead, Dir.;
Youth, Young Adult & Campus Ministry - Victoria Ramon, Dir.;
Finance & Administrative Services Department - Donald L. Wagner, CFO;
Cemeteries and Columbaria - Kevin O'Brien;
Claims and Risk Management - Catholic Mutual - Christina Ablorh;
Controller - Tracie Quan;
Financial Services - Donald L. Wagner; Kevin O'Brien; Christina Ybarra;
Property Management and Construction - Stephen Becht, Dir.; Tom Ross, Const. Prog. Mgr.; John Jackson;
Records Management & Archives Department (Vacant) -
Hospital Chaplaincy - Dcn. Bruce Corbett; Rev. Binoy Kurian, T.O.R.; Dcn. Don Warner;
Human Resources Department -
Chief Human Resources Officer - Gary R. Patton;
Human Resources Business Partner for PARISHES-VACANT -
Human Resources Business Partner for SCHOOLS - Faviola Carinci;
Senior Human Resources Business Partner (Talent Acquisition & Employee Relations) - Adrienne Howsare;
Liturgy and Worship Department - Rev. Thu Nguyen;
Missionary Childhood Association - Rev. Brijil Lawrence, S.A.C.;
Office of Child & Youth Protection - Sandra Schrader-Farry, Dir.; Patrick McGrail, Asst. Dir.;
Permanent Deacon Formation Program - Juan Rendon, Dir.; Dcn. Scott France, Coord. Inquiry, Admissions & Aspirants; Sr. Anne Frances Ai Le, Asst. Dir. Intellectual Formation;
Prison Ministry - Dcn. Don Warner; Rev. Richard Collins;
Safe Environment Program - Sandra Schrader-Farry, Dir.;
Scouting - Victoria Ramon;
Tribunal - Very Rev. D. Timothy Thompson, Judicial Vicar; Rev. Joy Joseph, T.O.R., Judge; Rev. Anh Tran, Judge;
Victim Assistance Ministry - t) (817) 945-9345
Vocations -
Director of Collegian Seminarian Formation - Rev. Maurice Moon;
Director of Theologian Seminarian Formation - Very Rev. Jonathan Wallis;
Director of Vocations - Rev. Brett Metzler;
Vocation Liaisons - Rev. Nghia Nguyen; Rev. Matthew Tatyrek; Rev. Pedro Javier Martinez;
Vocations- Administrative Assistant - Josie Geisler;

PARISHES, MISSIONS, AND CLERGY

STATE OF TEXAS

ABBOTT

Immaculate Heart of Mary - 601 W. Houston St., Abbott, TX 76621 t) 254-582-3092 ihom.rachel@gmail.com www.immaculateheartofmaryabbott.org/ Dcn. Denver Crawley; Dcn. Terry Timmons, DRE; CRP Stds.: 42

ALBANY

Jesus of Nazareth - 7950 W. US Hwy. 180, Albany, TX 76430; Mailing: 208 S. Miller St., Breckenridge, TX 76424 t) 254-559-2860 shofjcc@gmail.com Rev. Prakash Dias, SAC (India), Pst.; Janie Saucedo, DRE;

ALEDO

Holy Redeemer Parish - 16250 Old Weatherford Rd., Aledo, TX 76008 t) 817-441-3500 office@holyredeemeraledo.org; dre@holyredemeraledo.org www.holyredeemeraledo.org Rev. Msgr. Publius Xuereb, Pst.; Dcn. Scott France; Dcn. Steve Dixon; CRP Stds.: 249

ARGYLE

St. Mark - 6500 Crawford Rd., Argyle, TX 76226 t) 940-387-6223; 940-220-7160 (CRP) evasquez@stmarkdenton.org; kharbert@stmarkdenton.org www.stmarkdenton.org Rev. Baby George, Pst.; Dcn. James Dale Galbraith; Dcn. Victor Norton; Dcn. Edward Posvar; CRP Stds.: 646

ARLINGTON

Church of the Vietnamese Martyrs - 801 E. Mayfield Rd., Arlington, TX 76014 t) 817-466-0800; 817-917-7052 (CRP); 817-917-8703; 817-467-0690 vpgxtd@yahoo.com; johndiem2017@gmail.com www.cttdvn.net Rev. John M. Tinh Tran, CRM, Pst.; Dcn. John Ban Nguyen; CRP Stds.: 750

St. Joseph - 1927 S.W. Green Oaks Blvd., Arlington, TX 76017-2734 t) 817-472-5181 info@stjoe88.org stjoe88.org Rev. Ronaldo Mercado, Pst.; Dcn. Jimmy Garcia; Dcn. Bill Johnson; Dcn. Jose Roman; Dcn. Rodney Asebedo, Youth Min.; Michelle Ebambi, RCIA Coord.; CRP Stds.: 181

St. Joseph School - (Grades PreK-8) 2015 S.W. Green Oaks Blvd., Arlington, TX 76017-2399 t) 817-419-6800 info@stjosephtx.org www.stjosephtx.org Diane Price, Prin.; Stds.: 321; Sr. Tchrs.: 2; Lay Tchrs.: 35

St. Maria Goretti - 1200 S. Davis Dr., Arlington, TX 76013-2399 t) 817-274-0643; 817-274-0643 x226 (CRP) kmccoy@smgparish.org; kparker@smgparish.org www.smgparish.org Rev. Michael Ciski, T.O.R., Pst.; Rev. Stanley Holland, TOR, Par. Vicar; Keith Parker, DRE; CRP Stds.: 228

St. Maria Goretti School - (Grades PreK-8) t) 817-275-5081 secretary@smgschool.org www.smgschool.org Amy Utendorf, Prin.; Stds.: 176; Sr. Tchrs.: 1

St. Matthew - 2021 New York Ave., Arlington, TX 76010-6097 t) 817-860-0130 info@stmattcc.org www.stmattcc.org Rev. Ariel Sanchez, Pst.; Rev. Victor Manuel Contreras (Mexico), Par. Vicar; CRP Stds.: 806

Most Blessed Sacrament - 2100 N. Davis Dr., Arlington, TX 76012 t) 817-460-2751 info@mbs.church www.mbs.church Rev. Msgr. Joseph Pemberton, Pst.; Rev. Msgr. Joseph S. Scantlin, Pastor Emer.; Dcn. Willy Montano; Dcn. Michael Krempp; Dcn. Joe Ramos; Sallie Magallanez, Liturgy Dir.; Yvette Crumly, DRE; CRP Stds.: 285

St. Vincent de Paul - 5819 W. Pleasant Ridge Rd., Arlington, TX 76016 t) 817-478-8206 svdpcc.org Rev. Philip Brembah, Pst.; Dcn. Bruce Corbett; Kevin Keil, Dir., Liturgy & Music; Wendy Perez, Bus. Mgr.; Renee Bader, Dir.,Stewardship & Ministry; Michal Tincup, Dir., Adult Ministry; Michael Stratman, Youth Min.; Jessica Terry, Coord., Children's Ministry; CRP Stds.: 306

AZLE

Holy Trinity Catholic Church - 800 High Crest Dr., Azle, TX 76020 t) 817-444-3063 x4 briley@holytrinityazle.org www.holytrinityazle.org Brenda Riley, Bus. Mgr.; CRP Stds.: 165

BEDFORD

St. Michael - 3713 Harwood Rd., Bedford, TX 76021-4097 t) 817-283-8746; 817-510-2714 rharris@smcchurch.org; deaconwalt@smcchurch.org www.smcchurch.org Rev. Balaji Boyalla, S.A.C., Pst.; Dcn. Thomas Doran; Dcn. Harold Heinz; Dcn. Sangote Ulupano; Robin Harris, DRE; Dcn. Walter Stone, Bus. Mgr.; CRP Stds.: 249

BOWIE

St. Jerome - 1200 N. Matthews St., Bowie, TX 76230; Mailing: 105 S. Barrett St., Henrietta, TX 76365 t) 940-538-4214 stmaryhenrietta@yahoo.com stmarycatholichenrietta.org St. Mary, Henrietta. Rev. Albert Francis Kanjirathumkal, Pst.; CRP Stds.: 14

BRECKENRIDGE

Sacred Heart of Jesus - 208 S. Miller St., Breckenridge, TX 76424 t) 254-559-2860 shofjcc@gmail.com www.shojcc.org Rev. Prakash Dias, SAC (India), Pst.; Janie Saucedo, DRE; CRP Stds.: 80

BRIDGEPORT

St. John the Baptizer - 1801 Irvin, Bridgeport, TX 76426 t) 940-683-2743 main_office@jbdcatholics.org jbdcatholics.org Rev. Anto Vijayan Carloose, SAC (India), Pst.; Dcn. Eldon Gray; Dcn. Mauricio Hernandez; Dcn. Myles Miller; CRP Stds.: 128

BURKBURNETT

St. Jude Thaddeus - 600 Davey Dr., Burkburnett, TX 76354 t) 940-569-1222 stjudeburkburnett@gmail.com; dpoole746@gmail.com stjudeburkburnett.org Rev. Joseph George Moreno, Pst.; Dcn. David Poole; CRP Stds.: 25

BURLESON

St. Ann - 100 S.W. Alsbury Blvd., Burleson, TX 76028 t) 817-295-5621; 817-426-1101 (CRP) office@mystann.com; pastor@mystann.com stanninburleson.com Rev. Reehan Soosai Antony, SAC, Pst.; CRP Stds.: 364

CARROLLTON

St. Catherine of Siena - 1705 E. Peters Colony Rd., Carrollton, TX 75007-3704 t) 972-492-3237 info@stcatherine.org www.stcatherine.org Rev. Sushil William Tudu, T.O.R., Pst.; Dcn. Walter Stone; Dcn. David Robinett; CRP Stds.: 204

CISCO

Holy Rosary - 1108 Ave. F, Cisco, TX 76437; Mailing: 1109 Blackwell Rd., Ranger, TX 76470 t) 254-647-3163 stritaoffice2018@gmail.com stritacatholicranger.org St. Rita, Ranger. Rev. Vijaya Mareedu, SAC, Pst.;

CLEBURNE

St. Joseph - 807 N. Anglin St., Cleburne, TX 76031 t) 817-645-4478 stjo123@sbcglobal.net saintjosephcleburne,.com Rev. Sergio Rizo, Pst.; CRP Stds.: 236

CLIFTON

Holy Angels - 1915 W. Fifth St., Clifton, TX 76634 t) 254-675-8877 holyangels@holyangelstx.org holyangelsclifton.org Rev. Mariya James, S.A.C., Admin.; Cinthya Ernestina Fernandez, DRE; CRP Stds.: 56

COLLEYVILLE

Good Shepherd - 1000 Tinker Rd., Colleyville, TX 76034 t) 817-421-1387 www.gscc.net Rev. Michael Higgins, TOR, Pst.; Rev. Zachary Burns, TOR, Par. Vicar; Rev. John Mark Klaus, T.O.R., Par. Vicar; Rev. Ronald Mohnickey, T.O.R., Par. Vicar; Dcn. John Clark; Dcn. Al Mosco; Dcn. Richard Griego; Dcn. Rick Wright; CRP Stds.: 889

COMANCHE

Sacred Heart - 1206 N. Pearl St., Comanche, TX 76442; Mailing: 1444 W. Washington Ave., Stephenville, TX 76401 t) 254-965-5693; 325-356-2040 (CRP) stbrendancc@gmail.com www.stbrendanscc.org Rev. Matthew Sanka, S.A.C., Pst.; Rev. James Amasi, Pst. Assoc.; Martina Sierra, DRE; CRP Stds.: 52

CROWELL

St. Joseph - 1103 N. Main St., Crowell, TX 79227; Mailing: 2200 Roberts St, Vernon, TX 76384 t) 940-552-2895 church.accounting@att.net holyfamilyccvernon.org Holy Family, Vernon. Rev. Phil D Petta, Pst.; CRP Stds.: 4

DECATUR

Assumption of the Blessed Virgin Mary - 1305 Deer Park Rd., Decatur, TX 76234-9701 t) 940-683-2743 main_office@jbdcatholics.org jbdcatholics.org Rev. Reehan Soosai Antony, S.A.C., Pst.; Rev. Anto Vijayan Carloose, SAC (India), Par. Vicar; Dcn. Eldon Gray; Dcn. Mauricio Hernandez; Dcn. Myles Miller; Anna Boyles, DRE; CRP Stds.: 286

DELEON

Our Lady of Guadalupe - 6044 Hwy. 16, DeLeon, TX 76444; Mailing: 1444 W. Washington, Stephenville, TX 76401 t) 254-965-5693; 817-626-7421 (CRP) stbrendancc@gmail.com www.stbrendanscc.org St. Brendan, Stephenville. Rev. Matthew Sanka, S.A.C., Pst.; Rev. James Amasi, Pst. Assoc.; CRP Stds.: 20

DENTON

Immaculate Conception - 2255 N. Bonnie Brae St., Denton, TX 76207 t) 940-565-1770 margaret.casias@iccdenton.org www.iccdenton.org Rev. Matthew Tatyrek, Pst.; Rev. Jason Allan, Par. Vicar; Rev. Kheim Nguyen, Par. Vicar; Dcn. Angelo Lombardo; Dcn. Robert Moreno; Dcn. Alfonso Ramirez; Dcn. Barry Sweeden; Dcn. Art Cassias, DRE; CRP Stds.: 957

Immaculate Conception School - (Grades PreK-8) 2301 N. Bonnie Brae St., Denton, TX 76207 t) 940-381-1155 Elaine Schad, Prin.; Rebecca Bevilacqua, Librn.;

St. John Paul II Parish - 909 McCormick St., Denton, TX 76201; Mailing: 1303 Eagle Dr., Denton, TX 76201 t) 940-566-0004 stjohnpaulii@jp2denton.org jp2denton.org Catholic Church and Campus Ministry Rev. Kyle Walterscheid, Pst.; CRP Stds.: 12

DUBLIN

St. Mary - 12286 U.S. Hwy. 377, Dublin, TX 76446; Mailing: 1444 W. Washington St., Stephenville, TX 76401-4141 t) 254-965-5693; 254-445-0237 (CRP) catholic@embarqmail.com www.stbrendanscc.org St. Brendan, Stephenville. Rev. Matthew Sanka, S.A.C., Pst.; Rev. James Amasi, Assoc. Pst.; CRP Stds.: 240

EASTLAND

St. Francis Xavier - Halbryan and Foch St., Eastland, TX 76448; Mailing: 1109 Blackwell St., Ranger, TX 76470 t) 254-647-3163 stritacatholicranger.org St. Rita, Ranger. Rev. Vijaya Mareedu, SAC, Pst.; Leslie Boelter, Youth Min.; Leslie Boelter, DRE; CRP Stds.: 29

ELECTRA

St. Paul - 500 N. Bailey Ave., Electra, TX 76360; Mailing: 600 Davey Dr., Burkburnett, TX 76354 t) 940-569-1222 stjudeburkburnett@gmail.com; frjosephmoreno@gmail.com stjudeburkburnett.org/saint-paul-electra Rev. Joseph George Moreno, Pst.; Dcn. David Poole; CRP Stds.: 2

FLOWER MOUND

St. Philip the Apostle - 5201 Cross Timbers Rd., Flower Mound, TX 75022 t) 972-436-9581 stphilipcc.org/ Very Rev. Raymond McDaniel, Pst.; Rev. Msgr. Francis Boachie Tawiah, Par. Vicar; Dcn. Patrick Quinn; Dcn. Ramiro Rodriguez; Dcn. Joe Standridge; CRP Stds.: 375

FORT WORTH

St. Patrick Cathedral - 1206 Throckmorton St., Fort Worth, TX 76102; Mailing: 1300 Throckmorton St., Fort Worth, TX 76102 t) 817-332-4915 esmith@stpatrickcathedral.org www.stpatrickcathedral.org Most Rev. Michael F. Olson, Pst.; Very Rev. John Robert Skeldon, Rector; Dcn. Manuel Pereda; Dcn. James Crites; Dcn. Daniel Zavala; Dcn. Don Warner; Michele Baker, Dir.; Micheal Canfield, Dir.; Michael Waldon, Dir.; Aaron Medina, Dir.; Cintia Ventura, Dir.; Edward Robert Smith, COO; Carol Franko, Editor; Mary Lou Schulz, Admin. Asst. to Rector; Joseph Canfield, San Mateo Chapel of Ease Facilities Supvr.; Maria Rosales, DRE; Rev. Maurice Moon, In Res.; Rev. Binoy Kurian, T.O.R., In Res.; CRP Stds.: 167

All Saints - 214 N.W. 20th St., Fort Worth, TX 76104 t) 817-626-3055 allsaintscc.net/ Very Rev. D. Timothy Thompson, Pst.; Rev. Richard Collins, In Res.; Dcn. Ricardo De Leon, Bus. Mgr.; Dcn. Jesus Valadez, Liturgy Dir.; Dcn. Juan Escamilla; Sr. Diana Rodriguez, DRE; CRP Stds.: 243

All Saints School - (Grades PreK-8) 2006 N. Houston St., Fort Worth, TX 76164 t) 817-624-2670 aprado@ascsfw.org www.ascsfw.org Arica Prado, Prin.; Stds.: 130; Lay Tchrs.: 11

St. Andrew - 3314 Dryden Rd., Fort Worth, TX 76109; Mailing: 3312 Dryden Rd., Fort Worth, TX 76109 t) 817-927-5383 sachurch@standrewcc.org www.standrewcc.org Rev. James Gigliotti, T.O.R., Pst.; Rev. Daniel Pattee, TOR, Assoc. Pst.; Rev. John Shanahan, T.O.R., Assoc. Pst.; Dcn. Lynn Sowers; Dcn. Kevin Bagley; CRP Stds.: 130

St. Andrew Catholic School - (Grades PreK-8) 3304 Dryden Rd., Fort Worth, TX 76109-3799 t) 817-924-8917 Laura Behee, Prin.;

St. Bartholomew - 3601 Altamesa Blvd., Fort Worth, TX 76133 t) 817-292-7703 stbarts@stbartsfw.org www.stbartsfw.org Rev. Karl W. Schilken, Pst.; CRP Stds.: 531

St. Benedict Parish - 2920 Azle Ave., Fort Worth, TX 76106 t) 817-439-9944 pastor@stbensfw.org www.stbensfw.org Rev. Simon James Harkins, FSSP, Pst.;

Christ the King - 1112 Eagle Dr., Fort Worth, TX 76137 t) 817-386-5582 c) (817) 647-5419 chuakito1112@gmail.com www.chuakitovua.org Rev. Chau Van Nguyen, Pst.; Rev. Tien Van Ta, Lm., Assoc. Pst.; Dcn. Truat Van Nguyen; Peter Nguyen, DRE; Elaine Lai, Admin.; CRP Stds.: 403

St. George - 3500 Maurice Ave., Fort Worth, TX 76111; Mailing: 825 Karnes St., Fort Worth, TX 76111 t) 817-831-4404 parish.office@sgccftw-tx.org www.sgccftw-tx.org Rev. Nghia Nguyen, Pst.;

St. George School - (Grades PreK-8) 824 Hudgins St., Fort Worth, TX 76111-4799 t) 817-222-1221 fsollie@sgcsfwtx.org www.stgeorgecatholicschool.org/ Laura Leafgreen, Prin.; Stds.: 108; Lay Tchrs.: 11

Holy Family - 6150 Pershing Ave., Fort Worth, TX 76107 t) 817-737-6768; 817-737-6768 x107 (CRP) pastoraloffice@holyfamilyfw.org; gsayers@holyfamilyfw.org www.holyfamilyfw.org Very Rev. Hoa Nguyen, Pst.; Dcn. Mark Gannaway; Dcn. Michael Mocek; Genni Sayers, DRE; Dcn. David Kinch; CRP Stds.: 185

Holy Family School - (Grades PreK-8) 6146 Pershing Ave., Fort Worth, TX 76107 t) 817-737-4201 busmgr@hfcsfw.org www.hfcsfw.org Ann Walters, Prin.; Tracy Head, Bus. Mgr.; Stds.: 111; Sr. Tchrs.: 1; Lay Tchrs.: 10

Holy Name of Jesus - 2635 Burchill Rd., Fort Worth, TX 76105 t) 817-536-9604; 817-535-3068 (CRP) holyname2003@sbcglobal.net; sisterevasanchez@yahoo.com Rev. Francisco Alanis Gonzalez, Pst.; Sr. Eva Sanchez, M.C.S.H., DRE; Maribel Ruiz, Bus. Mgr.; CRP Stds.: 1,057

Immaculate Heart of Mary - 201 Thornhill Dr., Fort Worth, TX 76115; Mailing: 108 E. Hammond St., Fort Worth, TX 76115 t) 817-923-6323; 817-923-8582 (CRP) parishoffice@ihmfw.com ihmfw.com Rev. Oscar Sanchez Olvera, CORC, Pst.; Dcn. Marcelino Carranza; Sr. Silvia Gomez, MCSH, DRE; Maria Lorena Martinez, Bus. Mgr.; CRP Stds.: 1,677

St. Mary of the Assumption - 509 W. Magnolia Ave., Fort Worth, TX 76104 t) 817-923-1911 sylvia@stmarysftw.org; frjohn@stmarysftw.org www.stmarysftw.org Rev. John Perikomalayil, H.G.N., Pst.; CRP Stds.: 200

Our Lady of Fatima - 5109 E. Lancaster Ave., Fort Worth, TX 76112 t) 817-446-3980 c) 682-216-1735; 214-906-3438 ourladyoffatima160@gmail.com giaoxufatima.org Rev. Vinh Van Vu, C.M.C., Pst.; Dcn. Michael Hoang, DRE; Julie Do, Bus. Mgr.; CRP Stds.: 200

Our Lady of Guadalupe - 4100 Blue Mound Rd., Fort Worth, TX 76106 t) 817-626-7421; 817-624-3240 (CRP) churchoffice@ourladyguadalupefw.org; vrodriguez@ourladyguadalupefw.org ourladyguadalupefw.org/ Friar Luis Gerardo Arraiza, OFM, Cap., Pst.; Friar Federico Ortiz, OFM, Cap., Par. Vicar; Friar Jose Feliciano Torres, O.F.M.Cap., Par. Vicar; Virginia Rodriguez, DRE; Angelica Ruiz, Bus. Mgr.; CRP Stds.: 675

Our Mother of Mercy - 1001 E. Terrell Ave., Fort Worth, TX 76104-3788; Mailing: 1005 E. Terrell Ave., Fort Worth, TX 76104-3788 t) 817-335-1695 ourmother@omomftworth.org www.omomftworth.org Jennifer JB Rattliff, Bus. Mgr.; CRP Stds.: 30

St. Paul the Apostle - 5508 Black Oak Ln., Fort Worth, TX 76114 t) 817-738-9925; 817-738-9925 x18 (CRP) secretary@stpaulfw.org stpaulfw.org Rev. Thu Nguyen, Pst.; Dcn. Pedro Garcia; CRP Stds.: 222

St. Peter the Apostle - 1201 S. Cherry Ln., Fort Worth, TX 76108 t) 817-246-3622 x304 www.stpeterfw.com Rev. Pedro Javier Martinez, Pst.; Dcn. Wendell Geiger; Dcn. Steve Holton; Dcn. Rigoberto Leyva; Yasmin Cuevas, DRE; CRP Stds.: 519

St. Peter the Apostle School - (Grades PreK-8) t) 817-246-2032 x105 lgiardino@spsfw.org www.spsfw.org Lisa Giardino, Prin.; Stds.: 91; Sr. Tchrs.: 1; Lay Tchrs.: 10

St. Rita - 5550 E. Lancaster Ave., Fort Worth, TX 76112 t) 817-451-9395 www.stritafw.org Rev. Keith Hathaway, Pst.; CRP Stds.: 229

St. Rita School - (Grades PreK-8) 712 Weiler Blvd., Fort Worth, TX 76112-6398 t) 817-451-9383 mburns@saintritaschool.net www.saintritaschool.net Mary Burns, Prin.; Stds.: 135; Sr. Tchrs.: 1; Lay Tchrs.: 9

St. Thomas the Apostle - 5953 Bowman Roberts Rd., Fort Worth, TX 76179 t) 817-624-2184 dcnmike@sttafw.org; frbenjamin@sttafw.org www.sttafw.org Rev. Benjamin Hembrom, TOR, Pst.; Dcn. Mike Handler; Dcn. Humberto Serrano; Maria Rosales, Bus. Mgr.; CRP Stds.: 500

GAINESVILLE

St. Mary - 805 N. Weaver St., Gainesville, TX 76240; Mailing: 825 N. Weaver St., Gainesville, TX 76240 t) 940-665-5395 pam.hoedebeck@stmaryscatholic.com; silvia.lesko@stmaryscatholic.com www.stmarygainesvillecc.org Rev. John Pacheco, Pst.; Dcn. Jerome Caplinger; Dcn. David Finch; Dcn. Gelasio Garcia; Silvia Jo Lesko, M.T.S., DRE; CRP Stds.: 146

St. Mary School - (Grades PreK-8) 931 N. Weaver St., Gainesville, TX 76240-3299 kotto@smsmustangs.com smsmustangs.com Stds.: 128; Lay Tchrs.: 14

GLEN ROSE

St. Rose of Lima - 404 Mesquite St., Glen Rose, TX 76043; Mailing: P.O. Box 7324, Glen Rose, TX 76043 t) 817-326-2131 mespinosa@stfrances.net St. Frances Cabrini. Very Rev. Fernando Preciado, Pst.; CRP Stds.: 56

GRAFORD

St. Francis of Assisi - 14965 N. State Hwy. 16, Graford, TX 76449; Mailing: P.O. Box 404, Graford, TX 76449 t) 940-325-4789 pastoratoll@gmail.com Our Lady of Lourdes. Rev. Thomas Dsouza, SAC, Pst.;

GRAHAM

St. Mary - 1218 S. Rodgers Dr., Graham, TX 76450; Mailing: P.O.Box 547, Graham, TX 76450 t) 940-549-4314 stmarygm@sbcglobal.net Rev. Eugene Nyong, Admin.; Dcn. Adolfo Gonzalez; Vickie Keller, DRE; CRP Stds.: 173

GRANBURY

St. Frances Cabrini - 2301 Acton Hwy., Granbury, TX 76049 t) 817-326-2131 lgarcia@stfrances.net Very Rev. Fernando Preciado, Pst.; Dcn. Craig McAlister; CRP Stds.: 366

GRAPEVINE

St. Francis of Assisi - 861 Wildwood, Grapevine, TX 76051-3398 t) 817-481-2685 stfrancis@sfatx.org; emckuzes@sfatx.org www.sfatx.org Rev. Sojan George, H.G.N., Pst.; Rev. Mel Bessellieu, Par. Vicar; Dcn. William Johnson; Dcn. Tom Bates; Dcn. Paul Mahoney; Dcn. Perfecto Santiago; CRP Stds.: 550

HENRIETTA

St. Mary - 105 S. Barrett St., Henrietta, TX 76365 t) 940-538-4214 stmaryhenrietta@yahoo.com stmarycatholichenrietta.org Rev. Albert Francis Kanjirathumkal, Pst.; CRP Stds.: 3

HILLSBORO

Our Lady of Mercy - 107 Crestridge Dr., Hillsboro, TX 76645 t) 254-582-5640 olm@hillsboro.net www.ourladyofmercyhillsboro.org Magaly Pena, Bus. Mgr.; CRP Stds.: 224

HURST

Korean Martyrs - 415 Brown Tr., Hurst, TX 76053 t) 817-788-5530 jubo.kmcc@gmail.com www.cafe.daum.net/fortworthkmcc Rev. Chang-Jun Lee, Pst.; Youngmi Park, DRE; CRP Stds.: 21

IOWA PARK

Christ the King - 1008 N. First St., Iowa Park, TX 76367; Mailing: 600 Davey Dr., Burkburnett, TX 76354 t) 940-569-1222 stjudeburkburnett@gmail.com; frjosephmoreno@gmail.com stjudeburkburnett.org Rev. Joseph George Moreno, Pst.; Dcn. David Poole; CRP Stds.: 15

JACKSBORO

St. Mary - 1186 State Hwy. 148, Jacksboro, TX 76458; Mailing: 1801 Irvin St., Bridgeport, TX 76426 t) 940-683-2743 main_office@jbdcatholics.org; fatheranto@jbdcatholics.org jbdcatholics.org Rev. Anto Vijayan Carloose, SAC (India), Pst.; Dcn. Eldon Gray; Dcn. Mauricio Hernandez; Dcn. Myles Miller; CRP Stds.: 58

KELLER

St. Elizabeth Ann Seton - 2016 Willis Ln., Keller, TX 76248 t) 817-431-3857 Rev. James Flynn, Pst.; Rev. Linh Nguyen, Par. Vicar; Dcn. Normand Etienne; Dcn. Guido Serrano; Dcn. Larry Sandoval; Dcn. Jerry Rustand; Dcn. Nelson Petzold; Dcn. Michael Sutton; CRP Stds.: 650

St. Elizabeth Ann Seton School - (Grades PreK-8) t) 817-431-4845 svanderplas@seton.school; school@seton.school www.seascs.net Sam Vanderplas, Prin.; Stds.: 586; Lay Tchrs.: 41

KNOX CITY

Santa Rosa - 210 North Ave. G., Knox City, TX 79529; Mailing: P.O. Box 428, Knox City, TX 79529 t) 940-658-5062 stjosephrhineland@gmail.com St. Joseph, Rhineland. Rev. Francis Chinthamalla, Pst.;

LINDSAY

St. Peter - 424 W. Main St., Lindsay, TX 76250; Mailing: P.O. Box 148, Lindsay, TX 76250 t) 940-668-7609 x24 (CRP); 940-668-7609 stpeterschurch@ntin.net stpeterlindsay.org/ Dcn. Ralph Lira; CRP Stds.: 235

MANSFIELD

St. Jude - 500 E. Dallas St., Mansfield, TX 76063 t) 817-473-6709 d.kelley@stjudemansfieldtx.org www.stjudemansfieldtx.org Very Rev. Daniel P. Kelley, Pst.; Rev. Thomas Jones, Par. Vicar; Dcn. Jose Aragon; Dcn. Joel Rodriguez; Dcn. Kelly Canelo; CRP Stds.: 600

MEGARGEL

St. Mary - 13th St. & St. Mary St., Megargel, TX 76370; Mailing: 206 N. Cedar St., Seymour, TX 76380 t) 940-889-5252 shseymour@srcaccess.net sacredheartseymour.org Sacred Heart, Seymour. Rev. Bose Jujuvarapu, H.G.N., Par. Vicar; Dcn. James Novak, Admin.;

MINERAL WELLS

Our Lady of Lourdes - 108 N.W. 4th Ave., Mineral Wells, TX 76067 t) 940-325-4789 pastor@ollcatholicchurch.com; marlaourladyoflourdes@gmail.com www.ollcatholicchurch.com Rev. Thomas Dsouza, SAC, Pst.; Dcn. Jesus Cardenas; CRP Stds.: 150

MONTAGUE

St. William - 311 S. Union St., Montague, TX 76251; Mailing: 105 S. Barrett St., Henrietta, TX 76365 t) 940-538-4214 stmaryhenrietta@yahoo.com stmarycatholichenrietta.org St. Mary. Rev. Albert Francis Kanjirathumkal, Pst.; CRP Stds.: 23

MORGAN

Our Lady of Guadalupe - 304 Charles St., Morgan, TX 76671 t) 254-730-4942 rosafavela.olg@gmail.com; olgmorgantx@gmail.com Rev. Xavier Silvadasan, H.G.N., Pst.; CRP Stds.: 21

MUENSTER

Sacred Heart - 714 N. Main, Muenster, TX 76252; Mailing: 212 E. 6th St., Muenster, TX 76252 t) 940-759-2500 sforshee@shmuenster.com; joe.keating@fwdioc.org www.shchurchmuenster.com Rev. Joseph Keating, Pst.; Carmen Villa, DRE; CRP Stds.: 104

Preschool -

Sacred Heart School - (Grades K-8) 153 E. 6th St., Muenster, TX 76252 t) 940-759-2511 sforshee@shcmuenster.com

Sacred Heart High School - 153 E. 6th St., Muenster, TX 76252 sforshee@shcmuenster.com

MUNDAY

St. Joseph - 10180 County Rd. 6010, Munday, TX 76371 t) 940-422-4270; 940-422-4994 stjosephrhineland@gmail.com; jsdillard67@gmail.com stjosephrhineland.org Rev. Francis Chinthamalla, Pst.; Janet Dillard, DRE; CRP Stds.: 75

NOCONA

St. Joseph - 109 Denison St., Nocona, TX 76255; Mailing: 105 S. Barrett St., Henrietta, TX 76365 t) 940-538-4214 stmaryhenrietta@yahoo.com stmarycatholichenrietta.org St. Mary. Rev. Albert Francis Kanjirathumkal, Pst.; CRP Stds.: 8

NORTH RICHLAND HILLS

St. John the Apostle - 7341 Glenview Dr., North Richland Hills, TX 76180 t) 817-284-4811 church@sjtanrh.com sjtanrh.com Rev. Jack McKone, Pst.; Rev. Samuel Maul, Par. Vicar; Rev. Anh Tran, Par. Vicar; Dcn. Ruben Aguirre; Dcn. Matias Lagunas; Dcn. Juan Reyes; Dcn. Thien Ta; CRP Stds.: 34

St. John the Apostle School - (Grades PreK-8) 7421 Glenview Dr., North Richland Hills, TX 76180 t) 817-284-2228 afelton@stjs.org www.stjs.org Amy Felton, Prin.; Stds.: 165; Sr. Tchrs.: 2; Lay Tchrs.: 18

OLNEY

St. Theresa - Oak and Avenue E., Olney, TX 76374; Mailing: PO Box 547, Graham, TX 76450 t) 940-549-4314 stmarygm@sbcglobal.net St. Mary, Graham. Rev. Eugene Nyong, Admin.; CRP Stds.: 41

PENELOPE

Nativity of the Blessed Virgin Mary - 219 W. Magnolia St., Penelope, TX 76676; Mailing: P.O. Box 98, Penelope, TX 76676 t) 254-533-2325; 254-652-8802 c) 254-709-6003 penelopecatholicchurch@windstream.net nbvm.org Dcn. Denver Crawley; Dcn. Terry Timmons, DRE; CRP Stds.: 32

PILOT POINT

St. Thomas Aquinas - 400 St. Thomas Aquinas Ave., Pilot Point, TX 76258 t) 940-686-2088 office@sttpp.org; jwmartin5320@yahoo.com www.stthomaspilotpoint.org Rev. John Martin, Pst.; Dcn. Moises Camargo; Dcn. Francisco Leal; Dcn. Dave Garza; CRP Stds.: 313

PROSPER

St. Martin De Porres Parish - 3990 W. University, Prosper, TX 75078 t) 469-287-7624 office@saintmartindp.org; athomas@saintmartindp.org www.saintmartindp.org Very Rev. Stephen Hauck, Pst.; Dcn. Andrew Thomas, DRE; CRP Stds.: 262

St. Martin de Porres Catholic School - (Grades PreK-8) 4000 W. University, Prosper, TX 75078 t) 469-362-2400 office@smdpcatholic.org smdpcatholic.org Susan Flanagan, Prin.; Stds.: 288; Lay Tchrs.: 24

QUANAH

St. Mary - 609 Mercer St., Quanah, TX 79252; Mailing: 2200 Roberts, Vernon, TX 76384 t) 940-552-2895 church.accounting@att.net; catholic.secretary@att.net holyfamilyccvernon.org Holy Family, Vernon. Rev. Phil D Petta, Pst.; CRP Stds.: 12

RANGER

St. Rita - 1109 Blackwell Rd., Ranger, TX 76470 t) 254-647-3163 stritaoffice2018@gmail.com stritacatholicranger.org/ Rev. Vijaya Mareedu, SAC, Pst.; Dcn. Edward Ferguson; Leslie Boelter, Youth Min.; Leslie Boelter, DRE; CRP Stds.: 25

SEYMOUR

Sacred Heart - 206 N. Cedar St., Seymour, TX 76380 t) 940-889-5252 shseymour@srcaccess.net sacredheartseymour.org/ Rev. Bose Jujuvarapu, H.G.N., Par. Vicar; Dcn. Jim Novak, Admin.; Donna Carver,

DRE; CRP Stds.: 81

STEPHENVILLE

St. Brendan - 1444 W. Washington Ave., Stephenville, TX 76401 t) 254-965-5693 stbrendancc@gmail.com www.stbrendanscc.org Rev. Matthew Sanka, S.A.C., Pst.; Rev. James Amasi, Assoc. Pst.; Nathan Mena, Campus Min.; Melissa Winborn, Bus. Mgr.; CRP Stds.: 125

STRAWN

St. John - 126 Hickory St., Strawn, TX 76475; Mailing: 1109 Blackwell St., Ranger, TX 76470 t) 254-647-3163 stritaoffice2018@gmail.com stritacatholicranger.org St. Rita. Rev. Vijaya Mareedu, SAC, Pst.; Dcn. Edward Ferguson; Leslie Boelter, DRE; CRP Stds.: 10

THE COLONY

Holy Cross - 7000 Morning Star Dr., The Colony, TX 75056 t) 972-625-5252 x301; 972-625-5252 (CRP) jjoseph@holycrosscc.org holycrosscc.org Rev. Joy Joseph, T.O.R., Pst.; Karen da Costa, DRE; CRP Stds.: 170

VERNON

Holy Family of Nazareth - 2200 Roberts St., Vernon, TX 76384 t) 940-552-2895 catholic.secretary@att.net; church.accounting@att.net holyfamilyccvernon.org Rev. Philip Petta, Admin.; Debbie Frerich, Bus. Mgr.; CRP Stds.: 77

WEATHERFORD

St. Stephen - 1802 Bethel Rd., Weatherford, TX 76086 t) 817-596-9585 www.saintstephencc.org Rev. Emmet O'Hara, S.A.C, Pst.; Dcn. Carlos Frias; Dcn. Mauricio Hernandez; CRP Stds.: 611

WICHITA FALLS

Immaculate Conception of Mary - 2901 Barnett Rd., Wichita Falls, TX 76310 t) 940-692-1825 jimkhoi@juno.com Rev. Jim N. Khoi, Pst.; Thanh Ton, DRE;

Our Lady of Guadalupe - 421 Marconi, Wichita Falls, TX 76301 t) 940-766-2735 contact@guadalupewf.org; miriam.linares@guadalupewf.org www.guadalupewf.org Rev. Xavier Silvadasan, H.G.N., Pst.; Dcn. Davy Tolentino; Dcn. Brad Samuelson; Jessica Barron, DRE; Artemia Rodriguez, RCIA Coord.;

Our Lady Queen of Peace - 2601 Lansing Blvd., Wichita Falls, TX 76309; Mailing: 4040 York St., Wichita Falls, TX 76309 t) 940-696-1253 info@olqpwf.org www.olqpwf.org Very Rev. Alexander Ambrose, H.G.N., Pst.; Dcn. Jim Bindel; Dcn. Dennis Brent Catlin; CRP Stds.: 120

Sacred Heart - 1501 Ninth St., Wichita Falls, TX 76301; Mailing: 1504 Tenth St., Wichita Falls, TX 76301 t) 940-723-5288 sheart@sacredheartwf.org sacredheartwf.org Rev. Jonathan Demma, Pst.; Rev. Jose Francis, TOR (India), Par. Vicar; Dcn. David Bindel; Dcn. Manny Vasquez; Monica Robinson, DRE; CRP Stds.: 168

WINDTHORST

St. Boniface - Intersection of Hwy. 281 & 172, Windthorst, TX 76389; Mailing: P.O. Box 230, Windthorst, TX 76389 t) 940-423-6687 windscot@comcell.net www.stmarystboniface.org St. Boniface, Scotland, TX 76379. Rev. Michael Moloney, Pst.;

St. Mary - 101 Church St., Windthorst, TX 76389; Mailing: P.O. Box 230, Windthorst, TX 76389 t) 940-423-6687 windscot@comcell.net www.stmarysstboniface.org Rev. Michael Moloney, Pst.; CRP Stds.: 200

SCHOOLS: PRESCHOOL THRU HIGH SCHOOL

SCHOOLS

STATE OF TEXAS

DENTON

Immaculate Conception Catholic School - (PAR) (Grades PreK-8) 2301 N. Bonnie Brae St., Denton, TX 76207-1019 t) 940-381-1155 iccsoffice@gmail.com www.catholicschooldenton.org Frank Perez, Prin.; Stds.: 177; Lay Tchrs.: 11

GRAPEVINE

Holy Trinity Catholic School - (DIO) (Grades PreK-8) 3750 William D. Tate Ave., Grapevine, TX 76051 t) 817-421-8000 school@holytcs.org; admissions@holytcs.org www.holytcs.org Karen Ullman, Prin.; Cindy Rizzo, Vice Prin.; Stds.: 282; Lay Tchrs.: 23

MUENSTER

Sacred Heart School - (PAR) (Grades PreK-12) 153 E. Sixth St., Muenster, TX 76252-0588 t) 940-759-2511 nisalagle@shmuenster.com www.shmuenster.com Nisa Lagle, Prin.; Stds.: 195; Sr. Tchrs.: 1; Lay Tchrs.: 21

***Sacred Heart Teachers Trust Fund** -

HIGH SCHOOLS

STATE OF TEXAS

FORT WORTH

Cassata Catholic High School - (DIO) (Grades 9-12) 1400 Hemphill St., Fort Worth, TX 76104-4796 t) 817-926-1745 mharrison@cassatahs.org www.cassatahs.org (Coed Secondary). Maggie Harrison, Pres.; Stds.: 89; Lay Tchrs.: 7

Nolan Catholic High School - (DIO) (Grades 9-12) 4501 Bridge St., Fort Worth, TX 76103-1198 t) 817-457-2920 office@nolancatholichs.org www.nolancatholic.org/ (Coed) Oscar Ortiz, Prin.; Rev. Maurice Moon, Chap.; Kristy Webb, Pres.; Stds.: 689; Sr. Tchrs.: 1; Lay Tchrs.: 64

INSTITUTIONS LOCATED IN DIOCESE

CAMPUS MINISTRY / NEWMAN CENTERS [CAM]

ARLINGTON

University of Texas at Arlington University Catholic Community - 1010 Benge Dr., Arlington, TX 76013-2643 t) 817-460-1155 utacatholics.org Jeff Hedglen, Campus Min.;

FORT WORTH

Texas Christian University Catholic Community - 2704 W. Berry St., Fort Worth, TX 76109 t) 682-321-8827 www.tcucatholic.org Gabe Gutierrez, Campus Min.;

WICHITA FALLS

Catholic Campus Ministry - 3410 Louis J. Rodriguez Dr., Wichita Falls, TX 76308 t) 940-692-9778 msuccc@yahoo.com Debra Veitenheimer, Dir.;

CATHOLIC CHARITIES [CCH]

FORT WORTH

Catholic Charities Diocese of Fort Worth Endowment, Inc. - 249 W. Thornhill Dr., Fort Worth, TX 76115; Mailing: P.O. Box 15610, Fort Worth, TX 76119 t) 817-534-0814 info@ccdofw.org; lsotelo@ccdofw.org catholiccharitiesfortworth.org/ Catholic Charities, Diocese of Fort Worth, Inc. Debra McNamara, Chair; Staff: 1

Catholic Charities, Diocese of Fort Worth, Inc. - 249 W. Thornhill Dr., Fort Worth, TX 76115; Mailing: PO Box 15610, Fort Worth, TX 76119 t) 817-534-0814 infoccdofw@ccdofw.org www.catholiccharitiesfortworth.org An Independent Corporation Founded by the Diocese of Fort Worth. Rev. Anthony L. Chandler, CEO; Asstd. Annu.: 13,840; Staff: 301

CONVENTS, MONASTERIES, AND RESIDENCES FOR WOMEN [CON]

ARLINGTON

Monastery of the Most Holy Trinity, Discalced Carmelites - 5801 Mt. Carmel Dr., Arlington, TX 76017 t) 817-468-1781 arlingtoncarmel@gmail.com www.carmelnuns.com Mother Teresa Agnes Gerlach, OCD, Prioress; Srs.: 10

FORT WORTH

Hermanas Catequistas Guadalupanas - 9221 Jason Dr., Fort Worth, TX 76108 t) 817-945-9317 Sr. Diana Rodriguez, Supr.; Srs.: 2

Provincial House of the Western Province, Sisters of St. Mary of Namur. - 909 W. Shaw St., Fort Worth, TX 76110 t) 817-923-3091 patricia.ridgley@gmail.com www.ssmnwestern.com Sr. Patricia Ridgley, S.S.M.N., Supr.; Srs.: 24

Sisters of St. Mary of Namur - 909 W. Shaw, Fort Worth, TX 76110 t) (817) 923-3091 patricia.ridgley@gmail.com; frmstanton@sbcglobal.net www.ssmnwestern.com Sr. Patricia Ridgley, S.S.M.N., Supr.; Srs.: 24

ENDOWMENTS / FOUNDATIONS / TRUSTS [EFT]

FORT WORTH

Catholic Diocese of Fort Worth Advancement Foundation - 201 Main St., Ste. 1198, Fort Worth, TX 76102-3101 t) 817-533-3170 runderwood@adv-fdn.org www.advancementfoundation.org Rev. Msgr. E. James Hart, Chair; Clint J. Weber, Pres.; Cynthia Gordon, Treas.; Renee Underwood, Exec.; Most Rev. Michael F. Olson, Mem.; Ed Gray Jr., Dir.; John Michael Halloran, Dir.; Very Rev. Stephen Hauck, Dir.; Ryan F. Kagay, Dir.; Rosa Rios Navajar, Dir.;

Saint Thomas More Society of the Diocese of Fort Worth, Texas - 514 E. Belknap St., Ste. 200, Fort Worth, TX 76102

MISCELLANEOUS [MIS]

FORT WORTH

North Texas San Benito, Inc. - 800 W. Loop 820 S., Fort Worth, TX 76108 t) 817-945-9400 Most Rev. Michael F. Olson;

LEWISVILLE

Magnificat, Grapevine Chapter - 425 Misty Ln., Lewisville, TX 75067 t) 214-587-3478 registration@magnificat-ministry-grapevine.net Mary Trevino, Coord.;

MONASTERIES AND RESIDENCES FOR PRIESTS AND BROTHERS [MON]

CARROLLTON

***Third Order Regular of St. Francis, Province of St. Thomas** - 1705 E. Peters Colony Rd., Carrollton, TX 75005 t) 817-905-8632; 972-922-0422 Rev. Sushil William Tudu, T.O.R., Dir.; Rev. Benjamin Hembrom, TOR, Secy.; Rev. Joy Joseph, T.O.R., Treas.; Priests: 6

MUNDAY

Heralds of Good News Mother Theresa Province, Inc. - 10180 County Rd. 6010, Munday, TX 76371 t) 940-422-4990 hgnmtpusa@gmail.com www.heraldsofgoodnews.org Rev. John Perikomalayil, H.G.N., Pres.; Priests: 24

NURSING / REHABILITATION / CONVALESCENCE / ELDERLY CARE [NUR]

CROWLEY

St. Francis Village, Inc. - 4070 St. Francis Village Rd., Crowley, TX 76036 t) 817-292-5786 davidt@saintfrancisvillage.com www.saintfrancisvillage.com David Tolson, Exec.; Asstd. Annu.: 530; Staff: 23

Franciscan Tertiary Provinces Foundation - Sponsor corporation of St. Francis Village (retirement village) in Crowley, TX.

San Damiano, Inc. - 4070 St. Francis Village Rd.,

Crowley, TX 76036 t) 817-292-5786 davidt@saintfrancisvillage.com David Tolson, Exec.; Asstd. Annu.: 30

RETREAT HOUSES / RENEWAL CENTERS [RTR]

LAKE DALLAS

Montserrat Jesuit Retreat House - 600 N. Shady Shores Dr., Lake Dallas, TX 75065; Mailing: P.O. Box 1390, Lake Dallas, TX 75065 t) 940-321-6020 director@montserratretreat.org www.montserratretreat.org Rev. Anthony Rauschuber, SJ, Dir.; Rev. Joseph A. Tetlow, S.J., In Res.;

Montserrat Foundation, Inc. - Rev. Anthony R. Borrow, S.J., Chair;

An asterisk (*) denotes an organization that has established tax-exempt status directly with the IRS and is not covered by the USCCB Group Ruling.

Diocese of Fresno

(Dioecesis Fresnensis)

MOST REVEREND JOSEPH V. BRENNAN

Bishop of Fresno; ordained June 21, 1980; appointed Titular Bishop of Trofimiana and Auxiliary Bishop of Los Angeles July 21, 2015; ordained September 8, 2015; appointed Bishop of Fresno March 5, 2019; installed May 2, 2019.

Chancery Office: 1550 N. Fresno St., Fresno, CA 93703-3788. T: 559-488-7400; F: 559-488-7464.

ESTABLISHED DECEMBER 15, 1967.

Square Miles 36,072.

Formerly Diocese of Monterey-Fresno.

Comprises the Counties of Fresno, Inyo, Kern, Kings, Madera, Mariposa, Merced and Tulare in the State of California.

Diocesan Patroness: St. Therese of the Child Jesus.

Legal titles of parishes and institutions, the Roman Catholic Bishop of Fresno, a Corporation Sole, Diocese of Fresno Education Corporation (for schools).

STATISTICAL OVERVIEW

Personnel
Bishop....1
Retired Bishops....1
Priests: Diocesan Active in Diocese....63
Priests: Diocesan Active Outside Diocese....1
Priests: Diocesan in Foreign Missions....1
Priests: Retired, Sick or Absent....35
Number of Diocesan Priests....100
Religious Priests in Diocese....35
Total Priests in your Diocese....135
Extern Priests in Diocese....34
Ordinations:
Diocesan Priests....3
Transitional Deacons....5
Permanent Deacons....17
Permanent Deacons in Diocese....97
Total Brothers....1
Total Sisters....109

Parishes
Parishes....87
With Resident Pastor:
Resident Diocesan Priests....67
Resident Religious Priests....13
Without Resident Pastor:
Administered by Priests....20
Administered by Lay People....1
Completely vacant....4
Missions....44
Pastoral Centers....1
Professional Ministry Personnel:
Brothers....1
Sisters....105
Lay Ministers....150

Welfare
Catholic Hospitals....3
Total Assisted....573,615
Homes for the Aged....2
Total Assisted....201
Special Centers for Social Services....6
Total Assisted....283,609

Educational
Diocesan Students in Other Seminaries....24
Seminaries, Religious....1
Students, Religious....1
Total Seminarians....25
High Schools, Diocesan and Parish....2
Total Students....1,013
Elementary Schools, Diocesan and Parish....18
Total Students....4,400
Catechesis/Religious Education:
High School Students....9,431
Elementary Students....15,337
Total Students under Catholic Instruction....30,206
Teachers in Diocese:
Sisters....7
Lay Teachers....251

Vital Statistics
Receptions into the Church:
Infant Baptism Totals....13,277
Minor Baptism Totals....583
Adult Baptism Totals....261
Received into Full Communion....318
First Communions....6,988
Confirmations....5,735
Marriages:
Catholic....1,576
Interfaith....100
Total Marriages....1,676
Deaths....4,899
Total Catholic Population....1,114,805
Total Population....2,787,013

LEADERSHIP

Office of the Bishop - Most Rev. Joseph V. Brennan;
Chancellor - t) 559-493-2850 Cheryl Sarkisian;
Executive Assistant - t) 559-488-7400 msenteno@dioceseoffresno.org Mary Senteno, Secy.;
Vicar General/Moderator of the Curia - t) 559-488-7400 sgonzalez@dioceseoffresno.org Very Rev. Salvador Gonzalez Jr.;
Office of the Vicar General - t) 559-488-7400 sgonzalez@dioceseoffresno.org Very Rev. Salvador Gonzalez Jr., Vicar Gen./Mod. of the Curia;
Continuing Formation of Clergy - t) 209-383-3924 rborges@dioceseoffresno.org Rev. Robert B. Borges, Coord.;
Office of Canonical Services/Marriage Tribunal - t) (559) 488-7490 Estela Manzano; Rev. Jesus Del Angel, Contact; Rev. Msgr. Patrick Joseph McCormick, Dir.;
Office Of Permanent Diaconate - t) 559-493-2840 Dcn. Mark W Schultz (mschultz@dkoceseoffresno.org); Dcn. John Sousa, Dir. (jsousa@dioceseoffresno.org);
Accounting Manager - t) 559-488-7405 Rizza Pedrigal, Contact (rpedrigal@dioceseoffresno.org);
Office of Pastoral Services - t) 559-488-7400 sgonzalez@dioceseoffresno.org Very Rev. Salvador Gonzalez Jr.;
Vocations to the Priesthood - t) 559-488-7424 Rev. Daniel Avila, Dir. (vocations@dioceseoffresno.org);
Episcopal Delegate for Women Religious -
Office of Worship and Christian Initiation - t) 559-434-7701 Rev. Msgr. Patrick Joseph McCormick, Dir.;

ADVISORY BOARDS, COMMISSIONS, COMMITTEES, AND COUNCILS

Catholic Charities Board of Directors - Most Rev. Joseph V. Brennan; Bree Comstock, Mem.; Very Rev. Salvador Gonzalez Jr., Episcopal Delegate;
College of Consultors - Rev. Daniel Avila (vocations@dioceseoffresno.org); Rev. Robert B. Borges; Most Rev. Joseph V. Brennan;
Diocesan Finance Committee - Most Rev. Joseph V. Brennan; Very Rev. Salvador Gonzalez Jr.; Cynthia Martin, CFO, CDFM;
Diocesan Review Board - Very Rev. Salvador Gonzalez Jr.; Zetta A. Hadden; David Rodriguez;
Personnel Board - Most Rev. Joseph V. Brennan; Very Rev. Salvador Gonzalez Jr.;
Priests' Council - Most Rev. Joseph V. Brennan; Very Rev. Salvador Gonzalez Jr.; Rev. Michael Moore, Pst.;
Vicars Forane - Rev. Michael Andrade, Vicar; Rev. Juan Maldonado, Vicar;

CLERGY AND RELIGIOUS SERVICES

Clergy & Religious Women Services, Spanish Translations - t) 559-488-7400 Edith Maldonado, Contact;

COMMUNICATIONS

Office of Communications - t) 559-488-7457; 559-488-7413 cmarquez@dioceseoffresno.org Chandler Marquez, Dir.; Nick Cadena (ncadena@dioceseoffresno.org);
Central California Catholic Life (cccl) - t) 559-488-7448 srrosalie@dioceseoffresno.org Sr. Rosalie Rohrer, I.H.M., Editor;

EDUCATION

Office of Catholic Education - t) 559-488-7420 Joan Bouchard, Supt.;
Assistant Superintendent - t) 559-538-5012 Donna Smith, Asst. Supt.;
Health Ministries and Faith Community Nursing - t) 559-593-9757 Roxanna Stevens, Coord. (roxanna@dioceseoffresno.org); JoAnn LoForti, Contact (jloForti@dioceseoffresno.org);

EVANGELIZATION

Cursillo Movement - English - t) 661-391-4640 Dcn. Joe Parugrug, Spiritual Adv./Care Srvcs.;
Office of Formation and Evangelization - t) 559-488-7474 Rose M. Hernandez, Dir.;
Catechetical Ministry - t) 559-488-7474 x107 Roman Flores, Coord.;
School of Ministry - t) 559-488-7474 x104 drivas@dioceseoffresno.org Diana Rivas, Secy.;
Multicultural/Multilingual Collaborators - t) 559-488-7474 Rose M. Hernandez, Contact;

FACILITIES

Office of Risk Management/Safety - t) 559-488-7473 Denise McKenzie, Dir.; Maria Gonzalez, Contact (mgonzalez@dioceseoffresno.org);
Office of Property/Construction - t) 559-493-2872 Douglas DuRivage, Mgr.;
Cemeteries - t) 559-488-7459 crascon@dioceseoffresno.org Carlos Rascon, Dir. (cemeteries@dioceseoffresno.org);

FINANCE

Office of Finance and Administration - t) 559-488-7426 cmartin@dioceseoffresno.org Cynthia Martin, Dir.;

HUMAN RESOURCES

Safe Environment - t) 559-493-2882 Lucia Magana, Contact (lmagana@dioceseoffresno.org);
Office of Human Resources - t) 559-488-7488 Chel Nelson, Dir.;

ORGANIZATIONS

Fresno Traditional Latin Mass Society - Rev. Jose Zepeda, F.S.S.P.;

PASTORAL SERVICES

Hospital Chaplains - Rev. Chika Kamalu, Chap.; Rev. Emmanuel Ogbonnaya, Chap.;

SOCIAL SERVICES

Catholic Charities - Jeff Negrete, Exec. Dir. (jnegrete@ccdof.org);
Office of Child and Youth Protection - t) 559-488-7488 Chel Nelson, Dir.;
Victim Assistance - t) 559-493-2850 Cheryl Sarkisian, Coord.;
Office of Restorative Justice - t) 559-231-1533 cdavis@dioceseoffresno.org Dcn. Clyde Davis, Dir.;
Office of Social Justice - t) 661-664-4563 smfsccdf@hotmail.com Sr. Marie Francis Schroepfer, C.S.J., Assoc. Dir.;

SPIRITUAL LIFE

Diocesan Retreat Centers- St. Anthony Retreat Center - t) 559-561-4595 www.stanthonyretreat.org Rev. Msgr. John Griesbach, Dir.;
Santa Teresita Youth Conference Center - t) 559-561-1038 Cristal Juarez, Dir.;

MISCELLANEOUS / OTHER OFFICES

Monsignor James Culleton Archives - t) 559-488-7400 Cheryl Sarkisian, Archivist; Scott Alston, Archivist;
Pontifical Mission Societies - t) 559-488-7474 Anna Gonzalez, Apostolic Admin. (agonzalez@dioceseoffresno.org);

PARISHES, MISSIONS, AND CLERGY

STATE OF CALIFORNIA

ARVIN

St. Thomas the Apostle - 350 E. Bear Mountain Blvd., Arvin, CA 93203 t) 661-854-6150; 661-436-7130 (CRP) dmstthomas@gmail.com Rev. Walter Colocho, Admin.; Dcn. Rogelio Hernandez; Martha Verduzco, DRE; CRP Stds.: 311

ATWATER

St. Anthony - 1799 Winton Way, Atwater, CA 95301 t) 209-676-2076 (CRP); 209-358-5743 church.office@stanthonyatwater.org Rev. Paul Kado, Pst.; Dcn. Jesus Cisneros; Dcn. Rene Rubalcava Sr.; Agundis Lilliana, DRE; Shirley Rubalcava, Bus. Mgr.; CRP Stds.: 100
St. Anthony School - (Grades PreK-8) 1801 Winton Way, Atwater, CA 95301 t) 209-358-3341 office@stanthonyknights.org www.stanthonyknights.com Marianne Flynn, Prin.; Stds.: 139; Lay Tchrs.: 12
Immaculate Conception - 2988 N. Buhach Rd, Atwater, CA 95301; Mailing: 1799 Winton Way, Atwater, CA 95301 t) (209) 358-5743 Rev. Paul Kado, Pst.;

AVENAL

St. Joseph - 500 E. Kern St., Avenal, CA 93204; Mailing: 428 E. Kern St., Avenal, CA 93204 t) 559-386-9523 cdelarosa59@yahoo.com; stjosephchurchavenal@hotmail.com Rev. Henry Aguwa, Admin.; Carmen De La Rosa, DRE; CRP Stds.: 186
St. Cecilia - 800 Milham Ave., Kettleman City, CA 93239

BAKERSFIELD

Christ the King - 1800 Bedford Way, Bakersfield, CA 93308 t) 661-391-4640 ctk@christtheking.ws christtheking.ws Rev. Msgr. Stephen A. Frost, Pst.; Dcn. Fred Ansolabehere; Dcn. Joe Parugrug; CRP Stds.: 53
St. Elizabeth Ann Seton - 12300 Reina Rd., Bakersfield, CA 93312-6799 t) 661-587-3626 lizneuman@setoncatholicchurch.org; mpruett@setoncatholicchurch.org Rev. Msgr. Perry Kavookjian, Pst.; Dcn. Noel Delos Reyes; Dcn. Michael Richard; Megan Pruett, Youth Min.; Elizabeth Neuman, DRE; CRP Stds.: 584
St. Francis of Assisi - 900 H St., Bakersfield, CA 93304 t) 661-323-8800 (CRP); 661-327-4734 jetcheverry@stfran.org; dinah@stfran.org Rev. Theophane Antony, OCD, Admin.; Rev. Stanley Amburose, Par. Vicar; Rev. Joseph Lawrence Thottukadavil, OCD, Par. Vicar; Dinah Marquez, DRE; CRP Stds.: 408
St. Francis Parish School - (Grades PreK-8) 2516 Palm St., Bakersfield, CA 93304 t) 661-326-7955 info@stfrancisparishschool.com stfran.org Kelli Gruszka, Prin.; Mary Samson, Librn.; Stds.: 420; Lay Tchrs.: 32
St. Joseph - 1515 Baker St., Bakersfield, CA 93305 t) 661-327-2744 saintjosephbakersfield@gmail.com; stjosephchurchbakersfield@gmail.com stjosephbak.wixsite.com Rev. J. Jesus Reynaga, Pst.; Rev. Juan Carlos Reynoso, Par. Vicar; Angelina Flores-Moreno, DRE; CRP Stds.: 583
Our Lady of Perpetual Help - 124 Columbus St., Bakersfield, CA 93305 t) 661-323-3108 office@olphbakersfield.org www.olphbakersfield.org Rev. David Lopez, Admin.; CRP Stds.: 168
Our Lady of Perpetual Help School - (Grades PreK-8) t) 661-327-7741 nrebuck@olph1.org www.olph1.org Nicole Rebuck, Prin.; Stds.: 329; Lay Tchrs.: 31
St. Philip the Apostle - 7100 Stockdale Hwy., Bakersfield, CA 93309-1399 t) 661-834-7483 info@stphilipchurch.org stphilipchurch.org Rev. Hector Lopez, Pst.; Dcn. Raul Guarnizo; Dcn. Anthony Mendez; Dcn. Francis Moore; CRP Stds.: 360
Preschool - Karen Cerri, Dir.;
Sacred Heart - 9915 Ramos Ave., Bakersfield, CA 93307 t) 661-831-6223 (CRP); 661-831-8905 sacheartbks@gmail.com www.sacredheartbakersfield.org Rev. Juan Manuel Flores, Pst.; Teodora Pacheco, DRE; CRP Stds.: 271
San Clemente Mission Parish - 1305 Water St., Bakersfield, CA 93305 t) 661-871-9190 sanclementemission@gmail.com Rev. J. Jesus Reynaga, Pst.;
Shrine of Our Lady of Guadalupe, Co-Patroness of the Unborn - 601 E. California Ave., Bakersfield, CA 93307

t) 661-323-7642 (CRP); 661-323-3148 x202 office@guadalupebakersfield.org; aida@guadalupebakersfield.org guadalupebakersfield.org/es/home-es/ Rev. Shaji Athipozhi, Pst.; Rev. Gustavo Lopez, O.S.J., Par. Vicar; Aida Nunez, DRE; Angela Aguilar, Bus. Mgr.; Rev. Larry Toschi, O.S.J., Pst. Assoc.; CRP Stds.: 650

Our Lady of Guadalupe School - (Grades PreK-8) 609 E. California Ave., Bakersfield, CA 93307 t) 661-323-6059 olgs@olgsjs.org www.olgsjs.org Sr. Susana Del Toro, S.J.S., Prin.; Stds.: 203; Sr. Tchrs.: 3; Lay Tchrs.: 13

Holy Spirit - 720 E. Belle Terrace, Bakersfield, CA 93307

Worship Site - 4600 E. Brundage Ln., Bakersfield, CA 93307

BISHOP

Our Lady of Perpetual Help - 849 N. Home St., Bishop, CA 93514 t) 760-873-8862 (CRP); 760-872-7231 mike.olph@suddenlinkmail.com; olphsec@suddenlinkmail.com Rev. John Gracey, Pst.; Michael Holcomb, DRE; CRP Stds.: 92

St. Stephen - 461 S. Main St., Big Pine, CA 93513

BUTTONWILLOW

St. Mary - 420 N. Main St., Buttonwillow, CA 93206 t) 661-764-5486 stmarybw@gmail.com; stmarysbw@gmail.com Rev. Joachim Cheon, Pst.; Maria Pacheco, DRE; CRP Stds.: 45

CALIFORNIA CITY

Our Lady of Lourdes - 9970 California City Blvd., California City, CA 93505; Mailing: P.O. Box 2060, California City, CA 93504 t) 760-373-2256 ollcalcity@verizon.net ollcalcity.org Rev. Kris Sorenson, Pst.; Pam Jakobsen, DRE; CRP Stds.: 55

St. Joseph - 12456 Boron Ave., Boron, CA 93516

CHOWCHILLA

St. Columba - 213 Orange Ave., Chowchilla, CA 93610 t) 559-665-5104 (CRP); 559-665-3376 st_columba@sbcglobal.net Rev. John P. Fluetsch, Pst.; Dcn. Anthony DiMaggio; CRP Stds.: 162

St. George - 10760 S. Hwy. 59, El Nido, CA 95317; Mailing: 213 Orange Ave., Chowchilla, CA 93610

CLOVIS

Divine Mercy Catholic Church - 2525 Alluvial Ave. Ste. 271, Clovis, CA 93611 t) 559-374-2242 jcaiazza@divinemercyclovis.org Rev. Michael Cox, Pst.; Dcn. Rolando Nolasco; CRP Stds.: 95

Our Lady of Perpetual Help - 929 Harvard, Clovis, CA 93612 t) 559-299-4270 kmentlewski@hotmail.com; office@olphclovis.org olphclovis.org Rev. Michael Andrade, Pst.; Dcn. Ricardo DeLeon; Dcn. Michael Madrigal; Karen Mentlewski, DRE; Rev. Chimezie Patrick Okeke, Par. Vicar; Dcn. Mark W Schultz; CRP Stds.: 565

Our Lady of Perpetual Help School - (Grades PreSchool-8) 836 DeWitt, Clovis, CA 93612 t) 559-299-7504 pdodd@olphschool.net olphschool.net Patrick Dodd, Prin.; Stds.: 335; Lay Tchrs.: 16

COALINGA

St. Paul the Apostle - 637 Sunset St., Coalinga, CA 93210; Mailing: P.O. Box 812, Coalinga, CA 93210 t) 559-935-1872 st.paulcoalinga@att.net Rev. Viktor Perez, O.F.M.Conv., Pst.; Bro. Andres Amador, O.F.M.Conv.; CRP Stds.: 40

CORCORAN

Our Lady of Lourdes - 1404 Hanna Ave., Corcoran, CA 93212 t) 559-992-4414; 559-992-4698 (CRP) ourladyoflourdescorcoran@comcast.net Rev. Cesar Solorio, Admin.; CRP Stds.: 337

Sacred Heart - 3860 Ave. 54, Alpaugh, CA 93201 t) 559-949-8352

CUTLER

St. Mary - 12588 Ave. 407, Cutler, CA 93615 t) 559-590-5552 stmarycutler@att.net Rev. Juan Antonio Garcia, F.M.M., Pst.; Tere Fabionar, DRE; CRP Stds.: 452

DELANO

St. Mary of the Miraculous Medal - 916 Lexington St., Delano, CA 93215 t) 661-721-2921 (CRP); 661-725-8456 stmarydelanochurch@gmail.com Rev. Loji Pilones, Pst.; Nellie Sierra, DRE; CRP Stds.: 257

St. Vincent - 500 Richgrove Dr., Delano, CA 93215 Alicia Cantutay, Contact;

Our Lady of Guadalupe - 1015 Clinton St., Delano, CA 93215 t) 661-725-9087 x101; 661-725-9087 x103 (CRP); 661-725-2777 (CRP) guadalupechurchdelano@yahoo.com Rev. Miguel Campos, Pst.; Rev. Marlon Nicolas Gomez Alfaro, Par. Vicar; CRP Stds.: 269

DINUBA

St. Catherine of Siena - 356 N. Villa Ave., Dinuba, CA 93618 t) 559-591-2988 (CRP); 559-591-0931 laurallrllk@gmail.com; stcatherine356@yahoo.com Rev. Gonzalo Ramirez-Siller, Admin.; Dcn. Jose Contreras; Olivia Aguirre, Bus. Mgr.; Laura Rico, DRE; CRP Stds.: 500

DOS PALOS

Sacred Heart - 1655 Lucerne Ave., Dos Palos, CA 93620-2623 t) 209-392-2724 sacredheartchurch1655@comcast.net Rev. Anthony Iromenu, Pst.; Dcn. Jose Valenzuela; CRP Stds.: 180

EARLIMART

St. Jude Thaddeus - 1270 E. Washington Ave., Earlimart, CA 93219; Mailing: P. O. Box 12187, Earlimart, CA 93219 t) 661-849-3170 st.judescatholicchurch@yahoo.com www.stjudeearlimart.com Rev. Jose Valdez, MSC, Pst.; Rev. Jose de Jesus Valle Alvarez, MSC, Par. Vicar; Crystal Bueno, DRE; CRP Stds.: 197

EASTON

Catholic Community of St. Jude and Our Lady of the Assumption - 208 W. Jefferson, Easton, CA 93706 t) 559-485-3870 sjcc@stjude-easton.org; eastonstjude@gmail.com www.stjude-easton.org Rev. Bonaventure Chukwunomso Okoro, Admin.; Dcn. Salvador De La Torre; Joseph Hernandez, DRE; CRP Stds.: 366

Our Lady of the Assumption - 13540 S. Henderson Rd., Caruthers, CA 93609; Mailing: 208 W. Jefferson Ave., Fresno, CA 93706 Mary Rossotti, Contact;

EXETER

Sacred Heart - 417 North E St., Exeter, CA 93221 t) 559-592-2465 srrosalie@dioceseoffresno.org; sacredheart.stanthony@gmail.com Rev. Dominic Savio Yagappa Rajappa, Admin.; Dcn. Alex Herrera; Celia Maribel Sanchez, DRE; CRP Stds.: 333

St. Anthony of Egypt - 521 W. Visalia Rd., Farmersville, CA 93223 t) 559-747-0234

FIREBAUGH

St. Joseph - 1558 12th St., Firebaugh, CA 93622 t) 559-659-2225 stjosephfirebaugh@gmail.com Rev. Rayanna Pudota, Admin.; Pedro Vasquez, DRE; CRP Stds.: 309

FOWLER

St. Lucy - 512 S. 5th St., Fowler, CA 93625 t) 559-834-2624 stlucy1965@gmail.com stlucysfowler.org Rev. Adrian Kim, Pst.; CRP Stds.: 134

FRAZIER PARK

Our Lady of the Snows - 7115 Lakewood Dr., Frazier Park, CA 93225 t) 661-245-3741 c) 661-714-2482 (DRE); 559-612-9103 (Pastor) olsfrazierpark@gmail.com www.ourladyofthesnows.net (Quasi-parish) Rev. Joseph Xavier Warnakulasooriya, Pst.; Alma Castro, DRE; CRP Stds.: 23

FRESNO

St. John's Cathedral - 2814 Mariposa St., Fresno, CA 93721 t) 559-485-0161 (CRP); 559-485-6210 stjohnscathedral@sbcglobal.net www.stjohnsfresno.org Very Rev. Salvador Gonzalez Jr., Rector; Rev. Lenjenie Arcan (Phillipines), Par. Vicar; Rev. Ignacio Villafan, Par. Vicar; CRP Stds.: 392

St. Alphonsus - 351 E. Kearney Blvd., Fresno, CA 93706 t) 559-233-8275 stalphonsus_church@yahoo.com Rev. Carlos Serrano, Pst.; Rev. Oscar Anaya, Par. Vicar; Rev. Gasper Bautista, Par. Vicar; Suzanne Lopez, DRE; CRP Stds.: 139

St. Anthony Claret - 2494 S. Chestnut Ave., Fresno, CA 93725 t) 559-255-4260 mrodriguez@sanantonioclarefresno.org stanthonyclaretchurch.org/ Rev. Jose Sanchez, CMF, Admin.; Rev. Agustin Carrillo, CMF, Assoc. Pst.; Rev. Gerardo Rodriguez-Garibay, CMF, Par. Vicar; Salvador Macias, Youth Min.; Alberto Alvarez, DRE; CRP Stds.: 245

Christ the King - 3565 Calvin St., Malaga, CA 93725

St. Anthony of Padua - 5770 N. Maroa Ave., Fresno, CA 93704-2038 t) 559-439-0124 fatherrob@stanthonyfresno.org; cshiveley@stanthonyfresno.org Rev. Msgr. Robert D. Wenzinger, Pst.; Rev. Regino Quijano, Assoc. Pst.; Dcn. Edgar Briseno; Mary Briseno, DRE; CRP Stds.: 476

St. Anthony of Padua School - (Grades PreSchool-8) 5680 N. Maroa Ave., Fresno, CA 93704 t) 559-435-0700 www.sasfresno.com Tom Spencer, Prin.; Stds.: 539; Lay Tchrs.: 36

St. Agnes - 111 W. Birch, Pinedale, CA 93650-1111 t) 559-439-2100 Annette Amparano, Admin.;

St. Genevieve - 1127 Tulare St., Fresno, CA 93706 t) 559-486-2988 victortoandinh@yahoo.com; victordinh@yahoo.com Rev. Victor T. Dinh, Pst.; CRP Stds.: 12

St. Helen - 4875 E. Grant, Fresno, CA 93727 t) 559-255-3871 office.sthelens@sbcglobal.net Rev. Walter Martinez, Admin.; Rebecca Sanchez, DRE; CRP Stds.: 110

St. Helen School - (Grades PreSchool-8) 4888 E. Belmont Ave., Fresno, CA 93727 t) 559-251-5855 ppeterson@sthelensschool.org www.sthelensschool.org Patti Peterson, Prin.; Stds.: 162; Lay Tchrs.: 12

Holy Spirit - 355 E. Champlain Dr., Fresno, CA 93730-1273 t) 559-434-7701; 559-434-3522 (CRP) holyspirit@holyspiritfresno.org www.holyspiritfresno.org Rev. Msgr. Patrick Joseph McCormick, Pst.; Dcn. Pete Marquez; CRP Stds.: 358

St. Mary Queen of Apostles Catholic Church - 4636 W. Dakota, Fresno, CA 93722 t) 559-275-2022 stmaryfresno@gmail.com Rev. Timothy N. Cardoso, Pst.; Mary Eagan, DRE; Dcn. Naova Thao; CRP Stds.: 443

Our Lady of La Vang - 4144 N. Millbrook Ave., Fresno, CA 73726 t) 559-485-9467 victordinh03@netzero.net; victortoadinh@yahoo.com Rev. Victor T. Dinh, Pst.; Dcn. Hung Nguyen, Dir.; CRP Stds.: 79

Our Lady of Mt. Carmel - 816 Pottle Ave., Fresno, CA 93707 t) 559-264-2587 olmcfresno@gmail.com Rev. Carlos Serrano, Pst.; Rev. Gasper Bautista, Par. Vicar; Rev. Oscar Anaya, Par. Vicar; Adriana Figueroa, DRE; CRP Stds.: 246

Our Lady of Victory - 2838 N. West Ave., Fresno, CA 93705; Mailing: 2918 N. West Ave., Fresno, CA 93705 t) 559-226-1163 olvchurch@gmail.com olv-church.com/ Rev. Jesus Del Angel, Pst.; Dcn. Kenny Figueroa; Dcn. Kurt Neuhaus; Eva Gonzalez, DRE; CRP Stds.: 193

St. Paul Catholic Newman Center - 1572 E. Barstow St., Fresno, CA 93710 t) 559-436-3434 ncoffice@csufnewman.com www.csufnewman.com Rev. Byron Macias, C.M.F., Sacr. Min.; Rev. Paul Keller, CMF, Sacr. Min.; Dcn. John Supino; Dcn. William Lucido; Sr. Kathleen Drilling, S.S.N.D., DRE; CRP Stds.: 120

Sacred Heart - 2140 N. Cedar Ave., Fresno, CA 93703 t) 559-237-4121 sacredheartfresno@att.net Rev. Hilary Silva, Pst.; Rev. Joe Cooray, OMI, Par. Vicar; Dcn. Tom Ognibene; Dcn. Robert Sesma; CRP Stds.: 290

Shrine of St. Therese - 855 E. Floradora Ave., Fresno, CA 93728 t) 559-268-6388 info@shrineofsttherese.org shrineofsttherese.wordpress.com Rev. Msgr. Raymond C. Dreiling, Pst.; Dcn. Jess Avila; Dcn. Bryan G. Martin; Dee Schultz, Bus. Mgr.; CRP Stds.: 69

GUSTINE

Shrine of Our Lady of Miracles - 370 Linden Ave., Gustine, CA 95322 t) 209-854-0015 office.olmshrine@gmail.com; pastor.olmshrine@gmail.com www.shrineofourladyofmiracles.com Rev. Daniel Avila, Pst.; CRP Stds.: 181

Our Lady of Miracles Catholic School - (Grades PreK-8) t) 209-854-3180 office@olmiracles.com; cbrace@olmiracles.com olmiracles.com Julie Barcelos, Prin.; Stds.: 127; Lay Tchrs.: 10

HANFORD

St. Brigid - 1001 N. Douty St., Hanford, CA 93230; Mailing: 200 E. Florinda St., Hanford, CA 93230 t) 559-582-2533 office@stbrigid.org www.stbrigid.org Rev. Guadalupe Vargas, Pst.; Rev. Edgar Magana, Par. Vicar; Dcn. John Sousa; George Aguayo-Velez, Youth Min.; Elisua Medina, DRE; CRP Stds.: 144

St. Rose-McCarthy Catholic School - (Grades K-8) 1000 N. Harris St., Hanford, CA 93230 t) 559-584-5218 secretary@strosemccarthy.com www.strosemccarthy.com Rachel Manzo, Prin.; Stds.: 117; Lay Tchrs.: 10

St. Brigid Community Outreach Center - 115 W. 5th St., Hanford, CA 93230 t) 559-772-8213 stbrigid.coc@gmail.com Rosie Cervantes, Dir.;

Immaculate Heart of Mary - 10355 Hanford-Armona Rd., Hanford, CA 93230; Mailing: 10435 Hanford-Armona Rd., Hanford, CA 93230 t) 559-584-8576; 559-587-9292; 559-582-1149 admin@ihmhanford.org www.ihmhanford.org Rev. Efrain Martinez, Pst.; Dcn. Manuel Lababit; Dcn. Leonard Rodriguez; CRP Stds.: 403

HILMAR

Holy Rosary - 8471 Cypress St., Hilmar, CA 95324; Mailing: P.O. Box 429, Hilmar, CA 95324 t) 209-632-7163 (CRP); 209-667-8961 farmboys67@aol.com; info@hilmarholyrosary.org Rev. Isaque Meneses, Pst.; Dina Brindeiro, DRE; CRP Stds.: 270

St. Mary - 2809 Railroad, Stevinson, CA 95374

HURON

St. Frances Cabrini - 36986 Los Angeles St., Huron, CA 93234; Mailing: P.O. Box 939, Huron, CA 93234 t) 559-945-2507 s.cabrini@att.net Rev. Michael Moore, Pst.; Rev. Israel Avila, Par. Vicar; Marcilena Torres, DRE; CRP Stds.: 153

KERMAN

St. Patrick - 15437 W. Kearney Blvd., Kerman, CA 93630; Mailing: P.O. Box 375, Kerman, CA 93630 t) 559-846-8190 Rev. John Okeke Agwu, S.M.M.M., Assoc. Pst.; Rev. Bartholomew Ifionu, SMMM, Par. Vicar; Rosa Parra, DRE; CRP Stds.: 315

KINGSBURG

Holy Family - 1275 Smith St., Kingsburg, CA 93631-0798; Mailing: P.O. Box 798, Kingsburg, CA 93631-0798 t) 559-897-5953 holyfamily.kingsburg@comcast.net Rev. Mark Maxon, Pst.; Sr. Balbina Retama, DRE; CRP Stds.: 196

Santa Cruz - 5626 Ave. 378, London, CA 93631

St. John the Baptist Educational Center - 4204 Merritt Dr., Traver, CA 93673

LAMONT

St. Augustine - 10601 Myrtle Ave., Lamont, CA 93241-2111 t) 661-845-3622 (CRP); 661-845-0003 fjohndp@att.net; srrosalie@dioceseoffresno.org Rev. Milton Rene Acevedo-Fabian, Admin.; Margarita Colon, DRE; CRP Stds.: 385

LATON

Shrine of Our Lady of Fatima - 20855 S. Fatima Ave, Laton, CA 93242; Mailing: P.O. Box 119, Laton, CA 93242 t) 559-923-3715 (CRP); 559-923-4935 Rev. Athanasius Okure, Admin.; Dcn. Jesus Hernandez; Rita Alvarez, DRE; CRP Stds.: 96

LEMOORE

St. Peter Prince of Apostles - 870 N. Lemoore Ave., Lemoore, CA 93245 t) 559-924-2562; 559-924-2826 (CRP) office@stpeterslemoore.org Rev. Michael Moore, Pst.; Rev. Israel Avila, Par. Vicar; Patricia Garret, DRE; CRP Stds.: 482

Mary Immaculate Queen School - (Grades PreK-8) 884 N. Lemoore Ave., Lemoore, CA 93245 t) 559-924-3424 miqschool.com Rachael Manzo, Prin.; Stds.: 134; Lay Tchrs.: 15

St. Joseph - 19300 Empire St., Stratford, CA 93266

LINDSAY

Sacred Heart - 217 Lindero Ave., Lindsay, CA 93247-2623 t) 559-562-4008 shlindsay1@gmail.com Rev. Henry Rivera; Adriana Ochoa, DRE; CRP Stds.: 335

St. Anthony Church - 21631 Brooks Ave., Tonyville, CA 93247

St. James Catholic Church - 19752 Guthrie Rd., Strathmore, CA 93267; Mailing: P.O. Box 4010, Strathmore, CA 93267 t) 559-568-0435

Plainview, Santa Cruz -

LIVINGSTON

Shrine of Saint Jude Thaddeus - 330 Franci St., Livingston, CA 95334; Mailing: PO Box 77, Livingston, CA 95334 t) 209-394-7512 stjudethaddeus@frontiernet.net Rev. Msgr. Harvey Fonseca, Pst.; Dcn. David Torres; Elena Ramirez, DRE; CRP Stds.: 511

Saint Teresa of Calcutta - ; Mailing: P.O. Box 86, Delhi, CA 95315

LONE PINE

Santa Rosa - 311 E. Locust, Lone Pine, CA 93545; Mailing: PO Box 246, Lone Pine, CA 93545 t) 760-876-4350 santarosalonepine@gmail.com Rev. Douglas Walker, Pst.; Rev. Joel Aquino, Assoc. Pst.;

St. John the Baptist -

St. Vivian -

Furnace Creek -

Station -

St. Therese -

LOS BANOS

St. Joseph - 1621 Center Ave., Los Banos, CA 93635; Mailing: 1516 Center Ave., Los Banos, CA 93635 t) 209-826-1512 (CRP); 209-826-4246 stjosephlb@sbcglobal.net www.stjosephlosbanos.com Rev. John Schmoll, Obl. O.S.B. Cam., Pst.; Rev. Oscar Saul Medina Zermeno, Par. Vicar; Dcn. Leon Miller; CRP Stds.: 542

Our Lady of Fatima - (Grades PreK-8) 1625 Center Ave., Los Banos, CA 93635 t) 209-826-2709 kdarnell@olfdof.org olfdof.org Karen Forte, Prin.; Stds.: 195; Lay Tchrs.: 15

MADERA

St. Joachim - 401 W. Fifth St., Madera, CA 93637 t) 559-674-5871 (CRP); 559-673-3290 ccd@sjoachim.org; church@sjoachim.org www.sjoachim.org Rev. John Warburton, O.S.J., Pst.; Rev. John D Shearer, Rector; Rev. James Catalano, O.S.J., Assoc. Pst.; Rev. Carlos Esquivel, O.S.J., Assoc. Pst.; Diana Saenz, DRE; CRP Stds.: 562

St. Joachim School - (Grades K-8) 310 N. I St., Madera, CA 93637 t) 559-674-7628 school@sjoachim.org Heather Forcey, Prin.; Stds.: 290; Lay Tchrs.: 16

St. Agnes - 7308 Hwy. 145, Madera, CA 93637

St. Anne - Raymond-Knowles, Raymond, CA 93653

Convent - 310 N. J St., Madera, CA 93637 t) 559-674-4085 Sisters of the Immaculate Conception (RCM)

MARIPOSA

St. Joseph - 4985 Bullion St., Mariposa, CA 95338; Mailing: P.O. Box 215, Mariposa, CA 95338 t) 209-966-2522 sjccoff@yahoo.com Rev. Rodolfo Esmero-Carcueva, Admin.; Rebecca Soto, DRE; Diana Terra, RCIA Coord.; CRP Stds.: 19

St. Catherine of Siena - 7385 St. Catherine St., Hornitos, CA 95325

MCFARLAND

St. Elizabeth - 835 E. Perkins, McFarland, CA 93250 t) 661-792-3225; 661-792-3429 sisabel@msn.com; espi221@yahoo.com Rev. Antero Sanchez, M.S.C., Pst.; Esperanza Rios, DRE; CRP Stds.: 360

MENDOTA

Our Lady of Guadalupe - 484 Quince St., Mendota, CA 93640 t) 559-655-4237 c) 559-209-0541 ourladyofguadalupe.mendota@gmail.com Rev. Jorge Robles Cuevas, Pst.; Dcn. Luis Aguirre; CRP Stds.: 423

Our Lady of Lourdes - 16101 S. Derrick, Three Rocks, CA 93608

MERCED

St. Patrick's Parish and Our Lady of Mercy Church - 671 E. Yosemite Ave., Merced, CA 95340 t) 209-383-3924 info@olmstpatrick.org www.olmstpatrick.org/ Our Lady of Mercy Church is used by appointment only. Rev. Robert B. Borges, Pst.; Rev. Antonio Egiguren, OFM, Par. Vicar; Dcn. Jose Morales; Dcn. Charles Reyburn; Debbie Rosa, DRE; Rosemarie Pierce, Bus. Mgr.; CRP Stds.: 195

Our Lady of Mercy - 459 W. 21st St., Merced, CA 95340; Mailing: 671 E. Yosemite Ave., Merced, CA 95340 t) (209) 383-3924 www.olmstpatrick.org This Church is not active.

Our Lady of Mercy Elementary - (Grades PreSchool-8) 1400 E. 27th St., Merced, CA 95340 t) 209-722-7496 info@olmlancers.com www.olmlancers.com Judy Blackburn, Prin.; Stds.: 268; Lay Tchrs.: 20

Sacred Heart - 519 W. 12th St., Merced, CA 95341 t) 209-383-1528 (CRP); 209-383-6604 sacredheart1merced@sbcglobal.net www.sacredheartmerced.org Rev. Juan Maldonado, Pst.; Dcn. Trinidad Guadarrama; Dcn. Chong Moua; CRP Stds.: 626

OAKHURST

Our Lady of the Sierra - 40180 Indian Springs Rd., Oakhurst, CA 93644; Mailing: P.O. Box 2499, Oakhurst, CA 93644 t) 559-642-3452 ols.laura.h@gmail.com olscatholic.org Rev. Victor P. Hernando, Pst.; CRP Stds.: 30

St. Joseph the Worker - 56522 Rd. 200, North Fork, CA 93643

St. Dominic Savio - 40077 Rd. 222, Bass Lake, CA 93604

Our Lady of the Snows - 40180 Indian Springs Rd., Oakhurst, CA 93644; Mailing: P.O. Box 4299, Oakhurst, CA 93644 t) 559-342-3452 x100 monicaodols@gmail.com Under the administration of Our Lady of the Sierra, Oakhurst. Rev. Victor Hernando, Pst.;

ORANGE COVE

St. Isidore the Farmer - 480 Adams Ave., Orange Cove, CA 93646 t) 559-393-6313 (CRP); 559-626-4943 stisidore3802@sbcglobal.net; stisdore3802@sbcglobal.net Rev. Alfredo Arias, Pst.; Dcn. Alberto Gomez; Maria Chapa, DRE; CRP Stds.: 350

St. Rita - 30673 George Smith Rd., Squaw Valley, CA 93675

PARLIER

Our Lady of Sorrows (Nuestra Señora de Los Dolores) - 830 Tulare St., Parlier, CA 93648 t) 559-646-2161 ourladysorrows_church@yahoo.com Rev. Pedro Umana, Admin.; CRP Stds.: 272

PLANADA

Sacred Heart - 9317 Amistad St., Planada, CA 95365 t) 209-382-0459 sacredheartplanada@sbcglobal.net Rev. Joseph Govindu, Pst.; Dcn. Javier Higareda; Dcn. Higinio Yanez; Ana Maria Siifuentez, DRE; CRP Stds.: 206

Our Lady of Lourdes - 13145 Le Grand Rd., 9327 Amistad St., LeGrand, CA 95333 Juana Castillo, Contact;

PORTERVILLE

St. Anne's Parish - 378 N. F St., Porterville, CA 93257 t) 559-784-2800 x100 information@stannesparish.com www.stannesparish.com Rev. Msgr. Scott Daugherty, Pst.; Rev. Servio Alarcon (El Salvador), Par. Vicar; Dcn. James Dieterle; Dcn. Gregorio Echeveste, DRE; Dcn. John X. Rees; Dcn. Jorge Santoyo; Dcn. Jose Alfredo Ureno; CRP Stds.: 1,243

St. Anne School - (Grades PreK-8) 385 N. F St., Porterville, CA 93257 t) 559-784-4096 kaylat@stannesporterville.org Kayla Trueblood, Prin.; Stds.: 205; Lay Tchrs.: 17

Mater Dolorosa - 350 N. Reservation Road, Tule Indian Reservation, CA 93257

Blessed Miguel Agustin Pro - 9120 Rd. 236, Terra Bella, CA 93270 t) (559) 784-2800

St. Maximillian Kolbe - 35725 Hwy. 190, Springville, CA 93265

REEDLEY

St. Anthony of Padua - 1060 F. St., Reedley, CA 93654; Mailing: P.O. Box 188, Reedley, CA 93654 t) 559-638-5608 (CRP); 559-638-2012 stanthonychurch_reedley@comcast.net stanthonychurch-reedley.org Rev. Denny E. Joseph, R.C.J., Pst.; Rev. Thomas E. Michayel, R.C.J., Par. Vicar; Rev. Vito Di Marzio, RCJ, In Res.; CRP Stds.: 631

St. La Salle Grammar School - (Grades PreK-8) 404 E. Manning Ave., Reedley, CA 93654 t) 559-638-2621; 559-637-1446 hannibalmarylucy@yahoo.com Sr. Lucy Cassarino, F.D.Z., Prin.; Sr. Daisy DyTiaco, Librn.; Stds.: 283; Sr. Tchrs.: 3; Lay Tchrs.: 12

RIDGECREST

St. Ann - 446 W. Church Ave., Ridgecrest, CA 93555; Mailing: P.O. Box 127, Ridgecrest, CA 93556 t) 760-375-2110; 760-375-2110 x313 (CRP); 760-375-2110 x305 (CRP) ccd@parishofsaintann.org; office@parishofsaintann.org parishofsaintann.org Rev. Santiago Iriarte, Admin.; Jeannine McReynolds, DRE; Lilian Ramirez, 1st Year Confirmation Coord.; Bradley Kasberg, 2nd Year Confirmation Coord.; CRP Stds.: 52

St. Ann School - (Grades 1-1) t) 760-375-4713 school@parishofsaintann.org; principal@parishofsaintann.org www.school.parishofsaintann.org Tracy Sherrick, Prin.; Stds.: 141; Lay Tchrs.: 10

Santa Barbara - 72 Lexington Ave., Randsburg, CA 93554

RIVERDALE

St. Ann - 3047 W. Mt. Whitney, Riverdale, CA 93656; Mailing: P.O. Box 335, Riverdale, CA 93656 t) 559-867-3035 stannriverdale@yahoo.com; office@stannriverdale.org Rev. Athanasius Okure, Admin.; Rev. Pedro De Medeiros Cabral, OFM, Par. Vicar; Delia Maduena, DRE; CRP Stds.: 157

Holy Family Chapel -

ROSAMOND

St. Mary of the Desert - 3100 Fifteenth St. W., Rosamond, CA 93560; Mailing: P.O. Box 1359, Rosamond, CA 93560 t) 661-256-4505 st.mary3100@att.net; parishstmaryofthedesert@gmail.com Rev. Julian Policetti, Admin.; Pam Jakobsen, DRE; CRP Stds.: 75

St. Francis of Assisi Church - 15382 Meyer Rd., Mojave, CA 93501

SANGER

St. Mary - 828 O St., Sanger, CA 93657; Mailing: P.O. Box 335, Sanger, CA 93657 t) 559-875-2025 stmarysanger@gmail.com Rev. John Bruno, R.C.J., Pst.; Rev. Francisco Flores, RCJ, Par. Vicar; Dcn. Cesar Gonzales; Sr. Enedina Luna Lara, DRE; CRP Stds.: 394

St. Katherine - (Quasi-parish included with St. Mary, Sanger). Rev. Mark Robin Destura, Assoc. Pst.;

SELMA

St. Joseph - 2441 Dockery Ave., Selma, CA 93662 t) 559-896-2620 (CRP); 559-896-1052 stjosephsecretary@gmail.com Rev. Abel Loera, Admin.; Dcn. Ed Harmon III; Carol Moreno, DRE; CRP Stds.: 330

SHAFTER

St. Therese - 300 W. Lerdo, Shafter, CA 93263 t) 661-746-4471 sainttherese1952@yahoo.com sainttheresesshafter.com Rev. Jose Luis Rico, Pst.; CRP Stds.: 200

TAFT

St. Mary - 110 E. Woodrow St., Taft, CA 93268 t) 661-765-4292 stmarystaft@gmail.com Rev. Joachim Cheon, Pst.; Rosalba Romo, DRE; CRP Stds.: 117

TEHACHAPI

St. Malachy - 407 W. E St., Tehachapi, CA 93561-1642 t) 661-822-3060; 661-822-6327 (CRP) mcastillo@saintmalachy.church; jcorral@saintmalachy.church www.saintmalachy.church Rev. Gregory J. Beaumont, Pst.; Juana Corral, DRE; CRP Stds.: 102

TIPTON

St. John the Evangelist - 232 S. Adams Rd., Tipton, CA 93272 t) 559-752-4544; 559-466-6007 (CRP) stjohnevangelisttipton@gmail.com; stjohnevangelisttipton.re@gmail.com Rev. Miguel Angel Mancia Calderon, Admin.; CRP Stds.: 117

St. Francis of Assisi - 16410 Ave. 168, Woodville, CA 93258

Our Lady of the Assumption - 782 S. Main St., Pixley, CA 93256 t) (559) 752-4544 Rev. Miguel A. Mancia Calderon, Admin.;

TRANQUILLITY

St. Paul - 25592 Doughty St., Tranquillity, CA 93668; Mailing: P.O. Box 575, Tranquillity, CA 93668 t) 559-693-4320 (CRP); 559-698-7429 stpaultranquillity@gmail.com Rev. Marcelinus Ekenedo, Admin.; Rev. John Okeke Agwu, SMMM, Par. Vicar; Rev. Bartholomew Ifionu, SMMM, Par. Vicar; Cora Lopez, DRE; CRP Stds.: 137

St. Vincent de Paul -

TULARE

St. Aloysius - 125 E. Pleasant Ave., Tulare, CA 93274 t) 559-623-6298 (CRP); 559-688-1796 dmgtrans@hotmail.com; mtristao@sastulare.com sastulare.com Rev. Msgr. Richard Urizalqui, Pst.; Maralee Tristao, Admin.; CRP Stds.: 310

St. Aloysius School - (Grades 1-8) 627 Beatrice, Tulare, CA 93274 t) 559-686-6250 schooloffice@sastulare.com schoolsastulare.com Holly Zamora, Admin.; Stds.: 177; Lay Tchrs.: 10

St. Rita - 954 S. O St., Tulare, CA 93274 t) 559-686-0802 (CRP); 559-686-3847 benita@stritacatholicchurch.com; info@stritacatholicchurch.com Rev. Ivan Hernandez-Melchor, Pst.; Dcn. Mario Vasquez; CRP Stds.: 1,070

VISALIA

Good Shepherd Catholic Parish - 506 N. Garden St., Visalia, CA 93291 t) 559-734-9522 rparlier@gscparish.org www.gscparish.com Rev. Alex Chavez, Pst.; Rev. Dalton Rogers, Par. Vicar; Rev. Ferdinand Udeolisa, Par. Vicar; Dcn. Russ Bassett; Dcn. Francisco Javier Gomez; Dcn. Gary Hunt; Dcn. Paul Marquez; Dcn. Henry Medina; Dcn. Rick Miller; Ana Navarro, DRE; CRP Stds.: 1,220

The Catholic School of Visalia, George McCann Memorial Campus - (Grades PreSchool-8) 200 E. Race St., Visalia, CA 93291 t) 559-732-5831 krosa@ccsvgmc.org catholicschoolvisalia.org Karen Rosa, Prin.; Stds.: 209; Lay Tchrs.: 13

Holy Family Church - 1908 N. Court St., Visalia, CA 93291

St. Charles Borromeo - 5049 W. Caldwell Ave., Visalia, CA 93277

St. Thomas the Apostle - 6735 Ave. 308, Goshen, CA 93227

The Nativity of the Blessed Virgin Mary Church - 608 N. Church St., Visalia, CA 93291; Mailing: 506 N. Garden St., Visalia, CA 93291

Bethlehem Center - 1638 N. Dinuba Blvd., Visalia, CA 93291 t) 559-734-1572 ahernandez@gscparish.org www.bethlehemcentervisalia.com

WASCO

St. John the Evangelist - 1129 9th St., Wasco, CA 93280 t) 661-758-6668 (CRP); 661-758-6467 sjtewascooffice@gmail.com Rev. Miguel A. Mancia Calderon, Admin.; Alicia Gonzalez, DRE; Maggie Morales, DRE; CRP Stds.: 317

Nuestra Senora de la Paz - 14846 Hwy. 33, Blackwell's Corner, CA 93249

WOFFORD HEIGHTS

St. Jude - 86 Nellie Dent Dr, Wofford Heights, CA 93285; Mailing: P. O. Box 1190, Wofford Heights, CA 93285 t) 760-376-2416 ruthann.cookstj@gmail.com; ruthann.cooksj@gmail.com Rev. Showreddy Thirumalareddy, Admin.; Kimberly Kelso, DRE; CRP Stds.: 15

Station -

WOODLAKE

St. Frances Cabrini - 599 N. Valencia Blvd., Woodlake, CA 93286; Mailing: P.O. Box 459, Woodlake, CA 93286 t) 559-564-2647 scabrini@att.net Rev. Jesse C. Venzor, Pst.; CRP Stds.: 90

San Felipe de Jesus - 32809 Rd. 159, Ivanhoe, CA 93235

St. Clair - Alta Acres Dr., Three Rivers, CA 93271

SCHOOLS: PRESCHOOL THRU HIGH SCHOOL

HIGH SCHOOLS

STATE OF CALIFORNIA

BAKERSFIELD

Garces Memorial High School - (DIO) 2800 Loma Linda Dr., Bakersfield, CA 93305 t) 661-327-2578 mpeck@garces.org www.garces.org Rev. Msgr. Perry Kavookjian, Rector; Myka Peck, Prin.; Stds.: 496; Lay Tchrs.: 32

FRESNO

San Joaquin Memorial High School - (DIO) (Grades 9-12) 1406 N. Fresno St., Fresno, CA 93703-3789 t) 559-268-9251 info@sjmhs.org www.sjmhs.org Rev. Msgr. Robert D. Wenzinger, Rector; Michael C. Burke, Pres.; Stds.: 503; Lay Tchrs.: 35

INSTITUTIONS LOCATED IN DIOCESE

CATHOLIC CHARITIES [CCH]

BAKERSFIELD

Catholic Charities, Diocese of Fresno - 825 Chester Ave., Bakersfield, CA 93301 t) 661-281-2130; 661-616-4036 avorhees@ccdof.org www.ccdof.org Jeff Negrete, Dir.; Asstd. Annu.: 119,051; Staff: 8

FRESNO

Catholic Charities of the Diocese of Fresno - 149 N. Fulton St., Fresno, CA 93701 t) 559-237-0851 jnegrete@ccdof.org www.ccdof.org Jeff Negrete, Exec.; Asstd. Annu.: 92,547; Staff: 39

Senior Companion Program - 149 N. Fulton St., Fresno, CA 93701 t) 559-498-6377 lvalencia@ccdof.org Asstd. Annu.: 69; Staff: 3

MERCED

Catholic Charities, Diocese of Fresno - 336 W. Main #1, Merced, CA 95340 t) 209-383-2494 jnegrete@ccdof.org www.ccdof.org Dena Medeiros, Dir.; Asstd. Annu.: 58,350; Staff: 6

SANGER

Fr. Hannibal House Social Service Center - 1401 14th St., Sanger, CA 93657; Mailing: P.O. Box 37, Sanger, CA 93657 t) 559-217-8295 stmarysanger@verizon.net Ed Cuadros, Exec.; Asstd. Annu.: 8,633; Staff: 2

CEMETERIES [CEM]

FRESNO

Fresno Catholic Cemeteries - 264 N. Blythe Ave., Fresno, CA 93706 t) 559-488-7449 cemeteries@dioceseoffresno.org www.dioceseoffresno.org/cemeteries Carlos Rascon, Dir.;

CONVENTS, MONASTERIES, AND RESIDENCES FOR WOMEN [CON]

BAKERSFIELD

Sister Servants of the Blessed Sacrament (SJS) - 1100 S.

Kern St., Bakersfield, CA 93307 t) 661-869-1086 bakersfieldsjs@yahoo.com.mx Sr. Susana Del Toro, S.J.S., Prin.; Sr. Maria de los Remedios Aguilar, SJS, Supr.; Srs.: 3

FRESNO

Congregation of the Sisters of Nazareth - 2121 N. First St., Fresno, CA 93703 t) 559-237-2257 pmurphy@nazarethhousela.org Sr. Philomena Murphy, S.N., Supr.; Srs.: 5

Pious Disciples of the Divine Master - 3700 N. Cornelia Ave., Fresno, CA 93722 t) 559-275-1656; 559-275-9978 eugeniabpddm@aol.com Sr. Eugenia Pia Bianco, P.D.D.M., Supr.; Srs.: 13

LOS BANOS

Franciscan Hospitallers of the Immaculate Conception (FHIC) - 1441 Berkeley Dr., Los Banos, CA 93635-9599 t) 209-827-8933 confhic@sbcglobal.net www.fhiccalp.org Sr. Acacia Moises, FHIC, Supr.; Srs.: 13

MADERA

Sisters of the Immaculate Conception (RCM) - 310 N. J St., Madera, CA 93637 t) 559-674-4085 monikemsanz@hotmail.com www.concepcionistas.es Sr. Isabel Lopez, RCM, Contact; Srs.: 3

MERCED

***Apostoles de la Palabra of California** - 168 Cone Ave., Merced, CA 95341 t) 209-385-0795 srrosalie@dioceseoffresno.org Sr. Eri Rodriguez, IMAP, Supr.; Srs.: 5

REEDLEY

Daughters of Divine Zeal, Inc. (FDZ) - 379 E. Manning Ave., Reedley, CA 93654 t) 559-638-1916 c) 559-901-7675 hannibalmarylucy@yahoo.com www.figliedivinozelo.it Sr. Lucy Cassarino, F.D.Z., Prin.; Srs.: 3

TEHACHAPI

Norbertine Canonesses of the Bethlehem Priory of St. Joseph - 17831 Water Canyon Rd., Tehachapi, CA 93561 t) 661-823-1066 mothermarya@aol.com; norbertinecanonesses@gmail.com www.norbertinesisters.org Mother Mary Augustine Petit, Prioress; Srs.: 47

ENDOWMENTS / FOUNDATIONS / TRUSTS [EFT]

FRESNO

Our Faith, Our Family, Our Future Foundation, Inc. - 1550 N. Fresno St., Fresno, CA 93703 t) 559-488-7426 cmartin@dioceseoffresno.org Cynthia Martin, Contact;

HOSPITALS / HEALTH SERVICES [HOS]

BAKERSFIELD

Mercy Hospital (Dignity Health) - 2215 Truxtun Ave., Bakersfield, CA 93301 t) 661-632-5000 michal.yniguez@dignityhealth.org www.dignityhealth.org/mercy-bakersfield Mercy Southwest is a campus of Mercy Hospital. Sponsored by Catholic Health Care Federation. Bruce Peters, Pres.; Bed Capacity: 85; Asstd. Annu.: 18,806; Staff: 1,451

Mercy Foundation, Bakersfield (Friends of Mercy Foundation) - t) 661-663-6700 pam.koerner@commonspirit.org supportfriendsofmercy.org Toni Harper, Vice. Pres.;

Mercy Southwest Hospital (Dignity Health) - 400 Old River Rd., Bakersfield, CA 93311 t) 661-663-6000 pam.koerner@commonspirit.org Sponsored by Catholic Health Care Federation Benjamin Predum, CEO; Bed Capacity: 85; Asstd. Annu.: 18,806; Staff: 1,451

FRESNO

***Saint Agnes Medical Center (Trinity Health)** - 1303 E. Herndon Ave., Fresno, CA 93720 t) (559) 450-5213 nancy.hollingsworth@samc.com; pamela.steinhauer@samc.com www.samc.com Judge Robert Oliver, Chair; Bed Capacity: 436; Asstd. Annu.: 389,428; Staff: 3,100

Saint Agnes Medical Foundation - t) 559-449-3000 jarrell.williamson@samc.com

MERCED

Mercy Medical Center (Dignity Health) - 333 Mercy Ave., Merced, CA 95340 t) 209-564-5000 janice.wilkerson@commonspirit.org mercymercedcares.org Sponsored by Catholic Health Care Federation Dale Johns, CEO; Bed Capacity: 186; Asstd. Annu.: 165,331; Staff: 1,361

MISCELLANEOUS [MIS]

FRESNO

Catholic Professional & Business Club of the Fresno Diocese - c/o 1550 N. Fresno St., Fresno, CA 93703-3788 t) 559-434-2722 (Fresno Co.); 559-740-9599 (Tulare / Kings Co.) president@cpbcfresno.org; jjmartinusen@gmail.org Timothy Dodd, Dir.;

Catholic Professional and Business Club of Fresno - c/o 1550 N. Fresno St., Fresno, CA 93703-3788 t) 559-434-2722 president@cpbcfresno.org John Rast, Dir.;

NURSING / REHABILITATION / CONVALESCENCE / ELDERLY CARE [NUR]

FRESNO

Nazareth House of Fresno - 2121 N. First St., Fresno, CA 93703 t) 559-237-2257 rosemary@nazarethfresno.org Rosemary O'Neill, Admin.; Asstd. Annu.: 71; Staff: 80

LOS BANOS

New Bethany Residential Care and Skilled Nursing Community - 1441 Berkeley Dr., Los Banos, CA 93635 t) 209-827-8933 lucif@newbethanyconfhic.org www.newbethanyfhic.org Rev. Jose Carlos Santos, O.F.M., Chap.; Sr. Lucinda Fonseca, F.H.I.C., Admin.; Sr. Helen Petrovich, F.H.I.C., Pres.; Sr. Julia Fonseca, F.H.I.C., Dir.; Asstd. Annu.: 130; Staff: 101

RETREAT HOUSES / RENEWAL CENTERS [RTR]

THREE RIVERS

St. Anthony's Retreat Center - 43816 Sierra Dr., Hwy. 198, Three Rivers, CA 93271; Mailing: PO Box 249, Three Rivers, CA 93271 t) 559-561-4595 mike@stanthonyretreat.org stanthonyretreat.org Rev. Msgr. John Griesbach, Dir.; Rev. Rod L. Craig, Chap.; Cristal Juarez, Youth Min.; Mike Hand, Bus. Mgr.;

Santa Teresita Youth Center - 43816 Sierra Dr., Hwy. 198, Three Rivers, CA 93271 t) 559-561-4595 cristal@stteresitaycc.org www.stteresitaycc.org Rev. Msgr. John Griesbach, Dir.; Rev. Roderick L. Craig, Chap.; Cristal Juarez, Youth Min.; Mike Hand, Bus. Mgr.;

An asterisk (*) denotes an organization that has established tax-exempt status directly with the IRS and is not covered by the USCCB Group Ruling.

Diocese of Gallup

(Dioecesis Gallupiensis)

MOST REVEREND JAMES S. WALL, D.D.

Bishop of Gallup; ordained June 6, 1998; appointed Bishop of Gallup February 5, 2009; ordained and installed April 23, 2009. Office: 503 W. Historic 66, Ste. B, P.O. Box 1338, Gallup, NM 87301.

Chancery: 503 W. Historic 66, Ste. B, Gallup, NM 87301. Mailing Address: P.O. Box 1338, Gallup, NM 87305. T: 505-863-4406; F: 505-722-9131 (Bishop's Office); F: 505-863-2269.

ESTABLISHED DECEMBER 16, 1939.

Square Miles 55,468.

Comprises Apache, Navajo and those parts of the Navajo and Hopi Reservations in Coconino Counties in the State of Arizona; San Juan, McKinley, Catron, Cibola and those parts of Rio Arriba, Sandoval, Bernalillo and Valencia Counties lying west of 106, 52', 41" meridian in the State of New Mexico.

Legal Title: New Mexico: Roman Catholic Church of the Diocese of Gallup. Arizona: Bishop of the Roman Catholic Church of the Diocese of Gallup.

For legal titles of parishes and diocesan institutions, consult the Chancery Office.

STATISTICAL OVERVIEW

Personnel
Bishop 1
Priests: Diocesan Active in Diocese 19
Priests: Diocesan Active Outside Diocese 1
Priests: Retired, Sick or Absent 10
Number of Diocesan Priests 30
Religious Priests in Diocese 7
Total Priests in your Diocese 37
Extern Priests in Diocese 18
Permanent Deacons in Diocese 24
Total Brothers 6
Total Sisters 63

Parishes
Parishes 52
With Resident Pastor:
Resident Diocesan Priests 19
Resident Religious Priests 14
Without Resident Pastor:
Administered by Priests 19
Administered by Deacons 1
In the care of professed men religious other than priests or permanent deacons 1
Missions 22
Pastoral Centers 1
Professional Ministry Personnel:
Brothers 5
Sisters 57
Lay Ministers 8

Welfare
Homes for the Aged 1
Total Assisted 50

Educational
Diocesan Students in Other Seminaries 2
Total Seminarians 2
High Schools, Private 1
Total Students 119
Elementary Schools, Diocesan and Parish 8
Total Students 428
Elementary Schools, Private 3
Total Students 205
Catechesis/Religious Education:
High School Students 897
Elementary Students 1,411
Total Students under Catholic Instruction 3,062
Teachers in Diocese:
Lay Teachers 130

Vital Statistics
Receptions into the Church:
Infant Baptism Totals 260
Minor Baptism Totals 69
Adult Baptism Totals 61
Received into Full Communion 82
First Communions 423
Confirmations 593
Marriages:
Catholic 54
Interfaith 9
Total Marriages 63
Deaths 697
Total Catholic Population 107,653
Total Population 401,000

LEADERSHIP

Vicars General - Very Rev. Peter M. Short;
Moderator of the Curia - Very Rev. Peter M. Short;
Judicial Vicar - t) 505-863-4406 x13 Very Rev. Nathanael Z. Block;
Office of the Bishop - t) 505-863-4406
Chancery - t) 505-863-4406
Administrative Assistant to the Bishop - t) 505-863-4406 x24 vplacencio@dioceseofgallup.org Vera Placencio;
Chancellor - t) 505-863-4406 x18 chancellor@dioceseofgallup.org Dcn. Randolph Copeland;
Chief Financial Officer - t) 505-863-4406 x22 bhoracek@dioceseofgallup.org Bob Horacek;
Diocesan Tribunal (First Instance) - t) 505-863-4406
Adjutant Judicial Vicar - t) (505) 863-4406 x29 Rev. Augustine Laiju Kandanattuthara Mathew (framathew@dioceseofgallup.org);
Judge - Very Rev. Nathanael Z. Block, Vicar;
Defenders of the Bond - Very Rev. Thomas R. Maikowski;
 Secretary/Notary - t) 505-863-4406 x13 Rebecca Boucher;
Promoter of Justice -
Vicars Forane - Very Rev. Frank Chacon, San Juan Vicariate; Very Rev. Dale Jamison, O.F.M., McKinley Vicariate; Very Rev. Thomas R. Maikowski, Navajo Vicariate;
Bishop's Delegate for Religious - t) 505-863-4406 srrbacke@dioceseofgallup.org Sr. Rene Backe, C.S.A.;
Presbyteral Council - Most Rev. James S. Wall; Very Rev. Joshua Mayer; Very Rev. Florecito P.J. Pabatao, O.F.M.;
Diocesan Consultors - Very Rev. Frank Chacon; Very Rev. Dale Jamison, O.F.M.; Very Rev. Thomas R. Maikowski;
Vicar for Priests - Rev. Joachim Blonski;
Priests' Retirement Board - Rev. Timothy W. Farrell, Chair; Very Rev. Nathanael Z. Block; Very Rev. Daniel F. Kassis;
Priestly Life and Ministry Committee - Very Rev. Joshua Mayer; Very Rev. Nathanael Z. Block; Rev. David Tate;

OFFICES AND DIRECTORS

Archives - t) 505-863-4406 x25 archivist@dioceseofgallup.org Cathy McCarthy, Archivist;
Building Committee - Jeremy Boucher, Chair; Dcn. Randolph Copeland, Chancellor; Dcn. John Margis;
Catholic Charities of Gallup Inc. - t) 505-722-4407 v.trujillo@ccdioc.com Vicki Trujillo, Exec.;
Catholic Committee on Scouting - t) 505-330-3230 Rev. Jeffrey W. King, Chap.; Daniel Burnham; Carly Burnham;
Catholic Schools Office - t) 505-863-4406 x21 catholicschools@dioceseofgallup.org; friogba@dioceseofgallup.org Rev. Isaac Ogba, Supt.;
Communications Office - t) 505-863-4406 x20 media@dioceseofgallup.org Suzanne Hammons, Media Liaison, Coord. Web & Print Media Design;
 Newspaper - Voice of the Southwest - Suzanne Hammons;
Cursillos - t) 928-587-5210 Rev. Pio O'Connor, O.F.M., Spiritual Adv./Care Srvcs.; Very Rev. Peter M. Short, Spiritual Adv./Care Srvcs.; Larry Reyes, Dir.;
Diocesan Review Board for Sexual Abuse & Misconduct -
Finance Council - Tony Gonzales, Chair; Very Rev. Peter M. Short; Rev. Patrick N. McGuire, S.M.A.;
Finance Office - Bob Horacek, CFO;
Life, Peace, Justice and Creation Stewardship Office - t) 505-722-4407 Sr. Rose Marie Cecchini, M.M., Dir.;
Ministry Formation Office -
 Academic Formation - t) 505-863-6611 srrbacke@dioceseofgallup.org Sr. Rene Backe, C.S.A., Dir.;
 Builders of the New Earth & Native American Formation - Very Rev. Dale Jamison, O.F.M., Dir.;
 Diaconate Formation - diaconate@dioceseofgallup.org; dcntlujan@dioceseofgallup.org Dcn. Timoteo Lujan, Dir.;
Native American Ministries Office - Very Rev. Dale Jamison, O.F.M., Dir.;
Propagation of the Faith Office - Dcn. Randolph Copeland;
Religious Education and Youth Office - Kathleen Zelasko, Dir.;
Safe Environment Office - t) 505-863-4406 x17 safeenvironment@dioceseofgallup.org Cathy McCarthy; Anna Flores;
Search - search.christian.maturity@gmail.com Very Rev. Joshua Mayer, Spiritual Adv./Care Srvcs.; Mari Arreguin, Dir.;
Victim Assistance Coordinator - t) 505-906-7357 victimassistance@dioceseofgallup.org Elizabeth Mason Terrill, Dir.;
Vocations Office - Very Rev. Joshua Mayer, Dir.; Dcn. Timoteo Lujan, Dir.; Sr. Rene Backe, C.S.A., Dir.;
 Cure of Ars House of Discernment - t) 505-863-4406 x18 chancellor@dioceseofgallup.org Dcn. Randolph Copeland, Dir.;

PARISHES, MISSIONS, AND CLERGY

STATE OF ARIZONA

ALPINE

St. Helena - 42909 Hwy. 180, Alpine, AZ 85920; Mailing: P. O. Box 259, Alpine, AZ 85920-0259 t) 928-339-4363 sthelenaalpine@dioceseofgallup.org Rev. Anselm Amadi, Pst. Admin.; Dcn. Jorge Campos;

CHINLE

Our Lady of Fatima - Navajo Rt. 7, Chinle, AZ 86503-2119; Mailing: P.O. Box 2119, Chinle, AZ 86503-2119 t) 928-674-5413; 928-674-5254 (CRP) Very Rev. Florecito P.J. Pabatao, O.F.M., Pst.; Sr. Theresa Chato, S.B.S., DRE; CRP Stds.: 17
 St. Anthony - ; Mailing: P.O. Box 578, Many Farms, AZ 86538
 St. Mary of the Rosary - ; Mailing: P.O. Box 432, Pinon, AZ 86510

CIBICUE

St. Catherine - Human Services Rd., Cibicue, AZ 85911; Mailing: P.O. Box 679, Cibecue, AZ 85941 t) 928-338-4432 stfranciswhiteriver@dioceseofgallup.org Rev. John Cormack, Admin.;
 St. Anthony -

CONCHO

San Rafael - 35411 US 180 A, Concho, AZ 85924-0049; Mailing: P.O. Box 49, Concho, AZ 85924 t) 928-337-4390 Rev. Joachim Blonski, Pst.;

FT. DEFIANCE

Our Lady of Blessed Sacrament - 173 Main St., Ft. Defiance, AZ 86504-0070; Mailing: P.O. Box 70, Fort Defiance, AZ 86504-0070 t) 928-729-5068 Rev. Jose Femilou Gutay, O.F.M., Pst.; Rev. Edgardo Diaz, Assoc. Pst.; Rev. Blane Grein, O.F.M., Assoc. Pst.; Dcn. Daniel Martin; Sr. Zoe Brenner, S.B.S., DRE;

GANADO

All Saints - County Rd. 420, Ganado, AZ 86505; Mailing: P.O. Box 119, Ganado, AZ 86505 t) 928-755-3401 paulobofm@yahoo.com Bro. Paul O'Brien, O.F.M., Admin.; Sr. Monica Dubois, O.P., DRE; Teresa Gorman, DRE;
 St. Anne - ; Mailing: P.O. Box 366, Chambers, AZ 86502-0366 Bro. Charles Schilling, S.C.;
 Our Lady of the Rosary - ; Mailing: Box 119, Greasewood, AZ 86505
 Station - Cornfields, AZ
 Station - Wide Ruins, AZ

HOLBROOK

Our Lady of Guadalupe - 212 E. Arizona St., Holbrook, AZ 86025; Mailing: P.O. Box 849, Holbrook, AZ 86025-0849 t) 928-524-3261 dcnmashenfelder@dioceseofgallup.org; ologholbrook@dioceseofgallup.org Rev. Cyprian Okere, Admin.; Dcn. Michael Ashenfelder, DRE; CRP Stds.: 22

HOUCK

St. John the Evangelist - St. Anselm Rd., Houck, AZ 86506-0048; Mailing: P.O. Box 48, Houck, AZ 86506-0048 c) 650-605-5508 dcneschaub@dioceseofgallup.org Rev. Matthew A. Keller, Pst.;
 St. Rose - sjmwdc@gmail.com

KAYENTA

Our Lady of Guadalupe - ; Mailing: P.O. Box 517, Kayenta, AZ 86033 t) 928-697-3429 Rev. Jay Jung, C.M., Pst.;

KEAMS CANYON

St. Joseph's Indian Mission - E. Main St., Keams Canyon, AZ 86034; Mailing: P.O. Box 129, Keams Canyon, AZ 86034 t) 928-738-2325 peteshirley1214@gmail.com Rev. Cyprian Okere, Admin.;
 Station - Toyei, AZ

LUKACHUKAI

St. Isabel - 105 St. Isabel Ln., Lukachukai, AZ 86507-0128; Mailing: P.O. Box 128, Lukachukai, AZ 86507-0128 t) 928-674-5202 pjey54@yahoo.com Very Rev. Florecito P.J. Pabatao, O.F.M., Pst.;
 Our Lady of Guadalupe - Round Rock, AZ
 St. Ann - Tsaile, AZ
 Our Lady of the Lake - Wheatfields, AZ

MCNARY

St. Anthony - 33 N. McQuatters Ave., McNary, AZ 85930-0628; Mailing: P.O. Box 628, McNary, AZ 85930-0628 c) 520-373-8367 officeofbishsop@dioceseofgallup.org Rev. Robert A. Hyman, Pst.;

OVERGAARD

Our Lady of the Assumption - 3048 Hwy. 277, Overgaard, AZ 85933; Mailing: P.O. Box 628, Overgaard, AZ 85933 t) 928-535-5329 olaovergaard@dioceseofgallup.org Rev. Jerald (Jerry) W. Thompson, Pst. Admin.; Margaret Manchester, DRE;

PAGE

Immaculate Heart of Mary - 455 S. Lake Powell Blvd., Page, AZ 86040; Mailing: PO Box 1387, Page, AZ 86040-1387 t) 928-645-2301 Very Rev. Thomas R. Maikowski, Admin.; CRP Stds.: 54

PINETOP

St. Mary of the Angels - 1915 S. Penrod Ln., Pinetop, AZ 85935; Mailing: PO Box 819, Pinetop, AZ 85935 t) 928-367-2080 smoa@stmaryoftheangels.com; stmaryspinetop@frontiernet.net www.stmaryoftheangels.com Rev. Daniel P. Daley, Pst.; Michael Caruth, DRE; CRP Stds.: 40

PINON

St. Mary of the Rosary - Indian Rte. 8030, Pinon, AZ 86510; Mailing: P.O. Box 2119, Chinle, AZ 86503 t) 928-674-5202 pjey54@yahoo.com Very Rev. Florecito P.J. Pabatao, O.F.M., Pst.;
 Station - Tachee, AZ
 Station - Blue Gap, AZ
 Station - Forest Lake, AZ
 Station - Whippoorwill Spring, AZ
 Station - Hardrock, AZ
 Station - Kits'iiLi, AZ

SHOW LOW

St. Rita - 1400 E. Owens St., Show Low, AZ 85901; Mailing: PO Box 1449, Show Low, AZ 85902 t) 928-537-2543 stritadre@dioceseofgallup.org; stritashowlow@dioceseofgallup.org stritashowlow.com Very Rev. Daniel F. Kassis, Pst.; Rebecca Quintana, DRE; CRP Stds.: 56

SNOWFLAKE

Our Lady of the Snow - 1655 S. Main St., Snowflake, AZ 85937 t) 928-536-4559 olssnowflake@dioceseofgallup.org www.ourladyofthesnow.info Very Rev. Nathanael Z. Block, Pst.; CRP Stds.: 32

SPRINGERVILLE

St. Peter - 145 N. Papago St., Springerville, AZ 85938; Mailing: PO Box 1566, Springerville, AZ 85938 t) 928-333-4423 stpeterspringerville@dioceseofgallup.org stpeterchurchaz.com Rev. Anselm Amadi, Pst. Admin.; Dcn. Jorge Campos; CRP Stds.: 17

ST. JOHNS

St. John the Baptist - 203 E. Commercial St., St. Johns, AZ 85936-0309; Mailing: P.O. Box 309, St. Johns, AZ 85936 t) 928-337-4390 Rev. Joachim Blonski, Pst.; Dcn. Ronald Chavez; CRP Stds.: 52

ST. MICHAELS

St. Michael - 24 Mission Rd., St. Michaels, AZ 86511-0680; Mailing: P.O. Box 680, St. Michaels, AZ 86511-0680 t) 928-871-4171; 928-871-4172 missionsaintmichaels@gmail.com Very Rev. Florecito P.J. Pabatao, O.F.M., Par. Admin.; Rev. Edgardo Diaz, Par. Vicar; Rev. Pio O'Connor, O.F.M., In Res.; Bro. John Friebel, O.F.M., In Res.; CRP Stds.: 4

St. Michael's Mission for Navajo Indians - t) (928) 871-4171; (928) 871-4172

TUBA CITY

St. Jude - ; Mailing: P.O. Box 248, Tuba City, AZ 86045 t) 928-283-5391 stjudetubacity.org@gmail.com Rev. Faustinus Ibebuike, Pst.;

WHITERIVER

St. Francis - 9 W. Elm St., Whiteriver, AZ 85941; Mailing: P.O. Box 679, Whiteriver, AZ 85941 t) 928-338-4432 stfranciswhiteriver@dioceseofgallup.org Rev. John Cormack, Assoc. Pst.;

WINSLOW

St. Joseph's - 220 W. Second St., Winslow, AZ 86047; Mailing: 300 W. Hillview St., Winslow, AZ 86047 t) 928-289-2350 winslowparishes@dioceseofgallup.org catholiccommunityofwinslow.myfreesites.net Catholic Community of Winslow Very Rev. Peter M. Short, Pst.; Dcn. Greg Carlson; CRP Stds.: 35

Madre de Dios - 1015 Central St., Winslow, AZ 86047; Mailing: 300 W. Hillview St., Winslow, AZ 86047 t) 928-289-2350 winslowparishes@dioceseofgallup.org Catholic Community of Winslow Very Rev. Peter M. Short, Pst.; Dcn. Greg Carlson; Cathy Hernandez, DRE;

STATE OF NEW MEXICO

AZTEC

St. Joseph (Holy Trinity) - 501 N. Mesa Verde Ave., Aztec, NM 87410; Mailing: 424 N. Mesa Verde Ave., Father Owen Center, Aztec, NM 87410 t) 505-334-6535 www.stjosephaztec.org Rev. Rajasekhar Yeruva, Admin.; Dcn. James WurzbacK; CRP Stds.: 55

BLANCO

St. Rose of Lima - 7378 US Hwy. 64, Blanco, NM 87412; Mailing: 307 N. Church St., Bloomfield, NM 87413 t) 505-632-2014 Rev. Francis Akano, Admin.; Dcn. Roger Garcia; Dcn. Patrick R. Valdez; CRP Stds.: 25

Our Lady of Guadalupe - Los Martinez, NM

BLOOMFIELD

St. Mary - 307 N. Church St., Bloomfield, NM 87413 t) 505-632-2014 Rev. Francis Akano, Admin.; Dcn. Roger Garcia; Dcn. Patrick R. Valdez; Marilyn Benedict, DRE; CRP Stds.: 100

CEBOYETA

Our Lady of Sorrows - State Hwy. 279, Ceboyeta, NM 87014; Mailing: H.C. 77 Box 13, Ceboyeta, NM 87014 t) 505-552-6301 olsseboyeta@dioceseofgallup.org Very Rev. Alberto Avella, Pst.; Rev. Faustinus Ibebuike, Par. Vicar; Rev. John Sauter, Par. Vicar; Daniel Gonzales, DRE;

St. Joseph Mission - (Inactive)

Santa Rosalia - (Inactive)

Our Lady of Light - 17 Water Canyon Rd., Cubero, NM 87014; Mailing: P.O. Box 8098, Cubero, NM 87014-8098

CROWNPOINT

St. Bonaventure - ; Mailing: P.O. Box 268, Crownpoint, NM 87313 t) 505-786-7110 Rev. Gil Mangampo, Chap.;

St. Paul - 268 Church Rd., Crownpoint, NM 87313; Mailing: P O Box 268, Crownpoint, NM 87313 t) 505-786-5376 Rev. Gil Mangampo, Sacr. Min.; Dcn. John Margis; Dcn. Sherman Manuelito;

Risen Savior -

St. Bonaventure -

CUBA

Immaculate Conception - 6440 US-550, Cuba, NM 87013; Mailing: P.O. Box 40, Cuba, NM 87013 t) 575-289-3803 icccuba@dioceseofgallup.org Rev. Cornelius Onyigbuo, Admin.; Lynette R. Crespin, DRE;

Santo Nino -

Saint Aloysius Gonzaga -

San Jose -

FARMINGTON

St. Mary's - 2100 E. 20th St., Farmington, NM 87401 t) 505-325-0287 x101 stmarysfmt@dioceseofgallup.org www.stmarysfmt.org Very Rev. Frank Chacon, Pst.; Rev. Jeffrey W. King, Assoc. Pst.; Dcn. James Betts; Dcn. Martin Smith; CRP Stds.: 194

Sacred Heart - 414 N. Allen Ave., Farmington, NM 87401 t) 505-325-9743 shfarmington@dioceseofgallup.org; frtfarrell@dioceseofgallup.org sacredheartfarmington.weconnect.com/ Rev. Timothy W. Farrell, Pst.; CRP Stds.: 129

FLORA VISTA

Holy Trinity (St. Joseph Church) - 42 Road 3520, Flora Vista, NM 87415; Mailing: 424 N. Mesa Verde Ave., Aztec, NM 87410 t) 505-334-6535; 505-333-7366 www.stjosephaztec.org Administrated through St Joseph Church, Aztec, NM Rev. Rajasekhar Yeruva, Admin.; Dcn. James Wurzbach;

GALLUP

Cathedral of the Sacred Heart - 415 E. Green St., Gallup, NM 87301 t) 505-722-6644 shcathedral@dioceseofgallup.org sacredheartgallup.org Rev. Mitchell Athanasius Brown, Rector; Rev. Cornelius A Okere (Nigeria), Par. Vicar; Dcn. Randolph Copeland; CRP Stds.: 40

St. Francis of Assisi - 214 W. Wilson, Gallup, NM 87301; Mailing: 411 N. Second, Gallup, NM 87301 t) 505-863-3033 frjmayer@dioceseofgallup.org Very Rev. Joshua Mayer, Pst.; Rev. David Tate, Par. Vicar; CRP Stds.: 80

St. John Vianney - 3408 Zia Dr., Gallup, NM 87301 t) 505-722-3361 (CRP); 505-722-5085 sjv@dioceseofgallup.org Rev. Augustine Opara, Pst.; Dcn. John Margis; JoNell Becenti, DRE; CRP Stds.: 40

GRANTS

St. Teresa of Avila - 213 Smith St., Grants, NM 87020; Mailing: P.O. Box 668, Grants, NM 87020 t) 505-287-3549 (CRP); 505-285-6645 cibolacatholiccommunity.com Rev. Matthew A. Keller, Pst.; Rev. Augustine K.M. Laiju, Par. Vicar; Rev. John Sauter, Par. Vicar; Dcn. Larry Chavez; Velma Dees, DRE; CRP Stds.: 145

LAGUNA

St. Joseph - 1 Friar Rd., Laguna, NM 87026; Mailing: PO Box 1000, Laguna, NM 87026 t) 505-552-9330; 505-552-7464 (CRP) stjosephlaguna@dioceseofgallup.org Rev. Charles McCarthy, OFM, Pst.; Rev. Christopher Kerstiens, OFM, In Res.; Angela Riley, DRE; CRP Stds.: 60

Nativity of the Blessed Virgin Mary -

Sacred Heart -

St. Elizabeth of Hungary -

St. Margaret Mary -

St. Anne -

LUMBERTON

St. Francis of Assisi - 21 County Rd. 356, Lumberton, NM 87528; Mailing: P.O. Box 1147, 3760 Sandhill Dr., Dulce, NM 87528 t) 575-759-1307; 575-759-3252 valerielea711@gmail.com; frconyigbuo@dioceseofgallup.org Rev. Cornelius Onyigbuo, Admin.; Valerie Gomez, DRE; CRP Stds.: 40

St. Anthony - 3760 Sandhill Dr., Dulce, NM 87528; Mailing: PO Box 1147, Dulce, NM 87528 t) (575) 759-1307

MILAN

St. Vivian - 501 Sand St., Milan, NM 87201-2938; Mailing: P.O. Box 2938, Milan, NM 87201-2938 t) 505-287-9327 stvivianmilan@dioceseofgallup.org cibolacatholiccommunity.com Rev. Matthew A. Keller, Pst.; Rev. Augustine Laiju Kandanattuthara Mathew, Par. Vicar; Rev. John Sauter, Par. Vicar; CRP Stds.: 10

NAVAJO

St. Berard - ; Mailing: P.O. Box 1284, Navajo, NM 87328 t) 505-777-2490 (CRP); 928-729-5068 Very Rev. Florecito P.J. Pabatao, O.F.M., Pst.; Dcn. Wilson Gorman; Sr. Zoe Brenner, S.B.S., DRE;

St. Francis Mission - ; Mailing: P.O. Box 41, Sawmill, AZ 86549

Station - Crystal, NM

PINEHAVEN

Good Shepherd Catholic Mission - Hwy. 10A, Pinehaven, NM 87305; Mailing: P.O. Box 267, Vanderwagen, NM 87326 t) 505-782-2014 pastor@stanthonyzuni.org Rev. Patrick N. McGuire, S.M.A., Pst.;

PUEBLO OF ACOMA

San Esteban, Acoma Catholic Indian Mission - 266 Pueblo Rd., Pueblo of Acoma, NM 87034-0448; Mailing: P.O. Box 448, Pueblo of Acoma, NM 87034-0448 t) 505-552-6403 Rev. Charles McCarthy, OFM, Pst.; Rev. Christopher Kerstiens, OFM, In Res.; CRP Stds.: 15

St. Anne - t) 505-552-9403

Santa Maria de Acoma -

QUEMADO

Sacred Heart - 3 Parish Ln., Quemado, NM 87829-0339; Mailing: PO Box 339, Quemado, NM 87829 t) 575-773-4631 sacredheartquemado@dioceseofgallup.org Rev. Anthony O. Dike, Pst. Admin.; Rev. Divine Ekebe, Par. Vicar; Rev. Daniel P. Daley; Mark Hubbell, DRE;

Nativity of the Blessed Virgin Mary - Old Hwy. 60, Datil, NM 87821; Mailing: P.O. Box 339, Quemado, NM 87829-0039

RAMAH

San Lorenzo - HCC 1, Ramah, NM 87321; Mailing: P.O. Box 486, Zuni, NM 87327 t) 505-782-2014 pastor@stanthonyzuni.org Rev. Patrick N. McGuire, S.M.A., Pst.; CRP Stds.: 2

RESERVE

Santo Nino - 155 NM Hwy. 435, Reserve, NM 87830-0441; Mailing: P.O. Box 489, Reserve, NM 87830-0489 t) 575-533-6719 catronparishes@dioceseofgallup.org Rev. Anthony O. Dike, Admin.;

San Isidro -

St. Francis - t) (575) 533-6719

St. Anne -

Santo Nino - Cat Walk Rd., Glenwood, NM 88039; Mailing: P.O. Box 222, Glenwood, NM 88039 t) (575) 533-6719

SAN MATEO

San Mateo - 31 Main St., San Mateo, NM 87020; Mailing: P.O. Box 668, Grants, NM 87020 t) 505-285-6645 Rev. Matthew A. Keller, Pst.; Rev. Augustine Laiju Kandanattuthara Mathew, Par. Vicar; Rev. John Sauter, Par. Vicar; Dcn. Larry Chavez;

SAN RAFAEL

San Rafael - 100 Guadalupe Plz., San Rafael, NM 87051; Mailing: P.O. Box 2938, Milan, NM 87021 t) 505-287-9327 stvivianmilan@dioceseofgallup.org Rev. Matthew A. Keller, Pst.; Rev. Augustine K.M. Laiju, Par. Vicar; Rev. John Sauter, Par. Vicar; Dcn. Larry Chavez;

SHIPROCK

Christ the King - Hwy. 564 W., Shiprock, NM 87420; Mailing: P.O. Box 610, Shiprock, NM 87420 t) 505-368-4532 christkingparish@yahoo.com Rev. Patrick Wedeking, Pst.; Jerome Herbert, DRE;

TOHATCHI

St. Mary Church - 2 St. Mary Dr., Tohatchi, NM 87325;

Mailing: Box 39, Tohatchi, NM 87325 t) 505-733-2243 frdjamison@dioceseofgallup.org Very Rev. Dale Jamison, O.F.M., Pst.; Sr. Marlene Kochert, OSF, DRE;

St. Anthony -

St. Joseph -

VANDERWAGEN

St. Patrick - 549 Cousins Rd., Vanderwagen, NM 87326; Mailing: P.O. Box 267, Vanderwagen, NM 87326 t) 505-782-2014 pastor@stanthonyzuni.org (Navajo Mission) Rev. Patrick N. McGuire, S.M.A., Pst.; CRP Stds.: 6

WATERFLOW

Sacred Heart - 9 County Rd. 6820, Waterflow, NM 87421 t) 505-598-9856 (CRP); 505-598-5454 patricia.b.paul@gmail.com; patrickw515@earthlink.net Rev. Patrick Wedeking, Pst.; Patty Paul, DRE;

San Juan Catholic Center - 11 County Rd. 6446, Kirtland, NM 87417; Mailing: P.O. Box 857, Kirtland, NM 87417 patrick515@earthlink.net

Sacred Heart Missionary Cenacle - Sr. Ann Regis Barrett, M.S.B.T., Dir.;

ZUNI

St. Anthony - 11 St. Anthony Dr., Zuni, NM 87327; Mailing: P.O. Box 486, Zuni, NM 87327 t) 505-782-2014 pastor@stanthonyzuni.org www.stanthonyzuni.org Rev. Patrick N. McGuire, S.M.A., Pst.; Rev. Innocent Nzewuji (Nigeria), Assoc. Pst.;

SCHOOLS: PRESCHOOL THRU HIGH SCHOOL

SCHOOLS

STATE OF ARIZONA

PAGE

Immaculate Heart School - (PAR) (Grades PreK-K) 455 S. Lake Powell Blvd., Page, AZ 86040-1387; Mailing: P.O. Box 1387, Page, AZ 86040-1387 t) 928-645-2301 frtmaikowski@dioceseofgallup.org Very Rev. Thomas Maikowski, Prin.; Stds.: 40; Sr. Tchrs.: 3

SHOW LOW

St. Anthony Catholic School - (PRV) (Grades PreK-8) 1400 E. Owens St., Show Low, AZ 85901; Mailing: P.O. Box 789, Show Low, AZ 85902 t) 928-537-4497 admin@stantschool.org www.stantschool.org Bryan Yorksmith, Prin.; Stds.: 161; Bro. Tchrs.: 1; Lay Tchrs.: 10

ST. MICHAELS

St. Michael Indian School - (PRV) (Grades PreK-12) 1 Lupton Rd., St. Michaels, AZ 86511; Mailing: P.O. Box 650, St. Michaels, AZ 86511 t) 505-979-5590 tazbah.shortey@smischools.org www.stmichaelindianschool.org Tazbah Shortey, Prin.; Dot Teso, Pres.; Stds.: 400; Lay Tchrs.: 15

STATE OF NEW MEXICO

FARMINGTON

Sacred Heart Catholic School - (DIO) (Grades PreSchool-8) 404 N. Allen Ave., Farmington, NM 87401 t) 505-325-7152 office@shcsfarmington.org www.shcsfarmington.org Kami Donald, Prin.; Stds.: 119; Lay Tchrs.: 14

GALLUP

St. Francis of Assisi School - (PAR) (Grades PreK- 215 W. Wilson, Gallup, NM 87301; Mailing: P.O. Box 4060, Gallup, NM 87305 t) 505-863-3145 saintfrancisprincipal@gmail.com Sr. Liliana Garcia, H.N.S.G., Prin.; Stds.: 28

Sacred Heart Catholic School - (DIO) (Grades PreK-8) 555 S. Woodrow, Gallup, NM 87301 t) 505-863-6652 principal@gallupcatholicschool.org Rev. Mitchell Athanasius Brown, Pst.; Stds.: 49; Lay Tchrs.: 7

GRANTS

St. Teresa of Avila School - (PAR) (Grades PreK-8) 402 E. High St., Grants, NM 87020; Mailing: P.O. Box 729, Grants, NM 87020 t) 505-287-2261 brunson@stoscs.education www.stteresaschoolwarriors.com Angela Brunson, Prin.; Stds.: 66

LUMBERTON

St. Francis School - (PRV) (Grades K-8) 21 County Rd. 356, Lumberton, NM 87528 t) 575-759-3252 madeline.lyon@stfrancisoflumberton.org www.stfrancisoflumberton.org Madeline Lyon, Prin.; Valerie Gomez, DRE; Stds.: 80; Lay Tchrs.: 6

SAN FIDEL

St. Joseph School - (PAR) (Grades PreK-8) 26 School Rd., San Fidel, NM 87049; Mailing: P.O. Box 370, San Fidel, NM 87049-0370 t) 505-552-6362 atrujillo@stjosephmissionschool.org; contact@stjosephmissionschool.org www.stjosephmissionschool.com Antonio Trujillo, Prin.; Stds.: 37; Lay Tchrs.: 4

THOREAU

St. Bonaventure School - (PRV) (Grades PreK-8) 8 Lenore Ave., Thoreau, NM 87323; Mailing: P.O. Box 610, Thoreau, NM 87323 t) 505-862-7465 tlee@sbms.k12.nm.us www.stbonaventuremission.org Tracie Lee, Prin.; Stds.: 107; Scholastics: 20; Lay Tchrs.: 20

ZUNI

St. Anthony Indian Mission School - (PAR) (Grades PreK-8) 11 St. Anthony Dr., Zuni, NM 87327; Mailing: P.O. Box 486, Zuni, NM 87327 t) 505-782-4596 principal@stanthonyzuni.org www.stanthonyzuni.org Sr. Marsha Moon, RSC, Prin.; Stds.: 120; Sr. Tchrs.: 3; Lay Tchrs.: 10

INSTITUTIONS LOCATED IN DIOCESE

CONVENTS, MONASTERIES, AND RESIDENCES FOR WOMEN [CON]

BLANCO

Monastery of Our Lady of the Desert - 10258 Hwy. 64, Blanco, NM 87412; Mailing: P.O. Box 556, Blanco, NM 87412 t) 505-419-2938 kateriosb@ourladyofthedesert.org ourladyofthedesert.org Benedictine Nuns Subiaco-Cassinese Congregation Sr. Hilda Tuyuc, O.S.B., Prioress; Srs.: 15

GALLUP

Casa Reina - 711 S. Puerco Dr., Gallup, NM 87301; Mailing: P.O. Box 807, Gallup, NM 87305 t) 505-722-5511 sistershnsgj@gmail.com Sisters of Our Lady of Guadalupe and St. Joseph Perpetual Adoration Chapel. Mother Rosa Maria Zuniga, HNSG, Supr.; Srs.: 14

ENDOWMENTS / FOUNDATIONS / TRUSTS [EFT]

GALLUP

Catholic Peoples' Foundation, Inc. - 503 W. Historic Hwy. 66, Ste. A, Gallup, NM 87301; Mailing: PO Box 369, Gallup, NM 87305 t) 505-726-8295 amanda@catholicpeoplesfoundation.com www.catholicpeoplesfoundation.com Amanda Galaviz, Dir.; Herbert B. Mosher, Dir.;

Southwest Indian Foundation - 100 W. Coal Ave., Gallup, NM 87301; Mailing: P.O. Box 307, Gallup, NM 87305 t) 505-863-2837 bookkeeping@southwestindian.com www.southwestindian.com Most Rev. James S. Wall; James Mason, Pres.; John Dowling, Vice Pres.; William McCarthy, Exec.; Victoria Begay, Secy.;

MISCELLANEOUS [MIS]

GALLUP

Blue Army - 711 S. Puerco Dr., Gallup, NM 87301 t) 505-722-5511 garciamagda1219@gmail.com (Fatima Apostolate) Mother Magda Leticia Garcia, H.N.S.G., Dir.;

Catholic Charities of Gallup, Inc. - 503 W. Hwy. 66, Ste. C, Gallup, NM 87301; Mailing: P.O. Box 3146, Gallup, NM 87305 t) 505-722-4407 exectivedirector@catholiccharitiesgallup.org; accountant@catholiccharitiesgallup.org www.catholiccharitiesgallup.org Vicki Trujillo, Dir.;

St. Joseph's Shelter and Soup Kitchen - 207 Black Diamond Canyon Dr., Gallup, NM 87301 t) 505-722-5261 (Convent); 505-722-5156 (Soup Kitchen) officeofbishop@dioceseofgalluo.org Serving Native American clients. Missionaries of Charity. Sr. M. Elzeena, MC, Dir.;

PINETOP

St. Vincent DePaul Society - 1525 S. McCoy, Pinetop, AZ 85935; Mailing: P.O. Box 376, Pinetop, AZ 85935 t) 928-367-2029 (Shop); 928-367-3057 (Emergency Aid Office) svdp.pinetop@gmail.com Thrift Shop & Emergency Aid Office. Mike Pimper, Pres.;

THOREAU

St. Bonaventure Indian Mission & School - 25 Navarre Blvd. W., Thoreau, NM 87323; Mailing: P.O. Box 610, Thoreau, NM 87323 t) 505-862-7847 chaltar@stbonaventuremission.org www.stbonaventuremission.org Chris Halter, Dir.;

TUBA CITY

Life Sharing Center, Inc., St. Jude Food Bank - 100 Aspen Dr., Tuba City, AZ 86045; Mailing: P.O. Box 1277, Tuba City, AZ 86045 t) 928-283-6886 lsc.sjfb@gmail.com Sr. Pacita Calica, CEO;

WINSLOW

La Casa de Nuestra Senora (Madonna House) - 213 Jefferson St., Winslow, AZ 86047 t) 928-289-9284 mh.winslow@yahoo.com www.madonnahouse.org Mission of Madonna House Apostolate Combermere, Ontario, Canada; Prayer and Community Service Center. Public Association of the Faithful Julie Lynch, Mem.; Marian Moody, Mem.;

NURSING / REHABILITATION / CONVALESCENCE / ELDERLY CARE [NUR]

GALLUP

Villa Guadalupe Home for the Aged - 1900 Mark Ave., Gallup, NM 87301 t) 505-863-6894 msgallup@littlesistersofthepoor.org Sr. Rose Veronica Cantu, LSP, Admin.; Asstd. Annu.: 50; Staff: 46

RETREAT HOUSES / RENEWAL CENTERS [RTR]

GALLUP

Sacred Heart Retreat - Mile Marker 27, Gallup, NM 87301; Mailing: P.O. Box 1338, Gallup, NM 87305 t) 505-722-6755 shrc@dioceseofgallup.org retreat.dioceseofgallup.org Sr. Woohee Sofia Lee Sr., SFMA, Dir.;

SHRINES [SHR]

GALLUP

St. Kateri Tekakwitha Shrine Inc. - 162 Hwy. 602, Gallup, NM 87301; Mailing: P.O. Box 3637, Gallup, NM 87305 c) (575) 649-1185 katerirosary@dioceseofgallup.org www.saintkaterirosarywalk.org Dcn. Edward Schaub, Dir.;

Archdiocese of Galveston-Houston

(Archidioecesis Galvestoniensis-Houstoniensis)

HIS EMINENCE DANIEL CARDINAL DINARDO

Archbishop of Galveston-Houston; ordained July 16, 1977; appointed Coadjutor Bishop of Sioux City August 19, 1997; consecrated October 7, 1997; succeeded to Sioux City November 28, 1998; appointed Coadjutor Bishop of Galveston-Houston January 16, 2004; installed March 26, 2004; appointed Coadjutor Archbishop December 29, 2004; succeeded to the See February 28, 2006; elevated to Cardinal November 24, 2007. Mailing Address: P.O. Box 907, Houston, TX 77001-0907. T: 713-659-5461.

Chancery Office: P.O. Box 907, Houston, TX 77001-0907. T: 713-659-5461; F: 713-759-9151.

ESTABLISHED IN 1847.

Square Miles 8,880.

Redesignated Diocese of Galveston-Houston on July 25, 1959; created Archdiocese December 29, 2004.

Comprises the Counties of Austin, Brazoria, Fort Bend, Galveston, Grimes, Harris, Montgomery, San Jacinto, Walker and Waller in the State of Texas.

For legal titles of parishes and archdiocesan institutions, consult the Chancery Office.

MOST REVEREND ITALO DELL'ORO, C.R.S.

Auxiliary Bishop of Galveston-Houston; ordained Sept. 11, 1982; appointed Auxiliary Bishop of Galveston-Houston May 18, 2021; ordained July 2, 2021. Mailing Address: P.O. Box 907, Houston, TX 77001-0907. T: 713-659-5461.

STATISTICAL OVERVIEW

Personnel

Cardinals	1
Auxiliary Bishops	1
Priests: Diocesan Active in Diocese	145
Priests: Diocesan Active Outside Diocese	2
Priests: Diocesan in Foreign Missions	1
Priests: Retired, Sick or Absent	38
Number of Diocesan Priests	186
Religious Priests in Diocese	185
Total Priests in your Diocese	371
Extern Priests in Diocese	34
Ordinations:	
Diocesan Priests	3
Transitional Deacons	3
Permanent Deacons in Diocese	399
Total Brothers	6
Total Sisters	380

Parishes

Parishes	146
With Resident Pastor:	
Resident Diocesan Priests	99
Resident Religious Priests	36
Without Resident Pastor:	
Administered by Priests	11
Missions	7

Welfare

Health Care Centers	5
Total Assisted	62,663
Homes for the Aged	4
Total Assisted	646
Residential Care of Children	3
Total Assisted	974
Specialized Homes	4
Total Assisted	7,209
Special Centers for Social Services	9
Total Assisted	295,004

Educational

Seminaries, Diocesan	1
Students from This Diocese	27
Students from Other Dioceses	24
Diocesan Students in Other Seminaries	16
Seminaries, Religious	4
Total Seminarians	43
Colleges and Universities	1
Total Students	5,082
High Schools, Diocesan and Parish	11
Total Students	5,311
Elementary Schools, Diocesan and Parish	39
Total Students	10,510
Elementary Schools, Private	5
Total Students	1,886
Catechesis/Religious Education:	
High School Students	10,952
Elementary Students	26,450
Total Students under Catholic Instruction	60,234
Teachers in Diocese:	
Priests	12
Brothers	3
Sisters	25
Lay Teachers	1,844

Vital Statistics

Receptions into the Church:	
Infant Baptism Totals	5,866
Minor Baptism Totals	9,022
Adult Baptism Totals	1,506
Received into Full Communion	1,000
First Communions	8,237
Confirmations	7,043
Marriages:	
Catholic	2,190
Interfaith	528
Total Marriages	2,718
Deaths	4,614
Total Catholic Population	1,700,000
Total Population	7,430,555

LEADERSHIP

Chancery Office - t) 713-659-5461
Chancellor and Moderator of the Curia - Most Rev. Italo Dell`Oro, C.R.S.;
Vice Chancellor and Associate General Counsel - Christina Deajon;
Vicar General - Most Rev. Italo Dell`Oro, C.R.S.;
Personal Secretary to the Office of the Cardinal - Rev. Mark Hebert (frmark@shconroe.org);
Vicar for Clergy - t) 713-652-8241 Most Rev. Italo Dell`Oro, C.R.S., Vicar;
Ethnic Vicars - Rev. Reginald W. Samuels, Vicar; Rev. Thu Ngoc Nguyen, Vicar; Rev. Edmund P. Eduarte, Vicar;
Vicar for Religious - t) 713-741-8733 Sr. Francesca Kearns, C.C.V.I., Vicar;
Episcopal Vicars and Deans -
Central Vicariate - Rev. Albert Zanatta, C.R.S., Episcopal Vicar; Rev. Paul G. Felix, Central Deanery; Rev. Miguel A. Solorzano, Dean;
Northern Vicariate - Very Rev. Norbert J. Maduzia Jr., Vicar; Rev. Philip A. Wilhite, Northern Deanery; Rev. Terence P. Brinkman, Eastern Deanery;
Southern Vicariate - Rev. Chacko Puthumayil, Galveston-Mainland Deanery; Rev. Wencil C. Pavlovsky, Bay Area Deanery; Rev. John Kare Taosan;
Western Vicariate - Rev. Msgr. Daniel L. Scheel, Episcopal Vicar; Rev. John E. Cahoon, Western Deanery; Rev. Msgr. Bill Young, Southwest Deanery;
Secretariat Directors -
Secretariat For Administration - Most Rev. Italo Dell`Oro, C.R.S., Dir.;
Secretariat for Catholic Schools - t) 713-741-8704 Dr. Debra Haney, Supt.;
Secretariat For Clergy Formation and Chaplaincy Services - Rev. Thomas F. Rafferty, Dir.;
Secretariat For Communication - Jonah Dycus, Dir.;
Secretariat For Finance - t) 713-659-5461 Aad De Lange, Dir.;
Secretariat For Pastoral and Educational Ministries - t) 713-741-8786 Jim Barrette, Dir.;
Secretariat for Social Concerns - t) 713-741-8769 Sr. Maureen O'Connell, O.P., Dir.;
Tribunal Judicial -
Adjutant Judicial Vicar - t) 713-807-9286 Rev. Richard A. Wahl, C.S.B.;
Archdiocesan Judges - Very Rev. Trung V. Nguyen; Rev. Thu Ngoc Nguyen; Rev. Lawrence W. Jozwiak;
Defenders of the Bond - Rev. Alberto A. Maullon Jr.; Rev. Jose Garcia;
Director of the Tribunal - Anne Bryant;
Metropolitan Tribunal - t) 713-807-9286 Rev. R. Lucien (Luke) Millette, Judicial Vicar;
Promoter of Justice - Very Rev. Trung V. Nguyen;

OFFICES AND DIRECTORS

Archdiocesan Councils, Commissions and Committees
Archdiocesan Presbyteral Council -
Building and Planning Commission - t) 713-652-4456 Very Rev. Norbert J. Maduzia Jr.; Christina Deajon; Rev. Msgr. William L. Young;
College of Consultors - Rev. Msgr. Daniel L. Scheel; Rev. Msgr. Chester L. Borski; Very Rev. Norbert J. Maduzia Jr.
Ecumenism and Interreligious Affairs Office for the Archdiocese of Galveston/Houston - t) 281-342-3089 Rev. Orrin Halepeska, Chair;
Liturgical Commission - t) 281-497-1500 Rev. Richard R. Hinkley, Chair;
Presbyteral Council - His Eminence Daniel Cardinal DiNardo, Pres.; Most Rev. Italo Dell`Oro, C.R.S., Chancellor; Rev. Albert Zanatta, C.R.S.;
Priests Personnel Committee - His Eminence Daniel Cardinal DiNardo; Most Rev. Italo Dell`Oro, C.R.S.; Rev. Eurel S. P. Manzano;
Secretariat for Administration - Most Rev. Italo Dell`Oro, C.R.S., Dir.; Rev. Joseph Limanni, Special Projects;
Archives and Current Records - Lisa May, Dir.;
Catholic Cemeteries - t) 281-337-1641 Stephanie Nolan, Dir.;
Construction/Preventative Maintenance - t) 713-652-4456 Deanna Ennis, Dir.;
Human Resources - Charlie Pavlovsky, Dir.;
Information Services - Rory Murphy;
Internal Auditor - Katie Jaska, Dir.;
Legal Services - Frank Rynd, Gen. Counsel;
Real Estate - Ken Sykes;
Secretariat for Catholic Schools - t) 713-741-8704 Dr. Debra Haney, Supt.;
Catholic School Office - Dr. Debra Haney, Supt.;
School of Environmental Education - Camp Kappe - t) 936-894-2141 Randy Adams, Dir.; Michael Richmond, Dir.;
Secretariat for Clergy Formation and Chaplaincy Services - Most Rev. Italo Dell`Oro, C.R.S.;
Apostleship of the Sea (Port Ministry) - Rev. Jan Kubisa; Rev. Carlos V. de la Torre;
Catholic Chaplain Corps (Hospital Chaplains) - t) 713-747-8445 Denice Foose, Dir.;
Catholic Relief Services - Hilda Ochoa, Dir.;
Correctional Ministries (Jail Chaplains) - t) 713-741-8745; 713-755-5326 (Jail) Dcn. Alvin Lovelady, Dir.;
Diaconal Formation/Diaconal Ministry - Dcn. Phillip Jackson, Dir.; Dcn. Dominic Romaguera, Dir.; Dcn. George Silva, Dir.;
Director of Ministry to Priests - Rev. Phil (Skip) Negley, Dir.;
Mission Office - Hilda Ochoa, Dir.;
Seminarian Support - t) 713-659-5461 Rev. Richard McNeillie, Dir.;
Vocations Office - t) 713-659-5461 Rev. Richard McNeillie, Dir.;
Secretariat for Communication - Jonah Dycus, Dir.;
Radio - Madeline Johnson;
Texas Catholic Herald - Rebecca Torrellas, Editor;
Secretariat for Finance - t) 713-659-5461 Aad De Lange, Dir.;
Accounting Department - Rose Michalec, Controller;
Claims Risk Manager - t) 800-228-6108; 713-652-4469
Development Office - Michael Schillaci, Dir.;
Insurance & Risk Manager - J. Kirk Jenings;
Parish Accounting Services (PAS) - Margaret Woodrum, Dir.;
Secretariat for Pastoral and Educational Ministries - t) 713-741-8786 Jim Barrette, Dir.;
Adolescent Catechesis and Evangelization - t) 713-741-8723 Tim Colbert, Dir.;
Aging Ministry - t) 713-741-8712 Mark Ciesielski, Dir.;
Boy and Girl Scouts - Rev. Patrick Stuart Garrett;
Campus Ministry and Young Adults - t) 713-741-8780 Angela Pometto, Dir.;
Circle Lake Retreat Center - t) 281-356-6764 Ricardo Medina, Dir.;
Deaf Apostolate - t) 713-741-8721 Rev. Leonard R. Broniak, C.Ss.R., Dir.;
Evangelization and Catechesis - t) 713-741-8796 Julie Blevins, Dir.;
Family Life Ministry - t) 713-741-8710 Ricardo Medina, Dir.;
Pro-Life Activities - t) 713-741-8728 Julie Fritsch, Dir.;
Resource Center - t) 713-741-8781 Richard Lowell, Dir.;
Special Youth Services (Juvenile Detention Ministry) - t) 713-741-8725 Franchelle Lee, Dir.;
Worship - t) 713-741-8760
Secretariat for Social Concerns - t) 713-741-8769 Sr. Maureen O'Connell, O.P., Dir.;
Campaign for Human Development - Sr. Maureen O'Connell, O.P., Dir.;
Catholic Charities of the Archdiocese of Galveston-Houston - t) 713-526-4611 Cynthia Nunes Colbert, Pres.;
Chief Operating Officer - t) 713-874-6713 Bart Ferrell;
Communications - t) 713-874-6751 Betsy Ballard;
Galveston County Center - Elizabeth Kinard, Dir.; Norma Roche, Coord. Galveston; Annie Cazares, Coord. Texas City;
Mamie George Community Center/Fort Bend County - t) 281-202-6200 Gladys Brumfield-James, Dir.;
Refugee Resettlement Services - t) 713-874-6516 Ardiane Ademi;
St. Frances Cabrini Center for Immigrant Legal Assistance - t) 713-874-4145 Tammy Casey;
St. Jerome Emiliani's Home for Children - t) 713-874-6301 Chanica Brown;
St. Michael's Homes for Children - Sergio Cruz;
Senior Vice President of Programs - t) 713-874-6731 Natalie Wood, Vice. Pres.;
Vice President of Case Management and Poverty Alleviation - t) 713-874-6772 Shannon Strother, Vice. Pres.;
Vice President of Development & Stewardship - t) 713-874-6624 Brian Gillen;
Council of Catholic Women - t) 713-468-9555 Rev. Msgr. Daniel L. Scheel, Archdiocesan Moderator;
Cursillos in Christianity - t) 713-643-7682 Tin Ngo, Admin.; Rev. Eugene Canas, O.M.I., Dir.;
Disaster Relief - J. Kirk Jenings;
Justice and Peace - Sr. Maureen O'Connell, O.P., Dir.;
Rural Life Bureau (Vacant) -
***St. Vincent de Paul Society** - t) 832-538-0326 Ann Schorno, Exec.;
Victim Assistance Coordinator - t) 713-659-5461 x499; 713-654-5799 vac@archgh.org Diane Vines;

PARISHES, MISSIONS, AND CLERGY

STATE OF TEXAS

ALVIN

St. John the Baptist - 110 E. South St., Alvin, TX 77511-3570 t) 281-331-3751; 281-824-0877 (CCE) stjohns110@gmail.com stjohnalvin.org Rev. John Kare Taosan, Pst.; Dcn. David Bowman; Dcn. Allen James Stanton; CRP Stds.: 373

ANDERSON

St. Stanislaus - 1511 Hwy. 90 S., Anderson, TX 77830-0210; Mailing: P O Box 210, Anderson, TX 77830 t) 936-873-2291 ststan@embarqmail.com www.saintstans.org Rev. Giovanni Nguyen, Pst.; Dcn. Grant E. Holt; Dcn. Garry Janota; Dcn. Russell Pasket; Kirby Borski, DRE; CRP Stds.: 132

ANGLETON

Most Holy Trinity Catholic Church - 1713 N. Tinsley St., Angleton, TX 77515-3551 t) 979-849-2421 ccang@mhtangleton.org www.mhtangleton.org Rev. Khoi Le, Pst.; Dcn. Luis G. Hernandez; Dcn. Robert Ward; Cheryl Scott, Pst. Assoc.;

BARRETT STATION

St. Martin de Porres - 12606 Crosby-Lynchburg Rd., Barrett Station, TX 77532-8628 t) 281-328-4451; 281-691-4424 (CRP) Rev. Anthony Mbanefo, MSP, Pst.; Dcn. Martin Lemond; Mary Ligons, DRE;

BAYTOWN

St. John the Evangelist - 800 W. Baker Rd., Baytown, TX 77521-2311 t) 281-837-8180 a.medina@stjohnbaytown.org; office@stjohnbaytown.org stjohnbaytown.org Rev. Terence P. Brinkman, Pst.; Dcn. Mike Rodriguez; CRP Stds.: 150

St. Joseph - 1907 Carolina St., Baytown, TX 77520-6098

t) 281-420-3588 stjosephbaytown.org Rev. Yong Hyuk Lee, Pst.; Kristina Sommer, DRE; CRP Stds.: 60

St. Joseph School - 1811 Carolina St., Baytown, TX 77520-6099 t) 281-422-9749 c.carrizales@sjsbaytown.org www.stjosephbaytown.com Deborah Francis, Prin.;

Our Lady of Guadalupe - 1124 Beech St., Baytown, TX 77520-4143 t) 281-427-0810 (CRP); 281-428-1506; 281-428-1507 olg.baytown@yahoo.com www.olgbaytown.org Dcn. Fernando Gonzalez Bangs; Dcn. Samuel Martinez; Dcn. George Rincon; Dcn. Rudy Venegas; CRP Stds.: 680

BEASLEY

St. Wenceslaus Mission - 407 S. 3rd St., Beasley, TX 77417; Mailing: 1416 George St., Rosenberg, TX 77471 t) 281-342-3089 office@hrccr.com www.hrccr.com/st-wenceslaus Rev. Orrin Halepeska, Pst.; Rev. Vipin George, MSFS (India), Par. Vicar; Dcn. Carlito Buhay; Dcn. Jason Sulak; CRP Stds.: 13

BELLVILLE

Sts. Peter & Paul - 936 S. Front St., Bellville, TX 77418-0176; Mailing: PO Box 808, Bellville, TX 77418 t) 979-865-2368 stspandp@sbcglobal.net stsppbellvilletx.org/ Rev. Joseph A. Doran, Pst.; Dcn. Gerald W. DuPont; Kimberly Story, DRE; Cynthia Luongo, Youth Min.; David Montonati, Bus. Mgr.; CRP Stds.: 213

Immaculate Conception Catholic Church - 15994 Hwy. 159 W., Industry, TX 78944 t) (979) 865-2368 stsppbellvilletx.org/parish-imformation Heather Gross, DRE;

BRAZORIA

St. Joseph on the Brazos - 219 Country Rd. 762, Brazoria, TX 77422-7621 t) 979-798-4702 (CRP); 979-798-2288 Rev. Tin Cosmas Kim Pham, Pst.; Dcn. Jimmy Smith; Dcn. Jimmy T. Smith, DRE;

CHANNELVIEW

St. Andrew - 827 Sheldon Rd., Channelview, TX 77530-3511 t) 281-452-9865 standrew7067@comcast.net www.standrewchurch.net Rev. Christopher Shackelford, Pst.; Dcn. Javier Gomez; Dcn. Michael Muench; Ninfa Muench, DRE; Stephanie Ruiz Halleck, Youth Min.; CRP Stds.: 398

CLUTE

St. Jerome - 201 N. Lazy Ln., Clute, TX 77531-4001 t) 979-265-5179 Rev. James F. Lynes Jr., Pst.; Dcn. Agustin Cruz; Dina A. Tonche, DRE;

CONROE

Sacred Heart - 109 N. Frazier St., Conroe, TX 77301-2802; Mailing: 704 Old Montgomery Rd., Conroe, TX 77301 t) 936-756-8186 parishoffice@shconroe.org www.shconroe.org Rev. Philip A. Wilhite, Pst.; Rev. Joseph Manapuram, Par. Vicar; Rev. Jacob Ramirez, Par. Vicar; Dcn. Richard Lopez; Dcn. Alejandro Padilla; Dcn. Eddy Valbuena; CRP Stds.: 872

Sacred Heart School - 615 McDade St., Conroe, TX 77301-2758 t) 936-756-3848 dbrown@shconroe.org Deborah Brown, Prin.;

CROSBY

Sacred Heart - 915 Runneburg Rd., Crosby, TX 77532-5826 t) 281-328-4871 x10 parishoffice@shcrosby.org shcrosby.org Rev. Emmanuel Akpaidem, Admin.; Dcn. Pete Melancon; CRP Stds.: 180

Sacred Heart School - 907 Runneberg Rd., Crosby, TX 77532 t) 281-328-6561 sharris@sacredheartschoolcrosby.org Susan Harris, Prin.;

DAMON

Sts. Cyril and Methodius - 603 Parrott Ave., Damon, TX 77430-0309; Mailing: P.O. Box 309, Damon, TX 77430 t) 979-742-3383 c) 832-595-4963 patsystcyril@consolidated.net; patsypekar@gmail.com needvillecatholic.com Rev. Marty Pham, Pst.;

DANBURY

St. Anthony de Padua - 1523 Main St., Danbury, TX 77534-6004; Mailing: P.O. Box 299, Danbury, TX 77534 t) 979-922-1240; 979-922-1241 (CRP)

st1523@sbcglobal.net www.saopdtx.org Rev. Arnel B. Barrameda, Pst.; Dcn. Gerald Peltier; Monica Sebesta, DRE; CRP Stds.: 78

DEER PARK

St. Hyacinth - 2921 Center St., Deer Park, TX 77536-4997 t) 281-479-4298 info@sthyacinth.org sthyacinth.org Rev. Reginald W. Samuels, Pst.; Dcn. Charles Pitman; Dcn. John Rapacki, Admin.;

DICKINSON

Shrine of the True Cross - 300 FM 517 Rd. E., Dickinson, TX 77539 t) 281-337-4112 info@truecrosschurch.org www.truecrosschurch.org Rev. Lawrence C. Wilson, Pst.; Dcn. Robert George Alexander; Dcn. Raymundo Luna; Dcn. Pascual Velazquez; CRP Stds.: 213

Shrine of the True Cross School - (Grades PreK-8) 400 FM 517 E., Dickinson, TX 77539 t) 281-337-5212 yagrella@truecrosschurch.org www.truecrossschool.org Yolanda Agrella, Prin.; Stds.: 113; Lay Tchrs.: 16

FREEPORT

St. Mary: Star of the Sea - 1019 W. 6th St., Freeport, TX 77541-5423 t) 979-233-5271 secretary@stmarystarofthesea.org; pastor@stmarystarofthesea.org stmarystarofthesea.org Rev. Sebastine Okoye, Pst.; Dcn. Felipe Garza; Dcn. Wallace Shaw; Becki Pena, RCIA Coord.; CRP Stds.: 100

FRIENDSWOOD

Mary Queen Catholic Church - 606 Cedarwood Dr., Friendswood, TX 77546-4551 t) 281-482-1391 www.maryqueencatholicchurch.org Rev. James H. Kuczynski, M.S., Pst.; Rev. Sibi Kunninu, M.S., Par. Vicar; Dcn. Derick Soares; Dcn. Darrell Moulton; Dcn. Paul Robinson; Dcn. Charles Turner; CRP Stds.: 600

FRYDEK

St. Mary - 10471 Grotto Rd., Frydek, TX 77474-9055 t) 979-885-3131 stmary@twlt.net www.stmarysfrydek.org Rev. Thuy Quang Nguyen, Pst.; Dcn. Paul Franek; Dcn. Jerome D. Losack Sr.; Sarah Blundell, DRE; CRP Stds.: 100

FULSHEAR

St. Faustina Catholic Church - 28102 FM 1093, Fulshear, TX 77441 t) 346-773-3500; 346-773-3442 (CRP) info@saintfaustinachurch.org saintfaustinachurch.org Rev. Dat Hoang, Pst.; Rev. Christopher Meyer I, Par. Vicar; Brian Lennox, DRE; Dcn. Ernesto Abadejos; Dcn. Randy Graham; CRP Stds.: 1,614

GALENA PARK

Our Lady of Fatima - 1705 8th St., Galena Park, TX 77547-2924 t) 713-675-0981 info@olfparishgp.org www.olfparishgp.org Rev. Justin Cormie, Pst.; CRP Stds.: 360

Our Lady of Fatima School - (Grades PreSchool-7) 1702 Ninth St., Galena Park, TX 77547 t) 713-674-5832 kpham@olfatima-gp.org Khanh Pham, Prin.;

GALVESTON

St. Mary's Cathedral Basilica - 2011 Church St., Galveston, TX 77550-2091; Mailing: 1010 35th St., Galveston, TX 77550 t) 409-762-9646 secretaryhfp@gmail.com holyfamilygb.com Rev. Jude E. Ezuma, Rector; Rev. Chad Henry, Par. Vicar; Rev. Stephen J. Payne, Par. Vicar;

Holy Family - 1010 35th St., Galveston, TX 77550 t) 409-762-9646 theofficehfp@gmail.com www.holyfamilygb.com Rev. Jude E. Ezuma, Pst.; Rev. Chad Henry, Par. Vicar; Rev. Stephen J. Payne, Par. Vicar; Dcn. Sam Dell'Olio; Dcn. Douglas Matthews; Dcn. Kimble Nobles; Dcn. John Pistone; Dcn. Robert Standridge; Dcn. Jeff Willard; CRP Stds.: 186

Holy Family School - 2601 Ursuline Ave., Galveston, TX 77550 t) 409-765-6607 Rita Hesse, Prin.;

HEMPSTEAD

St. Katharine Drexel - 800 F.M. 1488 Rd., Hempstead, TX 77445-1700 t) 979-826-2275 info@skdcc.com www.skdcc.com Rev. Xavier Bilavendiran, Pst.; Marina Vasquez, Youth Min.; Norma Salinas, DRE;

HIGHLANDS

St. Jude Thaddeus - 800 S. Main St., Highlands, TX 77562-4236 t) 281-843-2422 sjudebus@comcast.net; sjudedre@comcast.net Rev. Daniel S. Baguio, Pst.; Maribel Chavez, Bus. Mgr.; CRP Stds.: 75

HITCHCOCK

Our Lady of Lourdes - 10114 Hwy. 6, Hitchcock, TX 77563-4515 t) 409-925-3579 ppersad@ololchurch.org www.ololchurch.org Rev. David G. Harris, Pst.; Dcn. Alvin Lovelady; Raquel Hinojosa, DRE; Alecia Lemelle, RCIA Coord.; Mike Comeaux, Music Min.; CRP Stds.: 178

Our Lady of Lourdes School - (Grades PreSchool-8) t) 409-925-3224 erobert@ololchurch.org ololcs.org Dr. Emilie Robert, Prin.; Stds.: 65; Scholastics: 5; Lay Tchrs.: 14

HOUSTON

Co-Cathedral of the Sacred Heart - 1111 St. Joseph Pkwy., Houston, TX 77002-8127 t) 713-659-1561 www.sacredhearthouston.org Rev. Jeffrey Bame, Pst.; Rev. Steven Son Tran, Par. Vicar; Dcn. John Carrara; Dcn. Jose M. Galvan; Dcn. Joseph J Millhouse; Dcn. Gil Vela; Steffani Aquila, Dir.; Mary Caprio, Dir.;

St. Albert of Trapani - 11027 S. Gessner Dr., Houston, TX 77071-3599 t) 713-771-3596 secretary@stalberthouston.org; mpeguero@stalberthouston.org www.stalbertoftrapani.org Rev. Vincent Vu Tran, Pst.; Dcn. Edwin F. Gosline; Dcn. Vicente Serrano; Dcn. Pedro Salas; Peggy Popkey, DRE;

All Saints - 215 E. 10th St., Houston, TX 77008-7025 t) 713-864-2653 fr.eli.lopez@allsaintscatholic.us www.allsaintsheights.com Rev. Elias Lopez, Pst.; Rev. Leon Strieder, In Res.;

St. Alphonsus - 9217 E. Ave. L, Houston, TX 77012-2727 t) 713-923-5843 Rev. Carlos V. de la Torre, Pst.; Mary Elizondo, DRE;

St. Ambrose - 4213 Mangum Rd., Houston, TX 77092-5599 t) 713-686-3497 gvalencia@stambrosehouston.org www.stambrosehouston.org Rev. Hieu Nguyen, Pst.; Rev. Joseph Tu Dinh, Par. Vicar; CRP Stds.: 352

St. Ambrose School - (Grades PreK-8) t) 713-686-6990 kpham@sashornets.org Khanh Pham, Prin.;

St. Andrew Kim - 1706 Bingle Rd., Houston, TX 77055-2336 t) 713-465-2682 standrewkimhouston@yahoo.com stakim.org Rev. Bong Ho Peter Ko, Pst.; CRP Stds.: 92

St. Anne - 2140 Westheimer, Houston, TX 77098-1419 t) 713-526-3276; 713-525-4273 (CRP) www.saintanne.org Rev. David J. Zapalac, C.S.B., Pst.; Rev. Eduardo Rivera, Par. Vicar; Dcn. Jean-Paul Budinger; Dcn. Thaddeus Kudela; Dcn. Jose Antonio Saucedo; CRP Stds.: 342

St. Anne School - 2120 Westheimer, Houston, TX 77098 t) 713-526-3279 dmartinez@stannecs.org Dawn Martinez, Prin.;

St. Anne de Beaupre - 2810 Link Rd., Houston, TX 77009-1196 t) 713-869-1319 Rev. Emmanuel Mbuk, Pst.;

Ascension Chinese Mission - 4605 Jetty Ln., Houston, TX 77072-1222 t) 281-575-8855 webmaster@ascensionchinesemission.org www.ascensionchinesemission.org Rev. Roger Shu-Xin Zhang, Pst.; Dcn. Benny Chang; Dcn. Paul Kiang; Bonnie Lee, DRE; CRP Stds.: 40

Assumption - 901 Rose Ln., Houston, TX 77037-4699 t) 281-445-1268 (CRP); 281-447-6381 acchurch@assumptionhouston.org www.assumptionhouston.org Rev. Osas A. Onaiwu, CRS, Admin.; Rev. Giulio Veronesi, S.J.E., Vicar; Dcn. Will Hunter; Dcn. Mario Ortega, DRE;

Assumption School - 801 Rose Ln., Houston, TX 77037 t) 281-447-2132 dpalomino@houstonassumption.org; jbates@houstonassumption.org John William Bates, Prin.;

St. Augustine - 5560 Laurel Creek Way, Houston, TX

77017-6746; Mailing: 5438 Laurel Creek Way, Houston, TX 77017 t) 713-946-8968 reception@staugustinecc.com www.staugustinecc.org Rev. Paul A. Foltyn, Pst.; Dcn. Benito Meza; Diana Ramirez, DRE; CRP Stds.: 157

St. Augustine School - (Grades PreK-8) 5500 Laurel Creek Way, Houston, TX 77017 t) 713-946-9050 tsanchez@staugustinecs.org www.staugustinecs.org Tracy Sanchez, Prin.;

St. Benedict the Abbot - 4025 Grapevine St., Houston, TX 77045-6320 t) 713-433-9836 stbenedictabbotcc@sbcglobal.net www.sbahouston.org Rev. Brandon Bay Nguyen, C.S.Sp., Pst.; Rev. Huy Quang Dinh, C.S.Sp., Par. Vicar; Dcn. David Johnson, DRE;

St. Bernadette Soubirous - 15500 El Camino Real, Houston, TX 77062-5793 t) 281-486-0337 office@stbchurch.org; honeycuttj@stbchurch.org www.stbchurch.org Rev. Robert S. Barras, Pst.; Dcn. Kevin Woodvine; Jason Honeycutt, Dir., Adult Faith Formation; CRP Stds.: 406

Blessed Sacrament - 4015 Sherman St., Houston, TX 77003-2695 t) 713-224-5291 office@bsccarchgh.org bsccarchgh.org Rev. Edmund P. Eduarte, Pst.;

St. Catherine of Siena - 10688 Shadow Wood Dr., Houston, TX 77043-2826 t) 713-467-8170 stcatherine-houston.org Rev. Niall Nolan, Pst.; Nicole Fair, Music Min.; Cathy Busald, DRE; CRP Stds.: 45

St. Cecilia - 11720 Joan of Arc Dr., Houston, TX 77024-2602 t) 713-465-3414 pastor@saintcecilia.org www.saintcecilia.org Rev. Francis M. Macatangay, Pst.; Rev. Michael A. Barrosa, Par. Vicar; Rev. Donald S. Nesti, C.S.Sp., In Res.; Dcn. Gregory Evans; Dcn. Sam Mancuso; Dcn. Jose Romay; CRP Stds.: 698

St. Cecilia School - (Grades PreK-8) 11740 Joan of Arc Dr., Houston, TX 77024 t) 713-468-9515 jmatthews@saintcecilia.org www.saintceciliacatholicschool.org Jeff Matthews, Prin.; Stds.: 611; Sr. Tchrs.: 1; Lay Tchrs.: 43

St. Charles Borromeo - 501 Tidwell, Houston, TX 77022-2121 t) 832-297-1315 (CRP); 713-692-6303 stcharleshouston.org Rev. Jesus Lizalde, Pst.; Dcn. Thomas Gandara; Rev. Antonio Cisneros-Luna, Par. Vicar; CRP Stds.: 345

Christ the King - 4419 N. Main St., Houston, TX 77009-5199 t) 832-338-3867 (CRP); 713-869-1449 ocoord@ctkcc.org; varkeycrs@hotmail.com www.ctkcc.org Rev. Julian Gerosa, C.R.S., Pst.; Rev. Varghese Arattukulam, Assoc. Pst.; Dcn. Tomas Cano, DRE; CRP Stds.: 255

Christ the Redeemer - 11507 Huffmeister Rd., Houston, TX 77065-1051 t) 281-469-5533 office@ctrcc.com www.ctrcc.com Rev. Sean P. Horrigan, Pst.; Rev. Vincent Vu Tran, Assoc. Pst.; Dcn. Kerry Bourque; Dcn. William Bradley; Dcn. Phillip Jackson; Dcn. Stephen Moses; Dcn. Jeff Speight; Dcn. David Carrasco; Dcn. Michael Jones; Dcn. Daniel Ruvalcaba; Dcn. Jack Alexander; Dcn. Lupe Trevino; Linda Watso, DRE; CRP Stds.: 2,050

Christ the Redeemer Catholic School - 11511 Huffmeister Rd., Houston, TX 77065 t) 281-469-8440 dan.courtney@ctrschool.com Dan Courtney, Prin.;

Christ, The Incarnate Word - 8503 S. Kirkwood Rd., Houston, TX 77099-4056 t) 281-495-8133 info@giaoxungoiloi.org www.giaoxungoiloi.org Rev. Thu Ngoc Nguyen, Pst.; Rev. Joseph T.P. Bui, Par. Vicar; Hien Le, DRE; Dcn. Harry Hung Pham; Bich Ngoc Nguyen, Prin.; CRP Stds.: 647

St. Christopher - 8150 Park Place Blvd., Houston, TX 77017-3033 t) 713-645-6142 (CRP); 713-645-6614 dtorres@stchristopherhouston.org www.stchristopherhouston.org Rev. Joseph Thu Le, Pst.; Rev. Gregory Cheo Ngwa, Par. Vicar; Dcn. Don Q. Hoang; Dcn. Benito Tristan; Nereida Medrano, DRE; CRP Stds.: 184

St. Christopher School - 8134 Park Place Blvd., Houston, TX 77017 t) 713-649-0009 principal@sccs1939.org www.sccs1939.org JoAnn Prater, Prin.;

St. Clare of Assisi - 3131 El Dorado Blvd., Houston, TX 77059-5100 t) 281-286-7729 www.stclarehouston.org Rev. Vincent Vuong-Quoc Nguyen, Pst.; Dcn. Robert Hebert; Dcn. Jose Trevino; Sandra Trevino, DRE; CRP Stds.: 100

St. Clare of Assisi School - t) 281-286-3395 al.varisco@stclarehouston.org Al Varisco, Prin.;

Corpus Christi - 9900 Stella Link Rd., Houston, TX 77025-4718 t) 713-667-0497 pastor@ccparishhouston.org ccparishhuston.org Rev. Thomas Smithson, SSS, Pst.; Rev. RaviEarnest Sebastin, SSS, Par. Vicar; Rev. Peter Tuong, SSS, Chap.; Christi Ayo, Pst. Assoc.; Claudia Sereno, DRE; Hilda Morales, CRE; Connie Rodriguez, CRE; Joseph Patrick, Music and Liturgy Dir.;

Corpus Christi School - 4005 Cheena St., Houston, TX 77025 t) 713-664-3351 www.corpuschristihouston.org Mazie McCoy, Prin.;

St. Cyril of Alexandria - 10503 Westheimer Rd., Houston, TX 77042-3502 t) 713-789-1250 stcyrilhouston.org/ Rev. Mario J. Arroyo, Pst.; Dcn. Eduardo M. Dolpher; Dcn. Arturo Mendoza; Sr. Rosalie Karstedt, C.D.P., Admin.; Beatriz Green, DRE; Sandra Russell, Admin.; CRP Stds.: 345

St. Dominic - 8215 Reservoir St., Houston, TX 77049-1728 t) 281-458-2910 www.stdominichouston.org Rev. Roger O. Estorque, Pst.; Rosana Gonzalez, DRE; Ana Martinez, DRE; Irma Galvan, Bus. Mgr.; CRP Stds.: 624

St. Elizabeth Ann Seton - 6646 Addicks-Satsuma Rd., Houston, TX 77084-1599 t) 281-463-7878 seasoffice@seascatholic.org; office@seascatholic.org www.seascatholic.org Rev. Stephen B. Reynolds, Pst.; Rev. Thomas Vu, CRM, Par. Vicar; Rev. Jose Alonso, Par. Vicar; Rev. Innocent Okhifo, Par. Vicar; Dcn. German Godoy, Pst. Assoc.; Dcn. Tom Jeffers; Dcn. Charles G. Pennell; Dcn. Heleodoro Rendon; CRP Stds.: 1,083

St. Elizabeth Ann Seton School - t) 281-463-1444 iaguilera@seascs.org Ignacio Aguilera, Prin.;

St. Frances Cabrini - 10727 Hartsook St., Houston, TX 77034-3523 t) 713-946-5768 nicolas.ramirez@cabrinihouston.org; isabel.rodriguez@cabrinihouston.org cabrinihouston.org Rev. Nicolas Ramirez, Pst.; Rev. Chacko Puthumayil, In Res.; Dcn. Freddy Ramirez, Bus. Mgr.; Dcn. Guadalupe Sanchez; CRP Stds.: 651

St. Francis de Sales - 8200 Roos Rd., Houston, TX 77036-6399 t) 713-774-7475 office@sfds-houston.org www.sfds-houston.org Rev. Joseph Son Thanh Phan, Pst.; Rev. Enrique V. Salen, In Res.; Dcn. Alberto Ospina; Dcn. Michael Quiray; Yolanda Salazar, DRE; CRP Stds.: 300

St. Francis de Sales School - (Grades PreK-8) 8100 Roos Rd., Houston, TX 77036 t) 713-774-4447 quatrinia@sfdsschool.org Anne Quatrini, Prin.;

St. Francis of Assisi - 5102 Dabney St., Houston, TX 77026-3015 t) 713-672-7773 stfrancisofassisihouston@gmail.com www.stfrancisofhouston.org Rev. Martin Eke, Pst.; Dcn. John Goodly; Dcn. Ignatius Joseph; Dcn. Michael St. Julian; Jamie Williams, DRE; CRP Stds.: 12

St. Francis Xavier - 4600 Reed Rd., Houston, TX 77051-2857 t) 713-738-2311; 713-731-2775 (CRP) stfrancishou@sfxhouston.com www.sfxhouston.com Rev. Michael Saah-Buckman, S.S.J., Pst.; Dcn. Michael V. Jenkins; Unella Baber, DRE;

St. Gregory the Great - 10500 Nold Dr., Houston, TX 77016-2921 t) 713-631-3681 stgregoryhouston@gmail.com www.stgregorygcc.com Rev. Noel Effiong, MSP, Pst.; Dcn. Rolando Rodriguez; Dr. Pertha Collette, DRE;

Holy Cross Chapel - 905 Main St., Houston, TX 77002-6408 t) 713-650-1323 info@holycrosschapel.org www.holycrosschapel.org Rev. Francisco Vera, Pst.;

Chapel -

Holy Ghost - 6921 Chetwood Dr., Houston, TX 77081-5697 t) 713-668-0463 office@holyghostchurch.net holyghostchurch.net Rev. William C. Bueche, C.Ss.R., Pst.; Rev. Andrew Meiners, C.Ss.R., Par. Vicar; Rev. Binh Ta, C.Ss.R., Par. Vicar; Rev. Leonard R. Broniak, C.Ss.R., Deaf Ministry; Bro. Clement J. Furno, C.Ss.R., Pst. Assoc.; Rev. Chuong Cao, C.Ss.R., In Res.; Rev. Peter H. Voelker, C.Ss.R., In Res.;

Holy Ghost School - 6920 Chimney Rock Rd., Houston, TX 77081 t) 713-668-5327 mendez@holyghostschool.com Christina Mendez, Prin.;

Holy Name - 1920 Marion St., Houston, TX 77009-8497; Mailing: 1917 Cochran St, Houston, TX 77009 t) 713-222-1255; 832-623-6180 (CRP) holynamehouston@gmail.com holynamecatholichouston.org/ Rev. Cocou Cyriaque Sounou, SVD, Pst.; Alicia Aviles, DRE;

Holy Rosary - 3601 Milam St., Houston, TX 77002-9591 t) 713-526-4389 (CRP); 713-529-4854 office@holyrosaryparish.org www.holyrosaryparish.org Friar Martin J. Gleeson, O.P., Pst.; Friar Peter Damian Harris, OP, Par. Vicar; Friar Nicholas Reynolds, O.P., Par. Vicar; Friar Martin Iott, O.P., In Res.; Friar Alberto Rodriguez Lopez, O.P., In Res.; Friar Juan M. Torres, OP, In Res.; Friar Anthony Hung N. Tran, O.P., In Res.; Friar Charles K. Johnson, OP, Campus Min.; Janet Hafernik, DRE;

Immaculate Conception - 7250 Harrisburg Blvd., Houston, TX 77011-4791 t) 713-921-1226 (CRP); 713-921-1261 rrodriguez@icchouston.church; tmartinez@icchouston.church www.icchouston.church Rev. Henry B. Walker, O.M.I., Pst.; Rev. Porfirio Garcia, Vicar; Rev. Salvatore DeGeorge, O.M.I., In Res.; Rev. Marco Antonio Ortiz, O.M.I., In Res.; Teresa Martinez, DRE; CRP Stds.: 344

Immaculate Heart of Mary - 7539 Ave. K, Houston, TX 77012-1033 t) 713-921-5431 (CRP); 713-923-2394 ihmhouston@hotmail.com immaculateheartofmary.org Rev. Timothy Paulsen, O.M.I., Pst.; Dcn. Martin Pena; Valerie Ponce, DRE; CRP Stds.: 222

St. Jerome - 8825 Kempwood, Houston, TX 77080-4199 t) 713-468-9555; (713) 464-5029 x203 (CCE) church@stjeromehou.org www.stjeromehou.org Rev. Rafael Becerra, C.S., Pst.; Rev. Alfonso Tran, Assoc. Pst.; Dcn. Jose Guadalupe Montoya Sr.; Dcn. Dan O'Dowd; Joel E Hernandez, Bus. Mgr.; Johana Ferro, DRE; CRP Stds.: 850

St. Jerome School - t) 713-468-7946 jkrametbauer@stjeromecs.org www.stjeromecs.org Jan Krametbauer, Prin.; Stds.: 149; Sr. Tchrs.: 1; Lay Tchrs.: 15

St. John Neumann - 2730 Nelwood Dr., Houston, TX 77038-1025 t) 281-931-1884 (CRP); 281-931-0684 www.sjnhouston.org Rev. Clair Antonio Orso, C.S., Pst.; Rev. Minh Nguyen, c.s., Par. Vicar; Blanca Dolpher, DRE; CRP Stds.: 610

St. John Vianney - 625 Nottingham Oaks Trail, Houston, TX 77079-6234 t) 281-497-1500 sjv@stjohnvianney.org www.stjohnvianney.org Rev. R. Troy Gately, Pst.; Rev. Joseph White, Par. Vicar; Dcn. Dale W. Steffes; Dcn. Gregory Stokes; Dcn. Albert E. Vacek Jr.; Rev. Charles J. Talar, In Res.; CRP Stds.: 1,195

St. Joseph Church - 1505 Kane St., Houston, TX 77007-7711 t) 713-222-6193 x31 (Reception) office@saintjoseph.org www.saintjoseph.org Rev. Victor C. Perez, Pst.; Dcn. Glen Pennell; CRP Stds.: 180

St. Justin Martyr - 13350 Ashford Point Dr., Houston, TX 77082-5100 t) 281-556-5116 sjm@sjmtx.com www.sjmtx.org Rev. Paul R. Chovanec, Pst.; Dcn. Cornelius C. Llorens; Dcn. Sean M. Nguyen; Rev. Joseph Phong Nguyen, Par. Vicar; CRP Stds.: 200

St. Leo the Great - 2131 Lauder Rd., Houston, TX 77039-3199 t) 281-449-2344 info@stleohouston.org; cceinfo@stleohouston.org www.stleohouston.org Rev. Jose Carmen Hernandez-Angulo, C.S., Pst.; Rev. Joseph Hieu The Nguyen, C.S., Par. Vicar; CRP Stds.: 246

St. Luke the Evangelist - 11011 Hall Rd., Houston, TX 77089-2999 t) 281-481-6816 information@stlukescatholic.com www.stlukescatholic.com Rev. Douglas J. Guthrie, Pst.; Rev. Kingsley Nwoko, Par. Vicar; Dcn. Adolfo Mejia;

Dcn. John Rapacki; Dcn. Jesse Tollett; Ben Hernandez, DRE; CRP Stds.: 266

St. Mark the Evangelist - 5430 W. Ridgecreek Dr., Houston, TX 77053-3211 t) 281-416-0186 (CRP); 281-437-9114 agarcia@stmarkshouston.org; admin@stmarkshouston.org www.stmarkshouston.org Rev. Oscar M. Castro, Pst.; Dcn. John Benoit; Dcn. Jorge Garcia; Dcn. Ramiro Silverio; Dcn. Miguel Zavala;

St. Mary of the Purification - 3006 Rosedale, Houston, TX 77004-6128 t) 713-528-0571 churchoffice@stmaryshouston.org; stmarysdre@stmaryshouston.org stmaryshouston.net Rev. Jaison Mangalath, SVD, Pst.; Rev. Francis Tri Tran, SVD, Par. Vicar; Dcn. Glen Pratt Sr.; Dcn. Andrew B. Malveaux Sr.; Valerie Harrison, DRE; CRP Stds.: 78

St. Mary of the Purification School - (Grades PreK-8) 3002 Rosedale, Houston, TX 77004 t) 713-522-9276 lgoudeau@stmaryshoustonschool.org stmaryshouston.net/school Lois Goudeau, Prin.;

St. Matthew the Evangelist - 9915 Hollister St., Houston, TX 77040-1702 t) 713-466-0510 (CRP); 713-466-4030 www.stmatthewhou.org Rev. Martial F. Oya, Pst.; Dcn. John W. Adams; Dcn. Thomas Piotrowski; Dcn. Thomas Whited; Francisco Fajardo, DRE; CRP Stds.: 371

St. Maximilian Kolbe - 10135 West Rd., Houston, TX 77064-5361 t) 281-955-7324 www.stmaximilian.org Rev. Lawrence W. Jozwiak, Pst.; Dcn. Dennis Hayes; Dcn. Joseph Steven Klak; Dcn. John Naber; Dcn. Matthew Rust; Dcn. Joseph Weir; CRP Stds.: 260

St. Michael - 1801 Sage Rd., Houston, TX 77056-3502 t) 713-621-4370 business@stmichaelchurch.net stmichaelchurch.net Rev. Wayne W. Wilkerson, Pst.; Rev. Thomas F. Rafferty, In Res.;

St. Michael School - 1833 Sage Rd., Houston, TX 77056-3502 t) 713-621-6847 kcox@stmichaelcs.org Kathleen Cox, Prin.;

St. Monica - 8421 W. Montgomery Rd., Houston, TX 77088-7116 t) 281-447-5837; 281-445-0334 (CCE) marilyn@stmonicahouston.com stmonicahouston.com Rev. Martins Emeh, Admin.; Dcn. John Lane, Pst. Assoc.; Dcn. Luis G. Hernandez; Irma L Navarro, DRE; CRP Stds.: 52

St. Nicholas - 2508 Clay St., Houston, TX 77003-4406 t) 713-223-5210 www..stnicholashouston.org Rev. Eliseus Ibeh, M.S.P., Pst.; CRP Stds.: 70

Notre Dame - 7720 Boone Rd., Houston, TX 77072-3595 t) 281-498-4653; 281-495-1256 (CCE Office) pastor@ndgh.org www.ndgh.org Rev. Angel Vincente Agila, Pst.; Blanca Plasencia, DRE; Dcn. Ernesto Abadejos; Dcn. Elie P. Calonge; Dcn. Anthony Olsovsky; Dcn. F.L. Ostrowski; CRP Stds.: 252

Our Lady of Czestochowa - 1712 Oak Tree Dr., Houston, TX 77080 t) 713-973-1081 proboszcz@parafiahouston.com www.parafiahouston.com Rev. Tadeusz Rusnak, Pst.; CRP Stds.: 95

Our Lady of Guadalupe - 2405 Navigation Blvd., Houston, TX 77003-1510 t) 713-222-0203 x113 (CRP); 713-222-0203 parish@olghouston.org www.olghouston.org Rev. Wojciech Adamczyk, Pst.; Rev. Jerzy Mordalski, S.C.J., Assoc. Pst.; Rev. Rafael Querobin, SCJ, Assoc. Pst.; Sr. Aida Ramirez, DRE; Bro. Andy Gancarczyk, S.C.J., Supr.;

Our Lady of Guadalupe School - t) 713-224-6904 iortiz@olgschoolhouston.org Irazema Ortiz, Prin.;

Our Lady of Lavang Church - 12401 Old Foltin Rd., Houston, TX 77086-3514; Mailing: 12320 Old Foltin Rd., Houston, TX 77086 t) 281-999-1672 lavangparishhouston@gmail.com www.lavangchurch.org Rev. Thomas Thien-An Tran, O.P., Pst.; Rev. Paul Hai Dang Nguyen, O.P., Par. Vicar; Rev. Liem Trung Tran, O.P., Par. Vicar; CRP Stds.: 950

Our Lady of Lourdes - 6550 Fairbanks N. Houston, Houston, TX 77040-4307 t) 713-939-1906 www.loduc.org Rev. Huy The Trinh, O.P., Pst.; Rev. Son Thanh Hoang, O.P., Par. Vicar; Rev. Liem Trung Tran, O.P., Par. Vicar; Dcn. J.B Dao; Dcn. Joseph Chuong Nguyen Do; Dcn. Vincent Nguyen; Dcn. Andy Dao, DRE;

Our Lady of Mt. Carmel - 6723 Whitefriars Dr., Houston, TX 77087-6598 t) 713-645-6673 mtcarmelalive.org Rev. J. Abelardo Cobos, Pst.;

Our Lady of Sorrows - 3006 Kashmere St., Houston, TX 77026-5999 t) 713-673-5600; 713-673-5601 (CRP) admin@olosch.com www.ourladyhouston.org Rev. David Garnier, Pst.; Oralia Guerrero, DRE; Berenice Alejandre, Bus. Mgr.; Dcn. Humberto Carrasco; Mathew Maldonado, Music Dir.; CRP Stds.: 76

Our Lady of St. John - 7500 Hirsch Rd., Houston, TX 77016-6215 t) 713-631-0810 olsjhouston@outlook.com sites.google.com/view/virgendesanjuanhouston/home Rev. Jhon Jaime Florez, Admin.; CRP Stds.: 163

Our Lady Star of the Sea - 1401 Fidelity St., Houston, TX 77029-4624 t) 713-674-9206 olsoshoustontx@gmail.com www.olsoshoustontx.com Rev. Thomas Robert Frank, SSJ, Pst.; CRP Stds.: 6

Our Mother of Mercy - 4000 Sumpter St., Houston, TX 77020-2497; Mailing: P.O. Box 15640, Houston, TX 77220-5640 t) 713-672-2037 (CRP); 713-672-0026 www.ourmotherofmercy.net Rev. Rodney J Armstrong, SSJ, Pst.; Dcn. Charles J. Allen Sr.; Dcn. Irvin Johnson Jr.; Gerald Joseph, DRE;

St. Patrick - 4918 Cochran St., Houston, TX 77009-2117 t) 713-697-4325 (CRP); 713-695-0631 (Office) www.stpatrickhouston.com Rev. Tom Hawxhurst, Pst.; Dcn. Reynaldo Torres; CRP Stds.: 240

St. Paul the Apostle - 18223 Point Lookout Dr., Houston, TX 77058-3594 t) 281-333-3891 www.stpaulcatholic.org/ Rev. Wencil C. Pavlovsky, Pst.; Dcn. Scott Bradley Daniel; Dcn. Arturo Monterrubio; Dcn. Servando Rojas; Dcn. Tom Spicer; Kathy Giannini, Liturgy Dir.; Beto Puebla, Youth Min.; Marisol Rojas, CRE; CRP Stds.: 324

St. Peter Claver - 6005 N. Wayside Dr., Houston, TX 77028-4494 t) 713-674-3338 parishoffice@stpeterclaverhouston.com stpeterclaverhouston.com Rev. Thomas Robert Frank, SSJ, Pst.; Leticia De La Cruz, DRE; CRP Stds.: 73

St. Peter the Apostle - 6220 La Salette Dr., Houston, TX 77021-1323 t) 713-747-7800 stpetercc@sbcglobal.net stpeterhouston.org Rev. Evaristus Chukwu, MSP, Pst.; Stephanie Jackson, DRE; CRP Stds.: 44

St. Peter the Apostle School -

St. Philip Neri - 10960 Martin Luther King Jr. Blvd., Houston, TX 77048-1896 t) 713-734-0320 (Parish Office); (832) 649-2524 (CCE Office); (832) 649-7704 (Parish Hall) officespn@yahoo.com; spnbulletin@yahoo.com www.stphilipnerichurch.org Rev. Christian Alimaji, M.S.P., Pst.; Dcn. Ronald Simon; Dcn. Orrin D. Burroughs;

St. Philip of Jesus - 9700 Villita St., Houston, TX 77013-3851 t) 713-672-6141 www.stphilipofjesus.net Rev. Hai Duc Dang, Pst.; Dcn. Roy Breaux; CRP Stds.: 430

Prince of Peace - 19222 Tomball Pkwy., Houston, TX 77070-3510 t) 281-469-2686 info@pophouston.org pophouston.org Rev. Thomas V. Ponzini, Pst.; Rev. Antonio Ortiz, Par. Vicar; Rev. Ebin Christopher Harris, MSFS (India), Par. Vicar; Dcn. William Barnes; Dcn. Kevin Cascarelli; Dcn. Timothy Hartnett; Dcn. Kenneth Henry; Dcn. Thomas Lattin; Dcn. William Sheffield; Dcn. Robert Trahan; CRP Stds.: 753

Queen of Peace - 3011 Telephone Rd., Houston, TX 77023-5312; Mailing: 2317 Craigmont St., Houston, TX 77023 t) 713-926-4494 (CRP); 713-921-6127 qop@qophouston.com www.qophouston.com/ Rev. Ruben Campbell, C.C., Pst.; Rev. Miguel Perez, Assoc. Pst.; Dcn. Luis Turcios; CRP Stds.: 303

St. Raphael the Archangel - 3915 Ocee St., Houston, TX 77263-5417 t) 713-781-9511 straphaelcc@comcast.net Rev. Ramon J. Arechua, Pst.; Maria Reyna, CRE;

Regina Caeli - 8121 Breen Dr., Houston, TX 77064 t) 832-328-0876 office@reginacaeliparish.org www.reginacaeliparish.org Rev. Charles Van Vliet, F.S.S.P., Pst.; Rev. Daniel Alloy, FSSP, Par. Vicar; Rev. William Rock, FSSP, Par. Vicar; CRP Stds.: 262

Church Of The Resurrection - 915 Zoe St., Houston, TX 77020-6898 t) 713-675-0350 (CRP); 713-675-5333 amesa@rcchouston.org www.rcchouston.org Rev. Oscar H. Dubon, Pst.; CRP Stds.: 124

Resurrection School - (Grades PreK-8) 916 Majestic St., Houston, TX 77020 t) 713-674-5545 dmartinez@rcchouston.org Dora Martinez, Prin.;

La Divina Providencia - 7913 Munn St, Houston, TX 77029 t) 713-360-7173 mbanda@rcchouston.org

St. Rose of Lima - 3600 Brinkman St., Houston, TX 77018-6329 t) 713-692-9123 www.stroselima.org Rev. Linh N. Nguyen, Pst.; Rev. John Samuel, Par. Vicar; Dcn. John T. Murrell, DRE; Dcn. Ed Herrera, Bus. Mgr.;

St. Rose of Lima School - (Grades PreK-8) t) 713-691-0104 bdrabek@stroselima.org Bernadette Drabek, Prin.;

The Church of the Annunciation - 1618 Texas Ave., Houston, TX 77003; Mailing: P.O. Box 214, Houston, TX 77001-0214 t) 713-222-2289 info@acchtx.org www.acchtx.org Rev. Paul G. Felix, Pst.; Dcn. Kenneth Curtis; Catherine Schaefer, Music Min.; Catherine O'Brien, CRE; Caryn Vukelich, RCIA Coord.;

St. Theresa - 6622 Haskell St., Houston, TX 77007-2097 t) 713-869-3783 info@sttheresa.cc www.sttheresa.cc Rev. Philip P. Lloyd, Pst.; Dcn. Larry A. Vaclavik; Dcn. Juan de Dios Perez; Tommy Cordova, DRE; CRP Stds.: 260

St. Theresa School - (Grades PreK-8) 6500 Durford St., Houston, TX 77007 t) 346-335-1700 k.mccarty@sttheresa.cc www.sttheresaschool.cc/ Melissa Ilski, Prin.;

St. Thomas More - 10330 Hillcroft St., Houston, TX 77096-4702 t) 713-729-0221 secretary@stmhouston.org stmhouston.org Rev. Clark Sample, Pst.; Rev. Thuc H. Nguyen, Par. Vicar; Dcn. John Krugh; Dcn. Danny Naranjo; Rev. Binny Philip, In Res.; Ryan Lambert, DRE; CRP Stds.: 299

St. Thomas More School - 5927 Wigton, Houston, TX 77096 t) 713-729-3434 jgentempo@stmorenews.com Kristin Thome, Prin.;

Vietnamese Martyrs - 10610 Kingspoint Rd., Houston, TX 77075-4114 t) 713-941-0521 vietnammartyrs.org Rev. John Kha Tran, Pst.; Rev. Loc Joseph Phan, Par. Vicar; Dcn. Joseph Ro Van Le; Dcn. Joseph Pham Nguyen; Dcn. Joseph Nguyen Pham, DRE; CRP Stds.: 455

St. Vincent de Paul - 6800 Buffalo Speedway, Houston, TX 77025-1405 t) 713-667-9111 info@svdp-houston.org www.svdp-houston.org Rev. Msgr. William L. Young, Pst.; Rev. Houston Ekene Okonma, Par. Vicar; Rev. Christopher M. Plant, Par. Vicar; Rev. Romanus Muoneke, In Res.; Dcn. Burt Martin; Laura Rivera, DRE; Dean Kovacs, Youth Min.; Patricia Rutz, Bus. Mgr.;

St. Vincent de Paul School - (Grades PreK-8) 6802 Buffalo Speedway, Houston, TX 77025 t) 713-666-2345 csears@svdp-edu.org Carolyn Sears, Prin.;

HUFFMAN

St. Philip the Apostle - 2308 3rd St., Huffman, TX 77336-2363; Mailing: P.O. Box 2363, Huffman, TX 77336-2363 t) 281-324-1478 parishoffice@stphilip.cc stphiliphuffmantx.org Rev. Richard E. Barker, Pst.; Becky Pursell, DRE; CRP Stds.: 69

HUMBLE

St. Mary Magdalene - 527 S. Houston Ave., Humble, TX 77338-4763 t) 281-446-2933 (CRP); 281-446-8211 tbutera@st-mm.com; saramburu@st-mm.com www.st-mm.com Rev. Felix I. Osasona, M.S.P., Pst.; Rev. Augustine Ogar, M.S.P., Par. Vicar; Mike Smith, DRE; Tony Butera, Bus. Mgr.; CRP Stds.: 203

St. Mary Magdalene School - (Grades PreK-8) 530 Ferguson, Humble, TX 77338 t) 281-446-8535 lgoudeau@smmcs.org Lois Goudeau, Prin.; Stds.: 196; Lay Tchrs.: 10

HUNTSVILLE

St. Thomas the Apostle - 1323 16th St., Huntsville, TX

77340-4431; Mailing: 1603 Ave. N, Huntsville, TX 77340 t) 936-295-8159 stthomashuntsville@sbcglobal.net; fvalone@saintthomashuntsville.org www.saintthomashuntsville.org Rev. Fred W. Valone, Pst.; Dcn. Felix Ramos; Kathy Boscarino, DRE; CRP Stds.: 205

KATY

St. Bartholomew the Apostle - 5356 11th St., Katy, TX 77493-1748 t) 281-391-4758 www.st-bart.org Rev. Miguel A. Solorzano, Pst.; Rev. Ricardo Arriola, Par. Vicar; Dcn. Rolando Garcia; Dcn. Gordon Robertson; Dcn. William C. Wagner; CRP Stds.: 1,059

St. Edith Stein - 3311 N. Fry Rd., Katy, TX 77449-6235 t) 281-492-7500 chris@stedithstein.org; mm@stedithstein.org Rev. Ryszard Kulma, Pst.; Dcn. Daniel Melchior; Dcn. Fernando Garcia; Dcn. Larry Biediger Jr.; Dcn. Leonard J. Broussard; Dcn. Ted F. Heap; Dcn. Glenn Jackson; Melissa Powell, DRE; CRP Stds.: 180

Epiphany of the Lord - 1530 Norwalk Dr., Katy, TX 77450-4918 t) 281-578-8271 (CRP); 281-578-0707 epiphany@epiphanycatholic.org www.epiphanycatholic.org Rev. Tom Lam, Pst.; Dcn. Don Kish; Dcn. Jose F Olascoaga; Matt Kiernan, DRE; CRP Stds.: 875

Epiphany of the Lord Catholic School - 20910 Highland Knolls Dr., Katy, TX 77450 t) 832-391-6500 epiphanycatholic.school Dr. Nicholas Morgan, Prin.; Stds.: 386; Lay Tchrs.: 25

LA MARQUE

Queen of Peace - 1220 Cedar Dr., La Marque, TX 77568; Mailing: 1224 Cedar Dr., La Marque, TX 77568 t) 409-938-7000; (409) 935-3535 (CRP) queenofpeacelamarque@gmail.com queenofpeacelamarque.org Rev. Msgr. James B. Anderson, Pst.; Dcn. Jose Duplan; Roger Frost, DRE; CRP Stds.: 117

LA PORTE

St. Mary - 816 Park Dr., La Porte, TX 77571-5811 t) 281-471-2000 stmaryslpcc@sbcglobal.net stmaryslaporte.com Rev. Antonio A. Castro, Pst.; Dcn. Stan Avallone; Dcn. Julio C. Matallana; Jessica Jaramillo, DRE;

LAKE JACKSON

St. Michael - 100 Oak Dr. S., Lake Jackson, TX 77566-5630 t) (979) 297-3041 (CRP); (979) 297-3043 www.smlj.org Rev. Dwight M. Canizares, Pst.; CRP Stds.: 181

LEAGUE CITY

St. Mary - 1612 E. Walker St., League City, TX 77573-4137 t) 281-332-3031 churchnews@saintmcc.org saintmcc.org Rev. John Rooney, M.R.E., Pst.; Dcn. George Blanford Jr.; Dcn. Russell Carroll; Dcn. Frank Fritz Claydon III; Dcn. Andrew DeYoung; CRP Stds.: 885

St. Mary School - t) 281-332-4014 lhalbardier@stmarylc.org Laura Halbardier, Prin.;

MAGNOLIA

St. Matthias the Apostle - 302 S. Magnolia Blvd., Magnolia, TX 77355-8535 t) 281-356-2000 gbrown@st-matthias.net; smedrano@st-matthias.net st-matthias.net Rev. J. Christopher C. Nguyen, Pst.; Marlene Grauvogl, DRE; CRP Stds.: 467

MANVEL

Sacred Heart of Jesus - 6502 County Rd. 48, Manvel, TX 77578-4146 t) 281-489-8720 www.sacredheartmanvel.org Very Rev. Trung V. Nguyen, Pst.; Dcn. Jose Luis Martinez; Dcn. Ricardo Reyes; Dcn. Robert Gregory Stevens; Dcn. Robert Reed Leicht Jr.; Rev. Augustine Obasi, In Res.; CRP Stds.: 1,193

MCNAIR

Holy Family - 7122 Whiting Rock St., McNair, TX 77521-1124 t) 281-421-7042 (CRP); 281-426-8448 hfrcc7122@verizon.net www.holyfamilycatholicchurchmcnairtx.org Rev. David Patrick Begany, S.S.J., Admin.; Vivian Randell-Alfred, DRE;

MISSOURI CITY

St. Angela Merici - 9009 Sienna Ranch Rd., Missouri City, TX 77549-3802; Mailing: 6140 Hwy. 6 PMB99, Missouri City, TX 77459 t) 281-778-0400 margaretmyers@stamericigh.com www.stamericigh.com Rev. John E. Cahoon, Pst.; Rev. Joy Thomas, M.S.F.S., Assoc. Pst.; Dcn. Jim Wright; CRP Stds.: 650

Holy Family - 1510 5th St., Missouri City, TX 77489-1298 t) 281-499-9688; 281-499-4612 (CRP) information@holyfamilychurch.us; holyfamilycce@holyfamilychurch.us www.holyfamilychurch.us Rev. Sunny Joseph Plammoottil, O.S.H., Pst.; Rev. Joy James, O.S.H., Par. Vicar; Dcn. William E. Seifert Jr.; Dcn. Jose Melendez; Dcn. Jeffrey Speight; Dcn. Cuong Nguyen; CRP Stds.: 700

NAVASOTA

Christ Our Light - 9677 Hwy. 6, Navasota, TX 77868-3926; Mailing: 510 Manley St., Navasota, TX 77868 t) 936-825-3920 fr.eli@christourlight.org; reboard@christourlight.org www.christourlight.org Rev. Eli Lopez, Pst.; Dcn. Grant E. Holt; Dcn. Garry Janota; Dcn. Russell Pasket; Carolyn Katkoski, DRE;

NEEDVILLE

St. Michael - 9214 Main St., Needville, TX 77461-0095; Mailing: P.O. Box 95, Needville, TX 77461 t) 979-793-4477 stmichaelschurch@consolidated.net needvillecatholic.com Rev. Marty Pham, Pst.; Jennifer Carlisle, DRE; CRP Stds.: 260

NEW CANEY

St. John of the Cross - 20000 Loop 494, New Caney, TX 77357-8213 t) 281-399-9008 office@sjotctx.org www.sjotctx.org Rev. Michael Applegate, Pst.; CRP Stds.: 458

NEW WAVERLY

St. Joseph - 101 Elmore, New Waverly, TX 77358-4105 t) 936-344-6104; 936-856-3713 (CRP) Rev. Daokim Nguyen, Pst.; Dcn. Klaus Petereit;

St. Stephen the Martyr - 101 Stagecoach, Pointblank, TX 77364 ststephenpb@gmail.com Dcn. Melvin Moulton;

PASADENA

St. Juan Diego - 3301 Pasadena Blvd., Pasadena, TX 77503-3201 t) 713-628-0183 (CRP); 713-477-6693 (Formerly Guardian Angel) Rev. Gerald Goodrum, Pst.; Rev. Jorge Rios, Assoc. Pst.; Dcn. Jose Jimenez; Gloria Raya, DRE;

St. Pius V - 824 S. Main St., Pasadena, TX 77506-3532 t) 713-473-9484 x106 (CRP); 713-473-9484 pastor@spvpasadena.org stpiusvchurch.com Rev. Benjamin Bueno Martinez, FM, Pst.; Rev. Kofi Adzaklui-Tume, FM, Par. Vicar; Dcn. Heath Hampton; Dcn. Daniel Seiler; Rev. Jan Kubisa, In Res.; Gina Pasket, DRE; Felicitas Palacios, CRE; CRP Stds.: 247

PATTISON

Sacred Heart - 4445 F.M. 359 N., Pattison, TX 77466; Mailing: P.O. Box 300, Pattison, TX 77466 t) 281-375-6799 Rev. David J. DuBois, Pst.; Juanita Camacho, DRE; Mary Ann Holdiman, Bus. Mgr.; CRP Stds.: 180

PEARLAND

St. Helen - 2209 Old Alvin Rd., Pearland, TX 77581-4499 t) 281-485-2421 shcc@sthelenchurch.org www.sthelenchurch.org Rev. Carl James Courville, Pst.; Rev. Jose Alonso, Pst. Assoc.; Dcn. Dale Almenario; Dcn. Jesus Davila; Dcn. Darryl Drenon; Dcn. Steven Griesmyer Sr.; Julie Martinez, DRE; CRP Stds.: 1,200

St. Helen School - 2213 Old Alvin Rd., Pearland, TX 77581 t) 281-485-2845 pcoleman@sthelencatholicschool.org www.shcssaints.org Phyliss Coleman, Prin.;

PLANTERSVILLE

St. Mary - 8227 County Rd. 205, Plantersville, TX 77363; Mailing: PO Box 388, Plantersville, TX 77363 t) 936-894-2223 info@smsj.org smsj.org Rev. Edward C. Kucera Jr., Pst.; Dcn. David Garvis; Cheryl Schratwieser, DRE; CRP Stds.: 256

St. Joseph - 11323 CR 304, Stoneham, TX 77363; Mailing: P.O. Box 388, Plantersville, TX 77363 t) (936) 894-2223

PORTER

St. Martha - 4301 Woodridge Pkwy., Porter, TX 77365-7709 t) 281-358-6637; 281-358-1959 x212 (CRP) indianaf@stmartha.com; thomask@stmartha.com www.stmartha.com Rev. Thomas J. Dolce, Pst.; Rev. Wayne Ly, Par. Vicar; Rev. Ralph O. Roberts, Par. Vicar; Dcn. Anthony Cardella; Dcn. Robert MacFarlane; Ruben Dario Manosalva; Rev. Miguel Perez; Dcn. Guy Puglia; Dcn. Gary Yepsen; CRP Stds.: 1,008

St. Martha School - 2411 Oakshores Dr., Kingwood, TX 77339 t) 281-358-5523 munscherj@stmarthacs.org stmarthacs.org Jessica Munscher, Prin.;

RICHMOND

St. John Fisher - 410 Clay St., Richmond, TX 77469-1708 t) 281-342-5092 office@stjohnfisher.info www.stjohnfisher.info/ Rev. Jose Luis Gutierrez, Pst.; Dcn. Gustavo Macha; Dcn. Hector R. Rodriguez; Dcn. Eric Suarez;

Sacred Heart Catholic Church - 507 S. Fourth St., Richmond, TX 77469-3599 t) 281-342-8371 (CRP); 281-342-3609 info@sacredhrt.com sacredhrt.com Rev. Joseph Ho, C.Ss.R., Pst.; Rev. Joseph Toan Lai, C.Ss.R., Par. Vicar; Dcn. John Placette; Dcn. Donald G. Ries; Kim Roy, DRE; CRP Stds.: 313

ROSENBERG

Holy Rosary - 1416 George St., Rosenberg, TX 77471-3198 t) 281-342-3089 office@hrccr.com www.hrccr.com Rev. Orrin Halepeska, Pst.; Rev. Vipin George, MSFS (India), Par. Vicar; Dcn. Carlito Buhay; Dcn. Jason Sulak; CRP Stds.: 136

Holy Rosary School - (Grades PreK-8) 1426 George St., Rosenberg, TX 77471 t) 281-342-5813 arodriguez@holyrosary-school.org www.holyrosary-school.org Adrienne Rodriguez, Prin.; Stds.: 153; Lay Tchrs.: 16

Our Lady of Guadalupe - 514 Carlisle St., Rosenberg, TX 77471; Mailing: 1600 Avenue D, Rosenberg, TX 77471 t) 281-232-5113 olgc.est1936@yahoo.com olgrosenberg.org Rev. Lee A. Flores, Pst.; Dcn. Enrique G. Avila; Dcn. Francisco Nunez; Dcn. Albert Yanez; CRP Stds.: 248

SEALY

Immaculate Conception - 600 4th St., Sealy, TX 77474-2607; Mailing: 608 5th St., Sealy, TX 77474-0337 t) 979-885-0018 (CRP); 979-885-3868 info@icc-sealy.org www.icc-sealy.org Rev. Jonathan More, Pst.; Dcn. Robert Kent; Dcn. Ben Munguia; Carl Floyd, Pst. Assoc.; Patricia Verm, DRE; CRP Stds.: 315

SOUTH HOUSTON

Our Lady of Grace - 1211 Michigan St., South Houston, TX 77587-0164 t) 713-946-6461 Rev. Maynard U. Parangan, Pst.; Maria Rosario Flores, DRE;

SPRING

Christ the Good Shepherd - 18511 Klein Church Rd., Spring, TX 77379-4998 t) 281-376-6831 jburkart@cgscc.church; mstakes@cgscc.church cgscc.church Rev. James Burkart, Pst.; Rev. David Michael Moses, Par. Vicar; Dcn. Mark Clancy; Dcn. Stacy Millsap; Dcn. Delores Villafranco; Michael Stakes, Bus. Mgr.; Jeremy Hearne, Liturgy Dir.; Ken Morrison, Music Min.; Ivana Meshell, DRE; CRP Stds.: 2,200

St. Edward - 2601 Spring Stuebner Rd., Spring, TX 77389-4824 t) 281-353-9774 info@saintedward.org www.saintedward.org Rev. Christian Bui, Pst.; Rev. Thomas Joseph, O.S.H., Par. Vicar; Dcn. Stuart Neck; Dcn. William Pitocco; Dcn. Dominic Romaguera; Annette O'Driscoll, DRE; CRP Stds.: 498

St. Edward School - (Grades PreK-8) t) 281-353-4570 emakel@stedwardschool.org www.stedwardschool.org Erin Makel, Prin.;

St. Ignatius of Loyola - 7810 Cypresswood Dr., Spring, TX 77379-7101 t) 281-370-3401 info@silcc.org www.silcc.org Very Rev. Norbert J. Maduzia Jr., Pst.; Rev. Jose Kumblolickal, MSFS (India), Par. Vicar; Dcn.

Peter Olivier; Dcn. Scott Glueck, Pst. Min./Coord.; Dcn. Joseph Wright, Pst. Min./Coord.; Dcn. Michael P Dargay; Dcn. Michael E. Higgins; Dcn. Larry Vines; Dcn. Greg Mouton; Ronald Svoboda, COO; Karla Jackson, Pst. Assoc.; CRP Stds.: 773

St. James the Apostle - 22800 Aldine Westfield Rd., Spring, TX 77373-6565 t) 281-353-5053 saintjta@stjta.com www.stjta.org Rev. Charles J. Samperi, Pst.; Rev. Thomas Devasahayam, D.S., In Res.; Dcn. Ray Oden, Bus. Mgr.; Dcn. Alfonso Chicas; Dcn. Paul Pinon; Dcn. Arthur Zepeda; CRP Stds.: 212

SUGAR LAND

St. Laurence - 3100 Sweetwater Blvd., Sugar Land, TX 77479-2630 t) 281-980-9812 toltremari@stlaurence.org www.stlaurence.org Rev. William Andrew Wood, Pst.; Rev. Jaison Thomas Pezhathinal, M.S.F.S., Assoc. Pst.; Rev. Truong Nguyen, Assoc. Pst.; Tony Oltremari, Admin.; Dcn. Renato Arellano; Dcn. Don Burns; Dcn. Dennis Henderson; Dcn. Charles Plant; Dcn. Timothy Cullen; Dcn. Tom Ruck; Christine Dunn, DRE; CRP Stds.: 1,166

St. Laurence School - 2630 Austin Pkwy., Sugar Land, TX 77479-2630 t) 281-980-0500 sbarto@stlaurence.org stlaurenceschool.org Suzanne Barto, Prin.;

St. Theresa - 705 St. Theresa Blvd., Sugar Land, TX 77498; Mailing: P.O. Box 968, Sugar Land, TX 77487-0968 t) 281-494-1156 diane@sugarlandcatholic.com sugarlandcatholic.com Rev. David Angelino, Pst.; Rev. Juan G. Pineda (Colombia), Par. Vicar; Rev. Jose J. Tharayil, Par. Vicar; Rev. Gregory Mirto, In Res.; Dcn. James Anderson; Dcn. John Kennedy; Dcn. Gilbert Rodriguez;

St. Theresa - t) 281-494-1157 mnewcomb@sttheresacatholicschool.org Mark Newcomb, Headmaster;

St. Thomas Aquinas - 12627 W. Bellfort Ave., Sugar Land, TX 77478-1844 t) 281-240-6721 frjoseph@stasugarland.com www.stasugarland.com Rev. Joseph Pottemmel, M.S.F.S., Pst.; Rev. Joseph Arulraj, MSFS, Par. Vicar; Matthew Falleri, CRE; Charles Sheffield (Chazz), Youth Min.; Russ Martinez, Music Min.; CRP Stds.: 105

SWEENY

Our Lady of Perpetual Help - 310 N. McKinney St., Sweeny, TX 77480-2899 t) 979-548-2020 x4; 979-548-6994 (CRP) olphsja.org Rev. Preston Quintela, Pst.;

St. John the Apostle - 807 Loggins, West Columbia, TX 77486-3843; Mailing: 310 N. McKinney St., Sweeny, TX 77480

TEXAS CITY

St. Mary of the Miraculous Medal - 1620 Ninth Ave. N., Texas City, TX 77590-5708; Mailing: 1604 9th Ave. N., Texas City, TX 77590 t) 409-948-8448 support@stmarycctc.org Rev. Clint C. Ressler, Pst.; Dcn. John Carrillo; Dcn. Stephen A. Mistretta; Dcn. Gerry Weiser; CRP Stds.: 185

Our Lady of Fatima - 1600 Ninth Ave. N., Texas City, TX 77590 t) 409-945-3326 grodgers@fatimatc.org Jennifer Lopez, Prin.;

THE WOODLANDS

St. Anthony of Padua - 7801 Bay Branch Dr., The Woodlands, TX 77382-5359 t) 281-296-2800 (CRP); 281-419-8700 communications@ap.church ap.church/ Rev. Jesus (Jesse) Garcia, Pst.; Rev. David Hust, Par. Vicar; Rev. Mathew Thottyil, MSFS, Par. Vicar; Dcn. Franco Knoepffler; Dcn. Mike Krall; Dcn. Dominic Madrid; Dcn. Eduardo Mejia; Dcn. Ralph F. Risk; Dcn. Tom Vicknair; Dcn. Richard Vogel; Rev. Ronnie Dela Cruz, Chap.; CRP Stds.: 870

St. Anthony of Padua School - 7901 Bay Branch Dr., The Woodlands, TX 77382 t) 281-296-0300 vtucker@ap.church Veronica Tucker, Prin.; Stds.: 488; Lay Tchrs.: 35

Sts. Simon and Jude - 26777 Glen Loch Dr., The Woodlands, TX 77381-2921 t) 281-367-9885 info@ssjwoodlands.com www.ssjwoodlands.com Rev. Patrick Stuart Garrett, Pst.; Rev. Kailas Hivale, M.S.F.S., Assoc. Pst.; Dcn. Dale Hayden; Dcn. Anthony G. Cantania; Dcn. John E. Charnisky Jr.; Dcn. Pat Kearns; Dcn. Joe Mignogna; CRP Stds.: 352

TOMBALL

St. Anne - 1111 S. Cherry St., Tomball, TX 77375-6675 t) 281-351-8106 parishoffice@stanne-tomball.org; kshamas@stanneschool-tomball.org www.stanne-tomball.org Rev. Thomas W. Hopper, Pst.; Dcn. Jose Gutierrez; CRP Stds.: 225

St. Anne School - (Grades PreK-8) t) 281-351-0093 edailey@stanneschool-tomball.org Kendall Shamas, Prin.;

WALLIS

Guardian Angel - 5610 Demel St., Wallis, TX 77485; Mailing: P.O. Box 487, Wallis, TX 77485 t) 979-478-6532 guardianangelwallis.org Rev. Thuy Quang Nguyen, Pst.; Dcn. Jerome D. Losack Sr.; CRP Stds.: 116

SCHOOLS: PRESCHOOL THRU HIGH SCHOOL

SCHOOLS

STATE OF TEXAS

GALVESTON

Holy Family Catholic School - (PAR) 2601 Ursuline Ave., Galveston, TX 77550-4398 t) 409-765-6607 rhesse@hfcsgalv.org hfcsgalv.org Rita Hesse, Prin.; Dawn Cromie, Librn.;

HOUSTON

Assumption Catholic School - (DIO) 801 Roselane St., Houston, TX 77037-4696 t) 281-447-2132 jbates@houstonassumption.org www.houstonassumption.org John William Bates, Prin.; Sr. Francis Marie Bordages, Librn.;

St. Catherine's Montessori, Inc. - (PRV) (Grades PreK-12) 9821 Timberside, Houston, TX 77025 t) 713-665-2195 ldelgado@stcathmont.org; hcopeland@stcathmont.org stcathmont.org Lina Delgado, Prin.; Stds.: 252; Sr. Tchrs.: 1; Lay Tchrs.: 16

St. John Paul II Catholic School - (PRV) (Grades PreK-8) 1400 Parkway Plaza Dr., Houston, TX 77077-1503 t) 281-496-1500 communications@jp2.org; principal@jp2.org www.jp2.org Rebecca Bogard, Prin.; Stds.: 710; Pr. Tchrs.: 1; Lay Tchrs.: 73

The Regis School - (PRV) 7330 Westview Dr., Houston, TX 77055-5122 t) 713-682-8383 dphillips@theregisschool.org www.theregisschool.org (Boys) Janna Roberson, Headmaster; Laura Dozier, Dir.; Beth Schneider, Dir.;

RICHWOOD

Our Lady Queen of Peace Catholic School - (PRV) (Grades PreK-8) 1600 Hwy. 2004, Richwood, TX 77531 t) 979-265-3909 nthomas@olqpschool.org www.olqpschool.org Serving the parishes of Most Holy Trinity, Angleton; St. Jerome, Clute; St. Anthony, Danbury; St. Mary Star of the Sea, Freeport. Nirmala Thomas, Prin.;

HIGH SCHOOLS

STATE OF TEXAS

GALVESTON

O'Connell College Preparatory School - (PRV) 1320 Tremont St., Galveston, TX 77550-4513 t) 409-765-5534 chantal.rodriguez@oconnellprep.com www.oconnellprep.com Patti Abbott, Prin.;

HOUSTON

St. Agnes Academy - (PRV) (Grades 9-12) 9000 Bellaire Blvd., Houston, TX 77036-4683 t) 713-219-5400 dwhalen@st-agnes.org www.st-agnes.org Carleen K. Raymond, Prin.; Deborah Whalen, Pres.; Stds.: 925; Sr. Tchrs.: 1; Lay Tchrs.: 93

Duchesne Academy of the Sacred Heart - (PRV) (Grades PreK-12) 10202 Memorial Dr., Houston, TX 77024-3299 t) 713-468-8211 admissions@duchesne.org www.duchesne.org (Girls) Religious of the Sacred Heart. Patricia Swenson, Head of School; Margaret Buza, Prin.; Suzy de Leon, Prin.; Donald Cramp, Prin.; Alye Inman, Dean; Stds.: 750; Lay Tchrs.: 98

Incarnate Word Academy - (PRV) (Grades 9-12) 609 Crawford St., Houston, TX 77002-3668 t) 713-227-3637 lbeck@incarnateword.org www.incarnateword.org Sr. Lauren Beck, C.V.I., Pres.; Cathy Stephen, Prin.; Stds.: 267; Lay Tchrs.: 24

Jesuit Cristo Rey High School of Houston, Inc. (Cristo Rey Jesuit College Preparatory School of Houston, Inc.) - 6700 Mount Carmel St., Houston, TX 77087 t) 281-501-1298 bdickson@cristoreyjesuit.org www.cristoreyjesuit.org (Co-Ed) Paul Beck, Pres.; Drew Hudson, Prin.; Bee Dickson, Exec. Dir.; Jill Ribbeck, Dir.; Rev. Randy Gibbens, Chap.; Stds.: 450; Scholastics: 1; Pr. Tchrs.: 1; Bro. Tchrs.: 1; Sr. Tchrs.: 1; Lay Tchrs.: 31

St. Pius X High School, Inc. - (PRV) 811 W. Donovan, Houston, TX 77091-5699 t) 713-692-3581 armisteadc@stpiusx.org www.stpiusx.org Diane Larsen, Prin.; Carmen G. Armistead, Headmaster;

Strake Jesuit College Preparatory Inc. - (PRV) (Grades 9-12) 8900 Bellaire Blvd., Houston, TX 77036-4699 t) 713-774-7651 sjcom@strakejesuit.org www.strakejesuit.org Ken Lojo, Prin.; Rev. Jeffrey C. Johnson, S.J., Pres.; Rev. R.V. Baylon, S.J., Teacher; Rev. Douglas J. Hypolite, S.J., Teacher; Stds.: 1,372; Scholastics: 2; Pr. Tchrs.: 3; Lay Tchrs.: 140

St. Thomas High School - (PRV) 4500 Memorial Dr., Houston, TX 77007-7332 t) 713-864-6348 www.sths.org Basilian Residence, Basilian Fathers. Aaron Dominguez, Prin.; Rev. James F. Murphy, C.S.B., Pres.; Stds.: 701; Lay Tchrs.: 59

KATY

St. John XXIII College Preparatory - (PRV) (Grades 9-12) 1800 W. Grand Pkwy. N., Katy, TX 77449 t) 281-693-1000 news@sj23lions.org www.sj23.org Rev. Jonathan Mitchican, Chap.; Joseph Noonan, Prin.; Elizabeth Dronet, Librn.; Stds.: 403; Pr. Tchrs.: 1; Sr. Tchrs.: 2; Lay Tchrs.: 30

SPRING

***Frassati Catholic High School (North Houston Catholic High School)** - (PRV) (Grades 9-12) 22151 Frassati Way, Spring, TX 77389 t) 832-616-3217 www.frassaticatholic.org Sr. John Paul, O.P., Prin.; Alissa Reynolds, Dean; Josh Moldiz, Dean; Robert Martin, Bus. Mgr.; Shayla Mullee, Librn.; Stds.: 283; Sr. Tchrs.: 4; Lay Tchrs.: 24

INSTITUTIONS LOCATED IN DIOCESE

CAMPUS MINISTRY / NEWMAN CENTERS [CAM]

GALVESTON

Galveston Newman Center - 602 Seawolf Pkwy., Ste. B, Pelican Island #5, Galveston, TX 77550 t) 409-740-3797 gal.newmancenterum@gmail.com www.archgh.org/galvestonnewman Texas A&M University at Galveston; University of Texas Medical Branch; Galveston College; College of the Mainland. Carl Erickson, Dir.;

HOUSTON

Catholic Newman Association at the University of Houston Central Campus - 4305 Martin Luther King Blvd., Houston, TX 77004 t) 713-748-2529 newman@central.uh.edu www.uhcatholic.org Salisha Miller, Campus Min.;

Catholic Student Center and St. Mary Chapel - 1703 Bolsover St., Houston, TX 77005 t) 713-526-3809

ministry@catholics.rice.edu catholics.rice.edu Newman Center for Rice University My Mimi Tran, Campus Min.; Rev. Raymond Cook, O.M.I., Dir.;
Texas Southern University Catholic Newman Center - 3535 Wheeler Ave., Houston, TX 77004 t) 713-747-7595 tsunewman@gmail.com www.tsunewmancenter.com Doris Barrow III, Campus Min.;
University of St. Thomas Campus Ministry - 3800 Montrose Blvd., Houston, TX 77006; Mailing: P.O. Box 27, Houston, TX 77006 t) 713-525-3589 campusministry@stthom.edu www.stthom.edu/campusministry Rev. Paul F English, CSB, Chap.; Pat Gunning, Campus Min.;
HUNTSVILLE
Catholic Student Center, S.H.S.U. - 1310 17th St., Huntsville, TX 77340-4415 t) 936-291-2620 info.shsucatholic@gmail.com www.shsu-catholic.org Simon Powell, Campus Min.;

CATHOLIC CHARITIES [CCH]

HOUSTON
Catholic Charities of the Archdiocese of Galveston-Houston - 2900 Louisiana St., Houston, TX 77006 t) 713-526-4611 hope@catholiccharities.org www.catholiccharities.org Cynthia Nunes Colbert, Pres.; Bart Ferrell, COO; Brian Gillen, Vice Pres., Develop. & Stewardship; Blanca Saldana, Vice. Pres.; Asstd. Annu.: 342,060; Staff: 450
Central Office -
Counseling Services -
Family Assistance Basic Needs - t) 713-227-9981
St. Frances Cabrini Center for Immigrant Legal Assistance - t) 713-874-6570
Guadalupe Center - 326 S. Jensen Dr., Houston, TX 77003; Mailing: 2900 Lousiana St., Houston, TX 77006 t) 713-227-9981 www.catholiccharities.org/basicneeds Greta Langley, Dir.;
St. Jerome Emiliani Home for Children - International Foster Care Program - t) 281-202-6315
Maime George Community Center - 1111 Collins Rd., Richmond, TX 77469 t) 231-202-6200 www.catholiccharities.org/mamiegeorge Gladys Brumfield-James, Exec.;
St. Michael's Homes for Children -
Moran Health Center - 2615 Fannin, Houston, TX 77002; Mailing: P.O. Box 1919, Houston, TX 77251-1919 christusfoundation.org
Parish Social Ministry - t) 713-874-6659
Pregnancy Services - Blessed Beginnings - t) 713-874-6632
Refugee Resettlement - t) 713-874-6516
Senior Services and Special Needs - Promoting independence for seniors, veterans and others.
Strengthening Families - Central Office -
Strengthening Families - Texas City/Galveston/Bay Area - 4700 Broadway, Ste. F-103, Galveston, TX 77551 t) 409-948-0405 Elizabeth Kinard, Exec. Dir.;

CEMETERIES [CEM]

DICKINSON
Mount Olivet - 7801 Gulf Fwy., Dickinson, TX 77539; Mailing: PO Box 965, Dickinson, TX 77539 t) 281-337-1641 snolan@archgh.org www.ccadgh.org Open for interments Stephanie Nolan, Exec. Dir.; Stacy Batey, Dir.;
GALVESTON
Old Catholic, Calvary - 2506 65th St., Galveston, TX 77551; Mailing: PO Box 965, Dickinson, TX 77539 t) 281-337-1641 snolan@archgh.org www.ccadgh.org Calvary Cemetery is open for interments Stephanie Nolan, Exec. Dir.; Stacy Batey, Dir.;
HOUSTON
Holy Cross - 3502 N. Main St., Houston, TX 77009; Mailing: PO Box 965, Dickinson, TX 77539 t) 281-337-1641 snolan@archgh.org www.ccadgh.org Open for future interments Stephanie Nolan, Exec. Dir.; Stacy Batey, Dir.;
St. Vincent - 2400 Navigation Blvd., Houston, TX 77003; Mailing: PO Box 965, Dickinson, TX 77539 t) 287-337-1641 snolan@archgh.org www.ccadgh.org Not open for burials Stephanie Nolan, Exec. Dir.; Stacy Batey, Dir.;

COLLEGES & UNIVERSITIES [COL]

HOUSTON
***University of St. Thomas** - 3800 Montrose Blvd., Houston, TX 77006-4696 t) 713-522-7911 president@stthom.edu; admissions@stthom.edu www.stthom.edu Richard Ludwick, Pres.; Chris Evans, Vice. Pres.; Spencer Conroy, Vice. Pres.; Dawn Koenning, Vice. Pres.; Jeff Olsen, Vice. Pres.; Arthur Ortiz, Vice. Pres.; Stds.: 3,691; Lay Tchrs.: 133; Pr. Tchrs.: 7; Sr. Tchrs.: 3; Scholastics: 1

CONVENTS, MONASTERIES, AND RESIDENCES FOR WOMEN [CON]

AUSTIN
Discipulas de Jesus - 5909 Reicher Dr, Austin, TX 78723 c) (281) 774-8963; (832) 820-2908 www.discipulasdejesus.org Sr. Olga Estrella Rivera Reyna, DJ, Supr.; Sr. Lucero Espitia, DJ, Vicar; Srs.: 3
CONROE
Missionary Catechists of Divine Providence (M.C.D.P.) - 704 Old Montgomery Rd., Conroe, TX 77301 t) 936-756-8186
Sacred Heart Convent - 105 N. Frazier St., Conroe, TX 77301 t) (713) 328-4871
HOUSTON
Carmelite Sisters of the Sacred Heart (C.S.H.) - 22 Farrell, Houston, TX 77022-2609 t) 713-697-6020 carmelitas200@hotmail.com Sr. Antonia Albarran, Supr.;
Casa Providencia - 3907 Rotman, Houston, TX 77003 t) 713-227-2555
Congregation of Divine Providence - 709 W. 34th St., Houston, TX 77018 t) 713-554-1556 rakcdp@gmail.com Sr. Rosalie Karstedt, C.D.P., Pastoral Formation, St. Mary's Seminary;
Congregation of the Incarnate Word & Blessed Sacrament (C.V.I.) (Houston) - Incarnate Word Convent, 3400 Bradford St., Houston, TX 77025-1398 t) 713-668-0423 lbeck@incarnateword.org Sr. Lauren Beck, C.V.I., Supr.; Srs.: 21
Incarnate Word Convent - 1217 Hogan St., Houston, TX 77009 t) 713-223-4143
Marian Convent - 3719 Glen Haven, Houston, TX 77025-1204; Mailing: 3400 Bradford Pl., Houston, TX 77025 t) 713-667-2238
Congregation of the Sisters of Charity of the Incarnate Word, Houston, Texas (CCVI) - 6510 Lawndale St., Houston, TX 77023-3913; Mailing: P.O. Box 230969, Houston, TX 77223-0969 t) 713-928-6053 ctrahan@ccvi-vdm.org www.sistersofcharity.org Sr. Celeste Trahan, Supr.; Sr. Ethel Puno, CCVI, Secy.; Srs.: 115
St. Anne Community - 6510 Lawndale St., Houston, TX 77023-3913; Mailing: P.O. Box 230969, Houston, TX 77223-0969 t) (713) 928-6053
Annunciation Community - 6510 Lawndale St., Houston, TX 77023-3913; Mailing: P.O. Box 230969, Houston, TX 77223-0969 t) (713) 928-6053
Bernice Place Community - 6510 Lawndale St., Houston, TX 77023-3913; Mailing: P.O. Box 230969, Houston, TX 77223-0969 t) (713) 928-6053
Casa de la Paz Community - 6641 Wildwood Way, Houston, TX 77023-4021 t) 713-921-4878
De Matel Community - 6510 Lawndale St., Houston, TX 77023-3913; Mailing: P.O. Box 230969, Houston, TX 77223-0969 t) (713) 928-6053
Dubuis Community - 6510 Lawndale St., Houston, TX 77023-3913; Mailing: P.O. Box 230969, Houston, TX 77223-0969 t) (713) 928-6053
Edith Stein Community - 6405 Pinehurst, Houston, TX 77023-3329 t) 713-926-6024
St. Jeanne Community - 6510 Lawndale St., Houston, TX 77023-3913; Mailing: P.O. Box 230969, Houston, TX 77223-0969 t) (713) 928-6053
Marian Community - 6510 Lawndale St., Houston, TX 77023-3913; Mailing: P.O. Box 230969, Houston, TX 77223-0969 t) (713) 928-6053
St. Placidus Community - 6510 Lawndale St., Houston, TX 77023-3913; Mailing: P.O. Box 230969, Houston, TX 77223-0969 t) (713) 928-6053
Placidus Place Community - 6510 Lawndale St., Houston, TX 77023-3913; Mailing: P.O. Box 230969, Houston, TX 77223-0969 t) (713) 928-6053
Shalom Community - 6510 Lawndale St., Houston, TX 77023-3913; Mailing: P.O. Box 230969, Houston, TX 77223-0969 t) 713-341-2723
Dominican Sisters of Houston, Texas, Inc. (O.P.) - Motherhouse Complex & Admin. Offices, 6501 Almeda Rd., Houston, TX 77021-2095 t) 713-747-3310 ewitrago@domhou.org www.domhou.org Sr. Donna M. Pollard, O.P., Prioress; Srs.: 49
Dominican Sisters of Mary Immaculate Province - Provincial House, 5250 Gasmer Dr., Houston, TX 77035 t) 713-723-8250 thukytinh@gmail.com www.houstondominicans.org Sr. Maria Theresa Kim-Hong Nguyen, Prov.; Srs.: 97
Dominican Sisters of Mary Immaculate Province (St. Catherine Convent) - 5250 Gasmer Dr., Houston, TX 77035
Holy Rosary Convent - 1602 Adams St., Missouri City, TX 77489 t) 281-403-9300
Mary Immaculate Convent - 5900 Chippewa Blvd., Houston, TX 77086 t) 281-445-9574; 281-591-6081
Marian Convent - 3719 Glenhaven Blvd., Houston, TX 77025-1204; Mailing: 3400 Bradford Pl., Houston, TX 77025 t) 713-667-2238 lbeck@incarnateword.org Sr. Lauren Beck, C.V.I., Pres.;
Missionary Carmelites of St. Teresa (C.M.S.T.) - Holy Family Provincial House, 9826 Marek Dr., Houston, TX 77038 t) 281-445-5520 hfamprovcmst@yahoo.com Sr. Margarita Castro, CMST, Prov.; Sr. Melania Garcia, CMST, Prov. Asst.; Sr. Maria Concepcion Perez, CMST, Secy.; Sr. Ivana A Menchaca, CMST, Treas.; Srs.: 37
Divine Providence Convent - 9600 Deer Trail Dr., Houston, TX 77038 t) 281-847-3328
Infant Jesus of Prague Convent - 9600 Deer Trail Dr., Houston, TX 77038 t) 281-445-8830
St. Joseph Convent - 9815 Marek Rd., Houston, TX 77038 t) 281-445-0056
Novitiate of St. Theresa of Lisieux - 9608 Deer Trail Dr., Houston, TX 77038 t) 281-999-4435
Missionary Sisters of the Eucharist - 7315 Brompton St. #266B, Houston, TX 77025 c) 713-584-8317 mseucharist@yahoo.com www.missionarysistersoftheeucharist.org Sr. Cristina Lopez Ralios, MSE, Supr.; Srs.: 3
Religious of the Sacred Heart (R.S.C.J.) - Duchesne Community, 10204 Memorial Dr., Houston, TX 77024 t) 713-467-5312 acaire@rscj.org www.rscj.org Sr. Ann Caire, Contact;
Convent - 2424 ETC Jester Blvd., Apt. 6102, Houston, TX 77008 t) 281-381-0467
Sisters of the Incarnate Word and Blessed Sacrament (C.V.I.) - 3719 Glen Haven, Houston, TX 77025-1204 t) 713-667-2738
MANVEL
***Sisters of St. Michael the Archangel (S.S.M.A.)** - 35 San Simeon Dr., Manvel, TX 77578 t) 281-692-1460 c) 832-259-3844 ssmahouston@aol.com; kejifash@yahoo.com ssmagen.org Sr. Morenikeji Francisca Faseemo, S.S.M.A., Supr.; Sr. Adenike Oke, SSMA, Supr. Gen.; Srs.: 15
NEW CANEY
Discalced Carmelite Nuns of New Caney, Texas - 1100 Parthenon Pl., New Caney, TX 77357-3276 t) 281-399-0270 x4 carmelnewcaney@gmail.com www.newcaneycarmel.com Sr. Angel Sweeney, Prioress;
PEARLAND
Congregation of the Handmaids of the Holy Child Jesus - 3614 Englewood Dr., Pearland, TX 77584 t) 281-692-0098 hhcjusam@gmail.com www.hhcjusa.org Sr. Gloriamary Agumagu, HHCJ, Supr.; Srs.: 35
Mission Development Office - 8011 Arletta St., Hoston, TX 77061; Mailing: P.O. Box 3321, Pearland,

TX 77588 t) (713) 485-6459 usamissiondev@hhcj.org

STAFFORD

Missionary Sisters of Mary Immaculate - 630 Easy Jet Dr., Stafford, TX 77477-6358 t) 281-499-0030 msmisisters@hotmail.com Sr. Reena Thonippara, Supr.;

ENDOWMENTS / FOUNDATIONS / TRUSTS [EFT]

HOUSTON

Catholic Clerical Student Fund - 9845 Memorial Dr, Houston, TX 77024 c) (281) 731-4376 catholicclericalstudentfund@gmail.com Higher learning for the priesthood.

The Catholic Endowment Foundation of Galveston-Houston - 5701 Woodway, Ste. 320, Houston, TX 77057 c) 713-857-3964 archgh.org Boone Schwartzel, Secy.;

The Claude Marie Dubuis Religious and Charitable Trust - 6510 Lawndale St., Houston, TX 77023-3913 t) 713-928-6053 Sr. Joyce Susan Njeri Mbataru, Chair;

Incarnate Word Religious and Charitable Trust - 6510 Lawndale St., Houston, TX 77023-3913 t) 713-928-6053 Sr. Joyce Susan Njeri Mbataru, Chair;

The St. Mary's Children's Relief Fund, Inc. - 1700 San Jacinto, Houston, TX 77001-0907; Mailing: P.O. Box 907, Houston, TX 77001-0907 t) 713-659-5461 adelange@archgh.org archgh.org His Eminence Daniel Cardinal DiNardo, Pres.;

St. Pius X High School Foundation, Inc. - 811 W. Donovan, Houston, TX 77091-5699 t) 713-692-3581 armisteadc@stpiusx.org www.stpiusx.org James Black, Pres.; Sr. Lavergne Schwender, O.P., Secy.;

The St. Thomas More Parish School Endowment Foundation - 10330 Hillcroft St., Houston, TX 77096 t) 713-729-0221 www.stmhouston.org Rev. Clark Sample, Admin.;

HOSPITALS / HEALTH SERVICES [HOS]

HOUSTON

***CHI St. Luke's Health - Baylor St. Luke's Medical Center** - 6720 Bertner Ave., Houston, TX 77030 t) 832-355-1000 www.chistlukeshealth.org/baylorstlukes Gay Nord, Pres.;

***CHI St. Luke's Health - The Vintage Hospital** - 20171 Chasewood Park Dr., Houston, TX 77070 t) 832-534-5000 www.chistlukeshealth.org/thevintagehospital Rob Heifner, Pres.;

***St. Luke's Health (System)** - 6624 Fannin St., Houston, TX 77030 t) 832-355-1000 giving@stlukeshealth.org www.stlukeshealth.org/ T. Douglas Lawson, CEO; Asstd. Annu.: 1,882,520; Staff: 11,200

Sisters of Charity of the Incarnate Word, Houston, Texas (SCH) - 6510 Lawndale St., Houston, TX 77023 t) 713-928-6053 Sr. Christina Murphy, CCVI, Pres.; Bed Capacity: 103; Asstd. Annu.: 185; Staff: 124

SUGAR LAND

***CHI St. Luke's Health - Sugar Land Hospital** - 1317 Lake Point Pkwy., Sugar Land, TX 77478 t) 281-637-7000 www.chistlukeshealth.org/sugarlandhospital Rob Heifner, Pres.;

MISCELLANEOUS [MIS]

GALVESTON

CHRISTUS Foundation for HealthCare - 2420 Winnie St., Galveston, TX 77550 t) 409-765-6971 christusfoundation.org Adult Learning Center for GED, English as a Second Language, Basic Computer Skills Jeannette Baughnman, Exec.; Angela Joseph, Dir.;

CHRISTUS Our Daily Bread - 2420 Winnie St., Galveston, TX 77550

HOUSTON

Angela House - 6725 Reed Rd., Houston, TX 77087 t) 281-445-9696 mhittinger@angelahouse.org www.angelahouse.org Kristin Guiney, CEO;

The Catholic Chaplain Corps - 4206 S. MacGregor Way, Houston, TX 77021 t) 713-747-8445 dthomas@archgh.org Romani Perera, Dir.; Rev. Ian Chris Balisnomo, F.L.P., Chap.; Rev. Rodolfo L. Cal-Ortiz Jr., Chap.; Rev. Desmond Daniels, Chap.; Rev. Ronnie De La Cruz, D.S., Chap.; Rev. Enrique V. Salen, Chap.; Rev. Ravi Earnest Sebastin, Chap.;

Catholic Charismatic Center - 1949 Cullen Blvd., Houston, TX 77023-0287; Mailing: P.O. Box 230287, Houston, TX 77223 t) 713-236-9977 ccc@cccgh.com www.cccgh.com Rev. Jorge Alvarado, C.C., Dir.; Rev. Juan Pablo Orozco, CC, Assoc. Dir.;

Charity Guild of Catholic Women - 1203 Lovett Blvd., Houston, TX 77006-3857 t) 713-529-0995 president@charityguildshop.org www.charityguildshop.org Peggy Idstein, Pres.;

Charity Guild of St. Joseph - 2132 Branard, Houston, TX 77098 t) 713-526-4239 Geralena Barone, Pres.;

St. Dominic Center, Inc. - 2403 Holcombe, Houston, TX 77021 t) 713-741-8743 wknight@archgh.org

Equestrian Order of the Holy Sepulchre of Jerusalem, Southwestern USA Lieutenancy - 2001 Kirby Dr., Ste. 902, Houston, TX 77019-1402 t) 713-524-5444 lieutenant@eohssouthwest.com eohssouthwest.com

Martha's Kitchen Food Services - 322 S. Jensen Dr., Houston, TX 77003 t) 713-224-2522; 281-358-6637 marthakitchen@stmartha.com Sr. Carmen Sanchez, Dir.;

Opus Dei - 5505 Chaucer Dr., Houston, TX 77005 t) 713-523-4351 www.opusdei.org Prelature of the Holy Cross and Opus Dei. Rev. Francisco Vera, Chap.; Rev. Christopher Schmitt; Rev. Jay Alvarez; Rev. Paul D. Kais;

UST Chapelle - 3034 Quenby Ave., Houston, TX 77005 t) 713-349-0921 ustchapelle.org Alain Maury, Contact;

MONASTERIES AND RESIDENCES FOR PRIESTS AND BROTHERS [MON]

HOUSTON

The Basilian Fathers of Dillon House - 1302 Kipling St., Houston, TX 77006-4212 t) 713-204-7383 bob.glass@sths.org Basilian Fathers. Rev. Jamie M. Abercrombie, C.S.B.; Rev. Philip Anthony Acquaro, C.S.B.; Rev. John L. Boscoe, C.S.B.; Rev. Wilfred S. Canning, C.S.B.; Rev. William Joseph Frankenberger, C.S.B.; Rev. James Joseph Gaunt, C.S.B.; Rev. Robert James Klem, C.S.B.; Rev. Roy Joseph Oggero, C.S.B.; Rev. Robert H. Glass, C.S.B., Supr.; Rev. Carl L. Belisch, C.S.B.; Rev. Paul F. O'Connor, C.S.B.; Rev. Richard Wahl, CSB;

The Companions of The Cross - 1949 Cullen Blvd., Houston, TX 77023; Mailing: 17330 Quincy St., Detroit, MI 48221 t) 866-885-8824 info@companionscross.org www.companionscross.org Rev. Roger Vandenakker, Moderator; Rev. Richard Jaworski, Treas.; Priests: 7

Congregation of the Passion, Holy Name Passionist Community and Retreat Center - 430 Bunker Hill Rd., Houston, TX 77024-6308 t) 713-464-4932 jschork@passionist.org; frcedric@frcedric.org www.passionist.org Rev. John Schork, C.P., Supr.; Rev. Antonio Curto, C.P.; Rev. Blaise Czaja, C.P.; Rev. Nicholas Divine, C.P.; Rev. Cedric Pisegna, C.P.; Priests: 5

Disciples of Hope (Texas) - 15403 Palmway St., Houston, TX 77071 t) 713-721-2894 www.thedisciplesofhope.org Rev. Thomas Devasahayam, D.S., Chap.;

Keon House - 4019 Yoakum Blvd., Basilian Fathers of Keon House, Houston, TX 77006-4833 c) 575-447-7785 penglish@basilian.org www.basilian.org Basilian Fathers of Keon House Rev. Paul F English, CSB, Supr.; Rev. James F. Murphy, C.S.B., Pres.; Rev. Edward J. Baenziger, C.S.B., Mem.; Rev. Mitch Dowalgo, C.S.B., Mem.; Rev. Janusz Ihnatowicz; John B Huber, CSB, In Res.;

US Foundation for the Congregation of the Holy Ghost and the Immaculate Heart of Mary, Inc. - 1700 W. Alabama St., Houston, TX 77098-2808 t) 713-522-2882 somacssptx@gmail.com; soma.gillespie@gmail.com www.spiritans.org (Sharelink - Spiritan Worldwide Aid Foundation) Rev. Michael T. Grey, C.S.Sp., Dir.; Rev. Honest Munishi, In Res.; Rev. Binh T. Quach, C.S.Sp., In Res.;

Vietnamese Dominican Vicariate of St. Vincent Liem - 12314 Old Foltin Rd., Houston, TX 77086 t) 281-999-4928 Rev. Huong Pham, O.P., Supr.; Rev. Martin Philip Nhan Thai Bui, O.P., In Res.;

MISSOURI CITY

The Society of the Oblates of Sacred Heart - 1510 Fifth St., Missouri City, TX 77489-1298 t) 832-798-8579 oblates.us@gmail.com www.oshsociety.org Rev. Lukose Manuel, O.S.H., Supr.; Rev. Joy James, O.S.H.; Rev. Thomas Joseph, O.S.H.; Rev. Sunny Joseph Plammoottil, O.S.H.;

SUGAR LAND

Basilian Fathers Missions - 414 Main St., Sugar Land, TX 77498; Mailing: PO Box 708, Sugar Land, TX 77487 t) 281-201-8690 central@basilianfathersmissions.com www.basilianfathersmissions.org Rev. Vincent J. Dulock, C.S.B., Dir., Mission Ctr.; Rev. Terence Kersch, C.S.B., Missionary; Aron Fernandez, Admin.; Priests: 2

Franciscan Missionary Brothers of North America, New York - 11710 Cobblestone Point Dr., Sugar Land, TX 77498 t) 281-495-1558 cmsfsugarland@gmail.com www.cmsfglobal.com Monastery / Religious Order of the congregation of the Missionary Brothers of Saint Francis of Assisi Bro. Joseph Chacko, C.M.S.F, Supr.; Bro. Jaison Augustine, C.M.S.F., Treas.; Brs.: 2

NURSING / REHABILITATION / CONVALESCENCE / ELDERLY CARE [NUR]

HOUSTON

St. Dominic Village - 2401 Holcombe Blvd., Houston, TX 77021 t) 713-741-8701 ashields@stdominicvillage.org www.stdominicvillage.org Amy Shields, CEO; Asstd. Annu.: 600; Staff: 105

Archbishop Joseph A. Fiorenza Priest Retirement Residence - 2407 Holcombe Blvd., Houston, TX 77021-2023 t) 713-440-3437 ghilbig@archgh.org Dcn. Gary Hilbig, Clergy Pastoral Outreach Min.;

St. Dominic Village Independent & Assisted Living - 2401A Holcombe Blvd., Houston, TX 77021 t) 713-741-8700 lgillespie@stdominicvillage.org

St. Dominic Village Rehabilitation and Nursing Center - 2409 Holcombe Blvd., Houston, TX 77021

PRESCHOOLS / CHILDCARE CENTERS [PRE]

PLANTERSVILLE

School of Environmental Education - Camp Kappe - 7738 Camp Kappe Rd., Plantersville, TX 77363 t) 936-894-2141 mrichmond@archgh.org Michael Richmond, Dir.;

RETREAT HOUSES / RENEWAL CENTERS [RTR]

DICKINSON

Christian Renewal Center (CRC Retreat Partners, Inc.) - 1515 Hughes Rd., Dickinson, TX 77539-0699; Mailing: PO Box 699, Dickinson, TX 77539 t) 281-337-1312 kbrown@retreatcentercrc.org www.retreatcentercrc.org Catholic Retreat Center. Kim Brown, Dir.;

HOUSTON

Holy Name Retreat Center - 430 Bunker Hill Rd., Houston, TX 77024-6399 t) 713-464-0211 holyname@passionist.org holynameretreatcenter Rev. Nicholas Divine, C.P., Dir. Ministry; Dcn. James Anderson, Admin.; Katherine Mims, Dir.;

SEMINARIES [SEM]

HOUSTON

St. Mary's Seminary - 9845 Memorial Dr., Houston, TX 77024-3498 t) 713-686-4345 sms@smseminary.com smseminary.com Rev. Matthew Gilbert Suniga, Admin.; Rev. Michael G Earthman, Liturgy Dir.; Kathi Kramer, Pst. Min./Coord.; Rev. Msgr. Chester L. Borski, Spiritual Adv./Care Srvcs.; Rev. Rafael R. Davila, M.M., Spiritual Adv./Care Srvcs.; Rev. Richard R. Hinkley, Spiritual Adv./Care Srvcs.; Very Rev. Eurel Manzano, Rector; Rev. Paul E. Lockey, Prof.; Rev.

Leon Strieder, Prof.; Rev. Charles J. Talar, Prof.; Stds.: 47; Lay Tchrs.: 2; Pr. Tchrs.: 8

SPECIAL CARE FACILITIES [SPF]

HOUSTON

Casa de Esperanza De Los Ninos, Inc. - ; Mailing: P.O. Box 66581, Houston, TX 77266-6581 t) 713-529-0639 casa@casahope.org www.casahope.org Homes for children in crisis situations, foster care, adoption. Kathleen Foster, Dir.;

Casa Juan Diego - ; Mailing: P.O. Box 70113, Houston, TX 77270 t) 713-869-7376 info@cjd.org www.cjd.org Louise Zwick, Dir.; Bed Capacity: 82; Asstd. Annu.: 54,720; Staff: 16

Casa Maria de Guadalupe Medical Clinic and Social Service Center - 6101 Edgemoor, Houston, TX 77270; Mailing: P. O. Box 70113, Houston, TX 77270

Covenant House Texas - 1111 Lovett Blvd., Houston, TX 77006 t) 713-523-2231 lkbourne@covenanthouse.org www.covenanthousetx.org Leslie Bourne, Contact;

Magnificat Houses Inc. - 3209 Austin St., Houston, TX 77004; Mailing: P.O. Box 8486, Houston, TX 77288 t) 713-529-4231 x4 apieniazek@mhihouston.org mhihouston.org/ Sr. Reena Thonippara, Contact; Bed Capacity: 130; Asstd. Annu.: 56,552; Staff: 28

San Jose Clinic - 2615 Fannin, Houston, TX 77252-2808; Mailing: P.O. Box 2808, Houston, TX 77252-2808 t) 713-490-2601 info@sanjoseclinic.org www.sanjoseclinic.org Maureen Sanders, Dir.;

Santa Maria Hostel - 2605 Parker Rd., Houston, TX 77093 t) 713-691-0900; 713-957-2413; 713-691-0900 www.santamariahostel.org Nadine Scamp, CEO; Bed Capacity: 231; Asstd. Annu.: 5,418; Staff: 149

SPLENDORA

Shalom Center, Inc. - 13516 Morgan Dr., Splendora, TX 77372-3121; Mailing: P.O. Box 1148, Splendora, TX 77372 t) 281-399-0520 info@shalomcenterinc.org www.shalomcenterinc.org A residential renewal and treatment center for priests, brothers and sisters. Also offers sabbatical and retreats. Daniel A. Kidd, CEO; Patricia Reed, Dir.; Bed Capacity: 20; Asstd. Annu.: 383; Staff: 30

Diocese of Gary

(Dioecesis Gariensis)

MOST REVEREND ROBERT J. MCCLORY

Bishop of Gary; ordained May 22, 1999; appointed Bishop of Gary November 26, 2019; installed February 11, 2020. Office: 9292 Broadway, Merrillville, IN 46410.

Chancery: 9292 Broadway, Merrillville, IN 46410. T: 219-769-9292; F: 219-738-9034. www.dcgary.org

ESTABLISHED DECEMBER 17, 1956.

Square Miles 1,807.

Comprises the Counties of Lake, LaPorte, Porter and Starke in the State of Indiana.

For legal titles of parishes and diocesan institutions, consult the Chancery.

STATISTICAL OVERVIEW

Personnel

Bishop	1
Priests: Diocesan Active in Diocese	43
Priests: Retired, Sick or Absent	34
Number of Diocesan Priests	77
Religious Priests in Diocese	47
Total Priests in your Diocese	124
Extern Priests in Diocese	5
Ordinations:	
Religious Priests	1
Transitional Deacons	1
Permanent Deacons	2
Permanent Deacons in Diocese	70
Total Brothers	12
Total Sisters	56

Parishes

Parishes	59
With Resident Pastor:	
Resident Diocesan Priests	35
Resident Religious Priests	7
Without Resident Pastor:	
Administered by Priests	16
Administered by Deacons	1
Missions	2
Pastoral Centers	6
Professional Ministry Personnel:	
Brothers	3
Sisters	20
Lay Ministers	129

Welfare

Catholic Hospitals	7
Total Assisted	2,374,799
Homes for the Aged	1
Total Assisted	25
Residential Care of Children	1
Total Assisted	16
Day Care Centers	1
Total Assisted	37
Specialized Homes	2
Special Centers for Social Services	7
Total Assisted	35,000
Residential Care of Disabled	1

Educational

Diocesan Students in Other Seminaries	13
Total Seminarians	13
Colleges and Universities	1
Total Students	664
High Schools, Diocesan and Parish	3
Total Students	1,248
High Schools, Private	1
Total Students	18
Elementary Schools, Diocesan and Parish	17
Total Students	4,397
Catechesis/Religious Education:	
High School Students	132
Elementary Students	4,870
Total Students under Catholic Instruction	11,342
Teachers in Diocese:	
Sisters	3
Lay Teachers	474

Vital Statistics

Receptions into the Church:	
Infant Baptism Totals	915
Minor Baptism Totals	59
Adult Baptism Totals	39
Received into Full Communion	79
First Communions	1,057
Confirmations	1,111
Marriages:	
Catholic	206
Interfaith	57
Total Marriages	263
Deaths	1,219
Total Catholic Population	170,144
Total Population	810,210

LEADERSHIP

Moderator of the Curia - Very Rev. Christopher M. Stanish;
Vicar General - Very Rev. Christopher M. Stanish;
Chancery - t) 219-769-9292 Rev. Kevin R. Huber, Chancellor; Valerie D. McManus, Chancery Specialist;
Bishop's Delegate for Sexual Misconduct Matters - Kelly Venegas;
Chief Financial Officer - Kathy Tomasik;
Executive Assistant to the Bishop - Carrie Martinez;
Deans -
Gary/North Lake Deanery - t) 219-844-3438 Rev. Charles A. Mosley;
LaPorte/Starke Deanery - t) 219-872-9196 Rev. David W. Kime;
Porter Deanery - t) 219-464-4831 Rev. Douglas J. Mayer;
South Lake Deanery - t) 219-836-8610 Rev. Michael J. Yadron;
Diocesan Tribunal - t) 219-769-9292
Auditor - Teri Kopil;
Defender of the Bond - Sr. Evelyn Ovalles; Msgr. John J. Siekierski; Rev. Ivan Carrillo;
Judge - Rev. Sammie L. Maletta;
Judicial Vicar - Very Rev. Brian D. Chadwick;
Notaries - Mildred Virus; Valerie McManus; Carrie Martinez;
Promoter of Justice - Msgr. John J. Siekierski;
Bishop's Council of Priests - Rev. Michael G. Heimer; Rev. Gregory A. Bim-Merle; Rev. Declan McNicholas;
Consultors - Rev. David W. Kime; Rev. Douglas J. Mayer; Rev. Michael J. Yadron;
Priests' Personnel Board - Very Rev. Christopher M. Stanish, Vicar; Rev. Peter J. Muha; Rev. Lourdu Pasala;

OFFICES AND DIRECTORS

Vicar for Canonical Services - Very Rev. Brian D. Chadwick;
Campus Ministry - t) 219-464-4042 Rev. Jacob McDaniel, Chap. (jacob.mcdaniel@valpo.edu);
Catholic Charities - t) 219-886-3549 Terry Seljan, Exec. Dir.;
Catholic Committee on Scouting -
Scouting - Boys - t) 219-838-5755 Rev. Benjamin J. Ross, Chap.; Susan Kresich, Chairperson;
Scouting - Girls - t) 219-365-5217 Rev. Theodore A. Nordquist, Chap.; Jackie Krilich, Chairperson;
Catholic Foundation for Northwest Indiana - t) 219-769-9292 Judy Holicky;
Catholic Relief Services - t) 219-886-3549 Terry Seljan, Contact;
Catholic Services Appeal - t) 219-769-9292 Judy Holicky;
Catholic Youth Organization (CYO) Office - t) 219-736-8931 John Curtin, Exec. Dir.;
Cemeteries - t) 219-844-9475 Michael P. Welsh;
Communications Office - t) 219-769-9292 Colleen Rabine, Dir.;
Cursillos in Christianity - Rev. Thomas E. Mischler, Chap. (English); Rev. Eduardo Malagon, Chap. (Spanish); Michele Daily, Co-Dir.;
Diaconate - Dcn. Thomas Gryzbek, Post-Ordination Dir.;
Employee Benefits - t) 219-769-9292 Rachel Green, Coord.;
Finance Council - t) 219-769-9292 Kathleen Tomasik, CFO; Rev. Joseph M. Pawlowski; Calvin E. Bellamy;
Human Resources - t) 219-769-9292 Kelly Venegas, Mgr.;
Indiana Catholic Conference - t) 219-769-9292 Gregory Sobkowski;
Intercultural Ministry - t) 219-769-9292 Erica Jimenez, Dir.;
Lay Ministry Formation Office - t) 219-769-9292 Rev. Leonardo Gajardo, Dir. (lgajardo@dcgary.org);
Legal Counsel - t) 219-841-5683 Robert M. Schwerd;
Marriage and Family Ministries - t) 219-769-9292 Sean Martin, Dir.;
Marriage Dispensations - t) 219-769-9292 Very Rev. Brian D. Chadwick;
Marriage Encounter - t) 800-442-3553 Rosanne Kouris, Dir.;
Mission Office - t) 219-789-2391 Rev. John J. Zemelko, Dir.;
Newspaper - t) 219-769-9292 Erin Ciszczon, Editor;
Persons with Disabilities - t) 219-769-9292 Erica Jimenez, Dir.;
Priestly Life Coordinator - t) 219-942-6441 Rev. Benjamin J. Ross, Coord.;
Priests' Pension Board - John J. Diederich; Rev. Ted J. Mauch (pastor@46410.org); Rev. James E. Wozniak;
Pro-Life Activities - t) 219-696-7307 Rev. Richard C. Holy;
Religious Education and Evangelization Office - t) 219-769-9292 Sean Martin, Dir.;
Retirement Plan of the Diocese of Gary, Indiana - t) 219-769-9292 Kelly Venegas, Admin.;
Safe Environment Program - t) 219-769-9292 Kathy Lafakis, Coord.;
St. Vincent de Paul Society - t) 219-845-7531 Mike Martinelli, Pres.;
Schools Office - t) 219-769-9292 Dr. Joseph Majchrowicz, Supt.; Julie Remschneider, Asst. Supt.;
Stewardship and Development Office - t) 219-769-9292 Judy Holicky;
Vicar for Clergy - t) 219-926-1282 Very Rev. Jon J. Plavcan;
Victim Assistance Coordinator - t) 219-512-4495 Cheryl Sopo;
Vocations - t) 219-464-4042 Very Rev. Christopher M. Stanish, Dir.; Rev. Nathaniel Edquist, Asst. Dir.; Rev. Jacob McDaniel, Asst. Dir.;
Worship and Spirituality, Office of - t) 219-769-9292 Rev. Martin J. Dobrzynski, Dir.;
Youth and Young Adult Ministry - t) 219-769-9292 Victoria Hathaway, Dir.;

PARISHES, MISSIONS, AND CLERGY

STATE OF INDIANA

BEVERLY SHORES

St. Ann - 433 E. Golfwood Rd., Beverly Shores, IN 46301; Mailing: P.O. Box 727, Beverly Shores, IN 46301 t) 219-879-7565 stannesdunnes@comcast.net www.st-ann-of-the-dunes.org Very Rev. Jon J. Plavcan, Admin.; Rev. Gediminas Kersys, Pastoral Care for the Lithuanian Community;

CEDAR LAKE

Holy Name - 11000 W. 133rd Ave., Cedar Lake, IN 46303 t) 219-374-7160; 219-232-2778 (CRP) office@holynamecl.org holynamecl.org Rev. Patrick Gawrylewski, O.F.M., Admin.; Dcn. John Bacon; Dcn. Barry Cummins; Dcn. Thomas R. Kubik; Mercedes Austgen, Pst. Assoc.; CRP Stds.: 185
Parish Center - 13209 Schneider St., Cedar Lake, IN 46303 t) 219-374-8798 discovermass.com/church/holy-name-cedar-lake-in

CHESTERTON

St. Patrick - 638 N. Calumet Rd., Chesterton, IN 46304-1502 t) 219-926-1282 churchoffice@stpatsparish.org www.stpatsparish.org Very Rev. Jon J. Plavcan, Pst.; CRP Stds.: 167
St. Patrick School - 640 N. Calumet Rd., Chesterton, IN 46304-1502 t) 219-926-1707 school@stpatsparish.org Richard Rupcich, Prin.; Stds.: 302; Lay Tchrs.: 14

CROWN POINT

Holy Spirit - 7667 E. 109th Ave., Crown Point, IN 46307 t) 219-661-0644 holyspirit.winfield@gmail.com; formationmcnamara@gmail.com catholicfamilyhs.org Rev. Thomas E. Mischler, Pst.; Dcn. Thomas Maicher; Rochelle McNamara, DRE; Suzanne K. Mycka, Bus. Mgr.; CRP Stds.: 121
St. Mary - 321 E. Joliet St., Crown Point, IN 46307 t) 219-663-0044 churchoffice@stmarycp.org www.stmarycrownpoint.org Rev. Kevin R. Huber, Pst.; CRP Stds.: 331
St. Mary School - 405 E. Joliet St., Crown Point, IN 46307 t) 219-663-0676 truiz@stmarycp.org stmarycrownpoint.org L. Thomas Ruiz, Prin.; Stds.: 493; Lay Tchrs.: 27
St. Matthias - 101 W. Burrell Dr., Crown Point, IN 46307 t) 219-663-2201; 219-663-4281 (CRP) office@stmatthiasparish.net; jackiemgentry@yahoo.com www.stmatthiasparish.net Rev. James E. Wozniak, Pst.; Dcn. Gregory Fabian; Dcn. Richard F. Hilbrich; Jackie Gentry, DRE; CRP Stds.: 300

DYER

St. Joseph - 440 Joliet St., Dyer, IN 46311 t) 219-865-2271 office@stjosephdyer.org www.stjosephdyer.org Rev. Peter J. Muha, Pst.; Dcn. Gary Blue, Pst. Assoc.; CRP Stds.: 15
St. Maria Goretti - 500 Northgate Dr., Dyer, IN 46311 t) 219-322-6124 (Christian Formation); 219-865-8956 info@smgdyer.org stmariagorettichurch.org Rev. Leonardo Gajardo, Admin.; Dcn. Phillip L. Muvich; Dcn. Daniel Ratliff; Kathy Hansen, DRE; CRP Stds.: 310

EAST CHICAGO

Holy Trinity - 4754 Carey St., East Chicago, IN 46312 t) 219-398-3061 holytrinitycroatian78@gmail.com Rev. Terrence J. Steffens, Admin.; Cynthia Rivas, DRE; Carmen Vasquez, DRE; CRP Stds.: 15
St. Mary - 4316 Indianapolis Blvd., East Chicago, IN 46312 t) 219-398-2409 office@stmaryec.com Rev. Nestor A. Varon, AIC, Pst.; CRP Stds.: 171
Our Lady of Guadalupe - 3510 Deodar St., East Chicago, IN 46312 t) 219-398-0253 olg.ec2020@gmail.com Rev. Diego Florez, A.I.C., Pst.; Rosalva Quintanilla, DRE; CRP Stds.: 101
St. Patrick Roman Catholic Church - 3814 Grand Blvd., East Chicago, IN 46312 t) 219-398-0253 (CRP); 219-398-1036 Rev. Diego Florez, A.I.C.; Dcn. Raymond E. Helfen; Rosalba Quintanilla, DRE; CRP Stds.: 16
St. Stanislaus Roman Catholic Church - 808 W. 150th St., East Chicago, IN 46312 t) 219-397-7059 (CRP); 219-398-2341 john_s96@yahoo.com Msgr. John J. Siekierski, Admin.; Sr. Gloria Jean Kozlowski, DRE; CRP Stds.: 8
St. Stanislaus School - 4930 Indianapolis Blvd., East Chicago, IN 46312 t) 219-398-1316 Anne Jackie Ruiz, Prin.; Stds.: 134; Lay Tchrs.: 11
Convent - 4914 Magoun Ave., East Chicago, IN 46312 Sr. Gloria Jean Kozlowski, SSJ-TOSF, DRE;

GARY

Cathedral of the Holy Angels - 640 Tyler St., Gary, IN 46402-2299 t) 219-882-6079 rector@garycathedral.org www.garycathedral.org Rev. Michael Surufka, OFM, Pst.; Dcn. Martin J. Brown; Dcn. Jose A. Serrano;
St. Ann - 6025 W. 25th Ave., Gary, IN 46406; Mailing: 525 N. Broad St., Griffith, IN 46319 t) 219-924-4163 stmarygriffith@comcast.net Rev. Keith Virus, Admin.; CRP Stds.: 5
St. Joseph the Worker - 330 E. 45th Ave., Gary, IN 46409 t) 219-980-1846 stjosephgary@gmail.com Rev. Michael Surufka, O.F.M., Admin.; Dcn. Christopher McIntire; Mildred Santos, DRE; CRP Stds.: 71
St. Mary of the Lake - 6060 Miller Ave., Gary, IN 46403 t) 219-938-1373 stmary_garyin@comcast.net stmaryofthelakegary.org Dcn. Stephen K. Grandfield;
SS. Monica-St. Luke - 645 Rhode Island, Gary, IN 46402 t) 219-883-1861 monicaluke@comcast.net Rev. Michael Surufka, O.F.M., Pst.; Rev. Juan Turcios, OFM, Assoc. Pst.;

GRIFFITH

St. Mary - 525 N. Broad St., Griffith, IN 46319-2225

t) 219-924-4163 stmarygriffith@comcast.net; st_mary_reled_griffith@yahoo.com www.smgriffith.org Rev. Keith M. Virus, Admin.; Liz Stadnik, DRE; CRP Stds.: 85

St. Mary School - (Grades PreK-8) t) 219-924-8633 st.marys@comcast.net Rebecca Maskovich, Prin.; Stds.: 200; Lay Tchrs.: 13

Convent - 508 N. Lafayette St., Griffith, IN 46319 t) 219-922-2278

HAMLET

Holy Cross - 6 W. Pearl St., Hamlet, IN 46532; Mailing: P.O. Box 234, Hamlet, IN 46532 t) 574-867-2461 spanleyhcsd@gmail.com Rev. Anthony L. Spanley, Pst.;

St. Dominic - 10440 E. SR 23, Walkerton, IN 46532

HAMMOND

All Saints - 570 Sibley St., Hammond, IN 46325-0836; Mailing: P.O. Box 836, Hammond, IN 46325-0836 t) 219-932-0204 Rev. Eduardo Malagon, Pst.; Rev. Stephen Gibson, Assoc. Pst.; CRP Stds.: 30

St. Casimir - 4340 Johnson St., Hammond, IN 46327 t) 219-931-2589; 219-932-2666 (CRP) saintcasimirchurch@comcast.net stcashammond.org Rev. Eduardo Malagon, Pst.; Rev. Stephen Gibson, Assoc. Pst.; CRP Stds.: 74

St. Casimir School - 4329 Cameron St., Hammond, IN 46327 t) 219-932-2686 mchico@stcasschool.org Matt Chico, Prin.; Stds.: 387; Lay Tchrs.: 22

St. John Bosco - 7113 Columbia Ave., Hammond, IN 46324 t) 219-844-9027 frjeff@st-johnbosco.org; deaconmatt@st-johnbosco.org www.sjbhammond.org Rev. Jeffrey D. Burton, Admin.; Dcn. Matthew Virus; Vickie Blackwood, DRE; CRP Stds.: 72

St. John Bosco - (Grades PreK-8) 1231 171st Pl., Hammond, IN 46324 t) 219-845-6226 nrepay@st-johnbosco.org www.stjohnboscoschool.org Nancy Repay, Prin.; Stds.: 207; Lay Tchrs.: 15

St. Joseph - 5304 Hohman Ave., Hammond, IN 46320-1808 t) 219-932-0702 saintjosephhammond@comcast.net www.stjoehmd.com Rev. Jeffrey D. Burton, Pst.; CRP Stds.: 20

St. Margaret Mary - 1445 Hoffman St., Hammond, IN 46327 t) 219-931-5229 stmargaretmary149@gmail.com Rev. Luis Ferneidy Cardona, AIC, Pst.; Sr. Rosa Valencia, DRE; CRP Stds.: 258

Our Lady of Perpetual Help - 7132 Arizona St., Hammond, IN 46323 t) 219-844-3438 x228 (CRP); 219-844-3438 frmosley@sbcglobal.net; olphfaith@sbcglobal.net olphparish.live Rev. Charles A. Mosley, Pst.; Alfredo Flores, DRE; CRP Stds.: 51

HEBRON

St. Helen - 302 N. Madison St., Hebron, IN 46341 t) 219-996-4611 sthelenchurch@comcast.net catholicfamilyhs.org/ Rev. Thomas E. Mischler, Pst.; CRP Stds.: 19

HIGHLAND

St. James the Less - 9640 Kennedy Ave., Highland, IN 46322 t) 219-924-4220; 219-924-4222 (CRP) stjames4220@sbcglobal.net www.stjameshighland.org Rev. Gregory A. Bim-Merle, Admin.; Dcn. Michael W. Halas; Emilija Lapas, DRE; Sr. Dcn. Martin Denkhoff; CRP Stds.: 98

Our Lady of Grace - 3025 Highway Ave., Highland, IN 46322; Mailing: 3005 Condit St., Highland, IN 46322 t) 219-934-7176 ourladygrace@sbcglobal.net; olgdre1@yahoo.com olgcatholicchurchhighland.org Very Rev. Brian D. Chadwick, Pst.; Donna Velez, DRE; CRP Stds.: 70

Our Lady of Grace School - (Grades PreK-8) t) 219-934-7178 olgracesecretary@gmail.com; principalolg@gmail.com www.olgraceschool.org Mark Topp, Prin.; Stds.: 153; Lay Tchrs.: 10

HOBART

Assumption of the Blessed Virgin Mary - 3530 Illinois St., Hobart, IN 46342 t) 219-962-6678 (CRP); 219-962-1073 lourdupasala54@gmail.com Rev. Lourdu Pasala, Pst.; Dorie Little, DRE; CRP Stds.: 21

St. Bridget - 107 Main St., Hobart, IN 46342-0408; Mailing: P.O. Box 408, Hobart, IN 46342-0408 t) 219-942-6441 x121 Rev. Benjamin J. Ross, Pst.; CRP Stds.: 75

KNOX

St. Thomas Aquinas - 406E. Washington St., Knox, IN 46534 t) 574-772-4134 c) (219) 617-1591 frloncars@gmail.com Rev. Stephen Loncar, O.F.M.Conv., Pst.; CRP Stds.: 9

KOUTS

St. Mary - 402 E. Indiana Ave., State Rd. 8, Kouts, IN 46347; Mailing: P.O. Box 663, Kouts, IN 46347 t) 219-766-3680 stmarykouts@frontier.com Rev. Thomas E. Mischler, Admin.; Dcn. Jim F. Knopf; CRP Stds.: 14

LA PORTE

Holy Family - 201 Bach St., La Porte, IN 46350 t) 219-362-2815 office@holyfamilylaporte.org www.holyfamilylaporte.org/ Rev. Nate Edquist, Admin.; Rev. Ian J. Williams, Pastor Emer.; Dcn. Robert J. Bucheit; Dcn. Frank J. Zolvinski; CRP Stds.: 250

LAKE STATION

St. Francis Xavier - 2447 Putnam St., Lake Station, IN 46405 t) 219-962-4507 (CRP); 219-962-8626 shirleyportega@gmail.com; st.francisxavierls@gmail.com francis-xavier-ls.net Rev. Jaime Perea; CRP Stds.: 165

LOWELL

St. Edward - 216 S. Nichols St., Lowell, IN 46356 t) 219-696-7307 stedwardchurch@sbcglobal.net www.stedlowell.com Rev. Richard C. Holy, Pst.; Dcn. Roberto Mendoza; Dcn. William Hathaway, DRE; CRP Stds.: 103

MERRILLVILLE

Holy Martyrs - 801 W. 73rd Ave., Merrillville, IN 46410 t) (219) 769-1755 (Parish Office) office@46410.org www.merrillvillecatholiccluster.org Rev. Ted J. Mauch, Pst.; Dcn. Thomas Gryzbek; Dcn. Robert J. Litavecz; Dcn. Malcolm Lunsford; Dcn. Steven Zubel; Melissa Novak, Pst. Min./Coord.; Cathy Scolaro, DRE; CRP Stds.: 67

St. Andrew School (Aquinas Catholic Community School) - (Grades PreK-8) t) (219) 769-2049 lgutierrez@aquinas.school www.aquinas.school Lisa Gutierrez, Prin.; Jennifer Marcheschi, Vice Prin.; Stds.: 211; Lay Tchrs.: 16

Our Lady of Consolation - 8303 Taft St., Merrillville, IN 46410 t) 219-769-1755 (Office); 219-769-2785 (Office); 219-769-2295 (CRP) church@olcweb.org; sacristan@olcweb.org www.olcweb.org Rev. Ted J. Mauch, Pst.; Dcn. Robert E. Gill; Dcn. Ralph J. Huber Jr.; Cathy Scolaro, DRE; CRP Stds.: 56

St. Stephen, Martyr - 5920 Waite St., Merrillville, IN 46410 t) 219-980-9348 ststephenmartyr@att.net Rev. Michael L. Maginot, Admin.;

MICHIGAN CITY

St. Mary of the Immaculate Conception - 411 W. 11th St., Michigan City, IN 46360 t) 219-872-9196 accounting@qas.org Rev. David W. Kime, Pst.; Dcn. Michael J. Green;

Notre Dame - 1010 Moore Rd., Michigan City, IN 46360 t) 219-872-4844 kcate@notredameparish.net Rev. Keith J. McClellan, Pst.;

Notre Dame School - (Grades PreK-8) 1000 Moore Rd, Michigan City, IN 46360 t) 219-872-6216 nmagnusen@notredameparish.net notredameparish.net Natasha Magnuson, Prin.; Stds.: 211; Lay Tchrs.: 11

Queen of All Saints - 606 S. Woodland Ave., Michigan City, IN 46360 t) 219-872-9196 qas.org Rev. David W. Kime, Pst.; Dcn. Michael J. Green; Rev. Jordan C. Fetcko, Sacr. Min.; CRP Stds.: 110

Queen of All Saints School - (Grades PreSchool-8) 1715 E. Barker Ave., Michigan City, IN 46360 t) 219-872-4420 principal@qas.org Kim Gondeck, Prin.; Stds.: 173; Lay Tchrs.: 16

St. Stanislaus Kostka - 1506 Washington St., Michigan City, IN 46360 t) 219-879-9281 sanctusstanislaus.com Rev. Walter M. Ciesla, Pst.; Bro. Shaun Gray, DRE; CRP Stds.: 12

St. Stanislaus Kostka School - t) 219-872-2258 office@ststansec.org santusstanislaus.com Christopher Evans, Prin.; Stds.: 114; Lay Tchrs.: 10

MUNSTER

St. Thomas More - 8501 Calumet Ave., Munster, IN 46321 t) 219-836-8610 parish.office@stm-church.com; ehackett@stm-church.com www.stm-church.com Rev. Michael J. Yadron, Pst.; Dcn. David J. Kapala; Dcn. Joseph Stodola; Dcn. Napoleon Tabion; Angie Lorandos, Music Min.; Emily Hackett, DRE; CRP Stds.: 232

St. Thomas More School - 8435 Calumet Ave., Munster, IN 46321 t) 219-836-9151 schooloffice@stm-school.com www.stm-school.com Samantha Hofferth-Francis, D.C., Prin.; Stds.: 424; Pr. Tchrs.: 1; Lay Tchrs.: 34

NORTH JUDSON

Ss. Cyril and Methodius - 303 Keller Ave., North Judson, IN 46366 t) 574-896-2195 peg@saintscyrilandmethodius.com scmccnj.org Rev. Terrence W. Bennis, Pst.; Peggy Okeley, Pst. Assoc.; Sue Dolezal, DRE; CRP Stds.: 18

OTIS

St. Mary - 101 N. Church St., Otis, IN 46391; Mailing: P.O. Box 386, Wanatah, IN 46390 t) 219-733-2955; 219-926-1639 (CRP) mtgroszek@gmail.com thecatholiccommunities.org Rev. Paul E. Quanz, Admin.; Dcn. Sherman Brown; Dcn. Jeffery L. Newburn; Dcn. Dale Walsh; Rev. John J. Zemelko, In Res.; Mary Ann Groszek, DRE; CRP Stds.: 35

PORTAGE

Nativity of Our Savior - 2949 Willowcreek Rd., Portage, IN 46368 t) 219-764-3143 (CRP); 219-762-4858 guernsey@nativityofoursavior.net; faithformation@nativityofoursavior.net nativityofoursavior.org Rev. Kevin P. McCarthy, Pst.; Dcn. Robert J. Bonta; Dcn. Stephen K. Grandfield; Dcn. Dennis M. Guernsey; Dcn. Richard Huber; Jason Yurechko, DRE; CRP Stds.: 107

Nativity of Our Savior School - (Grades PreK-8) 2929 Willowcreek Rd., Portage, IN 46368 t) 219-763-2400 principal@nativityofoursavior.net www.nativityofoursavior.net Sally Skowronski, Prin.; Stds.: 174; Lay Tchrs.: 10

SAINT JOHN

St. John the Evangelist - 10701 Olcott Ave., Saint John, IN 46373; Mailing: 11301 W. 93rd Ave., Saint John, IN 46373-9715 t) (219) 365-5678 x237; (219) 365-5678 x267 (CRP) hr@stjohnparish.org; khattar@stjohnparish.org stjohnparish.org Rev. Sammie L. Maletta, Pst.; Rev. Declan McNicholas, Assoc. Pst.; Dcn. Ray Carratini; Dcn. Philip Coduti; Dcn. Edwin J. Bodley; Dcn. Paul M. Krilich; Dcn. James McFarland; Dcn. William P. Sayre; Amy Goggin, DRE; CRP Stds.: 141

St. John the Evangelist School - (Grades PreK-8) 9400 Wicker Ave., St. John, IN 46373 t) 219-365-5451 kfredericksen@stjohnparish.org www.sjeschool.org Katie Fredericksen, Prin.; Stds.: 338; Lay Tchrs.: 23

SAN PIERRE

All Saints - 201 W. Eliza St., San Pierre, IN 46374; Mailing: 303 Keller Ave., North Judson, IN 46366 t) 574-896-2195 Rev. Terrence W. Bennis, Pst.;

SCHERERVILLE

St. Michael - 1 E. Wilhelm St., Schererville, IN 46375 t) 219-322-4505 x8220; 219-322-3077 (CRP) office@stmichaelparish.life; mjones@stmichaelparish.life www.stmichaelparish.life/ Rev. Martin J. Dobrzynski, Pst.; Dcn. Gary Wolfe; Dcn. Ronald L. Pyle; Kimberley Hoogeveen, DRE; CRP Stds.: 305

Preschool - 16 W. Wilhelm St., Schererville, IN 46375 stmichaelparish.life/school Colleen Kennedy, Prin.;

St. Michael School - (Grades K-8) 16 W. Wilhelm St., Schererville, IN 46375 t) 219-322-4531 ckennedy@stmichaelparish.life stmichaelparish.life/school Michelle Wacnik, Prin.; Stds.: 222; Sr. Tchrs.: 2; Lay Tchrs.: 18

VALPARAISO

St. Elizabeth Seton - 509 W. Division Rd., Valparaiso,

IN 46385 t) 219-464-1624 parishoffice@seseton.com www.seseton.com Rev. Michael J. Kopil, Pst.; Dcn. Brian Nosbusch; Dcn. Michael Prendergast; Dcn. Peter Znika; CRP Stds.: 97

Our Lady of Sorrows - 356 W. 700 N., Valparaiso, IN 46385 t) 219-299-3426 (CRP); 219-759-2400 admsorrows@gmail.com; ols.parish356@gmail.com www.ols-parish.org Rev. Paul E. Quanz, Pst.; CRP Stds.: 34

St. Paul - 1855 W. Harrison Blvd., Valparaiso, IN 46385; Mailing: P.O. Box 1475, Valparaiso, IN 46384-1475 t) 219-464-4831 (Parish Office); (219) 464-8502 (R.E. Office) office@saintpaulvalpo.org; stpaulre1755@gmail.com www.saintpaulvalpo.org Rev. Douglas J. Mayer, Pst.; Rev. Roque Meraz, Assoc. Pst.; Dcn. David A. Bergstedt; Dcn. James Caristi; Dcn. Michael Foster; Dcn. Kenneth Klawitter; Mark Chargualaf, Youth Min.; Catherine Dull, Middle School Youth Min.; Diane Marie Matthys, DRE; CRP Stds.: 273

St. Paul School - (Grades PreK-8) 1755 W. Harrison Blvd., Valparaiso, IN 46385 t) 219-462-3374 lhughes@stpaulvalpo.org www.stpaulvalpo.org Lisa Hughes, Prin.; Stds.: 238; Lay Tchrs.: 15

St. Agnes Adult Day Service Center - 1859 W. Harrison Blvd., Valparaiso, IN 46385 t) 219-477-5433 barbkubiszak@gmail.com www.stagnes@saintpaulvalpo.org Barbara Kubiszak, Dir.;

WALKERTON

St. Anthony of Padua - 7732 E. State Rd. 4, Walkerton, IN 46574 t) 219-369-1210 stanthony.kanty@frontier.com Rev. Michael G. Heimer, Pst.;

St. John Kanty - 7732 E. State Rd. 4, Walkerton, IN 46574 t) 219-369-1210 stanthony.kanty@frontier.com Rev. Michael G. Heimer, Admin.; Robert Chance, DRE; CRP Stds.: 70

WANATAH

Sacred Heart - 202 N. Ohio St., Wanatah, IN 46390; Mailing: PO Box 386, Wanatah, IN 46390 t) 219-733-2955 thecatholiccommunities.org Rev. Paul E. Quanz, Admin.; Dcn. Sherman Brown; Dcn. Jeffery L. Newburn; Dcn. Dale Walsh; Rev. John J. Zemelko, In Res.; Staci Bolakowski, DRE; CRP Stds.: 70

St. Martin - 118 Lowell St., LaCrosse, IN 46348

WHITING

St. Adalbert - 1340 121st St., Whiting, IN 46394; Mailing: 1849 Lincoln Ave., Whiting, IN 46394 t) 219-659-0023 cchurchparishoffice@stjohnbap.org Rev. Mark R. Peres, C.PP.S., Pst.; Jamie Sandona, DRE;

St. John the Baptist - 1849 Lincoln Ave., Whiting, IN 46394 t) 219-659-0023 churchparishoffice@stjohnbap.org; jsandona@stjohnbap.org stjohnbap.org Rev. Mark R. Peres, C.PP.S., Pst.; Dcn. Leo V. Barron Jr.; Dcn. Joseph Manchak; Jamie Sandona, DRE; Rebecca Flores, Bus. Mgr.; CRP Stds.: 90

St. John the Baptist School - (Grades PreK-8) 1844 Lincoln Ave., Whiting, IN 46394 t) 219-659-3042 jjones@stjohnbap.org Jessica Gonzalez, Prin.; Stds.: 260; Lay Tchrs.: 23

Sacred Heart - 1731 Laporte Ave., Whiting, IN 46394 t) 219-659-0733 sacredheart1889@gmail.com www.sacredheartwhiting.com Rev. Nuthulapati Jayababu, CPPS, Admin.; Rev. Selvaraj Selladurai, In Res.; Daniel R Mauch, DRE; CRP Stds.: 55

SCHOOLS: PRESCHOOL THRU HIGH SCHOOL

SCHOOLS

STATE OF INDIANA

ROLLING PRAIRIE

Sacred Heart Apostolic School, Inc. - (PRV) (Grades 8-12) 5901 N. 500 E., Rolling Prairie, IN 46371; Mailing: P.O. Box 7, Rolling Prairie, IN 46371 t) 219-778-4596 bmrprairie@arcol.org Rev. Ronald Conklin, L.C., Rector; Rev. Steven Liscinsky, L.C., Prin., Vice Supr.; Rev. Paul Silva, L.C., Admissions Dir.; Rev. Thomas Murphy, L.C., Dean of Students; Rev. Christopher Gronotte, L.C., Gen. Dean, Students; Rev. Robert DeCesare, Asst. Admissions Dir.; Rev. John Doyle, Prof.; Stds.: 18; Pr. Tchrs.: 1; Lay Tchrs.: 4

HIGH SCHOOLS

STATE OF INDIANA

HAMMOND

Bishop Noll Institute - (DIO) (Grades 9-12) 1519 Hoffman St., Hammond, IN 46327 t) 219-932-9058 lpastrick@bishopnoll.org; anunez-orozco@bishopnoll.org www.bishopnoll.org Lorenza Jara Pastrick, Prin.; Paul Mullaney, Pres.; Stds.: 547; Lay Tchrs.: 41

MERRILLVILLE

Andrean High School - (DIO) 5959 Broadway, Merrillville, IN 46410 t) 219-887-5959 jknazur@andreanhs.com www.andreanhs.org Jaycob Knazur, Prin.; Kelly Fitzgerald, Asst. Prin.; Stds.: 465; Lay Tchrs.: 36

MICHIGAN CITY

Marquette Catholic High School - (DIO) 306 W. Tenth St., Michigan City, IN 46360 t) 219-873-1325 jquinlan@marquette-hs.org www.marquette-hs.org Allyson Headd, Prin.; Stds.: 225; Lay Tchrs.: 23

INSTITUTIONS LOCATED IN DIOCESE

CAMPUS MINISTRY / NEWMAN CENTERS [CAM]

VALPARAISO

St. Teresa of Avila Catholic Student Center - 1511 LaPorte Ave., Valparaiso, IN 46383-5818 t) 219-464-4042 saintt.office@gmail.com www.saintt.com Rev. Jacob McDaniel, Chap.; Dcn. Edward Kozub; Dcn. Christopher Hawkins; Dcn. Robert W. Marben;

CATHOLIC CHARITIES [CCH]

GARY

Catholic Charities, Diocese of Gary, Inc. - 940 Broadway, Gary, IN 46402 t) 219-886-3549 info@catholic-charities.org www.catholic-charities.org Terry Seljan, CEO; Asstd. Annu.: 35,000; Staff: 17

CEMETERIES [CEM]

HAMMOND

Saint John-Saint Joseph - 1547 167th St., Hammond, IN 46320 t) 219-844-9475 mwelsh@garycathcems.org www.garycathcems.org Rev. Michael J. Yadron, Dir.; Michael P. Welsh, COO;

MICHIGAN CITY

Saint Stanislaus - 1015 Greenwood Ave., Michigan City, IN 46360 t) 219-874-4310 mwelsh@garycems.org Rev. Michael J. Yadron, Dir. Cemeteries; Michael P. Welsh, COO;

COLLEGES & UNIVERSITIES [COL]

WHITING

Calumet College of St. Joseph - 2400 New York Ave., Whiting, IN 46394 t) 219-473-7770 tmcfarland@ccsj.edu www.ccsj.edu Rev. Tim McFarland, C.PP.S., Exec.; Amy McCormack, Pres.; Derek Shouba, Dean; Dionne Jones-Malone, Dean; Diana Francis, Registrar; Lynn Miskus, Bus. Mgr.; Stds.: 664; Bro. Tchrs.: 1; Lay Tchrs.: 25; Pr. Tchrs.: 1; Sr. Tchrs.: 1

CONVENTS, MONASTERIES, AND RESIDENCES FOR WOMEN [CON]

EAST CHICAGO

St. Catherine Convent - 4325 Elm St., East Chicago, IN 46312 t) 219-398-0403 mdvorak@poorhandmaids.org www.poorhandmaids.org Sr. Michele Dvorak, PHJC, Contact; Srs.: 4

GARY

Missionaries of Charity - 509 W. Ridge Rd., Gary, IN 46408 t) 219-884-2140 Convent and emergency night shelter for women Sr. M.Celine Jhon MC, Supr.; Sr. M. Jonathan MC, Regl. Supr.; Srs.: 4

HAMMOND

Albertine Sisters (Prov. of Krakow, Poland) - 1501 Hoffman St., Hammond, IN 46327 t) 219-937-0575 albertineusa@att.net Sr. Danuta Karwacka, CSAPU, Supr.; Srs.: 9

ENDOWMENTS / FOUNDATIONS / TRUSTS [EFT]

CROWN POINT

Franciscan Health Foundation - Northern Indiana - 2050 N. Main St., Ste. A, Crown Point, IN 46307 t) 219-661-3401 nifoundation@franciscanalliance.org www.franciscanhealth.org/foundation Richard Peltier, Exec.;

HOSPITALS / HEALTH SERVICES [HOS]

CROWN POINT

Franciscan Health Crown Point - 1201 S. Main St., Crown Point, IN 46307-8483 t) 219-738-2100 daniel.mccormick@franciscanalliance.org www.franciscanalliance.org Franciscan Alliance, Inc. Rev. David Kelly, O.F.M., Chap.; Rev. Anthony F. Janik, O.F.M., Dir.; Dr. Daniel McCormick, Pres.; Sr. Ann Kathleen Magiera, OSF, Vice Pres., Mission Integration; Bed Capacity: 192; Asstd. Annu.: 464,269; Staff: 1,144

DYER

Franciscan Health Dyer - 24 Joliet, Dyer, IN 46311 t) 219-865-2141 www.franciscanhealth.org Franciscan Alliance, Inc. Rev. Gregory Holicky, Chap.; Rev. Selladurai Selvaraj, Chap.; Barbara Anderson, Pres.; Bed Capacity: 241; Asstd. Annu.: 178,498; Staff: 910

EAST CHICAGO

St. Catherine Hospital - 4321 Fir St., East Chicago, IN 46312 t) 219-392-1700 tpedroza@comhs.org www.comhs.org Leo Correa, CEO; Julie Latta, Dir., Finance; Teresa Pedroza, Dir., Mission Integration; Bed Capacity: 216; Asstd. Annu.: 94,986; Staff: 811

HOBART

St. Mary Medical Center - 1500 S. Lake Park Ave., Hobart, IN 46342 t) 219-942-0551 tpedroza@comhs.org www.comhs.org Janice Ryba, CEO; Mary Sudicky, CFO; Teresa Pedroza, Dir., Mission Integration; Bed Capacity: 200; Asstd. Annu.: 314,168; Staff: 1,139

MICHIGAN CITY

Franciscan Health Michigan City - 3500 N. Franciscan Way, Michigan City, IN 46360 t) 219-879-8511 dean.mazzoni@franciscanalliance.org www.franciscanhealth.org Franciscan Alliance, Inc. Rev. William F. O'Toole, Chap.; Rev. George Schopp, Chap.; Rev. Joseph Uko, Chap.; Dean Mazzoni, Pres.; Sr. M. Petra Nielsen, OSF, Vice. Pres.; Mark Grobner, Mgr. Spiritual Care; Bed Capacity: 113; Asstd. Annu.: 512,094; Staff: 1,243

MUNSTER

Franciscan Health Munster - 701 Superior Ave., Munster, IN 46321 t) 219-922-4200 www.franciscanhealth.org Barbara Anderson, Pres.; Rev. Francis Tebbe, O.F.M., Dir.; Bed Capacity: 78; Asstd. Annu.: 581,737; Staff: 956

MISCELLANEOUS [MIS]

GARY

Sojourner Truth House, Inc. - 410 W. 13th Ave., Gary, IN 46407 t) (219) 885-2282 acurtis@sojournertruthhouse.org www.sojournertruthhouse.org Angela Curtis, Exec. Dir.;

HAMMOND

***Alverno Provena Hospital Laboratories, Inc.** - 2434 Interstate Plaza Dr., Hammond, IN 46324 t) 219-989-3814; 800-937-5521 sam.terese@franciscanalliance.org Sam Terese, Pres.;

HealthVisions Midwest - 3700 179th St., Hammond, IN 46323 t) 219-844-2698 pwills@hvusa.org www.hvusa.org Paula Wills, Exec. Dir.;

MERRILLVILLE

Office of Intercultural Ministry - 9292 Broadway, Merrillville, IN 46410 t) 219-769-9292 x269 c) 219-769-9292 ejimenez@dcgary.org www.dcgary.org Erica Jimenez, Dir.;

VALPARAISO

Opus Dei - 359 W. 200 N., Valparaiso, IN 46385 t) 219-462-0931; 219-462-6594 shellbourne2@aol.com www.shellbourne.org Prelature of the Holy Cross and Opus Dei, Shellbourne Conference Center. Shareen Rador, Admin.;

MONASTERIES AND RESIDENCES FOR PRIESTS AND BROTHERS [MON]

CEDAR LAKE

Our Lady of Lourdes Friary - 14211 Garden Way, Cedar Lake, IN 46303; Mailing: P.O. Box 627, Cedar Lake, IN 46303 t) 219-374-5931 afjanik@yahoo.com Franciscan Friars of the Assumption of the Blessed Virgin Mary Province (Order of Friars Minor, O.F.M.), Franklin, Wisconsin. Rev. Juan de la Cruz Turcios, Pst.; Rev. Patrick Gawrylewski, O.F.M., Pst.; Rev. Tojy Josemandapathe, Pst.; Rev. Anthony F. Janik, O.F.M., Vicar; Rev. David Kelly, O.F.M., Chap.; Rev. Michael Surufka, O.F.M.; Priests: 7

MERRILLVILLE

Salvatorian Fathers (Society of the Divine Savior) - 5755 Pennsylvania St., Merrillville, IN 46410 t) 219-884-0714 merrillville@salwatorianie.us www.salwatorianie.us Mission House for Polish Priests and Brothers. Our Lady of Czestochowa Diocesan Marian Shrine. Rev. Mikolaj Markiewicz, S.D.S, Supr.; Rev. Stanislaw Pieczara, S.D.S.; Rev. Jozef Musiol, S.D.S.; Bro. Piotr Bogawski, S.D.S.; Brs.: 1; Priests: 4

MUNSTER

Discalced Carmelite Fathers Monastery - 1628 Ridge Rd., Munster, IN 46321 t) 219-838-7111 carmelmunster@yahoo.com www.carmelitefathers.com Rev. Franciszek Czaicki, O.C.D., Prior; Rev. Jacek Chodzynski, O.C.D.; Rev. Pawel Furdzik, O.C.D.; Rev. Andrzej Gbur, O.C.D.; Rev. Waclaw L. Lech, O.C.D.; Bro. Marian Leszewicz, O.C.D.; Rev. Bronislaw F. Socha, O.C.D.; Rev. Bartlomiej Stanowski, O.C.D.; Brs.: 1; Priests: 7

NURSING / REHABILITATION / CONVALESCENCE / ELDERLY CARE [NUR]

HAMMOND

Albertine Home - 1501 Hoffman St., Hammond, IN 46327 t) 219-937-0575 albertineusa@att.net Sr. Loretta Soja, Dir.; Asstd. Annu.: 25; Staff: 9

PRESCHOOLS / CHILDCARE CENTERS [PRE]

EAST CHICAGO

Carmelite Home for Girls/Holy Innocents Shelter - 4840 Grasselli Ave., East Chicago, IN 46312 t) 219-397-1085 srmgiuseppe.carmelite@gmail.com www.carmelitedcjnorth.org Sr. Maria Giuseppe Moxley, Supr.; Stds.: 16; Lay Tchrs.: 3

RETREAT HOUSES / RENEWAL CENTERS [RTR]

VALPARAISO

Camp Lawrence - 68 E. 700 N., Valparaiso, IN 46383; Mailing: 9292 Broadway, Merrillville, IN 46410 t) 219-769-9292 x286 camp.lawrence@dcgary.org Diocesan Spiritual Center and Youth Camp. David Moore, Contact;

An asterisk (*) denotes an organization that has established tax-exempt status directly with the IRS and is not covered by the USCCB Group Ruling.

Diocese of Gaylord

(Dioecesis Gaylordensis)

MOST REVEREND JEFFREY J. WALSH

Bishop of Gaylord; ordained June 25, 1994; appointed Bishop of Gaylord December 21, 2021; Episcopal ordination and installation March 4, 2022; Diocesan Pastoral Center: 611 W. North St., Gaylord, MI 49735-8349.

Diocesan Pastoral Center: 611 W. North St., Gaylord, MI 49735-8349. T: 989-732-5147; F: 989-705-3589. www.dioceseofgaylord.org

ESTABLISHED JULY 20, 1971.

Square Miles 11,171.

Comprises the following 21 Counties in the State of Michigan: Alcona, Alpena, Antrim, Benzie, Charlevoix, Cheboygan, Crawford, Emmet, Grand Traverse, Iosco, Kalkaska, Leelanau, Manistee, Missaukee, Montmorency, Ogemaw, Oscoda, Otsego, Presque Isle, Roscommon and Wexford.

For legal titles of parishes and diocesan institutions, consult the Chancery Office.

STATISTICAL OVERVIEW

Personnel

Bishop	1
Priests: Diocesan Active in Diocese	38
Priests: Diocesan Active Outside Diocese	4
Priests: Retired, Sick or Absent	14
Number of Diocesan Priests	56
Religious Priests in Diocese	1
Total Priests in your Diocese	57
Extern Priests in Diocese	20
Permanent Deacons in Diocese	26
Total Brothers	1
Total Sisters	21

Parishes

Parishes	75
With Resident Pastor:	
Resident Diocesan Priests	35
Without Resident Pastor:	
Administered by Priests	27
Administered by Deacons	4
Administered by Religious Women	2
Administered by Lay People	7
Professional Ministry Personnel:	
Sisters	2
Lay Ministers	4

Welfare

Catholic Hospitals	1
Total Assisted	181,394
Day Care Centers	14
Total Assisted	503
Special Centers for Social Services	16
Total Assisted	35,924

Educational

Diocesan Students in Other Seminaries	5
Total Seminarians	5
High Schools, Diocesan and Parish	4
Total Students	551
Elementary Schools, Diocesan and Parish	15
Total Students	2,039
Catechesis / Religious Education:	
High School Students	242
Elementary Students	977
Total Students under Catholic Instruction	3,814
Teachers in Diocese:	
Sisters	4
Lay Teachers	249

Vital Statistics

Receptions into the Church:	
Infant Baptism Totals	339
Minor Baptism Totals	30
Adult Baptism Totals	38
Received into Full Communion	98
First Communions	409
Confirmations	436
Marriages:	
Catholic	138
Interfaith	47
Total Marriages	185
Deaths	804
Total Catholic Population	43,361
Total Population	514,708

LEADERSHIP

College of Consultors - t) 989-732-5147 Rev. James P. Hayden (jhayden@dioceseofgaylord.org); Rev. Dennis R. Stilwell (dstilwell@dioceseofgaylord.org); Rev. Anthony M. Citro (acitro@dioceseofgaylord.org);

OFFICES AND DIRECTORS

Diocesan Pastoral Center - t) 989-732-5147 dioceseofgaylord.org

Office of the Bishop - t) (989) 705-3529 Patty Nemecek, Admin. Asst. to Bishop (pnemecek@dioceseofgaylord.org);

Vicar General/Moderator of the Curia - t) 989-705-3545 Rev. James P. Hayden, V.G., Moderator of the Curia (jhayden@dioceseofgaylord.org);

Chancellor - t) 989-705-3551 Julie Erhardt, Chancellor (jerhardt@dioceseofgaylord.org); Rev. Matthew A. Furgiuele, Asst. Chancellor (mfurgiuele@dioceseofgaylord.org);

Administrative Services - t) 989-705-3512 Kim A. Smith, Dir. (ksmith@dioceseofgaylord.org);

Catholic Schools - t) 989-705-3509 Erick Chittle, Supt. (echittle@gtacs.org); Caryn Jacobs, Admin. Asst. (cjacobs@dioceseofgaylord.org);

Communications - t) 989-732-5147 Renee Shimmel, Dir. (rshimmel@dioceseofgaylord.org);

Faith Formation - t) (989) 705-3539 Ami Peterson, Dir. (apeterson@dioceseofgaylord.org); Steven Sandoval, Pastoral & Admin. Asst. (ssandoval@dioceseofgaylord.org);

General Council, Diocesan - Sandra Jasinski, Atty. (sjasinski@bodmanlaw.com); Tim Clulo, Atty. (clulo@traverselaw.com);

Hispanic Apostolate - t) 989-705-3540 Silvia Cortes-Lopez, Dir. (scortes@dioceseofgaylord.org); Rev. Wayne H. Dziekan (wdziekan@dioceseofgaylord.org);

Human Resources - t) (989) 705-3511 Karina Bak, Dir. (kbak@dioceseofgaylord.org);

Native American Apostolate - t) 231-271-6651 Sr. Susan Gardner, O.P., Dir. (slg55us25@yahoo.com);

Permanent Deacon Formation - t) 231-347-8866 Dcn. Paul Fifer, Dir. (pfifer@dioceseofgaylord.org);

Stewardship and Development - t) (989) 732-5147 Mackenzie Ritchie, Dir. (mritchie@dioceseofgaylord.org); Hope Evans, Stewardship Coord. (hevans@dioceseofgaylord.org); Kelly Lauster, Database Coord. (klauster@dioceseofgaylord.org);

Tribunal, Diocesan - t) 989-705-3501 Rev. Daniel A. Smilanic, Judicial Vicar; Dr. John R. Amos, Dir. of Tribunal Svcs. (jamos@dioceseofgaylord.org); Lori Luckett, Tribunal Case Coord. (lluckett@dioceseofgaylord.org);

Judges - t) 989-732-5147 Rev. Daniel A. Smilanic, Judicial Vicar; Dr. John R. Amos, Dir. of Tribunal Svcs / Judge; Rev. Matthew A. Furgiuele, Judge;

Promoters of Justice / Defenders of the Bond - t) 989-732-5147 Rev. Benedetto J.J. Paris; Rev. John William;

Vicar for Clergy - t) 989-732-5147 Rev. Matthew A. Wigton (mwigton@dioceseofgaylord.org);

Vicar for Retired Clergy - t) 989-705-3545 Rev. James P. Hayden (jhayden@dioceseofgaylord.org);

Victim Assistance Coordinator - t) 989-705-9010 Larry LaCross (llacross@catholichumanservices.org);

Vocations, Seminarian and Priestly - t) (989) 705-3500 Rev. Benjamin Rexroat, Dir. (brexroat@dioceseofgaylord.org); Jenny Forman, Admin. Asst. (jforman@dioceseofgaylord.org);

Worship and Liturgical Formation - t) 989-705-3519 Cameron Diachun, Dir. (cdiachun@dioceseofgaylord.org); Steven Sandoval, Pastoral & Admin. Asst. (ssandoval@dioceseofgaylord.org);

ADVISORY BOARDS, COMMISSIONS, COMMITTEES, AND COUNCILS

Finance Council, Diocesan - t) 989-705-3512 Mark Eckhoff, Chair; Kim A. Smith, Dir. of Admin. Svcs. (ksmith@dioceseofgaylord.org); Rev. James P. Hayden, Vicar General (jhayden@dioceseofgaylord.org);

Pastoral Council, Diocesan - t) 989-732-5147 Seth Peters, Chair; Bethany Warner, Secy.; Rev. James P. Hayden, Vicar General (jhayden@dioceseofgaylord.org);

Presbyteral Council - t) (989) 705-3529 Rev. Tyler A. Bischoff, Chair (tbischoff@dioceseofgaylord.org); Rev. Mitchel Roman, Secy. (frroman@sfparish.org);

Priests' Retirement Fund Board - t) 989-732-5147 Donald Bartosh, Chair; Rev. James P. Hayden, Vicar for Retired Clergy (jhayden@dioceseofgaylord.org); Rev. Matthew A. Wigton, Vicar for Clergy (mwigton@dioceseofgaylord.org);

Review Board - t) (989) 732-5147 Thomas J. LaCross, Chair;

ORGANIZATIONS

Council of Catholic Women, Diocesan - c) (989) 858-5360 Ruth Munger (rmung71r@gmail.com);

Knights of Columbus - t) 989-766-2124 Joel Kendzorski, Dir.;

St. Vincent de Paul Society - t) 989-732-5147 Rev. Wayne H. Dziekan, Diocesan Rep. (wdziekan@dioceseofgaylord.org);

PARISHES, MISSIONS, AND CLERGY

STATE OF MICHIGAN

AFTON

Saint Monica of Afton - M-68 Hwy., Afton, MI 49705; Mailing: P.O. Box 130, Onaway, MI 49765-0130 t) 989-733-6053 parishoffice@stpaul-onaway.com www.stpaul-onaway.com/ Rev. Scott J. Lawler, Par. Admin.;

ALPENA

All Saints of Alpena - 817 Sable St., Alpena, MI 49707 t) 989-354-3019 jbenson@alpenacatholics.org; pjones@alpenacatholics.org www.alpenacatholics.org Rev. Tyler A. Bischoff, Admin.; Rev. Michael Anthony Lingaur, Par. Vicar; Dcn. Michael Roy; Jacqueline Benson, DRE; CRP Stds.: 80

ATLANTA

Jesus the Good Shepherd of Atlanta - 11483 County Rd. 487, Atlanta, MI 49709; Mailing: P.O. Box 216, Hillman, MI 49746 t) 989-742-4542 Rev. James Siler, Admin.;

BEAVER ISLAND

Holy Cross of Beaver Island - 37860 Kings Hwy., Beaver Island, MI 49782; Mailing: P.O. Box 145, Beaver Island, MI 49782 t) 231-448-2230 holycross@tds.net; filiomariae@gmail.com holycrossbeaverisland.com Rev. Peter T. Wigton, Admin.; CRP Stds.: 1

BELLAIRE

Saint Luke the Evangelist of Bellaire - 3088 M-88, Bellaire, MI 49615-0799; Mailing: Po Box 799, Bellaire, MI 49615-0799 t) 231-533-8121 stluke49615@gmail.com www.dioceseofgaylord.org Rev. James P. Hayden, Admin. Pro Tem; CRP Stds.: 6

BLACK RIVER

Saint Gabriel of Black River - 5570 N. Lake Shore Dr., Black River, MI 48721; Mailing: 2188 W. Nicholson Hill Rd., Ossineke, MI 49766-9736 t) 989-471-5121 stcatherine@resurrectionacgr.org www.resurrectionacgr.org Rev. John William, Admin.; Cathy MacFalda, DRE;

BOYNE CITY

Saint Matthew of Boyne City - 1303 Boyne Ave., Boyne City, MI 49712 t) 231-582-7718 parishoffice@jamcc.org; pafurtaw@gmail.com jamcc.org Rev. Dennis R. Stilwell, Canonical Pastor; Patricia A. Furtaw, Dir. Parish Life; Suzanne Dzwik, DRE; CRP Stds.: 63

BOYNE FALLS

Saint Augustine of Boyne Falls - 2347 Grove St., Boyne Falls, MI 49713; Mailing: 1303 Boyne Ave., Boyne City, MI 49712 t) 231-582-7718 parishoffice@jamcc.org; pafurtaw@gmail.com jamcc.org Rev. Dennis R. Stilwell, Pst.; Patricia A. Furtaw, Parish Life Coord.; CRP Stds.: 15

BRUTUS

Assumption of the Blessed Virgin Mary of Burt Lake - 3192 Indian Rd., Brutus, MI 49716; Mailing: PO Box 40, Cheboygan, MI 49721 t) 231-627-2105 info@cprparishes.org www.cprparishes.org Rev. Duane A. Wachowiak Jr., Pst.;

CADILLAC

Saint Ann of Cadillac - 800 W. 13th St., Cadillac, MI 49601-9281 t) 231-775-2471 x231 (CRP); 231-775-2471 x224 geigerj@stanncadillac.org; parish@stanncadillac.org stannparishcadillac.org Rev. Michael S. Janowski, Pst.; Rev. Bradley Nursey, Assoc. Pst.; Jennifer Geiger, DRE; CRP Stds.: 48

CEDAR

Holy Rosary of Cedar - 6982 S. Schomberg Rd., Cedar, MI 49621 t) 231-228-5429 holyrosarycedar@gmail.com www.holyrosarycedar.org Rev. Donald L. Libby, Pst.; Julie Anne Witkowski, DRE; CRP Stds.: 86

CHARLEVOIX

Saint Mary of the Assumption of Charlevoix - 1003 Bridge St., Charlevoix, MI 49720 t) 231-547-6652; 231-547-6652 x13 (CRP) mjoy@stmaryschoolchx.com; egengle@stmaryschoolcharlevoix.org stmarycharlevoix.com Rev. Peter T. Wigton, Pst.; Elizabeth Gengle, DRE; CRP Stds.: 77

CHEBOYGAN

Saint Mary-Saint Charles of Cheboygan - 120 N. D St., Cheboygan, MI 49721; Mailing: PO Box 40, Cheboygan, MI 49721-0040 t) 231-627-2105 info@cprparishes.org; kims@cprparishes.org www.cprparishes.org Rev. Duane A. Wachowiak Jr., Pst.; Kim Socolovitch, DRE; CRP Stds.: 33

Sacred Heart of Riggsville - 4989 Polish Line Rd., Cheboygan, MI 49721; Mailing: PO Box 40, Cheboygan, MI 49721-0040 t) 231-627-2105 info@cprparishes.org www.cprparishes.org Rev. Duane A. Wachowiak Jr., Pst.; Kim Socolovitch, DRE;

COPEMISH

Saint Raphael of Copemish - 18440 Cadillac Hwy., Copemish, MI 49625; Mailing: P.O. Box 150, Onekama, MI 49675-0150 t) 231-889-4254 office@stjosephonekama.com straphaelcopemish.com Rev. Ruben D. Munoz, Pst.;

CROSS VILLAGE

Holy Cross of Cross Village - 6624 N. Lake Shore Dr., Cross Village, MI 49723; Mailing: 150 W. Main St., Harbor Springs, MI 49740 t) 231-526-2017 secretary@cclcparishes.org cclcparishes.org Rev. James M. Bearss, Pst.;

EAST JORDAN

Saint John Nepomucene of Praga - 3804 St. John's Rd., East Jordan, MI 49727; Mailing: 1303 Boyne Ave., Boyne City, MI 49712-8920 t) 231-582-7718 parishoffice@jamcc.org; pafurtaw@gmail.com www.jamcc.org Patricia A. Furtaw, Admin.; Rev. Dennis R. Stilwell, Sacr. Min.;

Saint Joseph of East Jordan - 207 Nichols, East Jordan, MI 49727; Mailing: PO Box 379, East Jordan, MI 49727-0379 t) 231-536-2934 stjosephej@gmail.com stjosepheastjordan.org Rev. Matthew A. Furgiuele, Admin.; Mary Plude, DRE; CRP Stds.: 20

EAST TAWAS

Holy Family of East Tawas - 516 W. Lincoln St., East Tawas, MI 48730 t) 989-362-3162; 989-739-9511 (CRP) holyfamily@hf-sh.org hf-sh.org/holyfamily/ Rev. Nicholas Cooper, Admin.; CRP Stds.: 55

ELK RAPIDS

Sacred Heart of Elk Rapids - 143 Charles St., Elk Rapids, MI 49629 t) 231-264-8087; 231-264-8087 x204 (CRP) sacredheart@sacredheartelkrapids.org sacredheartelkrapids.org/ Rev. Robert J. Zuchowski, Pst.; CRP Stds.: 35

ELMIRA

Saint Thomas Aquinas of Elmira - 2567 Buell Rd., Elmira, MI 49730; Mailing: 606 N. Ohio Ave., Gaylord, MI 49735 t) 989-732-5448 parishoffice@stmarycathedral.org www.stmarycathedral.org/ Rev. Matthew Wigton, Pst.; Rev. Mitchel Roman, Par. Vicar;

EMPIRE

Saint Philip Neri of Empire - 11411 LaCore St., Empire, MI 49630; Mailing: P.O. Box 257, Empire, MI 49630-0257 t) 231-326-5255; 231-326-5888 (CRP) stphilipneriempire@gmail.com www.stphilipneriempire.org Rev. Kenneth R. Stachnik, Pst.; Carolyn Ballmer, DRE; CRP Stds.: 32

FIFE LAKE

Saint Aloysius of Fife Lake - 403 E. Merritt St., Fife Lake, MI 49633; Mailing: 438 County Rd. 612, N.E., Kalkaska, MI 49646 t) 231-258-5021; 231-258-2752 stmaryofthewoods@yahoo.com maryaloysius.com Rev. Michael Verschaeve, Sacr. Min.; Denise E. Elsenheimer, Dir. Parish Life; CRP Stds.: 4

FRANKFORT

Saint Ann of Frankfort - 508 Crystal Ave., Frankfort, MI 49635 t) 231-352-4421; 231-352-4421 x11 stannoffice1@gmail.com; stanneducation@gmail.com saintanninfrankfort.org Rev. Christopher B. Welsh, Sacr. Min.; Kristin Smeltzer, Dir., Parish Life; CRP Stds.: 3

GAYLORD

Saint Mary, Our Lady of Mt. Carmel Cathedral of Gaylord - 606 N. Ohio Ave., Gaylord, MI 49735-1999 t) 989-732-5448 parishoffice@stmarycathedral.org www.stmarycathedral.org Rev. Matthew Wigton, Rector; Rev. Mitchel Roman, Par. Vicar;

GOOD HART

Saint Ignatius of Good Hart - 101 N. Lamkin Rd., Good Hart, MI 49737; Mailing: 150 W. Main St., Harbor Springs, MI 49740 t) 231-526-2017 secretary@cclcparishes.org cclcparishes.org Rev. James M. Bearss, Pst.;

GRAYLING

Saint Mary of Grayling - 708 Peninsular Ave., Grayling, MI 49738; Mailing: 707 Spruce St., Grayling, MI 49738-1259 t) 989-348-7657 office@graylingstmary.org Rev. Gerard A. Hunko, Pst.; CRP Stds.: 9

HALE

Saint Pius X of Hale - 3901 N. M-65, Hale, MI 48739; Mailing: PO Box 428, Hale, MI 48739-0428 t) 989-728-2278; 989-728-6616 spxhale@gmail.com; bk2spx@gmail.com www.holythree.org/ Dcn. Brent H. Hemker, Admin.;

HARBOR SPRINGS

Holy Childhood of Jesus of Harbor Springs - 150 W. Main St., Harbor Springs, MI 49740 t) 231-526-2017 secretary@cclcparishes.org cclcparishes.org Rev. James M. Bearss, Pst.; CRP Stds.: 16

HARRIETTA

Saint Edward of Harrietta - 207 W. Gaston, Harrietta, MI 49638; Mailing: 800 W. 13th St., Cadillac, MI 49601 t) 231-775-2471 parish@stanncadillac.org stannparishcadillac.org Rev. Michael S. Janowski, Pst.; Rev. Bradley Nursey, Pst. Assoc.; Dcn. Frank P. Kopasz;

HARRISVILLE

Saint Anne of Harrisville - 110 S. State St., Harrisville, MI 48740; Mailing: P.O. Box 345, Harrisville, MI 48740-0345 t) 989-724-6713 stanne@resurrectionacgr.org Rev. John William, Admin.;

HERRON

Saint Rose of Lima of Herron - 3433 Herron Rd., Herron, MI 49744 t) 989-379-4316 strose@speedconnect.com Rev. Tyler A. Bischoff, Sacr. Min.; Rev. Michael Anthony Lingaur, Sacr. Min.; Dianne Blissland, DRE; Theresa M. Zbytowski, Dir. Parish Life; CRP Stds.: 16

HIGGINS LAKE

Saint Hubert of Higgins Lake - 7612 W. Higgins Lake Dr., Higgins Lake, MI 48627; Mailing: P.O. Box 75, Higgins Lake, MI 48627-0075 t) 989-821-5591 jambert2012@gmail.com jambert.org Rev. Peter O. Eke, Pst.; Rev. Bernard L. Tyler, Admin.; CRP Stds.: 2

HILLMAN

Saint Augustine of Hillman - 24138 Veteran's Memorial Hwy., Hillman, MI 49746; Mailing: PO Box 216, Hillman, MI 49746-0216 t) 989-742-4542 Rev. James Siler, Admin.; CRP Stds.: 29

HOUGHTON LAKE

Saint James the Greater of Houghton Lake - 7878 E. Houghton Lake Dr., Houghton Lake, MI 48629; Mailing: 7612 W. Higgins Lake Dr., P.O. Box 75, Higgins Lake, MI 48627-0075 t) 989-821-5591 jambert2012@gmail.com jambert.org Rev. Peter O. Eke, Pst.; Rev. Bernard L. Tyler, Admin.; CRP Stds.: 4

INDIAN RIVER

Cross in the Woods Catholic Shrine of Indian River - 7078 M-68 Hwy., Indian River, MI 49749 t) 231-238-8973 nationalshrine@crossinthewoods.com www.crossinthewoods.com Rev. T. Patrick Maher, Pst.; James Dean Nowka, Dir.; CRP Stds.: 15

KALKASKA

Saint Mary of the Woods of Kalkaska - 438 County Rd. 612, N.E., Kalkaska, MI 49646 t) 231-258-5021; 231-258-2752 stmaryofthewoods@yahoo.com maryaloysius.com Rev. Michael Verschaeve, Sacr. Min.; CRP Stds.: 13

KINGSLEY

Saint Mary of Hannah - 2912 W. M 113, Kingsley, MI 49649 t) 231-263-5640; 231-263-5288 rbelles@stmaryhannah.org; schoolsecretary@stmaryhannah.org www.stmaryhannah.org Rev. Joseph Muszkiewicz, Pst.; Dcn. Timothy Webb; CRP Stds.: 29

LAKE CITY

Saint Stephen of Lake City - 506 W. Union St., Lake City, MI 49651; Mailing: PO Box 379, Lake City, MI 49651-0379 t) 231-839-2121 ststephenlakecity@gmail.com ststephenlakecity.com Rev. Michael S. Janowski, Pst.; Rev. Bradley Nursey, Par. Vicar; Jeanne Johnson, Bus. Mgr.; CRP Stds.: 9

LAKE LEELANAU

Saint Mary of the Assumption of Lake Leelanau - 403 S. Saint Mary St., Lake Leelanau, MI 49653; Mailing: P.O. Box 340, Lake Leelanau, MI 49653 t) 231-256-9676 mkuznicki@stmarysll.org www.stmaryparishll.org Rev. Benjamin Martin, Admin.; Jude Thompson, DRE; CRP Stds.: 18

LEWISTON

Saint Francis of Assisi of Lewiston - 4086 Salling Ave., Lewiston, MI 49756; Mailing: P.O. Box 182, Lewiston, MI 49756-0182 t) 989-786-2235 stfrancisassisi@frontier.com stfrancislewiston.org Rev. Alfred M. Pillarelli, Pst.; Dcn. Arthur LoVetere; Cathy Grachal, Music Min.; Heather Runyan, Youth Min.; CRP Stds.: 10

MACKINAW CITY

Saint Anthony of Padua of Mackinaw City - 600 W. Central Ave., Mackinaw City, MI 49701; Mailing: PO Box 460, Mackinaw City, MI 49701-0460 t) 231-436-5561 chrisop@sbcglobal.net Sr. Chris Herald, O.P., Pastoral Admin.;

MANCELONA

Saint Anthony of Padua of Mancelona - 209 N. Jefferson St., Mancelona, MI 49659; Mailing: PO Box 677, Mancelona, MI 49659-0677 t) 231-587-8401 st.anthony1@charter.net; st.anthony209@gmail.com Rev. James P. Hayden, Admin. Pro Tem;

MANISTEE

Divine Mercy of Manistee - 254 Sixth St., Manistee, MI 49660 t) 231-723-2619; 231-723-2619 x114 (CRP) parish.office@divinemercymanistee.org www.divinemercymanistee.org Rev. Zeljko J. Guberovic, Pst.; Rev. Basil Lek, Par. Vicar; Michelle Hanson, DRE; CRP Stds.: 22

MANTON

Saint Theresa of Manton - 9475 14 & 1/4 Rd, Manton, MI 49663; Mailing: P.O. Box 379, Lake City, MI 49651-0379 t) 231-839-2121 ststephenlakecity@gmail.com ststephenlakecity.com/ Rev. Michael S. Janowski, Pst.; Rev. Bradley Nursey, Par. Vicar; Jeanne Johnson, Bus. Mgr.; CRP Stds.: 2

MAPLE CITY

Saint Rita-Saint Joseph of Maple City - 8707 Hill St., Maple City, MI 49664; Mailing: PO Box 75, Maple City, MI 49664-0075 t) 231-326-5255 stphilipneriempire@gmail.com www.strita-stjoseph.org Rev. Kenneth R. Stachnik, Pst.;

MIKADO

Saint Raphael of Mikado - 2531 E. F-30, Mikado, MI 48745; Mailing: P.O. Box 345, Harrisville, MI 48740-0345 t) 989-724-6713 stanne@resurrectionacgr.org www.resurrectionacgr.org Rev. John William, Admin.;

MIO

Saint Mary of Mio - 100 Deyarmond St., Mio, MI 48647; Mailing: PO Box 189, Mio, MI 48647-0189 t) 989-826-5509 stmarymio@m33access.com www.olwshrine.org/ Rev. Santiago M. Hoyumpa, Pst.; CRP Stds.: 6

NORTHPORT

Saint Gertrude The Great Of Northport - 701 Warren, Northport, MI 49670; Mailing: P.O. Box 9, Suttons Bay, MI 49682-0009 t) 231-271-3744 mary@stmichaelsb.com Rev. Leonard Paul, Admin.;

ONAWAY

Saint Paul of Onaway - 28011 Washington Ave., Onaway, MI 49765; Mailing: P.O. Box 130, Onaway, MI 49765-0130 t) 989-733-6053 parishoffice@stpaul-onaway.com stpaul-onaway.com Rev. Scott J. Lawler, Par. Admin.; CRP Stds.: 11

ONEKAMA

Saint Joseph of Onekama - 8380 Fifth St., Onekama, MI 49675; Mailing: P.O. Box 150, Onekama, MI 49675-0150 t) 231-889-4254 office@stjosephonekama.com stjosephonekama.com Rev. Ruben D. Munoz, Pst.; Tracy Daberkoe, DRE; CRP Stds.: 3

OSCODA

Sacred Heart of Oscoda - 5300 N. U.S.-23, Oscoda, MI 48750 t) 989-739-9511 rcopland@hf-sh.org; sacredheart@hf-sh.org www.hf-sh.org Rev. Charles G. Donajkowski, Pst.; Richard J. Copland, DRE; CRP Stds.: 11

OSSINEKE

Saint Catherine of Alexandria of Ossineke - 2188 W. Nicholson Hill Rd., Ossineke, MI 49766-9736 t) 989-471-5121 stcatherine@resurrectionacgr.org www.resurrectionacgr.org Rev. John William, Admin.; Cathy MacFalda, DRE; CRP Stds.: 12

PELLSTON

Saint Clement of Pellston - 202 N. Maple, Pellston, MI 49769; Mailing: P.O. Box 40, Cheboygan, MI 49721-0040 t) 231-627-2105 info@cprparishes.org www.cprparishes.org Rev. Duane A. Wachowiak Jr., Pst.; Kim Socolovitch, DRE;

Saint Nicholas of Larks Lake - 1987 Zulski Rd., Pellston, MI 49769; Mailing: 150 W. Main St., Harbor Springs, MI 49740 t) 231-526-2017 secretary@cclcparishes.org cclcparishes.org Rev. James M. Bearss, Pst.; CRP Stds.: 3

PESHAWBESTOWN

Saint Kateri Tekakwitha of Peshawbestown - 2753 N. West Bay Shore Dr., Peshawbestown, MI 49682; Mailing: PO Box 369, Suttons Bay, MI 49682-0369 t) 231-271-6651 slg55us25@yahoo.com Sr. Susan Gardner, O.P., Dir. Parish Life;

PETOSKEY

Saint Francis Xavier of Petoskey - 513 Howard St., Petoskey, MI 49770 t) 231-347-4133 (CRP); 231-347-4133 x410 judymkrussell@gmail.com; petoskeysfx@gmail.com www.petoskeysfx.org/ Rev. Gregory P. McCallum, Pst.; Craig Saunders, DRE; CRP Stds.: 75

St. Francis Xavier School - (Grades K-8) 414 Michigan St., Petoskey, MI 49770 t) 231-347-3651 adobrowolski@petoskeysfx.org petoskeysfxschool.org/ Adam Dobrowolski, Prin.; Stds.: 223; Lay Tchrs.: 27

POSEN

Saint Casimir of Posen - 10075 M-65 N., Posen, MI 49776; Mailing: P.O. Box 217, Posen, MI 49776-0217 t) 989-766-2660 stcasimir10075@gmail.com stcasimir-stdominic.org/ Rev. Arthur F. Duchnowicz, Pst.; Mary Hentkowski, DRE; CRP Stds.: 34

Saint Dominic of Metz - 9269 County Rd. 441, Posen, MI 49776; Mailing: P.O. Box 217, Posen, MI 49776 t) 989-766-2660 st_dominic_metz@i2k.com; stcasimir10075@gmail.com stccasimir-stdominic.org Rev. Arthur F. Duchnowicz, Pst.;

PRESCOTT

Saint Stephen, King of Hungary of Skidway Lake - 2811 E. Greenwood Rd., Prescott, MI 48756 t) 989-873-3340 office@ststephenofhungary.org www.holythree.org Dcn. Brent H. Hemker, Admin.;

PRUDENVILLE

Our Lady of the Lake of Prudenville - 1037 W. Houghton Lake Dr., Prudenville, MI 48651; Mailing: P.O. Box 800, Prudenville, MI 48651-0800 t) 989-366-5533; 989-366-5592 (School) ollsc@ollrcs.org ollrcs.org Rev. Peter Eke, Pst.; Tracey Haggart, DRE; CRP Stds.: 9

ROGERS CITY

Saint Ignatius of Loyola of Rogers City - 585 S. Third St., Rogers City, MI 49779 t) 989-734-3443 (CRP); 989-734-2753 parishoffice@stignatiuscs.org wwwstignatiusrc.org Rev. Rolando Silva, Pst.; Shannon Marie Wilbert, DRE; CRP Stds.: 11

ROSCOMMON

Saint Michael of Roscommon - 104 N. 6th St., Roscommon, MI 48653; Mailing: P.O. Box 9, Roscommon, MI 48653-0009 t) 989-275-5212 smym@stmichaelrosco.org; smcc@stmichaelsrosco.org Rev. Gerard A. Hunko, Pst.; Deborah Harris, DRE & Bus. Mgr.; CRP Stds.: 39

SAINT HELEN

Saint Helen of St. Helen - 737 N. St. Helen Rd., Saint Helen, MI 48656; Mailing: P.O. Box 318, Saint Helen, MI 48656-0318 t) 989-389-4959 sthelen737@gmail.com Rev. Gerard A. Hunko, Admin.;

SUTTONS BAY

Saint Michael the Archangel of Suttons Bay - 104 S. Elm St., Suttons Bay, MI 49682; Mailing: P.O. Box 9, Suttons Bay, MI 49682-0009 t) 231-271-3744 mary@stmichaelsb.com Rev. Leonard Paul, Admin.; CRP Stds.: 12

Saint Wenceslaus of Gills Pier - 8500 E. Kolarik Rd., Suttons Bay, MI 49682 t) 231-271-3574 stwenceslausgp@gmail.com Rev. Michael Class, S.J., Sacr. Min.; Dcn. Martin Korson, Pastoral Admin.;

TRAVERSE CITY

Saint Francis of Assisi of Traverse City - 1025 S. Union St., Traverse City, MI 49684 t) 231-947-4620; 231-947-4620 x222 (CRP) jim@sfparish.org; cheryl@sfparish.org www.sfparish.org Rev. Donald R. Geyman, Pst.; Rev. Innocent Zambua, Assoc. Pst.; Dcn. James L. Krupka; Cheryl A. Lee, DRE; Jim Belden, Bus. Mgr.; CRP Stds.: 36

Immaculate Conception of Traverse City - 308 N. Cedar St., Traverse City, MI 49684 t) 231-946-4211 office@immaculatetc.org immaculatetc.org Rev. Anthony M. Citro, Pst.; Rev. James P. Hayden, Pastor Emer.; Dcn. Jude F. Younker; CRP Stds.: 7

Saint Joseph of Mapleton - 12675 Center Rd., Traverse City, MI 49686 t) 231-421-7310 pastor@stjosephtc.org; businessmanager@stjosephtc.org stjosephtc.org Rev. Benjamin Rexroat, Admin.; Kelly O'Farrell, DRE; CRP Stds.: 46

Saint Patrick of Traverse City - 630 S. West Silver Lake Rd., Traverse City, MI 49685 t) 231-943-4633; 231-943-4633 x217 (CRP) skorson@shamrockchurchtc.org; sclutts@shamrockchurchtc.org www.stpatricktc.org Rev. Gerald C. Okoli, Pst.; Sherrie Clutts, DRE; CRP Stds.: 38

VANDERBILT

Holy Redeemer of Vanderbilt - 8075 Lincoln St., Vanderbilt, MI 49795; Mailing: 606 N. Ohio Ave., Gaylord, MI 49735-1999 t) 989-732-5448 parishoffice@stmarycathedral.org www.stmarycathedral.org Rev. Matthew Wigton, Pst.; Rev. Mitchel Roman, Par. Vicar;

WEST BRANCH

Holy Family of Klacking Creek - 402 W. Peters Rd., West Branch, MI 48661; Mailing: 961 W. Houghton Ave., West Branch, MI 48661 t) 989-345-0064 x302; 989-345-0064 x301 (CRP) holyfamily.klackingcreek@gmail.com; denemyjma@gmail.com sotncc.org Rev. Emmanual T Finbarr, Admin.; Maria Balser, Bus. Mgr.; Joan Denemy, DRE; CRP Stds.: 2

Saint Joseph of West Branch - 907 W. Houghton Ave., West Branch, MI 48661; Mailing: 961 W. Houghton Ave., West Branch, MI 48661 t) 989-345-0064; 989-345-0064 x304 (CRP) pc.stjoseph@gmail.com; denemyjma@gmail.com www.sotncc.org/ Rev. Emmanual T Finbarr, Admin.; Joan Denemy, DRE; CRP Stds.: 14

St. Joseph School - (Grades PreSchool-8) 935 W. Houghton Ave., West Branch, MI 48661 t) 989-345-0220 pclemens@wbstjoseph.com wbstjoseph.com Penny Clemens, Prin.; Stds.: 104; Lay Tchrs.: 6

WHITTEMORE

Saint James of Whittemore - 202 E. Sherman St., Whittemore, MI 48770; Mailing: PO Box 206, Whittemore, MI 48770-0206 t) 989-756-2591 stjames206@gmail.com www.holythree.org/ Dcn. Brent H. Hemker, Admin.;

WILLIAMSBURG

Christ the King of Acme - 3801 Shore Rd., Williamsburg, MI 49690; Mailing: P.O. Box 95, Acme, MI 49610 t) 231-938-9214 generalmail@christkingchurch.org christkingchurch.org/ Rev. Christopher A. Jarvis, Admin.; CRP Stds.: 98

SCHOOLS: PRESCHOOL THRU HIGH SCHOOL

SCHOOLS

STATE OF MICHIGAN

ALPENA

All Saints Catholic School - (PAR) (Grades PreK-8) 500 N. Second Ave., Alpena, MI 49707 t) 989-354-4911 mdoubek@alpenaallsaints.org; tkinney@alpenaallsaints.org alpenaallsaints.org Melissa Doubek, Prin.; Stds.: 88; Lay Tchrs.: 7

CADILLAC

St. Ann School - (DIO) (Grades PreSchool-6) 800 W. 13th, Cadillac, MI 49601 t) 231-775-1301 www.stanncadillac.org Ann Bush, Prin.; Stds.: 136; Lay Tchrs.: 9

CHARLEVOIX

St. Mary Elementary - (PAR) (Grades PreK-7) 1005 Bridge St., Charlevoix, MI 49720 t) 231-547-9441 mjoy@stmaryschoolchx.com; kdvoracek@stmaryschoolchx.com www.stmaryschoolcharlevoix.com Kathleen Dvoracek, Prin.; Stds.: 88; Lay Tchrs.: 5

CHEBOYGAN

Bishop Baraga Catholic School - (PAR) (Grades PreK-7) 623 W. Lincoln Ave., Cheboygan, MI 49721 t) 231-627-5608 ccloss@bbseduc.com www.bishopbaraga.com Chase Closs, Prin.; Stds.: 141; Lay Tchrs.: 8

EAST TAWAS

Holy Family Elementary School - (PAR) (Grades PreSchool-6) 411 N. Wilkinson, East Tawas, MI 48730 t) 989-362-5651 principal@hfs-tawas.org; secretary@hfs-tawas.org www.hfs-tawas.org Tim St. Aubin, Prin.; Stds.: 108; Lay Tchrs.: 4

GAYLORD

St. Mary Cathedral School - (PAR) (Grades PreK-12) 321 N. Otsego Ave., Gaylord, MI 49735 t) 989-732-5801 jbelanger@gaylordstmary.org; hglasby@gaylordstmary.org www.gaylordstmary.org Jerry Belanger, Prin.; Stds.: 324; Lay Tchrs.: 22

KINGSLEY

St. Mary - Hannah School - (PAR) (Grades PreK-8) 2912 W. M-113, Kingsley, MI 49649 t) 231-263-5288 lmedina@stmaryhannah.org www.stmaryhannah.org Lisa Swartz-Medina, Prin.; Stds.: 29; Lay Tchrs.: 2

LAKE LEELANAU

St. Mary School - (PAR) (Grades PreK-12) 303 S. St. Mary St., Lake Leelanau, MI 49653; Mailing: P.O. Box 340, Lake Leelanau, MI 49653 t) 231-256-9636 info@stmarysll.org www.stmarysll.org Rev. Benjamin Martin, Admin.; Megan Glynn, Prin.; Stds.: 181; Lay Tchrs.: 16

MANISTEE

Manistee Catholic Central School - (PAR) (Grades PreK-12) 1200 U.S. 31 S., Manistee, MI 49660 t) 231-723-2529 kgibson@sabers.org; sabersprincipal@gmail.com www.sabers.org Catherine Grinn, Prin.; Stds.: 186; Lay Tchrs.: 15

PRUDENVILLE

Our Lady of the Lake Regional Catholic School - (PAR) (Grades PreK-8) 1039 W. Houghton Lake Dr., Prudenville, MI 48651; Mailing: P.O. Box 800, Prudenville, MI 48651 t) 989-366-5592 ollsc@ollrcs.org www.ollrcs.org Michelle Johnson, Prin.; Stds.: 94; Lay Tchrs.: 6

ROGERS CITY

St. Ignatius - (PAR) (Grades PreK-8) 545 S. Third St., Rogers City, MI 49779 t) 989-734-3443 hryan@stignatiuscs.org www.stignatiusparishschool.com Heather Lyn Ryan, Prin.; Stds.: 97; Lay Tchrs.: 5

TRAVERSE CITY

St. Elizabeth Ann Seton Middle School - (PAR) (Grades 6-8) 1601 Three Mile Rd. N., Traverse City, MI 49696 t) 231-932-4810 mlundberg@gtacs.org; jbirney@gtacs.org www.gtacs.org Part of GTACS system John Birney, Prin.; Eric Mulvaney, Dir.; Stds.: 239; Lay Tchrs.: 18

Grand Traverse Area Catholic Schools - (PAR) (Grades PreK-12) 123 E. 11th St., Traverse City, MI 49684 t) 231-946-8100 emulvany@gtacs.org www.gtacs.org GTACS system consists of Immaculate Conception Elem School, St. Elizabeth Ann Seton Middle School & St. Francis HS. Michael R. Buell, Supt.; Erick Chittle, Prin.; Eric Mulvany, Dir. Oper.;

Immaculate Conception Elementary School - (PAR) (Grades PreK-5) 314 Vine St., Traverse City, MI 49684 t) 231-947-1252 mdeyoung@gtacs.org; jlesinski@gtacs.org www.gtacs.org Part of GTACS system Jessica Lesinski, Prin.; Maureen DeYoung, Vice Prin.; Eric Mulvaney, Dir., School Oper.; Stds.: 652; Sr. Tchrs.: 2; Lay Tchrs.: 37

HIGH SCHOOLS

STATE OF MICHIGAN

TRAVERSE CITY

St. Francis High School - (PAR) (Grades 9-12) 123 E. 11th St., Traverse City, MI 49684 t) 231-946-8038 echittle@gtacs.org www.gtacs.org Part of GTACS system Erick Chittle, Prin.; Eric Mulvaney, Dir.; Stds.: 359; Sr. Tchrs.: 2; Lay Tchrs.: 23

INSTITUTIONS LOCATED IN DIOCESE

CATHOLIC CHARITIES [CCH]

TRAVERSE CITY
Catholic Human Services - 1000 Hastings St., Traverse City, MI 49686 t) 231-947-8110 chstraverse@catholichumanservices.org www.catholichumanservices.org Edward Cieslinski, Pres.; Asstd. Annu.: 35,924; Staff: 89

Area Office - 154 S. Ripley Blvd., Alpena, MI 49707 t) 989-356-6385 chsalpena@catholichumanservices.org Kara Steinke, Admin.;

Area Office - 421 S. Mitchell, Cadillac, MI 49601 t) 231-775-6581 chscadillac@catholichumanservices.org

Area Office - 829 W. Main St., Ste. C-3, Gaylord, MI 49735 t) 989-732-6761 chsgaylord@catholichumanservices.org Kara Steinke, Admin.;

CONVENTS, MONASTERIES, AND RESIDENCES FOR WOMEN [CON]

CONWAY
Sacramentine Monastery of Perpetual Adoration - 2798 U.S. 31 N., Conway, MI 49722; Mailing: P.O. Box 86, Conway, MI 49722-0086 t) 231-347-0447 augustinecenter@gmail.com Sr. Mary Rosalie Smith, O.S.S., Prioress; Srs.: 1

TRAVERSE CITY
Infant Jesus of Prague Monastery (The Discalced Carmelite Nuns, Monastery of the Infant of Prague, Inc.) - 3501 Silver Lake Rd., Traverse City, MI 49684-8949 t) 231-946-4960 nuns@carmeltraversecity.org www.carmeloftraversecity.org Mother Perpetua Marie Aune, OCD, Prioress; Srs.: 9

ENDOWMENTS / FOUNDATIONS / TRUSTS [EFT]

GAYLORD
Northern Michigan Catholic Foundation, Inc. - 308 W. Main St., Gaylord, MI 49735 t) 231-922-9070 christie@nmcatholicfoundation.org nmcatholicfoundation.org Rev. James P. Hayden, Vice. Pres.; Christie Perdue, Exec. Dir.; Joel Myler, Chair; Tim Clulo, Vice Chair; John Puetz, Treas.;

HOSPITALS / HEALTH SERVICES [HOS]

TAWAS CITY
Ascension St. Joseph Hospital - 200 Hemlock Rd., Tawas City, MI 48764-0659; Mailing: P.O. Box 659, Tawas City, MI 48764-0659 t) 989-362-3411 christopher.mcclead@ascension.org healthcare.ascension.org A member of Ascension Michigan Bed Capacity: 47; Asstd. Annu.: 181,394; Staff: 301

MISCELLANEOUS [MIS]

ALPENA
Madonna House Apostolate - 114 S. 5th Ave., Alpena, MI 49707-2511 t) 989-354-4073 rhoran@hotmail.com Rosemary Horan, Dir.;

HARBOR SPRINGS
Christ Child Society of Northern Michigan, Inc. - 192 W. Third St., Harbor Springs, MI 49740; Mailing: P.O. Box 132, Harbor Springs, MI 49740-0132 t) 231-526-7271 dknachtrab@christchildsocietynorthernmichigan.org christchildsocietynorthernmichigan.com/ Dianne Creamer, Pres.; Deborah Nachtrab, Treas.;

Holy Childhood - New Beginnings Thrift and Resale - 650 Conway Rd., Harbor Springs, MI 49740 t) 231-348-2980 nbthrift@sbcglobal.net newbeginningsresale.com Carol Grissom, Mgr.;

JOHANNESBURG
Stella Maris Hermitage - 19466 Black River Rd., Johannesburg, MI 49751; Mailing: P.O. Box 315, Johannesburg, MI 49751-0315 c) (989) 858-8432 rwkropf@gmail.com www.stellamar.net Rev. Richard Kropf;

RETREAT HOUSES / RENEWAL CENTERS [RTR]

CONWAY
Augustine Center - 2798 U.S. 31 N., Conway, MI 49722; Mailing: P.O. Box 84, Conway, MI 49722-0084 t) 231-347-3657 augustinecenter@gmail.com Adam Chittle, Dir.;

GAYLORD
Camp Sancta Maria Trust - 5361 W. M-32, Gaylord, MI 49735; Mailing: P.O. Box 613, Washington, MI 48094 t) (248) 822-8199 (Sept. - May); (231) 546-3878 (June - Aug.) office@campsanctamaria.org www.campsanctamaria.org John David Kuhar, Exec. Dir.; Jan Klemm, Dir., Oper. & Devel.;

An asterisk (*) denotes an organization that has established tax-exempt status directly with the IRS and is not covered by the USCCB Group Ruling.

Diocese of Grand Island

(Dioecesis Insulae Grandis)

MOST REVEREND JOSEPH G. HANEFELDT

Bishop of Grand Island; ordained July 14, 1984; appointed Bishop of Grand Island January 14, 2015; ordained March 19, 2015. Office: 2708 Old Fair Rd., Grand Island, NE 68803.

Chancery Office: 2708 Old Fair Rd., Grand Island, NE 68803. T: 308-382-6565; F: 308-382-6569.

Square Miles 40,000.

Erected at Kearney, March 8, 1912; See Transferred to Grand Island, April 11, 1917.

Comprises the Counties of Arthur, Banner, Blaine, Box Butte, Brown, Buffalo, Cherry, Cheyenne, Custer, Dawes, Deuel, Garden, Garfield, Grant, Greeley, Hooker, Howard Keyapaha, Kimball, Logan, Loup, McPherson, Morrill, Rock, Scotts Bluff, Sheridan, Sherman, Wheeler, Sioux, Thomas, Valley, and those portions of Dawson, Hall, Lincoln and Keith lying north of the South Platte River in the State of Nebraska.

For legal titles of parishes and diocesan institutions, consult the Chancery Office.

STATISTICAL OVERVIEW

Personnel

Bishop	1
Retired Bishops	1
Priests: Diocesan Active in Diocese	31
Priests: Retired, Sick or Absent	25
Number of Diocesan Priests	56
Total Priests in your Diocese	56
Extern Priests in Diocese	5
Ordinations:	
Permanent Deacons	5
Permanent Deacons in Diocese	19
Total Sisters	19

Parishes

Parishes	36
With Resident Pastor:	
Resident Diocesan Priests	33
Without Resident Pastor:	
Administered by Priests	2
Administered by Deacons	1
Missions	36
New Parishes Created	1
Closed Parishes	1
Professional Ministry Personnel:	
Sisters	7
Lay Ministers	24

Welfare

Catholic Hospitals	2
Total Assisted	43,945
Homes for the Aged	1
Total Assisted	75

Educational

Diocesan Students in Other Seminaries	5
Total Seminarians	5
High Schools, Diocesan and Parish	4
Total Students	497
Elementary Schools, Diocesan and Parish	8
Total Students	1,040
Catechesis / Religious Education:	
High School Students	1,480
Elementary Students	2,930
Total Students under Catholic Instruction	5,952
Teachers in Diocese:	
Lay Teachers	132

Vital Statistics

Receptions into the Church:	
Infant Baptism Totals	707
Minor Baptism Totals	71
Adult Baptism Totals	49
Received into Full Communion	107
First Communions	697
Confirmations	597
Marriages:	
Catholic	101
Interfaith	66
Total Marriages	167
Deaths	546
Total Catholic Population	48,363
Total Population	280,181

LEADERSHIP

Vicar General - Very Rev. Donald A. Buhrman;
Chancery Office - t) 308-382-6565
Chancellor - Kathleen M. Hahn;
Diocesan Consultors - Very Rev. Donald A. Buhrman; Rev. Jorge Canela; Rev. Paul J. Colling;

OFFICES AND DIRECTORS

Catholic Relief Services - Most Rev. Joseph G. Hanefeldt, Dir. (jhanefeldt@gidiocese.org);
CEC (Catholics Encounter Christ) - Rev. Louis A. Nollette, Spiritual Adv./Care Srvcs.;
Communications - t) (308) 382-6565 Angie Fisher, Dir. (communications@gidiocese.org);
Community Mental Health -
Council of Catholic Women, Diocesan - Rev. Vijumon Choorackal, Spiritual Adv./Care Srvcs.;
Diocesan Magazine - t) (308) 382-6565 media@gidiocese.org Oscar Erives, Editor;
Episcopal Vicar for Clergy - Very Rev. Donald A. Buhrman;
Faith Formation & Evangelization - t) 308-382-6565 Michalene Iverson, Admin.;
Multimedia - t) (308) 382-6565 media@gidiocese.org Oscar Erives, Dir.;
Office of Child Protection - Elizabeth Heidt, Dir. (cpo@gidiocese.org); Cheryl Albright, Outreach Coord. (calbright@gidiocese.org);
Ongoing Formation for Clergy and Liturgy - c) (308) 455-7049 Rev. Vidya S. Arikotla, Dir.; Rev. Paul J. Colling, Dir.;
Operations and Human Resources - t) (308) 382-6565 Greg Fisher (gfisher@gidiocese.org);
Permanent Diaconate Formation - t) 308-660-1008 mirish@gidiocese.org Dcn. Matthew Irish, Dir. (m.irish@npcschools.org);
Personnel Board - Very Rev. Donald A. Buhrman, Pres.; Rev. Jose M. Chavez; Rev. Joseph A. Hannappel;
Priests' Advisory Board (Presbyteral Council) - Very Rev. Vincent L. Parsons, Pres.; Rev. Vidya S. Arikotla; Rev. Sidney B. Bruggeman;
Priests' Pension and Welfare Board - Rev. Jonathan D. Sorensen, Pres.; Rev. Michael Pampara; Rev. Martin L. Egging;
Pro Life - t) 308-390-1605 Michael Kube, Dir.;
Propagation of the Faith - t) 308-436-2290 Rev. Michael D. McDonald, Dir.;
Rural Life Conference - Rev. Bryan D. Ernest, Dir.;
Schools - t) 308-682-6565 Jordan C. Engle, Supt.;
Stewardship and Development - t) 308-382-6565 Amy Scheer, Admin. (stewardship@gidiocese.org);
Victim Assistance Coordinators - Elizabeth Heidt (cpo@gidiocese.org); Cheryl Albright (calbright@gidiocese.org);
Vocations - t) 308-234-1539 Rev. Neal J. Hock, Dir.;
Youth & Young Adult - t) 308-382-6565 L. Eric Heckman, Dir. (eheckman@gidiocese.org);

TRIBUNAL

Diocesan Tribunal - t) 308-382-6364
Vicar-Judicial - Very Rev. Vincent L. Parsons;
Associate Director-Notary - Marie Ryan;
Defenders of the Bond - Kathy Hahn; Rev. Richard L. Piontkowski Jr.;
Judges - Very Rev. Vincent L. Parsons; Rev. Jonathan D. Sorensen; Rev. Charles L. Torpey;
Procurator - Very Rev. Donald A. Buhrman; Rina Huntwork;
Advocates - Very Rev. Donald A. Buhrman; Rina Huntwork;

PARISHES, MISSIONS, AND CLERGY

STATE OF NEBRASKA

AINSWORTH

St. Pius X - 915 E. 3rd St., Ainsworth, NE 69210; Mailing: PO Box 7, Ainsworth, NE 69210 t) 402-387-1275; 402-387-2260 (CRP) stpiusxne@msn.com Rev. Michael E. Wetovick, Pst.; CRP Stds.: 81
Holy Cross - E. Hwy. 20, Bassett, NE 68714

ALLIANCE

Holy Rosary - 904 Cheyenne Ave., Alliance, NE 69301; Mailing: 1104 Cheyenne Ave., Alliance, NE 69301 t) 308-762-2009; 308-762-2830 (CRP) hrcsecretary@bbc.net www.bbccatholic.com Rev. Matthew J. Koperski, Pst.; Noreen Placek, DRE; Theresa Dykes, Pastoral Min.; CRP Stds.: 71
St. Agnes Academy - (Grades PreSchool-8) 1104 Cheyenne Ave., Alliance, NE 69301 t) 308-762-2315 merrelloa@saa.school www.stagnesacademy.com Orson Merrell, Prin.; Stds.: 138; Lay Tchrs.: 12
St. Bridget - 801 Niobrara Ave., Hemingford, NE 69348; Mailing: P.O. Box 67, Hemingford, NE 69348 t) 308-487-3617 stbridget@bbc.net

BRIDGEPORT

All Souls - 617 P St., Bridgeport, NE 69336; Mailing: 701 P St., Bridgeport, NE 69336 t) 308-262-0709 allsoulsbridgeport@gmail.com Rev. Timothy L. Stoner, Pst.; CRP Stds.: 94
St. Mary - 718 E. Francis St., Dalton, NE 69131 t) (308) 262-0709 smasshcatholics.org
Sacred Heart - 1003 Ave. B, Bayard, NE 69334 t) (308) 262-0709 smasshcatholics.org

BROKEN BOW

St. Joseph's - 1407 S. E St., Broken Bow, NE 68822; Mailing: P.O. Box 405, Broken Bow, NE 68822 t) 308-872-5809 stjoescatholic@msn.com www.stjoecatholic.org Rev. James M. Hunt, Pst.; Rashelle Ryan, DRE; CRP Stds.: 184
St. Anselm's - 201 W. Rolla Ave., Anselmo, NE 68813 t) (308) 872-5809 Lori Klein, DRE;
Assumption of the Blessed Virgin Mary - 300 N. 2nd St., Sargent, NE 68874 t) (308) 872-5809 Laura Kipp, DRE;

CHADRON

St. Patrick's - 340 Cedar St., Chadron, NE 69337; Mailing: PO Box 231, Chadron, NE 69337 t) 308-432-2626; 308-432-2161 (CRP) stpats@chadronstpatricks.org www.chadronstpatricks.org Rev. Todd K. Philipsen, Pst.; CRP Stds.: 93

CHAPPELL

St. Joseph's - 1049 2nd St., Chappell, NE 69129; Mailing: PO Box 586, Chappell, NE 69129 t) 308-874-3407 stjosephchappell@gmail.com Dcn. Dixon Powers, Admin.; CRP Stds.: 14
St. Elizabeth - 300 W. 4th, Oshkosh, NE 69154 t) (308) 874-3407
St. Gall - 307 1st St., Lisco, NE 69148 t) (308) 874-3407

COZAD

Christ the King - 613 W. 13th St., Cozad, NE 69130 t) 308-784-4161 secretaryckc.2016@gmail.com Rev. Michael Pampara, Pst.; CRP Stds.: 177
Our Lady of Good Counsel - 1915 Ave. J, Gothenburg, NE 69138 t) (308) 784-4161 Mary Meisinger, DRE;

CRAWFORD

St. John the Baptist - 808 4th St., Crawford, NE 69339 t) 308-665-1584; (308) 850-5235 (Arul Cell) stjohncrawford@bbc.net; stjohncrawford@gmail.com Rev. Arul Raj Innaiah, Pst.; CRP Stds.: 37
Church of the Nativity of the Blessed Virgin Mary - 280 Kate St., Harrison, NE 69339

ELM CREEK

Immaculate Conception - 310 N. Church St., Elm Creek, NE 68836; Mailing: P.O. Box 530, Elm Creek, NE 68836 t) 308-856-4375 Rev. Joseph K. Joseph, Pst.; Dcn. William O'Donnell; Cheska Hubbard, DRE; CRP Stds.: 20
Holy Rosary - 503 D St., Overton, NE 68863 t) (308) 856-4375 Sarah Luther, DRE;
St. John Capistran - 118 N. Ash, Amherst, NE 68812 t) (308) 856-4375 Annette Line, DRE;

GERING

Christ the King - 1345 18th St., Gering, NE 69341; Mailing: P.O. Box 33, Gering, NE 69341 t) 308-436-2290; 308-436-7272 christking@allophone.com Rev. Michael D. McDonald, Pst.; Micki Walker, DRE; Dcn. Leo (Lee) Trautman; CRP Stds.: 103

GORDON

St. Leo's - 300 N. Maverick, Gordon, NE 69343; Mailing: 228 N. Maverick, Gordon, NE 69343 t) 308-282-0427 stleosgordon@gmail.com Rev. Dan Gilbert, Pst.; Marvel Reeves, DRE; CRP Stds.: 51
Immaculate Conception - 606 Church St., Rushville, NE 69360; Mailing: P.O. Box 279, Rushville, NE 69360 t) 308-327-2430 ruthsch@pgcom.net Michelle Heck, DRE; Vicki Wellnitz, DRE;
St. Columbkille - 545 N. Main, Hay Springs, NE 69347; Mailing: PO Box 279, Rushvill, NE 69360 t) 308-327-2706 ruthsch@pgcom.net Miriam Kearns, DRE;

GRAND ISLAND

Cathedral of the Nativity of the Blessed Virgin Mary - 204 S. Cedar St., Grand Island, NE 68801; Mailing: 112 S. Cedar St., Grand Island, NE 68801 t) 308-384-2523 office@stmarysgi.com; parishadmin@stmarysgi.com www.stmarysgi.com Rev. Jorge Canela, Rector; Rev. Joseph G. Broudou, Assoc. Pst.; Dcn. John Farlee; Dcn. Matthew Lonnemann; Dcn. Frank Moreno; CRP Stds.: 324
Blessed Sacrament - 518 W. State St., Grand Island, NE 68801 t) 308-384-0532 blsachurch.net Rev. Martin L. Egging, Pst.; Sr. Bernadette Engelhaupt, O.S.F., Pst. Assoc.; CRP Stds.: 230
St. Leo - 2410 S. Blaine, Grand Island, NE 68801 t) 308-382-4753 office@saintleos.org www.saintleos.org Very Rev. Donald A. Buhrman, Pst.; Jenny Golka, DRE; Rita Hemmer, Youth Min.; Dcn. William Buchta; CRP Stds.: 192
Church of the Resurrection - 4130 Cannon Rd., Grand Island, NE 68803 t) 308-382-8644 adminassistant@giresurrection.com www.giresurrection.com Rev. Vijumon Choorackal, Pst.; Therese Stump, DRE; Dcn. John Willmes; CRP Stds.: 143

KEARNEY

St. James - 3801 A Ave., Kearney, NE 68847 t) 308-234-5536; 308-234-9695 (CRP) frjoe@stjameschurchkearney.org; kelley@stjameschurchkearney.org www.stjameschurchkearney.org Rev. Joseph A. Hannappel, Pst.; Dcn. Mark Bowman; Ron Dobesh, Admin.; Kelley Hendrickson, DRE; Sr. Catherine Bones, S.C.L., Pastoral Min.; CRP Stds.: 388
Kearney Catholic - (Grades 6-12) 110 E. 35th St., Kearney, NE 68847; Mailing: P.O. Box 1866, Kearney, NE 68848-1866 t) 308-234-2610 www.kearneycatholic.org Matthew Rogers, Prin.; Janet Anderson, Librn.; Stds.: 364; Lay Tchrs.: 27
Prince of Peace - 2407 W. 56th St., Kearney, NE 68845-4113 t) 308-236-9171 popoffice@kearneyprinceofpeace.org; pcolling@gidiocese.org www.princeofpeacekearney.com Rev. Paul J. Colling, Pst.; Dcn. Thomas Martin; Amy Lowe, DRE; Makayla Irwin, Youth Min.; Kathy Niedbalski, Music Min.; Mandy Mueting, Bus. Mgr.; CRP Stds.: 251

LEXINGTON

St. Ann's - 303 E. 6th St., Lexington, NE 68850; Mailing: P.O. Box 578, Lexington, NE 68850-0578 t) 308-324-4647 stannscatholic@gmail.com www.lexstanns.com Rev. Jose M. Chavez, Pst.; Sr. Mary Ann Flax, C.S.J., Pastoral Min.; Dcn. Jesus Alvarez; CRP Stds.: 250

LOUP CITY

St. Josaphat's - 704 N. 9th St., Loup City, NE 68853;

Mailing: P.O. Box 626, Loup City, NE 68853 t) 308-745-0315; 308-745-1235 (CRP) c) 308-530-5803 josaphatsaint@yahoo.com; rpiontkowski@gidiocese.org Rev. Richard L. Piontkowski Jr., Pst.; Rev. Mark Maresh, In Res.; Lorraine Panowicz, DRE; CRP Stds.: 75

St. Francis - 220 W. Carleton St., Ashton, NE 68817 t) (308) 745-0315 Marie Curlo, DRE;

St. Gabriel - 112 Market St., Hazard, NE 68844 t) (308) 745-0315 Jason Gross, DRE;

MITCHELL

St. Theresa's - 1715 17th St., Mitchell, NE 69357; Mailing: PO Box 217, Mitchell, NE 69357 t) 308-623-2245 sbcotriparishes@gmail.com Rev. Michael D. McDonald, Pst.; CRP Stds.: 18

St. Ann - Hwy. 26 & Walsh, Morrill, NE 69358 t) (308) 623-2245

MULLEN

St. Mary's - 304 S. Blaine Ave., Mullen, NE 69152; Mailing: P.O. Box 191, Mullen, NE 69152 t) 308-546-2250 mnash@gidiocese.org www.sandhillscatholic.org Rev. Matthew Nash, Pst.; CRP Stds.: 60

All Saint's - 201 S. Manderson, Hyannis, NE 69350 t) 308-544-6285

St. Thomas of Canterbury - 204 Main St., Thedford, NE 69166 t) (308) 546-2250

NORTH PLATTE

Holy Spirit - 2801 W. E St., North Platte, NE 69101 t) 308-534-6623 holy1spirit@allphone.com www.holyspiritcatholicchurch.com Rev. Vidya S. Arikotla, Pst.; Dcn. Michael Davis; Dcn. Mark Stadler; CRP Stds.: 61

Sacred Heart - 410 Poplar St., Sutherland, NE 69165; Mailing: P.O. Box 398, Sutherland, NE 69165 t) 308-386-4300

St. Patrick - 415 N. Chestnut, North Platte, NE 69101 t) (308) 532-0942 office@st-pats-online.org www.st-pats-online.org Rev. Jonathan D. Sorensen, Pst.; Rev. Joseph Kadaprayil, S.D.B., Sr. Assoc. Pst.; Makaela Lauderdale, DRE; Dcn. Matthew Irish; Dcn. Mark Lister; Dcn. Eric Parker; CRP Stds.: 85

McDaid Elementary - (Grades PreSchool-6) 1002 E. E St., North Platte, NE 69101; Mailing: P.O. Box 970, North Platte, NE 69101 t) 308-532-1874 p.wood@npcschools.org www.npcschools.org Kevin Dodson, Supt.; Pam Wood, Prin.; Stds.: 248; Lay Tchrs.: 20

St. Patrick High School - (Grades 7-12) 500 S. Silber, North Platte, NE 69101; Mailing: P.O. Box 970, North Platte, NE 69101 t) 308-532-1874 k.dodson@npcschools.org www.npcschools.org Kevin Dodson, Supt.; Stds.: 154; Lay Tchrs.: 14

OGALLALA

St. Luke's - 417 E. Third, Ogallala, NE 69153 t) 308-284-3196 frb@kccatholics.com; dre@kccatholics.com www.kccatholics.com Rev. Bryan D. Ernest, Pst.; CRP Stds.: 189

St. Luke's School - (Grades PreSchool-5) 406 E. 3rd St., Ogallala, NE 69153 t) 308-284-4841 stlukesschool@saintlukesschool.com Lynnette Powers, Prin.; Stds.: 77; Lay Tchrs.: 5

St. Patrick's Church - 301 E. 4th St., Paxton, NE 69153; Mailing: 417 E. 3rd St., Ogallala, NE 69165 t) (308) 284-3196 stpatricks@kccatholics.com Jan Spurgin, DRE;

ORD

Our Lady of Perpetual Help - 527 N. 19th St., Ord, NE 68862; Mailing: P.O. Box 123, Ord, NE 68862-0123 t) 308-728-3351 www.ordcatholicchurch.org Rev. Scott M. Harter, Pst.; Mattison Ference, DRE; Angela Cargill, Headmaster; Laura Pokorny, Bus. Mgr.; CRP Stds.: 135

St. Mary's School - (Grades K-6) 527 N. 20th St., Ord, NE 68862 t) 308-728-5389 acargill@stmarys.org Jordan C. Engle, Supt.; Stds.: 39; Lay Tchrs.: 4

Sacred Heart - 757 I St., Burwell, NE 68823; Mailing: PO Box 667, Burwell, NE 68823 t) 308-346-4190 shcburwell@gmail.com shcburwell.wixsite.com Kathy Carson, Bus. Mgr.;

RAVENNA

Our Lady of Lourdes - 515 Sicily Ave., Ravenna, NE 68869; Mailing: Box 90, Ravenna, NE 68869 t) 308-452-3109; 308-452-3903 (CRP) ourladyoflourdes324@gmail.com Rev. Richard L. Piontkowski Jr., Pst.; Joan Clifton, DRE; CRP Stds.: 97

St. Mary's - 504 N. Syracuse St., Pleasanton, NE 68866 t) (308) 452-3109

SCOTTSBLUFF

St. Agnes - 2314 3rd Ave., Scottsbluff, NE 69363; Mailing: P.O. Box 349, Scottsbluff, NE 69363 t) 308-632-2541; 308-632-6918 (CRP) office@st-agnes-church.com; dre@st-agnes-church.com www.st-agnes-church.com Rev. Rayappa Konka, Pst.; Terri Calvert, DRE; CRP Stds.: 129

St. Agnes School - (Grades PreK-5) 205 E. 23rd St., Scottsbluff, NE 69363 t) (308) 632-6918 Julie Brown, Headmaster; Stds.: 118; Lay Tchrs.: 7

Our Lady of Guadalupe - 1102 12th Ave., Scottsbluff, NE 69361; Mailing: P.O. Box 2485, Scottsbluff, NE 69363-2485 t) 308-632-2845 Rev. Joseph Thambi Bonagiri, Admin.; Eliza Rodriguez, DRE; CRP Stds.: 83

SIDNEY

St. Patrick's - 1039 14th Ave., Sidney, NE 69162 t) 308-254-2828 parish@sidneystpats.com www.sidneystpats.com Rev. C. P. Varghese, Pst.; Joan Falcon, DRE; Patricia Mertz, Pst. Assoc.; CRP Stds.: 84

St. Joseph's - 511 S. Howard St., Kimball, NE 69145; Mailing: P.O. Box 576, Kimball, NE 69145 t) 308-235-4031

SPALDING

St. Michael's - 150 W. Marguerite St., Spalding, NE 68665; Mailing: P.O. Box 310, Spalding, NE 68665 t) 308-497-2662 frantony@families-infaith.com; office@families-infaith.com Rev. Antony Thekkekara, Pst.; Dcn. Ronald Glaser; Dcn. Paul Nordhues; Holly Carraher, DRE; CRP Stds.: 166

Spalding Academy - (Grades PreK-12) 130 W. Marguerite, Spalding, NE 68665 t) 308-497-2103 amy.mckay@spaldingacademy.org Amy McKay, Prin.; Stds.: 68; Lay Tchrs.: 13

St. Theresa of the Child Jesus - 201 Chesapeake St., Ericson, NE 68637 t) (308) 497-2662 Jerilee Wright, DRE;

Sacred Heart - 302 W. Wicklow, Greeley, NE 68842; Mailing: PO Box 99, Greeley, NE 68842 t) 308-428-2855 Angie Pfeifer, DRE;

ST. LIBORY

St. Libory's - 505 Spruce St., St. Libory, NE 68872 t) 308-687-6276 sbruggeman@gidiocese.org; wieck.catherine@gmail.com www.stliborycatholic.com Rev. Sidney B. Bruggeman, Pst.; Cathy Wieck, DRE; CRP Stds.: 60

ST. PAUL

SS. Peter and Paul - 713 Elm St., St. Paul, NE 68873 t) 308-754-4002 office@howardcountycatholics.com www.howardcountycatholics.com Very Rev. Vincent L. Parsons, Pst.; Judi Baker, DRE; Dcn. Neil Baquet; CRP Stds.: 201

St. Joseph - 1803 Hwy. 11, Elba, NE 68835; Mailing: PO Box 156, Farwell, NE 68838 t) (308) 336-3351

St. Anthony of Padua - 103 Kearns Ave., Farwell, NE 68838; Mailing: PO Box 156, Farwell, NE 68838 t) (308) 336-3351

STAPLETON

St. John the Evangelist - 301 H St., Stapleton, NE 69163; Mailing: P.O. Box 309, Stapleton, NE 69163 t) 308-636-2421 stjohnscatholic@hotmail.com www.abjcatholic.org Rev. Thomas Gudipalli, Pst.; Jennifer Johnston, DRE; CRP Stds.: 70

St. Agnes - 503 N. Carroll, Arnold, NE 69120 t) (308) 848-2421 Aleta Ambler, DRE;

St. Boniface - 204 S. Morgan Ave., Callaway, NE 68825 t) (308) 836-2421 Mary Riddler, DRE;

VALENTINE

St. Nicholas - 400 W. 5th St., Valentine, NE 69201; Mailing: P.O. Box 510, Valentine, NE 69201 t) 402-376-1672 stnicholas.valentine@gmail.com Rev. Abraham Kaduthodiyil, Pst.; CRP Stds.: 90

St. Mary - Main St., Nenzel, NE 69219

WOOD RIVER

St. Mary's - 408 W. 11th St., Wood River, NE 68883; Mailing: PO Box 37, Wood River, NE 68883 t) 308-583-2464 Rev. Joshua S. Brown, Pst.; CRP Stds.: 104

Sacred Heart - 502 B St., Shelton, NE 68876; Mailing: P.O. Box 190, Shelton, NE 68876 t) (308) 647-5123

SCHOOLS: PRESCHOOL THRU HIGH SCHOOL

HIGH SCHOOLS

STATE OF NEBRASKA

GRAND ISLAND

Central Catholic Schools - (DIO) (Grades 6-12) 1200 Ruby Ave., Grand Island, NE 68803 t) 308-384-2440 jengle@gicc.org Jordan C. Engle, Prin.; Stds.: 297; Lay Tchrs.: 30

INSTITUTIONS LOCATED IN DIOCESE

CAMPUS MINISTRY / NEWMAN CENTERS [CAM]

CHADRON

Chadron State College-Newman House - 907 Main St., Chadron, NE 69337 t) 308-432-3673 L. Eric Heckman, Admin.;

KEARNEY

St. Teresa of Calcutta Newman Center - 821 W. 27th St., Kearney, NE 68845; Mailing: 2714 8th Ave., Kearney, NE 68845-4332 t) 308-234-1539 newmancenterunk@gmail.com; ncfinance.unk@gmail.com www.lopercatholic.org Rev. Neal J. Hock, Pst.; Monica Musil, Admin.;

HOSPITALS / HEALTH SERVICES [HOS]

GRAND ISLAND

Saint Francis Medical Center - 2620 W. Faidley Ave., Grand Island, NE 68802; Mailing: P.O. Box 9804, Grand Island, NE 68802 t) 308-384-4600 missionintegrationmidwest@commonspirit.org www.chihealth.com/st-francis Edward Hannon, Pres.; Andrew Santos, SVP Mission Integration; Bed Capacity: 153; Asstd. Annu.: 20,625; Staff: 844

KEARNEY

Good Samaritan Hospital - 10 E. 31st St., Kearney, NE 68848-1990; Mailing: P.O. Box 1990, Kearney, NE 68848-1990 t) 308-865-7100 missionintegrationmidwest@commonspirit.org www.chihealth.com/good-samaritan Curt Coleman, Pres.; Andrew Santos, SVP Mission Integration; Bed Capacity: 172; Asstd. Annu.: 22,000; Staff: 850

Richard H. Young Hospital - 4600 17th Ave., Kearney, NE 68847 t) 308-865-2000 Bed Capacity: 45; Asstd. Annu.: 1,320; Staff: 54

MISCELLANEOUS [MIS]

ALLIANCE

Magnificat Alliance, NE Chapter - 1104 Cheyenne Ave.,

Alliance, NE 69301 t) 308-762-2009; (308) 760-8324 (Debbie Zumbahlen) Deb Zumbahlen, Contact;

GRAND ISLAND

***The Family of the Good Shepherd, Inc.** - 611 S. Broadwell, Grand Island, NE 68803; Mailing: P.O. Box 911, Grand Island, NE 68802 t) 308-675-3002 c) 402-206-8088 catherine.nagl@gmail.com www.thefamilyofthegoodshepherd.org Sr. Catherine Nagl, Dir.;

PAXTON

Magnificat - Our Lady of the Harvest Chapter - Ogallala - 1051 Road East L N., Paxton, NE 69155 t) 308-289-5995 conniefrosh@opsd.org Connie Frosh, Contact;

NURSING / REHABILITATION / CONVALESCENCE / ELDERLY CARE [NUR]

KEARNEY

Mount Carmel Home-Keens' Memorial - 412 W. 18th St., Kearney, NE 68847 marycarmelite@hotmail.com ocarmtt.org Sr. Mary Florence Blavet, O.Carm., Supr.; Asstd. Annu.: 75; Staff: 120

An asterisk (*) denotes an organization that has established tax-exempt status directly with the IRS and is not covered by the USCCB Group Ruling.

Diocese of Grand Rapids

(Dioecesis Grandormensis)

MOST REVEREND DAVID J. WALKOWIAK, J.C.D.

Bishop of Grand Rapids; ordained June 9, 1979; appointed Bishop of Grand Rapids April 18, 2013; episcopal ordination June 18, 2013. Office: Cathedral Square Center, 360 Division Ave. S., Grand Rapids, MI 49503.

Administrative Offices of the Diocese of Grand Rapids: Cathedral Square Center, 360 Division Ave. S., Grand Rapids, MI 49503. T: 616-243-0491; F: 616-243-4910.
www.grdiocese.org

ESTABLISHED MAY 19, 1882.

Square Miles 6,795

Comprises the following counties of the lower peninsula of the State of Michigan: Ionia, Kent, Lake, Mason, Mecosta, Montcalm, Muskegon, Newaygo, Oceana, Osceola, Ottawa.

Consult the Chancery Office for legal titles of parishes and diocesan institutions.

STATISTICAL OVERVIEW

Personnel
Bishop....1
Retired Bishops....1
Priests: Diocesan Active in Diocese....57
Priests: Diocesan Active Outside Diocese....2
Priests: Retired, Sick or Absent....40
Number of Diocesan Priests....99
Religious Priests in Diocese....15
Total Priests in your Diocese....114
Extern Priests in Diocese....7
Ordinations:
Diocesan Priests....3
Transitional Deacons....2
Permanent Deacons....7
Permanent Deacons in Diocese....44
Total Brothers....1
Total Sisters....209

Parishes
Parishes....80
With Resident Pastor:
Resident Diocesan Priests....52
Resident Religious Priests....5
Without Resident Pastor:
Administered by Priests....21
Administered by Lay People....2
Missions....4

Professional Ministry Personnel:
Brothers....1
Sisters....184
Lay Ministers....165

Welfare
Catholic Hospitals....2
Total Assisted....2,268,585
Homes for the Aged....1
Total Assisted....105
Residential Care of Children....248
Total Assisted....371
Special Centers for Social Services....3
Total Assisted....53,241
Other Institutions....1
Total Assisted....1,837

Educational
Diocesan Students in Other Seminaries....20
Total Seminarians....20
Colleges and Universities....1
Total Students....1,467
High Schools, Diocesan and Parish....4
Total Students....1,257
High Schools, Private....1
Total Students....119
Elementary Schools, Diocesan and Parish....25
Total Students....4,782
Elementary Schools, Private....2
Total Students....313
Catechesis/Religious Education:
High School Students....924
Elementary Students....4,910
Total Students under Catholic Instruction....13,792
Teachers in Diocese:
Priests....1
Sisters....3
Lay Teachers....382

Vital Statistics
Receptions into the Church:
Infant Baptism Totals....1,415
Minor Baptism Totals....194
Adult Baptism Totals....98
Received into Full Communion....306
First Communions....1,545
Confirmations....1,317
Marriages:
Catholic....331
Interfaith....152
Total Marriages....483
Deaths....1,285
Total Catholic Population....179,098
Total Population....1,450,069

LEADERSHIP

Adjutant Judicial Vicar and Defender of the Bond - Dr. Christina Hip-Flores;
Adjutant Judicial Vicars - Rev. Douglas A. Braun;
Vicar General/Moderator of the Curia - t) 616-514-6050 Very Rev. Msgr. William H. Duncan;
Chief Financial Officer - t) 616-475-1247 Michael A. Lown;
Vicar for Priests - Rev. Thomas P. Page;
Chancellor - t) 616-475-1247 Michael A. Lown;
Tribunal - Very Rev. Kevin W. Niehoff, O.P.;
Judicial Vicar - t) 616-459-4509 Very Rev. Kevin W. Niehoff, O.P.;
Marriage Dispensations/Permissions - t) 616-514-6050 Very Rev. Msgr. William H. Duncan;
College of Consultors - Very Rev. Msgr. William H. Duncan; Rev. Stephen S. Dudek; Rev. John F. Vallier;
Presbyteral Council - Rev. Noah Thelen; Rev. Dat Tran, C.S.P.; Rev. Lawrence J. King;
Deans - Rev. Troy A. Nevins; Rev. Thomas J. Brown; Rev. Michael G. Hodges;
Diocesan Finance Council - Sr. Aquinas Weber, O.P.; Rev. Leonard A. Sudlik; Richard A. Wendt;

ADMINISTRATION

Secretary to the Bishop - t) 616-514-6050 Gail A. Welsh;
Building and Planning - t) 616-475-1247 Michael A. Lown;
Comptroller - t) 616-475-1253 Charles Fust;
Deposit and Loan Program - t) 616-475-1253 Charles Fust;
Facilities/Real Estate - t) 616-475-1247 Michael A. Lown;
Human Resources - t) 616-475-1242 Traci Douglas;
Parish Review Services - t) 616-288-0909 Cristine VanLinden;
Self-Insurance Program - t) 616-475-1247 Michael A. Lown;
Technology - t) 616-246-0593 Alec Saturley;

OFFICES AND DIRECTORS

Archives - t) 616-246-0596 Angela Yondo; Rev. Phillip A. Sliwinski;
Black Catholic Ministry - t) 231-744-3321 Rev. Godfrey C. Onyekwere;
Catholic Foundation of West Michigan - t) 616-475-1251 Greg Deja; Erinn Hill;
Catholic Services Appeal - t) 616-243-0491 Katie Olding;
Cemeteries - t) 616-453-1636 Connie Sacha;
Communications - t) 616-551-5629 Annalise Laumeyer;
Courage International - t) 616-288-0914 Rev. William R. Vander Werff;
Cursillo Movement - t) 616-243-0491 Rev. Jose Luis Quintana;
Diocesan Council of Catholic Women - t) 616-481-2529 Barb Vezino;
Ecumenical Affairs - t) (616) 243-0491
EnCourage Ministries - t) 616-288-0918 Rev. Thomas J. Cavera;
Faith Formation and Catechesis - t) 616-288-0912 Christine McCarty;
Family and Youth - t) 616-551-4748 D.J. Florian;
Hispanic Ministry - t) 616-246-0598 Juan Carlos Farias Gonzalez;
Immigration Legal Services - t) 616-551-5675 Nicole Iraola, Interim Dir.;
Liturgical Music - t) 616-243-5590 Dcn. Dennis Rybicki;
Missions Office - t) 616-243-0491 Rev. Stephen S. Dudek;
Native American Ministry - t) 616-551-4748 D.J. Florian;
Pastoral Services - t) 616-551-4748 D.J. Florian;
Prison/Jail Ministry - t) 616-475-1255 Tricia Worrell;
Pro-Life Ministry - t) 616-551-4748 D.J. Florian;
Safe Environment - t) 616-475-1246 Chris Castano;
Stewardship & Development - t) (616) 475-1251 Greg Deja;
Victim Assistance Coordinator - t) 616-840-2079 Allison Bush;
Vietnamese Ministry - t) 616-531-5213 Rev. Victor Kynam;
Worship - t) 616-475-1241 Dr. Aaron Sanders;

CATHOLIC CHARITIES

Catholic Charities West Michigan - t) 616-475-1252 David Bellamy;
- **Service Locations** -
- **Benton Harbor** - t) 269-757-7258
- **Big Rapids** - t) 231-796-1583
- **Grand Rapids** - t) 616-454-4110
- **Holland** - t) 616-796-9595
- **Ionia** - t) 616-522-0836
- **Kalamazoo** - t) 269-381-1234
- **Ludington** - t) 231-843-4899
- **Muskegon** - t) 231-726-4735
- **Stanton** - t) 616-855-5923
- **Traverse City** - t) 231-346-5250
- **White Cloud** - t) 231-689-6701

CLERGY AND RELIGIOUS SERVICES

Diaconate Formation - t) 616-288-0913 Rev. Mark C. Przybysz; Dcn. Gerald Roersma; Pattie L Reynolds;
Office of Continuing Formation for Priests - t) 616-288-0910 Rev. Lam T. Le; Pattie L Reynolds;
Office of Priestly Vocations - t) 616-288-0910 Rev. Stephen J. Durkee; Pattie L Reynolds;
Permanent Diaconate - t) 616-288-0910 Rev. Mark C. Przybysz;
Priest Retirement Fund - t) 616-243-0491 Rev. Troy A. Nevins;

EDUCATION

Superintendent of Catholic Schools - t) 616-233-5975 David A. Faber;
Assistant Superintendent of Catholic Schools - t) 616-551-5633 Sarah Grey;
Catholic Information Center - t) 616-459-7267 Rev. Mike Cruickshank, C.S.P.; Mark Mann;

PARISHES, MISSIONS, AND CLERGY

STATE OF MICHIGAN

ADA

St. Patrick - 4351 Parnell Ave. N.E., Ada, MI 49301 t) 616-691-8541; 616-691-8541 x803 (CRP) secretary@spparnell.org; rwelsh@spparnell.org spparnell.org Rev. Thomas J. Cavera, Pst.; CRP Stds.: 64

> **St. Patrick School** - (Grades PreK-8) 4333 Parnell Ave., N.E., Ada, MI 49301 t) 616-691-8833 assistant@spparnell.org; principal@spparnell.org www.stpatrickparnellschool.org Scott Czarnopys, Prin.; Stds.: 243; Lay Tchrs.: 11

St. Robert of Newminster - 6477 Ada Dr., S.E., Ada, MI 49301 t) 616-676-9111; 616-676-9111 x114 (CRP) parishmail@strobertchurch.org; tburns@strobertchurch.org strobertchurch.org Rev. Anthony S. Russo, Pst.; Rev. Logan Weber, Par. Vicar; Dcn. John Ashmore, Pst. Min./Coord.; Teri Burns, DRE; CRP Stds.: 511

BALDWIN

St. Ann - St. Ignatius - 1001 Michigan Ave., Baldwin, MI 49304; Mailing: PO Box 729, Baldwin, MI 49304 t) 231-745-7997 Rev. Matthew J. Barnum, Pst.;

BELDING

St. Joseph-St. Mary - 409 S. Bridge St., Belding, MI 48809; Mailing: 505 S. Lafayette St., Greenville, MI 48838 t) 616-754-4194 saintscjm.com Rev. James B. Wyse, Pst.; Dcn. Daniel Schneider; CRP Stds.: 16

> **St. Mary Chapel/Oratory** - 9041 Krupp Rd., Belding, MI 48809 t) 616-794-2145

BELMONT

Assumption of the Blessed Virgin Mary - 6390 Belmont Ave., N.E., Belmont, MI 49306 t) 616-361-5126 x200; 616-361-5126 x257 (CRP) ffd@assumptionbvm.com; dcowen@assumptionbvm.com www.assumptionbvm.com Rev. Anthony M. Pelak, Pst.; Dcn. Michael J. Mauer; Dcn. Paul S. Antor; Cheryl Sokolowski, DRE; CRP Stds.: 167

> **Assumption of the Blessed Virgin Mary School** - (Grades PreK-8) 6393 Belmont Ave., Belmont, MI 49306 t) 616-361-5483 schoolsecretary@abvmschool1.org www.schoolassumptionbvm.com Domenic Franconi, Prin.; Stds.: 205; Lay Tchrs.: 12

BIG RAPIDS

St. Mary-St. Paul Parish - 1009 Marion Ave., Big Rapids, MI 49307 t) 231-796-5202 mmendenhall@stmarystpaulbr.org; creed@stmarystpaulbr.org stmarystpaulbr.org Elizabeth Dake, Pst. Assoc.; Rev. Patrick Fickel, Pst.; CRP Stds.: 32

> **St. Mary Catholic School** - (Grades PreK-8) 927 Marion Ave., Big Rapids, MI 49307 t) 231-796-6731 jbwatters@stmarybr.org J.B. Watters, Prin.; Stds.: 172; Lay Tchrs.: 11

BYRON CENTER

St. Sebastian - 9408 Wilson Ave., S.W., Byron Center, MI 49315 t) 616-878-1619; 616-878-1619 x102 (CRP) sue@stsebastianmi.org www.stsebastianmi.org Very Rev. Msgr. William H. Duncan, Pst.; CRP Stds.: 273

CALEDONIA

Holy Family - 9669 Kraft Ave., S.E., Caledonia, MI 49316 t) 616-891-9259 parishoffice@holyfamilycaledonia.org www.holyfamilycaledonia.org Rev. Michael Cilibraise, Pst.; Deb Hazelbach, Bus. Mgr.; CRP Stds.: 301

CARSON CITY

St. Mary - 404 N. Division St., Carson City, MI 48811 t) 989-584-6044 nwoodcock@cmsinter.net; smsjchurch@cmsinter.net stmarystjohn.net Clustered with St. John the Baptist Parish, Hubbardston. Nancy Woodcock, Pastoral Min. & DRE; CRP Stds.: 49

CEDAR SPRINGS

Saint John Paul II - 3110 17 Mile Rd., N.E., Cedar Springs, MI 49319 t) 616-696-3904 kmendenhall@jp2-mqa.org jp2-mqa.org Rev. Lam T. Le, Pst.; Katie Mendenhall, DRE; CRP Stds.: 64

COMSTOCK PARK

Holy Trinity - 1200 Alpine Church Rd., N.W., Comstock Park, MI 49321 t) 616-784-0677; 616-784-0677 x152 (CRP) rdunneback@holytrinitycp.org; parishoffice@holytrinitycp.org www.holytrinitycp.org Rev. Chris W. Rouech, Pst.; Dcn. Gerald Roersma; Rebbeca Dunneback, DRE; CRP Stds.: 45

> **Holy Trinity School** - (Grades PreK-8) 1304 Alpine Church Rd., Comstock Park, MI 49321 t) (616) 784-0696 krand@holytrinitycp.org; jauchter@hotlytrinitycp.org holytrinityschoolcp.com Kathy Rand, Prin.; Stds.: 112; Lay Tchrs.: 10

CONKLIN

St. Francis Xavier - 2034 Gooding Rd., Conklin, MI 49403; Mailing: 3376 Thomas St., P.O. Box 216, Ravenna, MI 49451 t) 231-853-6222 stfrancisconklin@ourcluster.org ourcluster.org Clustered with St. Catherine, Ravenna and St. Joseph, Wright. Rev. Andrew Ayers, Pst.; CRP Stds.: 1

St. Joseph Wright - 18784 Eighth Ave., Conklin, MI 49403-9718 t) 616-899-2286; 231-853-6222 (CRP) clustersecretary@ourcluster.org ourcluster.org Clustered with St. Catherine-Ravenna and St. Francis Xavier-Conklin. Rev. Andrew Ayers, Pst.; CRP Stds.: 9

> **Divine Providence Academy of St. Joseph** - (Grades PreK-8) 18768 Eighth Ave., Conklin, MI 49403 t) 616-899-5300 kbeuschel@wingsdpa.org www.wingsdpa.org Two campuses; Divine Providence of St. Catherine and Divine Providence of St. Joseph. Kate Beuschel, Prin.; Stds.: 105; Lay Tchrs.: 10

COOPERSVILLE

St. Michael - 17150 88th Ave., Coopersville, MI 49404 t) 616-384-4026 secretary@saintmichaels.us;

childrensministry@saintmichaels.us www.saintmichaels.us Rev. Michael G. Hodges, Pst.; Dcn. Tom Roberts; CRP Stds.: 43

St. Michael School - (Grades PreSchool- t) (616) 384-4026 preschool@saintmichaels.us Cindy Lindberg, Dir.; Stds.: 7; Lay Tchrs.: 1

CUSTER

St. Mary-St. Jerome Parish - 85 S. Madison Ave, Custer, MI 49405; Mailing: P.O. Box 68, Custer, MI 49405 t) 231-757-4709; 231-757-3709 stjeromesc@sbcglobal.net stmarycuster.org Rev. Daniel R. DePew, Pst.; CRP Stds.: 21

EAST GRAND RAPIDS

St. Stephen Catholic Church - 750 Gladstone Dr., S.E., East Grand Rapids, MI 49506-2821; Mailing: 723 Rosewood Ave., S.E., East Grand Rapids, MI 49506 t) 616-243-8998 parishoffice@ststephenparish.com www.ststephenparish.com Rev. Scott T. Nolan, Pst.; Brittany Renne, DRE; CRP Stds.: 22

St. Stephen Catholic Church School - (Grades PreK-8) 740 Gladstone Dr., S.E., East Grand Rapids, MI 49506 t) (616) 243-8998 schooloffice@ststephenparish.com ststephenschoolgr.com Elizabeth Black, Prin.; Stds.: 48; Lay Tchrs.: 10

EVART

Sacred Heart - 9878 E. US 10, Evart, MI 49631; Mailing: P.O. Box 778, Evart, MI 49631 t) 231-734-3171 Rev. Loc Q. Trinh, Admin.;

FREE SOIL

St. John Cantius - 2845 E. Michigan, Free Soil, MI 49411 t) 231-464-5672; 231-757-4709 (Office) stjohncantiusfreesoil@gmail.com Rev. Daniel R. DePew, Pst.;

FREMONT

All Saints - 500 Iroquois Dr., Fremont, MI 49412 t) 231-924-7705; 231-924-7571 (CRP) office@allsaintsfremont.org; dre@allsaintsfremont.org www.allsaintsfremont.org Rev. Peter C. Schafer; Shannon Siuda, DRE; Cindy Nestle, Bus. Mgr.;

St. Michael - 6382 S. Maple Island Rd., Fremont, MI 49412 t) 231-924-3389 stmctk@ncats.net www.stmichaelctk.org Rev. Peter C. Schafer, Pst.; CRP Stds.: 40

Chapel/Oratory Christ the King - 263 Elm St., Hesperia, MI 49421 t) (231) 924-3389

GRAND HAVEN

St. Patrick - St. Anthony - 920 Fulton Ave., Grand Haven, MI 49417 t) 616-842-0001 parishoffice@stpatsgh.org www.stpatsgh.org Rev. Charles J. Schwartz, Pst.; Dcn. Lance Walters; Jimmy Beauchamp, Admin.; Tony Allen, DRE; CRP Stds.: 131

GRAND RAPIDS

Cathedral of St. Andrew - 301 Sheldon Blvd., S.E., Grand Rapids, MI 49503; Mailing: 215 Sheldon Blvd., S.E., Grand Rapids, MI 49503 t) 616-456-1454 www.cathedralofsaintandrew.org Rev. Dat Tran, C.S.P., Rector; Rev. Mike Cruickshank, C.S.P., Assoc. Pst.; Rev. William Edens, C.S.P., Assoc. Pst.; Rev. Joachim Lally, C.S.P., Senior Ministry; Sean Donovan, DRE; CRP Stds.: 131

St. Alphonsus - 224 Carrier St., N.E., Grand Rapids, MI 49505 t) 616-451-3043 stalphonsusgr@stalphonsusgr.org stalphonsusgr.org Rev. George E. Darling, Par. Admin.; Rev. Chung Tran, C.Ss.R., Assoc. Pst.; Rev. Eugene T. Batungbacal, C.Ss.R., In Res.; Bro. Leo Patin, C.Ss.R., In Res.; Rev. Thomas Santa, C.Ss.R., In Res.; CRP Stds.: 59

St. Anthony of Padua - 2510 Richmond St., N.W., Grand Rapids, MI 49504 t) 616-453-8229 x100 parishoffice@saparish.com; lhaley@saparish.com www.saparish.com Rev. Mark C. Przybysz, Pst.; Dcn. Leo Ferguson; Lynne Haley, DRE; CRP Stds.: 87

St. Anthony of Padua School - (Grades PreK-8) t) (616) 453-8229 schooloffice@saparish.com Jenny Pudelko, Prin.; Stds.: 267; Lay Tchrs.: 16

Basilica of St. Adalbert - 654 Davis N.W., Grand Rapids, MI 49504 t) 616-458-3065 ldavis@basilicagr.org; aanderson@basilicagr.org www.basilicagr.org Very Rev. Ronald Hutchinson, Pst.; Rev. David Sacha, Par. Vicar; Andrew Anderson, DRE; CRP Stds.: 27

Blessed Sacrament - 2275 Diamond Ave., N.E., Grand Rapids, MI 49505 t) 616-447-7554; 616-447-7554 (CRP) church@bsacrament.net; father@bsacrament.net www.bsacrament.net Rev. George E. Darling, Pst.; Jody DeGraw, DRE; CRP Stds.: 32

Holy Spirit - 2230 Lake Michigan Dr., N.W., Grand Rapids, MI 49504 t) 616-453-6369; 616-453-1591 (CRP) office@hsparish.org; dschoof@hsparish.org www.hsparish.org Rev. Mark E. Peacock, Pst.; Rev. David Jameson, Par. Vicar; Diane Schoof, DRE; CRP Stds.: 102

Holy Spirit School - (Grades PreK-8) 2222 Lake Michigan Dr., N.W., Grand Rapids, MI 49504 t) 616-453-2772 pkalahar@hsparish.org www.holyspiritschool.org Patrick Kalahar, Prin.; Stds.: 309; Lay Tchrs.: 16

Immaculate Heart of Mary - 1935 Plymouth Ave., S.E., Grand Rapids, MI 49506 t) 616-241-4477; 616-241-4477 x105 (CRP) parish@ihmparish.com; pa@ihmparish.com ihmparish.com Rev. Troy A. Nevins, Pst.; Stefanie Kay Iwan, DRE; CRP Stds.: 95

Immaculate Heart of Mary School - (Grades PreK-8) 1951 Plymouth, S.E., Grand Rapids, MI 49506 t) 616-241-4633 principal@ihmschoolgr.com ihmparish.com/school/ Holly Lake, Prin.; Stds.: 315; Lay Tchrs.: 21

St. Isidore - 628 Diamond Ave., N.E., Grand Rapids, MI 49503 t) 616-459-4731; 616-459-4731 x33 (CRP) directorfaithform@saintisidorechurch.org; parishsecretary@saintisidorechurch.org www.saintisidorechurch.org Rev. Msgr. Edward A. Hankiewicz, Pst.; CRP Stds.: 80

St. Jude - 1120 Four Mile Rd., N.E., Grand Rapids, MI 49525 t) 616-363-6885 x1150 lparks@stjudes.net Rev. Ayub Nasar, Pst.; Dcn. Daniel Esch; Dcn. Larry Hoogeboom; CRP Stds.: 38

St. Mary - 423 1st St., N.W., Grand Rapids, MI 49504 t) 616-459-7390 wanda@stmarygr.org stmarygr.org Very Rev. Ronald Hutchinson, Pst.; Rev. David Sacha, Par. Vicar; CRP Stds.: 8

Our Lady of Sorrows - 101 Hall St., S.E., Grand Rapids, MI 49507; Mailing: 116 Green St., S.E., Grand Rapids, MI 49507 t) 616-243-0222 office@ourladyofsorrows-gr.org www.ourladyofsorrows-gr.org Rev. Theodore Kozlowski, Pst.; Ana Becerra, DRE; Carlos Juarez, DRE; CRP Stds.: 36

St. Paul the Apostle - 2750 Burton St., S.E., Grand Rapids, MI 49546 t) 616-949-4170 mbreenan@spagr.org www.spagr.org Rev. Peter Damian, Pst.; Jeanne Winkelmann, DRE; Meghan Breenan, Bus. Mgr.; Rev. Michael J. Goodwin, Par. Vicar; CRP Stds.: 147

St. Paul the Apostle School - (Grades PreK-8) t) 616-949-1690 www.stpaul-school.org Michelle Morrow, Prin.; Stds.: 285; Lay Tchrs.: 19

SS. Peter and Paul - 520 Myrtle St., N.W., Grand Rapids, MI 49504-3277 t) 616-454-6000; 616-454-5611 dennisv@ssppgr.org; sallya@ssppgr.org www.ssppgr.com Rev. Mark F. Bauer, Pst.; Dennis Vainavicz, Bus. Mgr.; CRP Stds.: 11

Sacred Heart of Jesus - 156 Valley Ave., S.W., Grand Rapids, MI 49504 t) 616-459-8362 parishoffice@shgr.org; dre@shgr.org sacredheartgr.org Rev. Ronnie Floyd, Pst.; Rev. Donald E. Lomasiewicz, Pastor Emer.; Rev. Robert A. Sirico, Pastor Emer.; Rev. John Bosco Ssekkomo, In Res.; Michael Tober, DRE; CRP Stds.: 76

Sacred Heart Academy - (Grades PreK-12) 1200 Dayton, S.W., Grand Rapids, MI 49504 t) 616-459-0948 spoliskey@shgr.org; headmaster@sacredheartgr.org shgr.org Classical Catholic Academy for full-time students and part-time homeschool students Sean Maltbie, Headmaster; Stds.: 286; Sr. Tchrs.: 1; Lay Tchrs.: 16

Shrine of St. Francis Xavier and Our Lady of Guadalupe - 250 Brown St., S.E., Grand Rapids, MI 49507; Mailing: 245 Griggs St., S.E., Grand Rapids, MI 49507 t) 616-241-2485 x10 sfxolgoffice@sbcglobal.net; jcpaiz96@gmail.com sfxolg.org Rev. Edwin Carreño Carreño, Admin.; Fernando I. Gutierrez-Perez, Pst. Assoc.; Laura J. Brizio-Blas, Bus. Mgr.; Colleen Paiz, DRE; Steve VanderLaan, DRE; CRP Stds.: 135

St. Thomas the Apostle Parish - 1449 Wilcox Park Dr., S.E., Grand Rapids, MI 49506 t) 616-459-4662 x1202; 616-459-4662 x1209 (CRP) margodean@stthomasgr.org www.stthomasapostlegr.org Rev. James A. Chelich, Pst.; Patti Reynolds, DRE; Dcn. Dean Vernon; Dcn. Dennis Williams; CRP Stds.: 80

St. Thomas the Apostle School - (Grades PreK-8) 1429 Wilcox Park Dr., S.E., Grand Rapids, MI 49506 t) 616-458-4228 www.stthomasapostle.catholicweb.com Ryan Corcoran, Vice Prin.; Stds.: 340; Lay Tchrs.: 17

GRANDVILLE

St. Pius X - 3937 Wilson Ave., S.W., Grandville, MI 49418 t) 616-532-9344; 616-538-2600 (CRP) parishoffice@spxcatholic.org; formation@spxcatholic.org spxcatholic.org Rev. Stephen J. Durkee, Pst.; Elizabeth Post, DRE; CRP Stds.: 245

GREENVILLE

St. Charles Borromeo - 505 S. Lafayette, Greenville, MI 48838 t) 616-754-4194 admin@saintscjm.com saintscjm.com Rev. James B. Wyse, Pst.; Tessa Hoffman, DRE; Molly Scoby, DRE; CRP Stds.: 38

St. Charles Borromeo School - (Grades PreK-8) 502 S. Franklin St., Greenville, MI 48838 t) 616-754-3416 principal@saintscjm.com www.saintscjm.com/school Margaret Karpus, Prin.; Stds.: 115; Lay Tchrs.: 8

HART

St. Gregory-Our Lady of Fatima - 316 S. Peach Ave., Hart, MI 49420; Mailing: 214 S. Peach Ave., Hart, MI 49420 t) 231-873-2660 parish@stgregoryathart.org; officemanager@stgregoryathart.org www.stgregoryathart.org Rev. Daniel P. Schumaker, Pst.; Rev. Phillip A. Sliwinski, Admin.; Vickie Oomen, Bus. Mgr.; CRP Stds.: 71

St. Joseph - 2380 W. Jackson Rd., Hart, MI 49420 t) 231-873-5776 (Office); 231-869-2601 (Bus. Office) stjosephweare@comcast.net www.stjosephweare.org Rev. Phillip A. Sliwinski; Renee Dennert, DRE; CRP Stds.: 42

St. Vincent - 637 E. Sixth, Pentwater, MI 49449 t) (231) 873-5776

HOLLAND

St. Francis de Sales - 171 W. 13th St., Holland, MI 49423; Mailing: 195 W. 13th St., Holland, MI 49423 t) 616-392-6700 rvaldez@stfrancisholland.org www.stfrancisholland.org Rev. Luis F. Garcia, Pst.; Rev. Noah Thelen, Par. Vicar; Rev. Nicholas Monco, OP, Par. Vicar; CRP Stds.: 100

Our Lady of the Lake - 480 152nd Ave., Holland, MI 49424 t) 616-399-1062 office@oll.org www.oll.org Rev. Michael E. Burt, Pst.; Carla Niziolek, DRE; CRP Stds.: 107

HOWARD CITY

Christ the King-St. Francis de Sales - 9596 N. Reed Rd., Howard City, MI 49329 t) 231-937-5757 king-francis@ctknsf.org; faithformation@ctknsf.org www.ctknsf.org with St. Francis de Sales, Lakeview to form Christ the King-St. Francis de Sales, Howard City. Rev. James R. Vander Laan, Pst.; Dcn. Richard Dubridge; Julie Gould, DRE; CRP Stds.: 15

HUBBARDSTON

St. John the Baptist - 413 River St., Hubbardston, MI 48845; Mailing: 404 N. Division St., Carson City, MI 48811 t) 989-584-6044 smsjchurch@cmsinter.net; nwoodcock@cmsinter.net stmarystjohn.net Clustered with St. Mary, Carson City. Nancy Woodcock, Pastoral Min. & DRE; CRP Stds.: 18

IONIA

SS. Peter and Paul - 434 High St., Ionia, MI 48846 t) 616-527-3610 parishoffice@ssppcatholic.com www.saintspeterandpaulionia.org Rev. Thomas J. Brown, Pst.; Rev. Oscar Londono Builes, Assoc. Pst.;

Dcn. Zenon Cardenas Sr.; CRP Stds.: 30

SS. Peter and Paul School - (Grades PreK-8) 317 Baldie St., Ionia, MI 48846 t) 616-527-3561 jleik@ssppcatholic.com www.ssppcatholic.com Jennifer Leik, Prin.; Stds.: 122; Lay Tchrs.: 6

IRONS

St. Bernard - 5734 W. 10 1/2 Mile Rd., Irons, MI 49644; Mailing: P.O. Box 155, Irons, MI 49644 c) (231) 745-7997 Rev. Matthew J. Barnum, Pst.;

JENISON

Holy Redeemer - 2700 Baldwin St., Jenison, MI 49428 t) 616-669-9220 x1100 hrpsecr@holyredeemerparish.org holyredeemerparish.org Rev. Phong Pham, Pst.; CRP Stds.: 253

St. Luke University Parish - 10144 42nd Ave., Jenison, MI 49428 t) 616-895-2247 faithformation@lukespot.com; k.thomas@lukespot.com www.stlukegvsu.org Rev. Robert C. Mulderink, Pst.; CRP Stds.: 82

KENTWOOD

St. Mary Magdalen - 1253 52nd St., S.E., Kentwood, MI 49508 t) 616-455-9310 lcadorniga@stmmagdalen.org; witness@stmmagdalen.org www.stmmagdalen.org Rev. Peter G. Vu, Pst.; Molly Wisdom, DRE; CRP Stds.: 96

LAKE ODESSA

St. Edward - 531 Jordan Lake St., Lake Odessa, MI 48849 t) 616-374-7253 www.stedwardslakeodessa.org Rev. Thomas J. Brown, Pst.; Rev. Oscar Londono, Assoc. Pst.; Vanessa Booth, DRE; CRP Stds.: 39

LOWELL

St. Mary Great Mother of God Catholic Church - 402 Amity St., Lowell, MI 49331 t) 616-897-9820 office@stmarylowell.org; dre@stmarylowell.org www.stmarylowell.com/ Rev. Michael J. Goodwin, Admin.; Jennie Forney, DRE; CRP Stds.: 61

LUDINGTON

St. Simon - 702 E. Bryant Rd., Ludington, MI 49431 t) 231-843-8606; 231-843-3497 (CRP) stsimon@stsimonchurch.com www.stsimonchurch.com Rev. Wayne B. Wheeler Jr., Pst.; CRP Stds.: 80

Ludington Area Catholic School - (Grades PreK-8) 700 E. Bryant Rd., Ludington, MI 49431 t) 231-843-3188 mrsbigalke@lacschool.net Jan M. Bigalke, Prin.; Stds.: 108; Lay Tchrs.: 9

MARION

St. Agnes - 603 E. Main St, Marion, MI 49665; Mailing: PO Box 778, Evart, MI 49631 t) 231-734-3171 marciebennett999@gmail.com Rev. Loc Q. Trinh; Marcella Bennett, DRE; CRP Stds.: 25

MARNE

St. Mary - 15164 Juniper Dr., Marne, MI 49435 t) 616-677-3934; 616-677-5065 (CRP) secretary@saintmarysmarne.org; dre@saintmarysmarne.org www.saintmarysmarne.org Rev. Michael G. Hodges, Pst.; CRP Stds.: 115

MONTAGUE

St. James - 5149 Dowling St., Montague, MI 49437 t) 231-893-3085; 231-893-3085 x2 (CRP) faithformation@stjamescatholicparish.org; office.manager@stjamescatholicparish.org stjamescatholicparish.org Cluster with St. John the Baptist and Our Lady of Assumption, Rothbury Rev. Peter O. Omogo, Pst.; Dcn. Gregory Anderson; Kristin Schaub, Coord. Faith Formation; CRP Stds.: 54

St. John the Baptist - S. 50th Ave., Claybanks, MI 49446; Mailing: 5149 Dowling St., Montague, MI 49437 t) (231) 893-3085 (Business Office) Mary Lulofs, Bus. Mgr.;

MUSKEGON

St. Mary of the Immaculate Conception - 196 W. Webster Ave., Muskegon, MI 49440-1213; Mailing: 239 W. Clay Ave., Muskegon, MI 49440 t) 231-722-2803 stmarysmuskegon.org Rev. Kyle Kilpatrick, Admin.; Kacey Kersman, DRE; CRP Stds.: 143

St. Michael the Archangel - 1716 Sixth St., Muskegon, MI 49441 t) 231-722-3071 office@stmichaelmuskegon.org saintmichaelsmuskegon.com Rev. Charles D. Hall, Pst.; Sr. Agnes Mary Wojtkowiak, O.P., Pst. Assoc.;

St. Thomas the Apostle - 3252 Apple Ave., Muskegon, MI 49442 t) 231-773-3160 petersonsue5@gmail.com sacredheartmuskegon.org Rev. Douglas A. Braun, Pst.; Sue Peterson, DRE; CRP Stds.: 9

MUSKEGON HEIGHTS

Sacred Heart - 150 E. Summit Ave., Muskegon Heights, MI 49444-2161 t) 231-733-2440 admin@sacredheartmuskegon.org sacredheartmuskegon.org Rev. Douglas A. Braun, Pst.; Karen Edens, DRE; CRP Stds.: 15

NEWAYGO

St. Bartholomew - 599 W. Brooks St., Newaygo, MI 49337 t) 231-652-1286; 231-652-1286 x22 (CRP) parishoffice@stbart-stjoe.org; lkoester@stbart-stjoe.org stbart-stjoe.org Rev. Peter C. Schafer, Admin.; CRP Stds.: 74

NORTH MUSKEGON

Prince of Peace Parish North Muskegon - 1110 Dykstra Rd., North Muskegon, MI 49445-2014 t) 231-744-3321 tsteward@princeofpeacenm.org; office@princeofpeacenm.org princeofpeacenm.org Rev. Godfrey C. Onyekwere, Pst.; Dcn. Gregory Anderson, Bus. Mgr.; Dcn. James J. Schiltz; CRP Stds.: 91

NORTON SHORES

St. Francis de Sales - 2929 McCracken St., Norton Shores, MI 49441 t) 231-755-1953 x200; 231-755-1953 x225 (CRP) parish@stfrancisns.org www.stfrancisns.org Rev. Charles D. Hall, Pst.; CRP Stds.: 66

PEWAMO

St. Joseph - 126 East St., Pewamo, MI 48873; Mailing: P.O. Box 37, Pewamo, MI 48873 t) 989-593-3440; 989-593-3400 stewardship@stjosephpewamo.org rweber@stjosephpewamo.org www.stjosephpewamo.org Rev. Darrel C. Kempf, Pst.; CRP Stds.: 81

St. Joseph School - (Grades PreK-8) 160 East St., Pewamo, MI 48873; Mailing: P.O. Box 38, Pewamo, MI 48873 m.mowatt@stjosephpewamo.org Ryan Weber, Prin.; Stds.: 112; Lay Tchrs.: 6

PORTLAND

St. Patrick - 520 W. Grand River Ave., Portland, MI 48875; Mailing: 140 Church St., Portland, MI 48875 t) 517-647-6505; 517-647-6505 (CRP) parishoffice@portlandstpats.org; businessmanager@portlandstpats.org portlandstpats.com Rev. Michael J. Alber, Pst.; Carolyn Heckman, DRE; Carolyn Kwiecinski, RCIA Coord.; CRP Stds.: 187

St. Patrick School - (Grades PreK-8) 122 West St., Portland, MI 48875 t) 517-647-7551 office@portlandstpats.com Randy Hodge, Prin.; Cortney Smith, Prin.; Stds.: 281; Lay Tchrs.: 9

RAVENNA

St. Catherine - 3376 Thomas St., Ravenna, MI 49451; Mailing: P.O. Box 216, Ravenna, MI 49451 t) 231-853-6222 clustersecretary@ourcluster.org; jsokolowski@ourcluster.org ourcluster.org Clustered with St. Joseph, Wright and St. Francis Xavier, Conklin. Rev. Andrew Ayers, Pst.; Jeannie Sokolowski, DRE; CRP Stds.: 10

REED CITY

St. Philip Neri - 831 S. Chestnut St., Reed City, MI 49677 t) 231-832-5544 pneri831@stphilipanne.org www.stphilipanne.org Rev. Loc Q. Trinh, Par. Admin.; Elizabeth Dake, DRE; CRP Stds.: 15

St. Anne - 23949 22 Mile Rd., Paris, MI 49338 t) (231) 832-5544

REMUS

St. Michael the Archangel - 8929 50th Ave., Remus, MI 49340 t) 989-967-3520 elyseleach1@stmikes.us; parishoffice@stmikes.us www.stmichaelsremus.us Rev. Thomas F. Boufford, Pst.; Elyse Leach, Parish Life Coord.;

St. Michael the Archangel School - (Grades PreK-6) 8944 50th Ave., Remus, MI 49340 t) 989-967-3681 jerryward1@stmikes.us www.stmikes.us Jerry Ward, Prin.; Stds.: 85; Lay Tchrs.: 6

ROCKFORD

Our Lady of Consolation - 4865 Eleven Mile Rd., Rockford, MI 49341 t) 616-866-0931; 616-866-2577 (CRP) olcparish@olcparish.net www.olcparishrockford.com Rev. Dominic T Couturier, Pst.; Rev. Daniel Orris Jr., Assoc. Pst.; CRP Stds.: 293

Our Lady of Consolation School - (Grades PreK-8) t) 616-866-2427 kvarner@olcschoolrockford.org Kevin Varner, Prin.; Stds.: 214; Sr. Tchrs.: 1; Lay Tchrs.: 9

ROTHBURY

Our Lady of the Assumption - 3000 W. Winston Rd., Rothbury, MI 49452; Mailing: 5149 Dowling St., Montague, MI 49437 t) 231-893-3085 office.manager@stjamescatholicparish.org Cluster with St. James and St. John the Baptist, Montague Rev. Peter O. Omogo, Pst.; Dcn. Gregory Anderson;

SAND LAKE

Mary, Queen of Apostles - 1 Maple St., Sand Lake, MI 49343-0140; Mailing: P.O. Box 140, Sand Lake, MI 49343-0140 t) 616-636-5671 info@jp2mqa.org; mkloostra@jp2-mqa.org jp2-mqa.org Rev. Lam T. Le, Pst.; Katie Mendenhall, DRE;

SARANAC

St. Anthony - 6070 David Hwy., Saranac, MI 48881; Mailing: 3936 Jackson Rd., Saranac, MI 48881 t) 616-642-6119 stanthonyofsaranac.org Rev. Michael J. Goodwin; Susan Lauer, DRE; CRP Stds.: 21

SPARTA

Holy Family - 425 S. State St., Sparta, MI 49345 t) 616-887-8222; 616-887-8857 (CRP) srbgazda@holyfamilysparta.org; parishoffice@holyfamilysparta.org holyfamilysparta.org Rev. Msgr. Terrence L. Stewart, Pst.; Dcn. Greg Sokolowski; Sr. Bernadine Gazda, O.S.J., DRE; CRP Stds.: 42

SPRING LAKE

St. Mary - 406 E. Savidge St., Spring Lake, MI 49456 t) 616-842-1702; 616-842-2840 (CRP) parishoffice@stmarysl.org; clarson@slstm.org www.stmarysl.org Rev. William R. Vander Werff, Pst.; CRP Stds.: 144

St. Mary School - (Grades PreK-8) 430 E. Savidge St., Spring Lake, MI 49456 t) 616-842-1282 schooloffice@slstm.org www.slstm.org Maureen Turner, Prin.; Stds.: 207; Lay Tchrs.: 16

STANTON

St. Bernadette of Lourdes-St. Margaret Mary Alacoque - 991 E. Main St., Stanton, MI 48888 t) 989-831-5914 sbl.smm.church@gmail.com sbl-smm.net Rev. James VanderLaan;

WHITE CLOUD

St. Joseph - 965 Newell St., White Cloud, MI 49349; Mailing: 599 Brooks St., Newaygo, MI 49337 t) 231-652-1286 stbart-stjoe.org Rev. Peter C. Schafer, Admin.; CRP Stds.: 8

WYOMING

Holy Name of Jesus - 1630 Godfrey Ave., S.W., Wyoming, MI 49509; Mailing: 1048 Chicago Dr., S.W., Wyoming, MI 49509 t) 616-241-6489 dketchum@holynamewyoming.org holynameofjesuswyomingmichigan.com Rev. Charles D. Brown, Pst.; Luz Margarita Aguirre, DRE; CRP Stds.: 93

St. John Vianney - 4101 Clyde Park, S.W., Wyoming, MI 49509 t) 616-534-5449; 616-724-3123 (CRP) hcoppock@stjohnvianney.net; jhurst@stjohnvianney.net Rev. John F. Vallier, Pst.; Jim Hurst, Catechesis; CRP Stds.: 18

St. John Vianney School - (Grades PreK-8) t) 616-532-7001 lolejnik@stjohnvianney.net Linda Olejnik, Prin.; Stds.: 171; Lay Tchrs.: 9

St. Joseph the Worker - 225 32nd St., S.W., Wyoming, MI 49548; Mailing: 3138 Birchwood Ave., S.W., Wyoming, MI 49548 t) 616-456-7982; 616-456-7982 (CRP) padrejose@sanjoseobrero.net; oficina@sanjoseobrero.net sanjoseobrero.net Rev. Jose Luis Quintana, Pst.; Dcn. Martin Zapata, Pst. Assoc.;

Our Lady of LaVang - 2019 Porter St., S.W., Wyoming,

MI 49519 t) 616-531-5213 victorkynam@gmail.com Rev. Victor Kynam, Pst.; Dcn. Thu Le; CRP Stds.: 119

SCHOOLS: PRESCHOOL THRU HIGH SCHOOL

SCHOOLS

STATE OF MICHIGAN

ADA

St. Robert Catholic School - (Grades PreK-3) 6477 Ada Dr., S.E., Ada, MI 49301 t) 616-455-4966 lpeters@strobertschoolada.org www.strobertschoolada.org Greater Grand Rapids Independent Catholic Elementary Schools Liz Peters, Prin.; Stds.: 106; Lay Tchrs.: 7

GRAND RAPIDS

All Saints Academy - (PAR) (Grades PreK-8) 2233 Diamond Ave., N.E., Grand Rapids, MI 49505 t) 616-447-2997; 616-363-7725 mdebri@asagr.org www.asagr.org Michael Debri, Prin.; Stds.: 367; Lay Tchrs.: 24

HOLLAND

Corpus Christi School - (PAR) (Grades PreK-8) 12100 Quincy St., Holland, MI 49424 t) (616) 796-2300 jenniferliniewski@dogrschools.org www.corpuschristischool.us Jennifer M Liniewski, Prin.; Stds.: 124; Lay Tchrs.: 10

MUSKEGON

Muskegon Catholic Central Elementary School - (PRV) (Grades PreK-6) 1145 Laketon Ave., Muskegon, MI 49441 t) 231-755-2201 krasp@muskegoncatholic.org; scallow@muskegoncatholic.org www.muskegoncatholic.org Stephanie Callow, Prin.; Ken R. Rasp, Pres.; Rev. Kyle Kilpatrick, Chap.; Stds.: 207

WYOMING

San Juan Diego Academy - (PAR) (Grades K-8) 1650 Godfrey Ave., S.W., Wyoming, MI 49509 t) 616-243-1126 schooloffice@sjdaschool.org; jvergara@sjdaschool.org www.sanjuandiegoacademy.com Rev. Charles D. Brown, Pst.; Kristina Martinez-Precious, Prin.; Stds.: 182; Lay Tchrs.: 10

HIGH SCHOOLS

STATE OF MICHIGAN

GRAND RAPIDS

Catholic Central High School - (DIO) (Grades 9-12) 319 Sheldon Ave., S.E., Grand Rapids, MI 49503 t) (616) 233-5800 www.grcatholiccentral.org Tiffany Marrinan, Prin.; Terrence H. Tyrrell, Pres.; Stds.: 593; Pr. Tchrs.: 1; Lay Tchrs.: 34

Sacred Heart Academy - 1200 Dayton St., S.W., Grand Rapids, MI 49504 t) 616-459-0948 smaltbie@sacredheartgr.org; rarmock@shgr.org www.sacredheartacademygr.org Sean Maltbie, Headmaster; Stds.: 102; Sr. Tchrs.: 1; Lay Tchrs.: 10

West Catholic High School - (DIO) (Grades 9-12) 1801 Bristol Ave., N.W., Grand Rapids, MI 49504 t) 616-233-5900 erikavogel@grwestcatholic.org grwestcatholic.org Jill Annable, Pres.; Tony Fischer, Prin.; Stds.: 482; Lay Tchrs.: 30

MUSKEGON

Muskegon Catholic Central - (PRV) 1145 W. Laketon Ave., Muskegon, MI 49441 t) 231-755-2201 krasp@muskegoncatholic.org www.muskegoncatholic.org Rev. Kyle Kilpatrick; Matt Callow, Prin.; Ken R. Rasp, Pres.; Stds.: 119; Lay Tchrs.: 1

PORTLAND

St. Patrick High School - 122 West St., Portland, MI 48875 t) 517-647-7551 office@portlandstpats.com www.portlandstpats.com Randy Hodge, Prin.; Stds.: 80; Lay Tchrs.: 8

INSTITUTIONS LOCATED IN DIOCESE

CAMPUS MINISTRY / NEWMAN CENTERS [CAM]

JENISON

St. Luke University Parish and Catholic Campus Ministry - 10144 42nd Ave., Jenison, MI 49428 t) 616-895-2247 www.gvsucatholic.org Rev. Robert C. Mulderink, Pst.;

COLLEGES & UNIVERSITIES [COL]

GRAND RAPIDS

Aquinas College - 1700 Fulton St. E., Grand Rapids, MI 49506 t) 616-632-8900; (616) 632-2920 www.aquinas.edu Dr. Alicia Cordoba, Pres.; Rev. Stanley Drongowski, Chap.; Rev. Robert Keller, Chap.; Stds.: 1,467

CONVENTS, MONASTERIES, AND RESIDENCES FOR WOMEN [CON]

ADA (PARNELL)

Discalced Carmelite Nuns, Monastery of Our Lady of Guadalupe - 4300 Mount Carmel Dr., N.E., Ada (Parnell), MI 49301-9784 t) 616-691-7764; 616-691-7758 carmelparnell@mymailstation.com; carmelada@copper.net www.carmelitenuns.org Sr. Mary Angela, O.C.D., Prioress; Srs.: 9

BELMONT

Consolata Missionary Sisters - 6801 Belmont Rd., Belmont, MI 49306; Mailing: P.O. Box 371, Belmont, MI 49306 t) 616-361-2072 reusamc@consolatasisters.org www.consolatasisters.org Sr. Rosa Rosito, MC, Contact; Srs.: 5

GRAND RAPIDS

Motherhouse of the Dominican Sisters - 111 Lakeside Dr., N.E., Grand Rapids, MI 49503-3811 t) 616-459-2910 www.grdominicans.org Sisters of St. Dominic of the Congregation of Our Lady of the Sacred Heart (The Religious Institute), Sisters of the Order of St. Dominic of Grand Rap Sr. Sandra Delgado, O.P., Prioress; Sr. Maureen Geary, O.P., Treas.; Srs.: 148

Dominican Center - Marywood - Aquinas Bukowski Center, 1700 Fulton St., East, Grand Rapids, MI 49506 t) 616-454-1241 www.dominicancenter.com A ministry of the Dominican Sisters at the Motherhouse.

LOWELL

Franciscan Sisters of the Eucharist, Inc. - 11600 Downes St., N.E., Lowell, MI 49331 t) 616-897-5590 Sr. Colleen Ann Nagle, F.S.E., Dir.; Srs.: 10

ENDOWMENTS / FOUNDATIONS / TRUSTS [EFT]

GRAND RAPIDS

Basilica of St. Adalbert Education Foundation - 654 Davis N.W., Grand Rapids, MI 49504 t) 616-458-3065 basilicagr.org Very Rev. Ronald Hutchinson, Pst.;

Catholic Cemeteries Extended Care Fund - 2000 Walker N.W., Grand Rapids, MI 49504 t) 616-453-1636; 616-531-9320 connies@grcathcem.org Diocese of Grand Rapids Catholic Cemeteries Sacha Connie, Dir.;

The Catholic Foundation of West Michigan - 360 Division Ave. S., Grand Rapids, MI 49503 t) 616-475-1247 mlown@grdiocese.org; gdeja@cfwmi.org www.catholicfoundationwmi.org/ Michael A. Lown, Chancellor; Greg Deja, Dir.;

The Foundation for Catholic Secondary Education of Greater Grand Rapids, Inc. - 360 Division Ave., S., Grand Rapids, MI 49503 t) 616-458-1247 mlown@grdiocese.org Michael A. Lown, Chancellor;

Sisters of St. Dominic Charitable Trust - 111 Lakeside Dr., N.E., Grand Rapids, MI 49503-3811 t) 616-459-2910 www.grdominicans.org Sisters of St. Dominic of the Congregation of Our Lady of the Sacred Heart Charitable Trust (The Trust). Sr. Sandra Delgado, O.P., Prioress;

PORTLAND

The Father Flohe Foundation - 140 Church St., Portland, MI 48875 t) 517-647-6505 www.portlandstpats.com Rev. Michael J. Alber, Pst.;

HOSPITALS / HEALTH SERVICES [HOS]

GRAND RAPIDS

Mercy Health Saint Mary's - 200 Jefferson Ave., S.E., Grand Rapids, MI 49503 t) 616-685-5000 www.mercyhealth.com A member of Trinity Health, Livonia, MI Dr. Matthew Biersack, Pres.; Dr. Joanna Bailey, Spiritual Adv./Care Srvcs.; Michael E. Sanderl, Exec.; Bed Capacity: 303; Asstd. Annu.: 600,000; Staff: 3,400

MUSKEGON

Trinity Health - 1500 E. Sherman Blvd., Muskegon, MI 49444 t) (231) 672-4889 tricia.karnes@trinity-health.org Sponsored by Trinity Health. Gary Allore, Pres.; Bed Capacity: 331; Asstd. Annu.: 1,668,585; Staff: 3,961

MISCELLANEOUS [MIS]

GRAND RAPIDS

Cathedral Square, Inc. - 360 Division Ave., S., Grand Rapids, MI 49503 t) 616-514-6059 mlown@grdiocese.org Michael A. Lown, Chancellor;

Catholic Charities West Michigan - 360 Division Ave. S., Ste. 3A, Grand Rapids, MI 49503 t) 616-475-1252 www.ccwestmi.org David Bellamy, CEO;

Catholic Information Center - 360 Division Ave. S., Ste. 2A, Grand Rapids, MI 49503 t) 616-459-7267 cicoffice@catholicinformationcenter.org www.catholicinformationcenter.org/ Rev. Dat Tran, C.S.P., Exec. Dir.; Rev. Mike Cruickshank, C.S.P., Assoc. Dir.;

Chapel of Our Lady of Aglona, Latvian Apostolate - 504 Grand Ave., N.E., Grand Rapids, MI 49503 t) 616-363-4997 marybrons@comcast.net Brons Visockis, Admin.;

Christopher House - 360 Division Ave., S., Grand Rapids, MI 49503 t) 616-475-1247 mlown@grdiocese.org Michael A. Lown, Chancellor;

Marywood Academy - 111 Lakeside Dr., N.E., Grand Rapids, MI 49503-3811 t) 616-459-2910 www.grdominicans.org Sr. Maureen Geary, O.P., Treas.;

Ministry Ventures - 111 Lakeside Dr., N.E., Grand Rapids, MI 49503-3811 t) 616-514-3103 www.grdominicans.org Sr. Maureen Geary, O.P., Treas.;

Our Shepherds - Our Future - 360 Division Ave., S., Grand Rapids, MI 49503 t) 616-551-5635 mlown@grdiocese.org Michael A. Lown, Chancellor;

The Society For The Propagation Of The Faith - 360 Division Ave., S., Grand Rapids, MI 49503 t) 616-243-0491 gwelsh@grdiocese.org Rev. Stephen S. Dudek, Dir.;

The Society of the Redemptorists of the City of Grand Rapids - 224 Carrier St., N.E., Grand Rapids, MI 49505 t) 616-451-3043 stalphonsusgr@stalphonsusgr.org stalphonsusgr.org Rev. Thomas Santa, C.Ss.R., Local Supr.; Rev. Chung Tran, C.Ss.R., Assoc. Pst.; Rev. Eugene T. Batungbacal, C.Ss.R., In Res.; Bro. Leo Patin, C.Ss.R., In Res.;

LOWELL

Franciscan Life Center Network, Inc. - 11650 Downes St., Lowell, MI 49331 t) 616-897-7842 scanagle@lifeprocesscenter.org www.lifeprocesscenter.org A ministry of the Franciscan Sisters of the Eucharist Sr. Colleen Ann Nagle, F.S.E., Dir.;

MUSKEGON

The English Cursillo Movement of the Diocese of Grand Rapids, MI, Inc. - 1920 Whitehall Rd., Muskegon, MI

49445 t) 616-824-0701 sjhiltz42@gmail.com Tim Reno, Dir.; Steven Hiltz, Dir.;

ROCKFORD

Grand Rapids Catholic Committee on Scouting - 9380 Grange Ave. N.E., Rockford, MI 49341 t) 616-780-9088; 616-866-2767 scottharvey@prodigy.net www.grccscouting.org Scott Harvey, Treas.;

NURSING / REHABILITATION / CONVALESCENCE / ELDERLY CARE [NUR]

GRAND RAPIDS

St. Ann's Home - 2161 Leonard St., N.W., Grand Rapids, MI 49504 t) 616-453-7715 info@stannshome.com stannshome.com Carmelite Sisters of the Divine Heart of Jesus. Dana Prince, Dir.; Asstd. Annu.: 105; Staff: 180

An asterisk (*) denotes an organization that has established tax-exempt status directly with the IRS and is not covered by the USCCB Group Ruling.

Diocese of Great Falls-Billings

(Dioecesis Magnocataractensis-Billingensis)

MOST REVEREND MICHAEL W. WARFEL

Bishop of Great Falls-Billings; ordained April 26, 1980; appointed Bishop of Juneau November 19, 1996; ordained December 17, 1996; appointed Apostolic Administrator of Fairbanks October 23, 2001; resigned June 7, 2002; appointed Bishop of Great Falls-Billings November 20, 2007; installed January 16, 2008. 121 23rd St. S., Great Falls, MT 59401-3939. T: 406-727-6683.

Pastoral Office: 121 23rd St. S., Great Falls, MT 59401- 3939. Mailing Address: P.O. Box 1399, Great Falls, MT 59403-1399. T: 406-727-6683; T: 800-332-9998 (Toll Free); F: 406-454-3480.
www.diocesegfb.org
chancery@diocesegfb.org

ERECTED MAY 18, 1904.

Square Miles 94,158.

Corporation Title: "Roman Catholic Bishop of Great Falls, Montana, a corporation sole."

Comprises the eastern part of the State of Montana and is made up of the following Counties: Big Horn, Blaine, Carbon, Carter, Cascade, Chouteau, Custer, Daniels, Dawson, Fallon, Fergus, Garfield, Golden Valley, Hill, Judith Basin, Liberty, McCone, Musselshell, Park, Petroleum, Phillips, Powder River, Prairie, Richland, Roosevelt, Rosebud, Sheridan, Stillwater, Sweet Grass, Treasure, Valley, Wibaux, Yellowstone and parts of Toole.

For legal titles of parishes and diocesan institutions, consult the Pastoral Office.

Most Reverend Jeffrey M. Fleming
Coadjutor Bishop of Great Falls-Billings; ordained May 19, 1992; appointed Coadjutor Bishop of Great Falls-Billings April 19, 2022; ordained June 22, 2022.

STATISTICAL OVERVIEW

Personnel
Bishop ... 2
Priests: Diocesan Active in Diocese ... 23
Priests: Diocesan Active Outside Diocese ... 2
Priests: Retired, Sick or Absent ... 22
Number of Diocesan Priests ... 47
Religious Priests in Diocese ... 15
Total Priests in your Diocese ... 62
Extern Priests in Diocese ... 8
Ordinations:
Transitional Deacons ... 1
Permanent Deacons in Diocese ... 21
Total Brothers ... 1
Total Sisters ... 25

Parishes
Parishes ... 50
With Resident Pastor:
Resident Diocesan Priests ... 21
Resident Religious Priests ... 11
Without Resident Pastor:
Administered by Priests ... 16
Administered by Deacons ... 1
Missions ... 50
Professional Ministry Personnel:
Brothers ... 1
Sisters ... 8
Lay Ministers ... 35

Welfare
Catholic Hospitals ... 2
Total Assisted ... 206,738
Day Care Centers ... 1
Total Assisted ... 120
Specialized Homes ... 1
Total Assisted ... 25
Special Centers for Social Services ... 6
Total Assisted ... 1,347

Educational
Diocesan Students in Other Seminaries ... 2
Total Seminarians ... 2
Colleges and Universities ... 1
Total Students ... 955
High Schools, Diocesan and Parish ... 3
Total Students ... 496
High Schools, Private ... 1
Total Students ... 106
Elementary Schools, Diocesan and Parish ... 7
Total Students ... 1,597
Elementary Schools, Private ... 4
Total Students ... 360
Catechesis / Religious Education:
High School Students ... 324
Elementary Students ... 1,476
Total Students under Catholic Instruction ... 5,316
Teachers in Diocese:
Priests ... 1
Brothers ... 1
Lay Teachers ... 347

Vital Statistics
Receptions into the Church:
Infant Baptism Totals ... 273
Minor Baptism Totals ... 75
Adult Baptism Totals ... 37
Received into Full Communion ... 73
First Communions ... 450
Confirmations ... 470
Marriages:
Catholic ... 53
Interfaith ... 19
Total Marriages ... 72
Deaths ... 630
Total Catholic Population ... 29,422
Total Population ... 433,562

LEADERSHIP

Vicar General - Most Rev. Jeffrey M. Fleming, Coadjutor; Msgr. Daniel J. Wathen, Vicar;
Pastoral Office - t) 406-727-6683; 800-332-9998 (Toll Free)
Chancellor - Darren Eultgen (chancellor@diocesegfb.org);
Moderator of the Curia -
Fiscal Officer - t) 406-727-6683 Shanny Murphy;
Diocesan Tribunal - t) 406-727-6683; 800-332-9998 (Toll Free) tribunal@diocesegfb.org Terryal Ann Reavley, Dir.;
  Judicial Vicar - Rev. Robert D. Grosch, Judicial Vicar; Rev. David P. Wilkins, Adjunct Judicial Vicar;
Promoter of Justice - Rev. John W. Robertson;
Defenders of the Bond - Rev. Samuel Spiering; Rev. Michael Schneider;
Director of the Tribunal - t) 406-727-6683 x127 Terryal Ann Reavley;
Notary - Terryal Ann Reavley;
Diocesan Consultors - Msgr. Daniel J. Wathen; Rev. Jay H. Peterson (vicargeneral@diocesegfb.org); Rev. Ryan Erlenbush;
Personnel Board - Most Rev. Jeffrey M. Fleming; Msgr. Daniel J. Wathen; Rev. Antony Raj Kumar Arumugam, H.G.N. (frtonyhgn@gmail.com);
Vicars Forane - Rev. Stephen J. Zabrocki, Billings; Rev. Alphonsus Enelichi, M.S.P., Great Falls; Rev. James O'Neil, Wolf Point;
Cemetery Board - Most Rev. Michael W. Warfel; Rev. Barton K. Stevens;
Cum Christo/Cursillo - t) 406-989-1168 www.bigskycumchristo.org Lee Wegmann (lwegmann@midrivers.com); Rene Steinberger, Forsyth (rsteinberger@hotmail.com); Mark Brodhead, Sidney (bbtrailcrs@midrivers.com);

OFFICES AND DIRECTORS

Boy Scouts - t) 406-259-3389 Rev. Leo G. McDowell, Chap. (frleo@frleo.org);
Catechesis - t) 406-727-6683 H. Thomas Dotterweich, Dir.;
Catholic Campaign for Human Development - Darren Eultgen, Dir. (chancellor@diocesegfb.org);
Catholic Relief Services - Darren Eultgen (chancellor@diocesegfb.org);
Clerical Benefit Association - Most Rev. Michael W. Warfel; Msgr. Daniel J. Wathen; Rev. Stephen J. Zabrocki;
Continuing Formation of Clergy -
DCCW - Susan Fox, Rep.; Rev. Cory D. Sticha, Worship Comm. Rep.;
Diocesan Pastoral Council - t) 406-727-6683 Most Rev. Michael W. Warfel; Most Rev. Jeffrey M. Fleming; Shanny Murphy;
  Membership - Most Rev. Jeffrey M. Fleming; Rev. Ryan Erlenbush; Rev. Samuel Spiering;
Education - Angela Turoski, Supt. (aturoski@greatfallscentral.org);
Finance Council - Most Rev. Michael W. Warfel; Most Rev. Jeffrey M. Fleming; Msgr. Daniel J. Wathen, Vicar;
Fiscal Officer - t) 406-727-6683 Shanny Murphy;
Newspaper - Dcn. Peter Woelkers;
Office of Vocations - Msgr. Daniel J. Wathen, Dir.;
Office of Worship (Vacant) -
Pastoral Outreach - Dcn. Peter Woelkers, Editor; Matthew Brower, Mt. Catholic Conference (director@montanaacc.org); H. Thomas Dotterweich, Diocesan D.R.E.;
Priests' Council - Most Rev. Michael W. Warfel; Most Rev. Jeffrey M. Fleming; Msgr. Daniel J. Wathen, Vicar;
Sister's Council - Darren Eultgen, Rep. (chancellor@diocesegfb.org);

ORGANIZATIONS

Catholic Social Services of Montana - t) 406-442-4130 www.cssmt.org Scott Held, Exec. Dir. (scott@cssmt.org);
Montana Catholic Conference - t) 406-442-5761 Matthew Brower (director@montanaacc.org);
Safe Environment Coordinator - Barbara Haacke;
Victim Assistance Coordinator - t) 406-750-2373 Teresa Schmit;

PARISHES, MISSIONS, AND CLERGY

STATE OF MONTANA

ASHLAND

St. Labre - 112 St. Labre Campus Dr., Ashland, MT 59003; Mailing: P.O. Box 228, Ashland, MT 59003 t) 406-784-4516 jtimmers@stlabre.org sites.google.com/stlabre.org/st-labre-parish Rev. Jozef Timmers, OFM Cap., Pst.; CRP Stds.: 23

BAKER

St. John the Evangelist - 210 W Center Ave, Baker, MT 59313; Mailing: PO Box 1519, Baker, MT 59313 t) 406-778-2297 Rev. Philip Chinnappan, Pst.; Rita Breitbach, DRE; CRP Stds.: 56
  St. Joan of Arc - 100 Church Ave., Ekalaka, MT 59324 t) 406-775-6310
  St. Anthony - 201 W. Conser Ave., Plevna, MT 59344

BELT

St. Mark the Evangelist - 128 Castner St., Belt, MT 59412; Mailing: P.O. Box 213, Belt, MT 59412 t) (406) 277-3539; (406) 277-3366 (CRP) Rev. Rodrigo Mingollo, Admin.; Katrina Paulson, DRE; CRP Stds.: 27
  St. Clement - 62 Cascade Ave., Monarch, MT 59463 t) 406-727-6683 James Hoxter, Contact;
  St. Mary - 100 Main St., Raynesford, MT 59469
  Holy Trinity - 692 Stockett Rd., Centerville, MT 59480

BIG SANDY

St. Margaret Mary - 364 Johannes, Big Sandy, MT 59520; Mailing: PO Box 3009, Box Elder, MT 59521 t) 406-395-4380; 406-378-2369 (CRP) Rev. Joseph Tran, Pst.; Sr. Kathleen Kane, O.P., Pst. Assoc.; Sr. Margaret Mary O'Doherty, O.P., Pst. Assoc.; CRP Stds.: 50
  St. Anthony - 235 E Main, Box Elder, MT 59521
  St. Mary - 88 Church Hill Rd, RockyBoy, MT 59521

BIG TIMBER

St. Joseph - 910 McLeod St, Big Timber, MT 59011; Mailing: PO Box 871, Big Timber, MT 59011 t) 406-932-4728 Rev. Garrett J. Nelson, Pst.;

BILLINGS

St. Patrick Co-Cathedral - 215 N. 31st St., Billings, MT 59101 t) 406-259-3389 bulletin@stpatrickcocathedral.org www.stpatrickcocathedral.org Rev. Leo G. McDowell, Pst.; Rev. John Pankratz Jr., Par. Vicar; CRP Stds.: 42
St. Bernard - 226 Wicks Ln., Billings, MT 59105 t) 406-259-4350 brians@stbernardblgs.org; davidr@stbernardblgs.org www.stbernardblgs.org Rev. David Reichling, O.F.M.Cap., Pst.; Brian Shea, DRE; CRP Stds.: 155
  Sts. Cyril & Methodius - 16 S. Corner Rd., Ballantine, MT 59006
Mary Queen of Peace - 120 S. 34th St., Billings, MT 59101 t) 406-259-7611 info@maryqueenofpeacebillings.org www.maryqueenofpeacebillings.org Rev. Jose Marquez, Pst.; CRP Stds.: 7
St. Pius X - 717 18th St. W., Billings, MT 59102 t) 406-656-2522 shannonb@stpiusxblgs.org www.stpiusxblgs.org Rev. Gregory Staudinger, Pst.; Dcn. Tom Landry; Karyn Haider, Admin.; Jessica Rohrer, DRE; Matt Low, Formation Dir.; CRP Stds.: 88
St. Thomas the Apostle - 2055 Woody Dr., Billings, MT 59102 t) 406-656-5800 church@stthomasbillings.org www.stthomasbillings.org Rev. Stephen J. Zabrocki, Pst.; Joyce Hollowell, DRE; CRP Stds.: 204

BRIDGER

Sacred Heart - 209 S 4th St, Bridger, MT 59014-0309; Mailing: PO Box 309, Bridger, MT 59014-0309 t) 406-662-3550 Rev. Masilamani Suvakkin, Pst.; Amy Seymour, DRE; CRP Stds.: 24
  St. Joseph - 202 N Montana St, Fromberg, MT 59029 t) 406-663-3550
  St. John - 404 W Central, Joliet, MT 59041 t) 406-664-5355

BROADUS

St. David - 225 N. Wilbur, Broadus, MT 59317; Mailing: P.O. Box 1016, Miles City, MT 59301 t) 406-436-2430 shchurch@midrivers.com Rev. Jolly Ouseph Pathiyamoola, Pst.; CRP Stds.: 2

CHESTER

St. Mary - 11 W. Quincy Ave., Chester, MT 59522; Mailing: P.O. Box 647, Chester, MT 59522 t) 406-759-5377 stmolrsh@itstriangle.com Rev. Herbert Magaso, Admin.; CRP Stds.: 32

CHINOOK

St. Gabriel - 404 8th St W, Chinook, MT 59523; Mailing: PO Box 1089, Chinook, MT 59523 t) 406-357-2073 stgabriel@itstriangle.com stgabrielchinookmt.com Rev. Michael Schneider, Pst.;
  St. Thomas the Apostle - 210 1st Ave SE, Harlem, MT 59526; Mailing: PO Box 1125, Harlem, MT 59526
  St. Thomas Aquinas - 10610 Wing Rd, Hogeland, MT 59529

CIRCLE

St. Francis Xavier - 1100 C Ave., Circle, MT 59215; Mailing: PO Box 160, Circle, MT 59215-0160 t) 406-485-3520 stx@midrivers.com Rev. Joseph Ponessa, Pst.; Shanna Murnion, DRE; CRP Stds.: 25
  St. John the Baptist - 412 Leavitt Ave., Jordan, MT 59337
  St. Francis de Sales - 301 S. Main St., Richey, MT 59259

COLSTRIP

St. Margaret Mary - 320 Water Ave., Colstrip, MT 59323; Mailing: P.O. Box 305, Colstrip, MT 59323 t) 406-748-2234 stmargaretmary1@gmail.com www.stmargaretmarycolstrip.org Rev. Baskar Anandan, Pst.; CRP Stds.: 23

COLUMBUS

St. Mary - 240 4th Ave N, Columbus, MT 59019; Mailing: PO Box 956, Columbus, MT 59019 t) 406-322-5541 rriehl@stmarycolumbus.org mystmary.com Rev. Navil Rodrigues, Pst.; Mandy O'Connor, DRE;
  St. Michael - 307 S. Woodard St., Absarokee, MT 59001 t) (406) 322-5541

CROW AGENCY

St. Dennis - 76 Highway 1, Crow Agency, MT 59022; Mailing: PO Box 57, Crow Agency, MT 59022 t) 406-620-7500 Rev. Michael Dorn, OFM Cap., Pst.; Bro. Jerry Cornish, O.F.M.Cap., In Res.; CRP Stds.: 34
  St. Francis Xavier - 5936 W. 18300 S., St. Xavier, MT 59075; Mailing: P.O. Box 138, St Xavier, MT 59075 mjcoste@yahoo.com Rev. Mark Joseph Costello, O.F.M.Cap., Pst.;
  St. Katharine Friary - 96 Hwy. 1, Crow Agency, MT 59022 c) 773-447-2195 Rev. Tien Dinh, O.F.M.Cap., Vicar; Rev. Mark Joseph Costello, O.F.M.Cap., Supr.;

FORSYTH

Immaculate Conception - 521 N 12th Ave, Forsyth, MT 59327; Mailing: PO Box 166, Forsyth, MT 59327 t) 406-346-9239 immaculateconceptionforsyth@gmail.com Rev. Baskar Anandan, Pst.; Diane Wyrick, DRE; CRP Stds.: 12
  St. Joseph - 206 Orchard Ave, Hysham, MT 59038

FORT BENTON

Immaculate Conception - 1223 16th St. S., Fort Benton, MT 59442; Mailing: P.O. Box 849, Fort Benton, MT 59442 t) 406-622-3726 fralby1983@gmail.com iccfb.org

Rev. Mohan Raj, HGN, Pst.;

St. Margaret - 700 Brewster St., Geraldine, MT 59446-0050; Mailing: PO Box 50, Geraldine, MT 59446 t) 406-737-4573 7jeklund@itstriangle.com Trish Eklund, Contact;

FORT SHAW

St. Ann - 13327 MT Hwy. 200, Fort Shaw, MT 59443; Mailing: PO Box 82, Cascade, MT 59421 t) 406-264-5554 c) (406) 351-3251 frcory@frcory.org Rev. Cory D. Sticha, Pst.; CRP Stds.: 15

Sacred Heart - 22 2nd St NW, Cascade, MT 59421 Rev. Kiran Kumar Bernard, Assoc. Pst.;

GLASGOW

St. Raphael - 412 3rd Ave. N., Glasgow, MT 59230; Mailing: P.O. Box 471, Glasgow, MT 59230 t) 406-228-9800 faithformation@nemont.net Dcn. Eddie Malone; Rev. Jose Valliparambil, Pst.; CRP Stds.: 80

St. Albert - 304 Minnesota, Hinsdale, MT 59241

Queen of the Angels - 206 Hobart, Nashua, MT 59248

Holy Family - 116 1st Ave., N., Glentana, MT 59240

GLENDIVE

Sacred Heart - 320 W. Benham St., Glendive, MT 59330; Mailing: PO Box 36, Glendive, MT 59330 t) 406-377-2585 glendivesacredheart.com Rev. Francis Schreiber, Pst.; CRP Stds.: 71

Sacred Heart - 302 S. McDonald Ave., Terry, MT 59349

GREAT FALLS

St. Ann's Cathedral - 715 3rd Ave N, Great Falls, MT 59401; Mailing: PO Box 1708, Great Falls, MT 59403 t) 406-761-5456 office@stannscathedral.org; apxavi@gmail.com www.stannscathedral.org Rev. Xavier Arimboor, Pst.; Georgia Miller, Youth Min.; CRP Stds.: 14

Corpus Christi - 410 22nd Ave., N.E., Great Falls, MT 59404 t) 406-453-6546 corpuschristigreatfalls@gmail.com Rev. Ryan Erlenbush, Pst.; CRP Stds.: 50

Holy Spirit - 201 44th St S, Great Falls, MT 59405 t) 406-452-6491; 406-452-6491 (CRP) aubrey@holyspiritgf.org holyspiritgf.org Rev. Doug Krings, Pst.; Dcn. William Medved; Dcn. Peter Woelkers; Aubrey Rearden, DRE; CRP Stds.: 170

Holy Spirit School - (Grades PreK-8) 2820 Central Ave., Great Falls, MT 59401 t) 406-761-5775 www.holyspiritgfschool.org Melissa Hallahan, Prin.; Stds.: 160; Lay Tchrs.: 15

Holy Family - 2800 Central Ave, Great Falls, MT 59401

Sts. Peter & Paul Education Center - 200 44th St. S., Great Falls, MT 59405

Our Lady of Lourdes - 409 13th St. S., Great Falls, MT 59405 t) 406-452-6464 Rev. Alphonsus Enelichi, M.S.P., Pst.; Mary Stebbins, Youth Min.; CRP Stds.: 51

Our Lady of Lourdes School - (Grades PreK-8) 1305 5th Ave S, Great Falls, MT 59405 t) 406-452-0551 www.ollschoolgfmt.org Sherri Schmitz, Prin.; Stds.: 205; Lay Tchrs.: 12

HARDIN

St. Joseph - 710 N Custer, Hardin, MT 59034; Mailing: PO Box 510, Hardin, MT 59034 t) 406-665-1432 Rev. Callistus Igwenagu, Pst.; CRP Stds.: 11

St. Mary - 214 4th Ave, Custer, MT 59024; Mailing: PO Box 223, Custer, MT 59024 Rev. Thomas Selvaraj, Pst.;

HAVRE

St. Jude Thaddeus - 624 4th St, Havre, MT 59501; Mailing: PO Box 407, Havre, MT 59501 t) 406-265-4261 stjudehavre@gmail.com stjudehavre.org Msgr. Daniel J. Wathen, Pst.; Dcn. Timothy Maroney, DRE; CRP Stds.: 52

St. Jude Thaddeus School - (Grades PreK-8) 430 7th Ave, Havre, MT 59501 t) 406-265-4613 mhaugen@stjudeschoolmt.org stjudeschoolmt.org Michael Haugen, Prin.; Stds.: 162; Lay Tchrs.: 10

St. John the Baptist -

HAYS

St. Paul's Indian Mission - 301 Mission St, Hays, MT 59527; Mailing: PO Box 40, Hays, MT 59527 t) 406-673-3300 Rev. Michael Schneider, Pst.;

St. Paul's Indian Mission School - (Grades K-6) 761 Hays Rd, Hays, MT 59527 t) 406-673-3123 mgs@itstriangle.com

St. Joseph - 300 Azure Ave, Zortman, MT 59546 t) (406) 357-2073

St. Thomas - 8893 Lodgepole Rd, Lodgepole, MT 59524 t) (406) 673-3300

Sacred Heart, Fort Belknap - 210 Chipewa Ln, Harlem, MT 59526; Mailing: PO Box 236, Fort Belknap, MT 59526 t) 406-353-2257

HINGHAM

Our Lady of Ransom - 201 2nd St, Hingham, MT 59528; Mailing: St Mary Church, PO Box 647, Chester, MT 59522 t) 406-759-5377 stmolrsh@itstriangle.com Rev. Herbert Magaso, Pst.; Dianne Folk, DRE; CRP Stds.: 17

Sacred Heart - 630 Main, Inverness, MT 59530

LAME DEER

Blessed Sacrament - 630 Cheyenne Ave., Lame Deer, MT 59043; Mailing: PO Box 100, Lame Deer, MT 59043 t) 406-477-6384 dj@rangeweb.net; sjop@cdkc.edu Dcn. Joseph Kristufek, Admin.; Sr. Jean Glach, OP, Pst. Assoc.;

Christ the King - ; Mailing: P.O. Box 315, Busby, MT 59016 t) 406-592-3568 Lenora Wolfname, Contact;

LAUREL

St. Anthony - 715 4th Ave., Laurel, MT 59044; Mailing: 317 W 7th Ave., Laurel, MT 59044 t) 406-628-7182 (Office); 406-628-7484 (CRP) paduaoffice@gmail.com www.saintanthonycatholicchurch.org Rev. Barton K. Stevens, Pst.; Dcn. David Odermann; CRP Stds.: 80

LEWISTOWN

St. Leo - 102 W. Broadway St., Lewistown, MT 59457; Mailing: P.O. Box 421, Lewistown, MT 59457 t) 406-538-9306 saintleoscatholicchurch@gmail.com www.stleoscatholicchurch.org/ Rev. Samuel Spiering, Pst.; CRP Stds.: 64

Holy Family - 530 Main St., Winifred, MT 59489

LIVINGSTON

St. Mary - 41 View Vista Dr, Livingston, MT 59047-0646; Mailing: PO Box 646, Livingston, MT 59047 t) 406-222-1393 secretary@stmaryscommunity.org Rev. Garrett Nelson, Pst.; Bridget Yuvan, DRE; CRP Stds.: 12

St. Mary's School - (Grades PreK-8) 511 South F St, Livingston, MT 59047-0646 t) 406-222-3303 stmarys@stmaryscatholicschool.net Catherine Kirchner, Prin.; Stds.: 118; Lay Tchrs.: 7

St. Margaret - 206 1st Ave N, Clyde Park, MT 59018 Rev. Leo G. McDowell, Pst.; Rev. Felix Nayak, Assoc. Pst.;

St. William - 705 Scott St W, Gardiner, MT 59030 Rev. Leo G. McDowell, Pst.; Rev. Felix Nayak, Assoc. Pst.;

LODGE GRASS

Our Lady of Loretto - 11723 E. Helen St., Lodge Grass, MT 59050; Mailing: P.O. Box 57, Crow Agency, MT 59022 t) 406-620-7500; 406-639-2254 (CRP) Rev. Michael Dorn, OFM Cap., Pst.; CRP Stds.: 4

Blessed Kateri Tekakwitha - 309 S. Mondel Ave., Wyola, MT 59089; Mailing: PO Box 509, Lodge Grass, MT 59050 t) (406) 620-7500

MALTA

St. Mary - 27 S 7th St W, Malta, MT 59538; Mailing: PO Box 70, Malta, MT 59538 t) 406-654-1446 brenda@saintmarysmalta.org; office@saintmarysmalta.org www.saintmarysmalta.org Rev. Felix Nayak, Pst.; Brenda Rummel, DRE; CRP Stds.: 53

Sacred Heart - 225 2nd St. E., Dodson, MT 59524 t) (406) 654-1446

St. Francis of Assisi - 500 Wilson Ave., Saco, MT 59261 t) (406) 654-1446

St. John - 230 1st Ave. E., Whitewater, MT 59544 t) (406) 654-1446

MILES CITY

Sacred Heart - 120 N. Montana Ave., Miles City, MT 59301; Mailing: P.O. Box 1016, Miles City, MT 59301 t) 406-234-1691 shchurch@midrivers.com sacredheart.weconnect.com Rev. Jolly Ouseph Pathiyamoola, Pst.; CRP Stds.: 18

Sacred Heart School - (Grades PreSchool-8) 519 N. Center Ave., Miles City, MT 59301 t) 406-234-3850 shschool@midrivers.com www.midrivers.com/~shschool Bart Freese, Prin.; Stds.: 171; Sr. Tchrs.: 1; Lay Tchrs.: 12

St. David - 217 N. Wilbur, Broadus, MT 59317; Mailing: PO Box 52, Broadus, MT 59317 t) 406-436-2430 Rev. Jolly Pathiyamoola, Pst.;

PLENTYWOOD

St. Joseph - 301 N. Main, Plentywood, MT 59254; Mailing: PO Box 167, Plentywood, MT 59254-0167 t) 406-765-2250 stjoe@nemont.net Rev. Antony Raj Kumar Arumugam, H.G.N., Pst.; CRP Stds.: 28

St. Patrick - 401 Main St., Medicine Lake, MT 59247 Rev. Patrick Zabrocki, Pst.;

POPLAR

Our Lady of Lourdes - 105 F St. W., Poplar, MT 59255; Mailing: P.O. Box 187, Poplar, MT 59255 t) 406-768-3305 Rev. Anietie Ukanide, Pst.; Terry Romo, DRE; CRP Stds.: 3

Fort Kipp, St. Anthony - Rev. Baskar Anandan, Pst.;

St. Anthony - 413 3rd St., W., Culbertson, MT 59218; Mailing: PO Box 30, Culbertson, MT 59218 t) 406-787-6685

St. Thomas - 3022 BIA Rd. 173, Brockton, MT 59213 Rev. Baskar Anandan, Pst.;

Sacred Heart - 314 Clinton St., Bainville, MT 59212 Rev. Baskar Anandan, Pst.;

PRYOR

St. Charles Borromeo Church - 21228 S Pryor Gap Rd., Pryor, MT 59066; Mailing: PO Box 29, Pryor, MT 59066 t) 406-252-0993; 406-259-9747 (Convent) lilianchinwe7575@gmail.com Sr. Lilian Chinwe Onovo, Parish Life Coord.; CRP Stds.: 93

RED LODGE

St. Agnes - 1 N. Word Ave., Red Lodge, MT 59068; Mailing: P.O. Box 1067, Red Lodge, MT 59068 t) 406-322-5541; (406) 446-1237 stagnesrl@gmail.com www.stagnesrl.com Administered from St. Mary, Columbus. Rev. Navil Rodrigues, Pst.; CRP Stds.: 23

ROUNDUP

St. Benedict - 503 Main St., Roundup, MT 59072 t) 406-323-1019 Rev. Amulraj Yedanapalli, Pst.;

Our Lady of Mercy - 121 6th Ave., Melstone, MT 59054 t) (406) 323-1019

St. Aloysius - 112 W. Main St., Winnett, MT 59087

St. Theresa the Little Flower - 16638 Iowa, Broadview, MT 59015

St. Mathias - 305 Kemp St., Ryegate, MT 59074; Mailing: PO Box 30, Ryegate, MT 59074 t) 406-568-2335

St. Honorata - 22 3rd Ave., Musselshell, MT 59059

Our Lady of the Assumption -

SCOBEY

St. Philip Bonitus - 404 Timmons St., Scobey, MT 59263; Mailing: P.O. Box 827, Scobey, MT 59263-0827 t) 406-487-5525 stphilip@nemont.net LeRoy Nelson, DRE; Rev. Antony Raj Kumar Arumugam, H.G.N., Pst.; CRP Stds.: 7

SIDNEY

St. Matthew - 219 7th St. SE, Sidney, MT 59270; Mailing: 310 7th St. SE, Sidney, MT 59270 t) 406-433-1068 (Rectory); 406-433-2510 (Parish Center) stmattdre@midrivers.com; stmatt@midrivers.com www.stmattsidney.com Rev. Jim O'Neil, Pst.; Dcn. Mitchell Anderson; Mary Carda, Liturgy Dir.; Mary Quiroz, DRE; CRP Stds.: 61

St. Catherine - 317 7th St., W., Fairview, MT 59221; Mailing: PO Box 494, Fairview, MT 59221 t) 406-742-5293 stcatherns@midrivers.com Harriet Carico, Contact;

St. Theresa - 212 N. Main St., Lambert, MT 59243 t) 406-774-3360

St. Bernard - 31798 CR 148, Charlie Creek, MT 59270 t) 406-774-3422

St. Michael - 120 2nd Ave., Savage, MT 59262;

Mailing: 11123 CR 344, Savage, MT 59262

STANFORD

St. Rose of Lima - 101 4th St. W., Stanford, MT 59479; Mailing: P.O. Box 250, Stanford, MT 59479 t) 406-566-2531 fr.dom@live.com Rev. Domenico Pizzonia, Pst.; CRP Stds.: 2

St. Anthony - 1100 Main Ave., Denton, MT 59430; Mailing: P.O. Box 384, Denton, MT 59430 t) 406-567-2438

St. Cyril - 100 Hill Ave., Geyser, MT 59447; Mailing: R.R. 1 Box 50A, Geyser, MT 59447

St. Mathias - 310 2nd St., N.E., Moore, MT 59464; Mailing: P.O. Box 104, Moore, MT 59464

Sacred Heart - 100 2nd Ave. E., Hobson, MT 59452; Mailing: P.O. Box 225, Hobson, MT 59452

WIBAUX

St. Peter - 312 W 1st Ave S, Wibaux, MT 59353; Mailing: PO Box 217, 1st Ave SW, Wibaux, MT 59353 t) 406-769-2215; 406-796-8188 (CRP) Rev. Jose Panickomveli, Admin.; Dcn. Richard Miske; CRP Stds.: 27

St. Philip - 61 Lamesteer Rd, Wibaux, MT 59353 t) (406) 796-2215

WOLF POINT

Immaculate Conception - 513 Dawson St, Wolf Point, MT 59201; Mailing: PO Box 789, Wolf Point, MT 59201 t) 406-653-2610 iccreann@gmail.com Rev. Martin Ezeihuaku, M.S.P., Admin.; Ann Wienke, DRE; CRP Stds.: 81

Sacred Heart - 1022 Hwy. 201, Riverside, MT 59201

St. Ann - 102 Shell St., Vida, MT 59274

SCHOOLS: PRESCHOOL THRU HIGH SCHOOL

SCHOOLS

STATE OF MONTANA

ASHLAND

St. Labre Indian Catholic Elementary School - (PRV) (Grades PreK-4) 112 St. Labre Campus Dr., Ashland, MT 59003; Mailing: P.O. Box 77, Ashland, MT 59003 t) 406-784-4500 lsmall2@stlabre.org stlabreindianschool.org Lacee Small, Prin.; Leland Stocker, Dir.; Stds.: 76; Lay Tchrs.: 21

St. Labre Academy - (Grades PreK-4) t) (406) 784-4567 sewing@stlabre.org Steve Ewing, Prin.; Stds.: 69; Lay Tchrs.: 16

BILLINGS

St. Francis School - (DIO) (Grades PreK-5) 2202 Colton Blvd, Billings, MT 59102 t) 406-259-5037 billingscatholicschools.org Debra Hayes, Prin.; Jim Stanton, Prin.; Donna Petriccione, Librn.; Stds.: 617; Lay Tchrs.: 52

PRYOR

St. Charles Mission School - (PRV) (Grades PreK-8) 21228 Pryor Gap Rd., Pryor, MT 59066; Mailing: PO Box 29, Pryor, MT 59066 t) 406-259-9976 rraschkow@stlabre.org stlabreindianschool.org Rhonda Raschkow, Prin.; Leland Stocker, Dir.; Stds.: 78; Lay Tchrs.: 35

ST. XAVIER

Pretty Eagle Catholic Academy - (PRV) (Grades PreK-8) 212 Mission Loop, St. Xavier, MT 59075; Mailing: P.O. Box 257, St. Xavier, MT 59075 t) 406-666-2215 gwilliamson@stlabre.org stlabreindianschool.org Garla Williamson, Prin.; Leland Stocker, Dir.; Stds.: 137; Bro. Tchrs.: 1; Lay Tchrs.: 28

HIGH SCHOOLS

STATE OF MONTANA

ASHLAND

St. Labre Indian Catholic High School - (PRV) 112 St. Labre Campus Dr., Ashland, MT 59003; Mailing: P.O. Box 77, Ashland, MT 59003 t) 406-784-4500 mjoyce@stlabre.org stlabreindianschool.org Molly Joyce, Prin.; Leland Stocker, Dir.; Stds.: 106; Lay Tchrs.: 26

BILLINGS

Central Catholic High School - (PAR) 3 Broadwater Ave, Billings, MT 59101 t) 406-245-6651 shanser@billingscatholicschools.org; jhawbaker@billingscatholicschools.org www.billingscatholicschools.org Sheldon Hanser, Prin.; Stds.: 324; Pr. Tchrs.: 1; Lay Tchrs.: 30

GREAT FALLS

Great Falls Central Catholic High School - (DIO) 2800 18th Ave. S., Great Falls, MT 59405 t) 406-216-3344 mwoelkers@greatfallscentral.org greatfallscentral.org Monica J Woelkers, Admin.; Angela Turoski, Prin.; Stds.: 66; Lay Tchrs.: 8

INSTITUTIONS LOCATED IN DIOCESE

ASSOCIATIONS [ASN]

ASHLAND

St. Labre Indian School Educational Association - 112 St. Labre Campus Dr., Ashland, MT 59003; Mailing: P.O. Box 77, Ashland, MT 59003 t) 406-784-4500 www.stlabre.org A Nonprofit Corp. Four Catholic schools for Native Americans: St. Labre Indian School; Pretty Eagle Catholic Academy; St. Charles Mission School. Curtis Yarlott, Pres.;

CEMETERIES [CEM]

BILLINGS

Holy Cross - 1601 Mullowney Ln., Billings, MT 59101 c) 406-839-8387 Jerry Horton, Dir.;

GREAT FALLS

Calvary - Gibson Flats, Great Falls, MT 59405; Mailing: PO Box 1399, Great Falls, MT 59403 t) 406-727-6683 Jerry Horton, Dir.;

Mount Olivet - 2101 26th St S, Great Falls, MT 59405; Mailing: PO Box 1399, Great Falls, MT 59403 c) 406-453-8251 Eric Spragg, Family Svcs. Adv.;

COLLEGES & UNIVERSITIES [COL]

GREAT FALLS

University of Providence - 1301 20th St. S., Great Falls, MT 59405 t) 406-791-5300 admissions@uprovidence.edu www.uprovidence.edu Providence Ministries. Rev. Oliver Doyle, Pres.; Stds.: 955; Lay Tchrs.: 54

CONVENTS, MONASTERIES, AND RESIDENCES FOR WOMEN [CON]

BILLINGS

Sisters of Charity of Leavenworth - 1114 N. 30th St., Billings, MT 59101 t) 913-702-2049 Sr. Eileen Hurley, Contact; Srs.: 4

GREAT FALLS

Poor Clares of Montana, Inc. - 3020 18th Ave. S., Great Falls, MT 59405 t) 406-453-7891 sisters@poorclaresmt.org www.poorclaresmt.org Sr. Judith Ann Crosby, Abbess; Srs.: 6

ENDOWMENTS / FOUNDATIONS / TRUSTS [EFT]

BILLINGS

Billings Catholic Schools Foundation - 215 N 31st St, Billings, MT 59101; Mailing: PO Box 31158, Billings, MT 59107 t) 406-252-0252 info@billingscatholicschoolsfoundation.org billingscatholicschoolsfoundation.org (Formerly known as the Billings Area Catholic Education Trust). Adam Joseph Liberty, Pres.;

St. Vincent Healthcare Foundation - 1106 N. 30th St., Billings, MT 59101 t) 406-237-3600 tracy.neary@imail.org www.svfoundation.org Tyler Wiltgen, Vice. Pres.;

GREAT FALLS

The Catholic Foundation of Eastern Montana, Inc. - 121 23rd St. S., Great Falls, MT 59401; Mailing: P.O. Box 1345, Great Falls, MT 59403-1345 t) 406-315-1765 hello@catholicfoundationmt.org www.catholicfoundationmt.org Judy Held, Pres.;

Holy Spirit Catholic School Endowment Trust - 2820 Central Ave, Great Falls, MT 59401-3412 t) 406-761-5775 Jennifer Thomas, Development;

St. Joseph's Education Trust - 410 22nd Ave., N.E., Great Falls, MT 59404 t) 406-453-6546 corpuschristigreatfalls@gmail.com Rev. Ryan Erlenbush;

LEWISTOWN

St. Leo's Catholic Education Trust - 102 W. Broadway St., Lewistown, MT 59457; Mailing: PO Box 421, Lewistown, MT 59457 t) 406-538-9306 Rev. Samuel Spiering;

MALTA

St. Mary's Catholic Education Trust - 27 S 7th St W, Malta, MT 59538; Mailing: PO Box 70, Malta, MT 59538 t) 406-654-1446 office@saintmarysmalta.org www.saintmarysmalta.org Rev. Felix Nayak, Pst.;

MILES CITY

Holy Rosary Healthcare Foundation - 2600 Wilson St., Miles City, MT 59301 t) 406-233-2604 tracy.neary@imail.org www.supportholyrosary.com Tyler Wiltgen, Vice. Pres.;

HOSPITALS / HEALTH SERVICES [HOS]

BILLINGS

St. Vincent Healthcare - 1233 N. 30th St., Billings, MT 59101; Mailing: P.O. Box 35200, Billings, MT 59107-5200 t) 406-237-7000 svh-mt.org Sisters of Charity of Leavenworth, Kansas. Jennifer Alderfer, CEO; Tracy Neary, Vice. Pres.; Rev. Ayub Mwampela, Chap.; Bed Capacity: 286; Asstd. Annu.: 173,222; Staff: 1,451

MILES CITY

Holy Rosary Healthcare - 2600 Wilson St., Miles City, MT 59301 t) 406-233-2600; 800-843-3820 tracy.neary@imail.org www.sclhealth.org Dorothy Zabrocki, Dir.; Tracy Neary, Vice. Pres.; Karen Costello, Pres.; Jennifer Alderfer, CEO; Bed Capacity: 109; Asstd. Annu.: 33,516; Staff: 225

MISCELLANEOUS [MIS]

ASHLAND

St. Labre Youth & Family Services - 112 St. Labre Campus Dr., Ashland, MT 59003; Mailing: P.O. Box 458, Ashland, MT 59003 t) 406-784-4521; 877-785-4457 vanderson@stlabre.org www.stlabre.org Vicki Anderson, Dir.;

GREAT FALLS

Big Sky Cum Christo/Cursillo - 121 23rd St. S., Great Falls, MT 59403-1399; Mailing: c/o Lee Wegmann, P.O. Box 1399, Great Falls, MT 59403-1399 t) 406-989-1168 lwegmann@midrivers.com www.bigskycumchristo.org Carmen Thorsen, Treas.;

***Cascade County Council of the St. Vincent de Paul Society** - 426 Central Ave W, Great Falls, MT 59403 t) 406-761-0870 administrator@svdpncmt.org www.svdpncmt.org Doborah Kottel, Dir.;

Diocese of Great Falls-Billings Juridic Persons Capital Assets Support - 121 23rd St. S., Great Falls, MT 59403-1399; Mailing: P.O. Box 1399, Great Falls, MT 59403 t) 406-727-6683 Shanny Murphy, CEO;

Diocese of Great Falls-Billings Juridic Persons Real Property Support - 121 23rd St. S., Great Falls, MT 59403-1399; Mailing: P.O. Box 1399, Great Falls, MT 59403 t) 406-727-6683 Shanny Murphy, CEO;

Frank & Isabell Stites Memorial Center - 1701 26th St. S., Great Falls, MT 59403; Mailing: P.O. Box 1399,

Great Falls, MT 59403 t) 406-727-6683 business@diocesegfb.org www.diocesegfb.org (Retired Priests & Lay People Living) Shanny Murphy, CEO;

Heisey Community Center at St. Ann's - 313 7th St N, Great Falls, MT 59401 t) 406-453-1211 office@stannscathedral.org Rev. Xavier Arimboor, Pst.;

***St. Martin De Porres Mission of Great Falls** - 1920 10th Ave S, Great Falls, MT 59405 t) 406-771-6695

Regina Cleri - 121 23rd St. S., Great Falls, MT 59403; Mailing: P.O. Box 1399, Great Falls, MT 59403 t) 406-727-6683 business@diocesegfb.org www.diocesegfb.org Retired Priests Living. Shanny Murphy, Bus. Mgr.;

Retrouvaille of Montana - ; Mailing: P.O. Box 4, Great Falls, MT 59403-0004 t) 800-470-2330; 406-761-4830 retromt14@gmail.com Rev. Joseph Fleming;

MILES CITY

***Custer County Conference of the Society of Saint Vincent de Paul and Thrift Store** - 407 Main St., Miles City, MT 59301 t) 406-234-3011 info@stvincentsmilescity.com www.stvincentsmilescity.com/ Charlie Carranco, Dir.;

SHEPHERD

World Wide Marriage Encounter - 11739 EW Tenny Rd., Shepherd, MT 59079 t) 406-794-1582 dcsprojim@gmail.com www.wwme.org D'awn Ledgerwood; Greg Ledgerwood;

MONASTERIES AND RESIDENCES FOR PRIESTS AND BROTHERS [MON]

PLENTYWOOD

***Mary Queen of Apostles Province HGN, Inc.** - c/o St. Joseph Catholic Church, 301 N. Main St., Plentywood, MT 59254; Mailing: PO. Box 167, Plentywood, MT 59254-0167 c) 406-765-2250 frtonyhgn@gmail.com Rev. Antony Raj Kumar Arumugam, H.G.N., Supr.; Priests: 49

PRESCHOOLS / CHILDCARE CENTERS [PRE]

BILLINGS

Billings Catholic Schools Early Education Center - 1734 Yellowstone Ave., Billings, MT 59102 t) 406-656-2300 mtrafton@billingscatholicschools.org; ssaks@billingscatholicschools.org Child care for infants & pre-school for ages 3-6 Sue Saks, Dir.; Michelle Trafton, Dir.; Stds.: 164; Lay Tchrs.: 12

GREAT FALLS

Thieltges-St. Thomas Camp - 121 23rd St. S., Great Falls, MT 59401; Mailing: P.O. Box 1399, Great Falls, MT 59403 t) 406-727-6683 www.saintthomascamp.com Rev. Garrett J. Nelson, Chap.; Stds.: 171; Lay Tchrs.: 9

SPECIAL CARE FACILITIES [SPF]

GREAT FALLS

St. Thomas Child and Family Center - 1710 Benefis Ct., Great Falls, MT 59405 t) 406-761-6538 carrie@stthomaskids.org www2.providence.org/stthomas Providence Ministries. Kaleb Cunningham, Secy.; Melissa Kingsland, Pres.; Carrie Sammons, Exec.; Bed Capacity: 120; Asstd. Annu.: 120; Staff: 30

An asterisk (*) denotes an organization that has established tax-exempt status directly with the IRS and is not covered by the USCCB Group Ruling.

Diocese of Green Bay

(Dioecesis Sinus Viridis)

MOST REVEREND DAVID LAURIN RICKEN, D.D., J.C.L.

Bishop of Green Bay; ordained September 12, 1980; appointed Coadjutor Bishop of Cheyenne December 14, 1999; Episcopal Ordination January 6, 2000; succeeded to See September 26, 2001; appointed Bishop of Green Bay July 9, 2008; installed August 28, 2008. Office: 1825 Riverside Dr., Green Bay, WI 54301. Mailing Address: P.O. Box 23825, Green Bay, WI 54305-3825.

Chancery: 1825 Riverside Dr., Green Bay, WI 54301. T: 920-437-7531; F: 920-437-4067.
Mailing Address: P.O. Box 23825, Green Bay, WI 54305-3825.
www.gbdioc.org

ESTABLISHED MARCH 3, 1868.

Square Miles 10,728.

Incorporated January 16, 1907.

Comprises these 16 Counties: Brown, Calumet, Door, Florence, Forest, Kewaunee, Langlade, Manitowoc, Marinette, Menominee, Oconto, Outagamie, Shawano, Waupaca, Waushara and Winnebago in the State of Wisconsin.

Legal Title: Catholic Diocese of Green Bay, Inc.

For legal titles of parishes and diocesan institutions, consult the Chancery Office.

STATISTICAL OVERVIEW

Personnel

Bishop....1
Retired Bishops....2
Abbots....1
Retired Abbots....2
Priests: Diocesan Active in Diocese....62
Priests: Diocesan Active Outside Diocese....2
Priests: Retired, Sick or Absent....70
Number of Diocesan Priests....134
Religious Priests in Diocese....91
Total Priests in your Diocese....225
Extern Priests in Diocese....37
Ordinations:
Diocesan Priests....1
Religious Priests....1
Transitional Deacons....1
Permanent Deacons in Diocese....158
Total Brothers....8
Total Sisters....272

Parishes

Parishes....156
With Resident Pastor:
Resident Diocesan Priests....71
Resident Religious Priests....14
Without Resident Pastor:
Administered by Priests....57
Administered by Deacons....12
Administered by Religious Women....1
Administered by Lay People....1
Missions....2
Pastoral Centers....39
Professional Ministry Personnel:
Brothers....2
Sisters....6
Lay Ministers....204

Welfare

Catholic Hospitals....9
Total Assisted....1,969,621
Homes for the Aged....6
Total Assisted....2,660
Day Care Centers....8
Total Assisted....288
Special Centers for Social Services....3
Total Assisted....5,400

Educational

Diocesan Students in Other Seminaries....18
Students, Religious....5
Total Seminarians....23
Colleges and Universities....1
Total Students....1,882
High Schools, Diocesan and Parish....5
Total Students....1,254
High Schools, Private....1
Total Students....722
Elementary Schools, Diocesan and Parish....47
Total Students....7,157
Catechesis/Religious Education:
High School Students....4,039
Elementary Students....9,102
Total Students under Catholic Instruction....24,179
Teachers in Diocese:
Priests....2
Scholastics....2
Sisters....2
Lay Teachers....1,001

Vital Statistics

Receptions into the Church:
Infant Baptism Totals....2,195
Minor Baptism Totals....54
Adult Baptism Totals....54
Received into Full Communion....203
First Communions....2,268
Confirmations....1,961
Marriages:
Catholic....464
Interfaith....109
Total Marriages....573
Deaths....3,076
Total Catholic Population....252,352
Total Population....1,064,476

LEADERSHIP

Chancery - t) 920-437-7531

Office of the Bishop - Most Rev. David L. Ricken; Tania LeFevre, Exec. Asst.; Debra Adams, Exec. Asst.;

Bishops Emeritus - Most Rev. Robert J. Banks; Most Rev. Robert F. Morneau;

Vicar General/Moderator of the Curia - Very Rev. John W. Girotti, Vicar; Tania LeFevre, Exec. Asst.;

Vicar General - Very Rev. William O'Brien, Vicar;

Vicar for Canonical Services - Very Rev. John W. Girotti, Vicar;

Chancellor - Tammy Basten, Chancellor;

Associate Director of the Curia - Dr. Peter Murphy, Assoc. Dir.;

Censores Librorum - Very Rev. John W. Girotti;

Diocesan Tribunal - t) 920-272-8167 tribunal@gbdioc.org

Defender of the Bond - Very Rev. John W. Girotti;

Judge - Sr. Ann F. Rehrauer;

Judicial Vicar - Very Rev. Brian S. Belongia;

Promoter of Justice - Sr. Ann F. Rehrauer;

ADMINISTRATION

Office of Administration - t) 920-437-7531 Very Rev. John W. Girotti, Vicar General/Moderator of the Curia; Very Rev. William O'Brien, Vicar General; Dr. Peter Murphy, Assoc. Dir.;

Safe Environment - t) 920-272-8198 Courtney Coopman, Victim Asst. Coord.; Debra Knaus, Asst.;

Office of Canonical Services - t) 920-437-7531 Very Rev. John W. Girotti, Vicar; Jamie Kuhn, Compliance Monitor;

Office of the Chancellor - t) 920-272-8188 Tammy Basten, Chancellor; Mary Reynebeau, Admin. Asst.;

Archives - t) 920-272-8195 Olivia Wendt, Archivist; Bro. Steven J. Herro, O.Praem., Asst. Archivist;

Office of the Marriage Tribunal - t) 920-272-8169 tribunal@gbdioc.org Very Rev. Brian S. Belongia, Judicial Vicar; Kerry Adam, Tribunal Coord.;

OFFICES AND DIRECTORS

Mission Team Leader - Tammy Basten, Chancellor;

Office of Communications - t) 920-437-7531 Justine Lodl, Dir.; Matthew Livingstone, Media Production;

The Compass - t) 920-272-8208 Amy Kawula, Advertising & Mktg. Mgr.; Patricia Kasten, Assoc. Editor; Jeff Kurowski, Assoc. Editor;

Office of Information Technology - t) 920-272-8111 ithelpdesk@gbdioc.org Julie Ebben-Matzke, Dir.; Tim Rohloff, IT Mgr.; Nick Griffie, Systems Admin.;

Office of Finance & Accounting - t) (920) 272-8206 Paul Kolbach, CFO; Mike Speel, Dir.; Nick Speel, Controller;

Accounting - t) (920) 272-8298 Karen Rottier, Mgr.; Jackie Jocewicz, Supvr.;

Parish Financial Consulting - t) (920) 272-8273 Alyce Sauer; Jo Ann Eland;

Office of Human Resources - t) 920-437-7531 Becky Bond, Dir. (bbond@gbdioc.org); Bonnie Clancy, Benefits; Paul Doell, Staffing Mgr.;

Office of Facilities & Properties - t) 920-272-8314 Barbara Weiss, Dir.; Mike Gerrits, Mgr. Bldgs. & Grounds;

Allouez Catholic Cemetery & Chapel Mausoleum - t) 920-432-7585 Mary Breivogel, Admin.;

ADVISORY BOARDS, COMMISSIONS, COMMITTEES, AND COUNCILS

Diocesan Healthcare Services - t) (920) 272-8194 Very Rev. John W. Girotti;

College of Consultors - Most Rev. David L. Ricken; Very Rev. John Girotti;

Consultors - Rev. Joseph Dorner; Rev. Douglas E. LeCaptain; Rev. James W. Lucas;

Consultors - Rev. William A. Hoffman; Rev. Daniel J. Schuster; Rev. Larry J. Seidl;

Regional Vicars - Most Rev. David L. Ricken, Ex-Officio; Very Rev. John W. Girotti, Ex-Officio; Very Rev. Luke A. Ferris, Ex-Officio;

I-Northeast - Very Rev. Celestine Byekwaso;

II-Green Bay West - Very Rev. Mathew J. Simonar;

III-Southwest - Very Rev. Thomas Long;

IV-Fox Valley - Very Rev. Robert Kollath;

V-Southeast - Very Rev. David B. Beaudry;

VI-Green Bay East - Very Rev. Dennis M. Ryan;

VII-Peninsula - Very Rev. William O'Brien;

VIII-Northwest - Very Rev. Joel A. Sember;

Diocesan Pastoral Council -

Ex Officio Members - Most Rev. David L. Ricken, Bishop of Green Bay; Very Rev. John Girotti, Vicar General/Moderator of the Curia; Very Rev. William O'Brien, Vicar General;

Appointed Religious Representatives - Sr. Natalie Binversie, O.S.F., (Manitowoc); Very Rev. Brad Vanden Branden, O.Praem., (De Pere);

Appointed Representatives - Rev. Antonio de los Santos, (Green Bay); Dcn. David J. Scheuer, (Maribel); Dcn. Thomas (Chuck) Agnew, (Kewaunee);

Appointed Hispanic Representative - Javier Gomez;

Vicariate Representatives -

I-Northeast - Mary Poch; Paul Balzola;

II-Green Bay West - Travis Vanden Heuvel; Charles Grom;

III-Southwest - James Fay; Kristin Russell;

IV-Fox Valley - Walter Thomson; Jennifer Wood;

V-Southeast - Patrick Brandel; Dcn. Thomas Tomaszewski;

VI-Green Bay East - Lori Juza; David Wheeler;

VII-Peninsula - Dan Malcore; Mark Merkatoris;

VIII-Northwest - Susan Hickey; Thomas Koss;

Presbyteral Council Membership -

President - Most Rev. David L. Ricken, Pres.;

Chairman - Rev. William A. Hoffman, Chair;

Ex Officio - Very Rev. John Girotti; Very Rev. William O'Brien; Very Rev. Luke A. Ferris;

Appointed Members - Rev. Adam Bradley; Rev. Carl E. Schmitt, ; Rev. Larry Seidl; Rev. James T. Baraniak, O. Praem.;

Elected Members - Vicariates I, II, III - Rev. Francies Nusi, I-Northeast; Rev. James W. Lucas, II-Green Bay West; Rev. Matthew Rappl, III-Southwest;

Elected Members - Vicariates IV, V, VI - Rev. Joseph Dorner, IV-Fox Valley; Rev. Douglas E. LeCaptain, V-Southeast; Rev. William A. Hoffman, VI-Green Bay East;

Elected Members - Vicariate VII, VIII - Rev. Daniel J. Schuster, VII-Peninsula; Rev. Kennedy Gaspar, VIII-Northwest;

Bishop's Finance Council - Most Rev. David L. Ricken, Ex-Officio; Very Rev. John W. Girotti, Ex-Officio; Paul Kolbach, Resource;

Appointed Members - JoAnn Cotter; Joseph Varkoly; Thomas Vorpahl;

CATHOLIC CHARITIES

Mission Team Leader - Karmen Lemke;

Office of Catholic Charities - Karmen Lemke, Dir.;

Office of Living Justice - t) 920-272-8321 Peter Weiss, Dir., Living Justice;

Children and Family Services - t) 920-272-8234 Tara DeGrave, Assoc. Dir.; Chelsea Baucom-Young, Adoption Supvr.;

Social Ministry & Community Outreach - t) (920) 272-8234 Lori Paul;

Mental Health Counseling Services - t) 920-272-8234 Heather Novak, Mental Health Counselor; Amy Wetzler, Mental Health Counselor;

Financial Health Services - t) 920-272-8234 Kory Krauss, Financial Health Svcs. Mgr.; Kellie Dekarske, Community Engagement Specialist;

Immigrant and Refugee Services - t) 920-272-8234 Tara DeGrave, Dir.; Laurie Martinez, Immigrant & Refugee Svcs. Supvr.; Ruth Karakas, Immigration Counselor;

Fox Cities Office - t) 920-734-2601 Laurie Martinez, Immigration Svs Mgr; Julie Duffy, Mental Health Counselor; Megan Santkuyl, Financial Health Counselor;

Marinette Office - t) 715-735-7802 Tara DeGrave, Asst. Dir.; Lori Paul, Social Ministry & Comm. Outreach Mgr.; Debra Mullen, Mental Health Counselor;

CLERGY AND RELIGIOUS SERVICES

Mission Team Leader - Very Rev. Luke A. Ferris;

Office of Diaconate - t) (920) 272-8316 Shaun Johnson, Dir.; Dcn. Richard A. Hocking, Assoc. Dir.; Jennie Huettl, Admin. Asst.;

Office of Priest & Pastoral Leaders - t) 920-272-8189 Very Rev. Luke A. Ferris, Vicar for Clergy & Pastoral Leaders; Dcn. Peter J. Gard, Asst. to Vicar for Clergy & Pastoral Leaders; Jami Duvall, Administrative Asst.;

Priest Nurse & Health Care Advocate - Gloria Koth, Registered Nurse;

Rep for Religious - Sr. Leonette Kochan, O.S.F.;

Office of Vocations - t) (920) 272-8286 Rev. Mark Mleziva, Dir.; Rev. Adam Bradley, Asst. Dir.; Taylor Geiger, Vocation Coord.;

Office of Parish Operations & Mission Planning - t) 920-272-8295 Barry Metzentine, Dir.; Jennifer Buechel, Asst. Dir.; Patty Young, Parish Oper. & Mission Planning Support Coord.;

Analyst & Parish Census Software Tech. - Roy Verstegen, Analyst & Parish Census Software Tech.;

DEVELOPMENT

Catholic Foundation - t) 920-272-8181 Josh Diedrich, Exec.; Ali Kettner, Admin.;

Office of Bishop's Appeal - Tammy Danz, Dir.; Teresa Adler, Campaign Specialist; Debbie DeGrave, Database Coord.;

Office of Planned Giving - Janet Wagner, Dir.; Cindi Brawner, Senior Relationship Mgr.; Jarod Stoik, Relationship Mgr.;

Office of World Mission Services - t) 920-272-8192 Cynthia St. Aubin, Dir.;

EDUCATION

Mission Team Leader - t) (920) 272-8303 Todd Blahnik;

Office of Catholic Schools - t) 920-272-8303 Todd Blahnik, Supt.; Liz Goldman, Assoc. Supt., Instruction; Jamie Hahn, Assoc. Supt., Mission Effectiveness;

EVANGELIZATION

Mission Team Leader - Julianne Stanz;

Office of Divine Worship - t) 920-272-8341 Gerard Hall, Dir.; Arvilla Rusnak, Coord., Divine Worship; August Dittberner, Admin. Asst.;

Office of Evang. OCIA & Young Adult Ministry - t) 920-272-8229 Amy Deibert, Parish Evang. & OCIA Dir.; Katherine Summers, Young Adult Ministry Coord.;

Office of Missionary Discipleship - t) (920) 272-8329 Julianne Stanz, Dir., Parish Life & Evangelization; Eileen Gale, Missionary Discipleship Dir. (egale@holycrossmishicot.com);

Office of Lay Leader Formation - t) 920-272-8268 Jamie Whalen, Dir.;

Office of Hispanic Ministry - t) 920-272-8327 Sr. Martha Escobar, Hispanic Dir.;

FAITH FORMATION

Mission Team Leader (Interim) - Julianne Stanz;

Office of Children & Youth Faith Formation - t) (920) 272-8288 Maximus Cabey, Dir.; Tommy Nelson, Assist. Dir.;

Office of Marriage, Family Life & Pro-Life - t) 920-272-8315 Elisa Tremblay, Dir.;

Office of Camp Tekakwitha - t) 715-526-2316 Rebecca Sievers, Dir.; McKenna Runde, Communications & Alumni Rel. Coord.;

Office of Campus Ministry -

University of Wisconsin-Green Bay (UWGB) - Sr. Laura Zelten, O.S.F., Dir.; Rev. Ben Johnson, Campus Min.;

University of Wisconsin-Oshkosh (UWO) - t) 920-233-5555 Rev. Zachary Weber, Dir.; Sara Scheunemann, Pst. Assoc.;

PARISHES, MISSIONS, AND CLERGY

STATE OF WISCONSIN

ALGOMA

St. Mary - 214 Church St., Algoma, WI 54201-1035 t) 920-487-5005 x1 parishoffice@smsalgoma.com stmarysalgoma.com/ Rev. Andrew J. Kurz, Admin.;

AMBERG

St. Agnes - W8031 Wright Ave, Amberg, WI 54102; Mailing: P. O. Box 224, Amberg, WI 54102 t) 715-856-5276 c) 715-927-6735 stagnesamberg@gmail.com; staugustine@centurytel.net www.stagnes-staugustine-catholic-parishes.com Served from St. Mary in Crivitz Rev. David R. Schmidt, Pst.;

ANIWA

St. Boniface - W19104 Church St, Aniwa, WI 54414; Mailing: P.O. Box K, Birnamwood, WI 54414-0911 t) 715-449-0050 philboniface@charter.net Served from St. Philomena, Birnamwood. Vicente Llagas, Admin.;

ANTIGO

St. John - 415 6th Ave., Antigo, WI 54409-2104 t) 715-623-2024 stjohn@antigoareacatholicchurches.com antigoareacatholicchurches.com Also serves St. Mary & Hyacinth, Antigo and St. Wenceslaus, Neva Very Rev. Joel A. Sember, Pst.; Dcn. Andrew P. Bures; Kristen Rolling, DRE; CRP Stds.: 58

SS. Mary & Hyacinth - 819 3rd Ave., Antigo, WI 54409-1930 t) 715-623-5255 (CRP); 715-623-4938 ssmh@antigoareacatholicchurches.com antigoareacatholicchurches.com/ Served from St. John, Antigo. Has records for St. Mary & St. Hyacinth, Antigo. Very Rev. Joel A. Sember, Pst.; Dcn. Andrew P. Bures; Kristen Rolling, DRE; CRP Stds.: 35

APPLETON

St. Bernadette - 2331 E. Lourdes Dr., Appleton, WI 54915-3698 t) 920-739-4157 jlueck@saint-bernadette.org www.saint-bernadette.org/ Rev. Joseph Dorner, Pst.; Dcn. Scott David Pearce; CRP Stds.: 77

St. Francis Xavier Catholic School System, Inc. - 101 E. Northland Ave., Appleton, WI 54911 t) 920-735-9380 rduboise@xaviercatholicschools.org www.xaviercatholicschools.org Dcn. Ray DuBois, Pres.;

St. Bernard Congregation of Appleton - 1617 W. Pine St., Appleton, WI 54914-5118 t) 920-739-0331 stbernard@stbernardappleton.org stbernardappleton.org/ Dcn. Michael J. Eash, Dir.; Dcn. Gregory J. Humpal, Sacraments Coord.; Deb Holzem, CRE; Barbara Hoffman, Business Coord.; CRP Stds.: 57

St. Edward - N2926 State Rd. 47, Appleton, WI 54913-9564 t) 920-733-9266; 920-733-6070 (CRP) ne@stedwardmackville.org; parish@stedwardmackville.org www.stedwardmackville.org/ Served from St. Nicholas, Freedom. Rev. Robert K. Chinnapan, M.F., Admin.; Dcn. Jeffrey J. Hofacker; Celia J. McKee, DRE; CRP Stds.: 90

St. Edward School - (Grades PreSchool-5) N2944 State Rd. 47, Appleton, WI 54913-9564 t) 920-733-6276 office@stedwardk5.org www.stedwardk5.org Renee Cowart, Prin.; Stds.: 61; Lay Tchrs.: 6

St. Joseph - 404 W. Lawrence St., Appleton, WI 54911-5855 t) 920-738-7413 (CRP); 920-734-7195 dschmidt@stjoesparish.org www.saintjosephparish.org Rev. Raja Selvam, Admin.; Dcn. Mark J. Farrell; CRP Stds.: 126

St. Mary Congregation - 312 S. State St., Appleton, WI 54911-5926 t) 920-739-5119 stmary@stmaryparish.org stmaryparish.org Rev. William Swichtenberg, Pst.; Dcn. Gerard J. Schraufnagel; CRP Stds.: 545

St. Pius X - 500 W. Marquette St., Appleton, WI 54911-1996 t) 920-733-4919 (CRP); 920-733-0575 ffmiddlehigh@stpiusxappleton.com; administrator@stpiusxappleton.com www.stpiusappleton.org/ Rev. James R. Jugenheimer, Pst.; Dcn. Robert Seymour; Kathy Schommer, DRE; Dcn. Daniel W. Zajicek; Erin Buchholtz, DRE; Jennifer Buelow, DRE; CRP Stds.: 239

Sacred Heart - 222 E. Fremont St., Appleton, WI 54915-1890 t) 920-739-3196 office@sacredheartappleton.com www.sacredheartappleton.com Dcn. Daniel T. Koszalinski; Dcn. Gilbert F. Schmidt; Rev. John C. Katamba, Pst.; CRP Stds.: 39

St. Therese - 213 E. Wisconsin Ave., Appleton, WI 54911-4875 t) 920-733-8568 businessmgr@st-therese.com; secretary@st-therese.com www.st-therese.com Rev. Ryan Starks, Pst.; Dcn. Peter J. Gagnon; Dcn. Ernesto L. Gonzalez Jr.; CRP Stds.: 251

St. Francis Xavier Catholic School System, Inc. - (Grades PreK-12) 101 E. Northland Ave., Appleton, WI 54911-2104 t) 920-735-9380 priley@xaviercatholicschools.org www.xaviercatholicschools.org Philip R. Riley Jr., Pres.;

St. Thomas More - 1810B N. McDonald St., Appleton, WI 54911-3450 t) 920-739-7758; 920-739-8172 (CRP) stmparish@stmcath.org; greg@stmcath.org stmcath.org Dcn. Lincoln Wood, Admin.; Rev. Gerald R. Falk, Pastor Emer.; Greg Mohr, DRE; Dcn. Timothy E. Downey; Dcn. Donald J. Wetzel; CRP Stds.: 8

St. Francis Xavier Catholic School System - (Grades PreSchool-4) 1810 N. McDonald St., Appleton, WI 54911-3498; Mailing: 101 E. Northland Ave., Appleton, WI 54911 t) 920-739-2376 atapelt@xaviercatholicschools.org www.xaviercatholicschools.org (Part of the St. Francis Xavier Catholic School System, Inc.) Alena Tapelt, Prin.; Philip R Riley Jr., Pres.;

ARMSTRONG CREEK

St. Stanislaus Kostka - 521 U.S. Hwy. 8, Armstrong Creek, WI 54103-2334; Mailing: P.O. Box 39, Armstrong Creek, WI 54103-2334 t) 715-336-2334 ststanislausarmstrong@gmail.com Also serves St Joan of Arc-Goodman, and St Mary's in Florence Rev. Lourdu R. Madanu, M.F., Pst.; CRP Stds.: 8

AURORA

Sacred Heart - W782 County Hwy N, Aurora, WI 54151; Mailing: 1432 River St, Niagara, WI 54151 t) 715-251-3879 office.stanthonyniagara@gmail.com www.stanthonyniagara.org/ Served from St. Anthony, Niagara. Rev. Quentin A. Mann, C.D.L., Admin.;

BEAR CREEK

St. Mary - 207 W Tielky St., Bear Creek, WI 54922; Mailing: 140 Auto St., Clintonville, WI 54929-1712 t) 715-201-9913 sborlen@ssrmparishes.org ssrmparishes.org Served from St. Rose, Clintonville. Rev. Simon Minyati, Pst.; Dcn. Paul J. Brulla; CRP Stds.: 100

BIRNAMWOOD

St. Philomena - 432 State Road, Birnamwood, WI 54414; Mailing: P. O. Box K, Birnamwood, WI 54414 t) 715-449-0050 philboniface@charter.net Also serves St. Boniface, Aniwa. Vicente Llagas, Admin.; Jennifer Duranceau, DRE; CRP Stds.: 55

BLACK CREEK

St. Mary - 301 E. Burdick St., Black Creek, WI 54106; Mailing: P.O. Box 217, Black Creek, WI 54106-0217 t) 920-984-3319 Rev. David F. Greskowiak, Admin.; CRP Stds.: 50

BRILLION

Holy Family - 1100 W. Ryan St., Brillion, WI 54110-1074 t) 920-756-2535 office@holyfamily-parish.org www.holyfamilybrillion.org Formerly St. Mary, Brillion & St. Mary-St. Patrick, Reedsville/Maple Grove. Rev. Thomas Pomeroy, Pst.; Dcn. Mark Knipp; Dcn. Gregory Van Thiel; CRP Stds.: 180

Holy Family School - 209 N. Custer St., Brillion, WI 54110-1236 t) 920-756-2502 hfsc@holyfamily-parish.org www.hfcsbrillion.org Scott Smith, Prin.;

BRUSSELS

St. Francis & St. Mary Parish - 9716 Cemetery Rd., Brussels, WI 54204-9749 t) 920-825-7555 stfrancis@centurytel.net brusselscatholicchurch.com Formerly St. Francis Xavier, Brussels & St. Mary, Namur. Rev. Edward L. Looney, Pst.; CRP Stds.: 110

CASCO

Holy Trinity - 510 Church Ave, Casco, WI 54205-9712 t) 920-837-7531 office@holytrinitycasco.com www.holytrinitycasco.com Rev. Daniel J. Schuster, Pst.; Dcn. Robert J. Miller; Dcn. Thomas (Chuck) Agnew; CRP Stds.: 72

Holy Trinity School - (Grades PreK-7) t) (920) 837-7531 htprincipal@holytrinitycasco.com Curt Julian, Prin.; Stds.: 43; Lay Tchrs.: 5

St. Peter and St. Hubert - E3085 County Rd. X, Casco, WI 54205-9787 t) 920-837-2852 stpnh@centurytel.net www.stpeterandsthubert.com/ Rev. Edward L. Looney, Admin.; CRP Stds.: 90

CATO

Immaculate Conception - 15 S. County Rd. J, Cato, WI 54230-8329 t) 920-775-4365 stmarycm@tds.net Also serves St. Michael, Whitelaw. Rev. Richard H. Klingeisen, Pst.; Teresa Pederson, DRE; CRP Stds.: 63

CECIL

St. Martin of Tours Catholic Parish - 407 S. Warrington Ave., Cecil, WI 54111-9279 t) 715-745-6681 stmartin_cecil@frontiernet.net www.stmartin-cecil.org Previous Name: St. Martin Congregation Rev. Scott Valentyn, Moderator; Dcn. Kenneth J. Banker; Dcn. Todd Raether, Pst. Min./Coord.;

CHAMPION

St. Joseph - 5996 County Rd K, Champion, WI 54229; Mailing: 5930 Humboldt Rd., Luxemburg, WI 54217-9325 t) 920-863-6113 parish.office@threecatholicchurches.com Served from St. Thomas the Apostle, Humboldt. Rev. Carlo Villaluz, Admin.; Rebecca L Livingstone, DRE; CRP Stds.: 102

CHILTON

Good Shepherd - 62 E. Main St., Chilton, WI 53014-1428 t) 920-849-9363 goodshepherdbusinessmanager@gmail.com www.goodshepherdchilton.org Formerly St. Augustine, Chilton; St. Mary, Chilton; St. Charles Borromeo, Charlesburg; St. Martin, Charlestown; Holy Trinity, Jericho & St. Elizabeth. Rev. Jon Thorsen, Pst.; CRP Stds.: 130

Chilton Area Catholic School - (Grades PreK-8) 60 E. Washington St., Chilton, WI 53014-1297 t) 920-849-4141 smeyers@chiltonareacatholic.org chiltonareacatholic.org Samantha Meyers, Prin.; Stds.: 120; Lay Tchrs.: 13

CLINTONVILLE

St. Rose - 140 Auto St., Clintonville, WI 54929-1712 t) 715-201-9913 sborlen@ssrmparishes.org ssrmparishes.org Also serves St. Mary, Bear Creek. Dcn. Paul J. Brulla; Rev. Simon Minyati, Pst.; CRP Stds.: 100

COMBINED LOCKS

Saint Paul's Congregation of the Village of Combined Locks - 410 Wallace St., Combined Locks, WI 54113-1128 t) 920-788-4553 cvervoort@stpaulcl.com stpaulcl.com Maggie Melchior, Pst. Assoc.; Dcn. David V Hayden, Pastoral Leader; CRP Stds.: 80

COOPERSTOWN

St. James - 18228 County Rd. R, Cooperstown, WI 54208-9554 t) 920-863-2585 jessica@stjamescooperstown.org; office@stjamescooperstown.org Linked with St. Joseph, Kellnersville. Dcn. Daniel Gray; Rev. Santiago Turiano Jr., Pst.; Traci Hickey, DRE; CRP Stds.: 117

CRANDON

St. Joseph - 208 N. Park Ave., Crandon, WI 54520-1351 t) 715-478-3396 stjosephcrandon@gmail.com (Has records for St. Mary, Argonne & St. Michael Station, Hiles.) Rev. Kennedy Gaspar, Admin.; CRP Stds.: 61

CRIVITZ

St. Marys Congregation - 808 Henriette Ave., Crivitz, WI 54114-0159; Mailing: P.O. Box 159, Crivitz, WI 54114 t) 715-854-2501 saintmaryparishcrivitz@gmail.com www.stmarycrivitz.net Also serves Station at Caldron Falls. Rev. David R Schmidt, Pst.; CRP Stds.: 118

DE PERE

St. Francis Xavier - 220 S. Michigan St., De Pere, WI 54115-2794 t) 920-336-1813 sfxoffice@saintsdepere.org www.saintsdepere.org Served from St. Mary, De Pere, WI Rev. Michael L. Ingold, Pst.; Rev. Ben Johnson, Par. Vicar; Dcn. Mark G. Mullins; CRP Stds.: 300

Notre Dame School - (Grades PreK-8) 137 S. Superior St., De Pere, WI 54115 t) 920-337-1115 mmares@gracesystem.org www.notredameofdepere.com (Part of the GRACE, Inc. System) Molly Mares, Prin.;

Immaculate Conception - N5589 County Rd. E, De Pere, WI 54115; Mailing: 145 St. Joseph St., Oneida, WI 54155 t) 920-869-2244 parishsecsjic@gmail.com imconeida.org Served from St. Joseph, Oneida. Rev. Paul J. Paider, Pst.; Sandy Lezotte, DRE; Dcn. Donald F. Coenen; Barbara Geurts, Treas.;

St. Mary - 4805 Sportsman Dr., De Pere, WI 54115; Mailing: P.O. Box 70, De Pere, WI 54115-0070 t) 920-337-2330 smoffice@saintsdepere.org www.saintsdepere.org/ Also serves St. Francis Xavier, De Pere. Rev. Michael L. Ingold, Pst.; Rev. Ben Johnson, Par. Vicar; Dcn. Mark G. Mullins; CRP Stds.: 300

Notre Dame School - 137 S. Superior St., De Pere, WI 54115 t) 920-337-1115 mmares@gracesystem.org www.notredameofdepere.com (Part of the GRACE, Inc. System) Molly Mares, Prin.;

St. Norbert College Parish - 123 Grant St., De Pere, WI 54115-2002; Mailing: 100 GRANT ST, PARISH OFFICES, De Pere, WI 54115 t) 920-403-3010 parish@snc.edu www.snc.edu/parish Brian Fogarty, Liturgy Dir.; Jeff Koss, Bus. Mgr.; Rev. Michael Brennan, O. Praem., Pst.; Jennifer Rapavi, DRE; CRP Stds.: 105

Our Lady of Lourdes - 1307 Lourdes Ave., De Pere, WI 54115-1018 t) 920-336-4033; 920-337-0443 (CRP) parish@lourdesdepere.org www.lourdesdepere.org (Has records for St. Joseph, De Pere & St. Boniface, De Pere.) Rev. James T. Baraniak, O. Praem., Pst.; Dcn. Michael D. Vander Bloomen; CRP Stds.: 396

Our Lady of Lourdes School - 1305 Lourdes Ave., De Pere, WI 54115-1018 t) 920-336-3091 csmits@gracesystem.org www.lourdesschooldepere.org (Part of the GRACE, Inc. System) Jeffrey S. Young, Prin.; Stds.: 158; Lay Tchrs.: 13

DEERBROOK

St. Wenceslaus - N5340 Church RD, Deerbrook, WI 54424; Mailing: P.O. Box 50, Deerbrook, WI 54424-0050 t) 715-627-2126 stwencel@antigoareacatholicchurches.com antigoareacatholicchurches.com Served from St. John, Antigo. Very Rev. Joel A. Sember, Pst.; Dcn. Andrew P. Bures; Kristen Rolling, DRE; CRP Stds.: 23

All Saints Catholic School, Inc. - 419 6th Ave., Antigo, WI 54409-2104 t) 715-623-4835 pgaluska@ascscrusaders.org Paul Galuska, Prin.;

DENMARK

All Saints - 145 St. Claude St., Denmark, WI 54208 t) 920-863-5256 asden_parish@allsaintsschool.net www.denmarkareacatholic.com Also serves Holy Trinity Mission, New Denmark; St. Mary Parish, Glenmore/Stark. Rev. Xavier Amirtham, O. Praem., Admin.; Dcn. David J. Scheuer; Jessica Phillips, DRE; Alex Sekora, Bus. Mgr.; CRP Stds.: 173

All Saints School - (Grades PreK-8) 145 Saint Claude St., Denmark, WI 54208 t) 920-863-2449 asden_office@allsaintsschool.net www.allsaintsschooldenmark.net Lisa Gruber, Prin.; Stds.: 18; Lay Tchrs.: 3

Holy Trinity Mission - 145 St. Claude St., Denmark, WI 54208 t) 920-863-5256 asden_parish@allsaintsschool.net www.denmarkareacatholic.com Served from All Saints, Denmark. Rev. Xavier Amirtham, O. Praem., Admin.; Dcn. David J. Scheuer; Jessica Phillips, DRE;

St. Therese de Lisieux - N2085 County Rd. AB, Denmark, WI 54208-7705 t) 920-863-8747 stherese@netnet.net www.stthereseonline.com Also serves St. Isidore the Farmer, Tisch Mills. Rev. Dennis G. Drury, Pst.; Christal Wavrunek, Pst. Min./Coord.; Sandy Salentine, DRE; CRP Stds.: 126

DYCKESVILLE

St. Louis - N8726 County Line Rd., Dyckesville, WI 54217-8629 t) 920-866-2410 (Parish Office); 920-866-2842 (Faith Formation Office) parishoffice@stlouisdyckesville.com www.stlouisdyckesville.com Rev. Rommel Rodriguez Dacoco (Philippines), Pst.; CRP Stds.: 140

EGG HARBOR

Stella Maris - 7710 Hwy. 42, Egg Harbor, WI 54209; Mailing: P.O. Box 49, Egg Harbor, WI 54209-0049 t) 920-868-3241 churchofficesmdc@gmail.com www.stellamarisparish.com Merger: St. John's-Egg Harbor, St. Paul's-Fish Creek, St. Rosalia-Sister Bay, St. Mary's-Baileys Harbor, St. Michael's-Jacksonport & Washington Island Rev. Thomas J. Farrell, Pst.; Dcn. Tony Abts; CRP Stds.: 29

ELCHO

Holy Family - W10524 Cole St., Elcho, WI 54428; Mailing: PO Box 128, Elcho, WI 54428 t) 715-275-3750 holyfamilyelcho@frontiernet.net hfstm.org Also serves St. Mary Parish, Pickerel. Rev. Kennedy Gaspar, Pst.; CRP Stds.: 3

FLINTVILLE

SS. Edward and Isidore - 3667 Flintville Rd., Flintville, WI 54313-8330; Mailing: 3667 Flintville Rd., Green Bay, WI 54313-8330 t) 920-865-7844; 920-865-7677 (CRP) phendricks@stedwardisidore.org; kburkel@stedwardisidore.org www.stedwardisidore.org Rev. David J. Hoffman, Pst.; Dcn. Robert Hendricks; Phyllis Hendricks, DRE; Mary Walkenhorst, DRE; CRP Stds.: 459

FLORENCE

Immaculate Conception - 308 Florence Ave, Florence, WI 54121-0166; Mailing: PO Box 166, Florence, WI 54121 t) 715-528-3310 stmary@borderlandnet.net www.stmaryflorence.org Rev. Lourdu R. Madanu, M.F., Admin.; Carolyn Lemanski, DRE; CRP Stds.: 25

FRANCIS CREEK

St. Anne - 126 Packer Dr, Francis Creek, WI 54214; Mailing: P.O. Box 218, Francis Creek, WI 54214-0218 t) 920-755-2550 holycrossparish@holycrossmishicot.com Served from Holy Cross, Mishicot. Dcn. Michael Valenta; CRP Stds.: 58

St. Augustine - 202 S Packer Dr, Francis Creek, WI 54214; Mailing: P.O. Box 218, Francis Creek, WI 54214-0218 t) 920-755-2550 holycrossparish@hoycrossmishicot.com Served from Holy Cross, Mishicot. Eileen Gale, DRE;

FREEDOM

St. Nicholas - W2037 County Rd. S, Freedom, WI 54130-7565 t) 920-788-1492; 920-788-1451 (CRP) parish@stnicholasfreedom.org; businessmanager@stnicholasfreedom.org www.stnicholasfreedom.org Also serves St. Edward, Mackville. Rev. Robert K. Chinnapan, M.F., Admin.; Dcn. Jeffrey J. Hofacker; Dcn. Gary Vanness; CRP Stds.: 227

St. Nicholas School - W2035 County Rd. S., Freedom, WI 54130-7565 t) 920-788-9371 tgerritts@stnicholasfreedom.org www.stnicholasfreedom.org/school Travis Gerritts, Prin.;

GILLETT

St. John - 127 Garden St., Gillett, WI 54124-9413 t) 920-855-2542 stjohnsec@centurytel.net stjohnstmichael.com Also serves St. Michael, Suring & Chute Pond Station. Rev. Francis Xavier Dias, Admin.; Samantha Zeitler, DRE; CRP Stds.: 36

GLENMORE STARK

St. Mary - 5840 Big Apple Rd., Glenmore Stark, WI 54115-9766; Mailing: 5840 Big Apple Rd., De Pere, WI 54115-9766 t) 920-864-7641 secretarystmarysparish@gmail.com www.denmarkareacatholic.com Rev. Xavier Amirtham, O. Praem., Admin.; Dcn. David J. Scheuer; CRP Stds.: 77

GOODMAN

St. Joan of Arc - 602 Main St., Goodman, WI 54125-0218; Mailing: PO Box 218, Goodman, WI 54125-0218 t) 715-336-2334 Served from St. Stanislaus Kostka, Armstrong Creek. Rev. Lourdu R. Madanu, M.F., Pst.;

GREEN BAY

St. Francis Xavier Cathedral - 139 S Madison St., Green Bay, WI 54301-4501 t) 920-432-4348; 920-393-3773 (CRP) cathedral.sfx@gmail.com; faithformation.sfx.sje@gmail.com www.sfxcathedralgb.com Also serves St. John the Evangelist, Green Bay. Dcn. Conrad J. Kieltyka; Dcn. Thomas J. Mahoney; Very Rev. Brian S. Belongia, Pst.; Connie Demeuse, DRE;

St. Agnes - 1484 Ninth St., Green Bay, WI 54304-3061 t) 920-494-6450 (CRP); 920-494-2534 stagnesparishoffice@netnet.net; education@stagnesgreenbay.org www.stagnesgreenbay.org Rev. Patrick C Beno, Pst.; Dcn. Greg Rotherham; Donna Schuld, CRE; CRP Stds.: 81

Annunciation of the Blessed Virgin Mary - 1087 Kellogg St., Green Bay, WI 54303-3058 t) 920-496-2160 lverheyden@quad-parish.org www.quad-parish.org Also serves St. Joseph, Green Bay; St. Jude, Green Bay Rev. Antonio de los Santos, Admin.; Rev. Philip Dinh-Van-Thiep, Sacr. Min.; Dcn. Daniel Wagnitz; CRP Stds.: 33

St. Bernard - 2040 Hillside Ln., Green Bay, WI 54302-4098 t) 920-468-4811 adam@stbernardcong.org; office@stbernardcong.org www.stbernardgb.org Rev. Mark P. Vander Steeg, Pst.; Dcn. Keith P. Holschbach; Adam Horn, DRE; Dcn. Larry V. Mastalish; Dcn. Bernard Terrien; David A. Walters, Bus. Mgr.; CRP Stds.: 164

St. Bernard School - 2020 Hillside Ln., Green Bay, WI 54302-4099 t) 920-468-5026 cblahnik@gracesystem.org (Part of the GRACE, Inc. System) Crystal Blahnik, Prin.;

St. Elizabeth Ann Seton - 2771 Oakwood Dr., Green Bay, WI 54304-1699 t) 920-499-1546 seas@seasgb.org; mclercx@seasgb.org www.seasgb.org Dcn. Bill Gerl; Dcn. Steven J. Meyer; CRP Stds.: 73

Holy Cross - 3009 Bay Settlement Rd., Green Bay, WI 54311-7301 t) 920-468-0595 blsholycross@gmail.com www.holycrossgb.org Rt. Rev. Gary J. Neville, O. Praem., Pst.; Birdie Schantz, Parish Coordinator; CRP Stds.: 82

Holy Cross School - 3002 Bay Settlement Rd., Green Bay, WI 54311-7302 t) 920-468-0625 sgast@gracesystem.org www.holycrossfamily.org (Part of the GRACE, Inc. System) Sharon Gast, Prin.;

St. John the Evangelist - 413 St. John St., Green Bay, WI 54301-4116 t) 920-609-1826 (CRP); 920-436-6380 faithformation.sfx.sje@gmail.com; sjeoffice@sbcglobal.net www.stjohngb.org Served from St. Francis Xavier Cathedral, Green Bay. Very Rev. Brian S. Belongia, Pst.; Dcn. Conrad J. Kieltyka; Dcn. Thomas J. Mahoney; Dcn. Arthur Gerstner; Connie Demeuse, DRE; CRP Stds.: 4

St. Joseph - 936 Ninth St., Green Bay, WI 54304; Mailing: 1087 Kellogg St., Green Bay, WI 54303 t) 920-497-7042 (CRP); 920-496-2160 ckittell@quad-parish.org www.quad-parish.org Served from Annunciation of BVM, Green Bay. Rev. Antonio de los Santos, Admin.; Rev. Philip Dinh-Van-Thiep, Sacr. Min.; Dcn. Daniel Wagnitz; CRP Stds.: 33

St. Jude - 1420 Division St., Green Bay, WI 54303; Mailing: 1087 Kellogg St., Green Bay, WI 54303 t) 920-496-2160; 920-497-7042 (CRP) lverheyden@quad-parish.org; ckittell@quad-parish.org Served from Annunciation of the BVM, Green Bay. Rev. Antonio de los Santos, Admin.; Rev. Philip Dinh-Van-Thiep, Sacr. Min.; Dcn. Daniel Wagnitz; CRP Stds.: 33

St. Mary of the Angels - 650 S. Irwin Ave., Green Bay, WI 54301-3304 t) 920-437-1979; 920-432-2747 saintmaryfaith@gmail.com; stmarygb@gmail.com www.stmaryoftheangelsgb.org Rev. Finian Zaucha, ofm, Sacr. Min.; Beth Gajeski, DRE; Dcn. Paul P. Umentum, OFS, Parish Leader;

St. Thomas More School - 1420 Harvey St, Green Bay, WI 54302 t) 920-432-8242 oamor@gracesystem.org www.stmoregb.org (Part of the GRACE, Inc. System) Olgamar Amor, Prin.;

St. Matthew - 130 St. Matthews St., Green Bay, WI 54301-2910 t) 920-435-6811 mwestenberg@stmattsgb.org; parishoffice@stmattsgb.org www.stmattsgb.org Rev. Robert J. Kabat, Pst.; Dcn. Robert Hornacek; Michael Westenberg, DRE; CRP Stds.: 60

Father Allouez Catholic School, St. Matthew Campus - 2575 S. Webster Ave., Green Bay, WI 54301-2998 t) 920-432-5223 smsoffice@gracesystem.org www.fatherallouezschool.org (Part of the GRACE, Inc. System) Kay L. Franz, Prin.; Stds.: 191; Lay Tchrs.: 17

Nativity of Our Lord - 2270 S. Oneida St., Green Bay, WI 54304-4712 t) 920-499-5156; 920-499-6012 (CRP) natscene@nativitydisciples.org www.nativitydisciples.org/ Very Rev. Mathew J. Simonar, Pst.; Dcn. John J. Bundra; Dcn. Michael W. Dabeck; Angela R. Bieda, DRE; CRP Stds.: 253

St. Patrick - 211 N. Maple Ave, Green Bay, WI 54303 t) (920) 437-9660 institute-christ-king.org/greenbay-home Administered by Oratory of St. Patrick of Institute of Christ the King Rev. Antoine M. Boucheron, Admin.; CRP Stds.: 33

SS. Peter and Paul Catholic Congregation - 720 N. Baird St., Green Bay, WI 54302-1902 t) 920-435-7548; 920-437-0651 (Faith Formation); (920) 432-1321 (Hispanic Ministry) sspeterpaulgb@gmail.com sspeterpaulgb.org Rev. Jose Lopez, Admin.; CRP Stds.: 99

St. Philip the Apostle - 312 Victoria St., Green Bay, WI 54302-2818 t) 920-468-7848 bnoel@stphilipcong.org; jfiscal@stphilipcong.org www.stphilipgb.org Rev. Juan Zarate (Mexico), Admin.; Bill Noel, Bus. Mgr., CRP Stds.: 144

Prince of Peace - 3425 Willow Rd., Green Bay, WI 54311-8232 t) 920-468-5718; 920-468-5718 x103; 920-468-5718 x104 parish@popgb.org; re@popgb.org www.popgb.org Dcn. Jeff Prickette, Pastoral Leader; Very Rev. Dennis Ryan, Priest Celebrant; Theresa Williams, DRE; Neil Saindon, Youth Min.; Dcn. William J. Burkel; Dcn. Dennis Kozlovsky; CRP Stds.: 237

Resurrection - 333 Hilltop Dr., Green Bay, WI 54301-2799 t) 920-336-7768 resurrectionparish@gbres.org www.gbres.org Rev. Thomas J. Reynebeau, Pst.; Dcn. Kevin DeCleene; Susan K. Perrault, Pst. Min./Coord.; Wayne Efferson, Liturgy Dir.; Karolyn Efferson, DRE; Mary Vanden Busch, Bus. Mgr.; Sr. Dcn. Roger Vandervest; Sr. Dcn. Donald J. Ropson; Sr. Dcn. Michael G. Grzeca; CRP Stds.: 114

St. Willebrord - 209 S. Adams St., Green Bay, WI 54301-4584 t) 920-435-2016 frandy@stwillys.org; aidee@stwiilys.org www.stwillys.org Rev. Andrew G. Cribben, O. Praem., Pst.; Rev. John P. MacCarthy, O. Praem., Assoc. Pst.; Dcn. Luis Sanchez; Alma Vazquez, DRE;

GREENLEAF

St. Clare Parish Corporation - 2218 Day St., Greenleaf, WI 54126-9200 t) 920-864-2550; 920-864-2586 (CRP) lkohlman@stclareagw.org; stclarefaith@stclareagw.org stclareagw.org Rev. Brian Wideman, Pst.; Dcn. Kenneth J. Kabat; Dcn. Michael R. Zebroski; Anne P. Stemper, DRE; Kelly Bamke, Finance Mgr.; Theresa Reynders, Music & Liturgy Coord.; CRP Stds.: 197

St. Clare School - (Grades PreK-8) 425 Main St., Wrightstown, WI 54180-1057 t) 920-532-4833 stclareschool@stclareagw.org stclarek8.org/ Katie Stanczak, Prin.; Stds.: 117; Lay Tchrs.: 12

GREENVILLE

St. Mary - N2385 Municipal Dr., Greenville, WI 54942-9713 t) 920-757-6555 lgietman@stmarygreenville.org; parish@stmarygreenville.org Rev. Michael J. Warden, Pst.; Dcn. David L. DeYoung; Dcn. Brian Albers; CRP Stds.: 217

St. Mary School - (Grades PreK-8) N2387 Municipal Dr., Greenville, WI 54942-9713 dfuller@stmarygreenville.org Debra Fuller, Prin.;

GRESHAM

St. Francis Solanus - 1050 Main St., Gresham, WI 54128-0177; Mailing: P.O. Box 177, Gresham, WI 54128 t) 715-787-3250 sfrancis@livingwaterslivingfaith.org Served from St. Michael, Keshena. Rev. Timothy Machila, O.F.M. Conv.; Dcn. Mark Fuller;

HILBERT

St. Mary Congregation - 108 S. 6th St., Hilbert, WI 54129-0386; Mailing: P.O. Box 386, Hilbert, WI 54129-0386 t) 920-853-3252; (920) 989-2400 (CRP) stmary_hilbert@new.rr.com; triparishre@gmail.com www.ourtriparish.org Served from St. John-Sacred Heart, Sherwood. Rev. Michael E. Betley, Pst.; Dcn. Timothy Stevenson; Diane Wickersheim, Pst. Assoc.; Candace Gehl, DRE; CRP Stds.: 53

St. Mary School - (Grades PreK-6) 154 S. 6th St., Hilbert, WI 54129-0249; Mailing: P.O. Box 249, Hilbert, WI 54129-0249 t) 920-853-3216 chasro@stmaryhilbert.com www.stmaryhilbert.com Chandra L. Sromek, Prin.; Stds.: 30; Lay Tchrs.: 5

HOFA PARK

St. Stanislaus Congregation - W1888 Hofa Park Dr., Hofa Park, WI 54165-9510; Mailing: PO Box 379, Pulaski, WI 54162 t) 920-822-3279 parishoffice@abvm.org www.abvmcast.org Served from Assumption BVM, Pulaski. Rev. James Gerard Gannon, OFM, Admin.; Rev. David Kobak, OFM, Par. Vicar; Dcn. Dennis Majewski; Janet Maroszek, Pst. Assoc.; CRP Stds.: 10

HORTONVILLE

SS. Peter and Paul - 107 N. Olk St., Hortonville, WI 54944; Mailing: P.O. Box 238, Hortonville, WI 54944-0238 t) 920 779-6133; 920-779-0551 (CRP) parish@ssppp.org ssppp.org Greg Layton, Pastoral Leader; Rev. James R. Jugenheimer, Moderator; Lori Pugliese, DRE; CRP Stds.: 229

St. Mary School - N2387 Municipal Dr., Greenville, WI 54942-7801 t) 920-757-6555 dfuller@stmarygreenville.org Debra Fuller, Prin.;

HOWARD

St. John the Baptist Congregation - 2597 Glendale Ave., Howard, WI 54313-6899 t) 920-434-2145 swulf@sjbh.org; lpiechota@sjbh.org www.sjbh.org Rev. James W. Lucas, Pst.; Dcn. Manuel Torres; Dcn. Nicholas J. Williams; CRP Stds.: 301

St. John the Baptist School - 2561 Glendale Ave., Green Bay, WI 54313-6898 t) 920-434-3822 amulloy@gracesystem.org www.sjbhschool.org (Part of the GRACE, Inc. System) Andrew Mulloy, Prin.;

ISAAR

St. Sebastian - N9269 Isaar Rd., Isaar, WI 54165-9428 t) 920-833-2558 stseb2010@centurylink.net www.stsebastianseymour.com/ Served from St. John, Seymour. Rev. Sengole Arockia Dass, O. Praem., Admin.; Dcn. Richard J. Matuszak; CRP Stds.: 39

KAUKAUNA

Holy Cross - 309 Desnoyer St., Kaukauna, WI 54130-2187; Mailing: 112 W 8th St., Kaukauna, WI 54130 t) 920-766-1445; 920-766-5997 office@kaucp.org www.kaukaunacatholicparishes.org Rev. Donald E. Everts, Pst.; Rev. Krishnarao Mekala, M.F., Par. Vicar; Dcn. Jim Trzinski; Dcn. Steven Vande Hey; Dcn. Mark A. Ebben; Dcn. Randall A. Haak; CRP Stds.: 314

St. Katharine Drexel - 119 W. 7th St., Kaukauna, WI 54130-2356; Mailing: 112 W 8th St., Kaukauna, WI 54130 t) 920-766-1445; 920-766-5997 (CRP) office@kaucp.org www.kaukaunacatholicparishes.org Rev. Donald E. Everts, Pst.; Rev. Krishnarao Mekala, M.F., Par. Vicar; Dcn. Jim Trzinski; Dcn. Steven Vande Hey; Dcn. Mark A. Ebben; Dcn. Randall A. Haak; CRP Stds.: 314

KELLNERSVILLE

St. Joseph - 522 Tower Ave, Kellnersville, WI 54215-0027; Mailing: P.O. Box 27, Kellnersville, WI 54215-0027 t) 920-732-3770 Linked with St James Parish, Cooperstown. Rev. Santiago Turiano Jr., Pst.; Dcn. Daniel Gray; Lisa Vander Kelen, DRE; CRP Stds.: 49

KESHENA

St. Michael - N816 State Hwy. 47-55, Keshena, WI 54135; Mailing: PO Box 610, Keshena, WI 54135 t) 715-799-3811; 715-799-3234 (CRP) stmichaels@livingwaterslivingfaith.org www.stmichaelkeshena.org Also serves St. Mary, Leopolis, St. Francis Solanus, Gresham & St. Anthony, Neopit. Rev. Hanz Christian Borbor, Admin.; Lois Maczuzak, DRE; CRP Stds.: 24

KEWAUNEE

Holy Rosary - 521 Juneau St., Kewaunee, WI 54216-1397 t) 920-388-2285 x6; 920-388-2285 x33 (CRP) parishoffice@holyrosarykewaunee.com; jandfischer@holyrosarykewaunee.com www.holyrosarykewaunee.com Rev. Andrew J. Kurz, Admin.; Janet Fisher, DRE; CRP Stds.: 93

Holy Rosary School - (Grades PreK-8) 519 Kilbourn St., Kewaunee, WI 54216-1343 t) 920-388-2431 kstollberg@holyrosarykewaunee.com www.holyrosarykewaunee.com/school Kris Stollberg, Prin.;

KIEL

Holy Trinity - 11928 Marken Rd., Kiel, WI 53042-9750 t) 920-773-2380 holytrinityparish@tds.net holytrinityschoolhill.org Served from St. Gregory, St. Nazianz. Rev. William J. Brunner III, Admin.; Dcn. Gary Wilhelm; Patty Wilhelm, DRE;

SS. Peter & Paul Congregation - 413 Fremont St., Kiel, WI 53042-1398 t) 920-894-3553 daniellefaithformation@gmail.com; secretary@sspeternpaul.org Also serves Holy Rosary, New Holstein & St. Ann, St. Anna. Rev. Alvan Amadi, Pst.; Dcn. Dennis G. Bennin, Pst. Assoc.; Dcn. Bernard (Pat) P. Knier; Rev. Carl Diederichs, Sacr. Min.; CRP Stds.: 127

Divine Savior Catholic School - 423 Fremont St., Kiel, WI 53042-1316 t) 920-894-3533 dsprincipalsievert@gmail.com Kerry Sievert, Prin.;

KIMBERLY

Holy Spirit - 620 E. Kimberly Ave., Kimberly, WI 54136-1513 t) 920-788-7640 vandevoortp@holyspirit-parish.org holyspirit-parish.org Rev. Carl E. Schmitt, Pst.; Dcn. Clarence F. Dedman; Patricia Vande Voort, Bus. Mgr.; Dcn. Dennis G. Bennin; Margaret Franz, Liturgy Dir.; CRP Stds.: 507

Holy Spirit School - W2796 County Road KK, Appleton, WI 54915 t) 920-733-2651 mike.zuleger@holyspiritknights.org www.holyspiritknights.org Mike Zuleger, Prin.; Stds.: 284; Lay Tchrs.: 26

KRAKOW

St. Casimir Congregation - W146 Park St, Krakow, WI 54137; Mailing: PO Box 379, Pulaski, WI 54162 t) 920-822-3279; (920) 899-3621 (Mon., Tues., Wed., only) parishoffice@abvm.org www.abvmcast.org Served from Assumption Of The BVM, Pulaski. Rev. James Gerard Gannon, OFM, Admin.; Rev. Carmen Scuderi, OFM, Par. Vicar; Dcn. Dennis Majewski; Janet Maroszek, Pst. Assoc.; CRP Stds.: 30

LAKEWOOD

St. Mary of the Lake - 15232 County Road F, Lakewood, WI 54138; Mailing: P.O. Box 219, Lakewood, WI 54138-0219 t) 715-276-7364 stmary01@centurytel.net Also serves St. Ambrose, Wabeno & stations at Crooked Lake and Silver Cliff. Rev. Praveen Pamisetti (India), Admin.; Kendra

Yingling, CRE; CRP Stds.: 11

Crooked Lake, Crooked Lake Station -

LAONA

St. Leonard - 5330 Beech St., Laona, WI 54541-9340 t) 715-674-3862 (CRP); 715-674-3241 stleonardlaona@gmail.com; anilpolumari@gmail.com Also serves St. Norbert, Long Lake & St. Hubert Mission, Newald. Rev. Anil Polumari, Admin.;

LENA

St. Anne Parish - 221 E. Main St., Lena, WI 54139-0030; Mailing: P.O. Box 30, Lena, WI 54139-0030 t) 920-829-5222 lena@saintannesparish.com; maggie@saintannesparish.com www.saintannesparish.com Formerly SS. Francis-Wenceslaus, Coleman & Holy Cross, Lena. Rev. Felix Abano Jr., Admin.; Maggie Cook, DRE; CRP Stds.: 150

St. Patrick - 5246 St. Patrick Rd., Lena, WI 54139; Mailing: 253 N. Franklin St., Oconto Falls, WI 54154 t) 920-846-2276 lscanlan@holy3.org; secretary@holy3.org holy3.org Served from St. Anthony, Oconto Falls. Rev. Gregory Parent, Admin.; Theresa Blazer, Youth Min.;

LEOPOLIS

St. Mary - W11842 W. 3rd St., Leopolis, WI 54128; Mailing: P.O. Box 177, Gresham, WI 54128-0177 t) 715-787-3250 stfrancis@livingwaterslivingfaith.org Dcn. Howard R. Bricco; Bethany Grunewald, DRE; CRP Stds.: 22

LITTLE CHUTE

St. John Nepomucene (St. John Congregation) - 411 Vandenbroek St, Little Chute, WI 54140-1854 t) 920-788-9061; 920-788-9033 (CRP) stjnfaithdev@stjn.org; parishoffice@stjn.org www.stjn.org Rev. Ronald C. Belitz, Pst.; Dcn. David G. Van Eperen, Exec. Dir.; Dcn. Bruce H. Corey; CRP Stds.: 295

St. John Nepomucene School - 328 Grand Ave., Little Chute, WI 54140-1704 t) 920-788-9082 davidvaneperen@sjslc.net Kevin Flottmeyer, Prin.;

LITTLE SUAMICO

St. Pius - 1211 County Rd. J, Little Suamico, WI 54141; Mailing: P.O. Box 66, Suamico, WI 54173-0066 t) 920-434-2024; 920-434-1219 (CRP) sbsp@wi.twcbc.com www.st.piuslittlesuamico.com Served from St. Benedict Parish, Suamico. Rev. Demosthenes Olaso; Tammi LaLuzerne, DRE; CRP Stds.: 40

LONG LAKE

St. Norbert - 3402 State Hwy 139, Long Lake, WI 54542; Mailing: P.O. Box 101, Long Lake, WI 54542-0101 t) 715-674-3241 stnorbertlonglake@yahoo.com; anilpolumari@gmail.com Served from St. Leonard, Laona (Laona also serves St. Hubert Mission, Newald). Rev. Anil Polumari, Admin.;

LUXEMBURG

Immaculate Conception (St. Mary Parish) - 1412 Main St., Luxemburg, WI 54217-1308 t) 920-845-2056 parishoffice@stmarysluxemburg.org www.stmarysluxemburg.org Rev. Daniel J. Schuster, Pst.; Dcn. Robert J. Miller; Dcn. Thomas (Chuck) Agnew; CRP Stds.: 162

Immaculate Conception (St Mary School) - (Grades PreK-6) 1406 Main St, Luxemburg, WI 54217-1308 t) 920-845-2224 smsprincipal@stmarysluxemburg.org Curt Julian, Prin.; Stds.: 68; Lay Tchrs.: 11

St. Thomas the Apostle - 5930 Humboldt Rd., Luxemburg, WI 54217-9325 t) 920-863-6113 parish.office@threecatholicchurches.com www.threecatholicchurches.com Also serves St. Kilian, New Franken & St. Joseph, Champion. Rev. Carlo Villaluz, Admin.; Rebecca L Livingstone, DRE; CRP Stds.: 121

MANAWA

Sacred Heart - 614 S. Bridge St., Manawa, WI 54949-0010; Mailing: PO Box 10, Manawa, WI 54949 t) 920-596-3323 shmanawa@wolfnet.net sacredheartmanawa.org Rev. Matthew Rappl, Pst.; CRP Stds.: 18

MANITOWOC

St. Francis of Assisi - 601 N. 8th St., Manitowoc, WI 54220-3919 t) 920-684-3718 doug.lecaptain@sfamanitowoc.org www.sfamanitowoc.org Rev. Douglas E. LeCaptain, Pst.; Rev. Jason J. Blahnik, Pst. Assoc.; Rev. Matthew Colle, Pst. Assoc.; Dcn. Mark LeGreve, Bus. Mgr.; Andy Schmidt, DRE; Dcn. Alan L. Boeldt; Dcn. Bob Beehner; Dcn. Michael Dolezal; Dcn. Jeffery Wallander; CRP Stds.: 116

MAPLEWOOD

St. Mary (Holy Name of Mary) - 7491 County Rd. H, Maplewood, WI 54235-8757; Mailing: 7491 County Rd. H, Sturgeon Bay, WI 54235-8757 t) 920-856-6440 office@holynameofmary.church holynameofmary.church Served from Corpus Christi, Sturgeon Bay. Rev. Ryan E. Krueger, Pst.; Dcn. Mark R. Hibbs; June Gordon, DRE; CRP Stds.: 15

MARINETTE

Holy Family - 2715 Taylor St., Marinette, WI 54143-1537 t) 715-735-9100 holyfamily@holyfamparish.com www.holyfamparish.com Has records for St. Anthony, St. Joseph, Our Lady of Lourdes & Sacred Heart, Marinette. Very Rev. Celestine Byekwaso, Pst.; Dcn. David H Denby, Bus. Mgr.; Jeri Keepers, DRE; CRP Stds.: 71

MARION

St. Mary - 725 N.E. 7th St., Marion, WI 54950; Mailing: P.O. Box 106, Tigerton, WI 54486 t) 715-535-2571 office@catholicsupnorth.org wittomary.org Served from St. Anthony, Tigerton. Rev. Matthew W. Settle, Pst.; Dcn. Michael J. Brandt; Dcn. Howard R. Bricco; Tammy Wendler, DRE; CRP Stds.: 30

MENASHA

St. John the Baptist - 516 De Pere St., Menasha, WI 54952-3112; Mailing: 528 2nd St., Menasha, WI 54952-3112 t) 920-725-7714 ssiegel@smcatholicschools.org; cleduc@smcatholicschools.org www.menashacatholicparishes.org/ Served from St. Mary, Menasha. Rev. Michael Lightner, Admin.; Dcn. Donald E. Schultz; CRP Stds.: 35

St. Mary - 528 Second St., Menasha, WI 54952 t) 920-725-7714 ssiegel@smcatholicschools.org; cleduc@smcatholicschools.org menashacatholicparishes.org Also serves St. John the Baptist, Menasha. Dcn. Donald E. Schultz; Rev. Michael Lightner, Admin.; CRP Stds.: 36

St. Patrick Congregation - 324 Nicolet Blvd., Menasha, WI 54952-3334 t) 920-725-8381 x101 (Parish Office); 920-725-8381 x107 (CRP) stpatmen@gmail.com www.stpatricksmenasha.org Rev. Judah S. Pigon, M.F., Pst.; Anne Greif, Bus. Mgr.; CRP Stds.: 70

MISHICOT

Holy Cross - 423 S. Main St., Mishicot, WI 54228-9777 t) 920-755-2550; 920-755-2487 (CRP) holycrossparish@holycrossmishicot.com Also serves St. Anne, Francis Creek Dcn. Michael Valenta; CRP Stds.: 66

NAVARINO

St. Lawrence - W5125 State Hwy. 156, Navarino, WI 54107-8614 t) 715-758-8161 stlawrence@granitewave.com Rev. David F. Greskowiak, Admin.;

NEENAH

St. Gabriel the Archangel - 900 Geiger St., Neenah, WI 54956-2302 t) 920-722-4914; 920-725-0660 (CRP) stgabriel@smcatholicschools.org Very Rev. Robert Kollath, Pst.; Jenny Schneider, CRE; CRP Stds.: 215

St. Mary Catholic Schools - t) 920-725-4161 henglebert@smcatholicschools.org Includes: St. Mary Elementary; St. Margaret Mary Elementary; St. Mary Catholic Middle School; St. Mary Catholic High School. Helen Englebert, Prin.;

St. Margaret Mary - 620 Division St., Neenah, WI 54956-3398; Mailing: 439 Washington Ave, Neenah, WI 54956 t) 920-729-4560 smmneenah@smcatholicschools.org www.smmneenah.org Rev. Nonito Jesus Barra, Admin.; Dcn. Daniel Laurent; Amy M. Matz, DRE;

St. Mary Catholic Schools, Inc. - 610 Division St., Neenah, WI 54956-3094 t) 920-729-4565 kfairweather@smcatholicschools.org Eleanor Healy, Prin.;

NEOPIT

St. Anthony - W6799 Church St., Neopit, WI 54150-0241; Mailing: P.O Box 241, Neopit, WI 54150 t) 715-756-2361 stanthony@livingwaterslivingfaith.org Served from St. Michael, Keshena. Rev. Hanz Christian Borbor, Admin.; Dcn. Mark Fuller; Caroline Janz, DRE; CRP Stds.: 5

NEW FRANKEN

St. Kilian - 2508 Saint Kilian Rd, New Franken, WI 54229; Mailing: 5930 Humboldt Rd., Luxemburg, WI 54217-9325 t) 920-863-5180; 920-863-6113 parish.office@threecatholicchurches.com www.threecatholicchurches.com Served from St. Thomas the Apostle, Humboldt. Rev. Carlo Villaluz, Admin.; Rebecca L Livingstone, DRE; CRP Stds.: 2

NEW HOLSTEIN

St. Anna's Congregation - N188 School St., New Holstein, WI 53061-9776 t) 920-894-3147 stann1851@gmail.com threeparishesonefaith.org Linked with Ss. Peter & Paul, Kiel and Holy Rosary, New Holstein Rev. William J. Brunner III, Moderator; Dcn. Bernard (Pat) P. Knier, Pastoral Leader; Dcn. Dennis G. Bennin, Pst. Assoc.; Laura Winkel, DRE; CRP Stds.: 23

Holy Rosary - 1724 Madison St., New Holstein, WI 53061-1389 t) 920-898-4884; 920-898-9248 (CRP) holyrosaryreled@gmail.com; hrparish_1@charter.net threeparishesonefaith.org Rev. Alvan Amadi, Pst.; Dcn. Dennis G. Bennin, Pst. Assoc.; Dcn. Bernard (Pat) P. Knier; CRP Stds.: 56

Divine Savior Catholic School - 423 Fremont St., Kiel, WI 53042-1316 t) 920-894-3533 divinesaviorcatholicschool@gmail.com; mholst@divinesaviorschool.org www.divinesaviorschool.org Martha Holst, Prin.;

NEW LONDON

Most Precious Blood Parish - 712 S. Pearl St., New London, WI 54961-1861 t) 920-982-2346; 920-982-9025 (CRP) parish@mpbparishnl.org www.mostpreciousbloodchurch.com Rev. John Kleinschmidt, Admin.; CRP Stds.: 166

Most Precious Blood Parish - Catholic School - (Grades PreK-7) 120 E. Washington St., New London, WI 54961-1891 t) 920-982-2134 parish@mpbparishnl.org www.mostpreciousbloodschool.com/

St. Patrick - N5705 County Rd. T, New London, WI 54961-8464 t) 920-982-5475 stpatrickslebanon@charter.net www.stpatrickslebanon.com Rev. John Kleinschmidt, Admin.; Barbara Tate, Pst. Min./Coord.;

NEWALD

St. Hubert Mission - 5330 Beech St., Newald, WI 54541-9340 t) 715-674-3241; 715-674-3862 (CRP) stleonardlaona@gmail.com; anilpolumari@gmail.com Served from St. Leonard, Laona. Rev. Anil Polumari, Admin.;

NEWTON

St. Thomas the Apostle - 8100 Brunner Rd., Newton, WI 53063-9607 t) 920-726-4228 stthomasreceptionist@gmail.com; pfischer7662@gmail.com stthomasnewton.org Rev. David Beaudry, Pst.; Pamela Fischer, DRE; CRP Stds.: 165

NIAGARA

St. Anthony - 1432 River St., Niagara, WI 54151-1599 t) 715-251-3879 office.stanthonyniagara@gmail.com stanthonyniagara.org Also serves St. Margaret, Pembine & Sacred Heart, Aurora. Rev. Quentin A. Mann, C.D.L., Admin.; Dawn L. Johnson, DRE; CRP Stds.: 45

OCONTO

Holy Trinity - 716 Madison St., Oconto, WI 54153-1668 t) 920-835-5900 holytrinity@holy3.org www.holytrinityoconto.org Linked with St. Maximilian Kolbe, Sobieski, WI Rev. Francis Nusi, Admin.;

OCONTO FALLS

St. Anthony - 253 N. Franklin St., Oconto Falls, WI 54154-1042 t) 920-846-2276 lscanlan@holy3.org holy3.org Rev. Walter P. Stumpf, Pst.; CRP Stds.: 90

St. Anthony School - sbeschta@holy3.org

OMRO

St. Mary - 730 Madison Ave., Omro, WI 54963-1630 t) 920-685-2258 www.stmarychurches.org Rev. W. Thomas Long, Priest Moderator/Priest Celebrant; Rev. Kevin Ripley, Par. Vicar; Dcn. Paul Vidmar, Pst. Min./Coord.; Rose Unser, Pst. Assoc.; CRP Stds.: 75

ONEIDA

St. Joseph - 145 Saint Joseph Dr., Oneida, WI 54155-8914 t) 920-869-2244 parishffmary@gmail.com; parishsecsjic@gmail.com stjosephoneida.org Also serves Immaculate Conception, Oneida. Rev. Paul J. Paider, Pst.; Dcn. Everett L. Doxtator; Mary Van Schyndel, DRE; Barbara Geurts, Treas.;

OSHKOSH

St. Jude the Apostle - 1025 W. 5th Ave., Oshkosh, WI 54902 t) 920-235-7412 office@stjudeoshkosh.org Rev. Louis R. Golamari, Admin.; Dcn. Peter A. Cheskie; Dcn. Bradley E Gallenberg; Dcn. G. Patrick Gelhar; CRP Stds.: 160

Most Blessed Sacrament - 435 High Ave., Oshkosh, WI 54901-4708 t) 920-231-9782 info@mbsoshkosh.com mbsoshkosh.com Very Rev. Jerome P. Pastors, Pst.; Dcn. Richard A. Hocking; CRP Stds.: 46

St. Raphael the Archangel - 830 S Westhaven Dr., Oshkosh, WI 54904-7977 t) 920-233-8044 parish.office@raphael.org; jessie.adrians@raphael.org www.raphael.org Rev. W. Thomas Long, Pst.; Rev. Kevin Ripley, Par. Vicar; Dcn. Gregory A. Grey; Dcn. John Ingala; Dcn. Mark Leafgren; Jessica Adrians, DRE; CRP Stds.: 383

PEMBINE

St. Margaret - N18844 Hwy. 141 & 8, Pembine, WI 54156-0235; Mailing: P.O. Box 235, Pembine, WI 54156-0235 t) 715-324-5849 stmargaretpembine@gmail.com www.stanthonyniagara.org Rev. Quentin A. Mann, C.D.L., Admin.;

PESHTIGO

St. Mary - 171 S. Wood Ave., Peshtigo, WI 54157-1426; Mailing: 141 S. Wood Ave, Peshtigo, WI 54157 t) 715-582-3876 st.marypeshtigo@gmail.com; debra.meunier.faithformation@gmail.com www.stmaryjosephedwardparish.org Also serves SS. Joseph & Edward, Walsh. Dcn. Charles R. Schumacher; Rev. Edmundo Nachor Siguenza, Admin.; Debra Meunier, DRE; CRP Stds.: 51

PHLOX

St. Joseph-Holy Family Parish - W7365 State Hwy. 47, Phlox, WI 54464; Mailing: P.O. Box 73, W7365 State Hwy 47, Phlox, WI 54464-0073 t) 715-489-3330 sjhfphlox@granitewave.com sjhf-phlox.org Vicente Llagas, Admin.;

PICKEREL

St. Mary - N9155 State Rd. 55, Pickerel, WI 54465-0077; Mailing: P.O. Box 77, Pickerel, WI 54465 t) 715-484-4300 holyfamilyelcho@frontiernet.net hfstm.org Served from Holy Family, Elcho. Rev. Kennedy Gaspar, Pst.;

PLAINFIELD

St. Paul - 622 S. Beach St., Plainfield, WI 54966-9637 t) 715-335-4314 stpaul@uniontel.net Served from St. Joseph, Wautoma Dcn. James Hoegemeier, Pst. Assoc.; Rev. Kyle Sladek, Priest Celebrant;

PORTERFIELD

SS. Joseph & Edward - W3308 County Road G, Porterfield, WI 54159-9736 t) 715-789-2254 debra.meunier.faithformation@gmail.com; ssjosephedward@gmail.com www.stmaryjosephedwardparish.org Served from St. Mary, Peshtigo. (Has records for St. Edward, Wagner & St. Joseph, Walsh.) Rev. Edmundo Nachor Siguenza, Admin.; Dcn. Charles R. Schumacher; Debra Meunier, DRE;

POY SIPPI

Sacred Heart of Jesus - 2304 Liberty St, Poy Sippi, WI 54967; Mailing: PO Box 273, Redgranite, WI 54970-0273 t) 920-566-4442 sacredheartps@centurytel.net Served from St. Mark, Redgranite. Rev. Kyle Sladek, Admin.; CRP Stds.: 12

PULASKI

Assumption of the Blessed Virgin Mary Congregation - 119 E. Pulaski St, Pulaski, WI 54162-0379; Mailing: PO Box 379, Pulaski, WI 54162 t) 920-822-3279; 920-822-5650 (CRP) parishoffice@abvm.org; sara.mangold@abvm.org www.abvmcast.org Also serves St. Stanislaus, Hofa Park and St. Casimir, Krakow. Dcn. Dennis Majewski; Rev. James Gerard Gannon, OFM, Admin.; Rev. David Kobak, OFM, Par. Vicar; Janet Maroszek, Pst. Assoc.; Deanne Wilinski, DRE; Todd Skinkis, Youth Min.; Cathy Nampel, Music Min.; CRP Stds.: 223

Assumption of the Blessed Virgin Mary School - (Grades 1-5) 109 E. Pulaski St., Pulaski, WI 54162-9287 www.abvmeducation.org Sara Mangold, Prin.;

REDGRANITE

St. Mark - 228 Church Ave., Redgranite, WI 54970-0273; Mailing: PO Box 273, Redgranite, WI 54970-0273 t) 920-566-4442 stmarkredgranite@centurytel.net bitly.com/smshsite Also serves Sacred Heart of Jesus, Poy Sippi. Rev. Kyle Sladek, Admin.; CRP Stds.: 16

SEYMOUR

St. John - 915 Ivory St., Seymour, WI 54165-1629 t) 920-833-6140 office@stjohnseymour.com Rev. Sengole Arockia Dass, O. Praem., Admin.; Dcn. Richard J. Matuszak; John Steltz, CRE; CRP Stds.: 120

SHAWANO

Sacred Heart Parish - 302 S. Main St., Shawano, WI 54166-2437; Mailing: 321 S. Sawyer St, Shawano, WI 54166 t) 715-526-2023 lmathieu@sacredheartshawano.org www.sacredheartshawano.org Rev. Scott Valentyn, Admin.; Dcn. James Lonick; Kathleen Ruth, Youth Min.; CRP Stds.: 98

Sacred Heart School - 124 E. Center St., Shawano, WI 54166-2499 t) 715-526-5328 ayoung@sacredheartshawano.org; lmeisner@sacredheartshawano.org Aleta Young, Prin.;

SHERWOOD

St. John-Sacred Heart - N369 Military Rd, Sherwood, WI 54169-9661 t) 920-989-1515 triparish369@gmail.com; triparishre@gmail.com ourtriparish.org/ Rev. Michael E. Betley, Pst.; Dcn. Timothy Stevenson; Candace Gehl, DRE; CRP Stds.: 123

St. John-Sacred Heart School - (Grades PreK-8) N361 Military Rd., Sherwood, WI 54169-9661; Mailing: PO Box 78, Sherwood, WI 54169 t) 920-989-1373 sjshprincipal@gmail.com www.stjohnssacredheart.org Jacklyn Behnke, Prin.; Stds.: 55; Lay Tchrs.: 5

SHIOCTON

St. Denis - N5591 Second St., Shiocton, WI 54170; Mailing: N3686 State Rd. 76, Hortonville, WI 54944-8320 t) 920-757-5090 office@stdenis-shiocton.org www.stdenis-shiocton.org Served from St. Patrick, Stephensville. Rev. Michael Thiel, Admin.; CRP Stds.: 36

SOBIESKI

St. Maximilian Kolbe - 6051 Noble St., Sobieski, WI 54171-9724 t) 920-822-5255; 920-822-8795 (CRP) stmaxkolbeparish@gmail.com www.stmaximiliankolbe.com/ Rev. Francis Nusi, Admin.;

ST. NAZIANZ

St. Gregory - 214 Church St., St. Nazianz, WI 54232-0199; Mailing: PO Box 199, St. Nazianz, WI 54232 t) 920-773-2511 sgparishoffice@gmail.com www.stgregsparish.com Also serves Holy Trinity, School Hill. Rev. William J. Brunner III, Admin.; Dcn. Gary Wilhelm; Patty Wilhelm, DRE; Rita A. Steffen, Bus. Mgr.; CRP Stds.: 33

STEPHENVILLE

St. Patrick - N3686 State Rd. 76, Stephenville, WI 54944-8320 t) 920-757-5090 office@stpatrick-stephensville.org www.stpatrick-stephensville.org Also serves St. Denis, Shiocton. Rev. Michael Thiel, Admin.; CRP Stds.: 7

STOCKBRIDGE

St. Mary - ; Mailing: P.O. Box 8, Stockbridge, WI 53088-0008 t) 920-439-1515 stmarystockbridge@tds.net www.ourtriparish.org Served from St. John-Sacred Heart, Sherwood/Saint John. Rev. Michael E. Betley, Pst.; CRP Stds.: 34

STURGEON BAY

Corpus Christi - 25 N. Elgin Ave., Sturgeon Bay, WI 54235-2963 t) 920-743-4716 office@ccparish.net Rev. Ryan E. Krueger, Pst.; Dcn. Mark R. Hibbs; Laura Hoffman, DRE; Sarah Gavin, Youth Min.; CRP Stds.: 174

St. Joseph - 526 Louisiana St., Sturgeon Bay, WI 54235-1796 t) 920-743-2062 bwagner@stjosephsb.com stjosephsb.com Serves Ss. Peter & Paul Parish, Institute. Rev. Robert Stegmann, Pst.; Dcn. Mark Bortle; Dcn. Edward Winter; Sarah Gavin, DRE; Laura Hoffman, DRE; CRP Stds.: 67

SS. Peter and Paul - 4767 E. Dunn Rd., Sturgeon Bay, WI 54235-8822 t) 920-743-4842 ssppbusiness@sspeterpaulsb.org sspeterpaulsb.org/ Rev. Robert Stegmann, Pst.;

SUAMICO

St. Benedict - 3370 Deerfield W., Suamico, WI 54173-0066; Mailing: P.O. Box 66, Suamico, WI 54173-0066 t) 920-434-2024; 920-434-1219 (CRP) sbsp@wi.twcbc.com st.benedictsuamico.com Also serves St. Pius in Little Suamico, WI Rev. Demosthenes Olaso, Admin.; CRP Stds.: 60

SURING

St. Michael - 210 S Krueger St, Suring, WI 54174-0248; Mailing: PO Box 248, Suring, WI 54174 t) 920-842-2580 stmikesuring@centurytel.net www.stjohnstmichael.com Served from St. John, Gillett, with Station at Chute Pond. Rev. Francis Xavier Dias, Admin.; Sheelagh School, DRE; CRP Stds.: 9

TIGERTON

St. Anthony - 430 Swanke St., Tigerton, WI 54486-0106; Mailing: P.O. Box 106, Tigerton, WI 54486 t) 715-535-2571 office@catholicsupnorth.org wittomary.org Also serves St. Mary, Marion & Holy Family-St. William, Wittenberg. Rev. Matthew W. Settle, Pst.; Dcn. Michael J. Brandt; Tammy Wendler, DRE; CRP Stds.: 9

TISCH MILLS

St. Isidore the Farmer - 18424 Tisch Mills Rd., Tisch Mills, WI 54208-9508 t) 920-776-1555 st.isidore@tm.net Rev. Dennis G. Drury, Pst.; CRP Stds.: 60

TWO RIVERS

St. Peter the Fisherman - 3201 Mishicot Rd., Two Rivers, WI 54241-1501 t) 920-793-4531 parish@spfcp.org www.spfcp.org Dcn. John Vincent, Pst. Assoc.; Rev. David J. Pleier, Sacr. Min.; Dcn. Paul J. Gleichner, Pst. Min./Coord.; Dcn. Frank Birr; Dcn. Thomas Tomaszewski, DRE; CRP Stds.: 118

WABENO

St. Ambrose - 4265 N. Branch Ave, Wabeno, WI 54566; Mailing: PO Box 280, Wabeno, WI 54566-0280 t) 715-473-2511 stambrose@centurylink.net Served from St. Mary of the Lake, Lakewood. Rev. Praveen Pamisetti (India), Admin.; Amy Stefanovic, CRE;

WAUPACA

St. Mary Magdalene - N2845 Shadow Rd., Waupaca, WI 54981; Mailing: P.O. Box 409, Waupaca, WI 54981 t) 715-258-2088 info@smm-waupaca.org smm-waupaca.org Also has records for St. George, King. Rev. Xavier Santiago, Admin.; Robert Lewinski, Pst. Min./Coord.; Leann Ellenich, Bus. Mgr.; CRP Stds.: 113

WAUSAUKEE

St. Augustine - 507 Church St., Wausaukee, WI

54177-9749; Mailing: PO Box 137, Wausaukee, WI 54177-0137 t) 715-856-5276 secretarystaugustine2020@gmail.com www.stagnes-staugustine-catholic-parishes.com/ Also serves St. Agnes, Amberg. Rev. David R. Schmidt, Pst.; CRP Stds.: 13

WAUTOMA

St. Joseph - 364 S. Cambridge St., Wautoma, WI 54982-8101 t) 920-787-3848 office@stjosephwautoma.com Rev. William Evans, Admin.; Sr. Mary Ellen Doherty, SSND, Pst. Assoc.; Paula Caswell, DRE; CRP Stds.: 79

WEYAUWEGA

SS. Peter and Paul - 608 E Main St., Weyauwega, WI 54983-0548; Mailing: Po Box 548, Weyauwega, WI 54983 t) 920-867-2179; 920-867-2170 (CRP) sspeterpaulwega@gmail.com www.sspeterpaulchurch.org/ Rev. Matthew Rappl, Pst.; Stephanie A. Hansen, DRE; CRP Stds.: 93

WHITE LAKE

SS. James-Stanislaus - 235 Bissell St., White Lake, WI 54491-0036; Mailing: PO Box 36, White Lake, WI 54491 t) 715-882-2551 stjames2551@frontier.com Very Rev. Joel A. Sember, Pst.;

WHITELAW

St. Michael - 110 W. Menasha Ave., Whitelaw, WI 54247-0206; Mailing: PO Box 206, Whitelaw, WI 54247 t) 920-732-3901 stmichael3901@comcast.net Served from Immaculate Conception, Clarks Mills. Rev. Richard H. Klingeisen, Pst.; Dcn. Randy Meidl; Teresa Pederson, DRE; CRP Stds.: 60

St. Mary/St. Michael School - 19 S. County Rd., Reedsville, WI 54230-8329 t) 920-775-4366 rhamcher@stmarystmichael.com Rick Hamacher, Prin.;

WINNECONNE

St. Mary - 210 Pleasant Dr., Winneconne, WI 54986-0487; Mailing: PO Box 487, Winneconne, WI 54986-0487 t) 920-582-7712 stmarywinn@stmarychurches.org www.stmarychurches.org Also serves St. Mary Omro. Rev. W. Thomas Long, Pst.; Dcn. Paul Vidmar, Pst. Min./Coord.; Rose Unser, Pst. Assoc.; Andrea Krueger, CRE; CRP Stds.: 173

WITTENBERG

Holy Family-St. William - 106 N. Ellms St., Wittenberg, WI 54499-9099; Mailing: P.O. Box 106, Tigerton, WI 54486-0106 t) 715-535-2571 office@catholicsupnorth.org wittomary.org Rev. Matthew W. Settle, Pst.; Dcn. Michael J. Brandt; Dcn. Howard R. Bricco; Tammy Wendler, DRE; CRP Stds.: 24

SCHOOLS: PRESCHOOL THRU HIGH SCHOOL

SCHOOLS

STATE OF WISCONSIN

ANTIGO

All Saints Catholic Schools, Inc. - (PAR) (Grades PreK-8) 419 6th Ave., Antigo, WI 54409 t) 715-623-4835; 715-623-2211 pgaluska@ascscrusaders.org www.ascscrusaders.org Paul Galuska, Admin.; Stacy Beck, Vice Prin.; Jenny Thom, Librn.; Stds.: 213; Lay Tchrs.: 14

APPLETON

St. Francis Xavier Catholic School System, Inc. - 101 E. Northland Ave., Appleton, WI 54911 t) 920-735-9380 priley@xaviercatholicschools.org; tlarson@xaviercatholicschools.org www.xaviercatholicschools.org 4-schools: of St. Francis Xavier High School, St. Francis Xavier Middle School, St. Francis Xavier Elem-Marquette & St. Francis Xavier Elem-McDonald John Ravizza, Supt.; Philip R Riley Jr., Pres.; Stds.: 1,434; Lay Tchrs.: 108

St. Francis Xavier High School - 1600 W. Prospect Ave., Appleton, WI 54914 t) 920-733-6632 mmauthe@xaviercatholicschools.org Coed Mike Mauthe, Prin.; Stds.: 470; Lay Tchrs.: 44

St. Francis Xavier Middle School - 2626 N. Oneida St., Appleton, WI 54911 t) 920-730-8849 smeyer@xaviercatholicschools.org Sara Meyer, Prin.; Stds.: 364; Lay Tchrs.: 38

St. Francis Xavier Elementary - Marquette - 500 W. Marquette St., Appleton, WI 54911 t) 920-733-4918 kfairweather@xaviercatholicschools.org Tina Fairweather, Prin.; Stds.: 285; Lay Tchrs.: 27

St. Francis Xavier Elementary - McDonald - 1810 N. McDonald St., Appleton, WI 54911 t) 920-739-7826 atapelt@xaviercatholicschools.org Alena Tapelt, Prin.; Stds.: 315; Lay Tchrs.: 23

DE PERE

Notre Dame Catholic School of De Pere, Inc. - 137 S. Superior St., De Pere, WI 54115 t) (920) 337-2330 Steven Handrick, Accountant;

GREEN BAY

Green Bay Area Catholic Education, Inc. (GRACE) - (DIO) (Grades PreSchool-10) 1822 Riverside Dr., Green Bay, WI 54301 t) 920-499-7330 graceoffice@gracesystem.org www.gracesystem.org Kimberly Desotell, Pres.; Stds.: 2,346; Sr. Tchrs.: 1; Lay Tchrs.: 164

GRACE Holy Family School - (Grades PreSchool-10) 1204 S Fisk St, Green Bay, WI 54303-2299 t) 920-494-1931 hfsoffice@gracesystem.org holyfamilygreenbay.com/ Jere Kubuske, Prin.; Stds.: 206; Sr. Tchrs.: 1; Lay Tchrs.: 17

GRACE Father Allouez Catholic School, Resurrection Campus - (Grades PreSchool-10) 333 Hilltop Dr, Green Bay, WI 54301-2799 t) 920-336-3230 resoffice@gracesystem.org www.fatherallouezschool.org Kay L. Franz, Prin.; Stds.: 97; Lay Tchrs.: 9

GRACE Father Allouez Catholic School, St. Matthew Campus - (Grades PreSchool-10) 2575 S Webster Ave, Green Bay, WI 54301-2998 t) 920-432-5223 smsoffice@gracesystem.org www.fatherallouezschool.org Kay L. Franz, Prin.; Stds.: 192; Lay Tchrs.: 13

GRACE St. Bernard Catholic School - (Grades PreSchool-10) 2020 Hillside Ln, Green Bay, WI 54302-4099 t) 920-468-5026 cblahnik@gracesystem.org www.stbernardgb.org Crystal Blahnik, Prin.; Stds.: 434; Lay Tchrs.: 27

GRACE Holy Cross School, Bay Settlement - (Grades PreSchool-10) 3002 Bay Settlement Rd, Green Bay, WI 54311-7302 t) 920-468-0625 kpeterson@gracesystem.org www.holycrossfamily.org Kari Peterson, Prin.; Stds.: 121; Lay Tchrs.: 10

GRACE Notre Dame Elementary & Middle School, De Pere - (Grades PreSchool-10) 137 S Superior St, De Pere, WI 54115-2819 t) 920-337-1115 mmares@gracesystem.org notredameofdepere.com Molly Mares, Prin.; Stds.: 410; Lay Tchrs.: 25

GRACE Our Lady of Lourdes School, De Pere - (Grades PreSchool-10) 1305 Lourdes Ave, De Pere, WI 54115-1018 t) 920-336-3091 jyoung@gracesystem.org www.lourdesschooldepere.org Jeff Young, Prin.; Stds.: 200; Lay Tchrs.: 14

GRACE St. John the Baptist School - (Grades PreSchool-10) 2561 Glendale Ave., Green Bay, WI 54313-6821 t) 920-434-3822 dvance@gracesystem.org sjbhschool.org/ Dana Vance, Prin.; Stds.: 351; Lay Tchrs.: 23

GRACE St. Thomas More School - (Grades PreSchool-10) 1420 Harvey St, Green Bay, WI 54302 t) 920-432-8242 jfrohtyrrell@gracesystem.org www.stmoregb.org Dr. Jamie Froh Tyrrell, Prin.; Stds.: 175; Lay Tchrs.: 14

GRACE St. John Paul II Classical School - (Grades PreSchool-10) 320 Victoria St, Green Bay, WI 54302 t) 920-617-9542 sjpiioffice@gracesystem.org www.sjpclassicalschoolgreenbay.org Patrick McKeown, Headmaster; Alex Wolf, Headmaster; Stds.: 160; Lay Tchrs.: 12

KAUKAUNA

St. Ignatius of Loyola Catholic School - (PAR) (Grades PreK-12) 220 Doty St., Kaukauna, WI 54130-2108 t) 920-766-0186 www.stignatiuskaukauna.org Nathan Vandehey, System Pres.; Stds.: 281; Lay Tchrs.: 26

KIEL

Divine Savior Catholic Elementary School, Inc. - 423 Fremont St., Kiel, WI 53042 t) 920-894-3533 divinesaviorcatholicschool@gmail.com www.divinesaviorschool.org Rev. Alvan Amadi; Martha Holst, Prin.; Stds.: 77; Lay Tchrs.: 6

MANITOWOC

Roncalli Catholic Schools, Inc. - (PAR) 2000 Mirro Dr., Manitowoc, WI 54220-6799 t) 920-682-8801 barbara.strawn@roncallicatholicschools.org www.roncallicatholicschools.org John Stelzer, Pres.; Barbara Strawn, Dir.; Dianne Vadney, Campus Min.; Rev. David Beaudry, Spiritual Adv./Care Srvcs.; Stds.: 742; Lay Tchrs.: 60

Roncalli Elementary School - 1408 Waldo Blvd., Manitowoc, WI 54220 t) 920-683-6892 rems.roncallicatholicschools.org Adrienne Lundy, Prin.; Stds.: 315; Lay Tchrs.: 23

MARINETTE

St. Thomas Aquinas Academy - (Grades PreK-12) 1200 Main St., Marinette, WI 54143 t) 715-735-7481 jkeepers.staa@gmail.com www.thomas-aquinas.org Jon Keepers, Prin.; Stds.: 165; Lay Tchrs.: 15

St. Thomas Aquinas Academy - Secondary Campus - (Grades PreK-12) principal.staa@gmail.com Michael Cattani, Prin.; Stds.: 81; Lay Tchrs.: 7

St. Thomas Aquinas - Elementary - (Grades PreK-12) 171 S. Wood Ave., Peshtigo, WI 54157 t) 715-582-4041 principal.staa@gmail.com Michael Cattani, Prin.;

NEENAH

St. Mary Catholic Schools, Inc. - (Grades PreK-12) 1050 Zephyr Dr., Neenah, WI 54956 t) 920-722-7796 dmckenna@smcatholicschools.org; eknapinski@smcatholicschools.org www.smcatholicschools.org Five-school system: St. Gabriel, St. Margaret Mary, & St. Mary Elementary Schools; St. Mary Catholic Middle School; & St. Mary Catholic High School Dan McKenna, Supt.; Stds.: 988; Lay Tchrs.: 72

St. Mary Catholic High School - (Grades PreK-12) 1050 Zepher Dr., Neenah, WI 54956 patriciafouts@smcatholicschools.org smcatholicschools.org Stds.: 272; Lay Tchrs.: 22

St. Mary Catholic Middle School - (Grades PreK-12) 1000 Zephyr Dr., Neenah, WI 54956 jahles@smcatholicschools.org smcatholicschools.org Jill Ahles, Prin.; Stds.: 196; Lay Tchrs.: 17

St. Gabriel Elementary - (Grades PreK-12) 900 Geiger St., Neenah, WI 54956 jleege@smcatholicschools.org smcatholicschools.org Stds.: 168; Lay Tchrs.: 10

St. Margaret Mary Elementary - (Grades PreK-12) 610 Division St., Neenah, WI 54956 kfairweather@smcatholicschools.org smcatholicschools.org Stds.: 244; Lay Tchrs.: 17

St. Mary Elementary - (Grades PreK-12) 540 Second St., Menasha, WI 54952 spiotrowski@smcatholicschools.org smcatholicschools.org Stds.: 108; Lay Tchrs.: 10

OSHKOSH

Lourdes Academy of Oshkosh, Wisconsin, Inc. - (PAR) (Grades PreK-12) 250 N. Sawyer St., Oshkosh, WI 54902 t) 920-426-3626 jdinegan@lourdes.today www.lourdes.today John Dinegan, Pres.; Stds.: 638; Lay Tchrs.: 57

Lourdes Academy Middle & High School - (Grades PreK-12) 110 N. Sawyer St., Oshkosh, WI 54902

t) 920-235-5670 enroll@lourdes.today Coed David Mikesell, Prin.; Stds.: 358; Lay Tchrs.: 32

Lourdes Academy Elementary School - (Grades PreK-12) 110 N. Sawyer St., Oshkosh, WI 54902 t) 920-235-4060 enroll@lourdes.today Amy Geffers, Prin.; Reed Tyriver, Elementary & Middle School Assoc. Prin.; Stds.: 280; Lay Tchrs.: 20

STURGEON BAY

St. John Bosco Catholic School, Inc. - (DIO) (Grades PreK-8) 730 W. Maple St., Sturgeon Bay, WI 54235 t) 920-743-4144 vickie.dassler@johnboscoschool.org johnboscoschool.org Vickie Dassler, Prin.; Stds.: 117; Scholastics: 2; Lay Tchrs.: 12

HIGH SCHOOLS

STATE OF WISCONSIN

GREEN BAY

Notre Dame de la Baie Academy - (PAR) (Grades 9-12) 610 Maryhill Dr., Green Bay, WI 54303-2092 t) 920-429-6100; 920-429-6108 (Business Opers.) cdunlap@notredameacademy.com; jsidon@notredameacademy.com www.notredameacademy.com Andrea Hearden, Prin.; Thomas J Kiely, Pres.; Ken Flaten, Dir., Fin. & Bus. Opers.; Greg Masarik, Assoc. Prin.; Stds.: 722; Pr. Tchrs.: 1; Lay Tchrs.: 44

CAMPUS MINISTRY / NEWMAN CENTERS [CAM]

GREEN BAY

Catholic Campus Ministry, U.W.G.B. - 1825 Riverside Dr., Green Bay, WI 54305-3825; Mailing: P.O. Box 23825, Green Bay, WI 54305-3825 t) 920-288-0237; 920-272-8394 lzelten@gbdioc.org www.phoenixcatholic.org Sr. Laura Zelten, O.S.F., Campus Min.;

Lawrence University Newman Center -

Newman Center of Oshkosh, Inc. - 800 Elmwood Ave., Oshkosh, WI 54901-3518 t) 920-233-5555 titancatholics@gbdioc.org titancatholics.org Rev. Jason J. Blahnik, Dir.;

CEMETERIES [CEM]

GREEN BAY

Diocesan Cemeteries - 1825 Riverside Dr., Green Bay, WI 54301; Mailing: P.O. Box 23825, Green Bay, WI 54305-3825 t) (920) 432-7585 mbreivogel@gbdioc.org Mary Breivogel, Admin.;

Allouez Catholic Cemetery and Mausoleum - 2121 Riverside Dr., Green Bay, WI 54301 t) 920-432-7585 allouezcatholiccemetery.com

Calvary Cemetery of Manitowoc, Inc. - 2601 S. 14th St., Manitowoc, WI 54220-6467 t) 920-684-3646 calvarymausoleum@yahoo.com Jerry Schermetzler, Admin.;

COLLEGES & UNIVERSITIES [COL]

DE PERE

St. Norbert College - 100 Grant St., De Pere, WI 54115 t) 920-337-3181 oie@snc.edu www.snc.edu Carolyn Uhl, Dir.; Stds.: 1,882; Lay Tchrs.: 130; Pr. Tchrs.: 1

CONVENTS, MONASTERIES, AND RESIDENCES FOR WOMEN [CON]

DENMARK

Monastery of the Holy Name of Jesus, Ltd. - 6100 Pepper Rd., Denmark, WI 54208 t) 920-863-5055 mttabor@holynamecarmel.org Discalced Carmelite Nuns Very Rev. John Girotti, Chap.; Mother Mary Elizabeth, O.C.D., Prioress; Srs.: 17

GREEN BAY

Sisters of Our Lady of Charity of the Good Shepherd - Green Bay, Inc. - 2560 Shawano Ave., Green Bay, WI 54313; Mailing: 620 Roswell Rd., S.W., P.O. Box 340, Carrollton, OH 44615 t) 920-434-8208 sisterpat1165@gmail.com Sr. Patrick Dolan, Supr.; Srs.: 5

The Sisters of St. Francis of the Holy Cross, Inc. - 3110 Nicolet Dr., Green Bay, WI 54311-7212 t) 920-468-1828 sr.rose@gbfranciscans.org www.gbfranciscans.org Sr. Rose Jochmann, Pres.; Srs.: 43

MANITOWOC

St. Francis Convent - 6835 Calumet Ave., Manitowoc, WI 54220-9700 t) 920-684-7884 smaryannt@sfcc-calledtobe.org Franciscan Sisters of Christian Charity. Sr. Natalie Binversie, O.S.F., Prioress; Srs.: 33

Holy Family Convent of Franciscan Sisters of Christian Charity - 2409 S. Alverno Rd., Manitowoc, WI 54220-9320 t) 920-682-7728 snatalie@fscc-calledtobe.org fscc-calledtobe.org Motherhouse and Novitiate Rev. Gerald Prusakowski, O.F.M., Chap.; Rev. Placid Stroik, O.F.M., Chap.; Sr. Natalie Binversie, O.S.F., Dir.; Srs.: 178

INSTITUTIONS LOCATED IN DIOCESE

OSHKOSH

Sisters of the Sorrowful Mother St. Clare of Assisi Region - 815 S. Westhaven Dr., Ste. 100, Oshkosh, WI 54904 t) 920-230-2040 Sr. Lois Bush, Supr.; Srs.: 51

Sisters of the Sorrowful Mother - 2185 Abbey Ave., Oshkosh, WI 54904; Mailing: 815 S. Westhaven Dr., Ste. 100, Oshkosh, WI 54904-7978 t) (920) 230-2040

Sisters of the Sorrowful Mother - 2485 Arcadia Ave., Oshkosh, WI 54904

SSM Franciscan Courts - 815 S. Westhaven Dr., Ste. 100, Oshkosh, WI 54904-7978 t) 920-426-2440 john.fuller@ascension.org www.franciscancourts.org Sisters of the Sorrowful Mother. Sr. Lois Bush, Contact; Srs.: 33

ENDOWMENTS / FOUNDATIONS / TRUSTS [EFT]

APPLETON

Ascension St. Elizabeth Foundation, Inc. - 1506 S. Oneida St., Appleton, WI 54915-1397 t) 920-831-1475 timothy.waldoch@ascension.org healthcare.ascension.org/donate Sponsored by Ascension Health Ministries (Ascension Sponsor), a public juridic person Bernie Sherry, CEO; Timothy Waldoch, Exec.;

DE PERE

Augustine Stewardship Fund Trust - 1016 N. Broadway, De Pere, WI 54115-2610 t) 920-337-4300 jim.glover@norbertines.org www.norbertines.org Jim Glover, Treas.;

St. Norbert Abbey Seminary and Education Fund Trust - 1016 N. Broadway, De Pere, WI 54115-2610 t) 920-337-4300 jim.glover@norbertines.org www.norbertines.org Jim Glover, Treas.;

Norbertine Retirement Fund Trust - 1016 N. Broadway, De Pere, WI 54115-2610 t) 920-337-4300 jim.glover@norbertines.org www.norbertines.org Jim Glover, Treas.;

GREEN BAY

The Catholic Foundation for the Diocese of Green Bay, Inc. - 1825 Riverside Dr., Green Bay, WI 54305-2128; Mailing: P.O. Box 22128, Green Bay, WI 54305-2128 t) (920) 272-8197 catholicfoundation@gbdioc.org www.catholicfoundationgb.org Josh Diedrich, Dir.;

Catholic High School Foundation, L.T.D. - 610 Maryhill Dr, Green Bay, WI 54303; Mailing: P.O. Box 1117, Green Bay, WI 54305-1117 t) 920-337-4321 jglover@netnet.net; cdunlap@notredameacademy.com Thomas Konop, Pres.; Virginia Micksch, Secy.; Jim Glover, Treas.; William Micksch, Vice Pres.;

Notre Dame de la Baie Foundation, Inc. - 610 Maryhill Dr., Green Bay, WI 54303 t) 920-429-6110 (Exec. Asst.); 920-429-6108 (Bus. Opers.) cdunlap@notredameacademy.com; kflaten@notredameacademy.com Adrian Ulatowski, Pres.; Mary Pott, Vice. Pres.; John Frey, Secy.; Craig Darling, Treas.;

Sisters of St. Francis of the Holy Cross Retirement Fund Trust - 3110 Nicolet Dr., Green Bay, WI 54311 t) (920) 468-1828 mail@gbfranciscans.org www.gbfranciscans.org/ Sr. Rose Jochmann, Pres.;

NEENAH

St. Mary Catholic Schools Foundation, Inc. - 1050 Zephyr Dr., Neenah, WI 54956-1389 t) 920-722-7796 dmckenna@smcatholicschools.org www.smcatholicschools.org Dr. Tim Schigur, Supt.; Helen Englebert, Pres.;

HOSPITALS / HEALTH SERVICES [HOS]

ANTIGO

Langlade Hospital - Hotel Dieu of St. Joseph of Antigo Wisconsin (Aspirus Langlade Hospital) - 112 E. 5th Ave., Antigo, WI 54409 t) 715-623-2331 sherry.bunten@aspirus.org; dana.kulas@aspirus.org www.aspirus.org Religious Hospitallers of St. Joseph. Sherry Bunten, Pres.; Rev. Hillary Andebo, Chap.; Bed Capacity: 23; Asstd. Annu.: 112,000; Staff: 480

Religious Hospitalliers of St. Joseph - 650 Langlade Rd., Antigo, WI 55409 t) 715-623-4615 dolores.demulling@aspirus.org www.rhsj.org/

APPLETON

***Ascension Medical Group - Fox Valley Wisconsin, Inc. (Affinity Medical Group)** - 1506 S. Oneida St., Appleton, WI 54915 t) 920-738-2000 timothy.waldoch@ascension.org healthcare.ascension.org Sponsored by Ascension Health Ministries (Ascension Sponsor), a public juridic person Bernie Sherry, CEO; Timothy Waldoch, Chief Mission Integration Officer; Asstd. Annu.: 563,429; Staff: 665

Ascension NE Wisconsin, Inc (Ascension NE Wisconsin - St. Elizabeth Campus) - 1506 S. Oneida St., Appleton, WI 54915-1305 t) 920-738-2000 timothy.waldoch@ascension.org healthcare.ascension.org Sponsored by Ascension Health Ministries (Ascension Sponsor), a public juridic person. Bernie Sherry, CEO; Timothy Waldoch, Chief Mission Integration Officer; Bed Capacity: 172; Asstd. Annu.: 316,069; Staff: 918

CHILTON

Ascension Calumet Hospital, Inc. - 614 Memorial Dr., Chilton, WI 53014-1568 t) 920-849-2386 timothy.waldoch@ascension.org healthcare.ascension.org Bernie Sherry, CEO; Timothy Waldoch, Chief Mission Integration Officer; Bed Capacity: 12; Asstd. Annu.: 99,703; Staff: 113

GREEN BAY

St. Mary's Hospital Medical Center - 1726 Shawano Ave., Green Bay, WI 54303-3282 t) 920-498-4200 amy.bulpitt@hshs.org www.stmgb.org Hospital Sisters of Third Order of St. Francis. Brian Charlier, Pres.; Bed Capacity: 76; Asstd. Annu.: 264,265; Staff: 532

St. Vincent Hospital (Libertas) - 835 S. Van Buren, Green Bay, WI 54301 t) 920-433-0111 amy.bulpitt@hshs.org www.stvincenthospital.org St. Vincent Hospital of the Hospital Sisters of the Third Order of St. Francis Brian Charlier, Pres.; Bed Capacity: 277; Asstd. Annu.: 482,333; Staff: 1,769

MANITOWOC

Holy Family Memorial, Inc. - 2300 Western Ave., Manitowoc, WI 54221-1450; Mailing: P.O. Box 1450, Manitowoc, WI 54221-1450 t) 920-320-3481 (Exec. Asst.); 800-994-3662 sara.bashaw@froedtert.com; roxanne.miner@froedtert.com www.hfmhealth.org Roxanne Miner, Dir.; Bed Capacity: 60; Asstd. Annu.: 72,346; Staff: 735

OCONTO FALLS

***St. Clare Memorial Hospital, Inc.** - 855 S. Main St., Oconto Falls, WI 54154 t) 920-846-3444 amy.bulpitt@hshs.org www.stclarememorial.org Christopher Brabant, CEO; Bed Capacity: 22; Asstd. Annu.: 28,826; Staff: 142

STURGEON BAY

***Door County Memorial Hospital (Door County Medical Center)** - 323 S. 18th Ave., Sturgeon Bay, WI 54235-1401 t) 920-743-5566 brian.stephens@dcmedical.org www.dcmedical.org In partnership with Hospital Sisters Health System Brian Stephens, Pres.; Bed Capacity: 25; Asstd. Annu.: 30,650; Staff: 692

MISCELLANEOUS [MIS]

ANTIGO

Religious Hospitallers of St. Joseph Health Corporation "RHSJ Health Corporation" - 650, Langlade Rd., Antigo, WI 54409 t) (715) 623-2331 lstafford@rhsj.org www.rhsj.org Sr. Adele Demulling, R.H.S.J., Contact;

APPLETON

***Affinity Health System** - 1506 S. Oneida St., Appleton, WI 54915 t) 920-831-8912 timothy.waldoch@ascension.org healthcare.ascension.org Sponsored by Ascension Health Ministries (Ascension Sponsor), a public juridic person. Timothy Waldoch, Chief Mission Integration Officer; Bernie Sherry, CEO;

BAILEYS HARBOR

Catholic Youth Expeditions, Inc. - 3035 O'Brien Rd., Baileys Harbor, WI 54202 t) 920-573-0290 mail@cyexpeditions.org www.cyexpeditions.org Rev. Gregory Parent, Chap.; Mother Mary Catherine, M.W., Admin.;

Missionaries of the Word, Inc. - 3035 O'Brien Rd., Baileys Harbor, WI 54202-9132 t) 920-915-6592 mothermarycatherinemw@gmail.com; missionariesoftheword@gmail.com missionariesoftheword.com Mother Mary Catherine, M.W., Supr.;

DE PERE

Los Amigos del Peru, Inc. - 1016 N. Broadway, De Pere, WI 54115-2610 t) 920-337-4300 jim.glover@norbertines.org www.norbertines.org Jim Glover, Treas.;

NORBERT & CO. - 1016 N. Broadway, De Pere, WI 54115-2610 t) 920-337-4300 jim.glover@norbertines.org www.norbertines.org A nominee of The Premonstratensian Fathers Rt. Rev. Dane J. Radecki, O. Praem., Abbot; Rev. Bradley R. Vanden Branden, O. Praem., Prior; Jim Glover, Treas.;

Norbertine Generalate, Inc. - 1016 N. Broadway, De Pere, WI 54115-2610 t) 920-337-4300 www.premontre.org Rt. Rev. Jos Wouters, O.Praem., Pres.; Rt. Rev. Dane J. Radecki, O. Praem., Vice. Pres.; Rt. Rev. Gary J. Neville, O. Praem., Secy.;

DEERBROOK

***Living Waters International, Inc.** - N7544 County Rd. S., Deerbrook, WI 54424 t) 715-627-4782 livingh2o@livingwatersinternational.org www.livingwatersinternational.org Stephen L. Zimmerman, Exec. Dir.;

GREEN BAY

Catholic Charities of the Diocese of Green Bay, Inc. - 1825 Riverside Dr., Green Bay, WI 54305-3825; Mailing: P.O. Box 23825, Green Bay, WI 54305-3825 t) 920-272-8234 charitiesgb@gbdioc.org catholiccharitiesgb.org/ Karmen Lemke, Pres.;

St. Francis Xavier Investment Corp. - 1825 Riverside Dr., Green Bay, WI 54305-3825; Mailing: P.O. Box 23825, Green Bay, WI 54305-3825 t) 920-437-7531 x8206; 920-272-8206 pkolbach@gbdioc.org gbdioc.org Paul Kolbach, Pres.;

St. Gianna Clinic (St. Mary's Hospital Medical Center) - 1727 Shawano Ave., Green Bay, WI 54303 t) 920-884-3590 mary.salm@hshs.org www.stgiannaclinic.com/home/ Medical clinic. Andrew Bagnall, CEO; Dr. Rich Cooley, Exec.; Nicole Stapleton, Dir.;

The Green Bay Catholic Compass, Inc. - 1825 Riverside Dr., Green Bay, WI 54301; Mailing: P.O. Box 23825, Green Bay, WI 54305-3825 t) 920-437-7531 jlodl@gbdioc.org Justine Lodl, Pres.;

***HSHS Wisconsin Medical Group, Inc.** - 2710 Executive Dr., Green Bay, WI 54307; Mailing: 4936 Laverna Rd., Springfield, IL 62707 t) 217-492-5851 Megan Conkrite, Contract Specialist;

St. Joseph Real Estate Services Corporation - 1825 Riverside Dr., Green Bay, WI 54301; Mailing: P.O. Box 23825, Green Bay, WI 54305-3825 t) 920-272-8260 bweiss@gbdioc.org www.gbdioc.org Barbara Weiss, Pres.;

St. Luke Benefit & Insurance Services Corp. - 1825 Riverside Dr., Green Bay, WI 54301; Mailing: P.O. Box 23825, Green Bay, WI 54305-3825 t) 920-272-8343 bbond@gbdioc.org www.gbdioc.org Becky Bond, Pres.;

Oratory of St. Patrick - 211 N. Maple Ave., Green Bay, WI 54303 t) 920-437-9660 stpatrickgb@institute-christ-king.org institute-christ-king.org/greenbay/ Institute of Christ the King Sovereign Priest Rev. Antoine M. Boucheron, Rector;

Society for Faith and Children's Education, Inc. - 423 Woodfield Dr., Green Bay, WI 54313 t) 920-434-2420 sfacegreenbay@yahoo.com www.sfacemission.org June L. Ingold, Pres.; Rev. Savio J. Samala, Secy.;

St. Therese of the Little Flower, Inc. - 1825 Riverside Dr., Green Bay, WI 54301; Mailing: PO Box 23825, Green Bay, WI 54305-3825 t) 920-272-8206 pkolbach@gbdioc.org gbdioc.org Paul Kolbach, Pres.;

St. Thomas More Society of the Roman Catholic Diocese of Green Bay, Inc. - 1825 Riverside Dr., Green Bay, WI 54301; Mailing: P.O. Box 22336, Green Bay, WI 54305-2336 t) 920-593-2646 www.stmsgb.com Timothy Feldhausen, Contact;

***Tradivox, Inc.** - 1207 Mount Mary Dr., Green Bay, WI 54311; Mailing: 60613 Gentle Run Ct., South Bend, IN 46614 t) (574) 307-5307 Aaron Seng, Pres.;

MANITOWOC

Franciscan Sisters of Christian Charity Sponsored Ministries, Inc. - 2413 S. Alverno Rd., Manitowoc, WI 54220 t) 920-684-7071 smcconnaha@fsccm.org; bkane@fsccm.org www.fsccm.org Scott McConnaha, Pres.;

MENASHA

St. Gianna Molla Guild of Northeast Wisconsin, Inc. - C/O Hjortness and Associates, 851 Racine St., Ste. B, Menasha, WI 54952 t) (920) 378-2145 gail@simplewicpa.com; sgmgnew@gmail.com sgmgnew.com Robert McDonald, Pres.;

***Widows of Prayer, Inc.** - 414 Frances Way, Menasha, WI 54952 t) (920) 725-7768 widowsofprayer@yahoo.com Alice Peeters, Dir.;

NEW HOLSTEIN

Salvatorian Mission Warehouse - 1303 Milwaukee Dr., New Holstein, WI 53061 t) 920-898-5898 director@salvatorianmissionwarehouse.org salvatorianmissionwarehouse.org Mark Steiner, Dir.;

NEW LONDON

A New Genesis Community, Inc. - N6175 County Rd. W., New London, WI 54961; Mailing: P.O. Box 8642, Green Bay, WI 54308 t) 920-359-5176 dmbaumann15@gmail.com www.angcommunity.org A Public Association of the Faithful Sr. Diane Marie Baumann, ANG, Admin.;

OSHKOSH

Christ Child Society, Oshkosh Chapter - 830 S. Westhaven Dr., Oshkosh, WI 54903; Mailing: P.O. Box 2201, Oshkosh, WI 54903 c) 920-203-2632 ltkroening@gmail.com www.nationalchristchild.org Lori Kroening, Pres.;

Sisters of the Sorrowful Mother U.S. Region, Inc. - 815 S. Westhaven Dr., Ste. 100, Oshkosh, WI 54904-7978 t) 920-230-2040 www.sistersofthesorrowfulmother.org Sr. Lois Bush, Supr.;

SHAWANO

Camp Tekakwitha Retreat and Conference Center, Inc. - W5248 Lake Dr., Shawano, WI 54166 t) (715) 526-2316 camptekakwitha@gbdioc.org www.camptekakwitha.org Todd Blahnik, Pres.; Rebecca Sievers, Dir.;

STURGEON BAY

Christ Child Society of Door County - 4767 Dunn Rd., Sturgeon Bay, WI 54235-0572; Mailing: PO Box 572, Sturgeon Bay, WI 54235 c) 920-366-6013 purplebard77@gmail.com; doorcounty@nationalchristchild.org June Nirschl, Pres.;

MONASTERIES AND RESIDENCES FOR PRIESTS AND BROTHERS [MON]

APPLETON

St. Fidelis Friary - 1100 N. Ballard Rd., Appleton, WI 54911-5100 t) 920-954-8954; 920-231-0059 smaas@thecapuchins.org www.thecapuchins.org Order of Friars Minor Capuchin. Rev. Wilbert Lanser, Pst.; Rev. William Cieslak; Rev. Franklin Eichhorst; Rev. Ralph Fellenz, O.F.M.Cap.; Rev. David J. Funk, O.F.M.Cap.; Rev. Gerald Kessel; Rev. Ronald Rieder, In Res.; Rev. John F. Samsa; Rev. August Seubert, O.F.M.Cap.; Rev. Andre Weller; Rev. Joseph Wolf; Rev. James Zelinsk, O.F.M.Cap.; Bro. John Gau, O.F.M.Cap.; Bro. Lawrence Groeschel, O.F.M.Cap.; Bro. Paul Hanisko, In Res.; Brs.: 3; Priests: 25

St. Joseph Church - 404 W. Lawrence St., Appleton, WI 54911-5855 t) 920-734-7195 www.saintjosephparish.org Order of Friars Minor Capuchin. Rev. Raymond Stadmeyer, O.F.M. Cap, Admin.; Priests: 1

DE PERE

St. Norbert Abbey - 1016 N. Broadway, De Pere, WI 54115-2610 t) 920-337-4300 prior@norbertines.org www.norbertines.org The Premonstratensian Fathers, NORBERT & CO., a nominee of The Premonstratensian Fathers, Norbertine Fathers and St. Norbert Abbey, Inc. Rt. Rev. Dane J. Radecki, O. Praem., Abbot; Rt. Rev. Gary J. Neville, O. Praem., Abbot; Rev. Bradley R. Vanden Branden, O. Praem., Prior; Rt. Rev. Jerome G. Tremel, O. Praem., Abbot; Rev. Onwuham Akpa, O. Praem., Priest; Rev. Xavier Amirtham, O. Praem., Priest; Rev. Sengole Arockia Dass, O. Praem., Priest; Rev. James T. Baraniak, O. Praem., Priest; Rev. Michael Brennan, O. Praem., Priest; Rev. Richard Chiles, O. Praem., Priest; Rev. Andrew G. Cribben, O. Praem., Priest; Rev. Kenneth DeGroot, O. Praem., Priest; Rev. Matthew Dougherty, O. Praem., Priest; Rev. Mark D. Falcone, O. Praem, Priest; Rev. Roderick R. Fenzl, O. Praem., Priest; Rev. Robert K. Finnegan, O.Praem., Priest; Rev. Jay J. Fostner, O. Praem., Priest; Rev. Michael F. Frisch, O. Praem., Priest; Rev. John P. Kastenholz, O. Praem., Priest; Rev. David M. Komatz, O. Praem., Priest; Rev. Patrick LaPacz, O. Praem., Priest; Rev. John P. MacCarthy, O. Praem., Priest; Rev. David R. McElroy, O. Praem., Priest; Rev. Norbert N'Zilamba, O. Praem., Priest; Rev. Jordan S. Neeck, O. Praem., Priest; Rev. James P. Neilson, O. Praem., Priest; Rev. Peter J. Renard, O. Praem., Priest; Rev. William H. Ribbens, O. Praem., Priest; Rev. Stephen J. Rossey, O. Praem., Priest; Rev. Timothy D. Shillcox, O.Praem., Priest; Rev. Jeremy Tobin, O. Praem., Priest; Rev. Johnathan F. Turba, O. Praem., Priest; Rev. Steven J. Vanden Boogard, O. Praem., Priest; Rev. Michael J. Weber, O. Praem., Priest; Bro. Steven J. Herro, O.Praem., Brother; Bro. Terrence R. Lauerman, O. Praem., Brother; Bro. Jacob Sircy, O. Praem., Brother; Brs.: 3; Priests: 32

National Shrine of St. Joseph - 123 Grant St., De Pere, WI 54115 t) (920) 337-4300 norbertines.org/joseph

MANITOWOC

Blessed Giles Friary - 1820 Grand Ave., Manitowoc, WI 54220 t) 920-684-5201 friarski@gmail.com (Franciscan Friars, Sacred Heart Province) Rev. Raymond Rickels, OFM, In Res.; Bro. Thomas Eaton, OFM, Staff; Bro. Christopher Neuman, OFM, In Res.; Bro. Earl Benz, OFM, In Res.; Rev. Vincent Callaghan, O.F.M., In Res.; Rev. Michael Crosby, O.F.M., In Res.; Rev. Michael Grawe, O.F.M., In Res.; Rev. Frank Kordek, OFM, Staff; Rev. Lester Kochlin, OFM, In Res.; Bro. Leonard Lawrence, O.F.M., In Res.; Rev. Vernon Olmer, OFM, In Res.; Rev. Paul Pare, OFM, In Res.; Rev. Kenneth Rosswog, O.F.M., In Res.; Rev. John Dombrowski, Supr.; Brs.: 4; Priests: 10

OSHKOSH

Community of Our Lady - 2804 Oakwood Ln., Oshkosh,

WI 54904-8406 t) 920-233-5633 communityofourlady@gmail.com www.ourladyofoshkosh.com (Diocesan Pious Union) Rev. Augustine Serafini; Priests: 2

PULASKI

Assumption of B.V.M. Friary - 143 E. Pulaski St., Pulaski, WI 54162-0100; Mailing: P.O. Box 100, Pulaski, WI 54162-0100 t) 920-822-8125 janet.maroszek@abvm.org; jgannonofm@thefranciscans.net www.franciscan-friars.org (Order of Friars Minor). Rev. Finian Zaucha, OFM, Supr.; Rev. James Gerard Gannon, OFM, Prov.; Bro. Michael May, OFM, In Res.; Bro. Joseph Molinari, OFM, In Res.; Rev. Warren Rector, OFM, In Res.; Rev. Everard Scesney, O.F.M., In Res.; Rev. Gerald A. Prusakowski, O.F.M., Chap.; Rev. Placid Stroik, O.F.M., Chap.; Rev. James Esser, O.F.M., Sacr. Min.; Rev. Ponciano Macabalo, ofm, Sacr. Min.; Rev. Carmen Scuderi, OFM, Sacr. Min.; Rev. Brendan Wroblewski, O.F.M., Sacr. Min.; Priests: 5

Friary - 143 E Pulaski St., Pulaski, WI 54162 Bro. Anthony Gancarz, O.F.M.; Bro. Andrew Giba, O.F.M.; Bro. Henry Kolbok, O.F.M.; Bro. Peter Rydza, O.F.M.; Bro. Robert Sembrat, O.F.M.; Bro. Gregory Stasinski, O.F.M.; Rev. Joachim Swarick, O.F.M.; Bro. Gerald Tokarz, O.F.M.;

NURSING / REHABILITATION / CONVALESCENCE / ELDERLY CARE [NUR]

GREEN BAY

St. Paul Elder Services, Inc. (McCormick Assisted Living) - 212 Iroquois Ave., Green Bay, WI 54301-1918; Mailing: 316 E 14th St., Kaukauna, WI 54130 t) 920-437-0883 sondran@stpaulelders.org www.mccormickassistedliving.com Sondra Norder, CEO; Asstd. Annu.: 85; Staff: 50

KAUKAUNA

St. Paul Elder Services, Inc. - 316 E. 14th St., Kaukauna, WI 54130 t) 920-766-6020 sondran@stpaulelders.org stpaulelders.org Sondra Norder, Pres.; Becky Reichelt, Vice. Pres.; Asstd. Annu.: 1,600; Staff: 415

St. Paul Home - 316 E 14th St., Kaukauna, WI 54130

St. Paul Manor - 224 E. 14th St., Kaukauna, WI 54130

St. Paul Villa - 316 E. 14th St., Kaukauna, WI 54130 t) (920) 766-6020

MANITOWOC

Felician Village (St. Mary's Home for the Aged, Inc.) - 1635 S. 21st St., Manitowoc, WI 54220-5652 t) 920-684-7171 bfricke@felicianvillage.org www.felicianvillage.org Frank Soltys, Pres.; Asstd. Annu.: 405; Staff: 200

Felician Village Inc. (The Gardens at Felician Village) - felicianvillage.org

St. Mary's Home for the Aged, Inc. (The Court at Felician Village) - lvoda@felicianvillage.org felicianvillage.org

St. Mary's Home for the Aged, Inc. (The Villa at Felician Village) - lvoda@felicianvillage.org felicianvillage.org

St. Mary's Home for the Aged, Inc. (St. Mary's at Felician Village) - felicianvillage.org

NEW LONDON

St. Joseph Residence, Inc., New London - 107 E. Beckert Rd., New London, WI 54961 t) 920-982-5354 gblank@sjrcares.org www.stjosephresidence.com Gidget Blank, CEO; Asstd. Annu.: 335; Staff: 130

St. Joseph Residence - The Washington Center, Inc. - 500 Washington St., New London, WI 54961; Mailing: 107 E. Beckert Rd., New London, WI 54961 t) 920-982-9201 gblank@sjrcares.org www.stjosephresidence.com Gidget Blank, CEO; Asstd. Annu.: 150; Staff: 22

NIAGARA

Maryhill Manor (SNF) - 501 Madison Ave., Niagara, WI 54151 t) 715-251-3172 maryhill@borderlandnet.net; ckaldor@maryhillmanor.org www.maryhillmanor.org Sponsored by School Sisters of St. Francis, Milwaukee. Lynne Crockford, Admin./CEO; Christy Sanford, Dir., Nursing; Asstd. Annu.: 85; Staff: 77

RETREAT HOUSES / RENEWAL CENTERS [RTR]

DE PERE

Norbertine Center for Spirituality - St. Norbert Abbey, 1016 N. Broadway, De Pere, WI 54115-2610 t) 920-337-4315 ncs@norbertines.org www.norbertines.org An Apostolate of the Norbertine Community of St. Norbert Abbey Rt. Rev. Dane J. Radecki, O. Praem., Abbot; Rev. Bradley R. Vanden Branden, O. Praem., Dir.; Rev. James P. Neilson, O. Praem., Dir.; Kathie Tilot, Dir.; Michael Poradek, Dir.;

GREEN BAY

The Diocesan Charismatic Renewal Center - 650 S Irwin Ave., Green Bay, WI 54301 t) 920-405-1960 dcrcgb@gmail.com charismaticrenewal.org Maximus Cabey, Liaison to the Bishop;

Teens Encounter Christ (TEC), Green Bay Chapter - TEC/St Joseph Church, 936 Ninth St, Green Bay, WI 54304; Mailing: Anchor of Hope TEC, PO Box 5715, De Pere, WI 54115 t) 920-445-6121 tecgreenbay@gmail.com www.anchorofhopetec.org Very Rev. Joel A. Sember, Dir.;

MENASHA

Mount Tabor Center (SPIRITUS Ministries) - 522 2nd St., Menasha, WI 54952-3112 t) 920-722-8918 annettehovie@spiritusministries.org; edenfoord@spiritusministries.org www.spiritusministries.org Eden Foord, Dir.; Katherine Foord, Dir.;

OSHKOSH

Jesuit Retreat House - 4800 Fahrnwald Rd., Oshkosh, WI 54902-7598 t) 920-231-9060 office@jesuitretreathouse.org www.jesuitretreathouse.org Legal Title: Jesuit Retreat House of Oshkosh, Inc. Rev. Mark A. Carr, S.J., Exec. Dir.; Sr. Susan Kusz, SND, Assoc. Dir.; Bro. Lee Colombino, S.J., Asst. Dir.; Rev. Eugene L. Donahue, S.J., Asst. Dir.; Rev. James R. Shea, S.J., Asst. Dir.; Rev. John L. Treloar, S.J., Asst. Dir.;

SHRINES [SHR]

NEW FRANKEN

The National Shrine of Our Lady of Good Help, Inc. - 4047 Chapel Dr., New Franken, WI 54229 t) 920-866-2571 info@championshrine.org www.championshrine.org Rev. Joseph R Aytona, CPM, Rector; Rev. Michael O French, CPM, Chap.; Rev. Thomas Reagan, Chap.; Don Warden, Dir.;

SPECIAL CARE FACILITIES [SPF]

APPLETON

Global Outreach, Inc. - 4815 Whitetail Way, Appleton, WI 54914 t) 920-540-3085 barbara.tota-boryczka@globaloutreachprogram.com www.globaloutreachprogram.com Pam Mullins, Pres.; Barbara Tota-Boryczka, Dir.; Tom Kropidlowski, Vice Pres.; Asstd. Annu.: 22; Staff: 3

An asterisk (*) denotes an organization that has established tax-exempt status directly with the IRS and is not covered by the USCCB Group Ruling.

Diocese of Greensburg

(Dioecesis Greensburgensis)

MOST REVEREND LARRY J. KULICK, J.C.L.

Bishop of Greensburg; ordained May 16, 1992; appointed Bishop of Greensburg December 18, 2020; installed February 11, 2021. Pastoral Center: 723 E. Pittsburgh St., Greensburg, PA 15601. T: 724-837-0901; F: 724-837-0857.

Pastoral Center: 723 E. Pittsburgh St., Greensburg, PA 15601. T: 724-837-0901; F: 724-837-0857.
www.catholicgbg.org

ESTABLISHED MARCH 10, 1951.

Square Miles 3,334.

Comprises the Counties of Armstrong, Fayette, Indiana and Westmoreland in the State of Pennsylvania.

For legal titles of parishes and diocesan institutions, consult the Chancery Office.

STATISTICAL OVERVIEW

Personnel
Bishop 1
Retired Bishops 1
Abbots 1
Retired Abbots 1
Priests: Diocesan Active in Diocese 32
Priests: Retired, Sick or Absent 46
Number of Diocesan Priests 78
Religious Priests in Diocese 141
Total Priests in your Diocese 219
Extern Priests in Diocese 20
Ordinations:
Diocesan Priests 1
Religious Priests 3
Permanent Deacons in Diocese 11
Total Brothers 41
Total Sisters 258

Parishes
Parishes 78
With Resident Pastor:
Resident Diocesan Priests 37
Resident Religious Priests 6
Without Resident Pastor:
Administered by Priests 28
Administered by Deacons 2
In the care of professed men religious other than Priests or Permanent Deacons 5
Professional Ministry Personnel:
Sisters 18
Lay Ministers 38

Welfare
Homes for the Aged 2
Total Assisted 544
Special Centers for Social Services 2
Total Assisted 14,415
Residential Care of Disabled 1
Total Assisted 62

Educational
Students from This Diocese 4
Diocesan Students in Other Seminaries 6
Seminaries, Religious 1
Total Seminarians 10
Colleges and Universities 2
Total Students 3,683
High Schools, Diocesan and Parish 2
Total Students 480
Elementary Schools, Diocesan and Parish 10
Total Students 2,163
Elementary Schools, Private 2
Total Students 126
Non-residential Schools for the Disabled 1
Total Students 65
Catechesis / Religious Education:
High School Students 1,102
Elementary Students 4,668
Total Students under Catholic Instruction 12,297
Teachers in Diocese:
Priests 5
Brothers 6
Sisters 9
Lay Teachers 517

Vital Statistics
Receptions into the Church:
Infant Baptism Totals 742
Minor Baptism Totals 18
Adult Baptism Totals 31
Received into Full Communion 171
First Communions 753
Confirmations 858
Marriages:
Catholic 224
Interfaith 79
Total Marriages 303
Deaths 1,995
Total Catholic Population 109,931
Total Population 627,967

LEADERSHIP

Pastoral Center - t) 724-837-0901 Rev. Msgr. Raymond E. Riffle, Vicar; Rev. Msgr. William R. Rathgeb, Vicar; Sheila R. Murray, CFO;
Vicar General - t) 724-837-0901 x1220 Rev. Msgr. Raymond E. Riffle, Vicar;
Chief Financial Officer - t) 724-837-0901 smurray@dioceseofgreensburg.org Sheila R. Murray, CFO;
Deaneries - t) 724-837-0901 x1220 Rev. Eric J. Dinga, Dean; Rev. James B. Morley, Dean; Rev. Kenneth G. Zaccagnini, Deanery III;
Vicar for Clergy - t) 724-834-7350 x2020 Rev. Msgr. James T. Gaston, Dir.;
Bishop's Liaison for Consecrated Life - t) 724-837-0901 Rev. Anthony J. Carbone;
Bishop's Representative for Matters Pertaining to Celebration of Mass in the Extraordinary Form - t) 724-479-3881 Rev. Matthew J. Morelli;
Tribunal - t) 724-837-0901 x1550 kpolosky@dioceseofgreensburg.org Rev. Msgr. William R. Rathgeb, Vicar; Rev. Anthony J. Carbone; Kathleen Polosky;
Judicial Vicar - t) 724-837-0901 Rev. Msgr. William R. Rathgeb;
Defender of Bond - t) 724-837-0901 x1550 Rev. David Kelly, O.S.B. (dkelly@dioceseofgreensburg.org); Rev. Daniel J. Ulishney;
Judges - t) 724-837-0901 x1550 kpolosky@dioceseofgreensburg.org Rev. Anthony J. Carbone; Rev. Richard J. Kosisko; Kathleen Polosky, Contact;
Advocate - Kathleen Polosky, Contact;
Notaries - Cindy J. Ozzello; Kathleen Polosky;
Tribunal Coordinator and Auditor - Kathleen Polosky, Contact;

ADMINISTRATION

Chancellor - t) 724-837-0901 Rev. Msgr. Raymond E. Riffle, Chancellor;

OFFICES AND DIRECTORS

Archives - t) 724-837-0901 Cindy J. Ozzello, Contact;
Athletics - t) 724-837-0901 Amanda Iwinski, CYO Athletic;
Catholic Charities - t) 724-837-1840 Melaney Hegyes, Dir. (mhegyes@dioceseofgreensburg.org); Heather P. Rady, Assoc. Dir.;
Catholic Charities of the Diocese of Greensburg, PA, Inc. - t) 724-837-1840 Melaney Hegyes, Dir. (mhegyes@dioceseofgreensburg.org);
Board of Trust Members - t) 724-837-1840 Thomas Gothie, Pres.; Ralph May Jr., Vice. Pres.; Charles Deluzio, Treas.;
The Catholic Foundation for the Diocese of Greensburg - t) 724-837-0901 Paul Puleo, Dir.;
Board of Trustees - Paul Mongell, Pres.; Paul A. Rocker Jr., Vice. Pres.; Shirley A. Makuta, Secy.;
Ex-Officio Trustees - Rev. Kenneth G. Zaccagnini; Rev. Paul A. Lisik; Rev. Michael J. Crookston;
College of Deans - t) 724-837-0901 x1220 Rev. Tyler J. Bandura, Dean; Rev. Michael J. Crookston, Deanery VII; Rev. Eric J. Dinga, Dean;
Diocese of Greensburg - Managing Directors - t) 724-837-0901 Dr. Nancy Rottler, Supt.; Melaney Hegyes, Dir.; Paul Puleo, Dir.;
Members of the Corporation - Paul Puleo, Mem.; Most Rev. Larry J. Kulick; Rev. Msgr. Raymond E. Riffle, Vicar;
The Catholic Institute of Greensburg - t) 724-837-0901 Sheila R. Murray, Contact;
Board of Members of the Corporation - Rev. Msgr. Raymond E. Riffle, Mem.;
Board of Trustees - Mark E. Lopushansky, Pres.; Mara Bradford, Dir.; Rev. John A. Moineau;
Catholic Relief Services Representative - c) 724-837-0901 Rev. Anthony J. Carbone, Contact; Rev. Daniel Carr, Contact (dcarr@dioceseofgreensburg.org);
Engineering and Facility Management Office - t) 724-552-2570; 724-837-0901 James Garvin, Dir. (jgarvin@dioceseofgreensburg.org);
Greensburg Catholic Accent and Communications, Inc. - t) 724-834-4010 Jennifer Mielie, Contact; Clifford Gorski, Contact (cgorski@dioceseofgreensburg.org);
Missions - t) 724-837-0901 x1334 Rev. Anthony J. Carbone, Dir.;
Office for Priestly Vocations - t) 724-837-0901 Rev. Tyler J. Bandura, Dir.;
Office for the Permanent Diaconate - t) 724-837-0901 Dcn. William J. Hisker, Dir. (whisker@dioceseofgreensburg.org); Dcn. William M. Newhouse, Asst. Dir.;
Office for Worship - t) 724-837-0901 Rev. Michael P. Sikon, Dir.;
Office of Catholic Schools - t) 724-837-0901 Dr. Nancy Rottler, Supt.; Barbara Sabo, Asst. Supt.; Benjamin Althof, Dir., Curriculum & Instruction (balthof@dioceseofgreensburg.org);
The Office of Communications and Evangelization - t) 724-834-4010 Jennifer Mielie, Chief Communications Officer & Mng. Dir. Evangelization; Clifford Gorski (cgorski@dioceseofgreensburg.org); John Zylka, Dir.;
Diocesan Catholic Scoutmaster - t) 412-372-4577 gsaletrik@dioceseofgreensburg.org Rev. E. George Saletrik;
Diocesan Ecumenical Office - t) 724-423-3777 Rev. James F. Podlesny, O.S.B.;
Office of Information Technology - t) 724-552-2500; 724-834-4010 Daniel Kissel, IT Support Specialist; Kirstin Meyer, IT Support Specialist; Joshua Secrist, IT Support Specialist;
Youth & Young Adult Ministry and Adult Initiation - t) 724-837-0901 x1247 Vincent J. Reilly, Dir.;

ADVISORY BOARDS, COMMISSIONS, COMMITTEES, AND COUNCILS

Bishop's Priests Council - t) 724-837-0901 x1220 Rev. Msgr. Raymond E. Riffle, Contact; Rev. Eric J. Dinga, Mem.; Rev. James B. Morley, Mem.;
College of Consultors - t) 724-837-0901 x1220 Most Rev. Larry J. Kulick; Rev. Msgr. Raymond E. Riffle, Vicar; Rev. Msgr. Michael J. Begolly, Mem. (mbegolly@dioceseofgreensburg.org);
Diocesan Pastoral Council (Vacant) -
Finance Council - t) 724-837-0901 Most Rev. Larry J. Kulick; Rev. Msgr. Raymond E. Riffle, Vicar; Sheila R. Murray, CFO;
Diocesan Representatives - Dr. Nancy Rottler, Supt.; Melaney Hegyes, Dir.; Paul Pulo, Dir.;

MISCELLANEOUS / OTHER OFFICES

Apostleship of Prayer (Vacant) -
Apostolate for the Deaf (Vacant) -
Bishop's Delegate - t) 724-837-0901 x1221 Robert J. Specht, Contact;
Catholic Business and Professional Women's Association - t) 724-763-9141 Rev. Eric J. Dinga, Moderator;
Catholic Daughters of America - t) 724-838-9480 Rev. Daniel L. Blout, Chap.;
Cemeteries - t) 724-837-0901 Rev. Msgr. Raymond E. Riffle, Contact;
Charismatic - t) 724-837-7129 c) 412-817-5465 John Hutchins; Kim Hutchins (hutchins@hssop.org);
Cursillo - t) 724-837-0901
Diocesan Council of Catholic Women - t) 724-763-9141 Denise Pencola; Rev. Eric J. Dinga, Spiritual Adv./Care Srvcs.;
Holy Childhood Association - t) 724-837-0901 Rev. Anthony J. Carbone, Dir.;
Holy Name Society - t) 724-479-3881 Rev. Matthew J. Morelli;
Legion of Mary - t) 724-763-1089 Rev. Alan W. Grote;
Pilgrimages - t) 814-446-5759 wlechnar@dioceseofgreensburg.org Rev. Msgr. Raymond E. Riffle, Contact;
Priests' Eucharistic League (Vacant) -
St. Luke Society for Health Care Professionals - t) 724-834-3710 Dcn. William J. Hisker, Chap. (whisker@dioceseofgreensburg.org);
St. Thomas More Society for Lawyers - t) 724-785-7781 Shirley Makuta, Contact;
St. Vincent de Paul Society - t) 724-423-4431 Rev. John A. Sedlak, Chap.;
Victim Assistance Coordinator - t) 724-837-1840 Paul A. Niemiec (pniemiec@dioceseofgreensburg.org);

PARISHES, MISSIONS, AND CLERGY

COMMONWEALTH OF PENNSYLVANIA

APOLLO

St. James the Greater - 109 Owens View Ave., Apollo, PA 15613 t) 724-478-4958 Rev. Vincent Zidak, O.S.B., Pst.; Pamela McCauley, DRE; CRP Stds.: 24

AVONMORE

St. Ambrose - 505 Cambria Ave., Avonmore, PA 15618; Mailing: P.O. Box 617, Avonmore, PA 15618 t) 724-697-4129 jharrold@dioceseofgreensburg.org www.partnerparishesmas.org Rev. John J. Harrold, Pst.; Dcn. Craig Gilbert; Grace Sikora, DRE; CRP Stds.: 12
St. Matthew - 505 Cambria Ave., Avonmore, PA 15618; Mailing: P.O. Box 617, Avonmore, PA 15618 t) 724-697-4129 jharrold@dioceseofgreensburg.org Rev. John J. Harrold, Pst.; Dcn. Craig Gilbert; CRP Stds.: 34

BELLE VERNON

St. Sebastian - 801 Broad Ave., Belle Vernon, PA 15012 t) 724-929-9300 stsebastian@dioceseofgreensburg.org Rev. Michael J. Crookston, Pst.; CRP Stds.: 50

BLAIRSVILLE

SS. Simon and Jude - 155 N. Brady St., Blairsville, PA 15717 t) 724-459-7103 www.saintsimonandjude.org Rev. Stephen R. Bugay, Pst.; Elaine Scherer, Pst. Assoc.; CRP Stds.: 48

BROWNSVILLE

St. Cecilia - c/o 118 Church St., Brownsville, PA 15417 t) 724-785-7781 ssealy@dioceseofgreensburg.org Rev. Efren C. Ambre, Pst.; Patty Craig, DRE; CRP Stds.: 7
The Historic Church of St. Peter - 300 Shaffner Ave., Brownsville, PA 15417; Mailing: 118 Church St., Brownsville, PA 15417 t) 724-785-7781 stpeterbrownsville@dioceseofgreensburg.org www.historicchurchofstpeter.org Rev. Efren C. Ambre, Pst.; Patty Craig, DRE; CRP Stds.: 70

CLYMER

Church of the Resurrection - 349 Morris St., Clymer, PA 15728-1266 t) 724-254-3041 cor@dioceseofgreensburg.org www.churchresurrection.org Rev. Philip White OFM Cap, OFM Cap, Par. Vicar; Rev. James B. Morley, Pst.; Dcn. Stephen Black; CRP Stds.: 105
Cameron's Bottom, Chapel of Church of the Resurrection, Clymer - Suppressed June 21, 1995.

CONNELLSVILLE

Immaculate Conception - c/o 116 S. Second St., Connellsville, PA 15425 t) 724-628-6840 llauffer@dioceseofgreensburg.org www.youghcatholic.org Rev. Peter Guardiano, Par. Vicar; Rev. Paul A. Lisik, Pst.; Rev. Julius U. Capongpongan, Par. Vicar; CRP Stds.: 53
St. John the Evangelist - c/o 116 S. Second St., Connellsville, PA 15425 t) 724-628-6840 llauffer@dioceseofgreensburg.org www.youghcatholic.org Rev. Peter Guardiano, Par. Vicar; Rev. Paul A. Lisik, Pst.; Rev. Julius U. Capongpongan, Par. Vicar; CRP Stds.: 16
St. Rita - 116 S. Second St., Connellsville, PA 15425 t) 724-628-6840 llauffer@dioceseofgreensburg.org youghcatholic.org Rev. Peter Guardiano, Par. Vicar; Rev. Paul A. Lisik, Pst.; Rev. Julius U. Capongpongan, Par. Vicar; CRP Stds.: 29

CORAL

Our Lady of the Assumption - 2434 Neal Rd., Coral, PA 15731; Mailing: P.O. Box G, 2434 Neal Rd, Coral, PA 15731 t) 724-479-9542 cmarcoline@dioceseofgreensburg.org; khenry@dioceseofgreensburg.org www.olaparishpa.org Rev. John A. Pavlik, O.F.M. Cap., Pst.; Cindy Marcoline, DRE; CRP Stds.: 43

CRABTREE

St. Bartholomew - 2538 State Rte. 119, Crabtree, PA 15624; Mailing: P.O. Box A, Crabtree, PA 15624 t) 724-834-0709 jmatro@dioceseofgreensburg.org www.stbart@dioceseofgreensburg.org Rev. Justin M. Matro, O.S.B., Pst.; Rev. Thomas Acklin, O.S.B., In Res.; Eric Kocian, DRE; Becky Rock, Bus. Mgr.; CRP Stds.: 59

DELMONT

St. John Baptist de La Salle - 497 Athena Dr., Delmont, PA 15626; Mailing: 5900 Kennedy Ave, Export, PA 15632 t) 724-327-0647 dulishney@dioceseofgreensburg.org; mbloch@dioceseofgreensburg.org www.stjohnstmary.net Partnered with St. Mary, Export. Rev. Daniel J. Ulishney, Pst.; Dcn. F. Daniel Frescura; Xenia Yelovich, Music Min.; Joann Giuffre, DRE; Michele Bloch, Bus. Mgr.; CRP Stds.: 51

DERRY

St. Joseph - 117 S. Ligonier St., Derry, PA 15627 t) 724-694-5359 slamendola@dioceseofgreensburg.org Rev. Salvatore R. Lamendola, Pst.; Sr. Charlene Ozanick, C.S.S.F., Pst. Assoc.; Betty Wechtenhiser, DRE; CRP Stds.: 69

St. Martin - c/o 117 S. Ligonier St., Derry, PA 15627 t) 724-694-5359 slamendola@dioceseofgreensburg.org Sr. Charlene Ozanick, C.S.S.F., Pst. Assoc.; Rev. Salvatore R. Lamendola, Pst.; Betty Wechtenhiser, DRE; CRP Stds.: 30

DONEGAL

St. Raymond of the Mountains - 170 School House Ln., Donegal, PA 15628; Mailing: P.O. Box 330, Donegal, PA 15628 t) 724-593-7479 tfederline@dioceseofgreensburg.org www.straymondchurch.org Rev. Anthony A. Onoko, Pst.; Bill Pospisil, DRE; CRP Stds.: 37

DUNBAR

St. Aloysius - 459 Ranch Rd., Dunbar, PA 15431 t) 724-277-4236 plisik@dioceseofgreensburg.org Rev. Peter Guardiano, Par. Vicar; Rev. Paul A. Lisik, Pst.; Rev. Julius U. Capongpongan, Par. Vicar; CRP Stds.: 20

EAST BRADY

St. Patrick - 915 State Route 68, East Brady, PA 16028 t) 724-526-5079 stpatrick@dioceseofgreensburg.org; mseybert@dioceseofgreensburg.org www.stpatrickbradysbend.org Rev. Victor Baguna, Pst.; Mary Anne Seybert, DRE; CRP Stds.: 43

EAST VANDERGRIFT

Our Lady, Queen of Peace - 400 Kennedy Ave., East Vandergrift, PA 15629; Mailing: P.O. Box 429, East Vandergrift, PA 15629 t) 724-567-7603; 724-478-4958 (St. James) vzidek@dioceseofgreensburg.org; dsummerhill@dioceseofgreensburg.org Rev. Vincent E. Zidek, O.S.B., Pst.; Pamela McCauley, DRE; CRP Stds.: 11

EVERSON

St. Joseph - 200 Painter St., Everson, PA 15631; Mailing: c/o 416 S Broadway, Scottdale, PA 15683 t) 724-887-6321 ealforque@dioceseofgreensburg.org www.stjohnsandstjosephs.org Polish Rev. Elmer Alforque, Admin.; CRP Stds.: 6

EXPORT

St. Mary - 5900 Kennedy Ave., Export, PA 15632 t) 724-327-0647 dulishney@dioceseofgreensburg.org; mbloch@dioceseofgreensburg.org www.stjohnstmary.net Partnered with St. John Baptist de La Salle, Delmont Rev. Daniel J. Ulishney, Pst.; Dcn. F. Daniel Frescura; Xenia Yelovich, Music Min.; Joann Giuffre, DRE; Michele Bloch, Bus. Mgr.; CRP Stds.: 24

FAIRCHANCE

SS. Cyril and Methodius - 50 N Morgantown St., Fairchance, PA 15436 t) 724-564-7436 ddorula@dioceseofgreensburg.org Rev. Douglas E. Dorula, Pst.; Rev. Liberato Ortega, Par. Vicar; Rev. Michael J. Crookston, Admin.; CRP Stds.: 19

FARMINGTON

St. Joan of Arc - 3523 National Pike, Farmington, PA 15437; Mailing: PO Box 92, Farmington, PA 15437 t) 724-329-4522 stjoanofarcchurch@dioceseofgreensburg.org www.sjoafarmington.org Rev. James F. Petrovsky, Pst.; CRP Stds.: 7

FORD CITY

Christ, Prince of Peace Parish - 718 Fourth Ave., Ford City, PA 16226 t) 724-763-2521 (CRP); 724-763-9141 Rev. Eric J. Dinga, Pst.; Rev. Alan W. Grote, Par. Vicar; Darlene Scopel, DRE; CRP Stds.: 71

St. Lawrence - c/o 718 Fourth Ave., Ford City, PA 16226 t) 724-763-7973 (CRP); 724-763-9141 apolczynski@dioceseofgreensburg.org Rev. Eric J. Dinga, Pst.; Rev. Alan W. Grote, In Res.; Paula Sypulski, DRE; CRP Stds.: 26

Nicholson Run, Guardian Angel Cemetery and Chapel - Cadogan-Slatelick Rd., Kittanning, PA 16201

FREEPORT

St. Mary - 608 High St., Freeport, PA 16229 t) 724-295-2281 ggente@dioceseofgreensburg.org www.stmaryfreeport.com Rev. Msgr. Gilbert C. Gente, Pst.; CRP Stds.: 151

GREENSBURG

Blessed Sacrament Cathedral - 300 N. Main St., Greensburg, PA 15601 t) (724) 834-3710 blessedsacramentcathedral@dioceseofgreensburg.org www.blessedsacramentcathedral.org Rev. Msgr. Raymond E. Riffle, Rector; Rev. Christopher James Pujol, Par. Vicar; Katie Zuzik, Pst. Assoc.; Sr. Jean Marie Vonder Haar, ASCJ, DRE; Dcn. William J. Hisker; Christopher Pardini, Dir.; CRP Stds.: 216

St. Benedict - 260 Bruno Rd., Greensburg, PA 15601 t) 724-838-9480 asabol@dioceseofgreensburg.org stbenchurch.org Rev. Daniel L. Blout, Pst.; Rev. Samuel Pinheiro, OSB, Par. Vicar; Renie Prengaman, Youth Min.; Michele Ruby, Youth Min.; Paula Aiello, DRE; CRP Stds.: 51

St. Bruno - 1715 Poplar St., Greensburg, PA 15601 t) 724-836-0690 afiaschetti@dioceseofgreensburg.org www.stbruno@dioceseofgreensburg.org Rev. Lawrence L. Manchas, Admin.; Rev. Peter Augustine Pierjok, O.S.B., Sacr. Min.; Dcn. John D. Zombar; Emma B Sarsfield, DRE; CRP Stds.: 29

Our Lady of Grace - 1011 Mt. Pleasant Rd., Greensburg, PA 15601 t) 724-838-9480 dblout@dioceseofgreensburg.org www.ourladyofgracechurch.org Rev. Daniel L. Blout, Pst.; Rev. Samuel Pinheiro, OSB, Par. Vicar; Marisa Cazden, Music Min.; Katrina Coleman, DRE; CRP Stds.: 188

St. Paul - 824 Carbon Rd., Greensburg, PA 15601 t) 724-834-6880 jmosser@dioceseofgreensburg.org stpaul@dioceseofgreensburg.org Rev. Lawrence L. Manchas, Pst.; Rev. Peter Augustine Pierjok, O.S.B., Sacr. Min.; Dcn. John D. Zombar; CRP Stds.: 47

HARRISON CITY

St. Barbara - 111 Raymaley Rd., Harrison City, PA 15636 t) 724-744-7474 jshepherd@dioceseofgreensburg.org; smele@dioceseofgreensburg.org www.stbarbara.org Rev. Michael P. Sikon, Pst.; Joan Duncan, DRE; CRP Stds.: 408

HERMINIE

St. Edward - 120 St. Edward Ln., Herminie, PA 15637 t) 724-446-5197 stedward@dioceseofgreensburg.org www.saint-edward.org Rev. Vincent A. Yee Concepcion (Philippines), Pst.; Dcn. Robert W. Stauffer; CRP Stds.: 58

INDIANA

St. Bernard of Clairvaux - 200 Clairvaux Dr., Indiana, PA 15701 t) 724-465-2210 x113 (CRP); 724-465-2210 www.saintbernardparish.org Rev. Richard Owens, OFM, Cap, Pst.; Rev. Andrew Corriente, OFM Cap, Par. Vicar; Rachel Digmon, Youth Min.; Jessica Thompson, CRE; CRP Stds.: 143

St. Thomas More University Parish - 1200 Oakland Ave., Indiana, PA 15701 t) 724-463-2277 dcawley@dioceseofgreensburg.org www.stmup.org (Newman Center) Rev. Richard Owens, OFM, Cap, Pst.; Rev. Andrew Corriente, OFM Cap, Par. Vicar; Cindy Schillinger, Pst. Assoc.; Rachel Digmon, Youth Min.; Mary Beth Palko, DRE; CRP Stds.: 160

IRWIN

Immaculate Conception - 308 Second St., Irwin, PA 15642 t) 724-863-9550 jmoineau@dioceseofgreensburg.org www.icirwin.org/ Rev. John A. Moineau, Pst.; Rev. Roniel Bantugan Duenas, Assoc. Pst.; Dcn. Jeffrey Cieslewicz; CRP Stds.: 483

JEANNETTE

Ascension - 615 Division St., Jeannette, PA 15644; Mailing: C/o 504 Cowan Ave., Jeannette, PA 15644 t) 724-523-2560 www.ascensionsacredheartchurches.org Dcn. William M. Newhouse, Admin.; John Ridilla, DRE; Rev. Job J. Foote, O.S.B., Par. Vicar; CRP Stds.: 19

Sacred Heart - 504 Cowan Ave., Jeannette, PA 15644 t) 724-523-2560 shjeannette@dioceseofgreensburg.org Dcn. William M. Newhouse, Admin.; Rev. Job J. Foote, O.S.B., Par. Vicar; CRP Stds.: 14

KENT

Church of the Good Shepherd - 100 Good Shepherd Dr., Kent, PA 15752-0099; Mailing: P.O. Box 99, Kent, PA 15752-0099 t) 724-479-3881 goodshepherd@dioceseofgreensburg.org www.goodshepherdkent.org Rev. Matthew J. Morelli, Pst.; Carol Pike, Bus. Mgr.; CRP Stds.: 35

KITTANNING

St. Mary, Our Lady of Guadalupe - 101 W. High St., Kittanning, PA 16201 t) 724-548-7649 www.stmarykittanning.org Rev. Ronald Maquinana, Pst.; CRP Stds.: 81

LATROBE

Holy Family - 1200 Ligonier St., Latrobe, PA 15650 t) 724-539-3638 (CRP); 724-539-9751 ssutton@dioceseofgreensburg.org Rev. Richard J. Kosisko, Pst.; Rev. John M. Foriska, Sacr. Min.; Dcn. Michael J. Orange; Marlene Rafferty, DRE; CRP Stds.: 42

St. John the Evangelist - 306 St. John Dr., Latrobe, PA 15650 t) 724-537-8909 edinga@dioceseofgreensburg.org Rev. Richard J. Kosisko, Admin.; Eva Japalucci, DRE; CRP Stds.: 13

St. Rose - 4969 Rte. 982, Latrobe, PA 15650 t) 724-537-3709 edinga@dioceseofgreensburg.org Rev. Rodel Molina, Admin.; Rev. Daniel C. Mahoney, In Res.; Eva Japalucci, DRE; CRP Stds.: 25

St. Vincent Basilica - 300 Fraser Purchase Rd., Latrobe, PA 15650 t) 724-539-8629 rulam@dioceseofgreensburg.org Rev. Richard Ulam, O.S.B., Pst.; CRP Stds.: 98

LEECHBURG

Christ the King - 125 Park Rd., Leechburg, PA 15656 t) 724-845-8191 www.ctkleechburg.org Partner Parish with Saint Gertrude Vandergrift PA Rev. James H. Loew, O.S.B., Pst.; Rev. Michael J. Sciberras, In Res.; CRP Stds.: 38

LIGONIER

Holy Trinity - 342 W. Main St., Ligonier, PA 15658 t) 724-238-6434 aevangeliste@dioceseofgreensburg.org; acarbone@dioceseofgreensburg.org www.holytrinityligonier.org Rev. Anthony J. Carbone, Pst.; Dcn. Michael P. Dargay; CRP Stds.: 62

LOWER BURRELL

St. Margaret Mary - 3055 Leechburg Rd., Lower Burrell, PA 15068 t) 724-335-2336 ssmp@dioceseofgreensburg.org Rev. Kenneth G. Zaccagnini, Pst.; Rev. Roselo Melloria, Par. Vicar; Rev. Segundino R. Laude, Par. Vicar; Donna Misak, Pst. Assoc.; CRP Stds.: 106

MASONTOWN

Saint Francis of Assisi - 101 W. Church Ave., Masontown, PA 15461 t) 724-583-7866 sfoafayette@dioceseofgreensburg.org sfoafayette.org Rev. Marlon Libres Pates, Pst.; CRP Stds.: 31

MONESSEN

The Epiphany of Our Lord - 44 Pennsylvania Blvd., Monessen, PA 15062 t) 724-684-7661 mcrookston@dioceseofgreensburg.org www.eolparish.com Rev. Michael J. Crookston, Dean; CRP Stds.: 41

MOUNT PLEASANT

St. Pius X - 740 W Walnut St, Mount Pleasant, PA 15666 t) 724-547-1911 jklocek@dioceseofgreensburg.org www.mpcatholicchurches.org Rev. Paul A. Lisik, Admin.; Rev. Daniel Carr, Par. Vicar; Cheryl Hall, Youth Min.; CRP Stds.: 111

Visitation of the Blessed Virgin Mary - 740 W Walnut St., Mount Pleasant, PA 15666 t) 724-547-1911 jklocek@dioceseofgreensburg.org www.mpcatholicchurches.org Rev. Paul A. Lisik, Admin.; Rev. Daniel Carr, Par. Vicar; Cheryl Hall, Youth Min.; CRP Stds.: 53

MURRYSVILLE

Mother of Sorrows - 4202 Old William Penn Hwy., Murrysville, PA 15668 t) 724-733-8870 jretter@dioceseofgreensburg.org www.motherofsorrowschurch.org Rev. Msgr. Michael J. Begolly, Pst.; Jacob Gindhart, Pst. Assoc.; Elizabeth Haberstoh, Pst. Assoc.; Rev. Anthony W. Ditto, Sacr. Min.; Erin Colcombe, DRE; CRP Stds.: 400

NEW ALEXANDRIA

St. James - 306 Saint James Ln., New Alexandria, PA 15670 t) 724-668-2829 lkulick@dioceseofgreensburg.org www.stjamesnewalexandria.org Rev. Tyler J. Bandura, Pst.; CRP Stds.: 7

NEW KENSINGTON

St. Joseph - 1125 Leishman Ave., New Kensington, PA 15068; Mailing: 100 Freeport Rd., New Kensington, PA 15068 t) 724-337-6412 mbegolly@dioceseofgreensburg.org Rev. Kenneth G. Zaccagnini, Pst.; Rev. Roselo Melloria, Par. Vicar; Rev. Segundino R. Laude, Par. Vicar; CRP Stds.: 45

St. Mary of Czestochowa - 857 Kenneth Ave., New Kensington, PA 15068; Mailing: 100 Freeport Rd., New Kensington, PA 15068 t) 724-335-8212 mbegolly@dioceseofgreensburg.org Rev. Kenneth G. Zaccagnini, Pst.; Rev. Roselo Melloria, Par. Vicar; Rev. Segundino R. Laude, Par. Vicar; Sr. Mary Carol Kardell, C.S.S.F., Pst. Min./Coord.; Deborah Discello, DRE; CRP Stds.: 3

Mt. St. Peter - 100 Freeport Rd., New Kensington, PA 15068 t) 724-335-9877 mbegolly@dioceseofgreensburg.org Rev. Kenneth G. Zaccagnini, Pst.; Rev. Rodel Molina, Par. Vicar; Rev. Segundino R. Laude, Par. Vicar; CRP Stds.: 200

NORTH HUNTINGDON

St. Agnes - 11400 St. Agnes Ln., North Huntingdon, PA 15642 t) 724-863-2626 stagnes@dioceseofgreensburg.org www.stagneschurch.info Rev. Teodoro Cortezano, Admin.; Dcn. William Wilson; Mary Blythe, DRE; CRP Stds.: 222

St. Elizabeth Ann Seton - 200 Leger Rd, North Huntingdon, PA 15642 t) 724-864-6364 www.seasnh.org Rev. John A. Moineau, Pst.; Rev. Roniel Duenas, Par. Vicar; Dcn. Jeffrey Cieslewicz, DRE; CRP Stds.: 188

PERRYOPOLIS

St. John the Baptist - 3332 Pittsburgh Rd., Perryopolis, PA 15473 t) 724-736-4442 sjbperry@dioceseofgreensburg.org www.sjbperry.org Rev. Rodolfo P. Mejia Jr., Pst.; Scott Martin, DRE; Adelle Slebodnik, Bus. Mgr.; CRP Stds.: 135

POINT MARION

St. Hubert - 9 Sadler St., Point Marion, PA 15474; Mailing: 50 N Morgantown St, Fairchance, PA 15436 t) 724-564-7436 ddorula@dioceseofgreensburg.org Rev. Douglas E. Dorula, Pst.; Rev. Liberato Ortega, Par. Vicar; Rev. Michael J. Crookston, Admin.; CRP Stds.: 2

ROSTRAVER TOWNSHIP

St. Anne - 1870 Rostraver Rd., Rostraver Township, PA 15012 t) 724-872-3486 (CRP); 724-842-3555 stanne@dioceseofgreensburg.org www.stannerostraver.org Rev. David Nazimek, Pst.; CRP Stds.: 190

SCOTTDALE

St. John the Baptist - 500 S. Broadway, Scottdale, PA 15683; Mailing: c/o 416 S Broadway, Scottdale, PA 15683 t) 724-887-6321 ealforque@dioceseofgreensburg.org; sjbsje@dioceseofgreensburg.org stjosephsandstjohns.org/pages/default.aspx Rev. Elmer Alforque, Admin.; CRP Stds.: 31

SEWARD

Holy Family - 425 Bridge St., Seward, PA 15954 t) 814-446-5759 holyfamilysewardadmin@dioceseofgreensburg.org Rev. William J. Lechnar, Pst.; Danielle Cribbs, Parish Life Coord.; CRP Stds.: 44

SLICKVILLE

St. Sylvester - 3028 Rt. 819, Slickville, PA 15684; Mailing: Box 307, Slickville, PA 15684 t) 724-468-5794 jharrold@dioceseofgreensburg.org Rev. John J. Harrold, Admin.; Dcn. Craig Gilbert; CRP Stds.: 2

TRAFFORD

St. Regis - 517 Homewood Ave., Trafford, PA 15085 t) 412-372-4577 gsaletrik@dioceseofgreensburg.org; fgradisek@dioceseofgreensburg.org www.stregistrafford.org Florence Gradisek, Liturgy Dir.; Karen McDade, DRE; Alex Roman, Bus. Mgr.; CRP Stds.: 130

UNIONTOWN

St. John the Evangelist - 88 S. Pennsylvania Ave., Uniontown, PA 15401 t) 724-437-4441 bsabatini@dioceseofgreensburg.org Rev. Anthony J. Klimko, Pst.; Rev. Dick Anthony Cortado, Par. Vicar; Rev. Alvin B. Aberion, Par. Vicar; CRP Stds.: 99

St. Joseph - 180 Old Walnut Hill Rd., Uniontown, PA 15401 t) 724-438-2341 (CRP); 724-437-4441 aklimko@dioceseofgreensburg.org Rev. Anthony J. Klimko, Pst.; Rev. Dick Anthony Cortado, Par. Vicar; Rev. Alvin B. Aberion, Par. Vicar; Marlene Bandzuch, DRE; CRP Stds.: 62

Nativity of the Blessed Virgin Mary - 61 N. Mount Vernon Ave., Uniontown, PA 15401 t) 724-437-1512 aklimko@dioceseofgreensburg.org Rev. Anthony J. Klimko, Pst.; Rev. Dick Anthony Cortado, Par. Vicar; Rev. Alvin B. Aberion, Par. Vicar; CRP Stds.: 19

St. Therese, the Little Flower of Jesus - 61 Mill St., Uniontown, PA 15401 t) 724-438-2341 bsabatini@dioceseofgreensburg.org Rev. Anthony J. Klimko, Pst.; Rev. Dick Anthony Cortado, Par. Vicar; Rev. Alvin B. Aberion, Par. Vicar; Marlene Bandzuch, DRE; CRP Stds.: 119

UNITED

St. Florian - 4261 Rt. 981, United, PA 15689; Mailing: P.O. Box 187, United, PA 15689 t) 724-423-4431 jsedlak@dioceseofgreensburg.org www.saintflorian.org Rev. John A. Sedlak, Pst.; Joseph Dreliszak, Dir.; CRP Stds.: 21

VANDERGRIFT

St. Gertrude - 303 Franklin Ave., Vandergrift, PA 15690 t) 724-568-2331 sgcatholic.org Partner Parish with Christ the King Leechburg PA Rev. James H. Loew, O.S.B., Pst.; Rev. Michael J. Sciberras, Sacr. Min.; CRP Stds.: 44

WEST NEWTON

Holy Family - 225 N. Second St., West Newton, PA 15089 t) 724-872-2106 (CRP); 724-872-6123 dnazimek@dioceseofgreensburg.org Rev. David Nazimek, Pst.; Michalene Lovato, DRE; CRP Stds.: 16

WHITNEY

St. Cecilia - 218 St. Cecilia Rd., Whitney, PA 15693; Mailing: P.O. Box 80, Whitney, PA 15693 t) 724-423-3777 stceciliawhitney@dioceseofgreensburg.org www.saintcecilia.net Rev. James F. Podlesny, O.S.B., Admin.; Mary Stoner, DRE; CRP Stds.: 35

YATESBORO

St. Mary - 111 Second St., Yatesboro, PA 16263; Mailing: P.O. Box 327, Yatesboro, PA 16263 t) 724-783-7191 bfrailey@dioceseofgreensburg.org; sacredmary@dioceseofgreensburg.org www.stmaryyatesboro.org Rev. Ronald Maquinana, Pst.; Bonnie Frailey, DRE; CRP Stds.: 31

YOUNGSTOWN

Sacred Heart - 421 Main St, Youngstown, PA 15696; Mailing: P.O. Box 328, Youngstown, PA 15696 t) 724-537-7358; (724) 423-3777 (Parish Office) shyoungstown@dioceseofgreensburg.org www.sacredheart-online.com Rev. James F. Podlesny, O.S.B., Pst.; Mary Stoner, DRE; CRP Stds.: 12

YOUNGWOOD

Holy Cross - 711 Depot St., Youngwood, PA 15697 t) 724-925-7811 ssistek@dioceseofgreensburg.org; rrodriguez@dioceseofgreensburg.org www.holycrossyoungwood.org/ Rev. Rogelio Rodriguez, Pst.; Jennifer Kirshner, CRE; Scott C Sistek, Bus. Mgr.; CRP Stds.: 60

YUKON

Seven Dolors - 102 Center St., Yukon, PA 15698; Mailing: P.O. Box 308, Yukon, PA 15698 t) 724-722-3141 gsekerchak@dioceseofgreensburg.org Rev. Vincent A. Yee Concepcion (Philippines), Pst.; Dcn. Robert W. Stauffer; CRP Stds.: 9

SCHOOLS: PRESCHOOL THRU HIGH SCHOOL

SCHOOLS

COMMONWEALTH OF PENNSYLVANIA

BELLE VERNON

St. Sebastian Regional School - (PAR) (Grades PreK-7) 815 Broad Ave., Belle Vernon, PA 15012 t) 724-929-5143 caiello@sssbv.org Carole Aiello, Prin.; Stds.: 206; Lay Tchrs.: 16

CONNELLSVILLE

Conn-Area Catholic School - (PAR) (Grades PreK-6) 613 E. Crawford Ave., Connellsville, PA 15425 t) 724-628-5090 csolan@connareacatholic.org www.connareacatholic.org Cecilia Solan, Prin.; Stds.: 151; Lay Tchrs.: 11

FORD CITY

Divine Redeemer School - (PAR) (Grades PreK-6) 726 Fourth Ave., Ford City, PA 16226 t) 724-763-3761 Dr. John A. Giancola Jr., Prin.; Stds.: 128; Lay Tchrs.: 12

GREENSBURG

Aquinas Academy - (PAR) (Grades PreK-6) 340 N. Main St., Greensburg, PA 15601 t) 724-834-7940 info@aquinasacademy.org Kelly Watkins, Prin.; Michelle Finoli, Librn.; Stds.: 251; Lay Tchrs.: 19

Clelian Heights School for Exceptional Children (Clelian Heights, Inc., Apostles of the Sacred Heart of Jesus) - (PAR) (Grades K-12) 135 Clelian Heights Ln., Greensburg, PA 15601 t) 724-837-8120 clelian@aol.com www.clelianheights.org Rev. Anthony J. Grossi, O.S.B., Chap.; Sr. Charlene Celli, A.S.C.J., Prin.; Sr. Deborah Lopez, A.S.C..J., Pres.; Stds.: 62; Sr. Tchrs.: 7; Lay Tchrs.: 116

INDIANA

St. Bernard Regional School - (PAR) (Grades PreK-8) 300 Clairvaux Dr., Indiana, PA 15701 t) 724-465-7139 dswope@dioceseofgreensburg.org Tina Bucci, Prin.; Stds.: 132; Lay Tchrs.: 11

LATROBE

Christ the Divine Teacher School - (PAR) (Grades PreK-8) 323 Chestnut St., Latrobe, PA 15650 t) 724-539-3558 cdt@cdtschool.org www.cdtschool.org Teresa Tallarico, Prin.; Stds.: 205; Lay Tchrs.: 17

MURRYSVILLE
Mother of Sorrows School - (PAR) (Grades PreK-8) 3264 Evergreen Dr., Murrysville, PA 15668 t) 724-733-8840 tszmed@mosschool.org www.mosschool.org Theresa A. Szmed, Prin.; Stds.: 386; Lay Tchrs.: 27

NEW KENSINGTON
Mary Queen of Apostles - (PAR) (Grades PreK-8) 110 Elmtree Rd., New Kensington, PA 15068 t) 724-339-4411 mqa@mqaschool.org www.mqaschool.org (Regional School) Catherine M. Collett, Prin.; Stds.: 264; Lay Tchrs.: 19

NORTH HUNTINGDON
Queen of Angels School/The Bishop Anthony G. Bosco Center - (PAR) (Grades PreK-8) One Main St., North Huntingdon, PA 15642 t) 724-978-0144 info@queenofangelssch.org www.queenofangelssch.org Jennifer Filak, Prin.; Stds.: 228; Lay Tchrs.: 20

UNIONTOWN
St. John the Evangelist Regional Catholic School - (PAR) (Grades PreK-8) 52 Jefferson St., Uniontown, PA 15401 t) 724-438-8598 croskovensky@dioceseofgreensburg.org Christine Roskovensky, Prin.; Stds.: 213; Lay Tchrs.: 13

HIGH SCHOOLS

COMMONWEALTH OF PENNSYLVANIA

CONNELLSVILLE
Geibel Catholic Junior-Senior High School - (DIO) (Grades 7-12) 611 E. Crawford Ave., Connellsville, PA 15425 t) 724-628-5600 geibelinfo@geibelcatholic.org www.geibelcatholic.org Sr. Christine Kiley, A.S.C.J., Campus Min.; Rev. Julius U. Capongpongan, Chap.; Robert Fetter, Prin.; Stds.: 102; Lay Tchrs.: 13

GREENSBURG
Greensburg Central Catholic High School Jr./Sr. High School - (DIO) (Grades 7-12) 911 Armory Dr., Greensburg, PA 15601 t) 724-834-0310 info@gcchs.org www.gcchs.org Kevin Frye, Prin.; Carol Whalen, Librn.; Stds.: 378; Lay Tchrs.: 32

INSTITUTIONS LOCATED IN DIOCESE

COLLEGES & UNIVERSITIES [COL]

GREENSBURG
Seton Hill University - 1 Seton Hill Dr., Greensburg, PA 15601 t) 724-834-2200 admit@setonhill.edu www.setonhill.edu Sisters of Charity of Seton Hill. Mary C. Finger, Pres.; Sr. Susan Yochum, S.C., Provost; Sr. Maureen O'Brien, S.C., Dir.; Stds.: 2,308; Lay Tchrs.: 99; Sr. Tchrs.: 2

LATROBE
Saint Vincent College Corporation - 300 Fraser Purchase Rd., Latrobe, PA 15650-2690 t) 724-805-2271 president@stvincent.edu www.stvincent.edu Rev. Paul R. Taylor, O.S.B., Pres.; Rev. Philip Kanfush, OSB, CFO; Rt. Rev. Martin R. Bartel, O.S.B., Abbot; Bro. David Kelly, O.S.B., Librn.; Stds.: 1,375; Bro. Tchrs.: 3; Lay Tchrs.: 83; Pr. Tchrs.: 6

CONVENTS, MONASTERIES, AND RESIDENCES FOR WOMEN [CON]

GREENSBURG
Apostles of the Sacred Heart of Jesus - 135 Clelian Heights Ln., Greensburg, PA 15601-6665 t) 724-837-8120 www.clelianheights.org Sr. Charlene Celli, A.S.C.J., Supr.; Rev. Anthony J. Grossi, O.S.B., Chap.; Srs.: 9

Benedictine Nuns - St. Emma Monastery, 1001 Harvey Ave., Greensburg, PA 15601-1494 t) 724-834-3060 benedictinenuns@stemma.org www.stemma.org Sisters of St. Benedict of Westmoreland Co. Mother Mary Anne Noll, O.S.B., Prioress; Sr. Maria Johanna Uhlott, OSB, Subprior; Srs.: 5

Sisters of Charity of Seton Hill, United States Province - 144 DePaul Center Rd., Greensburg, PA 15601 t) 724-836-0406 ejohnston@scsh.org www.scsh.org Sr. Mary Norbert Long, SC, Pres.; Srs.: 111

Sisters of Charity of Seton Hill, United States Province Greensburg, Pennsylvania (DePaul Center) - 144 DePaul Center Rd., Greensburg, PA 15601 t) 724-836-0406 www.scsh.org Sr. Mary Norbert Long, SC, Prov.; Srs.: 111

Sisters of Charity of Seton Hill, Caritas Christi Motherhouse - 129 DePaul Center Rd., Greensburg, PA 15601 t) 724-853-7948 Sr. Donna Marie Leiden, SC, Admin.;

Sisters of Charity of Seton Hill, United States Province, Doran Hall - t) 724-837-8645

Sisters of Charity of Seton Hill, United States Province, Ennis Hall - 443 Mt. Thor Rd., Greensburg, PA 15601 t) (724) 836-7940 Rev. Msgr. William R. Rathgeb, Chap.;

LATROBE
Discalced Carmelite Nuns - 5206 Center Dr., Latrobe, PA 15650-5204 t) 724-539-1056 contact@latrobecarmel.org www.latrobecarmel.org Carmel of the Assumption Sr. Marie Elizabeth Krug, OCD, Prioress; Srs.: 9

LEECHBURG
Catechist Sisters of Mary Immaculate Help of Christians - 118 Park Rd., Leechburg, PA 15656 t) 724-845-2828 lbgsmi@gmail.com Sr. Jossy Jacob, Admin.; Srs.: 5

MOUNT PLEASANT
Sisters of Charity of the Immaculate Conception of Ivrea - Immaculate Virgin of Miracles Convent, 268 Prittstown Rd., Mount Pleasant, PA 15666 t) 724-887-6753 sr.letizia@vernamontessorischool.org Sr. Angelina Grimoldi, S.C.I.C., Supr.; Srs.: 8

ENDOWMENTS / FOUNDATIONS / TRUSTS [EFT]

GREENSBURG
Sisters of Charity of Seton Hill, United States Province Charitable Trust for the Aged, Infirmed and Disabled Vowed Members - 144 DePaul Center Rd., Greensburg, PA 15601 t) 724-836-0406 x6643 ejohnston@scsh.org www.scsh.org Sr. Eileen Johnston, SC, Contact;

LATROBE
Benedictine Society of St. Vincent Archabbey, O.S.B., Charitable Trust - 300 Fraser Purchase Rd., Latrobe, PA 15650 Rt. Rev. Martin R. Bartel, O.S.B., Abbot;

MISCELLANEOUS [MIS]

GREENSBURG
Christ Our Shepherd Center - 2900 Seminary Dr., Greensburg, PA 15601 t) 724-834-7350 jgarvin@dioceseofgreensburg.org www.christourshepherdcenter.org Diocesan Retreat and Conference Center, and Clergy Retirement Home James Garvin, Dir.; Rev. Msgr. Richard G. Curci, Dir., Neumann House Home for Retired Priests;

Elizabeth Seton Care Center - 129 DePaul Center Rd., Greensburg, PA 15601 t) 724-853-7948 x1192 tsalih@scsh.org Tonia Salih, Admin.;

Gilbert Straub Plaza - 620 Reamer Ave., Greensburg, PA 15601 t) 724-832-2280 jgrindle@scsh.org Sisters of Charity.

Magnificat - Greensburg, PA - 931 Mace St., Greensburg, PA 15601 c) 724-516-9955 plholtzer@gmail.com Patricia Holtzer, Coord.;

INDIANA
Clairvaux Commons - 100 Clairvaux Dr., Indiana, PA 15701 t) 724-349-2920 clairvau@verizon.net Christian Housing. Rev. Alan N. Polczynski, Dean;

LEECHBURG
Bishop Morrow Personal Care Home, Inc. - 118 Park Rd., Leechburg, PA 15656 t) 724-845-2828 lbgsmi@comcast.net Sisters of Mary Immaculate.

UNITED
Ladies of Charity - c/o St. Florian Church, United, PA 15689; Mailing: P.O. Box 187, United, PA 15689 t) 724-423-4431 jsedlak@dioceseofgreensburg.org Rev. John A. Sedlak, Spiritual Adv./Care Srvcs.;

MONASTERIES AND RESIDENCES FOR PRIESTS AND BROTHERS [MON]

BOLIVAR
Mount Carmel Hermitage - 244 Baileys Rd., Bolivar, PA 15923 t) 724-238-0423 smarr@winbeam.com Bro. Robert Ryba, O.Carm.; Brs.: 1

KITTANNING
Pauline Fathers Monastery - 543 Bunker Hill Rd., Kittanning, PA 16201; Mailing: P.O. Box 66, Kittanning, PA 16201 t) 724-763-1375 paulinefathers@comcast.net Rev. Raphael K. Glinkowski, O.S.P.P.E., In Res.; Rev. Edward Raymond Volz, O.S.P.P.E., Supr.; Rev. Mark Kreis, OSPPE, In Res.; Brs.: 3

LATROBE
Saint Vincent Archabbey - 300 Fraser Purchase Rd., Latrobe, PA 15650-2690 t) 724-532-6600 archabbot@stvincent.edu www.saintvincentarchabbey.org The Benedictine Society of Westmoreland County, Saint Vincent College Corporation, The Wimmer Corporation, The Saint Vincent Cemetery Corporation Rev. Thomas Acklin, O.S.B.; Rev. Joseph M. Adams, O.S.B., Subprior; Rev. Benoit Alloggia, O.S.B.; Rev. Shawn Matthew Anderson, O.S.B.; Rev. Michael Antonacci, O.S.B.; Rev. Kurt J. Belsole, O.S.B.; Rev. Brian D. Boosel, O.S.B.; Rev. Jude Brady, O.S.B.; Rev. Cristiano E. Brito, O.S.B.; Rev. Ananias G. Buccicone, O.S.B.; Rev. Aaron N. Buzzelli, O.S.B.; Rev. Cassian Edwards, OSB; Rev. Luke (Chien-Pang) Hsu, OSB; Rev. Augustine (Pinyu) Yang, OSB; Rev. Pio Adamonis, O.S.B., In Res.; Rev. Earl J. Henry, O.S.B., In Res.; Rt. Rev. Martin R. Bartel, O.S.B., Abbot; Rev. Frederick Byrne, O.S.B.; Rev. Ignatius Camello, O.S.B., In Res; Rev. Cornelius P. Chang, O.S.B.; Bro. Martinho Juan Jury Zevallos Chaves, O.S.B., In Res.; Rev. Athanasius C. Cherry, O.S.B.; Rev. Thomas More Sikora, O.S.B., In Res; Rev. Richard Chirichiello, O.S.B.; Rev. Wulfstan F. Clough, O.S.B.; Rev. Stephen P. Concordia, O.S.B.; Rev. Cyprian G. Constantine, O.S.B.; Rev. Lucas Torrell deAlmeida Costa, O.S.B.; Rev. Patrick T. Cronauer, O.S.B.; Rev. Vincent R. Crosby, O.S.B.; Rev. Thomas P. Curry, O.S.B.; Rev. Bonaventure J. Curtis, O.S.B.; Rev. Chad R. Ficorilli, O.S.B.; Rev. Job J. Foote, O.S.B.; Rev. Mario A. Fulgenzi, O.S.B.; Rev. Michael J. Gabler, O.S.B.; Rev. Ronald Gatman, O.S.B.; Rev. Campion P. Gavaler, O.S.B.; Rev. Joseph U. Gerg, O.S.B.; Rev. David R. Griffin, O.S.B.; Rev. Anthony J. Grossi, O.S.B.; Rev. Thomas M. Hart, O.S.B.; Rev. Isaac (Paul) Haywiser, O.S.B.; Rev. John Paul (Ryan) Heiser, O.S.B.; Rev. Boniface Hicks, O.S.B.; Rev. David Liang Ho, O.S.B.; Rev. Leon Hont, O.S.B.; Rev. Francis Jin, OSB; Rev. Philip M. Kanfush, O.S.B., Procurator; Rev. Robert Keffer, O.S.B., In Res.; Rev. Myron M. Kirsch, O.S.B.; David Klecker, O.S.B., In Res.; Rev. Rene M. Kollar, O.S.B.; Rev. Matthew T. Laffey, O.S.B.; Rev. Matthew Lambert, O.S.B.; Rev. Jeremiah (George) Lange, O.S.B.; Rev. Meinrad J. Lawson, O.S.B.; Bro. Dominic Leo, O.S.B., In Res.; Rev. Killian (Richard) Loch, O.S.B., Prior; Rev. James H. Loew, O.S.B.; Lawrence Shawn Machia, O.S.B, In Res.; Rev. Matthias Martinez, O.S.B.; Rev. Justin M. Matro, O.S.B.; Rev. Maximillian (Mark) Maxwell, O.S.B.; Rev. Edward M. Mazich, O.S.B.; Canice Daniel McMullen, O.S.B., In Res.; Joachim Joshua Morgan, O.S.B., In Res.; Rev. Paschal A. Morlino, O.S.B.; Rev. Maurus B. Mount, O.S.B.; Rev. Nathan J. Munsch, O.S.B.; Rev. Warren D. Murrman, O.S.B.; Rev. Justin Nolan, O.S.B.; Rt. Rev. Douglas R. Nowicki, O.S.B., Abbot; Rev. Jeffrey Nyardy, O.S.B.; Rev. Daniel Paul

O'Keefe, O.S.B.; Rev. Barnabas O'Reilly, OSB; Rev. Paulo Sergio Panza, O.S.B., Prior; Rev. Alfred Patterson, O.S.B.; Rev. John Peck, O.S.B.; Rev. Dominic J. Petroy, O.S.B.; Rev. Peter Augustine Pierjok, O.S.B., In Res.; Rev. Samuel Pinheiro, OSB; Rev. James F. Podlesny, O.S.B.; Rev. Nathanael R. Polinski, O.S.B.; Rev. Jerome J. Purta, O.S.B.; Rev. Donald Raila, O.S.B.; Rev. Thaddeus E. Rettger, O.S.B.; Rev. Chrysostom V. Schlimm, O.S.B.; Rev. Paul-Alexander Shutt, O.S.B.; Rev. Thomas More Sikora, OSB; Bruno Luiz Carlos da Silva, O.S.B., In Res.; Rev. Paul R. Taylor, O.S.B.; Rev. John Mary Tompkins, O.S.B.; Rev. Richard Ulam, O.S.B.; Rev. Eric Vogt, O.S.B.; Rev. Mark Edward Wenzinger, O.S.B.; Rev. Anthony Wesolowski, O.S.B.; Rev. Lee R. Yoakam, O.S.B.; Rev. Jean-Luc C. Zadroga, O.S.B.; Rev. Vincent E. Zidek, O.S.B.; Rev. Frank Ziemkiewicz, O.S.B.; Brs.: 37; Priests: 100

NURSING / REHABILITATION / CONVALESCENCE / ELDERLY CARE [NUR]

GREENSBURG

St. Anne Home - 685 Angela Dr., Greensburg, PA 15601 t) 724-837-6070 jlong@stannehome.org www.stannehome.org Jeffrey Long, Admin.; Sonia Kreig, Dir.; Christy Kremer, Dir.; Msgr. V. Paul Fitzmaurice, In Res.; Rev. Msgr. John A. Regoli, In Res.; Asstd. Annu.: 531; Staff: 222

Neumann House - 2900 Seminary Dr., Greensburg, PA 15601 t) 724-834-7350 jgarvin@dioceseofgreensburg.org Residence for retired priests. Rev. Msgr. Richard G. Curci, Dir - In Res.; Rev. Robert R. Byrnes, In Res.; Rev. James W. Clark, In Res.; Rev. John M. Foriska, In Res.; Rev. Msgr. James T. Gaston, In Res.; Rev. James M. Goldberg, In Res.; Rev. Thaddeus J. Kaczmarek, In Res.; Rev. Msgr. Lawrence R. Kiniry, In Res.; Rev. Emil S. Payer, In Res.; Rev. Peter L. Peretti, In Res.; Rev. Alexander L. Pleban, In Res.; Rev. Leonard W. Stoviak, In Res.; Rev. Douglas E. Dorula, In Res. While on Administrative Leave; Rev. Mark R. Dunmire, In Res. While on Sick Leave; Rev. Jeremy O'Shea, In Res; Asstd. Annu.: 16; Staff: 11

PRESCHOOLS / CHILDCARE CENTERS [PRE]

GREENSBURG

Elizabeth Seton Montessori School of Westmoreland County, Inc. - 294 Frye Farm Rd., Greensburg, PA 15601; Mailing: P.O. Box 268, Greensburg, PA 15601 t) 724-837-8500 esmontessori@comcast.net Sr. Anita Schulte, S.C., Admin.; Linda M. Fidazzo, Prin.; Stds.: 25; Lay Tchrs.: 1

MOUNT PLEASANT

Verna Montessori School - 268 Prittstown Rd., Mount Pleasant, PA 15666 t) 724-887-8810 office@vernamontessorischool.org Ivrea Sisters of Charity of the Immaculate Conception of Ivrea Sr. Letizia Tribuzio, SCIC, Prin.; Debora Witt, Librn.; Stds.: 101; Lay Tchrs.: 7

RETREAT HOUSES / RENEWAL CENTERS [RTR]

GREENSBURG

St. Emma Retreat House - 1001 Harvey Ave., Greensburg, PA 15601 t) 724-834-3060 benedictinenuns@stemma.org www.stemma.org Sisters of St. Benedict of Westmoreland Co. Mother Mary Anne Noll, O.S.B., Prioress; Sr. Maria Johanna Uhlott, OSB, Subprior;

SEMINARIES [SEM]

LATROBE

St. Vincent Seminary - 300 Fraser Purchase Rd., Latrobe, PA 15650 t) 724-805-2592 edward.mazich@stvincent.edu www.saintvincentseminary.edu Rev. Edward M. Mazich, O.S.B., Rector; Rev. John Mary Tompkins, O.S.B., Rector; Rev. Emmanuel Afunugo, Dean; Rev. Patrick T. Cronauer, O.S.B., Dean; Rev. Jude Brady, O.S.B., Dir.; Rev. Boniface Hicks, O.S.B., Dir.; Bro. David Kelly, O.S.B., Dir.; Dcn. Lawrence Sutton, Dir.; Rev. Cyprian G. Constantine, O.S.B., Dir., Liturgy; Stds.: 56; Bro. Tchrs.: 3; Lay Tchrs.: 1; Pr. Tchrs.: 13

An asterisk (*) denotes an organization that has established tax-exempt status directly with the IRS and is not covered by the USCCB Group Ruling.

Diocese of Harrisburg

(Dioecesis Harrisburgensis)

MOST REVEREND RONALD W. GAINER, D.D., J.C.L.

Bishop of Harrisburg; ordained May 19, 1973; appointed Bishop of Lexington December 13, 2002; consecrated February 22, 2003; appointed Bishop of Harrisburg January 24, 2014; installed March 19, 2014. Office: 4800 Union Deposit Rd., Harrisburg, PA 17111-3710.

Diocesan Center: 4800 Union Deposit Rd., Harrisburg, PA 17111-3710. T: 717-657-4804; F: 717-657-2453.
www.hbgdiocese.org
vicargeneraloffice@hbgdiocese.org

ESTABLISHED MARCH 3, 1868.

Square Miles 7,660.

Comprises the Counties of Dauphin, Lebanon, Lancaster, York, Adams, Franklin, Cumberland, Perry, Juniata, Mifflin, Snyder, Northumberland, Union, Montour and Columbia in the State of Pennsylvania.

Patron of Diocese: St. Patrick, Bishop and Confessor.

Legal Title: The Diocese of Harrisburg and each parish in the diocese are organized as unincorporated religious non-profit associations. Schools within the Diocese of Harrisburg are organized as non-profit corporations or unincorporated religious non-profit associations. The Diocese of Harrisburg, each parish, and each school has one or more separate supporting Pennsylvania Charitable Trusts. For further information, consult the Office of the Vicar General.

STATISTICAL OVERVIEW

Personnel

Bishop....1
Priests: Diocesan Active in Diocese....90
Priests: Diocesan Active Outside Diocese....3
Priests: Retired, Sick or Absent....29
Number of Diocesan Priests....122
Religious Priests in Diocese....31
Total Priests in your Diocese....153
Extern Priests in Diocese....15
Ordinations:
Diocesan Priests....5
Transitional Deacons....3
Permanent Deacons in Diocese....68
Total Brothers....16
Total Sisters....140

Parishes

Parishes....89
With Resident Pastor:
Resident Diocesan Priests....67
Resident Religious Priests....18
Without Resident Pastor:
Administered by Priests....1
In the care of professed men religious other than priests or permanent deacons....3
Missions....6
Professional Ministry Personnel:
Sisters....6
Lay Ministers....53

Welfare

Specialized Homes....3
Total Assisted....82
Special Centers for Social Services....1
Total Assisted....19

Educational

Diocesan Students in Other Seminaries....12
Total Seminarians....12
High Schools, Diocesan and Parish....6
Total Students....2,836
Elementary Schools, Diocesan and Parish....29
Total Students....6,607
Catechesis/Religious Education:
High School Students....709
Elementary Students....7,866
Total Students under Catholic Instruction....18,030
Teachers in Diocese:
Sisters....21
Lay Teachers....759

Vital Statistics

Receptions into the Church:
Infant Baptism Totals....1,142
Minor Baptism Totals....433
Adult Baptism Totals....184
Received into Full Communion....203
First Communions....1,732
Confirmations....1,881
Marriages:
Catholic....249
Interfaith....158
Total Marriages....407
Deaths....2,306
Total Catholic Population....201,186
Total Population....2,330,757

LEADERSHIP

Vicar General - Very Rev. William C. Forrey;
Director of the Office for Divine Worship - Very Rev. Joshua R. Brommer, Dir.;
Moderator of the Curia - Very Rev. William C. Forrey, Moderator;
Secretary for Catholic Charities - Kelly Gollick, Exec. Dir. (kgollick@hbgdiocese.org);
Secretary for Administrative Services - Donald J. Kaercher, CFO;
Secretary for Clergy and Consecrated Life - t) 717-657-4804 Very Rev. Mark M. Speitel, Secy.;
Secretariat for Public Relations - t) 717-657-4804 Rachel Bryson, Exec.;
Secretary for Education - t) 717-657-4804 Daniel Breen, Secy.;
Secretary for Catholic Life and Evangelization - t) 717-657-4804 Dcn. Gregory M. Amarante, Secy.;
Judicial Vicar - Very Rev. Paul M. Clark;
Chancellor - t) 717-657-4804 Barbara A. Bettwy, Dir.;
Vice Chancellor - Very Rev. Anthony R. Dill;

OFFICES AND DIRECTORS

Adult Education and Catechist Formation, Office of - Ryan Bolster, Dir.;
Buildings and Properties - t) 717-657-4804 Scott Udit, Dir. (sudit@hbgdiocese.org);
Campus Ministry - t) 717-657-4804 Zachary Haney, Dir. (zhaney@hbgdiocese.org);
Catholic Charities Administration, Department for - Kelly Gollick, Exec. Dir. (kgollick@hbgdiocese.org); Christopher Meehan, Dir. Devel.; Sean Miriello, Dir. (smiriello@hbgdiocese.org);
Catholic Charities Counseling/Field Services, Department for - Annette Martin; Patricia Tolle;
Catholic History and Archives, Office of - t) 717-657-4804 Barbara A. Bettwy, Chancellor; Alberto Rodriguez, Archivist;
Catholic Physicians Guild -
Catholic Schools, Department for - t) 717-657-4804 Margaret Barrett, Asst. Supt. (mbarrett@hbgdiocese.org); Daniel Breen, Supt.;
The "Catholic Witness" - Jennifer Reed, Editor;
Catholic Women, Diocesan Council of - t) 570-590-1116 Alycia Laureti;
Cemeteries - Vicki Kollar, Dir. (vkollar@hbgdiocese.org);
Charismatic Renewal - t) 570-339-1036 Very Rev. Francis J. Karwacki, Liaison;
Consecrated Life, Office of - t) 717-657-4804 Very Rev. Mark M. Speitel;
Consultors, College - Very Rev. William C. Forrey, Ex-Officio; Very Rev. Mark M. Speitel, Ex-Officio;
  College of Consultors - Rev. Leo M. Goodman III; Rev. James E. Lease; Very Rev. Timothy D. Marcoe;
  College of Consultors - Very Rev. Edward J. Quinlan; Very Rev. Thomas J. Rozman;
  College of Consultors - Rev. Kyle S. Sahd; Rev. Neil S. Sullivan;
Continuing Formation of Deacons, Office of - Very Rev. John B. Bateman Jr.;
Continuing Formation of Priests, Office of - t) 717-657-4804 Very Rev. Mark M. Speitel;
Cursillo Movement - t) 717-657-4804 Rev. William M. Weary;
Deans - Very Rev. William C. Forrey, Ex-Officio; Very Rev. Mark M. Speitel, Ex-Officio;
  College of Deans - Adams, Cumberland/Perry and Franklin - Rev. Msgr. James M. Lyons; Very Rev. Thomas J. Rozman; Very Rev. Allan F. Wolfe;
  College of Deans - Dauphin, North Lancaster and South Lancaster - Very Rev. Steven W. Fauser; Very Rev. Peter I. Hahn; Very Rev. Edward J. Quinlan;
  College of Deans - Lebanon and York - Very Rev. John B. Bateman Jr.; Very Rev. Anthony R. Dill;
  College of Deans - Northern and Northumberland - Very Rev. Francis J. Karwacki; Very Rev. Timothy D. Marcoe;
Development, Office of - t) 717-657-4804 Kim Roche, Dir.;
Diocesan Center - Curtis Wilson, Coord., Diocesan Ctr. Bldgs. (cwilson@hbgdiocese.org);
Ecumenical and Interreligious Affairs, Office for - Rev. James E. Lease, Dir.;
Finance Council - Most Rev. Ronald W. Gainer, Ex-Officio (brgainer@hbgdiocese.org); Very Rev. William C. Forrey, Ex-Officio;
  Finance Council - Mark B. Glessner; Very Rev. Edward J. Quinlan; Lora A. Kulick, Esq.;
  Finance Council - Lisa Rohrer; Kenneth R. Shutts, Esq.;
  Harrisburg Catholic Administrative Services, Inc. - Donald J. Kaercher, Diocesan Finance Officer & Sec. for Admin.;
Health Care Ministry - t) 717-657-4804 Marianne Weltmer, Dir. (mweltmer@hbgdiocese.org);
Holy Name Societies - t) 717-637-6491 Dcn. Thomas Aumen, Liaison;
Human Resources, Department for - Janet E. Jackson;
Knights of Columbus - Andrew Bacha (acb69ford@comcast.net);
Legion of Mary - t) 717-657-3147 Rev. Paul R. Shuda, Moderator;
Office of Life and Dignity - Marianne Weltmer, Dir. (mweltmer@hbgdiocese.org);
Mater Dei Community - t) 717-889-4217 Rev. James Smith, Chap. (frjsmith@hbgdiocese.org);
Ministry with People with Disabilities, Office for - Marianne Weltmer, Dir. (mweltmer@hbgdiocese.org);
Missions, Office of Pontifical - Rev. Robert F. Sharman, Dir.;
Office of Culture, Identity and Outreach - Dcn. Armando Torres, Dir. (atorres@hbgdiocese.org);
Permanent Diaconate, Office for - t) 717-657-4804 Very Rev. Mark M. Speitel;
Presbyteral Council -
  Adams, Lebanon and North Lancaster - Rev. Philip G. Burger; Rev. Kevin J. Coyle; Rev. Ryan M. Fischer;
  Appointed - Rev. Leo M. Goodman III; Rev. Stephen Fernandes, O.F.M.Cap., Pst.; Rev. Ryan M. Fischer, Pst.;
  Appointed - Rev. Charles L. Persing; Very Rev. Edward J. Quinlan; Rev. Michael W. Rothan;
  Appointed - Very Rev. Thomas J. Rozman; Rev. Kyle S. Sahd; Rev. Mark T. Wilke;
  Dauphin, Northern, South Lancaster - Rev. James E. Lease; Very Rev. Timothy D. Marcoe; Rev. Daniel F.X. Powell;
  Franklin - Very Rev. Allan F. Wolfe;
  Northumberland, Cumberland/Perry, Weiss - Rev. Joseph T. Scanlin; Rev. Neil S. Sullivan; Rev. Mark E. Weiss;
Prison Ministry - t) 717-657-4804 Marianne Weltmer, Dir. (mweltmer@hbgdiocese.org);
Saint Thomas More Society - t) 717-657-4804 x305 Linda Carroll;
Scout Chaplain - Rev. Keith M. Carroll, Chap.;
Tribunal - t) 717-657-4804 Barbara A. Bettwy, Chancellor;
  Advocates - Very Rev. John R. Bateman; Anita M. Paynter;
  Auditor - Very Rev. John R. Bateman;
  Canonical Consultants - Very Rev. John R. Bateman; Barbara A. Bettwy; Rev. Jordan Hite, T.O.R.;
  Case Services Administrator - Terry Dynako;
  Defenders of the Bond - Rev. Edward R. Lavelle; Very Rev. Anthony R. Dill;
  Diocesan Judges - Barbara A. Bettwy; Rev. Jordan Hite, T.O.R.; Rev. Msgr. William J. King;
  Judicial Vicar - Very Rev. Paul M. Clark;
  Notary - Terry Dynako, Case Svcs. Mgr.;
  Promoter of Justice - Very Rev. John R. Bateman;
Victim Assistance Coordinator - Kelly Gollick (kgollick@hbgdiocese.org);
Vocations, Office for - t) 717-657-4804 Rev. Jonathan P. Sawicki, Dir.;
World Apostolate of Fatima - t) 570-672-2122 Rev. John A. Szada Jr., Spiritual Adv./Care Srvcs.;
Youth and Young Adult Ministry, Office for - t) 717-657-4804 x327 Zachary Haney, Dir. (zhaney@hbgdiocese.org);
Youth Protection Program - Michelle Shae, Dir. (mshae@hbgdiocese.org); Kristen Lingle, Admin. (klingle@hbgdiocese.org);

PARISHES, MISSIONS, AND CLERGY

COMMONWEALTH OF PENNSYLVANIA

ABBOTTSTOWN

Immaculate Heart of Mary - 6084 W. Canal Rd., Abbottstown, PA 17301 t) 717-259-0611 p001immaculateheart@hbgdiocese.org ihmparadise.org Rev. Philip G. Burger, Pst.; Rev. Msgr. William M. Richardson, In Res.; CRP Stds.: 100

ANNVILLE

St. Paul the Apostle - 125 S. Spruce St., Annville, PA 17003 t) 717-867-1525 mlangan@stpaulsinannville.org; amattern@stpaulsinannville.org Rev. Kevin J. Coyle, Pst.; Mary Beazley, Music Min.; Anna M Mattern, DRE; CRP Stds.: 140

BERWICK

Immaculate Conception of the Blessed Virgin Mary - 1730 Fowler Ave., Berwick, PA 18603-1462 t) 570-759-9225 (CRP); 570-759-8113 frwbarbee@hbgdiocese.org Rev. William Barbee, Pst.;

St. Joseph's - 721 Monroe St., Berwick, PA 18603; Mailing: 730 Washington St., Berwick, PA 18603 t) 570-752-7000; 570-752-7000 x101 (CRP) www.stjosephberwick.com Rev. William Barbee, Pst.; Diane Kowalski, DRE;

BLOOMSBURG

St. Columba - 342 Iron St., Bloomsburg, PA 17815-1824 t) 570-784-0801 stcolumbaparishbloomsburg@hbgdiocese.org; dircye@saintcolumbachurch.org www.saintcolumbachurch.org Rev. Msgr. Robert E. Lawrence, Pst.; Helen McMenamin, DRE;

  St. Columba School - (Grades PreK-8) 40 E. Third St., Bloomsburg, PA 17815-1815 t) 570-784-5932 scsprincipal@saintcolumbaschool.org Peter Morisco, Prin.;

  Christ the King - ; Mailing: P.O. Box 297, Benton, PA 17814 t) 570-925-6969 ctkbenton.weebly.com/ Olusola Adewole, O.P., Admin.;

BLUE RIDGE SUMMIT

St. Rita - 13219 Monterey Ln., Blue Ridge Summit, PA 17214; Mailing: P O Box 365, Blue Ridge Summit, PA 17214 t) 717-642-8815; 717-794-2067 (CRP) www.stritacc.org Rev. Chidi Onwuka, MSSCC, Par. Vicar; Rev. Peter DiTomasso, M.SS.CC., Pst.; CRP Stds.: 20

CAMP HILL

Good Shepherd - 3435 Trindle Rd., Camp Hill, PA 17011-4489 t) 717-761-1167 frnsullivan@thegoodshep.org; hkantes@thegoodshep.org www.thegoodshep.com Rev. Neil S. Sullivan, Pst.; Helen Kantes, DRE; CRP Stds.: 165

CARLISLE

Saint Patrick - 152 E. Pomfret St., Carlisle, PA 17013 t) 717-243-4891 (CRP); 717-243-4411 po12stpatrickparishcarlisle@hbgdiocese.org www.saintpatrickchurch.org Rev. Donald H. Bender, Pst.; Rev. Gregory J. D'Emma, Assoc. Pst.; Rev. Javed Kashif, O.F.M.Cap., Par. Vicar; Alexandra Arp, Youth Min.; Stephanie Conrad, DRE;

  Saint Patrick School - 87 Marsh Dr., Carlisle, PA 17015 t) 717-249-4826 office@spscarlisle.org www.spscarlisle.org

  Pine Grove Furnace, St. Eleanor Regina -

St. Katherine Drexel Chapel - Perpetual Adoration -

CATAWISSA

Our Lady of Mercy - 304 Slabtown Rd., Catawissa, PA 17820 t) 717-799-5642 frddalesandro@hbgdiocese.org Rev. Dennis G. Dalessandro, Pst.; Margaret Jessick, DRE; CRP Stds.: 14

CHAMBERSBURG

Corpus Christi - 320 Philadelphia Ave., Chambersburg, PA 17201 t) 717-263-9541 (CRP); 717-264-6317 dmccarty@corpuschristichbg.org Dcn. Richard W. Ramsey; Rev. Luis R. Rodriguez, Pst.; Rev. Richard Lyons, Assoc. Pst.;

Corpus Christi School - 305 N. Second St., Chambersburg, PA 17201 t) 717-263-5036 tflohr@ccschambersburg.org www.cccschambersburg.org Mary A. Geesaman, Prin.;

Our Lady of Refuge - 21169 Cross Rd., Doylesburg, PA 17219 t) 717-349-7953

COAL TOWNSHIP

Our Lady of Hope - 863 W. Chestnut St., Coal Township, PA 17866-1995 t) 570-648-4432 p130ourladyhope2@hbgdiocese.org www.ourladyofhopepa.com Friar Michael Lasky, OFM, Conv., Pst.;

COLUMBIA

Holy Trinity - 409 Cherry St., Columbia, PA 17512 t) 717-684-2711 frskelley@hbgdiocese.org www.holytrinitycolumbiapa.com/ Rev. Stephen P. Kelley, Pst.; Sr. Anna Cosgrave, O.S.F., Pst. Assoc.;

Sisters of St. Francis of Philadelphia - 548 Cherry St., Columbia, PA 17512 t) 717-684-2232

Holy Trinity School - 404 Cherry St., Columbia, PA 17512 t) 717-684-2664 Kimberly S. Winters, Prin.;

St. Peter - 121 S. Second St., Columbia, PA 17512 t) 717-684-7070 dwickenheiser@hbgdiocese.org Rev. Anthony Swamy Anthappa, M.S.F.S., Pst.; Corrinne Eck, DRE;

Mother of Holy Purity Chapel - 217 Maple St., Wrightsville, PA 17368

CORNWALL

Sacred Heart of Jesus - 2596 Cornwall Rd., Cornwall, PA 17016-0136; Mailing: P.O. Box 136, Cornwall, PA 17016-0136 t) 717-273-2160 (CRP); 717-273-1574 phall@hbgdiocese.org Rev. Rodrigo A. Arrazola, Pst.;

DALLASTOWN

St. Joseph - 251 E. Main St., Dallastown, PA 17313 t) 717-246-9959 (CRP); 717-246-3007 ttracey@sjdrcc.org; frmweiss@hbgdiocese.org sjdrcc.org Dcn. Daniel L. Bernardy; Rev. Mark E. Weiss, Pst.; Timothy Tracey, DRE;

Holy Trinity Catholic School - 235 S. Beaver St., York, PA 17401 t) 717-854-8263 www.htcsyork.org St. Joseph, Dallastown & St. Patrick's Elementary Schools, York, Closed in June 2019 and formed Holy Trinity Catholic School, York, PA Kathleen Smith, Prin.; Margaret Snyder, Prin.;

DANVILLE

St. Joseph - 68 Center St., Danville, PA 17821 t) 570-275-2512 sjcd@verizon.net stjosephdanville.org Very Rev. Timothy D. Marcoe, Pst.; CRP Stds.: 71

St. Joseph School - (Grades K-8) 1027 Ferry St., Danville, PA 17821 t) 570-275-2435 kwinters@stjosephdanville.com; office@stjosephdanville.com www.stjosephdanville.com Kimberly S. Winters, Prin.;

DAUPHIN

St. Matthew, Apostle and Evangelist - 607 Stoney Creek Dr., Dauphin, PA 17018 t) 717-921-2363 p021stmatthew@hbgdiocese.org Very Rev. Paul M. Clark, Pst.; Dcn. Richard Aull; Dcn. Michael Derois; CRP Stds.: 50

DOYLESBURG

Our Lady of Refuge Mission - 21169 Cross Rd., Doylesburg, PA 17219-9707 t) 717-349-7953 frlrodriguez@hbgdiocese.org Rev. Luis R. Rodriguez, Pst.;

ELIZABETHTOWN

St. Peter - 1840 Marshall Dr., Elizabethtown, PA 17022 t) 717-367-1255 secretary@stpeteretown.org; cre@stpeteretown.org www.stpeteretown.org Rev. Bernard Mary Oniwe, Pst.;

ELYSBURG

Queen of the Most Holy Rosary - 599 W. Center St., Elysburg, PA 17824 t) 570-672-2302 frjscanlin@hbgdiocese.org www.qmhr.net Rev. Joseph T. Scanlin, Pst.;

ENOLA

Our Lady of Lourdes - 225 Salt Rd., Enola, PA 17025 t) 717-732-9642 frmowery@ourladyoflourdesenola.org www.ourladyoflourdesenola.org/ Rev. Richard Mowery, Pst.; Sarah Kling, Bus. Mgr.;

EPHRATA

Our Mother of Perpetual Help - 320 Church Ave., Ephrata, PA 17522 t) 717-733-9641 perpetualhelp@omph.org; omphreled@omph.org omphchurch.com Rev. John Murray, C.Ss.R., Pst.; Rev. James Szobonya, C.Ss.R., Par. Vicar; CRP Stds.: 103

Our Mother of Perpetual Help School - 330 Church Ave., Ephrata, PA 17522 t) 717-738-2414 office@omph.org www.omph.org Thomas Castner, Prin.;

Convent - 310 Church Ave., Ephrata, PA 17522 t) 717-733-1291

FAIRFIELD

Immaculate Conception of the Blessed Virgin Mary - 256 Tract Rd., Fairfield, PA 17320 t) 717-642-8815 www.stmarysfairfieldpa.org Rev. Peter DiTomasso, M.SS.CC., Pst.; Rev. Chidi Onwuka, MSSCC, Par. Vicar; CRP Stds.: 35

GETTYSBURG

St. Francis Xavier - 455 Table Rock Rd., Gettysburg, PA 17325 t) 717-334-1221 (CRP); 717-334-3919 sthresher@sfxcs-pa.org Rev. Daniel C. Mitzel, Pst.; Rev. Andrew St. Hilaire, Assoc. Pst.;

St. Francis Xavier School - 465 Table Rock Rd., Gettysburg, PA 17325 t) 717-334-4221 bsieg@sfxcs-pa.org www.sfxcs-pa.org Rebecca Sieg, Prin.;

St. Joseph the Worker - 12 E. Hanover St., Gettysburg, PA 17325-7750 t) 717-334-2510 stjosephget@comcast.net stjosephtheworkerpa.org Dcn. Richard J. Weaver; Rev. Benny Jose, M.SS.CC., Pst.; CRP Stds.: 26

GREENCASTLE

St. Mark the Evangelist - 395 S. Ridge Ave., Greencastle, PA 17225 t) 717-597-2705 stmkstlk@comcast.net www.stmarkstlukeparish.org Rev. Walter F. Guzman-Alvarez, Pst.; Dcn. Daniel Signore; Lucy Schemel, DRE; CRP Stds.: 97

St. Luke the Evangelist - Overhill Dr. & Black Rd., Mercersburg, PA 17236

HANOVER

Basilica of the Sacred Heart of Jesus - 30 Basilica Dr., Hanover, PA 17331-8924 t) 717-637-2721 www.sacredheartbasilica.org Rev. Dwight D. Schlaline, Pst.; Dcn. Christopher D. Livelsberger; CRP Stds.: 83

St. Joseph - 5125 Grandview Rd., Hanover, PA 17331; Mailing: 5055 Grandview Rd., Hanover, PA 17331 t) 717-637-5236 sgolden@hbgdiocese.org www.stjosephparishhanover.org Dcn. Thomas M. Aumen; Dcn. Timothy J. Shultis; Rev. Msgr. James M. Lyons, Pst.; Rev. Matthew Morelli, Assoc. Pst.; Rev. Lawrence J. McNeil, In Res.;

Saint Joseph Catholic School - t) 717-632-0118 office@sjshanover.org www.sjshanover.org Terrance Golden, Prin.;

St. Vincent de Paul - 220 Third St., Hanover, PA 17331 t) 717-637-4625 bmiller@hbgdiocese.org; secretary@svparish.org www.svparish.org Rev. Michael P. Reid II, Pst.; Rev. Joseph F. Gotwalt, In Res.; Rev. Ignacio Palomino, In Res.; Sandra Clark, DRE; CRP Stds.: 21

HARRISBURG

Cathedral Parish of St. Patrick - 212 State St., Harrisburg, PA 17101 t) 717-232-2169 x223 cathedralparish@comcast.net; cathedralsecretary@hbgdiocese.org www.stpatrickcathedral.com Rev. Joshua R. Brommer, Rector; Dcn. Lawrence R. Crudup, Pst. Assoc.; Dcn. Thomas A. Lang, Pst. Assoc.;

St. Catherine Laboure - 4000 Derry St., Harrisburg, PA 17111 t) 717-564-1321 frjlease@sclhbg.org www.sclhbg.org (Shrine of the Miraculous Medal) Rev. James E. Lease, Pst.; Rev. Jordan Hite, T.O.R., In Res.; Robert Jakielski, DRE; CRP Stds.: 53

St. Catherine Laboure School - 4020 Derry St., Harrisburg, PA 17111 t) 717-564-1760 www.sclhbg.org Sr. Mary Anne Sweeney, I.H.M., Prin.; Kelly Rogers, Dir.;

Convent - 4010 Derry St., Harrisburg, PA 17111 t) 717-745-4134 ihmsisters@sclhbg.org www.ihmimmaculata.org Sisters, Servants of the Immaculate Heart of Mary Sr. Bernard Agnes Smith, I.H.M., Supr.;

St. Francis of Assisi - 1439 Market St., Harrisburg, PA 17103 t) 717-233-7912 (CRP); 717-232-1003 cfagan@hbgdiocese.org stfrancishbg.org Rev. Orlando Reyes, O.F.M.Cap., Pst.; Rev. Philip White, OFM Cap., Par. Vicar; Bro. Michael Rubus, O.F.M.Cap., Chap.;

Holy Family - 555 S. 25th St., Harrisburg, PA 17104 t) 717-232-1003 cfagan@hbgdiocese.org Rev. Orlando Reyes, O.F.M.Cap., Pst.; Rev. Philip White, OFM Cap., Par. Vicar;

Holy Name of Jesus - 6150 Allentown Blvd., Harrisburg, PA 17112-2603 t) 717-657-1704 (CRP); 717-652-4211 www.holynameofjesus.com/parish Very Rev. Edward J. Quinlan, Pst.; Rev. Matthew E. Cannon, Par. Vicar; Dcn. Jerome T. Foerster; Dcn. Joseph J. Wrabel; Sr. Rita Smith, S.S.J., DRE;

Holy Name of Jesus School - (Grades PreK-8) 6190 Allentown Blvd., Harrisburg, PA 17112-2603 holynameofjesusschoolharrisburg@hbgdiocese.org (Lower Paxton Twp.) Elaine Tomeck, Librn.;

Convent - 6190 Allentown Blvd, Harrisburg, PA 17112 t) 717-545-4357 ssjhnj@ezonline.net

St. Margaret Mary Alacoque Parish and School Charitable Trust - 2800 Paxton Church Rd, Harrisburg, PA 17110; Mailing: 2848 Herr St., Harrisburg, PA 17103 t) 717-233-3062 prep@stmmparish.org; parishoffice@stmmparish.org Rev. Leo M. Goodman III, Pst.; Elizabeth Emery, DRE;

St. Margaret Mary Alacoque School - 2826 Herr St., Harrisburg, PA 17103 t) 717-232-3771 school.stmmparish.org Jean Fennessy, Prin.;

Worship Site -

Our Lady of the Blessed Sacrament - 2121 N. Third St., Harrisburg, PA 17110-1812 t) 717-233-1014 olbsparish@hbgdiocese.org www.olbsharrisburg.org/

HERSHEY

St. Joan of Arc - 359 W. Areba Ave., Hershey, PA 17033-1602 t) 717-533-7168 x100; 717-533-7168 x122 (CRP) etropp@stjoanhershey.org; srobison@stjoanhershey.org Rev. Alfred P. Sceski, Pst.; Rev. Kenneth Roth, Par. Vicar; Dcn. Joseph Gusherowski; Dcn. Rodrigue Mortel; Rev. Modestus Ngwu, O.P., Chap.; Earl Tropp, DRE; Marcie Warner, DRE;

St. Joan of Arc School - (Grades PreK-8) 1525 Sand Hill Rd., Hummelstown, PA 17036 t) 717-533-2854 sreileen@stjoanhershey.org Sr. Eileen M. McGowan, Prin.;

Convent - 301 W. Granada Ave., Hershey, PA 17033 t) 717-533-2864 sreileen@stjoanhershey.org

KULPMONT

Holy Angels - 855 Scott St., Kulpmont, PA 17834 t) 570-373-1221 oneangel@ptd.net www.holyangelskulpmont.org Rev. Andrew J. Stahmer, Pst.;

LANCASTER

St. Anne - 929 N. Duke St., Lancaster, PA 17602 t) 717-392-2225 stanneparishlancaster@hbgdiocese.org www.stannechurch.org Rev. Tri M. Luong, Pst.; Colleen Dougherty, DRE; CRP Stds.: 22

St. Anthony of Padua - 501 E. Orange St., Lancaster, PA 17602 t) 717-392-2930 (CRP); 717-394-0669

shlickes@hbgdiocese.org Rev. Matthew Christopher Morelli, Pst.; Patricia Meyer, DRE;

Conestoga View Nursing Home - t) 717-299-7850

Assumption of the Blessed Virgin Mary - 119 S. Prince St., Lancaster, PA 17603 t) 717-392-2578 alan@stmaryslancaster.org; info@stmaryslancaster.org www.stmaryslancaster.org Rev. Brian Olkowski, Pst.; Alan H. Schwartz, DRE;

San Juan Bautista Parish Lancaster Charitable Trust - 425 S. Duke St., Lancaster, PA 17602 t) 717-392-4118 p127sanjuan@hbgdiocese.org sanjuanbautistalancaster.com Rev. Luis R. Rodriguez, Pst.; Dcn. Jorge L. Nazario; Dcn. Expedito Santos-Santiago; Dcn. Armando Torres, DRE;

St. John Neumann - 601 E. Delp Rd., Lancaster, PA 17601 t) 717-569-8531 info@sjnlancaster.org www.sjnlancaster.org Dcn. Michael Oles; Rev. Daniel F.X. Powell, Pst.; Coleen Kibler, DRE;

St. Joseph Church - 440 St. Joseph St., Lancaster, PA 17603 t) 717-397-6921 x213 www.stjosephslanc.com Rev. Pang S. Tcheou, Pst.; Rev. Deogratias Rwegasira, A.J., In Res.; Dcn. Thomas Edward Owsinski; CRP Stds.: 56

St. Leo the Great - 2427 Marietta Ave., Lancaster, PA 17601-1942 t) 717-394-1742 dre@stleos.org; secretary@stleos.org www.stleos.org Very Rev. Peter I. Hahn, Pst.; Rev. Thomas Meinert, Par. Vicar; Dcn. Frank Kuchinski; Sr. Dorothy Wilkinson, S.S.C., DRE; Dcn. Eugene Vannucci; CRP Stds.: 169

St. Leo the Great School - (Grades PreK-8) secretary@stleoschool.org www.stleoschool.org Christine Sieg, Prin.;

St. Philip the Apostle - 2111 Millersville Pike, Lancaster, PA 17603 t) 717-872-2166 lneff@stphilipmillersville.com stphilipmillersville.com/ Rev. Lawrence W. Sherdel, Pst.; Dcn. Francis Phillips; CRP Stds.: 88

Sacred Heart of Jesus - 558 W. Walnut St., Lancaster, PA 17603 t) 717-394-0757 shparish@sacredheartsch.org www.sacredheartlanc.org Rev. Michael Metzgar, Pst.; Rev. Msgr. Richard A. Youtz, In Res.; Kathy Hauk, DRE;

Sacred Heart of Jesus School - (Grades PreK-8) 235 Nevin St., Lancaster, PA 17603 t) 717-393-8433 shschool@sacredheartsch.org www.sacredheartschlanc.org Sr. Danielle Truex, Prin.;

Convent - 565 W. Walnut St., Lancaster, PA 17603 t) 717-392-4522

LEBANON

Assumption of the Blessed Virgin Mary - 2 N. Eighth St., Lebanon, PA 17046 t) 717-272-5674 stm@abvmlebpa.org abvmlebpa.org Rev. Robert M. Gillelan Jr., Pst.; Dcn. Richard Wentzel, Pst. Assoc.; AnneMarie Boltz, DRE;

Our Lady of Fatima - US 22 & 560 N. Mill St., Jonestown, PA 17038 t) 717-865-7439

St. Benedict the Abbot - 1300 Lehman St., Lebanon, PA 17046-3331 t) 717-450-4506 stbenedictlebanon@hbgdiocese.org stbenedictlebanon.org Rev. Jose E. Mera-Vallejos, Admin.;

St. Cecilia - 120 E. Lehman St., Lebanon, PA 17046 t) 717-272-4412 x1 (CRP); 717-272-4352 stcecilia120@gmail.com Rev. Michael Laicha, Pst.; Sandi Rudegeair, DRE;

Convent - 200 E. Lehman St., Lebanon, PA 17046

LEWISBURG

Sacred Heart of Jesus - 814 St. Louis St., Lewisburg, PA 17837 t) 570-523-3104 sacredheart814@gmail.com; pkeller@hbgdiocese.org sacredheartofjesus.org Rev. Matthew R. Larlick, Pst.; Dcn. Richard D. Owen;

Saint George Church - 775 Forest Hill Rd., Mifflinburg, PA 17844 t) 570-966-3088

LEWISTOWN

Sacred Heart of Jesus - 9 N. Brown St., Lewistown, PA 17044 t) 717-242-2781 shparishoffice@sacredheartlewistown.com; office@sacredheartschool.com www.sacredheartlewistown.com Rev. William M. Weary, Pst.; Rev. Jayaseelan Amalanathan, Assoc. Pst.;

Sacred Heart of Jesus School - 110 N. Dorcas St., Lewistown, PA 17044 t) 717-248-5351 www.sacredheartschool.com Joseph Maginnis, Prin.;

LITITZ

St. James - 505 Woodcrest Ave., Lititz, PA 17543 t) 717-626-0244 (CRP); 717-626-5580 p060stjames@hbgdiocese.org; re060@hbgdiocese.org www.stjameslititz.org Rev. James O'Blaney, C.Ss.R., Pst.; Rose Barnas, DRE;

LITTLESTOWN

St. Aloysius - 29 S. Queen St., Littlestown, PA 17340 t) 717-359-4513 frcmiller@hbgdiocese.org Rev. Charles Anthony Miller, Pst.;

LYKENS

Our Lady Help of Christians - 732 E. Main St., Lykens, PA 17048 t) 717-453-7895 frmopoki@hbgdiocese.org Rev. Michael Opoki, A.J., Pst.;

Sacred Heart of Jesus - 140 E. Market St., Williamstown, PA 17098

MANCHESTER

Holy Infant - 535 Conewago Creek Rd., Manchester, PA 17345 t) 717-266-5286 holyinfantparish@gmail.com www.holyinfantparish.com Very Rev. William C. Forrey, Pst.; Dcn. Joseph J. Kramer; CRP Stds.: 94

MANHEIM

St. Richard - 110 N. Oak St., Manheim, PA 17545; Mailing: 201 Adele Ave., Manheim, PA 17545 t) 717-665-2465 rminieri@hbgdiocese.org Rev. Stephen D. Weitzel, Pst.; Dcn. William J. Jordan;

MARYSVILLE

Our Lady of Good Counsel - 121 Chestnut St., Marysville, PA 17053; Mailing: 121 William St., Marysville, PA 17053-1434 t) 717-957-2662 olgcsb.org Rev. Dijo Thomas, M.S.F.S., Pst.; Dcn. Patrick McCormack;

St. Bernadette - 901 N. High St., Duncannon, PA 17020 Dcn. John C. Heil;

MCSHERRYSTOWN

Annunciation of the Blessed Virgin Mary - 26 N. Third St., McSherrystown, PA 17344 t) 717-637-1191 parishoffice@abvmchurch.org www.abvmchurch.org Annunciation BVM Parish Charitable Trust Rev. Richard Lyons, Pst.; Sr. Ann Marie Wierman, S.S.J., Pst. Min./Coord.; CRP Stds.: 40

St. Teresa of Calcutta Catholic School -

MECHANICSBURG

St. Elizabeth Ann Seton - 310 Hertzler Rd., Mechanicsburg, PA 17055 t) 717-697-2614 frcpersing@hbgdiocese.org www.steas.net Rev. Charles L. Persing, Pst.; Rev. Samuel Dubois, Par. Vicar; Dcn. David L. Hall; Patricia Wargo, DRE;

Saint Joseph Catholic Church - 400 E. Simpson St., Mechanicsburg, PA 17055-6507; Mailing: 410 E Simpson St, Mechanicsburg, PA 17055-6507 t) 717-766-2472 (CRP); 717-766-9433 officemanager@stjosephmech.org; rep@stjosephmech.org www.stjosephmech.org Very Rev. Thomas J. Rozman, Pst.; Rev. Kenneth Roth, Par. Vicar; Dcn. Steven Auchey; Rudy Geisler, Bus. Mgr.; Justin Myers, Music Min.; Mark Rebuck, CRE;

Saint Joseph Catholic Church School - (Grades PreK-8) 420 E. Simpson St., Mechanicsburg, PA 17055 t) 717-766-2564 rbamberger@sjsmch.org Rebecca Bamberger, Prin.; Mary Earnest, Prin.;

Saint Katharine Drexel - 1 Peter Dr., Mechanicsburg, PA 17050 t) 717-697-8716 ksmith@skdparish.com; jkleponis@skdparish.com skdparish.com Rev. Kenneth G. Smith, Pst.; Rev. Jerome A. Kleponis, Par. Vicar; Dcn. Scott Root, DRE; Shannon Root, Music Min.; Susan Elter, Bus. Mgr.; CRP Stds.: 105

MIDDLETOWN

Seven Sorrows of the Blessed Virgin Mary - 280 N. Race St., Middletown, PA 17057 t) 717-944-3133; 717-944-5371 (CRP) frsahd@ssbvm.org www.ssbvm.org Rev. Timothy J. Sahd, Pst.; Ray Kerwin, DRE; CRP Stds.: 156

Seven Sorrows of the Blessed Virgin Mary School - (Grades PreK-8) 360 E. Water St., Middletown, PA 17057 pbyrnes@ssbvm.org Patricia A. Byrnes, Prin.;

MIFFLINTOWN

St. Jude - 3918 William Penn Hwy., Mifflintown, PA 17059; Mailing: P.O. Box 187, Mifflintown, PA 17059 t) 717-436-6722 gtreaster@hbgdiocese.org Rev. William M. Weary, Pst.;

St. Jude Thaddeus -

MILLERSBURG

Queen of Peace - 202 Zimmerman Rd., Millersburg, PA 17061 t) 717-692-3504 frdmoss@hbgdiocese.org Rev. Darius G. C. Moss, Pst.; J. Roadcap, DRE;

MILTON

St. Joseph - 109 Broadway St., Milton, PA 17847 t) 570-742-4356; 570-724-4302 (CRP) bgeiswite@hbgdiocese.org Rev. John D. Hoke, Pst.; Harold Prentiss, DRE;

MOUNT CARMEL

Divine Redeemer - 300 West Ave., Mount Carmel, PA 17851; Mailing: 438 West Ave., Mount Carmel, PA 17851 t) 570-339-3450 parishdrc@ptd.net; credrc@ptd.net www.divineredeemerpa.weconnect.com Mother Maria Kaupas Center Rev. Bernard Wamayose, A.J., Pst.; Dcn. Walter Joseph Kozlowski; Betty Ann Corrigan, DRE; CRP Stds.: 28

Our Lady of Mount Carmel - 47 S. Market St., Mount Carmel, PA 17851 t) 570-339-1031; 570-339-5091 (CRP) frankkarwacki@yahoo.com; olomcc@verizon.net revfrankkarwacki.net Active Territorial Parish Very Rev. Francis J. Karwacki, Pst.; CRP Stds.: 31

MOUNT JOY

Mary, Mother of the Church - 625 Union School Rd., Mount Joy, PA 17552-9712 t) 717-653-4903 www.marymotherparish.org/ Rev. Edward J. Keating Jr., Pst.; CRP Stds.: 116

MYERSTOWN

Mary, Gate of Heaven - 188 W. McKinley Ave., Myerstown, PA 17067 t) 717-866-5640 frmmessner@hbgdiocese.org Rev. Michael E. Messner, Dean;

NEW BLOOMFIELD

St. Bernard - 811 Shermans Valley Rd., New Bloomfield, PA 17068; Mailing: P.O. Box 25, New Bloomfield, PA 17068 t) 717-582-4113 stbernardcatholicchurch@embarqmail.com Rev. Robert F. Sharman, Pst.; Alice Vilk, DRE;

NEW CUMBERLAND

St. Theresa of the Infant Jesus - 1300 Bridge St., New Cumberland, PA 17070 t) 717-774-5918 redir@sainttheresaparish.org; eherald@sainttheresaparish.org Rev. Kyle S. Sahd, Pst.; Rev. William Barbee, Assoc. Pst.; Jane Monaghan, DRE;

St. Theresa of the Infant Jesus School - (Grades PreK-8) 1200 Bridge St., New Cumberland, PA 17070 t) 717-774-7464 mshore@sainttheresaschool.org Matthew Shore, Prin.;

NEW FREEDOM

St. John the Baptist - 315 N. Constitution Ave., New Freedom, PA 17349 t) 717-235-2156; 717-235-2439 (CRP) parish@sjbnf.org; reled@sjbnf.org www.sjbnf.org Rev. Robert A. Yohe Jr., Pst.; Rev. Benjamin Dunkelberger, Par. Vicar; Dcn. Frederick C. Horn, Pst. Assoc.;

St. John the Baptist School - (Grades PreK-6) t) 717-235-3525 smareck@sjbnf.org stjnschool.org Sue Mareck, Prin.;

NEW HOLLAND

Our Lady of Lourdes - 150 Water St., New Holland, PA 17557 t) 717-354-4686; 717-354-3338 (CRP) aoshea@hbgdiocese.org ourladyoflourdesnh.com Very Rev. Steven W. Fauser, Pst.;

NEW OXFORD

Immaculate Conception of the Blessed Virgin Mary - 106 Carlisle St., New Oxford, PA 17350 t) 717-624-4121; 717-887-5646 (CRP) frmletteer@hbgdiocese.org Rev. Michael C. Letteer, Pst.; Joanne Lauchman, DRE;

Immaculate Conception of the Blessed Virgin Mary School - 101 N. Peter St., New Oxford, PA 17350 t) 717-624-2061 Donna Hoffman, Prin.;

ORRTANNA

St. Ignatius Loyola - 1095 Church Rd., Orrtanna, PA 17353 t) 717-677-8012 stignatiusofloyola@hbgdiocese.org stignatiusofloyola.org Rev. Dominic M. DiBiccaro, Pst.; Dcn. Stephen M. Huete, Pst. Assoc.; CRP Stds.: 15

PALMYRA

Holy Spirit Parish Charitable Trust - 300 W. Pine St., Palmyra, PA 17078 t) 717-838-3369 manager@hspalmyra.com www.holyspiritpalmyra.com Very Rev. Anthony R. Dill, Pst.; CRP Stds.: 169

QUARRYVILLE

St. Catherine of Siena - 955 Robert Fulton Hwy., Quarryville, PA 17566-9543 t) 717-786-2695 stcatherinesiena@hbgdiocese.org stcatherinepa.com Rev. Olusola Adewole, OP, Pst.; Diane Dalgaard, DRE; CRP Stds.: 47

SELINSGROVE

St. Pius X - 112 Fairview Dr., Selinsgrove, PA 17870-9406 t) 570-374-4113 spxc@ptd.net stpiusxparish.net Rev. Joshua Cavender, Pst.; Dcn. Chris Darrup; CRP Stds.: 81

Susquehanna University - Selinsgrove Center -

SHAMOKIN

Mother Cabrini - 214 N. Shamokin St., Shamokin, PA 17872 t) 570-648-4512 x210 cabrini@ptd.net; judysurak@ptd.net www.mothercabrini.net Rev. Martin Kobos, OFM Conv., Pst.; Rev. Stephen King, OFM Conv, Par. Vicar; Judy Surak, DRE;

SHIPPENSBURG

Our Lady of the Visitation - 305 N. Prince St., Shippensburg, PA 17257 t) 717-532-2912 ourlady106@yahoo.com www.olvshippensburg.org Rev. Benjamin Dunkelberger, Pst.;

SPRING GROVE

Sacred Heart of Jesus - 146 N. Main St., Spring Grove, PA 17362; Mailing: 1031 Sprenkle Rd., Spring Grove, PA 17362 t) 717-225-1704 shjsg@hbgdiocese.org www.sacredheartsg.com Rev. Michael C. Letteer; Heather-Marie Merrill, Bus. Mgr.; CRP Stds.: 28

STEELTON

Prince of Peace - 815 S. Second St., Steelton, PA 17113 t) 717-985-1330 pop.parish@comcast.net popsteelton.org Rev. Jonathan P. Sawicki, Pst.; Dcn. Patrick M. Kiley; CRP Stds.: 13

SUNBURY

St. Monica Parish Sunbury Charitable Trust - 109 Market St., Sunbury, PA 17801 t) 570-286-1435 stmonicaparishsunbury@hbgdiocese.org stmonicasunbury.org Rev. Fred Wangwe, A.J., Pst.; Linda Walborn, Pst. Assoc.; Susan Bickhart, CRE; Monica Shovlin, Bus. Mgr.; CRP Stds.: 33

TREVORTON

St. Patrick - 331 W. Shamokin St., Trevorton, PA 17881-1523 t) 570-797-8251; 570-648-4432 (CRP) srevincent@hbgdiocese.org; stpats@ptd.net Sr. M. Emily Vincent, I.H.M., DRE;

WAYNESBORO

St. Andrew - 12 N. Broad St., Waynesboro, PA 17268 t) 717-762-1914 office@standrewwbo.org; dre@standrewwbo.org www.standrewwbo.org Rev. Christopher Onyeneke, M.SS.CC., Pst.; Margaret E. Wagaman, DRE; CRP Stds.: 53

St. Andrew School - 213 E. Main St., Waynesboro, PA 17268 t) 717-762-3221 nmiller@saintandrewschool.org www.saintandrewschool.org Lindsay Salmon, Prin.;

WILLIAMSTOWN

Sacred Heart of Jesus - E. Market St., Williamstown, PA 17098; Mailing: 732 Main St., Lykens, PA 17048 t) 717-453-7895; 717-647-2645 (CRP) ourladyhelpofchristiansparishlykens@hbgdiocese.org Rev. Michael Opoki, A.J., Pst.; Nora Valovage, DRE;

YORK

Immaculate Conception of the Blessed Virgin Mary - 309 S. George St., York, PA 17401 t) 717-846-6001 (CRP); 717-845-7629 mstarceski@stmarysyork.org www.stmarysyork.org Rev. John Kuchinski, Pst.; Rev. Charles Ocul, A.J., Chap.; Dcn. Catalino Gonzalez, Pst. Assoc.; Dcn. Stephen Paul Pichler, Pst. Assoc.; Marisa Starceski, DRE;

St. Joseph - 2935 Kingston Rd., York, PA 17402-4003 t) 717-755-7503 sjc@sjy.org www.sjy.org Rev. Stephen Fernandes, O.F.M.Cap., Pst.; Rev. Rigo Azanwi, OFM Cap., Par. Vicar; Dcn. Joe Shriver; CRP Stds.: 313

St. Patrick Parish York Charitable Trust - 231 S. Beaver St., York, PA 17401; Mailing: 219 S Beaver St, York, PW 17401 t) 717-848-2007; 717-854-6653 (CRP) frbateman@stpatrickyork.net; reled@stpatrickyork.net www.stpatrickyork.org Very Rev. John B. Bateman Jr., Pst.; Dcn. Michael V. DeVivo; Dcn. James Koch; Karen Bruskewicz, DRE; Rev. Hoa Van Nguyen, In Res.; Sr. Monica Imgrund, R.S.M., Pst. Assoc.; CRP Stds.: 70

Holy Trinity Catholic School - 235 S. Beaver St., York, PA 17401 t) 717-854-8263 ksmith@htcsyork.org

St. Rose of Lima - 950 W. Market St., York, PA 17401 t) 717-843-3043 (CRP); 717-846-4935 stroseoflimaparishyork@hbgdiocese.org www.saintroseoflimayork.org Rev. Dominic Azagbor, O.P., Pst.; Sharon Egan, DRE;

St. Rose of Lima School - 115 N. Biesecker Rd., Thomasville, PA 17364 t) 717-792-0889 Peggy Rizzuto, Prin.;

SCHOOLS: PRESCHOOL THRU HIGH SCHOOL

SCHOOLS

COMMONWEALTH OF PENNSYLVANIA

BERWICK

Holy Family Consolidated School - (PAR) 728 Washington St., Berwick, PA 18603 t) 570-752-2021 pmorisco@hfsberwick.org www.holyfamilyberwick.com/ David Brown, Prin.; Peter Morisco, Prin.; Laura Knorr, Librn.;

COLUMBIA

Our Lady of the Angels School - (PAR) 404 Cherry St., Columbia, PA 17512 t) 717-684-2433; 717-684-2664 ayoung@ourladyoftheangels.org www.ourladyoftheangels.org

HARRISBURG

Harrisburg Catholic Elementary School - (PAR) (Grades PreK-8) 225 North St., Harrisburg, PA 17101 t) 717-234-3797 jbearley@hbgcathelem.org www.hbgcathelem.org Joy Bearley, Prin.; Stds.: 206; Sr. Tchrs.: 1; Lay Tchrs.: 16

Harrisburg Catholic Elementary School - (Grades PreK-8) Stds.: 207; Sr. Tchrs.: 1; Lay Tchrs.: 12

Middle School - (Grades PreK-8) Stds.: 206; Sr. Tchrs.: 1; Lay Tchrs.: 12

LANCASTER

Resurrection Catholic School - (PAR) 521 E. Orange St., Lancaster, PA 17602 t) 717-392-3083 bweaver@resurrectioncatholicschool.net Brenda Weaver, Prin.; Robin Beutler, Librn.;

HIGH SCHOOLS

COMMONWEALTH OF PENNSYLVANIA

CAMP HILL

Trinity High School - (PAR) 3601 Simpson Ferry Rd., Camp Hill, PA 17011 t) 717-761-1116 jcominsky@thsrocks.us www.thsrocks.us Rev. Timothy J. Sahd, Chap.; John Cominsky, Prin.;

COAL TOWNSHIP

Our Lady of Lourdes Regional School - (PAR) (Grades PreK-12) 2001 Clinton Ave., Coal Township, PA 17866-1699 t) 570-644-0375 lourdes@ptd.net www.lourdes.k12.pa.us Rev. Andrew J. Stahmer, Chap.; Dcn. Martin P. McCarthy, Prin.;

HARRISBURG

Bishop McDevitt High School of Harrisburg - (PAR) 1 Crusader Way, Harrisburg, PA 17111 t) 717-236-7973 cpagliaro@bishopmcdevitt.org www.bishopmcdevitt.org Rev. Kevin J. Coyle, Chap.; Catherine Pagliaro, Prin.;

LANCASTER

Lancaster Catholic High School - (PAR) (Grades 9-12) 650 Juliette Ave., Lancaster, PA 17601 t) 717-509-0315 www.lchsyes.org Rev. Stephen Logue, Chap.; Terry Klugh, Prin.; Tim Hamer, Pres.; Stds.: 491; Lay Tchrs.: 37

LEBANON

Lebanon Catholic School - (PAR) (Grades PreK-12) 1400 Chestnut St., Lebanon, PA 17042 t) 717-273-3731 rosekury@lebanoncatholicschool.org; lebanoncatholic@hbgdiocese.org www.lebanoncatholicschool.org Rose Kury, Prin.; Megan Sanchez, Dir.; Cynthia Williams, Dir.;

MCSHERRYSTOWN

Delone Catholic High School - (PAR) 140 S. Oxford Ave., McSherrystown, PA 17344 t) 717-637-5969 information@delonecatholic.org www.delonecatholic.org Rev. Matthew Morelli, Chap.; Richard La Rocca, Prin.; John Fournie, Librn.;

YORK

York Catholic High School - (PAR) 601 E. Springettsbury Ave., York, PA 17403 t) 717-846-8871 info@yorkcatholic.org www.yorkcatholic.org Katie Seufert, Prin.;

INSTITUTIONS LOCATED IN DIOCESE

CAMPUS MINISTRY / NEWMAN CENTERS [CAM]

HARRISBURG

Catholic Campus Ministry - 4800 Union Deposit Rd., Harrisburg, PA 17111-3710 t) 717-657-4804 jjackson@hbgdiocese.org www.hbgdiocese.org Rev. David L. Danneker, Vicar;

Bloomsburg University of Pennsylvania - 353 E. Second St., Bloomsburg, PA 17815 t) 570-784-3123 Rev. Olusola Adewole, OP, Campus Min.;

Bucknell University - Newman Center, 610 St. George St., Lewisburg, PA 17837 t) 570-577-3766

Dickinson College - 152 E. Pomfret St., Carlisle, PA 17013 t) 717-243-4411 dickinsoncollegecampusministry@hbgdiocese.org Rev. Tiburtius Anthony Raja, Campus Min.;

Elizabethtown College - 1840 Marshall Dr., Elizabethtown, PA 17022 t) 717-367-1255 Rev. Bernard Mary Oniwe, Campus Min.;

Franklin and Marshall College, Lancaster - 558 W. Walnut St., Lancaster, PA 17603 t) 717-394-0757 Rev. Joshua Cavender, Campus Min.;

Gettysburg College - 300 N. Washington St., Gettysburg, PA 17325-0136; Mailing: Box 427, Gettysburg, PA 17325-0136 t) 717-337-6284 Rev. Andrew St. Hilaire, Campus Min.; Mary A. Geesaman, Campus Lay Minister;

Lebanon Valley College - 125 S. Spruce St., Annville, PA 17003 t) 717-867-1525 Rev. Kevin J. Coyle, Campus Min.;

Messiah College - 310 Hertzler Rd., Mechanicsburg, PA 17055 t) 717-766-2511 x7192 Rev. Msgr. William J. King, Campus Min.;

Millersville University - Newman Center, 227 N. George St., Millersville, PA 17551 t) 717-584-6447 Rev. Joshua Cavender, Campus Min.; Alicia Q. Spelfogel, Dir.;

Penn State University, Mont Alto Campus, South Mountain - 12 N. Broad St., Waynesboro, PA 17268 t) 717-762-1914

***Shippensburg University** - 1871 Old Main Dr., Rm.

215, Shippensburg, PA 17257 t) 717-477-1244 catholic@ship.edu Rev. Dwight D. Schlaline, Campus Min.; Nichole Schneider, Campus Min.;
Susquehanna University Catholic Campus Ministry - 112 Fairview Dr., Selinsgrove, PA 17870 t) 570-374-4113 frpius@ptd.net Rev. Tukura Pius Michael, O.P., Pst.;
York College - Catholic Campus Min. c/o Office of Spiritual Life, 441 Country Club Rd, York, PA 17403 t) 717-846-7591 Rev. Benjamin Dunkelberger, Campus Min.;

CATHOLIC CHARITIES [CCH]

HARRISBURG

Department for Catholic Charities Administrative Office - 4800 Union Deposit Rd., Harrisburg, PA 17111-3710 t) 717-657-4804; 717-657-4804 cklinger@hbgdiocese.org www.cchbg.org Peter A. Biasucci, Exec.; Carole Klinger, Exec.; Mark A. Totaro, Exec.;

Adoption Services - 939 E. Park Dr., Ste. 103, Harrisburg, PA 17111 t) 717-564-7115 gpfeifer@cchbg.org Gwen Needs Pfiefer, Dir.;
Capital Region Office - 939 E. Park Dr., Ste. 101, Harrisburg, PA 17111 t) 717-233-7978 kbolton@cchbg.org Kelly M. Bolton, Dir.;
Employment Services - t) 717-232-0568 ymohamed@cchbg.org Yusuf Mohamand, Dir.;
English As A Second Language - t) 717-232-0568 shbeck@cchbg.org Sara Beck, Dir.;
Evergreen House Program - 120 Willow Rd., Ste. B, Harrisburg, PA 17109 t) 717-412-4594 lthomas@cchbg.org Lydia Thomas, Dir.;
Immigration and Refugee Services - 939 E. Park Dr., Ste. 102, Harrisburg, PA 17111 t) 717-232-0568 ahabeeb@cchbg.org Annette Martin, Exec.;
Intensive Day Treatment - 47 S. Mulberry St., Lancaster, PA 17603 t) 717-295-9630 rdiamondstone@cchbg.org Rebecca Diamondstone, Dir.;
Interfaith Shelter for Homeless Families - 120 Willow Rd., Ste. C, Harrisburg, PA 17109 t) 717-652-8740 lpeck@cchbg.org Lisa Peck, Dir.;
Lancaster Office - 925 N. Duke St., Lancaster, PA 17602 t) 717-299-3659; 717-392-2113 (Spanish) kbolton@cchbg.org Kelly M. Bolton, Dir.;
Lourdeshouse Maternity Services - 120 Willow Rd., Ste. A, Harrisburg, PA 17109 t) 717-412-4865 amartin@cchbg.org
Paradise School - 6156 W. Canal Rd., Abbottstown, PA 17301-8982 t) 717-259-9537 dlangeheine@cchbg.org Dustin Langeheine, Dir.;
Resettlement Services - t) 717-232-0568 ahabeeb@cchbg.org Annette Martin, Exec.;
Specialized Foster Care - 939 E. Park Dr., Ste. 103, Harrisburg, PA 17111 t) 717-654-7115 gpfeifer@cchbg.org Suzanne Kearse, Dir.;
York Intensive Family Services - 253 E. Market St., York, PA 17401 t) 717-843-7986 skearse@cchbg.org Suzanne Kearse, Dir.;
York Office - 253 E. Market St., York, PA 17403 t) 717-845-2696 kbolton@cchbg.org Kelly M. Bolton, Dir.;
York/Adams Family Based Program - 6156 W. Canal Rd., Abbottstown, PA 17301-8982 t) 717-845-3373 rjacoby@cchbg.org Rebecca Jacoby, Dir.;

CONVENTS, MONASTERIES, AND RESIDENCES FOR WOMEN [CON]

COLUMBIA

Adorers of the Blood of Christ - 3954 Columbia Ave., Columbia, PA 17512-9714 t) 717-285-4536 www.adorers.org Sr. Joan Hornick, ASC, Contact; Srs.: 6

DANVILLE

Discalced Carmelite Nuns of Danville, PA - 190 Maria Hall Dr., Danville, PA 17821-1237 t) (570) 275-1120 Sr. Angela Pikus, O.C.D., Prioress; Srs.: 6
Sisters of Saints Cyril and Methodius - Villa Sacred Heart, 1002 Railroad St., Danville, PA 17821-1873 t) 570-275-3581 x300 jambresscm@hotmail.com www.sscm.org Sr. Barbara Sable, S.S.C.M., Supr.; Srs.: 53

St. Cyril Academy Preschool and Kindergarten - Villa Sacred Heart, 1002 Railroad St., Danville, PA 17821-1873 t) (570) 275-3581 x160 donnascasscm@hotmail.com www.stcyril1.vpweb.com Sr. Donna Marie, SS.C.M., Dir.;
St. Cyril Education and Spiritual Center - Villa Sacred Heart, 1002 Railroad St., Danville, PA 17821-1873 t) (570) 275-3581 x240 stcyrilspiritualcenter@gmail.com

HARRISBURG

Sisters of IHM Saint Catherine Laboure Convent - 4010 Derry St., Harrisburg, PA 17111 t) 717-745-4134 ihm4010@comcast.net Sr. Bernard Agnes, I.H.M., Supr.;

ENDOWMENTS / FOUNDATIONS / TRUSTS [EFT]

HARRISBURG

The Neumann Scholarship Foundation - 4800 Union Deposit Rd., Harrisburg, PA 17111-3710 t) 717-657-4804 frequinlan@hbgdiocese.org Very Rev. Edward J. Quinlan, Dir.;
Roman Catholic Diocese of Harrisburg Charitable Trust - 4800 Union Deposit Rd., Harrisburg, PA 17111 t) 717-657-4804 hbgdiocese.org Barbara A. Bettwy, Chancellor; Very Rev. Anthony R. Dill, Vice Chancellor; Very Rev. William C. Forrey, Vicar; Very Rev. Mark M. Speitel, Vicar; Alberto Rodriguez, Archivist;
Roman Catholic Diocese of Harrisburg Real Estate Trust - 4800 Union Deposit Rd., Harrisburg, PA 17111 t) 717-657-4804 Very Rev. William C. Forrey, Vicar;

LANCASTER

CHI St. Joseph Children's Health - 1929 Lincoln Hwy. E., Ste. 150, Lancaster, PA 17602 t) 717-397-7625 bethgrossmann@catholichealth.net www.chistjosephchildrenshealth.org (An affiliate of CommonSpirit Health) Beth Grossmann, Vice. Pres.;

HOSPITALS / HEALTH SERVICES [HOS]

CAMP HILL

***Holy Spirit Corporation** - 503 N. 21st St., Camp Hill, PA 17011 t) 717-763-2100 Rev. Robert F. Sharman, Dir.;
***Holy Spirit Health System** - 503 N. 21st St., Camp Hill, PA 17011-2288 t) 717-763-2100 Holy Spirit Corporation., Holy Spirit Hospital of the Sisters of the Christian Charity., Spirit Physician Services, Inc., West Shore ALS, Inc., Sister Kyle C. Snyder, Admin.;
***Holy Spirit Hospital of the Sisters of Christian Charity** - 503 N. 21st St., Camp Hill, PA 17011 t) 717-763-2100 see also Holy Spirit Health System Rev. Robert F. Sharman, Dir.;
***Spirit Physician Services, Inc.** - 503 N. 21st St., Camp Hill, PA 17011 t) 717-763-2100 Rev. Robert F. Sharman, Dir.;
***West Shore ALS, Inc.** - 503 N. 21st St., Camp Hill, PA 17011 t) 717-972-4491 Kyle C. Snyder, Admin.;

MISCELLANEOUS [MIS]

ELIZABETHTOWN

***Stewardship: A Mission of Faith** - 11 Black Hawk Ln., Elizabethtown, PA 17022 t) 717-367-0100 info@stewardshipmission.org www.stewardshipmission.org Chris Dipert, Exec.;

FAIRFIELD

Carmel of Jesus, Mary, & Joseph, Fairfield, Inc. - 327 Water St., Fairfield, PA 17320 t) 570-672-2122 fairfieldcarmelites@gmail.com www.fairfieldcarmelites.org/ Mother Stella Marie Gagne, Prioress;
Missionaries of the Sacred Hearts of Jesus & Mary House of Studies - 350 Tract Rd., Fairfield, PA 17320 t) 717-457-0114 fatherrobert356@gmail.com Rev. Peter DiTomasso, M.SS.CC., Rector;

HARRISBURG

Harrisburg Catholic Administrative Services, Inc. - 4800 Union Deposit Rd., Harrisburg, PA 17111 t) 717-657-4804 hkline@hbgdiocese.org Donald Kaercher, Exec.;
Kolbe Catholic Publishing, Inc. - 4800 Union Deposit Rd., Harrisburg, PA 17111-3710 t) 717-657-4804 x387 kolbepublishing@hbgdiocese.org
Pennsylvania Catholic Conference - 214 State St., Harrisburg, PA 17105; Mailing: PO Box 2835, Harrisburg, PA 17105 t) 717-238-9613 info@pacatholic.org www.pacatholic.org Eric Failing, Exec.;

MCSHERRYSTOWN

St. Joseph Village Corporation - 50 Academy St., McSherrystown, PA 17344; Mailing: Mt. St. Joseph Convent 9701 Germantown Ave., Philadelphia, PA 19118-2694 t) 215-248-7205 kshelly@ssjphila.org www.ssjphila.org Residence for Senior Citizens. Sisters of St. Joseph. Sr. Maureen Erdlen, SSJ, Pres.;

Village Location - t) 717-637-4441 Sr. Joanne Fehrenbach, S.S.J., Secy.;

MONASTERIES AND RESIDENCES FOR PRIESTS AND BROTHERS [MON]

EPHRATA

St. Clement's Mission House - 300 W. Pine St., Ephrata, PA 17522-2072 t) 717-733-6596 ledger@ptd.net Redemptorist Fathers and Brothers. Rev. Kevin Moley, C.Ss.R., Rector; Rev. Charles J. Brinkmann; Rev. Gordon Cannoles, C.Ss.R.; Rev. Richard Knappik, C.S.s.R.; Rev. John Murray, C.Ss.R.; Rev. Thomas Siconolfi, C.Ss.R.; Rev. James Szobonya, C.Ss.R.; Rev. Gerard J. Szymkowiak, C.Ss.R.; Rev. Arthur Tuttle, C.Ss.R.; Priests: 10

NURSING / REHABILITATION / CONVALESCENCE / ELDERLY CARE [NUR]

COLUMBIA

St. Anne's Retirement Community - 3952 Columbia Ave., Columbia, PA 17512-9715 t) 717-285-5443 mturnbaugh@stannesrc.org Adorers of the Blood of Christ. Rev. Norman C. Hohenwarter Jr., Chap.; Mary Turnbaugh, Pres.;

DANVILLE

Maria Hall, Inc. - 190 Maria Hall Dr., Danville, PA 17821 t) 570-275-1120 mhpcadm@yahoo.com Personal Care Home and Convent: Sisters of SS. Cyril & Methodius, Carmelites of Danville, Religious and Contemplatives of the Good Shepherd Rev. Gerard T. Heintzelman, Chap.; Sr. M. Philothea Fabian, SS.C.M., Admin.; Asstd. Annu.: 33; Staff: 23
Maria Joseph Manor - 1707 Montour Blvd., Danville, PA 17821 t) 570-275-4221 smaosscm@yahoo.com www.mariajosephccc.org Personal Care at Maria Joseph Continuing Care Community which includes Nazareth Memory Care, Emmanuel Skilled Care and Meadows Independent Living Sr. Sara Swayze, Treas.; Asstd. Annu.: 285; Staff: 502

The Meadows at Maria Joseph Manor - t) 570-271-1000 Sr. M. Christopher Godlewski, Dir.;

HARRISBURG

Bishop Dattilo Retirement Residence for Priests - 675 Rutherford Rd., Harrisburg, PA 17109 t) 717-657-3147 retirementresidence@hbgdiocese.org Mark A. Totaro, Exec.;

YORK

Misericordia Nursing & Rehabilitation Center - 998 S. Russell St., York, PA 17402 t) 717-755-1964 mbittner@mn-rc.org mn-rc.org Daughters of Our Lady of Mercy. Marion Bittner, Admin.;

An asterisk (*) denotes an organization that has established tax-exempt status directly with the IRS and is not covered by the USCCB Group Ruling.

Archdiocese of Hartford

(Archidioecesis Hartfortiensis)

MOST REVEREND LEONARD P. BLAIR, S.T.D., D.D.

Archbishop of Hartford; ordained June 26, 1976; appointed Titular Bishop of Voncariana and Auxiliary Bishop of Detroit July 9, 1999; ordained August 24, 1999; appointed Bishop of Toledo October 7, 2003; installed December 4, 2003; appointed Archbishop of Hartford October 29, 2013; installed December 16, 2013. Office: 134 Farmington Ave., Hartford, CT 06105-3784. T: 860-541-6491; F: 860-541-6293.

Chancery Office: The Hartford Roman Catholic Diocesan Corporation, 134 Farmington Ave., Hartford, CT 06105-3784. T: 860-541-6491; F: 860-541-6309. www.archdioceseofhartford.org

Square Miles 2,288.

ESTABLISHED NOVEMBER 28, 1843; CREATED ARCHDIOCESE AUGUST 6, 1953.

Corporate Title: "The Hartford Roman Catholic Diocesan Corporation."

Comprises the Counties of Hartford, Litchfield and New Haven in the State of Connecticut.

For legal titles of parishes and archdiocesan institutions, consult the Chancery Office.

MOST REVEREND JUAN MIGUEL BETANCOURT TORRES, S.E.M.V., S.S.L., M.DIV.

Auxiliary Bishop of Hartford; ordained April 21, 2001; appointed Auxiliary Bishop of Hartford and Titular See of Curzola September 18, 2018; ordained Bishop October 18, 2018. Office: 134 Farmington Ave., Hartford, CT 06105-3784. T: 860-541-6491; F: 860-541-6293.

STATISTICAL OVERVIEW

Personnel

Archbishops	1
Retired Archbishops	2
Auxiliary Bishops	1
Retired Bishops	2
Priests: Diocesan Active in Diocese	123
Priests: Diocesan Active Outside Diocese	5
Priests: Retired, Sick or Absent	103
Number of Diocesan Priests	231
Religious Priests in Diocese	18
Total Priests in your Diocese	249
Extern Priests in Diocese	14
Ordinations:	
Transitional Deacons	2
Permanent Deacons in Diocese	170
Total Brothers	63
Total Sisters	404

Parishes

Parishes	114
With Resident Pastor:	
Resident Diocesan Priests	103
Resident Religious Priests	10
Without Resident Pastor:	
Administered by Deacons	1
Professional Ministry Personnel:	
Brothers	1
Sisters	13
Lay Ministers	59

Welfare

Catholic Hospitals	2
Total Assisted	716,147
Health Care Centers	3
Total Assisted	1,575
Homes for the Aged	7
Total Assisted	1,277
Day Care Centers	11
Total Assisted	436
Special Centers for Social Services	15
Total Assisted	11,000
Residential Care of Disabled	8
Total Assisted	28
Other Institutions	2
Total Assisted	8,742

Educational

Diocesan Students in Other Seminaries	14
Seminaries, Religious	1
Students, Religious	51
Total Seminarians	65
Colleges and Universities	2
Total Students	5,227
High Schools, Diocesan and Parish	3
Total Students	1,251
High Schools, Private	5
Total Students	1,969
Elementary Schools, Diocesan and Parish	26
Total Students	5,427
Elementary Schools, Private	2
Total Students	267
Catechesis/Religious Education:	
High School Students	5,199
Elementary Students	15,044
Total Students under Catholic Instruction	34,449
Teachers in Diocese:	
Priests	4
Brothers	1
Sisters	9
Lay Teachers	634

Vital Statistics

Receptions into the Church:	
Infant Baptism Totals	3,699
Minor Baptism Totals	307
Adult Baptism Totals	69
Received into Full Communion	493
First Communions	3,459
Confirmations	3,635
Marriages:	
Catholic	666
Interfaith	90
Total Marriages	756
Deaths	6,534
Total Catholic Population	643,341
Total Population	1,949,519

LEADERSHIP

Chancery Office-Office of the Archbishop - t) 860-541-6491 www.archdioceseofhartford.org Most Rev. Leonard P. Blair, Archbishop of Hartford (archbishop@aohct.org); Bernadette Foley, Exec. Asst. to Archbishop (bernadette.foley@aohct.org);

Secretary to the Archbishop - t) 860-541-6491 Rev. John E. Gancarz, Secy.; Diana Tierinni, Admin. Asst. to Sec.;

Office of the Auxiliary Bishop - t) 860-541-6491 x1028 www.archdioceseofhartford.org Most Rev. Juan M. Betancourt, S.E.M.V., Auxiliary Bishop of Hartford; Michelle Harris, Exec. Asst. to Bishop;

ADMINISTRATION

Vicar General, Moderator of the Curia and Office for Administration - t) 860-541-6491 x3136 www.archdioceseofhartford.org Very Rev. Steven C. Boguslawski; Pamela Johnson, Exec. Asst.;

Chancellor - t) 860-541-6491 www.archdioceseofhartford.org Rev. Christopher M. Ford, Chancellor; Very Rev. Steven C. Boguslawski, Asst. Chancellor; Very Rev. George S. Mukuka, Asst. Chancellor (fr.mukuka@aohct.org);

Vicar for Clergy - t) 860-541-6491 x3150 www.archdioceseofhartford.org Rev. Msgr. James A. Shanley (msgr.shanley@aohct.org);

Delegate for Religious - t) 860-541-6491 x7492 www.archdioceseofhartford.org Sr. Barbara A. Mullen, C.S.J. (sbamcsj@gmail.com);

Office of the Permanent Diaconate - t) 860-541-6491 x7448 www.archdioceseofhartford.org Dcn. James J. McCormack, Asst. Vicar for Clergy;

OFFICES AND DIRECTORS

Archdiocesan Dispute Resolution Office - t) 860-541-6491 x3136 www.archdioceseofhartford.org Very Rev. Steven C. Boguslawski, Vicar Gen.;

Office of the Archdiocesan Archives - t) 860-541-6491 x3141 www.archdioceseofhartford.org Bridgette A. Woodall, Archivist (bridgette.woodall@aohct.org);

Office for Catholic Social Justice Ministry - t) 860-541-6491 www.archdioceseofhartford.org Lynn M. Campbell, Exec. (lynn.campbell@aohct.org);

Office for People with Disabilities (Vacant) - t) 860-541-6491 www.archdioceseofhartford.org

Office of Divine Worship - t) 860-541-6491 fr.ruminski@aohct.org www.archdioceseofhartford.org Rev. Michael A. Ruminski, Dir.;

Office of Faith and Culture - t) 860-541-6491 x3128 a.iriarte@aohct.org www.archdioceseofhartford.org Arturo Iriarte, Dir.;

Office of Human Resources - t) 860-541-6491 www.archdioceseofhartford.org Karen A. Kean, Dir. (karen.kean@aohct.org); Lesli Anderson, Group Benefits, Pension & Payroll Coord. (lesli.anderson@aohct.org);

Office of the Catholic Deaf Apostolate - t) 860-570-1806 (Voice); 860-965-0157 (Text) www.archdioceseofhartford.org Dcn. Dennis R. Ferguson, Dir. (dcn.ferguson@aohct.org);

Office of Safe Environment - t) 860-541-6491 www.archdioceseofhartford.org Ginamarie Garabedian, Dir. (ginamarie.garabedian@aohct.org); Theresa Hatfield, Background Check Coord. (theresa.hatfield@aohct.org);

Victim Assistance Coordinator - Faith Vos Winkel, Dir.;

Catholic Mission Aid Office - t) 860-541-6491 x3150 www.archdioceseofhartford.org Rev. Msgr. James A. Shanley, Dir. (msgr.shanley@aohct.org);

Office of Seminarians and Vocations - t) 860-761-7456 vocations@aohct.org www.archdioceseofhartford.org Most Rev. Juan M. Betancourt, S.E.M.V., Dir.; Rev. Michael T. Casey, Dir. (fr.casey@aohct.org); Ellen Tanguay, Admin. Asst.;

Associate Directors - t) 860-541-6491 Rev. Glen J. Dmytryszyn; Rev. Anthony Federico III; Rev. Jaime G. Maldonado-Aviles;

ADVISORY BOARDS, COMMISSIONS, COMMITTEES, AND COUNCILS

Episcopal Vicars - t) 860-541-6491 www.archdioceseofhartford.org Very Rev. John P. Melnick, Northern Vicariate; Very Rev. Daniel G. Keefe, Southern Vicariate; Very Rev. Robert M. Kwiatkowski, Western Vicariate;

Connecticut Catholic Conference - t) 860-541-6491 www.ctcatholic.org Christopher C. Healy, Exec. Dir. (chealy@ctcatholic.org); Anne Lamonica, Assoc. Dir., Educ. (anne.lamonica@aohct.org); Dcn. David Reynolds, Assoc. Dir., Public Policy (dcn.reynolds@aohct.org);

College of Consultors - t) 860-541-6491 bishop@aohct.org www.archdioceseofhartford.org Most Rev. Juan M. Betancourt, S.E.M.V.; Very Rev. Steven C. Boguslawski; Rev. Msgr. James A. Shanley (msgr.shanley@aohct.org);

Consultors - Canon 1742 - t) 860-541-6491 www.archdioceseofhartford.org Rev. Msgr. John J. Georgia (msgr.georgia@aohct.org); Rev. John S. Golas (fr.golas@aohct.org); Rev. Lawrence S. Symolon;

Presbyteral Council - t) 860-541-6491 www.archdioceseofhartford.org

Appointed Members - fr.ramirez@aohct.org Rev. Joseph P. Crowley, Dean Deanery 1; Rev. Matthew G. Gworek, Dean Deanery 2; Rev. Nicholas P. Melo, Dean Deanery 3;

Elected Members - Rev. Michael A. Santiago; Rev. Alvin J. LeBlanc; Rev. Joseph R. Cronin;

Ex Officio Members - bishop@aohct.org; fr.boguslawski@aohct.org Most Rev. Juan M. Betancourt, S.E.M.V., Auxiliary Bishop; Rev. Christopher M. Ford, Chancellor; Very Rev. Steven C. Boguslawski, Vicar;

Peritus Member - fr.mukuka@aohct.org Very Rev. George S. Mukuka;

CATHOLIC CHARITIES

Archdiocese of Hartford Catholic Charities - t) (860) 493-1841 www.ccaoh.org Marek Kukulka, CEO;

CLERGY AND RELIGIOUS SERVICES

Priest Retirement Board - t) 860-541-6491 www.archdioceseofhartford.org Rev. Msgr. James A. Shanley, Mem. (msgr.shanley@aohct.org); Rev. Msgr. Gerard G. Schmitz, Mem. (msgr.schmitz@aohct.org); Very Rev. Steven C. Boguslawski, Mem.;

Retirement Plan for Secular Priests of the Archdiocese of Hartford - t) 860-541-6491 www.archdioceseofhartford.org Rev. Shawn T. Daly, Ex Officio;

Office of Continuing Formation for Priests - t) 860-541-6491 fr.dolan@aohct.org www.archdioceseofhartford.org Rev. Michael J. Dolan, Dir.;

Minister for Priests - t) 860-541-6491 www.archdioceseofhartford.org Rev. Shawn T. Daly;

COMMUNICATIONS

Office of Communications and Public Relations - t) 860-541-6491 www.archdioceseofhartford.org Rev. Matthew G. Gworek, Dir.; David Elliott, Assoc. Dir.;

Office of Radio and Television/WJMJ-FM - t) 877-342-5956 ortv@aohct.org www.ortv.org Rev. John P. Gatzak, Exec. Dir.;

Magazine - Catholic Transcript - karen.avitabile@aohct.org Most Rev. Leonard P. Blair, Pres.; Karen A. Avitabile, Editor;

Photographer/Media Consultant - aaron.joseph@aohct.org Aaron Joseph;

Writer - shelley.wolf@aohct.org Shelley Wolf;

DEANERIES

Deanery 1 - t) 860-541-6491 www.archdioceseofhartford.org Rev. Gerald H. Dziedzic, Dean;

Deanery 2 - t) 860-541-6491 www.archdioceseofhartford.org Rev. Marcin P. Pluciennik, Dean;

Deanery 3 - t) 860-541-6491 www.archdioceseofhartford.org Rev. Daniel J. McLearen, Dean;

Deanery 4 - t) 860-541-6491 www.archdioceseofhartford.org Rev. Ivan D. Ramirez, Dean;

Deanery 5 - t) 860-541-6491 www.archdioceseofhartford.org Very Rev. James M. Sullivan, Dean;

Deanery 6 - t) 860-541-6491 www.archdioceseofhartford.org Rev. Jeffrey V. Romans, Dean;

Deanery 7 - t) 860-541-6491 www.archdioceseofhartford.org Rev. Jose Angel Mercado Jr., Dean;

DEVELOPMENT

Development Office - t) 860-761-7455 (William); 860-913-2673 (Amanda) www.archdioceseofhartford.org William McLean, Chief Devel. Officer; Amanda Martinelli, Dir. Oper.;

Forward with Faith - t) 860-541-6491 x2693 beth.wade@aohct.org www.archdioceseofhartford.org Elizabeth Wade, Devel. Officer - Major Gifts/Research for HBF;

The Hartford Bishops' Foundation - t) 860-541-6491 hbf@aohct.org Patricia Levandoski, Dir. Finance & Admin. for HBF; Suzan Bibisi, Mgr. Special Events for HBF; Kemche Michalic, Devel. Officer, Leadership Gifts for HBF;

Archbishop's Annual Appeal - t) 860-541-6491 www.archdioceseofhartford.org Rev. Jeffrey V. Romans, Chair; Tina Poet, Dir.; Timothy O'Shea, Data Admin., Archbishop's Annual Appeal;

EDUCATION

The Center for Catholic Education & Formation - t) 860-541-6491 www.archdioceseofhartford.org

Assistant Superintendent - eric.frenette@aohct.org Eric Frenette;

Faith Formation - kelly.henderschedt@aohct.org Kelly Henderschedt, Dir.;

Faith Formation Programs and Technology - jennifer.mcclintock@aohct.org Jennifer McClintock, Coord.;

Finance and Technology - laura.mccaffrey@aohct.org Laura McCaffrey, Exec. Dir.;

New England Catholic Biblical School - judy.kostelni@aohct.org Judy Kostelni, Dir.;

Superintendent of Catholic Schools - valerie.mara@aohct.org Valerie Mara;

Vicar for the Center for Catholic Education & Formation - fr.whyte@aohct.org Rev. Michael G. Whyte;

FACILITIES

Cathedral of Saint Joseph - t) (860) 249-8431 www.archdioceseofhartford.org

Library - t) 860-541-6491 www.archdioceseofhartford.org Rody Bazzano, Asst.; Rebecca Empoliti, Asst.;

The Chancery - t) 860-541-6491 www.archdioceseofhartford.org

The Saint Thomas Seminary of Hartford Corp - t) 860-541-6491 www.archdioceseofhartford.org Steven Rugens, Oper. Mgr.;

Archbishop Daniel A. Cronin Residence - t) 860-541-6491 www.archdioceseofhartford.org Sr. Cecelia Scaduto, A.S.C.J., Archbishop's Delegate for Senior Priests; Rev. Lawrence S. Symolon, Asst. to Vicar for Clergy for Senior Priests, Dir.;

FINANCE

Finance Office - t) 860-541-6491 www.archdioceseofhartford.org

Accounting Manager - deborah.grenier@aohct.org Deborah Grenier;

Accounts Payable Coordinator -

arlyn.page@aohct.org Arlyn Page;
Accounts Receivable Coordinator - cheryl.roaix@aohct.org Cheryl A. Roaix;
Chief Finance Officer - richard.braam@aohct.org Richard Braam;
Coordinator of Parish Financial Services and Parish Reporting and Analysis - dean.walford@aohct.org Dean W. Walford;
Director of Corporations, Offices, Agencies, and Financial Reporting - john.majkowski@aohct.org John Majkowski;
Executive Assistant To CFO - arlyn.page@aohct.org Arlyn Page;
Finance Manager - gene.munson@aohct.org Gene A. Munson;
Investment and Risk Management Officer - matt.byrne@aohct.org Matthew A. Byrne;
Parish Review Manager - veena.gowda@aohct.org Veena Gowda;
Staff Accountant for Corporations, Offices, Agencies, and Financial Reporting - asta.valionyte@aohct.org Asta Valionyte;
Treasury Management and Analyst - terry.mroczkowski@aohct.org Theresa Mroczkowski;

ORGANIZATIONS
Connecticut Catholic Cemeteries Association - t) 203-239-2557 jpinone@ccacem.org wwwccacem.org John Pinone, Exec. Dir.;

PASTORAL SERVICES
Campus Ministry - t) 860-541-6491 campmin@aohct.org www.archdioceseofhartford.org Theresa Bournique, Campus Min.;
Pastoral Planning - t) 860-541-6491 x7448 dcn.mccormack@aohct.org www.archdioceseofhartford.org Dcn. James J. McCormack, Asst. to Dir.;

PARISH SERVICES
Commission for Ecumenical Affairs - t) 860-541-6491 fr.donahue@aohct.org www.archdioceseofhartford.org Rev. Aidan N. Donahue, Ecumenical Officer;
Property and Assets - t) 860-541-6491 www.archdioceseofhartford.org Paul Connery, Dir.; Chris Kelly, Project Mgr.; Joanne Reilly, Property & Assets Assoc.;
Interreligious Affairs - t) 860-541-6491 fr.dolan@aohct.org www.archdioceseofhartford.org Rev. Michael J. Dolan, Dir.;

SPIRITUAL LIFE
Crossroads 4 Christ - t) 860-810-7956 www.crossroadsforchrist.org Alex Soucy, Exec. Dir.; Katie Purple, Dir. Formation;
Cursillo Movement - t) 860-482-4433 (Rev. Carlos M. Zapata); 203-756-4439 (Rev. Diego A. Jimenez) www.hartfordcursillo.org Rev. Carlos Zapata, Spiritual Adv., English & Portuguese; Rev. Diego A. Jimenez, Spiritual Adv., Spanish;
Family Life Office (Vacant) - t) 860-541-6491 www.archdioceseofhartford.org
Pro-Life Activities - t) 203-639-0833 prolife@flcenter.org www.archdioceseofhartford.org Rev. Glen J. Dmytryszyn, Dir.; Sr. Suzanne Gross, F.S.E., Respect Life Prog. Coord.; Sr. Amaris Salata, F.S.E., Respect Life Asst. Prog. Coord.;

TRIBUNAL
Metropolitan Tribunal - t) 860-541-6491 www.archdioceseofhartford.org
Assessor - t) 860-541-6491 Very Rev. Steven C. Boguslawski;
Defender of the Bond - t) 860-541-6491 msgr.kinnane@aohct.org Rev. Msgr. James F. Kinnane;
Ecclesiastical Judge/Canonists - t) 860-541-6491 justin.wachs@aohct.org; john.vizza@aohct.org Msgr. Thomas J. Barry; Rev. Christopher M. Ford; Justin Wachs;
Expert - t) 860-541-6491 Robert Swords;
Judicial Vicar (Officialis) - t) 860-541-6491 x7480 fr.mukuka@aohct.org Very Rev. George S. Mukuka, Vicar;
Moderator of the Metropolitan Tribunal - t) 860-541-6491 x7480 carol.hatten@aohct.org Carol M. Hatten;
Promoter of Justice - t) 860-541-6491 msgr.mccarthy@aohct.org Rev. Msgr. John J. McCarthy;
Tribunal Transcriptionist - t) 860-541-6491 x7490 linda.warks@aohct.org Linda Warks;

MISCELLANEOUS / OTHER OFFICES
Music Ministry - t) 860-578-1427 musicoffice@sjcct.org www.archdioceseofhartford.org Dr. Ezequiel Menendez;
Censor Librorum (Vacant) - t) 860-541-6491 www.archdioceseofhartford.org

PARISHES, MISSIONS, AND CLERGY

STATE OF CONNECTICUT

ANSONIA

The Church of the Assumption of the B.V. - 35 N Cliff St., Ansonia, CT 06401-1698; Mailing: 61 N Cliff St., Ansonia, CT 06401 t) 203-735-7857 welcome@assumptionansonia.church assumptionansonia.church Rev. Jeffrey A. Gubbiotti, Pst.; Dcn. Laurent Yergeau;
Assumption School - (Grades K-8) 51 N. Cliff St., Ansonia, CT 06401-1698 t) 203-734-0855 tbourke@assumptionschool.net assumptionansonia.com/ Torin Bourke, Prin.; Monica Masiero, Librn.; Stds.: 175; Lay Tchrs.: 11
Holy Rosary Church Corporation of Ansonia, Connecticut - 10 Fr. Salemi Dr., Ansonia, CT 06401 t) 203-735-7874 fff@holyrosaryansonia.org; holyrosary@aohct.org www.holyrosaryansonia.org Linked with Assumption Church, Ansonia, CT. 06401 Rev. Jeffrey A. Gubbiotti, Pst.; Robert Laccone, DRE; Dcn. Michael Lynch; CRP Stds.: 36
The St. Joseph Church Corporation of Ansonia - 32 Jewett St., Ansonia, CT 06401-2499 t) 203-734-0402 stjosephansonia@aohct.org; st.joseph.rectory@frontier.com Rev. Tadeusz Maciejewski, C.M., Pst.; Rev. Waclaw Hlond, C.M., In Res.; Rev. Mitchell Wanat, C.M., In Res.; CRP Stds.: 15

AVON

St. Ann's Church of Avon - 289 Arch Rd., Avon, CT 06001-4209 t) 860-673-9858; 860-673-2137 (CRP) stann@aohct.org www.stannavon.org Rev. Alphonso R. Fontana, Pst.; Dcn. Timothy Healy; Dcn. Jeffrey B. Sutherland; Rev. Joseph Cheah, O.S.M., In Res.; Rosemary Neamtz, DRE; Valerie St. Jean, DRE; CRP Stds.: 486

BEACON FALLS

The St. Michael's Church Corporation, Beacon Falls, Connecticut - 25 Maple Ave., Beacon Falls, CT 06403-1145 t) 203-729-2504 stmichaelbeaconfalls@gmail.com www.saintmichaelsonline.org Rev. Joy Jacob, SDB, Pst.; CRP Stds.: 155

BLOOMFIELD

Sacred Heart Church Corporation, Bloomfield - 26 Wintonbury Ave., Bloomfield, CT 06002 t) 860-242-4142 sacredheartbloomfield@aohct.org; sacredheartblct@gmail.com sacredheartbloomfieldct.com Rev. Michael A. Ruminski, Pst.; Dcn. Anthony Nwankwo; Dcn. Richard D. Santos; CRP Stds.: 40

BRANFORD

Saint John Bosco Parish Corporation - 731 Main St., Branford, CT 06405-3693 t) 203-488-1607; 203-488-2998 (CRP) stjohnbosco@aohct.org www.saintjohnboscobranford.org Very Rev. Daniel G. Keefe, Pst.; Rev. George Vellaplackil (India), Par. Vicar; Dcn. Robert J. Macaluso; Rev. Msgr. David M. Walker, Senior Status; Jenny Smith, DRE; CRP Stds.: 303
East Shoreline Catholic Academy - (Grades PreK-8) 62 Cedar St., Branford, CT 06405-3646 t) 203-488-8386 srannette@esca.eduk12.net www.eastshorelinecatholicacademy.org Separate legal entity; co-sponsored by St. John Bosco Parish (Branford), St. George Parish (Guilford), and St. Margaret Parish (Madison) Cheryl Panzo, Prin.; Sr. Annette D'Antonio, M.P.F., Vice Prin.; Stds.: 220; Sr. Tchrs.: 1; Lay Tchrs.: 14

BRISTOL

Saint Francis de Sales Parish Corporation - 180 Laurel St., Bristol, CT 06010-8078 t) 860-582-8169 stfrancisdesales@aohct.org; francisdesalesoffice@gmail.com www.stfrancisdesalesbristolct.org Rev. Philip R. Schulze, Pst.; CRP Stds.: 55
The Saint Gregory Roman Catholic Church Corporation of Bristol, Connecticut - 235 Maltby St, Bristol, CT 06010 t) 860-589-2295; (860) 973-7001 (CRP) rectory@stgregoryrcc.com; stgregorythegreat@aohct.org Rev. John James Dietrich, Pst.; Rev. Nathaniel C. Labarda, Par. Vicar; Maryann Wisniewski, DRE; CRP Stds.: 605
St. Joseph's Church, Bristol, Connecticut - 33 Queen St., Bristol, CT 06010-5115; Mailing: 149 Goodwin St., Bristol, CT 06010-5115 t) 860-583-1369; 860-582-2888 (CRP) stjosephbristol@aohct.org; parishoffice@stjosephbristol.org stjosephbristol.org Rev. Ivan D. Ramirez, Pst.; Kimberlee Donahue, DRE; CRP Stds.: 267
St. Joseph School - (Grades PreK-8) 335 Center St., Bristol, CT 06010 t) 860-582-8696 schooloffice@stjosephbristol.org; frenette@stjosephbristol.org www.schoolstjosephbristol.org Eric Frenette, Prin.; Stds.: 184; Lay Tchrs.: 13
The St. Stanislaus Church Corporation of Bristol - 510 West St., Bristol, CT 06010-1860; Mailing: PO Box 1860, Bristol, CT 06010-1860 t) 860-583-4242; 860-584-5378 (CRP) asiagrabowski@sbcglobal.net; ststanislausbristol@aohct.org www.ststanislausbristolct.org Rev. Tomasz Sztuber, Pst.; Joanna Grabowski, DRE; CRP Stds.: 153

BROAD BROOK

Saint Marianne Cope Parish Corporation - 6 Windsorville Rd., Broad Brook, CT 06016 t) 860-623-4636 stmariannecope@aohct.org www.smceastwindsor.org/ Rev. Ronald P. Zepecki, Pst.; CRP Stds.: 50

CANAAN

Saint Martin of Tours Parish Corporation - 4 Main St., Canaan, CT 06018-0897; Mailing: P.O. Box 897, Canaan, CT 06108-0897 t) 860-824-7078 stmartinoftours@aohct.org; fatherdawson@stmartinoftoursct.org www.stmartinoftoursct.org Rev. M. David Dawson Jr., Pst.; Christina Allyn, CRE; Dcn. Stephen Beecher; CRP Stds.: 29

CHESHIRE

Saint Bridget of Sweden Parish Corporation - 175 Main St., Cheshire, CT 06410-2446 t) 203-272-3531; 203-272-6504 (CRP) dyatcko@cheshirecatholic.org; rectory@cheshirecatholic.org www.cheshirecatholic.org/ Rev. Jeffrey V. Romans, Pst.; Rev. Piotr S. Buczek, Par. Vicar; Dcn. Richard Wilber; Donna Yatcko, DRE; CRP Stds.: 731
St. Bridget's School - (Grades PreK-8) 171 Main St., Cheshire, CT 06410 t) 203-272-5860 drtesta@stbridgetschool.org www.stbridgetschool.org Nancy Testa, Prin.; Stds.:

331; Sr. Tchrs.: 1; Lay Tchrs.: 23

COLLINSVILLE

St. Patrick's Church Corporation Collinsville, Connecticut - 50 Church St., Collinsville, CT 06019 t) 860-693-8727 stpatrickcollinsville@aohct.org; ps@sp4c.org www.sp4c.org Rev. Collins I. Anaeche, Pst.; Dcn. Kenneth Bangs; CRP Stds.: 100

DERBY

St. Michael the Archangel (The St. Michael's Church of Derby) - 75 Derby Ave., Derby, CT 06418-2098 t) 203-734-0005 stmichaelsderby@sbcglobal.net; stmichaelthearchangel@aohct.org www.saintmichaelsderby.org/ Rev. Marek Sadowski, C.M., Pst.; Rev. Marek Sobczak, CM, Par. Vicar; Dcn. Robert Carter; CRP Stds.: 44

St. Mary-St. Michael - (Grades PreK-8) 14 Seymour Ave., Derby, CT 06418-1491 t) 203-735-6471 gtorres@stmarystmichael.org www.stmarystmichaelct.eduk12.net Grace Torres, Prin.; Stds.: 168; Lay Tchrs.: 10

Our Lady, Queen of the Apostles Parish Corporation - 212 Elizabeth St., Derby, CT 06418-1615 t) 203-735-3341 stmarycre@sbcglobal.net queenoftheapostlesderby.org Rev. Carlos Castrillon, Pst.; Dcn. Robert C. Johnson; Dcn. Confesol Rodriguez; Kathleen Brouillette, DRE; CRP Stds.: 85

St. Mary-St. Michael - (Grades PreK-8) 14 Seymour Ave., Derby, CT 06418 t) 203-735-6471 gtorres@stmarystmichael.org Grace Torres, Prin.; Stds.: 164; Lay Tchrs.: 12

EAST HARTFORD

Saint Edmund Campion Parish Corporation - 538 Brewer St., East Hartford, CT 06118-2305 t) 860-568-5240 stedmundcampion@aohct.org www.stedmundcampionparish.org Rev. John P. Gwozdz, Pst.; Dcn. Philip Gosselin; Kristina Gillespie, Youth Min.; Leo Forte, CRE; CRP Stds.: 53

Saint Isaac Jogues Ghanaian Catholic Parish Corporation - 1 Community St., East Hartford, CT 06108 t) 860-290-1880 fr.baffuor-awuah@aohct.org; stisaacjoguesghanaian@aohct.org Rev. Paul Baffuor-Awuah, Pst.;

North American Martyrs Parish Corporation - 15 Maplewood Ave., East Hartford, CT 06108 t) 860-289-7916 northamericanmartyrs@aohct.org www.namct.org Rev. Timothy E Ryan, Pst.; Rev. Gustavo Lopez, Par. Vicar; CRP Stds.: 127

EAST HAVEN

Saint Pio of Pietrelcina Parish Corporation - 355 Foxon Rd., East Haven, CT 06513 t) 203-469-0764 stpioofpietrelcina@gmail.com www.stpioofpietrelcinaeh.com/ Rev. Jeremiah N. Murasso, Pst.; Rev. Patrick M. Kane, Par. Vicar; CRP Stds.: 402

St. Bernadette Church - 385 Townsend Ave., New Haven, CT 06512 t) (203) 469-0764 (Worship Site).

ENFIELD

Saint Jeanne Jugan Parish Corporation - 23 Simon Rd., Enfield, CT 06082 t) (860) 962-4001 stjeannejugan@aohct.org sjjenfield.org Rev. John S. Golas, Pst.; Rev. Mathew Kappalumakkel, Par. Vicar; Rev. Robert Villa, Par. Vicar; Dcn. Vincent J. Motto; Dcn. Paul Robert; Dcn. Michael Torres; Carolyn Dague, DRE; Lori Kedzior, Bus. Mgr.; CRP Stds.: 358

St. Bernard School - (Grades K-8) 232 Pearl St., Enfield, CT 06082-4399 t) 860-745-5275 principal@sbsenfield.org www.sbsenfield.org Charlene Mongillo, Prin.; Stds.: 175; Lay Tchrs.: 11

Little Angels Catholic Preschool - (Grades PreK-PreK) 424 Hazard Ave., Enfield, CT 06082 t) 860-745-6135 principal@sbsenfield.org sbsenfield.org Charlene Mongillo, Prin.; Stds.: 67; Lay Tchrs.: 2

Holy Family Church -

St. Adalbert Church - 90 Alden Ave., Enfield, CT 06082

St. Bernard Church - 426 Hazard Ave., Enfield, CT 06082

St. Martha Church - 214 Brainard Rd., Enfield, CT 06082

St. Patrick's Church - 64 Pearl St., Enfield, CT 06082

Saint Martha Parish Corporation - Merged Nov 2022 Subsumed into Saint Jeanne Jugan Parish. For sacramental records see St. Bernard Church.

Saint Raymond of Penafort Parish Corporation - Merged Nov 2022 Subsumed into Saint Jeanne Jugan Parish. For Sacramental Records see St. Bernard Church.

FARMINGTON

St. Patricks Church Society of Farmington, Connecticut - 110 Main St., Farmington, CT 06032-2236 t) 860-677-2639 farmingtondre@gmail.com; office@stpatsfarm.com stmarystpat.org Rev. Matthew G. Gworek, Pst.; Rev. Joshua Wilbur, Par. Vicar; Dcn. Robert J. Barry; Eileen Dignazio, DRE; CRP Stds.: 272

FORESTVILLE

The St. Matthew's Church Corporation of Forestville, Connecticut - 120 Church Ave., Forestville, CT 06011; Mailing: Box 9216, Forestville, CT 06011-9216 t) 860-583-1833 stmatthew@aohct.org; rectory@stmatthewrcc.com www.stmatthewrcc.com Rev. John James Dietrich, Pst.; Dcn. Brian Armstrong; CRP Stds.: 457

St. Matthew School - (Grades PreK-8) 33 Welch Dr., Forestville, CT 06010-6790 t) 860-583-5214 stmatthewschool.com Elizabeth Plasky, Prin.; Brett Bisson, Librn.; Stds.: 165; Lay Tchrs.: 10

Parish Center - 119 Church Ave., Forestville, CT 06010

GLASTONBURY

The Church of St. Dunstan of Glastonbury Corporation - 1345 Manchester Rd., Glastonbury, CT 06033 t) 860-633-3317 stdunstan@aohct.org; business@stdunstanparish.org www.stdunstanparish.org Rev. Kevin G. Donovan, Pst.; CRP Stds.: 384

Saints Isidore and Maria Parish Corporation - 2577 Main St., Glastonbury, CT 06033 t) 860-633-9419 contact@isidoreandmaria.org; fr.suslenko@aohct.org isidoreandmaria.org Rev. Mark S. Suslenko, Pst.; Dcn. William Dziatko; Dcn. Stephen L. Weaver; CRP Stds.: 376

GRANBY

Saint Therese Parish Corporation - 120 W. Granby Rd., Granby, CT 06035 t) 860-653-3371 sttherese@aohct.org; businessmanager@stthereségranby.com www.stthereségranby.com Rev. William Agyemang, Pst.; Maura L. Fleming, DRE; Deborah Havens Klotzman, Bus. Mgr.; CRP Stds.: 91

GUILFORD

St. George's Church - 33 Whitfield St., Guilford, CT 06437-1944 t) 203-453-2788; 203-453-3496 (CRP) info@stgeorgeguilford.org; stgeorge@aohct.org www.stgeorgeguilford.org Rev. Kevin M. Dillon, Pst.; CRP Stds.: 589

HAMDEN

Christ the Bread of Life Parish Corporation - Merged Feb 2022 Merged with Divine Mercy Parish Corporation and Our Lady of Mount Carmel Parish Corporation to form Saint Paul VI Parish Corporation.

Our Lady of Mt. Carmel Parish Corporation - Merged Feb 2022 Merged with Divine Mercy Parish Corporation and Christ, the Bread of Life Parish Corporation to form Saint Paul VI Parish Corporation.

Saint Paul VI Parish Corporation - 2819 Whitney Ave., Hamden, CT 06517-2024 t) 203-248-5513; (203) 248-0141 olmchamdenoffice@gmail.com www.hamdencatholic.org Rev. Christopher M. Tiano, Pst.; Rev. Lee Hellwig, Par. Vicar; Rev. Mauricio Galvis, Par. Vicar; Dcn. Dominic Corraro; Dcn. Ronald B. Gurr; Dcn. Tullio V. Ossa; Dcn. Joseph R. Ryzewski; Dcn. Anthony P. Solli; Dcn. John C. O'Donovan; Sr. Ann O'Neill, R.S.M., Pst. Assoc.; Megan Zinn, DRE; Betsy Fitzsimons, CRE; CRP Stds.: 350

St. Rita School - (Grades PreK-8) 1601 Whitney Ave., Hamden, CT 06517 t) 203-248-3114 ptiezzi.stritaschool@gmail.com stritaschool.org Patricia Tiezzi, Prin.; Stds.: 359; Lay Tchrs.: 22

St. Rita School Early Learning Center - 30 Gillies Rd., Hamden, CT 06517 t) 203-288-6828 stritaelc@gmail.com stritaschoolelc.com Colleen Dacey, Dir.;

Christ the Bread of Life Church - 321 Circular Ave., Hamden, CT 06514-3428 t) (203) 288-5228

Our Lady of Mt. Carmel Church - t) (203) 287-9017

HARTFORD

St. Joseph's Cathedral, Hartford, Connecticut - 140 Farmington Ave., Hartford, CT 06105-3708 t) 860-249-8431 cathedralofstjoseph@aohct.org www.hartfordcathedral.org Very Rev. John P. Melnick, Rector; Dcn. James J. McCormack; Dcn. Norris Taylor; CRP Stds.: 62

Saint Augustine Parish Corporation - 10 Campfield Ave., Hartford, CT 06114-1832 t) 860-522-7128; 860-249-3430 (CRP) staugustinehartford@gmail.com; staugustine@aohct.org www.staugustinehtfd.org Rev. Thomas J. Walsh, Pst.; Rev. Jose R. Linares, Par. Vicar; Dcn. Julio C. Maturana; Dcn. Carmelo Hernandez; Rosa Cartagena, DRE; CRP Stds.: 1

The Church of S.S. Cyril & Methodius of Hartford, Connecticut - 55 Charter Oak Ave., Hartford, CT 06106-1902 t) 860-522-9157 ss.cyril-meth@att.net Rev. Adam Hurbanczuk (Poland), Pst.; Cheryl Pietrycha, DRE; Rev. Andrzej Pogorzelski, In Res.; CRP Stds.: 54

Saint Justin - Saint Michael Parish Corporation - 230 Blue Hills Ave., Hartford, CT 06112-1836 t) 860-246-6897; 860-522-6184 (CRP) sjsmparish@stjustinstmichael.org stjustinstmichael.org/ Rev. Mathieu Isaac, Pst.; Dcn. Ramon Rosado; CRP Stds.: 19

Lithuanian Roman Catholic Church of the Most Holy Trinity - 53 Capitol Ave., Hartford, CT 06106-1798 t) 860-246-4162 fr.jacobs@aohct.org; holytrinity53@yahoo.com www.holytrinityhartford.org Rev. Charles E. Jacobs, Admin.;

Maria, Reina de la Paz Parish Corporation - 494 New Britain Ave., Hartford, CT 06106-3797 t) 860-522-1129 mariareinadelapaz@aohct.org; religiouseducation@mariareinadelapazct.com www.mrpct.org/ Rev. Henry Avendano, Pst.; Dcn. Edwin Ortiz; Dcn. Juan Zapata; Andrea Gil Espinosa, Pst. Assoc.; Rosa Vazquez-Bilbraut, DRE; Paul Ravita, Bus. Mgr.; CRP Stds.: 127

The Our Lady of Fatima Roman Catholic Church Corporation of Hartford - 50 Kane St - Fatima Square, Hartford, CT 06106 t) 860-236-1443 olfreligiouseducation@yahoo.com; olfchurch1958@yahoo.com www.ourladyoffatimachurch.org Rev. Antonio Jorge Tchingui (Angola), Pst.; CRP Stds.: 182

Our Lady of Sorrows Church Corporation of Parkville, Hartford - 79 New Park Ave., Hartford, CT 06106-2109; Mailing: 16 Greenwood St., Hartford, CT 06106-2109 t) 860-233-4424 rmarcano@olsparish.comcastbiz.net; fr.oneil.jm@aohct.org www.facebook.com/olschurchhartfordct Rev. Joseph O'Neil, m.s., Pst.; Rev. James J. Aherne, M.S., Par. Vicar; Rev. John F. Higgins, M.S., In Res.; Dcn. Victor Bilbraut; Dcn. Valentin Perez; Raquel Rios-Iverson, DRE; CRP Stds.: 104

St. Patrick and St. Anthony Roman Catholic Church Corporation - 285 Church St., Hartford, CT 06103 t) 860-756-4034 stpatrickstanthony@aohct.org www.spsact.org Rev. Timothy J. Shreenan, O.F.M., Pst.; Rev. William L. Beaudin, O.F.M., Par. Vicar; Rev. Michael Johnson, O.F.M., Par. Vicar; Rev. John J. Leonard, O.F.M., Par. Vicar; Rev. James P. Kelly, O.F.M., In Res.; Rev. John J. Kull, O.F.M., In Res.; Rev. A. Francis Soucy, Sr. Assoc. Friar in Res. & Parochial Vicar; Patricia Curtis, Pst. Assoc.; CRP Stds.: 201

Franciscan Center for Urban Ministry, Inc. -

KENSINGTON

Saint Paul Parish Corporation - 485 Alling St., Kensington, CT 06037-2170; Mailing: 467 Alling St., Kensington, CT 06037 t) 860-828-1934 (CRP); 860-828-0331 religioused@stpaulkensington.org;

ourchurch@stpaulkensington.org stpaulkensington.org Rev. Joseph Benicewicz, OFM Conv., Pst.; Rev. Martin Kobos, OFM Conv., Par. Vicar; Rev. Michael Englert, OFM Conv., Par. Vicar; Dcn. Donald Phillip; Rev. Raymond Borkowski, OFM Conv., In Res.; Daniel Tome, Youth Min.; Robin Veronesi, DRE; CRP Stds.: 538

Parish Center - 467 Alling St., Kensington, CT 06037

Saint Paul Parish School - (Grades PreK-8) 461 Alling St., Kensington, CT 06037-2170 t) 860-828-4343 ourschool@stpaulkensington.org ourschool.stpaulkensington.org Jill Conaway, Prin.; Stds.: 256; Lay Tchrs.: 12

KENT

Saint Kateri Tekakwitha Parish Corporation - 90 Cobble Rd., Kent, CT 06757-0186; Mailing: P.O. Box 186, Kent, CT 06757 t) 860-927-3003 office.stkaterict@gmail.com; stkateritekakwitha@aohct.org saintkaterict.org Merged with Sacred Heart, Kent, Saint Bernard, Sharon, and Saint Bridget, Cornwall Bridge. Rev. Robert N. Landback, Pst.; CRP Stds.: 25

LITCHFIELD

Saint Louis de Montfort Parish Corporation - 49 South St, Litchfield, CT 06759; Mailing: PO Box 97, Litchfield, CT 06759-0097 t) 860-567-5209 stlouisdemontfort@aohct.org; louisdemontfort@optonline.net www.stlouisdemontfortparish.org/ Rev. Stuart H. Pinette, Pst.; CRP Stds.: 78

MADISON

The St. Margaret's Church Corporation of Madison, Connecticut - 24 Academy St., Madison, CT 06443-0814 t) 203-245-7301 religiouseducation@stmargaretchurch.com; stmargaret@aohct.org www.stmargaretchurch.com Rev. Daniel J. McLearen; Dcn. Adam J. Michaele; CRP Stds.: 361

MANCHESTER

Saint James Parish Corporation - Merged Aug 2022 into St. Teresa of Calcutta Parish Corporation, Manchester.

Saint Teresa of Calcutta Parish Corporation - 80 Main St., Manchester, CT 06042 t) 860-643-2403 x100 stteresaofcalcutta@aohct.org; pastoroffice@saintteresacatholic.org saintteresacatholic.org Rev. Marcin P. Pluciennik, Pst.; Rev. Janusz Kukulka, Par. Vicar; Rev. Jaime Maldonado, Par. Vicar; Rev. Edward M. Moran, Par. Vicar; Dcn. Bill Gilles; Dcn. Leo R. LaRocque; John Ryan, Pst. Assoc.; Rachel Bursiewicz, DRE; Nancy Lastrina, Bus. Mgr.; CRP Stds.: 279

St. Bridget School - (Grades PreK-8) 74 Main St., Manchester, CT 06042-3140 t) 860-649-7731 principal@saintbridget-school.com saintbridget-school.com Joy Renner, Prin.; Stds.: 197; Lay Tchrs.: 19

St. James School - (Grades PreK-8) 73 Park St., Manchester, CT 06040 t) 860-643-5088 bzorger@saintjamesschool.net Bridget Zorger, Prin.; Lisa Anderson, Vice Prin.; Stds.: 375; Lay Tchrs.: 20

St. James Church - 896 Main St., Manchester, CT 06040

St. Bridget Church -

St. Bartholomew Church - 45 Ludlow Rd., Manchester, CT 06040

Assumption Church - 185 W. Center St., Manchester, CT 06040

MARLBOROUGH

The Church of St. John Fisher of Marlborough Corporation - 30 Jones Hollow Rd., Marlborough, CT 06447 t) 860-295-0001 stjohnfisher30@yahoo.com www.stjfchurch.org Rev. Thomas J. Sas, Pst.; Dcn. John W. McKaig; Jennifer O'Neill, Youth Min.; Melissa Jordan, CRE; CRP Stds.: 118

MERIDEN

Saint Faustina Parish Corporation - 82 Akron St., Meriden, CT 06450-5796 t) 203-235-6341 stfaustina@aohct.org www.stfaustinact.org/ Rev. Edward Ziemnicki, Pst.; CRP Stds.: 20

Our Lady Queen of Angels Parish Corporation - 109 Goodwill Ave., Meriden, CT 06450 t) 203-235-6381 ourladyqueenofangels@aohct.org; publicity@ourladyqueenofangels.net www.olqoa.org Rev. Dominic Anaeto, Admin.; Dcn. George W. Frederick; Dcn. Donald H. Smith Jr.; CRP Stds.: 119

Trustees of St. Roses Ch. Meriden, Connecticut - 35 Center St., Meriden, CT 06450-5685 t) 203-235-1644 stroseoflima@aohct.org; strosemeriden@gmail.com www.strosemeriden.org Rev. James C. Manship, Pst.; CRP Stds.: 186

MILFORD

Precious Blood Parish Corporation - 70 Gulf St., Milford, CT 06460 t) 203-878-3571 preciousblood@aohct.org preciousbloodparishmilford.org Rev. Aidan Donahue, Pst.; Rev. Lijo Thomas, Par. Vicar; Dcn. Nicholas A. Genovese; Dcn. Harold John Hoffman, Pst. Assoc.; CRP Stds.: 361

St. Mary School (Precious Blood Parish Corporation) - (Grades PreK-8) 72 Gulf St., Milford, CT 06460 t) 203-878-6539 dcorraro@smsmilford.com Dcn. Dominic Corraro, Prin.; Melissa Dubin, Vice Prin.; Stds.: 361; Pr. Tchrs.: 1; Lay Tchrs.: 25

Saint Raphael Parish Corporation - 501 Naugatuck Ave., Milford, CT 06460 t) 203-874-0634 straphael@aohct.org; secretary@saintraphaelmilford.org saintraphaelmilford.org Rev. John F. Brinsmade, Pst.; Dcn. George G. Sartor; CRP Stds.: 225

NAUGATUCK

Saint Francis of Assisi Parish Corporation - 318 Church St., Naugatuck, CT 06770; Mailing: 294 Church St., Naugatuck, CT 06770 t) 203-729-4543 stfrancisofassisinaugatuck@aohct.org stfrancisnaugatuck.org Rev. John Kuzhikottayil, SDB, Pst.; Michele LoRusso, DRE; Dcn. Thomas J. Clifford; Leonard Tiscia, DRE; CRP Stds.: 148

The Church of St. Vincent Ferrer of Naugatuck Corporation - 1006 New Haven Rd., Naugatuck, CT 06770-4731 t) 203-723-7497 stvincentferrer@aohct.org www.stvincentferrerchurch.org Rev. Binny Isaac Perumanamcheril, S.D.B, Pst.;

NEW BRITAIN

Divine Providence Parish Corporation (St. Joseph Church St. Peter Church) - 195 S. Main St., New Britain, CT 06051; Mailing: 1010 Slater Rd., New Britain, CT 06053 t) (860) 224-2411 stfrancisofassisinewbritain@aohct.org; fr.casey@aohct.org stfranciscatholic.org Rev. Michael T. Casey, Pst.;

St. Francis of Assisi Church Corporation of New Britain - 1755 Stanley St., New Britain, CT 06053-2099; Mailing: 1010 Slater Rd., New Britain, CT 06053 t) (860) 224-2411 stfrancisofassisinewbritain@aohct.org; fr.casey@aohct.org stfranciscatholic.org Rev. Michael T. Casey, Pst.; CRP Stds.: 53

Holy Apostles Parish Corporation - 655 East St., New Britain, CT 06051; Mailing: 1010 Slater Rd., New Britain, CT 06053 t) (860) 224-2411 fr.casey@aohct.org; stfrancisofassisinewbritain@aohct.org stfranciscatholic.org Rev. Michael T. Casey, Pst.;

The Church of the Holy Cross, New Britain - 31 Biruta St., New Britain, CT 06053-2899 t) 860-229-2011 holycross@aohct.org; hcfinance@sbcglobal.net www.holycrosschurchnb.org Rev. Dariusz Gosciniak, Pst.; Dcn. Michael Rubitz; Eva Fadgyas, DRE; CRP Stds.: 221

Saint Joachim Parish Corporation - 544 Main St., New Britain, CT 06051-1812 t) 860-229-4894 stjoachim@aohct.org; parish@stjoachimct.org www.stjoachimct.org Rev. Israel Rivera, Pst.;

Saint Katharine Drexel Parish Corporation - 1010 Slater Rd., New Britain, CT 06053 t) (860) 224-2411 stfrancisofassisinewbritain@aohct.org; fr.casey@aohct.org www.stfranciscatholic.org Rev. Michael T. Casey, Pst.;

St. Maurice Church - 100 Wightman Rd., New Britain, CT 06052

St. Jerome Church - parishoffice@stfranciscatholic.org stfranciscatholic.org

Church Corporation of the Sacred Heart of Jesus of New Britain - 158 Broad St., New Britain, CT 06053-4195 t) 860-229-0081; (860) 538-2840 www.sacredheartnb.org Rev. Msgr. Daniel J. Plocharczyk, Pst.; Rev. Stanislaus Dudek, O.F.M. Conv. (Poland), Par. Vicar; Dcn. Jacek Muszynski; Rev. William Baldyga, In Res.; Tory Lamore, DRE; CRP Stds.: 250

Sacred Heart of Jesus School - (Grades PreK-8) 35 Orange St., New Britain, CT 06053 t) 860-229-7663 kmuller@sacredheartnb.eduk12.net Katherine Muller, Prin.;

NEW HARTFORD

Our Lady of Hope Parish Corporation - 60 Town Hill Rd., New Hartford, CT 06057-0285; Mailing: P.O. Box 285, New Hartford, CT 06057 t) 860-379-5215 secretary@ourladyofhopeparish.com www.ourladyofhopeparish.com Rev. John Granato, Pst.; Dcn. David Reynolds; CRP Stds.: 140

NEW HAVEN

Saints Aedan and Brendan Parish Corporation - 112 Fountain St., New Haven, CT 06515-0156 t) 203-389-2619 ss.aedan.brendan@outlook.com; ssaedanandbrendan@aohct.org www.staedan-stbrendan-parishes.org Dcn. Martin J. O'Connor, Admin.; CRP Stds.: 11

Saint Anthony Parish Corporation - 70 Washington Ave., New Haven, CT 06519; Mailing: 25 Gold St., New Haven, CT 06519 t) 203-624-1418 stanthonynewhaven@aohct.org www.stanthony-church.org Rev. Hector G. Rangel, Pst.; CRP Stds.: 112

St. Anthony Food Pantry -

Saint Martin de Porres Church Corporation - 136 Dixwell Ave., New Haven, CT 06511-3400 t) 203-624-9944 saintmartindep@att.net smdp.org Rev. Joseph M. Elko, Admin.;

Saint Mary Parish Corporation - 5 Hillhouse Ave., New Haven, CT 06511; Mailing: P.O. Box 9286, New Haven, CT 06533 t) 203-562-6193 stmarynewhaven@aohct.org; fr.ryan@stmarysnewhaven.org www.stmarysnewhaven.org Rev. Ryan M. Lerner, Pst.; Rev. Anthony J. Federico III, Par. Vicar; Rev. Vincent J. Curran, In Res.; Dcn. Ernest Scrivani, T.O. Carm.; Dcn. Martin J. O'Connor; CRP Stds.: 71

The St. Michael's Church Corporation, N. Haven, Connecticut - 29 Wooster Pl., New Haven, CT 06511-6998 t) 203-562-7178 stmichaelnewhaven@aohct.org; smc1889@att.net stmichaelwoostersquare.org Rev. Robert P. Roy, Pst.;

Our Lady of Guadalupe Parish Corporation - 397 Ferry St, New Haven, CT 06513 t) 203-865-6149 ourladyofguadalupe@aohct.org Rev. Hector G. Rangel, Admin.; CRP Stds.: 161

St. Stanislaus' Church of New Haven Connecticut - 9 Eld St., New Haven, CT 06511-3815 t) 203-562-2828; 203-624-0850 ststanislausnewhaven@aohct.org www.ststanislaus-newhaven.com Rev. Sebastian K. Kos, Admin.; Rev. Ryan M. Lerner, Pst.; Dcn. Ernest Scrivani, T.O. Carm.; Toni Lucian, DRE; CRP Stds.: 19

St. Stanislaus Fraternity, Secular Franciscan Order -

NEW MILFORD

Saint Francis Xavier Parish Corporation - 26 Chestnut Land Rd., New Milford, CT 06776; Mailing: 1 Elm St., New Milford, CT 06776 t) 860-354-2202; 860-354-5372 (CRP) stfrancisxaviernewmilford@aohct.org; sfxparish@sfxnewmilford.org www.sfxnewmilford.org Rev. Francis Snell, Pst.; Rev. Chacko Kumplam, Par. Vicar; Dcn. Alfred Gambone; Karen O'Donnell, DRE; CRP Stds.: 463

Our Lady of the Lakes Church - 3 Old Town Park Rd., New Milford, CT 06776-4212

Saint Francis Xavier Church -

Our Lady of the Lakes Corporation - Merged Jul 2022 Merged with St. Francis Xavier, New Milford to form St. Francis Xavier Parish Corporation.

NEWINGTON

Annunciation Parish Corporation - 626 Willard Ave., Newington, CT 06111-2614 t) 860-666-1591

pastor@annunciationnewington.com www.annunciationnewington.com Rev. Robert A. Morgewicz II; Rev. Joseph Pullikattil; Dcn. James Blanchette; Dcn. James F. Tanguay; Rev. Lawrence R. Bock, In Res.; Rev. Msgr. James F. Kinnane, In Res.; CRP Stds.: 343

NORTH BRANFORD

Saint Ambrose Parish Corporation - 30 Caputo Rd., North Branford, CT 06471 t) 203-484-0403 stambrose@aohct.org nbcatholics.org Rev. Robert L. Turner, Pst.; Dcn. Joseph P. Marenna; CRP Stds.: 132

NORTH HAVEN

Saint Elizabeth of the Trinity Parish Corporation - 44 Washington Ave., North Haven, CT 06473 t) 203-239-5378 stelizabethofthetrin@aohct.org www.stelizabethofthetrinity.org Rev. Michael A. Santiago, Pst.; CRP Stds.: 620

St. Therese Nursery School - 555 Middletown Ave., North Haven, CT 06473 t) 203-234-9971 stns@etrinityparish.org Michele Adinolfi-Lucibello, Dir.; Stds.: 91

OAKVILLE

Roman Catholic Church of St. Mary Magdalen - Merged Jul 2022 Merged with The Corporation of St. Johns Church, Watertown to form Holy Disciples Parish Corporation.

ORANGE

The Church of the Holy Infant - 450 Racebrook Rd., Orange, CT 06477 t) 203-799-2417 (CRP); 203-799-2379 holyinfant@aohct.org; fr.brockett@aohct.org www.holyinfantorangect.com Rev. Norman L. Brockett, Pst.; CRP Stds.: 593

OXFORD

The Church of St. Thomas the Apostle of Oxford - 733 Oxford Rd., Oxford, CT 06478 t) 203-888-2382 stthomastheapostleoxford@aohct.org stthomastheapostleoxford.org Rev. Thomas B. Shepard, Pst.; Wanda Mascola, DRE; CRP Stds.: 225

PLAINVILLE

The Church of Our Lady of Mercy Corporation - 19 S. Canal St., Plainville, CT 06062-2756 t) 860-747-6825 olmct@sbcglobal.net; ourladyofmercy@aohct.org www.olmct.org Rev. Raymond S. Smialowski, Pst.; CRP Stds.: 64

PLANTSVILLE

The St. Aloysius Roman Catholic Church Corporation of Southington, Connecticut - Merged Jul 2022 Merged with St. Thomas, St. Dominic, Immaculate Conception, and Mary Our Queen to form Saint Luke Parish, Southington.

The Mary Our Queen Roman Catholic Church Corporation of Southington, Connecticut - Merged Jul 2022 Merged with St. Thomas, St. Dominic, Immaculate Conception, and St. Alyosius to form St. Luke's, Southington.

PROSPECT

The St. Anthony's Church Corporation of Prospect - 4 Union City Rd., Prospect, CT 06712-0117 t) 203-758-4848 (CRP); 203-758-4056 stanthonyprospect@aohct.org stanthonyprospect.org Rev. Grzegorz Jaworowski (Poland), Pst.; Dcn. Domenic N. Stolfi; CRP Stds.: 129

ROCKY HILL

Saint Josephine Bakhita Parish Corporation - 767 Elm St., Rocky Hill, CT 06067-1902 t) 860-529-8655 frgeorge@sjbrh.org; stjosephinebakhita@aohct.org www.saintjosephinebakhita.org St. Elizabeth Seton Church and St. James Church both in Rocky Hill, CT merged in 2017 Rev. George M. Couturier, Pst.; Dcn. Michael J. Ward; CRP Stds.: 354

SEYMOUR

Saint Nicholas Parish Corporation - 135 Mountain Rd., Seymour, CT 06483-2038 t) 203-888-9243 stnicholas@aohct.org stnicholasct.org Rev. Thomas J. Cieslikowski, Pst.; CRP Stds.: 300

SIMSBURY

The St. Mary's Church Corporation of Simsbury - 942 Hopmeadow St., Simsbury, CT 06070-0575; Mailing: P.O. Box 575, Simsbury, CT 06070-0575 t) 860-658-7627 stmarysimsbury@aohct.org www.stmarysimsbury.org Rev. Stephen M. Sledesky, Pst.; Dcn. Arthur L. Miller; Christine Simons, Youth Min.; Kathy Piggott, DRE; Lori Ryan, CRE; CRP Stds.: 261

St. Mary School - (Grades PreK-8) 946 Hopmeadow St., Simsbury, CT 06070 t) 860-658-9412 smsoffice@stmarysimsbury.eduk12.net stmarysschoolsimsbury.org Margaret R. Williamson, Prin.; Stds.: 174; Lay Tchrs.: 13

SOUTH WINDSOR

Saint Junipero Serra Parish Corporation - 80 Hayes Rd., South Windsor, CT 06074 t) 860-644-2411; 860-644-2549 (CRP) fr.castro@aohct.org; business@southwindsor.cc www.saintjuniperoserra.org Rev. Jorge E. Castro, Pst.; CRP Stds.: 352

SOUTHBURY

The Roman Catholic Parish of Middlebury and Southbury Church Corporation - 910 Main St., S., Southbury, CT 06488 t) 203-264-5071; 203-264-5065 (Faith Formation) sacredheartsouthbury@aohct.org www.middsouthcatholic.org Very Rev. Robert M. Kwiatkowski, Pst.; BJ Daly Horell, Pst. Assoc.; Ami Conlan, Pst. Assoc.; CRP Stds.: 480

***Seeds of Hope for Haiti, Inc.** - t) 203-206-3312 Bruce T. Palmatier, Treas.;

SOUTHINGTON

The Church of St. Dominic of Southington Corporation - Merged Jul 2022 Merged with St. Thomas, Immaculate Conception, St. Aloysius, and Mary Our Queen to form Saint Luke Parish, Southington.

The Immaculate Conception Church Corporation of Southington - Merged Jul 2022 Merged with St. Thomas, St. Dominic, St. Aloysius, and Mary Our Queen to form Saint Luke Parish, Southington.

Saint Luke Parish Corporation - 99 Bristol St., Southington, CT 06489-4599 t) 860-628-4713 www.stlukect.org Rev. Joseph R. Cronin, Pst.; Rev. David Madejski, Par. Vicar; Sr. Ellen Coates, Pst. Assoc.; Michael Pavano, Youth Min.; Adam Zangari, CRE; Dcn. Vincent Raby; Dcn. Paul J. Kulas; CRP Stds.: 804

Southington Catholic - (Grades PreK-8) 133 Bristol St., Southington, CT 06489 t) 860-628-2485 jmessina@southingtoncatholicschool.org Jim Messina, Prin.; Stds.: 113; Lay Tchrs.: 4

Religious Sisters Filippini - 20 Eden Pl., Southington, CT 06489-4599 t) 860-384-3301 mpfmr@att.net

The Church of St. Dominic of Southington Corporation - 1050 Flanders Rd., Southington, CT 06489-1344

The Immaculate Conception Church Corporation of Southington - 130 Summer St., Southington, CT 06489

The Mary Our Queen Roman Catholic Church Corporation of Southington, Connecticut - 248 Savage St., Plantsville, CT 06479

The St. Aloysius Roman Catholic Church Corporation of Southington, Connecticut - 254 Burritt St., Plantsville, CT 06489-4599

SUFFIELD

Sacred Heart Parish Corporation - 446 Mountain Rd., Suffield, CT 06078; Mailing: P.O. Box 626, Suffield, CT 06078-0626 t) 860-668-7766 (CRP); 860-668-4246 shc_dre@sbcglobal.net; sacredheartsuffield1@gmail.com www.sacredheartct.com Rev. Joseph F. Keough, Pst.; Donna Swols, DRE; CRP Stds.: 146

THOMASTON

Saint Maximillian Kolbe Parish Corporation - 19 Electric Ave., Thomaston, CT 06787-1852 t) 860-283-5817 stmaximiliankolbe@aohct.org; office@stmkp.org www.stmkp.org Rev. Joseph P. Crowley, Pst.; Dcn. Leo B. Conard III; CRP Stds.: 161

TORRINGTON

Saint John Paul the Great Parish Corporation - 160 Main St., Torrington, CT 06790-5201 t) 860-482-4433 c) 860-307-2291 stjohnpaulthegreat@aohct.org; johnpaulgreatreligioused@gmail.com www.johnpaulgreatparish.com Rev. Emmanuel I. Ihemedu, Pst.; Rev. Carlos Zapata, Par. Vicar; Dcn. Angel Garcia; Dcn. Richard H. Hamel; Carmelina Calabrese, Youth Min.; Jen Owens, DRE; Sr. Dcn. Roy C. Dungan; Sr. Dcn. Peter R. Hyde; CRP Stds.: 224

St John Paul the Great Academy - (Grades PreK-8) 360 Prospect St., Torrington, CT 06790 t) 860-489-4177 principal@sjptga.org Edward Goad, Prin.; Stds.: 192; Scholastics: 1; Lay Tchrs.: 10

UNIONVILLE

The Star of the Sea Church Corporation of Unionville, Connecticut - 145 Main St., Unionville, CT 06085-1116; Mailing: 16 Bidwell Square, Unionville, CT 06085 t) (860) 673-2422; (860) 677-2639 (CRP) stmarystaroftheseaunionville@gmail.com; stmarystarofthesea@aohct.org stmarystpat.org Rev. Matthew G. Gworek, Pst.; Rev. Joshua Wilbur, Par. Vicar; Dcn. Thomas S. Sutak; CRP Stds.: 235

WALLINGFORD

Most Holy Trinity Parish Corporation - 84 N. Colony St., Wallingford, CT 06492-3696; Mailing: 25 N. Whittlesey Ave., Wallingford, CT 06492 t) 203-269-8791; 203-269-8791 (CRP) mostholytrinity@aohct.org; church@mhtwallingford.org www.mhtwallingford.org Rev. Andres Mendoza Floyd, Pst.; Rev. Matthew Carl Collins, Par. Vicar; Dcn. Jose Alberto Robles; Dcn. Joseph S. Mazurek; Gail Bellucci, Pst. Assoc.; Tracy Blum, DRE; CRP Stds.: 320

Holy Trinity School - (Grades PreK-8) 11 N. Whittlesey Ave., Wallingford, CT 06492 t) 203-269-4476 school@myhts-wallingford.org hts-wallingford.org Dr. Michael J. Frechette, Prin.; Stds.: 196; Lay Tchrs.: 14

The Church of the Resurrection - 115 Pond Hill Rd., Wallingford, CT 06492-4836 t) 203-265-1694 resurrection@aohct.org; office@resurrectionct.org www.resurrectionct.org Rev. Msgr. John J. Georgia, Pst.; Rev. Hugh J. MacDonald, In Res.; Joseph R. Tatta, DRE & Pst. Assoc.; CRP Stds.: 450

WASHINGTON DEPOT

Our Lady of Perpetual Help Parish Corporation - 34 Green Hill Rd., Washington Depot, CT 06794-0303; Mailing: P. O. Box 303, Washington Depot, CT 06794-0303 t) 860-868-2600 churchofourlady@att.net www.ourlady-stpatrick.org Rev. Joseph Moonnanappallil (India), Admin.; CRP Stds.: 26

St. Patrick Church - 25 Church St., Roxbury, CT 06783

WATERBURY

All Saints Parish Corporation - 515 S. Main St., Waterbury, CT 06706-1089 t) 203-756-4439 allsaints@aohct.org; parishoffice@allsaintswtby.org www.allsaintswtby.org Rev. Diego A. Jimenez, Pst.; Rev. Eric Zuniga, Par. Vicar; Kimberly Pabey-Rivera, DRE; Cynthia Santiago, DRE; Angel Ruiz, RCIA Coord.; CRP Stds.: 327

The Corporation of the Church of the Blessed Sacrament in Waterbury - 182 Robbins St., Waterbury, CT 06708; Mailing: 12 Ardsley Rd., Waterbury, CT 06708 t) 203-753-3149 blessedsacrament@aohct.org; bscparishoffice@att.net www.bscwaterbury.com Rev. Vittorio Guerrera, Pst.;

Catholic Academy of Waterbury - (Grades PreK-8) 386 Robinwood Rd., Waterbury, CT 06708-2750 t) 203-756-5313 cchodkowski@catholicacademywaterbury.org www.catholicacademywaterbury.org/ Christa Chodkowski, Prin.; Stds.: 205; Lay Tchrs.: 11

St. Francis Xavier's Church Corporation of Waterbury, Connecticut - 625 Baldwin St., Waterbury, CT 06706-1597 t) 203-756-7804 sfxofficesecretary@yahoo.com; stfrancisxavierwaterbury@aohct.org www.sfxchurchwtby.weebly.com/ Rev. Diego A. Jimenez, Pst.; CRP Stds.: 1

Corporation of the Church of the Immaculate Conception, Waterbury, Connecticut - 74 W. Main St., Waterbury, CT 06702 t) 203-574-0017 info@waterburybasilica.org; rel.ed@waterburybasilica.org www.waterburybasilica.org Very Rev. James M. Sullivan, Rector; Rev. Joshy John (India), Par. Vicar; Rev. Msgr. John J. Bevins, In Res.; Rev. John R. Mariano, In Res.; CRP Stds.: 152

Saint Joseph Parish Corporation - 46 Congress Ave., Waterbury, CT 06708; Mailing: 785 Highland Ave, Waterbury, CT 06708 t) (203) 756-8981 officeolmcwtby@aol.com Rev. Frederick M. Aniello, Pst.;

Mary, Mother of the Church Parish Corporation - 67 Southmayd Rd., Waterbury, CT 06705-2096 t) 203-756-7919 mmcwaterbury@gmail.com; marymotherofthechurch@aohct.org www.mmcparish.com Rev. Msgr. Thomas M. Ginty, Pst.; CRP Stds.: 88

St. Michael's Church of Waterville, Connecticut - 62 St. Michael Dr., Waterbury, CT 06704-1295 t) 203-753-0689 stmichaelwaterbury@aohct.org www.stmichaelwtby.org/ Very Rev. James M. Sullivan, Pst.; CRP Stds.: 23

The Church of Our Lady of Fatima Corporation - 2071 Baldwin St., Waterbury, CT 06706 t) 203-753-1424 fr.eurico@aohct.org Rev. Francisco Eurico, Pst.; CRP Stds.: 160

The Church of Our Lady of Loreto of Waterbury Corporation - 12 Ardsley Rd., Waterbury, CT 06708-1825 t) 203-757-6112; 203-510-4263 (CRP) stephendre1@gmail.com; ourladyofloreto@aohct.org www.ourladyofloretowtby.org Rev. Vittorio Guerrera, Pst.; Stephen Derasmo, DRE; CRP Stds.: 34

The Church of Our Lady of Mount Carmel - 785 Highland Ave., Waterbury, CT 06708 t) 203-756-8981 officeolmcwtby@aol.com; fr.aniello@aohct.org www.olmcwtby.com Rev. Frederick M. Aniello, Pst.; Dcn. Ernest H. Pagliaro Jr.; CRP Stds.: 50

Our Lady of Mt. Carmel School - (Grades PreK-8) 645 Congress Ave., Waterbury, CT 06708-4198 t) 203-755-6809 jack.tavares@mtcarmelschool.net Joaquim (Jack) Tavares, Prin.; Stds.: 212; Lay Tchrs.: 13

Our Lady of Mount Carmel Child Care Center - 656 Congress Ave., Waterbury, CT 06708 t) 203-755-8278 kguerrera@olmcwtby.com olmcwtby.com

Saint Patrick Parish Corporation - 50 Charles St., Waterbury, CT 06708 t) 203-756-8837 stpatrick@icksp.org www.icksp.org/waterbury-home administered by the Institute of Christ the King Sovereign Priest, a Society of Apostolic Life of Pontifical Right Rev. Canon Joel Estrada, ICRSS, Pst.; CRP Stds.: 30

WATERTOWN

Holy Disciples Parish Corporation - 574 Main St., Watertown, CT 06795-2101; Mailing: 21 Academy Hill, Watertown, CT 06795 t) 860-274-8836; 860-274-4123 (CRP) stjohntheevangelist@aohct.org www.stjohn.weconnect.com Rev. Anthony J. Smith, Pst.; Rev. Joseph V. Carmel Napolitano, Par. Vicar; Rev. David C. Carey, Sr. Priest; Dcn. Victor C Mitchell Jr.; Dcn. Michael Malfitano; Dcn. George M. Pettinico; Sr. Dcn. Daniel Camerota; Sr. Dcn. Robert D. Gordon; Gintare Lopez, DRE; CRP Stds.: 368

St. Mary Magdalen School - (Grades PreK-8) 140 Buckingham St., Oakville, CT 06779 t) 860-945-0621 principal.smms@smmsoakville.org www.smmsoakville.org Deborah Mulhall, Prin.; Stds.: 202; Lay Tchrs.: 13

St. John the Evangelist School - (Grades PreK-8) 760 Main St., Watertown, CT 06795 t) 860-274-9208 sjsprincipal@stjohnwtn.org www.stjohnwtn.org Sherrie Gemmell, Prin.; Stds.: 111; Lay Tchrs.: 7

St. John the Evangelist Church - t) (860) 274-4123

St. Mary Magdalen Church - 16 Buckingham St, Oakville, CT 06779-1797 t) (860) 274-9273

WEST HARTFORD

Saint Andrew Dung-Lac Parish Corporation - 467 S. Quaker Ln., West Hartford, CT 06110 t) 860-830-8288 standrewdunglac@aohct.org www.saintandrewdunglac.org/ Rev. Tuan Anh Dinh Mai, Pst.; CRP Stds.: 78

Saint Gianna (Beretta Molla) Parish Corporation - 1088 New Britain Ave., West Hartford, CT 06110-2426 t) 860-236-5965 stgianna@aohct.org; karla@saintgiannaparish.org www.saintgiannaparish.org Rev. Joseph T. Devine, Pst.; Dcn. Robert J. Hilliard; CRP Stds.: 91

The St. Peter Claver Church Corporation of West Hartford - 47 Pleasant St., West Hartford, CT 06107-1625 t) 860-561-4235; 860-521-2904 spcoffice@spcwh.org; stpeterclaver@aohct.org www.stpeterclaverparish.com Rev. Christopher M. Ford, Pst.; Dcn. Kiley Robert; Dcn. Robert M. Pallotti; Carol Moriarty, DRE; Tim Stella, Music Min.; Gigi Frailey, Pst. Assoc.; CRP Stds.: 365

Saint Thomas & Saint Timothy Parish Corporation - 872 Farmington Ave., West Hartford, CT 06119-1499; Mailing: 1116 N. Main St., West Hartford, CT 06117 t) (860) 233-4580 jillc@stastm.org www.stastm.org Rev. Alvin J. LeBlanc, Pst.; Rev. Sam John, Par. Vicar; Dcn. Dennis R. Ferguson; CRP Stds.: 218

St. Thomas the Apostle School - (Grades PreK-5) 25 Dover Rd., West Hartford, CT 06119-1298 t) 860-236-6257 nhubert@stastmschool.org Natalie Hubert, Prin.; Janet Cashman, Librn.; Stds.: 204; Lay Tchrs.: 14

St. Timothy Middle School - 225 King Philip Dr., West Hartford, CT 06117-1497 t) 860-236-0614 stastmschool.org Thomas Menner, Prin.; Stds.: 104; Pr. Tchrs.: 1; Lay Tchrs.: 6

WEST HAVEN

Saint John XXIII Parish Corporation - 89 Bull Hill Ln., West Haven, CT 06516-3998 t) 203-934-5249 stjohnxxiii@aohct.org www.westhavencatholic.org Rev. Jose Angel Mercado Jr., Pst.; Rev. Ricardo Borja, Par. Vicar; Dcn. Frank J. Bevvino; Dcn. Dean A. Macchio; Loriann Ruiz, DRE; CRP Stds.: 616

St. Lawrence School - (Grades PreK-8) 231 Main St., West Haven, CT 06516 t) 203-933-2518 farnone@stlaw.eduk12.net www.stlaw.eduk12.net Frank Arnone, Prin.; Stds.: 192; Lay Tchrs.: 15

St. Lawrence Church - 207 Main St., West Haven, CT 06516

St. Louis Church -

St. John Vianney Church - 300 Captain Thomas Blvd., West Haven, CT 06516

Our Lady of Victory Parish Corporation - Merged Jan 2023 Subsumed into Saint John XXIII. For Inquiries or Sacramental Records see Saint Louis Church.

WEST SIMSBURY

The Church of St. Catherine of Siena of Simsbury Corporation - 265 Stratton Brook Rd., West Simsbury, CT 06092; Mailing: P.O. Box 184, West Simsbury, CT 06092-0184 t) 860-658-1642; 860-658-4737 stcatherineofsiena@aohct.org; stcathy@comcast.net www.stcatherine.info/ Rev. Michael G. Whyte, Pst.; CRP Stds.: 361

WETHERSFIELD

Christ the King Parish Corporation - 84 Somerset St., Wethersfield, CT 06109-3068 t) 860-529-2545 christtheking@aohct.org www.christthekingparishct.org/ Rev. Nicholas P. Melo, Pst.; Rev. Zacharias Pushpanathan, Par. Vicar; CRP Stds.: 2

Corpus Christi School - (Grades PreK-8) 581 Silas Deane Hwy., Wethersfield, CT 06109 t) 860-529-5487 schoolmail@corpuschristict.eduk12.net corpuschristischoolct.com Ann Theresa Sarpu, Prin.; Stds.: 355; Lay Tchrs.: 26

The Church of the Incarnation Corporation - 544 Prospect St., Wethersfield, CT 06109

Corpus Christi Church -

The Church of the Incarnation Corporation - Merged Jun 2022 Merged with Christ the King Parish Corporation, Wethersfield.

Sacred Heart of Jesus Korean Catholic Parish Corporation - 56 Hartford Ave., Wethersfield, CT 06109 t) 860-529-1456 (office) ctkoreancatholic@gmail.com; sacredheartkorean@aohct.org www.ctkoreancatholic.com Rev. Sang Sun Lee (Korea), Pst.; CRP Stds.: 38

WINDSOR

Saint Damien of Molokai Parish Corporation - 379 Broad St., Windsor, CT 06095-3004 t) 860-688-4905 office@windsorcatholic.org; stdamienofmolokai@aohct.org www.windsorcatholic.org Rev. Shawn T. Daly, Pst.; CRP Stds.: 134

St. Gabriel School - (Grades PreK-8) 77 Bloomfield Ave., Windsor, CT 06095 t) 860-688-6401 kneville@stgabrielschool.org www.stgabrielschool.org Karla Neville, Prin.; Stds.: 138; Lay Tchrs.: 14

WINDSOR LOCKS

Mary, Gate of Heaven Parish Corporation - 42 Spring St., Windsor Locks, CT 06096-2311 t) 860-623-2524 www.stmarystrobertwl.org Rev. Timothy A. O'Brien, Pst.; Dcn. Henry J. Szumowski; Marilyn Stratton, DRE; CRP Stds.: 152

Parish Center - 45 Church St., Windsor Locks, CT 06096 t) 860-627-9469

WINSTED

St. Josephs Roman Catholic Church Corporation, Winsted, Connecticut - 31 Oak St., Winsted, CT 06098-1715 t) 860-379-3369 stjosephwinsted@aohct.org; mvaccari@stjoseph-winsted.org www.stjoseph-winsted.org Rev. Bruce C. Czapla, O.F.M., Pst.; Rev. Roger L. Hall, O.F.M., Par. Vicar; CRP Stds.: 58

WOLCOTT

Saint Basil the Great Parish Corporation - 525 Woodtick Rd., Wolcott, CT 06617-2898 t) 203-879-2544 stbasilthegreat@aohct.org www.st-basilparish.org Rev. Msgr. Thomas M. Ginty, Pst.; CRP Stds.: 120

WOODBRIDGE

The Church of the Assumption, Woodbridge - 81 Center Rd., Woodbridge, CT 06525-1699 t) 203-387-7119; 203-389-9863 (CRP) assumptionwoodbridge@aohct.org www.assumptionchurch.com Rev. Glen J. Dmytryszyn, Admin.; Dcn. Victor M. Lembo; Dcn. John Mordecai; CRP Stds.: 324

WOODBURY

Prince of Peace Parish Corporation - 494 Main St. S., Woodbury, CT 06798; Mailing: P O Box 5001, Woodbury, CT 06798 t) 203-263-2008 princeofpeace@aohct.org www.princeofpeaceparish-aohct.org Rev. James T. Gregory, Pst.; CRP Stds.: 111

SCHOOLS: PRESCHOOL THRU HIGH SCHOOL

HIGH SCHOOLS

STATE OF CONNECTICUT

BRISTOL

St. Paul Catholic High School - (DIO) (Grades 9-12) 1001 Stafford Ave., Bristol, CT 06010-3894 t) 860-584-0911 cdupont@spchs.com www.spchs.com Cary Dupont, Pres.; Rev. Joshua Wilbur, Chap.; James Cooper, Dean; Albert Wallace, Dean; Stds.: 401; Sr. Tchrs.: 1; Lay Tchrs.: 31

HAMDEN

Sacred Heart Academy, Incorporated - (PRV) (Grades 9-12) 265 Benham St., Hamden, CT 06514-2833 t) 203-288-2309 www.sacredhearthamden.org Sr. Sheila O'Neill, A.S.C.J., Pres.; Sr. Kathleen Mary Coonan, A.S.C.J., Prin.; Sr. Judith Musco, ASCJ, Dean; Maureen Hayes, Librn.; Stds.: 350; Sr. Tchrs.: 2; Lay Tchrs.: 25

MANCHESTER

East Catholic High School - (DIO) (Grades 9-12) 115 New State Rd., Manchester, CT 06042-1898

t) 860-649-5336 brennans@echs.com www.echs.com Sean Brennan, Prin.; Stds.: 428; Lay Tchrs.: 38

MILFORD

Academy of Our Lady of Mercy (Sisters of Mercy of the Americas, N.E. Community) - (PRV) (Grades 9-12) Lauralton Hall, 200 High St., Milford, CT 06460-3262 t) 203-877-2786 nbenson@lauraltonhall.org www.lauraltonhall.org Elizabeth Miller, Pres.; Stds.: 278; Lay Tchrs.: 33

NEW MILFORD

Canterbury School - (PRV) (Grades 9-12) 101 Aspetuck Ave., New Milford, CT 06776-1739 t) 860-210-3800 admissions@cbury.org www.cbury.org Coed Boarding & Day Students Rachel E. Stone, Headmaster; Stds.: 333; Lay Tchrs.: 47

WATERBURY

Brothers of the Congregation of Holy Cross - (PRV) (Grades 9-12) 587 Oronoke Rd., Waterbury, CT 06708 t) 203-757-9248 tpellegrino@holycrosshs-ct.com www.holycrosshs-ct.com Dr. Thomas C. Pellegrino, Pres.; Thomas J. Pompei, Prin.; Todd Santa Maria, Dir.; Kyle Piatak, Campus Min.; Stds.: 493; Lay Tchrs.: 39

WEST HARTFORD

Northwest Catholic High School - (DIO) (Grades 9-12) 29 Wampanoag Dr., West Hartford, CT 06117-1299 t) 860-236-4221 frdolan@nwcath.org www.northwestcatholic.org Rev. Michael J. Dolan, Pres.; Jennifer Montoney, Dean; Stds.: 422; Pr. Tchrs.: 1; Bro. Tchrs.: 1; Lay Tchrs.: 35

WEST HAVEN

Notre Dame High School of West Haven, Inc. - (PRV) (Grades 9-12) 1 Notre Dame Way, West Haven, CT 06516-2499 t) 203-933-1673 development@notredamehs.com www.notredamehs.com Robert Curis, Pres.; Joseph Ramirez, Vice. Pres.; Ruben Valencia, Vice. Pres.; Kathleen Wielk, Vice. Pres.; Stds.: 518; Lay Tchrs.: 44

Notre Dame Loyalty & Endowment Fund, Inc. - colt@notredamehs.com Bro. George C. Schmitz, C.S.C., Dir.;

INSTITUTIONS LOCATED IN DIOCESE

ASSOCIATIONS [ASN]

HARTFORD

The Benevolent Association for Priests of The Archdiocese of Hartford, Incorporated - 134 Farmington Ave., Hartford, CT 06105-3784 t) 860-541-6491 msgr.shanley@aohct.org Rev. Msgr. James A. Shanley, Mem.;

NORTH HAVEN

Catholic Cemeteries Association of the Archdiocese of Hartford, Inc. - 700 Middletown Ave., North Haven, CT 06473-0517; Mailing: P.O. Box 517, North Haven, CT 06473-0517 t) 203-239-2557 cca@ccaem.org www.ccacem.org John Pinone, Dir.;

CAMPUS MINISTRY / NEWMAN CENTERS [CAM]

HAMDEN

Quinnipiac Catholic Chaplaincy - 275 Mt. Carmel Ave., Hamden, CT 06518-1908 t) 203-582-8257 admissions@qu.edu Rev. James Lenaghan, O.P., Chap.; Judy Olian, Pres.;

HARTFORD

University of Hartford Newman Center - 200 Bloomfield Ave., Hartford, CT 06117-1599 t) (860) 216-1254 uhacatholicmin@aol.com Rev. Tuan Anh Dinh Mai, Chap.;

Trinity College Chapel - 300 Summit St., Hartford, CT 06106-3186 t) 860-297-2015 campusministry5@aol.com www.trincoll.edu/orgs/newman-club Rev. Henry Avendano, Chap.;

NEW BRITAIN

Central Connecticut State University Newman House - 145 Paul J. Manafort Dr., New Britain, CT 06053-2552 t) 860-832-3795; 860-225-6449 fr.casey@aohct.org; fr.gutierrez@aohct.org www.ccsu.edu/campusministry/catholic.html Rev. Michael T. Casey, Chap.; Rev. Eduar Gutierrez, Chap.;

St. Francis of Assisi Friary - 1755 Stanley St., New Britain, CT 06053-2099 t) (860) 225-6449 stfranciscatholic.org

NEW HAVEN

Southern Connecticut State University Catholic Center - 129 Edwards St., New Haven, CT 06511 t) 203-392-5331 fr.dmytryszyn@aohct.org; armisteadb1@southernct.edu Rev. Glen J. Dmytryszyn, Chap.; Brooke Armistead, Campus Min.;

Saint Thomas More Catholic Chapel and Center at Yale University - 268 Park St., New Haven, CT 06511-4714 t) 203-777-5537 danielle.wilson@yale.edu; stmchapel@yale.edu www.stm.yale.edu Grace H. Carroll, Campus Min.; Allan Esteron, Campus Min.; David Rivera, Campus Min.; Rev. Ryan M. Lerner, Chap.; Sr. Jennifer Schaaf, O.P., Campus Min.;

CATHOLIC CHARITIES [CCH]

HARTFORD

Catholic Charities, Inc. - Archdiocese of Hartford - 839-841 Asylum Ave., Hartford, CT 06105 t) 860-493-1841 akarpiej@ccaoh.org www.ccaoh.org Marek Kukulka, CEO; Asstd. Annu.: 11,000; Staff: 312

WATERBURY

Spanish-Speaking Center - 515 S Main St, Waterbury, CT 06706, Waterbury, CT 06706 t) 203-756-4439 fr.jimenez@aohct.org Rev. Diego A. Jimenez, Pst.; Asstd. Annu.: 650; Staff: 3

CEMETERIES [CEM]

ANSONIA

St. Mary - 56 Burton St., Ansonia, CT 06401 t) 203-735-8026 sverespie@ccacem.org www.ccacem.org Scott Verespie, Dir.;

Old St. Mary - 56 Burton St., Ansonia, CT 06401; Mailing: 177 Wakelee Ave., Ansonia, CT 06401 t) 203-735-8026 sverespie@ccacem.org www.ccacem.org Scott Verespie, Dir.;

BLOOMFIELD

Mount Saint Benedict - 1 Cottage Grove Rd., Bloomfield, CT 06002-3398 t) 860-242-0738 bmccann@ccacem.org www.ccacem.org Bruce McCann, Dir.;

DERBY

Mount St. Peter - 219 New Haven Ave., Derby, CT 06418 t) 203-735-8026 sverespie@ccacem.org www.ccacem.org Scott Verespie, Dir.;

EAST HARTFORD

Old St. Mary Cemetery - 930 Burnside Ave., East Hartford, CT 06108 t) 860-646-3772 bralston@ccacem.org www.ccacem.org William Ralston, Contact;

GLASTONBURY

Holy Cross - 17 Wickham Rd., Glastonbury, CT 06033 t) 860-646-3772 bralston@ccacem.org www.ccacem.org William Ralston, Contact;

HARTFORD

Holy Trinity - 1821 Main St., Hartford, CT 06120 t) 860-242-0738 bmccann@ccacem.org www.ccacem.org Bruce McCann, Dir.;

St. Patrick - 470 Garden St., Hartford, CT 06112 t) 860-242-0738 bmccann@ccacem.org www.ccacem.org Bruce McCann, Dir.;

MANCHESTER

St. Bridget - 180 Oakland St., Manchester, CT 06040 t) 860-646-3772 bralston@ccacem.org www.ccacem.org William Ralston, Contact;

St. James - 368 Broad St., Manchester, CT 06040 t) 860-646-3772 bralston@ccacem.org www.ccacem.org William Ralston, Contact;

MERIDEN

St. Patrick - 94 Wall St., Meriden, CT 06450 t) 203-237-3226 jwallingford@ccacem.org www.ccacem.org John Wallingford, Dir.;

Sacred Heart - 250 Gypsy Ln., Meriden, CT 06450 t) 203-237-3226 jwallingford@ccacem.org www.ccacem.org John Wallingford, Dir.;

NAUGATUCK

St. Francis - 464 High St., Naugatuck, CT 06770 t) 203-754-9105 skomar@ccacem.org www.ccacem.org (New Haven Region) Steven Komar, Dir.;

St. James - 249 Cross St., Naugatuck, CT 06770 t) 203-754-9105 skomar@ccacem.org www.ccacem.org Steven Komar, Dir.;

NEW BRITAIN

St. Mary - 1309 Stanley St., New Britain, CT 06051; Mailing: 1141 Stanley St., New Britain, CT 06051 t) 860-225-1938 ppiscitelli@ccacem.org www.ccacem.org Paul Piscitelli, Dir.;

St. Mary - 1411 Stanley St., New Britain, CT 06051 t) 860-225-1938 ppiscitelli@ccacem.org www.ccacem.org Paul Piscitelli, Dir.;

Old St. Mary - 1141 Stanley St., New Britain, CT 06051 t) 860-225-1938 ppiscitelli@ccacem.org www.ccacem.org Paul Piscitelli, Dir.;

NEW HAVEN

St. Bernard - 520 Columbus Ave., New Haven, CT 06519 t) 203-624-3980 sverespie@ccacem.org www.ccacem.org Scott Verespie, Dir.;

NORTH HAVEN

All Saints - 700 Middletown Ave., North Haven, CT 06473; Mailing: P.O. Box 517, North Haven, CT 06473-0517 t) 203-239-2557 cgrzywacz@ccacem.org; cca@ccaem.org www.ccacem.org John Pinone, Contact;

TORRINGTON

St. Francis - 863 S. Main St, Torrington, CT 06070 t) 860-482-4670 mfrey@ccacem.org www.ccacem.org Michael Frey, Dir.;

Old St. Francis - 18 Willow St., Torrington, CT 06790 t) 860-482-4670 mfrey@ccacem.org www.ccacem.org Michael Frey, Dir.;

St. Peter - 236 E. Pearl Rd., Torrington, CT 06790 t) 860-482-4670 mfrey@ccacem.org www.ccacem.org Michael Frey, Dir.;

WALLINGFORD

Holy Trinity - 346 N. Colony St., Wallingford, CT 06492 t) 203-237-3226 jwallingford@ccacem.org www.ccacem.org John Wallingford, Dir.;

St. John - 400 Christian St., Wallingford, CT 06492 t) 203-237-3226 jwallingford@ccacem.org www.ccacem.org John Wallingford, Dir.;

WATERBURY

Calvary - 2324 E. Main St., Waterbury, CT 06705 t) 203-754-9105 skomar@ccacem.org www.ccacem.org Steven Komar, Dir.;

St. Joseph - 988 Hamilton Ave., Waterbury, CT 06706 t) 203-754-9105 skomar@ccacem.org www.ccacem.org Steven Komar, Dir.;

Old St. Joseph - 496 Hamilton Ave. & Silver St., Waterbury, CT 06706 t) 203-754-9105 skomar@ccacem.org www.ccacem.org Steven Komar, Dir.;

WATERTOWN

Mount Olivet - 669 Platt Rd., Watertown, CT 06795 t) 860-274-4641 rgambordella@ccacem.org www.ccacem.org Robert Gambordella, Dir.;

WEST HAVEN

St. Lawrence - 280 Derby Ave., West Haven, CT 06516 t) 203-624-3980 sverespie@ccacem.org www.ccacem.org Scott Verespie, Dir.;

COLLEGES & UNIVERSITIES [COL]

CHESHIRE

Legion of Christ College, Inc. - 475 Oak Ave., Cheshire, CT 06410 t) 203-271-0805 www.lccollege.org Rev. Frank Formolo, L.C., Contact; Stds.: 51; Lay Tchrs.: 5; Pr. Tchrs.: 5

HAMDEN

Mt. Sacred Heart College (Apostles of the Sacred Heart of Jesus, Incorporated) - 295 Benham St., Hamden, CT 06514-2801 t) 203-248-4225 secretary@ascjus.org Chartered by the State of Connecticut for Sisters of Community of Apostles of the Sacred Heart of Jesus. College closed in 1997 due to low enrollment. Sr. Sharon Kalert, A.S.C.J., Secy.; Sr. Barbara Thomas, ASCJ, Pres.;

NEW HAVEN

Albertus Magnus College (Dominican Sisters (Dominican Sisters of Peace, Columbus, OH)) - 700 Prospect St., New Haven, CT 06511-1189 t) 800-578-9160 admissions@albertus.edu www.albertus.edu Marc Camille, Pres.; Melissa DeLucia, Registrar; Anne Leeny-Panagrossi, Librn.; Stds.: 1,650

WEST HARTFORD

University of Saint Joseph - 1678 Asylum Ave., West Hartford, CT 06117 t) 860-232-4571 admissions@usj.edu www.usj.edu Chartered by the State of Connecticut. Parent: Sisters of Mercy Rhona Free, Pres.; Michelle Kalis, Admin.; Lucy Lucker, Exec.; Stds.: 2,132; Lay Tchrs.: 123; Pr. Tchrs.: 2

CONVENTS, MONASTERIES, AND RESIDENCES FOR WOMEN [CON]

BETHLEHEM

Abbey of Regina Laudis (Benedictine Nuns of the Primitive Observance) - 273 Flanders Rd., Bethlehem, CT 06751 t) 203-266-7727 sr.rachel@yahoo.com www.abbeyofreginalaudis.com Sr. Lucia Kuppens, O.S.B., Abbess; Sr. Olivia Frances Arnold, O.S.B., Prioress; Sr. Margaret Georgina Patton, O.S.B., Sub-Prioress; Sr. Maria Immaculata Matarese, O.S.B., Treas.; Sr. Rachel Morfesi, O.S.B., Secy.; Sr. Augusta Collins, O.S.B., Novice Mistress; Sr. Telchilde Hinckley, O.S.B., Vocation Dir.; Srs.: 33

BLOOMFIELD

Sisters of Mercy of the Americas Northeast Community - 5 Garrison Ter., Bloomfield, CT 06002-3005 t) 860-243-8524 lvh52@aol.com Sr. Irene Holowesko, R.S.M., Contact;

EAST HARTFORD

Sisters of Notre Dame de Namur - 21 Highview St., East Hartford, CT 06108-2983 t) 860-289-5295 peggy.evans@sndden.org Sr. Peggy Evans, S.N.D., Contact;

Sisters of Notre Dame de Namur - 50 Larrabee St., #G, East Hartford, CT 06108 t) 860-289-2421 spesnd@sbcglobal.net Sr. Mary Janson-LaPalme, S.N.D., Contact;

EAST HAVEN

Provincial House Sisters of Charity of Our Lady, Mother of Mercy - 32 Tuttle Pl., East Haven, CT 06512 t) 203-469-7872 scmm@comcast.net www.sistersofcharity.nl Sr. Barbara Connell, S.C.M.M., Contact;

ENFIELD

Felician Sisters - Our Lady of the Angels Convent (Felician Sisters of the Order of St. Francis of Connecticut) - 1315 Enfield St., Enfield, CT 06082-4929 t) 860-745-7791; 860-745-4946 sjudithmk@feliciansisters.org www.feliciansistersna.org Sr. Judith Marie Kubicki, Prov.; Srs.: 31

Enfield Convent (Felician Sisters) - 1315 Enfield St., Enfield, CT 06082-4929 t) (860) 745-7791; (860) 745-4946 www.feliciansisters.org Rev. Noel Danielewicz, O.F.M.Conv.; Sr. Mary Christopher Moore, C.S.S.F., Prov.;

Enfield Montessori School - 1325 Enfield St., Enfield, CT 06082-4929 t) 860-745-5847 info@enfieldmontessorischool.org www.enfieldmontessorischool.org Cliona Beaulieu, Dir.;

Felician Senior Services, Inc. (Felician Sisters) - 1333A Enfield St., Enfield, CT 06082-4929 t) 860-745-2542 enfieldccnurse@feliciansisters.org www.feliciansisters.org A day respite health care facility for caregivers of the frail, elderly and Alzheimer clients. Karen Enderle, Dir.;

Felician Sisters Care Center - 1315 Enfield St., Enfield, CT 06082-4929 t) 860-745-0217 enfieldccnurse@feliciansisters.org www.feliciansisters.org Sr. Mary Christopher Moore, C.S.S.F., Prov.;

Mother Angela Residence - 1333-B Enfield St., Enfield, CT 06082-4929 t) 860-745-5705; 860-745-0217 smchristopher@feliciansisters.org Sr. Mary Christopher Moore, C.S.S.F., Prov.;

Little Sisters of the Poor - 1365 Enfield St., Enfield, CT 06082-4925 t) 860-741-0791 enmothersuperior@littlesistersofthepoor.org www.littlesistersofthepoorconnecticut.org Sr. Maureen Weiss, Supr.; Srs.: 13

FARMINGTON

Maryknoll Sisters of St. Dominic - 275 Main St. #A1, Farmington, CT 06032-2930 t) 860-678-1971 kmageemm@yahoo.com www.maryknollsisters.org Kathleen A. Magee, Contact; Srs.: 1

Sisters of the Cross and Passion - St. Gabriel's House, 31 Colton St., Farmington, CT 06032-2381 t) 551-482-5729 marystrain1@mac.com passionistsisters.org Sr. Mary Ann Strain, Contact;

HAMDEN

Apostles of the Sacred Heart of Jesus, Inc. - 295 Benham St., Hamden, CT 06514 t) 203-248-4225 secretary@ascjus.org www.ascjus.org/ Sr. Barbara Thomas, ASCJ, Prov.; Srs.: 106

Mary, Mother of the Church Convent - 115 Denslow Hill Rd., Hamden, CT 06514 t) 203-407-1042 secretary@ascjus.org www.ascjus.org Sr. Luisa Fernanda Villegas, ASCJ, Supr.; Srs.: 4

Mount Sacred Heart Provincialate Convent (Apostles of the Sacred Heart of Jesus, Incorporated) - 295 Benham St., Hamden, CT 06514-2801 t) 203-248-4225 secretary@ascjus.org www.ascjus.org Sr. Sharon Kalert, A.S.C.J., Secy.; Sr. Barbara Thomas, ASCJ, Prov.; Sr. Mary Lee, A.S.C.J., Vice-Prov. & Treas.; Srs.: 25

Sacred Heart Academy Convent - 265 Benham St., Hamden, CT 06514 t) 203-288-9408 www.sacredhearthamden.org Sr. Kathleen Mary Coonan, ASCJ, Supr.; Srs.: 5

Sacred Heart Manor, Inc. - 261 Benham St., Hamden, CT 06514 t) 203-248-4031 secretary@ascjus.org Sr. Veronica Beato, ASCJ, Vice Pres. & Supr.; Sr. Mary Anne Sharron, Pres., Dir., Lay Staff & RCH; Srs.: 31

Sisters of Mercy of the Americas Northeast Community - 2809 Whitney Ave., Hamden, CT 06518-2544 t) 203-287-9017 annoneillrsm@juno.com Sr. Ann O'Neill, R.S.M., Contact;

Sr. Antonine Signorelli Formation House - 295 Benham St., Hamden, CT 06514 t) 203-281-2572 secretary@ascjus.org www.ascjus.org Sr. Mary Grace Giaimo, ASCJ, Novice Directress; Srs.: 3

HARTFORD

The Community of the Dominican Daughters of Our Lady of Nazareth Corporation - 510 New Britain Ave., Hartford, CT 06106 t) 860-249-2912 74srlucy@gmail.com Sr. Lucia Silva, O.P., Pres.;

Medical Mission Sisters - 100 Girard Ave., Hartford, CT 06105 t) 860-233-0875 mtwinter@hartsem.edu mtwinter.hartsem.edu

Sisters of Mercy of the Americas Northeast Community - 102 Putnam St., Hartford, CT 06106-1390 t) 860-560-9590 jgough@mercyhousing.org Sr. Mary Jennifer Carroll, D.M., Contact;

LITCHFIELD

Daughters of Wisdom - 12 Clark Rd., Litchfield, CT 06759 t) 860-866-8036 sptshc@gmail.com www.wisdomhouse.org Patricia Torre, Contact;

Daughters of Wisdom - 12 Clark Rd., Litchfield, CT 06759-2808 t) 860-529-8419 rg@wisdomhouse.org daughtersofwisdom.org Sr. Ann Casagrande, Contact;

MADISON

Sisters of Mercy of the Americas Northeast Community - 167 Neck Rd., Madison, CT 06443-2725 t) 203-245-4261 emmanuel115@juno.com

MERIDEN

Generalate of the Franciscan Sisters of the Eucharist (Franciscan Sisters of the Eucharist, Inc., The Institute of the Franciscan Sisters of the Eucharist) - 405 Allen Ave., Meriden, CT 06451 t) 203-237-0841 fseinfo@fsecommunity.org www.fsecommunity.org Mother Miriam Seiferman, F.S.E., Supr.; Sr. Barbara Johnson, F.S.E., Vicar; Sr. Suzanne Gross, F.S.E., Secy.; Mother Mary Richards, F.S.E., Treas.; Srs.: 84

Franciscan Sisters of the Eucharist - 275 Finch Ave., Meriden, CT 06451; Mailing: 405 Allen Ave., Meriden, CT 06451 t) 203-238-2400 chiaracenter@fsecommunity.org Sr. Mary Elizabeth Endee, F.S.E., Supr.;

Franciscan Sisters of the Eucharist - 269 Finch Ave., Meriden, CT 06451; Mailing: 405 Allen Ave., Meriden, CT 06451 t) 203-630-1771 fsepaulvi@fsecommunity.org

NEW BRITAIN

Daughters of Mary of the Immaculate Conception - 314 Osgood Ave., Suite 408, New Britain, CT 06053 t) 860-225-9406 conventheights@yahoo.com www.crossfire.org/daughtersofmary Mother Mary Janice Zdunczyk, DM, Supr.; Srs.: 20

St. Lucian's Residence - 532 Burritt St., New Britain, CT 06053-3699 t) 860-223-2123 stlucians@comcast.net; stluciansresidence@yahoo.com Rev. Joseph Tran, Chap.; Robert Skarba, Admin.;

Marian Heights - 314 Osgood Ave., New Britain, CT 06053 t) (877) 499-1351 smjanice@yahoo.com www.mariansenior living.com

Msgr. Bojnowski Manor - 50 Pulaski St., New Britain, CT 06053 t) 860-229-0336 smjanice@yahoo.com www.mbmanor.org

Sisters of Mercy of the Americas Northeast Community - 37 Carlton St., New Britain, CT 06053 t) 860-229-7575 info@mercyne.org Sr. Barbara Kowalski, R.S.M., Contact;

Sisters of St. Joseph of Chambery - 126 Texas Dr., New Britain, CT 06052; Mailing: 650 Willard Ave., Newington, CT 06111 t) 959-200-4086 x116 csjusa@yahoo.com Sr. Donna Hoffman, Community Services; Srs.: 1

Sisters of St. Joseph of Chambery - 407 McClintock St., New Britain, CT 06053; Mailing: 650 Willard Ave., Newington, CT 06111 t) 860-827-0479 csjusa@yahoo.com Sr. Annie P. O'Brien, Community Services; Sr. Barbara A. Mullen, C.S.J., Delegate for Religious; Srs.: 2

Sisters of St. Joseph of the Third Order of St. Francis - 85 Spring St., Apt. 211, New Britain, CT 06051 t) 860-229-0426 sbwanat@comcast.net Sr. Barbara Wanat, SSJ-TOSF, Contact;

NEW HAVEN

Dominican Sisters of Peace - 15 Lincoln St., New Haven, CT 06511 t) 203-865-7305 barbdecrosta@att.net Sr. Barbara DeCrosta, O.P., Contact;

Dominican Sisters of Peace - 15 Eld St., New Haven, CT 06511-3815

NORTH GUILFORD

Monastery of Our Lady of Grace (Dominican Contemplative Nuns (Cloistered)) - 11 Race Hill Rd., North Guilford, CT 06437-1099 t) 203-457-0599 olgracevocations@gmail.com; gracemonastery@gmx.com www.dominicannuns.org Sr. Maria of the Angels Heinemann, O.P., Prioress; Srs.: 26

NORTH HAVEN

Sisters of the Sacred Heart of Jesus Convent - 94 Chapel Hill Rd., North Haven, CT 06473 t) 203-239-8012 Sr. Jacinta A Ibe, Supr.; Srs.: 5

***Sisters of the Sacred Heart of Jesus of Ragusa** - 94 Chapel Hill Rd., North Haven, CT 06473 t) 203-239-8012 jakudo@sbcglobal.net www.sistersaremyteachers.com Sr. Jacinta A Ibe, Supr.; Srs.: 5

UNIONVILLE

Sisters of the Cross and Passion - 16 Hunters Ridge, Apt. 16, Unionville, CT 06085 t) 860-472-7260

maureenobriencp@gmail.com Sr. Ann Rodgers, C.P., Contact;

WALLINGFORD

Holy Trinity Convent (Sisters of Mercy of the Americas of Connecticut) - 247 S. Main St., Wallingford, CT 06492 t) 203-265-6999 sisterkatiekelly@snet.net Sr. Kathleen Kelly, R.S.M., Contact;

WATERBURY

Sisters of Notre Dame de Namur - 587 Oronoke Rd., Waterbury, CT 06708 t) 203-755-8828 pmccarthy@cnd-m.org Sr. Patricia McCarthy, Contact;

WATERTOWN

St. John the Evangelist Convent - 9 Academy Hill, Watertown, CT 06795-2101 t) 860-274-1820 bvaluckassnd@gmail.com Rev. Anthony J. Smith, Contact;

WEST HARTFORD

Convent of Mary Immaculate, Provincial House of the Sisters of St. Joseph of Chambery - 27 Park Rd., West Hartford, CT 06119; Mailing: 650 Willard Ave., Newington, CT 06111 t) 860-233-5734 csjusa@yahoo.com; sallycsj53@gmail.com www.sistersofsaintjoseph.org North American Province. Sr. Sally Hodgdon, C.S.J., Prov.; Srs.: 57

Religious Trust of the Sisters of St. Joseph of Chambery (the "Trust") - t) 860-231-8678

The Sisters of St. Joseph Corporation - ; Mailing: 650 Willard Ave., Newington, CT 06111 t) (860) 233-5734

Dominican Sisters - 78 Westpoint Ter., West Hartford, CT 06107 t) 860-521-8296 chancellor@aohct.org Sr. Magdalene Nguyen, O.P., Supr.;

Sisters of Mercy of the Americas - Northeast Community, Inc. - 25 Prescott St., 1st Fl., West Hartford, CT 06110-2335 t) 860-594-8619 jhardin@sistersofmercy.org Sr. Elizabeth deManbey, RSM, Local Coord.; Sr. Dorellen Sullivan, R.S.M., Sister Life Minister; Srs.: 69

Sisters of St. Joseph of Chambery - 27 Park Rd., West Hartford, CT 06119; Mailing: 650 Willard Ave., Newington, CT 06111 t) 860-233-5126; 860-233-5734 csjusa@yahoo.com www.sistersofsaintjoseph.org Sr. Sally Hodgdon, C.S.J., Prov.; Srs.: 57

Sisters of St. Joseph of Chambery - 27 Park Rd., West Hartford, CT 06119; Mailing: Prov. Admin. Offices, 650 Willard Ave., Newington, CT 06111 t) 860-233-5734 csjusa@yahoo.com www.sistersofsaintjoseph.org Mary D'Arcangelo, Contact; Srs.: 57

Convent - sbamcsj@gmail.com www.sistersofsaintjoseph.org Sr. Barbara A. Mullen, C.S.J., Prov.;

Visitation Plaza - 54 Boulanger Ave., #1, West Hartford, CT 06110 t) 203-755-7236 Sr. Mary Etta Higgins, R.S.M., Admin.;

WEST HAVEN

Sisters of Charity of St. Elizabeth, Convent Station - 101 W. Prospect St., West Haven, CT 06516 t) 203-397-5243 srjean@sbcglobal.net Sr. Jean Trainor, S.C., Contact;

WINCHESTER CENTER

Villa Ferretti, Religious Teachers Filippini - 438 Winchester Rd., Winchester Center, CT 06094; Mailing: Box 455, Winchester Center, CT 06094 t) 860-806-3059 villaferretti@gmail.com Sr. Angela Bulla, M.P.F., Contact;

WINDSOR

The Connecticut Province of the Sisters of Notre Dame de Namur, Inc. - 468 Poquonock Ave, Windsor, CT 06095-2473 t) 860-688-1832 elaine.bain@sndden.org Sr. Elaine Bain, Prov.; Sr. Barbara Barry, S.N.D.deN., Prov.; Sr. Eileen Burns, Prov.; Sr. Patricia Chappell, Prov.; Sr. Mary Farren, S.N.D.de.N., Prov.;

Julie House, Inc. - 425 Poquonock Ave., Windsor, CT 06095-2465 t) 860-298-8320 dina.karvelis@sndden.org Assisted living home for S.N.D.'s only. Dina Karvelis, Admin.;

Sisters of Notre Dame de Namur - 468 Poquonock Ave., Windsor, CT 06095 t) 860-688-1832 ellen.agritelley@sndden.org (Connecticut Province) Sr. Elanie Bain, SNDdeN, Prov. Asst.;

WOLCOTT

Contemplative Sisters of the Good Shepherd - 5 Carriage Hill Dr., Wolcott, CT 06716 t) 203-879-6330 www.sistersofthegoodshepherdcontemplatives.org Sr. Carol Anne Seigel, C.G.S., Contact; Srs.: 2

Daughters of Wisdom - 18 Munson Rd., #2, Wolcott, CT 06716 t) 203-879-3432 dguerettedw@comcast.net Sr. Diane Guerrette, D.W., Contact;

ENDOWMENTS / FOUNDATIONS / TRUSTS [EFT]

HAMDEN

Sacred Heart Academy Endowment Fund, Inc. - 265 Benham St., Hamden, CT 06514 t) 203-288-9408 www.sacredhearthamden.org Sr. Kathleen Mary Coonan, ASCJ, Prin.; Sr. Sheila O'Neill, A.S.C.J., Pres.;

HARTFORD

Archdiocese of Hartford Multi-Employer Health Benefits Trust - 134 Farmington Ave., Hartford, CT 06105 t) 860-541-6491 arlyn.page@aohct.org Richard Braam, CFO; Arlyn Page, Secy.;

Archdiocese of Hartford Retired Priests Health and Benefits Trust - 134 Farmington Ave., Hartford, CT 06105 t) 860-541-6491 richard.braam@aohct.org; chancellor@aohct.org Richard Braam, Dir.;

St. Augustine Foundation, Inc. - 134 Farmington Ave., Hartford, CT 06105 t) 860-541-6491 richard.braam@aohct.org Richard Braam, Dir.;

The Hartford Bishops' Foundation, Inc. - 134 Farmington Ave., Hartford, CT 06105 t) 860-541-6491 william.mclean@aohct.org www.hartfordbishopsfoundation.org William McLean, Admin.;

MLS Religious Trust - Missionaries of La Salette, 85B New Park Ave., Hartford, CT 06106-2184; Mailing: P.O. Box 331370, West Hartford, CT 06133 t) 860-956-8870 mlsprovinceoffice@gmail.com Cheryl Accinno, Contact;

The Archdiocese of Hartford Investment Trust - 134 Farmington Ave., Hartford, CT 06105-3784 t) 860-541-6491 matt.byrne@aohct.org

NEW BRITAIN

Charitable Trust of the Daughters of Mary of the Immaculate Conception - 314 Osgood Ave., Ste. 408, New Britain, CT 06053 c) (860) 612-9066 smjanice@yahoo.com Mother Mary Janice Zdunczyk, DM, Supr.;

Retirement Trust of the Daughters of Mary of the Immaculate Conception - 314 Osgood Ave., New Britain, CT 06053 c) (860) 612-9066 smjanice@yahoo.com Mother Mary Janice Zdunczyk, DM, Supr.;

WEATOGUE

Foundation for the Advancement of Catholic Schools - 92 Hopmeadow St., Weatogue, CT 06089 t) (860) 325-5096 cbhoward@facshartford.org; mdussult@facshartford.org www.facshartford.org Cynthia Basil Howard, Exec.; Marie M. Dussault, Dir.;

HOSPITALS / HEALTH SERVICES [HOS]

HARTFORD

Saint Francis Hospital and Medical Center (Catholic Health Ministries) - 114 Woodland St., Hartford, CT 06105-1299 t) 860-714-4000 www.trinityhealthofne.org Member of Trinity Health Of New England Regional Health Ministry of Trinity Health, Livonia MI Thomas Burke, Pres.; Gerald Galipeau, Exec.; Rev. Celillon Alteme, Chap.; Rev. Thomas Dekaa, Chap.; Sr. Nancy Donovan, Chap.; Dcn. Jacek Muszynski, Chap.; Bed Capacity: 617; Asstd. Annu.: 403,079; Staff: 2,980

Asylum Hill Family Medicine Center, Inc. - 99 Woodland St., Hartford, CT 06105-1299 t) 860-714-4212 www.asylumhillfamilymedicine.org Michael Grey, Exec.;

Saint Francis Hospital and Medical Center Foundation, Inc. - 95 Woodland St., Hartford, CT 06105-1299 t) 860-714-4900 Member of Trinity Health Of New England Regional Health Ministry of Trinity Health, Livonia MI Timothy R Stanton, Exec.;

Mount Sinai Rehabilitation Hospital, Inc. - 490 Blue Hills Ave., Hartford, CT 06112 Member of Trinity Health Of New England Regional Health Ministry of Trinity Health, Livonia MI Thomas Burke, Exec.; Bed Capacity: 30; Asstd. Annu.: 10,685; Staff: 150

Trinity Health of New England Corporation, Inc. - 1000 Asylum Ave., Hartford, CT 06105 t) (860) 714-5360 Regional Health Ministry of Trinity Health, Livonia MI D. Montez Carter, Pres.; Jennifer Schneider, CFO;

Trinity Health of New England Provider Network, Inc. - 114 Woodland St., Hartford, CT 06105 t) (860) 714-4000 Deborah Bitsoli, Pres.;

The Women's Auxiliary of Saint Francis Hospital and Medical Center - 114 Woodland St., Hartford, CT 06105 t) 860-714-4558 Linda Pendergast, Pres.; Mary Quish Smullen, Treas.;

WATERBURY

Saint Mary's Hospital - 56 Franklin St., Waterbury, CT 06706-1200 t) 203-709-6000 www.trinityhealthofne.org Rev. Amobi Atuegbu, Chap.; Sr. Nancy Donovan, Chap.; July Bellemare, Chap.; Bed Capacity: 347; Asstd. Annu.: 313,068; Staff: 1,349

Saint Mary's Hospital Foundation, Inc. - 56 Franklin St., Waterbury, CT 06706 t) 203-709-6390 Amanda Nardiello, Dir.;

MISCELLANEOUS [MIS]

BLOOMFIELD

The Catholic Mission Aid Society of Hartford, Inc. - 467 Bloomfield Ave., Bloomfield, CT 06002 t) 860-541-6491 missionoffice@aohct.org Rev. Msgr. James A. Shanley, Dir.;

HARTFORD

134 Farmington Avenue, Inc. - 134 Farmington Ave., Hartford, CT 06105 t) 860-541-6491 chancellor@aohct.org Diana Tierinni, Contact;

Cathedral Indemnity Company - 134 Farmington Ave., Hartford, CT 06105 t) 860-541-6491 arlyn.page@aohct.org Richard Braam, Contact;

Connecticut Catholic Conference, Inc. - 134 Farmington Ave., Hartford, CT 06105 t) 860-524-7882 ccc@ctcatholic.org www.ctcatholic.org Christopher C. Healy, Dir.;

Hartford Educational Broadband, Inc. - 134 Farmington Ave., Hartford, CT 06105-3784 t) 860-541-6491 Richard Braam, Contact;

The Hartford Roman Catholic Diocesan Corporation - 134 Farmington Ave., Hartford, CT 06105 t) 860-541-6491 richard.braam@aohct.org Richard Braam, Contact;

***House of Bread, Inc.** - 1453 Main St., Hartford, CT 06120-2726 t) 860-549-4188 hobread@aol.com Sr. Maureen Faenza, C.S.J., Dir.; Sr. Theresa Fonti, C.S.J., Dir.;

***Jubilee House, Inc.** - 40 Clifford St., Hartford, CT 06114 t) 860-247-3030 hobread@aol.com Sr. Theresa Fonti, CSJ, Dir.;

Mercy Housing and Shelter Corporation - 211 Wethersfield Ave, Hartford, CT 06114 t) 860-808-2048 amenald@mercyhousingct.org www.mercyhousingct.org Homeless Services Kara A. Capone, CEO; Kathleen Shaw, COO; Matthew Candiloro, Treas.;

North American La Salette Mission Center, Inc. - 915 Maple Ave., Hartford, CT 06114-2330 t) 860-956-8870 mlsprovinceoffice@gmail.com www.lsmc.org Rev. Thomas Vellappallil, M.S., Dir.;

KENSINGTON

St. Paul Friary (St. Paul Parish Corporation) - 479 Alling St., Kensington, CT 06037-2100 t) 860-828-0331 stpaul@aohct.org; ourchurch@stpaulkensington.org Rev. Raymond Borkowski, OFM Conv., In Res.; Rev. Joseph Benicewicz, OFM Conv., Pst.; Rev. Michael Englert, OFM Conv., Par. Vicar; Rev. Timothy Lyons, O.F.M.Conv., Par. Vicar;

LITCHFIELD

Lourdes Shrine Guild, Inc. - 83 Montfort Rd., Litchfield, CT 06759; Mailing: PO Box 667, Litchfield, CT 06759 t) 860-567-1041 lourdesshrinect@gmail.com Rev. Donald Gregory LaSalle, S.M.M., Supr.;

MANCHESTER

***Crossroads 4 Christ, Inc.** - 21 Adams St., S., Manchester, CT 06040 t) 860-810-7956 asoucy@crossroadsforchrist.org crossroads4christ.org Young Adult Apostolate Alex Soucy, Exec. Dir.;

MERIDEN

Franciscan Life Center Network, Inc. - 271 Finch Ave., Meriden, CT 06451 t) 203-237-8084 sbarbara@flcenter.org; sistersuzanne@communitysecretary.org www.flcenter.org Christina Caro, Dir.; Sr. Barbara Johnson, F.S.E., Dir.;

Franciscan Life Center Network, Incorporated - 405 Allen Ave., Meriden, CT 06451 t) (203) 237-0841 communitysecretary@fsecommunity.org www.flcenter.org Sr. Suzanne Gross, F.S.E., Secy.;

Franciscan Ever There Care - 273 Finch Ave., Meriden, CT 06451 t) 203-630-2881 clientservices@franciscanetc.org www.franciscanetc.org Christina Caro, Dir.;

Franciscan Life Center - 271 Finch Ave., Meriden, CT 06451 t) 203-237-8084 flc@flcenter.org Sr. Barbara Johnson, F.S.E., Exec. Dir.;

Franciscan Life Process Center - 11650 Downes St., Lowell, MI 49331; Mailing: 405 Allen Ave., Meriden, CT 06451 t) (616) 897-7842 flpc@lifeprocesscenter.org lifeprocesscenter.org Sr. Colleen Ann Nagle, F.S.E., Exec. Dir.;

Franciscan Montessori Earth School - 14750 S.E. Clinton St., Portland, OR 97236; Mailing: 405 Allen Ave., Meriden, CT 06451 t) (503) 760-8220 fmes.org Sr. Therese Gutting, F.S.E., Admin.;

NEW BRITAIN

Marian Heights, Incorporated - Daughters of Mary of the Immaculate Conception, 314 Osgood Ave., New Britain, CT 06053 t) (860) 515-5427 (Marian Heights); (860) 612-9066 (Mother Mary Janice) conventheights@yahoo.com www.crossfire.org Purpose: home is limited for low income elderly, adult day care, child day care, convent. Mother Mary Janice Zdunczyk, DM, Rel. Ord. Ldr.;

Siena Learning Center (Dominican Sisters of Peace, Inc.) - 29 Edson St., New Britain, CT 06051-3001 t) 860-348-0622 Nancy Rodriguez, Dir.; Sr. Virginia Bruen, Delegate;

NEW HAVEN

Apostle Immigrant Services, Corporation - 115 Blatchley Ave., New Haven, CT 06513 t) 203-752-9068 apostleimmigrantservices.org Sr. Mary Ellen Burns, ASCJ, Dir.;

Springs Learning Center (Dominican Sisters of Peace, Inc.) - 115 Blatchley Ave., New Haven, CT 06513-4206 t) 203-787-1025 springslearning@oppeace.org Sr. Margaret Mary Kennedy, Dir.;

PLANTSVILLE

Magnificat-Mother of Divine Mercy Corporation, Bristol, CT - 568 Mount Vernon Rd., Plantsville, CT 06479 t) 860-302-1349 janet.massa123@yahoo.com Purpose: to foster the work of intercession; to conduct prayer focused meetings and to serve the needy. Janet Massa, Pres.;

PROSPECT

ORTV, Inc. - 15 Peach Orchard Rd., Prospect, CT 06712 t) (860) 242-8800 (Hartford Area); (203) 758-7367 (Waterbury/New Haven Area); (877) 342-5956 (Outside the Calling Areas) ortv@ortv.org; programming@ortv.org www.ortv.org Rev. John P. Gatzak, Dir.;

WATERBURY

Francis Xavier Plaza, Inc. - 605 Baldwin St., Waterbury, CT 06706-1501; Mailing: 839-841 Asylum Ave., Hartford, CT 06105 t) 860-728-2562 akarpiej@ccaoh.org Alyson Karpiej, Contact;

***St. Vincent de Paul Mission of Waterbury, Inc.** - 34 Willow St., Waterbury, CT 06721; Mailing: P.O. Box 1612, Waterbury, CT 06721 t) 203-754-0000 st.vincent.depaul@snet.net svdpmission.org Gary Beaulieu, Dir.;

WEST HARTFORD

***Intensive Education Academy, Inc.** - 840 N. Main St., West Hartford, CT 06117-2026 t) 860-236-2049 lsusi@ie-academy.org ie-academy.org Lori Susi, Dir.;

Mercy Community Health, Inc. - 2021 Albany Ave., West Hartford, CT 06117-2796 t) 860-570-8301 mreardon@mchct.org; edana@mchct.org www.themercycommunity.org Eric Dana, Exec.;

MONASTERIES AND RESIDENCES FOR PRIESTS AND BROTHERS [MON]

CHESHIRE

Legionaries of Christ - 475 Oak Ave., Cheshire, CT 06410 t) 203-271-0805 twalsh@legionaries.org www.lccheshire.org Rev. Timothy Walsh, L.C., Rector; Rev. Jon Budke, L.C., Vice Rector; Rev. Bernardo Torres, L.C., Spiritual Adv./Care Srvcs.; Rev. Raymond Cosgrave, L.C., Prof.; Rev. Miguel de la Torre, LC, Prof.; Rev. Patrick Langan, Prof.; Rev. Christopher O'Connor, L.C., Prof.; Rev. John Pietropaoli, Prof.; Rev. Victor Jimenez, L.C. (Colombia), Asst. to Rector; Rev. John Bender, LC, Asst. to Rector for Humanities & Prof.; Rev. Nathan Torrey, LC, Asst. to Novice Dir.; Brs.: 42; Priests: 11

HARTFORD

Missionaries of La Salette Province of Mary, Mother of the Americas (The Missionaries of La Salette Corporation., MLS Religious Trust) - 85B New Park Ave., Hartford, CT 06106-2184; Mailing: P.O. Box 331370, West Hartford, CT 06133 t) 860-956-8870 mlsprovinceoffice@gmail.com www.lasalette.org Rev. Roland S. Nadeau, M.S., Vicar; Rev. William Kaliyadan, M.S., Prov.; Rev. Ronald B. Foshage, M.S., Prov. Asst.; Brs.: 17; Priests: 66

Missionaries of LaSalette - 85 New Park Ave., Hartford, CT 06106-2184 t) 860-523-8275 Rev. Jeffrey M. L'Arche, M.S., Supr.; Rev. Salvatore D. Altavista, M.S.; Rev. Paul N. Belhumeur, M.S.; Rev. Rene J. Butler, M.S.; Bro. David J. Cook, M.S.; Rev. James Dunphy, M.S.; Rev. Frederick R. Flaherty, M.S.; Rev. John Gabriel, M.S.; Bro. Andre J. Hamel, M.S.; Rev. Leo Holleran, M.S.; Rev. Thomas Huhn, M.S.; Bro. Edmund A. Normantowicz, M.S.; Rev. Manuel Pereira, M.S.; Rev. Paul G. Rainville, M.S.; Bro. Robert Russell, M.S.; Rev. Daniel J. Scott, M.S.; Rev. Thomas G. Sickler, M.S.; Rev. Donald D. Simonds, M.S.; Bro. Roger F. Clement, M.S.;

North American La Salette Mission Center - 85 New Park Ave., Hartford, CT 06106-2184 mlslprovinceoffice@gmail.com Rev. Thomas Vellappallil, M.S., Dir.;

Our Lady of Sorrows Rectory - 16 Greenwood St., Hartford, CT 06106-2109 t) 860-233-4424 fr.oneil.jm@aohct.org Rev. Joseph O'Neil, m.s., Pst.; Rev. James J. Aherne, M.S., Vicar; Rev. John F. Higgins, M.S., In Res.;

St. Patrick-St. Anthony Friary (Franciscan Friars) - 285 Church St., Hartford, CT 06103-1196 t) 860-249-7754 wbeaudin@gmail.com spsact.org (Holy Name Prov.) Rev. John J. Leonard, O.F.M., Par. Vicar; Rev. Timothy J. Shreenan, O.F.M., Pst.; Rev. Michael Johnson, O.F.M., Par. Vicar; Rev. William L. Beaudin, O.F.M., Guardian and Parochial Vicar; Rev. A. Francis Soucy, Sr. Assoc. Friar In Res. & Parochial Vicar; Priests: 5

LITCHFIELD

Montfort Missionaries - 83 Montfort Rd., Litchfield, CT 06759; Mailing: P.O. Box 667, Litchfield, CT 06759 t) 860-567-8434 lourdesshrinect@gmail.com www.shrinect.org Rev. Donald Gregory LaSalle, S.M.M., Supr.; Rev. William Considine, S.M.M., Assistant; Priests: 2

Lourdes in Litchfield (Lourdes Shrine Guild, Inc.) - t) 860-567-1041

Montfort House (Center for Spiritual Renewal) - t) (860) 567-8434

MANCHESTER

DePaul Provincial Residence (The New England Province of the Congregation of the Mission Incorporated, Congregation of the Mission, New England Province) - 234 Keeney St., Manchester, CT 06040-7048 t) 860-643-2828 nepcm1@cox.net cmnewengland.org (Vincentian Fathers and Brothers) Rev. Marek Sobczak, CM, Prov.; Priests: 16

Charitable Trust of the New England Province of the Congregation of the Mission - t) (860) 643-2828

St. Joseph Rectory - 32 Jewett St., Ansonia, CT 06401 t) 203-734-0402 fr.maciejewski@aohct.org Rev. Tadeusz Maciejewski, C.M., Pst.;

St. Michael the Archangel Rectory - 75 Derby Ave., Derby, CT 06418-2098 t) 203-734-0005 stmichaelsderby@sbcglobal.net

MERIDEN

Franciscan Brothers of the Eucharist - 173 Goodspeed Ave., Meriden, CT 06451 t) 203-235-4318 maryoftheangels@fbecommunity.org www.fbecommunity.org Bro. Leo Maneri, F.B.E., Treas.; Brs.: 2

NORTH GUILFORD

Our Lady of Grace Monastery (Order of Preachers (Dominicans)) - 11 Race Hill Rd., North Guilford, CT 06437-1099 t) 203-457-0599 gracemonastery@gmx.com www.dominicannuns.org Sr. Maria of the Angels, OP, Prioress; Brs.: 26

WATERBURY

Basilica of the Immaculate Conception Rectory - 74 W. Main St., Waterbury, CT 06702 t) 203-574-0017 info@wtbybasilica.org www.wtbybasilica.org Very Rev. James M. Sullivan, Rector; Rev. Lee Hellwig, Par. Vicar; Rev. Dennis J. Vincenzo, Par. Vicar; Priests: 4

WEST HARTFORD

Holy Family Monastery/Retreat - 303 Tunxis Rd., West Hartford, CT 06107 t) 860-521-0440 info@holyfamilyretreat.org www.holyfamilyretreat.org Rev. Terence J. Kristofak, C.P., In Res.; Bro. Michael Moran, C.P., Mem.; Bro. Terence Skorka, C. P., Mem.; Rev. David Cinquegrani, C.P., Dir.; Brs.: 2; Priests: 2

WEST HAVEN

Brothers of Holy Cross - 10 Ricardo St., West Haven, CT 06516-2499 t) 570-417-0638 gcscsc@gmail.com Bro. George C. Schmitz, C.S.C.; Brs.: 1

NURSING / REHABILITATION / CONVALESCENCE / ELDERLY CARE [NUR]

ENFIELD

The Home for the Aged of the Little Sisters of the Poor - 1365 Enfield St., Enfield, CT 06082-4925 t) 860-741-0791 enmothersuperior@littlesistersofthepoor.org Incorporated Operating as St. Joseph's Residence Thomas Ranstrom, Admin.; Rev. Edward O'Brien, In Res.; Kevin Jones, Grant Writer; Asstd. Annu.: 69; Staff: 98

NEW BRITAIN

St. Lucian's Residence, Inc. (Daughters of Mary of the Immaculate Conception) - 532 Burritt St., New Britain, CT 06053-3699 t) 860-223-2123 stlucians@comcast.net; stluciansresidence@yahoo.com Parent Entity: Daughters of Mary Rev. Joseph Tran, Chap.; Robert Skarba, Admin.; Asstd. Annu.: 24; Staff: 17

Monsignor Bojnowski Manor, Inc. - 50 Pulaski St., New Britain, CT 06053 t) 860-229-0336 mjulmisse@mbmanor.org www.mbmanor.org Owned and operated by the Daughters of Mary of the Immaculate Conception. Martin Julmisse, Admin.; Asstd. Annu.: 50; Staff: 90

WEST HARTFORD

Saint Mary Home - 2021 Albany Ave., West Hartford, CT 06117-2796 t) 860-570-8200 mreardon@mchc.org; brian.nyberg@trinity-health.org www.themercycommunity.org Brian Nyberg, Admin.; Eric Dana, Exec.; Patricia Russell, Dir.; Sr. Maureen Reardon, R.S.M., Senior Vice Pres.; Asstd. Annu.: 800; Staff: 296

Saint Mary Home, Incorporated - 2021 Albany Ave., West Hartford, CT 06117 t) 860-570-8200 edana@mchct.org www.themercycommunity.org Rachel DeMaida, Admin.; Eric Dana, Exec. Dir.; Patricia

Russell, Dir.; Srs.: 31; Asstd. Annu.: 825; Staff: 296

McAuley Center, Inc. - 275 Steele Rd., West Hartford, CT 06117 t) 860-920-6300 pmurray@mchct.org; edana@mchct.org www.themcauley.org Life Plan Community; Sisters of Mercy. Eric Dana, Regional Operations Dir.; Phillip Lemay, Dir.; Janice Hamilton-Crawford, Pres.; Asstd. Annu.: 250; Staff: 111

Sedgwick Cedars Corporation - 27 Park Rd., West Hartford, CT 06119 t) (860) 232-8252 sallycsj53@gmail.com Under the auspices of the Sisters of St. Joseph of Chambery. Sr. Sally Hodgdon, C.S.J., Pres.; Asstd. Annu.: 24; Staff: 18

RETREAT HOUSES / RENEWAL CENTERS [RTR]

FARMINGTON

Our Lady of Calvary Retreat Center - 31 Colton St., Farmington, CT 06032 t) 860-677-8519 olcretreat@sbcglobal.net www.ourladyofcalvary.net Conducted by the Sisters of the Cross and Passion for Religious and Lay Persons. Sr. Kathleen FitzSimons, C.N.D., Admin.; Sr. Ann Rodgers, C.P., Dir.;

LITCHFIELD

Wisdom House Retreat Center - 229 E. Litchfield Rd., Litchfield, CT 06759-3002 t) 860-567-3163 dkelly@wisdomhouse.org www.wisdomhouse.org Deborah Kelly, Exec.;

MADISON

Mercy Center, Incorporated (Sisters of Mercy-Northeast Community) - 167 Neck Rd., Madison, CT 06443 t) 203-245-0401 info@mercybythesea.org www.mercybythesea.org

NEW HARTFORD

Missionary Servants of the Most Blessed Trinity - 595 Town Hill Rd., New Hartford, CT 06057 t) 860-379-4329 trinita@charter.net msbt.org/trinita Trinita Retreat Center Sr. Deborah Wilson, Contact;

WEST HARTFORD

Holy Family Passionist Retreat Center (Passionist Fathers of CT, Inc.) - 303 Tunxis Rd., West Hartford, CT 06107 t) 860-521-0440 info@holyfamilyretreat.org www.holyfamilyretreat.org For laymen and laywomen. Conducted by the Passionist Community. Rev. David Cinquegrani, C.P., Dir.;

SEMINARIES [SEM]

BLOOMFIELD

St. Thomas Seminary - 467 Bloomfield Ave., Bloomfield, CT 06002-2999 t) 860-242-5573 stsevents@aohct.org www.archdioceseofhartford.org Very Rev. Steven C. Boguslawski, Moderator; Rev. Michael G. Whyte, Pres.; Stds.: 85; Lay Tchrs.: 1

CHESHIRE

Novitiate of the Legion of Christ - 475 Oak Ave., Cheshire, CT 06410 t) 203-271-0805 cheshire@legionaries.org www.facebook.com/lccheshire Rev. Bernardo Torres, L.C., Spiritual Adv./Care Srvcs.; Rev. Victor Jimenez, L.C. (Colombia), Assistant to the Rector; Rev. Timothy Walsh, L.C., Rector; Rev. John Budke, L.C., Vice Rector; Rev. Raymond Cosgrave, L.C., Prof.; Rev. Miguel Angel de la Torre, LC, Prof.; Rev. Patrick Langan, Prof.; Rev. Christopher O'Connor, L.C., Prof.; Rev. John Pietropaoli, Prof.; Rev. John Bender, LC, Asst. to Rector for Humanists; Rev. Nathan Torrey, LC, Asst. to Novitiate Dir.; Stds.: 9; Lay Tchrs.: 5; Pr. Tchrs.: 4

SPECIAL CARE FACILITIES [SPF]

HAMDEN

Apostles of the Sacred Heart Clelian Center, Incorporated - 261 Benham St., Hamden, CT 06514-2898 t) 203-288-4151 info@cleliancenter.com www.cleliancenter.com A day healthcare facility for the elderly (nondenominational) Lori Schommer, Dir.; Asstd. Annu.: 60; Staff: 10

HARTFORD

***Malta House of Care, Inc.** - 19 Woodland St., Ste. 21, Hartford, CT 06105 t) 860-725-0171 tcaputomd@maltahouseofcare.org www.maltahouseofcare.org Luis Diez-Morales, Pres.; Brian Sheehan, Chair; Asstd. Annu.: 1,265; Staff: 13

MERIDEN

Franciscan Family Care Center, Inc. - 267 Finch Ave., Meriden, CT 06451 t) 203-238-1441 ssuzanne@franciscanhc.org Sr. Suzanne Gross, F.S.E., Admin.; Asstd. Annu.: 250; Staff: 69

Diocese of Helena

(Dioecesis Helenensis)

MOST REVEREND AUSTIN A. VETTER

Bishop of Helena; ordained June 29, 1993; appointed Bishop of Helena October 8, 2019; consecrated November 20, 2019. Bishop's Office: 630 N. Last Chance Gulch, Suite 2200, P.O. Box 1729, Helena, MT 59624-1729.

Chancery: 630 N. Last Chance Gulch, Suite 2200, P.O. Box 1729, Helena, MT 59624-1729. T: 406-442-5820; F: 406-442-5191.
www.diocesehelena.org
chancery@diocesehelena.org

ERECTED MARCH 7, 1884.

Square Miles 51,922.

Comprises the western part of the State of Montana, and is made up of the following Counties: Lewis and Clark, Glacier, Pondera, Flathead, Lake, Lincoln, Missoula, Mineral, Sanders, Powell, Granite, Ravalli, Deer Lodge, Silver Bow, Jefferson, Broadwater, Gallatin, Madison, Beaverhead, Meagher, Wheatland and parts of Teton and Toole.

Diocesan Legal Title–Roman Catholic Bishop of Helena, Montana, a Corporation Sole.

For legal titles of parishes and diocesan institutions, consult the Chancery Office.

STATISTICAL OVERVIEW

Personnel
Bishop....1
Priests: Diocesan Active in Diocese....29
Priests: Diocesan Active Outside Diocese....1
Priests: Retired, Sick or Absent....23
Number of Diocesan Priests....53
Religious Priests in Diocese....11
Total Priests in your Diocese....64
Extern Priests in Diocese....2
Ordinations:
Diocesan Priests....2
Transitional Deacons....1
Permanent Deacons in Diocese....35
Total Brothers....4
Total Sisters....7

Parishes
Parishes....59
With Resident Pastor:
Resident Diocesan Priests....24
Resident Religious Priests....8
Without Resident Pastor:
Administered by Priests....24
Administered by Deacons....1
Administered by Lay People....2
Missions....38
Professional Ministry Personnel:
Sisters....3
Lay Ministers....24

Welfare
Catholic Hospitals....3
Total Assisted....304,246

Educational
Diocesan Students in Other Seminaries....15
Total Seminarians....15
Colleges and Universities....1
Total Students....1,210
High Schools, Diocesan and Parish....2
Total Students....261
High Schools, Private....1
Total Students....12
Elementary Schools, Diocesan and Parish....4
Total Students....887
Elementary Schools, Private....2
Total Students....188
Catechesis/Religious Education:
High School Students....581
Elementary Students....1,322
Total Students under Catholic Instruction....4,476
Teachers in Diocese:
Brothers....4
Sisters....1
Lay Teachers....227

Vital Statistics
Receptions into the Church:
Infant Baptism Totals....524
Minor Baptism Totals....63
Adult Baptism Totals....94
Received into Full Communion....167
First Communions....450
Confirmations....244
Marriages:
Catholic....96
Interfaith....42
Total Marriages....138
Deaths....546
Total Catholic Population....46,533
Total Population....667,785

LEADERSHIP

Vicar General - t) 406-442-5825 Rev. Msgr. Kevin S. O'Neill (koneill@sthelenas.org);
Delegate for Special Projects - t) 406-389-7059 Rev. Bart Tolleson (btolleson@diocesehelena.org);
Chancery Services - t) 406-442-5820 chancery@diocesehelena.org
Archivist - t) (406) 442-5820
Chancellor - Jim Carney, Chancellor; Matthew Brower, Vice Chancellor;
Pastoral and Renewal Services -
Financial Services - Jim Carney, Diocesan Financial Svcs. Officer;
Stewardship Services - Sharon Witham, Dir. (switham@diocesehelena.org);
Diocesan Tribunal - Rev. John W. Robertson;
Judicial Vicar - Rev. John W. Robertson;
Notary (Tribunal) - Raymond Shipman, Notary;
Associate Judge - Rev. Thomas P. Haffey;
Defenders of the Bond - Rev. Gary W. Reller;
Promoter of Justice - Rev. Robert Grosch;
Diocesan Consultors - Rev. Timothy J. Moriarty; Rev. Msgr. Kevin S. O'Neill; Raymond Shipman, Secy. (rshipman@diocesehelena.org);
Presbyteral Council - Rev. Msgr. Kevin S. O'Neill; Rev. Leo J. Proxell; Raymond Shipman, Secy. (rshipman@diocesehelena.org);
Diocesan Finance Council - Members - Terry B. Cosgrove; Jim Carney, Chancellor; Raymond Shipman, Secy. (rshipman@diocesehelena.org);
Deaneries -
Conrad - Rev. Roderick Ermatinger, Dean;
Helena - Rev. Msgr. Kevin S. O'Neill, Dean;
Bozeman - Rev. Valentine D. Zdilla, Dean;
Kalispell - Rev. Sean Raftis, Dean;
Butte - Rev. Patrick Beretta, Dean;
Missoula - Rev. Edward Hislop, Dean;
Personnel Board - Rev. Gary W. Reller; Rev. Msgr. Kevin S. O'Neill (koneill@sthelenas.org); Raymond Shipman, Secy. (rshipman@diocesehelena.org);

ADMINISTRATION

Human Resources - t) (406) 442-5820 chall@diocesehelena.org Cassie Hall, Dir.;

OFFICES AND DIRECTORS

Catholic Campaign for Human Development - Dcn. James Butts;
Catholic Committee on Scouting - t) 406-842-5085 Tolly Patten;
Catholic Youth Coalition - t) 406-442-5820 Kevin Molm, Contact;
Communications Director - Dan Bartleson (dbartleson@diocesehelena.org);
Continuing Formation of the Clergy - t) 406-389-7059 Rev. Bart Tolleson (btolleson@diocesehelena.org);
Cursillo Movement, Journey and Search - t) 406-442-5820 Dcn. Doug Cameron; Marilyn Cameron;
Daughters of Isabella (vacant) -
Coordinator for Religious - t) 406-442-5820 Raymond Shipman (rshipman@diocesehelena.org);
Diocesan Attorney - t) 406-442-0005 Terry B. Cosgrove; William Driscoll;
Diocesan Buildings - Jim Carney, CFO;
Diocesan Council of Catholic Women - Carol Endsley;
Diocesan Ecumenical Officer - t) 406-442-5820 Dan Bartleson (dbartleson@diocesehelena.org);
Office of Family Life, Pro Life, and Evangelization - t) 406-442-5820 Alex Kautzky, Dir. (akautzky@diocesehelena.org);
Guatemala Missions - t) 406-442-5820 Jim Carney, Interim Dir.; Rev. Kevin Christofferson, (Leave of Absence);
Legendary Lodge (Diocesan Summer Camp) - Alex Kautzky, Dir. (akautzky@diocesehelena.org);
Marriage Encounter - t) 406-534-2391 Alex Kautzky, Dir. (akautzky@diocesehelena.org);
Permanent Deacons - t) 406-442-5820 Rev. Bart Tolleson (btolleson@diocesehelena.org);
Program of Formation for Lay Ministry - Dan Bartleson (dbartleson@diocesehelena.org);
Program of Formation for the Permanent Diaconate - t) 406-442-5820 Rev. Bart Tolleson (btolleson@diocesehelena.org);
Propagation of the Faith - t) 406-442-5820 chancery@diocesehelena.org Jim Carney, Chancellor;
Third Order of St. Francis - Tony Poelman;
Victim Assistance Coordinator - t) 406-459-0513 Gabe Brennan;
Vocations Office - t) 406-442-5820 mlenneman@carroll.edu Rev. Marc J. Lenneman;

ORGANIZATIONS

Catholic Social Services for Montana, Inc. - t) 406-442-4130 www.cssmt.org Scott Held, Dir. (scott@cssmt.org);
Billings Office - t) 406-252-3399 Michelle Perlick, (Billings);
Helena Office - Scott Held, Dir.; Senja Linjanen, Exec. Asst.;
Montana Catholic Conference - t) 406-442-5761 director@montanacc.org www.montanacc.org Matthew Brower, Exec.;

PARISHES, MISSIONS, AND CLERGY

STATE OF MONTANA

ANACONDA

Anaconda Catholic Community: Series 204, LLC - 217 W. Pennsylvania, Anaconda, MT 59711 t) 406-563-8406 anacondacatholiccommunity.com Rev. Dougald McCallum, Pst.; CRP Stds.: 83
Holy Family - t) (406) 563-8406
St. Peter - 401 Alder St., Anaconda, MT 59711 t) (406) 563-8406

BELGRADE

Saint John Vianney Parish: Series 165, LLC - 609 N. Quaw Blvd., Belgrade, MT 59714 t) 406-388-1290 sjvbelgrade@gmail.com; sjvre.belgrade@gmail.com www.sjvbelgrade.org Rev. Eric C. Gilbaugh, Pst.; Dcn. Warner Holm; Dcn. Wayne Thompson; Krista B Baziak, DRE; CRP Stds.: 44

BIGFORK

Saint John Paul II Parish: Series 506, LLC - 195 Coverdell Rd., Bigfork, MT 59911; Mailing: P.O. Box 277, Bigfork, MT 59911 t) 406-837-4846 saintjp2church@gmail.com www.saintjp2.org Rev. Nicetas Msinge, ALCP/OSS, Admin.; Dcn. James Butts, Pst. Assoc.; Sierra Butts, DRE; Dawn Ella Lembke, Bus. Mgr.; CRP Stds.: 32
Our Lady of Swan Valley Mission - 210 E. Beck Rd., Swan Valley, MT 59826

BONNER

Saint Ann Parish: Series 607, LLC - 9015 Hwy. 200 E., Bonner, MT 59823; Mailing: P.O. Box 1008, Bonner, MT 59823 t) 406-258-6815 www.stannbonner.com Rev. Jozef Perehubka (Poland), Pst.; Doug Lawrence, Pres.; Jennifer Alexander, DRE; Heidi Gengo, Youth Min.; Anne Wright, Music Min.; CRP Stds.: 21
Living Water - 152 S.O.S. Rd., Seeley Lake, MT 59868; Mailing: P.O. Box 995, Seeley Lake, MT 59868 t) 406-677-2688 livingwatermission@diocesehelena.org Marilyn Niklas, Pres.; Chris Flinders, Music Min.; Velma Burnett, DRE;

BOULDER

Saint Catherine Parish: Series 208, LLC - 214 S. Elder St., Boulder, MT 59632; Mailing: P.O. Box 205, Boulder, MT 59632 t) 406-225-3222 Rev. John Crutchfield, Admin.;
St. John the Evangelist - Hwy. 69, Boulder Valley, MT 59632; Mailing: PO Box 205, Boulder, MT 59632 Rev. Bart Tolleson, Admin.;

BOZEMAN

Holy Rosary Parish: Series 109, LLC - 220 W. Main St., Bozeman, MT 59771-0096; Mailing: P.O. Box 96, Bozeman, MT 59771-0096 t) 406-587-4581 holyrosarybozeman.org Rev. Leo J. Proxell, Pst.; Croghan Laurie, Liturgy Dir.; Tim Bell, Music Min.; John Kawalski, Youth Min.; Cynthia M Deurmeier, DRE; CRP Stds.: 130
Resurrection Parish: Series 158, LLC - 1725 S. 11th Ave., Bozeman, MT 59715 t) 406-586-9243 office@resurrectionbozeman.org www.resurrectionbozeman.org Rev. Matthew Christiaens, Par. Vicar; Rev. Joseph Paddock, Pst.; CRP Stds.: 87
Resurrection Catholic Campus Ministry - t) (406) 586-9243 rccm@resurrectionbozeman.org

BROWNING

Saint Teresa of the Little Flower Parish: Series 310, LLC - 202 1st St., N.W., Browning, MT 59417; Mailing: P.O. Box 529, Browning, MT 59417 t) 406-338-5775 Rev. Roderick Ermatinger, Pst.; Dcn. John Gobert; Ronnalea Gallagher, DRE; CRP Stds.: 42
De La Salle Blackfeet Middle School - (Grades 4-8) 104 First St. N.W., Browning, MT 59417; Mailing: P.O. Box 1489, Browning, MT 59417 t) 406-338-5290 brodale@dlsbs.org www.dlsbs.org Bro. Dylan Perry, FSC, Prin.; Bro. Dale Mooney, F.S.C., Pres.; Stds.: 70; Lay Tchrs.: 10
Sacred Heart - Starr School Rd., Starr School, MT 59417; Mailing: PO Box 529, Browning, MT 59417 t) (406) 338-5775
Chapel of the Ascension - North East Corner, East Glacier, MT 59434 t) (406) 338-5775
St. Mary (Babb) - Hwy. 89 at Many Glacier turn, Babb, MT 59411 t) (406) 338-5775

BUTTE

Saint Ann Parish: Series 213, LLC - 2100 Farragut Ave., Butte, MT 59701 t) 406-723-4303 info@stannsbutte.org www.stannsbutte.org Rev. Craig Hanley, Pst.; Dcn. John Uggetti; Dcn. Bernard McCarthy, Admin.; Rosalie Stimatz-Richards, DRE; CRP Stds.: 49
Butte Catholic Community Central: Series 214, LLC - 1500 Cobban St., Butte, MT 59701 t) 406-782-8349 Includes St. Joseph and St. John the Evangelist Parishes. See individual listings. Rev. Craig Hanley, Admin.;
St. John the Evangelist - 1500 Majors Ave., Butte, MT 59701
St. Joseph - Utah & 2nd St., Butte, MT 59701
Butte Catholic Community North: Series 211, LLC - 102 S. Washington St., Butte, MT 59701 t) 406-723-5407 www.butteccn.org Includes Immaculate Conception and St. Patrick Parishes. See individual listings. Rev. Patrick Beretta, Pst.; Dcn. Bernard McCarthy; Seaneen Prendergast, DRE; John Brown, Bus. Mgr.; CRP Stds.: 35
Immaculate Conception -
St. Patrick - 329 W. Mercury St., Butte, MT 59701
Montana College of Mineral Science and Technology - t) (406) 723-5407 c) (406) 533-8852 mtechccm@gmail.com
Holy Spirit Parish: Series 219, LLC - 4400 Continental Dr., Butte, MT 59701; Mailing: 3930 E. Lake St., Butte, MT 59701 t) 406-494-5078 info@holyspiritbutte.org; rcrosby@q.com www.holyspiritbutte.org Rev. Craig Hanley, Pst.; Rev. William Dornbos, Sacr. Min.; Dcn. Doug Cameron; Rene Crosby, DRE & Music Min.; CRP Stds.: 31

CHOTEAU

Saint Joseph Parish: Series 319, LLC - 320 Main St. N., Choteau, MT 59422; Mailing: P.O. Box 640, Choteau, MT 59422 t) 406-466-2961; 406-463-2586 www.jmjparishes.com Rev. Yovin Shayo, Admin.; Laura Toeckes, DRE; CRP Stds.: 26

COLUMBIA FALLS

Saint Richard Parish: Series 520, LLC - 1210 9th St. W., Columbia Falls, MT 59912; Mailing: P.O. Box 2073, Columbia Falls, MT 59912 t) 406-892-5142 strichards@bresnan.net www.strichardsparish.org Rev. Sean Raftis, Pst.; Dcn. Doug Cordier, Pst. Assoc.; Angie Schubert, Youth Min.; CRP Stds.: 35

West Glacier Mission - Apgar Ampitheather, Apgar, MT 59936

CONRAD

Saint Michael the Archangel Parish: Series 321, LLC - 106 S. Maryland St., Conrad, MT 59425; Mailing: P.O. Box 577, Conrad, MT 59425 t) 406-278-7517 Dcn. Marcus Raba; Rev. Gasper Kyara, ALCP, Admin.; CRP Stds.: 35

CUT BANK

Saint Margaret Parish: Series 322, LLC - 129 Second Ave., S.E., Cut Bank, MT 59427; Mailing: P.O. Box 207, Cut Bank, MT 59427 t) 406-873-4413 www.stmargaretcatholiccommunity.org Rev. Peter Mikwabe, Admin.; Juanita Meeks, DRE; Pauline "Sissy" Nygaard, Music Min.; CRP Stds.: 32

DEER LODGE

Immaculate Conception Parish: Series 223, LLC - 611 Clark St., Deer Lodge, MT 59722; Mailing: P.O. Box 786, Deer Lodge, MT 59722 t) 406-846-4114 icdeerlodge@outlook.com www.icdeerlodge.org Rev. Joseph Fleming, Pst.; Joan Sewell, DRE; CRP Stds.: 13

St. Theodore Mission - Old Hwy Rd, Avon, MT 59713; Mailing: 611 Clark St., P.O. Box 786, Deer Lodge, MT 59722

DILLON

Saint Rose of Lima Parish: Series 224, LLC - 226 S. Atlantic St., Dillon, MT 59725 t) 406-683-4391 strosedillon@yahoo.com strosedillon.com Rev. Gregory Lively, Pst.; CRP Stds.: 41

St. John The Apostle - Frontage Rd., Melrose, MT 59743

Lima Mission - Lima Fire Hall, Lima, MT 59739; Mailing: 226 S. Atlantic St., Dillon, MT 59725 t) 406-276-3376 Kathy Stosich, Contact;

University of Montana - Western - t) (406) 683-4391

DRUMMOND

Flint Creek Catholic Community: Series 625, LLC - 12 W. Broad St., Drummond, MT 59832; Mailing: P.O. Box 329, Drummond, MT 59832 t) 406-241-3604 Dcn. Chris Burgmeier; Victoria K. Burgmeier, Parish Life Coord.;

St. Mary Mission (Gold Creek) -

St. Philip - 308 W. Kearney, Philipsburg, MT 59858

St. Michael -

DUTTON

Saint William Parish: Series 326, LLC - 20 1st Ave. N.E., Dutton, MT 59433; Mailing: P.O. Box 18, Dutton, MT 59433 t) 406-476-3429 c) 407-217-7996 marcus@3rivers.net Rev. Gasper Kyara, ALCP, Admin.; Dcn. Marcus Raba; CRP Stds.: 3

Guardian Angel - 104 Central Ave., Power, MT 59468; Mailing: P.O. Box 105, Power, MT 59468 t) 406-463-2450 deaconmarcus@me.com

EAST HELENA

Saints Cyril and Methodius Parish: Series 427, LLC - 120 W. Riggs St., East Helena, MT 59635; Mailing: PO Box 1110, East Helena, MT 59635 t) 406-227-5334 parishoffice@sscyril.org; marie@sscyril.org www.sscyril.org Rev. Christopher Lebsock, Pst.; Dcn. Iver Johnson; Suzanne Johnson, Pst. Assoc.; Caitlyn Van Horssen, Youth Min.; Marie Moran, DRE; Denice Volesky, Bus. Mgr.; CRP Stds.: 112

Our Lady of the Lake - 8375 Canyon Ferry Rd, Helena, MT 59602 t) (406) 227-5334

St. John's - 5 S. Main, Clancy, MT 59634

EUREKA

Our Lady of Mercy Parish: Series 528, LLC - 500 Dewey Ave., Eureka, MT 59917; Mailing: P.O. Box 626, Eureka, MT 59917-0626 t) 406-297-2118 olmeurekamt.org Lisa Stein, Admin.; CRP Stds.: 4

FAIRFIELD

Saint John the Evangelist Parish: Series 329, LLC - 519 First Ave. S., Fairfield, MT 59436; Mailing: P.O. Box 397, Fairfield, MT 59436 t) 406-466-2961; 406-463-2586 www.jmjparishes.com Rev. Yovin Shayo, Admin.; Laura Toeckes, DRE; CRP Stds.: 26

St. Matthias - 508 Broadway, Augusta, MT 59410 t) (406) 466-2961 jmjparishes.com

FRENCHTOWN

Saint John the Baptist Parish: Series 630, LLC - 16680 Main St., Frenchtown, MT 59834-9592; Mailing: P.O. Box 329, Frenchtown, MT 59834-0329 t) 406-626-4492 www.clarkforkcatholic.com Rev. David Severson, Pst.; CRP Stds.: 7

St. Mary Queen of Heaven - 204 2nd Ave. E., Superior, MT 59872 t) (406) 626-4492

St. Albert the Great - 117 Railroad St., Alberton, MT 59820-9491 t) (406) 626-4492

HAMILTON

Saint Francis of Assisi Parish: Series 631, LLC - 411 S. 5th St., Hamilton, MT 59840; Mailing: P.O. Box 593, Hamilton, MT 59840 t) 406-363-1385 www.stfrancishamilton.org Rev. James Connor, Pst.; Dcn. Jim Kaney; Sr. Margaret Hogan, S.C.L., Pst. Assoc.; George Lund, Youth Min.; Bonnie McKenna, RCIA Coord.; Nancy Bevins, Bus. Mgr.; CRP Stds.: 55

St. Philip Benizi - 312 Miles Ave., Darby, MT 59829 t) (406) 363-1385 Rev. Tom Lankenau, S.J., Admin.;

HARLOWTON

Saint Joseph Parish: Series 432, LLC - 26 Third St., N.W., Harlowton, MT 59036; Mailing: P.O. Box 286, Harlowton, MT 59036 t) 406-632-5538 stjosephmt@gmail.com Rev. Cody Williams, Pst.; Cindy Mauws, Bus. Mgr.; CRP Stds.: 5

Immaculate Conception - 304 Louis Ave., Judith Gap, MT 59453

Blessed Sacrament - 203 W. 1st St., Shawmut, MT 59078

HEART BUTTE

Saint Anne Parish: Series 333, LLC - BIA Rd. #1, Heart Butte, MT 59448; Mailing: P.O. Box 160, Heart Butte, MT 59448 t) 406-338-2312 stannes@3rivers.net Rev. Roderick Ermatinger, Pst.;

Holy Family Mission - Joe Show East Rd, Heart Butte, MT 59448; Mailing: P.O. Box 529, Browning, MT 59417 t) (406) 338-2312

HELENA

Cathedral of Saint Helena Parish: Series 401, LLC - 530 N. Ewing St., Helena, MT 59601 t) 406-442-5825 bfishman@sthelenas.org; tcorbett@sthelenas.org Rev. Msgr. Kevin S. O'Neill, Pst.; Dcn. Bob Fishman; Jonathan Embry, Music Min.; Michael Vreeberg, Pst. Assoc.; CRP Stds.: 123

Good Samaritan Thrift Store - 3067 N. Montana Ave., Helena, MT 59601 t) 406-442-0780 theresa@goodsamministries.org Assistance to those in need. Theresa Ortega, Dir.;

Saint Mary Catholic Community: Series 402, LLC - 1700 Missoula Ave., Helena, MT 59601 t) 406-442-5268 smcc@stmaryhelena.org; kboone@stmaryhelena.org www.stmaryhelena.org Rev. Timothy J. Moriarty, Pst.; Dcn. Michael Seipp; Dawn Brannman, DRE; CRP Stds.: 55

Our Lady of the Valley Parish: Series 460, LLC - 1502 Shirley Rd., Helena, MT 59602 t) 406-458-6114 www.olvmt.org Rev. Daniel B. Shea, Sacr. Min.; Dcn. Stephen Barry, Admin.; Dcn. Randy Fraser; Larry Thomas, Chair; Dennis Mayernik, Chair; Becky Tooke, CRE; Carleen Layne, RCIA Coord.; Dennis O'Reilly, RCIA Coord.; David Casey, Youth Min.; Margaret Brennan, Music Min.; Cathleen Lee Nelson, Bus. Mgr.; CRP Stds.: 97

Sacred Heart - 125 Walsh St, Wolf Creek, MT 59648 t) (406) 458-6114 olvmt.org

Santo Tomas - 630 N. Last Chance Gulch, Ste. 2200, Helena, MT 59601; Mailing: P.O. Box 1729, Helena, MT 59624 t) 406-442-5820 chancery@diocesehelena.org Rev. Kevin Christofferson, Dir.; Jim Carney, Interim Dir.;

Guatemala Mission Medical Fund - t) (406) 442-5820

HELMVILLE

Saint Thomas the Apostle Parish: Series 434, LLC - 108 Main St., Helmville, MT 59843; Mailing: P.O. Box 90, Helmville, MT 59843 t) 406-793-5697 www.thomasandjude.org Rev. Msgr. Kevin S. O'Neill, Admin.; Maureen Mannix, DRE;

St. Jude's - 100 Main St., Lincoln, MT 59639; Mailing: PO Box 802, Lincoln, MT 59639 t) 406-362-3210

KALISPELL

Saint Matthew Parish: Series 535, LLC - 602 S. Main St., Kalispell, MT 59901 t) 406-752-6788 www.saintmatthewskalispell.org/ Rev. Stanislaw Rog, Admin.; Dcn. Charles Harball; Jeanne O'Connell, Pst. Min./Coord.; Megan Holt, Treas.; John Bacon, DRE; Kim Maes, Bus. Mgr.; CRP Stds.: 102

Day Care Center (St. Matthew's Pre-K Academy) - t) (406) 249-7744 Sarah Baker, Dir.; Andrea Hanson, Dir.;

St. Matthew's Catholic School - (Grades PreK-8) t) (406) 752-6303 Susy Peterson, Prin.;

Risen Christ Parish: Series 536, LLC - 65 W. Evergreen Dr., Kalispell, MT 59901 t) 406-752-4219 risenchristkalispell.org Rev. Stanislaw Rog, Admin.; CRP Stds.: 17

LIBBY

Saint Joseph Parish: Series 537, LLC - 719 Utah Ave., Libby, MT 59923 t) 406-293-4322 Rev. Pius X Harding, O.S.B., Admin.; Leona LeRoy, Bus. Mgr.; Theresa Purdy, DRE; CRP Stds.: 30

Immaculate Conception - 756 Hwy. 2 W., Troy, MT 59935; Mailing: 719 Utah Ave, Libby, MT 59223

MISSOULA

Saint Anthony Parish: Series 639, LLC - 217 Tremont St., Missoula, MT 59801 t) 406-543-3129 office@stacp.org stacp.org Rev. Pascal Kasanziki, Pst.; Terry Jimmerson, Pst. Assoc.; Sarah Roberts, DRE; CRP Stds.: 29

Blessed Trinity Parish: Series 661, LLC - 1475 Eaton St., Missoula, MT 59801 t) 406-721-2405 judyc@blessedtrinitymissoula.org; jimm@blessedtrinitymissoula.org blessedtrinitymissoula.org Rev. Edward Hislop, Pst.; Sr. Mary Jo Quinn, S.C.L., Pst. Assoc.; Jim McDonald, Bus. Mgr.; Judy Cooney, DRE; Daniel Hampson, Music Min.; CRP Stds.: 10

Spirit of Christ - 5475 Farm Ln., Lolo, MT 59847; Mailing: 1475 Eaton St, Missoula, MT 59801-3224 t) 406-273-2748

Christ the King Parish: Series 638, LLC - 1400 Gerald Ave., Missoula, MT 59801 t) 406-728-3845 pcassidy@ctkmsla.org; office@ctkmsla.org ctkmsla.com (Newman Parish) Rev. Kirby Longo, Pst.; Rev. Tyler Frohlich, Par. Vicar; Patti Cassidy, DRE; Heidi Gengo, Youth Min.; CRP Stds.: 39

University of Montana - t) (406) 728-3845 www.umccm.org Genevieve G'Sell, Campus Min.;

Saint Francis Xavier Parish: Series 640, LLC - 420 W. Pine St., Missoula, MT 59802 t) 406-542-0321 stfrancisxavier@sfxmissoula.org www.sfxmissoula.org Rev. Craig Hightower, S.J., Pst.; Rev. Paul Cochran, S.J., Assoc. Pst.; Dcn. Michael Bloomdahl; Dcn. Carlton Quamme; Colin McCormack, Admin.; Brian Johnson, DRE; CRP Stds.: 48

PLAINS

Saint James Parish: Series 542, LLC - 109 W. Meany St., Plains, MT 59859; Mailing: P.O. Box 745, Plains, MT 59859 t) 406-826-3668 stwilliam@blackfoot.net www.parishesonline.com Rev. Jeffrey M. Benusa, Pst.; Linda Black, Youth Min.; CRP Stds.: 8

Sacred Heart - 22 First Ave., Hot Springs, MT 59845 Paula Morigeau, DRE;

POLSON

Immaculate Conception Parish: Series 543, LLC - 1002 4th Ave. E., Polson, MT 59860; Mailing: P.O. Box 1477, Polson, MT 59860 t) 406-883-2506 www.lakecountyromancatholic.org/ Rev. Kevin Christofferson, Pst.; Catherine Fansher, DRE; CRP Stds.: 65

RONAN

Sacred Heart Parish: Series 544, LLC - 35933 Round Butte Rd., Ronan, MT 59864; Mailing: P.O. Box 1477, Polson, MT 59860 t) 406-883-2506 lakecountyromancatholic.org Rev. Kevin Christofferson, Pst.; CRP Stds.: 7

St. Joseph's - 53099 Main St. N., Charlo, MT 59824

SHELBY

Saint William Parish: Series 346, LLC - 531 Main St., Shelby, MT 59474 t) 406-434-2988 stwilliamshelbymt.org Rev. Peter Mikwabe, Admin.; Emily McDermott, DRE; CRP Stds.: 30

St. Thomas Aquinas - 120 1st St. S., Sunburst, MT 59482; Mailing: PO Box 1010, Shelby, MT 59474 t) 406-434-9133

SHERIDAN

Madison County Catholic Community: Series 236, LLC - 105 Poppleton St., Sheridan, MT 59749; Mailing: P.O. Box 17, Sheridan, MT 59749 t) 406-842-5588 Comprised of St. Mary of the Assumption, Laurin; St. Joseph, Sheridan; and St. Patrick, Ennis. Rev. John Crutchfield, Pst.; Margaret Stecker, Youth Min.; CRP Stds.: 29

Notre Dame - N. Main and E. 8th St., Twin Bridges, MT 59754

ST. IGNATIUS

Saint Ignatius Mission Parish: Series 645, LLC - 300 Beartrack Ave., St. Ignatius, MT 59865; Mailing: P.O. Box 667, St. Ignatius, MT 59865 t) 406-745-2768 mission7@blackfoot.net; ashchurch@blackfoot.net www.stignatiusmission.org Rev. Victor Cancino, S.J., Assoc. Pst.; Rev. Craig Hightower, S.J., Pst.; CRP Stds.: 29

Sacred Heart - 112 Taelman, Arlee, MT 59821 t) 406-726-3540

St. John Berchman's - Agency Rd., Jocko, MT 59821; Mailing: P.O. Box 270, Arlee, MT 59821 t) 406-587-4581

STEVENSVILLE

Saint Mary Mission Parish: Series 647, LLC - 333 Charlos St., Stevensville, MT 59870 t) 406-777-5257 (Parish Office); (406) 777-5574 (Rectory Phone) www.stmarystevi.com Rev. David Severson, Admin.; Terri Todd, Bus. Mgr.; CRP Stds.: 19

St. Joseph - 224 Linder St., Florence, MT 59833 t) (406) 777-5257 (St. Mary Office)

THOMPSON FALLS

Saint William Parish: Series 549, LLC - 416 Preston Ave., Thompson Falls, MT 59873; Mailing: P.O. Box 186, Thompson Falls, MT 59873 t) 406-827-4433 www.parishesonline.com Rev. Jeffrey M. Benusa, Pst.; John Bennett, Youth Min.; Mandy Helvey, Youth Min.; Sherri Koskela, Youth Min.; Dcn. Ronald Kazmierczak; CRP Stds.: 22

Noxon Mission - 200 Broadway, Noxon, MT 59853

THREE FORKS

Holy Family Parish: Series 150, LLC - 104 E. Birch St., Three Forks, MT 59752; Mailing: P.O. Box 99, Three Forks, MT 59752 t) 406-285-3592 holyfamily@q.com www.holyfamilymt.org Rev. Eric C. Gilbaugh, Pst.; Dcn. Robert Lane;

TOWNSEND

Holy Cross Parish: Series 451, LLC - 101 S. Walnut St., Townsend, MT 59644; Mailing: P.O. Box 610, Townsend, MT 59644 t) 406-266-4811 holycrossmt.org Rev. Cody Williams, Pst.; Shawna Wickens, DRE; Meagan Poe, Bus. Mgr.; Buffy Woodring, Bus. Mgr.; CRP Stds.: 43

VALIER

Saint Francis Parish: Series 352, LLC - 616 4th St., Valier, MT 59486; Mailing: P.O. Box 338, Valier, MT 59486 t) 406-279-3327 Rev. Peter Mikwabe, Pst.; Mary Jean Brophy, Pst. Assoc.; Melissa Eagar Peebles, DRE; CRP Stds.: 21

Holy Cross -

WEST YELLOWSTONE

Our Lady of the Pines Parish: Series 163, LLC - 437 Madison Ave., West Yellowstone, MT 59758; Mailing: P.O. Box 577, West Yellowstone, MT 59758 t) 406-646-7755 olpineswy@gmail.com www.ourladypineswy.org/ Rev. Val Zdilla, Pst.;

St. Joseph of Big Sky - 510 Little Coyote Rd., Big Sky, MT 59716; Mailing: P.O. Box 161977, Big Sky, MT 59716 stjosephofbigsky@gmail.com stjosephbigsky.com Rev. Valentine D. Zdilla, Pst.;

WHITE SULPHUR SPRINGS

Saint Bartholomew Parish: Series 455, LLC - 407 Second Ave., S.E., White Sulphur Springs, MT 59645; Mailing: P.O Box 422, White Sulphur Springs, MT 59645 t) 406-547-3737 stbarthomewmt@gmail.com Rev. Cody Williams, Pst.; Lucy Zarr, Bus. Mgr.; CRP Stds.: 20

WHITEFISH

Saint Charles Borromeo Parish: Series 553, LLC - 230 Baker Ave., Whitefish, MT 59937; Mailing: P.O. Box 128, Whitefish, MT 59937 t) 406-862-2051 office@stcharleswhitefish.net www.stcharleswhitefish.org Rev. Sean Raftis, Pst.; Nikki MacLean, Youth Min.; CRP Stds.: 90

WHITEHALL

Saint Teresa of Avila Parish: Series 254, LLC - 107 Second Ave. E., Whitehall, MT 59759; Mailing: P.O. Box 337, Whitehall, MT 59759 t) 406-287-3893 stteresaavila@diocesehelena.org Rev. John Crutchfield, Admin.; CRP Stds.: 4

SCHOOLS: PRESCHOOL THRU HIGH SCHOOL

SCHOOLS

STATE OF MONTANA

BROWNING

De La Salle Blackfeet School - (PRV) (Grades 4-8) 104 First St., N.W., Browning, MT 59417; Mailing: P.O. Box 1489, Browning, MT 59417 t) 406-338-5290 (Office); 406-338-2434 (Bus. Office) info@dlsbs.org www.dlsbs.org Bro. Dale Mooney, F.S.C., Pres.; Stds.: 70; Lay Tchrs.: 10

BUTTE

Butte Central Catholic School - (DIO) (Grades PreK-12) 9 S. Idaho St., Butte, MT 59701 t) 406-782-6761; (406) 782-4500 (Elem.) info@buttecentralschools.org www.buttecentral.org Donald Peoples Jr., Pres.; DawnAnn Peterson, Prin.; Stds.: 390; Lay Tchrs.: 15

Central Junior High School - (PAR) (Grades 6-8) 1100 Delaware Ave., Butte, MT 59701 t) 406-782-4500 www.buttecentral.org DawnAnn Peterson, Prin.; Stds.: 288; Lay Tchrs.: 19

HELENA

***St. Andrew School** - (PRV) (Grades K-12) 1900 Flowerree St., Helena, MT 59601; Mailing: P.O. Box 231, Helena, MT 59624 t) 406-449-3201 standrew@standrewschool.org www.standrewschool.org Brian Barrett, Prin.; Stds.: 200; Lay Tchrs.: 17

MISSOULA

St. Joseph Elementary School - (PAR) (Grades PreK-8) 503 Edith St., Missoula, MT 59801 t) 406-549-1290 sjs.secretary@mcsmt.org www.mcsmt.org (Missoula Catholic Schools) Joanna Eichner, Prin.; Debra Jones, Dir.; Kristen Monroy, Early Education Dir.; Stds.: 355; Lay Tchrs.: 40

Child Care Center (St. Joseph School Early Childhood Program) - kristen.monroy@mcsmt.org www.mcsmt.org/sjs-early-education

HIGH SCHOOLS

STATE OF MONTANA

BUTTE

Central High School (Butte Central Catholic High School) - (DIO) (Grades 9-12) 9 S. Idaho St., Butte, MT 59701 t) 406-782-6761 www.buttecentralschools.org Don Peoples Jr., Prin.; Stds.: 104; Lay Tchrs.: 15

MISSOULA

Loyola Sacred Heart High School - (DIO) 320 Edith St., Missoula, MT 59801 t) 406-549-6101 www.mcsmt.org (Missoula Catholic Schools) Paul Richardson, Prin.; Stds.: 168; Lay Tchrs.: 26

INSTITUTIONS LOCATED IN DIOCESE

CEMETERIES [CEM]

HELENA

Resurrection Cemetery Association - 630 N. Last Chance Gulch, Helena, MT 59601; Mailing: P.O. Box 1729, Helena, MT 59604 t) (406) 442-5820 www.diocesehelena.org Jim Carney;

Holy Cross Cemetery - 4700 Harrison Ave., Butte, MT 59701

St. Mary Cemetery - 641 Turner St., Missoula, MT 59802

St. Patrick Cemetery - 4700 Harrison Ave., Butte, MT 59701

Resurrection Cemetery - 630 N. Last Chance Gulch, Ste. 2200, Helena, MT 59601

COLLEGES & UNIVERSITIES [COL]

HELENA

Carroll College - 1601 N. Benton Ave., Helena, MT 59625 t) 406-447-4300 kpaul@carroll.edu; president@carroll.edu www.carroll.edu Dr. John E. Cech, Pres.; Rev. Marc J. Lenneman, Dir.; Lori Peterson, Vice Pres. Finance & Admin.; Stds.: 1,210; Lay Tchrs.: 83

ENDOWMENTS / FOUNDATIONS / TRUSTS [EFT]

BUTTE

Central Education Foundation - 550 E. Mercury, Butte, MT 59701; Mailing: P.O. Box 634, Butte, MT 59703-0634 t) 406-723-6706 dpeoples@buttecentralfoundation.org www.buttecentral.org Don Peoples Jr., Exec.;

St. James Healthcare Foundation - 425 W. Porphyry St., Butte, MT 59701 t) 406-782-5640 kacie.bartholomew@imail.org; janel.morgan@imail.org sjh-mt.org/foundation Kacie Bartholomew, Dir.;

HELENA

***Foundation for the Diocese of Helena, Inc.** - 630 N. Last Chance Gulch, Ste. 2200, Helena, MT 59601; Mailing: P.O. Box 1729, Helena, MT 59624 t) 406-389-7051 dthies@diocesehelena.org www.fdoh.org John Talia, Pres.; Daniel Thies, Exec.;

***The Julius Foundation** - 3312 Dunlap Dr., Helena, MT 59602-7754 t) 406-465-8312 thejuliusfoundation@outlook.com thejuliusfoundation.org Teresa Kaiserski, Secy.;

MISSOULA

Missoula Catholic Schools Foundation - 300 Edith St., Missoula, MT 59801 t) 406-541-2858 www.mcsmt.org Serving Missoula Catholic Schools. Martin Lecholat, Chair; Debra Jones, Dir.;

Providence Montana Health Foundation - 502 W. Spruce St., Missoula, MT 59802; Mailing: P.O. Box 4587, Missoula, MT 59806 t) 406-329-5640; 406-327-3128 fran.albrecht@providence.org; janet.kaufman@providence.org www.supportpmhf.org Fran Albrecht, Exec.;

HOSPITALS / HEALTH SERVICES [HOS]

BUTTE

St. James Healthcare - 400 S. Clark St., Butte, MT 59701; Mailing: P.O. Box 3300, Butte, MT 59702 t) 406-723-2500 tracy.neary@imail.org www.stjameshealthcare.org Jennifer Alderfer, CEO; Jay Doyle, Pres.; Tracy Neary, Vice. Pres.; Rev. Robert G.

Porter, Chap.; Dcn. John Uggetti, Dir.; Bed Capacity: 100; Asstd. Annu.: 77,281; Staff: 452

MISSOULA

Providence Health & Services - Montana (St. Patrick Hospital) - 500 W. Broadway, Missoula, MT 59802; Mailing: Administration, 500 W. Broadway, Missoula, MT 59802 t) 406-329-5630 www.providence.org Joyce Dombrouski, CEO; Bed Capacity: 253; Asstd. Annu.: 175,676; Staff: 1,804

POLSON

St. Joseph Medical Center - #6 Thirteenth Ave. E., Polson, MT 59860; Mailing: P.O. Box 1010, Polson, MT 59860 t) 406-883-5680 montana.providence.org/hospitals/st-joseph/ Bed Capacity: 22; Asstd. Annu.: 50,289; Staff: 278

MISCELLANEOUS [MIS]

BROWNING

St. Vincent de Paul Thrift Store - 112 1st Ave., N.W., Browning, MT 59417; Mailing: P.O. Box 974, Browning, MT 59417 t) 406-338-5403 chall@dlsbs.org

BUTTE

***Maternal Life International** - 326A S. Jackson St., Butte, MT 59701-8804 t) 406-490-1998 gmuljones@gmail.com www.maternallifeint.com/ George Mulcaire-Jones, Dir.;

FRENCHTOWN

Regina Coeli Hermitage - 16680 Main St., Frenchtown, MT 59834; Mailing: P.O. Box 34, Frenchtown, MT 59834-0034 t) (406) 626-4492 pidacaritas@gmail.com reginacoelihermitage.com/ Bro. Timothy Marie Pida, Er.Dio., Brother;

HELENA

Catholic Social Services of Montana, Inc. - 630 N. Last Chance Gulch, Ste. 2200, Helena, MT 59624; Mailing: P.O. Box 907, Helena, MT 59624 t) 406-442-4130 adopt@cssmt.org www.cssmt.org Scott Held, Exec. Dir.;

The Montana Catholic Conference, Inc. - 630 N. Last Chance Gulch, Ste. 2200, Helena, MT 59601; Mailing: P.O. Box 1708, Helena, MT 59624 t) 406-442-5761 director@montanacc.org montanacc.org/ Matthew Brower, Exec. Dir.;

STEVENSVILLE

Historic St. Mary's Mission - 315 Charlo St., Stevensville, MT 59870; Mailing: P.O. Box 211, Stevensville, MT 59870-0211 t) 406-777-5734 stmary@cybernet1.com saintmarysmission.org Colleen Meyer, Dir.;

RETREAT HOUSES / RENEWAL CENTERS [RTR]

SWAN LAKE

Sycamore Tree Catholic Retreat: Series 680, LLC - 21592 Sycamore Tree Ln., Swan Lake, MT 59911 t) 406-754-2429 email@sycamoretreeretreat.org www.sycamoretreeretreat.org Michelle Jenkins, Dir.; Rev. Bart Tolleson, Priest Supvr.;

An asterisk (*) denotes an organization that has established tax-exempt status directly with the IRS and is not covered by the USCCB Group Ruling.

Diocese of Honolulu

(Dioecesis Honoluluensis)

MOST REVEREND CLARENCE R. SILVA

Bishop of Honolulu; ordained May 2, 1975; appointed Bishop of Honolulu May 17, 2005; consecrated July 21, 2005. Bishop's Office: 1184 Bishop St., Honolulu, HI 96813.

Chancery Office: 1184 Bishop St., Honolulu, HI 96813. T: 808-585-3300; F: 808-521-8428.
catholichawaii.org

Square Miles 6,435.

Corporate Title: The Roman Catholic Church In The State Of Hawaii.

Comprises all of the Hawaiian Islands.

The Hawaiian Islands were annexed as a Territory of the United States in 1898. Hawaii became the 50th State of the Union on August 21, 1959. In 1826, a Prefecture-Apostolic was erected for the Hawaiian Islands and entrusted to the Fathers of the Sacred Hearts of Jesus and Mary (Picpus). The Very Rev. Alexis Bachelot, SS.CC., was the first Prefect-Apostolic. He arrived with his companions in Honolulu on the 7th of July, 1827. In 1844, the Islands were erected a Vicariate Apostolic. Diocese erected Sept. 10, 1941.

For legal titles of parishes and diocesan institutions, consult the Chancery Office.

STATISTICAL OVERVIEW

Personnel

Bishop	1
Priests: Diocesan Active in Diocese	35
Priests: Diocesan Active Outside Diocese	3
Priests: Retired, Sick or Absent	25
Number of Diocesan Priests	63
Religious Priests in Diocese	39
Total Priests in your Diocese	102
Extern Priests in Diocese	20
Ordinations:	
Diocesan Priests	1
Permanent Deacons in Diocese	87
Total Brothers	17
Total Sisters	121

Parishes

Parishes	66
With Resident Pastor:	
Resident Diocesan Priests	29
Resident Religious Priests	18
Without Resident Pastor:	
Administered by Priests	19
Missions	25
Professional Ministry Personnel:	
Brothers	3
Sisters	17
Lay Ministers	57

Welfare

Health Care Centers	3
Total Assisted	700
Homes for the Aged	1
Total Assisted	182
Day Care Centers	1
Total Assisted	37
Special Centers for Social Services	2
Total Assisted	44,500
Residential Care of Disabled	1
Total Assisted	1,095

Educational

Diocesan Students in Other Seminaries	12
Total Seminarians	12
Colleges and Universities	1
Total Students	2,342
High Schools, Diocesan and Parish	5
Total Students	1,706
High Schools, Private	3
Total Students	2,031
Elementary Schools, Diocesan and Parish	12
Total Students	2,571
Elementary Schools, Private	1
Total Students	252
Catechesis / Religious Education:	
High School Students	551
Elementary Students	2,095
Total Students under Catholic Instruction	11,560
Teachers in Diocese:	
Priests	2
Brothers	3
Sisters	58
Lay Teachers	780

Vital Statistics

Receptions into the Church:	
Infant Baptism Totals	1,545
Minor Baptism Totals	115
Adult Baptism Totals	85
Received into Full Communion	85
First Communions	919
Confirmations	1,055
Marriages:	
Catholic	209
Interfaith	46
Total Marriages	255
Deaths	1,531
Total Catholic Population	122,652
Total Population	1,440,196

ADMINISTRATION

Office of the Bishop - t) 808-585-3356 Most Rev. Clarence (Larry) R. Silva (bishop@rcchawaii.org); Denise Oliveira, Admin. Asst./Public & Ecclesial Notary (doliveira@rcchawaii.org);
Chancellor - t) 808-203-6715 Dcn. Keith Cabiles (kcabiles@rcchawaii.org);
Vicar General and Moderator of the Curia - t) 808-585-3347 Rev. Msgr. Gary L. Secor (gsecor@rcchawaii.org); Brendan Porick, Secy. (bporick@rcchawaii.org);

OFFICES AND DIRECTORS

Vicars Forane - Very Rev. Lane K. Akiona, SS.CC., East Honolulu (lakiona@rcchawaii.org); Rev. Edmundo N. Barut Jr., Leeward Oahu (ebarut@rcchawaii.org); Rev. Konelio Faletoi, West Hawaii (lfaletoi@rcchawaii.org);
Deacon Formation - Dcn. John A. Coughlin, Dir. (jcoughlin@rcchawaii.org); Kathleen Coughlin, Dir.; Hazell Cabiles, Assoc. Dir.;
Vicar for Clergy - t) 808-585-3343 Rev. Gregorio S. Honorio, Vicar (ghonorio@rcchawaii.org); Darlene Cachola, Admin. Asst./Eccles. Notary (dcachola@rcchawaii.org);
Director of Vocations - t) 808-585-3355 Rev. Joseph A. Diaz (jodiaz@rcchawaii.org);
Worship - t) 808-585-3342 Rev. Alfred Guerrero, Dir.;
Hawaii Catholic Conference - t) 808-203-6704 Eva Marie Andrade, Dir. (eandrade@rcchawaii.org);
Finance - t) 808-585-3300 Lisa Sakamoto, Diocesan Finance Officer (lsakamoto@rcchawaii.org); Marvin Choy, Controller (marvin@rcchawaii.org); Diane Lamosao, Mgr., Financial & Systems Analysis (dlamosao@rcchawaii.org);
Land Asset Management - t) 808-585-3332 Marlene DeCosta, Dir. (mdecosta@rcchawaii.org);
Permanent Deacons - Dcn. Michael Weaver, Dir. (mweaver@rcchawaii.org);
Respect Life - t) 808-203-6722 Dcn. Gary Streff, Dir.; Valerie Streff, Dir. (gstreff@rcchawaii.org);
Safe Environment - t) 808-203-6719 Kristen Leandro, Dir. (kleandro@rcchawaii.org);

ADVISORY BOARDS, COMMISSIONS, COMMITTEES, AND COUNCILS

Hawaii Catholic Conference Board - Rev. Msgr. Gary L. Secor, Chair (gsecor@rcchawaii.org); Rev. Robert Stark, S.S.S., Vice Chair (rstark@rcchawaii.org); Eva Marie Andrade, Exec. (eandrade@rcchawaii.org);

COMMUNICATIONS

Hawaii Catholic Herald - t) 808-533-1791 Patrick Downes, Editor (pdownes@rcchawaii.org);
Information Technology - t) 808-203-6730 Francis Kung, Mgr. (ithelpdesk@rcchawaii.org);

COMMUNITY SERVICES

Social Ministry - Rev. Robert Stark, S.S.S., Dir. (rstark@rcchawaii.org); Iwie Tamashiro (itamashiro@rcchawaii.org); David Coleman (dcoleman@chaminade.edu);

CONSULTATIVE BODIES

College of Consultors - Rev. Msgr. Gary L. Secor (gsecor@rcchawaii.org); Rev. Msgr. Terrence A.M. Watanabe (twatanabe@rcchawaii.org); Very Rev. Mark J. Gantley (mgantley@rcchawaii.org);
Diocesan Finance Council - Diane Murakami, Chair; Paul Deville, Vice Chm.; Rick Stack Jr., Secy.;
Diocesan Pastoral Council - Zachary Ramones, Chair; Anne Matasci, Vice Chm.; Rev. Msgr. Gary L. Secor, Ex Officio (gsecor@rcchawaii.org);
Presbyteral Council - Rev. E.J. Resinto, Chair; Rev. Alfred Guerrero, Vice Chm.; Rev. Peter Miti, Secy. (pmiti@rcchawaii.org);

DEVELOPMENT

Stewardship and Development - t) 808-203-6728 Mark J. Clark, Dir. (mclark@rcchawaii.org);

EDUCATION

Hawaii Catholic Schools - t) 808-203-6764 Llewellyn Young, Supt. (lyoung@rcchawaii.org);

FACILITIES

Chancery - t) 808-585-3300
St. Stephen Diocesan Center - t) 808-203-6724 Sabrina Izaguirre, Asst. Admin. (sizaguirre@rcchawaii.org);

FAITH FORMATION

Religious Education - t) 808-203-6745 Jayne Mondoy, Dir. (jmondoy@rcchawaii.org);
Youth & Young Adult Ministry - t) 808-203-6743 Lisa Gomes, Dir. (lgomes@rcchawaii.org);

HUMAN RESOURCES

Human Resources - t) 808-585-3306 Dara Perreira, Dir. (dperreira@rcchawaii.org);

TRIBUNAL

Tribunal/Canonical Affairs - t) 808-203-6766 tribunal@rcchawaii.org www.catholichawaii.org/cic Very Rev. Mark J. Gantley, Judicial Vicar & Dir. Canonical Affairs (mgantley@rcchawaii.org); E. Roxanne Torres, Moderator of the Tribunal Chancery (rtorres@rcchawaii.org); Rev. Steve Nguyen, Defender of the Bond & Promoter of Justice (snguyen@rcchawaii.org);

PARISHES, MISSIONS, AND CLERGY

STATE OF HAWAII

AIEA

St. Elizabeth - 99-312 Moanalua Rd., Aiea, HI 96701 t) 808-487-2414 stelizabe001@hawaii.rr.com; umeristella@gmail.com stelizabethaiea.com Rev. Arnold Ortiz, Pst.; Rev. Paul John Camiring, Par. Vicar; Dcn. Frederico Carahasen Jr.; Dcn. Gary Streff; Sr. Meristella Umdor, MSMHC, DRE; CRP Stds.: 115
St. Elizabeth School - (Grades K-8) 99-310 Moanalua Rd., Aiea, HI 96701 t) 808-488-5322 info@steliz-hi.org steliz-hi.org Sr. Olive Fuentes, OP, Prin.; Stds.: 157; Sr. Tchrs.: 4; Lay Tchrs.: 7
Convent - t) 808-487-3131

CAPTAIN COOK

St. Benedict - 84-5140 Painted Church Rd., Captain Cook, HI 96704 t) 808-328-2227 st.benedict@rcchawaii.org thepaintedchurchhawaii.org Rev. Siegfred Dosdos, Admin.; Edwina Fujimoto, DRE; CRP Stds.: 5
St. John the Baptist - 81-6402 Mamalahoa Hwy., Kealakekua, HI 96750

EWA

Immaculate Conception Church - 91-1298 Renton Rd., Ewa, HI 96706 t) 808-681-3701; 808-954-1730 (CRP) iccewa@rcchawaii.org; ewaccd@gmail.com immaculateconceptionewa.org Dcn. Richard Abel; Rev. Nicholas Brown, Pst.; Shirley Sunio, DRE; CRP Stds.: 43

EWA BEACH

Our Lady of Perpetual Help - 91-1004 North Rd., Ewa Beach, HI 96706-2796 t) 808-689-8681 olph@rcchawaii.org; jtorres@rcchawaii.org olphewabeach.org Rev. Edmundo N. Barut Jr., Pst.; Dcn. Eric Kim; Dcn. Ronald Paglinawan; Dcn. Reynaldo Dinulong; Julia Torres, DRE; CRP Stds.: 112

HAIKU

St. Rita - 655 Haiku Rd., Haiku, HI 96708 t) 808-575-2601 stritahaiku@gmail.com stritahaiku.com Rita Bauldry, DRE; Rev. Chacko Muthoottil, M.F., Pst.; CRP Stds.: 10
St. Gabriel - Wailuanui Rd., Haiku, HI 96708 Keanae.

HANA

St. Mary - 5000 Hana Hwy., Hana, HI 96713; Mailing: P.O. Box 219, Hana, HI 96713 t) 808-248-8030; 808-248-8422 (CRP) hanastmary@gmail.com Rev. Roel delos Reyes, Pst.; Helen Cosma, DRE; CRP Stds.: 10
St. Peter - 47699 Hana Hwy., Puuiki, HI 96713
St. Paul - 41145 Hana Hwy., Kipahulu, HI 96713
St. Joseph - 33622 Piilani Hwy., Kaupo, HI 96790

HAWI

Sacred Heart - 55-3374 Akoni Pule Hwy., Hawi, HI 96719; Mailing: P.O. Box 220, Hawi, HI 96719-0220 t) 808-889-6436 shchawi@hawaii.twcbc.com sacredhearthawi.com John Pollard, DRE; Rev. Elias F. Escanilla, Admin.; CRP Stds.: 29

HILO

St. Joseph - 43 Kapiolani St., Hilo, HI 96720 t) 808-935-1465 dwatson@rcchawaii.org stjoehilo.com Rev. Ferdinand Tomo, SSS, Par. Vicar; Dcn. David Watson; Dcn. Berley Araceley; Rev. Apolinario Ty, SSS, Pst.;
St. Joseph School - (Grades PreK-12) 1000 Ululani St., Hilo, HI 96720 t) 808-961-0424 (Pre-school); 808-935-4935 (Elem.); 808-935-4936 (HS) tfuata@rcchawaii.org sjshilo.com Maile Kipapa, Prin.; Michael Eftink, Head of School; Stds.: 200; Lay Tchrs.: 24
Malia Puka O Kalani (Mary Gate of Heaven) - 326 Desha Ave., Hilo, HI 96721; Mailing: P.O. Box 222, Hilo, HI 96721 t) 808-935-9338 maliapastor@gmail.com; kmg2011@yahoo.com maliachurch.org Rev. Constantino T Atinaja Jr., Admin.; CRP Stds.: 12

HONOKAA

Our Lady of Lourdes - 54-5028 Plumeria St., Honokaa, HI 96727; Mailing: P.O. Box 129, Honokaa, HI 96727 t) 808-775-9591 ourladyof001@hawaii.rr.com honokaaoll.weebly.com Dcn. Keoki Wood; Rev. Anselmo Bobier, Admin.; Dolores Whaley, DRE; CRP Stds.: 6

HONOLULU

Cathedral Basilica of Our Lady of Peace - 1184 Bishop St., Honolulu, HI 96813-2838 t) 808-536-7036 coolop@rcchawaii.org; mbauer@rcchawaii.org honolulucathedral.com Rev. Pascual Abaya, Pst.; Rev. Leonardo Tubana, Par. Vicar; Dcn. Jose Almuena; Michael Bauer, DRE; CRP Stds.: 13
Co-Cathedral of St. Theresa of the Child Jesus - 712 N. School St., Honolulu, HI 96817 t) 808-521-1700 rmendoza@rcchawaii.org; mestrella@rcchawaii.org cocathedral.org Rev. Manuel A. Hewe, Pst.; Dcn. Raymond Lamb; Dcn. Francis Leasiolagi; Sr. Mercedita B. Estrella, S.P.C., DRE; CRP Stds.: 88
St. Theresa of the Child Jesus School - (Grades PreSchool-8) t) 808-536-4703 cgora@rcchawaii.org stshi.org Conception Gora, Prin.; Lauren Ramirez-Asaeda, Vice Prin.; Stds.: 225; Sr. Tchrs.: 1; Lay Tchrs.: 18
Convent - t) 808-533-3101 stccsj38@twc.com
Vietnamese Holy Martyrs Community - t) 808-536-0046 vietholymartyrs@gmail.com vietmartyrs-honolulu.net Rev. Dominic Hoan Nguyen, Chap.; Dcn. Jonathan Lam; Dcn. Anthony Nguyen;
St. Anthony - 640 Puuhale Rd., Honolulu, HI 96819 t) 808-845-3255 stanthonyhonolulu@gmail.com saintanthonykalihi.org Rev. Arlan Intal, M.S., Pst.; Dcn. Renier Torres; Rev. Francisco Nicomedes S. Sanchez, In Res.; Leeza Agpaoa, DRE; CRP Stds.: 5
St. Augustine by the Sea - 130 Ohua Ave., Honolulu, HI 96815 t) 808-923-7024; 808-367-0631 (Rectory) office@staugustinebythesea.com staugustinebythesea.com Very Rev. Lane K. Akiona, SS.CC., Pst.; Brandon Akiona, Bus. Mgr.; Dcn. Keith Cabiles; CRP Stds.: 50
Blessed Sacrament - 2124 Pauoa Rd., Honolulu, HI

96813 t) 808-531-6980 bscpauoa@rcchawaii.org blessedsacramentpauoa.blogspot.org Dcn. Ronald Choo; Violet Kondo, DRE; Rev. Steve Nguyen, Pst.; Dcn. Joseph Soon; CRP Stds.: 5

Holy Family - 830 Main St., Honolulu, HI 96818 t) 808-422-1135 info@holyfamilyhonolulu.org holyfamilyhonolulu.org Rev. Rheo Ofalsa, Pst.; Dcn. Michael Brown; CRP Stds.: 394

Holy Family Catholic Academy - (Grades K-8) t) 808-423-9611 lpatiak@rcchawaii.org hfcahawaii.org Celeste Akiu, Prin.;

Korean Catholic Community - 511 Main St., Honolulu, HI 96818 t) 808-422-1010 honolulukcc@gmail.com honolulukcc.org Rev. YoungKun Kim, Chap.;

Early Learning Center - t) 808-421-1265 elc@hfcahawaii.org hfcahawaii.org/e_l_c_website Allen Akiona, Dir.;

Holy Trinity - 5919 Kalanianaole Hwy., Honolulu, HI 96821 t) 808-396-0551 holytrinity@rcchawaii.org holytrinitychurchhi.org Vanessa Mark, DRE; Rev. Michel Dalton, O.F.M.Cap., Pst.; Dcn. Stephen Kula; CRP Stds.: 22

St. John the Baptist - 2324 Omilo Ln., Honolulu, HI 96819 t) 808-845-0984 sjbkalihi@gmail.com saintjohnthebaptisthawaii.org Rev. Jaroslaw Skrzypek, Admin.; Dcn. Ricardo Burgos; Dcn. Peter Soumwei; Danielle Burgos, DRE; CRP Stds.: 33

Mary, Star of the Sea - 4470 Aliikoa St., Honolulu, HI 96821 t) 808-734-0396; 808-349-2009 (CRP) sarahbryant.starofthesea@hawaii.rr.com; darlenealoha@gmail.com staroftheseahonolulu.com Rev. Francisco De Los Reyes, S.S.S., Pst.; Rev. Victor Diolata Jr., Par. Vicar; Rev. Robert Stark, S.S.S., In Res.; Dcn. Rafael Mendoza; Eliane Kuo, DRE;

Mary, Star of the Sea School - (Grades 1-8) 4469 Malia St., Honolulu, HI 96821 t) 808-734-0208 star@starofthesea.org starofthesea.org Margaret Rufo, Prin.; Marsee Williams, Librn.;

Early Learning Center - 4470 Aliikoa St., Ste. 100, Honolulu, HI 96821 t) 808-734-3840 elc@starofthesea.org staroftheseaelc.org Jill Kojima, Interim Dir.;

Newman Center-Holy Spirit Parish - 1941 East West Rd., Honolulu, HI 96822-2321 t) 808-988-6222 religioused@newmanhawaii.org; info@newmanhawaii.org newmanhawaii.org Rev. Alfred Omar B. Guerrero, Pst.; Fay Pabo, DRE; CRP Stds.: 25

Our Lady of the Mount - 1614 Monte St., Honolulu, HI 96819 t) 808-845-0828 olm@rcchawaii.org; srclemencespc@yahoo.com ourladyofthemountkalihi.org Rev. Edgar B. Brillantes, Pst.; Rev. Adrian R. Gervacio, Pastor Emer.; Francisca Kovaloff, CRE; CRP Stds.: 27

St. Patrick - 1124 Seventh Ave., Honolulu, HI 96816 t) 808-732-5565; 808-734-8979 (CRP) church@saintpatrickhawaii.org; adecosta@saintpatrickhawaii.org saintpatrickhawaii.org Rev. Clyde Guerreiro, SS.CC., Pst.; Rev. Bertram Lock, SS.CC., Par. Vicar; Sr. Anne Clare De Costa, SS.CC., DRE; CRP Stds.: 5

SS Peter and Paul - 800 Kaheka St., Honolulu, HI 96814-3728 t) 808-941-0675 sspeterandpaul@rcchawaii.org sspeterpaulhawaii.org Rev. Khanh Pham Nguyen, Pst.; Yvonne Toma, DRE; Dcn. Joel Narusawa; CRP Stds.: 58

St. Philomena - 3300 Ala Laulani St., Honolulu, HI 96818-2837 t) 808-839-1876; 808-834-6888 sp.hawaii.office@gmail.com; lforonda-ebia@rcchawaii.org stphilomenahawaii.org Rev. Dong Min (Paul) Li, Pst.; Dcn. Kin Shing Cheng; Rev. Antonio D. Bobis, In Res.; Rev. Mario Palanca, In Res.; CRP Stds.: 19

Early Learning Center - t) 808-833-8080 director@spelc-hawaii.com; admin@spelc-hawaii.com stphilomenaearlylearningcenter.com Angie Thomas, Vice Prin.; Peter Tedtaotao, Dir.;

St. Pius X - 2821 Lowrey Ave., Honolulu, HI 96822-1644 t) 808-988-3308 general@mp-cc.net stpiusxmanoa.com Rev. Norlito Concepcion, Admin.; CRP Stds.: 7

Sacred Heart - 1701 Wilder Ave., Honolulu, HI 96822 t) 808-973-2211; 808-952-7120 (CRP) general@mp-cc.net sacredhearthnl.online Rev. EJ Resinto, Pst.; Haley Calventas, DRE; CRP Stds.: 42

Maryknoll School - (Grades K-12) 1722 Dole St., Honolulu, HI 96822; Mailing: 1526 Alexander St., Honolulu, HI 96822 t) (808) 952-7300 admission@maryknollschool.org maryknollschool.org Shana Tong, Pres.; Cindy Lam, CFO; Stds.: 948; Lay Tchrs.: 74

St. Stephen - 2747 Pali Hwy., Honolulu, HI 96817 t) 808-595-3105 ssccpali@rcchawaii.org ssccpali.net Rev. Mario Raquepo, Pst.; Velma Mamuad, DRE; CRP Stds.: 32

KAHUKU

St. Roch - 56-350 Kamehameha Hwy., Kahuku, HI 96731; Mailing: P.O. Box 295, Kahuku, HI 96731 t) 808-293-5026; (808) 367-0631 (Rectory) saintrochkahuku@gmail.com strochkahuku.com Rev. Sebastian Kumar Soosai, MF, Pst.; CRP Stds.: 27

St. Joachim - 53-536 Kamekameha Hwy., Punaluu, HI 96717 Punaluu

KAHULUI

Christ the King - 20 W. Wakea Ave., Kahului, HI 96732 t) 808-877-6098; 808-877-3674 (CRP) info@ctkchurchmaui.org; mildred@ctkchurchmaui.org ctkchurchmaui.org Rev. Augustine Uthuppu, M.S., Pst.; Rev. Napoleon Andres, M.S., Par. Vicar; Dcn. Kenneth Bissen Jr.; Dcn. Cornelio Pulido; Sr. Angela Laurenzo, C.S.J, DRE; CRP Stds.: 74

Child Development Center (Pre-School) (Christ the King Child Development Center) - (Grades PreSchool-PreSchool) t) 808-877-3587 ctkps@hawaii.rr.com Carole Arakawa, Dir.;

KAILUA

St. Anthony of Padua - 148 Makawao St., Ste. A, Kailua, HI 96734-2334 t) 808-266-2222; 808-791-6523; 808-791-6525 (CRP) frontdesk@stanthonyskailua.org; accounting@atanthonyskailua.org stanthonyskailua.org Rev. William Kunisch II, Pst.; Rev. Clement Beeri, Par. Vicar; Dcn. Michael Weaver; Nicole Dewitt, DRE; CRP Stds.: 52

St. Anthony of Padua School - (Grades K-8) 148 Makawao St., Kailua, HI 96734-2334 t) 808-261-3331 info@saskailua.org saskailua.org Bridget Olsen, Prin.; Patricia Barros, Vice Prin.; MaryPat Kinsey, Librn.; Rev. Exsequel Tuyor, Parish Administrator;

Early Learning Center - 148 Makawao St., Kailua, HI 96734 t) 808-261-0090 bolsen@saskailua.org saskailua.org Bridget Olsen, Dir.;

St. John Vianney - 920 Keolu Dr., Kailua, HI 96734-3842 t) 808-262-8317 cclarke@rcchawaii.org saintjohnvianneyhawaii.org Rev. Vincent Vu, Pst.; Dcn. Jerry L. Tokars; Dcn. Clarence DeCaires; Steffanie Beissel, DRE; CRP Stds.: 57

St. John Vianney School - (Grades PreK-8) 940 Keolu Dr., Kailua, HI 96734-3842 t) 808-261-4651 sjvadmin@sjvkailua.org sjvkailua.org Caryn DeMello, Prin.;

KAILUA-KONA

St. Michael the Archangel - 75-5769 Alii Dr., Kailua-Kona, HI 96740 t) 808-326-7771 stmichaelarchangel@rcchawaii.org konacatholicchurch.net Rev. Konelio Faletoi, Pst.; Rev. William Quiamjot, Par. Vicar; Dcn. Craig Camello; Dcn. Sandor Hernandez-Morales; Margaret Essex, CRE; CRP Stds.: 108

Holy Rosary - 73-4179 Mamalahoa Hwy., Kailua Kona, HI 96740 Kalaoa

Immaculate Conception - 76-5960 Mamalahoa Hwy., Holualoa, HI 96725

St. Paul - 79-7234 St. Paul's Rd., Kailua Kona, HI 96740 Honalo

St. Peter by the Sea - 78-6684 Alii Dr., Kailua Kona, HI 96740 Kahaluu

KALAHEO

Holy Cross - 2-2370 Kaumualii Hwy., Kalaheo, HI 96741-0487; Mailing: P.O. Box 487, Kalaheo, HI 96741-0487 t) 808-332-8011 holycrosschurch@hawaii.rr.com holycrossrcckalaheo.weebly.com Rev. Danilo Corpuz Galang, M.S., Pst.; Dcn. Averiet Soto; Caroline Freudig, DRE; CRP Stds.: 23

Sacred Heart - 2626 Melemele Rd., Eleele, HI 96705

KALAUPAPA

St. Francis - Kamehameha St., Kalaupapa, HI 96742; Mailing: P.O. Box 9, Kalaupapa, HI 96742 t) 808-567-6238 pkilililea@rcchawaii.org damienchurchmolokai.org Rev. Patrick J. Killilea, SS.CC., Pst.; Rev. Patrick Fanning, Par. Vicar;

St. Philomena, Kalawao - Damien Rd., Kalaupapa, HI 96742

KANEOHE

St. Ann - 46-129 Haiku Rd., Kaneohe, HI 96744 t) 808-247-3092 x115; 808-247-3092 x104 (CRP) bhonda@saintannhawaii.org saintannhawaii.org Rev. Richard McNally, SS.CC., Pst.; Rev. Patrick Tukidia, sscc, Par. Vicar; Rev. Edward Popish, SS.CC., In Res.; Dcn. Billy Whitfield; Robert Noguchi, DRE; CRP Stds.: 92

Our Lady of Mt. Carmel - 48-422 Kamehameha Hwy., Kaneohe, HI 96744; Mailing: P.O. Box 6581, Kaneohe, HI 96744 t) 808-239-9269 olmc001@hawaii.rr.com; lsalas@rcchawaii.org mtcarmelhawaii.com Rev. Paulo R. Kosaka, O.F.M.Cap., Pst.; Lucy Salas, DRE; CRP Stds.: 12

KAPAA

St. Catherine - 5021-A Kawaihau Rd., Kapaa, HI 96746 t) 808-882-7900; 808-822-4804; 808-822-7900 (CRP) arapozo@rcchawaii.org; mcruz@rcchawaii.org kauaistcatherine.church Rev. Nicholas Apetorgbor, Admin.; Rev. Dario Rinaldi, Par. Vicar; Dcn. Alejandrino Ragasa; Michael Cruz, DRE; CRP Stds.: 30

St. Catherine School - (Grades PreK-12) 5021 Kawaihau Rd., Kapaa, HI 96746 t) 808-822-4212 scsoffice@st-catherineschool.org scskauai.com MaryAnn Bode, Prin.;

St. Sylvester, Kilauea - 2390 Kolo Rd., Kilauea, HI 96754 Kilauea

St. William, Hanalei - 5292-A Kuhio Hwy., Hanalei, HI 96714 Hanalei

KAPOLEI

St. Jude - 92-455 Makakilo Dr., Kapolei, HI 96707 t) 808-672-9041; 808-672-8669 (CRP) nwheeler@rcchawaii.org; bboquer@rcchawaii.org stjudehawaii.org Rev. Khanh Hoang, Pst.; Rev. Boniface Sakala, Par. Vicar; Dcn. John A. Coughlin; Dcn. William Friese; Dcn. Raul Perez; Rev. Clarence Zamora, In Res.; Bonnie Boquer, DRE; CRP Stds.: 164

KAUNAKAKAI

St. Damien - 115 Ala Malama St., Kaunakakai, HI 96748; Mailing: P.O. Box 1948, Kaunakakai, HI 96748-1948 t) 808-553-5220 molocath1@hawaiiantel.net damienchurchmolokai.org Rev. Patrick Fanning, Pst.; Dcn. James Krupka; Dcn. Michael K. Shizuma; Grace Kashiwamura, CRE; CRP Stds.: 43

Our Lady of Seven Sorrows, Kaluaaha - 8033 Kamehameha V Hwy., Kaunakakai, HI 96748

St. Vincent Ferrer, Maunaloa - 274 Maunaloa Rd., Maunaloa, HI 96770

St. Joseph, Kamalo - Kamehameha V Hwy., Kaunakakai, HI 96748

KEKAHA

St. Theresa - 8343 Kaumualii Hwy., Kekaha, HI 96752; Mailing: PO Box 159, Kekaha, HI 96752 t) 808-337-1548; (808) 337-1548 (CRP) sttheresac@yahoo.com kekahacatholic.com Rev. Edwin Conselva, MS, Pst.; Dcn. James E. Bostick; Dcn. Andres Emayo; Sr. Gloria Camitan, DRE; CRP Stds.: 9

St. Theresa School - (Grades PreK-8) 8320 Elepaio Rd., Kekaha, HI 96752; Mailing: PO Box 277, Kekaha, HI 96752 t) 808-337-1351 office@sttheresakanai.com sttheresakanai.com

Wendy Castillo, Prin.; Adela Chavez, Librn.; Stds.: 134; Sr. Tchrs.: 1; Lay Tchrs.: 12

Sacred Hearts - 9496 Kaumualii Hwy., Waimea, HI 96796 econselva@rcchawaii.org www.kekahacatholic.com Waimea

KIHEI

St. Theresa - 25 W. Lipoa St., Kihei, HI 96753 t) 808-879-2649; 808-879-4844 (CRP) mafalekaono@rcchawaii.org; kmartin@rcchawaii.org saint-theresa.com Rev. Arnel Soriano, M.S., Pst.; Rev. Ornoldo Cherrez, In Res.; Rev. John Hatcher, In Res.; Karen Powers, DRE; CRP Stds.: 87

KOLOA

St. Raphael - 3011 Hapa Rd., Koloa, HI 96756 t) 808-742-1955; (808) 320-8758 (Rectory) straphael@rcchawaii.org st-raphael-kauai.org Rev. Rizal Costa, Pst.; Allison Carveiro, DRE; CRP Stds.: 14

KULA

Our Lady Queen of the Angels - 9177 Kula Hwy., Kula, HI 96790-9464 t) 808-878-1261; 808-283-7545 (CRP) kccchurch@rcchawaii.org; dabegas@hotmail.com kulacatholiccommunity.org Rev. Anton Nyo, Pst.; Carol Mukai, DRE; CRP Stds.: 7

Holy Ghost - 4300 Lower Kula Rd., Kula, HI 96790 Waiakoa

St. James the Less - Piilani Hwy., Kula, HI 96790 Ulupalakua

LAHAINA

Maria Lanakila (Victorious Mary) - 712 Wainee St., Lahaina, HI 96761-1511 t) 808-661-0552 info@marialanakila.org; tlolesio@shsmaui.org marialanakila.org Rev. Kuriakose Nakooparambil, MF, Pst.; Rev. Robert Ni Ni, MF, Par. Vicar; Tonata Lolesio, DRE; CRP Stds.: 74

Sacred Hearts School - (Grades PreK-8) 239 Dickenson St., Lahaina, HI 96761 t) 808-661-4720 bspitznagel@shsmaui.org shsmaui.org Miguel Solis, Prin.;

Sacred Hearts - 500 Office Rd., Lahaina, HI 96761 Honokahua (Kapalua)

Convent - 239 Dickenson St., Lahaina, HI 96761

LANAI CITY

Sacred Hearts - 815 Fraser Ave., Lanai City, HI 96763; Mailing: P.O. Box 630784, Lanai City, HI 96763 t) 808-565-7070; 808-565-6837 (CRP) sacredheartslanai@yahoo.com sacredheartslanai.org Rev. Cipriano Alnas, Admin.; Dcn. Henry Costales; Wilma Koep, DRE; Jessie Myers, DRE; CRP Stds.: 30

LAUPAHOEHOE

St. Anthony - 35-2095 Old Mamalohoa Hwy., Laupahoehoe, HI 96764; Mailing: P.O. Box 339, Laupahoehoe, HI 96764 t) 808-962-6538 saintpadua@hotmail.com hamakuacatholic.org Merged with Immaculate Heart of Mary - Papaikou. St. Anthony is now a mission of IHM-Papaikou. Rev. Stephen A. Macedo, Pst.;

LIHUE

Immaculate Conception - 4453 Kapaia Rd., Lihue, HI 96766 t) 808-245-2432; 808-635-6874 (CRP) icchurchkauai@rcchawaii.org; sgina0814@yahoo.com icchurchlihue.com Rev. Edison Pamintuan, M.S., Pst.; Dcn. William A. Farias; Dcn. David E. Kane; Sr. Gina Senapio, O.P., DRE; CRP Stds.: 87

Convent - 3343 Kanakolu St., Lihue, HI 96766

MAKAWAO

St. Joseph - 1294 Makawao Ave., Makawao, HI 96768 t) 808-572-7652; 808-572-2273 (CRP) stjosephmakawao@rcchawaii.org; sharris@rcchawaii.org sjcmaui.org Rev. Michael Tolentino, Admin.; Sheri Harris, DRE; Dcn. Patrick Constantino; CRP Stds.: 24

St. Joseph Early Learning Center - (Grades PreSchool- t) 808-572-6235 stjoe@sjsmaui.org sjsmaui.org Helen Souza, Dir.;

MILILANI TOWN

St. John Apostle and Evangelist - 95-370 Kuahelani Ave., Mililani Town, HI 96789 t) 808-623-3332 sjaeinfo@rcchawaii.org stjohnmililani.org Rev. Anthony W. Rapozo, Pst.; Rev. John Gabriel, In Res.; Dcn. Romeo Ganibe; Kelly Higa, DRE; CRP Stds.: 73

St. John Catholic Preschool - mscat@sjcpmililani.org stjohnmililani.org/preschool Amytes Quiason, Dir.;

MOUNTAIN VIEW

St. Theresa - 18-1355 Volcano Hwy., Mountain View, HI 96771; Mailing: P.O. Box 37, Mountain View, HI 96771 t) 808-968-6233 stcmv1@gmail.com stcmv.org Rev. Samuel Loterte, Pst.; Dcn. Joseph Albert; Dcn. Jim Dougherty; Roquita Kaisen, DRE; CRP Stds.: 5

Holy Rosary - 16-537 Laukaki Pl., Keaau, HI 96749 t) 808-968-8233 Rev. Samuel E. Loterte, S.S.S.;

NAALEHU

Sacred Heart - 95-5558 Mamalahoa Hwy., Naalehu, HI 96772; Mailing: P.O. Box 760, Naalehu, HI 96772 t) 808-928-8208 hrc.shc@gmail.com Rev. William Tulua, Pst.; Dcn. Jay Cable; CRP Stds.: 1

NANAKULI

St. Rita - 89-318 Farrington Hwy., Nanakuli, HI 96792 t) 808-668-7833 strita_nanakuli@rcchawaii.org stritananakuli.org Rev. Alapaki Kim, Pst.; Dcn. Harold S. Levy Jr.; Karen Victor, DRE; CRP Stds.: 8

PAHALA

Holy Rosary - 96-3143 Pikake St., Pahala, HI 96777; Mailing: P.O. Box 760, Pahala, HI 96777 t) 808-928-8208 hrc.shc@gmail.com Rev. William Tulua, Pst.; Dcn. Joseph Aglia; Jeanette Castillo, DRE; CRP Stds.: 11

PAHOA

Sacred Heart - 15-3003 Pahoa Village Rd., Pahoa, HI 96778 t) 808-965-8202; 808-896-1148 (CRP) shpahoa@gmail.com; mnaiga03@gmail.com pahoasacredheart.com Rev. John Molina, Admin.; Dcn. Charles Mapa; CRP Stds.: 46

PAIA

Holy Rosary - 954 Baldwin Ave., Paia, HI 96779-9605 t) 808-579-9551 calnas@rcchawaii.org holyrosarypaia.org/ Cyrila Pascual, DRE; Rev. Jose Macoy, Pst.; Dcn. Christopher Ribucan; CRP Stds.: 10

PAPAIKOU

Immaculate Heart of Mary - 27-186 Kaapoko Homestead Rd., Papaikou, HI 96781; Mailing: P.O. Box 79, Papaikou, HI 96871 t) 808-964-1240; 808-938-3295 (CRP) ihmparish@hotmail.com; dcnandrews@gmail.com hamakuacatholic.org St. Anthony (Laupahoehoe) was merged with Immaculate Heart of Mary - Papaikou. St. Anthony is now a mission of IHM-Papaikou. Dcn. LeRoy Andrews, DRE; Rev. Stephen A. Macedo, Pst.; CRP Stds.: 40

Good Shepherd - 28-640 Government Main Rd., Honomu, HI 96728 Patricia Phillips, Contact;

PEARL CITY

Our Lady of Good Counsel - 1525 Waimano Home Rd., Pearl City, HI 96782 t) 808-455-3012 office@olgcchurchpc.org olgcchurch.org Rev. Santtosh Thotankara, Pst.; Rev. Herman Gomes, SS.CC., Par. Vicar; Dcn. Jeffrey Calamayan; Dcn. Thomas Miyashiro; Pamela Falasco, DRE; CRP Stds.: 56

Our Lady of Good Counsel School - (Grades PreK-8) 1530 Hoolana St., Pearl City, HI 96782 t) 808-455-4533 inquire@olgchawaii.org olgchawaii.org Chantelle Luarca, Prin.; Raynette Badua-Villamor, Librn.;

WAHIAWA

Our Lady of Sorrows - 1403-A California Ave., Wahiawa, HI 96786-2595 t) 808-621-5109 info@olswahiawa.org olswahiawa.org Rev. Falaniko Atonio, Admin.; Alan Kim, CRE; Dcn. Celestino Emwalu; CRP Stds.: 46

WAIALUA

St. Michael - 67-390 Goodale Ave., Waialua, HI 96791 t) 808-637-4040 stsmichaelpeter_paul@hawaii.rr.com stsmichaelpeterpaul.org Beverly Orillo, DRE; Rev. Romple Emwalu, Pst.; Dcn. Jonathan Ocampo; CRP Stds.: 30

St. Michael School - (Grades PreSchool-12) 67-340 Haona St., Waialua, HI 96791 t) 808-637-7772 stmichaelhi@hawaii.rr.com stmichaelschoolhi.com Kainoa Fukumoto, Prin.; Anvie Alcayde, Vice Prin.; Stds.: 103; Sr. Tchrs.: 2; Lay Tchrs.: 8

SS. Peter and Paul - 59-810 Kamehameha Hwy., Haleiwa, HI 96712 jpasala@rcchawaii.org

WAIANAE

Sacred Heart - 85-786 Old Government Rd., Waianae, HI 96792 t) 808-696-3773; 808-861-3747 (CRP) office.shcwaianae@gmail.com; lefua77@yahoo.com shcwaianae.churchspring.org Rev. Jaime Jose, Pst.; Dcn. Savili Bartley; Dcn. Jerome Vito; Dcn. Morton Zabala; Rosalina Lefu'a, DRE; CRP Stds.: 52

WAIHEE

St. Ann - 40 Kuhinia St., Waihee, HI 96793-9216 t) 808-244-3284 stannwaihee@gmail.com; info@saint-ann-maui.org Rev. Anastacio Postrano, Admin.; Dawn Kahalehau, DRE; CRP Stds.: 11

St. Francis Xavier - Kahekili Hwy., Wailuku, HI 96793 Kahakuloa

WAILUKU

St. Anthony of Padua - 1627 B Mill St., Wailuku, HI 96793-1999 t) 808-244-4148; 808-242-6040 (CRP) info@stanthonymaui.org stanthonymaui.org Rev. Msgr. Terrence A.M. Watanabe, Pst.; Rev. Ese'ese Tui, Par. Vicar; Dcn. Stephen Maglente; Tanya Barbero, DRE; CRP Stds.: 43

St. Anthony of Padua School - (Grades PreK-12) 1618 Lower Main St., Wailuku, HI 96793 t) 808-244-4976 (Elem.); 808-244-4190 (Middle & High School) sas@sasmaui.org sasmaui.org David Kenney, Prin.;

Saint Anthony Preschool - t) 808-242-9024 stanthonymaui.org/preschool Carlene Santos, Dir.;

WAIMANALO

St. George - 41-1323 Kalanianaole Hwy., Waimanalo, HI 96795 t) 808-259-7188 stgeorge@rcchawaii.org; kulani48@hawaii.rr.com stgeorge96795.com Rev. Raymund Ellorin, Pst.; Dcn. John Tolentino; Victoria DeSilva, DRE; CRP Stds.: 19

WAIMEA

Annunciation - 65-1235 Kawaihae Rd., Waimea, HI 96743 t) 808-887-1220; 808-887-1203 (CRP) annchhi@hawaiiantel.net; annunciationwaimeare@gmail.com bigislandcatholicchurch.org Rev. Anthony Pangan, SSS, Admin.; Jane Aganus, DRE; CRP Stds.: 37

Ascension - 69-1789 Puako Beach Dr., Kamuela, HI 96743 Puako

WAIPAHU

St. Joseph - 94-675 Farrington Hwy., Waipahu, HI 96797 t) 808-677-4276; 808-676-3493 (CRP) stjosephchurchwaipahu.org Rev. Efren A. Tomas, M.S., Pst.; Rev. Adondee Arellano, M.S., Par. Vicar; Rev. Geronimo Castro, M.S., Par. Vicar; Dcn. Keith Galang; Geraldine Simbahon, DRE; CRP Stds.: 127

St. Joseph School - (Grades PreK-8) 94-651 Farrington Hwy., Waipahu, HI 96797 t) 808-677-4475 sjs@stjosephwaipahu.org stjosephwaipahu.org Beverly Sandobal, Prin.;

Resurrection of the Lord - 94-1260 Lumikula St., Waipahu, HI 96797 t) 808-676-4700 zramones@rcchawaii.org; reanalex@hotmail.com resurrectionhawaii.org Rev. Peter Miti, Pst.; Dcn. Jose Ancheta; Anna Acebo, DRE; CRP Stds.: 105

SCHOOLS: PRESCHOOL THRU HIGH SCHOOL

SCHOOLS

STATE OF HAWAII

HONOLULU

***St. Louis School** - (PRV) (Grades PreK-12) 3142 Waialae Ave., Honolulu, HI 96816-1578 t) 808-739-7777 info@saintlouishawaii.org saintlouishawaii.org Glenn Medeiros, Pres.; Tim Los

Banos, Prin.; Brittany Souza, Vice Prin.; Stds.: 852; Bro. Tchrs.: 2; Lay Tchrs.: 100

St. Patrick School - (PRV) (Grades PreK-8) 3320 Harding Ave., Honolulu, HI 96816 t) 808-734-8979 adecosta@saintpatrickhawaii.org school.saintpatrickhawaii.org Rev. Clyde Guerreiro, SS.CC., Pres.; Sr. Anne Clare DeCosta, SS.CC., Prin. / Vice Pres.; Pattye Kim, Vice Prin.; Debra Corrales, Librn.; Stds.: 268; Lay Tchrs.: 25

Sacred Hearts Academy - (PRV) (Grades PreK-12) 3253 Waialae Ave., Honolulu, HI 96816 t) 808-734-5058 admissions@sacredhearts.org sacredhearts.org Dr. Scott Schroeder, Pres.; Carol Chong, Prin.; Kellie Fase, Librn.; Stds.: 584; Lay Tchrs.: 61

HIGH SCHOOLS

STATE OF HAWAII

HONOLULU

Damien Memorial School - (PRV) (Grades 6-12) 1401 Houghtailing St., Honolulu, HI 96817 t) 808-841-0195 damien.edu Dr. Arnold La'anui, Pres.; Dr. Kyle Atabay, Prin.;

INSTITUTIONS LOCATED IN DIOCESE

CATHOLIC CHARITIES [CCH]

HILO

Hope Services Hawaii - 296 Kilauea Ave., Hilo, HI 96720 t) 808-935-3050 info@hopeserviceshawaii.org hopeserviceshawaii.org Brandee Menino, CEO; Asstd. Annu.: 4,500

HONOLULU

***Catholic Charities Hawaii** - 1822 Keeaumoku St., Honolulu, HI 96822 t) 808-524-4673 info@catholiccharitieshawaii.org catholiccharitieshawaii.org Robert Van Tassell, CEO & Pres.; Tina Andrade, Vice Pres., Mission Integration; Paul Y Kobayashi Jr., Vice Pres., Fin.; Mary Leong Saunders, Vice Pres., Philanthropy; Stella Wong, Vice Pres., Progs.; Asstd. Annu.: 40,000

COLLEGES & UNIVERSITIES [COL]

HONOLULU

***Chaminade University of Honolulu** - 3140 Waialae Ave., Honolulu, HI 96816 t) 808-735-4711 admissions@chaminade.edu chaminade.edu Dr. Lynn Babington, Pres.; Stds.: 2,342; Bro. Tchrs.: 2; Lay Tchrs.: 278; Pr. Tchrs.: 2; Sr. Tchrs.: 1

CONVENTS, MONASTERIES, AND RESIDENCES FOR WOMEN [CON]

AIEA

Missionary Sisters of Mary Help of Christians of America - 98-218 Kanuku St., Aiea, HI 96701 c) 808-725-4080 umeristella@gmail.com Sr. Meristella Umdor, MSMHC, Local Superior;

HONOLULU

Congregation of the Sacred Hearts of Jesus and Mary and of Perpetual Adoration - 1120 Fifth Ave., Honolulu, HI 96816 t) 808-737-5822 reginasscc@cs.com www.ssccpicpus.com Sisters of the Congregation of the Sacred Hearts of Jesus and Mary and of Perpetual Adoration, SS.CC. Sr. Regina Mary Jenkins, SS.CC., Prov.; Srs.: 19

Malia o ka Malu Community - 1117 Fourth Ave., Honolulu, HI 96816 t) 808-734-2048 helenew@hawaii.rr.com Sr. Helene Wood, SS.CC., Supr.;

Moloka'i Sisters Community - 405 Palapalai Pl., Kaunakakai, HI 96748; Mailing: P.O. Box 1237, Kaunakakai, HI 96748 t) 808-553-4303 jessiealai@hotmail.com Sr. Jessie Kai, SS.CC., Supr.;

Paewalani Community - 45-901 Wailele Rd., Kaneohe, HI 96744 t) 808-247-3688 sisteranneclare@gmail.com sistersofthesacredhearts.org Sr. Anne Clare DeCosta, SS.CC., Contact;

Puawakea Community - 3351 Kalihi St., Honolulu, HI 96819 t) 808-845-4353 sisteranneclare@gmail.com Sr. Anne Clare DeCosta, SS.CC., Contact;

Regina Pacis Community -

Daughters of St. Paul Convent - 1143 Bishop St., Honolulu, HI 96813 t) 808-521-2731 honolulu@paulinemedia.com daughtersofstpaul.org The Daughters of St. Paul, ended their ministry to Hawaii and left the islands on June 16, 2022. Sr. Patricia Maresca, Supr.;

Sisters of St. Francis of the Neumann Communities - 2222 Liliha St., Honolulu, HI 96817 t) 808-595-2628 pschofield@sosf.org; wmeleniki@sosf.org Sisters of St. Francis of the Neumann Communities (O.S.F.); St. Francis Healthcare System of Hawaii; St. Francis School. Sr. Davilyn Ah Chick, O.S.F., Regional Minister; Sr. Joan of Arc Souza, O.S.F., Regional Minister;

Sisters of St. Joseph of Carondelet - 5311 Apo Dr., Honolulu, HI 96821-1829 t) 808-373-8801 hvpmae@gmail.com csjla.org Sr. Brenda Lau, C.S.J., Dir.;

St. Joseph by the Sea Community - 206 Kailua Rd., Kailua, HI 96734-2398 t) 808-262-0575

KAILUA

Maryknoll Sisters of St. Dominic - 125 Ainoni St., Kailua, HI 96734-2138 t) 808-261-6356 mkainoni@yahoo.com Sr. Bitrina Kirway, M.M., Contact;

Maryknoll Sisters Residence - 2880 Oahu Ave., Honolulu, HI 96822-1732 t) 808-988-6540 mkmanoa@hawaii.rr.com

Maryknoll Sisters Residence - 1570 Mokulua Dr., Kailua, HI 96734-3254 t) 808-261-1674 mkslanikai@yahoo.com

KANEOHE

Carmel of the Holy Trinity (Carmelite Monastery) - 6301 Pali Hwy., Kaneohe, HI 96744-5224 t) 808-261-6542 c) 808-466-5486 carmeltrinityhawaii@outlook.com; carith89@outlook.com Order of Discalced Carmelite Nuns of Our Lady of Mount Carmel (O.C.D.). Srs.: 8

WAIANAE

House of Aloha - 86-569 Paheehee Rd., Waianae, HI 96792 t) 808-696-3021 srermiet@yahoo.com Sr. Ermelinda Tagnipez, OP, Dir.;

WAIPAHU

Dominican Center Hawaii - 94-1249 Lumikula St., Waipahu, HI 96797 t) 808-676-1452; 808-677-1202 srbsindol@hotmail.com www.ophawiiregion.com Please refer to the following parish convents for additional residences: St. Elizabeth, Aiea; House of Aloha, Waianae Sr. Bernarda Sindol, O.P., Supr.;

ENDOWMENTS / FOUNDATIONS / TRUSTS [EFT]

HILO

The St. Joseph Legacy Foundation - 1000 Ululani St., Hilo, HI 96720; Mailing: P.O. Box 485, Hilo, HI 96721 t) 808-935-4936 James Tyrin, Pres.;

HONOLULU

Foundation for Maryknoll School - 1526 Alexander St., Honolulu, HI 96822 t) 808-952-7310 development@maryknollschool.org Stacey Wong, Chair;

***Hawaii Catholic Community Foundation** - 1184 Bishop St., Honolulu, HI 96813 t) 808-585-3307 marvin@rcchawaii.org; financeoffice@rcchawaii.org

KANEOHE

Augustine Educational Foundation - St. Stephen Diocesan Center, 6301 Pali Hwy., Kaneohe, HI 96744 t) 808-203-6736; 808-203-6748 sue@augustinefoundation.org; tonya@augustinefoundation.org augustinefoundation.org Tuition assistance and teacher curriculum development grants for Hawaii Catholic Schools. Susan Ferandin, Exec. Dir.; Tonya Stevenson, Assoc. Dir.;

WAILUKU

St. Anthony School of Maui Foundation - 1618 Lower Main St., Wailuku, HI 96793 t) 808-244-4190 mainoffice@sasmaui.org sasmaui.org

MISCELLANEOUS [MIS]

HONOLULU

***Marianist Center of Hawaii** - 3140 Waialae Ave., Honolulu, HI 96816 t) 808-738-5887 baldschmitz@aol.com; mch-wjcampbell@chaminade.edu marianisthawaii.com Bro. William Campbell, Dir.; Bro. Dennis Schmitz, S.M., Dir.;

Mystical Rose Oratory - Rev. Martin Solma, sm, Chap.;

MONASTERIES AND RESIDENCES FOR PRIESTS AND BROTHERS [MON]

HONOLULU

Christian Brothers of Ireland - 1840 Owawa St., Honolulu, HI 96819 c) (708) 833-6242 krj9491@gmail.com Bro. Bruce John Cullerton, cfc, Mem.; Bro. Liam Nolan, cfc, Mem.; Bro. James Keane, CFC, Contact; Brs.: 3

Marianist Communities - 3140 Waialae Ave., Honolulu, HI 96816-1578 t) 808-735-4835 broedsm@gmail.com; frankdamm31@gmail.com Bro. Edward Brink, Dir.; Bro. Dennis Schmitz, S.M., Spiritual Adviser / Care Svcs.;

Center Marianist Community - t) 808-739-8500 Rev. Martin Solma, sm, Chap.;

Marianist Hall Community - t) 808-739-8300 Rev. James Allen DeLong, S.M.; Bro. Frank Damm, SM, Dir.;

KANEOHE

Sacred Hearts Center, Congregation of the Sacred Hearts of Jesus and Mary and of Perpetual Adoration - 45-713 Pookela St., Kaneohe, HI 96744; Mailing: P.O. Box 1365, Kaneohe, HI 96744 t) 808-247-5035 usprovincial@sscc.org sscc.org Sacred Hearts Missions; Sacred Hearts Fathers. Additional residences: St. Anne, Kaneohe; St. Augustine, Honolulu; St. Damien, Kaunakakai. Very Rev. Lane K. Akiona, SS.CC., Prov.;

St. Patrick's Monastery - 1124-A 7th Ave., Honolulu, HI 96816 t) 808-732-0281 Rev. Paul Zaccone, SS.CC.; Rev. Albert Garcia, SS.CC., In Res.; Rev. William F. Petrie, SS.CC., In Res.; Rev. Herman Gomes, SS.CC., Prov.; Rev. Edward Popish, SS.CC., Dir.;

WAIALUA

Benedictine Monastery of Hawaii/Mary, Spouse of the Holy Spirit (Public Association of the Faithful of Diocesan Right) - 67-290 Farrington Hwy., Waialua, HI 96791; Mailing: P.O. Box 490, Waialua, HI 96791 t) 808-637-7887 monastery@hawaiibenedictines.org www.hawaiibenedictines.org Sr. Celeste Cabral, Contact;

PRESCHOOLS / CHILDCARE CENTERS [PRE]

EWA BEACH

St. Francis Preschool - 91-1758 Oohao St., Ewa Beach, HI 96706; Mailing: 2226 Liliha St., Ste. 227, Honolulu, HI 96817 t) 808-681-0100 info@stfrancishawaii.org stfrancishawaii.org/services/preschool-4

WAIPAHU

Rosary Preschool - 94-1249 Lumikula St., Waipahu, HI 96797 t) 808-676-1452 rosarypreschool@rcchawaii.org rosarypreschool.com Sr. Joy Garcia, O.P., Vice Prin.; Sr. Cecilia Fabular, O.P., Prin. & Dir.;

RETREAT HOUSES / RENEWAL CENTERS [RTR]

HONOLULU

St. Anthony Retreat Center - 3351 Kalihi St., Honolulu, HI 96819 t) 808-845-4353 sarc3351@gmail.com saintanthonyretreat.org Sr. Anne Clare DeCosta, SS.CC., Admin.;

KANEOHE

St. Stephen Diocesan Center - 6301 Pali Hwy., Kaneohe, HI 96744-5298 t) 808-203-6724 sizaguirre@rcchawaii.org Sabrina Izaguirre, Admin.;

SPECIAL CARE FACILITIES [SPF]

HONOLULU

St. Francis Healthcare System of Hawaii - 2228 Liliha St., Ste. 300, Honolulu, HI 96817 t) 808-547-6500 info@stfrancishawaii.org stfrancishawaii.org Melissa Ah Ho-Mauga, CEO; Staff: 220

Blessings House - 91-019 Popoi Pl., Ewa Beach, HI 96706; Mailing: 2226 Liliha St., Ste. 227, Honolulu, HI 96817 Sr. Beatrice Tom, O.S.F., Pres.;

St. Francis Adult Day Center (St. Francis Intergenerational Center) - 91-1758 Oohao St., Ewa Beach, HI 96706; Mailing: 2226 Liliha St., Ste. 227, Honolulu, HI 96817 t) 808-681-0100

St. Francis Community Health Services - 2228 Liliha St., Ste. 408, Honolulu, HI 96817 t) 808-595-7566 mahhomauga@stfrancishawaii.org

St. Francis Development Corporation - 2226 Liliha St., Ste. 227, Honolulu, HI 96817 Jerry Correa Jr., Pres.;

St. Francis Healthcare Foundation of Hawaii - 2228 Liliha St., Ste. 205, Honolulu, HI 96817; Mailing: 2226 Liliha St., Ste. 227, Honolulu, HI 96817

St. Francis Hospice Home Setting Program - 2226 Liliha St., Ste. 227, Honolulu, HI 96817

St. Francis Medical Center - 2226 Liliha St., Ste. 227, Honolulu, HI 96817 Jerry Correa Jr., Pres.;

St. Francis Residential Care Community (Franciscan Vistas) - 2226 Liliha St., Ste. 227, Honolulu, HI 96817 Jerry Correa Jr., Pres.;

Franciscan Care Services - 2226 Liliha St., Ste. 227, Honolulu, HI 96817 Jerry Correa Jr., Pres.;

Hawaii Bone Marrow Donor Registry - 2228 Liliha St., Ste. 105, Honolulu, HI 96817; Mailing: 2226 Liliha St., Ste. 227, Honolulu, HI 96817 t) 808-547-6154 rchung@stfrancis.org

Health Services for Senior Citizens - 2228 Liliha St., Ste. 408, Honolulu, HI 96817; Mailing: 2226 Liliha St., Ste. 227, Honolulu, HI 96817 t) 808-547-6121

The Maurice J. Sullivan Family Hospice Center - 91-2127 Fort Weaver Rd., Ewa Beach, HI 96706; Mailing: 2226 Liliha St., Ste. 227, Honolulu, HI 96817 t) 808-595-7566

MOB Management, LLC - 2226 Liliha St., Ste. 227, Honolulu, HI 96817 Jerry Correa Jr.;

Our Lady of Keaau, Waianae - Keaau Homesteads Rd., Waianae, HI 96792; Mailing: P.O. Box 1475, Waianae, HI 96792 t) 808-696-7255 Sr. Beatrice Tom, O.S.F., Pres.;

SFMC Joint Ventures, LLC - 2226 Liliha St., Ste. 227, Honolulu, HI 96817

Sister Maureen Intergenerational Learning Environment (Franciscan Adult Day Center) - 2715 Pamoa Rd., Honolulu, HI 96822; Mailing: 2226 Liliha St., Ste. 227, Honolulu, HI 96817 t) 808-988-5678

Sister Maureen Keleher Center St. Francis Hospice Nuuanu - 24 Puiwa Rd., Honolulu, HI 96817; Mailing: 2226 Liliha St., Ste. 227, Honolulu, HI 96817 t) 808-595-7566

An asterisk (*) denotes an organization that has established tax-exempt status directly with the IRS and is not covered by the USCCB Group Ruling.

Diocese of Houma-Thibodaux

(Dioecesis Humensis-Thibodensis)

(VACANT SEE)

Mailing Address: P.O. Box 505, Schriever, LA 70395. T: 985-868-7720; F: 985-868-7727.
htdiocese.org
bishop@htdiocese.org

ERECTED JUNE 5, 1977.

Square Miles 3,500.

Comprises the parishes of Lafourche, Terrebonne, parts of St. Mary, Jefferson, St. Martin and Assumption.

For legal titles of parishes and diocesan institutions, consult the Pastoral Center.

STATISTICAL OVERVIEW

Personnel
Retired Bishops....1
Priests: Diocesan Active in Diocese....52
Priests: Diocesan Active Outside Diocese....5
Priests: Retired, Sick or Absent....14
Number of Diocesan Priests....71
Total Priests in your Diocese....71
Ordinations:
Diocesan Priests....2
Transitional Deacons....3
Permanent Deacons in Diocese....32
Total Sisters....17

Parishes
Parishes....39
With Resident Pastor:
Resident Diocesan Priests....32
Resident Religious Priests....4
Without Resident Pastor:
Administered by Priests....3
Missions....6
Pastoral Centers....1

Professional Ministry Personnel:
Sisters....3
Lay Ministers....55

Welfare
Homes for the Aged....1
Total Assisted....58
Day Care Centers....1
Total Assisted....64
Specialized Homes....1
Total Assisted....53
Special Centers for Social Services....3
Total Assisted....5,435

Educational
Diocesan Students in Other Seminaries....9
Total Seminarians....9
High Schools, Diocesan and Parish....3
Total Students....1,653
Elementary Schools, Diocesan and Parish....8
Total Students....3,208
Catechesis/Religious Education:
High School Students....1,535
Elementary Students....2,583
Total Students under Catholic Instruction....8,988
Teachers in Diocese:
Lay Teachers....292

Vital Statistics
Receptions into the Church:
Infant Baptism Totals....650
Minor Baptism Totals....49
Adult Baptism Totals....13
Received into Full Communion....28
First Communions....682
Confirmations....697
Marriages:
Catholic....187
Interfaith....13
Total Marriages....200
Deaths....1,264
Total Catholic Population....76,115
Total Population....220,054

LEADERSHIP

Diocesan Pastoral Center - t) 985-868-7720 info@htdiocese.org

Vicar General for Administration - t) 985-850-3173 tclement@htdiocese.org Rev. Simon Peter Engurait V;

Vicar General for Parish Life - t) 985-850-3173 tclement@htdiocese.org Rev. Mark Toups;

Chancellor - t) 985-850-3124 bishopsec@htdiocese.org Rev. Jay L. Baker, Chancellor;

Judicial Vicar - t) 985-850-3126 eleyble@htdiocese.org Rev. Eric Leyble;

Vicar for Clergy - Rev. Vicente De La Cruz (vdelacruz@htdiocese.org);

Finance Officer - cvoisin@htdiocese.org Jon Toups, C.O.F.O.;

Victim Assistance Coordinator - t) 985-850-3172 Sr. Carmelita Centanni, M.S.C. (ccentanni@htdiocese.org);

ADMINISTRATION

Archives and Historical Research Center - t) 985-446-2383 Kevin Allemand, Admin. (kallemand@htdiocese.org);

Building Commission - t) 985-850-3150 James J. Danos, Dir. (jdanos@htdiocese.org);

Cemeteries Office - t) 985-446-0280 Kayla Brunet, Mgr. (kbrunet@htdiocese.org);

Child and Youth Protection - t) 985-850-3140 Melissa R. Robertson, Dir. (mrobertson@htdiocese.org); Michelle Ohmer, Safe Environment Coord. (mohmer@htdiocese.org);

College of Consultors - Rev. Jay Baker; Rev. Simon Peter Engurait V; Rev. Mark Toups;

Deans -

South Lafourche Deanery - Rev. Thankachan (John) Nambusseril, C.M.I.;

Terrebonne Deanery - Rev. Mike Tran;

Upper Lafourche Deanery - Rev. Vincente N. de la Cruz;

Diocesan Finance Council - Rev. Simon Peter Engurait V; Glenn Vice, Pastoral Council; April LeBouef, Dir. (amlebouef@htdiocese.org);

Human Resources & Employment Benefits - Melissa R. Robertson (mrobertson@htdiocese.org);

Insurance - Property, Casualty & Liability - t) 985-850-3135 Dawn Sevin (dsevin@htdiocese.org);

Legal Services - Jon Toups, Dir.;

Office of Finance and Accounting - t) 985-868-7720 April LeBouef, Dir. (amlebouef@htdiocese.org);

Operations - Computers & Technology - Holly Becnel, Dir. (hbecnel@htdiocese.org);

Priests Council - Rev. P. J. Madden; Rev. John David Matherne; Rev. Alexis Lazarra;

CATHOLIC CHARITIES

Adoption - t) 985-876-0490 Nicole M. Bourgeois;

Assisi Bridge House - t) 985-872-5529 Monique Albarado, Dir.;

Catholic Campaign for Human Development - t) 985-876-0490 Agnes Bitature, Assoc. Dir.;

Catholic Charities - t) 985-876-0490 Nicole M. Bourgeois, Dir.;

Catholic Community Center - t) 985-632-6859 Tricha Gross, Mgr.;

Catholic Housing Services - t) 985-876-0490 Paula Dawson-Ringo, Assoc. Dir.;

Catholic Relief Services - t) 985-876-0490 Agnes Bitature, Assoc. Dir.;

C.E.N.T.S. Micro Enterprise Program - t) 985-876-0490 Paula Dawson-Ringo, Assoc. Dir.;

Disaster Preparedness & Relief/Matthew 25 - t) 985-876-0490 Agnes Bitature, Assoc. Dir.;

Foster Grandparent Program - t) 985-876-0490 Van Johnson, Assoc. Dir.;

Good Samaritan Raceland Food Bank - t) 985-537-7706 Leslie Robichaux, Mgr.;

Good Samaritan Thibodaux Food Bank - t) 985-447-9776 Kristin Lafleur, Assoc. Dir.;

Individual and Family Assistance - t) 985-876-0490 Jennifer Gaudet, Assoc. Dir.;

Parish Social Ministry/Justice & Peace - t) 985-876-0490 Agnes Bitature, Assoc. Dir.;

Programs of Catholic Charities: -

St. Lucy Child Development Center - t) 985-876-1246 Danielle Davis-Coler, Dir.;

CLERGY AND RELIGIOUS SERVICES

Clergy Personnel - Rev. Jay Baker;

Continuing Education of the Clergy-Ministry to Priests Program - t) 985-868-7720; 985-850-3124 Rev. Mark Anthony Toups;

Coordinator - Rev. Jay Baker;

Office of Seminarians - t) 985-850-3157 Rev. Mitchel Semar, Dir. (agarcia@htdiocese.org);

Office of the Permanent Diaconate - t) 985-850-3145 Dcn. Stephen Brunet, Dir.;

Office of Vocations - t) 985-850-3157 vocations@htdiocese.org Rev. John David Matherne, Dir.;

Vicar for Priests - Rev. Vicente De La Cruz, Vicar (vdelacruz@htdiocese.org);

Women Religious - Sr. Carmelita Centanni, M.S.C. (ccentanni@htdiocese.org);

FAITH FORMATION

Bayou Catholic - Lawrence Chatagnier, Editor;

Campus Ministry - t) 985-446-6201 Rev. Mitchel Semar (agarcia@htdiocese.org);

Coordinator - Rev. Simon Peter Engurait V;

Office of Catholic Schools - t) 985-850-3114 Suzanne Troxclair, Supt. (stroxclair@htdiocese.org);

Office of Communications - t) 985-868-7720 Lonnie Thibodeaux, Dir.;

Office of Youth Formation - Rebecca Abboud;

Rite of Christian Initiation of Adults - t) 985-855-1063 Dcn. Lee Crochet;

Worship - Rev. Glenn LeCompte, Dir.;

ORGANIZATIONS

Catholic Daughters of the Americas - Rev. Carl Collins, Spiritual Adv./Care Srvcs.;

Catholic Foundation of South Louisiana - t) 985-850-3116 cfsl@htdiocese.org Amy Ponson, Dir.;

Diocesan Council of St. Vincent de Paul Societies - Murke Trahan Jr. (mptrahanjr@gmail.com);

Knights of Columbus - t) 985-384-3551 Rev. Clyde Mahler, Chap.;

St. Vincent de Paul Store - t) 985-872-9373 Pete Cavalier, Pres.; Janice Yakupzack, Vice. Pres.; Lacey Marcel, Secy.;

TRIBUNAL

Director of Tribunal - Rev. Eric Leyble;

Defender of the Bond - Rev. Jay L. Baker;

Diocesan Tribunal - t) 985-850-3126 Rev. Eric Leyble;

Judge - Rev. Vicente De La Cruz (vdelacruz@htdiocese.org);

Tribunal Specialist and Notary - Veronica Songe;

MISCELLANEOUS / OTHER OFFICES

Catholic Committee on Scouting - t) 985-868-7720 Dcn. Gary Lapeyrouse, Chap.; Kelly Rodrigue, Chair;

Charismatic Renewal - t) 985-856-4269 Penny Antill, Charismatic Renewal Liaison;

Cursillo - t) 985-850-3132 Dcn. Lloyd Duplantis, Dir.;

Ecumenism (Vacant) -

Lumen Christi Retreat Center - t) 985-868-1523 Chris Domingue, Dir.;

Pontifical Missionary Union of Priests and Religious - t) 985-850-0035 Rev. Robert Joel Cruz, Dir. (propfaith@htdiocese.org);

PARISHES, MISSIONS, AND CLERGY

STATE OF LOUISIANA

AMELIA

St. Andrew - 833 Julia St., Amelia, LA 70340; Mailing: P.O. Box 310, Amelia, LA 70340 t) 985-631-2333 st.andrewcentral.org Rev. Joseph Chacko, I.M.S., Pst.; Amber Cavalier, DRE; CRP Stds.: 58

BOURG

St. Ann - 4355 Hwy. 24, Bourg, LA 70343 t) 985-594-3548 stannchurch@htdiocese.org www.stannbourg.org Rev. Cody Chatagnier, Pst.; Dcn. Gerald Belanger; Dcn. Timothy White; Lisa Lapeyrouse, DRE; CRP Stds.: 270

CHAUVIN

St. Joseph - 5232 Hwy. 56, Chauvin, LA 70344 t) 985-594-5859 saintjosephchurch@charter.net saintjosephchurch5.wixsite.com Rev. Baby Kuruvilla, Pst.; Dcn. Gary Lapeyrouse; CRP Stds.: 134

CUT-OFF

The Congregation of the Sacred Heart Roman Catholic Church, Cut Off, LA (Sacred Heart Church) - 15300 W. Main, Cut-Off, LA 70345 t) 985-632-3858; 985-632-6322 mforet@htdiocese.org; cduet@htdiocese.org sacredheartcutoff.org Rev. Gregory Perkins Fratt, Pst.; Rev. Joey Lirette, Assoc. Pst.; CRP Stds.: 284

DULAC

Holy Family - 6641 Grand Caillou Rd., Dulac, LA 70353; Mailing: P.O. Box 87, Dulac, LA 70353 t) 985-563-2325; 985-563-2428 (CRP) www.holyfamilydulac.org Rev. Nathaniel Maria Gadalia, pfgm, Assoc. Pst.; Dcn. Bernard A. Harold Fanguy; Rev. Antonio Maria Speedy, pgsm, Admin.;

GALLIANO

St. Joseph - 17980 W. Main St., Galliano, LA 70354; Mailing: P.O. Box 519, Galliano, LA 70354 t) 985-242-4099 Rev. Peter Tai Thanh Le, Pst.; Lorey Autin, DRE; CRP Stds.: 56

GHEENS

Community of St. Anthony - 1701 Hwy. 654, Gheens, LA 70355; Mailing: 333 Twin Oaks Dr., Raceland, LA 70394 t) 985-537-6002 dmelancon@htdiocese.org sthilaryht.org (Quasi Parish) Rev. Rusty Paul Bruce, Pst.; Sarah Salinas, DRE; Diane Melancon, Bus. Mgr.; CRP Stds.: 130

GOLDEN MEADOW

Our Lady of Prompt Succor - 723 N. Bayou Dr., Golden Meadow, LA 70357 t) 958-475-5428 tduet@htdiocese.org Rev. Thankachan (John) Nambusseril, C.M.I., Pst.; Kritty Chouest, DRE; Greg Terrebonne, RCIA Coord.; Trisha G Duet, Bus. Mgr.; CRP Stds.: 60

GRAND ISLE

Our Lady of the Isle - 195 Ludwig Ln., Grand Isle, LA 70358; Mailing: P.O. Box 885, Grand Isle, LA 70358 c) 985-438-4162; 985-438-4164 oloti@htdiocese.org www.ourladyoftheisle.com Rev. Mark Anthony Toups, Pst.;

HOUMA

Cathedral of St. Francis De Sales - 400 Verret St., Houma, LA 70360; Mailing: P. O. Box 4014, Houma, LA 70361 t) 986-876-6904 (CRP); 985-876-6904 stfrancisdesaleshouma.org/ Rev. Jay L. Baker, Rector; Rev. Daniel Duplantis, Assoc. Pst.; Rev. Noas Kerketta, In Res.; Dcn. Lee Crochet; Cathy Butler, Pst. Min./Coord.; Jane Lirette, DRE; CRP Stds.: 128

Cathedral of St. Francis De Sales School - (Grades PreK-7) 300 Verret St., Houma, LA 70360 t) 985-868-6646 stfrancis@htdiocese.org www.sfcshouma.org Kelli Cazayoux, Prin.; Stds.: 668; Lay Tchrs.: 36

Annunziata - 2011 Acadian Dr., Houma, LA 70363 t) 985-876-2971 annunziatach@comcast.net; lbourg@htdiocese.org www.annunziatacatholic.org Rev. Paul Birdsall, Pst.; Maria Escabedo, Youth Min.; CRP Stds.: 112

St. Anthony of Padua - 3897 Bayou Black Dr., Houma, LA 70360 t) 985-872-0922 stanthonybayoublack@htdiocese.org stanthonybayoublack.org Rev. Carlos Talavera, Pst.;

Dcn. Brent Bergeron; Kayla Adams, DRE; Mary Massey, DRE; CRP Stds.: 85

St. Bernadette Soubirous Church - 409 Funderburk Ave., Houma, LA 70364 t) 985-879-1506 vbreaux@htdiocese.org; wfos@htdiocese.org stbernadettechurchhouma.com Rev. Andre Melancon, Pst.; Rev. James Rome, Assoc. Pst.; Dcn. James Brunet Jr.; Dcn. James Lefevre; Amanda Rodriguez Callais, Youth Min.; Wanda Fos, DRE; CRP Stds.: 316

St. Bernadette School - (Grades PreK-7) 309 Funderburk Ave., Houma, LA 70364 t) 985-872-3854 stbernelm@htdiocese.org saintbernadettepandas.org Dr. Elise LeBoeuf, Prin.; Stephanie Guidry, Vice Prin.; Dale Ford, Librn.; Stds.: 518; Lay Tchrs.: 26

St. Gregory Barbarigo - 1005 Williams Ave., Houma, LA 70364 t) 985-876-2047 stgregory@htdiocese.org stgregorybarbarigo.weconnect.com Rev. Alexis Lazarra, Pst.; Dcn. Dennis Dupre; CRP Stds.: 25

St. Gregory Barbarigo School - (Grades PreK-7) 441 Sixth St., Houma, LA 70364 t) 985-876-2038 stgregoryschool@htdiocese.org www.htdioceseschools.org Cindy Martin, Prin.; Stds.: 162; Lay Tchrs.: 10

St. Louis - 2226 Bayou Blue Rd., Houma, LA 70364 t) 985-876-3449; 985-976-3438 (CRP) stlouisch@comcast.net; stlouischurch@htdiocese.org Rev. Robert C. Rogers, Pst.; CRP Stds.: 178

St. Lucy - 1220 Aycock St., 1214 Aycock St., Houma, LA 70361 t) 985-879-2632 stlucychurch@htdiocese.org Rev. Msgr. Cletus Egbi, Pst.; Dcn. Martin Dickerson; Cynthia Moore, DRE;

Maria Immacolata - 246 Corporate Dr., Houma, LA 70360 t) 985-876-3313 mariaimmacolata@htdiocese.org www.micchouma.org Rev. Joseph Pilola, Pst.; Dcn. William Dunkelman; Dcn. Chris A. Prestenback; CRP Stds.: 146

Our Lady of the Most Holy Rosary - 8594 Main St., Houma, LA 70363 t) 985-876-7652; 985-876-7652 (CRP) angie.naquin@htdiocese.org; wmoore1048@aol.com www.holyrosaryhouma.com Rev. Romeo "Billy" Velasco, Admin.; Wanda Moore, DRE; CRP Stds.: 32

LAROSE

Our Lady of the Rosary - 12911 E. Main, Larose, LA 70373; Mailing: P.O. Box 10, Larose, LA 70373 t) 985-693-3433; 985-693-8850 olryff@htdiocese.org www.olrlarose.org Rev. Duc Bui, Pst.; Rev. Domingo Cruz, In Res.; CRP Stds.: 145

Holy Rosary - (Grades PreK-8) 12925 E. Main St., Larose, LA 70373 t) 985-693-3342; 985-693-8854 holyroselm@htdiocese.org www.htdioceseschools.org/holy-rosary Cathy Long, Prin.; Stds.: 162; Lay Tchrs.: 11

LOCKPORT

Holy Savior - 612 Main St., Lockport, LA 70374 t) 985-532-3533 holysaviorchurch@htdiocese.org www.holysaviorchurch.org Rev. Jean-Marie Nsambu, Pst.; Kecera Rodrigue, Youth Min.; CRP Stds.: 192

Holy Savior Catholic School - 201 Church St., Lockport, LA 70374

MONTEGUT

St. Charles Borromeo - 1237 Hwy. 665, Montegut, LA 70377 t) 985-594-6801 kdehart@htdiocese.org; stcharleschurchpac@htdiocese.org www.stcharlespac.com Rev. Evelio Buenaflor Jr., Pst.; Katie Dehart, DRE; CRP Stds.: 40

Sacred Heart - 1111 Hwy. 55, Montegut, LA 70377; Mailing: 1113 Hwy. 55, P.O. Box 2, Montegut, LA 70377 t) 985-594-5856 sacredheartch@htdiocese.org www.shmontegut.org Rev. Evelio Buenaflor Jr., Admin.; CRP Stds.: 21

MORGAN CITY

Holy Cross - 2100 Cedar St. Unit #3, Morgan City, LA 70380 t) 985-384-3551 holycrosschurch@htdiocese.org holycrossmc.org Rev. Mike Tran, Pst.; Rev. Francis Kayaye, Assoc. Pst.; CRP Stds.: 70

Central Catholic School - (Grades PreK-12) 2100 Cedar St., Unit 2, Morgan City, LA 70380 t) 985-384-1933 cceoffice@htdiocese.org holycrosselementary.org Amanda Talbot, Prin.; Stds.: 249; Lay Tchrs.: 19

St. Rosalie - 1315 Stephensville Rd., Morgan City, LA 70380; Mailing: 2100 Cedar St., Unit #3, Morgan City, LA 70380

Sacred Heart of Jesus - 415 Union St., Morgan City, LA 70381; Mailing: P.O. Box 632, Morgan City, LA 70381 t) 985-385-0770 shcsecretary@htdiocese.org; shcdre@htdiocese.org www.sacredheartmc.org Rev. Joseph Henry Sebastian, Pst.; Dcn. Larry Callais; Dcn. Randall Jennings; Christina Lange, DRE; CRP Stds.: 90

Thanh Gia - 1115 Lake Palourde Rd., Morgan City, LA 70340; Mailing: P.O. Box 338, Amelia, LA 70340 t) 985-631-3194 thanhgia@gmail.com Vietnamese. Rev. James Nguyen Van Thien, C.M.C., Pst.; Rev. John Bosco, Assoc. Pst.;

Vietnam's Martyrs - 406 N. Main Project Rd., Schriever, LA 70395 t) 985-714-9739

St. Holy Rosary - 3593 Friendswood Dr., Houma, LA 70363 t) 985-714-5167

St. Peter - 13040 Hwy. 308, Larose, LA 70373 t) 985-714-5167

RACELAND

St. Hilary of Poitiers - 333 Twin Oaks, Raceland, LA 70394 t) 985-537-6002 dmelancon@htdiocese.org sthilaryht.org/ Rev. Rusty Paul Bruce, Pst.; Sarah Matherne, Liturgy Dir.; Diane Melancon, Bus. Mgr.; CRP Stds.: 292

St. Mary's Nativity - 3500 Hwy. 1, Raceland, LA 70394 t) 985-537-3204; (985) 537-3205 bforet@htdiocese.org; cfalgoust@htdiocese.org www.stmnparish.org Rev. Clyde Mahler, Pst.; Rene Becnel, Youth Min.; Betty Ann Foret, Bus. Mgr.; CRP Stds.: 94

St. Mary's Nativity School - (Grades PreK-8) 3492 Nies St., Raceland, LA 70394 t) 985-537-7544 www.stmarysnativityschool.org Linda Henry, Prin.; Jackie Jackson, Librn.; Stds.: 262; Lay Tchrs.: 12

SCHRIEVER

St. Bridget - 100 Hwy. 311, Schriever, LA 70395; Mailing: 2076 W Main St, Schriever, LA 70395 t) 985-446-6801 stbridgetchurch@htdiocese.org; stbridgetccd@htdiocese.org www.stbridget-htdiocese.org Rev. Simon Peter Engurait, V.G., Pst.; Dcn. Stephen Brunet; Bernadette Mabile, DRE; CRP Stds.: 117

St. Lawrence - 2128 Bull Run Rd., Schriever, LA 70395 t) 985-448-2165 saintlawch@htdiocese.org; maleman@htdiocese.org Rev. Evelio Buenaflor Jr., Pst.; CRP Stds.: 13

THERIOT

St. Eloi - 1335 Bayou Dularge Rd., Theriot, LA 70397 t) 985-872-2946 steloichurch@htdiocese.org www.steloichurch.org Rev. Antonio Maria Speedy, pgsm, Admin.; Rev. Nathaniel Maria Gadalia, pfgm, Assoc. Pst.; Dcn. Glenn Porche; Dcn. Daniel Bascle; Jessica Marcus, CRE; CRP Stds.: 51

THIBODAUX

The Congregation of St. Joseph's Roman Catholic Cathedral - 721 Canal Blvd., Thibodaux, LA 70301; Mailing: P.O. Box 966, Thibodaux, LA 70302 t) 985-446-1387; 985-446-1388 stjosephcc@htdiocese.org www.stjoseph-cc.org Rev. Vincente DeLa Cruz, Pst.; Rev. Rholondo T. Grecia, Assoc. Pst.; Rev. Jackson Cleetus, Chap.; Dcn. Joseph Bourgeois; CRP Stds.: 111

St. Joseph Catholic Elementary School - (Grades PreK-7) 501 Cardinal Dr., Thibodaux, LA 70301 t) 985-446-1346 stjoelm@htdiocese.org www.stjosephcesthibodaux.org Gerard Rodrigue Jr., Prin.; Jami Chadwick, Vice. Pres.; Stds.: 672; Lay Tchrs.: 37

St. Charles Borromeo - 1985 Hwy. 308, Thibodaux, LA 70301 t) 985-446-6663 stcharles@htdiocese.org www.stcharlesthibodaux.org/ Rev. Carl Collins, Pst.; Dcn. Brent P. Bourgeois; Rev. Glenn LeCompte, In Res.; CRP Stds.: 89

Christ the Redeemer - 720 Talbot Ave., Thibodaux, LA 70301 t) 985-447-2013 ctrchurch@htdiocese.org www.ctr-htdiocese.org Rev. Alex Gerard Gaudet, Pst.; CRP Stds.: 160

St. Genevieve - 815 Barbier Ave., Thibodaux, LA 70301 t) 985-446-5127 (Formation); 985-446-5571 (Main) stgenevievechurch@htdiocese.org www.stgenevievechurch.com Rev. Eric Leyble, Pst.; Rev. Joseph Tregre, Assoc. Pst.; Justin L. Rodrigue, Exec. Dir.; Jacqueline M. Hebert, Bus. Mgr.; Jessica Harvey, Formation Dir.; CRP Stds.: 95

St. Genevieve School - (Grades PreK-7) 807 Barbier Ave., Thibodaux, LA 70301 t) 985-447-9291 stgenelm@htdiocese.org Cheryl Thibodaux, Prin.; Jamie Rodrigue, Asst. Prin.; Stds.: 515; Lay Tchrs.: 22

St. John the Evangelist - 2085 St. Mary St., Thibodaux, LA 70301 t) 985-447-3995 sjechurch@charter.net; sjechurch@charter.net Rev. Josekutty Varghese, Pst.; Sheryl Chauvin, Pst. Assoc.; Susie Richard, DRE; CRP Stds.: 95

St. Lawrence the Martyr - 3723 Hwy. 307, Thibodaux, LA 70301 t) 985-633-9431 stlstjchurch@htdiocese.org Rev. Thomas Kuriakose, Pst.; CRP Stds.: 61

St. James - 3086 Choctaw Rd., Thibodaux, LA 70301; Mailing: 3723 Hwy 307, Thibo, LA 70301

St. Luke - 1100 Bourbon St., Thibodaux, LA 70301; Mailing: 300 E. 11th St., Thibodaux, LA 70301 t) 985-446-0487 c) 985-688-2083 stlukecatholicchurch@htdiocese.org; bugsquire@aol.com stlukethibodaux.com Rev. Msgr. Cletus Egbi, Pst.; Carolyn Johnson, DRE;

Our Lady of Prompt Succor - 529 Hwy. 20, Thibodaux, LA 70301 t) 985-633-2903 nbenoit@htdiocese.org; priviere@htdiocese.org Rev. Patrick Riviere, Pst.; CRP Stds.: 266

St. Thomas Aquinas - 204 Madewood Dr. (Nicholls), Thibodaux, LA 70310; Mailing: P.O. Box 2051, Thibodaux, LA 70310 t) 985-446-6201 st.thomas@htdiocese.org www.nsucatholics.org/ Rev. Mitchel Semar, Pst.; Cissy Atzenhoffer, Campus Min.; Brandie Toups, Bus. Mgr.; CRP Stds.: 98

SCHOOLS: PRESCHOOL THRU HIGH SCHOOL

SCHOOLS

STATE OF LOUISIANA

MORGAN CITY

Central Catholic School - (DIO) (Grades PreK-12) 2100 Cedar St., Unit 1, Morgan City, LA 70380 t) 985-385-5372 centcathi@htdiocese.org www.cchseagles.org Peter Boudreaux, Prin.; Amanda Talbot, Prin.; Anna Saleme, Librn.; Stds.: 243; Lay Tchrs.: 20

HIGH SCHOOLS

STATE OF LOUISIANA

HOUMA

Vandebilt Catholic High School - (DIO) (Grades 8-12) 209 S. Hollywood Rd., Houma, LA 70360 t) 985-876-2551 communications@vchterriers.org www.vandebiltcatholic.org Jeremy Gueldner, Pres.; Ginny Medina-Hamilton, Prin.; Stds.: 687; Lay Tchrs.: 47

THIBODAUX

Edward Douglas White Catholic High - (DIO) (Grades 8-12) 555 Cardinal Dr., Thibodaux, LA 70301 t) 985-446-8486 edwhitehi@htdiocese.org www.edwhite.org (Coed) Michelle Chiasson, Prin.; Tim Robichaux, Pres.; Stds.: 723; Lay Tchrs.: 52

E.D. White Catholic High School Foundation, Inc. -

E.D. White Catholic High School Alumni Assn. - t) (985) 446-8486 edwalumni@htdiocese.org

INSTITUTIONS LOCATED IN DIOCESE

ENDOWMENTS / FOUNDATIONS / TRUSTS [EFT]

THIBODAUX

Cemeteries Trust - 949 Menard St, Thibodaux, LA 70301; Mailing: P.O. Box 505, Schriever, LA 70395 t) 985-850-3112 William Barbera, Chief Opers. & Fin. Officer;

MISCELLANEOUS [MIS]

GIBSON

The Chapel of the Blessed Sacrament - 138 Carroll St, Gibson, LA 70356; Mailing: P.O. Box 587, Gibson, LA 70356 t) 985-575-3551; 985-575-3551 (CRP) vconstant@htdiocese.org Rev. Van Constant, Chap.;

THIBODAUX

The Diocese of Houma-Thibodaux Historical Research Center - 205 Audubon Ave., Thibodaux, LA 70301 t) 985-446-2383 kallemand@htdiocese.org htdiocese.org/archives Kevin Allemand, Admin.; Rev. Jay L. Baker, Chancellor;

***St. Joseph Manor** - 1201 Cardinal Dr., Thibodaux, LA 70301 t) 985-446-9050 benb@stjosephmanor.org www.stjosephmanor.org (Assisted Living Community) Ann Thibodaux, Board Member; Ben Bolton, Admin.;

***Magnificat of the Houma-Thibodaux Diocese** - 515 Canal Blvd., Thibodaux, LA 70301 t) 985-446-1982 Jane Block, Dir.; Sally Masterson, Dir.;

***Marian Servants of the Word** - 506 Cardinal Dr., Thibodaux, LA 70301 t) 985-688-5578 marianservantsoftheword@gmail.com Monica Karns, Dir.; Sadie Bonvillain, Asst. Dir.;

PRESCHOOLS / CHILDCARE CENTERS [PRE]

HOUMA

St. Lucy Child Development Center - 1224 Aycock St., Houma, LA 70360; Mailing: 1220 Aycock St., Houma, LA 70360 t) 985-876-1246 stlucycdc@htdiocese.org catholiccharitiesht.org/otherhelp Courtney Virgin, Dir.; Stds.: 64; Lay Tchrs.: 5

RETREAT HOUSES / RENEWAL CENTERS [RTR]

SCHRIEVER

Lumen Christi Retreat Center - 100 Lumen Christi Ln., Hwy. 311, Schriever, LA 70395; Mailing: 100 Lumen Christi Ln., Schriever, LA 70395 t) 985-868-1523; 985-850-3152 lumenchristi@htdiocese.org Chris Domingue, Dir.;

An asterisk (*) denotes an organization that has established tax-exempt status directly with the IRS and is not covered by the USCCB Group Ruling.

Archdiocese of Indianapolis

(Archidioecesis Indianapolitana)

MOST REVEREND CHARLES C. THOMPSON

Archbishop of Indianapolis; ordained May 30, 1987; appointed Bishop of Evansville April 26, 2011; ordained June 29, 2011; appointed Archbishop of Indianapolis June 13, 2017; installed July 28, 2017. Office: 1400 N. Meridian St., Indianapolis, IN 46202-2367.

The Archbishop Edward T. O'Meara Catholic Center: 1400 N. Meridian St., Indianapolis, IN 46202-2367. T: 317-236-1400.
www.archindy.org
webmaster@archindy.org

Square Miles 13,758.

Established a Diocese in 1834; established an Archdiocese December 19, 1944 by decree of Pope Pius XII.

Comprises the Counties of Bartholomew, Brown, Clark, Clay, Crawford, Dearborn, Decatur, Fayette, Floyd, Franklin, Hancock, Harrison, Hendricks, Henry, Jackson, Jefferson, Jennings, Johnson, Lawrence, Marion, Monroe, Morgan, Ohio, Orange, Owen, Parke, Perry, Putnam, Ripley, Rush, Scott, Shelby, Switzerland, Union, Vermillion, Vigo, Washington and Wayne, and the township of Harrison in Spencer County, in the southern part of Indiana.

For legal titles of parishes and archdiocesan institutions, consult the Chancery Office.

STATISTICAL OVERVIEW

Personnel

Archbishops....1
Abbots....1
Retired Abbots....1
Priests: Diocesan Active in Diocese....72
Priests: Diocesan Active Outside Diocese....4
Priests: Retired, Sick or Absent....45
Number of Diocesan Priests....121
Religious Priests in Diocese....23
Total Priests in your Diocese....144
Extern Priests in Diocese....16
Ordinations:
Diocesan Priests....2
Religious Priests....2
Transitional Deacons....2
Permanent Deacons....15
Permanent Deacons in Diocese....43
Total Brothers....109
Total Sisters....363

Parishes

Parishes....126
With Resident Pastor:
Resident Diocesan Priests....83
Resident Religious Priests....16
Without Resident Pastor:
Administered by Priests....14
Administered by Deacons....2
Administered by Religious Women....3
Administered by Lay People....2
Administered by Pastoral Teams, etc.....6
Professional Ministry Personnel:
Brothers....5
Sisters....14
Lay Ministers....214

Welfare

Catholic Hospitals....2
Total Assisted....2,707,028
Homes for the Aged....2
Total Assisted....210
Day Care Centers....2
Total Assisted....930
Specialized Homes....2
Total Assisted....230
Special Centers for Social Services....8
Total Assisted....119,971

Educational

Seminaries, Diocesan....2
Students from This Diocese....28
Students from Other Dioceses....118
Diocesan Students in Other Seminaries....1
Total Seminarians....29
Colleges and Universities....2
Total Students....4,884
High Schools, Diocesan and Parish....7
Total Students....3,318
High Schools, Private....4
Total Students....2,348
Elementary Schools, Diocesan and Parish....56
Total Students....16,321
Elementary Schools, Private....1
Total Students....117
Catechesis/Religious Education:
High School Students....2,157
Elementary Students....9,036
Total Students under Catholic Instruction....38,210
Teachers in Diocese:
Sisters....5
Lay Teachers....1,288

Vital Statistics

Receptions into the Church:
Infant Baptism Totals....2,844
Minor Baptism Totals....362
Adult Baptism Totals....210
Received into Full Communion....447
First Communions....3,064
Confirmations....2,551
Marriages:
Catholic....519
Interfaith....229
Total Marriages....748
Deaths....2,023
Total Catholic Population....203,817
Total Population....2,794,392

LEADERSHIP

Archdiocesan Administration - t) 317-236-1400
Vicar General and Moderator of the Curia - Very Rev. Msgr. William F. Stumpf;
Chancellor - t) 317-236-1481 Christopher Walsh;
Archives - t) (317) 236-1538 archives@archindy.org www.archindy.org/archives Julie Motyka, Archivist;
Vice Chancellor - Very Rev. Eric M. Johnson;
Chief Financial Officer - Brian Burkert;
Board of Consultors - Most Rev. Charles C. Thompson, Chair; Very Rev. Msgr. William F. Stumpf; Very Rev. Eric M. Johnson;
Deaneries and Deans - Very Rev. Stephen W. Giannini, Indianapolis South; Very Rev. Richard Ginther, Indianapolis East; Very Rev. John P. McCaslin, Indianapolis West;
Finance Council - Most Rev. Charles C. Thompson, Chair; Very Rev. Msgr. William F. Stumpf, Vicar; Patrick Carney, Chair;

OFFICES AND DIRECTORS

Archdiocesan Review Board - Mary Catherine Horty, Chair; Rev. Todd Michael Goodson; Mary Ann Ransdell;
Council of Priests - Most Rev. Charles C. Thompson, Archbishop; Very Rev. Msgr. William F. Stumpf, Vicar Gen./Moderator of the Curia; Christopher Walsh, Chancellor;
Deacons' Personnel Board - Very Rev. Eric M. Johnson, Chair; Dcn. Michael East, Chair; Dcn. David Henn;
Priests' Personnel Board - Most Rev. Charles C. Thompson, Pres.; Very Rev. Eric M. Johnson; Very Rev. Douglas W. Marcotte;
Secretariat for Catholic Charities - t) 317-236-7325 David Bethuram, Exec.;
Catholic Charities Bloomington - t) 812-332-1262 Michael J Stribling, Clinical Dir.;
Catholic Charities Indianapolis - t) 317-236-1500 David Bethuram, Exec. Dir.;
Catholic Charities New Albany - t) 812-949-7305 Mark Casper, Dir.;
Catholic Charities Social Concerns - t) 317-473-0413 Theresa Chamblee;
Anti-Trafficking - Theresa Chamblee;
Catholic Campaign for Human Development -
Catholic Relief Services -
Justice for Immigrants -
Parish Social Ministry - Theresa Chamblee, Dir.;
Catholic Charities Tell City - t) 812-547-0903 Sr. Shellie Intravia, Dir.;
Catholic Charities Terre Haute - t) 812-232-1447 John C. Etling, Dir.;
Secretariat for Catholic Schools - t) 317-592-4051 Dr. Brian Disney, Exec.;
Catholic Education, School Improvement -
Office of Catholic Schools - Dr. Brian Disney, Supt.; Michelle Radomsky, Asst. Supt., Secondary Educ.; Sarah J. Watson, Asst. Supt., Elementary Educ.;
Secretariat for Communications - t) 317-236-1585 Michael A. Krokos, Editor;
Catholic Communications Center - Greg A. Otolski, Exec.;
Secretariat for Finance and Administrative Services - t) 317-236-1410 Brian Burkert, Exec.;
Accounting Services - Jenny Zelik, Controller;
Catholic Cemeteries Assoc. - t) 317-574-8898 Tony Lloyd, Buchanan Group;
Information Services - t) 317-261-3379 Kent Campbell, Dir.;
Management Services - t) 317-236-1452 Daniel Herbertz, Dir.;
Secretariat for Pastoral Ministries - Paul Sifuentes, Dir.;
Archdiocesan Office of Inter-Religious Affairs and Ecumenism - Very Rev. Richard Ginther, Dir.;
Office for Intercultural Ministry - t) 317-261-3380 Pearlette Springer, Coord., Black Catholic Ministry; Felix Navarette, Coord., Hispanic Ministry;
Office of Human Life and Dignity - t) 317-236-1543 Brie Anne Varick, Dir.;
Office of Marriage and Family Life - t) 317-236-1527 Gabriela Ross, Dir.;
Office of Youth Ministry - t) 317-236-1442 Paul Sifuentes, Dir.;
Parish Planning and Organizational Development -
Young Adult and College Campus Ministry - t) 317-592-4067 Meagan Morrisey, Dir.;
Secretariat for Stewardship and Development - t) 317-236-1462 Jolinda Moore, Exec.;
Mission Office - t) 317-236-1405 Very Rev. Msgr. William F. Stumpf, Dir.;
Office of Stewardship and Development - Jolinda Moore, Exec.; Kim Pohovey, Dir., Major & Planned Gifts; Dana Stone, Dir., Annual Appeals & Creative Designs;
Secretariat for Worship and Evangelization - t) 317-236-1483 Very Rev. Patrick J. Beidelman, Exec.;
Archdiocesan Cathedral - Very Rev. Patrick J. Beidelman, Pst.; Dcn. Stephen Hodges, Pst. Assoc.; Andrew Motyka, Music Min.;
Evangelization Commission - Very Rev. Patrick J. Beidelman, Exec.;
Ministry to Persons with Special Needs - t) 317-236-1448
Office of Catechesis - t) 317-236-1446 Ken Ogorek, Dir.;
Office of Worship - Very Rev. Patrick J. Beidelman, Exec.; Andrew Motyka, Dir.;
Retreat & Renewal Ministries and Fatima Retreat House - t) 317-545-7681 Georgene Beiriger, Dir.;
Vicar Judicial Metropolitan Tribunal - t) 317-236-1460 Very Rev. Joseph L. Newton;
Adjunct Vicar Judicial - Rev. Msgr. Frederick Easton; Rev. Robert J. Gilday; Rev. Paul M. Shikany;
Advocates - Kathryn Hubbard; Anthony Powers;
Archdiocesan Judge -
Auditor - Laura Torres, Ecclesiastical Notary/ Auditor;
Defender of the Bond/Promoter of Justice - Rev. Timothy M. Wyciskalla;
Ecclesiastical Notary - Maria Pietro;
Judge Instructors and Assessors - Joseph R. Gehret, Judge Instructor/Assessor; Daniel Ross, Judge Instructor/Assessor; Kay Summers, Assessor;
Vicariate for Clergy, Religious and Parish Life Coordinators - Very Rev. Eric M. Johnson, Vicar;
Deacon Formation, Office of - t) 317-236-1490 Dcn. Kerry Blandford, Dir.;
Deacons, Office of - Dcn. Michael East, Dir.;
Personnel: Priests, Religious and Parish Life Coordinators - t) 317-236-1495 Very Rev. Eric M. Johnson;
Priestly and Religious Vocations - t) 317-236-1490 Rev. Eric M. Augenstein, Dir.; Very Rev. Michael T. Keucher, Dir.;
Victim Assistance Coordinator - t) (317) 236-1548 victimsassistance@archindy.org

HUMAN RESOURCES

Human Resources - t) 317-236-1594 Andrea Wunnenberg, Dir.;

PARISHES, MISSIONS, AND CLERGY

STATE OF INDIANA

AURORA

St. Mary Immaculate Conception Catholic Church, Aurora, Inc. - 203 Fourth St., Aurora, IN 47001-1298 t) 812-926-0060 parish.office@dccatholics.com mystmarys.com/ Rev. Jonathan P. Meyer, Pst.; Rev. Daniel J. Mahan, Pst.; Anna Townsend, Bus. Mgr.; CRP Stds.: 8
St. Mary Immaculate Conception School - (Grades K-8) 211 Fourth St., Aurora, IN 47001 t) 812-926-1558 stmary@uswebmail.biz www.stmaryschoolaurora.com Randy Dennis, Prin.; Stds.: 98; Lay Tchrs.: 9

BATESVILLE

St. Louis Catholic Church, Batesville, Inc. - 13 St. Louis Pl., Batesville, IN 47006-1393 t) 812-934-3204 x249 (CRP); 812-934-3204 amytongesreligioused@st.louisschool.org www.stlouis-batesville.org Rev. Stanley Pondo, Pst.; Rev. Suresh Ganta, HGN (India), Par. Vicar; Dcn. Ronald Freyer; Amy Tonges, DRE; CRP Stds.: 177
St. Louis Catholic Church, Batesville, Inc. School - (Grades PreSchool-8) 17 St. Louis Pl., Batesville, IN 47006 t) 812-934-3310 cmoeller@st.louisschool.org Patty Mauer, Prin.; Stds.: 321; Lay Tchrs.: 21

BEDFORD

St. Vincent de Paul Catholic Church, Bedford, Inc. - 1723 I St., Bedford, IN 47421-4221 t) 812-275-6539 parish@svsbedford.org www.yourcclc.org Dcn. David Reising; Dcn. Matthew T. Scarlett; Rev. Jegan Peter, Admin.; CRP Stds.: 30
St. Vincent de Paul Catholic School - (Grades K-8) 923 18th St., Bedford, IN 47421 t) 812-279-2540 info@svsbedford.org www.svsbedford.org Teresa Underwood, Prin.; Stds.: 180; Lay Tchrs.: 10

BEECH GROVE

Holy Name of Jesus Catholic Church, Indianapolis, Inc. - 89 N. 17th Ave., Beech Grove, IN 46107-1531 t) 317-784-5454 x5 (CRP); 317-784-5454 jchrisman@holyname.cc www.holyname.cc Rev. Robert J. Robeson, Pst.; Dcn. Gary M. Blackwell; Joseph Chrisman, Pst. Assoc.; CRP Stds.: 37
Holy Name of Jesus School - 21 N. 17th Ave., Beech Grove, IN 46107 t) 317-784-9078 awright@holyname.cc www.holyname.cc/school.htm Amy Wright, Prin.; Stds.: 262; Sr. Tchrs.: 1; Lay Tchrs.: 19

BLOOMINGTON

St. Charles Borromeo Catholic Church, Bloomington, Inc. - 2222 E. 3rd St., Bloomington, IN 47401-5385 t) 812-336-6846; 812-334-1664 (CRP) frkovatch@stcharlesbloomington.org www.stcharlesbloomington.org Rev. Thomas G. Kovatch, Pst.; Rose Johnson, DRE; CRP Stds.: 98
St. Charles Borromeo School - (Grades PreK-8) 2224 E. 3rd St., Bloomington, IN 47401 t) 812-336-5853 Madonna Paskash, Prin.; Stds.: 348; Lay Tchrs.: 27
St. John the Apostle Catholic Church, Bloomington, Inc. - 4607 W. State Rd. 46, Bloomington, IN 47404-9255 t) 812-876-1974 info@sjabloomington.org; sjasecretary@sjabloomington.org www.sjabloomington.org Rev. Dennis M. Duvelius, Pst.; Dcn. Richard Stanford; CRP Stds.: 38
St. Paul Catholic Center, Bloomington, Inc. - 1413 E. 17th St., Bloomington, IN 47408-1602 t) 812-339-5561 www.hoosiercatholic.org Very Rev. Patrick F. Hyde, O.P., Pst.; Rev. Reginald Wolford, OP, Par. Vicar; Rev. Dennis C. Woerter, O.P., Par. Vicar; Rev. Simon-Felix Michalski, OP, Par. Vicar; Dcn. Ronald Reimer; Rev. Justus Marcel Pokrzewinski, OP, In Res.; CRP Stds.: 12

BRAZIL

Annunciation Catholic Church, Brazil, Inc. - 19 N. Alabama St., Brazil, IN 47834-2399 t) 812-448-1901 annunciationchurch@msn.com; secretary@annunciationbrazil.org www.annunciationbrazil.org Rev. John J. Hollowell, Pst.; Rev. Edward Suresh (India), Par. Vicar; Natalie Shonk, DRE; CRP Stds.: 28

BRISTOW

St. Isidore the Farmer Catholic Church, Bristow, Inc. - 6501 St. Isidore Rd., Bristow, IN 47515; Mailing: P.O. Box 54, Bristow, IN 47515 t) 812-843-5713 saintisidore@psci.net Rev. Luke Waugh, O.S.B., Admin.; Ashley Kellams, DRE; CRP Stds.: 50

BROOKVILLE

St. Michael the Archangel Catholic Church, Brookville, Inc. - 145 St. Michael Blvd., Brookville, IN 47012

t) 765-647-5462 bbertsch131@gmail.com brookvilleparishes.com/ Rev. Vincent P. Lampert, Pst.; Dcn. Steven C. Tsuleff; Brenda Bertsch, Faith Formation & Youth Min.; CRP Stds.: 41

St. Michael the Archangel School - (Grades PreK-8) t) 765-647-4961 Chad M. Moeller, Prin.; Stds.: 226; Lay Tchrs.: 13

Oratory of SS. Philomena and Cecilia Catholic Church, Brookville, Inc. - 16194 St. Mary's Rd., Brookville, IN 47012 t) 765-647-0310 priest1.sspc@gmail.com www.latinmassbrookville.com/ Rev. Howard Remski, F.S.S.P., Admin.;

St. Peter Catholic Church, Franklin County, Inc. - 1207 East Rd., Brookville, IN 47012-9365 t) 765-647-5462 brookvilleparishes@gmail.com www.brookvilleparishes.com/ Rev. Vincent P. Lampert, Pst.; Dcn. Steven C. Tsuleff; Susan Leffingwell, DRE; CRP Stds.: 27

BROWNSBURG

St. Malachy Catholic Church, Brownsburg, Inc. - 9833 E. Co. Rd. 750 N., Brownsburg, IN 46112-9633 t) 317-852-3195 jmccorkhill@stmalachy.org www.stmalachy.org/ Rev. Sean R. Danda, Pst.; Rev. Michael Clawson, Par. Vicar; Dcn. Daniel Collier; Dcn. Richard Renzi; Jean McCorkhill, Faith Formation Coord.; CRP Stds.: 442

St. Malachy Catholic Church, Brownsburg, Inc. School - (Grades PreK-8) 7410 N. Co. Rd. 1000 E., Brownsburg, IN 46112 t) 317-852-2242 abostrom@stmalachy.org Saundra Kennison, Prin.; Stds.: 494; Lay Tchrs.: 30

CAMBRIDGE CITY

St. Elizabeth of Hungary Catholic Church, Cambridge City, Inc. - 333 W. Maple St., Cambridge City, IN 47327-1130 t) 765-478-3242 frjhall@gmail.com; religioused.lawson@gmail.com www.st-eliz.org Rev. John M. Hall, Pst.; Patty Hughes, Bus. Mgr.; CRP Stds.: 6

CHARLESTOWN

St. Michael Catholic Church, Charlestown, Inc. - 101 St. Michael Dr., Charlestown, IN 47111-1635 t) 812-256-3200; 812-294-4682 (CRP) pastor@northclarkcountycatholic.org; stmichaelsecretary@northclarkcountycatholic.org stmichaelcharlestown.org Rev. Jeyaseelan W. Sengolraj, Admin.; Rita Poff, Prin.; Cherie Kopp, Bus. Mgr.; Jessica Sarver, Pst. Assoc.; CRP Stds.: 57

Child Care Center - 102 St. Michael Dr., Charlestown, IN 47111 t) 812-256-3503 (PreK-K)

CLARKSVILLE

St. Anthony of Padua Catholic Church, Clarksville, Inc. - 316 N. Sherwood Ave., Clarksville, IN 47129-2724 t) 812-282-2290 parishoffice@stanthony-clarksville.org www.stanthony-clarksville.org Rev. John Bamman, O.F.M.Conv., Pst.; Randy Munday, Bus. Mgr.; Edwin Jarboe, Youth Min.; Timothy Glasscock, Music Min.; Rev. Florian Tiell, O.F.M.Conv., In Res.; Rev. Robert St. Martin, O.F.M.Conv., In Res.; Rev. Mark Weaver, O.F.M.Conv., In Res.; CRP Stds.: 10

St. Anthony of Padua School - (Grades K-8) 320 N. Sherwood Ave., Clarksville, IN 47129 t) 812-282-2144 s.tucker@stanthony-clarksville.org www.stap.us Stephany Tucker, Prin.; Stds.: 249; Lay Tchrs.: 19

CLINTON

Sacred Heart Church, Clinton, Inc. - 610 S. 6th St., Clinton, IN 47842-2016 t) 765-832-8468 sacredheartclinton@sbcglobal.net Rev. Joby Abraham Puthussery, Admin.; CRP Stds.: 18

COLUMBUS

St. Bartholomew Catholic Church, Columbus, IN - 1306 27th St., Columbus, IN 47201-6375 t) 812-379-9353 mjanes@stbparish.net; mnieto@stbparish.net www.saintbartholomew.org Rev. Christopher Wadelton, Pst.; Rev. Clement T. Davis, Assoc. Pst.; Dcn. William Jones; Dcn. Juan Carlos Ramirez; CRP Stds.: 441

St. Bartholomew School - 1305 27th St, Columbus, IN 47201-6375 stbirish.net/ Julia King, Prin.; Stds.: 349; Lay Tchrs.: 23

CONNERSVILLE

St. Gabriel Catholic Church, Connersville, Inc. - 232 W. Ninth St., Connersville, IN 47331-2099 t) 765-825-8578; 765-285-8578 (CRP) mfronckowiak@stgabrielconnersville.com Rev. Dustin M. Boehm, Pst.; Pamela S. Rader, Bus. Mgr.; Melissa Fronckowiak, DRE; CRP Stds.: 63

St. Gabriel Catholic Church, Connersville, Inc. School - (Grades PreK-6) 224 W. Ninth St., Connersville, IN 47331 t) 765-825-7951 sbarth@stgabrielconnersville.org www.stgabriel.k12.in.us Michelle Struewing, Prin.; Stds.: 140; Lay Tchrs.: 8

CORYDON

St. Joseph Catholic Church, Corydon, Inc. - 312 E. High St., Corydon, IN 47112-1299 t) 812-738-2742 www.catholic-community.org/ Rev. Kyle Rodden, Admin.; Dcn. Timothy Elder; CRP Stds.: 52

St. Joseph Catholic Church, Corydon, Inc. School - (Grades PreSchool-7) 512 N. Mulberry St., Corydon, IN 47112 t) 812-738-4549 Brittany King, Prin.; Stds.: 165; Lay Tchrs.: 13

DANVILLE

Queen of Peace Catholic Church, Danville, Inc. - 1005 W. Main St., Danville, IN 46122-1025 t) 317-745-4284 x13 (CRP); 317-745-4284 lkhansen@bluemarble.net; info@mqpdanville.org www.mqpdanville.org/ Rev. Michael C. Fritsch, Pst.; Lynn Hansen, DRE; CRP Stds.: 109

DEPAUW

St. Bernard Catholic Church, Frenchtown, Inc. - 7600 Hwy 337 N.W., Depauw, IN 47115-8558 t) 812-347-2326 www.saintmichaelschurch.net Rev. Aaron J. Pfaff, Pst.; Dcn. John R. Jacobi, DRE; CRP Stds.: 36

EDINBURGH

Holy Trinity Catholic Church, Edinburgh, Inc. - 100 Keeley St., Edinburgh, IN 46124-0216; Mailing: P.O. Box 216, Edinburgh, IN 46124-0216 t) 812-526-9460 parishoffice@holytrinityedinburgh.net; rbwoodard@ameritech.net www.holytrinityedinburgh.net Rev. Todd Michael Goodson, Moderator; Rev. Ashok Valabazzi, HGN (India), Sacr. Min.; Rev. Clement T. Davis, Sacr. Min.; Sr. Donna M. Prickel, O.S.F., Parish Life Coord.; Dcn. Jorge Arturo Sanchez Leanos; CRP Stds.: 18

FLOYDS KNOBS

St. John the Baptist Catholic Church, Starlight, Inc. - 8310 St. John Rd., Floyds Knobs, IN 47119-8545 t) 812-923-5785 stjohnstarlight@aol.com www.stjohnstarlight.org/ Rev. Joseph West, O.F.M.Conv., Pst.; Rev. Wilfred E. Day, Sacr. Min.; Stephanie Willis, Pst. Assoc.; CRP Stds.: 26

St. Mary of the Annunciation Catholic Church, Navilleton, Inc. - 7500 Navilleton Rd., Floyds Knobs, IN 47119-8603 t) 812-923-5419 parish.navstar@gmail.com stmarysnavilleton.com/ Rev. Joseph West, O.F.M.Conv., Pst.; Rev. Wilfred E. Day, Sacr. Min.; Stephanie Willis, DRE; CRP Stds.: 50

St. Mary-of-the-Knobs Catholic Church, Floyds Knobs, Inc. - 3033 Martin Rd., Floyds Knobs, IN 47119-9107 t) 812-923-3011; 812-923-2459 (CRP) faithformation@yoursmk.org www.yoursmk.org/ Rev. William G. Marks, Pst.; CRP Stds.: 187

St. Mary-of-the-Knobs School - (Grades PreSchool-8) t) 812-923-1630 www.smkcatholicschool.com/ Tracy Jansen, Prin.; Stds.: 329; Lay Tchrs.: 18

FORTVILLE

St. Thomas the Apostle, Fortville, Inc. - 523 S. Merrill St., Fortville, IN 46040-1428 t) 317-485-5102 secretary@stthomasfortville.com stthomasfortville.com/ Rev. Aaron M. Jenkins; Leah Sears, DRE; CRP Stds.: 58

FRANKLIN

St. Rose of Lima Catholic Church, Franklin, Inc. - 114 Lancelot Dr., Franklin, IN 46131-8806 t) 317-736-6754 (CRP); 317-738-3929 info@stroselions.net strosechurch.saintrose.net/ Rev. Todd Michael Goodson, Pst.; Rev. Timothy DeCrane, Pst.; Claire Jackson, CRE; CRP Stds.: 73

St. Rose of Lima School - (Grades PreK-8) t) 317-738-3451 ktekippe@stroselions.net Kim Tekippe, Prin.; Stds.: 89; Lay Tchrs.: 11

FRENCH LICK

Our Lady of the Springs Catholic Church, French Lick, Inc. - 8796 W. State Rd. 56, French Lick, IN 47432-9391 t) 812-936-4568 www.occ-indy.org/ Rev. Randall R. Summers, Pst.; CRP Stds.: 11

FULDA

St. Boniface Catholic Church, Fulda, Inc. - 15519 N. State Rd. 545, Fulda, IN 47536; Mailing: P.O. Box 8, Saint Meinrad, IN 47577-0008 t) 812-357-5533 sbcatholic.church/ Rev. Anthony Vinson, O.S.B., Admin.; CRP Stds.: 60

GREENCASTLE

St. Paul the Apostle Catholic Church, Putnam County, Inc. - 202 E. Washington St., Greencastle, IN 46135-1549 t) 765-653-5678 www.stpaul-greencastle.com/ Rev. John J. Hollowell, Pst.; Rev. Edward Suresh (India), Par. Vicar; Tonya Welker, DRE; CRP Stds.: 52

GREENFIELD

St. Michael Catholic Church, Greenfield, Inc. - 519 Jefferson Blvd., Greenfield, IN 46140-1899 t) 317-462-4240 prichey@stmichaelsgrfld.org www.stmichaelsgrfld.org/ Rev. Aaron M. Jenkins, Pst.; Jonathan Higgins, Music Dir. & CRE; CRP Stds.: 56

St. Michael Catholic School - (Grades PreK-8) 515 Jefferson Blvd., Greenfield, IN 46140 t) 317-462-6380 rhittel@stmichaelsgrfld.org www.school-stmichaelsgrfld.org Ruth Hittel, Prin.; Stds.: 159; Lay Tchrs.: 10

GREENSBURG

St. Catherine of Siena Parish, Decatur County, Inc. - 9995 E. Base Rd., Greensburg, IN 47240-8406 t) 812-934-2880; 812-663-4754 (CRP) stcatherine47240@gmail.com www.stcatherinesparish.org Rev. William L. Ehalt, Pst.; Cynthia L Lamping, Bus. Mgr.; Kelly Bedel, DRE; CRP Stds.: 220

Immaculate Conception Catholic Church, Millhousen, Inc. - 2081 E. County Rd., 820 S., Greensburg, IN 47240-9636 t) 812-591-2362 sisterdonna@millhousenchurch.com; melea@millhousenchurch.com www.millhousenchurch.com Rev. Binu Mathew, Admin.; Melea Gault, DRE; CRP Stds.: 30

St. Mary Catholic Church, Greensburg, Inc. - 1331 E. Hunter Robbins Way, Greensburg, IN 47240-2197 t) 812-663-8427; 765-663-8427 (CRP) frmeyer@etczone.com; mgehrich@stmarysgreensburg.com church.stmarysgreensburg.com/ Rev. John A. Meyer, Pst.; Dcn. Bradley Anderson; Megan Gehrich, Youth Dir. & CRE; CRP Stds.: 146

St. Mary Catholic Church, Greensburg, Inc. School - (Grades PreK-8) t) 812-663-2804 nbuening@stmarysgreensburg.com Nancy Buening, Prin.; Stds.: 343; Lay Tchrs.: 23

GREENVILLE

St. Michael Catholic Church, Bradford, Inc. - 11400 Farmers Ln., N.E., Greenville, IN 47124 t) 812-364-6646; 812-364-6173 (CRP) stmichaels@mw.twcbc.com; johnjacobi@insightbb.com saintmichaelschurch.net Rev. Aaron J. Pfaff, Pst.; Dcn. John R. Jacobi, DRE; Dcn. Christopher Rainbolt; CRP Stds.: 116

GREENWOOD

SS. Francis and Clare of Assisi Catholic Church, Greenwood, Inc. - 5901 Olive Branch Rd., Greenwood, IN 46143-8181 t) 317-859-4673 ssfcparish@ss-fc.org; parishsecretary@ss-fc.org www.ss-fc.org Very Rev. Stephen W. Giannini, Pst.; Dcn. Ronald Pirau; Patricia McGill, DRE; CRP Stds.: 431

SS. Francis and Clare of Assisi Catholic Church, Greenwood, Inc. School - (Grades PreK-8) t) 317-215-2826 ssfcschool@ss-fc.org Betty Popp, Prin.; Stds.: 378; Lay Tchrs.: 23

Our Lady of the Greenwood Catholic Church, Inc. - 335 S. Meridian St., Greenwood, IN 46143-1698 t) 317-888-2861 becky@olgreenwood.org www.olgreenwood.org Rev. Todd Michael Goodson, Pst.; Rev. Timothy DeCrane, Pst.; Rev. Ashok Valabazzi, HGN (India), Par. Vicar; Dcn. Reynaldo Nava; Rev. Mauro G. Rodas, Sacr. Min.; Becky Cope, DRE; CRP Stds.: 255

Our Lady of the Greenwood Catholic Church, Inc. School - (Grades PreK-8) 399 S. Meridian St., Greenwood, IN 46143 t) (317) 881-1300 kclady@olg.org Kent Clady, Prin.; Stds.: 283; Lay Tchrs.: 23

GUILFORD

All Saints Catholic Church, Dearborn, Inc. - 25743 State Rte. 1, Guilford, IN 47022-8979 t) 812-576-4302 emilyalig.asp@gmail.com www.allssaintscatholic.net Rev. Jonathan P. Meyer, Pst.; Rev. Daniel J. Mahan, Pst.; Dcn. Robert W. Decker; Dcn. Mark Schmidl; CRP Stds.: 666

HENRYVILLE

St. Francis Catholic Church, Henryville, Inc. - 101 N. Ferguson St., Henryville, IN 47126; Mailing: 101 St. Michaels Dr., Charlestown, IN 47111 t) 812-294-4682 stfrancissecretary@northclarkcountycatholic.org; pastor@northclarkcountycatholic.org stfrancisxavierhenryville.org Rev. Jeyaseelan W. Sengolraj, Admin.; CRP Stds.: 25

INDIANAPOLIS

SS. Peter and Paul Cathedral, Indianapolis, Inc. - 1347 N. Meridian St., Indianapolis, IN 46202 t) 317-634-4519 www.ssppc.org Very Rev. Patrick J. Beidelman, Rector; Dcn. Stephen Hodges, Pst. Assoc.; Dcn. Nathan C. Schallert; Andrew Motyka, Music Min.; Very Rev. Eric M. Johnson, In Res.; Very Rev. Joseph L. Newton, In Res.;

St. Andrew the Apostle Catholic Church, Indianapolis, Inc. - 4052 E. 38th St., Indianapolis, IN 46218-1444 t) 317-546-1571 kblandford@archindy.org www.standrewindy.org Dcn. Kerry Blandford, Parish Life Coord.; Rev. Francis Joseph Kalapurackal, Moderator; Rev. Jeffrey H. Godecker, Sacr. Min.; CRP Stds.: 6

St. Ann Catholic Church, Indianapolis, Inc. - 6350 S. Mooresville Rd., Indianapolis, IN 46221-4519 t) 317-821-2909 saintannchurc@aol.com www.st-ann-rcindy.org Rev. Jude Meril Sahayam, Admin.; Dcn. Joseph J. Beauchamp; Lucy Castaneda, DRE; Mike McKay, Music Min.; Linda D Routon, Bus. Mgr.; CRP Stds.: 37

St. Anthony Catholic Church, Indianapolis, Inc. - 337 N. Warman Ave., Indianapolis, IN 46222-4094 t) 317-636-4828; 317-543-7729 (CRP) saintanthonybusiness@gmail.com; stanthonyreligioused19@gmail.com www.saintanthonyindy.org Rev. Juan Jose Valdes, Pst.; Dcn. Elvin Hernandez; Yadira Villatoro, DRE; David Sheets, Bus. Mgr.; CRP Stds.: 195

St. Barnabas Catholic Church, Indianapolis, Inc. - 8300 Rahke Rd., Indianapolis, IN 46217-4999 t) 317-882-0724 jsheehan@stbindy.org www.stbindy.org Rev. Guy R. Roberts, Pst.; Rev. Eustace Thang, Par. Vicar; Dcn. Jerome R. Matthews; Dcn. Thomas Hosty; Joe Sheehan, Dir., Faith Formation; CRP Stds.: 86

St. Barnabas School - (Grades PreK-8) t) 317-881-7422 Ryan Schnarr, Prin.; Stds.: 491; Lay Tchrs.: 29

Christ The King Catholic Church, Indianapolis, Inc. - 5884 Crittenden Ave., Indianapolis, IN 46220 t) 317-255-3666 cbeckerich@ctk-indy.org www.ctk-indy.org Rev. Robert Jason Hankee, Pst.; Rev. Msgr. Anthony R. Volz, Par. Vicar; Quanah Jeffries, DRE; Dominic Duray, Music Min.; CRP Stds.: 33

Christ the King School - 5858 Crittenden Ave., Indianapolis, IN 46220 t) 317-257-9366 info@ctk-indy.org Ed Seib, Prin.; Stds.: 367; Lay Tchrs.: 24

St. Christopher Catholic Church, Indianapolis, Inc. - 5301 W. 16th St., Indianapolis, IN 46224-6497 t) 317-241-6314 madefazio@stchrisindy.org; billsvv@stchrisindy.org www.stchrisindy.org Rev. Paul M. Shikany, Pst.; Rev. Tiago Vilanculo, CMM (Mozambique), Par. Vicar; Sr. Kathleen Morrissey, O.P., Pst. Assoc.; William Szolek-Van Valkenburgh, Pst. Assoc.; Sr. Mary DeFazio, S.P., Faith Formation & Youth Min.; Peter Kadeli, Music Dir.; CRP Stds.: 100

St. Christopher School - 5335 W. 16th St., Indianapolis, IN 46224 kking@stchrisindy.org Karen King, Prin.; Stds.: 176; Lay Tchrs.: 12

St. Gabriel the Archangel Catholic Church, Indianapolis, Inc. - 6000 W. 34th St., Indianapolis, IN 46224-1297 t) 317-299-9924 (CRP); 317-291-7014 www.stgabrielindy.org Rev. Cyprian Eranimus Fernandez (India), Admin.; Rev. Nicholas Ajpacaja Tzoc, Pst.; CRP Stds.: 180

Good Shepherd Roman Catholic Church, Indianapolis, Inc. - 2905 S. Carson Ave., Indianapolis, IN 46203-5216 t) 317-783-3158 goodshepherdcc@sbcglobal.net www.goodshepherdindy.org Rev. Robert J. Robeson, Admin.; Rev. Jeffery Moore, Sacr. Min.; Patricia Shepardson, Bus. Mgr.; CRP Stds.: 274

Holy Angels Catholic Church, Indianapolis, Inc. - 740 W. 28th St., Indianapolis, IN 46208-5099 t) 317-926-3324 holyangelsbulletin1@hotmail.com; canishalramsey@yahoo.com www.holyangelsindy.org Rev. John Ntawugashira, CMM, Admin.; Dcn. Wilfredo R. de la Rosa; Stephanie Whitley, DRE; Gayle Jones, Music Min.; CRP Stds.: 31

Holy Spirit Catholic Church, Indianapolis, Inc. - 7243 E. 10th St., Indianapolis, IN 46219-4990 t) 317-357-6915 (CRP); 317-353-9404 gtarter@holyspirit-indy.org www.holyspirit-indy.org Rev. Michael E. O'Mara, Pst.; Dcn. Michael Slinger; Gladys Tarter, DRE; Christian Kuphal, Music Min.; CRP Stds.: 396

Holy Spirit Catholic Church, Indianapolis, Inc. School - (Grades PreK-8) 7241 E. 10th St., Indianapolis, IN 46219 t) 317-352-1243 rparsons@holyspirit-indy.org Rita Parsons, Prin.; Stds.: 399; Lay Tchrs.: 25

Immaculate Heart of Mary Catholic Church, Indianapolis, Inc. - 5692 Central Ave., Indianapolis, IN 46220-3012 t) 317-257-2266 ueble@ihmindy.org www.ihmindy.org Rev. Robert W. Sims, Pst.; Ute Eble, DRE; Anna Harvey, Bus. Mgr.; CRP Stds.: 126

Immaculate Heart of Mary School - 317 E. 57th St., Indianapolis, IN 46220 t) 317-255-5468 schoolinfo@ihmindy.org Chris Kolakovich, Prin.; Stds.: 390; Lay Tchrs.: 27

St. Joan of Arc Catholic Church, Indianapolis, Inc. - 4217 Central Ave., Indianapolis, IN 46205-1896 t) 317-283-5508 kmurphy@sjoa.org www.sjoa.org Rev. Thomas L. Schliessmann, Pst.; Dcn. Mark Henry; Melinda Rivelli, Pst. Assoc.; Kyle Murphy, Pst. Assoc.; Joseph Burrows, Music Min.; CRP Stds.: 137

St. Joan of Arc School - (Grades PreK-8) 500 E. 42nd St., Indianapolis, IN 46205 t) 317-283-1518 jandriole@sjoa.org Nancy Kmiecik, Prin.; Stds.: 214; Lay Tchrs.: 14

St. John the Evangelist Catholic Church, Indianapolis, Inc. - 126 W. Georgia St., Indianapolis, IN 46225-1004 t) 317-635-2021 www.stjohnsindy.org/ Rev. Rick Nagel, Pst.; Dcn. David J. Bartolowits; Daniel Padilla, Music Min.; CRP Stds.: 65

St. Joseph Catholic Church, Indianapolis, Inc. - 1401 S. Mickley Ave., Indianapolis, IN 46241 t) 317-244-9002 stjosephschurch@hotmail.com www.stjosephindy.org Rev. Robert T. Hausladen, Pst.; Rev. Minh Quang Duong, Assoc. Pastor & Chap., Vietnamese Catholic Community; Judy Meyers, DRE; Mike McKay, Music Min.;

St. Jude Catholic Church, Indianapolis, Inc. - 5353 McFarland Rd., Indianapolis, IN 46227-7098 t) 317-786-4371 bulletin@stjudeindy.org; pmarshall@studeindy.org www.stjudeindy.org Rev. Peter Marshall, Pst.; Rev. Didier Sampungi, CMM (Congo), Par. Vicar; Dcn. David Henn; Dcn. Jim Kitchens; Tammy Stewart, CRE; CRP Stds.: 86

St. Jude Catholic Church, Indianapolis, Inc. School - 5375 McFarland Rd, Indianapolis, IN 46227 t) 317-784-6828 bmeece@sjsindy.org Beth Meece, Prin.; Stds.: 540; Lay Tchrs.: 27

St. Lawrence Catholic Church, Lawrence, Inc. - 6944 E. 46th St., Indianapolis, IN 46226-3704 t) 317-546-4065 www.saintlawrence.net Rev. Vincent M. Gillmore, Admin.; Rev. Jin Seung Pius Park, Assoc. Pst.; Claudia Diaz, CRE; CRP Stds.: 95

St. Lawrence Catholic Church, Lawrence, Inc. School - (Grades PreSchool-8) 6950 E. 46th St., Indianapolis, IN 46226 t) 317-543-4923 school.saintlawrence.net Andy Maxson, Prin.; Stds.: 224; Lay Tchrs.: 20

Saint Luke Catholic Church, Indianapolis, Inc. - 7575 Holliday Dr. E., Indianapolis, IN 46260-3697 t) 317-259-4373 www.stluke.org Rev. Msgr. Joseph F. Schaedel, Pst.; Rev. Jayaraju Bandari, HGN (India), Par. Vicar; Sr. Diane Carollo, S.G.L., DRE; Erin Jeffries, Spiritual Adv./Care Srvcs.; Thomas Nichols, Music Min.; Frank Loughery, Bus. Mgr.; CRP Stds.: 144

Saint Luke Catholic Church, Indianapolis, Inc. School - (Grades PreSchool-8) 7650 N. Illinois St., Indianapolis, IN 46260; Mailing: 7575 Holliday Dr E, Indianapolis, IN 46260 t) 317-255-3912 Johnathan Grismore, Prin.; Laurie Breen, Preschool Dir.; Stds.: 559; Lay Tchrs.: 43

St. Mark the Evangelist Catholic Church, Indianapolis, Inc. - 535 E. Edgewood Ave., Indianapolis, IN 46227-2099 t) 317-787-8246 aswiezy@stmarkindy.org Rev. Timothy M. Wyciskalla, Pst.; Rev. Hau Hawm John Mang (Myanmar), Par. Vicar; Dcn. James Martin; Dcn. Paul F. Fisherkeller; Angi Swiezy, Dir., Faith Formation; CRP Stds.: 94

St. Mark the Evangelist School - (Grades PreK-8) 541 E. Edgewood Ave., Indianapolis, IN 46227 t) 317-786-4013 jkocher@stmarkindy.org Jen Kocher, Prin.; Stds.: 509; Lay Tchrs.: 23

Saint Mary of the Immaculate Conception Catholic Church, Indianapolis, Inc. - 311 N. New Jersey St., Indianapolis, IN 46204-2174 t) 317-637-3983 www.saintmarysindy.org Very Rev. Patrick J. Beidelman, Pst.; Rev. Oscar Rivas, Par. Vicar; Andrew Motyka, Music Min.; Maureen Riley, Catechetical Leader; CRP Stds.: 112

St. Matthew Catholic Church, Indianapolis, Inc. - 4100 E. 56th St., Indianapolis, IN 46220-5599 t) 317-257-4297 x2215 (CRP); 317-257-4297 jlengerich@saintmatt.org www.saintmatt.org Rev. Msgr. William F. Stumpf, Pst.; Ann Tully, Pst. Assoc.; CRP Stds.: 24

St. Matthew School - (Grades PreK-8) t) 317-251-3997 David Smock, Prin.; Stds.: 367; Sr. Tchrs.: 1; Lay Tchrs.: 24

St. Michael the Archangel Catholic Church, Indianapolis, Inc. - 3354 W. 30th St., Indianapolis, IN 46222-2183 t) 317-926-7359 ddean@saintmichaelindy.org www.saintmichaelindy.org Rev. John Kamwendo, Pst.; Dcn. Michael Nygra; Angie Hyre, CRE & Youth Min.; CRP Stds.: 40

St. Monica Catholic Church, Indianapolis, Inc. - 6131 N. Michigan Rd., Indianapolis, IN 46228-1298 t) 317-253-2193 mjthomasday@stmonicaindy.org www.stmonicaindy.org Very Rev. John P. McCaslin, Pst.; Rev. Matthew Perronie, Par. Vicar; Dcn. Robert J. Beyke; Dcn. John R. McShea; Mary Jo Thomas-Day, DRE; CRP Stds.: 392

St. Monica School - 6131 N Michigan Rd, Indianapolis, IN 46228-1298 t) 317-255-7153 Eric Schommer, Prin.; Stds.: 353; Lay Tchrs.: 29

Nativity of Our Lord Jesus Christ Catholic Church, Indianapolis, Inc. - 7225 Southeastern Ave., Indianapolis, IN 46239-1209 t) 317-357-1200; 317-359-6075 (CRP) tmarlin@nativityindy.org www.nativityindy.org Rev. Eric M. Augenstein, Pst.; Dcn. John E. Hosier; CRP Stds.: 74

Nativity of Our Lord Jesus Christ School - 3310 S. Meadow Dr., Indianapolis, IN 46239 t) 317-357-1459 tbianchini@nativity.org Jenny Enrietto, Prin.; Stds.: 359; Lay Tchrs.: 24

Our Lady of Lourdes Catholic Church, Indianapolis, Inc. - 5333 E. Washington St., Indianapolis, IN 46219-6492 t) 317-356-7291 parish@ollindy.org www.ollindy.org Rev. Richard M. Ginther, Pst.; Dcn. Thomas Horn;

Matthew Fallon, DRE; CRP Stds.: 23

Our Lady of Lourdes School - 30 S. Downey Ave., Indianapolis, IN 46219 t) 317-357-3316 ckolakovich@ollindy.org Angie Therber, Prin.; Stds.: 161; Lay Tchrs.: 16

Our Lady of the Most Holy Rosary Catholic Church, Indianapolis, Inc. - 520 Stevens St., Indianapolis, IN 46203-1737 t) 317-636-4478 info@holyrosaryindy.org www.holyrosaryindy.org Rev. C. Ryan McCarthy, Pst.; Rev. Jeffrey Dufresne, In Res.; Elizabeth Welch, Music Min.; CRP Stds.: 128

St. Patrick Catholic Church, Indianapolis, Inc. - 950 Prospect St., Indianapolis, IN 46203-1897 t) 317-631-5824 www.stpatrickindy.org Rev. Dennis Schafer, O.F.M., Pst.; Rev. Duc Phan, OFM, Par. Vicar; Dcn. Emilio Ferrer-Soto; Sr. Karen Durliat, O.S.B., DRE; CRP Stds.: 177

St. Philip Neri Catholic Church, Indianapolis, Inc. - 550 N. Rural St., Indianapolis, IN 46201-2497 t) 317-631-8746 stphilipneri-indy.org/ Rev. Jeffrey Dufresne, Pst.; Amy Eggleston, Music Min.; CRP Stds.: 134

St. Pius X Catholic Church, Indianapolis, Inc. - 7200 Sarto Dr., Indianapolis, IN 46240-3599 t) 317-255-4534 kblandford@spxparish.org www.spxparish.org Rev. Francis Joseph Kalapurackal, Pst.; Rev. Hau Hawm John Mang (Myanmar), Sacr. Min.; Rev. Eustace Thang, Sacr. Min.; Dcn. Richard J. Wagner; Kaitlyn Blanford, Dir., Faith Formation; CRP Stds.: 138

St. Pius X Catholic Church School - (Grades K-8) 7200 Sarto Dr, Indianapolis, IN 46240-3599 t) 317-466-3361 Keely Beaudette, Prin.; Stds.: 426; Lay Tchrs.: 23

St. Rita Catholic Church, Indianapolis, Inc. - 1733 Dr. Andrew J. Brown Ave., Indianapolis, IN 46202-1998 t) 317-632-9349; 317-632-9346 (CRP) stritasecretary71@yahoo.com www.stritachurch-indy.org Rev. Jean Bosco Ntawugashira, CMM, Admin.; Dcn. Oliver L. Jackson; Anita Bardo, DRE; Angela Guynn, Bus. Mgr.; CRP Stds.: 31

St. Roch Catholic Church, Indianapolis, Inc. - 3600 S. Pennsylvania St., Indianapolis, IN 46227-1299 t) 317-784-1763 www.strochindy.org/ Rev. Douglas Hunter, Admin.; Dcn. Jerome Bessler; Meredith Elam, Music Min.; CRP Stds.: 40

St. Roch Catholic Church, Indianapolis, Inc. School - (Grades PreK-8) 3603 S. Meridian St., Indianapolis, IN 46217 t) 317-784-9144 Amy Wilson, Prin.; Stds.: 264; Sr. Tchrs.: 1; Lay Tchrs.: 22

Sacred Heart of Jesus Catholic Church, Indianapolis, Inc. - 1530 Union St., Indianapolis, IN 46225-1697 t) 317-638-5551 office@sacredheartindy.org www.sacredheartindy.org Rev. Ducanh Pham, O.F.M., Pst.; Rev. Dennis Schafer, O.F.M., Par. Vicar; Dr. R. Ryan Endris, Music Min.; Rev. Edward Boren, O.F.M., In Res.; Rev. Tom Fox, OFM, In Res.; Rev. Herb Jones, In Res.; CRP Stds.: 12

St. Simon the Apostle Catholic Church, Indianapolis, Inc. - 8155 Oaklandon Rd., Indianapolis, IN 46236-8578 t) 317-826-6000 x113 (CRP); 317-826-6000 . saintsimon.org/ Very Rev. Douglas W. Marcotte, Pst.; Dcn. James Wood; Dcn. Michael Braun; Kerry Schlimgen, DRE; CRP Stds.: 138

St. Simon the Apostle School - (Grades PreSchool-8) 8155 Oaklandon Rd, Indianapolis, IN 46236-8578 t) (317) 826-6000 x175 cdarragh@saintsimon.org Cathlene Darragh, Prin.; Stds.: 666; Lay Tchrs.: 40

St. Therese of the Infant Jesus Catholic Church, Indianapolis, Inc. - 4720 E. 13th St., Indianapolis, IN 46201-1798 t) 317-357-8352 littleflowerparish.org/ Rev. Robert J. Gilday, Pst.; CRP Stds.: 20

St. Therese of the Infant Jesus School - (Grades PreSchool-8) 1401 N. Bosart Ave, Indianapolis, IN 46202 t) 317-353-2282 kgawrys@littleflower.org www.littleflowerparish.org/school Kevin Gawrys, Prin.; Stds.: 291; Lay Tchrs.: 23

Saint Thomas Aquinas Catholic Church, Indianapolis, Inc. - 4625 N. Kenwood Ave., Indianapolis, IN 46208-3599 t) 317-253-1461 khudecek@staindy.org Rev. Varghese Maliakkal, Pst.; Karla Hudecek, Pst. Assoc.; CRP Stds.: 33

Saint Thomas Aquinas School - (Grades PreK-8) 4600 N. Illinois St., Indianapolis, IN 46208 t) 317-255-6244 nvaldiserri@staindy.org www.staschool-indy.org Nancy Valdiserri, Prin.; Stds.: 192; Lay Tchrs.: 19

JEFFERSONVILLE

St. Augustine Catholic Church, Jeffersonville, Inc. - 315 E. Chestnut St., Jeffersonville, IN 47131-0447; Mailing: P.O. Box 447, Jeffersonville, IN 47131-0447 t) 812-282-2677 faithformation@jeffersonvillecatholic.org www.jeffersonvillecatholic.org Rev. Adam L. Ahern; Dcn. John Thompson, Pst. Assoc.; Timothy Seman, Dir., Faith Formation; CRP Stds.: 26

Sacred Heart Catholic Church, Jeffersonville, Inc. - 1840 E. 8th St., Jeffersonville, IN 47130-4897 t) 812-282-2677 faithformation@jeffersonvillecatholic.org www.jeffersonvillecatholic.org/ Rev. Adam L. Ahern, Pst.; Dcn. John Thompson; Timothy Seman, Dir., Faith Formation; CRP Stds.: 31

Sacred Heart Catholic Church, Jeffersonville, Inc. School - (Grades PreK-8) 1842 E. 8th St., Jeffersonville, IN 47130 t) 812-283-3123 cbremmer@sacredheartschool.us Catherine Bremmer, Prin.; Stds.: 189; Lay Tchrs.: 10

LANESVILLE

St. Mary Catholic Church, Lanesville, Inc. - 2500 St. Mary's Dr., Lanesville, IN 47136 t) 812-952-2853 faithformation@frontier.com stmarylanesville.org/ Rev. Kyle Rodden, Pst.; Dcn. Richard Cooper; CRP Stds.: 42

LAWRENCEBURG

St. Lawrence Catholic Church, Lawrenceburg, Inc. - 542 Walnut St., Lawrenceburg, IN 47025-1861 t) 812-537-3992 parishoffice@dccatholics.com www.stlawrencechurch.us/ Rev. Jonathan P. Meyer, Pst.; Rev. Daniel J. Mahan, Pst.; Dcn. Kevin Daily; CRP Stds.: 19

St. Lawrence Catholic Church, Lawrenceburg, Inc. School - 524 Walnut St., Lawrenceburg, IN 47025 t) 812-537-3690 admin@sls-apps.org Randy Dennis, Prin.; Stds.: 266; Lay Tchrs.: 15

St. Teresa Benedicta of the Cross, Bright, Indiana - 23455 Gavin Ln., Lawrenceburg, IN 47025-8372 t) 812-656-8700 parishoffice@dccatholics.com; kim.s@stteresab.com stteresab.com/ Rev. Jonathan P. Meyer, Pst.; Rev. Daniel J. Mahan, Pst.; Kim Sprague, DRE; CRP Stds.: 11

LEOPOLD

St. Augustine Catholic Church, Leopold, Inc. - 18020 Lafayette St., Leopold, IN 47551 t) 812-843-5143 Rev. Brian G. Esarey, Pst.; CRP Stds.: 27

LIBERTY

St. Bridget Catholic Church, Liberty, Inc. - 404 E. Vine St., Liberty, IN 47353; Mailing: 232 W. 9th St., Connersville, IN 47331 t) 765-825-8578 Rev. Dustin M. Boehm, Pst.; CRP Stds.: 30

MADISON

Prince of Peace Catholic Church, Madison, Inc. - 413 E. 2nd ST, Madison, IN 47250; Mailing: 305 W. State St., Madison, IN 47250 t) 812-265-4166; 812-599-4883 (CRP) parishoffice@popeace.org www.popeace.org Rev. Christopher A. Craig, Pst.; Dcn. Michael Gardner; Dcn. Mike Boggs; CRP Stds.: 483

Pope John XXIII - 221 State St., Madison, IN 47250 t) 812-273-3957 bfewell@popeace.org Bethany Fewell, Prin.; Stds.: 280; Lay Tchrs.: 14

Shawe Memorial Junior-Senior High School - 201 W. State St., Madison, IN 47250 t) 812-273-2150 shaweprincipal@popeace.org Curt Gardner, Prin.; Stds.: 196; Lay Tchrs.: 16

MARENGO

St. Joseph Catholic Church, Marengo, Inc. - State Rd. 66, Marengo, IN 47115; Mailing: 7600 Hwy. 337, N.W., Depauw, IN 47115 t) 812-347-2326 saintbernardcatholicchurch@gmail.com; st.joseph.marengo.bulletin@gmail.com www.saintmichaelschurch.net Rev. Aaron J. Pfaff, Admin.; Rev. Frederick J. Denison, Sacr. Min.; CRP Stds.: 6

MARTINSVILLE

St. Martin of Tours Catholic Church, Martinsville, Inc. - 1709 E. Harrison St., Martinsville, IN 46151; Mailing: 1720 E. Harrison St., Martinsville, IN 46151 t) 765-349-7660 (CRP); 765-342-6379 tharte@rnetinc.net stmtours.org/ Very Rev. Stephen W. Giannini, Pst.; Dcn. David Urbanowski; Dcn. Tim Harte, CRE; CRP Stds.: 62

MILAN

St. Charles Catholic Church, Milan, Inc. - 213 Ripley St., Milan, IN 47031-0813; Mailing: P.O. Box 813, Milan, IN 47031-0813 t) 812-654-7015 (CRP); 812-654-7051 st.charleschurch@yahoo.com www.stcharlesmilan.com Rev. John A. Meyer, Moderator; Rev. Shaun P. Whittington, Pst.; Doug Bruner, DRE; CRP Stds.: 43

MITCHELL

St. Mary of the Assumption Catholic Church, Mitchell, Inc. - 777 S. 11th St., Mitchell, IN 47446-1643 t) 812-849-3570 www.yourcclc.org Rev. Jegan Peter, Pst.; Dcn. David Reising; Dcn. Thomas Scarlett; Melissa Epping, DRE; CRP Stds.: 11

MOORESVILLE

St. Thomas More Catholic Church, Mooresville, Inc. - 1200 N. Indiana St., Mooresville, IN 46158 t) 317-831-4142 mhawkins@stm-church.org Rev. Jude Meril Sahayam, Admin.; Marianne Hawkins, DRE; CRP Stds.: 105

MORRIS

St. Anthony of Padua Catholic Church, Morris, Inc. - 4781 E. Morris Church St., Morris, IN 47033; Mailing: PO Box 3, Morris, IN 47033-0003 t) 812-934-6218; 813-623-4618 (CRP) dre@stnicholas-sunman.org www.stanthonymorris.org Rev. Stanley Pondo, Pst.; Rev. Suresh Ganta, HGN (India), Sacr. Min.; Renee Jackson, DRE; CRP Stds.: 57

NAPOLEON

St. Maurice Catholic Church, Napoleon, Inc. - 8874 Harrison St., Napoleon, IN 47034-0017; Mailing: P.O. Box 17, Napoleon, IN 47034-0017 t) 812-852-4237 c) 812-621-7420 stmauricechurch.org/ Sr. Shirley Gerth, O.S.F., Parish Life Coord.; Rev. John A. Meyer, Moderator; Rev. William J. Turner, Sacramental Min.; CRP Stds.: 110

NASHVILLE

St. Agnes Catholic Church, Nashville, Inc. - 1008 McLary Rd., Nashville, IN 47448-0577; Mailing: P.O. Box 577, Nashville, IN 47448-0577 t) 812-988-2778; 812-325-9527 (CRP) stagnesnashville@gmail.com www.stagneschurchnashville.org Dcn. Russell B. Woodard, Parish Life Coord.; Very Rev. Eric M. Johnson, Sacr. Min.; Very Rev. Daniel J. Staublin, Moderator; Therese Chamblee, CRE; CRP Stds.: 34

NEW ALBANY

Holy Family Catholic Church, New Albany, Inc. - 129 W. Daisy Ln., New Albany, IN 47150 t) 812-944-8283 info@holyfamilynewalbany.org www.holyfamilynewalbany.org Very Rev. Jeremy M. Gries, Pst.; CRP Stds.: 33

Holy Family Catholic Church, New Albany, Inc. School - (Grades PreSchool-8) 217 W. Daisy Ln., New Albany, IN 47150 t) 812-944-6090 ahuber@holyfamilyeagles.com www.holyfamilyeagles.com Amy Huber, Prin.; Stds.: 301; Lay Tchrs.: 17

St. Mary of the Annunciation Catholic Church, New Albany, Inc. - 415 E. Eighth St., New Albany, IN 47150-3299 t) 812-944-0417 info@stmarysna.org www.stmarysna.org Rev. Mark Weaver, O.F.M.Conv., Pst.; Dcn. Martin Ignacio; Dcn. Jeffrey Powell, Pst. Assoc.; CRP Stds.: 139

Our Lady Of Perpetual Help Catholic Church, New Albany, Inc. - 1752 Scheller Ln., New Albany, IN 47150-2423 t) 812-944-1184 ecorrales@olphna.org www.olphna.org Rev. Joseph M. Feltz, Pst.; Dcn. Jeffrey Powell; Evonne Corrales, Youth & Children Min.; CRP Stds.: 46

Our Lady of Perpetual Help School - t) 812-944-7676 pmcguire@olphna.org school.olphna.org/school Pat McGuire, Prin.; Stds.: 378; Lay Tchrs.: 24

NEW CASTLE

St. Anne Catholic Church, New Castle, Inc. - 102 N. 19th St., New Castle, IN 47362-3999 t) 765-529-0933 religioused.lawson@gmail.com; frjhall@gmail.com Rev. John M. Hall, Pst.; Lawson Hunsicker, Coord., Faith Formation; CRP Stds.: 13

NORTH VERNON

St. Ann Catholic Church, Jennings County, Inc. - 629 Clay St., North Vernon, IN 47265 t) 812-346-3604 parishsecretary@stmarysnv.com; pastoralassoc@stmarysnv.com www.ccjc3.org Attended from St. Joseph, North Vernon. Rev. Jerry L. Byrd, Pst.; Dcn. Lawrence French; Joshua McNulty, Pst. Assoc.; CRP Stds.: 19

St. Joseph Catholic Church, Jennings County, Inc. - 629 Clay St, North Vernon, IN 47265 t) 812-346-4783; 812-346-3604 (CRP) pastoralassoc@stmarysnv.com www.ccjc3.org/ Rev. Jerry L. Byrd, Pst.; Dcn. Lawrence French; Joshua McNulty, Pst. Assoc.; CRP Stds.: 25

St. Mary Catholic Church, North Vernon, Inc. - 212 Washington St., North Vernon, IN 47265-1199 t) 812-346-3604 pastoralassoc@stmarysnv.com www.ccjc3.org/ Rev. Jerry L. Byrd, Pst.; Dcn. Lawrence French; Joshua McNulty, Pst. Assoc.; CRP Stds.: 102

St. Mary Catholic Church, North Vernon, Inc. School - (Grades PreK-8) 209 Washington St., North Vernon, IN 47265 t) 812-346-3445 stmarys@seidata.com www.stmarysnv.com Lisa Vogel, Prin.; Stds.: 227; Lay Tchrs.: 10

OLDENBURG

Holy Family Catholic Church, Oldenburg, Inc. - Main St., Oldenburg, IN 47036-0098; Mailing: P.O. Box 98, Oldenburg, IN 47036-0098 t) 812-934-3013 holyfamilybeth@gmail.com www.holyfamilychurcholdenburgin.com Rev. Carl Langenderfer, O.F.M., Admin.; Rev. Michael Chowning, O.F.M., In Res.; Rev. Joe Nelson, O.F.M., In Res.; Beth Geis, DRE; CRP Stds.: 370

OSGOOD

St. John the Baptist Catholic Church, Osgood, Inc. - 331 S. Buckeye St., Osgood, IN 47037-1305 t) 812-689-4244 stjohnsosgood@gmail.com Rev. Binu Mathew, Admin.;

PAOLI

Our Lord Jesus Christ the King Catholic Church, Paoli, Inc. - 833 S. Triangle Rd./Hwy 150 E, Paoli, IN 47454; Mailing: P O Box 544, Paoli, IN 47454 t) 765-932-3639 (CRP); 812-723-3900 christtheking1948@gmail.com; oconnellj53@frontier.com www.occ-indy.org/ Attended from Our Lady of the Springs, French Lick. Rev. Randall R. Summers, Pst.; Dcn. James O'Connell, DRE; CRP Stds.: 7

PLAINFIELD

St. Susanna Catholic Church, Plainfield, Inc. - 1210 E. Main St., Plainfield, IN 46168-1797 t) 317-838-7722 (CRP); 317-839-3333 jvandenbergh@saintsusanna.com www.saintsusannachurch.com Rev. Robert T. Hausladen, Pst.; Dcn. Martin May; CRP Stds.: 338

St. Susanna Catholic Church, Plainfield, Inc. School - (Grades PreSchool-8) 1212 E. Main St., Plainfield, IN 46168 t) 317-839-3713 jabdoulaye@saintsusanna.com Janet Abdoulaye, Prin.; Stds.: 253; Sr. Tchrs.: 1; Lay Tchrs.: 18

RICHMOND

St. Elizabeth Ann Seton Catholic Church, Richmond, Inc. - 240 S. 6th St., Richmond, IN 47374 t) 765-962-3902; 765-962-3902 (CRP) seas@setoncatholics.org; vroosa@setoncatholics.org www.setoncatholics.org Very Rev. Sengole Thomas Gnanaraj (India), Pst.; Dcn. James Miller; Susan Shaw, Bus. Mgr.; Vicky Roosa, DRE; Trinity Semler, Youth Min.; CRP Stds.: 102

Seton Catholic High School - (Grades PreK-12) 233 S. 5th St., Richmond, IN 47374; Mailing: 240 S. 6th St., Richmond, IN 47374 t) 765-962-4877 (Intermediate Campus); 765-962-5010 (Primary Campus); 765-965-6956 (Jr/Sr High Campus) kbecker@setoncatholics.org; jbrack@setoncatholics.org setonschools.org Kimberley Becker, Prin.; Jane Brack, Prin.; Stds.: 367; Lay Tchrs.: 19

ROCKVILLE

St. Joseph Catholic Church, Rockville, Inc. - 201 E. Ohio St., Rockville, IN 47872-1898 t) 765-569-5406 stjosephrockville.com Rev. Joby Abraham Puthussery, Admin.; CRP Stds.: 2

RUSHVILLE

St. Mary Catholic Church, Rushville, Inc. - 512 N. Perkins St., Rushville, IN 46173-1692 t) 765-932-2588 frbrockmeier@stmaryrush.org; akemple@stmaryrush.org stmaryrush.org/ Rev. James Brockmeier, Pst.; Amaranta Kemple, DRE; CRP Stds.: 113

St. Mary Catholic Church, Rushville, Inc. School - (Grades PreK-6) 226 E. 5th St., Rushville, IN 46173 t) 765-932-3639 www.stmaryrush.org Pam Wells, Prin.; Stds.: 123; Lay Tchrs.: 9

SALEM

St. Patrick Catholic Church, Salem, Inc. - 208 S. Shelby St., Salem, IN 47167-0273; Mailing: P.O. Box 273, Salem, IN 47167-0273 t) 812-752-3693 amartyrs@frontier.com amartyrs.org/ Rev. Santhosh Yohannan, Admin.; Judy Saunders, DRE; CRP Stds.: 19

SCOTTSBURG

Church of the American Martyrs, Scottsburg, Inc. - 270 S. Bond St., Scottsburg, IN 47170-2009 t) 812-752-3693 amartyrs@frontier.com www.amartyrs.org Rev. Santhosh Yohannan, Admin.; Cindy Light, DRE; CRP Stds.: 17

SELLERSBURG

St. John Paul II Catholic Church, Sellersburg, Inc. - 2605 W. St. Joe Rd., Sellersburg, IN 47172-1241 t) 812-246-2512 www.stjohnpaulparish.org Rev. Thomas E. Clegg, Pst.; Rev. Ronald Mervil (Haiti), Par. Vicar; CRP Stds.: 57

St. John Paul II Catholic School - (Grades PreK-8) 105 St. Paul St., Sellersburg, IN 47172 t) 812-246-3266 office@stjohnpaulschool.org www.stjohnpaulschool.org Karen Haas, Prin.; Stds.: 280; Lay Tchrs.: 14

SEYMOUR

St. Ambrose Catholic Church, Seymour, Inc. - 325 S. Chestnut St., Seymour, IN 47274-2329 t) 812-522-5304 smith@stambroseseymour.org www.stambroseseymour.org Very Rev. Daniel J. Staublin, Pst.; Dcn. John D. Cord; Dcn. Michael East; Christina Smith, CRE; CRP Stds.: 145

St. Ambrose Catholic Church, Seymour, Inc. School - (Grades PreK-8) 301 S. Chestnut St., Seymour, IN 47274 t) 812-522-3522 Michelle Neibert-Levine, Prin.; Stds.: 142; Lay Tchrs.: 11

SHELBYVILLE

St. Joseph Catholic Church, Shelbyville, Inc. - 125 E. Broadway, Shelbyville, IN 46176-1498; Mailing: 228 E. Hendricks St., Shelbyville, IN 46176-1498 t) 317-398-8227 rebecca@sjsshelbyville.org; bcross@sjsshelbyville.org www.stjoeshelby.org Very Rev. Michael T. Keucher, Pst.; Dcn. Charles J. Giesting; Dcn. Thomas Hill; William Cross, Pst. Assoc.; CRP Stds.: 77

St. Joseph Catholic Church, Shelbyville, Inc. School - (Grades PreK-5) 127 E. Broadway, Shelbyville, IN 46176 t) 317-398-4202 office@sjsshelbyville.org Beth Borland, Prin.; Stds.: 110; Lay Tchrs.: 8

St. Vincent De Paul Catholic Church, Shelby County, Inc. - 4218 E. Michigan Rd., Shelbyville, IN 46176-9242 t) 317-398-4028 Sr. Joan Miller, O.S.F., Parish Life Coord.; Rev. John A. Meyer, Moderator; Very Rev. Michael T. Keucher, Sacramental Min.; Dcn. Charles J. Giesting; CRP Stds.: 54

SPENCER

St. Jude Catholic Church, Spencer, Inc. - 300 W. Hillside Ave., Spencer, IN 47460-0317; Mailing: P.O. Box 317, Spencer, IN 47460-0317 t) 812-829-3082 stjudespencer@sbcglobal.net Rev. Dennis M. Duvelius, Pst.; CRP Stds.: 18

ST. CROIX

Holy Cross Catholic Church, St. Croix, Inc. - 12239 State Rd. 62, St. Croix, IN 47576-9999 t) 812-843-5701; 812-843-5143 (CRP) idhubert@psci.net www.holycross-saintcroix.com/ Rev. Brian G. Esarey, Pst.; Lesley Hubert, CRE; CRP Stds.: 25

ST. MARY OF THE WOODS

St. Mary-of-the-Woods Catholic Church, Inc. - 3827 N. Arms Pl., St. Mary of the Woods, IN 47876-0155; Mailing: P.O. Box 155, St. Mary of the Woods, IN 47876-0155 t) 812-535-1261 barb@shjth.org stmarysvillagechurch.org Barbara Black, Parish Life Coord.; Very Rev. Benjamin D. Syberg, Moderator; Rev. Darvin E. Winters, Sacr. Min.; CRP Stds.: 36

ST. MEINRAD

St. Meinrad Catholic Church, Inc. - 19570 N. 4th St., St. Meinrad, IN 47577; Mailing: PO Box 8, Saint Meinrad, IN 47577 t) 812-357-5533 smcatholic.church/ Rev. Anthony Vinson, O.S.B., Admin.; CRP Stds.: 44

SUNMAN

St. Nicholas Catholic Church, Sunman, Inc. - 6461 E. St. Nicholas Dr., Sunman, IN 47041 t) 812-623-2964; 812-623-4618 (CRP) dre@stnicholas-sunman.org stnicholas-sunman.org Rev. Shaun P. Whittington, Pst.; Renee Jackson, DRE; CRP Stds.: 90

St. Nicholas Catholic Church, Sunman, Inc. School - (Grades K-8) 6459 E. St. Nicholas Dr., Sunman, IN 47041 t) 812-623-2348 principal@stnicholas-sunman.org Eric Feller, Prin.; Stds.: 183; Lay Tchrs.: 9

TELL CITY

St. Mark's Catholic Church, Perry County, Inc. - 5377 Acorn Rd., Tell City, IN 47586-9738 t) 812-836-2481 Very Rev. Anthony P. Hollowell, Pst.; Bridgett Berger, CRE; CRP Stds.: 26

St. Michael Catholic Church, Cannelton, Inc. - c/o Catholic Ministry Center, 824 Jefferson St., Tell City, IN 47586-2114 t) 812-547-7994 Rev. Stephen D. Donahue, Pst.; Mandy Bauer, Bus. Mgr.;

St. Paul Catholic Church, Tell City, Inc. - Catholic Ministry Center, 824 Jefferson St., Tell City, IN 47586 t) 812-547-7994 meganrust@psci.net www.stpaultellcity.org/ Very Rev. Anthony P. Hollowell, Admin.; Rev. Kolbe Wolniakowski, OSB, Par. Vicar; Dcn. Kenneth C. Smith; Megan Rust, DRE; CRP Stds.: 147

St. Pius V Catholic Church, Troy, Inc. - Catholic Ministry Center, 824 Jefferson St., Tell City, IN 47586 t) 812-547-7994 st.piuschurch@yahoo.com Rev. Stephen D. Donahue, Pst.; Jeanne Harth, DRE; CRP Stds.: 26

TERRE HAUTE

St. Benedict Catholic Church, Terre Haute, Inc. - 111 S. Ninth St., Terre Haute, IN 47807-3711 t) 812-232-8421 rita@stbenedictth.org www.stbenedictth.org/ Rev. Robert St. Martin, O.F.M.Conv., Admin.; Rita Burns Senseman, Pst. Assoc.; CRP Stds.: 62

St. Benedict Soup Kitchen - 128 S. 9th St., Terre Haute, IN 47807 t) 812-238-9109 terran@stbenedictth.org

St. Joseph University Catholic Church, Terre Haute, Inc. - 113 S. 5th St., Terre Haute, IN 47807-3577 t) 812-232-7011 reled@stjoeup.org www.stjoeup.org/ Rev. Cyprian Uline, OFMConv, Admin.; Elizabeth Davis, DRE;

St. Joseph University Parish - 113 S. Fifth St., Terre Haute, IN 47807 t) 812-232-7011 www.stjoeup.org Rev. Robert G. Showers, O.F.M.Conv., Pst.; Rev. Cyprian Uline, OFMConv, Assoc. Pst.; Rev. Robert St. Martin, O.F.M.Conv., Assoc. Pst.; Elizabeth Davis, Pst. Assoc.; CRP Stds.: 63

St. Margaret Mary Catholic Church, Terre Haute, Inc. - 2405 S. Seventh St., Terre Haute, IN 47802-3599 t) 812-232-3512 mcoad@smmth.org; dre@saintpat.org www.smmth.org Very Rev. Benjamin D. Syberg, Pst.; Dcn. Michael Stratman; CRP Stds.: 18

St. Patrick Catholic Church, Terre Haute, Inc. - 1807 Poplar St., Terre Haute, IN 47803-2196 t) 812-232-8518 religioused@saintpat.org saintpat.org/parish/ Very Rev. Benjamin D. Syberg, Pst.; Dcn. Michael Stratman; Jared

Wuerzburger, DRE; Brittany Detamore, Bus. Mgr.; CRP Stds.: 39

St. Patrick Catholic Church, Terre Haute, Inc. School - (Grades PreK-8) 449 S. 19th St., Terre Haute, IN 47803 t) 812-232-2157 saintpat.school Corinne Cuffle, Prin.; Dallas Wright, Asst. Prin.; Stds.: 328; Lay Tchrs.: 23

Sacred Heart of Jesus Catholic Church, Terre Haute, Inc. - 2322 N. 13 1/2 St., Terre Haute, IN 47804-2498 t) 812-466-1231 www.shjth.org Barbara Black, Parish Life Coord.; Rev. Darvin E. Winters, Sacr. Min.; Very Rev. Benjamin D. Syberg, Moderator; CRP Stds.: 10

VEVAY

Most Sorrowful Mother of God Catholic Church, Vevay, Inc. - Ferry St., Vevay, IN 47043; Mailing: P.O. Box 257, Vevay, IN 47043 t) 812-265-4166 parishoffice@popeace.org Rev. Christopher A. Craig, Pst.; Dcn. Michael Gardner; Dcn. Mike Boggs;

SCHOOLS: PRESCHOOL THRU HIGH SCHOOL

SCHOOLS

STATE OF INDIANA

INDIANAPOLIS

Mother Theodore Catholic Academies, Inc. - 1400 N. Meridian St., Indianapolis, IN 46202-1410 t) 317-236-1400 rspringman@archindy.org Ronda Swartz, Exec. Dir.; Stds.: 830; Lay Tchrs.: 56

Holy Angels Catholic Church, Indianapolis, Inc. School - 2822 Dr. Martin Luther King, Jr. St., Indianapolis, IN 46208 t) 317-926-5211 jarmitage@holyangelscatholicschool.org www.holyangelscatholicschool.org Justin Armitage, Prin.; Stds.: 153; Lay Tchrs.: 9

St. Philip Neri School - 545 N. Eastern Ave., Indianapolis, IN 46201 t) 317-636-0134 Kari Buchinger, Prin.; Stds.: 280; Lay Tchrs.: 15

Central Catholic School - 1155 E. Cameron St., Indianapolis, IN 46203 t) 317-783-7759 rhurrle@centralcatholicindy.org Ruth Hurrle, Prin.; Stds.: 245; Sr. Tchrs.: 1; Lay Tchrs.: 22

West Deanery Unified Catholic Schools, Inc. - (Grades 7-12) 3360 W. 30th St., Indianapolis, IN 46222 t) 317-924-4333 jhoy@cardinalritter.org www.cardinalritter.org Kari Jost, Prin.; E. Jo Hoy, Pres.; Stds.: 1,182; Lay Tchrs.: 76

St. Michael-St. Gabriel Archangels School - (Grades 7-12) 3352 W. 30th St., Indianapolis, IN 46222 t) 317-926-0516 bulletin@saintmichaelindy.org www.smsgindy.org/ Liz Ramos, Prin.; Stds.: 333; Lay Tchrs.: 22

HIGH SCHOOLS

STATE OF INDIANA

CLARKSVILLE

Our Lady of Providence Junior - Senior High School, Inc. - (DIO) 707 Providence Way, Clarksville, IN 47129 t) 812-945-2538 mernstberger@providencehigh.net www.providencehigh.net Victor Beeler II, Pres.; Steve Beyl, Prin.; Rev. J. Daniel Atkins, Chap.; Stds.: 345; Lay Tchrs.: 24

INDIANAPOLIS

Bishop Chatard High School, Inc. - (DIO) 5885 Crittenden Ave., Indianapolis, IN 46220 t) 317-251-1451 jhansen@bishopchatard.org www.bishopchatard.org William Bill Sahm, Pres.; John Hasty, Prin.; Ben Reilly, Vice Prin.; Stds.: 702; Lay Tchrs.: 50

Brebeuf Jesuit Preparatory School, Inc. (Society of Jesus Community) - (PRV) (Grades 9-12) 2801 W. 86th St., Indianapolis, IN 46268-1926 t) 317-524-7050 ecrowell@brebeuf.org www.brebeuf.org Rev. William Verbryke, S.J., Pres.; Rev. Christopher Johnson, SJ, Vice. Pres.; Greg VanSlambrook, Prin.; Stds.: 824; Bro. Tchrs.: 5; Lay Tchrs.: 68

Cathedral High School (Cathedral Trustees, Inc.) - (PRV) 5225 E. 56th St., Indianapolis, IN 46226 t) 317-542-1481 www.gocathedral.com Julie Barthel, Prin.; Robert Bridges, Pres.; Stds.: 1,142; Sr. Tchrs.: 1; Lay Tchrs.: 88

Father Thomas Scecina Memorial High School, Inc. - (DIO) 5000 Nowland Ave., Indianapolis, IN 46201-1836 t) 317-356-6377 www.scecina.org Joseph Therber, Pres.; Dave Dellacca, Prin.; Rev. Aaron M. Jenkins, Chap.; Stds.: 470; Lay Tchrs.: 31

Providence Cristo Rey High School, Inc. - 2717 S. East St., Indianapolis, IN 46225 t) 317-860-1000 info@pcrhs.org www.cristoreyindy.org Tyler Mayer, Pres.; Leslie Napora, Prin.; Stds.: 202; Lay Tchrs.: 31

Roncalli High School, Inc. - (DIO) 3300 Prague Rd., Indianapolis, IN 46227 t) 317-787-8277 cweisenbach@roncalli.org www.roncalli.org Charles Weisenbach, Pres.; Kevin Banich, Prin.; Rev. Robert J. Robeson, Chap.; Stds.: 1,070; Lay Tchrs.: 61

OLDENBURG

Oldenburg Academy of the Immaculate Conception, Inc. - (PRV) (Grades 9-12) One Twister Cir., Oldenburg, IN 47036-0200; Mailing: PO Box 200, Oldenburg, IN 47036-0200 t) 812-934-4440 ahunger@oldenburgacademy.org www.oldenburgacademy.org Co-ed. Sponsored by the Sisters of St. Francis - Oldenburg Annette Hunger, Pres.; Angela Parmer, Prin.; Stds.: 155; Lay Tchrs.: 19

RICHMOND

Seton Catholic High School - (DIO) (Grades PreK-12) 233 S. 5th St., Richmond, IN 47374; Mailing: 240 S. 6th St., Richmond, IN 47374 t) 765-965-6956 (JH/HS Campus); (765) 962-5010 (Primary Campus); (765) 962-4877 (Intermediate) jbrack@setoncatholics.org; kbecker@setoncatholics.org setonschools.org Kimberley Becker, Prin.; Jane Brack, Prin.; Stds.: 369; Lay Tchrs.: 19

INSTITUTIONS LOCATED IN DIOCESE

ASSOCIATIONS [ASN]

OLDENBURG

Association of Contemplative Sisters - 22143 Main St., Oldenburg, IN 47036-0260; Mailing: P.O. Box 260, Oldenburg, IN 47036-0260 t) 812-932-2075 jeanmcgoff@gmail.com Marilyn Webb, Pres.;

CAMPUS MINISTRY / NEWMAN CENTERS [CAM]

BLOOMINGTON

St. Paul Catholic Center, Parish and Newman Center at Indiana University - 1413 E. 17th St., Bloomington, IN 47408 t) 812-339-5561 www.hoosiercatholic.org Very Rev. Patrick F. Hyde, O.P., Admin.;

FRANKLIN

Franklin College - 114 Lancelot Dr., Franklin, IN 46131 t) 317-738-3929 Rev. Todd Michael Goodson, Admin.;

GREENCASTLE

DePauw University - 202 E. Washington St., Greencastle, IN 46135 t) 765-653-5678 csa@depauw.edu depauwtigercatholic.wordpress.com/ Rev. John J. Hollowell, Chap.;

INDIANAPOLIS

Butler Catholic Community - 4600 Sunset Ave., Indianapolis, IN 46208; Mailing: 4615 Sunset Ave., Indianapolis, IN 46208 t) 317-236-1400 astankewitz@butler.edu www.butler-catholic.org Anna Stankewitz, Dir.;

University of Indianapolis Newman Center - 1400 Campus Dr., Indianapolis, IN 46227 t) 317-236-1400 shussey@archindy.org

MADISON

Hanover College - 305 W. State St., Madison, IN 47250 t) 812-265-4166 Rev. Christopher A. Craig;

RICHMOND

Earlham College - 240 S. 6th St., Richmond, IN 47374 t) 765-962-3902 Very Rev. Sengole Thomas Gnanaraj (India), Chap.;

CATHOLIC CHARITIES [CCH]

BLOOMINGTON

Catholic Charities Bloomington, Inc. - 803 N. Monroe St., Bloomington, IN 47404 t) 812-332-1262 occase@ccbin.org Michael J Stribling, Clinical Dir & Mental Health Therapist; Asstd. Annu.: 598; Staff: 16

INDIANAPOLIS

Catholic Charities Indianapolis, Inc. - 1400 N. Meridian St., Indianapolis, IN 46202 t) 317-236-1500 dbethuram@archindy.org www.catholiccharitiesindpls.org David Bethuram, Dir.; Asstd. Annu.: 69,535; Staff: 103

St. Elizabeth/Coleman Pregnancy & Adoption Services - 2500 Churchman Ave., Indianapolis, IN 46203 t) 317-787-3412 stelizabeths@stelizabeths.org www.stelizabeths.org David Bethuram, Dir.; Asstd. Annu.: 785; Staff: 7

Holy Family Services - 907 N. Holmes Ave., Indianapolis, IN 46222 t) 317-635-7830 bbickel@archindy.org www.catholiccharitiesindpls.org Bill Bickel, Dir.; Asstd. Annu.: 792; Staff: 13

NEW ALBANY

St. Elizabeth Catholic Charities, Inc. - 702 E. Market St., New Albany, IN 47150 t) 812-949-7305 mcasper@stecharities.org www.stelizabethcatholiccharities.org Mark Casper, Dir.; Asstd. Annu.: 3,707; Staff: 19

TELL CITY

Catholic Charities Tell City, Inc. - 802 9th St., Tell City, IN 47586 t) 812-547-0903 mintravia@cctcin.org www.catholiccharitiestellcity.org Sr. Shellie Intravia, Dir.; Asstd. Annu.: 5,804; Staff: 2

TERRE HAUTE

Catholic Charities Terre Haute, Inc. - 430 N 14th 1/2 St, Terre Haute, IN 47807; Mailing: PO Box 3318, Terre Haute, IN 47803 t) 812-232-1447 jetling@ccthin.org www.ccthin.org John C. Etling, Dir.; Asstd. Annu.: 38,750; Staff: 32

Bethany House - 1402 Locust Ave., Terre Haute, IN 47807 t) 812-232-4978 Danielle Elkins, Dir.;

Christmas House - 1440 Locust St., Terre Haute, IN 47807

Household Exchange - 1402 Locust St., Terre Haute, IN 47807 t) 812-232-4978

Ryves Youth Center at Etling Hall - 1356 Locust St., Terre Haute, IN 47807 t) 812-235-1265 Jim Edwards, Dir.;

***Terre Haute Catholic Charities Foodbank, Inc.** - ; Mailing: PO Box 3318, N Terre Haute, IN 47803 t) 812-235-3424 ccthin.org

CEMETERIES [CEM]

INDIANAPOLIS

Catholic Cemeteries - 9001 Haverstick Rd., Indianapolis, IN 46240; Mailing: 600 E. Ohio St., Indianapolis, IN 46202 t) 317-581-2643 tlloyd@catholiccemeteries.cc Tony Lloyd, Pres.;

COLLEGES & UNIVERSITIES [COL]

INDIANAPOLIS

Marian University (Sisters of the Third Order Regular of St. Francis) - 3200 Cold Spring Rd., Indianapolis, IN 46222 t) 317-955-6000 www.marian.edu (Coed) Rev. Barry Fischer, C.PP.S., Chap.; Daniel J. Elsener, Pres.; Stds.: 3,737; Lay Tchrs.: 190

Ancilla College - 20097 9B Rd., Plymouth, IN 46563; Mailing: P.O. Box 1, Donaldson, IN 46513 t) 574-936-8898 admissions@ancilla.edu www.ancilla.edu

ST. MARY OF THE WOODS

Saint Mary-of-the-Woods College - 1 St. Mary of the

Woods, St. Mary of the Woods, IN 47876 t) (812) 535-5151 smwc@smwc.edu www.smwc.edu Sponsored by the Sisters of Providence, St. Mary-of-the-Woods. Dottie King, Pres.; Stds.: 1,147; Lay Tchrs.: 59

CONVENTS, MONASTERIES, AND RESIDENCES FOR WOMEN [CON]

BEECH GROVE

Our Lady of Grace Monastery (Sisters of St. Benedict of Beech Grove, Ind., Inc.) - 1402 Southern Ave., Beech Grove, IN 46107-1197 t) 317-787-3287 olgprioress@benedictine.com www.benedictine.com Sr. Julie Sewell, Prioress; Srs.: 47

INDIANAPOLIS

F.I.H. Convent - Franciscan Sisters of the Immaculate Heart of Mary - 3356 W. 30th, Indianapolis, IN 46222 t) (317) 259-4097 srchristabelmary@gmail.com Sr. Christabel Yohannan, FIH, Contact; Srs.: 11

Missionaries of Charity - 2424 E. 10th St., Indianapolis, IN 46201 t) 317-916-6753 Convent with emergency night shelter for women Sr. Janita MC, MC, Supr.; Sr. M. Jonathan, MC, Regional Superior; Srs.: 4

Servants of the Gospel of Life, Inc. - 7575 Holliday Dr. E., Indianapolis, IN 46260 t) 317-509-3256 dcarollo@stluke.org Srs.: 1

OLDENBURG

Motherhouse of the Congregation of the Sisters of the Third Order of St. Francis - 22143 Main St., Oldenburg, IN 47036; Mailing: PO Box 100, Oldenburg, IN 47036 t) 812-934-2475 dkaimann@oldenburgosf.com www.oldenburgfranciscans.org Sr. Christa Franzer, Congregational Minister; Srs.: 138

Sisters of Our Lady of Mount Carmel Carmelite Monastery - 22143 Main St., Oldenburg, IN 47036; Mailing: P.O. Box 260, Oldenburg, IN 47036 t) 812-212-5901 jeanmcgoff@gmail.com Sr. Jean Alice McGoff, O.C.D., Prioress; Srs.: 3

ST. MARY OF THE WOODS

Sisters of Providence General Administration - 1 Sisters of Providence Rd., St. Mary of the Woods, IN 47876 t) 812-535-2864 generalsecretary@spsmw.org www.sistersofprovidence.org Rev. Terrence Johnson, Chap.; Sr. Dawn Tomaszewski, S.P., Supr.; Srs.: 147

TERRE HAUTE

Sisters of Our Lady of Mount Carmel of Terre Haute, Carmelite Monastery - Carmelite Monastery, 59 Allendale, Terre Haute, IN 47802-4751 t) 812-299-1410 carmelth@heartsawake.org www.heartsawake.org Mother Mary Joseph Nguyen, Prioress; Srs.: 12

ENDOWMENTS / FOUNDATIONS / TRUSTS [EFT]

NORTH VERNON

St. Vincent Jennings Hospital Foundation, Inc. - 301 Henry St., North Vernon, IN 47265 t) 812-352-4200 Jonathan Nalli, CEO; Ann Varner, Chief Mission Integration Officer;

HOSPITALS / HEALTH SERVICES [HOS]

BEDFORD

St. Vincent Dunn Hospital Inc. (Ascension St. Vincent Dunn) - 1600 23rd St., Bedford, IN 47421 t) 812-275-3331 www.healthcare.ascension.org Jonathan Nalli, CEO; Ann Varner, Chief Mission Integration Officer; Bed Capacity: 23; Asstd. Annu.: 28,320; Staff: 89

BRAZIL

***St. Vincent Clay Hospital, Inc. (Ascension St. Vincent Clay)** - 1206 E. National Ave., Brazil, IN 47834; Mailing: P.O. Box 489, Brazil, IN 47834 t) (317) 338-7060 www.healthcare.ascension.org Jonathan Nalli, CEO; Ann Varner, Chief Mission Integration Officer; Bed Capacity: 25; Asstd. Annu.: 32,524; Staff: 89

INDIANAPOLIS

Central Indiana Health System Cardiac Services, Inc. (Ascension St. Vincent Cardiac Services) - 10330 N. Meridian St., Indianapolis, IN 46290 t) 317-338-7060 www.healthcare.ascension.org Jonathan Nalli, CEO; Ann Varner, Chief Mission Integration Officer; Staff: 51

Franciscan Health - 8111 S. Emerson Ave., Indianapolis, IN 46237 t) 317-528-5000; 317-834-1160 james.callaghan@franciscanalliance.org www.franciscanalliance.org Franciscan Alliance Rev. James Barrand, Chap.; Rev. Michael E. Burns, S.D.S., Chap.; Rev. Jeffery Moore, Chap.; Rev. Thomas Perrin, Chap.; James Callaghan, Pres.; Sr. Marlene Shapley, OSF, Vice President Mission Integration; Bed Capacity: 555; Asstd. Annu.: 1,659,929; Staff: 4,260

Franciscan Health Mooresville - 1201 Hadley Rd., Mooresville, IN 46158 Sr. Lethia Marie Leveille, O.S.F., Contact;

St. Vincent Hospital and Health Care Center, Inc. (Ascension St. Vincent Hospital) - 2001 W. 86th St., Indianapolis, IN 46260 t) 317-338-7060 ann.varner@ascension.org www.healthcare.ascension.org Jonathan Nalli, CEO; Ann Varner, Chief Mission Integration Officer; Bed Capacity: 830; Asstd. Annu.: 919,567; Staff: 4,845

St. Vincent Seton Specialty Hospital, Inc. (Ascension St. Vincent Seton Specialty Hospital) - 8050 Township Line Rd., Indianapolis, IN 46260 t) 317-415-8500 www.healthcare.ascension.org Jonathan Nalli, CEO; Ann Varner, Chief Mission Integration Officer; Bed Capacity: 72; Asstd. Annu.: 265; Staff: 124

NORTH VERNON

***St. Vincent Jennings Hospital, Inc. (Ascension St. Vincent Jennings)** - 301 Henry St., North Vernon, IN 47265 t) 812-352-4200 www.healthcare.ascension.org Jonathan Nalli, CEO; Ann Varner, Chief Mission Integration Officer; Bed Capacity: 23; Asstd. Annu.: 34,603; Staff: 64

SALEM

St. Vincent Salem Hospital, Inc. (Ascension St. Vincent Salem) - 911 N. Shelby St., Salem, IN 47167 t) 812-883-5881 www.healthcare.ascension.org Jonathan Nalli, CEO; Ann Varner, Chief Mission Integration Officer; Bed Capacity: 25; Asstd. Annu.: 31,820; Staff: 72

MISCELLANEOUS [MIS]

BEECH GROVE

Franciscan Alliance Information Services - 1500 Albany St., Beech Grove, IN 46107 t) 317-532-7800 www.franciscanalliance.org Sponsored by Franciscan Alliance, Inc. Charles Wagner, Exec.;

INDIANAPOLIS

***Archdiocese of Indianapolis Cemeteries, Inc.** - 1400 N. Meridian St., Indianapolis, IN 46202 t) 317-236-1453 eatkins@archindy.org Eric L. Atkins, Dir.;

Batesville Deanery - 1400 N. Meridian St., Indianapolis, IN 46202 t) 317-236-1400 Very Rev. Michael T. Keucher, Dean;

St. Ann -
St. Anthony -
St. Cecilia -
Cemetery -
St. Charles -
Holy Family -
Holy Family Shrine -
Holy Guardian Angels -
Immaculate Conception -
St. John -
St. John -
St. John -
St. Joseph -
St. Joseph -
St. Louis -
St. Martin -
St. Mary -
St. Mary of the Rock -
St. Maurice -
St. Maurice -
St. Michael -
St. Paul -
St. Paul -
St. Peter -
St. Pius -
St. Raphael -
St. Vincent de Paul -

Bloomington Deanery - 1400 N. Meridian St., Indianapolis, IN 46202 t) 317-236-1400 Very Rev. Patrick F. Hyde, O.P., Dean;

Catholic -
St. Martin -
Our Lady of Springs -

***The Catholic Writers Guild Inc.** - ; Mailing: P.O. Box 39326, Indianapolis, IN 46239-0326 t) 877-829-5500 Carolyn Astfalk, Pres.;

Connersville Deanery - 1400 N. Meridian St., Indianapolis, IN 46202 t) 317-236-1400 Very Rev. Sengole Thomas Gnanaraj (India), Dean;

St. Andrew -
St. Anne -
St. Bridget -
Calvary -
St. Mary -

Criterion Press, Inc. - 1400 N. Meridian St., Indianapolis, IN 47206-1410 t) 317-236-1578 Mike Krokos, Editor;

Indianapolis North Deanery - 1400 N. Meridian St., Indianapolis, IN 46202 t) 317-236-1400 Very Rev. Douglas W. Marcotte, Dean;

Our Lady of Peace - 9001 Haverstick Rd., Indianapolis, IN 46240 t) 317-574-8898 tlloyd@catholiccemeteries.cc Indianapolis Tony Lloyd, Pres.;

Indianapolis South Deanery - 1400 N. Meridian St., Indianapolis, IN 46202 t) 317-236-1400 Very Rev. Stephen W. Giannini, Dean;

Calvary - 435 W. Troy St., Indianapolis, IN 46225 t) 317-784-4439 tlloyd@catholiccemeteries.cc Indianapolis Tony Lloyd, Pres.;

Holy Cross - 435 W. Troy St., Indianapolis, IN 46225 t) 317-784-4439 tlloyd@catholiccemeteries.cc Indianapolis Tony Lloyd, Pres.;

St. Joseph - 435 W. Troy St., Indianapolis, IN 46225 t) 317-784-4439 tlloyd@catholiccemeteries.cc Indianapolis Tony Lloyd, Pres.;

Indianapolis West Deanery - 1400 N. Meridian St., Indianapolis, IN 46202 t) 317-236-1400 Very Rev. John P. McCaslin, Dean;

St. Malachy - 56th St. & N. 267, Brownsburg, IN 46112 t) 317-271-3123 tlloyd@catholiccemeteries.cc Brownsburg Tony Lloyd, Pres.;

St. Malachy - State Road 136, Brownsburg, IN 46112 t) 317-271-3123 tlloyd@catholiccemeteries.cc Tony Lloyd, Pres.;

***Inter Mirifica, Inc.** - 7340 E. 82nd St., Ste. A, Indianapolis, IN 46256 t) 317-598-6700 bob@teipencpa.com www.catholicradioindy.org Robert C. Teipen, Chair;

Mount Saint Francis Sanctuary, Inc. - 3200 Cold Spring Rd., Indianapolis, IN 46222 t) 812-923-8817 Rev. Leopold Keffler, O.F.M.Conv., Secy.; Thomas A. Smith, O.F.M.Conv., Treas.; Tony Perkins, Pres.;

Seymour Deanery - 1400 N. Meridian St., Indianapolis, IN 46202 t) 317-236-1400 Very Rev. Daniel J. Staublin, Dean;

St. Ambrose -
St. Anne -
St. Anthony -
St. Bridget -
St. Catherine of Siena -
St. Dennis -
St. Joseph -
St. Joseph -
St. Magdalen -
St. Mary -
Old St. James -
St. Patrick -
St. Patrick -
St. Patrick -

Society of St. Vincent de Paul, Archdiocesan Council of Indianapolis, Inc. - 3001 E. 30th St., Indianapolis, IN 46218 t) 317-924-5769 www.svdpindy.org Paul Ainslie, Pres.;

Tell City Deanery - 1400 N. Meridian St., Indianapolis, IN 46202 t) 317-236-1400 Very Rev. Anthony P. Hollowell, Dean;

St. Augustine -
St. Boniface -
St. Croix -
Holy Cross -
St. Isidore -
St. John -
St. Joseph -
St. Joseph -
St. Joseph -
St. Martin -
St. Mary -
St. Mary -
St. Meinrad -
St. Michael -
Old St. Patrick -
St. Paul -
St. Peter -

Terre Haute Deanery - 1400 N. Meridian St., Indianapolis, IN 46202 t) 317-236-1400 Very Rev. Benjamin D. Syberg, Dean;

Annunciation -
Calvary -
Catholic -
Greek Catholic -
Immaculate Conception -
St. John Greek -
St. Joseph -
St. Mary-of-the-Woods -

***St. Vincent Health, Inc.** - 250 W. 96th St., Indianapolis, IN 46260 t) 317-583-3289 jonathan.nalli@ascension.org www.stvincent.org Jonathan Nalli, CEO; Ann Varner, Chief Mission Integration Officer;

St. Vincent Medical Group - 8333 Naab Rd., Ste. 200, Indianapolis, IN 46260 t) 317-338-7060 ann.varner@ascension.org Jonathan Nalli, CEO; Ann Varner, Chief Mission Integration Officer;

MOORESVILLE

St. Thomas More Free Clinic, Inc. - 1125 N. Indiana St., Mooresville, IN 46158; Mailing: P.O. Box 935, Mooresville, IN 46158 t) 317-831-1697 jbuckner@crowntech.com

NEW ALBANY

New Albany Deanery - 415 E. Eighth St., New Albany, IN 47150-3299; Mailing: 1400 N. Meridian St., Indianapolis, IN 46202 t) 812-944-0417 teri.ccna@gmail.com Very Rev. Jeremy M. Gries, Dean; Terri Popp, Cemetery Supervisor;

St. Anthony -
St. Bernard -
Cemetery - t) 317-944-0417
St. Francis -
Holy Trinity -
St. Joachim -
St. John -
St. Joseph -
St. Joseph -
St. Mary -
St. Mary -
St. Mary -
St. Mary of the Knobs -
Mary, Queen of Heaven -
St. Michael -
St. Michael -
St. Michael -
Most Precious Blood -
Old St. Bernard -
St. Peter -

SHELBYVILLE

Heart of Mercy Solitude, Inc. - 104 4th St., Shelbyville, IN 46176 c) 317-488-8988 Sr. Judith A. Ayers, HS, Dir.;

ST. MARY OF THE WOODS

Providence Health Care, Inc. - 1 Sisters of Providence Rd., St. Mary of the Woods, IN 47876; Mailing: P.O. Box 97, St. Mary of the Woods, IN 47876 t) 812-535-4001 mlynch@phcwoods.org phcwoods.com/ Sponsored by the Sisters of Providence of Saint Mary-of-the-Woods. Mandy Lynch, CEO;

Women of Providence in Collaboration, Inc. - 1 Sisters of Providence Rd., St. Mary of the Woods, IN 47876; Mailing: PO Box 721, Villa Maria, PA 16155 t) 812-535-3131 x2802 dweidenb@spsmw.org www.wpcweb.org Sr. Dawn Tomaszewski, S.P., Supr.;

ST. MEINRAD

Swiss-American Benedictine Congregation, Inc. - 100 Hill Dr., St. Meinrad, IN 47577; Mailing: 850 Butterfield Rd., Aurora, IL 60502-9743 t) 630-897-7215 jbrahill@marmion.org www.swissamericanmonks.org Rt. Rev. Vincent Bataille, O.S.B., Pres.;

TERRE HAUTE

Terre Haute Deanery Pastoral Center - 1801 Poplar St., Terre Haute, IN 47803 t) 812-232-8400 louise@thdeanery.org www.thdeanery.org Very Rev. Benjamin D. Syberg, Dean; Ray Veit, Admin. Coord.;

WARREN

***St. Paul Street Evangelization** - 26238 Ryan Rd., Warren, MI 48091 t) 657-777-2963 info@stpaulse.com Steve Dawson, Dir.;

WEST TERRE HAUTE

Providence Food Pantry of West Terre Haute, Indiana, Inc. - 701 W. National Ave., West Terre Haute, IN 47885 t) 812-535-2544 jfillenw@spsmw.org Sr. Joseph Fillenwarth, Dir.;

WHEATON

Indianapolis Ministries 1, Inc. - 26W171 Roosevelt Rd., Wheaton, IL 60187; Mailing: P.O. Box 667, Wheaton, IL 60187 t) 630-909-6933 Joe Rosenblum, Secy.;

Indianapolis Ministries 2, Inc. - 26W171 Roosevelt Rd., Wheaton, IL 60187; Mailing: P.O. Box 667, Wheaton, IL 60187 t) 414-271-6560 Melissa Clayton, Pres.; Joe Rosenblum, Secy.;

MONASTERIES AND RESIDENCES FOR PRIESTS AND BROTHERS [MON]

BLOOMINGTON

Marian Friary of Our Lady Coredemptrix, Franciscans of the Immaculate - 8212 W. Hendricks Rd., Bloomington, IN 47403 t) 812-825-4742 ffi.bloomington@gmail.com Rev. Ignatius Manfredonia, F.I., Father Guardian; Brs.: 2; Priests: 2

MOUNT ST. FRANCIS

Provincial Headquarters, Our Lady of Consolation Province, Conventual Franciscans (Province of Our Lady of Consolation) - 101 Anthony Dr., Mount St. Francis, IN 47146 t) 812-923-8444 secretaryolc@franciscansusa.org www.franciscansusa.org Rev. Martin Day, O.F.M.Conv., Prov.; Friar Mario L. Serrano, O.F.M. Conv., Secy.; Brs.: 15; Priests: 60

ST. MEINRAD

St. Meinrad Archabbey - 100 Hill Dr., St. Meinrad, IN 47577 t) 812-357-6611 abbot@saintmeinrad.edu www.saintmeinrad.org Archabbey of the Order of St. Benedict Rt. Rev. Kurt Stasiak, O.S.B., Abbot; Rev. Kolbe Wolniakowski, OSB, Par. Vicar; Rev. Anthony Vinson, O.S.B., Pst.; Rev. Luke Waugh, O.S.B., Pst.; Rev. Patrick Cooney, O.S.B., Vicar; Rev. Godfrey Mullen, O.S.B., Rector; Rev. Denis Robinson, O.S.B., Rector; Rev. Christian Raab, O.S.B., Par. Vicar; Rev. Ephrem Carr, O.S.B., In Res.; Rev. Matthias Neuman, O.S.B., In Res.; Rev. Aurelius Boberek, O.S.B., In Res.; Rev. Colman Grabert, O.S.B., In Res.; Rev. Louis Hacker, O.S.B., In Res.; Rev. Micheas Langston, O.S.B., In Res.; Rev. Louis Mulcahy, O.S.B., In Res.; Rt. Rev. Lambert Reilly, O.S.B., In Res.; Rev. Germain Swisshelm, O.S.B., In Res.; Rev. Nathaniel Szidik, OSB, Student; Rev. John McMullen, O.S.B., In Res.; Rev. Eugene Hensell, O.S.B., Chap.; Rev. Pius Klein, O.S.B., Chap.; Rev. Mark O'Keefe, O.S.B., Chap.; Rev. Denis Quinkert, O.S.B., Chap.; Rev. Tobias Colgan, O.S.B., Admin.; Rev. Jonathan Fassero, O.S.B., Admin.; Rev. Edward Linton, O.S.B., Admin.; Rev. Julian Peters, O.S.B., Admin.; Rev. Raymond Studzinski, O.S.B., Admin.; Rev. Samuel Weber, O.S.B., Admin.; Rev. Jeremy King, O.S.B., Pst. Min./Coord.; Rev. Adrian Burke, O.S.B., Spiritual Adv./Care Srvcs.; Rev. Noel Mueller, O.S.B., Spiritual Adv./Care Srvcs.; Rev. Thomas Gricoski, O.S.B., Headmaster; Rev. Guerric DeBona, O.S.B., Prof.; Rev. Harry Hagan, O.S.B., Prof.; Rev. Guy Mansini, O.S.B., Prof.; Rev. Paul Nord, O.S.B., Prof.; Rev. Bede Cisco, O.S.B., Prior; Rev. Joseph Cox, O.S.B., Subprior; Rev. Meinrad Brune, O.S.B., Archivist; Rev. Warren Heitz, O.S.B., Editor; Rev. Peduru Fonseka, Student; Rev. Simon Herrmann, OSB, Socius; Rev. Sean Hoppe, O.S.B., Guestmaster; Rev. Lorenzo Penalosa, OSB, Student; Rev. Mateo Zamora, O.S.B., Teacher; Brs.: 22; Priests: 46

NURSING / REHABILITATION / CONVALESCENCE / ELDERLY CARE [NUR]

INDIANAPOLIS

St. Augustine Home, Little Sisters of the Poor (Little Sisters of the Poor of Indianapolis, Inc.) - 2345 W. 86th St., Indianapolis, IN 46260 t) 317-415-5767 devindianapolis@littlesistersofthepoor.org www.littlesistersofthepoorindianapolis.org Mother Maria Christine, L.S.P., Mother Superior; Asstd. Annu.: 120; Staff: 120

PRESCHOOLS / CHILDCARE CENTERS [PRE]

INDIANAPOLIS

Catholic Youth Organization of the Archdiocese of Indianapolis, Inc. - 580 E. Stevens St., Indianapolis, IN 46203 t) 317-632-9311 www.cyoarchindy.org Bruce Scifres, Exec. Dir.;

***St. Mary's Early Childhood Center** - 901 Dr. Martin Luther King Jr. St., Indianapolis, IN 46202 t) 317-635-1491 kcavolick@stmarysecc.org www.smccindy.org A not-for-profit education center for at-risk young children. Kristin Cavolick, Exec. Dir.; Stds.: 130; Lay Tchrs.: 10

NASHVILLE

C.Y.O. Camp Rancho Framasa, Inc. - 2230 N. Clay Lick Rd., Nashville, IN 47448-8638 t) 888-988-2839 info@campranchoframasa.org www.campranchoframasa.org Kevin Sullivan, Dir.;

OLDENBURG

Camp River Ridge - 6145 Harvey Branch Rd., Oldenburg, IN 47036; Mailing: 8162 Chestershire Dr., Cincinnati, OH 45241 t) 513-497-1212 campriverridge@gmail.com www.campriverridge.org (Branch of Mission Networks Activities USA, Inc., Archdiocese of New York) Rev. Lucio Boccacci, Dir.; Stds.: 800

RETREAT HOUSES / RENEWAL CENTERS [RTR]

BEECH GROVE

Benedict Inn Retreat & Conference Center - 1402 Southern Ave., Beech Grove, IN 46107-1197 t) 317-788-7581 benedictinn@benedictinn.org www.benedictinn.org Retreats & workshops. Sr. Jennifer Mechtild Horner, OSB, Admin.;

INDIANAPOLIS

***Our Lady of Fatima Retreat House, Inc.** - 5353 E. 56th St., Indianapolis, IN 46226 t) 317-545-7681 fatima@archindy.org www.archindy.org/fatima Georgene Beiriger, Dir.;

MOUNT ST. FRANCIS

Mount Saint Francis Friary and Retreat Center - 101 St. Anthony Dr., Mount St. Francis, IN 47146-9999 t) 812-923-8817 retreats@mountsaintfrancis.org mountsaintfrancis.org Rev. Wayne Hellmann, O.F.M.Conv., Prov.; Rev. David Lenz, O.F.M.Conv., In Res.; Rev. Ken Bartsch, O.F.M.Conv., Chap.; Rev. John Elmer, O.F.M.Conv., Chap.; Bro. Paul Clark, O.F.M.Conv., Prof.; Bro. Dennes Moses, O.F.M.Conv., Archivist; Rev. Kenneth Davis, O.F.M.Conv., de Familia / Prof.; Rev. Leopold Keffler, O.F.M.Conv., de Familia / Prof.; Friar Nicholas Wolfla, O.F.M.Conv., Prov. Secy. / Guardian;

Province of Our Lady of Consolation, Inc. - 101 St. Anthony Dr., Mount St. Francis, IN 47146

t) 812-923-8444 secretaryolc@franciscansusa.org www.mountsaintfrancis.org (Provincial Office) Rev. Martin Day, O.F.M.Conv., Prov.;

ST. MEINRAD

Archabbey Guest House & Retreat Center - 200 Hill Dr., St. Meinrad, IN 47577 t) 812-357-6585; 800-581-6905; 812-357-6611 (Archabbey) mzoeller@saintmeinrad.edu; guestservices@saintmeinrad.edu www.saintmeinrad.edu Facilities available for Group Retreats, Workshops, Directed Retreats, and Private or Silent Retreats. Bro. Maurus Zoeller, O.S.B., Dir.;

SEMINARIES [SEM]

INDIANAPOLIS

Bishop Simon Bruté College Seminary, Inc. - 2500 Cold Spring Rd., Indianapolis, IN 46222 t) 317-924-4100 jmoriarty@archindy.org Very Rev. Joseph B. Moriarty, Rector; Rev. Andrew W. Syberg, Vice-Rector; Stds.: 24; Pr. Tchrs.: 3

ST. MEINRAD

Saint Meinrad School of Theology - 200 Hill Dr., St. Meinrad, IN 47577 t) 812-357-6611 rector@saintmeinrad.edu www.saintmeinrad.edu/ Rev. Denis Robinson, O.S.B., Pres.; Rev. Tobias Colgan, O.S.B., Vice Rector; Robert Alvis, Dean; Sr. Jeana Visel, O.S.B., Dir.; Lisa Castlebury, Treas.; Stds.: 193; Lay Tchrs.: 12; Pr. Tchrs.: 6

SPECIAL CARE FACILITIES [SPF]

INDIANAPOLIS

A Caring Place - Adult Day Services - c/o Fairview Presbyterian Church, 4609 N. Capitol Ave., Indianapolis, IN 46208 t) 317-466-0015 lsperry@archindy.org Lisa Sperry, Dir.; Asstd. Annu.: 19; Staff: 6

TERRE HAUTE

Gibault Children's Services - 6401 S. U.S. Hwy. 41, Terre Haute, IN 47802 t) 812-299-1156 gibault@gibault.org www.gibault.org Residential treatment facility for 6-21 year olds, sponsored by the Knights of Columbus of Indiana. Michele Madley, Pres.; Bed Capacity: 126; Asstd. Annu.: 211; Staff: 190

An asterisk (*) denotes an organization that has established tax-exempt status directly with the IRS and is not covered by the USCCB Group Ruling.

Diocese of Jackson

(Dioecesis Jacksoniensis)

MOST REVEREND JOSEPH R. KOPACZ, D.D., PH.D.

Bishop of Jackson; ordained May 7, 1977; appointed Bishop of Jackson December 12, 2013; consecrated and installed February 6, 2014. Mailing Address: P.O. Box 2248, Jackson, MS 39225-2248.

Chancery Office: 237 E. Amite St., P.O. Box 2248, Jackson, MS 39225-2248. T: 601-969-1880; F: 601-960-8455.
www.jacksondiocese.org
chancery@jacksondiocese.org

Square Miles 37,643.

Established July 28, 1837 as Diocese of Natchez. Name changed to Diocese of Natchez-Jackson, March 7, 1957. Name changed to Diocese of Jackson, June 6, 1977.

Comprises 65 Counties in the State of Mississippi, namely: Adams, Alcorn, Amite, Attala, Benton, Bolivar, Calhoun, Carroll, Chickasaw, Choctaw, Claiborne, Clarke, Clay, Coahoma, Copiah, De Soto, Franklin, Grenada, Hinds, Holmes, Humphreys, Issaquena, Itawamba, Jasper, Jefferson, Kemper, Lafayette, Lauderdale, Leake, Lee, Leflore, Lincoln, Lowndes, Madison, Marshall, Monroe, Montgomery, Neshoba, Newton, Noxubee, Oktibbeha, Panola, Pike, Pontotoc, Prentiss, Quitman, Rankin, Scott, Sharkey, Simpson, Smith, Sunflower, Tallahatchie, Tate, Tippah, Tishomingo, Tunica, Union, Warren, Washington, Webster, Wilkinson, Winston, Yalobusha and Yazoo.

Legal Title: "Catholic Diocese of Jackson".

STATISTICAL OVERVIEW

Personnel

Bishop....1
Priests: Diocesan Active in Diocese....24
Priests: Retired, Sick or Absent....25
Number of Diocesan Priests....49
Religious Priests in Diocese....19
Total Priests in your Diocese....68
Extern Priests in Diocese....12
Ordinations:
Diocesan Priests....1
Transitional Deacons....1
Permanent Deacons....6
Permanent Deacons in Diocese....14
Total Brothers....4
Total Sisters....38

Parishes

Parishes....72
With Resident Pastor:
Resident Diocesan Priests....22
Resident Religious Priests....28
Without Resident Pastor:
Administered by Priests....17
Administered by Deacons....2
Administered by Religious Women....1
Administered by Lay People....2
Missions....17
Pastoral Centers....2

Professional Ministry Personnel:
Sisters....9
Lay Ministers....9

Welfare

Catholic Hospitals....1
Total Assisted....494,350
Homes for the Aged....1
Total Assisted....490
Residential Care of Children....2
Total Assisted....70
Day Care Centers....2
Total Assisted....225
Specialized Homes....8
Total Assisted....750
Special Centers for Social Services....12
Total Assisted....720
Residential Care of Disabled....1
Total Assisted....9

Educational

Diocesan Students in Other Seminaries....8
Total Seminarians....8
High Schools, Diocesan and Parish....4
Total Students....1,610
Elementary Schools, Diocesan and Parish....10
Total Students....1,348
Elementary Schools, Private....2
Total Students....220
Non-residential Schools for the Disabled....1
Total Students....9
Catechesis / Religious Education:
High School Students....1,199
Elementary Students....2,453
Total Students under Catholic Instruction....6,847
Teachers in Diocese:
Sisters....3
Lay Teachers....303

Vital Statistics

Receptions into the Church:
Infant Baptism Totals....604
Minor Baptism Totals....75
Adult Baptism Totals....66
Received into Full Communion....152
First Communions....588
Confirmations....367
Marriages:
Catholic....86
Interfaith....55
Total Marriages....141
Deaths....381
Total Catholic Population....45,051
Total Population....2,303,500

LEADERSHIP

Chancery Office - t) 601-969-1880 chancery@jacksondiocese.org www.jacksondiocese.org Most Rev. Joseph R. Kopacz; Rev. Lincoln Dall, Vicar General; Mary Woodward, Chancellor;

Office of the Bishop - Most Rev. Joseph R. Kopacz;

Ecumenism - Mary Woodward;

Office of Vicar General - Rev. Lincoln Dall;

Moderator of the Curia - Rev. Lincoln Dall;

Parish Pastoral Councils - Rev. Lincoln Dall;

Propagation of the Faith - Rev. Lincoln Dall, Dir.;

Vicar for Priests - Rev. Kent Bowlds;

Chancellor - Mary Woodward;

Archivist - Mary Woodward, Archivist;

Office of Liturgy - Mary Woodward, Dir.;

Ecclesiastical Notaries - Mary Woodward; Rhonda Bowden; Rev. Matthew P. Simmons;

Victim Assistance Coordinator - t) 601-326-3736 Erika Rojas, Dir.;

Judicial Vicar - Rev. Jeffrey Waldrep; Rev. Msgr. Michael Flannery, Adjunct Judicial Vicar;

Vice Chancellor - Rev. Jeffrey Waldrep;

OFFICES AND DIRECTORS

Department of Social Services - t) 601-326-3724 Wanda Thomas, Exec. Dir.;

Department of Communications - Joanna King, Dir.;

Mississippi Catholic - Joanna King, Editor;

Department of Evangelization and Education - Karla Luke, Dir.;

Early Child Development, Health and Education Projects - Karla Luke;

Superintendent of Schools - Karla Luke;

Department of Faith Formation - Fran Lavelle, Dir.;

Campus Ministry/Young Adults - Amelia Rizor, Coord.;

Charismatic Renewal - Rev. William F. Henry;

Director of Spring Hill Theology Program - Fran Lavelle, Dir.;

Engaged Encounter - Debbie Tubertini, Coord.;

Intercultural Ministry - Sr. Amelia Breton, Coord.;

Marriage & Family Ministry - Debbie Tubertini, Coord.;

Youth Ministry - Abbey Schuhmann, Coord.;

Department of Stewardship - Development - Rebecca Harris, Dir.;

Catholic Foundation of Mississippi - t) 601-960-8477 Rebecca Harris, Dir.;

Department of Temporal Affairs - Carolyn Callahan, Dir.;

Director of Permanent Diaconate - Dcn. John T. McGregor, Dir.;

Office of Human Resources - Charles Tomlinson, Dir.;

Office of Child Protection - Jenifer Jenkins (jenifer.jenkins@jacksondiocese.org);

Office of Vocations - Rev. Nick Adam, Dir. (nick.adam@jacksondiocese.org);

CANONICAL SERVICES

Auditors/Assessors - Rev. Jason Johnston; Rev. Matthew P. Simmons; Rev. Joseph Tonos;

Judges - Rev. Jeffrey Waldrep; Rev. Msgr. Michael Flannery; Rev. David Szatkowski, S.C.J.;

Defenders of the Bond - Jacqueline Rapp; Rev. Kevin Slattery; Amy Jill Strickland;

Promoter of Justice - Rev. Thomas McGing;

CONSULTATIVE BODIES

Consultative Boards - Most Rev. Joseph R. Kopacz; Rev. Lincoln Dall, Vicar; Mary Woodward, Chancellor;

Association of Priests - Most Rev. Joseph R. Kopacz, Chair; Most Rev. Louis F. Kihneman III, Chair; Rev. Jason Johnston, Pres.;

Continuing Formation Committee - Rev. Nick Adam; Rev. Kent Bowlds; Dcn. John T. McGregor;

Diocesan Consultors - Most Rev. Joseph R. Kopacz, Pres.; Mary Woodward, Contact; Rev. Jeffrey Waldrep;

Finance Council - Most Rev. Joseph R. Kopacz; Bill Philipp, Chair; Carolyn Callahan, Ex Officio;

Personnel Board - Rev. Kent Bowlds, Dir.; Rev. Lincoln Dall, Ex Officio; Rev. Jason Johnston;

Priests' Council - Most Rev. Joseph R. Kopacz, Pres.; Rev. Timothy Murphy, Secy.; Rev. Jeffrey Waldrep, Treas.;

Deanery Representatives -

Deanery I -

Deanery II - Rev. Aaron Williams;

Deanery III - Rev. Jose de Jesus Sanchez;

Deanery IV - Rev. David Szatkowski, S.C.J.;

Deanery V - Rev. Timothy Murphy, Secy.;

Deanery VI - Rev. Augustine Palimattam Poulose;

Appointed Members - Rev. Joseph Dyer; Rev. Kent Bowlds; Rev. Adolfo Suarez-Pasillas;

Ex Officio - Rev. Lincoln Dall;

STATE OF MISSISSIPPI

PARISHES, MISSIONS, AND CLERGY

ABERDEEN

St. Francis of Assisi - 108 S. James St., Aberdeen, MS 39730-0134; Mailing: P.O. Box 134, Aberdeen, MS 39730-0134 t) 662-813-2295 Rev. Joseph Le, Pst.; CRP Stds.: 9

Immaculate Heart of Mary - 818 N. Jackson St., Houston, MS 38851-0309; Mailing: P.O. Box 309, Houston, MS 38851-0309 t) 662-456-5450 ihmhm2012@att.net; ihmcatholicchurch@att.net Lorenzo Aju, Lay Ecclesial Minister;

St. Theresa - 116 N. Fleming St., Okolona, MS 38860

AMORY

St. Helen - 401 Eighth Ave. S., Amory, MS 38821-0097; Mailing: P.O. Box 97, Amory, MS 38821-0097 t) 662-256-8392 Rev. Joseph Le, Pst.; Nancy Hoang, DRE; CRP Stds.: 32

BATESVILLE

St. Mary - 120 Hwy. 35 N., Batesville, MS 38606-0569; Mailing: P.O. Box 569, Batesville, ME 38606 t) 662-563-2273 saintmarycc1960@gmail.com Rev. Pradeep Kumar Thirumalareddy (India), Pst.; Robin Ridge, DRE; CRP Stds.: 62

St. John the Baptist - 110 N. Main St., Sardis, MS 38666; Mailing: P. O. Box 569, Batesville, MS 38606-0569 t) (662) 563-2273

BELZONI

All Saints - 200 Bowles St., Belzoni, MS 39038-3602 t) 662-247-1408 allsaintsbelzoni@att.net Rev. Panneer Selvam Arockiam, Pst.; CRP Stds.: 6

BOONEVILLE

St. Francis of Assisi - 721 N. College St., Booneville, MS 38829; Mailing: P.O. Box 654, Booneville, MS 38829 t) 662-728-7509 Rev. Timothy Murphy, Sacr. Min.; CRP Stds.: 3

St. Mary - 205 Eastport St. E., Iuka, MS 38852; Mailing: P.O. Box 651, Iuka, MS 38852 t) 662-423-9358 stmarycatho78710@bellsouth.net

BROOKHAVEN

St. Francis of Assisi - 227 E. Cherokee St., Brookhaven, MS 39602-0196; Mailing: P.O. Box 196, Brookhaven, MS 39602-0196 t) 601-754-0963 (CRP); 601-833-1799 stfrancisbrookhaven.org Rev. Manohar Thanugundla, Pst.; Erin Womack, DRE; CRP Stds.: 62

CAMDEN

Sacred Heart - 1493 Hwy. 17, Camden, MS 39045 t) 668-468-2354 (CRP); 662-468-2354; 662-468-2222 www.sacredheartcamden.com Rev. Guy Wilson, S.T., Pst.; Sr. Mary Anne Poeschl, R.S.M., DRE;

CANTON

Holy Child Jesus - 315 Garrett St., Canton, MS 39046-0366; Mailing: P.O. Box 366, Canton, MS 39046-0366 t) 601-859-2957 smapoeschl@hotmail.com; guywilst@gmail.com Rev. Guy Wilson, S.T., Pst.; Sr. Mary Anne Poeschl, R.S.M., DRE; CRP Stds.: 2

Sacred Heart - 238 E. Center St., Canton, MS 39046-0361; Mailing: P.O. Box 361, Canton, MS 39046-0361 t) 601-859-3749 Rev. Juan Chavajay, Pst.; Blanca Pealta, DRE; CRP Stds.: 50

CARTHAGE

St. Anne - 207 Red Dog Rd., Carthage, MS 39051-3113 t) 601-297-7190 Rev. Marco Sanchez, S.T. (Mexico), Pst.; Terrica Dawson, DRE; CRP Stds.: 7

CHARLESTON

St. John - 304 W. Cypress St., Charleston, MS 38921-0030; Mailing: P.O. Box 30, Charleston, MS 38921-0030 t) 662-647-3170 saintjohncharleston@gmail.com Rev. Lincoln Dall, Moderator; Rev. Arokia Savio, Sacr. Min.;

CLARKSDALE

St. Elizabeth - 130 Florence Ave., Clarksdale, MS 38614-2720 t) 662-624-4301 Rev. Raju Macherla, Pst.; Catelin Britt, DRE; CRP Stds.: 50

St. Elizabeth School - (Grades PreK-6) 150 Florence Ave., Clarksdale, MS 38614-2720 t) 662-624-4239 scauthen@seseagles.com Sarah Cauthen, Prin.; Stds.: 118; Lay Tchrs.: 16

Immaculate Conception - 510 Ritchie Ave., Clarksdale, MS 38614 t) 662-624-4029 Rev. Raju Macherla, Pst.;

CLEVELAND

Our Lady of Victories - 215 Bishop Rd., Cleveland, MS 38732-2446 t) 662-846-6273 olvcc@att.net www.olvcleveland.com Rev. Kent Bowlds, Pst.; CRP Stds.: 152

CLINTON

Holy Savior - 714 Lindale St., Clinton, MS 39056; Mailing: P.O. Box 85, Clinton, MS 39060-0085 t) 601-924-6344 re_holysavior@outlook.com; holysavior@att.net www.holy-savior-ms.org Rev. Lincoln Dall, Pst.; Rev. Thomas McGing, Pastor Emer.; Trish Ballard, DRE; CRP Stds.: 81

Immaculate Conception - 232 Main St., Raymond, MS 39154 t) (601) 924-6344

COLUMBUS

Annunciation - 823 College St., Columbus, MS 39701-5804 t) 662-327-2927 x11; 662-328-2927 x11 (CRP) Rev. Jeffrey Waldrep, Pst.; Dcn. David J. Gruseck; Erica Gruseck, DRE; CRP Stds.: 90

Annunciation School - (Grades PreK-8) 223 N. Browder St., Columbus, MS 39702-5236 t) 662-328-4479 Joni House, Prin.; Stds.: 200; Lay Tchrs.: 22

CORINTH

St. James the Less - 3189 N. Harper Rd., Corinth, MS 38835-0660; Mailing: P.O. Box 660, Corinth, MS 38835-0660 t) 601-331-5184 (CRP) stjamesc@comcast.net Rev. Mario Solorzano, Pst.; Peggy Clapp, DRE; CRP Stds.: 95

CRYSTAL SPRINGS

St. John the Evangelist - 221 E. Georgetown St., Crystal Springs, MS 39059-0167; Mailing: P.O. Box 167, Crystal Springs, MS 39059-0167 t) 601-892-1717 stjohnstmartin21@gmail.com Janice Stansell, Lay Ecclesial Min.; CRP Stds.: 13

St. Martin of Tours - 113 E. Conway, Hazlehurst, MS 39083

FAYETTE

St. Anne - 89 Harriston Rd., Fayette, MS 39069; Mailing: P.O. Box 159, Fayette, MS 39069 t) (601) 445-5700 stannefay@gmail.com Rev. Anthony Okwum, S.S.J., Admin.;

FLOWOOD

St. Paul - 5971 Hwy. 25, Flowood, MS 39232-7101 t) 601-992-9547 office@spaulcc.org Rev. Gerard Hurley, Pst.; Renee Borne, DRE; CRP Stds.: 188

Learning Center - 5969 Hwy. 25, Flowood, MS 39232-7101 t) 601-992-2876 Jennifer Henry, Dir.;

FOREST

St. Michael - Hwy. 80 E., Forest, MS 39074; Mailing: P. O. Box 388, Forest, MS 39074 t) 601-469-1916 Rev. Adolfo Suarez-Pasillas, Pst.; Liz Edmundson, DRE; CRP Stds.: 63

St. Anne - 608 Decatur St., Newton, MS 39345 t) (601) 469-1916

Centro San Martin De Porres - Hwy. 80 W., Morton, MS 39117 t) (601) 469-1916

GLUCKSTADT

St. Joseph - 127 Church Rd., Gluckstadt, MS 39110 t) 601-856-2054 carla@stjosephgluckstadt.com www.stjosephgluckstadt.com Rev. Matthew P. Simmons, Pst.; Karen Worrell, DRE; CRP Stds.: 255

GREENVILLE

St. Joseph - 412 Main St., Greenville, MS 38702-1220; Mailing: P.O. Box 1220, Greenville, MS 38702-1220 t) 662-335-5251 stjosephgreenville.org Rev. Jose de Jesus Sanchez, Pst.; Mary Ann Barker, DRE; CRP Stds.: 43

St. Joseph Catholic Unit School - (Grades PreK-12) 1501 VFW Rd., Greenville, MS 38701-5841 t) 662-378-9711 Craig Mandolini, Prin.; Christy Jonely, Elementary Prin.; Stds.: 273; Lay Tchrs.: 26

Sacred Heart - 560 E. Gloster St., Greenville, MS 38701-3836 t) 662-332-0891 Rev. Sebastian Myladiyil, SVD, Pst.; Rev. Thomas A. Mullally, S.V.D., In Res.; Bynarozelle Mitchell, DRE; CRP Stds.: 27

GREENWOOD

St. Francis of Assisi - 2613 Hwy. 82 E., Greenwood, MS 38930-5966 t) 662-453-0623 Rev. Joachim Studwell, O.F.M., Pst.; Rev. Camillus Janas, O.F.M., Assoc. Pst.; CRP Stds.: 52

St. Francis of Assisi School - (Grades PreK-6) 2607 Hwy. 82 E., Greenwood, MS 38930-5966 t) 662-453-9511 stfrancisgreenwood@gmail.com www.sfgwschool.org Jackie Lewis, Prin.;

Immaculate Heart of Mary - 511 W. Washington St., Greenwood, MS 38935-0313; Mailing: P.O. Box 313, Greenwood, MS 38935-0313 t) 662-453-3980 Rev. Andrew Nguyen, Pst.; Loretta Assini, DRE; CRP Stds.: 51

GRENADA

St. Peter - 320 College Blvd., Grenada, MS 38901-3808 t) 662-226-2490 stpeter38901@gmail.com stpetergrenadams.com Rev. Arokia Savio, Pst.; Annette Tipton, DRE; CRP Stds.: 20

HERNANDO

Holy Spirit - 545 E. Commerce St., Hernando, MS 38632-0424; Mailing: P.O. Box 424, Hernando, MS 38632-0424 t) 662-429-7851 www.holyspirit-catholic.com Rev. David Szatkowski, SCJ, Pst.; Rev. Hendrik Ardianto, S.C.J., Assoc. Pst.; Rev. Louis Mariano Fernandes, SCJ (India), Assoc. Pst.; Amanda Ready, DRE; CRP Stds.: 104

HOLLY SPRINGS

St. Joseph - 305 E. Van Dorn Ave., Holly Springs, MS 38635-0430; Mailing: P.O. Box 430, Holly Springs, MS 38635-0430 t) 662-252-3138 Rev. David Szatkowski, SCJ, Moderator; Rev. Louis Mariano Fernandes, SCJ (India), Assoc. Pst.; Rev. Hendrik Ardianto, S.C.J., Assoc. Pst.; Sr. Rose Hacker, S.S.S.F., Pst. Assoc.; Sr. Emily Morgan, R.S.M., DRE; CRP Stds.: 33

INDIANOLA

St. Benedict the Moor - 403 Church St., Indianola, MS 38751-0407; Mailing: P.O. Box 407, Indianola, MS 38751-0407 t) 662-887-4659 Rev. Sleeva Reddy Mekala (India), Admin.;

Immaculate Conception - 702 N. Sunflower Ext. Hwy. 448, Indianola, MS 38751-0944; Mailing: P.O. Box 944, Indianola, MS 38751 t) 662-887-4659 Rev. Sleeva Reddy Mekala (India), Admin.; Rosemary Miller, DRE;

JACKSON

St. Peter Cathedral - 123 N. West St., Jackson, MS 39201; Mailing: P O Box 57, Jackson, MS 39205-0057 t) 601-969-3125 info@cathedralsaintpeter.org www.cathedralsaintpeter.org Rev. Nick Adam, Rector; Hope Johnson, DRE; CRP Stds.: 11

Christ the King - 2303 John R. Lynch St., Jackson, MS 39209 t) 601-948-8867 christthekingjackson.org Rev. Joseph Dyer, Sacr. Min.; Dcn. Denzil Lobo, Ecclesial Min.;

Sister Thea Bowman School - (Grades PreK-6) 1217 Hattiesburg St., Jackson, MS 39209-7411 t) 601-352-5441 theabowmanschool.com Christopher Payne, Prin.; Stds.: 37; Lay Tchrs.: 5

Holy Family - 820 Forest Ave., Jackson, MS 39206-3299 t) 601-362-1888 Rev. Mario Roberto Rasonabe, SVD (Philippines), Admin.; Joyce Adams, DRE; Pamela Brown, DRE; CRP Stds.: 16

Holy Ghost - 1151 Cloister St., Jackson, MS 39202 t) 601-353-1339 holyghostcloister@gmail.com Rev. Nick Hien Nguyen, SVD (Vietnam), Pst.; Melanie Norwood, DRE; CRP Stds.: 3

St. Richard of Chichester - 1242 Lynnwood Dr., Jackson, MS 39236-6547; Mailing: P.O. Box 16547, Jackson, MS 39236-6547 t) 601-366-2335 Rev. Joseph Tonos, Pst.; Rev. Andrew Bowden, Par. Vicar; Tara Clifford, DRE; CRP Stds.: 193

St. Richard of Chichester School - (Grades PreK-6) 100 Holly Dr., Jackson, MS 39206-6037 t) 601-366-1157 jdavid@strichardschool.org www.strichardschool.org Jennifer David, Prin.; Stds.: 220; Lay Tchrs.: 25

St. Richard's School Special Kids Program - 100 Holly Dr., Jackson, MS 39206-6037 t) (601) 366-2335 sk@saintrichard.com Turner Kim, Dir.;

St. Therese - 329 W. McDowell Rd., Jackson, MS 39204; Mailing: P O Box 8642, Jackson, MS 39284-8642 t) 601-372-4481 www.sttheresejackson.org Rev. Kevin Slattery, Admin.; CRP Stds.: 88

KOSCIUSKO

St. Therese - 108 Bell St., Kosciusko, MS 39090-0628; Mailing: P.O. Box 628, Kosciusko, MS 39090-0628 t) 662-289-1193 Rev. Marco Sanchez, S.T. (Mexico), Pst.; Marline Tully, DRE; CRP Stds.: 10

LELAND

St. James - 312 E. Third St., Leland, MS 38756-0352; Mailing: P.O. Box 352, Leland, MS 38756-0352 t) 662-686-7352 Rev. Sleeva Reddy Mekala (India), Pst.;

Immaculate Conception - Hwy. 12 E., Hollandale, MS 38748 t) (662) 686-7352

LEXINGTON

St. Thomas - 200 Boulevard St., Lexington, MS 39095-3531 t) 662-453-0623 Rev. Joachim Studwell, O.F.M., Admin.;

Sacred Heart - 304 Jones St., Winona, MS 38967-2238 t) 601-591-8254

LOUISVILLE

Sacred Heart - 630 N. Spring Ave., Louisville, MS 39339-2222 t) 662-773-6062 sacredheart39339@yahoo.com Rev. Darnis Selvanayakam, Sacramental Min.;

MADISON

St. Francis of Assisi - 4000 W. Tidewater Ln., Madison, MS 39110-8942 t) 601-856-5556 contact.us@stfrancismadison.org www.stfrancismadison.org Rev. Albeenreddy Vatti, Pst.; Rev. Msgr. Elvin Sunds, In Res.; Mary Catherine George, DRE; CRP Stds.: 166

Assisi Early Learning Center - t) 601-856-9494 aelcmadison@jacksondiocese.org aelcmadison.org LaToya Kelly, Dir.;

St. Anthony Catholic School - (Grades PreK-6) 1585 Old Mannsdale Rd., Madison, MS 39110 t) 601-607-7054 www.stanthonyeagles.org Anne Cowger, Prin.; Stds.: 240; Lay Tchrs.: 21

MAGEE

St. Stephen - 594 Simpson Hwy. 149, Magee, MS 39111-0427; Mailing: P.O. Box 427, Magee, MS 39111-0427 t) 601-849-3237 office@ststephenchurchmagee.com www.ststephenchurchmagee.com Rev. Kevin Slattery, Sacr. Min.; Kirby Rivere, Lay Ecclesial Min.; Kenny McDonald, DRE; CRP Stds.: 8

MAGNOLIA

St. James the Greater Catholic Parish - 125 E. Bay St., Magnolia, MS 39652 t) (769) 327-2022 stalphonsusmccomb@gmail.com Rev. Suresh Reddy Thirumalareddy, Pst.; CRP Stds.: 5

MCCOMB

St. Alphonsus - 501 Delaware Ave., McComb, MS 39648; Mailing: PO Box 1105, McComb, MS 39649-1105 t) 601-684-5648 stalphonsusmccomb@gmail.com Rev. Suresh Reddy Thirumalareddy, Pst.; CRP Stds.: 111

MERIDIAN

St. Joseph - 1914 18th Ave., Meridian, MS 39302-0532; Mailing: P.O. Box 532, Meridian, MS 39302-0532 t) 601-484-8953 john@catholicmeridian.org www.catholicmeridian.org Rev. Augustine Palimattam Poulose, Pst.; Rev. Justin Joseph (India), Par. Vicar;

St. Patrick - 2601 Davis St., Meridian, MS 39301; Mailing: P.O. Box 529, Meridian, MS 39302-0529 t) 601-693-1321 john@catholicmeridian.org www.catholicmeridian.org Rev. Augustine Palimattam Poulose, Pst.; Rev. Justin Joseph (India), Par. Vicar; John Harwell, DRE; CRP Stds.: 114

St. Patrick School - (Grades PreK-6) 2700 Davis St., Meridian, MS 39301-5707 t) 601-482-6044 rcalcote@stpatrickcatholicschool.org www.stpatrickcatholicschool.org Rob Calcote, Prin.; Stds.: 117; Lay Tchrs.: 9

NATCHEZ

Assumption of the B.V.M. - 10 Morgantown Rd., Natchez, MS 39120-2788 t) 601-442-7250 office@assumption-bvm.org Rev. Aaron Williams, Pst.; CRP Stds.: 1

Holy Family - 16 Orange Ave., Natchez, MS 39120-3647 t) 601-445-5700 www.holyfamilynatchez.com Rev. Anthony Okwum, S.S.J., Admin.;

St. John the Baptist - 260 Cranfield Rd., Cranfield, MS 39661

St. Mary Basilica - 107 S. Union St., Natchez, MS 39121-1044; Mailing: P.O. Box 1044, Natchez, MS 39121-1044 t) 601-445-5616 Rev. Aaron Williams, Pst.; Ruth Powers, DRE; CRP Stds.: 14

Cathedral School - (Grades PreK-12) 701 N. Dr. Martin Luther King, Jr. St., Natchez, MS 39120-2962 t) 601-442-2531 www.cathedralgreenwave.com (Coed) Robin Branton, Prin.; Kimberly Burkley, Elem. Prin.; Stds.: 618; Lay Tchrs.: 52

NEW ALBANY

St. Francis of Assisi - 650 Hwy 15 S., New Albany, MS 38652-0887; Mailing: P.O. Box 887, New Albany, MS 38652-0887 t) 662-534-4654 Rev. Jesuraj Xavier, Pst.; Ronnie Rossetti, DRE; CRP Stds.: 38

St. Matthew Catholic Mission - 15710 Hwy. 15 N., Ripley, MS 38663; Mailing: P. O. Box 452, Ripley, MS 38663 t) 662-993-8862 stmatthewcatholicchurch@ripleycable.net Sr. Carol Ann Prenger, S.S.N.D., Parish Life Coord.;

OLIVE BRANCH

Queen of Peace - 8455 Germantown Rd., Olive Branch, MS 38654-0065; Mailing: P.O. Box 65, Olive Branch, MS 38654-0065 t) 662-895-5007 Rev. David Szatkowski, SCJ, Moderator; Rev. Hendrik Ardianto, S.C.J., Assoc. Pst.; Rev. Louis Mariano Fernandes, SCJ (India), Assoc. Pst.; Sr. Rose Hacker, S.S.S.F., Pst. Assoc.; Victoria Stirek, DRE; CRP Stds.: 122

OXFORD

St. John the Evangelist - 416 S. 5th St., Oxford, MS 38655-3806 t) 662-234-6073 Rev. Mark H Shoffner, Pst.; Jennifer Newsome, DRE; CRP Stds.: 120

PAULDING

St. Michael - 1823 Hwy. 503, Paulding, MS 39348; Mailing: P.O. Box 388, Forest, MS 39074-0388 t) 601-469-1916 Rev. Adolfo Suarez-Pasillas, Pst.; Liz Edmundson, Bus. Mgr.;

PEARL

St. Jude - 399 Barrow St., Pearl, MS 39288-5526; Mailing: P.O. Box 5526, Pearl, MS 39288-5526 t) 601-939-3181 ccd@stjudepearl.org; kmcgregor@stjudepearl.org Dcn. John T. McGregor, Ecclesial Minister; Rev. Jofin George (India), Sacr. Min.; CRP Stds.: 128

PHILADELPHIA

Holy Cross - 406 Wilson St., Philadelphia, MS 39350-2906 t) 601-656-1841 Rev. Darnis Selvanayakam, Pst.; Emily Moran, DRE; CRP Stds.: 75

Holy Rosary - 10131 Holy Rosary Rd., Philadelphia, MS 39350-0037; Mailing: PO Box 37, Philadelphia, MS 39350 t) 601-656-2880 www.holyrosaryindianmission.com Rev. Robert Goodyear, S.T., Pst.; CRP Stds.: 19

St. Catherine - 9857 Hwy. 489, Conehatta, MS 39057

St. Therese - 0110 BIA Rd. 2213, Choctaw, MS 39350

PORT GIBSON

St. Joseph - 411 Coffee St., Port Gibson, MS 39150; Mailing: P.O. Box 1012, Port Gibson, MS 39150-1012 t) 601-437-5790 Rev. Joseph C. Nguyen, SVD, Admin.;

ROBINSONVILLE

Good Shepherd Catholic Church - 1329 Casino Center Dr. Ext., Robinsonville, MS 38664; Mailing: 785 Church Rd. W, Southaven, MS 38671 t) 662-342-1073 ctkshaven@aol.com Rev. David Szatkowski, SCJ, Moderator; Dcn. Ted Schreck; Rev. Louis Mariano Fernandes, SCJ (India), Assoc. Pst.; Rev. Hendrik Ardianto, S.C.J., Assoc. Pst.;

Sacred Heart Chapel - 6473 Hwy. 161 N., Walls, MS 38680-0190; Mailing: P.O. Box 190, Walls, MS 38680-0190 t) 662-357-0250

ROSEDALE

Sacred Heart - 300 Riverside Dr., Rosedale, MS 38769-0307; Mailing: P.O. Box 307, Rosedale, MS 38769-0307 t) (662) 332-0891 Rev. Sebastian Myladiyil, SVD, Sacr. Min.;

SENATOBIA

St. Gregory the Great - 705 Strayhorn St., Senatobia, MS 38668; Mailing: 785 Church Rd. W., Southaven, MS 38671 t) 662-342-1073 ctkshaven@aol.com Rev. David Szatkowski, SCJ, Moderator; Rev. Hendrik Ardianto, S.C.J., Assoc. Pst.; Rev. Louis Mariano Fernandes, SCJ (India), Assoc. Pst.; Dcn. Ted Schreck; Sr. Rose Hacker, S.S.S.F., Pst. Assoc.; Sr. Emily Morgan, R.S.M., DRE; CRP Stds.: 75

SHAW

St. Francis of Assisi - 301 Dean Blvd., Shaw, MS 38773-0239; Mailing: P.O. Box 239, Shaw, MS 38773-0239 t) 662-754-5561 stfrancisassisi@gmail.com Rev. Sebastian Myladiyil, SVD, Sacr. Min.;

SHELBY

St. Mary - 900 Martin Luther King St., Shelby, MS 38774-0208; Mailing: P.O. Box 208, Shelby, MS 38774-0208 t) 662-719-5216 saintmary700@att.net Rev. Raju Macherla, Sacr. Min.;

SOUTHAVEN

Christ the King - 785 Church Rd. W., Southaven, MS 38671 t) 662-342-1073 ctkshaven@aol.com Rev. David Szatkowski, SCJ, Moderator; Rev. Hendrik Ardianto, S.C.J., Assoc. Pst.; Rev. Louis Mariano Fernandes, SCJ (India), Assoc. Pst.; Dcn. Ted Schreck; Sr. Rose Hacker, S.S.S.F., Pst. Assoc.; Sr. Emily Morgan, R.S.M., Pst. Assoc.; Donna Williamson, DRE; CRP Stds.: 160

STARKVILLE

St. Joseph - 607 University Dr., Starkville, MS 39759 t) 662-323-2257 deaconjeff@stjosephstarkville.org; office@stjosephstarkville.org www.stjosephstarkville.org Rev. Jason Johnston, Pst.; Dcn. Jeff Artiques; Dcn. John A. McGinley; CRP Stds.: 79

Corpus Christi - 206 N. Washington St., Macon, MS 39341; Mailing: P. O. Box 533, Macon, MS 39341 t) 662-323-2557

Chaplaincy - c) (662) 769-4948 Meg Ferguson, Campus Min.;

TUPELO

St. James - 1911 N. Gloster St., Tupelo, MS 38802-0434; Mailing: P.O. Box 734, Tupelo, MS 38802-0434 t) 662-842-4881 Rev. Timothy Murphy, Pst.; Rev. Cesar Sanchez, Par. Vicar; Rhonda Hanby, DRE; CRP Stds.: 508

Christ the King - 100 E. Main St., Fulton, MS 38843-0614; Mailing: P.O. Box 614, Fulton, MS 38843-0614 t) 662-862-2239 Joan Shell, Pst. Assoc.;

St. Thomas Aquinas - 612 County Rd. 683, Saltillo, MS 38866 t) (662) 842-4881

St. Christopher - 431 Pine Ridge Dr., Pontotoc, MS 38863; Mailing: P.O. Box 67, Tupelo, MS 38863 t) 662-637-7204

VICKSBURG

St. Mary - 1512 Main St., Vicksburg, MS 39183-2652 t) 601-638-0115 (CRP) stmaryvicksburg.org Rev. Joseph C. Nguyen, SVD, Pst.; Dr. Josephine Calloway, DRE;

St. Michael - 100 St. Michael Pl., Vicksburg, MS 39180-8246 t) 601-636-3445 stmichaelvicksburg.org/ Rev. Robert Dore, Pst.; Mimi Mitchell, DRE; CRP Stds.: 51

St. Paul - 713 Crawford St., Vicksburg, MS 39180-0646 t) 601-636-0140 stpaulvick@att.net www.stpaulvicksburg.org Rev. Roy Russel Vincent, Pst.; CRP Stds.: 55

WEST POINT

Immaculate Conception - 26707 E. Main St., West Point, MS 39773-7545 t) 662-494-3486 immaculateconception-wp.org Rev. Binh Chau Nguyen, Pst.; Penny Elliott, DRE; CRP Stds.: 19

WOODVILLE

St. Joseph - 338 Church St., Woodville, MS 39669-0668; Mailing: P.O. Box 668, Woodville, MS 39669-0668 t) 601-888-3261 Rev. Anthony Claret Onyeocha, Pst.; Ferguson Margo, DRE; CRP Stds.: 8

Holy Family - 242 Main St., Gloster, MS 39638-0548; Mailing: P.O. Box 548, Gloster, MS 39638-0548 t) 601-225-1298

YAZOO CITY

St. Mary - 129 N. Washington St., Yazoo City, MS 39194-0027; Mailing: P.O. Box 27, Yazoo City, MS 39194-0027 t) 662-746-1680 Rev. Panneer Selvam Arockiam, Pst.; Diane Melton, DRE;

Our Mother of Mercy - 119 Jefferson St., Anguilla, MS 38721 t) (662) 746-1680

SCHOOLS: PRESCHOOL THRU HIGH SCHOOL

SCHOOLS

STATE OF MISSISSIPPI

HOLLY SPRINGS

Holy Family School - (PAR) (Grades PreK-8) 395 N. West St., Holly Springs, MS 38635-1922 t) 662-252-1612 tsangster@shsm.org www.hfamilyschool.org Tunia Sangster, Prin.; Stds.: 126; Lay Tchrs.: 18

SOUTHAVEN

Sacred Heart School - (PAR) (Grades PreK-8) 5150 Tchulahoma Rd., Southaven, MS 38671-9726 t) 662-349-0900 bmartin@shsm.org www.sheartschool.org Bridget Martin, Prin.; Andrea Vincent, Dir.; Stds.: 281; Sr. Tchrs.: 1; Lay Tchrs.: 23

VICKSBURG

Vicksburg Catholic School - (PAR) (Grades PreK-12) 1900 Grove St., Vicksburg, MS 39183 t) 601-636-2256; 601-638-5810 mary.arledge@vicksburgcatholic.org; katherine.emfinger@vicksburgcatholic.org www.vicksburgcatholic.org (Coed), Interparochial Virgil "Buddy" Strickland, Prin.; Katherine Emfinger, Dir.; Mary Arledge, Elementary School Prin.; Stds.: 550; Lay Tchrs.: 47

HIGH SCHOOLS

STATE OF MISSISSIPPI

MADISON

St. Joseph Catholic School - (PAR) (Grades 7-12) 308 New Mannsdale Rd., Madison, MS 39110 t) 601-898-4800 www.stjoebruins.com (Coed) Dena Kinsey, Prin.; Stds.: 390; Lay Tchrs.: 46

INSTITUTIONS LOCATED IN DIOCESE

CAMPUS MINISTRY / NEWMAN CENTERS [CAM]

BOONEVILLE

Northeast Mississippi Community College Catholic Student Center - St. Francis of Assisi, Booneville, MS 38829; Mailing: P.O. Box 654, Booneville, MS 38829 t) 662-728-7509 www.stfrancisbooneville.com Rev. Timothy Murphy, Pst.;

BROOKHAVEN

Lincoln Junior College Newman Center - St. Francis of Assisi, Brookhaven, MS 39602; Mailing: P.O. Box 196, Brookhaven, MS 39602-0196 t) 601-833-1799 Rev. Manohar Thanugundla, Pst.;

CLEVELAND

Delta State University Newman Center - 215 Bishop Rd., Cleveland, MS 38732-2446 t) 662-846-6273 olvcc@att.net Rev. Kent Bowlds, Pst.;

CLINTON

Mississippi College Catholic Student Association - Holy Savior, Clinton, MS 39056; Mailing: P.O. Box 85, Clinton, MS 39060 t) 601-924-6344 holysavior@att.net Rev. Lincoln Dall, Pst.;

COLUMBUS

Mississippi University for Women Student Center - Annunciation Church, 823 College St., Columbus, MS 39701 t) 662-328-2927 www.annunciationcatholicchurch.com Rev. Jeffrey Waldrep, Pst.;

FOREST

East Central Community College Newman Center - St. Michael, Forest, MS 39074; Mailing: P.O. Box 388, Forest, MS 39074 t) 601-469-1916 foreststmichael@att.net Liz Edmundson, Dir.;

HOLLY SPRINGS

Rust College Newman Center - St. Joseph, Holly Springs, MS 38635; Mailing: P.O. Box 430, Holly Springs, MS 38635 t) 662-252-3138

JACKSON

Belhaven College Catholic Student Association - 123 North West St., Jackson, MS 39201; Mailing: P.O. Box 57, Jackson, MS 39205-0057 t) 601-969-3125 info@cathedralsaintpeter.org Rev. Nick Adam, Rector;

Millsaps College Catholic Student Association - St. Peter Cathedral, Jackson, MS 39201; Mailing: P.O. Box 57, Jackson, MS 39205-0057 t) 601-969-3125 info@cathedrdalsaintpeter.org Rev. Nick Adam, Campus Min.;

Tougaloo College Newman Center - 1151 Cloister St., Jackson, MS 39202-2296 t) 601-353-1339 holyghostcloister@gmail.com Rev. Nick Hien Nguyen, SVD (Vietnam), Chap.;

University of Mississippi Medical Center - Catholic Student Association - St. Peter Cathedral, Jackson, MS 39201; Mailing: P.O. Box 57, Jackson, MS 39205-0057 t) 601-969-3125 info@cathedralsaintpeter.org Rev. Nick Adam;

LEXINGTON

Holmes Community College Newman Center - 200 Boulevard St., Lexington, MS 39095 t) 662-453-0623 Rev. Joachim Studwell, O.F.M., Pst.;

OXFORD

Ole Miss Campus Ministries - 416 S. 5th St., Oxford, MS 38655 t) 662-234-6073 Rev. Mark H Shoffner, Pst.;

STARKVILLE

Mississippi State University Catholic Campus Ministry - St. Joseph Church, 607 University Dr., Starkville, MS 39759 t) 662-323-2257 msstateccm.org Megan Kanatzar, Campus Min.;

CATHOLIC CHARITIES [CCH]

RIDGELAND

Catholic Charities, Inc. - 731 S. Pear Orchard, Ste. 51, Ridgeland, MS 39157 t) (601) 355-8634 Wanda Thomas, Exec. Dir.; Asstd. Annu.: 2,374; Staff: 89

CONVENTS, MONASTERIES, AND RESIDENCES FOR WOMEN [CON]

JACKSON

St. Dominic Convent - 969 Lakeland Dr., Jackson, MS 39216 t) 601-200-6729 sisterd@stdom.com www.stdom.com Sr. Mary Dorothea Sondgeroth, O.P., Asst. Dir. Health Svcs. & Foundation; Srs.: 7

Our Lady of Mount Carmel and Little Flower Monastery (Discalced Carmelites) - 2155 Terry Rd., Jackson, MS 39204 t) 601-373-1460 carmelshop@aol.com Sr. Mary Jane Agonoy, O.C.D., Prioress; Srs.: 6

HOSPITALS / HEALTH SERVICES [HOS]

JACKSON

St. Dominic-Jackson Memorial Hospital - 969 Lakeland Dr., Jackson, MS 39216-4699 t) 601-200-6848 scott.kashman@stdom.com www.stdom.com Scott Kashman, Pres.; Bed Capacity: 571; Asstd. Annu.: 494,350; Staff: 3,067

MISCELLANEOUS [MIS]

JACKSON

Jackson Diocese Educational Services, Inc. - 237 E. Amite St., Jackson, MS 39201-2168; Mailing: P.O. Box 2248, Jackson, MS 39225-2248 t) 601-960-6930 karla.luke@jacksondiocese.org schools.jacksondiocese.org/ Karla Luke, Exec. Dir., School Opers.;

Parroquia De San Miguel Arcangel - Catholic Diocese of Jackson, Jackson, MS 39201; Mailing: P.O. Box 2248, Jackson, MS 39225-2248 t) 601-969-1880 chancery@jacksondiocese.org Saltillo Mission Sponsored by Dioceses of Jackson and Biloxi. Rev. David Martinez Rubio, Admin.;

Pax Christi Franciscans - LaVerna House, 2108 Alta Woods Blvd., Jackson, MS 39204 t) 601-373-4463 genfeyen2@yahoo.com; r.kalscheur@gmail.com A Private Association of the Christian Faithful Genevieve Feyem, Pres.; Rhoda Kalscheur, Vice. Pres.;

MADISON

***St. Catherine's Village, Inc.** - 200 Dominican Dr., Madison, MS 39110 t) 601-856-0100 scott.kashman@fmolhs.org www.stcatherinesvillage.com Scott Kashman, Pres.;

PONTOTOC

Catholic Committee of the South, Inc. - ; Mailing: P.O. Box 67, Pontotoc, MS 38863 t) 662-489-7749

WALLS

Sacred Heart Southern Missions Housing Corporation - 9260 McLemore Dr., Walls, MS 38680-0365; Mailing: P.O. Box 365, Walls, MS 38680-0365 t) 662-781-1516 avincent@shsm.org Andrea Vincent, Pres.;

Sacred Heart Southern Missions, Inc. - 6050 Hwy. 161 N., Walls, MS 38680-0190; Mailing: P.O. Box 190, Walls, MS 38680-0190 t) 662-781-1360 www.shsm.org Rev. Jack Kurps, S.C.J., Exec.;

MONASTERIES AND RESIDENCES FOR PRIESTS AND BROTHERS [MON]

GREENWOOD

St. Francis of Assisi Friary (Franciscan Friars - O.F.M.) - 2613 Hwy. 82 E., Greenwood, MS 38930-5966 t) 662-453-0623 Rev. Joachim Studwell, O.F.M., Pst.; Brs.: 1; Priests: 3

NESBIT

St. Michael Community House - 1360 Nesbit Rd., Nesbit, MS 38651; Mailing: P.O. Box 38, Nesbit, MS 38651 t) (662) 342-3325 jkurps@gmail.com Rev. David Szatkowski, SCJ, Pastoral Team; Rev. Hendrik Ardianto, S.C.J., Assoc. Pst.; Rev. Louis Mariano Fernandes, SCJ (India), Assoc. Pst.; Rev. Jack Kurps, S.C.J., Exec. Dir.; Priests: 4

PRESCHOOLS / CHILDCARE CENTERS [PRE]

JACKSON

St. Mary Orphan Home, Inc. - ; Mailing: P.O. Box 2248, Jackson, MS 39225 t) 601-355-8634 Most Rev. Joseph R. Kopacz, Bishop;

An asterisk (*) denotes an organization that has established tax-exempt status directly with the IRS and is not covered by the USCCB Group Ruling.

Diocese of Jefferson City

(Dioecesis Civitatis Jeffersoniensis)

MOST REVEREND W. SHAWN MCKNIGHT, S.T.D.

Bishop of Jefferson City; ordained May 28, 1994; appointed Bishop of Jefferson City November 21, 2017; consecrated February 6, 2018. Res.: 2207 W. Main St., Jefferson City, MO 65109-0914.

Catholic Center: Alphonse J. Schwartze Memorial, 2207 W. Main St., Jefferson City, MO 65109-0914. T: 573- 635-9127. www.diojeffcity.org

ESTABLISHED BY PAPAL BULL JULY 2, 1956.

Square Miles 22,127.

Comprises the Counties of Adair, Audrain, Benton, Boone, Callaway, Camden, Chariton, Clark, Cole, Cooper, Crawford, Gasconade, Hickory, Howard, Knox, Lewis, Linn, Macon, Maries, Marion, Miller, Moniteau, Monroe, Montgomery, Morgan, Osage, Pettis, Phelps, Pike, Pulaski, Putnam, Ralls, Randolph, Saline, Schuyler, Scotland, Shelby and Sullivan in the State of Missouri.

For legal titles of parishes and diocesan institutions, consult the Chancery Office.

STATISTICAL OVERVIEW

Personnel	
Bishop	1
Retired Bishops	1
Priests: Diocesan Active in Diocese	42
Priests: Diocesan Active Outside Diocese	1
Priests: Retired, Sick or Absent	33
Number of Diocesan Priests	76
Total Priests in your Diocese	76
Extern Priests in Diocese	19
Permanent Deacons in Diocese	93
Total Sisters	19
Parishes	
Parishes	92
With Resident Pastor:	
Resident Diocesan Priests	79
Without Resident Pastor:	
Administered by Priests	11
Administered by Deacons	1
Administered by Religious Women	1
Missions	12
Closed Parishes	2
Professional Ministry Personnel:	
Sisters	11
Lay Ministers	43
Welfare	
Catholic Hospitals	1
Total Assisted	210,373
Special Centers for Social Services	2
Total Assisted	19,800
Educational	
Diocesan Students in Other Seminaries	7
Total Seminarians	7
High Schools, Diocesan and Parish	3
Total Students	1,110
Elementary Schools, Diocesan and Parish	37
Total Students	5,702
Catechesis/Religious Education:	
High School Students	892
Elementary Students	2,142
Total Students under Catholic Instruction	9,853
Teachers in Diocese:	
Sisters	2
Lay Teachers	577
Vital Statistics	
Receptions into the Church:	
Infant Baptism Totals	753
Minor Baptism Totals	130
Adult Baptism Totals	87
Received into Full Communion	149
First Communions	1,085
Confirmations	1,589
Marriages:	
Catholic	190
Interfaith	72
Total Marriages	262
Deaths	804
Total Catholic Population	74,757
Total Population	925,262

LEADERSHIP

Chancery Office - t) 573-635-9127 diojeffcity.org

ADMINISTRATION

Vicar General - vicargeneral@diojeffcity.org Rev. Msgr. Robert A. Kurwicki;
Moderator of the Curia - mcuria@diojeffcity.org Very Rev. Jason T. Doke;
Canonical Services - broodhouse@diojeffcity.org Benjamin Roodhouse, Dir.;
Chancellor - broodhouse@diojeffcity.org Benjamin Roodhouse;
Vice Chancellor - badams@diojeffcity.org Bernadette Adams;
Ecclesiastical Notaries - Rev. Msgr. Robert A. Kurwicki; Very Rev. Jason T. Doke;
Episcopal Vicars -
Vicar for Priests - vicarforpriests@diojeffcity.org Rev. Christopher L. Cordes;
Vicar for Permanent Deacons - dmerz@diojeffcity.org Very Rev. Daniel J. Merz;
Vicar for Prison Ministry - jcorel@diojeffcity.org Very Rev. Joseph S. Corel;
Master of Ceremonies - bberhorst@diojeffcity.org Rev. Brad T. Berhorst, Head Master of Ceremonies;

OFFICES AND DIRECTORS

Buildings and Properties - property@diojeffcity.org Brad Copeland, Dir.;
Cemeteries - rtelthorst@diojeffcity.org Dcn. Ric Telthorst, Dir.;
Chief Financial Officer - cfo@diojeffcity.org Dcn. Joseph M. Braddock;
Communications - jluecke@diojeffcity.org Jacob Luecke, Dir.;
Newspaper--"The Catholic Missourian" - editor@diojeffcity.org Most Rev. W. Shawn McKnight, Publisher; Jay Nies, Editor; Kelly Martin, Advertising Coord.;
Development - development@diojeffcity.org Jake Seifert, Dir.;
Diaconate Office - deacon2@diojeffcity.org Very Rev. Daniel J. Merz, Vicar; Dcn. Michael W. Berendzen, Dir., Deacon Life & Ministry; Dcn. John A. Schwartze, Dir., Deacon Formation;
Human Resources - hrdir@diojeffcity.org Cheryl Hertfelder, Dir.; Gala Wolfmeier, Benefits Coord.;
Mission Office - development@diojeffcity.org Jake Seifert, Dir.;
Parish Services - dbarnes@diojeffcity.org Denise Barnes, Dir.;
Risk Management Contacts - cfo@diojeffcity.org Dcn. Joseph M. Braddock, Contact; Kathy Smith, Contact;
Safe Environment/Child and Youth Protection - flaverty@diojeffcity.org Fiona Laverty, Dir.;
Victim Assistance Coordinator - t) 573-694-3199 reportabuse@diojeffcity.org Jacqueline Baldwin;
School Office - evader@diojeffcity.org Erin Vader, Supt.;
Stewardship - stewardship@diojeffcity.org Rev. Stephen W. Jones, Dir.; Patricia Lutz, Assoc. Dir.;
Vocations Office - vocations@diojeffcity.org Rev. Paul J. Clark, Dir.;
Women's Ministry - bprasad@diojeffcity.org Barbara Prasad, Dir.;

ADVISORY BOARDS, COMMISSIONS, COMMITTEES, AND COUNCILS

Diocesan Consultors - vicargeneral@diojeffcity.org Rev. Msgr. Robert A. Kurwicki, Contact;
Liturgical Commission - dmerz@diojeffcity.org Very Rev. Daniel J. Merz, Chair;
Ministry to Priests - vicarforpriests@diojeffcity.org Rev. Christopher L. Cordes, Vicar;
Personnel Board - vicargeneral@diojeffcity.org Rev. Msgr. Robert A. Kurwicki, Chair;
Presbyteral Council - dmerz@diojeffcity.org Very Rev. Daniel J. Merz, Chair; Rev. William D. Debo, Vice Chair; Very Rev. Gregory C. Meystrik, Secy.;
Diocesan Pastoral Council - hosman@diojeffcity.org Helen Osman, Consultant;
Diocesan Finance Council - cfo@diojeffcity.org Dcn. Joseph M. Braddock, Contact;
Priestly and Religious Vocations Committee - vocations@diojeffcity.org Rev. Paul J. Clark, Chair;
Diocesan School Advisory Council - evader@diojeffcity.org Erin Vader, Supt.; Connie Hesse, Chair; Alan Lammers, Vice Chair;

DEANERIES

See City Deanery - lnelen@diojeffcity.org Very Rev. Louis M. Nelen, Dean;
North Deanery - mmakarewicz@diojeffcity.org Rev. Msgr. Marion J. Makarewicz, Dean;
Central Deanery - goligschlaeger@diojeffcity.org Very Rev. P. Gregory Oligschlaeger, Dean;
Southeast Deanery - gmeystrik@diojeffcity.org Very Rev. Gregory C. Meystrik, Dean;
Southwest Deanery - jcorel@diojeffcity.org Very Rev. Joseph S. Corel, Dean;
Missionary Priests - rike@diojeffcity.org Very Rev. Roberto M. Ike (Nigeria), Dean;

FAITH FORMATION

Department of Faith Formation - ecastro@diojeffcity.org Dcn. Enrique Castro, Exec. Dir.;
Marriage and Family Ministry - Rev. Francis W. Doyle, Moderator;
Marriage Enrichment and Marriage Encounter - Dcn. Jon M. Bequette, Marriage Enrichment Coord.; Dcn. James Farnell, Marriage Enrichment Coord.; Randy Wehmeyer, Marriage Encounter Liaison;
Marriage Preparation and Engaged Encounter - Dcn. Stephan J. Kliethermes, Marriage Preparation Coord.; Dcn. Burdett E. Wilson, Parish Outreach Coord. & Engaged Encounter Liaison;
Natural Family Planning - Dcn. Robert W. Reinkemeyer, Coord.;
Multicultural Ministry - ecastro@diojeffcity.org Dcn. Enrique Castro, Dir.;
Religious Education - maureenquinn@diojeffcity.org Maureen Quinn, Diocesan D.R.E.; Rev. Dylan Schrader, Moderator;
Youth and Young Adult Ministry - maureenquinn@diojeffcity.org Maureen Quinn, Dir.; Rev. Paul J. Clark, Moderator;
Camp Lolek - Junior High Camp - Maureen Quinn, Contact;
Camp Maccabee - Maureen Quinn, Contact;
Camp Sienna - Maureen Quinn, Dir.;
ChristPower Service Camp - Maureen Quinn, Contact;
Totus Tuus - Maureen Quinn, Dir.;
Teens Encounter Christ (TEC) - Dcn. Bruce Mobley, Dir.; Rev. Michael A. Coleman, Spiritual Adv./Care Srvcs.;
Scouting - Jerry Callahan, Scout Master; Dcn. Rick L. Vise Sr., Chap.;

ORGANIZATIONS

Campus Ministry - angelle.hall@comonewman.org Angelle Hall, Liaison;
Charismatic Renewal Program - Dcn. Kenneth Berry, English-Speaking Liaison; Ilsi Palacios, Spanish-Speaking Coord.;
Cursillo Movement - jeffcity.diocese.cursillo@gmail.com Susan Stolwyk, English-Speaking Lay Dir.; Luis Osvaldo Diaz, Spanish-Speaking Lay Dir.;
Legion of Mary - Dcn. David Thompson, Spiritual Dir.;
Priests' Mutual Benefit Society - Most Rev. W. Shawn McKnight; Rev. Msgr. Robert A. Kurwicki; Very Rev. Jason T. Doke;

TRIBUNAL

Judicial Vicar - ghigley@diojeffcity.org Rev. Msgr. Gregory L. Higley;
Adjutant Judicial Vicar - Rev. Brad T. Berhorst;
Promoter of Justice - Very Rev. Philip J. Bene;
Defenders of the Bond - Constance Schepers; Ashley Subler;
Judges - Rev. Michael F. Quinn; Benjamin Roodhouse;
Notary - Teresa Vignola;

PARISHES, MISSIONS, AND CLERGY

STATE OF MISSOURI

ARGYLE

St. Aloysius - 1 Church Ln., Argyle, MO 65001; Mailing: P.O. Box 6, Argyle, MO 65001 t) 573-728-6922 secretarysasb@gmail.com sasb.diojeffcity.org Attended from Visitation of the Blessed Virgin Mary, Vienna. Rev. Basil Tigga (India), Pst.; Dcn. Michael S. Brooks; Frank Neutzler, DRE; CRP Stds.: 42

St. Boniface - 3982 Hwy. T, Koeltztown, MO 65048 t) (573) 728-6922 sasb.diojeffcity.or

BARING

St. Aloysius - 402 Second St., Baring, MO 63531; Mailing: 509 N. Main St., Edina, MO 63537 t) 660-397-2183 stjoeal@marktwain.net knoxcountycatholic.org Rev. Simeon A. Etonu, Pst.; Dcn. Kenneth Berry; CRP Stds.: 7

BELLE

St. Alexander - 400 W. Third St., Belle, MO 65013; Mailing: PO Box 606, Belle, MO 65013 t) 573-859-6231 bellecatholic@gmail.com Attended from Immaculate Conception, Owensville. Rev. Philip F. Niekamp, Pst.; Rev. Derek J. Hooper, Assoc. Pst.; CRP Stds.: 8

BONNOTS MILL

St. Louis of France - 211 Church Hill St., Bonnots Mill, MO 65054; Mailing: PO Box 8, Loose Creek, MO 65054 t) 573-897-2922 icparish1845@gmail.com Attended from Immaculate Conception, Loose Creek. Rev. Anthony R. Rinaldo, Pst.; CRP Stds.: 6

BOONVILLE

SS. Peter and Paul - 322 7th St., Boonville, MO 65233 t) 660-882-6468 dre@ssppparish.net; secretary@ssppparish.net www.stsppchurch.net Rev. Mark S. Smith, Pst.; Dcn. David Miller; Theresa Krebs, DRE; CRP Stds.: 1

SS. Peter and Paul School - (Grades PreK-8) 502 7th St., Boonville, MO 65233 t) 660-882-2589 amartin@ssppschool.net www.stsppschool.net Abby Martin, Prin.; Stds.: 169; Lay Tchrs.: 15

BOURBON

St. Francis Caracciolo - 1050 N. Old Hwy. 66, Bourbon, MO 65441; Mailing: 415 School Ave., Cuba, MO 65453 t) 573-885-3520 hcccuba@gmail.com www.holycrosscubamo.org/ Attended from Holy Cross, Cuba Rev. Daniel I.J. Lueckenotte, Pst.; Sr. Karen Thein, S.S.N.D., Pst. Min./Coord.;

BRINKTOWN

Holy Guardian Angels - 37515 Highway N, Brinktown, MO 65443; Mailing: P.O. Box 226, Vienna, MO 65582 t) 573-422-3950 vgasecretary@att.net Attended from Visitation of the Blessed Virgin Mary, Vienna. Rev. Basil Tigga (India), Admin.; Dcn. Michael S. Brooks; CRP Stds.: 7

BROOKFIELD

Immaculate Conception - 313 N. Livingston St., Brookfield, MO 64628 t) 660-258-2507 rectory@icbrookfield.org icbrookfield.org Sr. Mary Rost, S.S.N.D., Parish Life Coord.; Rev. Paschal C. Ihediohamma (Nigeria), Sacr. Min.; CRP Stds.: 47

BRUNSWICK

St. Boniface - 203 E. Harrison St., Brunswick, MO 65236 t) 660-548-3267 stboniface@cvalley.net Rev. Boniface Kasiita Nzabonimpa (Uganda), Admin.; CRP Stds.: 5

CALIFORNIA

Annunciation - 310 S. Mill St., California, MO 65018;

Mailing: P.O. Box 204, California, MO 65018 t) 573-796-4842 annunciationcaliforniamo@gmail.com annunciation.diojeffcity.org/ Rev. Anthony J. Viviano, Pst.; Dcn. Robert W. Reinkemeyer; CRP Stds.: 60

CAMDENTON

St. Anthony - 1874 N. Business Rte. 5, Camdenton, MO 65020 t) 573-346-2716 stanthonysadmoffice@gmail.com camdenton.diojeffcity.org Rev. Daniel L. Vacca, Pst.; Dcn. Stanley J. Buczko; Dcn. Richard A. Von Gunten; CRP Stds.: 60

Our Lady of the Snows - Coffman Bend Rd & 51 Grace Ln, Climax Springs, MO 65324; Mailing: PO Box 21, Climax Spring, MO 65324 t) (573) 346-2716

CANTON

St. Joseph - 812 Lewis St., Canton, MO 63435 t) 573-288-3198 stjosephcanton@centurytel.net Rev. Callistus Okoroji (Nigeria), Pst.; CRP Stds.: 7

CENTRALIA

Holy Spirit - 404 S. Rollins St., Centralia, MO 65240 t) 573-682-2815 office@holyspiritcentralmo.org Rev. Michael A. Coleman, Pst.; Dcn. Jon M. Bequette; Nancy Robinson, DRE; CRP Stds.: 104

CHAMOIS

Most Pure Heart of Mary - 106 W. 2nd St., Chamois, MO 65024; Mailing: P.O. Box 156, Chamois, MO 65024 t) 573-763-5345 mphsec@mostpureheart.org www.mostpureheart.org Rev. David A. Means, Admin.; Dcn. Robert Schowengerdt; CRP Stds.: 11

CLARENCE

St. Patrick - 201 Grand St., Clarence, MO 63437; Mailing: PO Box 177, Clarence, MO 63437 t) (573) 501-0134 stpatricksclarence@gmail.com Attended from Immaculate Conception, Macon. Rev. R. William Peckman, Pst.; Dcn. Larry W. Mitchell;

COLUMBIA

Our Lady of Lourdes - 903 Bernadette Dr., Columbia, MO 65203 t) 573-445-7915 reddirector@ourladyoflourdes.org; office2@ourladyoflourdes.org www.ourladyoflourdes.org Rev. Christopher L. Cordes, Pst.; Rev. Simon Jude Kanyike (Uganda), Assoc. Pst.; Rev. Msgr. Michael T. Flanagan, In Res.; Dcn. Joseph M. Braddock; Dcn. James Leyden; Dcn. Joseph Puglis; CRP Stds.: 169

Our Lady of Lourdes Interparish School - (Grades K-8) 817 Bernadette Dr., Columbia, MO 65203 t) 573-445-6516 ehassemer@ollisk8.org ollisk8.org Elaine Hassemer, Prin.; Stds.: 620; Lay Tchrs.: 40

Sacred Heart - 105 Waugh St., Columbia, MO 65201 t) 573-443-3470 bhead@sacredheart-church.org www.sacredheart-church.org Rev. Msgr. Gregory L. Higley, Pst.; Dcn. Bill Caubet; CRP Stds.: 110

St. Thomas More Newman Center, University of Missouri - 602 Turner Ave., Columbia, MO 65201 t) 573-449-5424 reception@comonewman.org comonewman.org Very Rev. Daniel J. Merz, Pst.; Rev. Paulinus Aneke (Nigeria), Assoc. Pst.; Rev. Ignitius Nimwesiga (Uganda), In Res.; Dcn. Francis Ruggiero; CRP Stds.: 63

CROCKER

St. Cornelius - 115 State Hwy U, Crocker, MO 65452; Mailing: PO Box 668, Crocker, MO 65452 t) (573) 759-7521 st.corneliuscatholicchurch@gmail.com Attended from St. Theresa, Dixon. Rev. William Korte, Pst.;

CUBA

Holy Cross - 415 School Ave., Cuba, MO 65453 t) 573-885-3520 hccccuba@gmail.com www.holycrosscubamo.org/ Rev. Daniel I.J. Lueckenotte, Pst.; Dcn. Chad R. Lewis; Sr. Karen Thein, S.S.N.D., Pst. Min./Coord.; CRP Stds.: 45

Holy Cross School - (Grades PreK-4) t) 573-885-4727 holycrossschoolcuba@gmail.com www.holycrosscubamo.org Melinda Osentoski, Prin.; Stds.: 20; Lay Tchrs.: 3

DIXON

St. Theresa - 506 Oak St., Dixon, MO 65459 t) 573-336-3662 st.theresa@windstream.net Rev. William Korte, Admin.; Dcn. Chad R. Lewis;

EDINA

St. Joseph - 509 N. Main St., Edina, MO 63537-1239 t) 660-397-2183 stjoeal@marktwain.net sasj.diojeffcity.org Rev. Simeon A. Etonu, Pst.; Dcn. Kenneth Berry; CRP Stds.: 35

ELDON

Sacred Heart - 540 N. Mill St., Eldon, MO 65026 t) 573-392-5334 sacred540@sbcglobal.net sacredhearteldon.diojeffcity.org Rev. Alexius Ekka (India), Pst.; Dcn. Chet L. Zuck Jr.; CRP Stds.: 21

EWING

Queen of Peace - 307 N. Main St., Ewing, MO 63440; Mailing: PO Box 347, Ewing, MO 63440-0347 t) 573-209-3343 qofpeace@marktwain.net sites.google.com/view/qopewing/home Rev. Callistus Okoroji (Nigeria), Pst.; CRP Stds.: 26

FAYETTE

St. Joseph - 300 S. Cleveland Ave., Fayette, MO 65248 t) 660-248-2439 stjoseph-fayette@socket.net www.stjosephcath.org Rev. Joshua J. Duncan, Admin.; CRP Stds.: 9

FOLK

St. Anthony of Padua - 255 Hwy. EE, Folk, MO 65085; Mailing: PO Box 157, Westphalia, MO 65085 t) 573-455-2725 www.stjosephwestphalia.org/st-anthony.html Attended from St. Joseph Catholic Church, Westphalia. Rev. Dylan Schrader, Pst.; Dcn. James Haaf;

FRANKENSTEIN

Our Lady Help of Christians - 1665 Hwy. C, Frankenstein, MO 65016; Mailing: 1665 Hwy C, Bonnots Mill, MO 65016 t) 573-897-2587 olohc@hotmail.com olhoc.diojeffcity.org Rev. Colin P. Franklin, Pst.; Dcn. Robert Schowengerdt; Dcn. Anthony Valdes; CRP Stds.: 30

St. Mary School - (Grades 1-8) 1641 Highway C, Bonnots Mill, MO 65016 t) 573-897-2567 stmarymo@gmail.com Lisa Grellner, Prin.; Stds.: 16; Lay Tchrs.: 4

FREEBURG

Holy Family - 104 Oliver St., Freeburg, MO 65035; Mailing: PO Box 9, Freeburg, MO 65035 t) 573-744-5254 mbrandel@holyfamilyfreeburg.com www.holyfamilyfreeburg.com Rev. William D. Debo, Pst.; CRP Stds.: 8

Holy Family School - (Grades PreK-8) 110 W. Oliver St., Freeburg, MO 65035; Mailing: P.O. Box 156, Freeburg, MO 65035 t) 573-744-5200 dreinkemeyer@holyfamilyfreeburg.com school.holyfamilyfreeburg.com Debbie Reinkemeyer, Prin.; Stds.: 90; Lay Tchrs.: 7

FULTON

St. Peter - 700 State Rd. Z, Fulton, MO 65251-2342 t) 573-642-5562 (Office) stpeterparishoffice@stpeterfultonmo.org stpeterfulton.diojeffcity.org/ Rev. Joseph A. Abah (Nigeria), Pst.; Dcn. John L. Neudecker; CRP Stds.: 35

St. Peter School - (Grades PreK-8) t) (573) 642-2839 stpeterschooloffice@stpeterfultonmo.org Erin Polson, Prin.; Stds.: 110; Lay Tchrs.: 8

GLASGOW

St. Mary - 421 Third St., Glasgow, MO 65254 t) 660-338-2053 parishoffice@stmarysglasgow.org www.glasgowstmary.com Rev. Joshua J. Duncan, Pst.; CRP Stds.: 20

St. Mary School - (Grades K-8) 501 3rd St., Glasgow, MO 65254 t) 660-338-2258 kmonnigsms@gmail.com Kent Monnig, Prin.; Stds.: 116; Lay Tchrs.: 14

HANNIBAL

Holy Family - 1111 Broadway, Hannibal, MO 63401; Mailing: 218 S. Maple Ave., Hannibal, MO 63401 t) 573-221-1078 miller@myholyfamily.com; agabriel@diojeffcity.org www.myholyfamily.com Rev. Alexander Gabriel (India), Pst.; Dcn. Troy K. Egbert; Dcn. Luke Mahsman; CRP Stds.: 15

Holy Family School - (Grades PreK-8) 1113 Broadway, Hannibal, MO 63401 t) 573-221-0456 hooley@myholyfamily.com Sara Hooley, Prin.; Stds.: 140; Lay Tchrs.: 10

HERMANN

St. George Catholic Church - 128 W. 4th St., Hermann, MO 65041-1099 t) 573-486-5914 (CRP); 573-486-2723 church@sgs-hermann.com stghermann.diojeffcity.org Rev. Philip E. Niekamp, Pst.; Rev. Derek J. Hooper, Assoc. Pst.; CRP Stds.: 10

St. George School - (Grades PreK-8) 133 W. 4th St., Hermann, MO 65041-1099 t) (573) 486-5914 school@sgs-hermann.com stghermann.diojeffcity.org/school Amy Schebaum, Prin.; Stds.: 161; Lay Tchrs.: 18

HERMITAGE

St. Bernadette - Hwy. 254, Hermitage, MO 65668; Mailing: PO Box 167, Hermitage, MO 65668 t) 417-745-6361 stbernadettechurch@hotmail.com stbernadette.diojeffcity.org Attended from St. Ann, Warsaw. Rev. Benjamin E. Nwosu (Nigeria), Pst.;

HOLTS SUMMIT

St. Andrew - 400 St. Andrew Dr., Holts Summit, MO 65043 t) 573-896-5010 admin@standrewparishhs.org standrewparishhs.org Very Rev. Roberto M. Ike (Nigeria), Pst.; Dcn. Daniel J. Ramsay; Dcn. Edward D. Stroesser; CRP Stds.: 20

INDIAN CREEK

St. Stephen Catholic Church - 27519 Monroe Rd 533, Indian Creek, MO 63456; Mailing: 27519 Monroe Rd 533, Monroe City, MO 63456 t) 573-735-4718 churchst.stephen@gmail.com ststephenic.diojeffcity.org Very Rev. P. Gregory Oligschlaeger, Pst.; CRP Stds.: 11

INDIAN GROVE

St. Raphael - 23130 Raphael Rd., Indian Grove, MO 65236; Mailing: 409 S. Kansas Ave., Marceline, MO 64658 t) 660-376-3239 stbonmarceline@gmail.com Attended from St. Bonaventure, Marceline. Rev. Paschal C. Ihediohamma (Nigeria), Admin.; CRP Stds.: 2

JEFFERSON CITY

Cathedral of St. Joseph - 2305 W. Main St., Jefferson City, MO 65109 t) 573-635-7991 info@cathedraljc.org www.cathedral.diojeffcity.org Very Rev. Louis M. Nelen, Pst.; Dcn. R. Christopher Baker; Dcn. Alvin J. Brand; Dcn. Dana K. Joyce; Dcn. John A. Schwartze; CRP Stds.: 23

St. Joseph Cathedral School - (Grades PreK-8) 2303 W. Main St., Jefferson City, MO 65109 t) 573-635-5024 gbailey@sjcsmo.org www.sjcsmo.org Gina Bailey, Prin.; Jacob Akin, Vice Prin.; Stds.: 426; Lay Tchrs.: 34

Immaculate Conception - 1206 E. McCarty St., Jefferson City, MO 65101 t) 573-635-6143 icchurch@icangels.com www.icangels.com Rev. Matthew J. Flatley, Pst.; Rev. Anthony Onyeihe (Nigeria), Pst. Assoc.; Dcn. Mark Aulbur; Dcn. Raymond L. Purvis; Dcn. William Seibert Jr.; Dcn. Kenneth V. Wildhaber Jr.; CRP Stds.: 14

Immaculate Conception School - (Grades PreK-8) 1208 E. McCarty St., Jefferson City, MO 65101 t) 573-636-7680 hschrimpf@icangels.com Heather Schrimpf, Prin.; Stds.: 334; Lay Tchrs.: 35

St. Peters Church Parish - 216 Broadway, Jefferson City, MO 65101 t) 573-636-8159 parish@saintpeterjc.org www.saintpeterjc.org Rev. Jeremy A. Secrist, Pst.; Rev. Thomas L. Alber, Assoc. Pst.; Rev. Brad T. Berhorst, Assoc. Pst.; Dcn. Enrique Castro; Dcn. Thomas M. Fischer; Dcn. Ric Telthorst; Dcn. David Thompson; Dcn. Thomas M. Whalen; CRP Stds.: 51

St. Peter School - (Grades PreK-8) 314 W. High St., Jefferson City, MO 65101 t) 573-636-8922 saints@stpeterjc.org www.saintpeterjc.org/school/ Gayle Trachsel, Prin.; Heather Luebbert, Librn.; Stds.: 478; Lay Tchrs.: 40

JONESBURG

St. Patrick - 505 First St., Jonesburg, MO 63351 t) 636-488-5623 stpats@centurytel.net stpatricksjonesburg.org Rev. Ernest Dike (Nigeria), Admin.; Dcn. Ronald E. Deimeke; CRP Stds.: 6

KAHOKA

St. Michael the Archangel - 622 W. Exchange St., Kahoka, MO 63445 t) 660-727-3472 stmichel@centurytel.net Rev. Robert H. Fields, Pst.;

CRP Stds.: 31

KIRKSVILLE

Mary Immaculate - 716 E. Washington St., Kirksville, MO 63501 t) 660-665-2466 secretary@miparish.org www.miparish.org Rev. Msgr. Marion J. Makarewicz, Pst.; Dcn. Edwin Pacheco; Dcn. David D. Ream; Dcn. Chris Korte; CRP Stds.: 44

Mary Immaculate School - (Grades PreK-8) 712 E. Washington St., Kirksville, MO 63501 t) 660-665-1006 ann.gray@miparish.org www.miparishschool.org Ann Gray, Prin.; Stds.: 99; Lay Tchrs.: 7

St. Rose of Lima - 911 Rombauer, Novinger, MO 63559; Mailing: 716 E. Washington St., Kirksville, MO 63501 t) (660) 665-2466

LAKE OZARK

Our Lady of the Lake - 2411 Bagnell Dam Blvd., Lake Ozark, MO 65049; Mailing: PO Box 2390, Lake Ozark, MO 65049 t) 573-365-2241 office@ourladylakeozark.org ourladylake.diojeffcity.org/ Rev. Michael W. Penn, Pst.; Dcn. Paul Poulter; CRP Stds.: 148

LAURIE

St. Patrick - 176 Marian Dr., Laurie, MO 65037 t) 573-372-8594 (St. Patrick - CRP); 573-374-7855; 573-378-5958 (St. Philip Benizi - CRP) psr-dre@shrineofstpatrick.com; secretarystpatricks@gmail.com www.stpatrickcatholicchurch.org Rev. John J. Schmitz, Pst.; Dcn. David Lovell; Michele Haggerty, DRE; CRP Stds.: 14

St. Philip Benizi - 17034 Hwy. D, Versailles, MO 65084 t) 573-374-6835 Dcn. Mark A. Wand;

LINN

St. George - 613 E. Main St., Linn, MO 65051; Mailing: P.O. Box 49, Linn, MO 65051 t) 573-897-2293 stgeorgeparish@att.net stgeorgelinn.diojeffcity.org Rev. Colin P. Franklin, Pst.; Dcn. Robert Schowengerdt; Dcn. Anthony Valdes; Donna Zeilmann, DRE; CRP Stds.: 27

St. George School - (Grades PreK-8) 601 E. Main St., Linn, MO 65051; Mailing: P.O. Box 19, Linn, MO 65051 t) 573-897-3645 lgrellner@saint-george-parish.org school.saint-george-parish.org/school Lisa Grellner, Prin.; Stds.: 180; Sr. Tchrs.: 1; Lay Tchrs.: 9

LOOSE CREEK

Immaculate Conception - 121 County Rd. 402, Loose Creek, MO 65054; Mailing: PO Box 8, Loose Creek, MO 65054 t) 573-897-2922 icparish1845@gmail.com Rev. Anthony R. Rinaldo, Pst.; CRP Stds.: 64

Immaculate Conception School - (Grades K-8) 147 Co. Rd. 402, Loose Creek, MO 65054; Mailing: P.O. Box 68, Loose Creek, MO 65054 t) 573-897-3516 anne.luebbert@icloosecreek.org Anne Luebbert, Prin.; Stds.: 109; Lay Tchrs.: 10

LOUISIANA

St. Joseph - 508 N. 3rd St., Louisiana, MO 63353 t) 573-754-4757 st.joseph4757@gmail.com Rev. Henry Ussher (Ghana), Pst.; Dcn. Mark J. Dobelmann; Dcn. Wayne W. Korte; CRP Stds.: 10

Mary Queen of Peace - S. Second St., Clarksville, MO 63336; Mailing: 508 N. 3rd, Louisiana, MO 63353 t) (573) 754-4757

MACON

Immaculate Conception - 402 N. Rollins St., Macon, MO 63552 t) 660-385-3792 icchurchmacon@gmail.com Rev. R. William Peckman, Pst.; Dcn. Gregory Duffey; Dcn. Lloyd Collins; Dcn. Bruce Mobley; CRP Stds.: 25

Immaculate Conception School - (Grades K-8) 401 N Rubey St., Macon, MO 63552 t) 660-385-2711 principal@icsmaconk8.org Leigh A. Grant, Prin.; Stds.: 60; Lay Tchrs.: 11

Sacred Heart - 301 N. Macon St., Bevier, MO 63552; Mailing: 402 N. Rollins St., Macon, MO 63552 t) (660) 385-3792

MARCELINE

St. Bonaventure - 409 S. Kansas Ave., Marceline, MO 64658-1301 t) 660-376-3239 stbonmarceline@gmail.com stbon.net Rev. Paschal C. Ihediohamma (Nigeria), Admin.; Rev. Patrick G. Dolan, In Res.; CRP Stds.: 59

Fr. McCartan Memorial School - (Grades PreK-8) 327 S. Kansas Ave., Marceline, MO 64658 t) 660-376-3580 principal@fathermccartan.com Dick Davis, Prin.; Stds.: 40; Lay Tchrs.: 5

MARSHALL

St. Peter Catholic Church Marshall - 1801 S. Miami Ave., Marshall, MO 65340 t) 660-886-7960 stpeter.office@att.net www.stpeterchurch-marshallmo.org Rev. Francis W. Doyle, Pst.; Dcn. Pedro Almazan; Dcn. Jaime Medina; Dcn. Luis Reyes; Dcn. Santos Rubio; CRP Stds.: 40

St. Peter School - (Grades PreK-8) 368 S. Ellsworth St., Marshall, MO 65340 t) 660-886-6390 marmccoy@stpeterchurch-marshallmo.org stpetercatholicschool-marshallmo.org Mary McCoy, Prin.; Stds.: 193; Lay Tchrs.: 11

MARTINSBURG

St. Joseph - 408 E. Kellett St., Martinsburg, MO 65264 t) 573-492-6595 parish@stjosephmb.org www.stjosephmb.org Rev. Philip M. Kane, Pst.; Dcn. Ronald E. Deimeke; CRP Stds.: 29

St. Joseph School - (Grades PreK-8) 401 E. Kellett, Martinsburg, MO 65264 t) 573-492-6283 sjssecretary@stjosephmb.org; mhombs@stjosephmb.org stjosephmb.org Michelle Hombs, Prin.; Stds.: 64; Lay Tchrs.: 6

MARY'S HOME

Our Lady of the Snows - 274 Hwy. H, Mary's Home, MO 65032; Mailing: 274 Hwy H, Eugene, MO 65032 t) 573-498-3470 (CRP); 573-498-3820 carolannplank@gmail.com; olosparish@gmail.com ourladyofthesnows.diojeffcity.org/ Rev. Alexius Ekka (India), Pst.; Dcn. Chet L. Zuck Jr.; Carol Plank, DRE; Christy Evers, CFO; CRP Stds.: 82

Our Lady of the Snows School - (Grades PreK-8) 276 Hwy. H, Eugene, MO 65032 t) 573-498-3574 lvarner@olosschool.org; rbeck@olosschool.org Lucinda Varner, Prin.; Stds.: 57; Lay Tchrs.: 6

MEMPHIS

St. John - 547 N. Clay St., Memphis, MO 63555 t) 660-465-7130 stjohns@nemr.net www.nemr.net/~stjohns Rev. Simeon A. Etonu, Pst.; Laurie Jack, DRE; CRP Stds.: 5

META

St. Cecilia - 106 E. 6th St., Meta, MO 65058; Mailing: P.O. Box 146, St. Thomas, MO 65076 t) 573-477-3315 stceciliameta@gmail.com; dstumpeoffice@gmail.com stceciliameta.net Rev. Leonard Mukiibi (Uganda), Pst.; CRP Stds.: 10

MEXICO

St. Brendan - 615 S. Washington St., Mexico, MO 65265-2658 t) 573-581-4720 parishoffice@saintbrendans.org stbrendan.diojeffcity.org Rev. David J. Veit, Pst.; Dcn. James Farnell; Dcn. Louis J. Leonatti; CRP Stds.: 17

St. Brendan School - (Grades PreK-8) 620 S. Clark St., Mexico, MO 65265 t) 573-581-2443 kcoulson@saintbrendans.org Kathy Coulson, Prin.; Stds.: 184; Lay Tchrs.: 16

MILAN

St. Mary - 101 W. Baker St., Milan, MO 63556; Mailing: PO Box 147, Milan, MO 63556 t) 660-265-4110 office@stmarymilan.com www.stmary.church Dcn. John D. Weaver, Parish Life Coord.; Rev. Patrick G. Dolan, Sacramental Min.; Dcn. Jeronimo Chinchilla; CRP Stds.: 59

St. Mary - 1118 Main St., Hwy. 136 E., Unionville, MO 63565; Mailing: P.O. Box 147, Milan, MO 63556 t) (660) 947-2599 (Church Bldg.)

MOBERLY

St. Pius X - 201 S. Williams St., Moberly, MO 65270; Mailing: P.O. Box 310, Moberly, MO 65270 t) 660-263-5243 stpiusxchurch@mcmsys.com www.stpiusx.diojeffcity.org Rev. Joby Parakkacharuvil Thomas (India), Pst.; Dcn. John F. Hill Jr.; Dcn. William Christopher Sago; CRP Stds.: 32

St. Pius X School - (Grades K-8) 210 S. Williams St., Moberly, MO 65270 t) 660-263-5500 maulbur@spxmoberly.eduk12.net www.stpiusxmoberly.com Michael Aulbur, Prin.; Stds.: 132; Lay Tchrs.: 8

MOKANE

St. Jude Thaddeus - 401 Adams St., Mokane, MO 65059; Mailing: P.O. Box 128, Mokane, MO 65059 t) 573-690-7673 debakagg@gmail.com stjudemokane.diojeffcity.org Attended from St. Peter, Fulton. Rev. Joseph A. Abah (Nigeria), Pst.; Dcn. John L. Neudecker; CRP Stds.: 12

MONROE CITY

Holy Rosary - 405 S. Main St., Monroe City, MO 63456 t) 573-735-4718 hrosarymc@gmail.com; donnalong.hrss@gmail.com holyrosary.diojeffcity.org/ Very Rev. P. Gregory Oligschlaeger, Pst.; Dcn. L. Michael Long; Dcn. John Watkins; Donna Long, DRE; CRP Stds.: 65

Holy Rosary School - (Grades PreK-8) 415 S. Locust St., Monroe City, MO 63456 t) 573-735-2422 nancyshively@holyrosaryschool.com Nancy Shively, Prin.; Stds.: 194; Lay Tchrs.: 10

MONTGOMERY CITY

Immaculate Conception - 307 N. Walker St, Montgomery City, MO 63361 t) 573-564-2375 imm-con@sbcglobal.net www.mcicparish.org/ Rev. Ernest Dike (Nigeria), Admin.; Dcn. Ronald E. Deimeke; Bonnie Walker, DRE; CRP Stds.: 27

Immaculate Conception School - (Grades PreK-8) 407 W. Third St., Montgomery City, MO 63361 t) 573-564-2679 immaculateconception@icschool-mc.org immaculateconception@icschool-mc.org Dana Schroeder, Prin.; Aggie Baldetti, Librn.; Stds.: 34; Lay Tchrs.: 6

MORRISON

Assumption - 155 Morrison Ave., Morrison, MO 65061; Mailing: P.O. Box 156, Chamois, MO 65024 t) 573-763-5345 mphsec@mostpureheart.org www.assumptionmorrison.org Attended from Most Pure Heart of Mary, Chamois. Rev. David A. Means, Admin.; Dcn. Robert Schowengerdt; CRP Stds.: 3

OSAGE BEND

St. Margaret of Antioch - 12025 Rte. W., Osage Bend, MO 65101; Mailing: 12025 Rte. W., Jefferson City, MO 65101 t) 573-496-3404 stmargaretob@gmail.com Rev. Msgr. David D. Cox, Pst.; Dcn. Larry Hildebrand; CRP Stds.: 16

OWENSVILLE

Immaculate Conception - 103 E. Jefferson St., Owensville, MO 65066 t) 573-437-3086 icchurchowensvillemo@gmail.com Rev. Philip E. Niekamp, Pst.; Rev. Derek J. Hooper, Assoc. Pst.; Melinda Gibson, DRE; CRP Stds.: 32

PALMYRA

St. Joseph - 400 S. Lane St., Palmyra, MO 63461; Mailing: P.O. Box 606, Palmyra, MO 63461 t) 573-769-3270 office@stjoepalmyra.org sjpalmyra.diojeffcity.org/ Rev. Alexander Gabriel (India), Pst.; Rev. Gerald J. Kaimann, In Res.; Dcn. Troy K. Egbert; Dcn. Luke Mahsman; Andrea L Barnes, DRE; CRP Stds.: 111

PERRY

St. William - 602 E. Jefferson, Perry, MO 63462; Mailing: PO Box 339, Perry, MO 63462 t) 573-565-2852 stwill1901@gmail.com Rev. John A. Henderson, Pst.; CRP Stds.: 37

St. Frances Cabrini - 25560 Business Hwy. 24, Paris, MO 65275; Mailing: P.O. Box 339, Perry, MO 63462 t) (573) 565-2852 (Rectory)

St. Paul (Historic Church) - 22520 St. Paul Dr., Center, MO 63436; Mailing: P.O. Box 339, Perry, MO 63462 t) (573) 565-2852

PILOT GROVE

St. Joseph - 407 Harris St., Pilot Grove, MO 65276 t) 660-834-5600 agerling@stjosephcougars.com stjosephcougars.com Rev. Mark S. Smith, Pst.; CRP Stds.: 14

St. Joseph School - (Grades PreK-8) 405 Harris St., Pilot Grove, MO 65276 t) (660) 834-5600 nwatring@stjosephcougars.com www.stjosephcougars.com Nichole Watring, Prin.; Stds.: 92; Lay Tchrs.: 8

St. John the Baptist - t) (660) 834-5600

St. Joseph - t) (660) 834-5600 Rev. Mark S. Smith, Pst.;

RHINELAND

Church of the Risen Savior - 605 Bluff St., Rhineland, MO 65069 t) 573-236-4390 risensav@ktis.net Rev. Philip E. Niekamp, Pst.; Rev. Derek J. Hooper, Assoc. Pst.; Dcn. Joseph E. Horton; Dcn. Gerald W. Korman; CRP Stds.: 1

Shrine of Our Lady of Sorrows - 197 Hwy P, Starkenburg, MO 65069; Mailing: 605 Bluff St., Rhineland, MO 65069

RICH FOUNTAIN

Sacred Heart - 4277 Hwy. U, Rich Fountain, MO 65035; Mailing: 4277 Hwy U, Freeburg, MO 65035 t) 573-744-5987 shrf1838@sacredheartrf.com www.sacredheartrf.com Rev. William D. Debo, Pst.; CRP Stds.: 8

Sacred Heart School - (Grades PreK-8) 4309 Hwy. U, Freeburg, MO 65035 t) 573-744-5898 dreinkemeyer@sacredheartschoolrf.com www.schoolsacredheartrf.com Debbie Reinkemeyer, Prin.; Stds.: 38; Lay Tchrs.: 4

RICHLAND

St. Jude - 20063 s Hwy 7, Richland, MO 65556; Mailing: 367 Old Route 66, St. Robert, MO 65584 t) 573-336-3662 bellarminestrobert@gmail.com Attended from St. Robert Bellarmine, St. Robert Rev. Michael P. Murphy, Pst.; Dcn. Rick L. Vise Sr.; CRP Stds.: 15

ROLLA

St. Patrick - 17 St. Patrick Ln., Rolla, MO 65401 t) 573-364-1435 cbolbecher@stpatrickrolla.org; gmeystrik@stpatrickrolla.org stpatsrolla.diojeffcity.org/ Very Rev. Gregory C. Meystrik, Pst.; Dcn. Thomas C. Manion; Dcn. Matthew McLaughlin; CRP Stds.: 47

St. Patrick School - (Grades PreK-8) 19 St. Patrick Ln., Rolla, MO 65401 t) 573-364-1162 aarnold@stpatrickrolla.org school.stpatsrolla.org Tony Arnold, Prin.; Anna Starns, Dir.; Stds.: 204; Lay Tchrs.: 19

ROSATI

St. Anthony - 21670 County Rd. 3640, Rosati, MO 65559; Mailing: 316 E. Scioto St., St. James, MO 65559 t) 573-265-7250 Attended from Immaculate Conception, St. James. Very Rev. Gregory C. Meystrik, Pst.; Dcn. Lawrence L. Clark; Dcn. Thomas C. Manion; Dcn. Matthew McLaughlin;

RUSSELLVILLE

St. Michael - 5214 N. Hatler St., Russellville, MO 65074-1214; Mailing: 13321 Railroad Ave., Russellville, MO 65074 t) 573-782-3171 smcach@centurylink.net stmichael.diojeffcity.org Rev. Msgr. Robert A. Kurwicki, Pst.; CRP Stds.: 12

SALISBURY

St. Joseph - 301 W. Williams, Salisbury, MO 65281 t) 660-388-5590 saintjosephcatholicchurch@yahoo.com stjosephsalisbury.diojeffcity.org Rev. Boniface Kasiita Nzabonimpa (Uganda), Pst.; Dcn. Burdett E. Wilson; CRP Stds.: 42

St. Joseph School - (Grades PreK-8) 105 N. Willie Ave., Salisbury, MO 65281 t) 660-388-5518 kemmerich@school.stjoe.church www.school.stjoe.church Kelsey Emmerich, Prin.; Stds.: 143; Lay Tchrs.: 9

SEDALIA

St. Vincent de Paul - 421 W 3rd St., Sedalia, MO 65301 t) 660-827-2311; 660-826-2062 dianne.svdpparish@gmail.com svdpparish.diojeffcity.org Very Rev. Joseph S. Corel, Pst.; Rev. Cesar Anicama, Assoc. Pst.; Dcn. Jerome Connery; Dcn. Turf D. Martin; Dcn. Arvol Bartok; Dcn. Nestor Montenegro; Dcn. Amparo Orozco; Sr. Mary Ruth Wand, S.S.N.D., Pst. Min./Coord.; Mariela Messina, DRE; CRP Stds.: 84

Sacred Heart School - (Grades PreK-8) 416 W. Third St., Sedalia, MO 65301 t) 660-827-3800 www.gogremlins.com Nancy Manning, Prin.; Dr. Amanda Burdick, Dean; Stds.: 244; Lay Tchrs.: 24

Sacred Heart School - (Grades 9-12) 416 W. Third St., Sedalia, MO 65301 t) 660-827-3800 www.gogremlins.com Mark Register, Pres.; Nancy Manning, Prin.; Dr. Amanda Burdick, Dean; Stds.: 101; Lay Tchrs.: 19

St. John the Evangelist - Hwy V & M, Bahner, MO 65350; Mailing: 421 W. 3rd St., Sedalia, MO 65301 t) (660) 827-2311

St. Patrick - 415 E. Fourth St., Sedalia, MO 65301; Mailing: 421 W 3rd St., Sedalia, MO 65301 t) (660) 827-2311

Sacred Heart - t) (660) 827-2311

SHELBINA

St. Mary - 307 E. Chestnut St., Shelbina, MO 63468; Mailing: P.O. Box 306, Shelbina, MO 63468 t) 573-588-4540 stmaryshelbina@gmail.com stmaryshelbina.diojeffcity.org Attended from Immaculate Conception, Macon. Rev. R. William Peckman, Pst.; Dcn. Larry W. Mitchell; CRP Stds.: 92

SLATER

St. Joseph - 325 W. Emma St., Slater, MO 65349 t) 660-529-2588 stjoseph1927@sbcglobal.net www.stjosephslater.net Rev. Francis W. Doyle, Pst.;

ST. ANTHONY

St. Anthony - 132 Main St., St. Anthony, MO 65486; Mailing: 132 Main St., Iberia, MO 65486 t) 573-793-6550 stanthonyofpaduachurch@hotmail.com stanthonycatholicchurch.org Rev. Christopher M. Aubuchon, Admin.; Dcn. Stephen Schwartze; CRP Stds.: 55

ST. CLEMENT

St. Clement - 21509 Hwy. 161, St. Clement, MO 63334; Mailing: 21509 Hwy. 161, Bowling Green, MO 63334 t) 573-324-5545 stclementparish@gmail.com www.stclementmo.org Rev. Henry Ussher (Ghana), Pst.; Dcn. Mark J. Dobelmann; Dcn. Wayne W. Korte; CRP Stds.: 83

St. Clement School - (Grades PreK-8) 21493 Hwy. 161, Bowling Green, MO 63334 t) 573-324-2166 stclementschool@gmail.com stclementmo.org Laurie Schuckenbrock, Prin.; Stds.: 76; Lay Tchrs.: 7

ST. ELIZABETH

St. Lawrence - 246 Main St., St. Elizabeth, MO 65075; Mailing: PO Box 128, St. Elizabeth, MO 65075 t) (573) 493-2301 stlawrencegridiron@hotmail.com www.stlawrencecatholicchurch.org/ Rev. Christopher M. Aubuchon, Admin.; Dcn. Stephen Schwartze; CRP Stds.: 151

ST. JAMES

Immaculate Conception - 316 E. Scioto, St. James, MO 65559 t) 573-265-7250 icchurch@centurylink.net www.icchurchstjames.org Very Rev. Gregory C. Meystrik, Pst.; Dcn. Lawrence L. Clark; Dcn. Thomas C. Manion; Dcn. Matthew McLaughlin;

ST. MARTINS

St. Martin - 7148 Business 50 W., St. Martins, MO 65109; Mailing: 7148 St. Martins Blvd., Jefferson City, MO 65109 t) 573-893-2923 stmartinparishoffice@gmail.com www.stmartin.diojeffcity.org Very Rev. Jason T. Doke, Pst.; Dcn. Francis J. Butel; Dcn. Brad W Jones; Dcn. Stephan J. Kliethermes; CRP Stds.: 10

St. Martin School - (Grades PreK-8) 7206 St. Martins Blvd, Jefferson City, MO 65109 t) 573-893-3519 school@stmartinjc.org stmartin.diojeffcity.org/school/ Julie Clingman, Prin.; Heather Henley, Vice Prin.; Stds.: 213; Lay Tchrs.: 14

ST. PATRICK

The Shrine of St. Patrick - 2 Erin Cir, St. Patrick, MO 63445; Mailing: 622 W. Exchange St., Kahoka, MO 63445 t) 660-727-3472 stmichel@centurytel.net stpatrickshrine.com Attended from St. Michael, Kahoka Rev. Robert H. Fields, Pst.;

ST. ROBERT

St. Robert Bellarmine - 367 Old Rte. 66, St. Robert, MO 65584 t) 573-336-3662 bellarminestrobert@gmail.com strobert.diojeffcity.org Rev. Michael P. Murphy, Pst.; Dcn. Rick L. Vise Sr.; CRP Stds.: 63

ST. THOMAS

St. Thomas the Apostle - 14814 Rt. B, St. Thomas, MO 65076; Mailing: P.O. Box 146, St. Thomas, MO 65076 t) 573-477-3315 tveitoffice@gmail.com stthomasapostle.net Rev. Leonard Mukiibi (Uganda), Pst.; CRP Stds.: 32

St. Thomas the Apostle School - (Grades PreK-8) 14830 Rte. B, St. Thomas, MO 65076; Mailing: P.O. Box 211, St. Thomas, MO 65076 t) 573-477-3322 lheckemeyer@stacs.school www.stthomasapostleschool.net Leroy Heckemeyer, Prin.; Stds.: 78; Lay Tchrs.: 7

STEELVILLE

St. Michael - 81 Hwy 8 E., Steelville, MO 65559; Mailing: 415 School Ave, Cuba, MO 65453 t) 573-885-3520 hccccuba@gmail.com www.holycrosscubamo.org/ Attended from Holy Cross, Cuba. Rev. Daniel I.J. Lueckenotte, Pst.; Dcn. Chad R. Lewis; Sr. Karen Thein, S.S.N.D., Pst. Min./Coord.;

TAOS

St. Francis Xavier - 7319 Rte. M, Taos, MO 65101; Mailing: 7319 Rte. M, Jefferson City, MO 65101 t) 573-395-4401 sfxchurch1@embarqmail.com www.sfxtaosmo.org Rev. Kelechi Uzuegbu (Nigeria), Pst.; Dcn. Michael W. Berendzen; CRP Stds.: 68

St. Francis Xavier School - (Grades PreK-8) 7307 Rt. M., Jefferson City, MO 65101 t) 573-395-4612 jtobar@sfxtaos.com www.sfxtaos.com Jordan Tobar, Prin.; Stds.: 105; Lay Tchrs.: 13

TIPTON

St. Andrew - 106 W. Cooper St., Tipton, MO 65081-8210 t) 660-433-2162 sac_rectory@outlook.com www.standrewtipton.org Rev. Anthony J. Viviano, Pst.; Dcn. Robert W. Reinkemeyer; CRP Stds.: 13

St. Andrew School - (Grades K-8) 118 E. Cooper St., Tipton, MO 65081-0617 t) 660-433-2232 lgknipp@saintandrewpirates.com; khiggins@saintandrewpirates.com Kara Higgins, Prin.; Stds.: 94; Lay Tchrs.: 9

VANDALIA

Sacred Heart - 200 W. Home St., Vandalia, MO 63382; Mailing: PO Box 29, Vandalia, MO 63382 t) 573-594-2717 shccastj@windstream.net Rev. Philip M. Kane, Pst.; Rev. Louis E. Dorn, In Res.; Dcn. Ronald E. Deimeke; CRP Stds.: 10

St. John - 601 W. Elm St., Laddonia, MO 63352 t) (573) 594-2717

VIENNA

Visitation of the Blessed Virgin Mary - 101 N. Main St., Vienna, MO 65582; Mailing: P.O. Box 171, Vienna, MO 65582 t) 573-422-3950 vgabookkeeper@att.net Rev. Basil Tigga (India), Pst.; Dcn. Michael S. Brooks; CRP Stds.: 18

Visitation Inter-Parish School - (Grades K-8) 105 N. Coffey St., Vienna, MO 65582; Mailing: P.O. Box 269, Vienna, MO 65582 t) 573-422-3375 mbassett@visitationip.org Marilyn Bassett, Prin.; Stds.: 35; Lay Tchrs.: 5

WARDSVILLE

St. Stanislaus - 6418 Rte. W., Wardsville, MO 65101 t) 573-636-4925 ststansec@socket.net www.ststanislaus.net Rev. Msgr. David D. Cox, Pst.; Dcn. Larry Hildebrand; Mary Markway, DRE; CRP Stds.: 45

St. Stanislaus School - (Grades PreK-8) 6410 Rte. W., Wardsville, MO 65101 t) 573-636-7802 billyc@ststan.net www.ststan.net William Cannon, Prin.; Stds.: 182; Lay Tchrs.: 13

WARSAW

St. Ann - 30455 W. Dam Access Rd., Warsaw, MO 65355 t) 660-438-3844 stannwarsaw1@gmail.com stannwarsawmo.org Rev. Benjamin E. Nwosu (Nigeria), Pst.;

SS. Peter & Paul - 15042 Chat Ave., Cole Camp, MO 65325; Mailing: PO Box 248, Cole Camp, MO 65325 t) 660-285-0107 spapcolecampmo@gmail.com

WELLSVILLE

Church of the Resurrection - Merged Oct 2022 Merged

with St. Joseph, Martinsburg.

WESTPHALIA

St. Joseph - 125 E. Main St., Westphalia, MO 65085; Mailing: PO Box 116, Westphalia, MO 65085 t) 573-455-2320 (Office); 573-455-2725 (Rectory) parishoffice@stjosephwestphalia.org; dschrader@diojeffcity.org www.stjosephwestphalia.org Rev. Dylan Schrader, Pst.; Dcn. James Haaf; CRP Stds.: 30

St. Joseph School - (Grades K-8) 123 E. Main, Westphalia, MO 65085; Mailing: P.O. Box 205, Westphalia, MO 65085 t) 573-455-2339 schooloffice@stjosephwestphalia.org Patricia Kirk, Prin.; Stds.: 172; Lay Tchrs.: 13

WIEN

St. Mary of the Angels - 12520 Saint Mary's Ave., Wien, MO 63558-3418; Mailing: 12520 St. Marys Ave., New Cambria, MO 63558 t) 660-226-5243 parishstmaryoftheangels@gmail.com; reed.saintmaryoftheangels@gmail.com stmarywien.diojeffcity.org Rev. Boniface Kasiita Nzabonimpa (Uganda), Pst.; Dcn. Burdett E. Wilson; Joe Bertsch, DRE; CRP Stds.: 51

SCHOOLS: PRESCHOOL THRU HIGH SCHOOL

HIGH SCHOOLS

STATE OF MISSOURI

COLUMBIA

Fr. Augustine Tolton Regional Catholic High School - (PAR) (Grades 9-12) 3351 E. Gans Rd., Columbia, MO 65201 t) 573-445-7700 billing@toltoncatholic.org www.toltoncatholic.org Dr. Daniel Everett, Pres.; Jill McIntosh, Vice. Pres.; Rev. Michael A. Coleman, Chap.; Rev. Ignitius Nimwesiga (Uganda), Chap.; Stds.: 324; Pr. Tchrs.: 1; Lay Tchrs.: 26

JEFFERSON CITY

Helias Catholic High School - (DIO) (Grades 9-12) 1305 Swift's Hwy., Jefferson City, MO 65109 t) 573-635-6139 info@heliascatholic.com www.heliascatholic.com Spencer L. Allen, Prin.; John Knight, Pres.; Rev. Paul J. Clark, Chap.; Stds.: 685; Sr. Tchrs.: 1; Lay Tchrs.: 52

INSTITUTIONS LOCATED IN DIOCESE

CAMPUS MINISTRY / NEWMAN CENTERS [CAM]

COLUMBIA

St. Thomas More Newman Center - 602 Turner Ave., Columbia, MO 65201 t) 573-449-5424 reception@comonewman.org www.comonewman.org Very Rev. Daniel J. Merz, Pst.; Rev. Paulinus Aneke (Nigeria), Assoc. Pst.; Rev. Ignitius Nimwesiga (Uganda), Chap.; Angelle Hall, Dir.;

KIRKSVILLE

Catholic Newman Center, Truman State University - 709 S. Davis, Kirksville, MO 63501 t) 660-665-4357 info@newmantruman.org newmantruman.org A ministry of Mary Immaculate Catholic Church, Kirksville. Rev. Msgr. Marion J. Makarewicz, Pst.; Rev. Simeon A. Etonu, Chap.; Dcn. Chris Korte, Dir.;

ROLLA

Catholic Newman Center, Missouri University of Science and Technology - 1607 N. Rolla St., Rolla, MO 65402; Mailing: PO Box 838, Rolla, MO 65402 t) 573-364-2133 newman@mst.edu www.rollanewman.org Tom Kasza, Campus Min.; Very Rev. Gregory C. Meystrik, Chap.;

CATHOLIC CHARITIES [CCH]

JEFFERSON CITY

Catholic Charities of Central and Northern Missouri - 1015 Edmonds St., Jefferson City, MO 65109; Mailing: P.O. Box 104626, Jefferson City, MO 65110-4626 t) 573-635-7719 lprenger@cccnmo.org; dlester@cccnmo.org www.cccnmo.diojeffcity.org Daniel C. Lester, Exec.; Asstd. Annu.: 6,000; Staff: 52

Samaritan Center - 1310 E. McCarty St., Jefferson City, MO 65101; Mailing: PO Box 1687, Jefferson City, MO 65102 t) 573-634-7776 samaritan@midmosamaritan.org www.midmosamaritan.org Marylyn DeFeo, Exec.; Asstd. Annu.: 13,800; Staff: 10

CONVENTS, MONASTERIES, AND RESIDENCES FOR WOMEN [CON]

CLYDE

Discalced Carmelite Monastery - 31970 State Hwy P, Clyde, MO 64432 t) 573-635-9127 carmelofjc.prayers@gmail.com Mother Marie Therese DuBois, O.C.D., Prioress; Srs.: 3

ENDOWMENTS / FOUNDATIONS / TRUSTS [EFT]

COLUMBIA

Fr. Augustine Tolton Regional Catholic High School Foundation - 3351 E. Gans Rd., Columbia, MO 65201 t) 573-445-7700 deverett@toltoncatholic.org www.toltoncatholic.org Dr. Daniel Everett, Prin.;

JEFFERSON CITY

Catholic Diocese of Jefferson City Fund, Inc. - 2207 W. Main St., Jefferson City, MO 65109 t) 573-635-9127 cfo@diojeffcity.org www.diojeffcity.org Dcn. Joseph Braddock, Secy.;

Diocesan Excellence in Education Fund, Inc. - 2207 W. Main St., Jefferson City, MO 65109 t) 573-635-9127 cfo@diojeffcity.org www.diojeffcity.org Dcn. Joseph Braddock, Contact;

Diocese of Jefferson City Parish Development Corporation - 2207 W. Main St., Jefferson City, MO 65109 t) 573-635-9127 cfo@diojeffcity.org www.diojeffcity.org Dcn. Joseph Braddock, Contact;

Diocese of Jefferson City Real Estate Trust - 2207 W. Main St., Jefferson City, MO 65109 t) 573-635-9127 cfo@diojeffcity.org www.diojeffcity.org Dcn. Joseph Braddock, Contact;

Jefferson City Diocese Chancery Building Fund - 2207 W. Main St., Jefferson City, MO 65109 t) 573-635-9127 cfo@diojeffcity.org Dcn. Joseph M. Braddock, Contact;

Jubilee Retirement Trust Fund - 2207 W. Main St., Jefferson City, MO 65109 t) 573-635-9127 cfo@diojeffcity.org www.diojeffcity.org Dcn. Joseph Braddock, Contact;

St. Mary's Health Center, Jefferson City, Missouri, Foundation - 2505 Mission Dr., Jefferson City, MO 65109 t) 573-681-3743 www.ssmhealth.com Member of SSM Health Paul Ross, Vice. Pres.;

MARSHALL

St. Peter School Foundation - 368 S. Ellsworth St., Marshall, MO 65340 t) 660-886-6390 marmccoy@stpeterchurch-marshallmo.org Mary McCoy, Contact;

HOSPITALS / HEALTH SERVICES [HOS]

JEFFERSON CITY

SSM Health - St. Mary's Hospital - 2505 Mission Dr., Jefferson City, MO 65109 t) 573-681-3000 www.ssmhealthmidmo.com Joshua Allee, Chap.; Bed Capacity: 154; Asstd. Annu.: 210,373; Staff: 881

MISCELLANEOUS [MIS]

JEFFERSON CITY

Diocese of Jefferson City Real Estate Corporation - 2207 W. Main St., Jefferson City, MO 65109 t) 573-635-9127 cfo@diojeffcity.org www.diojeffcity.org Dcn. Joseph Braddock, Contact;

El Puente - Hispanic Ministry - 2709 Industrial Dr. Ste B, Jefferson City, MO 65109 t) (573) 680-8692 cristhia.castro@elpuentemo.org www.elpuentemo.org Cristhia Mariel Castro, Dir.;

Missouri Catholic Conference - 600 Clark Ave., Jefferson City, MO 65101; Mailing: PO Box 1022, Jefferson City, MO 65102 t) 573-635-7239; 800-456-1679 mocatholic@mocatholic.org www.mocatholic.org Jamie Morris, Exec. Dir.;

My Community Our Mission - 2207 W. Main St., Jefferson City, MO 65109 t) (573) 635-9127 Kathy Smith, Contact;

Priests' Mutual Benefit Society, Inc. - 2207 W. Main St., Jefferson City, MO 65109 t) 573-635-9127 cfo@diojeffcity.org Dcn. Joseph Braddock, Contact;

SHRINES [SHR]

GRAVOIS MILLS

***Mary, Mother of the Church Shrine** - 176 Marian Dr., Gravois Mills, MO 65037 t) 573-374-6279 info@thenationalshrineofmarymotherofthechurch.com thenationalshrineofmarymotherofthechurch.com Mary Carole Ducharme, Chair;

An asterisk (*) denotes an organization that has established tax-exempt status directly with the IRS and is not covered by the USCCB Group Ruling.

Diocese of Joliet in Illinois

(Dioecesis Joliettensis in Illinois)

MOST REVEREND RONALD A. HICKS

Bishop of Joliet; ordained May 21, 1994; appointed Auxiliary Bishop of Chicago July 3, 2018; consecrated September 17, 2018; appointed Bishop of Joliet July 17, 2020; installed September 29, 2020. Blanchette Catholic Center: 16555 Weber Rd., Crest Hill, IL 60403. T: 815-221-6100; F: 815-221-6101.

Blanchette Catholic Center, 16555 Weber Rd., Crest Hill, IL 60403. T: 815-221-6100; F: 815-221-6101.
www.dioceseofjoliet.org

ESTABLISHED BY BULL DATED DECEMBER 11, 1948.

Square Miles 4,218.

Canonically Erected March 24, 1949.

Comprises the Counties of Du Page, Kankakee, Will, Grundy, Ford, Iroquois and Kendall in the State of Illinois.

Patron of Diocese: St. Francis Xavier.

For legal titles of parishes and diocesan institutions, consult the Chancery.

STATISTICAL OVERVIEW

Personnel

Bishop	1
Retired Bishops	1
Abbots	1
Retired Abbots	2
Priests: Diocesan Active in Diocese	92
Priests: Diocesan Active Outside Diocese	4
Priests: Diocesan in Foreign Missions	1
Priests: Retired, Sick or Absent	70
Number of Diocesan Priests	167
Religious Priests in Diocese	93
Total Priests in your Diocese	260
Extern Priests in Diocese	14
Ordinations:	
Diocesan Priests	3
Transitional Deacons	3
Permanent Deacons	17
Permanent Deacons in Diocese	226
Total Brothers	38
Total Sisters	310

Parishes

Parishes	118
With Resident Pastor:	
Resident Diocesan Priests	73
Resident Religious Priests	25
Without Resident Pastor:	
Administered by Priests	4
Administered by Deacons	1
Missions	7
Professional Ministry Personnel:	
Brothers	6
Sisters	28
Lay Ministers	282

Welfare

Catholic Hospitals	2
Total Assisted	109,762
Homes for the Aged	14
Total Assisted	1,460
Day Care Centers	2
Total Assisted	79
Special Centers for Social Services	4
Total Assisted	3,309
Residential Care of Disabled	1
Total Assisted	123

Educational

Diocesan Students in Other Seminaries	24
Total Seminarians	24
Colleges and Universities	3
Total Students	13,669
High Schools, Diocesan and Parish	3
Total Students	1,426
High Schools, Private	5
Total Students	3,198
Elementary Schools, Diocesan and Parish	40
Total Students	11,387
Elementary Schools, Private	2
Total Students	402
Catechesis/Religious Education:	
High School Students	2,233
Elementary Students	22,023
Total Students under Catholic Instruction	54,362
Teachers in Diocese:	
Priests	6
Sisters	7
Lay Teachers	1,517

Vital Statistics

Receptions into the Church:	
Infant Baptism Totals	5,006
Minor Baptism Totals	120
Adult Baptism Totals	115
Received into Full Communion	203
First Communions	5,015
Confirmations	5,332
Marriages:	
Catholic	839
Interfaith	115
Total Marriages	954
Deaths	3,470
Total Catholic Population	507,455
Total Population	1,956,932

LEADERSHIP

Diocesan Bishop - t) 815-221-6185 Most Rev. Ronald A. Hicks, Bishop (jgrzadzinski@dioceseofjoliet.org);
Vicar General - Very Rev. Richard L. Smith (rsmith@dioceseofjoliet.org);
Episcopal Vicar for Clergy - Very Rev. John Balluff (jballuff@dioceseofjoliet.org);
Judicial Vicar - Very Rev. Grzegorz Podwysocki, Judicial Vicar; Dr. David Salvato, Moderator of Tribunal (dsalvato@dioceseofjoliet.org);
Tribunal - Very Rev. Grzegorz Podwysocki, Judge; Dr. David Salvato, Judge; Thomas E. Kerber, Judge;
Diaconate Office - Dcn. Dominic Cerrato, Dir. (dcerrato@dioceseofjoliet.org);
Vocations - Rev. Steven Borello, Dir. (sborello@dioceseofjoliet.org);
Chancellor - Dr. David Salvato (dsalvato@dioceseofjoliet.org);
Archives - archivist@dioceseofjoliet.org Rev. Scott M. McCawley, Archivist;
Office of Religious - Very Rev. John Balluff, Interim Dir. (jballuff@dioceseofjoliet.org);
Child and Youth Protection - Leah Heffernan, Dir. (lheffernan@dioceseofjoliet.org);
Communications - Mary Massingale, Dir. (mmassingale@dioceseofjoliet.org);
Deans -
East Dupage Deanery - Very Rev. Thomas Paul;
Ford-Iroquois Deanery - Very Rev. Douglas L. Hauber;
Joliet Deanery - Very Rev. Christopher Groh;
Kankakee Deanery - Very Rev. Matthew Pratscher;
North Will-Grundy Deanery - Very Rev. Grzegorz Podwysocki;
South Dupage Deanery - Very Rev. Daniel Bachner;
South Will-Grundy Deanery - Very Rev. John Lindsey;
West Dupage Deanery - Very Rev. Gregor Gorsic;
Diocesan Pastoral Council - Mary Galvan, Chair (mtgalvan87@gmail.com);

ADMINISTRATION

Chief Financial Officer - Brian Schroeder (bschroeder@dioceseofjoliet.org);
Legal Services - Mary Ann McLean, Attorney (mamclean@dioceseofjoliet.org);
Parish Finances - Mark Janus, Dir. (mjanus@dioceseofjoliet.org);
Diocesan Finance - Jeannette Bartosz, Dir., Accounting, Budgeting, Insurance & Pensions (jbartosz@dioceseofjoliet.org);
Building and Properties - Chris Nye, Dir. (cnye@dioceseofjoliet.org);
Development - Jane Lagger, Chief Devel. Officer (jlagger@dioceseofjoliet.org);
Cemeteries - Eric Holloway, Exec. Dir. (eholloway@dioceseofjoliet.org);
Human Resources - Pamela Geary, Dir. (pageary@dioceseofjoliet.org);
Information Technology - Thomas Fisher, IT Oper. Mgr. (tfisher@dioceseofjoliet.org);
Claims and Risk Management - James Wright, Claims/Risk Mgr. (jwright@catholicmutual.org);

EDUCATION

Superintendent of Catholic Schools - Dr. James Quaid, Interim (jquaid@dioceseofjoliet.org);
Catholic Education Foundation - Jennifer Georgis, Exec. Dir. (egeorgis@dioceseofjoliet.org);

PASTORAL SERVICES

Catechesis and Evangelization - Justin Reyes, Dir. (jreyes@dioceseofjoliet.org);
Catechetical Formation - aclishem@dioceseofjoliet.org Dcn. Anthony Clishem;
Divine Worship - sstola@dioceseofjoliet.org Sr. Sharon Marie Stola, O.S.B.;
Lifelong Lay Formation -
Ministries of Mercy - tsingh@dioceseofjoliet.org Tanya Singh;
Missions - bcarlson@dioceseofjoliet.org Dcn. Bruce Carlson;
Pastoral Services - rcichowicz@dioceseofjoliet.org Renata Cichowicz;

PARISHES, MISSIONS, AND CLERGY

STATE OF ILLINOIS

ADDISON

St. Joseph - 330 E. Fullerton Ave., Addison, IL 60101 t) 630-832-5514 (Rel. Ed.); 630-279-6553 x101 (Parish Office) carlo@stjosephaddison.org; parish@stjosephaddison.org www.stjoeaddison.com Rev. Luis Gutierrez, Pst.; Dcn. Philip Marrow; Carlo Zeffiro, DRE; CRP Stds.: 263

St. Philip the Apostle - 1223 W. Holtz Ave., Addison, IL 60101 t) 630-543-1754 (CRP); 630-628-0900 nmcknight@st-phil.org; jnoonan@st-phil.org www.st-phil.org Rev. Binu Varghese, O.Praem, Pst.; Dcn. Philip Heitz; Dcn. Sean McGreal; Nancy McKnight, DRE; CRP Stds.: 436

St. Philip the Apostle School - (Grades PreSchool-8) 1233 W. Holtz Ave., Addison, IL 60101 t) 630-543-4130 st-phil.org/school Julie Noonan, Prin.; Stds.: 250; Lay Tchrs.: 13

ASHKUM

Assumption of the Blessed Virgin Mary - 208 N. Second St., Ashkum, IL 60911; Mailing: PO Box 218, Ashkum, IL 60911 t) 815-698-2262 Very Rev. Douglas L. Hauber, Pst.; CRP Stds.: 15

St. John the Baptist - 1500 E. 2700 N. Rd., Clifton, IL 60927

AURORA

Our Lady of Mercy - 701 S. Eola Rd., Aurora, IL 60504 t) 630-851-3444 Rev. Michael Kearney, Pst.; Rev. James Guarascio, Par. Vicar; Dcn. Timothy Kueper; Dcn. Tony Leazzo; Dcn. Tony Martini; Dcn. Philip Rehmer; Dcn. Arturo Tiongson;

BEAVERVILLE

St. Mary - 308 St. Charles St., Beaverville, IL 60912; Mailing: P.O. Box 152, Beaverville, IL 60912 t) 815-435-2432 teacherdad79@yahoo.com; stmaryschurchbeaverville@yahoo.com www.stmaryschurchbeaverville.com Rev. Michael Powell, Pst.; Ryan Loy, Pst. Assoc.; CRP Stds.: 32

BENSENVILLE

St. Alexis - 400 W. Wood Ave., Bensenville, IL 60106 t) 630-766-4417 (CRP); 630-766-3530 secretaryalexis@yahoo.com; st.alexis.religious.education@gmail.com www.stalexisparish.org/ Rev. Jesus Oliveros, Pst.; Dcn. Anthony Holmes; Marco A. Esparza, Bus. Mgr.; CRP Stds.: 269

St. Charles Borromeo - 1135 Daniel Dr., Bensenville, IL 60106-3467 t) 630-860-1120; 630-766-8822 (CRP) officeadmin@stcbparish.org www.stcbparish.org Polish Mass Rev. Canon Michal Twaruzek, Pst.; Dcn. Timothy Taylor; CRP Stds.: 102

BLOOMINGDALE

St. Isidore - 427 W. Army Trail Rd., Bloomingdale, IL 60108-1390 t) 630-529-3045 jmcdaniel@stisidoreparish.org Rev. James Murphy, Pst.; Rev. Asirvadam Dandu, Vicar; Rev. Reynaldo B. Treyes, Vicar; Dcn. Daniel Defino; Dcn. Terry Neary; Dcn. Hung Nguyen; Joanna McDaniel, Admin.; CRP Stds.: 437

St. Isidore School - (Grades PreSchool-8) 431 W. Army Trail Rd., Bloomingdale, IL 60108-1390 t) 630-529-9323 cyndicollins@saintisidoreschool.org Corinne Alimento, Prin.; Stds.: 212; Lay Tchrs.: 17

BOLINGBROOK

St. Dominic - 440 E. Briarcliff Rd., Bolingbrook, IL 60440 t) 630-739-5703 stdominic@comcast.net; cherrera@stdominiccc.org www.stdominiccc.org Rev. Nestor Lopez (Colombia), Pst.; Rev. Ivan Carrillo, Par. Vicar; Rev. Sergio Rodriguez, Par. Vicar; Dcn. Armando Jaquez; Dcn. Arturo Chacon; Dcn. Lorenzo Chaidez; CRP Stds.: 402

St. Francis of Assisi - 1501 W. Boughton Rd., Bolingbrook, IL 60490 t) 630-759-7588 gmempin@stfrancisbb.org; jchamberlain@stfrancisbb.org stfrancisbb.org Rev. Herbert Essig, Pst.; Rev. Patrick Murphy, Assoc. Pst.; Dcn. John Blumenstein; Dcn. Raymond Hamilton; Dcn. Marco Lovero; Dcn. Michael McGuire; Dcn. Genaro Mempin; Dcn. Anthony Osei; April Johnson, Music Min.; Elizabeth Jesse Wagner, DRE; CRP Stds.: 311

BONFIELD

Sacred Heart - 588 S. 10000 W. Rd., Bonfield, IL 60913-7019; Mailing: 207 E 5th St, Herscher, IL 60941 t) 815-426-2550 smm_sja_sh@yahoo.mail Rev. Ron P. Neitzke, Pst.; Rhonda Berns, DRE; Julia Bisaillon, Bus. Mgr.; CRP Stds.: 7

BOURBONNAIS

St. George - 5272 E. 5000 North Rd., Bourbonnais, IL 60914-9725 t) 815-939-1851 stgeorge@stgeorgeil.com stgeorgeil.com Rev. Daniel R. Belanger, C.S.V., Pst.; Dcn. Milton Leppert; CRP Stds.: 102

Maternity of the Blessed Virgin Mary - 308 E. Marsile St., Bourbonnais, IL 60914 t) 815-933-8285 x326 (CRP); 815-933-8285 x310 mpallissard@mbvm.org; maternitybvm@mbvm.org www.mbvmchurch.org Rev. Jason Nesbit, C.S.V., Pst.; Rev. Moises Mesh, C.S.V., Par. Vicar; Dcn. Patrick Skelly; Maria Pallissard, DRE; CRP Stds.: 130

BRADLEY

St. Joseph - 211 N. Center Ave., Bradley, IL 60915 t) 815-939-3573 pstorer@stjosephbradley.org www.stjosephbradley.org Rev. Marcin Michalak, Pst.; Dcn. Gregory Clodi, Pst. Assoc.; Dcn. Leon Fritz; CRP Stds.: 101

BRAIDWOOD

Immaculate Conception - 110 S. School St., Braidwood, IL 60408 t) 815-458-2125 icparishbraidwood@gmail.com www.icparishbraidwood.org Rev. Joshua Miller, Pst.;

CAROL STREAM

Corpus Christi - 1415 W. Lies Rd., Carol Stream, IL 60188 t) 630-483-4222 (CRP); 630-483-4673 corpuschristicc@sbcglobal.net; cceducation@sbcglobal.net www.corpuschristicarolstream.org Rev. Marek Jurzyk, Pst.; Dcn. Andrew Jalove; Dcn. Phil Leonard; Dcn. Thomas R. Thiltgen; Dcn. William Thomas; Elizabeth Mazur, Pst. Assoc.; Mary Lou Conroy, DRE; CRP Stds.: 229

St. Luke - 421 Cochise Ct., Carol Stream, IL 60188 t) 630-668-1325 (Office); 630-665-2322 (RE) stloff@aol.com; stlgof@aol.com www.stlukecarolstream.weebly.com Rev. Michael Pennock, Admin.; Mary Liptak, DRE; CRP Stds.: 23

CHANNAHON

St. Ann Parish - 24500 S. Navajo Dr., Channahon, IL 60410 t) 815-467-6962 tom@stannchannahon.org; parishoffice@stannchannahon.org www.stannchannahon.org Rev. John Klein, Pst.; CRP Stds.: 240

CHEBANSE

SS. Mary and Joseph - 525 S. Chestnut, Chebanse, IL 60922; Mailing: P.O. Box 25, Clifton, IL 60927 t) 815-698-2262 Rev. Douglas Hauber, Pst.; CRP Stds.: 24

CLARENDON HILLS

Notre Dame - 64 Norfolk Ave., Clarendon Hills, IL 60514 t) 630-654-3365 x221 (CRP) parishoffice@notredameparish.org; notredamere@notredameparish.org notredameparish.org Rev. Mark Bernhard, Pst.; Dcn. Michael Januszewski; Dcn. Timothy Nickels; CRP Stds.: 568

Notre Dame School - (Grades PreK-8) 66 Norfolk

Ave., Clarendon Hills, IL 60514 t) 630-323-1642 school@notredameparish.org Amanda Paul, Prin.; Stds.: 189; Lay Tchrs.: 10

CLIFTON

St. Peter's - 450 E. Third Ave., Clifton, IL 60927-0025; Mailing: P.O. Box 25, Clifton, IL 60927-0025 t) 815-694-2027; 815-698-2262 debbie_assumption@comcast.net Very Rev. Douglas L. Hauber, Pst.; CRP Stds.: 18

COAL CITY

Assumption of the Blessed Virgin Mary - 195 S. Kankakee St., Coal City, IL 60416 t) 815-634-4171 deacon.bill.assumption@gmail.com; secretary@stmaryassumptionparish.org www.stmaryassumptionparish.org/ Rev. Joshua Miller, Pst.; Dcn. William E Dunn; CRP Stds.: 134

CREST HILL

St. Ambrose - 1711 Burry Cir., Crest Hill, IL 60403 t) 815-722-3222 stannestambrose@rcdoj.org www.stannestambrose.church Rev. Anthony Nyamai, Pst.; Sr. Mary Frances Werner, DRE; CRP Stds.: 85

St. Anne - 1800 Dearborn St., Crest Hill, IL 60403; Mailing: 1711 Burry Circle, Crest Hill, IL 60403 t) 815-722-3222 stannestambrose@rcdoj.org www.stannestambrose.church Rev. Anthony Nyamai, Pst.;

DARIEN

Our Lady of Mount Carmel - 8404 Cass Ave., Darien, IL 60561 t) 630-963-3053 (CRP); 630-852-3303 dre@ourladyofmtcarmel.org; receptionist@ourladyofmtcarmel.org Rev. Jeffery Smialek, O.Carm., Pst.; Rev. Gregory Houck, O.Carm, Par. Vicar; Rev. Robert Carroll, O.Carm., In Res.; Dcn. Edward Ptacek; Dcn. Guadalupe Villarreal; Sherry Rochford, DRE; CRP Stds.: 448

Our Lady of Peace - 709 Plainfield Rd., Darien, IL 60561 t) 630-986-8430 (CRP); 630-323-4333; 630-323-4392 mbaron@olopdarien.org; religioused@olopdarien.org Rev. Mark Baron, M.I.C., Par. Vicar; Dcn. Larry Fudacz; Dcn. Patrick Kenny; Dcn. Michael Murphy; Dcn. Frank Vonesh; Dcn. Joseph O'Donnell; Rev. Piotr Lach, MIC, In Res.; CRP Stds.: 200

DOWNERS GROVE

Divine Savior - 6700 Main St., Downers Grove, IL 60516 t) 630-969-1532; 630-969-1673 x132 (CRP) luis@divinesavior.net; connie@divinesavior.net divinesaviorparish.net/ Rev. Agustin Ortega-Ruiz, Pst.; Dcn. Paul S. Newey; Connie Rivas, DRE; Gonzalez Luis, Bus. Mgr.; CRP Stds.: 233

St. Joseph - 4801 Main St., Downers Grove, IL 60515; Mailing: 4824 Highland Ave., Downers Grove, IL 60515 t) 630-964-0216 bharbauer@sjpdg.org; jlackaff@sjpdg.org www.stjosephdg.org Rev. Albert J. Heidecke, Pst.; Rev. Michael Groth, Par. Vicar; Robert Valle, Liturgy Dir.; Marta Spiezio, Youth Min.; Jacqueline M Lackaff, DRE; CRP Stds.: 362

St. Joseph School - (Grades PreK-8) 4832 Main St., Downers Grove, IL 60515; Mailing: 4832 Highland Ave., Downers Grove, IL 60515 t) 630-969-4306 schooloffice@sjsdg.org www.stjosephdg.com/ Beth Cunningham, Prin.; Jessica Ranquist, Vice Prin.; Stds.: 464; Lay Tchrs.: 20

St. Mary of Gostyn - 445 Prairie Ave., Downers Grove, IL 60515 t) 630-969-1063 parish@stmarygostyn.org www.stmarygostyn.org Rev. James Schwab, Pst.; Rev. Shaun Cieslik, Par. Vicar; Dcn. Albert Agurkis; Dcn. Robert Miciunas; Jennifer Liszka, DRE; Kelly Johnson, CRE; CRP Stds.: 417

St. Mary of Gostyn School - (Grades PreSchool-8) 440 Prairie Ave., Downers Grove, IL 60515 t) 630-968-6155 school@stmarygostyn.org Christine Kalal, Prin.; Stds.: 472; Lay Tchrs.: 26

ELMHURST

Immaculate Conception - 134 Arthur St., Elmhurst, IL 60126 t) 630-530-8515 info@icelmhurst.org Dcn. John Feely; Very Rev. Thomas Paul, Pst.; Rev. Jose Cerna, Par. Vicar; CRP Stds.: 406

Immaculate Conception School - (Grades PreK-8) 132 Arthur St., Elmhurst, IL 60126 t) 630-530-3490 smeyer@icgradeschoolelmhurst.org Cathy Linley, Prin.; Stds.: 533; Lay Tchrs.: 58

IC Catholic Prep - (Grades 9-12) 217 Cottage Hill Ave., Elmhurst, IL 60126 t) 630-530-3460 sdavidson@iccatholicprep.org Steve Davidson, Prin.; Stds.: 362; Lay Tchrs.: 28

Mary, Queen of Heaven - 442 N. West Ave., Elmhurst, IL 60126-2128 t) 630-832-8962 (CRP); 630-279-5700; 630-833-9500 mglaudell@maryqueen.org; gpinkerton@maryqueen.org mqhelmhurst.org Rev. Santos Castillo, Pst.; Mary Gluadell, DRE; CRP Stds.: 230

Visitation - 779 S. York St., Elmhurst, IL 60126 t) 630-834-6700 visitationparish.org Rev. William Michael De Salvo, Pst.; Rev. Gregory Alberts, Par. Vicar; Dcn. James Eaker; Dcn. Michael Iozzo; Dcn. Michael O'Ryan; Dcn. Anthony Spatafore; CRP Stds.: 496

Visitation School - (Grades PreSchool-8) 851 S. York, Elmhurst, IL 60126 t) 630-834-4931 cmijal@visitationelmhurst.org; kmcvey@visitationelmhurst.org www.visitationelmhurst.org Carri Mijal, Prin.; Stds.: 464; Lay Tchrs.: 45

FRANKFORT

St. Anthony - 7659 W. Sauk Trail, Frankfort, IL 60423 t) 815-469-6198 (CRP); 815-469-3750 (Main Office) tony@stanthonyfrankfort.com; gwen@stanthonyfrankfort.com stanthonyfrankfort.com Rev. Dennis Paul, Pst.; Dcn. Joseph Johnson, Pst. Assoc.; Dcn. Anthony Schlott, DRE; Dcn. Paul Dirienzo; Dcn. William Boucek; Dcn. Daniel Danahey; CRP Stds.: 461

GIBSON CITY

Our Lady of Lourdes - 534 N. Wood St., Gibson City, IL 60936 t) 217-784-4671 office@ololgc.org ololgc.org Rev. Dong Bui, Pst.; Tannie Smith, DRE; CRP Stds.: 25

GILMAN

Immaculate Conception - 224 N. Secor St., Gilman, IL 60938 t) 815-383-5819 (CRP); 815-265-7236 (Our Lady of Guadalupe) Rev. Marek Herbut, Pst.; Krista Albrecht, DRE; CRP Stds.: 58

Immaculate Conception - 202 Green St., Roberts, IL 60962; Mailing: PO Box 186, Piper City, IL 60959 t) (815) 265-7236

St. Peter - 224 N. Secor St., Gilman, IL 60938 t) 815-265-7236 Rev. Marek Herbut, Pst.; CRP Stds.: 8

GLEN ELLYN

St. James the Apostle - 480 S. Park Blvd., Glen Ellyn, IL 60137 t) 630-858-5646 (CRP); 630-469-7540 lweesner@stjamesge.org Rev. Keith Wolfe, Pst.; Lisa Weesner, DRE; CRP Stds.: 289

St. James the Apostle School - (Grades PreK-8) 490 S. Park Blvd., Glen Ellyn, IL 60137 t) 630-469-8060 pkirk@stjamesge-school.org Paul Kirk, Prin.; Stds.: 151; Lay Tchrs.: 12

St. Petronille - 420 Glenwood Ave, Glen Ellyn, IL 60137-4506 t) 630-858-3796 x4000 (CRP); 630-469-0404 www.stpetschurch.org Rev. Thomas Milota, Pst.; Rev. Leslaw Prebendowski, Par. Vicar; Rev. John D. Sullivan, In Res.; Dcn. Bob Cassey; Dcn. John Spiezio; Dcn. Ronald Yurcus; Julie Knox, DRE; CRP Stds.: 267

St. Petronille School - (Grades K-8) 425 Prospect Ave., Glen Ellyn, IL 60137 t) 630-469-5041 gronwickk@stpetschool.org www.stpetschool.org Eric Schmidt, Prin.; Jennifer Wardynski, Vice Prin.; Stds.: 499; Lay Tchrs.: 27

Queenship of Mary - 219 Armitage Ave, Glen Ellyn, IL 60137; Mailing: 1379 Bloomingdale Rd., Glendade Heights, IL 60184 t) 630-752-0332 c) 847-833-0679; 630-890-3744 dahhh1@wowway.com; revtritran@hotmail.com Rev. Tri Van Tran, Pst.; Rev. Nguyen Huy Quyen, In Res.; CRP Stds.: 76

GLENDALE HEIGHTS

St. Matthew - 1555 Glen Ellyn Rd., Glendale Heights, IL 60139 t) 630-469-6300; 630-469-5178 (CRP) mruddle@stmatthewchurch.org; info@stmatthewchurch.org Very Rev. Gregor Gorsic, Pst.; Rev. Santiago (James) Corona Bernal, Par. Vicar; Dcn. Robert Malek; Dcn. Lindsey Parsons; Dcn. Michael Ruddle; Christine Balaty, DRE; CRP Stds.: 267

St. Matthew School - (Grades PreK-8) t) 630-858-3112 info@stmatthewschool.org AnnMarie Toutant, Prin.; Stds.: 127; Lay Tchrs.: 12

HERSCHER

St. Margaret Mary - 410 N Main, Herscher, IL 60941; Mailing: 207 E 5th St, Herscher, IL 60941 t) 815-426-2550 triparishcatholics.org Rev. Ron P. Neitzke, Pst.; Debbie Jensen, Admin.; Julia Bisaillon, Bus. Mgr.; Jill Fulton, DRE; CRP Stds.: 44

HINSDALE

St. Isaac Jogues - 306 W. Fourth St., Hinsdale, IL 60521 t) 630-323-0265 (CRP); 630-323-1248 cathy@sijhinsdale.com Rev. Burke Masters, Pst.; Rev. Raed Bader, Vicar; CRP Stds.: 1,000

St. Isaac Jogues School - (Grades K-8) 421 S. Clay St., Hinsdale, IL 60521 t) 630-323-3244 cburlinski@sijschool.org sijschool.org Carol Burlinski, Prin.; Stds.: 478; Lay Tchrs.: 44

HOMER GLEN

St. Bernard - 13030 W. 143rd St., Homer Glen, IL 60491; Mailing: 14135 Parker Rd., Homer Glen, IL 60491 t) 708-301-3020 st.bernardsrectory@comcast.net; st.bernardsrep@comcast.net stbernardhg.org Rev. Joseph McCormick, O.S.A., Pst.; Dcn. Kevin Ryan; Margie Wilson, DRE; CRP Stds.: 179

Our Mother of Good Counsel - 16043 S. Bell Rd., Homer Glen, IL 60491 t) 708-301-6246; 708-301-0214 mprincipe@omgccc.org www.omgccc.org Very Rev. Grzegorz Podwysocki, Pst.; Janet Litterio, DRE; CRP Stds.: 184

IRWIN

St. James the Apostle - 4372 Main St., Irwin, IL 60901; Mailing: 207 E. Fifth St., Herscher, IL 60941 t) 815-426-2153; 815-933-5443 (CRP); 815-426-2550 (Tri parish office) Rev. Ron P. Neitzke, Pst.; Allicia Miller, DRE; Julia Bisaillon, Bus. Mgr.; CRP Stds.: 72

ITASCA

St. Andrew Kim - 1275 N. Arlington Hts. Rd., Itasca, IL 60143 t) 630-250-0576 standrewkimchicago@gmail.com Rev. JooHyeon Kim, Pst.;

St. Peter the Apostle - 551 N. Rush St., Itasca, IL 60143-1698 t) 630-773-1272 x200; 630-773-1272 x201 office@stpeteritasca.com; business@stpeteritasca.com Dcn. Frederick Maier, Admin.; CRP Stds.: 223

JOLIET

The Cathedral of St. Raymond - 604 N. Raynor Ave., Joliet, IL 60435 t) 815-722-6653 info@straymond.net; re@straymond.net straymond.net Rev. William G. Dewan, Rector; Rev. John Abulag, Par. Vicar; Christine Pershey, DRE; CRP Stds.: 113

The Cathedral of St. Raymond School - (Grades PreSchool-8) 608 N. Raynor Ave., Joliet, IL 60435 t) 815-722-6626 cprieboy@csrn.org Marjorie Hill, Prin.; Stds.: 335; Lay Tchrs.: 18

St. Anthony - 100 N. Scott St., Joliet, IL 60432-4210 t) 815-722-1057 saintanthonyjoliet@hotmail.com Very Rev. John Balluff, Pst.;

St. Bernard - Sterling Ave & High St., Joliet, IL 60432; Mailing: 127 S. Briggs St., Joliet, IL 60433 t) 815-726-4474 Very Rev. Christopher Groh, Pst.; Margaret Trepal, Pst. Assoc.;

St. Francis Xavier - 2500 Arbeiter Rd., Joliet, IL 60431 t) 815-609-8077 pgiunta@sfxjoliet.org; office@sfxjoliet.org sfxjoliet.org Rev. Karl Langsdorf, Pst.; Penny Giunta, DRE; CRP Stds.: 223

Historic St. Joseph - 416 N. Chicago St., Joliet, IL 60432 t) 815-727-9378 cgimbel@stjosephjoliet.org; jhalsne@stjosephjoliet.org www.stjosephjoliet.org Rev. Timothy P. Andres, O.Carm., Pst.; Cherie Gimbal, DRE; CRP Stds.: 54

Holy Cross - 830 Elizabeth St., Joliet, IL 60435; Mailing: 901 Elizabeth St., Joliet, IL 60435 t) 815-726-4031 mnemanich@smncs.com; tricia@stmarynativity.org www.stmarynativityholycross.com Rev. Jerome Kish, Pst.; Rev. Tomasz Sielicki, Assoc. Pst.; CRP Stds.: 145

St. John the Baptist - 404 N. Hickory St., Joliet, IL 60435 t) 815-727-9077 (CRP); 815-727-4788; 815-727-4789 stjohnbap@church404.comcastbiz.net; stjohnsjolietym@yahoo.com sjbcatholic.org Rev. Larry Janezic, O.F.M., Pst.; Rev. Rommel Perez Flores, OFM, Assoc. Pst.; Dcn. Jose Lopez; Dcn. Artemio Martinez; Bro. Edward Arambasich, O.F.M., In Res.; CRP Stds.: 350

St. Jude - 2212 McDonough St., Joliet, IL 60436 t) 815-725-2209 parishsecretary@stjudejoliet.net stjudejoliet.org Rev. Michael Lane, Pst.; Paula Bucciferro, Bus. Mgr.; CRP Stds.: 103

St. Jude School - (Grades PreK-8) 2204 McDonough St., Joliet, IL 60436 t) 815-729-0288 lstangler@stjudejoliet.net stjudejoliet.net Lucas Stangler, Prin.; Stds.: 175; Sr. Tchrs.: 3; Lay Tchrs.: 11

St. Mary Magdalene - 127 S. Briggs St., Joliet, IL 60433 t) 815-727-4600 (CRP); 815-722-7653 www.stmarymagdalenechurch.com Very Rev. Christopher Groh, Pst.; Margaret Trepal, Pst. Assoc.; CRP Stds.: 46

St. Mary Nativity - 706 N. Broadway, Joliet, IL 60435 t) 815-726-4073 (CRP); 815-726-4031 frkish@outlook.com; mnemanich@smncs.com www.stmarynativityholycross.com Rev. Jerome Kish, Pst.; Rev. Tomasz Sielicki, Assoc. Pst.; CRP Stds.: 50

St. Mary Nativity School - (Grades PreK-8) 702 N. Broadway, Joliet, IL 60435 t) 815-722-8518 jmartinez@stmarynativity.org www.stmarynativity.org Stds.: 152; Lay Tchrs.: 11

Our Lady of Mount Carmel - 205 E. Jackson St., Joliet, IL 60432; Mailing: 407 Irving St., Joliet, IL 60432 t) 815-727-6330 (CRP); 815-727-7187 anamtzsolano@hotmail.com; mountcarmel@ourladymtcarmel.net www.ourladymtcarmel.net Rev. Enrique Varela-Nungaray II, O.Carm., Pst.; Rev. Jose Arisitides Menjivar, O.Carm., Par. Vicar; Rev. Edward Ward, O.Carm., Assoc. Pst.; Friar David Ulises Garcia, O.Carm., Youth Min.; Sr. Maria del Carmen Sotelo, MSCyMG, Pst. Assoc.; Sr. Francisca Serrano, MSCMG, CRE; Anatolia Martinez, DRE; Manuela Botello, Bus. Mgr.; CRP Stds.: 541

St. Patrick - 710 W. Marion St., Joliet, IL 60436-1556 t) 815-727-4746 stpatrectory0710@sbcglobal.net; pastorstpats@gmail.com www.stpatsjoliet.com Rev. Rodolphe Arty, C.S.C., Pst.; Dcn. Michael Doyle, Pst. Assoc.; Dcn. Fred Fillipo; CRP Stds.: 185

St. Paul the Apostle - 18 Woodlawn Ave., Joliet, IL 60435 t) 815-725-1527; 815-725-6927 (CRP) ekelch@stpauljoliet.com; parishoffice@stpauljoliet.com www.stpauljoliet.com Rev. Mark Cote, Pst.; Elizabeth Kelch, DRE; Dcn. John Freund; CRP Stds.: 195

St. Paul the Apostle School - (Grades PreSchool-8) 130 Woodlawn Ave., Joliet, IL 60435 t) 815-725-3390 calimento@stpauljoliet.com Kelly Kramerich, Prin.; Stds.: 167; Lay Tchrs.: 9

Sacred Heart - 337 S. Ottawa St., Joliet, IL 60436 t) 815-722-0295 pastorsacredheart337@gmail.com www.sacredheartjoliet.org Rev. William G. Dewan, Pst.; Rev. John Abulag, Par. Vicar; Dcn. Ralph Bias;

KANKAKEE

St. John Paul II Parish - 907 S. 9th Ave., Kankakee, IL 60901; Mailing: 956 S. 10th Ave., Kankakee, IL 60901 t) 815-933-7683; 815-932-7911 (CRP) sesparza@jp2kankakee.org; srevangeline@jp2kankakee.org jp2kankakee.org Very Rev. Matthew Pratscher, Pst.; Rev. Roy Jacob, Par. Vicar; Dcn. George Arocha; Dcn. Rocco Busato; Dcn. Gregory Clodi; Dcn. David Marlowe; Rev. John Horan, In Res.; Sr. Evangeline Kiambati, DRE; CRP Stds.: 240

St. Patrick - 428 S Indiana Ave, Kankakee, IL 60901 t) 815-932-6716 stpatskan@ameritech.net stpatrickkankakee.com Rev. John N. Peeters, C.S.V., Pst.; Rev. Patrick Render, C.S.V., In Res.; Rev. Donald R. Wehnert, C.S.V., In Res.; Marilyn Mulcahy, Pst. Assoc.; Eileen Kregor, DRE; CRP Stds.: 21

KINSMAN

Sacred Heart - 219 W. Emmett St., Kinsman, IL 60437; Mailing: P.O. Box 824, Kinsman, IL 60437 t) 815-392-4245 swkrcatholics.org Rev. Stanley Drewniak (Poland), Pst.; Lurelda Maier-Lorntz, DRE; CRP Stds.: 13

LISLE

St. Joan of Arc - 820 Division St., Lisle, IL 60532 t) 630-963-4500 caruso@sjalisle.org; agervacio@sjalisle.org www.sjalisle.org Rev. Gabriel Baltes, O.S.B., Pst.; Rev. James Radek, Sacr. Min.; Dcn. Paul Nappi; Barbara Caruso, DRE; Alex Gervacio, RCIA Coord. & Youth Min.; CRP Stds.: 100

St. Joan of Arc School - (Grades PreSchool-8) 4913 Columbia, Lisle, IL 60532 t) 630-969-1732 stjoanofarcschool@sjalisle.org school.sjalisle.org Michelle Picchione, Prin.; Stds.: 352; Lay Tchrs.: 22

LOCKPORT

St. Dennis - 1214 S. Hamilton St., Lockport, IL 60441 t) 815-838-2592 secretary@saint-dennis.org www.saint-dennis.org Rev. James Dvorscak, Pst.; CRP Stds.: 171

St. Dennis School - (Grades PreSchool-8) 1201 S. Washington St., Lockport, IL 60441 t) 815-838-4494 school@saint-dennis.org Lisa Smith, Prin.; Stds.: 174; Lay Tchrs.: 10

St. John Vianney - 401 Brassel, Lockport, IL 60441 t) 815-723-3291 sjvlockport@gmail.com Rev. Steven Bondi, Pst.; CRP Stds.: 31

St. Joseph - 410 S. Jefferson St., Lockport, IL 60441 t) 815-838-2112 (CRP); 815-838-0187 stjosephlockportdre@gmail.com; sjchurch@stjoeschool.com www.stjosephlockport.org Rev. Gregory Rothfuchs, Pst.; Dcn. Dennis Stolarz, DRE; CRP Stds.: 130

St. Joseph School - (Grades PreSchool-8) 529 Madison St., Lockport, IL 60441 t) 815-838-8173 blueribbonprincipal@stjoeschool.com www.stjoeschool.com Rita Stasi, Prin.; Stds.: 101; Lay Tchrs.: 9

Our Lady of Korean Martyrs Mission - 224 Bruce Rd., Lockport, IL 60441 t) 815-524-4502 c) 815-531-7921 olkmc7121@gmail.com iloveolkm.wixsite.com/ Rev. SeungWon Yoo, Admin.;

LOMBARD

Christ the King - 1501 S. Main St., Lombard, IL 60148 t) 630-396-6078 (CRP); 630-629-1717 loretta@ctklombard.org; carol@ctklombard.org Rev. Jeffery Stoneberg, Pst.; Dcn. Anthony Joseph Clishem; Dcn. Matthew Novak; Dcn. Peter Robinson; Vincent Zaprzal, Liturgy Dir.; Loretta Crotty, DRE; Dcn. Frank Lillig; CRP Stds.: 83

Divine Mercy Parish - 21W411 Sunset Ave., Lombard, IL 60148 t) 630-268-8766; 630-830-2669 (CRP) www.milosierdzie.us Rev. Andrzej Maslejak, Pst.; Rev. Krzysztof Janicki, Assoc. Pst.; Rev. Pawel Marek, Par. Vicar;

St. Pius X - 1025 E. Madison St., Lombard, IL 60148 t) 630-627-4526; 630-627-1551 (CRP) parishoffice@stpiuslombard.org stpiuslombard.org Rev. Jerzy Zieba, C.R., Pst.; Dcn. John Chan; Dcn. Armando Herrera; Dcn. Larry Lissak; Dcn. Thomas Rachubinski; Laura Mora, DRE; Laura May, DRE; CRP Stds.: 252

St. Pius X School - (Grades PreK-8) 601 S. Westmore, Lombard, IL 60148 t) 630-627-2353 schooloffice@stpiuslombard.org www.stpiuslombard.org/school/ Carrie Novak, Prin.; Stds.: 323; Lay Tchrs.: 25

Sacred Heart - 114 S. Elizabeth St., Lombard, IL 60148 t) 630-495-0843 (CRP); 630-627-0687 cthomas@shclombard.org www.sacredheartlombard.org Rev. Thomas Dunn, Pst.; Dcn. William H. Crane; Dcn. David Mahoney; Dcn. Christopher Mazzacano; Linda Andrejek, DRE; CRP Stds.: 205

Sacred Heart School - (Grades PreK-8) 322 W. Maple St., Lombard, IL 60148 t) 630-629-0536 info@shslombard.org www.shslombard.org Regina Pestrak, Prin.; Stds.: 177; Lay Tchrs.: 13

MANHATTAN

St. Joseph - 235 W. North St., Manhattan, IL 60442; Mailing: PO Box 25, Manhattan, IL 60442 t) 815-478-3341 (Parish Center) sjpoffice@sjpmanhattan.org; religioused@sjpmanhattan.org www.sjpmanhattan.org Very Rev. John Lindsey, Pst.; Dcn. Patrick Forsythe; Kelly Piasecki, DRE; CRP Stds.: 267

St. Joseph School - (Grades PreK-8) 275 W. North St., Manhattan, IL 60442; Mailing: P.O. Box 70, Manhattan, IL 60442 t) 815-478-3951 principal@sjsmanhaattan.org sjsmanhattan.org Colleen Domke, Prin.; Stds.: 186; Lay Tchrs.: 9

St. Patrick - 14936 Wilmington Peotone Rd., Manhattan, IL 60442 t) 815-478-3440 stpatrickwilton@aol.com www.stpatrickwiltoncenter.org Rev. Sebastian Gargol, Pst.; CRP Stds.: 10

MANTENO

St. Joseph Catholic Church - 175 S. Main St., Manteno, IL 60950; Mailing: 207 S. Main St., Manteno, IL 60950 t) 815-468-8116 (CRP); 815-468-3403 restjosephmanteno@gmail.com; stjosephmanteno@gmail.com Rev. Thomas Theneth, CMI, Pst.; CRP Stds.: 90

MINOOKA

St. Mary - 303 W. St. Mary St., Minooka, IL 60447; Mailing: P.O. Box 456, Minooka, IL 60447 t) 815-467-2769 (CRP); 815-467-2233 stmarysbusiness@gmail.com stmarysminooka.com Rev. Tuan Van Nguyen, Pst.; CRP Stds.: 325

MOKENA

St. Mary Church - 19515 S. 115th Ave., Mokena, IL 60448-0002 t) 708-326-9300 secretary@stmarymokena.org www.stmarymokena.org Rev. Dindo Billote, Pst.; Rev. Sam Conforti, Par. Vicar; Dcn. Gary Bednar; Dcn. Robert Kaminski; Dcn. Peter Manning; Dcn. Kevin Plankinton; Dcn. John Rex; Dcn. David Stanton; Stephen Warunek, Bus. Mgr.; Tami Brongiel, DRE; CRP Stds.: 562

St. Mary Church School - (Grades PreSchool-8) 11409 W. 195th St., Mokena, IL 60448 t) 708-326-9330 schoolsecretary@stmarymokena.org stmaryschoolmokena.org/ Dr. Michele Alday-Engelman, Prin.; Stds.: 467; Sr. Tchrs.: 1; Lay Tchrs.: 23

MOMENCE

St. Patrick - 119 N. Market St., Momence, IL 60954 t) 815-472-2864 stpatsrectory@mchsi.com www.stpatrickmomence.org/ Rev. Peter G. Jankowski, Admin.; CRP Stds.: 56

MONEE

St. Boniface - 5304 W. Main St., Monee, IL 60449; Mailing: P.O. Box 217, Monee, IL 60449 t) 708-534-9682 office@stboniface.comcastbiz.net stbonifacemonee.org Rev. Roger Kutzner, Pst.; Dcn. Mark Otten; CRP Stds.: 11

MORRIS

Immaculate Conception of the Blessed Virgin Mary - 600 E. Jackson St., Morris, IL 60450; Mailing: 516 E. Jackson St., Morris, IL 60450 t) 815-942-0620; 815-942-4177 (CRP) gfolkers@ics1.org; jdillenburg@ics1.org icmorris.org Rev. Jason Stone, Pst.; Dcn. Paul Jung; Dcn. Arnulfo Cisneros; Dcn. Santos H. Martinez; Rev. Gerald Watt, C.R., In Res.; Julie Dillenburg, DRE; CRP Stds.: 148

Immaculate Conception of the Blessed Virgin Mary School - (Grades PreK-8) 505 E. North St., Morris, IL 60450 t) 815-942-4111 sfriend@ics1.org www.ics1.org Stacey Swanson, Prin.; Stds.: 162; Sr. Tchrs.: 1; Lay Tchrs.: 11

NAPERVILLE

St. Elizabeth Seton - 2220 Lisson Rd., Naperville, IL 60565 t) 630-416-1992 (CRP); 630-416-3325 stelizabethseton@gmail.com sesnaperville.org Rev. Scott Huggins, Pst.; Dcn. Thomas Ross; Dcn. Gerard Erickson; Dcn. John Ripoll, RCIA Coord.; Dcn. Luciano Coson; Dcn. Matthew Napoli; CRP Stds.: 291

Holy Spirit Catholic Community - 2003 Hassert Blvd.,

Naperville, IL 60564 t) 630-922-0081 welcome@hscc.us www.hscc.us Rev. John Sponder, Pst.; CRP Stds.: 550

St. Margaret Mary - 1450 Green Trails Dr., Naperville, IL 60540 t) 630-369-0777 business@smmp.com smmp.com Rev. Max Behna, Pst.; Dcn. Joseph Ferrari; Dcn. Donald Helgeson; Dcn. Kenneth J. Miles; Dcn. Fred Straub; Dcn. Terry Taylor; CRP Stds.: 447

Sts. Peter and Paul - 36 N. Ellsworth St., Naperville, IL 60540 t) 630-355-1081 msalzman@sspeterandpaul.net www.sspeterandpaul.net Rev. Brad Baker, Pst.; Rev. Michael McMahon, Par. Vicar; Rev. Nestor Sanchez, Par. Vicar; Rev. Ryan Adorjan, In Res.; Rev. John T. McGeean, In Res.; Dcn. Michael Crowell; Dcn. Wilfredo Marrero; Dcn. Roger Novak; Dcn. Thomas Rehak; Dcn. Joseph Verdico; CRP Stds.: 287

Saints Peter and Paul School - (Grades PreSchool-8) 201 E. Franklin, Naperville, IL 60540 t) 630-355-0113 www.sspeterandpaulschool.com Stds.: 460; Sr. Tchrs.: 1; Lay Tchrs.: 29

St. Raphael - 1215 Modaff Rd., Naperville, IL 60540-7818 t) 630-355-4545 www.st-raphael.com Very Rev. Daniel Bachner, Pst.; Rev. Thomas Logue, Par. Vicar; Dcn. Ciro Afeltra; Dcn. Kurt Lange; Dcn. Leonard Penkala; CRP Stds.: 575

St. Raphael School - (Grades PreSchool-8) t) 630-355-1880 ejessen@st-raphaelschool.org Becky Ward, Prin.; Stds.: 293; Lay Tchrs.: 21

St. Thomas the Apostle - 1500 Brookdale Rd., Naperville, IL 60563 t) 630-355-8980; 630-305-6318 (CRP) jsimmons@stapostle.org; lkatz@stapostle.org www.stapostle.org Rev. Peter Infanger, Pst.; Rev. Joseph Kappilumakkal, C.M.I., Assoc. Pst.; Dcn. James Breen; Dcn. Joe Cuzzone; Dcn. Lawrence Kearney; CRP Stds.: 473

NEW LENOX

St. Jude - 241 W. Second Ave., New Lenox, IL 60451 t) 815-485-8049 dmcginn@stjudes.org www.stjudes.org Rev. Raymond Flores, OSA, Pst.; Rev. Jeff Rath, OSA, Par. Vicar; Rev. R. William Sullivan, O.S.A., Par. Vicar; Rev. John Sotak, Par. Vicar; Rev. John M. Ohner, O.S.A., In Res.; Dcn. Mark Armamentos; Dcn. William Ciston; Dcn. Robert Fitt; Dcn. George Goes; Dcn. Dennis Theriault; CRP Stds.: 1,280

St. Jude School - (Grades PreK-8) 241 W. 2nd Ave, New Lenox, IL 60451 t) 815-463-4254 kwinters@stjudes.org stjudes.org/school Kathy Winters, Prin.; Stds.: 146; Lay Tchrs.: 9

OAKBROOK TERRACE

Ascension of Our Lord - 1 S. 314 Summit Ave., Oakbrook Terrace, IL 60181 t) 630-629-5810 welcome@ascensionofourlord.net; mruddle@ascensionofourlord.net www.ascensionofourlord.net Rev. Jose Kadukunnel, C.M.I., Pst.; Dcn. Michael Ruddle, DRE; Edward Rylko, Bus. Mgr.; Sara Groppe, Music Min.; CRP Stds.: 42

OSWEGO

St. Anne - 551 Boulder Hill Pass, Oswego, IL 60543; Mailing: PO Box 670, Oswego, IL 60543-0670 t) 630-554-3331 stanne@stanneparish.org www.stanneparish.org Rev. Stephen Eickhoff, Pst.; Dcn. David Brockman; Dcn. James Perry; Dcn. Duane Wozek; Dcn. Gary Wooley; CRP Stds.: 597

PARK FOREST

St. Mary - 227 Monee Rd., Park Forest, IL 60466 t) 708-748-6686 cbartels@stmaryparkforest.org Rev. Greg Skowron, Pst.; CRP Stds.: 12

PAXTON

St. Mary - 407 W. Pells, Paxton, IL 60957-1290 t) 217-379-4033 frbui@stmarypaxton.org; jacob.brancaleon@gmail.co www.stmarypaxton.org/ Rev. Dong Bui, Pst.; Jacob Brancaleon, DRE; CRP Stds.: 42

St. Joseph -

PEOTONE

St. Paul the Apostle - 511 N. Conrad St., Peotone, IL 60468 t) 708-258-6917; 708-258-9580 stpaulre@att.net; stpauloffice@att.net stpaulpeotone.org Rev. Roger Kutzner, Pst.; Paula Prium, Bus. Mgr.; Dcn. James Kelly, CRE; CRP Stds.: 63

PLAINFIELD

St. Mary Immaculate - 15629 S. Rte. 59, Plainfield, IL 60544 t) 815-436-4501 (CRP); 815-436-2651 moleary@smip.org; gmorse@smip.org www.smip.org Rev. Patrick M. Mulcahy, Pst.; Rev. Ramon Sida III, Assoc. Pst.; Rev. John Regan, In Res.; Dcn. Patrick Lombardo; Dcn. Michael Perkins; Dcn. Thomas Schroeder; Dcn. James Sossong; Dcn. Glenn Vanek; Dcn. Manuel Perales; Denise Rowan, Bus. Mgr.; CRP Stds.: 857

St. Mary Immaculate School - (Grades PreSchool-8) t) 815-436-3953 jgarvey@smip.org Jennifer Errthum, Prin.; Lisa Kissel, Librn.; Stds.: 302; Lay Tchrs.: 19

PLANO

St. Mary - 901 N. Center St., Plano, IL 60545 t) 630-552-3448 emurillo@saintmaryplano.com; info@saintmaryplano.com saintmaryplano.com Rev. Andy Davy, M.I.C., Pst.; Rev. Matthew Lamoureux, M.I.C., In Res.; Dcn. Eduardo Murillo; CRP Stds.: 50

St. Mary School - (Grades K-8) 817 N. Center St., Plano, IL 60545 t) 630-552-3345 royals@saintmaryplano.com smplano.com Joseph Scarpino, Prin.; Stds.: 148; Lay Tchrs.: 10

ROCKDALE

St. Joseph Church - 1329 Belleview Ave., Rockdale, IL 60436-2577 t) 815-725-4469 (Office) stjosephrep@hotmail.com; michael_magiera@hotmail.com fsspjoliet.wordpress.com Rev. Michael Magiera, F.S.S.P, Pst.; Denise Lonigro, DRE; CRP Stds.: 47

ROMEOVILLE

St. Andrew the Apostle - 505 Kingston Dr., Romeoville, IL 60446; Mailing: 530 Glen Ave., Romeoville, IL 60446 t) 815-886-5962 (CRP); 815-886-4165 faithformation@andrewcc.org; adultff@andrewcc.org andrewcc.org Rev. Maciej Stelmach, Pst.; Rev. Eduardo Flores, Assoc. Pst.; Dcn. Ricardo Marquez; Dcn. Jesse Tagle; Dcn. Herb Waldron; Maria Jazowski, DRE; Barbara Sanders, RCIA Coord.; CRP Stds.: 230

St. Andrew the Apostle School - (Grades PreK-8) t) 815-886-5953 schooloffice@andrewcc.org; principal@andrewcc.org www.andrewcc.org Carol Albreski, Prin.; Stds.: 185; Lay Tchrs.: 11

ROSELLE

St. Walter - 130 W. Pine Ave., Roselle, IL 60172 t) 630-894-2461 rklemundt@stwalterchurch.com; dburke@stwalterchurch.com www.stwalterchurch.com Rev. Mario S. Quejadas, Pst.; Rev. Robert Basler, O.S.A., Par. Vicar; Dcn. Michael Kowalchik; Dcn. Joseph Pusateri; Dcn. Ron Searls; Valerie Della Penna, DRE; Richard T Klemundt, Bus. Mgr.; CRP Stds.: 245

St. Walter School - (Grades PreSchool-8) 201 W. Maple Ave., Roselle, IL 60172 t) 630-529-1721 swsoffice@stwalterschool.com www.stwalterschool.com Lauren Volk, Dean; Mary Kathryn Warco, Prin.; Stds.: 397; Lay Tchrs.: 24

SHOREWOOD

Holy Family - 600 Brook Forest Ave., Shorewood, IL 60404 t) 815-730-8691 (CRP); 815-725-6880 lkrauledis@holyfamilyshorewood.org; mnovak@holyfamilyshorewood.org holyfamilyshorewood.org Rev. John Phan, Pst.; Rev. Brian Geary, Par. Vicar; Dcn. Steve Gerding; Dcn. Manuel Guerrero; Dcn. John Gustin; Dcn. Karl Huebner; Dcn. Stephen Petrouske; Leslie Krauledis, DRE; CRP Stds.: 833

Holy Family School - (Grades PreK-8) t) 815-725-8149 asimone@holyfamilyshorewood.org Anthony Wilkinson, Prin.; Stds.: 336; Lay Tchrs.: 14

SOUTH WILMINGTON

St. Lawrence - 135 Rice St., South Wilmington, IL 60474; Mailing: Box 190, South Wilmington, IL 60474 t) 815-237-2230 swkrcatholics.org Rev. Stanley Drewniak (Poland), Pst.; Linette Hopwood, Bus. Mgr.; CRP Stds.: 46

St. Mary - 216 E. Lincoln St., Reddick, IL 60961; Mailing: PO Box 16, Reddick, IL 60961 t) (815) 237-2230 www.swkrcatholics.org Rev. Stanley Drewniak;

ST. ANNE

St. Anne - 230 N. Sixth Ave., St. Anne, IL 60964; Mailing: P.O. Box 470, St. Anne, IL 60964 t) 815-427-8265 stanneparish60964@gmail.com www.stannestanne.org Rev. Peter G. Jankowski, Admin.; CRP Stds.: 27

STEGER

St. Liborius - 71 W. 35th St., Steger, IL 60475 t) 708-754-3460 (CRP); 708-754-1363 parish@stliborius.org www.stliborius.org Dcn. Frank Ciscato; Dcn. David Prete, DRE; CRP Stds.: 95

Mother Teresa Catholic Academy - (Grades PreSchool-8) 24201 S. Kings Rd., Crete, IL 60417 t) 708-672-3093 info@mtcacademy.org www.mtcacademy.org (Steger Campus) Annie Murray, Prin.; Stds.: 141; Lay Tchrs.: 12

VILLA PARK

St. Alexander - 300 S. Cornell Ave., Villa Park, IL 60181 t) 630-833-7730 office@stalexanderparish.org www.stalexanderparish.org Rev. Mark Rosenbaum, Pst.; Dcn. Christopher Cochran; Dcn. Julio Jimenez; Dcn. James Krueger; Dcn. Mark Ranieri; Dcn. Matthew Tretina; Kathy Halloran, DRE; CRP Stds.: 100

St. John the Apostle - 330 N. Westmore, Villa Park, IL 60181 t) 630-279-7433 (CRP); 630-279-7404 (Rectory) sttacc@comcast.net www.stjohnvillapark.org Rev. Mark Rosenbaum, Pst.; Dcn. Ronald Madsen; Dolly Foley, DRE; CRP Stds.: 88

WARRENVILLE

St. Irene - 28 W. 441 Warrenville Rd., Warrenville, IL 60555 t) 630-393-2400 x110 parishoffice@st-irene.org www.st-irene.org/ Rev. Clive Otieno, Pst.; Dcn. Joseph Urso, Pst. Assoc.; Dcn. Bradley Hentz, Pst. Assoc.; Craig Mazur, DRE; Pamela Keating, Parish Life Coord.; Ryan Rump, Music Min.; Fred Schlick, Bus. Mgr.; CRP Stds.: 101

WATSEKA

St. Edmund - 219 E. Locust St., Watseka, IL 60970 t) 815-432-5569 (CRP); 815-432-3274 pattiduffy@ymail.com; sted1997@outlook.com www.stedstjoe.org Rev. Michael Powell, Pst.; CRP Stds.: 42

St. Joseph - 307 Union, Crescent City, IL 60928; Mailing: P.O. Box 173, Crescent City, IL 60928 t) (815) 432-3274

WAYNE

Resurrection Catholic Church - 30W350 Army Trail Rd., Wayne, IL 60184 t) 630-289-5400; 630-289-5400 x215 (CRP) clewis@resurrectioncc.com www.resurrectioncc.com Rev. Tri Van Tran, Pst.; CRP Stds.: 165

WEST CHICAGO

St. Mary - 140 N. Oakwood Ave., West Chicago, IL 60185 t) 630-231-0013 x233 (CRP); 630-231-0013 parish.office@stmarywc.org stmarywc.org Rev. David Lawrence, Pst.; Rev. Andrew Buchanan, Vicar; Dcn. Bruce Carlson; Dcn. Dan Culloton; Dcn. Luis Saltigerald; CRP Stds.: 327

WESTMONT

Holy Trinity - 111 S. Cass Ave., Westmont, IL 60559; Mailing: 25 E. Richmond St., Westmont, IL 60559 t) 630-968-1366 jgregoire@holytrinitywestmont.org www.holytrinitywestmont.org Rev. Rafal Wasilewski, C.R., Pst.; Dcn. Patrick Blaney; Dcn. Anthony Lenard; Joanne Gregoire, DRE; CRP Stds.: 131

Holy Trinity School - (Grades PreK-8) 108 S. Linden Ave., Westmont, IL 60559 t) 630-971-0184 schooloffice@holytrinitywestmont.org www.holytrinitywestmont.org/school Pamela Simon, Prin.; Stds.: 160; Lay Tchrs.: 14

WHEATON

St. Daniel the Prophet Church - 101 W. Loop Rd., Wheaton, IL 60189 t) 630-384-0123 info@stdaniel.org stdaniel.org Rev. John J. Ouper, Pst.; Karen Gulvas, DRE; William Runge, Bus. Mgr. & Music Min.; CRP Stds.: 73

St. Mark - 300 E. Cole Ave., Wheaton, IL 60187; Mailing: 303 E. Parkway Dr., Wheaton, IL 60187

t) 630-665-0030 office@stmarkwheaton.org Rev. Andrew Lewandowski, C.R., Pst.;

St. Michael - 310 S. Wheaton Ave., Wheaton, IL 60187 t) 630-682-3650 (CRP); 630-665-2250 churchoffice@stmichaelcommunity.org www.stmichaelcommunity.org/ Rev. Daniel Hoehn, Pst.; Rev. John Honiotes, Assoc. Pst.; Rev. Jacob Kolawole, Assoc. Pst.; Dcn. Daniel Aderholdt; Dcn. Daniel Simmet; Colleen Brodhead, DRE; CRP Stds.: 870

St. Michael School - (Grades PreSchool-8) 314 W. Willow Ave., Wheaton, IL 60187 t) 630-665-1454 schooloffice@stmichaelschoolwheaton.org www.stmichaelschoolwheaton.org Adam Ferguson, Prin.; Stds.: 592; Lay Tchrs.: 23

WILMINGTON

St. Rose - 603 S. Main St., Wilmington, IL 60481 t) 815-476-7491 strose603@aol.com Rev. Sebastian Gargol, Pst.; Dcn. Jay Plese; Jamie Hooper, CRE; Carol Treadman, Bus. Mgr.; CRP Stds.: 65

WINFIELD

St. John the Baptist - 0S233 Church St., Winfield, IL 60190-1244 t) 630-668-0918; 630-682-4400 x612 (CRP) contactus@stjohnwinfield.org www.stjohnwinfield.org Rev. Christopher Lankford, Pst.; Maureen Brennan, DRE; Jim Nolan, Bus. Mgr.; CRP Stds.: 217

St. John the Baptist School - (Grades PreK-8) O.S. 259 Church St., Winfield, IL 60190 t) 630-668-2625 terih@stjohnwinfield.org Joanne Policht, Prin.; Stds.: 203; Lay Tchrs.: 16

WOOD DALE

Holy Ghost - 254 N. Wood Dale Rd., Wood Dale, IL 60191 t) 630-766-1045 (CRP); 630-860-2975 nsiemers@holyghostparish.org; tbero@holyghostparish.org www.holyghostparish.org Rev. John Joseph Hornicak, Pst.; Dcn. Robbie Lasica, Pst. Assoc.; Dcn. Dino Franch; Nancy Siemers, DRE; CRP Stds.: 93

WOODRIDGE

Christ the Servant Parish - 8700 Havens Dr., Woodridge, IL 60517 t) 630-910-0770 ctsoffice@ctswoodridge.org www.ctswoodridge.org Rev. Robert Duda, Pst.; Dcn. Thomas Fricke; Dcn. Rod Accardi; CRP Stds.: 113

St. Scholastica - 7800 Janes Ave., Woodridge, IL 60517 t) 630-985-9255 (CRP); 630-985-2351 x122 bcartner@stscholasticaparish.org; mtrevino@stscholasticaparish.org www.stscholasticaparish.org Rev. Norbert Raszeja, C.R., Pst.; Rev. Edward Howe, C.R., Par. Vicar; Dcn. Rick Felts; Dcn. Thomas Marciani; Dcn. Bob Wallace; Jean Palasz, Bus. Mgr.; Beth Cartner, DRE; Jennifer Michalik-Olson, Youth Min.; CRP Stds.: 257

St. Scholastica School - (Grades K-8) 7720 Janes Ave., Woodridge, IL 60517 t) 630-985-2515 ldriscoll@stscholasticaschool.org Elizabeth Driscoll, Prin.; Barbara Stance, Librn.; Stds.: 212; Lay Tchrs.: 10

YORKVILLE

St. Patrick - 406 Walnut St., Yorkville, IL 60560 t) 630-553-6671 info@stpatrickyorkville.org www.stpatrickyorkville.org Rev. Matthew Lamoureux, M.I.C., Pst.; Dcn. Doug Wells; Dcn. Dale Metcalfe; Dcn. Victor Puscas; Dcn. Bill Johnson; Michele Gonzales, DRE; CRP Stds.: 415

SCHOOLS: PRESCHOOL THRU HIGH SCHOOL

SCHOOLS

STATE OF ILLINOIS

BOURBONNAIS

Bishop McNamara Catholic School - (PAR) (Grades PreK-5) 324 E. Marsile St., Bourbonnais, IL 60914 t) 815-933-7758 sgoselin@bmcss.org www.bishopmac.com Sue Goselin, Admin.; Stds.: 190; Lay Tchrs.: 13

BRADLEY

Bishop McNamara Catholic School - (PAR) (Grades PreK-5) 247 N. Center Ave., Bradley, IL 60915 t) 815-933-8013 dberg@bmcss.org www.bishopmac.com Dana Berg, Prin.; Stds.: 187; Lay Tchrs.: 13

KANKAKEE

Bishop McNamara Catholic School - (DIO) (Grades 6-12) 550 E. Brookmont Blvd., Kankakee, IL 60901 t) 815-932-7413 tgranger@bmcss.org www.bishopmac.com Terry Granger, Pres.; Stds.: 855; Pr. Tchrs.: 1; Lay Tchrs.: 35

NAPERVILLE

All Saints Catholic Academy - (DIO) (Grades PreSchool-8) 1155 Aurora Ave., Naperville, IL 60540 t) 630-961-6125 mmarshall@ascacademy.org ascacademy.org Marjorie Marshall, Prin.; Maggie Detwiler, Vice Prin.; Stds.: 465; Sr. Tchrs.: 1; Lay Tchrs.: 31

HIGH SCHOOLS

STATE OF ILLINOIS

JOLIET

Joliet Catholic Academy - (PRV) 1200 N. Larkin Ave., Joliet, IL 60435 t) 815-741-0500 jbudz@jca-online.org www.jca-online.org (Coed) Dr. Jeffrey Budz, Prin.; Laura Pahl, Vice Prin.; Stds.: 588; Bro. Tchrs.: 1; Lay Tchrs.: 40

LISLE

Benet Academy - (PRV) (Grades 9-12) 2200 Maple Ave., Lisle, IL 60532 t) 630-719-2782 wmyers@benet.org www.benet.org William Myers, Prin.; Dr. LoriAnne Frieri, Vice Prin.; Christopher Perez, Vice Prin.; Michelle Renicker, Bus. Mgr.; Stds.: 1,246; Lay Tchrs.: 63

***Chesterton Academy of the Holy Family NFP, Inc.** - (PRV) (Grades 9-12) 5205 Kingston Ave., Lisle, IL 60532 t) 630-442-1424 www.cathf.com Brenie Bowles, Chair; Stds.: 159; Pr. Tchrs.: 1; Lay Tchrs.: 15

LOMBARD

Montini Catholic High School - (PRV) (Grades 9-12) 19 W. 070 16th St., Lombard, IL 60148-4797 t) 630-627-6930 kbeirne@montini.org; jsegredo@montini.org www.montini.org James F. Segredo, Pres.; Kevin Beirne, Prin.; Sara Lhotka, Vice Prin.; Christopher Tiritilli, Vice Prin.; Stds.: 527; Lay Tchrs.: 38

NEW LENOX

Providence Catholic High School - (PRV) (Grades 9-12) 1800 W. Lincoln Hwy., New Lenox, IL 60451 t) 815-485-2136 jmerkelis@providencecatholic.org; ryoung@providencecatholic.org www.providencecatholic.org (Coed) Rev. John D. Merkelis, O.S.A., Pres.; Paul B Houston, Prin.; Rev. Gerald Nicholas, O.S.A., Prior; Rev. Richard Young, O.S.A., In Res.; Stds.: 740; Pr. Tchrs.: 2; Bro. Tchrs.: 1; Lay Tchrs.: 54

WHEATON

St. Francis High School - (PRV) (Grades 9-12) 2130 W. Roosevelt Rd., Wheaton, IL 60187 t) 630-668-5800 rhuhn@sfhscollegeprep.org www.sfhscollegeprep.org Raeann Huhn, Prin.; Stds.: 675; Lay Tchrs.: 52

INSTITUTIONS LOCATED IN DIOCESE

ASSOCIATIONS [ASN]

CREST HILL

National Association of Catholic Nurses, U.S.A. - 16555 Weber Rd., Crest Hill, IL 60403; Mailing: P.O. Box 4556, Wheaton, IL 60189 c) (609) 477-9547 (Pres.); (609) 410-4126 (Pres.-Elect) catholicnurses@nacn-usa.org www.nacn-usa.org Patricia Sayers, Pres.; Maria Arvonio, Pres.-Elect;

DARIEN

Association of Our Lady of Mount Carmel - 1313 N. Frontage Rd., Darien, IL 60561; Mailing: P.O. Box 1020, Westmont, IL 60559 t) 800-341-5950 info@associationofmtcarmel.org associationofmtcarmel.org/ Rev. Thomas Schrader, O.Carm., Pres.;

ROMEOVILLE

Association of Lasallian Catholic Colleges and Universities - 100 Faculty Ln., La Salle House, Romeoville, IL 60446 t) 815-836-5402 Bro. James Gaffney, F.S.C., Treas.;

CATHOLIC CHARITIES [CCH]

CREST HILL

Catholic Charities, Diocese of Joliet - 16555 Weber Rd., Crest Hill, IL 60403 t) 815-723-3405 info@cc-doj.org www.catholiccharitiesjoliet.org Kathleen Langdon, Exec.; Asstd. Annu.: 66,062; Staff: 250

DOWNERS GROVE

Catholic Charities, Diocese of Joliet - 3040 Finley Rd., Ste. 200, Downers Grove, IL 60515 t) 630-495-8008 info@cc-doj.org www.catholiccharitiesjoliet.org Regional Office for DuPage County. Kathleen Langdon, Exec.; Asstd. Annu.: 66,062; Staff: 250

KANKAKEE

Catholic Charities, Diocese of Joliet - 100 College Dr., Kankakee, IL 60901 t) 815-933-7791 info@cc-doj.org www.catholiccharitiesjoliet.org Regional Office for Kankakee, Ford, and Iroquois Counties. Kathleen Langdon, Exec.; Asstd. Annu.: 66,062; Staff: 250

CEMETERIES [CEM]

BOURBONNAIS

All Saints Cemetery - 1839 W. Rte. 102, Bourbonnais, IL 60914; Mailing: 200 W. Romeo Rd., Romeoville, IL 60446 t) 815-933-2342; 815-886-0750 eholloway@dioceseofjoliet.org www.dioceseofjoliet.org/cemeteries Eric Holloway, Exec. Dir.;

Maternity/BVM Cemetery - Canterberry Ln., Bourbonnais, IL 60914; Mailing: 200 W. Romeo Rd., Romeoville, IL 60446 t) 815-933-2342 eholloway@dioceseofjoliet.org www.dioceseofjoliet.org/cemeteries Eric Holloway, Exec. Dir.;

CAROL STREAM

St. Stephen Cemetery - 405 E. St. Charles Rd., Carol Stream, IL 60188; Mailing: 200 W. Romeo Rd., Romeoville, IL 60446 t) 815-886-0750 eholloway@dioceseofjoliet.org www.dioceseofjoliet.org/cemeteries Eric Holloway, Exec. Dir.;

CREST HILL

Holy Cross Cemetery - Theodore St., Crest Hill, IL 60403; Mailing: 200 W. Romeo Rd., Romeoville, IL 60446 t) 815-886-0750 eholloway@dioceseofjoliet.org Eric Holloway, Exec. Dir.;

St. Mary Nativity Cemetery - 601Caton Farm Rd. at Oakland Ave., Crest Hill, IL 60441; Mailing: 200 W. Romeo Rd., Romeoville, IL 60446 t) 815-886-0750 eholloway@dioceseofjoliet.org www.dioceseofjoliet.org/cemeteries Eric Holloway, Exec. Dir.;

DOWNERS GROVE

Holy Family Cemetery - 1501 Hobson Rd., Downers Grove, IL 60517; Mailing: 200 W. Romeo Rd., Romeoville, IL 60446 t) 815-886-0750 eholloway@dioceseofjoliet.org www.dioceseofjoliet.org/cemeteries Eric Holloway, Exec. Dir.;

ELMHURST

St. Mary Cemetery - 310 W. Alexander Blvd., Elmhurst, IL 60126; Mailing: 200 W. Romeo Rd., Romeoville, IL 60446 t) 630-668-3313 eholloway@dioceseofjoliet.org www.dioceseofjoliet.org/cemeteries Eric Holloway, Exec. Dir.;

JOLIET

SS. Cyril and Methodius Cemetery - Rte. 6 Maple Rd., Joliet, IL 60432; Mailing: 200 W. Romeo Rd., Romeoville, IL 60446 t) 815-886-0750 eholloway@dioceseofjoliet.org www.dioceseofjoliet.org/

cemeteries Eric Holloway, Exec. Dir.;
St. John the Baptist Cemetery - Ruby St. & Clements St., Joliet, IL 60435; Mailing: 200 W. Romeo Rd., Romeoville, IL 60446 t) 815-886-0750 eholloway@dioceseofjoliet.org www.dioceseofjoliet.org/cemeteries Eric Holloway, Exec. Dir.;
Mount Olivet Cemetery - 1320 E. Cass St., Joliet, IL 60432; Mailing: 200 W. Romeo Rd., Romeoville, IL 60446 t) (815) 886-0750 eholloway@dioceseofjoliet.org www.dioceseofjoliet.org/cemeteries Eric Holloway, Exec. Dir.;
St. Patrick Cemetery - Jefferson St. at Hunter St., Joliet, IL 60435; Mailing: 200 W. Romeo Rd., Romeoville, IL 60446 t) 815-886-0750 eholloway@dioceseofjoliet.org www.dioceseofjoliet.org/cemeteries Eric Holloway, Exec. Dir.;

KANKAKEE

Mt. Calvary Cemetery - 2000 E. Court St., Kankakee, IL 60901; Mailing: 200 W. Romeo Rd., Romeoville, IL 60446 t) 815-933-2342 eholloway@dioceseofjoliet.org www.dioceseofjoliet.org/cemeteries Eric Holloway, Exec. Dir.;
St. Rose Cemetery - Rte. 50, Kankakee, IL 60901; Mailing: 200 W. Romeo Rd., Romeoville, IL 60446 t) 815-933-2342; 815-886-0750 eholloway@dioceseofjoliet.org Eric Holloway, Exec. Dir.;

LOCKPORT

Calvary Cemetery - Rte. 171 & High Rd., Lockport, IL 60441; Mailing: 200 W. Romeo Rd., Romeoville, IL 60446 t) 815-886-0750 eholloway@dioceseofjoliet.org Eric Holloway, Exec. Dir.;
Lockport South Cemetery - 16th St. & Washington St., Lockport, IL 60441; Mailing: 200 W. Romeo Rd., Romeoville, IL 60446 t) 815-886-0750 eholloway@dioceseofjoliet.org Eric Holloway, Exec. Dir.;

LOMBARD

St. Mary Cemetery - Finley Rd., Lombard, IL 60148; Mailing: 200 W. Romeo Rd., Romeoville, IL 60446 t) 815-886-0750 eholloway@dioceseofjoliet.org Eric Holloway, Exec. Dir.;

NAPERVILLE

SS. Peter & Paul Cemetery - 911 North Ave. At Columbia, Naperville, IL 60563; Mailing: 200 W. Romeo Rd., Romeoville, IL 60446 t) 630-668-3313 eholloway@dioceseofjoliet.org www.dioceseofjoliet.org/cemeteries Eric Holloway, Exec. Dir.;

OSWEGO

Risen Lord Cemetery - 1501 Simons Rd., Oswego, IL 60543; Mailing: 200 W. Romeo Rd., Romeoville, IL 60446 t) 630-554-7590 eholloway@dioceseofjoliet.org www.dioceseofjoliet.org/cemeteries Eric Holloway, Exec. Dir.;

ROMEOVILLE

Resurrection Cemetery - 200 W. Romeo Rd., (135th) at Rt. 53, Romeoville, IL 60446 t) 815-886-0750 eholloway@dioceseofjoliet.org www.dioceseofjoliet.org/cemeteries Eric Holloway, Exec. Dir.;

WHEATON

Assumption Cemetery - 1S510 Winfield Rd., Wheaton, IL 60189; Mailing: 200 W. Romeo Rd., Romeoville, IL 60446 t) 630-668-3313; 815-886-0750 eholloway@dioceseofjoliet.org www.dioceseofjoliet.org/cemeteries Eric Holloway, Exec. Dir.;

WINFIELD

St. John the Baptist Cemetery - Garymills Rd. & Summit Dr., Winfield, IL 60190; Mailing: 200 W. Romeo Rd., Romeoville, IL 60446 t) 630-668-3313; 815-886-0750 eholloway@dioceseofjoliet.org www.dioceseofjoliet.org/cemeteries Eric Holloway, Exec. Dir.;

COLLEGES & UNIVERSITIES [COL]

JOLIET

University of St. Francis - 500 N. Wilcox, Joliet, IL 60435 t) 800-735-7500 information@stfrancis.edu www.stfrancis.edu Arvid C. Johnson, Pres.; Sr. Mary Elizabeth Imler, O.S.F., Vice Pres., Mission Integration; Sr. Gayle Rusbasan Sr., Campus Min.; Rev. Terry A. Deffenbaugh, O.S.A., Chap.; Rev. Michael Jennrich, Chap.; Stds.: 3,778; Lay Tchrs.: 87; Pr. Tchrs.: 2; Sr. Tchrs.: 2

LISLE

Benedictine University - 5700 College Rd., Lisle, IL 60532-0900 t) 630-829-6600 pariano@ben.edu www.ben.edu Charles Gregory, Pres.; Patricia Ariano, Chief of Staff Officer; Carrie Roberts, Dir., Campus Min.; Bro. Augustine Mallak, O.S.B., Prof.; Stds.: 3,378; Lay Tchrs.: 129

ROMEOVILLE

Lewis University - 1 University Pkwy., Romeoville, IL 60446-2200 t) 815-838-0500; 815-838-5561 dlivingston@lewisu.edu; hkrejci@lewisu.edu www.lewisu.edu/ (Coed University) Rev. Dennis Lewandowski, Chap.; Stds.: 6,513; Bro. Tchrs.: 4; Lay Tchrs.: 247

CONVENTS, MONASTERIES, AND RESIDENCES FOR WOMEN [CON]

FRANKFORT

Franciscan Sisters of the Sacred Heart - 9201 W. St. Francis Rd., Frankfort, IL 60423-8330 t) 815-469-4895 sisters@fssh.net www.fssh.net Sr. Joyce Shanabarger, Supr.; Srs.: 56

JOLIET

St. Clare House of Prayer - 1320 Franciscan Way, Joliet, IL 60435-3956 t) 815-725-1455 stclarehouse@aol.com Sr. Anita Beloin, OSF, Contact; Srs.: 3
Josephine Sisters - 351 N. Chicago St., Joliet, IL 60432 t) 815-727-1467 josephinesis@hotmail.com Sr. Judith Perez, Supr.; Srs.: 4
Sisters of St. Francis of Mary Immaculate (Congregation of the Third Order of St Francis of Mary Immaculate, Joliet, IL) - 1433 Essington Rd., Joliet, IL 60435-2873 t) 815-725-8735 jbessette@jolietfranciscans.org www.jolietfranciscans.org Sr. Jeanne Bessette, OSF, Pres.; Srs.: 102

KANKAKEE

Servants of the Holy Heart of Mary, Holy Family Prov., U.S.A. (Servants of the Holy Heart of Mary Charitable Trust) - 2041 W. State Rte. 113, Kankakee, IL 60901 t) 815-937-2380 ckarnitsky@sscm-usa.org; cshaw@sscm-usa.org www.sscm-usa.org Sr. Carol Karnitsky, Prov.; Srs.: 25

LISLE

Benedictine Sisters of the Sacred Heart, Sacred Heart Monastery - 1910 Maple Ave., Lisle, IL 60532-2164 t) 630-725-6000 mbratrsovsky@shmlisle.org www.shmlisle.org Sr. Mary Bratrsovsky, O.S.B., Prioress; Srs.: 16

MINOOKA

The Poor Clares of Joliet, Annunciation Monastery - 6200 E. Minooka Rd., Minooka, IL 60447 t) 815-467-0032 poorclaresofjoliet@att.net www.poorclaresjoliet.org Mother Maria Benedicta Murphy, Supr.; Srs.: 13

NEW LENOX

Mother of Good Counsel Monastery - 440 N. Marley Rd., New Lenox, IL 60451 t) (815) 462-0988 augustiniannuns@sbcglobal.net Augustinian Cloistered Nuns, Inc. Sr. Mary Grace Kuppe, O.S.A., Prioress; Srs.: 4

PLAINFIELD

Mantellate Sisters Servants of Mary of Plainfield - 16949 S. Drauden Rd., Plainfield, IL 60586-9168 t) 815-436-5796 srloustu@yahoo.com Sr. Marianne Talian, O.S.M., Supr.; Srs.: 6
Mantellate Sisters Servants of Mary, U.S.A. - 16949 S. Drauden Rd., Plainfield, IL 60586-9168 t) 815-436-5796 srloustu@yahoo.com Sr. Marianne Talian, O.S.M., Supr.; Srs.: 6

WHEATON

Convent of Our Lady of the Angels Motherhouse (Wheaton Franciscan Sisters Corporation (WFSC)) - 26 W. 171 Roosevelt Rd., Wheaton, IL 60187; Mailing: P.O. Box 667, Wheaton, IL 60187 t) 630-909-6600 rkennedy@wfsisters.org www.wheatonfranciscan.org Franciscan Sisters, Daughters of the Sacred Hearts of Jesus and Mary (Wheaton, IL) Sr. Melanie Paradis, O.S.F., Pres.; Srs.: 35
Religious of the Institute of the Blessed Virgin Mary - 26W171 Roosevelt Rd., Wheaton, IL 60187; Mailing: PO Box 508, Wheaton, IL 60187 t) 630-653-6113 ibvmbarb@aol.com www.ibvm.us Sr. Mary Carton, IBVM, Admin.; Sr. Judy Illig, I.B.V.M., Admin.; Sr. Helen Timothy, IBVM, Admin.; Sr. Barbara Nelson, Treas.; Srs.: 40

ENDOWMENTS / FOUNDATIONS / TRUSTS [EFT]

BURR RIDGE

Christian Brothers Fund, Inc. - 7650 S. County Line Rd., Burr Ridge, IL 60527-7959 t) 630-323-3725 info@cbmidwest.org cbmidwest.org Anthony Chimera, Pres.; Samantha VenHuizen, Secy.; Bro. Joseph Saurbier, F.S.C., Treas.;

CREST HILL

The Catholic Education Foundation of the Diocese of Joliet - 16555 Weber Rd., Crest Hill, IL 60403 t) 815-221-6127 jgeorgis@dioceseofjoliet.org cefjoliet.org Jennifer Georgis, Dir.;
Diocesan Educational Endowment Fund - 16555 Weber Rd., Crest Hill, IL 60403 t) 815-221-6100 mjanus@dioceseofjoliet.org Mark Janus, Dir.;
Diocese of Joliet Catholic Cemetery Perpetual Care Trust - 16555 Weber Rd., Crest Hill, IL 60403 t) 815-933-2342 eholloway@dioceseofjoliet.org Eric Holloway, Dir.;
Diocese of Joliet Parish Deposit & Loan Trust - 16555 Weber Rd., Crest Hill, IL 60403 t) (815) 221-6203 Most Rev. Ronald A. Hicks, Trustee; Brian Schroeder, Exec. Dir.; Michael Bava, Bd. Dirs.; Thomas Boler, Bd. Dirs.; Very Rev. Richard L. Smith, Bd. Dirs.; Randy Waring, Bd. Dirs.;
Diocese of Joliet Priests' Pension Plan - 16555 Weber Rd., Crest Hill, IL 60403 t) (815) 221-6203 Most Rev. Ronald A. Hicks, Chair; Brian Schroeder, CFO; Very Rev. John Balluff, Bd. Mem.; James Ceplecha, Bd. Mem.; Rev. Daniel Hoehn, Bd. Mem.; Rev. John Joseph Hornicak, Bd. Mem.; Rev. James Schwab, Bd. Mem.; Rev. Anthony Taschetta, Bd. Mem.;
Diocese of Joliet Retired Priests' Other Benefits Plan - 16555 Weber Rd., Crest Hill, IL 60403 t) (815) 221-6203 Most Rev. Ronald A. Hicks, Chair; Brian Schroeder, CFO; Very Rev. John Balluff, Vicar for Clergy Diocese of Joliet; James Ceplecha, Bd. Mem.; Rev. Daniel Hoehn, Bd. Mem.; Rev. John Joseph Hornicak, Bd. Mem.; Rev. James Schwab, Bd. Mem.; Rev. Anthony Taschetta, Bd. Mem.;
Diocese of Joliet Seminarian Education Endowment Trust - 16555 Weber Rd., Crest Hill, IL 60403 t) 815-221-6100 bschroeder@dioceseofjoliet.org Brian Schroeder, Contact;

MOMENCE

B.G.S. Charitable Trust - 114 W. Washington St., Momence, IL 60954-0736; Mailing: P.O. Box 736, Momence, IL 60954-0736 t) 815-472-3131 judy@sjog-na.org Bro. Michael Brown, Contact;

OAK BROOK

MV Benevolent Fund, Inc. - 1801 35th St., Oak Brook, IL 60523 t) 630-850-8232 lbanda@mayslake.com Joseph Saraceno, Pres.;

ROMEOVILLE

Charitable Trust of the Brothers of the Christian Schools - 1205 Windham Pkwy., Romeoville, IL 60446-1679 t) 630-378-2900 customerservice@cbservices.org www.cbservices.org Patrick Lynch, CEO;
Christian Brothers Employee Benefit Trust - 1205 Windham Pkwy., Romeoville, IL 60446-1679 t) 630-378-2900 info@cbservices.org www.cbservices.org Patrick Lynch, CEO; John Airola, Exec.;
Christian Brothers Employee Retirement Plan Trust - 1205 Windham Pkwy., Romeoville, IL 60446-1679 t) 630-378-2900 info@cbservices.org www.cbservices.org Patrick Lynch, CEO;
Christian Brothers Religious Medical Trust - 1205 Windham Pkwy., Romeoville, IL 60446-1679

t) 630-378-2900 info@cbservices.org www.cbservices.org Patrick Lynch, CEO;

Christian Brothers Retirement Savings Plan Trust - 1205 Windham Pkwy., Romeoville, IL 60446-1679 t) 630-378-2900 info@cbservices.org www.cbservices.org Patrick Lynch, CEO;

Religious & Charitable Risk Pooling Trust of the Brothers of the Christian Schools - 1205 Windham Pkwy., Romeoville, IL 60446-1679 t) 630-378-2900 info@cbservices.org www.cbservices.org Patrick Lynch, CEO;

WHEATON

St. Clare Region Charitable Trust - 26 W. 171 Roosevelt Rd., Wheaton, IL 60187-0667; Mailing: P.O. Box 667, Wheaton, IL 60187-0667 t) 630-909-6600 joliverio@wfsisters.org John D. Oliverio, Dir.;

Institute of the Blessed Virgin Mary Charitable Trust - 26 W. 171 Roosevelt Rd., Wheaton, IL 60187; Mailing: P.O. Box 508, Wheaton, IL 60187 t) 630-653-6113 ibvmbarb@aol.com www.ibvm.us Sr. Barbara Nelson, Treas.;

HOSPITALS / HEALTH SERVICES [HOS]

JOLIET

Presence Saint Joseph Medical Center - 333 N. Madison St., Joliet, IL 60435-6595 t) 815-725-7133 john.halstead1@ascension.org www.ascension.org Sponsored by Ascension Health Ministries (Ascension Sponsor), a public juridic person Polly Davenport, COO; John Halstead, Chief Mission Integration Officer; Bed Capacity: 478; Asstd. Annu.: 73,505; Staff: 1,303

KANKAKEE

Presence St. Mary's Hospital - 500 W. Court St., Kankakee, IL 60901 t) 815-937-2400 john.halstead1@ascension.org www.ascension.org Sponsored by Ascension Health Ministries (Ascension Sponsor), a public juridic person. DBA Ascension Saint Mary - Kankakee. Polly Davenport, COO; John Halstead, Chief Mission Integration Officer; Bed Capacity: 178; Asstd. Annu.: 36,257; Staff: 425

MOKENA

Presence Central and Suburban Hospitals Network - 18927 Hickory Creek Dr., Ste. 300, Mokena, IL 60448; Mailing: Alexian Brothers Health System, 200 S. Wacker Dr., Fl. 12, Chicago, IL 60606 t) 312-308-3200 john.halstead1@ascension.org www.ascension.org Sponsored by Ascension Health Ministries (Ascension Sponsor), a public juridic person Polly Davenport, COO; John Halstead, Chief Mission Integration Officer;

MISCELLANEOUS [MIS]

CREST HILL

Companions of Christ of the Diocese of Joliet - 16555 Weber Rd., Crest Hill, IL 60403; Mailing: 1409 Green Trails Dr., Naperville, IL 60540 t) (815) 216-8697 companionsofchristjoliet@gmail.com companionsofchrist.org Rev. Michael Groth, Treas.;

DARIEN

The League of the Miraculous Infant Jesus of Prague - 1313 N Frontage Rd, Darien, IL 60561; Mailing: P.O. Box 1045, Westmont, IL 60559-8245 t) 800-447-3436 info@infantprague.org infantprague.org/ Rev. Thomas Schrader, O.Carm., Pres.; Rev. Carl J. Markelz, O.Carm., Dir.;

National Shrine Museum of St. Therese of Lisieux - 8501 Bailey Rd., Darien, IL 60561 t) 800-621-2806 info@saint-therese.org www.littleflower.org/shrine Rev. Thomas Schrader, O.Carm., Pres.; Rev. Bernhard Bauerle, O.Carm., Dir.;

Provincial Office of Lay Carmelites and Scapular Center - 8501 Bailey Rd., Darien, IL 60561 t) 630-969-5050 laycarmelites@carmelnet.org laycarmelitespcm.org Sr. Libby Dahlstrom, O.Carm., Prov.; Cindy Perazzo, Prov.;

Society of the Little Flower - 1313 N. Frontage Rd., Darien, IL 60561-5340 t) 630-968-9400 carmelites@littleflower.org www.littleflower.org Rev. Thomas Schrader, O.Carm., Dir.;

JOLIET

Presence Home Care Joliet - 1060 Essington Rd., Joliet, IL 60435 t) 815-741-7371 ascension.org Polly Davenport, COO; John Halstead, CMIO;

***The Upper Room Crisis Hotline (TURCH)** - ; Mailing: P.O. Box 3572, Joliet, IL 60634 t) 815-727-4367; 888-808-8724 (Hotline) catholichotline@gmail.com www.theupperroomcrisishotline.org Terry Smith, Exec. Dir.;

LASALLE

***Assisi Homes - LaSalle Manor Inc.** - 1135 10th St., LaSalle, IL 61301 t) 815-223-0557 mrankin@mercyhousing.org www.mercyhousing.org Melissa Clayton, Pres.;

LISLE

Cursillo Movement - Diocese of Joliet - ; Mailing: P.O. Box 4247, Lisle, IL 60532 t) (815) 221-6174 www.jolietcursillo.org John Whitehouse, Dir.; Christina King, Chairperson;

Founders Woods, Ltd. - 5700 College Rd., Lisle, IL 60532 t) 630-829-6400 dturner@ben.edu Rev. David Turner, O.S.B., Contact;

***Friends of Imiliwaha, NFP** - 1910 Maple Ave., Lisle, IL 60532 t) 630-605-4760 www.friendsofimiliwaha.org Sr. Helen Jilek, Treas.; Alice Sima, Pres.;

MOKENA

Presence Care @ Home - 18927 Hickory Creek Dr., Mokena, IL 60448-8507; Mailing: AMITA Health, 2601 Navistar Dr., Legal, Lisle, IL 60532 t) 708-478-7900 john.halstead1@ascension.org www.ascension.org Polly Davenport, COO; John Halstead, Chief Mission Integration Officer;

MOMENCE

Little Brothers of the Good Shepherd, Inc. - 114 W. Washington St., Momence, IL 60954; Mailing: P.O. Box 736, Momence, IL 60954 t) 815-472-3131 judy@sjog-na.org www.sjog-na.org Bro. David Lynch, OH, Pres.; Bro. Richard MacPhee, Treas.;

OAK BROOK

Mayslake Center II, N.F.P. - 1801 35th St., Oak Brook, IL 60523 t) 630-850-8232 lbanda@mayslake.com Joseph Saraceno, Pres.;

ROMEOVILLE

Catholic Cemeteries Monument Sales - 200 W. Romeo Rd., Romeoville, IL 60446-2264 t) 815-886-0750 eholloway@dioceseofjoliet.org www.dioceseofjoliet.org/cemeteries Eric Holloway, Exec. Dir.;

***Christian Brothers Services** - 1205 Windham Pkwy., Romeoville, IL 60446-1679 t) 630-378-2900 info@cbservices.org www.cbservices.org

WEST CHICAGO

***The Society of St. Vincent de Paul of the Joliet Diocesan Council, Inc.** - 213 Main St., West Chicago, IL 60185; Mailing: 320 Windy Point Dr., Glendale Heights, IL 60139 t) 630-293-9755 svdpjoliet@sbcglobal.net Kent Sheldon, Dir.;

WHEATON

Canticle Place, Inc. - 26 W. 105 Roosevelt Rd., Wheaton, IL 60187; Mailing: 2126 W. Roosevelt Rd., Wheaton, IL 60187 t) 630-665-9100 mrankin@mercyhousing.org www.mercyhousing.org Melissa Clayton, Pres.;

Wheaton Franciscan Services, Inc. - 26 W. 171 Roosevelt Rd., Wheaton, IL 60187; Mailing: P.O. Box 667, Wheaton, IL 60187 t) 630-909-6600 joliverio@wfsisters.org John D. Oliverio, Pres.;

MONASTERIES AND RESIDENCES FOR PRIESTS AND BROTHERS [MON]

BURR RIDGE

Christian Brothers Provincial Office (Midwest Province) - 7650 S. County Line Rd., Burr Ridge, IL 60527-7959 t) 630-323-3725 info@cbmidwest.org www.cbmidwest.org Bro. Michael Fehrenbach, Prov.; Bro. Chris Englert, Prov. Asst.; Dr. Scott Kier, Supt.; Bro. Joseph Saurbier, F.S.C., Treas.; Anthony Chimera, Dir.; Brs.: 102

DARIEN

Carmelite Provincial Office - 1317 Frontage Rd., Darien, IL 60561 t) 630-971-0050 provincial@carmelnet.org; areynolds@carmelnet.org www.carmelnet.org Rev. Carl J. Markelz, O.Carm., Prov.; Rev. David McEvoy, O.Carm., Vice Prov.; Rev. Elias O'Brien, O.Carm., Treas.; Rev. Myron Judy, O.Carm., Dir.; Bro. Lawrence Fidelus, O.Carm., Dir.; Rev. Joseph P. O'Brien, O.Carm., Dir.; Rev. Thomas Schrader, O.Carm., Dir.; Rev. Gregory Houck, Second Councilor; Bro. Daryl Moresco, O.Carm., First Councilor; Rev. Jesus Paz, O.Carm., Third Councilor; Rev. Raul Maravi, O.Carm., Commissary Provincial of Perú; Rev. Gerald Payea, O.Carm., First Councilor of Perú; Rev. Eduardo Rivero, O.Carm., Second Councilor of Perú; Rev. Rolf Willemsen, Fourth Councilor; Rev. Edward Adelmann, O.Carm.; Rev. Marc Bell, O.Carm.; Rev. Robert Boley, O.Carm.; Rev. Alfredo Guillen, O.Carm.; Rev. Mario Loya, O.Carm.; Rev. Stanley Makacinas, O.Carm.; Rev. Craig Morrison, O.Carm.; Rev. Gerard Power, O.Carm.; Rev. Benjamin Salas, O.Carm.; Rev. Frank Weil, O.Carm.; Brs.: 40; Priests: 116

St. Simon Stock Priory - 8501 Bailey Rd., Darien, IL 60561 t) 630-971-0050 provincial@carmelnet.org Rev. Carl J. Markelz, O.Carm., Prov.; Rev. Robert E. Colaresi, O.Carm., Prior; Rev. Joseph Atcher, O.Carm.; Rev. Bernhard Bauerle, O.Carm.; Rev. Raymond Clennon, O. Carm.; Rev. David McEvoy, O.Carm.; Rev. Gavin Quinn, O.Carm.; Rev. Thomas Schrader, O.Carm.; Rev. Robert Traudt; Priests: 8

Titus Brandsma Priory (Society of Mount Carmel) - 8423 Bailey Rd., Darien, IL 60561-5361 t) 630-971-0050; 773-410-0211 pmcgarry@carmelnet.org www.carmelites.org Carmelite Priory of the Society of Mount Carmel Rev. Brian Henden, Prior; Rev. John J. Comerford, O.Carm.; Rev. Peter McGarry, O.Carm.; Priests: 3

JOLIET

St. Elias Carmelites - 3504 Lake Shore Dr., Joliet, IL 60431-8819 t) 815-439-8246 steliascarmelites@comcast.net Bro. Lawrence Fidelus, O.Carm., Prior; Rev. Donald W. Buggert, O.Carm.; Rev. Edward Ward, O.Carm.; Rev. John Welch, O.Carm.; Bro. Dominic Soganich, O.Carm.; Brs.: 2; Priests: 3

St. John the Baptist Friary - 404 N. Hickory St., Joliet, IL 60435-7554 t) 815-727-9783; 217-316-4335 eja1951@gmail.com Rev. Michael Jennrich, Guardian; Bro. Edward Arambasich, O.F.M.; Rev. Rommel Perez Flores, OFM; Brs.: 1; Priests: 2

LISLE

St. Procopius Abbey - 5601 College Rd., Lisle, IL 60532 t) 630-969-6410 secretary@procopius.org; gjelinek@procopius.org www.procopius.org Rt. Rev. Austin G. Murphy, O.S.B., Abbot; Rt. Rev. Hugh R. Anderson, O.S.B., Chap.; Rev. Gabriel Baltes, O.S.B., Pst.; Rev. Joseph Chang, O.S.B.; Rev. Thomas Chisholm, O.S.B.; Rev. James Flint, O.S.B., Subprior; Rev. T. Becket Franks, O.S.B., Chap.; Rev. Anthony J. Jacob, O.S.B.; Rev. Dismas B. Kalcic, O.S.B.; Rev. Philip S. Timko, O.S.B.; Rev. David Turner, O.S.B.; Rev. Julian von Duerbeck, O.S.B.; Rev. Kenneth Zigmond, O.S.B.; Bro. Kevin Coffey; Bro. Guy Jelinek, O.S.B., Prior; Bro. Augustine Mallak, O.S.B., Liturgy Dir.; Bro. Gregory Perron, Bus. Mgr.; Bro. Richard Poro, OSB, In Res.; Brs.: 5; Priests: 13

Benedictine Chinese Mission -

St. Procopius Abbey Endowment -

Slav Missions -

MOMENCE

Brother Mathias Barrett Inc. of Illinois - 114 W. Washington St., Momence, IL 60954; Mailing: P.O. Box 736, Momence, IL 60954 t) 815-472-3131 judy@sjog-na.org Bro. Alphonsus Brown, O.H., Pres.; Brs.: 2

Hospitaller Order of St. John of God Province of the Good Shepherd in NA, Inc. - 114 W. Washington St., Momence, IL 60954; Mailing: P.O. Box 736, Momence, IL 60954 t) 815-472-3131 judy@sjog-na.org www.sjog-na.org Bro. David Lynch, OH, Prov.;

NEW LENOX

Augustinian Friary - 1800 W. Lincoln Hwy., New Lenox, IL 60451 t) 815-485-6880 gnicholas@ameritech.net (See separate listing for Providence High School) Rev. Gerald Nicholas, O.S.A., Prior; Bro. David Relstab, OSA, Prof.; Rev. Joseph Roccasalva, OSA, Prof.; Rev. Richard Young, O.S.A., Chair; Rev. John D. Merkelis, O.S.A., Prov. Asst.; Brs.: 1; Priests: 4

ROMEOVILLE

La Salle Community - 100 Faculty Ln., Romeoville, IL 60446-1178 t) 815-836-5402 brjgaff@lewisu.edu Bro. James Gaffney, F.S.C., Dir.; Bro. Kenneth Arnold, F.S.C., Mem.; Bro. John Blease, F.S.C., Mem.; Bro. Thomas Dupre, F.S.C., Mem.; Bro. Christopher Ford, F.S.C., Mem.; Bro. Peter Hannon, F.S.C., Mem.; Bro. Philip Johnson, F.S.C., Mem.; Bro. Thomas Johnson, FSC, Mem.; Bro. Neil Kieffe, FSC, Mem.; Bro. David Kuebler, F.S.C., Mem.; Bro. Joseph Martin, F.S.C., Mem.; Bro. Raymond McManaman, F.S.C., Mem.; Bro. Sheferaw Mekonen, FSC, Mem.; Bro. Richard Merkel, FSC, Mem.; Bro. Steven Schonhoff, FSC, Mem.; Bro. Pierre St. Raymond, F.S.C., Mem.; Bro. Robert Veselsky, FSC, Mem.; Bro. John Vietoris, F.S.C., Mem.; Brs.: 18

NURSING / REHABILITATION / CONVALESCENCE / ELDERLY CARE [NUR]

CLIFTON

Arthur Merkle-Clara Knipprath Nursing Home - 1190 E. 2900 North Rd., Clifton, IL 60927-7103 t) 314-292-9308 ahscm-mission@ascension.org www.ascensionliving.org/ Apartment Community and Nursing Center. Ryan Endsley, COO;

HOMER GLEN

Franciscan Communities, Inc. (Marian Village) - 15624 Marian Dr., Homer Glen, IL 60491; Mailing: 11500 Theresa Dr., Lemont, IL 60439 t) 708-226-3780 csaysongkham@franciscancommunities.org www.franciscanministries.org A senior living and healthcare services ministry sponsored by the Franciscan Sisters of Chicago. Cari Saysongkham, Exec. Dir.; Rev. David Medow, Chap., Dir., Pastoral Care & Mission Integration; Staff: 55

JOLIET

Ascension Living Villa Franciscan Place - 210 N. Springfield Ave., Joliet, IL 60435 t) 314-292-9308 ahscm-mission@ascension.org www.ascensionliving.org/ Ryan Endsley, COO; Asstd. Annu.: 539; Staff: 78

Our Lady of Angels Retirement Home (Sisters of St. Francis of Mary Immaculate) - 1201 Wyoming Ave., Joliet, IL 60435 t) 815-725-6631 sbruno@olaretirement.org Sr. Sue Bruno, OSF, In Res.; Asstd. Annu.: 125; Staff: 130

KANKAKEE

Ascension Living Heritage Village - 901 N. Entrance Ave., Kankakee, IL 60901 t) 314-292-9308 ahscm-mission@ascension.org www.ascensionliving.org/ Ryan Endsley, COO; Asstd. Annu.: 91; Staff: 42

Presence Heritage Lodge (Presence Life Connections d/b/a Ascension Living Heritage Village) - 995 N. Entrance Ave., Kankakee, IL 60901 t) 314-292-9308 ahscm-mission@ascension.org www.ascensionliving.org/ Ryan Endsley, COO; Asstd. Annu.: 26; Staff: 11

LISLE

Villa St. Benedict - 1920 Maple Ave., Lisle, IL 60532 t) 630-725-7000 kbenjamin@villastben.org www.villastben.org Continuing Care Retirement Kathleen Benjamin, Dir. Nursing; Asstd. Annu.: 300; Staff: 133

NAPERVILLE

St. John Vianney Villa - 1464 Green Trails Dr., Naperville, IL 60540-8372 t) 630-983-0533 frscott@rcdoj.org Retirement home for priests. Rev. Lee Bacchi, In Res.; Rev. William Cullen, In Res.; Rev. James Curtin, In Res.; Rev. Martin M. Gabel, In Res.; Rev. Scott M. McCawley, In Res.; Rev. James Radek, In Res.; Rev. John Sebahar, In Res.; Rev. Danilo Soriano, In Res.; Rev. Daniel F. Stempora, In Res.; Asstd. Annu.: 9

St. Patrick's Residence - 1400 Brookdale Rd., Naperville, IL 60563-2126 t) 630-416-6565 info@stpatricksresidence.org www.stpatricksresidence.org Kate Marrero, Admin.; Staff: 186

OAK BROOK

Franciscan Tertiary Province of the Sacred Heart, Inc. (Mayslake Village Inc.) - 1801 35th St., Oak Brook, IL 60523 t) 630-850-8232 lbanda@mayslake.com www.mayslake.com Senior Citizen Retirement Community. Joseph Saraceno, Pres.; Asstd. Annu.: 156; Staff: 37

Mayslake Annex II, NFP - 1801 35th St., Oak Brook, IL 60523 t) 630-850-8232 lbanda@mayslake.com www.mayslake.com Joseph Saraceno, Pres.; Asstd. Annu.: 65; Staff: 37

Mayslake East Wing, Inc. - 1801 35th St., Oak Brook, IL 60523 t) 630-850-8232 lbanda@mayslake.com www.mayslake.com Joseph Saraceno, Pres.; Asstd. Annu.: 149; Staff: 37

Mayslake WAV, NFP - 1801 35th St., Oak Brook, IL 60523-2699 t) 630-850-8232 nferrari@mayslake.com Bro. Clarence Klingert, O.F.M., Chair; Michael A. Frigo, Pres.; Bro. Douglas Collins, O.F.M., Vice. Pres.; Katherine Maxwell, Secy.; James Fiore, Treas.;

PRESCHOOLS / CHILDCARE CENTERS [PRE]

JOLIET

Vilaseca Josephine Center - 351 N. Chicago St., Joliet, IL 60432 t) 815-727-1467 josemvilaseca@yahoo.com Sr. Araceli Perez, Dir.; Sr. Judith Perez, Dir.; Stds.: 79; Lay Tchrs.: 5

RETREAT HOUSES / RENEWAL CENTERS [RTR]

DARIEN

Carmelite Spiritual Center - 8419 Bailey Rd., Darien, IL 60561 t) 630-969-4141 retreats@carmelitespiritualcenter.org Rev. Robert E. Colaresi, O.Carm., Dir.;

FRANKFORT

Portiuncula Center for Prayer - 9263 W. St. Francis Rd., Frankfort, IL 60423-8330 t) 815-464-3880 marylou.nugent@fssh.net www.portforprayer.org Mary Lou Nugent, Dir.;

KANKAKEE

One Heart, One Soul Spirituality Center - 2041 W. State Rte. 113, Kankakee, IL 60901 t) 815-937-2380 cshaw@sscm-usa.org www.sscm-usa.org Sr. Carol Karnitsky, Prov.;

OAKBROOK TERRACE

Mayslake Ministries, Inc. - 1S314 Summit Ave., Oakbrook Terrace, IL 60181 t) 630-852-9000 mamore@mayslakeministries.org mayslakeministries.org Rev. Thomas Borkowski; Mary Amore, Exec.;

PLANO

La Salle Manor Christian Brothers Retreat House - 12480 Galena Rd., Plano, IL 60545 t) 630-552-3224 x101 info@lasallemanor.org lasallemanor.org Scott Baietti, Pres.;

SPECIAL CARE FACILITIES [SPF]

KANKAKEE

Azzarelli Clinic - 341 St. Joseph Ave., Kankakee, IL 60901 t) 815-928-6093 Kathy Wade, Dir.; Asstd. Annu.: 2,000; Staff: 1

Lisieux Pastoral Center - 371 N. St. Joseph Ave., Kankakee, IL 60901-2741 t) 815-939-2913 ksw1153@outlook.com Kathy Wade, Dir.; Asstd. Annu.: 1,200; Staff: 1

MOKENA

Presence Life Connections - 18927 Hickory Creek Dr., Ste. 300, Mokena, IL 60448-8507 t) 314-292-9308 ahscm-mission@ascension.org www.ascensionliving.org/ Ryan Endsley, COO;

MOMENCE

***Good Shepherd Manor** - 4129 N. State Rte. 1-17, Momence, IL 60954; Mailing: PO Box 260, Momence, IL 60954 t) 815-472-3700 info@goodshepherdmanor.org www.goodshepherdmanor.org Adult Male DD-MR. Rev. Wolf V.K. Werling, Chap.; Bro. Alphonsus Brown, O.H.; Kristen Stockle, Pres.; Bed Capacity: 120; Asstd. Annu.: 109; Staff: 130

Diocese of Kalamazoo

(Dioecesis Kalamazuensis)

MOST REVEREND PAUL J. BRADLEY, D.D., M.S.W.

Bishop of Kalamazoo; ordained May 1, 1971; appointed Titular Bishop of Afufenia and Auxiliary Bishop of Pittsburgh December 16, 2004; Episcopal ordination February 2, 2005; appointed Bishop of Kalamazoo April 6, 2009; installed June 5, 2009. officeofthebishop@diokzoo.org.

Diocesan Pastoral Center: 215 N. Westnedge Ave., Kalamazoo, MI 49007-3760. T: 269-349-8714; F: 269-349-6440. dioceseofkalamazoo.org

ESTABLISHED JULY 21, 1971.

Square Miles 5,337.

Comprises the following nine Counties in the State of Michigan: Allegan, Barry, Berrien, Branch, Calhoun, Cass, Kalamazoo, St. Joseph and Van Buren.

For legal titles of parishes and diocesan institutions, consult the Diocesan Pastoral Center.

STATISTICAL OVERVIEW

Personnel

Bishop....1
Priests: Diocesan Active in Diocese....39
Priests: Diocesan in Foreign Missions....1
Priests: Retired, Sick or Absent....17
Number of Diocesan Priests....57
Religious Priests in Diocese....9
Total Priests in your Diocese....66
Extern Priests in Diocese....9
Ordinations:
Diocesan Priests....1
Transitional Deacons....1
Permanent Deacons in Diocese....45
Total Brothers....1
Total Sisters....124

Parishes

Parishes....46
With Resident Pastor:
Resident Diocesan Priests....22
Resident Religious Priests....6
Without Resident Pastor:
Administered by Priests....4
Administered by Deacons....1
Administered by Religious Women....1
Administered by Lay People....1
Completely vacant....11
Missions....13
Pastoral Centers....1
Professional Ministry Personnel:
Brothers....1
Sisters....10
Lay Ministers....63

Welfare

Catholic Hospitals....3
Total Assisted....337,604
Health Care Centers....7
Total Assisted....25,000
Homes for the Aged....4
Total Assisted....582
Specialized Homes....3
Total Assisted....5,000
Special Centers for Social Services....2
Total Assisted....1,800
Other Institutions....1
Total Assisted....6,660

Educational

Diocesan Students in Other Seminaries....8
Total Seminarians....8
High Schools, Diocesan and Parish....3
Total Students....350
Elementary Schools, Diocesan and Parish....18
Total Students....2,034
Catechesis/Religious Education:
High School Students....747
Elementary Students....2,311
Total Students under Catholic Instruction....5,450
Teachers in Diocese:
Lay Teachers....166

Vital Statistics

Receptions into the Church:
Infant Baptism Totals....714
Minor Baptism Totals....77
Adult Baptism Totals....63
Received into Full Communion....89
First Communions....748
Confirmations....665
Marriages:
Catholic....151
Interfaith....51
Total Marriages....202
Deaths....943
Total Catholic Population....69,753
Total Population....966,198

LEADERSHIP

Diocesan Pastoral Center - t) 269-349-8714 www.dioceseofkalamazoo.org

Office of the Bishop - t) 269-349-8714 x1122 Most Rev. Paul J. Bradley;

Executive Assistant - Lexie Shoemaker-Fath;

Vicars General - Rev. Msgr. Michael Hazard; Rev. Msgr. Michael Osborn, Moderator of the Curia;

Chancellor - t) 269-903-0213 Very Rev. Robert Creagan;

Vicar for Canonical Concerns - t) 269-903-0179 Rev. Msgr. Thomas Martin, Vicar;

Chief Finance Officer - t) 269-349-8714 x1353 Timothy Meeker (tmeeker@diokzoo.org);

OFFICES AND DIRECTORS

General Secretariat - Rev. Msgr. Michael Osborn;

Deacon Formation - t) 269-903-0151 Rev. German Perez-Diaz, Dir.; Rev. Jose Haro, Dir.; Dcn. David Guido, Dir.;

Deacon Personnel - t) 269-903-0169 Dcn. John Ryder, Dir.; Dcn. James Mellen;

Society for the Propagation of Faith - Rev. Mark Vyverman;

Trauma Recovery Program - t) 269-779-5322 Rev. Kenneth Schmidt;

Victim Assistance Coordinator - t) 269-903-0175 Dcn. Patrick Hall;

Worship & Liturgy - t) 269-349-8714 x1123 Rev. Jeffrey David Hanley;

CATHOLIC CHARITIES

Catholic Charities Diocese of Kalamazoo - t) 269-381-9800 Toni Newell, Exec. Dir. (toninewell@ccdok.org);

Hispanic-Latino Ministry - t) 269-381-9800 Veronica Rodriguez, Dir.; Very Rev. Fabio Garzon, Clergy; Maria Marcella Trumm, Support Specialist;

The Ark Services for Youth -

Baraga Manor -

Immigration Assistance Program - t) 269-903-0135 Samantha Lindberg, Dir.;

Bridges Mental Health Counseling -

Caring Network -

Sanctity of the Human Person (Respect Life) - Lisa Irwin, Dir.;

Inner City Ministry - t) 269-926-6424

CLERGY AND RELIGIOUS SERVICES

Advocate for Priestly Ministry and Support - t) 269-779-5322 Rev. Kenneth Schmidt;

Vicar for Religious - t) 269-857-7951 Very Rev. Fabio Garzon;

COMMUNICATIONS

Secretariat for Communications and Public Affairs - t) 269-349-8714 x1350 Vicki Cessna, Exec. Dir. (vcessna@diokzoo.org);

Associate Director - Terry Hageman;

Communications Assistant - Sarah DeMott;

Legislative Relations/Public Affairs - Vicki Cessna;

Southwest Michigan Catholic - Editor - Vicki Cessna;

CONSULTATIVE BODIES

Diocesan Consultors - Very Rev. Fabio Garzon; Rev. Msgr. Michael Osborn; Rev. Msgr. Michael Hazard;

Presbyteral Council Members - Rev. R. Mathias, MSFS; Rev. Mark Vyverman, Secy.; Very Rev. Robert Creagan;

Diocesan Finance Council - t) 269-349-8714 x1353 David De Leeuw; Paul Hickey; Timothy Wenzel;

Diocesan Pastoral Council -

Clergy Members - Rev. Msgr. Michael Hazard; Rev. Msgr. Thomas Martin; Rev. Msgr. Michael Osborn;

Parish Members - Charles Young, Chair; Michelle Smith; Phil Green;

DEANERIES

Vicars Forane - Very Rev. Robert Creagan, Central Deanery; Very Rev. Daniel W. Hyman, Eastern Deanery; Very Rev. German Perez-Diaz, Western Deanery;

DEVELOPMENT

Director of Stewardship and Development - t) 269-903-0196 Jeannette Mattheis, Bishop's Annual Appeal;

EDUCATION

Secretariat for Catholic Education- Office of Schools - t) 269-349-8714 x1239 Margaret Erich, Supt. (merich@diokzoo.org);

Catholic Schools - Margaret Erich, Supt.; Jillian Kellough, Asst. Supt.;

Enrollment and Retention - Nina Laney;

Safe Environment/Child & Youth Protection - Marina Shoup;

EVANGELIZATION

Secretariat for Parish Life and Evangelization - t) 269-349-8714 x1234 Jamin Herold, Exec. Dir. (jherold@diokzoo.org); Joan Jaconette, Secy. (jjaconette@diokzoo.org);

Domestic Church (Marriage Preparation) - Socorro Truchan, Dir.;

Evangelization (Youth, Young Adult and Adult) - gdragan@diokzoo.org

Lay Ecclesial Ministry Formation - Jamin Herold;

Multicultural and Hispanic Ministry - Angelica Valdes, Contact;

FINANCE

Diocesan Business Office - t) 269-349-8714 x1353 Timothy Meeker, CFO (tmeeker@diokzoo.org); Tammi Wachterhauser, Accounting Clerk/Human Resources; Daniel Hughes, Sr. Accountant (dhughes@diokzoo.org);

TRIBUNAL

Diocesan Tribunal - t) 269-349-8714 x1117

Assessor - Rev. Kenneth Schmidt;

Court Experts - Carla Fallon; Phyllis Florian; Jillian Peyerk;

Defender of the Bond - Rev. Msgr. Thomas Martin;

Judge - Rev. Jeffrey David Hanley; Rev. Maxmilian Jacob Nightingale; Dcn. Hallie Bohan;

Judicial Vicar - Rev. Kenneth Schmidt;

Promoter of Justice - Rev. Msgr. Michael Osborn;

PARISHES, MISSIONS, AND CLERGY

STATE OF MICHIGAN

ALBION

St. John the Evangelist - 1020 Irwin Ave., Albion, MI 49224 t) 517-629-4532 churchoffice@stjohn-church.org; kesnyder@albion.edu www.stjohn-church.org Rev. Craig Lusk, Pst.; Rev. Joseph B. Gray, Pastor Emer.; Dcn. Kenneth Snyder, DRE; CRP Stds.: 26

ALLEGAN

Blessed Sacrament - 110 N. Cedar St., Allegan, MI 49010-1246 t) 269-673-4455 j_vmeer82@yahoo.com www.blessedsacrament-allegan.org Rev. Simon Joseph Chummar Manjooran, S.B.D. (India), Pst.; Dcn. Eugene Haas; Dcn. Fred Wall; Jolene Clearwater, DRE; CRP Stds.: 17

AUGUSTA

St. Ann - 12648 E. D Ave., Augusta, MI 49012 t) 269-731-4721 office@stannaugusta.org www.stannaugusta.org Rev. David Pinto, Pst.; Dcn. Michael Carl; Robert Kinkela, DRE; CRP Stds.: 49

Light of Christ Academy - (Grades PreK-8) t) 269-203-6808 office@lightofchristacademy.org lightofchristacademy.org Alane Fifelski, Prin.; Stds.: 73; Lay Tchrs.: 8

BANGOR

Sacred Heart of Jesus - 201 S. Walnut St., Bangor, MI 49013 t) 269-427-7514 sacredheartbangor@yahoo.com ichartford.com/ Rev. German Perez Diaz, Pst.; Dcn. Arthur Morsaw; CRP Stds.: 12

BATTLE CREEK

St. Jerome - 229 Collier Ave., Battle Creek, MI 49037 t) 269-968-2218 stjeromebc.org Rev. Christopher J. Ankley, Pst.; Rev. Pius Kei Cung, Par. Vicar; Rev. Kenneth Schmidt, Par. Vicar; Rev. Jacob Thomas, Par. Vicar; Dcn. Gary Wright;

St. Joseph - 61 23rd St. N., Battle Creek, MI 49015 t) 269-965-4079 (CRP); 269-962-0165 bkincaid@bcacs.org; frchris@bcacs.org stjosephbc.org Rev. Christopher J. Ankley, Pst.; Rev. Jacob Thomas, Par. Vicar; Rev. Pius Kei Cung, Par. Vicar; Dcn. David Krajewski; Dcn. James Nelson; CRP Stds.: 170

St. Joseph School - (Grades PreK-8) 47 N. 23rd, Battle Creek, MI 49015 t) 269-965-7749 bcacs.org Sara Myers, Prin.; Stds.: 183; Lay Tchrs.: 20

St. Philip - 112 Capital Ave., N.E., Battle Creek, MI 49017 t) 269-962-9506 (CRP); 269-968-6645 admin@stphilipbc.org www.stphilipbc.org Rev. James Richardson, Pst.; Dcn. Alfred Bell; CRP Stds.: 101

BENTON HARBOR

SS. John & Bernard - 600 Columbus Ave., Benton Harbor, MI 49022; Mailing: 580 Columbus Ave., Benton Harbor, MI 49022 t) 269-925-2425 ssjbbusmgr@gmail.com; religiousedoffice@att.net www.ssjohnandbernard.org Rev. James Adams, Pst.; CRP Stds.: 156

BRIDGMAN

Our Lady Queen of Peace - 3903 Lake St., Bridgman, MI 49106-0747 t) 269-465-6252 pastor@olqop.org Rev. Arthur Howard, Pst.; CRP Stds.: 20

BRONSON

St. Mary Assumption - 602 W. Chicago, Bronson, MI 49028 t) 260-829-6243 (CRP); 517-369-2120 stmarysbronson.org Very Rev. Daniel W. Hyman, Pst.; Dcn. Alan Sosinski; Dcn. John Wielgos; CRP Stds.: 130

St. Mary Assumption School - (Grades PreK-8) 204 Albers Rd., Bronson, MI 49028 t) 517-369-4625 ajohnston@stmarybronson.org stmarybronson.org Angela Johnston, Prin.; Stds.: 98; Lay Tchrs.: 7

BUCHANAN

St. Anthony - 509 W. 4th St., Buchanan, MI 49107 t) 269-695-3863 office@stanthonybuchanan.com Rev. Christian R. Johnston, Pst.; Rev. Leo Cartagena, Assoc. Pst.; Dcn. Alberto Rivera-Gutierrez; Patti Mitchell, DRE; CRP Stds.: 60

St. Gabriel Mission Church - 429 Rose Hill, Berrien Springs, MI 49103 t) (269) 471-2424 leocafra@gmail.com

BYRON CENTER

St. Mary's Visitation - 2459 146th Ave., Byron Center, MI 49315 t) 616-681-9701 x100 gandres@smvchurch.org; frderda@comcast.net www.smvchurch.org Rev. Stephen Rodrigo (India), Pst.; Dcn. Edward LaRoche; Rev. Christopher Derda, Admin.; CRP Stds.: 41

St. Mary's Visitation School - (Grades PreK-6) 2455 146th Ave., Byron Center, MI 49315 t) (616) 681-9607 smvschool.org Shannon Saxton-Murphy, Prin.; Stds.: 61; Lay Tchrs.: 7

CASSOPOLIS

St. Ann - 421 N. Broadway, Cassopolis, MI 49031; Mailing: P.O. Box 247, Cassopolis, MI 49031 t) 269-445-3000 stanncass@gmail.com stanncass.com Rev. Pangiraj Jabamalai Nathan, Pst.; CRP Stds.: 3

COLDWATER

St. Charles Borromeo - 150 Taylor St., Coldwater, MI 49036 t) 517-278-2650; 517-278-2650 x1004 (CRP) scbparishoffice@gmail.com; stcharlesdre@gmail.com st-charles-coldwater.org Very Rev. Daniel W. Hyman, Pst.; Dcn. James Lavelline; Dcn. Alan Sosinski; Dcn. John Wielgos; Angela Richards, DRE; CRP Stds.: 20

St. Charles Borromeo School - (Grades PreK-8) 79 Harrison St., Coldwater, MI 49036 t) 517-279-0404

www.scbcatholicschool.org/ Brenda Mescher, Prin.; Stds.: 161; Lay Tchrs.: 11

Our Lady of Fatima - 8220 M-60, Union City, MI 49094; Mailing: 150 Taylor St., Coldwater, MI 49036 t) (517) 741-7275 alichristo422@gmail.com

DECATUR

Holy Family - 500 W. St. Mary's St., Decatur, MI 49045 t) 269-783-4223 holyfamilydecatur@gmail.com; dan.northrup4@gmail.com holyfamilydecaturmi.com/ Rev. Arul Lazar; Dan Northrup, DRE; CRP Stds.: 30

DELTON

St. Ambrose - 11137 Floria Rd., Delton, MI 49046 t) 269-623-2490 stambrose@mei.net Sr. Constance Fifelski, O.P., Admin.; Rev. James Richardson, Pst.; CRP Stds.: 1

Our Lady of Great Oak - 6574 Lacey Rd., Bellevue, MI 49021 t) (269) 758-3636

DORR

St. Stanislaus - 1871 136th Ave., Dorr, MI 49323 t) 269-793-7268 rectory@st-stans.net; gandres@st-stans.net www.st-stanschurch.net Rev. Stephen Rodrigo (India), Pst.; Rev. Christopher Derda, Admin.; Dcn. Russell Pogodzinski; CRP Stds.: 13

St. Stanislaus School - (Grades PreK-8) 1861 136th Ave., Dorr, MI 49323 t) 269-793-7204 murphy@st-stans.net st-stans.net Shannon Saxton-Murphy, Prin.; Stds.: 85; Lay Tchrs.: 7

Sacred Heart - 2036 20th Ave., Allegan, MI 49010; Mailing: 1871 136th Ave., Dorr, MI 49323

DOUGLAS

St. Peter - 100 St. Peter Dr., Douglas, MI 49406-0248; Mailing: PO Box 248, Douglas, MI 49406 t) 269-857-7951 rick.hardy@stpeter-douglas.org stpeter-douglas.org Very Rev. Fabio Garzon, Pst.; Dcn. Anthony Nethercott; Rick Hardy, Pst. Assoc.; Alisha Giles, DRE; CRP Stds.: 73

San Felipe de Jesus - 5586 117th Ave., Fennville, MI 49408 t) 269-561-5029 joemarble328@gmail.com

DOWAGIAC

Holy Maternity of Mary - 210 N. Front St., Dowagiac, MI 49047 t) 269-782-2808; 269-782-9034 holymaternitydowagiac@gmail.com holymaternityofmary.com Rev. Arul Lazar, Admin.; CRP Stds.: 85

Sacred Heart of Mary - 51841 Leach Rd., Dowagiac, MI 49047 t) 269-782-8048 sacredheart2002b@gmail.com www.sacredheartsilvercreekmi.com Rev. Arul Lazar, Admin.; CRP Stds.: 10

EDWARDSBURG

Our Lady of the Lake - 24832 US Hwy. 12, Edwardsburg, MI 49112 t) 269-699-5870 ourlady49112@gmail.com www.ourladyedwardsburg.org Rev. Pangiraj Jabamalai Nathan, Pst.; CRP Stds.: 87

FENNVILLE

San Felipe de Jesus - 5586 117th Ave., Fennville, MI 49408; Mailing: P.O. Box 588, Fennville, MI 49408 t) 269-561-5029 joe.marble@stpeter-douglas.org www.sanfelipe-fennville.org Very Rev. Fabio Garzon, Pst.; Dcn. Maximino Rodriguez; Sr. Angee Bustos, msde, Pst. Min./Coord.; Joseph Marble, Parish Life Coord.; CRP Stds.: 94

GOBLES

St. Jude - 13809 M-40 N., Gobles, MI 49055; Mailing: P. O. Box 102, Gobles, MI 49055 t) 269-628-2219 st.judeparishgobles@gmail.com; deaconjimbauer@gmail.com www.stjudeparishgobles.com Rev. Alan P. Jorgensen, Pst.; Rev. Richard L. Altine, Par. Vicar; Dcn. James Bauer, Admin.; CRP Stds.: 26

HARTFORD

Immaculate Conception - 63559 60th Ave., Hartford, MI 49057 t) 269-621-4106 ic.hartfordchurch@gmail.com ichartford.com/ Rev. German Perez, Pst.; Dcn. Arthur Morsaw; CRP Stds.: 143

HASTINGS

St. Rose of Lima - 805 S. Jefferson Ave., Hastings, MI 49058 t) 269-945-4246 pastorstrose2015@gmail.com; syoungs48@sbcglobal.net strosehastings.com Rev. Stephan Philip, M.S.F.S., Pst.; Dcn. Gene Haas; Dcn. James Mellen; Steve Youngs, DRE; CRP Stds.: 36

St. Rose of Lima School - (Grades PreK-6) 707 S. Jefferson St., Hastings, MI 49058 t) 269-945-3164 info@srlsh.org stroseschoolhastings.com Diane Bennett, Prin.; Stds.: 70; Lay Tchrs.: 4

St. Cyril - 203 N. State St., Nashville, MI 49073; Mailing: 805 S Jefferson Ave, Hastings, MI 49058 t) (269) 945-4246 office.strose@gmail.com

KALAMAZOO

St. Augustine Cathedral - 542 W. Michigan Ave., -, Kalamazoo, MI 49007 t) (269) 345-5147 msaliwanchik@stakalamazoo.org www.stakalamazoo.org Very Rev. Robert Creagan, Rector; Rev. James Vinh Le, Par. Vicar; Rev. Robert J. Johansen, Par. Vicar; Dcn. Don Bouchard; Dcn. John R. Bodway;

St. Augustine Cathedral School - (Grades PreK-8) 600 W. Michigan Ave., Kalamazoo, MI 49007 t) 269-349-1945 azommers@stakzoo.org www.stakzoo.org Andra Zommers, Prin.; Stds.: 287; Lay Tchrs.: 17

St. Joseph - 936 Lake St., Kalamazoo, MI 49001 t) 269-343-6256 mail.stjoekal@gmail.com; dre.stjoekal@gmail.com Rev. Antony Rajesh, Pst.; Rev. Jeffrey David Hanley, Par. Vicar; Dcn. Timothy Kistka; Dcn. John Ryder; Nikki Smith, DRE; CRP Stds.: 122

St. Mary - 939 Charlotte Ave., Kalamazoo, MI 49048 t) 269-342-0621 office@stmarykzoo.org www.stmarykazoo.org Rev. Jose de Jesus Haro Gomez, Pst.; Dcn. Patrick Hall; Ursula Engebretsen, Music Min.; CRP Stds.: 29

St. Monica - 4408 S. Westnedge, Kalamazoo, MI 49008 t) 269-345-4389 facklerccd@gmail.com stmonicachurchkzoo.com Rev. Russell Homic, Pst.; Rev. Maxmilian Jacob Nightingale, Par. Vicar; Dcn. Kurt Lucas; Rev. Robert E. Consani, In Res.; Anne Fackler, DRE; CRP Stds.: 48

St. Monica School - (Grades PreK-8) 530 W. Kilgore Rd., Kalamazoo, MI 49008 t) 269-345-2444 jbeery@stmonicakzoo.org www.csgk.org\st-monica-welcome Jordan Beery, Prin.; Stds.: 236; Lay Tchrs.: 12

St. Thomas More Student Parish - 421 Monroe St., Kalamazoo, MI 49006 t) 269-381-8917 sttoms@sttomskazoo.org www.sttomskazoo.org Rev. Paul Redmond, Pst.; Dcn. Joe Schmitt, Pst. Assoc.; Dcn. Frank Sila, Pst. Assoc.; CRP Stds.: 129

MARSHALL

St. Mary - 212 W. Hanover St., Marshall, MI 49068 t) 269-781-5656 (CRP); 269-781-3949 stmaryschoolofreligion@gmail.com stmarymarshall.org Rev. Craig Lusk, Pst.; Sara Rodgers, DRE; CRP Stds.: 69

MATTAWAN

St. John Bosco - 23830 Front Ave., Mattawan, MI 49071 t) 269-668-3312 office@stjbparish.com stjohnbosco.com Rev. Alan P. Jorgensen, Pst.; Rev. John Tran, Par. Vicar; Dcn. Louis Zemlick; Johnna Makuch, DRE; CRP Stds.: 113

St. Margaret Mary - 296 E. Dibble St., Marcellus, MI 49067; Mailing: 23830 Front Ave., Mattawan, MI 49071 ltoso2015@outlook.com

MENDON

St. Edward - 332 W. State St., Mendon, MI 49072; Mailing: P.O. Box 368, Mendon, MI 49072 t) 269-496-3525 stedwardchurch@msn.com Rev. Msgr. Thomas Martin, Pst.; Lyn Wilson, DRE; CRP Stds.: 28

NEW BUFFALO

St. Mary of the Lake - 718 W. Buffalo St., New Buffalo, MI 49117 t) 269-469-2637 www.stmarynewbuffalo.org Rev. Basker Lopez, Pst.; CRP Stds.: 19

NILES

St. Mark - 3 N. 19th St., Niles, MI 49120-2117 t) 269-683-8650 stmark319@yahoo.com stmarkniles.org Rev. Peter Rocca, C.S.C., Pst.; Bro. Dennis Meyers, Pst. Assoc.; Eileen Toney, RCIA Coord.;

St. Mary of the Immaculate Conception Church - 203 S. Lincoln Ave., Niles, MI 49120; Mailing: 219 S. State St., Niles, MI 49120-2862 t) 269-683-5087 stmaryniles@sbcglobal.net stmarysniles.org/ Rev. Christian R. Johnston, Pst.; Dcn. Roger Gregorski, DRE; CRP Stds.: 54

St. Mary's School - (Grades PreK-8) 217 S. Lincoln Ave., Niles, MI 49120 t) 269-683-9191 l.conyers@stmarysniles.com www.stmarysschoolniles.org Leslie Conyers, Prin.; Stds.: 52; Lay Tchrs.: 4

Christian Service Center (CSC Food Pantry) - 322 Clay St., Niles, MI 49120 t) 269-684-0637 stmaryscsc2@gmail.com Nancy Gillespie, Dir.;

OTSEGO

St. Margaret - 766 S. Farmer St., Otsego, MI 49078 t) 269-694-6311 joyvlivingston@gmail.com www.stmargaret-otsego.com Rev. Simon Joseph Chummar Manjooran, S.B.D. (India), Pst.; Dcn. Eugene Haas; Dcn. Fred Wall; Joy Livingston, Youth Ministry; CRP Stds.: 62

St. Margaret School - (Grades PreK-8) 736 S. Farmer, Otsego, MI 49078 t) 269-694-2951 ewarnez@stmargaretschool.net www.stmargaretschool.net Erin Warnez, Prin.; Stds.: 17; Lay Tchrs.: 3

PARCHMENT

St. Ambrose - 1628 E. G Ave., Parchment, MI 49004 t) 269-385-4152 ambroseparchment@sbcglobal.net stambroseparchment.com Rev. Albert Kemboi, Par. Vicar; Dcn. Hallie Bohan; Dcn. Alfred Radford; Rev. Msgr. Michael Hazard, In Res.; CRP Stds.: 56

PAW PAW

St. Mary - 209 S. Brown St., Paw Paw, MI 49079; Mailing: 500 Paw Paw St., Paw Paw, MI 49079 t) 269-657-4459 drestmarypawpaw@bloomingdalecom.net stmarypawpaw.com Rev. Alan P. Jorgensen, Pst.; Dcn. Duane Poage; Jackie Marshall, DRE; CRP Stds.: 124

St. Mary School - (Grades PreK-5) 508 Paw Paw St., Paw Paw, MI 49079 t) 269-657-3750 www.saintmarypawpaw.org Margaret Erich, Admin.; Stds.: 78; Lay Tchrs.: 4

PORTAGE

St. Catherine of Siena - 1150 W. Centre St., Portage, MI 49024-5385 t) 269-327-5165 info@stcatherinesiena.org; kkelly@stcatherinesiena.org stcatherinesiena.org/ Rev. Mark Vyverman, Pst.; Rev. Benjamin Joseph Huynh, Par. Vicar; Rev. William Jacobs Jr., Par. Vicar; Dcn. Ronald Brown; Dcn. Brian Kaluzny; CRP Stds.: 233

SOUTH HAVEN

St. Basil - 513 Monroe Blvd., South Haven, MI 49090 t) 269-637-2404 aaleman@saintbasilcatholicchurch.org; mlittle4488@gmail.com Very Rev. Fabio Garzon, Pst.; Rev. Richard L. Altine, Par. Vicar; Dcn. John Lohrstorfer; Margie Little, DRE; CRP Stds.: 48

St. Basil School - (Grades PreK-6) 94 Superior St., South Haven, MI 49090 t) 269-637-3529 camilledelano@saintbasilcatholic.com www.saintbasilcatholic.com Camille DeLano, Prin.; Stds.: 137; Lay Tchrs.: 8

ST. JOSEPH

St. Joseph - 201 Church St., St. Joseph, MI 49085; Mailing: 220 Church St., St. Joseph, MI 49085 t) 269-983-1575 www.stjoestjoe.church Rev. John D. Fleckenstein, Pst.; Rev. Emmanuel MBah, In Res.; Rev. Joseph Abraham, In Res.; Dcn. Michael Gallagher; Dcn. Edward Nickel; Dcn. Philip Sirk; Stacey Nutting, Bus. Mgr.; CRP Stds.: 203

STURGIS

Holy Angels - 402 S. Nottawa St., Sturgis, MI 49091 t) 269-651-5520 (CRP); 269-651-5200 x101 dre@holyangelssturgis.org; angelica@holyangelssturgis.org www.holyangelssturgis.org/ Rev. Andrew Raczkowski, Pst.; Rev. Raul Gomez, Par. Vicar; Dcn. Lawrence M. Kasuboski; Rayito Tapia, DRE; CRP Stds.: 175

THREE OAKS

St. Mary of the Assumption - 28 W. Ash St., Three Oaks, MI 49128 t) 269-756-2041 stmaryassumptionstagnes@gmail.com Rev. Basker

Lopez, Pst.; CRP Stds.: 17

St. Agnes - 5760 Sawyer Rd., Sawyer, MI 49125; Mailing: 28 W. Ash St., Three Oaks, MI 49128 t) (269) 756-2041

THREE RIVERS

Immaculate Conception - 645 S. Douglas Ave., Three Rivers, MI 49093 t) 269-273-8953 iccollaborative.com Rev. R. Mathias, MSFS, Pst.; CRP Stds.: 15

St. Barbara - 479 S. Burr Oak Rd., Colon, MI 49040 t) (269) 273-8953 Rev. Rajain Mathais, Pst.;

Immaculate Conception School - (Grades PreK-5) 601 S. Douglas Ave., Three Rivers, MI 49093-2044 t) 269-273-2085 principal@iccatholicschool.com iccatholicschool.com Sharon Voege, Prin.; Stds.: 44; Lay Tchrs.: 4

St. Clare - 23126 M-86, Centreville, MI 49032; Mailing: 645 S. Douglas Ave., Three Rivers, MI 49093 t) (269) 273-8953 Rev. Rajain Mathais, Pst.;

VICKSBURG

St. Martin of Tours - 5855 E. W Ave., Vicksburg, MI 49097-0264; Mailing: P.O. Box 264, Vicksburg, MI 49097-0264 t) 269-649-1629 dre@stmartinvicksburg.org; ctakacs@stmartinvicksburg.org Rev. Msgr. Thomas Martin, Pst.; Dcn. David Guido; Dcn. Thomas Thamann; Tim McNamara, DRE; CRP Stds.: 40

WATERVLIET

St. Joseph - 157 Lucinda Ln., Watervliet, MI 49098 t) 269-463-5470 x100 stjcatholic.net Rev. John D. Fleckenstein, Pst.; Rev. Patrick H. Craig, Admin.; Julie Schmidt, DRE; CRP Stds.: 33

WAYLAND

SS. Cyril and Methodius - 159 131st Ave., Wayland, MI 49348 t) 269-792-3543 info@sscmparish.org www.sscmparish.org Rev. Evelio Ramirez, Pst.; Dcn. Jeffrey Ryan; Liz Ryan, DRE; CRP Stds.: 43

St. Therese of Lisieux - 128 Cedar St., Wayland, MI 49348 t) 269-792-2138 lizryandre@gmail.com; sttparish1@gmail.com sttparishwayland.org Rev. Evelio Ramirez, Pst.; Dcn. Mark Chrusciel; Dcn. Jeffrey Ryan; Liz Ryan, DRE; CRP Stds.: 42

St. Therese of Lisieux School - (Grades PreK-6) 430 S. Main St., Wayland, MI 49348 t) 269-792-2016 sttoffice1@gmail.com; sttprincipal1@gmail.com www.sttcatholicschool.org Sheryl O'Connor, Prin.; Stds.: 75; Lay Tchrs.: 5

WHITE PIGEON

St. Joseph - 16603 US Hwy. 12, White Pigeon, MI 49099 t) 269-483-7621 saintjoewp@comcast.net; lauren@holyangelssturgis.org www.stjosephwhitepigeon.org Rev. Andrew Raczkowski, Pst.; Lauren McDonald, DRE; CRP Stds.: 40

SCHOOLS: PRESCHOOL THRU HIGH SCHOOL

SCHOOLS

STATE OF MICHIGAN

ST. JOSEPH

Lake Michigan Catholic Schools - (PAR) (Grades PreK-5) 3165 Washington Ave., St. Joseph, MI 49085 t) 269-429-0227 lmclakers.org Larry Hoskins, Prin.; Stds.: 226; Lay Tchrs.: 13

HIGH SCHOOLS

STATE OF MICHIGAN

BATTLE CREEK

St. Philip Catholic Central High School - (DIO) 20 Cherry St., Battle Creek, MI 49017 t) 269-963-4503 vgroat@bcacs.org bcacs.org Vicky Groat, Prin.; Stds.: 78; Lay Tchrs.: 8

KALAMAZOO

Msgr. John R. Hackett High School - (DIO) (Grades 9-12) 1000 W. Kilgore Rd., Kalamazoo, MI 49008 t) 269-381-2646 bkosmerick@hackettcp.org; chaplain@hackettcp.org www.hackettcp.org Brian Kosmerick, Vice Prin.; Stds.: 210; Lay Tchrs.: 15

ST. JOSEPH

Lake Michigan Catholic Middle and High School - (DIO) (Grades 6-12) 915 Pleasant St., St. Joseph, MI 49085 t) 269-983-2511 jwhite@lmclakers.org www.lmclakers.org James White, Prin.; Stds.: 121; Lay Tchrs.: 9

INSTITUTIONS LOCATED IN DIOCESE

CAMPUS MINISTRY / NEWMAN CENTERS [CAM]

KALAMAZOO

Western Michigan University, Kalamazoo College, Kalamazoo Valley Community College - 421 Monroe St., Kalamazoo, MI 49006 t) 269-381-8917 sttoms@sttomskazoo.org www.sttomskazoo.org Rev. Paul Redmond, Pst.; Dcn. Joe Schmitt, Pst. Assoc.;

CATHOLIC CHARITIES [CCH]

KALAMAZOO

Catholic Charities Diocese of Kalamazoo - 1819 Gull Rd., Kalamazoo, MI 49048 t) 269-381-9800 info@ccdok.org www.ccdok.org Toni Newell, Exec. Dir.; Asstd. Annu.: 25,000; Staff: 47

CONVENTS, MONASTERIES, AND RESIDENCES FOR WOMEN [CON]

KALAMAZOO

Congregation of the Sisters of St. Joseph - 2929 Nazareth Rd., Kalamazoo, MI 49048 t) 269-381-6290 pwarbritton@csjoseph.org www.csjoseph.org Sr. Pam Owens, CSJ, Contact; Srs.: 115

ENDOWMENTS / FOUNDATIONS / TRUSTS [EFT]

BATTLE CREEK

BCACS Foundation, Inc. - 63 N. 24th St., Battle Creek, MI 49015 t) 269-963-4771 cerskine@bcacs.org bcacs.org/bcacs-foundation/ (Battle Creek Area Catholic Schools Foundation, Inc.) Abby Lumbard, Dir.;

HASTINGS

St. Rose Lima Trust Fund - 805 S. Jefferson St., Hastings, MI 49058 t) 269-945-4246 dbennett@srlsh.org Patricia Woods, Chair;

KALAMAZOO

The Catholic Foundation of Southwestern Michigan - 215 N. Westnedge Ave., Kalamazoo, MI 49007 t) 269-349-8714 lshoemaker@diokzoo.org Thomas Dowdall, Dir.;

Kalamazoo Regional Catholic Schools Foundation - 1000 W. Kilgore Rd., Kalamazoo, MI 49008 t) 269-381-2646 manderegg@csgk.org csgk.org Steven Johnson, Pres.;

SOUTH HAVEN

St. Basil Educational Endowment Fund - 94 Superior St., South Haven, MI 49090 t) 269-637-3529; 269-637-4272 principal@saintbasilcatholic.org www.saintbasilcatholic.org Frank Overton, Pres.; Megan Akami, Secy.; Chris Filbrandt, Treas.; Jim Marcoux, Contact;

ST. JOSEPH

Lake Michigan Catholic School Fund - 515 Ship St., Ste. #202, St. Joseph, MI 49085 t) 269-470-8891 lglendening@lmclakers.org Larry Glendenning, Dir.;

HOSPITALS / HEALTH SERVICES [HOS]

DOWAGIAC

Ascension Borgess-Lee Hospital (Borgess Lee Memorial Hospital, Lee Memorial Hospital, Lee Memorial Hospital Corporation) - 420 W. High St., Dowagiac, MI 49047 t) 269-782-8681 paula.caruso@ascension.org www.healthcare.ascension.org A member of Ascension Michigan Christopher McClead, Contact; Bed Capacity: 25; Asstd. Annu.: 38,035; Staff: 129

KALAMAZOO

Ascension Borgess Hospital (Borgess Medical Center, Borgess Hospital) - 1521 Gull Rd., Kalamazoo, MI 49048 t) 269-226-7000 paula.caruso@ascension.org healthcare.ascension.org A member of Ascension Michigan and operator of Ascension Borgess-Pipp Hospital Christopher McClead, Contact; Bed Capacity: 374; Asstd. Annu.: 299,569; Staff: 2,412

MISCELLANEOUS [MIS]

KALAMAZOO

Borgess Health Alliance, Inc. - 1521 Gull Rd., Kalamazoo, MI 49048

Catholic Schools of Greater Kalamazoo - 1000 W. Kilgore Rd., Kalamazoo, MI 49008 t) 269-381-2646 manderegg@csgk.org csgk.org/ Melissa Anderegg, Bus. Mgr.;

STEVENSVILLE

Diocesan Council of St. Vincent dePaul - 2400 Joni Ln., Stevensville, MI 49127 t) 269-449-8838 svdpkal@att.net Kathy Arendash, Pres.;

NURSING / REHABILITATION / CONVALESCENCE / ELDERLY CARE [NUR]

KALAMAZOO

Ascension Living Borgess Place (Borgess Nursing Home, Inc.) - 3057 Gull Rd., Kalamazoo, MI 49048 t) 314-292-9308 paula.caruso@ascension.org www.ascensionliving.org/ Skilled Nursing Facility Christopher McClead, Contact; Asstd. Annu.: 376; Staff: 85

Dillon Complex for Independent Living, Inc. - 3301 Gull Rd., #308, Kalamazoo, MI 49048 t) 269-342-0263 lisaw@lmc-mi.com; kdavis@csjinitiatives.org www.dillonhall.org Low Income Senior Housing (HUD). Sponsored by the Congregation of the Sisters of St. Joseph ministry CSJ Initiatives, Inc. Denise Gannon, CEO; Asstd. Annu.: 83; Staff: 5

Nazareth, Inc. - 2929 Nazareth Rd., Kalamazoo, MI 49048 t) 269-381-6290 dhasse@csjinitiatives.org Sr. Patricia Warbritton, CSJ, Treas.; Asstd. Annu.: 63; Staff: 50

OTSEGO

Otsego Senior Apts., Inc. - 301 Washington St., Baraga Manor Apts., Otsego, MI 49078 t) 269-694-9711 baraga@medallionmgmt.com catholicfamilyservices.org Managed by Medallion Management, Inc. Toni Newell, Exec. Dir.; Asstd. Annu.: 60; Staff: 3

Otsego Senior Apts. - 1819 Gull Rd., Kalamazoo, MI 49048 t) (269) 381-9800

Archdiocese of Kansas City in Kansas

(Archidioecesis Kansanopolitana in Kansas)

MOST REVEREND JOSEPH F. NAUMANN

Archbishop of Kansas City in Kansas; ordained May 24, 1975; appointed Titular Bishop of Caput Cilla and Auxiliary Bishop of St. Louis July 9, 1997; consecrated September 3, 1997; appointed Coadjutor Archbishop of Kansas City in Kansas January 7, 2004; installed March 19, 2004; succeeded to See January 15, 2005.

Catholic Chancery Offices: 12615 Parallel Pkwy., Kansas City, KS 66109. T: 913-721-1570; F: 913-721-1577.
www.archkck.org
archkck@archkck.org

Square Miles 12,524.

Established Vicariate Apostolic July 19, 1850. Diocese of Leavenworth established May 22, 1877.
See changed to Kansas City in Kansas May 10, 1947; created Archdiocese August 9, 1952.

Comprises the following 21 Counties of Kansas: Anderson, Atchison, Brown, Coffey, Doniphan, Douglas, Franklin, Jackson, Jefferson, Johnson, Leavenworth, Linn, Lyon, Marshall, Miami, Nemaha, Osage, Pottawatomie, Shawnee, Wabaunsee and Wyandotte.

Patrons of the Diocese: I. Blessed Virgin Mary (Immaculate Conception); II. St. John Baptist Vianney.

For legal titles of institutions, please contact the Catholic Chancery Offices.

STATISTICAL OVERVIEW

Personnel
Archbishops 1
Retired Archbishops 1
Abbots 1
Priests: Diocesan Active in Diocese 73
Priests: Diocesan Active Outside Diocese 4
Priests: Retired, Sick or Absent 26
Number of Diocesan Priests 103
Religious Priests in Diocese 44
Total Priests in your Diocese 147
Extern Priests in Diocese 19
Ordinations:
Diocesan Priests 2
Transitional Deacons 3
Permanent Deacons in Diocese 63
Total Brothers 16
Total Sisters 271

Parishes
Parishes 107
With Resident Pastor:
Resident Diocesan Priests 62
Resident Religious Priests 9
Without Resident Pastor:
Administered by Priests 36

Professional Ministry Personnel:
Sisters 12
Lay Ministers 93

Welfare
Health Care Centers 5
Total Assisted 6,615
Homes for the Aged 3
Total Assisted 908
Special Centers for Social Services 13
Total Assisted 421,249

Educational
Diocesan Students in Other Seminaries 25
Students, Religious 3
Total Seminarians 28
Colleges and Universities 3
Total Students 3,761
High Schools, Diocesan and Parish 5
Total Students 3,111
High Schools, Private 1
Total Students 178
Elementary Schools, Diocesan and Parish 36
Total Students 10,565
Elementary Schools, Private 2
Total Students 128

Catechesis/Religious Education:
High School Students 1,458
Elementary Students 8,477
Total Students under Catholic Instruction 27,706
Teachers in Diocese:
Sisters 1
Lay Teachers 900

Vital Statistics
Receptions into the Church:
Infant Baptism Totals 2,530
Minor Baptism Totals 222
Adult Baptism Totals 125
Received into Full Communion 279
First Communions 2,575
Confirmations 2,415
Marriages:
Catholic 438
Interfaith 218
Total Marriages 656
Deaths 1,432
Total Catholic Population 182,636
Total Population 1,404,470

LEADERSHIP

Catholic Chancery Offices - t) 913-721-1570 archkck.org/
Vicars General - Rev. John Riley (jriley@archkck.org); Rev. Brian Schieber (bschieber@archkck.org);
Episcopal Vicar for Ministry to Hispanics - Rev. Michael Hermes (frhermes@spcatholic.org);
Moderator of the Curia - Rev. Mark Mertes (mmertes@archkck.org);
Chancellor - Rev. John Riley, Chancellor (jriley@archkck.org);
Archdiocesan Finance Officer - Carla Mills, CFO;
Regional Pastoral Leaders - Rev. Jeremy Heppler, O.S.B., Atchison (jheppler@archkck.org); Rev. Adam Wilczak, Johnson Co. (awilczak@archkck.org); Rev. Jomon Palatty, M.S.F.S., Lawrence (jpalatty@archkck.org);
Archdiocesan Archivist -

OFFICES AND DIRECTORS

Administrative Services - Rita Herken, Dir.;
Black Catholics - t) 913-321-1958 babsbailey@yahoo.com Barbara Bailey, Dir.;
Communications - Anita McSorley, Media Liaison;
Deaf Ministry - Katie Locus, Cons. (deafministry@archkck.org);
Evangelization - Dcn. Dana Nearmyer, Dir. (dnearmyer@archkck.org);
Adult Evangelization - Emily Lopez, Lead Cons.;
Prairie Star Ranch - t) 785-746-5693 psoffice@archkck.org Gregory Wellnitz, Dir.;
Youth Evangelization - Rick Cheek, Consultant;
Hispanic Ministry - hispanic@archkck.org Rev. Ramiro Sanchez Chan, C.S., Dir. (rchan@archkck.org);
Human Resources - Bob Roper, Dir. (broper@archkck.org);
Liturgy and Sacramental Life - Michael Podrebarac, Cons.;
Marriage and Family Life - Dcn. Tony Zimmerman, Lead Cons. (famlife@archkck.org); Brad DuPont, Cons.; Libby DuPont, Cons.;
Newspaper "The Leaven" - Rev. Mark Goldasich, Editor; Anita McSorley, Mng. Editor;
Office for Protection and Care - Jenifer Valenti, Dir. (jvalenti@archkck.org);
Pontifical Mission Societies in the United States - Rev. Thomas Reddy Aduri, Dir.;
Missionary Childhood Association -
Pro-life/Respect Life - Debra Niesen, Cons.;
Religious & Consecrated Life - Sr. Eva-Maria Ackerman, F.S.G.M., Delegate (eackerman@archkck.org);
Schools - Dr. Vincent Cascone, Supt.; Allison Carney, Assoc. Supt.; Dr. Lorenzo Rizzi, Assoc. Supt. Student Svcs (lrizzi@archkckcs.org);
Social Justice - Dcn. Bill Scholl, Cons. (socialjustice@archkck.org);
Special Needs - Joshua Ruoff, Cons. (jruoff@archkck.org);
Stewardship and Development - William Maloney, Exec. Dir. (wmaloney@archkck.org);
Victim Assistance Coordinator - t) 913-298-9244 Amy Stork, Victim Care Advocate (astork@archkck.org);
Vocations Office - Rev. Daniel Morris, Dir. (dmorris@archkck.org);

ADVISORY BOARDS, COMMISSIONS, COMMITTEES, AND COUNCILS

Council for Catholic Charismatic Renewal - Rev. Anthony Ouellette, Spiritual Mod. (aouellette@archkck.org);
Archdiocesan College of Consultors - Rt. Rev. James R. Albers, O.S.B., Abbot; Rev. John Riley, Vicar General-Chancellor (jriley@archkck.org); Rev. Brian Schieber, Vicar General - Vicar for Clergy (bschieber@archkck.org);
Archdiocesan Council on Finances - Kelly Dubbert, Chair; Richard Enna; Beth Soukup;
Archdiocesan Pastoral Council - Steve Clark; Bro. Leven Harton, O.S.B.; Jeri McDonnell;
Presbyteral Council - Rev. Patrick Sullivan, Chair (psullivan@archkck.org);

FACILITIES

Savior Pastoral Center - t) 913-721-1097 savior@archkck.org www.saviorpastoralcenter.org Timothy Chik, Dir.;

ORGANIZATIONS

Archdiocesan Council of Catholic Women (ACCW) - t) 913-631-8872 Linda Oneslager, Pres.; Dcn. Tony Zimmerman, Chap. (famlife@archkck.org);
Catholic Committee on Scouting -
Kansas Catholic Conference - t) 785-227-9247 chuck@kansascatholic.org www.kansascatholic.org Gerald "Chuck" Weber Jr., Exec. Dir.;
Legion of Mary - Rev. Quentin Schmitz, Spiritual Dir. (qschmitz@archkck.org);

TRIBUNAL

Metropolitan Tribunal - t) 913-721-1570
Judicial Vicar - Rev. Joseph Arsenault, S.S.A.;
Adjutant Judicial Vicar - Rev. Bruce Ansems;
Judges - Rev. Anthony Saiki; Rev. Bruce Ansems; Rev. Joseph Arsenault, S.S.A.;
Defender of the Bond - Rev. Anthony Saiki;
Advocates - Selected priests and lay advocates -
Notary - Janie Snead;

PARISHES, MISSIONS, AND CLERGY

STATE OF KANSAS

ALMA

Holy Family - 1st & Kansas, Alma, KS 66401; Mailing: PO Box 128, Alma, KS 66401 t) 785-456-7869 (CRP); (620) 803-2570 (Bookkeeper) Served from Sacred Heart, Paxico. Dan Deiter, DRE; CRP Stds.: 47

ATCHISON

St. Benedict - 1001 N. 2nd St., Atchison, KS 66002 t) 913-367-0671 lcross@benedictine.edu www.stbenedictatchison.org Sacred Heart (1880), St. Benedict's (1857), St. Joseph (1948) and St. Patrick (1857) Churches consolidated in 2013 to form St. Benedict Parish Rev. Jeremy Heppler, O.S.B., Pst.; Rev. Meinrad Miller, O.S.B., Par. Vicar; Dcn. Jody Madden; Dcn. Charles Welte; CRP Stds.: 64
St. Benedict School - (Grades PreK-8) 201 Unity St., Atchison, KS 66002-1430 t) 913-367-3503 klunsford@benedictine.edu stbenedictatchison.org/school Kevin Lunsford, Prin.; Stds.: 211; Lay Tchrs.: 16
St. Joseph Church - 845 Spring Garden, Atchison, KS 66002; Mailing: 1001 N. 2nd St., Atchison, KS 66002
St. Patrick Church - 19384 234th Rd., Atchison, KS 66002; Mailing: 1001 N. 2nd St., Atchison, KS 66002 Merged with St. Joseph, St. Benedict's and Sacred Heart Churches in Atchison to form St. Benedict Parish in 2013
St. John Oratory - Doniphan County. For inquiries for parish records contact St. Benedict Parish, Atchison.
Corpus Christi - 18760 Rogers Rd., Atchison, KS 66002; Mailing: c/o St. Joseph, 221 N. Sycamore St., Nortonville, KS 66060 t) 913-886-2030; 913-774-2385 (CRP) Served from St. Joseph, Nortonville. Rev. Lazar Carasala (India), Par. Admin.; Lisa Kramer, DRE; CRP Stds.: 37

AXTELL

St. Michael - 504 6th St., Axtell, KS 66403; Mailing: P.O. Box K, Axtell, KS 66403 t) 785-736-2220 jshau47@gmail.com; jshaughnessy@archkck.org Rev. James Shaughnessy, Pst.; CRP Stds.: 102

BAILEYVILLE

Sacred Heart - 357 Third St., Baileyville, KS 66404; Mailing: P.O. Box 36, Baileyville, KS 66404 t) 785-336-6464 www.shbaileyville.com Rev. Reginald Saldanha, Pst.; Betsy Macke, DRE; CRP Stds.: 39

BALDWIN CITY

Annunciation - 740 N. 6th St., Baldwin City, KS 66006 t) 785-594-3700 annunciationchurchks.org Mission: St. Francis of Assisi, Lapeer. Rev. Jomon Palatty, M.S.F.S., Par. Admin.; Karla Wessling, DRE; CRP Stds.: 30

BASEHOR

Holy Angels - 15438 Leavenworth Rd., Basehor, KS 66007 t) 913-724-1665 pbaholyangels@gmail.com www.holyangelsbasehor.org Rev. Richard J. McDonald, Pst.; Paul R. Rittof, Admin.; Cathy Kern, DRE; CRP Stds.: 154

BEATTIE

St. Malachy - 1012 Main St, Beattie, KS 66406; Mailing: c/o St. Gregory, 207 N. 14th St., Suite B, Marysville, KS 66508 t) 785-562-3302 Served from St. Gregory, Marysville. Rev. Quentin Schmitz, Pst.;

BENDENA

St. Benedict - 676 St. Benedict Rd., Bendena, KS 66008; Mailing: P.O. Box 128, Bendena, KS 66008 t) 785-359-6725 Served from St. Joseph Parish in Wathena. Rev. Michael Guastello, Pst.; CRP Stds.: 29

BLAINE

St. Columbkille - 13311 Hwy. 16, Blaine, KS 66549; Mailing: 213 E. 5th St., Frankfort, KS 66427 t) 785-292-4462 Served from Annunciation in Frankfort. Rev. Anthony Chendumalli (India), Pst.; Sally Olson, DRE; CRP Stds.: 12

BLUE RAPIDS

St. Monica - St. Elizabeth - 1007 East Ave., Blue Rapids, KS 66411; Mailing: 213 E. 5th St., Frankfort, KS 66427 t) 785-292-4462 Served from Annunciation, Frankfort. St. Monica Church (1866) and St. Elizabeth Church (1913) were unified in 2003 to form St. Monica-St. Elizabeth Rev. Anthony Chendumalli (India), Pst.; Sarah Toerber, DRE; CRP Stds.: 50

BUCYRUS

Queen of the Holy Rosary - 22779 Metcalf Ave., Bucyrus, KS 66013 t) 913-533-2462; 913-533-2464 qhrwea.church Rev. Gerardo Arano-Ponce, Pst.; Dcn. Tom Rothermich; Kimberly Zubillaga, Pst. Assoc., Discipleship; CRP Stds.: 116
Queen of the Holy Rosary School - (Grades PreK-8) 22705 Metcalf Ave., Bucyrus, KS 66013 t) (913) 533-2462 nick@qhrwea.org qhrwea.school Nick Antista, Prin.; Stds.: 184; Lay Tchrs.: 19

BURLINGTON

St. Francis Xavier - 214 Juniatta, Burlington, KS 66839 t) 620-364-5671 st-francis-joseph-patrick-teresa.org/ Rev. Colin Haganey, Pst.; Kara Reynolds, DRE; Angela Myers, Youth Min.; CRP Stds.: 36

CORNING

St. Patrick - 6606 Atlantic, Corning, KS 66417; Mailing: 809 Clifton St., c/o St. Vincent de Paul, Onaga, KS 66521 t) 785-889-4896 3parishassistant@gmail.com www.facebook.com/groups/1699338376879407 Served from St. Vincent de Paul, Onaga. Rev. Mathew Francis (India), Pst.; Mindy Olberding, DRE; Candice Schmitz, DRE; CRP Stds.: 151

EASTON

St. Joseph-St. Lawrence - 211 W. Riley St., Easton, KS 66020; Mailing: P.O. Box 129, Easton, KS 66020 t) 913-773-5712 www.sjslparish.org St. Joseph of the Valley Church (1863) and St. Lawrence Church (1878) were merged in 2009 to form St. Joseph-St. Lawrence Parish. Rev. William McEvoy, Pst.; CRP Stds.: 61

EFFINGHAM

St. Ann - 301 Williams St., Effingham, KS 66023; Mailing: Box 54, Effingham, KS 66023 t) 913-833-5660 info@stanneffingham.org Rev. Hughes Sundeme, Par. Admin.; Jill Thorne, DRE; CRP Stds.: 31

EMPORIA

St. Catherine - 205 S. Lawrence St., Emporia, KS 66801 t) 620-342-1368 saintcatherineemporia@gmail.com Rev. Nicholas Ashmore; Sr. Guadalupe Jimenez Lopez,

DRE; CRP Stds.: 135

Sacred Heart - 27 Cottonwood St, Emporia, KS 66801 t) 620-342-1061 loiss@shemporia.org; emporiacatholics@gmail.com www.shemporia.org Rev. Carter Zielinski, Pst.; Dcn. Daniel Vehige; Joan Dold, Pst. Min./Coord.; Shawn Gerleman, Pst. Min./Coord.; CRP Stds.: 169

Sacred Heart School - (Grades K-5) 102 Cottonwood St., Emporia, KS 66801 t) 620-343-7394 ageitz@shemporia.org Ali Geitz, Prin.; Stds.: 53; Lay Tchrs.: 9

EUDORA

Holy Family - 409 E. 8th St., Eudora, KS 66025; Mailing: 820 Birch St., Eudora, KS 66025 t) 785-542-2788 holyfamilyeudora.com/ Rev. Michael Mulvany, Pst.; Dcn. William Graveman; Patricia Crable, DRE; CRP Stds.: 138

FRANKFORT

Annunciation - 213 E. Fifth St., Frankfort, KS 66427 t) 785-292-4462 Rev. Anthony Chendumalli (India), Pst.; Jan Stallbaumer, DRE; CRP Stds.: 95

GARDNER

Divine Mercy - 555 W. Main St., Gardner, KS 66030 t) 913-856-7781 office@divinemercyks.org www.divinemercyks.org Rev. Adam Wilczak, Pst.; Dcn. Vince Hallouer; Dcn. Jason Imlay; CRP Stds.: 307

Sacred Heart Church - info@divinemercyks.org Merged in 2011 with Assumption Church, Edgerton to form Divine Mercy Parish, Gardner

Assumption Church - 110 E. Nelson, Edgerton, KS 66021; Mailing: 555 W. Main, c/o Divine Mercy Parish, Gardner, KS 66030 t) (913) 856-7781 (Divine Mercy office) secretary@divinemercyks.org Merged with Sacred Heart Church to form Divine Mercy Parish, Gardner, Kansas

GARNETT

St. Boniface - 32292 N.E. Norton Rd., Garnett, KS 66032 t) 785-835-6273 www.stbonifacesttherese.com St. Therese Church in Richmond KS is served from St. Boniface Church in Garnett KS Rev. J. Gerald Williams, O.Carm., Pst.; Rev. David Simpson, O.Carm., In Res.; Carol Lutz, DRE; CRP Stds.: 75

Holy Angels - 500 E. 4th Ave., Garnett, KS 66032; Mailing: 520 E. 4th Ave., Garnett, KS 66032 t) 785-448-1686 hasjparishes.com/ Rev. Daniel Stover, Pst.;

GOOD INTENT

St. Louis - 11321 Morton Rd., Good Intent, KS 66002; Mailing: P.O. Box 54, c/o St. Ann, 301 William St., Effingham, KS 66023 t) 913-833-5660 info@stanneffingham.org Served from St. Ann, Effingham. Rev. Hughes Sundeme, Par. Admin.; Becky Finnegan, DRE; CRP Stds.: 51

GREELEY

St. John the Baptist - 427 S. Prairie, Greeley, KS 66033; Mailing: 520 E 4th Ave, Garnett, KS 66032 t) 785-448-1686 www.hasjparishes.com Served from Holy Angels, Garnett. Rev. Daniel Stover, Pst.;

HARTFORD

St. Mary - 507 Mechanic St, Hartford, KS 66854; Mailing: PO Box 147, Hartford, KS 66854 t) 620-343-6765 contact@diddecenter.org stmaryshartford.org Served from Didde Catholic Campus Center, Emporia, KS Rev. Matthew Nagle, Pst.; Loraine Zweimiller, DRE; CRP Stds.: 9

HIAWATHA

St. Ann - 800 Hiawatha Ave., Hiawatha, KS 66434 t) 785-742-3010 Rev. Daniel Gardner, Pst.; Hillary Boye, DRE; Paige Wilson, DRE; CRP Stds.: 75

HOLTON

St. Dominic - 115 E. 5th St., Holton, KS 66436 t) 785-364-3262 parish.jacocatholics@gmail.com www.jacocatholics.com Rev. Jonathan Dizon, Pst.; CRP Stds.: 86

Our Lady of the Snows Oratory - Potawatomi Reservation, Mayetta, KS 66509; Mailing: 115 E. 5th St, Holton, KS 66436

HORTON

St. Leo - 1340 First Ave. E., Horton, KS 66439 t) 785-486-3971 smslchurch@rainbowtel.net Served from St. Ann, Hiawatha. Rev. Daniel Gardner, Pst.; Rhonda Smith, DRE; CRP Stds.: 52

KANSAS CITY

Cathedral of St. Peter the Apostle - 416 N. 14th St., Kansas City, KS 66102; Mailing: 409 N. 15th St., Kansas City, KS 66102 t) 913-371-0840; 913-371-0840 (CRP) asaiki@archkck.org www.cathedralkck.org Rev. Anthony Saiki, Rector; Denise Fierro, Bus. Mgr.; CRP Stds.: 79

All Saints - 811 Vermont Ave, Kansas City, KS 66101; Mailing: 801 Vermont Ave, Kansas City, KS 66101 t) 913-371-1837; (913) 573-2067 secretary@allsaintsparishkck.org; allsaintsparishkc@gmail.com www.allsaintsparishkck.org Rev. Peter Jaramillo, S.S.A., Pst.; Lazara Beatriz Camareno, CRE; Nancy Luna-Loera, Pst. Min./Coord.; CRP Stds.: 57

Blessed Sacrament Church - 2203 Parallel Ave., Kansas City, KS 66104 t) 913-321-1958 contact@blessedsacramentkck.org www.blessedsacramentkck.org/ Rev. Nicholas Blaha, Pst.; Rev. Fredy Hernán Pinzon Palacio (Colombia), Par. Vicar; Maria Teresa Magana, DRE; CRP Stds.: 134

Christ the King - 3024 N. 53rd St., Kansas City, KS 66104 t) 913-287-8823 contact@ctkkck.org ctkclassical.org Rev. Nicholas Blaha, Pst.; Rev. Beyuo Kuukole (Ghana), In Res.; Sue Reaves, DRE; CRP Stds.: 37

Christ the King School - (Grades PreK-8) 3027 N. 54th St., Kansas City, KS 66104 t) 913-287-8883 www.ctkclassical.org Cathy Fithian, Prin.; Elizabeth Rebeck, Librn.; Stds.: 236; Sr. Tchrs.: 1; Lay Tchrs.: 18

Holy Family - 274 Orchard Ave., Kansas City, KS 66101; Mailing: 515 Ohio Ave., Kansas City, KS 66101 t) 913-413-0022 holyfamilychurch1925@gmail.com holyfamilychurchkck.org Rev. Joseph Arsenault, S.S.A., Pst.; CRP Stds.: 40

Holy Name of Jesus Parish - 1001 Southwest Blvd., Kansas City, KS 66103; Mailing: 16 S. Iowa, Kansas City, KS 66103 t) 913-236-9219 thayes@archkckcs.org www.holynameparishkc.org Rev. Anthony Ouellette, Pst.; Timothy Hayes, DRE; CRP Stds.: 11

Holy Name School - (Grades PreK-8) 1007 S.W. Blvd., Kansas City, KS 66103 t) 913-722-1032 holyname@archkckcs.org www.holynamecatholicschool.org Randall Smith, Prin.; Stds.: 127; Lay Tchrs.: 12

St. John the Baptist - 708 N. Fourth St., Kansas City, KS 66101 t) 913-371-0627 Rev. Joseph Arsenault, S.S.A., Pst.;

St. Mary-St. Anthony - 615 N 7th St., Kansas City, KS 66101; Mailing: 632 Tauromee, Kansas City, KS 66101 t) 913-371-1408; 913-621-2120 (CRP) St. Mary Church (1858) and St. Anthony Church (1859) were unified in 1980 to form St. Mary-St. Anthony Parish Rev. Peter Jaramillo, S.S.A., Pst.; Rev. Salvador Diaz Llamas, MNM, Par. Vicar; CRP Stds.: 47

Our Lady and St. Rose - 8th & Quindero, Kansas City, KS 66101; Mailing: 2203 Parallel Ave., Kansas City, KS 66104 t) 913-321-1958 olsr2300@gmail.com ourladyandsaintrose.org Rev. Msgr. Stuart Swetland, Pst.; Dcn. Bill Scholl; Barbara Bailey, Pst. Assoc.; Franchiel Nyakatura, DRE; CRP Stds.: 18

Our Lady of Unity - 2910 Strong Ave., Kansas City, KS 66106 t) 913-677-4621 Rev. John Cordes, Pst.; Rev. Fredy Hernán Pinzon Palacio (Colombia), Par. Vicar; Lety Fernandez, DRE; Diana Ortega, DRE; CRP Stds.: 250

St. Patrick's - 1086 N. 94th St., Kansas City, KS 66112 t) 913-299-3370 tsmith@archkckcs.org; stpatrickchurchkck@archkckcs.org Rev. Mark Mertes, Pst.; Rev. William Dun-Dery (Ghana), Par. Vicar; Rev. Michael Van Lian (Myanmar), Chin Burmese Ministry; Dcn. David Cresswell; Ramona Galvan, DRE; CRP Stds.: 152

St. Patrick's School - (Grades PreK-8) 1066 N. 94th, Kansas City, KS 66112 t) 913-299-8131 tconrad@stpatrickkck.org www.stpatrickkck.org Tim Conrad, Prin.; Emily Yantz, Librn.; Stds.: 336; Lay Tchrs.: 26

KELLY

St. Bede - 7344 Drought St., Kelly, KS 66538; Mailing: 809 Clifton St., Box 396, c/o St. Vincent de Paul, Onaga, KS 66521 t) 785-889-4896 3parishassistant@gmail.com www.facebook.com/stbedekelly Served from St. Vincent de Paul in Onaga. Rev. Mathew Francis (India), Pst.; Angie Lueger, DRE; CRP Stds.: 73

LA CYGNE

Our Lady of Lourdes - 819 N 5th St., La Cygne, KS 66040; Mailing: PO Box 4, Osawatomie, KS 66064 t) 913-755-2652 bclayton@archkck.org www.miamilinncatholics.org Served from St. Philip Neri, Osawatomie. Rev. Barry R. Clayton, Pst.; Sara Stevens, DRE; CRP Stds.: 5

LANCASTER

St. Mary, Purcell - 446 Hwy. 137, Lancaster, KS 66041; Mailing: Box 54, c/o St. Ann, Effingham, KS 66023 t) 913-833-5660 stmaryspurcell@rainbowtel.net Served from St. Ann, Effingham. Rev. Hughes Sundeme, Par. Admin.;

LANSING

St. Francis de Sales - 900 Ida St., Lansing, KS 66043 t) 913-727-3742 parishoffice@stfrancislansing.org stfrancislansing.org/ Rev. Balachandra Reddy Miriyala (India), Par. Admin.; McKinzie Horsley, DRE; CRP Stds.: 116

LAWRENCE

Corpus Christi - 6001 Bob Billings Pkwy., Lawrence, KS 66049-5200 t) 785-843-6286 Rev. Gerald Volz, Pst.; Dcn. Chris Allen; Sr. Doris Engeman, F.S.H.F., DRE; CRP Stds.: 60

Corpus Christi School - (Grades PreK-8) t) 785-331-3374 kirstenw@cccparish.org www.cccparish.org Kirsten Wondra, Prin.; Stds.: 290; Lay Tchrs.: 34

St. John the Evangelist Catholic Church - 1229 Vermont St., Lawrence, KS 66044 t) 785-843-0109 office@sjevangelist.com sjevangelist.com Rev. John Cousins, OFM, Cap., Pst.; Rev. John Kolencherry, O.F.M.Cap., Par. Vicar; CRP Stds.: 40

St. John the Evangelist School - (Grades PreK-8) 1208 Kentucky, Lawrence, KS 66044 t) 785-843-9511 creffett@sjeagles.com www.sjevangelist.com/school Chris Reffett, Prin.; Karen Rinke, Librn.; Stds.: 289; Lay Tchrs.: 22

LEAVENWORTH

Immaculate Conception-St. Joseph - 747 Osage, Leavenworth, KS 66048 t) 913-682-3953 icsj.org Immaculate Conception (Old Cathedral) and St. Joseph were unified in 2007 to form Immaculate Conception-St. Joseph Parish Rev. Glenn Snow, O.Carm., Pst.; Dcn. Patrick Hood, DRE; Dcn. Dean Gilbert, Pst. Assoc.; CRP Stds.: 62

Sacred Heart - 170th St. & Kickapoo Rd., Kickapoo, KS 66048; Mailing: c/o Immaculate Conception-St. Joseph Parish, 747 Osage, Leavenworth, KS 66048

Sacred Heart-St. Casimir - 521 Linn St., Leavenworth, KS 66048 t) 913-772-2424; 913-772-1787 (CRP) chelsie@shsc.org www.shsc.org/ Sacred Heart Parish (1886) and St. Casimir Parish (1888) were unified in 2007 to form Sacred Heart-St. Casimir Parish Rev. Marianand Mendem, Pst.; Dcn. James Skahan; Dcn. Robert D. Zbylut, DRE; CRP Stds.: 7

LEAWOOD

Church of the Nativity - 3800 W. 119th St., Leawood, KS 66209 t) 913-491-5017 info@kcnativity.org www.kcnativity.org Rev. Michael Hawken, Pst.; Rev. Sudeep Kodigandla, Par. Vicar; Dcn. Jim Mullin; Dcn. Ralph Schramp; Suzy Meinzenbach, DRE; CRP Stds.: 170

Church of the Nativity School - (Grades PreK-8) 3700 W. 119th St., Leawood, KS 66209 t) 913-338-4330 nativityparishschool@kcnativity.org www.nativityparishschool.com Luke Jennison, Prin.; Jean Stump, Librn.; Stds.: 365; Lay Tchrs.: 38

Cure of Ars - 9401 Mission Rd., Leawood, KS 66206 t) 913-649-1337 cureparish@cureofars.com cureofars.com Rev. Richard Storey, Pst.; Rev. Mohan Bathineni (India), Par. Vicar; Rev. Tam Nguyen (Vietnam), In Res.; Rev. Anthony Lickteig, In Res.; Dcn. Phillip Nguyen; Dcn. Kevin Cummings; Bernadette Myers, DRE; CRP Stds.: 116

Cure of Ars School - (Grades PreK-8) 9403 Mission Rd., Leawood, KS 66206 t) 913-648-2620 school@cureofars.com www.cureofars.org Natalie McDonough, Prin.; Stds.: 786; Lay Tchrs.: 45

LENEXA

Holy Trinity - 13615 W. 92nd St., Lenexa, KS 66215; Mailing: 9150 Pflumm Rd., Lenexa, KS 66215 t) 913-888-2770 htlenexa.org Rev. Michael Koller, Pst.; Rev. Keith Edward Chadwick, Par. Vicar; Rev. Travis Mecum, Par. Vicar; Dcn. Stuart Holland; Dcn. Steve Lemons; Dcn. Dana Nearmyer; CRP Stds.: 376

Holy Trinity School - (Grades K-8) 13600 W. 92nd St., Lenexa, KS 66215 t) 913-888-3250 smerfen@htslenexa.org htslenexa.org Scott Merfen, Prin.; Kelly Kinnan, Librn.; Stds.: 597; Lay Tchrs.: 44

LOUISBURG

Immaculate Conception - 602 S. Elm, Louisburg, KS 66053; Mailing: Box 118, Louisburg, KS 66053 t) 913-837-2295; 913-837-3309 (CRP) www.icclouisburg.com Rev. Bruce Ansems, Pst.; Rev. Francis Bakyor (Ghana), Par. Admin.; CRP Stds.: 75

MARYSVILLE

St. Gregory - 1310 Carolina St., Marysville, KS 66508; Mailing: 207 N. 14th St., Ste. B, Marysville, KS 66508 t) 785-562-3302 www.stgregorychurch.org Rev. Quentin Schmitz, Pst.; Allyson Lauer, DRE; CRP Stds.: 15

St. Gregory School - (Grades PreK-6) 207 N. 14th, Marysville, KS 66508 t) 785-562-2831 kfarrell@stgregorychurch.org www.stgregorychurch.org/school Karen Farrell, Prin.; Stds.: 139; Lay Tchrs.: 12

MAYETTA

St. Francis Xavier - 301 E. James, Mayetta, KS 66509; Mailing: 115 E. 5th St., Holton, KS 66436 t) 785-364-3262; 785-966-2690 (CRP) parish.jacocatholics@gmail.com www.jacocatholics.com Served from St. Dominic in Holton. Rev. Jonathan Dizon, Pst.; CRP Stds.: 24

MERIDEN

St. Aloysius - 615 Wyandotte St., Meriden, KS 66512; Mailing: P. O. Box 364, Meriden, KS 66512 t) 785-484-3312 staloysiusinmeriden.org Served from St. Theresa, Perry. Rev. Barnabas Eichor, O.F.M.Cap., Pst.; Linda Smith, DRE; CRP Stds.: 48

MISSION

St. Pius X - 5500 Woodson Rd., Mission, KS 66202 t) 913-432-4808 spxmission.org Rev. Gerard Alba, Pst.; Kathleen O'Bryan, DRE; CRP Stds.: 30

MOUND CITY

Sacred Heart Shrine to St. Philippine Duchesne - 729 W Main St, Mound City, KS 66056; Mailing: P.O. Box H, Mound City, KS 66056 t) 913-755-2652; 913-795-2724 (CRP) bclayton@archkck.org www.miamilinncatholics.org Attended by St. Philip Neri, Osawatomie. Rev. Barry R. Clayton, Pst.; Dcn. Don Poole; Jeff Dawson, DRE; CRP Stds.: 28

NORTONVILLE

St. Joseph - 221 N. Sycamore, Nortonville, KS 66060 t) 913-886-2030 www.stjosephsnortonville.com Rev. Lazar Carasala (India), Par. Admin.; Paula Larson, DRE; Becky Weishaar, DRE; CRP Stds.: 32

OLATHE

St. John Paul II Catholic Church - 18335 W. 168th Ter., Olathe, KS 66062 t) 913-747-9636 office@jp2kc.org www.jp2kc.org Rev. Brandon Farrar, Pst.; CRP Stds.: 119

St. Paul - 21650 W. 115th Ter., Olathe, KS 66061 t) 913-764-0323 (CRP); 913-764-0323 www.spcatholic.org Rev. Michael Hermes, Pst.; Rev. Agustin Martinez, Par. Vicar; Dcn. W.A. (Mike) Moffitt; Mayra Valadez, DRE; CRP Stds.: 450

St. Paul School - (Grades PreK-8) t) 913-764-0619 www.spcatholic.org/school Jenny Yankovich, Prin.; Stds.: 293; Lay Tchrs.: 27

Prince of Peace - 16000 W. 143rd St., Olathe, KS 66062 t) 913-782-8864 lmurray@popolathe.org popolathe.org Rev. Gregory Hammes, Pst.; Rev. Andrew Gaffney, Par. Vicar; Rev. Francis Hund, Sr. Par. Vicar, In Res.; Dcn. Gary (Mike) Denning; Dcn. Dan Ondracek; Dcn. Justin Reuter; April Bailey, DRE; CRP Stds.: 369

Prince of Peace School - (Grades K-8) t) 913-764-0650 jshriver@popolathe.org Jane Shriver, Prin.; Pam Schuetz, Librn.; Stds.: 494; Lay Tchrs.: 34

OLPE

St. Joseph - 306 Iowa, Olpe, KS 66865; Mailing: P.O. Box 165, Olpe, KS 66865 t) 620-475-3326 www.sjolpe.org Rev. Nicholas Ashmore, Pst.; Rose Redeker, DRE; CRP Stds.: 75

ONAGA

St. Vincent de Paul - 308 E. Third St., Onaga, KS 66521; Mailing: Box 396, 809 Clifton St., Onaga, KS 66521 t) 785-889-4896 3parishassistant@gmail.com www.facebook.com/profile.php?id=1000647074 Serves also St. Bede, Kelly and St. Patrick, Corning. Rev. Mathew Francis (India), Pst.; Sierra Valburg, DRE; CRP Stds.: 51

OSAGE CITY

St. Patrick - 303 S. 6th St., Osage City, KS 66523; Mailing: 309 S. 6th St., Osage City, KS 66523 t) 785-528-3424 office@stpatrickchurches.org; pmc@stpatrickchurches.org www.stpatrickchurches.org Rev. Konda Reddy Nusi, MSFS, Par. Admin.; CRP Stds.: 46

OSAWATOMIE

St. Philip Neri - 514 Parker Ave, Osawatomie, KS 66064; Mailing: PO Box 4, Osawatomie, KS 66064 t) 913-755-2652 bclayton@archkck.org www.miamilinncatholics.org Serves as Catholic Chaplain for Osawatomie State Hospital Rev. Barry R. Clayton, Pst.; Larry Goddard, DRE; CRP Stds.: 24

OTTAWA

Sacred Heart - 408 S. Cedar St., Ottawa, KS 66067 t) 785-242-2174 shcottawa@gmail.com www.sacredheartottawa.org Rev. Kenneth Clem, Pst.; Sandra Vrbas, DRE; CRP Stds.: 38

Sacred Heart School - (Grades PreK-5) 426 S. Cedar, Ottawa, KS 66067 t) 785-242-4297 sacredheartottawa.eduk12.net Patrick Greer, Prin.; Stds.: 92; Lay Tchrs.: 7

OVERBROOK

St. Francis of Assisi - 452 E. 300 Rd., Overbrook, KS 66524; Mailing: c/o Annunciation, 740 N 6th St., Baldwin City, KS 66006 t) 785-594-3700 Served from Annunciation in Baldwin City Rev. Jomon Palatty, M.S.F.S., Par. Admin.; CRP Stds.: 12

OVERLAND PARK

Church of the Ascension - 9510 W. 127th St., Overland Park, KS 66213 t) 913-681-3348 ascensionchurch@kcascension.org www.kcascension.org Rev. Gary Pennings, Pst.; Rev. Viet Nguyen, Par. Vicar; Rev. Brent Luke Stull, OP, Par. Vicar; Dcn. Kristopher Kuckelman; Dcn. John Stanley; William O'Leary, DRE; CRP Stds.: 543

Church of the Ascension School - (Grades PreK-8) t) 913-851-2531 bwright@acseagles.org www.acseagles.org Becky Wright, Prin.; Stds.: 581; Lay Tchrs.: 37

Holy Cross - 8311 W. 93rd St., Overland Park, KS 66212 t) 913-381-2755 holycrossopks.org Rev. Oswaldo Sandoval, Pst.; Rev. Raymond May Jr., Par. Vicar; Dcn. Timothy McEvoy; Patricia Argueta, DRE; CRP Stds.: 150

Holy Cross School - (Grades PreK-8) 8101 W. 95th, Overland Park, KS 66212 t) 913-381-7408 gradeschool@holycrosscatholicschool.com www.holycrosscatholicschool.com Melissa Wagner, Prin.; Stds.: 191; Lay Tchrs.: 20

Holy Spirit - 11300 W. 103rd St., Overland Park, KS 66214 t) 913-492-7382 (CRP); 913-492-7318 Rev. Andrew Strobl, Pst.; Rev. Msgr. Thomas Tank, Par. Vicar; Dcn. Michael Schreck; Dcn. John Williams; CRP Stds.: 161

Holy Spirit School - (Grades PreK-8) t) 913-492-2582 koshea@hscatholic.org www.hscatholic.org Kevan O'Shea, Prin.; Stds.: 307; Lay Tchrs.: 25

St. Michael the Archangel - 14251 Nall Ave., Overland Park, KS 66223 t) 913-402-3900 stmichaelcp.org/ Rev. Brian Schieber, Pst.; Rev. Edward Ahn, Par. Vicar; Rev. Luke Doyle, Par. Vicar; Dcn. Mark Stukel; Dcn. John Weist; CRP Stds.: 503

St. Michael the Archangel School - (Grades K-8) 14201 Nall Ave., Leawood, KS 66223 t) 913-402-3950 diana.tate@stmichaelcp.org edu.stmichaelcp.org Diana Tate, Prin.; Elaine Glenski, Librn.; Stds.: 545; Lay Tchrs.: 36

Queen of the Holy Rosary - 7023 W. 71st St., Overland Park, KS 66204 t) 913-722-2206 (CRP); 913-432-4616 queenoftheholyrosary.org Rev. William Bruning, Pst.; Dcn. Jim Lavin; Denise Godinez, DRE; CRP Stds.: 50

PAOLA

Holy Trinity - 509 E. Chippewa St., Paola, KS 66071 t) 913-557-2067 holytrinity.weconnect.com Rev. Joseph Sellas (India), Par. Admin.; CRP Stds.: 43

Holy Trinity School - (Grades PreK-8) 601 E. Chippewa, Paola, KS 66071 t) 913-294-3286 htsecretary@holytrinitypaola.org Michelle Gavin, Prin.; Stds.: 100; Lay Tchrs.: 11

PAXICO

Sacred Heart - 22298 Newbury Rd., Paxico, KS 66526 t) 785-636-5578; 785-636-5547 (Rectory) sacredheartparishpaxico@gmail.com sacredheartpaxico.com Rev. Ratna Swamy Nannam, MSFS, Par. Admin.; Renee Spellman, DRE; CRP Stds.: 35

PERRY

St. Theresa - 209 Third, Perry, KS 66073; Mailing: P. O. Box 42, Perry, KS 66073 t) 785-597-5558 rellis107@yahoo.com sttheresainperry.org Rev. Barnabas Eichor, O.F.M.Cap., Pst.; Kim Alshahri, DRE; CRP Stds.: 27

PRAIRIE VILLAGE

St. Ann - 7231 Mission Rd., Prairie Village, KS 66208 t) (913) 660-1184 (CRP); (913) 660-1182 stanncatholicchurch@stannpv.org www.stannpv.org Rev. Craig Maxim, Pst.; Dcn. Todd Brower; Dcn. Stephen Nguyen; CRP Stds.: 135

St. Ann School - (Grades K-8) 7241 Mission Rd., Prairie Village, KS 66208 t) 913-660-1101 kminshall@stannpv.org www.school.stannpv.org Kelli Minshall, Prin.; Donna O'Connor, Librn.; Stds.: 376; Lay Tchrs.: 31

RICHMOND

St. Therese - 544 E Central, Richmond, KS 66080; Mailing: 32292 N E Norton Rd., Garnett, KS 66032 t) 785-835-6273 www.stbonifacesttherese.com Served from St. Boniface, Scipio. Rev. J. Gerald Williams, O.Carm., Pst.; Rev. David Simpson, O.Carm., In Res.; Carol Lutz, DRE; CRP Stds.: 75

ROELAND PARK

St. Agnes - 5250 Mission Rd., Roeland Park, KS 66205 t) 913-262-2400 youngstrom.teresa@stagneskc.org www.stagneskc.org Rev. William Porter, Pst.; Sr. Patricia Lynch, O.S.U., Pst. Assoc.; Jennifer Hense, DRE; CRP Stds.: 48

St. Agnes School - (Grades PreK-8) 5130 Mission Rd., Roeland Park, KS 66205 t) 913-262-1686 sullivan.jane@stagneskc.org school.stagneskc.org Jane Sullivan, Prin.; Stds.: 329; Lay Tchrs.: 26

ROSSVILLE

St. Stanislaus - 701 S. Main St., Rossville, KS 66533; Mailing: PO Box 794, Rossville, KS 66533 t) 785-584-6612 www.ststansrossville.org Served from Immaculate Conception, St. Marys. Rev. Justin Hamilton, Pst.; Connie Fischer, DRE; CRP Stds.: 97

SABETHA

St. Augustine - 1948 Acorn Rd., Sabetha, KS 66534; Mailing: 1031 S. 12th St., Sabetha, KS 66534 t) 785-284-0888 jzarse@archkck.org Served from Sacred Heart, Sabetha Rev. Jaime Zarse, Pst.; CRP Stds.: 21

Sacred Heart - 1031 S. 12th St., Sabetha, KS 66534 t) 785-284-0888 info@nekansascatholics.org www.nekansascatholics.org Rev. Jaime Zarse, Pst.; Gina Sallman, Director of Faith Formation; CRP Stds.: 79

SCRANTON

St. Patrick - 400 E. Bracken St., Scranton, KS 66537; Mailing: 309 S. 6th St., Osage City, KS 66523 t) 785-528-3424 office@stpatrickchurches.org; pmc@stpatrickchurches.org www.stpatrickchurches.org Served from St. Patrick's, Osage City. Rev. Konda Reddy Nusi, MSFS, Par. Admin.; CRP Stds.: 29

SENECA

SS. Peter and Paul - 411 Pioneer, Seneca, KS 66538 t) 785-336-2128 www.saintspeterandpaul-seneca.com Rev. Arul Carasala (India), Pst.; Shannon Holthaus, DRE; CRP Stds.: 105

SS. Peter and Paul School - (Grades PreK-8) 409 Elk St., Seneca, KS 66538 t) 785-336-2727 tleonard@stspeterandpaulschool.com www.sppschool.com Todd Leonard, Prin.; Stds.: 216; Lay Tchrs.: 18

SHAWNEE

Good Shepherd - 12800 W. 75th St., Shawnee, KS 66216 t) 913-563-5303 (CRP); 913-631-7116 info@gsshawnee.org www.gsshawnee.org Rev. Kent O'Connor, Pst.; Rev. Anthony Mersmann, Par. Vicar; Dcn. Marcos Navarro; Dcn. Tom Greer; CRP Stds.: 324

Good Shepherd School - (Grades PreK-8) t) 913-631-0400 amcguff@gsshawnee.org Ann McGuff, Prin.; Jennifer Smith, Librn.; Stds.: 363; Lay Tchrs.: 29

St. Joseph - 11311 Johnson Dr., Shawnee, KS 66203; Mailing: 5901 Flint St., Shawnee, KS 66203 t) 913-631-8923 (CRP); 913-631-5983 church.stjoeshawnee.org/ Rev. Scott Wallisch, Pst.; Rev. Joel Haug, Par. Vicar; Rev. Mark Ostrowski, Par. Vicar; Dcn. Mark Mies; Dcn. Tom Mulvenon; Beth Bracken, DRE; CRP Stds.: 82

St. Joseph School - (Grades K-8) 11505 Johnson Dr., Shawnee, KS 66203 t) 913-631-7730 jmaddox@stjoeshawnee.org www.stjoeshawnee.org Jodie Maddox, Prin.; Stds.: 375; Lay Tchrs.: 28

Early Education Center - 11525 Johnson Dr., Shawnee, KS 66203 t) 913-631-0004 (Day Care & Preschool) Theresa Gavila, Dir.;

Sacred Heart - 5501 Monticello Rd., Shawnee, KS 66226 t) 913-422-5700 www.shoj.org Rev. Patrick Sullivan, Pst.; Rev. John Riley, Sacr. Min.; Dcn. Nicholas Moragues; Emily Dumler, D.R.E. (K-6); CRP Stds.: 425

Sacred Heart School - (Grades K-8) 21801 Johnson Dr., Shawnee, KS 66218 t) 913-422-5520 kathy.rhodes@shoj.org Kathy Rhodes, Prin.; Kathy Clevinger, Librn.; Stds.: 396; Lay Tchrs.: 25

ST. BENEDICT

St. Mary's Catholic Church - 9208 Main St., St. Benedict, KS 66538 t) 785-336-6464 Served from Sacred Heart, Baileyville. Rev. Reginald Saldanha, Pst.; Diane Schmitz, DRE; CRP Stds.: 22

ST. GEORGE

St. Joseph - 8965 Flush Rd., St. George, KS 66535; Mailing: 17665 Old Post Rd., Wamego, KS 66547 t) 785-456-7869 Served from St. Bernard in Wamego. Rev. Michael Peterson, Pst.; CRP Stds.: 142

ST. MARYS

Immaculate Conception - 208 W. Bertrand, St. Marys, KS 66536 t) 785-437-2408 icparish1848@gmail.com immaculateconceptionstmarys.com Rev. Justin Hamilton, Pst.; Alice Bordelon, DRE; CRP Stds.: 98

SUMMERFIELD

Holy Family - 601 Main, Summerfield, KS 66541; Mailing: PO Box K, Axtell, KS 66403 t) 785-736-2220 jshau47@gmail.com; jshaughnessy@archkck.org Served from St. Michael, Axtell. All Religious Ed. is at St. Michael. Rev. James Shaughnessy, Pst.;

TONGANOXIE

Sacred Heart - 1100 West St., Tonganoxie, KS 66086-0539; Mailing: P.O. Box 539, Tonganoxie, KS 66086-0539 t) 913-369-2851 cfoure6@msn.com; mgoldy@sunflower.com www.shcct.com Rev. Mark Goldasich, Pst.; Dcn. Ron Zishka; Jennifer Eastes, DRE; Nancy Lanza, DRE; CRP Stds.: 112

TOPEKA

Christ the King - 5973 S.W. 25th St., Topeka, KS 66614 t) 785-273-0710 ctktopeka.org Rev. Matthew Schiffelbein, Pst.; Rev. Thomas Maddock, Par. Vicar; Dcn. John Langer; Dcn. Chris Seago; Connie Fischer, Bus. Mgr.; CRP Stds.: 179

Christ the King School - (Grades K-8) t) 785-272-2220 reynosor@ctktopeka.eduk12.net ctkschooltopeka.org Relynn Reynoso, Prin.; Stds.: 219; Lay Tchrs.: 24

Mater Dei - 911 S.W. Clay, Topeka, KS 66606 t) 785-232-7744 www.materdeiparish.org Rev. John Pilcher, Pst.; Dcn. Robert Ortiz; CRP Stds.: 15

Mater Dei School - (Grades PreK-8) 934 S.W. Clay St., Topeka, KS 66606 t) 785-233-1727 hilleberta@materdeischool.org materdeischool.org Andrea Hillebert, Prin.; Stds.: 141; Lay Tchrs.: 13

Mater Dei Assumption Church - 8th & Jackson St., Topeka, KS 66603; Mailing: 911 S.W. Clay, Topeka, KS 66606

Mater Dei Holy Name Church - 10th & Clay St., Topeka, KS 66604; Mailing: 911 S.W. Clay St., Topeka, KS 66606

St. Matthew Catholic Church Topeka - 2700 S.E. Virginia Ave., Topeka, KS 66605 t) 785-232-5012 parishoffice@saintmatthews.org; jtorrez@archkck.org www.saintmatthews.org Rev. John Torrez, Pst.; Dcn. David Auten; Sonya Sparks, DRE; Bob Broxterman, Bus. Mgr.; CRP Stds.: 83

St. Matthew School - (Grades K-8) 1000 S.E. 28th, Topeka, KS 66605 t) 785-235-2188 school@saintmatthews.org Theresa Lein, Prin.; Debbie Otting, Librn.; Stds.: 150; Lay Tchrs.: 15

Most Pure Heart of Mary - 3601 S.W. 17th St., Topeka, KS 66604 t) 785-272-5590 www.mphm.com Rev. Nathan Haverland, Pst.; CRP Stds.: 107

Most Pure Heart of Mary School - (Grades K-8) 1750 S.W. Stone, Topeka, KS 66604 t) 785-272-4313 ewhite@mphm.com www.mphm.com/school Eric White, Prin.; Stacey McBride, Vice Prin.; Stds.: 360; Lay Tchrs.: 22

Mother Teresa of Calcutta - 2014 N.W. 46th St., Topeka, KS 66618 t) 785-286-2188 office@mtcctopeka.org mtcctopeka.org Rev. Thomas Reddy Aduri, Pst.; Dcn. Timothy Ruoff; Dcn. Bradley Sloan; Beth Mercer, DRE; CRP Stds.: 175

Our Lady of Guadalupe - 201 N.E. Chandler St., Topeka, KS 66616; Mailing: 134 N.E. Lake St., Topeka, KS 66616 t) 785-232-5088 www.olg-parish.com Rev. Daniel Coronado, Pst.; Rev. Romulo Real-Linares (Colombia), Par. Vicar; CRP Stds.: 110

Sacred Heart-St. Joseph - 227 S.W. Van Buren, Topeka, KS 66603 t) 785-232-2863; 785-234-3338 www.sacredheartstjosephcatholic.org/ Sacred Heart Parish (1919) and St. Joseph Parish (1887) were unified in 2006 to form Sacred Heart-St. Joseph Parish Rev. Timothy A. Haberkorn, Pst.; Maggie Carey, DRE; Sabrina Seidl, DRE; CRP Stds.: 127

TROY

St. Charles - 520 W. Chestnut, Troy, KS 66087; Mailing: PO Box 456, Troy, KS 66087 t) 785-985-2271; 785-985-2113 (CRP) Served from St. Joseph Parish, Wathena. Rev. Michael Guastello, Pst.; Barb Greaser, DRE;

VALLEY FALLS

St. Mary's Immaculate Conception - 905 Broadway St, Valley Falls, KS 66088; Mailing: PO Box 176, Valley Falls, KS 66088 t) 913-886-2030; 785-945-3787 (CRP) Served from St. Joseph, Nortonville. Rev. Lazar Carasala (India), Par. Admin.; Jolina Wildeman, DRE; CRP Stds.: 36

WAMEGO

St. Bernard - 17665 Old Post Rd., Wamego, KS 66547 t) 785-456-7869 Rev. Michael Peterson, Pst.; CRP Stds.: 200

WATHENA

St. Joseph - 102 S. 7th St., Wathena, KS 66090; Mailing: P.O. Box 159, Wathena, KS 66090 t) 785-989-4818 stjosephwathena@outlook.com www.stjosephwathena.com Rev. Michael Guastello, Pst.; Mary Kay Nold, DRE; CRP Stds.: 20

WAVERLY

St. Joseph - 508 Pearson Ave., Waverly, KS 66871; Mailing: 214 Juniatta, Burlington, KS 66839 t) 620-364-5671 st-francis-joseph-patrick-teresa.org/ Served from St. Francis Xavier, Burlington. Rev. Colin Haganey, Pst.; Jill Barnhart, DRE; CRP Stds.: 37

WESTPHALIA

St. Teresa - 404 Garrison Ave., Westphalia, KS 66093; Mailing: 214 Juniatta St., Burlington, KS 66839 t) 620-364-5671 st-francis-joseph-patrick-teresa.org/ Served from St. Francis Xavier, Burlington. Rev. Colin Haganey, Pst.; Jennifer Blaufuss, DRE; CRP Stds.: 36

WETMORE

St. James - 512 Kansas Ave., Wetmore, KS 66550 t) 785-284-0888 info@nekansascatholics.org www.nekansascatholics.org Served from Sacred Heart, Sabetha. Rev. Jaime Zarse, Pst.; CRP Stds.: 37

WILLIAMSBURG

St. Patrick - 33721 N.W. Crawford Rd., Williamsburg, KS 66095; Mailing: 214 Juniatta, Burlington, KS 66839 t) 620-364-5671 st-francis-joseph-patrick-teresa.org/ Served by St. Francis Xavier, Burlington. Known as St. Patrick in Emerald. Rev. Colin Haganey, Pst.;

SCHOOLS: PRESCHOOL THRU HIGH SCHOOL

SCHOOLS

STATE OF KANSAS

GARNETT

St. Rose Philippine Duchesne School - (PAR) (Grades PreK-8) 530 E. Fourth, Garnett, KS 66032 t) 785-448-3423 kwolken@archkckcs.org strosegarnett.eduk12.net/ Kelli Woelken, Prin.; Stds.: 112; Lay Tchrs.: 6

KANSAS CITY

Our Lady of Unity School - (PAR) (Grades K-8) 2646 S. 34th, Kansas City, KS 66106 t) 913-262-7022 www.olucs.org Cally Dahlstrom, Prin.; Linda Hutzenbuhler, Librn.; Stds.: 180; Lay Tchrs.: 15

Our Lady's Montessori School - (PRV) (Grades PreK-6) 3020 S. 7th St., Kansas City, KS 66103 t) 913-403-9550 srmarymediatrix@gmail.com; srlaudem@olmskc.org olmskc.org Catholic Montessori Preschool and Elementary Sr. Laudem Gloriae Dolan, S.O.L.T, Dir.; Stds.: 73; Sr. Tchrs.: 2; Lay Tchrs.: 9

Resurrection Catholic School at the Cathedral - (Grades PreK-8) 425 N. 15th St., Kansas City, KS 66102 t) 913-371-8101 kobrien@rcskck.org www.rcskck.org Kevin O'Brien, Prin.; Allie Dorsey, Librn.; Stds.: 321; Sr. Tchrs.: 1; Lay Tchrs.: 28

LEAVENWORTH

Xavier Elementary School - (Grades PreK-8) 541 Muncie Rd., Leavenworth, KS 66048; Mailing: 1409 2nd Ave., c/o Administrative Office, Leavenworth, KS 66048 t) 913-682-7801; 913-682-3135 lrcsadmin@leavenworthcatholicschools.org leavenworthcatholicschools.org Janelle Hartegan, Prin.; Cindi Thiele, Librn.; Stds.: 228; Lay Tchrs.: 21

MAPLE HILL

St. John Vianney School - (PRV) (Grades K-6) 14611A Waterman Crossing Rd., Maple Hill, KS 66507 t) 785-207-5927 sjvs.cristeros@gmail.com Rev. Eric Flood, F.S.S.P., Chap.; Stds.: 55

OVERLAND PARK

John Paul II Catholic School - (Grades PreK-8) 6915 W. 71st., Overland Park, KS 66204 t) 913-432-6350 eharmon@johnpaul2opks.com johnpaul2opks.com Dr.

Eva Harmon, Prin.; Joanne Rineman, Librn.; Stds.: 175; Lay Tchrs.: 25

TOPEKA

Holy Family Catholic School - (PAR) (Grades PreK-8) 1725 N.E. Seward Ave., Topeka, KS 66616 t) 785-234-8980; 785-233-9171 holyfamilytopeka.net Travis Lamb, Prin.; Stds.: 164; Sr. Tchrs.: 1; Lay Tchrs.: 11

HIGH SCHOOLS

STATE OF KANSAS

ATCHISON

Maur Hill - Mount Academy - (PRV) (Grades 9-12) 1000 Green St., Atchison, KS 66002 t) 913-367-5482 admissions@mh-ma.com mh-ma.com A Benedictine, boarding and day high school. Phil Baniewicz, Pres.; Dr. Cameron Carlson, Prin.; Whitney McGinnis, Vice Prin.; Stds.: 173; Pr. Tchrs.: 1; Bro. Tchrs.: 1; Lay Tchrs.: 16

KANSAS CITY

Bishop Ward High School - (PAR) (Grades 9-12) 708 N. 18th St., Kansas City, KS 66102 t) 913-371-1201 wardhigh@wardhigh.org www.wardhigh.org Rev. Joel Haug, Chap.; Michelle Olson, Prin.; James (Jay) Dunlap Jr., Pres.; Stds.: 315; Lay Tchrs.: 24

Bishop Ward High School Foundation -

LENEXA

St. James Catholic Academy, Inc. - (PAR) (Grades 9-12) 24505 Prairie Star Pkwy., Lenexa, KS 66227 t) 913-254-4200 cpeterson@sjakeepingfaith.org; atylicki@sjakeepingfaith.org www.sjakeepingfaith.org Andy Tylicki, Pres.; Shane Rapp, Prin.; Rev. Mark Ostrowski, Chap.; Stds.: 920; Sr. Tchrs.: 1; Lay Tchrs.: 59

OVERLAND PARK

Saint Thomas Aquinas High School, Inc. - (PAR) (Grades 9-12) 11411 Pflumm Rd., Overland Park, KS 66215 t) 913-345-1411 bschenck@stasaints.net www.stasaints.net Brian Schenck, Pres.; Craig Moss, Prin.; Michael Sullivan, Prin.; Rev. Andrew Gaffney, Chap.; Amanda Davis, Librn.; Stds.: 882; Lay Tchrs.: 74

St. Thomas Aquinas High School Foundation -

SHAWNEE MISSION

Bishop Miege High School - (PAR) (Grades 9-12) 5041 Reinhardt Dr., Shawnee Mission, KS 66205 t) 913-262-2700 mjaksa@bishopmiege.com www.bishopmiege.com Randy Salisbury, Pres.; Maureen Engen, Prin.; Rev. Anthony Mersmann, Chap.; Joe Schramp, Assoc. Prin./Athletic Dir.; Alex Keith, Dean of Students; Stds.: 648; Lay Tchrs.: 42

Bishop Miege High School Foundation - t) (913) 222-5814 drjpass@bishopmiege.com Dr. Joseph Passantino, Pres.;

TOPEKA

Hayden High School - (PAR) (Grades 9-12) 401 Gage Blvd., Topeka, KS 66606 t) 785-272-5210 sandstromj@haydencatholic.net www.haydencatholic.org Shelly Buhler, Pres.; James Sandstrom, Prin.; Rev. Thomas Maddock, Chap.; Stds.: 346; Lay Tchrs.: 32

Hayden High School Foundation -

INSTITUTIONS LOCATED IN DIOCESE

ASSOCIATIONS [ASN]

OVERLAND PARK

Catholic Cemeteries Association of Northeast Kansas, Inc. - 9290 Bond St., Suite 211, Overland Park, KS 66214; Mailing: PO Box 19203, Lenexa, KS 66285 t) 913-371-4040; 785-272-0820 svallejo@cathcemks.org www.cathcemks.org Sharon Vallejo, Dir.;

CAMPUS MINISTRY / NEWMAN CENTERS [CAM]

EMPORIA

Didde Catholic Campus Center, Emporia State University - Office: 1415 Merchant St., Emporia, KS 66801 t) 620-343-6765 contact@diddecenter.org www.diddecenter.org Rev. Matthew Nagle, Chap.;

LAWRENCE

Haskell Catholic Campus Center - Tekakwitha House, 2301 Barker Ave., Lawrence, KS 66046-4813 t) 785-979-3296 katerihcsc@gmail.com Rev. Michael Scully, O.F.M.Cap., Chap.; Jean Finch, Dir.;

St. Lawrence Catholic Campus Center at the University of Kansas and Residence - 1631 Crescent Rd., Lawrence, KS 66044 t) 785-843-0357 kucatholic@kucatholic.org www.kucatholic.org Rev. Mitchel Zimmerman, Chap.; Rev. Daniel Morris, In Res.;

TOPEKA

Catholic Campus Center at Washburn University - 1633 S.W. Jewell, Topeka, KS 66604 t) 785-233-2204 wucatholic@hotmail.com www.wucatholic.com Jessica Hammer, Dir.; Rev. Ratna Swamy Nannam, MSFS, Chap.;

CATHOLIC CHARITIES [CCH]

LENEXA

Catholic Community Hospice of Northeast Kansas, Inc. - 16201 W. 95th St., Lenexa, KS 66219 t) 913-621-5090 info@catholiccommunityhealth.org Duke Onkoba, Exec. Dir.; Asstd. Annu.: 238; Staff: 45

Catholic Community Service, In-Home Support of Northeast Kansas, Inc. - 16201 W. 95th St., Ste. 220, Lenexa, KS 66219 t) (913) 433-2000 kdickerson@catholiccommunityhealth.org catholiccommunityhospice.com Duke Onkoba, Admin.; Asstd. Annu.: 209; Staff: 36

OVERLAND PARK

Catholic Charities of Northeast Kansas, Inc. - 9720 W. 87th St., Overland Park, KS 66212 t) 913-433-2100 info@catholiccharitiesks.org catholiccharitiesks.org Provides help, hope and hospitality to the most vulnerable of all faiths. Lauren Solidum, Pres. & CEO; Asstd. Annu.: 421,249; Staff: 147

Catholic Charities Foundation of Northeast Kansas - 9720 W. 87th St., Overland Park, KS 66212 t) (913) 433-2100

Catholic Neighborhood Outreach, Inc. - 9750 W. 87th St., Overland Park, KS 66212 t) 913-648-6795 TurnStyles Thrift Store location.

Catholic Neighborhood Outreach, Inc. - 5304 Martway, Mission, KS 66205 t) (913) 416-4090

Catholic Neighborhood Outreach, Inc. - 11310 W. 135th St., Overland Park, KS 66221 t) 913-909-2485 TurnStyles location

Family Support Center - Topeka - 234 S. Kansas Ave., Topeka, KS 66603 t) 785-233-6300

Family Support Center (FSC) - Lawrence - 1525 W. 6th St., Lawrence, KS 66044 t) 785-856-2694

Family Support Center (FSC) - North Johnson County - 9806 W. 87th St., Overland Park, KS 66212 t) 913-384-6608

Family Support Center (FSC) - South Johnson County - 333 E. Poplar, Olathe, KS 66061 t) 913-782-4077

Family Support Center (FSC) - Wyandotte County - 600 Minnesota Ave., Kansas City, KS 66101 t) 913-621-3445

Family Support Center (FSC) - Leavenworth - 716 N. 5th St., Leavenworth, KS 66048 t) 913-651-8060

Family Support Center (FSC) - Atchison - 502 Kansas Ave., Atchison, KS 66002 t) 913-367-5070 www.catholiccharitiesks.org

Hope Distribution Center - 1708 Steele Rd., Kansas City, KS 66106 t) 913-432-3141

Morning Glory Estate Sales - 9720 W. 87th St., Overland Park, KS 66212 t) (913) 433-2100

Shalom House Men's Shelter - 2601 Ridge Ave., Kansas City, KS 66102; Mailing: 9720 W. 87th St., c/o Catholic Charities, Overland Park, KS 66212 t) 913-321-2206

CEMETERIES [CEM]

OVERLAND PARK

Gate of Heaven, St. John, Mount Calvary - 9290 Bond St., Ste. 211, Catholic Cemeteries, Overland Park, KS 66214; Mailing: PO Box 19203, Lenexa, KS 66255 t) 913-371-4040 www.cathcemks.org Sharon Vallejo, Dir.;

Resurrection, Shawnee, St. Joseph's, Shawnee, St. John, Lenexa, Mount Calvery, Olathe - Catholic Cemeteries Association of Northeast Kansas, Inc., 9290 Bond St., Ste 211, Overland Park, KS 66214 t) 913-371-4040 Sharon Vallejo, Dir.;

COLLEGES & UNIVERSITIES [COL]

ATCHISON

Benedictine College - 1020 N. 2nd St., Atchison, KS 66002 t) 913-367-5340 www.benedictine.edu Coed College of St. Benedict's & Mount St. Scholastica. Stephen D. Minnis, Pres.; Rev. Ryan Richardson, L.C., Chap.; Rev. Marion Charboneau, O.S.B., Prof.; Rev. Meinrad Miller, O.S.B., Adj. Prof.; Dcn. Dana Nearmyer, Adj. Prof.; Dcn. Charles Welte, IT Dir.; Bro. Joseph Ryan, O.S.B., Mailroom; Steven Gromatzky, Librn.; Kimberly C. Shankman, Dean; Stds.: 2,134; Lay Tchrs.: 115

KANSAS CITY

Donnelly College - 608 N. 18th St., Kansas City, KS 66102 t) 913-621-8700 admissions@donnelly.edu www.donnelly.edu Rev. Msgr. Stuart Swetland, Pres.; Jennifer Bales, Registrar; Elizabeth Strother, Librn.; Stds.: 360; Lay Tchrs.: 13

LEAVENWORTH

University of Saint Mary - 4100 S. 4th St., Leavenworth, KS 66048 t) 913-682-5151 sharron.lucas@stmary.edu www.stmary.edu Sr. Diane Steele, S.C.L., Pres.; Michelle Metzinger, Provost & Academic Vice Pres.; Stds.: 1,267; Lay Tchrs.: 82; Sr. Tchrs.: 1

CONVENTS, MONASTERIES, AND RESIDENCES FOR WOMEN [CON]

ATCHISON

Mount St. Scholastica - 801 S. 8th St., Atchison, KS 66002 t) 913-360-6200 www.mountosb.org Motherhouse of the Sisters of St. Benedict. Sr. Esther Fangman, O.S.B., Prioress; Srs.: 92

KANSAS CITY

Little Sisters of the Lamb - 36 S. Boeke St., Kansas City, KS 66101 t) 913-621-1727 lumenchristi@communityofthelamb.org Sr. Judith Chazelle, Prioress; Srs.: 7

Servants of Mary, Ministers to the Sick - 800 N. 18th St., Kansas City, KS 66102 t) 913-371-3423; 913-621-1147 mprovincialsdemkc@yahoo.com; superiorasdemkc@gmail.com Mother Alicia Hermosillo, S.deM., Prov.; Mother Ema Munoz, S.deM., Supr.; Rev. Joseph Arsenault, S.S.A., Chap.; Srs.: 17

LEAVENWORTH

Motherhouse of the Sisters of Charity of Leavenworth - 4200 S. 4th St., Leavenworth, KS 66048-5054 t) 913-758-6501 communications@scls.org www.scls.org Sr. Eileen Haynes, SCL, Dir.; Rev. Dennis Schaab, C.PP.S., Chap.; Sr. Rita McGinnis, SCL, Admin.; Sherry Wickenhauser, Coord., Motherhouse & Ross Hall; Srs.: 124

OLATHE

Province of the Sisters of St. Anne, Inc. - 1901 E. Sunvale Dr., Olathe, KS 66062 t) (913) 829-3548 Sr. Anne Annakatty Varghese, CSSA, Supr.; Srs.: 6

ENDOWMENTS / FOUNDATIONS / TRUSTS [EFT]

ATCHISON

The Maur Hill Prep School Endowment Association, Inc. - 1000 Green St., Atchison, KS 66002 t) 913-367-5482 philb@mh-ma.com Phil Baniewicz, Pres.;

Maur Hill-Mount Academy School Endowment Association, Inc. - 1000 Green St., Atchison, KS 66002

t) 913-367-5482 philb@mh-ma.com Phil Baniewicz, Pres.;

KANSAS CITY

Catholic Education Foundation - 12615 Parallel Pkwy., Kansas City, KS 66109 t) (913) 721-1570 vanch@archkck.org www.cefks.org Vincent Anch, Exec. Dir.;

The Catholic Foundation of Northeast Kansas - 12615 Parallel Pkwy., Kansas City, KS 66109 t) 913-647-3062 cfnek@archkck.org; wmaloney@archkck.org www.cfnek.org (Formerly known as Archdiocesan Foundation) William Maloney, Dir.;

MISCELLANEOUS [MIS]

KANSAS CITY

Archdiocese of Kansas City in Kansas Deposit and Loan Fund - 12615 Parallel Pkwy., Kansas City, KS 66109 t) 913-721-1570 x177 cmills@archkck.org Carla Mills, Trustee;

Catholic Housing of Wyandotte County - 2 S. 14th St., Kansas City, KS 66102 t) 913-342-7580 bcrawford@chwckck.org www.chwckck.org Rev. John Riley, Mem.;

Duchesne Clinic - 636 Tauromee Ave., Kansas City, KS 66101 t) 913-321-2626 michele.surber@caritasclinics.org; richard.martin@imail.org www.duchesneclinic.org A division of Caritas Clinics, Inc., Leavenworth, KS. Michele Surber, Exec. Dir.;

***El Centro, Inc.** - 650 Minnesota Ave., Kansas City, KS 66101 t) 913-677-0100 icaudillo@elcentroinc.com www.elcentroinc.com Irene Caudillo, Pres.;

Lay and Deacon and Priest Retirement Plans of the Archdiocese of Kansas City in Kansas - 12615 Parallel Pkwy., Kansas City, KS 66109 t) 913-721-1570 cmills@archkck.org www.archkck.org Carla Mills, CFO;

Little Brothers of the Lamb, Inc. - 921 Homer, Kansas City, KS 66101 t) 913-998-6644 littlebrotherskansas@communityofthelamb.org Bro. Louis Marie Dupont, Pres.; Bro. Jean-Marie Thierry D'Argenlieu, Treas.;

***Society of St. Augustine - Public Association of the Faithful** - 615 N. 7th St., Kansas City, KS 66101 t) 913-371-1408 augustinian11@hotmail.com www.augustinian.us Public Association of the Faithful Rev. Peter Jaramillo, S.S.A., Prior; Rev. Joseph Arsenault, S.S.A.;

LEAVENWORTH

Caritas Clinics, Inc. (Sisters of Charity of Leavenworth Health System) - 818 N. 7th St., Leavenworth, KS 66048 t) 913-651-8860 michele.surber@caritasclinics.org; richard.martin@imail.org www.caritasclinics.org Administrative structure for Saint Vincent Clinic, Leavenworth, Duchesne Clinic, Kansas City. Michele Surber, Exec.;

Saint Vincent Clinic - 818 N. 7th St., Leavenworth, KS 66048 t) 913-651-8860 jennifer.wewers@caritasclinics.org; michele.surber@caritasclinics.org www.saintvincentclinic.org (A division of Caritas Clinics, Inc., Leavenworth, KS) Michele Surber, Exec. Dir.; Jennifer Wewers, Admin.;

Xavier Corporation - 4200 S. 4th St., Ste. 309, Leavenworth, KS 66048 t) 913-758-6502 katherinefranchett@yahoo.com Sr. Katherine Franchett, Chair;

OLATHE

Catholic Care Campus, Inc. (Santa Marta) - 13800 W. 116th St., Olathe, KS 66062 t) 913-906-0990 csurmaczewicz@santamartaretirement.com www.santamartaretirement.com Independent, assisted living, memory support, skilled nursing. Chet Surmaczewicz, Dir.; Rev. Francis Burger, Chap.;

Villa St. Francis Real Estate Holdings, Inc. - 16600 W. 126th St., Olathe, KS 66062 t) (913) 829-5201 Jackie Longston, Interim Admin.;

OVERLAND PARK

Holy Family School of Faith - 13240 Craig St., Overland Park, KS 66213 t) 913-310-0014 support@schooloffaith.com www.schooloffaith.com Michael Scherschligt, Exec.;

School of Love, Inc. - 10412 Cody St., Overland Park, KS 66214 t) 913-583-0007 info@schooloflovekc.com www.schooloflovekc.com Mike Dennihan, Exec. Dir.;

RAYMORE

Franciscan Servants of the Holy Family - Public Association of the Faithful - 1204 N. Jeter Rd., Raymore, MO 64083; Mailing: P.O. Box 7251, Shawnee Mission, KS 66207 t) 785-218-2894 srdoris@kcfranciscans.org www.kcfranciscans.org Mission: Helping families grow in holiness and unity.

ROELAND PARK

Catholic Youth Organization of Johnson and Wyandotte Counties, Inc. - 5041 Reinhardt Dr., Roeland Park, KS 66205 t) (913) 915-0139 www.cyojwa.org John McGoldrick, Exec. Dir.;

Heart of the Redeemer, Inc. - 3220 W. 53rd St., Roeland Park, KS 66205; Mailing: 5842 N. Spruce, Kansas City, MO 64119 t) 913-433-8181 brad@heartoftheredeemer.org www.heartoftheredeemer.org Brad Schleeter, Pres.;

SHAWNEE

The Cursillo Movement of the Archdiocese of Kansas City in Kansas - 6525 Larsen Ln., Shawnee, KS 66203 t) 913-220-5566 mhill@archkck.org www.cursillo.org/kckcursillo Dcn. Michael Hill, Spiritual Adv./Care Srvcs.; Rev. Peter Jaramillo, S.S.A., Asst. Spiritual Adv.; Richard Sulzen, Lay Dir.;

TOPEKA

El Centro de Servicios Para Hispanos - 134 N.E. Lake St., Topeka, KS 66616 t) 785-232-8207 lmunoz@elcentrooftopeka.org www.elcentrooftopeka.org Immigrant services Lalo Munoz, Dir.;

Marian Clinic, Inc. - 3164 S.E. 6th Ave., Topeka, KS 66607 t) 785-233-2800 michele.surber@caritasclinics.org; richard.martin@imail.org www.mariandental.org Affiliate of Sisters of Charity of Leavenworth Health System Michele Surber, Exec. Dir.;

MONASTERIES AND RESIDENCES FOR PRIESTS AND BROTHERS [MON]

ATCHISON

St. Benedict's Abbey - 1020 N. 2nd St., Atchison, KS 66002 t) 913-367-7853 jalbers@kansasmonks.org; levenharton@gmail.com www.kansasmonks.org Rt. Rev. James R. Albers, O.S.B., Abbot; Rev. Jeremy Heppler, O.S.B., Pst.; Rev. Jay Kythe, O.S.B., Subprior; Rev. Joaquim Carvalho, O.S.B.; Rev. Marion Charboneau, O.S.B.; Rev. Josias Dias da Costa, O.S.B.; Rev. Roderic Giller, O.S.B.; Rev. Matthew Habiger, O.S.B.; Bro. Placidus Lee, O.S.B.; Rev. Daniel McCarthy, O.S.B.; Bro. Timothy McMillan, O.S.B.; Rev. Meinrad Miller, O.S.B.; Rev. Rodrigo Perissinotto, O.S.B.; Rev. Aaron Peters, O.S.B.; Bro. John Peto, O.S.B.; Bro. Maximilian Anderson, OSB; Bro. Angelus Atkinson, OSB; Bro. Florian Rumpza, OSB; Rev. Vinicius de Queiroz Rezende; Rev. Brendan Rolling, O.S.B.; Rev. Duane Roy, O.S.B.; Bro. Joseph Ryan, O.S.B.; Bro. Karel Soukup, O.S.B.; Rev. Benjamin Tremmel, O.S.B.; Rev. Michael Zoellner, O.S.B.; Rev. Maurice C. Haefling, O.S.B., Treas.; Bro. Leven Harton, O.S.B., Prior; Rev. Simon Baker, O.S.B., Junior Master; Bro. Jean-Marie Hogan, O.S.B., Novice; Rev. Gabriel Landis, O.S.B., Advancement Office; Rev. Thiago Ferreira Silva, O.S.B., Subprior of Brazil Community; Rev. Luke Turner, O.S.B., Benedictine Monk; Brs.: 10; Priests: 22

LAWRENCE

St. Conrad Friary - 745 Tennessee, Lawrence, KS 66044 t) 785-843-0188 dfreinert@gmail.com www.capuchins.org (Capuchins) Rev. John Cousins, OFM, Cap., Pst.; Rev. John Kolencherry, O.F.M.Cap., Par. Vicar; Rev. Barnabas Eichor, O.F.M.Cap., In Res.; Rev. Duane F. Reinert, O.F.M.Cap., In Res.; Rev. Michael Scully, O.F.M.Cap., In Res.; Priests: 5

NURSING / REHABILITATION / CONVALESCENCE / ELDERLY CARE [NUR]

ATCHISON

Dooley Center, Inc. (Benedictine Sisters of Mount St. Scholastica, Inc., Atchison, KS) - 801 S.8th St., Atchison, KS 66002 t) 913-360-6200 www.mountosb.org Nursing care facility for the aged/infirm members of this religious community. Sr. Esther Fangman, O.S.B., Prioress; Asstd. Annu.: 35; Staff: 41

OLATHE

Villa St. Francis Catholic Care Center, Inc. - 16600 W. 126th St., Olathe, KS 66062 t) 913-829-5201 contactus@villasf.org www.villasf.org Owned & operated by Villa St. Francis, Inc. skilled nursing care; memory care, long term care, respite care, rapid recovery with PT/OT speech therapy. Jackie Longston, Interim Admin.; Asstd. Annu.: 332; Staff: 329

OVERLAND PARK

Ascension Living St. Joseph Place - 11901 Rosewood St., Overland Park, KS 66209 t) 314-292-9308 ahscm-mission@ascension.org www.ascensionliving.org/ Legal entity: Carondelet Long Term Care Facilities, Inc. Ryan Endsley, COO; Asstd. Annu.: 178; Staff: 71

RETREAT HOUSES / RENEWAL CENTERS [RTR]

EASTON

Christ's Peace House of Prayer - 22131 Meagher Rd., Easton, KS 66020 t) 913-773-8255 info@christspeace.com www.christspeace.com Vincent Eimer, Dir.;

SHRINES [SHR]

MAYETTA

Our Lady of the Snows Oratory - Potawatomi Reservation, Mayetta, KS 66509; Mailing: 115 E. 5th St., c/o St. Dominic, Holton, KS 66436 t) 785-364-3262 jacocatholics.com Attended by: St. Dominic, Holton, KS. Rev. Jonathan Dizon, Chap.;

SPECIAL CARE FACILITIES [SPF]

KANSAS CITY

St. Joseph Adoption Referral Service, Inc. - 8160 Parallel Pkwy., Ste. 103, Kansas City, KS 66112 t) 913-299-5222; 800-752-1737 apeacefulblessing@yahoo.com www.catholicadoptionministry.org Sr. Dolora May, Dir.; Asstd. Annu.: 6; Staff: 6

An asterisk (*) denotes an organization that has established tax-exempt status directly with the IRS and is not covered by the USCCB Group Ruling.

Diocese of Kansas City-St. Joseph

(Dioecesis Kansanopolitanae Sancti Josephi)

MOST REVEREND JAMES V. JOHNSTON, JR., D.D., J.C.L.

Bishop of Kansas City-Saint Joseph; ordained June 9, 1990; appointed Bishop of Springfield-Cape Girardeau January 24, 2008; ordained March 31, 2008; appointed Bishop of Kansas City-Saint Joseph September 15, 2015; installed November 4, 2015. Chancery: 20 W. 9th St., Ste. 200, Kansas City, MO 64105. Mailing Address: P.O. Box 419037, Kansas City, MO 64141-6037. T: 816-756-1850; F: 816-756-2105; bishopsoffice@diocesekcsj.org.

Chancery: 20 W. 9th St., Ste. 200, Kansas City, MO 64105. T: 816-756-1850. Mailing Address: P.O. Box 419037, Kansas City, MO 64141-6037. www.kcsjcatholic.org

Square Miles 15,429.

Diocese of Kansas City Established September 10, 1880; Diocese of St. Joseph Established March 3, 1868. Redesignated Diocese of Kansas City-St. Joseph August 29, 1956.

Comprises the Counties of Andrew, Atchison, Bates, Buchanan, Caldwell, Carroll, Cass, Clay, Clinton, Daviess, DeKalb, Gentry, Grundy, Harrison, Henry, Holt, Jackson, Johnson, Lafayette, Livingston, Mercer, Nodaway, Platte, Ray, St. Clair, Vernon and Worth in the State of Missouri.

For legal titles of parishes and diocesan institutions, consult the Chancery Office.

STATISTICAL OVERVIEW

Personnel	
Bishop	1
Retired Bishops	1
Abbots	1
Priests: Diocesan Active in Diocese	70
Priests: Retired, Sick or Absent	28
Number of Diocesan Priests	98
Religious Priests in Diocese	33
Total Priests in your Diocese	131
Extern Priests in Diocese	2
Ordinations:	
Diocesan Priests	1
Transitional Deacons	1
Permanent Deacons	16
Permanent Deacons in Diocese	84
Total Brothers	20
Total Sisters	133
Parishes	
Parishes	86
With Resident Pastor:	
Resident Diocesan Priests	63
Resident Religious Priests	9
Without Resident Pastor:	
Administered by Priests	13
Administered by Lay People	1
Missions	9
Closed Parishes	1
Professional Ministry Personnel:	
Sisters	3
Lay Ministers	268
Welfare	
Homes for the Aged	10
Total Assisted	7,783
Day Care Centers	8
Total Assisted	433
Special Centers for Social Services	8
Total Assisted	138,242
Residential Care of Disabled	1
Total Assisted	1,022
Other Institutions	1
Total Assisted	423
Educational	
Seminaries, Diocesan	1
Students from This Diocese	7
Students from Other Dioceses	26
Diocesan Students in Other Seminaries	9
Total Seminarians	16
Colleges and Universities	2
Total Students	5,032
High Schools, Diocesan and Parish	3
Total Students	946
High Schools, Private	4
Total Students	2,050
Elementary Schools, Diocesan and Parish	23
Total Students	5,349
Elementary Schools, Private	1
Total Students	273
Catechesis/Religious Education:	
High School Students	1,223
Elementary Students	3,213
Total Students under Catholic Instruction	18,102
Teachers in Diocese:	
Priests	5
Sisters	7
Lay Teachers	1,105
Vital Statistics	
Receptions into the Church:	
Infant Baptism Totals	1,657
Minor Baptism Totals	172
Adult Baptism Totals	130
Received into Full Communion	256
First Communions	1,607
Confirmations	1,518
Marriages:	
Catholic	344
Interfaith	154
Total Marriages	498
Deaths	1,019
Total Catholic Population	120,756
Total Population	1,583,646

LEADERSHIP

Chancery - t) 816-756-1850
Vicar General - Chancellor & Moderator of the Curia - Very Rev. Kenneth A. Riley;
Vicar General - Vicar for Clergy - Very Rev. Charles N. Rowe;
Finance Officer - Angela E. Laville;
Judicial Vicar - Very Rev. Kenneth A. Riley;
Presbyteral Council - Rev. Matthew Brumleve, Chair; Rev. Andres Moreno, Vice Chm.; Rev. Gabriel Lickteig, Sec./Treas.;

OFFICES AND DIRECTORS

Archivist - Zachary Daughtrey, Archivist;
Bright Futures Fund - Jeremy Lillig, Exec. Dir.;
Building Commission - Dcn. Michael Lewis, Chair;
Catholic Charities Foundation - t) 816-221-4377 Karen Noel, CEO;
Catholic Charities of Kansas City-St. Joseph, Inc. - t) 816-221-4377 Karen Noel, CEO; Sunny Jones, COO;
Catholic Community Foundation - Jeremy Lillig, Exec. Dir.;
Catholic Healthcare Office - John F. Morris, Dir.;
Catholic Key - The Magazine of the Diocese of Kansas City-St. Joseph - Ashlie Hand, Editor;
Cemeteries (Catholic Cemeteries Associated, Diocese of Kansas City-St. Joseph, Inc.) - Stephen Reyes, Gen. Mgr.; Charlie Passatino, Mng. Partner; Steve Pierce, Mng. Partner;
College Campus Ministry - Abigail Byron-Goslin, Dir.;
Communications - Ashlie Hand, Dir.; Megan Marley, Digital/Social Media Coord.;
Consecrated Life Office - Sr. Connie Boulch, O.S.F., Dir.;
Construction Management Office/Building Commission - Martha C. Kauffman, Construction Mgr.;
Diocesan Special Events Office - Dcn. Ralph L. Wehner, Coord.;
Disability & Deaf Services - Lisa Wagner-Carollo, Coord.;
Divine Worship - Rev. Paul Turner, Dir.; Lorie Sage, Office Mgr.; Mario Pearson, Music Coord.;
Domestic Church & Discipleship - Dino Durando, Dir.;
Ecumenical/Interreligious Commission - Teresa Albright, Chair;
Endowment Trust Fund for Catholic Education - Jeremy Lillig, Exec. Dir.;
Facilities and Real Estate Management - Bill Gagnon, Dir.;
Family Life Office - Dino Durando, Dir.;
Finance Council - Most Rev. James V. Johnston Jr., Presider; Angela E. Laville;
Finance Office - Angela E. Laville, Finance Officer; Monica Adams, Internal Auditor; Donna Lewis, Accounting Mgr.;
General Counsel - Patrick Miller;
Hispanic Ministry - Leyden Rovelo-Krull, Dir.;
Human Resources - Bob Roper, Dir.; Carol Anne Hoppins, HR Mgr.;
Human Rights Office - Bill Francis, Dir.;
Insurance Office - Monica Adams, Risk Mgr.;
Legion of Mary - Rev. Alex Kreidler, Chap.;
Office of Child and Youth Protection - Carrie Cooper, Dir.; Whitney True-Francis, Victim Assistance Coord.; Don Stubbings, Safe Environment Prog. Coord.;
Permanent Diaconate - Dcn. Paul Muller, Dir.;
Priestly Life and Ministry - Rev. David L. Holloway, Dir.; Rev. Justin E. Hoye, Vicar for Priests;
Priests' Pension Plan - Very Rev. Charles N. Rowe, Chair;
Priests' Purgatorial Society - Very Rev. Charles N. Rowe;
Propagation of the Faith - Very Rev. Charles N. Rowe, Dir.;
Respect Life Office - Bill Francis, Dir.;
School Office - Karen Kroh, Supt.;
Stewardship and Development - Jeremy Lillig, Exec. Dir.; Ken Kremer, Dir.; Theresa Schuman, Dir.;
Tribunal - t) 816-756-1850 tribunal@diocesekcsj.org Dcn. Julio Lara, Dir. & Auditor; Very Rev. Kenneth A. Riley, Judicial Vicar;
Vocation Office - Rev. Adam Johnson, Dir., Seminarians; Rev. Andrew Kleine, Promoter;
Youth Office - Michael Nations, Dir.;

ORGANIZATIONS

Journey to Bethany - Jennifer Prusa, Dir.;

MISCELLANEOUS / OTHER OFFICES

Ombudsman:Sexual Abuse - c) 816-812-2500 crayon@ombudsmankcsj.org Joseph Crayon;

PARISHES, MISSIONS, AND CLERGY

STATE OF MISSOURI

BELTON

St. Sabina Catholic Church, Belton - 700 Trevis Ave., Belton, MO 64012 t) 816-331-4713 frjeff@stsabinaparish.org www.stsabinaparish.org Rev. M. Jeffrey Stephan, Pst.; Dcn. Michael Gates; CRP Stds.: 135

BETHANY

Blessed Sacrament - 1208 S. 25th St., Bethany, MO 64424; Mailing: P.O. Box 166, Bethany, MO 64424 t) 660-425-8160 kevdrew11@yahoo.com Rev. Devasahayam Gudime, Pst.;

BLUE SPRINGS

St. John LaLande Catholic Church, Blue Springs, MO - 805 N.W. R.D. Mize Rd., Blue Springs, MO 64015 t) 816-229-3378 parishoffice@sjlparish.org www.stjohnlalande.com Rev. Sean P. McCaffery, Pst.; Dcn. Shane Voyles; Dcn. Richard Isaacks; CRP Stds.: 133

St. John LaLande School - (Grades PreSchool-8) 801 N.W. R.D. Mize Rd., Blue Springs, MO 64015 t) 816-228-5895 smartin@sjlparish.org www.stjohnlalandeschool.com Susan Martin, Prin.; Stds.: 227; Lay Tchrs.: 13

St. John LaLande Early Childhood Learning Academy - 801 N.W. R.D. Mize Rd., Blue Springs, MO 64015 t) 816-229-8343 mmcanerney@sjlparish.org Education for children 6 weeks through PreK. Molly McAnerney, Dir.;

St. Robert Bellarmine - 4313 S.W. State Rte. 7, Blue Springs, MO 64014-5701 t) 816-229-5168; 816-229-3552 rena@srbcatholic.org; susan@srbcatholic.org www.srbcatholic.org Rev. Richard D. Rocha, Pst.; Dcn. Joseph Zagar; CRP Stds.: 101

BUCKNER

Church of the Santa Fe - 231 S. Sibley St., Buckner, MO 64016-0317; Mailing: PO Box 317, Buckner, MO 64016-0317 t) 660-259-3043 paterursi@yahoo.com Rev. Jayson Becker, Par. Admin.;

BUTLER

St. Patrick's - 400 W. Nursery St., Butler, MO 64730 t) 660-679-4482 stpatrickbutler@embarqmail.com Rev. Jason Koch, Pst.; CRP Stds.: 15

CAMERON

St. Munchin - 301 N. Cedar St., Cameron, MO 64429 t) 816-632-2768 stmunchinparish@gmail.com www.munchin.net Rev. Thomas K. Ludwig, Pst.; Mary Morgan, DRE; CRP Stds.: 37

St. Aloysius - 301 S. Water, Maysville, MO 64469; Mailing: 301 N. Cedar, Cameron, MO 64429 t) (816) 632-2768 (St Munchin)

CARROLLTON

St. Mary's - 211 E. Shanklin St., Carrollton, MO 64633 t) 660-542-1259 Rev. J. Kenneth Criqui, Pst.; Dcn. Gary Kappler; CRP Stds.: 55

· **Sacred Heart** - 403 S. Walnut, Norborne, MO 64668

CHILLICOTHE

St. Columban - 1111 Trenton St., Chillicothe, MO 64601-1499 t) 660-646-0190 stcolumbanonline.org Rev. Ryan Koster, Pst.;

Bishop Hogan Memorial School - (Grades PreSchool-8) 1114 Trenton St., Chillicothe, MO 64601 t) 660-646-0705 kidsareus@bishophogan.org www.bishophogan.org Pam Brobst, Prin.; Stds.: 157; Lay Tchrs.: 10

CLINTON

Holy Rosary - 610 S. 4th St., Clinton, MO 64735 t) 660-885-4523 www.trumanlakecatholic.com/ Rev. James Taranto, Pst.; Dcn. Steven Carter;

Holy Rosary School - 400 E. Wilson, Clinton, MO 64735 t) 660-885-4412 hrsecretary@hrclinton.net Zach Maxon, Prin.;

St. Catherine's - 605 Walnut St., Osceola, MO 64776; Mailing: 610 S. 4th, Clinton, MO 64735 www.trumanlakecatholic.com

St. Bartholomew - 504 E. Benton, Windsor, MO 65360; Mailing: 610 S. 4th, Clinton, MO 64735 trumanlakecatholic.com

CONCEPTION JUNCTION

St Columba Catholic Church Conception Junction, MO - 311 Roosevelt St., Conception Junction, MO 64434 t) 660-944-2301 Rev. Peter Ullrich, O.S.B., Pst.; CRP Stds.: 86

EASTON

St. Joseph's - 107 S. Shortridge, Easton, MO 64443; Mailing: P.O. Box 197, Easton, MO 64443 t) 816-473-2011 baskets105@gmail.com; stjosepheaston@gmail.com stjosepheaston.org Rev. Eric Schneider, Admin.; Christine Ottinger, Music Min.;

EXCELSIOR SPRINGS

St. Ann - 1503 Tracy Ave., Excelsior Springs, MO 64024 t) 816-630-6659 x3 c) 417-257-9401 (Dcn Bandy); 816-810-5035 (Fr Drew) stannparishoffice@gmail.com www.stanncatholicchurch.net Rev. Kevin Drew, Pst.; Dcn. George "Alan" Bandy; CRP Stds.: 49

GALLATIN

Mary Immaculate - 409 S. Main, Gallatin, MO 64640; Mailing: P.O. Box 188, Hamilton, MO 64644-0188 t) 660-663-2146 (Office); 816-583-1117 (Rectory) shmichurch@gmail.com www.maryimmaculategallatin.org Rev. Thomas W. Hermes, Pst.; Mary Jarboe, DRE; Sarah Clark, Bus. Mgr.; CRP Stds.: 6

GLADSTONE

St. Andrew the Apostle - 6415 NE Antioch Rd., Gladstone, MO 64119 t) 816-454-7377 x311; 816-453-2089 spalmarine@sataps.com; lbuckner@sataps.com www.sataps.com Rev. Vincent M. Rogers, Pst.; Rev. Garrett King, Assoc. Pst.; Dcn. Brian Buckner; CRP Stds.: 191

St. Andrew the Apostle School - (Grades PreK-8) Tony Calcara, Prin.;

GRANDVIEW

Coronation of Our Lady - 13000 Bennington Ave., Grandview, MO 64030 t) 816-761-8811 office.coronation@gmail.com www.coronationofourlady.com Rev. Adam Haake, Pst.; Dcn. Ralph Joseph McNeal, Pst. Assoc.; Dcn. Michael Dennis; CRP Stds.: 20

HAMILTON

Sacred Heart - 205 E. Middle St., Hamilton, MO 64644; Mailing: PO Box 188, Hamilton, MO 64644-0188 t) 816-583-1117 (Rectory); 660-663-2146 (Office) shmichurch@gmail.com www.sacredheart-hamilton.org Rev. Thomas W. Hermes, Pst.; Sabrina Banks, DRE; Sarah Clark, Bus. Mgr.; CRP Stds.: 12

HARRISONVILLE

Our Lady of Lourdes Catholic Church, Harrisonville - 2700 E. Mechanic, Harrisonville, MO 64701 t) 816-380-5744 info@ollhv.org www.ollhv.org Rev. Daniel Reardon, Pst.; CRP Stds.: 31

Holy Trinity Catholic Church, Urich - 1372 N.W. Graham Rd., Urich, MO 64788; Mailing: 2700 E. Mechanic St., Harrisonville, MO 64701

HIGGINSVILLE

St. Mary's - 401 W. Broadway, Higginsville, MO 64037 t) 660-584-3038 Rev. Thomas J. D. Hawkins, Pst.;

HOLDEN

St. Patrick's - 703 S. Olive St., Holden, MO 64040-1443; Mailing: 2103 Lexington Rd., St. Bridget Catholic Church, Pleasant Hill, MO 64080 t) 816-540-4563 www.stpatrickholden.org Betsy Bentsen, DRE; Rev. Curt Vogel, Pst.; CRP Stds.: 7

HURLINGEN

Seven Dolors - 12750 N.E. Hurlingen Rd., Hurlingen, MO 64443; Mailing: P.O. Box 197, Easton, MO 64443 t) (816) 473-2011 stjosepheaston@gmail.com; mbartulica@hotmail.com Rev. Matthew Bartulica, Pst.;

INDEPENDENCE

St. Ann's - 10113 E. Lexington Ave., Independence, MO 64053 t) 816-252-1160 saintanns64053@yahoo.com Rev. Kendall Ketterlin, Par. Admin.;

St. Joseph the Worker - 2200 N. Blue Mills Rd., Independence, MO 64058 t) 816-796-6877 pastor@sjtw.us www.sjtw.us Rev. Kendall Ketterlin, Par. Admin.; CRP Stds.: 3

St. Mark - 3736 S. Lees Summit Rd., Independence, MO 64055 t) 816-373-2600 jarthur@stmarksparish.com; jpowers@stmarksparish.com www.stmarksparish.com Rev. Joseph Powers, Pst.; Dcn. Kenneth Fuenfhausen, Dir., Youth Ministry; CRP Stds.: 126

St. Mary's - 600 N. Liberty St., Independence, MO 64050 t) 816-252-0121 pastor@saintmarysparish.org; smoffice@saintmarysparish.org www.saintmarysparish.org Rev. Kendall Ketterlin, Par. Admin.; Janice McQuillan, DRE; CRP Stds.: 9

Nativity of Mary Parish - 10017 E. 36th Ter. S., Independence, MO 64052 t) 816-353-2184 parish@nativityofmary.org nativityofmary.org Rev. Robert Stone, Pst.;

Nativity of Mary Parish School - (Grades PreK-8) 10021 E. 36th Ter. S., Independence, MO 64052 t) 816-353-0284 school@nativityofmary.org www.nativityofmary.org Dr. Lisa Lauck, Prin.;

KANSAS CITY

Cathedral of Immaculate Conception - 416 W. 12th St., Kansas City, MO 64105 t) 816-842-0416 info@kcgolddome.org kcgolddome.org/ Rev. Paul Turner, Pst.; Dcn. Julio Lara; Dcn. Stephen W. Livingston; Dcn. Jim Olshefski;

St. Anthony - 318 Benton Blvd., Kansas City, MO 64124 t) 816-231-5445 stanthony318@gmail.com www.stanthonykc.org Rev. Andres Moreno, Pst.; Dcn. Thomas D. Powell; Dcn. Juan Garcia; Dcn. Julio Lara; Dcn. Jordan Schiele; CRP Stds.: 85

St. Bernadette Catholic Church - 9020 E. 51st Ter., Kansas City, MO 64133 t) 816-356-3700 stbkcmo@gmail.com www.stbernadettekcmo.org Rev. Robert Stone, Pst.; CRP Stds.: 5

St. Catherine of Siena - 4101 E. 105th Ter., Kansas City, MO 64137-1649 t) 816-761-5483 anitaosb@saintcatherine.com www.saintcatherine.com Rev. Justin E. Hoye, Pst.; Dcn. David Healy;

St Charles Borromeo Catholic Church Kansas City - 900 N.E. Shady Lane Dr., Kansas City, MO 64118-4742 t) 816-436-0880 bharmon-vaughan@stcharleskc.com; frsthomas@stcharleskc.com www.stcharleskc.com Rev. Sunoj Thomas, O.S.B., Pst.; Dcn. Joseph Whiston; Dcn. Victor Quiason;

St. Charles Borromeo School - (Grades PreSchool-8) 804 N.E. Shady Lane Dr., Oakview, MO 64118 t) 816-436-1009 cstracener@stcharleskc.com borromeoacademy.com Stds.: 218; Lay Tchrs.: 17

Christ the King - 8510 Wornall Rd., Kansas City, MO 64114 t) 816-363-4888 justinbolson1987@gmail.com; frlock@ctkkcmo.org www.ctkkcmo.org Rev. Gregory J. Lockwood, Pst.; Rev. Louis Farley, Par. Vicar; Susan Dietchman, DRE; Justin Olson, RCIA Coord.;

Church of the Holy Martyrs - 7801 Paseo Blvd., Kansas City, MO 64131 t) 816-333-3214 c) 832-651-7401 giaoxukcmo.org The Vietnamese Holy Martyrs parish in Kansas City: Giáo Xứ Các Thánh Tử Đạo Việt Nam Kansas City Rev. Francis Hau Pham, C.Ss.R., Pst.; Rev. Thanh Nguyen, C.Ss.R., Par. Vicar; Dcn. Paul H Nguyen; Dcn. Doan Tran; Dcn. Diem Nguyen; CRP Stds.: 250

St. Elizabeth - 2 E. 75th St., Kansas City, MO 64114 t) 816-523-2405 info@stekc.org www.stekc.org Rev. Gregory Haskamp, Pst.; Dcn. Michael McLean, Pst. Assoc.; CRP Stds.: 21

St. Elizabeth's School - (Grades PreSchool-8) 14 W. 75th St., Kansas City, MO 64114 t) 816-523-7100 mriley@stekcschool.org stekcschool.org Michael Riley, Prin.; Stds.: 417; Lay Tchrs.: 31

St. Francis Xavier - 1001 E. 52 St., Kansas City, MO 64110 t) 816-523-5115 parish@sfx-kc.org www.sfx-kc.org Rev. James N. Caime, S.J., Pst.; Ann Sheridan, Pst. Admin.; Mariann Mccormally, DRE;

St. Gabriel Archangel - 4737 N. Cleveland Ave., Kansas City, MO 64117 t) 816-453-1183 x200 www.stgabrielskc.net Rev. Alex Kreidler, Pst.; Dcn. Daniel Brink; CRP Stds.: 26

St. Gabriel Archangel School - (Grades K-8) t) 816-453-4443 www.stgabrielskc.com/ Stacey Bresette, Prin.; Stds.: 120; Lay Tchrs.: 9

Early Childhood Learning Center - t) (816) 453-4443

Guardian Angels - 1310 Westport Rd., Kansas City, MO 64111 t) 816-931-4351 csaballo@guardianangelskc.org; finance@guardianangelskc.org guardianangelskc.org/ Rev. Carlito Saballo, S.O.L.T., Par. Admin.; Dcn. John Purk;

Holy Cross - 5106 St. John Ave., Kansas City, MO 64123 t) 816-231-4845 holycrosskc@juno.com www.holycrosskcmo.org Rev. Olvin Giron, Pst.; Dcn. Daniel Esteban; CRP Stds.: 40

Holy Family - 919 N.E. 96th St., Kansas City, MO 64155 t) 816-436-9200 www.holyfamily.com Rev. Philip Egan, Pst.; CRP Stds.: 312

Holy Rosary - 911 Missouri Ave., Kansas City, MO 64106 t) 816-842-5440 www.hrkcmo.org Rev. Abner Marcelo Ables Jr., C.S., Pst.; Rev. Ramiro Sanchez Chan, C.S., In Res.;

St. James - 3909 Harrison St., Kansas City, MO 64110 t) 816-561-8512 parish@stjkc.org www.stjkc.org Rev. Donald P. Farnan, Pst.; Rev. Garry Richmeier, C.PP.S., Sacramental Min.; CRP Stds.: 23

St. John Francis Regis - 8941 James A. Reed Rd., Kansas City, MO 64138 t) 816-761-1608 cmelchior@regischurch.org www.stregischurch.com Rev. Thomas Holder, Par. Admin.; Rev. Emmanuel Garduno Lopez, Par. Vicar; Dcn. Samuel Adams; Dcn. Kenneth Albers; Dcn. Robert Falke; CRP Stds.: 81

St. John Francis Regis School - (Grades PreK-8) t) 816-763-5837 www.regisacademy.org Robin Fisher, Prin.; Stds.: 152; Lay Tchrs.: 15

St. Louis Catholic Church - 5930 Swope Pkwy., Kansas City, MO 64130 t) 816-444-6535 saintlouiskcmo@yahoo.com Rev. Carlito Saballo, S.O.L.T., Pst.; Dcn. John Purk;

St. Monica - 1616 Paseo Blvd., Kansas City, MO 64108; Mailing: 1400 E. 17th St., Kansas City, MO 64108 t) 816-471-3696 stmonica1616kc@hotmail.com Rev. Leonard Gicheru, Par. Admin.; Dcn. Darwin Dupree; Dcn. Kenneth Greene;

Oratory of Old St. Patrick (Institute of Christ the King) - 806 Cherry St., Kansas City, MO 64106; Mailing: P.O. Box 414237, Kansas City, MO 64141-4237 t) 816-931-5612 oldstpatrick@institute-christ-king.org www.institute-christ-king.org/kansascity/ Traditional Latin Mass Community. Rev. Canon Andrew Todd, ICRSS, Rector;

Our Lady of Good Counsel - 3934 Washington, Kansas City, MO 64111-2904 t) 816-561-0400 www.goodcounselkc.org/ Rev. Adam Johnson, Pst.; Rev. Andrew Mattingly, Assoc. Pst.; Dcn. Ralph L. Wehner; Michael Mills, Liturgy Dir.; Mark Sappington, Parish Life Coord.; Hope Piernick, Bus. Mgr.;

Our Lady of Peace - 1029 Bennington Ave., Kansas City, MO 64126-2299 t) 816-231-0953 frandres@stanthonykc.org; olopkcmo2014@gmail.com www.ourladyofpeacekc.org Rev. Andres Moreno, Par. Admin.; CRP Stds.: 20

Our Lady of Perpetual Help - 3333 Broadway Blvd., Kansas City, MO 64111 t) 816-561-3771 info@olphkc.org; pmcdonald@olphkc.org www.redemptoristkc.org/ Rev. Gary Ziuraitis, C.Ss.R., Pst.; Rev. Andrew Thompson, C.Ss.R., Assoc. Pst.; Rev. James White, C.Ss.R., Local Superior; Bro. William Cloughley, C.Ss.R., In Res.; Rev. Francis Thomas Danielsen, C.Ss.R., In Res.; Rev. Michael McAndrew, C.Ss.R., In Res.; Rev. Thanh Nguyen, C.Ss.R., In Res.; Rev. Francis Hau Pham, C.Ss.R., In Res.; Rev. Gregory Schmitt, C.Ss.R., In Res.; CRP Stds.: 25

Our Lady of Sorrows - 2552 Gillham Rd., Kansas City, MO 64108 t) 816-421-2112 oloskc@oloskc.org oloskc.org Dcn. Tyrone Gutierrez, Admin.;

St. Patrick - 1357 N.E. 42nd Ter., Kansas City, MO 64116 t) 816-453-0971 info@stpatrickkc.com www.saintpatrickkc.com Rev. Matthew Brumleve, Pst.; Dcn. Jim Koger, Pst. Assoc.; Dcn. Michael Lewis, Pst. Assoc.; CRP Stds.: 18

St. Patrick School - (Grades PreK-8) 1401 N.E. 42nd Ter., Kansas City, MO 64116 kmonaghan@stpatrickkc.com stpatrickkc.com Kaci Monaghan, Prin.; Stds.: 154; Lay Tchrs.: 14

St. Peter's - 701 E. Meyer Blvd., Kansas City, MO 64131; Mailing: 815 E. Meyer Blvd., Kansas City, MO 64131 t) 816-363-2320 communications@stpeterskc.org www.stpkc.org Rev. Matthew Rotert, Pst.; CRP Stds.: 9

St. Peter's School - (Grades PreK-8) 6400 Charlotte St., Kansas City, MO 64131 t) 816-523-4899 ameyer@stpeterskc.org; mstewart@stpeterskc.org Angie Meyer, Prin.; Mary Stewart, Vice Prin.;

Sacred Heart-Guadalupe - 2544 Madison Ave., Kansas City, MO 64108 t) 816-842-6146 x22 (Admin.); 816-599-7242 x21 (DRI) ramonaarroyo@sacredheartguadalupe.org; frfelipes@sacredheartguadalupe.org www.sacredheartguadalupe.org Shrine: 901 Avenida Cesar E Chavez, Kansas City, MO 64108. Rev. Luis Felipe Suarez, Par. Vicar; Ramona Arroyo, DRE; Araceli Bernardino, Bus. Mgr.; Rev. Paul Turner, Par. Admin.; CRP Stds.: 30

St. Therese Little Flower - 5814 Euclid Ave., Kansas City, MO 64130 t) 816-444-5406 dfarnan@stlfkc.org; busmgr@stlfkc.org www.stlfkc.org Rev. Donald P. Farnan, Par. Admin.; CRP Stds.: 8

St. Therese Parish - 7207 Hwy. 9, N.W., Kansas City, MO 64152 t) 816-741-5400 x219 (RE); 816-741-2800 (Church); 816-741-5400 (School); 816-746-1500 (Early Education) jdavis@sttheresenorth.org; sttheresenorth@sttheresenorth.org www.sttheresenorth.org Rev. Joseph Cisetti, Pst.; Rev. Randolph Sly, Assoc. Pst.; Dcn. Rick Boyle; Dcn. Tony Zimmerman; Dcn. Scott McKellar, Pst. Assoc.; Sam Ford, Youth Min.; Jennifer Davis, DRE; Dcn. Doug Warrens, RCIA Coord.; CRP Stds.: 260

St. Therese Parish School - (Grades K-8) 7277 Hwy. 9, N.W., Kansas City, MO 64152 ahogan@sttheresenorth.org www.saintthereseschool.org Amy Hogan, Prin.; Kathy Hadel-Racy, Vice Prin.; Elizabeth Ann Sharp, Vice Prin.; Stds.: 636; Lay Tchrs.: 39

St. Thomas More - 11822 Holmes Rd., Kansas City, MO 64131 t) 816-942-2492 information@stmkc.com stmkc.com Rev. Justin E. Hoye, Pst.; Rev. Andrew Kleine, Par. Vicar; Rev. Paul Sappington, In Res.; Dcn. Benjamin Fenlon; CRP Stds.: 4

St. Thomas More School - (Grades PreK-8) 11800 Holmes Rd., Kansas City, MO 64131 t) 816-942-5581 crosthwait_linda@stmcyclones.org www.stmkcschool.org Linda Crosthwait, Prin.; Meredith Blair, Vice Prin.; Stds.: 463; Sr. Tchrs.: 1; Lay Tchrs.: 41

Visitation of the Blessed Virgin Mary - 5141 Main St., Kansas City, MO 64112 t) 816-753-7422 joni@church.visitation.org www.visitation.org Rev. Msgr. Bradley S. Offutt, Pst.; CRP Stds.: 32

Visitation of the Blessed Virgin Mary School - (Grades K-8) 5134 Baltimore Ave., Kansas City, MO 64112 t) 816-531-6200 mkallman@school.visitation.org www.visitationschoolkc.org/ Mary Kallman, Prin.; Stds.: 450; Lay Tchrs.: 30

KEARNEY

Church of the Annunciation - 701 N. Jefferson, Kearney, MO 64060-0599; Mailing: P.O. Box 599, Kearney, MO 64060-0599 t) 816-628-5030 annunciation.kearney@gmail.com annunciationkearney.com Rev. Ravindranath Jose Talari (India), Par. Admin.; CRP Stds.: 129

LEES SUMMIT

Holy Spirit - 1800 S.W. State Rte. 150, Lees Summit, MO 64082 t) 816-537-6990 parish@holyspiritmo.org www.holyspiritmo.org Rev. Joseph M. Sharbel, Pst.; Dcn. Tyrone Gutierrez; Dcn. Richard Akins; Dcn. Fred Lange; Dcn. Don Schmidt; CRP Stds.: 131

St. Margaret of Scotland Catholic Church - 777 N.E. Blackwell Rd., Lees Summit, MO 64086 t) 816-246-6800 business.manager@stmos.org; jsharbel@stmos.org www.stmos.org Rev. Joseph M. Sharbel, Pst.; Rev. Samuel Miloscia, Par. Vicar; Dcn. David Rennicke, Pst. Assoc.; Cristen M Huntz, Bus. Mgr.; Dcn. Paul Muller;

Our Lady of the Presentation - 130 N.W. Murray Rd., Lees Summit, MO 64081 t) 816-251-1100 clauderdale@olpls.org www.olpls.org Rev. Thomas Holder, Pst.; Rev. Angel Randolfo Lemus, Par. Vicar; Dcn. Keith Hoffman; Dcn. Dave Talken; CRP Stds.: 251

Our Lady of the Presentation School - -8) 150 N.W. Murray Rd., Lees Summit, MO 64081 t) 816-251-1150 jbriggs@olpls.org Marianne Organ, Prin.;

Our Lady of the Presentation Early Childhood Center - 100 S.W. Murray Rd., Lee's Summit, MO 64081 t) 816-251-1140 ckoob@olpls.org Cathy Koob, Dir.;

LEXINGTON

Immaculate Conception - 107 N. 18th St., Lexington, MO 64067 t) 660-259-3043 iccc@embarqmail.com Rev. Jayson Becker, Par. Admin.;

LIBERTY

St. James - 309 S. Stewart Rd., Liberty, MO 64068 t) 816-781-4343 kirsten.maggi@stjames-liberty.org www.stjames-liberty.org Rev. Michael Roach, Pst.; Rev. Michael Volkmer, C.PP.S., In Res.; Dcn. Charles Koesterer; CRP Stds.: 286

St. James School - (Grades PreK-8) t) 816-781-4428 jennifer.smith@stjames-school.org www.stjames-school.org Jennifer Scanlon-Smith, Prin.; Stds.: 323; Lay Tchrs.: 23

MARYVILLE

St. Gregory Barbarigo - 333 S. Davis St., Maryville, MO 64468 t) 660-582-3833 rankindevinsg@gmail.com www.stgregorysmaryville.org Rev. Albert Bruecken, O.S.B., Pst.;

St. Gregory Barbarigo School - (Grades PreK-8) 315 S. Davis St., Maryville, MO 64468 t) 660-582-2462 kellyq@stgregorysschool.org; kcoleman@stgregorysschool.org www.stgregorysschool.org Karma Coleman, Prin.;

MONTROSE

Immaculate Conception - 606 Kansas Ave., Montrose, MO 64770-9601 t) 660-693-4651 jkoch1224@gmail.com; theresam.iccmo@embarqmail.com Rev. Jason Koch, Pst.; CRP Stds.: 35

St. Mary School - (Grades PreK-8) 608 Kansas Ave., Montrose, MO 64770 t) 660-693-4502 Angela Steward, Prin.;

NEVADA

St. Mary - 330 N. Main St., Nevada, MO 64772 t) 417-667-7517 abcdhab@gmail.com Rev. Peter M. Savidge, Pst.; Colleen Haberkorn, DRE; Amanda Prine, Dir.;

St. Mary's Early Childhood Center -

St. Bridget's - 9th & E. Walnut St., Rich Hill, MO 64779

OAK GROVE

St. Jude the Apostle - 2001 S. Broadway, Oak Grove, MO 64075; Mailing: P.O. Box 590, Oak Grove, MO 64075 t) 816-690-3165 contact@stjudeoakgrove.com www.stjudeoakgrove.org Rev. Bryan C. Amthor, Pst.; CRP Stds.: 30

ODESSA

St. George - 716 S. Third, Odessa, MO 64076 t) 816-230-4127; 816-633-7475 stgeorgeodessamo.org Rev. Bryan C. Amthor, Admin.; CRP Stds.: 40

PARNELL

St. Joseph's - 411 S. Main, Parnell, MO 64475; Mailing: P.O. Box 78, Parnell, MO 64475 t) 660-986-3305 Rev. Peter Ullrich, O.S.B., Pst.; CRP Stds.: 44

PLATTE CITY

Twelve Apostles Parish - 17900 Humphrey's Rd., Platte City, MO 64079; Mailing: 407 Cherry St., Weston, MO 64098 t) 816-640-2206 swishon@ht12.org www.twelveapostlescatholic.org Rev. Steven C. Rogers, Pst.; CRP Stds.: 85

PLATTSBURG

St. Ann's - 700 W. Maple St., Plattsburg, MO 64477 t) 816-539-2634 stannplattsburg@gmail.com stannplattsburg.org Rev. Eric Schneider, Pst.; CRP Stds.: 58

PLEASANT HILL

St. Bridget Catholic Church, Pleasant Hill - 2103 N. Lexington, Pleasant Hill, MO 64080 t) 816-540-4563 stbridgetparish@stbridgetph.org stbridgetph.weconnect.com Rev. Curt Vogel, Pst.; Betsy Bentsen, DRE; Timothy Long, Bus. Mgr.; Dcn. Corey Morgan; CRP Stds.: 14

RAYTOWN

Our Lady of Lourdes - 7009 Blue Ridge Blvd., Raytown, MO 64133; Mailing: 7049 Blue Ridge Blvd, Raytown, MO 64133 t) 816-353-2380 office@ollraytown.com www.ollraytown.com Rev. Adam Haake, Pst.; Wanda Demoss, Sr. Damiana; Dcn. Richard Gross;

RICHMOND

Immaculate Conception - 602 S. Camden, Richmond, MO 64085 t) 816-776-6870 Rev. Kevin Drew, Pst.; CRP Stds.: 13

SAVANNAH

St. Rose of Lima - 707 S. Hall Ave., Savannah, MO 64485 t) 816-324-5700 saintroseparishoffice@gmail.com; fr.barlett@yahoo.com www.saintroseoflima.org/ Rev. Joshua Barlett, Pst.; Ashleigh Eisiminger, DRE; CRP Stds.: 65

St. Patrick - 303 Grand Ave., Forest City, MO 64451; Mailing: 707 S Hall Ave, Savannah, MO 64485

SMITHVILLE

Good Shepherd Catholic Church - 18601 N. 169 Hwy., Smithville, MO 64089 t) 816-532-4344 gsccmo@gmail.com www.gsccmo.org Rev. Terrell M. Finnell, Pst.; Dcn. Michael Koile; Dcn. John Wichmann; CRP Stds.: 85

ST. JOSEPH

Cathedral of St. Joseph - 519 N. 10th St., St. Joseph, MO 64501 t) 816-232-7763 ecobb@cathedralsj.org www.cathedralsj.org Rev. Stephen Hansen, Pst.; Rev. Benjamin Armentrout, Par. Vicar; Joshua Fultz; CRP Stds.: 29

Co-Cathedral of St. Joseph School - (Grades PreK-8) t) 816-232-8486 cneumayr@cathedralsj.org Catherine Neumayr, Prin.;

St. Gianna Early Childhood Center - 509 N. 9th St., St. Joseph, MO 64501 t) 816-233-9794 lpuett@cathedralsj.org Lisa Puett, Dir.;

Saint Francis Xavier Catholic Church - 2618 Seneca St., St. Joseph, MO 64507 t) 816-232-8449 rwhite@sfxstjoe.com www.sfxstjoe.com Rev. Aloys Ebach, C.PP.S., Par. Admin.; Rev. Lau Pham, C.PP.S., Par. Vicar; Rev. William Walter, C.PP.S., In Res.; CRP Stds.: 26

St. Francis Xavier School - (Grades PreK-8) 2614 Seneca St., St. Joseph, MO 64507 t) 816-232-4911 admissions@sfxstjoe.com www.stfranstjo.com Darin Pollard, Prin.;

St. James - 5814 King Hill Ave, St. Joseph, MO 64504 t) 816-238-0853 fgirard@saintjamessaintjoseph.org; fgirard@saintjamescatholic.church www.saintjamescatholic.church Rev. Joseph Totton, Pst.; CRP Stds.: 29

St. James School - (Grades PreSchool-8) 120 Michigan Ave., St. Joseph, MO 64504 t) 816-238-0281 James Hosler, Dean; Stds.: 100; Lay Tchrs.: 11

St. Mary Catholic Church - 1606 N. 2nd St., St. Joseph, MO 64505 t) 816-279-1154 email.stmary@gmail.com Rev. Stephen Hansen, Pst.; Rev. Benjamin Armentrout, Par. Vicar; CRP Stds.: 6

Our Lady of Guadalupe - 4503 Frederick Blvd., St. Joseph, MO 64506 t) 816-232-2847 cmalewski@olog.org; kpowers@olog.org www.olog.org Rev. Christian J. Malewski, Pst.; Erin Goettemoeller, DRE; Kathy Powers, Pst. Assoc.; Mandy Jo Fultz, Bus. Mgr.; CRP Stds.: 7

St. Patrick Catholic Church, St. Joseph - 1723 S. 12th St., St. Joseph, MO 64503 t) 816-279-2594 office@stpatrickstj.org www.stpatrickstj.org/ Rev. Jonathan Davis, Pst.; Dcn. Marcelino Canchola; Dcn. John Nash;

STANBERRY

St. Peter's - 614 N. Alanthus Ave., Stanberry, MO 64489 t) 660-783-2159 Rev. Sebastian Allgaier, O.S.B., Pst.; CRP Stds.: 86

St. Patrick's - 4201 State Hwy. AA, King City, MO 64463

SUGAR CREEK

St. Cyril's Catholic Church - Sugar Creek - 11401 Chicago Ave., Sugar Creek, MO 64054 t) 816-252-9564 john_bolderson@msn.com saintcyrilsparish.org/ Rev. John D. Bolderson, Par. Admin.;

TARKIO

St. Paul the Apostle - 908 Elm St., Tarkio, MO 64491 t) 660-736-4342 Rev. Duc Nguyen, Pst.; CRP Stds.: 10

St. Benedict Catholic Church - 621 Custer St., Burlington Junction, MO 64428; Mailing: 908 Elm St., Tarkio, MO 64491

TRENTON

St. Joseph's Catholic Church - 1728 St. Joseph St., Trenton, MO 64683 t) 660-359-2841 stjosephtrenton@gmail.com Rev. William Fox, Admin.; CRP Stds.: 12

Immaculate Heart of Mary Catholic Church - 606 N. Broadway St., Princeton, MO 64673; Mailing: 1728 Saint Joseph St., Trenton, MO 64683

WARRENSBURG

Sacred Heart - 300 S. Ridgeview Dr., Warrensburg, MO 64093 t) 660-747-6154 parish@shcatholic.com www.shcatholic.com Rev. Gabriel Lickteig, Par. Admin.; CRP Stds.: 65

WESTON

Holy Trinity - 407 Cherry St., Weston, MO 64098 t) 816-640-2206 swishon@ht12.org www.holytrinitycatholic.org Rev. Steven C. Rogers, Pst.; CRP Stds.: 24

SCHOOLS: PRESCHOOL THRU HIGH SCHOOL

SCHOOLS

STATE OF MISSOURI

KANSAS CITY

Holy Cross School - (PAR) (Grades PreK-8) 121 N. Quincy Ave., Kansas City, MO 64123-1399 t) 816-231-8874 shenn@hcskcmo.org www.hcskcmo.org Shelley Henn, Prin.; Stds.: 163; Lay Tchrs.: 14

Notre Dame de Sion Elementary School - (PRV) (Grades PreK-8) 3823 Locust St., Kansas City, MO 64109-2697 t) 816-753-3810 www.ndsion.edu Patricia Gray, Prin.; Alicia Herald Kotarba, Pres.; Annie Riggs, Mission Dir.; Stds.: 273; Lay Tchrs.: 42

Our Lady of Hope School (Our Lady of the Angels) - (PAR) (Grades K-8) 4232 Mercier, Kansas City, MO

64111 t) 816-931-1693 mdelac@olhkcmo.org www.olhkcmo.org Mary Delac, Prin.; Stds.: 148; Lay Tchrs.: 9

ST. JOSEPH

St. Joseph Catholic Academy - 3529 Frederick Ave., St. Joseph, MO 64506

HIGH SCHOOLS

STATE OF MISSOURI

KANSAS CITY

Cristo Rey Kansas City High School - (PRV) 211 W. Linwood Blvd., Kansas City, MO 64111-1327 t) 816-457-6044 joconnor@cristoreykc.org www.cristoreykc.org Steve Belen, Prin.; John O'Connor, Pres.;

Notre Dame de Sion High School - (PRV) 10631 Wornall Rd., Kansas City, MO 64114-5096 t) 816-942-3282 www.ndsion.edu Ellen Carmody, Prin.; Alicia Herald Kotarba, Pres.; Elizabeth Middleton, Registrar; Annie Riggs, Mission Dir.; Stds.: 284; Lay Tchrs.: 47

St. Pius X High School - (DIO) (Grades 9-12) 1500 N.E. 42nd Ter., Kansas City, MO 64116 t) 816-453-3450 jmonachino@spxkc.org www.spxkc.org Joseph Monachino Jr., Prin.; Joseph Ross, Pres.; Stds.: 367; Pr. Tchrs.: 1; Lay Tchrs.: 28

Rockhurst High School - (PRV) (Grades 9-12) 9301 State Line Rd., Kansas City, MO 64114-3229 t) 816-363-2036 vgiacabazi@rockhursths.edu; kherdlick@rockhursths.edu www.rockhursths.edu/ Rev. Vincent Giacabazi, S.J., Prin.; David Laughlin, Pres.; Stds.: 925; Scholastics: 3; Pr. Tchrs.: 3; Lay Tchrs.: 138

St. Teresa's Academy - (PRV) (Grades 9-12) 5600 Main St., Kansas City, MO 64113-1298 t) 816-501-0011 lbaker@stteresasacademy.org; bmccormick@stteresasacademy.org www.stteresasacademy.org Siabhan May-Washington, Pres.; Elizabeth Baker, Prin., Student Affairs; Barbara McCormick, Prin., Academic Affairs; Stds.: 571; Lay Tchrs.: 58

LEES SUMMIT

St. Michael the Archangel Catholic High School - 2901 N.W. Lees Summit Rd., Lees Summit, MO 64064 t) 816-763-4800; 816-499-8601 contact@smacatholic.org; jbriggs@smacatholic.org www.smacatholic.org Jodi Briggs, Prin.; Rev. Randy Sly, Pres.; Stacy Needels, Bus. Mgr.; Lamar Hunt Jr., Interim Pres.;

ST. JOSEPH

Bishop LeBlond High School - (DIO) 3529 Frederick Ave, St. Joseph, MO 64506 t) 816-279-1629 khuss@bishopleblondhs.com www.bishopleblond.com Rev. Jonathan Davis, Chap.; Kimberly Huss, Prin.; Stds.: 174; Lay Tchrs.: 15

INSTITUTIONS LOCATED IN DIOCESE

ASSOCIATIONS [ASN]

KANSAS CITY

***De La Salle Alumni Association** - ; Mailing: P.O. Box 380083, Kansas City, MO 64138 t) 816-767-9800 johnlouis1945@gmail.com John Delgado, Contact;

RAYMORE

St. Francis de Sales Association - 1800 N. Jeter Rd., Raymore, MO 64083 t) 816-331-4831 willabird1@juno.com Barbara McClung, Dir.;

CAMPUS MINISTRY / NEWMAN CENTERS [CAM]

KANSAS CITY

Avila University Campus Ministry - 11901 Wornall Rd., Kansas City, MO 64145 t) 816-501-2423 david.armstrong@avila.edu; julie.cowley@avila.edu www.avila.edu David Armstrong, Dir.;

University of Missouri - Kansas City Newman Center at JPII Commons - 5220 Troost Ave., Kansas City, MO 64110 t) 816-714-2328 abgoslin@diocesekcsj.org; umkccatholics@diocesekcsj.org www.jp2commons.org/newman Rev. Andrew Mattingly, Chap.; Abigail Byron-Goslin, Dir.;

MARYVILLE

Newman Catholic Center, Northwest Missouri State University - 606 College Ave., Maryville, MO 64468 t) 660-582-7373 newman@nwmissouri.edu; nwmocatholics@diocesekcsj.org www.northwestnewman.com Rev. Joshua Barlett, Chap.; Maximilian Kolbe Pawlowski, Campus Min.; Abigail Byron-Goslin, Dir.;

ST. JOSEPH

MOWEST Campus Ministry - 4518 Mitchell, St. Joseph, MO 64507 t) 816-396-8410 mowestcatholics@diocesekcsj.org www.mowestcatholic.org/ Ally Goetz, Campus Min.; Abigail Byron-Goslin, Dir.;

WARRENSBURG

Newman Center Catholic Campus Ministry for University of Central Missouri - 307 S. Holden St., Warrensburg, MO 64093 t) 660-864-3136 ucmcatholics@diocesekcsj.org www.ucmcatholic.com/ Rev. Gabriel Lickteig, Chap.; Kevin O'Reilly, Campus Min.; Abigail Byron-Goslin, Dir.;

CATHOLIC CHARITIES [CCH]

KANSAS CITY

Bishop Sullivan Center - 6435 Truman Rd., Kansas City, MO 64126 t) 816-231-0984; 816-561-8515; 913-906-8938 donations@bishopsullivan.org www.bishopsullivan.org Michelle Carlstedt, Dir.;

Catholic Charities Foundation - 4001 Blue Pkwy, Kansas City, MO 64130 t) 816-221-4377 knoel@ccharities.com www.catholiccharities-kcsj.org Karen Noel, CEO;

Redemptorist Social Services Center, Inc. - 207 W. Linwood Blvd., Kansas City, MO 64111-1327 t) 816-931-9942 info@kcsocialservices.org www.kcsocialservices.org Diana Kennedy, Dir.;

CEMETERIES [CEM]

KANSAS CITY

Mount Olivet & Mount St. Mary - 7601 Blue Ridge Blvd, Kansas City, MO 64506 t) 816-353-1900 kgilbert@cemeterieskcsj.org Kenny Lee Gilbert, Bus. Mgr.;

Resurrection - 5001 N.E. Cookingham Dr., Kansas City, MO 64156; Mailing: 7601 Blue Ridge Blvd., Kansas City, MO 64138 t) 816-734-2356 kgilbert@cemeterieskcsj.org www.cemeterieskcsj.org Kenny Lee Gilbert, Bus. Mgr.;

ST. JOSEPH

Mount Olivet - 26th & Lovers Ln., St. Joseph, MO 64506 t) 816-353-1900 kgilbert@cemeterieskcsj.org www.cemeterieskcsj.org Kenny Lee Gilbert, Bus. Mgr.;

COLLEGES & UNIVERSITIES [COL]

KANSAS CITY

Avila University - 11901 Wornall Rd., Kansas City, MO 64145-1698 t) 816-942-8400 david.armstrong@avila.edu www.avila.edu Darby Gough, Dean; Ronald A. Slepitza, Pres.; David Armstrong, Dir.;

Rockhurst University - 1100 Rockhurst Rd., Kansas City, MO 64110-2561 t) 816-501-4000 decla.tyler-simpson@rockhurst.edu www.rockhurst.edu Douglas Dunham, Provost, Sr. Vice Pres. Academic Affairs; Kris Pace, Comptroller; Matthew Quick, Vice Pres., Student Devel. & Athletics, Dean of Students; Gerald Moench, CFO;

College of Arts and Sciences - t) 816-501-4075 thomas.curran@rockhurst.edu www.rockhurst.edu Pedro Maligo, Dean;

Helzberg School of Management - t) 816-501-4087 thomas.curran@rockhurst.edu www.rockhurst.edu/hsom/index.asp Cheryl McConnell, Dean;

St. Luke's College of Nursing and Health Sciences - t) 816-501-4686 thomas.curran@rockhurst.edu www.rockhurst.edu/academic/sgps/index.asp

Research College of Nursing - 2525 E. Meyer Blvd., Kansas City, MO 64132 t) 816-995-2800 info@rockhurst.edu www.researchcollege.edu Nancy DeBasio, Pres.;

CONVENTS, MONASTERIES, AND RESIDENCES FOR WOMEN [CON]

CLYDE

Benedictine Convent of Perpetual Adoration - 31970 State Hwy. P, Clyde, MO 64432 t) 660-944-2221 sister@benedictinesisters.org www.benedictinesisters.org Attended by Conception Abbey Sr. Dawn Mills, Prioress General; Srs.: 41

GOWER

Benedictines of Mary, Queen of Apostles - 8005 N.W. 316th St., Gower, MO 64454 t) 816-424-3194 benedictinesofmary.org Abbey of Our Lady of Ephesus Mother Cecilia Snell, O.S.B., Abbess; Srs.: 47

INDEPENDENCE

St. Francis Convent Novitiate and Prayer Center - 2100 N. Noland Rd., Independence, MO 64050 t) 816-252-1673 www.osfholyeucharist.org Motherhouse of the Sisters of St. Francis of the Holy Eucharist. Sr. M. Connie Boulch, O.S.F., Supr.; Srs.: 13

KANSAS CITY

Sisters of the Society of Our Lady of the Most Holy Trinity - 3738 Tracy Ave., Kansas City, MO 64109 t) 816-561-8849 kcecclesialteam@gmail.com; conventkansascity@gmail.com solt.net Society of Apostolic Life. Sr. Megan Mary Thibodeau, SOLT, Gen. Sister Servant;

LIBERTY

Mercedarian Missionaries of Berriz (M.M.B.) - 2115 Maturana Dr., 101B, Liberty, MO 64068-7985 t) 816-781-8202 mmbus@sbcglobal.net mmberriz.com

Mercedarian Missionaries of Berriz - 2116 Maturana Dr., Liberty, MO 64068-9102 t) 816-415-3024 lcteegarden808@gmail.com

Mercedarian Missionaries of Berriz - 2120 Maturana Dr., Liberty, MO 64068 t) 816-415-3133 sf_thib@att.net

SAVANNAH

Sisters of St. Francis Provincial House - 908 Franciscan Way, Savannah, MO 64485-0488; Mailing: P.O. Box 488, Savannah, MO 64485-0488 t) 816-324-3179 sistersofstfrancis.org Sr. Christine Martin, O.S.F., Prov.;

ST. JOSEPH

Sisters in Jesus the Lord - 512 N 11th St., St. Joseph, MO 64501 t) 816-689-0837 info@cjd.cc www.cjd.cc Mother M. Stella Whittier, CJD, Prioress; Srs.: 4

ENDOWMENTS / FOUNDATIONS / TRUSTS [EFT]

CONCEPTION

***The St. Benedict Education Foundation** - 37174 State Hwy. V V, Conception, MO 64433; Mailing: P.O. Box 16, Conception, MO 64433 t) 660-944-2832 jacob@conception.edu www.stbenedictfoundation.org Rev. Benedict Neenan, O.S.B.;

KANSAS CITY

Diocese of Kansas City-St. Joseph Real Estate Trust - 20 W. 9th St., Ste. 200, Kansas City, MO 64105; Mailing: P.O. Box 419037, Kansas City, MO 64141 t) 816-756-1850 laville@diocesekcsj.org Angela E. Laville, Finance Officer;

Endowment Trust Fund for Catholic Education - 20 W. 9th St., Ste. 200, Kansas City, MO 64105; Mailing: P.O. Box 419037, Kansas City, MO 64141-6037 t) 816-756-1850 lillig@diocesekcsj.org www.diocese-kcsj.org Jeremy Lillig, Dir.;

St. Joseph Medical Center Foundation - 1000 Carondelet Dr., Kansas City, MO 64114

Our Lady of Perpetual Help Charitable Trust - 3333 Broadway, Kansas City, MO 64111 t) 816-561-3771 www.redemptoristkc.org Rev. Gary Ziuraitis, C.Ss.R., Pst.;

LIBERTY

***Queen of Angels Foundation, Inc.** - 23615 N.E. 100th St., Liberty, MO 64068; Mailing: 7526 N. Kentucky Ave., Kansas City, MO 64158 t) 816-797-3837 anitabenedictine@gmail.com Sr. Anita Helgenberger, Treas.;

HOSPITALS / HEALTH SERVICES [HOS]

ST. LOUIS

Carondelet Health - 4600 Edmundson Rd., St. Louis, MO 63134

MISCELLANEOUS [MIS]

CLYDE

The American Benedictine Review - 31970 State Hwy. P, Clyde, MO 64432 t) 660-944-2221 abenedictinereview@gmail.com www.americanbenedictinereview.org Sr. Colleen Maura McGrane, O.S.B., Editor;

KANSAS CITY

***Alexandra's House** - 638 W. 39th Ter., Kansas City, MO 64111-2914 t) 816-931-2539 care@alexandrashouse.com www.alexandrashouse.com Perinatal hospice and infant care system. Patti Lewis, Dir.;

Catholic Community Hospice - 8510 Wornall Rd., Kansas City, MO 64114 t) 816-523-5634 emark@catholiccommunityhospice.com www.catholiccommunityhospice.com Edra Mark, Dir.;

Catholic Diocese of Kansas City-St. Joseph Deposit and Loan Fund - 20 W. 9th St., Ste. 200, Kansas City, MO 64105; Mailing: P. O. Box 419037, Kansas City, MO 64141 t) 816-756-1850 malanowski@diocesekcsj.org Angela E. Laville, Dir.;

Cristo Rey Kansas City Corporate Internship Program - 211 W. Linwood Blvd., Kansas City, MO 64111 t) 816-457-6044 joconnor@cristoreykc.org www.cristoreykc.org John O'Connor, Pres.;

Cursillo - 7724 N. Broadway, Kansas City, MO 64118 t) 816-803-3517 gabelick@gmail.com www.diocese-kcsj.org Rev. William Fox, Spiritual Adv./Care Srvcs.; Dcn. Michael Dennis, Asst. Spiritual Dir.;

Diocesan Council of Catholic Women - 20 W. 9th St., Ste. 200, Kansas City, MO 64105; Mailing: P.O. Box 419037, Kansas City, MO 64141-6037 t) 816-756-1850 blando@diocesekcsj.org Kathy Philpott, Pres.;

Diocese of Kansas City-St. Joseph Real Estate Corporation - 20 W. 9th St., Ste. 200, Kansas City, MO 64105; Mailing: P.O. Box 419037, Kansas City, MO 64141-6037 t) 816-756-1850 rowe@diocesekcsj.org Very Rev. Charles N. Rowe, Vice Pres.;

***Face of Mercy** - ; Mailing: P.O. Box 481641, Kansas City, MO 64148

***If U Love Me** - 905 Carnoustie Dr., Kansas City, MO 64145

***The Ignatian Spirituality Center of Kansas City** - 1001 E. 52nd St., Kansas City, MO 64110

***Jerusalem Farm, Inc.** - 520 Garfield Ave., Kansas City, MO 64124 t) 816-421-1855 community@jerusalemfarm.org www.jerusalemfarm.org Jessie Schiele, Dir.; Dcn. Jordan Schiele, Dir.;

Ladies of Charity of Metropolitan Kansas City - ; Mailing: P.O. Box 480753, Kansas City, MO 64148-0753 t) 913-268-8652 rosemary.nelson17@gmail.com www.ladiesofcharitykc.org Rosemary Nelson, Pres.;

Marillac Home for Children - ; Mailing: P.O. Box 419037, Kansas City, MO 64141-6037 t) 816-756-1850 laville@diocesekcsj.org Angela E. Laville, Dir.;

***Seton Center** - 2816 E. 23 St., Kansas City, MO 64127; Mailing: 4600 Edmundson Rd., St. Louis, MO 63134 t) 816-231-3955; 314-733-8000 john.tersigni@ascension.org www.setonkc.org Total Assisted Annually: 7204 Total Staff: 17 John Tersigni, Chief Mission Integration Officer; Craig Cordola, Exec. Vice Pres. & COO;

LIBERTY

***St. Gaspar Society** - 2130 Saint Gaspar Way, Liberty, MO 64068; Mailing: P.O. Box 339, Liberty, MO 64069 t) 816-781-4344 communications@preciousbloodkc.org Rev. Jeffrey Kirch, C.PP.S., Pres.; Rev. John Wolf, C.PP.S., Secy.; Rev. William Nordenbrock, C.PP.S., Treas.; Rev. Lau Pham, C.PP.S., Mem.; Rev. Ron Will, C.PP.S., Mem.; Rev. Timothy Armbruster, C.PP.S., Mem.; Rev. Michael Goode, C.PP.S., Mem.;

Our Lady of Mercy Home - 2115 Maturana Dr., Liberty, MO 64068-9469 t) 816-781-5711 dtrimmer@ourladyofmercy.net Sr. Sandra Thibodeaux, M.M.B., Regl. Coord.;

MONASTERIES AND RESIDENCES FOR PRIESTS AND BROTHERS [MON]

CONCEPTION

Conception Abbey (Benedictine Monks) - 37174 State Hwy. V V, Conception, MO 64433 t) 660-944-3100 communications@conception.edu www.conceptionabbey.org Rt. Rev. Benedict Neenan, O.S.B., Abbot; Rev. Sebastian Allgaier, O.S.B.; Rev. Albert Bruecken, O.S.B.; Rev. Richard Cleary, O.S.B.; Rev. Martin DeMeulenaere, O.S.B.; Rev. Donald Grabner, O.S.B.; Rev. Rene Guesnier, O.S.B.; Most Rev. Jerome Hanus; Rev. Etienne Huard, O.S.B.; Rt. Rev. Edmund Boyce; Rev. Pachomius Meade, O.S.B.; Rev. Daniel Petsche, O.S.B.; Rev. Robert Schoofs; Rev. Macario Martinez, O.S.B.; Rev. Xavier Nacke, O.S.B.; Rev. Kenneth Reichert, O.S.B.; Rt. Rev. Marcel Rooney, O.S.B.; Rev. Paul Sheller, O.S.B.; Rev. Samuel Russell, O.S.B.; Rev. Aquinas Keusenkothen, O.SB.; Rev. Quentin Kathol, O.S.B.; Rev. Adam Ryan, O.S.B.; Rev. Norbert Schappler, O.S.B.; Rev. Reginald Sander, O.S.B.; Rev. Allan Stetz, O.S.B.; Rev. Roger Schmit, O.S.B.; Rev. Peter Ullrich, O.S.B.; Very Rev. Victor Schinstock, O.S.B.; Bro. Cyprian Langlois, O.S.B.; Bro. Justin Hernandez, O.S.B.; Bro. Jacob Kubajak, O.S.B.; Bro. Michael Marcotte, O.S.B.; Bro. Luke Kral, O.S.B.; Bro. Placid Dale, O.S.B.; Bro. Maximilian Burkhart, O.S.B.; Bro. Simeon Johnson; Bro. Bernard Montgomery, O.S.B.; Bro. Matthew Marie; Bro. Jude Person, O.S.B.; Bro. Blaise Bonderer, O.S.B.; Bro. David Wilding, O.S.B.; Bro. Elias Zaczkiewicz, O.S.B.; Bro. Jonathan Clark, O.S.B., Prior; Bro. Thomas Sullivan, O.S.B., Subprior; Bro. Anselm Broom, O.S.B., Educ.; Brs.: 18; Priests: 34

KANSAS CITY

St. Peter Claver Jesuit Community - 5133 Forest Ave., Kansas City, MO 64110-2513 t) 816-501-3232 derricksj@yahoo.com www.rockhurst.edu/jesuitcommunity Rev. James N. Caime, S.J., Pst.; Rev. Derrick Weingartner, S.J., Rector; Rev. Vincent Giacabazi, S.J., Prin.; Rev. Gary Menard, Teacher; Rev. Daniel J. Tesvich, S.J., Teacher; Rev. Stephen M. Hess, SJ; Rev. Thomas A. Pesci, S.J.; Rev. James J. White, S.J.; Rev. Michael Sheeran, S.J., In Res.; Brs.: 3; Priests: 9

Redemptorists Fathers of Kansas City, Missouri - 3333 Broadway Blvd., Kansas City, MO 64111 t) 816-561-3771 info@olphkc.org Rev. Gary Ziuraitis, C.Ss.R., Pst.; Rev. Andrew Thompson, C.Ss.R., Assoc. Pst.; Rev. James White, C.Ss.R., Local Supr.; Rev. Francis Hau Pham, C.Ss.R., Pastor, Holy Martyrs; Rev. Thanh Nguyen, C.Ss.R., Assoc., Holy Martyrs; Rev. Thomas Danielsen, C.Ss.R., In Res.; Rev. Michael McAndrew, C.Ss.R., In Res.; Rev. Gregory Schmitt, C.Ss.R., In Res.; Bro. William Cloughley, C.Ss.R., In Res.; Brs.: 1; Priests: 8

Society of Our Lady of the Most Holy Trinity - 3705 Tracy Ave., Kansas City, MO 64109 t) 816-868-8254 frcarlito64@yahoo.com.ph; padrescottsolt3@yahoo.com www.solt.net Rev. Scott Brossart, S.O.L.T., Chap.; Rev. Carlito Saballo, S.O.L.T., Mission Servant;

LIBERTY

Precious Blood Center - 2130 Saint Gaspar Way, Liberty, MO 64068-7941 t) 816-781-4344 communications@preciousbloodkc.org Rev. Michael Goode, C.PP.S., Property Mgr.; Rev. Michael Volkmer, C.PP.S., In Res.; Rev. Ron Will, C.PP.S., In Res.; Priests: 2

Society of the Precious Blood - 2130 Saint Gaspar Way, Liberty, MO 64068; Mailing: P.O. Box 339, Liberty, MO 64069-0339 t) 816-781-4344 communications@preciousbloodkc.org preciousbloodkc.org Rev. William Walter, C.PP.S., Mem.; Rev. Ron Will, C.PP.S., Mem.; Rev. John Wolf, C.PP.S., Mem.; Rev. Keith Branson, C.PP.S., Mem.; Rev. Aloys Ebach, C.PP.S., Mem.; Rev. Michael Goode, C.PP.S., Mem.; Rev. Mark Miller, C.PP.S., Mem.; Rev. Paul Sanders, C.PP.S., Mem.; Rev. Garry Richmeier, C.PP.S., Mem.; Rev. Richard Bayuk, C.PP.S., Mem.; Rev. Michael Volkmer, C.PP.S., Mem.; Brs.: 1; Priests: 14

NURSING / REHABILITATION / CONVALESCENCE / ELDERLY CARE [NUR]

CAMERON

St. Patrick's Manor - 514 Northland Dr., Cameron, MO 64429 t) 816-632-1684 stpatricksmanor@dalmarkgroup.com Christopher Freeman, Mgr.;

KANSAS CITY

St. Anthony's Senior Living - 1000 E. 68th St., Kansas City, MO 64131 t) 816-846-0870 mledomjr@stanthonyskc.com stanthonyskc.com Mark Ledom Jr., Bus. Mgr.;

St. Joseph Place - 1900 E. 10th St., Kansas City, MO 64127

Red Bridge Place - 11300 Colorado Ave., Kansas City, MO 64137 t) 816-761-4667 redbridge@dalmarkgroup.com

Tremont Place - 6161 N. Chatham Ave., Kansas City, MO 64151 t) 816-587-7637 tremontapts01@gmail.com A 50-unit apartment residence for the elderly and disabled. Must be sixty-two or over.

LIBERTY

Our Lady of Mercy Country Home (Mercedarian Missionaries of Berriz) - 2115 Maturana Dr., Liberty, MO 64068 t) 816-781-5711 jwalters@ourladyofmercy.net ourladyofmercy.net

RAYTOWN

Jeanne Jugan Center (Little Sisters of the Poor) - 8745 James A. Reed Rd., Raytown, MO 64138-4490 t) 816-761-4744 adkansascity@littlesistersofthepoor.org www.littlesistersofthepoorkansascity.org Home for the elderly, nursing, independent living and assisted living. Rev. Timothy Leete, Chap.; Mother Margaret Patricia Lennon, psdp, Supr.; Asstd. Annu.: 150; Staff: 86

ST. JOSEPH

Benedictine Living Community | St. Joseph - 1202 Heartland Rd., St. Joseph, MO 64506 t) 816-671-8500 amy.byrom@benedictineliving.org www.benedictineliving.org/st-joseph-mo/ Amy J. Byrom, Exec. Dir.; Asstd. Annu.: 2,158; Staff: 130

St. Charles Place - 3240 Pear St., St. Joseph, MO 64503

WARRENSBURG

Murphy Lake Apartments - 107 E. Hale Lake Rd., Warrensburg, MO 64093

SEMINARIES [SEM]

CONCEPTION

Conception Seminary College - 37174 State Hwy. VV, Conception, MO 64433-0502; Mailing: P.O. Box 502, Conception, MO 64433-0502 t) 660-944-3105 seminary@conception.edu conception.edu Very Rev. Victor Schinstock, O.S.B., Rector; Rev. Benedict Neenan, O.S.B., Abbot; Most Rev. Jerome Hanus, O.S.B., Prof.; Rev. Pachomius Meade, OSB, Vice Rector - Dean of Students; Rev. Paul Sheller, O.S.B., Dir. Spiritual Formation; Rev. Etienne Huard, O.S.B., Prof.; Rev. Patrick Caveglia, O.S.B., Librn.; Rev. Stephen Keusenkothen, Spiritual Advisor; Rev. Xavier Nacke, O.S.B., Spiritual Advisor; Rev. Msgr. Patrick J. Gaalaas, Spiritual Adv./Care Srvcs.; Rev. Duane F. Reinert, O.F.M.Cap., Dir. Counseling Srvcs.; Stds.: 27; Bro. Tchrs.: 10; Lay Tchrs.: 8; Pr. Tchrs.: 11

KANSAS CITY

Gaspar Mission House - 5221 Rockhill Rd., Kansas City, MO 64110 t) 816-333-7980 Rev. Richard Bayuk,

C.PP.S., In Res.; Rev. Garry Richmeier, C.PP.S., In Res.;

LIBERTY

Society of the Precious Blood Provincial Offices - 2130 Saint Gaspar Way, Liberty, MO 64068; Mailing: P.O. Box 339, Liberty, MO 64069-0339 t) 816-781-4344 communications@kcprovince.org preciousbloodkc.org Rev. Michael Goode, C.PP.S., Property Mgr.;

SPECIAL CARE FACILITIES [SPF]

LIBERTY

Life Unlimited - 2135 Manor Way, Liberty, MO 64068-9397 t) 816-781-4332 info@imanor.org Residential and day habilitation services for people with developmental disabilities, Operated by the Life Unlimited of Directors. Julie Edlund, Exec.;

An asterisk (*) denotes an organization that has established tax-exempt status directly with the IRS and is not covered by the USCCB Group Ruling.

Diocese of Knoxville

MOST REVEREND RICHARD F. STIKA

Third Bishop of Knoxville; ordained December 14, 1985; appointed third Bishop of Knoxville January 12, 2009; ordained and installed March 19, 2009. Office: 805 S. Northshore Dr., Knoxville, TN 37919.

Chancery Office: 805 S. Northshore Dr., Knoxville, TN 37919. T: 865-584-3307
www.dioknox.org

Tribunal of the Diocese of Knoxville. Office: 214 E. 8th St., Chattanooga, TN 37402. T: 865-584-3307, Ext. 8001 or 865-381-0200.
office@tribunal.dioknox.org
dioknox.org/tribunal

ESTABLISHED SEPTEMBER 8, 1988.

Square Miles 14,242.

Comprises the Counties of Anderson, Bledsoe, Blount, Bradley, Campbell, Carter, Claiborne, Cocke, Cumberland, Fentress, Grainger, Greene, Hamblen, Hamilton, Hancock, Hawkins, Jefferson, Johnson, Knox, Loudon, McMinn, Marion, Meigs, Monroe, Morgan, Pickett, Polk, Rhea, Roane, Scott, Sequatchie, Sevier, Sullivan, Unicoi, Union and Washington in the State of Tennessee.

For legal titles of parishes and diocesan institutions, consult the Chancery Office.

STATISTICAL OVERVIEW

Personnel
Bishop....1
Priests: Diocesan Active in Diocese....49
Priests: Diocesan Active Outside Diocese....4
Priests: Retired, Sick or Absent....15
Number of Diocesan Priests....68
Religious Priests in Diocese....18
Total Priests in your Diocese....86
Extern Priests in Diocese....5
Ordinations:
Transitional Deacons....3
Permanent Deacons....23
Permanent Deacons in Diocese....100
Total Brothers....11
Total Sisters....44

Parishes
Parishes....50
With Resident Pastor:
Resident Diocesan Priests....33
Resident Religious Priests....6
Without Resident Pastor:
Administered by Priests....8
Administered by Deacons....3
Missions....1
Pastoral Centers....2
Professional Ministry Personnel:
Brothers....3
Sisters....39
Lay Ministers....49

Welfare
Catholic Hospitals....1
Total Assisted....101,454
Health Care Centers....1
Total Assisted....578
Homes for the Aged....1
Total Assisted....578
Specialized Homes....2
Total Assisted....90
Special Centers for Social Services....7
Total Assisted....24,223

Educational
Diocesan Students in Other Seminaries....13
Total Seminarians....13
High Schools, Diocesan and Parish....2
Total Students....1,065
Elementary Schools, Diocesan and Parish....8
Total Students....2,481
Catechesis / Religious Education:
High School Students....844
Elementary Students....3,330
Total Students under Catholic Instruction....7,733
Teachers in Diocese:
Priests....1
Scholastics....5
Sisters....11
Lay Teachers....326

Vital Statistics
Receptions into the Church:
Infant Baptism Totals....1,093
Minor Baptism Totals....146
Adult Baptism Totals....119
Received into Full Communion....242
First Communions....1,226
Confirmations....1,231
Marriages:
Catholic....210
Interfaith....54
Total Marriages....264
Deaths....455
Total Catholic Population....71,274
Total Population....2,538,487

LEADERSHIP

Vicars General - Very Rev. David Boettner, V.G.; Very Rev. Douglas Owens, V.G., M.O.C.;
Episcopal Vicar for Priests - Rev. Michael E. Cummins, Episcopal Vicar for Priests;
Deans of the Diocese - Rev. Michael E. Cummins, Five Rivers Deanery; Rev. Michael Nolan, Chattanooga Deanery; Rev. Brent A. Shelton, Cumberland Mtn. Deanery;
Chancery Office - t) 865-584-3307
Moderator of the Curia - Very Rev. Douglas Owens, V.G., M.O.C.;
Chancellor and Chief Operating Officer - ssmith@dioknox.org Dcn. Sean K. Smith;
Assistant to the Bishop - Dcn. Sean K. Smith;
Vice Chancellor for Canonical Affairs - office@tribunal.dioknox.org Very Rev. J. David Carter, Judicial Vicar;
Vice Chancellor for Administration - psimoneau@dioknox.org Paul Simoneau;
Auditors - All priests on assignment in the diocese -
Presbyteral Council - Rev. Joseph Reed, Chair; Rev. Mark Schuster, Vice Chmn.; Rev. Ray Powell, Secy. (fatherraypoweell@gmail.com);
Diocesan Consultors - Very Rev. David Boettner, V.G.; Very Rev. Douglas Owens, V.G., M.O.C.; Rev. Msgr. T. Allen Humbrecht;
Diocesan Finance Council - Shannon Hepp, Ex Officio, Diocesan Finance Officer; Sharon Folk, Chair; J. Michael Connor;

OFFICES AND DIRECTORS

Archives - t) 865-584-3307 ssmith@dioknox.org Dcn. Sean K. Smith, Chancellor;
Campus Ministries -
East Tennessee State University - t) 423-926-7061 Rev. Bede C. Aboh, Chap.;
University of Tennessee-Chattanooga -
Chattanooga Deanery Priests (Sacramental Ministry) - t) 423-618-9062 Rev. Valentin Iurochkin, Chap.; Donna Gabor, Campus Min.; Dcn. Brian Gabor, Campus Min.;
University of Tennessee-Knoxville - t) 865-523-7931 Rev. Donald Andrie, C.S.P., Dir.;
Catholic Campaign for Human Development - t) 865-524-9896 Lisa Healy, Dir.;
Catholic Schools Office - t) 865-584-3307 Dr. Sedonna Prater, Supt.;
Cemeteries - Dcn. Sean K. Smith, Dir.; Very Rev. J. David Carter, Contact; Rev. Charles Donahue, C.S.P., Contact;
Censor Librorum - t) 865-584-3307 Dcn. Sean K. Smith, Contact; Sr. Mary Timothea Elliott, R.S.M.;
Chancellor and Chief Operating Officer - t) 865-584-3307 ssmith@dioknox.org Dcn. Sean K. Smith;
Christian Formation - t) 865-584-3307 Dcn. James Bello, Dir. (jbello@dioknox.org); Sr. Mary Timothea Elliott, R.S.M., Theological Consultant;
Communications Office - jwogan@dioknox.org Jim Wogan, Dir.;
Diaconate and Deacon Formation - Dcn. Tim Elliott, Dir.;
Diocesan Catholic Committee on Scouting - t) 423-282-6367 Rev. Dustin Alan Collins, Chap.; Christopher J. Manning, Chair;
Diocesan Council of Catholic Women - t) 423-470-2560 Rev. Dan G. Whitman, Diocesan Spiritual Moderator; Susan Collins, Pres.;
The East Tennessee Catholic - Bill Brewer, Editor;
Ecumenism - Rev. Msgr. T. Allen Humbrecht, Dir.;
Finance Office - Shannon Hepp, Diocesan Finance Officer;
Hispanic Ministry - t) 865-637-4769 Blanca Primm, Dir.;
Human Resources Office - t) 865-584-3307 Jennifer Mills, Dir.;
Justice and Peace Office - Paul Simoneau, Dir.;
Marriage Preparation and Enrichment - t) 865-584-3307 x6002 Dcn. Al Forsythe, Dir.;
Ministries of the Chattanooga Deanery - t) 423-476-8123 Rev. Michael Nolan, V.F.;
Ministries of the Cumberland Mtn. Deanery - t) 865-482-2875 Rev. Brent A. Shelton, V.F.;
Ministries of the Five Rivers Deanery - t) 423-288-8101 Rev. Michael E. Cummins, V.F.;
Ministries of the Smoky Mtn. Deanery - t) 865-982-3672 Rev. Peter J. Iorio, V.F.;
Moderator of the Curia - t) 865-584-3307 Very Rev. Douglas Owens, V.G., M.O.C.;
Priestly Life and Ministry - t) (423) 480-7072 Rev. Michael E. Cummins, Dir.;
Propagation of the Faith - Paul Simoneau, Dir.;
Scouting - t) 423-282-6367 Rev. Dustin Alan Collins, Chap.;
Stewardship and Strategic Planning - harmor@dioknox.org Dcn. Hicks Armor, Dir.; Allison DiGennaro, Asst. Dir.;
Tribunal of the Diocese of Knoxville - office@tribunal.dioknox.org Very Rev. J. David Carter, Judicial Vicar;
Victim Assistance Coordinator - t) (865) 321-9080 (McNabb Ctr. Victims Svcs.)
Vocations - t) 865-584-3307 Rev. Christopher Floersh, Dir.; Rev. Arthur Torres, Assoc. Vocations Dir. & Intl. Liaison;
Worship and Liturgy - t) 865-584-3307 Rev. Randy Stice, Dir.;
Youth, Young Adult and Pastoral Juvenil Ministry - t) 865-584-3307 Brittany Garcia, Diocesan Dir.; Magdiel Argueta, Coord. Pastoral Juvenil Hispana (margueta@dioknox.org); Donna L. Jones, Coord. Middle School Ministry;

PARISHES, MISSIONS, AND CLERGY

STATE OF TENNESSEE

ALCOA

Our Lady of Fatima - 858 Louisville Rd., Alcoa, TN 37701 t) 865-982-3672 lramos@ourladyoffatoma.org; dprugh@ourladyoffatima.org ourladyoffatima.org Rev. Peter J. Iorio, Pst.; Rev. Adam Royal, Assoc. Pst.; Dcn. Leon Dodd Jr.; Dcn. William Jacobs; Luis Ramos, Youth Min.; CRP Stds.: 192

ATHENS

St. Mary - 1291 E. Madison Ave., Athens, TN 37303 t) 423-745-4277 stmaryathenstn.org Rev. John Arthur Orr, Pst.; Dcn. Al Forsythe; Dcn. Erasmo Hernandez; Sandra Hartert, DRE; CRP Stds.: 54

CHATTANOOGA

Basilica of Sts. Peter and Paul - 214 E. 8th St., Chattanooga, TN 37402 t) 423-266-1618 dre@stspeterandpaulbasilica.com; business@stspeterandpaulbasilica.com www.stspeterandpaulbasilica.com Very Rev. J. David Carter, Rector; Rev. Valentin Iurochkin, Par. Vicar; Dcn. Hicks Armor; Dcn. Gaspar DeGaetano; Dcn. Joe Hartz; Rev. Nick Tran, In Res.; Florence Porter, DRE; Sr. Eloisa Torralba-Aquino, M.A.G., DRE; CRP Stds.: 279

St. Jude - 930 Ashland Ter., Chattanooga, TN 37415 t) 423-870-2386 info@stjudechattanooga.org Rev. Charles Burton, Pst.; Rev. Alex Waraska, Assoc. Pst.; Dcn. Bernard (Butch) Feldhaus; Dcn. Brian Gabor; Dcn. Paul Nelson; Kyra Niemann King, DRE; CRP Stds.: 102

St. Jude School - (Grades PreK-8) t) 423-877-6022 info@mysjs.com www.mysjs.com Dr. Joshua Overton, Prin.; Stds.: 321; Lay Tchrs.: 30

Our Lady of Perpetual Help - 501 S. Moore Rd., Chattanooga, TN 37412 t) 423-622-7232 pfranklin@myolph.com www.myolph.com Rev. Arthur Torres Barona, Pst.; Rev. Zachary Griffith, Assoc. Pst.; Dcn. Wade Eckler; Dcn. Dennis Meinert; CRP Stds.: 124

Our Lady of Perpetual Help School - (Grades PreK-8) 505 S. Moore Rd., Chattanooga, TN 37412 t) 423-622-1418 ccarlin@myolph.com Caroline Carlin, Prin.; Stds.: 277; Scholastics: 5; Lay Tchrs.: 37

St. Stephen - 7111 Lee Hwy., Chattanooga, TN 37421 t) 423-892-1261 x4; 423-486-9909 secretary@ststephenchatt.org; bookkeeper@ststephenchatt.org ststephenchatt.org Rev. Manuel Perez, Pst.; Rev. Christopher Manning, Assoc. Pst.; Dcn. Gary Brinkworth; Dcn. David Waguespack; Karen Underwood, CRE; CRP Stds.: 187

CLEVELAND

St. Therese of Lisieux - 900 Clingan Ridge Dr., N.W., Cleveland, TN 37312 t) 423-476-8123 dre@sttheresecIevelandtn.org; secretary@stthereseclevelandtn.org www.sttheresecatholicchurch.org Rev. Michael Nolan, Pst.; Dcn. Barry Maples; Dcn. Stephen Ratterman; Marietta Giraldo, DRE; CRP Stds.: 162

CLINTON

St. Therese - 701 S. Charles G. Seivers Blvd., Clinton, TN 37716 t) 865-457-4073 office@sainttheresecIinton.org www.sainttheresecIinton.org Dcn. Peter J Chiaro, Par. Admin.;

COPPERHILL

St. Catherine Laboure - 115 E. Main St., Copperhill, TN 37317; Mailing: P.O. Box 1165, Copperhill, TN 37317 t) 423-496-3498 sclcchurch@etcmail.com www.sclccopperhill.org Rev. Jerry Daniels, Pst.; Rev. Thomas W. Moser, In Res.; CRP Stds.: 42

CROSSVILLE

St. Alphonsus - 151 St. Alphonsus Way, Crossville, TN 38555 t) 931-484-2358 (Church); (931) 484-2358 x105 (Rel. Educ.) office@stalonline.org; sara@stalonline.org stalonline.org Rev. Mark Schuster, Pst.; Dcn. Peter Minneci; Sara Carey, Asst. Dir., Faith Formation; CRP Stds.: 77

DAYTON

St. Bridget - 320 Walnut Grove Church Rd., Dayton, TN 37321; Mailing: P.O. Box 106, Dayton, TN 37321 t) 423-775-2664 Rev. James L. Vick, Pst.; Rachel Velez, DRE; CRP Stds.: 28

DUNLAP

Shepherd of the Valley - 6191 Hwy. 28, Dunlap, TN 37327-1747; Mailing: P.O. Box 1747, Dunlap, TN 37327-1747 t) 423-949-6903 shepherdofthevalleyindunlap@yahoo.com www.sotvcc.weebly.com Rev. Mark A. Scholz, Pst.; Lisa Tuggle, DRE; CRP Stds.: 23

ELIZABETHTON

St. Elizabeth - 510 W. C St., Elizabethton, TN 37643-2522; Mailing: P. O. Box 7, Elizabethton, TN 37644 t) 423-543-3412; 423-518-1166 www.stelizabethsparish.org Rev. Dennis Kress, Pst.; Dcn. Richard Carner; Dcn. Michael Gray; CRP Stds.: 23

ERWIN

St. Michael the Archangel Catholic Church - 657 N. Mohawk Dr., Erwin, TN 37650; Mailing: P.O. Box 1009, Erwin, TN 37650 t) 423-735-0484 stmichaelthearchangeluc@gmail.com www.stmichaelthearchangeluc.org Rev. Thomas Charters, G.H.M., Pst.; Rev. Kenneth Wandera, GHM, Pst. Assoc.; CRP Stds.: 112

FAIRFIELD GLADE

St. Francis of Assisi - 7501 Peavine Rd., Fairfield Glade, TN 38558; Mailing: 7503 Peavine Rd., Fairfield Glade, TN 38558 t) 931-484-3628 office@saintfrancisfairfield.org saintfrancisfairfield.org/ Rev. Michael Woods, Pst.;

FARRAGUT

St. John Neumann - 633 St. John Ct., Farragut, TN 37934-1555 t) 865-966-4540 sjncoffice@sjnknox.org sjnknox.org Rev. Joseph Reed, Pst.; Rev. Christopher

Floersh, Par. Vicar; Rev. Michael R. Maples, Par. Vicar; Rev. Joseph Hammond, C.H.S. (Ghana), In Res.; Dcn. Donald Amelse; Dcn. Shawn Ballard; Dcn. Mike Gouge; Dcn. Greg Larson; Dcn. Agustin Ortega; Dcn. Marquis Syler; Gretchen Micio, DRE; Sr. Elizabeth Wanyoike, E.S.M., RCIA Coord.; Marilyn Derbyshire, DRE; CRP Stds.: 109

St. John Neumann School - (Grades PreK-8) 625 St. John Ct., Farragut, TN 37934-1555 t) 865-777-0077 sjns@sjncs-knox.org www.sjncs-knox.org Bill Derbyshire, Prin.; Sabrina Talley, Dean; Mallory Nygard, Librn.; Stds.: 420; Sr. Tchrs.: 1; Lay Tchrs.: 32

GATLINBURG

St. Mary - 304 Airport Rd., Gatlinburg, TN 37738 t) 865-436-4907 saintmarygatlinburg.org Rev. Moises Moreno-Urzua, Sacr. Min.; Stacy Champagne, DRE; CRP Stds.: 45

GREENEVILLE

Notre Dame - 212 Mt. Bethel Rd., Greeneville, TN 37745 t) 423-639-9381 info@notredametn.org; susan@notredametn.org notredamechurchtn.org Rev. Joseph Kuzhupil, M.S.F.S. (India), Pst.; Dcn. Wil Johnson; Susan Collins, DRE; CRP Stds.: 59

HARRIMAN

Blessed Sacrament - 535 Margrave Dr., Harriman, TN 37748-2118 t) 865-882-9838 www.blessedsacramentchurchandmissions.com Rev. Michael Sweeney, Pst.; Dcn. Henning Vic Landa; Alicia Laffoon, DRE; CRP Stds.: 14

HELENWOOD

St. Jude Parish - 13067 Scott Hwy., Helenwood, TN 37755 t) 423-562-0312 Rev. Samuel L. Sturm, Pst.;

JAMESTOWN

St. Christopher Catholic Church - 160 Holt Spur Dr., Jamestown, TN 38556; Mailing: P.O. Box 1332, Jamestown, TN 38556-1332 t) 931-879-4146 stchris38556@gmail.com www.saintchristopherjamestown.com Rev. Michael Sweeney, Pst.; CRP Stds.: 11

JEFFERSON CITY

Holy Trinity Catholic Church - 475 N. Hwy. 92, Jefferson City, TN 37760; Mailing: P.O. Box 304, Jefferson City, TN 37760 t) 865-471-0347 holytrinity.jeffcity@gmail.com htjctn.org Rev. James P. Harvey II, Pst.; Rev. Andres Cano, In Res.; Dcn. David Oatney; Dcn. Matt Pidgeon; Dcn. Jim Prosak; Dcn. Jack Raymond; Cindy Giardiello, DRE; CRP Stds.: 36

JOHNSON CITY

St. Mary's Catholic Church - 2211 E. Lakeview Dr., Johnson City, TN 37601 t) 423-282-6367 church.secretary@stmarysjc.org stmarysjc.org Rev. Dustin Alan Collins, Pst.; Rev. Jesus Guerrero Rodriguez, Assoc. Pst.; Dcn. Donald Griffith; Dcn. James Haselsteiner; Dcn. George Fredericks III; Dcn. Michael Jacobs; Judy Holt, DRE; Mary Klug, Youth Min.; CRP Stds.: 234

St. Mary's Catholic Church School - (Grades PreK-8) t) 423-282-3397 becky.frye@stmarysjc.org Becky Frye, Prin.; Stds.: 190; Lay Tchrs.: 20

ETSU Catholic Center - 734 W. Locust St., Johnson City, TN 37601 t) 423-926-7061 bchinonyeaboh@yahoo.com Rev. Bede C. Aboh, Campus Min.;

KINGSPORT

St. Dominic - 2517 John B. Dennis Hwy., Kingsport, TN 37660 t) 423-288-8101 www.saintdominickpt.org/ Rev. Michael E. Cummins, Pst.; Rev. Emmanuel Massawe, A.J. (Kenya), Assoc. Pst.; Dcn. Humberto Collazo; Dcn. Frank Fischer; Dcn. Stephan Helmbrecht; Dcn. Robert Lange; Rosa Mondragon, DRE; CRP Stds.: 122

St. Dominic School - (Grades PreK-5) 1474 E. Center St., Kingsport, TN 37664; Mailing: 2517 John B. Dennis Hwy, Kingsport, TN 37660 t) 423-245-8491 saintdominiccatholicschool.com Andrew Cooper, Prin.; Stds.: 120; Lay Tchrs.: 8

KNOXVILLE

Cathedral of the Most Sacred Heart of Jesus - 711 S. Northshore Dr., Knoxville, TN 37919; Mailing: 417 Erin Dr. Ste 120, Knoxville, TN 37919 t) 865-588-0249 wotey@shcknox.org shcathedral.org/ Very Rev. David Boettner, Rector; Rev. Jhon Mario Garcia, Assoc. Pst.; Rev. Martin Gladysz, Assoc. Pst.; Mary Mac Wilson, CEO; Dcn. Mike Mescall; Dcn. Fredy Vargas; Glenn Kahler, Dir. Liturgy & Music; Rick Grinstead, Youth Min.; Scott Barron, Parish Life Coord.; Dcn. Walt Otey, CFO; CRP Stds.: 231

Sacred Heart Cathedral School - (Grades PreK-8) t) 865-588-0415 mkosky@shcknox.org www.shcschool.org Mary Sue Kosky, Prin.; Emily Broussard, Vice Prin.; Stds.: 720; Lay Tchrs.: 76

St. Albert the Great Church - 7200 Brickey Ln., Knoxville, TN 37918 t) 865-689-7011 office@satgknox.org; maria@satgknox.org www.satgknox.org Rev. Chris Michelson, Pst.; Rev. Msgr. G. Patrick Garrity, Sacr. Min.; Dcn. Michael Eiffe; Dcn. John Elshaw; Dcn. Michael Duncan; Dcn. Robert Smearing; Maria Armento, Ministries Coordinator; Michael Persicano, Office/Finance Manager; CRP Stds.: 81

All Saints Catholic Church - 620 N. Cedar Bluff Rd., Knoxville, TN 37923 t) 865-531-0770 admin@allsaintsknoxville.com; carrie.manabat@allsaintsknoxville.com www.allsaintsknoxville.com Very Rev. Douglas Owens, Pst.; Rev. Alex Hernandez, Assoc. Pst.; Rev. Jorge Mejia, Assoc. Pst.; Dcn. Tim Elliott; Dcn. Robert Hunt; Dcn. David J. Lucheon; Dcn. Salvador Soriano; Carrie Manabat, DRE; CRP Stds.: 562

Church of Divine Mercy - 10919 Carmichael Rd., Knoxville, TN 37932 t) 865-454-8317 www.divinemercyknox.org Rev. Dominic Nguyen, C.R.M., Admin.; Dcn. Joseph Vinh; CRP Stds.: 19

Holy Ghost - 1041 N. Central St., Knoxville, TN 37917; Mailing: 111 Hinton Ave, Knoxville, TN 37917 t) 865-522-2205 holyghostknoxville.org Rev. William J. McNeeley, Pst.; Rev. Michael Hendershott, Assoc. Pst.; Dcn. Gordon Lowery; Dcn. Scott Maentz; Dcn. David Venesky; Mark Ghost Williamson, DRE; CRP Stds.: 154

Immaculate Conception - 414 W. Vine Ave., Knoxville, TN 37902-1327 t) 865-522-1508 icknoxoffice@gmail.com www.icknoxville.org Rev. Charles Donahue, C.S.P., Pst.; Rev. Timothy Sullivan, C.S.P., Par. Vicar; Dcn. Doug Bitzer; Dcn. Patrick Murphy-Racey; Dcn. Joe Stackhouse; Brigid Johnson, DRE; Wendy Waxmonsky, Youth Min.; CRP Stds.: 28

Saint John XXIII University Parish/Catholic Center - 1710 Melrose Pl., Knoxville, TN 37916 t) 865-523-7931 andrea@john23rd.org; john23@utk.edu john23rd.org (Non-territorial parish for the University of Tennessee at Knoxville). Rev. Donald Andrie, C.S.P., Pst.; Rev. Richard Whitney, CSP, Assoc. Pst.; Rev. Robert J. O'Donnell, CSP, In Res.; Andrea Sirek, DRE; CRP Stds.: 16

LA FOLLETTE

Our Lady of Perpetual Help - 1142 E. Elm St., La Follette, TN 37766 t) 423-562-0312 olphlafollette@dioknox.org our-lady-of-perpetual-help-church-lafollette Rev. Samuel L. Sturm, Pst.; CRP Stds.: 22

LANCING

St. Ann - 198 Ridge Rd., Lancing, TN 37770; Mailing: 535 Margrave Dr., Harriman, TN 37748 t) 865-882-9838 saintannlancing@gmail.com Blessed Sacrament, Harriman. Rev. Michael Sweeney, Pst.;

LENOIR CITY

St. Thomas the Apostle - 1580 St. Thomas Way, Lenoir City, TN 37772 t) 865-986-9885 receptionist@sthomaslc.com www.sthomaslc.com Rev. Ray Powell, Pst.; Rev. Julian Cardona, Assoc. Pst.; Dcn. James Bodine; Dcn. Roberto Cortes; Dcn. David Egan; Dcn. John Krepps; Dcn. Rafael Pubillones; Dcn. Sean K. Smith; Arlene Maresca, DRE; CRP Stds.: 227

MADISONVILLE

St. Joseph the Worker - 649 Old Tellico Hwy. N., Madisonville, TN 37354 t) 423-442-7273 office@sjtwrrc.org www.sjtwrcc.org Rev. Julius Abuh (Nigeria), Pst.; CRP Stds.: 58

MAYNARDVILLE

Saint Teresa of Kolkata Church - 3445 Maynardville Hwy., Maynardville, TN 37807; Mailing: P.O. Box 1076, Maynardville, TN 37807-3329 t) 865-992-7222 st_teresa@att.net www.stkchurch.org Rev. Neil Pezzulo, G.H.M., Pst.; Bro. Joe Steen, G.H.M.; Dcn. Larry Rossini; CRP Stds.: 40

MORRISTOWN

St. Patrick - 2518 W. Andrew Johnson Hwy., Morristown, TN 37814 t) 423-586-9174 x7 churchofficestpat@gmail.com stpatrickmorristowntn.org Rev. Miguel Velez-Cardona, Pst.; Rev. Adam Kane, Assoc. Pst.; Dcn. Frank Bosh; Dcn. Gerald James Fage; Marivel Villa, DRE; Colleen Marie Jacobs, Bus. Mgr.; CRP Stds.: 310

MOUNTAIN CITY

St. Anthony of Padua Catholic Church - 833 W. Main St., Mountain City, TN 37683 t) 423-727-5156 (CRP) stanthonyofpaduamountaincitytn.org Rev. Dennis Kress, Pst.; Dcn. Joseph Herman; CRP Stds.: 18

NEWPORT

Good Shepherd - 2361 Cosby Hwy., Newport, TN 37821; Mailing: P.O. Box 1894, Newport, TN 37821 t) 423-623-5051 goodshepherdtn.org/ Dcn. Eric Dadey; Dcn. Otto F. Preske; Sonja Pliscott, DRE; Valerie Mulligan, Bus. Mgr.;

NORRIS

St. Joseph - 3425 Andersonville Hwy. 61, Norris, TN 37828; Mailing: P.O. Box 387, Norris, TN 37828 t) 865-494-7746 www.sjnorris.org Dcn. Dan Hosford, Admin.; Lynette Currie, DRE; CRP Stds.: 23

OAK RIDGE

St. Mary - 327-B Vermont Ave., Oak Ridge, TN 37830 t) 865-482-2875; 865-482-2875 x8386 (CRP) officesecretary@stmarysoakridge.org; dre@stmarysoakridge.org www.stmarysoakridge.org Rev. James Brent Shelton, Pst.; Rev. Pontian Kiyimba, A.J. (Uganda), Assoc. Pst.; Dcn. John DeClue; Dcn. David Duhamel; Dcn. Gary Sega; Cyndi Panter, DRE; CRP Stds.: 95

St. Mary School - (Grades PreK-8) 323 Vermont Ave., Oak Ridge, TN 37830 t) 865-483-9700 kdoogan@stmarysoakridge.org; smsprincipal@stmarysoakridge.org school.stmarysoakridge.org/ Sr. Mary John Slonkosky, OP, Prin.; Kendall Doogan, Vice Prin.; Stds.: 188; Sr. Tchrs.: 4; Lay Tchrs.: 16

PIGEON FORGE

Holy Cross - 144 Wears Valley Rd., Pigeon Forge, TN 37863 t) 865-429-5587 www.holycrosscatholicchurchtn.org/ Rev. Ronald Stone, Pst.; Dcn. David William Anderson; Dcn. Stephen May; Patty Whaley, DRE; CRP Stds.: 76

ROGERSVILLE

St. Henry - 112-114 Hwy. 70 N., Rogersville, TN 37857-4000 t) 423-272-6897 sainthenrychurch.org Rev. Bartholomew Okere (Nigeria), Pst.; CRP Stds.: 5

RUTLEDGE

Saint John Paul II Catholic Mission - 161 Bryan Rd., Rutledge, TN 37861 t) 865-992-7222 c) (423) 231-3216 jp2catholicmission@gmail.com; st_teresa@att.net stjohnpaulcatholic.com Rev. Neil Pezzulo, GHM, Pst.; Clarisia Chavarria, Pst. Assoc.; CRP Stds.: 31

SEYMOUR

Holy Family - 307 Black Oak Ridge Rd., Seymour, TN 37865 t) 865-573-1203; 865-573-4597 (CRP) www.holyfamilyseymour.org Rev. Gilbert M. Diaz, Pst.; Dcn. Dean Burry; Dcn. Gil Campos; Dcn. Robert Denne; Todd David DeGroot, DRE; CRP Stds.: 39

SIGNAL MOUNTAIN

St. Augustine - 1716 Anderson Pike, Signal Mountain, TN 37377 t) 423-886-3424 parishoffice@staugustinecatholic.org www.staugustinecatholic.org Rev. John R. Dowling, Pst.; Rev. Albert C. Sescon (Philippines), In Res.; Dcn. Gordon Kilburn; Dcn. Tom Tidwell; Heather Chapman, DRE; CRP Stds.: 82

SNEEDVILLE
St. James the Apostle - 3652 Main St., Sneedville, TN 37869; Mailing: 112-114 Hwy. 70 N., c/o St. Henry Church, Rogersville, TN 37857 t) 423-272-6897 Attended by St. Henry, Rogersville Rev. Bartholomew Okere (Nigeria), Pst.;
SODDY DAISY
Holy Spirit Catholic Church - 10768 Dayton Pike, Soddy Daisy, TN 37379; Mailing: P. O. Box 1015, Soddy Daisy, TN 37384 t) 423-332-5300 hscc_parish@holyspirittn.com www.holyspiritsoddydaisy.com Rev. Msgr. T. Allen Humbrecht, Pst.; Dcn. James Bello, Dean; Dcn. Michael Kucharzak; Dcn. Noel W. Spencer Jr.; CRP Stds.: 65
SOUTH PITTSBURG
Our Lady of Lourdes - 704 Holly Ave., South Pittsburg, TN 37380 t) 423-837-7068 ourladyoflourdesparish.org Rev. Mark A. Scholz, Pst.; Dcn. Michael Butz; CRP Stds.: 6
Virgin of the Poor Shrine - t) (423) 837-7068
TAZEWELL
Christ the King - 816 Blue Top Rd., Tazewell, TN 37879; Mailing: P.O. Box 404, Tazewell, TN 37879 t) 423-562-0312 joan.rowectk@gmail.com Our Lady of Perpetual Help Church, LaFollette Rev. Samuel L. Sturm, Pst.;
TOWNSEND
St. Francis of Assisi - 7719 River Rd., Townsend, TN 37882 t) 865-448-6070 stfrancistownsend7717@gmail.com stfrancistownsend.org Rev. Antonio Giraldo; Julie Dew, DRE;

SCHOOLS: PRESCHOOL THRU HIGH SCHOOL

SCHOOLS

STATE OF TENNESSEE

KNOXVILLE
Saint Joseph School of Knoxville - (PAR) (Grades PreK-8) 1810 Howard Dr., Knoxville, TN 37918 t) 865-689-3424 azengel@sjsknox.org www.sjsknox.org Parochial-Regional School for Holy Ghost Church, Immaculate Conception Church, & St. Albert the Great Church. Andy Zengel, Prin.; Rev. Chris Michelson, Pres.; Kelley Griffin, Librn.; Stds.: 245; Lay Tchrs.: 18

HIGH SCHOOLS

STATE OF TENNESSEE

CHATTANOOGA
Notre Dame High School - (DIO) (Grades 9-12) 2701 Vermont Ave., Chattanooga, TN 37404 t) 423-624-4618 www.myndhs.com Dcn. Hicks Armor, Pres.; Jamie Goodhard, Prin.; Rev. Christopher Manning, Campus Min.; Leigh Broxton, Librn.; Stds.: 393; Sr. Tchrs.: 2; Lay Tchrs.: 29

KNOXVILLE
Knoxville Catholic High School - (DIO) (Grades 9-12) 9245 Fox Lonas Rd., Knoxville, TN 37923 t) 865-560-0313 info@knoxvillecatholic.com knoxvillecatholic.com Dickie Sompayrac, Pres.; Dawn Harbin, Librn.; Stds.: 672; Sr. Tchrs.: 2; Lay Tchrs.: 60
Knoxville Catholic High School Development Board of Trust - 9245 Fox Lonas Rd., Knoxville, TN 37923 t) 865-560-0509

INSTITUTIONS LOCATED IN DIOCESE

CAMPUS MINISTRY / NEWMAN CENTERS [CAM]

CHATTANOOGA
Newman Foundation of Chattanooga, Inc. - 514 Palmetto St., Chattanooga, TN 37403 t) 423-618-9062 bjgabor@comcast.net www.utccatholic.com Rev. Valentin Lurochkin, Chap.; Dcn. Brian Gabor, Campus Min.; Donna Gabor, Campus Min.;
JOHNSON CITY
ETSU-Catholic Center - 734 W. Locust St., Johnson City, TN 37604 t) 423-926-7061 etsucatholiccenter@yahoo.com www.catholiccenteratetsu.com Rev. Bede C. Aboh, Chap.;
KNOXVILLE
UT-Knoxville, Newman Foundation, Inc. - 1710 Melrose Pl., Knoxville, TN 37916 t) 865-523-7931 john23@utk.edu www.john23rd.org Rev. Donald Andrie, C.S.P., Pst.; Rev. Richard Whitney, CSP, Assoc. Pst.; Rev. Robert J. O'Donnell, CSP, In Res.;

CATHOLIC CHARITIES [CCH]

KNOXVILLE
Catholic Charities of East Tennessee, Inc. - 119 Dameron Ave., Knoxville, TN 37917 t) 865-524-9896 www.ccetn.org The umbrella agency for the Catholic Charities of the diocese. Lisa Healy, Contact; Asstd. Annu.: 3,044; Staff: 60

CEMETERIES [CEM]

CHATTANOOGA
Mount Olivet Cemetery - One Mount Olivet Dr., Chattanooga, TN 37412; Mailing: 214 E. 8th St., Chattanooga, TN 37402 t) 423-622-0728; 423-266-1618 encompass@prodigy.net; business@stspeterandpaulbasilica.com www.mountolivet.com Very Rev. J. David Carter; David E. Hale, Supt.;
KNOXVILLE
Calvary Cemetery - 1916 Martin Luther King Jr. Ave., Knoxville, TN 37915; Mailing: 414 W. Vine Ave., Knoxville, TN 37902-1327 t) 865-522-1508 icknoxoffice@gmail.com Rev. Charles Donahue, C.S.P., Contact;

CONVENTS, MONASTERIES, AND RESIDENCES FOR WOMEN [CON]

KNOXVILLE
Mary, Mother of Mercy Convent (Religious Sisters of Mercy of Alma, Michigan (R.S.M.) - 6832 S. Northshore Dr., Knoxville, TN 37919 t) 865-690-9266 knoxvillersm@gmail.com www.rsmofalma.org Sr. Mary Lisa Renfer, R.S.M., Supr.; Srs.: 6
NEW MARKET
Handmaids of the Precious Blood Corp. - 596 Callaway Ridge Rd., New Market, TN 37820-3446 t) 423-241-7065 sistersarahmichael@gmail.com www.nunsforpriests.org Mother Sarah Michael, H.P.B., Prioress; Srs.: 14
OAK RIDGE
Dominican Sisters (St. Cecilia Congregation) - 323 Vermont Ave., Oak Ridge, TN 37830 t) 865-220-0922 oakridge@op-tn.org nashvilledominican.org Sr. Scholastica Niemann, O.P., Supr.; Srs.: 6

ENDOWMENTS / FOUNDATIONS / TRUSTS [EFT]

KNOXVILLE
The Catholic Diocese of Knoxville Foundation, Inc. - 805 S. Northshore Dr., Knoxville, TN 37919 t) 865-584-3307 shepp@dioknox.org Dcn. Sean K. Smith, Chancellor;
Catholic Foundation of East Tennessee - 805 S. Northshore Dr., Knoxville, TN 37919 t) 865-584-3307 Dcn. Hicks Armor, Dir.;
St. Mary's Legacy Foundation of East Tennessee, Inc. - 805 S. Northshore Dr., Knoxville, TN 37919 t) 865-584-3307 harmor@dioknox.org dioknox.org Most Rev. Richard F. Stika, Chair; Sally Sefton, Pres.; Dcn. Hicks Armor, Dir.; Very Rev. David Boettner; Dcn. David J. Lucheon; Dcn. Sean K. Smith;

HOSPITALS / HEALTH SERVICES [HOS]

CHATTANOOGA
Memorial Health Care System, Inc. (CHI Memorial) - 2525 De Sales Ave., Chattanooga, TN 37404 t) 423-495-2525 lisa_sheets@memorial.org; kathryn_davis@memorial.org www.memorial.org (Member of CommonSpirit Health) Janelle Reilly, CEO; Betsy Kammerdiener, Dir.; Bed Capacity: 459; Asstd. Annu.: 101,454; Staff: 4,558
Memorial Health Care System Foundation, Inc. - jennifer_nicely@memorial.org Jennifer Nicely, Pres.;
SIGNAL MOUNTAIN
Alexian Village Health and Rehabilitation Center - 635 Alexian Way, Signal Mountain, TN 37377 t) 314-292-9308 ahscm-mission@ascension.org www.ascensionliving.org Parent: Alexian Village of Tennessee Ryan Endsley, COO; Bed Capacity: 471; Asstd. Annu.: 578; Staff: 159

MISCELLANEOUS [MIS]

CHATTANOOGA
Ladies of Charity - 2821 Rossville Blvd., Chattanooga, TN 37407 t) (423) 624-3222 cshipp0810@gmail.com
St. Alexius Outreach Ministries, Inc. - 250 E. 10th St., Chattanooga, TN 37402-4241 t) (423) 755-3446 info@stalexiusoutreach.org stalexiusoutreach.org Bro. Steve Fogt, C.F.A., Chmn. & Pres.; Bro. Thomas Klein, C.F.A., Sec. & Treas.; Bro. Richard Lowe, C.F.A., Asst. Chair & Vice Pres.;
KNOXVILLE
Diocesan Council of Catholic Women - 805 S. Northshore Dr., Knoxville, TN 37919 t) 423-470-2560 scollins51@hotmail.com Susan Collins, Pres.; Rev. Msgr. T. Allen Humbrecht, Deanery Spiritual Mod.; Rev. Ray Powell, Deanery Spiritual Mod.; Rev. Dan G. Whitman, Deanery Spiritual Mod.; Rev. Joseph Kuzhupil, M.S.F.S. (India), Sacr. Min.;
The Diocese of Knoxville Paraclete Bookstore, Inc. - 417 Erin Dr., Ste. 110, Knoxville, TN 37919 t) 865-588-0388 theparaclete@dioknox.org www.paracletecatholic.org Catholic Book and Gift store Dcn. Walt Otey, Dir.; Sara Lauer, Bus. Mgr.;
***Ladies of Charity Knoxville** - 120 W. Baxter Ave., Knoxville, TN 37917-6401 t) 865-247-5790 (Thrift Shop); 865-247-6217 (Exec. Dir.) ladiesofcharityknox@locktown.org ladiesofcharityknox.org We serve those in need. Rev. Timothy Sullivan, C.S.P., Spiritual Adv./Care Srvcs.;
St. Mary's Legacy Clinic, Inc. - 805 S. Northshore Dr., Knoxville, TN 37919 t) 865-212-5570 srmarylisa@dioknox.org; mvargas@dioknox.org www.smlcares.com Provides holistic primary healthcare to the medically underserved in East Tennessee. Martin Vargas, Exec. Dir.;

MONASTERIES AND RESIDENCES FOR PRIESTS AND BROTHERS [MON]

KNOXVILLE
Paulist Fathers (Missionary Society of St. Paul the Apostle) - 707 E. Scott Ave., Knoxville, TN 37917 c) 865-300-5499 frcharlie@paulist.org www.paulistfathers.org Rev. Charles Donahue, C.S.P., Supr.; Rev. Robert J. O'Donnell, CSP, Vicar; Rev. Donald Andrie, C.S.P., In Res.; Rev. James A. Haley, C.S.P., In Res.; Rev. Timothy Sullivan, C.S.P., In Res.; Rev. Richard Whitney, CSP, In Res.; Priests: 6
Paulist Fathers (Missionary Society of St. Paul the Apostle) - 110 E. Scott Ave., Knoxville, TN 37917 c) (865) 300-5499 Rev. Charles Donahue, C.S.P., Supr.;
SIGNAL MOUNTAIN
Alexian Brothers - 198 James Blvd., Signal Mountain,

TN 37377-1816 t) 423-551-3969 blowe@alexianbrothers.net www.alexianbrothers.org/ Bro. Lawrence Krueger, C.F.A., Supr.; Bro. Richard Lowe, C.F.A., Dir.; Brs.: 8

NURSING / REHABILITATION / CONVALESCENCE / ELDERLY CARE [NUR]

SIGNAL MOUNTAIN

Ascension Living Alexian Village Tennessee - 437 Alexian Way, Signal Mountain, TN 37377 t) 314-292-9308 ahscm-mission@ascension.org www.ascensionliving.org Ryan Endsley, COO; Asstd. Annu.: 578; Staff: 159

RETREAT HOUSES / RENEWAL CENTERS [RTR]

BENTON

Christ Prince of Peace Retreat Center - 250 Locke Ln., Benton, TN 37307; Mailing: 805 S. Northshore Dr., Knoxville, TN 37919 t) 865-584-3307 x6002; 865-806-1343 (Dcn. Forsythe) psimoneau@dioknox.org; aforsythe@dioknox.org dioknoxretreat.org/ Retreat House/Renewal Center/ Resurrection Cemetery Rev. Jerry Daniels, Chap.; Dcn. Al Forsythe, Prog. & Devel. Mgr.;

SPECIAL CARE FACILITIES [SPF]

KNOXVILLE

Columbus Home - 3227 Division St., Knoxville, TN 37919; Mailing: 119 Dameron Ave., Knoxville, TN 37917 t) 865-971-3560 paul@ccetn.org ccetn.org Paul Ritter, Contact; Bed Capacity: 6; Asstd. Annu.: 83; Staff: 10

An asterisk (*) denotes an organization that has established tax-exempt status directly with the IRS and is not covered by the USCCB Group Ruling.

Diocese of La Crosse

(Dioecesis Crossensis)

MOST REVEREND WILLIAM P. CALLAHAN, O.F.M.CONV.

Bishop of La Crosse; ordained April 30, 1977; appointed Auxiliary Bishop of Milwaukee and Titular Bishop of Lares October 30, 2007; ordained December 21, 2007; appointed Bishop of La Crosse June 11, 2010; installed August 11, 2010. Chancery Office: 3710 East Ave. S., P.O. Box 4004, La Crosse, WI 54602-4004.

Holy Cross Diocesan Center: 3710 East Ave. S., P.O. Box 4004, La Crosse, WI 54602-4004. T: 608-788-7700; F: 608-788-8413.
diolc.org
info@diolc.org

Square Miles 15,078.

Erected March 3, 1868. Subdivided May 3, 1905. Subdivided January 15, 1946.

Comprises the following 19 Counties in the State of Wisconsin: Adams, Buffalo, Chippewa, Clark, Crawford, Dunn, Eau Claire, Jackson, Juneau, La Crosse, Marathon, Monroe, Pepin, Pierce, Portage, Richland, Trempealeau, Vernon and Wood.

For legal titles of parishes and diocesan institutions, consult the Chancery Office.

STATISTICAL OVERVIEW

Personnel

Bishop	1
Priests: Diocesan Active in Diocese	84
Priests: Diocesan Active Outside Diocese	1
Priests: Diocesan in Foreign Missions	1
Priests: Retired, Sick or Absent	43
Number of Diocesan Priests	129
Religious Priests in Diocese	10
Total Priests in your Diocese	139
Extern Priests in Diocese	30
Ordinations:	
Diocesan Priests	2
Transitional Deacons	4
Permanent Deacons	9
Permanent Deacons in Diocese	68
Total Brothers	2
Total Sisters	156

Parishes

Parishes	156
With Resident Pastor:	
Resident Diocesan Priests	91
Resident Religious Priests	4
Without Resident Pastor:	
Administered by Priests	60
Administered by Religious Women	1
Closed Parishes	1

Professional Ministry Personnel:	
Sisters	6
Lay Ministers	70

Welfare

Catholic Hospitals	4
Total Assisted	185,672
Homes for the Aged	8
Total Assisted	702
Day Care Centers	4
Total Assisted	193
Special Centers for Social Services	5
Total Assisted	7,876

Educational

Diocesan Students in Other Seminaries	13
Total Seminarians	13
Colleges and Universities	1
Total Students	2,457
High Schools, Diocesan and Parish	7
Total Students	1,310
High Schools, Private	1
Total Students	20
Elementary Schools, Diocesan and Parish	58
Total Students	5,522
Elementary Schools, Private	1
Total Students	79
Non-residential Schools for the Disabled	1
Total Students	8
Catechesis/Religious Education:	
High School Students	2,745
Elementary Students	6,834
Total Students under Catholic Instruction	18,988
Teachers in Diocese:	
Sisters	1
Lay Teachers	807

Vital Statistics

Receptions into the Church:	
Infant Baptism Totals	1,002
Minor Baptism Totals	29
Adult Baptism Totals	68
Received into Full Communion	88
First Communions	1,698
Confirmations	2,022
Marriages:	
Catholic	248
Interfaith	84
Total Marriages	332
Deaths	1,898
Total Catholic Population	135,268
Total Population	875,018

LEADERSHIP

Holy Cross Diocesan Center - t) 608-788-7700 diolc.org
Bishop's Office - t) (608) 788-7700 dbrannon@diolc.org Deborah Brannon, Exec. Asst.;
Chancellor - t) 608-791-2655 wdhein@diolc.org diolc.org/chancery Very Rev. William A. Dhein, Chancellor; Rev. Kurt J. Apfelbeck, Vice Chancellor; Maryjo Wilson, Admin. Asst. (mwilson@diolc.org);
College of Consultors - t) 608-788-7700 Most Rev. William P. Callahan, O.F.M.Conv., Pres.; Very Rev. William A. Dhein, Vicar Gen.; Rev. Msgr. Michael J. Gorman, Vicar Gen.;
College of Deans - t) 608-791-2655 mwilson@diolc.org Very Rev. William A. Dhein, Vicar General; Very Rev. Woodrow H. Pace, Vicar for Clergy; Rev. Msgr. Steven J. Kachel, La Crosse;
Diocesan Pastoral Council - t) 608-791-2655 wdhein@diolc.org Very Rev. William A. Dhein, Exec. Secy.;
Finance (See Temporalities) -
Personnel Council - t) 608-791-2652 Most Rev. William P. Callahan, O.F.M.Conv., Pres.; Very Rev. Samuel A. Martin, Chair;
Personnel Council Ex Officio - Very Rev. Woodrow H. Pace, Vicar for Clergy; Rev. Msgr. Michael J. Gorman, V.G./Secy.;
Presbyteral Council - t) (608) 791-2655 mwilson@diolc.org Most Rev. William P. Callahan, O.F.M.Conv., Pres.;
Presbyteral Council Ex Officio - Very Rev. William A. Dhein, V.G./College of Consultors; Rev. Msgr. Joseph G. Diermeier, V.G./College of Consultors; Very Rev. Woodrow H. Pace, Vicar for Clergy;
Vicars General - t) (608) 791-2655 Very Rev. William A. Dhein; Rev. Msgr. Joseph G. Diermeier; Rev. Msgr. Michael J. Gorman;

OFFICES AND DIRECTORS

Archive - t) 608-791-0162 archives@diolc.org diolc.org/archives Rev. Kurt J. Apfelbeck, Archivist;
Buildings & Grounds - t) 608-791-2692 khaverland@diolc.org Kathy Haverland, Admin. Asst.;
Catechesis and Evangelization - t) 608-791-2658 diolc.org/catechesis Ann C. Lankford, Dir.; Beth Johnson, Admin. Asst. (bjohnson@diolc.org);
Catholic Schools - t) 608-788-7707 diolc.org/schools/ Thomas Reichenbacher, Supt. (treichenbacher@diolc.org); Nathan Schams, School Finance Coord.; Darla Jereczek, Admin. Asst.;
Communications and Public Relations - t) (608) 791-2661 earcher@diolc.org diolc.org/communications Erik Archer, Dir.;
Catholic Life- Diocesan Magazine - t) 608-788-1524 catholiclife@diolc.org Jack Felsheim, Editor; Pam Willer, Advertising Rep.; Danelle Bjornson, Graphic Designer;
Information Technology - t) (608) 791-2662 nlichter@diolc.org Nick Lichter, Project Leader; Sr. Donna Krzmarzick, I.S.S.M., Database Admin.; Zach Tudahl, Tech Support Specialist;
Consecrated Life - t) 608-791-2690 diolc.org/consecratedlife Sr. Donna Krzmarzick, I.S.S.M., Dir. (dkrzmarzick@diolc.org);
Deacon Program for Education & Formation - t) 608-791-0161 ministries@diolc.org diolc.org/diaconate/permanent-deacon-formation Rev. William P. Felix, Dir. (wfelix@diolc.org); Christopher J. Ruff, Asst. Dir.; Jen Mickschl, Admin. Asst.;
Diaconate Office - t) 608-791-2665 diolc.org/diaconate Dcn. Bryan K. Hilts, Dir. (bhilts@diolc.org);
Deacon Community Board Members - Dcn. Bryan K. Hilts, Ex Officio; Rev. William P. Felix; Christopher J. Ruff;
Ecumenism - t) 715-842-4543 Very Rev. Samuel A. Martin, Diocesan Officer, Ecumenical Questions;
Hmong Ministry - t) 608-791-2658 diolc.org/catechesis/hmong-ministry/ Rev. Alan T. Burkhardt, Wausau (aburkhardt@diolclergy.org); Ann C. Lankford, Coord.;
Hmong Pastoral Care-Wausau - t) 715-298-9055 info@marymotherofgoodhelp.org www.marymotherofgoodhelp.org/ Sean Lo, Coord., Pastoral Care; Lor Thao, Coord., Faith Formation;
Hospitals and Health Affairs - t) 715-223-3048 dredfern@diolclergy.org
Letters of Suitability for Clergy - t) 608-791-2679 tbrown@diolc.org diolc.org/vicarforclergy/ Teresa Brown;
Marriage & Family Life - t) 608-791-2673 familylife@diolc.org www.diolc.org/marriage Christopher J. Rogers, Dir.; Beth Johnson, Admin. Asst. (bjohnson@diolc.org);
Natural Family Planning Program - t) 608-791-2673 nfp@diolc.org diolc.org/marriage/natural-family-planning Christy Kitzhaber, Coord.;
Matrimonial Tribunal - t) 608-791-2684 tribunal@diolc.org www.diolc.org/tribunal
Auditor - Sr. Donna Krzmarzick, I.S.S.M.;
Defender of the Bond - Rev. William J. Kulas;
Judges - Rev. Msgr. Robert P. Hundt; Rev. Msgr. Michael J. Gorman;
Judicial Vicar - t) (608) 791-2684 tribunal@diolc.org Rev. Msgr. Robert P. Hundt;
Promoter of Justice - Rev. Msgr. Joseph G. Diermeier;
Ministries - t) 608-791-0161 ministries@diolc.org diolc.org/ministries Christopher J. Ruff, Dir.; Jen Mickschl, Admin. Asst.;
Mission Office/Propagation of the Faith - t) 608-791-2676 mapel@diolc.org diolc.org/missions Very Rev. Woodrow H. Pace, Dir.; Marga Apel, Admin. Asst.;
Casa Hogar- home for youth in Lima, Peru - t) 608-791-2677 nfurger@frjoesguild.org www.homeajpm.org Noel Furger, Contact;
Father Joseph Walijewski Legacy Guild, Inc. - t) 608-791-2677 nfurger@frjoesguild.org frjoesguild.org/the-cause/the-guild Noel Furger, Contact;
Moderator of the Curia - t) 608-791-2655 Very Rev. William A. Dhein;
Sacred Worship - t) 608-791-2674 worship@diolc.org diolc.org/sacredworship Christopher J. Carstens, Dir.;
Safe Environment - t) 608-791-2679 safeenvironment@diolc.org diolc.org/safe-environment/ Teresa Brown, Dir.;
Social Concerns - t) 608-791-0161 ministries@diolc.org diolc.org/social-concerns Christopher J. Ruff, Dir.; Jen Mickschl, Admin. Asst.;
Stewardship & Development - t) 608-791-2653 diolc.org/stewardship Jeffrey Reiter, Dir. (jreiter@diolc.org);
Temporalities - t) 608-791-2668 kjereczek@diolc.org diolc.org/temporalities/ James Rieder, CFO (jrieder@diolc.org); Claudia Weinberger, Auditor/Parish Support (cweinberger@diolc.org); Kurt Jereczek, Staff Accountant;
Vicar for Clergy - t) 608-791-2652 wpace@diolc.org diolc.org/vicarforclergy/ Very Rev. Woodrow H. Pace;
Vicar for Senior Priests - t) 608-788-5483 bkonopa@diolclergy.org Very Rev. Brian D. Konopa;
Victim Assistance Coordinator - t) 608-792-9684 intakeagent@diolc.org diolc.org/safe-environment/reporting Teresa Brown, Complaint Intake Agent; Dcn. Thomas H. Skemp, Coord.;
Vocations - t) (608) 791-2667 vocations@diolc.org diolc.org/priesthood/ Rev. Nathaniel W. Kuhn, Dir.; Renee Orth, Admin. Asst.;
Journey & Regency Programs (House of Formation) - t) 608-791-2667 vocations@diolc.org diolc.org/priesthood Rev. Nathaniel W. Kuhn, Vocation Dir.; Andrew Brueggen, Asst. Dir., Vocational Formation;
Youth & Young Adult Ministry - t) 608-791-2652 crogers@diolc.org diolc.org/yya/ Christopher J. Rogers, Dir.; Laura Boden, Admin. Asst.;

ADVISORY BOARDS, COMMISSIONS, COMMITTEES, AND COUNCILS

Diocesan Council of Catholic Women - www.ldccw.org Susan Tully, Pres.; Marie Fleisner, Pres.-Elect (dre@stpaulmosinee.org); Candace McGrath, Vice. Pres. (re@stmarysrc.com);
Rural Life Committee - t) 608-780-4751 rzietlow@diolc.org diolc.org/social-concerns/rural-life Dcn. Robert J. Zietlow, Liaison to the Bishop;
Scouting Committee - t) 608-783-4911 catholicscoutslacrossediocese@gmail.com www.diolc.org/yya/scouting Cindy Sjolander, Chair; Dcn. Jason C. Hutzler, Chap.;

CATHOLIC CHARITIES

Catholic Charities of the Diocese of La Crosse, Inc. - t) 608-782-0710 info@cclse.org cclse.org/ Roberto Partarrieu, Exec. Dir. (rpartarrieu@cclse.org);

EDUCATION

Biblical Studies - www.diocesanschoolofbiblicalstudies.com
Lay Formation Institute - t) 608-791-0161 ministries@diolc.org diolc.org/ministries Christopher J. Ruff, Dir.; Jen Mickschl, Admin. Asst.;

MISCELLANEOUS / OTHER OFFICES

Catholic Foundation of West Central Wisconsin, Inc. - t) 608-519-9892 jreiter@cfwcw.org cfwcw.org Jeffrey Reiter, Interim Exec. Dir. (jreiter@diolc.org); Matt Binsfeld, Pres.;
St. Joseph's Priest Fund, Inc., (Benevolent Society) - t) 608-791-2655 mgorman@diolc.org Rev. Msgr. Michael J. Gorman, Exec. Sec.;
St. Ambrose Financial Services, Inc. - t) 608-791-2669 dherricks@stambrosefinancial.com www.stambrosefinancial.com Dennis Herricks, Exec. Dir.;

PARISHES, MISSIONS, AND CLERGY

STATE OF WISCONSIN

ABBOTSFORD

St. Bernard - 400 N. 2nd Ave., Abbotsford, WI 54401 t) 715-223-4026 abbydoreparish@gmail.com www.abbydore.org Also serves St. Louis, Dorchester. Rev. Timothy L. Oudenhoven, Pst.; CRP Stds.: 194

ALMA

St. Lawrence - 206 S. 2nd St., Alma, WI 54610; Mailing: PO Box 246, Alma, WI 54610 t) 608-687-8418 tresecclesiae@gmail.com tresecclesiae.org Serves Immaculate Conception Parish, Fountain City & St. Boniface Parish, Waumandee. Rev. Aruldoss Savarimuthu (India), Pst.; Dcn. Edward D. Wendt; CRP Stds.: 9

ALMA CENTER

Immaculate Conception Parish - 341 W. Main St., Alma Center, WI 54611; Mailing: P.O. Box 188, Alma Center, WI 54611 t) 715-964-5201 office@icpstj.diolcparish.org www.catholic-parishes-of-almacenter-fairchild.org Also serves St. Joseph-Fairview, Fairchild; St. John Cantius, Fairchild (Oratory) Very Rev. Peter J. Kieffer, Par. Admin.; CRP Stds.: 37

ALMOND

St. Maximilian Maria Kolbe - 8611 State Rd. 54, Almond, WI 54909 t) 715-824-3380 secretary@stmaxkolbe.org; finance@stmaxkolbe.org www.stmaxkolbe.org Merger of Holy Guardian Angels, Almond (1914), St. Martin, Buena Vista (1862), St. John, Heffron (1967), St. Patrick, Lanard (1888). Rev. Peter M. Manickam, Pst.; Dcn. James Trzinski; CRP Stds.: 69

ALTOONA

St. Mary - 1812 Lynn Ave., Altoona, WI 54720

t) 715-855-1294 www.stmarys-altoona.com Also serves St. Raymond of Penafort Parish in Fall Creek. Rev. Derek J. Sakowski, Pst.; Rev. Levi J. Schmitt, Pst. Assoc.; CRP Stds.: 125

AMHERST

St. James - 453 S. Main St., Amherst, WI 54406; Mailing: PO Box 280, Amherst, WI 54406 t) 715-824-3455 catholiccentral54406@gmail.com; sjsmparishlife@gmail.com sjsmmcc.weconnect.com Also serves St. Mary of Mount Carmel Parish, Fancher. Rev. Jerzy Rebacz, Pst.; Dcn. Arthur J. Schaller; Ann Hemmy, Parish Life Coord.; CRP Stds.: 50

St. Mary of Mount Carmel - 3995 County Rd. K, Amherst, WI 54406; Mailing: 453 S. Main St., P.O. Box 280, Amherst, WI 54406 t) 715-316-7056 (CRP); 715-824-3455 sjsmparishlife@gmail.com; catholiccentral54406@gmail.com sjsmmcc.weconnect.com Also serves St. James, Amherst. Rev. Jerzy Rebacz, Pst.; Dcn. Arthur J. Schaller; Ann Hemmy, Parish Life Coord.; CRP Stds.: 37

ARCADIA

Holy Family - 223 E. Maple St., Arcadia, WI 54612 t) 608-323-7116 secretary@holyfam.com; dre@holyfam.com www.holyfam.com Also serves Most Sacred Heart, Pine Creek (Dodge). Rev. Kyle N. Laylan, Par. Admin.; Rev. Arturo Vigueras, Assoc. Pst.; Dcn. Michael Kamrowski, DRE; CRP Stds.: 61

Holy Family Catholic School (Arcadia Catholic School) - (Grades PreK-8) 532 Mc Kinley St., Arcadia, WI 54612 t) 608-323-3676 barb@holyfam.com arcadiahfcs.wixsite.com/holyfamily Leanne Haines, Acting Prin.; Stds.: 190; Lay Tchrs.: 11

ARKANSAW

St. Joseph - W7805 County Rd. Z, Arkansaw, WI 54721 t) 715-647-2901 saintjoseph@nelson-tel.net Also serves St. John the Baptist Parish, Plum City. Rev. Junabe Villaflor Villapaz (Philippines), Pst.;

ATHENS

St. Anthony de Padua - 417 Caroline St., Athens, WI 54411; Mailing: PO Box 206, Athens, WI 54411 t) 715-257-7684 www.stanthonyathens.com Rev. George Nelson Graham (Ghana), Pst.; Sharon Westfall, DRE; CRP Stds.: 57

St. Anthony de Padua School - (Grades PreK-8) 309 Mueller St., Athens, WI 54411; Mailing: PO Box i, Athens, WI 54411 t) 715-257-7541 Donna Conley, Prin.; Stds.: 62; Lay Tchrs.: 5

St. Thomas - 232451 Vilas St, Athens, WI 54411; Mailing: 417 Caroline St, PO Box 206, Athens, WI 54411 t) 715-257-7684 tricia.cowan@staathens.org www.stanthonyathens.com Also serves St. Anthony Parish, Athens. The church is located in the unincorporated community of Milan. Rev. George Nelson Graham (Ghana), Pst.; CRP Stds.: 5

AUBURNDALE

Nativity of the Blessed Virgin Mary - 5866 Main St., Auburndale, WI 54412; Mailing: PO Box 177, Auburndale, WI 54412 t) 715-652-2806 saintsmmk@gmail.com; stmaryre1.10@gmail.com www.saintsmmk.com Also serves St. Kilian, Blenker and St. Michael, Hewitt. Rev. Murali Anand Rayappan (India), Pst.; Sharon Schaefer, DRE; CRP Stds.: 55

BLACK RIVER FALLS

Guardian Angels - 507 Main St., Black River Falls, WI 54615 t) 715-284-5613 parishoffice@guardianangelscathparish.org www.guardianangelscathparish.org Founded in 2017, the merger of St. Joseph Parish in Black River Falls (1857) and St. Kevin Parish in Melrose (1963). Rev. Arivu Mariappan (India), Par. Admin.; CRP Stds.: 40

BLAIR

St. Ansgar - 607 E. Olson St., Blair, WI 54616; Mailing: 22650 Washington St., Ettrick, WI 54627 t) 608-525-3811 stbridgets@centurytel.net Also serves St. Bridget, Ettrick. Rev. Jeyaseelan Yobu (India), Par. Admin.; Delrose Patzner-Hansen, DRE; CRP Stds.: 4

BLENKER

St. Kilian - 3872 County Rd. P, Blenker, WI 54415; Mailing: 5866 Main St., PO Box 177, Auburndale, WI 54412 t) 715-652-2806 saintsmmk@gmail.com www.saintsmmk.com Also serves Nativity of the BVM Parish, Auburndale and St. Michael Parish, Hewitt. Rev. Murali Anand Rayappan (India), Pst.; Joyce Martin, DRE; CRP Stds.: 47

BLOOMER

St. John the Baptist - 4540 State Hwy. 40, Bloomer, WI 54724 t) 715-568-3778 stjohns@bloomer.net stjohns.bloomertel.net Also serves St. Paul Parish, Bloomer Rev. Victor C. Feltes, Pst.; Rev. Chinnappan Pelavendran (India), Assoc. Pst.; CRP Stds.: 53

St. Paul - 1222 Main St., Bloomer, WI 54724 t) 715-568-3255; 715-568-3256 (CRP) stpaulrecoffice@bloomer.net stpauls.bloomertel.net Also serves St. John the Baptist Parish, Bloomer (Cooks Valley) Rev. Victor C. Feltes, Pst.; Rev. Chinnappan Pelavendran (India), Assoc. Pst.; Dcn. Richard J. Kostner; CRP Stds.: 93

St. Paul School - (Grades PreK-8) 1210 Main St., Bloomer, WI 54724 t) 715-568-3233 stpaulpr@bloomer.net Jacqueline Peterson, Prin.;

BOYCEVILLE

St. Luke - 919 Center St., Boyceville, WI 54725; Mailing: PO Box 316, Boyceville, WI 54725 t) 715-643-3081 stlukeboyceville@gmail.com www.saintlukebv.org Also serves Sacred Heart Parish, Elmwood; Sacred Heart of Jesus Parish, Spring Valley. Mary Byrne, DRE; CRP Stds.: 8

CADOTT

St. Anthony - 13981 250th St., Cadott, WI 54727; Mailing: 13989 195th St., P.O. Box 68, Jim Falls, WI 54748 t) 715-382-4422 sacredheartparishjimfalls@yahoo.com Also serves Holy Cross, Cornell and Sacred Heart, Jim Falls Rev. Eric G. Linzmaier, Pst.; Dcn. Kurt G. Zakrzewski;

CAMP DOUGLAS

St. James - 100 Bartell St., Camp Douglas, WI 54618; Mailing: P.O. Box 199, Camp Douglas, WI 54618 t) 608-427-6762 stjames@mwt.net www.mjpcatholic.com Also serves St. Michael Parish, Indian Creek and St. Paul Parish, New Lisbon. Rev. Peter Raj Mariasamy;

CASHTON

Sacred Heart of Jesus - 1205 Front St., Cashton, WI 54619 t) 608-654-5654 secretary@smash3p.org www.smash3p.org Also serves St. Augustine, Norwalk and Nativity of the BVM, St. Mary's Ridge Rev. Michael E. Klos, Pst.; Dcn. Samuel G. Schmirler;

Sacred Heart of Jesus School - (Grades PreK-8) 710 Kenyon St, Cashton, WI 54619 t) 608-654-7733 smash3pschool@mwt.net Jayme Klinge, Head Teacher;

CAZENOVIA

St. Anthony de Padua - 32505 County Hwy. V, Cazenovia, WI 53924 t) 608-983-2367 grrottwi@gmail.com Also serves Sacred Heart Parish, Lone Rock and St. Mary Parish, Keyesville. Very Rev. Irudayanathan Thainase, Pst.;

CHIPPEWA FALLS

St. Bridget - 2801 N 110th Ave, Chippewa Falls, WI 54729; Mailing: 412 S Main St, Chippewa Falls, WI 54729 t) 715-723-4890 yhiess@ssndcp.org www.parishesonline.com/find/st-bridget Also serves Holy Ghost, Chippewa Falls and Notre Dame, Chippewa Falls. Very Rev. Jesse D. Burish, Pst.; Rev. Brandon Guenther, Assoc. Pst.; Allison Burch, DRE; Paula Hanson, DRE; CRP Stds.: 21

St. Charles Borromeo - 810 Pearl St, Chippewa Falls, WI 54729 t) 715-723-4088 centraloffice@stcharles-cf.com; dre@stcharles-cf.com www.stcharles-cf.com Also serves St. Peter Parish, Tilden. Rev. Msgr. Michael J. Gorman, Pst.; Rev. Ethan Hokamp, Par. Vicar; Dcn. Daniel J. Rider; Alexis Pomietlo, DRE; Abigail Lynch, Music Min.; Janet Wolfe, Bus. Mgr.; CRP Stds.: 42

Holy Ghost - 412 S Main St, Chippewa Falls, WI 54729 t) 715-723-4890 www.holyghostchurchcf.com Also serves Notre Dame in Chippewa Falls and St. Bridget in Springfield. Very Rev. Jesse D. Burish, Pst.; Rev. Brandon Guenther, Assoc. Pst.; Paula Hanson, DRE; CRP Stds.: 78

Notre Dame - 117 Allen St., Chippewa Falls, WI 54729 t) 715-723-7108 akatz@ourladyofthefalls.org www.ourladyofthefalls.org Also serves Holy Ghost Parish in Chippewa Falls and St. Bridget Parish in Springfield. Very Rev. Jesse D. Burish, Pst.; Rev. Brandon Guenther, Assoc. Pst.; CRP Stds.: 53

St. Peter - 11358 County Hwy. Q, Chippewa Falls, WI 54729; Mailing: 810 Pearl St., Chippewa Falls, WI 54729 t) 715-723-4088 centraloffice@stcharles-cf.com www.stpetertilden.com Served from St. Charles Borromeo, Chippewa Falls. Rev. Msgr. Michael J. Gorman, Pst.; Rev. Ethan Hokamp, Par. Vicar; Dcn. Daniel J. Rider; Alexis Pomietlo, DRE; Janet Wolfe, Bus. Mgr.; CRP Stds.: 4

St. Peter School - (Grades 1-8) 11370 County Hwy. Q, Chippewa Falls, WI 54729 t) 715-288-6250 principal@stpetersschooltilden.com www.stpeterschooltilden.com Janelle Dachel, Head Teacher; Stds.: 33; Lay Tchrs.: 3

COLBY

St. Mary Help of Christians - 205 S. 2nd St., Colby, WI 54421; Mailing: P.O. Box 436, Colby, WI 54421 t) 715-223-3048; 715-223-3048 x4 (CRP) catholiccentral@gmail.com Rev. D. Joseph Redfern, Pst.; Dcn. Michael J. Schaefer; Jenessa Freidhof, CRE; CRP Stds.: 85

St. Mary Help of Christians School - (Grades PreK-8) 209 S. 2nd St., Colby, WI 54421-0408; Mailing: P.O. Box 408, Colby, WI 54421-0408 t) 715-223-3033 stmoff@gmail.com stmaryschoolcolby.org/ Paul Klinkhammer, Prin.; Stds.: 90; Lay Tchrs.: 10

COON VALLEY

St. Mary - 904 Central Ave., Coon Valley, WI 54623 t) 608-452-3841 c) (608) 606-9787 stmaryscv@mwt.net www.stmarycv.org Also serves Annunciation of the Blessed Virgin Mary Parish, Viroqua Rev. Joseph M. Richards, Pst.; Dcn. Anthony F. Shay; CRP Stds.: 24

CORNELL

Holy Cross - 107 S. 8th St., Cornell, WI 54732; Mailing: P.O. Box 68, Cornell, WI 54732 t) 715-239-6826 holycross107@centurytel.net Also serves: St. Anthony, Drywood and Sacred Heart, Jim Falls Rev. Eric G. Linzmaier, Pst.; Dcn. Kurt G. Zakrzewski; Kayla Olmstead, DRE; CRP Stds.: 49

CUSTER

Immaculate Conception - 7176 Esker Rd., Custer, WI 54423 t) 715-592-4330 stmary@wi-net.com www.stmaryscuster.com Also serves Sacred Heart, Polonia (Custer). Rev. Mark A. Miller, Pst.; CRP Stds.: 21

Sacred Heart - 7379 Church St., Custer, WI 54423 t) (715) 600-6942 parishoffice@sacredheartpolonia.com www.sacredheartpolonia.com Rev. Mark A. Miller, Pst.; Dcn. James J. Sniadajewski; CRP Stds.: 91

Sacred Heart School - (Grades PreK-6) principal@sacredheartpolonia.com www.sacredheartpolonia.com/sacred-heart-school Thomas McCann, Prin.; Stds.: 52; Lay Tchrs.: 4

DODGE

Most Sacred Heart - N20555 County Rd. G, Dodge, WI 54625-9721 t) 608-539-3704 rmspittler@triwest.net sacredheartpc.wixsite.com/sacredheartpc Also serves Holy Family Parish, Arcadia. Rev. Kyle N. Laylan, Par. Admin.; Rev. Arturo Vigueras, Assoc. Pst.; CRP Stds.: 17

DORCHESTER

St. Louis - 133 N. 3rd St., Dorchester, WI 54425; Mailing: 400 N. 2nd Ave., Abbotsford, WI 54405 t) 715-223-4026 abbydoreparish@gmail.com abbydore.org Also serves St. Bernard, Abbotsford. Rev. Timothy L. Oudenhoven, Pst.; CRP Stds.: 6

DURAND

Holy Rosary - N6235 County Rd. V, Durand, WI 54736; Mailing: 911 W. Prospect St., PO Box 188, Durand, WI 54736 t) 715-672-5640; 715-672-4668 (CRP) secretary@catholictriparish.org www.catholictriparish.org Also serves St. Mary's

Assumption, Durand and Sacred Heart, Mondovi. Rev. Emmanuel Kofi Asamoah-Bekoe (Ghana), Pst.; Rev. Timothy M. Reither, Assoc. Pst.; Dcn. James A. Weingart; Benjamin Mitchell, DRE; CRP Stds.: 41

Holy Rosary School - (Grades K-3) N6217 County Rd. V, Durand, WI 54736 t) 715-672-4276 assumptionk-3@nelson-tel.net catholictriparish.org/catholic-school.html Mary Lansing, Prin.; Stds.: 44; Lay Tchrs.: 4

St. Mary's Assumption - 911 W. Prospect St., Durand, WI 54736; Mailing: P.O. Box 188, Durand, WI 54736 t) 715-672-5640; 715-672-4668 (CRP) secretary@catholictriparish.org www.catholictriparish.org Rev. Emmanuel Kofi Asamoah-Bekoe (Ghana), Pst.; Rev. Timothy M. Reither, Assoc. Pst.; Dcn. James A. Weingart; Benjamin Mitchell, DRE; Susan Wolf, Bus. Mgr.; CRP Stds.: 50

St. Mary's Assumption School - (Grades 4-8) 901 W. Prospect St., Durand, WI 54736 t) 715-672-5617 assumption4-8@nelson-tel.net catholictriparish.org/catholic-school.html Mary Lansing, Prin.; Stds.: 60; Lay Tchrs.: 7

EASTMAN

St. Patrick - 21140 State Hwy. 27, Eastman, WI 54626; Mailing: 106 Main St., PO Box 35, Seneca, WI 54654 t) 608-734-3252; 608-734-3931 (Bus. Office) stpatricks.seneca.bookkeeper@gmail.com www.catholicchurchesofncc.com Also serves St. Mary Parish, Gays Mills and St. Philip Parish, Rolling Ground. Rev. Thomas M. Huff, Pst.; Sue Garfoot, DRE; CRP Stds.: 25

St. Wenceslaus - 57975 Baer Ct., Eastman, WI 54626; Mailing: PO Box 109, Eastman, WI 54626 t) 608-874-4151 stwenceslaus@centurytel.net Also serves Sacred Heart of Jesus Parish, Wauzeka. Very Rev. Rajendran Anandan, Pst.; Jane Achenbach, DRE; CRP Stds.: 11

EAU CLAIRE

Immaculate Conception - 1712 Highland Ave., Eau Claire, WI 54701 t) 715-835-9935 parishoffice@icpeau.diolcparish.org www.ic-ec.us Rev. Francis Thadathil, MSFS (India), Pst.; Dcn. Gregory J. Power; Rev. Amalraj Roche (India), In Res.; CRP Stds.: 113

St. James the Greater - 2502 11th St. Ste. 1, Eau Claire, WI 54703 t) 715-835-5887 stjameseac@aol.com stjameseauclaire.org Rev. Thomas J. Krieg, Pst.; Christine Warloski, Pst. Min./Coord.; Patrice Taft, Pst. Min./Coord.; Anne Henriksen, Bus. Mgr.; Kelly Beaudrie, DRE; Elizabeth Cerny, CRE; Mary Felton-Kolstad, Music Min.; CRP Stds.: 191

Newman Community - 110 Garfield Ave., Eau Claire, WI 54701 t) 715-834-3399 parishoffice@newmanec.com www.newmanec.com Rev. Daniel E. Oudenhoven, Pst.; CRP Stds.: 52

St. Olaf - 3220 Monroe St., Eau Claire, WI 54702; Mailing: PO Box 1203, Eau Claire, WI 54702 t) 715-832-2504 solaf@saintolafparish.org www.saintolafparish.org Very Rev. James R. Kurzynski, Pst.; Robin Johengen, DRE; CRP Stds.: 64

Sacred Heart of Jesus-St. Patrick - 448 N. Dewey St., Eau Claire, WI 54703 t) 715-832-0925 office@shspec.org www.shspec.org Merger of St. Patrick, Eau Claire (1865) and Sacred Heart of Jesus, Eau Claire (1875). Rev. Antony Joseph (India), Pst.; CRP Stds.: 23

Sacred Heart Church - 418 N. Dewey St., Eau Claire, WI 54703

St. Patrick Church - 316 Fulton St., Eau Claire, WI 54703

EAU GALLE

St. Henry - N460 County Rd. D, Eau Galle, WI 54737 t) 715-283-4448 sthenry@wwt.net Rev. Jerome G. Hoeser, Pst.; Kay Weinzirl, DRE; CRP Stds.: 39

EDGAR

Holy Family - 125074 County Rd. U, Edgar, WI 54426 t) 715-507-1975 parishoffice@hfppon.diolcparish.org Also serves St. John the Baptist, Edgar. Rev. Alan P. Wierzba, Pst.; Lori Gajewski, DRE; CRP Stds.: 40

St. John the Baptist - 103 N. 4th Ave., Edgar, WI 54426; Mailing: P.O. Box 35, Edgar, WI 54426 t) 715-352-3011 parishadmin@stjohnedgar.org stjohn-edgar.org Also serves Holy Family Parish, Poniatowski. Rev. Alan P. Wierzba, Pst.; Dcn. Gregory W. Kaiser; Nancy Hackel, DRE; CRP Stds.: 133

St. John the Baptist School - (Grades PreSchool-8) 125 N. 4th Ave., Edgar, WI 54426; Mailing: PO Box 66, Edgar, WI 54426 t) 715-352-3000 secretary@stjohnedgar.org Renee Fait, Prin.; Stds.: 55; Lay Tchrs.: 9

ELK MOUND

St. Joseph - 417 W. Menomonie St., Elk Mound, WI 54739; Mailing: PO Box 275, Elk Mound, WI 54739 t) 715-875-4539 stjosephemwi@gmail.com Also serves St. Joseph Parish, Rock Falls. Rev. Timothy J. Welles, Pst.; Ann Hoffman, DRE; CRP Stds.: 42

ELLSWORTH

St. Francis of Assisi - 264 S. Grant St., Ellsworth, WI 54011; Mailing: PO Box 839, Ellsworth, WI 54011 t) 715-273-4774 stfrancisrectory@sbcglobal.net www.stfrancisellsworth.com

St. Francis School - (Grades PreK-5) 244 W. Woodworth St., Ellsworth, WI 54011; Mailing: PO Box 250, Ellsworth, WI 54011 t) 715-273-4391 cbuckel@stfrancisellsworth.org Charles Buckel, Prin.;

ELMWOOD

Sacred Heart - 106 W. Wilson Ave., Elmwood, WI 54740; Mailing: S105 Sabin Ave., PO Box 456, Spring Valley, WI 54767 t) 715-778-5519 admin@svecatholic.org www.svecatholic.org Also serves St. Luke, Boyceville and Sacred Heart of Jesus, Spring Valley Rev. Anbalagan Shanmugam, Par. Admin.; CRP Stds.: 20

ELROY

St. Patrick - 110 Spring St., Elroy, WI 53929; Mailing: 307 Spring St., Box 155, Kendall, WI 54638 t) 608-463-7120 stjosephkendall@centurytel.net Also serves St. Joseph Parish, Kendall and St. John the Baptist Parish, Wilton Rev. John Ofori-Domah (Ghana), Pst.; CRP Stds.: 38

ETTRICK

St. Bridget - 22650 Washington St., Ettrick, WI 54627 t) 608-525-3811 stbridgets@centurytel.net Also serves St. Ansgar Parish, Blair. Rev. Jeyaseelan Yobu (India), Pst.; CRP Stds.: 12

FAIRCHILD

St. Joseph - N13740 Fairview Rd., Fairchild, WI 54741 t) 715-964-5201 office@icpstj.diolcparish.org www.catholic-parishes-of-almacenter-fairchild.org Also serves Immaculate Conception Parish, Alma Center and St. John Cantius (Oratory), Fairchild Very Rev. Peter J. Kieffer, Par. Admin.; CRP Stds.: 4

FALL CREEK

St. Raymond of Penafort - E10455 E. Mallard Rd., Fall Creek, WI 54742 t) 715-877-3400 bfirkus@smsrcatholic.com www.straymond.us Also serves St. Mary, Altoona. Merger of St. Anthony, Augusta (1857), Holy Guardian Angels, Brackett (1903), St. John the Apostle, Fall Creek (1967). Rev. Derek J. Sakowski, Pst.; Rev. Levi J. Schmitt, Assoc. Pst.; CRP Stds.: 45

FOUNTAIN CITY

Immaculate Conception - 2 N. Hill St., Fountain City, WI 54629; Mailing: P.O. Box 218, Fountain City, WI 54629 t) 608-687-8418 tresecclesiae@gmail.com tresecclesiae.org Also serves St. Lawrence, Alma and St. Boniface, Waumandee. Rev. Aruldoss Savarimuthu (India), Pst.; Dcn. Edward D. Wendt; CRP Stds.: 47

FRIENDSHIP

St. Joseph - 807 W. Lake St., Friendship, WI 53934; Mailing: 712 N. Godwin Cir., Friendship, WI 53934 t) 608-339-3485 stjosephcc@frontier.com stjoseph-friendship.org Founded as St. Leo's in Friendship. In 1922, St. Joseph Church in Adams was formed. In 2005, St. Joseph Church in Friendship was constructed. Rev. David P. Bruener, Pst.; Theresa David, DRE; CRP Stds.: 32

GALESVILLE

St. Mary - 20344 W. Ridge Ave., Galesville, WI 54630; Mailing: 11646 South St., Trempealeau, WI 54661 t) 608-534-6652 secretary@stmstb.diolcparish.org www.saintbartholomew.net Also serves St. Bartholomew Parish, Trempealeau. Rev. Sebastian S. Saleth-Pitchai (India), Par. Admin.; Dcn. Kent L. Jacobson; CRP Stds.: 46

GAYS MILLS

St. Mary - 115 School St., Gays Mills, WI 54631; Mailing: 106 Main St., PO Box 35, Seneca, WI 54654 t) 608-735-4420; 608-734-3931 stpatricks.seneca.bookkeeper@gmail.com www.catholicchurchesofncc.com Also serves St. Philip Parish, Rolling Ground & St. Patrick Parish, Seneca. Rev. Thomas M. Huff, Pst.;

GENOA

St. Charles Borromeo - 701 Walnut St., Genoa, WI 54632; Mailing: PO Box 130, Genoa, WI 54632 t) 608-689-2642 office@stcharlesgenoa.org www.mwt.net/~st.charl/ Rev. Daniel J. Sedlacek, Pst.; Kelly Hutchinson, DRE; CRP Stds.: 24

St. Charles School - (Grades PreK-6) 707 Eagle St., Genoa, WI 54632 phytry@stcharle.org Patricia Hytry, Head Teacher; Stds.: 24; Lay Tchrs.: 4

GREENWOOD

St. Mary Help of Christians - 121 N. Main St., Greenwood, WI 54437; Mailing: P.O. Box 129, Greenwood, WI 54437 t) 715-255-8017 stap1931@gmail.com; sharonls1963@yahoo.com stanthonyloyal.org/st-mary-parish Also serves St. Anthony Parish, Loyal and Holy Family Parish, Willard. Rev. Emmanuel Famiyeh, Pst.; CRP Stds.: 23

HATLEY

St. Florian - 500 Church Ln, Hatley, WI 54440; Mailing: PO Box 100, Hatley, WI 54440 t) 715-446-3085 officemanager@stflos.org www.stflos.org Also serves St. Agnes Parish, Weston. Rev. Gregory J. Bohren, Pst.;

St. Ladislaus - 173141 State Hwy. 153, Hatley, WI 54440 t) 715-446-3060 sisterme@stladislaus.org; parishsecretary@stladislaus.org stladislaus.weebly.com Also serves St. Joseph Parish, Galloway (Wittenberg). Rev. Augustine Kofi Bentil (Ghana), Pst.; Sr. Mary Ellen Diermeier, S.S.J.-T.O.S.F., Pst. Assoc.; CRP Stds.: 96

HEWITT

St. Michael - 11100 Main St., Hewitt, WI 54441 t) 715-652-2806 saintsmmk@gmail.com www.saintsmmk.com Also serves Nativity of the BVM Parish, Auburndale and St. Kilian Parish, Blenker. Rev. Murali Anand Rayappan (India), Pst.; CRP Stds.: 24

HILLSBORO

St. Aloysius - 545 Prairie Ave., Hillsboro, WI 54634; Mailing: PO Box 466, Hillsboro, WI 54634 t) 608-489-2580 saintals@mwt.net Also serves St. Jerome, Wonewoc & St. Teresa of Avila Oratory, Union Center. Rev. Donald J. Bauer, Pst.; Rachel Smith, DRE; CRP Stds.: 12

HOLMEN

St. Elizabeth Ann Seton - 515 N. Main St., Holmen, WI 54636 t) 608-526-4424 office@seasholmen.org www.seasholmen.org Rev. James C. Weighner, Pst.; Mary Luebke, DRE; CRP Stds.: 239

INDEPENDENCE

SS. Peter and Paul - 36028 Osseo Rd., Independence, WI 54747; Mailing: PO Box 430, Independence, WI 54747 t) 715-985-2227 www.ssppwi.org Also serves St. John the Apostle Parish, Whitehall. Rev. George Kutty Thayilkuzhithottu, M.S.F.S. (India), Pst.; CRP Stds.: 85

SS. Peter and Paul School - (Grades PreK-8) 36100 Osseo Rd, Independence, WI 54747 t) 715-985-3719 kpronschinske@ssppwi.org Amanda Gierok, Prin.; Stds.: 56; Lay Tchrs.: 9

JIM FALLS

Sacred Heart of Jesus - 14065 195th St., Jim Falls, WI 54748; Mailing: P.O. Box 68, Jim Falls, WI 54748 t) 715-382-4422 sacredheartparishjimfalls@yahoo.com Also serves Holy Cross, Cornell and St. Anthony, Drywood Rev. Eric G. Linzmaier, Pst.; Dcn. Kurt G.

Zakrzewski;

JUNCTION CITY

St. Michael - 324 Main St., Junction City, WI 54443; Mailing: 146 Main St., Milladore, WI 54454 t) 715-457-2314 kmwparishes@tds.net Also serves St. Bartholomew Parish, Mill Creek and St. Wenceslaus Parish, Milladore. Rev. Mariapackiam Pitchai-Savari (India), Pst.; Kim Rusch, DRE; Jennifer Zarecki, DRE; CRP Stds.: 31

KENDALL

St. Joseph - 307 Spring St., Kendall, WI 54638; Mailing: PO Box 155, Kendall, WI 54638 t) 608-463-7120 stjosephkendall@centurytel.net Also serves St. Patrick Parish, Elroy, and St. John the Baptist Parish, Wilton. Rev. John Ofori-Domah (Ghana), Pst.;

LA CROSSE

St. Joseph the Workman Cathedral - 530 Main St., La Crosse, WI 54601 t) 608-782-0322 office@cathedralsjworkman.org www.cathedralsjworkman.org Rev. Msgr. Richard W. Gilles, Rector; Dcn. Joseph A. Richards; Dcn. Thomas H. Skemp;

Blessed Sacrament Parish - 130 Losey Blvd. S., La Crosse, WI 54601 t) 608-782-2953 x2 office@bsplacrosse.org bsplacrosse.org Rev. Billy J. Dodge, Pst.; Rev. Samuel C. McCarty, Assoc. Pst.; Dcn. David J. Allen; CRP Stds.: 21

Holy Trinity - 1333 13th St. S., La Crosse, WI 54601 t) 608-782-2028; 608-782-2028 (CRP) htparish@outlook.com www.htparishlax.com Rev. G. Richard Roberts, Pst.; CRP Stds.: 50

St. James the Less - 1032 Caledonia St., La Crosse, WI 54603 t) 608-782-7557 saintjameslacrosse@gmail.com www.saintjameslax.com Rev. Robert M. Letona, Pst.; Dcn. Jason C. Hutzler; CRP Stds.: 16

St. Joseph - W2601 State Rd. 33, La Crosse, WI 54601 t) 608-788-1646 sjrp2601@gmail.com www.saintjosephridgeparish.com Also serves St. Peter Parish, Middle Ridge (Rockland). Rev. Biju Chennala Kunjukutty, M.S.F.S. (India), Pst.; Stacy Burns, DRE; CRP Stds.: 34

Mary, Mother of the Church - 2006 Weston St, La Crosse, WI 54601 t) 608-788-5483 secretary@mmoclacrosse.org www.mmoclacrosse.org Very Rev. Brian D. Konopa, Pst.; Dcn. Terrence L. Bell; Kristin Johnson, DRE; CRP Stds.: 102

Roncalli Newman Parish - 1732 State St., La Crosse, WI 54601 t) 608-784-4994 office@newmanlc.org www.roncallinewmancenter.com Rev. Billy J. Dodge, Pst.; Rev. Samuel C. McCarty, Assoc. Pst.; Dcn. David J. Belland; CRP Stds.: 65

LONE ROCK

Sacred Heart - 417 S Oak St, Lone Rock, WI 53556; Mailing: 32505 County Hwy V, Cazenovia, WI 53924 t) 608-983-2367 grrottwi@gmail.com Also serves St. Anthony Parish, Cazenovia and Nativity of the BVM Parish, Keyesville. Very Rev. Irudayanathan Thainase, Pst.; CRP Stds.: 4

LOYAL

St. Anthony of Padua - 407 N Division St, Loyal, WI 54446-0069; Mailing: PO Box 69, Loyal, WI 54446-0069 t) 715-255-8017 (CRP); 715-255-8017 stap1931@gmail.com www.stanthonyloyal.org Also serves St. Mary Help of Christians Parish, Greenwood and Holy Family Parish, Willard. Rev. Emmanuel Famiyeh, Pst.; Janet Boh, DRE; CRP Stds.: 50

St. Anthony of Padua School - (Grades K-6) 208 W Spring St, Loyal, WI 54446 t) 715-255-8636 Barbara Kingsbury, Prin.; Stds.: 23; Lay Tchrs.: 3

LYNDON STATION

St. Mary - 117 N. Juneau St., Lyndon Station, WI 53944; Mailing: P.O. Box 303, Lyndon Station, WI 53944 t) 608-666-2421 office@stmlys.diolcparish.org stmaryparishlyndon.com Rev. Cryton Outschoorn (Sri Lanka), Par. Admin.; Sandra Madland, DRE; CRP Stds.: 18

MARATHON

Nativity of the Blessed Virgin Mary - 712 Market St, Marathon, WI 54448; Mailing: PO Box 7, Marathon, WI 54448 t) 715-443-2045 bvmparish@stmarysmarathon.org stmarysmarathon.weconnect.com Rev. Msgr. Joseph G. Diermeier, Pst.; Dcn. John P. Bourke; Dcn. Bryan K. Hilts; Dcn. Gordon J. Ruplinger; Steve Kreager, DRE; CRP Stds.: 144

St. Mary's School - (Grades K-8) 716 Market St., Marathon, WI 54448; Mailing: P.O. Box 102, Marathon, WI 54448 t) 715-443-3430 tglobensky@stmarysmarathon.org Terese Globensky, Prin.; Stds.: 182; Lay Tchrs.: 17

Sacred Heart - 222761 County Rd S, Marathon, WI 54448 t) 715-443-3675 sacredheartcassel@gmail.com Also serves St. Patrick, Halder. Rev. Joseph C. Nakwah (Ghana), Pst.;

MARSHFIELD

Corpus Christi - 10075 County Hwy. BB, Marshfield, WI 54449; Mailing: 112 E. 11th St., Marshfield, WI 54449 t) 715-384-3213 sacredheartmarshfield@gmail.com sacredheartmarshfield.org Also serves Sacred Heart, Marshfield. Rev. Keith J. Kitzhaber, Pst.; Dcn. Raymond R. Draeger; CRP Stds.: 10

St. John the Baptist - 201 W. Blodgett St., Marshfield, WI 54449 t) 715-384-3252 mjgouin@frontier.com; sjbcp_fin@frontier.com www.stjohnsmarshfield.org Rev. Daniel L. Thelen, Pst.; Rev. Daniel R. Williams, Assoc. Pst.; Dcn. Jeffrey L. Austin; CRP Stds.: 90

Our Lady of Peace - 1414 W. 5th St., Marshfield, WI 54449 t) 715-384-9414 office@olpmarshfield.com; teachdisciples@gmail.com olpmarshfield.com Very Rev. Douglas C. Robertson, Pst.; David Alcott, DRE; CRP Stds.: 89

Sacred Heart of Jesus - 112 E. 11th St., Marshfield, WI 54449 t) 715-384-3213 sacredheartmarshfield@gmail.com sacredheartmarshfield.org Also serves Corpus Christi, Bakerville. Rev. Keith J. Kitzhaber, Pst.; Dcn. Raymond R. Draeger; CRP Stds.: 38

MAUSTON

Our Lady of the Lake - 6865 Evergreen St., Mauston, WI 53948; Mailing: 2001 S. Main St., Necedah, WI 54646 t) 608-565-2488 stfrancisnecedah@tds.net stfrancisnecedah.org Also serves St. Francis, Necedah. Rev. Wesley Janowski, Pst.; Dcn. Glen J. Heinzl; Dcn. Paul J. Arbanas;

St. Patrick - 401 Mansion St., Mauston, WI 53948 t) 608-847-6054 stpatrickparishmauston@gmail.com www.stpatricksmauston.com Very Rev. John A. Potaczek, Pst.; CRP Stds.: 57

St. Patrick School - (Grades PreK-8) 325 Mansion St., Mauston, WI 53948 t) 608-847-5844 toniross@stpatricksmauston.com Toni Ross, Prin.; Stds.: 135; Lay Tchrs.: 11

MENOMONIE

St. Joseph - 921 Wilson Ave., Menomonie, WI 54751; Mailing: 910 Wilson Ave., Menomonie, WI 54751 t) 715-232-4922 jen.engel@menomoniecatholic.org; mark.wacek@menomoniecatholic.org www.menomoniecatholic.org Rev. John Muthu Vijayan (India), Pst.; Jennifer Engel, DRE; CRP Stds.: 149

St. Joseph School - (Grades PreK-6) 910 Wilson Ave., Menomonie, WI 54751 t) 715-232-4920 mary.kiefer@menomoniecatholc.org menomoniecatholic.org Mary Kiefer, Prin.; Stds.: 66; Lay Tchrs.: 10

MILLADORE

St. Wenceslaus - 146 Main St., Milladore, WI 54454 t) 715-457-2314 kmwparishes@tds.net Also serves St. Bartholomew Parish, Mill Creek and St. Michael Parish, Junction City. Rev. Mariapackiam Pitchai-Savari (India), Admin.; Kathy Smrz, DRE; CRP Stds.: 51

MONDOVI

St. Joseph - E9265 State Rd. 85, Mondovi, WI 54755 t) 715-875-4539 stjosephrf@gmail.com Also serves St. Joseph Parish, Elk Mound. Rev. Timothy J. Welles, Pst.; CRP Stds.: 15

Sacred Heart of Jesus - 453 W. Hudson St., Mondovi, WI 54755; Mailing: 911 W. Prospect St., PO Box 188, Durand, WI 54736 t) 715-672-5640; 715-672-4668 (CRP) secretary@catholictriparish.org; dre@catholictriparish.org catholictriparish.org Also serves St. Mary's Assumption, Durand and Holy Rosary, Lima. Rev. Emmanuel Kofi Asamoah-Bekoe (Ghana), Pst.; Rev. Timothy M. Reither, Assoc. Pst.; Dcn. James A. Weingart; Benjamin Mitchell, DRE; Susan Wolf, Bus. Mgr.; CRP Stds.: 66

MOSINEE

St. Francis Xavier - 150051 Mead Ln., Mosinee, WI 54455 t) 715-693-3120 sfxknowl@mtc.net stfrancisxavier-knowlton.org Also serves St. John the Baptist Parish, Peplin. Rev. James F. Trempe, Pst.; CRP Stds.: 72

St. John the Baptist - 3308 State Hwy. 153, Mosinee, WI 54455; Mailing: 150051 Mead Ln., Mosinee, WI 54455 t) 715-693-3120 sfxknowl@mtc.net Parish suppressed May 15, 2022. Please direct all mail and sacramental record requests to St. Francis Xavier Church, Knowlton (Mosinee). Rev. James F. Trempe, Contact;

St. Patrick - 136058 Halder Dr., Mosinee, WI 54455 t) 715-693-2765 stpats@mtc.net stpatshalder@gmail.com Also serves Sacred Heart Parish, Cassel. Rev. Joseph C. Nakwah (Ghana), Pst.; Ann Ehster, Music Min.; CRP Stds.: 29

St. Paul - 603 4th St., Mosinee, WI 54455 t) 715-693-2650 parish@stpaulmosinee.org www.stpaulmosinee.org Rev. Aaron Becker, Par. Admin.; Dcn. Kevin J. Breit; Dcn. Russell Maples; Marie Fleisner, DRE; CRP Stds.: 124

NECEDAH

St. Francis of Assisi - 2001 S. Main St., Necedah, WI 54646 t) 608-565-2488 stfrancisnecedah@tds.net www.saintfrancisnecedah.org Also serves Our Lady of the Lake, Castle Rock Lake. Rev. Wesley Janowski, Pst.; Dcn. Paul J. Arbanas; Dcn. Glen J. Heinzl; Therese McNally, CRE; CRP Stds.: 74

NEILLSVILLE

St. Mary - 1813 Black River Rd., Neillsville, WI 54456 t) 715-743-3840 parishoffice@stmaryneillsville.org stmaryneillsville.weebly.com Rev. Gregory A. Michaud, Pst.; Judith A Conner, CRE; CRP Stds.: 103

NEKOOSA

Sacred Heart of Jesus - 711 Prospect Ave., Nekoosa, WI 54457 t) 715-886-3422; 715-886-3952 (CRP) sacredht@wctc.net sachtnek.com Also serves St. Alexander, Port Edwards. Rev. R. John Swing, Pst.; Dcn. Mark C. Quayhackx; Dcn. Richard A. Skifton; Peggy Wettstein, DRE; CRP Stds.: 81

NEW LISBON

St. Paul - 408 W. River St., New Lisbon, WI 53950 t) 608-562-3125 parishoffice@stpnewl.diolcparish.org www.mjpcatholic.com Also serves St. James Parish, Camp Douglas and St. Michael Parish, Indian Creek. Rev. Peter Raj Mariasamy, Pst.; Sue La Budda, DRE; CRP Stds.: 22

NORWALK

St. Augustine of Hippo - W109 County Hwy. U, Norwalk, WI 54648; Mailing: 1205 Front St., Cashton, WI 54619 t) 608-654-5654 secretary@smash3p.org www.smash3p.org Also serves Sacred Heart of Jesus Parish, Cashton and Nativity of the BVM Parish, St. Mary's Ridge. Rev. Michael E. Klos, Pst.; Dcn. Samuel G. Schmirler;

St. John the Baptist - 16585 Kellogg Ave., Norwalk, WI 54648; Mailing: 319 W. Main St., Sparta, WI 54656 t) 608-269-2655 rectorysec@stpatricksparta.net www.stpatricksparish.weconnect.com Also serves St. Patrick Parish, Sparta. Rev. Eric R. Berns, Pst.; Rev. Fernando E. Lara-Hernandez, Assoc. Pst.;

Nativity of the Blessed Virgin Mary - 26400 County Rd. U, Norwalk, WI 54648; Mailing: 1205 Front St., Cashton, WI 54619 t) 608-654-5654 secretary@smash3p.org www.smash3p.org Also serves Sacred Heart, Cashton; St. Augustine, Norwalk. Rev. Michael E. Klos, Pst.; Dcn. Samuel G. Schmirler; CRP Stds.: 3

ONALASKA

St. Patrick - 1031 Main St., Onalaska, WI 54650 t) 608-783-5535 www.stpatsonalaska.com Rev. Msgr.

Steven J. Kachel, Pst.; Dcn. Frank J. Abnet; CRP Stds.: 213

OWEN

Holy Rosary - 415 W. 3rd St., Owen, WI 54460; Mailing: P.O. Box 309, Owen, WI 54460-0309 t) 715-229-0606 holyrosaryowen@gmail.com stbernardsthedwig.org Also serves St. Bernard-St. Hedwig Parish, Thorp Rev. Stanislaus Michael Antony (India), Par. Admin.; James Mauel, DRE; CRP Stds.: 18

PITTSVILLE

St. Joachim - 5312 3rd Ave., Pittsville, WI 54466; Mailing: PO Box 69, Pittsville, WI 54466 t) 715-884-6815 friarjo@tds.net Also serves Holy Rosary Parish, Sigel and St. James Parish, Vesper. Rev. Amalanathan Malaiyappan (India), Pst.; Cindy Schooley, DRE; CRP Stds.: 64

PLOVER

St. Bronislava - 3200 Plover Rd., Plover, WI 54467; Mailing: PO Box 158, Plover, WI 54467 t) 715-344-4326; 715-341-6700 (CRP) parishoffice@stbrons.com stbrons.com Very Rev. Edward J. Shuttleworth, Pst.; Rev. Juan Pedro Roblez-Baltazar, Assoc. Pst.; Dcn. Vernon R. Linzmeier; Jody Glodowski, DRE; Anna McCarty, DRE; CRP Stds.: 240

PLUM CITY

St. John the Baptist - 212 Church Rd., Plum City, WI 54761 t) 715-647-2901 11stjohn@centurylink.net Also serves St. Joseph Parish, Arkansaw. Rev. Junabe Villaflor Villapaz (Philippines), Pst.; Robyn Trannel, DRE; CRP Stds.: 33

PORT EDWARDS

St. Alexander - 880 1st St, Port Edwards, WI 54469 t) 715-887-3012 stalexander@wctc.net saintalexander.weebly.com/ Also serves Sacred Heart of Jesus, Nekoosa. Rev. R. John Swing, Pst.; Dcn. Mark C. Quayhackx; Dcn. Richard A. Skifton; CRP Stds.: 10

PRAIRIE DU CHIEN

Holy Family Parish - 710 S. Wacouta Ave., Prairie Du Chien, WI 53821 t) 608-326-6511 cvorwald@prairiecatholic.org prairiecatholic.org Merger of St. Gabriel Church (1817) and St. John Nepomucene Church (1891). Rev. Msgr. Charles D. Stoetzel, Pst.; Dcn. Mark Grunwald; CRP Stds.: 69

Prairie Catholic School - (Grades PreK-8) 515 N. Beaumont Rd., Prairie du Chien, WI 53821 t) 608-326-8624 bspindler@prairiecatholic.org Brenda Spindler, Prin.; Stds.: 115; Lay Tchrs.: 11

PRESCOTT

St. Joseph - 269 Dakota St. S., Prescott, WI 54021 t) 715-262-5310 parishoffice@stjosephprescott.com stjosephprescott.com Rev. Zacharie Beya-Tshingimba (Democratic Republic of Congo), Pst.; Dcn. Gerald T. Rynda; CRP Stds.: 169

St. Joseph School - (Grades PreK-6) 281 Dakota St. S., Prescott, WI 54021 t) 715-262-5912 school.office@stjosephprescott.com Chris Magee, Prin.; Stds.: 76; Lay Tchrs.: 6

RICHLAND CENTER

St. Mary (Assumption of B.V.M.) - 160 W. 4th St., Richland Center, WI 53581 t) 608-647-2621; 608-647-0400 (CRP) cheryl.blankenship@stmarysrc.com; re@stmarysrc.com stmarysrc.com Rev. Msgr. Roger J. Scheckel, Pst.; Dcn. Donald Tully; Candace McGrath, DRE; CRP Stds.: 77

St. Mary (Assumption of B.V.M.) School - (Grades K-8) 155 W. 5th St., Richland Center, WI 53581 t) 608-647-2422 stacia.kohlstedt@stmaryrc.com Stacia Kohlstedt, Prin.; Stds.: 167; Lay Tchrs.: 10

Nativity of the Blessed Virgin Mary - 32605 Durst Ln, Richland Center, WI 53581 t) 608-585-4846 www.facebook.com/stmarykeyesville Also serves St. Anthony de Padua, Cazenovia and Sacred Heart, Lone Rock Very Rev. Irudayanathan Thainase, Pst.; CRP Stds.: 19

RIVER FALLS

Nativity of the Blessed Virgin Mary - W10137 570th Ave., River Falls, WI 54022 t) (715) 425-5806 parishoffice@stmbigriver.diolcparish.org www.stmarysbigriver.com Rev. William D. Brenna, Par. Admin.; Dcn. Daniel A. Gannon;

ROCKLAND

St. Peter - W697 State Rd. 33, Rockland, WI 54653 t) 608-486-2180 parishoffice@stpmr.diolcparish.org www.saintpetersparish.net Also serves St. Joseph Parish in St. Joseph's Ridge (La Crosse). Rev. Biju Chennala Kunjukutty, M.S.F.S. (India), Pst.; CRP Stds.: 47

ROSHOLT

St. Adalbert - 3315 St. Adalberts Rd., Rosholt, WI 54473 t) 715-677-4519 parish@rosholtcatholic.org; bookkeeper@rosholtcatholic.org www.rosholtcatholic.org Also serves St. Mary (Immaculate Conception) Parish, Torun. Rev. Thomas Nirappel, MSFS (India), Pst.; CRP Stds.: 48

St. Adalbert School - (Grades PreK-8) 3314 St. Adalberts Rd., Rosholt, WI 54473 t) 715-677-4517 principal@rosholtcatholic.org www.rosholtcatholic.org/school Orsolya Gosztony, Prin.; Stds.: 31; Lay Tchrs.: 3

ROTHSCHILD

St. Mark - 602 Military Rd., Rothschild, WI 54474-1523 t) 715-359-5206 stmarkroths@smproths.org www.smproths.org Rev. Allan L. Slowiak, Pst.; Dcn. Patrick J. McKeough; Mary Hart, DRE; CRP Stds.: 90

St. Therese of the Child Jesus - 113 Kort St. W., Rothschild, WI 54474; Mailing: 112 Kort St. W., Schofield, WI 54476 t) 715-359-2421; 715-359-2421 x110 (CRP) secretary@sttheresecc.org sttheresecc.org Rev. Joseph Albert Saleth (India), Pst.; Dcn. Michael Lambrecht, DRE; CRP Stds.: 98

RUDOLPH

St. Philip - 6957 Grotto Ave., Rudolph, WI 54475; Mailing: PO Box 165, Rudolph, WI 54475 t) 715-435-3286 stphilipchurch@gmail.com www.saint-philip.org Also serves St. Lawrence Parish, Wisconsin Rapids. Rev. Janusz A. Kowalski, Pst.; Dcn. Jonathan A. Anderson; CRP Stds.: 17

SOLDIERS GROVE

St. Philip - 42678 Church Rd., Soldiers Grove, WI 54655; Mailing: 106 Main St., PO Box 35, Seneca, WI 54654 t) 608-734-3931 stpatricks.seneca.bookkeeper@gmail.com www.catholicchurchesofncc.com Also serves St. Mary Parish, Gays Mills and St. Patrick Parish, Seneca. Rev. Thomas M. Huff, Pst.; CRP Stds.: 10

SPARTA

St. Patrick - 118 S. K St., Sparta, WI 54656; Mailing: 319 W. Main St., Sparta, WI 54656 t) 608-269-2655 (CRP); 608-269-2655 x1 (Rectory) rectorysec@stpatricksparta.net www.spartacatholic.com Also serves St. John the Baptist Parish, Summit Ridge. Rev. Eric R. Berns, Pst.; Rev. Fernando E. Lara-Hernandez, Assoc. Pst.; CRP Stds.: 100

St. Patrick School - (Grades PreSchool-8) 100 S. L St., Sparta, WI 54656 t) 608-269-4748 principal@stpatricksparta.net spartacatholic.com/ Jessica Williams, Prin.; Stds.: 130; Lay Tchrs.: 11

SPENCER

Christ the King - 306 S. LaSalle St., Spencer, WI 54479 t) 715-659-4480 office@ctk.diolcparish.org; dre@ctk.diolcparish.org www.ctkspencer.net Rev. Barry P. Saylor, Pst.; Debra Mlsna, DRE; CRP Stds.: 82

SPRING VALLEY

Sacred Heart of Jesus - S105 Sabin Ave., Spring Valley, WI 54767; Mailing: PO Box 456, Spring Valley, WI 54767 t) 715-778-5519 admin@svecatholic.org www.svecatholic.org Also serves St. Luke, Boyceville and Sacred Heart, Elmwood. Rev. Anbalagan Shanmugam, Par. Admin.; CRP Stds.: 65

STANLEY

All Saints - 226 E. 3rd Ave., Stanley, WI 54768; Mailing: P.O. Box 125, Stanley, WI 54768 t) 715-644-5435 info@allsaintscathcom.com allsaintscathcom.com Merger of St. Joseph, Boyd (1890), Sacred Heart of Jesus, Edson (1876), St. Rose of Lima, Cadott (1883), and Holy Family, Stanley (1967) Rev. William P. Felix, Pst.; Dcn. Ned L. Willkom; LouAnn Willkom, DRE; CRP Stds.: 138

Saint Joseph Catholic School - (Grades PreK-6) 813 E. Patten St., Boyd, WI 54726; Mailing: PO Box 129, Boyd, WI 54726 t) 715-703-1034 rjensen@stjosephboyd.com www.allsaintscathcom.com Russell M Jensen, Prin.; Stds.: 30; Lay Tchrs.: 4

STEVENS POINT

St. Bartholomew - 2493 County Rd. M, Stevens Point, WI 54481 t) 715-344-3003 stbartsmc@gmail.com Also serves St. Michael Parish, Junction City and St. Wenceslaus Parish, Milladore Rev. Mariapackiam Pitchai-Savari (India), Pst.; Rev. Dennis P. Stanchik, In Res.; CRP Stds.: 50

St. Casimir (Township of Hull) - 203 Casimir Rd, Stevens Point, WI 54481 t) 715-344-9582 saintcasimirparish@gmail.com Also serves St. Peter, Stevens Point. Rev. Arul Joseph Visuvasam, Pst.; Dcn. Ray J. Heitzinger; CRP Stds.: 4

Holy Spirit Parish - 2151 Stanley St., Stevens Point, WI 54481 t) 715-344-9117 contact@holyspiritstevenspoint.org www.holyspiritstevenspoint.org Merger of St. Stanislaus Kostka, Stevens Point (1917) and Newman University Parish, Stevens Point (1970) Rev. Steven J. Brice, Pst.; Rev. Todd A. Mlsna, Assoc. Pst.; Dcn. William J. Holzhaeuser; Dcn. Richard Letto; CRP Stds.: 135

St. Joseph - 1709 Wyatt Ave., Stevens Point, WI 54481-3615 t) 715-341-1617 x101; 715-344-3319 (CRP) secretary@pointcatholicfaith.org www.pointcatholicfaith.org Also serves St. Stephen, Stevens Point. Rev. Jeffrey W. Hennes, Pst.; Rev. Todd A. Mlsna, Assoc. Pst.; Dcn. Michael Horgan; CRP Stds.: 54

St. Mary (Immaculate Conception) - 5589 Dewey Dr., Stevens Point, WI 54482 t) 715-344-2599 parish@toruncatholic.org www.toruncatholic.org Also serves St. Adalbert Parish, Rosholt. Rev. Thomas Nirappel, MSFS (India), Pst.;

St. Peter - 800 4th Ave., Stevens Point, WI 54481 t) 715-344-6115 stpeters@pacellicatholicschools.com stpeter.us Also serves St. Casimir Parish, Stevens Point. Rev. Arul Joseph Visuvasam, Pst.; Rev. Todd A. Mlsna, Assoc. Pst.; Dcn. Ray J. Heitzinger, DRE; CRP Stds.: 38

St. Stephen - 1401 Clark St., Stevens Point, WI 54481 t) 715-344-3319 x103; (715) 341-1617 x101 pastor@pointcatholicfaith.org pointcatholicfaith.org Also serves St. Joseph Parish, Stevens Point. Rev. Jeffrey W. Hennes, Pst.; Rev. Todd A. Mlsna, Assoc. Pst.; Dcn. Michael Horgan; CRP Stds.: 43

STRATFORD

St. Andrew - 122726 County Rd. C, Stratford, WI 54484; Mailing: P.O. Box 6, Stratford, WI 54484 t) 715-687-2404 stjosephoffice1@gmail.com www.stjosephstratford.org Also serves St. Joseph Parish, Stratford. Rev. Sengole V. Vethanayagam (India), Pst.; CRP Stds.: 24

St. Joseph - 119200 Larch St., Stratford, WI 54484; Mailing: P.O. Box 6, Stratford, WI 54484 t) 715-687-2404 stjosephoffice1@gmail.com www.stjosephstratford.org Also serves St. Andrew Parish, Rozellville (Stratford). Rev. Sengole V. Vethanayagam (India), Pst.; CRP Stds.: 99

St. Joseph Catholic School - (Grades PreK-8) 119210 Larch St, Stratford, WI 54484; Mailing: PO Box 6, Stratford, WI 54484 t) 715-687-4145 principal@stjstratford.org Sally Wenzel, Prin.; Stds.: 26; Lay Tchrs.: 5

THORP

St. Bernard-St. Hedwig Parish - 109 N. Church St., Thorp, WI 54771; Mailing: P.O. Box 329, Thorp, WI 54771 t) 715-669-5526 busmgr.stbernhed@gmail.com; ccd@thorpcatholicschool.org www.stbernardsthedwig.org Also serves Holy Rosary, Owen. Rev. Stanislaus Michael Antony (India), Parochial Admin.; Patrick Conley, DRE; CRP Stds.: 79

St. Bernard-St. Hedwig Parish School (Thorp Catholic School) - (Grades PreK-8) 411 E. School St., Thorp,

WI 54771; Mailing: PO Box 329, Thorp, WI 54771 t) 715-669-5530 administrator@thorpcatholicschool.org Kendra Conley, Prin.; Stds.: 60; Lay Tchrs.: 7

TOMAH

St. Michael - 18316 County Hwy. N., Tomah, WI 54660; Mailing: 100 Bartell St., P.O. Box 199, Camp Douglas, WI 54618 t) 608-427-6762 stjames@mwt.net www.mjpcatholic.com Also serves James Parish, Camp Douglas and St. Paul Parish, New Lisbon. Rev. Peter Raj Mariasamy, Pst.; Deb Granger, DRE; CRP Stds.: 19

Queen of the Apostles Parish - 303 W. Monroe St., Tomah, WI 54660 t) 608-372-4516 dre@queenoftheapostlestomah.com; psecretary@queenoftheapostlestomah.com www.queenoftheapostlestomah.com Merger of Immaculate Conception (St. Mary), Tomah (1867) and St. Andrew the Apostle, Warrens (1896). Rev. Msgr. David C. Kunz, Pst.; Rev. Matthew L. Bowe, Assoc.; Dcn. Robert G. Riedl; Joh Burbach, DRE; CRP Stds.: 97

Queen of the Apostles Parish School - (Grades PreK-5) 315 W. Monroe St., Tomah, WI 54660 t) 608-372-5765 school@queenoftheapostlestomah.com Debra Pfab, Prin.; Stds.: 96; Lay Tchrs.: 10

TREMPEALEAU

St. Bartholomew - 11646 South St., Trempealeau, WI 54661 t) 608-534-6652 secretary@stmstb.diolcparish.org saintbartholomew.net Also serves St. Mary Parish, Galesville. Rev. Sebastian S. Saleth-Pitchai (India), Par. Admin.; Dcn. Kent L. Jacobson; CRP Stds.: 82

VESPER

St. James - 6631 Church Ave., Vesper, WI 54489; Mailing: PO Box 68, Vesper, WI 54489 t) 715-884-6815; 715-569-3978 (CRP) stjames@tds.net www.parishesonline.com Also serves Holy Rosary Parish, Sigel and St. Joachim Parish, Pittsville. Rev. Amalanathan Malaiyappan (India), Pst.; David Ecke, DRE; CRP Stds.: 11

VIROQUA

Annunciation of the Blessed Virgin Mary - 400 Congress Ave., Viroqua, WI 54665 t) 608-637-7711 stmaryparish@mwt.net saintmaryviroqua.org Rev. Joseph M. Richards, Pst.; Dcn. Anthony F. Shay; CRP Stds.: 14

WAUMANDEE

St. Boniface - S2022 County Rd. U, Waumandee, WI 54622 t) 608-626-2611 tresecclesiae@gmail.com tresecclesiae.org Serves St. Lawrence Parish, Alma and Immaculate Conception Parish, Fountain City Rev. Aruldoss Savarimuthu (India), Pst.; Dcn. Edward D. Wendt; CRP Stds.: 18

St. Boniface School - (Grades PreK-8) S2026 County Rd. U, Waumandee, WI 54622 t) (608) 626-2611 Olivia Wick, Head Teacher; Stds.: 17; Lay Tchrs.: 3

WAUSAU

St. Anne - 700 W. Bridge St., Wausau, WI 54401 t) 715-849-3930 mail@stanneswausau.org; finance@stanneswausau.org www.stanneswausau.org Rev. Thomas F. Lindner, Pst.; Dcn. Ervin A. Burkhardt; CRP Stds.: 174

Church of the Resurrection - 621 N. 2nd St., Wausau, WI 54403 t) 715-845-6715 croffice@eastsideparishes.org eastsideparishes.org Merger of St. Mary (Immaculate Conception) (1851) and St. James (1905). Also serves St. Michael Parish, Wausau. Rev. Thomas F. Lindner, Par. Admin.; Rev. Eric J Mashak, Assoc. Pst.; Dcn. Peter A. Burek; Dcn. John P. McDonnell; CRP Stds.: 23

Holy Name of Jesus - 1104 S. 9th Ave., Wausau, WI 54401 t) 715-842-4543 judy@holynamewausau.com holynamewausau.com Very Rev. Samuel A. Martin, Pst.; Dcn. Michael Maher Jr.; Rev. Alan T. Burkhardt, In Res.;

Mary, Mother of Good Help Parish - 2221B Grand Ave., Wausau, WI 54403 t) 715-298-9055 info@marymotherofgoodhelp.org marymotherofgoodhelp.org Especially serving the Hmong community. Rev. Alan T. Burkhardt, Pst.; CRP Stds.: 20

St. Matthew - 229 S. 28th Ave., Wausau, WI 54401 t) 715-842-3148 patl@stmatthewwausau.org www.stmatthewwausau.org Rev. Sebastian J. Kolodziejczyk, Pst.; Dcn. Thomas J. Tierney; Maria Joy Orozco, DRE; CRP Stds.: 152

St. Michael - 611 Stark St., Wausau, WI 54403 t) 715-842-4283 smoffice@eastsideparishes.org; faithform@eastsideparishes.org www.eastsideparishes.org Rev. Thomas F. Lindner, Par. Admin.; Rev. Eric J Mashak, Assoc. Pst.; Dcn. Peter A. Burek; Dcn. John P. McDonnell; Michelle Fischer, DRE; CRP Stds.: 66

WAUZEKA

Sacred Heart - 711 E. Main St., Wauzeka, WI 53826; Mailing: PO Box 237, Wauzeka, WI 53826 t) 608-874-4151 shwauzeka@gmail.com Also serves St. Wenceslaus, Eastman. Rev. Rajendran Anandan, Pst.; CRP Stds.: 27

WEST SALEM

St. Teresa of Kolkata Parish - 210 Hamlin St. W., West Salem, WI 54669 t) 608-786-0610 stteresaoffice@wsbcwi.org www.westsalembangorcatholic.org Rev. Msgr. Jeffrey D. Burrill, Pst.; Dcn. Robert J. Zietlow; Karla Schams, CRE; CRP Stds.: 95

WESTON

St. Agnes - 6101 Zinser St., Weston, WI 54476 t) 715-359-5675 deb@stagnescatholicparish.com www.stagnescatholicparish.com Also serves St. Florian Parish, Hatley. Rev. Gregory J. Bohren, Pst.; Amy Martin, DRE; CRP Stds.: 219

WHITEHALL

St. John the Apostle - 35900 Lee St., Whitehall, WI 54773; Mailing: PO Box 566, Whitehall, WI 54773 t) 715-538-4607 sjawhitehall@gmail.com www.ssppwi.org Also serves SS. Peter & Paul, Independence Rev. George Kutty Thayilkuzhithottu, M.S.F.S. (India), Pst.;

WILLARD

Holy Family - W8170 Main St., Willard, WI 54493; Mailing: 407 N. Division St., PO Box 69, Loyal, WI 54446 t) 715-255-8017 stap1931@gmail.com stanthonyloyal.org/holy-family-parish Also serves St. Mary Help of Christians, Greenwood and St. Anthony, Loyal. Rev. Emmanuel Famiyeh, Pst.; CRP Stds.: 9

WILTON

St. John the Baptist - 504 Enderby St., Wilton, WI 54670; Mailing: 307 Spring St., PO Box 155, Kendall, WI 54638 t) 608-463-7120 stjosephkendall@centurytel.net Also serves St. Patrick Parish, Elroy and St. Joseph Parish, Kendall. Rev. John Ofori-Domah (Ghana), Pst.; CRP Stds.: 32

WISCONSIN RAPIDS

Holy Rosary - 6190 Chapel Rd., Wisconsin Rapids, WI 54495; Mailing: 5312 3rd Ave., PO Box 69, Pittsville, WI 54466 t) 715-884-6815 friarjo@tds.net Also serves St. Joachim, Pittsville and St. James, Vesper. Rev. Amalanathan Malaiyappan (India), Pst.;

St. Lawrence - 550 10th Ave. N., Wisconsin Rapids, WI 54495 t) 715-421-5777 slparishwr@gmail.com www.saintlawrencewr.org Also serves St. Philip Parish, Rudolph. Rev. Janusz A. Kowalski, Pst.; Dcn. Jonathan A. Anderson; CRP Stds.: 11

Our Lady, Queen of Heaven - 750 10th Ave. S., Wisconsin Rapids, WI 54495 t) (715) 423-1251 parishoffice@our-lady.org; reoffice@our-lady.org www.our-lady.org Rev. Alan M. Guanella, Pst.; Rev. Steven J. Weller, Assoc. Pst.; CRP Stds.: 73

SS. Peter and Paul - 1150 2nd St. N., Wisconsin Rapids, WI 54494 t) 715-423-1351 kaitlyn@ssppwisrapids.org www.ssppwisrapids.org Very Rev. Robert A. Schaller, Pst.; Dcn. Jerome Ruesch; Dcn. Tony C. Biolo; CRP Stds.: 65

St. Vincent de Paul - 820 13th St. S., Wisconsin Rapids, WI 54494 t) 715-423-2111 stvin@wctc.net stvincentdepaulparish.weebly.com Rev. Jerome Patric Maria Francis, Pst.; Mary Jo Sigourney, DRE; CRP Stds.: 61

WITTENBERG

St. Joseph - 182590 County Rd. C, Wittenberg, WI 54499 t) 715-454-6431 stjosephchurchgalloway@gmail.com www.stjosephgalloway.com Also serves St. Ladislaus Parish, Bevent. Rev. Augustine Kofi Bentil (Ghana), Pst.; Sr. Mary Ellen Diermeier, S.S.J.-T.O.S.F., Pst. Assoc.; Mary Uttecht, DRE; CRP Stds.: 85

WONEWOC

St. Jerome - 528 Center St., Wonewoc, WI 53968; Mailing: 545 Prairie Ave., PO Box 466, Hillsboro, WI 54634-0466 t) 608-489-2580 saintals@mwt.net Also serves St. Aloysius, Hillsboro and St. Theresa Adoration Chapel, Union Center. Rev. Donald J. Bauer, Pst.; CRP Stds.: 12

SCHOOLS: PRESCHOOL THRU HIGH SCHOOL

SCHOOLS

STATE OF WISCONSIN

CHIPPEWA FALLS

McDonell Area Catholic Schools - (DIO) (Grades PreK-12) 1316 Bel Air Blvd., Chippewa Falls, WI 54729 t) 715-723-0538 k.adams@macs.k12.wi.us; m.bushman@macs.k12.wi.us www.macs.k12.wi.us Central Office Molly K Bushman, Pres.; Stds.: 448; Lay Tchrs.: 41

Holy Ghost Elementary School - (Grades PreK-12) 436 S. Main St., Chippewa Falls, WI 54729 t) 715-723-6478 j.smith@macs.k12.wi.us Jerry Smith, Prin.; Stds.: 120; Lay Tchrs.: 6

McDonell Central Catholic High School - (Grades PreK-12) t) 715-723-9126 x2200 principal@macs.k12.wi.us; e.wedemeyer@macs.k12.wi.us www.mcdonellareacatholicschools.org/ Eric Wedemeyer, Prin.; Rev. Ethan Hokamp, Chap.; Stds.: 178; Lay Tchrs.: 20

Notre Dame Middle School - (Grades PreK-12) t) 715-723-4777 e.wedemeyer@macs.k12.wi.us Eric Wedemeyer, Prin.; Rev. Ethan Hokamp, Chap.; Stds.: 117; Lay Tchrs.: 9

St. Charles Primary School - (Grades PreK-12) 429 W. Spruce St., Chippewa Falls, WI 54729 t) 715-723-5827 j.smith@macs.k12.wi.us Jerry Smith, Vice Prin.; Stds.: 94; Lay Tchrs.: 6

EAU CLAIRE

Regis Catholic Schools - (DIO) (Grades PreK-12) 2728 Mall Dr., Ste. 200, Eau Claire, WI 54701 t) 715-830-2273 x1403 ppedersen@regiscatholicschools.com; enelson@regiscatholicschools.com www.regiscatholicschools.org Central Office Paul Pedersen, Pres.; Stds.: 785; Lay Tchrs.: 42

Genesis Child Development Center - 418 N. Dewey St., Eau Claire, WI 54703-3241 t) 715-830-2275 gflaig@regiscatholicschools.com www.regiscatholicschools.com Gayle Flaig, Exec. Dir.;

Immaculate Conception School - (Grades PreK-12) 1703 Sherwin Ave., Eau Claire, WI 54701 t) 715-830-2276 kbahnub@regiscatholicschools.com www.regiscatholicschools.com Kayla Bahnub, Prin.; Stds.: 206; Lay Tchrs.: 8

Regis Child Development Center - 418 N. Dewey St., Eau Claire, WI 54703 t) 715-830-2274 gflaig@regiscatholicschools.com www.regiscatholicschools.com Gayle Flaig, Exec. Dir.;

Regis Middle School - (Grades PreK-12) 2100 Fenwick Ave., Eau Claire, WI 54701 t) 715-830-2272 www.regiscatholicschools.com Christi Machler, Prin.; Rev. Levi J. Schmitt, Chap.; Stds.: 171; Lay Tchrs.: 13

Regis High School - (Grades PreK-12) 2100 Fenwick Ave., Eau Claire, WI 54701 t) 715-830-2271 cmachler@case.k12.wi.us www.regiscatholicschools.com Christi Machler, Prin.; Rev. Levi J. Schmitt, Chap.; Stds.: 195; Lay Tchrs.: 18

St. James School - (Grades PreK-12) 2502 11th St., Eau Claire, WI 54703 t) 715-830-2277 jlutz@regiscatholicschools.com www.regiscatholicschools.com Kelly Mechelke, Prin.; Stds.: 102; Lay Tchrs.: 6

St. Mary School - (Grades PreK-12) 1828 Lynn Ave., Altoona, WI 54720 t) 715-830-2278 csmiskey@regiscatholicschools.com www.regiscatholicschools.com Carisa Smiskey, Prin.; Stds.: 106; Lay Tchrs.: 7

LA CROSSE

Aquinas Catholic Schools, Inc. - (DIO) (Grades PreK-12) 315 11th St. S., Ste. 2200, La Crosse, WI 54601 t) 608-784-8585 ted.knutson@aquinasschools.org www.aquinasschools.org Ted Knutson, Pres.; Stds.: 2,029; Pr. Tchrs.: 1; Lay Tchrs.: 99

Aquinas Middle School - (Grades PreK-12) 315 11th St. S, La Crosse, WI 54601 t) 608-784-0156 andrew.bradley@aquinasschools.org www.aquinascatholicschools.org Andrew Bradley, Prin.; Rev. Samuel C. McCarty, Chap.; Stds.: 172; Lay Tchrs.: 18

Aquinas High School - (Grades PreK-12) 315 11th St. S., La Crosse, WI 54601 t) 608-784-0287 andrew.bradley@aquinasschools.org Andrew Bradley, Prin.; Rev. Daniel J. Sedlacek, Chap.; Stds.: 313; Lay Tchrs.: 32

Blessed Sacrament School - (Grades PreK-12) 2404 King St., La Crosse, WI 54601 t) 608-782-5564 kate.moll@aquinasschools.org www.aquinascatholicschools.org Kate Moll, Prin.; Stds.: 175; Lay Tchrs.: 18

St. Joseph Cathedral School - (Grades PreK-12) 1319 Ferry St., La Crosse, WI 54601 t) 608-782-5998 Tara Key, Prin.; Stds.: 168; Lay Tchrs.: 17

St. Patrick School - (Grades PreK-12) 127 11th Ave. N., Onalaska, WI 54650 t) 608-783-5483 angela.koblitz@aquinasschools.org Angela Koblitz, Prin.; Stds.: 184; Lay Tchrs.: 18

MARSHFIELD

Columbus Catholic Schools (CCS) - (DIO) (Grades PreK-12) 710 S. Columbus Ave., Marshfield, WI 54449 t) 715-387-1177 eaton.david@columbusdons.org; admissions@columbusdons.org www.columbuscatholicschools.org David Eaton, Pres.; Stds.: 643; Pr. Tchrs.: 1; Lay Tchrs.: 65

Columbus Catholic High School - (Grades PreK-12) t) (715) 387-1177 lambrecht.michael@columbusdons.org Rev. Daniel R. Williams, Chap.; Michael Lambrecht, Prin.; Stds.: 145; Lay Tchrs.: 20

Columbus Catholic Middle School - (Grades PreK-12) t) (715) 387-1177 lambrecht.michael@columbusdons.org www.columbusdons.org Michael Lambrecht, Prin.; Rev. Daniel R. Williams, Chap.; Stds.: 122; Lay Tchrs.: 9

Our Lady of Peace School - (Grades PreK-12) 1300 W. 5th St., Marshfield, WI 54449 t) 715-384-5474 giza.sara@columbusdons.org Sara Giza, Prin.; Stds.: 106; Lay Tchrs.: 5

St. John the Baptist Primary School - (Grades PreK-12) 307 N. Walnut Ave., Marshfield, WI 54449 t) 715-384-4989 fortin.jill@columbusdons.org Jill Fortin, Prin.; Stds.: 237; Lay Tchrs.: 7

STEVENS POINT

Pacelli Catholic Schools - (DIO) (Grades PreK-12) 1301 Maria Dr., Stevens Point, WI 54481 t) 715-341-2445 cweber@pacellicatholicschools.com www.pacellicatholicschools.com Cindy Weber, Pres.; Stds.: 695; Lay Tchrs.: 58

Pacelli Catholic Elementary School-St. Bronislava - (Grades PreK-12) 3301 Willow Dr., Plover, WI 54467 t) 715-342-2015 llarkin@pacellicatholicschools.com pacellicatholicschools.com Lyndsey Larkin, Prin.; Stds.: 152; Lay Tchrs.: 8

Pacelli Catholic High School - (Grades PreK-12) t) 715-341-2442 ltheiss@pacellicatholicschools.com pacellicatholicschools.com Lawrence Theiss, Prin.; Rev. Todd A. Mlsna, Chap.; Stds.: 169; Lay Tchrs.: 15

Pacelli Catholic Middle School - (Grades PreK-12) 708 First St., Stevens Point, WI 54481 t) 715-344-1890 elopas@pacellicatholicschools.com pacellicatholicschools.com Ellen Lopas, Prin.; Rev. Todd A. Mlsna, Chap.; Stds.: 145; Lay Tchrs.: 13

Pacelli Catholic Schools Tim Copps Early Childhood Center - (Grades PreK-12) 2150 High St., Stevens Point, WI 54481 t) 715-341-2878 cosullivan@pacellicatholicschools.com pacellicatholicschools.com Cindy O'Sullivan, Dir.; Stds.: 154; Lay Tchrs.: 6

Pacelli Catholic Elementary School-St. Stephen - (Grades PreK-12) 1335 Clark St., Stevens Point, WI 54481 t) 715-344-3751 jnowinski@pacellicatholicschools.com pacellicatholicschools.com Jamie Nowinski, Prin.; Stds.: 162; Lay Tchrs.: 15

WAUSAU

Newman Catholic Schools - (DIO) (Grades PreK-12) 619 Stark St., Wausau, WI 54403 t) 715-845-5735 jgulan@newmancatholicschools.com www.newmancatholicschools.com Jeff Gulan, Pres.; Stds.: 566; Lay Tchrs.: 53

Newman Catholic High School (NCS) - (Grades PreK-12) 1130 W. Bridge St., Wausau, WI 54401 t) 715-845-8274 cfech@newmancatholicschools.com Carl Fech, Prin.; Stds.: 126; Lay Tchrs.: 15

Newman Catholic Elementary School at St. Anne Parish - (Grades PreK-12) 604 N. 6th Ave., Wausau, WI 54401 t) 715-845-5754 tvechinski@newmancatholicschools.com Terry Vechinski, Prin.; Stds.: 158; Lay Tchrs.: 16

Newman Catholic Elementary School at St. Mark Parish - (Grades PreK-12) 602 Military Rd., Rothschild, WI 54474 t) 715-359-9662 sheise@newmancatholicschools.com Shirley Heise, Prin.; Stds.: 92; Lay Tchrs.: 8

Newman Catholic Early Childhood Center: St. Michael - (Grades PreK-12) 615 Stark St., Wausau, WI 54403 t) 715-848-0206 swelch@newmancatholicschools.com Sara Welch, Interim Site Dir.; Stds.: 75; Lay Tchrs.: 6

Newman Catholic Middle School (NCMS) - (Grades PreK-12) 1130 W. Bridge St., Wausau, WI 54401 t) 715-845-8274 cfech@newmancatholicschools.com Carl Fech, Prin.; Stds.: 115; Lay Tchrs.: 8

WISCONSIN RAPIDS

Assumption Catholic Schools, Inc. (ACS-WR) (Wisconsin Rapids Area Catholic Schools) - (DIO) (Grades PreK-12) 445 Chestnut St., Wisconsin Rapids, WI 54494 t) 715-422-0900 dminter@assumptioncatholicschools.org www.assumptioncatholicschools.org Central Office Daniel Minter, Pres.; Stds.: 429; Lay Tchrs.: 45

Assumption Middle School - (Grades PreK-12) 440 Mead St., Wisconsin Rapids, WI 54494 t) 715-422-0950 jlynch@assumptioncatholicschools.org assumptioncatholicschools.org James Lynch, Prin.; Rev. Steven J. Weller, Chap.; Stds.: 117; Lay Tchrs.: 12

Assumption High School - (Grades PreK-12) 445 Chestnut St., Wisconsin Rapids, WI 54494 t) 715-422-0910 jlynch@assumptioncatholicschools.org assumptioncatholischools.org James Lynch, Prin.; Rev. Steven J. Weller, Chap.; Stds.: 140; Lay Tchrs.: 19

Our Lady Queen of Heaven School - (Grades PreK-12) 750 10th Ave. S., Wisconsin Rapids, WI 54495 t) 715-422-0982 sbruley@assumptioncatholicschools.org assumptioncatholicschool.org Shelley Bruley, Prin.; Stds.: 85; Lay Tchrs.: 8

St. Lawrence Early Childhood Center - 551 10th Ave. N., Wisconsin Rapids, WI 54495 t) 715-422-0990 jwendels@assumptioncatholicschools.org assumptioncatholicschools.org JoAnn Wendels, Dir.;

St. Vincent de Paul School - (Grades PreK-12) 831 12th St. S., Wisconsin Rapids, WI 54494 t) 715-422-0962 pfochs@assumptioncatholicschools.org assumptioncatholicschools.org Pam Fochs, Prin.; Stds.: 87; Lay Tchrs.: 8

INSTITUTIONS LOCATED IN DIOCESE

ASSOCIATIONS [ASN]

LA CROSSE

La Crosse Guild of the Catholic Medical Association - W5560 County Rd. MM, La Crosse, WI 54601 t) (608) 799-4473 slpavela@gmail.com Stephen Pavela, Pres.;

CAMPUS MINISTRY / NEWMAN CENTERS [CAM]

EAU CLAIRE

Newman Parish - 110 Garfield Ave., Eau Claire, WI 54701 t) 715-834-3399 parishoffice@newmanec.com www.newmanec.com Serving UW-Eau Claire and Chippewa Valley Technical College. Rev. Daniel E. Oudenhoven, Pst.;

LA CROSSE

Roncalli Newman Parish - 1732 State St., La Crosse, WI 54601-3756 t) 608-784-4994 office@newmanlc.org www.roncallinewmancenter.com Serving Univ. of Wisconsin-La Crosse and Western Technical College. Rev. Billy J. Dodge, Pst.; Rev. Samuel C. McCarty, Assoc. Pst.; Dcn. David J. Belland;

MENOMONIE

Newman Center at University of Wisconsin - Stout - 710 2nd St. E., Menomonie, WI 54751-1808 t) 715-235-4258 director@stoutcatholic.org stoutcatholic.org Rev. John Muthu Vijayan (India), Chap.; Becca Sheahan, Dir.;

CATHOLIC CHARITIES [CCH]

LA CROSSE

Catholic Charities of the Diocese of La Crosse, Inc. - 3710 East Ave. S., La Crosse, WI 54602-0266; Mailing: PO Box 266, La Crosse, WI 54602-0266 t) 608-782-0710 info@cclse.org www.cclse.org Adoption Services, Disability Services, Disaster Relief, Emergency Svcs., Fin. Counseling, Pregnancy & Parenting Svcs., Adoption Placement. Roberto Parterrieu, Exec. Dir.; Asstd. Annu.: 10,381; Staff: 110

CEMETERIES [CEM]

CHIPPEWA FALLS

Chippewa Catholic Cemetery Assoc., Inc. - 418 N. State St., Chippewa Falls, WI 54729 t) 715-723-0792 cfcatholiccemetery@gmail.com Peter J. Danielson, Supt.;

EAU CLAIRE

Calvary Cemetery Association - 4100 S. Hastings Way, Eau Claire, WI 54702-0633; Mailing: PO Box 633, Eau Claire, WI 54702-0633 t) 715-831-2156 managercccec@gmail.com Jim Theisen, Pres.; Rev. Derek J. Sakowski, Vice. Pres.; Diane Dingman, Treas.; Peter Wagener, Mgr.;

LA CROSSE

Catholic Cemetery - 519 Losey Blvd. S., La Crosse, WI 54601 t) 608-782-0238 jreinhart1@yahoo.com Gate of Heaven Cemetery; French Island Cemetery; Catholic Cemetery; Woodlawn Cemetery. Jeffrey Reinhart, Supt.;

MARSHFIELD

Gate of Heaven - 1100 N. St. Joseph Ave., Marshfield, WI 54449; Mailing: 7883 State Hwy. 80, Marshfield, WI 54449 t) 715-486-2098; 715-676-2629 zif00@hotmail.com; dan.rogers@ci.marshfield.wi.us John Pritzl, Pres.; Dan Rogers, Sexton;

STEVENS POINT

Stevens Point Area Catholic Cemetery Association, Inc. - 1232 Wilshire Blvd., Stevens Point, WI 54481 t) 715-341-3236 spacca@att.net www.stevenspointcatholiccemetery.com Serves St. Bronislava, St. Joseph, St. Peter, St. Stephen & Holy Spirit parishes. John Okonek, Supt.;

COLLEGES & UNIVERSITIES [COL]

LA CROSSE

Viterbo University - 900 Viterbo Dr., La Crosse, WI 54601-8804 t) 608-796-3000 maranscht@viterbo.edu www.viterbo.edu Founded by the Franciscan Sisters of Perpetual Adoration Rev. Conrad Targonski, OFM, Chap.; Sr. Laura Nettles, FSPA, Exec. Dir.; Emilio Alvarez, Dir. Campus Ministry; Sheila Severson, Admin.; Stds.: 2,457; Lay Tchrs.: 117; Sr. Tchrs.: 1

CONVENTS, MONASTERIES, AND RESIDENCES FOR WOMEN [CON]

LA CROSSE

St. Rose Convent (Congregation of the Sisters of Third Order of St. Francis of Perpetual Adoration) - 912 Market St., La Crosse, WI 54601 t) 608-782-5610 fspa@fspa.org www.fspa.org Motherhouse for the congregation of the Franciscan Sisters of Perpetual Adoration. Sr. Sue Ernster, FSPA, Pres.; Sr. Georgia Christensen, Vice. Pres.; Sr. Marcia Baumert, Mission Councilor; Sr. Marie DesJarlais, Mission Councilor; Sr. Julie Tydrich, FSPA, Mission Councilor; Srs.: 156

Villa St. Joseph - W2658 State Rd. 33, La Crosse, WI 54601-2625 t) 608-788-5100 jtydrich@fspa.org www.fspa.org A Retirement home for aged and convalescent Franciscan Sisters of Perpetual Adoration. Sr. Julie Tydrich, FSPA, Admin.; Srs.: 28

MARSHFIELD

Franciscan Association of Divine Mercy, Inc. - 118065 Kraus St., Marshfield, WI 54449; Mailing: PO Box 243, Marathon, WI 54448-0243 t) 715-451-2395 mmercifulheartofjesus@gmail.com www.faofdivinemercy.org Sr. Mary Veronica Fitch, Foundress; Srs.: 3

STEVENS POINT

Seraphic Adorers of the Child Jesus, Inc. - 807 Tommys Tpke., Stevens Point, WI 54481; Mailing: PO Box 550, Plover, WI 54467-0550 c) 715-899-0768 m.agnesofjesus@seraphicadorers.com; prayers@seraphicadorers.com seraphicadorers.com Mother Mary Agnes, Foundress & Pres.; Srs.: 5

The Sisters of St Joseph of the Third Order of St Francis, Inc - 2801 Hoover Rd., Unit 1, Stevens Point, WI 54481; Mailing: P.O. Box 305, Stevens Point, WI 54481-0305 t) 715-341-8457 x5 cindy@ssj-tosf.org www.ssj-tosf.org Cindy Matteson, CAO; Srs.: 137

ENDOWMENTS / FOUNDATIONS / TRUSTS [EFT]

ALMOND

St. Maximilian Kolbe Church Endowment Trust - 8611 State Rd. 54, Almond, WI 54909 t) 715-824-3380 angie@stmaxkolbe.org www.stmaxkolbe.org Rev. Peter M. Manickam, Contact;

ALTOONA

St. Mary Parish Endowment Trust - 1812 Lynn Ave., Altoona, WI 54720 t) 715-855-1294 bfirkus@smsrcatholic.com Rev. Derek J. Sakowski, Contact;

ARCADIA

Arcadia Catholic School to Holy Family School - 532 E. McKinley St., Arcadia, WI 54612-1522 t) 608-323-3676 barb@holyfam.com www.holyfam.com Rev. Kyle N. Laylan, Contact;

ATHENS

Saint Anthony Parish Endowment Trust - 417 Caroline St., Athens, WI 54411; Mailing: PO Box 206, Athens, WI 54411 t) 715-257-7684 Rev. George Nelson Graham (Ghana), Contact;

AUBURNDALE

St. Mary Education Endowment Trust - 5866 Main St., Auburndale, WI 54412-0177; Mailing: P.O. Box 177, Auburndale, WI 54412-0177 t) 715-652-2806 saintsmmk@gmail.com www.saintsmmk.com Rev. Murali Anand Rayappan (India), Pst.;

BLAIR

The St. Ansgar Catholic Church Endowment Trust - 607 E. Olson St., Blair, WI 54616; Mailing: 22650 Washington St., Ettrick, WI 54627 t) 608-525-3811 stbridgets@centurytel.net Rev. Jeyaseelan Yobu (India), Contact;

BLOOMER

St. Paul Catholic Parish of Bloomer Wisconsin Endowment Trust - 1222 Main St., Bloomer, WI 54724 t) 715-568-3255 stpaulrecoffice@bloomer.net stpauls.bloomertel.net Rev. Victor C. Feltes, Contact;

CASHTON

Holy Family Endowment Trust Fund - 1205 Front St., Cashton, WI 54619-8029 t) 608-654-5654 mklos@diolclergy.org Rev. Michael E. Klos, Contact;

Sacred Heart of Jesus Education Endowment Trust - 1205 Front St., Cashton, WI 54619 t) 608-654-5654 smash3pfinance@mwt.net Rev. Michael E. Klos, Contact;

CHIPPEWA FALLS

St. Charles Future Fund Trust - 810 Pearl St., Chippewa Falls, WI 54729-1729 t) 715-723-4088 centraloffice@stcharles-cf.com Rev. Msgr. Michael J. Gorman, Contact;

The Education/Sustaining Endowment Trust (Holy Ghost Parish Trust) - 412 S. Main St., Chippewa Falls, WI 54729 t) 715-723-4890 Very Rev. Jesse D. Burish, Contact;

St. Joseph's Foundation - 2661 County Hwy. I, Chippewa Falls, WI 54729 t) 715-717-7397 cheryl.halida@hshs.org www.stjoeschipfalls.com Cheryl Halida, Contact;

McDonell Catholic Schools Endowment Trust - 1316 Bel Air Blvd., Chippewa Falls, WI 54729 t) 715-723-0538 x3305 m.bushman@macs.k12.wi.us Molly K Bushman, Pres.;

Notre Dame Children's Endowment Trust - 117 Allen St., Chippewa Falls, WI 54729 t) 715-723-7108 akatz@ourladyofthefalls.org Very Rev. Jesse D. Burish, Pst.;

Notre Dame Parish Endowment Trust - 117 Allen St., Chippewa Falls, WI 54729-2899 t) 715-723-7108 akatz@ourladyofthefalls.org Very Rev. Jesse D. Burish, Pst.;

St. Peter Parish Endowment Trust - 11358 County Hwy. Q, Chippewa Falls, WI 54729; Mailing: 810 Pearl St., Chippewa Falls, WI 54729-1729 t) 715-723-4088 centraloffice@stcharles-cf.com Rev. Msgr. Michael J. Gorman, Contact;

COLBY

St. Mary's Catholic School, Colby Endowment Trust - 205 S. 2nd St., Colby, WI 54421; Mailing: P.O. Box 436, Colby, WI 54421 t) 715-223-3048 catholiccentral@gmail.com Rev. D. Joseph Redfern, Contact;

CUSTER

Sacred Heart School, Polonia Endowment Trust - 7379 Church St., Custer, WI 54423 t) 715-592-4902 parishoffice@sacredheartpolonia.com Rev. Mark A. Miller, Pst.; Thomas McCann, Prin.;

DURAND

St. Mary Catholic School Endowment Trust - 901 W. Prospect St., Durand, WI 54736; Mailing: P.O. Box 188, Durand, WI 54736 t) 715-672-5640 secretary@catholictriparish.org Rev. Emmanuel Kofi Asamoah-Bekoe (Ghana), Pst.; Rev. Timothy M. Reither, Assoc. Pst.;

EAU CLAIRE

Friends of St. James the Greater Catholic School at Eau Claire Tuition Endowment Trust - 2502 11th St., Ste. 1, Eau Claire, WI 54703-2700 t) 715-835-5887 stjameseac@aol.com www.stjameseauclaire.org Rev. Thomas J. Krieg, Contact;

Hospital Sisters of St. Francis Foundation, Inc. - 900 W. Clairemont Ave., Eau Claire, WI 54701 t) 715-717-4925 amy.bulpitt@hshs.org www.sacredhearteauclaire.org HSHS Sacred Heart Foundation (a division of Hospital Sisters of St. Francis Foundation, Inc.) Daniel McCormack, Pres.;

The St. James the Greater Catholic Church Endowment Trust - 448 N. Dewey St., Eau Claire, WI 54703 t) 715-835-5887 stjameseac@aol.com Rev. Thomas J. Krieg, Pst.;

St. Olaf Parish Endowment Trust - 3220 Monroe St., Eau Claire, WI 54703-1203; Mailing: PO Box 1203, Eau Claire, WI 54703-1203 t) 715-832-2504 solaf@saintolafparish.org www.saintolafparish.org Very Rev. James R. Kurzynski, Contact;

St. Patrick of Eau Claire Endowment Trust - 448 N. Dewey St., Eau Claire, WI 54703 t) 715-832-0925 office@shspec.org Rev. Antony Joseph (India), Contact;

Regis Catholic Schools Educational Endowment Trust - 2728 Mall Dr., Ste. 200, Eau Claire, WI 54701 t) 715-830-2273 x1407 jbachmeier@regiscatholicschools.com www.regiscatholicschools.com Jackie Bachmeier, Contact;

Regis Catholic Schools Foundation - 2728 Mall Dr., Ste. 200, Eau Claire, WI 54701 t) (715) 830-2273 x1407 foundation@regiscatholicschools.com www.regiscatholicschoolsfoundation.com Provides funds to support the greatest needs of our schools-tuition asst., capital improve, curriculum etc. Jackie Bachmeier, Exec. Dir.;

The Sacred Heart Parish Endowment Trust - 448 N. Dewey St., Eau Claire, WI 54703 t) 715-832-0925 office@shspec.org Rev. Antony Joseph (India), Contact;

ELLSWORTH

The St. Francis Parish Endowment Trust - 264 S. Grant, Ellsworth, WI 54011; Mailing: PO Box 839, Ellsworth, WI 54011 t) 715-273-4774 office@stfrancisellsworth.com Very Rev. David P. Olson, Contact;

HATLEY

St. Ladislaus Parish Bevent Endowment Trust - 173141 State Hwy. 153, Hatley, WI 54440 t) 715-446-3060 sisterme@stladislaus.org; parishsecretary@stladislaus.org Rev. Augustine Kofi Bentil (Ghana), Pst.; Sr. Mary Ellen Diermeier, S.S.J.-T.O.S.F., Pst. Assoc.;

HOLMEN

St. Elizabeth Ann Seton Endowment Trust - 515 N. Main St., Holmen, WI 54636 t) 608-526-4424 office@seasholmen.org Sandy Jerue, Contact;

INDEPENDENCE

The SS. Peter & Paul Parish-Independence Education Endowment Trust - 36028 Osseo Rd., Independence, WI 54747; Mailing: PO Box 430, Independence, WI 54747 t) 715-985-2227 Rev. George Kutty Thayilkuzhithottu, M.S.F.S. (India), Contact;

LA CROSSE

Aquinas Catholic Schools Foundation - 315 S. 11th St., La Crosse, WI 54601 t) 608-784-8585 (Bus. Office); 608-784-0707 (Devel. Office) ted.knutson@aquinasschools.org Ted Knutson, Admin.; Rev. Msgr. Steven J. Kachel, Dean;

Bishop John J. Paul Scholarship Endowment Trust - 3710 East Ave. S., La Crosse, WI 54601; Mailing: PO Box 4004, La Crosse, WI 54601 t) 608-791-0171 Kurt Jereczek, Contact;

Bishop's Education Endowment Trust - 3710 East Ave. S., La Crosse, WI 54601; Mailing: PO Box 4004, La Crosse, WI 54602 t) 608-791-0171 Kurt Jereczek, Contact;

Blessed Sacrament Parish Endowment Trust - 130 Losey Blvd. S., La Crosse, WI 54601 t) 608-782-2953 office@bsplacrosse.org www.bsplacrosse.org Rev. Billy J. Dodge, Contact;

Caritas Endowment Trust - 3710 East Ave. S., La Crosse, WI 54602-0266; Mailing: PO Box 266, La Crosse, WI 54602-0266 t) 608-782-0710 lnigon@cclse.org Lori Nigon, Dir.;

Cathedral of St. Joseph the Workman Endowment Trust - 530 Main St., La Crosse, WI 54601 t) 608-782-0322 office@cathedralsjworkman.org Rev. Msgr. Richard W. Gilles, Contact;

Catholic Foundation of West Central Wisconsin, Inc. - 3710 East Ave. S., La Crosse, WI 54601; Mailing: PO Box 4004, La Crosse, WI 54602-4004 t) (608) 519-9892 jreiter@cfwcw.org cfwcw.org Jeffrey Reiter, Interim Exec. Dir.;

Diocese of La Crosse Youth Ministry Endowment Trust - 3710 East Ave. S., La Crosse, WI 54601; Mailing: PO Box 4004, La Crosse, WI 54602 t) 608-791-0171 Kurt Jereczek, Contact;

Father Joseph Walijewski Orphanage Endowment Trust - 3710 East Ave. S., La Crosse, WI 54601; Mailing: PO Box 4004, La Crosse, WI 54602 t) 608-791-2685 jreiter@diolc.org www.frjoesguiild.org Jeffrey Reiter, Devel. Dir.;

Franciscan Skemp Foundation of Arcadia, Inc. - 700 West Ave. S., La Crosse, WI 54601 t) 608-392-9710 bortnem.mark@mayo.edu www.mayoclinichealthsytems.org Mark Bortnem, CFO;

Holy Cross Seminary Education Fund Endowment Trust - 3710 East Ave. S., La Crosse, WI 54601; Mailing: PO Box 4004, La Crosse, WI 54601 t) 608-791-0171 Kurt Jereczek, Contact;

Holy Trinity Catholic Church Endowment Trust - 1333 13th St. S., La Crosse, WI 54601 t) 608-782-2028 htparish@outlook.com Rev. G. Richard Roberts, Contact;

St. James Parish Endowment Trust - 1032 Caledonia St., La Crosse, WI 54603 t) 608-782-7557 saintjameslacrosse@gmail.com www.saintjameslax.com Rev. Robert M. Letona, Contact;

La Crosse Deanery Catholic Education Endowment Trust - 3710 East Ave. S., La Crosse, WI 54601; Mailing: PO Box 4004, La Crosse, WI 54602-4004 t) 608-788-7700 treichenbacher@diolc.org diolc.org Thomas Reichenbacher, Supt.;

Mary, Mother of the Church Parish Endowment Trust - 2006 Weston St., La Crosse, WI 54601 t) 608-788-5483 secretary@mmoclacrosse.org www.mmoclacrosse.org Very Rev. Brian D. Konopa, Contact;

Mayo Clinic Health System - Franciscan Healthcare Foundation, Inc. - 700 West Ave. S., La Crosse, WI 54601 t) 608-785-0940 grabow.peter@mayo.edu; bortnem.mark@mayo.edu www.mayohealthsystem.org Peter Grabow, Admin.; Mark Bortnem, CFO;

Roncalli Newman Parish Student Endowment Trust - 1732 State St., La Crosse, WI 54601 t) 608-784-4994 office@newmanlc.org www.roncallinewmancenter.com Rev. Billy J. Dodge, Contact;

MARATHON

Nativity of the Blessed Virgin Mary, Marathon Endowment Trust - 712 Market, Marathon, WI 54448-0007; Mailing: PO Box 7, Marathon, WI 54448-0007 t) 715-443-2045 bvmparish@stmarysmarathon.org stmarysmarathon.weconnect.com Rev. Msgr. Joseph G. Diermeier, Contact;

MARSHFIELD

Columbus High School Foundation - 710 S. Columbus Ave., Marshfield, WI 54449 t) 715-387-2444 loucks.angela@columbusdons.org www.columbuscatholicschools.org David Eaton, Pres.;

St. John the Baptist Educational Endowment Trust - 201 W. Blodgett St., Marshfield, WI 54449 t) 715-384-3252 mjgouin@frontier.com Rev. Daniel L. Thelen, Contact;

St. John the Baptist Maintenance Endowment Trust - 201 W. Blodgett St., Marshfield, WI 54449 t) 715-384-3252 mjgouin@frontier.com Rev. Daniel L. Thelen, Contact;

Marshfield Area Catholic Schools Endowment Trust - 710 S. Columbus Ave., Marshfield, WI 54449 t) 715-387-2444 eaton.david@columbusdons.org David Eaton, Pres.;

The Our Lady of Peace Endowment Trust - 1414 W. 5th St., Marshfield, WI 54449 t) 715-384-9414 office@olpmarshfield.com Very Rev. Douglas C. Robertson, Pst.;

MAUSTON

St. Patrick's Congregation Trust - 401 Mansion St., Mauston, WI 53948 t) 608-847-6054 stpatrickparishmauston@gmail.com www.stpatricksmauston.com Very Rev. John A. Potaczek, Contact;

MENOMONIE

The St. Joseph School at Menomonie Endowment Trust - 910 Wilson Ave., Menomonie, WI 54751 t) 715-232-4922 Rev. John Muthu Vijayan (India), Pst.; Mark Wacek, Admin.;

MOSINEE

St. Paul Parish Endowment Trust - 603 4th St., Mosinee, WI 54455 t) 715-693-2650 parish@stpaulmosinee.org Rev. Aaron Becker, Contact;

NEILLSVILLE

The St. Mary's Catholic Church Endowment Trust - 1813 Black River Rd., Neillsville, WI 54456 t) 715-743-3840 parishoffice@stmaryneillsville.org stmaryneillsville.weebly.com Rev. Gregory A. Michaud, Contact;

ONALASKA

Father John Rossiter and Friends Endowment Trust of St. Patrick Parish - 1031 Main St., Onalaska, WI 54650 t) 608-783-5535 skachel@diolclergy.org www.stpatsonalaska.com Rev. Msgr. Steven J. Kachel; Dcn. Frank J. Abnet;

PITTSVILLE

St. Joachim's Parish Endowment Trust - 5312 3rd Ave., Pittsville, WI 54466; Mailing: PO Box 69, Pittsville, WI 54466 t) 715-884-6815 friarjo@tds.net Rev. Amalanathan Malaiyappan (India), Contact;

PLOVER

St. Bronislava Parish, Plover Endowment Trust - 3200 Plover Rd., Plover, WI 54467-0158; Mailing: PO Box 158, Plover, WI 54467-0158 t) 715-344-4326 parishoffice@stbrons.com Very Rev. Edward J. Shuttleworth, Contact;

PORT EDWARDS

St. Alexander's Church, Port Edwards Endowment Trust - 880 1st St., Port Edwards, WI 54469 t) 715-887-3012 stalexander@wctc.net saintalexander.weebley.com Rev. R. John Swing, Pst.;

PRAIRIE DU CHIEN

The St. Gabriel's Endowment Trust - 710 S. Wacouta Ave., Prairie du Chien, WI 53821 t) 608-326-6511 sgp@prairiecatholic.org; cvorwald@prairiecatholic.org Rev. Msgr. Charles D. Stoetzel, Pst.;

The St. John's Endowment Trust - 710 S. Wacouta Ave., Prairie du Chien, WI 53821 t) 608-326-6511 sgp@prairiecatholic.org Rev. Msgr. Charles D. Stoetzel, Pst.;

RICHLAND CENTER

The Assumption of the Blessed Virgin Mary Parish Endowment Trust - 160 W. 4th St., Richland Center, WI 53581 t) 608-647-2621 cheryl.blankenship@stmarysrc.com Rev. Msgr. Roger J. Scheckel, Pst.;

RIVER FALLS

The St. Mary's-Big River Endowment Trust - W10137 570th Ave., River Falls, WI 54022 t) 715-425-5806 parishoffice@stmbigriver.diolcparish.org Dcn. Daniel A. Gannon;

ROTHSCHILD

The St. Mark Catholic Parish Endowment Trust - 602 Military Rd., Rothschild, WI 54474 t) 715-359-5206 stmarkroths@smproths.org Rev. Allan L. Slowiak, Contact;

SCHOFIELD

St. Therese Catholic Church Endowment Fund - 112 Kort St. W., Schofield, WI 54476 t) 715-359-2421 colleen@sttheresecc.org sttheresecc.org Rev. Joseph Albert Saleth (India), Pst.;

SPARTA

Endowment Trust of the Friends and Parishioners of St. Patrick Parish - 319 W. Main St., Sparta, WI 54656 t) 608-269-2655 stpatricksparish.weconnect.com Rev. Eric R. Berns, Contact;

Mayo Clinic Health System - Franciscan Healthcare Foundation of Sparta, Inc. - 310 W. Main St., Sparta, WI 54656-2142; Mailing: 700 West Ave. S., La Crosse, WI 54601 t) 608-269-2132 meyer.tia@mayo.edu www.mayohealthsystem.org Tia Meyer, Admin.;

STANLEY

St. Rose of Lima Catholic Church Endowment Trust - 226 E. 3rd Ave., Stanley, WI 54768; Mailing: P.O. Box 125, Stanley, WI 54768 t) 715-644-5435 info@allsaintscathcom.com Rev. William P. Felix, Contact;

STEVENS POINT

Catholic Schools Endowment Trust in Portage County, Wisconsin - 1301 Maria Dr., Stevens Point, WI 54481 t) 715-341-2445 cweber@pacellicatholicschools.com www.pacellicatholicschools.com Hannah Testin, Devel. Dir.;

Newman Campus Ministry Endowment Trust - 2151 Stanley St., Stevens Point, WI 54481 t) 715-344-9117 contact@holyspiritstevenspoint.org www.holyspiritstevenspoint.org Rev. Steven J. Brice, Contact;

Pacelli High School Foundation - 1301 Maria Dr., Stevens Point, WI 54481 t) 715-341-2445 schulfer@wi-net.com www.pacellicatholicschools.com LouAnn Shulfer, Pres.;

St. Joseph Parish, Stevens Point Endowment Trust - 1709 Wyatt Ave., Stevens Point, WI 54481 t) 715-341-1617 x103 pastor@pointcatholicfaith.org www.pointcatholicfaith.org Rev. Jeffrey W. Hennes, Contact;

St. Stanislaus Kostka Congregation, Stevens Point Endowment Trust - 2151 Stanley St., Stevens Point, WI 54481 t) 715-344-9117 contact@holyspiritstevenspoint.org Rev. Steven J. Brice, Pst.;

St. Stephen Parish Endowment Trust - 1401 Clark St., Stevens Point, WI 54481 t) 715-344-3319 x103 pastor@pointcatholicfaith.org pointcatholicfaith.org Rev. Jeffrey W. Hennes, Contact;

STRATFORD

St. Joseph Parish Endowment Trust - 119200 Larch St., Stratford, WI 54484; Mailing: P.O. Box 6, Stratford, WI 54484 t) 715-687-2404 stjosephoffice1@gmail.com Rev. Sengole V. Vethanayagam (India), Contact;

TOMAH

The St. Mary's Catholic Church Educational Endowment Trust - 303 W. Monroe St., Tomah, WI 54660 t) 608-372-4516 cbailey@queenoftheapostlestomah.com Rev. Msgr. David C. Kunz, Contact;

VIROQUA

St. Mary's Parish Viroqua Endowment Trust - 400 Congress Ave., Viroqua, WI 54665 t) 608-637-7711 stmaryparish@mwt.net Rev. Joseph M. Richards, Contact;

WAUMANDEE

St. Boniface Parish Catholic School Endowment Trust Fund - S2022 County Rd. U, Waumandee, WI 54622 t) 608-626-2621 tresecclesiae@gmail.com Rev. Aruldoss Savarimuthu (India), Contact;

WAUSAU

Church of the Resurrection Parish Church Building Endowment Trust - 621 N. 2nd St., Wausau, WI 54403 t) 715-845-6715 finance@eastsideparishes.org Rev. Thomas F. Lindner, Par. Admin.;

St. Michael Parish Endowment Trust - 611 Stark St., Wausau, WI 54403 t) 715-842-4283 finance@eastsideparishes.org www.eastsideparishes.org Rev. Thomas F. Lindner, Admin.;

***Newman Catholic Schools Endowment Trust** - 619 Stark St., Wausau, WI 54403 t) 715-842-4283 www.newmancatholicschools.com Rev. Thomas F. Lindner, Contact; Jeff Gulan, Pres.;

WHITEHALL

St. John Parish Endowment Trust - 35900 Lee St., Whitehall, WI 54773; Mailing: PO Box 566, Whitehall, WI 54773 t) 715-538-4607 sjawhitehall@gmail.com Rev. George Kutty Thayilkuzhithottu, M.S.F.S. (India), Contact;

WILLARD

Holy Family Parish, Willard Endowment Trust - W8170 Main St., Willard, WI 54493; Mailing: 407 N. Division St., PO Box 69, Loyal, WI 54446 t) 715-255-8017 sharonls1963@yahoo.com Rev. Emmanuel Famiyeh, Contact;

WISCONSIN RAPIDS

Assumption Catholic Schools Endowment - 445 Chestnut St., Wisconsin Rapids, WI 54494 t) 714-422-0902 assumptioncatholicschools.org Daniel Minter, Pres.;

St. Lawrence Parish, Wisconsin Rapids Endowment Trust - 530 10th Ave. N., Wisconsin Rapids, WI 54495 t) 715-421-5777 slparishwr@gmail.com Rev. Janusz A. Kowalski, Contact;

Our Lady Queen of Heaven Parish Endowment Trust - 750 10th Ave. S., Wisconsin Rapids, WI 54495 t) 715-423-1251 jsievers@our-lady.org www.our-lady.org Rev. Alan M. Guanella, Contact;

St. Vincent de Paul Parish, Wisconsin Rapids Endowment Trust - 820 13th St. S., Wisconsin Rapids, WI 54494 t) 715-423-2111 stvin@wctc.net Rev. Jerome Patric Maria Francis, Pst.;

HOSPITALS / HEALTH SERVICES [HOS]

CHIPPEWA FALLS

St. Joseph's Hospital of the Hospital Sisters of the Third Order of St. Francis - 2661 County Hwy. I, Chippewa Falls, WI 54729 t) 715-717-7200 amy.bulpitt@hshs.org www.stjoeschipfalls.com Hospital Sisters Health System. John Wagnor, Pres.; Rev. Amalraj Roche (India), Chap.; Rev. John A. Schultz, Chap.; Bed Capacity: 102; Asstd. Annu.: 137,058; Staff: 264

EAU CLAIRE

HSHS Sacred Heart Hospital - 900 W. Clairemont Ave., Eau Claire, WI 54701 t) 715-717-4131 amy.bulpitt@hshs.org www.sacredhearteauclaire.org Hospital Sisters Health System John Wagnor, Pres.; Rev. John A. Schultz, Chap.; Bed Capacity: 185; Asstd. Annu.: 265,484; Staff: 864

LA CROSSE

Mayo Clinic Health System - Franciscan Healthcare, La Crosse Campus Medical Center - 700 West Ave. S., La Crosse, WI 54601-4783 t) 608-785-0940 bortnem.mark@mayo.edu www.mayohealthsystem.org Dr. Paul Mueller, Pres.;

SPARTA

Mayo Clinic Health System - Franciscan Healthcare, Sparta Campus Hospital - 310 W. Main St., Sparta, WI 54656; Mailing: 700 West Ave. S., La Crosse, WI 54601 t) 608-269-2132 bortnem.mark@mayo.edu www.mayohealthsystem.org Tia Meyer, Admin.; Bed Capacity: 25; Asstd. Annu.: 8,796; Staff: 80

MISCELLANEOUS [MIS]

BOYD

Institute of St. Joseph - 31360 County Hwy. MM, Boyd, WI 54726-5988 t) 715-667-3372 frwilliamfelix.isj@gmail.com instituteofstjoseph.com Rev. John Mary Gilbert, Chap.; Rev. William P. Felix, Moderator;

EASTMAN

Society of the Oblates of Wisdom - 119 Sheridon Rd., Eastman, WI 54626-8702; Mailing: P.O. Box 13230, St. Louis, MO 63157 t) 608-874-5221 c) (618) 741-9308 materdei82@hotmail.com www.rtforum.org James Hooper Jr., OHT, Contact; Rev. Brian W. Harrison, O.S., Dir.; Rev. Msgr. John F. McCarthy, Asst. Dir.;

Marian Academy of the Oblates of Holy Tradition - ; Mailing: 1118 Butternut Ln, OFallon, IL 62269 c) 618-741-9308 hooperje12@yahoo.com www.rtforum.org/oht/index.html

EAU CLAIRE

Hospital Sisters Health Care-West, Inc. - 851 University Dr., St. Francis Apartments, Eau Claire, WI 54701 t) 217-523-4747 amy.bulpitt@hshs.org Affordable senior living apartments. Damond Boatwright, CEO;

GENOA

The Hermitage of St. Mary, Inc. - W1498 Spring Coulee Rd., Genoa, WI 54632 t) 608-386-5143 hermitageofstmary@hotmail.com Sr. Mary Dawiczyk, H.S.M., Foundress/Pres.;

GLENDALE

Ascension St. Clare's Hospital, Inc. - 40 W. River Woods Pkwy., c/o Ascension Wisconsin Main Office, Glendale, WI 53212; Mailing: P.O. Box 45998, c/o Tax Dept., St. Louis, MO 63145-5998 t) (414) 465-3000 timothy.waldoch@ascension.org Bernie Sherry, Sr. Vice Pres.;

LA CROSSE

St. Ambrose Financial Services, Inc. - 3710 East Ave. S., La Crosse, WI 54602-4004; Mailing: PO Box 4004, La Crosse, WI 54602 t) 608-791-2669 dherricks@stambrosefinancial.com stambrosefinancial.com Dennis Herricks, Dir.;

Father Joseph Walijewski Legacy Guild, Inc. - 3710 East Ave. S., La Crosse, WI 54601 t) (608) 791-2685 jreiter@diolc.org frjoesguild.org/ Very Rev. Woodrow H. Pace, Secy.; Jeffrey Reiter, Treas.;

Holy Cross (Seminary) Diocesan Center - 3710 East Ave. S., La Crosse, WI 54602-4004; Mailing: PO Box 4004, La Crosse, WI 54602-4004 t) 608-788-7700 jreider@diolc.org diolc.org Rev. Kurt J. Apfelbeck; Rev. Paul N. Check; Rev. Robert J. Cook; Very Rev. William A. Dhein; Rev. Msgr. Robert P. Hundt; Rev. Nathaniel W. Kuhn; Very Rev. Woodrow H. Pace; Rev. John L. Parr; Rev. Eugene J. Wolf;

The Marian Catechist Apostolate - 5250 Justin Rd., La Crosse, WI 54602; Mailing: PO Box 637, La Crosse, WI 54602 t) 608-782-0011 internationaloffice@mariancatechist.com mariancatechist.com His Eminence Raymond Leo Cardinal Burke, Intl. Dir.;

***Mayo Clinic Health System - Franciscan Healthcare, Inc., Corporate Office** - 700 West Ave. S., La Crosse, WI 54601-4783 t) 608-785-9710 hansen.julie@mayo.edu www.mayohealthsystem.org Sponsored by the Congregation of the Sisters of the Third Order of St. Francis of Perpetual Adoration (Franciscan Sisters of Perpetual Adoration) and Timothy Johnson, Pres.;

***Mayo Clinic Health System - Franciscan Medical Center, Inc.** - 700 West Ave. S., La Crosse, WI 54601-4796 t) 608-785-0940 hansen.julie@mayo.edu www.mayohealthsystem.org Timothy Johnson, Regl. Vice Pres.;

St. Clare Health Mission - 916 Ferry St., La Crosse, WI 54601 t) 608-519-4633 schmschedule@aol.com www.stclarehealthmission.org A non-profit organization run by volunteers to bring free health care to those most in need. Jason Larsen, Exec. Dir.;

SPRING VALLEY

Brothers of St. Pius X - S830 Westland Ave., Spring Valley, WI 54767 t) (608) 791-0177 Bro. Michael Mandernach, C.S.P.X., Co-founder; Brs.: 1

WAUSAU

St. Mary's Roman Catholic Oratory - 408 Seymour St., Wausau, WI 54403-6266 t) 715-842-9995 stmarysoratory@institute-christ-king.org www.institute-christ-king.org Rev. Canon Aaron Huberfeld, ICRSS, Rector; Rev. Canon Heitor Matheus, Vicar;

WILLARD

The Christine Center - W8303 Mann Rd, Willard, WI 54493 t) 715-267-7507 welcome@christinecenter.org christinecenter.org A spirituality retreat center founded on Franciscan values. Kathleen Yosko, Exec.;

NURSING / REHABILITATION / CONVALESCENCE / ELDERLY CARE [NUR]

EAU CLAIRE

St. Francis Apartments (Hospital Sisters Health Care-West, Inc.) - 851 University Dr, Eau Claire, WI 54701 t) 715-834-1338 info@saintfrancisapartments.com Therese Quick, Contact; Asstd. Annu.: 64; Staff: 4

LA CROSSE

Benedictine Manor (Catholic Residential Services, Inc.) - 2902 East Ave. S., La Crosse, WI 54601 t) 608-788-9870 leslie.thompson@benedictineliving.org www.benedictineliving.org/la-crosse-wi/ Sponsored by the Benedictine Sisters of St. Scholastica Monastery. Leslie Thompson, Exec. Dir.; Asstd. Annu.: 180; Staff: 130

Benedictine Villa (Catholic Residential Services, Inc.) - 2904 East Ave. S., La Crosse, WI 54601 t) 608-788-7489 leslie.thompson@benedictineliving.org www.benedictineliving.org/la-crosse-wi/ Assisted Living Apartments. Sponsored by the Benedictine Sisters of St. Scholastica Monastery. Leslie Thompson, Exec. Dir.; Asstd. Annu.: 50; Staff: 20

Bethany St. Joseph Care Center - 2501 Shelby Rd., La Crosse, WI 54601 t) 608-788-5700 info@bsjcorp.com www.bsjcorp.com Craig Ubbelohde, Admin.; Asstd. Annu.: 65; Staff: 120

WAUSAU

Benedictine Living Community of Wausau (Catholic Residential Services, Inc.) - 1821 N. 4th Ave., Wausau, WI 54401 t) 715-675-9451 gary.hixon@benedictineliving.org www.benedictineliving.org/wausau-wi/ Sponsored by the Benedictine Sisters of St. Scholastica Monastery. Gary Hixon, Exec. Dir.; Asstd. Annu.: 250; Staff: 93

RETREAT HOUSES / RENEWAL CENTERS [RTR]

LA CROSSE

Franciscan Spirituality Center (Franciscan Sisters of Perpetual Adoration) - 920 Market St., La Crosse, WI 54601-8809 t) 608-791-5295 fscenter@fspa.org www.fscenter.org A sacred place that welcomes everyone. We are rooted in the Gospels and sponsored by the FSPA Jean Pagliaro, Dir.;

MARATHON

St. Anthony's of Marathon, Inc. - 300 E. 4th St., Marathon, WI 54448; Mailing: PO Box 86, Marathon, WI 54448 t) 715-443-2236 info@sarcenter.com; lrandall@sarcenter.com www.sarcenter.com Jacqueline Kellner, Dir.;

SEMINARIES [SEM]

LA CROSSE

Holy Cross Seminary House of Formation - 3710 East Ave. S., La Crosse, WI 54602-4004; Mailing: PO Box 4004, La Crosse, WI 54602-4004 t) 608-791-2667 rorth@diolc.org diolc.org/vocations Rev. Nathaniel W. Kuhn, Dir.; Stds.: 8; Lay Tchrs.: 1; Pr. Tchrs.: 1

SHRINES [SHR]

LA CROSSE

Shrine of Our Lady of Guadalupe - 5250 Justin Rd., La Crosse, WI 54602-1237; Mailing: PO Box 1237, La Crosse, WI 54602-1237 t) 608-782-5440 frcheck@guadalupeshrine.org www.guadalupeshrine.org Rev. Paul N. Check, Exec. Dir.;

SPECIAL CARE FACILITIES [SPF]

CHIPPEWA FALLS

L.E. Phillips Libertas Treatment Center - 2661 County Hwy. I, Chippewa Falls, WI 54729 t) 715-723-5585; 800-680-4578 infosjcf@hshs.org www.libertascenter.org Andrew Bagnall, Pres.; Toni Simonson, Exec. Dir.; Bed Capacity: 38; Asstd. Annu.: 1,400; Staff: 45

An asterisk (*) denotes an organization that has established tax-exempt status directly with the IRS and is not covered by the USCCB Group Ruling.

Diocese of Lafayette

(Dioecesis Lafayettensis)

MOST REVEREND J. DOUGLAS DESHOTEL

Bishop of Lafayette; ordained priest May 13, 1978; appointed Auxiliary Bishop of Dallas and Titular Bishop of Cova, March 11, 2010; Episcopal ordination April 27, 2010; appointed Bishop of Lafayette February 17, 2016; installed April 15, 2016. Office: 1408 Carmel Dr., Lafayette, LA 70501.

Administrative Office: Diocesan Office Building, 1408 Carmel Dr., Lafayette, LA 70501. T: 337-261-5500; F: 337-261-5603.
www.diolaf.org
lleblanc@diolaf.org

ESTABLISHED JANUARY 11, 1918.

Square Miles 5,777.

Comprises the civil parishes (Counties) of Acadia, Evangeline, Iberia, Lafayette, St. Landry, St. Martin and St. Mary (west of Atchafalaya River) and Vermilion in the south central part of the State of Louisiana.

For legal titles of Diocese, parishes and diocesan institutions, consult the Chancery Office.

STATISTICAL OVERVIEW

Personnel

Bishop	1
Retired Bishops	1
Priests: Diocesan Active in Diocese	96
Priests: Diocesan Active Outside Diocese	10
Priests: Diocesan in Foreign Missions	1
Priests: Retired, Sick or Absent	35
Number of Diocesan Priests	142
Religious Priests in Diocese	51
Total Priests in your Diocese	193
Extern Priests in Diocese	14
Ordinations:	
Diocesan Priests	2
Transitional Deacons	3
Permanent Deacons in Diocese	105
Total Brothers	2
Total Sisters	64

Parishes

Parishes	122
With Resident Pastor:	
Resident Diocesan Priests	84
Resident Religious Priests	16
Without Resident Pastor:	
Administered by Priests	22
Missions	27
Professional Ministry Personnel:	
Sisters	3
Lay Ministers	217

Welfare

Catholic Hospitals	1
Total Assisted	299,847
Health Care Centers	1
Total Assisted	352
Homes for the Aged	31
Total Assisted	4,978
Day Care Centers	1
Total Assisted	163
Specialized Homes	1
Total Assisted	25
Special Centers for Social Services	18
Total Assisted	271,549

Educational

Diocesan Students in Other Seminaries	23
Students, Religious	12
Total Seminarians	35
High Schools, Diocesan and Parish	9
Total Students	3,170
High Schools, Private	1
Total Students	130
Elementary Schools, Diocesan and Parish	26
Total Students	9,154
Elementary Schools, Private	1
Total Students	310
Catechesis / Religious Education:	
High School Students	4,039
Elementary Students	7,914
Total Students under Catholic Instruction	24,752
Teachers in Diocese:	
Sisters	1
Lay Teachers	882

Vital Statistics

Receptions into the Church:	
Infant Baptism Totals	2,198
Minor Baptism Totals	111
Adult Baptism Totals	66
Received into Full Communion	170
First Communions	2,254
Confirmations	2,264
Marriages:	
Catholic	562
Interfaith	73
Total Marriages	635
Deaths	3,317
Total Catholic Population	276,452
Total Population	630,574

LEADERSHIP

Bishop's Office - t) 337-261-5614 Most Rev. J. Douglas Deshotel, Bishop of Lafayette; Leslie LeBlanc, Secy. (lleblanc@diolaf.org);

Vicar General - t) 337-261-5611 Msgr. W. Curtis Mallet;

Judicial Vicar - t) (337) 261-5623 Very Rev. Ken Broussard, Judicial Vicar;

Tribunal - t) 337-261-5623 Very Rev. Ken Broussard, Judicial Vicar; Very Rev. Kevin P. Bordelon, Adjutant Judicial Vicar;

Vicar for Clergy - t) 337-261-5690 Very Rev. Jared G. Suire;

Chancellor - t) 337-261-5613 Maureen K. Fontenot, Chancellor;

Finance Officer - t) 337-261-5632 Dcn. Jeff Trumps, CFO;

Diocesan Consultors - Msgr. William Curtis Mallet, Vicar General; Very Rev. Jared G. Suire, Vicar for Clergy; Rev. Steven C. LeBlanc;

Office of Dean - Very Rev. Chester C. Arceneaux, Central Deanery; Very Rev. William C. Blanda, South Deanery; Very Rev. Brent Smith, West Deanery (bsmith@diolaf.org);

Administrative Offices - t) 337-261-5614

Moderator of the Curia - Msgr. W. Curtis Mallet, Vicar General;

Victims' Assistance Coordinator - t) 337-298-2987 Joseph Pisano Jr.;

OFFICES AND DIRECTORS

Catholic Education - t) 337-261-5568 Anna Larriviere, Supt.;

Office of Catholic Schools - Anna Larriviere, Supt.;

Chancellor - t) 337-261-5613 Maureen K. Fontenot;

Archives - Research and Information - t) 337-261-5639 bdejean@diolaf.org Barbara C. DeJean, Archivist;

Auxiliary Services - t) 337-261-5600 Patsy Arwood, Coord.;

Human Resources - t) 337-261-5526 mfontenot@diolaf.org Maureen K. Fontenot, Chancellor;

Pontifical Mission Societies - t) (337) 261-5613 Maureen K. Fontenot, Dir.;

Safe Environment - t) (337) 735-9434 Lisa Frederick, Dir.; Joseph Pisano Jr., Victim Asst. Coord.;

Communications - t) 337-261-5612 Blue Rolfes, Dir.;

Acadiana Catholic Magazine - t) 337-261-5512 Stephanie Martin, Editor;

Media/Public Relations - Blue Rolfes, Dir.;

Social Media - t) 337-261-5518 jmire@diolaf.org Julie D. Mire, Social Media Specialist;

Financial Affairs - t) 337-261-5632 Dcn. Jeff Trumps, CFO;

Building & Renovations - t) (337) 261-5674 Ben Mann, Dir.;

Facilities Manager - t) 337-261-5605; (337) 261-5625 Todd Broussard, Contact; Anthony Boudreaux, Prog. Coord.;

Financial Affairs - Dcn. Jeff Trumps, CFO;

Accounting - t) 337-261-5627 Eric Guidry, Controller;

Information Technology - t) 337-261-5516 Robin Stevenson, Dir.;

Parish & School Finance - t) (337) 261-5554 Eric Guidry, Dir.;

Property Management - t) (337) 261-5532 Jack Bienvenu, Risk Mgr.; Dcn. Jeff Trumps, CFO;

Risk Management - t) (337) 735-9449 Jack Bienvenu, Mgr.;

Stewardship & Development - t) 337-261-5641 Margaret Trahan, Dir.;

Ministries - t) 337-261-5609 Dcn. James Kincel, Dir.;

Black Catholic Ministry - t) 337-261-5694 Stephanie Bernard, Prog. Coord.;

Catechetics - t) 337-261-5550 Chad Judice, Dir.;

Diaconal Formation - Dcn. James "Jim" Kincel;

Hispanic Ministry - t) 337-261-5542 Dcn. Juan Carlos Pagan, Prog. Coord.;

Justice, Peace & Prison Ministry - t) 337-261-5694 Stephanie Bernard, Prog. Coord.;

Marriage and Family Life Ministry & Pro-Life Apostolate - t) 337-261-5653 Kelley Chapman, Dir.; Rev. Jude Halphen, Counselor;

Office of Worship - t) (337) 261-5609 Rev. Alexander Albert, Dir.;

Religious Brothers and Sisters - t) (337) 261-5609 Sr. Celeste D. Larroque, S.E.C., Dir.;

Vietnamese Catholic Ministry - t) (337) 740-4659 Dcn. Tam Minh Tran, Prog. Coord.;

Vicar for Clergy - t) (337) 261-5690 Very Rev. Jared G. Suire, Vicar;

Clergy - t) (337) 261-5690 Very Rev. Jared G. Suire;

Ongoing Formation of Priests - t) 337-261-5690 Very Rev. Jared G. Suire;

Permanent Diaconate - t) 337-261-5609 Dcn. James "Jim" Kincel;

Seminarians - t) 337-261-5690 Rev. Blake Dubroc, Dir.;

Vocations - t) 337-261-5690 Rev. Blake Dubroc, Dir.;

ADVISORY BOARDS, COMMISSIONS, COMMITTEES, AND COUNCILS

Presbyteral Council - t) 337-261-5611 Rev. John Breaux, Chair;

Diocesan Pastoral Council - t) 337-261-5613 Maureen K. Fontenot, Chancellor;

Clergy Personnel Advisory Board - t) 337-261-5690 Very Rev. Jared G. Suire, Chair;

Abuse Review Board - t) 337-261-5611 Msgr. William Curtis Mallet;

CATHOLIC CHARITIES

Catholic Charities of Acadiana - t) 337-235-4972 Kim Boudreaux, Dir.;

Catholic Relief Services - Kim Boudreaux, Diocesan Coord.;

Migration and Refugee Services - t) 337-235-4972

Persons with Disabilities - t) 337-232-3463; 337-235-4972 Julie Caillouet, Prog. Coord.;

Rebuilding Together Acadiana - sarah@catholiccharitiesacadiana.org

Catholic Charities of Acadiana - sarah@catholiccharitiesacadiana.org

FoodNet Food Bank - sarah@catholiccharitiesacadiana.org

Immigration Legal Services - sarah@catholiccharitiesacadiana.org

Disaster Response - sarah@catholiccharitiesacadiana.org

TRIBUNAL

Advocate - t) (337) 261-5623

Assessors - t) 337-261-5623 Dcn. Michael Raymond Morrison; Dcn. William Merrill Vincent; Dcn. Adam Conque;

Auditor/Instructor - t) (337) 261-5671 Leah Guidry, Auditor;

Defender of the Bond - t) (337) 261-5623 Rev. Joshua P. Guillory; Rev. Michael Richard;

Judges - t) 337-261-5623 Very Rev. Kevin P. Bordelon, Adjutant Judicial Vicar (kbordelon@diolaf.org); Very Rev. Ken Broussard, Judicial Vicar;

Judicial Vicar - t) 337-261-5623 Very Rev. Ken Broussard, Judicial Vicar;

Notaries - t) (337) 261-5623 Diane Prejean; Betty Sampay;

Promoter of Justice - Msgr. W. Curtis Mallet;

MISCELLANEOUS / OTHER OFFICES

Catholic Charismatic Renewal - t) 337-288-9402 John V. Listi, Admin. (johnvlisti@gmail.com);

Catholic Committee on Scouting - Robert T. Clements, Chair;

Catholic Daughters of America - Rev. Herbert Bennerfield, Chap.; Rev. Cedric Sonnier, Chap.;

Credit Union - Pelican State Credit Union - t) 337-261-1151

Cursillo - Rev. Theodore Broussard Jr., Dir.;

Diocesan Disaster Coordinator - t) 337-235-4972 Kim Boudreaux;

Knights of Columbus - Rev. Mark Derise, Chap.;

Retreats - t) 337-662-5410 oloaks@centurytel.net Albert S. Cain III, Exec. Dir. (olodirector@centurytel.net); Rev. Steven E. Kimmons, S.J., Retreat Dir. (skimmons@jesuits.org);

Scouting - Rev. Kenneth J. Domingue, Assoc. Scout Chap.;

PARISHES, MISSIONS, AND CLERGY

STATE OF LOUISIANA

ABBEVILLE

Saint Andrew Dung-Lac Roman Catholic Church - 1201 N. Lafitte Rd., Abbeville, LA 70510; Mailing: P O Box 715, Abbeville, LA 70511 t) 337-740-4659 nnguyenstandrewdunglac@gmail.com Rev. James B. Nguyen, Pst.; Dcn. Tam Minh Tran; CRP Stds.: 13

St. Anne - 17315 Lionel Rd., Abbeville, LA 70510 t) 337-643-7714 stanne@kaplantel.net Rev. Matthew Barzare, Pst.; CRP Stds.: 121

Sacred Heart - 28220 W. Hwy. 82, Pecan Island, LA 70510; Mailing: 17315 Lionel Rd., Abbeville, LA 70510

St. Mary Magdalen - 300 Pere Megret, Abbeville, LA 70510; Mailing: P O Box 1507, Abbeville, LA 70511 t) 337-893-0244 parish@stmarymagdalenparish.org; rlivers@diolaf.org www.stmarymagdalenparish.org Very Rev. Louis J. Richard, Pst.; Dcn. Khang Francis Xavier Van Cao; Dcn. William Merrill Vincent; Renella Livers, DRE; CRP Stds.: 254

Vermilion Catholic, a legacy of Mount Carmel - (Grades PreSchool-12) 425 Park Ave., Abbeville, LA 70510 t) 337-893-6636 sarabie@diolaf.org www.vermilioncatholic.com Dr. Stella Arabie, Prin.; Stds.: 494; Lay Tchrs.: 32

Mt. Carmel School - (Grades PreK-8) 405 Park Ave., Abbeville, LA 70510 t) 337-898-0859 carmel@mceschool.org; jtrahan@mceschool.com www.mceschool.org Jackie Trahan, Prin.; Sr. Janet LeBlanc, O.Carm., Pres.; Tiffany Abshire, Librn.;

St. Mary Magdalen Christian Service Center - 701 Chevis St., Abbeville, LA 70510

St. Theresa of the Child Jesus - 101 N. Leonard St., Abbeville, LA 70510; Mailing: P.O. Box 609, Abbeville, LA 70511-0609 t) 337-893-5631 lgayneaux@diolaf.org; lorettagayneaux@yahoo.com sttheresaabbeville.com Rev. Francois Sainte-Marie, Pst.; Loretta Gayneaux, DRE; CRP Stds.: 92

ARNAUDVILLE

St. Catherine - 242 Pine St., Arnaudville, LA 70512; Mailing: PO Box 351, Arnaudville, LA 70512 t) 337-754-5912 pastor@arnaudvillecatholic.org; bsanders@arnaudvillecatholic.org arnaudvillecatholic.org Rev. Travis Abadie, Pst.; Betty V. Sanders, Bus. Mgr.; Sheila Gresko, DRE; CRP Stds.: 17

St. John Francis Regis - 232 Main St., Arnaudville, LA 70512; Mailing: PO Box 649, Arnaudville, LA 70512 t) 337-754-5912 pastor@arnaudvillecatholic.org; bsanders@arnaudvillecatholic.org arnaudvillecatholic.org Rev. Travis Abadie, Pst.; Betty V. Sanders, Bus. Mgr.; Sheila Gresko, DRE; CRP Stds.: 143

BALDWIN

Sacred Heart - 414 Martin Luther King, Baldwin, LA 70514; Mailing: P. O. Box 308, Baldwin, LA 70514 t) 337-923-7781 sacred_heart07@bellsouth.net Rev. Christopher B. Cambre, Pst.; Dcn. Richard Picard; Kathy Sanders, DRE; CRP Stds.: 20

BASILE

St. Augustine - 2717 Dr. Bobby Deshotel Ave., Basile, LA 70515 t) 337-432-6817 kbrown@diolaf.org; staugustinecc@ymail.com Rev. Keenan Wynn Brown, Pst.; Deneen Ortego, DRE; CRP Stds.: 200

BAYOU VISTA

St. Bernadette - 1112 Saturn Rd., Bayou Vista, LA 70380 t) 985-395-2470 stbern@teche.net stbern-bv.org Rev. Thainese Alphonse, Pst.; Becky Blanchard, DRE; CRP Stds.: 88

BERWICK

St. Stephen - 3217 Second St., Berwick, LA 70342 t) 985-385-1280; 985-385-1283 (CRP) ststephenchurch@atvci.net ststephenberwick.org Rev. Msgr. J. Douglas Courville, Pst.; Peggy Acosta, DRE; CRP Stds.: 142

BREAUX BRIDGE

St. Bernard - 204 N. Main St., Breaux Bridge, LA 70517 t) 337-332-2159 stbernardcatholicchurch.com Rev. Garrett K. McIntyre, Pst.; Dcn. Jim Davis; Dcn. Marcel P. Hebert Jr.; Kelli LeBlanc, DRE; CRP Stds.: 261

St. Bernard School - (Grades PreK-8) 251 E. Bridge St., Breaux Bridge, LA 70517 t) 337-332-5350 jpmasterson@sbscrusaders.com www.sbscrusaders.com John Paul Masterson, Prin.; Stds.: 396; Lay Tchrs.: 27

St. Francis of Assisi - 610 N. Main St., Breaux Bridge, LA 70517 t) 337-332-2250 nwaigwejerome@yahoo.com Rev. George Bede Ajuruchi, SSJ, Pst.; Cheryl Ozen, DRE; CRP Stds.: 67

BROUSSARD

St. Joseph - 232 St. DePorres St., Broussard, LA 70518; Mailing: PO Box 278, Broussard, LA 70518-0278 t) 337-837-6218; 337-714-9327 stjosant@yahoo.com; pbellow@diolaf.org www.stjosant.org Rev. Ryszard Zawadzki, S.V.D., Pst.; Charlotte Milson, DRE; CRP Stds.: 26

St. Anthony - 1639 Old Spanish Hwy., Cade, LA 70519

Sacred Heart of Jesus - 200 W. Main St., Broussard, LA 70518 t) 337-837-1864 marsha@shbroussard.org shbroussard.org Rev. Michael L. Delcambre, Pst.; CRP Stds.: 273

St. Cecilia - (Grades PreK-8) 302 W. Main St., Broussard, LA 70518 t) 337-837-6363 ehenry@scsbluejays.org scsbluejays.org Stds.: 475; Sr. Tchrs.: 1; Lay Tchrs.: 25

CANKTON

St. John Berchmans - 552 Main St., Cankton, LA 70584-5922 t) 337-668-4413 stjb@centurytel.net stjberchmans.com Rev. Kenneth J. Domingue, Pst.; CRP Stds.: 188

CARENCRO

Our Lady of the Assumption - 410 N. Michaud St., Carencro, LA 70520-0130; Mailing: P.O. Box 430, Carencro, LA 70520 t) 337-896-8304 secretaryolac@yahoo.com; deaconsenegal@yahoo.com Rev. Msgr. Ronald Broussard, Pst.; Dcn. Nolton J. Senegal; Sarah Robert, DRE; CRP Stds.: 30

St. Peter - 102 N. Church St., Carencro, LA 70520; Mailing: P.O. Box 40, Carencro, LA 70520 t) 337-896-9408 mledoux@diolaf.org www.sprcc.org Rev. Mark Ledoux, Pst.; CRP Stds.: 27

Carencro Catholic - (Grades PreK-8) 200 W. St. Peter St., Carencro, LA 70520 t) 337-896-8973 dsoeseno@diolaf.org www.carencrocatholic.org Devin Soeseno, Prin.; Morgen Landry, Dir.; Jill Myers, Librn.; Stds.: 201; Lay Tchrs.: 18

CECILIA

St. Joseph - 2250 Cecilia High School Hwy., Cecilia, LA 70521; Mailing: P. O. Box 279, Cecilia, LA 70521 t) 337-667-6344 pastor@stjosephcecilia.com www.stjosephcecilia.com Rev. Gregory P. Cormier, Pst.; Dcn. Kenneth E. Soignier; CRP Stds.: 236

St. Rose of Lima - 2184 Bushville Hwy., Cecilia, LA 70521; Mailing: P.O. Box 126, Cecilia, LA 70521 t) 337-667-6555 st.roseoflimacatholicchurch@yahoo.com; pastor@stjosephcecilia.com Rev. Gregory P. Cormier, Pst.; Traci Sassau, DRE; CRP Stds.: 22

CENTERVILLE

St. Joseph - 132 Hwy. 317, Centerville, LA 70522; Mailing: P.O. Box 280, Centerville, LA 70522 t) 337-836-5659 sjcc@cox-internet.com Rev. Joel Christopher Faulk, Pst.; Rev. Seth Lemaire, Par. Vicar; CRP Stds.: 51

CHARENTON

Immaculate Conception - 3041 Chitamacha Tr., Charenton, LA 70523; Mailing: P. O. Box 278, Charenton, LA 70523 t) 337-923-4281 ccambre@diolaf.com www.icsee.com Rev. Christopher Cambre, Pst.;

CHATAIGNIER

Our Lady of Mount Carmel - 5706 Vine St., Chataignier, LA 70524; Mailing: P.O. Box 100, Chataignier, LA 70524 t) 337-885-3223 fr.d.b.clement@gmail.com; seldridge@diolaf.org Rev. D. Blaine Clement, Pst.; CRP Stds.: 21

CHURCH POINT

Assumption of the Blessed Virgin Mary - 6080 Mire Hwy., Church Point, LA 70525 t) 337-873-6574 emeche@diolaf.org Rev. Msgr. Russell J. Harrington, Pst.; Edna Meche, DRE; CRP Stds.: 146

St. Edward - 1463 Charlene Hwy., Church Point, LA 70525 t) 337-684-5991 Rev. Korey LaVergne, Pst.; Monica Rougeau, DRE; CRP Stds.: 142

St. Thomas - 802 Tasso Loop, Savoy, LA 70525 Rev. Wayne J. Duet, Pst.;

Our Lady of the Sacred Heart - 102 Church Blvd., Church Point, LA 70525 t) 337-684-5494 jwyble@diolaf.org Rev. Brian Harrington, Pst.; Rev. David Rozas, Assoc. Pst.; Dcn. Francis Douglas Wimberly; Dcn. Jerry Wayne Wyble; CRP Stds.: 135

Our Mother of Peace - (Grades PreK-8) 218 N. Rogers St., Church Point, LA 70525 t) 337-684-5780 gkirkpatrick@ompwildcats.com www.ompwildcats.com Genny Kirkpatrick, Prin.; Jill Myers, Librn.; Stds.: 216; Lay Tchrs.: 14

Lewisburg, St. John Chapel - 374 Bourque Rd., Church Point, LA 70525

Our Mother of Mercy - 693 N. Main St., Church Point, LA 70525; Mailing: P.O. Box 237, Church Point, LA 70525 t) 337-684-6832 (CRP); 337-684-2319 ourmotherofmercychurchpoint41@gmail.com; praisehouse@centurytel.net Rev. Pius Titus Ajiki (NIgeria), Pst.; Linda Brooks, DRE; CRP Stds.: 23

CROWLEY

Immaculate Heart of Mary - 901 E. Elm St., Crowley, LA 70526 t) 337-783-3498 ihmcatholicchurch@cox-internet.com; parish@ihmcrowley.org Rev. Johnathan J. Janise, Pst.; Dcn. Joshua Reed LeBlanc; James Franke, DRE; CRP Stds.: 55

St. John the Baptist - 8021 Lyons Point Hwy., Crowley, LA 70526 t) 337-783-2968 icc-sjtb@outlook.com icc-sjtb.org Rev. Arockia Doss Palthasar, HGN, Pst.; Deanna Spell, DRE; CRP Stds.: 52

St. Michael Archangel - 224 W. 5th St., Crowley, LA 70526; Mailing: P.O. Box 406, Crowley, LA 70527 t) 337-783-7394 stmichaelcrowley@gmail.com stmichaelcrowley.org Rev. Mikel Anthony Polson, Pst.; Dcn. Daniel Peter Didier; Eva Cormier, DRE; CRP Stds.: 37

St. Michael's Catholic School - (Grades PreK-8) 805 E. Northern Ave., Crowley, LA 70526 t) 337-783-1410 hbroussard@stmike.net Terri Hebert, Prin.; Jeanne Nickel, Librn.; Stds.: 491; Lay Tchrs.: 31

St. Theresa - 417 W. 3rd St., Crowley, LA 70526 t) 337-783-1880 st.theresachurch@hotmail.com www.josephites.org Rev. Mark Alewo Odoguje, SVD, Pst.; Verila Cormier, DRE; CRP Stds.: 68

DELCAMBRE

Saint Martin de Porres - 608 Martin Luther King Dr., Delcambre, LA 70528; Mailing: 206 W. Church St., Delcambre, LA 70528 t) 337-685-4426 mike.reeser2@yahoo.com; frbbreaux@gmail.com www.delcambrechurches.weconnect.com Rev. John Breaux, Pst.; CRP Stds.: 24

Castel School of Religion - 208 S. Peter St., Delcambre, LA 70528

Our Lady of the Lake - 206 W. Church St., Delcambre, LA 70528 t) 337-685-4426 delcambrechurches@yahoo.com; mike.reeser2@yahoo.com Rev. John Breaux, Pst.; Dcn. Russell James Hayes; Dcn. Patrick Douglas Burke; CRP Stds.: 201

DUSON

St. Basil - 1803 Duhon Rd. (Judice), Duson, LA 70529 t) 337-984-2179 stbasil@glacoxmail.com stbasiljudice.org Rev. Steven C. LeBlanc, Pst.; Cindy Richardson, DRE; CRP Stds.: 82

St. Benedict the Moor - 9135 Cameron St., Duson, LA 70529; Mailing: P O Box 8, Duson, LA 70529-0008 t) 337-873-6772; 337-873-4962 (CRP) Rev. Aaron Melancon, Pst.; CRP Stds.: 78

St. Theresa of the Child Jesus - 209 C St., Duson, LA 70529; Mailing: P O Box 8, Duson, LA 70529-0008 t) 337-873-4962 sbcdus@bellsouth.net none Rev. Aaron Melancon, Pst.; Dcn. Steve Simon; CRP Stds.: 59

ERATH

St. John - 18534 LA Hwy. 689, Erath, LA 70533 t) 337-937-5108 Rev. Emmanuel Fernandez, Pst.; Linda Choate, DRE; CRP Stds.: 25

St. James - 21125 LA Hwy. 333, Abbeville, LA 70510

Our Lady of Lourdes - 700 S. Broadway, Erath, LA 70533 t) 337-937-6888 ftoups@gmail.com Rev. Clinton M. Sensat, Pst.; Dcn. Timothy Isidore Marcantel; Frances Toups, DRE; CRP Stds.: 500

EUNICE

Annunciation of the B.V.M. - 4476 Duralde Hwy., Eunice, LA 70535 t) 337-457-4849 annunciationduralde@gmail.com Rev. D. Blaine Clement, Pst.; Maggie Vidrine, DRE; CRP Stds.: 85

St. Anthony of Padua - 310 W. Vine Ave., Eunice, LA 70535 t) 337-457-5285; 337-457-7505 (CRP) stanthony@stanthonyeunice.org; dreangieag@yahoo.com stanthonyeunice.org Rev. F. Hampton Davis III, Pst.; Rev. Raymond Ssebina (Uganda), Assoc. Pst.; Rev. Nicholas Ware, Assoc. Pst.; Dcn. Gary Michael Gaudin; Angie Aguillard, DRE; CRP Stds.: 100

St. Edmund Catholic School - (Grades PreK-12) 351 W. Magnolia St., Eunice, LA 70535 t) 337-457-2592; 337-457-3777 fhdavis3@bellsouth.net stedmund.com Rev. Hampton Davis III, Prin.; Callie Reiners, Librn.; Stds.: 423; Lay Tchrs.: 31

St. Edmund Catholic School - (Grades 7-12) 351 W. Magnolia St., Eunice, LA 70535 t) 337-457-2592 charles.hazard@stedmund.com

St. Lawrence - 29031 Crowley-Eunice Hwy., Eunice, LA 70535 t) 337-457-2739 Rev. Michael M. Sucharski, S.V.D., Pst.; Tina Johnson, DRE; CRP Stds.: 50

St. Mathilda - 800 E. Laurel Ave., Eunice, LA 70535; Mailing: PO Box 346, Eunice, LA 70535 t) 337-457-3286 stmathildaeunice@gmail.com Rev. Hampton Davis III, Pst.; Rev. Raymond Ssebina (Uganda), Par. Vicar; Rev. Nick Ware, Par. Vicar; Eltra Jordan, DRE; CRP Stds.: 41

St. Thomas More - 1011 Sittig St., Eunice, LA 70535 t) 337-457-8107; 337-457-8101 (CRP) stmeunice.com Rev. Clinton M. Sensat, Pst.; Yolanda Thibodeaux, DRE; CRP Stds.: 186

EVANGELINE

St. Joseph - 1400 Old Evangeline Hwy., Evangeline, LA 70537; Mailing: P.O. Box 183, Evangeline, LA 70537 t) 337-824-4995 plafleur@diolaf.org Rev. Paul J. LaFleur, Pst.; CRP Stds.: 80

St. Jules - 5469 Riverside Rd., Petit Mamou, LA 70537

FRANKLIN

Assumption B.V.M. - 211 Iberia St., Franklin, LA 70538 t) 337-828-3869; 337-828-9499 (CRP) marysassumption@yahoo.com www.churchofassumption.com Rev. Joel Christopher Faulk, Pst.; CRP Stds.: 54

St. John Elementary - (Grades PreK-5) 924 Main St., Franklin, LA 70538 t) 337-828-2648

shigdon@stjohnelem.com www.stjohnelem.com Sheri Higdon, Prin.; Stds.: 130; Lay Tchrs.: 8

Hanson High School - (Grades 6-12) 903 Anderson St., Franklin, LA 70538 t) 337-828-3487 cdaigle@hansonmemorial.com www.hansonmemorial.com Connie Daigle, Prin.; Stds.: 164

St. Helena - 108 St. Helen's Church Ln., Franklin, LA 70538; Mailing: Post Office Box 369, Lydia, LA 70569 t) 337-867-4378 sacred_heart07@bellsouth.net Rev. Randy Courville, Pst.;

St. Francis -

St. Jules - 601 Magnolia St., Franklin, LA 70538 t) 337-828-1714 pemusa@diolaf.org Rev. Peter Emusa, Pst.; CRP Stds.: 12

Immaculate Conception -

St. Peter the Apostle - 1325 Big Four Corners Rd., Franklin, LA 70538 t) 337-276-5256 spta4c@yahoo.com; akedati@diolaf.org Rev. Francis Damoah, S.V.D., Pst.; CRP Stds.: 14

GRAND COTEAU

St. Charles Borromeo - 174 Church St., Grand Coteau, LA 70541; Mailing: P.O. Box A, Grand Coteau, LA 70541 t) 337-662-5279 matte@st-charles-borromeo.org www.st-charles-borromeo.org Rev. Mark Kramer, S.J., Pst.; Rev. Clyde LeBlanc, S.J., Assoc. Pst.; Dcn. David Wayne Menard; CRP Stds.: 200

St. Ignatius School - (Grades PreK-8) 180 Church St., Grand Coteau, LA 70541; Mailing: P.O. Drawer J, Grand Coteau, LA 70541 t) 337-662-3325 cindyp@siscardinals.org siscardinals.org Cynthia Prather, Prin.; Stds.: 327; Lay Tchrs.: 24

Christ the King - 369 Christ the King Rd, Opelousas, LA 70570

GUEYDAN

St. Peter the Apostle - 603 Main, Gueydan, LA 70542; Mailing: PO Box 28, Gueydan, LA 70542 t) 337-536-9258 www.saintpeterchurch.org Rev. Corey Campeaux, Pst.; CRP Stds.: 63

St. David - 13022 Hwy. 3093, Kaplan, LA 70548 saintpeterchurch.org

HENDERSON

Our Lady of Mercy - 1454 Henderson Hwy., Henderson, LA 70517; Mailing: PO Box 587, Breaux Bridge, LA 70517 t) 337-228-2352 lbenoit@diolaf.org Dcn. Perry John Guidry; Donna Lacombe, DRE; CRP Stds.: 50

Sacred Heart - 1718 Herman Dupre Rd., Butte LaRose, LA 70517; Mailing: P.O. Box 587, Breaux Bridge, LA 70517

IOTA

St. Joseph - 604 St. Joseph Ave., Iota, LA 70543 t) 337-779-2627 stjosephiota@gmail.com www.stjosephiota.org Rev. Jude W. Thierry, Pst.; CRP Stds.: 242

St. Francis - (Grades PreK-8) 490 St. Joseph Ave., Iota, LA 70543 t) 337-779-2527 st_francis@centurytel.net stfranciswolves.com Michael Darbonne, Admin.; Stds.: 132; Lay Tchrs.: 11

St. Michael - 2106 Egan Hwy., Egan, LA 70543

JEANERETTE

St. John the Evangelist - 1510 Church St., Jeanerette, LA 70544 t) 337-276-4576 stjohnev@stjohnjeanerette.org www.stjohnjeanerette.org Rev. Alexander Albert, Pst.; Becki Landry, Dir., Discipleship & Evangelization; CRP Stds.: 42

Our Lady of the Rosary - 11200 Old Jeanerette Rd., Jeanerette, LA 70544 t) 337-276-6900 olrjean@yahoo.com Rev. Francis Damoah, S.V.D., Pst.; CRP Stds.: 5

KAPLAN

Our Lady of the Holy Rosary - 603 N. Herbert Ave., Kaplan, LA 70548 t) 337-643-6472 hrcc@kaplantel.net; hrcc3@kaplantel.net www.holyrosarycabrini.org Rev. Mark H. Miley, Pst.; Rev. Matthew Hebert, Par. Vicar; Dcn. Bryan Kade Istre; Jerry Abshire, DRE; CRP Stds.: 219

Maltrait Memorial - (Grades PreK-8) One Crusader Sq., Kaplan, LA 70548; Mailing: 612 N. Hebert, Kaplan, LA 70548 t) 337-643-7765 mmcscrusader@kaplantel.net Renee C. Meaux, Prin.; Stds.: 110; Lay Tchrs.: 10

St. Frances Xavier Cabrini - 901 N. Frederick Ave., Kaplan, LA 70548

KROTZ SPRINGS

St. Anthony of Padua - 219 8th Ave., Krotz Springs, LA 70750; Mailing: PO Box 425, Krotz Springs, LA 70750 t) 337-566-3527 mdeblanc@diolaf.org; parish@saintanthonyks.org Rev. Michael DeBlanc III, Pst.; Sabrina Ardoin, DRE; CRP Stds.: 48

LAFAYETTE

Cathedral of St. John the Evangelist - 515 Cathedral St., Lafayette, LA 70501 t) 337-232-1325 (CRP); 337-232-1322 bprimeaux@saintjohncathedral.org; dhuval@saintjohncathedral.org Very Rev. Chester C. Arceneaux, Pst.; Dcn. George Bernard Jourdan; Dcn. Albert George Alexander; Dcn. Todd Michael McKee; Rev. Cyprian Eze, In Res.; Brittany Primeaux, DRE; CRP Stds.: 167

Cathedral-Carmel Elementary - (Grades PreK-8) 848 St. John St., Lafayette, LA 70501 t) 337-235-5577 kaillet@cathedralcarmel.com www.cathedralcarmel.com Menard Christine, Admin.; Jill Spikes, Admin.; Nicole White, Admin.; Mary Catherine "Kay" Aillet, Prin.; Jan Johnson, Librn.; Stds.: 789; Lay Tchrs.: 47

St. Anthony Catholic Church - 615 Edison St., Lafayette, LA 70501 t) 337-234-5855; 337-852-0157 (CRP) stanthonychurch@bellsouth.net; taym822@gmail.com Rev. Rick Andrus, SVD, Pst.; Dcn. Albert Marcel Jr.; Tammy Marcel, DRE; CRP Stds.: 53

St. Edmond - 4131 W. Congress St., Lafayette, LA 70506 t) 337-981-0874 secretary@st-edmond.org; religioused@st-edmond.org Rev. Joseph Campion, Pst.; Rev. Francis Kwasi Agbley, Assoc. Pst.; Dcn. Ricky Castaneda; Dcn. Frank Alex Cormier; CRP Stds.: 165

St. Elizabeth Seton - 610 Raintree Tr., Lafayette, LA 70507 t) 337-235-1483 nelsonschexnayder@yahoo.com; pastor@setonchurch.org www.setonchurch.org Rev. David B. Hebert, Pst.; Dcn. Nelson Joseph Schexnayder Jr.; Dcn. Ronald Paul Chauvin; Gerry Baumboree, DRE; CRP Stds.: 185

Sts. Leo-Seton Catholic School - 502 St. Leo. St., Lafayette, LA 70501 t) 337-234-5510 Kimberly Gothreaux, Prin.;

St. Genevieve - 417 E. Simcoe, Lafayette, LA 70501 t) 337-234-5147 x121 (CRP); 337-234-5147 info@stgens.net www.stgens.net Rev. Brian Taylor, Pst.; Dcn. Arthur Francis Bakeler Jr.; Dcn. Kyle Joseph Faber; Nicole Osmer, DRE; CRP Stds.: 11

St. Genevieve Elementary School - (Grades PreK-4) 201 Elizabeth St., Lafayette, LA 70501 t) 337-234-5257 sgscardinals@stgen.net www.stgen.net Michelle Melancon, Prin.; Stds.: 321; Lay Tchrs.: 13

St. Genevieve Middle School - (Grades 5-8) 91 Teurlings Dr., Lafayette, LA 70501 t) 337-266-5553 sgscardinals@stgen.net www.stgen.net Julie Zaunbrecher, Prin.; Stds.: 245; Lay Tchrs.: 11

St. Genevieve School Foundation, Inc. - 91 Teurlings Dr., Lafayette, LA 70501 t) 337-266-5553

Holy Cross - 415 Robley Dr., Lafayette, LA 70503 t) 337-984-9636 kborah@holycrosslafayette.com www.holycrosslafayette.com/ Rev. Mario P. Romero, Pst.; Rev. Ravi Jampangi (India), Assoc. Pst.; Dcn. Scotty James Baudoin; Dcn. Robert Charles Klingman Jr., Bus. Mgr.; Dcn. James "Jim" Kincel, Liturgical Appointment; Dcn. Kenneth James David; CRP Stds.: 301

Immaculate Heart of Mary - 818-12th St., Lafayette, LA 70501 t) 337-235-4518; 337-235-6323 (CRP) ihm818@bellsouth.net Rev. Augustine Wall, SVD, Pst.; Rev. Arockia Sabastian Mariasusai, SVD, Par. Vicar; Rev. Alfred Ayem, SVD, Par. Vicar; Dcn. Michael Raymond Morrison; Rev. Ryszard Kalinowski, S.V.D., In Res.; Lana Pierre, DRE; CRP Stds.: 66

St. Jules - 116 St. Jules St., Lafayette, LA 70506 t) 337-234-2727 gporche@diolaf.org; church@stjuleschurch.org stjuleschurch.org Rev. Gregory Chauvin, Admin.; Rev. Joseph Sai Tran, S.V.D.; Dcn. Jose Vicente Blanco; Dcn. Reginald A. Bollich; Dcn. Barney Dale Lejeune; Dcn. Jose Luna-Becerra; Rev. Thomas Finley, In Res.; Corine M Porche, DRE; CRP Stds.: 192

St. Leo the Great - 300 W. Alexander St., Lafayette, LA 70501 t) 337-232-2404 cherie@stleolafayette.com; frwhite@stleolafayette.com www.stleolafayette.com Rev. Kyle White, Pst.; Rev. Jared G. Suire, In Res.; CRP Stds.: 73

Sts. Leo-Seton - (Grades PreK-8) 502 St. Leo St., Lafayette, LA 70501 t) 337-234-5510 mbagala@diolaf.org Marissa Bagala, Prin.; Kathy Schaub, Bus. Mgr.; Kellie Plaisance, Librn.; Stds.: 472; Lay Tchrs.: 27

St. Mary Mother of the Church - 419 Doucet Rd., Lafayette, LA 70503 t) 337-981-3379 deb58@cox.net Rev. Cedric Sonnier, Pst.; Dcn. Michael Wayne Crain; Denise Gesser, DRE; CRP Stds.: 143

St. Mary Early Learning Center - t) 337-984-3750 dlcastille@diolaf.org Dina Castille, Prin.;

Our Lady of Fatima - 2319 Johnston St., Lafayette, LA 70503 t) 337-235-2464 (CRP); 337-232-8945 lmelancon@olf.org; administrator@fatimalafayette.org www.fatimalafayette.org Rev. Msgr. Jefferson J. DeBlanc Jr., Pst.; Rev. Randy Moreau, Par. Vicar; Dcn. Timothy Maragos; Lisa Melancon, DRE; Dcn. Randy Eugene Hyde, Liturgical Appointment; CRP Stds.: 50

Our Lady of Fatima School - (Grades PreK-8) 2315 Johnston St., Lafayette, LA 70503 aisaacs@olf.org www.fatimawarrior.com Special Ed. offered. Angela Isaacs, Prin.; Stds.: 883; Lay Tchrs.: 56

Our Lady of Wisdom, University of Louisiana - 501 E. Saint Mary Blvd., Lafayette, LA 70503; Mailing: P.O. Box 43599, Lafayette, LA 70504-3599 t) 337-232-8742 wisdom@ourladyofwisdom.org www.ourladyofwisdom.org Rev. Patrick Broussard, Pst.; Rev. Stephen Pellessier, Par. Vicar; Dcn. Juan Carlos Pagan; Dcn. Kyle Patrick Polozola; Dcn. Coby Brandon Thomas; Veronica Pagan, DRE; CRP Stds.: 175

Our Lady Queen of Peace - 145 Martin Luther King Jr. Dr., Lafayette, LA 70501 t) 337-233-1591 fhdavis3@bellsouth.net; queenofpeace1969@gmail.com Rev. Edward Duhon Jr., Pst.; Dcn. Louis J. Lloyd; Gail Lee, DRE; CRP Stds.: 110

St. Patrick - 406 E. Pinhook Rd., Lafayette, LA 70501 t) 337-237-0988 stpat.org@gmail.com stpat.org Rev. Joshua P. Guillory, Pst.;

St. Paul the Apostle - 326 S. Washington St., Lafayette, LA 70501 t) 337-235-0272 tonanala@yahoo.com; lmoten@diolaf.org Rev. Anthony A. Anala, S.V.D., Pst.; Bobbette Castille, DRE; CRP Stds.: 45

Our Lady of Good Hope -

St. Pius X - 600 Kaliste Saloom Rd., Lafayette, LA 70508; Mailing: P.O. Box 80489, Lafayette, LA 70598-0489 t) 337-232-4656 skleinpeter@stpiusxchurch.org www.stpiusxchurch.org Rev. James Brady, Pst.; Rev. Connor Poirrier, Par. Vicar; Dcn. Philip Lizotte; Dcn. Samuel Joseph Russo Jr.; Dcn. Jeffrey Paul Trumps; CRP Stds.: 180

St. Pius Elementary School - (Grades PreK-8) 205 E. Bayou Pkwy., Lafayette, LA 70508 t) 337-237-3139 jamie_hebert@stpiuselementary.org www.stpiuselementary.org Kellie DesOrmeaux, Prin.; Judice Kay, Librn.; Stds.: 641; Lay Tchrs.: 34

LAWTELL

St. Ann - 8348 Hwy. 190, Lawtell, LA 70550; Mailing: P.O. Box 310, Lawtell, LA 70550 t) 337-543-2366 baubespin@diolaf.org Rev. Stanley Jawa, S.V.D., Pst.; Antoinette Rene, DRE; CRP Stds.: 64

St. Bridget - 3933 Hwy. 35, Lawtell, LA 70550; Mailing: P.O. Box 156, Lawtell, LA 70550 t) 337-543-7591 tjbroussard@diolaf.org Rev. Ted Broussard, Pst.; Lisa Thibodeaux, DRE; CRP Stds.: 80

Sacred Heart - 3681 Hwy. 104, Opelousas, LA 70570 stbridgetsacredheart@gmail.com Rev. Theodore Broussard Jr., Pst.;

Holy Family - 283 Thibodeaux St., Lawtell, LA 70550; Mailing: P.O. Box 310, Lawtell, LA 70550 t) 337-543-2366 www.holyfamilysaintann.org Rev. Stanley Jawa, S.V.D., Pst.; Antoinette Rene, DRE;

LEBEAU

Immaculate Conception - 103 Lebeau Church Rd., Lebeau, LA 71345 t) 337-623-0303 jfallon@diolaf.org; jpfallon@hotmail.com www.lebeauchurch.com Rev. James P. Fallon, S.S.J., Admin.; Jane Edwards, DRE; CRP Stds.: 19

LEONVILLE

St. Catherine - 4399 Hwy. 31, Leonville, LA 70551; Mailing: PO Box 547, Leonville, LA 70551 t) 337-879-2365 Rev. Darren J. Eldridge, Pst.; Dcn. Dwayne Boudreaux; CRP Stds.: 35

St. Jules - 6098 Hwy. 31, Prairie Laurent, LA 70551 t) (337) 879-2365

St. Leo the Great - 126 Church Rd., Leonville, LA 70551; Mailing: PO Box 544, Leonville, LA 70551 t) 337-879-2365 Rev. Darren J. Eldridge, Pst.; Dcn. Dwayne Boudreaux; Peggy Lalonde, DRE; CRP Stds.: 86

LOREAUVILLE

St. Joseph - 117 S. Main St., Loreauville, LA 70552; Mailing: P.O. Box 365, PO Box 365, Loreauville, LA 70552 t) 337-229-4254 bcrochet@diolaf.org stjosephparishonline.org Rev. Barry F. Crochet, Pst.; Rev. Godwin O. Nzeh, C.M.F., Assoc. Pst.; CRP Stds.: 277

Our Lady of Victory - 120 Daigre St., Loreauville, LA 70552; Mailing: P.O. Box 387, Loreauville, LA 70552 t) 337-229-8284 olv_loreauville@yahoo.com; bcrochet@diolaf.org ourladyofvictory-loreauville.com Rev. Barry F. Crochet, Pst.; Rev. Godwin O. Nzeh, C.M.F., Assoc. Pst.; Dcn. Roland James Jeanlouis; Mary Claire Collins, DRE; CRP Stds.: 53

MAMOU

St. Ann - 716 Sixth St., Mamou, LA 70554 t) 337-543-2366 (CRP); 337-468-3159 baubespin@diolaf.org www.saintannmamou.org Rev. William Massie, Pst.; Rev. Bala Prabhakar Rayapati, Par. Vicar; Antoinette Rene, DRE; CRP Stds.: 83

Holy Spirit - 5023 Vidrine Rd., Ville Platte, LA 70586; Mailing: 716 6th St., Mamou, LA 70554

MAURICE

St. Alphonsus - 8700 Maurice Ave., Maurice, LA 70555; Mailing: P.O. Box 190, Maurice, LA 70555 t) 337-893-4099 stalphonsus@cox-internet.com Rev. Paul G. Bienvenu, Pst.; Dcn. Joseph Hebert; Dcn. Byron James Soley; Chris Guidry, DRE; CRP Stds.: 567

St. Joseph - 8005 Maurice Ave., Maurice, LA 70555-0250; Mailing: P.O. Box 250, Maurice, LA 70555-0250 t) 337-893-5428 stjosephchurchmaurice@yahoo.com; sjawa@diolaf.org Rev. Joseph Sai Tran, S.V.D., Pst.; Rev. Clifton Labbe, S.V.D., In Res.; CRP Stds.: 36

Our Lady of Perpetual Help - 12995 LA Hwy. 699, Maurice, LA 70555 t) 337-893-0610 petitema51@yahoo.com Rev. Paul G. Bienvenu, Pst.; Abbie Bergeron, DRE;

MELVILLE

St. John the Evangelist - 318 First St., Melville, LA 71353-0256; Mailing: P.O. Box 256, Melville, LA 71353 t) 337-623-4957 sjstcc@gmail.com Rev. Stephen Chibunda Ugwu, Pst.; CRP Stds.: 28

St. Thomas, the Apostle -

MERMENTAU

St. John the Evangelist - 707 Orange St., Mermentau, LA 70556; Mailing: P.O. Box 340, Mermentau, LA 70556 t) 337-824-2278 kbenoit@diolaf.org Rev. Andrew Schumacher, Pst.; Amy Mouton, DRE; CRP Stds.: 123

St. Margaret - 322 Miller St., Estherwood, LA 70534 Katrina Benoit, Contact;

MILTON

St. Joseph - 100 E. Milton Ave., Milton, LA 70558; Mailing: P. O. Box 299, Milton, LA 70558 t) 337-856-5997 secretary@stjo-milton.org www.stjo-milton.org Rev. William Schambough, Pst.; Dcn. Keith Anthony Duhon; Kayla Robles, DRE; CRP Stds.: 373

MORROW

St. Peter - 111 St. Peter Ln., Morrow, LA 71356; Mailing: P.O. Box 319, Morrow, LA 71356 t) 318-346-7010 tsylvester@diolaf.org Rev. Donavan J. Labbe, Pst.;

Resurrection -

MORSE

Immaculate Conception - 123 N. Jules Ave., Morse, LA 70559; Mailing: 8021 Lyons Point Hwy., Crowley, LA 70526 t) 337-783-2968 icc-sjtb@outlook.com www.icc-sjtb.org Rev. Arockia Doss Palthasar, HGN, Pst.; Deanna Spell, DRE;

St. Aloysius - 218 2nd St., Midland, LA 70559

NEW IBERIA

St. Edward - 201 Ambassador W. Lemelle Dr., New Iberia, LA 70560 t) 337-369-3101; 337-412-7881 (CRP) stedwardcc@cox.net www.stedwardstjudeni.com Rev. Donald Bernard, Pst.; Dcn. Steve Anthony Rogers; Elizabeth Harris, DRE; CRP Stds.: 109

St. Edward School - (Grades PreK-3) 175 Porter St., New Iberia, LA 70560 t) 337-369-6764 questions@sespandas.com www.sespandas.com Karen Bonin, Prin.; Stds.: 301; Lay Tchrs.: 20

St. Jude -

St. Marcellus - 6100 Avery Island Rd., New Iberia, LA 70560 t) 337-364-0818; 337-364-9419 (CRP) ylhebert@diolaf.org; stmarcellusc@aol.com www.stmarcellus.org Rev. James B. Nguyen, Pst.; Yvonne Hebert, DRE; CRP Stds.: 68

Nativity of Our Lady - 130 N. Richelieu Cir., New Iberia, LA 70560 t) 337-365-3759 (Barsen Hall Faith Formati); 337-364-8360 nativityccd@ni.brcoxmail.com; nativity@ni.brcoxmail.com www.nativityni.org Rev. Msgr. J. Robert Romero, Pst.; Janet Viator, DRE; CRP Stds.: 98

St. Nicholas - 7809 Weeks Island Rd., New Iberia, LA 70560; Mailing: P. O. Box 369, Lydia, LA 70569 t) 337-369-7510; 337-369-3837 (CRP) Rev. Randy Courville, Pst.; Dcn. Christopher Doumit; CRP Stds.: 94

Our Lady of Perpetual Help - 1303 St. Jude Ave., New Iberia, LA 70560 t) 337-365-5481 olphni@gmail.com Rev. Garrett Savoie, Pst.; Rev. Anselm I. Ofodum, Par. Vicar; Dcn. Durwood Gerard Viator; Peggy Tauzin, DRE; CRP Stds.: 60

Our Lady of Prompt Succor - 2409 Coteau Rd., New Iberia, LA 70560 t) 337-369-6993 cmouton@diolaf.org; secretary@olps-coteau.org Rev. Matthew Hebert, Pst.; Cathy Mouton, DRE; CRP Stds.: 252

St. Peter - 108 E. St. Peter St., New Iberia, LA 70562; Mailing: P.O. Box 12507, New Iberia, LA 70562 t) 337-369-3816 stpeter@cox-internet.com www.stpetersofnewiberia.com Very Rev. William C. Blanda, Pst.; Rev. Nathan A. Comeaux, Sacr. Min.; Dcn. Wynard Joseph Mitchell Boutte, DRE; CRP Stds.: 119

Sacred Heart of Jesus - 2514 Old Jeanerette Rd., New Iberia, LA 70563 t) 337-364-4439 Rev. Michael Keith Landry, Pst.; Peter Derouen, Youth Min.; Robin Landry, DRE; CRP Stds.: 304

OPELOUSAS

Holy Ghost - 747 N. Union St., Opelousas, LA 70570; Mailing: P.O. Box 1785, Opelousas, LA 70571-1785 t) 337-945-3824 (CRP); 337-942-2732 dre@hgcatholic.org; pastor@hgcatholic.org www.hgcatholic.org Rev. Lambert Lein, S.V.D., Pst.; Rev. Dilip Soreng, SVD, Par. Vicar; Rev. Hai Hgoc Pham, SVD, Par. Vicar; Dcn. Charles Richard; Rev. Thomas James, S.V.D., In Res.; Tamara Broussard, DRE; Barbara Butler, DRE; CRP Stds.: 122

St. Joseph - 3283 Hwy. 167, Opelousas, LA 70570 t) 337-826-3395 Rev. Taj Van Courtlan Glodd, Pst.;

St. Ann -

St. Landry - 1020 N. Main St., Opelousas, LA 70570 t) 337-942-6552; 337-942-6552 x101 (CRP) djoubert@diolaf.org; ljoubert@diolaf.org stlandrycatholicchurch.com Rev. Neil Pettit, Pst.; Dcn. Samuel Diesi; Dcn. Dwayne Paul Joubert; Dcn. John W. Miller; CRP Stds.: 20

Our Lady of Mercy - 1432 W. Landry St., Opelousas, LA 70570; Mailing: 207 N. Camille St., Opelousas, LA 70570 t) 337-942-4174 (CRP); 337-942-4174 gsimien@diolaf.org; olomcamille@yahoo.com Rev. Gregory M. Simien, Pst.; Dcn. J. Ulysse Joubert; Dcn. Thomas Lindsey; CRP Stds.: 50

Our Lady Queen of Angels - 2125 S. Union St., Opelousas, LA 70570-5742 t) 337-942-5628 kjdmartin@aol.com; secretary@queenofangelschurch.org Rev. Msgr. Keith J. DeRouen, Pst.; Dcn. Jerome Collins; CRP Stds.: 97

PARKS

St. Joseph - 1034 Bridge St., Parks, LA 70582 t) 337-845-4168 parkschurches@gmail.com parkschurches.org Rev. David Rozas, Pst.; Dcn. Dennis Joseph Landry; Dcn. Joseph Philip Liuzza III; CRP Stds.: 87

St. Louis -

PATTERSON

St. Joseph - 1011 First St., Patterson, LA 70392 t) 985-395-3881 (CRP); 985-395-3616 stjoedre@teche.net Rev. Herbert Bennerfield, Pst.; Mamie Perry, DRE; CRP Stds.: 58

PINE PRAIRIE

St. Peter - 1325 1st St., Pine Prairie, LA 70576; Mailing: P.O. Box 709, Pine Prairie, LA 70576 t) 337-599-2224 kmayne@diolaf.org; stpeterinpineprairie@yahoo.com Rev. Kenneth Mayne, Pst.; Barry Bonnett, DRE; CRP Stds.: 106

St. Theresa - 2117 St. Landry Hwy., St. Landry, LA 71367

PORT BARRE

St. Mary - 4827 Hwy. 103, Port Barre, LA 70577; Mailing: P.O. Box 338, Port Barre, LA 70577 t) 337-585-2315 smc_pb@yahoo.com Rev. Clint James Trahan, Pst.; CRP Stds.: 7

Sacred Heart of Jesus - 417 Salzan St., Port Barre, LA 70577; Mailing: P.O. Box 129, Port Barre, LA 70577 t) 337-585-2279 sacredrectory@bellsouth.net Rev. Clint James Trahan, Pst.; Dcn. Clifford Mitchell Hebert Jr.; Dee Jesclard, DRE; CRP Stds.: 170

RAYNE

St. Joseph - 401 S. Adams, Rayne, LA 70578 t) 337-334-2193; 337-334-5657 (CRP) stjoseph1872@diolaf.org Very Rev. Brent Smith, Pst.; Dcn. Denis Francis LaCroix; Dcn. Barry Joseph LeBlanc; Dcn. Timothy Francis Ledet; CRP Stds.: 452

Rayne Catholic Elementary - (Grades PreK-8) 407 S. Polk St., Rayne, LA 70578 t) 337-334-5658 rdaigle@raynecatholic.org www.raynecatholic.org Alicia Ardoin, Prin.; Stds.: 206; Lay Tchrs.: 14

St. Leo IV - 7166 Roberts Cove Rd., Rayne, LA 70578-8912 t) 337-334-5056 jdupuis@diolaf.org; josette@stsleoandedmund.org Rev. Paul Broussard, Pst.; CRP Stds.: 41

St. Edmund Chapel -

Our Mother of Mercy - 707 Lyman Ave., Rayne, LA 70578 t) 337-334-3516; 337-207-4092 (CRP) shrineomomrayne@gmail.com; omomrayne24@gmail.com Rev. Pius Titus Ajiki (NIgeria), Pst.; CRP Stds.: 27

SCOTT

Saint Martin de Porres - 1100 Chaisson St., Scott, LA 70583; Mailing: P.O. Box 1347, Scott, LA 70583-1347 t) 337-232-1968 deporres@bellsouth.net; deaconsenegal@yahoo.com Rev. Msgr. Ronald Broussard, Pst.; Dcn. Nolton J. Senegal; Norma Arceneaux, DRE; Brenda Dugas, DRE; CRP Stds.: 30

Sts. Peter and Paul - 1110 Old Spanish Tr., Scott, LA 70583; Mailing: P.O. Box 610, Scott, LA 70583 t) 337-235-2433; 337-262-6167 (CRP) stspeterandpaulscott@hotmail.com; mderise@diolaf.org www.stspeterandpaulscott.org Rev. Mark Derise, Pst.; Rev. Suresh Mathangi, Par. Vicar; Dcn. Clifford Jude Tanner; Most Rev. Michael Jarrell, Bishop Emeritus - In Res.; CRP Stds.: 95

Sts. Peter and Paul Catholic School - (Grades PreK-8) 1301 Old Spanish Tr., Scott, LA 70583 t) 337-504-3400 info@sts-peter-paul.org www.stspeter-paul.org Danielle Babineaux, Prin.; Stds.: 379; Lay Tchrs.: 25

ST. MARTINVILLE

St. Elizabeth - 1006 St. Elizabeth St., St. Martinville, LA 70582 t) 337-394-6684 dcnrhayes@aol.com Rev. Bill John Melancon, Pst.; CRP Stds.: 1

St. Martin de Tours - 133 S. Main St., St. Martinville, LA 70582; Mailing: PO Box 10, St. Martinville, LA 70517 t) 337-394-6021 saintmartin1765@gmail.com; rrichard@diolaf.org www.saintmartindetours.org Rev. Jason Vidrine, Pst.; Tilly Duplechein, DRE; Dcn. Adam Conque; Dcn. Joshua Reed LeBlanc; CRP Stds.: 79

Notre Dame de Perpetuel Secours - 201 Gary St., St. Martinville, LA 70582; Mailing: PO Box 677, St. Martinville, LA 70582 t) 337-394-3084 Rev. Abelardo Gabriel, SVD, Pst.; Rev. Cocou Cyriaque Sounou, SVD, Assoc. Pst.; Dcn. Richard Chambers; Glenda Sonnier, DRE;

St. Rita - 1006 St. Rita Hwy., St. Martinville, LA 70582 t) 337-394-4030 (CRP); 337-394-4679 rlatiolais67@gmail.com; bmelancon@diolaf.org Rev. Bill John Melancon, Pst.; Raymond Latiolais Jr., DRE; CRP Stds.: 120

VILLE PLATTE

St. Joseph - 1107 Martin Luther King Jr. Dr., Ville Platte, LA 70586; Mailing: 708 E. Main St., Ville Platte, LA 70586 t) 337-363-2989 frtom@sacredheartvp.com Very Rev. Thomas P. Voorhies, Pst.; Rev. Andrew Killeen, Par. Vicar; CRP Stds.: 1

Our Lady Queen of All Saints - 1012 Dardeau St., Ville Platte, LA 70586 t) 337-363-5167 olqassec@centurytel.net; pereguidry@yahoo.com Rev. Mitchell Guidry, Pst.; Dcn. John Bennett Soileau Jr.; Tiffany Alfred, DRE; CRP Stds.: 92

Sacred Heart of Jesus - 708 E. Main St., Ville Platte, LA 70586 t) 337-363-2989 frtom@sacredheartvp.com www.sacredheartvp.com Very Rev. Thomas P. Voorhies, Pst.; Rev. Andrew Killeen, Par. Vicar; Tiffany Alfred, DRE; CRP Stds.: 47

Sacred Heart Elementary School - (Grades K-8) 161 Bourgeois St., Ville Platte, LA 70586 t) 337-363-3445 virginia.morein@shsvp.com Virginia Morein, Prin.; Rebecca Buller, Librn.; Stds.: 444; Lay Tchrs.: 18

Sacred Heart High School - (Grades 9-12) 114 Trojan Ln., Ville Platte, LA 70586 t) 337-363-1475 dawn.shipp@shsvp.com www.shsvp.com Dawn C. Shipp, Prin.; Sadie Fontenot, Contact; Lynn Landreneau, CRE; Stds.: 177; Lay Tchrs.: 14

Belaire Cove Chapel - 2003 Belaire Cove Rd., Ville Platte, LA 70586

WASHINGTON

Holy Trinity - 414 E. St. Mitchell St., Washington, LA 70589; Mailing: PO Box 186, Washington, LA 70589 t) 337-826-3376; 337-826-7396 (CRP) sherolyn.boutte@diolaf.org; mhigginbotham@diolaf.org Rev. Matthew P. Higginbotham, Pst.; CRP Stds.: 6

Immaculate Conception - 330 E. Moundville St., Washington, LA 70589; Mailing: P.O. Box 116, Washington, LA 70589 t) 337-826-7396 immaculateconceptionchurch@yahoo.com Rev. Matthew P. Higginbotham, Pst.; CRP Stds.: 36

St. Peter - 1074 Hwy. 748 (Grand Prairie), Washington, LA 70589-4541 t) 337-826-3870 (CRP); 337-826-5635 secretarystpeter@outlook.com Rev. Jude Halphen, Pst.; Dcn. Shawn Malcolm Melancon; CRP Stds.: 37

YOUNGSVILLE

St. Anne - 201 Church St., Youngsville, LA 70592 t) 337-856-8212; 337-857-6382 (CRP) officemanager@stannechurch.net; dre@stannechurch.net www.stannechurch.net Rev. Michael Russo, Pst.; Dcn. Martin Ancil Cannon; Dcn. Edward Jules Boustany; Dcn. Cody Miller, Liturgical Appointment; Jessica Currier, DRE; CRP Stds.: 224

SCHOOLS: PRESCHOOL THRU HIGH SCHOOL

SCHOOLS

STATE OF LOUISIANA

ABBEVILLE

Mt. Carmel School - (PRV) (Grades PreK-8) 405 Park Ave., Abbeville, LA 70510 t) 337-898-0859 jtrahan@mceschool.com www.mceschool.org Jackie Trahan, Prin.; Sr. Janet LeBlanc, O.Carm., Pres.; Nanette Cope, Librn.;

GRAND COTEAU

Academy of the Sacred Heart (Academy of the Sacred Heart of Grand Coteau, Inc.) - (PRV) (Grades PreK-12) 1821 Academy Rd., Grand Coteau, LA 70541; Mailing: PO Box 310, Grand Coteau, LA 70541 t) 337-662-5275 yadler@sshcoteau.org www.sshcoteau.org Yvonne Adler, Headmaster; Jeanne-Marie Meaux, Librn.; Stds.: 267; Lay Tchrs.: 26

Berchmans Academy of the Sacred Heart (Academy of the Sacred Heart of Grand Coteau, Inc.) - (Grades PreK-12) aboagni@sshcoteau.org (Day school for boys) Angie Boagni, Contact; Stds.: 173; Lay Tchrs.: 23

LAFAYETTE

Holy Family School - (PAR) (Grades PreK-8) 200 St. John St., Lafayette, LA 70501 t) 337-235-0267 rgriffin@holyfamilycs.com www.hfcsonline.com Roger Griffin, Prin.; Cynthia Cluse, Librn.; Stds.: 312; Sr. Tchrs.: 2; Lay Tchrs.: 13

HIGH SCHOOLS

STATE OF LOUISIANA

CROWLEY

Notre Dame High School of Acadia Parish - (PAR) (Grades 9-12) 910 N. Eastern Ave., Crowley, LA 70526 t) 337-783-3519 cistre@ndpios.com; jmouton@ndpios.com www.ndpios.com Very Rev. Brent Smith, Chancellor; Cindy M. Istre, Prin.; Stds.: 313; Lay Tchrs.: 29

LAFAYETTE

Teurlings Catholic High School - (PAR) (Grades 9-12) 139 Teurlings Dr., Lafayette, LA 70501 t) 337-235-5711 mboyer@tchs.net www.tchs.net Michael H. Boyer, Prin.; Stds.: 836; Lay Tchrs.: 52

St. Thomas More High School - (PAR) (Grades 9-12) 450 E. Farrel Rd., Lafayette, LA 70508 t) 337-988-3700 kelley.leger@stmcougars.net www.stmcougars.net Rev. Michael Russo, Chancellor; Kelley Leger, Prin.; Stds.: 987; Lay Tchrs.: 78

NEW IBERIA

Catholic High School - (PAR) (Grades 4-12) 1301 DeLaSalle Dr., New Iberia, LA 70560 t) 337-364-5116 esegura@chspanthers.com chspanthers.com Kyle Bourque, Prin.; Penny Smith, Librn.; Stds.: 602; Lay Tchrs.: 43

OPELOUSAS

Opelousas Catholic School - (PAR) (Grades PreK-12) 428 E. Prudhomme St., Opelousas, LA 70570 t) 337-942-5404 mheintz@diolaf.org www.ocsvikings.com Marty Heintz, Prin.; Stds.: 635; Lay Tchrs.: 47

INSTITUTIONS LOCATED IN DIOCESE

CAMPUS MINISTRY / NEWMAN CENTERS [CAM]

EUNICE

Catholic Student Center-Louisiana State Univ.-Eunice - 2048 Johnson Hwy., Eunice, LA 70535; Mailing: P.O. Box 1129, Eunice, LA 70535 t) 337-457-8107 lsuecatholic.stm@gmail.com www.lsuecatholic.com Kassie R. Rougeau, Admin.;

LAFAYETTE

Our Lady of Wisdom Catholic Student Center - 501 E. Saint Mary Blvd., Lafayette, LA 70503; Mailing: P.O. Box 43599, Lafayette, LA 70504 t) 337-232-8741; 337-232-8742 wisdom@ourladyofwisdom.org ragincajuncatholics.org Rev. Patrick Broussard, Pst.; Rev. Stephen Pellessier, Par. Vicar;

CATHOLIC CHARITIES [CCH]

CROWLEY

Crowley Christian Care Center - 726 W. 7th St., Crowley, LA 70527-0686; Mailing: P.O. Box 686, Crowley, LA 70527-0686 t) 337-783-5811 edboustany@diolaf.org Dcn. Edward Jules Boustany, Contact;

LAFAYETTE

Catholic Charities of Acadiana, Inc. - 501 W. Saint Mary Blvd., Lafayette, LA 70506; Mailing: P.O. Box 3177, Lafayette, LA 70502 t) 337-235-4972 www.catholiccharitiesacadiana.org Kim Boudreaux, Exec.; Sarah Clement, Dir.; Asstd. Annu.: 9,534; Staff: 63

Disaster Response -

FoodNet Food Bank -

Immigration Legal Services -

St. Joseph Diner - 613 W. Simcoe, Lafayette, LA 70501 kboudreaux@catholicservice.org www.catholicservice.org

St. Joseph Shelter for Men - 425 St. John St., Lafayette, LA 70501 t) 337-233-6816 mhinman@catholicservice.org www.catholicservice.org

St. Michael Center for Veterans - 425 St. John St., Lafayette, LA 70501 t) 337-233-6816 mhinman@catholicservice.org www.catholicservice.org

Msgr. A. O. Sigur Service Center - 401 St. John St., Lafayette, LA 70501; Mailing: P.O. Box 3177, Lafayette, LA 70502 kboudreaux@catholicservice.org www.catholicservice.org

New Life Center (Emily House) - 1000 E. Willow St., Lafayette, LA 70501; Mailing: P.O. Box 3177, Lafayette, LA 70502 michelle@catholiccharitiesacadiana.org www.catholicservice.org

Rebuilding Together Acadiana -

Stella Maris Center - 615 Simcoe St., Lafayette, LA 70501 mhinman@catholicservice.org www.catholicservice.org

NEW IBERIA

Social Service Center - 432 Bank Ave., New Iberia, LA 70560 t) 337-369-6384 eboustany@diolaf.org Shirley DeClouet, Dir.;

VILLE PLATTE

Christian Care and Share Center - 129 W. Main St., Ville Platte, LA 70586; Mailing: P.O. Box 901, Ville Platte, LA 70586 t) 337-363-8041 eboustany@diolaf.org Eugene S. Fontenot, Chair;

CONVENTS, MONASTERIES, AND RESIDENCES FOR WOMEN [CON]

ABBEVILLE

Sisters of Mt. Carmel - 2326 Camella Ave., Abbeville, LA 70510 t) 337-385-2834 leahsellers@cox.net Sr. Leah Sellers, Contact;

GRAND COTEAU

Religious of the Sacred Heart - 376 E. Martin Luther King Dr., Grand Coteau, LA 70541; Mailing: P.O. Box 4292, Grand Coteau, LA 70541 t) 337-662-5526 slasseigne@rscj.org www.rscj.org Sr. Sheila Hammond, Prov.;

LAFAYETTE

The Carmelite Monastery of Lafayette, Louisiana, Inc. - 1250 Carmel Dr., Lafayette, LA 70501-5299

t) 337-232-4651 srmj@lafayettecarmel.com lafayettecarmelites.org Monastery of Mary, Mother of Grace. Very Rev. Ken Broussard, Chap.; Mother Mary John Billeaud, Prioress; Srs.: 16

Franciscan Missionaries of Our Lady - 101 Sandbar Ln., Lafayette, LA 70508 t) 337-504-5949 uyen.vu@fmolhs.org Sr. Uyen Vu, Contact; Srs.: 2

Marianites of Holy Cross - 1417 St. John St., Lafayette, LA 70506 t) 337-234-5454 joelmillermsc@aol.com Sr. Joel Miller, msc, Contact;

Marianites of the Holy Cross - 1417 St. John St., Lafayette, LA 70501 t) 337-234-5454 smrcno@yahoo.com Sr. Margaret Cano, Contact;

Missionaries of Charity - 904 Jack St., Lafayette, LA 70501 t) 337-233-3929 Sr. M. Jessiline MC, Supr.; Sr. M. Jonathan, MC, Regl. Supr.; Srs.: 4

Sisters of the Most Holy Sacrament - 313 Corona Dr., Lafayette, LA 70509-0037; Mailing: P.O. Box 90037, Lafayette, LA 70509-0037 t) 337-981-8475 dmholysisters@bellsouth.net Srs.: 6

LEBEAU

Sisters of the Holy Spirit - ; Mailing: P.O. Box 115, Lebeau, LA 71345 t) 337-623-5540 smr28@bellsouth.net Sr. Martha Readore, Contact;

NEW IBERIA

School Sisters of Notre Dame - 501 Darby Ln., Apt. 102, New Iberia, LA 70560 t) 337-256-5988 sthompson@diolaf.org Sr. Barbara Kraus, S.S.N.D., Admin.;

Sisters of Providence - 213 Oak Hill Rd., New Iberia, LA 70563 t) 337-364-3142 jbacon@diolaf.org Sr. Helen Vinton, SP, Contact;

OPELOUSAS

Hospitaler Sisters of Mercy - 168 Monastery Ln., Opelousas, LA 70570 t) 335-999-5087 villaraffaella@msn.com www.motherofmercyretreathouse.com Mother of Mercy Retreat House Sr. Normita Nunez, Contact; Srs.: 5

ENDOWMENTS / FOUNDATIONS / TRUSTS [EFT]

LAFAYETTE

St. Augustine Trust Fund (Sisters of the Most Holy Sacrament) - ; Mailing: P.O. Box 90037, Lafayette, LA 70509-0037 t) 337-981-8475 srddornan@gmail.com Sr. Diane Dornan, M.H.S., Pres.;

Lourdes Foundation, Inc. - 4801 Ambassador Caffery Pkwy., Lafayette, LA 70508 t) 337-470-4610 jeigh.stipe@fmolhs.org www.lourdes.net Jeigh O. Stipe, Exec.;

HOSPITALS / HEALTH SERVICES [HOS]

LAFAYETTE

Our Lady of Lourdes Regional Medical Center, Inc. - 4801 Ambassador Caffery Pkwy., Lafayette, LA 70508 t) 337-470-2100 www.lourdesrmc.com Donna Landry, COO; Bed Capacity: 385; Asstd. Annu.: 299,847; Staff: 2,400

MISCELLANEOUS [MIS]

ABBEVILLE

***Family Missions Company** - 12611 Everglade Rd., Abbeville, LA 70510 t) (337) 893-6111 Kevin Granger, Exec. Dir.; Sarah Granger, Exec. Dir.;

BREAUX BRIDGE

***Red Bird Ministries, Inc.** - 333 Waterford Pl., Breaux Bridge, LA 70517; Mailing: PO Box 266, Breaux Bridge, LA 70517 t) 337-223-2019 kelly@redbird.love; hello@redbird.love www.redbird.love Catholic Grief Support Ministry Kelly Breaux, Contact;

LAFAYETTE

Come Lord Jesus! Inc. - 1804 W. University Ave., Lafayette, LA 70506 t) 337-233-6277 comelordjesusprogram@gmail.com www.comelordjesus.com Rev. Conley Bertrand, Dir.;

Sisters of the Eucharistic Covenant - 105 Upperline Ave., Lafayette, LA 70501 t) (337) 278-9498 (Mobile phone) clarr0101@gmail.com secsisters.org Sr. Celeste D. Larroque, S.E.C., Pres.;

OPELOUSAS

Cursillo Center - 3651 Hwy. 104 (Prairie Ronde), Opelousas, LA 70570 t) 337-543-7425 rctomlinson@bellsouth.net www.whowillsit.com Rev. Theodore Broussard Jr., Dir.;

ST. MARTINVILLE

Community of Jesus Crucified - 103 Railroad Ave., St. Martinville, LA 70582 t) 337-394-6550 frchampagne@yahoo.com www.jesuscrucified.net Lay Association Rev. John Joseph Bourque, CJC; Rev. Michael Champagne, C.J.C., Spiritual Adv./Care Srvcs.;

Community of Jesus Crucified - Priest Brother and Sister Servants - 103 Railroad Ave., St. Martinville, LA 70582 t) 337-394-6550 frchampagne@yahoo.com www.jesuscrucified.net Consecrated Priests, Brothers, and Sisters of Jesus Crucified Rev. Michael Champagne, C.J.C., Supr.; Rev. John Joseph Bourque, CJC, Mem.;

***Witness to Love Marriage Prep Renewal Ministry** - 1039 Rue Maline, St. Martinville, LA 70582 t) 337-282-0446 info@witnesstolove.org Most Rev. Gregory M. Aymond, Bd. Mem.;

MONASTERIES AND RESIDENCES FOR PRIESTS AND BROTHERS [MON]

GRAND COTEAU

St. Charles College - 313 E. Martin L. King Dr., Grand Coteau, LA 70541-1003; Mailing: P.O. Box C, Grand Coteau, LA 70541-1003 t) 337-662-5251 office@jesuitspiritualitycenter.org A Jesuit Community for men working in the region Rev. Mark Kramer, S.J., Pst.; Rev. Clyde LeBlanc, S.J., Pst. Assoc.; Rev. Walter Sidney, S.J., Rector; Rev. William J. Snyders, S.J., Pastoral Min.; Rev. Michael E. Chesney, S.J., Dir., St. Alphonsus Rodriguez Pavilion; Rev. Paul Deutsch, S.J., Dir., Jesuit Spirituality Center; Rev. James P. Bradley, S.J., Asst. Dir., St. Alphonsus Rodriguez Pavilion; Rev. Anthony H. Ostini, S.J., Retreat Dir.; Rev. John R. Payne, S.J., Retreat Dir.; Rev. John Lan Tran, S.J., Retreat Dir.; Brs.: 1; Priests: 25

NURSING / REHABILITATION / CONVALESCENCE / ELDERLY CARE [NUR]

LAFAYETTE

Village du Lac, Inc. - 1404 Carmel Dr., Lafayette, LA 70501 t) 337-234-5106 sleger@diolaf.org Sebastian Leger, Dir.; Asstd. Annu.: 2,400; Staff: 5

NEW IBERIA

Consolata Home - 2319 E. Main St., New Iberia, LA 70560 t) 337-365-8226 chasdel@cox.net Rev. Charles Langlois, Chap.; Charles L. Delahoussaye, Admin.; Asstd. Annu.: 107; Staff: 18

OPELOUSAS

C'est La Vie Center of the Sisters Marianites of Holy Cross - 960 E. Prudhomme St., Opelousas, LA 70570 t) 337-942-8154 mike@promptsuccor.com; brandie@promptsuccor.com www.promptsuccor.com Brandie Perry, Admin.; Michael Purser, Admin.; Asstd. Annu.: 15; Staff: 6

Prompt Succor Nursing Home Corporation - 954 E. Prudhomme St., Opelousas, LA 70570 t) 337-948-3634 mike@promptsuccor.com www.promptsuccor.com Brandie Perry, Admin.; Michael Purser, Admin.; Asstd. Annu.: 130; Staff: 133

RETREAT HOUSES / RENEWAL CENTERS [RTR]

GRAND COTEAU

Jesuit Spirituality Center (St. Charles College) - 313 E. Martin Luther King Dr., Grand Coteau, LA 70541-1003; Mailing: P.O. Box C, Grand Coteau, LA 70541-1003 t) 337-662-5251 office@jesuitspiritualitycenter.org jesuitspiritualitycenter.org Joan Broussard, Dir.; Rev. Paul Deutsch, S.J., Dir.; Easton Hebert, Dir.; Rev. Anthony H. Ostini, S.J., Dir.; Rev. John R. Payne, S.J., Dir.; Rev. Walter Sidney, S.J., Dir.; Sr. Kathleen Stakelum, MSC, Dir.; Rev. John Lan Tran, S.J., Dir.; Nelda Turner, Dir.;

Our Lady of the Oaks Retreat House - 214 Church St., Grand Coteau, LA 70541-1004; Mailing: P.O. Box D, Grand Coteau, LA 70541-1004 t) 337-662-5410 oloaks@centurytel.net www.ourladyoftheoaks.com For men, women and married couples. Albert S. Cain III, Exec. Dir.; Janeth M. Harrington, Admin. Asst.; Rev. Lou McCabe, S.J., Retreat Dir.; Rev. Donald E. Saunders, S.J., Retreat Dir.;

ST. MARTINVILLE

Our Lady of Sorrows Retreat Center - 103 Railroad Ave., St. Martinville, LA 70582 t) 337-394-6550 frchampagne@yahoo.com www.jesuscrucified.net Rev. Michael Champagne, C.J.C., Spiritual Adv./Care Srvcs.;

SEMINARIES [SEM]

GRAND COTEAU

Jesuit Novitiate of St. Stanislaus Kostka at St. Charles College - 313 E. Martin Luther King Dr., Grand Coteau, LA 70541-1003; Mailing: P.O. Box C, Grand Coteau, LA 70541-1003 t) 337-662-5253 office@jesuitspiritualitycenter.org Novitiate of U.S. Central and Southern Province of the Society of Jesus. Rev. Andrew Kirschman, Novice Dir.; Rev. Hanh D. Pham, S.J., Socius to Novice Dir.; Stds.: 12; Pr. Tchrs.: 2

Diocese of Lafayette in Indiana

(Dioecesis Lafayettenis in Indiana)

MOST REVEREND TIMOTHY L. DOHERTY, S.T.L., PH.D.

Bishop of Lafayette in Indiana; ordained Priest June 26, 1976; appointed Sixth Bishop of Lafayette in Indiana May 12, 2010; ordained and installed as Bishop July 15, 2010. Office: P.O. Box 260, Lafayette, IN 47902-0260.

Office of Bishop and Chancery: P.O. Box 260, Lafayette, IN 47902-0260. T: 765-742-0275; F: 765-742-7513.
www.dol-in.org

CANONICALLY ERECTED OCTOBER 21, 1944.

Square Miles 9,832.

Comprises the Counties of Benton, Blackford, Boone, Carroll, Cass, Clinton, Delaware, Fountain, Fulton, Grant, Hamilton, Howard, Jasper, Jay, Madison, Miami, Montgomery, Newton, Pulaski, Randolph, Tippecanoe, Tipton, Warren and White in the State of Indiana.

For legal titles of parishes and diocesan institutions, consult the Bishop's Office (Chancery).

STATISTICAL OVERVIEW

Personnel
Bishop 1
Retired Bishops 1
Priests: Diocesan Active in Diocese 55
Priests: Diocesan Active Outside Diocese 6
Priests: Retired, Sick or Absent 24
Number of Diocesan Priests 85
Religious Priests in Diocese 5
Total Priests in your Diocese 90
Extern Priests in Diocese 5
Ordinations:
Diocesan Priests 1
Transitional Deacons 2
Permanent Deacons in Diocese 23
Total Sisters 30

Parishes
Parishes 61
With Resident Pastor:
Resident Diocesan Priests 56
Resident Religious Priests 1
Without Resident Pastor:
Administered by Priests 4
Professional Ministry Personnel:
Brothers 1
Sisters 12

Welfare
Catholic Hospitals 12
Total Assisted 1,389,234
Health Care Centers 2
Total Assisted 817

Educational
Diocesan Students in Other Seminaries 13
Total Seminarians 13
Colleges and Universities 1
High Schools, Diocesan and Parish 2
Total Students 1,214
Elementary Schools, Diocesan and Parish 17
Total Students 3,699
Catechesis/Religious Education:
High School Students 1,684
Elementary Students 5,822
Total Students under Catholic Instruction 12,432
Teachers in Diocese:
Priests 1
Lay Teachers 338

Vital Statistics
Receptions into the Church:
Infant Baptism Totals 1,157
Minor Baptism Totals 65
Adult Baptism Totals 107
Received into Full Communion 115
First Communions 1,594
Confirmations 1,346
Marriages:
Catholic 206
Interfaith 86
Total Marriages 292
Deaths 851
Total Catholic Population 99,034
Total Population 1,290,812

LEADERSHIP

Executive Assistant to the Bishop - Rhonda Chyall;
Vicar General - Very Rev. Theodore C. Dudzinski;
Chancellor and Moderator of the Curia - Very Rev. Theodore C. Dudzinski;
Executive Assistant to the Vicar General and Ecclesiastical Notary - Caroline Cooper Ching;
Vicar for Clergy - Very Rev. Dominic C. Petan, Vicar;
Judicial Vicar - Very Rev. David L. Rasner, Vicar;
Office of Bishop and Chancery - t) 765-742-0275
Deans - Very Rev. Andrew J. Dudzinski; Very Rev. Christopher R. Shocklee; Very Rev. Eric C. Underwood;
Diocesan Consultors - Very Rev. Theodore C. Dudzinski; Rev. Anthony T. Rowland; Rev. Michael A. McKinney;

ADMINISTRATION

Department of Finance and Administration - Matthew McKillip, Dir.;
Office of Administration - t) 765-742-4852 Cathy Ramer, Staff Accountant; Andrew A. Guljas, Facilities Mgmt. Mgr.; Robin Caldanaro, Controller;

ADVISORY BOARDS, COMMISSIONS, COMMITTEES, AND COUNCILS

Building Commission - Norbert Stransky, Chair; Very Rev. Theodore C. Dudzinski, Ex Officio; Andrew A. Guljas, Facilities Mgmt. Coord. & Ex Officio (aguljas@dol-in.org);
Finance Council - Most Rev. Timothy L. Doherty, Ex Officio; Very Rev. Theodore C. Dudzinski, Ex Officio; Matthew McKillip, Dir.;

CLERGY AND RELIGIOUS SERVICES

Ecumenical & Interreligious Officer - t) 765-742-2107 Dcn. James B. Rush;
Office of the Permanent Diaconate - Dcn. Timothy Perry, Dir.; Dcn. Christopher Bock, Vocational Recruitment; Very Rev. Dominic C. Petan, Dir. Office of Vocations;
Vicars for Clergy - Very Rev. Dominic C. Petan; Beth Facemyer, Administrative Asst.;
Vocation Director - t) 765-269-4652 Rev. Derek Aaron, Dir. Vocations; Very Rev. Dominic C. Petan, Dir. Office of Vocations; Beth Facemyer, Admin. Asst.;

COMMUNICATIONS

Office of Communications - t) 765-742-2050 Gabby Hlavek, Dir.; Katharine Calabro, Content Producer; Melinda McPherson, Social Media & Website Coord.;
Newspaper "The Catholic Moment" - Gabby Hlavek, Editor;
Publisher- "The Catholic Moment" - Most Rev. Timothy L. Doherty;

EDUCATION

Greater Lafayette Area Catholic School Foundation, Inc. - Michael L. Gibson;
Greater Lafayette Catholic School Board - t) 765-474-7500 Mike Seeley, Exec.;
Office of Catholic Schools - Trudy Young, Supt.;
Schools - t) 765-269-4670

EVANGELIZATION

Department of Evangelization, Family Life and Pastoral Ministries - Robert Hartley, Dir.; Claudia Castillo, Admin. Asst.;
Office of Catechesis - Jonathan Sullivan, Formation Specialist; Jessica Wade, Youth & Young Adult Formation Specialist;
Office of Divine Worship & The Catechumenate - t) 765-269-4677
Office of Family Life - t) 765-269-4675 Susan Hoefer, NFP Coord.; Elsa Samora, Hispanic Project Rachel; Kathy Lehe, English Project Rachel;
Office of Hispanic Ministry - Dora Tobar, Mgr.; Claudia Sadowski, Hispanic Ministry Specialist; Dcn. Jose D. Munoz;

HUMAN RESOURCES

Human Resources Department - t) 765-742-0275 Jeanne K. Lausten, Dir.; Erica Wetli, Payroll & Benefits Coord.;

PASTORAL SERVICES

Office of Planning - Melissa Krockover, Dir.; Very Rev. Theodore C. Dudzinski;
St. Joseph Retreat & Conference Center - t) 765-551-9570 www.stjosephretreat.org Rev. David G. Huemmer, Spiritual Dir./Chap.; Twyla Arnold, Mktg. Specialist; Terence Connelly, Dir.;

STEWARDSHIP

Catholic Ministries Office - t) 765-269-4608
Office of Stewardship, Development & Charity - t) 765-742-7000 Tim Bobillo; Mike MacNulty, Dir.;

TRIBUNAL

Tribunal - t) 765-474-0506
Administrative Causes - Very Rev. Theodore C. Dudzinski;
Judicial Vicar - Very Rev. David L. Rasner;
Ecclesiastical Tribunal -
Auditor - Dcn. John R. Jezierski;
Defender of the Bond - Rev. Timothy M. Alkire;
Ecclesiastical Notary - Niall Hickey;
Full-Time Advocates - Linda O'Gara; Lou Coffing;
Judge - Rev. Samuel J. Kalu; Rev. Stephen J. Duquaine;
Judge Instructor - Rev. Samuel J. Kalu;
Office Manager - Linda O'Gara;

MISCELLANEOUS / OTHER OFFICES

Aquinas Educational Foundation, Inc. - t) 765-743-4653 Rev. Thomas McDermott, O.P., Res. Agent;
Censor Librorum - t) 765-474-0506 Very Rev. David L. Rasner;
Corporation - Most Rev. Timothy L. Doherty, Pres.; Very Rev. Theodore C. Dudzinski, Vice. Pres.; Matthew McKillip, Vice. Pres.;
Corporation - Hamilton County Catholic High School Corporation - Most Rev. Timothy L. Doherty, Pres.; Very Rev. Theodore C. Dudzinski, Vice. Pres.; Matthew McKillip, Secy.;
D.C.C.W. - Beth Keele, Pres.;
Newman Apostolate, Purdue University - t) 765-743-4652 Rev. Thomas McDermott, O.P., Dir.;
Newman Foundation, Ball State, Inc. - t) 765-288-6180 Very Rev. Eric C. Underwood;
Presbyteral Council - Most Rev. Timothy L. Doherty, Pres.; Rev. Clayton D. Thompson, Chair; Rev. Samuel J. Kalu, Vice Chmn.;
Members - Very Rev. Theodore C. Dudzinski; Very Rev. Eric C. Underwood; Very Rev. Dominic C. Petan;
Propagation of the Faith - Very Rev. Theodore C. Dudzinski, Dir.; Rhonda Chyall, Dir.;
Victim Assistance Coordinator - t) 765-464-4988 Jackie Montrie;

PARISHES, MISSIONS, AND CLERGY

STATE OF INDIANA

ALEXANDRIA

St. Mary - 820 W. Madison St., Alexandria, IN 46001-1520 t) 765-724-2483 fr.tmetzger@dol-in.org; tgates@stmaryalex.net maryandjosephchurches.com Rev. Thomas H. Metzger, Pst.; Rev. Martin J. Sandhage, Assoc. Pst.; Rev. Matthew Jakupco, Assoc. Pst.; CRP Stds.: 29
St. Mary School - (Grades PreK-8) t) 765-724-4459 stmary820@comcast.net; mbudzenski@maryandjosephchurches.com

AMBIA

St. Mary - 2961 South SR71, Ambia, IN 47917; Mailing: 107 E. Main St., Fowler, IN 47944 t) 765-884-1818 sheart18@sacredheartsite.com; jgoetz@parish.dol-in.org swnewtonbentoncopastorate Rev. Richard J. Weisenberger, Pst.; Rev. Peter J. Vanderkolk, Assoc. Pst.;

ANDERSON

St. Ambrose - 2801 Lincoln St., Anderson, IN 46016-5068 t) 765-644-5956 amboffice@anderson-alexandriapastorate.org www.stambrosestmary.org Rev. Thomas H. Metzger, Pst.; Rev. Martin J. Sandhage, Assoc. Pst.; Rev. Matthew Jakupco, Assoc. Pst.; CRP Stds.: 2
Holy Cross School - (Grades PreK-8) 2825 Lincoln St., Anderson, IN 46016; Mailing: 1115 Pearl St., Anderson, IN 46016 t) 765-642-8428; 765-642-1848 rfrey@holycrossschool-anderson.org www.holycrossschool-anderson.com Combined St. Mary and St. Ambrose, Anderson. Rob Frey, Prin.; Stds.: 174; Lay Tchrs.: 15
St. Mary - 305 E. 11th St., Anderson, IN 46016-1789; Mailing: 2801 Lincoln St., Anderson, IN 46016 t) 765-644-8467 smaoffice@anderson-alexandriapastorate.org stambrosestmary.org Rev. Thomas H. Metzger, Pst.; Rev. Martin J. Sandhage, Assoc. Pst.; Rev. Matthew Jakupco, Assoc. Pst.; CRP Stds.: 79
Holy Cross School - (Grades PreK-8) 321 E. 11th St., Anderson, IN 46016 t) 765-642-1848 agranger@holycrossschool-anderson.org; rfrey@holycrossschool-anderson.org www.holycrossschool-anderson.com/ with St. Ambrose, Anderson. Rob Frey, Prin.; Stds.: 174; Lay Tchrs.: 15

ATTICA

St. Francis Xavier - 407 S. Perry St., Attica, IN 47918-0001; Mailing: PO Box 55, Attica, IN 47918 t) 765-762-3330 stfj-parish@stfrancisxstjoseph.org Very Rev. David L. Rasner, Admin.; CRP Stds.: 48

BRYANT

Holy Trinity - 7321 E. SR 67, Bryant, IN 47326-9636 t) 260-997-6450 www.jayandrandolphcatholic.com Rev. Peter F. Logsdon, Pst.; Rev. Matthew J. Arbuckle, Assoc. Pst.; CRP Stds.: 140

CARMEL

St. Elizabeth Seton - 10655 Haverstick Rd., Carmel, IN 46033-3800 t) 317-846-3850 (Office); 317-816-0045 (Formation Office) parish@setoncarmel.org setoncarmel.org Rev. Brian M. Doerr, Pst.; Rev. David J. Newton, Assoc. Pst.; Rev. John R. Johnson, Assoc. Pst.; Dcn. William T. Reid; CRP Stds.: 450
Our Lady of Mount Carmel - 14598 Oak Ridge Rd., Carmel, IN 46032-1201 t) 317-846-3475 olmcparish@olmc1.org www.olmc1.org Rev. Richard J. Doerr, Pst.; Rev. Daniel B. Gartland, Assoc. Pst.; Rev. Joseph Vargese, Assoc. Pst.; Dcn. Paul S. Lunsford; CRP Stds.: 676
Our Lady of Mount Carmel School - (Grades K-8) 14596 Oak Ridge Rd., Carmel, IN 46032-1198 t) 317-846-1118 www.school.olmc1.org
Dominican Sisters of St. Cecilia Congregation - 40 Bennet Rd., Carmel, IN 46032

CICERO

Sacred Heart of Jesus - 410 S. Pearl St., Cicero, IN 46034-0889; Mailing: P.O. Box 889, Cicero, IN 46034-0889 t) 317-984-2115 (Office); 317-606-8153 (Pastor) shjc@dol-in.org www.sacredheartcicero.org Rev. Sean V. Pogue, Pst.; Dcn. John P. Etter; CRP Stds.: 65

COVINGTON

St. Joseph - 308 Pearl St., Covington, IN 47932-1062 t) 765-793-3289 stfj-parish@stfrancisxstjoseph.org Very Rev. David L. Rasner, Admin.; CRP Stds.: 8

CRAWFORDSVILLE

St. Bernard - 1306 E. Main St., Crawfordsville, IN 47933-2001 t) (765) 362-6121; (765) 362-6121 x212 (CRP) parish@stbernardcville.org stbernardcville.org Rev. Michael Bower, Pst.; CRP Stds.: 115

DE MOTTE

St. Cecilia - 334 Fifteenth St., S.W., De Motte, IN 46310-0700; Mailing: PO Box 700, DeMotte, IN 46310 t) 219-987-3511 saintcecilia@parish.dol-in.org; htokarz@parish.dol-in.org www.stceciliademotte.org Rev. Michael A. McKinney, Pst.; CRP Stds.: 107

DELPHI

St. Joseph - 207 N. Washington St., Delphi, IN 46923-1297 t) 765-564-2407 (Office); (574) 583-5724 (Rectory); (765) 564-3601 (DRE) dre@stjosephdelphi.org; office@stjosephdelphi.org www.stjosephdelphi.org Rev. Christopher T. Miller, Pst.; Dcn. Michael Booth; CRP Stds.: 86

DUNKIRK

St. Mary - 346 S. Broad St., Dunkirk, IN 47336-0286; Mailing: P.O. Box 286, Dunkirk, IN 47336 t) 765-768-1283 stmaryjohn@att.net stmaryjohn.org Rev. Kevin H. Hurley, Pst.; CRP Stds.: 9

EARL PARK

St. John the Baptist - 203 S. Chestnut St., Earl Park, IN 47942; Mailing: 107 E. Main St., Fowler, IN 47944 t) 219-474-5514; 765-884-1818 Rev. Richard J. Weisenberger, Pst.; Rev. Peter J. Vanderkolk, Assoc. Pst.; CRP Stds.: 4

ELWOOD

St. Joseph - 1306 S. A St., Elwood, IN 46036-1941 t) 765-552-6753 stsjohnandjoseph.com Rev. Dennis J. Goth, Pst.; CRP Stds.: 42

FISHERS

Holy Spirit Church - 10350 Glaser Way, Fishers, IN 46037 t) 317-849-9245; 317-849-8016 (CRP) Rev. Dale W. Ehrman, Pst.; Rev. Cole Daily, Par. Vicar; Rev. Andrew Thornton, Par. Vicar; CRP Stds.: 738

St. John Vianney Parish - 15176 Blessed Mother Blvd., Fishers, IN 46037 t) 317-485-0150 dduquaine@parish.dol-in.org; sboulet@parish.dol-in.org www.sjvfishers.org Rev. Dale W. Ehrman, Pst.; Rev. Cole Daily, Par. Vicar; Rev. Andrew Thornton, Par. Vicar; Rev. Derek Aaron, In Res.; CRP Stds.: 157

St. Louis de Montfort - 11441 Hague Rd., Fishers, IN 46038-1876 t) 317-842-6778 www.sldmfishers.org Rev. Thomas J. Haan, Pst.; Rev. Sean Aaron, Assoc. Pst.; CRP Stds.: 354

St. Louis de Montfort School - (Grades K-8) 11421 Hague Rd., Fishers, IN 46038 t) 317-842-1125 sstewart@sldmfishers.org Scott Stewart, Prin.;

FOWLER

Sacred Heart of Jesus - 107 E. Main St., Fowler, IN 47944-1148 t) 765-884-1818 sheart18@sacredheartsite.com; jgoetz@parish.dol-in.org swnewtonbentoncopastorate Rev. Richard J. Weisenberger, Pst.; Rev. Peter J. Vanderkolk, Assoc. Pst.; CRP Stds.: 5

Sacred Heart of Jesus School - (Grades PreK-6) 607 N. Washington Ave., Fowler, IN 47944-1148 t) 765-884-0710 kgross@sacredheartsite.com www.sacredheartschoolfowler.org Kristina Gross, Prin.;

St. Mary's Church - 2961 S. State Rd. 71, Ambia, IN 47917-8516; Mailing: 107 E. Main St., Fowler, IN 47944

FRANCESVILLE

St. Francis Solano - 217 W. Montgomery St., Francesville, IN 47946; Mailing: 401 N. Monticello St, Winamac, IN 46996 t) 574-946-4906 rmorris@dol-in.org Rev. Andrew R. DeKeyser, Pst.; Rev. Daniel P. Shine, Assoc. Pst.;

FRANKFORT

St. Mary - 600 St. Mary's Ave., Frankfort, IN 46041-2735 t) 765-654-5796 stmaryfrankfort@gmail.com saintmarysfrankfort.org Pastorate with St. Joseph, Lebanon, Indiana Rev. Paul W. Cochran, Pst.; Rev. Daniel J. Duff, Assoc. Pst.; CRP Stds.: 310

GAS CITY

Holy Family - 325 E. North A St., Gas City, IN 46933-1431 t) 765-674-2605 hcatholicchurch@indy.rr.com Rev. Kevin H. Hurley, Pst.; CRP Stds.: 28

GOODLAND

SS. Peter and Paul - 421 S. Newton St., Goodland, IN 47948-8156; Mailing: 318 N. McKinley Ave, Rensselaer, IN 47978 t) 219-866-5351 fr.jbennett@dol-in.org; stpeterandpaul@parish.dol.in.org stmichaelpastorate.org/ Rev. Joshua Tobias Bennett, Admin.;

HARTFORD CITY

St. John the Evangelist - 209 S. Spring St., Hartford City, IN 47348-2551 t) 765-348-3889 stmaryjohn@att.net stmaryjohn.org Rev. Kevin H. Hurley, Pst.; CRP Stds.: 52

KENTLAND

St. Joseph - 409 E. Allen St., Kentland, IN 47951-1322; Mailing: 107 E Main St, Fowler, IN 47944 t) 219-474-5514; 765-884-1818 swnewtonbentoncopastorate Rev. Richard J. Weisenberger, Pst.; CRP Stds.: 21

St. Joseph School Foundation, Inc. - ; Mailing: P.O. Box 131, Kentland, IN 47951-1322 Rev. Robert J Bernotas, Chair;

KEWANNA

St. Ann - 415 Logan St., Kewanna, IN 46939; Mailing: 401 N Monticello St., Winamac, IN 46996 t) 574-223-2808; 574-946-4906 rmorris@dol-in.org Rev. Andrew R. DeKeyser, Pst.; Rev. Daniel P. Shine, Pst. Assoc.;

KOKOMO

St. Joan of Arc - 3155 S. 200 W., Kokomo, IN 46902-9611 t) 765-865-9964 bwillis@parish.dol-in.org saintjoan.org Very Rev. Christopher R. Shocklee, Pst.; Rev. Stephen J. Duquaine, Assoc. Pst.; Rev. Elliot D Zak, Assoc. Pst.; CRP Stds.: 136

Sts. Joan of Arc & Patrick - (Grades PreK-8) t) 765-865-9960 stsjp@stsjp.org stsjp@stsjp.org Consolidated school with St. Patrick Parish in Kokomo. Bradley Willis, Dir.; Stds.: 264; Lay Tchrs.: 20

St. Patrick - 1201 N. Washington St., Kokomo, IN 46901; Mailing: 1204 N. Armstrong St., Kokomo, IN 46901 t) 765-452-6021 bwillis@parish.dol-in.org stpatrick-kokomo.org Very Rev. Christopher R. Shocklee, Pst.; Rev. Stephen J. Duquaine, Assoc. Pst.; Rev. Elliot D Zak, Assoc. Pst.; Dcn. Ronald L. Morrow; Dcn. Steve Seitz; Dcn. Charles "Chuck" L. Springer; CRP Stds.: 91

Sts. Joan of Arc & Patrick - (Grades PreSchool-8) 1230 N. Armstrong St., Kokomo, IN 46901 t) 765-459-4769 www.stsjp.org (St. Patrick Campus) Nick Kanable, Prin.; Stds.: 264; Lay Tchrs.: 21

LAFAYETTE

Cathedral of St. Mary of the Immaculate Conception - 1207 Columbia St., Lafayette, IN 47901-1521; Mailing: 1212 South St., Lafayette, IN 47901 t) 765-742-4440 saintmarycathedral.org/ Rev. Anthony T. Rowland, Rector; Rev. Dennis A. Faker, Assoc. Pst.; Rev. Dennis J. O'Keeffe, Assoc. Pst.; Dcn. John R. Jezierski; Dcn. Ronald D. Nevinger; Dcn. Joseph Poremski; CRP Stds.: 121

St. Mary Cathedral School - (Grades K-3) 1200 South St., Lafayette, IN 47901 t) 765-742-6302 social@lcss.org www.lcss.org/ Governed by the Lafayette Catholic School System. Katie Christopher, Prin.; Stds.: 147; Lay Tchrs.: 8

St. Ann - 612 Wabash Ave., Lafayette, IN 47905-1096 t) (765) 742-4440 www.stannlafayette.org/ Rev. Anthony T. Rowland, Pst.; Rev. Dennis A. Faker, Par. Vicar; Rev. Dennis J. O'Keeffe, Par. Vicar; Dcn. John R. Jezierski; Dcn. Ronald D. Nevinger; Dcn. Joseph Poremski; CRP Stds.: 29

St. Boniface - 318 N. Ninth St., Lafayette, IN 47904-2597 t) 765-742-1351 (CRP); 765-742-5063 haroreled@comcast.net Very Rev. Andrew J. Dudzinski, Pst.; Rev. Matthew Kalu, Assoc. Pst.; Rev. Jeffrey D. Martin, Assoc. Pst.; Rev. William Summerlin, Assoc. Pst.; Dcn. Stanislaw Zak; Dcn. Jose D. Munoz; CRP Stds.: 285

St. Boniface Middle School - (Grades 4-6) 813 North St., Lafayette, IN 47901 t) 765-742-7913 social@lcss.org www.lcss.org/ Marybeth Fabian, Prin.; Stds.: 123; Sr. Tchrs.: 2; Lay Tchrs.: 12

Sisters of St. Francis of Perpetual Adoration Convent - 1106 State St., Lafayette, IN 47905 t) 765-742-8081

St. Lawrence - 1916 Meharry St., Lafayette, IN 47904-1442 t) 765-742-2107 hillman@saintlawrencechurch.net; hsyouth@saintlawrencechurch.net www.saintlawrencechurch.net Very Rev. Andrew J. Dudzinski, Pst.; Rev. Matthew Kalu, Par. Vicar; Rev. Jeffrey D. Martin, Par. Vicar; Rev. William Summerlin, Par. Vicar; Dcn. Edward Boes; Dcn. Jim B. Rush; CRP Stds.: 195

St. Lawrence School - (Grades K-6) 1902 Meharry St., Lafayette, IN 47904-1497 t) 765-742-4450 social@lcss.org www.lcss.org/ Governed by the Lafayette Catholic School System Pam Myers, Prin.; Stds.: 191; Lay Tchrs.: 18

LAKE VILLAGE

St. Augusta - 3228 W. St. Rd. 10, Lake Village, IN 46349-9465 t) 219-992-3220 staugusta@parish.dol-in.org; htokarz@parish.dol-in.org www.staugustalv.org Rev. Michael A. McKinney, Pst.; CRP Stds.: 3

LEBANON

St. Joseph - 319 E. South St., Lebanon, IN 46052 t) 765-482-5558 stjoe@stjoeleb.org www.stjoeleb.org Pastorate with St. Mary, Frankfort, Indiana Rev. Paul W. Cochran, Pst.; Rev. Daniel J. Duff, Assoc. Pst.; CRP Stds.: 104

LOGANSPORT

All Saints - 112 E. Market St., Logansport, IN 46947-3428 t) 574-722-4080 reception.allsaints@parish.dol-in.org cassmiamicatholic.org/ Rev. Adam G. Mauman, Pst.; Rev. Gustavo Lopez, Assoc. Pst.; Rev. Kyle Neterer, Assoc. Pst.; CRP Stds.: 275

MARION

St. Paul - 1031 W. Kem Rd., Marion, IN 46952; Mailing: 1009 W. Kem Rd., Marion, IN 46952 t) (765) 664-6345 x117 (CRP); 765-664-6345 x107 stpaulcatholicmarion.org Rev. Theodore D. Rothrock, Pst.; CRP Stds.: 56

St. Paul School - (Grades PreK-7) 1009 Kem Rd., Marion, IN 46952 t) (765) 662-2883 info@stpaulcatholicmarion.com stpaulcatholicmarion.org/ Stds.: 143; Lay Tchrs.: 9

MONTEREY

St. Anne - 6894 N. Walnut St., Monterey, IN 46960-0096; Mailing: 401 N. Monticello St., Winamac, IN 46996 t) 574-223-2808; 574-946-4906 rmorris@dol-in.org Rev. Andrew R. DeKeyser, Pst.; Rev. Daniel P. Shine, Assoc. Pst.;

MONTICELLO

Our Lady of the Lakes - 543 S. Main St., Monticello, IN 47960-2948 t) 574-583-5724 (Rectory); 574-583-6790 (Parish Office) frchris93@yahoo.com; ololm@gmail.com www.ololm.org Rev. Christopher T. Miller, Pst.; Dcn. Michael Booth; CRP Stds.: 132

MUNCIE

St. Francis of Assisi - 1200 W. Riverside Ave., Muncie, IN 47303-3650 t) 765-288-6180 stfrancisnewman@parish.dol-in.org www.stfrancisnewman.org (Ball State University Parish) Very Rev. Eric C. Underwood, Pst.; Rev. Christian Michael DeCarlo, Par. Vicar; Rev. Coady Owens, Par. Vicar; CRP Stds.: 96

St. Lawrence - 820 E. Charles St., Muncie, IN 47305-2699 t) 765-288-9223 fr.eunderwood@dol-in.org; pmcpherson@parish.dol-in.org stlawrencemuncie.com Very Rev. Eric C. Underwood, Pst.; Rev. Christian Michael DeCarlo, Assoc. Pst.; Rev. Coady Owens, Assoc. Pst.; Rev. Robert Williams, In Res.; CRP Stds.: 41

St. Mary - 2300 W. Jackson St., Muncie, IN 47303-4797 t) 765-288-5308 parishoffice@stmarymuncie.org stmarymuncie.org Very Rev. Eric C. Underwood, Pst.; Rev. Christian Michael DeCarlo, Par. Vicar; Rev. Coady Owens, Par. Vicar; CRP Stds.: 38

St. Michael School - (Grades PreSchool-8) 2301 W.

Gilbert St., Muncie, IN 47303 t) 765-288-5878 Stds.: 169; Scholastics: 2; Lay Tchrs.: 12

NOBLESVILLE

Our Lady of Grace - 9900 E. 191st St., Noblesville, IN 46060-1520 t) 317-773-4275 churchoffice@ologn.org ologn.org Rev. Clayton D. Thompson, Pst.; Rev. Michael Block, Assoc. Pst.; CRP Stds.: 432

Our Lady of Grace School - (Grades PreSchool-8) t) 317-770-5660 schooloffice@ologn.org ologs.org/ Michelle Boyd, Prin.; Stds.: 452; Lay Tchrs.: 31

OTTERBEIN

St. Charles - 109 N. Meadow St., Otterbein, IN 47970; Mailing: 502 S. Michigan St., Oxford, IN 47971 t) 765-385-2587 www.swnewtonbentoncopastorate.org Rev. Richard J. Weisenberger, Pst.; Rev. Peter J. Vanderkolk, Par. Vicar; CRP Stds.: 65

OXFORD

St. Patrick - 502 S. Michigan St., Oxford, IN 47971-8562 t) 765-385-2587 www.swnewtonbentoncopastorate.org Rev. Richard J. Weisenberger, Pst.; Rev. Peter J. Vanderkolk, Par. Vicar; CRP Stds.: 69

PERU

St. Charles Borromeo - 58 W. 5th St., Peru, IN 46970; Mailing: 80 W. 5th St., Peru, IN 46970 t) 765-473-5543 pstaso@parish.dol-in.org cassmiamicatholic.org/ Rev. Adam G. Mauman, Pst.; Rev. Gustavo Lopez, Assoc. Pst.; Rev. Kyle Neterer, Assoc. Pst.; Dcn. Steve Seitz, Dir.; CRP Stds.: 37

PORTLAND

Immaculate Conception - 506 E. Walnut St., Portland, IN 47371-1599 t) 260-726-7055 fr.plogsdon@dol-in.org; jjohnston2@parish.dol-in.org www.jayandrandolphcatholic.com Rev. Peter F. Logsdon, Pst.; Rev. Matthew J. Arbuckle, Assoc. Pst.; CRP Stds.: 169

REMINGTON

Sacred Heart of Jesus - 124 New York St., Remington, IN 47977-0159; Mailing: P.O. Box 159, Remington, IN 47977 t) 219-261-2302 sacredheartremington.org/ Rev. Joshua Tobias Bennett, Pst.; CRP Stds.: 45

RENSSELAER

St. Augustine - 318 N. McKinley Ave., Rensselaer, IN 47978-2599 t) 219-866-5351 staugustine@parish.dol-in.org saugustineparish.org/ Rev. Joshua Tobias Bennett, Pst.; CRP Stds.: 61

St. Augustine School - (Grades PreK-5) 328 N. Mckinley Ave., Rensselaer, IN 47978 t) 219-866-5480 nagel@s-augustine.org www.s-augustine.org Angela Nagel, Prin.;

REYNOLDS

St. Joseph - 601 S. Kenton St., Reynolds, IN 47980-8098; Mailing: 543 S Main St, Monticello, IN 47960 t) 574-583-5724 (Rectory); 574-583-6790 (Office) frchris93@yahoo.com Rev. Christopher T. Miller, Pst.; Dcn. Michael Booth; CRP Stds.: 28

ROCHESTER

St. Joseph - 1310 Main St., Rochester, IN 46975-2108; Mailing: 401 N. Monticello St., Winamac, IN 46996 t) 574-223-2808; 574-946-4906 rmorris@dol-in.org Rev. Andrew R. DeKeyser, Pst.; Rev. Daniel P. Shine, Assoc. Pst.; CRP Stds.: 49

STAR CITY

St. Joseph - 5895 S. State Rd. 119, Star City, IN 46985; Mailing: 401 N. Monticello St., Winamac, IN 46996 t) 574-946-4906 rmorris@dol-in.org Rev. Andrew R. DeKeyser, Pst.; Rev. Daniel P. Shine, Assoc. Pst.;

TIPTON

St. John the Baptist - 336 Mill St., Tipton, IN 46072-1403; Mailing: 335 Mill St., Tipton, IN 46072 t) 765-675-2422 slpowell_2000@yahoo.com; k.leininger@stjohnstipton.com www.stsjohnandjoseph.com Rev. Dennis J. Goth, Pst.; CRP Stds.: 36

St. John the Baptist School - (Grades PreSchool- 323 Mill St., Tipton, IN 46072 g.king@stjohnstipton.com

UNION CITY

St. Mary - Corner of Plum & Hickory Sts., Union City, IN 47390; Mailing: 425 W. Hickory St., Union City, IN 47390 t) 765-964-4202 fr.plogsdon@dol-in.org jayandrandolphcatholic.com Rev. Peter F. Logsdon, Pst.; Rev. Matthew J. Arbuckle, Assoc. Pst.; CRP Stds.: 44

WEST LAFAYETTE

Blessed Sacrament - 2224 Sacramento Dr., West Lafayette, IN 47906-1998 t) 765-463-5733 www.blessedsacramentwl.org Very Rev. Theodore C. Dudzinski, Admin.; Dcn. Michael D. Gray, Parish Life Coord.; Rev. Samuel J. Kalu, In Res.; CRP Stds.: 192

Indiana Veterans' Home - 3851 N. River Rd., West Lafayette, IN 47906 t) (765) 463-1502

St. Thomas Aquinas - 535 W. State St., West Lafayette, IN 47906-3541 t) 765-743-4652 mailbox@boilercatholics.org; communications@boilercatholics.org www.boilercatholics.org (Purdue University Parish) Rev. Thomas McDermott, O.P., Pst.; Rev. Steve Kuhlmann, Assoc. Pst.; Rev. Ben Keller, Assoc. Pst.; Rev. Brent Bowen, Assoc. Pst.; CRP Stds.: 288

WESTFIELD

St. Maria Goretti - 17102 Spring Mill Rd., Westfield, IN 46074 t) 317-867-3213 m.bruce@smgonline.org www.smgonline.org Rev. Brian A. Dudzinski, Pst.; Rev. Kevin J. Haines, Assoc. Pst.; Rev. Michael McKinley, Assoc. Pst.; Dcn. Sid Cammeresi; Dcn. Stephen P. Miller; CRP Stds.: 539

St. Maria Goretti School - (Grades K-8) 17104 Spring Mill Rd., Westfield, IN 46074 t) 317-896-5582 e.kissel@smgonline.org Elizabeth Kissel, Prin.; Stds.: 438; Lay Tchrs.: 30

WHEATFIELD

Sorrowful Mother - 165 Grace St., Wheatfield, IN 46392-0248; Mailing: P.O. Box 248, Wheatfield, IN 46392 t) 219-956-3343 htokarz@parish.dol-in.org; fr.mmckinney@dol-in.org www.sorrowfulmotherwheatfield.org Rev. Michael A. McKinney, Pst.; CRP Stds.: 34

WINAMAC

St. Peter - 401 N. Monticello St., Winamac, IN 46996-1327 t) 574-946-4906 rmorris@dol-in.org Rev. Andrew R. DeKeyser, Pst.; Rev. Daniel P. Shine, Assoc. Pst.; CRP Stds.: 45

WINCHESTER

St. Joseph - 514 W. Washington St., Winchester, IN 47394; Mailing: 425 W. Hickory St., Union City, IN 47390 t) 765-964-4202 fr.plogsdon@dol-in.org jayandrandolphcatholic.com Rev. Peter F. Logsdon, Pst.; Rev. Matthew J. Arbuckle, Assoc. Pst.; CRP Stds.: 32

ZIONSVILLE

St. Alphonsus Liguori - 1870 W. Oak St., Zionsville, IN 46077-1894 t) 317-873-2885 parishsecretary@zionsvillecatholic.com www.zionsvillecatholic.com Rev. Travis R. Stephens, Pst.; Dcn. Timothy Perry; CRP Stds.: 552

SCHOOLS: PRESCHOOL THRU HIGH SCHOOL

SCHOOLS

STATE OF INDIANA

LAFAYETTE

Lafayette Catholic School System - 2410 S. 9th St., Lafayette, IN 47909 t) 765-474-7500 social@lcss.org www.lcss.org/ Mike Seeley, Pres.;

St. Francis Early Learning Academy - 1223 N. 16th St., Lafayette, IN 47904

HIGH SCHOOLS

STATE OF INDIANA

LAFAYETTE

Central Catholic Junior-Senior High School - (PAR) (Grades 7-12) 2410 S. Ninth St., Lafayette, IN 47909-2499 t) 765-474-2496 mrobertson@lcss.org; spatacsil@lcss.org www.lcss.org Governed by the Lafayette Catholic School System. Caitie Beardmore, Campus Min.; Melissa Robertson, Prin.; Sam Patacsil, Vice Prin.; Stds.: 440; Lay Tchrs.: 31

Emmaus House - 2500 S. Ninth St., Lafayette, IN 47909; Mailing: 2410 S. 9th St, Lafayette, IN 47909 t) (765) 474-7500 social@lcss.org www.lcss.org/ Mike Seeley, Pres.;

NOBLESVILLE

Hamilton County Catholic High School Corporation (St. Theodore Guerin High School) - (DIO) (Grades 9-12) 15300 N. Gray Rd., Noblesville, IN 46062 t) 317-582-0120 www.guerincatholic.org James M. McNeany Jr., Prin.; Dcn. Richard Wagner, Pres.; Stds.: 774; Pr. Tchrs.: 1; Sr. Tchrs.: 2; Lay Tchrs.: 56

INSTITUTIONS LOCATED IN DIOCESE

CAMPUS MINISTRY / NEWMAN CENTERS [CAM]

MUNCIE

Newman Foundation-Ball State University - 1200 W. Riverside Ave., Muncie, IN 47303 t) 765-288-6180 stfrancisnewman@parish.dol-in.org www.stfrancisnewman.org Rev. Coady Owens, Pst.;

WEST LAFAYETTE

St. Thomas Aquinas Parish and Foundation for Catholic Students Attending Purdue University - 535 W. State St., West Lafayette, IN 47906-3541 t) 765-743-4652 mailbox@boilercatholics.org; communications@boilercatholics.org www.boilercatholics.org Rev. Thomas McDermott, O.P., Pst.; Rev. Steve Kuhlmann, Assoc. Pst.; Rev. Ben Keller, Assoc. Pst.; Rev. Brent Bowen, Assoc. Pst.;

COLLEGES & UNIVERSITIES [COL]

RENSSELAER

Saint Joseph's College (The Society of the Precious Blood) - 1027 S. College Ave., Rensselaer, IN 47978 t) 219-866-6000 www.saintjoe.edu Bro. Robert Reuter, C.PP.S.;

CONVENTS, MONASTERIES, AND RESIDENCES FOR WOMEN [CON]

ANDERSON

Sisters of the Holy Cross, Inc. - 2115 Meridian St., Anderson, IN 46016 t) 765-642-2427 Sr. Kathleen Moroney, C.S.C., Treas.; Srs.: 2

KOKOMO

Maria Regina Mater Monastery (Monastery of Poor Clares of the Reform of St. Colette) - 1175 N. 300 W., Kokomo, IN 46901-1799 t) 765-457-5743 www.thepoorclares.org Mother Miriam P.C.C., Abbess; Srs.: 15

ENDOWMENTS / FOUNDATIONS / TRUSTS [EFT]

ANDERSON

St. Vincent Anderson Regional Hospital Foundation, Inc. - 2015 Jackson St., Anderson, IN 46016 t) 765-646-8373 jonathan.nalli@ascension.org www.stvincent.org/ andersonregional Parent entity: St. Vincent Anderson Regional Hospital, Inc. Jonathan Nalli, CEO; Ann Varner, Chief Mission Integration Officer;

LAFAYETTE

***Franciscan Health Foundation Western Indiana** - 1501 Hartford St., Lafayette, IN 47904 t) 765-423-6810 wifoundation@franciscanalliance.org www.franciscanhealth.org/foundation A regional office

& division of Franciscan Alliance Foundation, Inc. Susan Howarth, Exec.;

Lafayette Diocesan Foundation, Inc. - 610 Lingle Ave., Lafayette, IN 47901-1740; Mailing: P.O. Box 1687, Lafayette, IN 47902-1687 t) 765-742-7000 dol-in.org William Gettings, Chair; Mike MacNulty, Dir.;

WEST LAFAYETTE

Aquinas Educational Foundation, Inc. - 535 W. State St., West Lafayette, IN 47906 t) (765) 743-4652 Thomas Ryba, Pres.;

HOSPITALS / HEALTH SERVICES [HOS]

ANDERSON

St. Vincent Anderson Regional Hospital, Inc. - 2015 Jackson St., Anderson, IN 46016 t) 765-649-2511 jonathan.nalli@ascension.org www.healthcare.ascension.org Margaret Johnson, Pres.; Jonathan Nalli, CEO; Ann Varner, Chief Mission Integration Officer; Bed Capacity: 147; Asstd. Annu.: 218,599; Staff: 655

CARMEL

Franciscan Health Indianapolis at Carmel - 12188B N. Meridian St., Carmel, IN 46032 t) 317-705-4520 sharon.annee@franciscanalliance.org www.franciscanhealth.org Sharon Annee, Dir.; Bed Capacity: 6; Asstd. Annu.: 4,754; Staff: 50

Franciscan Health Orthopedic Hospital Carmel - 10777 N. Illinois St., Carmel, IN 46032 t) (317) 528-5400 www.franciscanhealth.org Sharon Annee, Dir.; Bed Capacity: 20; Asstd. Annu.: 2,235; Staff: 150

St. Vincent Carmel Hospital, Inc. - 13500 N. Meridian St., Carmel, IN 46032-1903 t) 317-582-7000 jonathan.nalli@ascension.org www.healthcare.ascension.org Margaret Johnson, Pres.; Jonathan Nalli, CEO; Ann Varner, Chief Mission Integration Officer; Bed Capacity: 124; Asstd. Annu.: 75,439; Staff: 454

CRAWFORDSVILLE

Franciscan Health Crawfordsville - 1710 Lafayette Rd., Crawfordsville, IN 47933 t) 765-362-2800 terrence.klein@franciscanalliance.org www.franciscanhealth.org Franciscan Alliance, Inc. Sr. Cheryl Dazey, Dir.; Terrence L. Klein, Vice Pres. & COO; Bed Capacity: 40; Asstd. Annu.: 117,867; Staff: 284

ELWOOD

St. Vincent Madison County Health System, Inc. - 1331 S. A St., Elwood, IN 46036-1942 t) 765-552-4600 jonathan.nalli@ascension.org www.healthcare.ascension.org Ann Varner, Chief Mission Integration Officer; Jonathan Nalli, CEO; Bed Capacity: 13; Asstd. Annu.: 30,041; Staff: 81

FISHERS

St. Vincent Fishers Hospital, Inc. - 13861 Olio Rd., Fishers, IN 46037 t) 317-415-9000 jonathan.nalli@ascension.org www.healthcare.ascension.org Margaret Johnson, Pres.; Jonathan Nalli, CEO; Ann Varner, Chief Mission Integration Officer; Bed Capacity: 46; Asstd. Annu.: 61,314; Staff: 167

KOKOMO

St. Joseph Hospital & Health Care Center, Inc. - 1907 W. Sycamore St., Kokomo, IN 46901 t) 765-456-5433 www.healthcare.ascension.org Jonathan Nalli, Exec.; Ann Varner, Exec.; Bed Capacity: 129; Asstd. Annu.: 196,768; Staff: 540

Saint Joseph Foundation of Kokomo, Indiana, Inc. - t) 765-456-5406 stvincent.org/stjoseph

LAFAYETTE

Franciscan Health Lafayette Central (Franciscan Alliance, Inc.) - 1501 Hartford St., Lafayette, IN 47904; Mailing: P.O. Box 7501, Lafayette, IN 47904 t) 765-423-6011 terry.wilson@franciscanalliance.org www.franciscanhealth.org Terrance E. Wilson, CEO; Asstd. Annu.: 92,560; Staff: 179

Franciscan Health Lafayette East - 1701 S. Creasy Ln., Lafayette, IN 47904 t) 765-502-4000 terry.wilson@franciscanalliance.org www.franciscanhealth.org Owned by Franciscan Alliance, Inc. Terrance E. Wilson, Pres.; Rev. David J. Buckles, Chap.; Sr. Aline Shultz, Vice. Pres.; Sr. Marcene Franz OSF, Vice Pres., Mission Integration; Bed Capacity: 231; Asstd. Annu.: 455,036; Staff: 1,602

St. Elizabeth School of Nursing - 1501 Hartford St., Lafayette, IN 47904 t) 765-423-6400 michelle.gerrety@franciscanalliance.org www.steson.org Michelle L. Gerrety, Dir.; Stds.: 144; Lay Tchrs.: 18

RENSSELAER

Franciscan Health Rensselaer - 1104 E. Grace St., Rensselaer, IN 47978-3296 t) 219-866-5141 carlos.vasquez@franciscanalliance.org www.franciscanhealth.org Carlos Vasquez, Vice Pres. & COO; Bed Capacity: 25; Asstd. Annu.: 76,870; Staff: 132

WILLIAMSPORT

St. Vincent Williamsport Hospital, Inc. - 412 N. Monroe St., Williamsport, IN 47993-1097 t) 765-762-4000 jonathan.nalli@ascension.org www.healthcare.ascension.org Jonathan Nalli, CEO; Ann Varner, Chief Mission Integration Officer; Bed Capacity: 16; Asstd. Annu.: 57,739; Staff: 107

MISCELLANEOUS [MIS]

NOBLESVILLE

Hamilton County Catholic High School Corporation (St. Theodore Guerin High School; Guerin Catholic High School) - 15300 N. Gray Rd., Noblesville, IN 46062 t) 317-582-0120 www.guerincatholic.org Most Rev. Timothy L. Doherty, Pres.; Very Rev. Theodore C. Dudzinski, Vice. Pres.; Very Rev. Christopher R. Shocklee, At Large Member;

PERU

St. Charles Conference of the Society of St. Vincent DePaul, Inc. - 30 W. 7th St., Peru, IN 46970; Mailing: PO Box 1332, Peru, IN 46970 t) 765-472-1855 Sara Welke, Contact;

WEST LAFAYETTE

Dominicans, Community of St. Thomas Aquinas, Inc. - 2535 Newman Rd., West Lafayette, IN 47906-4537 c) (207) 462-9161 (Fr. Brent Bowen) Rev. Brent Bowen, O.P., Supr.; Rev. Steven F. Kuhlmann, O.P., Vicar;

NURSING / REHABILITATION / CONVALESCENCE / ELDERLY CARE [NUR]

LAFAYETTE

St. Anthony Health Care Inc., - 1205 N. 14th St., Lafayette, IN 47904 t) 765-423-4861 admin@sahc.net; pwindler@sahc.net www.saintanthonycares.com Skilled nursing facility. Rev. Samuel J. Kalu, Liturgy Dir.; Asstd. Annu.: 400; Staff: 154

WEST LAFAYETTE

***University Place, Inc.** - 1700 Lindberg Rd., West Lafayette, IN 47906; Mailing: 11500 Theresa Dr., Lemont, IL 60439 t) 765-464-5600 dkinder@franciscancommunities.org www.franciscanministries.org Continuing Care Retirement Community. A senior living and healthcare services ministry sponsored by the Franciscan Sisters of Chicago. David Kinder, Exec. Dir.; Melissa Smith, Rev., Dir. Mission Integration & Pastoral Care; Asstd. Annu.: 417; Staff: 88

An asterisk (*) denotes an organization that has established tax-exempt status directly with the IRS and is not covered by the USCCB Group Ruling.

Diocese of Lake Charles

MOST REVEREND GLEN JOHN PROVOST

Bishop of Lake Charles; ordained June 29, 1975; appointed Bishop of Lake Charles March 6, 2007; ordained April 23, 2007. Chancery Office: 414 Iris St., P.O. Box 3223, Lake Charles, LA 70602. T: 337-439-7400; F: 337-439-7413.

Chancery Office: 414 Iris St., P.O. Box 3223, Lake Charles, LA 70602. T: 337-439-7400; F: 337-439-7413.
lcdiocese.org
info@lcdiocese.org

ESTABLISHED APRIL 25, 1980.

Square Miles 5,313.

Comprises the civil parishes (or counties) of Allen, Beauregard, Calcasieu, Cameron and Jefferson Davis in the State of Louisiana.

For legal titles of parishes and diocesan institutions, consult the Chancery Office.

STATISTICAL OVERVIEW

Personnel
Bishop....1
Priests: Diocesan Active in Diocese....29
Priests: Retired, Sick or Absent....13
Number of Diocesan Priests....42
Religious Priests in Diocese....19
Total Priests in your Diocese....61
Extern Priests in Diocese....3
Ordinations:
Transitional Deacons....1
Permanent Deacons in Diocese....30
Total Brothers....1
Total Sisters....12

Parishes
Parishes....37
With Resident Pastor:
Resident Diocesan Priests....20
Resident Religious Priests....15
Without Resident Pastor:
Administered by Priests....2
Missions....6

Professional Ministry Personnel:
Sisters....12
Lay Ministers....217

Welfare
Catholic Hospitals....2
Total Assisted....214,701
Homes for the Aged....1
Total Assisted....60
Day Care Centers....1
Total Assisted....125
Special Centers for Social Services....3
Total Assisted....28,078

Educational
Diocesan Students in Other Seminaries....9
Total Seminarians....9
Colleges and Universities....1
Total Students....6,236
High Schools, Diocesan and Parish....1
Total Students....524
Elementary Schools, Diocesan and Parish....5
Total Students....1,771
Catechesis/Religious Education:
High School Students....1,679
Elementary Students....3,921
Total Students under Catholic Instruction....14,140
Teachers in Diocese:
Priests....4
Sisters....2
Lay Teachers....217

Vital Statistics
Receptions into the Church:
Infant Baptism Totals....746
Adult Baptism Totals....45
Received into Full Communion....277
First Communions....627
Confirmations....558
Marriages:
Catholic....180
Interfaith....50
Total Marriages....230
Deaths....800
Total Catholic Population....54,917
Total Population....318,221

LEADERSHIP

Bishop's Office - t) 337-439-7400 x204 bishop@lcdiocese.org Most Rev. Glen John Provost; Dcn. George Stearns, Chancellor; Rev. Msgr. Daniel A. Torres, Vicar;

Chancery Office - t) 337-439-7400

Bishop Perry Building - t) 337-439-7426 Very Rev. Ruben J. Buller, Vicar;

Vicar General (Pastoral Services) - t) 337-439-7400; 337-477-1236 Rev. Msgr. Daniel A. Torres;

Moderator of the Curia and Vicar General (Administration) - t) 337-439-7400 Very Rev. Ruben J. Buller, Moderator;

Chancellor - t) 337-439-7400 Dcn. George Stearns, Chancellor; Very Rev. Ruben Villarreal, Vice Chancellor;

Vice Chancellor - t) 337-439-7400 ruben.villarreal@lcdiocese.org Very Rev. Ruben Villarreal;

Tribunal - t) 337-439-7400 x210 ruben.villarreal@lcdiocese.org Very Rev. Ruben Villarreal, Vicar;

Judges - Rev. Msgr. Jace F. Eskind; Bonnie Landry; Rev. John Payne;

Advocates - t) 337-439-7400

Notary - t) 337-439-7400 Ann Vincent, Secy. (ann.vincent@lcdiocese.org);

Defenders of the Bond - t) 337-439-7400 Rev. Albert W. Borel; Rev. Msgr. Harry D. Greig II;

Promoter of Justice - Rev. John Payne;

Deans - Very Rev. Matthew Cormier, North Central Deanery; Very Rev. Rojo Antony Palatty Koonathan, H.G.N., South Central Deanery; Very Rev. Keith Pellerin, East Deanery;

Presbyteral Council - Very Rev. Aubrey V. Guilbeau, Chair; Very Rev. Rojo Antony Palatty Koonathan, H.G.N.; Very Rev. Ruben J. Buller, Secy.;

Diocesan Consultors - Very Rev. Matthew Cormier; Rev. Msgr. Daniel A. Torres; Very Rev. Aubrey V. Guilbeau;

ADVISORY BOARDS, COMMISSIONS, COMMITTEES, AND COUNCILS

Black Catholics - t) 337-439-7436 Dcn. Edward Lavine (edward.lavine@lcdiocese.org);

Camp Karol of Saint Charles Center - t) 337-855-1232 Dcn. Brian Soileau, Dir.;

Catholic Charities - t) 337-439-7436 Sr. Miriam MacLean, R.S.M., Dir.;

Clergy Formation - t) 337-725-3719 jeffrey.starkovich@lcdiocese.org Rev. Jeffery Paul Starkovich;

Communications - t) 337-439-7400 morris.lebleu@lcdiocese.org; pamela.seal@lcdiocese.org Morris LeBleu, Dir.; Pamela Seals, Assoc. Dir.;

Counseling - t) 337-436-7275 x231 whitney.miller@lcdiocese.org Rev. Whitney Miller;

Deaf Apostolate - t) 337-439-4373 aubrey.guilbeau@lcdiocese.org Very Rev. Aubrey V. Guilbeau, Chap.;

Development Office - t) 337-439-7400 stephanie.rodrigue@lcdiocese.org; morris.lebleu@lcdiocese.org Stephanie Rodrigue, Dir.; Morris LeBleu, Assoc. Dir.;

Diocesan Building Commission - t) 337-439-7400 george.stearns@lcdiocese.org Dcn. George Stearns, Chair;

Education - t) 337-439-7426 Kimberlee Gazzolo, Supt.;

Evangelization - t) 337-439-7400 Sr. Marirose Rudek, R.S.M.;

Fiscal Administration - t) 337-439-7400 Dcn. George Stearns, CFO; Jacob Troutman, Dir. (jacob.troutman@lcdiocese.org);

Hispanic Ministry - t) 337-436-7223 Very Rev. Matthew Cormier, Dir.; Rev. Joseph Caraway, Chap. (joseph.caraway@lcdiocese.org); Ricardo Ruvalcaba, Pst. Assoc. (spanish@sthenry.church);

Office of Liturgy - t) 337-439-7400 x217 sam.bond@lcdiocese.org Rev. Samuel E. Bond, Dir.;

Parish Boundaries Commission - Rev. Msgr. Daniel A. Torres, Chair;

Pastoral Services, Catholic - t) 337-439-7436 miriam.maclean@lcdiocese.org Sr. Miriam MacLean, R.S.M., Secy.;

Permanent Diaconate - Dcn. Patrick LaPoint, Chair;

Personnel Board - Rev. Msgr. Daniel A. Torres; Very Rev. Aubrey V. Guilbeau; Very Rev. Keith Pellerin;

Propagation of the Faith - t) 337-582-3503 anthony.fontenot@lcdiocese.org Rev. Anthony M. Fontenot, Dir.;

Relief Services Catholic - t) 337-439-7436 Sr. Miriam MacLean, R.S.M. (miriam.maclean@lcdiocese.org);

Religious Education - t) 337-439-7400 Sr. Maura Clare Mayock, R.S.M., DRE;

St. Charles Retreat Center - t) 337-855-1232 Dcn. Brian Soileau, Dir.;

Scouting - t) 337-824-1164 trey.ange@lcdiocese.org Rev. Sam Ange III, Chap.;

Sea, Apostleship of the - t) 337-436-1315 Raymond Fontenot, Dir.; Rev. Rommel P. Tolentino, Chap.;

Vocation Director - t) 337-527-5261 michael.caraway@lcdiocese.org Rev. Michael Eugene Caraway;

Vocation Director & Director of Seminarians - t) 337-527-5261 michael.caraway@lcdiocese.org Rev. Michael Eugene Caraway;

PARISHES, MISSIONS, AND CLERGY

STATE OF LOUISIANA

BELL CITY

St. John Vianney - 7120 Hwy. 14 E., Bell City, LA 70630; Mailing: 7128 Hwy. 14 E., Bell City, LA 70630 t) 337-622-3218 stjohnvianney1939@yahoo.com; sjvcbk@gmail.com www.sjv-bc.com Rev. John Payne, Pst.; CRP Stds.: 50

CAMERON

Our Lady Star of the Sea - 135 Our Lady's Rd., Cameron, LA 70631; Mailing: 5250 W. Creole Hwy., Cameron, LA 70631 t) 337-542-4795 Rev. Jerish George, MOC, Pst.;

Sacred of Heart of Jesus Catholic Church - 5250 W. Creole Hwy., Cameron, LA 70631 t) 337-542-4795 shjbookkeeper@gmail.com; stephaniedrodrigue@gmail.com Rev. Jerish George, MOC, Admin.; Stephanie Rodrigue, DRE; CRP Stds.: 40

DEQUINCY

Our Lady of La Salette - 203 S. Grand, DeQuincy, LA 70633 t) 337-786-3500 lasalettedequincy@yahoo.com olldq.com Rev. Luis Tigga, HGN, Pst.; Melissa Sonnier, Admin.; Mary McMahon, DRE; CRP Stds.: 64

DERIDDER

St. Joseph's - 1125 Blankenship Dr., DeRidder, LA 70634 t) 337-463-6878 stjosephderidder.org Rev. V. Wayne LeBleu, Pst.; CRP Stds.: 133

ELTON

St. Joseph's - 209 Al Woods St., Elton, LA 70532; Mailing: P.O. Box 789, Elton, LA 70532 t) 337-584-2818 jose.vattakunnel@lcdiocese.org Rev. Jose Vattakunnel, M.C., Pst.; Lezlie LaFosse, DRE;

St. Paul - 1100 St. Mary St., Elton, LA 70532; Mailing: P.O. Box 129, Elton, LA 70532 t) 337-584-2818 stpaul-elton@hotmail.com Rev. Jose Vattakunnel, M.C., Pst.; Dcn. Michael Paul Guillory; Lezlie LaFosse, DRE; CRP Stds.: 120

FENTON

St. Charles Borromeo - 804 Third Ave., Fenton, LA 70640; Mailing: P.O. Box 309, Fenton, LA 70640 t) 337-756-2529; 337-588-4606 (CRP) stcharles02@yahoo.com; scbccd@gmail.com Rev. Jom Joseph, HGN, Pst.; Susan Augustine, DRE; Cindy Scharff, DRE; CRP Stds.: 45

St. John the Evangelist - 306 Ann St., Lacassine, LA 70650; Mailing: P. O. Box 124, Lacassine, LA 70650 t) (337) 588-4606

GRAND CHENIER

St. Eugene - 5035 Grand Chenier Hwy., Grand Chenier, LA 70643 t) 337-538-2245 Rev. Jerish George, MOC, Pst.;

HACKBERRY

St. Peter the Apostle - 1210 Main St., Hackberry, LA 70645; Mailing: P.O. Box 372, Hackberry, LA 70645 t) 337-762-3365 Rev. Arvind Minz, Pst.; Trisha Savoie, DRE; CRP Stds.: 58

Our Lady of the Assumption - 6470 Gulf Beach Hwy., Johnsons Bayou, LA 70631 t) (337) 762-3365 Cheyenne Sandifer, DRE; Selina Trahan, DRE;

IOWA

St. Raphael - 213 S. Thomson Ave., Iowa, LA 70647; Mailing: P.O. Box 849, Iowa, LA 70647 t) 337-582-3503 Rev. Anthony M. Fontenot, Pst.; Emilie McCown, Music Min.; CRP Stds.: 284

St. Joseph -

JENNINGS

Immaculate Conception - 515 Bryan St., Jennings, LA 70546 t) 337-824-1164 icchurchjennings@yahoo.com icchurchjennings.com/ Rev. Sam A. Trey Ange III, Pst.; CRP Stds.: 30

St. Lawrence - 5505 Pine Island Hwy., Jennings, LA 70546 t) 337-584-2700 Rev. William Miller, Pst.; CRP Stds.: 128

Our Lady Help of Christians - 710 State St., P.O. Drawer 1170, Jennings, LA 70546 t) 337-824-0168 olhcjennings.com Very Rev. Keith Pellerin, Pst.; Elaine Walker, Liturgy Dir.; Richard Mark Sellers, Music Min.; Angie Comeaux, DRE; CRP Stds.: 166

Our Lady Help of Christians School - 600 Roberts Ave., Jennings, LA 70546 t) 337-824-1743 rchapman@olischool.org Rebecca Chapman, Prin.;

Our Lady of Perpetual Help - 920 S. Broadway, Jennings, LA 70546; Mailing: P.O. Box 1331, Jennings, LA 70546 t) 337-824-3703 (CRP); 337-824-3182 olphjennings@att.net Rev. Jude Fernando, T.O.R., Pst.; Ella Dartest-Williams, DRE; CRP Stds.: 18

KINDER

St. Philip Neri - 607 4th Ave., Kinder, LA 70648; Mailing: P.O. Box 146, Kinder, LA 70648 t) 337-738-5612; 337-738-5535 (CRP) pastor@spncatholic.com www.spnerichurch.com Rev. Alan P. Trouille, Pst.; Dcn. Roy Nash; Laurie Pickle, DRE; CRP Stds.: 226

LAKE ARTHUR

Our Lady of the Lake - 203 Commercial Ave., Lake Arthur, LA 70549 t) 337-774-2614; 337-774-2675 (CRP) www.ourladyofthelake.church Rev. Jay Alexius, Pst.; CRP Stds.: 157

LAKE CHARLES

Christ the King - 7680 Gulf Hwy., Lake Charles, LA 70605 t) 337-478-0213 ctkbk7680@gmail.com www.ctkcatholic.org Rev. Rojo Anthony Palatty Koonathan, H.G.N., Pst.; Shane M. Swire, Bus. Mgr.; Kim G. Trahan, DRE; Becky DesOrmeaux, DRE; Jeanette Fontenot, RCIA Coord.; Jenny Slaydon, Music Min.; CRP Stds.: 64

St. Henry - 1021 8th Ave., Lake Charles, LA 70601 t) 337-436-7223 pkittling@sthenry.church www.sthenry.church Very Rev. Matthew Cormier, Pst.; Rev. Joseph Caraway, Par. Vicar; Dcn. Josue Canelo; Dcn. Patrick Hebert; CRP Stds.: 183

Immaculate Conception Cathedral - 935 Bilbo St., Lake Charles, LA 70601; Mailing: P.O. Box 1029, Lake Charles, LA 70602 t) 337-436-7251 iccathedral@structurex.net immaculateconceptioncathedral.com Very Rev. Ruben J. Buller, Pst.; Rev. Samuel Bond, Par. Vicar; Dcn. Christopher Fontenot; CRP Stds.: 375

Immaculate Heart of Mary - 2031 Opelousas St., Lake Charles, LA 70601 t) 337-436-8093 ihmchurch@suddenlink.net ihmp.weconnect.com Rev. Rommel P. Tolentino, Pst.; Rev. Shaji Jose, In Res.; Rev. D.B. Thompson, In Res.; Jacqueline Mathews, DRE; CRP Stds.: 71

Our Lady of Fatima Chapel - 1700 Graham St., Lake Charles, LA 70601

St. Margaret - 2500 Enterprise Blvd., Lake Charles, LA 70601 t) 337-439-4585; 337-436-6358 (CRP) info@stmargaret.church www.stmargaret.church Rev. Nathan Long, Pst.; Rev. Andrew M DeRouen, Par. Vicar; Dcn. Raymond Menard; Dcn. Anthony Pousson; Denise Jones, DRE; CRP Stds.: 85

St. Margaret School - (Grades PreK-8) t) 337-436-7959

St. Martin de Porres - 5495 Elliott Rd., Lake Charles, LA 70605 t) 337-478-3845 www.smdpcatholic.com Rev. Msgr. Jace F. Eskind, Pst.; Dcn. Richard E. Donahoe; CRP Stds.: 163

St. Mary of the Lake - 11054 Hwy. 384 (Big Lake), Lake Charles, LA 70607 t) 337-598-3101 stmarysla@aol.com Rev. Msgr. James M. Gaddy, Pst.; CRP Stds.: 149

Our Lady of Good Counsel - 221 Aqua Dr., Lake Charles, LA 70605 t) 337-477-1434 paul.jussen@lcdiocese.org Rev. Paul Jussen, M.S., Pst.; Sr. Shirley Gobert, S.E.C., Pst. Assoc.; Dcn. Paul Gregory; CRP Stds.: 60

Our Lady Queen of Heaven - 617 W. Claude St., Lake Charles, LA 70605 t) 337-477-1236; 337-477-3937 (CRP) olqh@lcdiocese.org olqh.org Rev. Msgr. Daniel A. Torres, Pst.; Rev. Levi Thompson, Par. Vicar; Dcn. Harold Nixon; Rev. Charles Okorougo, In Res.; Dcn. George K. Carr; Very Rev. Ruben Villarreal, In Res.; Robin Suire, DRE; Charlotte Spicer, DRE; CRP Stds.: 312

Our Lady Queen of Heaven School - (Grades PreK-8) 3908 Creole St., Lake Charles, LA 70605 t) 337-477-7349 Diane Oden, Librn.;

Sacred Heart of Jesus - 1100 Mill St., Lake Charles, LA 70601 t) 337-439-2646 Rev. Joby Kaniyamparambil Mathew, H.G.N., Pst.; Dcn. Erroll Joseph DeVille; Dcn. Edward Lavine; Barbara Batiste, DRE; CRP Stds.: 20

St. Theodore - 785 Sam Houston Jones Pkwy., Lake Charles, LA 70611; Mailing: P O Box 12726, Lake Charles, LA 70612 t) 337-855-6662 theodoreccd@yahoo.com mossbluffcatholic.org Very Rev. Aubrey V. Guilbeau, Pst.; Dcn. Leo Anthony Hebert; Sandi Robinson, DRE; CRP Stds.: 387

OAKDALE

Sacred Heart - 1208 7th Ave., Oakdale, LA 71463-0926; Mailing: P.O. Box 926, Oakdale, LA 71463 t) 318-335-3780 Rev. Vijaya Peddoju, HGN, Pst.; Diane Bacon, DRE;

St. Frances - 204 Poplar St., Elizabeth, LA 70638

OBERLIN

St. Joan of Arc - 112 S. Seventh St., Oberlin, LA 70655; Mailing: P.O. Box 479, Oberlin, LA 70655 t) 337-639-4399 Rev. Pradeep Gali, HGN, Admin.; Dcn. Norris Chapman; Dcn. James Dale Deshotel; CRP Stds.: 60

RAGLEY

St. Pius X Catholic Church - 16816 Hwy. 171, Ragley, LA 70657 t) 337-725-3719 secretary@spx.church; bookkeeper@spx.church spx.church Rev. Jeffery Paul Starkovich, Pst.; CRP Stds.: 278

SULPHUR

Immaculate Conception of the B.V.M. - 2700 Maplewood Dr., Sulphur, LA 70663 t) 337-625-3364; 337-625-9719 (CRP) church@icsulphur.org icsulphur.org Rev. Timothy Goodly, Pst.; Rev. Whitney Miller, In Res.; Paula Hunter, DRE; CRP Stds.: 259

Our Lady of LaSalette - 602 N. Claiborne St., Sulphur, LA 70663 t) 337-527-6722; 337-527-8307 (CRP) olls@suddenlinkmail.com Rev. John Welch, MS, Pst.; Rev. Lawrence A. Kohler, M.S., In Res.; Cay Gibson, DRE; CRP Stds.: 136

Our Lady of Prompt Succor - 1109 Cypress St., Sulphur, LA 70663 t) 337-527-5261 olps1@olpssulphur.com; olps6@olpssulphur.com www.olpssulphur.com Very Rev. Edward J. Richard, M.S., Pst.; Rev. Michael Beverung, Par. Vicar; Rev. Msgr. Arthur B Calkins, In Res.; Rev. Jude Brunnert, M.S., In Res.; Dcn. Patrick LaPoint; Hanna Beard, DRE; CRP Stds.: 149

Our Lady's School - (Grades PreK-8) 1111 Cypress St., Sulphur, LA 70663 t) 337-527-7828 hdouglas@ourladysschool.org Hank Douglas, Prin.; Joan Habetz, Treas.; Stephanie Viator, Librn.;

St. Theresa - 4822 Carlyss Dr., Sulphur, LA 70665 t) 337-583-4800 sthresa1@camtel.net st-theresa-parish.org Rev. Sibi Kunninu Chacko, M.S., Pst.; Dcn. Keith Ellender; Angie Clark, DRE; CRP Stds.: 341

VINTON

St. Joseph - 1502 Industrial St., Vinton, LA 70668 t) 337-589-7358 Dcn. Jesse Menard; Rev. Carlos Garcia Cardona, Pst.; Rhonda Guidry, DRE;

WELSH

St. Joseph - 310 N. Sarah St., Welsh, LA 70591 t) 337-434-3673 Rev. Pradeep Gali, HGN, Pst.;

St. Peter Claver - 400 W. 2nd St., Iowa, LA 70547

Our Lady of Seven Dolors - 209 N. Adams St., Welsh, LA 70591; Mailing: P.O. Box 515, Welsh, LA 70591 t) 337-734-3446 susilfernando@yahoo.com Rev. Susil Fernando (Sri Lanka), Pst.; Dcn. Wayne Chapman; Laurie Pickle, DRE; CRP Stds.: 198

WESTLAKE

St. John Bosco - 1301 Sampson St., Westlake, LA 70669 t) 337-433-2467 bhogan@st.johnboscochurch.com Rev. Jenesh Joseph, HGN, Pst.; Rev. Michael J. Barras, In Res.; Dcn. Garrett Caraway Jr.; Dcn. Fred Reed Jr.; Barbara Hogan, DRE; CRP Stds.: 150

SCHOOLS: PRESCHOOL THRU HIGH SCHOOL

HIGH SCHOOLS

STATE OF LOUISIANA

LAKE CHARLES

St. Louis Catholic High School - (PAR) 1620 Bank St., Lake Charles, LA 70601 t) 337-436-7275 morgeron@slchs.org www.slchs.org Rev. Nathan Long, Rector; Very Rev. Ruben Villarreal, Chap.; Melanie Lejeune, Librn.; Mia Orgeron, Admin.; Stds.: 524; Pr. Tchrs.: 2; Sr. Tchrs.: 1; Lay Tchrs.: 54

INSTITUTIONS LOCATED IN DIOCESE

CAMPUS MINISTRY / NEWMAN CENTERS [CAM]

LAKE CHARLES

Catholic Student Center - McNeese State University, 221 Aqua Dr., Lake Charles, LA 70605 t) 337-477-1434 paul.jussen@lcdiocese.org www.cowboycatholics.com Rev. Paul Jussen, M.S., Pst.; Dcn. Paul Gregory; Sr. Shirley Gobert, S.E.C., Pst. Assoc.;

Center for Catholic Studies - 221 Aqua Dr., Lake Charles, LA 70605 t) 337-477-1434 Sr. Maura Clare Mayock, R.S.M., Diocesan D.R.E.;

Vianney House of Discernment - 206 Aqua Dr., Lake Charles, LA 70605 t) (337) 439-7400 x226 michael.caraway@lcdiocese.org lcvocations.com Rev. Michael J Caraway, Dir.;

CATHOLIC CHARITIES [CCH]

LAKE CHARLES

***Catholic Charities of Southwest Louisiana in the Roman Catholic Diocese of Lake Charles, Inc.** - 1225 2nd St., Lake Charles, LA 70601 t) 337-439-7436 director@catholiccharitiesswla.org catholiccharitiesswla.com Sr. Miriam MacLean, R.S.M., Exec. Dir.; Asstd. Annu.: 8,500; Staff: 11

CONVENTS, MONASTERIES, AND RESIDENCES FOR WOMEN [CON]

LAKE CHARLES

The Congregation of the Sisters of Charity of the Incarnate Word, Houston, Texas (CCVI) - 609 Orchard Dr., Lake Charles, LA 70605-4451

ENDOWMENTS / FOUNDATIONS / TRUSTS [EFT]

LAKE CHARLES

CHRISTUS St. Patrick Foundation (CHRISTUS Ochsner Southwestern Louisiana Foundation) - 524 Doctor Michael DeBakey Dr., Lake Charles, LA 70601 t) 337-430-5353 patricia.prudhomme@christushealth.org www.christusochsnerswlafoundation.org Patricia Prudhomme, Dir.;

The St. Louis High School Foundation - 1620 Bank St., Lake Charles, LA 70681 t) (337) 436-7275 mtouchet@slchs.org Mia Orgeron, Prin.;

HOSPITALS / HEALTH SERVICES [HOS]

LAKE CHARLES

CHRISTUS Health Southwestern Louisiana - 524 Dr. Michael DeBakey Dr., Lake Charles, LA 70601 t) 337-436-2511; 337-474-6370 paul.trevino@christushealth.org; james.davidson@christushealth.org www.christusochsner.org Sponsored by Christus Health System, Irving, TX Paul Trevino, CEO; Rev. Felix Okey Alaribe (Nigeria), Vice. Pres.; Rev. Brian Madison King, Chap.; Rev. Charles Okorougo, Chap.; Bed Capacity: 318; Asstd. Annu.: 214,701; Staff: 1,295

MISCELLANEOUS [MIS]

BATON ROUGE

Catholic Daughters of America - 7506 Cardiff Ave., Baton Rouge, LA 70808 t) 225-769-0122 conniecda@yahoo.com Very Rev. Edward J. Richard, M.S., Chap.;

JENNINGS

Magnificat Lake Charles Chapter Inc. - 18057 D.A. LeDoux Rd., Jennings, LA 70546 t) (337) 368-3612 sharlaprejean@yahoo.com Sharla Prejean, Coord.;

LAKE CHARLES

School Food Services of Lake Charles, Inc. - 1112 Bilbo St., Lake Charles, LA 70601 t) 337-433-9640 x402 edrie.durio@lcdiocese.org Edrie Durio, Dir.;

Society of Roman Catholic Church of the Dioceses of Lake Charles - 414 Iris St., Lake Charles, LA 70601; Mailing: P. O. Box 3223, Lake Charles, LA 70602-3223 t) 337-439-7400 daniel.torres@lcdiocese.org; ruben.buller@lcdiocese.org www.lcdiocese.org Dcn. George Stearns, Chancellor; Very Rev. Ruben J. Buller, Vicar; Very Rev. Aubrey V. Guilbeau, Vicar; Rev. Msgr. Daniel A. Torres, Vicar; Very Rev. Ruben Villarreal, Vicar;

SULPHUR

Saint Francis de Sales Oratory - 802 Huntington St., Sulphur, LA 70663 t) 337-564-2867 canon.moreau@institute-christ-king.org Rev. Canon Jean Marie Moreau, Rector;

RETREAT HOUSES / RENEWAL CENTERS [RTR]

LAKE CHARLES

St. Charles Center - 2151 Sam Houston Jones Pkwy., Lake Charles, LA 70611 t) 337-855-1232 michelle.monceaux@lcdiocese.org www.stcharlescenter.com Dcn. Brian Soileau;

SPECIAL CARE FACILITIES [SPF]

LAKE CHARLES

Our Lady Queen of Heaven Manor - Villa Maria, 3905 Kingston St., Lake Charles, LA 70605 t) 337-478-4780 villamaria@suddenlinkmail.com Becky See, Dir.; Bed Capacity: 118; Asstd. Annu.: 55; Staff: 33

An asterisk (*) denotes an organization that has established tax-exempt status directly with the IRS and is not covered by the USCCB Group Ruling.

Diocese of Lansing

(Dioecesis Lansingensis)

MOST REVEREND EARL A. BOYEA

Bishop of Lansing; ordained May 20, 1978; appointed Auxiliary Bishop of Detroit and Titular Bishop of Siccenna July 22, 2002; consecrated September 13, 2002; appointed Bishop of Lansing February 27, 2008; installed April 29, 2008. Chancery: 228 N. Walnut St., Lansing, MI 48933. T: 517-342-2452; F: 517-342-2505.

Chancery: 228 N. Walnut St., Lansing, MI 48933. T: 517-342-2440; F: 517-342-2519.
www.dioceseoflansing.org
chancery@dioceseoflansing.org

ESTABLISHED MAY 22, 1937.

Square Miles 6,218.

Canonically Erected August 4, 1937.

Comprises the Counties of Clinton, Eaton, Genesee, Hillsdale, Ingham, Jackson, Lenawee, Livingston, Shiawassee and Washtenaw, in the State of Michigan.

For legal titles of parishes and diocesan institutions, consult the Chancery Office.

STATISTICAL OVERVIEW

Personnel

Bishop	1
Retired Bishops	1
Priests: Diocesan Active in Diocese	72
Priests: Diocesan Active Outside Diocese	5
Priests: Retired, Sick or Absent	58
Number of Diocesan Priests	135
Religious Priests in Diocese	26
Total Priests in your Diocese	161
Extern Priests in Diocese	11
Ordinations:	
Diocesan Priests	2
Transitional Deacons	2
Permanent Deacons in Diocese	146
Total Brothers	1
Total Sisters	356

Parishes

Parishes	72
With Resident Pastor:	
Resident Diocesan Priests	55
Resident Religious Priests	4
Without Resident Pastor:	
Administered by Priests	10
Administered by Deacons	1
Pastoral Centers	2
Professional Ministry Personnel:	
Sisters	27
Lay Ministers	192

Welfare

Catholic Hospitals	4
Total Assisted	1,433,879
Health Care Centers	2
Total Assisted	11,499
Homes for the Aged	1
Total Assisted	3
Day Care Centers	1
Special Centers for Social Services	6
Total Assisted	334,551
Residential Care of Disabled	1
Total Assisted	60

Educational

Diocesan Students in Other Seminaries	26
Total Seminarians	26
Colleges and Universities	1
Total Students	1,856
High Schools, Diocesan and Parish	4
Total Students	1,927
High Schools, Private	1
Total Students	31
Elementary Schools, Diocesan and Parish	29
Total Students	5,242
Elementary Schools, Private	6
Total Students	846
Catechesis / Religious Education:	
High School Students	1,415
Elementary Students	6,268
Total Students under Catholic Instruction	17,611
Teachers in Diocese:	
Priests	1
Sisters	24
Lay Teachers	665

Vital Statistics

Receptions into the Church:	
Infant Baptism Totals	1,533
Minor Baptism Totals	129
Adult Baptism Totals	146
Received into Full Communion	336
First Communions	1,665
Confirmations	1,667
Marriages:	
Catholic	363
Interfaith	116
Total Marriages	479
Deaths	2,025
Total Catholic Population	172,717
Total Population	1,813,445

LEADERSHIP

Chancery - t) 517-342-2440

Bishop's Office - t) 517-342-2452 Michael Andrews, Chancellor; Lisa Kutas, Chief of Staff; William R. Bloomfield, General Counsel;

Office of Missions - Anne Rivet, Coord. Mission Appeals;

Vicar General - t) 517-783-2748 Rev. Timothy E. MacDonald;

Vicar for Priests - Rev. Karl L. Pung;

Delegate for Consecrated Life - t) 517-342-2506 Dawn Hausmann;

Liaison for Charismatic Communities - t) 734-878-3161 Rev. Daniel J. Kogut;

Commissions and Councils -

Presbyteral Council - Rev. Mathias D. Thelen, Chair; Rev. Steven M. Mattson, Vice Chair; Rev. Karl L. Pung;

Board of Education and Catechesis - Rev. Steven M. Mattson, Pres.;

Building Commission - Rev. Andrew A. Czajkowski;

Finance Council - t) 517-377-0866 Tom Smith, Chair;

Priest Pension Board - Rev. Ryan L. Riley;

Priests' Assignment Commission - Rev. Robert Crowley Bacik; Rev. Edward O. Fride; Rev. Todd W. Koenigsknecht;

OFFICES AND DIRECTORS

Department of Communications - t) 517-342-2475 David Kerr, Chair; Michelle Hildebrandt, Creative Svcs. Mgr.; Matt Riedl, Multi-Media Journalist;

Department of Discipleship Formation - t) 517-342-2479 Jeremy Priest, Chair;

Campus Ministry - t) 517-337-9778 Katie Diller Gleason;

Christian Initiation Advisory Committee - t) 517-342-2476 Jeremy Priest, Chair;

Fertility and Life Ministries - Jenny Ingles, Dir.;

Marriage and Family Life - Richard Budd, Dir.;

Natural Family Planning - t) 517-342-2587 Jenny Ingles;

Worship Commission - Rev. Anthony J. Strouse;

Worship Office - t) 517-342-2476 Jeremy Priest, Dir.;

Young Adult Ministry - t) 517-342-2506 Dawn Hausmann, Dir.;

Youth Ministry - t) 517-342-2584 Brian Flynn;

Department of Education - t) 517-342-2483 Thomas P. Maloney, Chair;

Associate Superintendent - t) 517-342-2481 Sarah Salow; Amanda Wildern;

Superintendent of Schools - Thomas P. Maloney;

Department of Evangelization and Catechesis - Craig Pohl, Chair;

Hispanic Ministry - Susana Chapa-Vargas, Dir.;

New Evangelization - Craig Pohl, Dir.;

Parish Youth Discipleship - Brian Flynn, Dir.;

Department of Finance - t) 517-342-2442 George Landolt, Chair;

Accounting - Kim Poupard;

Diocesan Cemeteries - t) 517-484-2500 Brian Epkey, Dir.;

Director of Properties - t) 517-342-2534 Alan Olsen;

Technology Administrator - t) 517-342-2538 Peter Frahm;

Department of Human Resources - t) 517-342-2511 Lisa Kutas, Dir.;

HR Generalist - Rebecca Swift;

Office of Child & Youth Protection - t) 517-342-2551 Reba Sommer, Coord.;

Victim Assistance Coordinator - t) 888-308-6252 Lisa Veenstra;

Department of Vocations - t) 517-342-2507 Rev. John J. Whitlock, Chair;

Consecrated Vocations - t) 517-342-2506 Dawn Hausmann, Dir.;

Director of Vocations/Seminarians - Rev. John J. Whitlock;

Life Justice - t) 517-342-2587 Jenny Ingles;

Permanent Diaconate - Dcn. Kenneth Preiss; Dcn. Randal Desrochers, Diaconal Formation;

Priestly Life and Ministry - t) 810-229-9863 Rev. Karl L. Pung, Dir.;

Restorative Justice - t) 517-342-2451 Dcn. Kenneth Preiss;

Diocesan Archivist - t) 517-342-2540 Rev. Msgr. George C. Michalek (gmichalek@dioceseoflansing.org);

Diocesan Missions Office - t) 517-342-2510 Ann Rivet;

Diocesan Tribunal - Rev. Msgr. George C. Michalek, Judicial Vicar (gmichalek@dioceseoflansing.org);

Adjunct Judicial Vicar - Rev. Nathaniel J. Sokol;

Assessors - Rev. David Michael Fons;

Court Experts - Rev. George R. Daisy; Angela Fowler; Paul Johnston;

Defender of the Bond - Dcn. John M. Cameron;

Judicial Vicar - t) 517-342-2560 Rev. Msgr. George C. Michalek;

Moderator of the Tribunal Chancery - Heidi Gonzales;

Notary - Susan Bartold, Ecclesiastical Notary; Linda Skiba, Ecclesiastical Notary;

Promoter of Justice - Rev. David Michael Fons;

Tribunal Judges - Rev. Msgr. Raymond J. Goehring; Rev. Msgr. George C. Michalek; Rev. Nathaniel J. Sokol;

Discernment Houses -

Emmaus House - t) 517-342-2506 Dawn Hausmann, Dir.;

St. Catherine House - t) 734-761-8606 Rev. William A. Ashbaugh, Dir.;

PARISHES, MISSIONS, AND CLERGY

STATE OF MICHIGAN

ADRIAN

Holy Family Parish Adrian - 305 Division St., Adrian, MI 49221 t) 517-263-4681 office@holyfamilyadrian.org; officecoordinator.hfa@gmail.com holyfamilyadrian.org Rev. Michael Newman, OSFS, Pst.; Dcn. Leonard C. Brown; Dcn. Richard Bayes Jr., Senior Status; Kurt Weber, Liturgy Dir.; Kathryn G Love, DRE; CRP Stds.: 85

St. Joseph Oratory - 415 Ormsby St, Adrian, MI 49221

ANN ARBOR

Christ the King Parish Ann Arbor - 4000 Ave Maria Dr., Ann Arbor, MI 48105 t) 734-665-5040 info@ctkcc.net www.ctkcc.net Rev. Edward O. Fride, Pst.; Dcn. Daniel R. Foley; Dcn. Pete Hansen; Dcn. Gerald P. Holowicki; Dcn. John Ozog; Dcn. Larry Randolph; Dcn. Louis J. Russello; CRP Stds.: 376

St. Francis of Assisi Parish Ann Arbor - 2250 E. Stadium Blvd., Ann Arbor, MI 48104; Mailing: 2150 Frieze Ave., Ann Arbor, MI 48104 t) 734-821-2132 (CRP); 734-821-2125 (CRP); 734-821-2100 ward@stfrancisa2.org; parishoffice@stfrancisa2.org www.stfrancisa2.com Rev. James P. Conlon, Pst.; Rev. John Vinton, Assoc. Pst.; Dcn. Richard Badics; Dcn. Gene Leger; Ellen Ward, DRE; CRP Stds.: 481

St. Francis of Assisi School - (Grades PreK-8) 2270 E. Stadium Blvd., Ann Arbor, MI 48104 t) 734-821-2200 school@stfrancisaa.org www.stfrancisa2.com/school/ Julia Pritzel, Prin.; Stds.: 481; Lay Tchrs.: 36

St. Mary Student Parish Ann Arbor - 331 Thompson St., Ann Arbor, MI 48104-2295 t) 734-663-0557 x240; 734-663-0557 (CRP) stmarys@umich.edu www.stmarystudentparish.org Serving students, faculty, and staff at the University of Michigan. Rev. James Gartland, SJ, Pst.; Rev. Patrick Casey, S.J., Pst. Assoc.; Rev. Robert Karle, Pst. Assoc.; Rev. Joseph F. Wagner, S.J., Campus Min.; Rev. Kyle Shinseki, Pst. Assoc.; CRP Stds.: 216

St. Patrick Parish Ann Arbor - 5671 Whitmore Lake Rd., Ann Arbor, MI 48105 t) 734-662-8141 info@stpatricka2.org www.stpatricka2.org Rev. Thomas Wasilewski, Pst.; Dcn. Frank Joseph Papp; CRP Stds.: 35

St. Thomas the Apostle Parish Ann Arbor - 530 Elizabeth St., Ann Arbor, MI 48104 t) 734-761-8606 frontdesk@sta2.org sta2.org/ Rev. William A. Ashbaugh, Pst.; Rev. Gerald Gawronski, Par. Vicar; Dcn. Thomas Loewe; Dcn. James Miles; Dcn. James Thibodeau; CRP Stds.: 78

St. Thomas the Apostle School - (Grades PreK-9) 540 Elizabeth St., Ann Arbor, MI 48104 t) 734-769-0911 sta2.org/school/ Stds.: 145; Lay Tchrs.: 14

BRIGHTON

Holy Spirit Parish Brighton - 9565 Musch Rd, Brighton, MI 48116 t) 810-231-9199; 810-231-9199 x209 (CRP) parishoffice@holyspiritrcs.org; mabastian@holyspiritrcs.org holyspiritparishbrighton.org/ Rev. John George Rocus, Pst.; Dcn. Gerald Brennan; Mary Anne Bastian, DRE; CRP Stds.: 72

Holy Spirit School - (Grades PreK-8) t) 810-900-9050 office@holyspiritrcs.org holyspiritschoolbrighton.org Stds.: 67; Lay Tchrs.: 6

St. Mary Magdalen Parish Brighton - 2201 S. Old U.S. 23 Hwy., Brighton, MI 48114 t) 810-229-8624 perickson@saintmarymagdalen.org www.saintmarymagdalen.org Rev. Paul Erickson, Admin.; Dcn. P. Devon Wolfe; Joshua Kenny, DRE; Kathy Grisdela, Bus. Mgr.; Erin Wolfe, RCIA Coord.; CRP Stds.: 227

St. Patrick Parish Brighton - 711 Rickett Rd., Brighton, MI 48116 t) 810-229-9863 cklebba@stpatchurch.org; busmgr@stpatchurch.org www.stpatrickcatholicparish.org Rev. Mathias D. Thelen, Pst.; Rev. Miguel Colunga, Par. Vicar; Dcn. Michael Gilbert; Dcn. Patrick A. McDonald; Stephen Royal, Pst. Min./Coord.; Anne Guminik, RCIA/ Adult Faith Formation; CRP Stds.: 247

St. Patrick School - (Grades PreK-8) 1001 Orndorf Dr., Brighton, MI 48116 t) 810-229-7946 principal@stpatschool.org www.stpatschool.org Carley Dunphey, Prin.; Stds.: 465; Lay Tchrs.: 25

BROOKLYN

St. Joseph Shrine Parish Brooklyn - 8743 U.S. 12, Brooklyn, MI 49230 t) 517-467-2106 (Family Center); 517-467-2183 (Parish) faithformationsjs@gmail.com; sjshrine@frontiernet.net www.stjosephbrooklynmi.com Rev. Zachary M. Mabee, Pst.; Dcn. Gene Hausmann; Deb Falk, Music Min.; Diane Dover, RCIA Coord.; Debbie Schirmacher, DRE; Rose Noble, Bus. Mgr.; Elizabeth Girdham, Admin.; CRP Stds.: 25

BURTON

Holy Redeemer Parish Flint - 1227 E. Bristol Rd., Burton, MI 48529 t) 810-743-3050 holyredeemercatholic@gmail.com holyredeemerburton.org Rev. Steven D. Anderson, Pst.; Dcn. Omar Odette; Dcn. Kenneth Preiss; John Mira, Youth Min.; Molly Muxlow, Bus. Mgr.; Daniel Schmit, Music Min.; Emily Arthur, RCIA Coord.; Rafael Urgino, DRE; CRP Stds.: 78

CHARLOTTE

St. Mary Parish Charlotte - 807 St. Mary Blvd., Charlotte, MI 48813 t) 517-543-4319 parishoffice@stmarycharlotte.org www.stmarycharlotte.org Rev. Dwight M. Ezop, Pst.; Dcn. Thomas Fogle; CRP Stds.: 46

St. Mary School - (Grades K-8) 905 St. Mary Blvd., Charlotte, MI 48813 t) 517-543-3460 eharbor@stmarycharlotte.org stmarycharlotte.org Erin Gutierrez-Harbor, Prin.; Stds.: 147; Lay Tchrs.: 8

St. Ann Oratory - 312 S. Main St., Bellevue, MI 49021; Mailing: 807 St. Marys Blvd., Charlotte, MI 48813

CHELSEA

St. Mary Parish Chelsea - 14200 E. Old U.S. Hwy. 12,

Chelsea, MI 48118 t) 734-475-8164 (CRP); 734-475-7561 smcch@aol.com stmarychelsea.org Rev. William J. Turner, Pst.; Dcn. Thomas Franklin; Dcn. D. Michael Martin; Dcn. Wayne Slomiany; Marita Martin, DRE; CRP Stds.: 165

CLARKLAKE

St. Rita Parish Clarklake - 10516 Hayes Rd., Clarklake, MI 49234 t) 517-592-5718 (DRE); 517-592-5470 nancy.carter.dre.strita@gmail.com; stritasclarklake@gmail.com www.stritacatholicparish.com Rev. Thomas J. Helfrich, O.S.F.S., Pst.; Dcn. Christopher Vida; CRP Stds.: 76

CLIO

SS. Charles and Helena Parish Clio - 230 E. Vienna St., Clio, MI 48420-1423 t) 810-686-9861 parish@sscharlesandhelena.org Rev. Kenneth F. Coughlin, Pst.; Grace Guzowski, DRE; CRP Stds.: 62

CONCORD

St. Catherine Parish Concord - 211 Harmon Ave., Concord, MI 49237 t) 517-524-7578 www.stcatherinelaboureconcord.org Rev. Timothy E. MacDonald, Admin.; Dcn. Thomas Arehart; Leslie Reagle, DRE; CRP Stds.: 34

DAVISON

St. John the Evangelist Parish Davison - 404 N. Dayton St., Davison, MI 48423-1397 t) 810-653-2377; 810-653-4056 (CRP) sschroeder@stjohndavison.org; lmiles@stjohndavison.org www.stjohndavison.org Rev. Andrew A. Czajkowski, Pst.; Rev. Dieudonne Ntakarutimana, Par. Vicar; Dcn. Daniel Fairweather; Becky Beck, Youth Min.; Janet Gravel, DRE; CRP Stds.: 178

Blessed Sacrament Oratory - 6340 Roberta St., Burton, MI 48509; Mailing: 404 N. Dayton St., Davison, MI 48423 t) (810) 653-2377 parishoffice@stjohndavison.org Merged with St. John the Evangelist Parish, Davison.

DEERFIELD

Light of Christ Parish Deerfield - 222 Carey St., Deerfield, MI 49238 t) 517-447-3500 lightofchristparish@gmail.com www.lightofchristparish.com Rev. Jeffrey A. Poll, Pst.; Deanna Burke, DRE; CRP Stds.: 37

St. Peter the Apostle - 309 S. Ln., Blissfield, MI 49228-1244 t) (517) 447-3500 (Parish Office)

DEWITT

St. Jude Parish DeWitt - 801 N. Bridge St., DeWitt, MI 48820 t) 517-669-8335 info@stjudedewitt.com www.stjudedewitt.com Rev. David J. Speicher, Pst.; Dcn. Kevin Orth; Dcn. Robert Nieman; Dcn. Robert Strouse; CRP Stds.: 236

DEXTER

St. Joseph Parish Dexter - 6805 Mast Rd., Dexter, MI 48130; Mailing: 3430 Dover St., Dexter, MI 48130 t) 734-426-2674 (CRP); 734-426-8483 michelle_hochrein@stjos.com; info@stjos.com www.stjos.com Rev. Brendan J. Walsh, Pst.; Dcn. Randal Desrochers; Dcn. Larry Deford; Dcn. Romolo Leone; Donaldneil James Dalgleish, Youth Min.; Michelle Hochrein, DRE; Marinell High, RCIA Coord.; CRP Stds.: 161

DURAND

St. Mary and St. Joseph Parish Durand - 700 Columbia Dr., Durand, MI 48429 t) 855-288-6701; 989-271-8434 (CRP) stmarydurand@gmail.com; stjosephgaines@gmail.com stmarystjoseph.org Dcn. Wayne Walter Corrion, Admin.; Mollie Shay, CRE; Pamela Schaefer, Music Min.; Paul Williamson, Bus. Mgr.; CRP Stds.: 15

St. Joseph Oratory - 9450 Duffield Rd., Gaines, MI 48436

EAST LANSING

St. Thomas Aquinas Parish East Lansing - 955 Alton Rd., East Lansing, MI 48823 t) 517-351-7215 jderengoski@elcatholics.org; dzakerski@elcatholics.org www.elcatholics.org Rev. Gordon P. Reigle, Pst.; Rev. Michael Cassar, Par. Vicar; Rev. Peter Joseph Ludwig, Par. Vicar; Dcn. David Drayton; Dcn. James Kasprzak; Dcn. David Zygmontowicz; Debra Lewis, DRE; CRP Stds.: 367

St. Thomas Aquinas School - (Grades PreK-8) 915 Alton Rd., East Lansing, MI 48823 t) 517-332-0813 enobach@elcatholics.org Erin Nobach, Prin.; Stds.: 113; Lay Tchrs.: 24

St. John the Evangelist Church and Student Center - 327 M.A.C., East Lansing, MI 48823 t) (517) 337-9778 stjohnmsu@org Katie Diller Gleason, Campus Min.;

EATON RAPIDS

St. Peter Parish Eaton Rapids - 515 E. Knight St., Eaton Rapids, MI 48827 t) 517-663-4735 spceatonrapidsoffice@gmail.com; spceatonrapidspastor@gmail.com www.spceatonrapids.org Rev. George Puthenpeedika, Pst.; CRP Stds.: 32

FENTON

St. John the Evangelist Parish Fenton - 600 N. Adelaide St., Fenton, MI 48430 t) 810-629-2251 mfrench@stjohnfenton.org; cward@stjohnfenton.org www.stjohnfenton.org Rev. Robert F. Copeland, Pst.; Dcn. Lawrence Blondin; Dcn. Richard Stoolmaker; CRP Stds.: 141

St. John the Evangelist School - (Grades PreK-8) 514 Lincoln St., Fenton, MI 48430 t) 810-629-6551 aschmit@sjseducation.com www.stjohnfenton.com Andrew Schmit, Prin.; Stds.: 308; Lay Tchrs.: 26

FLINT

Christ the King Parish Flint - 1811 Seymour Ave., Flint, MI 48503 t) 810-233-0402 christthekingflint@gmail.com www.christthekingparishflint.org Rev. Thomas Firestone, Admin.;

Holy Rosary Parish Flint - 5199 Richfield Rd., Flint, MI 48506 t) 810-736-4040 holyrosaryflint@yahoo.com holyrosaryflint.com Rev. Roy Horning, Pst.; Kimberly Murawski, DRE; CRP Stds.: 83

Holy Rosary School - (Grades K-8) t) 810-736-4220 kkallas@holyrosarycatholic.com holyrosaryflint.org Karen West-Aiello, Prin.; Stds.: 83; Lay Tchrs.: 6

St. John Vianney Parish Flint - 2415 Bagley St., Flint, MI 48504-4613 t) 810-235-1812 stjohnvianney@flintcatholic.org www.flintcatholic.org Rev. Thomas Firestone, Pst.; Rev. Matthew Bonk, Par. Vicar; Dcn. Sean Costello; Dcn. Michael Dear; Dcn. Anthony Verdun; Rev. Anthony Smela, In Res.; CRP Stds.: 25

St. John Vianney School - (Grades PreK-8) 2319 Bagley St., Flint, MI 48504 t) 810-235-5687 stjohnvianney@sjvkids.org www.sjvkids.org Dr. Theresa Marshall, Prin.; Stds.: 165; Lay Tchrs.: 15

St. Mary Oratory - 2500 N. Franklin, Flint, MI 48506; Mailing: 2415 Bagley St, Flint, MI 48504 t) 810-232-4012

St. Matthew - 706 Beach St., Flint, MI 48502 t) 810-232-0880 www.flintcatholic.org/stmatthew Rev. Anthony J. Strouse, Pst.; CRP Stds.: 5

Our Lady of Guadalupe Parish Flint - G-2316 W. Coldwater Rd., Flint, MI 48505 t) 810-787-5701 ologflint@gmail.com Dcn. Michael Dear; Vikey Gonzalez, DRE; CRP Stds.: 25

St. Pius X Parish Flint - G-3139 Hogarth Ave., Flint, MI 48532 t) 810-235-8574 www.spxparish.com Rev. Anthony J. Strouse, Pst.; Dcn. Mark Danaho; Dcn. David Jansen; CRP Stds.: 11

FLUSHING

St. Robert Bellarmine Parish Flushing - 310 N. Cherry St., Flushing, MI 48433 t) 810-659-8556 (CRP); 810-659-2501 hturchi@strobertschool.com; jrymar@srbcatholic.com srbcatholic.com Rev. Jonathan P. Perrotta, Pst.; Dcn. Richard Rymar; Hannah Turchi, DRE; Rev. Prabhu Lakra, Par. Vicar; CRP Stds.: 122

St. Robert School - (Grades PreK-8) 214 E. Henry, Flushing, MI 48433 t) 810-659-2503 srsoffice@aol.com www.strobertschool.com Sarah Bushey, Prin.; Stds.: 208; Lay Tchrs.: 12

FOWLER

Most Holy Trinity Parish Fowler - 545 N. Maple St., Fowler, MI 48835 t) 989-593-2162 office@mhtparish.com www.mhtparish.com/ Rev. Eric C. Weber, Pst.; Rev. Peter Lawrence, P.V., Assoc. Pst.; Jordan Spitzley, Admin.; Aaron Epkey, DRE; Andrea Schneider, Parish Life Coord.; Chris Groves, Youth Min.; CRP Stds.: 207

Most Holy Trinity School - (Grades 1-8) 11144 Kent St., Fowler, MI 48835 t) 517-593-2616 principal@mhtparish.com Anne K. Hufnagel, Prin.; Stds.: 93; Lay Tchrs.: 5

FOWLERVILLE

St. Agnes Parish Fowlerville - 855 E. Grand River Ave., Fowlerville, MI 48836 t) 517-223-8684 msheridandre@gmail.com; stagnesfowlerville@sbcglobal.net www.stagnesmi.com Rev. Nathaniel J. Sokol, Pst.; Dcn. Roger Cahaney; Dcn. Peter Guditas; Marie Sheridan, DRE; CRP Stds.: 101

GRAND BLANC

Holy Family Parish Grand Blanc - 11804 S. Saginaw St., Grand Blanc, MI 48439 t) 810-694-4891 holyfamily@hfgb.org hfgb.org Rev. Joseph J. Krupp, Pst.; CRP Stds.: 83

Holy Family School - (Grades PreK-8) 215 Orchard St., Grand Blanc, MI 48439 t) 810-694-9072 info@hfsgb.org hfsgb.org Theresa Purcell, Prin.; Stds.: 434; Lay Tchrs.: 25

St. Mark the Evangelist Parish Grand Blanc - 7296 Gale Rd., Grand Blanc, MI 48439 t) 810-636-2216 sgriffith@stmarkgoodrich.org; rkenney@stmarkgoodrich.org www.stmarkgoodrich.org St. Mark the Evangelist is clustered with Holy Family Parish. Both are in Grand Blanc. Rev. Joseph Krupp, Pst.; Rev. David F. Howell, Sacr. Min.; Dcn. Ronald Kenney, DRE; CRP Stds.: 50

GRAND LEDGE

St. Michael Parish Grand Ledge - 345 Edwards St., Grand Ledge, MI 48837 t) 517-627-8493 (CRP); 517-627-8493 x11 terimarshall@stmichaelgl.org www.stmichaelgl.org/ Rev. James F. Eisele, Pst.; CRP Stds.: 68

St. Michael School - (Grades PreK-8) 325 Edwards St., Grand Ledge, MI 48837 t) 517-627-2167 nathansweet@stmichaelgl.org Nathan Sweet, Prin.; Stds.: 117; Lay Tchrs.: 7

HILLSDALE

St. Anthony Parish Hillsdale - 11 N. Broad St., Hillsdale, MI 49242 t) 517-437-3305 office@stanthonyhillsdale.com stanthonyhillsdale.com Rev. David M. Reamsnyder, Pst.; Amy Miller, DRE; CRP Stds.: 174

HOWELL

St. Augustine Parish Howell - 6481 Faussett Rd., Howell, MI 48855 t) 517-546-9807 st.augustinechurch@att.net (Quasi Parish) Rev. Gregg Pleiness, Pst.; Dcn. Jeffrey Southerland; Shannon Scherba, Pst. Assoc.; Timothy Asher, DRE; CRP Stds.: 59

St. John the Baptist Parish Howell - 2099 N. Hacker Rd., Howell, MI 48855 t) 517-546-7200 fgeorge@stjohnhowell.com; wburke@stjohnhowell.com www.stjohnhowell.com Rev. Francis M. George, Pst.; Dcn. David Piggot; Dcn. William Russell; Wendi Burke, DRE; CRP Stds.: 177

St. Joseph Parish Howell - 440 E. Washington St., Howell, MI 48843 t) 517-546-0090 x400 (CRP); 517-546-0090 michelle@stjosephhowell.org; jessicam@stjosephhowell.org www.stjosephhowell.com Rev. Gary K. Koenigsknecht, Pst.; Dcn. Endre Doran; Dcn. Ray Kunik; Dcn. Frank Wines Sr.; Timothy Carpenter, DRE; CRP Stds.: 136

St. Joseph Catholic School - (Grades PreK-8) 425 E. Washington St., Howell, MI 48843 t) (517) 546-0090 x200 school.stjosephhowell.com/ Sandra Ford, Prin.; Stds.: 57; Lay Tchrs.: 5

HUDSON

Sacred Heart Parish Hudson - 207 S. Market St., Hudson, MI 49247 t) 517-448-3811 info@sacredhearthudson.org www.sacredhearthudson.org Rev. Todd W. Koenigsknecht, Admin.; Dcn. John Amthor, DRE; CRP Stds.: 64

Sacred Heart School - (Grades PreK-6) 208 S. Market St., Hudson, MI 49247 t) 517-448-6405 aatkin@sacredhearthudson.org Anne Atkin, Prin.; Stds.: 93; Lay Tchrs.: 5

JACKSON

St. John the Evangelist Parish Jackson - 711 N. Martin Luther King Jr. Dr., Jackson, MI 49201 t) 517-784-0553 x7007 saintjohnjackson.org Rev. Charles Canoy, Pst.; Dcn. David Etters; Dcn. Albert Krieger; Dcn. Michael McCormick; Shayne Slough, Parish Life Coord.; Kathleen Blanchard, DRE; CRP Stds.: 173

St. John the Evangelist School - (Grades PreSchool-6) 405 E. North St., Jackson, MI 49202 t) 517-784-1714 sjsoffice@myjacs.org www.jcsstjohn.org/ Renee Hornby, Prin.; Stds.: 173; Lay Tchrs.: 14

St. Joseph the Worker - 705 N. Waterloo Ave., Jackson, MI 49202

St. Mary Star of the Sea Parish Jackson - 120 E. Wesley St., Jackson, MI 49201 t) 517-784-7184 stmaryjackson.com Rev. Timothy A. Nelson, Pst.; Rev. Tyler Lee Arens, Par. Vicar; Dcn. Matthew Shannon; Dcn. Carol Franssen; Bernice Haglund, DRE; CRP Stds.: 39

St. Mary Star of the Sea School - (Grades PreK-6) 116 E. Wesley St., Jackson, MI 49201 t) 517-784-8811 stmaryschool@myjacs.org Nancy O'Neill, Prin.; Stds.: 127; Lay Tchrs.: 9

St. Stanislaus Kosta Oratory - 608 S. Elm Ave., Jackson, MI 49203 t) 517-784-0551 ststanschapel@gmail.com

Queen of the Miraculous Medal Parish Jackson - 606 S. Wisner, Jackson, MI 49203 t) 517-783-2748 x1002; 517-783-2748 (CRP) jlienhart@queenschurch.com; bkoval@queenschurch.com queenschurch.com Rev. Timothy E. MacDonald, Pst.; Dcn. Patrick Gorczyca; Betsy Koval, DRE; CRP Stds.: 90

Queen of the Miraculous Medal School - (Grades K-6) 811 S. Wisner, Jackson, MI 49203 t) 517-782-2664 lhartley@myjacs.org Elizabeth Hartley, Prin.; Stds.: 256; Lay Tchrs.: 17

LAINGSBURG

St. Isidore Parish Laingsburg - 310 Crum St., Laingsburg, MI 48848 t) 517-651-6722 marystevens@stisidorechurch.org; office@stisidorechurch.org stisidorechurch.org/ Rev. Anthony Brooks, Pst.; Mary Stevens, DRE; CRP Stds.: 48

Holy Family - 510 N. Mabbit Rd., Ovid, MI 48866

LANSING

St. Mary Cathedral Lansing - 219 Seymour, Lansing, MI 48933 t) 517-484-5331 kpung@stmarylansing.org; mvillarreal@stmarylansing.org stmarylansing.org Rev. Karl L. Pung, Pst.; Dcn. Joseph Jong; Rev. William R. Lugger, In Res.; CRP Stds.: 20

St. Andrew Dung Lac Parish Lansing - 1611 W. Oakland Ave., Lansing, MI 48915 t) 517-580-7557 Rev. Joseph S. Kim, Pst.; Hang Pham, DRE; CRP Stds.: 30

Cristo Rey Parish Lansing - 201 W. Miller Rd., Lansing, MI 48911 t) 517-394-4639 olgadlt@cristoreychurch.org; silviam@cristoreychurch.org www.cristoreychurch.org Rev. Vincent Richardson, Admin.; Olga De La Torre, DRE; CRP Stds.: 84

St. Gerard Parish Lansing - 4437 W. Willow Hwy., Lansing, MI 48917 t) 517-323-2379 stgerard.org Rev. Robert Crowley Bacik, Pst.; Rev. Mark Martin, Par. Vicar; Dcn. Jim Corder; Dcn. Phil Guyeskey; Kathy Warriner, DRE; CRP Stds.: 250

St. Gerard School - (Grades PreK-8) 4433 W. Willow Hwy., Lansing, MI 48917 t) 517-321-6126 kmarshall@stgerardlansing.org stgerardlansing.org Karen Marshall, Prin.; Stds.: 417; Lay Tchrs.: 30

Immaculate Heart of Mary Parish Lansing - 3815 S. Cedar, Lansing, MI 48910 t) 517-393-3030 dowsettm@ihmlansing.org; marshb@ihmlansing.org www.ihmlansing.org Rev. James R. Rolph, Pst.; Dcn. John M. Cameron; Rev. George R. Daisy, In Res.; Mary Dowsett, DRE; CRP Stds.: 34

Immaculate Heart of Mary School - (Grades PreK-8) 3830 Rosemont St., Lansing, MI 48910-4525 t) 517-882-6631 wilcoxc@ihmlansing.org Michael Olds, Prin.; Stds.: 110; Lay Tchrs.: 8

Resurrection Parish Lansing - 1505 E. Michigan Ave., Lansing, MI 48912; Mailing: 1514 E. Michigan Ave., Lansing, MI 48912-2221 t) 517-482-4749; 517-482-4749 x120 (CRP) www.corlansing.org Rev. Steven M. Mattson, Pst.; Debbie McPherson, Faith Formation/ Sacraments; Liz O'Neill, Coord. Healing & Women's Ministry; Sean O'Neill, Dir. Outreach Formation & Ministry; CRP Stds.: 40

Resurrection School - (Grades PreK-8) 1527 E. Michigan Ave., Lansing, MI 48912 t) 517-487-0439 jallstott@corlansing.org www.corlansing.org/ Jacob Allstott, Prin.; Stds.: 199; Sr. Tchrs.: 2; Lay Tchrs.: 9

St. Therese Parish Lansing - 102 W. Randolph St., Lansing, MI 48906 t) 517-487-3730 (CRP); 517-487-3749 secretary@sttherese.org; ssmithdre@gmail.com www.sttherese.org Rev. John M. Fain, Pst.; Stephanie Smith, DRE; Dcn. David Borzenski; CRP Stds.: 41

MANCHESTER

St. Mary Parish Manchester - 210 W. Main St., Manchester, MI 48158; Mailing: P.O. Box 249, Manchester, MI 48158-0249 t) 734-428-8811 stmarymanchester@gmail.com stmarymanchester.org Rev. Bosco Padamattummal (India), Admin.; Dcn. Dennis Walters; CRP Stds.: 15

MANITOU BEACH

St. Mary on the Lake Parish Manitou Beach - 450 Manitou Rd., Manitou Beach, MI 49253 t) 517-547-7496 ssinkovitz@saintmarymanitoubeach.org www.saintmarymanitoubeach.org/ Rev. Todd W. Koenigsknecht, Pst.; Dcn. John Amthor, DRE; CRP Stds.: 18

MASON

St. James Parish Mason - 1010 S. Lansing St., Mason, MI 48854 t) 517-676-9111 saintsjcc.org Rev. Kusitino Cobona, Pst.; Dcn. Chuong Nguyen; Dcn. Albert Turkovich; Maureen Stockwell, DRE; CRP Stds.: 103

SS. Cornelius and Cyprian Oratory - 1320 Catholic Church Rd., Leslie, MI 49251; Mailing: 1010 S. Lansing St., Catholic Community of Ss. James, Cornelius and Cyprian, Mason, MI 48854 Bonnie Sweet, Bus. Mgr.;

MICHIGAN CENTER

Our Lady of Fatima Parish Michigan Center - 913 Napoleon Rd., Michigan Center, MI 49254 t) 517-764-2088 (CRP); 517-764-1321 linda@fatimaparish.net www.fatimaparish.net Rev. Satheesh C. Alphonse, S.D.C., Pst.; CRP Stds.: 66

MILAN

Immaculate Conception Parish Milan - 420 North St., Milan, MI 48160 t) 734-439-2030 valeriew@live.com; iccmilanparishoffice@gmail.com www.iccmilan.com Rev. Vincent VanDoan, Pst.; Dcn. John Flanagan; Valerie Wilson, DRE; CRP Stds.: 43

MONTROSE

Good Shepherd Parish Montrose - 400 N. Saginaw, Montrose, MI 48457-0974; Mailing: P.O. Box 3274, Montrose, MI 48457-0974 t) 810-639-7600 goodshepherdofmontrose@gmail.com www.goodshepherdmontrose.org Rev. Jonathan P. Perrotta, Pst.; Rev. Prabhu Lakra, Par. Vicar; Dcn. Bryan Root; Jacqueline Danaho, DRE; CRP Stds.: 49

MORRICE

St. Mary Parish Morrice - 509 N. Main St., Morrice, MI 48857; Mailing: P.O. Box 310, Morrice, MI 48857 t) 517-625-4260 lnebo115@gmail.com; cgarrison4118@gmail.com www.stmarymorrice.org Rev. Msgr. George C. Michalek, Pst.; Susan Baldwin, DRE; CRP Stds.: 38

MOUNT MORRIS

St. Mary Parish Mt. Morris - 11110 Saginaw St., Mount Morris, MI 48458 t) 810-686-3920 stmarymountmorris@gmail.com stmarymountmorris.org Rev. Roy Theodore Horning, Pst.;

OKEMOS

St. Martha Parish Okemos - 1100 W. Grand River Ave., Okemos, MI 48864 t) 517-349-1763 jrosalez@st-martha.org; ilolson@st-martha.org www.st-martha.org Rev. Michael A. Murray, Pst.; Dcn. Carl Boehlert; Rev. John J. Whitlock, In Res.; Donald Morgan, Bus. Mgr.; IvyLynn Olson, Admin. Asst; Marriage Prep Coord.; Hallie Card, Dir. Discipleship; Jackie Rosalez, DRE; Tony Andorfer, Liturgy Dir.; Joey DiMenno, Children's Choir Dir.; Claudia Fountain, Youth Min.; Sr. Pat Newhouse, S.C., Senior Ministry Coord.; CRP Stds.: 124

St. Martha School - (Grades PreK-8) t) 517-349-3322 Andrea Patton, Prin.; Stds.: 120; Lay Tchrs.: 14

OTISVILLE

St. Francis Xavier Parish Otisville - 212 Center St., Otisville, MI 48463 t) 810-631-6305; 810-686-9861; 810-631-8306 office212.sfx@gmail.com; parish@sscharlesandhelena.org www.sfxotisville.org Rev. Kenneth F. Coughlin, Pst.; Grace Guzowski, DRE; CRP Stds.: 19

OWOSSO

St. Paul Parish Owosso - 111 N. Howell St., Owosso, MI 48867 t) 989-723-4277; 989-723-4765 (CRP) secretary@stpaulowosso.org; religioused@stpaulowosso.org www.stpaulowosso.org Rev. Michael O'Brien, Pst.; Dcn. Gary Edington; CRP Stds.: 42

St. Paul School - (Grades K-8) 811 E. Oliver St., Owosso, MI 48867 t) 989-725-7766 stpaulschool@spsowosso.org www.spsowosso.org Laura Heatwole, Prin.; Stds.: 38; Lay Tchrs.: 3

St. Joseph Oratory - 915 E. Oliver St., Owosso, MI 48867 t) 989-725-5215 St. Joseph Church merged with and became an Oratory, July 1, 2018, with St. Paul Church, Owosso

PINCKNEY

St. Mary Parish Pinckney - 10601 Dexter-Pinckney Rd., Pinckney, MI 48169 t) 734-878-5616 (CRP); 734-878-3161 mrskinsey@stmarypinckney.org; info@stmarypinckney.org www.stmarypinckney.org Rev. Daniel J. Kogut, Pst.; Dcn. Randy Coffelt; Dcn. Daniel Hall; Dcn. Tom Rea; Dcn. Kevin Wiley; CRP Stds.: 63

St. Mary School - (Grades PreK-8) t) (734) 878-5616 mrskinsey@stmarypinckey.org www.stmarypinckney.org/school Stds.: 150; Lay Tchrs.: 11

SALINE

St. Andrew Parish Saline - 910 Austin Dr., Saline, MI 48176 t) 734-429-5210 k-8@standrewsaline.org; office@standrewsaline.org www.standrewsaline.org Rev. John A. Linden, Pst.; Dcn. Douglas Cummings; Dcn. Gordon Prepsky; Janet Cook, DRE; CRP Stds.: 288

ST. JOHNS

St. Joseph Parish St. Johns - 109 Linden St., St. Johns, MI 48879 t) 989-224-8537 (CRP); 989-224-8994 dre.stjoseph@gmail.com; stjosephchurchstjohns@gmail.com www.stjoecatholic.com/ Rev. Michael J. Williams, Pst.; Dcn. Eric Elstro; Dcn. Gerald Fust; Dcn. Marvin Robertson; Jennifer Nelson, DRE; CRP Stds.: 83

St. Joseph School - (Grades K-6) 201 E. Cass St., Saint Johns, MI 48879 t) 989-224-2421 principal@stjoecatholicschool.org www.stjoecatholic.com Christopher O. Wells, Prin.; Stds.: 218; Lay Tchrs.: 12

SWARTZ CREEK

St. Mary Queen of Angels Parish Swartz Creek - 4413 Morrish Rd., Swartz Creek, MI 48473 t) 810-635-3240 vstandley@smqa.net; info@smqa.net www.smqa.net Rev. Louis T. Ekka (India), Pst.; Valerie Standley, DRE; CRP Stds.: 41

TECUMSEH

St. Elizabeth Parish Tecumseh - 506 N. Union St., Tecumseh, MI 49286 t) 517-423-2447 steliz50@aol.com www.stelizabethstdominic.org/ Rev. Daniel F. Wheeler, Pst.; Dcn. Ray Pizana; Dcn. David Hammer; Heather Marsh, DRE; CRP Stds.: 87

St. Dominic Oratory - (Clinton)

WESTPHALIA

St. Mary Parish Westphalia - 201 N. Westphalia St., Westphalia, MI 48894; Mailing: PO Box 267, Westphalia, MI 48894 t) 989-587-4201 office@stmarychurch.net; jltrierweiler@stmarychurch.net www.stmarychurch.net Rev. Eric C. Weber, Pst.; Rev. Peter Lawrence, P.V., Assoc. Pst.; Dcn. Chuck Thelen; CRP Stds.: 521

St. Mary School - (Grades K-6) 209 N. Westphalia St., Westphalia, MI 48894; Mailing: P.O. Box 270, Westphalia, MI 48894 t) 989-587-3702 principal@stmaryschool.us Helen Hengesbach, Prin.; Stds.: 321; Lay Tchrs.: 16

WILLIAMSTON

St. Mary Parish Williamston - 157 High St., Williamston, MI 48895 t) 517-655-2620 smwilliamston@gmail.com stmarywilliamston.org Rev. David Michael Fons, Pst.; Dcn. Stephen Hilker, Bus. Mgr.; CRP Stds.: 180

St. Mary School - (Grades PreK-8) 220 N. Cedar St., Williamston, MI 48895 t) 517-655-4038 stmarywilliamston.rj@gmail.com; stmarys@wowway.biz R. J. Lomas, Prin.; Stds.: 137; Lay Tchrs.: 10

YPSILANTI

St. John the Baptist Parish Ypsilanti - 411 Florence St., Ypsilanti, MI 48197 t) 734-483-3360 info@ypsicatholic.org www.ypsicatholic.org Rev. Daniel J. Westermann, Pst.; Dcn. Wayne Charlton; Dcn. Mark Millage; Dcn. Curtis Scholl; CRP Stds.: 62

St. Joseph Parish Ypsilanti - 9425 Whittaker Rd., Ypsilanti, MI 48197 t) 734-461-6555 annan@stjosephypsilanti.com; office@stjosephypsilanti.com stjosephypsilanti.com Rev. Pieter vanRooyen, Pst.; Dcn. Stanley Kukla; Dcn. Gary Perrydore; Anna Nowaczewski, DRE; Nathan Everts, Bus. Mgr.; CRP Stds.: 115

SCHOOLS: PRESCHOOL THRU HIGH SCHOOL

SCHOOLS

STATE OF MICHIGAN

ANN ARBOR

***Spiritus Sanctus Academy** - (PRV) (Grades PreK-8) 4101 E. Joy Rd., Ann Arbor, MI 48105 t) 734-996-3855 annarbor@spiritussanctus.org www.spiritussanctus.org Independent Catholic School owned and administered by the Dominican Sisters of Mary, Mother of the Eucharist Stds.: 181; Sr. Tchrs.: 6; Lay Tchrs.: 6

BURTON

St. Thomas More Academy - (PRV) (Grades K-12) 6456 E. Bristol Rd., Burton, MI 48519 t) 810-742-2411; 810-742-5906 k12.stma@gmail.com stma-mi.org Douglas A Weisbrod, Prin.; Stds.: 96; Lay Tchrs.: 11

JACKSON

Jackson Catholic Schools - 3483 Spring Arbor Rd., Jackson, MI 49203 t) (517) 841-9203 jacksoncatholicschools.org Stephanie Kristovic, Provost, Chief Acad. Officer;

PLYMOUTH

***Spiritus Sanctus Academy** - (PRV) (Grades K-8) 10450 Joy Rd., Plymouth, MI 48170 t) 734-414-8430 srmariafaustina@spiritussanctus.org; larena@spiritussanctus.org www.spiritussanctus.org Sr. Maria Faustina, O.P., Prin.; Stds.: 192; Sr. Tchrs.: 4; Lay Tchrs.: 8

YPSILANTI

***HVS Corp. (Huron Valley Catholic School)** - (PRV) (Grades PreK-8) 1300 N. Prospect Rd., Ypsilanti, MI 48198-3093 t) 734-483-0366 khall@hvcatholicschool.org; msmith@hvcatholicschool.org www.huronvalleycatholicschool.org Michael Smith, Prin.; Becky Tepen, Bus. Mgr.; Stds.: 240; Lay Tchrs.: 12

HIGH SCHOOLS

STATE OF MICHIGAN

ANN ARBOR

Father Gabriel Richard High School - (DIO) (Grades 9-12) 4333 Whitehall Dr., Ann Arbor, MI 48105 t) 734-662-0496 communications@fgrhs.org www.fgrhs.org Regional High School serving Washtenaw, western Wayne, and Livingston Counties Rev. Ryan L. Riley, Chap.; Christopher Dotson, Prin.; Joe Jordano, Pres.; Stds.: 477; Sr. Tchrs.: 5; Lay Tchrs.: 36

FLINT

Powers Catholic High School - (DIO) (Grades 9-12) 1505 W. Court St., Flint, MI 48503 t) 810-591-4741 bsheeran@powerscatholic.org www.powerscatholic.org Rev. Anthony Smela, Pst. Min./Coord.; Brian Sheeran, Prin.; Stds.: 588; Pr. Tchrs.: 1; Lay Tchrs.: 27

JACKSON

Lumen Christi Catholic School - (DIO) (Grades 7-12) 3483 Spring Arbor Rd., Jackson, MI 49203 t) 517-787-0630 lcadv@myjacs.org www.jcslumenchristi.org Rev. Brian Lenz, P.V., Chap.; Timothy Dewitt, Pres.; Stds.: 432; Lay Tchrs.: 43

LANSING

Lansing Catholic High School - (DIO) (Grades 9-12) 501 Marshall St., Lansing, MI 48912 t) 517-267-2100 dominic.iocco@lansingcatholic.org www.lansingcatholic.org Rev. Joseph Campbell, Chap.; Dominic Iocco, Pres.; Stds.: 430; Sr. Tchrs.: 3; Lay Tchrs.: 32

INSTITUTIONS LOCATED IN DIOCESE

ASSOCIATIONS [ASN]

LANSING

Catholic Lay Association of the Holy Spirit Oratory - 3815 S. Cedar St., Lansing, MI 48910 t) 517-393-3030 frjbyers@ihmlansing.org Rev. John Byers, Chap.;

CAMPUS MINISTRY / NEWMAN CENTERS [CAM]

ADRIAN

Siena Heights University - 1247 E. Siena Heights Dr., Adrian, MI 49221 t) 517-264-7192 tpuszcze@sienaheights.edu www.sienaheights.edu Kateri Sullivan Golbiw, Campus Min.; Tom Puszczewicz, Campus Min.; Sr. Mary Jones OP, Dir. Mission & Ministry;

ANN ARBOR

St. Mary Student Parish - 331 Thompson St., Ann Arbor, MI 48104-2295 t) 734-663-0557 stmarys@umich.edu www.stmarystudentparish.org Serving the University of Michigan. Rev. James Gartland, SJ, Pst.; Rev. Joseph F. Wagner, S.J., Campus Min.; Rev. Patrick Casey, S.J., Pst. Assoc.; Rev. Robert Karle, Pst. Assoc.; Rev. Kyle Shinseki, Pst. Assoc.;

CATHOLIC CHARITIES [CCH]

ANN ARBOR

Catholic Charities of Michigan - 4925 Packard St., Ann Arbor, MI 48108 t) 734-223-1844 ceo@catholiccharities-mi.org www.catholiccharities-mi.org Outpatient Mental Health and Addiction Services. Roberto M. Javier, CEO; Asstd. Annu.: 9,000; Staff: 3

Catholic Social Services of Washtenaw County - 4925 Packard St., Ann Arbor, MI 48108 t) 734-971-9781 marketing@csswashtenaw.org; pbravo@csswashtenaw.org www.csswashtenaw.org Peg Bravo, Pres.; Asstd. Annu.: 6,400; Staff: 69

FLINT

Catholic Charities of Shiawassee and Genesee Counties - 901 Chippewa St., Flint, MI 48503 t) (810) 232-9950 kbaxter@ccsgc.org www.ccsgc.org Services available: Counseling, Adoption, Foster Care, Prevention, Housing, Soup Kitchens, Community Closets, St. Christopher Medical Transport. Katherine Baxter, CEO; Asstd. Annu.: 228,650; Staff: 118

HOWELL

Livingston County Catholic Charities - 2020 E. Grand River Ave., Ste. 104, Howell, MI 48843 t) 517-545-5944 mark@livingstoncc.org www.livingstoncc.org Mark T. Robinson, Exec.; Asstd. Annu.: 3,100; Staff: 45

JACKSON

Catholic Charities of Jackson, Lenawee & Hillsdale Counties - 3425 Francis St., Jackson, MI 49203 t) 517-263-2191; 517-782-2551 slewis@catholiccharitiesjlhc.org www.catholiccharitiesjlhc.org Sue Lewis, Exec.; Asstd. Annu.: 18,251; Staff: 71

LANSING

***Cristo Rey Community Center** - 1717 N. High St., Lansing, MI 48906 t) 517-372-4700 jgarcia@cristoreycommunity.org; jgardner@cristoreycommunity.org www.cristoreycommunity.org Joseph Garcia, Exec.; Asstd. Annu.: 77,730; Staff: 47

***Cristo Rey Family Health Center** - t) 517-371-1700

St. Vincent Catholic Charities - 2800 W. Willow, Lansing, MI 48917 t) 517-323-4734 www.stvcc.org Andrea Boruta, CFO; Asstd. Annu.: 420; Staff: 70

Adoption - cooperd@stvcc.org

Counseling Services - carrerj@stvcc.org

Foster Care - cooperd@stvcc.org Includes case management and licensing

Immigration Law Clinic - glennol@stvcc.org

Refugee Resettlement - harrisj@stvcc.org Includes Reception, Placement, Health & Employment

CEMETERIES [CEM]

FLINT

St. Michael Byzantine - Groveland Ave., Flint, MI 48505 t) 810-732-2620 bepkey@dioceseoflansing.org Brian Epkey, Dir.;

New Calvary - 4142 Flushing Rd., Flint, MI 48504 t) 810-732-2620 bepkey@dioceseoflansing.org Brian Epkey, Dir.;

Old Calvary - Ballenger Hwy., Flint, MI 48504 t) 810-732-2620 bepkey@dioceseoflansing.org Brian Epkey, Dir.;

LAINGSBURG

St. Patrick - Shiawassee St., Laingsburg, MI 48848 t) 517-651-5374 bepkey@dioceseoflansing.org Brian Epkey, Dir.;

LANSING

St. Joseph - 2520 W. Willow St., Lansing, MI 48917 t) 517-484-2500 bepkey@dioceseoflansing.org Brian Epkey, Dir.;

COLLEGES & UNIVERSITIES [COL]

ADRIAN

Siena Heights University - 1247 E. Siena Heights Dr., Adrian, MI 49221-1796 t) 517-264-7100 kbarnes3@sienaheights.edu www.sienaheights.edu Sponsored by the Adrian Dominican Sisters. Sr. Peg Albert, O.P., Pres.; Stds.: 1,856; Lay Tchrs.: 86; Sr. Tchrs.: 2

CONVENTS, MONASTERIES, AND RESIDENCES FOR WOMEN [CON]

ADRIAN

Adrian Dominican Office of Development (Adrian Dominican Sisters) - 1257 E. Siena Heights. Dr., Adrian, MI 49221-1793 t) 517-266-3480 development@adriandominicans.org www.adriandominicans.org Amy Palmer, Dir.; Srs.: 265

Adrian Dominican Sisters, Inc. - 1257 E. Siena Heights Dr., Adrian, MI 49221

Motherhouse of the Sisters of St. Dominic, Congregation of the Most Holy Rosary - 1257 E. Siena Heights Dr., Adrian, MI 49221-1793 t) 517-266-3400 info@adriandominicans.org adriandominicans.org/ Sr. Elise Daniele Garcia, Prioress; Rev. James Hug, S.J., Chap.; Srs.: 265

Dominican Life Center - 1277 E. Siena Heights Dr., Adrian, MI 49221-1755 t) 517-266-3650 cpickney@adriandominicans.org Cheryl Pickney, Admin.;

ANN ARBOR

Dominican Sisters of Mary, Mother of the Eucharist - 4597 Warren Rd., Ann Arbor, MI 48105 t) 734-994-7437 secretary@sistersofmary.org www.sistersofmary.org Mother Amata Veritas Ellenbecker, OP, Prioress; Srs.: 148

Dominican SMME Corporation - 4597 Warren Rd., Ann Arbor, MI 48105 t) 734-994-7437 secretary@sistersofmary.org Mother Amata Veritas Ellenbecker, OP, Pres.; Srs.: 148

***Servants of God's Love** - 4399 Ford Rd., Ann Arbor, MI 48105 t) 734-663-6128 srsarahb@gmail.com www.servantsofgodslove.net/ Sr. Sarah Burdick, Supr.; Srs.: 17

DE WITT

St. Albert the Great Convent - 217 Schavey Rd., De Witt, MI 48820 t) 517-669-2277 saintalbertdewitt@gmail.com rsmofalma.org Sr. Mary Rafqa, Supr.; Srs.: 7

LANSING

Congregation of the Passion - St. Therese Convent, 109 E. Randolph, Lansing, MI 48906-4042 t) (517) 974-3310 mavialfaro@hotmail.com Sr. Marcella Oloarte, Prioress; Srs.: 2

ENDOWMENTS / FOUNDATIONS / TRUSTS [EFT]

ANN ARBOR

The Sister Mary Richard Rhea Foundation - 1257 E. Siena Heights Dr., Ann Arbor, MI 49221

LANSING

The Catholic Foundation of the Diocese of Lansing - 101 S. Washington Sq., Ste. 620, Lansing, MI 48933 t) 517-253-8787 mhufnagel@dioceseoflansing.org Matthew Hufnagel, Pres.;

Parish Savings & Loan Trust - 228 N.Walnut St., Lansing, MI 48933 t) 517-342-2445 George Landolt, Admin.;

HOSPITALS / HEALTH SERVICES [HOS]

ANN ARBOR

Catherine McAuley Health Services Corporation - 5305 E. Huron River Dr., Ann Arbor, MI 48106; Mailing: P.O. Box 992, Ann Arbor, MI 48106 t) 734-712-3791 www.stjoeshealth.org (Subsidiary of Trinity Health), Health Care Center, Ancillary Care Systems: (Primary Care Physician Practices) Robert Casalou, CEO;

St. Joseph Mercy Hospital - 5301 E. Huron River Dr., Admin. Ste., Ann Arbor, MI 48106 t) 734-712-4307 david.nantais@trinity-health.org Alonzo Lewis, Pres.; David Nantais, Mission Leader; Bed Capacity: 548; Asstd. Annu.: 862,298; Staff: 5,856

CHELSEA

Saint Joseph Mercy Chelsea, Inc. - 775 S. Main St., Chelsea, MI 48118 t) 734-398-0628 david.nantais@trinity-health.org (A Member of Trinity Health) David Nantais, Admin.; Bed Capacity: 133; Asstd. Annu.: 139,738; Staff: 1,455

GRAND BLANC

Ascension Genesys Hospital - 1 Genesys Pkwy., Grand Blanc, MI 48439 t) 810-606-5000 paula.caruso@ascension.org healthcare.ascension.org A member of Ascension Michigan Christopher McClead, Contact; Bed Capacity: 412; Asstd. Annu.: 216,649; Staff: 2,203

Genesys Ambulatory Health Services, Inc. - 5445 Ali Dr., Grand Blanc, MI 48439-5193 t) 810-603-8686 paula.caruso@ascension.org genesys.org An affiliate of Genesys Health System, Provides private duty home care services and manages shared services. Christopher McClead, Contact; Staff: 1

PACE - Program of All Inclusive for the Elderly - 412 E. First St., Flint, MI 48503 t) (810) 236-7500 annette.sivertson@ascension.org Annete Siverston, Dir.;

Genesys Health System - 1 Genesys Pkwy., Grand Blanc, MI 48439 t) 810-603-8686 paula.caruso@ascension.org ascension.org Christopher McClead, Contact;

HOWELL

Saint Joseph Mercy Livingston Hospital - 620 Byron Rd., Howell, MI 48843-1093 t) 517-545-6000 jessica.gobbo@stjoeshealth.org; david.nantais@stjoeshealth.org trinity-health.org/ stjoeshealth.org (A member of Trinity Health) David Nantais, Admin.; John O'Malley, Pres.; Bed Capacity: 66; Asstd. Annu.: 215,194; Staff: 1,121

MISCELLANEOUS [MIS]

ADRIAN

Adrian Dominican Montessori Teacher Education Institute - 1257 E. Siena Heights Dr., Adrian, MI 49221 t) 517-266-3415 info@admtei.org www.admtei.org Sr. Leonor J. Esnard, O.P., Dir.;

Adrian Rea Literacy Center - 1257 E. Siena Heights Dr., Adrian, MI 49221-1793 t) 517-264-7320 cmaly@adriandominicans.org Sr. Carleen Maly, O.P., Dir.;

ANN ARBOR

Catholic Men's Movement - 1 Ave Maria Dr., Ann Arbor, MI 48106; Mailing: P.O. Box 466, Ann Arbor, MI 48106 t) 734-930-4524 cmmdesk@gmail.com www.catholic-men.org Bob Roleke, Admin.; Peter Ziolkowski, Dir.;

Education in Virtue - 4597 Warren Rd., Ann Arbor, MI 48105; Mailing: 4101 E. Joy Rd., Ann Arbor, MI 48105 t) 734-996-4245 sjdr@educationinvirtue.com educationinvirtue.com Sr. John Dominic Rasmussen, O.P., Pres.;

Lumen Ecclesiae Press - 4597 Warren Rd., Ann Arbor, MI 48105; Mailing: 4101 E. Joy, Ann Arbor, MI 48105 t) 734-996-4245 sjdr@sistersofmary.org Sr. John Dominic Rasmussen, OP, Dir.;

The Marnee and John DeVine Foundation - 4925 Packard, Ann Arbor, MI 48108 t) 734-971-9781 development@csswashtenaw.org; janw@csswashtenaw.org www.csswashtenaw.org Philanthropic arm of Catholic Social Services of Washtenaw County. Jan Wisniewski, Contact;

Renewal Ministries Inc. - 24 Frank Lloyd Wright Dr., Ste. L-2000, Ann Arbor, MI 48105; Mailing: P.O. Box 491, Ann Arbor, MI 48106-0491 t) 734-662-1730 gseromik@renewalministries.net www.renewalministries.net Dedicated to Catholic Renewal and Evangelization Ralph Martin, Pres.;

BROOKLYN

***Holley Family Village, Inc.** - 1142 DeSales Dr., Brooklyn, MI 49230

FENTON

Alma Redemptoris Mater - 7381 Turner Rd., Fenton, MI 48430 t) 810-397-4657 tmf734@netzero.com Bro. Gary Pearce; Rev. Thomas Firestone, Contact;

FLINT

St. Luke N.E.W. Life Center - 3115 Lawndale Ave., Flint, MI 48504 t) 810-239-8710 mmotley@stlukenewlifecenter.com Sr. Judith Blake, Dir.; Sr. Carol Weber, Dir.;

FLUSHING

Mt. Zion Catholic Community - 8228 N. McKinley Rd., Flushing, MI 48433 t) 810-639-7175 mtzion@centurytel.net www.mtzioncatholiccommunity.com Pastoral Center. Salvador Barba, Dir.;

Residence - 8236 N. McKinley Rd., Flushing, MI 48433 t) 810-639-5262

GRASS LAKE

The Pious Union of St. Joseph - 953 E. Michigan Ave., Grass Lake, MI 49240-9210 t) 517-522-8017 piousunion@pusj.org www.piousunionofstjoseph.org Rev. Leo Joseph Xavier, S.D.C., Admin.; Rev. Satheesh C. Alphonse, S.D.C.;

Now and at the Hour Magazine - pusj.org

JACKSON

Sacred Heart Chapel - 608 Elm Ave., Jackson, MI 49203 t) 517-783-2772 sacred.heart32@gmail.com Sr. Clareth Chavarrio Porras, C.F.P., Pst. Assoc.; Angeline V. Medina, Treas.;

LANSING

Catholic Lawyers Guild - 228 N. Walnut St., Lansing, MI 48933 t) 517-402-1562 lclguild@gmail.com www.lansingcatholiclawyersguild.com Diane Arzberger, Exec.;

Chancery Office - 300 W. Ottawa, Lansing, MI 48933 t) 517-342-2440

Blessed Sacrament Educational Trust Fund - 228 N. Walnut, Lansing, MI 48933 t) 810-742-3151 (Blessed Sacrament Parish, Burton)

Church of the Resurrection Educational Trust Fund (Church of the Resurrection, Lansing) - t) 517-482-4749

Father Al Miller Educational Trust Fund (St. Mary Parish, Westphalia) - t) 517-587-4201

Father Gabriel Richard High School Trust Fund (Fr. Gabriel Richard H.S., Ann Arbor) - t) 734-662-0496

St. Francis of Assisi Educational Trust Fund (St. Francis of Assisi Parish, Ann Arbor) - t) 734-821-2200

St. Gerard Educational Trust Fund (St. Gerard Parish, Lansing) - t) 517-323-2379

Holy Redeemer Educational Trust Fund (Holy Redeemer Parish, Burton) - t) 810-743-3050

Immaculate Heart of Mary St. Casimir School Mary Goeddeke Educational Trust Fund - t) 517-882-6631 (IHM-St. Casimir School, Lansing)

St John School Educational Foundation, Inc. (St. John Parish, Fenton) - t) 810-629-2251

St. John the Evangelist Parish Educational Trust Fund (St. John the Evangelist Parish, Jackson) - t) 517-784-0553

St. John Vianney Educational Trust Fund (St. John Vianney Parish, Flint) - t) 810-235-1812

St. Joseph Church of Howell Trust Fund (St. Joseph Church, Howell) - t) 517-546-0090

St. Joseph Educational Trust Fund (St. Joseph Church, Owosso) - t) 517-725-5215

St. Joseph Educational Trust Fund (St. Joseph Church, St. Johns) - t) 517-224-8994

St. Louis Center for Exceptional Children & Adults Endowment Trust Agreement - t) 734-475-8430 (St. Louis Center, Chelsea)

Luke M. Powers Educational Trust Fund (Flint) - t) 810-591-4741

Lumen Christi High School Endowment Fund (Lumen Christi H.S., Jackson) - t) 517-787-0630

St. Mary Parish Educational Trust Fund (St. Mary Parish, Charlotte) - t) 517-543-4319

St. Mary Star of the Sea Educational Trust Fund (St. Mary Star of the Sea Parish, Jackson) - t) 517-784-7184

St. Michael's School Endowment Fund Policy (St. Michael School, Grand Ledge) - t) 517-627-2167

Most Holy Trinity Educational Trust Fund (Most Holy Trinity Church, Fowler) - t) 517-593-2616

Msgr. Lawrence H. Soest Educational Trust Fund (St. Mary Parish, Flint) - t) 810-232-4012

St. Patrick Parish Educational Trust Fund (St. Patrick Parish, Brighton) - t) 810-229-9863

St. Paul's School Education Trust Fund (St. Paul Parish, Owosso) - t) 517-723-4277

St. Pius X Church Educational Trust Fund (St. Pius X Church, Flint) - t) 810-235-8574

Rev. Joseph R. Robb Educational Trust Fund (Holy Rosary Parish, Flint) - t) 810-736-4040

St. Robert Bellarmine/Fr. Charles Jacobs Educational Trust Fund (St. Robert Bellarmine Parish, Flushing) - t) 810-659-2501

Sacred Heart Educational Fund (Sacred Heart Parish, Hudson) - 300 W. Ottawa, Lansing, MI 49247;

Mailing: 207 S. Market St., hudson, MI 49247 t) 517-448-3811 sacredhearthudson.org Rev. Todd W. Koenigsknecht, Pst.;

St. Thomas Scholarship Trust for Father Gabriel Richard H.S. - 517 Elizabeth St., Ann Arbor, MI 48104 t) 734-769-0911 (St. Thomas the Apostle Parish, Ann Arbor)

St. Therese Educational Trust Fund (St. Therese Parish, Lansing) - t) 517-487-3749

St. Thomas Aquinas Educational Foundation Trust (St. Thomas Aquinas Parish, East Lansing) - t) 517-351-7215

St. Thomas Grade School Trust Agreement (St. Thomas the Apostle Parish, Ann Arbor) - t) 734-761-8606

Charismatic Renewal Diocesan Service Committee - 835 Maycroft Rd., Lansing, MI 48917 t) 517-256-7223 rstamford@hotmail.com (Catholic Charismatic Renewal) Rev. Benjamin B. Hawley, S.J.; Connie McClanahan, Secy.; Ralph Stamford, Treas.;

FAITH Catholic - 1500 E. Saginaw St., Lansing, MI 48906 t) 517-853-7600 esolsburg@faithcatholic.com www.faithcatholic.com Publisher of Catholic magazines Elizabeth Solsburg, Pres./CEO; Kris Conley, Controller;

FAITH Magazine - Rev. Dwight M. Ezop, Editor;

Mass Times Trust - t) 517-853-7610 masstimes.org

St. Gregory the Great Community - 3020 S. Washington Ave, Lansing, MI 48910 t) 517-574-4921 fr@gregorythegreat.com www.gregorythegreat.com Rev. Jeffrey Robideau, Chap.;

Michigan Catholic Conference - 510 S. Capitol Ave., Lansing, MI 48933 t) 517-372-9310 plong@micatholic.org www.micatholic.org Paul A. Long, Pres.;

***Mother Teresa House for the Care of the Terminally Ill** - 308 N. Walnut St., Lansing, MI 48933; Mailing: PO Box 13004, Lansing, MI 48901 t) 517-484-5494 info@motherteresahouse.org motherteresahouse.org Karen Bussey, Dir.;

MONASTERIES AND RESIDENCES FOR PRIESTS AND BROTHERS [MON]

ANN ARBOR

USA Midwest Province of the Society of Jesus - Jesuit Residence - 1919 Wayne St., Ann Arbor, MI 48104 t) 734-663-0557 a2jesuits@gmail.com Rev. Joseph F. Wagner, S.J., Supr.; Rev. Richard Baumann, S.J., In Res.; Rev. Patrick Casey, S.J., In Res.; Rev. James Gartland, SJ; Rev. Robert Karle, In Res.; Rev. Kyle Shinseki, In Res.; Priests: 6

BROOKLYN

Oblate Fathers of St. Francis De Sales, Inc. - 1198 DeSales Dr., Brooklyn, MI 49230 t) 517-592-2074 c) 517-414-0784 mckenna@oblates.us; jloughran@oblates.us www.oblates.us Owners of Camp DeSales, Site of North American Oblate novitiate. Rev. John Loughran, OSFS, Prov.; Rev. Kenneth N. McKenna, O.S.F.S., Treas.; Priests: 8

Thorrez Vocational Trust, Ltd. - t) 517-592-8218 mcintire@oblates.us; loughran@oblates.us

NURSING / REHABILITATION / CONVALESCENCE / ELDERLY CARE [NUR]

ANN ARBOR

Servants of God's Love Ministries: Emmanuel House - 475 Evergreen, Ann Arbor, MI 48103 t) 734-780-7667 emmanuelhse@gmail.com emmanuel-house.org Sr. Fran DePuydt, S.G.L., Admin.; Asstd. Annu.: 3; Staff: 48

GRAND BLANC

Genesys Short Term Rehabilitation Center - 8481 Holly Rd., Grand Blanc, MI 48439 t) 810-694-1711 ascension.org A member of Ascension Michigan and subsidiary of Genesys Ambulatory Services, Inc. Raquel Largent, Admin.;

PRESCHOOLS / CHILDCARE CENTERS [PRE]

CHELSEA

St. Louis Center for Exceptional Children & Adults - 16195 W. Old U.S. Hwy. 12, Chelsea, MI 48118 t) 734-475-8430 frenzo@stlouiscenter.org; afielder@stlouiscenter.org www.stlouiscenter.org Operated by the Servants of Charity. Rev. Enzo Addari, S.D.C., Admin.; Rev. Rayapillai Amalorpavanathan, S.D.C., Chap.; Rev. Michael Irudayanathan Franklin Arolaiadoss, S.D.C., Chap.; Rev. David Stawasz, S.D.C.; Stds.: 60; Lay Tchrs.: 90

JACKSON

St. Joseph Home for Children, Inc. (Felician Sisters (C.S.S.F.) - 205 Seymour Ave., Jackson, MI 49202; Mailing: P.O. Box 532437, Livonia, MI 48153 t) 517-841-3876 tjackson@feliciansisters.org felicianchildrenscenter.org Child care center for children, Preschool & Montessori Preschool and Kindergarten. Tracy Smith-Jackson, Pres.; Stds.: 171; Sr. Tchrs.: 2; Lay Tchrs.: 32

RETREAT HOUSES / RENEWAL CENTERS [RTR]

ADRIAN

Weber Retreat Center - 1257 E. Siena Heights Dr., Adrian, MI 49221-1793 t) 517-266-4000 webercenter@adriandominicans.org www.adriandominicans.org/weber Sr. Janet Doyle, O.P., Dir.;

BROOKLYN

Lake Vineyard Camps, Inc., (De Sales Center) - 1198 DeSales Dr., Brooklyn, MI 49230-9078 c) 517-414-0784; 517-592-2074 mckenna@oblates.us; jloughran@oblates.us www.desales.org Operated by Lake Vineyard Camps, Inc. for the Oblates of St. Francis de Sales, Inc. Rev. Kenneth N. McKenna, O.S.F.S., Dir.; Rev. John Loughran, OSFS, Treas.;

DE WITT

St. Francis Retreat Center DeWitt - 703 E. Main St., De Witt, MI 48820 t) 517-669-8321 info@stfrancis.ws www.stfrancis.ws Michael Kutas, Dir.;

Bethany House (Spiritual Life Center for Youth) - information@stfrancis.ws

An asterisk (*) denotes an organization that has established tax-exempt status directly with the IRS and is not covered by the USCCB Group Ruling.

Diocese of Laredo

MOST REVEREND JAMES A. TAMAYO, D.D.

Bishop of Laredo; ordained Priest June 11, 1976; appointed Titular Bishop of Ita and Auxiliary Bishop of Galveston-Houston January 26, 1993; consecrated March 10, 1993; appointed first Bishop of Diocese of Laredo July 3, 2000; installed August 9, 2000. Office: 1901 Corpus Christi St., Laredo, TX 78043. T: 956-727-2140; F: 956-727-2777.

Chancery Office: 1901 Corpus Christi St., Laredo, TX 78043. T: 956-727-2140; F: 956-727-2777. Mailing Address: P.O. Box 2247, Laredo, TX 78044-2247

ESTABLISHED AUGUST 9, 2000.

Square Miles 10,905.

Comprises the Counties of Webb, Zapata, Jim Hogg, La Salle, Maverick, Zavala and Dimmitt.

STATISTICAL OVERVIEW

Personnel

Bishop	1
Priests: Diocesan Active in Diocese	28
Priests: Diocesan Active Outside Diocese	1
Priests: Retired, Sick or Absent	7
Number of Diocesan Priests	36
Religious Priests in Diocese	16
Total Priests in your Diocese	52
Extern Priests in Diocese	5
Ordinations:	
Diocesan Priests	1
Transitional Deacons	1
Permanent Deacons in Diocese	44
Total Brothers	5
Total Sisters	37

Parishes

Parishes	32
With Resident Pastor:	
Resident Diocesan Priests	23
Resident Religious Priests	7
Without Resident Pastor:	
Administered by Priests	2
Missions	17

Professional Ministry Personnel:

Brothers	1
Sisters	6
Lay Ministers	20

Welfare

Health Care Centers	1
Total Assisted	29,344
Residential Care of Children	1
Total Assisted	30
Specialized Homes	1
Total Assisted	2,117
Special Centers for Social Services	2
Total Assisted	37,529

Educational

Diocesan Students in Other Seminaries	3
Total Seminarians	3
High Schools, Diocesan and Parish	1
Total Students	325
Elementary Schools, Diocesan and Parish	3
Total Students	920
Elementary Schools, Private	1
Total Students	422

Catechesis/Religious Education:

High School Students	1,892
Elementary Students	2,601
Total Students under Catholic Instruction	6,163
Teachers in Diocese:	
Sisters	2
Lay Teachers	107

Vital Statistics

Receptions into the Church:

Infant Baptism Totals	1,577
Minor Baptism Totals	156
Adult Baptism Totals	44
Received into Full Communion	61
First Communions	1,312
Confirmations	1,013
Marriages:	
Catholic	353
Interfaith	8
Total Marriages	361
Deaths	1,232
Total Catholic Population	328,508
Total Population	360,998

LEADERSHIP

Chancery - t) 956-727-2140

Vicar General - t) (956) 727-2140 franthonym@dioceseoflaredo.org Very Rev. R. Anthony Mendoza;

Chancellor - t) 956-727-2140 frfquiroz@dioceseoflaredo.org Very Rev. Francisco M. Quiroz;

Vice Chancellor -

Tribunal - t) 956-727-2140 frbello@dioceseoflaredo.org Very Rev. Iden J. Bello Miquilena, Judicial Vicar;

Fiscal Officer - t) 956-727-2140 cmoreno@dioceseoflaredo.org Cecilia Moreno, CFO;

Presbyteral Council - Most Rev. James A. Tamayo, Pres.; Very Rev. R. Anthony Mendoza, Vicar; Very Rev. Iden J. Bello Miquilena, Chair;

College of Consultors - Very Rev. R. Anthony Mendoza, Mem.; Very Rev. Iden J. Bello Miquilena, Mem.; Rev. Jose Maria Guevara, Mem.;

OFFICES AND DIRECTORS

Adult Faith Formation - t) 956-727-2140 frfquiroz@dioceseoflaredo.org Very Rev. Francisco M. Quiroz, Dir.;

Archives - t) 956-727-2140 Very Rev. Francisco M. Quiroz, Chancellor; Rev. Jose Angel De Leon Jr.; Celia H. Reyna, Asst. Archivist;

Calvary Catholic Cemetery - t) 956-723-6811 mkazen@calvarycemeterylaredo.org Michael A Kazen, Dir.;

Catholic Charities - t) 956-722-2443 Rebecca Solloa, Exec. Dir.;

Catholic Charities Humanitarian Relief Center - t) 956-722-3629 sramirez@ccdol.org Sandra Ramirez, Contact;

Immigration Services-Servicios Para Immigrantes - tdelagarza@ccdol.org Teresa De La Garza;

Social and Human Services - emartinez@ccdol.org Edgar Martinez, Contact;

Catholic Schools - t) 956-753-5208 gperez@dioceseoflaredo.org Guadalupe M. Perez;

Superintendent's Office - t) 956-753-5208 gperez@dioceseoflaredo.org Guadalupe M. Perez, Supt.;

Charismatic Renewal -

Cursillo Movement - t) 956-285-4839 frtobyguerrero@dioceseoflaredo.org Rev. Toribio C. Guerrero, Spiritual Dir.;

Diocesan Finance Council - Hector J. Cerna, Chair; Saul Fernandez, Mem. (extact98@hotmail.com); Pedro Saenz Jr., Mem.;

Family Life Ministry - t) 956-727-2140 mmiller@dioceseoflaredo.org Martha E. Miller, Dir.;

Human Resources - t) 956-727-2140 msepulveda@dioceseoflaredo.org Melinda Sepulveda, Dir.;

Laredo Catholic Communications, Inc. - t) 956-722-4167 khoy@khoy.org Bennett McBride, Exec. (bmcbride@dioceseoflaredo.org);

Communications Department - t) (956) 722-4167 Anselmo Guarneros, Dir.; Bennett McBride, Dir.; Melissa Pici, Editor;

Natural Family Planning and Understanding Sexuality - t) 956-727-2140 Martha E. Miller, Dir.;

Office of Respect Life - Very Rev. R. Anthony Mendoza, Dir.;

Our Lady of Refuge Cemetery - t) 830-773-4247 Celina M. Cardenas, Admin.;

Persons with Special Needs - t) 956-727-2140 ramgarza@dioceseoflaredo.org Dcn. Ramiro Garza, Dir.;

Priests Personnel Board - Very Rev. Iden J. Bello Miquilena, Mem.; Very Rev. Francisco M. Quiroz, Mem.; Rev. Msgr. Alejandro Salazar, Mem.;

Sacramental Preparation Office - t) 956-727-2140 ramgarza@dioceseoflaredo.org Dcn. Ramiro Garza;

Sacred Heart Church Cemetery - t) 830-879-2658 Rev. Pawel Antoszewski, Admin.;

Safe Environment Coordinator - t) 956-727-2140 Isabel Rodriguez, Contact (irodriguez@dioceseoflaredo.org);

Stewardship and Development - t) 956-727-2140 kibarra@dioceseoflaredo.org Karla Ibarra, Dir.;

Victim Assistance Coordinator - t) (956) 727-2140 x7868 msepulveda@dioceseoflaredo.org Melinda Sepulveda, Contact;

Vocations Office - t) 956-727-2140 frfquiroz@dioceseoflaredo.org Very Rev. Francisco M. Quiroz, Dir.;

Casa Guadalupe House of Discernment - t) (956) 727-2140 frfquiroz@dioceseoflaredo.org Very Rev. Francisco M. Quiroz, Dir.;

Youth Ministry - t) 956-727-2140 Most Rev. James A. Tamayo, Contact;

C.Y.O. - t) 956-727-2140 cyo@dioceseoflaredo.org Most Rev. James A. Tamayo, Contact;

ORGANIZATIONS

Catholic Daughters of the Americas - t) 956-436-4222 Elva Medina, District Deputy #15;

Equestrian Order of the Holy Sepulcher of Jerusalem - Saul Fernandez, Contact (extact98@hotmail.com); Rosantina Fernandez, Contact (quichy_4@yahoo.com);

Southwestern Lieutenancy - Saul Fernandez, KC HS; Rosantina Fernandez, DC HS;

Knights of Columbus - t) 830-325-1788 Angel Luna, Diocesan Deputy;

PARISHES, MISSIONS, AND CLERGY

STATE OF TEXAS

ASHERTON

Immaculate Conception - 579 Crockett St., Asherton, TX 78827-0008; Mailing: PO Box 8, Asherton, TX 78827 t) 830-468-3343; (830) 468-3343 (CRP) sec@immaculateconceptionasherton.org; cre@immaculateconceptionasherton.org Very Rev. Francisco M. Quiroz, Admin.; CRP Stds.: 80

St. Michael - t) (830) 457-2693

St. Henry -

CARRIZO SPRINGS

Our Lady of Guadalupe - 1003 N. 6th St., Carrizo Springs, TX 78834 t) 830-876-2239; 830-876-0153 (CRP) sec@ourladyofguadalupecarrizo.org; olog.ccd@sbcglobal.net Rev. Jerzy Krzywda, Admin.; Monica Castillo, CRE; Dcn. Rogelio Ortiz; CRP Stds.: 139

COTULLA

Sacred Heart - 307 S. Main St., Cotulla, TX 78014 t) 830-879-2658 sec@sacredheartcotulla.org www.sacredheartcotulla.org Rev. Pawel Antoszewski, Pst.; CRP Stds.: 64

CRYSTAL CITY

Sacred Heart - 115 E. Kinney St., Crystal City, TX 78839 t) 830-374-3148 sec@sacredheartcrystalcity.org Rev. Gerardo Silos, Admin.; Dcn. Frank Huerta; Dcn. Antonio Rivera; Dcn. Frank Solansky; Moises Garcia Jr., CRE; CRP Stds.: 155

EAGLE PASS

St. Joseph - 800 Comal St., Eagle Pass, TX 78852-4029 t) 830-773-6114; 830-773-6515 (CRP) cre@stjosepheaglepass.org Rev. Richard Kulwiec, O.M.I., Pst.; Dcn. Benito Ibarra; Dcn. David Joseph Even; Maria R. Hernandez, DRE; CRP Stds.: 120

Our Lady of Refuge - 815 Webster, Eagle Pass, TX 78852 t) 830-773-8451 (Office); 830-773-8421 (Res.) bk@ourladyofrefgueeaglepass.org Rev. Stanislaw Zowada, O.M.I., Admin.; Dcn. Keith Ayers; Dcn. Michael Castillo; Dcn. Carlos G. de la Pena; Dcn. Juan Martinez; Rev. Jerry Orsino, OMI, In Res.; CRP Stds.: 250

Our Lady of Lourdes - t) 956-765-4216 sec@ourladyoflourdeszapata.org

Our Lady of Guadalupe - sec@ourladyofrefugeeaglepass.org

Sacred Heart (Parroquia Sagrado Corazon) - 2055 Williams St., Eagle Pass, TX 78852-5099 t) 830-773-2451; 830-758-1681 (CRP); 830-773-3628 sacredheartchurch-eaglepass.org Rev. Peter Antonisamy, OMI, Admin.; Rev. Robert Hickl, OMI, In Res.; Dcn. Manuel Rene Cardona; Dcn. Leandro Contreras Jr.; Dcn. Hector Ricardo Martinez; Dcn. Carlos Enrique Hernandez; Maria Guadalupe Tovar, DRE; CRP Stds.: 332

Our Lady of San Juan - 18779 El Indio Hwy., El Indio, TX 78860 Sonia Belmonte, Contact;

ENCINAL

Immaculate Heart of Mary - 400 Santa Fe St, Encinal, TX 78019; Mailing: PO Box 5, Encinal, TX 78019-0005 t) 956-948-5328 sec@immaculateheartofmaryencinal.org; ihmcce@yahoo.com www.immaculateheartofmaryencinal.org Rev. P. Nolasco Hinojosa Jr., Admin.; Herlinda R. Mancha, DRE; CRP Stds.: 2

HEBBRONVILLE

Our Lady of Guadalupe - 504 E. Santa Clara St., Hebbronville, TX 78361 t) 361-527-3865 sec@ourladyofguadalupehebbronville.org www.dioceseoflaredo.org Rev. Juan Jose Ibarra, O.F.M, Pst.; Rev. Pablo Cesar Cisneros, O.F.M., Par. Vicar; Bro. Alberto Alvarado Vasquez, O.F.M., Admin.; CRP Stds.: 63

St. Agnes - 324 Liner St., Mirando City, TX 78369 t) 361-586-4449

St. Bridget - 115 Laurel Ave., Oilton, TX 78371 t) 361-527-2865

Sacred Heart - 211 N. Ave. G, Bruni, TX 78344

LA PRYOR

St. Joseph - 620 W. Benson St., La Pryor, TX 78872-0436; Mailing: P.O. Box 436, La Pryor, TX 78872 t) 830-365-4107 frgusortega@dioceseoflaredo.org; sec@stjosephlapryor.org stjosephlapryor.org Dcn. Eugene F. Corrigan; Dcn. Juan Gallegos; Juanita Cazares, DRE; CRP Stds.: 46

St. Patrick - Old Loma Vista Rd., Batesvillle, TX 78829 t) (830) 365-4107 Rev. Gustavo Ortega, Pst.;

LAREDO

San Agustin Cathedral - 201 San Agustin Ave., Laredo, TX 78040; Mailing: 214 San Bernardo Ave., Laredo, TX 78040 t) 956-722-1382 sec@sanagustincathedrallaredo.org Rev. Iden Jose Bello, Rector; Rev. Jose Luis Restrepo Prisco, Par. Vicar; Dcn. Leonardo Aguillon; Miroslava Vargas, DRE; CRP Stds.: 63

Blessed Sacrament - 2219 Galveston St., Laredo, TX 78043 t) 956-722-1231 sec@blessedsacramentlaredo.org; frwojciechp@dioceseoflaredo.org www.blessedsacramentlaredo.org Rev. Wojciech Przystasz, Admin.; Dcn. Rogelio Martinez Jr.; Patricia Lopez, DRE; CRP Stds.: 148

Christ the King - 1105 Tilden Ave., Laredo, TX 78040 t) 956-723-4267 sec@christthekinglaredo.org; frjcadena@dioceseoflaredo.org www.christthekinglaredo.org Rev. Jose G. Cadena, Admin.; Rev. Juan Mercado, Par. Vicar; Dcn. Enrique Marte Avila; Dcn. Alberto Brizuela; Maria Virginia Ramirez, DRE; CRP Stds.: 233

San Carlos Mission - Hwy. 359, Laredo, TX 78046 t) 956-286-6298

Divine Mercy - 9350 Amber Ave., Laredo, TX 78045 t) 956-726-0210 x100; 956-726-0210 x113 (CRP) frmichael@dioceseoflaredo.org; sec@divinemercylaredo.org divinemercylaredo.com/ Rev. Michael De Leon, Pst.; Rev. Luis E. Mares, Par. Vicar; Veronica Garcia, DRE; CRP Stds.: 199

St. Frances Cabrini - 3018 Davis Ave., Laredo, TX 78040 t) 956-722-2919; 956-722-8315 (CRP); 956-722-3481 sec@stfrancescabrinilaredo.org www.stfrancescabrinilaredo.org Rev. Msgr. James E.

Harris, Admin.; Rev. Noel Davis, Vicar; Dcn. Raymundo Guevara Jr.; CRP Stds.: 74
Holy Family - 2702 Stone Ave., Laredo, TX 78040; Mailing: 2705 McPherson Ave., Laredo, TX 78040-5432 t) 956-724-6881 www.holyfamilylaredo.org Rev. P. Nolasco Hinojosa Jr., Pst.; Dcn. Hector D. Hernandez; Antonieta Palacios, DRE; CRP Stds.: 7
Holy Redeemer - 1602 Garcia St., Laredo, TX 78040; Mailing: P.O. Box 1087, Laredo, TX 78042 t) 956-723-7171 bk@holyredeemerlaredo.org www.holyredeemerlaredo.org Rev. Francisco Leon, O.S.A., Pst.; Dcn. Edmundo Lopez Jr.; Cristina Lozano, DRE; CRP Stds.: 130
Santa Cruz - 2002 Lee Ave., Laredo, TX 78040 t) (956) 723-7171
St. John Neumann - 102 W. Hillside Rd., Laredo, TX 78041 t) 956-726-9488 sec@sjnlaredo.org; bk@sjnlaredo.org www.sjnlaredo.org Rev. Salvador Pedroza, Pst.; Rev. Jose Luis Balderas, In Res.; Dcn. Gerardo Morales; CRP Stds.: 66
St. Joseph - 109 N. Meadow Ave., Laredo, TX 78040 t) 956-723-4172; 956-286-9779 (CRP) Rev. Janusz Glabinski, Pst.; Julissa Liendo, DRE; CRP Stds.: 110
St. Jude - 2031 Lowry Rd., Laredo, TX 78045 t) 956-722-2280 sec@stjudelaredo.org Rev. Jose Maria Guevara, Pst.; Aracely Juarez, DRE; CRP Stds.: 196
Sagrado Corazon de Jesus -
Nuestra Senora del Rosario - 420 Sierra Vista Blvd., Laredo, TX 78046-7765 t) 956-753-8764 sec@nuestrasenoradelrosariolaredo.org www.dioceseoflaredo.org Rev. Francisco Stodola, Pst.; Rev. Wojciech Kosowicz, In Res.; Dcn. Jerry Gutierrez; Guadalupe Rivera De Medina, DRE; CRP Stds.: 264
Our Lady of Guadalupe - 1718 San Jorge Ave., Laredo, TX 78040 t) 956-723-6954; 956-723-6954 Rev. Leszek J. Waclawik, Pst.; Dcn. Ignacio Valdez; Dcn. Juan Agustin Zamarripa; Amanda Cantu, DRE; CRP Stds.: 84
St. Patrick - 555 E. Del Mar Blvd., Laredo, TX 78041 t) 956-722-6215; (956) 722-6225 x103 (Secy.); (956) 722-1251 x102 (Secy.); 956-726-4644 (CRP) sec@stpatricklaredo.org; reception@stpatricklaredo.org www.stpatricklaredo.org Very Rev. R. Anthony Mendoza, Pst.; Rev. Francisco Javier Hernandez, Par. Vicar; Rev. Esteban Gonzalez, C.S.J., Par. Vicar; Rev. Jacinto Olguin, In Res.; Dcn. Ramiro Garza; Dcn. Steve Landin; Dcn. Joe Longoria; Dcn. Miguel Robles; CRP Stds.: 426
St. Peter the Apostle - 1510 Matamoros St., Laredo, TX 78040 t) 956-723-6301; 956-286-6488 (CRP); 956-231-4786 (CRP) sec@stpetertheapostlelaredo.org Rev. Agustin Escalante, Pst.; Patricia Reyes Morales, DRE; CRP Stds.: 50
San Francisco Javier - 2502 Zaragoza St., Laredo, TX 78042-1175; Mailing: P.O. Box 1175, Laredo, TX 78042-1175 t) 956-723-3850; 956-285-3850 (CRP) sec@sanfranciscojavierloredo.org; frtobyguerrero@dioceseoflaredo.org Rev. Toribio C. Guerrero, Pst.; CRP Stds.: 28
San Luis Rey - 3502 Sanders Ave, Laredo, TX 78040-1346 t) 956-723-6587; 956-722-3323 (CRP) cre@sanluisreylaredo.org www.dioceseoflaredo.org Rev. Jose F. Lucero, Pst.; Dcn. Enrique Peñuñurri; Dcn. Jose Rodriguez; Rev. Luis Flores, SDB (Chile), Pst. Assoc.; Carlos Ochoa, DRE; CRP Stds.: 320
San Martin de Porres - 1704 Sandman St., Laredo, TX 78041; Mailing: P.O. Box 2666, Laredo, TX 78044-2666 t) 956-723-5215; 956-725-2440 (CRP) smartinccd@hotmail.com www.sanmartincatholicchurch.org Rev. Msgr. Alejandro Salazar, Pst.; Rev. Pedro Mercado Jr., Par. Vicar; Dcn. Frank Idrogo; Dcn. Enrique Mejia; Dcn. Luis E. Raines; Dcn. Gabriel Vargas; CRP Stds.: 308
Santa Teresita - Hwy. 59, Laredo, TX 78044 smpyvonne@gmail.com
Santa Margarita de Escocia - 320 Segovia Dr., Laredo, TX 78046 t) 956-724-9669 sec@santamargaritadeescocialaredo.org Rev. Alirio Corrales, Admin.; Laura Villanueva, DRE; CRP Stds.: 70
Santo Nino de Atocha Catholic Church - 2801 Cross St., Laredo, TX 78046 t) 956-724-6638 sec@santoninolaredo.org; cre@santoninolaredo.org Rev. Joel Perez, Pst.; CRP Stds.: 133
St. Vincent de Paul - 2710 Boulanger St., Laredo, TX 78043 t) 956-722-3034; 956-726-4134 (CRP) Rev. Leonel Martinez, O.S.A., Pst.; Dcn. Miguel Vallarta; Rita Diaz, DRE; CRP Stds.: 265

RIO BRAVO

Santa Rita de Casia - 1001 Espejo Molina, Rio Bravo, TX 78046 t) 956-725-7215 Rev. Jan Ziemniek, Pst.; CRP Stds.: 84
Santa Monica Mission - 507 Morales (El Cenizo), Rio Bravo, TX 78046

ZAPATA

Our Lady of Lourdes - 1610 Hidalgo Blvd., Zapata, TX 78076 t) 956-765-4216 sec@ourladyoflourdeszapata.org Rev. Daniel Ramirez-Portugal, Pst.; Rev. Alan Sanchez, Par. Vicar; Sr. Maria de Jesus Callejas, HMRF, DRE;
Our Lady of Refuge -
San Pedro -
Santa Ana -

SCHOOLS: PRESCHOOL THRU HIGH SCHOOL

SCHOOLS

STATE OF TEXAS

EAGLE PASS

Our Lady of Refuge - (PAR) (Grades PreK-8) 577 Washington St., Eagle Pass, TX 78852 t) 830-773-3531 ana.bermea@olorschoolep.org oloroschoolep.org Ana Bermea, Prin.; Stds.: 261; Lay Tchrs.: 14

LAREDO

St. Augustine (Elementary School) - (DIO) (Grades PreK-8) 1300 Galveston St., Laredo, TX 78040 t) 956-724-1176 bzurita@st-augustine.org; romo@st-augustine.org www.st-augelem.org Barbra Zurita, Prin.; Rodrigo Romo, Prin.; Leonor Roriguez, Admin.; Stds.: 342; Lay Tchrs.: 20
Blessed Sacrament School - (PAR) (Grades PreK-8) 1501 N. Bartlett Ave., Laredo, TX 78043 t) 956-722-1222 ssantos@bsacramentschool.com; greyes@bsacramentschool.com www.bsacramentschool.com Selma J. Santos, Prin.; Stds.: 317; Lay Tchrs.: 16
Mary Help of Christians School - (PRV) (Grades PreK-8) 10 E. Del Mar Blvd., Laredo, TX 78041 t) 956-722-3966 srpn@mhcslaredo.org; anita.averill@mhcslaredo.org www.mhcslaredo.org Sr. Phuong Nguyen, FMA, Prin.; Ann Macdonald, Vice Prin.; Alberto Perez, Vice Prin.; Anita Averill, Dir.; Alheyda Guerra, Bus. Mgr.; Stds.: 422; Sr. Tchrs.: 2; Lay Tchrs.: 33

HIGH SCHOOLS

STATE OF TEXAS

LAREDO

St. Augustine High School - (DIO) (Grades 9-12) 1300 Galveston St., Laredo, TX 78040 t) 956-724-8131 ogentry@st-augustine.org st-augustine.org Olga P. Gentry, Prin.; Stds.: 325; Lay Tchrs.: 24

INSTITUTIONS LOCATED IN DIOCESE

CAMPUS MINISTRY / NEWMAN CENTERS [CAM]

LAREDO

Campus Ministry - 1901 Corpus Christi, Laredo, TX 78043 t) 956-727-2140 bishoptamayo@dioceseoflaredo.org www.newmanclub.us Laredo College; Texas A&M International University. Most Rev. James A. Tamayo, Contact;

CEMETERIES [CEM]

EAGLE PASS

Our Lady of Refuge Cemetery - 1679 Flowers, Eagle Pass, TX 78852 t) 830-773-4247 cemetery@ourladyofrefugeeaglepass.org Celina M. Cardenas, Admin.;

CONVENTS, MONASTERIES, AND RESIDENCES FOR WOMEN [CON]

EAGLE PASS

Missionary Sisters of Our Lady of Perpetual Help - 895 Webster, Eagle Pass, TX 78852 t) 830-773-8915 garzamps@yahoo.com Sr. Ma. Ana Popo, MPS, DRE; Srs.: 3
Order of St. Benedict - 1080 Vista Hermosa, Eagle Pass, TX 78852 t) 830-758-0812 sisursie@hotmail.com Sr. Ursula Herrera, Contact; Srs.: 1

LAREDO

Daughters of Mary Help of Christians Convent - 10 E. Del Mar Blvd., Laredo, TX 78041-2368 t) 956-791-8617 suosec@salesiansisterswest.org www.mhcslaredo.org Sr. Phuong Nguyen, FMA, Supr.; Srs.: 4
Daughters of Saint Joseph - 8986 Foggy Loop, Laredo, TX 78045 t) 956-717-5944 laredotexasfsj@yahoo.com Sr. Guadalupe Guarneros, FSJ, Dir.; Srs.: 3
Religious Sisters of Mercy Convent - 2905 Monterrey St., Laredo, TX 78046 t) 956-744-5312 c) 956-693-0697 mvera@sistersofmercy.org Sr. Maria Luisa Vera, R.S.M., Dir.; Srs.: 3
Servants of the Sacred Heart of Jesus and the Poor - 3310 S. Zapata Hwy., Laredo, TX 78046 t) 956-723-3343 regionyermousa@gmail.com Sr. Elia Lucia Hernandez Arroyo, SSHJP, Supr.; Srs.: 17

ZAPATA

Hermanas Misioneras del Rosario de Fatima - 1609 Glenn St., Zapata, TX 78076; Mailing: 1610 Hidalgo Blvd., Zapata, TX 78076 t) 956-765-4216 mjcsmrf@hotmail.com Sr. Maria de Jesus Callejas, DRE; Srs.: 3

ENDOWMENTS / FOUNDATIONS / TRUSTS [EFT]

LAREDO

St. Augustine School Endowment Fund, Inc. - 1300 Galveston St., Laredo, TX 78040 t) 956-724-8131 ogentry@st-augustine.org www.st-augustine.org Olga P. Gentry, Prin.;
Diocese of Laredo Deposit and Loan Fund, Inc. - 1901 Corpus Christi St., Laredo, TX 78043 t) 956-727-2140 cmoreno@dioceseoflaredo.org Maria Moreno, Admin.;
Diocese of Laredo Perpetual Benefit Endowment Fund, Inc. - 1901 Corpus Christi St., Laredo, TX 78043 t) 956-727-2140 cmoreno@dioceseoflaredo.org Maria Moreno, Admin.;

MISCELLANEOUS [MIS]

LAREDO

Casa de Misericordia - 1000 Mier, Laredo, TX 78040; Mailing: 14528 S. Outer 40 Rd., Ste. 100, Mercy - Corporate Paralegal Legal Dept., Chesterfield, MO 63017 t) 956-712-9590; 877-782-2722 marambula@casademisericordia.org; marynell.ploch@mercy.net www.casademisericordia.org Domestic Violence Shelter Maria Elena Arambula, Admin.; Sr. Rosemary Welsh, R.S.M., Dir.;
Mercy Ministries of Laredo - 2500 Zacatecas, Laredo, TX 78046; Mailing: 14528 S. Outer 40 Rd., Ste. 100, Mercy c/o Corporate Paralegal-Legal Dept.,

Chesterfield, MO 63017 t) 956-718-6810 marynell.ploch@mercy.net; mercyministriesoflaredo2@mercy.net mercy.net Elizabeth Casso, Pres.;

National Nocturnal Adoration Society (Congregation of the Blessed Sacrament) - 2308 Maya Rd., Laredo, TX 78041 t) 956-608-3434 info@nashqusa.org; nashqusadm@gmail.com nationalnocturnaladorationsociety.org Raul Mendoza, Pres.; Rev. Alirio Corrales, Dir.;

MONASTERIES AND RESIDENCES FOR PRIESTS AND BROTHERS [MON]

LAREDO

Congregation of St. John - 505 Century Dr., S., Laredo, TX 78046 t) (956) 324-6473 laredo@stjean.com www.csjohn.org Rev. Johannes Pio Van Elshout, C.S.J., Prior; Rev. Victor Shoemaker, C.S.J., Mem.; Rev. Felipe de Jesus Marroquin, C.S.J., Mem.; Bro. John of the Cross Lix, C.S.J., Mem.; Bro. Jose Luis Hernandez, C.S.J., Mem.; Brs.: 2; Priests: 3

Marist Brothers - 1511 Cherry Hill Dr., Laredo, TX 78041-3807 t) 956-724-2651 brojoeh@prodigy.net Bro. Philip R. Degagne, F.M.S.; Bro. Joseph E. Herrera, F.M.S., Dir.; Brs.: 2

PRESCHOOLS / CHILDCARE CENTERS [PRE]

LAREDO

Sacred Heart Children's Home - 3310 S. Zapata Hwy., Laredo, TX 78046 t) 956-723-3343 magdasofiasscjp@gmail.com; misidrav2010@gmail.com www.sacredheartchildrenhome.org/ Mother Magdalena Juarez, Supr.; Sr. Maria Isidra Valdez, S.S.H.J.P., Admin.; Stds.: 30

RETREAT HOUSES / RENEWAL CENTERS [RTR]

LAREDO

Holy Spirit Retreat and Conference Center - 501 Century Dr., S., Laredo, TX 78046 t) (956) 324-6473 laredo@st.jean.com www.csjohn.org Rev. Johannes Pio Van Elshout, C.S.J., Dir.;

An asterisk (*) denotes an organization that has established tax-exempt status directly with the IRS and is not covered by the USCCB Group Ruling.

Diocese of Las Cruces

(Dioecesis Las Cruces)

MOST REVEREND PETER BALDACCHINO, D.D.

Bishop of Las Cruces; ordained May 25, 1996; appointed Titular Bishop of Vatarba and Auxiliary Bishop of Miami February 20, 2014; ordained March 19, 2014; appointed Bishop of Las Cruces May 15, 2019; installed July 23, 2019. The Pastoral Center, 1280 Med Park Dr., Las Cruces, NM 88005.

The Pastoral Center: 1280 Med Park Dr., Las Cruces, NM 88005. T: 575-523-7577; F: 575-524-3874.

www.rcdlc.org

ESTABLISHED OCTOBER 18, 1982.

Square Miles 44,483.

Comprises the Counties of Dona Ana, Hidalgo, Grant, Luna, Sierra, Otero, Lincoln, Chaves, Eddy and Lea in the State of New Mexico.

For legal titles of parishes and diocesan institutions, consult The Pastoral Center.

STATISTICAL OVERVIEW

Personnel

Bishop	1
Retired Bishops	1
Priests: Diocesan Active in Diocese	15
Priests: Diocesan Active Outside Diocese	2
Priests: Retired, Sick or Absent	11
Number of Diocesan Priests	28
Religious Priests in Diocese	23
Total Priests in your Diocese	51
Extern Priests in Diocese	21
Permanent Deacons in Diocese	53
Total Sisters	61

Parishes

Parishes	47
With Resident Pastor:	
Resident Diocesan Priests	27
Resident Religious Priests	14
Without Resident Pastor:	
Administered by Priests	6
Missions	36
Professional Ministry Personnel:	
Lay Ministers	23

Welfare

Day Care Centers	1
Total Assisted	55
Other Institutions	1
Total Assisted	1,750

Educational

Diocesan Students in Other Seminaries	4
Total Seminarians	4
Elementary Schools, Diocesan and Parish	4
Total Students	607
Catechesis/Religious Education:	
High School Students	1,825
Elementary Students	3,240
Total Students under Catholic Instruction	5,676
Teachers in Diocese:	
Sisters	3
Lay Teachers	56

Vital Statistics

Receptions into the Church:	
Infant Baptism Totals	1,149
Minor Baptism Totals	138
Adult Baptism Totals	54
Received into Full Communion	154
First Communions	912
Confirmations	967
Marriages:	
Catholic	195
Interfaith	16
Total Marriages	211
Deaths	1,469
Total Catholic Population	105,000
Total Population	582,742

LEADERSHIP

Bishop's Office - t) 575-222-4229 Most Rev. Peter Baldacchino (pbaldacchino@rcdlc.org); Martha Beasley, Secy. (mbeasley@rcdlc.org);
Pastoral Center - t) 575-523-7577 rcdlc.org
Vicar General - t) (575) 222-4228 Very Rev. Kevin Waymel (kwaymel@rcdlc.org);
Judicial Vicar - t) 575-222-4224 Very Rev. Joseph L. Pacquing (jpacquing@rcdlc.org);
Chancellor - t) (575) 222-4228 Very Rev. Kevin Waymel, Chancellor (kwaymel@rcdlc.org);
Diocesan Consultors - Rev. Richard Catanach (rcatanach@rcdlc.org); Rev. Martin G. Cordero (mcordero@rcdlc.org); Very Rev. Carlos A. Espinoza (cespinoza@rcdlc.org);
Vicars Forane - Very Rev. Martin Cornejo (mcornejo@rcdlc.org); Very Rev. Carlos A. Espinoza (cespinoza@rcdlc.org); Very Rev. Carlos Martinez, O.F.M. (cmartinez@rcdlc.org);
Priest Personnel Board - Most Rev. Peter Baldacchino (pbaldacchino@rcdlc.org); Very Rev. Kevin Waymel, Vicar General (kwaymel@rcdlc.org); Very Rev. Oliver Obele, Vicar for Priest Personnel (oobele@rcdlc.org);
Presbyteral Council - Most Rev. Peter Baldacchino, Pres. (pbaldacchino@rcdlc.org); Very Rev. Kevin Waymel, Vicar General (kwaymel@rcdlc.org); Very Rev. Joseph L. Pacquing, Judicial Vicar (jpacquing@rcdlc.org);
Deacons' Council - Dcn. Melvin Balderrama, Carlsbad Vicariate; Dcn. Roberto Garcia, Roswell Vicariate; Dcn. Arthur Gutierrez, Copper Vicariate;
Director of Permanent Deacons - t) 575-222-4231 Very Rev. Carlos A. Espinoza, Dir. (cespinoza@rcdlc.org);

ADMINISTRATION

Finance Office - t) 575-523-0928 Andrew Marshall, Controller (amarshall@rcdlc.org);
Human Resources - t) 575-222-4254 Dcn. John Eric Munson, Dir. (jemunson@rcdlc.org);
Payroll Office - t) 575-222-4250 Brenda Clark, Mgr. (bclark@rcdlc.org);
Insurance Office - t) 575-222-4254 Dcn. John Eric Munson, Dir. (jemunson@rcdlc.org);
Victim Assistance - t) (575) 222-4235 Mary Frances Garcia, Coord. (mgarcia@rcdlc.org);
Diocesan Archives - t) 575-222-4230 archivist@rcdlc.org Donna Vargas, Archivist;

CATHOLIC CHARITIES

Catholic Charities of Southern New Mexico - t) 575-527-0500 catholiccharitiesdlc.org Kenneth Ferrone, Exec. Dir. (kf@catholiccharitiesdlc.org);

CLERGY AND RELIGIOUS SERVICES

Episcopal Vicar for Priest Personnel - t) (575) 538-9373 Very Rev. Oliver Obele (oobele@rcdlc.org);
Episcopal Vicar for Consecrated Life - t) 575-526-8171 Very Rev. Valentine M. Jankowski, O.F.M.Conv. (vjankowski@rcdlc.org);
Director of Permanent Deacon Formation - t) (575) 222-4231 Very Rev. Carlos A. Espinoza, Dir. (cespinoza@rcdlc.org);

COMMUNICATIONS

Communications - t) (575) 523-7577

CONSULTATIVE BODIES

Priestly Life and Ministry Committee - t) 575-523-0167 Rev. Richard Catanach (rcatanach@rcdlc.org);
Finance Council - Most Rev. Peter Baldacchino (pbaldacchino@rcdlc.org); Christine Wright, Chair; Greg Carrasco;
Priests Retirement Board - Rev. Richard Catanach, Chair (rcatanach@rcdlc.org); Rev. Martin G. Cordero (mcordero@rcdlc.org); Rev. Ruben Romero (rromero@rcdlc.org);

DEVELOPMENT

Development, Stewardship and Foundation - t) 575-222-4236 Anthony Casaus, Dir. (acasaus@rcdlc.org);

EDUCATION

Catholic Schools - t) 575-222-4229 Dr. Frances Gallo, Supt.;

EVANGELIZATION

Vocations - t) 575-526-9545 Rev. Ruben Romero, Dir. (rromero@rcdlc.org);
Campus Ministry - t) 575-522-6202 Very Rev. Kevin Waymel, Dir. (kwaymel@rcdlc.org);
Evangelization and Parish Life Office - t) (575) 523-7577
Holy Childhood Association - Rev. Msgr. John E. Anderson (frjohn@zianet.com);
Propagation of the Faith - t) 575-523-0167 Rev. Richard Catanach (rcatanach@rcdlc.org);
Ecumenical Liaison - Dcn. Leonel Briseno (lbriseno@rcdlc.org);
Youth, Young Adults and Pastoral Juvenile Ministry - t) (575) 523-7577
Prison and Jail Ministry - t) 575-222-4244 Dcn. John Eric Munson, Dir. (jemunson@rcdlc.org);

FACILITIES

Buildings and Properties - t) (575) 222-4241 Oscar Javier Padilla, Coord., Property & Risk Mgmt. (opadilla@rcdlc.org);

SPIRITUAL LIFE

Cursillo - t) 575-910-2564 Dcn. Jesus Herrera, Spiritual Adv./Care Srvcs.;
Charismatic Renewal Liaison - Rev. Martin G. Cordero (mcordero@rcdlc.org);

TRIBUNAL

Diocesan Tribunal - t) 575-523-7577 Very Rev. Joseph L. Pacquing, Judicial Vicar (jpacquing@rcdlc.org); Very Rev. Christopher E. Williams, Adjutant Judicial Vicar (cwilliams@rcdlc.org);
Judge - t) 575-392-7551 Very Rev. Joseph L. Pacquing, Judicial Vicar (jpacquing@rcdlc.org); Very Rev. Christopher E. Williams, Adjutant Judicial Vicar (cwilliams@rcdlc.org); Rev. Ephraim Ezulike (Nigeria), Judge (fr.ephraim.roswell@gmail.com);
Promoter of Justice -
Defenders of the Bond - Rev. Emmanuel Ezenneh (eezenneh@rcdlc.org); Rev. Richard Catanach (rcatanach@rcdlc.org); Rev. Msgr. John E. Anderson (frjohn@zianet.com);
Notary - t) (575) 222-4237 Deborah Herrera (dherrera@rcdlc.org);

PARISHES, MISSIONS, AND CLERGY

STATE OF NEW MEXICO

ALAMOGORDO

Immaculate Conception Parish, Alamogordo, Inc. - 705 Delaware Ave., Alamogordo, NM 88310 t) 575-437-3291 iccalamogordo@gmail.com; iccreligiousedu7@gmail.com www.iccalamogordo.org Very Rev. Martin Cornejo, Pst.; Rev. Emmanuel O. Okoye (Nigeria), Par. Vicar; Dcn. Gary Perkins; Sr. Elvis Obodo, CRE; Lucas Gallegos, Bus. Mgr.; CRP Stds.: 45
St. Jude Parish, Inc. - 1404 College Ave., Alamogordo, NM 88310-4860 t) 575-437-0238 sjalamo@zianet.com Rev. Marcel Okonkwo, Pst.; Dcn. Andy Weiss; Cecilia Woosley, DRE; CRP Stds.: 70

ANTHONY

St. Anthony Parish, Anthony, Inc. - 310 Lincoln St., Anthony, NM 88021; Mailing: PO Box 2624, 324 Lincoln St., Anthony, NM 88021 t) 575-882-2239; 575-882-4100 office@stanthonysnm.org; rep@stanthonysnm.org stanthonysnm.org Rev. Jesus M. Mena, O.A.R., Par. Admin.; Rev. Jesus Antonio Lasheras Gonzalez, Par. Vicar; Dcn. Jesse Sanchez; Rev. Ricardo Hinojal, O.A.R., In Res.; CRP Stds.: 124
Our Lady of Refuge Mission, Inc. - 1320 Mercantil, La Union, NM 88021 t) 575-589-0542 info@olrmission.com
Immaculate Conception - 205 Conception Ave., Mequite, NM 88048 c) 575-201-5019 stanthonysnm@gmail.com

ARTESIA

St. Anthony Parish, Artesia, Inc. - 502 S. Ninth St., Artesia, NM 88253 t) 575-746-4471 stanthonyartesia@yahoo.com Rev. Francis Lazer, Pst.; Dcn. Antonio Torrez; Dcn. Roberto Garcia; CRP Stds.: 64
Our Lady of Grace Parish, Artesia, Inc. - 1111 N. Roselawn Ave., Artesia, NM 88210 t) 575-748-1356 ourlady@pvtnetworks.net www.ourladyofgraceartesia.org Rev. Lurdhu Vijaya Amarlapudi, Admin.; Dcn. Pablo Merjil; Dcn. Richard Rodriguez; CRP Stds.: 250

BAYARD

Our Lady of Fatima Parish, Inc. - 340 Mayo St., Bayard, NM 88023; Mailing: P.O. Box 1425, Bayard, NM 88023 t) 575-537-2421 ourladyoffatimabayard@gmail.com Rev. Martin Okonkwo, Admin.; CRP Stds.: 15
St. Anthony - 287 Fierro Rd., Fierro, NM 88041
Holy Family - t) (575) 537-2421
San Lorenzo - ; Mailing: Box 385, San Lorenzo, NM 88049 t) 575-313-7137

CARLSBAD

St. Edward Parish, Inc. - 205 N. Guadalupe St., Carlsbad, NM 88220 t) 575-885-6600 workingforjesus@saint-edward.net; dre@saint-edward.net Very Rev. Hriday K. Pasala, Par. Admin.; CRP Stds.: 115
San Jose Parish, Carlsbad, Inc. - 1002 De Baca, Carlsbad, NM 88220 t) 575-885-5792 sjcatholicchurch@windstream.net; office@sanjoseparish.org www.sanjoseparish.org Rev. Juan Carlos Ramirez, Pst.; Dcn. Melvin Balderrama; Dcn. Manuel Chavez; Dcn. Antonio Dominguez; CRP Stds.: 273

CARRIZOZO

St. Rita Parish, Inc. - 213 Birch St., Carrizozo, NM 88301; Mailing: Box 727, Carrizozo, NM 88301 t) 575-648-2853 santaritaparish@yahoo.com Rev. Thadayoose Lazar, HGN (India), Admin.; Dcn. Gilbert Chavez; CRP Stds.: 19
Sacred Heart -
St. Therese of the Little Flower -

CHAMBERINO

San Luis Rey - 204 S. San Luis Ave., Chamberino, NM 88027; Mailing: 353 E. Josephine St., La Mesa, NM 88044 t) 575-233-3191 Very Rev. Carlos A. Espinoza, Pst.; Yolanda Gonzalez, DRE; CRP Stds.: 32

CHAPARRAL

St. Thomas More Parish, Inc. - 568 E. Lisa, Chaparral, NM 88081 t) 575-824-4433 parishst.thomasmore@yahoo.com Rev. Jose Rodolfo Yela, OAR, Pst.; Dcn. Roberto Mata; CRP Stds.: 70

DEMING

St. Ann Parish, Inc. - 400 S. Ruby St., Deming, NM 88030 t) 575-546-3343 saintanndeming@me.com www.santaanademing.com Rev. Aloysius Orekie, Par. Admin.; Marisol Perez, DRE; CRP Stds.: 125
Holy Family Parish, Inc. - 615 S. Copper St., Deming, NM 88030-4115 t) 575-546-9783 hfcdeming@gmail.com Rev. Prakasham Babu Naripogula, Admin.; Rochelle Aquino, DRE; CRP Stds.: 57

DEXTER

Immaculate Conception Parish, Dexter, Inc. - 400 W. Sixth St., Dexter, NM 88230; Mailing: P.O. Box 189, Dexter, NM 88230 t) 575-734-5478 (Parish office) c) 470-955-9076 (Priest's number); (575) 626-2169 (Parish secretary) rnwosu@rcdlc.org dexterimmaculate.org Rev. Raphael Chinedu Nwosu, Admin.; Maria Ramirez, DRE; CRP Stds.: 156
Our Lady of Guadalupe - 204 Broadway, Lake Arthur,

NM 88253 t) 575-308-3818 acsalcido2002@yahoo.com Adelina Salcido, Contact;

St. Catherine - 200 S. Texas, Hagerman, NM 88232 t) 575-840-6720 munozmrosario@yahoo.com Mary Varela, Contact;

DONA ANA

Our Lady of Purification Parish, Inc. - 5525 Cristo Rey St., Dona Ana, NM 88032; Mailing: P.O. Box 706, Dona Ana, NM 88032 t) 575-526-2114 www.ourladyofpurification.org Rev. Martin G. Cordero, Pst.; Dcn. Leonel Briseno; CRP Stds.: 93

San Isidro - 3875 San Isidro Rd., Las Cruces, NM 88007 t) (575) 526-2114

GARFIELD

San Isidro Parish, Inc. - 2003 Loma Parda, Garfield, NM 87936-9701; Mailing: HC 31, Box 43, Garfield, NM 87936-9701 t) 575-267-5111 Rev. Michael J. Williams, Admin.;

San Jose -

Our Lady of Guadalupe -

HATCH

Our Lord of Mercy Parish, Inc. - 117 Hartman St., Hatch, NM 87937; Mailing: PO Box 321, Hatch, NM 87937 t) 575-267-4983 olmsecretary@gmail.com; itorres@rcdlc.org hatchvalleycatholic.com/ Rev. Mario Ivan Torres, Admin.; Dcn. Timothy Flynn; Debbie Cordero, DRE; CRP Stds.: 194

Our Lady of All Nations - 1992 Rincon Rd., Rincon, NM 87940

HOBBS

St. Helena Parish, Inc. - 100 E. Bender Blvd., Hobbs, NM 88240 t) 575-392-7551 x100; 575-392-7552 x101 (CRP) parishoffice@sthelenaparish.org Very Rev. Joseph L. Pacquing, Admin.; Yvonne Gomez, DRE; CRP Stds.: 244

Our Lady of Guadalupe Parish, Inc. - 914 S. Selman St., Hobbs, NM 88240 t) 575-393-4991 ourladyparish@yahoo.com olgparishhobbs.com Rev. Jorge Santiago Vargas La Rosa, Admin.; CRP Stds.: 256

HURLEY

Infant Jesus Parish, Inc. - 204 Cortez Ave., Hurley, NM 88043; Mailing: PO Box 97, Hurley, NM 88043 t) 575-537-3691 infantjesushurley@gmail.com Rev. Casmir Anozie (Nigeria), Admin.; Dcn. Arthur Gutierrez; Dcn. Richard Maynes Jr.; Dcn. David M. Castanon; CRP Stds.: 58

San Juan - 2281 Hwy. 61, San Juan, NM 88041; Mailing: 100 De La O, San Lorenzo, NM 88041 t) 505-259-9523 dgurule1027@gmail.com

San Jose - 1071 Hwy. 61, Faywood, NM 88034; Mailing: 100 De La O, San Lorenzo, NM 88041 t) 505-259-9523 dgurule1027@gmail.com

JAL

St. Cecilia Parish, Inc. - 500 S. 5th St., Jal, NM 88252; Mailing: P.O. Box 430, 500 S 5th St, Jal, NM 88252 t) 575-395-2431 stceciliajal@gmail.com Rev. Christopher Amojo, C.M. (Nigeria), Admin.; CRP Stds.: 82

St. Clare - 3000 N. Main St., Eunice, NM 88252; Mailing: P.O. Box 1464, Eunice, NM 88252 t) 575-394-2198 stclairemission1@gmail.com

LA LUZ

Our Lady of the Light, La Luz, Inc. - 4 La Luz Rd., La Luz, NM 88337; Mailing: P.O. Box 236, La Luz, NM 88337 t) 575-434-9460 olofthelt@hotmail.com www.ourladyofthelight.org Rev. Patrick Montgomery, Pst.; Alicia McAninch, DRE; CRP Stds.: 20

LA MESA

San Jose Parish, La Mesa, Inc. - 353 E. Josephine St., La Mesa, NM 88044 t) 575-233-3191 c) (575) 993-3647 Very Rev. Carlos A. Espinoza, Pst.; Dcn. Roger Montes; CRP Stds.: 13

San Pedro (Del Cerro) - 137 Lomas Ave., Vado, NM 88072 t) (575) 233-3191 Rev. Carlos A. Espinoza, Par. Vicar;

LAS CRUCES

Immaculate Heart of Mary Cathedral Parish, Inc. - 1240 S. Espina St., Las Cruces, NM 88001 t) 575-524-8563 ihm@ihmcathedral.com; apascua@ihmcathedral.com www.ihmcathedral.com Rev. Alejandro Reyes, Rector; Rev. Emmanuel Ezenneh, Par. Vicar; Dcn. Ed Fierro; Dcn. Ruben Gutierrez; CRP Stds.: 75

St. Albert the Great Newman Parish, Inc. - 2615 S. Solano Dr., Las Cruces, NM 88001 t) 575-522-6202 isabel@stalbertnewmancenter.org www.stalbertnewmancenter.org Serving New Mexico State University. Very Rev. Kevin Waymel, Admin.; Dcn. David McNeill Jr.; CRP Stds.: 210

St. Genevieve Parish, Inc. - 100 S. Espina, Las Cruces, NM 88001 t) 575-524-9649 sgcchurch@stgen.info www.stgen.info Rev. Theophine Okafor, Par. Admin.; Rev. Juan Moreno, In Res.; Rev. Peter Okonkwo (Nigeria), In Res.; Dcn. Roberto Gallo; Dcn. Louis A. Roman; Veronica Garcia, DRE; CRP Stds.: 105

Holy Cross Parish, Inc. - 1327 N. Miranda, Las Cruces, NM 88005 t) 575-523-0167 info@hcclc.org Rev. Richard Catanach, Pst.; Dcn. Francisco Gurrola; Dcn. Randolph Rivas; Irene M. Gomez, DRE; CRP Stds.: 165

Our Lady of Health Parish, Inc. - 1178 N. Mesquite St., Las Cruces, NM 88001 t) 575-526-9545 oloh1178@yahoo.com www.ourladyofhealthchurch.org Rev. Ruben Romero, Pst.; Rev. Alonso Quinonez, Par. Vicar; Dcn. John Eric Munson; Gina Burgos, DRE; CRP Stds.: 42

Santa Rosa de Lima Parish, Inc. - 5035 Holsome Rd., Las Cruces, NM 88011 t) 575-382-8123 santarosadelimachurch@yahoo.com santarosadelimalc.org Rev. Gino Wilcox, Rev., Admin.; CRP Stds.: 62

Shrine and Parish of Our Lady of Guadalupe, Inc. - 3600 Parroquia St., Las Cruces, NM 88001; Mailing: Box 298, Mesilla Park, NM 88047 t) 575-526-8171; 575-525-1966 (CRP) pazkathy60@yahoo.com olgtortugas.com Very Rev. Valentine M. Jankowski, O.F.M.Conv., Pst.; Dcn. Emilio Ramos; Margie Graham, DRE; CRP Stds.: 79

LORDSBURG

St. Joseph Parish, Lordsburg, Inc. - 416 E. Second St., Lordsburg, NM 88045 t) 575-542-3268 stjosephcatholicparish416@gmail.com Rev. Jude M. Okonkwo (Nigeria), Admin.; CRP Stds.: 57

St. Jude -

San Felipe de Neri -

LOVING

Our Lady of Grace - 302 S. 4th St., Loving, NM 88256; Mailing: P.O. Box 428, Loving, NM 88256 t) 575-745-3341 workingforjesus@saint-edward.net Very Rev. Hriday K. Pasala, Admin.; CRP Stds.: 46

LOVINGTON

St. Thomas Aquinas Parish, Inc. - 1301 N. Ninth St., Lovington, NM 88260 t) 575-396-4206 stthomasholyrosary@gmail.com; st.thomaslovington@gmail.com stalovington.org/ Rev. Samuel Ameh, Admin.; CRP Stds.: 362

Our Lady of the Holy Rosary - 610 W. 2nd, Tatum, NM 88267; Mailing: 1301 N. 9th, Lovington, NM 88260 t) (575) 396-4206

MESCALERO

St. Joseph Parish, Mescalero, Inc. - 626 Mission Tr., Mescalero, NM 88340; Mailing: P. O. Box 187, Mescalero, NM 88340 t) 575-464-4473 st.josephapachemission@gmail.com www.stjosephapachemission.org Rev. David Mercer, Admin.; Sr. Robert-Ann Hecker, OSF, Pst. Assoc.; Harry Vasile, Youth Min.; CRP Stds.: 50

St. Patrick -

MESILLA

San Albino Parish, Inc. - 2280 Calle Principal, Mesilla, NM 88046; Mailing: P O Box 26, Mesilla, NM 88046 t) 575-526-9349 basilica@sanalbino.org sanalbino.org Very Rev. Christopher E. Williams, Pst.; Rev. Francis Gyau, Par. Vicar; CRP Stds.: 93

San Jose Mission - ; Mailing: P.O. Box 502, Fairacres, NM 88033 t) 575-312-4215 Sr. Marie-Paule Willem, F.M.M., Parish Life Coord.;

ROSWELL

Assumption Parish Inc. - 2808 N. Kentucky Ave., Roswell, NM 88201 t) 575-622-9895 x101 assumptionbvm@hotmail.com assumption-roswell.org Rev. Jaroslaw Nowacki, Admin.; Rev. Ephraim Ezulike (Nigeria), Par. Vicar; Carol Dutchover, DRE; CRP Stds.: 139

St. John Parish, Inc. - 506 S. Lincoln, Roswell, NM 88203; Mailing: 510 S. Lincoln Ave., Roswell, NM 88203 t) 575-622-3531; 575-623-1438 (CRP) spsjbreled@gmail.com sanjuannm.org Rev. Eduardo Espinosa, O.F.M., Pst.; Rev. Jose Abel Olivas, Assoc. Pst.; Dcn. Ernesto Martinez; Lorena Valencia, DRE; CRP Stds.: 468

St. Peter Parish, Inc. - 111 E. Deming St., Roswell, NM 88203 t) 575-622-5092 stpeterchurchroswellnm@gmail.com www.stpeterchurchroswell.org Very Rev. Carlos Martinez, O.F.M., Pst.; Dcn. Howard Herring, Pst. Assoc.; Dcn. Christopher Gutierrez; Lorena Valencia, DRE; CRP Stds.: 152

RUIDOSO

St. Eleanor Parish, Inc. - 140 Junction Rd., Ruidoso, NM 88355; Mailing: P.O. Box 8300, Ruidoso, NM 88355 t) 575-652-5950 steleanorparish@gmail.com www.steleanorparish.org Rev. Emmanuel Eche Stephen, Admin.; CRP Stds.: 60

St. Jude Thaddeus - 28110 Peter Hurd Loop, San Patricio, NM 88348 t) (575) 652-5950 steleanor@valornet.com; steleanor140@gmail.com www.steleanor.org

St. Joseph - Hwy. US 380, Picacho, NM 88343 t) (575) 652-5950 steleanor@valornet.com; steleanor140@gmail.com www.steleanor.org

San Ysidro - Hwy. US 380, San Ysidro Ln., Glencoe, NM 88324 t) (575) 652-5950 steleanor@valornet.com; steleanor140@gmail.com www.steleanor.org

SAN MIGUEL

San Miguel Parish, Inc. - 19217 S. Hwy. 28, San Miguel, NM 88058; Mailing: P.O Box E, San Miguel, NM 88058 t) 575-233-3191 Very Rev. Carlos A. Espinoza, Pst.; Dcn. Roger Montes; Claudia Pareyra, DRE; CRP Stds.: 19

Our Lady of Perpetual Help - 125 W. Mesquite St., Mesquite, NM 88048 t) (575) 233-3191 Rev. Chudy Peter Sixtus;

SANTA CLARA

Santa Clara Parish, Inc. - 707 Ft. Bayard St., Santa Clara, NM 88026; Mailing: PO Box 215, Santa Clara, NM 88026 t) 575-537-3713 santaclara_church13@yahoo.com Rev. Casmir Anozie (Nigeria), Admin.; Dcn. Richard Rodriguez, DRE; CRP Stds.: 39

SANTA TERESA

St. John Paul II Parish, Inc. - 6100 McNutt Rd., Santa Teresa, NM 88008 t) 575-332-4496; 575-502-4723 (CRP) johnpauliifamily@gmail.com; st.johnpaul2.rel.edu@gmail.com www.saintjpiiparish.org Rev. Francisco M. Tovar, Admin.; Dcn. Ramon Lozano, DRE; CRP Stds.: 128

SILVER CITY

St. Francis Newman Center Parish, Inc. - 914 W. 13th St., Silver City, NM 88061; Mailing: 1303 N. Florida St., Silver City, NM 88061 t) 575-538-3662 stfrancisnewman@msn.com www.stfrancisnewman.wix.com Serving Western New Mexico University. Rev. Bartholomew Ezenwelem (Nigeria), Admin.; Sylvia Misquez, DRE; CRP Stds.: 87

St. Vincent de Paul Parish, Inc. - 420 Market St., Silver City, NM 88061; Mailing: P.O. Box 1189, Silver, NM 88062-1189 t) 575-538-9373 svdp_nm@comcast.net svdpsc.com/ Very Rev. Oliver Obele, Pst.; Dcn. William Holguin; CRP Stds.: 82

St. Isidore - Hwy. 211 N. #9 Turkey Creek, Gila, NM 88038 t) (575) 538-9373

Holy Cross - 4814 Hwy. 15, Pinos Altos, NM 88053 t) (575) 538-9373

SUNLAND PARK

San Martin de Porres Parish, Inc. - 1885 McNutt Rd., Sunland Park, NM 88063 t) 575-589-2106 sanmartin@saintly.com Rev. Guillermo Rivera, O.P.,

Admin.; Dcn. Jesus Favela, DRE; CRP Stds.: 132

TRUTH OR CONSEQUENCES

Our Lady of Perpetual Help Parish, Inc. - 103 E. 6th Ave., Truth or Consequences, NM 87901 t) 575-894-7804; 575-894-7805; 575-894-0451 olphviola@gmail.com Rev. Michael J. Williams, Pst.; Dcn. James R. Winder; CRP Stds.: 18

St. Jose - t) (575) 894-7804

St. Ignatius - t) (575) 894-7804

San Lorenzo - t) (575) 894-7804

St. Gregory, Chapels Chiz - t) (575) 894-7804

San Miguel, Rancho de San Miguel - t) (575) 894-7804

St. Jude - t) (575) 894-7804

TULAROSA

St. Francis de Paula Parish, Inc. - 303 Encino St., Tularosa, NM 88352 t) 575-585-2793 stfrancisdepaula@gmail.com stfrancisdepaulachurch.org Rev. Patrick Montgomery, Pst.; Dcn. Mariano C. Melendrez; Janie Aragon, DRE; CRP Stds.: 27

Santo Nino -

SCHOOLS: PRESCHOOL THRU HIGH SCHOOL

SCHOOLS

STATE OF NEW MEXICO

ALAMOGORDO

St. Frances Cabrini Catholic School (Father James B. Hay School) - (PRV) (Grades PreK-8) 1000 E. Eighth St., Alamogordo, NM 88310 t) 575-437-7821 office@stfccatholic.org www.stfccatholic.org Victor Gonzales, Prin.; Sr. Noblyne Aldo, SJS, Faculty; Stds.: 95; Sr. Tchrs.: 1; Lay Tchrs.: 8

HOBBS

St. Helena School of Hobbs, Inc. - (PRV) (Grades PreK-5) 105 E. St. Anne Pl., Hobbs, NM 88240 t) 575-392-5405 office@sthelenaschool.net www.sthelenaschool.net Waverly Roan; Stds.: 80; Lay Tchrs.: 7

LAS CRUCES

Las Cruces Catholic School, Inc. - (PRV) (Grades PreK-8) 1331 N. Miranda, Las Cruces, NM 88005 t) 575-526-2517 wdrake@lascrucescatholicschool.com lccsonline.org Windy Drake, Prin.; Adrian Galaz, Prin.; Stds.: 297; Sr. Tchrs.: 2; Lay Tchrs.: 25

ROSWELL

All Saints Catholic School - (PRV) (Grades PreK-8) 2700 N. Kentucky, Roswell, NM 88201 t) 575-627-5744 principal2700@gmail.com www.allsaintsroswell.com Anna Pabst, Librn.; Stds.: 80; Lay Tchrs.: 8

INSTITUTIONS LOCATED IN DIOCESE

CATHOLIC CHARITIES [CCH]

LAS CRUCES

Catholic Charities of Southern New Mexico, Inc. - 125 W. Mountain Ave., Las Cruces, NM 88005 t) 575-527-0500 kf@catholiccharitiesdlc.org www.catholiccharitiesdlc.org Provider of social, legal, and economic assistance to people in need. Most Rev. Peter Baldacchino, Pres.; Kenneth Ferrone, Exec. Dir.; Asstd. Annu.: 1,750; Staff: 10

CONVENTS, MONASTERIES, AND RESIDENCES FOR WOMEN [CON]

CHAPARRAL

Dominicas De La Doctrina Cristiana - 124 Tornillo Flats Dr., Chaparral, NM 88081 t) 575-824-0508 gutierrezgloria451@gmail.com; ramirezgloria23@yahoo.com.mx Sr. Araceli Lopez, Contact; Srs.: 7

Religious of the Assumption - 629 Mesilla View Dr., Chaparral, NM 88081; Mailing: 300-2 McCombs Rd., PMB #43, Chaparral, NM 88081 t) 575-824-2850 rachaparral02@gmail.com assumptionsisters.org Sr. Mary Ann Azanza, RA, Supr.; Sr. Nha Trang Thi Nguyen, RA, Treas.; Srs.: 6

LAS CRUCES

The Discalced Carmelite Nuns of Las Cruces, Inc. - Monastery of St. Joseph and St. Teresa Benedicta of the Cross, 2011 Glass Rd., Las Cruces, NM 88005 t) 575-520-3515 edithlcnm@gmail.com www.carmelitenunsoflascruces.org Srs.: 11

ROSWELL

The Community of Poor Clares of New Mexico, Inc. - 809 E. 19th St., Roswell, NM 88201 t) 575-622-0868 www.poorclares-roswell.org Sr. Therese Passo, Vicar; Sr. Angela Kelly, P.C.C., Abbess; Srs.: 25

SILVER CITY

Sisters of St. Joseph - 1410 W. 6th St., Apt. 2, 602 N. Arizona St., Silver City, NM 88061 t) 575-313-2206 c) 575-538-3350 rplante@csjkansas.org; rafarrell@csjkansas.org Srs.: 2

ENDOWMENTS / FOUNDATIONS / TRUSTS [EFT]

LAS CRUCES

Catholic Diocese of Las Cruces Foundation, Inc. - 1280 Med Park Dr., Las Cruces, NM 88005 t) 575-523-7577 jemunson@rcdlc.org www.rcdlc.org Matthew Seltzer, Chair; Anthony Casaus, Dir.;

MISCELLANEOUS [MIS]

ALAMOGORDO

***Order of Secular Discalced Carmelites** - 776 Montwood Ct., Alamogordo, NM 88810; Mailing: P.O. Box 1509, Mesilla, NM 88046 t) 575-430-2106 1littlepoet@gmail.com Therese Wiley, Pres.;

Shroud Exhibit and Museum, Inc. - 923 N. New York Ave., Alamogordo, NM 88310; Mailing: P.O. Box 1711, Alamogordo, NM 88310 t) 575-921-3505 andy@shroudnm.com shroudnm.com Dcn. Andy Weiss;

LAS CRUCES

The Priests' Retirement Plan of the Catholic Diocese of Las Cruces, Inc. - 1280 Med Park Dr., Las Cruces, NM 88005; Mailing: 5024 4th St. NW, Albuquerque, NM 87101 t) 505-503-8637 jen@jcantrellcpa.com Rev. Richard Catanach, Pres.;

Secular Institute of Missionaries of the Kingship of Christ - 5344 Isabella Ct, Las Cruces, NM 88012 c) 575-635-9807 iojinaga@yahoo.com simkc.org Ida C Ojinaga, Contact;

MESILLA

Magnificat-Our Lady of the Cross Chapter, Inc. - ; Mailing: P.O. Box 1387, Mesilla, NM 88046 c) 575-636-3339; 575-571-5090 dnecek@yahoo.com; magnificatlascruces@gmail.com Rev. Alejandro Reyes, Spiritual Advisor; Denise Anderson, Chapter Coord.;

MONASTERIES AND RESIDENCES FOR PRIESTS AND BROTHERS [MON]

ANTHONY

Augustinian Recollect Fathers - 224 Lincoln St., Anthony, NM 88021; Mailing: P.O. Box 2624, Anthony, NM 88021 c) (915) 474-9707 www.agustinosrecoletos.org Province of St. Nicholas of Tolentine, Provincial Delegation in the South of U.S.A. Rev. Jesus M. Mena, O.A.R.; Priests: 5

LAS CRUCES

The Basilian Fathers of Las Cruces - 1682 Alta Vista Pl., Las Cruces, NM 88011 t) 575-521-4269 c) 575-520-0578 ed.heidt@gmail.com Rev. Ed Heidt, C.S.B., Pres.; Rev. Donald F. Hyatt, C.S.B.; Rev. David O. Klein, C.S.B.; Rev. David L. Sharp, C.S.B.; Priests: 4

PRESCHOOLS / CHILDCARE CENTERS [PRE]

CARLSBAD

San Jose Child Care Inc. - 421 W. Fox St., Carlsbad, NM 88220 t) 575-628-1346 sanjosedaycare1@windstream.net Patsy Grantner, Prin.; Stds.: 55; Lay Tchrs.: 8

RETREAT HOUSES / RENEWAL CENTERS [RTR]

MESILLA PARK

Holy Cross Retreat and Friary (Franciscan Fathers) - 600 Holy Cross Rd., Mesilla Park, NM 88047 t) 575-524-3688 director@holycrossretreat.org www.holycrossretreat.org Very Rev. Valentine M. Jankowski, O.F.M.Conv., Pst.; Rev. Thomas A. Smith, O.F.M.Conv., Dir.; Friar Peter Massengill, Sacramental Min.; Rev. Camillus Gott, OFM Conv., In Res.; Friar Charles Henkle, In Res.;

An asterisk (*) denotes an organization that has established tax-exempt status directly with the IRS and is not covered by the USCCB Group Ruling.

Diocese of Las Vegas

(Dioecesis Campensis)

MOST REVEREND GEORGE LEO THOMAS, PH.D.

Bishop of Las Vegas; ordained May 22, 1976; appointed Auxiliary Bishop of Seattle November 19, 1999; appointed Bishop of Helena March 23, 2004; installed June 4, 2004; appointed Bishop of Las Vegas February 28, 2018; installed May 15, 2018. Catholic Center, 336 Cathedral Way, Las Vegas, NV 89109.

Catholic Center: 336 Cathedral Way, Las Vegas, NV 89109. T: 702-735-3500; F: 702-735-8941.

Square Miles 39,088.

Established by His Holiness Pope Saint John Paul II on 21 March 1995.

Comprises the counties of Clark, Esmeralda, Lincoln, Nye, and White Pine in the State of Nevada.

For legal titles of parishes and diocesan institutions, consult the Chancery Office.

MOST REVEREND GREGORY W. GORDON
Auxiliary Bishop of Las Vegas; ordained January 16, 1988; appointed Auxiliary Bishop of Las Vegas May 28, 2021; installed July 16, 2021. Catholic Center, 336 Cathedral Way, Las Vegas, NV 89109.

STATISTICAL OVERVIEW

Personnel

Bishop	1
Auxiliary Bishops	1
Retired Bishops	1
Priests: Diocesan Active in Diocese	21
Priests: Diocesan Active Outside Diocese	1
Priests: Retired, Sick or Absent	17
Number of Diocesan Priests	39
Religious Priests in Diocese	29
Total Priests in your Diocese	68
Extern Priests in Diocese	19
Ordinations:	
Transitional Deacons	2
Permanent Deacons in Diocese	21
Total Brothers	2
Total Sisters	10

Parishes

Parishes	30
With Resident Pastor:	
Resident Diocesan Priests	13
Resident Religious Priests	7
Without Resident Pastor:	
Administered by Priests	10
Missions	5
Pastoral Centers	4
Professional Ministry Personnel:	
Brothers	1
Sisters	6
Lay Ministers	80

Welfare

Catholic Hospitals	3
Total Assisted	162,661
Specialized Homes	1
Total Assisted	30,000
Special Centers for Social Services	15
Total Assisted	38,000

Educational

Diocesan Students in Other Seminaries	9
Total Seminarians	9
High Schools, Diocesan and Parish	1
Total Students	1,568
High Schools, Private	1
Total Students	330
Elementary Schools, Diocesan and Parish	6
Total Students	2,020
Catechesis / Religious Education:	
High School Students	2,735
Elementary Students	4,495
Total Students under Catholic Instruction	11,157
Teachers in Diocese:	
Lay Teachers	257

Vital Statistics

Receptions into the Church:	
Infant Baptism Totals	2,922
Minor Baptism Totals	598
Adult Baptism Totals	126
Received into Full Communion	134
First Communions	1,644
Confirmations	1,281
Marriages:	
Catholic	342
Interfaith	77
Total Marriages	419
Deaths	907
Total Catholic Population	620,000
Total Population	2,350,718

LEADERSHIP

Catholic Center - t) 702-735-3500 www.dioceseoflasvegas.org

Chancellor - t) 702-735-3500 chancellor@dolv.org Very Rev. Robert M. Herbst, O.F.M.Conv.;

Vicar General - t) 702-629-4776 vg@dolv.org Most Rev. Gregory W. Gordon;

ADVISORY BOARDS, COMMISSIONS, COMMITTEES, AND COUNCILS

College of Consultors - t) 702-735-3500 Most Rev. George Leo Thomas; Most Rev. Gregory W. Gordon; Very Rev. Robert M. Herbst, O.F.M.Conv.;

Presbyteral Council for the Diocese of Las Vegas - t) 702-735-3500 Rev. William J.M. Kenny (wjmkenny2@gmail.com); Rev. John T. Assalone; Very Rev. Ronald Zanoni;

Priests' Pension Board - t) 702-735-3500 Most Rev. George Leo Thomas; Most Rev. Gregory W. Gordon; Dcn. Aruna I. Silva, CFO;

CATHOLIC CHARITIES

Catholic Charities of Southern Nevada - t) 702-385-2662 Dcn. Thomas A. Roberts, Pres.;

Board of Directors - t) 702-385-2662 Most Rev. George Leo Thomas, Chair; John P. Hester, Chair; Dcn. Thomas A. Roberts, Pres.;

CLERGY AND RELIGIOUS SERVICES

Director of Clergy Education - t) 702-735-3500 Very Rev. Ronald Zanoni, Dir.;.

Vocations - t) 702-735-3500 Very Rev. Ronald Zanoni, Dir.; Rev. Miguel Corral, Asst. Dir. (frmiguel@stannelvnv.org);

COMMUNICATIONS

Information, Communications and Media - t) 702-697-5918 webmaster@dolv.org Donna O'Callaghan;

DEANERIES

Deaneries -

Northern Deanery - t) 702-735-3500 Rev. James Michael Jankowski, Dean;

Rural Deanery - t) 702-735-3500 Rev. Charles B. Urnick, Dean;

Southern Deanery - t) 702-735-3500 Rev. William J.M. Kenny, Dean;

FACILITIES

Property Management - t) 702-735-7865 Jonathan Batista (JBatista@dolv.org);

FAITH FORMATION

Faith and Ministry Formation - t) 702-735-6044 Connie Clough, Dir.;

Hispanic Ministry - t) 702-735-3500 Rev. Miguel Corral, Vicar;

Youth Ministry - t) 702-735-6044 Hector Bautista;

FINANCE

Chief Financial Officer - t) 702-735-7865 silva@dolv.org Dcn. Aruna I. Silva;

Diocesan Finance Committee Members - t) 702-735-7865 silva@dolv.org Most Rev. George Leo Thomas; Most Rev. Gregory W. Gordon; Dcn. Aruna I. Silva, CFO;

HUMAN RESOURCES

Human Resources Department - t) 702-735-4570 lfinchio@dolv.org Judith Simon-Kohl, Dir. (kohl@dolv.org);

PASTORAL SERVICES

Hospital Apostolate (Vacant) -

SOCIAL SERVICES

Natural Family Planning/Fertility Care (Vacant) -

Pro Life/Respect Life - t) 702-735-3500 Kathleen Miller; Rev. Steven R. Hoffer; Dcn. Timothy O'Callaghan (lvsocialaction@gmail.com);

TRIBUNAL

Diocesan Tribunal Office - t) 702-735-1210 Very Rev. Robert M. Herbst, O.F.M.Conv., Judicial Vicar; Margarita Hernandez, Secy. (margarita@dolv.org);

Tribunal - Defenders of the Bond - Rev. Jaime Ponce; Bro. Christopher Douglas Garcia; Bro. Manuel Ruiz;

Tribunal - Diocesan Advocates - Rev. Samuel Martinez; Dcn. Felipe Rivas; Dcn. Jim L. Wiggins;

Tribunal - Diocesan Judges - Rev. Msgr. Charles J. Chaffman; Very Rev. Robert M. Herbst, O.F.M.Conv.;

Tribunal - Promoter of Justice - Most Rev. Joseph A. Pepe;

MISCELLANEOUS / OTHER OFFICES

Archivist - t) 702-735-2744 Argia Kopa (archivist@dolv.org);

Coordinator for Catholic Campaign for Human Development, Catholic Relief Services - t) 702-293-7500 lvsocialaction@gmail.com Dcn. Tim O'Callaghan, Dir.;

Home and Foreign Missions - t) 702-735-3500 Most Rev. Gregory W. Gordon;

Legal Department - t) 702-735-2512 kohl@dolv.org Judith Simon-Kohl (kohl@dolv.org);

Missionary Childhood Association - t) 702-735-3500 Most Rev. Gregory W. Gordon;

Native American and Colored People Commission - t) 702-735-3500 Most Rev. Gregory W. Gordon;

Propagation of the Faith - t) 702-735-3500 Most Rev. Gregory W. Gordon;

Victim Advocate & Safe Environment Coordinator - t) 702-235-7723 Ronald Vallance (AssistMin@dolv.org);

PARISHES, MISSIONS, AND CLERGY

STATE OF NEVADA

AMARGOSA VALLEY

Christ of the Desert Catholic Church - 3405 E. White Sands, Amargosa Valley, NV 89020; Mailing: 2381 N. Joshua Rd., Amargosa Valley, NV 89020 t) 775-372-5337; 775-727-4044; 775-372-5501 (CRP) amargosarose@yahoo.com; frbrunomauricci@yahoo.com christofthedesertmissionchurch.com Mission Church-Priest from Our Lady of the Valley, Pahrump NV-Diocese of Las Vegas, NV Rev. Bruno Mauricci, Pst.;

BOULDER CITY

St. Andrew Catholic Community - 1399 San Felipe Dr., Boulder City, NV 89005 t) 702-293-7500 standrewbc@gmail.com; tim.standrewsbc@gmail.com standrewbc.org Rev. Ron Zanoni, Pst.; Dcn. Tim O'Callaghan, Parish Life Coord.; CRP Stds.: 1

CALIENTE

Holy Child - 80 Tennille St., Caliente, NV 89008-0748; Mailing: P.O. Box 748, Caliente, NV 89008-0748 t) 775-726-3669 Margaret Bushman, DRE; Rev. Elias V. Kabuk (Nigeria), Admin.; CRP Stds.: 10

ELY

Sacred Heart - 1100-1198 E. 11th St., Ely, NV 89301; Mailing: P.O. Box 151026, Ely, NV 89315 t) 775-289-2201 sacredheartchurchely@yahoo.com sacredheartchurchely.org/ Rev. Elias V. Kabuk (Nigeria), Admin.; Sr. Sandy DiCianno, DRE; CRP Stds.: 67

St. Michael's - 40 Second St., McGill, NV 89301; Mailing: P O Box 151026, Ely, NV 89315 t) (775) 289-2201

HENDERSON

St. Francis of Assisi - 2300 Sunridge Heights Pkwy., Henderson, NV 89052 t) 702-914-3563 (CRP); 702-914-2175 king@sfahdnv.org; sfa@sfahdnv.org www.sfahdnv.org Rev. John T. Assalone, Pst.; Rev. Vicente Panaligan, Par. Vicar; Rev. John Minde, Par. Vicar; Craig King, DRE; David Hall, Youth Min.; CRP Stds.: 827

St. Anthony of Padua Roman Catholic School - (Grades PreK-8) 2320 Sunridge Heights Pkwy., Henderson, NV 89052 t) 702-331-9050 stanthonyschool@sapsaints.org www.sapsaints.org Rick Blanc, Prin.; Cynthia McNeal, Vice Prin.; Stds.: 375; Scholastics: 14; Lay Tchrs.: 20

St. Peter the Apostle - 204 S. Boulder Hwy., Henderson, NV 89015 t) 702-970-2525 (CRP); 702-970-2500 info@stpahend.org www.stpeterhenderson.org Rev. Samuel Martinez, Pst.; Anthony Sperduti, Faith Formation Supvr.; CRP Stds.: 170

St. Thomas More - 130 N. Pecos Rd., Henderson, NV 89074 t) 702-361-3022 staceys@stmlv.org; jeniferj@stmlv.org www.stmlv.org Rev. Edmund Nnadozie, MSP (Nigeria), Par. Admin.; Rev. Joseph Trong Nguyen, Par. Vicar; Dcn. William McManus; Dcn. Robert Rudloff Jr.; Jenifer Jefferies, DRE; CRP Stds.: 496

LAS VEGAS

Guardian Angel Cathedral - 302 Cathedral Way, Las Vegas, NV 89109; Mailing: 336 Cathedral Way, Las Vegas, NV 89109 t) 702-735-5241 www.gaclv.org Rev. Robert E. Stoeckig, Rector; Colleen Bevilacqua, Bus. Mgr.; William Paul Freeman, Pst. Assoc.;

St. Anne - 1901 S. Maryland Pkwy., Las Vegas, NV 89104 t) 702-735-0510; 702-866-0008 (CRP) parish@stannelvnv.org; dre@stannelvnv.org www.stannelvnv.org Rev. Miguel Corral, Pst.; Rev. Gregorio Leon, Assoc. Pst.; Dcn. Santiago Guerrero; Silvia Corral, DRE; CRP Stds.: 886

St. Anne School - (Grades K-8) 1813 S. Maryland Pkwy., Las Vegas, NV 89104 t) 702-735-2586 school@stannelvnv.org Abigale Carpenter, Prin.; Sheila Solomon, Librn.; Susan McDonald, Office Mgr.; Stds.: 184; Lay Tchrs.: 12

St. Anthony of Padua - 6350 N. Fort Apache Rd., Las Vegas, NV 89149 t) 702-399-6897 egeorge@saplv.com; josephw@saplv.com www.saplv.com Rev. Robert W. Puhlman, Pst.; Joseph Wattendarger, DRE; CRP Stds.: 363

St. Bridget Roman Catholic Church - 220 N. 14th St., Las Vegas, NV 89101-4312 t) 702-384-3382 info@stbridgetc.org Rev. Faustinus Okeyikam, MSP, Pst.; CRP Stds.: 228

Christ the King - 4925 S. Torrey Pines Dr., Las Vegas, NV 89118 t) 702-871-1904; 702-871-1904 x230 (CRP) fr.shawn@ctkccnv.org; ginap@ctkccnv.org www.ctklv.org Rev. Shawn Dresden, Pst.; CRP Stds.: 229

St. Catherine of Siena - 47 Pearl, Sandy Valley, NV 89109; Mailing: P.O. Box 19789, Sandy Valley, NV 89019 t) 702-858-3792 rminch2@sbcglobal.net Dcn. Rick Minch;

St. Elizabeth Ann Seton - 1811 Pueblo Vista Dr., Las Vegas, NV 89128 t) 702-228-8311 seaschurch@seaslv.org www.seaslv.org Rev. James Michael Jankowski, Pst.; Rev. Joseph Le, C.Ss.R., Par. Vicar; Rev. Luis Van Dam, Minister to the Sick; Dcn. Steve Doucet; Dcn. Aruna I. Silva; Marcie Wilske, Pst. Assoc.; CRP Stds.: 289

St. Elizabeth Ann Seton School - (Grades PreK-8) 1807 Pueblo Vista Dr., Las Vegas, NV 89128 t) 702-804-8328 seasschool@seaslv.org www.seascatholicschool.org/ Len Urso, Prin.; Stds.: 409; Lay Tchrs.: 26

St. Francis de Sales - 1111 Michael Way, Las Vegas, NV 89108 t) 702-647-3440; 702-646-2266 (CRP) parishinfo@sfdslv.org www.stfrancisdesaleslv.org Rev. Rogelio Molina, Pst.; Rev. Lucas Kimario, Vicar; Charlene Domschot, DRE; CRP Stds.: 738

St. Francis de Sales School - (Grades K-8) t) 702-647-2828 frbruno@sfdslv.org Carol Wilson, Prin.; Stds.: 234; Lay Tchrs.: 13

Holy Family - 4490 Mountain Vista, Las Vegas, NV

89121 t) 702-458-2211 esmesaldiaz@yahoo.com; fr.steve.hoffer@gmail.com www.holyfamilylv.org Rev. Steven R. Hoffer, Pst.; Rev. Tony Udoh, MSP, Assoc. Pst.; Esmeralda Saldivar, DRE; Dcn. Daniel Maier, RCIA Coord.; Patti R Kelly, Bus. Mgr.; CRP Stds.: 366

Holy Spirit Catholic Church - 5830 Mesa Park Dr., Las Vegas, NV 89135 t) 702-459-7778 holyspiritlv@holyspiritlv.org; louiel@holyspiritlv.org www.holyspiritlv.org Rev. William J.M. Kenny, Pst.; Anna Forsberg, Dir.; Louie Latina, Dir.; Rev. Jose Unlayao, C.J.D., Pst. Assoc.; CRP Stds.: 600

St. James the Apostle - 1920 N. Martin Luther King Blvd., Las Vegas, NV 89106 t) 702-648-6606 aeagan@sjtac.org; stjames@sjtac.org sjtac.org Rev. Binoy Akkalayil-Lucka, O.SS.T, Admin.; Dcn. Timothy Byrnes; Dcn. James Marek; Arsenia Eagan, DRE; CRP Stds.: 48

St. Joan of Arc - 315 S. Casino Center Blvd., Las Vegas, NV 89101 t) 702-382-9909 st.joanlv@gmail.com stjoanlv.org Rev. Siarhei Anhur, S. Chr, Pst.;

St. Joseph, Husband of Mary - 7260 W. Sahara Ave., Las Vegas, NV 89117 t) 702-363-1902 mameh@stjosephhom.org; gsinclair@stjosephhom.org www.stjosephhom.org Rev. Eugene M Kinney, Par. Vicar; Rev. Mark Thomas Ameh, M.S.P., Admin.; Dcn. Vince Murone, Treas.; Barbara Finn, Music Min.; Greg Sinclair, Pst. Assoc.; Kristin Mulligan, DRE; CRP Stds.: 381

Our Lady of La Vang - 4835 S. Pearl St., Las Vegas, NV 89121 t) 702-821-1459 melavanglasvegas@gmail.com www.lavanglasvegas.com Rev. Thomas Ha, Admin.; Gia Nguyen, DRE;

Our Lady of Las Vegas - 3050 Alta Dr., Las Vegas, NV 89107 t) 702-802-2300 lizwilliams1234@hotmail.com; ollvparish@ollv.org ollvchurch.org Rev. Gerald Grupczynski, S.Chr., Pst.; Elizabeth Williams, DRE; CRP Stds.: 100

Our Lady of Las Vegas School - (Grades PreK-8) 3046 Alta Dr., Las Vegas, NV 89107 t) 702-802-2323 ollvschool@ollv.org www.ollvschool.org Marisa Bello, Prin.; Stds.: 466; Lay Tchrs.: 29

St. Paul Jung-Ha-Sang Korean Catholic Church - 6080 S. Jones Blvd., Las Vegas, NV 89118 t) 702-222-4349 daysys2018@gmail.com Jungyob Yun, Admin.;

Prince of Peace - 5485 E. Charleston Blvd., Las Vegas, NV 89142 t) 702-431-2233; 702-431-2233 x106 (CRP) cathy@poplv.org; guadalupe@poplv.org princeofpeacelasvegas.org Rev. Jose Rolando Rivera, Pst.; Rev. Mugagga Lule, Par. Vicar; Dcn. David Walker; Guadalupe Munoz-Haas, DRE; CRP Stds.: 673

St. Viator Catholic Community - 2461 E. Flamingo Rd., Las Vegas, NV 89121 t) 702-733-0392 (CRP); 702-733-8323 info@stviator.org www.stviator.org Rev. Richard A. Rinn, C.S.V., Pst.; Dcn. Michael Underwood; Rosy Hartz, DRE; Susan Lockett, Bus. Mgr.; CRP Stds.: 153

St. Viator Catholic Community School - (Grades PreK-8) 4246 S. Eastern Ave., Las Vegas, NV 89119-5426 t) 702-732-4477 tbrunelle@stviator.org; svsschool@stviator.org stviatorschool.org Tracy L. Brunelle, Prin.; Carolyn Wells, Librn.; Stds.: 352; Lay Tchrs.: 24

LAUGHLIN

St. John the Baptist Catholic Church - 3055 El Mirage Way, Laughlin, NV 89029; Mailing: P.O. Box 31230, Laughlin, NV 89028 t) 702-298-0440; 702-726-7014 (CRP) sjblaughlin@gmail.com laughlincatholic.com Rev. Charles B. Urnick, Admin.; Dcn. Richard Lambert; Dcn. Daniel McHugh; Hope Castillo, DRE; CRP Stds.: 5

LOGANDALE

St. John the Evangelist - 2955 St. Joseph St., Logandale, NV 89021; Mailing: P.O. Box 457, Overton, NV 89040 t) 702-398-3998 stjohn@mvdsl.com Rev. Henry P. Salditos, Admin.; CRP Stds.: 47

MESQUITE

La Virgen de Guadalupe - 401 Canyon Crest Blvd., Mesquite, NV 89027; Mailing: P O Box 300, Mesquite, NV 89024 t) 702-346-7065; 702-346-4460 (CRP) lvdgoffice@mesquiteweb.com catholicchurches89027.org Rev. Blaise R. Baran, Admin.; Dcn. Jaime Marquez; Dcn. John Lawrence Smith; Miriam Flores, DRE; CRP Stds.: 112

Education Center - 93 W. First S., Bunkerville, NV 89007; Mailing: P.O. Box 300, Mesquite, NV 89024 floresnev@yahoo.com

NORTH LAS VEGAS

St. Christopher - 1840 N. Bruce St., North Las Vegas, NV 89030 t) 702-642-1154; (702) 685-4063 x106 (Business Office) reoffice@stchrisnlv.org stchristophernlv.org/ Rev. Michael Rolland, OP, Par. Admin.; CRP Stds.: 943

St. John Neumann - 2575 W. El Campo Grande Ave., North Las Vegas, NV 89031 t) 702-657-0200; 702-657-0200 x210 (CRP) cathy.trawinski@sjnc.org www.sjnc.org Rev. Marc C. Howes, Pst.; Rev. Roy Kurian, Assoc. Pst.; Dcn. Patrick Cater; Dcn. James Pittman; Cathy Trawinski, DRE; CRP Stds.: 393

PAHRUMP

Our Lady of the Valley - 781 E. Gamebird, Pahrump, NV 89048 t) 775-727-4044 ourladyofthevalleychurch.org/ Rev. Bruno Mauricci, Pst.; Maria Gonzalez, DRE; CRP Stds.: 124

TONOPAH

St. Patrick - 144 South St., Tonopah, NV 89049; Mailing: P.O. Box 325, Tonopah, NV 89049 t) 775-482-6746 stpatrickstonopah@frontier.com Rev. Alex Thomas Viruthakulangara, Par. Admin.; CRP Stds.: 7

St. Barbara - 91 Hadley Cir., Round Mountain, NV 89045; Mailing: PO Box 325, Tonopah, NV 89049 Dana Friel, Secy.;

Our Lady of Guadalupe - SR 264, Fish Lake Community Center, Dyer, NV 89010 Dana Friel, Secy.;

SCHOOLS: PRESCHOOL THRU HIGH SCHOOL

HIGH SCHOOLS

STATE OF NEVADA

LAS VEGAS

Bishop Gorman High School - (DIO) 5959 S. Hualapai Way, Las Vegas, NV 89148 t) 702-732-1945 kkiefer@bishopgorman.org; jkilduff@bishopgorman.org www.bishopgorman.org Kevin Kiefer, Prin.; John Kilduff, Pres.; Stds.: 1,568; Lay Tchrs.: 106

NORTH LAS VEGAS

Cristo Rey St. Viator Las Vegas Preparatory, Inc. - (PRV) (Grades 9-12) 2880 N. Van Der Meer St., North Las Vegas, NV 89030 t) 702-844-2019 tvonbehren@crsvlv.org; stsutahara@crsvlv.org www.cristoreystviator.org Rev. Thomas von Behren, C.S.V., Pres.; Bro. Carlos Ernesto Florez, C.S.V., Dir. of Viatorian & Catholic Identity; Stds.: 330; Lay Tchrs.: 27

INSTITUTIONS LOCATED IN DIOCESE

CAMPUS MINISTRY / NEWMAN CENTERS [CAM]

LAS VEGAS

St. Thomas Aquinas Catholic Newman Community at UNLV - 4765 Brussels St., Las Vegas, NV 89119-6602 t) 702-736-0887 info@unlvnewman.com unlvnewman.com Rev. Daniel Rolland, O.P., Dir.;

CATHOLIC CHARITIES [CCH]

LAS VEGAS

Catholic Charities of Southern Nevada - 1501 Las Vegas Blvd., N., Las Vegas, NV 89101 t) 702-385-2662 abeltran@catholiccharities.com www.catholiccharities.com Dcn. Thomas A. Roberts, Pres.; Asstd. Annu.: 38,000; Staff: 239

Adoption Services - 1511 Las Vegas Blvd. N., Las Vegas, NV 89101 t) 702-385-3351 Dcn. Thomas A Roberts, Pres.;

CCSN McFarland Housing Development Corporation, Inc. - 4988 Jeffreys St., Las Vegas, NV 89119 t) 702-736-7596 ncoleaia2@cox.net Dcn. Thomas A Roberts;

CCSN McFarland Housing, Inc. - 4988 Jeffreys St., Las Vegas, NV 89119 t) 702-736-9596 ncoleaia2@cox.net Dcn. Thomas A Roberts;

CCSN Mojave Project, Inc. - 561 N. Mojave Rd., Las Vegas, NV 89101 t) 702-384-2643 ncoleaia2@cox.net Dcn. Thomas A Roberts;

Emergency Shelter - 1511 Las Vegas Blvd. N., Las Vegas, NV 89101 t) 702-387-2282 Dcn. Thomas A Roberts, Pres.;

English Language Program - 1511 Las Vegas Blvd. N., Las Vegas, NV 89101 t) 702-215-4732 Dcn. Thomas A Roberts, Pres.;

Immigration Services - 1511 Las Vegas Blvd. N., Las Vegas, NV 89101 t) 702-383-8387 Dcn. Thomas A Roberts, Pres.;

Migration and Refugee Services - 1511 Las Vegas Blvd. N., Las Vegas, NV 89101 t) 702-383-8387 Dcn. Thomas A Roberts, Pres.;

NCWB Housing, Inc. - 400 Brush St., Las Vegas, NV 89107 t) 702-878-5398 ncoleaia2@cox.net Dcn. Thomas A Roberts, Pres.;

Resident Empowerment Program - 1511 Las Vegas Blvd. N., Las Vegas, NV 89101 t) 702-387-2282 Dcn. Thomas A Roberts, Pres.;

Senior Nutrition & Meals-on-Wheels - 531 N. 30th St., Las Vegas, NV 89101 t) 702-385-5284 Dcn. Thomas A Roberts, Pres.;

Social Services - 1511 Las Vegas Blvd. N., Las Vegas, NV 89101 t) 702-387-2291 Dcn. Thomas A Roberts, Pres.;

St. Vincent CCSN SRO Inc. - 1521 Las Vegas Blvd. N., Las Vegas, NV 89101 t) 702-366-2090 Dcn. Thomas A Roberts, Pres.;

St. Vincent Lied Dining Facility - 1501 Las Vegas Blvd. N., Las Vegas, NV 89101 t) 702-215-4727 Dcn. Thomas A Roberts, Pres.;

Women, Infants, and Children (WIC) - 1511 Las Vegas Blvd. N., Las Vegas, NV 89101 t) 702-366-2069 Dcn. Thomas A Roberts, Pres.;

ENDOWMENTS / FOUNDATIONS / TRUSTS [EFT]

HENDERSON

St. Rose Dominican Health Foundation - 2865 Siena Hts. Dr., Ste. 300, Henderson, NV 89052; Mailing: 3001 St. Rose Pkwy., Henderson, NV 89052 t) 702-616-5750 pam.koerner@commonspirit.org www.supportstrose.org Charles Guida, Pres.;

HOSPITALS / HEALTH SERVICES [HOS]

HENDERSON

St. Rose Dominican Hospital, Rose de Lima Campus - 102 E. Lake Mead Pkwy., Henderson, NV 89015 t) 702-616-5000 pam.koerner@commonspirit.org www.strosehospitals.org Sponsored by Catholic Health Care Federation Thomas Burns; Bed Capacity: 110; Asstd. Annu.: 20,449; Staff: 171

St. Rose Dominican Hospital, San Martin Campus - 8280 W. Warm Springs Rd., Las Vegas, NV 89015 t) 702-492-8000 thomas.burns@commonspirit.org Sponsored by Catholic Health Care Federation Kim Shaw, Pres.; Bed Capacity: 147; Asstd. Annu.: 36,916; Staff: 827

St. Rose Dominican Hospital, Siena Campus - 3001 St.

Rose Pkwy., Henderson, NV 89052-6178 t) 702-616-5000 pam.koerner@commonspirit.org www.strosehospitals.org Sponsored by Catholic Health Care Federation Jon Van Boening, Pres.; Bed Capacity: 326; Asstd. Annu.: 105,296; Staff: 2,284

MISCELLANEOUS [MIS]

HENDERSON

Saint Therese Center - 215 Palo Verde, Henderson, NV 89015; Mailing: P.O. Box 90625, Henderson, NV 89015 t) 702-564-4224 aidsproject@dolv.org sainttheresecenter.org HIV/AIDS Outreach Program Rev. Joseph O'Brien, O.P., Exec.; Rev. Joseph Sergott, OP, Assoc.; Bro. Michael James Rivera, OP, Assoc.;

St. Therese HIV/AIDS Executive Office -

St. Therese HIV/AIDS Little Flower House - 241 Palo Verde Dr., Henderson, NV 89015; Mailing: P.O. Box 90625, Henderson, NV 89009-0625 t) (702) 564-4224

LAS VEGAS

Bishop Gorman Assistance Corporation - 336 Cathedral Way, Las Vegas, NV 89109 t) 702-735-3500 silva@dolv.org Dcn. Aruna Silva, Exec.;

Bishop Gorman Development Corp. - 336 Cathedral Way, Las Vegas, NV 89109 t) 702-735-7865 silva@dolv.org Dcn. Aruna I. Silva, Exec.;

Catholic Diocese of Las Vegas Capital Funding Corporation - 336 Cathedral Way, Las Vegas, NV 89109 t) 702-735-3500 silva@dolv.org Dcn. Aruna I. Silva, Exec.;

Catholic Diocese of Las Vegas Capital Management Corporation - 336 Cathedral Way, Las Vegas, NV 89109 t) 702-735-7865 silva@dolv.org Dcn. Aruna I. Silva, Exec.;

Diocesan Residence - Diocese of Las Vegas, 336 Cathedral Way, Las Vegas, NV 89109 t) 702-735-7865 silva@dolv.org Dcn. Aruna I. Silva, Exec.;

St. Thomas More Society of Nevada - ; Mailing: P.O. Box 97404, Las Vegas, NV 89193 t) 702-361-7480 katrina@stmnevada.org www.stmnevada.org Richard Gordon, Pres.;

MONASTERIES AND RESIDENCES FOR PRIESTS AND BROTHERS [MON]

LAS VEGAS

Canons Regular of Jesus the Lord of Nevada, Inc. - 1811 Pueblo Vista Dr., Las Vegas, NV 89128 c) 725-244-7344 luisnvd@yahoo.com Rev. Luis Van Dam, Contact; Priests: 1

Clerics of St. Viator Retirement Home - 4219 Pinecrest Cir. E., Las Vegas, NV 89121; Mailing: 2028 Heritage Oaks St., Las Vegas, NV 89119 c) 847-772-8800 tvonbehren@viatorians.com Rev. William F. Haesaert, C.S.V., In Res.; Priests: 1

Dominican Rectory, Fra Angelico House - 1701 Chapman Dr., Las Vegas, NV 89104-3516 t) 702-369-1215 aidsproject@dolv.org (Western Dominican Province) Rev. Joseph O'Brien, O.P., Supr.; Bro. Michael James Rivera, OP, In Res.; Rev. Joseph Sergott, OP, In Res.; Rev. Daniel Rolland, O.P., In Res.; Rev. Albert Felice-Pace, O.P., In Res.; Brs.: 1; Priests: 4

SHRINES [SHR]

LAS VEGAS

Shrine of the Most Holy Redeemer - 55 E. Reno Ave., Las Vegas, NV 89119 t) 702-891-8600 x229 (Rector) frmanuel@shrinelv.org; mthompson@shrinelv.org www.shrinelv.org Rev. Manuel Quintero, Rector; Merlyn Thompson, Dir.;

An asterisk (*) denotes an organization that has established tax-exempt status directly with the IRS and is not covered by the USCCB Group Ruling.

Diocese of Lexington

MOST REVEREND JOHN STOWE, O.F.M. CONV.

Bishop of Lexington; ordained September 16, 1995; appointed Bishop of Lexington March 12, 2015; installed May 5, 2015.
The Catholic Center: 1310 W. Main St., Lexington, KY 40508-2048.

The Catholic Center: 1310 W. Main St., Lexington, KY 40508-2048. T: 859-253-1993; F: 859-254-6284.
www.cdlex.org
webmaster@cdlex.org

ESTABLISHED MARCH 2, 1988.

Square Miles 16,423.

Comprises the counties of Anderson, Bath, Bell, Bourbon, Boyd, Boyle, Breathitt, Carter, Clark, Clay, Elliott, Estill, Fayette, Floyd, Franklin, Garrard, Greenup, Harlan, Jackson, Jessamine, Johnson, Knott, Knox, Laurel, Lawrence, Lee, Leslie, Letcher, Lincoln, McCreary, Madison, Magoffin, Martin, Menifee, Mercer, Montgomery, Morgan, Nicholas, Owsley, Perry, Pike, Powell, Pulaski, Rockcastle, Rowan, Scott, Wayne, Whitley, Wolfe and Woodford.

For legal titles of parishes and diocesan institutions, consult the Chancellor.

STATISTICAL OVERVIEW

Personnel	
Bishop	1
Priests: Diocesan Active in Diocese	39
Priests: Diocesan Active Outside Diocese	4
Priests: Retired, Sick or Absent	15
Number of Diocesan Priests	58
Religious Priests in Diocese	14
Total Priests in your Diocese	72
Extern Priests in Diocese	3
Ordinations:	
Diocesan Priests	1
Permanent Deacons in Diocese	82
Total Sisters	36
Parishes	
Parishes	49
With Resident Pastor:	
Resident Diocesan Priests	43
Resident Religious Priests	11
Without Resident Pastor:	
Administered by Deacons	1
Administered by Lay People	5
Missions	10
Professional Ministry Personnel:	
Sisters	18
Lay Ministers	48
Welfare	
Catholic Hospitals	10
Total Assisted	532,837
Health Care Centers	4
Total Assisted	38,273
Homes for the Aged	1
Total Assisted	82
Special Centers for Social Services	1
Total Assisted	377
Educational	
Students from This Diocese	4
Total Seminarians	4
High Schools, Diocesan and Parish	1
Total Students	710
High Schools, Private	1
Total Students	33
Elementary Schools, Diocesan and Parish	12
Total Students	2,721
Catechesis/Religious Education:	
High School Students	351
Elementary Students	1,715
Total Students under Catholic Instruction	5,534
Teachers in Diocese:	
Priests	5
Lay Teachers	304
Vital Statistics	
Receptions into the Church:	
Infant Baptism Totals	343
Minor Baptism Totals	301
Adult Baptism Totals	145
Received into Full Communion	148
First Communions	603
Confirmations	641
Marriages:	
Catholic	95
Interfaith	45
Total Marriages	140
Deaths	352
Total Catholic Population	38,673
Total Population	1,604,276

LEADERSHIP

The Catholic Center - t) 859-253-1993
Bishop of Lexington - Most Rev. John Stowe, O.F.M.Conv.;
Vicar General - t) 859-253-1993 x1027 dnoll@cdlex.org Rev. Daniel J. Noll;
Chancellor - t) 859-253-1993 x1002 kabbey@cdlex.org Karen Abbey;
Bishop's Delegate for Administration - t) 859-253-1993 x1003 dculp@cdlex.org Doug Culp;
Executive Administrative Assistant To The Bishop - t) 859-253-1993 x1002 kabbey@cdlex.org Karen Abbey;
Secretariat for Stewardship - t) 859-253-1993 x1043 dswisher@cdlex.org Debbie Swisher, Diocesan Finance Officer;
College of Consultors - Rev. Paul Prabell; Rev. Linh Nguyen; Rev. Robert H. Nieberding;
Regional Councillors - Rev. Anthony McLaughlin (amclaughlin@cdlex.org); Rev. Tom Farrell; Rev. Michael D. Flanagan;
Diocesan Tribunal - t) 859-253-1993 Renata Babicz-Baratto, Dir. (ribabicz@cdlex.org);
 Judicial Vicar - t) 859-253-1993 x1032 Rev. John E. List;
 Tribunal Director - t) 859-253-1993 x1031 ribabicz@cdlex.org Renata Babicz-Baratto;
 Associate Judges - Rev. Victor Finelli; Rev. Barry Windholtz; Rev. Michael Hack;
 Defenders of the Bond - t) 859-253-1993 arockiadoss@cdlex.org Rev. Arokodias Das; Rev. Anthony McLaughlin;
 Promoter of Justice - t) 859-253-1993 pprabell@cdlex.org Rev. Paul Prabell;
 Notaries - t) 859-253-1993 dgoodman@cdlex.org; llee@cdlex.org Donna Goodman; Lorraine Lee;
Priests' Retirement Committee - t) 859-253-1993 Rev. Michael J. Ramler, Mem.; Rev. Richard Watson, Mem.; Rev. Frank C. Osburg, Mem.;
Secretariat for Catholic Schools - t) 859-253-1993 x1015 klee@cdlex.org Dr. Kyle Lee, Supt.;

OFFICES AND DIRECTORS

Archives - t) 859-253-1993 x1002 kabbey@cdlex.org Karen Abbey, Archivist;
Campus Ministry (Vacant) - t) 859-253-1993
Catholic Charities of Lexington - t) 859-253-1993 x1036 Cheryl Bogarty, Exec. Dir. (cbogarty@cdlex.org);
Catholic Scouting - t) 859-253-1993 Rev. Chris Clay, Dir. (cclay@cdlex.org);
Commission for African American Catholic Concerns - Theresa Hawkins-Jones, Chair;
Deaf Ministry - t) 859-253-1993
Development Office - t) 859-253-1993 x1049 rwatts@cdlex.org Robert Watts, Dir.;
Ecumenical Liaison - mholland@cdlex.org Melissa Holland, Contact;
Father Beiting Appalachian Mission Center - t) 606-638-0219 emichael@cdlex.org Ed Michael, Dir.;
HIV/AIDS Ministry - t) 859-253-1993 Rev. John C. Curtis, Diocesan Coord.;
Liturgy - t) 859-253-1993 x1010 krood@cdlex.org Karen Rood, Dir.;
Magazine "Cross Roads" - t) 859-253-1993 x1005 Dcn. Paul "Skip" Olson (solson@cdlex.org);
Magnificat-Lexington - t) 859-229-1801 Laura Westbrook, Coord. (lauralkw@twc.com);
Ministry for Persons with Disabilities - t) 859-253-1993 disability@cdlex.org
Mission Office, Propagation of the Faith and The Holy Childhood - t) 859-253-1993 x1049 rwatts@cdlex.org Robert Watts, Dir.;
Peace & Justice - t) 859-253-1993 x1011 jvancleef@cdlex.org Joshua van Cleef, Dir.;
Permanent Diaconate - t) 859-253-1993 x1030 mlynch@cdlex.org Dcn. Michael Joseph Lynch, Dir.;
Priests' Personnel - t) (859) 252-0738 rwatson@cdlex.org Rev. Richard Watson, Vicar;
R.C.I.A. - t) 859-253-1993 x1010 krood@cdlex.org Karen Rood, Coord.;
Regina Pacis Community - t) 859-268-5159 Rev. Mark Fischer, FSSP, Chap. (mfischer@cdlex.org);
Religious - t) 859-509-2662 cfehringer@cdlex.org Sr. Clara Fehringer, O.S.U., Delegate;
Secretariat for Pastoral Life - t) 859-253-1993 x1003 dculp@cdlex.org Doug Culp, Secy.;
 Communications - t) 859-253-1993 Ed Bauer, Dir.; Dcn. Skip Olson, Assoc. Dir.;
 Director of Family Life - t) (859) 253-1993 x1009 mallen@cdlex.org Michael Allen;
 Director of Religious Formation & Adult Faith Formation - rstearn@cdlex.org Rod Stearn;
 Director of Youth & Young Adult Ministry - t) (859) 253-1993 x1008 Michael Armstrong, Youth Min.;
 Hispanic Ministry - efortini@cdlex.org Doug Culp, Dir.; Dcn. Eduardo Fortini, Coord. Hispanic Ministry;
 Human Resources - Greg Hodge, Dir.;
Secretariat for Stewardship - t) 859-253-1993 x1043 dswisher@cdlex.org Debbie Swisher, Diocesan Finance Officer;
Secretariat of the Vicar General - t) 859-253-1993 x1027 dnoll@cdlex.org Rev. Daniel J. Noll;
Victim Assistance Coordinator - t) 859-338-5695 Laura Napora (victimsassistance@cdlex.org);
Vocations - t) 859-253-1993 x1029 Rev. Daniel Schwendeman, Dir. (dschwendeman@cdlex.org);

PARISHES, MISSIONS, AND CLERGY

COMMONWEALTH OF KENTUCKY

ASHLAND

Holy Family - 900 Winchester Ave., Ashland, KY 41101-7497 t) 606-329-1607 holyfamily@cdlex.org hfchurchashland.weebly.com/ Rev. Andy Garner, Pst.; Rev. Ronald Sagum, Par. Vicar; CRP Stds.: 90
 Holy Family School - (Grades PreK-12) 932 Winchester Ave., Ashland, KY 41101 t) 606-324-7040 akempf@cdlex.org holyfamilyashland.weebly.com Ann Kempf, Prin.;
 St. Lawrence - 500 Laurel St., Greenup, KY 41144; Mailing: 900 Winchester Ave., Ashland, KY 41101 t) (606) 329-1607

BARBOURVILLE

St. Gregory - 329 N. Sycamore Dr., Barbourville, KY 40906-1540 t) 606-546-4461 pverunkal@cdlex.org Rev. Mani George, M.C., Pst.; CRP Stds.: 6

BEATTYVILLE

Queen of All Saints - 90 Railroad St., Beattyville, KY 41311-0563; Mailing: P.O. Box 617, Beattyville, KY 41311-0563 t) 606-464-8695 qas@cdlex.org Rev. Mark Ouma, In Res.;
 Booneville Catholic Church of the Holy Family - 1439 KY 11 S., Booneville, KY 41314 t) 606-593-6948 meilermanosf@yahoo.com Sr. Marge Eilerman, O.S.F, Pst. Assoc.; Sr. Angie Keil, O.S.F., Pst. Assoc.;

BEREA

St. Clare - 622 Chestnut St., Berea, KY 40403 t) 859-986-4633 stclare@cdlex.org Rev. Gary Simpson, Pst.; CRP Stds.: 18
 St. Paul - 469 Main St. North, McKee, KY 40447; Mailing: P. O. Box 189, McKee, KY 40456 t) 606-287-7601 mckee@cdlex.org Rebecca Nixon, Pst. Assoc.; Harold Nixon, Pst. Assoc.;
 Our Lady of Mt. Vernon - 425 Williams St., Mt. Vernon, KY 40456; Mailing: P. O. Box 1006, Mt. Vernon, KY 40456 t) 606-256-4170 olmv@cdlex.org

CARLISLE

Shrine of Our Lady of Guadalupe - 617 E. Main St., Carlisle, KY 40311 t) 859-289-5586 (CRP); 859-289-5502 dfister@cdlex.org Rev. Daniel Fister, Pst.; Amy Switzer, DRE; CRP Stds.: 5

CORBIN

Sacred Heart - 703 Master St., Corbin, KY 40702; Mailing: P.O. Box 455, Corbin, KY 40702 t) 606-528-5222 sacredheart@cdlex.org corbin.cdlex.org Rev. Damian Anumba, Pst.; Dcn. Kevin Gerald Meece; Dcn. Kurt Sosa; CRP Stds.: 18

CUMBERLAND

St. Stephen - 304 Central St., Cumberland, KY 40823; Mailing: 2536 S. US Hwy. 421, Harlan, KY 40831 t) 606-573-6311 tdesilva@cdlex.org Rev. Terrence de Silva, Pst.;

DANVILLE

SS. Peter & Paul - 117 W. Main St., Danville, KY 40422 t) 859-236-2111 ssppchurch@cdlex.org; cunderwood@cdlex.org ssppdanville.org Rev. Anthony K. W. McLaughlin, Pst.; Dcn. Dennis Chatham; Dcn. Jeremy Watson; CRP Stds.: 137

FRANKFORT

Good Shepherd - 70 Shepherd Way, Frankfort, KY 40601 t) 502-227-4511 gsc@gssfrankfort.org frankfortgoodshepherd.org Rev. John Lijana, Pst.; Dcn. Thomas Wilhelm Kaldy; Dcn. Michael Joseph Lynch; Dcn. Thomas Snyder; Dcn. Robert A. Amato; CRP Stds.: 40
 Good Shepherd School - (Grades PreK-8) 75 Shepherd Way, Frankfort, KY 40601 t) 502-223-5041 office@gssfrankfort.org; larmstrong@gssfrankfort.org www.gssfrankfort.org Kelly Rowe, Prin.; Stds.: 149; Lay Tchrs.: 17

GEORGETOWN

SS. Francis & John Catholic Church - 806 Cincinnati Rd., Georgetown, KY 40324 t) 502-863-3404 parishoffice@ssfrancisjohn.org www.ssfrancisjohn.org Rev. Linh Nguyen, Pst.; Dcn. John Calandrella; Dcn. Dallas Kelley; Dcn. Tim Stout; CRP Stds.: 112
 St. John Catholic School - (Grades PreK-8) 810 Cincinnati Rd., Georgetown, KY 40324 t) 502-863-2607 office@stjohnschoolonline.org www.stjohnschoolonline.org Brent Mayer, Prin.; Stds.: 175; Lay Tchrs.: 22

GRAYSON

Ss. John & Elizabeth - 799 State Hwy. 1947, Grayson, KY 41143 t) 606-474-9979 mbentley@cdlex.org; sje1947@cdlex.org graysoncatholic.weebly.com/ Rev. Marc Bentley, Pst.; Taunya Carpenter, DRE; CRP Stds.: 10

HARLAN

Holy Trinity - 2536 S. U.S. Hwy. 421, Harlan, KY 40831-1798 t) 606-573-6311 tdesilva@cdlex.org Rev. Terrence deSilva, Pst.; CRP Stds.: 6
 The Preschool and Learning Center - t) 606-573-3570 holytrinitylearningcenter@gmail.com

HARRODSBURG

St. Andrew - 1125 Danville Rd., Harrodsburg, KY 40330-9671 t) 859-734-4270 www.harrodsburgcatholic.com Rev. Edwin Netlas, CMF (India), Pst.; Dcn. Richard L. Abbey; Dcn. Bruce Browning; Dcn. Brian Wayne Wentz; Mary Jane Trimble, Bus. Mgr.; CRP Stds.: 67
 St. Mary - 307 S. Buell St., Perryville, KY 40468; Mailing: 1125 Danville Rd., Harrodsburg, KY 40330

HAZARD

Mother of Good Counsel - 329 Poplar St., Hazard, KY 41701 t) 606-436-2533 c) 606-233-3012 lhelfrich@cdlex.org mgccc.org/ Rev. Robert Damron, Sacr. Min.; Lori Helfrich, Parish Life Coord.; CRP Stds.: 13

JACKSON

Holy Cross - 51 Brewers Dr., Jackson, KY 41339-9616 t) 606-666-7871 jvancleef@cdlex.org www.holycrossjackson.org Rev. John Curtis, Moderator; Kirsten Thorstad, Parish Life Coord.;
 Catholic Church of the Good Shepherd - 532 Main St., Campton, KY 41301; Mailing: P.O. Box 742, Campton, KY 41301 t) 606-668-3731 spleiss@cdlex.org Sr. Susan Marie Pleiss, O.S.F., Parish Life Dir.;

JENKINS

St. George - 22 Dotty Ln., Jenkins, KY 41537; Mailing: P.O. Box 787, Jenkins, KY 41537 t) 606-437-6117 radams@cdlex.org Rev. Rob Adams, Pst.;

LANCASTER

St. William - 224 Lexington St., Lancaster, KY 40444; Mailing: P.O. Box 269, Lancaster, KY 40444 t) 859-792-4009 stwlcath@cdlex.org www.cdlex.org/stwilliam Rev. John E. List, Pst.; Dcn. Mark Averett; Dcn. Dennis Arthur Dever; CRP Stds.: 5

LAWRENCEBURG

St. Lawrence - 120 N. Gatewood St., Lawrenceburg, KY 40342 t) 502-839-6381 stlawrencenews@cdlex.org www.saintlawrencecatholicchurch.org/ Rev. Jeffrey Estacio, Pst.; Dcn. Chris Cecil; CRP Stds.: 26

LEXINGTON

Cathedral of Christ the King - 299 Colony Blvd., Lexington, KY 40502 t) (859) 268-2861 ctkoffice@cdlex.org cathedralctk.org Rev. John Moriarty, Rector; Rev. Albert J. DeGiacomo, Par. Vicar; Rev. David Wheeler, Par. Vicar; Dcn. Lee Ferguson; Dcn. John Hinkel; Dcn. Paul Root; Dcn. Mark Stauffer; Dcn. Al Wiemann; Dcn. Timothy Weinmann, DRE; Karen Kirkland, Youth Min.; Jennifer McKenna, Bus. Mgr.; Gabrielle Manion, Music Min.; Robert Whitaker, Music Min.; Rebecca Whitney, Youth Min.; CRP Stds.: 229

Cathedral of Christ the King School - (Grades PreK-8) 412 Cochran Rd., Lexington, KY 40502 t) 859-266-5641 office@ckslex.org; abruggemann@ckslex.org ctkschool.net Ann Bruggemann, Prin.; Stds.: 516; Lay Tchrs.: 34

St. Elizabeth Ann Seton - 1730 Summerhill Dr., Lexington, KY 40515 t) 859-273-1318 www.setonchurch.com Rev. Charles W. Howell, Pst.; Dcn. Matthew C. Coriale; Dcn. Robert S. Joice; Dcn. Spencer Parrott; Dcn. Mark T. Woelfel; CRP Stds.: 55

Seton Catholic School - (Grades PreK-8) 1740 Summerhill Dr., Lexington, KY 40515 t) 859-273-7827 abrown@cdlex.org www.setonstars.com Amy Brown, Prin.; Susan Whalen, Librn.;

Holy Spirit Church - the Newman Center - 320 Rose Ln., Lexington, KY 40508 t) 859-255-8566 dsmith@cdlex.org; psutherland@cdlex.org www.uknewman Parish for Students, Faculty and Staff of the University of Kentucky. Rev. Stephen Roberts, Pst.; Rev. Prashanth Lobo, M.SS.CC., Assoc. Pst.; Sr. Ellen Kehoe, S.P., DRE; CRP Stds.: 71

Mary, Queen of the Holy Rosary - 601 Hill N Dale Rd., Lexington, KY 40503 t) 859-278-7432 mqhr@cdlex.org www.mqhr.org Rev. Miguel Alvizures, Pst.; Rev. Ben Horn, Par. Vicar; Rev. Ramiro Reyes, Par. Vicar; Dcn. John Becerra, Pst. Assoc.; Dcn. Nick Nickl; Dcn. Bill Rood; Tara Kaufmann, Dir.; CRP Stds.: 378

Mary, Queen of the Holy Rosary School - (Grades PreK-8) 605 Hill N Dale Rd., Lexington, KY 40503 t) 859-277-3030 kpedroche@maryqueenschool.org www.maryqueenschool.org Rebecca Brown, Prin.; Christine Hayes, Librn.;

St. Paul - 425 W. Short St., Lexington, KY 40507-1254; Mailing: 501 W. Short St., Lexington, KY 40507-1254 t) 859-252-0738 saintpaul@cdlex.org saintpaul.cdlex.org Rev. Richard Watson, Pst.; Dcn. Ramon Alfaro, Pst. Assoc.; Dcn. Steven Hester, Pst. Assoc.; CRP Stds.: 301

Sts. Peter & Paul Regional Elementary School - Main Campus - (Grades K-8) 501 W. Short St., c/o St. Paul Parish, Lexington, KY 40507-1254; Mailing: 423 W. Short St., Lexington, KY 40507 t) 859-254-9257 jpica@cdlex.org Jamie Burch, Prin.;

Pax Christi Catholic Church - 4001 Victoria Way, Lexington, KY 40515 t) 859-273-9999 pstewart@cdlex.org; tparsons@cdlex.org paxchristilex.org Rev. Patrick F. Stewart, Pst.; Dcn. John Robert Brannen, Pst. Assoc.; Dcn. Thomas Edward Parsons; CRP Stds.: 95

St. Peter - 141 Barr St., Lexington, KY 40507; Mailing: 125 Barr St., Lexington, KY 40507-1321 t) 859-252-7551 st.peter@cdlex.org stpeterlex.org/ Rev. Peter Kizhakkeparambil, Pst.; Dcn. Ted Fraebel; Dcn. Philip Latiff; CRP Stds.: 35

Sts. Peter & Paul Regional School - Early Childhood Campus - 125 Barr St., c/o St. Peter Parish, Lexington, KY 40507-1321; Mailing: 133 Barr St., Lexington, KY 40507 t) 859-233-2235 price@sppslex.org Pam Rice, Dir.;

St. Peter Claver - 485 W. 4th St., Lexington, KY 40508-1319 t) 859-254-0030 jweathers@cdlex.org; nfischer@cdlex.org cdlex.org/stpeterclaver Rev. Norman Fischer, Pst.; Dcn. James Weathers, Parish Life Coord.; Dcn. Eddie H. Grider; Nita Clarke, DRE; Christina Weathers, Bus. Mgr.; CRP Stds.: 65

LONDON

St. William - 521 W. 5th St., London, KY 40741 t) 606-864-7500 stwilliamlondon@cdlex.org cdlex.org/london Rev. Mani George, M.C.; Dcn. Charles Kevin Black; Sr. Marjorie Manning, Pst. Assoc.; CRP Stds.: 41

St. Ann - 222 Town Branch Rd., Manchester, KY 40962-1322 t) 606-598-2718 stannmanchester@cdlex.org Sr. Alice Schmersal, Pst. Assoc.;

St. Sylvester, East Bernstadt -

LOUISA

St. Jude - 1121 Meadowbrook Ln., Louisa, KY 41230 t) 606-638-3409; 606-638-0418 (Rectory) churchstjude@yahoo.com; stjude@cdlex.org www.cdlex.org/stjude Rev. Michael J. Ramler, Pst.; Dcn. James Leonard Dalton; Sr. Patricia Cataldi, C.P.S., DRE; CRP Stds.: 3

LYNCH

Church of the Resurrection - 200 Church St., Lynch, KY 40855; Mailing: 2536 S. U.S. Hwy 421, Harlan, KY 40831 t) 606-573-6311 tdesilva@cdlex.org Rev. Terrence deSilva, Pst.; CRP Stds.: 2

MIDDLESBORO

St. Julian - 118 E. Chester Ave., Middlesboro, KY 40965 t) 423-869-9255 (CRP); 606-248-2068 saintjuliancatho@bellsouth.net www.saintjuliancatholicchurch.com Rev. Maria Salethu Jesuraj, HGN, Pst.; Theresa Tanner, DRE; CRP Stds.: 5

St. Anthony - 309 Virginia Ave., Pineville, KY 40977 t) (606) 248-2068 stjuliancatholicchurch.com

MONTICELLO

St. Peter - 1139 Hwy. #3106, Monticello, KY 42633; Mailing: P.O. Box 669, Monticello, KY 42633 t) 606-348-9416 c) 773-595-5481 Rev. Danny Taylor, Sacr. Min.; Clarita Lilia Encomio, Dir.; CRP Stds.: 17

MOREHEAD

Church of Jesus Our Savior - 315 Battson-Oates, Morehead, KY 40351; Mailing: P.O. Box 307, Morehead, KY 40351 t) 606-784-4392 morehead@cdlex.org www.cdlex.org/morehead Rev. Arturo Molina, Pst.; Dcn. Daniel Joseph Connell; Dcn. William R. Grimes; Susette Redwine, DRE; Dcn. William T. Buelterman; CRP Stds.: 39

Morehead, St. Claire Medical Center - 222 Medical Cir., Morehead, KY 40351 t) 606-783-6500 smjudilambert@yahoo.com www.st-claire.org Sr. Judi Lambert, OSB, Pastoral Care Dir.;

St. Julie Catholic Church - 77 E. Main St., Owingsville, KY 40360; Mailing: PO Box 248, Owingsville, KY 40360 t) 606-674-3261 stjulie@gmail.com

MOUNT STERLING

St. Patrick - 139 W. Main St., Mount Sterling, KY 40353 t) 859-498-0300 stpatrickmtsterling@cdlex.org stpatmtsterling.wix.com/stpat Rev. James J. Kinney, Pst.; Rev. Arokiades Arokisamy, Par. Vicar; CRP Stds.: 31

NICHOLASVILLE

St. Luke - 304 S. Main St., Nicholasville, KY 40356 t) 859-885-4892 cdlex.org/nichlolasville Rev. Aldrin Tayag, Pst.; Dcn. David James; Dcn. Gary Rudemiller; CRP Stds.: 66

PAINTSVILLE

St. Michael Catholic Church - 720 Washington Ave., Paintsville, KY 41240 t) 606-789-4455 c) 606-792-7114 mflanagan@cdlex.org Rev. Michael D. Flanagan, Pst.; Dcn. Paul David Brown; CRP Stds.: 4

Our Lady of the Mountains - (Grades PreK-5) 405 3rd St., Paintsville, KY 41240 t) 606-789-3661 sites.google.com/view/ourladyofthemountainsschool

PARIS

Annunciation of the Blessed Virgin Mary - 1007 Main St., Paris, KY 40361 t) 859-987-1571 annunciation@cdlex.org annunciationparis.org Rev. Daniel Fister, Pst.; Dcn. Phil Hanrahan; Dcn. Kenneth Rayfield; Dcn. Ronald Sparks; Jennifer Frye, DRE; CRP Stds.: 30

St. Mary - (Grades PreK-5) 1121 Main St., Paris, KY 40361 t) 859-987-3815 stmary@cdlex.org; kleer@cdlex.org sms-ky.org Lucy Marsh, Admin.;

PIKEVILLE

St. Francis of Assisi - 137 Bryan St., Pikeville, KY 41501-1656 t) 606-437-6117 radams@cdlex.org Rev. Rob Adams, Pst.; Dcn. Joseph Byron Jacobs; CRP Stds.: 5

PRESTONSBURG

St. Martha - 60 Marthas Vineyard, Prestonsburg, KY 41653 t) 606-874-9526 stmarthaprestonsburg@cdlex.org Rev. Brandon J. Bigam, Pst.; CRP Stds.: 5

St. Luke - 1221 Parkway Dr., Salyersville, KY 41465; Mailing: P.O. Box 129, Salyersville, KY 41465 t) 606-349-5320 stlukesalyersville@cdlex.org

RAVENNA

St. Elizabeth of Hungary - 316 5th St., Ravenna, KY 40472-1312 t) 606-723-8216 st.elizabeth@windstream.net Rev. Albert Fritsch, S.J., Pst.; CRP Stds.: 10

RICHMOND

St. Mark - 608 W. Main St., Richmond, KY 40475 t) 859-623-2989 x1851 tfarrell@cdlex.org www.saintmarkcatholicchurch.net Rev. Thomas P. Farrell, Pst.; Dcn. James D. Bennett; Dcn. Anthony R. Fritz; CRP Stds.: 95

St. Mark School - (Grades PreK-5) 115 Parrish Ave., Richmond, KY 40475 cathycornett@saintmarkcatholicschool.com www.saintmarkcatholicschool.com

SOMERSET

St. Mildred - 203 S. Central Ave., Somerset, KY 42501 t) 606-678-5051 mmckinney@cdlex.org www.saintmildred.com Rev. Jay Von Handorf, Pst.; Rev. Danny Taylor, Par. Vicar; Dcn. Vincent E. Cheshire; Dcn. Larry Cranfill; CRP Stds.: 98

Good Shepherd Chapel - 130 N. Main St., Whitley City, KY 42653 t) 606-376-8728

STANTON

Our Lady of the Mountains - 1093 E. College Ave., Stanton, KY 40380-2354; Mailing: P.O. Box 727, Stanton, KY 40380-2354 t) (606) 737-0826 fbrawner@cdlex.org Rev. Frank Brawner, Pst.; CRP Stds.: 4

VERSAILLES

St. Leo - 295 Huntertown Rd., Versailles, KY 40383 t) 859-873-4573 stleo@cdlex.org saintleoparishky.org Rev. Catesby Clay Jr., Pst.; Dcn. Patrick David DeLuca; Dcn. Jim Lafser; Dcn. Lawrence Todd; CRP Stds.: 94

St. Leo School - (Grades K-8) 255 Huntertown Rd., Versailles, KY 40383 t) 859-873-4591 hdibiasie@saintleoky.org saintleoky.org Helena DiBiasie, Prin.;

WAYNESBURG

St. Sylvester - 100 Kentucky 1948, Waynesburg, KY 40489; Mailing: P.O. Box 269, Lancaster, KY 40444-1183 t) 859-792-4009 stwlcath@cdlex.org Rev. John E. List, Pst.; Dcn. Mark Averett; Dcn. Dennis Arthur Dever; MaryAnn Adams, Music Min.; Emily Abee, DRE; CRP Stds.: 16

WEST LIBERTY

Prince of Peace - 163 Pine Acres Dr., West Liberty, KY 41472; Mailing: P.O. Box 393, West Liberty, KY 41472-0393 t) 606-743-3266 mbentley@cdlex.org Rev. Marc Bentley, Pst.;

WILLIAMSBURG
St. Boniface - 98 Catholic Ave., Williamsburg, KY 40769; Mailing: 76 W. Sycamore St., P.O. Box 330, Williamsburg, KY 40769 t) 606-549-2156 olph.boniface@gmail.com Rev. Prashanth Lobo, M.SS.CC., Pst.;
Our Lady of Perpetual Help - 76 W. Sycamore St., Williamsburg, KY 40769; Mailing: P. O. Box 330, Williamsburg, KY 40769 t) 606-549-2156 olph.boniface@gmail.com Rev. Prashanth Lobo, M.SS.CC., Pst.;
WINCHESTER
St. Joseph - 248 S. Main St., Winchester, KY 40391 t) 859-744-4917 stjospeh@cdlex.org stjosephwinchester.com Rev. Frank Brawner, Pst.; Rev. Arockiadoss Arockiasamy, Assoc. Pst.; Dcn. Ron Allen; Dcn. Larry Pierce Durbin; Dcn. John Roche; CRP Stds.: 52
St. Agatha Academy - (Grades K-8) 244 S. Main St., Winchester, KY 40391 t) 859-744-6484 stagatha@bellsouth.net saintagathaacademy.org John Pica, Prin.; Christy Hisle, Librn.;

SCHOOLS: PRESCHOOL THRU HIGH SCHOOL

HIGH SCHOOLS

COMMONWEALTH OF KENTUCKY

HAGAR HILL
The Piarist School - (PRV) (Grades 7-12) 7279 S. Rt. 321, Hagar Hill, KY 41222; Mailing: P.O. Box 369, Hagerhill, KY 41222 t) 606-789-1967 piarist_adm@bellsouth.net www.piaristschool.org Rev. Thomas R. Carroll, Sch.P., Prin.; Stds.: 33; Pr. Tchrs.: 1; Lay Tchrs.: 11
LEXINGTON
Lexington Catholic High School - (DIO) (Grades 9-12) 2250 Clays Mills Rd., Lexington, KY 40503 t) 859-277-7183 lchsprincipal@lexingtoncatholic.com www.lexingtoncatholic.com Mathew George, Prin.; Stds.: 710; Lay Tchrs.: 73

INSTITUTIONS LOCATED IN DIOCESE

CAMPUS MINISTRY / NEWMAN CENTERS [CAM]

BARBOURVILLE
St. Gregory Church-Union College - 329 N. Sycamore Dr., Barbourville, KY 40906-1540 t) 606-546-4461 c) 606-733-3211 tmgeorge@cdlex.org www.facebook.com Rev. Mani George, M.C., Pst.;
BEREA
St. Clare Church-Berea College - 622 Chestnut St., Berea, KY 40403 t) 859-986-4633 stclare@cdlex.org Rev. Gary Simpson;
LEXINGTON
Holy Spirit Parish Newman Center, University of Kentucky - 320 Rose Ln., Lexington, KY 40508 t) 859-255-8566 jmusgove@cdlex.org Rev. Stephen Roberts, Pst.; Rev. Ronald Sagum, Par. Vicar;
MOREHEAD
Catholic Student Center-Morehead State University - 315 Battson-Oates Dr., Morehead, KY 40351; Mailing: P.O. Box 307, Morehead, KY 40351 t) 606-784-4392 morehead@cdlex.org www.cdlex.org/morehead Rev. Arturo Molina;
RICHMOND
Catholic Campus Ministry of St. Mark (St. Stephen the Martyr Newman Center) - Eastern Kentucky University, 405 University Dr., Richmond, KY 40475-2154 t) 859-623-2989 asininger@cdlex.org; stmarkrichmond@cdlex.org www.saintmarkcatholicchurch.net Rev. Thomas P. Farrell, Pst.; Alanna Sininger, Campus Min.;

CEMETERIES [CEM]

ASHLAND
Calvary - 3801 13th St., Ashland, KY 41102 t) 606-329-1607 holyfamily@cdlex.org Rev. Andy Garner, Pst.;
LEXINGTON
Calvary - 874 W. Main St., Lexington, KY 40508 t) 859-252-5415 ccemetery@cdlex.org www.cdlex.org/calvary-cemetery/ Doug Culp, Dir.;
MT. STERLING
St. Thomas - 612 N. Maysville Rd., US 460, Mt. Sterling, KY 40353; Mailing: 139 W. Main St., Mt. Sterling, KY 40353 t) 859-498-0300 stpatmtsterling@gmail.com Rev. Frank Brawner, Pst.;

CONVENTS, MONASTERIES, AND RESIDENCES FOR WOMEN [CON]

JENKINS
Missionaries of Charity - 44 Cove Rd., Jenkins, KY 41537; Mailing: P.O.Box 883,, Jenkins, KY 41537 t) 606-832-4824 scadiz7@hotmail.com Sr. M. Jonathan MC, Prov.; Srs.: 4
MARTIN
Mt. Tabor Benedictines-The Dwelling Place Monastery - 150 Mt. Tabor Rd., Martin, KY 41649 t) 606-886-9624; 606-886-6598 kathycurtis.osb@gmail.com www.mtabor.com Sr. Kathleen Curtis, OSB, Prioress; Srs.: 7

ENDOWMENTS / FOUNDATIONS / TRUSTS [EFT]

LEXINGTON
Catholic Education Opportunities Foundation, Inc. - 100 W. Main St., Ste. 700, Lexington, KY 40507 t) 859-303-9555 kthompson@ceoflex.org www.ceoflex.org Kim Thompson, Dir.;

HOSPITALS / HEALTH SERVICES [HOS]

BEREA
Saint Joseph-Berea - 305 Estill St., Berea, KY 40403 t) 859-986-3151 emily.ruble@commonspirit.org A member of Catholic Health Initiatives. John Yanes, Pres.; Bed Capacity: 25; Asstd. Annu.: 48,828; Staff: 190
FRENCHBURG
St. Claire Family Medicine-Frenchburg - 732 Hwy. 36, Frenchburg, KY 40322 t) 606-768-2191 wcwhitt@st-claire.org st-claire.org (Div. of St. Claire Regional Medical Center). Asstd. Annu.: 8,795; Staff: 7
IRVINE
Mercy Health - Marcum and Wallace Hospital, LLC - 60 Mercy Ct., Irvine, KY 40336 t) 606-723-2115 www.mercy.com Trena Stocker, Pres.; Bed Capacity: 25; Asstd. Annu.: 10,274; Staff: 146
LEXINGTON
Continuing Care Hospital, Inc. - 1 St. Joseph Dr., 3rd & 4th Fls., Lexington, KY 40504 t) 859-967-5744 bob.desotelle@commonspirit.org Robert Desotelle, Pres.; Bed Capacity: 25; Asstd. Annu.: 245; Staff: 72
Saint Joseph Health System - 150 N. Eagle Creek Dr., Lexington, KY 40509 t) 859-967-5000 katherine.love@commonspirit.org www.sjhlex.org/east Katherine Love, Pres.; Bed Capacity: 433; Asstd. Annu.: 108,048; Staff: 1,309
St. Joseph Health System, Inc. - 1 St. Joseph Dr., Lexington, KY 40504 t) 859-313-1000 (Member of Catholic Health Initiatives). Anthony A Houston, CEO; Bruce Tassin, Pres.; Bed Capacity: 433; Asstd. Annu.: 76,514; Staff: 1,258
LONDON
Saint Joseph London - 1001 Saint Joseph Ln., London, KY 40741 t) 606-330-6000 debra.moore520@commonspirit.org saintjoseph-london.org (Member of Catholic Health Initiatives). John Yanes, Pres.; Bed Capacity: 150; Asstd. Annu.: 128,638; Staff: 730
MOREHEAD
Saint Claire Regional Medical Center (Sisters of Notre Dame) - 222 Medical Cir., Morehead, KY 40351 t) 606-783-6500 mark.neff@st-claire.org st-claire.org Mark Neff, Pres.; Bed Capacity: 159; Asstd. Annu.: 33,487; Staff: 1,110
MOUNT STERLING
St. Joseph Hospital Mt. Sterling - 225 Falcon Dr., Mount Sterling, KY 40353 t) 859-497-5000 amanda.spurling@commonspirit.org John Yanes, Pres.; Sr. Janet Carr, C.D.P., Chap.; Bed Capacity: 42; Asstd. Annu.: 63,950; Staff: 299
OLIVE HILL
St. Claire Family Medicine-Olive Hill - 155 Bricklayer St., Olive Hill, KY 41164; Mailing: P.O. Box 1268, Olive Hill, KY 41164 t) 606-286-4152 gloria.riggs@st-claire.org (Div. of St. Claire Medical Center). Asstd. Annu.: 14,079; Staff: 9
OWINGSVILLE
St. Claire Family Medicine - Owingsville - 632 Slate Ave., Owingsville, KY 40360; Mailing: P.O. Box 1120, Owingsville, KY 40360 t) 606-674-6386 angela.fryman@st-claire.org (Div. of St. Claire Medical Center). Asstd. Annu.: 9,320; Staff: 7
SANDY HOOK
St. Claire Family Medicine-Sandy Hook - 390 KY Hwy. 7 S., Sandy Hook, KY 41171; Mailing: P.O. Box 748, Sandy Hook, KY 41171 t) 606-738-5155 donna.conkright@st-claire.org (Div. of St. Claire Medical Center). Asstd. Annu.: 9,919; Staff: 9

MISCELLANEOUS [MIS]

CARLISLE
Our Lady of Guadalupe Shrine - 617 E. Main St., Carlisle, KY 40311 t) 859-987-1571 cfrye@cdlex.org Rev. Daniel Fister;
DAVID
***St. Vincent Mission Inc.** - 6369 Hwy. 404, David, KY 41616; Mailing: PO Box 232, David, KY 41616 t) 606-886-2513 c) 606-339-5928; 606-339-0445 stvm@stvincentmission.org; kathleen@stvincentmission.org stvincentmission.org Erin Bottomlee, CEO; Sr. Kathleen Weigand, Contact;
LEXINGTON
Catholic Way Bible Study - 299 Colony Blvd., Lexington, KY 40502; Mailing: P.O. Box 22324, Lexington, KY 40522-2324 t) 859-552-6484 teachingleader@cwbs.org www.cwbs.org
CDLEX Management Services, Inc. - 1310 W. Main St., Lexington, KY 40508 t) 859-253-1993 dswisher@cdlex.org Debbie Swisher, Admin.;
***Newman Foundation, Inc.** - 528 N. Broadway, Ste. 303, Lexington, KY 40508 t) 859-255-0880 newmandirector@gmail.com www.newmanfnd.org Peggy Gabriel, Office Mgr.;
Society of St. Vincent de Paul - 1730 Summerhill Dr., Lexington, KY 40515 t) 859-266-8003 svdplex@yahoo.com Tim Lewis, Pres.;
MARTIN
The Catholic Committee of Appalachia - 150 Mt. Tabor Rd., Martin, KY 41649 t) 304-927-5798 cca@ccappal.org www.ccappal.org Jeannie Kirkhope, Exec. Dir.;

MONASTERIES AND RESIDENCES FOR PRIESTS AND BROTHERS [MON]

LEXINGTON
Jesuit Fathers & Brothers - 153 Barr St., Lexington, KY 40507 t) 859-940-8306 wbado@cdlex.org Rev. Walter Bado, S.J., Supr.; Priests: 1
MARTIN
Piarist Fathers - ; Mailing: P.O. Box 369, Martin, KY

41222 t) 606-789-1967 tcarroll@cdlex.org Rev. Thomas R. Carroll, Sch.P.; Priests: 1

NURSING / REHABILITATION / CONVALESCENCE / ELDERLY CARE [NUR]

VERSAILLES

Taylor Manor - 300 Berry Ave., Versailles, KY 40383 t) 859-873-4201 srmaryfaustina@taylormanor.org www.taylormanor.org Rev. Frank Sherry, C.P.M., Chap.; Sr. Mary Faustina Zugelder, S.J.W., Admin.; Asstd. Annu.: 55; Staff: 55

RETREAT HOUSES / RENEWAL CENTERS [RTR]

HAZARD

Father Farrell Spiritual Life Center - 329 Poplar at Cedar, Hazard, KY 41701 t) 606-436-2533 lhelfrich@cdlex.org Lori Helfrich, Parish Life Coord.;

MARTIN

Mt. Tabor Retreat Center - 150 Mt. Tabor Rd., Martin, KY 41649 t) 606-886-9624 mtabor150@hotmail.com Sr. Jan Barthel, Admin.;

An asterisk (*) denotes an organization that has established tax-exempt status directly with the IRS and is not covered by the USCCB Group Ruling.

Diocese of Lincoln

(Dioecesis Lincolnensis)

MOST REVEREND JAMES D. CONLEY, D.D., S.T.L.

Bishop of Lincoln; ordained May 18, 1985; appointed Titular Bishop of Cissa and Auxiliary Bishop of Denver April 10, 2008; ordained May 30, 2008; appointed Bishop of Lincoln September 14, 2012; installed November 20, 2012. Mailing Address: 3400 Sheridan Blvd., Lincoln, NE 68506-6125.

Chancery: 3400 Sheridan Blvd., Lincoln, NE 68506-6125. T: 402-488-0921; F: 402-488-3569.

ERECTED AUGUST 2, 1887.

Square Miles 23,844.

Comprises that part of the State of Nebraska south of the Platte River.

Legal Title: "The Catholic Bishop of Lincoln."

For legal titles of parishes and diocesan institutions, consult the Chancery.

STATISTICAL OVERVIEW

Personnel

Bishop	1
Retired Bishops	1
Priests: Diocesan Active in Diocese	138
Priests: Diocesan Active Outside Diocese	8
Priests: Retired, Sick or Absent	19
Number of Diocesan Priests	165
Religious Priests in Diocese	10
Total Priests in your Diocese	175
Extern Priests in Diocese	2
Ordinations:	
Diocesan Priests	4
Religious Priests	7
Transitional Deacons	3
Total Brothers	10
Total Sisters	136

Parishes

Parishes	134
With Resident Pastor:	
Resident Diocesan Priests	82
Resident Religious Priests	1
Without Resident Pastor:	
Administered by Priests	51
Missions	1
Pastoral Centers	8
Professional Ministry Personnel:	
Sisters	70
Lay Ministers	15

Welfare

Catholic Hospitals	4
Total Assisted	121,098
Homes for the Aged	2
Total Assisted	210
Day Care Centers	1
Total Assisted	50
Specialized Homes	1
Total Assisted	150
Special Centers for Social Services	20
Total Assisted	25,000
Residential Care of Disabled	1
Total Assisted	16
Other Institutions	1
Total Assisted	5,476

Educational

Seminaries, Diocesan	1
Students from This Diocese	12
Students from Other Dioceses	16
Diocesan Students in Other Seminaries	16
Seminaries, Religious	1
Students, Religious	76
Total Seminarians	104
High Schools, Diocesan and Parish	6
Total Students	1,652
Elementary Schools, Diocesan and Parish	23
Total Students	4,544
Non-residential Schools for the Disabled	1
Total Students	16
Catechesis / Religious Education:	
High School Students	1,150
Elementary Students	3,600
Total Students under Catholic Instruction	11,066
Teachers in Diocese:	
Priests	43
Sisters	34
Lay Teachers	594

Vital Statistics

Receptions into the Church:	
Infant Baptism Totals	1,236
Minor Baptism Totals	56
Adult Baptism Totals	59
Received into Full Communion	84
First Communions	1,192
Confirmations	1,462
Marriages:	
Catholic	240
Interfaith	160
Total Marriages	400
Deaths	685
Total Catholic Population	94,428
Total Population	630,315

LEADERSHIP

Chancery - t) 402-488-0921

Moderator of the Curia - Rev. Nicholas A. Kipper;

Vicar General - Rev. Justin R. Fulton;

Chancellor - chancellor@lincolndiocese.org Rev. Daniel J. Rayer;

Vice-Chancellor - Rev. Caleb J. LaRue;

Finance Officer - Tracy Lockwood;

Diocesan Consultors - Rev. Msgr. Mark D. Huber; Rev. Msgr. Robert G. Tucker; Rev. Daniel J. Rayer;

Diocesan Tribunal - t) 402-488-0921 Rev. Steven P. Snitily, Vicar;

Officialis - Rev. Steven P. Snitily;

Adjutant Judicial Vicar - Rev. Maurice H. Current;

Promoters Justitiae - Rev. Msgr. Mark D. Huber; Rev. Caleb J. LaRue;

Defensores Vinculi - Rev. Msgr. Timothy J. Thorburn; Rev. Gary L. Coulter;

Judges - Rev. Daniel J. Rayer; Rev. Msgr. Timothy J. Thorburn; Rev. Craig A. Doty;

Advocates - Rev. Corey R. Harrison; Rev. Ryan A. Kaup; Rev. Denton R. Morris;

Notaries - Rev. Gary L. Coulter; Sr. Kathryn Maney, M.S.; Marilyn L. Friesen;

Presbyteral Council - Rev. Justin R. Fulton; Rev. Nicholas A. Kipper; Rev. Daniel J. Rayer;

Vicar for Clergy - Rev. Douglas D. Dietrich;

Vicars For Religious - Rev. Gary L. Coulter; Rev. Msgr. Timothy J. Thorburn;

Vicar for Hispanic Ministry - Rev. Rafael Rodriguez-Fuentes, Vicar;

Deaneries and Deans - Rev. Robert K. Barnhill, Crete; Rev. Jay M. Buhman, David City; Rev. John B. Birkel, Fairbury;

OFFICES AND DIRECTORS

Apostleship of Prayer - Rev. Michael J. Morin, Dir.;

Apostolate to the Spanish Speaking - Ricardo Izquierdo, Dir.; Rev. Rafael Rodriguez-Fuentes; Rev. Craig J. Clinch;

Archivist - Sr. Patricia Radek, M.S., Archivist;

Bishop's Pastoral Plan for Pro-Life Activities - t) 402-477-7517 Tom Venzor, Dir.;

Building Commission - Rev. Msgr. John J. Perkinton, Chair; Rev. Troy J. Schweiger; Rev. Msgr. Mark D. Huber;

Cemeteries - Rev. Msgr. Timothy J. Thorburn;

Censores Librorum - Rev. M. James Divis; Rev. Sean P. Kilcawley; Rev. Msgr. Timothy J. Thorburn;

Child and Youth Protection Office - t) 402-613-2488 Jeff Hohlen, Safe Environment Coord. & Victim Assistance Coord.;

Clergy Relief Society--The Saint John Vianney Association - Rev. Justin R. Fulton, Vice. Pres.;

Commission for Sacred Liturgy and Sacred Music - Rev. Daniel J. Rayer, Chair; Rev. Msgr. Timothy J. Thorburn; Rev. Brendan R.J. Kelly;

Commission on Alcohol and Drug Abuse - t) 402-483-1941 Rev. M. James Divis, Dir.; Rev. John C. Rooney;

Deaf Ministry - t) 402-488-2040 Rev. Robert K. Barnhill, Dir.; Rev. Michael S. Stec, Asst. Dir.;

Diocesan Council of Catholic Women - Kathy Rowell, Pres.; Rev. Thomas J. Lux, Moderator; Rev. Thomas D. McGuire, Asst. Moderator;

Diocesan Education Office - t) 402-473-0610 Rev. Msgr. John J. Perkinton, Supt.; Rev. Lawrence J. Stoley; Sr. Collette, O.S.F., Asst. Supt.;

Diocesan Finance Council - Most Rev. James D. Conley; Tony Fulton, Chair; Tracy Lockwood, CFO;

Ecumenical Affairs, Commission for - Rev. Douglas D. Dietrich, Chair; Rev. Matthew F. Eickhoff; Rev. M. James Divis, Chair;

Family Life Office - t) 402-488-2040 Rev. Sean P. Kilcawley, Dir.;

Insurance - Marsha Bartek; Rev. Justin R. Fulton, Dir.;

Liturgical Ministries - Rev. Christopher M. Eckrich, Dir.;

Mission Office - t) 402-473-0635 K. William Holoubek, Dir. (fr.william-holoubek@cdolinc.net);

Natural Family Planning - t) 402-473-0630 Rev. Sean P. Kilcawley, Dir.; Kealey Butler, Diocesan Coord.; Marilyn Klein;

Nebraska Catholic Conference - t) 402-477-7517 Tom Venzor, Exec.;

Newspaper - t) 402-488-0090 Cathy Bender, Editor;

Office of Communications - t) 402-488-0921 Rev. Nicholas A. Kipper, Dir.;

Office of Religious Education (CCD) - t) 402-488-2040 Rev. Andrew J. Heaslip, Diocesan D.R.E.;

Office of Stewardship & Development - t) 402-488-0921 Katie Ostgren, Dir.;

Pro Life - Jeff Schinstock, Dir.; Rev. Jonathan J. Haschke, Asst. Dir.;

Project Rachel - t) 800-964-3787

Rural Life Conference - Rev. Brian Wirth, Dir.;

Scouting - Rev. Denton R. Morris;

Serra Club - t) 402-474-7914 Rev. Robert A. Matya, Chap.;

Teens Encounter Christ (TEC) - Jeff Schinstock, Dir.;

Vocations - t) 402-474-7914 Rev. Robert A. Matya, Dir.; Rev. Alec J. Sasse, Asst.;

PARISHES, MISSIONS, AND CLERGY

STATE OF NEBRASKA

ASHLAND

St. Mary's - 1625 Adams St., Ashland, NE 68003 t) 402-944-3554 stmaryashland@windstream.net Rev. William Holoubek, Pst.;

St. Joseph's -

AUBURN

St. Joseph's - 1306 23rd St., Auburn, NE 68305; Mailing: PO Box 406, Auburn, NE 68305 t) 402-274-3733 stjoseph@kc.twcbc.com auburnstjoseph.org Rev. Timothy Danek, Pst.;

St. Clara - 604 6th St., Peru, NE 68421; Mailing: P.O. Box 406, c/o St. Joseph Catholic Church, Auburn, NE 68305

AURORA

St. Mary's - 1420 9th St., Aurora, NE 68818; Mailing: P.O. Box 291, Aurora, NE 68818 t) 402-694-3427 stmarysaurora.org Rev. Loras K. Grell, Pst.;

St. Joseph's - 209 Derby Ave., Giltner, NE 68841 Rev. Loras Grell, Pst.;

BEATRICE

St. Joseph's - 612 High St., Beatrice, NE 68310 t) 402-223-2923 Rev. Leo D. Kosch, Pst.; Rev. Joseph J. Faulkner, In Res.;

St. Joseph's School - (Grades PreK-5) 420 N. 6th St., Beatrice, NE 68310; Mailing: 612 High St., Beatrice, NE 68310 t) 402-223-5033 emily-lohr@cdolinc.net

BEAVER CROSSING

Sacred Heart - 401 Dimery Ave., Beaver Crossing, NE 68313; Mailing: P.O. Box 208, Beaver Crossing, NE 68313 t) 402-532-2545 www.sacredheartcatholicbc.org Rev. Msgr. Mark D. Huber, Pst.; CRP Stds.: 18

St. Patrick's - 110 Third St., Utica, NE 68456; Mailing: PO Box 208, Beaver Crossing, NE 68313-0208 t) (402) 532-2545

BEE

St. Wenceslaus - 350 Elm St., Bee, NE 68314; Mailing: P.O. Box 146, Bee, NE 68314 t) 402-643-9107 stwenceslaus@lmnetworks.net Rev. Raymond L. Jansen, Pst.;

BELLWOOD

St. Peter's - 211 Esplanade St., Bellwood, NE 68624-2402 t) 402-538-3135 saintpetersaintjoseph@gmail.com Rev. Benjamin P. Holdren, Pst.;

St. Joseph's -

Presentation - 1291 41 Rd., Bellwood, NE 68624 t) 402-367-3001 presentationparish-bellwood@lincolndiocese.org Rev. Michael A. Ventre, Pst.;

BENKELMAN

St. Joseph's - 817 Cheyenne St., Benkelman, NE 69021; Mailing: P.O. Box 447, Benkelman, NE 69021 t) 308-423-2329 mfeickhoff@hotmail.com Rev. Matthew F. Eickhoff, Pst.;

St. Joseph's - 419 County Rd., Stratton, NE 69043

BRAINARD

Holy Trinity - 108 E. Brainard St., Brainard, NE 68626; Mailing: P.O. Box 39, Brainard, NE 68626 t) 402-545-2691 www.holytrinitybrainard.com Rev. Steven P. Snitily, Pst.; CRP Stds.: 36

BRUNO

St. Anthony - 405 Pine St., Bruno, NE 68014 t) 402-543-2233 (Rectory) abiebrunochurches@gmail.com Rev. Ronald G. Homes, Pst.; CRP Stds.: 21

SS. Peter and Paul - 222 Maple, Abie, NE 68036; Mailing: 405 Pine St, Bruno, NE 68014-2030

CAMBRIDGE

St. John's - 815 Nelson, Cambridge, NE 69022; Mailing: P.O. Box F, Cambridge, NE 69022 t) 308-697-3722 cchurch@swnebr.net Rev. Kenneth J. Wehrs, Pst.;

St. Germanus -

CAMPBELL

St. Anne - 518 S. Stewart, Campbell, NE 68932; Mailing: P.O. Box 156, Campbell, NE 68932-0156 t) 402-756-8006 fr.adam-sparling@lincolndiocese.org Rev. Adam M. Sparling, Pst.;

Holy Trinity - 513 S. Liberty, Blue Hill, NE 68930

COLON

St. Joseph's - 111 Cherry St., Colon, NE 68018; Mailing: P.O. Box 58, Colon, NE 68018 t) 402-647-4901 fr.cole-kennett@cdolinc.net Rev. Timothy Cole Kennett, Pst.;

St. Mary -

CORTLAND

St. James - 500 W. First St., Cortland, NE 68331; Mailing: 155 N. Lincoln Ave, Cortland, NE 68331 t) 402-798-7335 stjamescortland@gmail.com stjamescortland.com Rev. Thomas J. Lux, Pst.;

CRETE

Sacred Heart - 515 E. 14th St., Crete, NE 68333 t) 402-826-2044 jsec@cdolinc.net www.sacred-heart-crete.org Rev. Christopher Stoley, Pst.; Rev. Allan N. Phan, Par. Vicar; CRP Stds.: 126

St. James School - (Grades PreK-6) t) 402-826-2318 sr.mary-alma@cdolinc.net Sr. Mary Alma Linscott, C.K., Prin.;

CURTIS

St. James - 313 E. 6th St., Curtis, NE 69025; Mailing: P.O. Box 144, Curtis, NE 69025 t) 308-367-4280 stjames@curtis-ne.com Rev. Thomas Walsh, Admin.;

St. Joseph's -

St. William's -

DAVEY

St. Mary's - 17630 N. 3rd St., Davey, NE 68336; Mailing: P.O. Box 37, Davey, NE 68336 t) 402-785-3445 stmarydavey@gmail.com www.facebook.com/stmaryscatholicchurchdavey/ Rev. Douglas D. Dietrich, Pst.;

DAVID CITY

St. Francis - 3071 P Rd., David City, NE 68632; Mailing: PO Box 82, David City, NE 68632 t) 402-367-4202 Rev. Adam M. Sughroue, Pst.;

St. Mary's - 580 I St., David City, NE 68632 t) 402-367-3579 stmarysdavidcity@gmail.com www.stmarysdavidcity.org Rev. Brian P. Connor, Pst.; Rev. Tony Schukei, Assoc. Pst.; CRP Stds.: 20

Assumption - t) 402-641-1542 stmarysdavidcity.org

DAWSON

St. Mary's - 312 4th St., Dawson, NE 68337; Mailing: PO Box 96, Dawson, NE 68337 t) 402-855-3595 www.lincolndiocese.org Rev. Kenneth F. Hoesing, Pst.;

St. Anne's - 507 Main St., Shubert, NE 68437; Mailing: P.O. Box 96, Dawson, NE 68337 www.lincolndiocese.org

DENTON
St. Mary's - 7105 Cass, Denton, NE 68339; Mailing: P.O. Box 406, Denton, NE 68339 t) 402-797-2105 pastor@dentonstmarys.com dentonstmarys.com/ Rev. Craig A. Doty, Pst.; CRP Stds.: 55
DONIPHAN
St. Ann's - 202 N. 5th St., Doniphan, NE 68832; Mailing: Box 407, Doniphan, NE 68832 t) 402-845-2707 stannsdoniphan.org Rev. David A. Oldham, Pst.;
Sacred Heart - 103 W. Pine St., Kenesaw, NE 68956
DWIGHT
Assumption - 336 W. Pine, Dwight, NE 68635; Mailing: P.O. Box 70, Dwight, NE 68635 t) 402-566-2765 snatrectory@hotmail.com Rev. Raymond L. Jansen, Pst.;
EXETER
St. Stephen's - 207 N. Union Ave., Exeter, NE 68351 t) 402-266-5581 Rev. Brendan R.J. Kelly, Pst.; CRP Stds.: 30
St. Wenceslaus - 703 Main St., Milligan, NE 68406; Mailing: 207 N Union Ave, Exeter, NE 68351
FAIRBURY
St. Michael's - 807 F St., Fairbury, NE 68352; Mailing: P.O. Box 406, Fairbury, NE 68352 t) 402-729-2058 st.michael.fairbury@gmail.com www.stmichaelsfairbury.org/ Rev. John B. Birkel, Pst.;
St. Mary's - 511 Amanda, Alexandria, NE 68303
FALLS CITY
SS. Peter and Paul - 1820 Fulton St., Falls City, NE 68355 t) 402-245-3002 deb-lem@cdolinc.net; fr.james-meysenburg@cdolinc.net Rev. Lawrence J. Stoley, Pst.; CRP Stds.: 12
FRIEND
St. Joseph's - 405 S. Main St., Friend, NE 68359 t) 402-947-3651 st.joseph-friend@lincolndiocese.org Rev. Leo V. Seiker, Admin.; CRP Stds.: 13
GENEVA
St. Joseph's - 831 E St., Geneva, NE 68361; Mailing: P.O. Box 383, Geneva, NE 68361 t) 402-759-3225 Rev. Harlan D. P. Waskowiak, Pst.; CRP Stds.: 61
St. Mary - 703 Swartzendruber Dr., Shickley, NE 68436; Mailing: PO Box 383, Geneva, NE 68361-0383
GRANT
Mother of Sorrows - 745 Garfield Ave., Grant, NE 69140; Mailing: PO Box 536, Grant, NE 69140 t) 308-352-4803 Rev. Thomas B. Bush, Pst.; Diana Tate, DRE; CRP Stds.: 46
Resurrection of Our Lord - t) (308) 352-4803
HARVARD
St. Joseph's - 605 N. Kearney Ave., Harvard, NE 68944; Mailing: P.O. Box 70, Harvard, NE 68944 t) 402-772-3511 st.joseph.cc.hrvrd.ne@gmail.com Rev. Denton Morris, Pst.;
HASTINGS
St. Cecilia's - 301 W. 7th St., Hastings, NE 68901 t) 402-462-2105 (CRP); 402-463-1336 stcbulletin@windstream.net stceciliahastings.org Rev. Craig J. Clinch, Pst.; Rev. Douglas Daro, Par. Vicar; Rev. Dominic T.H. Phan, Par. Vicar;
St. Michael's - 715 Creighton Ave., Hastings, NE 68901 t) 402-463-1023 fr.jeremy-hazuka@cdolinc.net; office@stmichaelshastings.com Rev. Jeremy L. Hazuka, Pst.; Rev. Liam O'Shea-Creal, Par. Vicar; CRP Stds.: 81
HEBRON
Sacred Heart - 436 N. 3rd St., Hebron, NE 68370 t) 402-768-1764 sacredhearthebron@gmail.com; sacredheartdove@gmail.com Rev. Steven P. Major, Pst.; CRP Stds.: 84
HOLDREGE
All Saints - 1204 Logan St., Holdrege, NE 68949 t) 308-995-4590 church@asholdrege.org www.ascholdrege.com Rev. Jay M. Buhman, Pst.; CRP Stds.: 62
St. John's - 105 E. Niobrara St., Smithfield, NE 68976; Mailing: 1204 Logan St., c/o All Saints, Holdrege, NE 68949 www.ascholdrege.com/st.john
All Saints Catholic School - (Grades PreK-4) 1206 Logan St., Holdrege, NE 68949 school@asholdrege.org www.ascholdrege.com/ascs Stds.: 62; Lay Tchrs.: 3
IMPERIAL
St. Patrick - 128 E. 7th St., Imperial, NE 69033; Mailing: P.O. Box 96, Imperial, NE 69033 t) 308-882-4995 Rev. Lothar Gilde, Pst.;
INDIANOLA
St. Catherine's - 815 D St., Indianola, NE 69034; Mailing: P.O. Box O, Indianola, NE 69034 t) 308-364-2428 st.catherine.church@hotmail.com Rev. Michael K. Houlihan;
KENESAW
Sacred Heart - 100 W. Pine St., Kenesaw, NE 68956; Mailing: P.O. Box 407, Doniphan, NE 68832 t) 402-752-8149 (CRP); 402-845-2707 stannsdoniphan.org Rev. Adam M. Sughroue, Pst.;
LAWRENCE
Sacred Heart - 141 E. 2nd St., Lawrence, NE 68957; Mailing: 250 N. Phillips, P.O. Box 247, Lawrence, NE 68957 t) 402-756-7393 Rev. Corey R. Harrison, Pst.; Barb Janda, DRE;
Assumption - 506 Liberty St., Deweese, NE 68934
St. Stephen's - 1838 Rd. 2600, Lawrence, NE 68957; Mailing: P.O. Box 247, Lawrence, NE 68957
LINCOLN
Cathedral of the Risen Christ - 3500 Sheridan Blvd., Lincoln, NE 68506 t) 402-488-0948 church@crchrist-parish.org Rev. Msgr. Thomas J. Fucinaro, Pst.; Rev. Caleb D. Hile, Par. Vicar; Rev. Joseph J. Bernardo, In Res.; Rev. Christopher M. Eckrich, In Res.;
Cathedral of the Risen Christ School - (Grades PreK-8) 3245 S. 37th, Lincoln, NE 68506 t) 402-489-9621 jeremy-ekeler@cdolinc.net www.cathedraleagles.com Jeremy Ekeler, Prin.;
St. Andrew Dung Lac and Companions Catholic Church of Lincoln - 9230 1st St., Lincoln, NE 68526 t) 402-423-2005 josthanh24@yahoo.com www.andrewdunglac.org Rev. Joseph Nguyen, Pst.;
Bishop Bonacum Chancery - 3400 Sheridan Blvd., Lincoln, NE 68506-6125 t) 402-488-0921 fr.dan-rayer@lincolndiocese.org www.lincolndiocese.org Rev. Justin R. Fulton, Vicar;
Blessed Sacrament - 1720 Lake St., Lincoln, NE 68502 t) 402-474-4249 cindyuhing@bsc.church; frjohnsullivan@blessedsacramentlincoln.org www.blessedsacrmentlincoln.org Rev. Michael J. Morin, Pst.; Rev. Matthew Kovar, Assoc. Pst.;
Blessed Sacrament School - (Grades PreK-8) 1725 Lake St., Lincoln, NE 68502; Mailing: 1720 Lake St., c/o Blessed Sacrament Parish, Lincoln, NE 68502 t) 402-476-6202 blessed-sacrament-school.com/ Danielle Miller, Prin.;
Cristo Rey - 4245 J St., Lincoln, NE 68510 t) 402-488-5087 pastor@cristoreylincoln.org; office@cristoreylincoln.org cristoreylincoln.com Rev. Brian Wirth, Par. Vicar; Melania Palacios de Izquierdo, DRE;
Immaculate Heart of Mary - 6345 Madison Ave., Lincoln, NE 68507; Mailing: 6405 Madison Ave., Lincoln, NE 68507 t) 402-465-8541 giaoxukhiettamme@gmail.com giaoxukhiettamme.org Rev. Thomas Tuan Van Nguyen, C.M.C., Pst.; CRP Stds.: 212
St. John the Apostle - 7601 Vine St., Lincoln, NE 68505 t) 402-489-1946 jnel-bulletin@cdolinc.net Rev. Lyle Johnson, Pst.; Rev. Robert J. Froeschl, Par. Vicar; Rev. Steven A. Mills, In Res.;
St. John the Apostle School - (Grades PreK-8) t) 402-486-1860 dennis-martin@cdolinc.net Dennis Martin, Prin.;
St. Joseph - 7900 Trendwood Dr., Lincoln, NE 68506 t) 402-483-2288 www.stjosephlnk.org Rev. Michael G. McCabe, Pst.; Rev. Robert Johnson, Assoc. Pst.; Rev. Joseph J. Bernardo, In Res.; CRP Stds.: 86
St. Joseph School - (Grades K-8) 1940 S. 77th St., Lincoln, NE 68506 t) 402-489-0341 school.stjosephlnk.org Stds.: 426; Sr. Tchrs.: 4; Lay Tchrs.: 33
St. Mary - 1420 K St., Lincoln, NE 68508 t) 402-435-2125 stmarylincoln@gmail.com stmarylincoln.org Rev. Joseph M. Walsh, Pst.; Rev. Joseph P. Finn, In Res.; Rev. Stephen A. Cooney, In Res.; CRP Stds.: 14
St. Michael - 9101 S. 78th St., Lincoln, NE 68516 t) 402-488-1313 stmichaelchurch@cdolinc.net stmichaellincoln.org Rev. Kenneth A. Borowiak, Pst.; Rev. Luke Fleck, Par. Vicar;
St. Michael School - (Grades K-8) denise-ray@cdolinc.net
North American Martyrs - 1101 Isaac Dr., Lincoln, NE 68521 t) 402-476-8088 fr.brian.connor@cdolinc.net www.namartyrs.org Rev. Nathan Hall, Pst.; Rev. Joseph Wahlmeier, Par. Vicar;
North American Martyrs School - (Grades PreK-8) t) 402-476-7373 sr.janelle-buettner@cdolinc.net Sr. Janelle Buettner, M.S., Prin.;
St. Patrick's - 6111 Morrill Ave., Lincoln, NE 68507 t) 402-466-2752 Rev. Troy J. Schweiger, Pst.; Rev. Christopher J. Miller, Assoc. Pst.; Rev. David F. Bourek, In Res.; CRP Stds.: 69
St. Patrick's School - -8) 4142 N. 61st St., Lincoln, NE 68507 t) 402-466-3710 www.stpatricklincolnschool.com
St. Peter - 4500 Duxhall Dr., Lincoln, NE 68516 t) 402-423-1239 stpeterchurch@cdolinc.net www.saintpeterlincoln.com Rev. Eric A Clark, Pst.; Rev. Jason Doher, Assoc. Pst.; Rev. Brian Wirth, Assoc. Pst.;
St. Peter School - (Grades PreK-8) t) 402-421-6299 margaret-aldridge@cdolinc.net www.saintpeterslincoln.com/school.html
Sacred Heart - 3128 S St., Lincoln, NE 68503 t) 402-476-2610 sacredheartlincoln@outlook.com sacredheartlincoln.org Rev. Msgr. Timothy J. Thorburn, Pst.; Rev. Valerian Bartek, Assoc. Pst.; CRP Stds.: 33
St. Teresa Catholic Church - 735 S. 36th St., Lincoln, NE 68510 t) 402-477-3979 jeanne-kee@cdolinc.net Rev. Nicholas A. Kipper, Pst.; Rev. Christian Schwenka, Par. Vicar; Rev. Samuel Beardslee, Par. Vicar;
St. Teresa Catholic School - (Grades PreK-8) 616 S. 36th St., Lincoln, NE 68510 t) 402-477-3358 sr.mary-cecilia@cdolinc.net stlfschool.org/ Sr. Mary Cecilia Mills, Prin.;
St. Thomas Aquinas - 320 N. 16th St., Lincoln, NE 68508 t) 402-474-7914 newmancenter@unl.edu newmancenter.unl.edu Rev. Robert A. Matya, Pst.; Rev. Alec J. Sasse, Par. Vicar; Emily Gratopp, DRE; Rev. Caleb J. LaRue, In Res.;
MANLEY
St. Patrick's - 101 N. Broadway, Manley, NE 68403; Mailing: P.O. Box 27, 107 Broadway St., Manley, NE 68403 t) 402-234-3595 Rev. Thomas L. Wiedel, Pst.;
St. Mary's - 505 W. G St., Elmwood, NE 68349 t) 402-994-2485
MCCOOK
St. Patrick - 612 E. 4th St., McCook, NE 69001; Mailing: P.O. Box 1040, McCook, NE 69001 t) 308-345-6734 Rev. Bernard Kimminau, Pst.; Rev. Dale Jonathan Allder, Par. Vicar; Rev. Bernard A. Lorenz, In Res.; CRP Stds.: 70
St. Patrick School - (Grades PreK-8) 401 E. F St., McCook, NE 69001 becky-redl@cdolinc.net
Sacred Heart -
St. Ann's -
MEAD
St. James - 213 E. 8th St., Mead, NE 68041 t) 402-624-3555 office@stjamesmead.com Rev. Gary Gross, Pst.; CRP Stds.: 15
MINDEN
St. John the Baptist - 624 N. Garber Ave., Minden, NE 68959; Mailing: P.O. Box 245, Minden, NE 68959 t) 308-832-1626 (CRP); 308-832-1245 Rev. James E. Winter, Pst.;
Holy Family -
MORSE BLUFF
St. George - 260 Short St., Morse Bluff, NE 68648; Mailing: PO Box 98, Morse Bluff, NE 68648 t) 402-666-5280 stgmbne.com Rev. Dennis Hunt, Pst.; CRP Stds.: 15

Sacred Heart -

NEBRASKA CITY

St. Benedict's - 411 5th Rue, Nebraska City, NE 68410 t) 402-873-3047 stbenedicts1856@gmail.com stbens.org Rev. Ryan A. Kaup, Pst.; CRP Stds.: 55

St. Joseph's - 5592 O Rd., Nebraska City, NE 68410 t) 402-873-4569 Rev. Stephen L. Graeve, Pst.;

St. Bernard's - On Hwy. 75 1 mile South of Julian exit, Julian, NE 68379; Mailing: 5592 O Rd., Nebraska City, NE 68410 Rev. Michael A. Ventre, Pst.;

St. Mary Catholic Church of Nebraska City - 520 1st Ave., Nebraska City, NE 68410; Mailing: 218 N. 6th St., Nebraska City, NE 68410 t) 402-873-3024 stmbulletin@windstream.net stmarysnebraskacity.com Rev. Thomas J. Schultes, Pst.; Rev. Mark S. Pfeiffer, Assoc. Pst.; Rev. Jonathan J. Haschke, In Res.; CRP Stds.: 26

NORTH PLATTE

St. Elizabeth Ann Seton - 3301 Echo Dr., North Platte, NE 69101; Mailing: PO Box 1558, North Platte, NE 69103 t) 308-534-5461 rectory-office@seas-np.org seas-np.org Rev. Randall Langhorst, Pst.;

ORLEANS

St. Mary's - 109 W. Linn St., Orleans, NE 68966 t) 308-473-3475 Rev. Maurice H. Current, Pst.;

St. Joseph's - 810 4th St., Alma, NE 68920; Mailing: P.O. Box 764, Alma, NE 68920 t) 308-928-2575 Rev. Nicholas J. Baker, In Res.;

St. Michael's - 510 Central Ave., Oxford, NE 68967

OSCEOLA

St. Vincent Ferrer - 751 S. Nance, Osceola, NE 68651; Mailing: P.O. Box 212, Osceola, NE 68651 t) 402-747-3491 cr62313@windstream.net Rev. Thomas Au, Admin.;

St. Mary's -

PALMYRA

St. Leo's - 330 W. 8th St., Palmyra, NE 68418-2537 t) 402-780-5535 leomartinpastor@gmail.com; leomartinsecretary@gmail.com www.stleoandstmartin.com Rev. Sean P. Kilcawley, Pst.;

St. Martin's -

PLATTSMOUTH

Church of the Holy Spirit - 520 S. 18th St., Plattsmouth, NE 68048 t) 402-296-3139 plattsmouthhsc@cdolinc.net www.holyspiritplattsmouth.com Rev. Sean M. Timmerman, Pst.; Rev. Anthony Bedient, Par. Vicar; CRP Stds.: 32

St. John the Baptist School - (Grades PreSchool-8) 500 S. 18th St., Plattsmouth, NE 68048 t) 402-296-6230 www.stjbcatholic.com Stds.: 135; Lay Tchrs.: 13

PRAGUE

St. John's - 122 W. Center Ave., Prague, NE 68050; Mailing: P.O. Box 96, Prague, NE 68050 t) 402-663-4615 Rev. Carson Kain, Pst.;

SS. Cyril and Methodius - 2880 County Rd. O, Plasi, NE 68050

RED CLOUD

Sacred Heart - 413 N. Seward St., Red Cloud, NE 68970 t) 402-746-3750 rcsacredheart@gmail.com Rev. Paul G. Frank, Pst.;

St. Katharine Drexel - 358 9th Ave., Franklin, NE 68939 t) 308-746-3750

ROSELAND

Sacred Heart - 11818 W. Alexander, Roseland, NE 68973; Mailing: P.O. Box 67, Roseland, NE 68973 t) 402-756-6251 shcc@gtmc.net Rev. Corey Harrison, Pst.;

Assumption - 12620 W. Assumption Rd., Roseland, NE 68973

RULO

Immaculate Conception - 601 W. Rouleau St., Rulo, NE 68431 t) 402-245-4731 fr.ben-rynearson@cdolinc.net Rev. Benjamin J. Rynearson, Pst.; CRP Stds.: 5

St. Mary's -

SEWARD

St. Vincent de Paul - 152 Pinewood Ave., 152 Pinewood Ave, Seward, NE 68434 t) 402-643-3421 gloria-schneider@cdolinc.net Rev. Msgr. Robert G. Tucker, Pst.; Rev. Shravankumar Raminedi, Par. Vicar; CRP Stds.: 128

St. Vincent de Paul School - (Grades K-5) t) 402-643-9525

SHELBY

Sacred Heart - 210 S. Walnut St., Shelby, NE 68662-8002; Mailing: P.O. Box 340, Shelby, NE 68662-0340 t) 402-527-5425 sacredheartshelby@windstream.net www.sacredheartshelby.org/ Rev. Andrew Litt, Pst.;

STEINAUER

St. Anthony - 310 Hickory St., Steinauer, NE 68441 t) 402-869-2256 mschmit@windstream.net pcocatholics.com Rev. Michael R. Christensen, Pst.;

Sacred Heart -

SUPERIOR

St. Joseph's - 1415 California, Superior, NE 68978-1019 t) 402-879-3735 stjoseph@gtmc.net Rev. Ferdinand J. Boehme, Pst.;

Sacred Heart -

SUTTON

St. Mary's - 312 S. Saunders Ave., Sutton, NE 68979; Mailing: P.O. Box 406, Sutton, NE 68979 t) 402-773-5346 stmaryssutton@gmail.com Rev. Michael J. Zimmer, Pst.;

St. Helena's - 172 Jackson St., Grafton, NE 68365

SYRACUSE

St. Paulinus - 863 5th St., Syracuse, NE 68446-9504 t) 402-269-3382 stpaulinuschurch@gmail.com paulinustrinity.weebly.com Rev. Ryan L. Salisbury, Pst.;

Holy Trinity - 4456 Arbor Rd., Avoca, NE 68307

TECUMSEH

St. Andrew's - 186 N. 5th St., Tecumseh, NE 68450; Mailing: P.O. Box 656, Tecumseh, NE 68450 t) 402-335-3742 Rev. Christopher K. Kubat, Pst.; Rev. Thomas D. McGuire, In Res.; CRP Stds.: 54

St. Andrew's School - (Grades PreK-6) t) 402-335-2234 Stds.: 13; Lay Tchrs.: 3

St. Mary's - 61518 Hwy. 41, St Mary, NE 68443; Mailing: Box 656, Tecumseh, NE 68450 t) (402) 335-3742

TRENTON

St. James - 117 W. B St., Trenton, NE 69044; Mailing: P.O. Box 488, Trenton, NE 69044 t) 308-334-5328 stjames@gpcom.net Rev. Gary G. Brethour, Pst.;

St. John's -

Holy Family -

ULYSSES

Immaculate Conception - 215 S. 6th St., Ulysses, NE 68669; Mailing: P.O. Box 128, Ulysses, NE 68669 t) 402-549-2437 Rev. Michael S. Stec, Pst.; CRP Stds.: 30

VALPARAISO

Sts. Mary and Joseph's - 637 Iver St., Valparaiso, NE 68065 t) 402-784-2511 www.stsmaryandjosephval.com/ Rev. Matthew Zimmer, Pst.;

WAHOO

St. Wenceslaus - 211 E. 2nd St., Wahoo, NE 68066; Mailing: 256 N. Linden, Wahoo, NE 68066 t) 402-443-4235 stwencoffice@wahoocatholic.org www.wahoocatholic.org Rev. Jeffrey R. Eickhoff, Pst.; Rev. Andrew Schwenka, Par. Vicar; Rev. Lee T. Jirovsky, In Res.; CRP Stds.: 80

St. Wenceslaus School - (Grades PreK-6) 108 N. Linden, Wahoo, NE 68066-1953 t) 402-443-3336 Mike Weiss, Admin.; Rev. Michael J. Morin, Supt.;

WALLACE

St. Mary's - 209 N. Commercial Ave., Wallace, NE 69169; Mailing: PO Box 191, Wallace, NE 69169 t) 308-387-4441 Rev. Thomas B. Bush, Pst.; Kim Sullivan, DRE; CRP Stds.: 10

WESTON

St. John Nepomucene - 450 School St., Weston, NE 68070; Mailing: PO Box 10, Weston, NE 68070 t) 402-642-5245 www.stjohnschurchweston.com/ Rev. Matthew J. Vandewalle, Pst.; CRP Stds.: 11

St. John Nepomucene School - (Grades PreK-6) 130 N. Front St., Weston, NE 68070 t) 402-642-5234 fr.matthew-vandewalle@cdolinc.net stjohnschoolweston.com/ Linda Maly, Headmaster; Stds.: 84; Lay Tchrs.: 6

St. Vitus - N. Main St., Touhy, NE 68065 t) (402) 642-5245 www.stjohnschurchweston.com

WILBER

St. Wenceslaus - 501 N. Wilson, Wilber, NE 68465; Mailing: PO Box 706, Wilber, NE 68465 t) 402-821-2689 Rev. Robert K. Barnhill, Pst.; CRP Stds.: 80

St. Joseph's - 511 N. Elm St., Tobias, NE 68465 t) 402-821-8269 Rev. Randall Langhorst, Pst.;

WYMORE

St. Mary's - 115 N. 11th St., Wymore, NE 68466; Mailing: 107 N. 11th St., P.O. Box 13, Wymore, NE 68466 t) 402-645-3160 fathergrell@gmail.com Rev. Loras K. Grell, Pst.; CRP Stds.: 28

St. Joseph's - 406 Wyatt St., Barneston, NE 68466

St. Mary's - 521 Perry St., Odell, NE 68415

YORK

St. Joseph's - 505 N. East Ave., York, NE 68467 t) 402-362-4595 stjoeyork@gmail.com www.stjosephyork.com Rev. John R. Sullivan, Pst.; Rev. Janusz Marzynski, Assoc. Pst.; Katie Burger, DRE; CRP Stds.: 104

St. Joseph's School - (Grades PreK-8) t) 402-362-3021 office@stjosephyork.org Mary Jo Leininger, Prin.;

St. Patrick's - 305 E. M St., Mc Cool Junction, NE 68401; Mailing: 505 N. East Ave., York, NE 68467 t) (402) 362-4595 (Same as Parent)

SCHOOLS: PRESCHOOL THRU HIGH SCHOOL

SCHOOLS

STATE OF NEBRASKA

HASTINGS

St. Michael's Elementary, Hastings Catholic Schools - (PAR) (Grades K-5) 721 Creighton Ave., Hastings, NE 68901 t) 402-462-6310 chelsey-mangers@cdolinc.net Chelsey Mangers, Admin.; Stds.: 195; Sr. Tchrs.: 1; Lay Tchrs.: 16

NEBRASKA CITY

Lourdes Elementary - (PAR) (Grades PreK-5) 412 2nd Ave., Nebraska City, NE 68410 t) 402-873-3739 lourdes-office@cdolinc.net lourdescentralcatholic.org Curt Feilmeier, Prin.; Rev. Jonathan Haschke, Pres.; Kim Esser, Librn.;

HIGH SCHOOLS

STATE OF NEBRASKA

DAVID CITY

Aquinas/St. Mary's Schools - (PAR) (Grades PreK-12) 3420 MN Rd., David City, NE 68632; Mailing: P.O. Box 149, David City, NE 68632 t) 402-367-3175 fr.sean-timmerman@cdonlinc.net www.aquinas-catholic.com Rev. Michael A. Ventre, Admin.; David G. McMahon, Prin.;

St. Mary's School - (Grades PreK-12) 1026 5th St., David City, NE 68632 t) 402-367-3669 www.aquinas-catholic.com/st-marys Sarah Zook, Prin.;

FALLS CITY

Sacred Heart School - (PAR) 1820 Fulton St., Falls City, NE 68355 t) 402-245-4151 doug-goltz@cdolinc.net www.fcsacredheart.org Douglas Goltz, Prin.;

High School -

Elementary School - Angela Simon, Librn.;

HASTINGS

St. Cecilia's Middle School/High School - (PAR) (Grades 6-12) 521 N. Kansas Ave., Hastings, NE 68901; Mailing: 604 N. St. Joseph Ave., Hastings, NE 68901

t) 402-462-6566 fr.tom-brouillette@cdolinc.net www.hastingscatholicschools.org Rev. Thomas S. Brouillette, Admin.; Rev. Cyrus Rowen, Prin.; Marilyn Zysset, Librn.; Stds.: 218; Pr. Tchrs.: 5; Sr. Tchrs.: 3; Lay Tchrs.: 18

LINCOLN

Pius X Catholic High School - (PAR) (Grades 9-12) 6000 A St., Lincoln, NE 68510 t) 402-488-0931; 402-473-5970 x56120 communications@piusx.net www.piusx.net Rev. Msgr. John J. Perkinton, Chancellor; Tom Korta, CEO; Terry Kathol, Prin.; Rev. Steven A. Mills, Vice Prin.; Kelsey Bugarin, Vice Prin.; Rev. Joseph J. Bernardo, Chap.; Rev. Samuel Beardslee, Chap.; Victoria (Tori) Roberts, Campus Min.; Erin Rose Willis, Librn.; Stds.: 1,091; Pr. Tchrs.: 2; Sr. Tchrs.: 2; Lay Tchrs.: 58

NEBRASKA CITY

Lourdes Central Catholic Schools - (PAR) (Grades 6-12) 412 2nd Ave., Nebraska City, NE 68410 t) 402-873-6154 lourdes-office@cdolinc.net lourdescentralcatholic.org Curt Feilmeier, Prin.; Rev. Jonathan J. Haschke, Pres.; Kim Esser, Librn.;

WAHOO

Bishop Neumann Jr.-Sr. High School - (PAR) 202 S. Linden, Wahoo, NE 68066 t) 402-443-4151 jennifer-benes@cdolinc.net bishopneumann.com Rev. Lee T. Jirovsky, Admin.;

INSTITUTIONS LOCATED IN DIOCESE

CAMPUS MINISTRY / NEWMAN CENTERS [CAM]

LINCOLN

University of Nebraska, Newman Club - 320 N. 16th St., Lincoln, NE 68508 t) 402-474-7914 newmancenter@unl.edu newmancenter.unl.edu See also: St. Thomas Aquinas, Lincoln, NE. Rev. Alec J. Sasse, Par. Vicar; Rev. Robert A. Matya, Dir.;

CATHOLIC CHARITIES [CCH]

LINCOLN

Catholic Social Services - Admin. Offices 2241 O St., Lincoln, NE 68510 t) 402-474-1600 info@cssisus.org; kpatrick@cssisus.org www.cssisus.org Rev. Justin R. Fulton, Vice. Pres.; Asstd. Annu.: 25,500; Staff: 73

Apostolate of Suffering - 2241 O St., Lincoln, NE 68510

Catholic Social Services - 333 W. 2nd St., Hastings, NE 68901 t) 402-463-2112; 888-826-9629 Katie Patrick, Dir.;

Counseling Services - 3700 Sheridan Blvd., Lincoln, NE 68506 t) 402-489-1834; 800-961-6277 Katie Patrick, Dir.;

St. Francis Thrift Store and Services - 1014 Central Ave., Auburn, NE 68305 t) 402-274-4818

St. Isidore Thrift Store and Services - 527 Broadway St., Imperial, NE 69033; Mailing: P.O. Box 1085, Imperial, NE 69033 t) 308-882-3065

CEMETERIES [CEM]

LINCOLN

Calvary Cemetery and Mausoleum - 3880 L St., Lincoln, NE 68510 t) 402-476-8787 calvary@cdolinc.net www.calvarycatholic.com Joint cemetery for Lincoln parishes. Rev. Msgr. Timothy J. Thorburn, Dir.;

CONVENTS, MONASTERIES, AND RESIDENCES FOR WOMEN [CON]

CRETE

Secular Institute of the Schoenstatt Sisters of Mary, ISSM - 340 State Hwy. 103, Crete, NE 68333-5020; Mailing: W284N404 Cherry Ln., Waukesha, WI 53188-9416 t) 402-826-3346 cor.mariae.shrine@gmail.com www.schoenstatt-nebraska.us/ Sr. M. Emily Kenkel, Prov.; Srs.: 1

LINCOLN

Adoration Convent and Church of Christ the King (Sister Servants of the Holy Spirit of Perpetual Adoration) - 1040 S. Cotner Blvd., Lincoln, NE 68510 t) 402-489-0765 adorechristk@gmail.com Rev. Nicholas A. Kipper, Chap.; Sr. Cecilia M. Hocbo, Supr.; Srs.: 6

St. Agnes Convent - 3405 Sheridan Blvd., Lincoln, NE 68506 t) 402-484-7348 sr.collette@cdolinc.net Sr. Collette Bruskewitz, O.S.F., Contact;

Congregation of Missionary Sisters of the Blessed Virgin Mary, Queen of Mercy - 9141 S. 78th St., Lincoln, NE 68516 t) 402-421-1704 srsqueenmercy@hotmail.com www.queenmercysisters.org Sr. Samantha Nguyen, Supr.; Srs.: 14

School Sisters of Christ the King, Villa Regina Motherhouse & Novitiate - 4100 S.W. 56th St., Lincoln, NE 68522-9261 t) 402-477-5232 m.margaret-mary@cdolinc.net www.cksisters.org Most Rev. Robert W. Finn, Chap.; Mother Margaret Mary Waldron, Supr.; Srs.: 29

NEBRASKA CITY

The Franciscan Sisters of the Sorrowful Mother - 347 N. 62nd Rd., Nebraska City, NE 68410-6195 t) 402-873-3052 fs93813@gmail.com www.franciscansisters.net Sr. Kathleen Kilp, O.S.F., Supr.; Srs.: 3

VALPARAISO

Carmel of Jesus, Mary, and Joseph - 9300 W. Agnew Rd., Valparaiso, NE 68065 t) 402-784-0375 Sr. Teresa of Jesus, O.C.D., Prioress;

WAVERLY

Marian Sisters of the Diocese of Lincoln Motherhouse and Novitiate - 6765 N. 112th St., Waverly, NE 68462-9762 t) 402-786-2750 srannmarie-zierke@cdolinc.net www.mariansisters.org Mother Ann Marie Zierke, Supr.; Srs.: 40

ENDOWMENTS / FOUNDATIONS / TRUSTS [EFT]

DAVID CITY

Aquinas High School Endowment Fund - 3420 MN Rd., David City, NE 68632 t) 402-367-3175 www.aquinas-catholic.net Rev. Sean M. Timmerman, Supt.;

FALLS CITY

Falls City Sacred Heart Catholic School Foundation - 1820 Fulton St., Falls City, NE 68355 t) 402-245-4151 fr.lawrence-stoley@cdolinc.net Rev. Lawrence J. Stoley, Secy.;

HASTINGS

Hastings Catholic Schools Foundation - 521 N. Kansas, Hastings, NE 68901 t) 402-462-2105 fr.tom-brouillette@cdolinc.net www.hastingscatholicschools.org Rev. Thomas S. Brouillette, Secy.;

LINCOLN

Lincoln Diocesan Investment Trust and Loan - 3400 Sheridan Blvd., Lincoln, NE 68506 t) 402-488-0921 tracy-lockwood@lincolndiocese.org Rev. Justin R. Fulton, Vice. Pres.;

Pius X Foundation and Pius X Endowment Fund - 6000 A St., Lincoln, NE 68510 t) 402-488-1046 courtney.johnson@piusx.net; emily.moore@piusx.net www.piusx.net/foundation Courtney Johnson, Dir.; Tom Korta, Secy.;

NEBRASKA CITY

Lourdes Central High School Endowment Fund - 412 Second Ave., Nebraska City, NE 68410 t) 402-873-6154 lourdes-office@cdolinc.net www.lourdescentralcatholic.org Rev. Jonathan J. Haschke, Secy.;

WAHOO

Bishop Neumann High School Endowment Fund - 202 S. Linden, Wahoo, NE 68066 t) 402-443-4151 jennifer-benes@cdolinc.net bishopneumann.com Rev. Lee Thomas Jirovsky, Secy.;

HOSPITALS / HEALTH SERVICES [HOS]

LINCOLN

CHI Health Nebraska Heart - 7500 S. 91st St., Lincoln, NE 68526 t) (402) 327-2700 missionintegrationmidwest@commonspirit.org www.chihealth.com/nebraska-heart Affiliate of Catholic Health Initiatives. Dr. Richard Thompson, Pres.; Andrew Santos, SVP Mission Integration; Bed Capacity: 63; Asstd. Annu.: 9,744; Staff: 221

CHI Health St. Elizabeth - 555 S. 70th St., Lincoln, NE 68510 t) 402-219-8000 missionintegrationmidwest@commonspirit.org www.chihealth.com/st-elizabeth Affiliate of Catholic Health Initiatives. Derek Vance, Pres.; Andrew J. Santos III, SVP, Mission Integration; Andrew Santos; Bed Capacity: 259; Asstd. Annu.: 65,098; Staff: 778

NEBRASKA CITY

CHI Health St. Mary's - 1301 Grundman Blvd., Nebraska City, NE 68410; Mailing: P.O. Box 70, Nebraska City, NE 68410 t) (402) 873-3321 missionintegrationmidwest@commonspirit.org www.chihealth.com/st-marys Affiliate of Catholic Health Initiatives. Daniel J DeFreece, Pres.; Andrew J. Santos III, SVP, Mission Integration; Andrew Santos; Bed Capacity: 18; Asstd. Annu.: 45,000; Staff: 210

MISCELLANEOUS [MIS]

LINCOLN

Chancery - 3400 Sheridan Blvd., Lincoln, NE 68506 t) 402-488-0921 www.lincolndiocese.org Rev. Caleb J. LaRue, Chancellor;

The Catholic Foundation of Southern Nebraska - 3700 Sheridan Blvd., Ste. 9, Lincoln, NE 68506 t) 402-488-2142 chris-raun@catholicgift.org catholicgift.org Chris Raun, Dir.;

Diocesan Health Ministries - 3400 Sheridan Blvd., Lincoln, NE 68506 t) 402-488-0921 chancellor@lincolndiocese.org Most Rev. James D. Conley, Pres.;

Diocesan Housing Ministries, Inc. - 3400 Sheridan Blvd., Lincoln, NE 68506 t) 402-488-0921 chancellor@lincolndiocese.org Rev. Justin R. Fulton, Contact;

Ecclesial Carmelite Movement - 3745 S. 44th St., Lincoln, NE 68506 t) 402-430-3163 carmelitemovement@gmail.com Rev. Msgr. Timothy J. Thorburn, Chap.;

St. Francis of Assisi Church - 1145 South St., Lincoln, NE 68502 t) (402) 477-5145; (402) 477-5159 rector@stfrancislincoln.org www.stfrancislincoln.org Rev. Joseph Heffernan, Rector;

John XXIII Diocesan Center - 3700 Sheridan Blvd., Lincoln, NE 68506 t) 402-488-2040 joan-penn@cdolinc.net Rev. Justin R. Fulton, Moderator;

Madonna Rehabilitation Hospitals - 5401 South St., Lincoln, NE 68506 t) 402-413-3000; 800-676-5448 info@madonna.org www.madonna.org Physical Medicine and Rehabilitation, Inpatient and Outpatient Services, Long-Term Care. Rev. Joseph S. Steele, Chap.; Paul Dongilli Jr., CEO; Rev. John R. Sullivan, Vice Pres.;

Magnificat-Lincoln - 1101 N. 79th St., Lincoln, NE 68505-2008 t) 402-489-3819 rhonda33.praising.him.4ever@gmail.com

***Society of St. Vincent de Paul - Lincoln Council** - ; Mailing: P.O. Box 30145, Lincoln, NE 68503-0145 t) 402-435-7986 svdplincolncouncil@gmail.com lincoln.svdcouncil.org Denise Dean, Pres.; Angela Reiling, Secy.;

WAVERLY

***Knights of the Holy Eucharist, Inc.** - 7303 N. 112th St., Waverly, NE 68462 t) 402-786-2705 knightsinfo@gmail.com www.knightsoftheholyeucharist.com/ Bro. David Mary Fazzini, KHE, Supr.;

NURSING / REHABILITATION / CONVALESCENCE / ELDERLY CARE [NUR]

LINCOLN

Bonacum House - 3301 Sheridan Blvd., Lincoln, NE

68506 t) 402-483-0391 priestshome@gmail.com Residence for retired priests. Sr. Andrea Goeckner, Contact; Rev. Justin R. Fulton, Admin.;

PRESCHOOLS / CHILDCARE CENTERS [PRE]

MC COOL JUNCTION

Camp Kateri Tekakwitha - 1305 Rd. 3, Mc Cool Junction, NE 68401; Mailing: P.O. Box 127, Mc Cool Junction, NE 68401 t) 402-366-9337 campkaterit@gmail.com www.campkateri.org Russell Koos, Dir.;

RETREAT HOUSES / RENEWAL CENTERS [RTR]

WAVERLY

Our Lady of Good Counsel Retreat House - 7303 N. 112th St., Waverly, NE 68462 t) 402-786-2705 office@goodcounselretreat.org goodcounselretreat.org/ Rev. Gary L. Coulter, Dir.; Rev. Msgr. John J. Perkinton, In Res.;

SEMINARIES [SEM]

DENTON

Our Lady of Guadalupe Seminary, Inc. - 7880 W. Denton Rd., Denton, NE 68339; Mailing: P.O. Box 147, Denton, NE 68339 t) 402-797-7700 seminary@fsspolgs.org; vocations@fsspolgs.org www.fsspolgs.org Rev. Josef Bisig, F.S.S.P., Rector; Rev. Robert Ferguson, F.S.S.P., Prof./Vice-Rector; Rev. Anthony Uy, F.S.S.P., Prof.; Rev. Benoit Guichard, F.S.S.P., Prof.; Rev. William Lawrence, F.S.S.P., Prof.; Rev. Joseph Lee, F.S.S.P., Prof.; Rev. Rhone Lillard, F.S.S.P., Prof.; Rev. Charles Ryan, F.S.S.P., Prof.;

SEWARD

St. Gregory the Great Seminary - 800 Fletcher Rd., Seward, NE 68434 t) 402-643-4052 sggs@sggs.edu sggs.edu Rev. Brian P. Kane, Rector; Rev. John Cletus Rooney, Vice Rector; Rev. M. James Divis, Spiritual Dir.; Rev. Matthew M. Rolling, Academic Dean; Terrence Nollen, Librn.;

Newman Institute for Catholic Thought and Culture - t) (785) 813-2547 John Freeh, Dir.;

SHRINES [SHR]

CRETE

Schoenstatt Shrine - 340 State Hwy. 103, Crete, NE 68333-5020 t) 402-826-3346 cor.mariae.shrine@gmail.com www.cormariae.org Sr. M. Emily Kenkel, Prov.;

LOMA

St. Luke's Czech Catholic Shrine - Main St., Loma, NE 68635; Mailing: P.O. Box 39, Brainard, NE 68626 t) 402-545-2691 Rev. Steven P. Snitily, Dir.;

SPECIAL CARE FACILITIES [SPF]

WAVERLY

Villa Marie School and Home for the Educable Mentally Handicapped - 7205 N. 112th, Waverly, NE 68462 t) 402-786-3625 sr.jeanette-rerucha@cdolinc.net Rev. Msgr. John J. Perkinton, Dir.;

An asterisk (*) denotes an organization that has established tax-exempt status directly with the IRS and is not covered by the USCCB Group Ruling.

Diocese of Little Rock

(Dioecesis Petriculana)

MOST REVEREND ANTHONY BASIL TAYLOR

Bishop of Little Rock; ordained August 2, 1980; appointed seventh Bishop of Little Rock March 18, 2008; consecrated & installed June 5, 2008. Office: 2500 N. Tyler St., Little Rock, AR 72207. Res.: 1201 S. Van Buren, Little Rock, AR 72204. T: 501-664-0340. Mailing Address: P.O. Box 7565, Little Rock, AR 72217.

Chancery: 2500 N. Tyler St., P.O. Box 7565, Little Rock, AR 72217. T: 501-664-0340
www.dolr.org

ESTABLISHED NOVEMBER 28, 1843.

Square Miles 52,068.

Comprises the State of Arkansas.

For legal titles of parishes and diocesan institutions, consult the Chancery Office.

STATISTICAL OVERVIEW

Personnel

Bishop	1
Abbots	1
Priests: Diocesan Active in Diocese	70
Priests: Diocesan Active Outside Diocese	2
Priests: Retired, Sick or Absent	17
Number of Diocesan Priests	89
Religious Priests in Diocese	26
Total Priests in your Diocese	115
Extern Priests in Diocese	17
Ordinations:	
Diocesan Priests	2
Transitional Deacons	2
Permanent Deacons	46
Permanent Deacons in Diocese	133
Total Brothers	25
Total Sisters	115

Parishes

Parishes	91
With Resident Pastor:	
Resident Diocesan Priests	67
Resident Religious Priests	23
Without Resident Pastor:	
Administered by Priests	39
Administered by Deacons	1
Completely vacant	1
Missions	39
Professional Ministry Personnel:	
Brothers	4
Sisters	5
Lay Ministers	157

Welfare

Catholic Hospitals	12
Total Assisted	1,239,360
Health Care Centers	6
Total Assisted	5,433
Homes for the Aged	29
Total Assisted	1,012
Day Care Centers	20
Total Assisted	804
Specialized Homes	1
Total Assisted	126
Special Centers for Social Services	8
Total Assisted	2,149
Other Institutions	1
Total Assisted	3,000

Educational

Diocesan Students in Other Seminaries	26
Total Seminarians	26
High Schools, Diocesan and Parish	3
Total Students	870
High Schools, Private	3
Total Students	693
Elementary Schools, Diocesan and Parish	22
Total Students	4,843
Elementary Schools, Private	1
Total Students	21
Catechesis/Religious Education:	
High School Students	2,792
Elementary Students	6,529
Total Students under Catholic Instruction	15,774
Teachers in Diocese:	
Priests	6
Brothers	1
Sisters	1
Lay Teachers	527

Vital Statistics

Receptions into the Church:	
Infant Baptism Totals	2,146
Minor Baptism Totals	187
Adult Baptism Totals	133
Received into Full Communion	252
First Communions	1,836
Confirmations	1,794
Marriages:	
Catholic	343
Interfaith	132
Total Marriages	475
Deaths	930
Total Catholic Population	166,293
Total Population	3,011,524

LEADERSHIP

Vicar General - Rev. John M Connell;

Chancery Offices - t) 501-664-0340 x313

Chancellor for Canonical Affairs - t) 501-664-0340 x361 Dcn. Matthew Glover;

Chancellor for Administrative Affairs - t) 501-664-0340 x308 Dennis P. Lee;

Finance Officer - t) 501-664-0340 x377 Gregory C. Wolfe, CFO;

Diocesan Tribunal - t) 501-664-0340 x367 Rev. Gregory T. Luyet, Judicial Vicar; Rev. Andrew P. Hart, Adjutant Judicial Vicar; Rev. Juan Manjarrez, Assessor;

Defenders of the Bond - Dcn. Matthew Glover; Rev. John K. Antony;

Judges - Rev. Gregory T. Luyet; Rev. Andrew P. Hart; Msgr. Scott L. Marczuk;

Notaries - Maria Velazquez; Amanda Crawford; Veronica Mendez-Mathey;

Promoter of Justice - Rev. John K. Antony;

Tribunal Moderator - Amanda Crawford;

Diocesan Consultors - Rev. John M Connell; Rev. Msgr. Scott Friend; Rev. Msgr. Jack D. Harris;

Deans - Rev. John K. Antony, West River Valley Deanery; Rev. Mauricio Carrasco, River Valley Deanery; Rev. Stephen Elser, North Delta Deanery (frstephenelser@gmail.com);

OFFICES AND DIRECTORS

Adoption Services, Inc. - t) 501-664-0340 x347 Antje Harris, Dir.;

Building Commission - t) 501-664-0340 x307 Jim Driedric, Exec. Sec.;

Calvary Cemetery, Greater Little Rock - t) 501-517-6453 Michael Cagle, Supt.;

Catholic Campus Ministry - t) 501-664-0340 x333 Liz Tingquist, Dir.;

Catholic Charities Medical Clinic - t) 501-664-0340 x356 Janice Bohac;

Catholic Charities of Arkansas, Vacant -

Catholic Immigration Services - Little Rock Office - t) 501-664-0340 x396 Jennifer Verkamp-Ruthven, Dir.;

Catholic Immigration Services - NW Arkansas Office - t) 479-927-1996 Jennifer Verkamp-Ruthven, Dir.;

Catholic Youth Ministry - t) 501-664-0340 x333 Liz Tingquist, Dir.;

Charismatic Movement - Rev. Norbert F. Rappold, (English); Rev. Salvador Vega-Alvarenga (El Salvador), (Spanish);

Clergy Personnel Advisory Board (Diocesan) - Most Rev. Anthony B. Taylor, Chair; Rev. John M Connell; Dcn. Matthew Glover;

Continuing Education for the Clergy - Rev. Jason Tyler, Dir.;

Cursillo Movement - Rev. Martin Siebold, Spiritual Advisor; Dcn. Timothy James Costello, Asst. Spiritual Advisor; Nancy Christian, Dir.;

Diocesan Council for Black Catholics - Rev. Warren Harvey, Bishop's Liaison;

Faith Formation - t) 501-664-0340 x359 Jeff Hines, Dir.;

Family Life Office: (Pre-Cana, Marriage Encounter, Retrouvaille, Natural Family Planning) - t) 501-664-0340 x373 Elizabeth Reha, Dir.;

Hispanic Ministry - Sr. Esperanza Micaela Espinoza Tamayo, M.C.P., Dir.; Sr. Silvia Patricia Nava Munoz, M.C.P.; Sr. Ana Luisa Diaz Vazquez, M.C.P.;

Minister to Deacons - Dcn. Timothy James Costello, Min. to Permanent Deacons;

Minister to Priests -

Coordinator of Retreats and Days of Recollection - Rev. Msgr. Scott Friend, CRE;

Minister to Priests at St. John Manor - Rev. Warren Harvey;

Minister to Religious - Sr. Cecilia Nguyen, OSB;

Minister to Senior and Infirm Priests - Rev. William Elser;

Newspaper "Arkansas Catholic" - t) (501) 664-0340 x369 Malea Hargett, Editor;

Office of Divine Worship - t) 479-783-7745 Rev. Juan J. Guido;

Parish Outreach - t) 501-664-0340 x403 Sr. Iliana Aponte Colon, D.C., Dir.;

Permanent Diaconate Formation Program - Dcn. Mark Joseph Verkamp, Dir.;

Presbyteral Council - Most Rev. Anthony B. Taylor; Rev. John M. Connell, Ex-officio, West Ozark Deanery; Rev. William Wyatt Burmester, Ouachita Deanery;

Prison Ministry - t) 501-664-0340 x336 Rev. Phillip A. Reaves;

Propagation of the Faith - t) 501-664-0340 x308 Dennis P. Lee;

Refugee Resettlement Program - Jennifer Verkamp-Ruthven, Dir.;

Respect Life Office and Project Rachel - t) 501-664-0340 x326 Catherine Phillips, Dir.;

Safe Environment Office - t) 501-664-0340 x332 Susan David;

St. John Catholic Center/Office Services - t) 501-665-4034 x390 Dcn. Timothy James Costello, Dir.;

Schools - t) 501-664-0340 x321 Theresa Hall, Supt.;

Stewardship and Development Office - t) 501-664-0340 x391 Dianne Brady, Dir.;

Victim Assistance Coordinator - Laura Gottsponer;

Vocations - Rev. Jeffrey Hebert, Dir.;

Assistant Director for Development and Academic Advising - Dcn. Charles Victor Ashburn;

PARISHES, MISSIONS, AND CLERGY

STATE OF ARKANSAS

ALTUS

St. Mary - 5118 St. Mary's Ln., Altus, AR 72821 t) 479-468-2585 stmarysparish@centurytel.net www.stmarysaltus.org Attended from St. Joseph Church, Paris AR Rev. Reginald Udouj, OSB, Sacr. Min.; Dcn. Brian Albert Lachowsky, Admin.; CRP Stds.: 49

ARKADELPHIA

St. Mary - 249 N. 14th St., Arkadelphia, AR 71923; Mailing: P. O. Box 26, Arkadelphia, AR 71923 t) 870-246-7575 stmarysarkadelphia@gmail.com www.stmarysarkadelphia.org/ Also attends St. John Church, Malvern Rev. D. Mark Wood, Pst.; Dcn. David Henry Evans; CRP Stds.: 32

ASHDOWN

St. Elizabeth Ann Seton Church - 1910 Rankin St., Ashdown, AR 71822; Mailing: P O Box 966, Ashdown, AR 71822 t) (870) 772-1115 office@saintedwardstexarkana.com Attended from St. Edward, Texarkana. Rev. William Wyatt Burmester, Pst.;

ATKINS

Assumption B.V.M. - 118 Ave. 3 N.E., Atkins, AR 72823; Mailing: P.O. Box 337, Atkins, AR 72823 t) 479-641-7179 assumptionchurchatkins@gmail.com assumptionbvmchurch.weebly.com Rev. Mauricio Carrasco, Pst.; CRP Stds.: 27

BALD KNOB

St. Richard Church - 101 W. Cleveland St., Bald Knob, AR 72010; Mailing: P.O. Box 172, Searcy, AR 72145 t) 501-268-5252 stjames172@sbcglobal.net Attended from St. James, Searcy. Rev. Nelson Rubio, Admin.;

BARLING

Sacred Heart of Mary - 1301 Frank St., Barling, AR 72923 t) 479-452-1795 shmbarling@gmail.com shmbarling.org Also attends Sts. Sabina and Mary Church, Jenny Lind Rev. G. Matthew Garrison, Pst.; Rev. Peter Quang Le, Assoc. Pst.; CRP Stds.: 51

BATESVILLE

St. Mary - 3800 Harrison St., Batesville, AR 72501 t) 870-793-7717 secretary@stmarysbatesville.com www.stmarysbatesville.com Also attends St. Cecilia, Newport Rev. Jon Miskin, Admin.; CRP Stds.: 120

BELLA VISTA

St. Bernard of Clairvaux - 1 Saint Bernard Ln., Bella Vista, AR 72715 t) 479-855-9069 office@bvstbernard.org www.bvstbernard.org Rev. Barnabas Maria Susai, I.M.S. (India), Pst.; Dcn. Al Genna; Dcn. Stephen Brunet; CRP Stds.: 34

BENTON

Our Lady of Fatima - 900 W. Cross St., Benton, AR 72015 t) 501-315-5186 churchsecretary@olfbenton.org www.olfbenton.org Rev. Luke Womack, Pst.; Dcn. Marcelino Luna, Hispanic Min.; CRP Stds.: 212

Our Lady of Fatima School - (Grades PreK-8) 818 W. Cross St., Benton, AR 72015 t) 501-315-3398 holydays@swbell.net www.ourladyoffatimaschool.com Jan Cash, Prin.; Stds.: 65; Lay Tchrs.: 6

Our Lady of Fatima School Endowment Trust Fund - t) 501-315-3398 holydays@swbell.net

BENTONVILLE

St. Stephen - 1300 N.E. J St., Bentonville, AR 72712 t) 479-273-1240 ststephen@ststephenbentonville.com www.ststephenbentonville.com Rev. Msgr. Scott L. Marczuk, Pst.; Rev. Polycarp Ssebbowa (Uganda), Assoc. Pst.; CRP Stds.: 423

BERRYVILLE

St. Anne - 614 S. Main St., Berryville, AR 72616 t) 870-423-3927 secretary@stannesberryville.com www.stannesberryville.com Rev. Joseph Archibong, Pst.; Dcn. Elias Rangel Flores; Pam Richter, DRE; CRP Stds.: 167

BIGELOW

St. Boniface - 20 St. Boniface Dr., Bigelow, AR 72016 t) 501-759-2371 stbnewdixie@gmail.com Attends St. Elizabeth, Oppelo. and St. Francis of Assisi, Little Italy Rev. Taryn Whittington, Pst.;

BLYTHEVILLE

Immaculate Conception - 1301 W. Main St., Blytheville, AR 72315; Mailing: P.O. Box 747, Blytheville, AR 72316 t) 870-762-2506 icccbly@gmail.com www.icbly.com Also attends St. Matthew Church, Osceola and St. Norbert in Marked Tree Rev. Francis Madanu (India), Pst.; Dcn. William G. Brandon Jr.; Dcn. Robert Edward Ward; CRP Stds.: 6

BOONEVILLE

Church of Our Lady of the Assumption - 616 Cherry St., Booneville, AR 72927; Mailing: P.O. Box 298, Booneville, AR 72927 t) 479-675-3371 assumptionboone@yahoo.com Also attends St. Jude Thaddeus, Waldron. Rev. Leslie A. Farley, Pst.; Dcn. Kenneth Edward Stengel; CRP Stds.: 21

BRINKLEY

St. John the Baptist - 203 W. Ash, Brinkley, AR 72021-3201 t) 870-734-1202 stjohnbrinkley@gmail.com Attended from St. Mary Church, Helena. Rev. Gilbert Tairo, C.S.Sp. (Tanzania), Pst.; Rev. James Uzoma Ibeh, C.S.Sp., Assoc. Pst.; CRP Stds.: 5

CABOT

St. John the Baptist Catholic Church - 602 E. Main St., Cabot, AR 72023; Mailing: PO Box 1288, Cabot, AR 72023 t) 501-941-1566 secretary@arkansaslatinmass.com www.arkansaslatinmass.com Rev. Paul McCambridge, FSSP, Pst.; CRP Stds.: 40

CAMDEN

St. Louis - 202 Adams, N.W., Camden, AR 71701 t) 870-836-2426 stlouiscc1234@sbcglobal.net Rev. Michael Johns, Pst.; CRP Stds.: 16

CARLISLE

St. Rose of Lima Church - 603 E. Park, Carlisle, AR 72024; Mailing: P.O. Box M, Carlisle, AR 72024 t) 870-552-3601 strose011@centurytel.net Also attends SS. Cyril and Methodius Church, Slovak Rev. Shaun C. Wesley, Pst.; CRP Stds.: 40

CENTER RIDGE

St. Joseph - 343 Catholic Point Rd., Center Ridge, AR

72027 t) 501-893-2889 stjosephoffice2889@gmail.com Attended from Sacred Heart, Morrilton Rev. Msgr. Jack D. Harris, Pst.; Rev. Joseph S. Friend, Assoc. Pst.; CRP Stds.: 27

CHARLESTON

Sacred Heart - 18 Prairie St., Charleston, AR 72933-9334; Mailing: P.O. Box 1087, Charleston, AR 72933 t) 479-965-2532 sacredheartcharleston@gmail.com Rev. Norman McFall, Pst.; Dcn. Mark Joseph Verkamp; CRP Stds.: 91

CHEROKEE VILLAGE

St. Michael - 49 Tekakwitha Dr., Cherokee Village, AR 72529; Mailing: P.O. Box 970, Cherokee Village, AR 72525 t) 870-257-2850 stmichaelcv@yahoo.com www.stmichaelscv.org Also attends St. Mary of the Mount, Horseshoe Bend. Rev. Amal Raju Punganoor, Pst.; CRP Stds.: 25

St. Michael Memorial Garden (Columbarium) -

CLARKSVILLE

Holy Redeemer - 103 E. Main St., Clarksville, AR 72830 t) 479-754-3610 wgwosb@suddenlinkmail.com www.hrclarksville.org Rev. William Wewers, O.S.B., Pst.; CRP Stds.: 226

CLINTON

St. Jude Church - 3178 Hwy. 65 S., Clinton, AR 72031; Mailing: P O Box 526, Clinton, AR 72031 t) 501-745-5716 bookkeeper.stjtcc@gmail.com Attended from St. Francis of Assisi, Fairfield Bay. Rev. Luke Womack, Admin.; Toni (Marie A.) Loudon, DRE;

CONWAY

St. Joseph - 1115 College Ave., Conway, AR 72032 t) 501-327-6568 sjoffice@sjparish.org www.sjparish.org Attends St. Oscar de Romero Catholic Community - Greenbrier Rev. Anthony M. Robbins, Pst.; Rev. Balaraju Desam (India), Assoc. Pst.; Dcn. David Bruce French; Dcn. Richard John Papini; Dcn. David Kirby Westmoreland; Dcn. Ramon Argueta; Dcn. Calvin Pearcy; Dcn. Doug Adams; CRP Stds.: 284

St. Joseph School - (Grades PreK-6) 502 Front St., Conway, AR 72032 t) 501-329-5741 dwolfe@sjbulldogs.org www.stjosephconway.org Diane Wolfe, Prin.; Stds.: 290; Sr. Tchrs.: 3; Lay Tchrs.: 5

CORNING

St. Joseph the Worker Church - 1415 Harb St., Corning, AR 72422; Mailing: 800 11th St., Corning, AR 72422 t) 870-892-3319 stjosephcatholic67@gmail.com Attended from St. Paul the Apostle, Pocahontas. Rev. Stephen Elser, Pst.;

CRAWFORDSVILLE

Sacred Heart Church - 216 S Main St, Crawfordsville, AR 72327; Mailing: P.O. Box 899, West Memphis, AR 72303 t) 870-733-1212 westmemphiscatholic@gmail.com Attended by St. Michael, West Memphis. Rev. Charles Thessing, Pst.;

CROSSETT

Holy Cross - 2400 S. Main St., Crossett, AR 71635; Mailing: P.O. Box 1184, Crossett, AR 71635 t) 870-364-4847 dutchw@live.com Our Lady of the Lake, Lake Village. Rev. Stephen Hart, Pst.; Dcn. Timothy Gelio Sampolesi;

DANVILLE

Saint Andrew Church - 1810 E 8th St., Danville, AR 72833; Mailing: P.O. Box 1262, Danville, AR 72833 t) 479-495-3404 (Main); (479) 229-3972 catholicstandrew@gmail.com Attended from St. Augustine, Dardanelle, AR. Rev. Maurico Carrasco, Pst.; Dcn. Jose Noe Morales; CRP Stds.: 98

DARDANELLE

St. Augustine - 1001 N. 2nd St., Dardanelle, AR 72834; Mailing: P.O. Box 460, Dardanelle, AR 72834 t) 479-229-3972 staugustcatholic@gmail.com; staugustine@sjccr.org Rev. Mauricio Carrasco, Pst.; Dcn. Jose Noe Morales; CRP Stds.: 68

DE QUEEN

St. Barbara - 503 W. DeQueen Ave., De Queen, AR 71832 t) 870-642-2256 st.barbaraparish@yahoo.com Also attends St. Juan Diego Church, Wickes Rev. Ramses Abian Mendieta Lacayo, Pst.; Dcn. Israel Sanchez; CRP Stds.: 322

St. Juan Diego - 113 Main St., Wickes, AR 71973; Mailing: 503 W De Queen Ave, De Queen, AR 71832 t) 870-385-7402 Rev. Ramses Abian Mendieta Lacyo, Pst.;

DECATUR

Blessed Stanley Rother Catholic Church - 758 Hill Ave., Decatur, AR 72722; Mailing: P.O. Box 118, Siloam Springs, AR 72761 t) 479-524-8526 secretary@stmarysiloam.com Rev. Balaraju Akkala, Admin.; CRP Stds.: 10

DUMAS

Holy Child Church - 807 E. Waterman, Dumas, AR 71639; Mailing: 1016 N. Hyatt, Monticello, AR 71655 t) 870-367-2848 stmkoff@gmail.com Mission of St. Mark, Monticello. Rev. Mark Abban (Ghana), Pst.; CRP Stds.: 20

EL DORADO

Holy Redeemer - 440 W. Main St., El Dorado, AR 71730 t) 870-863-3620 holyredeemer@holyredeemereldorado.org www.holyredeemereldorado.org Also attends St. Luke Church, Warren Rev. Edward P. D'Almeida, Pst.; Dcn. Jose Guadalupe Luebanos; CRP Stds.: 93

ENGELBERG

St. John the Baptist - 4650 Engelberg Rd., Engelberg, AR 72455 t) 870-892-3319 stjohns4650@gmail.com Attended from St. Paul the Apostle Church, Pocahontas. Rev. Stephen Elser, Pst.;

ENGLAND

Holy Trinity Church - 1240 AR Hwy. 161 W., England, AR 72046; Mailing: P.O. Box 243, England, AR 72046 t) 870-552-3601 holyrose1234@gmail.com Attended from Holy Rosary, Stuttgart Rev. Babu Battula (India), Pst.;

EUREKA SPRINGS

St. Elizabeth of Hungary - 30 Crescent Dr., Eureka Springs, AR 72632; Mailing: 232 Passion Play Rd., Eureka Springs, AR 72632 t) 479-253-2222; 479-253-6742 (CRP) secretary@stelizabetheureka.com stelizabethar.org Attended from St. Anne, Berryville. Rev. Joseph Archibong, Pst.;

FAIRFIELD BAY

St. Francis of Assisi - 250 Woodlawn Dr., Fairfield Bay, AR 72088 t) 501-884-3349 stfrancis@artelco.com Also attends St. Jude Thaddeus Church, Clinton Rev. Thomas Joseph Hart, Pst.;

FAYETTEVILLE

St. Joseph - 1722 N. Starr Dr., Fayetteville, AR 72701 t) 479-442-0890 www.sjfay.com Rev. Jason Tyler, Pst.; Rev. Alexander Xavier Smith, Assoc. Pst.; Dcn. Bud Baldwin III; Dcn. Marcelino Vazquez; Dcn. William Curry; CRP Stds.: 403

St. Joseph School - (Grades PreK-8) t) 479-442-4554 jpohlmeier@sjfay.com www.sjfayschool.com Stds.: 358; Lay Tchrs.: 28

St. Joseph Endowment and Educational Trust Fund - t) 479-442-4554 jpohlmeier@sjfay.com

St. Thomas Aquinas University Parish - 603 N. Leverett Ave., Fayetteville, AR 72701-3220; Mailing: P.O. Box 4840, Fayetteville, AR 72702 t) 479-444-0223 info@catholichogs.com www.catholichogs.com Rev. Jason Sharbaugh, Pst.; Dcn. Timothy Paul Cronan; Dcn. Norman Francis DeBriyn;

FORDYCE

Good Shepherd - 410 N. Oak St., Fordyce, AR 71742; Mailing: P.O. Box 565, Fordyce, AR 71742 t) 870-352-2328 sjccpb1838@gmail.com Attended from St. Joseph, Pine Bluff Rev. Joseph P. Marconi, Pst.;

FOREMAN

Sacred Heart Church - 415 S. Bell St., Foreman, AR 71836; Mailing: P O Box 43, Foreman, AR 71836 t) (870) 772-1115 (St. Edward parish office) office@saintedwardstexarkana.com Attended from St. Edward, Texarkana. Rev. William Wyatt Burmester, Pst.; CRP Stds.: 4

FORREST CITY

St. Francis of Assisi - 621 S. Washington St., Forrest City, AR 72335; Mailing: PO Box 786, Forrest City, AR 72336 t) 870-633-1665 stfrancis621@gmail.com Attended from St. Mary Church, Helena. Rev. Gilbert Tairo, C.S.Sp. (Tanzania), Pst.; Rev. James Uzoma Ibeh, C.S.Sp., Assoc. Pst.;

FORT SMITH

St. Boniface - 1820 N. B St., Fort Smith, AR 72901 t) 479-783-6711 stbfaceoffice@gmail.com www.stbonifacefortsmith.com Rev. Mario Jacobo, Pst.; Dcn. Thomas Bradney Brown; Dcn. Jaime Flores; CRP Stds.: 230

St. Boniface Catholic School Endowment Fund -

Christ the King - 2112 S. Greenwood Ave., Fort Smith, AR 72901 t) 479-783-7745 ctk@ctkparishfs.com ctkparishfs.com Rev. Brian Cundall, Admin.; Rev. Jack Sidler, Assoc. Pst.; Dcn. Thomas Jakobs; CRP Stds.: 300

Christ the King School - (Grades PreK-5) 1918 S. Greenwood Ave, Fort Smith, AR 72901 t) 479-782-0614 mkeyton@ctkparishfs.com; kkratzberg@ctkparishfs.com www.ctkschoolfs.com Myndi Keyton, Prin.; Katie Suzanne Kratzberg, Vice Prin.; Stds.: 231; Lay Tchrs.: 18

Christ the King Catholic School Trust and Endowment Fund - 1918 S. Greenwood Ave., Fort Smith, AR 72901 t) (479) 782-0614 www.ctkschoolfs.com

Immaculate Conception - 22 N. 13th St., Fort Smith, AR 72901; Mailing: P O Box 1866, Fort Smith, AR 72902 t) 479-783-7963 ic@icchurch.com www.icchurch.com Also attends Our Lady of the Ozarks Shrine, Winslow Rev. John K. Antony, Pst.; Rev. Balaraju Akkala, Assoc. Pst.; Dcn. Candelario Galvan; Dcn. Charles Edward Kuehl; Dcn. Greg Pair; Dcn. Cesar Augusto Villafranca; CRP Stds.: 599

Immaculate Conception School - (Grades PreK-6) 223 S. 14th St., Fort Smith, AR 72901 t) 479-783-6798 sblentlinger@icschoolfs.org www.icschoolfs.org Sharon Blentlinger, Prin.; Stds.: 275; Lay Tchrs.: 27

Immaculate Conception School Educational Trust - t) (479) 783-7963

SS. Sabina and Mary Church - 14304 Old Jenny Lind Loop, Fort Smith, AR 72916; Mailing: 1301 Frank St., Barling, AR 72923 t) 479-452-1795 shmbarling@gmail.com shmbarling.org Attended from Sacred Heart of Mary, Barling. Rev. G. Matthew Garrison, Pst.;

GLENWOOD

Our Lady of Guadalupe Church - 43 Kennedy Cut off Rd., Glenwood, AR 71943; Mailing: P O Box 426, Glenwood, AR 71943 c) (870) 200-4078 ologglenwood@outlook.com Rev. Salvador Vega-Alvarenga (El Salvador), Pst.; CRP Stds.: 15

HAMBURG

Holy Spirit Church - 1138 S. Main St., Hamburg, AR 71646; Mailing: P.O. Box 188, Hamburg, AR 71646 t) 870-265-5439 frstephenhart@gmail.com ourladyofthelake.us Attended from Our Lady of the Lake, Lake Village. Rev. Stephen Hart, Pst.; Dcn. Timothy Gelio Sampolesi;

HARRISON

Mary, Mother of God - 1614 Maplewood Rd., Harrison, AR 72601 t) 870-741-5234 mmgchurch@yahoo.com www.harrisoncatholic.org Also attends St. Andrew Church, Yellville Rev. Benjamin A Riley; Dcn. Mark Allen Scouten; CRP Stds.: 55

HARTFORD

St. Leo - 101 Locust St., Hartford, AR 72938; Mailing: 1018 Mourning Dove Way, Barling, AR 72923 c) 479-652-6454 fatherjosephchan@gmail.com Rev. Joseph Chan, Pst.; CRP Stds.: 3

HATTIEVILLE

St. Mary - 11 Kaufman Ln., Hattieville, AR 72063 t) 501-354-3206 saintmary411@yahoo.com Rev. James Burnie, C.S.Sp., Pst.; CRP Stds.: 60

HEBER SPRINGS

St. Albert Church - 21 Park Rd., Heber Springs, AR 72543 t) 501-362-2914 stalbert21@suddenlinkmail.com stalhsar.com Rev. Paul F. Worm, Pst.; Dcn. Robert L. Morris; CRP Stds.: 23

HELENA

St. Mary - 123 Columbia St., Helena, AR 72342 t) 870-338-6990 86stmary@gmail.com www.stmaryshelena.org Also attends St. John the Baptist, Brinkley; St. Francis of Assisi, Forrest City; St. Mary of the Lake, Horseshoe Lake; and St. Andrew, Marianna. Rev. Gilbert Tairo, C.S.Sp. (Tanzania), Pst.; Rev. James Uzoma Ibeh, C.S.Sp., Assoc. Pst.; CRP Stds.: 15

HOPE

Our Lady of Good Hope - 315 W. Walker St., Hope, AR 71801; Mailing: P O Box 517, Hope, AR 71802-0517 t) 870-777-3202 ourladyofgoodhope@sbcglobal.net Rev. Nirmalraj Mariadass Kambala, C.P.P.S. (India), Pst.; CRP Stds.: 41

HORSESHOE BEND

St. Mary of the Mount - 1002 First St., Horseshoe Bend, AR 72512 t) 870-670-5896 mounts1002@gmail.com Attended from St. Michael, Cherokee Village. Rev. Amal Raju Punganoor, Pst.;

HORSESHOE LAKE

St. Mary of the Lake Church - 626 Horseshoe Cir., Horseshoe Lake, AR 72348; Mailing: 123 Columbia St., Helena, AR 72342 t) 870-338-6990 86stmary@gmail.com Attended from St. Mary, Helena. Rev. Gilbert Tairo, C.S.Sp. (Tanzania), Pst.; Rev. James Uzoma Ibeh, C.S.Sp., Assoc. Pst.;

HOT SPRINGS

St. John the Baptist - 589 W. Grand Ave., Hot Springs, AR 71901; Mailing: 583 W. Grand Ave., Ste. A, Hot Springs, AR 71901 t) 501-623-6201 saintjohn.secretary@gmail.com www.stjohnshotsprings.net Rev. George W. Sanders, Pst.; Rev. Jules Norbert Njopmo (Cameroon), Assoc. Pst.; Dcn. Robert James Standridge; Dcn. Robert E. Wanless; Edith Ochoa, DRE; CRP Stds.: 130

St. John the Baptist School - (Grades PreK-8) 583 W. Grand Ave., Hot Springs, AR 71901 t) 501-624-3147 sjhsprincipal@gmail.com Janet Edgar, Prin.; Stds.: 108; Lay Tchrs.: 13

St. John's School Endowment - t) 501-624-3171 saintjohnhotsprings@gmail.com

St. Mary of the Springs - 100 Central Ave., Hot Springs, AR 71901 t) 501-623-3233 stmcc@hotsprings.net; stmccadmin@hotsprings.net www.stmaryofthesprings.org Rev. Ravi Rayappa Gudipalli, Pst.; Dcn. Greg Beeber; Dcn. Thomas Michael Cumnock; Dcn. Joe Dale Harrison; Dcn. Lee Leckner; CRP Stds.: 118

Sacred Heart of Jesus - 295 Balearic Rd., Hot Springs, AR 71909 t) 501-922-2062 c) 501-209-2502 sacredheart@hsvsacredheart.com www.hsvsacredheart.com Rev. William Elser, Pst.; Dcn. B.J. Bowen; Dcn. Larry Lipsmeyer; CRP Stds.: 16

HUNTSVILLE

St. John the Evangelist - 411 Crossbow Rd., Huntsville, AR 72740; Mailing: PO Box 755, Huntsville, AR 72740-0755 t) 479-442-0890 Attended from St. Joseph Church in Fayetteville Rev. Jason Tyler, Pst.; Rev. Chandra Kodavatikanti, Admin.; CRP Stds.: 10

JACKSONVILLE

St. Jude the Apostle - 2403 McArthur Dr., Jacksonville, AR 72076 t) 501-982-4891 stjudeapostle@gmail.com stjudejax.com Rev. Martin Siebold, Pst.; Dcn. Ernesto Corona Gallegos; CRP Stds.: 155

JONESBORO

St. John Newman University Parish - 2800 E. Johnson Ave., Jonesboro, AR 72401 t) 870-972-1888 director@astatecnc.com www.astatecnc.com Rev. Tuyen Do, Pst.; Dcn. Bob Bennett; Patricia McCaughan, Treas.; CRP Stds.: 54

Blessed Sacrament - 1101 E. Highland Dr., Jonesboro, AR 72401; Mailing: P.O. Box 1735, Jonesboro, AR 72403-1735 t) 870-932-2529 office@catholicjonesboro.com www.catholicjonesboro.com Rev. Msgr. Scott Friend, Pst.; Rev. Martin Amaro, Assoc. Pst.; Dcn. Ramon Ramirez Fernandez; Dcn. Martin Huss; CRP Stds.: 133

Blessed Sacrament School - (Grades PreK-6) 1105 E. Highland Dr., Jonesboro, AR 72401 t) 870-932-3684 school@catholicjonesboroschool.com; principal@catholicjonesboroschool.com www.catholicjonesboroschool.com Mary Kay Jones, Prin.; Stds.: 133; Lay Tchrs.: 9

Blessed Sacrament Educational Endowment Fund - t) 870-935-2871 Rev. Msgr. Scott Friend;

LAKE VILLAGE

Our Lady of the Lake - 314 S. Lake Shore Dr., Lake Village, AR 71653; Mailing: P.O. Box 272, Lake Village, AR 71653 t) 870-265-5439; 870-265-5663 ourladyofthelaker@gmail.com Rev. Stephen Hart, Pst.; Dcn. Timothy Gelio Sampolesi; CRP Stds.: 71

LINCOLN

SS. Peter and Paul Catholic Church - 113 Boyer Ave., Lincoln, AR 72744; Mailing: 1722 N. Starr Dr., St. Joseph Church, Fayetteville, AR 72701 t) 479-442-0890 lvazquez@sjfay.com Attended from St. Joseph Church, Fayetteville Rev. Jason Tyler, Pst.; Rev. Alexander Xavier Smith, Assoc. Pst.; Dcn. Marcelino Vazquez, Admin.; CRP Stds.: 41

LITTLE ROCK

Cathedral of St. Andrew - 617 Louisiana St., Little Rock, AR 72201 t) 501-374-2794 info@csalr.org www.csalr.org Rev. Joseph de Orbegozo, Admin.; Dcn. Charles Victor Ashburn; Dcn. William J. Bowen; Dcn. Marc Rios; CRP Stds.: 25

St. Bartholomew - 1622 Marshall St., Little Rock, AR 72202 t) 501-372-4682 stbartholomew72202@yahoo.com stbartholomewchurch-lr.org Attend from St. Augustine Church, North Little Rock Rev. Leon Ngandu, SVD, Pst.;

Christ the King - 4000 N. Rodney Parham Rd., Little Rock, AR 72212 t) 501-225-6774 parishsecretary@ctklr.org; ccole@ctklr.org www.ctklr.org Rev. Juan J. Guido, Pst.; Rev. Chanda Pillai PJ, I.M.S., Pst. Assoc.; Rev. Taryn Whittington, Assoc. Pst.; Dcn. Tom Cannon; Dcn. Greg Donaldson; Dcn. Matthew Glover; Dcn. Joe Lukacs; Dcn. Jerome Ngundue; Dcn. Randall Spellins; Dcn. John Suskie; Dcn. Angelo Volpi; Dcn. Curtis Don Greenway; Dcn. Daniel Thomas Hartnedy; Dcn. Richard Lewis Patterson; Dcn. Michael Lynn Rector; CRP Stds.: 125

Christ the King School - (Grades PreK-8) 4002 N. Rodney Parham Rd., Little Rock, AR 72212 t) 501-225-7883 khouse@ctklr.org Kathy House, Prin.; Stds.: 554; Lay Tchrs.: 38

Msgr. Hebert Endowment Fund - t) 501-225-7883 Kathy House, Prin.;

St. Edward - 801 Sherman St., Little Rock, AR 72202 t) 501-374-5767 office@saintedwards.net www.stedwardchurchlr.com Rev. Juan Manjarrez, Pst.; Dcn. Efrain Antonio Vargas Rodriguez; CRP Stds.: 152

Our Lady of Good Counsel - 1321 S. Van Buren St., Little Rock, AR 72204 t) 501-666-5073 office@goodcounsellr.com www.goodcounsellr.com Rev. Gregory T. Luyet, Pst.; CRP Stds.: 175

Our Lady of the Holy Souls - 1003 N. Tyler St., Little Rock, AR 72205 t) 501-663-8632 office@holysouls.org www.holysouls.org Rev. Daniel Velasco-Perez, Admin.; Rev. Bhaskararao Malapolu, Assoc. Pst.; Dcn. John Wesley Hall; Dcn. Jim Goodhart; Dcn. Ted Saer; CRP Stds.: 32

Our Lady of the Holy Souls School - (Grades PreK-8) 1001 N. Tyler St., Little Rock, AR 72205 t) 501-663-4513 hss@holysouls.org arcathsch.org/hs/ Amber Bagby, Prin.; Sarah Richards, Vice Prin.; Stds.: 460; Lay Tchrs.: 33

Monsignor Allen Trust Fund for Holy Souls School - 1001 N. Tyler St., Little Rock, AR 72205 t) (501) 663-8632 coker@holysouls.org Samantha Coker, Dir.;

St. Theresa - 6219 Baseline Rd., Little Rock, AR 72209 t) 501-565-9198 office@stclr.org www.stclr.org Rev. D. Mark Wood, Pst.; Rev. Nelson Rubio, Assoc. Pst.; Dcn. William Robert Wrape; CRP Stds.: 325

St. Theresa School - (Grades PreK-8) 6311 Baseline Rd., Little Rock, AR 72209 t) 501-565-3855 schooloffice@stslr.org www.stslr.org Kristy Dunn, Prin.; Stds.: 228; Sr. Tchrs.: 1; Lay Tchrs.: 20

MAGNOLIA

Immaculate Heart of Mary - 2114 N. Jackson St., Magnolia, AR 71753; Mailing: PO Box 365, Magnolia, AR 71754 t) 870-901-3173 ihom1949@yahoo.com Attended from St. Louis, Camden Rev. Michael Johns, Admin.; CRP Stds.: 40

MALVERN

St. John the Baptist - 1114 Pine Bluff St., Malvern, AR 72104; Mailing: P. O. Box 6, Malvern, AR 72104 t) 870-246-7575 stmarysarkadelphia@gmail.com www.stmarysarkadelphia.org/ Attended from St. Mary Church, Arkadelphia Rev. D. Mark Wood, Pst.; CRP Stds.: 24

MARIANNA

St. Andrew - 54 W. Tennessee St., Marianna, AR 72360; Mailing: P O Box 724, Marianna, AR 72360 t) 870-338-6990 86stmary@gmail.com Attended from St. Mary, Helena. Rev. Gilbert Tairo, C.S.Sp. (Tanzania), Pst.; Rev. James Uzoma Ibeh, C.S.Sp., Assoc. Pst.;

MARKED TREE

St. Norbert - 501 Normandy St., Marked Tree, AR 72365; Mailing: P O Box 265, Marked Tree, AR 72365 t) 870-762-2506 icccbly@gmail.com Attended from Immaculate Conception Church, Blytheville Rev. Francis Madanu (India), Admin.; Dcn. Robert Edward Ward;

MCCRORY

St. Mary Church - 29 Woodruff 413, McCrory, AR 72101; Mailing: P O Box 517, Wynne, AR 72396 t) 870-238-2613 alfhones.perikala@gmail.com; jhamrick0717@gmail.com Mission of St. Peter, Wynne. Rev. Alfhones Perikala, Pst.; CRP Stds.: 2

MCGEHEE

St. Mary - 401 N. 3rd St., McGehee, AR 71654 t) 870-367-2848 stmarysmcgeheear@yahoo.com Attended from St. Mark, Monticello Rev. Mark Abban (Ghana), Pst.; CRP Stds.: 13

MENA

St. Agnes - 203 8th St., Mena, AR 71953 t) 479-394-1017 saintagnesmena@sbcglobal.net www.stagneschurchmena.org Also attends All Saints Church, Mount Ida Rev. Joseph Shantiraj (India), Pst.; Dcn. James Tony Salamone;

MONTICELLO

St. Mark - 1016 N. Hyatt St., Monticello, AR 71655 t) 870-367-2848 stmkoff@gmail.com www.stmkcatholic.com Also attends Holy Child of Jesus Church, Dumas, St. Mary Church, McGehee Rev. Mark Abban (Ghana), Pst.; CRP Stds.: 40

MORRILTON

Sacred Heart - 506 E. Broadway, Morrilton, AR 72110 t) 501-354-4181 sacred_heart@hotmail.com sacredheartmorrilton.org Also attends St. Joseph Church, Center Ridge Also attends St. Elizabeth Church, Oppelo Rev. Msgr. Jack D. Harris, Pst.; Rev. Joseph S. Friend, Assoc. Pst.; Dcn. Stephen Bradley Mallett; CRP Stds.: 27

Sacred Heart School - (Grades PreK-6) 106 N. St. Joseph, Morrilton, AR 72110 t) 501-354-8113 bgreeson@sacredheartmorrilton.org Buddy Greesom, Prin.; Stds.: 160; Lay Tchrs.: 17

MORRISON BLUFF

SS. Peter and Paul - 2216 N. State Hwy. 109, Morrison Bluff, AR 72863; Mailing: P O Box 87, Scranton, AR 72863 t) 479-938-2821 3parishes@gmail.com www.stspeterpaulchurch.org Attended from St. Ignatius, Scranton. Rev. John Miranda (India), Pst.; CRP Stds.: 15

MOUNT IDA

All Saints Church - 708 Hwy. 270 E, Mount Ida, AR 71957; Mailing: P.O. Box 724, Mount Ida, AR 71957 t) 479-394-1017 saintagnesmena@sbcglobal.net allsaintsmountida.org Mission of St. Agnes, Mena. Rev. Joseph Shantiraj (India), Pst.; Dcn. Tony Salamone;

MOUNTAIN HOME

St. Peter the Fisherman - 249 Dyer St., Mountain Home, AR 72653; Mailing: P O Box 298, Mountain Home, AR

72654 t) 870-425-2832 stpeters@spccmtnhome.org www.spccmtnhome.org Rev. Norbert F. Rappold, Pst.; CRP Stds.: 65

MOUNTAIN VIEW

St. Mary Church - 17068 Hwy. 66 W., Mountain View, AR 72560; Mailing: P.O. Box 926, Mountain View, AR 72560 t) 870-269-5194 saintmarybulletin@gmail.com Attended from St. Albert, Heber Springs, AR Rev. Paul F. Worm, Pst.;

NASHVILLE

St. Martin Church - 1011 Leslie St., Nashville, AR 71852; Mailing: P O Box 1039, Nashville, AR 71852 t) 870-451-9695 clubcobb@sbcglobal.net Also attends Our Lady of Guadalupe Church, Glenwood Rev. Salvador Vega-Alvarenga (El Salvador), Pst.; CRP Stds.: 60

NEW BLAINE

St. Scholastica - 288 St. Scholastica Rd., New Blaine, AR 72851 t) 479-938-7566 c) (479) 438-5072 stscholcreek@yahoo.com Rev. Mark Stengel, O.S.B., Pst.;

NEWPORT

St. Cecilia - 2475 Galeria Dr., Newport, AR 72112 t) 870-523-6542 stmarys@suddenlinkmail.com Attended from St. Mary Church, Batesville. Rev. Jon Miskin, Pst.; CRP Stds.: 14

NORTH LITTLE ROCK

St. Anne - 6150 Remount Rd., North Little Rock, AR 72118 t) 501-753-3977 secretary@saintannenlr.org www.saintannenlr.org Rev. Alejandro Puello, Pst.; CRP Stds.: 31

St. Augustine - 1400 E. 2nd St., North Little Rock, AR 72114; Mailing: 1421 E. 2nd St., North Little Rock, AR 72114 t) 501-375-9617 staugustine1929@att.net www.staugustinechurch-nlr.org Attended from St. Bartholomew, Little Rock Rev. Leon Ngandu, SVD, Pst.; CRP Stds.: 12

Immaculate Conception - 7000 John F. Kennedy Blvd., North Little Rock, AR 72116 t) 501-835-4323 administrativeassistant@iccnlr.org www.iccnlr.org Rev. John Wakube, A.J. (Uganda), Pst.; Dcn. Chuck Arthur Farrar; Dcn. Edward Joseph Sweeden; CRP Stds.: 25

Immaculate Conception School - (Grades PreK-8) t) 501-835-0771 x300 principal@icsnlr.org; info@icsnlr.org icsnlr.org Marcia Brucks, Prin.; Stds.: 342; Lay Tchrs.: 29

Immaculate Conception School Endowment Fund - mkoch@icsnlr.org Carmen Sellinger, Bus. Mgr.;

Immaculate Heart of Mary - 7006 Jasna Gora Dr., North Little Rock, AR 72118 t) 501-851-2763 parish@ihmnlr.org www.ihmnlr.org Rev. Ruben Quinteros, Pst.; Rev. Emmanuel Torres, Assoc. Pst.; Dcn. Timothy James Costello; Dcn. John Augustine Hartnedy; CRP Stds.: 12

Immaculate Heart of Mary School - (Grades PreK-8) 7025 Jasna Gora Dr., North Little Rock, AR 72118 t) 501-851-2760 principal@ihmnlr.org ihmnlr.org Daniel Smith, Prin.; Stds.: 125; Lay Tchrs.: 13

Immaculate Heart of Mary Educational Trust Fund for Immaculate Heart of Mary School - t) (501) 851-2763 school@ihmnlr.org

St. Mary - 1516 Parker St., North Little Rock, AR 72114 t) 501-374-7123 secretary@stmarysnlr.org Attended from Immaculate Heart of Mary Church, North Little Rock Rev. Ruben Quinteros, Pst.; Rev. Emmanuel Torres, Assoc. Pst.; CRP Stds.: 240

North Little Rock Catholic Academy - (Grades PreK-8) 1518 Parker St., North Little Rock, AR 72114 t) 501-374-5237 sharpmelody6@gmail.com www.nlrca.org Denise Troutman, Prin.; Stds.: 200; Lay Tchrs.: 13

St. Mary's School Endowment Fund - t) 501-758-2220

St. Patrick Catholic Church - 211 W. 19th St., North Little Rock, AR 72114 t) 501-758-1155 stpatrickschurch@comcast.net saintpatricknlr.com Rev. Jack Vu (Vietnam), Pst.; CRP Stds.: 60

St. Patrick's Educational Endowment Fund - t) 501-605-0008

OPPELO

St. Elizabeth - St. Elizabeth Rd., Oppelo, AR 72110; Mailing: 20 St. Boniface Dr., Bigelow, AR 72016 t) 501-759-2371 stbnewdixie@gmail.com St. Boniface Church, Bigelow. Rev. Msgr. Jack D. Harris, Pst.;

OSCEOLA

St. Matthew - 501 S. Ermen Ln., Osceola, AR 72370; Mailing: P.O. Box 583, Osceola, AR 72370 t) 870-762-2506 icccbly@gmail.com Attended from Immaculate Conception, Blytheville. Rev. Francis Madanu (India), Pst.; Dcn. William G. Brandon Jr.; Dcn. Robert Edward Ward;

PARAGOULD

St. Mary - 220 N. 2nd St., Paragould, AR 72450 t) 870-236-2568 secretary@stmaryparagould.org www.stmaryparagould.org Also attends Immaculate Heart of Mary Church, Walnut Ridge Rev. Nazarus Maduba (Nigeria), Admin.; Dcn. John Charles Drake; Dcn. Ricardo Jose Puello Brenes; CRP Stds.: 25

St. Mary School - (Grades PreK-6) 310 N. 2nd St., Paragould, AR 72450 t) 870-236-3681 principal@stmarysparagould.org www.stmarysparagould.org Sharon Warren, Prin.; Stds.: 58; Lay Tchrs.: 6

St. Mary Educational Trust Fund - stmryoff@grnco.net

PARIS

St. Joseph - 15 S. Spruce St., Paris, AR 72855 t) 479-963-2131 secretary@saintjosephschoolar.org www.stjosephparis.org Rev. Reginald Udouj, OSB, Pst.; Dcn. Thomas J. Pohlmeier; CRP Stds.: 21

St. Joseph School - (Grades PreK-8) 25 S. Spruce St., Paris, AR 72855 t) 479-963-2119 principal@saintjosephschoolar.org www.saintjosephschoolar.org Stds.: 75; Lay Tchrs.: 7

St. Joseph Endowment Fund - 25 S. Spruce St., Paris, AR 72855 t) (479) 963-2119 www.saintjosephschoolar.org Michelle O'Neal, Prin.;

PINE BLUFF

St. Joseph - 412 W. 6th Ave., Pine Bluff, AR 71601; Mailing: PO Box 7434, Pine Bluff, AR 71611-7434 t) 870-534-4701 sjccpb1838@gmail.com www.stjosephpinebluff.org Also attends Holy Cross Church, Sheridan, Good Shepherd Church, Fordyce Rev. Joseph P. Marconi, Pst.; Dcn. Garry Boccarossa; Dcn. Noel F. "Bud" Bryant; CRP Stds.: 21

St. Mary Plum Bayou - Saint Mary Church Rd., Plum Bayou, AR 71611 t) (870) 534-4701

St. Peter - 207 E. 16th Ave., Pine Bluff, AR 71601 t) 870-794-8029 st.peterpinebluff@gmail.com www.saintpeterpinebluff.com Attends St. Raphael, Pine Bluff and St. Justin, Star City Rev. Andreas Kedati; CRP Stds.: 22

St. Raphael - t) (870) 536-8277

POCAHONTAS

St. Paul the Apostle - 1002 Convent St., Pocahontas, AR 72455 t) 870-892-3319 catholichillssecretary@gmail.com www.saintpaulcatholicchurchpocahontas.com Attends St. John the Baptist, Engelberg and St Joseph the Worker, Corning Rev. Stephen Elser, Pst.; CRP Stds.: 101

St. Paul the Apostle School - (Grades PreK-6) 311 Cedar St., Pocahontas, AR 72455 t) 870-892-5639 principal@stpaulsabers.com www.stpaulsabers.com Rebecca Steimel, Prin.; Stds.: 145; Lay Tchrs.: 19

PRAIRIE VIEW

St. Meinrad Church - 35 Saint Meinrad Loop, Prairie View, AR 72863; Mailing: P.O. Box 87, Scranton, AR 72863 t) 479-938-2821 3parishes@gmail.com; canoffood@aol.com Attended from St. Ignatius, Scranton and St. Peter and Paul Rev. John Miranda (India), Pst.;

RATCLIFF

St. Anthony - 470 W. Wilson St., Ratcliff, AR 72951; Mailing: P.O. Box 60, Ratcliff, AR 72951 t) 479-970-3063 kstengel75@gmail.com Attended from Sacred Heart, Charleston Rev. Norman McFall, Sacr. Min.; Dcn. Kenneth Edward Stengel, Admin.; CRP Stds.: 15

ROGERS

St. Vincent de Paul - 1416 W. Poplar St., Rogers, AR 72758 t) 479-636-4020 information@svdprogers.com www.svdprogers.com Rev. Msgr. David LeSieur, Pst.; Rev. Rodolphe Balthazar, Assoc. Pst.; Rev. Keith Higginbotham, Assoc. Pst.; Dcn. Sergio Aguilar; Dcn. Rob Brothers; Dcn. Jose Fabio Cruz; Dcn. Dan Grelle; Dcn. Larry Grelle; Dcn. Arturo Hernandez; Dcn. Byron Newton; Dcn. Tom Parks; Dcn. Arturo Castrejon; Dcn. Silvestre Duran; Dcn. John Ray Pate; Dcn. Ronald William Hoyt; CRP Stds.: 882

St. Vincent de Paul School - (Grades PreK-8) 1315 W. Cypress St., Rogers, AR 72758 t) 479-636-4421 svdpinfo@svdpschool.net www.svdpschool.net Alice Stautzenberger, Prin.; Stds.: 391; Lay Tchrs.: 22

St. Vincent de Paul Endowment Fund - t) (479) 636-4020 Glenn Kelley, Chair; Sandra Dominguez, Secy.;

ROLAND

St. Francis of Assisi Church - 33223 Hwy. 300, Roland, AR 72135; Mailing: 4000 N. Rodney Parham Rd., c/o Christ the King, Little Rock, AR 72212 t) (501) 225-6774 parishsecretary@ctklr.org stfrancislittleitaly.org/ Attended from Christ the King, Little Rock Rev. Juan J. Guido, Pst.; Rev. Chanda Pillai PJ, I.M.S., Assoc. Pst.; Dcn. Chris Dorer;

RUSSELLVILLE

St. John - 1900 W. Main St., Russellville, AR 72801 t) 479-967-3699 churchoffice@sjccr.org www.sjccr.org Rev. Daniel Ramos, Admin.; Rev. Jayarayu Sure, Assoc. Pst.; CRP Stds.: 220

St. John School - (Grades PreK-5) 1912 W. Main St., Russellville, AR 72801 t) 479-967-4644 principal@sjccr.org Vivian Fox, Prin.; Stds.: 104; Lay Tchrs.: 9

St. John's Educational Trust - Rev. Daniel Ramos, Pst.;

St. Leo the Great University Parish - 509 W. L St., Russellville, AR 72801; Mailing: P.O. Box 9033, Russellville, AR 72811 t) 479-968-8249 stleosatu@gmail.com www.stleosatu.org Rev. Daniel Ramos; Rev. Jayaraju Sure (India); CRP Stds.: 5

SCRANTON

St. Ignatius - 108 S. Main St., Scranton, AR 72863; Mailing: P.O. Box 87, Scranton, AR 72863 t) 479-938-2821 3parishes@gmail.com Also attends SS. Peter and Paul Church, Morrison Bluff and St. Meinrad Church, Prairie View Rev. John Miranda (India), Pst.; CRP Stds.: 61

SEARCY

St. James - 1102 Pioneer Rd., Searcy, AR 72143; Mailing: PO Box 172, Searcy, AR 72143 t) 501-268-5252 stjames172@sbcglobal.net www.stjamessearcy.org Rev. Nelson Rubio; CRP Stds.: 80

SHERIDAN

Holy Cross - 921 W. Vine St., Sheridan, AR 72150; Mailing: PO Box 624, Sheridan, AR 72150 t) 870-534-4701 (St. Joseph phone number) joesaia6@gmail.com Mission of St. Joseph, Pine Bluff. Rev. Joseph P. Marconi, Pst.; CRP Stds.: 12

SILOAM SPRINGS

St. Mary - 1998 Hwy. 412 E, Siloam Springs, AR 72761; Mailing: P.O. Box 118, Siloam Springs, AR 72761 t) 479-524-8526 secretary@stmarysiloam.com www.stmarysiloamsprings.com Rev. Salvador Marquez-Munoz, Pst.; Dcn. Moisés Colón; CRP Stds.: 222

SPRINGDALE

Our Lady of Sorrows Catholic Church - 1600 W. Graham Rd., Springdale, AR 72762; Mailing: P.O. Box 1871, Springdale, AR 72765 t) 479-935-2858 parishoffice@ourladyofsorrowsnwa.org; admin@ourladyofsorrowsnwa.org ourladyofsorrowsnwa.org/ Rev. Joshua Passo, FSSP, Pst.; Rev. Edgar Ramirez, FSSP, Assoc. Pst.;

St. Raphael - 1386 S. West End St., Springdale, AR 72764 t) 479-756-6711 x230 info@straphaelcc.org www.straphaelcc.org Rev. John M. Connell, Pst.; Rev. Omar Galvan Gonzalez, Assoc. Pst.; Rev. Daniel

Wendel, Assoc. Pst.; Dcn. Dan Cashman; Dcn. Jesus Ramos; Dcn. Eduardo Andrade; Dcn. Oscar Lopez; Dcn. Robert Phillips; Dcn. Luis Sanchez; CRP Stds.: 846

STAR CITY

St. Justin - 400 N. Drew St., Star City, AR 71667; Mailing: 207 E. 16th Ave., Pine Bluff, AR 71601 t) 870-794-8029 st.peterpinebluff@gmail.com Attended from St. Peter, Pine Bluff. Rev. Andreas Kedati, Pst.;

STUTTGART

SS. Cyril and Methodius - 1852 Hwy. 86 W., Stuttgart, AR 72160 t) 870-241-3359 Rev. Shaun C. Wesley, Pst.; CRP Stds.: 14

Holy Rosary - 1815 S. Prairie St., Stuttgart, AR 72160 t) 870-673-8351 holyrose1234@gmail.com www.holyrosarystuttgart.net Rev. Babu Battula (India), Pst.; CRP Stds.: 30

Holy Rosary School - (Grades PreK-6) 920 W. 19th St., Stuttgart, AR 72160 t) 870-673-3211 holyrosary@centurytel.net wwww.holyrosarystuttgart.come Kathy Lorince, Prin.; Stds.: 54; Lay Tchrs.: 4

SUBIACO

St. Benedict - 81 W. Parish Dr., Subiaco, AR 72865 t) 479-934-1169 c) 479-438-5072 stengelmark@gmail.com Rev. Mark Stengel, O.S.B., Pst.; CRP Stds.: 80

TEXARKANA

St. Edward - 407 Beech St., Texarkana, AR 71854; Mailing: 410 Beech St., Texarkana, AR 71854 t) 870-772-1115 office@saintedwardstexarkana.com www.saintedwardstexarkana.com Also attends St. Elizabeth Ann Seton Church, Ashdown and Sacred Heart Church, Foreman Rev. William Wyatt Burmester, Pst.; Dcn. Greg Casteel; Dcn. Leon Pesek; CRP Stds.: 210

TONTITOWN

St. Joseph - 154 E Henri de Tonti Blvd., Tontitown, AR 72770; Mailing: P.O. Box 39, Tontitown, AR 72770 t) 479-361-2612 mwhinnery@stjoetontitown.org www.stjoetontitown.org Attended from St. Raphael, Springdale Rev. Arokiasamy Madhichetty Irudayaraj, Pst.; Dcn. Dan Joseph Daily; Rev. Omar Galvan Gonzalez, Assoc. Pst.; CRP Stds.: 123

VAN BUREN

St. Michael - 1019 E. Pointer Trl., Van Buren, AR 72956 t) 479-471-1211 secretary@stmichaelvanburen.com; officemgr@stmichaelvanburen.com www.stmichaelvanburen.com Rev. Charles R. Hobbs, Pst.; CRP Stds.: 205

WALDRON

St. Jude Thaddeus Church - 680 St. Jude Dr., Waldron, AR 72958; Mailing: P.O. Box 1688, Waldron, AR 72958 t) 501-358-1238 waldronstjudecatholicchurch@yahoo.com www.waldronar.catholicweb.com Attended from Church of the Assumption, Booneville. Rev. Leslie A. Farley, Pst.; CRP Stds.: 12

WALNUT RIDGE

Immaculate Heart of Mary - 320 W. Free St., Walnut Ridge, AR 72476; Mailing: P O Box 70, Walnut Ridge, AR 72476 t) 870-886-2119; 870-236-2568 (Paragould Office) Attended by St. Mary, Paragould. Rev. Nazarus Maduba (Nigeria), Admin.; Dcn. Marlyn Glenn Tate;

WARREN

St. Luke Church - 200 N. Bradley St., Warren, AR 71671; Mailing: 440 W. Main St., El Dorado, AR 71730 t) 870-863-3620 holyredeemer@holyredeemereldorado.org www.dolr.org Attended from Holy Redeemer, El Dorado. Rev. Edward P. D'Almeida, Pst.; CRP Stds.: 74

WEINER

St. Anthony - 407 Kings Hwy., Weiner, AR 72479; Mailing: P.O. Box 76, Weiner, AR 72479 t) 870-684-2656 stanthonychurchweiner@gmail.com Rev. Tuyen Do, Pst.;

WEST MEMPHIS

St. Michael - 411 N. Missouri St., West Memphis, AR 72301; Mailing: P O Box 899, West Memphis, AR 72303 t) 870-733-1212 westmemphiscatholic@gmail.com Attends Sacred Heart of Jesus Church - Crawfordsville Rev. Charles Thessing, Pst.;

St. Michael School - (Grades PreK-6) 405 N. Missouri St., West Memphis, AR 72301 t) 870-735-1730 smcswm@sbcglobal.net stmichaelwm.org Kimberly Odom, Prin.;

St. Michael's School Endowment and Charitable Trust -

WINSLOW

Our Lady of the Ozarks Shrine - 22741 N. Hwy. 71, Winslow, AR 72959; Mailing: 3436 Breckenridge Dr., Fayetteville, AR 72703 c) 479-530-3792 mhenry@coldwellbanker.com ourladyoftheozarksshrine.org/ Attended from Immaculate Conception Church, Fort Smith. Rev. John K. Antony, Pst.; Rev. Balaraju Akkala, Assoc. Pst.; Dcn. Grant Michael Henry, Admin.; CRP Stds.: 10

WYNNE

St. Peter - 1695 N. Falls Blvd., Wynne, AR 72396; Mailing: P.O. Box 517, Wynne, AR 72396 t) 870-238-2613 stpeterswynne@outlook.com Rev. Alfhones Perikala, Pst.; CRP Stds.: 28

YELLVILLE

St. Andrew Church - 1486 Hwy. 62 W., Yellville, AR 72687; Mailing: P.O. Box 197, Yellville, AR 72687 t) 870-449-4850 mmgchurch@yahoo.com harrisoncatholic.org Attended from Mary Mother of God Church, Harrison. Rev. Benjamin A Riley; Dcn. George Gussy; CRP Stds.: 16

SCHOOLS: PRESCHOOL THRU HIGH SCHOOL

SCHOOLS

STATE OF ARKANSAS

CONWAY

St. Joseph School - (DIO) (Grades 7-12) 502 Front St., Conway, AR 72032-5408 t) 501-329-5741 www.stjosephconway.org Matthew Tucker, Prin.; Stds.: 484; Lay Tchrs.: 42

HIGH SCHOOLS

STATE OF ARKANSAS

FORT SMITH

Trinity Catholic School - (DIO) (Grades 6-8) 1205 S. Albert Pike, Fort Smith, AR 72903 t) 479-782-2451 office@thinktrinity.org www.trinitycatholicjh.org Rev. John K. Antony, Admin.; Stds.: 221; Lay Tchrs.: 21

Trinity Educational Trust Fund - 1205 Albert Pike, Fort SMith, AR 72903 t) (479) 782-2451

LITTLE ROCK

Catholic High School of Little Rock, AR - (DIO) (Grades 9-12) 6300 Father Tribou St., Little Rock, AR 72205 t) 501-664-3939 chs@lrchs.org www.lrchs.org Rev. Msgr. Lawrence A. Frederick, Rector; Steve Straessle, Prin.; Stds.: 682; Pr. Tchrs.: 1; Bro. Tchrs.: 1; Lay Tchrs.: 46

Mount St. Mary Academy - (PRV) (Grades 9-12) 3224 Kavanaugh Blvd., Little Rock, AR 72205 t) 501-664-8006 kwewers@mtstmary.edu www.mtstmary.edu (Girls) Rev. Msgr. Lawrence A. Frederick, Chap.; Rev. Leon Ngandu, SVD, Chap.; Sara Jones, Headmaster; Stds.: 460; Lay Tchrs.: 36

Mount St. Mary Foundation Corporation - 3224 Kavanaugh Blvd., Little Rock, AR 72205 t) (501) 664-8006 x121 Mary Catherine Burney, Dir.;

MORRILTON

Sacred Heart Catholic School - (DIO) (Grades PreSchool-12) 106 N. St. Joseph St., Morrilton, AR 72110 t) 501-354-8113; (501) 354-4358 akoonce@sacredheartmorrilton.org; jroscoe@sacredheartmorrilton.org www.sacredheartmorrilton.org Stds.: 251; Lay Tchrs.: 30

SUBIACO

***Subiaco Academy** - (PRV) (Grades 7-12) 405 N. Subiaco Ave., Subiaco, AR 72865 t) (479) 934-1000 dwright@subi.org www.subiacoacademy.us David Wright, Headmaster; Stds.: 135; Pr. Tchrs.: 4; Bro. Tchrs.: 3; Lay Tchrs.: 17

INSTITUTIONS LOCATED IN DIOCESE

CAMPUS MINISTRY / NEWMAN CENTERS [CAM]

BATESVILLE

Lyons College Catholic Campus Ministry - 3800 Harrison St., Batesville, AR 72501 t) 870-793-7717 laurengunderman@gmail.com Rev. Jon Miskin, Pst.; Lauren Gunderman, Campus Min.;

BEEBE

Harding University In Searcy/Arkansas State University at Beebe, Campus Ministry - 109 Campbell Dr., Beebe, AR 72012 t) 501-230-2890 flofitch@gmail.com Flo Fitch, Campus Min.;

CLARKSVILLE

University of Ozarks Catholic Campus Ministry (Clarksville) - 415 N. College Ave., Clarksville, AR 72830 c) 479-264-7929; 501-681-8156 mfrizzell@ozarks.edu; aoatis@ozarks.edu Monica Frizzell, Campus Min.; Amy Oatis, Campus Min.;

CONWAY

University of Central Arkansas & Hendrix College Catholic Campus Ministry - 1902 South Blvd., Conway, AR 72034 t) 501-336-9091 catholic@cyberback.com; kaseymillerccm@gmail.com www.conwaycatholic.com (Conway) Rev. Msgr. Jack D. Harris, Chap.; Kasey Miller, Campus Min.; Dcn. Richard John Papini, Dir.;

FAYETTEVILLE

University of Arkansas, St. Thomas Aquinas University Parish - 603 N. Leverett Ave., Fayetteville, AR 72701 t) 479-444-0223 ccm@uark.edu www.catholichogs.com Rev. Jason Sharbaugh, Pst.; Adam Koehler, Campus Min.;

FORT SMITH

University of Arkansas at Fort Smith, Catholic Campus Ministry - 22 N. 13th St., Fort Smith, AR 72901 t) 479-785-7972 deacongreg@icchurch.com www.uafscatholic.org Dcn. Greg Pair, Campus Min.;

JONESBORO

Arkansas State University, St. John Newman University Parish - 2800 E. Johnson Ave., Jonesboro, AR 72401 t) 870-972-1888 director@astatecnc.com; finance@astatecnc.com www.astatecnc.com Rev. Tuyen Do, Pst.; Dcn. Bob Bennett;

LITTLE ROCK

Catholic Campus Ministry - 2500 N. Tyler St., Little Rock, AR 72207 t) 501-664-0340 x333 Liz Tingquist, Dir.;

MAGNOLIA

Campus Ministry, Southern Arkansas University - 2114 N. Jackson St., Magnolia, AR 71753 t) 870-901-3173 almagt2013@gmail.com Alma Garcia, Campus Min.;

RUSSELLVILLE

St. Leo the Great University Parish - 509 W. L St., Russellville, AR 72801; Mailing: P.O. Box 9033, Russellville, AR 72811 t) 479-968-8249 stleoatu@gmail.com www.stleoatu.homestead.com/

homepage Rev. Daniel Ramos, Pst.; Mary Buford Corkins, Campus Min.; Pat Buford, Dir.;

CEMETERIES [CEM]

FORT SMITH

Calvary - c/o Immaculate Conception Church, Fort Smith, AR 72902; Mailing: P.O. Box 1866, Fort Smith, AR 72902 t) 479-783-7963 ic@icchurch.com Rev. John K. Antony, Pst.;

LITTLE ROCK

Calvary - Wright Ave. & S. Woodrow St., Little Rock, AR 72205; Mailing: 2500 N. Tyler St., Little Rock, AR 72207 t) 501-664-0340 calvarycemetery@dolr.org Dennis P. Lee, Admin.;

CONVENTS, MONASTERIES, AND RESIDENCES FOR WOMEN [CON]

FORT SMITH

St. Scholastica Monastery-Motherhouse - 1315 S. Albert Pike, Fort Smith, AR 72903; Mailing: P.O. Box 3489, Fort Smith, AR 72903-3489 t) 479-783-4147; 479-783-7086 x246 (Prioress) monastery@stscho.org www.stscho.org Rev. Leslie A. Farley, Chap.; Sr. Kimberly Rose Prohaska, OSB, Prioress; Srs.: 30

JONESBORO

Holy Angels Convent-Motherhouse (Olivetan Benedictine Sisters) - 1699 County Rd. 766, Jonesboro, AR 72405-6981; Mailing: P.O. Box 1209, Jonesboro, AR 72403-1209 t) 870-935-5810 secretary@olivben.org www.olivben.org Mother Mary Clare Bezner, O.S.B., Prioress; Rev. Benignus Wego, SVD, Chap.; Srs.: 27

LITTLE ROCK

Discalced Carmelite Nuns of Little Rock, Inc. - 7201 W. 32nd St., Little Rock, AR 72204 t) 501-565-5121 lrcarmel@comcast.net www.littlerockcarmel.org Sr. Lucia Ellender, OCD, Prioress; Sr. Andrea Fulmer, OCD, Subprioress; Sr. Mercia M Bowie, OCD, 2nd Councilor, Novice Dir.; Sr. Stephanie Turner, OCD, 3rd Councilor; Srs.: 12

Missionaries of Charity - 1014 S. Oak St., Little Rock, AR 72204 t) 501-663-3596 (convent); 501-666-9718 Convent and home for expectant mothers, homeless women & children. Sr. M. Jonathan, MC, Regl. Supr.; Sr. Dominga M.C., Supr.; Srs.: 5

ENDOWMENTS / FOUNDATIONS / TRUSTS [EFT]

JONESBORO

Arkansas State Univ. St. John Newman Univ. Parish Trust Fund Agreement - 2800 E. Johnson Ave., Jonesboro, AR 72401 t) (870) 972-1888 Rev. Tuyen Do;

LITTLE ROCK

***Catholic Foundation of Arkansas** - 2500 N. Tyler St., Little Rock, AR 72207 t) (501) 664-0340

Clergy Welfare Fund, Inc. - 2500 N. Tyler St., Little Rock, AR 72207 t) 501-664-0340 gwolfe@dolr.org Gregory C. Wolfe, Dir.;

Diocese of Little Rock Catholic Schools Education Trust - 2500 N. Tyler St., Little Rock, AR 72207 t) 501-664-0340 thall@dolr.org Theresa Hall, Supt.; Ileana Dobbins, Asst. Supt.; Marguerite Olberts, Asst. Supt.;

The Mary Raymond Trust - 2500 N Tyler, Little Rock, AR 72217-7565; Mailing: P O Box 7565, Little Rock, AR 72217-7565 t) 501-664-0340 gwolfe@dolr.org Gregory C. Wolfe, Dir.;

MORRILTON

Sacred Heart Catholic School Endowment Fund - 406 E. Elm, Morrilton, AR 72110; Mailing: PO Box 426, Morrilton, AR 72110 t) 501-354-4358 akoonce@sacredheartmorrilton.org www.sacredheartmorrilton.org Supports Sacred Heart Catholic School in Morrilton, AR Rev. Msgr. Jack D. Harris, Pst.;

HOSPITALS / HEALTH SERVICES [HOS]

BOONEVILLE

Mercy Hospital Booneville - 880 W. Main St., Booneville, AR 72927; Mailing: 14528 S Outer 40 Rd., Ste 100, Mercy Corporation Paralegal-Legal, Chesterfield, MO 63017 t) (479) 675-2800 x1600 Jacquelynn K. Richmond, Vice-Pres., Deputy Gen. Counsel; Bed Capacity: 25; Asstd. Annu.: 16,452; Staff: 73

FORT SMITH

Mercy Hospital Fort Smith - 7301 Rogers Ave., Fort Smith, AR 72903 t) 479-314-6000 www.mercy.net Jacquelynn K. Richmond, Contact; Bed Capacity: 372; Asstd. Annu.: 398,013; Staff: 1,639

Mercy Health Foundation, Fort Smith - t) 479-314-1133 patrick.pendleton@mercy.net; taylor.martinez2@mercy.net Martin Schreiber, Admin.;

HOT SPRINGS

CHI St. Vincent Hot Springs - 300 Werner St, Hot Springs, AR 71913 t) 501-622-1000 mwmillard@stvincenthealth.com www.chistvincent.com Rev. George W. Sanders, Chap.; Dr. Douglas Ross, Pres.; Bed Capacity: 279; Asstd. Annu.: 16,300; Staff: 2,200

JONESBORO

St. Bernard Medical Center - 225 E. Washington Ave. #84, Jonesboro, AR 72401 t) 870-972-4100; 870-207-4230 mpolk@sbrmc.org stbernards.info Chris Barber, Pres.; Benjamim Barylske, VP/CFO; Bed Capacity: 440; Asstd. Annu.: 185,577; Staff: 2,953

LITTLE ROCK

St. Vincent Infirmary Medical Center - No. 2 St. Vincent Cir., Little Rock, AR 72205 t) 501-552-3676 mwmillard@stvincenthealth.com Rev. Warren Harvey, Chap.; Shawn Barnett, Pres.; Bed Capacity: 615; Asstd. Annu.: 18,316; Staff: 2,159

MORRILTON

CHI St. Vincent Morrilton (St. Anthony's Hospital Association) - 4 Hospital Dr., Morrilton, AR 72110-4510 t) 501-977-2300 mwmillard@stvincenthealth.com Sponsored by St. Vincent Health System, a division of Catholic Health Initiatives. Leslie Bubba Arnold, Pres.; Bed Capacity: 25; Asstd. Annu.: 36,768; Staff: 137

OZARK

Mercy Hospital Ozark - 801 W. River St., Ozark, AR 72949 t) 479-667-4138 Bed Capacity: 25; Asstd. Annu.: 13,583; Staff: 45

PARIS

Mercy Hospital Paris - 500 E. Academy, Paris, AR 72855 t) 479-963-6101 Bed Capacity: 16; Asstd. Annu.: 29,485; Staff: 63

ROGERS

Mercy Hospital Rogers - 2710 Rife Medical Ln., Rogers, AR 72756 t) 479-338-2903 Eric Pianalto, CEO; Bed Capacity: 245; Asstd. Annu.: 328,720; Staff: 1,387

Mercy Health Foundation Northwest Arkansas - t) 479-338-8000

SHERWOOD

St. Vincent Medical Center/Sherwood - 2215 Wildwood Ave., Sherwood, AR 72120 t) 501-552-7107 mwmillard@stvincenthealth.com Shawn Barnett, Pres.; Bed Capacity: 69; Asstd. Annu.: 36,053; Staff: 189

WALDRON

Mercy Hospital Waldron - 1341 W. 6th St., Waldron, AR 72958 t) 479-637-4135 Jacquelynn K. Richmond, Contact; Bed Capacity: 25; Asstd. Annu.: 15,736; Staff: 65

WYNNE

St. Bernard Community Hospital Corporation (CrossRidge Community Hospital) - 310 S. Falls Blvd., Wynne, AR 72396 t) 870-238-3300 mpolk@sbrmc.org stbernards.info Chris Barber, Pres.; Benjamim Barylske, VP Finance; Bed Capacity: 25; Asstd. Annu.: 70,662; Staff: 169

MISCELLANEOUS [MIS]

BERRYVILLE

Brothers and Sisters of Charity at Little Portion - 350 County Rd. 248, Berryville, AR 72616 t) 479-253-0253 info@littleportion.org; violatalbot40@gmail.com www.littleportion.org Public Association of the Faithful Viola Talbot, Vicar; John Michael Talbot, Gen. Min.;

CHEROKEE VILLAGE

Magnificat - Mary Ark of the Covenant Corp. - 49 Tekakwitha Dr., Cherokee Village, AR 72529; Mailing: P.O. Box 970, Cherokee Village, AR 72525 t) 870-257-2850 stmichaelcv@yahoo.com Niki Elizabeth McDaniel, Contact;

CONWAY

Magnificat - Central Arkansas Chapter - 1440 Brookfield Dr., Conway, AR 72032 t) 501-392-2690 susan.denys50@gmail.com Rev. Anthony M. Robbins, Pst.;

FORT SMITH

West River Valley Deanery Council (Council of Catholic Women) - 3005 S. 106th Cir., Fort Smith, AR 72903 t) (479) 719-2368 Debbie Bogner, Treas.;

LITTLE ROCK

Diocese of Little Rock House of Formation - 1201 S. Van Buren, Little Rock, AR 72204 t) 501-418-8525 Rev. Jeffrey Hebert, Prefect;

Ladies of Charity of Arkansas - 2500 N. Tyler St., Little Rock, AR 72207; Mailing: PO Box 7565, Little Rock, AR 72217 t) 501-664-0340 lcark@dolr.org Cheryl Smith, Pres.;

Monsignor James E. O'Connell Diocesan Seminarian Fund, Inc. - 2500 N. Tyler St., Little Rock, AR 72207; Mailing: PO Box 7565, Little Rock, AR 72217-7565 t) 501-664-0340 x331 jhebert@dolr.org Rev. Jeffrey Hebert, Dir.;

NORTH LITTLE ROCK

MVL-VLM, Inc. - 6150 Remount Rd., North Little Rock, AR 72118 t) 501-753-3977 catecismo@saintannenlr.org Guillermo Bruzatori, Dir.;

MONASTERIES AND RESIDENCES FOR PRIESTS AND BROTHERS [MON]

CABOT

Priestly Fraternity of St. Peter - 106 Pin Oak Dr., Cabot, AR 72023 t) 501-941-1566 pastor@arkansaslatinmass.com Rev. Paul McCambridge, FSSP, Contact; Priests: 1

LITTLE ROCK

St. John Manor - 2414 N. Tyler St., Little Rock, AR 72207; Mailing: 2500 N. Tyler St., Little Rock, AR 72207 t) 501-664-0340 tcostello@dolr.org Rev. Warren Harvey, Asst. Min to Priests; Rev. John Marconi, In Res.; Rev. Nho Duy Do, In Res.; Rev. Clayton Gould, In Res.; Rev. Edwin Graves, In Res.; Rev. Thomas W. Keller, In Res.; Rev. Thomas C Marks, In Res.; Rev. John Oswald, In Res.; Rev. Msgr. Richard S. Oswald, In Res.; Priests: 9

SUBIACO

Subiaco Abbey - 405 N. Subiaco Ave., Subiaco, AR 72865 t) 479-934-1000 abbot@subi.org www.subi.org Rt. Rev. Elijah Owens, O.S.B., Abbot; Rev. Richard Walz, O.S.B., Prior; Bro. Adrian Strobel, OSB, Subprior; Glenn Constantino, CEO; Karla Kennedy, CFO; David Wright, Headmaster; Rev. Mark Stengel, O.S.B., Pst.; Rev. Reginald Udouj, OSB, Pst.; Rev. William Wewers, O.S.B., Pst.; Stds.: 135; Bro. Tchrs.: 1; Lay Tchrs.: 17; Pr. Tchrs.: 5

NURSING / REHABILITATION / CONVALESCENCE / ELDERLY CARE [NUR]

BARLING

Mercy Crest Housing, Inc. - 1300 Strozier Ln., Barling, AR 72923 t) 479-478-3000 administrator@mercycrest.com www.mercycrest.com Sponsored by the Religious Sisters of Mercy Cindy Taylor, Admin.; Asstd. Annu.: 128; Staff: 57

BERRYVILLE

Mercy Home Health Berryville - 804 W. Freeman, Ste. 4, Berryville, AR 72616 t) 866-433-6078 marynell.ploch@mercy.net Jacquelynn K. Richmond, Vice-Pres., Deputy Gen. Counsel; Asstd. Annu.: 400; Staff: 15

JONESBORO

Benedictine Manor I - 312 S. Bridge St., Jonesboro, AR 72401 t) 870-932-8141 stbseniorhousing.com (Affiliated with Olivetan Benedictine Sisters, Inc., Jonesboro, AR)

Asstd. Annu.: 20; Staff: 1

Benedictine Manor II - 310 S. Bridge St., Jonesboro, AR 72401 t) 870-932-8141 stbseniorhousing.com (Affiliated with Olivetan Benedictine Sisters, Inc., Jonesboro, AR) Asstd. Annu.: 20; Staff: 1

St. Bernard Village, Inc. - 1606 Heern Dr., Jonesboro, AR 72401 t) 870-932-8141 www.stbseniorhousing.com Affiliated with Olivetan Benedictine Sisters, Inc., Jonesboro, AR Chris Barber, CEO; Asstd. Annu.: 350; Staff: 98

LITTLE ROCK

Christopher Homes of Arkansas, Inc. - 2417 N. Tyler St., Little Rock, AR 72207 t) 501-664-1881 llopez@dolr.org www.christopherhomesofarkansas.org Elizabeth Lopez, Dir.; Staff: 7

Christopher Homes of Augusta, Inc. - 900 Carver N. St., Augusta, AR 72006 t) 870-497-2191 aug@christopherhomesofarkansas.org Christopher Homes of Augusta, Inc.

Christopher Homes of Camden, Inc. - 900 Sharp Ave., Camden, AR 71701 t) 870-837-1911 cam@christopherhomesofarkansas.org

Christopher Homes of Brinkley, Inc. - 900 W. 6th St., Brinkley, AR 72021 t) 870-734-2201 bri@christopherhomesofarkansas.org Christopher Homes of Brinkley, Inc.

Christopher Homes of Hot Springs, Inc. - 1010 Cones Rd., Hot Springs, AR 71901 t) 501-318-1317 hot@christopherhomesofarkansas.org

Christopher Homes of Little Rock - 9216 Lanehart Rd., Little Rock, AR 72204 t) 501-812-3442 lit@christopherhomesofarkansas.org

Christopher Homes of Monette, Inc. - 21 Christopher Pl., Monette, AR 72447 t) 870-486-2748 mon@christopherhomesofarkansas.org

Christopher Homes of North Little Rock, Inc. - 656 Donovan Briley Blvd., North Little Rock, AR 72118 t) 501-758-8582 nlr@christopherhomesofarkansas.org

Christopher Homes of Palestine, Inc. - 21 Christopher Pl., Palestine, AR 72372 t) 870-581-2023 pal@christopherhomesofarkansas.org

Christopher Homes of Strong, Inc. - 21 Christopher Pl., Strong, AR 71765 t) 870-277-2439 str@christopherhomesofarkansas.org Christopher Homes of Strong, Inc

Christopher Homes of Clarendon, Inc. - 400 Meadow Ln., Clarendon, AR 72029 t) 870-277-0621 cla@christopherhomesofarkansas.org

The Cottages at Delta Acres Inc. - 721 N. 7th St., Clarendon, AR 72029 t) 870-497-2201

Christopher Homes of De Queen, Inc. - 119 S. Lakeside Dr., De Queen, AR 71832 t) 870-642-6211 deq@christopherhomesofarkansas.org

Christopher Homes of De Valls Bluff, Inc. - 119 W. Sycamore, De Valls Bluff, AR 72041 t) 870-340-2272 dev@christopherhomesofarkansas.org

Christopher Homes of El Dorado, Inc. - 1323 W. 5th St., El Dorado, AR 71730 t) 870-862-9711 eld@christopherhomesofarkansas.org

Christopher Homes of Elaine, Inc. - 500 N. Pecan, Elaine, AR 72333; Mailing: P.O. Box 43, Elaine, AR 72333 t) 870-340-2271 ela@christopherhomesofarkansas.org Christopher Homes of Elaine, Inc.

Christopher Homes of Forrest City, Inc. - 805 Dawson Rd., Forrest City, AR 72335 t) 870-633-4804 for@christopherhomesofarkansas.org

Christopher Homes of Horatio, Inc. - 408 Bruce St., Horatio, AR 71842 t) 870-832-4014 hor@christopherhomesofarkansas.org Christopher Homes of Horatio, Inc.

Christopher Homes of Jacksonville, Inc - 2417 N. Tyler St., Little Rock, AR 72207 t) (501) 664-0340

Christopher Homes of Jonesboro, Inc. - 2204 Crescendo Dr., Jonesboro, AR 72401 t) 870-931-9575 jon@christopherhomesofarkansas.org

Christopher Homes of Marianna, Inc. - 238 Christopher Cove #1, Marianna, AR 72360 t) 870-295-6345 mar@christopherhomesofarkansas.org Christopher Homes of Marianna, Inc.

Christopher Homes of Paragould, Inc. - 1612 S. 9th St., Paragould, AR 72450 t) 870-239-8609 par@christopherhomesofarkansas.org Christopher Homes of Paragould, Inc

Christopher Homes of Parkin, Inc. - 100 College St., Parkin, AR 72373; Mailing: P.O. Box 586, Parkin, AR 72373 t) 870-340-2252 pkn@christopherhomesofarkansas.org Christopher Homes of Parkin, Inc.

Christopher Homes of Searcy, Inc. - 17 Christopher Cir., Searcy, AR 72143 t) 501-268-7804 ser@christopherhomesofarkansas.org Christopher Homes of Searcy, Inc.

Christopher Homes of West Helena, Inc. - 13 Christopher Pl., West Helena, AR 72390 t) 870-572-9433 whl@christopherhomesofarkansas.org Christopher Homes of West Helena, Inc.

Christopher Homes of Wynne, Inc. - 21 Christopher Pl., Wynne, AR 72396 t) 870-238-3388 wyn@christopherhomesofarkansas.org Christopher Homes of Wynne, Inc.

RETREAT HOUSES / RENEWAL CENTERS [RTR]

BERRYVILLE

Little Portion Hermitage (Brothers and Sisters of Charity at Little Portion, Inc.) - 350 CR 248, Berryville, AR 72616-8505 t) 479-253-7710 info@littleportion.org www.littleportion.org (Public Association of the Faithful) Viola Talbot, Vicar; John Michael Talbot, Gen. Min.;

NEW BLAINE

Hesychia House of Prayer - 204 St. Scholastica Rd., New Blaine, AR 72851 t) 479-938-7375 hesychia@stscho.org www.seektheholy.org Attended from Subiaco Abbey, Subiaco, AR. Sr. Lisa Elaine Atkins, RSM, Dir.; Rev. Mark Stengel, O.S.B., Pst.;

SEMINARIES [SEM]

LITTLE ROCK

Discalced Carmelite Friars of St. Therese, Little Rock - 5151 Marylake Dr., Little Rock, AR 72206 t) 501-888-3052 executivedirector@carmelitefriarsocd.com www.carmelitefriarsocd.com Friar Jerome Earley, O.C.D., Supr.; Friar Bonaventure Sauer, O.C.D., In Res.; Friar Stephen Sanchez, O.C.D., In Res.; Pr. Tchrs.: 3

SPECIAL CARE FACILITIES [SPF]

DUMAS

Ascension DePaul Services - 161 S. Main St., Dumas, AR 71639; Mailing: P.O. Box 158, Dumas, AR 71639 t) 870-382-3080; 314-733-8000 john.tersigni@ascension.org John Tersigni, Chief Mission Integration Officer; Michael Griffin, CEO; Staff: 26

DePaul Health Center - 145 S. Waterman St., Dumas, AR 71639; Mailing: P.O. Box 158, Dumas, AR 71639 t) (870) 382-3080 www.depaularkansas.org

St. Elizabeth Health Center - 407 S. Gould Ave., Gould, AR 71643; Mailing: P.O. Drawer 370, Gould, AR 71643 t) 870-263-4317 www.depaularkansas.org

Wellness Center - 405 S. Gould Ave., Gould, AR 71643; Mailing: P.O. Box 370, Gould, AR 71643 t) 870-263-4748 www.depaularkansas.org

JONESBORO

St. Bernard Healthcare - 225 Washington Ave., #84, Jonesboro, AR 72401 t) 870-207-4230 mpolk@sbrmc.org www.stbernards.info Chris Barber, Pres.; Benjamim Barylske, VP CFO; Asstd. Annu.: 259,272; Staff: 952

Jonesboro Real Estate Holding Company, Inc. - 225 Washington Ave., #84, Jonesboro, AR 72401 t) 870-207-4230 mpolk@sbrmc.org Benjamim Barylske, VP CFO;

Total Life Healthcare, Inc. - 505 E. Matthews Ave., Jonesboro, AR 72401 t) 870-207-7500; 870-207-4230 Chris Barber, Pres.; Benjamim Barylske, VP CFO; Asstd. Annu.: 440; Staff: 70

Archdiocese of Los Angeles

(Archidioecesis Angelorum in California)

MOST REVEREND JOSE H. GOMEZ

Archbishop of Los Angeles; ordained August 15, 1978; appointed Auxiliary Bishop of Denver and Titular See of Belali January 23, 2001; ordained March 26, 2001; appointed Archbishop of San Antonio December 29, 2004; installed February 15, 2005; Pallium conferred June 29, 2005; appointed Coadjutor Archbishop of Los Angeles April 6, 2010; Succeeded to the See March 1, 2011. Office: 3424 Wilshire Blvd., Los Angeles, CA 90010- 2241. T: 213-637-7534; F: 213-637-6510.

Archdiocesan Catholic Center Office: 3424 Wilshire Blvd., Los Angeles, CA 90010-2241. T: 213-637-7000; F: 213-637-6000. www.LA-Archdiocese.org; info@LA-Archdiocese.org

Square Miles 8,636.

Diocese Established 1840; an Archbishopric July 11, 1936.

Comprises the Counties of Los Angeles, Santa Barbara and Ventura in the State of California. Patroness of the Archdiocese: Our Lady of the Angels. Secondary Patroness and Patrons: St. Vibiana; St. Emydius; and St. Patrick.

Legal Titles: The Roman Catholic Archbishop of Los Angeles, a Corporation Sole; Archdiocese of Los Angeles Education and Welfare Corporation; Archdiocese of Los Angeles Insurance Company; Archdiocese of Los Angeles Risk Management Corporation; Archdiocese of Los Angeles Funeral and Mortuary Services Corporation; Our Lady Queen of Angels; St. John's Seminary in California; The Cardinal McIntyre Fund for Charity; Catholic Charities of Los Angeles, Inc.; Catholic Charities Community Development Corporation; The Tidings Vida Nueva; Catholic Education Foundation; Opus Caritatis; Cathedral of Our Lady of the Angels.

For legal titles of parishes and archdiocesan institutions, consult the Chancery Office.

Most Reverend Marc V. Trudeau, D.D., V.G.
Auxiliary Bishop of Los Angeles; ordained June 8, 1991; appointed Titular Bishop of Tinis in Proconsular and Auxiliary Bishop of Los Angeles April 5, 2018; ordained June 7, 2018. Office: Regional Bishop, San Pedro Pastoral Region: 3555 St. Pancratius Pl., Lakewood, CA 90712-1416. T: 562-634-0456; F: 562-531-4783.

Most Reverend Alejandro D. Aclan, D.D., V.G.
Auxiliary Bishop of Los Angeles; ordained June 5, 1993; appointed Titular Bishop of Rusicade and Auxiliary Bishop of Los Angeles March 5, 2019; ordained May 16, 2019. Office: Regional Bishop, San Fernando Pastoral Region, 15101 San Fernando Mission Blvd., Mission Hills, CA 91345. T: 818-361-6009; F: 818-361-6270.

STATISTICAL OVERVIEW

Personnel
Retired Cardinals....1
Archbishops....1
Auxiliary Bishops....2
Retired Bishops....6
Abbots....1
Retired Abbots....1
Priests: Diocesan Active in Diocese....320
Priests: Diocesan Active Outside Diocese....2
Priests: Retired, Sick or Absent....140
Number of Diocesan Priests....462
Religious Priests in Diocese....455
Total Priests in your Diocese....917
Extern Priests in Diocese....114
Ordinations:
Diocesan Priests....8
Religious Priests....5
Transitional Deacons....8
Permanent Deacons....18
Permanent Deacons in Diocese....410
Total Brothers....49
Total Sisters....1,116

Parishes
Parishes....288
With Resident Pastor:
Resident Diocesan Priests....213
Resident Religious Priests....71
Without Resident Pastor:
Administered by Priests....38
Administered by Deacons....3
Administered by Lay People....1
Missions....10
Pastoral Centers....15
Professional Ministry Personnel:
Brothers....18
Sisters....147
Lay Ministers....803

Welfare
Catholic Hospitals....11
Total Assisted....1,546,054
Homes for the Aged....11
Total Assisted....1,204
Residential Care of Children....2
Total Assisted....168
Day Care Centers....19
Total Assisted....919
Specialized Homes....2
Total Assisted....54
Special Centers for Social Services....31
Total Assisted....184,116

Educational
Seminaries, Diocesan....1
Students from This Diocese....44
Students from Other Dioceses....41
Diocesan Students in Other Seminaries....9
Seminaries, Religious....2
Students, Religious....17
Total Seminarians....70
Colleges and Universities....3
Total Students....12,728
High Schools, Diocesan and Parish....24
Total Students....10,723
High Schools, Private....26
Total Students....11,334
Elementary Schools, Diocesan and Parish....191
Total Students....40,597
Elementary Schools, Private....17
Total Students....2,456
Catechesis/Religious Education:
High School Students....30,893
Elementary Students....53,829
Total Students under Catholic Instruction....162,630
Teachers in Diocese:
Priests....21
Brothers....19
Sisters....60
Lay Teachers....4,707

Vital Statistics
Receptions into the Church:
Infant Baptism Totals....46,601
Minor Baptism Totals....2,099
Adult Baptism Totals....1,146
Received into Full Communion....2,131
First Communions....29,065
Confirmations....19,950
Marriages:
Catholic....4,739
Interfaith....475
Total Marriages....5,214
Deaths....12,117
Total Catholic Population....3,851,636
Total Population....11,132,330

LEADERSHIP

Archdiocesan Catholic Center Office - t) 213-637-7000 info@la-archdiocese.org

Office of the Archbishop - t) 213-637-7534 office.archbishop@la-archdiocese.org Most Rev. Jose H. Gomez; Rev. Raymont Medina, Priest Sec. & Master of Ceremonies; Beatriz Velazquez, Exec. Coord.;

Moderator of the Curia and Vicar General - t) 213-637-7255 frbnunes@la-archdiocese.org Rev. Brian Nunes;

Chancellor - t) 213-637-7460 sracostello@la-archdiocese.org Sr. Mary Anncarla Costello, S.N.D.;

OFFICES AND DIRECTORS

African-American Catholic Center for Evangelization - t) 323-777-2106 aaccfe@sbcglobal.net Anderson Shaw, Dir.;

Angelus (Archdiocesan Magazine) - t) (213) 637-7327 pkay@la-archdiocese.org Pablo Kay, Editor;

Annual Catholic Appeals - t) 213-637-7461 dsmith@la-archdiocese.org Deirdre Smith, Dir.;

Apostleship of the Sea - t) 310-833-3541 parish-6080@la-archdiocese.org Rev. Diego Menniti, Chap.;

Applied Technology - t) 213-637-7526 dschmitt@la-archdiocese.org David Schmitt, Dir.;

Archdiocesan Council of Catholic Women - t) 213-637-7394 accw-info@la-archdiocese.org Carol Westlake, Pres.;

Archives - t) 818-365-1501 ttamberg@la-archdiocese.org Tod Tamberg, Exec. Dir.;

Brothers Council, Religious - t) 323-337-6776 lmoen@la-archdiocese.org Bro. Larry J. Moen, C.M.F., Chair;

- **Liaison to Brothers' Council** - t) (213) 637-7592 sr.mcarlos@la-archdiocese.org Sr. Maria Carlos, E.I.N.;

Canonical Services, Vicar for - t) (213) 637-7210 frjfox@la-archdiocese.org Rev. Joseph Fox, O.P.;

Cardinal Manning House of Prayer for Priests - t) (323) 662-0092 houseofprayer@la-archdiocese.org Rev. Msgr. Lorenzo Miranda, Dir.; Rev. Msgr. John D. Stoeger, Assoc. Dir.;

Cardinal McIntyre Fund for Charity - t) (213) 637-7506 mecapers@la-archdiocese.org Mary Ann E. Capers, Contact;

Catholic Campaign for Human Development - t) 213-637-7047 mpdonaldson@la-archdiocese.org Michael Donaldson, Dir.;

Catholic Charities of Los Angeles, Inc. - t) 213-251-3400

- **Executive Director** - t) 213-251-3464 Rev. Msgr. Gregory A. Cox;
- **Chief Financial Officer** - t) 213-251-3410 Daniel P. O'Brien;
- **Chief Development and Communications Officer** - t) 213-251-3495 Alexandria (Sandi) Arnold;
- **Department of Human Resources** - t) 213-251-3414 Leland R. Ratleff;
- **Director of Intra-Agency Programs** - t) 213-251-3412 Brenda Thomas;

Catholic Charities Regional Offices -

- **Our Lady of the Angels Region** - t) 310-392-8701 alalaian@ccharities.org Armine Lalain, Dir.;
- **San Fernando Region** - t) 213-251-3549 syanez@ccharities.org Sandra Yanez, Dir.;
- **San Gabriel Region** - t) 213-251-3582 xzendejas@ccharities.org Xochitl Zendejas, Dir.;
- **San Pedro Region** - t) 213-251-3429 bhackman@ccharities.org Bruce Hackman, Dir.;
- **Santa Barbara Region** - t) 805-965-7045 yvasquez@ccharities.org Yolanda Vasquez, Dir.;

Catholic Education Foundation - t) 213-637-7319 djcooper@la-archdiocese.org Douglas Cooper, Dir.;

Catholic Relief Services - t) 213-637-7047 mpdonaldson@la-archdiocese.org Michael Donaldson, Dir.;

Cemeteries and Mortuaries, Catholic - t) 213-637-7800

- **Chief Operating Officer** - t) 213-637-7808 dsfarruggia@catholiccm.org Douglas S. Farruggia;
- **Director of Community Outreach** - t) 213-637-7815 bmcmahon@catholiccm.org Brian McMahon;
- **Director of Operations - Eastern Region** - t) 213-637-7817 ogallarzo@catholiccm.org Omar Gallarzo;
- **Director of Operations - Western Region** - t) 213-637-7818 mperez@catholiccm.org Mauricio Perez;

Clergy, Vicar for - t) 213-637-7284 vfco@la-archdiocese.org Rev. James M. Anguiano, Vicar; Rev. Joel Henson, Assoc. Vicar;

Communication Office - t) 213-637-7253 cguevara@la-archdiocese.org Carolina Guevara, Chief Communication Officer;

Construction - t) (213) 637-7855 curibe@la-archdiocese.org Cecilia Uribe, Dir.;

Deacons in Ministry - t) 213-637-7734 dnshanecuda@la-archdiocese.org Dcn. Shane Cuda, Dir.;

Development Department - t) 213-637-7240 cvfraser@la-archdiocese.org Catherine Fraser, Chief Devel. Officer;

Diaconate Formation Office - t) 213-637-7282 dnbconroy@la-archdiocese.org Dcn. Brian Conroy, Dir.;

Digital Office - t) 213-637-7251 syaklic@la-archdiocese.org Sarah Yaklic, Chief Digital Officer;

Divine Worship - t) (213) 637-7513 frjuanochoa@la-archdiocese.org Rev. Juan Jose Ochoa, Dir.;

Ecumenical and Interreligious Affairs - t) 310-322-1892 frarsmith@la-archdiocese.org Rt. Rev. Alexei R. Smith, Dir.;

Ethnic Ministry - t) 213-637-7230 frpsandoval@la-archdiocese.org Rev. Parker Sandoval, Dir.;

Financial Services - t) (213) 637-7218 resteiner@la-archdiocese.org Randy Steiner, CFO;

Fingerprinting Department - t) 213-637-7680 dnjbarry@la-archdiocese.org Dcn. John William Barry, Dir.;

General Counsel - t) 213-637-7511 legal@la-archdiocese.org Margaret G. Graf;

Government Funded Programs - t) 213-637-7915 lschavez@la-archdiocese.org Lilia Chavez, Dir.;

H.I.V./AIDS Ministry - t) 323-223-9047 frcponnet@la-archdiocese.org Rev. Christopher D. Ponnet, Dir.;

Human Resources - t) 213-637-7596 abaltierra@la-archdiocese.org Annabelle Baltierra, Dir.;

Instructional Television - t) 213-637-7312 dmoore@la-archdiocese.org David G. Moore, Dir.;

Insurance - t) 213-637-7279 ltomacan@la-archdiocese.org Levontine Tomacan, Dir.;

Life, Justice, and Peace - t) 213-637-7047 mpdonaldson@la-archdiocese.org Michael Donaldson, Dir.;

Marriage and Family Life Office - t) 213-637-7227 jvienna@la-archdiocese.org Joan T. Vienna, Dir.;

Mission Office - t) 213-637-7244 tfleming@la-archdiocese.org Rev. Msgr. Terrance L. Fleming, Exec. Dir.;

New Evangelization and Parish Life, Office of - t) 213-637-7366 Bobby Vidal, Dir.;

Newman Centers (Campus Ministry Sites) -

- **Claremont Colleges - McAllister Religious Activities** - t) 909-625-0369 Rev. Joseph Fenton, S.M., Dir.;
- **Loyola Law School** - t) 213-736-1000 Rev. Wayne R. Negrete, S.J., Dir.;
- **Loyola Marymount University - Malone Student Ctr.** - t) 310-338-4571 Rev. Marc Reeves, S.J., Dir.;
- **Mount St. Mary's University** - t) 310-954-4125 Gaile Krause, Dir.;
- **University of California at Los Angeles** - t) 310-208-5015 Rev. Jamie Baca, C.S.P., Dir.;
- **University of California at Santa Barbara - St. Mark University Parish** - t) 805-968-1078 Rev. Ryan Thornton, O.F.M., Dir.;
- **University of Southern California - Our Saviour University Parish** - t) 213-749-5341 Rev. Richard Sunwoo, Pst.;

Operations - t) 213-637-7618 eeobrien@la-archdiocese.org Eileen O'Brien, Dir.;

Purchasing/Mail Center - t) 213-637-7281 pmcstaff@la-archdiocese.org John Marmolejo, Purchasing Mgr.;

Queen of Angels Center for Priestly Formation - t) 310-516-6671 frpmgarcia@la-archdiocese.org Rev. Paolo Garcia, Dir.;

Real Estate - t) 213-637-7273 mtdavitt@la-archdiocese.org Michael T. Davitt, Dir.;

Religious Education - t) 213-637-7309 rosaliameza@la-archdiocese.org Sr. Rosalia Meza, V.D.M.F., Dir.; Giovanni Perez, Assoc. Dir. (goperez@la-archdiocese.org); Paulette Smith, Assoc. Dir. (pasmith@la-archdiocese.org);

Restorative Justice - t) 818-201-3100 gdevivero@la-archdiocese.org Gonzalo De Vivero, Dir.;

Safeguard the Children - t) 213-637-7227 jvienna@la-archdiocese.org Joan T. Vienna, Dir.;

Schools, Department of Catholic - t) 213-637-7300 dcs@la-archdiocese.org Paul Escala, Supt.;

Scouting, Camp Fire Ministry -

- **Catholic Committee for Girl Scouts and Camp Fire (Girls)** - t) 562-862-8309 cathscoutdg@ca.rr.com Diane Garcia, Chair;
- **Los Angeles Catholic Committee on Scouting (Boys)** - t) 323-255-3824 mab4swim@aol.com Maureen Brown, Chair;

Society of St. Vincent de Paul - t) 800-974-3571; (323) 226-1762 rsweet@svdpla.org David Garcia, Exec. Dir.; Ray Sweet, Pres.;

Special Services - t) 213-637-7636 jbrooks@la-archdiocese.org Judy DeRosa Brooks, Dir.;

Tribunal - t) 213-637-7245 marriagetribunal@la-archdiocese.org Rev. Reynaldo B. Matunog, Judicial Vicar; Rev. Gerardo Galaviz, Adjutant Judicial Vicar;

Vice Chancellor - t) 213-637-7230 frpsandoval@la-archdiocese.org Rev. Parker Sandoval;

Vice Chancellor for Communications - t) 213-637-7259 dscott@la-archdiocese.org David Scott;

Victims Assistance Ministry - t) 213-637-7650 (Office); 800-355-2545 (Toll Free) hbanis@la-archdiocese.org Dr. Heather Banis, Dir.;

Vida Nueva (Archdiocesan Spanish Newspaper) - t) (213) 637-7310 valeman@la-archdiocese.org Victor Aleman, Editor;

Vocations - t) 213-637-7248 frmikeperucho@la-archdiocese.org Rev. Michael Perucho, Dir.; Rev. Pedro Saucedo, Assoc. Dir. (frpsaucedo@la-archdiocese.org);

Women Religious, Vicar for - t) 213-637-7592 Sr. Maria Carlos, E.I.N. (sr.mcarlos@la-archdiocese.org);

ADVISORY BOARDS, COMMISSIONS, COMMITTEES, AND COUNCILS

Archdiocesan Pastoral Council - Most Rev. Jose H. Gomez, Pres.; Virginia Tanawong, Moderator; David Kennedy, Secy.;

Cardinal McIntyre Fund for Charity - Board of Directors - Most Rev. Jose H. Gomez, Chair; Rev. Brian Nunes, Pres.; Sr. Mary Anncarla Costello, S.N.D., Secy.;

Clergy Misconduct Oversight Board - Dr. Kathleen McKenna, Chair; Rhoda Conde, Admin.;

Council of Priests - Most Rev. Jose H. Gomez, Pres.; Rev. Nabor Rios, Chair; Rev. Jose Magana, Vice Chair;

Deacon Council - Dcn. Jorge Ramos, Chair; Dcn. James Carper, Secy.;

Finance Council - Monica Luechtefeld, Chair;

H.I.V./AIDS Ministry Advisory Board - Rev. Christopher D. Ponnet, Co-Chair; Nick Jordan, Co-Chair;

Liturgical Commission - Rev. Marc Reeves, S.J., Chair;

Personnel Board - Rev. Parker Sandoval, Chair;

Priests' Pension Board - Rev. Paul K. Fitzpatrick, Chair;

Sisters' Coordinating Council - Sr. Tracey Sharp, S.C.R.H., Chair;

Theological Commission - Sr. Mary Leanne Hubbard, S.N.D., Co-Chair; Dr. David Albertson, Co-Chair;

DEANERIES

Archdiocesan Pastoral Regions -

- **Santa Barbara Region** - t) 805-682-0442 Rev. Leon Hutton;
  - **Deanery 01** - Rev. Altaire Fernandez;
  - **Deanery 02** - Rev. Lawrence Seyer;

Deanery 03 - Rev. Leon Hutton;
Deanery 04 - Rev. Rizalino J. Carranza;
San Fernando Region - t) 818-361-6009 Most Rev. Alejandro Aclan;
Deanery 05 - Rev. Eben MacDonald;
Deanery 06 - Rev. James M. Bevacqua;
Deanery 07 - Rev. Jose Magana;
Deanery 08 - Rev. Msgr. Craig A. Cox;
San Gabriel Region - t) 626-960-9344
Deanery 09 - Rev. Msgr. John T. Moretta;
Deanery 10 - Rev. John Kyebasuuta;
Deanery 11 - Rev. William T. Easterling;
Deanery 12 - Rev. Msgr. Timothy E. Nichols;
Our Lady of the Angels Region - t) 310-215-0703 Rev. Msgr. Terrance L. Fleming;
Deanery 13 - Rev. Msgr. Liam J. Kidney;
Deanery 14 - Rev. Msgr. Terrance L. Fleming;
Deanery 15 - Rev. Luis Espinoza;
Deanery 16 - Rev. Ever Quintero;
San Pedro Region - t) 562-634-0456 Most Rev. Marc V. Trudeau;
Deanery 17 - Rev. Nabor Rios;
Deanery 18 - Rev. Vicente Raymond Decipeda, M.M.H.C.;
Deanery 19 - Rev. Msgr. Michael W. Meyers;
Deanery 20 - Rev. George Aguilera;

PARISHES, MISSIONS, AND CLERGY

STATE OF CALIFORNIA

ALHAMBRA

All Souls - 1500 W. Main St., Alhambra, CA 91801; Mailing: 29 S. Electric Ave., Alhambra, CA 91801 t) (626) 281-0466 allsoulscc@allsouls-la.org; parish-4320@la-archdiocese.org www.allsouls-la.org/ Rev. Patrick Mbazuigwe, Pst.; CRP Stds.: 64

All Souls Catholic School - (Grades PreK-8) 29 S. Electric Ave., Alhambra, CA 91801 t) (626) 282-5695 school-7530@la-archdiocese.org www.allsoulsla.org Dr. Patrick Allison, Prin.; Maria-Elena Navarro, Prin.; Stds.: 370; Lay Tchrs.: 18

St. Therese - 1110 E. Alhambra Rd., Alhambra, CA 91801; Mailing: 510 N. El Molino St., Alhambra, CA 91801 t) (626) 284-0020 x225 (CRP); (626) 282-2744 parish-4460@la-archdiocese.org www.sttheresechurchalhambra.org (Little Flower) Rev. Philip Sullivan, O.C.D., Pst.; Rev. David Guzman, O.C.D., Assoc. Pst.; Rev. Bernard Perkins, O.C.D., Assoc. Pst.; Rhonda Storey, DRE; CRP Stds.: 127

St. Therese School - (Grades PreK-8) 1106 E. Alhambra Rd., Alhambra, CA 91801 t) (626) 289-3364 admin@sainttheresecarmeliteschool.com; school-7650@la-archdiocese.org www.sainttheresecarmeliteschool.com Alma Cornejo, Prin.; Stds.: 100; Lay Tchrs.: 10

St. Thomas More - 2510 S. Fremont Ave., Alhambra, CA 91803 t) (626) 284-8333 parish-4470@la-archdiocese.org; frthaile@yahoo.com www.stmcatholicalhambra.org/ Rev. Thai Le, Pst.; Dcn. Rogelio Garcia; Sr. Andrea Johnson, C.S.H., Liturgy Dir.; Francisco Ramos, Youth Min.; Gabriella Ramos, DRE; CRP Stds.: 80

St. Thomas More School - (Grades PreK-8) t) (626) 284-5778 school-7660@la-archdiocese.org www.stmcsa.org Norma Gibson, Prin.; Stds.: 156; Lay Tchrs.: 10

ALTADENA

St. Elizabeth of Hungary - 1879 N. Lake Ave., Altadena, CA 91001 t) (626) 797-1167; (626) 797-1167 x15 (CRP) mgalindo@saintelizabethchurch.org; eviramontes@saintelizabethchurch.org www.saintelizabethchurch.org Rev. Modesto Lewis Perez, Pst.; Dcn. Douglas Cremer; Dcn. Jose Gallegos; Dcn. Charles A. Mitchell; Cary Novellas, Admin.; CRP Stds.: 225

St. Elizabeth of Hungary School - (Grades PreK-8) 1840 N. Lake Ave., Altadena, CA 91001 t) (626) 797-7727 school-7600@la-archdiocese.org www.saint-elizabeth.org Richard Gruttadaurio, Prin.; Stds.: 221; Lay Tchrs.: 10

Sacred Heart - 2889 N. Lincoln Ave., Altadena, CA 91001; Mailing: 600 W. Mariposa St., Altadena, CA 91001 t) (626) 794-2046; (626) 798-6961 (CRP) parish-4350@la-archdiocese.org; sacredheart.91001@gmail.com www.sacredheartaltadena.com Rev. Gilbert Guzman; Dcn. Jose Diaz; CRP Stds.: 184

ARCADIA

Annunciation - 1307 E. Longden Ave., Arcadia, CA 91006-5501; Mailing: 2701 S. Peck Rd., Monrovia, CA 91016-5004 t) (626) 447-6202; (626) 446-1625 (CRP) parish-4510@la-archdiocese.org; togetherinfaith@gmail.com www.annunciationchurch.net Rev. Freddie T. Chua, Pst.; Rev. Eugene Herbert, Pastor Emer.; Rev. Msgr. Timothy P. O'Connell, In Res.; Arcie Reza, DRE; CRP Stds.: 136

Holy Angels - 370 Campus Dr., Arcadia, CA 91007 t) (626) 447-1671; (626) 445-2967 (CRP) ha@holyangelsarcadia.org; parish-4530@la-archdiocese.org www.holyangelsarcadia.org Rev. Kevin E. Rettig, Pst.; Rev. Blaise N. Brockman, Assoc. Pst.; Dcn. Arnaldo Lopez; Dcn. Raymond Jaurequi; JoLynn Ann Shehee, DRE; Barbara Ferris, Pst. Min./Coord.; Enrique Reyes, Bus. Mgr.; CRP Stds.: 151

Holy Angels School - (Grades PreK-8) 360 Campus Dr., Arcadia, CA 91007 t) (626) 447-6312 admin@holyangelsarcadia.org; school-7700@la-archdiocese.org www.holyangelsarcadia.net/ Aimee Dyrek, Prin.; Stds.: 305; Lay Tchrs.: 10

ARTESIA

Holy Family - 18708 S. Clarkdale Ave., Artesia, CA 90701 t) (562) 865-2185; (562) 860-5973 (CRP) parish-5910@archdiocese.org www.holyfamilyartesia.org/ Rev. John Cordero, M.M.H.C., Pst.; Rev. Melvin Denina, Assoc. Pst.; Rev. Matthew Fernandez, M.M.H.C., Assoc. Pst.; CRP Stds.: 612

Our Lady of Fatima - (Grades PreK-8) 18626 S. Clarkdale Ave., Artesia, CA 90701 t) (562) 865-1621 olfbusinessoffice@olfartesia.org; school-8970@la-archdiocese.org www.olfartesia.org/ Luis Hayes, Prin.; Stds.: 246; Lay Tchrs.: 10

AVALON

St. Catherine of Alexandria - 800 Beacon St., Avalon, CA 90704; Mailing: P.O. Box 735, Avalon, CA 90704 t) (310) 510-0192 parish-6130@la-archdiocese.org; stcatherineofavalon@gmail.com www.stcatherineoncatalinaisland.org Hermida Hernandez, DRE; Lynda Poindexter, DRE; CRP Stds.: 115

AZUSA

St. Frances of Rome - 501 E. Foothill Blvd., Azusa, CA 91702; Mailing: P.O. Box 637, Azusa, CA 91702 t) (626) 969-1829; (626) 969-1829 x120 (CRP) parish-4610@la-archdiocese.org www.sfrchurch.org Rev. Richard Vega, Pst.; Rev. Roque A.D. Fernandes, Assoc. Pst.; Rev. Michael S. Grieco, Assoc. Pst.; Lupe Roberts, DRE; CRP Stds.: 720

St. Frances of Rome School - (Grades PreK-8) 734 N. Pasadena Ave., Azusa, CA 91702 t) (626) 334-2018 school-7760@la-archdiocese.org Brian Wagner, Prin.; Stds.: 210; Lay Tchrs.: 10

BALDWIN PARK

St. John the Baptist - 3848 Stewart Ave., Baldwin Park, CA 91706; Mailing: 3883 Baldwin Park Blvd., Baldwin Park, CA 91706 t) (626) 962-1004 (CRP); (626) 960-2795 parish-4620@la-archdiocese.org; info@stjohnsbp.org www.stjohnsbp.org Rev. Ismael R. Robles, Par. Admin.; Rev. Emmanuel Sylvester, CMF, Assoc. Pst.; Rev. Jude Uche, Assoc. Pst.; Rev. Juan Gutierrez, Assoc. Pst.; Briceida Bugarin, DRE; CRP Stds.: 637

St. John the Baptist School - (Grades K-8) 3870 Stewart Ave., Baldwin Park, CA 91706 t) (626) 337-1421 school-7770@la-archdiocese.org Deborah Escalera, Prin.; Stds.: 266; Sr. Tchrs.: 1; Lay Tchrs.: 12

Convent - 3963 Baldwin Park Blvd., Baldwin Park, CA 91706 t) (626) 337-0527 loveofgodstjohn@hotmail.com

BELL GARDENS

St. Gertrude - 7025 Garfield Ave., Bell Gardens, CA 90201 t) (562) 927-4495 (Office); (562) 927-3185 (CRP) parish-5820@la-archdiocese.org; stgertrude@verizon.net www.stgertrudethegreatchurch.org Rev. Nabor Rios, Pst.; Rev. Justin Oh, Assoc. Pst.; CRP Stds.: 413

St. Gertrude School - (Grades PreK-8) 6824 Toler Ave., Bell Gardens, CA 90201 t) (562) 927-1216 peggy.weber@stgertrudethegreat.org; school-8860@la-archdiocese.org www.stgertrudethegreat.org Peggy A Weber, Prin.; Stds.: 265; Lay Tchrs.: 10

BELLFLOWER

St. Bernard - 9627 Beach St., Bellflower, CA 90706; Mailing: 9647 Beach St., Bellflower, CA 90706 t) (562) 867-2337 parish-5790@la-archdiocese.org; office@saintbernardcc.org www.saintbernardcc.org Rev. Toribio Gutierrez, C.M., Pst.; Dcn. Ralph Riera; Avelina Jimenez, DRE; CRP Stds.: 109

St. Bernard School - (Grades PreK-8) 9626 Park St., Bellflower, CA 90706 t) (562) 867-9410 school-8830@la-archdiocese.org; sbsoffice@stbernardcatholicschool.com www.stbernardcatholicschool.com Aaron De Loera, Prin.; Stds.: 225; Lay Tchrs.: 11

St. Dominic Savio - 13400 Bellflower Blvd., Bellflower, CA 90706 t) (562) 920-7796 x317 (CRP); (562) 920-7796 saviores24@gmail.com; parish-5800@la-archdiocese.org www.saintdominicsavio.org Rev. Michael Gergen, SDB, Pst.; Rev. Jesse Montes, S.D.B., Assoc. Pst.; Rev. Andrew Ng, S.D.B., Assoc. Pst.; Sr. Cynthia Salas, DRE; CRP Stds.: 400

St. Dominic Savio School - (Grades PreK-8) 9750 Foster Rd., Bellflower, CA 90706 t) (562) 866-3617 mwatson@sdss-bellflower.org; school-8840@la-archdiocese.org www.sdss-bellflower.org Maria Watson, Prin.; Stds.: 290; Sr. Tchrs.: 5; Lay Tchrs.: 13

BEVERLY HILLS

Good Shepherd - 504 N. Roxbury Dr., Beverly Hills, CA 90210 t) (310) 285-5425 info@gsbh.org; parish-4800@la-archdiocese.org www.gsbh.org Rev. Edward C. Benioff, Pst.; Rev. Colm O'Ryan, In Res.; Wendy Rappe, DRE; CRP Stds.: 52

Good Shepherd School - (Grades PreK-8) 148 S. Linden Dr., Beverly Hills, CA 90212 t) (310) 275-8601 admissions@gsbh.net www.gsbh.net Lisa Widmann, Prin.; Stds.: 195; Lay Tchrs.: 10

BURBANK

St. Finbar - 2010 W. Olive Ave., Burbank, CA 91506 t) (818) 940-3921 sally@stfinbarburbank.org; parish-3740@la-archdiocese.org www.stfinbarburbank.org Rev. Francis Mendoza, Pst.; Veronica Hernandez, DRE; CRP Stds.: 330

St. Finbar School - (Grades PreK-8) 2120 W. Olive Ave., Burbank, CA 91506 t) (818) 848-0191 finbar4545@yahoo.com; school-7070@la-archdiocese.org www.saintfinbar.org Michael Marasco, Prin.; Stds.: 300; Lay Tchrs.: 10

St. Francis Xavier - 3801 Scott Rd., Burbank, CA 91504 t) (818) 504-4411 (CRP); (818) 504-4400 religioused@sfxburbank.com; parish-3760@la-archdiocese.org www.sfxburbank.com Rev. Sebastian Vettickal, C.M.I., Pst.; Dcn. Jaime Abrera; Dcn. James Roope; Rita Recker, Pst. Assoc.; Rosie Roope, DRE; CRP Stds.: 93

St. Francis Xavier School - (Grades PreK-8) 3601 Scott Rd., Burbank, CA 91504 t) (818) 504-4422

school-7090@la-archdiocese.org www.sfxschool.org Paul Sullivan, Prin.; Stds.: 235; Lay Tchrs.: 18

St. Robert Bellarmine - 143 N. Fifth St., Burbank, CA 91501; Mailing: 520 E. Orange Grove Blvd., Burbank, CA 91501 t) (818) 846-3443 parish-3800@la-archdiocese.org; accounting@srbburbank.org www.srbburbank.org Rev. Marco Antonio Ortiz, Pst.; Carol Gallagher, DRE; CRP Stds.: 90

St. Robert Bellarmine School - (Grades PreK-8) 154 N. Fifth St., Burbank, CA 91501 t) (818) 842-5033 info@strobertbellarmineburbank.com; school-7130@la-archdiocese.org www.srbburbankschool.com Angite Riggio, Prin.; Stds.: 200; Lay Tchrs.: 10

CAMARILLO

St. Junipero Serra - 5205 Upland Rd., Camarillo, CA 93012 t) (805) 482-6417 parish-3320@la-archdiocese.org; parish@padreserra.org www.padreserra.org Rev. Patrick Mullen, Pst.; Dcn. John Picard; Dcn. William Spies; Dcn. Robert Fargo; Dcn. Neil Joseph Kingsley; Dcn. Jack William Redmond II; Dcn. Arnold Peter Reyes; Dcn. Joseph Felix Torti; Dcn. Genaro Roy Gacasan; Dcn. Luc Papillon; Tere Delgado, DRE; Teresa Runyon, Pst. Assoc.; CRP Stds.: 315

St. Mary Magdalen - 25 Las Posas Rd., Camarillo, CA 93010; Mailing: 2532 Ventura Blvd., Camarillo, CA 93010 t) (805) 482-1219 (CRP); (805) 484-0532 redirector@smmcam.org; office@smmcam.org www.smmcam.org Rev. Preston P. Passos, Pst.; Rev. Francis V. Aguilar, Assoc. Pst.; Rev. Lawrence J. Dowdel Jr., Assoc. Pst.; Dcn. George Bednar; Dcn. Patrick Dale Carman; Dcn. Andrew Cottam; Dcn. George J. Esseff Jr.; Dcn. Manuel J. Martinez; Dcn. Ronald Dale Moon; Jeremiah Shoop, Youth Min.; CRP Stds.: 318

St. Mary Magdalen School - (Grades PreK-8) 2534 Ventura Blvd., Camarillo, CA 93010 t) (805) 482-2611 school-6670@la-archdiocese.org; office@smmschool.net www.smmschool.net Michael Ronan, Prin.; Stds.: 301; Lay Tchrs.: 15

CANOGA PARK

Our Lady of the Valley - 22021 Gault St., Canoga Park, CA 91303-1804 t) (818) 592-2880 receptionist@olvcp.org; parish-3400@la-archdiocese.org www.ourladyofthevalley.org Rev. Alejandro A. Amayun (Philippines), Pst.; Rev. Samuel Aceves Cuarto, M.I, Assoc. Pst.; Estrela del Bando, C.H.S., DRE; CRP Stds.: 300

Our Lady of the Valley School - (Grades PreK-8) 22041 Gault St., Canoga Park, CA 91303-1804 t) (818) 592-2894 principal@olvcrusaders.org; school-6760@la.archdiocese.org www.olvcrusaders.org Miguel Beltran, Prin.; Stds.: 148; Lay Tchrs.: 10

CARPINTERIA

St. Joseph - 1532 Linden Ave., Carpinteria, CA 93013 t) (805) 684-2181; (805) 684-2181 x225 (CRP) c) (805) 696-3773 stjoseph@stjosephchurch.org; nancy@stjosephchurch.org www.stjosephchurch.org Rev. Msgr. Richard Martini, Pst.; Rev. Manuel Ramos, Assoc. Pst.; Dcn. Genaro Aispuro; Dcn. Michael Joseph Betliskey; Rev. Rafael Marin-Leon, In Res.; Nancy Perez, DRE; CRP Stds.: 170

St. Joseph Chapel - 4691 7th St., Carpinteria, CA 93103

CARSON

St. Philomena - 21900 S. Main St., Carson, CA 90745-2998 t) (310) 830-6180 (CRP); (310) 835-7161 rmgrosa@yahoo.com; parish-6210@la-archdiocese.org www.stphilomenaparish.org Rev. Francis Ilano, Pst.; Rev. Gregorio Hidalgo, Assoc. Pst.; Rev. Mikaele Mataafa, Assoc. Pst.; Rosa Garcia, DRE; CRP Stds.: 832

St. Philomena School - (Grades PreK-8) 21832 S. Main St., Carson, CA 90745 t) (310) 835-4827 school-9240@la-archdiocese.org www.stphilomenaschool.org Sr. Mary John Schik, Prin.; Stds.: 325; Lay Tchrs.: 10

Convent - 21832 1/2 S. Main St., Carson, CA 90745 t) 310-834-9180 sr.maryjohn@la-archdiocese.org Sr. Mary John Schik, Sr.;

CHATSWORTH

St. John Eudes - 9901 Mason Ave., Chatsworth, CA 91311 t) (818) 341-3680 parish-3450@la-archdiocese.org www.sjeparish.net Rev. Ethan Southard, Admin.; CRP Stds.: 454

St. John Eudes School - (Grades PreK-8) 9925 Mason Ave., Chatsworth, CA 91311 t) (818) 341-1454 lstrom@stjohneudes.org; school-6810@la-archdiocese.org sjeschool.net/ Lizette Strom, Prin.; Stds.: 231; Lay Tchrs.: 12

CLAREMONT

Our Lady of the Assumption - 435 Berkeley Ave., Claremont, CA 91711 t) (909) 626-3596 reception@olaclaremont.org; parish-4670@la-archdiocese.org www.olaclaremont.org Rev. Charles J. Ramirez, Pst.; Rev. Paul Phan, Assoc. Pst.; Rev. Matthew T. Cumberland; Dcn. Joe Domond; Dcn. Rodolfo R. Leyva; Dcn. Robert Steighner; CRP Stds.: 417

Our Lady of the Assumption School - (Grades PreK-8) 611 W. Bonita Ave., Claremont, CA 91711 t) (909) 626-7135 school-7840@la-archdiocese.org www.ola-ca.org Bernadette Boyle, Prin.; Stds.: 415; Lay Tchrs.: 10

COMMERCE

St. Marcellinus - 2349 Strong Ave., Commerce, CA 90040 t) (323) 269-2733; (323) 266-4938 (CRP) adq311@yahoo.com; parish-4270@la-archdiocese.org www.stmarcellinus.org Rev. Gilbert Cruz, Sacramental Min.; Dr. Humberto Ramos, Dir.; Alejandra Duarte, DRE; CRP Stds.: 150

COMPTON

Our Lady of Victory - 519 E. Palmer St., Compton, CA 90221 t) (310) 631-1831 (CRP); (310) 631-3233 parish-5740@la-archdiocese.org; office@olvcompton.org olvcompton.org/ Rev. Gilberto Rodriguez, S.T., Pst.; Rev. Roberto Mena, S.T., Assoc. Pst.; Rev. Domingo Rodriguez, S.T., Assoc. Pst.; Rev. Carlos Zacarias, S.T., Assoc. Pst.; Ana Aguilar, DRE; CRP Stds.: 440

Our Lady of Victory School - (Grades K-8) 601 E. Palmer St., Compton, CA 90221 t) (310) 631-1320 principal@ourladyofvictorycatholicschool.org; school-8790@la-archdiocese.org www.ourladyofvictorycatholicschool.org Dcn. Arturo Gonzalez, Prin.; Stds.: 218; Lay Tchrs.: 9

Sagrado Corazon, Sacred Heart - 1720 N. Culver Ave., Compton, CA 90222 t) (310) 635-5436 parish-5750@la-archdiocese.org Rev. Victor Raul Ramos, Pst.; CRP Stds.: 290

COVINA

St. Louise de Marillac - 1720 E. Covina Blvd., Covina, CA 91724 t) (626) 915-7873; (626) 332-5822 (CRP) info@stlouisedm.org; faithformation@stlouisedm.org www.stlouisedm.org Rev. Robert P. Fulton, Pst.; Rev. Emmanuel Francis, Assoc. Pst.; Dcn. Peter Brause; Dcn. Alan Holderness; Dcn. Omar Uriarte; CRP Stds.: 206

St. Louise de Marillac School - (Grades PreK-8) 1728 E. Covina Blvd., Covina, CA 91724 t) (626) 966-2317 principal@stlouisedm.org; school-7790@la-archdiocese.org www.stlouisedmschool.org Catherine Ossa, Prin.; Stds.: 229; Lay Tchrs.: 10

Sacred Heart - 344 W. Workman St., Covina, CA 91723 t) (626) 331-7914 (CRP); (626) 332-3570 parish-4580@la-archdiocese.org; info@sacredheart.cc www.sacredheart.cc Rev. William T. Easterling, Pst.; Rev. Msgr. Brian M. Cavanagh, Assoc. Pst.; Rev. James J. Kelly, Assoc. Pst.; Dcn. Ronald Butler; Dcn. John G. Horn; CRP Stds.: 690

Sacred Heart School - (Grades PreK-8) 360 W. Workman St., Covina, CA 91723 t) (626) 332-7222 shscovina@hotmail.com; school-7730@la-archdiocese.org www.shs.cc Claudia Tice, Prin.; Stds.: 204; Lay Tchrs.: 10

CUDAHY

Sagrado Corazon y Santa Maria de Guadalupe - 4235 Clara St., Cudahy, CA 90201 t) (323) 562-3356 parish-6040@la-archdiocese.org websitedesignwebhosting.com/sagcor/ Rev. Miguel Angel Gutierrez, M.S.C., Pst.; Rev. Raul Silva, MSC, Par..Vicar; CRP Stds.: 201

CULVER CITY

St. Augustine - 3850 Jasmine Ave., Culver City, CA 90232 t) (310) 838-2477; (310) 838-2477 x209 (DRE / CRP) businessmgr@staugustineadla.org; socorro@staugustineadla.org www.st-augustine-church.org Rev. Christopher B. Fagan, Pst.; Rev. Esteban Marquez, Pst. Assoc.; Dcn. Sonal Seneviratne, Bus. Mgr.; Socorro Parrales, DRE; CRP Stds.: 250

St. Augustine School - (Grades PreK-8) 3819 Clarington Ave., Culver City, CA 90232 t) (310) 838-3144 bnguyen@la-archdiocese.org; mbriseno@sasmail.org www.staugustineschool.com Dr. Beate Nguyen, Prin.; Stds.: 206; Lay Tchrs.: 10

St. Augustine Licenced Preschool - 3819 Clarington Ave., Culver City, CA 90232 t) (310) 838-3144 bnguyen@sasmail.org www.staugustineschool.com Dr. Beate Nguyen, Prin.;

DIAMOND BAR

St. Denis - 2151 S. Diamond Bar Blvd., Diamond Bar, CA 91765-2981 t) (909) 861-7106 jtorres@stdenis.org; parish-4690@la-archdiocese.org www.stdenis.org Rev. John Palmer, Pst.; Rev. Dennis Mongrain, Assoc. Pst.; Dcn. Alfred Guerrero; Dcn. Dennis Shin; Celia Flores, DRE; Jay Duller, Dir., Adult Faith Formation & Christian Initiation; CRP Stds.: 240

DOWNEY

Our Lady of Perpetual Help - 10727 Downey Ave., Downey, CA 90241 t) (562) 923-3246 parish-5720@la-archdiocese.org; office@olphdowney.com www.olphdowney.com Rev. Daniel Garcia, Admin.; Rev. Joseph Aline Dadiri, Assoc. Pst.; Dcn. Carlos Origel; Dcn. John Saavedra; Theresa Nicholas, DRE; CRP Stds.: 580

Our Lady of Perpetual Help School - (Grades PreK-8) 10441 Downey Ave., Downey, CA 90241 t) (562) 869-9969 school-8770@la-archdiocese.org www.ourladyschool.com Douglas Rynerson, Prin.; Stds.: 328; Lay Tchrs.: 18

St. Raymond - 12348 Paramount Blvd., Downey, CA 90242 t) (562) 862-6959 (CRP); (562) 923-4509 parish-5870@la-archdiocese.org www.saintraymond.org Rev. Samuel Ward, Pst.; Rev. Solomon Nwokocha, Assoc. Pst.; Rev. Justin Ordoveza, Assoc. Pst.; Rev. John Higgins, Pastor Emer.; Jennifer Quinones, DRE; CRP Stds.: 450

St. Raymond School - (Grades PreK-8) 12320 Paramount Blvd., Downey, CA 90242 t) (562) 862-3210 school-8900@la-archdiocese.org www.straymondschool-downey.org Claudia Rodarte, Prin.; Stds.: 350; Lay Tchrs.: 10

EL MONTE

Nativity - 3743 N. Tyler Ave., El Monte, CA 91731 t) (626) 448-8895 (CRP); (626) 444-2511 parish-4550@la-archdiocese.org; parish@nativityelmonte.org www.nativityelmonte.org Rev. Roberto F. Jaranilla Jr., Pst.; Rev. Joseph Dang Kim Nguyen, Assoc. Pst.; Sandra Jinesta, DRE; CRP Stds.: 253

Nativity School - (Grades PreK-8) 10907 St. Louis Dr., El Monte, CA 91731 t) (626) 448-2414 principal@nativityschoolelmonte.org; school-7720@la-archdiocese.org www.nativityschoolelmonte.org Sr. Stacy Reiniman, Prin.; Stds.: 185; Sr. Tchrs.: 1; Lay Tchrs.: 11

Nativity Convent - 10929 Saint Louis Dr., El Monte, CA 91731 t) (626) 448-6575 Sr. Stacy Reineman, Contact;

Our Lady of Guadalupe - 11359 Coffield Ave., El Monte, CA 91731 t) (626) 448-7137 (CRP); (626) 448-1795 parish-4560@la-archdiocese.org www.olglupita.org Rev. Julio Cesar Ramos Ortega, M.G., Pst.; Rev. Carlos May Correa, M.G, Assoc. Pst.; Jenny Areas, DRE; CRP Stds.: 2,100

EL SEGUNDO

St. Andrew - 538 Concord St., El Segundo, CA 90245 t) 310-322-1892 frarsmith@la-archdiocese.org Rt. Rev. Alexei R. Smith, Pst.;

St. Anthony - 720 E. Grand Ave., El Segundo, CA 90245; Mailing: 215 Lomita St., El Segundo, CA 90245 t) (310) 322-4392 (CRP); (310) 322-4392 dre.stanthonyes@outlook.com; parish-6120@la-archdiocese.org www.stanthonyes.com Rev. Paul E. Vigil, Pst.; Timothy Rodrick, DRE; CRP Stds.: 100

ENCINO

St. Cyril - 15520 Ventura Blvd., Encino, CA 91436; Mailing: 4601 Firmament Ave., Encino, CA 91436 t) (818) 986-8234 parish@st-cyril.org; parish-3440@la-archdiocese.org www.st-cyril.org Rev. Eben MacDonald, Pst.; Rev. Cyprian Carlo, In Res.; Dianne Eusebio, Youth Min.; Ray Perry, DRE; CRP Stds.: 48

St. Cyril School - (Grades PreK-8) 4548 Haskell Ave., Encino, CA 91436 t) (818) 501-4155 school-6800@la-archdiocese.org www.stcyril.net Ryan Halverson, Prin.; Angelica Pugliese, Prin.; Stds.: 280; Lay Tchrs.: 10

Our Lady of Grace - 5011 White Oak Ave., Encino, CA 91316; Mailing: 5001 White Oak Ave, Encino, CA 91316 t) (818) 342-4686 administrator@ourladyofgrace.org; dre@ourladyofgrace.org www.ourladyofgrace.org Rev. Marinello Saguin, Admin.; Jeannie Rogers, Liturgy Dir.; Anisha Virgen, Parish Life Coord.; Jesse Rodriguez, DRE; CRP Stds.: 380

Our Lady of Grace School - (Grades PreSchool-8) 17720 Ventura Blvd., Encino, CA 91316 t) (818) 344-4126 principal@ourladyofgrace.co; school-6740@la-archdiocese.org www.ourladyofgrace.co Thomas Ambriz, Prin.; Stds.: 320; Lay Tchrs.: 15

FILLMORE

St. Francis of Assisi - 1048 W. Ventura St., Fillmore, CA 93015 t) (805) 524-1306 stfrancisoffice@spcglobal.net; parish-3210@la-archdiocese.org www.stfrancisfillmore.wordpress.com Rev. Alejandro A. Amayun (Philippines), Pst.; Raymond Rodriguez; Leti Olvera, Youth Min.; Gloria Ordaz, DRE; CRP Stds.: 175

San Salvador Mission - 4045 E. Carter St., Piru, CA 93040; Mailing: PO Box 805, Piru, CA 93040 Rev. Eben MacDonald, Pst.;

GARDENA

St. Anthony of Padua - 1050 W. 163rd St., Gardena, CA 90247 t) (310) 323-0860 (CRP); (310) 327-5830 jcastaneda@saintanthonygardena.org; msgrspilato@la-archdiocese.org www.saintanthonygardena.org Rev. Msgr. Sabato "Sal" A. Pilato, Pst.; Rev. Roberto Pirrone, Assoc. Pst.; Sr. Luz Maria Hernandez, CRE; Jose Luis Castaneda, Bus. Mgr.; Nely Go, DRE; CRP Stds.: 270

St. Anthony of Padua School - (Grades K-8) 1003 W. 163rd St., Gardena, CA 90247 t) (310) 329-7170 contact@stanthonygardena.org; school-8820@la-archdiocese.org www.stanthonygardena.org Angela Grey, Prin.; Stds.: 220; Sr. Tchrs.: 1; Lay Tchrs.: 8

St. Anthony of Padua Convent - 1050 W. 161st St., Gardena, CA 90247 t) (310) 323-9942 maryvc82@gmail.com Sr. Mary Valadez, M.C., Contact;

St. Francis Korean Center - 2040 W. Artesia Blvd., Torrance, CA 90504 t) (310) 324-8159 stfranciskcc@hotmail.com Rev. Byeong Hoon Kim, O.F.M. Conv., Chap.; Rev. Soonhyun Macario Koh, O.F.M.Conv., Chap.; Rev. Changwoo Lee, O.F.M.Conv., Chap.;

St. Anthony's Day Nursery - 1044 W. 163rd St., Gardena, CA 90247 t) (310) 329-8654 stanthonyspreschoolg@gmail.com Sr. Gisela Pedrasa, M.C., Dir.;

Maria Regina - 2150 W. 135th St., Gardena, CA 90249 t) (310) 323-0030 office@mariareginagardena.net; parish-5710@la-archdiocese.org www.mariareginagardena.net Rev. Sang V. Tran (Vietnam), Pst.; Rev. Martin Enyinna Akanaefu, Assoc. Pst.; Dcn. Ramon Nunez; Dcn. Matthew Phuoc Van Nguyen; Yolanda Marquez, DRE; CRP Stds.: 177

Maria Regina School - (Grades PreK-8) 13510 S. Van Ness Ave., Gardena, CA 90249 t) (310) 327-9133 school-8760@la-archdiocese.org www.mregina.org Lynette Lino, Prin.; Stds.: 225; Lay Tchrs.: 11

GLENDALE

Holy Family - 209 E. Lomita Ave., Glendale, CA 91205 t) (818) 247-2222 parish@hfglendale.org; rel-ed@hfglendale.org www.hfglendale.org Rev. Anthony Garcias, Admin.; Rev. Michael Samuel Mesa, Assoc. Pst.; Rev. Alexander Chukwuemeka Okondu-Ugba (Nigeria), Assoc. Pst.; Dcn. Ron Baker; Dcn. Neon Recuenco; Dcn. John Steele; Marietta Rogers, DRE; CRP Stds.: 298

Holy Family Grade School - (Grades PreK-8) 400 S. Louise St., Glendale, CA 91205 t) (818) 243-9239 school-6890@la-archdiocese.org; fsuelto@la-archdiocese.org www.hfgsglendale.org Dr. Fidela Suelto, Prin.; Stds.: 240; Lay Tchrs.: 15

Holy Family High School - (Grades 9-12) 400 E. Lomita Ave., Glendale, CA 91205 t) (818) 241-3178 school-9830@la-archdiocese.org www.hfhsglendale.org (Girls) College Prep Robert Bringas, Headmaster; Stds.: 79; Lay Tchrs.: 8

Incarnation - 1001 N. Brand Blvd., Glendale, CA 91202; Mailing: 121 W. Glenoaks Blvd., Glendale, CA 91202 t) (818) 242-2579 receptionist@incaglendale.org; religioused@incaglendale.org www.incaglendale.org Rev. Rodel G. Balagtas, Pst.; Rev. Ramon Reyes, Assoc. Pst.; Dcn. Dominic Pontrelli; Dcn. Michael Morgan, Bus. Mgr.; Rev. Parker Sandoval, In Res.; Ruben Castorena, DRE; CRP Stds.: 207

Incarnation School - (Grades PreK-8) 123 W. Glenoaks Blvd., Glendale, CA 91202-2908 t) (818) 241-2269 school-6920@la-archdiocese.org www.incaschool.org Colby Boysen, Prin.; Stds.: 267; Lay Tchrs.: 14

Pre-School - 214 W. Fairview Ave., Glendale, CA 91202 t) (818) 241-2264 preschool@incaschool.org Rosemarie Muscarella, Dir.;

GLENDORA

St. Dorothy - 241 S. Valley Center, Glendora, CA 91741-3854 t) (626) 914-3941 (CRP); (626) 914-3941 x117 parish-4600@la-archdiocese.org; fr.ron@stdorothy.org www.stdorothy.org Rev. Ronald Lee Clark, Pst.; Rev. Daniel Vega, Assoc. Pst.; Rev. Msgr. Norman F. Priebe, In Res.; Dcn. Philip Luevanos; Bernadette M. Martin, DRE; CRP Stds.: 281

St. Dorothy School - (Grades PreK-8) 215 S. Valley Center Ave., Glendora, CA 91741 t) (626) 335-0772 info@stdorothyschool.com; school-7750@la-archdiocese.org www.stdorothyschool.com Adrienne Ferguson, Prin.; Stds.: 208; Lay Tchrs.: 11

GRANADA HILLS

St. Euphrasia - 11779 Shoshone Ave., Granada Hills, CA 91344 t) (818) 360-4611; (818) 831-9239 (CRP) sredominguez@stemail.org; fralden@stemail.org www.steuphrasia.org Rev. Alden J. Sison, Admin.; Sr. Elizabeth Dominguez, DRE; CRP Stds.: 196

St. Euphrasia School - (Grades PreK-8) 17637 Mayerling St., Granada Hills, CA 91344 t) (818) 363-5515 school-7200@la-archdiocese.org www.steuphrasiaschool.org Jean Ornelaz, Prin.; Stds.: 188; Lay Tchrs.: 11

St. John Baptist de la Salle - 10738 Hayvenhurst Ave., Granada Hills, CA 91344 t) (818) 368-1514 (CRP); (818) 363-2535 x225 (Bus. Mgr.) dre@sjbdls.org; parish-3910@la-archdiocese.org www.sjbdls.com Rev. Ramon G. Valera, Pst.; Rev. Tovia Lui, Assoc. Pst.; Rev. Msgr. Robert L. Milbauer, Pastor Emer.; Dcn. Dan Revetto; Sandy Cole, DRE; CRP Stds.: 446

St. John Baptist de la Salle School - (Grades PreK-8) 16535 Chatsworth St., Granada Hills, CA 91344 t) (818) 363-2270 office@sjbdls.org; school-7220@la-archdiocese.org www.sjbdls.org Monica Castaneda, Prin.; Stds.: 380; Lay Tchrs.: 10

GUADALUPE

Our Lady of Guadalupe - 1164 Obispo St., Guadalupe, CA 93434; Mailing: P.O. Box 897, Guadalupe, CA 93434 t) (805) 343-4404 (CRP); (805) 343-2181 dfunkhouser@la-archdiocese.org; parish-2920@la-archdiocese.org www.olg-guadalupe.org Rev. Rolando A. Sierra, Pst.; Dawn Funkhouser, DRE; CRP Stds.: 229

HACIENDA HEIGHTS

St. John Vianney - 1345 Turnbull Canyon Rd., Hacienda Heights, CA 91745 t) (626) 330-2269 parish-4710@la-archdiocese.org www.sjvhh.org Rev. Msgr. Timothy E. Nichols, Pst.; Rev. Joseph Choi, Assoc. Pst.; Rev. James Tin Mg Htwe, Assoc. Pst.; Dcn. Jesse Martinez; Dcn. Richard Noon; CRP Stds.: 344

HAWAIIAN GARDENS

St. Peter Chanel - 12001 214th St., Hawaiian Gardens, CA 90716 t) (562) 924-7591 parish-6020@la-archdiocese.org www.spcomv.com Rev. Lino Estadilla, O.M.V., Pst.; Rev. Edward Broom, O.M.V., Assoc. Pst.; Rev. David Yankaukas, O.M.V., Assoc. Pst.; Dcn. Jonas Verdeflor, OMV, In Res.; Rev. Gerald Wright, OMV, In Res.; Rev. Lawrence T. Darnell, O.M.V., In Res.; CRP Stds.: 1,320

HAWTHORNE

St. Joseph - 11901 Acacia Ave., Hawthorne, CA 90250 t) (310) 679-1139; (310) 679-1139 x103 (CRP) parish-6170@la-archdiocese.org; info@stjoseph-haw.org www.stjosephhawthorne.org/ Rev. Arturo Velasco, Pst.; Rev. Roberto Rueda Catetano, Assoc. Pst.; Rev. Kamil Ziolkowski, Assoc. Pst.; Luz Maria Salgado, DRE; CRP Stds.: 1,256

St. Joseph School - (Grades PreK-8) 11886 Acacia Ave., Hawthorne, CA 90250 t) (310) 679-1014 kgutierrez@saintjosephsschool.org; school-9210@la-archdiocese.org www.saintjoe.online Kevin Donohue, Prin.; Stds.: 310; Lay Tchrs.: 12

HERMOSA BEACH

Our Lady of Guadalupe - 440 Massey Ave., Hermosa Beach, CA 90254; Mailing: 244 Prospect Ave., Hermosa Beach, CA 90254 t) (310) 372-7077 office@olgmail.org; parish-6100@la-archdiocese.org www.ourladyofguadalupechurch.org Rev. Paul Gawlowski, O.F.M. Conv, Pst.; Rev. Carlos Morales, O.F.M.Conv., Assoc. Pst.; Bro. John Fleming, O.F.M.Conv., In Res.; Rev. Joseph Kim, O.F.M.Conv., In Res.; Rev. Peter Mallin, O.F.M.Conv., In Res.; Theresa Avila, DRE; CRP Stds.: 175

Our Lady of Guadalupe School - (Grades PreK-8) 320 Massey Ave., Hermosa Beach, CA 90254 t) (310) 372-7486 school-9150@la-archdiocese.org; info@ourladyofguadalupeschool.org www.ourladyofguadalupeschool.org April Beuder, Prin.; Stds.: 237; Lay Tchrs.: 12

Our Lady of Guadalupe Preschool - 340 Massey Ave., Hermosa Beach, CA 90254 t) (310) 372-7486 info@ourladyofguadalupeschool.org; school-9150@la-archdiocese.org www.ourladyofguadalupeschool.org/preschool Maritza Corleto, Dir.;

HUNTINGTON PARK

St. Martha - 6000 Seville St., Huntington Park, CA 90255; Mailing: P.O. Box 2127, Huntington Park, CA 90255 t) (323) 585-0386 parish-5840@la-archdiocese.org; stamartha@aol.com www.stmarthaparishhp.org Rev. Julio Cesar Ramos Ortega, M.G., Pst.; Rev. Alejandro Cortez, MG, Assoc. Pst.; Dcn. Ciro Augusto Garza; CRP Stds.: 493

St. Matthias - 3095 E. Florence Ave., Huntington Park, CA 90255; Mailing: 7105 Mission Pl., Huntington Park, CA 90255 t) (323) 588-2134; (323) 588-2134 x13 (CRP) sanmatias.hp@gmail.com; parish-5850@la-archdiocese.org stmatthiashp.org/ Rev. Ruben D. Restrepo, C.M., Pst.; Rev. Franklin Cubas, Assoc. Pst.; CRP Stds.: 413

St. Matthias School - (Grades PreK-8) 7130 Cedar St., Huntington Park, CA 90255 t) (323) 588-7253 school-8880@la-archdiocese.org www.saintmatthiasschool.org Joe Gallardo, Prin.; Stds.: 171; Lay Tchrs.: 10

INGLEWOOD

St. John Chrysostom - 546 E. Florence Ave., Inglewood, CA 90301 t) (310) 677-2736; (310) 677-2736 x500 (CRP) dresjc@gmail.com; sjcparish.559@gmail.com www.stjohnchrysostomparish.org Rev. Alexis Ibarra, Admin.; Rev. Alfonso Abarca, S.D.B., Assoc. Pst.; Rev. Paul A. Sustayta, Assoc. Pst.; Rev. Daniel Lopez, Assoc. Pst.; Rev. Gerardo Galaviz, In Res.; Dcn. Juan Villaseñor; CRP Stds.: 395

St. John Chrysostom School - (Grades PreK-8) 530 E. Florence Ave., Inglewood, CA 90301 t) (310) 677-5868 info@stjohninglewood.org; school-8660@la-archdiocese.org www.stjohninglewood.org Miguel Arizmendi, Prin.; Stds.: 238; Lay Tchrs.: 10

IRWINDALE

Our Lady of Guadalupe - 16025 E. Cypress St., Irwindale, CA 91706 t) (626) 962-3649 x221; (626) 962-3649 (CRP) olgirwindale@earthlink.net; parish-4570@la-archdiocese.org www.olgirwindale.org Rev. Hector William Rodriguez, Admin.; Ana Juarez, DRE; CRP Stds.: 1,269

ISLA VISTA

St. Mark University Parish - 6550 Picasso Rd., Isla Vista, CA 93117 t) (805) 968-1078 parish-3070@la-archdiocese.org www.saint-marks.net Serving the Catholic community in Isla Vista and at the University of California-Santa Barbara (UCSB) Rev. Ryan Thornton, O.F.M., Admin.;

LA CANADA FLINTRIDGE

St. Bede the Venerable - 215 Foothill Blvd., La Canada Flintridge, CA 91011 t) (818) 949-4300 lisa@bede.org; jamie@bede.org www.bede.org Rev. James M. Bevacqua, Pst.; Andre Nicdao, Youth Min.; Moira Arjani, DRE; CRP Stds.: 244

St. Bede the Venerable School - (Grades PreK-8) 4524 Crown Ave., La Canada Flintridge, CA 91011 t) (818) 790-7884 school-6940@la-archdiocese.org; contact@stbedeschool.net www.stbedeschool.net Elizabeth Bozzo, Prin.; Stds.: 265; Lay Tchrs.: 15

LA CRESCENTA

St. James the Less - 4625 Dunsmore Ave., La Crescenta, CA 91214; Mailing: 4651 Dunsmore Ave, La Crescenta, CA 91214 t) (818) 249-2008 (CRP); (818) 248-3442 parish-3650@la-archdiocese.org www.hrsjcatholic.com Twinned parish and school with Holy Redeemer, Montrose Rev. Olin Mayfield, Admin.; Rev. Michael S. Grieco, Assoc. Pst.; CRP Stds.: 110

St. James the Less - Holy Redeemer Elementary School - (Grades PreK-8) 4635 Dunsmore Ave., La Crescenta, CA 91214 t) (818) 248-7778 jwick@hrsjs.org; school-6990@la-archdiocese.org www.hrsjs.org Combined school of Holy Redeemer, Montrose and St James, La Crescenta Dr. John Wick, Prin.; Stds.: 80; Lay Tchrs.: 7

LA MIRADA

Beatitudes of Our Lord - 13013 S. Santa Gertrudes Ave., La Mirada, CA 90638 t) (562) 943-1521 (Office); (562) 943-5678 (CRP) bol@ca.rr.com; parish-5900@la-archdiocese.org www.bolchurch.net Rev. Edward R. Dover, Pst.; Rev. Anthony J. Page, Pastor Emer.; Dcn. Bruce Allen Clark; Dcn. Hector M. Hidalgo; CRP Stds.: 113

Beatitudes of Our Lord School - (Grades PreK-8) 13021 S. Santa Gertrudes Ave., La Mirada, CA 90638 t) (562) 943-3218 office@bolschool.org; school-8960@la-archdiocese.org www.bolschool.org Andre Villegas, Prin.; Stds.: 278; Lay Tchrs.: 16

St. Paul of the Cross - 14020 Foster Rd., La Mirada, CA 90638 t) (562) 445-4542 x2 (CRP); (562) 921-2914 parish-6010@la-archdiocese.org www.stpaulofthecross.org Rev. Joseph Visperas, Pst.; Dcn. Mark Orcutt; Dcn. Timothy J. Roberto; Theresa Bartolone, DRE; CRP Stds.: 172

St. Paul of the Cross School - (Grades PreK-8) 14030 Foster Rd., La Mirada, CA 90638 t) (562) 445-4542 x1 school-9050@la-archdiocese.org www.stpaulofthecrosslamirada.org Sandra Hernandez, Prin.; Stds.: 112; Lay Tchrs.: 8

LA PUENTE

St. Joseph - 550 N. Glendora Ave., La Puente, CA 91744 t) (626) 709-4832 (CRP); (626) 336-2001 bvargas@la-archdiocese.org; st.joseph.secretary@gmail.com www.stjosephchurch-lapuente.org Rev. Miguel Angel Menjivar (El Salvador), Admin.; Rev. Jean Tattegrain, Assoc. Pst.; CRP Stds.: 302

St. Joseph School - (Grades PreK-8) 15650 E. Temple Ave., La Puente, CA 91744 t) 626-336-2821 stjoseph1@gmail.com; school-7870@la-archdiocese.org www.st-josephschool-lp.org Roger Ranney, Prin.; Stds.: 194; Lay Tchrs.: 10

St. Louis of France - 13935 E. Temple Ave., La Puente, CA 91746; Mailing: 630 Ardilla Ave., La Puente, CA 91746 t) (626) 918-7002 (CRP); (626) 918-8314 saintlouisoffrance@gmail.com; parish-4630@la-archdiocese.org www.stlouisoffrancechurch-lapuente.org Rev. Julio Domenech, Admin.; Rev. Lawrence J. Dowdel Jr., Assoc. Pst.; Dcn. Jose Rodriguez; Dolores Lazcano, DRE; CRP Stds.: 965

St. Louis of France School - (Grades PreK-8) 13901 E. Temple Ave., La Puente, CA 91746-2021 t) (626) 918-6210 slfoffice@saintlouisoffrance.org; school-7780@la-archdiocese.org www.slfschool.org Lorraine Ovalle, Prin.; Stds.: 89; Lay Tchrs.: 6

LAKE BALBOA

St. Bridget of Sweden - 7100 Whitaker Ave., Lake Balboa, CA 91406; Mailing: 16707 Gault St., Van Nuys, CA 91406 t) 818-312-3142 (CRP); (818) 782-7181 dresbos91406@gmail.com; parish-3420@la-archdiocese.org www.sbos.org Rev. Rufino Carlos Nava, O.M.I., Pst.; Rev. Rajan Sengol, Assoc. Pst.; Elizabeth Escamilla-Cruz, DRE; CRP Stds.: 227

St. Bridget of Sweden School - (Grades PreK-8) 7120 Whitaker Ave., Lake Balboa, CA 91406 t) (818) 785-4422 school-6780@la-archdiocese.org www.stbridgetofswedenschool.org Robert Pawlak, Prin.; Stds.: 215; Lay Tchrs.: 10

LAKEWOOD

St. Pancratius - 3519 Saint Pancratius Pl., Lakewood, CA 90712 t) (562) 634-1611 (CRP); (562) 634-6111 stpanre@sbcglobal.net; parish-6360@la-archdiocese.org www.stpancratius.org Rev. Andrew Chung, Admin.; Dcn. Romeo (Romy) Ligot; Dcn. Samuel Montoya; Rev. Christopher Iloha, In Res.; Andrew Coffey, DRE; CRP Stds.: 309

St. Pancratius School - (Grades PreK-8) 3601 St. Pancratius Pl., Lakewood, CA 90712 t) (562) 634-6310 school-9400@la-archdiocese.org www.stpanschool.org Jennifer Anderson, Prin.; Stds.: 152; Lay Tchrs.: 13

LANCASTER

St. Junipero Serra - 42121 60th St. W., Lancaster, CA 93536-3767 t) (661) 943-9314; (661) 943-5912 (CRP) ldechant@fatherserra.org; cortiz@fatherserra.org www.saintserra.org Rev. Leo Dechant, C.S.J., Pst.; Rev. Norbert Joseph, CSJ, Assoc. Pst.; Rev. Sylvan Schiavo, C.S.J., Assoc. Pst.; Rev. Giampietro Gasparin, C.S.J., In Res.; Dcn. Marvin Castillo, Pst. Min./Coord.; Dcn. Rito R. Lopez, Pst. Min./Coord.; Dcn. Paul Schwerdt, Pst. Min./Coord.; Dcn. Gary D. Poole; Cassandra Ortiz, DRE; CRP Stds.: 710

St. Elizabeth - 13845 Johnson Rd., Lake Hughes, CA 93532; Mailing: 42121 60th St. W., Lancaster, CA 93536 info@fatherserra.org Rev. Claudio Iori, C.S.J., Admin.;

Sacred Heart - 565 W. Kettering St., Lancaster, CA 93534 t) (661) 948-3011 (CRP); (661) 942-7122 sacredheartdre@yahoo.com; parish-3840@la-archdiocese.org www.sacredheartlancaster.org Rev. Gerald Osuagwu, Assoc. Pst.; Rev. Hieu Chi Tran, Assoc. Pst.; Dcn. Fermin Herrera; Rosa Anna Cruz, DRE; CRP Stds.: 926

Sacred Heart School - (Grades PreK-8) 625 W. Kettering St., Lancaster, CA 93534 t) (661) 948-3613 school-7170@la-archdiocese.org; sacredheartschool@shsav.org www.shsav.org David Schatz, Prin.; Stds.: 275; Lay Tchrs.: 10

LOMITA

St. Margaret Mary Alacoque - 25511 Eshelman Ave., Lomita, CA 90717 t) (310) 326-3364 x17 (CRP); (310) 326-3364 smmcym@yahoo.com; parish-6190@la-archdiocese.org www.smmlomita.org Rev. Long Nguyen, Admin.; Rev. John Palmer, Assoc. Pst.; Rev. Marinello Saguin, Assoc. Pst.; Joe Voight, DRE; CRP Stds.: 760

St. Margaret Mary Alacoque School - (Grades PreK-8) 25515 Eshelman Ave., Lomita, CA 90717 t) (310) 326-9494 school-9230@la-archdiocese.org www.smmsspartans.org Elisa Zimmerman, Prin.; Stds.: 305; Lay Tchrs.: 10

The 103 Saints Korean Catholic Center - 2701 W. 237th St., Torrance, CA 90505-5271 t) (310) 326-4350 x100 103skccusa@gmail.com www.103skcc.org/ Dcn. Francis Tchoi;

LOMPOC

La Purisima Concepcion - 213 W. Olive Ave., Lompoc, CA 93436 t) (805) 735-3068 x23 (CRP); (805) 735-3068 leticia.diaz@lapurisima.org; parish-2910@la-archdiocese.org www.lapurisima.org Rev. Oscar Daniel Martinez, Admin.; Leticia Diaz, DRE; CRP Stds.: 208

La Purisima Concepcion School - (Grades K-8) 219 W. Olive Ave, Lompoc, CA 93436 t) (805) 736-6210 school-6430@la-archdiocese.org; lpsoffice@lapurisimaschool.org www.lapurisimaschool.org Orlando Leon, Prin.; Stds.: 53; Lay Tchrs.: 9

Little Saints Preschool - 219 W. Olive Ave, Lompoc, CA 93436 t) (805) 736-6210 lapurisimaschool.org/preschool Terese Hill, Dir.;

Our Lady Queen of Angels - 3495 Rucker Rd., Lompoc, CA 93436 t) (805) 733-3155 (CRP); (805) 733-2735 queenofangelsparish@la-archdiocese.org; parish-2930@la-archdiocese.org www.queenofangelslompoc.org Rev. Joshua Diener, Admin.; Dcn. Michael Lujan; Mary Lujan, DRE; CRP Stds.: 195

LONG BEACH

St. Anthony - 540 Olive Ave., Long Beach, CA 90802 t) (562) 590-9229 x105 (CRP); (562) 590-9229 x101 secretary@saintanthonylongbeach.org; verbumdei@saintanthonylongbeach.org www.stanthonylb.org Rev. George Aguilera, Pst.; Rev. Victor Ozoufuanya, In Res.; Rev. Joseph Yang, In Res.; Dcn. Jorge Ramos; Sr. Zulma Esquivel, DRE; CRP Stds.: 440

St. Anthony School - (Grades PreK-8) 855 E. 5th St., Long Beach, CA 90802 t) (562) 432-5946 office@saintanthonylongbeach.org; school-9320@la-archdiocese.org www.stanthonyelemlb.org Francisco Lim, Prin.; Stds.: 201; Lay Tchrs.: 11

Our Lady of Mt. Carmel Cambodian Catholic Center - 1851 Cerritos Ave., Long Beach, CA 90806 Rev. George Aguilera, Pst.;

St. Athanasius - 5390 Linden Ave., Long Beach, CA 90805; Mailing: 5369 Linden Ave., Long Beach, CA 90805 t) (562) 423-7986 church@stathanasius-lb.org; parish-6270@la-archdiocese.org www.stathanasius.us Rev. Alfredo Vargas, CMF, Pst.; Dcn. Faustino Ciau; Victoria H. Ciau, Bus. Mgr.; CRP Stds.: 232

St. Athanasius School - (Grades PreK-8) 5377 Linden Ave., Long Beach, CA 90805 t) (562) 428-7422 school-9330@la-archdiocese.org; office@sharkslongbeach.com www.sharkslongbeach.com/ Sonia Nunez, Prin.; Stds.: 88; Lay Tchrs.: 4

St. Barnabas - 3955 Orange Ave., Long Beach, CA 90807 t) (562) 988-6855 (CRP); (562) 424-8595 (Main) parish-6280@la-archdiocese.org; church@stbarnabaslb.org www.stbarnabaslb.org Rev. Antony J. Gaspar, Pst.; Rev. Bernard Shaw Santiago, Assoc. Pst.; CRP Stds.: 345

St. Barnabas School - (Grades PreK-8) 3980 Marron Ave., Long Beach, CA 90807 t) (562) 424-7476 school-9340@la-archdiocese.org; stbarnabasschool@yahoo.com www.school.stbarnabaslb.org Jennifer Kellam, Prin.;

Stds.: 301; Lay Tchrs.: 10

St. Bartholomew - 5100 E. Broadway, Long Beach, CA 90803; Mailing: 252 Granada Ave., Long Beach, CA 90803 t) (562) 438-3826 kdeleo@la-archdiocese.org; kflood@la-archdiocese.org www.stbartholomewcclb.org Rev. Mark A. Strader, Pst.; Kathleen Flood, Bus. Mgr.; CRP Stds.: 66

St. Cornelius - 5500 Wardlow Rd., Long Beach, CA 90808 t) (562) 420-7613 (CRP); (562) 421-8966 secretary@stcorneliuslb.org; parish-6300@la-archdiocese.org www.stcorneliuslb.org Rev. Jarlath Cunnane, Pst.; Rev. George Reynolds, Assoc. Pst.; Dcn. Richard Boucher; Dcn. Joseph Hamamoto; Cristy Hull, Youth Min.; Ana Lopez, DRE; CRP Stds.: 244

St. Cornelius School - (Grades PreK-8) 3330 Bellflower Blvd., Long Beach, CA 90808 t) (562) 425-7813 school-9350@la-archdiocese.org; nhayes@stcornelius.net www.stcornelius.net Nancy Hayes, Prin.; Stds.: 323; Lay Tchrs.: 12

St. Cyprian - 4714 Clark Ave., Long Beach, CA 90808 t) (562) 421-9487 parish-6310@la-archdiocese.org; parish@stcyprianchurch.org www.stcyprianchurch.org Rev. Alidor Mikobi, Admin.; CRP Stds.: 140

St. Cyprian School - (Grades PreK-8) 5133 Arbor Rd., Long Beach, CA 90808 t) (562) 425-7341 principal@stcyprianschool.org; school-9360@la-archdiocese.org www.stcyprianschool.org Rachelle Riemersma, Prin.; Stds.: 268; Lay Tchrs.: 13

Holy Innocents - 425 E. 20th St., Long Beach, CA 90806 t) (562) 591-6924 office@lbcatholic.com; parish-6230@la-archdiocese.org www.lbcatholic.com Rev. G. Peter Irving III, Pst.; Rev. Robert McGowan, Assoc. Pst.; Maria Gonzalez, DRE; CRP Stds.: 111

Holy Innocents School - (Grades PreK-8) 2500 Pacific Ave., Long Beach, CA 90806 t) (562) 424-1018 school-9300@la-archdiocese.org; info@lbcatholicschool.com www.lbcatholicschool.com Cyril Cruz, Prin.; Stds.: 197; Sr. Tchrs.: 3; Lay Tchrs.: 7

Holy Innocents Convent - 2556 Pacific Ave., Long Beach, CA 90806 t) (562) 427-6924 contacts@carmelitesistersocd.com www.carmelitesistersocd.com Sr. Mary Patrice Matamoros, O.C.D., Supr.;

St. Joseph - 6180 E. Willow St., Long Beach, CA 90815 t) (562) 594-4657; (562) 598-0519 (CRP) stjoseph@stjosephlb.org; religioused@stjosephlb.org www.stjosephlb.org Rev. Msgr. Kevin J. Kostelnik, Pst.; Dcn. Shane Cuda; Dcn. Thomas L. Halliwell; Joe Voight, DRE; CRP Stds.: 155

St. Joseph School - (Grades PreK-8) 6200 E. Willow St., Long Beach, CA 90815 t) (562) 596-6115 school-9370@la-archdiocese.org www.sjknights.net Margaret Alvarez, Prin.; Stds.: 308; Lay Tchrs.: 16

St. Lucy - 2344 Cota Ave., Long Beach, CA 90810 t) (562) 997-0511 (CRP); (562) 424-9051 santarb@hotmail.com; parish-6330@la-archdiocese.org www.saintlucyparish.org Rev. John Quy V. Tran, Pst.; Rev. Francis Espiga, Assoc. Pst.; Rev. Joseph Van Vu, Assoc. Pst.; Dcn. Francisco J. Gonzalez; Dcn. Thien Joseph Pham; Santa Rivera, DRE; CRP Stds.: 355

St. Lucy School - (Grades PreK-8) 2320 Cota Ave., Long Beach, CA 90810 t) (562) 424-9062 principal@stlucyschoollb.org; school-9380@la-archdiocese.org www.stlucyschoollb.org Angelica Izquierdo, Prin.; Stds.: 178; Lay Tchrs.: 10

St. Maria Goretti - 3954 Palo Verde Ave., Long Beach, CA 90808-2298 t) (562) 425-7459 parish-6340@la-archdiocese.org; smgsecretary@gmail.com www.smgchurch.com Rev. John Schiavone, Pst.; Debra Palzer, Rel. Educ. Coord.; Albert Valdespino, Confirmation Coord.; CRP Stds.: 78

St. Maria Goretti School - (Grades PreK-8) 3950 Palo Verde Ave., Long Beach, CA 90808 t) (562) 425-5112 principal@smgschool.com; school-9390@la-archdiocese.org www.smgschool.com Kathleen Hernandez, Prin.; Stds.: 165; Lay Tchrs.: 10

St. Matthew - 672 Temple Ave., Long Beach, CA 90814 t) (562) 439-0931 parish-6350@la-archdiocese.org; stmatt@stmatthewlb.org www.stmatthewlb.org Rev. Randy Raul Campos, Pst.; Rev. Norman A. Supancheck, In Res.; Sr. Virginia Stewart, SDSH, DRE; Tricia Mora, RCIA Coord.; Julia A Castaneda, Bus. Mgr.; CRP Stds.: 215

Our Lady of Refuge - 5195 E. Stearns St., Long Beach, CA 90815 t) (562) 597-3102 (CRP); (562) 498-6641 (Office) parish@start.olrs.org; sre@start.olrs.org www.ourladyofrefuge.org Rev. Gerard O'Brien, Pst.; CRP Stds.: 120

Our Lady of Refuge School - (Grades PreK-8) 5210 Los Coyotes Diagonal, Long Beach, CA 90815 t) 562-597-0819 admin@start.olrs.org; school-9310@la-archdiocese.org www.olrs.org Margaret Kennedy, Prin.; Stds.: 157; Lay Tchrs.: 12

LOS ANGELES

Cathedral of Our Lady of the Angels - 555 W. Temple St., Los Angeles, CA 90012 t) (213) 680-5200 cathedralinfo@olacathedral.org; parish-5460@la-archdiocese.org www.olacathedral.org Rev. Msgr. Antonio Cacciapuoti, Pst.; Most Rev. Jose H. Gomez, In Res.; Rev. Raymont Medina, In Res.; Rev. Brian Nunes, In Res.; Rev. Pedro Saucedo, In Res.; Bro. Hilarion O'Connor, O.S.F., Dir.; Eileen Bonaduce, Bus. Mgr.; CRP Stds.: 5

St. Agatha - 2646 S. Mansfield Ave., Los Angeles, CA 90016 t) (323) 933-0963 (CRP); (323) 935-8127 tamezcua@stagathas.org; parish-5320@la-archdiocese.org www.stagathas.org Rev. Anthony S. Lee, Admin.; Rev. Joseph Martin Palacios, In Res.; Teresa Amezcua, DRE; Gricelda de la Cerda, DRE; CRP Stds.: 257

St. Agnes - 2625 S. Vermont Ave., Los Angeles, CA 90007 t) (323) 731-2464; (323) 731-2464 x120 (CRP) lizbetholiva2004@yahoo.com; stagneschurchla@yahoo.com www.stagnes-la.org/ Rev. Luis Espinoza, Pst.; Rev. David Matz, C.PP.S., Admin.; Rev. Timothy Guthridge, C.PP.S., Assoc. Pst.; Rev. DaeJe Choi, S.J., In Res.; Rev. Chang Hyon Lee, S.J., In Res.; Rev. Dien Truong, C.PP.S., In Res.; Miriam Oliva, DRE; CRP Stds.: 317

St. Agnes School - (Grades PreK-8) 1428 W. Adams Blvd., Los Angeles, CA 90007 t) (323) 734-6441 c) (323) 537-7051 (Office Cell) principal@stagnesschool.org; school-8460@la-archdiocese.org www.stagnesschool.org Will Summer, Prin.; Stds.: 110; Lay Tchrs.: 9

All Saints - 3431 Portola Ave., Los Angeles, CA 90032-2215 t) (213) 216-2361 (CRP); (323) 223-1101 allsaintschurch@earthlink.net; parish-4310@la-archdiocese.org www.allsaintsla.com Dcn. Pedro Rojas; Rev. Thomas C. Francis, O.M., Pst.; Rev. Mario Pisano, O.M., Assoc. Pst.; Rev. Jose L. Vega, O.M., Assoc. Pst.; Ana Sanchez, DRE; CRP Stds.: 89

St. Aloysius Gonzaga - 2023 E. Nadeau St., Los Angeles, CA 90001; Mailing: 7814 Crocket Blvd., Los Angeles, CA 90001 t) (323) 585-4485 parish-5770@la-archdiocese.org www.staloysiusgonzagachurchla.org Rev. Pedro Antonio Esteban, Pst.; Rev. Avelino S. Crisanto, O.deM., Assoc. Pst.; Gricelda Garibay, Bus. Mgr.; CRP Stds.: 229

St. Aloysius Gonzaga School - (Grades PreK-8) t) 323-582-4965 school-8810@la-archdiocese.org; n.johnson@staloysiusla.org www.staloysiusla.org Nicole Johnson, Prin.; Stds.: 237; Lay Tchrs.: 11

St. Alphonsus - 532 S. Atlantic Blvd., Los Angeles, CA 90022; Mailing: 5223 Hastings St., Los Angeles, CA 90022 t) 323-266-0855 (CRP); 323-264-3353 restalphonsus@gmail.com; parish-4230@la-archdiocese.org Rev. Alfonso Borgen, O.F.M.Conv., Pst.; Rev. Omoldo Cherrez, Assoc. Pst.; Rev. Gerardo Galaviz, In Res.; Maria Elena Jauregui, DRE; CRP Stds.: 459

St. Alphonsus School - (Grades PreK-8) 552 S. Amalia Ave., Los Angeles, CA 90022 t) (323) 268-5165 school-7470@la-archdiocese.org; mmunguia-sanchez@la-archdiocese.org www.saintalphonsusschool.org Minerva Munguia-Sanchez, Prin.; Stds.: 315; Lay Tchrs.: 10

St. Anastasia - 7390 W. Manchester Ave., Los Angeles, CA 90045 t) (310) 670-2243; (310) 670-2243 x36 (CRP) parish@st-anastasia.org; parish-4820@la-archdiocese.org www.st-anastasia.org Rev. Leszek Semik, Pst.; Rev. Grzegorz Rozborski (Poland), Pst. Assoc.; Rev. Msgr. Gregory A. Cox, In Res.; CRP Stds.: 99

St. Anastasia School - (Grades PreK-8) 8631 S. Stanmoor Dr., Los Angeles, CA 90045 t) (310) 645-8816 school@st-anastasia.org; school-7960@la-archdiocese.org www.school.st-anastasia.org Angelica Izquierdo, Prin.; Stds.: 285; Lay Tchrs.: 10

St. Ann - 2302 Riverdale Ave., Los Angeles, CA 90031; Mailing: 1365 Blake Ave., Los Angeles, CA 90031 t) 323-225-9181 (CRP); 323-221-6368 ccuevas@dssala.org; office@dssala.org www.dssala.org Rev. Albert Susai Pragasam, O.S.M, Pst.; Rev. SamyDurai Arockiam, O.S.M, Assoc. Pst.; Dcn. Juan Corletto; Claudia Cuevas, DRE; Theresa Salas, Bus. Mgr.; CRP Stds.: 43

St. Anselm - 2222 W. 70th St., Los Angeles, CA 90043 t) (323) 758-6729 soniamay59@yahoo.com; frfidelisomeaku@la-archdiocese.org www.stanselmla.org Rev. Fidelis C. Omeaku, Admin.; Sonia Hernandez, DRE; CRP Stds.: 110

St. Anthony - 712 N. Grand Ave., Los Angeles, CA 90012 t) (213) 628-2938 parish-5340@la-archdiocese.org; croatsvantela@sbcglobal.net www.croatianchurchla.org (Croatian) Rev. Zvonimir Coric, Pst.; CRP Stds.: 14

Ascension - 517 W. 112th St., Los Angeles, CA 90044 t) (323) 754-2978 ascens@pacbell.net; parish-5480@archdiocese.org www.ascensionla.org Rev. Joseph Lal, Admin.; Maria Lupe Sanchez, DRE; CRP Stds.: 450

Ascension School - (Grades PreK-8) 500 W. 111th Pl., Los Angeles, CA 90044 t) (323) 756-4064 ascjcastellanos@gmail.com; school-8580@la-archdiocese.org www.ascensionschoolla.org Jesse Castellanos, Prin.; Stds.: 213; Lay Tchrs.: 10

Assumption - 2832 Blanchard St., Los Angeles, CA 90033 t) (323) 269-8171; (323) 269-5920 (CRP) mapacheco@la-archdiocese.org; parish-4060@la-archdiocese.org assumptionchurchlosangeles.webstarts.com/ Rev. Arturo Lopez, OFM, Pst.; Rev. Javier Alvarez, O.F.M., Assoc. Pst.; Sr. Maria Calvillo, E.I.N., DRE; CRP Stds.: 140

St. Basil's Roman Catholic Church - 3611 Wilshire Blvd, Los Angeles, CA 90010; Mailing: 637 S. Kingsley Dr., Los Angeles, CA 90005 t) (213) 381-6191 eccristobal@la-archdiocese.org; parish-5090@la-archdiocese.org www.stbasilchurch-la.org Rev. Msgr. Francis J. Hicks, Pst.; Rev. Miguel B. Java (Philippines), In Res.; Rev. Victor J. Ruvalcaba, In Res.; Dcn. Thomas E. Brandlin; Dcn. Carlos Ortega; Edna Cristobal, DRE; CRP Stds.: 70

St. Bernadette - 3825 Don Felipe Dr., Los Angeles, CA 90008 t) (323) 293-4877 parish-5350@la-archdiocese.org; j.carper@la-archdiocese.org www.stbernadettela.org Dcn. James Carper, Parish Life Dir.; Rev. Msgr. Loreto Gonzales, In Res.; CRP Stds.: 21

St. Bernard - 2516 W. Ave. 33, Los Angeles, CA 90065; Mailing: 2515 W. Ave. 33, Los Angeles, CA 90065 t) (323) 256-6242 (CRP); (323) 255-6142 parish-3620@la-archdiocese.org www.stbernard-parish.com Rev. Perry D. Leiker, Pst.; Victor Mojica, DRE; CRP Stds.: 206

St. Bernard School - (Grades PreK-8) 3254 Verdugo Rd., Los Angeles, CA 90065 t) 323-256-4989 school-6950@la-archdiocese.org; info@stbernard-school.com www.stbernard-school.com Claudia Montiel, Prin.; Stds.: 191; Lay Tchrs.: 17

Blessed Sacrament - 6657 Sunset Blvd., Los Angeles, CA 90028 t) (323) 462-6311 parish-5010@archdiocese.org; info@blessedsacramenthollywood.org www.blessedsacramenthollywood.org Rev. John C Bentz, SJ, Pst.; Rev. John Tanner, S.J., Assoc. Pst.; Rev.

Michael Manalastas, S.J., Assoc. Pst.; Jan Sooter, Pst. Assoc.;

St. Brendan - 310 S. Van Ness Ave., Los Angeles, CA 90020 t) (323) 936-4656 info@stbrendanchurch.org; parish-5100@la-archdiocese.org www.stbrendanla.org Rev. Brian Castaneda, Pst.; Rev. Msgr. Terrance L. Fleming, Pastor Emer.; CRP Stds.: 100

St. Brendan School - (Grades PreK-8) 238 S. Manhattan Pl., Los Angeles, CA 90004 t) (213) 382-7401 school-8220@la-archdiocese.org; cyoung@la-archdiocese.org www.stbrendanschoolla.org Sr. Maureen O'Connor, C.S.J., Prin.; Stds.: 310; Lay Tchrs.: 10

St. Bridget - 510 Cottage Home St., Los Angeles, CA 90012; Mailing: 445 Cottage Home St., Los Angeles, CA 90012 t) (323) 222-5518 parish-5110@la-archdiocese.org; wanching-law@yahoo.com www.stbridgetccc.com Rev. John Lam, S.D.B., Pst.; Sr. Maria Lai, C.S.J., DRE;

St. Brigid - 5214 S. Western Ave., Los Angeles, CA 90062 t) (323) 292-0781 floy@floyhawkins.com; parish-5550@la-archdiocese.org www.stbrigidchurchla.com Rev. Michael Okechukwu, S.S.J., Pst.; Rev. Emmanuel Awe, S.S.J., Assoc. Pst.; Floy Hawkins, DRE; CRP Stds.: 56

St. Camillus de Lellis - 1911 Zonal Ave., Los Angeles, CA 90033-1032 t) (323) 225-4461 parish-4250@la-archdiocese.org; cponnet@stcamilluscenter.org www.stcamilluscenter.org Rev. Christopher D. Ponnet, Pst.; Arely Deras, Chap.; Rev. John Carlos Greeley, MSP, Chap.; Sr. Janet Husung, CSJ, Chap.; Nick Jordan, Chap.; Rev. Quyen Nguyen, CMF, Chap.; Stephanie Ramos, Chap.; Dcn. Orlando Rubio, Chap.; Rita Rubio, Chap.; Luis Manuel Torres, Chap.; CRP Stds.: 18

Catholics Against the Death Penalty Center - t) (323) 225-4461 x221 Rev. Christopher Ponnet, Pst.;

Catholic HIV/AIDS Office - t) (323) 225-4461 x221 Rev. Christopher Ponnet, Pst.;

Pax Christi Los Angeles - Rev. Christopher Ponnet, Pst.;

Catholic Ministry with Lesbian & Gay Persons - t) (323) 225-4461 x221 info@stcamilluscenter.org Rev. Christopher Ponnet, Pst.;

Consistent Life Ethics Institute - t) (323) 225-4461 x221 Rev. Christopher Ponnet, Pst.;

St. Casimir - 2718 St. George St., Los Angeles, CA 90027 t) (323) 664-4660 tkaranauskas@gmail.com; st.casimir@gmail.com www.stcasimirchurchla.org Rev. Tomas Karanauskas, Pst.; CRP Stds.: 50

Cathedral Chapel of St. Vibiana - 923 S. La Brea Ave., Los Angeles, CA 90036; Mailing: 926 S. Detroit St., Los Angeles, CA 90036 t) (323) 930-5976 religioused@cathedralchapel.org; parish-5020@la-archdiocese.org www.cathedralchapel.org Rev. Doan The Pham, Pst.; Nancy G. Sheehan, Bus. Mgr.; Sr. Anna Tom, S.D.S.H., DRE; CRP Stds.: 47

Cathedral Chapel of St. Vibiana School - (Grades PreK-8) 755 S. Cochran Ave., Los Angeles, CA 90036 t) (323) 938-9976 school-8150@la-archdiocese.org www.cathedralchapelschool.org Tina Kipp, Prin.; Stds.: 271; Lay Tchrs.: 25

St. Cecilia - 4230 S. Normandie Ave., Los Angeles, CA 90037 t) (323) 298-7721 (CRP); (323) 294-6628 parish-5370@la-archdiocese.org; parish@stcecilia-la.org www.stceciliachurch-la.org Rev. Roman Arzate, Pst.; Sr. Olivia Ramirez, H.A., DRE; CRP Stds.: 434

St. Cecilia School - (Grades PreK-8) 4224 S. Normandie Ave., Los Angeles, CA 90037 t) (323) 293-4266 stceciliasprincipal@gmail.com; school-8480@la-archdiocese.org www.stceciliaschoolla.org Norma Guzman, Prin.; Stds.: 175; Lay Tchrs.: 10

Christ the King - 624 N. Rossmore Ave., Los Angeles, CA 90004; Mailing: 616 N. Rossmore Ave., Los Angeles, CA 90004 t) (323) 465-7605; (323) 465-7084 (CRP) parish@ctkla.org; parish-5030@la-archdiocese.org www.ctkla.org Rev. Juan Jose Ochoa, Admin.; Sr. Maria Alice Hernandez, C.V.D., DRE; CRP Stds.: 151

Christ the King School - (Grades PreK-8) 617 N. Arden Blvd., Los Angeles, CA 90004 t) (323) 462-4753 principal@cksla.com; school-8160@la-archdiocese.org www.ctkschool.org Patty Hager, Prin.; Stds.: 200; Lay Tchrs.: 10

St. Columban - 125 Loma Dr., Los Angeles, CA 90026 t) (213) 250-8818 stcolumbanla@gmail.com; parish-5130@la-archdiocese.org www.stcolumbanla.org Rev. Anh-Tuan D. Nguyen, Admin.; Rev. Francis Espiga, Par. Vicar; Rev. Joel Henson, In Res.; Dcn. Felix Dumlao; CRP Stds.: 37

St. Columbkille - 6315 S. Main St., Los Angeles, CA 90003 t) (323) 758-5540; (323) 789-3344 (CRP) parish-5560@la-archdiocese.org; stcolumbkillechurchla@yahoo.com www.columbkille.org Rev. Ever Quintero, Pst.; CRP Stds.: 455

St. Columbkille School - (Grades PreK-8) 145 W. 64th St., Los Angeles, CA 90003 t) (323) 758-2284 office@columbkille.org; school-8630@la-archdiocese.org www.columbkille.org/ Dr. Karen Holyk-Casey, Prin.; Stds.: 265; Lay Tchrs.: 10

Cristo Rey - 4343 Perlita Ave., Los Angeles, CA 90039 t) (323) 245-4585 parish-3530@la-archdiocese.org www.cristoreyla.com Rev. Michael Stechmann, O.A.R., Pst.; Bro. Jorge Valdivia, O.A.R., Pst. Assoc.; Jose Torres, DRE; CRP Stds.: 197

Divine Saviour - 610 Cypress Ave., Los Angeles, CA 90065; Mailing: 2911 Idell St., Los Angeles, CA 90065 t) (323) 225-9181 x128 (CRP); (323) 225-9181 ccuevas@dssala.org; office@dssala.org www.dssala.org Rev. Albert Susai Pragasam, O.S.M, Pst.; Rev. SamyDurai Arockiam, O.S.M, Assoc. Pst.; Claudia Cuevas, DRE; Theresa Salas, Bus. Mgr.; CRP Stds.: 200

Divine Saviour School - (Grades PreK-8) 624 Cypress Ave., Los Angeles, CA 90065 t) (323) 222-6077 school-6880@la-archdiocese.org; office@divinesaviourschool.org www.dsschoolla.org/ Alejandra Alvarez, Prin.; Stds.: 72; Lay Tchrs.: 5

Dolores Mission - 171 S. Gless St., Los Angeles, CA 90033 t) (323) 881-0039 aislas@dolores-mission.org; parish-4070@la-archdiocese.org www.dolores-mission.org Rev. Ted Gabrielli, S.J., Pst.; Rev. Brendan P. Busse, S.J., Assoc. Pst.; Rev. Justin Claravall, S.J., Assoc. Pst.; Rev. Michael Lee, S.J., Assoc. Pst.; Rev. Gregory Boyle, S.J., In Res.; Rev. Tri M. Dinh, S.J., In Res.; Rev. Mark Torres, In Res.; Ellie Hidalgo, Pst. Assoc.; Alma Islas, DRE; Jody Lozano, Bus. Mgr.; CRP Stds.: 205

Dolores Mission School - (Grades PreK-8) 170 S. Gless St., Los Angeles, CA 90033 t) (323) 881-0001 school-7330@la-archdiocese.org www.doloresmissionschool.org Karina Moreno, Prin.; Stds.: 245; Lay Tchrs.: 10

St. Dominic - 2002 Merton Ave., Los Angeles, CA 90041 t) (323) 254-2519 parish-3630@la-archdiocese.org; info@saintdominics.org www.saintdominics.org Rev. Peter Rogers, O.P., Pst.; Rev. Francis Goode, O.P., Assoc. Pst.; Rev. Isaiah Mary Molano, O.P., Assoc. Pst.; Sr. Joyanne Sullivan, SND, RCIA Coord.; Bro. Xavier Marie Wu, Pst. Assoc.; Christina Garcia, DRE; Michelle Perez, DRE; Rev. Donald Bramble, O.P., In Res.; Rev. Michael Carey, O.P., In Res.; Rev. Jude Eli, O.P., In Res.; Rev. Vincent Lopez, OP; Rev. Anthony Patalano, OP; CRP Stds.: 175

St. Dominic School - (Grades PreK-8) 2005 Merton Ave., Los Angeles, CA 90041 t) (323) 255-5803 school-6960@la-archdiocese.org www.stdominicla.us Tiffany Sawyer, Prin.; Stds.: 235; Sr. Tchrs.: 1; Lay Tchrs.: 9

Pre-School - 2005 Merton Ave., Los Angeles, CA 90041 t) (323) 255-5803 school-6960@la-archdiocese.org www.stdominicla.us Danielle Serafin, Dir.;

St. Eugene - 9505 Haas Ave., Los Angeles, CA 90047 t) (323) 757-3121 steugenechurch@sbcglobal.net; parish-5570@la-archdiocese.org www.steugeneparish.org Rev. Jude Umeobi, Pst.; Anthony Ikebudu, DRE; CRP Stds.: 65

St. Eugene School - (Grades PreK-8) 9521 Haas Ave., Los Angeles, CA 90047 t) (323) 754-9536 ckingsby@steugene.net www.steugene.net Celynda Kingsby, Prin.; Stds.: 225; Lay Tchrs.: 10

St. Frances Xavier Cabrini - 1440 W. Imperial Hwy., Los Angeles, CA 90047; Mailing: 1430 W. Imperial Hwy., Los Angeles, CA 90047 t) (323) 757-0271 nora_stfrances@yahoo.com; sfxcabrini@gmail.com www.sfxcabrini.org Rev. Juan Bosco Jimenez, S.D.B., Pst.; CRP Stds.: 442

St. Frances Xavier Cabrini School - (Grades PreK-8) 1428 W. Imperial Hwy., Los Angeles, CA 90047 t) (323) 756-1354 school-8650@la-archdiocese.org www.sfxcabrini.org/ Carmen A. Orinoco-Hart, Prin.; Stds.: 220; Lay Tchrs.: 10

St. Francis of Assisi - 1523 Golden Gate Ave., Los Angeles, CA 90026 t) (323) 662-3345 (CRP); (323) 664-1305 vilmasierra77@yahoo.com; sfaparish@gmail.com stfrancischurchla.wordpress.com/ Rev. Enrique Huerta, Pst.; Vilma Sierra, DRE; CRP Stds.: 50

St. Francis Xavier Chapel - 222 S. Hewitt St., Los Angeles, CA 90012 t) (213) 626-2279 parish-5380@la-archdiocese.org; info@sfxcjcc.org www.sfxcjcc.org Rev. Doan T. Hoang, S.J., Pst.; CRP Stds.: 8

St. Gerard Majella - 4439 Inglewood Blvd., Los Angeles, CA 90066 t) (310) 391-9637 (CRP); (310) 390-5034 stgerardmajella@ca.rr.com; parish-4860@la-archdiocese.org www.stgerardla.com Rev. Gerardo Padilla, Pst.; Rev. Juan Carlos Garcia Lomeli, MSE, Assoc. Pst.; Gabriela Gudino, DRE; Frances Gomez, Bus. Mgr.; CRP Stds.: 81

St. Gregory Nazianzen - 900 S. Bronson Ave., Los Angeles, CA 90019 t) (323) 935-4224 parish-5150@la-archdiocese.org; stgregory1923@yahoo.com stgregoryla.org Rev. Augustine Chang, Pst.; Rev. Hae In Kim (Korea), Pst. Assoc.; Jenny Menendez, DRE; CRP Stds.: 102

Holy Cross - 4705 S. Main St., Los Angeles, CA 90037 t) (323) 234-5984; (323) 325-7413 (CRP) parish-5490@la-archdiocese.org; ore@holycrossla.org www.iglesiasantacruzla.com Rev. Mariano Tibaldo, M.C.C.J, Pst.; Rev. Domenico Guarino, M.C.C.J, Assoc. Pst.; Rev. Jose Angel Santos Romero Morales, M.C.C.J, Assoc. Pst.; Rev. Xavier Colleoni, M.C.C.J. (Italy), In Res.; Dcn. Leonel Yoque; CRP Stds.: 242

Holy Name of Jesus - 2186 W. 31st St., Los Angeles, CA 90018 t) (323) 734-8888 holynameofjesus@gmail.com; parish-5240@la-archdiocese.org www.holynameofjesus-la.org Rev. Kenneth C. Ugwu, S.S.J., Pst.; Dcn. Hosea Alexander Sr.; Dcn. Douglass R. Johnson Sr.; Dcn. Jose Ines Penate Mojica; Catherine Brown, DRE; CRP Stds.: 45

Holy Name of Jesus School - (Grades PreK-8) 1955 W. Jefferson Blvd., Los Angeles, CA 90007 t) (323) 731-2255 school-8420@la-archdiocese.org www.hnojla.org Marva Belisle, Prin.; Stds.: 185; Lay Tchrs.: 10

Holy Spirit - 1425 S. Dunsmuir Ave., Los Angeles, CA 90019-4031 t) (323) 935-1333 srluzdelcarmen@holyspiritla.org; parish-5250@la-archdiocese.org www.hs-smm.org Rev. Arturo Valadez, Admin.; Sr. Luz Del Carmen Perez, DRE; CRP Stds.: 160

Holy Spirit School - (Grades PreK-8) 1418 S. Burnside Ave., Los Angeles, CA 90019 t) (323) 926-9419 holyspiritschoolla@yahoo.com; school-8430@la-archdiocese.org www.holyspiritstem.org/ James Ryan, Prin.; Stds.: 102; Lay Tchrs.: 7

Holy Trinity - 3722 Boyce Ave., Los Angeles, CA 90039 t) (323) 664-4723 parish-3570@la-archdiocese.org www.holytrinityla.org Rev. Ricardo Henry Viveros, Pst.; Rev. Jaehun Song, Assoc. Pst.; Dcn. Rolando Bautista; Dcn. Ray Chris Emnace; Msgr. Joseph Herres, In Res.; CRP Stds.: 100

Holy Trinity School - (Grades PreK-8) 3716 Boyce Ave., Los Angeles, CA 90039 t) (323) 663-2064 klloyd@la-archdiocese.org; school-6910@la-archdiocese.org www.holytrinityla.com Karen Lloyd, Prin.; Stds.: 125; Lay Tchrs.: 10

Sung Sam Korean Catholic Center - 1230 N. San Fernando Rd., Los Angeles, CA 90065 t) (323) 221-8874 office@sungsamkcc.com www.sungsamkcc.com/online/ Rev. Taehyun Gregory Yang, Chap.;

St. Ignatius of Loyola - 322 N. Ave. 61, Los Angeles, CA 90042; Mailing: 6024 Terrace Dr., Los Angeles, CA 90042 t) (323) 254-9073 (CRP); (323) 256-3041 stignatiusre@gmail.com; parish-3640@la-archdiocese.org www.saintignatiusparish.com Rev. Edwin C. Duyshart, Pst.; Sr. Gemma de la Trinidad, E.F.M.S., DRE; CRP Stds.: 350

St. Ignatius of Loyola School - (Grades PreK-8) 6025 Monte Vista St., Los Angeles, CA 90042 t) (323) 255-6456 admin@stignatiusla.org; school-6970@la-archdiocese.org www.stignatiusla.org Ileana Wade, Prin.; Stds.: 187; Lay Tchrs.: 10

Immaculate Conception - 1433 James M. Wood Blvd., Los Angeles, CA 90015 t) (213) 384-1019; (213) 389-7277 (CRP) immaconc@sbcglobal.net; parish-5260@la-archdiocese.org www.inmaculadaconcepla.org Rev. Jesus Francisco Garcia Aguilar, C.O.R.C. (Mexico), Pst.; Rev. Abdias Gonzalez Gonzalez, C.O.R.C. (Mexico), Assoc. Pst.; Rev. Miguel Jimenez Nieto, C.O.R.C. (Mexico), Assoc. Pst.; Rev. Michael Saso, SJ, In Res.; Sonia Ruiz, Bus. Mgr.; Edith Cruz, DRE; CRP Stds.: 268

Immaculate Conception School - (Grades PreK-8) 830 Green St., Los Angeles, CA 90017 t) (213) 382-5931 principal@ics-la.org; school-8440@la-archdiocese.org www.ics-la.org Mary Ann Murphy, Prin.; Stds.: 250; Lay Tchrs.: 10

Immaculate Heart of Mary - 4950 Santa Monica Blvd, Los Angeles, CA 90029; Mailing: 4954 Santa Monica Blvd, Los Angeles, CA 90029 t) (323) 660-0034; (323) 660-0034 x17 (CRP) m.martinez@la-archdiocese.org; ihmcla@gmail.com www.ihmc-la.org Rev. Rolando Clarin, Pst.; Rev. Florentino Victorino, M.S.C., Assoc. Pst.; Maria L Martinez, Bus. Mgr.; Mariela Morales, DRE; CRP Stds.: 269

Immaculate Heart of Mary School - (Grades PreK-8) 1055 N. Alexandria Ave., Los Angeles, CA 90029 t) (323) 663-4611 ihm1@pacbell.net www.ihmla.org Stds.: 170; Lay Tchrs.: 8

St. Jerome - 5550 Thornburn St., Los Angeles, CA 90045 t) (310) 348-8212; (310) 670-1678 (CRP) parish-4870@la-archdiocese.org www.stjeromelax.org Rev. Bill Bolton, S.D.B., Pst.; CRP Stds.: 187

St. Jerome School - (Grades PreSchool-8) 5580 Thornburn St., Los Angeles, CA 90045 principal@stjeromewestchester.org; school-8010@la-archdiocese.org www.st-jeromeschool.org Stds.: 142; Lay Tchrs.: 10

St. Joan of Arc - 11534 Gateway Blvd., Los Angeles, CA 90064 t) (310) 479-5111 parish-4880@la-archdiocese.org; parish@stjoanchurch.com www.stjoanchurch.com Rev. Joseph Q. Nguyen, Pst.; Nuria Gordillo, DRE; CRP Stds.: 150

St. John the Evangelist - 6028 S. Victoria Ave., Los Angeles, CA 90043 t) 323-758-9161; 323-758-9161 x300 (CRP) parish-5600@la-archdiocese.org; office@johnevangelist.org www.johnevangelist.org Rev. Alexander Sila, S.V.D., Admin.; Rev. Frank Tinajero, SVD, In Res.; CRP Stds.: 63

St. Joseph - 1202 S. Los Angeles St., Los Angeles, CA 90015; Mailing: 218 E. 12th St., Los Angeles, CA 90015 t) (213) 663-6995 (CRP); (213) 748-5394 stjosephschurch@sbcglobal.net; parish-5390@la-archdiocese.org stjosephschurchla.com/ Rev. Rafael Casillas, Pst.; Dcn. Miguel Cruz; Ambrocio Alonso, DRE; CRP Stds.: 160

St. Turibius School - (Grades PreK-8) 1524 Essex St., Los Angeles, CA 90021 t) (213) 749-8894 info@stturibius.org; school-8500@la-archdiocese.org www.stturibius.org Karina Mendez, Prin.; Stds.: 165; Lay Tchrs.: 10

St. Turibius Mission - 1530 Essex St., Los Angeles, CA 90021

St. Kevin - 4072 Beverly Blvd., Los Angeles, CA 90004; Mailing: 202 N. Alexandria Ave., Los Angeles, CA 90004 t) (213) 909-1801 parish-5160@la-archdiocese.org; stkevin.cc@gmail.com www.stkevinchurchla.org Rev. Crespo Lape, M.J., Pst.; Rev. Manuel Gacad, M.J., Assoc. Pst.; Rev. Freddie B Pinuela, MJ, Assoc. Pst.; CRP Stds.: 84

St. Lawrence of Brindisi - 10122 Compton Ave., Los Angeles, CA 90002 t) (323) 567-4698 (CRP); (323) 567-1439 parish-5610@la-archdiocese.org; pastor@stlawrenceofbrindisi.org www.stlawrenceofbrindisi.org Rev. Matthew Elshoff, O.F.M.Cap., Pst.; Rev. Michael Ronayne, O.F.M., Assoc. Pst.; Bro. Mark Mance, O.F.M.Cap., Pst. Assoc.; Rayito Ruelas, DRE; CRP Stds.: 555

St. Lawrence of Brindisi School - (Grades PreK-8) 10044 Compton Ave., Los Angeles, CA 90002 t) (323) 564-3051 school-8680@la-archdiocese.org www.stlawrencebrindisi.com Alicia Camacho, Prin.; Stds.: 300; Lay Tchrs.: 10

St. Lucy - 3945 City Terrace Dr., Los Angeles, CA 90063; Mailing: 1419 N. Hazard Ave., Los Angeles, CA 90063 t) (323) 266-0451 parish-4260@la-archdiocese.org; santalucy@sbcglobal.net www.stlucyschurchla.org Rev. Roberto Morales, Sch.P., Pst.; Rev. Josep M. Margalef, Sch.P., Assoc. Pst.; Leticia Robles, DRE; CRP Stds.: 180

St. Malachy - 1228 E. 81st St., Los Angeles, CA 90001 t) (323) 585-1437; (323) 582-3024 (CRP) st.malachychurch@gmail.com; ordazmartha14@yahoo.com stmalachyla.org Rev. Luis R. Lucchetti (Peru), Pst.; Martha Ordaz, DRE; CRP Stds.: 350

St. Malachy School - (Grades PreK-8) 1200 E. 81st St., Los Angeles, CA 90001 t) (323) 582-3112 stmalachyschl@sbcglobal.net; school-8690@la-archdiocese.org www.saintmalachyschool.com Rocio Orozco, Prin.; Stds.: 162; Lay Tchrs.: 9

St. Martin of Tours - 11967 W. Sunset Blvd., Los Angeles, CA 90049 t) (310) 476-7403 parish-4900@la-archdiocese.org; frpaul@la-archdiocese.org www.saintmartinoftours.com Rev. Paul K. Fitzpatrick, Pst.; CRP Stds.: 32

St. Martin of Tours School - (Grades PreK-8) 11955 W. Sunset Blvd., Los Angeles, CA 90049 t) (310) 472-7419 school-8040@la-archdiocese.org www.smtschool.net Debbie Margulis, Prin.; Stds.: 174; Lay Tchrs.: 17

St. Mary - 407 S. Chicago St., Los Angeles, CA 90033 t) (323) 268-7432 parish-4280@la-archdiocese.org; stmarysalesian@gmail.com www.stmaryschurchla.com Rev. Jesse Montes, S.D.B., Pst.; Rev. Alberto Chavez, S.D.B., Assoc. Pst.; Rev. Joseph Farias, S.D.B., Assoc. Pst.; Carlos Flores, DRE; Ramon Rodriguez, DRE; CRP Stds.: 243

St. Mary Magdalen - 1241 S. Corning St., Los Angeles, CA 90035 t) (310) 652-2444 srluzdelcarmen@holyspiritla.org; parish-4910@la-archdiocese.org www.hs-smm.org Rev. Joseph Okech Adhunga, A.J. (Kenya), Pst.; Rev. Macdonald Akuti, A.J., Assoc. Pst.; Rev. John Montag, S.J., Assoc. Pst.; Sr. Luz Del Carmen Perez, DRE; CRP Stds.: 22

St. Michael - 1016 W. Manchester Ave., Los Angeles, CA 90044 t) (323) 753-2696 parish-5630@la-archdiocese.org; info.stmichaella@gmail.com www.stmichaella.org Rev. Peter Thang C. Ngo, Pst.; CRP Stds.: 260

St. Michael School - (Grades PreK-8) 1027 W. 87th St., Los Angeles, CA 90044 t) (323) 752-6101 principal@stmichaelguardians.org; school-8700@la-archdiocese.org www.stmichaelguardians.org Anabel Rodriguez, Prin.; Stds.: 284; Lay Tchrs.: 10

Mother of Sorrows - 114 W. 87th St., Los Angeles, CA 90003 t) (323) 789-6316 (CRP); (323) 758-7697 moscatholicch@yahoo.com; parish-5500@la-archdiocese.org www.moscatholicla.org Rev. Brian Chung, Pst.; Sr. Marta Elena Molina, DRE; CRP Stds.: 231

Mother of Sorrows School - (Grades PreK-8) 100 W. 87th Pl., Los Angeles, CA 90003 t) (323) 758-6204 school-8590@la-archdiocese.org www.motherofsorrowsla.org Griselda Villarreal, Prin.; Stds.: 250; Sr. Tchrs.: 1; Scholastics: 3; Lay Tchrs.: 10

Nativity - 953 W. 57th St., Los Angeles, CA 90037; Mailing: 937 W. 57th St., Los Angeles, CA 90037 t) (323) 759-1562; (323) 753-9802 (CRP) parish-5510@la-archdiocese.org; columbkille-nativityconfirmation@yahoo.com www.nativitychurchla.org Rev. Ever Quintero, Admin.; Rev. Jorge Onofre Salazar, Assoc. Pst.; Juan Carlos Alvarado, DRE; CRP Stds.: 330

Nativity School - (Grades PreK-8) 944 W. 56th St., Los Angeles, CA 90037 t) (323) 752-0720 school-8600@la-archdiocese.org www.nativityla.org Yanira Gomez, Prin.; Stds.: 327; Lay Tchrs.: 11

St. Odilia - 5222 Hooper Ave., Los Angeles, CA 90011 t) (323) 231-5930 odiliaccd2011@yahoo.com; parish-5640@la-archdiocese.org www.stodiliaschool-la.org/about/our-parish/ Rev. Juan Silva, Pst.; Rosa Enriquez, DRE; CRP Stds.: 181

St. Odilia School - (Grades PreK-8) 5300 S. Hooper Ave., Los Angeles, CA 90011 t) (323) 232-5449 school-8710@la-archdiocese.org www.stodiliaschool-la.org Sima Saravia-Perez, Prin.; Stds.: 280; Lay Tchrs.: 10

St. John Bosco - 5516 Duarte St., Los Angeles, CA 90058 parish-5640@laarchdiocese.org

Our Lady Help of Christians (Maria Auxiliadora) - 512 S. Ave. 20, Los Angeles, CA 90031 t) (323) 225-2846 (CRP); (323) 223-4153 chuy200@yahoo.com; parish-4080@la-archdiocese.org mariaauxiliadorala.org/ Rev. Manuel Sanahuja, Sch.P., Pst.; Rev. Federico Castillo, Sch.P., In Res.; Jesse Arellano, DRE; CRP Stds.: 150

Our Lady of Guadalupe - 4018 Hammel St., Los Angeles, CA 90063 t) (323) 526-8397 (CRP); (323) 261-8051 (Rectory) olghammel@aol.com; parish-4090@la-archdiocese.org www.olghammel.org Rev. Marco Solis, Pst.; Sr. Sandra Martinez, M.J.C., DRE; CRP Stds.: 171

Our Lady of Guadalupe School - (Grades PreK-8) 436 N. Hazard Ave., Los Angeles, CA 90063 t) (323) 269-4998 nfigueroa@la-archdiocese.org; school-7350@la-archdiocese.org www.olglions.org Nancy Figueroa, Prin.; Stds.: 142; Lay Tchrs.: 6

San Felipe - 738 N. Geraghty Ave., Los Angeles, CA 90063

Our Lady of Guadalupe - 4509 Mercury Ave., Los Angeles, CA 90032; Mailing: 4504 Browne Ave., Los Angeles, CA 90032 t) (323) 225-4202; (323) 225-4201 srtherese@olgrosehill.com; parish-4100@la-archdiocese.org www.olgrosehill.com Rev. Nelson Trinidad, Pst.; Sr. Theresa Marie Cedillo, DRE; CRP Stds.: 126

Our Lady of Guadalupe School - (Grades PreK-8) 4522 Browne Ave., Los Angeles, CA 90032 t) (323) 221-8187 school-7360@la-archdiocese.org www.olgrhschool.org Evie Lopez, Prin.; Stds.: 81; Lay Tchrs.: 5

Our Lady of Guadalupe Sanctuary - 4100 E. 2nd St., Los Angeles, CA 90063 t) (323) 261-4365 parish-4110@la-archdiocese.org Rev. Leslie N. Delgado (Panama), Pst.; Manuel S. Chavez, DRE; Alfredo Diaz, DRE; CRP Stds.: 176

Our Lady of Loretto - 250 N. Union Ave., Los Angeles, CA 90026 t) (213) 483-3013; (213) 483-5251 (CRP); (213) 483-8137 (CRP) mevelynmo@gmail.com; lorettola@aol.com www.lorettola.org Rev. Anh-Tuan D. Nguyen, Pst.; Rev. Francis Espiga, Par. Vicar; Evelyn Mendoza, DRE; CRP Stds.: 161

Our Lady of Loretto School - (Grades PreK-8) 258 N. Union Ave., Los Angeles, CA 90026 office@ourladyofloretto.org; school-8190@la-archdiocese.org www.ourladyofloretto.org Carlos Loaiza Sr., Prin.; Stds.: 97; Lay Tchrs.: 7

Our Lady of Lourdes - 3772 E. 3rd St., Los Angeles, CA 90063-2408 t) (323) 526-3800; (323) 526-3800 x122 (CRP) fmendez@ollourdes.com; parish-4120@la-archdiocese.org www.ollourdes.com Rev. Jesus Zamarripa, S.V.D., Pst.; Rev. Ricardo Gonzalez Delgadillo, SVD, Assoc. Pst.; Francisco Mendez, DRE; CRP Stds.: 183

Our Lady of Lourdes School - (Grades PreK-8) 315 S. Eastman Ave., Los Angeles, CA 90063 t) (323) 526-3813 school-7370@la-archdiocese.org www.la-ourladyoflourdes.org Veronica Carrillo, Prin.; Stds.: 138; Lay Tchrs.: 10

Our Lady of Solitude - 4561 E. Cesar Chavez Ave., Los Angeles, CA 90022 t) (323) 407-3623 (CRP); (323) 269-7248 parish-4140@la-archdiocese.org; lasoledad@sbcglobal.net www.ourladyofsolitude.org Rev. Efrain Villalobos, MSP, Pst.; Rev. Israel Ramirez, MSP, Assoc. Pst.; Dcn. Sergio A. Perez; Martha Quijano, DRE; CRP Stds.: 390

Our Lady of the Bright Mount - 3424 W. Adams Blvd., Los Angeles, CA 90018 t) (323) 734-5249; (323) 734-5249 (CRP) parish-5280@la-archdiocese.org www.polskaparafiala.org/en Rev. Rafal Dygula, Pst.; Teresa Lezak, DRE; CRP Stds.: 130

Our Lady of the Rosary of Talpa - 2914 E. 4th St., Los Angeles, CA 90033 t) (323) 268-9176 parish-4150@la-archdiocese.org www.talpachurchla.org Rev. Jorge Luis Chalaco Vega, Admin.; CRP Stds.: 93

Our Lady of the Rosary of Talpa School - (Grades PreK-8) 411 S. Evergreen Ave., Los Angeles, CA 90033 t) 323-261-0583 school-7400@la-archdiocese.org www.ourladyoftalpaschool.org John Rojas, Prin.; Stds.: 280; Lay Tchrs.: 10

La Purisima Chapel - 3236 Inez St., Los Angeles, CA 90023 t) 323-268-9177

Our Lady of Victory - 4168 Union Pacific Ave., Los Angeles, CA 90023; Mailing: 1317 S. Herbert Ave., Los Angeles, CA 90023 t) (323) 262-2101 (CRP); (323) 268-9502 elavictory@adelphia.net; parish-4160@la-archdiocese.org www.nuestrasenoradelavictoria.org Rev. Armando Lopez, O.F.M., Pst.; Mary Valentino, DRE; CRP Stds.: 305

Our Lady Queen of Angels - 535 N. Main St., Los Angeles, CA 90012 t) (213) 629-3101 info@laplacita.org; parish-5290@la-archdiocese.org www.laplacita.org Rev. Arturo N. Corral, Pst.; Rev. Jesus Garcia, Assoc. Pst.; Rev. Juan Francisco Gonzalez, Assoc. Pst.; Elisa Nevarez, Asst. to Pastor; CRP Stds.: 155

Our Mother of Good Counsel - 2060 N. Vermont Ave., Los Angeles, CA 90027-1919 t) (323) 664-2111 office@omgcla.org; dre.omgcparish@gmail.com www.omgcla.org Rev. Alvin Paligutan, O.S.A., Pst.; Rev. Mark Menegatti, O.S.A., Assoc. Pst.; Rev. James A. Mott, O.S.A., In Res.; John Dinh, Youth Min.; Dr. Ava Haylock, DRE; CRP Stds.: 112

Our Mother of Good Counsel School - (Grades PreK-8) 4622 Ambrose Ave., Los Angeles, CA 90027 t) 323-664-2131 school@omgcschool.org; school-8180@la-archdiocese.org www.omgcschool.org Kevin Komenkul, Prin.; Stds.: 75; Lay Tchrs.: 10

Our Savior Parish & U.S.C. Caruso Catholic Center - 844 32nd St., Los Angeles, CA 90007 t) (213) 516-3959 x205 info@catholictrojan.org; parish-5300@la-archdiocese.org www.catholictrojan.org Rev. Richard Sunwoo, Pst.; Rev. Joseph Kim, O.F.M.Conv., Campus Min.; Dcn. Paul Pesqueira; Tricia Tembreull, Campus Min.; James Cappetta, Pres.; Yvette Cardona, Bus. Mgr.;

St. Patrick - 1046 E. 34th St., Los Angeles, CA 90011 t) (323) 232-5460 (CRP); (323) 234-5963 parish-5400@la-archdiocese.org www.stpatrickparishla.org Rev. Msgr. Timothy J. Dyer, Pst.; Rev. Moises R. Apolinar Jr., Assoc. Pst.; Enedina Perez, DRE; CRP Stds.: 540

St. Paul - 1920 S. Bronson Ave., Los Angeles, CA 90018 t) (323) 737-1784 (CRP); (323) 730-9490 parish-5410@la-archdiocese.org; stpaulchurchla1920@gmail.com www.stpaulsla.org Rev. Erasmus B. Soriano, Pst.; Rev. Isaac Arrieta Viloria, Assoc. Pst.; Rev. Ho Seok Jin, Assoc. Pst.; Sr. Antonieta M. Zapata, M.G.Sp.S., DRE; Mary Marquez, Bus. Mgr.; CRP Stds.: 249

St. Paul School - (Grades PreK-8) 1908 S. Bronson Ave., Los Angeles, CA 90018 t) (323) 734-4022 school-8510@la-archdiocese.org; lindaguzman@la-archdiocese.org www.stpaulschoolla.org Linda Guzman, Prin.; Stds.: 185; Lay Tchrs.: 10

St. Paul the Apostle - 10750 Ohio Ave., Los Angeles, CA 90024 t) (310) 474-1527 parishoffice@sp-apostle.org; parish-4930@la-archdiocese.org www.sp-apostle.org Rev. Gilbert S. Martinez, C.S.P., Pst.; Rev. Gerard Tully, C.S.P., Assoc. Pst.; Rev. Peter Abdella, C.S.P., In Res.; Rev. Jamie Baca, C.S.P., In Res.; Rev. Robert Cary, CSP, In Res.; Rev. Thomas J. Clerkin, C.S.P., In Res.; Rev. Thomas C. Gibbons, C.S.P., In Res.; Rev. Paul A. Lannan, In Res.; Rev. Theodore A. Vierra, In Res.; Rev. Mark Villano, C.S.P., In Res.; CRP Stds.: 130

St. Paul the Apostle School - (Grades PreK-8) 1536 Selby Ave., Los Angeles, CA 90024 t) (310) 474-1588 info@sp-apostle.org; school-8070@la-archdiocese.org Crystal Pinkofsky, Prin.; Stds.: 552; Lay Tchrs.: 33

St. Peter - 1039 N. Broadway, Los Angeles, CA 90012-1429 t) (323) 225-8119 stpeterit@yahoo.com; parish-5170@la-archdiocese.org www.stpeteritalianchurchla.org Rev. Gianantonio Baggio, C.S., Pst.; Rev. Firmo Mantovani, C.S., Assoc. Pst.; Michelle Fanara, DRE; CRP Stds.: 25

San Conrado - 1820 Bouett St., Los Angeles, CA 90012; Mailing: 1039 N. Broadway St., Los Angeles, CA 90012

Precious Blood - 435 S. Occidental Blvd., Los Angeles, CA 90057 t) (213) 389-8439 parish-5070@la-archdiocese.org; preciousblood.la@gmail.com www.preciousbloodchurchla.org Rev. Crespo Lape, M.J., Pst.; Rev. Manuel Gacad, M.J., Assoc. Pst.; Rev. Freddie Pinuela, MJ, Assoc. Pst.; Dcn. Carlos Magos; CRP Stds.: 66

Precious Blood School - (Grades K-8) 307 S. Occidental Blvd., Los Angeles, CA 90057 t) (213) 382-3345 school-8200@la-archdiocese.org; info@preciousbloodschool.net www.preciousbloodschool.net Maria Cunanan, Prin.; Stds.: 93; Lay Tchrs.: 7

Presentation of Mary - 6406 Parmelee Ave., Los Angeles, CA 90001 t) (323) 585-0570 parish-5520@la-archdiocese.org; presentationofmaryparish@gmail.com Rev. Fredy B. Rosales, Pst.; Rev. Jorge Onofre Salazar; Martin Pardo, DRE; CRP Stds.: 514

St. Raphael - 942 W. 70th St., Los Angeles, CA 90044 t) (323) 752-5965 (CRP); (323) 758-7100 reled@straphaelchurchla.org; office@straphaelchurchla.org www.straphaelchurchla.org Rev. Stan Bosch, ST, Pst.; Dcn. Miguel Angel Martinez; Carmen Carbajal, DRE; CRP Stds.: 255

St. Raphael School - (Grades PreK-8) 924 W. 70th St., Los Angeles, CA 90044 t) (323) 751-2774 school-8720@la-archdiocese.org www.straphaella.org Martha Flores, Prin.; Stds.: 225; Lay Tchrs.: 10

Resurrection - 3324 E. Opal St., Los Angeles, CA 90023; Mailing: 3340 E. Opal St., Los Angeles, CA 90023 t) (323) 264-1963 (CRP); (323) 268-1141 resurrectionla@yahoo.com; parish-4170@la-archdiocese.org www.resurrectionla.com Rev. Msgr. John T. Moretta, Pst.; Rev. Christopher M. Felix, Assoc. Pst.; Letty Pinon, DRE; CRP Stds.: 145

Resurrection School - (Grades PreK-8) 3360 E. Opal St., Los Angeles, CA 90023 t) (323) 261-5750 principal@resurrection-school.org; school-7410@la-archdiocese.org www.resurrection-school.org Catalina Saenz, Prin.; Stds.: 247; Sr. Tchrs.: 1; Lay Tchrs.: 10

Convent for Franciscan Sisters of Mary Immaculate - 3346 E. Opal St., Los Angeles, CA 90023 t) (323) 526-6980

Sacred Heart - 2200 Sichel St., Los Angeles, CA 90031; Mailing: 2210 Sichel St., Los Angeles, CA 90031 t) (323) 223-7571 (CRP); (323) 221-3179 parish-4180@la-archdiocese.org; sacredheartreled@att.net www.sacredheartchurchla.org Rev. Tesfaldet Asghedom, Pst.; Rev. Tesfaldet Tekie Tsada (Eritrea), Assoc. Pst.; Wendy Jones, DRE; Rev. George E. Horan, In Res.; Rev. Reynaldo B. Matunog, In Res.; CRP Stds.: 124

Sacred Heart School - (Grades PreK-8) 2109 Sichel St., Los Angeles, CA 90031 t) (323) 225-4177 adbronzina@la-archdiocese.org; abronzina@sacredheartla.org www.sacredheartla.org Adriana Bronzina, Prin.; Stds.: 217; Lay Tchrs.: 10

San Antonio de Padua - 555 N. Fairview Ave., Los Angeles, CA 90033 t) (323) 225-1301 parish-4190@la-archdiocese.org sanantoniodepaduachurchla.org/ Rev. Gustavo J. Ramon, Pst.; CRP Stds.: 108

San Antonio de Padua Preschool Academy - 1500 Bridge St., Los Angeles, CA 90033 t) (323) 226-0227 school-4191@la-archdiocese.org www.sanantonioacademypreschool.com Sr. Mary Magdalene Acuna, O.S.F., Dir.;

San Francisco - 4800 E. Olympic Blvd., Los Angeles, CA 90022 t) (323) 262-4253; (323) 261-2447 (CRP) rel.ed.sfchurch@gmail.com; parish-4200@la-archdiocese.org www.sfchurchla.org Rev. Mario Arellano, Pst.; Eduviges Cerda, DRE; CRP Stds.: 250

San Miguel - 2214 E. 108th St., Los Angeles, CA 90059; Mailing: 2216 E. 108th St., Los Angeles, CA 90059 t) (323) 569-5951 parish-5530@la-archdiocese.org; sanmiguel-church@hotmail.com Rev. Oscar Esquivel Esquivel, M.S.C., Pst.; Rev. Emiliano Pozas Perez, MSC, Par. Vicar; Elba Rosales, CRE; Sr. Jane Bonar, P.B.V.M., RCIA Coord.; Sr. Catherine Burke, RCIA Coord.; CRP Stds.: 299

San Miguel School - (Grades PreK-8) 2270 E. 108th St., Los Angeles, CA 90059 t) (323) 567-6892 info@sanmiguelcatholicschool.com; school-8610@la-archdiocese.org www.sanmiguelcatholicschool.com Maryann Reynoso-Davis, Prin.; Stds.: 202; Lay Tchrs.: 10

Santa Isabel - 918 S. Soto St., Los Angeles, CA 90023 t) (323) 268-4065 santaisabelrectory@sbcglobal.net; parish-4210@la-archdiocese.org www.santaisabelchurch.org Rev. James Nieblas, SDB, Pst.; Rev. Luis Alfredo Oyarzo, S.D.B., Assoc. Pst.; Rachel Silva, DRE; CRP Stds.: 125

Santa Isabel School - (Grades PreK-8) 2424 Whittier Blvd., Los Angeles, CA 90023 t) (323) 263-3716 school-7450@la-archdiocese.org www.santaisabelsaints.org Hilda Orozco, Prin.; Stds.: 149; Lay Tchrs.: 8

Santa Teresita - 2645 Zonal Ave., Los Angeles, CA 90033 t) (323) 221-2511 (CRP); (323) 221-2446 parish-4220@la-archdiocese.org; steresita38@yahoo.com santateresitala.org Rev. Carlos E. Rojas, Sch.P., Pst.; Rev. Josep M. Margalef, Sch.P., Assoc. Pst.; Jenny Areas, DRE; CRP Stds.: 88

Santa Teresita School - (Grades K-8) 2646 Zonal Ave., Los Angeles, CA 90033 t) (323) 221-1129 office@santateresitaschool.org; school-7460@la-archdiocese.org www.santateresitaschool.org Vernice Grajeda, Prin.; Stds.: 144; Lay Tchrs.: 5

St. Sebastian - 1453 Federal Ave., Los Angeles, CA 90025; Mailing: 11607 Ohio Ave., Los Angeles, CA 90025 t) (310) 479-7380 (CRP); (310) 478-0136 stsebastianoffice@gmail.com; parish-4940@la-archdiocese.org www.stsebastianla.org Rev. German Sanchez, Admin.; Sr. Posada Leidy, DRE; Sr. Ivon Bruno, CRE; CRP Stds.: 71

St. Sebastian School - (Grades PreK-8) 1430 Federal Ave., Los Angeles, CA 90025 t) (310) 473-3337 principal@saintsebastianschool.com; school-8110@la-archdiocese.org www.saintsebastianschool.com Karisa Avalos, Prin.; Stds.: 106; Lay Tchrs.: 10

St. Stephen of Hungary - 3705 Woodlawn Ave., Los

Angeles, CA 90011; Mailing: 1046 E. 34th St., Los Angeles, CA 90011 t) (323) 234-5963 parish-4450@la-archdiocese.org www.saintstephencatholic.org Rev. Msgr. Timothy J. Dyer, Pst.;

St. Teresa of Avila - 2216 Fargo St., Los Angeles, CA 90039 t) (323) 664-8426 parish-5180@la-archdiocese.org www.saintteresaofavilala.org Rev. Roberto Pirrone, Pst.; Francis Calderon, DRE; CRP Stds.: 30

St. Teresa of Avila School - (Grades PreK-8) 2215 Fargo St., Los Angeles, CA 90039 t) (323) 662-3777 stapanthers@gmail.com; school-8260@la-archdiocese.org www.stapanthers.org Christina Fernandez-Caso, Prin.; Stds.: 71; Lay Tchrs.: 10

St. Thomas the Apostle - 2760 W. Pico Blvd., Los Angeles, CA 90006; Mailing: 2727 W. Pico Blvd., Los Angeles, CA 90006 t) (323) 737-3325 parishofficela@gmail.com; parish-5420@la-archdiocese.org www.saintthomasla.org/about/our-parish/ Rev. Mario Torres, Pst.; CRP Stds.: 480

St. Thomas the Apostle School - (Grades PreK-8) 2632 W. 15th St., Los Angeles, CA 90006 t) (323) 737-4730 office@saintthomasla.org; school-8520@la-archdiocese.org www.saintthomasla.org Adrian Xavier Cuevas, Prin.; Stds.: 304; Lay Tchrs.: 10

St. Timothy - 10425 W. Pico Blvd., Los Angeles, CA 90064 t) (310) 474-1216 parish-4950@la-archdiocese.org; sttimothychurchla@gmail.com www.sttimothyla.org Rev. Joseph Visperas, Pst.; CRP Stds.: 75

St. Timothy School - (Grades PreK-8) 10479 W. Pico Blvd., Los Angeles, CA 90064 t) (310) 474-1811 school-8080@la-archdiocese.org www.sttimothy.org Lena Randle, Prin.; Stds.: 224; Lay Tchrs.: 20

Transfiguration - 2515 W. Martin Luther King Blvd., Los Angeles, CA 90008 t) (323) 291-1136 missmrg2@yahoo.com; parish-5530@la-archdiocese.org www.transfigchurchla.com Rev. Godwin Akpan, SSJ, Pst.; Dcn. Gregory Patterson; Refugio Godinez, DRE; CRP Stds.: 15

Transfiguration School - (Grades PreK-8) 4020 Roxton Ave., Los Angeles, CA 90008 t) (323) 292-3011 school-8540@la-archdiocese.org www.transfigurationla.org Evelyn Rickenbacker, Prin.; Stds.: 225; Lay Tchrs.: 10

St. Vincent De Paul - 621 W. Adams Blvd., Los Angeles, CA 90007 t) (213) 749-8950 (CRP); (213) 749-8950 stvincentparishla@gmail.com; parish-5440@la-archdiocese.org www.stvincentla.net Rev. David G. Nations, C.M., Pst.; Rev. Scott D. Jakubowski, C.M., Assoc. Pst.; Dcn. Juan Francisco Ascencio; Miriam Cruz, DRE; Silvia Macias, Liturgy Dir.; CRP Stds.: 220

St. Vincent De Paul School - (Grades PreK-8) 2333 S. Figueroa St., Los Angeles, CA 90007 t) (213) 748-5367 principal@stvincentla.net; school-8530@la-archdiocese.org www.stvincentla.net/school Erika Avila, Prin.; Stds.: 249; Lay Tchrs.: 10

Visitation - 6561 W. 88th St., Los Angeles, CA 90045 t) (310) 216-1145 visitationchurch497@gmail.com; parish-4970@la-archdiocese.org www.visitationchurch-la.com Rev. William Matthew Wheeler, Admin.; Rev. Msgr. James Forsen, Pastor Emer.; Rev. Timothy McGowan, In Res.; Rev. Msgr. Charles E. Hill, In Res.; CRP Stds.: 114

Visitation School - (Grades PreK-8) 8740 Emerson Ave., Los Angeles, CA 90045 t) (310) 645-6620 school-8100@la-archdiocese.org; visitationschool810@gmail.com www.visitationschool.org Christopher Watson, Prin.; Stds.: 244; Lay Tchrs.: 15

LOS NIETOS

Our Lady of Perpetual Help - 8545 S. Norwalk Blvd., Los Nietos, CA 90606 t) (562) 463-3389 (CRP); (562) 692-3758 parish-5920@la-archdiocese.org olphwhittier.org/ Rev. Jose A. Bautista, Pst.; Rev. Josef Draugialis, Assoc. Pst.; Virginia Farias, DRE; CRP Stds.: 800

LYNWOOD

St. Emydius - 10900 California Ave., Lynwood, CA 90262; Mailing: P.O. Box 100, Lynwood, CA 90262 t) (310) 639-1249 (CRP); (310) 637-7095 stemydius@hotmail.com; parish-5810@la-archdiocese.org www.saintemydius.org Rev. Rigoberto Rodriguez, Pst.; Rev. Cesar Guardado Marin, Assoc. Pst.; Rev. Jose Castaneda, Assoc. Pst.; Rev. David Ochoa (Mexico), In Res.; Adela Saucedo, DRE; CRP Stds.: 595

St. Emydius School - (Grades K-8) 10990 California Ave., Lynwood, CA 90262 t) (310) 635-7184 school-8850@la-archdiocese.org; saintemydius84@yahoo.com www.saintemydiuscatholicschool.org Erika Melendez, Prin.; Stds.: 180; Lay Tchrs.: 10

Convent - 10950 California Ave., Lynwood, CA 90262 t) (310) 635-3264

St. Philip Neri - 4311 Olanda St., Lynwood, CA 90262 t) (310) 632-7179; (310) 632-7179 x27 (CRP) parish-5860@la-archdiocese.org www.spneri.com Rev. Ernesto Jaramillo, Pst.; Rev. Jose Maria Cuahutemoc Ramirez, Assoc. Pst.; Rev. Louie Reyes, Assoc. Pst.; Maria Refugio Rosas, DRE; CRP Stds.: 821

St. Philip Neri School - (Grades K-8) 12522 Stoneacre Ave., Lynwood, CA 90262 t) (310) 638-0341 school-8890@la-archdiocese.org; agonzales@stphilipneri.net www.stphilipneri.net Elvia Villasenor, Prin.; Stds.: 217; Lay Tchrs.: 10

MALIBU

Our Lady of Malibu - 3625 Winter Canyon Rd., Malibu, CA 90265 t) (310) 456-2361 parish-4810@la-archdiocese.org www.olmalibu.org Rev. William F. Kerze, Pst.; Marie Slaton, DRE; CRP Stds.: 90

Our Lady of Malibu School - (Grades K-8) t) (310) 456-8071 school-7950@la-archdiocese.org www.olmalibuschool.org Michael A. Smith, Prin.; Stds.: 111; Lay Tchrs.: 10

MANHATTAN BEACH

American Martyrs - 1431 Deegan Pl., Manhattan Beach, CA 90266; Mailing: 700 15th St., Manhattan Beach, CA 90266 t) (310) 546-4734 (CRP); (310) 545-5651 pwilliams@americanmartyrs.org; rectory@americanmartyrs.org www.americanmartyrs.org Rev. Msgr. John F. Barry, Pst.; Rev. Joseph Kammerer, Assoc. Pst.; Rev. Richard Prindle, Assoc. Pst.; Dcn. Chris Amantea; Dcn. Derek A. Brown; Dcn. Richard (Dick) Williams; Patti Williams, DRE; CRP Stds.: 911

American Martyrs School - (Grades PreK-8) 1701 Laurel Ave., Manhattan Beach, CA 90266-4805 t) (310) 545-8559 ams@americanmartyrs.org; school-9100@la-archdiocese.org www.americanmartyrsschool.org Camryn Friel, Prin.; Stds.: 714; Lay Tchrs.: 12

Spirituality Center - 770 17th St., Manhattan Beach, CA 90266-4805

MAYWOOD

St. Rose of Lima - 4450 E. 60th St., Maywood, CA 90270; Mailing: 4430 E. 60th St., Maywood, CA 90270 t) (323) 560-2381 parish-5880@la-archdiocese.org; sroflima@sroflima.org www.sroflima.org Rev. R. Dario Miranda, Pst.; Rev. Isaac Arrieta Viloria, Par. Vicar; Rev. Freddy D. Gonzalez, Par. Vicar; Alvaro Guardado, DRE; CRP Stds.: 266

St. Rose of Lima School - (Grades PreK-8) 4422 E. 60th St., Maywood, CA 90270 t) (323) 560-3376 school-8910@la-archdiocese.org; lguzman@sroflimaschool.org www.sroflimaschool.org Laura Guzman, Prin.; Stds.: 155; Lay Tchrs.: 10

MISSION HILLS

San Fernando Rey Mission - 15151 San Fernando Mission Blvd., Mission Hills, CA 91345 t) (818) 361-0186 x1003 kevin@archivalcenter.org Kevin Feeney, Dir.;

MONROVIA

Immaculate Conception - 740 S. Shamrock Ave., Monrovia, CA 91016 t) (626) 357-3010 (CRP); (626) 358-1166 mmota@icmonrovia.org; information@icmonrovia.org www.icmonrovia.org Rev. Joachim Lepcha, Admin.; Rev. Martin Gonzalez, Assoc. Pst.; Dcn. Michael Salcido; Dcn. Ronald Sanchez; Margarita Mota, DRE; Maria E Natera, Bus. Mgr.; CRP Stds.: 110

Immaculate Conception School - (Grades PreK-8) 726 S. Shamrock Ave., Monrovia, CA 91016 t) (626) 358-5129 clovano@icschoolmonrovia.org; office@icschoolmonrovia.org www.icschoolmonrovia.org Carmela Lovano, Prin.; Stds.: 100; Lay Tchrs.: 8

MONTEBELLO

St. Benedict - 1022 W. Cleveland Ave., Montebello, CA 90640 t) (323) 721-1184; (323) 720-5760 (CRP) stbenedict1022@hotmail.com; parish-4240@la-archdiocese.org Rev. Fredric Abiera, O.A.R., Pst.; Rev. Dionisio C. Cacherco, O.A.R., Assoc. Pst.; Rev. Galo Espinoza, O.A.R. (Ecuador), Assoc. Pst.; Dcn. Alfonso Castillo; Dcn. David J. Estrada; Raymundo Garcia, DRE; CRP Stds.: 505

St. Benedict School - (Grades PreK-8) 217 N. 10th St., Montebello, CA 90640 t) (323) 721-3348 school-7480@la-archdiocese.org www.st-benedict.com Frank Loya, Prin.; Stds.: 470; Lay Tchrs.: 10

Our Lady of the Miraculous Medal - 820 N. Garfield Ave., Montebello, CA 90640 t) (323) 725-7578 x312 (CRP); (323) 725-7578 irmamontreal@yahoo.com; parish-4130@la-archdiocese.org www.olmmparish.com Rev. John M. Vianney, Admin.; Dcn. Frederick Peter Lara; Dcn. Fred Rios; Irma Montreal, DRE; CRP Stds.: 274

Our Lady of the Miraculous Medal School - (Grades PreK-8) 840 N. Garfield Ave., Montebello, CA 90640 t) (323) 728-5435 school-7380@la-archdiocese.org; schoolcommunication@olmmschool.com www.olmmschool.com Dominique Preciado, Prin.; Stds.: 450; Lay Tchrs.: 23

MONTEREY PARK

St. Stephen Martyr - 320 W. Garvey Ave., Monterey Park, CA 91754; Mailing: 122 S. Ramona Ave., Monterey Park, CA 91754 t) (626) 573-0427 parish-4440@la-archdiocese.org www.ststephenmpk.org Rev. Joseph Magdaong, Pst.; CRP Stds.: 99

St. Stephen Martyr School - (Grades PreK-8) 119 S. Ramona Ave., Monterey Park, CA 91754 t) (626) 573-1716 frontoffice@stsmc.org; school-7640@la-archdiocese.org www.stsmc.org Debora Cilio, Prin.; Stds.: 138; Lay Tchrs.: 10

St. Thomas Aquinas - 1501 S. Atlantic Blvd., Monterey Park, CA 91754 t) (323) 264-1338 (CRP); (323) 264-4447 parish-4290@la-archdiocese.org; stareligioused@stampk.org stampk.org Rev. John Kyebasuuta, Pst.; Rev. Justin Liu Zhen Tian, Assoc. Pst.; Ana Martinez, CRE; CRP Stds.: 109

St. Thomas Aquinas School - (Grades PreK-8) t) (323) 261-6583 school-7500@la-archdiocese.org; info@stampkschool.org www.stampkschool.org Stephanie Lutero, Prin.; Stds.: 150; Lay Tchrs.: 12

MONTROSE

Holy Redeemer - 2411 Montrose Ave., Montrose, CA 91020 t) (818) 249-2008 parish-3560@la-archdiocese.org www.hrsjcatholic.com Twinned parish and school with St James the Less, La Crescenta. Rev. Olin Mayfield, Admin.; Rev. Michael S. Grieco, Assoc. Pst.; CRP Stds.: 30

MOORPARK

Holy Cross - 13955 Peach Hill Rd., Moorpark, CA 93021 t) (805) 529-1397; (805) 529-0283 (CRP) church@holycross-moorpark.org; parish-3260@la-archdiocese.org www.holycross-moorpark.org Rev. Msgr. Joseph F. Hernandez, Pst.; Dcn. J. Trinidad Andrade; Dcn. Eduardo Castillo; Dcn. Patrick Coulter; Dcn. Kevin Barry Mauch; Sue Jones, DRE; CRP Stds.: 425

NEW CUYAMA

Immaculate Conception - 4595 Hwy. 166, New Cuyama, CA 93254; Mailing: P.O. Box 265, New Cuyama, CA 93254 t) (661) 766-2741; (805) 682-0442 (CRP) parish-2900@la-archdiocese.org Dcn. Ricardo

Barragan, DRE & Parish Life Coord.;

NEWBURY PARK

St. Julie Billiart - 2475 Borchard Rd., Newbury Park, CA 91320 t) (805) 498-3602; (805) 498-3602 x105 (CRP) parish-3270@la-archdiocese.org; parish@stjulieschurch.org www.stjulieschurch.org Rev. William Ian-Vincent Hagan, Admin.; Dcn. Claudio Selame; Dcn. David Nicholas Smith; CRP Stds.: 196

NORTH HILLS

Our Lady of Peace - 15444 Nordhoff St., North Hills, CA 91343 t) (818) 894-1176 parish-3700@la-archdiocese.org ourladyofpeace.church Rev. Jose Manuel Baeza Gama, M.C.C.J., Admin.; Rev. Filadelfo Segundo Angulo Viloria, Assoc. Pst.; Rev. Hoai Phong Vu, S.D.B., Assoc. Pst.; Dcn. Rey Guiao; CRP Stds.: 170

Our Lady of Peace School - (Grades PreK-8) 9022 Langdon Ave., North Hills, CA 91343 t) (818) 894-4059 office@olpeaceschool.org; school-7030@la-archdiocese.org www.olpeaceschool.org Joanne Testacross, Prin.; Stds.: 104; Lay Tchrs.: 9

NORTH HOLLYWOOD

St. Charles Borromeo - 10834 Moorpark St., North Hollywood, CA 91602 t) (818) 766-3838; (818) 980-1826 (CRP) parish-3720@la-archdiocese.org www.stcharlesborromeochurch.org Rev. Jose Magana, Pst.; His Eminence Roger Michael Mahony, In Res.; Dcn. Louis N. Roche Jr.; Sony Carlos, Bus. Mgr.; Jean Essa, DRE; James Drollinger, Liturgy & Music Dir.; Richard Klee, Confirmation Coord.; CRP Stds.: 160

St. Charles Borromeo School - (Grades PreK-8) 10850 Moorpark St., North Hollywood, CA 91602 t) (818) 508-5359 school-7050@la-archdiocese.org; frontoffice@scb.school www.scb.school John Genova, Prin.; Stds.: 276; Lay Tchrs.: 10

St. Jane Frances de Chantal - 13001 Victory Blvd., North Hollywood, CA 91606; Mailing: 12930 Hamlin St., North Hollywood, CA 91606 t) (818) 985-8600 sjfdechantal@yahoo.com; parish-3780@la-archdiocese.org www.stjanefranceschurch.org Rev. Antonio Carlucci, R.C.J., Pst.; Rev. Jupeter Quinto, R.C.J., Assoc. Pst.; Rev. Santi Scibilia, RCJ, In Res.; CRP Stds.: 424

St. Jane Frances de Chantal School - (Grades PreK-8) 12950 Hamlin St., North Hollywood, CA 91606 t) (818) 766-1714 school-7110@la-archdiocese.org; office@stjanefrancesschool.org www.stjanefrancesschool.org Ashley Giron, Prin.; Stds.: 334; Lay Tchrs.: 16

St. Patrick - 6160 Cartwright Ave., North Hollywood, CA 91606; Mailing: 6153 Cahuenga Blvd., North Hollywood, CA 91606 t) (818) 752-3240; (818) 752-3240 (CRP) nicolas.sanchez@la-archdiocese.org; parish-3790@la-archdiocese.org www.stpatrickcatholicchurch.net Rev. Nicolas Sanchez, Pst.; Ricardo Sifontes, DRE; CRP Stds.: 248

St. Patrick School - (Grades PreK-8) 10626 Erwin St., North Hollywood, CA 91606 t) (818) 761-7363 school-7120@la-archdiocese.org www.stpatrickcatholicschool.com Raquel Shin, Prin.; Stds.: 248; Sr. Tchrs.: 1; Lay Tchrs.: 13

NORTHRIDGE

Our Lady of Lourdes - 18400 Kinzie St., Northridge, CA 91325; Mailing: 18405 Superior St., Northridge, CA 91325 t) (818) 349-1500; (818) 349-2836 (CRP) parishcenter@ollnr.org; re@ollnr.org www.ollnr.org Rev. David C. Loftus, Pst.; Rev. Filiberto Cortez, Assoc. Pst.; Rev. Jeremiah E. O'Keeffe, In Res.; Sr. Frances Kennedy, S.D.S.H., DRE; Sr. Sharon Richards, S.D.S.H., RCIA Coord.; CRP Stds.: 129

Our Lady of Lourdes School - (Grades PreK-8) 18437 Superior St., Northridge, CA 91325 t) 818-349-0245 school-6750@la-archdiocese.org; school@ollnr.org www.ollnr.org/school Kris Brough, Prin.; Stds.: 197; Lay Tchrs.: 9

NORWALK

St. John of God - 13819 Pioneer Blvd., Norwalk, CA 90650 t) (562) 863-5721 x221 frontoffice@sjogparish.org; parish-5970@la-archdiocese.org www.sjogparish.org Rev. Vicente Raymond Decipeda, M.M.H.C., Pst.; Rev. Joachim E. Ablanida, M.M.H.C., Assoc. Pst.; CRP Stds.: 280

St. John of God School - (Grades PreK-8) 13817 S. Pioneer Blvd., Norwalk, CA 90650 t) (562) 863-5722 school@sjogschool.com; school-9010@la-archdiocese.org www.sjogschool.com Lina Vidal-Calderon, Prin.; Stds.: 134; Lay Tchrs.: 7

St. Linus - 13915 Shoemaker Ave., Norwalk, CA 90650 t) (562) 921-6649; (562) 921-5179 (CRP) cmay@stlinus.org; a.engquist@stlinus.org stlinus-church.org Rev. Erasmus B. Soriano, Pst.; Rev. Ambrose Udoji, Assoc. Pst.; Rev. Marco D. Reyes, In Res.; Christina May, DRE; CRP Stds.: 350

St. Linus School - (Grades PreK-8) 13913 Shoemaker Ave., Norwalk, CA 90650 t) (562) 921-0336 schooloffice@stlinuslions.com; school-9020@la-archdiocese.org www.stlinuslions.com Greg Climaco, Prin.; Stds.: 260; Lay Tchrs.: 10

OJAI

St. Thomas Aquinas - 185 Saint Thomas Dr., Ojai, CA 93023 t) (805) 646-4338 stacojai@gmail.com; parish-3230@la-archdiocese.org www.stacojai.org Rev. Kirk Davis, O. S. A., Pst.; Rev. Fernando Lopez, O.S.A., Assoc. Pst.; Rev. Emmanuel Isaac, O.S.A., In Res.; Aina Yates, DRE; CRP Stds.: 92

OXNARD

St. Anthony - 2511 S. C St., Oxnard, CA 93033; Mailing: 2635 Maywood Way, Oxnard, CA 93033 t) (805) 486-7301 x120 parish-3200@la-archdiocese.org; saintanthonyreo@gmail.com www.stanthonyoxnard.org Rev. Joshua Diener, Pst.; Rev. Arthur Najera Jr., Par. Vicar; Rev. Emmanuel Delfin, Par. Vicar; Dcn. Roy Edward Sadowski; Dcn. Joe Kennedy; Dcn. George Angel Garcia; Dcn. Donald Pinedo; CRP Stds.: 460

St. Anthony School - (Grades PreK-8) 2421 S. C St., Oxnard, CA 93033 t) (805) 487-5317 office@sasoxnard.org; school-6600@la-archdiocese.org www.sasoxnard.org Dcn. Henry Barajas Jr., Prin.; Stds.: 260; Lay Tchrs.: 10

Mary Star of the Sea - 463 W. Pleasant Valley Rd., Oxnard, CA 93033 t) (805) 483-9313 (CRP); (805) 486-6133 marystar@marystaroxnard.com; parish-3120@la-archdiocese.org www.marystarchurchoxnard.com Rev. Felizardo J. Daganta, Pst.; Dcn. Alfonso Flores; Sr. Rosa Hernandez, C.V.D., DRE; CRP Stds.: 896

Our Lady of Guadalupe Parish - 500 N. Juanita Ave., Oxnard, CA 93030; Mailing: P.O. Box 272, Oxnard, CA 93032 t) (805) 483-0987 olggladislemus@gmail.com; parish-3150@la-archdiocese.org www.olgoxnard.org Rev. Celso Marquez, M.Sp.S., Admin.; Rev. Jose Gerardo Alberto, M.Sp.S., Assoc. Pst.; Rev. Vincente Gutierrez-Franco, M.Sp.S., Assoc. Pst.; Rev. Rodolfo Martinez, M.Sp.S., Assoc. Pst.; Rev. Eugenio Cardenas, M.Sp.S., In Res.; Dcn. Henry Barajas Jr.; Dcn. Arturo Godinez; Dcn. Alejandro Zendejas Marron; Sr. Nora Estrada, H.B.C.V.D., DRE; CRP Stds.: 671

Our Lady of Guadalupe Parish School - (Grades PreK-8) 530 N. Juanita Ave., Oxnard, CA 93030 t) (805) 483-5116 school-6560@la-archdiocese.org www.guadalupeschool.com Julio Tellez, Prin.; Stds.: 207; Lay Tchrs.: 10

Christ the King - 535 Cooper Rd., Oxnard, CA 93030

Santa Clara - 323 S. E St., Oxnard, CA 93030 t) (805) 487-3891 parish-3190@la-archdiocese.org; church@santaclaraparish.org www.santaclaraparish.org Rev. John W. Love, Pst.; Rev. Patrick Ayala, Assoc. Pst.; Rev. Carlos Villasano, Assoc. Pst.; Dcn. Vincent Crawford; Dcn. Michael Holguin; Dcn. Leonardo Lacbain; Dcn. Lawrence James Lopez; Dcn. Fidel Ramirez; Dcn. Dano L. Ramos; Dcn. Milton Rosenberg; Dcn. Raymond Vasquez Jr.; Sr. Estela Pina, DRE; CRP Stds.: 1,265

Santa Clara School - (Grades PreK-8) 324 S. E St., Oxnard, CA 93030 t) (805) 483-6935 school-6590@la-archdiocese.org; mrslozano@scesoxnard.org www.scesoxnard.weebly.com Jennifer Lozano, Prin.; Stds.: 243; Lay Tchrs.: 10

Santa Clara Chapel - 1333 Ventura Blvd., Oxnard, CA 93036

Ventura Korean Catholic Church - 601 S. D St., Oxnard, CA 93030 t) 805-263-6215 venturakcc@gmail.com venturakcc.org/ Rev. Sang Man Han, Chap.;

PACIFIC PALISADES

Corpus Christi - 15100 Sunset Blvd., Pacific Palisades, CA 90272; Mailing: 880 Toyopa Dr., Pacific Palisades, CA 90272 t) (310) 454-1328 parishmail@corpuschristichurch.com; parish-4790@la-archdiocese.org www.corpuschristichurch.com Rev. Msgr. Liam J. Kidney, Pst.; Rev. Larry Neumeier, Assoc. Pst.; Rev. Xavier Lourdu, In Res.; Jane Young, DRE; CRP Stds.: 75

Corpus Christi School - (Grades PreK-8) 890 Toyopa Dr., Pacific Palisades, CA 90272 t) (310) 454-9411 school@cchristi.org; school-7930@la-archdiocese.org www.corpuschristi-school.com Suzanne Duffy, Prin.; Stds.: 172; Lay Tchrs.: 10

PACOIMA

Guardian Angel - 10886 Lehigh Ave., Pacoima, CA 91331; Mailing: 10919 Norris Ave., Pacoima, CA 91331 t) (818) 899-8907 (CRP); (818) 485-5207 parish-3680@la-archdiocese.org www.guardianangelparish.com/en/home Rev. Rafael Lara, Pst.; Dcn. Raul Chavez; Dcn. Ruben Ochoa; Dcn. Ruben A. Cordero, DRE; CRP Stds.: 230

Guardian Angel School - (Grades PreK-8) 10919 Norris Ave., Pacoima, CA 91331 t) (818) 485-5000 office@guardianangelcs.com; principal@guardianangelcs.com www.guardianangelcs.com Mario Landeros, Prin.; Stds.: 232; Lay Tchrs.: 10

Mary Immaculate - 10390 Remick Ave., Pacoima, CA 91331 t) (818) 899-2111 (CRP); (818) 899-0278 parish-3690@la-archdiocese.org; hermanaraquel@hotmail.com www.maryimmaculateparish.org Rev. Julio Domenech, Admin.; Rev. Jeyaraj Joseph Williams, Assoc. Pst.; Rev. Walter Paredes, Assoc. Pst.; Raquel Arroyo, DRE; Javier Hinojoza, DRE; Carlos Ruiz, RCIA Coord.; CRP Stds.: 803

Mary Immaculate School - (Grades PreK-8) t) (818) 834-8551 school-7020@la-archdiocese.org; info@maryimmaculateschool.org www.maryimmaculateschool.org Federina Gullano, Prin.; Stds.: 200; Lay Tchrs.: 10

PALMDALE

St. Mary - 1600 E Ave., R-4, Palmdale, CA 93550 t) (661) 947-3306; (661) 273-5554 (CRP) agasca@saintmarys-ave.org; info@saintmarys-ave.org www.saintmarys-ave.org Rev. Vaughn P. Winters, Pst.; Rev. Esteban Marquez, Assoc. Pst.; Rev. Eder Tamara, Assoc. Pst.; Rev. Efren Franco, M.S.P., Assoc. Pst.; Dcn. Efrain Calderon; Dcn. Elvys C. Perez; Astrid Gasca, DRE; CRP Stds.: 1,800

St. Mary School - (Grades K-8) t) (661) 273-5555 school-7230@la-archdiocese.org www.stmaryspalmdale.org Anna Maria Rios, Prin.; Stds.: 250; Lay Tchrs.: 10

Our Lady of the Desert - 35647 87th St. E, Littlerock, CA 93543 t) (661) 269-8837 mcamacho@saintmarys-ave.org Maria Iboa, Secy.;

St. John Paul II Mission - 16310 E. Ave. Q, Palmdale, CA 93591 t) (661) 264-9166 mcamacho@saintmarys-ave.org (at Lake Los Angeles School) Maria Iboa, Secy.;

Acton Mission at High Desert Jr. High School - 3620 Antelope Woods Rd., Acton, CA 93510 t) (661) 877-7528 quiltingnani@gmail.com Maria Iboa, Secy.;

PANORAMA CITY

St. Genevieve - 14061 Roscoe Blvd., Panorama City, CA 91402 t) (818) 894-2261 jmorales@stgenparish.org; parish-3770@la-archdiocese.org www.stgenchurch.org Rev. Joy Lawrence Santos, Pst.; Rev. Yesupadam Teneti, Assoc. Pst.; Rev. Guillermo Alonso, Assoc. Pst.; Dcn. Paulino Juarez-Ramirez; Rebecca Chan, DRE; CRP Stds.: 985

St. Genevieve Elementary School - (Grades PreK-8) 14024 Community St., Panorama City, CA 91402 t) (818) 892-3802 school-7100@la-archdiocese.org www.sgps.org Daniel Horn, Prin.; Stds.: 400; Lay Tchrs.: 16

St. Genevieve High School - (Grades 9-12) 13967 Roscoe Blvd., Panorama City, CA 91402 t) (818) 894-6417 school-9860@la-archdiocese.org; jasso@sgps.org www.valiantspirit.com Daniel Horn, Pres.; Amanda Allen, Dir.; Stds.: 550; Lay Tchrs.: 25

PARAMOUNT

Our Lady of the Rosary - 14815 S. Paramount Blvd., Paramount, CA 90723 t) (562) 633-1126 parish-5730@la-archdiocese.org; parish@myladyolr.com www.myladyolr.com Rev. Julio Gonzalez, Pst.; Dcn. Oscar A. Corcios; Dcn. Ezequiel Martinez; Dcn. Jorge Perez; Dcn. Victor Manuel Ramos; CRP Stds.: 884

Our Lady of the Rosary School - (Grades PreK-8) 14813 S. Paramount Blvd., Paramount, CA 90723 t) (562) 633-6360 school-8780@la-archdiocese.org; olrcontact_us@olrwarriors.org www.olrcatholicschool.com/home Vanessa Rivas, Prin.; Stds.: 285; Lay Tchrs.: 10

PASADENA

St. Andrew - 311 N. Raymond Ave., Pasadena, CA 91103; Mailing: 140 Chestnut St., Pasadena, CA 91103 t) (626) 768-9376 (CRP); (626) 792-4183 (Office) janderson@standrewpasadena.org; saintandrewpasadena@gmail.com www.saintandrewpasadena.org Rev. Marcos J. Gonzalez, Pst.; Rev. Martin Rodriguez, Assoc. Pst.; Dcn. Juan Jose Gomez, Dean; CRP Stds.: 289

St. Andrew School - (Grades PreK-8) 42 Chestnut St., Pasadena, CA 91103 t) (626) 796-7697 school-7580@la-archdiocese.org www.saspasadena.com Jae Kim, Prin.; Stds.: 180; Lay Tchrs.: 15

Assumption of the Blessed Virgin Mary - 2640 E. Orange Grove Blvd., Pasadena, CA 91107 t) (626) 792-6844 (CRP); (626) 792-1343 cvaldez@abvmpasadena.org; church@abvmpasadena.org www.abvmpasadena.org Rev. Michael Ume, Pst.; Cheli Valdez, DRE; CRP Stds.: 116

Assumption of the Blessed Virgin Mary School - (Grades PreK-8) 2660 E. Orange Grove Blvd., Pasadena, CA 91107 t) (626) 793-2089 school-7540@la-archdiocese.org; school@abvmpasadena.org www.abvm-school.org Rosalinda Navarro, Prin.; Stds.: 192; Lay Tchrs.: 27

St. Philip the Apostle - 151 S. Hill Ave., Pasadena, CA 91106 t) (626) 793-0693 parish-4420@la-archdiocese.org; pbm@stphiliptheapostle.org www.stphiliptheapostle.org Rev. Anthony J. Gomez, Pst.; Dcn. William Landa; Susie Arevalos, CRE; CRP Stds.: 350

St. Philip the Apostle School - (Grades PreK-8) 1363 Cordova St., Pasadena, CA 91106 t) (626) 795-9691 school-7620@la-archdiocese.org school.stphiliptheapostle.org/ Jennifer Ramirez, Prin.; Stds.: 558; Lay Tchrs.: 14

PICO RIVERA

St. Francis Xavier - 4245 Acacia Ave., Pico Rivera, CA 90660 t) (562) 699-8527; (562) 699-7517 (CRP) parish-5940@la-archdiocese.org Rev. Martin Madero, Sch.P., Admin.; Rev. Patrick Torres, M.C., Assoc. Pst.; Dcn. Joseph Bernal; Dcn. Sergio Islas; Dcn. Carlos R. Rivas; Sr. Petra Lopez, DRE; CRP Stds.: 245

St. Hilary - 5465 Citronell Ave., Pico Rivera, CA 90660 t) (562) 942-7300; (562) 942-7310; (562) 942-7018 (CRP) st.hilarydre@gmail.com; parish-5960@la-archdiocese.org www.st-hilary.com Rev. Diego Cabrera Rojas, S.S.C., Pst.; Rev. Gerard O'Shaughnessy, S.S.C., Assoc. Pst.; Dcn. Salvador Aviles; Rev. Thomas Reynolds, S.S.C., In Res.; Carlos Loaiza Sr., Youth Min.; Mia Gonzalez, DRE; Theresa Salas, Bus. Mgr.; CRP Stds.: 316

St. Hilary School - (Grades PreK-8) 5401 Citronell Ave., Pico Rivera, CA 90660 t) (562) 942-7361 school-9000@la-archdiocese.org; office@sthilarycougars.org www.sthilaryschool.com Patricia Contreras-McJunkin, Prin.; Stds.: 172; Lay Tchrs.: 10

St. Mariana de Paredes - 7930 Passons Blvd., Pico Rivera, CA 90660; Mailing: 7922 Passons Blvd., Pico Rivera, CA 90660 t) (562) 949-8240 parish-5990@la-archdiocese.org; parish@stmariana.org www.stmariana.org Rev. Lazaro Revilla, Pst.; Rev. Juan Carrasco, Assoc. Pst.; Pablo Palacios, DRE; Moises Vargas, RCIA Coord.; CRP Stds.: 268

St. Mariana de Paredes School - (Grades PreK-8) 7911 Buhman Ave., Pico Rivera, CA 90660 t) (562) 949-1234 school-9030@la-archdiocese.org; stmarianne@stmarianne.org www.stmarianne.org Frank Montejano, Prin.; Stds.: 194; Lay Tchrs.: 10

POMONA

St. Joseph - 1150 W. Holt Ave., Pomona, CA 91768 t) (909) 629-1404 (CRP); (909) 629-4101 parish-4720@la-archdiocese.org; cervantesstjosephchurch@gmail.com www.stjosephchurchpomona.org/ Rev. Steven Guitron, Pst.; Rev. Everardo Soto Montoya, Assoc. Pst.; Rev. Ala Alamat, In Res.; Rev. John Montejano, In Res.; Lilian Cervantes, DRE; CRP Stds.: 216

St. Joseph School - (Grades PreK-5) 1200 W. Holt Ave., Pomona, CA 91768 t) (909) 622-3365 school-7860@la-archdiocese.org; principal@stjosephschoolpomona.org www.stjosephschoolpomona.org Diane Marie Gehner, Prin.; Stds.: 73; Lay Tchrs.: 10

St. Madeleine - 931 E. Kingsley Ave., Pomona, CA 91767 t) (909) 629-9495 vrincon91@gmail.com; parish-4740@la-archdiocese.org www.stmadeleinechurch.org Rev. Manuel Leon Bravo, Pst.; Veronica Rincon, Youth Min.; Rev. Vivian B. Lima, In Res.; CRP Stds.: 21

Sacred Heart - 1215 S. Hamilton Blvd., Pomona, CA 91766 t) (909) 622-4553 parish-4680@la-archdiocese.org www.sacredheartpomona.com Rev. Alberto Arreola, Pst.; Dcn. Miguel Galvez; Silvia Contreras, DRE; CRP Stds.: 928

RANCHO DOMINGUEZ

St. Albert the Great - 804 E. Compton Blvd., Rancho Dominguez, CA 90220 t) (310) 323-1599 (CRP); (310) 329-7548 parish-5760@la-archdiocese.org; st.albertthegreatchurch@yahoo.com www.stalbertthegreatchurch.org Rev. Humberto Bernabe, Pst.; Rev. Michael E. Kennedy, S.J., Assisting Priest; Marilyn De La Rosa, Bus. Mgr.; Macrina Garcia, DRE; CRP Stds.: 316

St. Albert the Great Elementary School - (Grades PreK-5) t) (310) 323-4559 school-8800@la-archdiocese.org; stalbertms@aol.com www.stalbertthegreatschool.org Tina Johnson, Prin.; Stds.: 120; Lay Tchrs.: 6

St. Albert the Great Middle School - (Grades 6-8) 823 E. Compton Blvd., Rancho Dominguez, CA 90220 t) (310) 515-3891 school-9410@la-archdiocese.org; stalbertms@aol.com www.stalbertthegreatms.com Tina Johnson, Prin.; Stds.: 285; Lay Tchrs.: 10

RANCHO PALOS VERDES

St. John Fisher - 5448 Crest Rd., Rancho Palos Verdes, CA 90275 t) (310) 377-5571; (310) 377-4573 (CRP) parish-6160@la-archdiocese.org; info@sjf.org www.sjf.org Rev. Msgr. David A. Sork, Pst.; Rev. Bernard Kalu, Assoc. Pst.; CRP Stds.: 298

St. John Fisher School - (Grades PreK-8) 5446 Crest Rd., Rancho Palos Verdes, CA 90275 t) (310) 377-2800 school-9200@la-archdiocese.org; principal@sjf.org www.sjfpv.org Christine Gurrola, Prin.; Stds.: 170; Lay Tchrs.: 13

REDONDO BEACH

St. James - 415 Vincent St., Redondo Beach, CA 90277; Mailing: 124 N. Pacific Coast Hwy., Redondo Beach, CA 90277 t) (310) 372-5228 office@stjamesparish.org; parish-6150@la-archdiocese.org www.saintjames.church Rev. Msgr. Michael W. Meyers, Pst.; Rev. Thaddeus Agbasonu, SMMM, Assoc. Pst.; Rev. James F. Kavanagh, Pastor Emer.; Dcn. Robert J. Miller; Gretchen Nobleza, Youth Min.; Andrea Sullivan, DRE; CRP Stds.: 249

St. James School - (Grades PreK-8) 4625 Garnet St., Torrance, CA 90503 t) (310) 371-0416 office@sjscatholicschool.org; school-9190@la-archdiocese.org www.sjscatholicschool.org/ Noreen Maricich, Prin.; Stds.: 240; Lay Tchrs.: 12

St. James Preschool - 126 N. Pacific Coast Hwy., Redondo Beach, CA 90277 t) (310) 376-5550 saintjamespreschool123@gmail.com www.saintjames.church/preschool/ Wendy Bell, Dir.;

St. Lawrence Martyr - 1900 S. Prospect Ave., Redondo Beach, CA 90277; Mailing: 1940 S. Prospect Ave., Redondo Beach, CA 90277 t) (310) 540-0329 info@stlm.org; parish-6180@la-archdiocese.org www.stlm.org Rev. Msgr. Paul T. Dotson, Pst.; Rev. Charles Balamaze, Assoc. Pst.; Rev. Msgr. Peter A. O'Reilly, In Res.; Dcn. Donald Burt; Dcn. James A. Egnatuk; Dcn. Dale Sheckler; Susan Mills, DRE; Jenny Attanasio, Bus. Mgr.; CRP Stds.: 650

St. Lawrence Martyr School - (Grades PreK-8) 1950 S. Prospect Ave., Redondo Beach, CA 90277 t) (310) 316-3049 school-9220@la-archdiocese.org www.stlmschool.org Janell O'Dowd, Prin.; Stds.: 316; Lay Tchrs.: 10

RESEDA

St. Catherine of Siena - 18115 Sherman Way, Reseda, CA 91335 t) (818) 996-4588 (CRP); (818) 343-2110 parish-3430@la-archdiocese.org; receptionist@catherineofsiena.org www.catherineofsienaparish.org Rev. Mauricio O. Goloran III (Philippines), Pst.; Rev. Fufa Ensermu Wakuma, Assoc. Pst.; Adrian Aralar, DRE; Dcn. Son Hoang; Dcn. Pedro Lira; CRP Stds.: 200

ROWLAND HEIGHTS

St. Elizabeth Ann Seton - 1835 Larkvane Rd., Rowland Heights, CA 91748 t) (626) 964-3629; (626) 965-5792 (CRP) parish-4700@la-archdiocese.org; stelizabethannseton@yahoo.com www.seasrh.org Rev. John H. Keese, Pst.; Rev. Mark Martinez, Assoc. Pst.; Rev. Dominic Su, Assoc. Pst.; Rev. Msgr. Michael F. Killeen, Pastor Emer.; Dcn. Steven V. Hillmann; Fe Musgrave, Pst. Assoc.; CRP Stds.: 293

St. Gabriel Korean Center - 2035 Otterbein Ave., Rowland Heights, CA 91748-3950 t) (626) 965-7553 stgabrielkcc@gmail.com www.stgabrielkcc.com/

SAN DIMAS

Holy Name of Mary - 724 E. Bonita Ave., San Dimas, CA 91773 t) (909) 599-1243 cosme@hnmparish.org; parish-4660@la-archdiocese.org www.hnmparish.org Rev. Christopher Santangelo, SS.CC., Pst.; Rev. Micheal Kumar, SS.CC, Assoc. Pst.; Rev. John Roache, SS.CC, Assoc. Pst.; Dcn. Marv Estey; Dcn. Alfred H. Austin; Dcn. Amante Pulido; Dcn. Mario Lopez; Dcn. Jose Guadamuz; Melanie Bailey, DRE; Cosme Garcia, Bus. Mgr.; CRP Stds.: 625

Holy Name of Mary School - (Grades PreK-8) 124 S. San Dimas Cyn. Rd., San Dimas, CA 91773 t) (909) 542-0449 hnmschool@hnmschool.org; school-7830@la-archdiocese.org www.hnmschool.org Deborah Marquez, Prin.; Stds.: 355; Lay Tchrs.: 10

SAN FERNANDO

St. Ferdinand - 1044 Pico St., San Fernando, CA 91340; Mailing: 1109 Coronel St., San Fernando, CA 91340 t) (818) 365-3967; (818) 361-1813 (Religious Ed); (818) 361-1814 (Youth/Confirmation); (818) 540-9786 (RCIA) parish-3900@la-archdiocese.org; mariacalzada1109@gmail.com www.stferdinandchurch.org Rev. Juan Ayala, O.M.I., Pst.; Rev. Feliciano Lopez Ortiz, O.M.I., Assoc. Pst.; Daniel Enriquez, Youth Min.; Estella Fajardo Pompa, DRE; CRP Stds.: 249

Santa Rosa - 668 S. Workman St., San Fernando, CA 91340 t) (818) 361-4617; (818) 933-1978 (CRP) parish-3860@la-archdiocese.org www.santarosacatholic.church Rev. Alberto Arreola, Pst.; Rev. Mario F. Cabrera, Assoc. Pst.; Rev. Heriberto Serrano, Assoc. Pst.; Rev. Jeejo K. Vazhappilly, Sch.P.,

Assoc. Pst.; Rev. Sergio Hidalgo, Assoc. Pst.; Alexis Davila-Rodriguez, Youth Min.; Magdalena Reynoso, RCIA Coord.; Maricela Lopez, Bus. Mgr.; CRP Stds.: 309

Santa Rosa de Lima Catholic School - (Grades PreK-8) 1316 Griffith St., San Fernando, CA 91340 t) (818) 361-5096 aaceves@srdlcs.com; school-7180@la-archdiocese.org www.srdlcs.com Alexandra Aceves, Prin.; Stds.: 132; Lay Tchrs.: 6

St. Vitus - 607 4th St., San Fernando, CA 91340 t) 626-424-1962 email@fssp.la www.fssp.la Traditional Latin Mass apostolate staffed by the Priestly Fraternity of St. Peter Rev. James Fryar, F.S.S.P., Pst.; Rev. John Kodet, FSSP, Par. Vicar; Rev. Michael Kokoszka, Par. Vicar; CRP Stds.: 75

SAN GABRIEL

St. Anthony - 1901 S. San Gabriel Blvd., San Gabriel, CA 91776 t) (626) 288-8912 dre@saintanthonyparishsg.org; parish-4390@la-archdiocese.org www.stanthonysg.org Rev. Spencer Lewerenz, Admin.; Rev. Nahum Gutierrez, M.G., Assoc. Pst.; Rev. James Clarke, In Res.; Jonah Zeko, Youth Min.; Gustavo Lemus, DRE; CRP Stds.: 231

St. Anthony School - (Grades K-8) 1905 S. San Gabriel Blvd., San Gabriel, CA 91776 t) (626) 280-7255 agutierrez@saintanthonysg.com; school-7590@la-archdiocese.org www.stanthonyschoolsg.org Angela Mastantuono, Prin.; Stds.: 109; Lay Tchrs.: 8

Convent - 626 E. Marshall St., San Gabriel, CA 91776 t) (626) 288-2200 callaway@ramonaconvent.org Sr. Kathleen Callaway, S.N.J.M., Contact; Sr. Eddy Miriam Mark, Contact;

San Gabriel Mission - 428 S. Mission Dr., San Gabriel, CA 91776 t) (626) 457-3035 parish-4360@la-archdiocese.org www.sangabrielmissionchurch.org (Old Mission) Rev. John Molyneux, CMF, Pst.; Rev. Gerald Kumar Balavendra, CMF, Assoc. Pst.; Rev. Gabriel Ruiz, CMF, Assoc. Pst.; Rev. Emmanuel Sylvester, CMF, In Res.; Gigi Galardi, DRE; Terri Valadez, Bus. Mgr.; CRP Stds.: 393

San Gabriel Mission Elementary School - (Grades PreK-8) 416 S. Mission Dr., San Gabriel, CA 91776 t) (626) 281-2454 egarcia@sgmission.org; school-7560@la-archdiocese.org www.sgmission.org Sr. Sharon Dempsey, Prin.; Stds.: 205; Lay Tchrs.: 10

San Gabriel Mission High School - (Grades 9-12) 254 S. Santa Anita St., San Gabriel, CA 91776 t) (626) 282-3181 school-9880@la-archdiocese.org www.sgmhs.org Girls College Prep. Parish School Raquel Cagigas, Prin.; Stds.: 206; Lay Tchrs.: 8

Convent - 412 S. Mission Dr., San Gabriel, CA 91776 t) (626) 284-9585 Rev. Theo Fuentes, C.M.F., Pst. Assoc.;

SAN MARINO

Ss. Felicitas and Perpetua - 1190 Palomar Rd., San Marino, CA 91108 t) (626) 796-0432 jackiew@ssfp.org; parish-4370@la-archdiocese.org www.ssfp.org Rev. John Collins, Pst.; Jackie Whitenack, DRE; Annette Early, Bus. Mgr.; CRP Stds.: 75

Saints Felicitas and Perpetua School - (Grades PreK-8) 2955 Huntington Dr., San Marino, CA 91108 t) (626) 796-8223 school-7570@la-archdiocese.org; jpringle-starr@ssfp.org Jennifer Pringle-Starr, Prin.; Stds.: 138; Lay Tchrs.: 11

SAN PEDRO

Holy Trinity - 1292 W. Santa Cruz St., San Pedro, CA 90732; Mailing: 209 N. Hanford Ave., San Pedro, CA 90732 t) (310) 548-6535; 310-833-3500 (CRP) parishoffice@holytrinitysp.org; parish-6070@la-archdiocese.org www.holytrinitysp.org Rev. Kevin L. Nolan, Pst.; Dcn. Walter John Lauderdale; Dcn. Gaspar Munoz; Molly Slaught, DRE; Dr. Joy Jones, Pst. Assoc.; CRP Stds.: 178

Holy Trinity School - (Grades PreK-8) 1226 W. Santa Cruz St., San Pedro, CA 90732 t) (310) 833-0703 school-9120@la-archdiocese.org; secretary@holytrinityschoolsp.com www.school.holytrinitysp.org Lisa Monique Luna, Prin.; Stds.: 447; Lay Tchrs.: 27

Mary Star of the Sea - 877 W. 7th St., San Pedro, CA 90731; Mailing: 870 W. 8th St., San Pedro, CA 90731 t) 310-833-3541 office@marystar.org; parish-6080@la-archdiocese.org www.marystar.org Rev. Maurice D. Harrigan, Pst.; Rev. Raymond Perez, Assoc. Pst.; Rev. Ignatius Harsha, O.Praem., Assoc. Pst.; Dcn. John Burgos Salazar; Rev. Menniti Diego, In Res.; Rev. Ivan Gerovac, S.J., In Res.; Sr. Mary J. Glynn, S.J.C., DRE; CRP Stds.: 255

Mary, Star of the Sea School - (Grades PreK-8) 717 S. Cabrillo Ave., San Pedro, CA 90731 t) (310) 831-0875 office@marystarelementary.com; school-9130@la-archdiocese.org www.marystarelementary.com James Cordero, Prin.; Stds.: 227; Lay Tchrs.: 10

Mary, Star of the Sea High School - (Grades 9-12) 2500 N. Taper Ave., San Pedro, CA 90731 t) (310) 547-1138 principal@marystarhigh.com; info@marystarhigh.com www.marystarhigh.com Rev. Nicholas Tacito, Rector; Rita Dever, Prin.; Stds.: 549; Lay Tchrs.: 18

St. Peter - 338 N. Grand Ave., San Pedro, CA 90731 t) (310) 831-5360 parish-6200@la-archdiocese.org Rev. Joseph Scalco, C.S.J., Pst.; CRP Stds.: 380

SANTA BARBARA

Holy Cross - 1740 Cliff Dr., Santa Barbara, CA 93109 t) (805) 962-7311 (CRP); (805) 962-0411 cre@holycross.sbcoxmail.com; parish-3000@la-archdiocese.org www.holycrosssantabarbara.org Rev. Egren Gomez, Admin.; CRP Stds.: 65

Old Mission Santa Barbara - 2201 Laguna St., Santa Barbara, CA 93105 t) (805) 682-4151 (Office); (805) 682-4713 (Porter) parishoffice@saintbarbaraparish.org; parish-3050@la-archdiocese.org www.saintbarbaraparish.org Rev. Daniel Lackie, O.F.M., Pst.; Rev. Larry Gosselin, O.F.M., Assoc. Pst.; CRP Stds.: 75

Our Lady of Guadalupe - 221 N. Nopal St., Santa Barbara, CA 93103; Mailing: 227 N. Nopal St., Santa Barbara, CA 93103 t) (805) 962-4441 (CRP); (805) 965-4060; (805) 965-4060 x207 (CRP) rcanseco@olgsb.org; info@olgsb.org www.olgsb.org Rev. Pedro J. Lopez, Pst.; Rev. Alberto Cuevas, Assoc. Pst.; Rafaela Canseco, DRE; CRP Stds.: 234

Our Lady of Mount Carmel - 1300 E. Valley Rd., Santa Barbara, CA 93108 t) (805) 969-6868 (Parish Office); (805) 969-4868 (RE Office) info@mtcarmelsb.com; parish-3020@la-archdiocese.org www.mtcarmelsb.com Rev. Lawrence Seyer, Pst.; Rev. Msgr. Stephen N. Downes, Pastor Emer.; Rev. Maurice K. O'Mahony, Pastor Emer.; Sr. Rosalie Callen, C.S.J., DRE; CRP Stds.: 97

Our Lady of Mount Carmel School - (Grades PreK-8) 530 Hot Springs Rd., Santa Barbara, CA 93108 t) (805) 969-5965 info@mountcarmelschool.net; school-6480@la-archdiocese.org www.mountcarmelschool.net Tracie Simolon, Prin.; Stds.: 226; Lay Tchrs.: 12

Our Lady of Sorrows - 21 E. Sola St., Santa Barbara, CA 93101 t) (805) 966-4941 (CRP); (805) 963-1734 religioused@olssb.org; coordinator@olssb.org www.our-lady-of-sorrows-santa-barbara.com Rev. Cesar Magallon, Pst.; Maria Moreno, DRE; Cara Crosetti, Bus. Mgr.; CRP Stds.: 322

Notre Dame - (Grades PreSchool-8) 33 E. Micheltorena St., Santa Barbara, CA 93101 t) (805) 965-1033 info@notredamesb.org; school-6490@la-archdiocese.org www.notredamesb.org Timothy Flanagan, Prin.; Stds.: 125; Lay Tchrs.: 15

St. Raphael - 5444 Hollister Ave., Santa Barbara, CA 93111 t) (805) 967-5641 parish-3080@la-archdiocese.org; office@straphaelsb.org www.straphaelsb.org Rev. Msgr. Jon F. Majarucon, Pst.; Rev. Rajan Sengol, Assoc. Pst.; Dcn. Sergio Lopez Macias; Dcn. Stephen Montross; Ana Solis-Cervantes, CRE; CRP Stds.: 389

St. Raphael School - (Grades PreSchool-8) 160 St. Joseph St., Santa Barbara, CA 93111 t) (805) 967-2115 mlimb@la-archdiocese.org; office@straphaelschoolsb.org www.straphaelschoolsb.org Michelle Limb, Prin.; Stds.: 251; Lay Tchrs.: 13

San Roque - 325 Argonne Cir., Santa Barbara, CA 93105 t) (805) 682-1097 (CRP); (805) 687-5215 education@sanroqueparish.org; office@sanroqueparish.org www.sanroqueparish.org Rev. Bruce Correio, Pst.; Noel Fuentes, DRE; CRP Stds.: 29

SANTA CLARITA

St. Clare - 19606 Calla Way, Santa Clarita, CA 91351; Mailing: 27341 Camp Plenty Rd., Santa Clarita, CA 91351 t) (661) 252-3353 office@st-clare.org; parish-3870@la-archdiocese.org www.st-clare.org Rev. Olin Mayfield, Pst.; CRP Stds.: 694

St. Kateri Tekakwitha - 22508 Copper Hill Dr., Santa Clarita, CA 91350 t) (661) 296-3180 parish-3960@la-archdiocese.org; parishoffice@saintkateriparish-scv.org www.saintkateriparish.org Rev. Vaughn P. Winters, Pst.; Rev. Jihoon Kim, Assoc. Pst.; Rev. Msgr. Michael J. Slattery, Pastor Emer.; Dcn. Gabriel Aguilera; Dcn. Terry Irwin; Dcn. Kevin McCarthy; Dcn. Robert Seidler; Mindy Irwin, CRE; Jennifer Cummings-Martin, Dir.; CRP Stds.: 588

Our Lady of Perpetual Help - 23233 Lyons Ave., Santa Clarita, CA 91321; Mailing: 23045 Lyons Ave., Santa Clarita, CA 91321 t) 661-259-4266 (CRP); (661) 259-2276 olph@olphscv.org; parish-3830@la-archdiocese.org www.olphscv.org Rev. Msgr. Craig A. Cox, Pst.; Rev. Jonathan Nestico, Assoc. Pst.; Rev. Luther Alvaro Diaz, Assoc. Pst.; Dcn. Richard Karl; Dcn. Terry Irwin, Bus. Mgr.; Dcn. Jay Reiser; Iris Samson, DRE; CRP Stds.: 557

Our Lady of Perpetual Help School - (Grades PreK-8) 23225 Lyons Ave., Santa Clarita, CA 91321 t) (661) 259-1141 principal@olphsc.org; school-7160@la-archdiocese.org www.olphsc.org Sharon Krahl, Prin.; Stds.: 260; Lay Tchrs.: 10

SANTA FE SPRINGS

St. Pius X - 10827 Pioneer Blvd., Santa Fe Springs, CA 90670 t) (562) 863-8734; (562) 868-2389 (CRP); (562) 567-7242 (CRP) ra0926@gmail.com; parish-6030@la-archdiocese.org Rev. Artur Gruszka, Pst.; Rev. Pedro Valdez, Assoc. Priest; Dcn. Ron Elchert; Rita Amador, DRE; Susanna Espinosa, DRE; Rita K. Freeborg, Bus. Mgr.; CRP Stds.: 383

St. Pius X School - (Grades PreK-8) 10855 S. Pioneer Blvd., Santa Fe Springs, CA 90670 t) (562) 864-4818 office@spxraiders.com; school-9060@la-archdiocese.org www.spxraiders.com Christine Huerta Soler, Prin.; Stds.: 200; Lay Tchrs.: 10

St. Pius X Preschool - 10855 S. Pioneer Blvd., Santa Fe Springs, CA 90670 t) 562-864-4818 preschool@spxraiders.com; office@spxraiders.com www.spxraiders.com/preschool Kristin Muniz, Dir.;

SANTA MARIA

St. John Neumann - 966 W. Orchard St., Santa Maria, CA 93458-2063 t) (805) 922-7099 stjohnneumannchurch966@gmail.com; parish-2950@la-archdiocese.org www.sjnsantamaria.org Rev. Rolando A. Sierra, Pst.; Dcn. Ricardo Berumen; Dcn. Romeo Mabansag; Dcn. Jose Ojeda; Rosalba Iniguez, Bus. Mgr.; CRP Stds.: 620

St. Louis de Montfort - 1190 E. Clark Ave., Santa Maria, CA 93455; Mailing: 5075 Harp Rd., Santa Maria, CA 93455 t) (805) 937-4555 sldmchurch@sldm.org; aidanpeter@sldm.org www.sldm.org Rev. Aidan Peter Rossiter, C.J., Pst.; Rev. Armand Bopda, CJ, Assoc. Pst.; Rev. John A. Mayhew, C.J., Assoc. Pst.; Rev. Alfred Verstreaken, C.J., Assoc. Pst.; Dcn. Raul Blanco; Dcn. Christopher Boerger; Dcn. Richard Carmody; Dcn. Alfredo Espinoza; Dcn. Antonio Mejia; Rev. Gerardo Toscano, C.J., In Res.; CRP Stds.: 505

St. Louis de Montfort School - (Grades PreK-8) 5095 Harp Rd., Santa Maria, CA 93455 t) (805) 937-5571 school_office@sldmschool.org; school-6410@la-archdiocese.org www.sldmschool.org Regina Fox, Prin.; Stds.: 275; Lay Tchrs.: 12

St. Anthony's Church - 270 Helena St., Los Alamos,

CA 93440 t) (805) 344-1604 david@sldm.org www.sldm.org/st-anthonys

San Ramon Chapel - Forest Rte. 10N06, Santa Maria, CA 93454 t) (805) 895-3933 mexmara@aol.com www.sanramonchapel.info/

St. Mary of the Assumption - 414 E. Church St., Santa Maria, CA 93454 t) (805) 922-5826; (805) 925-2007 (CRP) parish@stmary-sm.org; parish-2970@la-archdiocese.org www.stmary-sm.org Rev. Thomas S. Cook, Pst.; Rev. Jesus Silva Ortega, CMH, Assoc. Pst.; Dcn. Dennis Pearson; Dcn. Jesus Rico; CRP Stds.: 358

St. Mary of the Assumption School - (Grades K-8) 424 E. Cypress St., Santa Maria, CA 93454 t) 805-925-6713 school@stmarysschoolsm.com; principal@stmarysschoolsm.com www.stmarysschoolsm.com Erica Stevens, Prin.; Stds.: 220; Lay Tchrs.: 9

St. Mary's Preschool - 309 S. School St., Santa Maria, CA 93454 t) (805) 346-6541 preschool@stmarysschoolsm.com www.stmarysschoolsm.com/preschool Lupe Fernandez, Dir.;

SANTA MONICA

St. Anne - 2011 Colorado Ave., Santa Monica, CA 90404 t) (310) 829-4040 (CRP); (310) 829-4411 stannere@gmail.com; parish-4830@la-archdiocese.org www.smtriparish.org Rev. Jorge Guillen, S.D.B., In Res.; Rev. Christopher Onyenobi, In Res.; Dcn. Raul Molina, Parish Life Coord.; Carolina Badillo, DRE; CRP Stds.: 200

St. Anne School - (Grades PreK-8) 2015 Colorado Ave., Santa Monica, CA 90404 t) (310) 829-2775 school-7970@la-archdiocese.org; admin@saintanneschool.com www.saintanneschool.com Michael Browning, Prin.; Stds.: 250; Lay Tchrs.: 10

St. Clement - 3102 3rd Ave., Santa Monica, CA 90405 t) (310) 396-2679 parish-4850@la-archdiocese.org stclementcatholic.church/ Rev. Michael Joseph Wu, O.Carm., Admin.; Lorena Pina, DRE; CRP Stds.: 40

St. Monica - 725 California Ave., Santa Monica, CA 90403 t) (310) 566-1500 info@stmonica.net; parish-4920@la-archdiocese.org www.stmonica.net Rev. Msgr. Lloyd A. Torgerson, Pst.; Rev. Prosper Hedagbui, Assoc. Pst.; Rev. David Guffey, C.S.C., In Res.; Rev. Vincent A. Kuna, C.S.C., In Res.; Suzette Sornborger, DRE; CRP Stds.: 260

St. Monica Elementary School - (Grades PreK-8) 1039 Seventh St., Santa Monica, CA 90403 t) (310) 451-9801 school@stmonicaelem.com; school-8060@la-archdiocese.org www.saintmonicaprep.org Neil Quinly, Prin.; Dcn. Kevin Francis McCardle, Pres.; Stds.: 270; Lay Tchrs.: 10

St. Monica High School - (Grades 9-12) 1030 Lincoln Blvd., Santa Monica, CA 90403 t) (310) 394-3701 jspellman@smprep.org; school-9870@la-archdiocese.org www.saintmonicaprep.org Dcn. Kevin Francis McCardle, Pres.; James Spellman, Prin.; Stds.: 377; Lay Tchrs.: 31

SANTA PAULA

Our Lady of Guadalupe - 427 N. Oak St., Santa Paula, CA 93060 t) (805) 525-3716; (805) 525-2225 (CRP) parish-3160@la-archdiocese.org www.guadalupechurchsp.com Rev. Canon Thomas J. Dome, C.R.I.C., Admin.; Sr. Encarnacion de los Santos, O.P., DRE; CRP Stds.: 450

Convent - 432 N. Oak St., Santa Paula, CA 93060 t) (805) 525-9207 opolgs@aol.com www.crmsdusadelegation.org Rev. Charles R. Lueras, C.R.I.C., Admin.;

St. Sebastian - 235 N. 9th St., Santa Paula, CA 93060 t) (805) 525-3201 (CRP); (805) 525-2149 stsebastianccd@verizon.net; parish-3220@la-archdiocese.org www.stsebastiansp.com Rev. Pasquale Vuoso, C.R.I.C., Pst.; Rev. Thaddeus Haynes, C.R.I.C., Assoc. Pst.; Dcn. Alfonso A. Guilin; Marisela Favila, DRE; CRP Stds.: 145

St. Sebastian School - (Grades K-8) 325 E. Santa Barbara St., Santa Paula, CA 93060 t) (805) 525-1575 principal@spsaints.org; school-6620@la-archdiocese.org www.spsaints.weebly.com Grace Kelly, Prin.; Stds.: 127; Lay Tchrs.: 9

St. Sebastian Preschool - 325 E. Santa Barbara St., Santa Paula, CA 93060 t) (805) 933-5518 school-6620@la-archdiocese.org Grace Kelly, Prin.; Annette Romero, Dir.;

SHERMAN OAKS

St. Francis de Sales - 13360 Valleyheart Dr., Sherman Oaks, CA 91423 t) (818) 784-0105; (818) 782-7846 (CRP) lathuras@msn.com; parish-3750@la-archdiocese.org www.sfdsparish.com Rev. Michael Wakefield, Pst.; Jack Lathuras, DRE; CRP Stds.: 140

St. Francis de Sales School - (Grades PreSchool-8) 13368 Valleyheart Dr., Sherman Oaks, CA 91423 t) (818) 784-9573 school-7080@la-archdiocese.org; lreising@stfrancisds.org www.saintfrancisdesalesschool.com Myra Goethals, Prin.; Stds.: 313; Lay Tchrs.: 10

SIERRA MADRE

St. Rita - 318 N. Baldwin Ave., Sierra Madre, CA 91024; Mailing: 50 E. Alegria Ave., Sierra Madre, CA 91024 t) (626) 355-1292 parishadministrator@st-rita.org; parish-4430@la-archdiocese.org www.st-rita.org Rev. Thomas E. Baker, Pst.; Theresa Costanzo, DRE; Paul Puccinelli, Liturgy Dir.; CRP Stds.: 126

St. Rita School - (Grades PreK-8) 322 N. Baldwin Ave., Sierra Madre, CA 91024 t) (626) 355-6114 school-7630@la-archdiocese.org www.st-ritaschool.org Adela Solis, Prin.; Stds.: 196; Lay Tchrs.: 10

SIMI VALLEY

St. Peter Claver - 2380 Stow St., Simi Valley, CA 93063; Mailing: 5649 Pittman St., Simi Valley, CA 93063 t) (805) 526-0680 (CRP); (805) 526-6499 faithformation@saintpeterclaver.org; saintpeterclaver@aol.com www.saintpeterclaver.org Rev. Rizalino J. Carranza, Pst.; Rev. Michael J. Sezzi, Assoc. Pst.; Dcn. Melecio Zamora; Dcn. Brian Clements; Laura Diaz, DRE; CRP Stds.: 256

St. Peter Claver Preschool and Kindergarten - (Grades PreK-k) 5670 Cochran St., Simi Valley, CA 93063 t) (805) 526-2244 lbalcaceres@stpeterclaverschool.org; ameyer@stpeterclaverschool.org www.stpeterclaverschool.org Lauren Balcaceres, Prin.; Stds.: 77; Lay Tchrs.: 9

St. Rose of Lima - 1305 Royal Ave., Simi Valley, CA 93065 t) (805) 526-5513 (CRP); (805) 526-1732 parish@strosesv.com; parish-3310@la-archdiocese.org www.strosesv.com Rev. Joseph P. Shea, Pst.; Rev. Luis Rivera Estrada, Assoc. Pst.; Dcn. Terence Reibenspies; Dcn. Peter Wilson Jr.; Rev. John Moloney, In Res.; Lucy Bolgonino, DRE; CRP Stds.: 340

St. Rose of Lima School - (Grades PreK-8) 1325 Royal Ave., Simi Valley, CA 93065 t) (805) 526-5304 office@srls.org; school-6690@la-archdiocese.org www.srls.org Molly Harding, Prin.; Stds.: 197; Lay Tchrs.: 11

SOLVANG

Old Mission Santa Ines - 1760 Mission Dr., Solvang, CA 93463; Mailing: P.O. Box 408, Solvang, CA 93464 t) (805) 688-4138 (CRP); (805) 688-4815 x222 office@missionsantaines.org; parish-2940@la-archdiocese.org www.missionsantaines.org Rev. Robert A. Barbato, O.F.M.Cap., Pst.; Rev. Peter M Banks, OFM Cap, In Res.; Rev. Robert E. Kose, OFM, Cap, In Res.; Sr. Carmen Acosta, S.D.S.H., DRE; Dcn. Ancelmo Aguirre; CRP Stds.: 134

SOUTH EL MONTE

Epiphany - 10911 Michael Hunt Dr., South El Monte, CA 91733 t) (626) 442-6262; (626) 444-8809 (CRP) parish-4520@la-archdiocese.org; epiphanysem@att.net www.epiphanychurch-elmonte.org Dr. Humberto Ramos, Parish Life Coord.; Rev. Gilbert Cruz, Sacr. Min.; CRP Stds.: 228

Epiphany School - (Grades PreK-8) 10915 Michael Hunt Dr., South El Monte, CA 91733 t) (626) 442-6264 school-7690@la-archdiocese.org; eschool213@aol.com www.epiphanyeagles.org/ Gabriela Negrete, Prin.; Stds.: 98; Lay Tchrs.: 9

SOUTH GATE

St. Helen - 8912 S. Gate Ave., South Gate, CA 90280 t) (323) 569-9550 (CRP); (323) 563-3522 parish-5830@la-archdiocese.org; info@sthelencc.org www.sthelencc.org Rev. Angel Castro, Pst.; Rev. Michael Masteller, Assoc. Pst.; Dcn. Rogelio Ramirez; Dcn. Cecilio G. Pena; CRP Stds.: 299

St. Helen School - (Grades PreK-8) 9329 Madison Ave., South Gate, CA 90280 t) (323) 566-5491 sthelen9329@yahoo.com; school-8870@la-archdiocese.org www.sthelensg.net/ Kurt Spanel, Prin.; Stds.: 305; Lay Tchrs.: 10

SOUTH PASADENA

Holy Family - 1501 Fremont Ave., South Pasadena, CA 91030; Mailing: 1527 Fremont Ave., South Pasadena, CA 91030 t) (626) 403-6118 (CRP); (626) 799-8908 parish-4340@la-archdiocese.org; reception@holyfamily.org www.holyfamily.org Msgr. Albert M. Bahhuth, Pst.; Rev. Andrew Daniel Hedstrom, Pst. Assoc.; Msgr. Clement J. Connolly, Pastor Emer.; Colette Villegas, DRE; CRP Stds.: 290

Holy Family School - (Grades PreK-8) 1301 Rollin St., South Pasadena, CA 91030 t) (626) 799-4354 school-7550@la-archdiocese.org; info@holyfamily.org www.school.holyfamily.org Jennifer Garzia, Prin.; Stds.: 316; Lay Tchrs.: 17

SUN VALLEY

Our Lady of the Holy Rosary - 7800 Vineland Ave., Sun Valley, CA 91352 t) (818) 982-4248 (CRP); (818) 765-3350 parishoffice@olhr.org; parish-3710@la-archdiocese.org www.olhr.org Rev. Luiz Kendzierski, Pst.; Rev. Gildardo Blanco, Assoc. Pst.; Diana Cruz, DRE; CRP Stds.: 570

Our Lady of the Holy Rosary School - (Grades PreK-8) 7802 Vineland Ave., Sun Valley, CA 91352 t) (818) 765-4897 school-7040@la-archdiocese.org; olhrschooloffice@olhr.org www.olhrschool.org Maria Aguilar, Prin.; Stds.: 233; Lay Tchrs.: 10

Our Lady of Zapopan - 7824 Lankershim Blvd., North Hollywood, CA 91605 t) (818) 503-8920 Rev. Marvin Ajic, C.S., Pst.;

Our Lady of the Holy Rosary Convent - 7757 Cleon Ave., Sun Valley, CA 91352 t) (818) 764-9857 Rev. Marvin Ajic, C.S., Pst.;

SYLMAR

St. Didacus - 14339 Astoria St., Sylmar, CA 91342; Mailing: 14337 Astoria St., Sylmar, CA 91342 t) (818) 367-4155 (CRP); (818) 367-6181 theresagross01@gmail.com; parish-3880@la-archdiocese.org www.stdidacus.org Rev. Robert E. J. Garon, Pst.; Rev. Daniel M. Martinez (Mexico), Assoc. Pst.; Dcn. Fermin Gomez; Rev. Msgr. Peter L. Amy, In Res.; Theresa Gross, DRE; CRP Stds.: 822

St. Didacus School - (Grades K-8) 14325 Astoria St., Sylmar, CA 91342 t) (818) 367-5886 school-7190@la-archdiocese.org; sdoffice@stdidacus.org www.stdidacusschool.org Krishana Gonzales, Prin.; Stds.: 143; Lay Tchrs.: 9

St. Didacus Preschool - 14325 Astoria St., Sylmar, CA 91342 t) (818) 367-5296; (818) 367-5886 sdoffice@stdidacus.org; school-7190@la-archdiocese.org www.stdidacusschool.org Dolores Hernandez, Dir.;

TEMPLE CITY

St. Luke the Evangelist - 5605 Cloverly Ave., Temple City, CA 91780 t) (626) 291-5900 parish-4410@la-archdiocese.org; barbara@stluketemplecity.org www.stluketemplecity.org Rev. Msgr. James L. Halley, Pst.; Barbara Hansen, DRE; CRP Stds.: 52

St. Luke the Evangelist School - (Grades PreK-8) 5521 Cloverly Ave., Temple City, CA 91780 t) (626) 291-5959 school-7610@la-archdiocese.org; office@stluketemplecity.org www.stlukelions.org Yvette Jefferys, Prin.; Stds.: 83; Lay Tchrs.: 7

THOUSAND OAKS

St. Paschal Baylon - 155 E. Janss Rd., Thousand Oaks,

CA 91360 t) (805) 496-0222 x115 (CRP); (805) 496-0222 x101 liliana@stpaschal.org; parish@stpaschal.org www.stpaschal.org Rev. Michael Rocha, Pst.; Rev. Danilo Guinto, Assoc. Pst.; Rev. Pedro Valdez, Assoc. Pst.; Dcn. Mitchell Ito; Liliana Rivas, DRE; CRP Stds.: 214

St. Paschal Baylon School - (Grades K-8) 154 E. Janss Rd., Thousand Oaks, CA 91360 t) (805) 495-9340 principal@stpaschal.org; school-6680@la-archdiocese.org www.stpaschalbaylonschool.org Ryan Bushore, Prin.; Stds.: 217; Lay Tchrs.: 11

TORRANCE

St. Catherine Laboure - 3846 Redondo Beach Blvd., Torrance, CA 90504 t) (310) 323-8900; (310) 515-6033 (CRP) parish-6140@la-archdiocese.org; mchew@stcatchurch.org www.stcatchurch.org Rev. Alfred Hernandez, Pst.; Rev. Hoang Dang, Assoc. Pst.; Angela Morvice, DRE; CRP Stds.: 408

St. Catherine Laboure School - (Grades PreK-8) t) (310) 324-8732 school-9180@la-archdiocese.org; administration@stcat.org www.stcat.org Jennifer Meyer Bagheri, Prin.; Stds.: 470; Lay Tchrs.: 10

Nativity - 1447 Engracia Ave., Torrance, CA 90501 t) (310) 320-6673 (CRP); (310) 328-2776 parish-6090@la-archdiocese.org; nativitytorrance@nativitytorrance.org www.nativitytorrance.org Rev. Hung Ba Tran, Pst.; Bertha Melendres, DRE; CRP Stds.: 419

Nativity School - (Grades PreK-8) 2371 Carson St., Torrance, CA 90501 t) (310) 328-5387 school-9140@la-archdiocese.org; principal.wechsler@la-archdiocese.org www.nativitybruins.org Michelle Wechsler, Prin.; Stds.: 269; Lay Tchrs.: 10

Nativity Convent - 1421 Cota Ave., Torrance, CA 90501 t) (310) 328-6725 efms@earthlink.net Eucharistic Franciscan Missionary Sisters Linda Plaza, Secy.;

TUJUNGA

Our Lady of Lourdes - 7315 Apperson St., Tujunga, CA 91042; Mailing: 7344 Apperson St., Tujunga, CA 91042 t) (818) 352-3218; (818) 352-2084 (CRP) parish-3590@la-archdiocese.org; frrolly106@gmail.com www.ollchurch.us Rev. Roland Astudillo, Pst.; Dcn. Marciano Enriquez; Gloriann McGowan, DRE; CRP Stds.: 174

Our Lady of Lourdes School - (Grades PreK-8) 7324 Apperson St., Tujunga, CA 91042 t) (818) 353-1106 school-6930@la-archdiocese.org www.ollschooltujunga.org/ Evelyn Cortez, Prin.; Stds.: 115; Lay Tchrs.: 8

St. Matthew Korean Catholic Center - 7245 Valmont St., Tujunga, CA 91042 t) (818) 951-0879 jiwankim@la-archdiocese.org; stmatthewkcc@hanmail.net www.stmatthewkcc.org Rev. Jiwan Kim, Dir.;

VALINDA

St. Martha - 444 N. Azusa Ave., Valinda, CA 91744 t) (626) 912-2581 (CRP); (626) 964-4313 parish-4750@la-archdiocese.org; walmanzor@yahoo.com www.stmarthavalinda.org Rev. Thomas Frederick Asia, Pst.; Rev. Benito Armenta, Par. Vicar; Dcn. Jesse Batacan; Rev. Msgr. Aidan M. Carroll, In Res.; Eduardo Macalalad, Youth Min.; Sara Monte, DRE; Willie Almanzor, Bus. Mgr.; CRP Stds.: 339

St. Martha School - (Grades PreK-8) 440 N. Azusa Ave., Valinda, CA 91744-4299 t) (626) 964-1093 school-7890@la-archdiocese.org www.saintmarthaschool.org Sr. Carmen Fernandez, Prin.; Stds.: 296; Lay Tchrs.: 10

VAN NUYS

St. Elizabeth - 14655 Kittridge St., Van Nuys, CA 91405; Mailing: 6635 Tobias Ave., Van Nuys, CA 91405 t) (818) 779-1756 x200 parish-3730@la-archdiocese.org; st.elisabethchurchvn@gmail.com www.stelisabethchurch.org Rev. Shinto Sebastian, R.C.J., Pst.; Rev. Dileep Sebastian, RCJ, Assoc. Pst.; Rev. Antonio Fiorenza, R.C.J., In Res.; Sr. Angelie Inoferio, F.D.Z., DRE; CRP Stds.: 242

St. Elizabeth School - (Grades PreK-8) 6635 Tobias Ave., Van Nuys, CA 91405 t) (818) 779-1766 school-7060@la-archdiocese.org; administrator@stelisabethchurch.org www.stelisabethschool.org Sr. Marita A. Olango, F.D.Z., Prin.; Stds.: 184; Lay Tchrs.: 10

VENICE

St. Mark - 940 Coeur d'Alene Ave., Venice, CA 90291 t) (310) 822-1201 (CRP); (310) 821-5058 info@stmarkvenice.com; parish-4890@la-archdiocese.org www.stmarkvenice.com/ Rev. Albert Van der Woerd, Admin.; Judy Girard, DRE; CRP Stds.: 280

St. Mark School - (Grades PreK-8) 912 Coeur d'Alene Ave., Venice, CA 90291 t) (310) 821-6612 school-8030@la-archdiocese.org www.stmarkschool.com Mary Ann McQueen, Prin.; Stds.: 268; Lay Tchrs.: 10

VENTURA

Mission Basilica San Buenaventura - 211 E. Main St., Ventura, CA 93001 t) (805) 643-4318 sistermaryrose@sanbuenaventuramissiin.org; parish-3180@la-archdiocese.org www.sanbuenaventuramission.org Rev. Thomas J. Elewaut, Pst.; Rev. Peter Damian Fernando, In Res.; Dcn. Mark Lawrence Banda; Dcn. Gustavo Catipon; Dcn. Alfonso Cruz Mendez; Sr. Mary Rose Chinn, J.M.J., DRE; Lynzi Rivera, Youth Min.; CRP Stds.: 278

Holy Cross School - (Grades PreK-8) t) (805) 643-1500 principal@holycrossventura.org; school-6580@la-archdiocese.org www.holycrossventura.org Jessica Reddick, Prin.; Stds.: 86; Lay Tchrs.: 7

Our Lady of the Assumption - 3175 Telegraph Rd., Ventura, CA 93003 t) (805) 642-7966 x100 (CRP); (805) 642-7966 parish-3140@la-archdiocese.org; parish@ola-vta.org www.olaventura.com Rev. Leon Hutton, Pst.; Rev. Matthew Miguel, Par. Vicar; Dcn. Daniel Bojorquez; Dcn. Michael Burns; Dcn. Donald Huntley; Dcn. Philip Joerger; Dcn. Charles Philip Wessler; Rev. Lawrence David Ahyuwa (Nigeria), Chap.; CRP Stds.: 490

Our Lady of the Assumption School - (Grades PreK-8) 3169 Telegraph Rd., Ventura, CA 93003 t) (805) 642-7198 school-6550@la-archdiocese.org; pgroff@olaventura.org www.olaventura.org Patricia Groff, Prin.; Stds.: 252; Lay Tchrs.: 10

Sacred Heart - 10800 Henderson Rd., Ventura, CA 93004 t) (805) 647-3235 x306 (CRP); (805) 647-3235 re@sacredheartventura.org; rectory@sacredheartventura.org www.sacredheartventura.org Rev. Aloysius Ezeonyeka, Pst.; Rev. Marco D. Reyes, Assoc. Pst.; Rev. Daniel A. O'Sullivan, Pastor Emer.; Dcn. John William Barry; Dcn. Philip Conforti; Dcn. Fernando M. Flores; Dcn. Humberto Guzman; CRP Stds.: 169

Sacred Heart School - (Grades K-8) 10770 Henderson Rd., Ventura, CA 93004 t) (805) 647-6174 office@sacredheartschoolventura.org; principal@sacredheartschoolventura.org www.sacredheartschoolventura.org Christine Benner, Prin.; Stds.: 192; Lay Tchrs.: 11

VERNON

Holy Angels Parish of the Deaf - 4433 S. Santa Fe Ave., Vernon, CA 90058; Mailing: P.O. Box 58423, Vernon, CA 90058 t) (323) 230-9582 deacontomas@hacofthedeaf.org; info@hacofthedeaf.org www.hacofthedeaf.org Rev. Thomas Schweitzer, Pst.; Dcn. Tomas Garcia Jr.; Dcn. Roger Gomez; Dcn. Lawrence McGloin; Dcn. David Rose; Joanna Hinojosa-Martinez, DRE; CRP Stds.: 25

WALNUT

St. Lorenzo Ruiz - 747 Meadowpass Rd., Walnut, CA 91789 t) (909) 468-1812 (CRP); (909) 595-9545 gabycoria@saintlorenzo.org; parish-4760@la-archdiocese.org www.saintlorenzo.org Rev. Tony P. Astudillo, Pst.; Rev. Martin Madero, Sch.P., Assoc. Pst.; Gaby Coria, DRE; CRP Stds.: 428

WEST COVINA

St. Christopher - 629 S. Glendora Ave., West Covina, CA 91790 t) 626-960-1805 parish-4590@la-archdiocese.org www.sccwestcovina.net Rev. Ben Le, Pst.; Rev. Joseph Aline Dadiri, Assoc. Pst.; Dcn. Taejun Cho; Sr. Annuncia Thu Mai, LHC, DRE; CRP Stds.: 213

St. Christopher School - (Grades PreK-8) 900 W. Christopher St., West Covina, CA 91790 t) (626) 960-3079 school-7740@la-archdiocese.org; info@scpswc.com www.saintchristopherparishschoolwc.com Lucia Saborio, Prin.; Stds.: 207; Lay Tchrs.: 10

WEST HOLLYWOOD

St. Ambrose - 1281 N. Fairfax Ave., West Hollywood, CA 90046 t) 323-656-4433 stambrosech@aol.com; parish-5080@la-archdiocese.org www.stambroseweho.org Rev. Dennis P. Marrell, Pst.; CRP Stds.: 4

St. Victor - 8634 Holloway Dr., West Hollywood, CA 90069 t) (310) 652-6477 saintvictorparish@saintvictor.org; parish-4960@la-archdiocese.org www.saintvictor.org Rev. John-Paul Gonzalez, Pst.; Rev. Joseph Fox, O.P., In Res.;

WESTLAKE VILLAGE

St. Jude - 32032 Lindero Canyon Rd., Westlake Village, CA 91361 t) (818) 889-0612 (CRP); (818) 889-1279 cindy@saintjudetheapostle.org; parish@saintjudetheapostle.org www.saintjudetheapostle.org Rev. James Stehly, Pst.; Dcn. Jerome Bettencourt; Dcn. Dick Dornan; Cindy Kozal, DRE; CRP Stds.: 372

St. Jude School - (Grades K-8) 32036 W. Lindero Canyon Rd., Westlake Village, CA 91361 t) (818) 889-9483 school-6830@la-archdiocese.org; mschulte@stjudeschool.org www.stjudeschool.org Michele Schulte, Prin.; Stds.: 216; Lay Tchrs.: 10

St. Maximilian Kolbe - 5801 Kanan Rd., Westlake Village, CA 91362 t) (818) 991-3915; (818) 991-3915 x137 (CRP) kolbe@stmaxchurch.org; parish-3330@la-archdiocese.org www.stmaxchurch.org Rev. Msgr. Paul M. Albee, Pst.; Dcn. John Kruer; Dcn. Christopher Laliberte; Dcn. Gary Mallaley; CRP Stds.: 175

Kolbe's Korner Preschool - t) (818) 874-1241 pkkorner@la-archdiocese.org Paula Kruer, Dir.;

WHITTIER

St. Bruno - 15740 Citrustree Rd., Whittier, CA 90603 t) (562) 947-5637 x114 teresa@stbrunochurch.org; jason@stbrunochurch.org www.stbrunochurch.org Rev. David Heney, Pst.; Dcn. P. Michael Freeman, Pst. Assoc.; Jason Manley, DRE; Dcn. Gabriel Saavedra, RCIA Coord.; CRP Stds.: 472

St. Bruno School - (Grades PreK-8) 15700 Citrustree Rd., Whittier, CA 90603 t) (562) 943-8812 school-8980@la-archdiocese.org; schooloffice@saintbrunoschool.com www.saintbrunoschool.com Nancy Chavana, Prin.; Stds.: 310; Lay Tchrs.: 15

St. Gregory the Great Church - 13935 Telegraph Rd., Whittier, CA 90604 t) (562) 944-8311 (CRP); (562) 941-0115 (Main Line) info@sggcatholic.org; parish-5950@la-archdiocese.org www.sggcatholic.org Rev. Jeffrey Baker, Pst.; Rev. Huy Nhat Nguyen, Assoc. Pst.; Dcn. William Pilkington; CRP Stds.: 339

St. Gregory the Great School - (Grades PreK-8) 13925 Telegraph Rd., Whittier, CA 90604 t) (562) 941-0750 school-8990@la-archdiocese.org; mainoffice@sggknights.org www.stgregorythegreatschoolwhittier.org Paulette Clagon, Prin.; Stds.: 306; Lay Tchrs.: 10

St. Mary of the Assumption - 7215 Newlin Ave., Whittier, CA 90602 t) (562) 698-0107 manager@stmaryschurch-whittier.org; parish-6000@la-archdiocese.org www.stmaryschurch-whittier.org Rev. Patrick Keyes, C.Ss.R., Pst.; Rev. Tuan Pham, C.Ss.R., Assoc. Pst.; Dcn. Dennis Lee, C.Ss.R.; CRP Stds.: 589

St. Mary of the Assumption School - (Grades K-8) 7218 S. Pickering Ave., Whittier, CA 90602 t) (562)

698-0253 school-9040@la-archdiocese.org www.stmaryswhittier.org Maria Isabel Ortiz-Lopez, Prin.; Stds.: 232; Lay Tchrs.: 9

WILMINGTON

Holy Family - 1011 East L St., Wilmington, CA 90744 t) (310) 834-6333 (Office); (310) 549-0011 (CRP) mainoffice@holyfamilywilmington.org; parish-6060@la-archdiocese.org www.holyfamilywilmington.org Rev. Ruben Rocha (Mexico), Pst.; Rev. Carlos Mesa, Assoc. Pst.; Rev. Salvador Vazquez, Assoc. Pst.; Dcn. Benoni Neftali Tahuite; CRP Stds.: 617

SS. Peter and Paul - 515 W. Opp St., Wilmington, CA 90744 t) (310) 834-5215; (310) 834-5216 (CRP) sppc@sbcglobal.net; parish-6110@la-archdiocese.org www.sppc.us Rev. Claude Williams, O. Praem., Pst.; Rev. Michael U. Perea, O.Praem., Assoc. Pst.; Rev. Adrian Sanchez, O.Praem, Assoc. Pst.; Rev. Jacob Hsieh, O. Praem, Rector; Rev. Anselm Rodriguez, O. Praem., In Res.; CRP Stds.: 298

SS. Peter and Paul School - (Grades PreK-8) 706 Bay View Ave., Wilmington, CA 90744 t) (310) 834-5574 school-9160@la-archdiocese.org www.sppschool.org Nancy Kuria, Prin.; Stds.: 210; Lay Tchrs.: 10

WINNETKA

St. Joseph the Worker - 19855 Sherman Way, Winnetka, CA 91306; Mailing: 19808 Cantlay St., Winnetka, CA 91306 t) (818) 341-6634 parish-3460@la-archdiocese.org; parish@sjwchurch.com www.sjwchurch.com Rev. Alberto Villalobos, Pst.; Rev. Rufino Carlos Nava, O.M.I., Assoc. Pst.; Rev. Thuan Nguyen, Assoc. Pst.; Bill Sparks, DRE; CRP Stds.: 190

St. Joseph the Worker School - (Grades PreK-8) 19812 Cantlay St., Winnetka, CA 91306 t) (818) 341-6616 school-6820@la-archdiocese.org; mr.kruska@sjwschool.net www.sjwschool.net C.J. Kruska, Prin.; Stds.: 235; Lay Tchrs.: 12

WOODLAND HILLS

St. Bernardine of Siena - 24410 Calvert St., Woodland Hills, CA 91367 t) (818) 888-8200 parishoffice@stbernardine.org; parish-3410@la-archdiocese.org stbernardine.org Rev. Michael J. Evans, Pst.; Rev. William R. Crowe, Assoc. Pst.; Cathy Barkes, Stewardship & Devel.; Jill Moore, Elementary Faith Formation Coord.; Alejandra Gasser, Youth Ministry & Confirmation Coord.; Bob Nicholas, Initiation for Adults & Children, Adult Faith Formation; CRP Stds.: 155

St. Bernardine of Siena School - (Grades K-8) 6061 Valley Cir. Blvd., Woodland Hills, CA 91367 t) (818) 340-2130 office@stbernardine.org; school-6770@la-archdiocese.org stbernardineschool.org/ Katy Kruska, Prin.; Stds.: 247; Lay Tchrs.: 12

St. Bernardine of Siena Preschool - 24425 Calvert St., Woodland Hills, CA 91367 t) (818) 716-4730 sbscc@stbernardine.org stbpreschool.com/ Charlene Barkes, Dir.;

St. Mel - 20870 Ventura Blvd., Woodland Hills, CA 91364 t) (818) 340-6020 (CRP); (818) 340-6020 mmatthews@stmel.org; parish-3480@la-archdiocese.org www.stmelparish.org Rev. Stephen Davoren, Pst.; Rev. Francis Beth Kim, Pst. Assoc.; Dcn. Brian Conroy; Lisa Beth Feliciano, DRE; Monica Matthews, RCIA Coord.; CRP Stds.: 554

St. Mel School - (Grades K-8) 20874 Ventura Blvd., Woodland Hills, CA 91364 t) (818) 340-1924 school-6840@la-archdiocese.org www.stmel.org Mary Beth Lutz, Prin.; Stds.: 550; Lay Tchrs.: 10

St. Mel Preschool - (Grades PreK- 5130 Serrania Ave., Woodland Hills, CA 91364; Mailing: 20870 Ventura Blvd., Woodland Hills, CA 91364 t) (818) 340-3180 cpowell@stmel.org www.stmel.org/ preschool Stds.: 119; Lay Tchrs.: 1

SCHOOLS: PRESCHOOL THRU HIGH SCHOOL

SCHOOLS

STATE OF CALIFORNIA

LOS ANGELES

Notre Dame Academy Schools of Los Angeles - (PRV) (Grades PreK-8) 2911 Overland Ave., Los Angeles, CA 90064 t) 310-287-3895 mmartinez@ndala.com elementary.ndasla.org Sponsored by the Sisters of Notre Dame (SND). Lilliam Paetzold, Pres.; Brianna Berlin, Prin.; Stds.: 276; Lay Tchrs.: 18

MONTROSE

***St. Monica Academy, Inc.** - (PRV) (Grades 1-12) 2361 Del Mar Rd., Montrose, CA 91020 t) 818-369-7310 admissions@stmonicaacademy.com www.stmonicaacademy.com Marguerite Grimm, Headmaster; Stds.: 287; Lay Tchrs.: 39

PASADENA

Mayfield Junior School of the Holy Child Jesus - (PRV) (Grades 6-8) 405 S. Euclid Ave., Pasadena, CA 91101 t) 626-796-2774 school-2803@la-archdiocese.org www.mayfieldjs.org Joseph J. Gill, Headmaster; Stds.: 180; Lay Tchrs.: 4

SANTA PAULA

***Saint Augustine Academy, Inc.** - (PRV) (Grades K-4) 121 Davis St., Santa Paula, CA 93060 t) 805-672-0411 office@saintaugustineacademy.com www.saintaugustineacademy.com Michael Van Hecke, Pres.; Stds.: 47; Lay Tchrs.: 4

VENTURA

***Saint Augustine Academy, Inc.** - (PRV) (Grades 5-12) 130 S. Wells Rd., Ventura, CA 93004 t) 805-672-0411 office@saintaugustineacademy.com www.saintaugustineacademy.com Michael Van Hecke, Pres.; Stds.: 120; Lay Tchrs.: 20

HIGH SCHOOLS

STATE OF CALIFORNIA

ALHAMBRA

Ramona Convent Secondary School, Ramona Convent of the Holy Names - (PRV) (Grades 9-12) 1701 W. Ramona Rd., Alhambra, CA 91803-3080 t) 626-282-4151 lwolffe@ramonaconvent.org; school-2703@la-archdiocese.org www.ramonaconvent.org (Girls) Sr. Kathleen Callaway, S.N.J.M., Pres.; Mary Mansell, Prin.; Halina Szymanski, Vice Prin.; Stds.: 284; Lay Tchrs.: 27

BELLFLOWER

St. John Bosco High School - (PRV) (Grades 9-12) 13640 S. Bellflower Blvd., Bellflower, CA 90706 t) 562-920-1734 school-2723@la-archdiocese.org www.bosco.org (Boys) Brian Wickstrom, Pres.; Dr. Christian DeLarkin, Prin.; Rev. Ted Montemayor, S.D.B., Dir.; Stds.: 831

BURBANK

Providence High School - (PRV) (Grades 9-12) 511 S. Buena Vista St., Burbank, CA 91505 t) 818-846-8141 school-2693@la-archdiocese.org; info@providencehigh.org www.providencehigh.org/ Scott McLarty, Head of School; Annie Matthews, Interim Asst. Head of School; Kerry Martin, Dean of Curriculum; Joseph Granado, Dean of Student Life; Shanica Dale, Dean of Equity & Wellbeing; Stds.: 500

CHATSWORTH

Chaminade College Preparatory - (PRV) (Grades 6-12) 10210 Oakdale Ave., Chatsworth, CA 91311-3533 t) 818-360-4211 rwebb@chaminade.org; egluvna@chaminade.org www.chaminade.org Robert S. Webb, Pres.; Stds.: 1,831; Pr. Tchrs.: 2; Bro. Tchrs.: 4; Lay Tchrs.: 198

Chatsworth Campus (Middle School) - (Grades 6-12) t) 818-363-8127 school-2830@la-archdiocese.org Michael Valentine, Prin.; Stds.: 620; Lay Tchrs.: 32

West Hills Campus (High School, Grades 9-12) - (Grades 6-12) t) 818-347-8300 Louis Guerra, Prin.; Stds.: 1,200; Bro. Tchrs.: 1; Lay Tchrs.: 68

DOWNEY

St. Pius X-St. Matthias Academy - (DIO) (Grades 9-12) 7851 E. Gardendale St., Downey, CA 90242 t) 562-861-2271 principal@piusmatthias.org; pmamarketing@piusmatthias.org www.piusmatthias.org Dr. Christian DeLarkin, Pres.; Stds.: 424; Lay Tchrs.: 29

ENCINO

Crespi Carmelite High School - (PRV) (Grades 9-12) 5031 Alonzo Ave., Encino, CA 91316 t) 818-345-1672 info@crespi.org; bforray@crespi.org www.crespi.org Dr. Kenneth A Foersch, Pres.; Dr. Liam Joyce, Prin.; Stds.: 547; Pr. Tchrs.: 1; Bro. Tchrs.: 1; Lay Tchrs.: 45

GARDENA

Junipero Serra High School - (DIO) (Grades 9-12) 14830 S. Van Ness Ave., Gardena, CA 90249 t) 310-324-6675 bramos@la-serrahs.org; school-9620@la-archdiocese.org www.la-serrahs.org Michael J. Guzman, Prin.; Nadi Wissa, Vice Prin.; Stds.: 565

GLENDORA

St. Lucy's Priory High School (Benedictine Sisters of St. Lucy's Priory) - (PRV) (Grades 9-12) 655 W. Sierra Madre Ave., Glendora, CA 91741 t) 626-335-3322 info@stlucys.com; school-2733@la-archdiocese.org www.stlucys.com (Girls) Judy Hartranft, Prin.; Stds.: 480

INGLEWOOD

St. Mary's Academy - (PRV) (Grades 9-12) 701 Grace Ave., Inglewood, CA 90301 t) 310-674-8470 school-9990@la-archdiocese.org; smaprincipal@smabelles.org www.smabelles.org (Girls) Sr. Ann Patricia O'Connor, CSJ, Co-Prin.; Sr. Ann Bernard O'Shea, CSJ, Co-Prin.; Stds.: 227; Lay Tchrs.: 20

LA CANADA FLINTRIDGE

Flintridge Sacred Heart Academy, A Corporation - (PRV) (Grades 9-12) 440 St. Katherine Dr., La Canada Flintridge, CA 91011 t) 626-685-8500 info@fsha.org; school-2593@la-archdiocese.org www.fsha.org (Girls) Sr. Carolyn McCormack, Pres.; Stds.: 366; Lay Tchrs.: 51

St. Francis High School of La Canada-Flintridge - (PRV) (Grades 9-12) 200 Foothill Blvd., La Canada Flintridge, CA 91011 t) 818-790-0325 martit@sfhs.net; school-2713@la-archdiocese.org sfhs.net (Boys) Rev. Antonio (Tony) Marti, O.F.M.Cap., Pres.; Thomas G. Moran, Prin.; Stds.: 645

LA PUENTE

Bishop Amat Memorial High School - (DIO) (Grades 9-12) 14301 Fairgrove Ave., La Puente, CA 91746 t) 626-962-2495 school-9520@la-archdiocese.org www.bishopamat.org Richard Beck, Pres.; Gabriel Escovar, Prin.; Ivette Salcedo, Vice Prin.; Rev. John Montejano, Chap.; Deborah Oswald, Dir., Finance & Devel.; Stds.: 1,028; Pr. Tchrs.: 1; Lay Tchrs.: 62

LA VERNE

Damien High School - (DIO) (Grades 9-12) 2280 Damien Ave., La Verne, CA 91750 t) 909-596-1946 info@damien-hs.edu; school-9590@la-archdiocese.org www.damien-hs.edu Dr. Joseph Siegmund, Pres.; Dr. Mike Castillo, Prin.; Jeff Coray, Vice Prin.; Angela Curry, Dean; Chris Douglas, Dean; Eric McElrea, Dean; Jocelle Reyes, Bus. Mgr.; Stds.: 725; Lay Tchrs.: 45

LAKEWOOD

St. Joseph High School - (DIO) (Grades 9-12) 5825 N. Woodruff Ave., Lakewood, CA 90713 t) 562-925-5073 glogsdon@sj-jester.org; school-9730@la-archdiocese.org www.sj-jester.org (Girls) Terri Mendoza, Prin.; Stds.: 484; Sr. Tchrs.: 1; Lay Tchrs.: 35

LANCASTER

Paraclete High School - (DIO) (Grades 9-12) 42145 30th St. W., Lancaster, CA 93536 t) 661-943-3255 janson@paracletehs.org; school-9640@la-archdiocese.org www.paracletehs.org John W. Anson, Prin.; Kathleen Troisi, Vice Prin.; Rev. Giampietro Gasparin, C.S.J., Campus Min.; Stds.: 560; Pr. Tchrs.:

2; Lay Tchrs.: 35

LONG BEACH

St. Anthony High School - (DIO) (Grades 9-12) 620 Olive Ave., Long Beach, CA 90802 t) 562-435-4496 president@longbeachsaints.org; school-9850@la-archdiocese.org www.longbeachsaints.org Michael Brennan, Pres.; Marcelo Eureste, Prin.; Stds.: 430; Lay Tchrs.: 30

LOS ANGELES

Bishop Conaty-Our Lady of Loretto High School - (DIO) (Grades 9-12) 2900 W. Pico Blvd., Los Angeles, CA 90006-3802 t) 323-737-0012 rcarroll@bishopconatyloretto.org www.bishopconatyloretto.org (Girls) Robyn Patricia Carroll, Prin.; Dr. Joshua Brian Ornelas, Vice Prin.; Alejandra Frutos-Silva, Vice Prin.; Stds.: 350; Lay Tchrs.: 25

Bishop Mora Salesian High School (Salesians of Don Bosco) - (DIO) (Grades 9-12) 960 S. Soto St., Los Angeles, CA 90023 t) 323-261-7124 school-9560@la-archdiocese.org www.mustangsla.org (Boys) Alex Chacon, Pres.; Mark Johnson, Prin.; Rev. Jim Nieblas, SDB, Dir.; Stds.: 465; Pr. Tchrs.: 1; Lay Tchrs.: 21

Cathedral High School of Los Angeles, Incorporated (Conducted by the Brothers of the Christian Schools (F.S.C.)) - (PRV) (Grades 9-12) 1253 Bishops Rd., Los Angeles, CA 90012 t) 323-225-2438 brjohnm@chsla.org; school-9580@la-archdiocese.org www.cathedralhighschool.org (Boys) Bro. John Montgomery, F.S.C., Prin.; Stds.: 600; Bro. Tchrs.: 4; Lay Tchrs.: 40

***Immaculate Heart High School** - (PRV) (Grades 9-12) 5515 Franklin Ave., Los Angeles, CA 90028 t) 323-461-3651 kjohnsonbrown@ihs.immaculateheart.org; school-2603@la-archdiocese.org www.immaculateheart.org (Girls) Maureen Diekmann, Pres.; Naemah Morris, Prin.; Stds.: 459; Lay Tchrs.: 37

Loyola High School of Los Angeles - (PRV) (Grades 9-12) 1901 Venice Blvd., Los Angeles, CA 90006 t) 213-381-5121 ggoethals@loyolahs.edu; school-2643@la-archdiocese.org loyolahs.edu Boys. Sponsored by the California Province of the Society of Jesus. Rev. Gregory M. Goethals, S.J., Pres.; Frank Kozakowski, Prin.; Stds.: 1,246

Marymount High School (Religious of the Sacred Heart of Mary.) - (PRV) (Grades 9-12) 10643 Sunset Blvd., Los Angeles, CA 90077 t) 310-472-1205 admission@mhs-la.org; school-2653@la-archdiocese.org www.mhs-la.org (Girls) Jacqueline L. Landry, Prin.; Stds.: 373

Notre Dame Academy Schools of Los Angeles - (PRV) (Grades 9-12) 2851 Overland Ave., Los Angeles, CA 90064 t) 310-839-5289 mmartinez@ndala.com; school-9960@la-archdiocese.org academy.ndasla.org Girls. Sponsored by the Sisters of Notre Dame (SND). Lilliam Paetzold, Pres.; Brad Fuller, Prin.; Stds.: 258; Sr. Tchrs.: 1; Lay Tchrs.: 22

Sacred Heart High School - (DIO) (Grades 9-12) 2111 Griffin Ave., Los Angeles, CA 90031 t) 323-225-2209 mr.saborio@shhsla.org; school-9690@la-archdiocese.org www.shhsla.org (Girls) Raymond Saborio, Prin.; Luz Vivas, Vice Prin.; Stds.: 260; Lay Tchrs.: 25

Verbum Dei Jesuit High School - (PRV) (Grades 9-12) 11100 S. Central Ave., Los Angeles, CA 90059 t) (323) 564-6651 info@verbjesuit.org verbumdei.us Rev. Travis Dean Russell, SJ, Pres.; Stds.: 316; Pr. Tchrs.: 1; Bro. Tchrs.: 1; Lay Tchrs.: 27

VDHS Work Study, Inc. - info@verbumdei.us www.verbjesuit.org Jesse Jovel, Corp. Secy.;

MISSION HILLS

Bishop Alemany High School - (DIO) (Grades 9-12) 11111 N. Alemany Dr., Mission Hills, CA 91345 t) 818-365-3925 school-9510@la-archdiocese.org; aarnold@alemany.org www.alemany.org Alexis Arnold-Cox, Prin.; Andrea Chavez, Vice Prin.; Miguel A Pimentel, Vice Prin.; Theresa Salas, Bus. Mgr.; Stds.: 719; Pr. Tchrs.: 1; Lay Tchrs.: 42

MONTEBELLO

Cantwell Sacred Heart of Mary High School - (DIO) (Grades 9-12) 329 N. Garfield Ave., Montebello, CA 90640 t) 323-887-2066 school-9570@la-archdiocese.org; rfraley@cshm.org www.cshm.org Robert Fraley, Prin.; Stds.: 400; Lay Tchrs.: 20

MONTROSE

***St. Monica Academy, Inc.** - (PRV) (Grades 9-12) 2361 Del Mar Rd., Montrose, CA 91020 t) (818) 369-7310 admissions@stmonicaacademy.com; school-30040@la-archdiocese.org www.stmonicaacademy.com Marguerite Grimm, Headmaster; Stds.: 122

OJAI

Villanova Preparatory School in California, Conducted by Augustinians (Order of St. Augustine). - (PRV) (Grades 9-12) 12096 N. Ventura Ave., Ojai, CA 93023-3999 t) 805-646-1464 info@villanovaprep.org; school-2753@la-archdiocese.org www.villanovaprep.org Nancy O'Sullivan, Pres.; Stds.: 262

OXNARD

Santa Clara High School - (DIO) (Grades 9-12) 2121 Saviers Rd., Oxnard, CA 93033 t) 805-483-9502 guzman@santaclarahighschool.com; palmisano@santaclarahighschool.com www.santaclarahighschool.com Rev. Juan Jose Guzman, O.A.R., Admin.; Stds.: 200; Lay Tchrs.: 20

PASADENA

La Salle High School - (PRV) (Grades 9-12) 3880 E. Sierra Madre Blvd., Pasadena, CA 91107 t) 626-351-8951 principal@lasallehs.org; school-2623@la-archdiocese.org lasallehs.org Courtney Kassakhian, Prin.; Stds.: 643

Mayfield Senior School of the Holy Child Jesus - (PRV) (Grades 9-12) 500 Bellefontaine St., Pasadena, CA 91105-2439 t) 626-799-9121 school-2663@la-archdiocese.org www.mayfieldsenior.org (Girls) Kate Morin, Prin.; Cynthia Riegsecker, Dir.; Toi Treister, Asst. Dir., Academics; Stds.: 330

PLAYA DEL REY

St. Bernard High School - (DIO) (Grades 9-12) 9100 Falmouth Ave., Playa del Rey, CA 90293 t) 310-823-4651 rbillups@stbernardhs.org; school-9700@la-archdiocese.org www.stbernardhs.org Richard Billups, Prin.; Rosalie Roberts, Vice Prin.; Carter Paysinger, Exec. Dir.; Stds.: 200; Lay Tchrs.: 11

POMONA

Pomona Catholic High School - (DIO) (Grades 9-12) 533 W. Holt Ave., Pomona, CA 91768 t) 909-623-5297 admissions@pomonacatholic.org; school-9670@la-archdiocese.org www.pomonacatholic.org (Girls) Rebecca Arteaga, Prin.; Stds.: 200; Sr. Tchrs.: 1; Lay Tchrs.: 15

Pomona Catholic Middle School - (Grades 9-12) rarteaga@pomonacatholic.org; admissions@pomoancatholic.org Stds.: 105

ROSEMEAD

Don Bosco Technical Institute - (PRV) (Grades 9-12) 1151 San Gabriel Blvd., Rosemead, CA 91770-4251 t) 626-940-2000 school-2580@la-archdiocese.org; generalinfo@boscotech.edu www.boscotech.edu (Boys), Secondary Section. Sponsored by Salesians of St. John Bosco. Memo Gutierrez, Pres.; Jeff Krynen, Prin.; Eric Tom, Asst. Prin.; Phil Raul Consuegra, Vice Pres., Devel. & Strategic Initiatives; Thomas Hogan, Dir. Admissions; Stds.: 326; Lay Tchrs.: 30

SANTA BARBARA

Bishop Garcia Diego High School Inc. - (PRV) (Grades 9-12) 4000 La Colina Rd., Santa Barbara, CA 93110 t) 805-967-1266 bishop@bishopdiego.org; school-9540@la-archdiocese.org www.bishopdiego.org Karen Regan, Headmaster; Jennifer Winnewisser, Campus Min.; Stds.: 280

SANTA FE SPRINGS

St. Paul High School - (DIO) (Grades 9-12) 9635 S. Greenleaf Ave., Santa Fe Springs, CA 90670 t) 562-698-6246 rmiller@stpaulhs.org; school-9760@la-archdiocese.org www.stpaulhs.org Robert Miller, Prin.; Christopher Aquino, Admin.; Gregory Dixon, Admin.; Stds.: 500; Pr. Tchrs.: 1; Lay Tchrs.: 23

SANTA MARIA

St. Joseph High School - (DIO) (Grades 9-12) 4120 S. Bradley Rd., Santa Maria, CA 93455 t) 805-937-2038 sjhs@sjhsknights.com; school-9720@la-archdiocese.org www.sjhsknights.com Joanne Poloni, Prin.; Jennifer Perez, Vice Prin.; Rev. Edward Jalbert, C.J., Chap.; Stds.: 398

SHERMAN OAKS

Notre Dame High School - (PRV) (Grades 9-12) 13645 Riverside Dr., Sherman Oaks, CA 91423 t) 818-933-3600 school-2673@la-archdiocese.org; president@ndhs.org www.ndhs.org Alice Cotti, Prin.; Samuel Carl Lagana, Pres.; Stds.: 1,250; Lay Tchrs.: 96

SIERRA MADRE

Mt. Alverno High School - (PRV) (Grades 9-12) 200 N. Michillinda Ave., Sierra Madre, CA 91024 t) 626-355-3463 school-2550@la-archdiocese.org; admissions@alvernoheightsacademy.org alvernoheightsacademy.org (Girls) Julia Fanara, Prin.; Kari Irvin, Asst. Prin.; Sara McCarthy, Dir. Admissions; Stds.: 185; Lay Tchrs.: 18

THOUSAND OAKS

La Reina High School & Middle School - (PRV) (Grades 6-12) 106 W. Janss Rd., Thousand Oaks, CA 91360 t) 805-495-6494 tguevara@lareina.com; school-2613@la-archdiocese.org www.lareina.com (Girls) Anthony Guevara, Pres.; Margaret Marschner, Prin.; Sr. Regina Robbins, Dean; Stds.: 271; Sr. Tchrs.: 2; Lay Tchrs.: 28

TORRANCE

Bishop Montgomery High School - (DIO) (Grades 9-12) 5430 Torrance Blvd., Torrance, CA 90503 t) 310-540-2021 school-9550@la-archdiocese.org www.bmhs-la.org Dr. James C Garza, Prin.; Yvette Vigon-Morffi, Vice Prin.; Stds.: 828; Lay Tchrs.: 61

VENTURA

St. Bonaventure High School - (DIO) (Grades 9-12) 3167 Telegraph Rd., Ventura, CA 93003-3281 t) 805-648-6836 office@sbhsvta.org; school-9710@la-archdiocese.org www.sbhsvta.org Christina Castro, Prin.; Stds.: 367; Lay Tchrs.: 29

WOODLAND HILLS

Louisville High School - (PRV) (Grades 9-12) 22300 Mulholland Dr., Woodland Hills, CA 91364 t) 818-346-8812 kvercillo@louisvillehs.org; school-2633@la-archdiocese.org louisvillehs.org (Girls) Sr. Donna Hansen, S.S.L., Pres.; Kathleen Vercillo, Prin.; Stds.: 350

INSTITUTIONS LOCATED IN DIOCESE

CATHOLIC CHARITIES [CCH]

LOS ANGELES

Catholic Charities Community Development Corporation, Inc. - 1531 James M. Wood Blvd., Los Angeles, CA 90015-0095; Mailing: P.O. Box 15095, Los Angeles, CA 90015-0095 t) (213) 251-3400 mruvalcaba@ccharities.org Rev. Msgr. Gregory A. Cox, Dir.; Asstd. Annu.: 1; Staff: 1

Catholic Charities of Los Angeles, Inc. - 1531 James M. Wood Blvd., Los Angeles, CA 90015-0095; Mailing: P.O. Box 15095, Los Angeles, CA 90015-0095 t) (213) 251-3400 mruvalcaba@ccharities.org catholiccharitiesla.org Most Rev. Jose H. Gomez; Rev. Msgr. Gregory A. Cox, Exec. Dir.; Daniel P. O'Brien, CFO; Asstd. Annu.: 184,289; Staff: 358

Archdiocesan Youth Employment Services - 3250 Wilshire Blvd., Ste. 1010, Los Angeles, CA 90010 t) (213) 736-5456 rgutierrez@ccharities.org Robert L. Gutierrez, Dir.;

Catholic Youth Organization - 1530 James M. Wood Blvd., Los Angeles, CA 90015 t) 213-251-3454 James

McGoldrick, Prog. Dir. I;
Central Administrative Offices - 1531 James M. Wood Blvd., Los Angeles, CA 90015-0095; Mailing: P.O. Box 15095, Los Angeles, CA 90015-0095 info@catholiccharitiesla.org
Continuous Quality Improvement - 1530 James M. Wood Blvd., Los Angeles, CA 90015 t) (213) 251-3468 alalaian@ccharities.org Maria Ruvalcaba, Contact;
Esperanza Immigrant Rights Project - 1530 James M. Wood Blvd., Los Angeles, CA 90015 t) 213-251-3505 portiz@ccharities.org Patricia Ortiz, Dir.;
Immigration & Refugee Services - 1530 James M. Wood Blvd., Los Angeles, CA 90015 t) 213-251-3411 slee@ccharities.org Evenson (Steve) Lee, Prog. Dir.;
Catholic Immigration Services - 1530 James M. Wood Blvd., Los Angeles, CA 90015 mruvalcaba@ccharities.org Maria Ruvalcaba, Secy.;
Our Lady of the Angels Region - 211 Third Ave., Venice, CA 90291 t) 213-318-5757 alalaian@ccharities.org Armine Lalaian, Dir.;
ADESTE Child Care Program - 211 Third Ave., Venice, CA 90291 t) 310-392-8701 lpearreault@ccharities.org
ADESTE Child Care Program at El Santo Nino Community Services Center - 601 E. 23rd St., Los Angeles, CA 90011 t) (213) 318-5705 Elizabeth Soriano, Dir.;
Angel's Flight at My Club at El Santo Nino Community Services Center - 357 S. Westlake Ave., Los Angeles, CA 90057 t) (213) 413-2311; (800) 833-2499 pchaidez@ccharities.org Patricia Chaidez, Dir.;
Angel's Flight - At Risk Youth Services - 357 S. Westlake Ave., Los Angeles, CA 90057 t) (213) 413-2311; (800) 833-2499 (Hotline) Patricia Chaidez, Dir.;
Archdiocesan Youth Employment Services (AYES) - 3965 S. Vermont Ave., Los Angeles, CA 90037 t) (213) 736-5456; (888) 463-6293 robert@aye-la.org; gail@aye-la.org www.ayela.org Gail Guenther, Office Mgr.; Rosa Penaloza, Prog. Dir.;
Catholic Counseling Services - 10217 S. Inglewood Ave., Inglewood, CA 90304 t) (310) 392-8701
Good Shepherd Center for Homeless Women and Children - 1671 Beverly Blvd., Los Angeles, CA 90026 t) 213-235-1460; 213-250-5241 evaldes@gschomeless.org Sr. Anne Tran, L.H.C., Dir.; Elvia Valdez, Dir.;
St. Margaret's Community Services Center - 10217 S. Inglewood Ave., Inglewood, CA 90304 t) 310-672-2208 Mary Agnes Erlandson, Dir.;
My Club Program - 8705 S. Vermont Ave., Los Angeles, CA 90044 t) 323-751-2582 pchaidez@ccharities.org Patricia Chaidez, Dir.;
Refugee Resettlement Program - 1530 James M. Wood Blvd., Los Angeles, CA 90015 t) (213) 318-5757
St. Robert's Community Services Center - 211 Third Ave., Venice, CA 90291 t) 310-392-8701
San Fernando Region - 21600 Hart St., Canoga Park, CA 91303 t) 213-251-3578; 213-251-3549 syanez@ccharities.org Sandra Yanez, Dir.;
Angel's Flight My Club at Guadalupe Center - 21600 Hart St., Canoga Park, CA 91303 t) (213) 251-3566 Patricia Chaidez, Dir.;
Employment Support Partnership - 4322 San Fernando Rd., Glendale, CA 91204 t) (213) 318-5716
Employment Support Partnership - 21600 Hart St., Canoga Park, CA 91303 t) (213) 251-3586 Sandra Yanez, Dir.;
Glendale Community Services Center - 4322 San Fernando Rd., Glendale, CA 91204 t) 213-318-5707
Guadalupe Community Services Center - 21600 Hart St., Canoga Park, CA 91303
Refugee Resettlement Program - 4322 San Fernando Rd., Glendale, CA 91204 t) 818-409-0057
Loaves and Fishes Community Services - 7309 Van Nuys Blvd., Van Nuys, CA 91405 t) 818-997-0943
Temporary Skilled Worker Center - 1190 Flower St., Burbank, CA 91502 t) 818-566-7148 (Day Laborer Program)
San Gabriel Region - 1307 Warren St., Los Angeles, CA 90033 t) 213-251-3582 xzendejas@ccharities.org Xochitl Zendejas, Dir.;
Brownson House Community Center - 1307 Warren St., Los Angeles, CA 90033 t) (213) 251-3512 mruvalcaba@ccharities.org
Catholic Charities Parish Liaison Program (CCPal) - 1307 Warren St., Los Angeles, CA 90033 t) (213) 251-3520 mruvalcaba@ccharities.org
McGill Street House - 1460 E. Holt Ave., Ste. 98, Pomona, CA 91767 t) 909-629-1335
Pomona Community Services - 1460 E. Holt Ave., Ste. 98, Pomona, CA 91767 t) 909-629-1331
San Juan Diego Center - 4171 N. Tyler Ave., El Monte, CA 91731 t) 626-575-7652
San Pedro Region - 123 E. 14th St., Long Beach, CA 90813 t) 213-251-3429 bhackman@ccharities.org Bruce Hackman, Dir.;
Elizabeth Ann Seton Residence - 2198 San Gabriel Ave., Long Beach, CA 90810 t) (562) 388-7670
Gatekeeper Project - 123 E. 14th St., Long Beach, CA 90813 t) 213-251-3432
Long Beach Community Services Center - 123 E. 14th St., Long Beach, CA 90813 t) 213-251-3432
Mahar House - My Club - 1115 Mahar Ave., Wilmington, CA 90744 t) 213-251-3458
Pico Rivera Food Pantry and Resource Center - 5014 Passons Blvd., Pico Rivera, CA 90660 t) 562-949-0937
Project Achieve Emergency Shelter - 1368 Oregon Ave., Long Beach, CA 90813 t) 562-218-9864
Santa Barbara Region: Santa Barbara County - 609 E. Haley St., Santa Barbara, CA 93103 t) 805-965-7045 yvasquez@ccharities.org Yolanda Vasquez, Dir.;
Carpinteria Community Services - 1500 Linden Ave., Carpinteria, CA 93013 t) (805) 684-8621
Cuyama Valley Mobile Food Distribution Site - 4711 Hwy. 166, New Cuyama, CA 93254 t) (805) 922-2059
Guadalupe Mobile Food Distribution Site - 4681 11th St., Guadalupe, CA 93434 t) 805-922-2059
Isla Vista Mobile Food Distribution Site - 6647 El Colegio Rd., Isla Vista, CA 93117 t) (805) 965-7045
Lompoc Community Services Center - 325 N. 2nd St., Lompoc, CA 93436 t) 805-736-6226
Santa Barbara Community Services Center - 609 E. Haley St., Santa Barbara, CA 93103
Santa Maria Community Services Center - 607 W. Main St., Santa Maria, CA 93454 t) 805-922-2059
Catholic Charities Thrift Stores - 609 E. Haley St., Santa Barbara, CA 93103 t) (805) 966-9659
Catholic Charities Thrift Stores (Santa Maria) - 607 W. Main St., Santa Maria, CA 93454 t) (805) 922-4174
Santa Barbara Region: Ventura County - 303 N. Ventura Ave., Ste. A, Ventura, CA 93001-1961 t) 805-965-7045 yvasquez@ccharities.org Yolanda Vasquez, Dir.;
Moorpark Community Services - 612 Spring Rd., Ste. 101, Moorpark, CA 93021 t) 805-529-0720; 805-520-3017
Older Adult Services and Intervention System (OASIS) - Camarillo - 2532 Ventura Blvd., Camarillo, CA 93010 t) 805-987-2083; 805-914-4277
Ventura Community Services Center - 303 N. Ventura Ave., Ventura, CA 93001 t) 805-643-4694

CEMETERIES [CEM]

CULVER CITY
Holy Cross Cemetery & Mortuary - 5835 W. Slauson Ave., Culver City, CA 90230 t) 310-836-5500 holycrosscc@catholiccm.org Ramon Nunez, Mortuary Mgr.; Kathy Silva, Cemetery Mgr.;
LANCASTER
Good Shepherd Cemetery & Mausoleum - 43121 70th St. W., Lancaster, CA 93536 t) 661-722-0887 goodshepherd@catholiccm.org www.catholiccm.org Iris Soriano-Ross, Interim Cemetery Mgr.;
LONG BEACH
All Souls Cemetery and Mortuary - 4400 Cherry Ave., Long Beach, CA 90807 t) 562-424-8601 allsouls@catholiccm.org www.allsoulsmortuary.com/ Mary Ann McAdams, Cemetery Mgr.; Ashley Menear, Mortuary Mgr.;
LOS ANGELES
Calvary Cemetery and Mortuary - 4201 Whittier Blvd., Los Angeles, CA 90023 t) 323-261-3106 calvaryla@catholiccm.org www.calvarymortuary.com/ Sonyaann Sandoval-Carreon, Mortuary Mgr.; Olga Medina, Cemetery Mgr.;
MISSION HILLS
San Fernando Cemetery and Mission Hills Catholic Mortuary - 11160 Stanwood Ave., Mission Hills, CA 91345 t) 818-361-7387 sanfernando@catholiccm.org www.missionhillsmortuary.com Mark Neander, Mortuary Mgr.; Iris Soriano-Ross, Cemetery Mgr.;
OXNARD
Santa Clara Cemetery and Mortuary - 2370 N. H St., Oxnard, CA 93036 t) 805-485-5757 sclara@catholiccemeteriesla.org; sclara@catholiccm.org www.santaclaramortuary.com/ Ruby Barrios, Gen. Mgr.;
POMONA
Holy Cross Cemetery - 444 E Lexington Ave., Pomona, CA 91766 t) 909-627-3602 holycrosspom@catholiccemeteriesla.org Edel Cabrera, Cemetery Mgr.;
ROSEMEAD
Resurrection Cemetery & Mausoleum - 966 N. Potrero Grande Dr., Rosemead, CA 91770 t) 323-887-2024 resurrection@catholiccemeteriesla.org www.lacatholiccemeteries.org Eva Gamboa, Cemetery Mgr.;
ROWLAND HEIGHTS
Queen of Heaven Cemetery and Mortuary - 2161 S. Fullerton Rd., Rowland Heights, CA 91748 t) 626-964-1291 queenofheaven@catholiccm.org www.queenofheavenmortuary.org/ Sylvia Dizon, Cemetery Mgr.; Ruth Rincon, Gen. Mgr.;
SANTA BARBARA
Calvary Cemetery & Mausoleum - 199 N. Hope Ave., Santa Barbara, CA 93110 t) 805-687-8811 calvarysb@catholiccm.org Amanda Caracheo, Cemetery Mgr.;
SIMI VALLEY
Assumption Cemetery - 1380 Fitzgerald Rd., Simi Valley, CA 93065 t) 805-583-5825 assumption@catholiccm.org catholiccm.org/assumption-cemetery Mauricio Perez, Dir.; Kathy Silva, Interim Cemetery Mgr.; Roxana Cordero, Asst. Mgr.;

COLLEGES & UNIVERSITIES [COL]

LOS ANGELES
***Loyola Marymount University** - One LMU Dr., Ste. 4844, Los Angeles, CA 90045-2659 t) 310-338-2700 president@lmu.edu www.lmu.edu Timothy Law Snyder, Pres.; Rev. Patrick J. Cahalan, S.J., Chancellor; Rev. Albert P. Koppes, O.Carm., Chancellor; Rev. Robert V. Caro, S.J., Vice Pres., Mission & Min.; Stds.: 9,392; Pr. Tchrs.: 8
Jesuit Community - One L.M.U. Dr., Los Angeles, CA 90045; Mailing: P.O. Box 45041, Los Angeles, CA 90045 t) 310-338-7445 esiebert@lmu.edu Rev. Edward J. Siebert, S.J., Rector; Rev. Michael Engh, S.J., Chancellor; Rev. Roy Antunez, S.J., In Res.; Rev. Michael Braden, S.J., In Res.; Bro. Michael E. Breault, S.J., In Res.; Rev. Julian Climaco, S.J., In Res.; Rev. Patrick Connolly, S.J., In Res.; Rev. John Guyol, S.J., In Res.; Rev. James McDermott, S.J., In

Res.; Rev. Martin Ngo, S.J., In Res.; Rev. Amaechi M. Ugwu, S.J., In Res.; Rev. Richard A. Robin, S.J., Chap.; Rev. Randall Roche, S.J., Chap.; Rev. Marc Reeves, S.J., Campus Min.; Rev. Paul H. Vu, S.J., Dean; Rev. Jose Ignacio Badenes, S.J., Prof.; Rev. Mark Bandsuch, S.J., Prof.; Rev. Philip J. Chmielewski, S.J., Prof.; Rev. Allan Figueroa Deck, S.J., Prof.; Rev. Sean T. Dempsey, S.J., Prof.; Rev. Lan Ngo, S.J., Prof.; Rev. Thomas P. Rausch, S.J., Prof.; Rev. Kenneth Rudnick, S.J., Prof.; Rev. Tri M. Dinh, S.J., Dir.;

Loyola School of Law - 919 S. Albany St., Los Angeles, CA 90015; Mailing: P.O. Box 15019, Los Angeles, CA 90015 t) 213-736-1000 admissions@lls.edu www.lls.edu Michael Waterstone, Dean; Stds.: 1,000

The Sacred Heart of Mary and Sisters of St. Joseph of Orange - One LMU Dr., Ste. 4844, Los Angeles, CA 90045-2659 t) (310) 338-2700 sr.ellen.jordan@csjorange.org Sr. Eileen McNerney, Supr.;

Mount Saint Mary's University - 12001 Chalon Rd., Los Angeles, CA 90049 t) 310-954-4010 amcelaney@msmu.edu www.msmu.edu Dr. Ann McElaney-Johnson, Pres.; Stds.: 3,554

Doheny Campus - 10 Chester Pl., Los Angeles, CA 90007 t) 213-477-2500 onlineadmissions@msmu.edu Robert J. Perrins, Provost & Academic Vice Pres.; Chris McAlary, Vice Pres. Admin. & Fin.; Ruth Jackson, Librn.; Stds.: 2,897

SANTA PAULA

***Thomas Aquinas College** - 10000 Ojai Rd., Santa Paula, CA 93060 t) 805-525-4417; 800-634-9797 pr@thomasaquinas.edu www.thomasaquinas.edu Paul O'Reilly, Pres.; Dennis McCarthy, Vice. Pres.; John Goyette, Dean; Rev. Robert Marczewski, Chap.; Rev. John Mary Chung, Chap.; Rev. Jorge Jesus Lopez (Argentina), Chap.; Richena Curphey, Librn.; Stds.: 358; Lay Tchrs.: 38

CONVENTS, MONASTERIES, AND RESIDENCES FOR WOMEN [CON]

ALHAMBRA

Carmel of St. Teresa of Los Angeles (Discalced Carmelite Nuns of the Order of the Blessed Virgin Mary of Mt. Carmel.) - 215 E. Alhambra Rd., Alhambra, CA 91801 t) 626-282-2387 teresacarm1913@gmail.com www.carmelteresa.org Sr. Brenda Marie Schroeder, O.C.D., Prioress; Srs.: 13

Carmelite Sisters of the Most Sacred Heart of Los Angeles - 920 E. Alhambra Rd., Alhambra, CA 91801-2799 t) 626-289-1353 gensecretary@carmelitesistersocd.com www.carmelitesistersocd.com Sr. Elizabeth Therese Shively, OCD, Secy.; Srs.: 120

ALTADENA

Franciscan Sisters of the Sacred Heart - 579 W. Mariposa St., Altadena, CA 91001 t) 805-451-0365; 213-381-2931 californiasister72@yahoo.com www.fssh.com Sr. Joyce Shanabarger, O.S.F., Supr.; Srs.: 1

BELLFLOWER

***Sisters of the Blessed Korean Martyrs, S.B.K.M.** - 16276 California Ave., Bellflower, CA 90706 t) 562-461-8100 sbkm.americas@gmail.com www.sbkm.kr Sr. Hang Soon Agnes Park, Prov.; Srs.: 4

CULVER CITY

Daughters of St. Paul - 3908 Sepulveda Blvd., Culver City, CA 90230 t) 310-390-4699 culvercity@paulinemedia.com pauline.org Sr. Pauline Brooks, Supr.; Srs.: 1

Religious Sisters of Charity - 10668 St. James Dr., Culver City, CA 90230-5461 t) 310-559-0176 bermorganrsc@gmail.com www.rsccaritas.org Sr. Bernadette Morgan, R.S.C., Pres.; Srs.: 36

Religious Sisters of Charity - 830 1/2 W. 14th St., San Pedro, CA 90731 t) (310) 519-0721 evabryrsc@gmail.com

DOWNEY

Sisters of the Holy Faith in California - 12322 S. Paramount Blvd., Downey, CA 90242 c) (504) 621-4530 usregion2017@yahoo.com www.holyfaithsisters.com Sr. Teresa Ann Rooney, Supr.; Srs.: 10

Visitation Congregation of North America - 7845 Quill Dr., Downey, CA 90242 t) 562-862-7472 lasvm2000@yahoo.com Sr. Meera Parayil, Contact; Srs.: 1

ENCINO

Sisters of Social Service of Los Angeles, Inc. - 4316 Lanai Rd., Encino, CA 91436 t) 818-285-3358 sisterssocialservice@gmail.com www.sssla.org Sr. Maribeth Larkin, Dir.; Srs.: 60

GARDENA

Lovers of the Holy Cross Sisters - 14700 S. Van Ness Ave., Gardena, CA 90249 t) 310-516-0271 srgracele@lhcla.org www.lhcla.org Sr. Grace Duc Le, LHC-LA, Supr.; Srs.: 74

St. Anselm Convent - 7023 Arlington Ave., Los Angeles, CA 90043 t) 323-455-2103 srvannenguyen@lhcla.org; stanselm@lhcla.org Sr. Vanne Hong Nguyen, LHC-LA, Contact;

St. Bruno Convent - 10734 S. Widener Ave., Whittier, CA 90603 t) 562-947-1177 stbruno@lhcla.org; srteresadao@lhcla.org Sr. Thu Hong Dao, LHC-LA, Contact;

Poor Clare Missionary Sisters, Inc. - 1050 W. 161st St., Gardena, CA 90247 t) 310-323-9942 blanca_lopez90@yahoo.com Sr. Yanory Zuniga, M.C., Supr.; Srs.: 14

Poor Clare Missionary Sisters - 13026 Angeles Trail Way, Sylmar, CA 91342; Mailing: P.O. Box 922046, Sylmar, CA 91392 t) (818) 365-8307 www.cmswr.org Sr. Elvira Duron, M.C., Supr.;

GLENDORA

St. Lucy's Priory of Glendora California, Inc. - 19045 E. Sierra Madre Ave., Glendora, CA 91741 t) 626-335-1682 stlucysebrown@aol.com www.stlucys.com Sr. Elizabeth Brown, Prioress; Srs.: 4

LONG BEACH

***Little Handmaids of the Most Holy Trinity, M.A.S.T.** - 3716 Arabella St., Long Beach, CA 90805 t) 562-633-0640 holytrinitylb@yahoo.com Sr. Monica D Bermiso, M.A.S.T., Supr.; Srs.: 2

The Medical Sisters of St. Joseph - 3627 Lemon Ave., Long Beach, CA 90807 t) 562-426-8825 msjnirmala@aol.com www.msjnirmala.org Sr. Dennis Punchakunnel, M.S.J., Contact; Srs.: 3

LOS ANGELES

***The Blessed Sacrament Sisters of Charity, Inc.** - 248 S. Mariposa Ave., Los Angeles, CA 90004 t) 213-389-7760 inbousa@yahoo.com Sr. Theresa Kong, Supr.; Srs.: 4

California Institute of the Sisters of the Immaculate Heart Mary - 3424 Wilshire Blvd., 5th Fl., Office of the Archbishop, Los Angeles, CA 90010-2241 t) 213-637-7000 info@la-archdiocese.org Pontifical Commissary of the Archbishop. Most Rev. Jose H. Gomez; Srs.: 3

Congregation of the Sisters of Nazareth Motherhouse, U.S.A. - 3333 Manning Ave., Los Angeles, CA 90064 t) 310-839-2361 c) 310-733-8378 regional@nazarethhousela.org www.nazarethhouse.org Sr. Marie McCormack, C.S.N., Supr.; Srs.: 1

Esclavas de la Inmaculada Nina - 350 S. Boyle Ave., Los Angeles, CA 90033 t) 323-685-9210 Sr. Maria R CarlosValdez, EIN, Supr.; Sr. Petra Lopez, Treas.; Srs.: 5

Eucharistic Franciscan Missionary Sisters - 943 S. Soto St., Los Angeles, CA 90023 t) 213-264-6556; 310-328-6725 efms@earthlink.net Sr. Rose Seraphim, Supr.; Srs.: 1

Hermanas Carmelitas de San Jose - 141 W. 87th Pl., Los Angeles, CA 90003 t) (424) 208-9264 lupagoz@yahoo.com Sr. Lucia Padilla, C.S.J., Supr.; Srs.: 4

Missionary Benedictine Sisters of Tutzing in Los Angeles, Inc. - 912 S. Bronson Ave., Los Angeles, CA 90019-1935 t) 323-939-3977; 323-937-7971 osbgregory@hanmail.net Sr. Pachomia Kim, O.S.B., Supr.; Srs.: 1

Missionary Guadalupanas of the Holy Spirit, Inc. - 5467 W. 8th St., Los Angeles, CA 90036 t) 323-424-7208 province@guadalupeusa.org www.mgsps.org Sr. Ana Gabriela Castro, M.G.Sp.S., Prov.; Sr. Frances Aldama, Vicar; Sr. Yesenia Fernandez, M.G.Sp.S., Treas.; Srs.: 4

Novitiate - novitiate@guadalupeusa.org Sr. Lorena Sandoval, Contact;

Missionary Sisters of Christ the King (Poland) - 3424 W. Adams Blvd., Los Angeles, CA 90018 t) 323-734-5249 plchurchla@earthlink.net Sr. Anna Kalinowski, M.S.C.K., Supr.; Sr. Jadwiga Kokolus, M.C.H.R., Secy.; Srs.: 3

Monastery of the Angels (Contemplative) (Nuns of the Order of Preachers) - 1977 Carmen Ave., Los Angeles, CA 90068 t) 323-466-2186 monasteryprioress@gmail.com Sr. Mary St. Pius, O.P., Prioress; Rev. Michael Carey, O.P., Chap.; Srs.: 17

Pious Disciples of the Divine Master - 501 N. Beaudry Ave., Los Angeles, CA 90012-1509 t) 213-250-7962 (Center); 213-977-0893 (Community) lalitcenter@aol.com www.pddm.us Sr. M. Lucille Van Hoogmoed, P.D.D.M., Supr.; Srs.: 7

Sisters of St. Joseph of Carondelet in California - 11999 Chalon Rd., Los Angeles, CA 90049-1524 t) 310-889-2100 mmckay@csjla.org www.csjla.org (St. Mary's Provincialate, Carondelet Center) Sr. Mary McKay, C.S.J., Prov.; Sr. Rosanne Belpedio, C.S.J., Prov. Asst.; Sr. Ingrid Honore-Lallande, C.S.J., Prov. Asst.; Srs.: 208

Sisters of St. Joseph in California - t) 310-889-2158 communications@csjla.org; info@csjla.org csjla.org/

Sisters of St. Joseph Ministerial Services - t) (310) 889-2100 communications@csjla.org csjla.org/

Sisters of St. Joseph of Orange - One L.M.U. Dr., Los Angeles, CA 90045; Mailing: 440 S. Batavia St., Orange, CA 92868 t) 714-633-8121 x7704 sr.ellen.jordan@csjorange.org csjorange.org/ Sr. Ellen Jordan, C.S.J., Secy.; Srs.: 5

Sisters of the Company of Mary - 2634 Monmouth Ave., Los Angeles, CA 90007 t) 213-747-3542 kschneider@odn-la.org www.cdm.edu.co Sr. Gloria Liliana Franco, Prov.; Sr. Kathy Schneider, O.D.N., Supr.; Srs.: 8

Sisters of the Good Shepherd - 2561 W. Venice Blvd., Los Angeles, CA 90019 t) 323-737-6111 rgsla1@aol.com www.goodshepherdsisters.org Sr. Regina Do, Supr.; Srs.: 7

Sisters of the Guardian Angel - 4529 New York St., Los Angeles, CA 90022 t) 323-266-4431 regipenin@yahoo.com Jenny Areas, Dir.; Srs.: 5

Sisters of the Immaculate Heart of Mary of Mirinae, I.H.M.M. - 423 S. Commonwealth Ave., Los Angeles, CA 90020 t) 213-738-1020 laihmm@hanmail.net Sr. Cyrilla Kim, I.H.M.M., Supr.; Srs.: 7

MONROVIA

Maryknoll Sisters of St. Dominic, Inc. - 340 Norumbega Dr., Monrovia, CA 91016-2445 t) 626-358-1825 mkmonrovia340@gmail.com Sr. Arlene Trant, Contact; Srs.: 19

MONTEBELLO

Religious of the Sacred Heart of Mary - 441 N. Garfield Ave., Montebello, CA 90640-2901 t) 323-887-8821 rshmwap@earthlink.net www.rshm.org Sr. Kathleen Kelemen, R.S.H.M., Prov.; Srs.: 35

MONTEREY PARK

Theresian Sisters - 901 W. El Repetto Dr., Monterey Park, CA 91754 t) 213-637-7559 mgreyes@la-archdiocese.org Sr. Anna Thaolu, C.S.T., Contact; Srs.: 1

NORTHRIDGE

Mother of Mercy Convent (Sister of Mercy Burlingame) - 9329 Crebs Ave., Northridge, CA 91324 t) 818-882-4095 info@dmmmg.com Sr. Patricia Beirne, R.S.M., Supr.; Srs.: 1

Sisters of the Society Devoted to the Sacred Heart - 9814 Sylvia Ave., Motherhouse, Northridge, CA 91324 t) 818-772-9961 mhsdsh2@sbcglobal.net www.sacredheartsisters.com Sr. Mary Tomasella,

S.D.S.H., Supr.; Srs.: 46

Sisters of the Society Devoted to the Sacred Heart - 869 S. Rimpau Blvd., Los Angeles, CA 90005 t) (323) 935-2372 sdshtreasurer@gmail.com Sr. Rosemarie Karl, S.D.S.H., Treas.;

Sisters of the Society Devoted to the Sacred Heart - 1762 Mission Dr., Solvang, CA 93463 t) (805) 688-6158 sdshtreasurer@gmail.com Sr. Rosemarie Karl, S.D.S.H., Treas.;

NORWALK

***Lovers of the Holy Cross of Nha Trang** - 12323 Alondra Blvd., Norwalk, CA 90650 t) (562) 809-1570 anhtram69@yahoo.com Sr. Anh Tram, L.H.C.N.T., Supr.; Srs.: 1

OJAI

Sisters of Mary Mother of the Church - 431 Montana Cir., Ojai, CA 93023 t) 805-640-1798 contact@sistersofmarymc.org Sr. Kathryn Duddy, Supr.; Srs.: 11

OXNARD

Servants of Mary, Ministers to the Sick - 140 N. G St., Oxnard, CA 93030-5214 t) 805-486-5502 superioraox@gmail.com Sr. Elvia Navarro, S.deM., Contact; Srs.: 15

Servants of Mary, Ministers to the Sick - 2131 W. 27th St., Los Angeles, CA 90018-3018 t) (323) 731-5747 servantsofmaryla@aol.com Sr. Lourdes Garcia, S.deM., Supr.;

RANCHO PALOS VERDES

Daughters of Mary & Joseph, D.M.J. - 5300 Crest Rd., Rancho Palos Verdes, CA 90275-5004 t) 310-377-9968 leadershipteam@dmjca.org www.daughtersofmaryandjoseph.org Sr. Linda Webb, D.M.J., Supr.; Srs.: 32

Sisters of Charity of Rolling Hills - 28600 Palos Verdes Dr. E., Rancho Palos Verdes, CA 90275 t) 310-831-4104 scrh1964@gmail.com Sr. Virginia Buchholz, S.C.R.H., Supr.; Srs.: 6

SAN PEDRO

Little Sisters of the Poor - 2100 S. Western Ave., San Pedro, CA 90732 t) 310-548-0625 adsanpedro@littlesistersofthepoor.org Sr. Margaret Lennon, L.S.P., Supr.; Srs.: 1

SANTA BARBARA

Monastery of Poor Clares - 215 E. Los Olivos St., Santa Barbara, CA 93105 t) 805-682-7670 john@thynelaw.com www.poorclaressantabarbara.org Sr. Aimee Marie of the Eucharist, Contact; Srs.: 13

SYLMAR

Franciscan Sisters of the Immaculate Conception - 13367 Borden Ave., Unit A, Sylmar, CA 91342 t) 818-364-5557 provstclare@outlook.com Sr. Yolanda Yanez, O.S.F., Supr.; Srs.: 1

THOUSAND OAKS

Sisters of Notre Dame - 1776 Hendrix Ave., Thousand Oaks, CA 91360 t) 805-496-3243 mgorman@sndusa.org Sr. Margaret Gorman, S.N.D., Prov.; Srs.: 46

TORRANCE

Little Company of Mary Convent - 20552 Mansel Ave., Torrance, CA 90503 t) 310-214-3190 srmildred@sbcglobal.net www.lcmglobal.org Sr. Terrence Landini, Supr.; Srs.: 1

VENTURA

Sisters of the Holy Cross, Inc. - 1931 Poli St., Ventura, CA 93001-2360 t) 805-652-1700 yhatt@cscsisters.org Sr. Kathleen Moroney, C.S.C., Treas.; Srs.: 15

***Handmaids of the Triune God** - 2509 Pawnee Ct., Ventura, CA 93001-1442; Mailing: P.O. Box 2957, Ventura, CA 93002-2957 t) 805-613-7503 handmaidsjmj@gmail.com Sr. Mary Joseph Mei, JMJ, Rel. Ord. Ldr.; Srs.: 2

WILMINGTON

The Congregation of the Norbertine Sisters - 943 Lagoon Ave., Wilmington, CA 90744 t) 310-952-0144 norbertinesrswilm@gmail.com www.congregationofnorbertinesisters.org/ Sr. Adriana Gacikova, Supr.; Srs.: 5

WOODLAND HILLS

Sisters of St. Louis (Monaghan) - 22300 Mulholland Dr., Woodland Hills, CA 91364-4933 t) 818-883-1678 sslca4@sistersofsaintlouis.com www.stlouissisters.org Sr. Judith Dieterle, S.S.L., Rel. Ord. Ldr.; Srs.: 1

ENDOWMENTS / FOUNDATIONS / TRUSTS [EFT]

ALHAMBRA

Carmelite Sisters Foundation, Inc. - 920 E. Alhambra Rd., Alhambra, CA 91801 t) 626-289-1353 srscholastica@carmelitesistersocd.com Sr. Mary Scholastica Lee, O.C.D., Dir.;

LA VERNE

Picpus Charitable Trust - 2150 Damien Ave., La Verne, CA 91750 t) 909-227-9346 ptravers37@gmail.com Rev. Patrick Travers, SS.CC., Trustee;

LONG BEACH

St. Mary Medical Center Foundation - 1050 Linden Ave., Long Beach, CA 90813 t) 562-491-9225 supportstmarylb@dignityhealth.org www.supportstmary.org Michael Neils, Pres.;

LOS ANGELES

***Friends of John Paul II Foundation of California** - 3424 W. Adams Blvd., Los Angeles, CA 90018 t) 805-796-0960 bogusia.doerr@gmail.com fjp2la.com Boguslawa Doerr, Pres.;

Notre Dame Academy Schools Foundation - 2851 Overland Ave., Los Angeles, CA 90064 t) 310-839-5289 mmartinez@ndala.com James Tomchak, CEO; Cathy Kaiser, CFO;

Sisters of Nazareth Foundation, Inc. - 3333 Manning Ave., Los Angeles, CA 90064 t) 310-839-2361 mwashington@nazarethhousela.org Melanie Washington, Dir.;

NORTHRIDGE

***John Paul II Foundation for the New Evangelization** - 9227 Reseda Blvd., Apt. 260, Northridge, CA 91324 t) 747-224-1229 info@parishevangelizationleaders.org www.parishevangelizationleaders.org/ Sylvia Acayan, Contact;

OJAI

***St. Joseph's H. & RC Foundation** - 2464 Ojai Ave., Ojai, CA 93023 t) 805-646-1466 igi@ojai.net Rev. Ignatius Sudol, O.H., CEO;

OXNARD

St. John's Healthcare Foundation (Oxnard and Pleasant Valley) - 1600 N. Rose Ave., Oxnard, CA 93030 t) 805-988-2868 pam.koerner@commonspirit.org supportstjohns.org Gail Summers, Vice. Pres.;

SANTA MARIA

American Region of the Josephite Fathers Charitable Trust - 180 Patterson Rd., Santa Maria, CA 93455 t) 805-937-5378 frcharles71@gmail.com www.josephite.community Rev. Ludovic DeClippel, Supr.; Rev. Charles L. Hofschulte, C.J., Contact;

SUNLAND

***Tierra del Sol Foundation** - 9919 Sunland Blvd., Sunland, CA 91040 t) 818-352-1419 jestrada@tierradelsol.org tierradelsol.org Community Program/Supported Employment for Adults with Developmental Disabilities. Stephen J. Miller, Exec.; Nancy Bissonette-Andrew, Dir.;

THOUSAND OAKS

University Series Foundation, Inc. - 155 E. Janss Rd., Thousand Oaks, CA 91360 t) 805-496-0222 parish-3290@la-archdiocese.org; office@theuniversityseries.org theuniversityseries.org/ Bob Jordan, Pres.; Rev. Michael Rocha, Dir.;

TORRANCE

Providence Little Company of Mary Foundation - 4101 Torrance Blvd., Torrance, CA 90503 t) 310-303-5340 plcmfoundation@providence.org Joseph M. Zanetta, Pres.;

WESTLAKE VILLAGE

***Conrad N. Hilton Fund for Sisters** - 1 Dole Dr., Westlake Village, CA 91362 t) 818-483-0485 info@hiltonfundforsisters.org www.hiltonfundforsisters.org Sr. Gina Blunck, S.N.D., Dir.;

HOSPITALS / HEALTH SERVICES [HOS]

BURBANK

Providence Saint Joseph Medical Center - 501 S. Buena Vista St., Burbank, CA 91505 t) 818-843-5111 psjmc@providence.org www.providence.org Samuel Scrivens, Dir.; Rev. Mark Ciccone, S.J., Chap.; R. Phillip Kiehl, Chap.; Claire Richardson, Chap.; Bed Capacity: 392; Asstd. Annu.: 74,326; Staff: 2,185

CAMARILLO

St. John's Pleasant Valley Hospital - 2309 Antonio Ave., Camarillo, CA 93010 t) 805-389-5800 pam.koerner@commonspirit.org www.dignityhealth.org/pleasantvalley Sponsored by Catholic Health Care Federation Rev. William C.B. Lowe, Chap.; Kate Lewis, Supvr., Spiritual Care; George West, Vice. Pres.; Bed Capacity: 132; Asstd. Annu.: 22,927; Staff: 617

LONG BEACH

St. Mary Medical Center - 1050 Linden Ave., Long Beach, CA 90813 t) 562-491-9000 carolyn.caldwell@commonspirit.org www.stmarymedicalcenter.org Sponsored by Catholic Health Care Federation Rev. Jose Pazhevetti, M.S.T., Chap.; Rev. Manuel A. Sundaram, Chap.; Bed Capacity: 360; Asstd. Annu.: 93,255; Staff: 1,500

MISSION HILLS

Providence Holy Cross Medical Center - 15031 Rinaldi St., Mission Hills, CA 91345-1207 t) 818-365-8051 phcfoundation@providence.org www.providence.org/holycross Bernie Klein, Exec.; Samuel Scrivens, Dir.; Bed Capacity: 329; Asstd. Annu.: 354,909; Staff: 2,282

OXNARD

St. John's Regional Medical Center - 1600 N. Rose Ave., Oxnard, CA 93030 t) 805-988-2500 pam.koerner@commonspirit.org www.dignityhealth.org/stjohnsregional Sponsored by Catholic Health Care Federation Barry Wolfman, Interim CEO; George West, Vice Pres., Mission Integration; Bed Capacity: 269; Asstd. Annu.: 135,902; Staff: 1,422

SAN PEDRO

Providence Little Company of Mary Medical Center San Pedro - 1300 W. 7th St., San Pedro, CA 90732 t) 310-832-3311 plcmfoundation@providence.org www.providence.org/sanpedro Sponsored by Providence Ministries. Rev. Peter Mallin, O.F.M.Conv., Chap.; Sr. Nancy Jurecki, O.P., Dir.; Paul White, Spiritual Adv./Care Srvcs.; Bed Capacity: 356; Asstd. Annu.: 49,582; Staff: 1,171

Providence Little Company of Mary Peninsula Diagnostic Center - 1360 W. 6th St., Ste. 100, San Pedro, CA 90732 t) 310-831-0371 plcmfoundation@providence.org Garry Olney, CEO;

Providence Little Company of Mary Peninsula Recovery Center - 1386 W. 7th St., San Pedro, CA 90732 t) 310-832-3311 plcmfoundation@providence.org Garry Olney, CEO;

SANTA MARIA

Marian Regional Medical Center - 1400 E. Church St., Santa Maria, CA 93454 t) 805-739-3000 pam.koerner@commonspirit.org www.marianmedicalcenter.org Sponsored by Catholic Health Care Federation Sue Anderson, Pres.; Heidi Summers, Dir.; Flora Washburn, B.C.C., Mgr., Spiritual Care; Bed Capacity: 351; Asstd. Annu.: 437,628; Staff: 2,602

Marian Regional Medical Center Extended Care Facility - t) 805-739-3650 Skilled Nursing Facility Jill Ledbetter, Dir.;

Marian Regional Medical Center Foundation - t) 805-739-3595 www.supportmarianmedical.org Jessa Brooks, Pres.;

Marian Residence Retirement Home - 124 S. College Dr., Santa Maria, CA 93454 t) 805-922-7731

SANTA MONICA

Providence Saint John's Health Center - 2121 Santa Monica Blvd., Santa Monica, CA 90404 t) 310-829-5511 saintjohnshealthcenter@providence.org california.providence.org/saint-johns/ Rev. Anthony Mbaegbu, Chap.; Michael Ricks, Exec. Dir.; Bed Capacity: 266; Asstd. Annu.: 165,682; Staff: 1,660

TARZANA

Tarzana Medical Center, LLC (Providence Cedars-Sinai Tarzana Medical Center) - 18321 Clark St., Tarzana, CA 91356 t) 818-881-0800 ptzfoundation@providence.org Shawn Kiley, Chap.; Rev. Anselm Nwakuna, Chap.; Sr. Nancy Jurecki, O.P., Dir.; Bed Capacity: 249; Asstd. Annu.: 142,558; Staff: 1,415

TORRANCE

Providence Little Company of Mary Medical Center - 4101 W. Torrance Blvd., Torrance, CA 90503 t) 310-540-7676 plcmfoundation@providence.org www.providence.org Sponsored by Providence Ministries. Garry Olney, CEO; Rev. Peter Mallin, O.F.M.Conv., Chap.; Paul White, Spiritual Adv./Care Srvcs.; Bed Capacity: 442; Asstd. Annu.: 123,578; Staff: 2,229

WEST COVINA

***Emanate Health Medical Center** - 1115 S. Sunset Ave., West Covina, CA 91790; Mailing: P.O. Box 1980, West Covina, CA 91790 t) 626-962-4011 www.emanatehealth.org Rev. Daniel Malaver, Chap.; Robert Curry, CEO; Ana Haffner, Mgr., Spiritual Care; Roger Sharma, Pres. & CFO; Bed Capacity: 325; Asstd. Annu.: 61,080; Staff: 1,059

MISCELLANEOUS [MIS]

ALHAMBRA

***Carmelite Educational Centers, Inc.** - 920 E. Alhambra Rd., Alhambra, CA 91801 t) 626-289-1353 gensecretary@carmelitesistersocd.com www.carmelitesistersocd.com Sr. Marisa Ducote, Dir.;

Flos Carmeli Formation Centers, Inc. - 920 E. Alhambra Rd., Alhambra, CA 91801 t) 626-289-1353 gensecretary@carmelitesistersocd.com Sr. Elizabeth Therese Shively, OCD, Contact;

Mount Carmel Health Ministries, Inc. - 920 E. Alhambra Rd., Alhambra, CA 91801 t) 626-289-1353 gensecretary@carmelitesistersocd.com Sr. Elizabeth Therese Shively, OCD, Contact;

BALDWIN PARK

The Redemptorist Vietnamese Mission Corporation - 3452 N. Big Dalton Ave., Baldwin Park, CA 91706 t) 626-851-9020 chaqhung@yahoo.com Rev. Pham Quoc Hung, C.Ss.R., Pres.;

BURBANK

SCRC (Southern California Renewal Communities) - 9795 Cabrini Dr., Ste. 208, Burbank, CA 91504-1740 t) 818-771-1361 spirit@scrc.org www.scrc.org Serving Catholic Charismatic Renewal Dominic Berardino, Pres.; Rev. William K. Delaney, S.J., Pastoral Coord.;

CARPINTERIA

***International Theological Institute for Studies on Marriage and the Family** - 3299 Padaro Ln., Carpinteria, CA 93013 t) 805-649-2346 betty-itius@msn.com Betty Hartmann, Contact;

CHATSWORTH

***El Sembrador Ministries** - 20720 Marilla St., Chatsworth, CA 91311 t) 773-777-7773 rosiegomez@elsembrador.org www.elsembrador.org Evangelization through Mass Media Noel Diaz, CEO; Rosie Sayes, Dir.;

Sacred Heart Retreat Apostolate - 10480 1/2 Winnetka Ave., Chatsworth, CA 91311 t) 818-488-1357 sdshtreasurer@gmail.com www.sacredheartretreatcamp.com Sr. Rosemarie Karl, S.D.S.H., Treas.;

COVINA

Comboni Mission Center - 645 S. Aldenville Ave., Covina, CA 91723 t) 626-339-1914 comboni@verizon.net Rev. Jorge Ochoa, M.C.C.J., Supr.; Rev. Gerardo De Tomasi, M.C.C.J.; Rev. Paul Ewers; Rev. Modi Abel Nyorko; Rev. Aldo Pozza, M.C.C.J.;

Scouting and Camp Fire Ministry/Catholic Youth Camps - 4811 Rimhurst Ave., Covina, CA 91724 t) 626-825-6436 info@nfcym.org Diane Garcia, Chair; Dcn. Christopher Laliberte, Chap.;

Sacred Heart Retreat Camp - 896 Cienega Rd., Big Bear Lake, CA 92315-1795; Mailing: 4811 Rimhurst Ave., Covina, CA 91724 t) 323-935-2372; 909-866-5696 office@sacredheartretreatcamp.com www.sacredheartretreatcamp.com Girls Sessions ages 8-17 years. Owned and operated by the Sisters of the Society Devoted to the Sacred Heart. Sr. Mary Tomasella, S.D.S.H., Supr.;

St. Vincent dePaul Ranch Camp - 210 N. Ave. 21, Los Angeles, CA 90031 t) 323-224-6213 rlopez@svdpla.org Boys, ages 7-13. Raymond P. Lopez, Dir.;

CULVER CITY

***Catholics in Media Associates** - 3908 Sepulveda Blvd., Culver City, CA 90230 t) 818-907-2734 info@catholicsinmedia.org www.catholicsinmedia.org Sr. Rose Pacatte, F.S.P., Pres.; Andrea Setterstrom, Treas.;

Christus Ministries - 10775 Deshire Pl., Culver City, CA 90230; Mailing: P.O. Box 4525, Culver City, CA 90231-4525 t) 310-919-8485 contact@christusministries.org www.christusministries.org Rev. Tri M. Dinh, S.J., Dir.;

DOWNEY

St. Louise Resource Services - 8535 Florence Ave., Ste. 100, Downey, CA 90240 t) 424-220-6647; 424-220-6645 lramirez@stlrs.org stlouiseresourceservices.org Lydia Ines Ramirez, Exec.;

EL MONTE

***Hombre Nuevo** - 12036 Ramona Blvd., El Monte, CA 91732 t) 626-444-4442 contacto@guadaluperadio.com www.guadaluperadio.com/ Rev. Frank Formolo, Secy.;

ENCINO

Camp Mariastella - 4316 Lanai Rd., Encino, CA 91436 t) 818-285-1555 campmariastella@aol.com www.campmariastella.com/ Girls ages 7-15, coed teen retreats. Owned & Chartered by Sisters of Social Service. Located in Wrightwood. Sr. Jennifer Gaeta, S.S.S., Exec.;

Works in New Directions, Inc. (WIND) - 4316 Lanai Rd., Encino, CA 91436 t) 818-285-3355 officemanager@hsrcenter.com Sr. Celeste Arbuckle, S.S.S., Contact;

GARDENA

***LHC Ministries, Inc.** - 14700 S. Van Ness Ave., Gardena, CA 90249 t) 310-516-0271 srgracele@lhcla.org Sr. Jennifer HongMai Nguyen, LHC-LA, Contact;

GLENDALE

***Together in Christ** - 311 E. Stocker St., Ste. 102, Glendale, CA 91207 t) 818-246-5582 togetherchrist1@gmail.com Nancy Barona, Pres.;

GLENDORA

Magnificat - San Gabriel Valley Chapter, Inc. - 1352 Valeview Ave., Glendora, CA 91740 t) 626-963-5532 sgvmagnificat@yahoo.com Clara Luera, Contact;

LAKE BALBOA

Maria Auxiliadora Magnificat Chapter - 6738 Aldea Ave., Lake Balboa, CA 91406 t) 818-708-9702 terithompson@sbcglobal.net Rosemarie Leon, Contact;

LANCASTER

Antelope Valley Magnificat - 42018 Purplebush Ave., Apt. 25F, Lancaster, CA 93536 t) 661-943-6402 trabjack@yahoo.com magnificat-ministry.net Rita Trabold, Contact;

***Our Lady of Charity, Conference of St. Vincent de Paul Society** - 45058 Trevor, Ste. B, Lancaster, CA 93534; Mailing: P.O. Box 412, Lancaster, CA 93584 t) 661-942-3222; 661-946-0125 dfields@svdpla.org David R. Fields, Dir.; Donald Willey, Pres.;

LONG BEACH

St. Mary Catholic Housing Corp. (St. Mary Tower) - 1050 Linden Ave., Long Beach, CA 90813 t) 562-491-9929 robert.sahagian@dignityhealth.org Robert Sahagian, Contact;

St. Mary Professional Building, Inc. - 1050 Linden Ave., Long Beach, CA 90813 t) 562-491-9000 pam.koerner@commonspirit.org Sponsored by Catholic Health Care Federation Carolyn Caldwell, CEO;

LOS ANGELES

Archdiocesan Catholic Center - 3424 Wilshire Blvd., Los Angeles, CA 90010-2241 t) 213-637-7000 info@la-archdiocese.org www.lacatholics.org Most Rev. Jose H. Gomez; Rev. Brian Nunes, Moderator; Sr. Mary Anncarla Costello, S.N.D., Chancellor;

Archdiocese of Los Angeles Education & Welfare Corporation - 3424 Wilshire Blvd., Los Angeles, CA 90010 t) (213) 637-7218 resteiner@la-archdiocese.org Randolph Steiner, CFO;

***Archdiocese of Los Angeles Funeral and Mortuary Services Corporation** - 3424 Wilshire Blvd., Los Angeles, CA 90010 t) (213) 637-7808 dsfarruggia@la-archdiocese.org Douglas S. Farruggia, Dir.;

***Archdiocese of Los Angeles Insurance Company** - 3424 Wilshire Blvd., Los Angeles, CA 90010 t) (213) 637-7218 resteiner@la-archdiocese.org Randy Steiner, CFO;

***Archdiocese of Los Angeles Risk Management Corporation** - 3424 Wilshire Blvd., Los Angeles, CA 90010 t) (213) 637-7218 resteiner@la-archdiocese.org Randy Steiner, CFO;

Bethany House - 850 N. Hobart Blvd., Los Angeles, CA 90029 t) 323-665-6937 hmas.bethania@hotmail.com Sr. Leticia Gomez, C.V.D., Dir.;

The Cardinal McIntyre Fund for Charity - 3424 Wilshire Blvd., Los Angeles, CA 90010 t) (213) 637-7255 frbnunes@la-archdiocese.org Rev. Brian Nunes, Pres.;

***Catholic Association of Latino Leaders** - 3424 Wilshire Blvd., 4th Fl., Los Angeles, CA 90010 t) (213) 637-7400 administration@call-usa.org; rosie@call-usa.org www.call-usa.org Rosie Shawver, Exec. Dir.;

Catholic Big Brothers Big Sisters, Inc. - 1530 James M. Wood Blvd., Los Angeles, CA 90015 t) 213-251-9800; 213-251-7760 (TTY) info@catholicbigbrothers.org www.catholicbigbrothers.org Ken Martinet, Pres.;

Catholic Kolping House - 1225 S. Union Ave., Los Angeles, CA 90015 t) 213-388-9438 losangeleskolpinghouse@yahoo.com www.kolping.org Mary Freidonni, Dir.;

Charisma in Missions, La Porciuncula - 1059 S. Gage Ave., Los Angeles, CA 90023 t) 323-260-7031 charismisn@aol.com Catholic Center of Evangelization and renewal ministries. A service for Hispanic people through ongoing affirmation and growth seminars and courses. Esther Garzon, Dir.;

***Estrella del Mar de Los Angeles, Inc. (Regis House Community Center)** - 2212 W. Beverly Blvd., Los Angeles, CA 90057 t) 213-380-8168 regishousecc@att.net www.regishousecommunitycenter.org/ Sr. Albertina Morales, S.S.S., Dir.; Sr. Teresita Saavedra, S.S.S., Dir.;

***Federation of Oases of Koinonia John the Baptist** - 1016 W. Manchester Ave., Los Angeles, CA 90044 t) 310-990-6362 leg@koinoniagb.org Sr. Maire S. Close, Contact;

The Focolare Movement, Men's Branch (California) (Work of Mary) - 8016 Cowan Ave., Los Angeles, CA 90045-1405 t) 310-670-6736 focolare.mla@gmail.com www.focolare.us Giampiero Sciutto, Dir.;

The Focolare Movement, Women's Branch - 4560 Mount Vernon Dr., Los Angeles, CA 90043 t) 323-815-9315 wla.focolare@gmail.com www.focolare.us Catherine G De Guzman, Dir.;

St. Francis Center - 1835 S. Hope St., Los Angeles, CA 90015 t) 213-747-5347 info@sfcla.org www.sfcla.org Serving the homeless and low-income people in downtown Los Angeles. Jasmine Bravo, Exec.;

Hotel Dieu - 265 S. Lake St., Ste. 202, Los Angeles, CA 90057 t) 213-487-7006 veronica@hoteldieu.org Senior Housing Apartments Veronica Dover, CEO;

***Ignatians West** - 1 LMU Dr., Center for Catholic Education, Los Angeles, CA 90045; Mailing: 8601 Lincoln Bl. Ste. 180-306, Los Angeles, CA 90045 c) 805-443-0812; (310) 703-2733 ahansen@ignatianswest.org www.ignatianswest.org Volunteer service by adults (50 years+) in Ignatian tradition to people in need. Anne Hansen, Dir.;

***The Institute for Advanced Catholic Studies** - 3601 Watt Way, #304, Los Angeles, CA 90089-0751 t) 213-740-3055; 213-740-1864 iacss@comcast.net www.instituteforadvancedcatholicstudies.com Rev. Dorian Llywelyn, S.J., Pres.;

Korean Catholic Renewal Movement of Southern California - 1230 San Fernando Rd., Los Angeles, CA 90065 t) 323-221-8874 office@sungsamkcc.com Rev. Taehyun Gregory Yang, Chap.;

***Lay Mission-Helpers Association** - 6102 S. Victoria Ave., Los Angeles, CA 90043 t) 213-368-1870 info@laymissionhelpers.org www.laymissionhelpers.org Janice England, Dir.; Damian Kabot, Exec. Dir.;

***Loyola Productions, Inc.** - 1 LMU Dr. MS 8427, Los Angeles, CA 90045 t) 310-338-7884 c) 310-962-8089 esiebert@loyolaproductions.com; enid@loyolaproductions.com www.loyolaproductions.com Rev. Edward J. Siebert, S.J., Pres.;

***Mission Doctors Association** - 6102 S. Victoria Ave., Los Angeles, CA 90043 t) 213-368-1872 info@missiondoctors.org www.missiondoctors.org Elise Frederick, Exec.;

Notre Dame Academy Facilities Corporation - 2851 Overland Ave., Los Angeles, CA 90064 t) 310-839-5289 mmartinez@ndala.com A subsidiary of the Notre Dame Academy Schools of Los Angeles. Michael Shore, CEO; Cathy Kaiser, CFO;

Opus Caritatis, Inc. - 1531 James M. Wood Blvd., Los Angeles, CA 90015-0095 t) 213-251-3464 mruvalcaba@ccharities.org Rev. Msgr. Gregory A. Cox, Contact;

***Parish Catalyst** - 11100 Santa Monica Blvd., Ste. 1910, Los Angeles, CA 90025 t) 310-500-4286 info@parishcatalyst.org William Simon, Dir.;

Paulist Pictures - 6430 Sunset Blvd., Ste. 1220, Los Angeles, CA 90028 t) 310-454-0688 paulistmail@paulistproduction.org www.paulistproductions.org Mike Sullivan, Pres.;

Paulist Productions - 10866 Wilshire Blvd., Ste. 830, Los Angeles, CA 90024 t) 310-454-0688 assistant@paulistproductions.com www.paulistproductions.org Michael O'Sullivan, Pres.; Rev. Tom Gibbons, Dir.; David Moore, Admin.;

Prelature of the Holy Cross and Opus Dei - 770 S. Windsor Blvd., Los Angeles, CA 90005 t) 323-930-2844 la.priest.scheduler@gmail.com Offices of the Prelature in California Rev. Luke Mata, Vicar; Rev. John R. Meyer, In Res.;

Tilden Study Center - 655 Levering Ave., Los Angeles, CA 90024-2308 t) 310-208-0941 office@tildensc.org; info@tildensc.org www.tildensc.org Rev. Mark Mannion, Dir.; Rev. Paul A. Donlan, In Res.;

Presentation Learning Center - 10843 Gorman Ave., Los Angeles, CA 90059 t) (323) 383-8126 preslearningctr@gmail.com Sr. Jane Bonar, P.B.V.M., Admin.;

The Roman Catholic Archbishop of Los Angeles, a corporation sole - 3424 Wilshire Blvd., Los Angeles, CA 90010 t) (213) 637-7000 info@la-archdiocese.org lacatholics.org Most Rev. Jose H. Gomez;

Serra Institute - 2060 N. Vermont Ave., Los Angeles, CA 90027 t) 323-664-9292 gcrye@aol.com quantumtheology.org Rev. Alvin Paligutan, O.S.A., Dir.;

***Society of Saint Vincent de Paul Council of Los Angeles** - 210 N. Ave. 21, Los Angeles, CA 90031 t) 323-224-6287 csariego@svdpla.org www.svdpla.org David Garcia, Exec. Dir.;

***St. Vincent de Paul Ranch Camp & Retreat Center** - 2550 Hwy. 154, Santa Barbara, CA 93105; Mailing: 210 N. Ave. 21, Los Angeles, CA 90031 t) 323-224-6213 circlev@svdpla.org Raymond P. Lopez, Dir.;

***St. Vincent de Paul Stores** - t) 323-224-6280 dfields@svdpla.org David R. Fields, Dir.;

***St. Vincent's Cardinal Manning Center** - 231 Winston St., Los Angeles, CA 90013 t) 213-229-9963 dfields@svdpla.org Lawrence Hurst, Dir.;

***South Central Los Angeles Ministry Project** - 892 E. 48th St., Los Angeles, CA 90011 t) 323-234-1471 social@southcentrallamp.org www.southcentrallamp.org Diana Z. Pinto, Exec.;

The Tidings - 3424 Wilshire Blvd., Los Angeles, CA 90010 t) (213) 637-7327 pkay@angelusnews.com Pablo Kay, Editor;

***Western U.S.A. Lieutenancy of the Equestrian Order of the Holy Sepulchre of Jerusalem** - 555 W. Temple St., Los Angeles, CA 90012 t) 213-680-5200 contact@eohsjwestern.org www.eohsjwesternusa.org Most Rev. Jose H. Gomez, Grand Prior; Michael Scottfeeley, Lieutenant;

MONTEREY PARK

Filipino Pastoral Ministry - 320 W. Garvey Ave., Monterey Park, CA 91754 t) 213-587-2226 fr.albert@yahoo.com Rev. Albert H. Avenido, Contact;

PALMDALE

***Koinonia John the Baptist California** - 30451 Aliso Canyon Rd., Palmdale, CA 93550 t) 310-990-6362 losangeles@koinonia-la.org koinonia-la.org Rev. Artur Bilski, Supr.;

PASADENA

***The Association of Catholic Student Councils** - 530 S. Lake Ave., Ste. 889, Pasadena, CA 91101-3515 t) 925-954-7048 tacsc@tacsc.org www.tacsc.org Heidi Johnson, Dir.;

GRACE - 85 S. Grand Ave., Pasadena, CA 91105 t) 626-356-4200 info@grace-inc.org grace-inc.org Shimica Gaskins, CEO;

PICO RIVERA

Margaret Aylward Center - 4270 Acacia Ave., Pico Rivera, CA 90660 t) 562-695-6621 maylwardonline@gmail.com Leticia Solis, Dir.;

RANCHO PALOS VERDES

Congregazione delle Figlie di Maria e di Giuseppe, Inc. - 5300 Crest Rd., Rancho Palos Verdes, CA 90275-5004 t) 310-377-9968 lpeters@dmjca.org Sr. Linda Peters, D.M.J., Dir.;

Filles de Marie et de Joseph en Afrique, Inc. - 5300 Crest Rd., Rancho Palos Verdes, CA 90275-5004 t) 310-377-9968 lpeters@dmjca.org Sr. Linda Peters, D.M.J., Dir.;

SAN FERNANDO

***Valley Family Center (Religious Sisters of Charity)** - 302 S. Brand Blvd., San Fernando, CA 91340 t) 818-365-8588 info@valleyfamilycenter.org www.valleyfamilycenter.com Counseling services. Sr. Carmel Somers, R.S.C., Exec.;

SAN PEDRO

Apostleship of the Sea, Catholic Maritime Ministry - 870 W. 8th St., San Pedro, CA 90731 t) 310-833-3541 aoslalb@gmail.com Rev. Raja Selvam, Dir.;

Center - Berth 93A, World Cruise Center, Port of Los Angeles, San Pedro, CA 90731

SANTA BARBARA

***The Cause of Blessed Junipero Serra** - 2201 Laguna St., Old Mission Santa Barbara, Santa Barbara, CA 93105-3611 t) 805-682-4713 kjlofm@aol.com Rev. Ken Laverone, O.F.M., Dir.;

St. Vincent's Institution - 4200 Calle Real, Santa Barbara, CA 93110-1454 t) 805-683-6381 info@sv-sb.org www.stvincents-sb.org Rosa Paredes, CEO;

***De Marillac, LLC** -

Early Childhood Education Center - t) (805) 683-6381 x211 For infants, toddlers, and preschoolers. Susy Del Toro, Dir.;

Family Strengthening Program - For single or pregnant moms and their children 5 years and under on welfare and/or very low income.

Fr. Virgil Cordano Center - 4020 Calle Real, Santa Barbara, CA 93110-1454; Mailing: 4200 Calle Real, Santa Barbara, CA 93110-1454 t) 805-563-1051 frvirgilcordanocenter.org

Ladies of Charity of Santa Barbara - ladiesofcharity-sb.org Providing Vincentian Leadership to women acting together against all forms of poverty.

San Vicente Mobile Home Park - 340 Old Mill Rd. #135A, Santa Barbara, CA 93110-1454 t) 805-964-9662 Seniors 55 and over under Santa Barbara County Rent Control. Mary Manzo, Vice. Pres.;

Villa Caridad - 4202 Calle Real, Santa Barbara, CA 93110-1454 t) 805-683-4375 Affordable apartments for 95 low-income seniors. Ruth Torres, Dir.;

St. Vincent's Gardens - 4234 Pozzo Cir., Santa Barbara, CA 93110-1454 t) 805-967-4340 svg@pshhc.org Affordable apartments for 75 families. Vivian Chavez, Dir.;

St. Vincent's Heart - Campus outreach program for Seniors. Includes Aging Well Program.

Vincent's Ministries, LLC - 4200 Calle Real, Santa Barbara, CA 93110 t) 805-683-6381 info@sv-sb.org www.stvincents-sb.org Rosa Paredes, CEO;

SANTA MARIA

***Servants and Handmaids of the Sacred Heart of Jesus, Mary and Joseph** - 4421 Boardwalk Ln, Santa Maria, CA 93455; Mailing: P.O. Box 2309, Santa Maria, CA 93457-2309 t) 805-524-5890 admin@theservantsandhandmaids.net www.theservantsandhandmaids.net Jerrie Castro, Pres.; Mary Ann Armstrong, Vice. Pres.;

SANTA PAULA

***JM Educational Group (Catholic Textbook Project)** - 144 Davis St., Santa Paula, CA 93060; Mailing: P.O. Box 4638, Ventura, CA 93007 t) (805) 302-6716 mvh@catholictextbookproject.com; office@catholicliberaleducation.org www.jmeducational.org dba: Institute for Catholic Liberal Education and Catholic Textbook Project Michael Van Hecke, Pres.; Matt Sumers, Vice. Pres.; Elisabeth R. Sullivan, Exec.;

SANTA SUSANA KNOLLS

Magnificat, A Ministry to Catholic Women West San Fernando Valley Chapter - 6202 Wisteria Dr., Santa Susana Knolls, CA 93063 t) 805-527-3745 terithompson@sbcglobal.net; teri@magnificatsfv.org www.magnificatsfv.org Teri Thompson, Dir.; Espe Martin, Admin.; Debbie Haywood, Secy.; Leslie Ozark, Treas.; Rev. Robert E. J. Garon, Contact;

SIMI VALLEY

Society of Our Lady of the Way of Southern California, Inc. - 2725 Tumbleweed Ave., Simi Valley, CA 93065 t) 805-520-6942 pearlinea@hotmail.com; solw@cwjamaica.com Pearline Archer, Dir.; Marlene Holman, Dir.;

TEMPLE CITY

Claretian Teaching Ministry - 10203 Lower Azusa Rd., Temple CIty, CA 91780 t) 310-782-6408 ctmonline@catholicbooks.net www.catholicbooks.net Rev. Rosendo Urrabazo, CMF, Pres.;

VENICE

St. Joseph Center - 204 Hampton Dr., Venice, CA 90291-8633 t) 310-396-6468 vadams@stjosephctr.com; community@stjosephctr.org www.stjosephctr.org Sr. Catherine Mary Bundon, C.S.J., Contact;

VENTURA

***CAREGIVERS: Volunteers Assisting the Elderly** - 1765 Goodyear Ave., #205, Ventura, CA 93003 t) 805-658-8530 info@vccaregivers.org; administrativeassistant@vccaregivers.org www.vccaregivers.org Tammy Glenn, Dir.;

***Servants of the Father of Mercy, Inc.** - 4744 Telephone Rd., Ste. 3, Ventura, CA 93003; Mailing: P.O. Box 42001, Los Angeles, CA 90042 t) 310-595-4175 contact@servantsofthefather.org www.servantsofthefather.org/ Bro. Gary Joseph, Dir.;

Trinitas - 10332 Darling Rd., Ventura, CA 93004-2425 t) 805-659-4158 trinitascom@juno.com Mary Ann Wixted, Dir.;

WEST COVINA

Luz De Cristo USA - 1151 E. Grovecenter St., West Covina, CA 91790 t) 626-966-7594 aidaimiranda@gmail.com www.luzdecristousa.org Aida Miranda, Dir.;

WEST HILLS

Missionary Community of the Holy Spirit - 22749 Strathern St., West Hills, CA 91304 t) 818-687-5685;

424-208-4752; 562-296-8254 sollano_aurora@yahoo.com; jjhs106@aol.com www.missionarycommunityoftheholyspirit.org Association of the Faithful Sr. Aurora Sollano, Supr.;

MONASTERIES AND RESIDENCES FOR PRIESTS AND BROTHERS [MON]

BALDWIN PARK

Vietnamese Redemptorist Mission - 3452 N. Big Dalton Ave., Baldwin Park, CA 91706 t) 626-851-9020; 626-377-6540 chaqhung@yahoo.com Rev. Chau Xuan Bau, C.Ss.R., In Res.; Rev. Ngo Van Dao, C.Ss.R., In Res.; Bro. Nguyen Tran Duc, C.Ss.R., In Res.; Rev. Nguyen Quoc Dung, C.Ss.R., In Res.; Rev. Nguyen Tat Hai, C.Ss.R., In Res.; Rev. Dinh Minh Hai, C.Ss.R., In Res.; Rev. Pham Quoc Hung, C.Ss.R., In Res.; Rev. Le Trong Hung, C.Ss.R., In Res.; Rev. Phan Phat Huon, C.Ss.R., In Res.; Bro. Nguyen Ngoc Khanh, C.Ss.R., In Res.; Rev. Nguyen Phi Long, C.Ss.R., In Res.; Rev. Nguyen Truong Luan, In Res.; Rev. Nguyen Duc Mau, C.Ss.R., In Res.; Rev. Quang Minh Nguyen, In Res.; Rev. Dat Tan Nguyen, C.Ss.R., In Res.; Bro. Hanh Phuoc Nguyen, C.Ss.R., In Res.; Rev. Dominic Pham, C.Ss.R., In Res.; Rev. Tran Dinh Phuc, C.Ss.R., In Res.; Rev. Dang Phuoc Hoa, C.Ss.R., In Res.; Rev. Dinh Ngoc Que, C.Ss.R., In Res.; Rev. Doan Trong Son, C.Ss.R., In Res.; Rev. Ngo Dinh Thoa, C.Ss.R., In Res.; Rev. Nguyen Dinh Trung, C.Ss.R., In Res.; Rev. Bui Quang Tuan, C.Ss.R., In Res.; Bro. Martin Nguyen Van Moi, C.Ss.R., In Res.; Bro. John M. Viet Hien, C.Ss.R., In Res.; Rev. John Cuong Ba Vu, C.Ss.R., In Res.; Rev. Tung Duc Vu, C.Ss.R., In Res.; Bro. Sang Thanh Vu, C.Ss.R., In Res.; Brs.: 6; Priests: 23

CUDAHY

Misioneros del Sagrado Corazon y Santa Maria de Guadalupe - 4235 Clara St., Cudahy, CA 90201 t) 323-562-3356 miguelgmsc@hotmail.com Rev. Antero Sanchez, M.S.C., Supr.; Priests: 1

ENCINO

Our Lady of Mount Carmel Priory (Fathers of the Order of Mount Carmel, Corporation) - 4966 Alonzo Ave., Encino, CA 91316 t) 818-345-6055 jsprissler@crespi.org Rev. Benjamin Aguilar, O.Carm, Treas.; Rev. Matt J. Ewing, O.Carm.; Priests: 3

FILLMORE

***Friars of the Sick Poor of Los Angeles, Inc.** - 576 Hunter Dr., Fillmore, CA 93015; Mailing: P.O. Box 861, Fillmore, CA 93016-0861 t) 562-822-6499 rhirbefsp@gmail.com friarsofthesickpoor.org Bro. Richard A. Hirbe, f.s.p., Contact; Brs.: 1

LA VERNE

Congregation of the Sacred Hearts of Jesus and Mary - 2150 Damien Ave., La Verne, CA 91750-5114; Mailing: P.O. Box 668, San Dimas, CA 91773 t) 909-593-5441 ssccwest@gmail.com www.ssccusawest.org Rev. Richard J. Danyluk, SS.CC., Supr.; Rev. Martin P. O'Loghlen, SS.CC., Treas.; Rev. Brian Guerrini, SS.CC., Pst.; Rev. Christopher Santangelo, SS.CC., Assoc. Pst.; Rev. Peadar Cronin, SS.CC., Pst. Assoc.; Rev. Michael W. Barry, SS.CC., Dir.; Rev. Patrick J. Crowley, SS.CC., Healing Ministry; Rev. William C. Moore, SS.CC., Ministry of the Arts; Rev. Patrick Fanning, SS.CC., Novice Master; Rev. Jeremiah Holland, SS.CC., Asst. Novice Master; Rev. John Roche, SS.CC., Campus Min.; Rev. Paul Carl Zaccone, SS.CC., Campus Min.; Rev. Pasquale Laghezza, SS.CC., In Res.; Rev. Michael N. Maher, SS.CC, In Res.; Rev. Peter K. Dennis, SS.CC., In Res.; Rev. Henry Paul Murtagh, SS.CC., In Res.; Rev. Patrick Travers, SS.CC., In Res.; Rev. Patrick P. Coyle, SS.CC., In Res.; Priests: 20

LOS ANGELES

Brothers of St. John of God, Inc., The - 2425 S. Western Ave., Los Angeles, CA 90018-2608 t) 323-734-0233 usaprov-office@sbcglobal.net www.stjog.org Bro. Stephen de la Rosa, O.H., Prov.; Brs.: 1

Grande Apartments-Los Angeles - 2446 S. St. Andrews Pl., Los Angeles, CA 90018 t) 323-730-4100 evasquez@stjog.org Edemidia Vasquez, Admin.;

Helper's Club, Inc. - 2468 S. St. Andrew's Pl., Los Angeles, CA 90018 t) 323-731-7141 arlene@hospitallerfoundation.org Bro. Stephen de la Rosa, O.H., Prov.;

Hospitaller Brothers Healthcare, Inc. - 2468 S. St. Andrews Pl., Los Angeles, CA 90018 t) (323) 731-7141 stephenoh@sbcglobal.net Bro. Stephen de la Rosa, O.H., Contact;

Hospitaller Brothers of St. John of God - 2468 S. St. Andrew's Pl., Los Angeles, CA 90018 t) (323) 731-0641

Hospitaller Foundation of California, Inc. - 2468 S. St. Andrews Pl., Los Angeles, CA 90018 t) 323-731-7141 info@hospitallerfoundation.org hospitallers.org Bro. Patrick Corr, O.H., Pres.;

St. John of God Health Care Services - 2425 S. Western Ave., Los Angeles, CA 90018-2608 t) 760-241-4917 gbarnes@sjghcs.org Bro. Stephen de la Rosa, O.H., Prov.;

St. John of God Retirement and Care Center - 2468 S. St. Andrews Pl., Los Angeles, CA 90018 t) (323) 731-0641 Bro. Pablo Lopez, O.H.;

St. Joseph's Novitiate - 2468 S. St. Andrews Pl., Los Angeles, CA 90018 t) (323) 734-0233

Women's League of St. John of God, Inc. - 2468 S. St. Andrew's Pl., Los Angeles, CA 90018 t) 323-731-7141 Bro. Stephen de la Rosa, O.H., Prov.;

Women's League of St. Joseph's Health & Retirement Center - 2464 E. Ojai Ave., Ojai, CA 93023 t) 805-646-1466 rjensen@stjog.org stjhrc.org/ Rev. Ignatius Sudol, O.H., Prior;

Colombiere House (Jesuit Fathers) - 5322 Franklin Ave., Los Angeles, CA 90027 t) 323-466-3723 wdelaney@jesuits.org Formerly Connolly House. Rev. Mark Ciccone, S.J., Supr.; Rev. John Bentz, S.J., Pst.; Rev. Michael Manalastas, S.J., Assoc. Pst.; Rev. John Tanner, S.J., Assoc. Pst.; Rev. Frank C. Buckley, S.J., clinical psychologist, Homeboy Industries; Rev. William K. Delaney, S.J., Chap.; Rev. Timothy J Meier, SJ, Hospital Chaplain; Bro. Henry Perez, SJ, Graduate Student in Art Therapy at Loyola Marymount University; Rev. Augusto Berrio, S.J., In Res.; Rev. Leo P. Prengaman, S.J., In Res.; Brs.: 1; Priests: 9

Dominic Savio Salesian Residence - 510 Cottage Home St., Los Angeles, CA 90012; Mailing: P.O. Box 331059, Los Angeles, CA 90033 t) 323-493-3135 jimnieblas@yahoo.com www.donboscowest.org Rev. John Lam, S.D.B., Supr.; Rev. James Nieblas, SDB, Dir.; Bro. Steven Standard, S.D.B., In Res.; Rev. Steven Way, SDB, In Res.; Brs.: 1; Priests: 3

Franciscan Brothers of the Third Order Regular - 4522 Gainsborough Ave., Los Angeles, CA 90027-1227 c) 213-216-2218 jhoconnor@yahoo.com; btfahy@yahoo.com www.franciscan-brothers.com Bro. Hilarion O'Connor, O.S.F., Supr.; Brs.: 6

Guadalupe Missioners Procure - 4714 W. 8th St., Los Angeles, CA 90005 t) 323-937-2780 guadalupemissionersla@gamil.com.com Rev. Victor Manuel Zavala Contreras, MG, Dir.; Rev. Lucas Gyu Whan Cheong, MG, In Res.; Priests: 2

Maryknoll Fathers and Brothers - 222 S. Hewitt St. #6, Los Angeles, CA 90012-4309 t) 213-747-9676 losangeles@maryknoll.org www.maryknoll.org (Catholic Foreign Mission Society of America) Rev. Michael G. Callanan, M.M., Supr.; Rev. Gerald J. Persha, M.M., Mem.; Priests: 2

Minim Fathers - 3431 Portola Ave., Los Angeles, CA 90032 t) 323-223-1101 allsaintschurch@earthlink.net www.allsaintsla.com Rev. Mario Pisano, O.M., Supr.; Rev. Thomas C. Francis, O.M., In Res.; Rev. Gino Vanzillotta, O.M., In Res.; Rev. Jose L. Vega, O.M., In Res.; Priests: 4

Missionary Brothers of Charity, Inc. - 1316 S. Westlake Ave., Los Angeles, CA 90006 t) 213-380-5225 brosla@aol.com www.mcbrothers.org Bro. Peter Upendranath, MC, Supr.; Bro. Manoj Ekka, MC, Treas.; Brs.: 3

***Missionaries of Jesus, Inc.** - 435 S. Occidental Blvd., Los Angeles, CA 90057 t) 213-389-8439 info@missionariesofjesus.com www.missionariesofjesus.com Rev. Joseph Ricardo Guerrero, M.J., Supr.; Rev. Michael Montoya, M.J., Supr.; Rev. Manuel Gacad, M.J., Pst.; Rev. Enrique Ymson, M.J., Assoc. Pst.; Rev. Melanio Viuya Jr., M.J., Dir.; Priests: 5

Piarist Fathers - 3940 Perry St., Los Angeles, CA 90063 t) (424) 208-4223 hilof@yahoo.com Rev. Federico Castillo, Sch.P., In Res.; Rev. Pedro Lucia, Sch.P., In Res.; Rev. Josep M. Margalef, Sch.P., In Res.; Rev. Roberto Morales, Sch.P., In Res.; Rev. Carlos E. Rojas, Sch.P., In Res.; Rev. Jeejo K. Vazhappilly, Sch.P., In Res.; Priests: 6

The Society of St. Paul - 112 Herbert St., Los Angeles, CA 90063 t) (213) 440-8279 admin@sspusa.org Rev. Gilberto Martinez, S.S.P., Supr.; Rev. Arnulfo Gomez, S.S.P., Treas.; Priests: 2

MONTEBELLO

Congregation of the Mission Western Province (DePaul Center Residence) - 1105 Bluff Rd., Montebello, CA 90640-6198 c) 504-610-9406 phenry@vincentian.org www.vincentian.org Rev. Perry F. Henry, C.M., Supr.; Rev. Hoan N. Nguyen, C.M., Chap.; Rev. Jeffrey Harvey, CM, Faculty/St. John's Seminary; Rev. Juan Antonio Ruiz, C.M., In Res.; Priests: 4

Nuestra Senora de Los Angeles House - 641 W. Adams Blvd., Los Angeles, CA 90007 t) (504) 610-9406

OXNARD

Order of Augustinian Recollects (O.A.R.), St. Augustine Priory - 400 Sherwood Way, Oxnard, CA 93033-7510 t) 805-486-7433 saprovince@yahoo.com www.agustinosrecolectos.com Rev. Marlon Beof, O.A.R., Prior; Rev. John Michael Rafferty, O.A.R., Subprior; Bro. Mario Alvarez, O.A.R., In Res.; Rev. James V. Brown, O.A.R., In Res.; Rev. Joaquin Goni, O.A.R., In Res.; Rev. Fidel Hernandez, O.A.R., In Res.; Rev. Robert Huse, O.A.R., In Res.; Rev. Frank T. Wilder, O.A.R., In Res.; Brs.: 1; Priests: 7

PASADENA

Legionaries of Christ - 1455 Sierra Madre Villa Ave., Pasadena, CA 91107 c) 213-454-2938 dokeeffe@legionaries.org www.legionofchrist.org Rev. Donal O'Keeffe, LC, Supr.; Rev. Agustin De la Vega, L.C., In Res.; Rev. Lorenzo Gomez Sotres, L.C., In Res.; Rev. Kevin Meehan LC, L.C., In Res.; Rev. John Hopkins, In Res.; Priests: 5

Ramona Blvd., Inc. - 1455 Sierra Madre Villa Ave., Pasadena, CA 91107 t) 770-828-4950 fformolo@legionaries.org Rev. Frank Formolo, Secy.; Priests: 5

SANTA BARBARA

Franciscan Friary, Order of Friars Minor (Old Mission) - 2201 Laguna St., Santa Barbara, CA 93105 t) 805-682-4713 Rev. Larry Gosselin, O.F.M., Pst.; Bro. Angelo Cardinalli, O.F.M., In Res.; Bro. Regan Chapman, O.F.M., In Res.; Bro. John Gutierrez, O.F.M., In Res.; Bro. Arturo Noyes, O.F.M., In Res.; Rev. Kenan Osborne, O.F.M., In Res.; Rev. Adrian Peelo, O.F.M., In Res.; Bro. Freddy Rodriguez, O.F.M., In Res.; Bro. Nicholas Ronalter, O.F.M., In Res.; Brs.: 6; Priests: 3

SANTA MARIA

St. Joseph Seminary (Josephite Fathers' Novitiate) - 180 Patterson Rd., Santa Maria, CA 93455 t) 805-937-5378 cjvocationseu@josephite.community josephite.community Rev. Ludo DeClippel, C.J. (Belgium), In Res.; Rev. Charles L. Hofschulte, C.J., In Res.; Rev. Edward Jalbert, C.J., In Res.; Rev. Timothy R. Lane, C.J., In Res.; Rev. Mark L. Newman, C.J., In Res.; Bro. Romualdo Orozco, C.J., In Res.; Rev. Gerardo Toscano, C.J., In Res.; Pr. Tchrs.: 6; Brs.: 1

SANTA PAULA

Canons Regular of the Immaculate Conception - 601 Glade Dr., Santa Paula, CA 93060-1640 t) 805-420-0099 cricusa@icloud.com cricusa.com Rev. Thomas J. Dome, C.R.I.C., Supr.; Rev. Pasquale Vuoso, C.R.I.C., Supr.; Rev. Thaddeus Haynes, C.R.I.C., In Res.; Rev. Charles R. Lueras, C.R.I.C., In Res.; Bro. Emil C Palafox, C.R.I.C., In Res.; Bro. Roger M. Proulx, C.R.I.C., In Res.; Rev. Christopher A. Reeve, C.R.I.C., In Res.; Rev.

William B. Ustaski, C.R.I.C., In Res.; Brs.: 2; Priests: 6

Canons Regular of the Immaculate Conception, (C.R.I.C.) Dom Grea House (House of Formation) -

SIERRA MADRE

Passionist Residence - 700 N. Sunnyside Ave., Sierra Madre, CA 91024 t) 626-355-1740 dbrunocp@materdolorosa.org Rev. Bruno D'Souza, C.P., Supr.; Rev. Clemente Barron, In Res.; Rev. Michael Higgins, C.P., In Res.; Bro. John Rockenbach, C.P., In Res.; Brs.: 1; Priests: 3

SUN VALLEY

Scalabrini House of Discernment - 10651 Vinedale St., Sun Valley, CA 91352-2825 t) 818-504-9561 parish-3710@la-archdiocese.org Rev. Giovanni Bizzotto, C.S., Dir.; Rev. Ramiro V. Sanchez Chan, C.S., Dir.; Pr. Tchrs.: 2

TEMPLE CITY

Claretian Missionaries - Western Province, Inc. - 10203 Lower Azusa Rd., Temple City, CA 91780 t) 626-443-2009 moralese@claretians.org www.claretiansusa.org Affiliated with Claretian Missionaries - U.S.A. Province, Inc. (Chicago, IL) Edith Morales, Contact; Brs.: 4; Priests: 15

Dominguez Seminary Inc. - 18127 S. Alameda St., Rancho Dominguez, CA 90220 t) 323-636-6030; 310-631-8484 bricully@yahoo.com Rev. Brian Culley, CMF, Supr.; Rev. Robert Billett, C.M.F., Vicar; Bro. Rene LePage, C.M.F., Admin.; Rev. Milton Alvarez, C.M.F., In Res.; Rev. Robert Bishop, C.M.F., In Res.; Rev. James Curran, CMF, In Res.; Rev. Alberto Domingo, C.M.F., In Res.; Rev. Frank Ferrante, C.M.F., In Res.; Rev. Matthias Nwaiwu, CMF, In Res.; Rev. John Raab, CMF, In Res.; Rev. Stephen Sherwood, CMF, In Res.; Rev. Albert Vazquez, CMF, In Res.; Bro. Thomas Haerle, C.M.F., In Res.; Bro. Paul Roy, C.M.F., In Res.;

Educational and Renewal Center, Inc. - Rev. Rosendo Urrabazo, CMF, Prov.;

Tepeyac House - 6104 York Blvd., Los Angeles, CA 90042 Bro. Larry J. Moen, C.M.F., Supr.; Rev. Quyen Nguyen, CMF, Chap.; Rev. Darrin Merlino, CMF, In Res.; Rev. William Paiz, CMF, In Res.;

VALYERMO

St. Andrew's Abbey (Benedictine Monks) - 31001 N. Valyermo Rd., Valyermo, CA 93563-0040; Mailing: P.O. Box 40, Valyermo, CA 93563-0040 t) 661-944-2178 information@saintandrewsabbey.com www.saintandrewsabbey.com Rt. Rev. Damien Toilolo, O.S.B., Abbot; Rev. Joseph (Dennis) Brennan, O.S.B., Prior; Rev. Patrick Sheridan, O.S.B., Subprior; Rt. Rev. Francis Benedict, O.S.B., Abbot Emeritus; Bro. Benedict Dull, O.S.B.; Rev. Luke Dysinger, O.S.B.; Rev. Angelus Echeverry, O.S.B.; Rev. Philip Edwards, O.S.B.; Bro. Dominic Guillen, O.S.B.; Bro. Joseph Iarrobino, O.S.B.; Rev. Francois Kabalisa, O.S.B.; Rev. Isaac Kalina, O.S.B.; Rev. Carlos Lopez, O.S.B.; Bro. John Mark Matthews, O.S.B.; Rev. Aelred Niespolo, O.S.B.; Bro. Paul Ortega, O.S.B.; Bro. John Baptist Santa Ana, O.S.B.; Rev. Martin Yslas, O.S.B.; Brs.: 6; Priests: 12

VAN NUYS

Congregation of Rogationists, Inc. - 6635 Tobias Ave., Van Nuys, CA 91405-4614 t) 818-782-0184; 818-782-1762 info@vocationsandprayer.org; info@rogationists.org www.rogationists.org Rev. Antonio Fiorenza, R.C.J., Supr.; Rev. John Bruno, RCJ, Pst.; Rev. Antonio Carlucci, R.C.J., Pst.; Rev. Denny Joseph, R.C.J., Pst.; Rev. Shinto Sebastian, R.C.J., Pst.; Rev. Javier E. Flores, R.C.J., Assoc. Pst.; Rev. Vito Di Marzio, R.C.J., Assoc. Pst.; Rev. Renato Panlasigui, R.C.J., Assoc. Pst.; Rev. Jupeter Quinto, R.C.J., Assoc. Pst.; Rev. Mark Robin Destura, Youth Min.; Bro. Eduardo Lopez Rodriguez, R.C.J., In Res.; Rev. Thomas Kannampuzha, In Res.; Rev. Santi Scibilia, RCJ, In Res.; Brs.: 1; Priests: 12

WEST COVINA

Fr. Kolbe Missionaries of the Immaculata - 531 E. Merced Ave., West Covina, CA 91790 t) 626-917-0040 fkmissionaries@gmail.com Anna Brizzi, Dir.;

WHITTIER

Redemptorists of Whittier - 7215 S. Newlin Ave., Whittier, CA 90602-1266 t) 562-698-0107 tuaphm@gmail.com www.stmaryschurch-whittier.org Rev. Tuan Pham, C.Ss.R., Local Supr.; Rev. Patrick Keyes, C.Ss.R., Pst.; Rev. Mark Scheffler, C.Ss.R., Chap.; Rev. Robert A. Ruhnke, C.Ss.R., Marriage Prep. Min.; Rev. William Adams, C.Ss.R., In Res.; Rev. Paul Coury, C.Ss.R., In Res.; Dcn. Dennis Lee, C.Ss.R., In Res.; Brs.: 1; Priests: 6

NURSING / REHABILITATION / CONVALESCENCE / ELDERLY CARE [NUR]

CULVER CITY

***Marycrest Manor** - 10664 St. James Dr., Culver City, CA 90230-5498 t) 310-838-2778 admin@marycrestculvercity.com marycrestculvercity.com/ Sr. Veronica Maldonado, O.C.D., Admin.; Asstd. Annu.: 87; Staff: 85

LOS ANGELES

St. John of God Retirement and Care Center - 2468 S. St. Andrews Pl., Los Angeles, CA 90018 t) 323-731-0641 contactus@stjog.org stjog.org Bro. Br. Michael Bassemier, O.H., CEO; Bro. Stephen de la Rosa, O.H., Prov.; Bro. Pablo Lopez, O.H., Prior; Rev. Thaddeus Bui, O.H., Chap.; Rev. Donald J. Ours, C.M., Chap.; Asstd. Annu.: 285; Staff: 289

Nazareth House - 3333 Manning Ave., Los Angeles, CA 90064 t) 310-839-2361 www.sistersofnazareth.com William Boles, Exec. Dir.; Asstd. Annu.: 133; Staff: 94

NEWBURY PARK

Mary Health of the Sick Convalescent and Nursing Hospital (Sisters Servants of Mary) - 2929 Theresa Dr., Newbury Park, CA 91320 t) 805-498-3644 office@maryhealth.com maryhealth.com Skilled Nursing Facility. Sr. Yesenia Perea, S de M, Exec. Dir.; Bed Capacity: 61; Asstd. Annu.: 93; Staff: 104

NORTH HOLLYWOOD

Providence St. Elizabeth Care Center - 10425 Magnolia Blvd., North Hollywood, CA 91601 t) 818-980-3872 psjfoundation@providence.org Samuel Scrivens, Chap.; Bed Capacity: 52; Asstd. Annu.: 60; Staff: 50

SAN FERNANDO

Mother Gertrude Home for Senior Citizens - 11320 Laurel Canyon Blvd., San Fernando, CA 91340 t) 818-898-1546 email@mothergertrudehome.org www.mothergertrudehome.org (Franciscan Missionary Sisters of the Immaculate Conception, Inc.) Sr. Yolanda Yanez, O.S.F., Admin.; Asstd. Annu.: 25; Staff: 13

SAN PEDRO

Little Sisters of the Poor of Los Angeles - 2100 S. Western Ave., Jeanne Jugan Res., San Pedro, CA 90732 t) 310-548-0625 mssanpedro@littlesistersofthepoor.org www.littlesistersofthepoorsanpedro.org Sr. Margaret Hogarty, LSP, Supr.; Asstd. Annu.: 103; Staff: 87

Providence Little Company of Mary San Pedro Peninsula Hospital Pavilion - 1322 W. Sixth St., San Pedro, CA 90732 t) 310-832-3311 plcmfoundation@providence.org Skilled Nursing Facility. Garry Olney, CEO; Paul White, Spiritual Adv./Care Srvcs.; Bed Capacity: 128; Asstd. Annu.: 128

Providence Little Company of Mary Sub-Acute Center-South Bay - 1322 W. 6th St., San Pedro, CA 90732 t) 310-732-6700 plcmfoundation@providence.org Skilled Nursing Facility., Sponsored by Providence Ministries. Garry Olney, CEO; Paul White, Spiritual Adv./Care Srvcs.; Bed Capacity: 120; Asstd. Annu.: 120

SUN VALLEY

Villa Scalabrini (Missionary Fathers of St. Charles) - 10631 Vinedale St., Sun Valley, CA 91352 t) 818-768-6500 laura@villascalabrini.com www.villascalabrini.com Retirement Center and Special Care Unit, Augustinian Recollect Sisters. Rev. Adlso Luis Balen, C.S., Exec.; Asstd. Annu.: 85; Staff: 64

PRESCHOOLS / CHILDCARE CENTERS [PRE]

LOS ANGELES

***Salesian Boys & Girls Club of Los Angeles** - 3218 Wabash Ave., Los Angeles, CA 90063 t) 323-980-8551 jc@salesianclubs-la.org www.salesianclubs-la.org Juan Montenegro, Exec.;

Salesian Family Youth Center - tmass@salesianclubs-la.org

SYLMAR

Poverello of Assisi Preschool - 13367 Borden Ave., Sylmar, CA 91342 t) 818-364-7446 principal@poverelloschool.com Sr. Patricia Cerrillo, Prin.; Stds.: 120; Lay Tchrs.: 1

THOUSAND OAKS

Notre Dame Learning Center - 1776 Hendrix Ave., Thousand Oaks, CA 91360 t) 805-494-0304 cpapet@sndusa.org; bbienlein@sndusa.org www.ndlcpreschool.com/ Sr. Carol Papet, Dir.; Stds.: 40; Lay Tchrs.: 1

RETREAT HOUSES / RENEWAL CENTERS [RTR]

ALHAMBRA

***Sacred Heart Retreat House, Inc.** - 920 E. Alhambra Rd., Alhambra, CA 91801 t) 626-289-1353 gensecretary@carmelitesistersocd.com www.sacredheartretreathouse.com Carmelite Sisters of the Most Sacred Heart of Los Angeles. Sr. Marie Andre Petit, O.C.D., Dir.;

ENCINO

***Holy Spirit Retreat Center** - 4316 Lanai Rd., Encino, CA 91436 t) 818-784-4515 officemanager@hsrcenter.org www.hsrcenter.com Sisters of Social Service. Sr. Chris Machado, S.S.S., Dir.;

MALIBU

Serra Retreat - 3401 Serra Rd., Malibu, CA 90265; Mailing: P.O. Box 127, Malibu, CA 90265 t) 310-456-6631 frmel@serraretreat.com www.serraretreat.com Franciscan Friars of California. Friar Melvin A. Jurisich, O.F.M., Dir.; Rev. Warren Rouse, O.F.M., Dir.; Bro. Samuel Cabot, O.F.M., In Res.; Bro. Regan Chapman, O.F.M., In Res.; Rev. Michael Doherty, O.F.M., In Res.; Rev. Raymond Tintle, O.F.M., In Res.;

RANCHO PALOS VERDES

Mary & Joseph Retreat Center - 5300 Crest Rd., Rancho Palos Verdes, CA 90275-5004 t) 310-377-4867 pcraig@maryjoseph.org www.maryjoseph.org Daughters of Mary and Joseph. Paul Craig, Dir.;

ROSEMEAD

St. Joseph's Salesian Youth Renewal Center - 8301 Arroyo Dr., Rosemead, CA 91770; Mailing: P.O. Box 1639, Rosemead, CA 91770 t) 626-280-8622 pcnguyensdb@sjscenter.org sjscenter.org Conducted by Salesians of St. John Bosco. Rev. Paul Chuong Nguyen, S.D.B., Dir.;

SAN FERNANDO

Poverello of Assisi Retreat House - 1519 Woodworth St., San Fernando, CA 91340 t) 818-365-1071 poverelloretreathouse@hotmail.com Sr. Mary Jesus Ochoa, O.S.F., Dir.;

SIERRA MADRE

***Mater Dolorosa Passionist Retreat Center, Inc.** - 700 N. Sunnyside Ave., Sierra Madre, CA 91025 t) 626-355-7188 materdolorosa@materdolorosa.org www.materdolorosa.org Conducted by the Passionist Community. Elizabeth Welch Velarde, Admin.; Rev. Michael Higgins, C.P., Retreat Dir.; Dcn. Manuel Valencia, Retreat Dir.; Dr. Michael Downey, Retreat Dir.; Rev. Bruno D'Souza, C.P., In Res.; Rev. Michael Hoolahan, C.P., In Res.; Bro. John Rockenbach, C.P., In Res.;

VALYERMO

St. Andrew's Abbey Retreat Center - 31001 N. Valyermo Rd., Valyermo, CA 93563; Mailing: P.O. Box 40, Valyermo, CA 93563 t) 661-944-2178 retreats@valyermo.com www.saintandrewsabbey.com Conducted by the Benedictine Monks. Rita Jones, Dir.; Rev. Patrick Sheridan, O.S.B., Dir.; Rev. Philip Edwards, O.S.B., Chap.;

SEMINARIES [SEM]

CAMARILLO

St. John's Seminary - 5012 Seminary Rd., Camarillo, CA 93012-2500 t) 805-482-2755 rector@stjohnsem.edu www.stjohnsem.edu Major Seminary of the Archdiocese of Los Angeles. Rev. Marco Antonio Durazo, Rector; Rev. Gustavo Castillo, Faculty/Dir., Spiritual Formation; Rev. John P. Brennan, S.M.A., Faculty; Rev. Eugenio Cardenas, M.Sp.S., Faculty; Rev. Luke Dysinger, O.S.B., Faculty; Rev. Jeffrey Harvey, CM, Faculty; Rev. Raymond Marquez, Faculty; Rev. Aelred Niespolo, O.S.B., Faculty; Rev. John Joseph O'Brien, Faculty; Rev. Leo Ortega, Faculty; Rev. Timothy Peters, Faculty; Rev. Thinh Duc Pham, Faculty; Rev. Slawomir Szkredka, Faculty; Rev. Steven Thoma, C.R., Faculty; Sr. Leanne Hubbard, Faculty; Stds.: 87; Lay Tchrs.: 8; Pr. Tchrs.: 14; Sr. Tchrs.: 1

CULVER CITY

Ignatius House, The Novitiate of the U.S. West Province, Society of Jesus - 10775 Deshire Pl., Culver City, CA 90230; Mailing: P.O. Box 5166, Culver City, CA 90231-5166 t) 310-815-0166 x235 scoble@jesuits.org www.jesuitswest.org Rev. Scott W Coble, S.J., Minister; Rev. Andrew Rodriguez, S.J., Dir., Novices; Rev. Anton F Harris, S.J., Asst. Dir., Novices; Stds.: 7; Pr. Tchrs.: 3

SANTA YNEZ

San Lorenzo Seminary - Novitiate - 1802 Sky Dr., Santa Ynez, CA 93460-0247; Mailing: P.O. Box 247, Santa Ynez, CA 93460-0247 t) 805-688-5630 stjw@slseminary.org; finance@olacapuchins.org www.sanlorenzoseminary.org Capuchin Franciscan Friars. Rev. John Celichowski, OFM Cap., Dir.; Bro. Kip Ledger, OFM Cap., In Res.; Bro. Miguel Ramirez, OFM Cap., In Res.; Rev. Bill Talentino, OFM Cap., In Res.; Stds.: 10; Bro. Tchrs.: 2; Pr. Tchrs.: 2

SPECIAL CARE FACILITIES [SPF]

CHATSWORTH

***Rancho San Antonio Boys Home, Inc.** - 21000 Plummer St., Chatsworth, CA 91311 t) 818-882-6400 info@ranchosanantonio.org Aubree Sweeney, CEO; Bro. John Crowe, C.S.C., Treas.; Bed Capacity: 106; Asstd. Annu.: 400; Staff: 150

LOS ANGELES

St. Anne's Family Services - 155 N. Occidental Blvd., Los Angeles, CA 90026 t) 213-381-2931 stannes@stannes.org www.stannes.org Felician Sponsored Ministry; Residential Treatment Program; Transitional Housing; Mental Health; Family Based Services; Early Learning Center Svcs. Lorna Little, Dir.; Bed Capacity: 50; Asstd. Annu.: 1,150; Staff: 300

St. Anne's Foundation -

St. Anne's Guild -

Loretta Young Auxiliary -

Mabel Mosler Auxiliary -

Sister Winifred Auxiliary -

Convent of the Good Shepherd-Good Shepherd Shelter - 2561 Venice Blvd., Los Angeles, CA 90019; Mailing: P.O. Box 19487, Los Angeles, CA 90019 t) 314-381-3400 akelley@goodshepherdshelter.org; tponder@gspmna.org www.goodshepherdshelter.org Shelter for Battered Women and Their Children. Conducted by Sisters of the Good Shepherd. Sr. Madeleine Munday, Prov.; Bed Capacity: 73; Asstd. Annu.: 73; Staff: 3

Good Shepherd Center for Homeless Women and Children - 267 N. Belmont Ave., Languille Emergency Shelter, Los Angeles, CA 90026 t) 213-250-5241; 213-482-1834 srannetran@gsohomeless.org www.gschomeless.org (A Program of Catholic Charities of Los Angeles, Inc.) Sr. Anne Tran, L.H.C., Dir.; Bed Capacity: 93; Asstd. Annu.: 1,283; Staff: 28

Angel Guardian Home/Women's Village - 1660 Rockwood St., Los Angeles, CA 90026 t) 213-483-6654 srannetran@gschomeless.org

Good Shepherd Center Farley House/Women's Village - 1671 Beverly Blvd., Los Angeles, CA 90026 t) 213-235-1460 srannetran@gschomeless.org (A Program of Catholic Charities of Los Angeles, Inc.)

Good Shepherd Center Hawkes Transitional Residence/ Women's Village - 1640 Rockwood St., Los Angeles, CA 90026 t) 213-482-0281 srannetran@gschomeless.org (A Program of Catholic Charities of Los Angeles, Inc.)

St. Joseph's Residence - 1124 W. Adams Blvd., Los Angeles, CA 90007; Mailing: 16791 E. Main St., Tustin, CA 92780 t) 714-541-3125 srglondono@odnusa.org Sponsored by Sisters of the Company of Mary. Sr. Beatriz Guzman, O.D.N., Dir.; Bed Capacity: 32; Asstd. Annu.: 25; Staff: 1

***Order of Malta Los Angeles Clinic, Inc.** - 2222 W. Ocean View, #112, Los Angeles, CA 90057 t) 213-384-4323 freemed112@sbcglobal.net Primary Health Care for the frail elderly, the working poor and medically underserved children. Conducted by Order of Malta Los Angeles Clinic, Inc. Dr. David Frelinger, Dir.; David Johnson, Admin.; Asstd. Annu.: 2,217; Staff: 12

St. Vincent Senior Citizen Nutrition Program, Inc. (St. Vincent Meals on Wheels) - 2303 Miramar St., Los Angeles, CA 90057 t) 213-484-7778 vdover@stvincentmow.org stvincentmow.org Veronica Dover, CEO; Asstd. Annu.: 3,000; Staff: 73

ROSEMEAD

Maryvale - 7600 E. Graves Ave., Rosemead, CA 91770-1003; Mailing: P.O. Box 1039, Rosemead, CA 91770-1003 t) 626-280-6510 sgunther@maryvale.org www.maryvale.org Steve Gunther, Pres.; Bed Capacity: 72; Asstd. Annu.: 555; Staff: 120

The Los Angeles Orphan Asylum - 7600 E. Graves Ave., Rosemead, CA 91770-1003 t) (626) 280-6510

Los Angeles Orphanage Guild - 7600 E. Graves Ave., Rosemead, CA 91770-1003 t) (626) 280-6510 www.laorphanageguild.com

SANTA MONICA

Saint John's Child Study Center, Saint John's Hospital & Health Center - 1339 20th St., Santa Monica, CA 90404-2033 t) 310-829-8921 saintjohnshealthcenter@providence.org Affiliated with Saint John's Hospital. Conducted by Sisters of Charity of Leavenworth. Rebecca Refuerza, Dir.; Asstd. Annu.: 1,800; Staff: 2

TORRANCE

***Providence Trinity Care Hospice** - 5315 Torrance Blvd., Ste. B1, Torrance, CA 90503 t) 800-829-8660; 310-543-3400 plcmfoundation@providence.org www.trinitycarehospice.org Liz Dunne, Dir.; Asstd. Annu.: 1,677; Staff: 160

An asterisk (*) denotes an organization that has established tax-exempt status directly with the IRS and is not covered by the USCCB Group Ruling.

Archdiocese of Louisville

(Archidioecesis Ludovicopolitana)

MOST REVEREND SHELTON J. FABRE

Archbishop of Louisville; ordained August 5, 1989; appointed Auxiliary Bishop of the Archdiocese of New Orleans December 16, 2006; installed Auxiliary Bishop of New Orleans February 8, 2007; appointed Bishop of Houma-Thibodaux on September 23, 2013; installed on October 30, 2013; appointed Archbishop of Louisville February 8, 2022; installed March 30, 2022.

Pastoral Center, 3940 Poplar Level Rd., Louisville, KY 40213. T: 502-585-3291; F: 502-585-2466.
www.archlou.org
pastoralcenter@archlou.org

Square Miles 8,124.

Established at Bardstown April 8, 1808; Transferred to Louisville Feb. 13, 1841; created an Archdiocese Dec. 10, 1937.

Comprises the following twenty-four Counties in central Kentucky: Adair, Barren, Bullitt, Casey, Clinton, Cumberland, Green, Hardin, Hart, Henry, Jefferson, Larue, Marion, Meade, Metcalfe, Monroe, Nelson, Oldham, Russell, Shelby, Spencer, Taylor, Trimble and Washington.

For legal titles of parishes and archdiocesan institutions, consult the Office of the Archbishop.

STATISTICAL OVERVIEW

Personnel
Archbishops 1
Retired Archbishops 1
Priests: Diocesan Active in Diocese 64
Priests: Diocesan Active Outside Diocese 4
Priests: Diocesan in Foreign Missions 1
Priests: Retired, Sick or Absent 51
Number of Diocesan Priests 120
Religious Priests in Diocese 39
Total Priests in your Diocese 159
Extern Priests in Diocese 7
Ordinations:
Diocesan Priests 1
Permanent Deacons in Diocese 131
Total Brothers 22
Total Sisters 251

Parishes
Parishes 101
With Resident Pastor:
Resident Diocesan Priests 79
Resident Religious Priests 23
Without Resident Pastor:
Administered by Priests 7
Administered by Deacons 1
Missions 9
Professional Ministry Personnel:
Sisters 3
Lay Ministers 165

Welfare
Catholic Hospitals 1
Total Assisted 20,309
Homes for the Aged 3
Total Assisted 2,232
Residential Care of Children 2
Total Assisted 989
Day Care Centers 1
Total Assisted 155
Specialized Homes 2
Total Assisted 571
Special Centers for Social Services 4
Total Assisted 175,111
Residential Care of Disabled 1
Total Assisted 12

Educational
Diocesan Students in Other Seminaries 11
Total Seminarians 11
Colleges and Universities 2
Total Students 4,339
High Schools, Diocesan and Parish 4
Total Students 2,022
High Schools, Private 9
Total Students 3,432
Elementary Schools, Diocesan and Parish 33
Total Students 12,125
Elementary Schools, Private 5
Total Students 764
Non-residential Schools for the Disabled 1
Total Students 94
Catechesis/Religious Education:
High School Students 386
Elementary Students 3,485
Total Students under Catholic Instruction 26,658
Teachers in Diocese:
Sisters 4
Lay Teachers 1,430

Vital Statistics
Receptions into the Church:
Infant Baptism Totals 1,518
Minor Baptism Totals 183
Adult Baptism Totals 143
Received into Full Communion 197
First Communions 1,844
Confirmations 1,791
Marriages:
Catholic 279
Interfaith 90
Total Marriages 369
Deaths 1,519
Total Catholic Population 164,724
Total Population 1,319,621

LEADERSHIP
Vicar General - Rev. Martin A. Linebach;
Pastoral Center - t) 502-585-3291
Chancellor - Brian B. Reynolds;
Vice Chancellor - Richard "Tink" Guthrie;
Secretary to Archbishop - Connie DuPlessis;
Vicar for Priests - Rev. Jeffrey P. Shooner, Vicar;
Archivist - ttomes@archlou.org archlou.org Tim Tomes;
Chief Financial Officer - Robert Cecil;
Metropolitan Tribunal - t) 502-585-3291 Rev. R. Paul Beach, Dir.;
Judicial Vicar and Director - Rev. R. Paul Beach;
Defenders of the Bond - Rev. Patrick J. Dolan; Rev. Robert E. Osborne; Rev. Frederick W. Klotter;
Associate Judges - Very Rev. Philip Lee Erickson; Lisabeth Walsh; Rev. R. Paul Beach;
Assessor and Associate Director -
Ecclesiastical Notaries - Kim McDaniel; Carmen Rendon; Linda D. Thoman;
Adjutant Judicial Vicar - tribunal@archlou.org
College of Consultors - Rev. R. Paul Beach; Rev. William M. Bowling; Rev. Terry L. Bradshaw;
Deans - Rev. Terry L. Bradshaw, Bardstown Deanery; Rev. Mark M. Hamilton, Lebanon Deanery; Rev. Michael T. Wimsatt, Elizabethtown Deanery;
Priest Personnel Board - Rev. Kevin J. Bryan (kevin40108@bbtel.com); Rev. Peter Quan Do; Rev. Steven D. Henriksen;
Priests' Council - Rev. R. Paul Beach; Rev. Gerald L. Bell; Rev. William M. Bowling;
Archdiocesan Examiners - Rev. Gary T. Padgett;

OFFICES AND DIRECTORS
Byzantine Rite Faithful - t) 502-459-8900
Catholic Campus Ministry - University of Louisville Interfaith Center - t) 502-852-6598 info@uoflcatholic.org Rev. John Baptist Hoang, O.P.;
Catholic Cemeteries Office - t) 502-451-7710 cemeteries@archlou.org Javier Fajardo, Exec.;
Catholic Charities - t) 502-637-9786 charities@archlou.org Lisa DeJaco Crutcher, CEO;
Archdiocesan Communications Center - t) 502-636-0296 archlou.org Cecelia Price, Chief Communications Officer;
Clerical Aid - t) 502-585-3291 Rev. Jeffrey P. Shooner;
Continuing Education for Clergy-Ministry to Priests - Rev. Jeffrey P. Shooner;
Cursillo Movement - t) 502-448-8581 Pat Williams, Dir.;
Ecumenical and Interreligious Relations Officer - Rev. Mark M. Hamilton;
Family Ministries Office - t) 502-636-0296 Dcn. T. Stephen Bowling, Exec.;
Holy Childhood Association - Brian B. Reynolds, Dir.;
L.A.M.P. - t) 502-585-3291 Most Rev. Shelton Fabre (archbp@archlou.org);
Office of Catholic Schools - t) 502-585-3291 Mary Beth Bowling, Supt. (mbowling@archlou.org); Amy Nall, Asst. Supt.;
Office of Facilities Management - t) 502-636-0296 Bill Zoeller, Dir.;
Office of Faith Formation - t) 502-636-0296 Arthur Turner, Dir.;
Office of Mission and Advancement - t) 502-585-3291 Molly Keene Smith, Dir.;
Office of Multicultural Ministry - t) 502-636-0296 M. Annette Turner, Dir.;
Office of the Diaconate - t) 502-636-0296 Dcn. Dennis M. Nash, Dir.;
Office of Worship - t) 502-636-0296 Karen Shadle, Dir.;
Office of Youth and Young Adult - t) 502-636-0296 Karl Dolson, Dir.;
Opportunities for Life - t) 502-637-9786 Cydnei Dean, Dir.;
Personnel Office - t) 502-585-3291 Andrea Colpo, Dir.;
Priest Personnel Office - Rev. Jeffrey P. Shooner, Dir.;
Pro-Life Ministries - t) 502-636-0296 Stuart Hamilton, Pro-Life Event Coord.;
Propagation of the Faith - Brian B. Reynolds, Dir.;
Sacred Heart Enthronement Center - Rev. Jeffery G. Hooper, Dir.;
Vicar for Retired Clergy - t) 502-377-0610 Rev. Gerald L. Bell;
Victim Assistance Coordinator - t) 502-636-1044 Martine Siegel;
Vocations - t) 502-636-0296 Rev. Martin A. Linebach, Dir.; Rev. Kien Nguyen, Assoc. Dir.;

PARISHES, MISSIONS, AND CLERGY

COMMONWEALTH OF KENTUCKY

ALBANY
Emmanuel Catholic - 2546 Hwy. 127 N., Albany, KY 42602; Mailing: P.O. Box 160, Albany, KY 42602 t) 606-387-7251 Rev. Joel C. Rogers, C.P.M., Sacr. Min.;
Holy Cross Catholic Church - 264 Glasgow Rd., Burkesville, KY 42717 t) 270-864-4107 Rev. Devassya P. Kanattu, C.M.I., Pst.;

BARDSTOWN
Basilica of St. Joseph Proto-Cathedral - 310 W. Stephen Foster Ave., Bardstown, KY 40004; Mailing: P.O. Box 548, Bardstown, KY 40004 t) 502-348-3126 stjoe@bardstown.com www.stjosephbasilica.org Rev. Terry L. Bradshaw, Pst.; Rev. C. Joseph Batcheldor, In Res.; CRP Stds.: 46
Basilica of St. Joseph Proto-Cathedral School - (Grades PreK-8) 320 W. Stephen Foster Ave., Bardstown, KY 40004 t) 502-348-5994 mbowen@stjoeelem.org Margaret Bowen, Prin.; Tricia Payne, Librn.;
St. Joseph Montessori Children's Center - 300 W John Fitch Ave, Bardstown, KY 40004 t) (502) 203-3510 www.stjosephmontessori.org/
St. Vincent de Paul Outreach Ministries - 118 E. Broadway, Bardstown, KY 40004
St. Monica - 407 S. Third St., Bardstown, KY 40004 t) 502-348-5250 saintmonicabardstown@gmail.com stmonicabardstown.org Rev. Steven Reeves, Pst.; Dcn. Scott R. Turner; CRP Stds.: 6
St. Thomas - 870 Saint Thomas Ln., Bardstown, KY 40004 t) 502-348-3717 saintthomasoffice@gmail.com; stthomasformation@gmail.com www.saintthomasbardstown.org Rev. Steven Reeves, Admin.; Dcn. Scott R. Turner; Olivia Seeger, DRE; Kim Hall, Bus. Mgr.; CRP Stds.: 90

BRANDENBURG
St. John the Apostle - 515 Broadway, Brandenburg, KY 40108 t) 270-422-2196 sjsecretary@bbtel.com stjohnonline.org Rev. Toan Do, Pst.; Dcn. J. Michael Jones; Regina Bennett, DRE; CRP Stds.: 115

CAMPBELLSVILLE
Our Lady of Perpetual Help - 425 N. Central Ave., Campbellsville, KY 42719; Mailing: 213 University Dr., Campbellville, KY 42718 t) 270-465-4282 www.onfirecatholic.com Rev. Saju M. Vadakumpadan, C.M.I., Pst.; CRP Stds.: 26
Our Lady of Fatima - 7066 Calvary Rd., Campbellsville, KY 42718; Mailing: 213 University Dr, Campbellsville, KY 42718

CECILIA
St. Ambrose - 609 E. Main St., Cecilia, KY 42724; Mailing: 611 E. Main St., Cecilia, KY 42724 t) 270-862-5343 stambrose@windstream.net Rev. Benedict J. Brown, Admin.;

COX'S CREEK
St. Gregory - 330 Samuels Loop, Cox's Creek, KY 40013 t) 502-348-6337 clara.fulkerson@stgregoryparish.org; stgregory@stgregoryparish.org www.stgregoryparish.org Rev. Kien Nguyen, Pst.; Andrew Salsman, RCIA Coord.; Clara Fulkerson, DRE; CRP Stds.: 55
St. Gregory School - (Grades PreK-8) 350 Samuels Loop, Cox's Creek, KY 40013 t) 502-348-9583 camille.boone@stgregoryparish.org Camille Boone, Prin.; Sr. Rosemary Rule, Librn.;

EDMONTON
Christ the Healer - 1610 W. Stockton St., Edmonton, KY 42129; Mailing: P.O. Box 599, Edmonton, KY 42129 t) 270-452-5024 (CRP); 270-432-5024; 270-432-0686 christtheheale@scrtc.com Rev. Joseph Thomas, C.M.I., Admin.; Dcn. John Froehlich; CRP Stds.: 5
Christ the King - 1000 Celina Rd., Tompkinsville, KY 42167 t) (270) 432-5024 Kenneth Michael Scheller, Bus. Mgr.;

ELIZABETHTOWN
St. James - 307 W. Dixie Ave., Elizabethtown, KY 42701 t) 270-765-6268 parishoffice@stjames-etown.org www.stjames-etown.org Rev. Michael T. Wimsatt, Pst.; Rev. Juan Luis Gomez, Assoc. Pst.; Rev. Loi D. Pham, Assoc. Pst.; Dcn. William Clark; Dcn. Karl A. Drerup; CRP Stds.: 60
St. James School - (Grades PreK-8) 401 Robinbrooke Blvd., Elizabethtown, KY 42701 t) 270-765-7011 info@sjschoolonline.org Martha West, Librn.;
St. John the Baptist - 657 St. John Church Rd., Elizabethtown, KY 42701 t) 270-735-6930 (CRP); 270-877-2461 frdaniel@bbtel.com Rev. Jeffrey D. Gatlin, Pst.; Dcn. Mike Ryan;

FAIRDALE
Saint Teresa of Calcutta Parish - 903 Fairdale Rd., Fairdale, KY 40118 t) 502-363-9929 btoc.dre@att.net; parishstoc@gmail.com www.teresaofcalcuttafairdale.weebly.com Rev. Benni Pengiperambil, CMI, Pst.; Theresa Watson, DRE; CRP Stds.: 51

FAIRFIELD
St. Michael - 111 Church St., Fairfield, KY 40020; Mailing: PO Box 27, Fairfield, KY 40020 t) 502-252-0106 stmichaelfairfield.com/ Rev. Brandon DeToma, Admin.; Gilly Simpson, DRE; CRP Stds.: 49

FINLEY
Our Lady of the Hills - 9259 Old Lebanon Rd., Finley, KY 42718; Mailing: 213 University Dr., Campbellsville, KY 42718 t) 270-465-4282 olph@windstream.net www.onfirecatholic.com Rev. Saju M. Vadakumpadan, C.M.I., Pst.; CRP Stds.: 15

GLASGOW
St. Helen - 103 W. Brown St., Glasgow, KY 42141; Mailing: 230 Cavalry Dr., Glasgow, KY 42141 t) 270-651-5263 www.sthelenolc.org Rev. Joel Rogers, C.P.M., Pst.; CRP Stds.: 84
Our Lady of the Caves Church - 1010 S. Dixie St., Horse Cave, KY 42749; Mailing: 103 W. Brown St., St. Helen Catholic Church, Glasgow, KY 42141-2101

GREENSBURG
Holy Redeemer - 110 Industrial Dr., Greensburg, KY 42743; Mailing: P.O. Box 247, Jamestown, KY 42629 t) 270-343-3346 www.southernkycatholics.org Rev. Patrick J. Dolan, Pst.;

HODGENVILLE
Our Lady of Mercy - 208 Walters Ave., Hodgenville, KY 42748 t) 270-325-3801 (CRP); 270-358-4697 olmparish@windstream.net Rev. Brian A. Kenney, Pst.; Dcn. James A. Cecil; CRP Stds.: 10

HOWARDSTOWN
St. Ann - 7490 Howardstown Rd., Howardstown, KY 40051 t) 502-286-3181 staschool@hughes.net www.facebook.com/st-ann-church-howardstown Rev. Brian A. Kenney, Pst.; CRP Stds.: 25
St. Ann School - -8) t) 502-549-7210 stannhowardstown@gmail.com Lois Cecil, Prin.;

JAMESTOWN
Holy Spirit - 406 N. Main St., Jamestown, KY 42629; Mailing: P.O. Box 247, Jamestown, KY 42629 t) 270-343-3346 mucl@hotmail.com Rev. Patrick J. Dolan, Admin.; CRP Stds.: 9
Good Shepherd - 1221 Greensburg St., Columbia, KY 42728 c) 502-322-2857

LAGRANGE

Immaculate Conception - 502 N. Fifth Ave., LaGrange, KY 40031 t) 502-222-0255 monica.breitholle@iclagrange.org www.iclagrange.org Rev. Robert Barnell, Pst.; Dcn. Robert R. Caruso; Dcn. Thomas M. McNally; CRP Stds.: 220

Kentucky State Reformatory - t) 502-222-9441

Cedar Lake Lodge - t) 502-222-7157

Baptist Hospital Northeast - t) 502-222-5388

Richwood Nursing Home - t) 502-222-3186

LEBANON

St. Augustine - 235 S. Spalding Ave., Lebanon, KY 40033 t) 270-692-3019 www.stagustinechurch.net Rev. Mark M. Hamilton, Pst.; Dcn. Joseph R. Dant; Dcn. Dennis May; CRP Stds.: 55

St. Augustine School - (Grades PreK-8) 236 S. Spalding Ave., Lebanon, KY 40033 t) 270-692-2063 cbland@saintaschool.net Cindy Bland, Prin.; Stds.: 189; Lay Tchrs.: 11

St. Charles - 675 Hwy. 327, Lebanon, KY 40033 t) 270-692-4513 saintcharles@windstream.net Rev. David W. Naylor, Pst.; Lisa Sandusky, CRE; CRP Stds.: 88

Holy Name of Mary - 3295 Hwy. 208, Lebanon, KY 40033; Mailing: 235 S. Spalding Ave., Lebanon, KY 40033 t) 270-692-3019; 270-692-6491 andreaw@staugustinechurch.net; staugustinechurch@staugustinechurch.net Rev. Mark M. Hamilton, Pst.; Dcn. Joseph R. Dant; Dcn. Dennis May; Andrea Willett, DRE; CRP Stds.: 93

LEBANON JUNCTION

St. Benedict - 211 W. Oak St., Lebanon Junction, KY 40150 t) 502-543-5918 secretary@stafalcons.com www.sta-stb.com Rev. Terry L. Langford, Pst.; CRP Stds.: 3

LIBERTY

St. Bernard - 5075 KY 551, Liberty, KY 42539 t) 606-787-7570 sbchurch1@windstream.net Rev. George Otuma, A.J., Admin.; CRP Stds.: 8

Sacred Heart -

LORETTO

St. Francis of Assisi Church - 6785 Hwy. 52, Loretto, KY 40037; Mailing: 200 School Dr., P.O. Box 74, Loretto, KY 40037 t) 270-865-2521 office@sfahc.com sfahc.com Rev. Richard Goodin, Admin.; CRP Stds.: 67

Holy Cross - 59 New Haven Rd., Loretto, KY 40037; Mailing: 200 School Dr., P.O. Box 74, Loretto, KY 40037 t) 270-865-2521 office@sfahc.com sfahc.com Rev. Richard Goodin, Admin.; CRP Stds.: 14

LOUISVILLE

Cathedral of the Assumption - 433 S. 5th St., Louisville, KY 40202 t) 502-657-5213 (Admin.); 502-582-2971 (Office) administrator@cathedraloftheassumption.org www.cathedraloftheassumption.org Most Rev. Shelton Fabre; Rev. Martin A. Linebach, Rector; Dcn. Christopher F. McDonell; CRP Stds.: 29

St. Agnes - 1920 Newburg Rd., Louisville, KY 40205 t) 502-451-2220 mmuncy@stagneslouisville.org Rev. Justin Nelson, Pst.; CRP Stds.: 11

St. Agnes School - (Grades K-8) 1800 Newburg Rd., Louisville, KY 40205 t) 502-458-2850 ageorge@stagneslouisville.org Aundrea George, Prin.;

St. Albert the Great - 1395 Girard Dr., Louisville, KY 40222 t) 502-425-3940 office@stalbert.org stalbert.org Rev. David W. Harris, Pst.; Dcn. Stephen Marks, Admin.; CRP Stds.: 62

St. Albert the Great School - (Grades PreK-8) t) 502-425-1804 school@stalbert.org Ellen Martin, Prin.;

Ascension of Our Lord - 4600 Lynnbrook Dr., Louisville, KY 40220 t) 502-451-3860 x10 dschabel@ascension-parish.com www.ascension-parish.com Rev. Adam Carrico, Pst.; CRP Stds.: 24

Ascension of Our Lord School - (Grades PreK-8) t) 502-451-2535 terry@ascension-parish.com Terry Mullaney, Prin.; Stds.: 217; Scholastics: 17; Lay Tchrs.: 17

St. Athanasius - 5915 Outer Loop Dr., Louisville, KY 40219 t) 502-969-3332 dminton@staparish.com; secretary@staparish.com Rev. Minh Vu, Pst.; Dcn. Sam King; CRP Stds.: 30

St. Athanasius School - (Grades PreK-8) t) 502-969-2345 reecem@athanasiusschool.org saintathanasiuslouisville.com Margie Reece, Prin.;

St. Augustine - 1310 W. Broadway, Louisville, KY 40203 t) 502-584-4602 staugustine@mw.twcbc.com staugustinelou.org Rev. Christopher S. Rhodes, Pst.; Dcn. Keith L. McKenzie;

St. Bartholomew - 2042 Buechel Bank Rd., Louisville, KY 40218 t) 502-499-0883 chayslette@saintbarths.org www.saintbarths.org Rev. Pablo A. Hernandez, Pst.; CRP Stds.: 55

St. Bernard - 7500 Tangelo Dr., Louisville, KY 40228 t) 502-239-5178 x2302 (Principal); 502-239-5178 rneal@stbernardlou.com Rev. Charles Walker, Pst.; CRP Stds.: 49

St. Bernard School - (Grades PreK-8) fklausing@stbernardlou.com Julie Perdue, Prin.;

St. Boniface - 531 E. Liberty St., Louisville, KY 40202-1107 t) 502-584-4279 patty@stbonifaceparish.com www.stbonifaceparish.com Rev. Jeffrey P. Shooner, Pst.; Rev. Quan Nguyen, Assoc. Pst.; Dcn. David R. Tomes;

St. Brigid - 1520 Hepburn Ave., Louisville, KY 40204 t) 502-584-5565 info@stbrigidlou.org Rev. Gary T. Padgett, Pst.; Dcn. Will Tribbey; CRP Stds.: 5

Christ the King - 718 S. 44th St., Louisville, KY 40211 t) 502-772-7851 (CRP); 270-432-5024 Rev. Christopher S. Rhodes, Pst.; Loueva Moss, DRE;

St. Edward - 9608 Sue Helen Dr., Louisville, KY 40299 t) 502-267-7494 churchoffice@stedward.church www.stedwardchurch.com Rev. Scott Murphy, Pst.; Dcn. James McCarty; CRP Stds.: 106

St. Edward School - (Grades PreK-8) 9610 Sue Helen Dr., Louisville, KY 40299 t) 502-267-6633; 502-267-1122 www.stedward.school/ Karen Loper, Prin.; Diane Walsh, Librn.; Stds.: 315; Lay Tchrs.: 21

St. Elizabeth Ann Seton - 11501 Maple Way, Louisville, KY 40229 t) 502-969-0004 parishoffice@easeton.com easeton.com Rev. Albert C Anover, Pst.; CRP Stds.: 23

St. Elizabeth of Hungary - 1020 E. Burnett Ave., Louisville, KY 40217; Mailing: 747 Harrison Ave., Louisville, KY 40217 t) 502-637-7600 parishoffice@paxchristilou.org www.paxchristilou.org Very Rev. Philip Lee Erickson, Pst.; Dcn. Timothy E. Stewart;

Epiphany Catholic Church - 914 Old Harrods Creek Rd., Louisville, KY 40223 t) 502-245-9733 office@epiphanycatholicchurch.org www.epiphanycatholicchurch.org Rev. J. Randall Hubbard, Pst.; CRP Stds.: 111

St. Frances of Rome - 2119 Payne St., Louisville, KY 40206 t) 502-896-8401 stfranrome@sfrlou.org saintfrancesofrome.org/ Rev. Louis J. Meiman, Pst.; Steve King, Admin.; Sharon Coonan, Pst. Assoc.; Rick Knoop, Music Min.; CRP Stds.: 15

St. Francis of Assisi - 1960 Bardstown Rd., Louisville, KY 40205-1572 t) 502-456-6394 susellis@ccsfa.org; drenauer@ccsfa.org www.ccsfachurch.org Dcn. Michael Sowers; JoAnn Jones, DRE; CRP Stds.: 9

St. Francis of Assisi School - (Grades PreK-8) 1938 Alfresco Pl., Louisville, KY 40205-1876 t) 502-459-3088 sfrommeyer@ccsfa.org www.sfalouisville.org/ Steve Frommeyer, Prin.;

St. Gabriel the Archangel - 5505 Bardstown Rd., Louisville, KY 40291 t) 502-239-5481 parish@stgabriel.net www.stgabriel.net Rev. James Jason Harris, Pst.; Dcn. T. Stephen Bowling; Dcn. Michael Fitzmayer; Kathleen Abell, DRE; CRP Stds.: 97

St. Gabriel the Archangel School - (Grades PreK-8) 5503 Bardstown Rd., Louisville, KY 40291 t) 502-239-5535; 502-239-1298 (Preschool) school@stgabriel.net; preschool@stgabriel.net Lara Krill, Prin.;

Good Shepherd - 3525 Rudd Ave., Louisville, KY 40212 t) 502-749-9780 secretary@goodshepherdchurch.us www.goodshepherdchurch.us Rev. Deogratias Ssamba, A.J., Pst.; Dcn. Christopher J Herbert; CRP Stds.: 7

Guardian Angels - 6000 Preston Hwy., Louisville, KY 40219 t) 502-968-5421 guardangels@att.net guardianangelslouisville.org Rev. Jeffrey P. Leger, Pst.;

Holy Family - 3938 Poplar Level Rd., Louisville, KY 40213-1463 t) 502-459-6066 holyfamilyky.org Rev. George Munjanattu, Pst.; Rev. John Pozhathuparambil, O.F.M.Conv., Sacr. Mod.; Dcn. J. Patrick Wright; CRP Stds.: 3

Holy Name - 2914 S. 3rd St., Louisville, KY 40208 t) 502-637-5560 info@holynamelouisville.org www.holynamelouisville.org/ Rev. William M. Bowling, Pst.; Dcn. Frank Villalobos; CRP Stds.: 45

Holy Spirit - 3345 Lexington Rd., Louisville, KY 40206 t) 502-893-3982 jhertzman@hspirit.org www.hspirit.org Rev. Frederick W. Klotter, Pst.; Dcn. Bryan Bush; CRP Stds.: 12

Holy Spirit School - (Grades PreK-8) 322 Cannons Ln., Louisville, KY 40206 t) 502-893-7700 dswenson@hspiritschool.org hspirit.org Doris Swenson, Prin.; Stds.: 424; Lay Tchrs.: 31

Holy Trinity - 501 Cherrywood Rd., Louisville, KY 40207 t) 502-897-5207 x125 (CRP) bcobb@htparish.org; csmith@htparish.org Rev. Shayne R. Duvall, Pst.; CRP Stds.: 39

Holy Trinity School - (Grades PreK-8) 423 Cherrywood Rd., Louisville, KY 40207 t) 502-897-2785 jrichards@ht-school.org Jack Richards, Prin.; D. Dee Hill, Librn.; Stds.: 835; Lay Tchrs.: 50

St. Ignatius Martyr - 1818 Rangeland Rd., Louisville, KY 40219 t) 502-964-5904; 502-964-5904 x110 (CRP) marysecsti@yahoo.com stignatiusmartyrlou.org Dcn. Lucio A. Caruso, Pst. Assoc.;

Immaculate Heart of Mary - 1545 Louis Coleman Jr. Dr., Louisville, KY 40211 t) 502-774-5772 irectory@bellsouth.net Rev. Christopher S. Rhodes, Pst.;

Incarnation - 2229 Lower Hunters Trace Rd., Louisville, KY 40216 t) 502-447-2013 incarnationcatho@bellsouth.net www.icclou.org Rev. Shaju Puthussery, O.F.M. Conv; CRP Stds.: 16

St. James - 1826 Edenside Ave., Louisville, KY 40204 t) 502-451-1420 info@sbsjlou.org Rev. Gary T. Padgett, Pst.;

St. James School - (Grades PreSchool-8) 1818 Edenside Ave., Louisville, KY 40204 t) 502-454-0330 stjames@stjamesbluejays.com www.stjamesbluejays.com Jennifer Zimmerman, Admin.;

St. John Paul II - 3042 Hikes Ln., Louisville, KY 40220-2017 t) 502-459-4251 cmeyers@stjpiiparish.com; dhoard@stjpiiparish.com www.stjpiiparish.com Rev. Peter Quan Do, Pst.; Dcn. James I. McGoff; Dcn. Bruce Warren;

St. John Vianney - 4839 Southside Dr., Louisville, KY 40214 t) 502-366-5517 franthonyngo@yahoo.com Rev. Anthony Chinh N'go, Assoc. Pst.;

Sitio Clothing Ministry - t) (502) 969-0018 asimplepath@sitioministry.org Linda Gottbrath, Volunteer Dir.;

St. Joseph - 1406 E. Washington St., Louisville, KY 40206 t) 502-583-7401 (Office); 502-583-0892 (Parish Hall) parish@sjosephcatholic.org; wfernandez@sjosephcatholic.org sjosephcatholic.org Rev. L. Wilfredo Fernandez, Pst.;

St. Lawrence - 1925 Lewiston Dr., Louisville, KY 40216 t) 502-448-2122 stlsusang@gmail.com stl-lawrence.org Rev. William P. Burks, Pst.; Dcn. David S. Maxwell; William (Bill) Unruh, DRE; CRP Stds.: 6

St. Leonard - 440 Zorn Ave., Louisville, KY 40206 t) 502-897-2595 stlparish@stleonardlouisville.org www.stleonardlouisville.org Rev. Louis J. Meiman, Pst.; Sharon Coonan, Pst. Assoc.; Sharon Bidwell, DRE; Steve King, Bus. Mgr.; CRP Stds.: 10

St. Louis Bertrand - 1104 S. 6th St., Louisville, KY 40203 t) 502-583-4448 stlouisbertrand@stlb.org www.stlb.org Rev. Bernard Timothy, O.P., Pst.; Rev. Martin Martiny, O.P., Prior; Rev. Pier Giorgio Dengler, O.P., Par. Vicar; Rev. John Baptist Hoang, O.P., Chap.; Dcn. William Klump; Rev. Emmanuel Bertrand, O.P., In Res.; Rev. Joseph Anthony Breen, O.P., In Res.; CRP Stds.: 31

Lourdes Rosary Shrine, Inc. -

Blessed Margaret Castello Shrine -

St. Luke - 4211 Jim Hawkins Dr., Louisville, KY 40229 t) 502-969-3291 stluke40229@gmail.com www.stlukelouisville.org Rev. T. Michael Tobin, Pst.; Rev. Joseph M. Rankin, In Res.;

St. Margaret Mary - 7813 Shelbyville Rd., Louisville, KY 40222 t) 502-426-1588 parish@stmm.org www.stmm.org Rev. William D. Hammer, Pst.; CRP Stds.: 75

St. Margaret Mary School - (Grades K-8) t) 502-426-2635 wsims@stmm.org Wendy Sims, Prin.;

St. Martha - 2825 Klondike Ln., Louisville, KY 40218 t) 502-491-8535 efrederick@stmarthachurch.org; abergamini@stmarthachurch.org www.stmarthalouisville.org Rev. Seejo Thandiackal, C.M.I., Pst.; Dcn. Daniel G. Bisig Sr.; Dcn. John P. Maher; CRP Stds.: 22

St. Martha School - (Grades PreK-8) t) 502-491-3171 sbarnett@stmarthschool.org www.stmartharocks.com

St. Martin de Porres - 3112 W. Broadway, Louisville, KY 40211 t) 502-778-1118 c) 502-594-5054 parishoffice@stmartindeporrescatholic.org; michael@stmartindeporrescatholic.org www.stmartindeporrescatholic.org Rev. William M. Bowling, Pst.;

St. Martin of Tours - 639 S. Shelby St., Louisville, KY 40202 t) 502-582-2827 cindyheckmann@stmartinoftourschurch.org; secretary@stmartinoftourschurch.org www.stmartinoftourslouisville.org Rev. R. Paul Beach, Pst.; Rev. David J. Carr, Assoc. Pst.; Dcn. Richard P. Zoldak; Dcn. Scott Hedges; Dcn. Robert C. Bryant; Cindy Heckmann, DRE; Jackie Carlin, Bus. Mgr.; CRP Stds.: 78

Mary Queen of Peace Parish - 4005 Dixie Hwy., Louisville, KY 40216 t) 502-448-4008 mqop@twc.com www.maryqueenofpeace.net Rev. Thomas E. Gentile, Admin.; CRP Stds.: 1

St. Michael - 3705 Stone Lakes Dr., Louisville, KY 40299 t) 502-266-5611 skrieger@stmichaellouisville.org; shenriksen@stmichaellouisville.org www.stmichaelchurch.org/ Rev. Steven D. Henriksen, Pst.; Dcn. Kenneth J. Carter; Dcn. Mark Kelley; CRP Stds.: 42

St. Michael School - (Grades K-8) 3703 Stone Lakes Dr., Louisville, KY 40299 t) 502-267-6155 stackett@stmichaellouisville.org Stacy Tackett, Prin.;

Most Blessed Sacrament - 3509 Taylor Blvd., Louisville, KY 40215; Mailing: 4335 Hazelwood Ave., Louisville, KY 40215 t) 502-361-0149 blanford@louisville.edu; mbs3509@aol.com Rev. Nicholas J. Brown, Pst.; Sandra Blanford, DRE; CRP Stds.: 20

Our Lady of Lourdes - 508 Breckenridge Ln., Louisville, KY 40207 t) 502-896-0241; 502-895-5122 (School) olol@ourlourdes.org ourlourdes.org Rev. Scott J. Wimsett, Pst.; Doug Doug Wolz, DRE; CRP Stds.: 27

Our Lady of Lourdes School - (Grades PreSchool-8) 510 Breckenridge Ln., Louisville, KY 40207 jeffb@ourlourdes.org www.ourlourdes.org/school Jeffrey Beavin, Prin.; Morgan Wissing, Vice Prin.; Stds.: 400; Lay Tchrs.: 33

Our Lady of Mount Carmel - 5505 New Cut Rd., Louisville, KY 40214 t) 502-366-5651 cmay@southendcatholic.com Rev. Troy D. Overton, Pst.; Dcn. Johnny Fellonneav; Dcn. W. Timothy Johnson; Dcn. Terry Maguire; Dcn. Michael A. Tolbert; CRP Stds.: 42

Our Mother of Sorrows - 760 Eastern Pkwy., Louisville, KY 40217; Mailing: 747 Harrison Ave., Louisville, KY 40217 t) 502-637-7600 parishoffice@paxchristilou.org www.paxchristilou.org Very Rev. Philip Lee Erickson, Pst.; Dcn. Timothy E. Stewart;

St. Patrick - 1000 N. Beckley Station Rd., Louisville, KY 40245 t) 502-244-6083 ourparish@stpatlou.org www.stpatlou.org/ Rev. Jeffrey P. Shooner, Pst.; Rev. Quan Nguyen, Assoc. Pst.; Rev. Robert E. Osborne, Assoc. Pst.; Dcn. Gregory M. Gitschier; Dcn. Scott R. Haner; Dcn. Mark J. Rougeux; Rev. T. Anthony Smith, In Res.; Carrie Williamson, Pst. Assoc.; Dave Naber, Bus. Mgr.; R. Tim Grove, Dir.; Lynne Marshall, Dir.; Jonna O'Bryan, Dir.; Julie Roth, Dir.; CRP Stds.: 100

St. Patrick School - (Grades PreK-8) t) 502-244-7083 nsturtzel@stpatlou.org www.school.stpatlou.org Nathan Sturtzel, Prin.; Stds.: 688; Lay Tchrs.: 41

St. Paul - 6901 Dixie Hwy., Louisville, KY 40258 t) 502-935-1223 office@stpaulparishlouisvilleky.org www.stpaulparishlouisvilleky.org Friar Shaju Puthussery, O.F.M.Conv., Pst.; Friar Leo Payyappilly, OFM Conv., Assoc. Pst.; Friar Mario Serrano, OFM Conv., In Res.; Rev. Adam Bunnell, O.F.M.Conv., In Res.; Dcn. Gary W. Fowler; Pat Garlitz, DRE; CRP Stds.: 95

St. Paul School - (Grades PreK-8) t) 502-935-5511 jen.burba@saintpaulschool.net Jennifer Burba, Prin.;

St. Peter the Apostle Parish - 5431 Johnsontown Rd., Louisville, KY 40272 t) 502-937-5920 x232 athieneman@saintpeterapostle.org; bcolyer@saintpeterapostle.org saintpeterapostle.org Rev. Christopher B. Lubecke, Pst.; Dcn. Gregory L. Klinglesmith; Dcn. Stephen Smith; Betty Rowland, DRE; CRP Stds.: 60

St. Andrew Academy - (Grades PreK-8) 7724 Columbine Dr., Louisville, KY 40258 t) 502-935-4578 barbaraschrader@saintandrewacademy.com Sponsored by St. Peter the Apostle Parish. Stuart Cripe, Prin.; Doris Baines, Librn.;

St. Raphael the Archangel - 2141 Lancashire Ave., Louisville, KY 40205 sleon@sraparish.org Rev. Anthony Leo Cecil Jr., STB, Admin.; CRP Stds.: 7

St. Raphael the Archangel School - (Grades K-8) 2131 Lancashire Ave., Louisville, KY 40205 t) 502-456-1541 jtabor@straphaelschool.org Jill Tabor, Prin.;

St. Rita - 8709 Preston Hwy., Louisville, KY 40219 t) 502-969-4579 wpuga@saintrita.net Rev. T. Michael Tobin, Pst.; Dcn. Aurelio A. Puga; Dcn. Kenneth J. Mitchell; Rev. Joseph M. Rankin, In Res.; CRP Stds.: 91

St. Rita School - (Grades PreK-8) t) 502-969-7067 nhulsewede@stritacatholicschool.com Neil Hulsewede, Prin.;

SS. Simon and Jude - 4335 Hazelwood Ave., Louisville, KY 40215 t) 502-368-4887 blanford@louisville.edu; mbs3509@aol.com Rev. Nicholas J. Brown, Pst.; Sandra Blanford, DRE; CRP Stds.: 20

St. Stephen, Martyr - 2931 Pindell Ave., Louisville, KY 40217 t) 502-635-5813 mlotz@ssmartyr.org; cfautz@ssmartyr.org www.ssmartyr.org Rev. Peter Bucalo, Pst.; Dcn. Stephen J. DaPonte; Dcn. Sylvester Nitzken; Dcn. Ken Roberts; CRP Stds.: 10

St. Stephen, Martyr School - (Grades PreK-8) t) 502-635-7141 bbritt@ssmartyr.org www.ssmartyr.org/ Bridget Britt, Prin.; Stds.: 289; Lay Tchrs.: 17

St. Therese - 1010 Schiller Ave., Louisville, KY 40204; Mailing: 747 Harrison Ave., Louisville, KY 40217 t) 502-637-7600 parishoffice@paxchristilou.org www.paxchristilou.org Very Rev. Philip Lee Erickson, Pst.; Dcn. Timothy E. Stewart;

St. Thomas More - 6105 S. Third St., Louisville, KY 40214 t) 502-366-1463 jstieren@southendcatholic.com; bcrask@southendcatholic.com Rev. Troy Overton, Pst.; Dcn. Johnny Fellonneau; Dcn. W. Timothy Johnson; Dcn. Terry Maguire; Dcn. Michael A. Tolbert; Julie Stieren, DRE; CRP Stds.: 34

St. William - 1226 W. Oak St., Louisville, KY 40210 t) 502-635-6307 stwilliamchurchlouisville@gmail.com stwilliamchurch.org Rev. William D. Hammer, Pst.; Dawn Dones, Pst. Assoc.; Rev. John R. Burke, Senior Assoc.; CRP Stds.: 28

MOUNT WASHINGTON

St. Francis Xavier - 155 Stringer Ln., Mount Washington, KY 40047 t) 502-538-4933 lauren.battcher@sfxmw.com; jennifer.sweeney@sfxmw.com sfxmw.com Rev. R. Dale Cieslik, Pst.; Dcn. Stephen A. Age; Dcn. Earl Baker; Dcn. Gerald J. Mattingly; Paula Silliman, Pst. Assoc.; Helen Hagan, Bus. Mgr.; Lauren Battcher, DRE; CRP Stds.: 142

NEW HAVEN

St. Catherine - 174 N. Main St., New Haven, KY 40051; Mailing: 413 N. First St., New Haven, KY 40051 t) 502-549-3680 parishoffice@saintcatherineschool.com www.stcatherinenewhaven.org Rev. Matthew T. Hardesty, Pst.; Dcn. Dean Giulitto; CRP Stds.: 8

St. Catherine School - (Grades PreK-8) 413 N. 1st St., New Haven, KY 40051 jreed@saintcatherineschool.com louisvillecatholicschools.com Jessie Reed, Prin.; Stds.: 67

Immaculate Conception - 8191 New Haven Rd., New Haven, KY 40051-6030; Mailing: 413 N. 1st St., c/o St. Catherine Church, New Haven, KY 40051 t) 502-549-3680 parishoffice@saintcatherineschool.com www.archlou.org Rev. Matthew T. Hardesty, Pst.; Dcn. Dean Giulitto;

NEW HOPE

St. Vincent de Paul - 104 Church St., New Hope, KY 40052; Mailing: c/o St. Catherine Church, 413 N. 1st St., New Haven, KY 40051 t) 502-549-3680 parishoffice@saintcatherineschool.com www.stvincentdepaulnewhope.org/ Rev. Matthew T. Hardesty, Pst.; Dcn. Dean Giulitto; CRP Stds.: 26

PAYNEVILLE

St. Mary Magdalen of Pazzi - 110 Hwy. 376, Payneville, KY 40157; Mailing: P.O. Box 110, Payneville, KY 40157 t) 270-496-4333 stmarymag@bbtel.com www.stmarypayneville.org Rev. George Illikkal, C.M.I. (India), Pst.; Dcn. Gregory A. Beavin; Dcn. Dean Sears; CRP Stds.: 62

St. Theresa - 9245 Rhodelia Rd., Payneville, KY 40157 t) 270-496-4362 sttheresa@bbtel.com www.sttheresarhodelia.org Rev. George Illikkal, C.M.I. (India), Pst.; Dcn. Gregory A. Beavin; Dcn. Dean Sears; CRP Stds.: 62

PEWEE VALLEY

St. Aloysius - 212 Mount Mercy Dr., Pewee Valley, KY 40056 t) 502-241-8452 x1000 (CRP); 502-241-8516 x1013 parishoffice@staloysiuspwv.org; schooloffice@staloysiuspwv.org Rev. John J. Stoltz, Pst.; Dcn. Phillip L. Noltemeyer; Dcn. Thomas L. Roth; CRP Stds.: 8

St. Aloysius School - (Grades PreK-8) 122 Mount Mercy Dr., Pewee Valley, KY 40056 Paula Smith, Prin.; Stds.: 356; Lay Tchrs.: 26

Korean Catholic Community - t) (502) 241-8452

PROSPECT

St. Bernadette Parish - 6500 St. Bernadette Ave., Prospect, KY 40059 t) 502-245-2210 tinal@stb2008.org; elizabetha@stb2008.org www.stb2008.org Rev. Jeffrey Scott Nicolas, Pst.; Rev. A. Biju Chathely, C.M.I., Assoc. Pst.; Dcn. Todd C. Auffrey; Dcn. Jerome L. Buehner; Dcn. Jim Shields; Elizabeth Auffrey, DRE; CRP Stds.: 150

RADCLIFF

St. Christopher - 1225 S. Wilson Rd., Radcliff, KY 40160 t) 270-351-3706 church@stchristopherparish.org www.stchristopherparish.org/ Rev. Jeffrey G. Hopper, Pst.; CRP Stds.: 69

RAYWICK

St. Francis Xavier Church - 108 Main St., Raywick, KY 40060 t) 270-692-2245 raywickchurch@windstream.net Rev. David W. Naylor, Pst.;

SHELBYVILLE

Annunciation of the Blessed Virgin Mary - 105 Main St., Shelbyville, KY 40065 t) 502-633-1547 office@annunciationky.org www.annunciationky.org Rev. David Sanchez, Pst.; Dcn. Robert J. Hart; Dcn. John P. Strain; Wilson Wilder, Music Min.; CRP Stds.:

182

St. John Chrysostom - 122 Penn St., Eminence, KY 40019; Mailing: P.O. Box 74, Eminence, KY 40019 t) 502-518-0154

SHEPHERDSVILLE

St. Aloysius - 187 S. Plum St., Shepherdsville, KY 40165 t) 502-543-5918 www.sta-stb.com Rev. Terry L. Langford, Pst.;

SPRINGFIELD

St. Dominic - 303 W. Main St., Springfield, KY 40069 t) 859-336-3569 stdom@stdomparish.org Rev. David Farrell, Pst.; CRP Stds.: 83

St. Dominic School - (Grades PreK-8) 312 W. High St., Springfield, KY 40069 t) 859-336-7165 pbreunig@stdominicelementary.org Pamela Breunig, Prin.; Stds.: 216; Lay Tchrs.: 15

Holy Rosary - 378 Rosary Heights, Springfield, KY 40069; Mailing: P.O. Box 146, Springfield, KY 40069 t) (859) 284-5242 kyholyrosary3860@att.net Rev. Michael Martin, Pst.; CRP Stds.: 7

Holy Trinity - 306 Fredericktown Rd., Springfield, KY 40069 t) (859) 284-5242 htr@bardstown.com Rev. Michael Martin, Pst.; Dcn. John Hamilton; Judy Gordon, DRE; CRP Stds.: 40

Holy Rosary-Manton - 6964 Cissellville Rd., Springfield, KY 40069; Mailing: 306 Fredericktown Rd., Springfield, KY 40069 t) 859-284-5242 Rev. Michael Martin, Pst.;

St. Rose - 868 Loretto Rd., Springfield, KY 40069; Mailing: P.O. Box 71, Springfield, KY 40069 t) 859-336-3121 strose3121@att.net Rev. Kevin Anthony McGrath, O.P., Pst.; Rev. Edmund Augustine Ditton, O.P., Assoc. Pst.; Dcn. William D. Coulter; Bro. Gerard Thayer, In Res.; CRP Stds.: 49

VINE GROVE

St. Brigid - 314 E. Main St., Vine Grove, KY 40175 t) 270-877-2461 Rev. Jeffrey D. Gatlin, Pst.; Dcn. Michael A. Ryan; CRP Stds.: 33

St. Martin of Tours - 440 Saint Martin Rd., Vine Grove, KY 40175 t) 270-828-2552; 270-317-0985 (CRP) stmartinfl@bbtel.com; faithformation@stchristopherparish.org Rev. Jeffrey G. Hopper, Pst.; Dcn. Joseph D. Calvert; CRP Stds.: 76

WHITE MILLS

St. Ignatius - 7786 Sonora Hardin Springs Rd., White Mills, KY 42788; Mailing: P. O. Box 67, White Mills, KY 42788-0067 c) 270-763-3856 stignatiuscc@outlook.com Rev. Benedict J. Brown, Admin.; CRP Stds.: 10

SCHOOLS: PRESCHOOL THRU HIGH SCHOOL

SCHOOLS

COMMONWEALTH OF KENTUCKY

LOUISVILLE

***Holy Angels Academy, Inc.** - (PRV) (Grades PreK-12) 12201 Old Henry Rd., Louisville, KY 40223 t) 502-254-9440 info@holyangelsacademy.org holyangelslouisville.com Rev. Robert M. Gregor, C.P.M., Chap.; Stds.:-100; Pr. Tchrs.: 1; Lay Tchrs.: 12

John Paul II Academy - (PAR) (Grades PreK-8) 3525 Goldsmith Ln., Louisville, KY 40220 t) 502-452-1712 aconliffe@jp2a.org Conliffe Alicia, Prin.; Stds.: 119; Lay Tchrs.: 15

***Nativity Academy** - (Grades 5-8) 529 E. Liberty St., Louisville, KY 40202 t) 502-855-3300 tkallay@nativitylouisville.org nativitylouisville.org Roni Witherspoon, Prin.; Stds.: 44; Lay Tchrs.: 5

St. Nicholas Academy - (PAR) (Grades PreK-8) 5501 New Cut Rd., Louisville, KY 40214 t) 502-368-8506 kwallitsch@sna-panthers.org www.sna-panthers.org Katie Wallitsch Oehmann, Prin.; Stds.: 254; Lay Tchrs.: 23

Notre Dame Academy - (PAR) (Grades PreK-8) 1927 Lewiston Dr., Louisville, KY 40216 t) 502-447-3155 a.titus@ndasaints.com ndasaints.org Ashley Titus, Prin.; Stds.: 259; Lay Tchrs.: 20

Pitt Academy - 7515 Westport Rd., Louisville, KY 40222 t) 502-966-6979 rdoty@pitt.com www.pitt.com Special needs school. Renee Doty, Prin.; Stds.: 25; Lay Tchrs.: 9

Sacred Heart Model School - (PRV) (Grades PreK-8) 3107 Lexington Rd., Louisville, KY 40206 t) 502-896-3931 mbratcher@shslou.org www.shslou.org Michael L. Bratcher, Prin.; Stds.: 398; Lay Tchrs.: 35

Sacred Heart School for the Arts - 3105 Lexington Rd., Angela Hall Buidling #17, Louisville, KY 40206 t) 502-897-1816 www.shslou.org Kathie Davis, Exec. Dir.; Stds.: 350

PROSPECT

Saint Mary Academy - (Grades PreK-8) 11311 Saint Mary Ln., Prospect, KY 40059 t) 502-315-2555 julie.speer@saintmaryacademy.com www.saintmaryacademy.com Trevor Timmerberg, Prin.; Stds.: 509; Lay Tchrs.: 28

HIGH SCHOOLS

COMMONWEALTH OF KENTUCKY

BARDSTOWN

Bethlehem High School - (DIO) 309 W. Stephen Foster Ave., Bardstown, KY 40004 t) 502-348-8594 pmontgomery@bethlehemhigh.org www.bethlehemhigh.org Thurmond Sarah, Prin.; Stds.: 294; Lay Tchrs.: 24

LOUISVILLE

Academy of Our Lady of Mercy - (PRV) (Grades 9-12) 5801 Fegenbush Ln., Louisville, KY 40228 t) 502-671-2010 csmith-ough@mercyjaguars.com www.mercyacademy.com Becky Montague, Pres.; Stds.: 508; Lay Tchrs.: 46

Assumption High School (Sisters of Mercy) - (PRV) 2170 Tyler Ln., Louisville, KY 40205 t) 502-458-9551 martha.tedesco@ahsrockets.org; mary.lang@ahsrockets.org www.ahsrockets.org Martha Tedesco, Prin.; Mary Lang, Pres.; Stds.: 835; Lay Tchrs.: 73

St. Francis DeSales High School - (DIO) (Grades 9-12) 425 W. Kenwood Dr., Louisville, KY 40214 t) 502-368-6519 rick.blackwell@desaleshs.com; anastasia.quirk@desaleshs.com www.desaleshighschool.com College Preparatory School Dr. Anastasia Quirk, Prin.; Dr. Rick Blackwell, Pres.; Stds.: 320; Lay Tchrs.: 32

Holy Cross High School - (DIO) 5144 Dixie Hwy., Louisville, KY 40216 t) 502-447-4363 kbuerger@holycrosshs.com www.holycrosshs.com Jennifer Barz, Prin.; Stds.: 236; Lay Tchrs.: 25

***Presentation Academy** - (PRV) (Grades 9-12) 861 S. 4th St., Louisville, KY 40203 t) 502-583-5935 bnoonan@presentationacademy.org; khartman@presentationacademy.org www.presentationacademy.org Becca Noonan, Prin.; Kelly Hartman, Assoc. Prin.; Amy Skretny Fowler, Dir., External Affairs; Stds.: 155; Sr. Tchrs.: 1; Lay Tchrs.: 22

Sacred Heart Academy - (PRV) (Grades 9-12) 3175 Lexington Rd., Louisville, KY 40206 t) 502-897-6097 katemple@shslou.org www.shslou.org/academy Kelly Lanza, Prin.; Dr. Karen McNay, Pres.; Stds.: 748; Lay Tchrs.: 73

Trinity High School - (DIO) 4011 Shelbyville Rd., Louisville, KY 40207 t) 502-895-9427 snyder@trinityrocks.com www.trinityrocks.com Daniel J. Zoeller, Prin.; Stds.: 1,073; Sr. Tchrs.: 1; Lay Tchrs.: 92

St. Xavier High School, Xaverian Brothers - (PRV) 1609 Poplar Level Rd., Louisville, KY 40217 t) 502-637-4712 pcolistra@saintx.com www.saintx.com Amy Sample, Prin.; Paul Colistra, Pres.; Michele Metcalfe, Librn.; Stds.: 1,090; Lay Tchrs.: 106

CEMETERIES [CEM]

LOUISVILLE

Calvary (Archdiocesan Catholic Cemeteries) - 1600 Newburg Rd., Louisville, KY 40205; Mailing: P.O. Box 4096, Louisville, KY 40204 t) 502-451-7710 cemeteries@archlou.org www.catholiccemeterieslouisville.org Francisco Javier Fajardo-Ocana, Dir.;

St. John - 2601 Duncan St., Louisville, KY 40212; Mailing: P.O. Box 4096, Louisville, KY 40204 t) 502-451-7710 cemeteries@archlou.org www.catholiccemeterieslouisville.org Francisco Fajardo-Ocana, Dir.;

St. Louis - 1167 Barret Ave., Louisville, KY 40204 t) 502-451-7710 cemeteries@archlou.org www.catholiccemeterieslouisville.org Francisco Fajardo-Ocana, Dir.;

St. Michael - 1153 Charles St., Louisville, KY 40204 t) 502-451-7710 cemeteries@archlou.org www.catholiccemeterieslouisville.org Francisco Fajardo-Ocana, Dir.;

COLLEGES & UNIVERSITIES [COL]

INSTITUTIONS LOCATED IN DIOCESE

LOUISVILLE

Bellarmine University - 2001 Newburg Rd., Louisville, KY 40205-0671 t) 502-272-8291 president@bellarmine.edu www.bellarmine.edu Rev. Clyde F. Crews; Rev. Isaac McDaniel; Susan Donovan, Pres.; John Stemmer, Librn.; Stds.: 2,978

***Spalding University** - 845 S. 3rd St., Louisville, KY 40203 t) 502-585-9911 ekrumhansl@spalding.edu www.spalding.edu Tori Murden McClure, Pres.; Stds.: 1,361; Lay Tchrs.: 52

CONVENTS, MONASTERIES, AND RESIDENCES FOR WOMEN [CON]

LOUISVILLE

Discalced Carmelite Nuns - 1907 Lauderdale Rd., Louisville, KY 40205 t) 812-841-6731 nreynolds@spsmw.org Sr. Nancy Reynolds, S.P., Prioress; Srs.: 5

The Sisters of Mercy of the Americas - 3112 Commander Dr., Louisville, KY 40220 t) 502-963-5473 c) 502-774-0839 pdiebold@sistersofmercy.org Sr. Paulanne Diebold, R.S.M., Contact; Srs.: 4

Ursuline Sisters of the Immaculate Conception - 3115 Lexington Rd., Louisville, KY 40206 t) (502) 515-7524 webmaster@ursulineslou.org www.ursulinesisterslouisville.org Jean Anne Zappa, Pres.; Srs.: 44

NAZARETH

Generalate, Motherhouse and Novitiate of the Sisters of Charity of Nazareth - 200 Nazareth Dr., Nazareth, KY 40048; Mailing: PO Box 172, Nazareth, KY 40048 t) 502-348-1555 (Center & Generalate); 502-348-1500 (Motherhouse) sangeeta@scnky.org www.nazareth.org Rev. Gary Young, C.R., Chap.; Sr. Sangeeta Ayithamattam, Pres.; Srs.: 474

NERINX

Motherhouse and Novitiate of the Sisters of Loretto at the Foot of the Cross - 515 Nerinx Rd., Nerinx, KY 40049 t) 270-865-5811 bnicholas@lorettocommunity.org www.lorettocommunity.org Sr. Barbara Nicholas, SL, Pres.; Srs.: 62

ST. CATHARINE

Dominican Sisters of Peace - 2645 Bardstown Rd., St. Catharine, KY 40061 t) 859-336-9303 barbara.sullivan@oppeace.org www.oppeace.org St. Catharine Motherhouse Sr. Barbara Sullivan, Mission Group Coord.; Srs.: 41

Sansbury Care Center, Inc. - 2625 Bardstown Rd., St.

Catharine, KY 40061 t) 859-336-3974 mfinnie@sansburycare.org Megan Finnie, Admin.; Srs.: 15

ENDOWMENTS / FOUNDATIONS / TRUSTS [EFT]

BARDSTOWN

Flaget Hospital Foundation, Inc. - 4305 New Shepherdsville Rd., Bardstown, KY 40004 t) 502-350-5058 foundation@flaget.com www.kentuckyonehealth.org Jennifer Nolan, Pres.;

LORETTO

Holy Cross Cemetery Trust, Inc. - 7945 Loretto Rd., Loretto, KY 40037 t) 502-348-5404 fballard@holycrosscemeterytrust.org Fabian Ballard, Dir.;

LOUISVILLE

***Catholic Education Foundation** - 401 W. Main St., Ste. 806, Louisville, KY 40202 t) 502-585-2747 gwentzel@ceflou.org www.ceflou.org Richard A. Lechleiter, Pres.;

Catholic Foundation of Louisville, Inc. - 3940 Poplar Level Rd., Louisville, KY 40213 t) 502-585-3291 bash@archlou.org Rev. Martin A. Linebach, Vicar; Brian B. Reynolds, Dir.;

***Center for Interfaith Relations** - 415 W. Muhammad Ali Blvd., Ste. 101, Louisville, KY 40202-2334 t) 502-583-3100 interfaithrelations@interfaithrelation.org interfaithrelations.org Sarah Riggs, Dir.;

***The St. Francis de Sales High School Foundation, Inc.** - 425 Kenwood Dr., Louisville, KY 40214 t) 502-368-6519 joshua.blandford@desaleshs.com Stephen James, Chair;

The Franciscan Foundation, Inc. - 400 W. Market St., Ste. 2000, WT&C Corp. Svcs. Inc., Louisville, KY 40202; Mailing: 1104 Kentucky Ave., San Antonio, TX 78201 c) 502-432-7993 secretary@francisfound.org www.francisfound.org Sr. Georgette Lehmuth, OSF, Pres.; Rev. Charles McCarthy, O.F.M.Conv., Vice Pres.; Friar Paul Gregory Schloemer, OFM Conv., Secy.; Paul Tillman, Treas.;

St. Patrick School Foundation, Inc. - 1000 N. Beckley Station Rd., Louisville, KY 40245 t) 502-244-7083 rmarkpage@aol.com www.stpatlou.org R. Mark Page, Pres.; Dave Naber, Bus. Mgr.;

Trinity High School Foundation, Inc. - 4011 Shelbyville Rd., Louisville, KY 40207 t) 502-736-2100 ths.foundation@thsrock.net Joe Landenwich, Chair;

Ursuline Sisters of Louisville Charitable Trust - 3115 Lexington Rd., Louisville, KY 40206 t) 502-515-7524 x3104 bphillips@ursulineslou.org Trust for Retired Religious Sr. Janet Marie Peterworth, Trustee;

NERINX

Sisters of Loretto Charitable Trust - 515 Nerinx Rd., Nerinx, KY 40049-9999 t) 270-865-5811 www.lorettocommunity.org Sr. Barbara Nicholas, SL, Pres.;

HOSPITALS / HEALTH SERVICES [HOS]

BARDSTOWN

Flaget Healthcare, Inc. (Catholic Health Initiatives) - 4305 New Shepherdsville Rd., Bardstown, KY 40004 t) 502-350-5000 www.chisaintjosephhealth.org/flaget Attended from St. Joseph Church. Jennifer Nolan, Pres.; Bed Capacity: 52; Asstd. Annu.: 20,309; Staff: 306

MISCELLANEOUS [MIS]

FRANKFORT

Catholic Conference of Kentucky - 1042 Burlington Ln., Frankfort, KY 40601 t) (502) 875-4345 cckstaff@ccky.org

LEBANON

The Laura - 220 Laura Ln., Lebanon, KY 40033 t) 270-692-1790 mheleneking@windstream.net Sr. Marilyn King, R.S.M., Dir.; Sr. Genevieve Durcan, O.C.S.O., In Res.; Sr. Mary Louise Yurik, R.S.M., In Res.;

LOUISVILLE

Archdiocesan Marian Committee - 639 S. Shelby St., Louisville, KY 40202 t) 502-582-2827 secretary@stmartinoftourschurch.org Dcn. Joseph D. Calvert, Dir.;

CHI Kentucky, Inc. - 1850 Bluegrass Ave., Louisville, KY 40215 t) 303-383-2746 peggymartin@commonspirit.org Sr. Peggy Martin, O.P., Senior Vice Pres.;

***Community Catholic Center, Inc.** - 3525 Rudd Ave., Louisville, KY 40212; Mailing: PO Box 11065, Louisville, KY 40251 t) 502-424-9398 www.communitycatholicenter.org Sarah Weatherwax, Dir.;

Franciscan Shelter House - 748 S. Preston St., Louisville, KY 40203 t) 502-589-0140 franciscankitchen@gmail.com franciscankitchen.org Heather Benjamin, Bus. Mgr.;

Saint Luke Center - 9400 Williamsburg Plaza, Ste. 300, Louisville, KY 40222-6016 t) 502-632-2471 slcadmin@sli.org www.stlukecenter.org Professional counseling center Dr. Emily Cash, Dir.;

Mass of the Air - 1200 S. Shelby St., Louisville, KY 40203 t) 502-893-5120 massoftheair@gmail.com Dcn. Mark J. Rougeux, Dir.;

Our Lady's Rosary Makers - 4611 Poplar Level Rd., Louisville, KY 40213; Mailing: P.O. Box 37080, Louisville, KY 40233 t) 502-968-1434 mikeford@olrm.org; info@olrm.com www.olrm.org Michael Ford, Pres.;

Perpetual Eucharistic Adoration - 3940 Poplar Level Rd., Louisville, KY 40213 t) 502-853-2915; 502-968-2933 lmclemore@archlou.org Rev. Gary T. Padgett, Admin.;

Publication: "The Record" - 1200 S. Shelby St., Maloney Center, Louisville, KY 40203-2600 t) 502-636-0296 record@archlou.org therecordnewspaper.org Official newspaper of the Archdiocese of Louisville (Weekly). Marnie McAllister, Editor;

Sacred Heart Schools, Inc. - 3177 Lexington Rd., Louisville, KY 40206 t) 502-896-3910 shs@shslou.org www.shslou.org Sponsored by Ursuline Sisters. Cynthia Crabtree, Pres.;

Secular Franciscan Order - Holy Trinity Region - 3111 Oriole Dr., Louisville, KY 40213 c) 502-541-2764 drjoeedwards@iglou.com Holy Trinity Regional Fraternity of the Secular Franciscan Order Joseph Francis Edwards, Pres.;

Ursuline Society and Academy of Education - 3115 Lexington Rd., Louisville, KY 40206 t) (502) 515-7524 webmaster@ursulineslou.org www.ursulinesisterslouisville.org Sr. Jean Anne Zappa, Pres.;

NAZARETH

Sisters of Charity of Nazareth, Inc. - 135 West Dr., Nazareth, KY 40048; Mailing: P.O. Box 187, Nazareth, KY 40048 t) 502-331-4072 Sr. Barbara Flores Sr., SCN, Prov.;

Nazareth Retreat Center - ; Mailing: P.O. Box 7, Nazareth, KY 40018

SPRINGFIELD

World Apostolate of Fatima (Blue Army) - 306 Fredericktown Rd., Springfield, KY 40069 t) 502-968-2933 mhardesty@archlou.org Rev. Matthew T. Hardesty, Dir.;

Sacred Heart Apostolate - 1225 S. Wilson Rd., Radcliff, KY 40160 t) 270-351-3706 church@stchristopherparish.org Rev. Jeffrey G. Hopper, Dir.;

MONASTERIES AND RESIDENCES FOR PRIESTS AND BROTHERS [MON]

LOUISVILLE

St. Francis of Assisi Friary - 2225 Lower Hunters Trace, Louisville, KY 40216 t) 502-447-5566 fran.voc@aol.com Brs.: 3; Priests: 3

St. Louis Bertrand Priory - 1104 S. Sixth St., Louisville, KY 40203 t) 502-583-4448 stlouisbertrand@stlb.org Rev. Bernard Timothy, O.P., Pst.; Priests: 5

Sacred Heart Retreat - 1924 Newburg Rd., Louisville, KY 40205 t) 502-451-2330 monzykcp@passionist.org www.passionist.org (Corporate Title: Congregation of the Passion, Sacred Heart Community) Rev. Justin Nelson, Pst.; Rev. John Patrick Day, Pastor, Diocese of Nashville; Rev. Febin Barose, Assoc. Pst.; Rev. Robert Weiss, C.P., Asst. Supr.; Rev. Chris Gibson, In Res.; Rev. Eric Meyer, C.P., In Res.; Rev. Joseph Mitchell, C.P., In Res.; Rev. Richard L. Parks, C.P., In Res.; Rev. Kenneth O'Malley, In Res.; Rev. Robert Crossmyer, C.P., In Res.; Bro. Vimal Backiyaraj, In Res.; Bro. Jerome Milazzo, C.P., In Res.; Bro. John Monzyk, C.P., Supr.; Bro. Kurt Wernert, C.P., Dir., Sr. Care; Bro. Kurt Newbold, In Res.;

TRAPPIST

Abbey of Our Lady of Gethsemani, of the Order of Cistercians of the Strict Observance - 3642 Monks Rd., Trappist, KY 40051 t) 502-549-3117 trappists@monks.org Rt. Rev. Elias Dietz, O.C.S.O., Abbot; Rev. Michael Casagram, O.C.S.O.; Rev. James Conner, O.C.S.O.; Rev. Alan Gilmore, O.C.S.O.; Rev. Joachim Johnson, O.C.S.O.; Rt. Rev. Timothy Kelly, O.C.S.O.; Rev. Andrew McAughan, O.C.S.O.; Rev. Carlos Rodriguez, O.C.S.O.; Rev. Anton Rusnak, O.C.S.O.; Rev. David Altman; Rev. Casimir Bernas; Rev. Raphael Hodari; Rev. Lawrence Morey; Rev. Peter Tong, O.C.S.O.; Brs.: 22; Priests: 14

NURSING / REHABILITATION / CONVALESCENCE / ELDERLY CARE [NUR]

LOUISVILLE

St. Joseph Home for the Aged (Little Sisters of the Poor) - 15 Audubon Plaza Dr., Louisville, KY 40217 t) 502-636-2300 adlouisville@littlesistersofthepoor.org www.littlesistersofthepoorlouisville.org Kelly Mahoney, Dir.; Asstd. Annu.: 80; Staff: 55

Nazareth Home, Inc. (Sisters of Charity of Nazareth) - 2000 Newburg Rd., Louisville, KY 40205 t) 502-459-9681 mbuckman@nazhome.org nazhome.org Mary Haynes, Pres.; Asstd. Annu.: 526; Staff: 248

PRESCHOOLS / CHILDCARE CENTERS [PRE]

LOUISVILLE

St. Joseph Catholic Orphan Society - 2823 Frankfort Ave., Louisville, KY 40206 t) 502-893-0241 gracea@sjkids.org; kathyo@sjkids.org www.sjkids.org Grace Akers, CEO; Stds.: 69; Lay Tchrs.: 5

St. Joseph Child Development Center - 2823 Frankfort Ave., Louisville, KY 40206 t) 502-893-0241 aprilm@sjkids.org www.sjkids.org April Manning, Dir.;

St. Joseph Children's Home - 2823 Frankfort Ave., Louisville, KY 40206 t) 502-893-0241 gracea@sjkids.org www.sjkids.org Grace Akers, Exec.; Stds.: 185; Lay Tchrs.: 40

Sacred Heart Preschool - 3105 Lexington Rd., Louisville, KY 40206 t) 502-896-3941 anikolich@shslou.org www.shslou.org Lisa Bell Houghlin, Dir.; Stds.: 251; Lay Tchrs.: 40

St. Thomas Orphan Society, Inc. - 3940 Poplar Level Rd., Louisville, KY 40213 t) 502-585-3291 pastoralcenter@archlou.org Brian B. Reynolds, Chancellor;

St. Vincent's Orphan Society, Inc. - 3940 Poplar Level Rd., Louisville, KY 40213 t) 502-585-3294 lmclemore@archlou.org archlou.org Brian B. Reynolds, Chancellor;

RETREAT HOUSES / RENEWAL CENTERS [RTR]

CRESTWOOD

Lake St. Joseph Center - 5800 Old LaGrange Rd., Crestwood, KY 40014 t) 502-241-4469 Sr. Martha Leis, Admin.;

LOUISVILLE

Catholic Charismatic Renewal - 1200 S. Shelby St., Maloney Center, Louisville, KY 40203 t) 502-636-0296 mlarison@archlou.org Maureen Larison, Contact;

Flaget Center - 1935 Lewiston Dr., Louisville, KY 40216 t) 502-448-8581 krobbins@archlou.org Kim Robbins,

Contact;

NERINX

Knobs Haven - 515 Nerinx Rd., Nerinx, KY 40049 t) 270-865-2621 knobshaven@lorettomotherhouse.org lorettoretreatcenters.com Jo Ann Gates, Dir.;

SPECIAL CARE FACILITIES [SPF]

LOUISVILLE

Boys & Girls Haven - 2301 Goldsmith Ln., Louisville, KY 40218 t) 502-458-1171 amasterson@boyshaven.org; vperronteau@boyshaven.org www.boysandgirlshaven.org For dependent, neglected, or abused boys, 12 to 23 years of age, and females, 17 to 23 years of age. Amanda Masterson, CEO; Bed Capacity: 46; Asstd. Annu.: 900; Staff: 75

Nazareth Home Clifton (Mercy Sacred Heart, Inc., Sisters of Mercy) - 2120 Payne St., Louisville, KY 40206 t) 502-895-9425 cjennings@nazhome.org Craig Jennings, CEO; Bed Capacity: 125; Asstd. Annu.: 478; Staff: 130

Sacred Heart Village I, Inc. - 2110 Payne St., Louisville, KY 40206 t) 502-895-6409 tsteiden@mercyhousing.org (Senior Housing Apartments) Bed Capacity: 55; Asstd. Annu.: 110; Staff: 9

***Sacred Heart Village II, Inc.** - 2108 Payne St., Louisville, KY 40206 t) 502-895-8085 tsteiden@mercyhousing.org (Senior Housing Apartments) Bed Capacity: 55; Asstd. Annu.: 110; Staff: 9

***Sacred Heart Village III, Inc.** - 3101 Wayside Dr., Louisville, KY 40216 t) 502-776-5004 tsteiden@mercyhousing.org (Senior Housing Apartments) Bed Capacity: 55; Asstd. Annu.: 109; Staff: 9

An asterisk (*) denotes an organization that has established tax-exempt status directly with the IRS and is not covered by the USCCB Group Ruling.

Diocese of Lubbock

MOST REVEREND ROBERT M. COERVER

Bishop of Lubbock; ordained June 27, 1980; appointed Third Bishop of Lubbock September 27, 2016; installed Nov. 21, 2016. Res.: 3505 37th St., Lubbock, TX 79413. Office: The Catholic Pastoral Center, 4620 4th St., Lubbock, TX 79416. F: 806-792-2953; rcoerver@catholiclubbock.org.

The Catholic Pastoral Center: 4620 4th St., Lubbock, TX 79416. T: 806-792-3943; F: 806-792-8109.
www.catholiclubbock.org
lflores@catholiclubbock.org

ESTABLISHED AND CREATED A DIOCESE, JUNE 17, 1983.

Square Miles 23,382.

Comprises the Counties of Bailey, Lamb, Hale, Floyd, Motley, Cottle, Cochran, Hockley, Lubbock, Crosby, Dickens, King, Yoakum, Terry, Lynn, Garza, Kent, Stonewall, Haskell, Gaines, Dawson, Borden, Scurry, Fisher and Jones.

Legal Title: Roman Catholic Diocese of Lubbock.

STATISTICAL OVERVIEW

Personnel
Bishop 1
Retired Bishops 1
Priests: Diocesan Active in Diocese 27
Priests: Diocesan Active Outside Diocese 2
Priests: Retired, Sick or Absent 16
Number of Diocesan Priests 45
Religious Priests in Diocese 14
Total Priests in your Diocese 59
Extern Priests in Diocese 1
Permanent Deacons in Diocese 73
Total Sisters 21

Parishes
Parishes 61
With Resident Pastor:
Resident Diocesan Priests 29
Resident Religious Priests 9
Without Resident Pastor:
Administered by Priests 20
Administered by Deacons 3
Pastoral Centers 1

Professional Ministry Personnel:
Sisters 21
Lay Ministers 55

Welfare
Catholic Hospitals 2
Total Assisted 617,211
Health Care Centers 8
Total Assisted 62,378
Homes for the Aged 2
Total Assisted 52,000
Day Care Centers 2
Total Assisted 196

Educational
Seminaries, Diocesan 1
Students from This Diocese 2
Diocesan Students in Other Seminaries 4
Total Seminarians 6
High Schools, Diocesan and Parish 1
Total Students 70
Elementary Schools, Diocesan and Parish 1
Total Students 238

Catechesis / Religious Education:
High School Students 1,872
Elementary Students 3,103
Total Students under Catholic Instruction 5,289
Teachers in Diocese:
Sisters 2
Lay Teachers 36

Vital Statistics
Receptions into the Church:
Infant Baptism Totals 275
First Communions 322
Confirmations 374
Marriages:
Catholic 45
Total Marriages 45
Deaths 208
Total Catholic Population 138,800
Total Population 532,275

LEADERSHIP

The Catholic Pastoral Center - t) 806-792-3943 www.catholiclubbock.org Most Rev. Robert M. Coerver, Bishop of Lubbock; Rev. Msgr. David Cruz, Chancellor (stjohnbaptistlbk@gmail.com); Dcn. Adrian Jimenez, Chancellor;
Chancellor - t) 806-792-3943 x238 www.catholiclubbock.org Dcn. Adrian Jimenez, Chancellor; Judy Leos Rodriguez, Exec.;
Moderator of the Curia - www.catholiclubbock.org Most Rev. Robert M. Coerver;
Bishop/Chancellor's Executive Assistant - www.catholiclubbock.org Most Rev. Robert M. Coerver, Contact; Judy Leos Rodriguez, Exec.;
Diocesan Tribunal - t) 806-792-3943 www.catholiclubbock.org Rita Ortiz, Dir.; Elizabeth O'Balle, Tribunal Assessor & Auditor (elizabeth@catholiclubbock.org);
Officialis - www.catholiclubbock.org Rev. Msgr. David Cruz, Chancellor (stjohnbaptistlbk@gmail.com);
Tribunal Director - www.catholiclubbock.org Rita Ortiz, Tribunal Dir.; Elizabeth O'Balle, Tribunal Assessor & Auditor (elizabeth@catholiclubbock.org); Belinda L. Aguirre, Immigration/Safe Environment;
Promoter of Justice - Rev. Msgr. David Cruz (stjohnbaptistlbk@gmail.com);
Defender of the Bond - www.catholiclubbock.org Rev. William J. Anton (wjanton@gmail.com);
Defender of the Bond-Appeal - Rev. William J. Anton (wjanton@gmail.com);
Notaries - Rita Ortiz; Judy Leos Rodriguez; Belinda L. Aguirre;
Presbyteral Council - www.catholiclubbock.org Most Rev. Robert M. Coerver; Rev. Msgr. David Cruz, Chancellor (stjohnbaptistlbk@gmail.com); Very Rev. Jose Matthew Kochuparambil, Vicar;
Priests Personnel Board - www.catholiclubbock.org Most Rev. Robert M. Coerver; Rev. Msgr. David Cruz, Chancellor (stjohnbaptistlbk@gmail.com); Very Rev. Jose M Kochuparambil (jkochuparambil@catholiclubbock.org);
Vicar General - www.catholiclubbock.org Rev. Msgr. David Cruz, Vicar (stjohnbaptistlbk@gmail.com); Judy Leos Rodriguez;
Vicar of Priests - www.catholiclubbock.org Rev. William J. Anton (wjanton@gmail.com);
Vicar of Retired Priests - www.catholiclubbock.org Rev. William J. Anton (wjanton@gmail.com);
Vicars Forane - www.catholiclubbock.org Rev. James McCartney, Vicar (mccartneyjim27@yahoo.com); Rev. Selva Nayagam, H.G.N., Snyder Deanery; Rev. George Poonely, Plainview Deanery (georgepoonely@gmail.com);

OFFICES AND DIRECTORS

Campus Ministry - t) 806-762-5225 Peggy Klein, Dir.;
Catholic Campaign for Human Development - Dcn. Robert Hogan;
Catholic Charities, Diocese of Lubbock, Inc. - t) 806-765-8475 Cynthia Quintanilla, Dir.;
Cursillo Movement - www.catholiclubbock.org Rev. Ernesto Lopez (priestosky@hotmail.com);
Diocesan Attorney - www.catholiclubbock.org Victor Wanjura;
Diocesan Building Commission - Dcn. Martin Miranda; Ray Arias; Lyle Fetterly;
Diocesan Council of Catholic Women - Angie Cervantez, Pres.;
Diocesan Pastoral Liturgy Commission - Most Rev. Robert M. Coerver; Dcn. Juan Cavazos, Chair;
Diocesan Rural Life Office - Doug Hlavaty;
Director of Communications - www.catholiclubbock.org Lucas Flores;
Director of the Permanent Diaconate - t) 806-792-3943 www.catholiclubbock.org Dcn. Juan Cavazos;
Director of Vocations - Rev. Jeremy Trull (jtrull17@yahoo.com);
Director of Youth - www.catholiclubbock.org Peggy Klein, Dir.;
Evangelization & Family Faith Formation - t) 806-792-3943 Sr. Peggy Szeljack, C.V.;
Facilities Director - t) 806-792-3943 www.catholiclubbock.org Dcn. Martin Miranda, Dir.;
Finance Office - t) 806-797-3943 www.catholiclubbock.org B. Marty Martin, CFO;
Newspaper - t) 806-792-3943 Lucas Flores, Editor;
Office of Stewardship & Development - t) 806-792-3943 Kathreena Thompson, Dir. (kthompson@catholiclubbock.org);
Priests' Pension Board - www.catholiclubbock.org Most Rev. Robert M. Coerver; B. Marty Martin, CFO; Rev. Jacob Jacob Powell, Pst. (fatherjpowell@gmail.com);
Superintendent of Schools - www.catholiclubbock.org Christine Wanjura;
Victim Assistance Coordinator - t) 806-543-9178 www.catholiclubbock.org Oscar Reyes, Victim's Assistance Coord.; Belinda L. Aguirre, Safe Environment;

PARISHES, MISSIONS, AND CLERGY

STATE OF TEXAS

ABERNATHY

St. Isidore - 17813 N. I-27, Abernathy, TX 79311 t) 806-298-4278 fr.brianwood@yahoo.com; st.isidoreabernathy@gmail.com Rev. Brian Wood, Pst.; Manuel & Rita Prieto, DRE; Gloria Garibay, DRE; CRP Stds.: 40

ANSON

St. Michaels Church Anson - 2010 County Rd. 477, Anson, TX 79501 t) 325-823-2777 Rev. Arockia dhass Jeganathan, HGN; Rev. Alexander Amburose, HGN;
Holy Trinity - 1400 N. Hwy. 83, Hamlin, TX 79520

BROWNFIELD

St. Anthony's - 1902 Levelland Hwy., Brownfield, TX 79316; Mailing: P.O. Box 671, Brownfield, TX 79316 t) (806) 637-6626; 806-637-6626 saintanthonycatholicchurch@yahoo.com stanthonybrownfield.org Rev. John M. Ohlig, Pst.; Dcn. George Holguin; Dcn. Israel Limon Jr.; Dcn. Martin Miranda; CRP Stds.: 150
San Francisco de Asis - ; Mailing: P.O. Box 92, Ropesville, TX 79358

DENVER CITY

St. William - 401 Mustang Ave., Denver City, TX 79323-2749 t) 806-592-2063 stwilliamcc@gmail.com Rev. Heriberto Mercado, Pst.; Dcn. Angel Hernandez, DRE;
Sacred Heart - 1305 11th St., Plains, TX 79355 t) 806-456-7002

FLOYDADA

St. Mary Magdalen - 309 S. Wall, Floydada, TX 79235 t) 806-983-5878; 806-983-3496 Rev. Joseph Kurumbel, O.S.B.;
Our Lady of Guadalupe - 701 Bundy St., Matador, TX 79244 t) (806) 790-4212 www.catholiclubbock.org Rev. Renato Cruz, Pst.;
St. Elizabeth - Second St. & Clare St., Paducah, TX 79348 t) (806) 790-4212 www.catholiclubbock.org Rev. Renato Cruz, Pst.;
San Jose de Calasanz - 303 S.E. Fourth, Lockney, TX 79241 t) 806-652-2321 www.catholiclubbock.org Rev. Sylvester Dsouza;

IDALOU

St. Philip Benizi - 8002 E. Hwy. 62/82, Idalou, TX 79329 t) 806-892-2928 www.catholiclubbock.org Rev. Rene Perez, Pst.; Dcn. Steve Padilla; CRP Stds.: 50
San Lorenzo - 508 5th St., Lorenzo, TX 79343; Mailing: P.O. Box 129, Lorenzo, TX 79343 t) (806) 893-2928

LAMESA

St. Margaret Mary - 908 S. 2nd St., Lamesa, TX 79331 t) 806-872-7100 stmmolg@yahoo.com Rev. Chacko Thadathil, Pst.; Maria Casillas, DRE; Sara Del Busto, DRE; CRP Stds.: 124
Our Lady of Guadalupe - 407 N. Hartford, Lamesa, TX 79331; Mailing: P.O. Box 599, Lamesa, TX 79331 www.catholiclubbock.org

LEVELLAND

St. Michael's - 319 E. Washington St., Levelland, TX 79336-2611 t) 806-894-2268 stmichaellevelland@gmail.com stmichaellevelland.org Rev. Jonathan Phillips, Pst.; Dcn. Jesse Moreno; Dcn. Sergio Vidales; Dcn. Frankie Ruiz;

LITTLEFIELD

Sacred Heart - 1309 W. 8th St., Littlefield, TX 79339-4234; Mailing: P.O. Box 1347, Littlefield, TX 79339-4234 t) 806-385-6043 sacheart@windstream.net sacredheartlittlefield.org Rev. Angelo R. Consemino, Pst.;

LUBBOCK

Cathedral Christ the King - 4011 54th St., Lubbock, TX 79413-4699 t) 806-792-6168 www.ctkcathedral.org Very Rev. Jose Matthew Kochuparambil, Rector; CRP Stds.: 236
Christ the King Cathedral School - (Grades PreK-12) t) 806-795-8283 cwanjura@ctkcathedralschool.org; achaloupka@ctkcathedralschool.org www.ctkcathedralschool.org Christine Wanjura, Supt.; Alicea Chaloupka, Prin.; Stds.: 225; Sr. Tchrs.: 1; Lay Tchrs.: 29
Early Childhood Development Center - 5502 Nashville, Lubbock, TX 79413 t) 806-771-2077 ecdcchristtheking@gmail.com Katie Huey, Dir.;
St. Elizabeth University Parish - 2305 Main St., Lubbock, TX 79401 t) 806-762-5225 x7294; 806-762-5225 x7304 (CRP) stelubbock@gmail.com www.stelizabethlubbock.com Rev. John Restrepo, OP, Pst.; Rev. Emiliano Zapata, OP, Pst.; Dcn. Jeffrey J. Church; Dcn. Waldo Martinez; Dcn. Richard McCann; Dcn. Alex Toralba; Rev. Robert U. Perry, O.P., In Res.; Rev. R.B. Williams, O.P., In Res.; Sr. Sylvia Salvan, M.S.L.T., DRE; Kassidy Allen, Dir.; Kevin Mantooth, Campus Min.; CRP Stds.: 83
Holy Spirit - 9821 Frankford Ave., Lubbock, TX 79424 t) 806-698-6400 parish@holyspiritlubbock.org www.holyspiritcathparish.org Rev. Wesley Beal, Pst.; Dcn. Robert Hogan; Dcn. Mick Irving; Dcn. Brad Brooks; Mary Ellen Doskocill, DRE; CRP Stds.: 471
St. John Neumann - 5802 22nd, Lubbock, TX 79407-1721 t) 806-799-2649 stjneumann79@gmail.com www.sjnlubbock.org/ Rev. James McCartney, Pst.; Dcn. Kyle Broderson; Dcn. Ed Sears; Dcn. Victor Guzman Jr.;
St. John the Baptist Catholic Church - 10805 Indiana Ave., Lubbock, TX 79423; Mailing: 3410 98th St., Ste. 4-363, Lubbock, TX 79423 t) 806-771-2673 stjohnbaptistlbk@gmail.com www.stjohnbaptistlbk.org Rev. Msgr. David Cruz, Pst.; Dcn. Severo Alvarado; RoseMary Cardenas, Bus. Mgr.; CRP Stds.: 165
St. Joseph's - 102 N. Ave. P, Lubbock, TX 79401-1199 t) 806-317-1309; 806-763-9695 (CRP) stjosephchurchlbk@gmail.com Rev. Raymundo Manriquez, Pst.; Dcn. Jesse Cantu; Dcn. Santos Chavez Jr.; CRP Stds.: 261
Our Lady of Grace - 3111 Erskine St., Lubbock, TX 79415 t) 806-763-4156 ourladyofgrace@yahoo.com olgracelubbock.org Rev. Rudolf Crasta, Pst.; Dcn. Ted Hernandez; Dcn. Ernest Hernandez; Dcn. Manuel R. Lopez Jr.; Dcn. Joe Morin; Dcn. Daniel Romo; Melinda Garcia, RCIA Coord.; Karen Macha, Admin.; CRP Stds.: 85
Our Lady of Guadalupe - 1120 52nd St., Lubbock, TX 79412 t) 806-763-0710 jmora@lubbockolg.org; info@lubbockolg.org www.lubbockolg.org Rev. Martin Pina, Pst.; Dcn. Isaac Aguilar; Dcn. Robert Cardona; Dcn. Joe Martinez; Dcn. Isaac McDonald; Dcn. Jose Mora; Dcn. Gregg Morgan;
St. Patrick - 1603 Cherry Ave., Lubbock, TX

79403-6001 t) 806-765-5123 saintpatrickchurch@yahoo.com Rev. Joseph Thanavelil, Pst.; CRP Stds.: 31

San Ramon - 15706 Loop 493, Lubbock, TX 79423 t) 806-863-2201 Dcn. Ron Vowels; Rev. Msgr. Timothy Schwertner, Pst.; CRP Stds.: 42

St. Francis of Assisi - ; Mailing: P.O. Box 785, Wolfforth, TX 79382 t) 806-866-9007

St. Theresa's - 2202 Upland Ave., Lubbock, TX 79407 c) (806) 292-5288 www.sttheresalubb.com Rev. Nahum Lopez, Pst.; Dcn. Pedro Juarez; Dcn. Jose Luis Rodriguez;

MORTON

St. Ann - 105 N.E. 8th St., Morton, TX 79346 t) 806-266-8693 stannchurchmorton@gmail.com Rev. Robert Williams, Sacr. Min.;

St. Philip Neri - Farm Rd. 303, Pep, TX 79353; Mailing: P.O. Box 395, Pep, TX 79353 t) 806-933-4355 Marcy Demel, Contact;

MULESHOE

Immaculate Conception - 805 E. Hickory Ave., Muleshoe, TX 79347 t) 806-272-4384; 806-272-4167 (CRP) iccmuleshoe@gmail.com Rev. Leonardo Pahamtang (Philippines), Pst.; Patsy Garcia, DRE; Alma Orozco, DRE;

St. Mary Magdalen - 806 E. Hwy. 70, Earth, TX 79031 t) (806) 272-4384 www.catholiclubbock.org Rev. Heriberto Mercado, Pst.;

O'DONNELL

St. Pius X - 3025 CR.P, O'Donnell, TX 79351 t) 806-428-3224 www.catholiclubbock.org Rev. John Stephen Rathinam, I.M.S., Pst.;

St. Jude Thaddeus Catholic Church - 1829 S. 4th St., Tahoka, TX 79373 c) (806) 241-0086

OLTON

St. Peter the Apostle - 206 E. 11th St., Olton, TX 79064-0655; Mailing: P.O. Box 655, Olton, TX 79064-0655 saintpeterolton@gmail.com Rev. George Poonely; Dcn. Natividad Santoval, Admin.;

PLAINVIEW

St. Alice - 1114 Houston St., Plainview, TX 79072-7124 t) 806-293-2891 staliceplainview@gmail.com Rev. George Poonely;

Our Lady of Guadalupe - 211 W. 7th St., Plainview, TX 79072; Mailing: PO Box 1269, Plainview, TX 79073 c) (806) 281-7247 wjanton@gmail.com www.catholiclubbock.org Rev. William John Anton; Dcn. Arturo Hinojosa; Dcn. Ruben Moran; Dcn. Jaime Salinas; Maribel DeLaRosa, Youth Min.; Sheila Ramirez, DRE; CRP Stds.: 115

Sacred Heart - 2801 N. Columbia, Plainview, TX 79072; Mailing: 400 W. 29th St., Plainview, TX 79072 c) (806) 782-4410; (806) 445-7105 shplainview@gmail.com www.catholiclubbock.org Rev. George Poonely, Pst.; Rev. Angelo R. Consemino; CRP Stds.: 175

St. Theresa - 504 E. 13th St., Hale Center, TX 79041; Mailing: P.O. Box 528, Hale Center, TX 79041 t) 806-839-2892; 806-292-5592 (CRP)

POST

Holy Cross - 205 Main St., Post, TX 79356; Mailing: Box 190, Post, TX 79356-0190 t) 806-990-9130 holycrosscatholicchurch6@gmail.com Rev. Jacob Jacob Powell, Pst.; Dcn. Adam V. Behnke;

Blessed Sacrament - 15th & Culpepper, Wilson, TX 79356 c) (806) 773-8889 www.catholiclubbock.org Debbie Hernadez, DRE;

RALLS

St. Michael - 1210 4th St., Ralls, TX 79357-0906; Mailing: P.O. Box 906, Ralls, TX 79357-0906 t) 806-253-2008 Rev. Samuel B. Oracion, Pst.; Virginia Torres, DRE;

St. Joseph - 115 W Fir, Crosbyton, TX 79322 c) (806) 224-5806 www.catholiclubbock.org Rev. Jeganathan Arulsamy, HGN, Pst.;

ROTAN

St. Joseph - 303 E. Lee, Rotan, TX 79546-3011 t) 325-267-6413; 325-267-6412; 325-735-3517 (CRP) stjosephrotan@yahoo.com Rev. Santhiago Selvaraj, HGN, Pst.; Dcn. Valentin Morin, Youth Min.;

Sacred Heart - 1146 FM Rd. 3339, Ranchito, TX 79520 t) (325) 257-6413 www.catholiclubbock.org

St. Mary - 510 Swenson Ave., Aspermont, TX 79546 t) (325) 267-6413 www.catholiclubbock.org

SEMINOLE

St. James - 1010 Hobbs Hwy., Seminole, TX 79360; Mailing: P.O. Box 898, Seminole, TX 79360-0898 t) 432-758-2371; 432-847-9493 (CRP); 432-238-3478 (CRP) stjamescatholic@sbcglobal.net; gomez_lucinda@att.net Rev. Jose de Dios Gonzalez, Pst.;

St. Paul's - 805 12th St., Seagraves, TX 79359 Cindy M Davila, Contact;

SHALLOWATER

St. Philip Benizi - 1314 6th St., Shallowater, TX 79363 t) 806-832-4088 Rev. Ernesto Lopez, Pst.;

St. Anthony of Padua - 4th S. Lawrence, Anton, TX 79313; Mailing: Box 545, Anton, TX 79313 t) (806) 832-4088 www.catholiclubbock.org Dcn. Frank Lopez;

SLATON

St. Joseph's - 205 S. 19th St., Slaton, TX 79364-3755 t) (806) 828-3644 c) (806) 300-1520 sjcslaton@gmail.com www.catholiclubbock.org Rev. Jacob P. Puthuparambil, O.S.B. (India), Pst.;

St. Joseph's School - (Grades PreK-8) 1305 W. Division St., Slaton, TX 79364 t) 806-828-6761 Sr. Brenda Haynes, S.N.D., Prin.;

Our Lady of Guadalupe - 705 S. Fourth, Slaton, TX 79364-5406 c) (806) 300-1520 olgslaton@yahoo.com www.catholiclubbock.org Rev. Jacob P. Puthuparambil, O.S.B. (India); Dcn. Phillip Maldonado;

SNYDER

St. Elizabeth's - 3005 Ave. A, Snyder, TX 79549-3909 t) 325-573-8824 snyderstelizabeth@gmail.com Rev. Msgr. Arsenio C. Redulla, Pst.;

St. John - 4125 County Rd., Hermleigh, TX 79526; Mailing: 3005 Ave. A, Snyder, TX 79549 Rev. Msgr. Arsenio C. Redulla, Pst.;

Our Lady of Guadalupe - 1311 Ave. K, Snyder, TX 79549-9533 t) 325-573-3866 (Office); 325-573-1569 (Res.); 325-574-1022 (CRP) ologsny@sbcglobal.net Rev. Raj Arokiasamy, Pst.; Irma Guerero, DRE;

SPUR

St. Mary - 402 E. 6th St., Spur, TX 79370; Mailing: Box 189, Spur, TX 79370-0189 t) 806-271-4830 Rev. Jeganathan Arulsamy, HGN, Pst.; Dcn. Eddie Morales;

Epiphany -

STAMFORD

St. Ann - 104 New Braunfels, Stamford, TX 79553-6415 t) 325-773-2659 stannschurch1@gmail.com Rev. Arockia dhass Jeganathan, HGN, Pst.;

St. George - 901 N. 16th St., Haskell, TX 79521-3340 t) 940-864-3171

WOLFFORTH

St. Francis of Assisi Mission - 8202 CR 7700, Wolfforth, TX 79382 t) (806) 866-9007 See San Ramon, Woodrow for details. Rev. Nahum Lopez, Pst.;

INSTITUTIONS LOCATED IN DIOCESE

CONVENTS, MONASTERIES, AND RESIDENCES FOR WOMEN [CON]

LUBBOCK

Our Lady of Grace Convent - 3101 Erskine, Lubbock, TX 79415; Mailing: 3111 Erskine St., Lubbock, TX 79415-1623 t) 806-747-7472 ourladyofgrace@yahoo.com www.catholiclubbock.org Sr. Antonieta Salazar, Rel. Ord. Ldr.; Srs.: 1

WOLFFORTH

St. Francis Mission Community - Our Lady of the Angels Motherhouse, 8202 CR 7700, Wolfforth, TX 79382 t) 806-863-4904 franciscan@erfwireless.net Sr. Martha Jane Venhaus, OSF, Prov.; Srs.: 14

ENDOWMENTS / FOUNDATIONS / TRUSTS [EFT]

LUBBOCK

Catholic Foundation of the South Plains - 4620 4th St., Lubbock, TX 79416; Mailing: P.O. Box 64845, Lubbock, TX 79464 c) 806-777-2089 tvowels@catholicfoundationlubbock.org www.catholicfoundationlubbock.org Tricia Vowels, Dir.;

Christ the King Diocesan Schools Foundation - 4011 54th St., Lubbock, TX 79413 t) 806-795-8283 cduran@ctkcathedralschool.org; cwanjura@ctkcathedralschool.org www.ctkcathedralschool.org Christine Wanjura, Supt.;

MONASTERIES AND RESIDENCES FOR PRIESTS AND BROTHERS [MON]

LUBBOCK

Southern Dominican Fathers of Lubbock - 2305 Main St., Lubbock, TX 79401 t) 806-762-5225 x7343 stelubbock@gmail.com Rev. Robert U. Perry, O.P., Mem.; Rev. R.B. Williams, O.P., Mem.; Rev. Emiliano Zapata, OP, Mem.; Rev. Carl Paustian, O.P., Mem.; Priests: 5

RETREAT HOUSES / RENEWAL CENTERS [RTR]

LUBBOCK

Catholic Renewal Center - 4620 4th St., Lubbock, TX 79416 t) 806-792-3943 x228 mmiranda@catholiclubbock.org www.dioceseoflubbock.org Dcn. Martin Miranda, Dir.;

Office for Cursillo Movement - ; Mailing: P.O. Box 98303, Lubbock, TX 79499-8296 t) 806-792-4308 Dcn. Joe Morin;

SLATON

Our Lady of Mercy Retreat Center - 605 S. 19th St., Slaton, TX 79364-0744; Mailing: PO Box 744, Slaton, TX 79364 t) 806-828-6428 mercyslaton@gmail.com mercyrc.com Rev. Msgr. Joseph W. James; Mark Meurer, Dir.;

Diocese of Madison

(Dioecesis Madisonensis)

MOST REVEREND DONALD J. HYING

Bishop of Madison; ordained Priest May 20, 1989; appointed Auxiliary Bishop of Milwaukee and Titular Bishop of Regiae May 26, 2011; ordained Bishop July 20, 2011; appointed Bishop of Gary November 24, 2014; installed January 6, 2015; appointed Bishop of Madison April 25, 2019; installed June 25, 2019. Chancery: Holy Name Heights, 702 S. High Point Rd., Ste. 225, Madison, WI 53719.

Chancery: Holy Name Heights, 702 S. High Point Rd., Ste. 225, Madison, WI 53719. T: 608-821-3000; F: 608-440-2809.
www.madisondiocese.org
diocese@madisondiocese.org

ESTABLISHED 1946.

Square Miles 8,002.

Corporate Title: "Roman Catholic Diocese of Madison, Inc."

Comprises the Counties of Columbia, Dane, Grant, Green, Green Lake, Iowa, Jefferson, Lafayette, Marquette, Rock and Sauk in the State of Wisconsin.

For legal titles of parishes and diocesan institutions, consult the Chancery.

STATISTICAL OVERVIEW

Personnel

Bishop....1
Priests: Diocesan Active in Diocese....75
Priests: Diocesan Active Outside Diocese....8
Priests: Retired, Sick or Absent....46
Number of Diocesan Priests....129
Religious Priests in Diocese....9
Total Priests in your Diocese....138
Extern Priests in Diocese....18
Ordinations:
Diocesan Priests....1
Transitional Deacons....2
Permanent Deacons....2
Permanent Deacons in Diocese....29
Total Brothers....5
Total Sisters....263

Parishes

Parishes....102
With Resident Pastor:
Resident Diocesan Priests....101
Resident Religious Priests....1
Missions....1
Pastoral Centers....2
Professional Ministry Personnel:
Brothers....4
Sisters....4
Lay Ministers....238

Welfare

Catholic Hospitals....4
Total Assisted....576,375
Health Care Centers....2
Total Assisted....2,814
Homes for the Aged....12
Total Assisted....545
Day Care Centers....20
Total Assisted....682
Specialized Homes....1
Total Assisted....160
Special Centers for Social Services....15
Total Assisted....15,735
Residential Care of Disabled....64
Total Assisted....472
Other Institutions....4
Total Assisted....16,198

Educational

Diocesan Students in Other Seminaries....19
Total Seminarians....19
Colleges and Universities....1
Total Students....1,907
High Schools, Private....3
Total Students....709
Elementary Schools, Diocesan and Parish....39
Total Students....6,008
Elementary Schools, Private....3
Total Students....537
Catechesis/Religious Education:
High School Students....2,440
Elementary Students....6,620
Total Students under Catholic Instruction....18,240
Teachers in Diocese:
Sisters....4
Lay Teachers....613

Vital Statistics

Receptions into the Church:
Infant Baptism Totals....1,572
Minor Baptism Totals....89
Adult Baptism Totals....72
Received into Full Communion....198
First Communions....1,783
Confirmations....1,646
Marriages:
Catholic....231
Interfaith....101
Total Marriages....332
Deaths....1,517
Total Catholic Population....145,089
Total Population....1,122,750

LEADERSHIP

Office of the Bishop - t) 608-821-3002 officeofbishop@madisondiocese.org Most Rev. Donald J. Hying; Rev. Gregory S. Ihm, Master of Ceremonies to the Bishop; Paul Merline, Exec. Dir. Devel.;
Vicar General - t) 608-821-3015 vicargeneral@madisondiocese.org Rev. Msgr. James R. Bartylla;
Chancellor - t) 608-821-3061 Timothy J. Cavanaugh;
Vice Chancellor - Michael Wick, Vice Chancellor/Chief of Staff;

OFFICES AND DIRECTORS

Apostolate for Persons with Disabilities - t) 608-821-3050 apd@madisondiocese.org Megan Wedwick, Assoc. Dir. (megan.wedwick@madisondiocese.org); Rev. Msgr. Lawrence M. Bakke, Dir.;
Apostolate to the Deaf (Vacant) -
Archives - t) (608) 440-2811 Timothy J. Cavanaugh;
Building Commission - t) 608-821-3010 madisondiocese.org/real-estate Lang Paul, Chair (Paul.Lang@madisondiocese.org);
Holy Name Heights (Catholic Pastoral Center) - t) 608-821-3000 Tom Bartoszek, Admin.;
Catholic Schools - t) 608-821-3180 Michael Lancaster, Supt.; Therese Milbrath, Asst. Supt.;
Cemeteries - t) 608-238-5561 Damian Lenshek, Dir.;
Chief Development Officer - Paul Merline, Dir.;
Communications - t) 608-821-3033 communication@madisondiocese.org Brent King, Dir.;
Continuing Formation of Priests - t) 608-821-3006 Rev. Scott M. Jablonski, Dir.;
Evangelization and Catechesis - t) 608-821-3160 Michelle Nilsson, Assoc. Dir.; Marie Lins, Assoc. Coord.;
Finance - t) 608-821-3021 Maggie Opichka, CFO;
Hispanic Ministry - t) 608-821-3139 lorianne.aubut@madisondiocese.org Lorianne Aubut, Dir.;
Human Life and Dignity - t) (608) 821-3021 Dr. Christopher McAtee, Dir.;
Human Resources - t) 608-821-3024 Adam Markert, Dir.;
Permanent Deacons - t) 608-821-3083 Dcn. Christopher Schmelzer, Dir.;
Rural Life Ministry - t) 608-438-7154 Tom Nelson, Dir.;
Safe Environment - t) 608-821-3133 ose@madisondiocese.org Anna Delaney, Dir.;
Stewardship and Development - t) 608-821-3039 Jill McNally, Dir.;
Tribunal - t) 608-821-3060 tribunal@madisondiocese.org

- **Judicial Vicar** - Very Rev. Gabriel A. Lopez-Betanzos;
- **Judges** - Very Rev. Gabriel A. Lopez-Betanzos; Rev. Scott J. Emerson; Katherine Beall;
- **Promoter of Justice** - Timothy J. Cavanaugh;
- **Defender of the Bond** - Timothy J. Cavanaugh;
- **Advocate/Procurator (cc.1481-1490)** - Jenna M. Cooper; Vincent M. Gardiner; Aldean B. Hendrickson;
- **Notaries** - Mary Kate DeBroux; Rebecca Fischer; Nate Simmons;

Vicar for Priests - t) 608-821-5121 Rev. Msgr. James L. Gunn, Dir.;
Vicar for Religious - t) 608-821-3015 Rev. Msgr. James R. Bartylla; Rebecca Fischer, Contact;
Victim Assistance Coordinator - t) 608-821-3162 CJ Grahn;
Vocations - t) 800-833-8452 Rev. Jared J. Holzhuter, Dir. (jaredholzhuter@gmail.com); Lorie Ballweg, Contact;
Worship - t) 608-821-3080 Rev. Gregory S. Ihm, Dir.; John Sittard, Liturgy Dir.;

ADVISORY BOARDS, COMMISSIONS, COMMITTEES, AND COUNCILS

Diocese of Madison Clergy Health and Welfare Trust Fund - t) 608-821-3000 Rev. Msgr. James R. Bartylla; Timothy J. Cavanaugh; Maggie Opichka;
Finance Council - t) 608-821-3000 Rev. Msgr. James R. Bartylla; Maggie Opichka, Contact;
Priest Personnel Board - t) 608-821-3015 Rev. Msgr. James R. Bartylla, Chair; Rebecca Fischer, Contact;
Saint Raphael Society Clergy Retirement Plan of the Diocese of Madison - t) 608-821-3000 Most Rev. Donald J. Hying, Ex Officio; Rev. Msgr. James R. Bartylla, Ex Officio; Maggie Opichka, Authorized Plan Rep.;

CATHOLIC CHARITIES

Catholic Charities - t) 608-826-8000 Shawn Carney, Exec. Dir.;
Catholic Multicultural Center - t) 608-661-3512 Steve Maurice, Dir.;

- **Centro Pastoral Guadalupano** - Steve Maurice, Coord.;
- **St. Martin House** - Steve Maurice, Coord.;

CONSULTATIVE BODIES

College of Consultors - t) 608-821-3015 Rev. Msgr. James R. Bartylla; Rebecca Fischer, Contact;
Diocesan Ethicist - t) 608-821-3000 Rev. Joseph Baker;
Presbyteral Council - t) 608-821-3015 Rev. Msgr. James R. Bartylla; Rebecca Fischer, Contact;
Vicariates Forane - t) 608-821-3015 Rev. Msgr. James R. Bartylla; Rebecca Fischer, Contact;

ORGANIZATIONS

Camp Gray - t) 608-356-8200 bigfun@campgray.com Jeff Hoeben, Exec. Dir.;
Catholic Committee on Scouting - t) 608-275-3344 stephen.brunner@madisondiocese.org Aaron Teche, Chair; Rev. Stephen Brunner, Chap.;
Catholic Herald - t) 608-821-3070 Kevin Wondrash, Editor;
Council of Catholic Women - Rev. Msgr. Duane R. Moellenberndt, Spiritual Adv./Care Srvcs.;
Madison Diocesan Choir - diocesanchoir@madisondiocese.org John Sittard, Liturgy Dir.;
Propagation of the Faith - t) (608) 821-3052 Rev. Chad M. Droessler, Dir.;
Wisconsin Catholic Conference - t) 608-257-0004 Barbara Sella, Exec. Dir.;

STATE OF WISCONSIN

PARISHES, MISSIONS, AND CLERGY

BARABOO

St. Joseph - 300 2nd St., Baraboo, WI 53913 t) 608-356-4773; 608-356-5353 (CRP) beckyt@stjosephbaraboo.com; jayp@stjosephbaraboo.com baraboocatholic.org Very Rev. James M. Poster, Pst.; Rev. Luke Powers, Par. Vicar; Becky Thompson, Dir.; CRP Stds.: 91

- **St. Joseph School** - (Grades PreK-8) 310 2nd St., Baraboo, WI 53913 t) 608-356-3083 info@stjosephbaraboo.org Denise Brinker, Prin.; Stds.: 215; Lay Tchrs.: 11

BELLEVILLE

St. Francis of Assisi - 338 S. Harrison St., Belleville, WI 53508; Mailing: P.O. Box 349, Belleville, WI 53508 t) 608-424-3831; 608-558-4998 (CRP) stfrancisbell@gmail.com www.stfrancisbelleville.com Rev. Mark W. Miller, Pst.; Janet M Carley, Admin.; Pamela Burke, DRE; Teresa Miller, Bus. Mgr.; CRP Stds.: 58

BELMONT

St. Philomena - 338 Chestnut St., Belmont, WI 53510; Mailing: P.O. Box 345, Belmont, WI 53510 t) 608-762-5446; 608-987-2026 st.philomena5446@gmail.com belmontcatholic.weebly.com/ (Linked with St. Mary/St. Paul, Mineral Point) Rev. Joseph Michael Tarigopula (India), Pst.; Jamie Dreger, DRE; CRP Stds.: 61

BELOIT

St. Jude - 737 Hackett St., Beloit, WI 53511 t) 608-364-2820 office@stjudeandstthomas.com; re@stjudeandstthomas.com stjudeandstthomas.com (Linked with St. Thomas the Apostle, Beloit) Rev. Bala Kasipogu (India), Par. Admin.; Dcn. James Davis; Erin Olver, DRE; DeAnne Gile, Admin.; CRP Stds.: 171

Our Lady of the Assumption - 2222 Shopiere Rd., Beloit, WI 53511 t) 608-362-9066 miker@olabeloit.com; amym@olabeloit.com www.olabeloit.com Rey. Michael A. Resop, Pst.; CRP Stds.: 113

- **Our Lady of the Assumption School** - (Grades PreK-8) t) 608-365-4014 tseivert@olaschool.ws www.olaschool.ws Stds.: 163; Lay Tchrs.: 12

St. Thomas Congregation - 822 E. Grand Ave., Beloit, WI 53511 t) 608-362-1034 office@stjudeandstthomas.com; re@stjudeandstthomas.com stjudeandstthomas.com (Linked with St. Jude, Beloit) Rev. Bala Kasipogu (India), Par. Admin.; Dcn. James Davis; Erin Olver, DRE; CRP Stds.: 170

BENTON

St. Patrick - 237 E. Main St., Benton, WI 53803; Mailing: P.O. Box 3, Benton, WI 53803 t) 608-759-2131; 608-778-3577 (CRP) stpatrickbenton@gmail.com (Linked with St. Rose of Lima, Cuba City) Rev. David J. Flanagan, Pst.; Karrie Steinhart, DRE; CRP Stds.: 22

BERLIN

All Saints Catholic Congregation - N8566 State Rd. 49, Berlin, WI 54923-0269; Mailing: P.O. Box 269, Berlin, WI 54923 t) 920-361-5252 parishoffice@allsaintsberlin.org allsaintsberlin.org Very Rev. John A. Silva, Pst.; Rev. Anthony Thirumalareddy (India), Par. Vicar; Rev. Andrew J. Showers, Assoc. Pst.; Michelle Wolff, DRE; Kari A Clark, Bus. Mgr.; CRP Stds.: 150

- **All Saints School** - (Grades K-8) 151 S. Grove St., Berlin, WI 54923 t) 920-361-1781 school.allsaintsberlin.org Jana Dahms, Prin.; Stds.: 165; Lay Tchrs.: 12

BLOOMINGTON

St. Mary - 535 Congress St., Bloomington, WI 53804-0035; Mailing: P.O. Box 35, Bloomington, WI 53804 t) 608-994-2526 swwicatholicparishes.com (Linked with St. John, Patch Grove; St. Charles, Cassville; St. Mary, Glen Haven) Rev. Gregory S. Ihm, Pst.; CRP Stds.: 51

- **St. Mary School** - (Grades PreK-8) 531 Congress St., Bloomington, WI 53804 t) 608-994-2435 stmarybl@tds.net Kelly Copsey, Prin.; Stds.: 39; Lay Tchrs.: 4

BOSCOBEL

Corpus Christi Parish, Boscobel, WI - 405 E. LeGrand St., Boscobel, WI 53805-1150 t) 608-375-4257 corpuschristi53805@gmail.com Rev. Christopher Padilla, Pst.; Rev. Cristian Valenzuela, S.J.S., Par. Vicar; Dcn. Lawrence Schmitt; Peggy Schmitt, DRE; CRP Stds.: 81

BRIGGSVILLE

St. Mary Help of Christians - N565 Hwy. A, Briggsville, WI 53920-0127; Mailing: Box 127, Briggsville, WI 53920-0127 t) 608-981-2282 stmaryhofc@maqs.net www.stmaryoticandhoc.org/ (Linked with St. Mary of the Immaculate Conception, Portage) Rev. Gary L. Krahenbuhl, Pst.; Sr. Anita Henning, Pst. Min./Coord.; CRP Stds.: 16

CAMBRIDGE

St. Pius X - 701 W. Water St., Cambridge, WI 53523 t) 608-423-3015 x102 (Office); 608-423-3015 x103 (CRP); (608) 423-3015 x101 (Father David Timmerman) parishstpiusx@gmail.com stpiusxcp.org/ Rev. David W. Timmerman, Pst.; Hannah Thompson, DRE; CRP Stds.: 71

CASSVILLE

St. Charles Borromeo - 521 E. Dewey St., Cassville, WI 53806; Mailing: P.O. Box 166, Cassville, WI 53806 t) 608-725-5595 stchas@tds.net (Linked with St. Mary

Help of Christians, Glen Haven, St. John, Patch Grove & St. Mary, Bloomington) Rev. Gregory S. Ihm, Pst.; Cheryl Junk, Admin.; CRP Stds.: 34

St. Charles Borromeo School - (Grades 1-8) t) 608-725-5173 Dianne Makovec, Prin.; Stds.: 6; Lay Tchrs.: 1

St. Mary Help of Christians - 8808 4th St., Glen Haven, WI 53810

CLINTON

St. Stephen - 716 Shu-Lar Ln., Clinton, WI 53525; Mailing: P.O. Box 399, Clinton, WI 53525 t) 608-676-2241; 608-676-2242 parish@ststephensclinton.com ststephen.weconnect.com Rev. Prabhakar Singareddy (India); CRP Stds.: 45

COLUMBUS

St. Jerome - 1550 Farnham St., Columbus, WI 53925 t) 920-623-3753 cgrahn@stjeromecolumbus.org; parish@stjeromecolumbus.org www.sjcolumbus.org/parish (Linked with St. Patrick, Doylestown) Rev. Grant Thies, Pst.; CRP Stds.: 72

St. Jerome School - (Grades PreK-8) t) 920-623-5780 sjsoffice@stjeromecolumbus.org www.sjcolumbus.org/school Adrienne Van Norman, Prin.; Stds.: 122; Lay Tchrs.: 10

COTTAGE GROVE

St. Patrick - 434 N. Main St., Cottage Grove, WI 53527-0400 t) 608-839-3969 father@st-patrick-parish.com www.st-patrick-parish.com Rev. Brian D. Dulli, Pst.; Kristia Loeder, DRE; John Walsh III, DRE; CRP Stds.: 63

CROSS PLAINS

St. Francis Xavier - 2947 Thinnes St., Cross Plains, WI 53528 t) 608-798-0100 info@sfxcrossplains.org www.sfxcrossplains.org Rev. Scott M. Jablonski, Pst.; Marc Laudonio, DRE; CRP Stds.: 90

St. Francis Xavier School - (Grades PreK-8) 2939 Thinnes St., Cross Plains, WI 53528 t) 608-798-2422 petrece.klein@sfxcrossplains.org www.sfxcatholicshool.org Petrece Klein, Prin.; Stds.: 196; Lay Tchrs.: 13

St. Martin of Tours - 5959 St. Martin Cir., Cross Plains, WI 53528-9312 t) 608-798-2815 martinsvillesmtp@straphael.org martinsville.saintpetersaintmartin.org (Linked with St. Peter, Ashton) Rev. Christopher Gernetzke, Pst.; Michelle Leveque, DRE; CRP Stds.: 4

St. Mary of Pine Bluff - 3673 County Rd. P, Cross Plains, WI 53528-9179 t) 608-798-2111 catholic@tds.net www.stmarypb.org Rev. Richard M. Heilman, Pst.; CRP Stds.: 32

CUBA CITY

St. Rose of Lima - 519 W. Roosevelt, Cuba City, WI 53807 t) 608-744-2010 c) 608-778-3577 strosech@lagrant.net strosecubacity.weconnect.com (Linked with St. Patrick, Benton) Rev. David J. Flanagan, Pst.; Karrie Steinhart, DRE; CRP Stds.: 157

St. Rose of Lima School - (Grades PreK-8) 218 N. Jackson St., Cuba City, WI 53807 t) 608-744-2120 schneiderm@strose.us www.strose.us Mary Schneider, Prin.; Stds.: 118; Lay Tchrs.: 9

DARLINGTON

Our Lady of Fatima Congregation, Lafayette County, WI, Inc. - 206 E. Harriet St., Darlington, WI 53530 t) 608-776-4059 olfhrosary@gmail.com darlingtoncatholic.org Rev. Luke Syse, Pst.; CRP Stds.: 90

Holy Rosary School - (Grades PreK-4) 744 Wells St., Darlington, WI 53530; Mailing: 730 Wells St., Darlington, WI 53530 t) 608-776-3710 hrschool@mediacombb.net olfhrschool.org Tanya Horne, Prin.; Stds.: 85; Lay Tchrs.: 5

St. Peter, Elk Grove -

St. Michael, Calamine -

Our Lady of Hope, Seymour -

Immaculate Conception, Truman -

Holy Rosary, Darlington -

DE FOREST

St. Olaf - 623 Jefferson St., De Forest, WI 53532 t) 608-846-5726; 608-839-7149 (CRP) pastor@saintolafchurch.org; dre@saintolafchurch.org www.saintolafchurch.org (Linked with St. Joseph, East Bristol) Rev. Jared J. Holzhuter, Pst.; Paula Hill, DRE; CRP Stds.: 266

DICKEYVILLE

Holy Ghost - 305 W. Main St., Dickeyville, WI 53808; Mailing: P.O. Box 429, Dickeyville, WI 53808 t) 608-568-7519; 608-568-7530 (CRP) hgparishdickeyville@gmail.com; icparishkieler@gmail.com www.hgicchurches.org (Linked with Immaculate Conception, Kieler) Rev. Bernard E. Rott, Pst.; Dcn. Lawrence F. Tranel; Angela Snyder, DRE; CRP Stds.: 86

Holy Ghost-Immaculate Conception School - (Grades PreK-8) 325 W. Main St., Dickeyville, WI 53808; Mailing: P.O. Box 40, Dickeyville, WI 53808 t) 608-568-7790; 608-568-7220 mullerm@hgicschool.com hgicschool.com Megan Muller, Prin.; Stds.: 123; Lay Tchrs.: 10

DODGEVILLE

St. Joseph - 305 E. Walnut St., Dodgeville, WI 53533-1799 t) 608-930-3392 x1 jackie.boley@stjoedodge.org; parishsecretary@stjoedodge.org www.stjoedodge.org Rev. Bill Van Wagner, Pst.; Jackie Boley, DRE; CRP Stds.: 37

St. Joseph School - (Grades PreSchool-8) t) (608) 930-3392 x2 principal@stjoedodge.org Dana Graber, Prin.; Stds.: 93; Lay Tchrs.: 9

DOYLESTOWN

St. Patrick - N4085 Bruce St., Doylestown, WI 53928; Mailing: P.O. Box 40, Doylestown, WI 53928 t) 920-992-3343; 920-992-3549 (CRP) (Linked with St. Jerome, Columbus) Rev. Grant Thies, Pst.; Marcia Vange, DRE; CRP Stds.: 19

EDGERTON

St. Joseph - 590 S. Saint Joseph's Cir., Edgerton, WI 53534-1243 t) 608-884-3038 admin@stjoeedgerton.org; cre@stjoeedgerton.org www.stjoeedgerton.org Rev. David A. Wanish, Pst.; Laura Kisting, Bus. Mgr.; Kim Jensen, DRE; CRP Stds.: 99

EVANSVILLE

St. Paul - 39 Garfield Ave., Evansville, WI 53536 t) 608-882-4138 stpaul@rockcountycatholic.org; stpdre@rockcountycatholic.org www.rockcountycatholic.org (Linked with St. Augustine, Footville) Amanda Adams, DRE; CRP Stds.: 37

FENNIMORE

Queen of All Saints - 960 Jefferson St., Fennimore, WI 53809 t) 608-822-3520 creinoso@slsonline.org; cvalenzuela@slsonline.org queenofallsaints.net Rev. Carlos Ernesto Reinoso (Ecuador), Pst.; Mary Ann Catherine Carmody, Bus. Mgr.; Barbara Kohout, DRE; CRP Stds.: 59

St. John Nepomuc - 15055 Shemak Rd., Muscoda, WI 53573 Rev. Cristian Valenzuela, S.J.S., Par. Vicar;

St. Lawrence O'Toole - 13814 Irish Ridge Rd., Mount Hope, WI 53816 Rev. Cristian Valenzuela, S.J.S., Par. Vicar;

St. Mary - Rev. Cristian Valenzuela, S.J.S., Par. Vicar;

FOOTVILLE

St. Augustine - 280 Haberdale Dr., Footville, WI 53537; Mailing: PO Box 325, Footville, WI 53537-0325 t) 608-876-6252 staugustine@rockcountycatholic.org www.rockcountycatholic.org (Linked with St. Paul, Evansville) Rev. Lawrence K. Oparaji (Nigeria), Pst.; Janet Kassel, DRE; CRP Stds.: 20

FORT ATKINSON

St. Joseph - 1660 Endl Blvd., Fort Atkinson, WI 53538 t) 920-563-3029 parish@stjosephfort.org stjosephfort.org Very Rev. Timothy J. Renz, Pst.; Gina McDonald, DRE; Norma Mayans, Youth Min.; CRP Stds.: 71

St. Joseph School - (Grades PreK-8) 1650 Endl Blvd., Fort Atkinson, WI 53538 khomb@stjosephfort.org Kari Homb, Prin.; Stds.: 123; Lay Tchrs.: 11

GLEN HAVEN

St. Mary Help of Christians - 8808 4th St., Glen Haven, WI 53810; Mailing: P.O. Box 166, Cassville, WI 53806 t) 608-725-5595 stchas@tds.net (Linked with St. Charles Borromeo, Cassville, St. John, Patch Grove & St. Mary, Bloomington) Rev. Gregory S. Ihm, Pst.;

GRATIOT

St. Joseph - 5695 Main St., Gratiot, WI 53541; Mailing: 344 N. Judgement St., Shullsburg, WI 53586 t) (608) 491-1035 stmathewschurch@centurytel.net shullsburghcatholic.com (Linked with St. John, South Wayne & St. Matthew's, Shullsburg) Rev. Peter John Lee, Pst.; CRP Stds.: 3

GREEN LAKE

Our Lady of the Lake - 530 Ruth St., Green Lake, WI 54941 t) 920-294-6440 olglcatholic@gmail.com www.olol.center Very Rev. John A. Silva, Pst.; Rev. Anthony Thirumalareddy (India), Assoc. Pst.; Michelle Wolff, DRE;

HAZEL GREEN

St. Francis de Sales - 2720 N. Percival St., Hazel Green, WI 53811-9681 t) (608) 854-2392 www.hgschurches.com (Linked with St. Joseph, Hazel Green) Rev. Peter Auer, Pst.; CRP Stds.: 54

Parish Center - 1720 26th St., Hazel Green, WI 53811

St. Joseph - 780 County Hwy. Z, Hazel Green, WI 53811-9709 t) 608-854-2392 www.hgschurches.com (Linked with St. Francis de Sales, Hazel Green) Rev. Peter Auer, Pst.;

St. Joseph School - (Grades PreK-8) t) 608-748-4442 principalwills@stjosephscs.info www.stjosephscs.info Barbara Wills, Prin.; Stds.: 79; Lay Tchrs.: 6

HIGHLAND

Saints Anthony and Philip Parish - 726 Main St., Highland, WI 53543; Mailing: P.O. Box 306, Highland, WI 53543 t) 608-929-7490; 608-929-7701 deggers@centurylink.net; mhebgen@centurylink.net ssanthonyphilip.com (Linked with St. Thomas, Montfort) Rev. James H. Murphy, Pst.; Delores Eggers, DRE; CRP Stds.: 105

HOLLANDALE

Congregation of St. Isidore - 601 Grover St., Hollandale, WI 53544; Mailing: P.O. Box 37, Hollandale, WI 53544 t) 608-967-2344 stisidore@mhtc.net stisidorecatholicparish.com/ Rev. Michael Johnson, Pst.; CRP Stds.: 50

JANESVILLE

St. John Vianney Cure of Ars - 1250 E. Racine St., Janesville, WI 53545; Mailing: 1245 Clark St., Janesville, WI 53545 t) 608-752-8708 (Office); 608-755-1476 (Faith Formation) parish@sjv.org www.sjv.org Very Rev. Paul Ugo Arinze, Pst.; Rev. Vincent Racanelli, Par. Vicar; Rev. Matthew Gregory Pearson, Par. Vicar; Rev. Thomas P. Marr, In Res.; George Wollinger, Pst. Min./Coord.; Emily Wallace, DRE; Kris Kranenburg, RCIA Coord.; Jeanne Vogt, Bus. Mgr.; CRP Stds.: 63

St. John Vianney School - (Grades PreK-8) t) 608-752-6802 school@sjv.org Heidi Miller, Prin.; Stds.: 211; Lay Tchrs.: 16

St. Mary's Congregation - 313 E. Wall St., Janesville, WI 53545 t) 608-752-7861 psec@nativitymary.org; re@nativitymary.org www.nativitymary.org Very Rev. Paul Ugo Arinze; Rev. Vincent Racanelli; Rev. Matthew Gregory Pearson; CRP Stds.: 20

Nativity of St. Mary School - (Grades PreK-8) 307 E. Wall St., Janesville, WI 53545 t) 608-754-5221 principal@stmaryschoolwi.com www.stmaryschoolwi.com Dr. Kim Ehrhardt, Prin.; Stds.: 97; Lay Tchrs.: 7

St. Patrick - 315 Cherry St., Janesville, WI 53548 t) 608-754-8193 info@saintpatrickofjanesville.org www.saintpatrickofjanesville.org Rev. Drew Gregory Olson, Pst.; Dcn. John Houseman, Pst. Assoc.; CRP Stds.: 141

St. William - 456 N. Arch St., Janesville, WI 53548; Mailing: 445 N. Arch St., Janesville, WI 53548 t) 608-755-5180; 608-755-5183 (CRP) parish@stwilliam.net www.stwilliam.net Rev. James R. Leeser, Pst.; Terri Runde, Bus. Mgr.; Melissa Lentz,

DRE; CRP Stds.: 61

St. William School - (Grades PreK-8) 1822 Ravine St., Janesville, WI 53548 t) 608-755-5184 info@stwilliam.net Diane Rebout, Prin.; Stds.: 197; Lay Tchrs.: 10

JEFFERSON

St. Francis of Assisi - 214 N. Sanborn Ave., Jefferson, WI 53549; Mailing: P.O. Box 269, Jefferson, WI 53549 t) (920) 674-2025; (920) 674-5433 (CRP) ttopel@stjohnbaptist.net; jelberi@stjohnbaptist.net www.stfranciscommunity.net Merger of St. John the Baptist Church, Jefferson, and St. Lawrence Church, Jefferson Rev. Thomas J. Coyle, Pst.; CRP Stds.: 149

St. John the Baptist School - (Grades PreK-8) 333 E. Church St., Jefferson, WI 53549 t) 920-674-5821 bbare@stjohnbaptist.net www.stjohnbaptist.net William Bare, Prin.; Stds.: 97; Lay Tchrs.: 11

KIELER

Immaculate Conception - 3685 County Rd. HHH, Kieler, WI 53812; Mailing: P.O. Box 57, Kieler, WI 53812 t) 608-568-7530 icparishkieler@gmail.com hgicchurches.org (Linked with Holy Ghost, Dickeyville) Rev. Bernard E. Rott, Admin.; Dcn. Lawrence F. Tranel; CRP Stds.: 150

Immaculate Conception School - ; Mailing: P.O. Box 129, Kieler, WI 53812 t) 608-568-7220 hesselingr@hgicschool.com Rita Hesseling, Prin.; Stds.: 123; Lay Tchrs.: 12

LA VALLE

Holy Angels Congregation, Sauk County WI, Inc. - 310 Bluff St., La Valle, WI 53941; Mailing: P.O. Box 166, La Valle, WI 53941 t) 608-985-7558 holyangels7558@gmail.com holyangelslavalle.org Rev. Sanctus K. Ibe, Pst.; Kami Clary, CRE; Margaret Hewitt, CRE; CRP Stds.: 14

St. Boniface - 105 Church St., Lime Ridge, WI 53942; Mailing: PO Box 166, La Valle, WI 53941

St. Patrick - S8284 County Rd. G, Plain, WI 53577; Mailing: PO Box 166, La Valle, WI 53941

Holy Family -

LAKE MILLS

St. Gabriel the Archangel Parish (Saint Gabriel Congregation, Jefferson County WI, Inc.) - 602 College St., Lake Mills, WI 53551; Mailing: 242 Williams St., Johnson Creek, WI 53038 t) 920-648-2468 saintgabriel.lmjc@yahoo.com stgabriellmjc.com Rev. Alex Carmel (India), Pst.; Natalie Raupp, DRE; Mary Paulowske, Youth Min.; CRP Stds.: 140

LANCASTER

St. Clement - 135 S. Washington St., Lancaster, WI 53813 t) 608-723-4990 st_clement@tds.net saintclementparish.com Rev. William F. Vernon, Pst.; Nick Crosby, CRE; Rebecca Dean, CRE; Melissa Wiest, CRE; CRP Stds.: 78

St. Clement School - (Grades PreK-6) 330 W. Maple St., Lancaster, WI 53813 t) 608-723-7474 school@saintclementschool.com www.saintclementschool.com Parent Entity is Saint Clement Congregation Joshua Jensen, Prin.; Stds.: 114; Lay Tchrs.: 8

LODI

Blessed Trinity Parish - 521 Fair St., Lodi, WI 53555 t) 608-592-5711; 608-592-5711 x4 (CRP) www.btcatholic.us Rev. Joseph Baker, Pst.; Stephen Zepp, DRE; CRP Stds.: 114

Blessed Trinity School - (Grades PreK-8) 109 S. Military Rd., Dane, WI 53529 t) (608) 592-5711 x7 azepp@btcatholic.us Alicia Zepp, Prin.; Stds.: 75; Lay Tchrs.: 5

MADISON

Cathedral Parish of St. Raphael - 404 E. Main St., Madison, WI 53703 t) 608-257-5000; 608-257-5000 x12 (CRP) madisonsrcp@madisoncathedral.org www.madisoncathedral.org Rev. Msgr. Kevin D. Holmes, Rector; Rev. Jose Luis Vazquez (Mexico), Par. Vicar; Dcn. Todd R. Burud; Dcn. Raymond Lukesic; Dcn. Christopher Schmelzer; Amber Cerrato, DRE; CRP Stds.: 119

Lumen House, LLC - 142 W. Johnson St., Madison, WI 53703; Mailing: 404 E. Main St., Madison, WI 53703

St. Bernard - 2462 Atwood Ave., Madison, WI 53704; Mailing: 2438 Atwood Ave., Madison, WI 53704 t) 608-249-9256 pastor@sbmsn.org; office@sbmsn.org www.sbmsn.org Rev. Michael R. Radowicz, Pst.; CRP Stds.: 15

Blessed Sacrament - 2121 Rowley Ave., Madison, WI 53726-3958; Mailing: 2116 Hollister Ave., Madison, WI 53726-3958 t) 608-238-3471; 608-238-3471 x134 (DRE) info@blsacrament.org; fr.andy@blsacrament.org www.blsacrament.org Rev. Andrew McAlpin, O.P., Pst.; Bro. Jordan David Coonen, OP, In Res.; Bro. Edward van Merrienboer, O.P., In Res.; Donna Roeck, Dir.; Maria Habib, Pst. Assoc.; Peggie Hansen, DRE; Carl Buttke, Music Min.; CRP Stds.: 71

Blessed Sacrament School - (Grades PreK-8) 2112 Hollister Ave., Madison, WI 53726 t) 608-233-6155 efirst@school.blsacrament.org Steve Castrogiovanni, Prin.; Elizabeth First, Bus. Mgr.; Stds.: 220; Lay Tchrs.: 16

Saint Dennis Congregation - 505 Dempsey Rd., Madison, WI 53714; Mailing: 413 Dempsey Rd., Madison, WI 53714 t) 608-246-5124; 608-246-5123 (CRP) office@stdennisparish.org www.stdennisparish.org Very Rev. Randy J. Timmerman, Pst.; Rev. Joji R. Allam (India), Par. Vicar; Dcn. David J. Hendrickson; Lisa Harms, DRE; CRP Stds.: 218

St. Dennis School - (Grades K-8) 409 Dempsey Rd., Madison, WI 53714 t) 608-246-5121 principal@st-dennisschool.org www.st-dennisschool.org Matt Beisser, Prin.; Stds.: 250; Lay Tchrs.: 24

Good Shepherd Parish - 1128 St. James Ct., Madison, WI 53715-1363 t) 608-268-9931 (CRP); 608-268-9930 parish@goodshepherdmadison.org www.thegoodshepherdmadison.org Rev. David A. Carrano, Pst.; Rev. Manuel Mendez-Cobos (Mexico), Par. Vicar; CRP Stds.: 206

St. James School - (Grades PreK-8) 1204 St. James Ct., Madison, WI 53715 t) 608-268-9935 www.stjamesschool.org Randall Enders, Prin.; Stds.: 114; Lay Tchrs.: 13

St. Maria Goretti Congregation - 5313 Flad Ave., Madison, WI 53711 t) 608-271-7421 parish@stmariagoretti.org www.stmariagoretti.org/ Rev. Scott J. Emerson, Pst.; Rev. Enan Zelinski, Par. Vicar; Sr. Denise Herrmann Sr., Pst. Assoc.; Melissa Coleman, CRE; CRP Stds.: 125

St. Maria Goretti Congregation - (Grades PreSchool-8) 5405 Flad Ave., Madison, WI 53711 t) 608-271-7551 school@stmariagoretti.org stmariagoretti.org/school/ Robert J. Schell, Prin.; Stds.: 111; Lay Tchrs.: 12

Our Lady, Queen of Peace - 401 S. Owen Dr., Madison, WI 53711 t) 608-231-4600 qpmail@qopc.org www.qopc.org Rev. Msgr. Lawrence M. Bakke, Par. Admin.; Dcn. Mark Zwolski, Liturgy Dir.; Cheryl Horne, Pst. Assoc.; CRP Stds.: 94

Our Lady, Queen of Peace School - (Grades PreK-8) 418 Holly Ave., Madison, WI 53711 t) 608-231-4580 maryjovitale@qopc.org www.qopcschool.org Mary Jo Vitale, Prin.; Stds.: 481; Lay Tchrs.: 30

St. Paul University Parish - 723 State St., Madison, WI 53703 t) 608-258-3140 welcomedesk@uwcatholic.org uwcatholic.org/ Rev. Eric H. Nielsen, Pst.; Rev. Timothy Mergen, Par. Vicar;

St. Peter Catholic Church - 5001 N. Sherman Ave., Madison, WI 53704-1440 t) 608-249-6651 sue.whooley@stpetermadison.org; office@stpetermadison.org stpetermadison.org Very Rev. Gabriel A. Lopez-Betanzos, Pst.; Dcn. Todd Martin; CRP Stds.: 21

St. Thomas Aquinas - 602 Everglade Dr., Madison, WI 53717 t) 608-833-2600 parish@stamadison.org stamadison.org Rev. Bart D. Timmerman, Pst.; Rev. Steven J. Kortendick, In Res.; Dcn. Jerome Buhman; Dcn. Richard Martin; CRP Stds.: 389

MARKESAN

Holy Family Parish - 41 St. Joseph St., Markesan, WI 53946; Mailing: 318 S. Main St., Pardeeville, WI 53954 t) 608-429-3030 stfaustina.holyfamily@sfhfcatholic.org; hfreligiousedu2019@gmail.com www.sfhfparish.com Rev. Joji Reddy Thirumalareddy (India), Admin.; Patty Bartz, DRE; CRP Stds.: 31

St. Joseph Church -

St. Mary Church - 177 W. Pearl St., Kingston, WI 53939; Mailing: 318 S. Main St, Pardeeville, WI 53954

MAZOMANIE

Holy Cross Parish (St. Barnabas Parish) - 410 Cramer St., Mazomanie, WI 53560; Mailing: P.O Box 68, Mazomanie, WI 53560 t) 608-795-4321 c) 608-909-1959 holycrossparish113@gmail.com holycrossparishmazo.com Rev. Osvaldo Briones, S.J.S., Pst.; Rev. Miguel Galvez, S.J.S. (Ecuador), Admin.;

St. John the Baptist - County Hwy. H, Arena, WI 53503

MCFARLAND

Christ the King - 5306 Main St., McFarland, WI 53558; Mailing: P.O. Box 524, McFarland, WI 53558 t) 608-838-9797 ctk@myparish.com www.myparish.com Rev. Stephen Brunner, Pst.; Mary Karels, Pst. Min./Coord.; Andrea Wiltzius, Music Min.; CRP Stds.: 73

MIDDLETON

St. Bernard - 2015 Parmenter St., Middleton, WI 53562-2627 t) 608-831-6531; 608-831-6531 x328 (CRP) parish@stbmidd.org www.stbmidd.org Rev. Brian J. Wilk, Pst.; Barbara A Harrington, Bus. Mgr.; CRP Stds.: 193

St. Peter Catholic Church - 7121 County Rd. K, Middleton, WI 53562 t) 608-831-4843; 608-831-4846 (School) info@ashtoncatholic.org; faithformation@ashtoncatholic.org ashtoncatholic.org (Linked with St. Martin of Tours, Martinsville) Rev. Christopher Gernetzke, Pst.; Michelle Leveque, DRE; CRP Stds.: 64

St. Peter Catholic Church School - (Grades PreK-6) 7129 County Rd. K, Middleton, WI 53562-3912 principal@ashtoncatholic.org www.ashtoncatholic.org/school Dcn. Michael Pipitone, Prin.; Stds.: 84; Lay Tchrs.: 5

MILTON

St. Mary - 837 Parkview Dr., Milton, WI 53563 t) (608) 868-3337; 608-868-3334 (Faith Formation) stmarymilton@gmail.com; victoria.kersten1@gmail.com www.saintmarymilton.org Rev. David A. Wanish, Pst.; Vicki Kersten, Bus. Mgr.; Sabrina Elsen, DRE; CRP Stds.: 162

MINERAL POINT

Congregation of St. Mary-St. Paul - 224 Davis St., Mineral Point, WI 53565 t) 608-987-2026; 608-987-3361 stmarypaul@msn.com; stmarypaulccd@gmail.com stmarysstpauls.org Rev. Joseph Michael Tarigopula (India), Pst.; Paula Schuette, DRE; CRP Stds.: 121

MONONA

Immaculate Heart of Mary - 5101 Schofield St., Monona, WI 53716 t) 608-221-1521 ihmoffice@ihmparish.org www.ihmcatholicparish.org Rev. Chad M. Droessler, Pst.; CRP Stds.: 194

Immaculate Heart of Mary School - (Grades PreK-8) 4913 Schofield St., Madison, WI 53716 t) 608-222-8831 cmeiller@ihm-school.org www.ihmcatholicschool.org Callie Meiller, Prin.; Stds.: 212; Sr. Tchrs.: 1; Lay Tchrs.: 14

MONROE

St. Clare of Assisi Parish - 1760 14th St., Monroe, WI 53566-2149 t) 608-325-9506 www.stclaregreencounty.org (Linked with St. Victor Church, Monroe & St. Rose of Lima Church, Brodhead) Rev. Tafadzwa Kushamba, Pst.; CRP Stds.: 125

St. Victor School - (Grades PreK-6) 1416 20th Ave., Monroe, WI 53566-2149 t) 608-325-3395 joepeters@stvictormonroe.org www.stvictormonroe.org Joseph Peters, Prin.; Stds.: 128; Lay Tchrs.: 8

MONTELLO

St. John the Baptist - 277 E. Montello St., Montello, WI 53949 t) 608-297-7423 sjbgsparishoffice@gmail.com www.marquettecountycatholic.org/ (Linked with Good Shepherd, Westfield) Rev. Savio Yerasani (India), Pst.; Marianne Biedrzycki, DRE; Steve Zoulek, Bus. Mgr.; CRP Stds.: 33

MONTFORT

St. Thomas - 104 Park St., Montfort, WI 53569; Mailing: P.O. Box 68, Montfort, WI 53569 t) 608-943-6944 officestthomasmontfort@gmail.com stthomasmontfort.org (Linked with SS. Anthony and Philip, Highland) Rev. James H. Murphy, Pst.; Julie Hawes, DRE; CRP Stds.: 55

MOUNT HOREB

St. Michael the Archangel - 107 S. Seventh St., Mount Horeb, WI 53572-2050 t) 608-437-5348 stihr@mhtc.net stmichaelwi.com/ Rev. Chahm Gahng, Pst.; Sonja Preimesberger, DRE; Jennifer Stoddard, DRE; CRP Stds.: 167

NESHKORO

St. James - 315 N. Main, Neshkoro, WI 54960; Mailing: 1211 W. Main, Princeton, WI 54968 t) 920-293-4211 stjamesneshkoro@gmail.com www.stjamesneshkoro.com (Linked with St. John the Baptist, Princeton) Rev. Dale W. Grubba, Pst.;

OREGON

Holy Mother of Consolation - 651 N. Main St., Oregon, WI 53575 t) (608) 835-5763; 608-835-5764 (CRP) gary.wankerl@hmocchurch.org holymotherchurch.weconnect.com Rev. Gary A. Wankerl, Pst.; CRP Stds.: 303

PALMYRA

St. Mary - 919 W. Main St., Palmyra, WI 53156; Mailing: P.O. Box P, Palmyra, WI 53156 t) 262-495-2395 smarypal@gmail.com (Linked with St. Mary Help of Christians) Rev. Mariadas Bekala (India), Pst.;

PARDEEVILLE

St. Faustina Congregation - 312 S. Main St., Pardeeville, WI 53954; Mailing: 318 S. Main St., Pardeeville, WI 53954 t) 608-429-3030 stfaustina.holyfamily@sfhfcatholic.org; religioused@sfhfcatholic.org www.sfhfparish.com/ Rev. Joji Reddy Thirumalareddy (India), Par. Admin.; Alfred Nickel, DRE; CRP Stds.: 24

PATCH GROVE

St. John - 213 N. Wyalusing St., Patch Grove, WI 53817; Mailing: 535 Congress St., P.O. Box 35, Bloomington, WI 53804 t) 608-994-2526 sunday7@tds.net www.swwicatholicparishes.com (Linked with St. Mary, Bloomington; St. Charles, Cassville; St. Mary's, Glen Haven) Rev. Gregory S. Ihm, Pst.;

PLAIN

St. Luke - 1240 Nachreiner Ave., Plain, WI 53577 t) 608-546-2482; 608-546-2963 x312 (CRP) www.stlukecatholicchurchplain.com/ (Linked with St. John the Evangelist, Spring Green) Rev. Garrett B. Kau, Pst.; Meg Aspinwall, Youth Min.; CRP Stds.: 45

St. Luke School - (Grades PreK-8) 1290 Nachreiner Ave., Plain, WI 53577 t) (608) 546-2963 stlukes-plain.org Diane C Mueller, Prin.; Stds.: 75; Lay Tchrs.: 8

PLATTEVILLE

St. Augustine University Parish - 135 S. Hickory St., Platteville, WI 53818-3316 t) 608-383-5574 office@pioneercatholic.org pioneercatholic.org Dcn. William Bussan, Pst. Min./Coord.;

St. Mary - 130 W. Cedar St., Platteville, WI 53818-2457 t) 608-496-1058 info@saintmaryplatteville.com www.saintmaryplatteville.com (Linked with St. Augustine University Parish, Platteville) Rev. John Patrick Blewett, S.J.S., Pst.; Dcn. Lee Eggers; Dcn. William Bussan; Katie Leahy, DRE; CRP Stds.: 34

PORTAGE

St. Mary of the Immaculate Conception - 309 W. Cook St., Portage, WI 53901-2107 t) 608-742-6998 portage@stmaryotic.org www.stmaryoticandhoc.org (Linked with St. Mary Help of Christians, Briggsville) Rev. Gary L. Krahenbuhl, Pst.; CRP Stds.: 48

St. Mary School - (Grades PreK-8) 315 W. Cook St., Portage, WI 53901 t) 608-742-4998 www.stmaryportage.org Josh Schuenemann, Prin.; Stds.: 185; Lay Tchrs.: 15

POTOSI

SS. Andrew and Thomas - 101 Church St., Potosi, WI 53820-9654 t) 608-763-2671 frleffler@tds.net www.ss-andrew-thomas.org Rev. Richard J. Leffler, Pst.; Dcn. Roger W. Scholbrock; CRP Stds.: 70

SS. Andrew and Thomas School - (Grades PreK-8) 100 Hwy. 61 N., Potosi, WI 53820; Mailing: P.O. Box 160, Potosi, WI 53820 t) 608-763-2120 ssandrew@ss-andrew-thomas.org www.ssandrew-thomas.org Stds.: 30; Lay Tchrs.: 3

POYNETTE

St. Thomas - 655 S. Main St., Poynette, WI 53955-0310; Mailing: P.O. Box 310, Poynette, WI 53955-0310 t) 608-635-4326; 608-635-8375 (CRP) office@prcatholic.org; rereligionclass7@gmail.com prcatholic.org (Linked with St. Joseph, Rio) Rev. Kumud Chandra Nayak, C.J.D., Pst.; Melinda Murray, CRE; CRP Stds.: 73

PRINCETON

St. John the Baptist - 1211 W. Main, Princeton, WI 54968 t) 920-295-6209 grubba@centurytel.net www.stjohnprince.org (Linked with St. James, Neshkoro) Rev. Dale W. Grubba, Pst.;

REEDSBURG

Sacred Heart - 624 N. Willow St., Reedsburg, WI 53959 t) 608-524-2412 sheart@shcreedsburg.org; faithformation@shcreedsburg.org www.shcreedsburg.org Rev. Patrick J. Wendler, Pst.; Dcn. Ronald Pickar; CRP Stds.: 60

Sacred Heart School - (Grades PreK-8) 545 N. Oak St., Reedsburg, WI 53959 t) 608-524-3611 shs@rucls.net shsreedsburg.org Karen Marklein, Prin.; Stds.: 169; Lay Tchrs.: 9

RIDGEWAY

St. Bernadette - 106 North St., Ridgeway, WI 53582 t) 608-924-2441 saintbernadette2010@aol.com; steve.petrica@gmail.com www.facebook.com/groups/stbernadetteparish/ Very Rev. Stephen C. Petrica, Pst.; CRP Stds.: 45

RIO

St. Joseph - 514 Lincoln Ave., Rio, WI 53960; Mailing: 655 Main St., P.O. Box 310, Poynette, WI 53955-0310 t) 608-635-4326 c) 608-698-4339 parishstjoseph@gmail.com; office@prcatholic.org prcatholic.org (Linked with St. Thomas the Apostle, Poynette) Rev. Kumud Chandra Nayak, C.J.D., Pst.; Peggy Lapacek, DRE; CRP Stds.: 16

SAUK CITY

Divine Mercy Parish - 115 Madison St., Sauk City, WI 53583 t) 608-643-4062 (CRP); 608-643-2449 secretary@divinemercy-parish.org; sharon.schoepp@divinemercy-parish.org www.divinemercy-parish.org Rev. Miguel Galvez, S.J.S. (Ecuador), Admin.; Rev. Pedro Escribano (Ecuador), Par. Vicar; Rev. Osvaldo Briones, S.J.S., Par. Vicar; Rev. James Kotch, Par. Vicar; Sharon Schoepp, CRE; CRP Stds.: 48

Divine Mercy Parish School - (Grades PreK-5) 608 Oak St., Sauk City, WI 53583 t) 608-643-6868 info@saintaloysiusschool.org www.saintaloysiusschool.org Daniela Saldana, Prin.; Stds.: 84; Bro. Tchrs.: 1; Sr. Tchrs.: 1; Lay Tchrs.: 5

St. Norbert - 8944 County Rd. Y, Sauk City, WI 53583-9510 t) 608-643-3661; 608-643-6611 (RE Center & Parish Hall) silvanna.navarro@gmail.com; jkotch@slsonline.org www.saint-norbert.org Rev. Osvaldo Briones, S.J.S., Par. Vicar; Rev. Pedro Escribano (Ecuador), Par. Vicar; Rev. James Kotch, Par. Vicar; Rev. Faustino Ruiz, Par. Vicar; Silvanna Navarro, DRE; CRP Stds.: 71

SHULLSBURG

St. Matthew - 344 Judgment St., Shullsburg, WI 53586 t) 608-491-1035 c) 608-208-2126 stmathewschurch@centurytel.net shullsburgcatholic.com (Linked with St. John's, South Wayne & St. Joseph's, Gratiot) Rev. Peter John Lee, Pst.; Diane Weiskircher, DRE; CRP Stds.: 50

SOUTH WAYNE

St. John - 304 E. Pleasant St., South Wayne, WI 53587; Mailing: 344 N. Judgement St., Shullsburg, WI 53586 t) (608) 491-1035 stmathewschurch@centurytel.net shullsburgcatholic.com (Linked with St. Joseph, Gratiot & St. Matthew's, Shullsburg) Rev. Peter John Lee, Pst.; CRP Stds.: 8

SPRING GREEN

St. John the Evangelist - 129 W. Daley St., Spring Green, WI 53588; Mailing: P.O. Box 628, Spring Green, WI 53588 t) 608-588-2028; 608-574-1880 (CRP) stjohnspringgreen@gmail.com www.stjohnspringgreen.com (Linked with St. Luke, Plain) Rev. Garrett B. Kau, Pst.; Meg Aspinwall, Parish Life Coord.; CRP Stds.: 28

STOUGHTON

St. Ann - 323 N. Van Buren, Stoughton, WI 53589 t) 608-873-7633 tamarah.fleres@stanns-school.org stannparish.weconnect.com/ Rev. Randy J. Budnar, Pst.; CRP Stds.: 129

St. Ann School - (Grades PreK-8) 324 N. Harrison St., Stoughton, WI 53589 t) 608-873-3343 stanns@stanns-school.org www.stanns-school.org Kara Roisum, Prin.; Stds.: 135; Lay Tchrs.: 10

SULLIVAN

St. Mary Help of Christians - W856 Hwy. 18, Sullivan, WI 53178-0418; Mailing: P.O. Box 418, Sullivan, WI 53178 t) 262-593-2250 smaryhoc@gmail.com Rev. Mariadas Bekala (India), Pst.; Anne Auger, DRE; CRP Stds.: 21

SUN PRAIRIE

St. Albert the Great - 2420 St. Albert Dr., Sun Prairie, WI 53590 t) 608-837-3798 www.saintalberts.org Rev. Msgr. Donald J. Heiar Jr., Pst.; Dcn. Joseph Stafford; Joanna Rogers, Pst. Min./Coord.; CRP Stds.: 230

St. Joseph - 1935 Hwy. V, Sun Prairie, WI 53590; Mailing: 630 Jefferson St., DeForest, WI 53532 t) 608-846-5726 x1100; 608-825-4934 (CRP) pastor@saintolafchurch.org; dre@stjosepheastbristol.org saintolafchurch.org (Linked with St. Olaf, De Forest) Rev. Jared J. Holzhuter, Pst.; Bill Ringelstetter, DRE; Dom Godard, Bus. Mgr.; CRP Stds.: 35

Sacred Hearts of Jesus and Mary - 221 Columbus St., Sun Prairie, WI 53590 t) 608-837-7381; 608-837-8509 x244 (CRP) sacredhearts@sacred-hearts.org www.sacred-hearts.org Very Rev. Thomas L. Kelley, Pst.; Rev. Miroslaw Szynal (Poland), Par. Vicar; Sarah King, DRE; Paul Jozwiak, Youth Min.; CRP Stds.: 102

Sacred Hearts of Jesus and Mary School - (Grades PreK-8) 219 Columbus St., Sun Prairie, WI 53590 t) 608-837-8508 kim.frederick@shjms.org; dianne.metz@shjms.org www.shjms.org/ Kimberlee Frederick, Prin.; Stds.: 393; Lay Tchrs.: 35

VERONA

St. Christopher Parish - 301 N. Main St., Verona, WI 53593 t) 608-845-6613 pastor@sainthristopherparish.com; office@saintichristopherparish.com www.saintchristopherparish.com Rev. Robert J. Butz, Pst.; CRP Stds.: 180

WATERLOO

Holy Family Parish - 387 S. Monroe St., Waterloo, WI 53594-1329 t) 920-478-2032 pastor@holyfamily.info www.holyfamily.info Rev. Jorge A. Miramontes, Pst.; CRP Stds.: 69

Holy Family Parish School - (Grades PreK-7) t) 920-478-3221 monica.jacobsen@holyfamily.info; penny.hilgendorf@holyfamily.info Penny Hilgendorf, Prin.; Stds.: 30; Lay Tchrs.: 5

WATERTOWN

St. Bernard - 114 S. Church St., Watertown, WI 53094-4399 t) (920) 261-7273; 920-261-5133 x168 (CRP) parishoffice@watertowncatholic.org www.watertowncatholic.org Rev. Vincent Brewer, Pst.; Rev. Michael Wanta, Par. Vicar; Michele McFarland,

DRE; CRP Stds.: 99

St. Bernard School - (Grades PreK-k) 111 S. Montgomery St., Watertown, WI 53094-4399 t) 920-261-7204 secretarystb@watertowncatholic.org Sherry Harms, Prin.; Stds.: 26; Lay Tchrs.: 3

St. Henry - 412 N. 4th St., Watertown, WI 53094 t) 920-261-7273 parishoffice@watertowncatholic.org www.watertowncatholic.org Rev. Vincent Brewer, Pst.; Rev. Michael Wanta, Par. Vicar; Todd Weissenborn, DRE; CRP Stds.: 98

St. Henry School - (Grades 1-8) 300 E. Cady St., Watertown, WI 53094 t) 920-261-2586 sharms@watertowncatholic.org Sherry Harms, Prin.; Stds.: 122; Sr. Tchrs.: 1; Lay Tchrs.: 10

WAUNAKEE

St. John the Baptist - 209 South St., Waunakee, WI 53597 t) 608-849-5121 stjohnparish@stjb.org www.stjb.org Rev. Msgr. James L. Gunn, Pst.; Rev. Joseph Bellamkonda (India), Par. Vicar; Eileen Daley, DRE; Jackie Nerat, Bus. Mgr.; CRP Stds.: 410

St. John the Baptist School - (Grades PreK-8) 114 E. 3rd St., Waunakee, WI 53597 t) 608-849-5325 kkozinski@stjb.org Kalee Kozinski, Prin.; Stds.: 214; Lay Tchrs.: 19

St. Mary of the Lake - 5460 Mary Lake Rd., Waunakee, WI 53597; Mailing: 209 South St., Waunakee, WI 53597 t) (608) 849-5121 stmaryparish@stjb.org Rev. Msgr. James L. Gunn, Pst.; Rev. Joseph Bellamkonda (India), Par. Vicar; Jackie Nerat, Bus. Mgr.;

WESTFIELD

Good Shepherd - 241 E. 6th St., Westfield, WI 53964; Mailing: 277 E. Montello St., Montello, WI 53949 t) 608-296-3631; 608-297-7423 sjbgsparishoffice@gmail.com www.marquettecountycatholic.org (Linked with St. John the Baptist, Montello) Rev. Savio Yerasani (India), Pst.; Marianne Biedrzycki, DRE; Annette LaVia, DRE; Steven Zoulek, Bus. Mgr.; CRP Stds.: 49

WISCONSIN DELLS

Saint Cecilia - 603 Oak St., Wisconsin Dells, WI 53965 t) 608-254-8381 pastor@dellscatholic.com; secretary@dellscatholic.com www.dellscatholic.com Rev. Eric G. Sternberg, Pst.; Elizabeth Monaghan, Parish Life Coord.; Tracey Tolzmann, Music Min.; CRP Stds.: 132

SCHOOLS: PRESCHOOL THRU HIGH SCHOOL

SCHOOLS

STATE OF WISCONSIN

EDGERTON

Oaklawn Academy - (PRV) (Grades 6-9) 432 Liguori Rd., Edgerton, WI 53534 t) 608-884-3425 info@oaklawnacademy.org www.oaklawnacademy.org Rev. Luis Felipe Rivero, LC (Mexico), Dir.; Rev. Agustin De la Vega, L.C., Supr.; Rev. David Kluk, LC (Chile), Chap.; Rev. Chad Everts, Regional Vocations Dir.; Stds.: 146; Pr. Tchrs.: 3; Lay Tchrs.: 5

MADISON

Edgewood Campus School, Inc. - (PRV) (Grades PreK-8) 829 Edgewood College Dr., Madison, WI 53711 t) 608-663-4100 apalzkill@edgewoodk8.com; lcostello@edgewoodk8.com www.edgewoodk8.org Sponsored by the Catholic Dominican Sisters of Sinsinawa Anne Palzkill, Pres.; Lauren Costello, Admin.; Stds.: 400; Lay Tchrs.: 35

HIGH SCHOOLS

STATE OF WISCONSIN

MADISON

***St. Ambrose Academy** - (PRV) (Grades 6-12) 3 Point Pl., Ste. 150, Madison, WI 53719 t) 608-827-5863 info@ambroseacademy.org www.ambroseacademy.org David Stiennon, Pres.; Scott Schmiesing, Prin.; Stds.: 165; Lay Tchrs.: 9

Edgewood High School of the Sacred Heart, Inc. - (PRV) (Grades 9-12) 2219 Monroe St., Madison, WI 53711 t) 608-257-1023 jen.trost@edgewoodhs.org www.edgewoodhs.org Jerome Zander, Prin.; Kevin Rea, Pres.; Stds.: 569; Lay Tchrs.: 52

INSTITUTIONS LOCATED IN DIOCESE

CAMPUS MINISTRY / NEWMAN CENTERS [CAM]

PLATTEVILLE

St. Augustine Newman Center - 135 S. Hickory St., Platteville, WI 53818-3316 t) 608-383-5574 frjohn@pioneercatholic.org pioneercatholic.org Rev. John Del Priore, S.J.S. (Spain), Admin.;

CATHOLIC CHARITIES [CCH]

JEFFERSON

St. Coletta of Wisconsin, Inc. - N4637 County Rd. Y, Jefferson, WI 53549 t) 920-674-4330 rbaker@stcolettawi.org www.stcolettawi.org Residential housing, day programs, transportation and employment for special needs. Sponsored by the Sisters of St. Francis of Assisi, Milwaukee. Ted Behncke, Pres.; Robin Baker, Vice. Pres.; Asstd. Annu.: 425; Staff: 408

MADISON

Catholic Charities, Inc., Diocese of Madison - 702 S. High Point Rd., Ste. 201, Madison, WI 53719 t) 608-826-8000 ccharities@ccmadison.org www.catholiccharitiesofmadison.org Serve as a visible present of the Church, by providing compassionate services, meeting the physical, mental, emotional needs of the community. Shawn Carney, Exec. Dir.; Asstd. Annu.: 20,333; Staff: 214

Catholic Multicultural Center - 1862 Beld St., Madison, WI 53713 t) 608-661-3512 laura@cmcmadison.org; steve@cmcmadison.org www.cmcmadison.org Our Lady Queen of Peace Parish / Catholic Multicultural Center. Steve Maurice, Dir.; Asstd. Annu.: 6,300; Staff: 13

CEMETERIES [CEM]

BELOIT

Calvary Cemetery - 1801 Colley Rd., Beloit, WI 53511; Mailing: 1827 N. Washington St., Janesville, WI 53547 t) 608-754-3472 calvary@madisondiocese.org madisondiocese.org/cemeteries Damian X. Lenshek, Dir.;

Mount Thabor Cemetery - 2138 Shopiere Rd., Beloit, WI 53511; Mailing: 1827 N. Washington St., Mt. Olivet Cemetery, Janesville, WI 53548 t) 608-754-3472 thabor@madisondiocese.org madisondiocese.org/cemeteries Damian X. Lenshek, Dir.;

JANESVILLE

Mount Olivet Cemetery - 1827 N. Washington St., Janesville, WI 53548 t) (608) 754-3472 olivet@madisondiocese.org madisondiocese.org/cemeteries Damian X. Lenshek, Dir.;

MADISON

Resurrection Cemetery - 2705 Regent St., Madison, WI 53705 t) 608-238-5561 resurrection@madisondiocese.org madisondiocese.org/cemeteries Damian X. Lenshek, Dir.;

COLLEGES & UNIVERSITIES [COL]

MADISON

Edgewood College, Inc. - 1000 Edgewood College Dr., Madison, WI 53711-1997 t) (608) 663-2262 (Pres.); (608) 663-6714 (CFO) amanion@edgewood.edu; amberg@edgewood.edu www.edgewood.edu Sponsored by the Dominican Sisters of Sinsinawa, Edgewood College, rooted in the Dominican tradition, engages students within a community of learners. Dr. Andrew Manion, Pres.; Dr. Milton J. Bravo, Vice Pres., Mission, Values & Inclusion; Laurin Dodge, Asst. Dir. Campus Ministry; Stds.: 1,907; Lay Tchrs.: 86

CONVENTS, MONASTERIES, AND RESIDENCES FOR WOMEN [CON]

BELOIT

Auxiliaries of the Blessed Sacrament - 916 Bluff St., Beloit, WI 53511 t) 608-466-9751 pamala31@juno.com Sr. Pauline Labrecque, Admin.; Srs.: 2

MADISON

Secular Institute of Schoenstatt Sisters of Mary - 5901 Cottage Grove Rd., Madison, WI 53718-1397 t) 608-222-7208 schoenstattheights@schsrsmary.org Sr. Gabriella Maschita, Admin.; Srs.: 3

PRAIRIE DU SAC

Valley of Our Lady Monastery (Cistercian Nuns) - E11096 Yanke Dr., Prairie du Sac, WI 53578-9737 t) 608-643-3520 cistercian nuns@valleyofourlady.org www.valleyofourlady.org Mother Anne-Marie Joerger, O.Cist., Prioress; Srs.: 22

SINSINAWA

Sinsinawa Dominican Congregation of the Most Holy Rosary. - 585 County Rd. Z, Sinsinawa, WI 53824-9701 t) 608-748-4411 tharris@sinsinawa.org www.sinsinawa.org Dominican Motherhouse Sr. Antoinette Harris, O.P., Prioress of the Congregation; Sr. Georgia Acker, O.P., Prioress, Mound Community; Sr. Mary Ann Nelson, O.P., Prioress, St. Elizabeth Manor; Sr. Deborah Bomyea, O.P., Co-Prioress, St. Dominic Villa; Sr. Diane Marie Skibicki, O.P., Co-Prioress, St. Dominic Villa; Sr. Maryann Lucy, O.P., Asst. Prioress, Siena; Rev. Daniel Davis, O.P., Chap.; Rev. John C. Risley, O.P., Chap.; Srs.: 294

ENDOWMENTS / FOUNDATIONS / TRUSTS [EFT]

BARABOO

St. Clare Health Care Foundation, Inc. - 707 14th St., Baraboo, WI 53913 t) 608-356-1449 www.stclare.com/foundation Primarily for the maintenance and benefit of St. Clare Hospital and St. Clare Meadows Care Center of Baraboo, WI. Julia Randles, Dir.;

JANESVILLE

St. Mary's Janesville Foundation, Inc. - 3400 E. Racine St., Janesville, WI 53546 t) 608-373-8015 www.stmarysjanesville.com Organized to provide gifts, grants or other payments to SSM Health Care of Wisconsin, Inc. Dona Hohensee, Dir.;

MADISON

The Catholic Diocese of Madison Foundation, Inc. - 702 S. High Point Rd., Ste. 223, Madison, WI 53719 t) (608) 821-3003 paul.merline@diocesemadisonfoundation.org www.diocesemadisonfoundation.org Operating exclusively for religious, charitable, and educational purposes within the meaning of 501(C)(3) per IRS code or subsequent law. Paul Merline, Devel. Consultant;

St. Mary's Foundation, Inc. - 700 S. Park St., Madison, WI 53715 t) 608-258-5600 ssmhealth.com/donatemadison To solicit, manage, invest and expend endowment funds and other gifts, grants and bequests primarily for the maintenance and benefit of St. Mary's. Dina Boyle, Exec. Dir.;

St. Paul University Catholic Foundation, Inc. - 723 State St., Madison, WI 53703-1087 t) 608-258-3140 welcomedesk@uwcatholic.org; enielsen@uwcatholic.org uwcatholic.org/ Rev. Eric H. Nielsen, Dir.; Daniel Hartung, Chair; Augustine Redington, Secy.; John Drake, Treas.;

MONROE

***Monroe Clinic and Hospital Foundation, Inc.** - 515 22nd Ave., Monroe, WI 53566; Mailing: 10101 Woodfield Ln., St. Louis, MO 63132 t) 608-324-2868 SSM Health Care of Wisconsin, Inc. Jane Sybers, Exec. Dir.;

SINSINAWA

The Dominican Outreach Foundation - 585 County Rd. Z, Sinsinawa, WI 53824 t) 608-748-4411 aendter@sinsinawa.org www.sinsinawa.org Organized to support the sisters educational, religious and charitable ministries. Andrea L. Endter, Secy.;

Mother Samuel Coughlin Charitable Trust - 585 County Rd. Z, Sinsinawa, WI 53824-9701 t) 608-748-4411 aendter@sinsinawa.org www.sinsinawa.org To provide financial support to the aged, infirm or disabled vowed members of the Sinsinawa Dominicans. Sr. Anne Sur, O.P., Secy.;

HOSPITALS / HEALTH SERVICES [HOS]

BARABOO

St. Clare Hospital - 707 14th St., Baraboo, WI 53913 t) 608-356-1400 www.stclare.com Member of SSM Health Care. Kyle Nondorf, Pres.; Bed Capacity: 43; Asstd. Annu.: 92,383; Staff: 420

JANESVILLE

SSM Health, St. Mary's Hospital - Janesville - 3400 E. Racine St., Janesville, WI 53546 t) 608-373-8010 www.stmarysjanesville.com A division of SSM Health Care of Wisconsin, Inc. Sponsored by Franciscan Sisters of Mary (St. Louis, MO). Eric Thornton, Pres.; Bed Capacity: 50; Asstd. Annu.: 91,141; Staff: 387

MADISON

SSM Health St. Mary's Hospital-Madison - 700 S. Park St., Madison, WI 53715 t) 608-251-6100 A division of SSM Health Care of Wisconsin, Inc. Sponsored by Franciscan Sisters of Mary (St. Louis, MO). Rev. Patrick F. Norris, O.P., Chap.; Susan Leet, Team Leader; Bed Capacity: 440; Asstd. Annu.: 118,347; Staff: 2,575

MONROE

The Monroe Clinic, Inc. - 515 22nd Ave., Monroe, WI 53566; Mailing: 10101 Woodfield Ln., St. Louis, MO 63132 t) 608-324-1000 www.monroeclinic.org A division of SSM Health Care of Wisconsin, Inc. Jane Curran-Meuli, Pres.; Bed Capacity: 95; Asstd. Annu.: 274,504; Staff: 1,121

MISCELLANEOUS [MIS]

BLANCHARDVILLE

Wisconsin Catholic Medical Guilds, Inc. - N8604 Hay Hollow Rd., Blanchardville, WI 53516 t) 608-209-2763 madisonguild.cathmed.org/ Dr. Robin Goldsmith, Pres.; Dr. Elizabeth Anderson, Vice. Pres.; Dr. Stephen Pavela, Treas.;

Wisconsin Catholic Conference - 106 E. Doty St., Ste. 300, Madison, WI 53703

CROSS PLAINS

Dead Theologians Society - 3673 County Rd. P, Cross Plains, WI 53528; Mailing: P.O. Box 368, Black Earth, WI 53515-0368 t) 608-843-2907 eddie@deadtheologianssociety.com www.deadtheologianssociety.com Eddie Cotter Jr., Exec.;

EDGERTON

Oaklawn Incorporated - 432 Liguori Rd., Edgerton, WI 53534 t) 608-884-3425 oaklawnusa@aol.com oaklawnacademy.org Rev. Agustin De la Vega, L.C., Supr.; Rev. Luis Felipe Rivero, LC (Mexico), Prin.;

MADISON

Apostolate to the Handicapped, Inc. - 702 S. High Point Rd., Ste. 225, Madison, WI 53719 t) 608-821-3050 apd@madisondiocese.org www.apdmadisondiocese.com dba Apostolate for Persons with Disabilities - Diocese of Madison Rev. Msgr. Lawrence M. Bakke, Dir.; Megan Wedwick, Dir.; Kayla Schiesser, Admin.;

***District Council of Madison Inc., Society of St. Vincent de Paul** - 2033 Fish Hatchery Rd., Madison, WI 53713 t) 608-442-7200 manager@svdpmadison.org svdpmadison.org Catholic lay organization providing services to people in need. Julie Bennett, CEO;

***The Evangelical Catholic, Inc.** - 6602 Normandy Ln., Fl.2, Madison, WI 53719 t) 608-820-1288 ec@evangelicalcatholic.org www.evangelicalcatholic.org Jason J. Simon, Pres.; Andrew Ochalek, Vice. Pres.; Robert Koonce, Sr. Dir., Mission Advancement;

Holy Name Catholic Center, Inc. - 702 S. High Point Rd., Ste. 225, Madison, WI 53719 t) 608-821-3000 vicargeneral@madisondiocese.org www.madisondiocese.org Most Rev. Donald J. Hying; Rev. Msgr. James R. Bartylla, Vicar;

Holy Name Seminary, Inc. (St. Joseph Fund) - 702 S. High Point Rd., Ste. 225, Madison, WI 53719 t) 608-821-3000 www.madisondiocese.org Rev. Msgr. James R. Bartylla, Vicar;

Roman Catholic Diocese of Madison Cemeteries, Inc. - 702 S. High Point Rd., Ste. 225, Madison, WI 53705 t) 608-821-3000 damian.lenshek@madisondiocese.org www.madisondiocese.org Damian X. Lenshek, Dir.;

SSM Health Care of Wisconsin, Inc. (Franciscah Sisters of Mary) - 1808 W. Beltline Hwy., Madison, WI 53713 t) 608-260-3500 To provide either directly or in conjunction with other persons or organizations health care, health education and related facilities. Sue Anderson, Pres.;

Tridentine Mass Society of the Diocese of Madison - 733 Struck St., Madison, WI 53711-6145; Mailing: P.O. Box 44603, Madison, WI 53711-6145 t) 608-228-5063 james@litewire.net www.latinmassmadison.org James Howard, Vice Pres. & Treas.;

SINSINAWA

Sinsinawa Housing, Inc. - 585 County Rd. Z, Sinsinawa, WI 53824-9701 t) 608-748-4411 aendter@sinsinawa.org www.sinsinawa.org To provide low- to moderate-income housing for senior residents of southwestern Wisconsin. Andrea L. Endter, Secy.;

MONASTERIES AND RESIDENCES FOR PRIESTS AND BROTHERS [MON]

EDGERTON

Koshkonong Pastoral Center - 432 Liguori Rd., Edgerton, WI 53534 t) 608-884-3425 Rev. Luis Felipe Rivero, LC (Mexico), Prin.; Priests: 3

MADISON

Holy Name Heights - 702 S. High Point Rd., Madison, WI 53719 t) 608-821-3000 vicargeneral@madisondiocese.org www.madisondiocese.org Most Rev. Donald J. Hying, In Res.; Rev. Msgr. James R. Bartylla, In Res.; Priests: 2

NURSING / REHABILITATION / CONVALESCENCE / ELDERLY CARE [NUR]

BARABOO

SSM Health St. Clare Meadows Care Center - 1414 Jefferson St., Baraboo, WI 53913 t) 608-356-4838 www.stclare.com/meadows Member of SSM Health Care. Ronnie E. Schaetzl, Dir.; Douglas Trost, Vice. Pres.; Asstd. Annu.: 87; Staff: 82

JANESVILLE

St. Elizabeth Home - 109 S. Atwood Ave., Janesville, WI 53545 t) 608-752-6709; (920) 261-0400 (Marquardt Management) www.stelizabethcampus.com/ Part of the St. Elizabeth Campus. Nicole Chwala, CFO; Drew Flores, Admin.; Asstd. Annu.: 95; Staff: 30

MADISON

All Saints Assisted Living Center, Inc. - 519 Commerce Dr., Madison, WI 53719; Mailing: 702 S. High Point Rd., Ste. 201, Madison, WI 53719 t) 608-827-2990; (608) 826-8000 hstringham@elderspan.com ww.allsaintsneighborhood.org Own & operate assisted living facilities for seniors, serving the needs of residents. Parent: Catholic Charities, Inc., Diocese of Madison Shawn Carney, Exec. Dir.; Asstd. Annu.: 195; Staff: 100

All Saints Retirement Center, Inc. - 8202 Highview Dr., Madison, WI 53719; Mailing: 702 S. High Point Rd., Ste. 201, Madison, WI 53719 t) 608-827-2222; (608) 826-8000 mnaegle@elderspan.com www.allsaintsneighborhood.org Apartments for seniors, in the tradition of the Church, serving the needs of the residents. Parent: Catholic Charities, Inc., Diocese of Madison Shawn Carney, Exec. Dir.; Asstd. Annu.: 192; Staff: 3

St. Mary's Care Center - 3401 Maple Grove Dr., Madison, WI 53719 t) 608-845-1000 Member of SSM Health Care. Douglas Trost, Vice. Pres.; Karen Hayden, Dir.; Asstd. Annu.: 647; Staff: 273

An asterisk (*) denotes an organization that has established tax-exempt status directly with the IRS and is not covered by the USCCB Group Ruling.

Diocese of Manchester

(Dioecesis Manchesteriensis)

MOST REVEREND PETER A. LIBASCI

Bishop of Manchester; ordained April 1, 1978; appointed Titular Bishop of Satafis and Auxiliary Bishop of Rockville Centre April 3, 2007; installed June 1, 2007; appointed Bishop of Manchester September 19, 2011; installed December 8, 2011. Chancery Office: 153 Ash St., Manchester, NH 03104.

Chancery Office: 153 Ash St., Manchester, NH 03104. T: 603-669-3100; F: 603-669-0377.
www.catholicnh.org
webmaster@rcbm.org

ESTABLISHED 1884.

Square Miles 9,305.

Comprises the State of New Hampshire.

For legal titles of parishes and diocesan institutions, consult the Chancery Office.

STATISTICAL OVERVIEW

Personnel

Bishop	1
Retired Bishops	1
Abbots	1
Priests: Diocesan Active in Diocese	68
Priests: Diocesan Active Outside Diocese	2
Priests: Retired, Sick or Absent	41
Number of Diocesan Priests	111
Religious Priests in Diocese	35
Total Priests in your Diocese	146
Extern Priests in Diocese	34
Ordinations:	
Diocesan Priests	3
Permanent Deacons	7
Permanent Deacons in Diocese	70
Total Brothers	15
Total Sisters	226

Parishes

Parishes	88
With Resident Pastor:	
Resident Diocesan Priests	72
Resident Religious Priests	10
Without Resident Pastor:	
Administered by Priests	6
Missions	11

Welfare

Catholic Hospitals	2
Total Assisted	350,501
Health Care Centers	6
Total Assisted	851
Homes for the Aged	6
Total Assisted	107
Specialized Homes	2
Total Assisted	122
Special Centers for Social Services	8
Total Assisted	130,411
Other Institutions	1
Total Assisted	26

Educational

Diocesan Students in Other Seminaries	12
Total Seminarians	12
Colleges and Universities	4
Total Students	4,624
High Schools, Diocesan and Parish	4
Total Students	1,054
High Schools, Private	3
Total Students	911
Elementary Schools, Diocesan and Parish	13
Total Students	2,588
Elementary Schools, Private	5
Total Students	1,135
Catechesis/Religious Education:	
High School Students	314
Elementary Students	4,053
Total Students under Catholic Instruction	14,691
Teachers in Diocese:	
Priests	5
Brothers	1
Sisters	11
Lay Teachers	457

Vital Statistics

Receptions into the Church:	
Infant Baptism Totals	1,306
Minor Baptism Totals	31
Adult Baptism Totals	19
Received into Full Communion	113
First Communions	1,224
Confirmations	1,827
Marriages:	
Catholic	260
Interfaith	80
Total Marriages	340
Deaths	2,312
Total Catholic Population	210,850
Total Population	1,377,529

LEADERSHIP

Vicars General - Rev. Shawn M. Therrien; Very Rev. Jason Y. Jalbert (jjalbert@rcbm.org);
Vicar for Canonical Affairs - Rev. Georges F. de Laire;
Episcopal Master of Ceremonies - Very Rev. Jason Y. Jalbert (jjalbert@rcbm.org);
Priest Secretary - Very Rev. Jason Y. Jalbert (jjalbert@rcbm.org);

ADMINISTRATION

Operations and Administration - Dennis Honan, Dir.;
Chancellor - Meredith P. Cook (mcook@rcbm.org);
Bishop's Secretary - Louise LeDuc (lleduc@rcbm.org);

OFFICES AND DIRECTORS

Archivist - Dennis W. Pedley;
Legal Services - Meredith P. Cook (mcook@rcbm.org); Briand T. Wade; Robert E. Dunn;
Office for Healing and Pastoral Care - t) 603-663-0125 Marc F. Guillemette;
Office for Ministerial Conduct - James Kinney, Bishop's Delegate for Ministerial Conduct (jkinney@rcbm.org);
Office of Information Technologies - John Ashworth-King, Dir.;
Office of Public Policy - Robert E. Dunn Jr., Dir.;
Safe Environment - Mary Ellen D'Intino, Bishop's Delegate;

CATHOLIC CHARITIES

New Hampshire Catholic Charities, Inc. - t) 603-669-3030 Thomas E. Blonski, Pres. (tblonski@nh-cc.org); Dominique A. Rust, Vice. Pres. (drust@nh-cc.org); Alain Bernard, Asst. Vice Pres. Healthcare Svcs. (abernard@nh-cc.org);

CLERGY AND RELIGIOUS SERVICES

Coordinator for International Priests - Rev. Christopher M. Martel;
Coordinator for Retired Priests - Rev. Msgr. C. Peter Dumont;
Liaison for Women Religious - Rev. Georges F. de Laire;
Office for Ordained Ministry & Formation - Rev. Shawn M. Therrien; Very Rev. Jason Y. Jalbert (jjalbert@rcbm.org);
Office for Worship - Very Rev. Jason Y. Jalbert, Dir. (jjalbert@rcbm.org);
Office of Vocations - Rev. Matthew J. Mason, Dir. (mmason@rcbm.org); Rev. Volney J. DeRosia, Dir.; Rev. Charles H. Pawlowski, Dir.;

COMMUNICATIONS

Communications Director - Tara Bishop;
Parable Magazine - Rosemary Ford, Editor;

COMMUNITY SERVICES

Secretariat for Multicultural Ministries - Dcn. Ramon Andrade, Secy.;

CONSULTATIVE BODIES

College of Consultors - Very Rev. Michael S. Taylor; Very Rev. Jason Y. Jalbert (jjalbert@rcbm.org); Rev. Shawn M. Therrien;
Diocesan Review Board - Mark Collopy, Chair; Robert Carey; Rev. Michael E. Gendron;
Finance Council - Eva Martel, Chair; Rev. Michael E. Gendron; Anthony Annino;
Presbyteral Council - Rev. Michael E. Gendron, Chair; Rev. Marcel I. Martel, Vice Chmn.; Very Rev. Kyle F. Stanton, Secy.;

DEVELOPMENT

Secretariat for Development and Communications - Bevin Kennedy, Cabinet Sec. (bkennedy@rcbm.org);
Development - Bevin Kennedy, Dir.;

EDUCATION

Superintendent of Catholic Schools - David Thibault;
Assistant Superintendent of Catholic Schools - Lisa Zolkos;
Marketing, Enrollment and Development - Alison Mueller, Dir.;
Director of Operations - Steven R. McManis;

FAITH FORMATION

Secretariat for Catholic Formation - Mary Ellen Mahon, Secy. (memahon@rcbm.org);
Adult Faith Formation - Mary Jane Silvia, Dir.;
Family Life & Respect Life Ministries - Derek McDonald, Dir.;
Parish Faith Formation -
Catholic Scouting - Rev. Raymond A. Ball, Dir.;
Catholic Youth Organization - Charles Cook, Dir.;
Office of Pastoral Ministry - Mary Ellen Mahon, Dir.;

FINANCE

Finance - Rolla "Mac" McFall Bryant, Finance Officer; Christine Bogacz, Dir. (cbogacz@rcbm.org); Patricia Goneau, Controller (pgoneau@rcbm.org);
Cemetery Operations - David A. Gabert, Dir. (dgabert@rcbm.org);
Office of Real Estate and Construction - Robert Eib, Dir. (reib@rcbm.org);

HUMAN RESOURCES

Office of Human Resources - Christine L. Hagen, Dir.;

TRIBUNAL

Judicial Vicar - Rev. Georges F. de Laire;
Moderator of Tribunal Office - Winifred McGrath, Dir.;
Adjutant Judicial Vicar - Very Rev. Michael S. Taylor;
Diocesan Judges - Rev. Georges F. de Laire; Very Rev. Michael S. Taylor; Winifred McGrath;
Advocates - Rev. Eric T. Delisle; Rev. John W. Fleming; Rev. Michael E. Gendron;
Defender of the Bond - Rev. Msgr. Paul L. Bouchard;
Promoter of Justice - Rev. Msgr. Paul L. Bouchard;

PARISHES, MISSIONS, AND CLERGY

STATE OF NEW HAMPSHIRE

ALTON

St. Katharine Drexel - 40 Hidden Springs Rd., Alton, NH 03809; Mailing: P.O. Box 180, Wolfeboro, NH 03894-0180 t) 603-875-2548 office@stkdrexel.org stkdrexel.org Very Rev. Robert F. Cole, Pst.; Dcn. Christopher E. Conley; Dcn. Rick Hilton; Dcn. Charles Ferraro; Gertrude Hammond, DRE;

AUBURN

St. Peter - 567 Manchester Rd., Auburn, NH 03032-3123 t) 603-623-5429 stpeteraub@comcast.net stpeteraub.org Rev. Michael E. Gendron, Pst.; Rev. Roarke Traynor, Par. Vicar; Dcn. Sean C. Magee;

BEDFORD

St. Elizabeth Seton - 190 Meetinghouse Rd., Bedford, NH 03110-6027 t) 603-669-7444 sesparish@comcast.net www.stelizabethsetonchurch.org Rev. Msgr. John P. Quinn, Pst.; Gertrude Hammond, DRE; Christine Saltzman, DRE; CRP Stds.: 263

BELMONT

St. Joseph - 6 High St., Belmont, NH 03220-0285; Mailing: P.O. Box 285, Belmont, NH 03220-0285 t) 603-267-8174; 603-286-9995 (CRP) stjoebel@metrocast.net stjosephbelmont.org Very Rev. Marc B. Drouin, Pst.; Rev. Richard B. Thompson, Pst. Assoc.; Dcn. Mark DeRosch; CRP Stds.: 22

BERLIN

Good Shepherd - 151 Emery St., Berlin, NH 03570 t) 603-752-2880 frkfstanton@gmail.com Very Rev. Kyle F. Stanton, Pst.; Rev. Joseph Moynahan, Par. Vicar; Rev. Stephen Savarimuthu, H.G.N. (India), Par. Vicar; Dcn. Michael C. Couture; Ben Robertson, DRE;

CENTER OSSIPEE

St. Joseph - 23 Moultonville Rd., Center Ossipee, NH 03814; Mailing: P.O. Box 248, Center Ossipee, NH 03814-0248 t) 603-539-5036 stanthony239@gmail.com www.stanthonystjoseph.org (Twinned with St. Anthony Parish, Sanbornville, N.H.) Very Rev. Patrick N. Gilbert, Pst.; CRP Stds.: 1

CHARLESTOWN

All Saints Parish - 285 Main St., Charlestown, NH 03603-0332; Mailing: P.O. Box 332, Charlestown, NH 03603-0332 t) 603-826-3359 allsaints3@comcast.net Rev. John B. Loughnane, Pst.;
St. Catherine of Siena Church -
St. Peter Church - 38 Church St., North Walpole, NH 03609-1715

CLAREMONT

St. Joseph - 58 Elm St., Claremont, NH 03743-0824; Mailing: P.O. Box 824, Claremont, NH 03743-0824 t) 603-542-5732 stjosephsclaremont@gmail.com Rev. Sebastian Susairaj, H.G.N., Pst.;
St. Mary - 32 Pearl St., Claremont, NH 03743-2552 t) 603-542-9518 stmarysclaremont@comcast.net Rev. Sebastian Susairaj, H.G.N., Pst.;
Old St. Mary - Old Church Rd., Claremont, NH 03743

COLEBROOK

North American Martyrs Parish - 55 Pleasant St., Colebrook, NH 03576-0065 t) 603-237-4342 frchenenamp@myfairpoint.net Rev. Craig I. Cheney, Pst.;
St. Albert Church - 15 Church St., West Stewartstown, NH 03597
St. Brendan Church -
St. Pius the Tenth - 108 Colebrook Rd., Errol, NH 03579

CONCORD

Christ the King Parish - 72 S Main St, Concord, NH 03301-4830 t) 603-224-2328 parish@christthekingnh.org www.christthekingnh.org/ Rev. Richard A. Roberge, Pst.; Dcn. Winton P. DeRosia; Rev. Maurice Abasilim (Nigeria), In Rcs.;
Immaculate Heart of Mary - 180 Loudon Rd., Concord, NH 03301-6028 t) 603-224-4393; 603-225-2026 (CRP) recoffice@ihmnh.org Rev. Raymond A. Ball, Pst.; Dcn. John Morrow;

DERRY

St. Thomas Aquinas - 26 Crystal Ave., Derry, NH 03038-1799 t) 603-432-5000 staderry@stthomasderry.org stthomasderry.org Rev. Joseph Powell, O.F.M., Pst.; Rev. Christopher Gaffrey, O.F.M., Par. Vicar; Bro. Damian Johnson, O.F.M., Pst. Assoc.; Dcn. Joseph Dion;

DOVER

Parish of the Assumption - 150 Central Ave., Dover, NH 03820-3464 t) 603-742-4837 office@assumptiondovernh.org www.assumptiondovernh.org Rev. Agapit H. Jean Jr., Pst.; Rev. Daniel Mikolajewski, Par. Vicar; Dcn. David C. Deutsch; Dcn. Arnold J. A. Gustafson; Dcn. James P. Wilton; Sheila Cronin, DRE; Megan Licata, DRE;
Chapel of the Nativity - Rte. 9, Barrington, NH 03820

DURHAM

St. Thomas More - 6 Madbury Rd., Durham, NH 03824-0620; Mailing: Box 620, Durham, NH 03824-0620 t) 603-868-2666; 603-868-2666 x117 (CRP) stmdurham@comcast.net; stmfaith@comcast.net stmdurham.org Rev. Andrew W. Cryans, Pst.; Rev. John P. Rosson, Supply Min.; Ann McGurty, DRE; CRP Stds.: 60

ENFIELD

St. Helena - 36 Shaker Hill Rd., Enfield, NH 03766; Mailing: P.O. Box 1363, Enfield, NH 03766 t) 603-632-4263; 603-448-1262 (CRP) dffsheartlebanon@gmail.com; sthstm@gmail.com Rev. Charles H. Pawlowski, Pst.;
St. Mary - 1157 Rte. 4, Canaan, NH 03741

EPPING

St. Joseph - 200 Pleasant St., Epping, NH 03042-0337;

Mailing: P.O. Box 337, Epping, NH 03042-0337 t) 603-679-8805 nh337@comcast.net stjosepheppingnh.com Rev. David Gagnon, Admin.; Ann Ryan, DRE;

EXETER

St. Michael Parish - 93 Front St., Exeter, NH 03833-3297; Mailing: 9 Lincoln St., Exeter, NH 03833 t) 603-772-2494 business@stmnh.org; admin@stmnh.org www.stmichaelparish.org Rev. Matthew J. Mason, Pst.; Rev. Bartholomew I. Okonkwo (Nigeria), Par. Vicar; Dcn. Eric M. Lambert; CRP Stds.: 246

FARMINGTON

St. Peter - 88 Central St., Farmington, NH 03835; Mailing: 71 Lowell St., Rochester, NH 03867 t) 603-755-3921 stmary@metrocast.net Rev. Thomas L. Duston, Pst.; Dcn. Richard A. Falardeau; CRP Stds.: 4

FRANKLIN

St. Gabriel - 110 School St., Franklin, NH 03235-0490; Mailing: PO Box 490, Franklin, NH 03235 t) 603-934-5013 Rev. Adrian Frackowiak, Admin.; Dcn. David D. Hemeon III; Dcn. Thomas F. Matzke; Christine Dzujna, DRE;

St. Mary of the Assumption - 16 Chestnut St., Tilton, NH 03276

St. Paul - 108 School St., Franklin, NH 03235; Mailing: P.O. Box 490, Franklin, NH 03235

GOFFSTOWN

St. Lawrence - 1 E. Union St., Goffstown, NH 03045-1644 t) 603-497-2651 office@stlawrencegoffstown.org www.stlawrencegoffstown.org Rev. David L. Kneeland, Pst.; Dcn. Geoffrey L. Ashman;

GONIC

St. Leo - 32 Pickering Rd., Gonic, NH 03839-5220; Mailing: 189 N. Main St., Rochester, NH 03867 t) 603-332-1863 pgousse@hrsl.org www.hrsl.org Rev. Matthew Schultz, Pst.; Sr. Mary Rose Reddy, D.M.M.L., DRE; CRP Stds.: 10

St. Leo Catholic Children's Center - ; Mailing: 189 N Main St., Rochester, NH 03867

GORHAM

Holy Family - 7 Church St., Gorham, NH 03581-1695; Mailing: 151 Emery St., Berlin, NH 03570 t) 603-752-2880 ben@berlingorhamcatholics.org; bgoudreau@berlingorhamcatholics.org berlingorhamcatholics.org Very Rev. Kyle F. Stanton, Pst.; Rev. Joseph Moynahan, Par. Vicar; Rev. Stephen Savarimuthu, H.G.N. (India), Par. Vicar; Dcn. Michael C. Couture; Ben Robertson, DRE;

Salve Regina Academy - 9 Church St., Gorham, NH 03570 t) 603-707-5893 Michael Timberlake, Prin.;

GREENVILLE

Sacred Heart of Jesus - 15 High St., Greenville, NH 03048-3121 t) 603-878-1121; 603-878-2274 (CRP) sacredheartgreenvillenh@comcast.net Rev. Wilfred H. Deschamps, Pst.; Lisa Kouropoulos, DRE;

GROVETON

St. Marguerite d'Youville Parish - 11 State St., Groveton, NH 03582-0247; Mailing: P.O. Box 247, Groveton, NH 03582-0247 t) 603-636-1047 stfxsh11@gmail.com Rev. Daniel R. Deveau, Pst.; Dcn. Michael H. Johnson;

Sacred Heart Church - 59 Main St., North Stratford, NH 03590

St. Francis Xavier Church -

HAMPSTEAD

St. Anne - 26 Emerson Ave., Hampstead, NH 03841-0339; Mailing: P.O. Box 339, Hampstead, NH 03841-0339 t) 603-329-5886 psmith@saintannechurchnh.org www.saintannechurchnh.org Rev. Marc R. Gagne, Pst.; Dcn. William E. Mullen; Dcn. Terry Sullivan; Cheryl Gottwald, DRE; Pam Walsh, DRE;

HAMPTON

Our Lady of the Miraculous Medal - 289 Lafayette Rd., Hampton, NH 03842-2109 t) 603-926-2206; 603-926-5573 (CRP) office@olmmparish.org Rev. Gary J. Kosmowski, Pst.; Rev. Boniface Agbata, Par. Vicar; Dcn. Stephen J. Kaneb; Rev. Robert G. Biron, In Res.; Sherry Impostato, DRE;

St. Elizabeth of Hungary -

St. Patrick - 5 Williams St., Hampton, NH 03842-2722 t) 603-926-2205 m.dunker@yahoo.com For all records contact O.L.M.M. Parish, Hampton. Very Rev. Jason Y. Jalbert, Admin.;

HANOVER

St. Denis - 8 Sanborn Rd., Hanover, NH 03755-2182 t) 603-643-2166 admin.stdenis@gmail.com; faithformation.stdenis@gmail.com www.saindenisparish.org Rev. Jacob Bertrand Janczyk, O.P., Pst.; Jessica DePrizio Cole, DRE;

HENNIKER

St. Theresa - 158 Old W. Hopkinton Rd., Henniker, NH 03242-0729; Mailing: P. O. Box 729, Henniker, NH 03242 t) 603-428-3325 parish.office@tds.net www.showerofroses.org Rev. Marcel I. Martel, Pst.; Dcn. Wayne R. Bolduc;

HILLSBOROUGH

St. Mary - 38 Church St., Hillsborough, NH 03244-0907; Mailing: P. O. Box 729, Henniker, NH 03242 t) 603-428-3325 parish.office@tds.net www.showerofroses.org Rev. Marcel I. Martel, Pst.; Dcn. Wayne R. Bolduc;

HOOKSETT

Holy Rosary - 21 Main St., Hooksett, NH 03106-1685 t) 603-485-3523 hrparishhook@comcast.net Rev. Michael E. Gendron, Pst.; Rev. Steven M. Lepine, Par. Vicar; Dcn. William R. Lavallee;

HUDSON

St. Kathryn - 4 Dracut Rd., Hudson, NH 03051-5006 t) 603-882-7793 fr.michael@stkathryns.org www.stkathryns.org Rev. Michael R. Monette, Pst.; Sr. Janice Rooney, S.N.D.deN., DRE; Dcn. Raymond V. Marcotte; CRP Stds.: 59

JAFFREY

St. Patrick - 87 Main St., Jaffrey, NH 03452-6139 t) 603-532-6634 laurie@myfairpoint.net; stpatric@myfairpoint.net www.stpatricksjaffrey.com/ Rev. Wilfred H. Deschamps, Pst.; Laurie Mathieu, DRE;

KEENE

Parish of the Holy Spirit - 161 Main St., Keene, NH 03431 t) 603-352-3525 swymerken@gmail.com; holyspirit.peace@gmail.com swnhcatholics.com Rev. Alan C. Tremblay, Pst.; Rev. Cuong Van Nguyen, Par. Vicar; Dcn. Fintan Moore Jr.; Dcn. Kenneth J. Swymer;

St. Bernard Church - 185 Main St., Keene, NH 03431

St. Margaret Mary Church - 33-35 Arch St., Keene, NH 03431

Immaculate Conception Church - 37 School St., Troy, NH 03465

LACONIA

St. Andre Bessette - 277 Union Ave., Laconia, NH 03246-3122 t) 603-524-9609 standrebessette.org Very Rev. Marc B. Drouin, Pst.; Rev. Richard B. Thompson; Dcn. Mark DeRosch; CRP Stds.: 56

St. Joseph - 30 Church St., Laconia, NH 03246

Sacred Heart - 291 Union Ave., Laconia, NH 03246 t) (603) 524-9609

LANCASTER

Gate of Heaven - 163 Main St., Lancaster, NH 03584-3032 t) 603-788-2083 gateofheavennh@aol.com Rev. Britto Adaikalam, Pst.;

St. Agnes -

St. Matthew Church - 9 Jefferson Rd., Whitefield, NH 03598-3101

St. Patrick - 65 St. Patrick Church Rd., Twin Mountain, NH 03595

Bretton Woods, Our Lady of the Mountains - 2470 Rte. 302 E., Bretton Woods, NH 03575 Diane Caruso, DRE; Susan Tibbetts, DRE;

LEBANON

Sacred Heart - 2 Hough St., Lebanon, NH 03766-0482; Mailing: P.O. Box 482, Lebanon, NH 03766-0482 t) 603-448-1262 sheartlebanon@gmail.com Rev. Charles H. Pawlowski, Pst.;

LINCOLN

St. Joseph - 25 Church St., Lincoln, NH 03251-0128; Mailing: P.O. Box 128, Lincoln, NH 03251 t) 603-745-2266 Rev. John J. Mahoney Jr., Pst.; Paula King, DRE; CRP Stds.: 7

LITCHFIELD

St. Francis of Assisi - 9 St. Francis Way, Litchfield, NH 03052-8050 t) 603-424-9061 (CRP); 603-424-3456 parish@stfrancisofassisi.net Rev. Jeffrey P. Statz, Pst.; Dcn. Frank Ottaviano; Vicki Isabelle, DRE;

LITTLETON

St. Rose of Lima - 77 Clay St., Littleton, NH 03561 t) 603-444-2593 strosechurchnh.org Rev. Ryan C. Amazeen, Admin.; Dcn. Stephen M. Noyes; Allison Culver, DRE; CRP Stds.: 49

Our Lady of the Snows -

LONDONDERRY

St. Jude - 435 Mammoth Rd., Londonderry, NH 03053-2304 t) 603-432-3333 (Office); 603-437-7026 (Faith Formation); 603-425-1795 (Adult Faith Formation) sgreen@stjudenh.com; twoodward@stjudenh.com stjudenh.com Rev. Robert E. Gorski, Pst.; Dcn. Jay L. Cormier; Trish Woodward, DRE; CRP Stds.: 81

St. Mark the Evangelist - One South Rd., Londonderry, NH 03053-3814 t) 603-432-8711; 603-432-5711 (CRP) info@stmarksnh.org Rev. Michael S. Zgonc, Pst.; Dcn. Thomas Lavallee;

MANCHESTER

St. Joseph Cathedral - 145 Lowell St., Manchester, NH 03104-6135 t) 603-622-6404 office@stjosephcathedralnh.org www.stjosephcathedralnh.org Very Rev. Jason Y. Jalbert, Rector; Rev. Msgr. C. Peter Dumont, In Res.; Most Rev. Francis J. Christian, In Res.; Rev. Eric T. Delisle, In Res.; Rev. Elson Kattookkaran, M.S., In Res.; Rev. Jeffrey P. Statz, In Res.; Dcn. Karl Cooper; CRP Stds.: 36

Most Blessed Sacrament Chapel - Lowell St., Manchester, NH 03104

St. Anne-St. Augustin - 383 Beech St., Manchester, NH 03103-5350 t) 603-623-8809; 603-625-5655; 603-625-4603 parishoffice@stasta.org Rev. Shawn M. Therrien, Pst.; Dcn. Ramon Andrade; Dcn. Lam Tran; CRP Stds.: 61

St. Anthony of Padua - 172 Belmont St., Manchester, NH 03103-4452 t) 603-625-6409 saintanthony@comcast.net stanthonyofpaduanh.org Rev. Richard H. Dion, Pst.; Dcn. Michael Brunette; Rev. Roger L. Lascelle, In Res.; Rev. Theodore Mbaegbu, In Res.;

Cardinal Lacroix Academy - 148 Belmont St., Manchester, NH 03103 t) 603-622-0414 Beverly Broomhall, Prin.;

Blessed Sacrament - 14 Elm St., Manchester, NH 03103-7242 t) 603-622-5445 lisa@blessedsacramentnh.org www.blessedsacramentnh.org Rev. John Bucchino, O.F.M., Pst.; Stephen Donohue, DRE; Martha Donohue, DRE;

Chapel: St. Theresa of Lisieux Adoration Chapel -

St. Catherine of Siena - 207 Hemlock St., Manchester, NH 03104-3248 t) 603-622-4966; 603-622-6264 (CRP) yff@scsnh.com; parishoffice@scsnh.com www.saintcatherineparishnh.com Rev. Christopher M. Martel, Pst.; Dcn. Edward P. Munz; Lisa Daugherty, DRE; CRP Stds.: 49

St. Hedwig - 147 Walnut St., Manchester, NH 03104-4225 t) 603-623-4835 parishoffice@sthedwigparish.comcastbiz.net sainthedwignh.org Rev. Eric T. Delisle, Pst.;

Ste. Marie - 378 Notre Dame Ave., Manchester, NH 03102-3793 t) 603-622-4615 mandy@stemariechurch.com Rev. Maurice R. Larochelle, Pst.; Dcn. Kevin Cody; Rev. Paul M. Gousse, In Res.; Rev. Bartholomew Ogumelo, In Res.; Terry Bolduc, DRE;

Chapel of North American Martyrs -

St. Joan of Arc -

Mother Rivier Eucharist Adoration Chapel - 133 Wayne St., Manchester, NH 03102

Parish of the Transfiguration - 107 Alsace St., Manchester, NH 03102-3006 t) 603-623-4715; 603-622-0504 (CRP) office.transfiguration@comcast.net transfigurationparish.org Rev. John W. Fleming, Pst.; Dcn. Richard J. Shannon;

St. Pius X - 575 Candia Rd., Manchester, NH 03109-4735 t) 603-622-6510 sdahlberg@saintpiusxnh.org; parishoffice@saintpiusxnh.org saintpiusxnh.org/ Rev. Georges F. de Laire, Pst.; Dcn. James E. Patterson; Samuel Dahlberg, DRE; CRP Stds.: 35

St. Raphael - 103 Walker St., Manchester, NH 03102-4566 t) 603-623-2604 srp@st-raphael-parish.org www.st-raphael-parish.org Rev. Anselm Smedile, O.S.B, Pst.; CRP Stds.: 20

Sacred Heart Parish - 265 S. Main St., Manchester, NH 03102-4890; Mailing: 247 S. Main St., Manchester, NH 03102 t) 603-625-9525 sacredheartmanchester@comcast.net www.sacredheartchurch-nh.com Rev. Stephen Marcoux III, Pst.;

MEREDITH

St. Charles Borromeo - 300 NH Rte. 25, Meredith, NH 03253-0237; Mailing: PO Box 237, Meredith, NH 03253 t) 603-279-4403 office@stcharlesnh.org www.stcharlesnh.org Rev. Msgr. Gerald R. Belanger, Pst.; De-Anne Porter, DRE; CRP Stds.: 37

MERRIMACK

St. John Neumann - 708 Milford Rd., Merrimack, NH 03054 t) 603-880-0825 (CRP); 603-880-4689 office@sjnnh.org Very Rev. Robert K. Glasgow, Pst.; Dcn. Brian W. Lester;

Our Lady of Mercy - 16 Baboosic Lake Rd., Merrimack, NH 03054-3603 t) 603-424-3757 frpaul@olmnh.org; mcoughline@olmnh.org www.olmnh.org Rev. Msgr. Paul L. Bouchard, Pst.; Dcn. John B. Castelot;

MILFORD

St. Patrick - 34 Amherst St., Milford, NH 03055 t) 603-673-1311; 603-673-4797 (CRP) diane.st.patoffice@gmail.com saintpatrickmilfordnh.org Rev. Dennis J. Audet, Pst.;

NASHUA

St. Aloysius of Gonzaga - 48 W. Hollis St., Nashua, NH 03060-3286 t) 603-882-4362; 603-821-5192 (CRP) businessmanager@stlouisnashua.org Rev. Marcos A. Gonzalez-Torres, Pst.;

St. Christopher - 60 Manchester St., Nashua, NH 03064 t) 603-882-0632 cmercurio@stchrisparishnh.org; info@stchrisparishnh.org Rev. David Harris, Pst.; Dcn. James P. Daly; Christine Mercurio, DRE;

Immaculate Conception - 216 E. Dunstable Rd., Nashua, NH 03062-2344 t) 603-888-0321 (Office); 603-888-0608 (CRP) office@iccnashuanh.org iccnashuanh.org/ Rev. Ray J. Labrie, Pst.; Rev. Remo Zanatta, Weekend Priest Asst.; Dcn. Christopher M. Everhart; Dcn. William McDermott; Rev. Paul D. Montminy, In Res.;

Saint John XXIII Parish - 121 Allds St., Nashua, NH 03060-6395 t) 603-882-2462 x4 office@stjohnxxiiinh.org www.stjohnxxiiinh.org Rev. George Mattathilani, Pst.; Dcn. Edmund C. Hilston; Rev. Ethelbert C. Orabuche, In Res.;

Brazilian Outreach Office -

Infant Jesus Church -

St. John the Evangelist Church - 25 Library St., Hudson, NH 03051-4239

St. Joseph the Worker - 777 W. Hollis St., Nashua, NH 03062-3553 t) 603-883-0757; 603-883-0757 x4 (CRP) janicemercure@stjoenash.org; parishoffice@stjoenash.org www.stjoenash.org Most Rev. Francis J. Christian, Pst.; Dcn. Roland Leduc; Dcn. Douglas Hoffer; Dcn. Raymond A. Wheeler; Janice Mercure, DRE; CRP Stds.: 43

Parish of the Resurrection - 449 Broad St., Nashua, NH 03063-3412 t) (603) 882-0925 rezparish@comcast.net www.parishoftheresurrection.org Rev. John M. Grace, Pst.; Dcn. Steven Veneman; Terry Root, DRE;

St. Patrick - 29 Spring St., Nashua, NH 03060-3490 t) 603-882-2262; 603-882-5417 (CRP) office@stpatricksnashua.org; faithformation.st.patrick@gmail.com www.stpatricksnashua.org/ Rev. Michael Kerper, Pst.; Rev. Edmund G. Crowley, In Res.; Rev. John E. Healey, In Res.; CRP Stds.: 10

St. Stanislaus Parish - 43 Franklin St., Nashua, NH 03064; Mailing: 5 Green St., Nashua, NH 03064 t) 603-598-0400 office@latinmassnashua.org www.latinmassnashua.org Rev. John Brancich, F.S.S.P., Pst.; Rev. Edward Brodsky, FSSP, Par. Vicar; CRP Stds.: 57

NEW LONDON

Our Lady of Fatima - 724 Main St., New London, NH 03257-7821 t) 603-526-4484 parishoffice@olfic.org www.olfic.org Rev. Donald E. Clinton, Pst.; Dcn. Gregory R. McGinn;

Immaculate Conception -

NEWMARKET

St. Mary Church - 182 Main St., Newmarket, NH 03857-0337; Mailing: PO Box 337, Newmarket, NH 03857 t) 603-659-3643 business@stmnh.org stmarynh.org Rev. Matthew J. Mason, Pst.; Rev. Bartholomew I. Okonkwo (Nigeria), Par. Vicar; Dcn. Eric M. Lambert; CRP Stds.: 25

NEWPORT

St. Patrick - 32 Beech St., Newport, NH 03773-1416; Mailing: 40 School St., Newport, NH 03773-1416 t) 603-863-1422 office@saintpatrickparish.net www.saintpatrickparish.net Rev. Michael L. Sartori, Pst.;

St. Joachim - 5 Old Georges Mills Rd., Sunapee, NH 03782 Rev. Michael R. Monette, Pst.;

NORTH CONWAY

Our Lady of the Mountains - 2905 White Mountains Hwy., North Conway, NH 03860 t) 603-356-2535; 603-986-7582 x18 (CRP) ourladynh@myfairpoint.net; olmreligioused@myfairpoint.net ourladyofthemountainsnh.org Rev. Joshua M. Livingston, Admin.; Dcn. John Carey;

PELHAM

St. Patrick - 12 Main St., Pelham, NH 03076-3724 t) 603-635-3525; 603-635-1447 (CRP) faithlifeformation@comcast.net; therese42852@comcast.net Rev. Volney J. DeRosia, Pst.; Rev. Msgr. Richard J. Kelley, In Res.; Adam Castor, DRE;

PENACOOK

Immaculate Conception - 9 Bonney St., Penacook, NH 03303-1654 t) 603-753-4413 pastor@icpenacook.org www.icpenacook.org/ Rev. David Wong, Admin.;

PETERBOROUGH

Divine Mercy Parish - 12 Church St., Peterborough, NH 03458 t) 603-924-7647; 603-547-8607 (CRP) maplemanse@aol.com; divinemercynh@comcast.net divinemercynh.org Very Rev. Michael S. Taylor, Pst.; Dcn. Dennis W. Marquis; Jackie Capes, DRE; CRP Stds.: 61

PITTSFIELD

Our Lady of Lourdes - 20 River Rd., Pittsfield, NH 03263-3314 t) 603-435-6242; 603-942-8716 (CRP) ololstjoseph@metrocast.net; stjgar@outlook.com ourladyoflourdes-stjosephs.org Very Rev. John B. MacKenzie, Pst.; Regina Garcia, DRE;

St. Joseph - 844 1st NH Tpke. (Rte. 4), Northwood, NH 03261; Mailing: 20 River Rd., Pittsfield, NH 03263-3314 Jeannie Garcia, DRE;

PLAISTOW

St. Luke the Evangelist Parish - 8 Atkinson Depot Rd., Plaistow, NH 03865-3103 t) 603-382-8324 purchase@stluketheevangelist.net www.stlukenh.org Rev. Albert J. Tremblay, Pst.; Joyce Szczapa, DRE;

Holy Angels Church -

Mary, Mother of the Church - 12 Amesbury Rd., Newton, NH 03858

Holy Angels Pre-School - t) 603-382-9783 jtremblay@stluketheevangelist.net Jean Lanctot, Dir.;

Convent - 6 Atkinson Depot Rd., Plaistow, NH 03865

PLYMOUTH

Holy Trinity Parish - 46 Langdon St., Plymouth, NH 03264-1438 t) 603-536-4700 holytrinitynh@gmail.com holytrinityparishnh.org Rev. Mark E. Dollard; Dcn. Michael Guy;

St. Matthew Church - 11 School St., Plymouth, NH 03264 Maureen Ebner, DRE; Amy Ulricson, DRE;

Our Lady of Grace - 2 W. Shore Rd., Bristol, NH 03222

PORTSMOUTH

Corpus Christi Parish - 845 Woodbury Ave., Portsmouth, NH 03801-3213 t) 603-436-4555; 603-436-0344 parishmail.ccnh@gmail.com www.corpuschristinh.org Rev. Gary J. Belliveau, Pst.; Rev. David M. Affleck, Assisting Priest; CRP Stds.: 76

Immaculate Conception Church - 98 Summer St., Portsmouth, NH 03801-4398

ROCHESTER

St. Mary - 71 Lowell St., Rochester, NH 03867-5002 t) 603-332-1869 stmary@metrocast.net www.stmarychurchnh.org Rev. Thomas L. Duston, Pst.; Dcn. Richard A. Falardeau; CRP Stds.: 15

Our Lady of the Holy Rosary - 189 N. Main St., Rochester, NH 03867-1299 t) 603-332-1863 srmaryrose@hrsl.org; pgousse@hrsl.org www.hrsl.org Rev. Matthew Schultz, Pst.; Sr. Mary Rose Reddy, D.M.M.L., DRE;

St. Leo Catholic Children's Center - 32 Pickering Rd., Gonic, NH 03839-5220; Mailing: 189 N. Main St., Rochester, NH 03867 t) (603) 332-9840 Rebecca Croteau, Dir.;

ROLLINSFORD

St. Mary - Church St., Rollinsford, NH 03869; Mailing: 404 High St., St. Ignatius of Loyola Parish, Somersworth, NH 03878 t) 603-692-4367; 603-749-1666 (CRP); 603-692-2172 www.stignatius-stmary.org Rev. Andrew Nelson, Pst.; Dcn. David Divins; Laurie Lambert, DRE; CRP Stds.: 20

RYE BEACH

St. Theresa - 815 Central Rd., Rye Beach, NH 03871-0482; Mailing: P.O. Box 482, Rye Beach, NH 03871-0482 t) 603-964-6440; 603-964-9878 (CRP) ljoyce@sainttheresachurchrye.org Rev. Gary J. Kosmowski, Pst.;

SALEM

Saints Mary and Joseph - 200 Lawrence Rd., Salem, NH 03079-3978 t) 603-893-8661 officeadmin@saintsmaryandjoseph.org Rev. Msgr. Marc R. Montminy, Pst.; Rev. Charles Aruldurai, H.G.N., Par. Vicar; Susan Levesque, DRE;

Mary, Queen of Peace Church -

St. Joseph Church - 40 Main St., Salem, NH 03079

SANBORNVILLE

St. Anthony - 239 Meadow St., Sanbornville, NH 03872; Mailing: P.O. Box 490, Sanbornville, NH 03872-0490 t) 603-552-3304; 603-522-8632 (CRP) stanthony239@gmail.com www.stanthonystjoseph.org (Twinned with St. Joseph Parish, Center Ossipee, N.H.) Very Rev. Patrick N. Gilbert, Pst.; CRP Stds.: 10

SOMERSWORTH

Saint Ignatius of Loyola - 404 High St., Somersworth, NH 03878 t) 603-692-2172 www.stignatius-stmary.org Rev. Andrew Nelson, Pst.; Dcn. David Divins; Janet Jacobson, DRE;

Holy Trinity Church -

St. Martin Church - 120 Maple St., Somersworth, NH 03878

SUNCOOK

St. John the Baptist - 10 School St., Suncook, NH 03275-1817 t) 603-485-3113 stjohnthebaptist@comcast.net www.catholicsuncook.org Rev. Michael E. Gendron, Pst.; Rev. Roarke Traynor, Par. Vicar; Dcn. William R. Lavallee; Dcn. Sean C. Magee;

WINCHESTER

St. Stanislaus Parish - 80 Richmond St., Winchester, NH 03470 t) 631-612-1285 hbeaugrand@rcbm.org Rev. Hugues Beaugrand, I.B.P., Pst.; CRP Stds.: 10

WINDHAM

St. Matthew - 2 Searles Rd., Windham, NH 03087-1206 t) 603-893-3336 officemanager@stmattwind.org www.stmatthew-nh.org Rev. Msgr. Anthony R. Frontiero, Pst.; Dcn. Leland Fastnacht;

WOODSVILLE

St. Catherine of Siena - c/o 21 Pine St., Woodsville, NH 03785-1215 t) 603-747-2038 stjoseph_church@yahoo.com Rev. Arockia Antony, H.G.N., Pst.;

St. Joseph - 21 Pine St., Woodsville, NH 03785-1215 t) 603-747-2038; 603-747-8071 stjoseph_church@yahoo.com stjoseph-stcatherine.org Rev. Arockia Antony, H.G.N., Pst.;

SCHOOLS: PRESCHOOL THRU HIGH SCHOOL

SCHOOLS

STATE OF NEW HAMPSHIRE

CONCORD

St. John Regional School - (PAR) (Grades PreK-8) 61 S. State St., Concord, NH 03301 t) 603-225-3222 x100 mrdonohue@stjohnregional.org stjohnregional.org Lisa Zolkos, Interim Prin.;

DOVER

St. Mary Academy - (PAR) (Grades PreK-8) 222 Central Ave., Dover, NH 03820 t) 603-742-3299 mmckernan@stmaryacademy.org www.saintmaryacademy.org Brandy Houle, Prin.;

HAMPTON

Sacred Heart School - (PAR) (Grades PreK-8) 289 Lafayette Rd., Hampton, NH 03842 t) 603-926-3254 mkoelker@shshampton.org www.shshampton.org Maegan Koelker, Prin.; Stds.: 242; Lay Tchrs.: 12

HUDSON

Presentation of Mary Academy - (PRV) (Grades PreK-8) 182 Lowell Rd., Hudson, NH 03051 t) 603-889-6054 principal@pmaschool.org www.pmaschool.org Sr. Maria Rosa, P.M., Prin.; Stds.: 498; Sr. Tchrs.: 1; Lay Tchrs.: 30

KEENE

Saint Joseph Regional School - (PAR) (Grades PreK-8) 92 Wilson St., Keene, NH 03431 t) 603-352-2720 csmith@stjosephkeene.org stjosephkeene.org Christopher D. Smith, Prin.;

LACONIA

Holy Trinity School - (PAR) (Grades PreK-8) 19 Gilford Ave., Laconia, NH 03246 t) 603-524-3156 www.holytrinitynh.com Vincent Schuck, Prin.;

LITCHFIELD

St. Francis of Assisi School - (PAR) (Grades PreSchool-6) 9 St. Francis Way, Litchfield, NH 03052-8050 t) 603-424-3312 schwerdtm@stfrancisschoolnh.org Mark Schwerdt, Prin.;

MANCHESTER

St. Benedict Academy - (PAR) (Grades PreK-8) 85 Third St., Manchester, NH 03102 t) 603-669-3932 officeadmin@st.benedictacademy.org stbenedictacademy.org Tanya Paiva, Prin.;

St. Catherine School - (PAR) (Grades PreK-6) 206 North St., Manchester, NH 03104 t) 603-622-1711 office@scsnh.com; kmeehan@scsnh.com www.scsnh.com Katie Knight, Prin.;

Mount Saint Mary Academy - (PRV) (Grades PreK-6) 2291 Elm St., Manchester, NH 03104 t) 603-623-3155 principal@mtstmary.org www.mtstmary.org Dr. Theresa Kirk, Prin.;

St. Joseph Regional Junior High - (PAR) (Grades 7-8) 148 Belmont St., 2nd Fl., Manchester, NH 03103 t) 603-624-4811 dmailloux@stjoesjrhs.org www.stjoesjrhs.org Michael Gaumont, Prin.;

NASHUA

St. Christopher Academy, Inc. - 20 Cushing Ave., Nashua, NH 03064 t) (603) 882-7442 Cynthia Vita Clarke, Prin.;

SALEM

St. Joseph Regional Catholic School - (DIO) (Grades PreK-8) 40 Main St., Salem, NH 03079 t) 603-893-6811 mainoffice@sjrcs.com www.stjosepheagles.org Mary Croteau, Prin.; Stds.: 196; Lay Tchrs.: 17

SUNAPEE

Mount Royal Academy - (PRV) (Grades PreK-12) 26 Seven Hearths Ln., Sunapee, NH 03782; Mailing: PO Box 362, Sunapee, NH 03782 t) 603-763-9010 dtremblay@mountroyalacademy.com www.mountroyalacademy.com Derek Tremblay, Headmaster;

HIGH SCHOOLS

STATE OF NEW HAMPSHIRE

CONCORD

Bishop Brady High School - (DIO) 25 Columbus Ave., Concord, NH 03301 t) 603-224-7418 info@bishopbrady.edu; aelliot@bishopbrady.edu www.bishopbrady.edu Keith Bergeron, Dean; Andrea Elliot, Prin.; Sara Smith, Campus Min.; Stds.: 238; Lay Tchrs.: 24

DOVER

St. Thomas Aquinas High School, Inc. - (DIO) 197 Dover Point Rd., Dover, NH 03820 t) 603-742-3206 sta@stalux.org www.stalux.org Paul Marquis, Prin.;

MANCHESTER

Trinity High School - (DIO) 581 Bridge St., Manchester, NH 03104-5395 t) 603-668-2910 webmaster@trinity-hs.org www.trinity-hs.org Steven Gadecki, Prin.; Nathan Stanton, Pres.;

NASHUA

Bishop Guertin High School - (PRV) (Grades 9-12) 194 Lund Rd., Nashua, NH 03060 t) 603-889-4107 brodeurl@bghs.org; strnistej@bghs.org www.bghs.org (Coed) Jason Strniste, Prin.; Linda Brodeur, Pres.;

SUNAPEE

Mount Royal Academy - (PRV) (Grades PreK-12) 26 Seven Hearths Ln., Sunapee, NH 03782; Mailing: P.O. Box 362, Sunapee, NH 03782 t) 603-763-9010 dtremblay@mountroyalacademy.com www.mountroyalacademy.com Derek Tremblay, Headmaster;

INSTITUTIONS LOCATED IN DIOCESE

CAMPUS MINISTRY / NEWMAN CENTERS [CAM]

DURHAM

St. Thomas More Catholic Student Center at the University of New Hampshire - 6 Madbury Rd., Durham, NH 03824-0620; Mailing: P.O. Box 620, Durham, NH 03824-0620 t) 603-868-2666 stmdurham@comcast.net Rev. Andrew W. Cryans, Chap.;

HANOVER

***The Catholic Student Center at Dartmouth, Aquinas House, Aquinas at Dartmouth, Inc.** - 2 Occom Ridge, Hanover, NH 03755; Mailing: P.O. Box 147, Hanover, NH 03755 t) 603-643-2154 aq@dartmouth.edu www.dartmouthcatholic.com Rev. Timothy Danaher, O.P., Chap.;

KEENE

Catholic Newman Center for Keene State College - 161 Main St., Ste. 11, Keene, NH 03431 t) 603-357-1444 director@newmancenterkeene.com Cynthia Cheshire, Campus Min.;

PLYMOUTH

Plymouth State University Catholic Campus Ministry - 19 Highland Ave., Ste. A6, Plymouth, NH 03264 t) 603-535-2673 kmtardif@plymouth.edu Kate Neal, Campus Min.;

CATHOLIC CHARITIES [CCH]

MANCHESTER

Catholic Charities Administration (New Hampshire Catholic Charities, Inc.) - 100 William Loeb Dr., Unit 3, Manchester, NH 03109 t) 603-669-3030 info@nh-cc.org www.nh-cc.org Thomas E. Blonski, Pres. & CEO; Alain Bernard, Asst. Vice Pres. Healthcare Svcs.; Laura Brusseau, Dir. Devel. Opers.; Danielle Capelle, Dir. Mental Health Svcs.; Elsy Cipriani, Exec. Dir. New Generation; Marc Cousineau, Dir. Community Svcs.; David Danielson, Ethics, Compliance & Privacy Of.; Sandra Faber, Exec. Dir. Monadnock at Home; Neil Funcke, Dir. Tech.; David Hildenbrand, CFO; Steven Knight, Asst. Vice Pres., Prog. & Mission Integrity; Jeff Lefkovich, Exec. Dir. Real Estate & Bus. Devel.; Eileen Groll Liponis, Exec. Dir. NH Food Bank; Karen Schoch, Ch. HR; Brian May, Dir. Acctg.; Michael McDonough, Exec. Dir. Mktg. & Comm.; Karen Moynihan, Vice Pres. Philanthropy; Jeffrey O. Nelson, Exec. Dir. Liberty House; Dominique A. Rust, COO; Michal Waterman, Dir. HR; James Wilkie, Exec. Dir. The CareGivers; Asstd. Annu.: 131,517; Staff: 850

The CareGivers - 700 E. Industrial Park Dr., Manchester, NH 03109 t) 603-622-4948 james@caregiversnh.org www.caregiversnh.org Assists the frail, elderly, and disabled to maintain independence and dignity by providing rides to appointments and grocery deliveries.

St. Charles School - 19 Grant St., Rochester, NH 03867-3001 t) 603-332-4768 sma@stcharleshome.net www.cc-nh.org/programs/stcharles/ School behavioral services Thomas Hayward, Prin.; Sr. Mary Agnes Dombrowski, Exec. Dir.;

District Office - 2 Main St., Berlin, NH 03570-0182 t) 603-752-1325 berlin@nh-cc.org Nicole Plourde, Parish and Community Services - Dep. Director;

District Office - 176 Loudon Rd., Concord, NH 03301-6025 t) 603-228-1108 Su McKinnon, Community Services Coordinator;

District Office - 248 Main St., #11, Keene, NH 03431-3722 t) 603-357-3093 keene@nh-cc.org Judith Case, Community Services Coordinator;

District Office - 17 Gilford Ave., Laconia, NH 03246-2827 t) 603-528-3035 laconia@nh-cc.org Leonard B. Campbell, Admin.;

District Office - 24 Hanover St., #8, Lebanon, NH 03766-1334 t) 603-448-5151

District Office - 41 Cottage St., Littleton, NH 03561-0323; Mailing: P.O. Box 323, Littleton, NH 03561-0323 t) 603-444-7727 littleton@nh-cc.org Janice MacKenzie, Admn. Mgr., LCSW;

District Office - 587 Maple St., Manchester, NH 03104-4351 t) 603-624-4717 manchester@nh-cc.org

District Office - 3 Crown St., Nashua, NH 03060-4127 t) 603-889-9431 nashua@nh-cc.org

District Office - 23 Grant St., Rochester, NH 03867-3001 t) 603-332-7701 rochester@nh-cc.org

Guardian Angel Thrift Store - 153 Grafton St., Berlin, NH 03570 t) 603-752-4844 Nicole Plourde, Dir.;

Healthcare Services - 100 William Loeb Dr., Unit 3, Manchester, NH 03109 t) 603-641-0577 kblain@nh-cc.org

Immigration and Refugee Services - 3 Crown St., Nashua, NH 03060-4127 t) 603-889-9431 kgeorge@nh-cc.org Legal and case management services for immigrants and refugees. Kimberly George, Dir.;

Liberty House - 221 Orange St., Manchester, NH 03104 t) 603-669-0761 jeff@libertyhouse.org Housing and support for homeless and struggling veterans.

Monadnock at Home - ; Mailing: P.O. Box 422, Jaffrey, NH 03452 t) 603-371-0809 sfaber@nh-cc.org www.monadnockathome.org/

New Generation - 568 Portsmouth Ave., Greenland,

NH 03840 t) 603-436-4989 office@newgennh.org www.newgennh.org/ Shelter and transitional housing for pregnant women, mothers and children experiencing homelessness.

New Hampshire Food Bank - 700 E. Industrial Park Dr., Manchester, NH 03109 t) 603-669-9725 www.nhfoodbank.org Statewide food distribution to soup kitchens, food pantries and direct service programs.

Our Place - 16 Oak St., Manchester, NH 03104-4319 t) 603-647-2244 A pregnancy and parenting ed. program, which empowers first-time parents with the knowledge and skills needed to provide a loving, caring & safe home. Karen A. Munsell, Supvr. & Social Worker;

Our Place - 3 Crown St., Nashua, NH 03060 t) (603) 889-9431 A pregnancy and parenting Ed. program, which empowers first-time parents with the knowledge and skills needed to provide a loving, caring & safe home. Karen Munsell, Contact;

Searles Place at Warde - 21 Searles Rd., Windham, NH 03087 t) 603-890-1290 x302 whc.activitydir@nh-cc.org

CEMETERIES [CEM]

MANCHESTER

Diocesan Cemetery Office - 153 Ash St., Manchester, NH 03105; Mailing: P.O. Box 310, Manchester, NH 03105 t) 603-669-3100 dgabert@rcbm.org David A. Gabert, Dir.;

All Saints Cemetery - Water St., Lancaster, NH 03584; Mailing: 163 Main St., Gate of Heaven Parish, Lancaster, NH 03584-3032 t) 603-788-2083 gateofheavennh@aol.com; mschultz@rcbm.org

St. Anne Cemetery - E. Milan Rd., Berlin, NH 03570; Mailing: 151 Emery St., Good Shepherd Parish, Manchester, NH 03570 t) 603-752-2880 Bridget Goudreau, Secy.;

St. Augustin Cemetery - S. Beech St., Manchester, NH 03103; Mailing: 383 Beech St., St. Anne-St Augustin Parish, Manchester, NH 03103-5350 t) 603-860-0386 cornerstone.kr@comcast.net; sta.sta@stannestaug.org Keith Racine, Contact;

St. Brendan Cemetery - S. Main St., Colebrook, NH 03576; Mailing: 55 Pleasant St., North American Martyrs Parish, Colebrook, NH 03576-3250 t) 603-237-4342 frcheneynamp@myfairpoint.net Edward Poulin, Contact;

Calvary Cemetery - E. Milan Rd., Berlin, NH 03570; Mailing: 151 Emery St., Good Shepherd Parish, Berlin, NH 03570 t) 603-752-2880 Bridget Goudreau, Secy.;

Calvary Cemetery - 378 N. Main St., Lancaster, NH 03584; Mailing: 163 Main St., Gate of Heaven Parish, Lancaster, NH 03584-3032 t) 603-788-2083 gateofheavennh@aol.com; mschultz@rcbm.org

Calvary Cemetery - Rte. 108, Newmarket, NH 03857; Mailing: 182 Main St., PO Box 337, St. Mary Parish, Newmarket, NH 03587-0337 t) 603-659-3344 info@kentandpelczarfh.com Michael Pelczar, Admin.;

Calvary Cemetery - Village St. Rte. 3, Penacook, NH 03303; Mailing: 9 Bonney St., Immaculate Conception Parish, Penacook, NH 03582-1654 t) 603-753-4413 (Pastor); 603-225-3911 (Burial Info; Concord) pastor@icpenacook.org Rev. Raymond J. Potvin;

Calvary Cemetery - Intersection of Greenland Rd., Islington St. & Middle Rd., Portsmouth, NH 03804; Mailing: 845 Woodbury Ave., Corpus Christi Parish, Portsmouth, NH 03801 t) 603-436-9239; 603-436-4555 businessmgr.ccnh@gmail.com Kate Gordon, Bus. Mgr.;

Cathedral Cemetery - 145 Lowell St., Manchester, NH 03104 t) 603-622-6404 Very Rev. Jason Y. Jalbert, Rector;

St. Catherine Cemetery - S. West St., Charlestown, NH 03603; Mailing: 285 Main St., PO Box 332, All Saints Parish, Charlestown, NH 03603-0332 t) 603-826-3359 allsaints3@comcast.net Rev. John B. Loughnane;

St. Charles Cemetery - Old Rochester Rd., Dover, NH 03822; Mailing: 150 Central St., Parish of the Assumption Parish, Dover, NH 03820-3464 t) 603-742-4837 cemeteries@assumptiondovernh.org Angela Fahy, Contact;

St. Denis - Nelson Rd., Harrisville, NH 03450 t) 603-924-7647 divinemercynh@comcast.net Very Rev. Michael S. Taylor, Pst.;

St. Francis Xavier Cemetery - Brown Rd., Groveton, NH 03582; Mailing: 11 State St., PO Box 247, St. Marguerite d'Youville Parish, Groveton, NH 03582-0247 t) 603-636-1047 deveau.d.r@gmail.com Rev. Daniel R. Deveau, Pst.;

St. Francis Xavier Cemetery - 32 Pine Hill Rd., Nashua, NH 03064; Mailing: 752 W. Hollis St., St. Aloysius of Gonzaga Parish - Cemetery Office, Nashua, NH 03060-3519 t) 603-886-1302 cemetery@stlouisnashua.org Donna Pratt, Contact;

St. Hedwig Cemetery - Old Bedford Rd., Bedford, NH 03110; Mailing: 147 Walnut St., St. Hedwig Parish, Manchester, NH 03104-4225 t) 603-623-4835 parishoffice@sthedwigparish.comcastbiz.net Eleanor Felch, Contact;

Holy Angels Cemetery - 22 East Rd., Plaistow, NH 03865; Mailing: 8 Atkinson Depot Rd., St. Luke the Evangelist Parish, Plaistow, NH 03865-3103 t) 603-382-8324 jtremblay@stluketheevangelist.net Jackie Tremblay, Contact;

Holy Cross Cemetery - 1 Carr St., Franklin, NH 03235; Mailing: 100 School St., PO Box 490, St. Gabriel Parish, Franklin, NH 03235-0490 t) 603-934-5013 office@stgabrielnh.org Claire Connify, Secy.;

Holy Cross Cemetery - Ledge Rd., Hudson, NH 03051; Mailing: 29 Spring St., St. Patrick Parish, Nashua, NH 03060-3490 t) 603-881-8131 mmgray@stpatricksnashua.org Diane Duffy, Contact;

Holy Cross Cemetery - Gilcrest Rd., Londonderry, NH 03053; Mailing: 133 Wayne St., St. Marie Parish, Manchester, NH 03102-3740 t) 603-622-3215 kccody@mtcalvarycem.org Dcn. Kevin W. Cody, Dir.;

Holy Family Cemetery - 9 Church St., Gorham, NH 03581; Mailing: 151 Emery St., Holy Family Parish, Berlin, NH 03570 t) 603-752-2880 Bridget Goudreau, Secy.;

Holy Rosary Cemetery - 21 Main St., Hooksett, NH 03106 t) 603-485-3523 hrparishhook@comcast.net Rev. Edmund G. Crowley;

Holy Rosary Cemetery - 133 Brook St., Rochester, NH 03839; Mailing: 189 N. Main St., Our Lady of the Holy Rosary Parish, Rochester, NH 03867-1299 t) 603-332-1863 nhamann@hrsl.org Norbert Hamann, Contact;

Holy Trinity Cemetery - 333 High St., Somersworth, NH 03878; Mailing: 404 High St., St. Ignatius of Loyola Parish, Somersworth, NH 03878-1011 t) 603-692-0524; 603-692-2172 Denise Gauthier, Contact;

St. Joseph Cemetery - Rte. 302, Bartlett, NH 03812; Mailing: 2905 White Mountain Hwy., Our Lady of the Mountains Parish, North Conway, NH 03860-5111 t) 603-356-2535 ourladynh@myfairpoint.net Louise Michaud, Bus. Mgr.;

St. Joseph Cemetery - Monroe Rd., Bath, NH 03740; Mailing: 21 Pine St., St. Joseph Parish, Woodsville, NH 03785-1215 t) 603-747-2038 stjoseph_church@yahoo.com Rev. Maria Susairaj;

St. Joseph Cemetery - 448 Donald St., Bedford, NH 03110; Mailing: 145 Lowell St., St. Joseph Cathedral, Manchester, NH 03104-6315 t) 603-860-0386 director@stjcem.org Keith Racine, Contact;

St. Joseph Cemetery - Rte. 27, Epping, NH 03042; Mailing: 198 Pleasant St., St. Joseph Parish, Epping, NH 03042-0337 t) 603-679-8805 nh337@comcast.net Mike Kappler, Contact;

St. Joseph Cemetery - Plain Rd., Hinsdale, NH 03451; Mailing: 161 Main St., Ste. 201, Mary, Queen of Peace Parish, Keene, NH 03431-3772 t) 603-336-7090; 603-352-3525 holyspirit.peace@gmail.com Mike Abbott, Contact;

St. Joseph Cemetery - 600 Main St., Keene, NH 03435; Mailing: 161 Main St., Parish of the Holy Spirit, Keene, NH 03431 t) 603-352-3525 holyspirit.peace@gmail.com Heather Houle, Contact;

St. Kieran Cemetery - E. Milan Rd., Berlin, NH 03570; Mailing: 151 Emery St., Good Shepherd Parish, Manchester, NH 03570 t) 603-752-2880 Bridget Goudreau, Secy.;

St. Lambert Cemetery - Province St., Laconia, NH 03247; Mailing: 277 Union Ave., St. Andre Bessette, Laconia, NH 03246-3122 t) 603-524-9609 cjohnson@eternalrestlaconia.com Cory Johnson, Contact;

St. Louis de Gonzaga Cemetery - 752 W. Hollis St., Nashua, NH 03064 t) 603-886-1302 cemetery@stlouisnashua.org Donna Pratt, Contact;

St. Margaret Cemetery - St. Margaret's Rd. (off Rte. 3), Carroll, NH 03598; Mailing: Gate of Heaven Parish, 163 Main St., Lancaster, NH 03884-3032 t) 603-788-2083

St. Mary Cemetery - Plains Rd., Claremont, NH 03743; Mailing: 32 Pearl St., St. Mary Parish, Claremont, NH 03743-2552 t) 603-542-9518 stmarysclaremont@comcast.net Rev. Shawn M. Therrien;

St. Mary Cemetery - Dover Point Rd., Dover, NH 03822; Mailing: 150 Central St., Parish of the Assumption, Manchester, NH 03820-3464 t) 603-742-4837 cemeteries@assumptiondovernh.org Angela Fahy, Contact;

St. Mary Cemetery - Intersection of Greenland Rd., Islington St. & Middle Rd., Portsmouth, NH 03804; Mailing: Corpus Christi Parish, 845 Woodbury Ave., Portsmouth, NH 03801 t) 603-436-9239; 603-436-4555 businessmgr.ccnh@gmail.com Kate Gordon, Bus. Mgr.;

St. Mary Cemetery - Center Rd., Hillsborough, NH 03244-0729; Mailing: PO Box 729, St. Mary Parish, Henniker, NH 03242 t) 603-464-3325 parish.office@tds.net Dolores Megans, Contact;

St. Mary's Cemetery - Lowell St., Rochester, NH 03839; Mailing: 71 Lowell St., St. Mary Parish, Rochester, NH 03867-5002 t) 603-332-1869 tduston@rcbm.org Rev. Thomas L. Duston, Contact;

Mount Calvary Cemetery - Old Stagecoach Rd., Bennington, NH 03442; Mailing: 12 Church St., Divine Mercy Parish, Peterborough, NH 03458 t) 603-924-7647 divinemercynh@comcast.net Very Rev. Michael S. Taylor, Pst.; Brenda Wesoly, Bus. Mgr.;

Mount Calvary Cemetery - Cates Hill Rd., Berlin, NH 03570; Mailing: 151 Emery St., Good Shepherd Parish, Manchester, NH 03570 t) 603-752-2880 Bridget Goudreau, Secy.;

Mount Calvary Cemetery - Cemetery Rd. (Gonic), Rochester, NH 03839; Mailing: 189 N. Main St., Our Lady of the Holy Rosary Parish, Rochester, NH 03867-1299 t) 603-332-1863 nhamann@hrsl.org Norbert Hamann, Contact;

Mount Calvary Cemetery - 474 Goffstown Rd., Manchester, NH 03102 t) 603-622-3215 kccody@mtcalvarycem.org Dcn. Kevin W. Cody;

Mount Calvary Cemetery - (End of) Ling St., Marlborough, NH 03455 t) 603-352-3525 holyspirit.peace@gmail.com Heather Houle, Contact;

Mount Calvary Cemetery - Norris Rd., Pittsfield, NH 03263; Mailing: 20 River Rd., Our Lady of the Lourdes, Pittsfield, NH 03263-3314 t) 603-435-6242 ololstjoseph@metrocast.net Very Rev. John B. MacKenzie;

Mount Calvary Cemetery - St. Anthony's Rd.,

Sanbornville, NH 03872; Mailing: PO Box 490, St. Anthony Parish, Sanbornville, NH 03872-0490 t) 603-522-3304 stanthony239@gmail.com Very Rev. Patrick N. Gilbert;
Mount Calvary Cemetery - Maple St., Somersworth, NH 03878; Mailing: 404 High St., St. Ignatius of Loyola Parish, Somersworth, NH 03878-1011 t) 603-692-2172; 603-692-0524 Denise Gauthier, Contact;
Mount Calvary Cemetery - Abbott Hill Rd., Wilton, NH 03086; Mailing: 15 High St., Sacred Heart of Jesus Parish, Greenville, NH 03048-3121 t) 603-878-1121 sacredheartgreenvillenh@comcast.net Kathy Caron, Secy.;
Mount Carmel Cemetery - Marlborough Rd., Troy, NH 03465; Mailing: 161 Main St., Parish of the Holy Spirit, Keene, NH 03431 t) 603-352-3525 holyspirit.peace@gmail.com Heather Houle, Contact;
New St. Rose of Lima Cemetery - W. Main St., Littleton, NH 03561; Mailing: 77 Clay St., St. Rose of Lima Parish, Littleton, NH 03561-4800 t) 603-444-2680 Paul Harvey, Contact;
Old St. Rose of Lima Cemetery - Brook Rd., Bethlehem, NH 03574; Mailing: 77 Clay St., St. Rose of Lima Parish, Littleton, NH 03561-4800 t) 603-444-2593 Rev. Mark E. Dollard;
Our Lady of the Mountains Cemetery - Rte. 16, North Conway, NH 03860; Mailing: 2905 White Mountain Hwy., Our Lady of the Mountains Parish, North Conway, NH 03860-5111 t) 603-356-2535 ourladynh@myfairpoint.net Louise Michaud, Bus. Mgr.;
St. Patrick Cemetery - 71 Derry Rd., Hudson, NH 03051; Mailing: 29 Spring St., St. Patrick Parish, Nashua, NH 03060-3490 t) 603-881-8131 mmgray@stpatricksnashua.org Diane Duffy, Contact;
St. Patrick Cemetery - Hillcrest Rd., Jaffrey, NH 03452; Mailing: 87 Main St., St. Patrick Parish, Jaffrey, NH 03452-6139 t) 603-305-4825; 603-532-6634 stpatric@myfairpoint.net John LaCroix, Contact;
St. Patrick Cemetery - Summer St., Newport, NH 03773; Mailing: 32 Beech St., St. Patrick Parish, Newport, NH 03773-1416 t) 603-863-1422 office@saintpatrickparish.net; msartori@rcbm.org Rev. Michael L. Sartori, Contact;
St. Patrick Cemetery - Silver St., Rollinsford, NH 03805; Mailing: 404 High St., St. Mary Parish, Somersworth, NH 03878-1011 t) 603-692-0524; 603-692-2172 Denise Gauthier, Contact;
St. Peter Cemetery - Rte. 123, Walpole, NH 03604; Mailing: 285 Main St., PO Box 332, All Saints Parish, Charlestown, NH 03603-0332 t) 603-826-3359 allsaints3@comcast.net Rev. John B. Loughnane;
St. Peter Cemetery (new) - 313 High St., Peterborough, NH 03458; Mailing: 12 Church St., Divine Mercy Parish, Peter, NH 03458 t) 603-924-7647 divinemercynh@comcast.net Very Rev. Michael S. Taylor, Pst.;
St. Peter Churchyard Cemetery (old) - 18 Vine St., Peterborough, NH 03458; Mailing: 12 Church St., Divine Mercy Parish, Peterborough, NH 03458 t) 603-924-7647 divinemercynh@comcast.net Very Rev. Michael S. Taylor, Pst.;
St. Pius Forest Lawn Cemetery - Main St., Errol, NH 03579; Mailing: 55 Pleasant St., North American Martyrs Parish, Manchester, NH 03576-3250 t) 603-237-4342 frcheneynamp@myfairpoint.net Louise Cote, Contact;
Sacred Heart Cemetery - Garfield St., Laconia, NH 03247; Mailing: 277 Union Ave., St. Andre Bessette, Laconia, NH 03246-3122 t) 603-524-9609 cjohnson@eternalrestlaconia.com Cory Johnson, Contact;
Sacred Heart Cemetery - Rte. 3, North Stratford, NH 03590; Mailing: 11 State St., PO Box 247, St. Marguerite d'Youville Parish, Groveton, NH 03582-0247 t) 603-636-1047 deveau.d.r@gmail.com Rev. Daniel R. Deveau;
Sacred Heart of Jesus Cemetery - High St., New Ipswich, NH 03071; Mailing: 15 High St., Sacred Heart of Jesus Parish, Greenville, NH 03048-3121 t) 603-878-1121 sacredheartgreenvillenh@comcast.net; dirtnapnh@gmail.com Larry Legere, Contact;
St. Albert Cemetery - Rte. 3, West Stewartstown, NH 03597; Mailing: 55 Pleasant St., North American Martyrs Parish, Colebrook, NH 03576-3250 t) 603-237-4342 frcheneynamp@myfairpoint.net Suzanne Madore, Contact;
St. John the Baptist Cemetery - River Rd., Suncook, NH 03275; Mailing: 10 School St., St. John the Baptist Parish, Suncook, NH 03275-1917 t) 603-485-3113 stjohnthebaptist@comcast.net Michelle Petit, Contact;
St. John the Baptist Old Cemetery - Granite St. Ext., Suncook, NH 03275; Mailing: 10 School St., St. John the Baptist Parish, Sunccok, NH 03275-1917 t) 603-485-3113 stjohnthebaptist@comcast.net Michelle Petit, Contact;
St. John's Cemetery - Sanborn Rd., Rte. 132, Tilton, NH 03299; Mailing: 110 School St., PO Box 490, St. Gabriel Parish, Franklin, NH 03235-0490 t) 603-934-5013 office@stgabrielnh.org Claire Connifey, Secy.;
St. Margaret Cemetery - St. Margaret Rd. (off Rte. 3), Carroll, NH 03595 t) 603-788-2083 gateofheavennh@aol.com Kathi Marshall, Secy.;
St. Matthew Cemetery - Whitefield Rd., Whitefield, NH 03598; Mailing: 163 Main St., Gate of Heaven Parish, Lancaster, NH 03584-3032 t) 603-788-2083 gateofheavennh@aol.com; mschultz@rcbm.org Rev. Matthew Schultz, Contact;
St. Patrick Cemetery - Merrimack Rd., Amherst, NH 03031; Mailing: 34 Amherst St., Milford, NH 03055-0027 t) 603-673-1311; 603-672-1254 diane.st.patoffice@gmail.com Jerry Guthrie, Contact;
St. Peter Cemetery - Rte. 123 Whitcomb Rd., Walpole, NH 03608 t) 603-826-3359 allsaints3@comcast.net (Drewsville) Rev. John B. Loughnane;
St. Stanislaus Cemetery - 61 Pine Hill Rd., Nashua, NH 03064; Mailing: 752 W. Hollis St., St. Aloysius of Gonzaga Parish - Cemetery Office, Nashua, NH 03060-3519 t) 603-886-1302 cemetery@stlouisnashua.org Donna Pratt, Contact;

COLLEGES & UNIVERSITIES [COL]

MANCHESTER

Saint Anselm College - 100 Saint Anselm Dr., Manchester, NH 03102 t) 603-641-7000 jfavazza@anselm.edu www.anselm.edu Rt. Rev. Mark A. Cooper, O.S.B., Chancellor; Dr. Joseph A Favazza, Pres.; Stds.: 1,977; Lay Tchrs.: 153; Pr. Tchrs.: 2

MERRIMACK

The Thomas More College of Liberal Arts - 6 Manchester St., Merrimack, NH 03054 t) 603-880-8308 mschneider@thomasmorecollege.edu www.thomasmorecollege.edu William E. Fahey, Pres.;

NASHUA

Rivier University - 420 S. Main St., Nashua, NH 03060-5086 t) 603-888-1311; 603-897-8202 pbuley@rivier.edu; dtilders@rivier.edu www.rivier.edu Sr. Paula Marie Buley, I.H.M., Pres.; Daniel Speidel, Dir.;

WARNER

Magdalen College of the Liberal Arts - 511 Kearsarge Mountain Rd., Warner, NH 03278-9206 t) 603-456-2656 administration@magdalen.edu magdalen.edu Dr. Ryan Messmore, Pres.; Dr. Brian FitzGerald, Dean; Stds.: 59; Lay Tchrs.: 4

CONVENTS, MONASTERIES, AND RESIDENCES FOR WOMEN [CON]

CONCORD

Monastery of Discalced Carmelites - 275 Pleasant St., Concord, NH 03301-2590 t) 603-225-5791 sisters@concordcarmel.org Sr. Claudette M. Blais, O.C.D., Prioress;

LITTLETON

Daughters of the Charity of the Sacred Heart of Jesus - 226 Grove St., Littleton, NH 03561 t) 603-444-5346 www.fcscj.org Sr. Juanita Durgin, Delegate; Srs.: 18

MANCHESTER

***Daughters of Mary, Mother of Healing Love** - 279 Cartier St., Manchester, NH 03102 c) 603-817-0540 motherpaulmarie@gmail.com; daughtersofmarydmml@gmail.com www.motherofhealinglove.org (Private Association of the Christian Faithful) Mother Paul Marie Santa Lucia, DMML, Supr.; Sr. Maximilian Cote, DMML, Vice. Pres.; Sr. Mary Rose Rose Reddy, DMML, Secy.; Sr. Mary Agnes Dombroski, DMML, Treas.;
St. George Manor / Holy Cross Health Center - 357 Island Pond Rd., Manchester, NH 03109 t) 603-624-4557 chcll2@aol.com Rev. Roland P. Cote, Pst.;
Holy Cross Health Center, Inc. - 357 Island Pond Rd., Manchester, NH 03109-4811 t) 603-628-3550 sosiek@holycrosshc.org Nursing home for women religious, managed by Sisters of Holy Cross Rev. Roland P. Cote, Pst.;
Monastery of the Precious Blood - 700 Bridge St., Manchester, NH 03104-5495 t) 603-623-4264 superior@srspreciousbloodnh.org Sr. Mary Clare, A.P.B., Supr.;
 Missionary Rosebushes of St. Theresa - Sr. Mary Clare Bergeron, Supr.;
Sisters of Holy Cross, No. American Region / U.S. Sector Office - 365 Island Pond Rd., Manchester, NH 03109 t) 603-622-9504 dydupere@srsofholycross.com sistersofholycross.org Sr. Diane Dupere, Sector Leader; Srs.: 67
 Sisters of Holy Cross - 136 Lynwood Ln., Manchester, NH 03109
 Sisters of Holy Cross - 113 Wedgewood Ln., Manchester, NH 03109
 Sisters of Holy Cross - 5 Crosswoods Path Blvd., #13, Merrimack, NH 03054
 Sisters of Holy Cross - 11 Crosswoods Path Blvd., #11 & #12, Merrimack, NH 03054
Sisters of the Presentation of Mary - 495 Mammoth Rd., Manchester, NH 03104-5494 t) 603-669-1080 pmtreasurer209@gmail.com www.presentationofmary-usa.org See School Section for related schools. Sr. Annette Laliberte, P.M., Treas.; Srs.: 44
 St. Joseph Residence - t) 603-627-5831; 603-668-6011 Sr. Lorraine Letourneau, Supr.; Sr. Cecile Plasse, Supr.;
 St. Marie Residence - t) 603-623-0671 stemarieres@yahoo.com Sr. Colette Barbeau, Supr.;
 Presentation of Mary Academy - 182 Lowell Rd., Hudson, NH 03051-4987 t) (603) 883-8192 pmaschool.org Sr. Maria Rosa, P.M., Prin.; Sr. Jacqueline Levreault, Supr.; Stds.: 498; Sr. Tchrs.: 1; Lay Tchrs.: 30
 Presentation of Mary House of Formation - 186 Lowell Rd., Hudson, NH 03051-4908 t) 603-882-1347 camiremargaret@hotmail.com Sr. Margaret Camire, p.m., Supr.;

NASHUA

Sisters of Mercy of the Americas-Northeast Community, Inc. - 11 Trafalgar Sq., Ste. 203, Nashua, NH 03063 t) 603-402-2883 jhardin@sistersofmercy.org See Schools Section for related school. Sr. Rosemary Burnham, RSM, Local Coord.; Sr. Cecelia Ferland, RSM, Local Coord.;
 Frances Warde House - 21 Searles Rd., Windham, NH 03087; Mailing: P.O. Box 420, Windham, NH 03087 t) 603-893-6550; 603-641-2163 mfastnacht@nh-cc.org Bret Pomeroy, Admin.;
 McAuley Commons - 37 Searles Rd., #207, Windham, NH 03087 t) 603-641-2163 fmckone@mercyne.org

Mount St. Mary Academy, Inc. - 2291 Elm St., Manchester, NH 03104 t) 603-623-3155 ksegalk@mtstmary.org Kate Segal, Prin.;

ENDOWMENTS / FOUNDATIONS / TRUSTS [EFT]

MANCHESTER

Bishop's Charitable Assistance Fund - 153 Ash St., Manchester, NH 03104 t) 603-669-3100 menglish@rcbm.org Melanie English, Contact;

Diocesan Priest Retirement Plan and Trust - 153 Ash St., Manchester, NH 03105 t) 603-669-3100 webmaster@rcbm.org Rolla Bryant, Contact;

Friends of Saint Patrick School Trust Fund - 153 Ash St., Manchester, NH 03105-0310 t) 603-669-3100 mbryant@rcbm.org Rolla Bryant, Contact;

Friends of the St. Thomas Aquinas School Trust Fund - 153 Ash St., Manchester, NH 03104 t) 603-669-3100 mbryant@rcbm.org www.catholicnh.org c/o Roman Catholic Bishop of Manchester, a corporation sole Rolla Bryant, Contact;

Saint Jude Parish Capital Campaign Trust - 153 Ash St., Manchester, NH 03104 t) 603-669-3100 mbryant@rcbm.org catholicnh.org c/o Roman Catholic Bishop of Manchester, a corporation sole Rolla Bryant, Contact;

St. Thomas Aquinas High School Capital Campaign Trust Fund - 153 Ash St., Manchester, NH 03105-0310 t) 603-669-3100 mbryant@rcbm.org Rolla Bryant, Contact;

St. Thomas Aquinas High School Tuition Endowment Trust Fund - 153 Ash St., Manchester, NH 03105-0310 t) 603-669-3100 mbryant@rcbm.org Rolla Bryant, Contact;

Trinity High School Endowment Trust - 153 Ash St., Manchester, NH 03104 t) 603-669-3100 mbryant@rcbm.org catholicnh.org c/o Roman Catholic Bishop of Manchester, a corporation sole Rolla Bryant, Contact;

HOSPITALS / HEALTH SERVICES [HOS]

MANCHESTER

Catholic Medical Center - 100 McGregor St., Manchester, NH 03102 t) 603-668-3545 carrie.perry@cmc-nh.org www.catholicmedicalcenter.org Alex J. Walker Jr., Pres.;

NASHUA

St. Joseph Hospital - 172 Kinsley St., Nashua, NH 03061 t) 603-882-3000 dmoen@stjosephhospital.com www.stjosephhospital.com Sponsored by Covenant Health Inc., Tewksbury, MA. John Jurczyk, Pres.;

MISCELLANEOUS [MIS]

CENTER HARBOR

L.C. Center Harbor, Inc. - 109 Dane Rd., Center Harbor, NH 03226; Mailing: P.O. Box 936, Center Harbor, NH 03226 t) (770) 828-4950 jbudke@legionaries.org Rev. Frank Formolo, L.C., Secy.;

KEENE

Catholic Faith Formation Center - 161 Main St., Ste. 118, Keene, NH 03431 t) 603-352-7662 cffc.keene@gmail.com Ann Ball, Contact;

MANCHESTER

Catholic Lawyers Guild of New Hampshire, Inc. - 153 Ash St., Manchester, NH 03105 t) 603-410-1704 rdunn@rcbm.org Robert E. Dunn Jr., Pres.;

CMC Healthcare System - 100 McGregor St., Manchester, NH 03102 t) 603-668-3545 carrie.perry@cmc-nh.org Joseph Pepe, Pres.;

Alliance Ambulatory Services, Inc. - dorothy.welsh@cmc-nh.org

Alliance Resources Inc. - t) 608-663-6850 dorothy.welsh@cmc-nh.org

Catholic Medical Center -

St. Peter's Home - 300 Kelly St., Manchester, NH 03102 t) 603-669-1219 lisa_stpeters@hotmail.com www.stpetershome.com Sr. Florence Therrien, S.C.S.H., Contact;

The NH Guild for Catholic Healthcare Professionals - 153 Ash St., Manchester, NH 03108-4538; Mailing: P.O. Box 4538, Manchester, NH 03108-4538 t) 603-663-8706 nancy.malo@cmc-nh.org Nancy Malo, Pres.;

NASHUA

Corpus Christi Food Pantry and Assistance, Inc. - 3 Crown St., Nashua, NH 03060 t) 603-882-6372 (Pantry); 603-598-1641 (Assistance) corpuschristifp@outlook.com www.corpuschristifoodpantry.org Susan Dignan, Dir.;

MONASTERIES AND RESIDENCES FOR PRIESTS AND BROTHERS [MON]

COLEBROOK

Shrine of Our Lady of Grace - ; Mailing: P.O. Box 35, Colebrook, NH 03576 t) 978-458-9912 provsec@omiusa.org Rev. James Chambers, Treas.;

ENFIELD

Shrine of Our Lady of La Salette (La Salette of Enfield, Inc.) - 410 N.H. Rte. 4A, Enfield, NH 03748-0420; Mailing: P.O. Box 420, Enfield, NH 03748-0420 t) 603-632-4301 (Shop); 603-632-7087 lasalette-enfield@comcast.net www.lasaletteofenfield.org Rev. Joseph Gosselin, Supr.; Rev. John Sullivan, M.S., Dir.;

HANOVER

Order of Preachers - 2 Occom Ridge, Hanover, NH 03755; Mailing: P.O. Box 147, Hanover, NH 03755 t) 603-643-2154 aq@dartmouth.edu Rev. Brian Mulcahy, O.P.; Rev. D. Brendan Murphy, O.P.;

MANCHESTER

St. Anselm Abbey - 100 St. Anselm Dr., Manchester, NH 03102 t) 603-641-7652 abbey@anselm.edu www.saintanselmabbey.org Of the Order of St. Benedict including seminary and formation program. Rt. Rev. Mark A. Cooper, O.S.B., Chancellor; Rev. Bede Camera, O.S.B., In Res.; Rev. Jerome J. Day, O.S.B., In Res.; Rev. Jonathan DeFelice, O.S.B., In Res.; Rev. Bernard Disco, O.S.B., In Res.; Rev. Cecil J. Donahue, O.S.B., In Res.; Rev. Mathias D. Durette, O.S.B., In Res.; Bro. Dunstan Enzor, O.S.B., In Res.; Rev. John R. Fortin, O.S.B, In Res.; Rev. Benedict M. Guevin, O.S.B., In Res.; Bro. Celestine Hettrick, O.S.B., In Res.; Rev. Augustine G. Kelly, O.S.B, In Res.; Bro. Thomas Lacourse, OSB, In Res.; Rev. Stephen Lawson, O.S.B., In Res.; Rt. Rev. Matthew K. Leavy, O.S.B., In Res.; Rev. Iain G. MacLellan, O.S.B., In Res.; Bro. Ignatius Membrino, O.S.B., In Res.; Bro. Isaac S. Murphy, O.S.B., In Res.; Rev. Benet C. Phillips, O.S.B., In Res.; Rev. Anselm Smedile, O.S.B, In Res.; Rev. Patrick M. Sullivan, O.S.B., In Res.; Bro. Andrew Thornton, O.S.B., In Res.; Rev. Deacon Basil Franciose, O.S.B., In Res.; Rev. Francis McCarty, O.S.B., In Res.; Rev. Deacon Titus Phelan, O.S.B., In Res.; Rev. Aloysius Sarasin, O.S.B., In Res.; Brs.: 8; Priests: 20

NASHUA

Brothers of the Sacred Heart - 196 Lund Rd., Nashua, NH 03060; Mailing: 4600 Elysian Fields Ave., New Orleans, LA 70122 t) 504-301-4758 unitedstatesprovince@gmail.com Bro. Laurent Beaunoyer, S.C., Dir.; Bro. Ralph Lebel, S.C., In Res.; Bro. Bertrand Ouellette, S.C., In Res.; Bro. Gerald Provencher, S.C., In Res.; Brs.: 4

NURSING / REHABILITATION / CONVALESCENCE / ELDERLY CARE [NUR]

BERLIN

St. Vincent de Paul Rehabilitation and Nursing Center - 29 Providence Ave., Berlin, NH 03570-3130 t) 603-752-1820 stv.administrator@nh-cc.org New Hampshire Catholic Charities. Jeff Lacroix, Admin.;

DOVER

St. Ann Rehabilitation and Nursing Center - 195 Dover Point Rd., Dover, NH 03820-4693 t) 603-742-2612 sta.administrator@nh-cc.org New Hampshire Catholic Charities. Rev. Donald McAllister, Chap.; Kathleen McCracken, Admin.;

Bishop Gendron Senior Living Community -

LACONIA

St. Francis Rehabilitation and Nursing Center - 406 Court St., Laconia, NH 03246-3600 t) 603-524-0466 stf.administrator@nh-cc.org New Hampshire Catholic Charities. Brenda Buttrick, Admin.;

Bishop Bradley Senior Living Community - Deb Sturgeon, Apt. Mgr.;

MANCHESTER

Mt. Carmel Rehabilitation and Nursing Center - 235 Myrtle St., Manchester, NH 03104-4314 t) 603-627-3811 jbohunicky@nh-cc.org New Hampshire Catholic Charities. Joe Bohunicky, Admin.;

St. Teresa Rehabilitation and Nursing Center - 519 Bridge St., Manchester, NH 03104-5337 t) 603-668-2373 stt.administrator@nh-cc.org New Hampshire Catholic Charities Luanne Rogers, Admin.;

Bishop Primeau Senior Living Community - Linda Illg, Contact;

WINDHAM

Warde Rehabilitation & Nursing Center - 21 Searles Rd., Windham, NH 03087-1203; Mailing: P.O. Box 420, Windham, NH 03087-1203 t) 603-890-1290 whc.administrator@nh-cc.org Owned by New Hampshire Catholic Charities. Bret Pomeroy, Admin.;

PRESCHOOLS / CHILDCARE CENTERS [PRE]

ALLENSTOWN

Pine Haven Boys Center - 133 River Rd., Allenstown, NH 03275; Mailing: P.O. Box 162, Allenstown, NH 03275 t) 603-485-7141 paulriva68@hotmail.com www.pinehavenboyscenter.org Rev. Remo Zanatta, Exec. Dir.;

EFFINGHAM

Camp Marist - 22 Abel Blvd., Effingham, NH 03882 t) 603-539-4552 office@campmarist.org www.campmarist.org Stds.: 400

GILMANTON IRON WORKS

Camp Fatima - 32 Fatima Rd., Gilmanton Iron Works, NH 03837 t) (603) 931-5500 dthibault@rcbm.org www.bfcamp.com (Boys) Most Rev. Peter A. Libasci, Chair; Leonard (Budd) Ryer, Exec. Dir.; Stds.: 500; Lay Tchrs.: 1

MANCHESTER

St. Augustin Pre-School - 251 Merrimack St., Manchester, NH 03103 t) 603-623-8800 sapreschool@comcast.net Crystal Elie, Dir.;

Holy Cross Early Childhood Center - 420 Island Pond Rd., Manchester, NH 03109-4812 t) 603-668-0510 holycrossecc@yahoo.com Cindy Wallace, Dir.;

St. Peter's Home - 300 Kelley St., Manchester, NH 03102-3093 t) 603-625-9313 sft@stpeterhome.com www.stpeterhome.com Sr. Florence Therrien, S.C.S.H., Dir.;

ROCHESTER

St. Charles School - 19 Grant St., Rochester, NH 03867-3099 t) 603-332-4768 sma@stcharleshome.net; jgilbert@stcharleshome.net www.cc-nh.org/programs/stcharles/ New Hampshire Catholic Charities. Sr. Mary Agnes Dombroski, D.M.M.L., Exec. Dir.; Thomas Hayward, Prin.;

WOLFEBORO

Camp Bernadette (Girls) - 83 Richards Rd., Wolfeboro, NH 03894; Mailing: 32 Fatima Rd., Gilmanton Iron Works, NH 03837 t) (603) 931-5500 dthibault@rcbm.org www.bfcamp.com Most Rev. Peter A. Libasci, Chair; Stds.: 600; Lay Tchrs.: 1

Summer Business Office for Camp Bernadette - 32 Fatima Rd., Gilmanton Iron Works, NH 03837 t) 603-569-1692 info@bfcamp.com

RETREAT HOUSES / RENEWAL CENTERS [RTR]

ENFIELD

Shrine of Our Lady of La Salette (La Salette of Enfield, Inc) - 417 N.H. Rte. 4A, Enfield, NH 03748; Mailing: P.O. Box 420, Enfield, NH 03748 t) 603-632-7087; 603-632-4301 (Shop) lasalette-enfield@comcast.net www.lasaletteofenfield.org Rev. Joseph Gosselin, Supr.;

Rev. John Sullivan, M.S., Dir.;

SEMINARIES [SEM]

MANCHESTER

St. Anselm Abbey Seminary - 100 St. Anselm Dr., Manchester, NH 03102 t) 603-641-7652 webmaster@anselm.edu www.anselm.edu Rt. Rev. Mark A. Cooper, O.S.B.;

SPECIAL CARE FACILITIES [SPF]

LACONIA

Bishop Bradley Senior Living Community - 406 Court St., Laconia, NH 03246 t) 603-524-0466 stf.administrator@nh-cc.org Deborah Sturgeon, Secy.;

MANCHESTER

St. Joseph Residence - 495 Mammoth Rd., Manchester, NH 03104-5463 t) 603-668-6011 mjm@presmarynh.org A managed home of New Hampshire Catholic Charities sponsored by the Sisters of the Presentation of Mary. Marlene Makowski, Admin.;

NASHUA

Marguerite's Place - 87 Palm St., Nashua, NH 03060 t) 603-598-1582 balves@margueritesplace.org www.margueritesplace.org Barbara A. Alves, CEO;

An asterisk (*) denotes an organization that has established tax-exempt status directly with the IRS and is not covered by the USCCB Group Ruling.

Diocese of Marquette

(Dioecesis Marquettensis)

MOST REVEREND JOHN F. DOERFLER, S.T.D., J.C.L.

Bishop of Marquette; ordained July 13, 1991; appointed Bishop of Marquette; installed February 11, 2014. Chancery: 1004 Harbor Hills Dr., Marquette, MI 49855.

Chancery: 1004 Harbor Hills Dr., Marquette, MI 49855. T: 906-225-1141; F: 906-225-0437. www.dioceseofmarquette.org

VICARIATE-APOSTOLIC JULY 29, 1853; DIOCESE 1857.

Square Miles 16,281.

Comprises the Upper Peninsula of the State of Michigan.

For legal titles of parishes and diocesan institutions, consult the Chancery.

STATISTICAL OVERVIEW

Personnel
Bishop....1
Retired Bishops....1
Priests: Diocesan Active in Diocese....40
Priests: Diocesan Active Outside Diocese....3
Priests: Retired, Sick or Absent....23
Number of Diocesan Priests....66
Religious Priests in Diocese....4
Total Priests in your Diocese....70
Extern Priests in Diocese....16
Ordinations:
Diocesan Priests....2
Transitional Deacons....1
Permanent Deacons in Diocese....34
Total Sisters....34

Parishes
Parishes....73
With Resident Pastor:
Resident Diocesan Priests....60
Resident Religious Priests....7
Without Resident Pastor:
Administered by Priests....4
Administered by Religious Women....2
Missions....20
Pastoral Centers....4
Professional Ministry Personnel:
Sisters....13
Lay Ministers....16

Welfare
Catholic Hospitals....1
Total Assisted....128,450
Homes for the Aged....1
Total Assisted....23,393
Specialized Homes....3
Total Assisted....52
Special Centers for Social Services....2
Total Assisted....8,918
Residential Care of Disabled....1
Other Institutions....1
Total Assisted....8,485

Educational
Diocesan Students in Other Seminaries....7
Total Seminarians....7
High Schools, Diocesan and Parish....1
Total Students....13
Elementary Schools, Diocesan and Parish....8
Total Students....1,060
Catechesis/Religious Education:
High School Students....725
Elementary Students....1,618
Total Students under Catholic Instruction....3,423
Teachers in Diocese:
Sisters....1
Lay Teachers....82

Vital Statistics
Receptions into the Church:
Infant Baptism Totals....275
Minor Baptism Totals....35
Adult Baptism Totals....20
Received into Full Communion....38
First Communions....340
Confirmations....210
Marriages:
Catholic....107
Interfaith....33
Total Marriages....140
Deaths....830
Total Catholic Population....52,337
Total Population....301,396

OFFICES AND DIRECTORS

Chancery - t) 906-225-1141

Administration & Finance, Dept. of - t) 906-227-9105 Timothy D. Thomas, Exec. Dir.; Casey Banks, Dir.;

Bishop, Office of - t) 906-227-9115 mbernier@dioceseofmarquette.org MaryAnn Bernier, Vice Chancellor;

Canonical Services, Tribunal & Divine Worship -

Chancellor & Vicar for Religious - t) 906-227-9154 dmoll@dioceseofmarquette.org Very Rev. Daniel J. Moll;

Diocesan Tribunal - t) 906-227-9131

Judicial Vicar - Very Rev. Daniel J. Moll;

Adjunct Judicial Vicar - Very Rev. Timothy T. Ferguson, Vicar;

Defenders of the Bond - Rev. Benedetto J.J. Paris; Rev. John J. Shiverski;

Notaries - Martha Tomasi; Valerie Bailey;

Promoter of Justice - Rev. Benedetto J.J. Paris;

Advocates - Rev. Michael D. Chenier; Rev. Francis J. DeGroot; Rev. Ryan T. Ford;

Advocates (cont.) - Rev. Bradley S. Sjoquist;

Divine Worship - t) (906) 227-9126 tfoye@dioceseofmarquette.org Dcn. Thomas E. Foye, Dir.;

Sacred Music - t) (906) 227-9122 bobrien@dioceseofmarquette.org Benjamin O'Brien, Dir.;

Communication Office - t) 906-227-9129 jfee@dioceseofmarquette.org John Fee, Exec. Dir.;

Newspaper "The U.P. Catholic" - John Fee, Editor;

Evangelization and Education - t) 906-227-9127 msalisbury@dioceseofmarquette.org Mark Salisbury, Exec. Dir.;

Catechesis, Youth and Young Adult Ministry and Adult Faith Formation - t) (906) 227-9127 msalisbury@dioceseofmarquette.org Mark Salisbury, Exec. Dir.;

Family Ministry - t) 906-863-7460 sgretzinger@dioceseofmarquette.org Dcn. Stephen S. Gretzinger, Contact;

Stewardship & Development, Dept. of - t) 906-227-9108 rtaylor@dioceseofmarquette.org Rob Taylor, Exec. Dir.;

Vicar General, Office of -

Vicar General - t) 906-227-9107 tekaitis@dioceseofmarquette.org Very Rev. Timothy M. Ekaitis;

Vicar for Senior Priests - t) 906-227-9155 Rev. Michael A. Woempner;

Administrative Services - t) 906-227-9155 mtomasi@dioceseofmarquette.org Martha Tomasi, Admin.;

Ministry Personnel Services -

Permanent Diaconate Formation Program -

Safe Environment Program - t) 906-227-9155 mtomasi@dioceseofmarquette.org Martha Tomasi, Coord.;

Victim Assistance Coordinators - t) 844-495-4330 (Steve Lynott); 844-694-4362 (Diane Tryan)

Vocations Office - t) 906-482-5530 c) 906-290-2434 Rev. Benjamin J. Hasse, Dir. (benjhasse@yahoo.com);

ADVISORY BOARDS, COMMISSIONS, COMMITTEES, AND COUNCILS

College of Consultors - t) 906-227-9115 mbernier@dioceseofmarquette.org MaryAnn Bernier, Contact;

Diocesan Building Commission - t) 906-227-9135 imccauley@dioceseofmarquette.org Timothy D. Thomas; Irene McCauley, Contact;

Diocesan Finance Council - t) 906-227-9135 imccauley@dioceseofmarquette.org Timothy D. Thomas, Contact; Irene McCauley, Contact;

Diocesan Review Board - t) 906-227-9155 mtomasi@dioceseofmarquette.org Martha Tomasi, Contact;

Priests' Council - t) 906-227-9115 mbernier@dioceseofmarquette.org MaryAnn Bernier, Contact;

Executive Board - Rev. Ryan T. Ford, Chair;

St. Joseph Association - t) 906-227-9135 imccauley@dioceseofmarquette.org Rev. Larry P. Van Damme, Pres.; Irene McCauley, Contact;

Vicariate-Holy Name of Mary - Very Rev. Timothy W. Hruska, Vicar; Rev. Bradley S. Sjoquist, Priests Council;

Vicariate-Most Holy Name of Jesus - Very Rev. Corey J. Litzner, Vicar; Rev. John E. Martignon, Priests Council;

Vicariate-St. John Neumann - Rev. Abraham J. Mupparathara, M.C.B.S. (India), Priests Council (smuparra@hotmail.com);

Vicariate-St. Joseph & St. Patrick - Very Rev. Timothy T. Ferguson, Vicar; Rev. James C. Ziminski, Priests Council;

Vicariate-St. Mary Norway - Very Rev. Janusz Romanek, Vicar; Rev. Michael A. Woempner, Priests Council;

Vicariate-St. Mary Rockland - Very Rev. Brian C. Gerber, Vicar; Rev. Dominic Agyapong, Priests Council;

Vicariate-St. Peter Cathedral - Rev. Msgr. Michael J. Steber, Vicar; Rev. Ryan T. Ford, Priests Council;

Vicars Forane - t) 906-227-9155 mtomasi@dioceseofmarquette.org Martha Tomasi, Contact;

CATHOLIC CHARITIES

Catholic Social Services, Dept. of - t) 906-227-9119 Kyle Rambo, Exec.;

ORGANIZATIONS

Bishop Baraga Association - t) (906) 227-9117 lmckeen@bishopbaraga.org www.bishopbaraga.org/ Very Rev. Timothy T. Ferguson, Chap.; Lenora McKeen, Exec. Dir.;

Charismatic Prayer Groups - t) 906-226-6548 Rev. Msgr. Michael J. Steber, Liaison;

Cursillo - t) 906-475-9969 Rev. Larry P. Van Damme, Chap.;

Irving Houle Association - t) (906) 786-0727 www.irvingfrancishoule.org/ Dcn. Terrance J. Saunders, Contact;

Knights of Columbus - t) 906-524-6424 Very Rev. Corey J. Litzner, Chap.;

Youth Retreats - t) 906-486-6212 Rev. Ryan T. Ford, Chap.;

MISCELLANEOUS / OTHER OFFICES

Archives - t) 906-225-9115 mbernier@dioceseofmarquette.org MaryAnn Bernier, Vice Chancellor;

Cemeteries - t) 906-225-0191 nnewcomb@dioceseofmarquette.org Neil Newcomb, Dir.;

Propagation of the Faith - t) 906-227-9155 mtomasi@dioceseofmarquette.org Martha Tomasi, Admin.;

PARISHES, MISSIONS, AND CLERGY

STATE OF MICHIGAN

AHMEEK

Our Lady of Peace - 2854 US Hwy. 41, Ahmeek, MI 49901; Mailing: P.O. Box 546, Calumet, MI 49913 t) 906-337-0810 www.keweenawcc.org (Keweenaw Catholic Missions) Rev. Gracious Joseph Pulimoottil, M.C.B.S., Pst.; Dcn. Jeremiah Mason; Dcn. Arthur Stancher; CRP Stds.: 7

Holy Redeemer - 507 South St., Eagle Harbor, MI 49950; Mailing: P. O. Box 546, Calumet, MI 49913 t) (906) 337-0810 keweenawcc.org

Our Lady of the Pines - 443 1st St., Copper Harbor, MI 49918; Mailing: P. O. Box 546, Calumet, MI 49913 t) (906) 337-0810 keweenawcc.org

BARAGA

St. Ann - 322 Lyons St., Baraga, MI 49908; Mailing: 16 6th St., L'Anse, MI 49946 t) 906-524-6424 x3 www.baragacatholic.org Very Rev. Corey J. Litzner, Pst.; Wayne Schwartz, Bus. Mgr.; CRP Stds.: 5

The Most Holy Name of Jesus-Saint Kateri Tekakwitha - 14808 Assinins Rd., Baraga, MI 49908; Mailing: 16 Sixth St., L'Anse, MI 49946 t) 906-524-6424 www.baragacatholic.org Very Rev. Corey J. Litzner, Pst.; Wayne Schwartz, Bus. Mgr.; CRP Stds.: 5

BARBEAU

Holy Family Mission - 4585 E. 15 Mile Rd., Barbeau, MI 49710; Mailing: P.O. Box 39, Barbeau, MI 49710 t) 906-248-1077 siskholyfamily.org Rev. Dominic Afrifa Yamoah, Pst.; CRP Stds.: 4

BARK RIVER

St. Elizabeth Ann Seton - 1216 12th Rd., Bark River, MI 49807; Mailing: P.O. Box 187, Bark River, MI 49807 t) 906-466-9938 Formerly St. George, Bark River, Sacred Heart of Jesus, Schaffer & St. Michael, Perronville. Rev. Darryl J. Pepin, Pst.; Kelley VanLanen, DRE; CRP Stds.: 113

St. Joseph - W2332 Cemetery Rd., Foster City, MI 49834 t) (906) 466-9938

BAY MILLS

Saint Kateri Tekakwitha - 12014 W. Lakeshore Dr., Bay Mills, MI 49715 t) 906-248-1077 c) 571-317-8905 katayieafrifa1974@gmail.com; stshokajogues3missions17@gmail.com siskholyfamily.org Rev. Dominic Afrifa Yamoah, Pst.; CRP Stds.: 4

BESSEMER

St. Sebastian - 210 E. Iron St., Bessemer, MI 49911 t) 906-667-0952 dre@stsebastianparish.com; office@stsebastianparish.com www.tri-catholicgogebic.com/ Rev. Dominic Agyapong, Pst.; Michelle R Fink, Admin.; Angie Mazurek, DRE; CRP Stds.: 19

BRIMLEY

St. Francis Xavier - 6769 S. Bay St. M-221, Brimley, MI 49715; Mailing: 11509 W H-40, Rudyard, MI 49780 t) 906-478-4331 stjosephsofrudyardmi@gmail.com; 3parishaa@gmail.com Very Rev. Timothy W. Hruska, Pst.; CRP Stds.: 5

CALUMET

St. Paul the Apostle - 301 Eight St., Calumet, MI 49913; Mailing: P. O. Box 546, Calumet, MI 49913 t) 906-337-2044; 906-337-0810 www.keweenawcc.org Rev. Gracious Joseph Pulimoottil, M.C.B.S., Pst.; Dcn. Jeremiah Mason; Dcn. Arthur Stancher; CRP Stds.: 23

Sacred Heart - 56512 Rockland St., Calumet, MI 49913; Mailing: P. O. Box 546, Calumet, MI 49913 t) 906-337-0810 www.keweenawcc.org Rev. Gracious Joseph Pulimoottil, M.C.B.S., Pst.; Dcn. Jeremiah Mason; Dcn. Arthur Stancher; CRP Stds.: 35

CASPIAN

St. Cecilia - 510 Brady St., Caspian, MI 49915; Mailing: 702 N. 4th Ave., Iron River, MI 49935 t) 906-265-4557 (St. Agnes Office) stagnesstcecilia@gmail.com www.catholicyooperfaithful.org Rev. Jose Cherian, Pst.; Dcn. Terry Verville; CRP Stds.: 6

CHAMPION

Sacred Heart - 1723 Main St., Champion, MI 49814; Mailing: P.O. Box 99, Champion, MI 49814 t) 906-376-8475 smargey@att.net Rev. Ryan T. Ford, Moderator; Rev. Christian Flagstadt, Sacr. Min.; Sr. Margey Schmelzle, O.S.F., Pst. Min./Coord.;

CHANNING

St. Rose - 703 Bell Ave., Channing, MI 49815; Mailing: P.O. Box 235, Channing, MI 49815 t) 906-542-3215 st.rosechurch@sbcglobal.net Rev. Daniel L. Malone, Pst.; Nancy Reese, DRE; CRP Stds.: 4

CHASSELL

St. Anne - 41903 Willson Memorial Dr., Chassell, MI 49916; Mailing: 411 MacInnes Dr., Houghton, MI 49931 t) 906-523-4912 office@mtucatholic.org www.stannechassell.org Rev. Benjamin J. Hasse; Sr. Linda Brandes, Pst. Assoc.; Sr. Jacqueline Spaniola, DRE; Rev. Thomas Merkel, Assoc. Pst.; Dcn. Thomas F. Corrigan; CRP Stds.: 33

COOKS

St. Mary Magdalene - 1130S County Rd. 442, Cooks, MI 49817; Mailing: P.O. Box 68, Garden, MI 49835 t) 906-644-2626 stjohns@centurytel.net Rev. James C. Ziminski, Pst.; Rev. Brandon S Yanni, Par. Vicar;

CRYSTAL FALLS

Guardian Angels - 412 Crystal Ave., Crystal Falls, MI 49920 t) 906-875-3019 guardang@up.net Rev. Daniel L. Malone, Pst.; Claudia Alexa, DRE; Krystal Kudwa, DRE; CRP Stds.: 26

DETOUR VILLAGE

Sacred Heart - 245 N. Ontario St., DeTour Village, MI 49725; Mailing: P.O. Box 325, Hessel, MI 49745 t) 906-484-3825 4parishoffice@gmail.com Rev. Jernej Sustar, Pst.;

St. Florence - 34138 S. Townline Rd., Drummond Island, MI 49726 t) (906) 484-3828

ESCANABA

St. Anne - 817 S. Lincoln Rd., Escanaba, MI 49829 t) 906-786-1421; 906-786-6202 (CRP) stanne@chartermi.net; stanneformation@gmail.com Rev. Francis J. DeGroot, Pst.; Dcn. Terrance J. Saunders; Dcn. Lewis Vailliencourt; Matt Buchmiller, DRE; Nick Moreno, DRE; CRP Stds.: 92

St. Joseph & St. Patrick - 709 1st Ave. S., Escanaba, MI 49829 t) 906-789-6244 sjspoffice709@gmail.com (Formerly St. Joseph, Escanaba; Formerly St. Patrick, Escanaba). Very Rev. Timothy T. Ferguson, Pst.; CRP Stds.: 17

St. Thomas the Apostle - 1820 Ninth Ave. N., Escanaba, MI 49829 t) 906-786-4627; 906-233-9566 (CRP) beth.sviland@stanthonystthomas.org dioceseofmarquette.org/stthomasescanaba Rev. Rick L. Courier, Pst.; CRP Stds.: 35

EWEN

Sacred Heart - 201 S. Birch St., Ewen, MI 49925; Mailing: P.O. Box 427, White Pine, MI 49971 t) 906-885-5763 shcewen@jamadots.com ontonagoncountycatholics.com Rev. Michael J. Jacobus, Pst.; CRP Stds.: 10

St. Ann - 480 Forest Ave., Bergland, MI 49910 t) (906) 885-5763

GARDEN

St. John the Baptist - 6410 State St., Garden, MI 49835; Mailing: P.O. Box 68, Garden, MI 49835 t) 906-644-2626 stjohns@centurytel.net Rev. James C. Ziminski, Pst.; Rev. Brandon S Yanni, Par. Vicar; CRP Stds.: 2

GLADSTONE

All Saints - 715 Wisconsin Ave., Gladstone, MI 49837; Mailing: P.O. Box 392, Gladstone, MI 49837 t) 906-428-3199 www.allsaintsgladstone.org Rev. James C. Ziminski, Pst.; Rev. Brandon S Yanni, Par. Vicar; Dcn. John Bedard; Dcn. Michael LeBeau; Kathy Kohtala, DRE; CRP Stds.: 203

Holy Family - 4011 CO 416-20th Rd., Gladstone, MI 49837 t) 906-786-1209 secretary@holyfamilyparish.net www.holyfamilyparish.net Rev. Sebastian Kavumkal, M.S.T. (India), Pst.; CRP Stds.: 30

GOETZVILLE

St. Stanislaus Kostka - 12841 E. Traynor Rd., Goetzville, MI 49736; Mailing: P.O. Box 325, Hessel, MI 49745 t) 906-484-3825 4parishoffice@gmail.com Rev. Jernej Sustar, Pst.; Barbara Storey, DRE; CRP Stds.: 4

Our Lady of the Snows - 261 Island View Rd., Hessel, MI 49745 t) (906) 297-5211

GRAND MARAIS

Holy Rosary Church - E21907 Grand Marais Ave., Grand Marais, MI 49839; Mailing: P.O. Box 424, Grand Marais, MI 49839 t) 906-494-2589 hrosary@gmail.com Rev. Michael Ocran, Pst.;

GWINN

St. Anthony - 280 N. Boulder, Gwinn, MI 49841 t) 906-346-5312 stanthonygwinn@gmail.com www.dioceseofmarquette.org/stanthonygwinn Rev. Sebastian Oppong, Assoc. Pst.; Danyl Winkler, DRE; Rev. Larry P. Van Damme, Temp. Admin.; CRP Stds.: 17

St. Joseph - County Rd. 426, Northland, MI 49801; Mailing: 280 N. Boulder St., Gwinn, MI 49841

HANCOCK

Church of the Resurrection - 900 Quincy St., Hancock, MI 49930 t) 906-482-0215 secretary@resurrectionhancock.org www.resurrectionhancock.com Rev. Jubish Joseph, Pst.; Dcn. Martin Thompson; CRP Stds.: 44

St. Francis of Assisi - 23176 Fir Ave., Dollar Bay, MI 49922 t) 906-482-6489 stfrancisdollarbay@gmail.com

HOUGHTON

St. Albert the Great University Parish - 411 MacInnes Dr., Houghton, MI 49931 t) 906-482-5530 office@mtucatholic.org www.mtucatholic.org (Michigan Technological University) Rev. Benjamin J. Hasse, Pst.; Sr. Linda Brandes, Pst. Assoc.; Sr. Jacqueline Spaniola, Pst. Assoc.; Rev. Thomas Merkel, Assoc. Pst.;

St. Ignatius Loyola - 305 Portage St., Houghton, MI 49931 t) 906-482-0212 annette_bookkeeper@stignatius-houghton.org www.stignatius-houghton.org/ Rev. John E. Martignon, Pst.; Annette Butina, DRE; CRP Stds.: 122

IRON MOUNTAIN

Immaculate Conception of the Blessed Virgin Mary - 500 E. Blaine St., Iron Mountain, MI 49801-1840 t) 906-774-0511 icparishoffice@gmail.com; fathermikechenier@gmail.com Rev. Michael D. Chenier, Pst.; Dcn. Donald R. Christy; Rev. Mark A. McQuesten, In Res.; CRP Stds.: 34

St. Mary and St. Joseph - 411 W. B St., Iron Mountain, MI 49801 t) 906-774-2046 office@stmarystjosephchurch.org stmarystjosephchurch.org Very Rev. Janusz Romanek, Pst.; CRP Stds.: 64

IRON RIVER

St. Agnes - 702 N. Fourth Ave., Iron River, MI 49935-1304 t) 906-265-4557 www.catholicyooperfaithful.org Rev. Jose Cherian, Pst.; Dcn. Terry Verville; CRP Stds.: 28

IRONWOOD

Our Lady of Peace - 108 S. Marquette St., Ironwood, MI 49938 t) 906-932-0174 ktlolop@gmail.com Very Rev. Brian C. Gerber, Pst.; Alison Schlag, Faith Formation Coord.; CRP Stds.: 82

ISHPEMING

St. John the Evangelist - 325 S. Pine St., Ishpeming, MI 49849-2339 t) 906-486-6212 stjohnschurch325@yahoo.com; ishpemingfaithformation@gmail.com www.ishpemingcatholic.com Rev. Ryan T. Ford, Pst.; Rev. Christian Flagstadt, Assoc. Pst.; Alizabeth Ogle, DRE; CRP Stds.: 51

St. Joseph - 1889 Prairie Ave., Ishpeming, MI 49849-1045 t) 906-485-4200 stjoeparish@outlook.com www.ishpemingcatholic.com Rev. Ryan T. Ford, Pst.; Rev. Christian Flagstadt, Assoc. Pst.; Dcn. Steven M. Schaffer; Alizabeth Ogle, DRE; CRP Stds.: 38

KINGSFORD

American Martyrs - 908 W. Sagola Ave., Kingsford, MI 49802 t) 906-774-0630 frjoe@att.net americanmartyrskg.org Rev. Msgr. Joseph O. Gouin, Pst.; Kelly Bruns, DRE; CRP Stds.: 102

St. Mary Queen of Peace - 600 Marquette Blvd., Kingsford, MI 49802 t) 906-774-6122 st.maryqueenofpeacechurch@chartermi.net; qofpoffice@gmail.com Rev. Michael A. Woempner, Pst.; Mary Beth Casanova, DRE; CRP Stds.: 77

LAKE LINDEN

St. Joseph - 701 Calumet St., Lake Linden, MI 49945 t) 906-296-6851 churchlady@saintjosephll.com saintjosephll.com Rev. Raju Jose, M.S.T., Pst.; CRP Stds.: 44

L'ANSE

Sacred Heart - 16 6th St., L'Anse, MI 49946 t) 906-524-6424 www.baragacatholic.org Very Rev. Corey J. Litzner, Pst.; Wayne Schwartz, Bus. Mgr.; CRP Stds.: 30

MACKINAC ISLAND

Ste. Anne de Michilimackinac - 6836 Main St., Mackinac Island, MI 49757; Mailing: P.O. Box 537, Mackinac Island, MI 49757 t) 906-847-3507 steannes@gmail.com steanneschurch.org Rev. John Essel, Par. Admin.;

MANISTIQUE

St. Francis de Sales - 330 Oak St., Manistique, MI 49854 t) 906-341-5355 sfparish1@gmail.com stfrancisofmanistique.weconnect.com Rev. Benedetto J.J. Paris, Pst.; Dcn. Gary Prise; CRP Stds.: 8

Divine Infant of Prague - US Hwy. 2, Gulliver, MI 49840; Mailing: 330 Oak St., Manistique, MI 49854 t) (906) 341-5355

MARQUETTE

St. Peter Cathedral - 311 Baraga Ave., Marquette, MI 49855 t) 906-226-6548 www.stpetercathedral.org Rev. Msgr. Michael J. Steber, Pst.; Rev. Benjamin Rivard, Par. Vicar; Dcn. Thomas E. Foye; Dcn. Dean J. Jackson; Dcn. Lawrence H. Londo; Dcn. Donald Thoren; Dcn. Gregg R. St. John; Annalisa Ogle, DRE; Katelyn McKeen, Youth Min.; CRP Stds.: 50

St. Mary - 305 Bensinger, Big Bay, MI 49808; Mailing: P.O. Box 342, Big Bay, MI 49808 t) (906) 226-6548

St. Christopher - 2372 Badger St., Marquette, MI 49855 t) 906-226-2265 stchristopher49855@gmail.com www.stchristophermqt.org Very Rev. Daniel J. Moll, Pst.; Dcn. Steven M. Gualdoni; CRP Stds.: 8

St. Louis the King (Harvey) - 264 Silver Creek Rd., Marquette, MI 49855 t) 906-249-1438 secretary@sltkchurch.org sltkchurch.org Very Rev. Timothy M. Ekaitis, Temp. Admin.; Rev. Daniel Fosu (Ghana), Par. Vicar; Dcn. Scott A Jamieson; Dcn. Paul Lochner; Dcn. William McKnight; CRP Stds.: 150

St. Michael - 401 W. Kaye Ave., Marquette, MI 49855 t) 906-228-8180 stmichaelmqt@gmail.com www.stmichaelmqt.com Rev. Gregory R. Heikkala, Pst.; Dcn. Dennis R. Maki; CRP Stds.: 30

MENOMINEE

Holy Redeemer - W-5541 Birch Creek Rd., Menominee, MI 49858 t) 906-863-6920 holyredeemer1@gmail.com www.hrcmenominee.com Rev. Abraham J. Mupparathara, M.C.B.S. (India), Pst.; Dcn. Stephen S. Gretzinger; CRP Stds.: 10

Holy Spirit - 1016 10th Ave., Menominee, MI 49858 t) 906-863-5239 office@holyspiritonline.org www.holyspiritonline.org Rev. Abraham J. Mupparathara, M.C.B.S. (India), Pst.; Dcn. Charles H. Gervasio; CRP Stds.: 8

Resurrection - 2607 18th St., Menominee, MI 49858 t) 906-863-3405 (CRP) office@resurrectionparishonline.org www.resurrectionparishonline.org Rev. Joseph Boakye Yiadom (Ghana), Pst.; Dcn. Charles H. Gervasio; Dcn. Robert J. Kostka; CRP Stds.: 29

MORAN

Immaculate Conception - W1934 Church St., Moran, MI 49760; Mailing: 120 Church St., St. Ignace, MI 49781 t) 906-643-7671 stigchurch@lighthouse.net www.stigchurch.org Rev. Francis Ricca, Pst.; Dcn. Thomas McClelland; CRP Stds.: 12

MUNISING

Sacred Heart - 110 W. Jewell St., Munising, MI 49862; Mailing: P.O. Box 99, Munising, MI 49862 t) 906-387-4901; 906-387-4900 (Main Line) bullofc@gmail.com Rev. Michael Ocran, Pst.; CRP Stds.: 35

St. Therese - E5420 Woodland Ave., Autrain, MI 49806 t) (906) 387-4900 (Main office)

NADEAU

St. Bruno - N13770 Old US Hwy. 41, Nadeau, MI 49863; Mailing: P.O. Box 95, Nadeau, MI 49863 t) 906-639-2388 stbruno@alphacomm.net Rev. Benny Mathew, M.S.T., Pst.; Cindy Swille, DRE; Lynette M

Verbisky, Bus. Mgr.; CRP Stds.: 27

NAHMA

St. Andrew - 8236 River St., Nahma, MI 49864; Mailing: PO Box 68, Garden, MI 49835 t) 906-644-2626 stjohns@centurytel.net Rev. James C. Ziminski, Pst.; Rev. Brandon S Yanni, Par. Vicar; CRP Stds.: 1

NEGAUNEE

St. Paul - 202 W. Case St., Negaunee, MI 49866 t) 906-475-9969 parish@stpaulchurchneg.net www.dioceseofmarquette.org/stpaulnegaunee Rev. Larry P. Van Damme, Pst.; Mary Evans, DRE; Katelyn McKeen, DRE; CRP Stds.: 46

Our Lady Perpetual Help - 201 Nicholas Ave., Palmer, MI 49871; Mailing: 202 W. Case St., Negaunee, MI 49866 t) (906) 475-9969

NEWBERRY

St. Gregory - 212 W. Harrie St., Newberry, MI 49868 t) 906-293-5511 stgreg@sbcglobal.net stgregorysmissions.com/ Rev. Jacek S. Wtyklo, Pst.; Dawn Stephenson, DRE; CRP Stds.: 47

St. Stephen - Hwy. U.S. 2, Naubinway, MI 49762; Mailing: P.O. Box 134, Naubinway, MI 49762 t) 906-477-6117 sawicker@lighthouse.net Rev. Jacek S. Wtyklo, Pst.;

Our Lady of Victory - 7208 N M123, Paradise, MI 49768; Mailing: P.O. Box 13, Paradise, MI 49768 t) (906) 477-6117 Rev. Jacek S. Wtyklo, Pst.;

NORWAY

St. Mary - 401 Main St., Norway, MI 49870 t) 906-563-9845 saintmary@norwaymi.com; religioused@norwaymi.com www.stmarybarbara.org Rev. Martin Flynn, Pst.; Nancy Degnan, DRE; CRP Stds.: 44

ONTONAGON

Holy Family - 515 Pine St., Ontonagon, MI 49953 t) 906-884-2569 hfcc@up.net ontonagoncountycatholics.com/ Rev. Michael J. Jacobus, Pst.; CRP Stds.: 26

PERKINS

St. Joseph - 5803 Hwy. M-35, Perkins, MI 49872; Mailing: P.O. Box 22, Perkins, MI 49872 t) 906-359-4701 perkins_stjoes@hotmail.com Rev. William Ssozi, Pst.; CRP Stds.: 34

RAPID RIVER

St. Charles Borromeo - 7860 River St., Rapid River, MI 49878; Mailing: P.O. Box 247, Rapid River, MI 49878 t) 906-474-6606 stcharles@stcharleschurch-rr.org Rev. William Ssozi, Pst.; Michelle Loper, DRE; CRP Stds.: 15

REPUBLIC

St. Augustine - 626 Kloman Ave., Republic, MI 49879; Mailing: 574 Kloman Ave., Republic, MI 49879 t) 906-376-8475 smargey@att.net Rev. Ryan T. Ford, Moderator; Rev. Christian Flagstadt, Sacr. Min.; Sr. Margey Schmelzle, O.S.F., Pastoral Coord.;

ROCKLAND

St. Mary - 11 Elm St., Rockland, MI 49953; Mailing: 515 Pine St., Holy Family Parish, Ontonagon, MI 49953 t) 906-884-2569 smcc@up.net ontonagoncountycatholics.com/ Rev. Michael J. Jacobus, Pst.;

RUDYARD

St. Joseph - 11509 W. H-40, Rudyard, MI 49780 t) 906-478-4331 stjosephsofrudyardmi@gmail.com; 3parishaa@gmail.com Very Rev. Timothy W. Hruska, Pst.; CRP Stds.: 22

St. Mary, Trout Lake - 21481 Beech St., Trout Lake, MI 49793; Mailing: 11509 W H 40, Rudyard, MI 49780 t) (906) 478-4331

SAULT SAINTE MARIE

Holy Name of Mary - 377 Maple St., Sault Sainte Marie, MI 49783 t) 906-632-3381 stmary377@gmail.com www.holymarywebsite.org Very Rev. Allen P. Mott, Pst.; CRP Stds.: 40

St. Isaac Jogues Mission - 1529 Marquette Ave., Sault Sainte Marie, MI 49783 t) 906-259-0584 c) 571-317-8905 Rev. Dominic Afrifa Yamoah, Pst.; Leslie Ruditis, DRE;

St. Joseph - 606 E. Fourth Ave., Sault Sainte Marie, MI 49783 t) 906-632-9625 stjosephsault@gmail.com stjosephssm.org Rev. Bradley S. Sjoquist, Pst.; Rev. Romeo Cappella, Assoc. Pst.; CRP Stds.: 60

SOUTH RANGE

Holy Family - 107 Atlantic Ave., South Range, MI 49963; Mailing: 305 Portage St., Houghton, MI 49931 t) 906-482-0212 annette_bookkeeper@stignatius-houghton.org www.holyfamily-southrange.org/ Rev. John E. Martignon, Pst.; CRP Stds.: 28

SPALDING

St. John Neumann - N16150 Maple St., Spalding, MI 49886; Mailing: P.O. Box 135, Spalding, MI 49886 t) 906-497-4578 (Rectory); 906-497-5800 (Office) spiritu@att.net (Formerly St. Mary, Hermansville; St. Francis Xavier, Spalding). Rev. Benny Mathew, M.S.T., Pst.; Mariah Martin, DRE; CRP Stds.: 59

ST. IGNACE

St. Ignatius Loyola - 120 Church St., St. Ignace, MI 49781 t) 906-643-7671 stigchurch@lighthouse.net www.stigchurch.org Rev. Francis Ricca, Pst.; Dcn. Thomas McClelland; CRP Stds.: 59

STEPHENSON

Precious Blood Church - S. 304 Bluff St., Stephenson, MI 49887 t) 906-753-2562; 906-753-4771 (CRP) pbchurch@304att.net Rev. Edward Baah Baafi, Pst.; Dcn. Thomas J. Rivard; Kris Wangerin, DRE; CRP Stds.: 41

SUGAR ISLAND

Sacred Heart - 3001 S. Westshore Dr., Sugar Island, MI 49783; Mailing: 377 Maple St., Sault Sainte Marie, MI 49783 t) 906-632-3381 stmary377@gmail.com www.holymarywebsite.org Indian Missionaries, East. Very Rev. Allen P. Mott, Pst.;

TRENARY

St. Rita - N1048 First Ave. E., Trenary, MI 49891; Mailing: P.O. Box 207, Trenary, MI 49891 t) 906-446-3350 strita@tds.net Rev. William Ssozi, Pst.;

VULCAN

St. Barbara - W5058 Main St., Vulcan, MI 49892; Mailing: 401 Main St., Norway, MI 49870 t) 906-563-9845 saintmary@norwaymi.com; religioused@norwaymi.com www.stmarybarbara.org Rev. Martin Flynn, Pst.; Nancy Degnan, DRE; CRP Stds.: 15

WAKEFIELD

Immaculate Conception of the Blessed Virgin Mary - 407 Ascherman St., Wakefield, MI 49968; Mailing: 210 E. Iron St., Bessemer, MI 49911 t) 906-667-0952 office@stsebastianparish.com www.tri-catholicgogebic.com/ Rev. Dominic Agyapong, Pst.; Michelle R Fink, Admin.; Laura Yuchasz, DRE; CRP Stds.: 17

St. Catherine - 406 Main St., Marenisco, MI 49947 t) (906) 667-0952

WATERSMEET

Immaculate Conception - E23933 D Ave., Watersmeet, MI 49969; Mailing: 702 N. 4th Ave., Iron River, MI 49935 t) 906-265-4557 (Office) stagnesstcecilia@gmail.com www.catholicyooperfaithful.org Rev. Peter H. Fosu (Ghana), Par. Admin.; Dcn. Terry Verville;

WELLS

St. Anthony of Padua - 6596 N. 3rd St., Wells, MI 49894; Mailing: 1820 9th Ave. N., Escanaba, MI 49829 t) 906-786-4627; 906-233-9566 (CRP) beth.sviland@stanthonystthomas.org www.dioceseofmarquette.org/stanthony.org Rev. Rick L. Courier, Pst.; CRP Stds.: 37

WHITE PINE

St. Jude - 8 Cedar St., White Pine, MI 49971; Mailing: P.O. Box 427, White Pine, MI 49971 t) 906-885-5763 ontonagoncountycatholics.com Rev. Michael J. Jacobus, Pst.;

SCHOOLS: PRESCHOOL THRU HIGH SCHOOL

SCHOOLS

STATE OF MICHIGAN

ESCANABA

Holy Name Catholic School - (PAR) (Grades PreK-11) 409 S. 22nd St., 2203 7th Ave. S., Escanaba, MI 49829 t) 906-786-7550 office@holynamecrusaders.com holynamecrusaders.com Joseph L. Carlson, Prin.; Mark Surrell, Headmaster; Stds.: 284; Lay Tchrs.: 24

IRON MOUNTAIN

Bishop Baraga Catholic School - (PAR) (Grades PreK-8) 406 W. B St., Iron Mountain, MI 49801 t) 906-774-2277 office@baragaup.com; aoller@baragaup.com www.baragaup.com Angela Oller, Prin.; Stds.: 140; Lay Tchrs.: 8

L'ANSE

Sacred Heart School - (PAR) (Grades PreK-8) 433 Baraga Ave., L'Anse, MI 49946 t) 906-524-5157 principal@sacredheartlanse.org; secretary@sacredheartlanse.org www.sacredheartlanse.org Christy Miron, Prin.; Stds.: 59; Sr. Tchrs.: 1; Lay Tchrs.: 4

MANISTIQUE

St. Francis de Sales School - (PAR) (Grades PreK-8) 210 Lake St., Manistique, MI 49854 t) 906-341-5512 lisamarie.burnis@sfdsraiders.com www.sfdsraiders.com Lisa Marie Burnis, Prin.; Karen Mooi, Librn.; Stds.: 151; Lay Tchrs.: 11

MARQUETTE

Father Marquette Catholic Academy - (PAR) (Grades PreK-8) 500 S. Fourth St., Marquette, MI 49855 t) 906-225-1129 jbetz@fathermarquette.org www.fathermarquette.org Serving the following parishes: St. Peter's Cathedral; St. Louis; St. Michael; St. Christopher. Dr. Jessica N. Betz, Prin.; Stds.: 162; Lay Tchrs.: 13

MENOMINEE

St. John Paul II Catholic Academy - (PAR) (Grades PreK-8) 2701 17th St., Menominee, MI 49858 t) 906-863-3190 secretary@jpiicatholicacademy.org; principal@jpiicatholicacademy.org www.jpiicatholicacademy.org Michael Muhs, Prin.; Diane Mielke, Librn.; Stds.: 125; Lay Tchrs.: 8

NORWAY

Holy Spirit Central School - (PAR) (Grades PreSchool-8) 201 Saginaw St., Norway, MI 49870 t) 906-563-8817 office@hscsnorway.org hscsnorway.org Catherine Menghini, Prin.; Stds.: 72; Lay Tchrs.: 6

SAULT SAINTE MARIE

St. Mary School - (DIO) (Grades K-8) 360 Maple St., Sault Sainte Marie, MI 49783 t) 906-635-6141 tvail-stm@eupschools.org www.stmarysup.org/ Timothy Vail, Prin.; Stds.: 86; Lay Tchrs.: 8

INSTITUTIONS LOCATED IN DIOCESE

CAMPUS MINISTRY / NEWMAN CENTERS [CAM]

HOUGHTON

St. Albert the Great University Parish (Catholic Campus Ministry at Michigan Tech) - 411 MacInnes Dr., Houghton, MI 49931 t) 906-482-5530 office@mtucatholic.org www.mtucatholic.org Rev. Benjamin J. Hasse, Pst.; Rev. Thomas Merkel, Assoc. Pst.; Sr. Jacqueline Spaniola, Pst. Assoc.; Joseph Rushlau, Bus. Mgr.;

MARQUETTE

Catholic Campus Ministry-Northern Michigan University - 1200 Hebard Ct., Marquette, MI 49855; Mailing: 401 W. Kaye Ave., Marquette, MI 49855 t) 906-228-3302 office@nmucatholic.org; fatherdustin@nmucatholic.org www.nmucatholic.org Rev. Dustin Larson, Chap.;

SAULT SAINTE MARIE

Lake Superior State University, Newman Center - 517 W. Easterday Ave., Sault Sainte Marie, MI 49783 t) 906-253-1285 newmanlakerstudents@gmail.com; frsjoquist@gmail.com Rev. Bradley S. Sjoquist, Pst.; Rev. Romeo Cappella, Par. Vicar; Caroline Partyka, Campus Min.;

CEMETERIES [CEM]

ESCANABA

Holy Cross Catholic Cemetery - 3026 Lake Shore Dr., Escanaba, MI 49829 t) 906-786-4685 tstannard@dioceseofmarquette.org Tom Stannard, Bus. Mgr.;

MARQUETTE

Holy Cross Catholic Cemetery - 1400 Wright St., Marquette, MI 49855 t) 906-225-0191 nnewcomb@dioceseofmarquette.org Neil Newcomb, Dir.;

CONVENTS, MONASTERIES, AND RESIDENCES FOR WOMEN [CON]

IRON MOUNTAIN

Monastery of the Holy Cross - N4028 Hwy. U.S. 2, Iron Mountain, MI 49801; Mailing: P.O. Box 397, Iron Mountain, MI 49801-0397 t) 906-774-0561 vocation@holycrosscarmel.com www.holycrosscarmel.com Mother Maria of Jesus, O.C.D., Prioress; Srs.: 18

MARQUETTE

Sisters of Saint Paul de Chartres - 1300 County Rd. 492, Marquette, MI 49855 t) 906-226-3932 malaurin9@aol.com sistersofstpaulus.org Sr. Mary Ann Laurin, Supr.; Srs.: 12

ENDOWMENTS / FOUNDATIONS / TRUSTS [EFT]

ESCANABA

Holy Name Endowment Fund - 409 S. 22nd St., Escanaba, MI 49829 t) 906-786-7550 office@holynamecrusaders.com Joseph L. Carlson, Prin.;

Holy Name Scholarship Foundation - 409 S. 22nd St., Escanaba, MI 49829 t) 906-786-7550 office@holynamecrusaders.com Joseph L. Carlson, Prin.;

IRON MOUNTAIN

Bishop Baraga Catholic School Foundation - 406 W. B St., Iron Mountain, MI 49801 t) 906-774-2277 office@baragaup.com; aoller@baragaup.com www.baragaup.com Angela Oller, Prin.; Jerry Brien, Chair;

MANISTIQUE

St. Francis de Sales Education Foundation - 330 Oak St., Manistique, MI 49854 t) 906-341-5355 jimjweber52@gmail.com www.sfdsraiders.com James Weber, Pres.;

MARQUETTE

Marquette Area Catholic Education Fund - 401 W. Kaye Ave., Marquette, MI 49855 t) 906-226-3900 mhdavenport54@hotmail.com Maura Davenport, Pres.;

Upper Peninsula Catholic Foundation, Inc. - 1004 Harbor Hills Dr., Marquette, MI 49855 t) 906-227-9108 rtaylor@dioceseofmarquette.org upcatholicfoundation.org Rob Taylor, Exec. Dir.;

MENOMINEE

Menominee Catholic Education Fund - 2701 17th St., Menominee, MI 49858-2604 t) 906-863-3190 bookkeeper@jpiicatholicacademy.org Mary Fox, Bus. Mgr.;

NEGAUNEE

Negaunee St. Paul Endowment Fund - 202 W. Case St., Negaunee, MI 49866 t) 906-475-9969 parish@stpaulchurchneg.net Rev. Larry P. Van Damme, Pst.;

SAULT SAINTE MARIE

St. Mary School Endowment Fund - 360 Maple St., Sault Sainte Marie, MI 49783 t) 906-635-6141 tvail-stm@eupschools.org Timothy Vail, Prin.;

HOSPITALS / HEALTH SERVICES [HOS]

ESCANABA

OSF HealthCare St. Francis Hospital & Medical Group - 3401 Ludington, Escanaba, MI 49829 t) 906-786-3311 robert.brandfass@osfhealthcare.org www.osfhealthcare.org OSF Healthcare System Kelly Jefferson, Pres.; Rev. Robb M. Jurkovich, Chap.; Bed Capacity: 25; Asstd. Annu.: 128,450; Staff: 478

MISCELLANEOUS [MIS]

ESCANABA

Irving C. "Francis" Houle Association - 709 1st Ave., S., Escanaba, MI 49829 t) 906-786-0727 tjsaunders1955@gmail.com Dcn. Terrance J. Saunders, Moderator;

PARADISE

Companions of Christ the Lamb - 12161 N. Whitefish Point Rd., Paradise, MI 49768; Mailing: P.O. Box 12, Paradise, MI 49768 t) 906-492-3647 communityofccl@gmail.com Operates a Retreat Center in Paradise, Michigan Rev. Gregory L. Veneklase, Chap.; Rev. John Fabian; Rev. Daniel S. Zaloga;

NURSING / REHABILITATION / CONVALESCENCE / ELDERLY CARE [NUR]

ESCANABA

Bishop Noa Home for Senior Citizens - 2900 3rd Ave. S., Escanaba, MI 49829 t) 906-786-5810 director@bishopnoahome.com www.bishopnoahome.com Jamie LaFave, Admin.; Asstd. Annu.: 23,393; Staff: 109

An asterisk (*) denotes an organization that has established tax-exempt status directly with the IRS and is not covered by the USCCB Group Ruling.

Diocese of Memphis

(Memphitana in Tennesia)

MOST REVEREND DAVID P. TALLEY

Bishop of Memphis; ordained June 3, 1989; appointed Titular Bishop of Lambaesis and Auxiliary Bishop of Atlanta January 3, 2013; ordained April 2, 2013; appointed Coadjutor Bishop of Alexandria September 21, 2016; installed November 7, 2016; Succeeded February 2, 2017; appointed Bishop of Memphis March 5, 2019; installed April 2, 2019.

Catholic Center: 5825 Shelby Oaks Dr., Memphis, TN 38134. T: 901-373-1200; F: 901-373-1269.
www.cdom.org

ESTABLISHED JUNE 20, 1970.

Square Miles 10,682.

Comprises the Counties of Benton, Carroll, Chester, Crockett, Decatur, Dyer, Fayette, Gibson, Hardeman, Hardin, Haywood, Henderson, Henry, Lake, Lauderdale, McNairy, Madison, Obion, Shelby, Tipton and Weakley in the State of Tennessee.

For legal titles of parishes and diocesan institutions, consult the Chancery Office.

STATISTICAL OVERVIEW

Personnel
Bishop.....1
Retired Bishops.....2
Priests: Diocesan Active in Diocese.....43
Priests: Retired, Sick or Absent.....23
Number of Diocesan Priests.....66
Religious Priests in Diocese.....10
Total Priests in your Diocese.....76
Extern Priests in Diocese.....8
Ordinations:
Diocesan Priests.....2
Permanent Deacons in Diocese.....62
Total Brothers.....16
Total Sisters.....21

Parishes
Parishes.....41
With Resident Pastor:
Resident Diocesan Priests.....35
Resident Religious Priests.....6
Missions.....6
Pastoral Centers.....1
Professional Ministry Personnel:
Brothers.....16
Sisters.....21
Lay Ministers.....40

Welfare
Homes for the Aged.....2
Total Assisted.....193
Special Centers for Social Services.....1
Total Assisted.....49,000

Educational
Diocesan Students in Other Seminaries.....13
Total Seminarians.....13
Colleges and Universities.....1
Total Students.....1,730
High Schools, Diocesan and Parish.....1
Total Students.....468
High Schools, Private.....3
Total Students.....1,129
Elementary Schools, Diocesan and Parish.....8
Total Students.....2,545
Elementary Schools, Private.....1
Total Students.....304
Catechesis/Religious Education:
High School Students.....679
Elementary Students.....4,020
Total Students under Catholic Instruction.....10,888
Teachers in Diocese:
Priests.....2
Brothers.....1
Sisters.....8
Lay Teachers.....590

Vital Statistics
Receptions into the Church:
Infant Baptism Totals.....964
Minor Baptism Totals.....91
Adult Baptism Totals.....98
Received into Full Communion.....163
First Communions.....927
Confirmations.....1,061
Marriages:
Catholic.....177
Interfaith.....50
Total Marriages.....227
Deaths.....440
Total Catholic Population.....69,863
Total Population.....1,553,201

LEADERSHIP

Vicar General - Very Rev. J. Keith Stewart;
Chancellor - Very Rev. James M. Clark, Judicial Vicar;
Director of Vocations - Very Rev. Robert Szczechura;
Chief Financial Officer - David Zaleski;
Director of Human Resources - Sandra Goldstein;
Office of the Bishop - Most Rev. James Terry Steib, Bishop Emeritus; Margaret Scott, Exec. Asst.; Kari Olesen, Admin. Asst.;
Deaneries -
Central Deanery - Very Rev. Joey Kaump, Dean;
Northern Deanery - Very Rev. Robert Ballman, Dean;
Southeastern Deanery - Rev. James J. Martell, Dean;
Western Deanery - Rev. Juan Antonio Romo-Romo, S.V.D., Dean;
Continuing Formation for Clergy - Rev. Patrick M. Gallagher, Chair;
Permanent Diaconate - Dcn. William Pettit, Dir.; Dcn. Rick Martin, Assoc. Dir.;
Deacon Formation - Dcn. Justin Mitchell, Dir.; Dcn. David Woolley, Assoc. Dir.;
Ministry to Priests - Rev. James J. Martell, Coord.;

OFFICES AND DIRECTORS

Canonical Services - Very Rev. James M. Clark, Chancellor; Anna M. Lynn, Vice Chancellor; Angela Canale, Exec. Asst.;
Catholic Schools - Pierre Nic Antoine, Supt.; Colleen Butterick, Dir., Counseling Svcs.; Tallie Hodges, Admin. Asst.;
Divine Worship - Very Rev. Robert Szczechura, Dir.; Steve Peterson, Sacristan; Candace Campbell, Admin. Asst.;
Evangelization - Sam Mauck, Dir.; Rebecca Talarico, Assoc. Dir., Youth Ministry; Corey Kieffer, Assoc. Coord., Campus & Young Adult Ministry;
Multicultural Ministries - Sam Mauck;
Facilities and Risk Management - Bill Hecht, Dir.; Ed Enright;
Faith Formation - Sam Mauck, Dir.; Dcn. Jeffrey Drzycimski, Assoc. Dir., Catechetical & Sacramental Formation; Dcn. Rick Martin, Assoc. Dir., Pastoral Care;
Finance - Patti Morris, Controller; Pamela Greenwood, Regional Accounting Mgr.; Cynthia Steele, Bookkeeper;
Communications - Rick Ouellette, Dir.; Megan Rogers, Admin. Asst.;
Development - Jim Marconi, Dir.; Allison Thron, Assoc. Dir.; Megan Rogers, Admin. Asst.;
Human Resources - Sandra Goldstein, Dir.; Heather Beeckman, Generalist; Sharon Ichniowski, Benefits Coord.;
Justice, Peace & Human Development - Dcn. Henry P. Littleton, Dir.; Dcn. James Schmall, Assoc. Dir.;
Technical Support Services - Kathy Saba, Dir.; Karin Starnes, Technical Support Analyst;
Tribunal - Anna M. Lynn, Judge; Rev. Carlos Donato Da Silva, Defender of the Bond; Lynn Cozart, Moderator of the Tribunal Chancery;
Vocations - Rev. Dennis L. Schenkel, Asst. Dir.; Lysette Candia, Admin. Asst.;

ADVISORY BOARDS, COMMISSIONS, COMMITTEES, AND COUNCILS

Clergy Personnel Board - Rev. Msgr. Victor P. Ciaramitaro; Rev. Gerald Azike; Rev. Carl J. Hood;
College of Consultors - Very Rev. Joey Kaump; Very Rev. Robert Szczechura; Very Rev. James M. Clark;
Diocesan Finance Council - Joe Evangelisti, Chair; Jim McMahon, Budget Chair; Tom Scherer, RBIF Chair;
Diocesan Review Board - Dr. Pat Lawler, Chair; Tina Burns; John Campbell;
Pastoral Council - Irma Hernandez, Chair; Donny Bearden, Secy.; Rob MacMain, Vice Chair;
Presbyteral Council - Rev. Dennis L. Schenkel, Chair; Rev. Michael E. Werkhoven, Vice Chmn.; Rev. Joseph P. Hastings, Secy.;

ORGANIZATIONS

Catholic Charities - t) 901-722-4700 ccwtn.org/ Kelley Henderson, Exec. Dir.; Brenda O'Looney, CFO; Dana Brooks, Sr. Dir., Homeless Svcs.;
Catholic Cemeteries - t) 901-948-1529 Patrick Posey Sr., Dir.;
Our Lady Queen of Peace Retreat Center - t) 731-548-2500 Dcn. Ernest Albonetti, Dir.;
Villa Vianney Senior Priests Residence - t) 901-752-0766 Rev. Richard L. Mickey, Dir.;

PARISHES, MISSIONS, AND CLERGY

STATE OF TENNESSEE

BARTLETT

St. Ann - 6529 Stage Rd., Bartlett, TN 38134 t) 901-373-6011 info@stannbartlett.org; susan.hunt@stannbartlett.org www.stannbartlett.org Rev. Ernie DeBlasio, Pst.; Susan Hunt, Admin.; CRP Stds.: 276

St. Ann School - (Grades PreSchool-8) t) 901-386-3328 didier.aur@sascolts.org www.sascolts.org Didier Aur, Prin.; Stds.: 293; Lay Tchrs.: 25

Church of the Nativity - 5955 St. Elmo Rd., Bartlett, TN 38135-1516 t) 901-382-2504 www.nativitybartlett.org Rev. Jose Cruz Zapata-Torres, Pst.; Dcn. Christopher Frame; Dcn. Chip Jones; Dcn. Franklin O. Larker; CRP Stds.: 106

BOLIVAR

St. Mary Church - 223 Mecklenburg Dr., Bolivar, TN 38008-1736 t) 901-658-4627; 731-658-4627 (CRP) stmary9@bellsouth.net Rev. Wayne H. Arnold, Pst.; Sue Certain, DRE; CRP Stds.: 15

BROWNSVILLE

St. John's Church - 910 N. Washington, Brownsville, TN 38012; Mailing: 1665 Hwy. 45 By-Pass, Jackson, TN 38305-4414 t) 731-668-2596 kate.todd@stmarys.tn.org Very Rev. David Graham, Pst.; Rev. Jonathan Perez, Par. Vicar; CRP Stds.: 31

CAMDEN

St. Mary Church - 220 W. Main St., Camden, TN 38320 t) 731-584-6459 stmaryscamden.org/ Rev. Herbert Ene (Nigeria), Pst.; Dcn. Wayne Tedford; Tessa Walker, DRE; CRP Stds.: 12

Holy Family Church - 265 Cotham Dr., Huntingdon, TN 38344; Mailing: 220 W. Main St., c/o St. Mary Church, Camden, TN 38320 t) (731) 584-6459

COLLIERVILLE

Church of the Incarnation - 360 Bray Station Rd., Collierville, TN 38017-3263 t) 901-853-7468; 901-853-0135 (CRP) lea.weaver@incarnationcollierville.org; front.desk@incarnationcollierville.org www.incarnationchurch.com Rev. Michael E. Werkhoven, Pst.; Rev. Scott Bahrke, Assoc. Pst.; Lea Weaver, DRE; CRP Stds.: 411

CORDOVA

St. Francis of Assisi - 8151 Chimneyrock Blvd., Cordova, TN 38016-5157 t) 901-756-1213 office@stfrancismemphis.org www.stfrancismemphis.org Rev. Carl J. Hood, Pst.; Rev. Carlos Donato, Par. Vicar; Rev. Joseph P. Hastings, Par. Vicar; Very Rev. James M. Clark, In Res.; Dcn. Norman Alexander; Dcn. William (Bill) Davis; Dcn. Mick Hovanec; Dcn. Anthony (Tony) Rudolph; Betty Siano, DRE; CRP Stds.: 391

St. Francis of Assisi Catholic School - (Grades PreK-8) 2100 N. Germantown Pkwy., Cordova, TN 38016 t) 901-388-7321 alicia.brown@sfawolves.org www.sfawolves.org Alicia Brown, Prin.; Antonia Corzine, Asst. Prin.; Cynthia Lopez, Librn.; Stds.: 376; Lay Tchrs.: 34

COVINGTON

St. Alphonsus Church - 1225 Hwy. 51 S., Covington, TN 38019; Mailing: P.O. Box 430, Covington, TN 38019 t) 901-476-8140 www.stalphonsuscovington.org Very Rev. Robert Dale Ballman, Pst.; Elizabeth A. Teer, DRE; CRP Stds.: 23

Ave Maria - 664 S. Washington St., Ripley, TN 38063 t) (901) 476-8140

DYERSBURG

Holy Angels Catholic Church - 535 Tucker St., Dyersburg, TN 38024 t) (731) 287-8000; (731) 334-5181 c) (731) 589-8302 (Emergency Number) info.holyangels@holyangels.cdom.org; pastor.holyangels@holyangels.cdom.org www.holyangelscc.com Rev. Patrick Hirtz, Pst.; Jamie Patrick McGowan, DRE; Sarah Jean, Music Min.; CRP Stds.: 63

GERMANTOWN

Our Lady of Perpetual Help - 8151 Poplar Ave., Germantown, TN 38138 t) 901-754-1204 x325; 901-754-1204 x319 (CRP) kpesce@olphgermantown.org; lcotros@olphgermantown.org www.olphgermantown.org Rev. Jolly Sebastian, MCBS, Pst.; Rev. Peter Nguyen, Par. Vicar; Rev. Msgr. Victor P. Ciaramitaro, Senior Priest; Dcn. John Moskal; Dcn. Stephen Mangin; Laurie Cotros, DRE; Shane Cole, Music Min.; CRP Stds.: 196

Our Lady of Perpetual Help School - (Grades PreK-8) t) (901) 753-1181 www.olphowls.org Cristy Sneed, Prin.; Elise Rodriguez, Vice Prin.; Barbara Moranville, Librn.; Stds.: 248; Lay Tchrs.: 22

HUMBOLDT

Sacred Heart - 2887 E. Main St., Humboldt, TN 38343 t) 731-784-3904 sacredheart@aeneas.com www.sacredhearthumboldttn.org/ Rev. Mauricio Abeldaño, Pst.; Dcn. James Hobbs; Dcn. Ed Kutz; CRP Stds.: 50

St. Matthew Mission - 9060 Telecom Dr., Milan, TN 38358 t) (731) 784-3904

JACKSON

St. Mary's Church - 1665 Hwy. 45 Bypass, Jackson, TN 38305 t) 731-668-2596 kate.todd@stmarys.tn.org www.stmarys.tn.org Very Rev. David Graham, Pst.; Rev. Jonathan Perez, Par. Vicar; Dcn. Dale Brown; Dcn. Eddy Koonce; Dcn. Jim Moss; Dcn. Robert Russell; Dcn. William Winston; CRP Stds.: 169

St. Mary Church School - (Grades PreK-8) t) 731-668-2525 becky.dearmitt@stmarys.tn.org www.stmarysschool.tn.org Jo-Ann Wormer, Prin.; Stds.: 229; Sr. Tchrs.: 3; Lay Tchrs.: 14

Our Lady of Guadalupe Mission - Bells - 172 W. Main St., Bells, TN 38006; Mailing: 1665 Hwy. 45 Bypass, Jackson, TN 38305-4414 t) (731) 668-2596 fr.david@stmarys.tn.org

LEXINGTON

St. Andrew the Apostle - 895 N. Broad St., Lexington, TN 38351 t) 731-968-6393 finsecstandrew@outlook.com saintandrewcatholicchurch.org Rev. Anthony Onyekwe (Nigeria), Pst.; Lois Freeland, DRE; CRP Stds.: 33

St. Regina - 108 Skyline Ln., Parsons, TN 38363 t) 731-847-2054 saintregina@outlook.com streginacatholicchurch.org

MARTIN

St. Jude Catholic Church - 435 Moody Ave., Martin, TN 38237 t) 731-587-9777 office@stjudemartin.org www.stjudemartin.org Rev. David Michael Orsak, Pst.; Dcn. Rodney Freed; Stacy Freed, DRE; CRP Stds.: 85

MEMPHIS

Cathedral of the Immaculate Conception - 1695 Central Ave., Memphis, TN 38104; Mailing: 1669 Central Ave., Memhis, TN 38104 t) 901-725-2700 parish.office@ic.cdom.org www.iccathedral.org Very

Rev. Robert Szczechura, Pst.; Rev. Casey C. Weber, Par. Vicar; Dcn. Alan Crone; Dcn. Rick Martin; Dcn. William Pettit; Courtney Winter, DRE; CRP Stds.: 60

Cathedral of the Immaculate Conception School - (Grades PreK-8) 1669 Central Ave., Memphis, TN 38104 t) 901-725-2710 info.iccs@ic.cdom.org myiccs.org Kadesha Gordon, Prin.; Nancy Miller, Librn.; Stds.: 167; Lay Tchrs.: 22

St. Anne's - 706 S. Highland St., Memphis, TN 38111 t) 901-323-3817 evaloftin@hotmail.com; sandra.swain@stannechurch.cdom.org stannehighland.net Rev. R. Bruce Cinquegrani, Pst.; Dcn. David Woolley; Rev. Gary Lamb, In Res.; Rev. Thomas P. Thomas, In Res.; CRP Stds.: 59

St. Augustine - 1169 Kerr Ave., Memphis, TN 38106 t) 901-774-2298 (CRP); 901-774-2297 staug.info@staugustine.cdom.org; nixise@comcast.net www.staugustinememphis.net Rev. Francis Chiawa (Nigeria), Pst.; Dcn. Curtiss J. Talley; Dcn. Andrew Terry Jr.; Annye Hughes, DRE; CRP Stds.: 2

Blessed Sacrament - 2564 Hale Ave., Memphis, TN 38112; Mailing: 1644 Jackson Ave., c/o St. Therese Little Flower Church, Memphis, TN 38107-5053 t) 901-276-1412 x5 blessed.sacrament@stlfchurch.cdom.org memphismidtowncatholic.com Rev. Yoelvis Aloysius Gonzalez, Pst.;

St. Brigid - 7801 Lowrance Rd., Memphis, TN 38125-2825 t) 901-758-0128 frjoeykaump@gmail.com; frcain@stbrigidmemphis.org www.stbrigidmemphis.org Very Rev. Joey Kaump, Pst.; Rev. Cain Galicia-Ramirez, Par. Vicar; Galvez Cecilia, DRE; Tyler Griffis, Music Min.; CRP Stds.: 410

Church of the Ascension - 3680 Ramill Rd., Memphis, TN 38128-3245 t) 901-372-1364 dre@ascensionmemphis.org; office@ascensionmemphis.org ascensionmemphis.org Rev. Dennis L. Schenkel, Pst.; Rev. Rito De Santiago-Carreon, Par. Vicar; CRP Stds.: 60

Church of the Holy Spirit - 2300 Hickory Crest Dr., Memphis, TN 38119-6805 t) 901-754-7146 x30 (CRP); 901-754-7146 eleanor.vinson@hspirit.cdom.org; wendy.gabb@hspirit.cdom.org www.hspirit.com Rev. Mathew Panackachira, M.C.B.S., Pst.; Dcn. Werner Rose; Dcn. Richard Griffith; Wendy Gabb, DRE; CRP Stds.: 103

Church of the Resurrection - 5475 Newberry Ave., Memphis, TN 38115-3629 t) 901-794-8970 resurrectionmemphis@comcast.net; predirector@comcast.net resurrectionmemphis.org Rev. Robert D. Favazza, Pst.; Rev. Enrique Granados-Garcia, Par. Vicar; Dcn. Justin Mitchell; Leticia Gonzalez-Garcia, DRE; CRP Stds.: 182

Holy Rosary - 4851 Park Ave., Memphis, TN 38117 t) 901-767-6949; 901-685-1231 (School) stephanie.schadrack@holyrosarymemphis.org www.holyrosarychurchmphs.org Rev. Patrick M. Gallagher, Pst.; Rev. Jeo Poulose, M.C.B.S., Assoc. Pst.; Dcn. Jeffrey Drzycimski; Dcn. James McBride; Dcn. Greg Thomas; Dcn. G. Richmond Quinton; Landon Hayes Boone, DRE; CRP Stds.: 15

Holy Rosary School - (Grades PreK-8) 4841 Park Ave., Memphis, TN 38117 darren.mullis@holyrosarymemphis.org Darren Mullis, Prin.; Anne Gardino, Vice Prin.; Stds.: 409; Lay Tchrs.: 46

St. James - 4180 Leroy Ave., Memphis, TN 38108 t) 901-767-8672 stjamescatholic@bellsouth.net stjamesmemphis.org Rev. Gerald Azike, Pst.; CRP Stds.: 125

St. John's - 2742 Lamar Ave., Memphis, TN 38114 t) 901-480-7055 stjohnmemphis@gmail.com Rev. Fausta Odinwankpa, Pst.; Dcn. Walt Bolton, Pst. Assoc.; CRP Stds.: 52

St. Joseph Catholic Church - 3825 Neely Rd., Memphis, TN 38109 t) 901-396-9996 m_darrichon@yahoo.com.ar; stjoseph-secretary@hotmail.com www.stjosephccmemphis.org Rev. Juan Antonio Romo-Romo, S.V.D., Pst.; Dcn. James Calicott; CRP Stds.: 120

St. Louis - 203 S. White Station Rd., Memphis, TN 38117 t) 901-255-1950 jan.odonnell@stlouis.cdom.org stlouischurchmphs.org Very Rev. J. Keith Stewart, Pst.; Rev. Jins Mathew, MCBS, Assoc. Pst.; Rev. Michael Okata, Assoc. Pst.; Rev. Joseph Sax, Assoc. Pst.; Dcn. Michael d'Addabbo; Dcn. David Dierkes; Dcn. Bob Skinner; CRP Stds.: 122

St. Louis School - (Grades PreK-8) 5192 Shady Grove Rd., Memphis, TN 38117 t) 901-255-1900 www.stlouismemphis.org Teddi Niedzwiedz, Prin.; Stds.: 521; Lay Tchrs.: 44

St. Mary Church - 155 Market St., Memphis, TN 38105 t) 901-522-9420 nancythielemier@gmail.com www.stmarymemphistn.com Rev. Gary Lamb, Pst.; Dcn. Ernest Albonetti; Dcn. Jerry Horne; CRP Stds.: 7

St. Michael Church - 3863 Summer Ave., Memphis, TN 38122 t) 901-323-0896 stmichaelmemphis.org Rev. Benjamin Bradshaw, Pst.; Rev. Francisco Franquiz, Assoc. Pst.; CRP Stds.: 620

Our Lady of Sorrows - 3700 Thomas St., Memphis, TN 38127 t) 901-353-1530 carolyn.roberts@ols.cdom.org Rev. Ruben Villalon-Rivera, Pst.; Dcn. Henry P. Littleton; Daniel Sanchez, DRE; CRP Stds.: 75

St. Patrick's - 287 S 4th St., Memphis, TN 38126 t) 901-527-2542 julie.boland@stpat.cdom.org; shannon.curtis@stpat.cdom.org www.stpatsmemphis.org Rev. Msgr. Valentine Handwerker, Pst.; Dcn. Eugene Champion; Dcn. Frank Williams; Shannon Curtis, Pst. Assoc.; CRP Stds.: 68

St. Paul the Apostle - 1425 E. Shelby Dr., Memphis, TN 38116 t) 901-346-2380 jackie@stpaulmemphis.org; m.jimenez@stpaulmemphis.org www.stpaulmemphis.org Rev. Stephen K. Kenny, Pst.; Rev. William Gabriel Bouck, Par. Vicar; Dcn. Patrick Lyons; Maria Jimenez, DRE; CRP Stds.: 160

St. Paul the Apostle School - (Grades PreK-8) t) 901-346-0862 tondra.davis@stpaulsmemphis.com www.stpaulsmemphis.com Sr. Mary Lawrence Wright, O.P., Prin.; Stds.: 302; Sr. Tchrs.: 3; Lay Tchrs.: 18

St. Peter Church - 190 Adams Ave., Memphis, TN 38103 t) 901-527-8282 secretary@stpeterchurch.org www.stpeterchurch.org Rev. John Dominic Sims, O.P., Pst.; Very Rev. James Martin Nobles, O.P., Par. Vicar; Friar John Lydon, O.P., In Res.; Dcn. Eddie Ramsey; Christina Klyce, DRE; Jane Sharding Smedley, Music Min.; Peter Longoria, Youth Min.; CRP Stds.: 105

Sacred Heart Church - 1336 Jefferson Ave., Memphis, TN 38104; Mailing: 1324 Jefferson Ave., Memphis, TN 38104-2012 t) 901-726-1891 contactus@sacredheartmemphis.org sacredheartmemphis.org Rev. Brandon Nguyen, Pst.; CRP Stds.: 117

St. Therese the Little Flower - 1644 Jackson Ave., Memphis, TN 38107 t) 901-276-1412 sttherese@stlfchurch.cdom.org littleflowermemphis.org Rev. Yoelvis Aloysius Gonzalez, Pst.; Dcn. Bill Lifsey; CRP Stds.: 44

<u>MILAN</u>

St. Matthew Mission - 9060 Telecom Dr., Milan, TN 38358; Mailing: 2887 E. Main St., Humboldt, TN 38343 t) 731-784-3904 sacredheart@aeneas.com Rev. Mauricio Abeldaño, Pst.; Dcn. Ed Kutz; Dcn. James Hobbs;

<u>MILLINGTON</u>

St. William - 4932 Easley St., Millington, TN 38053 t) 901-872-4099 lisa.rhodes@stwilliam.cdom.org; debbiebreckenridge@earthlink.net stwilliamcc.org Rev. John J. Hourican, Pst.; Dcn. James Schmall; Debbie Breckenridge, DRE; CRP Stds.: 66

<u>PARIS</u>

Holy Cross - 1210 E. Wood St., Paris, TN 38242 t) 731-642-4681 dre@holycrossparis.org; officemanager@holycrossparis.org www.holycrossparis.org Rev. Martin M. Orjianioke (Nigeria), Pst.; Dcn. Rodney Seyller; CRP Stds.: 70

Holy Cross School - (Grades PreK-PreK) t) (731) 642-4681 Stds.: 24; Lay Tchrs.: 1

<u>SAVANNAH</u>

St. Mary Church - 2315 Pickwick St., Savannah, TN 38372 t) 731-925-4852 smccsavannah1@gmail.com www.saintmarysavannah.com Rev. Tojan Abraham, M.C.B.S., Pst.; CRP Stds.: 39

Our Lady of the Lake - 10645 Hwy. 57, Counce, TN 38326 t) (731) 925-4852 www.saintmarysavannah.com/

<u>SELMER</u>

St. Jude the Apostle Catholic Church - 1318 E. Poplar Ave., Selmer, TN 38375-1913 t) 731-645-4188 stjude9@bellsouth.net Rev. Wayne H. Arnold, Pst.;

<u>SOMERVILLE</u>

St. Philip the Apostle - 11710 Hwy. 64, Somerville, TN 38068 t) 901-465-8685 spacc@saintphilipcc.org; ycarroll@saintphilipcc.org www.saintphilipcc.org Dcn. Joseph (Joe) Kuzio; Dcn. David Rosenthal; Yissel Carroll, DRE; Rev. James J. Martell, Pst.; CRP Stds.: 56

<u>UNION CITY</u>

Immaculate Conception - 1303 E. Reelfoot Ave., Union City, TN 38261 t) 731-885-0963 icuctnmaster@gmail.com www.icuctn.org Rev. Carl Gregorich, Pst.; Teresa Vallee, DRE; CRP Stds.: 97

SCHOOLS: PRESCHOOL THRU HIGH SCHOOL

SCHOOLS

<u>STATE OF TENNESSEE</u>

<u>MEMPHIS</u>

St. Agnes Academy - St. Dominic School - (PRV) (Grades PreSchool-12) 4830 Walnut Grove Rd., Memphis, TN 38117 t) 901-767-1356 thood@saa-sds.org; communications@saa-sds.org www.saa-sds.org Tom Hood, Pres.; Beth Odom, DRE; Stds.: 778; Scholastics: 5; Lay Tchrs.: 140

HIGH SCHOOLS

<u>STATE OF TENNESSEE</u>

<u>CORDOVA</u>

St. Benedict at Auburndale High School - (DIO) (Grades 9-12) 8250 Varnavas Dr., Cordova, TN 38016 t) 901-260-2840 morriss@sbaeagles.org www.sbaeagles.org Special programs for gifted and learning disabled. Sondra Morris, Prin.; Rev. Dexter Noblefranca, Chap.; Stds.: 468; Pr. Tchrs.: 1; Sr. Tchrs.: 2; Lay Tchrs.: 46

<u>JACKSON</u>

Sacred Heart of Jesus High School - (PRV) (Grades 9-12) 146 McClellan Rd., Jackson, TN 38305 t) 731-660-4774 office@shjhs.org www.shjhs.org Adam M. Rust, Prin.; Nicole Livelli, Vice Prin.; Stds.: 106; Lay Tchrs.: 15

<u>MEMPHIS</u>

***Christian Brothers High School** - (PRV) (Grades 9-12) 5900 Walnut Grove Rd., Memphis, TN 38120-2174 t) 901-261-4900 info@cbhs.org www.cbhs.org Title of Incorporation: Christian Brothers (LaSalle) High School. Bro. David Poos, F.S.C., Pres.; Dr. Jamie Brummer, Prin.; Stds.: 719; Bro. Tchrs.: 1; Lay Tchrs.: 56

INSTITUTIONS LOCATED IN DIOCESE

CAMPUS MINISTRY / NEWMAN CENTERS [CAM]

MEMPHIS

Catholic Campus Ministry - 3625 Mynders Ave., Memphis, TN 38111 t) 901-323-3051 info@ccm.cdom.org memphisccm.org Sam Mauck, Dir.; Rebekah Zachary, Assoc. Dir.; Corey Kieffer, Assoc. Dir.;

CATHOLIC CHARITIES [CCH]

MEMPHIS

Catholic Charities of West Tennessee - 1325 Jefferson Ave., Memphis, TN 38104-2013 t) 901-722-4700 director@acc.cdom.org; development@acc.cdom.org www.ccwtn.org Emergency services, homeless services, community support services, and volunteerism. S. Kelley Henderson, Exec. Dir.; Asstd. Annu.: 49,000; Staff: 37

CEMETERIES [CEM]

MEMPHIS

All Saints - 1663 Elvis Presley Blvd., c/o Calvary Cemetery, Memphis, TN 38106 t) 901-948-1529 pat.posey@cemeteries.cdom.org cdom.org/catholic-cemeteries-office Patrick Posey Sr., Dir.;

Calvary - 1663 Elvis Presley Blvd., Memphis, TN 38106 t) 901-948-1529 pat.posey@cemeteries.cdom.org cdom.org Patrick Posey Sr., Dir.;

Mount Calvary - 1663 Elvis Presley Blvd., c/o Calvary Cemetery, Memphis, TN 38106; Mailing: 1665 Hwy. 45 Bypass, Jackson, TN 38305-4414 t) 731-668-2596 pat.posey@cemeteries.cdom.org cdom.org Patrick Posey Sr., Dir.; Callie Carpenter, Contact;

COLLEGES & UNIVERSITIES [COL]

MEMPHIS

***Christian Brothers University** - 650 E. Pkwy. S., Memphis, TN 38104 t) 901-321-3000 admissions@cbu.edu www.cbu.edu David Archer, Pres.; Ron Brandon, CFO & Vice Pres., Admin. & Fin.; Paul Haught, Vice Pres., Academics; Mark Billingsley, Vice Pres., Advancement; Bro. Dominic Ehrmantraut, F.S.C., Special Asst. to Pres., Mission & Identity; Stds.: 1,730; Lay Tchrs.: 107; Pr. Tchrs.: 1

CONVENTS, MONASTERIES, AND RESIDENCES FOR WOMEN [CON]

MEMPHIS

Missionaries of Charity - 700 N. 7th St., Memphis, TN 38107 t) 901-527-4947 Convent with emergency shelter for women and children Sr. Alphina Maria, MC, Supr.; Sr. M. Jonathan, MC, Regl. Supr.; Srs.: 4

Missionary Sisters Servants of the Holy Spirit, S.Sp.S. - 5280 Brenton Ave., Memphis, TN 38120 c) 901-230-3279; 847-800-8174 monicad@ssps-usa.org Sr. Monica P. Darrichon, S.Sp.S., Supr.; Srs.: 1

ENDOWMENTS / FOUNDATIONS / TRUSTS [EFT]

MEMPHIS

The Catholic Foundation of West Tennessee, Inc. - 5825 Shelby Oaks Dr., Memphis, TN 38134 t) (901) 373-1200 Jim Marconi, Contact; David Zaleski, CFO;

MISCELLANEOUS [MIS]

ARLINGTON

The Catholic Cafe, Inc. - 30 Clover Leaf Dr., Arlington, TN 38002 t) (901) 240-7649 www.thecatholiccafe.com Dcn. Jeffrey Drzycimski, Exec. Dir.;

MEMPHIS

St. Anne Lay Carmelite Community - 2929 Baskin St., Memphis, TN 38127 t) 901-830-7824 carmemphis@gmail.com Deanna Caswell, Admin.;

The Dominican Friars of Memphis, Inc. (St. Peter Dominican Community) - 190 Adams Ave., Memphis, TN 38103 t) 901-527-8282 dominicanmemphis@gmail.com Friar John Dominic Sims, O.P., Supr.; Friar John Lydon, O.P., Mem.; Very Rev. James Martin Nobles, O.P., Mem.; Priests: 3

Knights of St. Peter Claver (3rd Degree St. Benedict the Black Council No. 188 & Assembly 26 Bishop James P. Lyke 4th Degree) - 1169 Kerr Ave., Memphis, TN 38106 c) 901-270-8164 geowens1@comcast.net George Owens, Exec.;

Ladies of Charity of Memphis - 2300 Hickory Crest Dr., Memphis, TN 38119; Mailing: P.O. Box 17699, Memphis, TN 38187-0699 t) 901-767-0207 rosemariep@comcast.net Patti Ricossa, Pres.;

***Lumen Civitatis Inc.** - 2542 Ridgeway Rd., Ste. 7, Memphis, TN 38119; Mailing: PO Box 771692, Memphis, TN 38177-1692 t) 901-219-4591 andrew@lumencivitatis.org www.lumencivitatis.com Andrew Bowie, Contact;

***Madonna Circle, Inc.** - 2300 Hickory Crest Dr., Memphis, TN 38119 t) 901-479-7870 madonnacirclememphis@gmail.com www.madonnacircle.org (Catholic Women's Service Organization) Amy Ryan, Pres.;

St. Patrick's Center - 297 S. Fourth St., Memphis, TN 38126 t) (901) 527-2542 julie.boland@stpat.cdom.org www.stpatsmemphis.org Dcn. Eugene Champion, Exec.;

Serra Club of Memphis - 5825 Shelby Oaks Dr., Memphis, TN 38134; Mailing: 186 E. Pecan Valley, Collierville, TN 38117 c) 901-336-7475 Barbara Meehan, Pres.; Rev. Yoelvis Aloysius Gonzalez, Chap.;

***Society of St. Vincent DePaul** - 1306 Monroe Ave., Memphis, TN 38104 t) 901-722-4703; 901-274-2137 ozanamcentercoord@gmail.com www.svdpmemphis.org Rev. Richard D. Coy; Richard Peyton, Pres.;

MONASTERIES AND RESIDENCES FOR PRIESTS AND BROTHERS [MON]

CORDOVA

Villa Vianney Senior Priests Residence - 10605 Bishop Dozier Dr., Cordova, TN 38016-5559 t) 901-752-0766 rick.mickey@cc.cdom.org Rev. Richard L. Mickey, Dir.; Priests: 7

MEMPHIS

Brothers of the Christian Schools (Mid-West Prov.), F.S.C., #343 - Christian Brothers Univ., 650 E. Pkwy. S., Memphis, TN 38104 t) 901-321-3520 Bro. Alan Parham, F.S.C., Dir.; Brs.: 16

Society of the Divine Word (Chicago Province) - 1324 Jefferson Ave., Memphis, TN 38104 t) 901-726-1891 Rev. Antonio Romo-Romo, S.V.D.; Priests: 2

RETREAT HOUSES / RENEWAL CENTERS [RTR]

STANTON

Our Lady Queen of Peace Retreat Center - 3630 Dancyville Rd., Stanton, TN 38069-4711 t) 731-548-2500 deacon.ernie@olqp.cdom.org; deacon.ernie@olqp.cdom.org www.olqpretreats.com Dcn. Ernest Albonetti, Dir.;

SHRINES [SHR]

MEMPHIS

St. Martin de Porres National Shrine & Institute - 190 Adams Ave., Memphis, TN 38103 t) 901-578-2643 rector@stmartinshrine.org www.stmartinshrine.org A Ministry of the Dominican Province of St. Martin de Porres Very Rev. James Martin Nobles, O.P., Rector;

An asterisk (*) denotes an organization that has established tax-exempt status directly with the IRS and is not covered by the USCCB Group Ruling.

Diocese of Metuchen

MOST REVEREND JAMES F. CHECCHIO, J.C.D., M.B.A.

Bishop of Metuchen; ordained June 20, 1992; appointed Rector of the Pontifical North American College 2006-2016; appointed Bishop of Metuchen March 8, 2016; installed May 3, 2016. 146 Metlars Lane, Piscataway, NJ 08854. Res.: 10 Library Pl., Metuchen, NJ 08840.

146 Metlars Lane, Piscataway, NJ 08854. T: 732-562-1990; F: 732-562-1399.
Mailing Address: St. John Neumann Pastoral Center, P.O. Box 191, Metuchen, NJ 08840.
www.diometuchen.org

ESTABLISHED NOVEMBER 19, 1981.

Square Miles 1,425.

Legal Corporate Title: The Diocese of Metuchen.

Comprises the Counties of Warren, Hunterdon, Somerset and Middlesex in the State of New Jersey.

STATISTICAL OVERVIEW

Personnel

Bishop	1
Retired Bishops	1
Priests: Diocesan Active in Diocese	119
Priests: Diocesan Active Outside Diocese	6
Priests: Retired, Sick or Absent	31
Number of Diocesan Priests	156
Religious Priests in Diocese	34
Total Priests in your Diocese	190
Extern Priests in Diocese	13
Ordinations:	
Diocesan Priests	1
Transitional Deacons	1
Permanent Deacons	15
Permanent Deacons in Diocese	176
Total Brothers	7
Total Sisters	202

Parishes

Parishes	90
With Resident Pastor:	
Resident Diocesan Priests	77
Resident Religious Priests	11
Without Resident Pastor:	
Administered by Priests	2
Pastoral Centers	4
Professional Ministry Personnel:	
Brothers	6
Sisters	87
Lay Ministers	341

Welfare

Catholic Hospitals	1
Total Assisted	242,528
Health Care Centers	4
Total Assisted	23,107
Homes for the Aged	4
Total Assisted	107
Day Care Centers	2
Total Assisted	279
Specialized Homes	1
Total Assisted	12
Special Centers for Social Services	8
Total Assisted	35,145
Residential Care of Disabled	1
Total Assisted	5

Educational

Diocesan Students in Other Seminaries	24
Total Seminarians	24
High Schools, Diocesan and Parish	2
Total Students	1,058
High Schools, Private	2
Total Students	804
Elementary Schools, Diocesan and Parish	22
Total Students	5,246
Catechesis/Religious Education:	
High School Students	956
Elementary Students	16,575
Total Students under Catholic Instruction	24,663
Teachers in Diocese:	
Priests	2
Brothers	1
Sisters	5
Lay Teachers	548

Vital Statistics

Receptions into the Church:	
Infant Baptism Totals	2,970
Minor Baptism Totals	229
Adult Baptism Totals	88
Received into Full Communion	174
First Communions	2,880
Confirmations	3,084
Marriages:	
Catholic	537
Interfaith	103
Total Marriages	640
Deaths	3,310
Total Catholic Population	662,256
Total Population	1,447,109

LEADERSHIP

Office of the Bishop - Most Rev. James F. Checchio; Rev. Roy Quesea, Sec. to Bishop & Vice Chancellor;
St. John Neumann Pastoral Center - t) 732-562-1990
Vicar General - Very Rev. Jonathan S. Toborowsky;
Episcopal Vicars - Rev. Msgr. William Benwell, Episcopal Vicar for Canonical Svcs.; Rev. Msgr. John N. Fell, Health Care Apostolate; Rev. Antony Arockiadoss, Hunterdon & Warren Counties;

ADMINISTRATION

Episcopal Vicar - Rev. Msgr. Joseph G. Celano, Vicar;
Executive Director - Carol Purcell;
Office of Cemeteries - Jeffrey Mager, Dir.;
Office of Finance - Patricia Murtha, Controller;
Office of Human Resources - Melissa Pujols, Dir.;
Office of Information Systems - Leonardo G. Cortelezzi, Dir.;
Office of Insurance - Jacqueline Glackin, Dir.;
Office of Parish Financial Services - Oscar Montalvo, Internal Auditor;
Office of Property & Facility Ownership & Management - Steve Michalek Jr., Dir.;

OFFICES AND DIRECTORS

Office of Bishop Emeritus - Most Rev. Paul G. Bootkoski;
Office of the Vicar General - Very Rev. Jonathan S. Toborowsky;
Office of Child and Youth Protection - Doranne Rossiter, Dir.;
Victim Assistance Coordinator - t) 732-439-4730 Paule Galette;
Moderator of the Curia - t) 732-562-2439 Very Rev. Jonathan S. Toborowsky;
Office of the Chancellor - t) 732-562-2439 chancellor@diometuchen.org Anthony P. Kearns III, Chancellor; Rev. Roy Quesea, Vice Chancellor;
Office of the Diocesan General Counsel - Anthony P. Kearns III; Christopher J. Fusco, Assoc. Gen. Counsel, St. Thomas More Society;
Office of Development - Richard Lanahan, Dir.;
Office of Stewardship - Sue Mantarro, Dir.;

CLERGY AND RELIGIOUS SERVICES

Board for Seminary Education - Rev. Mauricio Tabera-Vasquez, Chair;
Office for Priest Personnel - Rev. Msgr. John N. Fell, Dir.;
Office for Religious - Sr. Anna Nguyen, S.S.C., Delegate for Rel.;
Office of Hospital Chaplaincy - Rev. Sean G. Winters, Coord.;
Office of Ministry to Priests - Rev. Msgr. Joseph M. Curry, Dir.;
Office of Prison Ministry - Rev. Sean G. Winters, Dir.;
Office of the Diaconate - Dcn. Stephen F. Kern, Dir.;
Office of Vocations - Rev. Msgr. John N. Fell, Dir. Seminarians; Rev. Mauricio Tabera-Vasquez, Vocations Recruiter;
Vicariate for Clergy and Consecrated Life - Rev. Msgr. Edward C. Puleo, Episcopal Vicar;

CONSULTATIVE BODIES

College of Consultors - Most Rev. James F. Checchio; Rev. Msgr. Joseph G. Celano, Secy.; Very Rev. Timothy A. Christy;
Council for Financial Affairs - Most Rev. James F. Checchio; John Papa, Chair; Very Rev. Timothy A. Christy, Ex Officio;
Deans - Rev. Anthony Siranni, Cathedral Deanery; Rev. Charles T. O'Connor, Forsgate Deanery; Rev. John J. Barbella, Morris Canal Deanery;
Diocesan Pastoral Council - Most Rev. James F. Checchio; Maria Hunter, Chair; Rev. Msgr. John N. Fell;
Diocesan Review Board - Anthony P. Kearns III, Chancellor; Hon. Richard S. Rebeck, Chair; Rev. Msgr. William Benwell, Promoter of Justice;
Presbyteral Council - Most Rev. James F. Checchio, Pres.;

EDUCATION

Catholic Scouting Apostolate - Rev. John J. Barbella, Moderator; Doreen Sekora, Girl Scout Committee; Nora Burke Klippstein, Coord. Boy Scout Min.;
Office of the Schools - Barbara Stevens, Supt.;
Secretary for Education -

EVANGELIZATION

Catholic Charismatic Renewal - Robert Walker, Moderator; Bro. Jude Lasota, B.H., Spiritual Adv./Care Srvcs.;
The Catholic Spirit - Very Rev. Jonathan S. Toborowsky, Editor; Rev. Glenn J. Comandini, Mng. Editor;
Diocesan Holy Name Societies - metuchenhns@gmail.com Michael W. Corbin, Pres.; Rev. Chester H. Carina, Moderator;
Diocesan Liturgical Commission - Very Rev. Robert B. Kolakowski, Chair; Tony Varas, Ex Officio;
Divine Mercy Apostolate - Rev. John C. Grimes, Moderator; James Dimino, Coord.;
Episcopal Vicar - Very Rev. Timothy A. Christy, Vicar;
Legion of Mary, Metuchen Comitium - Rev. John J. Barbella, Dir.;
Office of Evangelization & Communication - Adam Carlisle, Secy.; Gerald Wutkowski, Asst. Dir.;
Office of Pontifical Mission Societies - Rev. John G. Hillier, Dir.;
Office of RCIA -
Office of Worship - Rev. Timothy Mark Eck II, Dir.;
Diocesan Eucharistic League - Rev. Robert G. Gorman, Dir.;

FAMILY LIFE

Campus Ministry Apostolate - Rev. Jason Pavich, Admin.; Bro. Patrick Reilly, B.H., Dir.; Colleen Donahue, Office Mgr.;
The Catholic Center at Rutgers University - t) 732-545-6663 www.rutgerscatholic.org Rev. Jason Pavich, Admin.; Bro. Patrick Reilly, B.H., Dir.;
Catholic Rural Ministry - Rev. Michael C. Saharic, Coord.;
Courage - Rev. Thomas A. Odorizzi, C.O., Chap.;
Ecumenical & Interfaith Affairs - Rev. Guy W. Selvester, Diocesan Ecumenical Officer;
EnCourage - Rev. David V. Skoblow, Chap.;
Family and Pastoral Life - Jennifer A. Ruggiero, Secy.;
Office for Cultural Diversity Ministries -
African-American, African & Caribbean Apostolate - Rev. Alphonsus Kariuki, Coord.; Dcn. Enock Berluche Sr., Coord.;
Chinese Apostolate - Eugene Ho, Coord.;
Filipino Apostolate - Rev. Gerardo B. Paderon, Coord.;
Hispanic Evangelization & Ministry - Dcn. Edgar R. Chaves, Director, Office of Hispanic Ministry; Rev. Gustavo Rodriguez-Perez, Coordinator of Hispanic Lay Ministry; Rev. Juan Carlos Gaviria, Coord., Hispanic Lay Formation;
Hungarian Apostolate - Rev. Imre Juhasz, Coord.;
Indian and Sri-Lankan Apostolate -
Indonesian Apostolate - Triana Prijadi, Co-Coord.; Deivy Worotitjan, Co-Coord.;
Korean Apostolate - Rev. Namwoong Lee, Coord.;
Polish Apostolate -
Portuguese & Brazilian Apostolate -
Vietnamese Apostolate - Rev. Peter Tran, Coord.;
Office for Persons with Disabilities - Rev. John G. Hillier, Dir.;
Office of Discipleship Formation for Children - Carol Mascola, Dir.;
Office of Family Life Ministry - Cristina D'Averso-Collins, Dir.;
Office of Human Life & Dignity - Jennifer A. Ruggiero, Dir.;
Office of Ongoing Faith Formation -
Office of Youth & Young Adult Ministry - Megan Callahan, Dir.;

SOCIAL SERVICES

Secretariat of Charity - Anthony P. Kearns III, Secy.;
Catholic Charities Solidarity Team - www.ccsolidarity.org Dcn. Peter Barcellona, Dir.;
Catholic Charities, Diocese of Metuchen - Julio Coto, Exec. Dir.;

TRIBUNAL

The Diocesan Center - t) 732-562-1990 Very Rev. Robert B. Kolakowski, Judicial Vicar; Rev. Msgr. Richard J. Lyons, Judicial Vicar Emeritus; Christopher J. Fusco, Moderator of the Tribunal;
Canonical Staff - Rev. Msgr. William Benwell, Promoter of Justice; Very Rev. Robert B. Kolakowski; Christopher J. Fusco;
Auditor - Sara T. Acevedo;
Psychological Consultants - Sr. Elizabeth Monica Acri, I.H.M.; Sr. Mary Aquinas Szott, C.S.S.F.; Dr. John Halloran;
Notary - Margaret Manza;

PARISHES, MISSIONS, AND CLERGY

STATE OF NEW JERSEY

ALPHA

St. Mary - 830 Fifth Ave., Alpha, NJ 08865 t) 908-454-0444; 908-454-5264 office@stmaryrc.org; alphareled@verizon.net www.stmaryrc.org Rev. Dawid Wejnerowski, Admin.; Gina Talijan, DRE; Dcn. John B. Van Haute; CRP Stds.: 207

ANNANDALE

Immaculate Conception - 316 Old Allerton Rd., Annandale, NJ 08801 t) 908-735-7319; 908-735-0478 (CRP) parishoffice@iccannadale.org; prep@iccannandale.org www.iccannandale.org Rev. Keith Cervine, Admin.; Rev. Ariel Bautista Jr., Par. Vicar; Dcn. Joseph P. Campbell; Dcn. Michael R. Martini; Dcn. Mark van Duynhoven; Dcn. Bill Bauer; Coleen D'Amato, DRE; CRP Stds.: 432
Immaculate Conception School - (Grades PreK-8) 314 Old Allerton Rd., Annandale, NJ 08801 t) 908-735-6334 info@icsclinton.org www.icsannandale.org Connie Fortunato, Prin.; Stds.: 404; Lay Tchrs.: 28

AVENEL

St. Andrew - 244 Avenel St., Avenel, NJ 07001 t) 732-634-4355; 732-636-4261 (CRP) our.church@standrewparish.com www.standrewparish.com Rev. David B. Kosmoski, Pst.; Elizabeth Vitale, DRE; CRP Stds.: 85

BAPTISTOWN

Our Lady of Victories - 1005 Rte. 519, Baptistown, NJ 08803; Mailing: P.O. Box 127, Baptistown, NJ 08803 t) 908-996-2068 olvkris@yahoo.com www.olvbaptistown.com Rev. Krzysztof Kaczynski, Pst.; Dcn. John T. Monahan; Dcn. Michael Semko; Gloria Nardone, DRE; CRP Stds.: 117

BASKING RIDGE

St. James - 184 S. Finley Ave., Basking Ridge, NJ 07920; Mailing: P.O. Box 310, Basking Ridge, NJ 07920 t) 908-766-0888; 908-766-4774 x230 (CRP) administration@saintjamesbr.org; parishmanager@saintjamesbr.org www.saintjamesbr.org Rev. Msgr. Sylvester J. Cronin III, Pst.; Rev. Gregory Zannetti, Par. Vicar; Dcn. Frank Sinatra; Dcn. Peter J. DePrima Jr.; Sr. Faustina Nguyen, SCC, Pst. Assoc.; Sr. Marie Luu, SCC, DRE; Sr. Annelyth Pandi, SCC, DRE; CRP Stds.: 616
St. James School - (Grades PreK-8) 200 S. Finley Ave., Basking Ridge, NJ 07920 soffice@sjsbr.org

www.sjsbr.org Suzanne Florendo, Prin.; Stds.: 319; Sr. Tchrs.: 1; Lay Tchrs.: 21

BELVIDERE

St. Patrick - 327 Greenwich St., Belvidere, NJ 07823 t) 908-475-2559; 908-475-2559 (CRP) kkelly1@comcast.net www.stpatrickrose.org Rev. Charles A. Sabella, Pst.; Michele Beha, DRE; CRP Stds.: 80

BERNARDSVILLE

Our Lady of Perpetual Help - 111 Claremont Rd., Bernardsville, NJ 07924 t) 908-766-0079; 908-766-5638 (CRP) olphreligiousedf@aol.com www.olphbernardsville.org Rev. John C. Siceloff, Pst.; Rev. Ronal Vega Pastrana, Par. Vicar; Dcn. Lawrence J. Duffy; Dcn. Benigno Ruiz-Diaz; Michele Lobo, DRE; CRP Stds.: 292

School of St. Elizabeth - (Grades PreK-8) 30 Seney Dr., Bernardsville, NJ 07924 t) 908-766-0244 principal.stelizabeth@diometuchen.org www.steschool.org Debra Ostrowski, Prin.; Stds.: 181; Sr. Tchrs.: 1; Lay Tchrs.: 11

Bernardsville, Sacred Heart (Chapel of Convenience) - Bernards Ave., Bernardsville, NJ 07924 t) (908) 766-0079

St. Elizabeth Convent - 30 Seney Dr., Bernardsville, NJ 07924 t) 908-766-0266 Sr. Martha Kavanagh, Pst. Assoc.;

BLOOMSBURY

Church of the Annunciation - 80 Main St., Bloomsbury, NJ 08804-0136; Mailing: P O Box 136, Bloomsbury, NJ 08804-0136 t) 908-479-4905; 908-479-6708 (CRP) annunication80@gmail.com; annunciationccd64@gmail.com www.annunciationrcc.org Rev. Roberto Coruna, Pst.; Donna Perrone, DRE; CRP Stds.: 36

BOUND BROOK

St. Joseph - 111 E. High St., Bound Brook, NJ 08805; Mailing: P.O. Box 72, Bound Brook, NJ 08805 t) 732-356-0027 ana.valencia@sjcbb.net; reled@sjcbb.net www.dreamsofstjoseph.org Rev. Msgr. Joseph J. Kerrigan, Pst.; Ana Valencia, Contact; Dcn. Gustavo Sandoval; Dcn. Gary Newton; CRP Stds.: 198

St. Mary of Czestochowa - 201 Vosseller Ave., Bound Brook, NJ 08805 t) 732-356-0358 stmarybb1@verizon.net Rev. John Stec, Admin.;

BRIDGEWATER

St. Bernard of Clairvaux - 500 Rte. 22, Bridgewater, NJ 08807 t) 908-725-0552 office@stbernardbridgewater.org www.stbernardbridgewater.org Rev. Msgr. Randall J. Vashon, Pst.; Rev. Tholitho Tholitho, Par. Vicar; Dcn. Patrick J. Cline; Dcn. Gerard C. Sims; Denise Metzgar, DRE; CRP Stds.: 436

Holy Trinity - 60 Maple St., Bridgewater, NJ 08807 t) 908-526-2394 office@holytrinitynj.org; reoffice@holytrinitynj.org www.holytrinitynj.org Rev. Jeffrey Calia, C.O., Pst.; Dcn. Michael A. Forrestall; Dcn. John Phalen; Briana George, DRE; CRP Stds.: 69

CALIFON

St. John Neumann - 398 Country Rd. 513, Califon, NJ 07830; Mailing: P.O. Box 455, Califon, NJ 07830 t) 908-832-2513; 908-832-2162 (CRP) ccsjn.org Rev. Richard M. Rusk, Pst.; Dcn. Michael Wojcik; Karen Verso, DRE; CRP Stds.: 95

CARTERET

Divine Mercy Parish - 213 Pershing Ave., Carteret, NJ 07008 t) 732-541-5768 dmpcarteret@aol.com divinemercycarteret.org Rev. Edmund J. Shallow, Pst.;

St. Joseph - 7 Locust St., Carteret, NJ 07008 t) 732-541-8946; 732-969-8767 (CRP) stjosephparishcarteret@sjps.net www.sjps.net Rev. Msgr. John B. Gordon, Pst.; Rev. Msgr. Pafnouti Wassef, Par. Vicar; Rev. Sean G. Winters, In Res.; Dcn. George F. Kimball; Dcn. Ramon L. Torres; Marcelle Doherty, DRE; CRP Stds.: 103

St. Joseph School - (Grades PreK-8) 865 Roosevelt Ave., Carteret, NJ 07008 t) 732-541-7111 jmcknight@sjps.net Joanne McKnight, Prin.; Lonie Yuschik, Librn.;

COLONIA

St. John Vianney - 420 Inman Ave., Colonia, NJ 07067 t) 732-574-0150; 732-388-1424 (CRP) jdrevelus@sjvs.net; snoto@sjvs.net parish.sjvianney.com Rev. John C. Gloss, Pst.; Rev. Robert G. Gorman, Par. Vicar; Rev. Bede Kim, Par. Vicar; Dcn. Vincent C. Brigande; Jordan Drevelus, DRE; Dcn. Thomas S. Michnewicz; Dcn. Joseph D. Ragucci; CRP Stds.: 209

St. John Vianney School - (Grades PreK-8) t) 732-388-1662 ntannucilli@sjvs.net www.sjvs.net Nancy Tannucilli, Prin.; Stds.: 306; Lay Tchrs.: 21

COLUMBIA

St. Jude - St. Jude Church, 7 Eisenhower Rd, Columbia, NJ 07832-2716; Mailing: PO Box N, Blairstown, NJ 07825-0973 t) 908-362-6444; 908-362-1431 (CRP) stjudech@ptd.net; stjudecrosstrainingyouth@gmail.com stjudech.org Rev. Ronald L. Jandernoa, Pst.; Elizabeth Thornton, DRE; CRP Stds.: 134

DUNELLEN

St. John the Evangelist - 317 First St., Dunellen, NJ 08812 t) 732-968-2621 stjohnpcl@gmail.com; stjev@verizon.net www.stjohnsdunellen.org Rev. Alphonsus Kariuki, Pst.; Dcn. Glenn Robitaille; Patricia Hummel, DRE; CRP Stds.: 123

EAST BRUNSWICK

St. Bartholomew - 470 Ryders Ln., East Brunswick, NJ 08816 t) 732-257-7722 www.stbartseb.org Rev. Thomas J. Walsh, Pst.; Rev. Timothy Mark Eck II, Par. Vicar; Dcn. Anthony J. Gostkowski; Dcn. John F. Kenny; Dcn. Filippo Tartara; Barbara Fitzgerald, DRE; CRP Stds.: 581

St. Bartholomew School - (Grades PreK-8) t) 732-254-7105 Theresa Craig, Prin.; Stds.: 425; Lay Tchrs.: 26

EDISON

St. Helena - 950 Grove Ave., Edison, NJ 08820 t) 732-494-3399; 732-549-4660 (CRP) parishoffice@sthelenaedison.org; cff@sthelenaedison.org www.sthelenaedison.org Rev. Anthony M. Sirianni, Pst.; Rev. Joseph Kubiak, O.F.M.Cap., Par. Vicar; Dcn. Robert G. Yunker; Dr. Mary Kay Cullinan, DRE; CRP Stds.: 103

St. Helena School - (Grades PreK-8) 930 Grove Ave., Edison, NJ 08820 t) 732-549-6234 school@sthelenaedison.org Sr. Mary Charles Wienckoski, C.S.S.F., Prin.; Stds.: 190; Lay Tchrs.: 14

St. Matthew the Apostle - 81 Seymour Ave., Edison, NJ 08817 t) 732-985-5063 frgeorge@stmatthewtheapostle.com; pcl@stmatthewtheapostle.com stmatthewtheapostle.com Rev. George Targonski, Pst.; Rev. Joseph Kabali, Par. Vicar; Dcn. Edward F. Ciszewski; Dcn. Richard Ferreira; David Jules, DRE; CRP Stds.: 173

St. Matthew School - (Grades PreK-8) 100 Seymour Ave., Edison, NJ 08817 t) 732-985-6633 stmatthewtheapostle.com/school Joyce Schaefer, Prin.; Stds.: 115; Lay Tchrs.: 10

Our Lady of Peace - 26 Maple Ave., Edison, NJ 08837; Mailing: P.O. Box 69, Fords, NJ 08863 t) 732-738-7940; 732-738-7940 x27 (CRP) mail@olpfords.org; prep@olpfords.org www.olpfords.org Rev. Matthew R. Paratore, Pst.; Rev. James Gregory Tucker, Par. Vicar; Rev. Sebastian D. Kaithackal, C.M.I., In Res.; Candida Gonzalez, DRE; Dcn. John A. Raychel; CRP Stds.: 116

FLEMINGTON

St. Magdalen de Pazzi - 105 Mine St., Flemington, NJ 08822 t) 908-782-2922 ckinney@stmagdalen.org www.stmagdalen.org Rev. James De Fillipps, Admin.; Rev. Matthew Marinelli, Par. Vicar; Dcn. Michael J. Bachynsky; Dcn. Anthony Cozzi; Dcn. Stephen F. Kern; Dcn. Hernando Patino; Dcn. David L. Urcinas; Dcn. Thaddeus Wislinski; Rod deVillers, DRE; Bill Tackett, DRE; CRP Stds.: 369

St. Magdalen Convent - 83 Bonnell St., Flemington, NJ 08822 t) (907) 822-9220

GREAT MEADOWS

Ss. Peter and Paul - 360 U.S. Hwy. 46, Great Meadows, NJ 07838 t) 908-637-4269 stpeterandpaul@comcast.net peterpaulgm.com Rev. Grzegorz Podsiadlo, S.D.S., Admin.; Diane Francis, DRE; CRP Stds.: 93

HACKETTSTOWN

Assumption of the Blessed Virgin Mary - 302 High St., Hackettstown, NJ 07840-0547 t) 908-852-3320; 908-852-3220 (CRP) faithformation@assumptionbvmnj.org; secretary@assumptionbvmnj.org olofa.org/ Rev. Leopoldo S. Salvania, Admin.; Dcn. Daniel Gallagher; Dcn. Walter H. Pidgeon; Rose Strohmaier, DRE; CRP Stds.: 159

HAMPTON

St. Ann - 6 Church St., Hampton, NJ 08827; Mailing: P.O. Box 405, Hampton, NJ 08827 t) 908-537-2221; 908-537-1070 (CRP) Rev. Michael C. Saharic, Pst.; Kelly Vacca, DRE; CRP Stds.: 115

HELMETTA

Holy Trinity - 100 Main St., Helmetta, NJ 08828 t) 732-521-0172 htc100jmj@gmail.com Rev. Andrzej Wieliczko, Pst.; Kathy Mangano, DRE; CRP Stds.: 39

HIGH BRIDGE

St. Joseph - 59 Main St., High Bridge, NJ 08829 t) 908-638-6211 parishoffice@sjchb.org www.sjchb.org Rev. James A. Kyrpczak, Pst.; Dcn. Steven Fortier; Dcn. Thomas McGovern; Shari Shultz, DRE; CRP Stds.: 90

HIGHLAND PARK

Transfiguration of the Lord Parish - 23 S. Fifth Ave., Highland Park, NJ 08904-2604 t) 732-572-0977; 732-985-5804 transfiguration.parish@verizon.net; transfigurationofthelordhp@gmail.com transfiguration-parish.com Rev. Abraham Lotha, Pst.; Dcn. Edward Krupa; Bridget O'Connor, DRE; CRP Stds.: 78

St. Paul the Apostle - 502 Raritan Ave., Highland Park, NJ 08904 (Worship Site)

Guardian Angels - 37 Plainfield Ave., Edison, NJ 08818 (Worship Site)

HILLSBOROUGH

St. Joseph - 34 Yorktown Rd., Hillsborough, NJ 08844 t) 908-874-3141; 908-874-3141 x40383 (CRP) sjmillstone.com/ Rev. Francis G. Hilton, S.J., Pst.; James Jungels, DRE; CRP Stds.: 305

Mary, Mother of God - 157 S. Triangle Rd., Hillsborough, NJ 08844 t) 908-874-8220; 908-874-8604 (CRP) office@marymotherofgod.org; dre@marymotherofgod.org marymotherofgod.org Rev. Msgr. Joseph M. Curry, Pst.; Rev. Alexander J. Carles, Par. Vicar; Dcn. William Chirinos; Dcn. Salvatore J. Bonfiglio; Rev. Sean A. Broderick, C.S.Sp., In Res.; CRP Stds.: 510

Mary, Mother of God School - (Grades PreSchool-) t) 908-874-8489 preschool@marymotherofgod.org Kelly Longobardi, Dir.; Stds.: 52; Scholastics: 2; Lay Tchrs.: 5

HOPELAWN

Good Shepherd Parish - 625 Florida Grove Rd., Hopelawn, NJ 08861 t) 732-826-4859 goodshepherd20@verizon.net goodshepherdpanj.org Rev. Krystian S. Burdzy, Admin.; Dcn. Samuel J. Costantino; Dcn. Albert Coppola; CRP Stds.: 68

ISELIN

St. Cecelia - 45 Wilus Way, Iselin, NJ 08830 t) 732-283-2300; 732-283-2816 (CRP) stcre@yahoo.com; ceceliaparish@gmail.com www.stcecelia.com Rev. Deniskingsley Nwagwu, SDV, Admin.; Rev. Cyril Offiong, SDV, Par. Vicar; Dcn. Anthony J. Pepe; Sr. Anna Tran, DRE; CRP Stds.: 157

JAMESBURG

St. James the Less - 36 Lincoln Ave., Jamesburg, NJ 08831 t) 732-521-0100; 732-521-1188 (CRP) sjtlccd@gmail.com; jamestheless1880@gmail.com stjamesthelesschurch.org Rev. Juan Carlos Gaviria, Admin.; Dcn. Patrick J. Smith; Rev. Peter Akkanath, CMI, In Res.; Linda Rondinelli, DRE; CRP Stds.: 229

KENDALL PARK

St. Augustine of Canterbury - 45 Henderson Rd.,

Kendall Park, NJ 08824 t) 732-297-3000; 732-297-3011 (CRP) www.staugustinenj.org Rev. Robert G. Lynam, Pst.; Dcn. Denis Mayer; Dcn. James Rivera; Sr. Ruthann McGoldrick, Pst. Assoc.; Sr. Barbara Takacs, MPF, DRE; CRP Stds.: 140

St. Augustine of Canterbury School - (Grades PreK-8) t) 732-297-6042 www.staugustinenj.org/school/ Edward Modzelewski Jr., Prin.; Stds.: 326; Lay Tchrs.: 20

St. Augustine of Canterbury Convent - t) 732-798-6950

LAMBERTVILLE

St. John the Evangelist - 44 Bridge St., Lambertville, NJ 08530; Mailing: 13 N. Main St., Lambertville, NJ 08530 t) 609-397-3350 stjohndre@gmail.com; stjohnlamb.office@gmail.com parishofsaintjohn.org Very Rev. Robert B. Kolakowski, Pst.; Veronica McCabe, DRE; CRP Stds.: 100

LAURENCE HARBOR

St. Lawrence - 109 Laurence Pkwy., Laurence Harbor, NJ 08879 t) 732-566-1093 saintlawrenceharbor@gmail.com Rev. Mark Kehoe, Pst.; Dcn. Michael Abriola; Dcn. Stephen J. Gajewski; Dcn. Gregory Ris; Judy Logan, DRE; CRP Stds.: 84

MANVILLE

Christ the Redeemer Parish - 98 S. Second Ave., Manville, NJ 08835; Mailing: P.O. Box 924, Manville, NJ 08835 t) 908-725-0072 www.ctrmanville.com Rev. Stanislaw Slaby, C.Ss.R., Pst.; Rev. Piotr Grzeskiewicz, C.Ss.R. (Poland), Par. Vicar; Dcn. Thomas J. Giacobbe; Dcn. William G. Stefany; Charlotte Snow, DRE; CRP Stds.: 105

Christ the King Church - 211 Louis St., Manville, NJ 08835 t) 908-231-1330

Sacred Heart Church -

MARTINSVILLE

Blessed Sacrament - 1890 Washington Valley Rd., Martinsville, NJ 08836; Mailing: 852 Newmans Ln., Martinsville, NJ 08836 t) 732-356-4405 x2 kslattery@blessedsacramentnj.org www.blessedsacramentnj.org Rev. Brian J. Nolan, Pst.; Rev. Pawel Michalowski, SDB, Par. Vicar; Dcn. Louis Pizzigoni III; Mary Foy, DRE; CRP Stds.: 330

MATAWAN

Most Holy Redeemer - 133 Amboy Rd., Old Bridge Township, Matawan, NJ 07747 t) 732-566-9334; 732-566-5630 (CRP) mhrccd1993@aol.com; mhr1985@optimum.net www.mhr-parish.org Rev. Chester H. Carina, Pst.; Rev. Joseph L. Desmond, In Res.; Dcn. Robert T. McGovern; Dcn. A. Keith Berg; Deborah Dyson, DRE; CRP Stds.: 200

METUCHEN

Cathedral of St. Francis of Assisi - 32 Elm Ave., Metuchen, NJ 08840; Mailing: 45 Library Pl., Metuchen, NJ 08840 t) 732-548-0100; 732-548-0100 x226 (CRP) religioused@stfranciscathedral.org; info@stfranciscathedral.org www.stfranciscathedral.org Very Rev. Timothy A. Christy, Rector; Rev. Jun Joseph Alquiros, Par. Vicar; Rev. Edgar Madarang, Par. Vicar; Rev. Roy Quesea, In Res.; Dcn. Guido J. Brossoni; Dcn. Kenrick Fortune; Dcn. Kenneth Hamilton; Dcn. Eduardo Olegario; Dcn. Joseph P. Saggese; Debra Schurko, DRE; CRP Stds.: 920

St. Francis Cathedral School - (Grades PreK-8) 528 Main St., Metuchen, NJ 08840 t) 732-548-3107 www.stfranciscathedralschool.org Ann Major, Prin.; Judi Monteleone, Vice Prin.; Angela Hajduk, Librn.; Stds.: 422; Sr. Tchrs.: 2; Lay Tchrs.: 22

MIDDLESEX

Our Lady of Mount Virgin - 600 Harris Ave., Middlesex, NJ 08846 t) 732-356-2149 pmarshall@olmv.net www.olmv.net Rev. David V. Skoblow, Pst.; Rev. Louis A. Mattina, Par. Vicar; Dcn. Thomas G. Sommero; Dcn. Edgar R. Chaves; Dorothy Zmigrodski, DRE; CRP Stds.: 196

MILFORD

St. Edward the Confessor - 61 Mill St., Milford, NJ 08848 t) 908-995-4723 stedgrowingfaith@gmail.com www.stedwardmilford.com Rev. Krzysztof Kaczynski, Pst.; Dcn. William J. Barr; Kristine Menard, DRE; CRP Stds.: 59

MILLTOWN

Our Lady of Lourdes - 233 N. Main St., Milltown, NJ 08850 t) 732-828-0011 ololchurch233@gmail.com ololchurchnj.org Rev. Edward A. Czarcinski, Pst.; Rev. Michael E. Crummy, In Res.; Dcn. Robert Gerling; Dcn. Stephen Holzinger; Renee Young, DRE; CRP Stds.: 90

MONMOUTH JUNCTION

St. Cecilia - 10 Kingston Ln., Monmouth Junction, NJ 08852 t) 732-329-2893 drescc@yahoo.com; parishsect@stceciliaparish.net www.stceciliaparish.net Rev. Charles T. O'Connor, Pst.; Christine Slovensky, DRE; CRP Stds.: 165

MONROE TOWNSHIP

Nativity of Our Lord - 185 Applegarth Rd., Monroe Township, NJ 08831 t) 609-371-0499 x10; 609-371-2518 x14 (CRP) admin@nativitymonroe.org; pcl@nativitymonroe.org www.nativitymonroe.org Rev. Nalaka Silva, O.M.I., Pst.; Rev. Lancelot Mc Grath, Par. Vicar; Dcn. John H. Shelton; Tara Vigario, DRE; Dcn. Robert E. Gatto; CRP Stds.: 216

Blessed Pauline Convent - 59A Essex Rd., Monroe Twp., NJ 08831 Sr. Marie Colette Martelli, SCC, Pst. Assoc.;

NEW BRUNSWICK

Holy Family Parish - 56 Throop Ave., New Brunswick, NJ 08901 t) 732-545-1681 hfpcenter@holyfamilyforall.org www.holyfamilyforall.org Rev. Thomas F. Ryan, Pst.; Rev. Imre Juhasz, Par. Vicar; Rev. Walter Wiktorek, Par. Vicar; Dcn. Nelson Torres; Catherine Kovarcik, DRE; CRP Stds.: 170

St. Joseph Church - Somerset and Maple Sts., New Brunswick, NJ 08901; Mailing: 56 Throop Ave., New Brunswick, NJ 08901 (Worship Site)

Sacred Heart Church - t) (732) 545-1681 (Holy Family Parish) (Worship Site)

St. Ladislaus Church - 215 Somerset St., New Brunswick, NJ 08901 (Worship Site)

Our Lady of Mt. Carmel - 75 Morris St., New Brunswick, NJ 08901; Mailing: PO Box 1372, New Brunswick, NJ 08903 t) 732-846-5873 mtcarmel@verizon.net www.olmtcarmelonline.com Rev. Raymond L. Nacarino, SJS, Pst.; Rev. Bonfilio Enriquez, SJS, Par. Vicar; Rev. Jose Lorente, In Res.; CRP Stds.: 803

Parish of the Visitation - 192 Sandford St., New Brunswick, NJ 08901 t) 732-545-5090 parishofthevisitation@gmail.com www.parishofthevisitation.org Rev. Michael Fragoso, Pst.; Rev. Edmund A. Luciano III, Par. Vicar; Rev. Michael Tabernero, In Res.; Amelia Johnson, DRE; CRP Stds.: 240

St. John the Baptist Church - 29 Abeel St., New Brunswick, NJ 08901 (Worship Site)

St. Mary of Mt. Virgin Church - 190 Sandford St., New Brunswick, NJ 08901 (Worship Site)

St. Theresa of the Infant Jesus - 15 Fox Rd., Edison, NJ 08817 (Worship Site)

St. Mary of Mount Virgin Convent - 198 Sandford St., New Brunswick, NJ 08901 t) 732-545-0514

St. Peter the Apostle - 94 Somerset St., New Brunswick, NJ 08901 t) 732-545-6820; (609) 661-2409 (Emergency contact) parishoffice@stpeternewbrunswick.org www.stpeternewbrunswick.org Rev. Jason Pavich, Admin.; Rev. Thomas Lanza, Chap.; Dcn. Patrick J. Gutsick; Dcn. Helmut Wittreich; CRP Stds.: 36

NORTH BRUNSWICK

Our Lady of Peace - 1730 U.S. Hwy. Rte. 130, North Brunswick, NJ 08902 t) 732-297-9680; 732-821-1581 (CRP) office@olopnb.org; religioused@olopnb.org olopnb.org Rev. Michael G. Krull, Pst.; Rev. Kenneth R. Kolibas, In Res.; Dcn. Francis D'Mello; Alicia Marie DeFrange, DRE; CRP Stds.: 195

NORTH PLAINFIELD

St. Joseph - 41 Manning Ave., North Plainfield, NJ 07060; Mailing: 99 Westervelt Ave., North Plainfield, NJ 07060 t) 908-756-3383 info@sjnp.org www.sjnp.org Rev. Mauricio Tabera-Vasquez, Admin.; Rev. Gustavo Rodriguez-Perez, Par. Vicar; Rev. Msgr. Richard J. Lyons, In Res.; Sr. Susana Islas, MCSH, DRE; CRP Stds.: 204

St. Luke - 300 Clinton Ave., North Plainfield, NJ 07063 t) 908-754-8812 stlukesinfo@gmail.com www.stlukenp.weconnect.com Jeanne Enteman, DRE; CRP Stds.: 45

OLD BRIDGE

St. Ambrose - 83 Throckmorton Ln., Old Bridge, NJ 08857 t) 732-679-5666; 732-679-5580 (CRP) joan.abitabile@saintambroseparish.com Rev. John C. Grimes, Pst.; Rev. David E. Keyes, Par. Vicar; CRP Stds.: 450

St. Ambrose School - (Grades PreK-8) 81 Throckmorton Ln., Old Bridge, NJ 08857 t) 732-679-4700 principal@stambroseschool.net www.stambroseschool.net Rita Naviello, Prin.; Stds.: 270; Lay Tchrs.: 26

St. Thomas the Apostle - One St. Thomas Plaza, Old Bridge, NJ 08857 t) 732-251-4000; 732-251-1660 (CRP) dyesis@sttaob.com; lsorrentino@saintthomasob.com www.saintthomasob.com Rev. Jerome A. Johnson, Pst.; Rev. Paulus Marandi, C.M.F., Par. Vicar; Rev. John M. Rozembajgier; Dcn. Robert Bonfante Sr.; Dcn. Patrick W. Hearty; Dcn. Scott D. Titmas; Dcn. Joseph C. Tobin; Debbie Yesis, DRE; CRP Stds.: 502

St. Thomas the Apostle School - (Grades PreK-8) 333 Hwy. 18, Old Bridge, NJ 08857 t) 732-251-4812 apioppo@diometuchen.org www.sttaob.com Annette Pioppo, Prin.; Diane Zarate, Vice Prin.; Stds.: 373; Lay Tchrs.: 25

OXFORD

St. Rose of Lima - 85 Academy St., Oxford, NJ 07863; Mailing: 327 Greenwich St., Belvidere, NJ 07823 t) 908-475-2559 kkelly1@comcast.net www.stpatrickrose.org Rev. Charles A. Sabella, Pst.; Dcn. Lawrence V. D'Andrea;

PARLIN

St. Bernadette - 20 Villanova Rd., Parlin, NJ 08859 t) 732-721-2772; 732-727-4343 (Rel. Ed.) stbernsecy@gmail.com saintbernadettechurch.net Rev. James W. Hagerman, Pst.; Rev. Msgr. Andrew L. Szaroleta, Senior Priest; Dr. Mary Kay Cullinan, DRE; CRP Stds.: 201

PEAPACK

St. Elizabeth - St. Brigid - 129 Main St., Peapack, NJ 07977; Mailing: PO Box 33, Peapack, NJ 07977 t) 908-234-1265; 908-234-0079 parishlife@sainteb.org; reled@sainteb.org www.sainteb.org Rev. Msgr. Edward C. Puleo, Pst.; Rev. John G. Hillier, In Res.; Sr. Phyllis Vella, DRE; CRP Stds.: 194

St. Brigid - t) (908) 234-1265

St. Elizabeth - 34 Peapack Rd., Far Hills, NJ 07931

PERTH AMBOY

Saint John Paul II Parish - 490 State St., Perth Amboy, NJ 08861-3541 t) 732-826-1395 office@johnpaulsecond.com; pastor@johnpaulsecond.com www.johnpaulsecond.com Rev. Slawomir Romanowski, C.Ss.R, Pst.; Rev. Waldemar Wieladek, C.Ss.R, Par. Vicar; Dcn. Basilio A. Perez; Ana Maria Zevallos, DRE; CRP Stds.: 285

Our Lady of the Rosary of Fatima - 188 Wayne St., Perth Amboy, NJ 08861 (Worship Site)

St. Stephen - (Worship Site)

Most Holy Name of Jesus Parish - 777 Cortlandt St., Perth Amboy, NJ 08861-2843 t) 732-442-3457 (CRP); 732-442-0512 mostholynameofjesus@gmail.com mostholynameofjesus.org Rev. Ronald Machado, Admin.; Rev. Nicholas Norena, Par. Vicar; Dcn. Noe Cortez; Dcn. Enrique Garcia; Teresa Galen, DRE; CRP Stds.: 321

Our Lady of Hungary Church - 691 Cortland St., Perth Amboy, NJ 08861; Mailing: 697 Cortlandt St., Perth Amboy, NJ 08861 (Worship Site)

Holy Trinity Church - 315 Lawrie St., Perth Amboy, NJ 08861 (Worship Site)

La Asuncion Church - (Worship Site) Rev. Nicolas F Norena, Par. Vicar;

Our Lady of Fatima - 380 Smith St., Perth Amboy, NJ 08861 t) 732-442-6634 x21; 732-442-6637 olfperthamboy@gmail.com www.ourladyoffatimaperthamboy.com/ Rev. Gilles D. Njobam, C.M.F., Admin.; Dcn. Jose R. Diaz; Dcn. Sergio Diaz; Dcn. Pablo Bencosme; Dcn. Gregorio A. Rios; Rev. Thomasaiah Mallavarapu, In Res.; Rev. Alberto Ruiz, C.M.F., In Res.; Rev. Manuel Diaz, In Res.; Fe Morales, DRE; CRP Stds.: 384

PHILLIPSBURG

St. Philip & St. James - 430 S. Main St., Phillipsburg, NJ 08865-3094 t) 908-454-0112; 908-859-1244 x9 (CRP) pastor@spsj.org; secretary@spsj.org www.spsj.org Rev. John J. Barbella, Pst.; Rev. Gilbert Starcher, Par. Vicar; Dcn. Enock Berluche Sr.; Dcn. Larry M. Bevilacqua; Dcn. Robert Fisher; Dcn. John T. Flynn; Jo-Ann Scott, DRE; CRP Stds.: 200

St. Philip and St. James School - (Grades PreK-8) 137 Roseberry St., Phillipsburg, NJ 08865 sspjschool@spsj.org sspjnj.org Donna Kucinski, Prin.; Stds.: 147; Lay Tchrs.: 15

PISCATAWAY

St. Frances Cabrini - 208 Bound Brook Ave., Piscataway, NJ 08854-4097 t) 732-885-5313; 732-885-8996 (CRP) sfc208@yahoo.com stfrancab.com Rev. James F. Considine, Pst.; Dcn. Roger Ladao; Terri Abano, DRE; CRP Stds.: 105

Our Lady of Fatima - 50 Van Winkle Pl., Piscataway, NJ 08854 t) 732-968-5555 x1104; 732-968-5555 (CRP); 732-968-5556 rdelillo@olfparish.org wwwolfparish.org Rev. Arlindo Paul DaSilva, Pst.; Rev. Robert V. Meyers, Par. Vicar; Rev. David J. Pekola, Par. Vicar; Rev. A. David Chalackal, C.M.I., In Res.; Dcn. Lawrence P. Reilly; Dcn. William P. Rider; Sr. Alina Marie Nieser, P.V.M.I., DRE; CRP Stds.: 161

PITTSTOWN

St. Catherine of Siena - 2 White Bridge Rd., Pittstown, NJ 08867-0245; Mailing: P.O. Box 245, Pittstown, NJ 08867 t) 908-735-4024; 908-735-5086 (CRP) scoscoffice@gmail.com; office@scoschurch.org www.scoschurch.org Rev. Czeslaw Zalubski, Pst.; Dcn. Michael A. Meyer; Sandra Kopka, DRE; CRP Stds.: 123

PLAINSBORO

Queenship of Mary - 16 Dey Rd., Plainsboro, NJ 08536 t) 609-779-5511; 609-799-1428 (CRP) parishoffice@qomchurch.org www.qomchurch.org Rev. Gerardo B. Paderon, Pst.; Dcn. Thomas P. Boccellari; Dcn. Hugo Simao; CRP Stds.: 82

PORT MURRAY

St. Theodore - 855 Rte. 57, Port Murray, NJ 07865; Mailing: P.O. Box 146, Port Murray, NJ 07865 t) 908-689-8318 sttheodorenj@gmail.com www.sttheodorenj.org Rev. Damian Tomiczek, S.D.S., Admin.; Elizabeth Saam, DRE; CRP Stds.: 51

PORT READING

St. Anthony of Padua - 436 Port Reading Ave., Port Reading, NJ 07064 t) 732-634-1403 info.stanthony1@gmail.com www.saintanthonypadua.org Rev. William J. Smith, Pst.; Rev. Msgr. Pafnouti Wassef, Par. Vicar; Dcn. Peter Barcellona; Dcn. Michael Brucato; Dcn. Kenneth J. Perlas; CRP Stds.: 115

Our Lady of Mount Carmel - 267 E. Smith St., Woodbridge, NJ 07095 (Worship Site)

RARITAN

The Catholic Church of St. Ann - 45 Anderson St., Raritan, NJ 08869 t) 908-725-1008 info@stannparish.com www.stannparish.com Rev. Thomas A. Odorizzi, C.O., Pst.; Dcn. Roy Rabinowitz; Sr. Ella Mae McDonald, MPF, DRE; Dcn. Salvatore J. Bonfiglio, Bus. Mgr.; CRP Stds.: 195

St. Ann Classical Academy - (Grades PreK-8) 40 Second Ave., Raritan, NJ 08869 t) 908-725-7787 principal.stannschool@diometuchen.org stannclassical.org Stds.: 78; Lay Tchrs.: 7

St. Ann Convent - 29 Second Ave., Raritan, NJ 08869 t) 908-725-2256 Sr. Phyllis Vella, Supr.; Sr. Charlyne Greene, MPF, Pst. Min./Coord.; Sr. Dolores Toscano, Pst. Assoc.;

St. Joseph - 16 E. Somerset St., Raritan, NJ 08869 t) 908-725-0163 parishoffice@sjraritan.org sjraritan.com Rev. Kevin Patrick Kelly, C.O., Admin.;

SAYREVILLE

Our Lady of Victories - 42 Main St., Sayreville, NJ 08872 t) 732-257-0077; 732-238-9222 (CRP) www.olvsayrenj.com Rev. David J. Pekola, Pst.; Dcn. Edward J. Majkowski; Sr. Alice Ivanyo, DRE; CRP Stds.: 185

St. Stanislaus Kostka - 225 MacArthur Ave., Sayreville, NJ 08872 t) 732-254-0212 saintstanislaus@optonline.net Rev. Kenneth R. Murphy, Pst.; Dcn. David Mikolai; Dcn. Andrew Ozga; Kathleen Krolick, DRE; CRP Stds.: 66

St. Stanislaus Kostka School - (Grades K-8) 221 MacArthur Ave., Sayreville, NJ 08872 t) 732-254-5819 emalinconico@diometuchen.org www.sskschool.org Lori Hodder, Prin.; Stds.: 168; Lay Tchrs.: 15

SKILLMAN

St. Charles Borromeo - 47 Skillman Rd., Skillman, NJ 08558; Mailing: 376 Burnt Hill Rd., Skillman, NJ 08558 t) 609-466-0300 jdimeglio@borromeo.org www.borromeo.org Rev. Msgr. Gregory E. S. Malovetz, Pst.; Cathy Souto, DRE; CRP Stds.: 158

SOMERSET

St. Matthias - 168 John F. Kennedy Blvd., Somerset, NJ 08873 t) 732-828-1400 www.stmatthias.net Rev. Abraham Orapankal, Pst.; Rev. Msgr. Seamus F. Brennan, Senior Priest; Dcn. Russell B. Demkovitz; Dcn. John M. Radvanski; Dolores Nann, DRE; CRP Stds.: 287

St. Matthias School - (Grades PreK-8) 170 J.F. Kennedy Blvd., Somerset, NJ 08873 t) 732-828-1402 www.stmatthias.info Mary Lynch, Prin.; Joseph Gidaro, Vice Prin.; Stephanie Lanzalotto, Librn.; Stds.: 275; Sr. Tchrs.: 1; Lay Tchrs.: 22

St. Matthias Convent - 1 Leupp Ln., Somerset, NJ 08873 t) 732-828-9545 Sr. Marie Therese Sherwood, Pst. Min./Coord.;

SOMERVILLE

Church of the Immaculate Conception - 35 Mountain Ave., Somerville, NJ 08876 t) 908-725-1112; 908-725-1112 x1119 (CRP) cjanuse@icsomerville.org; kbohler@icsomerville.org www.immaculateconception.org Rev. Msgr. Joseph G. Celano, Pst.; Rev. Joseph Joseph Illes, Par. Vicar; Rev. Mhonchan Ezung, Par. Vicar; Dcn. John R. Czekaj; Dcn. Reynaldo Lopez; Dcn. Frank J. Quinn; Karen Bohler, DRE; CRP Stds.: 437

Immaculate Conception School - (Grades PreK-8) 41 Mountain Ave., Somerville, NJ 08876 t) 908-725-6516 dberger@ics41mtn.org www.icsschool.org Katie Parsells, Prin.; Kelly Seccamanie, Vice Prin.; Victoria Proctor, Dean; Stds.: 356; Lay Tchrs.: 27

Immaculata High School - (Grades 9-12) 240 Mountain Ave., Somerville, NJ 08876 t) 908-722-0200 ewebber@immaculatahighschool.org www.immaculatahighschool.org Ed Webber, Prin.; Kristen Boczany, Vice Prin., Academic Affairs; Sonja Gasko, Vice Prin., Campus Affairs; Stds.: 514; Lay Tchrs.: 56; Pr. Tchrs.: 1

SOUTH AMBOY

St. Mary - 256 Augusta St., South Amboy, NJ 08879 t) 732-721-0179; 732-721-1514 (CRP) saintmarysa@aol.com saintmarysa.org Rev. Dennis R. Weezorak, Pst.; Dcn. Stephen N. Laikowski; Dcn. Richard O'Brien; John Kobiernicki IV, DRE; CRP Stds.: 160

Sacred Heart - 531 Washington Ave., South Amboy, NJ 08879 t) 732-721-0040 sheart224@aol.com www.sacredheartsa.org Rev. Stanley G. Gromadzki, Pst.; Rev. Lukasz Blicharski, Par. Vicar; Shannon Able-Liana, DRE; CRP Stds.: 225

SOUTH BOUND BROOK

Our Lady of Mercy - 122 High St., South Bound Brook, NJ 08880 t) 732-356-1037 olmsecretary@optonline.net; edisonkcc@gmail.com www.olmsbb.org Rev. Namwoong Lee, Admin.; Suwan Kim, DRE; CRP Stds.: 26

SOUTH PLAINFIELD

Our Lady of Czestochowa - 857 Hamilton Blvd., South Plainfield, NJ 07080; Mailing: 120 Kosciusko Ave., South Plainfield, NJ 07080 t) 908-756-1333 olcchurch@verizon.net www.olcsouthplainfield.weconnect.com Rev. Peter Tran, Pst.; Sr. Maria Goretti Nguyen, SCC, DRE & Pst. Assoc.; CRP Stds.: 67

Sacred Heart - 149 S. Plainfield Ave., South Plainfield, NJ 07080; Mailing: 200 Randolph Ave., South Plainfield, NJ 07080 t) 908-756-0633 x110; 908-756-0633 x143 (CRP) admin@churchofthesacredheart.net www.churchofthesacredheart.net Rev. John Paul Alvarado, Pst.; Rev. Pervais Indrias, Par. Vicar; Dcn. Gregory Caruso; Louise Timko, DRE; CRP Stds.: 276

SOUTH RIVER

Corpus Christi - 100 James St., South River, NJ 08882 t) 732-254-1800 x10 corpuschristichurch5@gmail.com; corpuschristisouthriver@yahoo.com www.corpuschristisouthriver.org Rev. Damian B. Breen, Pst.; Jane Magliulo, DRE; Cathy Ondrejack, DRE; CRP Stds.: 100

St. Mary of Ostrabrama - 30 Jackson St., South River, NJ 08882 t) 732-254-2220 ostrabrama@stmarysr.org stmarysr.org Rev. Michael J. Gromadzki, Pst.; Dcn. Thomas F. Dominiecki; Dcn. Mark J. Hennicke; Rosemary Eckert, DRE; CRP Stds.: 131

St. Stephen Protomartyr - 20 William St., South River, NJ 08882 t) 732-257-0100; 732-766-3452 (Spanish) saintstephen1@aol.com ststephennj.com Rev. John Szczepanik, Pst.; CRP Stds.: 87

SPOTSWOOD

Immaculate Conception - 23 Manalapan Rd., Spotswood, NJ 08884; Mailing: 18 South St., Spotswood, NJ 08884 t) 732-251-3110; 732-251-5973 (CRP) www.chicspotswood.com Rev. John J. O'Kane, Pst.; Rev. James W. McGuffey, Par. Vicar; Mark Sahli, DRE; Dcn. Thomas Griffoul; CRP Stds.: 337

Immaculate Conception School - (Grades PreK-8) t) 732-251-3090 rfornaro@icsspotswood.com www.icsspotswood.org Rocco Fornaro, Prin.; Shannon Chadwick, Librn.; Stds.: 126; Lay Tchrs.: 16

Convent - 21 Manalapan Rd., Spotswood, NJ 08884 t) 732-251-3446 Sr. Antonella Chunka, CSSF, Local Min.;

THREE BRIDGES

St. Elizabeth Ann Seton - 105 Summer Rd., Three Bridges, NJ 08887-2307 t) 908-782-1475; 908-284-2929 (CRP) parishoffice@easeton.net; seasrf@easeton.net easeton.net Rev. Thomas J. Serafin, Pst.; Dcn. Michael S. Tomcho; Dcn. Kevin M. Kilcommons; Dcn. William P. Weber Jr.; Mariam Nawab, DRE; CRP Stds.: 464

WARREN

Our Lady of the Mount - 167 Mount Bethel Rd., Warren, NJ 07059; Mailing: 170 Mount Bethel Rd., Warren, NJ 07059 t) 908-647-1075 parishoffice@olmwarren.org ourladyofthemount.org Rev. Sean W. Kenney, OFS, Pst.; CRP Stds.: 251

WASHINGTON

St. Joseph - 200 Carlton Ave., Washington, NJ 07882 t) 908-689-0058; 908-689-0093 (CRP) stjosephwashingtonnj.org Rev. Guy W. Selvester, Pst.; Dcn. Paul Flor; Dcn. Edmund Hartmann Jr.; Joyce Rock, DRE; CRP Stds.: 100

WATCHUNG

St. Mary-Stony Hill - 225 Mountain Blvd., Watchung, NJ 07069 t) 908-756-6524 www.stmaryswatchung.org Rev. Msgr. William Benwell, Pst.; Dcn. Peter D'Angelo; Dcn. Walter S. Maksimik; Catherine Cooney, DRE; Karen Dill, CRE; CRP Stds.: 215

WHITEHOUSE STATION

Our Lady of Lourdes - 390 County Rd. 523, Whitehouse Station, NJ 08889; Mailing: P.O. Box 248, Whitehouse Station, NJ 08889 t) 908-534-2319 pastor@ollwhs.org; faithformation@ollwhs.org www.ollwhs.org Rev.

Leonard F.A. Rusay, Pst.; Dcn. Sylvan Webb; Dcn. John Scansaroli; Rev. Maurice T. Carlton, In Res.; Nina Forestiere, DRE; CRP Stds.: 238

WOODBRIDGE

St. James - 369 Amboy Ave., Woodbridge, NJ 07095; Mailing: 149 Grove St., Woodbridge, NJ 07095 t) 732-634-0500 x100; 732-634-3026 (CRP) stjameschurch@stjamesonline.org; ccd@stjamesonline.org www.stjamesonline.org/ Rev. Thomas Naduviledathu, S.D.V., Pst.; Rev. Ignacio Cogollodo Jr., SDV, Par. Vicar; Dcn. William F. Lange; Dcn. Roel S. Mercado; Dcn. Carl E. Psota; Dorothy Zmigrodski, DRE; CRP Stds.: 216

St. James School - (Grades PreK-8) 341 Amboy Ave., Woodbridge, NJ 07095 t) 732-634-2090 John Maresca, Prin.; Stds.: 161; Lay Tchrs.: 13

SCHOOLS: PRESCHOOL THRU HIGH SCHOOL

SCHOOLS

STATE OF NEW JERSEY

MARTINSVILLE

Little Friends of Jesus Nursery School - (PRV) (Grades PreSchool-k) 1881 Washington Valley Rd., Martinsville, NJ 08836 t) 732-667-5272 littlefriendsnursery@gmail.com www.littlefriendsmartinsville.com Sr. Ermelita Gella, S.D.V., Prin.; Stds.: 62; Scholastics: 41; Lay Tchrs.: 3

PERTH AMBOY

Perth Amboy Catholic School - (PAR) (Grades K-8) 500 State St., Perth Amboy, NJ 08861 t) 732-442-9533 www.pacatholicschool.org Anacelis Diaz, Prin.; Stds.: 141; Lay Tchrs.: 12

SOUTH PLAINFIELD

Holy Savior Academy - (PAR) (Grades PreK-8) 149 S. Plainfield Ave., South Plainfield, NJ 07080-1179 t) 908-822-5890 mhaluszka@holysavioracademy.com; cwoodburn@holysavioracademy.com www.holysavioracademy.com Carol Woodburn, Prin.; Stds.: 141; Lay Tchrs.: 14

HIGH SCHOOLS

STATE OF NEW JERSEY

EDISON

St. Thomas Aquinas High School - (DIO) (Grades 9-12) One Tingley Ln., Edison, NJ 08820 t) 732-549-1108 dtrukowski@diometuchen.org; hziegler@stahs.net www.stahs.net Harry Ziegler, Prin.; Peter G. Kane, Pres.; Rev. Michael Tabernero, Chap.; Stds.: 544; Pr. Tchrs.: 1; Lay Tchrs.: 51

METUCHEN

Saint Joseph High School - (PRV) 145 Plainfield Ave., Metuchen, NJ 08840-1099 t) 732-549-7600 mhutnick@stjoes.org www.stjoes.org Anne Rivera, Prin.; John Nolan, Pres.; Stds.: 532; Bro. Tchrs.: 1; Lay Tchrs.: 36

WATCHUNG

Mount St. Mary Academy - (PRV) (Grades 9-12) 1645 U.S. Hwy. 22 W., Watchung, NJ 07069 t) 908-757-0108 lgambacorto@mountsaintmary.org www.mountsaintmary.org College preparatory day school for girls. A sponsored work of the Sisters of Mercy of the Americas. Rev. Msgr. William Benwell, Chap.; Sr. Lisa D. Gambacorto, R.S.M., Pres.; Stds.: 272; Lay Tchrs.: 32

INSTITUTIONS LOCATED IN DIOCESE

ASSOCIATIONS [ASN]

FLEMINGTON

St. Joseph's Association, Inc. - 26 Harmony School Rd., Flemington, NJ 08822 t) 908-782-4800 Sr. Gabriela of the Incaration Hicks, 1st Councilor;

CAMPUS MINISTRY / NEWMAN CENTERS [CAM]

NEW BRUNSWICK

Catholic Center at Rutgers University - 84 Somerset St., New Brunswick, NJ 08901 t) 732-545-6663 www.rutgerscatholic.org Rev. Thomas Lanza, Chap.; Rev. Jason Pavich, Pst.; Sr. Lorraine Doiron, S.J.H., Campus Min.; Bro. Joseph Donovan, B.H., Campus Min.; Sr. Anna Palka, SJH, Campus Min.; Bro. Brennan Robinson, Campus Min.; Bro. Patrick Reilly, B.H., Dir.;

CATHOLIC CHARITIES [CCH]

PERTH AMBOY

Catholic Charities Central Office - 319 Maple St., Perth Amboy, NJ 08861 t) 732-324-8200 aplace@ccdom.org www.ccdom.org Marci Booth, Exec.; Christine Salimbene, Exec.; Marie Zissler, Exec.; Julio Coto, Dir.; Asstd. Annu.: 11,128; Staff: 98

Bridgewater Family Service Center - 540 U.S. Rte. 22 E., Bridgewater, NJ 08807 t) 908-722-1881 ccdom.org LuAnn Dias, Dir.;

Catholic Charities, Edison Family Service Center - 26 Safran Ave., Edison, NJ 08837 t) 732-738-1323 ccdom.org Jessica Polizzotto, Dir.;

Catholic Charities, Ozanam Inn - 20-22 Abeel St., New Brunswick, NJ 08901 t) 732-729-0850 ccdom.org Nicole Fernandez, Dir.;

Community Child Care Solutions - 103 Center St., Perth Amboy, NJ 08861 t) 732-324-4357 Mary Jane DiPaolo, Dir.;

Community House at St. Thomas - 124 Bentley Ave., Old Bridge, NJ 08857 t) 732-251-0022

East Brunswick Family Service Center - 288 Rues Ln., East Brunswick, NJ 08816 t) 732-257-6100 ccdom.org Angela Orth, Dir.;

Flemington Family Service Center - 6 Park Ave., Flemington, NJ 08822 t) 908-782-7905 ccdom.org Brooke Rekens, Dir.;

Metuchen Community Services Corporation - 103 Center St., Perth Amboy, NJ 08861 t) 732-324-4357

The Ozanam Shelter for Families and Single Women - 89 Truman Dr., Edison, NJ 08817 t) 732-985-0327 ccdom.org Nicole Fernandez, Dir.;

Phillipsburg Family Service Center - 700 Sayre Ave., Phillipsburg, NJ 08865 t) 908-454-2074 ccdom.org Brooke Rekens, Dir.;

Social Service Center - 387 South St., Phillipsburg, NJ 08865 t) 908-859-5447 ccdom.org Brooke Renkens, Dir.;

CEMETERIES [CEM]

JAMESBURG

The Crematory at Holy Cross Burial Park - 840 Cranbury-S. River Rd., Jamesburg, NJ 08831; Mailing: P.O. Box 191, Metuchen, NJ 08840 t) 732-640-1533 cemeteries@diometuchen.org Jeffrey Mager, Dir.;

Holy Cross Burial Park - 840 Cranbury-S. River Rd., Jamesburg, NJ 08831; Mailing: P.O. Box 191, Metuchen, NJ 08840 t) 732-463-1424 cemeteries@diometuchen.org Jeffrey Mager, Dir.;

PISCATAWAY

Resurrection Burial Park - 899 Lincoln Ave., Piscataway, NJ 08854 t) 732-463-1424 cemeteries@diometuchen.org Jeffrey Mager, Dir.;

CONVENTS, MONASTERIES, AND RESIDENCES FOR WOMEN [CON]

BELVIDERE

Immaculate Conception Convent - Augustinian Recollect Sisters - 743 Water St., Belvidere, NJ 07823; Mailing: 20 Manunka Chunk Rd., Belvidere, NJ 07823 t) 908-475-9947 Mother Beatriz Aguirre Oro, Supr.; Srs.: 6

BLOOMSBURY

Sisters of Jesus Our Hope - 376 Bellis Rd., Bloomsbury, NJ 08804 t) 908-995-7261 sisterchristine@sistersofjesusourhope.org www.sistersofjesusourhope.org Sr. Christine Quense, S.J.H., Supr.; Srs.: 10

EDISON

St. Thomas Aquinas Convent - 15 Wren Ct., Edison, NJ 08820; Mailing: 871 Mercer Rd., Beaver Falls, PA 15010 t) 732-321-0137 srcynthia@stahs.net www.feliciansistersna.org Sr. Cynthia Marie Babyak, C.S.S.F., Contact; Srs.: 4

FLEMINGTON

The Carmel of Mary Immaculate and St. Mary Magdalen - 26 Harmony School Rd., Flemington, NJ 08822 t) 908-782-4802 friendsofcarmel@gmail.com www.flemingtoncarmel.org Rev. John Primich, Chap.; Mother Mary Elizabeth of the Trinity, Prioress; Srs.: 11

Dominican Sisters of Divine Providence - 25 Harmony School Rd., Flemington, NJ 08822 t) 908-782-1504 srmcath25@gmail.com Sr. Mary Catherine Baidy, O.P., Prioress; Srs.: 1

MARTINSVILLE

Vocationist Sisters Convent - 1881 Washington Valley Rd., Martinsville, NJ 08836 t) 732-667-5272 vocationistsisters@gmail.com; srperpetua@hotmail.com Sr. Maria P DaConceicao, S.D.V., Supr.; Srs.: 8

METUCHEN

St. Clare Convent - 52 Elm Ave., Metuchen, NJ 08840 t) 732-549-7598 kkwiatkowski@stfranciscathedral.org Srs.: 2

St. Francis Convent - 44 Elm Ave., Metuchen, NJ 08840 t) 732-662-5729 Sr. Mary Elizabeth McCauley, Supr.; Srs.: 3

NEW BRUNSWICK

Sisters of Jesus Our Hope - 51 Jefferson Ave., New Brunswick, NJ 08901 t) 732-570-1540 sisterlorraine@sistersofjesusourhope.org www.sistersofjesusourhope.org Sr. Lorraine Doiron, SJH, Supr.; Srs.: 3

NORTH PLAINFIELD

Congregation of the Servants of the Holy Child Jesus of the Third Order Regular of Saint Francis - 99 Harrison Ave., North Plainfield, NJ 07060 t) 908-370-3616 antoniavm@aol.com Sr. Antonia Cooper, OSF, Contact; Srs.: 5

WATCHUNG

McAuley Hall Inc. - 1633 U.S. Hwy. 22, Watchung, NJ 07069-6505 t) 908-754-3663 mdavis@mcauleyhall.org Dcn. James McGovern; Srs.: 43

Sisters of Mercy of the Americas, Mid-Atlantic Community - 1645 U.S. Hwy. 22 W., Watchung, NJ 07069-6587 t) 908-756-0994 x4006 lcavallo@sistersofmercy.org www.sistersofmercy.org Sr. Patricia McDermott, RSM, Pres.; Srs.: 36

WOODBRIDGE

St. Joseph Convent - 184 Amboy Ave., Woodbridge, NJ 07095 t) 732-634-0415 Sr. Lucyna Zugaj, LSIC, Supr.; Srs.: 16

St. Joseph Home Convent - 3 St. Joseph Ter., Woodbridge, NJ 07095 t) 732-750-0077 Sr. Teresa Jradowska, Supr.; Srs.: 11

ENDOWMENTS / FOUNDATIONS / TRUSTS [EFT]

PISCATAWAY

The Foundation for Catholic Education - 146 Metlars Ln., Piscataway, NJ 08854; Mailing: P.O. Box 191, Metuchen, NJ 08840 t) 732-562-1990 Carol Purcell, Contact;

The Fund for the Future, Inc. - 146 Metlars Ln.,

Piscataway, NJ 08854; Mailing: P.O. Box 191, Metuchen, NJ 08840 t) 732-562-1990

The Priestly Education Fund, Inc. - 146 Metlars Ln., Piscataway, NJ 08854; Mailing: P.O. Box 191, Metuchen, NJ 08840 t) 732-562-1990

HOSPITALS / HEALTH SERVICES [HOS]

NEW BRUNSWICK

Saint Peter's University Hospital - 254 Easton Ave., New Brunswick, NJ 08901 t) 732-745-8600 lhirsch@saintpetersuh.com www.saintpetershcs.com Leslie D. Hirsch, Pres. & CEO; Dcn. Vincent C. Brigande, Dir., Pastoral Care; Rev. A. David Chalackal, C.M.I., Chap.; Rev. Peter Suhaka, Chap.; Dcn. William P. Weber Jr., Chap.; Bed Capacity: 478; Asstd. Annu.: 119,610; Staff: 3,415

MISCELLANEOUS [MIS]

NEW BRUNSWICK

Saint Peter's Healthcare System, Inc. - 254 Easton Ave., New Brunswick, NJ 08901 t) 732-745-8600 x8581 lhirsch@saintpetersuh.com www.saintpetershcs.com Leslie D. Hirsch, Pres. & CEO;

Saint Peter's Foundation - t) (732) 745-8542 spfoundation@saintpetersuh.com www.saintpetershcs.com\donate Emily Lyssikatos, Dir.; James Choma, Vice President for Catholic Mission and Chief Development Officer;

Saint Peter's Health & Management Services Corporation - t) (732) 745-8600 x8588

Saint Peter's Properties Corporation, Inc. - t) (732) 745-8600 x8588

OXFORD

The Anawim Community - 354 Jonestown Rd., Oxford, NJ 07863-3137 t) 908-453-3886 oxford@anawim.com www.anawim.com Rev. Daniel H. Healy, Dir.; Rev. Richard M. Rusk, Dir.;

PISCATAWAY

The Retirement Plan for the Priests of the Diocese of Metuchen - 146 Metlars Ln., Piscataway, NJ 08854; Mailing: P.O. Box 191, Metuchen, NJ 08840 t) 732-562-1990 Carol Purcell, Contact;

SOMERSET

The Center for Great Expectations, Inc. - 19 B Dellwood Ln., Somerset, NJ 08873 t) 732-247-7003 x356 (V. Finlay, Dir. of Dev.) pegw@cge-nj.org; rsmith@cge-nj.org www.cge-nj.org Care for substance use and mental health disorders Peg Wright, Pres.;

WATCHUNG

All-Africa Conference: Sister to Sister, Inc. - 1645 U.S. Hwy. 22 W., Mount Saint Mary, Watchung, NJ 07069 c) 732-539-2171 rjeffries@aacss.net www.allafrica-sistertosister.org Provides assistance and support to Women Religious in Sub-Saharan Africa. Sr. Rosemary Elizabeth Jeffries, RSM, Exec.;

WOODBRIDGE

Mt. Carmel Home Nursing Service - 184 Amboy Ave., Woodbridge, NJ 07095 t) 732-277-8569 info@stjosephseniorhome.com Sr. Maria Dziuban, L.S.I.C., Dir.;

MONASTERIES AND RESIDENCES FOR PRIESTS AND BROTHERS [MON]

EDISON

Brothers of the Sacred Heart - 103 Buchanan Rd., Edison, NJ 08820; Mailing: 4600 Elysian Fields Ave., New Orleans, LA 70122 t) 504-301-4758 unitedstatesprovince@gmail.com Bro. Daniel St. Jacques, S.C., Dir.; Bro. Richard Leven, S.C., In Res.; Bro. Gary Humes, S.C., In Res.; Brs.: 3

NORTH BRUNSWICK

Consolata Society for Foreign Missions - 2624 Rte. 27, North Brunswick, NJ 08902; Mailing: P.O. Box 5550, Somerset, NJ 08875-5550 t) 732-297-9191 cimcrao@aol.com www.consolata.us Rev. Paolo Fedrigoni, I.M.C., Moderator; Rev. Timothy Kinyua Gatitu, I.M.C., Mem.; Rev. James Kingori, I.M.C. (Kenya), Mem.; Priests: 3

RARITAN

Clairvaux House - 52 W. Somerset St., Raritan, NJ 08869 t) 908-300-8167 blessedsacrametnshrine@blessedsacramentshrine.org blessedsacramentshrine.com Rev. Peter R. Cebulka, C.O., Rector; Rev. John Fredy Triana Beltran, C.O., Vice Rector; Priests: 2

The Raritan Congregation of the Oratory of St. Philip Neri - 45 Anderson St., Raritan, NJ 08869 t) 908-725-1008 oratorians@raritanoratory.org www.raritanoratory.org Rev. Jeffrey Calia, C.O., Supr.; Rev. Peter Cebulka, C.O., Vicar; Rev. Thomas A. Odorizzi, C.O., Secy.; Rev. Kevin Kelly, C.O., Mem.; Rev. John Fredy Triana Beltran, C.O., Mem.; Bro. Steven Bolton, Mem.; Brs.: 1; Priests: 5

SOMERSET

Maria Regina Residence - 5 Dellwood Ln., Somerset, NJ 08873 t) 732-828-6800 Retirement home for Diocesan priests. Rev. John C. Gloss; Rev. Msgr. Edward M. O'Neill; Rev. Msgr. Robert J. Zamorski; Rev. Marco A. Caceres; Rev. Vincent P. Chen; Rev. George A. Farrell; Rev. Henry L. Hemmerling; Rev. John R. Pringle; Rev. Daniel Sloan; Rev. Louis F. Stingel; Rev. Edward J. Struzik; Rev. A. Gregory Uhrig; Priests: 11

STEWARTSVILLE

Society of Jesus Christ the Priest - 70 Edison Rd., Stewartsville, NJ 08886; Mailing: PO Box 157, Stewartsville, NJ 08886 t) 908-213-1447 meadwater@slsonline.org; rnacarino@slsonline.org Rev. Lope Pascual de La Parte, SJS, Dir.; Rev. Bonfilio Enriquez, SJS, Assoc. Pst.; Rev. Jose Lorente, Assoc. Pst.; Rev. Raymond L. Nacarino, SJS, Treas.; Priests: 4

NURSING / REHABILITATION / CONVALESCENCE / ELDERLY CARE [NUR]

WOODBRIDGE

St. Joseph Assisted Living - 1 St. Joseph Ter., Woodbridge, NJ 07095 t) 732-634-0004 Sr. Zdzislawa Krukowska, L.S.I.C., Admin.; Asstd. Annu.: 49; Staff: 56

St. Joseph Nursing Home - 3 St. Joseph Ter., Woodbridge, NJ 07095 t) 732-750-0077 Sr. Teresa Gradowska, Supr.; Sr. Elzbieta Lopatka, L.S.I.C., Admin.;

RETREAT HOUSES / RENEWAL CENTERS [RTR]

BELVIDERE

Augustinian Recollect Sisters - 20 Manunka Chunk Rd., Belvidere, NJ 07823 t) 908-475-9947 Mother Beatriz Aguirre Oro, Supr.; Sr. Beatriz Garcia Sanchez, Subprior;

FLEMINGTON

Our Lady of Providence (Little Sisters of the Poor) - 31 Britton Dr., Flemington, NJ 08822 t) 908-581-4297 fllsp@littlesistersofthepoor.org Sr. Bernice Marie, l.s.p., Dir.;

WATCHUNG

Mt. St. Mary House of Prayer - 1651 U.S. Hwy. 22, Watchung, NJ 07069-6587 t) 908-753-2091 msmhope@msmhope.org www.msmhope.org Retreat House Sr. Laura Arvin, O.P., Dir.; Sr. Eileen P. Smith, R.S.M., Assoc. Dir.;

SHRINES [SHR]

ASBURY

National World Apostolate of Fatima, USA, Inc. National Blue Army Shrine of Our Lady of Fatima Dedicated to the Immaculate Heart of Mary - 674 Mountain View Rd. E., Asbury, NJ 08802; Mailing: P.O. Box 976, Washington, NJ 07882 t) 908-689-1700 vendoradmin9722@bluearmy.com www.bluearmy.com David Carollo, Exec. Dir.;

RARITAN

Shrine Chapel of the Blessed Sacrament - 50 W. Somerset St., Raritan, NJ 08869 t) 908-300-8167 blessedsacramentshrine@blessedsacramentshrine.org blessedsacramentshrine.com Associated with Clairvaux House Rev. Peter R. Cebulka, C.O., Rector; Rev. John Fredy Triana Beltran, C.O., Vice Rector;

Archdiocese of Miami

(Archidioecesis Miamiensis)

MOST REVEREND THOMAS G. WENSKI

Archbishop of Miami; ordained May 15, 1976; appointed Titular Bishop of Kearney and Auxiliary Bishop of Miami June 24, 1997; ordained September 3, 1997; appointed Coadjutor Bishop of Orlando cum jure successionis, July 1, 2003; welcomed August 22, 2003; took office as fourth Bishop of Orlando November 13, 2004; appointed Archbishop of Miami April 20, 2010; installed June 1, 2010.

Pastoral Center: 9401 Biscayne Blvd., Miami Shores, FL 33138. T: 305-757-6241; F: 305-754-1897.

information@theadom.org; www.miamiarch.org

ESTABLISHED AUGUST 13, 1958.

Square Miles 4,958.

Created an Archbishopric, June 13, 1968.

Comprises the Counties in the southern part of the State of Florida, namely, Broward, Miami-Dade and Monroe.

For legal titles of Parishes and Archdiocesan institutions, consult the Pastoral Center.

MOST REVEREND ENRIQUE DELGADO

Auxiliary Bishop of Miami; ordained June 29, 1996; appointed Titular Bishop of Aquae Novae in Proconsulari and Auxiliary Bishop of Miami October 12, 2017; ordained December 7, 2017.

STATISTICAL OVERVIEW

Personnel

Archbishops....1
Retired Archbishops....1
Auxiliary Bishops....1
Priests: Diocesan Active in Diocese....149
Priests: Diocesan Active Outside Diocese....3
Priests: Retired, Sick or Absent....80
Number of Diocesan Priests....232
Religious Priests in Diocese....25
Total Priests in your Diocese....257
Extern Priests in Diocese....42

Ordinations:

Diocesan Priests....3
Transitional Deacons....6
Permanent Deacons in Diocese....121
Total Brothers....37
Total Sisters....210

Parishes

Parishes....102

With Resident Pastor:

Resident Diocesan Priests....90
Resident Religious Priests....12
Missions....6
Pastoral Centers....1

Professional Ministry Personnel:

Brothers....13
Sisters....28
Lay Ministers....156

Welfare

Catholic Hospitals....5
Total Assisted....871,139
Health Care Centers....5
Total Assisted....483,149
Homes for the Aged....6
Total Assisted....4,120
Day Care Centers....15
Total Assisted....3,465
Specialized Homes....1
Total Assisted....249
Special Centers for Social Services....19
Total Assisted....196,817
Residential Care of Disabled....3
Total Assisted....646
Other Institutions....7
Total Assisted....10,253

Educational

Seminaries, Diocesan....2
Students from This Diocese....23
Students from Other Dioceses....25
Diocesan Students in Other Seminaries....27
Total Seminarians....50
Colleges and Universities....2
Total Students....13,370
High Schools, Diocesan and Parish....8
Total Students....9,189
High Schools, Private....5
Total Students....4,058
Elementary Schools, Diocesan and Parish....48
Total Students....19,444
Elementary Schools, Private....2
Total Students....538
Non-residential Schools for the Disabled....1
Total Students....26

Catechesis/Religious Education:

High School Students....2,534
Elementary Students....15,825
Total Students under Catholic Instruction....65,034

Teachers in Diocese:

Priests....17
Scholastics....1
Brothers....13
Sisters....28
Lay Teachers....2,740

Vital Statistics

Receptions into the Church:

Infant Baptism Totals....8,505
Minor Baptism Totals....623
Adult Baptism Totals....335
Received into Full Communion....629
First Communions....6,125
Confirmations....5,482

Marriages:

Catholic....1,320
Interfaith....114
Total Marriages....1,434
Deaths....3,519
Total Catholic Population....487,506
Total Population....4,676,170

LEADERSHIP

Office of the Archbishop - t) 305-762-1231 Most Rev. Thomas G. Wenski (archbishop@theadom.org);
Priest Secretary to the Archbishop - t) (305) 762-1232 Rev. Ryan Saunders (priestsecretary@theadom.org);
Pastoral Center - t) 305-762-1220 www.miamiarch.org/
Vicar General - t) 305-762-1194 Most Rev. Enrique Delgado, Auxiliary Bishop & Vicar Gen. (edelgado@theadom.org);
Chancellor for Canonical Affairs - t) 305-762-1221; 305-762-1262 c) 786-604-6453 Msgr. Dariusz J. Zielonka (dzielonka@theadom.org);
Chancellor for Administration and Chief Operating Officer - t) 305-762-1284 c) 305-450-6420 Sr. Elizabeth Anne Worley, S.S.J. (eworley@theadom.org);
Consultors - Most Rev. Enrique Delgado (edelgado@theadom.org); Msgr. Dariusz J. Zielonka (dzielonka@theadom.org); Msgr. Pablo A. Navarro (rector@sjvcs.edu);
Priests' Personnel Board - Msgr. Pablo A. Navarro, Chair (rector@sjvcs.edu); Most Rev. Enrique Delgado, Auxiliary Bishop (edelgado@theadom.org); Rev. Michael W. Davis;
Deans and Deaneries -
- **East Dade Deanery** - Very Rev. Luis Roger Largaespada;
- **Monroe Deanery** - Very Rev. John C. Baker;
- **Northeast Broward Deanery** - Very Rev. Michael J. Greer;
- **Northeast Dade Deanery** - Very Rev. Christopher B. Marino;
- **Northwest Broward Deanery** - Very Rev. Kenneth D. Whittaker;
- **Northwest Dade Deanery** - Very Rev. Israel E. Mago;
- **South Dade Deanery** - Very Rev. Jose N. Alfaro;
- **Southeast Broward Deanery** - Very Rev. Javier Barreto Medina;
- **Southwest Broward Deanery** - Very Rev. Ernest Biriruka;
- **West Dade Deanery** - Very Rev. Marcos A. Somarriba;

Presbyteral Council -
- **President** - Most Rev. Thomas G. Wenski;
- **Chairman** - Rev. Michael W. Davis;
- **Secretary** - Rev. Bryan Anthony Garcia;
- **Ex Officio** - Most Rev. Enrique Delgado, Vicar Gen. & Auxiliary Bishop; Msgr. Dariusz J. Zielonka, Chancellor; Msgr. Pablo A. Navarro, Seminary Rector;
- **Age Group I** - Rev. Ivan Maximiliano Rodriguez;
- **Age Group II** - Msgr. Michael A. Souckar;
- **Age Group III** - Rev. Juan J. Sosa;
- **Incardinated Priests** - Rev. Michael W. Davis;
- **Religious Priests** - Rev. Eduardo Alvarez, S.J. (Cuba);
- **Non-Incardinated Priests** - Rev. Juan Antonio Tupiza (Ecuador);
- **Incardinated Retired Priests** - Rev. Federico Capdepon;
- **Appointed by the Archbishop** - Very Rev. Jose N. Alfaro; Very Rev. John C. Baker; Very Rev. Javier Barreto Medina;

Archdiocesan Attorney - t) 305-443-9162 Patrick Fitzgerald;

ADMINISTRATION

Chancellor / Chief Operating Officer - t) 305-762-1284 Sr. Elizabeth Anne Worley, S.S.J. (eworley@theadom.org);
Finance Office - t) 305-762-1242 Michael A. Casciato, CFO (mcasciato@theadom.org);
Building and Property Office - t) 305-762-1032 David Prada, Senior Dir. (dprada@theadom.org); Carlos Sanabria, Project Mgr. (csanabria@theadom.org);
Human Resources Office - t) 305-762-1201 Lisa Pinto, Senior Dir. (lpinto@theadom.org);
- **Archdiocese of Miami Health Plan Trust** - t) 305-762-3001 Sr. Elizabeth Anne Worley, S.S.J., Vice Chair, Trust Bd.; Susan Waddell, Dir.;
- **Pension** - t) 954-527-1616 Most Rev. Thomas G. Wenski; Msgr. Kenneth K. Schwanger, Chair; Pam Painter, Plan Admin.;
- **Safe Environment Program** - t) 305-762-1043 Mary Ross Agosta, Dir.; Peter Routsis-Arroyo, Victim Asst. Coord.;
- **Fingerprinting Office** - t) 305-762-1059

Office of Ecumenical and Inter-Faith Relations - t) 305-762-1254 Rev. Patrick O'Neill, Dir.;

CANONICAL SERVICES

Metropolitan Tribunal - t) 305-762-1161 tribunal@theadom.org
- **Judicial Vicar** - Msgr. Gregory C. Wielunski;
- **Adjutant Judicial Vicar** - Msgr. Michael A. Souckar;
- **Judges** - Rev. Francis Cancro; Rev. Emmanuel J. Essiet; Rev. Jude O. Ezeanokwasa (Nigeria);
- **Promoter of Justice** - Msgr. Kenneth K. Schwanger;
- **Defenders of the Bond** - Rev. Ivan Carrillo-Paris, A.I.C.; Chorbishop Michael G. Thomas; Rev. Juan Antonio Tupiza (Ecuador);
- **Notaries** - Goretti Anthony; Maite Lenoz;
- **Assessor** - Roberto Aguirre;
- **Advocates** - Pauline Cervantes; Charles D'Como; Juan Del Sol;
- **Counsel-Assistant to the Tribunal** - t) 305-443-9162 x17 J. Patrick Fitzgerald, Archdiocesan Attorney;

CATHOLIC CHARITIES

Catholic Charities of the Archdiocese of Miami (corporate listing in INSTITUTIONS section) - t) 305-754-2444 www.ccadm.org Peter Routsis-Arroyo, CEO (parroyo@ccadm.org); Msgr. Roberto Garza, Chair (rgarza@paxcc.org); Jules Jones, CFO (jjones@ccadm.org);
- **Counseling Services** - t) (866) 758-0025 counseling@ccadm.org
- **Centro Hispano Catolico** - t) 305-573-9093 centrohispano@ccadm.org; feccentrohispano@ccadm.org
- **Good Shepherd Child Development Center** - t) 305-235-1756 goodshepherd@ccadm.org
- **Holy Redeemer Child Development Center** - t) 305-836-4971 holyredeemer@ccadm.org
- **Notre Dame Child Development Center** - t) 305-751-6778 notredame@ccadm.org
- **Sagrada Familia Child Development Center** - t) 305-324-5424 sagradafam@ccadm.org
- **South Dade Child Development Center** - t) 305-245-0979 southdade@ccadm.org
- **Unaccompanied Refugee Minors Program** - t) 305-883-3383 urmp@ccadm.org
- **Unaccompanied Minors Programs** - t) 305-380-0141 ump@ccadm.org
- **Boystown of Florida** - t) (954) 315-2601 Peter Routsis-Arroyo, CEO;
- **Refugee Resettlement and Employment Services** - t) 305-883-4555 refugee@ccadm.org
- **Homeless Prevention/Rapid Re-Housing, Miami Dade** - t) 305-573-3333
- **Homeless Prevention/Rapid Re-Housing, Broward** - t) (954) 630-9793 browardhousingservices@ccadm.org
- **Homeless Prevention/Rapid Re-Housing, Monroe** - t) 305-272-9790
- **New Life Family Center, Miami Dade** - t) 305-573-3333 newlife@ccadm.org
- **St. Bede's Village, Monroe** - t) 305-292-9790 stbedes@ccadm.org
- **Theresa House, Monroe** - t) 305-292-9790
- **Pierre Toussaint Haitian Center, Miami** - t) (305) 573-3333 pierretoussaint@ccadm.org
- **Elderly Services Congregate Meals, Miami Dade** - t) 305-751-5203 congregatemeals@ccadm.org
- **Wilton Manors, Broward** - t) 954-630-9501 browardelderly@ccadm.org
- **St. Luke's Center of Miami / Substance Abuse Program** - t) 305-795-0077 stlukes@ccadm.org

CLERGY AND RELIGIOUS SERVICES

Vicar for Priests - t) 305-318-9938 Msgr. Roberto Garza, Vicar (rgarza@paxcc.org);
Office for Permanent Diaconate - t) 305-762-1024 Dcn. Victor M. Pimentel, Dir. (vpimentel@theadom.org);
Permanent Diaconate Advisory Board - Most Rev. Thomas G. Wenski (archbishop@theadom.org); Msgr. Kenneth K. Schwanger, Chair; Dcn. Victor M. Pimentel (vpimentel@theadom.org);
Office for Religious - t) 305-762-1082 Sr. Ana Margarita Lanzas, S.C.T.J.M., Dir. (alanzas@theadom.org);
Vocations Office - t) 305-762-1137 Rev. Matthew Gomez, Dir. (mgomez@theadom.org);
Vocations Review Board - Very Rev. Jose N. Alfaro; Rev. Manuel Alvarez; Dcn. Ernesto Del Riego;
Serra Club Miami-Dade - t) 305-321-7947 Peter Jude, Pres. (petertjude@gmail.com); Rev. Matthew Gomez, Chap. (mgomez@theadom.org); Rev. Elvis Antonio Gonzalez, Chap. (EGonzalez@stmacs.org);
Serra Club Broward - c) 207-831-0385 Rev. Sahayanathan Nathan, Chap. (frnathan@stagathaonline.org); Malcolm Meikle, Pres. (malcolm@meikle.com);

COMMUNICATIONS

Communications - Media Relations - t) 305-762-1043 Mary Ross Agosta, Dir. (mragosta@theadom.org); Maria Alejandra Rivas, Media Coord. & Digital Media Specialist (mrivas@theadom.org);
The Florida Catholic - t) 305-762-1131 Ana Rodriguez-Soto, Editor (arsoto@theadom.org);
La Voz Catolica - Ana Rodriguez-Soto, Exec. (arsoto@theadom.org); Rocio Granados, Editor (rgranados@theadom.org);

COMMUNITY SERVICES

Catholic Health Services - t) 954-484-1515 www.catholichealthservices.org/ Aristides Pallin, CEO (apallin@chsfla.com); Ralph Lawson, Chair (ralphlawsoncpa@gmail.com);
- **See INSTITUTIONS section for listing of Skilled Nursing and Assisted Living facilities and services provided** -
- **See INSTITUTIONS section for a listing of Rehabilitation Hospitals and outpatient services provided** -
- **See INSTITUTIONS section for Hospice and Home Health Care services provided** -
- **See INSTITUTIONS section for listing of Senior Housing facilities and services provided** -

Archdiocesan Cemeteries - Mary Jo Frick, Exec. Dir. (mjfrick@chsfla.com);
- **Our Lady of Mercy Cemetery, Miami-Dade County** - t) 305-592-0521 Maria Trujillo, Mgr.;
- **Our Lady Queen of Heaven Cemetery, Broward County** - t) 954-972-1234 Ofelia Spardy, Mgr.;

CONSULTATIVE BODIES

Finance Council - t) 305-762-1242 Most Rev. Thomas G. Wenski (archbishop@theadom.org); Sr. Elizabeth Anne Worley, S.S.J. (eworley@theadom.org); Sean Clancy;

EDUCATION

Office of Catholic Schools - t) 305-762-1070 Dr. Jim Rigg, Supt. (jrigg@theadom.org); Brenda Cummings, Asst. Supt. (bcummings@theadom.org); Dr. Donald Edwards, Asst. Supt. (dedwards@theadom.org);
Archdiocese of Miami and Private Catholic High Schools, see listing in INSTITUTIONS Section -
Marian Center School and Services, see listing in INSTITUTIONS section - t) 305-200-8927
Archdiocese of Miami Catholic Virtual School, see listing in INSTITUTIONS Section -
Office of Catechesis - t) 305-762-1090 Sr. Karen Muniz, S.C.T.J.M., Dir. (kmuniz@theadom.org);
Office of Lay Ministry - t) 305-762-1187
Centro Mater Child Care Services - t) 305-357-4395 Aristides Pallin, CEO (apallin@chsfla.com); Madelyn Rodriguez-Llanes, Exec. Dir.;

Centro Mater Child Care Center - t) 305-545-6049 Soledad Serrano, Prog. Admin.;
Centro Mater Child Care Center II - t) 305-545-6049 Soledad Serrano, Prog. Admin.;
Centro Mater Walker Park - t) 305-887-1140 Jaime Caro, Prog. Mgr.;
Centro Mater West Child Care Center - Julietta Riveron-Bello, Prog. Dir.;
Centro Mater West II Child Care Center - t) 305-362-9701 Dayra Pla, Prog. Dir.;

PASTORAL SERVICES

Office of Evangelization and Parish Life - t) (305) 762-1140 Susanna Diaz, Mgr. (sdiaz@theadom.org); Stephen Colella (scolella@theadom.org);
Office of Marriage and Family Life - t) 305-762-1123 Claudia Shaw, Mgr. (cshaw@theadom.org);
Respect Life Ministry - t) 954-981-2922 info@respectlifemiami.org www.respectlifemiami.org Angela Curatalo, Dir. (acuratalo@theadom.org);
Project Joseph Men's Ministry - projectjoseph@pregnancyhelpsfl.org
Project Rachel - t) (954) 981-2984 projectrachel@theadom.org
Respect Life Pregnancy Help Centers - information@pregnancyhelpsfl.org www.pregnancyhelpsfl.org
Central Broward Pregnancy Help Center - t) 954-565-0229
South Broward Pregnancy Help Center - t) 954-963-2229
South Dade Pregnancy Help Center - t) 305-273-8508; 305-273-8507 southdadepregnancyhelp@gmail.com
Office of Youth and Young Adult Ministry - t) 305-762-1123 Stephen Colella, Dir. (scolella@theadom.org);
Scouting - t) 305-762-1245 Dcn. Emilio Blanco, Chap.;
Office of Campus Ministry - t) 305-762-1123 Stephen Colella, Dir. (scolella@theadom.org);
Campus Ministry - Directory of Universities -
Barry University - Rev. Cristobal Torres, O.P., Chap.; Karen J. Stalnaker, Dir. Campus Ministry;
FIU - University Park Campus - Rev. Luis Pavon, Campus Min.; Very Rev. Marcos A. Somarriba, Dir. Campus Ministry;
St. Thomas University - Rev. Rafael Capo, Vice Pres., Mission;
University of Miami - Rev. Richard J. Vigoa, Pst.; Michelle Ducker-Lopez, Assoc. Campus Min.;
Mission Office - t) (305) 762-1140 Stephen Colella, Dir. (scolella@theadom.org);
Society for the Propagation of the Faith - Msgr. Dariusz J. Zielonka, Dir.;
Holy Childhood Association - Msgr. Dariusz J. Zielonka, Dir.;
Ministry of Worship and Spiritual Life - t) 305-762-1104 Rev. Richard J. Vigoa, Dir. (rvigoa@theadom.org);
Committee on Popular Piety - t) 305-866-6567 Rev. Juan J. Sosa, Chair;
Liturgical Music - t) 305-759-4531 Gustavo Zayas, Dir.;
Sacred Art & Architecture - t) 305-635-1331 corpuschristi@corpuschristimiami.org Rev. Jose Luis Menendez;
Office of Black Catholic Ministry - t) 305-762-1120 blackcatholicministry@theadom.org Katrenia C. Reeves-Jackman, Dir.;
Rural Life Ministry - t) 305-258-6998 Rev. Rafael Cos, Dir.;
Cristo Rey South Dade Camp Chapel -
Everglades San Juan Diego Chapel -
St. Ann Mission - misionsantaananaranja@gmail.com www.misionsantaana.org Rev. Rafael Cos, Pst.;
Redland Camp Chapel -
Apostleship of the Sea -
Airport Ministry - t) 305-372-0250 reception@blessed-trinity.org
Port Everglades Seafarer's House - t) 954-734-1580 c) 305-283-7207 Rev. Peter Yunping Lin (China), Chap.; Dcn. Randy Millikin; Dcn. Gerald McGuinn;
Stella Maris Seamen Center, Port of Miami - t) 305-372-0250 Rev. Roberto M. Cid, Chap.;
Ministry to the Deaf or Disabled - Schott Memorial Center - t) 954-434-3306 www.schottcommunities.org Ileana Ramirez-Cueli, Exec. Dir.;
Ministry for Catholic Law Enforcement -
City of Miami Beach - Dcn. Jose Antonio Santos, Chap.;
City of Miami Police - Rev. Elvis Antonio Gonzalez, Chap.; Rev. Reginald Jean-Mary, Chap.;
Neocatechumenal Way - Rev. Edivaldo Da Silva Oliviera (Brazil), Responsible (father.edivaldo@gmail.com);
Ministry to (Non-Hispanic) Cultural Groups - t) 305-872-2537 Rev. Jesus S. (Jets) Medina, Dir. (frjets@stpeterbpk.org);
Brazilian and Portuguese Apostolate - t) 954-972-0434 stvincentcatholicchurch@gmail.com www.stvincentcatholicchurchmargate.org Rev. Isaia Birollo, C.S.;
Caribbean Apostolate - Prince Smith, (Jamaica); John West, (Trinidad & Tobago);
Chinese Apostolate - Rev. Peter Yunping Lin (China); Bernadette Chik;
Filipino Apostolate - t) 954-907-0299 Janet Macasero, Coord.;
Haitian Apostolate - Rev. Reginald Jean-Mary; Annette Decius;
Indian Apostolate - t) 630-202-2989 Rev. John Thomas;
Italian Apostolate - Very Rev. Christopher B. Marino;
Korean Apostolate - t) 954-474-9091 miamikoreanmission@gmail.com Rev. Sukhun Koo (Korea), Chap.;
Nigerian Apostolate - t) 305-705-2010 Rev. Fidelis Nwankwo, C.S.Sp. (Nigeria);
Polish Apostolate - t) 954-946-6347 Rev. Hubert Zasada, S.Ch.R. (Poland);
Vietnamese Apostolate - t) 954-374-9100 Rev. Joseph Long Nguyen; Tam Truong;
Knights of Columbus (English and Spanish) - t) 305-762-1161 www.floridakofc.org Msgr. Gregory C. Wielunski, Chap. (gwielunski@theadom.org);
Prison Ministry - t) 305-762-1093 Dcn. Edgardo Farias, Dir. (efarias@theadom.org);
Radio Paz - t) 305-638-9729 Msgr. Roberto Garza, Gen. Mgr. (rgarza@paxcc.org);

STEWARDSHIP

Archdiocese of Miami Development and Stewardship Office - t) 305-762-1053 Katie Blanco Bourdeau, Exec. Dir. (kblancobourdeau@theadom.org);

MISCELLANEOUS / OTHER OFFICES

Amor en Accion (Love in Action) - t) 305-762-1226 amor.en.accion@theadom.org Carlos Cueto, Dir.;
Catholic Legal Services - t) 305-373-1073 Randolph P. McGrorty, CEO (rmcgrorty@cclsmiami.org);
Downtown Senior Citizens' Community Center at Gesu Church - t) 305-374-6099 Sr. Julia Barreto, O.P.; Sr. Maria Isabel Rincon, O.P.;

PARISHES, MISSIONS, AND CLERGY

STATE OF FLORIDA

BIG PINE KEY

St. Peter Catholic Church - 31300 Overseas Hwy., Big Pine Key, FL 33043 t) 305-872-2537 frjets@stpeterbpk.org; nancy@stpeterbpk.org www.stpeterbpk.org Rev. Jesus S. (Jets) Medina, Pst.; Rosalinda Hally, CRE; Rowena Garcia-Frank, RCIA Coord.; CRP Stds.: 20

CORAL GABLES

St. Augustine - 1400 Miller Rd., Coral Gables, FL 33146 t) 305-661-1648 education@saintaugustinechurch.org; mgarcia@saintaugustinechurch.org www.saintaugustinechurch.org Rev. Richard J. Vigoa, Pst.; Rev. Leandro Freitas Siqueira, Par. Vicar; Rev. Oscar Perez-Dudamel (Venezuela), Par. Vicar; Dcn. Jose Chirinos; Diana Rojas, DRE; CRP Stds.: 198
Little Flower - 2711 Indian Mound Tr., Coral Gables, FL 33134 t) 305-446-9950; 305-446-9950 x307 (CRP) jsantibanez@cotlf.org; frmanny@cotlf.org Rev. Manuel Alvarez, Pst.; Rev. Andrew James Tomonto, Par. Vicar; Rev. Juan Escamez, In Res.; Rev. Stephen Sawuaan, In Res.; Rev. Fidelis Uko, In Res.; Dcn. Roberto Fleitas; Dcn. Miguel Parlade; Dcn. Jorge Alvarez; Jorge Santibanez, DRE; CRP Stds.: 279
Little Flower School - (Grades PreK-8) 2701 Indian Mound Tr., Coral Gables, FL 33134 t) 305-446-1738 principal@stscg.org stscg.org Sr. Rosalie Nagy, O.C.D., Prin.; Stds.: 904; Sr. Tchrs.: 3; Lay Tchrs.: 48

CORAL SPRINGS

St. Andrew - 9950 N.W. 29th St., Coral Springs, FL 33065-6103 t) 954-752-3950; (954) 905-6322 (CRP); 954-905-6332 (CRP) parish@saccs.org; bcastro@saccs.org www.standrewparish.org Msgr. Michael A. Souckar, Pst.; Rev. Isaac Arickappalil (India), Par. Vicar; Rev. Yosbany Alfonso, Par. Vicar; Dcn. Frank Gonzalez; Dcn. Stephen Rynkiewicz; Beatriz Castro, DRE; Cecelia Sousa, DRE; CRP Stds.: 337
St. Andrew School - (Grades PreK-8) 9990 N.W. 29th St., Coral Springs, FL 33065 t) 954-753-1280 khughes@saccs.org www.standrewcatholicschool.com Kristen Hughes, Prin.; Stds.: 333; Lay Tchrs.: 31
St. Elizabeth Ann Seton - 1401 Coral Ridge Dr., Coral Springs, FL 33071 t) 954-753-3330; 954-345-7071 (CRP) setonparishoffice@seasrc.org; setonre@seasrc.org www.stelizabethannseton.org Rev. Edward M. Kelly, Pst.; Rev. Mathew Varghese (India), Par. Vicar; Gladys Jacobs, DRE; CRP Stds.: 304

DANIA

St. Maurice at Resurrection - 441 N. E. 2nd St., Dania, FL 33004 t) 954-961-7777; (954) 547-4562 (CRP) saintmauriceatresurrection.org Rev. Luis R. Rivera, Pst.; Ashley Ronnan, DRE; CRP Stds.: 38

DAVIE

St. Bonaventure - 1301 S.W. 136th Ave., Davie, FL 33325-4300 t) 954-236-7981; 954-424-9504 cdaiber@stbonaventurechurch.com; smccrea@stbonaventurechurch.com www.stbonaventurechurch.com Rev. Edmond Prendergast, Pst.; Dcn. Joseph M. Pearce; Dcn. Nestor Cardenas; Dcn. Stephen James Pyle; Dcn. Domingo Vasquez; Susan McCrea, DRE; CRP Stds.: 732
St. Bonaventure School - (Grades PreK-8) t) 954-476-5200 sbcs.weconnect.com/ Lisa Kempinski, Prin.; Stds.: 701; Lay Tchrs.: 38
Saint David - 3900 S. University Dr., Davie, FL 33328 t) 954-475-8046 stdavidchurch@saintdavid.org; mcarterwaren@yahoo.com Rev. Steven O'Hala, Pst.; Rev. Joseph Kottayil, Par. Vicar; Rev. Edivaldo Da Silva Oliviera (Brazil), In Res.; Char Lea Gutierrz, DRE; Dr. Mary Carter Waren, RCIA Coord.; CRP Stds.: 188
Saint David School - (Grades PreK-8) t) 954-472-7086 schoolinformation@saintdavid.org www.saintdavid.org Michelle Chimineti, Prin.; Breanna Becker, Vice Prin.; Stds.: 394; Lay Tchrs.: 33

DEERFIELD BEACH

St. Ambrose - 380 S. Federal Hwy., Deerfield Beach, FL 33441 t) 954-427-2225 stambrosedeerfield@yahoo.com; mcguinnjerry@yahoo.com stambrosedeerfieldbeach.com Rev. Dariusz Zarebski, S.D.S (Canada), Pst.; Rev. Long Do, Par. Vicar; Dcn. Randy Millikin; CRP Stds.: 72

St. Ambrose School - (Grades PreK-8) 363 S.E. 12th Ave., Deerfield Beach, FL 33441 t) 954-427-2226 principal.stambrose@gmail.com stambrosecs.org Lisa Dodge, Prin.; Stds.: 205; Lay Tchrs.: 15

Our Lady of Mercy - 5201 N. Military Tr., Deerfield Beach, FL 33064 t) 954-421-3246 ourladyofmercycatholicchurch.org Very Rev. Kenneth D. Whittaker, Pst.; Dahlia Steele-Huie, DRE; CRP Stds.: 39

DORAL

Our Lady of Guadalupe - 11691 N.W. 25 St., Doral, FL 33172 t) 305-593-6123; 305-593-6123 x204 (CRP) info@guadalupedoral.org; miguel.ruiz@guadalupedoral.org www.guadalupedoral.org Very Rev. Israel E. Mago, Pst.; Rev. Mebounou Gbedey (Brazil), Par. Vicar; Rev. Alexander Narvaez (Colombia), Par. Vicar; Dcn. Manuel Jimenez; Dcn. William Bertot, Admin.; Dcn. Vincente Crespo; Dcn. Alvaro Velasco; Miguel Ruiz, DRE; CRP Stds.: 1,090

FORT LAUDERDALE

St. Anthony - 901 N.E. 2nd St., Fort Lauderdale, FL 33301 t) 954-463-4614; 954-467-7749 (CRP) churchoffice@stanthonyftl.org www.saintanthonyfl.org Rev. Michael Grady, Pst.; Rev. Jeremy Lully, Par. Vicar; Patricia Solenski, DRE; CRP Stds.: 137

St. Anthony School - (Grades PreK-8) 820 N.E. Third St., Fort Lauderdale, FL 33301 t) 954-467-7747 j.mcintosh@stanthonyftl.org www.saintanthonyschoolfl.org Jenna McIntosh, Prin.; Stds.: 435; Lay Tchrs.: 27

St. Clement - 2975 N. Andrews Ave., Fort Lauderdale, FL 33311 t) 954-563-1183; 954-563-2838 (CRP) stclement@ymail.com; stclement@ymail.com Rev. Patrick Charles, Pst.; Sr. Anne Stinfil, DRE; CRP Stds.: 93

St. Jerome - 2533 S.W. 9th Ave., Fort Lauderdale, FL 33315 t) 954-525-4133; 954-525-4133 x3040 (CRP) church@stjfl.org stjfl.org Rev. Joseph Maalouf, Pst.; CRP Stds.: 58

St. Jerome School - 2601 S.W. 9th Ave., Fort Lauderdale, FL 33315 t) 954-524-1990 office@stjfl.org; school@stjfl.org www.stjfl.org Tara Marino, Prin.; Stds.: 190; Lay Tchrs.: 16

St. John the Baptist Catholic Church - 4595 Bayview Dr., Fort Lauderdale, FL 33308 t) 954-771-8950 church@stjohncc.org www.stjohncc.org Rev. Patrick J. Naughton, Par. Vicar; Rev. Edgardo S. De Los Santos, Par. Admin.; Meg Cairns, CRE; CRP Stds.: 145

Our Lady Queen of Martyrs - 2731 S.W. 11 Ct., Fort Lauderdale, FL 33312 t) 954-583-8725 pastor@ourlqm.com; olqmbulletins@gmail.com www.ourlqm.com Rev. Ivan Maximiliano Rodriguez, Pst.; Regina Medina, DRE; CRP Stds.: 110

Our Lady Queen of Martyrs School - (Grades PreK-8) 2785 S.W. 11th Ct., Fort Lauderdale, FL 33312 t) 954-583-8112 ourlqm.com Althea Mossop, Prin.; Stds.: 320; Lay Tchrs.: 16

St. Pius X - 2500 N.E. 33rd Ave., Fort Lauderdale, FL 33305; Mailing: 2511 N. Ocean Blvd., Ft Lauderdale, FL 33305 t) 954-564-1763 office@stpiusxfl.org www.stpiusxfl.org Rev. Jean Jadotte, Pst.; Dcn. Philip J. Newton;

St. Sebastian - 2000 S.E. 25th Ave., Fort Lauderdale, FL 33316 t) 954-524-9344 info@stsebastianfl.org; annie@stsebastianfl.org www.stsebastianfl.org Msgr. James F. Fetscher, Pst.; Anne M. Gardner, DRE; CRP Stds.: 8

HALLANDALE BEACH

St. Matthew - 542 Blue Heron Dr., Hallandale Beach, FL 33009 t) (954) 458-1590; (954) 458-0612 (Religious Education) lois@smatt.org; pastor@smatt.org www.smatt.org Rev. Lazarus J. Govin, Pst.; Barbara Woroniecki, DRE; CRP Stds.: 52

Our Lady of La Vang Vietnamese Catholic Mission - 123 N.W. 6th Ave., Hallandale Beach, FL 33009 t) 954-374-9100; 954-665-7572 (CRP) longknguyen14@gmail.com; bnc7897@gmail.com Rev. Joseph Long Nguyen, Pst.; Kim Chung Nguyen, DRE; CRP Stds.: 250

HIALEAH

St. Benedict - 701 W. 77th St., Hialeah, FL 33014 t) 305-558-2150; 305-557-2511 (CRP) sori.stbenedictreled@gmail.com Rev. Julio Enrique De Jesus, Pst.; Dcn. Emilio Blanco; Dcn. Carlos Ramirez; Sori Govin, DRE; CRP Stds.: 61

St. Cecilia - 1040 W. 29th St., Hialeah, FL 33012 t) 305-883-0003; 786-355-5423 (CRP) saintceciliacatholicchurch@gmail.com Rev. Emanuele DeNigris (Italy), Pst.; Rev. Pedro Luis Durango Agudelo, Par. Vicar; Lisellot Casasnovas, DRE; CRP Stds.: 62

Immaculate Conception - 4497 W. First Ave., Hialeah, FL 33012 t) 305-822-2011; 305-823-9563 (CRP) icrectory@icsmiami.org; nstanley@icsmiami.org Rev. Rolando Cabrera (Cuba), Pst.; Rev. Enzo Rosario Prendes, Par. Vicar; Dcn. Manuel Alfonso; Dcn. Felix Gonzalez; Nubia Stanley, DRE; CRP Stds.: 205

Immaculate Conception School - (Grades PreK-8) 125 W. 45th St., Hialeah, FL 33012 t) 305-822-6461 icschool@miamiarch.org Victoria Leon, Prin.; Stds.: 340; Lay Tchrs.: 25

St. John the Apostle - 475 E. 4th St., Hialeah, FL 33010 t) 305-888-9769 sjamiami@gmail.com www.sjamiami.com/ Rev. Hector A. Perez, Pst.; Rev. Julio Fernandez Triana, Par. Vicar; Janet Quintana, DRE; CRP Stds.: 58

St. John the Apostle School - t) 305-888-6819 bacosta@sjacs.org www.sjacs.org/ Bianca Acosta, Prin.; Stds.: 170; Lay Tchrs.: 12

Mother of Our Redeemer - 8445 N.W. 186th St., Hialeah, FL 33015 t) (786) 480-9858 (CRP); (305) 829-6141 lmartorella@motherofourredeemer.org www.motherofourredeemer.org Rev. Juan P. Hernandez-Alonso (Spain), Pst.; Dcn. Orlando Rojo; Liliana Martorella, DRE; CRP Stds.: 185

Mother of Our Redeemer School - (Grades PreK-8) t) (305) 829-3988 acasariego@moorsch.org www.moorsch.org Ana Casariego, Prin.; Stds.: 277; Lay Tchrs.: 14

San Lazaro - 4400 W. 18 Ave., Hialeah, FL 33012 t) 305-556-1717; 305-558-4078 (CRP) mquintana@sanlazaro17.org sanlazaro17.org Rev. Luis A. Perez, Pst.; Dcn. Jorge Arencibia; Dcn. Carlos Lamas; Dcn. Miguel Benitez; Maritza Bonachea, DRE; CRP Stds.: 102

Santa Barbara - 6801 W. 30th Ave., Hialeah, FL 33018 t) 305-556-4442; 305-556-4442 x104 (CRP) info@santabarbaradn.org santabarbaradn.org Rev. Alvaro Huertas (Colombia), Pst.; Sr. Monica Sanchez Espindola, DIC, DRE; CRP Stds.: 170

HOLLYWOOD

St. Bernadette - 7450 Stirling Rd., Hollywood, FL 33024 t) 954-432-5313; 954-432-6300 (CRP) dbuschman@stbernadettefl.com; sstettner@stbcs.org www.saintbernadettefl.org Rev. Biju Vells, Pst.; Rev. Mario Avila Vivero (Chile), Par. Vicar; Stacey Stettner, DRE; CRP Stds.: 82

St. Bernadette School - (Grades PreK-8) t) (954) 432-7022 principal@stbcs.org Maria Wagner, Prin.; Stds.: 190; Lay Tchrs.: 14

Little Flower - 1805 Pierce St., Hollywood, FL 33020 t) 954-922-3517 susan@littleflowerhollywood.org littleflowerhollywood.org Very Rev. Javier Barreto Medina, Pst.; Rosalie Modzelewski, DRE; CRP Stds.: 96

Little Flower School - (Grades PreK-8) 1843 Pierce St., Hollywood, FL 33020 t) 954-922-1217 macosta@littleflowerleopards.com littleflowerhollywood.org/school/ Omayra Roy, Prin.; Stds.: 163; Sr. Tchrs.: 1; Lay Tchrs.: 15

Nativity - 5220 Johnson St., Hollywood, FL 33021 t) 954-987-3300; 954-987-3300 x203 (CRP) office@nativityhollywood.org; victoria@nativityhollywood.org www.nativityhollywood.org Rev. Robert M. Ayala, Pst.; Rev. Victor J. Babin, Par. Vicar; Rev. Victor Garcia (Dominican Republic), Par. Vicar; Dcn. Timothy Smith; Dcn. Jorge Reyes; Victoria Molina, DRE; CRP Stds.: 152

Nativity School - (Grades PreK-8) 5200 Johnson St., Hollywood, FL 33021 t) 954-987-3301 x221 office@nativitysch.com www.nativityknights.com Heidi Suero, Prin.; Judy Skehan, Vice Prin.; Stds.: 813; Lay Tchrs.: 42

HOMESTEAD

Sacred Heart - 106 S.E. First Dr., Homestead, FL 33030-7322 t) 305-247-4405 x230 www.sacredhearthomestead.org Rev. Robes C. Charles, Pst.; Rev. Manuel Galvan Vargas, Vicar; Dcn. Alpha Fleurimond; Dcn. Ramon Grille; Sebastian Zapata, Youth Min.; Mary See, DRE; CRP Stds.: 304

KEY BISCAYNE

St. Agnes - 100 Harbor Dr., Key Biscayne, FL 33149 t) 305-361-2351; 305-361-1378 (CRP) info@stagneskb.org www.stakb.org Rev. Juan Carlos Paguaga, Pst.; Rev. Andrzej Foltyn (Poland), Par. Vicar; Dcn. Edgardo Farias; Sr. Maria Andrea Oliver, S.C.T.J.M., DRE; Anabel Stevens, Bus. Mgr.; CRP Stds.: 386

St. Agnes School - (Grades PreK-8) 122 Harbor Dr., Key Biscayne, FL 33149 t) 305-361-3245 ctorres@stagneskb.us; jfleitas@stagneskb.us stakb.org Jorge Fleitas, Prin.; Isabela Morales, Vice Prin.; Cristina Torres, Registrar; Stds.: 479; Sr. Tchrs.: 2; Lay Tchrs.: 36

KEY LARGO

St. Justin Martyr - 105500 Overseas Hwy., Key Largo, FL 33037 t) 305-451-1316 parishsecretary@sjmkeylargo.org Rev. Stephen J. Hilley, Pst.; CRP Stds.: 63

KEY WEST

St. Mary Star of the Sea Basilica - 1010 Windsor Ln., Key West, FL 33040 t) 305-294-1018 stmary@stmarykeywest.com www.stmarykeywest.com Very Rev. John C. Baker, Pst.; Rev. Feliere Louis, C.S., Par. Vicar; Dcn. Peter H. Batty; Dcn. Robert Magnuson; CRP Stds.: 42

The Basilica School of Saint Mary Star of the Sea - (Grades PreK-9) 700 Truman Ave., Key West, FL 33040 t) 305-294-1031 office@basilicaschool.com www.basilicaschoolkeywest.com Robert M. Wright, Prin.; Stds.: 396; Sr. Tchrs.: 2; Lay Tchrs.: 28

Star of the Sea Outreach Mission - 5640 Mac Donald Ave., Key West, FL 33040 t) 305-292-3013 thomasmcallahan@gmail.com Thomas Callahan, Contact;

St. Mary, Star of the Sea Convent, Holy Spirit Sisters - t) (305) 294-1018 Sr. Elizabeth Gati, Contact;

LAUDERDALE LAKES

St. Helen - 3033 N.W. 33rd Ave., Lauderdale Lakes, FL 33311 t) 954-731-7314 x1002; 954-731-7314 (CRP) dphan@sainthelen.net; fatherlucien@sainthelen.net www.sthelencatholicchurch.net Rev. Lucien Eugene Pierre, Pst.; Sr. Duong Therese Phan, DRE; CRP Stds.: 206

Saint Helen Catholic School - (Grades PreK-8) 3340 W. Oakland Park Blvd., Fort Lauderdale, FL 33311 t) 954-739-7094 fbarrat@sainthelen.net; fbarrat@sainthelen.net Farah Barrat, Prin.; Stds.: 206; Sr. Tchrs.: 3; Lay Tchrs.: 14

LAUDERDALE-BY-THE-SEA

Assumption Church - 2001 S. Ocean Blvd., Lauderdale-by-the-Sea, FL 33062 t) 954-941-7647 gallman.assumption@gmail.com; m.costa@assumptionlauderdale.org www.assumptionlauderdale.org Very Rev. Michael J. Greer, Pst.; CRP Stds.: 19

LEISURE CITY

St. Martin de Porres Catholic Church - 14881 S.W. 288th St., Leisure City, FL 33033 t) 305-248-5355 stmartindeporrescc@gmail.com www.stmartindeporrescc.org Rev. Joaquin Rodriguez, Pst.; Dcn. Santos Rodriguez; Debbie Serrano, DRE; CRP Stds.: 481

LIGHTHOUSE POINT

St. Paul the Apostle - 2700 N.E. 36th St., Lighthouse

Point, FL 33064 t) 954-943-9154; 954-943-9155; 954-571-3852 (CRP) stpaultheapostlechurch@gmail.com; lorimilano@comcast.net stpaulslhp.org Msgr. William Dever, Pst.; Rev. Mathew Padickal Thomas (India), Par. Vicar; Lori Milano, DRE; CRP Stds.: 63

MARATHON

San Pablo - 550 122nd St. Ocean, Marathon, FL 33050 t) 305-289-0636 (Parish) c) (305) 731-3343 (Office Mgr.) info@sanpablomarathon.org; faithformation-children@sanpablomarathon.org www.sanpablomarathon.org Rev. Kris Bartos, Par. Admin.; Therese Walters, DRE; CRP Stds.: 34

MARGATE

St. Vincent - 6350 N.W. 18th St., Margate, FL 33063-2320 t) 954-972-0434 stvincentcatholicchurch@gmail.com www.stvincentcatholicchurchmargate.org Rev. Carlos Andres Reyes, CS (Mexico), Pst.; Rev. Hugo Santana Cardoso, C.S., Par. Vicar; Rev. Isaia Birollo, C.S., In Res.; Blanca Hernandez, O.P., DRE; CRP Stds.: 245

Our Lady Aparecida Mission -

MIAMI

St. Mary's Cathedral - 7525 N.W. 2nd Ave., Miami, FL 33150 t) 305-759-4531 frontoffice@thecathedralofstmary.org www.thecathedralofstmary.org Very Rev. Christopher B. Marino, Rector; Rev. Reynold Brevil, Par. Vicar; Rev. Oswaldo Agudelo, In Res.; Rev. Matthew Gomez, In Res.; Dcn. Sergio Rodicio, Bus. Mgr.; Dcn. Raul Flores; Sr. Teresa Urioste, SCTJM, DRE; CRP Stds.: 10

St. Mary's Cathedral School - (Grades K-8) 7485 N.W. 2nd Ave., Miami, FL 33150 t) 305-795-2000 info@stmarycathedralschool.org www.stmarycathedralschool.org/ Julie Perdomo, Prin.; Stds.: 414; Bro. Tchrs.: 2; Lay Tchrs.: 24

St. Mary's Cathedral Foundation Trust - 9401 Biscayne Blvd., Miami Shores, FL 33138 t) 305-762-1242 mcasciato@theadom.org Michael A. Casciato, Contact;

St. Agatha - 1111 S.W. 107th Ave., Miami, FL 33174 t) 305-222-1500; 305-222-8067 (CRP) pauline@stagathaonline.org stagathaonline.org Very Rev. Marcos A. Somarriba, Pst.; Rev. Luis Pavon, Par. Vicar; Rev. Raul S. Soutuyo, In Res.; Dcn. Ernesto Del Riego; Dcn. Santos Feliciano; Dcn. Hector Norat; Sr. Teresa Urioste, SCTJM, DRE; CRP Stds.: 160

St. Agatha School - (Grades PreK-8) 1125 S.W. 107th Ave., Miami, FL 33174 t) 305-222-8751 office@stagathaonline.com school.stagathaonline.org Patricia Hernandez, Prin.; Stds.: 363; Lay Tchrs.: 23

St. Brendan - 8725 S.W. 32nd St., Miami, FL 33165 t) 305-221-0881; 305-221-2861 (CRP) pastor@sbrendan.org www.stbrendanmiami.org Rev. Miguel A. Sepulveda, Pst.; Rev. Juan Alberto Gomez Franyutty, Par. Vicar; Gerardo Gonzalez, DRE; CRP Stds.: 94

St. Brendan School - (Grades PreK-8) 8755 S.W. 32 St., Miami, FL 33165 t) 305-221-2722 mcapote@stbrendanmiami.org Maria Cristina Capote-Alonso, Prin.; Stds.: 874; Lay Tchrs.: 59

St. Catherine of Siena - 9200 S.W. 107th Ave., Miami, FL 33176 t) 305-274-6333; 305-274-6333 x229 (CRP) hfujita@scsmiami.org; fr.tolosa@scsmiami.org www.scsmiami.org/ Rev. Armando Tolosa, Par. Admin.; Dcn. Raimundo Santos Matos; Dcn. Jose Villena, DRE; CRP Stds.: 191

Christ the King - 16000 S.W. 112th Ave., Miami, FL 33157 t) 305-238-2485; 305-235-0293 (CRP) ctkcatholic@bellsouth.net; alphaglardia@yahoo.com ctkcatholicmiami.com Rev. Joseph Jean-Louis, Pst.; Dcn. George Gibson; Dcn. Alpha Fleurimond, DRE; CRP Stds.: 27

Corpus Christi - 3220 N.W. 7th Ave., Miami, FL 33127 t) 305-635-1331 corpuschristi@corpuschristimiami.org www.corpuschristimiami.org Rev. Jose Luis Menendez, Pst.; Rev. Adelson Silvestre Moreira, Par. Vicar; Rev. Federico Capdepon, In Res.; Rev. John O'Leary, In Res.; Dcn. Antonio Perez; Sr. Carmen Alvarez, R.M.I., DRE; CRP Stds.: 402

San Francisco y Santa Clara - 402 N.E. 29th St., Miami, FL 33137; Mailing: 3220 N.W. 7 Ave., Miami, FL 33127 t) (305) 635-1331

San Juan Bautista - 3116 N.W. 2nd Ave., Miami, FL 33127; Mailing: 3220 N.W. 7th Ave., Miami, FL 33127 t) (305) 635-1331

Nuestra Senora de Altagracia - 1779 N.W. 28th St., Miami, FL 33142; Mailing: 3220 N.W. 7th Ave., Miami, FL 33127 t) (305) 635-1331

La Milagrosa - 1860 N.W. 18th Ter., Miami, FL 33125; Mailing: 3220 N.W. 7th Ave., Miami, FL 33127 t) (305) 635-1331

St. Robert Bellarmine - 3405 N.W. 27th Ave., Miami, FL 33142; Mailing: 3220 N.W. 7th Ave., Miami, FL 33127 t) (305) 635-1331

St. Dominic - 5909 N.W. 7th St., Miami, FL 33126 t) 305-264-0181 elogiste@gmail.com; stdominicmiami2020@gmail.com www.stdominicmiami.com Rev. Eduardo Logiste, O.P. (Dominican Republic), Pst.; Rev. Orlando Cardozo, O.P. (Colombia), Par. Vicar; Robert Cruz, DRE; CRP Stds.: 113

Epiphany - 8080 S.W. 54 Ct., Miami, FL 33143 t) 305-667-4911; 305-665-0037 (CRP) info@epiphanycatholicchurch.com epiphanycatholicchurch.com Rev. Jose Alvarez, Pst.; Rev. Ireneusz Ekiert, Par. Vicar; Dcn. Thomas V. Eagan; Dcn. Jose Martinez; Dcn. Marcos Perez; Dcn. Norman Ruiz-Castaneda; Dcn. Eduardo Smith; Susana Yllanes, DRE; CRP Stds.: 176

Epiphany School - (Grades PreK-8) 5557 S.W. 84th St., Miami, FL 33143 t) 305-667-5251 www.epiphanycatholicschool.com Ana Oliva, Prin.; Stds.: 797; Lay Tchrs.: 78

Church of the Epiphany Parish Endowment Trust - 9401 Biscayne Blvd., Miami Shores, FL 33138 t) 305-762-1294 mcasciato@theadom.org Michael A. Casciato, Contact;

Gesu - 118 N.E. 2nd St., Miami, FL 33132 t) 305-379-1424; 305-374-6099 (CRP) gesuchurch@yahoo.com gesuchurch.org Rev. Eduardo Alvarez, S.J. (Cuba), Pst.; Rev. Sergio Figueredo, S.J. (Cuba), Par. Vicar; Dcn. William Bertot; Sr. Julia Barreto, O.P., DRE; CRP Stds.: 24

Good Shepherd - 14187 S.W. 72nd St., Miami, FL 33183 t) 305-385-4320 sue@gscatholic.org; angelica@gscatholic.org www.gscatholic.org Rev. Jesus J. Arias, Pst.; Rev. Jaime Antonio Guardado Delgado (El Salvador), Par. Vicar; Dcn. Guillermo Dutra; Angelica Martinez, CRE; CRP Stds.: 493

Good Shepherd School - (Grades PreK-8) t) 305-385-7002 www.good-shepherd-school.org Melissa Hernandez, Prin.; Stds.: 226; Lay Tchrs.: 25

Holy Redeemer - 1301 N.W. 71st St., Miami, FL 33147 t) 305-691-1701 www.holyredeemercatholicchurch.com Rev. Alexander Ekechukwu, C.S.Sp. (Nigeria), Pst.; Bernadette Poitier, DRE; CRP Stds.: 14

St. Hugh - 3460 Royal Rd., Miami, FL 33133 t) (305) 444-8363 (Main Office) sthughchrurch@st-hugh.org sthughmiami.org Very Rev. Luis Roger Largaespada, Pst.; Rev. Paul Pierce, Par. Vicar; Dcn. Frank Alvarez Gil; Patricia Zapatero, DRE; CRP Stds.: 206

St. Hugh School - (Grades PreK-8) t) 305-448-5602 sthugh@sthugh.org www.sthughmiami.org Mary E. Fernandez, Prin.; Stds.: 297; Lay Tchrs.: 30

St. James - 540 N.W. 132nd St., Miami, FL 33168 t) 305-681-7428 businessmanager@stjamesnorthmiami.org www.stjamesnorthmiami.org Msgr. Chanel Jeanty, Pst.; Rev. Edwin Diesen, Par. Vicar; CRP Stds.: 42

St. James School - (Grades PreK-8) 601 N.W. 131st St., North Miami, FL 33168 t) 305-681-3822 admin@stjamesmiami.net; lori.bryant@stjamesmiami.net stjamesmiami.net Lori Bryant, Prin.; Stds.: 444; Lay Tchrs.: 26

St. Joachim - 11740 S.W. 192nd St., Miami, FL 33177 t) 305-233-1278 parish@stjoachimcc.org www.saintjoachimmiami.org Msgr. Roberto Garza, Pst.; Rev. Ivan Toledo (Cuba), Par. Vicar; Gloria Torres, DRE; CRP Stds.: 169

St. John Bosco - 1349 W. Flagler St., Miami, FL 33135; Mailing: 1358 N.W. 1 St., Miami, FL 33125 t) 305-649-5464 religiouseducation@sjbmiami.org Rev. Yader F. Centeno, Pst.; Rev. Salvador Diaz Guerra (Cuba), Par. Vicar; Dcn. Alfredo Valle; Sr. Monica Arguello, DRE; CRP Stds.: 198

St. John Neumann - 12125 S.W. 107th Ave., Miami, FL 33176 t) 305-255-6642; 305-253-3081 (CRP) parishoffice@sjn-miami.org; dre@sjn-miami.org www.sjn-miami.org Very Rev. Jose N. Alfaro, Pst.; Rev. Cesar Yohel Betancourt Suriel, Par. Vicar; Rev. Nicholas Rafael Toledo, D., Par. Vicar; Dcn. Marco Fernandez; Dcn. Ralph Gazitua; Dcn. Jose Felipe Gomez; Dcn. Jose M. Naranjo; Dcn. Louis Phang Sang; John Fernandez, DRE; CRP Stds.: 528

St. John Neumann School - 12115 S.W. 107th Ave., Miami, FL 33176 t) 305-255-7315 info@sjncs.org www.sjncs.org Cristina R Rodriguez, Prin.; Stds.: 362; Lay Tchrs.: 28

St. Kevin - 12525 S.W. 42nd St., Miami, FL 33175 t) 305-223-0633 (Parish); 305-223-2469 (Rel. Ed. Prog.) stkevin@stkevinchurch.org; reled@stkevinrep.org Rev. Jesus Saldana, Pst.; Rev. Miguel Angel Blanco, Par. Vicar; Dcn. Robert B. Dinsmore; Dcn. Michael Fresneda; Daniel Mercado, DRE; CRP Stds.: 347

St. Kevin School - (Grades PreK-8) 4001 S.W. 127 Ave., Miami, FL 33175 t) 305-227-7571 stkevin@stks.org www.stks.org Dr. Mayra R. Constantino, Prin.; Dr. Sharyn D. Henderson, Vice Prin.; Stds.: 674; Lay Tchrs.: 62

St. Kieran - 3605 S. Miami Ave., Miami, FL 33133 t) 786-254-2543 secretary@stkierancatholicchurch.org; principal@ilsroyals.com www.stkierancatholicchurch.org Rev. Jesus Ferras, I.S.P. (Cuba), Pst.; Rev. Carlos J. Cabrera, In Res.; Sr. Kim Keraitis, FMA, DRE; Rev. Sterling Laurent, In Res.; CRP Stds.: 45

St. Michael the Archangel - 2987 W. Flagler St., Miami, FL 33135 t) 305-649-1811; 305-649-1811 x7011 (CRP) agonzalez@stmacs.org; ramonrivero@stmacs.org www.stmichaelmiami.org Rev. Elvis Antonio Gonzalez, Pst.; Rev. Esney Munoz (Cuba), Par. Vicar; Dcn. Ernesto Rodriguez; Ramon Rivero, DRE; CRP Stds.: 240

St. Michael the Archangel School - (Grades PreK-8) 300 N.W. 28th Ave., Miami, FL 33125 t) 305-642-6732 fermo@stmacs.org stmacs.org Lissette Naranjo, Prin.; Stds.: 363; Lay Tchrs.: 36

Mother of Christ - 14141 S.W. 26th St., Miami, FL 33175 t) 305-559-0163 (CRP); 305-559-6111 ccd@motherofchrist.net; info@motherofchrist.net motherofchrist.info/ Rev. Jorge A. Carvajal (Colombia), Par. Admin.; Rev. James Arriola, Vicar; Dcn. Enrique Ferrer; Dcn. Jose Leroy Martinez; Dcn. Jose F. Rosado; Sylvia Lopez, DRE; CRP Stds.: 250

Mother of Christ School - (Grades PreK-8) t) 786-497-6111 moc.principal@motherofchrist.net www.motherofchristcatholicschool.net Yesenia De La Torre, Prin.; Stds.: 254; Lay Tchrs.: 20

Notre Dame d'Haiti - 110 N.E. 62nd St., Miami, FL 33138 t) 305-751-6289 info@notredamedhaiti.org www.notredamedhaiti.org Rev. Reginald Jean-Mary, Par. Admin.; Rev. Youry Jules (Haiti), Par. Vicar; Dcn. Mesmin Augustin; Rosel Lebreton, DRE; CRP Stds.: 165

Our Lady of Divine Providence - 10205 W. Flagler St., Miami, FL 33174 t) 305-551-8113 x104 (CRP); 305-551-8113 zmurgado@oldpmiami.org; office@oldpmiami.org www.oldpmiami.org Rev. Enrique J. Estrada, Pst.; Rev. Pedro M. Corces, Par. Vicar; Dcn. Eduardo Panellas; Zoila M. Murgado, DRE; CRP Stds.: 220

Our Lady of Lourdes - 11291 S.W. 142nd Ave., Miami, FL 33186 t) 305-386-4121 doris@ololourdes.org; sandra@ololourdes.org Msgr. Kenneth K. Schwanger, Pst.; Rev. Alberto Jose Chavez Godoy, Par. Vicar; Rev.

Francisco Garcia Fernandez, Par. Vicar; Dcn. Erick Cinco; Dcn. Jorge Matamala; Dcn. Michael Plummer; Dcn. Ricardo Rauseo; Dcn. Isidoro Villa; CRP Stds.: 403

Our Lady of Lourdes School - (Grades PreK-8) 14000 S.W. 112th St., Miami, FL 33186 t) 305-386-8446 thalfaker@ololjaguars.org www.ololjaguars.org Thomas Halfaker, Prin.; Stds.: 573; Lay Tchrs.: 30

SS. Peter and Paul - 900 S.W. 26th Rd., Miami, FL 33129 t) 305-858-2621 elvylengyel@gmail.com; ltm310@yahoo.com www.stspeter-paul.weebly.com Rev. Luis Flores, Admin.; Rev. Darwin Daniel Ramirez La Cruz (Venezuela), Par. Vicar; Rev. Juan Luis Sanchez, In Res.; Dcn. Steven Lee; Leyla Mazpule, DRE; CRP Stds.: 60

SS. Peter and Paul School - (Grades PreK-8) 1435 S.W. 12th Ave., Miami, FL 33129 t) 305-858-3722 jzlatkin@stspeter-paul.org www.stspeter-paul.org Jocelyn Zlatkin, Prin.; Stds.: 340; Lay Tchrs.: 24

Prince of Peace - 12800 N.W. 6th St., Miami, FL 33182 t) 305-559-3171; 305-559-3171 x110 (CRP) ccd@popmiami.net; info@popmiami.net www.popmiami.net Rev. Giovanni de Jesus Pena, Pst.; Dcn. Jorge Prieto; Dcn. Lazaro Ulloa; Vivian Lorenzo, DRE; CRP Stds.: 119

St. Raymond - 3475 S.W. 17th St., Miami, FL 33145 t) 305-446-2427; 305-646-1130 (CRP) pastor@straymondchurch.com; officemanager@straymondchurch.com www.straymondchurch.com Rev. Francisco J. Hernandez, Pst.; Dcn. Eduardo Blanco; Sr. Elena A. Castillo, S.C.T.J.M., DRE; CRP Stds.: 165

St. Thomas the Apostle Church - 7377 S.W. 64th St., Miami, FL 33143 t) 305-665-5600; 305-665-6862 (CRP) pastor@stamiami.org; mcahensol@stamiami.org www.stamiami.org Rev. Alejandro J. Rodriguez Artola, Pst.; Rev. Adonis Gonzalez Betancourt, Par. Vicar; Dcn. Carlos Charur Jr.; Dcn. Carlos Pulido; Dcn. Sebastian Grisales; CRP Stds.: 138

St. Thomas the Apostle School - (Grades PreK-8) 7303 S.W. 64th St., c/o St. Thomas the Apostle Parish, Miami, FL 33143 t) 305-661-8591 x301 lfigueredo@stamiami.com stamiami.org Lisa Figueredo, Prin.; Stds.: 556; Lay Tchrs.: 45

St. Timothy - 5400 S.W. 102nd Ave., Miami, FL 33165 t) 305-274-8224; 305-274-8225 (CRP) frontdesk@sainttimothycatholic.org; frvega@sainttimothycatholic.org www.sainttimothycatholic.org Rev. Carlos Vega, Pst.; Rev. Angel Renato Calderon Espinoza, Par. Vicar; Rev. Alberto Petroff (Argentina), Par. Vicar; Dcn. Nelson Diaz; Dcn. Fernando Bestard; Annie Seiglie, Parish Life Coord.; Hilda Bonet, DRE; CRP Stds.: 262

St. Timothy School - (Grades PreK-8) t) 305-274-8229 information@sttimothymiami.org www.sttimothymiami.org Susana T. Rivera, Prin.; Stds.: 482; Sr. Tchrs.: 1; Lay Tchrs.: 29

Sister Carolyn Learning Center - t) 305-274-8229 information@sttimothymiami.org www.sttimothymiami.org PreK-2 and PreK-3 Barbara Perdomo, Dir.;

Visitation - 100 N.E. 191st St., Miami, FL 33179 t) 305-652-3624 ccddre@visitationmiami.org; office@visitationmiami.org www.visitationmiami.org Msgr. George Puthusseril, Pst.; Roslyn Taylor, DRE; CRP Stds.: 14

MIAMI BEACH

St. Francis de Sales - 621 Alton Rd., Miami Beach, FL 33139 t) 305-672-0093; 305-767-6582 (CRP) secretary@saintfrancisonthebeach.com www.saintfrancisonthebeach.com Rev. Juan Alberto Aviles, Par. Admin.; Dcn. Jose Irrizarry; Alicia Martinez, DRE; CRP Stds.: 77

St. Joseph - 8670 Byron Ave., Miami Beach, FL 33141 t) 305-866-6567; 305-866-6566 (CRP) framirez@stjosephmiamibeach.com; glodos@stjosephmiamibeach.com www.stjosephmiamibeach.com Rev. Juan J. Sosa, Pst.; Rev. Juan Rumin Dominguez, Par. Vicar; Dcn. John T. Ermer; Dcn. Roberto Pineda; Gipsy Lodos, DRE; CRP Stds.: 163

St. Patrick - 3716 Garden Ave., Miami Beach, FL 33140 t) 305-531-1124 parish@stpatrickmiamibeach.com stpatrickmiamibeach.com Rev. Roberto M. Cid, Pst.; Rev. Fernando Carmona (Argentina), Par. Vicar; Dcn. James Dugard; Dcn. Tony Santos; Dcn. Adrian Zapatero; CRP Stds.: 100

St. Patrick School - (Grades K-8) 3700 Garden Ave., Miami Beach, FL 33140 t) 305-534-4616 school@stpatrickmiamibeach.com www.stpatrickmiamibeach.com Bertha Moro, Prin.; Stds.: 300; Lay Tchrs.: 31

MIAMI GARDENS

St. Monica - 3490 N.W. 191st St., Miami Gardens, FL 33056 t) 305-621-9846 pastor@saintmonica.org www.saintmonica.org Rev. Samuel Muodiaju, C.S.Sp. (Nigeria), Pst.; Rev. Alfred Cioffi, In Res.; Dcn. Marco Rosales; Auxiliadora Castillo, DRE; CRP Stds.: 45

St. Philip Neri Catholic Church - 15700 N.W. 20th Ave. Rd., Miami Gardens, FL 33054 t) 305-705-2010 stphilipneri15700@comcast.net stphilipnerimiamigardens.org Rev. Fidelis Nwankwo, C.S.Sp. (Nigeria), Pst.; Tricia Hendricks, DRE; CRP Stds.: 9

MIAMI LAKES

Our Lady of the Lakes - 15801 N.W. 67th Ave., Miami Lakes, FL 33014 t) 305-558-2202 mdelpozo@ollnet.com www.ollnet.com Rev. Flavio Montes Colon, Par. Admin.; Rev. Hector Perez, Par. Vicar; Dcn. Juan Gonzalez; Dcn. Luis Verdecia; Josefina Vazquez, DRE; CRP Stds.: 232

Our Lady of the Lakes School - 6600 Miami Lakeway N., Miami Lakes, FL 33014 t) 305-362-5315 bpicazo@ollnet.com Barbara Picazo, Prin.; Stds.: 563; Lay Tchrs.: 45

MIAMI SHORES

St. Martha - 9221 Biscayne Blvd., Miami Shores, FL 33138 t) 305-751-0005 frontoffice@stmarthamiami.com www.stmarthamiami.com Rev. Juan Carlos Salazar Gomez, Par. Admin.; Danilo Recinos, DRE; CRP Stds.: 56

St. Rose of Lima - 415 N.E. 105th St., Miami Shores, FL 33138 t) 305-758-0539 mpinder@srlschool.com; frgeorge@srlchurch.com www.stroseoflimamiamishores.org Rev. George Packuvettithara, Pst.; Rev. Juan Antonio Tupiza (Ecuador), Par. Vicar; Sr. Rachel Lucia Kottoor, SCTJM, DRE; CRP Stds.: 190

St. Rose of Lima School - (Grades PreK-8) 425 N.E. 105th St., Miami Shores, FL 33138 t) 305-751-4257 sbrown@srlschool.com www.srlschool.com Dr. Stephen Brown, Prin.; Stds.: 509; Sr. Tchrs.: 1; Lay Tchrs.: 29

MIRAMAR

St. Bartholomew - 8005 Miramar Pkwy., Miramar, FL 33025 t) 954-431-3600 office@stbartholomew.com; religiouseducation@stbartholomew.com www.stbartholomew.com Rev. Andrew Chan-A-Sue, Pst.; Rev. Pierre Listo Charles, Par. Vicar; Dcn. David Bowen; Dcn. Michel du Chaussee; Mercedes Brown, DRE; CRP Stds.: 110

St. Bartholomew School - (Grades PreK-8) 8003 Miramar Pkwy., Miramar, FL 33025 t) 954-431-5253 office@stbartschool.org Christine M. Gonzalez, Prin.; Stds.: 175; Lay Tchrs.: 14

Saint John XXIII Church - 16800 Miramar Pkwy., Miramar, FL 33027 t) 954-392-5062 popestjohn23@gmail.com www.john23parish.org Very Rev. Ernest Biriruka, Pst.; Rev. Pedro Torres Samudio, Par. Vicar; Dcn. Victor Lopez; Dcn. Ismar Martinez; Kathryn Cabrisas, DRE; CRP Stds.: 158

St. Stephen - 6044 S.W. 19th St., Miramar, FL 33023 t) 954-987-1100; 954-260-8169 (CRP) pastor@ststephenparish.net; joanne_day@bellsouth.net Rev. Franky Jean, Pst.; Rev. Freddy Alexander Yara, Par. Vicar; Dcn. Emilio Infante; Joann Day, DRE; CRP Stds.: 152

NARANJA

St. Ann Mission - 13875 S.W. 264th St., Naranja, FL 33032; Mailing: P.O. Box 924884, Princeton, FL 33092-4884 t) 305-258-6998 Rev. Rafael Cos, Pst.; Sr. Carmen Ors, DRE; CRP Stds.: 161

NORTH LAUDERDALE

Our Lady Queen of Heaven - 1400 S. State Rd. 7, North Lauderdale, FL 33068 t) 954-971-5400 olqhcc.org Rev. Kidney M. Saint Jean, Pst.; Dcn. Antonio Bobadilla; CRP Stds.: 145

NORTH MIAMI

Holy Family - 14500 N.E. 11 Ave., North Miami, FL 33161 t) 305-947-5043; 305-947-7739 (CRP) secretary.holyfamilynorthmiami@gmail.com www.holyfamilynorthmiami.com Rev. Fritzner Bellonce, Pst.; Dcn. Valentine Onuigbo; Kettly Alphonse, Youth Min.; CRP Stds.: 75

Holy Family School - (Grades PreSchool-8) 14650 N.E. 12th Ave., North Miami, FL 33161 t) 305-947-6535 ndaniel@holyfamilynorthmiami.org www.holynorthmiami.org Daniel Nyce, Prin.; Stds.: 275; Lay Tchrs.: 14

NORTH MIAMI BEACH

St. Lawrence - 2200 N.E. 191st St., North Miami Beach, FL 33180 t) 305-932-3560 religious.education@stlawrencemiami.org; frcletus@stlaw.org www.stlawrencemiami.org/ Rev. Cletus Oluwafemi Omode, Par. Admin.; Dcn. Clyde McFarland; Eliecer Moises Franchi, CRE; CRP Stds.: 134

St. Lawrence School - (Grades K-8) t) 305-932-4912 schooloffice@stlaw.org www.stlaw.org Dr. Stephanie Paguaga, Prin.; Stds.: 194; Lay Tchrs.: 13

Child Care Center - t) 305-932-5366 stlawrenceccc@stlawrencemiami.org www.stlawrencechildcarecenter.com Iliana Medolla, Dir.;

OAKLAND PARK

Blessed Sacrament - 1701 E. Oakland Park Blvd., Oakland Park, FL 33334 t) 954-564-1010 bscc1701@bellsouth.net blessedsacramentrcc.org Rev. Robert F. Tywoniak, Pst.; Dcn. Dan Blaha; CRP Stds.: 21

PALMETTO BAY

Our Lady of the Holy Rosary - St. Richard Church - 7500 S.W. 152nd St., Palmetto Bay, FL 33157 t) 305-233-8711 potero@hrsrcs.org; info@hrsrcs.org www.hrsrcs.org Rev. Daniel Houde, O.SS.T., Pst.; Dcn. Robert F. O'Malley Jr.; Paul Otero, DRE; CRP Stds.: 279

Our Lady of the Holy Rosary - St. Richard Catholic School - (Grades PreK-8) 18455 Franjo Rd., Cutler Bay, FL 33157 t) 305-235-5442 Floredenis Brown, Prin.; Stds.: 384; Lay Tchrs.: 24

PARKLAND

Mary Help of Christians Church - 5980 University Dr., Parkland, FL 33067 t) 954-323-8025 (CRP); 954-323-8012 parish@mhocrc.org mhocrc.org/ Rev. Harry Loubriel, Pst.; Rev. Julio R. Solano, Par. Vicar; Dcn. Charles Edel; Dcn. Ricardo Longueira; Dcn. Mark Luttio; CRP Stds.: 514

Mary Help of Christians Church School - (Grades PreK-8) 6000 University Dr., Parkland, FL 33067 t) 954-323-8006 panthers@mhocschool.org mhocschool.org Eric Palacio, Prin.; Stds.: 443; Lay Tchrs.: 29

PEMBROKE PINES

St. Boniface - 8330 Johnson St., Pembroke Pines, FL 33024 t) 954-432-2750 ehenchy@saintboniface.us; frgilberto@saintboniface.us www.saintboniface.us Rev. Fernando Orejuela, A.I.C. (Colombia), Pst.; Rev. Gilberto Amortegui, A.I.C, Par. Vicar; Dcn. Khatchig Chirinian; CRP Stds.: 75

St. Edward - 19000 Pines Blvd., Pembroke Pines, FL 33029 t) 954-436-7944; 954-436-7944 x213 (DRE) info@stedward.net; camille@stedward.net www.stedward.net Rev. Albert Lahens Jr., Par. Admin.; Rev. John Aduseh Poku (Ghana), Par. Vicar; Dcn. Carl R. Cramer; Camille Laurino, DRE; CRP Stds.: 283

St. Maximilian Kolbe - 701 N. Hiatus Rd., Pembroke Pines, FL 33026-4034 t) 954-885-7260 (CRP); 954-432-0206 reled@stmax.cc; office@stmax.cc www.stmax.cc Rev. Jeffrey McCormick, Pst.; Rev. Octavio Gomez (Colombia), Par. Vicar; Dcn. Carl Carrieri; Dcn. Pierre Douyon; Dcn. Scott Joiner; Dcn. Manuel Mendoza; Maryann Hotchkiss, DRE; CRP Stds.: 286

St. Maximilian Kolbe Pre-School - (Grades PreSchool-PreK) 601 N. Hiatus Rd., Pembroke Pines, FL 33026 t) 954-885-7250 preschool@stmax.cc www.stmax.cc/pres-school-2 Jimena Hibbard, Dir.; Stds.: 77; Lay Tchrs.: 14

PINECREST

St. Louis - 7270 S.W. 120th St., Pinecrest, FL 33156 t) 305-238-7562; 305-238-7562 x1500 (CRP) information@stlcatholic.org; mildred@stlcatholic.org stlcatholic.org Rev. Gabriel Vigues, Pst.; Rev. Elkin Sierra, Par. Vicar; Rev. Hector Troche (Dominican Republic), Par. Vicar; Dcn. Thomas Hanlon; Dcn. Alex Lam; Dcn. John Peremenis; Dcn. Mark Westman; Mildred Ratcliff, DRE; CRP Stds.: 472

St. Louis Covenant School - (Grades PreK-8) egarcia@stlcatholic.org Edward Garcia, Prin.; Stds.: 520; Lay Tchrs.: 36

PLANTATION

St. Gregory - 200 N. University Dr., Plantation, FL 33324 t) 954-473-6261 x1001; 954-473-8169 x1149 (CRP) avomvolakis@saintgreg.org; rectory@saintgreg.org www.saintgreg.org Rev. Michael W. Davis, Pst.; Rev. Agustin Estrada, Par. Vicar; Rev. Gustavo Barrios, Par. Vicar; Dcn. William Horton; Antonio Vomvolakis Jr., DRE; CRP Stds.: 241

St. Gregory School - (Grades PreSchool-8) dmasters@saintgreg.org; lyoung@saintgreg.org Lisa Young, Prin.; Stds.: 704; Lay Tchrs.: 44

POMPANO BEACH

St. Coleman - 1200 S. Federal Hwy., Pompano Beach, FL 33062 t) 954-942-3533 churchacct@stcoleman.org www.saintcoleman.org Rev. Michael A. Garcia, Pst.; Rev. Franklin Ifeanyichukwu Ekezie, Par. Vicar; Rev. Hans Chamorro, Par. Vicar; Edward Shannon Burns, DRE; CRP Stds.: 103

St. Coleman School - (Grades PreK-8) 2250 S.E. 12th St., Pompano Beach, FL 33062 t) 954-942-3500 admissions@stcoleman.org Lori St. Thomas, Prin.; Stds.: 474; Lay Tchrs.: 36

St. Elizabeth of Hungary Catholic Church - 3331 N.E. 10th Ter., Pompano Beach, FL 33064-5298 t) 954-941-8117; 954-943-6801 (CRP) stelizabeth@bellsouth.net; religioused.ste@att.net www.saintelizabethofhungary.org Rev. Fenly E. Saint-Jean (Haiti), Par. Admin.; Rev. Martin Munoz Escamilla, Par. Vicar; Dcn. Blaise Augustin; Dcn. Willie Harris Sr.; Alicia McDermott, Bus. Mgr.; Nadine Destine, DRE; CRP Stds.: 248

St. Joseph - 1210 N.W. 6th Ave., Pompano Beach, FL 33060; Mailing: 3331 NE 10th St., Pompano Beach, FL 33064 t) (954) 941-8117

St. Gabriel - 731 N. Ocean Blvd., Pompano Beach, FL 33062 t) 954-943-3684 st_gabriel@bellsouth.net Rev. Sahayanathan Nathan, Pst.;

St. Henry - 1500 S. Andrews Ave., Pompano Beach, FL 33069 t) 954-785-2450 amy@sainthenrys.org; pastor@sainthenrys.org www.sainthenrys.org Rev. Francis Akwue, C.S.Sp. (Nigeria), Pst.; Rev. Warren Escalona (Venezuela), Par. Vicar; Dcn. Eduardo Martinez; Gus Maldonado, DRE; CRP Stds.: 53

Our Lady of Czestochowa Mission - 2400 N.E. 12th St., Pompano Beach, FL 33062 t) 954-545-3861 polishchurch@bellsouth.net www.polishchurch.com Rev. Hubert Zasada, S.Ch.R. (Poland), Pst.; CRP Stds.: 51

San Isidro - 2310 Martin Luther King Blvd., Pompano Beach, FL 33069-1591 t) 954-971-8780 x201; 954-971-8780 x204 (CRP) fatherwilfredo@sanisidro.org; gildakawano@sanisidro.org www.sanisidro.org Rev. Wilfredo Contreras, Pst.; Rev. Pedro Freitez (Venezuela), Par. Vicar; Dcn. Vincent Eberling Jr.; Luz Lopez, DRE; CRP Stds.: 230

SOUTHWEST RANCHES

St. Mark - 5601 S. Flamingo Rd., Southwest Ranches, FL 33330 t) 954-434-3777; 954-252-9899 (CRP) religiondirector@stmarkparish.org; info@stmarkparish.org www.stmarkparish.org Rev. Jaime H. Acevedo, Pst.; Rev. Paul G. Karenga (Burkina Faso), Par. Vicar; Dcn. Jose Escudero; Dcn. Jose Manuel Gordillo; Dcn. Jose David Mercado; Donna Villavisanis, DRE; CRP Stds.: 510

St. Mark School - (Grades PreK-8) t) 954-434-3887 principal@stmarklions.com stmarklions.com Teresita Wardlow, Prin.; Stds.: 556; Lay Tchrs.: 30

SUNNY ISLES BEACH

St. Mary Magdalen - 17775 N. Bay Rd., Sunny Isles Beach, FL 33160 t) 305-931-0600 stmmsib.org Rev. Damian Flanagan, Par. Admin.; Rev. Francis Chidi Nwakile, F.J.S., In Res.; Sr. Maria Elena Larrea, osf, DRE; CRP Stds.: 168

SUNRISE

All Saints - 10900 W. Oakland Park Blvd., Sunrise, FL 33351 t) 954-742-7742 (CRP); 954-742-2666 info@allsaintsvillage.com www.allsaintsvillage.com Rev. Yamil Alejandro Miranda Perez, Pst.; Rev. Eliseus Ezeuchenne (Nigeria), Par. Vicar; Sr. Michelle Fernandez, S.C.T.J.M., DRE; Dcn. Ramon Gonzalez; Dcn. Benjamin Roa; CRP Stds.: 120

All Saints School - (Grades PreK-8) t) 954-742-4842 www.allsaintscatholicschool.net Kristen B Whiting, Prin.; Stds.: 315; Lay Tchrs.: 31

St. Bernard - 8279 Sunset Strip, Sunrise, FL 33322 t) 954-741-7800 accounting@stbernardsunrise.org www.stbernardsunrise.org Rev. Jorge L. Rodriguez de la Viuda, Pst.; Dcn. Armando Martinez; CRP Stds.: 35

TAMARAC

St. Malachy - 6200 John Horan Terr., Tamarac, FL 33321 t) 954-726-1237 stmalachychurch@comcast.net; crestmalachychurch@gmail.com www.stmalachy.church Rev. Alfredo A. Rolon Ortiz, Pst.; Dcn. Edoualdo Desmornes; Zoraida Perez, DRE; Dcn. Humberto Reyes Anciano; CRP Stds.: 72

TAVERNIER

San Pedro - 89500 Overseas Hwy., Tavernier, FL 33070; Mailing: P.O. Box 456, Tavernier, FL 33070 t) 305-852-5372 office@sanpedroparish.org www.sanpedroparish.org Rev. Ferry Brutus, Pst.; Amy Pope Brown, DRE; CRP Stds.: 81

VIRGINIA GARDENS

Blessed Trinity - 4020 Curtiss Pkwy., Virginia Gardens, FL 33166 t) 305-871-5780 reception@blessed-trinity.org www.blessed-trinity.org/ Rev. Matias Hualpa, Pst.; Rev. Attila Frohlich, Par. Vicar; Dcn. Jose Aleman; Dcn. Javier Inda; Dcn. Ernesto Sosa; Olga Venegas, DRE; CRP Stds.: 99

Blessed Trinity School - (Grades PreK-8) t) 305-871-5766 btschool@blessed-trinity.org www.blessed-trinity.org Susy Del Riego, Prin.; Stds.: 200; Sr. Tchrs.: 1; Lay Tchrs.: 24

WEST PARK

Annunciation - 3781 S.W. 39th St., West Park, FL 33023 t) 954-989-0606 www.annuncatholicchurch.com Rev. John Wladyslaw Juszczak, C.Ss.R. (Poland), Par. Admin.; CRP Stds.: 188

Annunciation School - (Grades PreK-8) 3751 S.W. 39th St., West Park, FL 33023 t) 954-989-8287 www.annun.org Maria Jebian, Prin.; Stds.: 188; Lay Tchrs.: 13

St. Paul Chung Ha Sang Korean Mission - 3600 S.W. 32nd Blvd., West Park, FL 33023; Mailing: 14344 S. Royal Cove Cir., Davie, FL 33325 t) 954-474-9091 miamikoreanmission@gmail.com Rev. Sukhun Koo (Korea), Par. Admin.; CRP Stds.: 7

WESTON

St. Katharine Drexel - 2501 S. Post Rd., Weston, FL 33327 t) 954-389-5003 veronicar@skdrexel.org skdrexel.org Rev. Yonhatan Londoño, Par. Vicar; Rev. Omar Ayubi, Par. Admin.; Hedalys Anton, CRE; CRP Stds.: 490

SCHOOLS: PRESCHOOL THRU HIGH SCHOOL

SCHOOLS

STATE OF FLORIDA

MIAMI

Leadership Learning Center at St. John Bosco, Inc. - 1366 N.W. 1st St., Miami, FL 33125 t) 305-649-4730 yamador@sjbmiami.org www.leadershiplearningcenter.org After-School and Summer Camp Program K - 12 Yannet Amador, Exec. Dir.; Most Rev. Thomas G. Wenski, Pres.; Stds.: 240; Lay Tchrs.: 1

MIAMI GARDENS

Marian Center School and Services, Inc. - (PRV) (Grades 1-12) 15701 N.W. 37th Ave., Miami Gardens, FL 33054 t) (305) 200-8927 x200 lidia.valli@mariancenterschool.org www.mariancenterschool.org Marian Center provides day and residential programs for adults with developmental disabilities. Sr. Lidia Valli, SSJBC, Prin.; Stds.: 26; Sr. Tchrs.: 1; Lay Tchrs.: 6

MIAMI SHORES

Archdiocese of Miami Catholic Virtual School - (DIO) (Grades K-12) 9401 Biscayne Blvd., Miami Shores, FL 33138 t) 305-508-5556 principal@adomvirtual.com www.adomvirtual.com Dr. Rebeca Bautista, Prin.; Stds.: 923; Lay Tchrs.: 21

HIGH SCHOOLS

STATE OF FLORIDA

FORT LAUDERDALE

Cardinal Gibbons High School, Inc. - (DIO) (Grades 9-12) 2900 N.E. 47th St., Fort Lauderdale, FL 33308 t) 954-491-2900 cghs@cghsfl.org www.cghsfl.org Oscar Cedeno, Prin.; Dr. Katrina Azevedo, Vice Prin.; Kim Eichholtz, Campus Min.; Stds.: 1,059; Sr. Tchrs.: 1; Lay Tchrs.: 81

St. Thomas Aquinas High School, Inc. - (PAR) 2801 S.W. 12th St., Fort Lauderdale, FL 33312 t) 954-581-0700 denise.aloma@aquinas-sta.org www.aquinas-sta.org Rev. Khiet Huu Manh Pham, S.J. (Vietnam), Chap.; Dr. Denise Aloma, Prin.; Stds.: 2,058; Pr. Tchrs.: 1; Lay Tchrs.: 106

HOLLYWOOD

Chaminade-Madonna College Preparatory - (PRV) (Grades 9-12) 500 E. Chaminade Dr., Hollywood, FL 33021-5800 t) 954-989-5150 info@cmlions.org www.cmlions.org Dr. Judith Mucheck, Pres.; Rev. Robert Bouffier, S.M., Chap.; Raiza Echemendia, Prin.; Michael Eaton, Dean; Stds.: 547; Lay Tchrs.: 30

MIAMI

Archbishop Coleman F. Carroll High School, Inc. - (DIO) (Grades 9-12) 10300 S.W. 167th Ave., Miami, FL 33196 t) 305-388-6700 principal@colemancarroll.org www.archbishopcolemancarroll.org Sr. Margaret Ann, O.C.D., Prin.; Stds.: 443; Sr. Tchrs.: 4; Lay Tchrs.: 29

Belen Jesuit Preparatory School, Inc. - (PRV) (Grades 6-12) 500 S.W. 127th Ave., Miami, FL 33184 t) 305-223-8600 tmartinez@belenjesuit.org; communications@belenjesuit.org www.belenjesuit.org Rev. Alberto Garcia, Supr.; Rev. Guillermo Garcia-Tunon, S.J., Pres.; Rev. Guillermo Arias, S.J., Spiritual Adv./Care Srvcs.; Rev. Pedro A. Suarez, S.J., Spiritual Adv./Care Srvcs.; Rev. Christian A. Saenz, S.J., Chap.; Rev. Vincent Capuano, S.J., Campus Min.; Rev. Pedro Cartaya, S.J., Faculty; Rev. Lionel Lopez, Faculty; Bro. Hunter D'Armond, S.J., Campus Min.; Jose Roca, Prin.; Stds.: 1,375; Scholastics: 1; Pr. Tchrs.: 1; Sr. Tchrs.: 1; Lay Tchrs.: 120

Our Lady of Belen Jesuit Foundation, Inc. - t) 786-621-4043

Covadonga Group, LLC - 2100 Salzedo St., Ste. 303, Coral Gables, FL 33134 t) (305) 665-3400

St. Brendan High School, Inc. - (DIO) (Grades 9-12) 2950 S.W. 87th Ave., Miami, FL 33165 t) (305) 223-5181 info@stbhs.org www.stbrendanhigh.org Ivette G. Alvarez, Prin.; Stds.: 1,267; Lay Tchrs.: 87

Carrollton School of the Sacred Heart - (PRV) (Grades PreK-12) 3747 Main Hwy., Miami, FL 33133 t) 305-446-5673 tcheleotis@carrollton.org; hgillingham@carrollton.org www.carrollton.org Tom Cheleotis, Exec.; Rev. Robert Vallee, Chap.; Stds.: 865; Pr. Tchrs.: 2; Lay Tchrs.: 109

Christopher Columbus High School - (PRV) (Grades 9-12) 3000 S.W. 87 Ave., Miami, FL 33165 t) 305-223-5650 info@columbushs.com; ccruz@columbushs.com www.columbushs.com Thomas Kruczek, Pres.; David Pugh, Prin.; Stds.: 1,731; Bro. Tchrs.: 11; Lay Tchrs.: 122

Immaculata La Salle High School, Inc. - (DIO) (Grades 9-12) 3601 S. Miami Ave., Miami, FL 33133 t) 305-854-2334 x2113 principal@ilsroyals.com www.ilsroyals.com Please note remove Mrs. Catherine Campos no longer the Dean of Technology. Mrs. Alishea Jurado's new position is Dean of Innovation & Technology. Sr. Kim Keraitis, FMA, Prin.; Monica Orelle, Asst. Prin.; Ana Lourdes Garcia, Dean, Faculty; James Rydborn, Dean, Students; Rebecca Shaw, Dean, STEAM; Alishea Jurado, Dean, Innovation & Tech.; Gaston Arellano, Dir., Campus Opers.; Marlen Medina, Financial Admin.; Stds.: 882; Sr. Tchrs.: 3; Lay Tchrs.: 75

Our Lady of Lourdes Academy, Inc. - (DIO) (Grades 9-12) 5525 S.W. 84th St., Miami, FL 33143 t) 305-667-1623 scarmen@bobcats.olla.org www.olla.org Sr. Carmen T. Fernandez, I.H.M., Prin.; Sr. Maryanne Lynch, I.H.M., Vice Prin.; Stds.: 840; Sr. Tchrs.: 1; Lay Tchrs.: 56

MIAMI GARDENS

Msgr. Edward Pace High School, Inc. - (DIO) (Grades 9-12) 15600 Spartan Blvd., N.W. 32nd Ave., Miami Gardens, FL 33054 t) 305-623-7223 agarcia@pacehs.com; ldubon@pacehs.com www.pacehs.com Ana Garcia, Prin.; Lillian Dubon, Admin.; Melanie Otero, Admin.; Stds.: 867; Lay Tchrs.: 54

NORTH MIAMI

***Cristo Rey Miami High School** - (PRV) (Grades 9-12) 125 N.E. 119th St., North Miami, FL 33161 t) 305-495-4232 info@cristoreymiami.org www.cristoreymiami.org Anamarie Moreiras, Pres.; Cesar D. Munoz, Prin.; Stds.: 73; Lay Tchrs.: 3

SOUTHWEST RANCHES

Archbishop Edward A. McCarthy High School, Inc. - (DIO) (Grades 9-12) 5451 S. Flamingo Rd., Southwest Ranches, FL 33330 t) 954-434-8820 x202 maverick@mccarthyhigh.org; cthomas@mccarthyhigh.org www.mccarthyhigh.org Richard P. Jean, Prin.; Rev. Edivaldo Da Silva Oliviera (Brazil), Chap.; Stds.: 1,742; Lay Tchrs.: 81

INSTITUTIONS LOCATED IN DIOCESE

CATHOLIC CHARITIES [CCH]

TALLAHASSEE

Catholic Charities of Florida, Inc. - 201 W. Park Ave., Tallahassee, FL 32301 t) 305-762-1284 eworley@theadom.org Sr. Elizabeth Anne Worley, S.S.J., Chancellor;

WILTON MANORS

Catholic Charities of the Archdiocese of Miami, Inc. - 1505 N.E. 26 St., 2nd Fl., Wilton Manors, FL 33305 t) 305-754-2444 parroyo@ccadm.org www.ccadm.org Peter Routsis-Arroyo, CEO; Most Rev. Thomas G. Wenski, Mem.; Asstd. Annu.: 4,387; Staff: 388

CEMETERIES [CEM]

MIAMI

Catholic Cemeteries of the Archdiocese of Miami, Inc. - 11411 N.W. 25 St., Miami, FL 33172 t) 305-592-0521 mjfrick@chsfla.com catholiccemeteriesmiami.org Mary Jo Frick, Exec. Dir.;

COLLEGES & UNIVERSITIES [COL]

MIAMI

Barry University - 11300 N.E. 2nd Ave., Miami, FL 33161 t) 305-899-3010 officeofthepresident@barry.edu www.barry.edu Michael S. Allen, Pres.; Rev. George Boudreau, Prof.; Rev. Jose David Padilla, O.P., Prof.; Rev. Jorge L. Presmanes, O.P., Prof.; Rev. Cristobal Torres, O.P., Chap.; John D. Murray, Provost; Sr. Linda Bevilacqua, O.P., Pres. Emerita & Dir., Adrian Dominican Institute for Mission & Leadership; Stds.: 7,000; Lay Tchrs.: 270; Pr. Tchrs.: 2; Sr. Tchrs.: 2

MIAMI GARDENS

St. Thomas University, Inc. - 16401 N.W. 37th Ave., Miami Gardens, FL 33054 t) 305-474-6800 www.stu.edu Most Rev. Thomas G. Wenski, Mem.; David A. Armstrong, Pres.; Rev. Rafael Capo, Vice Pres., Mission; Rev. Alfred Cioffi, Prof.; Dr. Michelle Johnson-Garcia, Provost; Stds.: 6,427; Lay Tchrs.: 81; Pr. Tchrs.: 2; Sr. Tchrs.: 1

CONVENTS, MONASTERIES, AND RESIDENCES FOR WOMEN [CON]

HIALEAH

Dominicas de la Inmaculada Concepcion - 571 W. 33rd Pl., Hialeah, FL 33012 t) 305-823-3282 Sr. Monica Sanchez Espindola, DIC, Supr.; Srs.: 3

Servants of Jesus of Charity, Inc. - 126 W. 45th St., Hialeah, FL 33012 t) 305-231-2063 tostadodeanda.yolanda@yahoo.com.mx Sr. Yolanda de Anda, Prioress; Srs.: 4

HOMESTEAD

Daughters of Mary, Mothers of Mercy (Nigeria), Inc. - 18444 S.W. 293rd Ter., Homestead, FL 33030 t) 317-716-0485 fofoma5@yahoo.com Sr. Chidi Nwanya, D.M.M.M., Supr.; Srs.: 18

Mercy Convent - 1618 Polk St., Hollywood, FL 33020; Mailing: 9751 S.W. 15th St., Pembroke Pines, FL 33025 t) 954-895-3005 bernadettedike44@gmail.com www.dmmmsisters-usa.org Sr. Sochima Mgbeokwere, DMMM, Councilor;

Discalced Carmelite Nuns, Inc. - 29190 S.W. 209 Ave., Homestead, FL 33030 t) 305-558-7122 madrescarmelitasmiami2001@gmail.com Mother Teresa Lopez, O.C.D., Prioress; Srs.: 11

Monastery of the Most Holy Trinity, (Discalced Carmelite Nuns) - 29190 S.W. 209 Ave., Homestead, FL 33030 t) 305-558-7122 madrescarmelitasmiami2001@gmail.com Mother Teresa Lopez, O.C.D., Prioress; Mother Blanca Flor Caracheo, O.C.D., Dir.; Srs.: 11

MIAMI

Claretian Missionary Sisters of Florida, Inc. - 7080 S.W. 99th Ave., Miami, FL 33173 t) 305-274-6148 vivian.gonzalez@claretianas.org www.claretiansisters.org Sr. Vivian Gonzalez, R.M.I., Prov.; Srs.: 11

Congregation of the French-Cuban Dominican Sisters of Holy Rosary, Inc. - 7920 S.W. 23rd St., Miami, FL 33155 t) 305-265-9759 cecilia.alonso1416@gmail.com Sr. Mary Cecilia Alonso, O.P., Pres.; Srs.: 3

Daughters of Charity of St. Vincent de Paul - 500 N.W. 63rd Ave., Miami, FL 33126 t) 305-266-6485 eperezpuelles@yahoo.com; hijasdelacaridadmiami@yahoo.com (Santo Domingo, R.D.), Mision San Vicente de Paul., Asociacion Hijas de la Caridad de San Vicente de Paul del Estado de la Florida, Inc. Sr. Eva Perez Puelles, Dir.; Srs.: 10

Daughters of Charity of St. Vincent de Paul - 3609 S. Miami Ave., Miami, FL 33133 t) 305-854-2404 sorines@ermita.org Sr. Ines Espinosa, Prioress;

Daughters of St. Paul Convent - 11117 S.W. 2nd St., Miami, FL 33174 t) 305-227-2125 miami@paulinemedia.com www.pauline.org Sr. Maria Teresa Meza, F.S.P., Supr.; Srs.: 4

Handmaids of the Sacred Heart of Jesus A.C.J. - 1615 N.E. 108th St., Miami, FL 33161 c) 786-616-0641 sistermargarita@gmail.com www.acjusa.org Sr. Margarita Maria Martin, Supr.; Srs.: 4

Missionaries of Charity - 727 N.W. 17th St., Miami, FL 33136 t) 305-545-5699 weberag@att.net Sr. M. Ajaya, M.C., Supr.; Srs.: 6

***Siervas de los Corazones Traspasados de Jesus y Maria, Inc. (Servants of the Pierced Hearts of Jesus and Mary)** - 3098 S.W. 14th St., Miami, FL 33145 t) 305-444-7437 c) 786-554-7970 sisterana@piercedhearts.org www.piercedhearts.org Mother Adela I. Galindo, S.C.T.J.M., Supr.; Sr. Ana M. Lanzas, S.C.T.J.M., Dir.; Rev. Joseph Everett Rogers, Chap.; Srs.: 70

Theatine Sisters of the Immaculate Conception, Co. - 12261 S.W. 6th St., Miami, FL 33184 t) 786-409-5212 teatinasmia@att.net religiosasteatinas.com Sr. Esther Samudio, Supr.; Srs.: 3

ENDOWMENTS / FOUNDATIONS / TRUSTS [EFT]

COOPER CITY

Schott Memorial Center Foundation, Inc. - 6591 S. Flamingo Rd., Cooper City, FL 33330 c) 239-877-9883 rgschott@comcast.net Msgr. Roberto Garza, Trustee; Jose Rementeria, Exec.; Greg Schott, Exec.;

CORAL GABLES

Foundation Order of Malta, Inc. - 2655 S. LeJeune Rd., Ste. 918, Coral Gables, FL 33134 t) 786-888-6494 president@foundationorderofmalta.org; presidente@ordendemaltacuba.org www.ordendemaltacuba.org Part of the Sovereign Military and Hospitaler Order of St. John of Jerusalem, of Rhodes and of Malta. Juan T. O'Naghten, Pres.; Mauricio Fernandez y Ferran, Treas.; Jose Joaquin Centurion, Dir.;

***Roman Catholic Archdiocese of Nassau Foundation, Inc.** - 110 Merrick Way, Ste. 3-B, Coral Gables, FL 33134 t) 305-443-9162 x17 jpf@jpfitzlaw.com Patrick Fitzgerald, Legal Counsel;

MIAMI

***ADOM Health Foundation, Inc. (SSJ Health Foundation, Inc.)** - 730 N.W. 34th St., Miami, FL 33127 t) 305-854-0533 anthony.pinto@ssjhealthfoundation.org ssjhealthfoundation.org Jorge Uribe, Chair; Anthony Pinto, Exec. Dir.; Sr. Elizabeth Anne Worley, S.S.J., Bd. Mem.;

Archdiocese of Miami Endowment Fund, Inc. - 9401 Biscayne Blvd., Miami, FL 33138 t) 305-762-1053 kblancobourdeau@theadom.org William G. Benson, Chair;

Archdiocese of Miami Health Plan Trust - 9401 Biscayne Blvd., Miami, FL 33138 t) 305-757-6241 swaddell@adomhealthplan.org Sr. Elizabeth Anne Worley, S.S.J., Vice. Pres.;

Charity Unlimited Foundation, Inc. - 1603 N.W. 7th Ave., Miami, FL 33136 t) 305-374-1065 x220 hfernandez@camillus.org; judy@sjog-na.org Bro. Richard MacPhee, O.H., Pres.;

Charity Unlimited of Florida, Inc. - 1603 N.W. 7th Ave., Miami, FL 33136 t) 305-374-1065 x220 rmacphee@gsc.ca; judy@sjog-na.org Bro. Richard MacPhee, O.H., Pres.;

Father Amando Llorente, S.J. Foundation, Inc. - 12805 S.W. 6th St., Miami, FL 33184 t) 786-360-8004 evieira@estovir.org; acuinfo@estovir.org Rev. Christian A. Saenz, S.J., Trustee;

Father Tino Foundation, Inc. - 12725 S.W. 6th St., Miami, FL 33184 c) 305-972-9499 cdlt1948@yahoo.com Rev. Eduardo Alvarez, S.J. (Cuba), Dir.; Rev. Alberto

Garcia, Dir.; Carlos de la Torre, CEO;
Hurley Heritage Trust - 9401 Biscayne Blvd., Miami, FL 33138 t) 305-762-1284 eworley@theadom.org Sr. Elizabeth Anne Worley, S.S.J., Vice Chancellor;
SEPI Evangelization and Education Foundation, Inc. - 7700 S.W. 56th St., Miami, FL 33155 t) 305-279-2333 director@sepi.us Most Rev. Thomas G. Wenski, Trustee; Most Rev. Gregory M. Aymond, Trustee; Most Rev. Thomas J. Rodi, Trustee; Most Rev. Shelton Fabre, Trustee; Olga Lucia Villar, Exec. Dir.;

MIAMI SHORES

Catholic Community Foundation in the Archdiocese of Miami, Inc. - 9401 Biscayne Blvd., Miami Shores, FL 33138 t) 305-762-1053 Katie Blanco Bourdeau, CEO; William G. Benson, Chair;
St. John Vianney College Seminary in Florida Inc. Endowment Trust - 9401 Biscayne Blvd., Miami Shores, FL 33138 t) 305-762-1284 eworley@theadom.org Most Rev. Thomas G. Wenski, Pres.;

NORTH MIAMI

***Villa Maria Foundation, Inc.** - 1050 N.E. 125 St., North Miami, FL 33161 t) (954) 484-1515 dlogue@chsfla.com Aristides Pallin, CEO;

HOSPITALS / HEALTH SERVICES [HOS]

FORT LAUDERDALE

Holy Cross Primary Care, Inc. - 4725 N. Federal Hwy., Fort lauderdale, FL 33308 t) 954-771-8000 x3293 mark.e.doyle@trinity-health.org; mary.carterwaren@trinity-health.org holycross.com James Moffett, Admin.; Asstd. Annu.: 483,035; Staff: 743

FORT LAUDERDALE

Holy Cross Hospital, Inc. - 4725 N. Federal Hwy., Fort Lauderdale, FL 33308 t) 954-771-8000 mark.e.doyle@trinity-health.org; mary.carterwaren@trinity-health.org www.holy-cross.com Mark E. Doyle, CEO; Dr. Mary Carter Waren, Mission Leader; Rev. James A. Quinn, Chap.; Rev. Michael Hoyer, Chap.; Sr. Xiomara Mendez-Hernandez, Chap.; Bed Capacity: 557; Asstd. Annu.: 751,512; Staff: 3,064
Holy Cross Outpatient Services, Inc. - 4725 N. Federal Hwy., Fort Lauderdale, FL 33308 t) 954-771-8000 mark.e.doyle@trinity-health.org Mark E. Doyle, CEO; Bed Capacity: 25; Asstd. Annu.: 476,414; Staff: 743
Holy Cross Senior Services, Inc. - 4725 N. Federal Hwy., Fort Lauderdale, FL 33368 t) 954-771-8000 mark.e.doyle@trinity-health.org Mark E. Doyle, CEO; Asstd. Annu.: 6,479; Staff: 2

MIAMI

Mercy Hospital, Inc. - 3663 S. Miami Ave., Miami, FL 33133 t) 305-854-4400 www.mercymiami.com A Catholic hospital owned and operated by HCA. Sponsored by the Sisters of St. Joseph of St. Augustine, FL. Rev. Chidiebere Ogbuagu, Vice Pres., Mission; Rev. Carlos J. Cabrera, Chap.; Rev. Pedro Toledo, Chap.; Rev. Sterling Laurent, Chap.; Sr. Elizabeth Anne Worley, S.S.J., Trustee; Sr. Stephanie Flynn, SSJ, Trustee; Sr. Kathleen Carr, SSJ, Trustee; Bed Capacity: 488; Asstd. Annu.: 79,049; Staff: 1,497

MISCELLANEOUS [MIS]

CORAL GABLES

House of the Divine Will, Inc. - 5900 Leonardo St., Coral Gables, FL 33146-3332 t) 305-667-5714 casadivinavoluntad@msn.com www.casadivinavoluntad.org Rev. Carlos Massieu, Pres.; Mother Marianela Perez, Treas.;

CORAL SPRINGS

***St. Andrew Towers, Inc.** - 2700 N.W. 99 Ave., Coral Springs, FL 33065 t) (954) 484-1515 x5200 dlogue@chsfla.com Aristides Pallin, CEO; Aldea Smith, Mgr.;

CUTLER BAY

Magnificat, Miami Chapter, Inc. - 9822 S.W. 222 St., Cutler Bay, FL 33190 t) 305-753-8380 mariabl003@gmail.com Maria Luque, Pres.; Valli Leoni, Vice. Pres.; Lisette Fernandez, Secy.; Judith Johnson, Treas.;

HIALEAH

***Opus Caritatis Corp.** - 998 W. 65 St., Hialeah, FL 33012 t) 786-312-4234 susi@corpuschristimiami.org; father.oscar@yahoo.com Rev. Oscar F. Castaneda, Dir.;

HIALEAH GARDENS

Centro Mater Child Care Services, Inc. - 8298 N.W. 103 St., Hialeah Gardens, FL 33016 t) 954-484-1515 Aristides Pallin, CEO; Madelyn Rodriguez-Llanes, Exec. Dir.;

HOMESTEAD

Brother Keily Place, Inc. - 27940 S. Dixie Hwy., Homestead, FL 33032 t) 305-374-1065 hfernandez@camillus.org; judy@sjog-na.org Bro. Richard MacPhee, O.H., Pres.;
***Centro de Artes y Oficios De La Salle, Inc.** - 13350 S.W. 314 St., Homestead, FL 33033-5617 t) 305-245-5810 center@celasalleh.org www.celasalleh.org Vocational Center for adults. Also after school for children K-9. Rev. Jose Espino, Pres.; Bro. Daniel Aubin, F.S.C., Dir.;

LAUDERDALE LAKES

CHS St. Joseph Manor II, Inc. - 4790 N. State Rd. 7, Lauderdale Lakes, FL 33319 t) (954) 484-1515 x5200 Aristides Pallin, CEO; Juana Mejia, Exec. Dir.;
Catholic Health Care Transitions Services, Inc. - 3075 N.W. 35 Ave., Lauderdale Lakes, FL 33311 t) 954-484-1515 dlogue@chsfla.com Aristides Pallin, CEO; Carol Hylton, Exec. Dir.;
Catholic Elderly Services, Inc. - 4790 N. State Rd. 7, Lauderdale Lakes, FL 33319 t) 954-484-1515 dlogue@chsfla.com Aristides Pallin, CEO;
Catholic Health Services, Inc. - 4790 N. State Rd. 7, Lauderdale Lakes, FL 33319 t) 954-484-1515 x5200 Ralph Lawson, Chair; Aristides Pallin, CEO; David D'Amico, CFO;
CHS St. Joseph Manor II Development, LLC - t) (954) 484-1515 x5200 Juana Mejia, Exec. Dir.;
CHS Casa Sant'Angelo Apartments Development, LLC - t) (954) 484-1515 x5200 Juana Mejia, Exec. Dir.;
CHS Miami Beach Marian Towers Development, LLC - t) (954) 484-1515 x5200 Juana Mejia, Exec. Dir.;
CHS Palmer House, LLC - t) (954) 484-1515 x5200
CHS St. Andrew Towers I Development, LLC - t) (954) 484-1515 x5200 Juana Mejia, Exec. Dir.;
CHS St. Andrew Towers II Development, LLC - t) (954) 484-1515 x5200 Juana Mejia, Exec. Dir.;
CHS St. Elizabeth Gardens Development, LLC - t) (954) 484-1515 x5200 Juana Mejia, Exec. Dir.;
CHS St. Mary Towers Development, LLC - t) (954) 484-1515 x5200
CHS Stella Maris, LLC - t) (954) 484-1515 x5200 www.catholichealthservices.org/
Catholic Home Health Medicare Services, Inc. - 4790 N. State Rd. 7, Lauderdale Lakes, FL 33319 t) 954-484-1515 dlogue@chsfla.com Carol Hylton, Exec. Dir.; Aristides Pallin, CEO;
Catholic Home Health Services, Inc. - 3075 N.W. 35 Ave., Lauderdale Lakes, FL 33311 t) (954) 484-1515 x5200 Carol Hylton, Exec. Dir.; Aristides Pallin, CEO;
Catholic Home Health Services of Broward, Inc. - 4790 No. State Rd. 7, Lauderdale Lakes, FL 33319 t) 954-484-1515 dlogue@chsfla.com Carol Hylton, Exec. Dir.; Aristides Pallin, CEO;
Catholic Hospice of Broward, Inc. - 4790 N. State Rd. 7, Lauderdale Lakes, FL 33319 t) 954-484-1515 dlogue@chsfla.com Aristides Pallin, CEO; Dian Backoff, Exec. Dir.;
CHS St. Mary Towers, Inc. - 4790 N. State Rd. 7, Lauderdale Lakes, FL 33319 t) (954) 484-1515 x5200 dlogue@chsfla.com www.catholichealthservices.org/ Ralph Lawson, Chair; Aristides Pallin, CEO; David D'Amico, CFO;
St. Joseph Residence, Inc. - 3485 N.W. 30 St., Lauderdale Lakes, FL 33311 t) (954) 484-1515 x5200 Rev. Antony Vayalikarottu (India); Aristides Pallin, CEO; Rosemarie Bailey, Exec. Dir.;
St. Joseph Towers, Inc. - 3475 N.W. 30 St., Lauderdale Lakes, FL 33311 t) (954) 484-1515 x5200 dlogue@chsfla.com Juana Mejia, Exec. Dir.; Aristides Pallin, CEO;
Magnificat Broward County, Florida Chapter, Inc. - 2998 N.W. 48th Terr., Apt 221, Lauderdale Lakes, FL 33313 c) 754-234-1847 julianafindley@yahoo.com Rev. Paul G. Karenga (Burkina Faso), Chap.;
Miami-Dade Nursing Center, Inc. - 4790 N. State Rd. 7, Lauderdale Lakes, FL 33319 t) 954-484-1515 x5200 dlogue@chsfla.com Aristides Pallin, CEO;
Miramar Senior Housing Project, Inc. - 4790 N. State Rd. 7, Lauderdale Lakes, FL 33319 t) (954) 484-1515 x5200 dlogue@chsfla.com Juana Mejia, Exec. Dir.; Aristides Pallin, CEO;

MIAMI

Agrupacion Catolica Universitaria, Inc. - 12805 S.W. 6th St., Miami, FL 33184 t) 786-360-8004 evieira@estovir.org; acuinfo@estovir.org www.estovir.org Rev. Christian A. Saenz, S.J., Trustee;
St. Anne's Gardens, Inc. - 11800 Quail Roost Dr., Miami, FL 33177 t) (954) 484-1515 x5200 dlogue@chsfla.com Aristides Pallin, CEO; Juana Mejia, Exec. Dir.;
***Archbishop Carroll Manor, Inc.** - 3667 S. Miami Ave., Miami, FL 33133; Mailing: 9401 Biscayne Blvd., Miami, FL 33138 t) (954) 484-1515 x5200 Juana Mejia, Exec. Dir.; Aristides Pallin, CEO; Ramon Lopez Pena, Mgr.;
***Archbishop Hurley Hall, Inc.** - 11410 N. Kendall Dr., Ste. 306, Miami, FL 33176 t) (954) 484-1515 x5200 Aristides Pallin, CEO; Juana Mejia, Exec. Dir.;
***Archbishop McCarthy Residence, Inc.** - 11410 N. Kendall Dr., Ste. 306, Miami, FL 33176 t) (954) 484-1515 x5200 Juana Mejia, Exec. Dir.; Aristides Pallin, CEO; Janetta Mora-Olivera, Mgr.;
Archdiocese of Miami Development Corporation - 9401 Biscayne Blvd., Miami, FL 33138 t) 305-762-1053 kblancobourdeau@theadom.org
Brother Mathias Barrett, Inc. - 680 N.E. 52nd St., Miami, FL 33137 t) 815-472-3131 judy@sjog-na.org Bro. David Lynch, OH, Prov.;
Brownsville Housing, Inc. - 4700 N.W. 32nd Ave., Miami, FL 33142; Mailing: 1603 N.W. 7th Ave., Miami, FL 33136 t) 305-374-1065 x220 hfernandez@camillus.org; judy@sjog-na.org Bro. Richard MacPhee, O.H., Pres.;
Catholic Hospice, Inc. - 14875 N.W. 77 Ave., Ste. 100, Miami, FL 33014 t) (954) 484-1515 x5200 Rev. Oswaldo Agudelo; Rev. Andy Lorenzo-Puga; Rev. Pierre-Louis Joseph (Haiti), Chap.; Dian Backoff, Exec. Dir.; Aristides Pallin, CEO;
Catholic Housing for the Elderly and Handicapped, Inc. (Catholic Housing Management) - 11410 N. Kendall Dr., Ste. 306, Miami, FL 33176 t) (954) 484-1515 x5200 Aristides Pallin, CEO; Juana Mejia, Exec. Dir.;
Catholic Legal Services, Archdiocese of Miami, Inc. - 28 W. Flagler St., Miami, FL 33130 t) 305-373-1073 rmcgrorty@cclsmiami.org www.cclsmiami.org Randolph P. McGrorty, CEO; Myriam Mezadieu, COO;
Claretian Missions, Inc. - 7080 S.W. 99th Ave., Miami, FL 33173 t) 305-274-6148 ondina.cortes@claretianas.org; chiquirmi@gmail.com www.claretiansisters.org Sr. Ondina Cortes, R.M.I., Pres.;
St. Dominic Gardens, Inc. - 5849 N.W. 7th St., Miami, FL 33126 t) (954) 484-1515 x5200 Juana Mejia, Exec. Dir.; Aristides Pallin, CEO;
Emmaus Place, Inc. - 432 N.W. 4th Ave., Miami, FL 33128; Mailing: 1603 N.W. 7th Ave., Miami, FL 33136 t) 305-374-1065 hfernandez@camillus.org; judy@sjog-na.org Bro. Richard MacPhee, O.H., Pres.;
Federacion de Institutos Pastorales, Inc. - 7700 S.W. 56th St., Miami, FL 33155 t) 305-279-2333 x3 pductram@cathdal.org fipusa.org Peter J. Ductram, Pres.; Rev. Rafael Capo, Vice. Pres.; Juan Escarfuller, Treas.; Maria Antonia Amao, Member At Large; Olga Lucia Villar, Secy.;
Good Shepherd Villas, Inc. - 3036 N.W. 77th St., Miami,

FL 33147; Mailing: 1603 N.W. 7th Ave., Miami, FL 33136 t) 305-374-1065 x220 hfernandez@camillus.org; judy@sjog-na.org Bro. Richard MacPhee, O.H., Pres.;

Hijas de la Caridad de San Vincente de Paul Mision de Miami, LLC - 3609 S. Miami Ave., Miami, FL 33133 t) 305-266-6485 c) 786-367-1657 hijasdelacaridad@yahoo.com; eperezpuelles@yahoo.com Sr. Eva Perez Puelles, Dir.;

Jesus Maestro, Inc. - 12805 S.W. 6th St., Miami, FL 33184 t) 786-360-8004 acuinfo@estovir.org; evieira@estovir.org www.estovir.org Rev. Christian A. Saenz, S.J., Trustee;

Labre Place, Inc. - 350 N.W. 4th St., Miami, FL 33128; Mailing: 1603 N.W. 7th Ave., Miami, FL 33136 t) 305-374-1065 hfernandez@camillus.org; judy@sjog-na.org Bro. Richard MacPhee, O.H., Pres.;

***St. Mary Towers, Inc.** - 7615 N.W. 2nd Ave., Miami, FL 33150 t) (954) 484-1515 x5200 Juana Mejia, Exec. Dir.; Aristides Pallin, CEO; Fabio Ladino, Mgr.;

***New Camillus House Campus, Inc.** - 1603 N.W. 7th Ave., Miami, FL 33136 t) 305-374-1065 hfernandez@camillus.org; judy@sjog-na.org Bro. Richard MacPhee, O.H., Pres.;

Palmer House, Inc. - 1225 S.W. 107th Ave., Miami, FL 33174 t) (954) 484-1515 x5200 Juana Mejia, Exec. Dir.; Aristides Pallin, CEO;

Pauline Books & Media - 145 S.W. 107th Ave., Miami, FL 33174 t) 305-559-6715 miami@paulinemedia.com www.pauline.org Sr. Maria Teresa Meza, F.S.P., Supr.;

Paulinas Spanish Distribution Center - t) 305-225-2513; 800-872-5852 paulinas@paulinemedia.com

Pax Catholic Communications, Inc. - 1779 N.W. 28 St., Miami, FL 33142 t) 305-638-9729 rgarza@theadom.org Msgr. Roberto Garza, Dir.;

Peruvian Mission, Inc. - 9360 S.W. 87 Ave., #N4, Miami, FL 33176; Mailing: P.O. Box 432745, Miami, FL 33143 c) (786) 492-2112 aprilis2@bellsouth.net (A Florida Not-for-Profit Corporation) Most Rev. Luis Alberto Barrera Pacheco, M.C.C.I., Pres.; Most Rev. Pedro Barreto, S.J., Trustee; Most Rev. Jorge Carrion, Trustee; Most Rev. Javier del Rio Alba, Trustee; Most Rev. Enrique Delgado, Trustee;

Pierre Toussaint Leadership and Learning Center, Inc. - 130 N.E. 62 St., 2nd Fl., Miami, FL 33138; Mailing: 110 N.E. 62nd St., Miami, FL 33138 t) 305-751-6289; (305) 751-3880 info@ptllc.org ptllc.org Most Rev. Thomas G. Wenski; Most Rev. Enrique Delgado, Secy./Dir.; Rev. Reginald Jean-Mary, Pres.; Sr. Elizabeth Anne Worley, S.S.J., Vice. Pres.; J. Patrick Fitzgerald, AS;

Prelature of the Holy Cross and Opus Dei - 4415 S.W. 88th Ave., Miami, FL 33165 t) 305-551-7956 www.tekesta.org Rev. William Shaughnessy, Chap.; Rev. Juan R. Velez, Chap.;

Somerville Residence, Inc. - 400 N.W. 3rd Ct., Miami, FL 33128; Mailing: 1603 N.W. 7th Ave., Miami, FL 33136 t) 305-374-1065 hfernandez@camillus.org; judy@sjog-na.org Bro. Richard MacPhee, O.H., Pres.;

Southeast Regional Office for Hispanic Ministry, Inc. - 7700 S.W. 56th St., Miami, FL 33155 t) 305-279-2333 director@sepi.us www.sepi.us Most Rev. Thomas G. Wenski; Most Rev. Gregory M. Aymond, Trustee; Most Rev. Thomas J. Rodi, Trustee; Most Rev. Shelton Fabre, Trustee;

Southeast Pastoral Institute - t) (305) 279-2333 x3 Olga Lucia Villar, Exec. Dir.;

Stella Maris Seamen Center, Inc. - Port of Miami, 1172 S. America Way, Miami, FL 33132 t) 305-531-1124; 305-372-0250 parish@stpatrickmiamibeach.com Rev. Roberto M. Cid, Dir.;

Teresian Institute, (Rome, Italy), Teresian Institute of Florida, Inc. - 3400 S.W. 99 Ave., Miami, FL 33165 t) 305-554-0035; 513-559-9498 c) (305) 799-5384 marbona@fuse.net www.instituciontheresiana.org An International Association of the Faithful of Pontifical Rite. Rachel Portell, Secy.;

St. Thomas Foreign Missions, LLC - 9401 Biscayne Blvd., Miami, FL 33138 t) 305-762-1284 eworley@theadom.org Most Rev. Thomas G. Wenski, Mem.;

Vida Humana Internacional (Hispanic Division of Human Life International) - 45 S.W. 71st Ave., Miami, FL 33144 t) 305-260-0525 vhi@vidahumana.org; adriana@vidahumana.org www.vidahumana.org Rev. Shenan Boquet, Pres.;

St. Vincent de Paul Gardens, Inc. - 10160 N.W. 19th Ave., Miami, FL 33147 t) (954) 484-1515 x5200 Juana Mejia, Exec. Dir.; Aristides Pallin, CEO;

MIAMI BEACH

***Stella Maris House, Inc.** - 8638 Harding Ave., Miami Beach, FL 33141 t) (954) 484-1515 x5200 Aristides Pallin, CEO; Juana Mejia, Exec. Dir.;

MIAMI GARDENS

Congregation of the Holy Spirit Province of Nigeria South East, Inc. - 3490 N.W. 191 St., Miami Gardens, FL 33056 t) 305-621-9846 smuodiaju@yahoo.com Rev. Francis Akwue, C.S.Sp. (Nigeria), Dir.; Rev. Samuel Muodiaju, C.S.Sp. (Nigeria), Secy.;

***Fundacion Ramon Pane, Inc.** - 1335 N.W. 179th Ter., Miami Gardens, FL 33169 t) 305-323-9257 c) 786-473-9027 presidencia@fundacionpane.org; emailme@fundacionpane.org www.fundacionpane.org Bro. Ricardo Grzona, F.R.P., Pres.;

St. Monica Gardens, Inc. - 3425 N.W. 189 St., Miami Gardens, FL 33056 t) (954) 484-1515 x5200 dlogue@chsfla.com Juana Mejia, Exec. Dir.; Aristides Pallin, CEO;

MIAMI LAKES

Catholic Palliative Care Services, Inc. - 14875 N.W. 77 Ave., Ste. 100, Miami Lakes, FL 33014 t) (954) 484-1515 x5200 Dian Backoff, Exec. Dir.; Aristides Pallin, CEO;

***Villa Maria Health Care Services, Inc.** - 14875 N.W. 77th Ave., Ste. 201, Miami Lakes, FL 33014 t) (954) 484-1515 x5200 Carol Hylton, Exec. Dir.; Aristides Pallin, CEO;

Catholic Home Health Services of Miami-Dade County - 14875 N.W. 77 Ave., Ste. 101, Miami Lakes, FL 33014 t) (954) 484-1515 x5200 Beatrice Voltaire, Admin.;

MIAMI SHORES

Archdiocese of Miami Millennium Appeal, Inc. - 9401 Biscayne Blvd., Miami Shores, FL 33138 t) 305-757-6241 eworley@theadom.org Most Rev. Thomas G. Wenski, Pres.; Sr. Elizabeth Anne Worley, S.S.J., Treas.;

Archdiocese of Miami Mission Services, Inc. - 9401 Biscayne Blvd., Miami Shores, FL 33138 t) 305-762-1284 eworley@theadom.org Most Rev. Thomas G. Wenski, Pres.; Sr. Elizabeth Anne Worley, S.S.J., Treas.;

Archdiocese of Miami, Inc. - 9401 Biscayne Blvd., Miami Shores, FL 33138 t) 305-762-1284 eworley@theadom.org Most Rev. Thomas G. Wenski, Pres.; Sr. Elizabeth Anne Worley, S.S.J., Vice Pres.; Michael A. Casciato, Treas.;

Asociacion Nacional de Diaconos Hispanos, Inc. - 9401 Biscayne Blvd., Miami Shores, FL 33138 t) 305-762-1024 vpimentel@theadom.org Dcn. Fernando Bestard, Pres.;

Bahamas Mission of Florida, Inc. - 9401 Biscayne Blvd., Miami Shores, FL 33138 t) 305-762-1284 eworley@theadom.org Sr. Elizabeth Anne Worley, S.S.J., Chancellor;

Colonial Heritage of Florida, LLC - 9401 Biscayne Blvd., Miami Shores, FL 33138 t) 305-762-1284 eworley@theadom.org Sr. Elizabeth Anne Worley, S.S.J., Chancellor;

DOM, Inc. - 9401 Biscayne Blvd., Miami Shores, FL 33138 t) 305-762-1284 eworley@theadom.org Sr. Elizabeth Anne Worley, S.S.J., Pres.;

Dominican Leadership Conference Inc./Dominican Sisters Conference - Barry University Campus, 11415 N.E. 2nd Ave., Miami Shores, FL 33161-6629; Mailing: 8521 Greenway Blvd., #204, Middleton, WI 53562 c) (517) 990-2720 sisters@domlife.org www.dominicansistersconference.org Dominican Leadership Conference of elected Dominican leaders in the United States of America. Sr. Xiomara Mendez-Hernandez, Exec. Dir.;

Ecclesiastical Province of Miami, Inc. - 9401 Biscayne Blvd., Miami Shores, FL 33138 t) 305-762-1284 eworley@theadom.org Sr. Elizabeth Anne Worley, S.S.J., Chancellor;

Francis Realty Corporation - 9401 Biscayne Blvd., Miami Shores, FL 33138 t) 305-762-1284 eworley@theadom.org Sr. Elizabeth Anne Worley, S.S.J., Pres.;

Hospitalite de Miami, LLC - 9401 Biscayne Blvd., Miami Shores, FL 33138 t) 305-762-1284 eworley@theadom.org Most Rev. Thomas G. Wenski, Pres.; Msgr. Kenneth K. Schwanger;

***North American Friends of the Venerable English College** - 9401 Biscayne Blvd., Miami Shores, FL 33138 c) (305) 814-8504 mbatey@nafvec.org; mark@markbatey.net www.nafvec.org Dr. Paul Beresford-Hill, Chair; Mark Batey, CEO;

P.O.M., Inc. - 9401 Biscayne Blvd., Miami Shores, FL 33138 t) 305-762-1284 eworley@theadom.org Sr. Elizabeth Anne Worley, S.S.J., Pres.;

Provincial Realty Associates, Inc. - 9401 Biscayne Blvd., Miami Shores, FL 33138 t) 305-762-1284 eworley@theadom.org (A Florida Not-for-Profit Corporation), Land Holding Corporation. Sr. Elizabeth Anne Worley, S.S.J., Pres.;

***Society of Saint Vincent de Paul Archdiocesan Council of Miami, Inc.** - 9401 Biscayne Blvd., Miami Shores, FL 33138; Mailing: P.O. Box 8307, Coral Springs, FL 33075 t) 305-741-5163 svdp-adom@4svdp.org www.4svdp.org Claudia Luedeking, Pres.;

St. Vincent de Paul Food Pantry - 14205 S.W. 142 Ave., Miami, FL 33186 t) 305-282-4253 svpmoc@hotmail.com Jim Werle, Treas.;

PEMBROKE PINES

***St. Boniface Gardens, Inc.** - 8200 Johnson St., Pembroke Pines, FL 33024 t) (954) 484-1515 x5200 Juana Mejia, Exec. Dir.; Aristides Pallin, CEO;

POMPANO BEACH

***St. Elizabeth Gardens, Inc.** - 801 N.E. 33rd St., Pompano Beach, FL 33064 t) (954) 484-1515 x5200 Aristides Pallin, CEO; Juana Mejia, Exec. Dir.;

St. Joseph Haitian Mission Manor, Inc. - 1220 N.E. 6th Ave., Pompano Beach, FL 33060 t) (954) 484-1515 x5200 Juana Mejia, Exec. Dir.; Aristides Pallin, CEO;

SUNNY ISLES BEACH

***Miami Beach Marian Towers, Inc.** - 17505 N. Bay Rd., Sunny Isles Beach, FL 33160 t) (954) 484-1515 x5200 Aristides Pallin, CEO; Juana Mejia, Exec. Dir.;

WILTON MANORS

Boystown of Florida, Inc. - 1505 N. E. 26 St., 2nd Fl., Wilton Manors, FL 33305 t) 954-630-9404 parroyo@ccadm.org Peter Routsis-Arroyo, Dir.;

St. Luke's Center of Miami, Inc. - 1505 N.E. 26th St., Wilton Manors, FL 33305 t) (954) 315-2602 eworley@theadom.org Peter Routsis-Arroyo, Dir.;

St. Martin de Porres Housing Project, Inc. - 1505 N.E. 26th St., Wilton Manors, FL 33305; Mailing: 4790 N. State Rd. 7, Lauderdale Lakes, FL 33319 t) (954) 484-1515 x5200 dlogue@chsfla.com www.catholichealthservices.org/ Ralph Lawson, Chair; Aristides Pallin, CEO; David D'Amico, CFO;

MONASTERIES AND RESIDENCES FOR PRIESTS AND BROTHERS [MON]

MIAMI

Belen Jesuit Fathers, Inc. - 12725 S.W. 6th St., Miami, FL 33184 c) (305) 205-1017 Rev. Alberto Garcia, Pres.; Brs.: 1; Priests: 11

Compania de Jesus, Provincia de las Antillas, LLC - Rev. Guillermo Garcia-Tunon, S.J.;

Brothers of the Good Shepherd of Florida, Inc. - 680 N.E. 52nd St., Miami, FL 33137 t) 815-472-3131 judy@sjog-na.org Bro. Richard MacPhee, O.H., Pres.; Brs.: 2

Edmund Rice Christian Brothers of North America - 471 N.E. 53rd St., Miami, FL 33137 t) 914-636-6194 gguarente@cbinstitute.org Bro. Joseph Payne, C.F.C.; Brs.: 5

Dominican Fathers of Miami, Inc. - 5909 N.W. 7th St.,

Miami, FL 33126 t) 305-264-0181 x25 c) 305-613-8265 jpresmanes@barry.edu www.opsouth.org Rev. Eduardo Logiste, O.P. (Dominican Republic); Rev. Charles Gerard Austin, O.P.; Rev. George Boudreau; Rev. Orlando Cardozo, O.P. (Colombia); Rev. David G. Caron, O.P.; Rev. Jose David Padilla, O.P.; Rev. Restituto Perez, O.P.; Rev. Jorge L. Presmanes, O.P.; Rev. Cristobal Torres, O.P.; Priests: 9

Marist Brothers of the Schools, Inc. - 3000 S.W. 87th Ave., Miami, FL 33165 t) 305-223-5650 x2247 Bro. Herbert Baker, F.M.S., Dir.; Bro. Richard Van Houten, Mem.; Brs.: 23

Piarist Fathers, Province of the USA & Puerto Rico - 7700 S.W. 56 St., Miami, FL 33155; Mailing: P.O. Box 11822, Fort Lauderdale, FL 33339 t) 954-771-6525 piaristfl@bellsouth.net www.piarist.info Rev. Ricardo Rivera, Sch.P., Rector; Rev. Francisco Anaya, Sch.P., Mem.; Rev. Mario Vizcaino, Sch.P., Mem.; Priests: 3

Villa Javier - 12725 S.W. 6th St., Miami, FL 33184-1305 c) (305) 205-1017 psuarezsj@belenjesuit.org Rev. Pedro A. Suarez, S.J., Admin.; Rev. Alberto Garcia, Supr.; Brs.: 1; Priests: 10

NURSING / REHABILITATION / CONVALESCENCE / ELDERLY CARE [NUR]

LAUDERDALE LAKES

***St. John's Rehabilitation Hospital and Nursing Center, Inc.** - 3075 N.W. 35th Ave., Lauderdale Lakes, FL 33311 t) 954-484-1515 dlogue@chsfla.com Aristides Pallin, CEO; Rev. Santhosh Thomas (India); Rev. Antony Vayalikarottu (India); Rosemarie Bailey, Exec. Dir.; Asstd. Annu.: 1,326; Staff: 198

MIAMI

***St. Anne's Nursing Center, St. Anne's Residence, Inc.** - 11855 Quail Roost Dr., Miami, FL 33177 t) (954) 484-1515 x5200 Rev. Edmund Aku (Cameroon); Rev. Francis Whatley; Aristides Pallin, CEO; Sandra Cabezas, Exec. Dir.; Asstd. Annu.: 945; Staff: 172

NORTH MIAMI

Villa Maria Nursing and Rehabilitation Center, Inc. - 1050 N.E. 125 St., North Miami, FL 33161 t) 954-484-1515 Nathaniel Johnson, Exec. Dir.; Aristides Pallin, CEO;

St. Catherine's Rehabilitation Hospital - t) (954) 484-1515

St. Catherine's West Rehabilitation Hospital - 8850 N.W. 122nd St., Hialeah, FL 33018 t) (954) 484-1515 Msgr. M. Parker Ogboe (Nigeria);

Villa Maria Nursing Center - t) (954) 484-1515 x5200

Villa Maria West Skilled Nursing Facility - 8850 N.W. 122nd St., Hialeah, FL 33016 t) (954) 484-1515 x5200 Rev. Esteker Elyse, S.M.M. (Haiti); Msgr. M. Parker Ogboe (Nigeria);

RETREAT HOUSES / RENEWAL CENTERS [RTR]

MIAMI

***Ignatian Spirituality Center, Inc. - Manresa Retreat House** - 12190 S.W. 56th St., Miami, FL 33175; Mailing: P.O. Box 651512, Miami, FL 33265 t) 305-596-0001 mgarciasj@belenjesuit.org; info@ceimiami.org ceimiami.org Ignatian Retreat, Religious and psychological workshops, seminars on Papal documents, Family Encounters, services for the Dioceses. Rev. Marcelino Garcia, S.J., Dir.;

PINECREST

MorningStar Renewal Center, Inc. - 7275 S.W. 124th St., Pinecrest, FL 33156-5324 t) 305-238-4367 info@morningstarrenewal.org www.morningstarrenewal.org Sue DeFerrari, Dir.;

SEMINARIES [SEM]

HIALEAH

The Redemptoris Mater Seminary Archdiocese of Miami, Inc. - 1040 W. 29th St., Hialeah, FL 33012 t) 305-882-1728 seminary@rmmiami.org www.rmmiami.org Most Rev. Thomas G. Wenski, Archbishop; Rev. Emanuele DeNigris (Italy), Rector; Rev. Pedro Luis Durango Agudelo, Vice Rector; Rev. Juan Alfredo Sanchez Leandro (Spain), Spiritual Dir.; Stds.: 33; Pr. Tchrs.: 3

MIAMI

St. John Vianney College Seminary, Inc. - 2900 S.W. 87th Ave., Miami, FL 33165 t) 305-223-4561 rector@sjvcs.edu www.sjvcs.edu Most Rev. Thomas G. Wenski, Archbishop; Msgr. Pablo A. Navarro, Rector; Rev. Bryan Anthony Garcia, Vice Rector; Rev. Konrad Jozef Zaborowski, S.D.S (Poland), Prof.; Rev. Daniel P. Martin, Chair, Philosophy Dept. & Coord., Spiritual Formation; Rev. Jorge Perales, Chair & Prof., Theology & Dir. Liturgy Asst.; Rev. Luis Ardiel Rivero, Asst. Admin.; Rev. Joseph Everett Rogers, Spiritual Dir.; Stds.: 49; Lay Tchrs.: 4; Pr. Tchrs.: 6

SHRINES [SHR]

MIAMI

National Shrine of Our Lady of Charity - 3609 S. Miami Ave., Miami, FL 33133-4205 t) 305-854-2404 santuario@ermita.org www.ermita.org Rev. Jose Espino, Rector; Rev. Carlos J. Cespedes (Cuba), Par. Vicar;

***Schoenstatt Movement of Florida, Inc.** - 22800 S.W. 187 Ave., Miami, FL 33170 t) 305-248-4800 www.schoenstattmiamiusa.org Rev. Raimundo Costa, I.S.P., Spiritual Adv./Care Srvcs.;

SPECIAL CARE FACILITIES [SPF]

COOPER CITY

Ministry to the Deaf or Disabled - Schott Memorial Center Inc. - 6591 S. Flamingo Rd., Cooper City, FL 33330 t) 954-434-3306 iramirez@schottcommunities.org www.schottcommunities.org Ileana Ramirez-Cueli, Exec. Dir.; Pablo A. Cuadra, DRE; Bed Capacity: 19; Asstd. Annu.: 130; Staff: 26

MIAMI

Camillus Health Concern, Inc. (Good Shepherd Health Center) - 336 N.W. 5th St., Miami, FL 33128 t) 305-577-4840 info@camillushealth.org www.camillushealth.org Provides medical, dental, mental health and social services to persons who are homeless, mentally ill, &/or poor. John Dubois, Chair; Francis Afram-Gyening, CEO; Asstd. Annu.: 5,870; Staff: 82

Camillus House, Inc. - 1603 N.W. 7th Ave., Miami, FL 33136 t) 305-374-1065 x308 hfernandez@camillus.org www.camillus.org Services to the homeless. Hilda Fernandez, CEO; Bed Capacity: 1,874; Asstd. Annu.: 25,927; Staff: 214

Gift of Hope, Missionaries of Charity - 724 N.W. 17th St., Miami, FL 33136 t) 305-326-0032; 305-545-5699 weberag@att.net Sr. M. Ajaya, M.C., Supr.; Bed Capacity: 24; Asstd. Annu.: 70,297; Staff: 1

Soup Kitchen - t) (305) 326-0032

Women's and Children's Shelter - t) (305) 326-0032

St. John Bosco Clinic Inc. - 730 N.W. 34th St., Miami, FL 33127 t) 305-635-1335 luz.gallardo@sjbclinic.org stjohnboscoclinicmiami.org Free clinic for underserved. Sr. Rosa M. Lopez, S.S.J., Chair; Luz Gallardo, Dir.; Asstd. Annu.: 1,077; Staff: 7

An asterisk (*) denotes an organization that has established tax-exempt status directly with the IRS and is not covered by the USCCB Group Ruling.

Archdiocese for the Military Services, U.S.A.

Ordinariatus Castrensis

MOST REVEREND TIMOTHY P. BROGLIO, J.C.D., S.T.B.

Archbishop for the Military Services; ordained May 19, 1977; appointed Titular Archbishop of Amiternum & Apostolic Nuncio to the Dominican Republic February 27, 2001; ordained a bishop March 19, 2001; appointed Archbishop for the Military Services November 19, 2007; installed January 25, 2008.

Chancery: Edwin Cardinal O'Brien Pastoral Center, 1025 Michigan Ave., N.E., P.O. Box 4469, Washington, DC 20017-0469. T: 202-719-3600; F: 202-269-9022.
www.milarch.org
info@milarch.org

Established as the Archdiocese For The Military Services, U.S.A. (Ordinariatus Castrensis) March 25, 1985.

Serving U.S. Catholics of the Army, Navy, Marine Corps, Air Force, Space Force, Coast Guard, Department of Veterans Affairs and those in Government Service outside the USA.

Most Reverend F. Richard Spencer, M.A., D.D.
Auxiliary Bishop for the Military Services; ordained May 14, 1988; appointed Titular Bishop of Auzia and Auxiliary Bishop of the Archdiocese for the Military Services May 22, 2010; ordained September 8, 2010.

Most Reverend William J. Muhm, D.D.
Auxiliary Bishop for the Military Services; ordained May 13, 1995; appointed Titular Bishop of Capsus and Auxiliary Bishop of the Archdiocese for the Military Services January 22, 2019; ordained March 25, 2019.

Most Reverend Neal J. Buckon, D.D.
Auxiliary Bishop for the Military Services; ordained May 25, 1995; appointed Titular Bishop of Vissalsa and Auxiliary Bishop of the Archdiocese for the Military Services January 3, 2011; ordained February 22, 2011.

Most Reverend Joseph L. Coffey, D.D.
Auxiliary Bishop for the Military Services; ordained May 18, 1996; appointed Titular Bishop of Arsacal and Auxiliary Bishop of the Archdiocese for the Military Services January 22, 2019; ordained March 25, 2019.

STATISTICAL OVERVIEW

Personnel

Archbishops	1
Auxiliary Bishops	4
Retired Bishops	1
Permanent Deacons in Diocese	2

Vital Statistics

Receptions into the Church:

Infant Baptism Totals	816
Minor Baptism Totals	328
Adult Baptism Totals	182
Received into Full Communion	102
First Communions	1,094
Confirmations	911
Marriages:	
Catholic	125
Interfaith	25
Total Marriages	150

LEADERSHIP

Vicar General & Moderator of the Curia - Rev. Msgr. Jeffrey G. Laible;

Episcopal Vicars -

Episcopal Vicar for Installations in Europe and Asia - Most Rev. William J. Muhm;

Episcopal Vicar for Installations in the AMS Eastern Vicariate of the United States - Most Rev. F. Richard Spencer;

Episcopal Vicar for Installations in the AMS Western Vicariate of the United States - Most Rev. Neal J. Buckon;

Episcopal Vicar for Veteran Affairs - Most Rev. Joseph L. Coffey;

OFFICES AND DIRECTORS

Chancery - t) 202-719-3600 info@milarch.org www.milarch.org

Chancellor - Very Rev. Robert R. Cannon;

Vice Chancellor & Archivist - Sr. Helen Sumander, M.C.S.T.;

Office of Evangelization -

Vice Chancellor for Evangelization - Dr. Mark Moitoza;

Director of Faith Formation - Jose M. Amaya;

Office of Vocations -

Director of Vocations - Rev. S. Matthew Gray;

Assistant to the Archbishop - Sr. Lisa Marie Drover, O.S.F.;

Chief Financial Officer - William Biggs;

Director of Advancement - Salvador Perez;

Tribunal -

Judicial Vicar - Very Rev. Mark Rutherford;

Judges - Rev. Thomas J. Petro; Rev. Pius Pietrzyk, O.P.; Rev. John B. Ward; Linda E. Price; Mateusz A. Makowski;

Defenders of the Bond - Rev. Jordan F. Hite, T.O.R.; Rev. Joseph G. Mulroney; Zabrina Decker; Michele M. McAloon; Elisa Ugarte; Adrienne A. Yates;

Notary - Leslie A. Floeter;

General Counsel - Elizabeth Tomlin;

Presbyteral Council - Most Rev. F. Richard Spencer; Most Rev. Neal J. Buckon; Most Rev. William J. Muhm; Most Rev. Joseph L. Coffey; Rev. Msgr. Jeffrey G. Laible; Rev. Msgr. Gerald D. McManus; Very Rev. Mark Rutherford; Very Rev. Robert R. Cannon; Rev. Alejandro De Jesus; Rev. Curtiss Dwyer; Rev. Gary Fukes; Rev. Alan Irizarry; Rev. Robert Monagel;

United States Army Chaplains -

Army Chaplains - Rev. Philip Agber; Rev. Raymond A. Akeriwe, S.M.A. (Ghana); Rev. Alwyn M. Albano (Philippines); Rev. Eric J. Albertson; Rev. Lito D. Amande (Philippines); Rev. Christopher C. Anumata (Nigeria); Rev. Daniel Asue; Rev. Dominik Bakowski; Rev. John F. Barkemeyer; Rev. Joseph R. Brankatelli; Rev. Marcin J. Bulinski; Rev. Yuen Servanez Caballejo; Rev. Joseph C. Campbell; Rev. James B. Collins; Rev. Stephen D. Cotter; Rev. Jason Dechenne; Rev. Christopher E. Doering; Rev. Christopher Dorsey; Rev. Sampson U. Etim, M.S.P. (Nigeria); Rev. Matthew Faucett; Rev. John Michael Fletcher; Rev. Joseph M. Fleury, S.M.; Rev. John B. Gabriel (India); Rev. Grantley DaCosta Gaskin; Rev. Daniel R. Goulet; Rev. Frantisek A. Halka; Rev. Paul A. Halladay; Rev. Anselmo Hernandez, L.C.; Rev. Jason E. Hesseling; Rev. John Vianney Ijeoma (Nigeria); Rev. Sylvester Ileka; Rev. Alan M. Irizarry; Rev. Lyndon A. Jong (Philippines); Rev. Thomas N. Kelly; Rev. Andriy Khomyn; Rev. Claudes Kilumbu (Congo); Rev. David R. Kirk; Rev. Rajmund Kopec; Rev. Piotr Koziolkiewicz; Rev. Lukasz Kozlowski; Rev. Felix K. Kumai (Nigeria); Rev. Andrew F. Lawrence; Rev. Joseph P. Lea; Rev. Kiskama Lemor, C.S.Sp.; Rev. Benjamin Letran; Rev. Michael P. Lindsay; Rev. Jhon Madrid; Rev. Edward Martin; Rev. Stephen C. McDermott; Rev. John Michael Metz; Rev. Bolivar G. Molina; Rev. Guillermo Leon Mora Gomez; Rev. Leo Moras (India); Rev. Adam Muda; Rev. Killian Muli (Kenya); Rev. Adolphus Muoghalu; Rev. Maciej Napieralski (Poland); Rev. Martin Novitzky; Rev. Przemyslaw J. Nowak; Rev. Anselm Nwagbara (Nigeria); Rev. Peter Nwokoye; Rev. Arkadiusz Ochalek; Rev. Francis I. Oforka (Nigeria); Rev. George Okoth (Kenya); Rev. Isaac Opara (Nigeria); Rev. Emanuel Otiaba (Nigeria); Rev. Michael Palmer; Rev. Joel Panzer; Rev. Jeffrey Paveglio; Rev. James Peak; Rev. Peter A. Pomposello; Rev. Joseph Reffner; Rev. Jerzy Rzasowski (Poland); Rev. Eugene Savarimuthu; Rev. Mikolaj L. Scibbior (Poland); Rev. Alexander Scott; Rev. Gerald Sherbourne; Rev. Romelo B. Somera (Philippines); Rev. Denis Ssekannyo (Uganda); Rev. Philip P. Tah (Nigeria); Rev. David M. Voss; Rev. James Walling; Rev. Matthew Whitehead; Rev. Jeffrey T. Whorton; Rev. Lukasz J. Willenberg; Rev. Jeremi C. Wodecki; Rev. Bernardino S. Yebra (Philippines); Rev. Pawel Zemczak;

Army National Guard Chaplains - Rev. Adam L. Ahern; Very Rev. Richard J. Allen; Rev. Patrick P. Brownell; Rev. Christopher S. Butera; Rev. Kevin P. Cavanaugh; Rev. Van Constant; Rev. Brian J. Converse; Rev. Michael Creagan; Rev. Chad O. Gion; Rev. Scott Gratton; Rev. Adam Hofer; Rev. Dominic Ibok; Rev. Glennon Jones; Rev. Brian P. Kane; Rev. Raymond J. LaVoie; Rev. Robert Edward Lacey; Rev. Joseph Marcoux; Rev. David L. Meinzen; Rev. Kevin T. Peek; Rev. Angel Sanchez; Rev. Alejandro Sanchez-Munoz; Rev. David Severson; Rev. Mark Tracy; Rev. Julio Angel Vera Gonzalez; Very Rev. John R. Worster;

Army Reserve Chaplains - Rev. Joseph M. Adams, O.S.B.; Rev. James Akpan; Rev. Jose-Angel Anaya Estrada; Rev. Boguslaw Adam Augustyn, C.Ss.R.; Rev. Vasyl S. Behay; Rev. Anthony N. Bernas (Philippines); Rev. Minhyun Cho; Rev. Biju Chitteth Cleatus; Rev. Cecil C. Corneille; Rev. Andrew De Silva; Rev. Cathal Doherty; Rev. Rafael E. Esquen; Rev. Miguel Flores-Perez; Rev. Bartlomiej L. Gadaj; Rev. Peter Gevera (Kenya); Rev. Jay Horning; Rev. Hilary Ike (Nigeria); Rev. Ishmael O. Iwuala (Nigeria); Rev. Sudash Joseph Kokeram; Rev. Severyn Kovalyshin; Rev. James J. Krische; Rev. Dawid Krzeszowski (Poland); Rev. Denis M. Mandamuna, C.F.I.C. (Congo); Rev. Adam Marchese; Rev. Wankie-Dean Mbuzi; Rev. Kristoffer T. McKusky; Rev. Junot Nelvy; Rev. Filbert Ngwila; Rev. Przemyslaw J. Nowak; Rev. Alexander Nwagwu; Rev. Cosmas Nzeabalu (Nigeria); Rev. Dilio A. Onyejiuwa (Nigeria); Rev. Mario Palanca (Philippines); Rev. Robert Pamula (Poland); Rev. Sojan Parappilly Xavier; Rev. Brian Ray; Rev. Teji John Thanippilly; Rev. Henry Tutuwan; Rev. Sinisa Ubiparipovic; Rev. Valentine C. Ugwuanya; Rev. Martin Vavrak; Rev. M. Paul Weberg, O.S.B.; Rev. Dane Westhoff; Rev. Michael Wimsatt; Rev. Zbigniew Zielinski (Poland);

United States Air Force Chaplains -

Air Force Chaplains - Rev. Abraham O. Adejoh; Rev. Paul Obi Amaliri; Rev. Kwaku John Appiah; Rev. Dariusz P. Barna, O.F.M.Cap.; Rev. Ryan Boyle; Rev. Mario T. Catungal, O.C.D. (Philippines); Rev. Ruben Covos; Rev. Dennis De Guzman; Rev. Robbie Deka; Rev. Peter Dumag; Rev. Akajiaku Eluka (Nigeria); Rev. Emmanuel Enoh; Rev. Basil Eruo (Nigeria); Rev. Aaron R. Ferris; Rev. Thomas S. Foley; Rev. Oscar D. Fonseca; Rev. Piotr J. Gajda; Rev. Edwin A. Gomez; Rev. James A. Hamel; Rev. Joseph Hoang; Rev. Joseph O. Idomele (Nigeria); Rev. Jesryll Intes (Philippines); Rev. Joshua Janko; Rev. Pedro Jimenez Barros (Spain); Rev. Guy Kagere (Zambia); Rev. Zachary Kautzky; Rev. Ihar Labacevic; Rev. Jose Nestor P. Lachica (Philippines); Rev. John Machiorlatti; Rev. Brendan O. Mbagwu (Nigeria); Rev. David V. McGuire; Rev. Robert J. Monagle; Rev. Gustavo Montanez; Rev. Jesus Navarrete (Spain); Rev. Hoang Peter Nguyen; Rev. Son Nguyen, S.V.D.; Rev. Laserian Nwoga; Rev. Philip O'Neill; Rev. Nelson Ogwuegbu, S.M.M.M. (Nigeria); Rev. Kizito R. Okhuoya; Rev. Onyema Okorie; Rev. Emmanuel Okwaraocha (Nigeria); Rev. Brandon W. Oman; Rev. Cyriacus N. Onyejegbu; Rev. George Patauave; Rev. Jerzy Pikulinski; Rev. Richard C. Poole; Rev. Nicholas J. Reid; Rev. John F. Reutemann III; Rev. Donald Romero; Rev. Mario S. Rosario (Philippines); Rev. Joshua R. Stevens; Rev. Arkadiusz Szyda (Poland); Rev. Michael C. Tenorio, O.F.M.Cap.; Rev. Khoi Tran; Rev. Bedemoore Udechukwu (Nigeria); Rev. Charles Chidindu Ugo; Rev. Lambert Ulinzwenimana (Rwanda); Rev. William J. Vit Jr.; Rev. Peter Son Vo; Rev. Christopher M. Yakkel;

Air National Guard Chaplains - Rev. Ilie Babota; Very Rev. John B. Bateman Jr.; Rev. Aaron Bayless; Rev. Vincent Bryan Brewer; Rev. Msgr. Michael T. Butler; Rev. James W. Cheney; Rev. Darin V. Colarusso; Rev. Douglas D. Cunningham; Very Rev. Michael G. Dandurand; Rev. Bernard Thomas Donovan; Rev. Thomas L. Duston; Rev. John P. Echert; Rev. Timothy M. Fuller; Rev. Gary M. Garrison; Rev. Anthony Giamello; Rev. Walter Salomon Gomez-Baca; Rev. Samuel M. Gray; Rev. Andrew Jaspers; Rev. Peter Julia; Rev. Anthony Kathawa; Rev. John W. Love; Rev. Thomas Ludwig; Rev. Michael Martinez; Rev. Ryan McDaniel; Rev. John P. McDonough; Rev. Brian J. McNamara; Rev. Michael B. Medas; Rev. David Meinzen; Rev. John J. Mink; Rev. Jeffrey Scott Nicolas; Rev. German Osorio Hernandez; Rev. Rory K. Pitstick; Very Rev. Francis J. Rella; Rev. David G. Thurber Jr.; Rev. Ramon Orlando Tirado; Rev. Justin P. Waltz; Rev. Andrew Young; Rev. Peter Zalewski; Rev. Michael Zimmer;

Air Force Reserve Chaplains - Rev. Jeffrey A. Ballou; Rev. Gregg Caggianelli; Rev. Dairo E. Diaz; Rev. Daniel Duplantis; Rev. Xavier Edet, S.S.J.; Rev. Michal A. Falgowski; Rev. Tyler Harris; Rev. Madison Hayes; Rev. Joseph L. Kim; Rev. Stuart King; Rev. Louis A. Mattina; Rev. Timothy Mergen; Rev. Hung Van Nguyen, S.O.L.T.; Rev. Clive Otieno; Rev. John Phan; Rev. William Robinson; Rev. Wieslaw P. Strzadala; Rev. Daniel Sweeney, S.J.; Very Rev. Raju Thottankara (India); Rev. Raju Thottankara; Rev. Joseph Tran; Rev. Joseph Dang Hai Vu, S.D.D.; Rev. Henry M. Yanju;

United States Navy Chaplains -

Navy Chaplains - Rev. Eduardo B. Amora (Philippines); Rev. William A. Appel; Rev. Emmanuel Banico; Rev. Imad N. Barakeh, B.S.O.; Rev. Thomas Barry II; Rev. Matthew Benjamin; Rev. Mark C. Bristol; Rev. Jason C. Burchell; Rev. Jude C. Caliba (Philippines); Rev. Andrew Colvin; Rev. David A. Daigle; Rev. Luke R. Dundon; Rev. Curtiss Dwyer; Rev. John Fitzpatrick; Rev. Daniel J. Fullerton; Rev. Benton Lee Garrett; Rev. Edward M. Gorman, O.P.; Rev. Brad D. Guillory; Rev. David I. Hammond; Rev. James Harper; Rev. James Hinkle; Rev. Thomas Ianucci; Rev. Charles W. Johnson; Rev. Robert J. Keener; Rev. Jay J. Kersten; Rev. Bradley Lawrence; Rev. Gregory L. Lesher; Rev. Tomasz Maka; Rev. Michael Marcelli; Rev. Adam McMillan; Rev. Jacob A. Meyer; Rev. David Miloscia; Rev. Daniel L. Mode; Rev. Thomas P. O'Flanagan; Rev. Celsius Offor (Nigeria); Rev. Philemon Okoh; Rev. Rene J. Pellessier; Rev. Benjamin Pitre; Rev. Patrick J. Riffle; Rev. Samuel F. Schneider; Rev. Leszek Sikorski; Rev. Daniel Swartz; Rev. Donelson Thevenin; Rev. Ulysses L. Ubalde; Rev. Steven R. Walker; Rev. Erich J. Weiss;

Navy Reserve Chaplains - Rev. Carmelo A. Romanello; Rev. Jacque Beltran; Rev. Santo Cricchio, O.F.M.Conv.; Rev. Carlo B. Davantes (Philippines); Rev. Paul Guzman; Rev. Paul Kostka; Rev. Sean J. LaBat; Very Rev. Jose I. Lavastida; Rev. John H. McKenzie, O.S.B.; Rev. Ron P. Neitzke; Rev. Emmanuel Ochigbo; Rev. Francis Okoli; Rev. Thomas T. Pham, C.Ss.R.; Rev. Michael Plona; Rev. Brian Reedy, S.J.; Rev. Joseph Totton; Rev. Thanh Tran Tung; Very Rev. Matthew J. Westcott; Rev.

Keith Wolfe; Rev. Matthew C. Worthen; Rev. Kurt Young;

Chaplains at non-Catholic Institutions -

Department of Veterans Affairs Hospitals and Chaplains - Rev. Lawrence N. Abara; Rev. Ray G. Abella; Rev. Patrick O. Adejoh (Nigeria); Rev. Stephen Adu-Kwaning (Ghana); Rev. Anthony Aduaka; Rev. Pius Akajiofor (Nigeria); Rev. Ronnie Alvero; Rev. Jude Anyaeche (Nigeria); Rev. Cosmas P. Archibong (Nigeria); Rev. Phil Audet; Rev. Romeo J. Axalan (Philippines); Rev. Charles Barnes, S.J.; Rev. James R. Bastian; Rev. B. Jeffrey Blangiardi, S.J.; Rev. Mario W. Blas (Philippines); Rev. Glenn Breed; Rev. Paul A. Burke; Rev. Frederick K. Byaruhanga (Uganda); Rev. Diego Cadri (Uganda); Rev. Joseph Chacko (India); Rev. Vincent Lazar Chembakassery (India); Rev. Martin Chevalier; Rev. Chijioke A. Chigbo (Nigeria); Rev. Benjamin Chinnappan (India); Rev. Bruce R. Clapham; Rev. Dustin A. Collins; Rev. James M.T. Connolly; Rev. Diego O. Cuevas; Rev. Maurice D'Souza, C.S.C.; Rev. Craig David; Rev. Alejandro DeJesus, O.S.B.; Rev. Lenin Delgado, C.Ss.R.; Rev. Philip P. Denig; Rev. Hector Diaz; Rev. Lawrence Ejiofo; Rev. Edwin O. Emeli (Nigeria); Rev. Barry C. Eneh (Nigeria); Rev. Mathew Eraly (India); Rev. Juan Escamez; Rev. Ignacio M Estrada; Rev. Jose Ferroni; Rev. Patrick Fitzsimons; Rev. Thomas J. Foster; Rev. Bijoy Francis, O.Praem. (India); Rev. R. Peter Francis, O.F.M.; Rev. Gary M. Fukes; Rev. Jacob George (India); Rev. Leonard M. Gicheru; Rev. Joseph A. Grasso, C.PP.S.; Rev. John T. Hannigan; Rev. Fidelis Igwenwanne (Nigeria); Rev. Peter C. Igwilo (Nigeria); Rev. Emmanuel K. Iheaka (Nigeria); Rev. Anthony Ike (Nigeria); Rev. Damian O. Ilokaba (Nigeria); Rev. Alexander Inke, A.J. (Uganda); Rev. Paulinus Iwuji (Nigeria); Very Rev. James P. Jaeger; Rev. James A. Kaczmarek; Rev. John Kelly, O.S.F.S.; Rev. Andrzej Kielkowski, S.D.S.; Rev. Thomas A. Kirchhoefer; Rev. Michael J. Kloton; Rev. Edward Kopec; Rev. Steve Kortendick; Rev. Peter Raphael Kunnalakattu; Rev. Sean J. LaBat; Rev. Michael G. Lankford; Rev. Karl-Albert Lindblad; Rev. Michael A. Lipareli; Rev. Richard A. Lopes, O.F.M.Cap; Rev. Anthony Madu (Nigeria); Rev. Denis M. Mandamuna, C.F.I.C. (Congo); Rev. Richard F. Mattox; Rev. David Meinzen; Rev. Isaac Ebo Mensah (Ghana); Rev. Tony Kyere Mensah (Ghana); Rev. Abraham Miller; Very Rev. Jonathan K. Morse; Rev. James E. Moster; Rev. Douglas L. Mullin; Rev. Patrick E. Murphy; Rev. Christopher P. Myers, S.O.L.T.; Rev. Innocent E. Njoku, C.S.Sp (Nigeria); Rev. Austin Charles Ochu, S.M.A.; Rev. Emmanuel Okeiyi, C.C.C.E. (Nigeria); Rev. Theophilus T. Okpara (Nigeria); Rev. Joseph Olikkara, M.S.T. (India); Rev. Christopher Onuoha; Rev. Leonard Onwumere, J.P. (Nigeria); Rev. Paul Oye (Nigeria); Rev. Theodore K. Parker; Rev. Juan C. Perez; Rev. Thomas Pesaresi, M.M.; Rev. Marian A. Piekarczyk, S.D.S.; Rev. Brian Plate; Rev. Antony W. Rajayan (India); Rev. Edward F. Ramatowski; Rev. Richard J. Rath; Rev. Joseph Repko; Rev. John A. Rich, M.M.; Rev. Randall Roberts, O.F.M.; Rev. Robert E. Roetzel; Rev. Richard Rojas; Rev. Romain Rurangirwa (Rwanda); Rev. Ramon Saavedra (Philippines); Rev. Gerald F. (Damien) Schill; Rev. Bowan M. Schmitt; Rev. Andrew Sioleti, I.V.Dei.; Rev. Charles F. Smith, S.V.D.; Very Rev. Hugo C. Soutus; Rev. Jerome R. Steinbrunner, C.PP.S.; Very Rev. Archpriest Thomas P. Steinmetz; Rev. Thomas P. Steinmetz; Rev. Reynaldo S. Taylor; Rev. Bruce Teague; Rev. Ivan J. Torres; Rev. Ivan R. Trujillo; Rev. Tarasisio Tumuhereze, A.J. (Uganda); Rev. Ivan Tyhovych; Rev. Chrysanthus F. Udoh, M.S.P. (Nigeria); Rev. John Ugobueze (Nigeria); Rev. Sebastian A. Ugochukwu (Nigeria); Rev. Marcellinus U. Uwandu (Nigeria); Rev. Carl E. Vacek, T.O.R.; Rev. Donald J. Van Alstyne, M.I.C.; Rev. Vincent VanDoan; Rev. George Varkey; Rev. Dominic J. Vitaliano; Rev. Joseph B. Westfall; Rev. Tyson J. Wood;

Civil Air Patrol - Rev. Belen Gonzalez y Perez; Rev. John M. Harth; Rev. Jeffrey G. Hopper; Rev. Dennis J. Mercieri; Rev. Ross Syracuse, O.F.M.Conv.;

Auxiliary Priests - GS and non-GS Full Time Contract - Rev. Joseph Okech Adhunga, A.J. (Kenya); Rev. Christopher Adunchezor (Nigeria); Rev. Aaron Bayless; Rev. Antony N. Berchmanz (Philippines); Rev. Michael Booth; Rev. Rafael Britanico (Philippines); Rev. Longin Buhake (Congo); Rev. Msgr. Michael T. Butler; Rev. Dominic Joseph Castro; Rev. Biju Chitteth Cleatus; Rev. James M. Coindreau, L.C.; Rev. Jamilcar Cruz; Rev. Msgr. William F. Cuddy; Rev. Joseph Deichert; Rev. Dairo E. Diaz; Rev. Raphael Eke; Rev. Elbert A. Fadallan; Rev. Thomas J. Fey; Rev. Kevin Fimian; Rev. Richard Flores; Rev. Gildardo Garcia; Rev. Luis Garcia-Chavez; Rev. Tadeusz Gegotek; Rev. Linn S. Harbour; Rev. John Paul Ryan Heiser; Rev. Jeffrey F. Henry; Rev. Thomas Hoar, S.S.E.; Rev. Eric R. Hoog, C.Ss.R.; Rev. Simon Ignacio (Philippines); Rev. David Ivey; Rev. Gerald Kasule (Uganda); Rev. Stuart King; Rev. John M. Kinney; Rev. David Klecker; Rev. Hermes LosBanes (Philippines); Rev. Ignatius Madumere, O.P. (Nigeria); Rev. Philip A. Mahalic; Rev. Peter McLaughlin; Rev. Msgr. Gerald D. McManus; Rev. Adam McMillan; Rev. Gerald Glorioso Metal; Rev. Msgr. Ronald W. Metha; Rev. Patrick Mockler; Rev. John Monahan; Rev. Bhaskar Morugudi (India); Rev. Donald Moss; Rev. John Bosco Musinguzi (Rwanda); Rev. Michael E. Nolan; Rev. Martin Okoro (Nigeria); Rev. Samuel Oloyede, O.P.; Rev. Max B. Omana (Philippines); Rev. Gilbert Omolo, C.P.; Rev. Benedict M Opara (Nigeria); Rev. Matthew Pawlikowski; Rev. Rory Pitstick; Rev. Alexander Ramos (Philippines); Rev. Tomy Raphel; Rev. Redmond P. Raux; Rev. Jovy Roldan; Rev. Juan S. Salonga; Rev. Jude Serfino (Philippines); Rev. Keith J. Shuley; Rev. Stephan Silipigni; Rev. Dawid Stelmach; Rev. Paul Stewart; Rev. Steven Thomlison; Rev. Joselito S. Tiongson (Philippines); Rev. Nelson T. Toledo (Philippines); Rev. John Tran; Rev. Adam Frederick Travis; Rev. Joseph Udeze; Rev. Franklin Watts (United Kingdom); Rev. William Waun; Rev. Joseph Yamaoka; Rev. Paul Zaccone, SS.CC.;

INSTITUTIONS LOCATED IN DIOCESE

MISCELLANEOUS [MIS]

ALEXANDRIA

Catholic War Veterans, USA, Inc. - 441 N. Lee St., Alexandria, VA 22314-2301 t) 703-549-3622 admin@cwv.org Most Rev. Joseph L. Coffey, Contact;

SAN FRANCISCO

National Conference of Veterans Affairs Catholic Chaplains, Inc. - 4150 Clement St., San Francisco, CA 94121 t) 415-221-4810 x24505 c) 415-370-4011 ncvacc.catholic@gmail.com Rev. Alejandro De Jesus, Contact;

WASHINGTON

The Chaplains Aid Association - ; Mailing: P.O. Box 4469, Washington, DC 20017

Father Capodanno Guild - 1025 Michigan Ave., N.E., Washington, DC 20017; Mailing: P.O. Box 29424, Washington, DC 20017 t) 202-719-3642 Mary Preece, Contact; P. Stephen Stanley, Chair;

The Saint John XXIII Foundation, Inc. - 1025 Michigan Ave., N.E., Washington, DC 20017 t) (202) 230-4316 www.stjohnxxiiifoundation.org

Military Council of Catholic Women (MCCW) - 1025 Michigan Ave., NE, Washington, DC 20017; Mailing: P.O. Box 4456, Washington, DC 20017 t) (785) 341-4540 admin@mccw.org Bevin Landrum, Pres.;

21st Century Centurions - ; Mailing: P.O. Box 4469, Washington, DC 20017

An asterisk (*) denotes an organization that has established tax-exempt status directly with the IRS and is not covered by the USCCB Group Ruling.

Archdiocese of Milwaukee

(Archidioecesis Milvauchiensis)

MOST REVEREND JEROME E. LISTECKI

Archbishop of Milwaukee; ordained May 14, 1975; appointed Auxiliary Bishop of Chicago and Titular Bishop of Nara November 7, 2000; consecrated January 8, 2001; appointed Bishop of La Crosse December 29, 2004; installed March 1, 2005; appointed Archbishop of Milwaukee November 14, 2009; installed January 4, 2010. Chancery Office: 3501 S. Lake Dr., P.O. Box 070912, Milwaukee, WI 53207-0912. T: 414-769-3497.

Chancery Office: 3501 S. Lake Dr., P.O. Box 070912, Milwaukee, WI 53207-0912. T: 414-769-3340; F: 414-769-3408.
www.archmil.org
chancery@archmil.org

Square Miles 4,758.

Established November 28, 1843; Created Archbishopric February 12, 1875.

Corporate Title: Archdiocese of Milwaukee.

Comprises the Counties of Dodge, Fond du Lac, Kenosha, Milwaukee, Ozaukee, Racine, Sheboygan, Walworth, Washington and Waukesha in the State of Wisconsin.

For legal titles of parishes and archdiocesan institutions, consult the Chancery Office.

Most Reverend Jeffrey R. Haines
Auxiliary Bishop of Milwaukee; ordained May 17, 1985; appointed Titular Bishop of Thagamuta and Auxiliary Bishop of Milwaukee January 25, 2017; consecrated March 17, 2017. Chancery Office: 3501 S. Lake Dr., P.O. Box 070912, Milwaukee, WI 53207-0912. T: 414-769-3594.

Most Reverend James T. Schuerman
Auxiliary Bishop of Milwaukee; ordained May 17, 1986; appointed Titular Bishop of Girba and Auxiliary Bishop of Milwaukee January 25, 2017; consecrated March 17, 2017. Chancery Office: 3501 S. Lake Dr., P.O. Box 070912, Milwaukee, WI 53207-0912. T: 414-769-3594.

STATISTICAL OVERVIEW

Personnel

Archbishops	1
Auxiliary Bishops	2
Retired Bishops	1
Retired Abbots	1
Priests: Diocesan Active in Diocese	120
Priests: Diocesan Active Outside Diocese	13
Priests: Diocesan in Foreign Missions	5
Priests: Retired, Sick or Absent	133
Number of Diocesan Priests	271
Religious Priests in Diocese	343
Total Priests in your Diocese	614
Extern Priests in Diocese	111
Ordinations:	
Diocesan Priests	6
Religious Priests	7
Transitional Deacons	5
Permanent Deacons	16
Permanent Deacons in Diocese	169
Total Brothers	94
Total Sisters	1,898

Parishes

Parishes	189
With Resident Pastor:	
Resident Diocesan Priests	77
Resident Religious Priests	36
Without Resident Pastor:	
Administered by Priests	63
Administered by Deacons	8
Administered by Lay People	5
Professional Ministry Personnel:	
Brothers	2
Sisters	17
Lay Ministers	594

Welfare

Catholic Hospitals	9
Total Assisted	2,911,479
Health Care Centers	1
Total Assisted	250
Homes for the Aged	19
Total Assisted	4,118
Day Care Centers	4
Total Assisted	549
Specialized Homes	4
Total Assisted	8,863
Special Centers for Social Services	12
Total Assisted	413,326
Residential Care of Disabled	2
Total Assisted	460
Other Institutions	19
Total Assisted	291,617

Educational

Seminaries, Diocesan	1
Students from This Diocese	42
Students from Other Dioceses	34
Diocesan Students in Other Seminaries	8
Seminaries, Religious	2
Students, Religious	8
Total Seminarians	58
Colleges and Universities	5
Total Students	17,743
High Schools, Diocesan and Parish	7
Total Students	2,677
High Schools, Private	9
Total Students	3,983
Elementary Schools, Diocesan and Parish	81
Total Students	18,729
Elementary Schools, Private	4
Total Students	1,638
Non-residential Schools for the Disabled	1
Total Students	27
Catechesis/Religious Education:	
High School Students	6,905
Elementary Students	12,357
Total Students under Catholic Instruction	64,117
Teachers in Diocese:	
Priests	31
Brothers	2
Sisters	17
Lay Teachers	3,953

Vital Statistics

Receptions into the Church:	
Infant Baptism Totals	4,084
Minor Baptism Totals	287
Adult Baptism Totals	159
Received into Full Communion	420
First Communions	4,038
Confirmations	3,258
Marriages:	
Catholic	890
Interfaith	275
Total Marriages	1,165
Deaths	4,479
Total Catholic Population	509,903
Total Population	2,367,407

LEADERSHIP

Vicars General - Most Rev. Jeffrey R. Haines (bishophaines@archmil.org); Most Rev. James T. Schuerman (bishopschuerman@archmil.org); Very Rev. Nathan D. Reesman (reesmann@archmil.org);

Archdiocesan Consultors - Most Rev. Jeffrey R. Haines (bishophaines@archmil.org); Most Rev. James T. Schuerman (bishopschuerman@archmil.org); Rev. Dennis Ackeret;

Archdiocesan Council of Priests - Most Rev. Jeffrey R. Haines (bishophaines@archmil.org); Most Rev. James T. Schuerman (bishopschuerman@archmil.org); Very Rev. Phillip A. Bogacki (bogackip@archmil.org);

Archdiocesan Pastoral Council - Kathi Andreoni; Rick Bigus; Tim Cincotta;

Archbishop's Executive Council - Most Rev. Jeffrey R. Haines (bishophaines@archmil.org); Most Rev. James T. Schuerman (bishopschuerman@archmil.org); Very Rev. Phillip A. Bogacki (bogackip@archmil.org);

Moderator of the Curia - Very Rev. Phillip A. Bogacki (bogackip@archmil.org);

Chief of Staff - t) 414-769-3590 Jerome T. Topczewski (topczewskij@archmil.org);

Chief Operating Officer - t) 414-769-3360 Brad Berghouse (berghouseb@archmil.org);

Executive Secretary - t) 414-769-3497 Gwen Fastabend (fastabendg@archmil.org);

Auxiliary Bishops - Most Rev. Jeffrey R. Haines (bishophaines@archmil.org); Most Rev. James T. Schuerman (bishopschuerman@archmil.org);

Executive Assistant to Auxiliary Bishops - t) 414-769-3594 Nancy Kerns;

Bishop Emeritus - t) 414-769-3594 Most Rev. Richard J. Sklba;

Director of Community Relations - t) 414-769-3588 Lydia LoCoco (lococol@archmil.org);

Director - Archdiocesan Events & Special Projects - t) 414-769-3585 Jennifer Oliva (olivaj@archmil.org);

Chancery Office - chancery@archmil.org

Chancellor - t) 414-769-3341 Barbara Anne Cusack;

Vice Chancellor - t) 414-769-3307 Very Rev. Ricardo Martin Pinillos;

Archivist - t) 414-769-3407 Shelly Taylor;

Associate Director of Archives - t) 414-769-3431 Amy Lisinski;

Office of Communications - communication@archmil.org

Director - t) 414-769-3461 Sandra Peterson;

Associate Director of Communications & Marketing - t) 414-769-3453 Melissa Bishop;

Associate Director of Communications - t) 414-769-3435 Amy Taylor;

Associate Director of Communications - t) (414) 769-3452 John Bruns;

Associate Director of Content - t) (414) 769-3504 Kathleen McGillis Drayna;

Associate Director for Creative Services - t) 414-769-3436 Gina Rupcic;

Graphic Designer for Creative Services - t) 414-769-3437 Meghan Endter;

Coordinator for Communications - t) 414-769-3494 Heidi Heistad;

Financial Services -

Treasurer/Finance Officer - t) 414-769-3325 Chris Brown;

Diocesan Controller - t) 414-769-3347 Deanna Chernouski;

General Counsel - t) 414-769-3379 Sharon Hanson;

Director, Parish & School Financial Consulting - t) 414-769-3377 Katherine Esterle;

Parish & School Financial Consultant - t) 414-769-3336 Denise Montpas;

Parish & School Financial Consultant - t) 414-769-3335 Michael Waddell;

Manager of Business Analysis - t) 414-769-3346 Anne Levendoski;

Senior Accountant - t) 414-769-3314 Carol Abuya;

Financial Analyst - t) 414-769-3316 Nancy Lechuga;

Treasury Analyst - t) 414-769-3326 Kim Kasten;

Lay Pension Coordinator - t) 414-769-3317 Bridget Fischer;

Payroll Coordinator - t) 414-769-3318 Donna Steffan;

Victim Assistance and Employee Support Coordinator - t) 414-758-2232 Sofia Thorn;

Safe Environment Program Manager - t) 414-769-3449 Suzanne Nickolai;

Safe Environment Program Training Coordinator - t) 414-769-3447 Cynthia Rivera Garcia;

Building Services - t) 414-769-3491 Steve Jupp (jupps@archmil.org);

Coordinator for Maintenance - t) 414-769-3566 Larry Schwartz;

Maintenance Assistant - t) 414-769-3566 Steve Kelliher;

Director for Cemeteries and Mausoleums - t) 414-438-4420 Mary Thiel (mthiel@cfcmission.org);

Spiritual Director for Cemeteries and Mausoleums - t) 414-645-0611 Rev. Aurelio H. Perez;

Director of Outreach for Cemeteries and Mausoleums - t) 414-769-3492 Dcn. Jorge Benavente;

Archdiocesan Marian Shrine - t) 414-640-5590 Dcn. Steven F. Pemper, Dir.;

Human Resource Services -

Director for Central Offices and Agencies - t) 414-769-3328 Susan Gorski;

Human Resources and Benefits Administrator - t) 414-769-3423 Maureen Wurster;

Director for Parish and School Personnel - t) 414-769-3370 Jenny Moyer;

Human Resources Coordinator - t) (414) 769-3356 Rachel Uchytil;

Associate Director of Recruitment and Engagement - t) (414) 769-3470 Jennifer Pollock;

Apostolate for the Deaf, Director - Rev. Christopher L. Klusman (klusmanc@archmil.org);

Missionary Planning and Leadership Office -

Director, Missionary Planning & Leadership - t) (414) 769-3354 Laura Engel;

Director, Missionary Planning & Leadership - t) (414) 758-2216 Michael Laird;

Associate Director for Missionary Planning & Leadership -

Office of Catholic Social Responsibility -

Director - t) 414-758-2214 Susan McNeil;

Director, Office for Catholic Social Action - t) 414-758-2286 Robert Shelledy;

Director, Office for Hispanic Ministry - t) 414-769-3397 Eva J. Diaz;

Associate Director, Office for Hispanic Ministry - t) 414-769-3398 Maria Prado;

Director, Office for Respect Life and Jail Ministries - t) 414-769-3454 Dcn. James Matthias;

Director, Office for Lay Ministry - t) 414-758-2214 Susan McNeil;

Director, Office for Urban Ministry - t) (414) 758-2215 Shanedra Johnson;

Bilingual Programs and Events Coordinator - t) 414-769-3395 Allie Karos;

Project Rachel Coordinator - t) (414) 769-3448 Colleen Kremer;

Metropolitan Tribunal -

Judicial Vicar - t) (414) 769-3376 Very Rev. Mark C. Payne;

Adjutant Judicial Vicar -

Tribunal Chancellor - t) 414-769-3302 Zabrina R. Decker;

Judges - Very Rev. Phillip A. Bogacki; Very Rev. Mark C. Payne; Zabrina R. Decker;

Judges for the Appellate Court - Very Rev. Phillip A. Bogacki; Very Rev. Mark C. Payne; Rev. James E. Connell;

Defender of the Bond - Rebecca Ruesch;

Procurators and Advocates - Natalia Penaloza Ferreira; Andrew R. J. Vaughn;

Promoter of Justice - Very Rev. Phillip A. Bogacki; Zabrina R. Decker;

Office for Marital Reconciliation-Separation - Zabrina R. Decker;

Archdiocesan Court of Equity - Zabrina R. Decker;

Canonical Consultant - t) 414-769-3442 Rebecca Ruesch;

Office of Evangelization & Catechesis -

Director of Evangelization & Catechesis - t) 414-758-2219 Pete Burds;

Director of Evangelization & Catechesis - Childhood - t) (414) 758-2242 Gary Pokorny;

Associate Director of Evangelization & Catechesis - Adult & Family - t) 414-758-2211 Doug Ulaszek;

Associate Director of Evangelization & Catechesis - Campus/Young Adult - t) 414-758-2221 Micah Pfundstein;

Associate Director of Evangelization & Catechesis - Parish Renewal - t) 414-758-2218 Margaret Rhody;

Associate Director of Evangelization & Catechesis - Middle/High School Youth - t) (414) 758-2223 Meg Aspinwall;

Special Projects Coordinator - t) (414) 758-2213 Emily Burds;

Natural Family Planning Coordinator - t) (414) 758-2241 Tori Franke;

Campus & Young Adult Coordinator - t) 414-758-2201 Anna Kozlowski;

Program and Event Coordinator - t) 414-758-2240 Jennifer Murphy;

Office Event Coordinator - t) (414) 758-2222 Jaclyn Thompson;

Campus Ministry -

UW-Milwaukee Campus Ministry Director - t) 414-332-9220 Rev. Andrew Infanger;

UW-Milwaukee Campus Ministry Coordinator - Amy Rebholz;

UW-Whitewater Campus Ministry Coordinator - t) 262-473-5555 Andrew Schueller;

UW-Whitewater Campus Ministry Administrative Assistant - t) 262-473-5555 Kim Weiss;

Ordained and Lay Ecclesial Ministry -

Vicar for Ordained, Lay Ecclesial Ministry - t) 414-769-3490 reesmann@archmil.org Very Rev. Nathan D. Reesman;

Vicar for Senior Priests - t) 414-769-3496 Very Rev. James E. Lobacz;

Manager of Priest Placement - t) 414-769-3458 Brenda Cline;

Minister to Priests - t) 414-305-3384 Rev. Alan D. Veik, O.F.M.Cap.;

Vocations Director - t) 414-747-6425 Rev. John C. LoCoco;

Vocations Promoter - t) 414-747-6400 Rev. John Burns;

Director for Deacon Services - t) 414-769-3409 Dcn. James J. Starke;

Director, Diaconate Formation - t) 414-758-2212 Dcn. Dale T. Nees;

Associate Director, Diaconate Formation - t) 414-758-2207 Dcn. Manuel Maldonado;

Associate Director, Pastoral Formation - t) 414-758-2205 Maria Espino;

Schools Office -

Superintendent - t) 414-758-2251

Associate Superintendents - Susan Nelson; John Soper; Bruce Varick;

Stewardship and Development -

Director for Development - t) 414-769-3322 Andy Gaertner;

Director, Catholic Stewardship Appeal - t) 414-769-3320 Jenny Mendenhall;

Director of Planned Giving - t) 414-769-3583 Robert Pfundstein;

Director of Stewardship - t) 414-769-3572 Cindy Lukowitz;

Director for Systems and Operations - t) 414-769-3323 Michele Nabih;

Associate Director Catholic Schools Development - t) 414-769-3451 Paige Rohr;

Synod Implementation -

Director - t) 414-758-2214 Susan McNeil;

World Mission Ministries Director - t) 414-758-2282

Antoinette Mensah (mensaha@archmil.org);
Office for Worship -
Office for Worship Director - t) 414-769-3349 Kim Mandelkow;
Office for Worship Coordinator - t) 414-769-3355 Laurie Cosson;
Catholic Charities -
Vicar - t) 414-769-3400 Very Rev. David H. Reith;
Chief Operating Officer - t) 414-769-3400 Ricardo Cisneros;
Executive Assistant - t) 414-769-3401 Colleen Schmidt;
Director of Mission Advancement - t) 414-769-3400 Jackie Rekowski;
Director of Adult Day Services - t) 414-771-6063 Annette Jankowski;
Director of Behavioral Health - t) 414-771-2881 Laura Ramos;
Director of Child Welfare Services - t) 414-771-2881 Jennifer Layton;
Director of In-Home Support Services - t) 414-771-2881 Carla Alejo;
Director of Outreach and Case Management - t) 414-771-2881 Susan Howland;
Director of Refugee & Immigration Services - t) 414-643-8570 Barbara Graham;
Director of Supported Parenting - t) 262-547-2463 Sarah Matson;
Director of Human Resources - t) 414-769-3400 Nate Braun;
Catholic Herald -
Publisher - t) 414-769-3497 Most Rev. Jerome E. Listecki;
Managing Editor - t) 414-769-3466 Larry Hanson;

PARISHES, MISSIONS, AND CLERGY

STATE OF WISCONSIN

ALLENTON

Congregation of the Resurrection - 209 Main St., Allenton, WI 53002; Mailing: P.O. Box 96, Allenton, WI 53002 t) 262-629-5240 office@resurrectionallenton.org; childandfamily@resurrectionallenton.org resurrectionallenton.org Very Rev. Richard J. Stoffel, Pst.; Rev. Russell L. Arnett, Assoc. Pst.; CRP Stds.: 65

BEAVER DAM

St. Katharine Drexel Parish - 408 S. Spring St., Beaver Dam, WI 53916 t) 920-887-2082 tischlerj@stkatharinedrexelbd.org www.stkatharinedrexelbd.org Rev. William Arnold, Admin.; Rev. Onildo Orellana Diaz, MFM (Guatemala), Assoc. Pst.; Kristin Adsit, DRE; John Pryme, DRE; CRP Stds.: 125

St. Katharine Drexel School - (Grades PreK-8) 503 S. Spring St., Beaver Dam, WI 53916 t) 920-885-5558 ellefsont@stkds.com www.skds.org Tina Ellefson, Prin.; Kimberly Lopas, Librn.; Stds.: 191; Lay Tchrs.: 14

BIG BEND

St. Joseph's Congregation - S89 W22650 Milwaukee Ave., Big Bend, WI 53103 t) 262-662-2832; 262-662-3317 (CRP) parish@stjoesbb.com; cfm@stjoesbb.com www.stjoesbb.com Rev. Andrew T. Kysely, Pst.; Erika Evans, CRE; CRP Stds.: 112

St. Joseph Catholic School - (Grades K-8) t) 262-662-2737 school@stjoesbb.com stjoesbb.com/ Jeffrey Van Rixel, Prin.; Stds.: 92; Lay Tchrs.: 8

BRISTOL

Holy Cross Parish - 18700 116th St., Bristol, WI 53104 t) (262) 857-2068 (Office) holycross.christianformation@gmail.com; holycrossparish.wi@gmail.com www.holycrosscatholicchurch.net Sandra J. Schmitt, Dir.; Shelby Miller, DRE; CRP Stds.: 33

BROOKFIELD

St Dominic's Congregation - 18255 W. Capitol Dr., Brookfield, WI 53045-1422 t) 262-781-3480; 262-781-3480 x251 (CRP); 262-781-3480 x252 (CRP) info@stdominic.net; parish@stdominic.net www.stdominic.net Rev. Dennis J. Saran, Pst.; Rev. Timothy R. Schumaker, Assoc. Pst.; Dcn. Gregory H. Diciaula; Dcn. Jeff Kucharski; Paul Burzynski, Liturgy & Music; Emily Nolan, Youth Min.; Samantha Taylor, Youth Min.; CRP Stds.: 321

St. Dominic Catholic School - (Grades PreK-8) 18105 W. Capitol Dr., Brookfield, WI 53045-1425 t) 262-783-7565 school@stdominic.net; francis.dempsey@stdominic.net www.stdominic.net/school Francis Dempsey, Prin.; Stds.: 408; Lay Tchrs.: 24

St. John Vianney Congregation - 1755 N. Calhoun Rd., Brookfield, WI 53005-5036 t) 262-796-3940; 262-796-3944; 262-796-3946 www.stjohnv.org Very Rev. Edwin M. Kornath, Pst.; Rev. Marco Valentini (Italy), Assoc. Pst.; Dave Baudry, Dir., Adult, Child & Youth Min; Angela Bravata, Dept. Dir., Liturgy, Communications & The Weekend Experience; Janlyn Carvahlo, Assoc. Dir., Adult, Child & Youth Ministry; Joshua Chandra, Dir. Music; Robb Lied, Dir., Admin. Svcs.; Sharon Roberts, Assoc. Dir., Accounting & Human Resources; Peter Thomas, Assoc. Dir. Devel.; John Thompson, Dept. Dir., Formation & Human Concerns; CRP Stds.: 294

St. John Vianney School - (Grades PreK-8) 17500 W. Gebhardt Rd., Brookfield, WI 53045-5096 t) 262-796-3942 Kathy Davis, Prin.; Stds.: 274; Pr. Tchrs.: 2; Lay Tchrs.: 16

St. Luke Congregation - 18000 W. Greenfield Ave., Brookfield, WI 53045 t) 262-782-0032; 262-782-0032 x106 (CRP) stluke@stlukebrookfield.org; csmith@stlukebrookfield.org stlukebrookfield.org Rev. Kenneth J. Augustine, Pst.; Cathy Smith, DRE; CRP Stds.: 36

BURLINGTON

St. Charles Congregation - 441 Conkey St., Burlington, WI 53105; Mailing: 440 Kendall St., Burlington, WI 53105 t) 262-763-2260 jmorrow@ourblcc.org www.ourblcc.org Very Rev. James T. Volkert, Pst.; Rev. Sergio Rodriguez, Assoc. Pst.; Rita VanSchyndel, DRE; Elle Schultz, DRE; CRP Stds.: 176

Congregation of the Immaculate Conception (St. Mary) - 108 McHenry St., Burlington, WI 53105 t) 262-763-1500; 262-763-2260; 262-763-1500; 262-763-2050 stmaryoffice@ourblcc.org; eschultz@ourblcc.org www.ourblcc.org Very Rev. James T. Volkert, Pst.; Rev. Sergio Rodriguez, Assoc. Pst.; Rita Van Schyndel, DRE; Susan Vrzan, Bus. Mgr.; Elle Schultz, DRE; CRP Stds.: 176

BUTLER

St. Agnes Congregation - 12801 W. Fairmount Ave., Butler, WI 53007 t) 262-781-9521; 262-781-6998 (CRP) info@stagnesparish.org; fellinm@stagnesparish.org stagnesparish.org Rev. Joy A. Thachil, S.A.C., Admin.; Dcn. Raymond Waitrovich; Michelle Fellin, DRE; CRP Stds.: 58

St. Agnes School - (Grades PreK-8) t) 262-781-4996 www.stagnesparish.org Rachel Kolbeck, Prin.; Stds.: 143; Lay Tchrs.: 11

CALEDONIA

St. Louis' Congregation - 13207 County Rd. G, Caledonia, WI 53108-9531 t) 262-835-4533 office@stlouisparishwi.com; tclowney@stpaulracine.org www.stlouisparishwi.com Rev. Yamid Blanco, Pst.; Dcn. Jim Zdeb; Mary Beth Clowney, DRE; Ronnie Quella, Music Min.; Thomas Clowney, Bus. Mgr.; CRP Stds.: 45

CAMPBELLSPORT

St. Matthew's Congregation - 419 Mill St., Campbellsport, WI 53010; Mailing: P.O. Box 740, Campbelllsport, WI 53010 t) 920-533-4441 swerth@stmattcport.org; ddoll@sothparish.org www.stmatthewofcsport.org Includes St. Martin Chapel, Ashford & St. Kilian Chapel, St. Kilian. Rev. Mark R. Jones, Pst.; Dawn Doll, DRE; Shawn Woodhead Werth, Bus. Mgr.; CRP Stds.: 113

St. Matthew School - (Grades PreK-7) 423 Mill St., Campbellsport, WI 53010; Mailing: P.O. Box 639, Campbellsport, WI 53010 t) 920-533-4103 office@stmattsschoolcampbellsport.com; jschlaefer@stmattsschoolcampbellsport.com www.stmattschoolcampbellsport.com Joan Schlaefer, Prin.; Stds.: 93; Lay Tchrs.: 8

CEDARBURG

Congregation of St. Francis Borgia - 1375 Covered Bridge Rd., Cedarburg, WI 53012 t) 262-377-1070 parish@sfbchurch.org; ferchm@sfbchurch.org www.saintfrancisborgia.org Rev. Patrick J. Burns, Pst.; Rev. Matthew Ferch, Pst. Assoc.; KC Kranich, Youth Min.; Laura Lindemann, Youth Min.; Catie Weasler, Youth Min.; CRP Stds.: 357

St. Francis Borgia School - (Grades PreK-8) 1425 Covered Bridge Rd., Cedarburg, WI 53012 t) 262-377-2050 office@sfbschool.org www.sfbschool.org Jordan Last, Prin.; Stds.: 289; Lay Tchrs.: 18

CLYMAN

St. John's Congregation - 714 Church St., Clyman, WI 53016; Mailing: 302 Prairie St., P.O. Box 277, Reeseville, WI 53579-0277 t) 920-927-3102 triparish@charter.net www.triparishwi.com Also serves Holy Family, Reeseville & St. Columbkille, Elba. Rev. William Arnold, Admin.; Rev. Onildo Orellana Diaz, MFM (Guatemala), Assoc. Pst.; John Pryme, Youth Min.; Connie Caine, DRE; Mary Hensen, Bus. Mgr.; CRP Stds.: 6

COLUMBUS

St. Columbkille - W10802 County Rd. TT, Columbus, WI 53925; Mailing: P O Box 277, 302 Prairie St., Reeseville, WI 53579 t) 920-623-3989; 920-927-3102 triparish@charter.net www.triparishwi.com Also serves Holy Family, Reeseville and St. John the Baptist, Clyman. Rev. William Arnold, Admin.; Rev. Onildo Orellana Diaz, MFM (Guatemala), Assoc. Pst.; John Pryme, Youth Min.; Connie Caine, DRE; Mary Hensen, Bus. Mgr.; CRP Stds.: 8

CUDAHY

Nativity of the Lord Congregation - 3672 E. Plankinton Ave., Cudahy, WI 53110; Mailing: 4611 S. Kirkwood Ave., Cudahy, WI 53110 t) (414) 482-2920 parishoffice@nativitycudahy.org www.nativitycudahy.org/ Very Rev. Carmelo Giuffre, Pst.; Sr. Sylvia Anne Sheldon, OSF, COO; Karen Bushman, DRE; Dr. Delano Kahlstorff, Music Min.; CRP Stds.: 35

DELAVAN

St. Andrew's Congregation - 714 E. Walworth Ave., Delavan, WI 53115 t) 262-728-5922 stewardship@saspcatholics.org; faithformation@saspcatholics.org www.standrews-delavan.org Rev. Oriol Regales, Pst.; Rev. Josegerman Zapata-Ramirez, Assoc. Pst.; Dcn. Philip O. Kilkenny; Sr. Monica Semper, Dir., Hispanic Ministry; Ray Henderson, DRE; Jennifer Paul, DRE; Becky Baker, Bus. Mgr.; CRP Stds.: 77

St. Andrew School - (Grades PreK-8) 115 S. 7th St., Delavan, WI 53115 t) 262-728-6211 office@standrewsparishschool.com standrews-delavan.org David Wieters, Prin.; Stds.: 150; Lay Tchrs.: 9

DOUSMAN

St. Bruno's Congregation - 226 W. Ottawa Ave., Dousman, WI 53118 t) 262-965-2332 stbruno226@gmail.com; steve.spiegelhoff@gmail.com www.stbrunoparish.com Rev. Daniel P. Volkert, Admin.; Dcn. Joseph M. Senglaub, Parish Life Coord.; Mary Kral, DRE; Steve Spiegelhoff, Bus. Mgr.; CRP Stds.: 54

St. Bruno School - (Grades PreK-8) 246 W. Ottawa Ave., Dousman, WI 53118 t) 262-965-2291 mary.macdonald@stbrunoparishschool.com; tammy.price@stbrunoparishschool.com stbrunoparish.com/st-bruno-parish-school Mary MacDonald, Prin.; Stds.: 91; Lay Tchrs.: 10

EAGLE

St. Theresa's Congregation - 136 W. Waukesha Rd., Eagle, WI 53119-2026 t) 262-594-5200 judyh@sttheresaeagle.com www.sttheresaeagle.com Rev. Jordan Berghouse, Admin.; CRP Stds.: 64

EAST TROY

St. Peters Congregation - 1975 Beulah Ave., East Troy, WI 53120 t) 262-642-7225 x3 (CRP); 262-642-7225 religioused@stpetersschoolet.org; office@stpeterset.org stpeterset.org Rev. Mark L. Molling, Pst.; Susan Bashynski, DRE; CRP Stds.: 100

St. Peter School - (Grades PreK-5) 3001 Elm St., East Troy, WI 53120 t) 262-642-5533 msagat@stpetersschoolet.org Megan Prudom, Prin.; Stds.: 29; Pr. Tchrs.: 1; Lay Tchrs.: 5

EDEN

Good Shepherd Congregation - W1562 Cty. B, Eden, WI 53019 t) 920-477-3201; 920-477-3551 (CRP) sgitter@sothparish.org www.sothparish.org Rev. Mark R. Jones, Pst.; CRP Stds.: 89

St. Michael Chapel - N3604 Scenic Dr., Cascade, WI 53011 t) (920) 477-3201

Shepherd of the Hills (Good Shepherd) - (Grades PreK-8) W1562 County Rd. B, Eden, WI 53019 t) (920) 477-3551 Ronald Smyczek, Prin.; Stds.: 95; Lay Tchrs.: 9

ELKHART LAKE

St. Thomas Aquinas Congregation - 94 N. Lincoln St., Elkhart Lake, WI 53020; Mailing: P.O. Box 396, Elkhart Lake, WI 53020-0396 t) 920-876-2457 c) 920-980-7622 st.thomas.aquinas@frontier.com; ljochmann@wi.rr.com stthomasaquinasel.org Very Rev. Philip D. Reifenberg, Pst.; Lynnette Jochmann, DRE; CRP Stds.: 50

ELKHORN

St. Patrick's Congregation - 107 W. Walworth St., Elkhorn, WI 53121 t) 262-723-5565 office@stpatrickselkhorn.org; business@stpatrickselkhorn.org www.stpatrickselkhorn.org Rev. Oriol Regales, Pst.; Rev. Josegerman Zapata-Ramirez, Assoc. Pst.; Dcn. Arnold Bryson; Ray Henderson, DRE; Becky Baker, Bus. Mgr.; Dcn. Philip O. Kilkenny; CRP Stds.: 194

ELM GROVE

St. Mary's Congregation - 1260 Church St., Elm Grove, WI 53122 t) 262-782-4575 stmaryeg@stmaryeg.org stmaryeg.org Rev. Peter J. Berger, Pst.; Rev. Patrick Behling, Assoc. Pst.; Dcn. Richard T. Piontek; Joshua Dieterich, DRE; Erica Nelson, DRE; Monica Hiller, Bus. Mgr.; CRP Stds.: 118

St. Mary's Visitation School - (Grades PreK-8) 13000 Juneau Blvd., Elm Grove, WI 53122 t) 262-782-7057 info@stmaryeg.org www.stmaryeg.org Mary Tretow, Prin.; Stds.: 322; Lay Tchrs.: 21

FOND DU LAC

Holy Family Congregation - 271 Fourth St. Way, Fond du Lac, WI 54937-7508 t) 920-921-0580 info@hffdl.org; scarter@hffdl.org www.hffdl.org Rev. Ryan J. Pruess, Pst.; Rev. Edward Joseph Sanchez, Assoc. Pst.; Rev. Justin Weber, Assoc. Pst.; Rev. Pedro Javier Ruiz-Aular, Assoc. Pst.; Rev. Michael J. Malucha, Assoc. Pst.; Sabina Carter, Dir.; CRP Stds.: 519

Sons of Zebedee: Ss. James and John Congregation - W5882 Church Rd., Fond du Lac, WI 54937-8602 t) 920-266-9873; 920-979-4656 (CRP) lstaehlerdre@gmail.com; stmarylomira@gmail.com www.smsoz.org Rev. Nathaniel J. Miniatt, Pst.; Lesa Staehler, DRE; CRP Stds.: 18

FONTANA

St. Benedict's Congregation - 137 Dewey Ave., Fontana, WI 53125-1239 t) 262-275-2993 (CRP); 262-275-2480 office@stbensparish.org www.stbensparish.org Rev. Mark J. Danczyk, Pst.; Ben Janssen, DRE; CRP Stds.: 64

FOX LAKE

Annunciation Congregation - 305 W. Green St., Fox Lake, WI 53933-9472 t) 920-928-3513 annunciationparish305@gmail.com; annunciationparishdre@gmail.com visitannunciationparish.org Rev. John J. Radetski, Pst.; CRP Stds.: 28

FOX POINT

St. Eugene Congregation - 7600 N. Port Washington Rd., Fox Point, WI 53217 t) 414-918-1102 seoffice@stme.church; childministry@stme.church steugenecongregation.org Half of Cluster Parish - with St. Monica, Whitefish Bay, WI Very Rev. Mark C. Payne, Pst.; Rev. Tonny Kizza, Pst. Assoc.; Jeanette Lambrecht, DRE; Joyce Swietlik, DRE; CRP Stds.: 124

St. Eugene School - (Grades PreSchool-8) t) 414-918-1120 schooloffice@steugene.school www.steugene.school/ Rebecca Jones, Prin.; Stds.: 163; Lay Tchrs.: 16

FRANKLIN

St. James Congregation - 7219 S. 27th St., Franklin, WI 53132 t) 414-761-0480; 414-761-0480 x116 (CRP) donna@stjames-franklin.org; maryjo@stjames-franklin.org www.stjames-franklin.org Rev. Robert Betz, Admin.; Rev. Msgr. T. George Gajdos, Assisting Priest; Steven Fluur, Pst. Min./Coord.; Carl Reyes, Liturgy Dir.; Mary Jo Hennemann, DRE; CRP Stds.: 57

St. Martin of Tours Congregation - 7963 S. 116th St., Franklin, WI 53132 t) 414-425-1114 parish@stmoftours.org; kdelemont@stmoftours.org www.stmoftours.org Rev. Andrzej Sudol, SCJ, Pst.; Rev. Son Thai Nguyen, SCJ, Assoc. Pst.; Dcn. Bruno Long H. Nguyen; Dcn. Charles G. Schneider; Katherine Delemont, DRE; CRP Stds.: 76

FREDONIA

Divine Savior Congregation - 305 Fredonia Ave., Fredonia, WI 53021-0250; Mailing: P.O. Box 250, Fredonia, WI 53021 t) 262-692-9994 divinesavior@dsoll.org; triesselmann@dsoll.org www.dsoll.org/ Rev. Donald H. Thimm, Supervising Priest; Rev. Stephen J. Lampe, Assisting Priest; Debbie Hamm, Dir.; Terri Riesselmann, DRE; CRP Stds.: 90

Divine Savior School - (Grades PreSchool-8) t) 262-692-2141 dscsschool@dscsfredonia.org divinesavior.weconnect.com Lynn Sauer, Prin.; Stds.: 114; Lay Tchrs.: 10

GERMANTOWN

St. Bonifacius Congregation - W204 N11940 Goldendale Rd., Germantown, WI 53022 t) 262-628-2040; 262-628-8143 (CRP) parish@stbonifacewi.org; das@stbonifacewi.org www.stbonifacewi.org Rev. Michael J. Petrie, Pst.; CRP Stds.: 199

St. Boniface School - (Grades PreK-8) W204 N11968 Goldendale Rd., Germantown, WI 53022 t) 262-628-1955 derlandson@stbonifacewi.org Diana Erlandson, Prin.; Stds.: 72; Sr. Tchrs.: 1; Lay Tchrs.: 8

GRAFTON

St. Joseph's Congregation - 1619 Washington St., Grafton, WI 53024 t) 262-375-6500 (Main); 262-375-6500 x175 (Pst. Assoc.); (262) 375-6500 x103 (Pst./Admin.); (262) 375-6500 x102 (Dir. Admin.) shanson@stjosephgrafton.org; swiese@stjosephgrafton.org stjosephgrafton.org Rev. Nicholas Baumgardner, Admin.; Dcn. Scott T. Wiese, Dir. Admin.; Dcn. Alfred C. Lazaga; Sheri Hanson, Pst. Assoc.; CRP Stds.: 221

St. Joseph School - (Grades PreK-8) t) 262-375-6505 schooloffice@stjosephgrafton.org stjosephgrafton.org/school/ Stds.: 138; Lay Tchrs.: 11

GREENDALE

St. Alphonsus Congregation - 6060 W. Loomis Rd., Greendale, WI 53129; Mailing: 5960 W. Loomis Rd., Greendale, WI 53129 t) 414-421-2442 stals@st-alphonsus.org; christianformation@st-alphonsus.org www.st-alphonsus.org Rev. Kevin P. McManaman, Pst.; Rev. Patrick J. Magnor, Assoc. Pst.; Dcn. James Leggett; Rev. Walter J. Vogel, In Res.; Sr. Eileen Kazmierowicz, Pst. Assoc.; Karen Farrell, DRE; CRP Stds.: 402

St. Alphonsus School - (Grades PreK-8) 6000 W. Loomis Rd., Greendale, WI 53129 t) 414-421-1760 school@st-alphonsus.org Russ Johnston, Prin.; Stds.: 167; Lay Tchrs.: 13

GREENFIELD

St. John, The Evangelist, Congregation - 8500 W. Cold Spring Rd., Greenfield, WI 53228 t) 414-321-8922 (CRP); 414-321-1965 rectory@stjohns-grfd.org; arahill@stjohns-grfd.org www.stjohns-grfd.org Very Rev. Michael F. Merkt, Pst.; Dcn. Steven F. Pemper; Austin Rahill, DRE; CRP Stds.: 61

St. John the Evangelist School - (Grades PreK-8) t) 414-321-8540 boberdorf@sje.school www.sje.k12.wi.us Bob Oberdorf, Prin.; Stds.: 161; Lay Tchrs.: 10

HALES CORNERS

St. Mary Congregation - 9520 W. Forest Home Ave., Hales Corners, WI 53130 t) 414-425-2174 kacalaj@stmaryhc.org www.stmaryhc.org Rev. Aaron R. Laskiewicz, Admin.; Jeff Kacala, DRE; Dcn. John R. Burns; Dcn. William Goulding; CRP Stds.: 300

St. Mary School - (Grades PreK-8) 9553 W. Edgerton Ave., Hales Corners, WI 53130 t) 414-425-3100 mroczenskim@stmaryhc.org Dr. Mark Joerres, Prin.; Stds.: 357; Lay Tchrs.: 29

HARTFORD

St. Kilians Congregation - 264 W. State St., Hartford, WI 53027 t) 262-673-4831; 262-673-4831 x7406 (CRP) parishoffice@stkiliancong.org; dcf@stkiliancong.org www.stkiliancong.org Rev. Britto Raja Suresh, Pst.; CRP Stds.: 176

St. Kilian School - (Grades PreK-8) 245 High St., Hartford, WI 53027 t) 262-673-3081 trimbergerj@stkiliancong.org www.stkiliancong.org/school Jenny Trimberger, Prin.; Stds.: 73; Lay Tchrs.: 10

St. Lawrence Congregation - 4886 Hwy. 175, Hartford, WI 53027 t) 262-644-5701 stlawrenceoffice@gmail.com www.stlawrence-parish.com Very Rev. Richard J. Stoffel, Pst.; Rev. Russell L. Arnett, Assoc. Pst.; Dcn. Robert Derks; Nancy Pfeifer, Bus. Mgr.; CRP Stds.: 106

HARTLAND

St. Charles Congregation - 313 Circle Dr., Hartland, WI 53029-1824 t) 262-367-0800; 262-367-0800 x201 (CRP) parish@stcharleshartland.org www.stcharleshartland.com Rev. Kenneth E. Omernick, Pst.; Rev. Ariel F. Orozco, Assoc. Pst.; CRP Stds.: 360

St. Charles School - (Grades PreK-8) 526 Renson Rd., Hartland, WI 53029 t) 262-367-2040 school@stcharleshartland.com school.stcharleshartland.com/site/school Daniel Garvey, Prin.; Stds.: 286; Lay Tchrs.: 17

HORICON

Sacred Heart Congregation - 950 Washington St., Horicon, WI 53032; Mailing: P.O. Box 27, Horicon, WI 53032 t) 920-485-0694 office@sheart.org www.sheart.org (Clustered with St. Matthew, Neosho) Rev. Justin L. Lopina, Admin.; CRP Stds.: 115

HUBERTUS

St. Gabriel Congregation - 1200 St. Gabriel Way, Hubertus, WI 53033 t) 262-628-1141; 262-628-1141 x223 (CRP) stgabriel@stgabrielhubertus.org; gwolf@stgabrielhubertus.org www.stgabrielhubertus.org Rev. Timothy C. Bickel, Pst.; Gerry Wolf, DRE; CRP Stds.: 198

St. Gabriel School - (Grades PreK-8) t) 262-628-1711 klestina@sgabriel.org www.sgabriel.org Kim Lestina, Prin.; Stds.: 136; Lay Tchrs.: 10

St. Mary's of the Hill Congregation - 1515 Carmel Rd., Hubertus, WI 53033-9770 t) 262-628-3606 (CRP); 262-673-7505 (CRP) secretary@stmaryhh.org www.stmaryhh.org Rev. Jude Peters, O.C.D., Pst.; Melinda Diels, DRE; Grace Marie Urlakis, RCIA Coord.; CRP Stds.: 51

KANSASVILLE

St. Francis Xavier - 1704 240th Ave., Kansasville, WI

53139 t) 262-878-2267 business@krcatholics.org www.krcatholics.org Dcn. Anton B. Nickolai, Parish Dir.; Kathi Andrioni, Dir., Faith Formation; Sheryl Miller, Dir., Finance; Troy J Temple, Dir., Oper.; Maria Wargolet, Dir., Liturgy & Music; CRP Stds.: 40

St. Marys Congregation - 23211 Church Rd., Kansasville, WI 53139-9518; Mailing: 3320 S. Colony Ave., Union Grove, WI 53182 t) 262-878-3476 business@krcatholics.org www.krcatholics.org Dcn. Anton B. Nickolai, Parish Dir.; Kathi Andrioni, Dir., Faith Formation; Sheryl Miller, Dir., Finance; Troy J Temple, Dir., Oper.; Maria Wargolet, Dir., Liturgy & Music; CRP Stds.: 18

KENOSHA

St. Anthony's Congregation - 5100 22nd Ave., Kenosha, WI 53140; Mailing: 2223 51st St., Kenosha, WI 53140 t) 262-652-1844 paduakenosha@gmail.com stanthonykenosha.org Rev. Todd Belardi, Pst.; CRP Stds.: 15

Congregation of St. Elizabeth - 4801 8th Ave., Kenosha, WI 53140; Mailing: 4816 7th Ave., Kenosha, WI 53140 t) 262-657-1156 office@dtkc.org www.downtownkenoshacatholic.org Rev. Sean S. Granger, Pst.; Dcn. Daniel F. Kehrer; CRP Stds.: 107

St. James Congregation - 5804 Sheridan Rd., Kenosha, WI 53140; Mailing: 4816 7th Ave., Kenosha, WI 53140 t) 262-657-1156 sean@dtkc.org; office@dtkc.org www.downtownkenoshacatholic.org Rev. Sean S. Granger, Admin.;

St. Mark's Congregation - 7117 14th Ave., Kenosha, WI 53143 t) 262-656-7373 stmarkfaithk8@gmail.com; saintmark.kenosha@gmail.com stmark-kenosha.org Rev. Carlos A. Florez-Ardila, Pst.; Gema Soria, DRE; Camille Dacak Florez, Confirmation Formation; CRP Stds.: 293

St. Mark Outreach Center - t) 262-656-7370 stmarkoutreachbetty@gmail.com Betty Regalado, Social Outreach Dir.;

St. Mary's Congregation - 7300 39th Ave., Kenosha, WI 53142; Mailing: 7307 40th Ave., Kenosha, WI 53142-1923 t) 262-694-6018 www.stmarycatholic.org Rev. Roman Stikel, Pst.; Dcn. Brent Enwright; Dcn. James S. Francois; Dcn. Ronald F. Lesjak; Dcn. Wilson A. Shierk; Sandy Schwalbe, DRE; Sandy Slivon, DRE; CRP Stds.: 261

Our Lady of Mount Carmel - 1919 54th St., Kenosha, WI 53140 t) 262-925-3187 (CRP); 262-652-7660 parishoffice@olmckenosha.org; religiouseducation@olmckenosha.org www.olmckenosha.org Rev. Dwight P. Campbell, Pst.; Rev. Robert T. McDermott, Assoc. Pst.; Heather Kathlene Schweitzer, DRE; CRP Stds.: 36

Mt. Carmel Preschool - (Grades PreK-K) 5400 19th Ave., Kenosha, WI 53140; Mailing: 1919 54th St., Kenosha, WI 53140 t) 262-653-1464 Lori Lux, Dir.; Stds.: 55; Lay Tchrs.: 4

Congregation of the Holy Rosary of Pompeii - 2224 45th St., Kenosha, WI 53140 t) 262-652-2771 krozzoni@hrosarykenosha.org; finance@hrosarykenosha.org www.hrosarykenosha.org Rev. Joseph L. Lappe, M.I.C., Admin.; Rev. John L. Larson, MIC, Par. Vicar; Kathy DelConte, DRE; CRP Stds.: 114

St. Peter's Congregation - 2224 30th Ave., Kenosha, WI 53144 t) 262-551-9004; 262-551-9006 stpeterskenosha@gmail.com www.stpeterskenosha.com Rev. Ireneusz Chodakowski, M.I.C., Pst.; Rev. Michael Allen Baker, M.I.C., Assoc. Pst.; Dcn. Terry Maack; CRP Stds.: 27

St. Therese Congregation - 2020 91st St., Kenosha, WI 53143-6699 t) 262-694-4695; 262-694-0118 (CRP) valang@tds.net Rev. Dwight P. Campbell, Pst.; Rev. Robert T. McDermott, Assoc. Pst.; CRP Stds.: 32

KEWASKUM

Holy Trinity Congregation - 331 Main St., Kewaskum, WI 53040; Mailing: P.O. Box 461, Kewaskum, WI 53040 t) 262-626-2650 (CRP); 262-626-2860 htparish@htschool.net; faithformation@htschool.net www.kewaskumcatholicparishes.org/ Rev. Jacob A. Strand, Pst.; Dcn. Ralph E. Horner; Mary Breuer, DRE; CRP Stds.: 93

Holy Trinity School - (Grades PreK-8) 305 Main St., Kewaskum, WI 53040; Mailing: P. O. Box 464, Kewaskum, WI 53040 t) 262-626-2603 principal@htschool.net www.htschool.net Amanda Longden, Prin.; Stds.: 141; Lay Tchrs.: 15

St. Michaels' Congregation - 8883 Forestview Rd., Kewaskum, WI 53040 t) 262-334-5270; 262-626-2650 (CRP) stmickew@htschool.net; faithformation@htschool.net www.kewaskumcatholicparishes.org/ Rev. Jacob A. Strand, Pst.; Dcn. Ralph E. Horner; Mary Breuer, DRE; CRP Stds.: 69

KOHLER

St. John Evangelist Congregation - 601 Valley Rd., Kohler, WI 53044 t) 920-452-9623; 920-452-9623 x218 (CRP); 920-452-9623 x220 (CRP) stjohnev@btsje.org; jeanne@btsje.org stjohnkohler.org Rev. Jonathon A. Schmeckel, Admin.; Teresa Bettag, DRE; Jeanne Bitkers, DRE; CRP Stds.: 121

LAKE GENEVA

Congregation of St. Francis de Sales - 148 W. Main St., Lake Geneva, WI 53147 t) 262-248-8524 parish@sfdslg.org www.sfdslg.org Rev. Raymond Guthrie, Admin.; CRP Stds.: 107

St. Francis de Sales School - (Grades PreK-8) 130 W. Main St., Lake Geneva, WI 53147 t) 262-248-2778 principal@sfdslg.org Kelly Sykora, Prin.; Stds.: 148; Lay Tchrs.: 11

LOMIRA

St. Andrews Congregation - W3081 County Rd. Y, Lomira, WI 53048 t) 920-583-4125; 920-387-3130 jdominic@stmarymayville.org www.stsandrewmarytheresa.org Also serves St. Mary, Mayville and St. Theresa, Theresa. Rev. Joseph Dominic, S.A.C., Pst.; CRP Stds.: 34

St. Mary's Congregation - 699 Milwaukee St., Lomira, WI 53048 t) 920-979-4656 (CRP); 920-269-4429 lstaehlerdre@gmail.com; stmarylomira@gmail.com www.smsoz.org Rev. Nathaniel J. Miniatt, Pst.; Lesa Staehler, DRE; CRP Stds.: 62

LYONS

St. Joseph's Congregation - 1540 Mill St., Lyons, WI 53148; Mailing: P.O. Box 60, Lyons, WI 53148-0060 t) 262-763-2050; 262-763-2260 (CRP) stjosephoffice@ourblcc.org; eschultz@ourblcc.org www.ourblcc.org Very Rev. James T. Volkert, Pst.; Rev. Sergio Rodriguez, Assoc. Pst.; Dcn. Anton B. Nickolai; Elle Schultz, DRE; Rita VanSchyndel, DRE; CRP Stds.: 176

MAYVILLE

Saint Mary's Congregation - 302 S. German St., Mayville, WI 53050; Mailing: P.O. Box 22, Mayville, WI 53050-0022 t) 920-387-3130 jdominic@stmarymayville.org www.stsandrewmarytheresa.org Also serves St. Andrew, LeRoy & St. Theresa, Theresa. Rev. Joseph Dominic, S.A.C., Pst.; CRP Stds.: 85

St. Mary School - (Grades PreK-2) 28 Naber St., Mayville, WI 53050 t) 920-387-2920 info@stmarymayville.org www.stmarymayville.org Mary Yauck, Prin.; Stds.: 46; Lay Tchrs.: 5

MENOMONEE FALLS

St. Anthony's Congregation - N74 W13604 Appleton Ave., Menomonee Falls, WI 53051 t) 262-251-5910 scosentino@stam.church; shecterlemsgr@stam.church www.stanthony-parish.org Rev. Msgr. Ross A. Shecterle, Admin.; Rev. Andrew J.T. Linn, Assoc. Pst.; Dcn. James P. Goetter; Steve Cosentino, Bus. Mgr.; Karissa Tousignant, DRE; CRP Stds.: 81

Good Shepherd Congregation - N88 W17658 Christman Rd., Menomonee Falls, WI 53051-2630 t) 262-255-2035 goodshepherd@gdinet.com www.mygoodshepherd.org Rev. Peter C. Drenzek, Assisting Priest; Rev. Thomas M. Suriano, Assisting Priest; Dcn. Sanford Sites, Parish Dir.; Marguerite Thompson, Adult Form. /Social Justice; Andy Kukec, Dir., Liturgy & Music; Corinna Ramsey, Dir., Child & Youth Min.; Bryan Ramsey, Community Engagement Mgr.; Marge Beck, Bus. Mgr.; CRP Stds.: 101

St. James Congregation - W220 N6588 Town Line Rd., Menomonee Falls, WI 53051 t) 262-251-3944; 262-253-2259 stjameschurch@bizwi.rr.com; sdevine-simon@stjames-parish.com www.stjames-parish.com Rev. John D. Hemsing, Pst.; Kristin Kebis, Youth Min.; David Weber, Youth Min.; Barbara Schuelke, Liturgy Dir.; Sue Devine-Simon, DRE; Theresa Weber, Bus. Mgr.; CRP Stds.: 513

St. Mary's Congregation - N89 W16297 Cleveland Ave., Menomonee Falls, WI 53051 t) 262-251-0220 scosentino@stam.church; shecterlemsgr@stam.church stmaryparish.net Rev. Msgr. Ross A. Shecterle, Admin.; Rev. Andrew J.T. Linn, Assoc. Pst.; Karissa Tousignant, DRE; Dcn. James P. Goetter; Steve Cosentino, Bus. Mgr.; CRP Stds.: 123

St. Mary Parish School - (Grades PreK-8) N89 W16215 Cleveland Ave., Menomonee Falls, WI 53051 t) 262-251-1050 schooloffice@stmp.school www.stmaryparishschool.org Linda Joyner, Prin.; Stds.: 219; Lay Tchrs.: 19

MEQUON

Lumen Christi Congregation - 2750 W. Mequon Rd., Mequon, WI 53092 t) 262-242-7967; 262-512-8985 (CRP) receptionist@lumenchristiparish.org www.lumenchristiparish.org Rev. Matthew Jacob, Pst.; Rev. Stephen Buting, Assoc. Pst.; Dcn. David W. Grambow; Dcn. Anthony Monfre; Dcn. John P. Shaughnessy; Dcn. Joseph P. Wenzler; CRP Stds.: 378

Lumen Christi School - (Grades PreK-8) 11300 N. St. James Ln., Mequon, WI 53092 t) 262-242-7960 lcschool@lumenchristiparish.org www.lumenchristiparish.org/school/ Kelly Fyfe, Prin.; Stds.: 370; Lay Tchrs.: 36

MILWAUKEE

St. Adalbert's Congregation - 1923 W. Becher St., Milwaukee, WI 53215 t) 414-988-0228 x100 businessoffice@adalbertschool.org; parishoffice@adalbertschool.org www.stadalbertmke.org/ Rev. Angel Anaya, Admin.; Manuel Camacho Santos, Parish Life Coord.; Lidia Bonilla, DRE; Jorge Bravo, Trustee; Victos M Cobos, Trustee; CRP Stds.: 182

St. Adalbert School - (Grades PreK-8) 1913 W. Becher St., Milwaukee, WI 53215-2688 t) 414-645-5450 info@adalbertschool.org stadalbertmke.com/ Daniel Heding, Prin.; Stds.: 397; Lay Tchrs.: 28

Congregation of All Saints Catholic Church - 4051 N. 25th St., Milwaukee, WI 53209; Mailing: 4060 N. 26th St., Milwaukee, WI 53209-6695 t) 414-444-5610 allsaintsmke@gmail.com allsaintsmke.org Rev. James Arthur, Pst.; CRP Stds.: 3

St. Anthonys Congregation - 1711 S. 9th St., Milwaukee, WI 53204 t) 414-645-1455 andac@stanthonymilwaukee.org; info@stanthonymilwaukee.org www.stanthony-sthyacinth.org Rev. Hugo A. Londono, Admin.; Rev. Erick Cassiano-Amaya, F.M.M., Assoc. Pst.; Rev. Jaime E. Charuc Mox, F.M.M., Assoc. Pst.; Dcn. Carlos Cornejo; Dcn. Rogelio Macias; Dcn. Henry O. Reyes; Sr. Maria del Carmen de Anda, R.M., DRE; Martha Andrade, Bus. Mgr.; CRP Stds.: 98

St. Anthony of Padua School - (Grades PreK-12) 1727 S. 9th St., Milwaukee, WI 53204 t) 414-384-6612 www.stanthonymilwaukee.org Dr. Rosana Mateo, Pres.; Stds.: 1,482; Lay Tchrs.: 75

St. Augustinus Congregation - 2530 S. Howell Ave., Milwaukee, WI 53207 t) 414-744-0808; 414-481-0777 x1117 (CRP) info@staugies.org; karen@secatholic.org www.staugies.org Affiliated with St. Thomas Aquinas Academy, Milwaukee operated by Seton Catholic Schools, Inc. Rev. Philip J. Schumaker, Pst.; Karen Bushman, DRE; Paul Weisenberger, Liturgy Dir.; Christine Stemwell, Bus. Mgr.; CRP Stds.: 13

St. Josaphat Congregation - 601 W. Lincoln Ave., Milwaukee, WI 53215; Mailing: 2333 S. 6th St., Milwaukee, WI 53215-3203 t) 414-645-5623; 414-645-5623 x232 (CRP) lmarindanay@thebasilica.org; sjbdome@thebasilica.org www.thebasilica.org Rev. James Ciaramitaro, O.F.M. Conv., Admin.; Dcn. William A. Banach; Dcn. Theodore Faust; Sr. Lucy Marindany, DRE; CRP Stds.: 66

St. Josaphat Parish School - (Grades PreK-8) 801 W. Lincoln Ave, Milwaukee, WI 53215-3222 t) 414-645-4378 kstrasser@sjpsmke.org www.sjpsmke.com/ Karin Strasser, Prin.; Stds.: 225; Lay Tchrs.: 16

Basilica of Saint Josaphat Endowment Fund - 2333 S. 6th St., Milwaukee, WI 53215-3203 t) (414) 645-5623

Saint Josaphat Parish School Endowment Fund - 2333 S. 6th St., Milwaukee, WI 53215 t) (414) 645-5623

St. Benedict the Moor - 930 W. State St., Milwaukee, WI 53233 t) 414-271-0135 stbensparish@thecapuchins.org www.stbensparishmilwaukee.org Rev. Michael Bertram, O.F.M.Cap, Pst.; Dcn. John I. Champagne; Dcn. Francisco Javier Rodriguez;

St. Bernadette Congregation - 8200 W. Denver Ave., Milwaukee, WI 53223 t) (414) 358-4600; (414) 365-2020 (CRP) stbernadette@nwmcp.org; lmaples@stcatherinemke.org www.stbweb.com Affiliated with Northwest Catholic School, Milwaukee operated by Seton Catholic Schools, Inc. Rev. Gregory J. Greiten, Pst.; Sr. Jane Mary Lorbiecki, S.S.N.D., Pst. Min./Coord.; Lorrie Maples, Dir., Christian Formation; CRP Stds.: 6

Blessed Sacrament Congregation - 3100 S. 41st St., Milwaukee, WI 53215 t) 414-649-4720 michael.federman@blessedsacramentmke.org; parish@blessedsacramentmke.org www.blessedsacramentmke.org Rev. Glenn E. Powers, Pst.; Rev. Ekene (Alex) Nwosu, Assoc. Pst.; Dcn. Paul Klingseisen; Bro. James Scarpace, S.A.C., Pst. Min./Coord.; Sr. Theresa Engel, O.S.F., Pastoral Coord.; Michael Federman, DRE; Nancy Petoskey Ahern, Youth Min.; Sam Skogstad, Music Min.; Claudia Plascencia, Bus. Mgr.; CRP Stds.: 25

Blessed Sacrament School - (Grades K-8) 3126 S. 41st St., Milwaukee, WI 53215 t) 414-649-4730 vile.carlos@blessedsacramentmke.org Megan Cerbins, Prin.; Stds.: 180; Lay Tchrs.: 14

Blessed Savior Congregation - 8545 W. Villard Ave., Milwaukee, WI 53225; Mailing: 8607 W. Villard Ave., Milwaukee, WI 53225 t) 414-464-5033 parish@blessedsavior.org www.blessedsaviorparish.org Rev. Romanus N. Nwaru, Pst.; Yolanda Coly, DRE; CRP Stds.: 7

Blessed Savior Catholic School - (Grades PreK-8) 8607 W. Villard Ave., Milwaukee, WI 53225 t) 414-438-2745 (E. Campus); 414-463-3878 (S. Campus); 414-464-5775 (W. Campus) eodonnell@blessedsavior.org; crooney@blessedsavior.org www.blessedsaviorcatholicschool.org Erin O'Donnell, Prin.; Sarah Radiske, Prin.; Colleen Rooney, Prin.; Stds.: 456; Lay Tchrs.: 38

Congregation of St. John's Cathedral - 812 N. Jackson St., Milwaukee, WI 53202; Mailing: 831 N. Van Buren St., Milwaukee, WI 53202-3918 t) 414-276-9814; 414-276-9814 x302 cathedral@stjohncathedral.org; tbeach@stjohncathedral.org www.stjohncathedral.org Affiliated with Catholic East Elementary School operated by Seton Catholic Schools, Inc. Most Rev. Jeffrey R. Haines, Rector; Rev. Jose Gonzalez, Par. Vicar; Dcn. Thomas N. Hunt; Trevor Beach, DRE; CRP Stds.: 73

St. Catherine's Congregation - 5101 W. Center St., Milwaukee, WI 53210 t) 414-445-5115; 414-445-5449 (CRP) mlee@saintsebs.org; secretary@saintcatherine.org www.saintcatherine51.org Rev. Peter Patrick Kimani, Pst.; Dcn. Ralph W. Kornburger Jr.; Margaret Lee, DRE; CRP Stds.: 7

St. Catherine - 8661 N. 76th Pl., Milwaukee, WI 53223-2697 t) 414-365-2020; 414-365-2020 x14 (CRP) lmaples@stcatherinemke.org; greiteng@archmil.org www.stcatherinemke.org Affiliated with Northwest Catholic School, Milwaukee operated by Seton Catholic Schools, Inc Rev. Gregory J. Greiten, Admin.; Lorrie Maples, DRE; CRP Stds.: 16

St. Charles Borromeo Congregation - 5571 S. Marilyn St., Milwaukee, WI 53221 t) 414-281-8115 info@scbmil.org www.scbmil.org Affiliated with St. Charles Borromeo School operated by Seton Catholic Schools, Inc. Rev. Gideon K. Buya, Pst.; Rev. Carlos Alberto Zapata, Assoc. Pst.; CRP Stds.: 70

Congregation of the Great Spirit - 1000 W. Lapham Blvd., Milwaukee, WI 53204; Mailing: 1050 W. Lapham Blvd., Milwaukee, WI 53204 t) 414-672-6989 greatspirit59@yahoo.com www.greatspirit.net/ Rev. Edward J. Cook, Pst.; Sally A LaFountain, Bus. Mgr.; Michelle Boyd, Treas.;

S.S. Cyril and Method's Congregation - 2427 S. 15th St., Milwaukee, WI 53215 t) 414-383-3973 pastor@cmmk.org www.cmmk.org Rev. Edward W. Traczyk, S.Chr., Pst.; CRP Stds.: 20

St. Francis of Assisi - 1937 Vel R. Phillips Ave., Milwaukee, WI 53212 t) 414-374-5750 stfrancismil@gmail.com www.stfrancismil.org Rev. Michael Bertram, O.F.M.Cap., Pst.; Bro. Kent Bauer, O.F.M.Cap, Guardian; Rev. Myron Kowalsky, OFM Cap., In Res.; Rev. Jibin James, O.F.M.Cap., In Res.; Rev. Perry McDonald, O.F.M.Cap., In Res.; Rev. Thomas Skowron, OFM Cap, In Res.; Rev. Lawrence Webber, OFMCap, In Res.; Bro. Arnauld Dad, In Res.; Bro. David Hirt, O.F.M.Cap., In Res.; Bro. T.L. Michael Auman, O.F.M.Cap., In Res.; Bro. Brenton Ertel, OFM Cap., In Res.; Bro. Jerome Johnson, O.F.M.Cap., In Res.; Bro. Carl Schaefer, O.F.M.Cap., In Res.; Bro. Mark Romanowski, O.F.M.Cap., In Res.; Dcn. Francisco Javier Rodriguez, In Res.; CRP Stds.: 30

Gesu Parish - 1210 W. Michigan St., Milwaukee, WI 53233; Mailing: PO Box 495, Milwaukee, WI 53201 t) 414-288-7101 gesuparish@gmail.com www.gesuparish.org Rev. R. Benjamin Osborne, S.J., Pst.; Rev. Thomas S. Anderson, S.J., Assoc. Pst.; CRP Stds.: 58

St. Gregory the Great Congregation - 3160 S. 63rd St., Milwaukee, WI 53219 t) 414-543-8292 lgkenny@stgregsmil.org; salonso@stgregsmil.org www.stgregsmil.org Rev. Todd Budde, Pst.; CRP Stds.: 33

St. Gregory the Great School - (Grades PreK-8) 3132 S. 63rd St., Milwaukee, WI 53219 t) 414-321-1350 aschlegel@stgregsmil.org gregthegreat.org Amy Schlegel, Prin.; Stds.: 177; Lay Tchrs.: 12

St. Hyacinth's Congregation - 1414 W. Becher St., Milwaukee, WI 53215; Mailing: 1711 S. 9th St., Milwaukee, WI 53204 t) 414-645-1455 parishoffice@stanthonymilwaukee.org; andac@stanthonymilwaukee.org www.stanthony-sthyacinth.org Rev. Hugo A. Londono, Admin.; Rev. Erick Cassiano-Amaya, F.M.M., Assoc. Pst.; Rev. Jaime E. Charuc Mox, F.M.M., Assoc. Pst.; Dcn. Carlos Cornejo; Dcn. Rogelio Macias; Dcn. Henry O. Reyes; Sr. Maria del Carmen de Anda, R.M., DRE; CRP Stds.: 36

The Congregation of the Immaculate Conception - 1023 E. Russell Ave., Milwaukee, WI 53207; Mailing: 2530 S. Howell Ave., Milwaukee, WI 53207 t) 414-481-0777 x1117 (CRP); 414-769-2480 (Office) icbayview@gmail.com; karen@secatholic.org icbayview.org Affiliated with St. Thomas Aquinas Academy, Milwaukee operated by Seton Catholic Schools, Inc. Rev. Philip J. Schumaker, Pst.; Karen Bushman, DRE; Paul Weisenberger, Liturgy Dir.; Christine Stemwell, Bus. Mgr.; CRP Stds.: 11

St. John Paul II Congregation - 3307 S. 10th St., Milwaukee, WI 53215 t) 414-744-3695 dahles@sjp2cs.org www.sjpii-parish.org Rev. Michael A. Ignaszak, Pst.; Amelia Avila, DRE; CRP Stds.: 185

St. John Paul II School - (Grades PreK-8) 3329 S. 10th St., 3344 S. 16th St., Milwaukee, WI 53215 t) 414-744-7188 (Grades K4-4); 414-383-3453 (Grades 5-8) eichmanb@sjp2cs.org Beth Eichman, Prin.; Stds.: 232; Lay Tchrs.: 13

St. Margaret Mary Congregation - 3970 N. 92nd St., Milwaukee, WI 53222-2506 t) 414-461-6073 adminasst@stmmp.org; frpatn@stmmp.org stmmp.org Affiliated with St. Margaret Mary School operated by Seton Catholic Schools, Inc. Rev. Patrick Nelson, S.D.S., Pst.; Dcn. Frank Pemper; CRP Stds.: 11

Congregation of St. Martin de Porres Catholic Church - 128 W. Burleigh St., Milwaukee, WI 53212-2046 t) 414-372-3090 smdp@smdpmilw.com smdpmilw.org Rev. James Arthur, Admin.; Peggy Bowles, DRE; CRP Stds.: 15

St. Mary Magdalen Congregation - 1854 W. Windlake Ave., Milwaukee, WI 53215 t) 414-810-1405 stmarymagdalen@archmil.org; stmarymagdalen.mke@gmail.com Rev. Seungwon John Yoo (Korea), Pst.; CRP Stds.: 5

St. Mathias Congregation - 9306 W. Beloit Rd., Milwaukee, WI 53227 t) 414-321-0893 lowes@stmatthias-milw.org; cpfeifer@stmatthias-milw.org stmatthias-milw.org/ Rev. Jerome G. Herda, Pst.; Dcn. Stanley J. Lowe, Pst. Min./Coord.; CRP Stds.: 115

St. Matthias School - (Grades PreK-8) 9300 W. Beloit Rd., Milwaukee, WI 53227 t) 414-321-0894 aturner@stmatthias-milw.org Alissa Turner, Prin.; Stds.: 183; Lay Tchrs.: 12

St. Michael's Congregation - 1445 N. 24th St., Milwaukee, WI 53205 t) 414-933-3143 stmichaelstrose@gmail.com stmichael-strose.org Rev. Rafael G. Rodriguez, Pst.; Rev. Chakrit Micaphitak, C.Ss.R., Assoc. Pst.; Dcn. Eugenio Ramirez-Murphy; Sr. Alice Thepouthay, Faith Formation; CRP Stds.: 142

Mother of Good Counsel Congregation - 6924 W. Lisbon Ave., Milwaukee, WI 53210-1259 t) 414-442-7600 x102 reedcmungovan@hotmail.com; konzal@mgcparish.org www.mgcparish.org Rev. Reed C. Mungovan, S.D.S., Pst.; Dcn. Dean J. Collins; Dcn. Andrew Meuler; Mariza Konzal, DRE; CRP Stds.: 58

Mother of Good Counsel School - (Grades PreK-8) 3001 N. 68th St., Milwaukee, WI 53210-1299 t) (414) 442-7600 x118 johnston@mgcparish.org Rachel Johnston, Prin.; Stds.: 190; Lay Tchrs.: 14

St. Mary's Congregation - 835 N. Milwaukee St., Milwaukee, WI 53202-3605 t) 414-271-6180 drivera@ffpmke.org; familyformation@ffpmke.org www.oldsaintmary.org Affiliated with Catholic East Elementary School operated by Seton Catholic Schools, Inc. Rev. Timothy L. Kitzke, Pst.; Rev. Carlos L. Londono, Assoc. Pst.; Most Rev. Richard J. Sklba, In Res.; Rev. Joseph J. Juknialis, In Res.; Chad Griesel, Pst. Assoc.; Margaret Moyer, Liturgy Dir.; Christine D'Amato, Dir.; Terri Balash, Dir.; Sarah Haus, Dir.; Anh Clausen, DRE; CRP Stds.: 14

Our Lady of Divine Providence Congregation - 2600 N. Bremen St., Milwaukee, WI 53212; Mailing: 1716 N. Humboldt Ave., Milwaukee, WI 53202 t) 414-962-2443 (CRP); 414-264-0049 familyformation@ffpmke.org; lablackmer@ffpmke.org www.ourladyofdivineprovidence.org Affiliated with Catholic East Elementary School operated by Seton Catholic Schools, Inc. Rev. Timothy L. Kitzke, Pst.; Rev. Carlos L. Londono, Assoc. Pst.; Chad Griesel, Pst. Assoc.; Anh Clausen, DRE; Christine D'Amato, Bus. Mgr.; Mary Robertson, Dir. Liturgy & Music; CRP Stds.: 5

Our Lady of Good Hope Congregation - 7152 N. 41st St., Milwaukee, WI 53209 t) 414-352-1148; 414-365-2020 (CRP) parish.office@olghparish.org; lmaples@stcatherinemke.org www.olghparish.org Affiliated with Northwest Catholic School, Milwaukee operated by Seton Catholic Schools, Inc. Rev. Gregory J. Greiten, Admin.; Lorrie Maples, DRE; CRP Stds.: 6

Our Lady of Guadalupe Congregation - 723 W. Washington St., Milwaukee, WI 53204 t) 414-645-7624 guadalupe@archmil.org Rev. Timothy T. Manatt, S.J., Pst.; Rev. Richard P. Abert, S.J., Asst. Pastor; Silvia Jiminez, Prog. Coord.; CRP Stds.: 38

Our Lady of Lourdes Congregation - 3722 S. 58th St., Milwaukee, WI 53220 t) 414-545-4316 office@ololmke.org www.ololmke.org Very Rev. Mark C. Payne, Supervising Priest; Rev. William C. Burkert, Assisting Priest; Deb Steppe, Liturgy Dir.; Nancie Chmielewski, Parish Dir.; Margaret Elizabeth Russell, DRE; Steve Szymanski, DRE; Maryrose M Wolf, Bus. Mgr.; Anne Van Deusen, Music Min.; CRP Stds.: 66

Our Lady, Queen of Peace Congregation - 3222 S. 29th St., Milwaukee, WI 53215 t) 414-672-0313 x113 (Laura); (414) 672-0313 x111 (DAS) c) 414-807-6830 (Rafa); 414-429-2235 (Pastor) fkleczka@olqpmke.org; rafamedina07@yahoo.com www.ourladyqueenofpeaceparish.org Very Rev. Javier Bustos-Lopez, Pst.; CRP Stds.: 118

St. Patricks Congregation - 723 W. Washington St., Milwaukee, WI 53204 t) 414-645-7624 stpats@archmil.org Rev. Timothy T. Manatt, S.J., Pst.; Rev. Richard P. Abert, S.J., Asst. Pastor; CRP Stds.: 39

St. Paul's Congregation - 1720 E. Norwich Ave., Milwaukee, WI 53207 t) (414) 482-2920 (CRP) stpaulmilwaukee@gmail.com Affiliated with St. Thomas Aquinas Academy, Milwaukee operated by Seton Catholic Schools, Inc. Very Rev. Carmelo Giuffre, Pst.; Karen Bushman, DRE; Dr. Delano Kahlstorff, Music Min.; CRP Stds.: 35

SS. Peter and Paul - 2490 N. Cramer St., Milwaukee, WI 53211; Mailing: 2491 N. Murray Ave., Milwaukee, WI 53211 t) 414-962-2443; 414-962-2443 (CRP); 414-962-3776 (CRP) ssppmilw@ffpmke.org; familyformation@ffpmke.org www.ssppmilw.org Affiliated with Catholic East Elementary School operated by Seton Catholic Schools, Inc. Rev. Timothy L. Kitzke, Pst.; Rev. Carlos L. Londono, Assoc. Pst.; Dcn. Gary J. Nosacek; Chad Griesel, Pst. Assoc.; Christine D'Amato, Dir.; Margaret Moyer, Liturgy Dir.; Terri Balash, Dir.; Sarah Haus, Dir.; Anh Clausen, DRE; CRP Stds.: 32

Prince of Peace/Principe de Paz Congregation - 1138 S. 25th St., Milwaukee, WI 53204 t) 414-645-8786 parishoffice@princeofpeaceschool.org Operated by Seton Catholic Schools, Inc. Rev. Fabian F. Rodas Aguilar, M.F.M. (Guatemala), Pst.; Rev. Alejandro Umul Chopox, M.F.M. (Guatemala), Assoc. Pst.; Betel M Garcia, DRE; Rosario Mendez, DRE; Lisamarie Lukowski, Bus. Mgr.; CRP Stds.: 197

St. Rafael the Archangel Congregation - 2059 S. 33rd St., Milwaukee, WI 53215 t) 414-645-9172 parish@strafael.org Affiliated with St Rafael the Archangel School operated by Seton Catholic Schools, Inc. Rev. Fabian F. Rodas Aguilar, M.F.M. (Guatemala), Pst.; Rev. Alejandro Umul Chopox, M.F.M. (Guatemala), Assoc. Pst.; Silvia Gomez, DRE; Lisamarie Lukowski, Bus. Mgr.; CRP Stds.: 169

St. Roman Congregation - 1710 W. Bolivar Ave., Milwaukee, WI 53221 t) 414-282-9063 das@stromans.com; vcamarillo@stromans.com www.stromans.com Rev. Gideon K. Buya, Pst.; Rev. Carlos Alberto Zapata, Assoc. Pst.; Dcn. Jorge Zuniga; CRP Stds.: 132

The Congregation of St. Rose - 540 N. 31st St., Milwaukee, WI 53208 t) 414-342-1778 stmichaelstrose@gmail.com stmichael-strose.org Rev. Rafael G. Rodriguez, Pst.; Rev. Chakrit Micaphitak, C.Ss.R., Assoc. Pst.; CRP Stds.: 17

Sacred Heart Congregation - 917 N. 49th St., Milwaukee, WI 53208 t) 414-774-9418 sh.croatian@yahoo.com sacredheartmilwaukee.org Rev. Dragan Bolcic, OFM, Admin.; CRP Stds.: 5

St. Sebastian's Congregation - 5400 W. Washington Blvd., Milwaukee, WI 53208 t) 414-453-1061; 414-453-7150 (CRP) saintsebs@saintsebs.org; mlee@saintsebs.org www.saintsebastianonline.net/ Rev. Peter Patrick Kimani, Pst.; Dcn. Warren D. Braun; Dcn. James Matthias; Dcn. James J. Peterson; Margaret Lee, DRE; CRP Stds.: 48

St. Sebastian School - (Grades PreK-8) 1747 N. 54th St., Milwaukee, WI 53208 t) 414-453-5830 school@saintsebs.org school.saintsebs.org/home Kathleen Immen, Prin.; Stds.: 320; Lay Tchrs.: 24

St. Sebastian School Foundation, Inc. - t) (414) 453-1061

The St. Stanislaus Congregation - 524 W. Historic Mitchell St., Milwaukee, WI 53204 t) 414-226-5490 ststanislaus@institute-christ-king.org www.institute-christ-king.org/milwaukee Rev. Canon Benoit Jayr, I.C.R.S.S., Pst.; CRP Stds.: 158

St. Therese Congregation - 9525 W. Bluemound Rd., Milwaukee, WI 53226 t) 414-771-2500 info@sttheresemke.org www.sttheresemke.org Rev. Thomas Varkey, SAC (India), Admin.; Heather Goeden, Dir.; CRP Stds.: 58

Three Holy Women Congregation - 1716 N. Humboldt Ave., Milwaukee, WI 53202-1697 t) 414-271-6577; 414-962-2443 (CRP) lablackmer@ffpmke.org; familyformation@ffpmke.org www.threeholywomenparish.org Affiliated with Catholic East Elementary School operated by Seton Catholic Schools, Inc. Rev. Timothy L. Kitzke, Pst.; Rev. Carlos L. Londono, Assoc. Pst.; Chad Griesel, Pst. Assoc.; Anh Clausen, DRE; Christine D'Amato, Bus. Mgr.; Mary Robertson, Dir. Liturgy & Music; CRP Stds.: 28

St. Veronica's Congregation - 353 E. Norwich St., Milwaukee, WI 53207 t) 414-482-2920 parishoffice@stvmke.org parishoffice@stvmke.org Affiliated with St. Thomas Aquinas Academy, Milwaukee operated by Seton Catholic Schools, Inc. Very Rev. Carmelo Giuffre, Pst.; Karen Bushman, DRE; Dr. Delano Kahlstorff, Music Min.; CRP Stds.: 35

The St. Vincent a Paulo Congregation - 2100 W. Mitchell St., Milwaukee, WI 53204; Mailing: 1138 S. 25th St., Milwaukee, WI 53204-1940 t) 414-645-8786 parishoffice@princeofpeaceschool.org Affiliated with Prince of Peace School operated by Seton Catholic Schools, Inc. Rev. Fabian F. Rodas Aguilar, M.F.M. (Guatemala), Pst.; Rev. Alejandro Umul Chopox, M.F.M. (Guatemala), Assoc. Pst.; Betel M Garcia, DRE; Rosario Mendez, DRE; Lisamarie Lukowski, Bus. Mgr.;

St. Vincent Pallotti Congregation - 201 N. 76th St., Milwaukee, WI 53213 t) 414-453-5344 vpallotti@stvpc.org www.stvincentpallotti.org Rev. Thomas Manjaly, S.A.C., Admin.; Jan Grosschadl, DRE; CRP Stds.: 8

St. Vincent Pallotti Catholic School - (Grades PreK-8) t) 414-258-4165 jfryda@stvps.org; ljones@stvps.org www.stvincentpallottischool.org Joseph Fryda, Prin.; Lirse Jones, Bus. Mgr.; Stds.: 165; Lay Tchrs.: 10

MOUNT CALVARY

Our Lady of the Holyland - 308 S. County. Rd. W., Mount Calvary, WI 53057; Mailing: P.O. Box 176, Mount Calvary, WI 53057-0716 t) 920-753-3311 llemke@ourladyoftheholyland.org ourladyoftheholyland.org Rev. Paul J. Koenig, OFM Cap, Pst.; CRP Stds.: 71

MUKWONAGO

St. James Congregation - 830 E. Veterans Way, Mukwonago, WI 53149 t) 262-363-7615 parish@stjmuk.org www.stjamesmukwonago.org Rev. Jordan Berghouse, Admin.; CRP Stds.: 296

MUSKEGO

St. Leonard Congregation - W173S7743 Westwood Dr., Muskego, WI 53150-9160 t) 262-679-1773; 262-679-0880 (CRP) parish@stleonards.org; lisa.jachimiec@stleonards.org www.stleonards.org Very Rev. Daniel R. Janasik, Pst.; Dcn. Larry Ramsey; Dcn. Rick J. Wirch; Bridget Klawitter, Pst. Assoc.; Lisa Jachimiec, DRE; Bethanne Maus-Schaefer, Youth Min.; Bryan Staedler, Music Min.; Karen Tenfel, Bus. Mgr.; CRP Stds.: 347

St. Leonard Congregation School - (Grades PreK-8) W173S7777 Westwood Dr., Muskego, WI 53150 t) 262-679-0451 school@stleonards.org Laura Bisher, Prin.; Stds.: 159; Lay Tchrs.: 11

NASHOTAH

St. Joan of Arc Congregation - 120 Nashotah Rd., Nashotah, WI 53058 t) 262-646-5979 (CRP); 262-646-8078; 262-646-5821 sj-office@scsjcluster.org; eheitman@scsjcluster.org www.scsjcluster.org Rev. Michael D. Strachota, Pst.; Leisha Smith, Bus. Mgr.; CRP Stds.: 76

St. Joan of Arc School - (Grades PreK-8) school-office@scsjcluster.org Holly Cerveny, Prin.; Stds.: 83; Lay Tchrs.: 6

NEOSHO

St. Matthew's Congregation - 148 W. Lehman St., Neosho, WI 53059; Mailing: P.O. Box 27, Horicon, WI 53032 t) 920-485-0694 office@sheart.org www.sheart.org Clustered with Sacred Heart, Horicon. Rev. Justin L. Lopina, Admin.; CRP Stds.: 8

NEW BERLIN

St. Elizabeth Ann Seton - 12700 W. Howard Ave., New Berlin, WI 53151 t) 262-782-6760; 262-782-8982 (CRP) office@mystelizabeth.com mystelizabeth.com Rev. Joseph A. Aufdermauer, Admin.; Dcn. Jeffrey J. Copson; Dcn. Richard Winkowski; Susan Switalski, Pst. Min./Coord.; Linda Noel Halverson, Music Min.; Skylar Kumprey, Youth Min.; Barbara Lee, DRE; Ann Ryan, DRE; David Fennelly, Bus. Mgr.; CRP Stds.: 184

Congregation of the Holy Apostles - 16000 W. National Ave., New Berlin, WI 53151 t) 262-786-7330 jfredrickson@hanb.org; aponnaiyan@hanb.org www.hanb.org Rev. Arul Ponnaiyan, Pst.; CRP Stds.: 240

Holy Apostles School - (Grades PreK-8) 3875 S. 159 St., New Berlin, WI 53151 t) 262-786-7331 www.hanbschool.org Lori Suarez, Prin.; Stds.: 415; Lay Tchrs.: 24

NEW MUNSTER

St. Alphonsus's Congregation - 6211 344th Ave., New Munster, WI 53152; Mailing: P.O. Box 767, New Munster, WI 53152 t) 262-537-4370 office.staljohn@gmail.com; staljohnevdas@gmail.com staljohn.org Rev. Arthur W. Mattox, Admin.; CRP Stds.: 50

NEWBURG

Holy Trinity Congregation - 521 Congress St., Newburg, WI 53060-0016; Mailing: P.O. Box 16, Newburg, WI 53060-0016 t) 262-675-6256 holytrinitynewburgoffice@gmail.com holytrinitynewburg.org Rev. Howard G. Haase, Supervising Priest; Rev. Thomas D. DeVries, Assisting Priest; Dcn. Michael S. Koebel, Dir.;

NORTH LAKE

Saint Teresa of Calcutta Congregation - W314N7462 State Rd. 83, North Lake, WI 53064; Mailing: PO Box 68, North Lake, WI 53064-0068 t) 262-966-2191 cashaw@stteresaofcalcutta.org; jen@stteresaofcalcutta.org www.stteresaofcalcutta.org Dcn. Allen B. Olson, Parish Director; Jennifer Ishizaki, DRE; CRP Stds.: 124

OAK CREEK

St. Matthews Congregation - 9303 S. Chicago Rd., Oak Creek, WI 53154 t) 414-762-4200 x117 (Administrative Assistant); 414-762-4200 x120 (Parish Office) kfelske@stmattoc.org; parish@stmattoc.org www.stmattocparish.org Rev. Patrick J. O'Loughlin, Pst.; Dcn. Steven L. Kramer; Dcn. John Stodola; CRP Stds.: 186

St. Matthew Parish School - (Grades PreK-8) 9329 S. Chicago Rd., Oak Creek, WI 53154 t) 414-762-6820 school@stmattocparish.org stmattoc.org Laura Fleischmann, Prin.; Stds.: 210; Lay Tchrs.: 10

St. Stephens Congregation - 1441 W. Oakwood Rd., Oak Creek, WI 53154 t) 414-762-0552; 414-762-0552 x224 (CRP) adminasst@saintstephenmil.org; rkacalo@saintstephenmil.org www.saintstephenmil.org Rev. Robert C. Kacalo, Pst.; Dcn. Stanley J. Lowe; Dcn. Robert G. Starr; CRP Stds.: 94

OCONOMOWOC

St. Catherine's Congregation - W359 N8512 Brown St., Oconomowoc, WI 53066 t) 920-474-7000 sc-office@scsjcluster.org; hcerveny@scsjcluster.org www.scsjcluster.org Rev. Michael D. Strachota, Pst.; Holly Cerveny, DRE; CRP Stds.: 60

St. Jerome's Congregation - 995 S. Silver Lake St.,

Oconomowoc, WI 53066 t) 262-569-3020 parish@stjerome.org www.stjerome.org Rev. John S. Gibson, Pst.; Dcn. Luis Pena; Dcn. James Casserly; CRP Stds.: 232

St. Jerome School - (Grades PreK-8) 1001 S. Silver Lake St., Oconomowoc, WI 53066 t) 262-569-3030 school@stjerome.org Theresa Chudy, Prin.; Stds.: 198; Lay Tchrs.: 13

PEWAUKEE

St. Anthony Congregation - W 280 N 2101 Prospect Ave., Pewaukee, WI 53072 t) 262-691-1173; 262-691-9170 (CRP) parish@stanthony.cc www.stanthony.cc Rev. Anthony J. Zimmer, Pst.; Dcn. Michael J. Finley; Dcn. Dennis J. Petrie; Kathie Amidei, Pst. Assoc.; Vincent LaTona, Liturgy & Music Dir.; CRP Stds.: 482

St. Anthony on the Lake School - (Grades PreK-8) t) 262-691-0460 principal@stanthony.cc www.stanthony.cc/school Marty Van Hulle, Prin.; Stds.: 225; Lay Tchrs.: 17

Queen of Apostles Congregation - N35 W23360 Capitol Dr., Pewaukee, WI 53072 t) 262-691-1535; 262-691-1535 x108 (CRP) lizk@queenofapostles.net; lisak@queenofapostles.net www.queenofapostles.net Rev. Charles T. Hanel, Pst.; Liz Kuhn, DRE; CRP Stds.: 85

PLEASANT PRAIRIE

Congregation of St. Anne - 9091 Prairie Ridge Blvd., Pleasant Prairie, WI 53158-1934 t) 262-942-8300 parishoffice@saint-anne.org; mmowry@saint-anne.org www.saint-anne.org Very Rev. Robert J. Weighner, Pst.; Dcn. Richard J. Stanula; Dcn. Todd Benzschawel; Mary Mowry, DRE; CRP Stds.: 174

PLYMOUTH

Congregation of St. John the Baptist - 115 Plymouth St., Plymouth, WI 53073 t) 920-892-4006; 920-892-6015 (CRP) sjbparish@sjbplymouth.org www.sjbplymouth.org Very Rev. Philip D. Reifenberg, Pst.; Amy Albers, DRE; Lisa Schoneman, Bus. Mgr.; CRP Stds.: 186

St. John the Baptist School - (Grades PreK-8) 116 Pleasant St., Plymouth, WI 53073 t) 920-893-5961 sjbschool@sjbplymouth.org Amy Nelson, Prin.; Stds.: 124; Lay Tchrs.: 10

PORT WASHINGTON

St. John XXIII Congregation - 1800 N. Wisconsin St., Port Washington, WI 53074 t) 262-284-4266; 262-284-2102 (CRE) parish@stjohn23rd.org; goodnod@stjohn23rd.org www.st.john23rd.org Rev. Patrick R. Wendt, Pst.; Dcn. Michael F. Burch; Bill Henkle, Bus. Mgr.; Dawn Goodno, DRE; Maureen Rotramel, DRE; CRP Stds.: 244

St. John XXIII Catholic School - (Grades PreK-8) 1802 N. Wisconsin St., Port Washington, WI 53074 t) 262-284-2682 kklein@stjohn23rd.school; sgraykowski@stjohn23rd.school stjohn23rd.school Kristine Klein, Prin.; Stds.: 189; Lay Tchrs.: 15

RACINE

St. Edward's Congregation - 1401 Grove Ave., Racine, WI 53405 t) 262-636-8040; 262-636-8040 x1006 (CRP) karen@cccracine.org www.saintedwardracine.org Affiliated with Our Lady of Grace Academy operated by Siena Catholic Schools of Racine, Inc. Rev. Juan Manuel Camacho, Admin.; Rev. Jose Mario Nieto Restrepo (Colombia), Assoc. Pst.; CRP Stds.: 8

St. John Nepomucene Congregation - 1903 Green St., Racine, WI 53402; Mailing: 700 English St., Racine, WI 53402 t) 262-634-5647 (Office) stjohnnepomuk@wi.rr.com; faithformationsjsjn@gmail.com Rev. Stephen K. Varghese, Pst.; Amber Fay, DRE; Dcn. Edward Sosa; CRP Stds.: 11

St. Joseph's Congregation - 1533 Erie St., Racine, WI 53402; Mailing: 1532 N. Wisconsin St., Racine, WI 53402 t) 262-633-8284; 262-633-9005 (CRP) info@st-joes.org; faithformationsjsjn@gmail.com Affiliated with St. Joseph School operated by Siena Catholic Schools of Racine, Inc. Rev. Stephen K. Varghese, Pst.; Amber Fay, DRE; CRP Stds.: 32

St. Lucy Congregation - 3101 Drexel Ave., Racine, WI 53403-3408 t) 262-554-1801 x601 (Parish); 262-554-1801 x208 (Children's Formation); 262-554-1801 x205 (Youth & Adult Formation); (262) 554-1801 x201 (Business Mgr.) parishoffice@stlucychurch.org; lfeiler@stlucychurch.org www.stlucychurch.org Affiliated with St. Lucy School operated by Siena Catholic Schools of Racine, Inc. Rev. Thomas Vathappallil, M.C.B.S., Pst.; Dcn. Eric M. Sewell; Patrick McLeod, Bus. Mgr.; Eric Antrim, Youth Min.; Sarah Amason, DRE; CRP Stds.: 85

St. Marys Congregation - 7605 Lakeshore Dr., Racine, WI 53402 t) 262-639-3616; 262-639-4493 (CRP) stmarybl@wi.twcbc.com; jwiseman@stmarybythelake.org www.stmarybythelake.org Rev. Patrick J. O'Loughlin, Pst.; Jennifer Wiseman, Bus. Mgr.; Heather Warner, DRE; CRP Stds.: 25

St. Patrick's Congregation - 1100 Erie St., Racine, WI 53402 t) 262-632-8808; 262-898-5651 (CRP) church@stpatrickracine.com; gabyenmilwaukee1@hotmail.com www.stpatrickracine.com/ Rev. Juan Manuel Camacho, Admin.; Rev. Jose Mario Nieto Restrepo (Colombia), Assoc. Pst.; Bro. Michael Kadow, Exec.; Dcn. Roberto Fuentes; Dcn. Leonides Rocha; Dcn. Julio Lopez; Eloy Contreras, Youth Min.; Laura Gabriela Cabrera, DRE; CRP Stds.: 339

John the 23rd Educational Center - 1101 Douglas Ave., Racine, WI 53402 t) 262-898-7250 mike_kadow@john23center.org (After School Program). Served by Casa Benedicta Community, Racine (Christian Brothers of the Midwest). Bro. Michael Kadow, Dir.;

St. Paul The Apostle Congregation - 6400 Spring St., Racine, WI 53406 t) 262-886-0530; 262-886-0531 (CRP) tclowney@stpaulracine.org www.stpaulracine.org Rev. Yamid Blanco, Pst.; Dcn. Keith A. Hansen; Dcn. Dale T. Nees; Ronnie Quella, Music Min.; Mary Beth Clowney, DRE; Thomas Clowney, Bus. Mgr.; CRP Stds.: 172

Congregation of St. Richard - 1503 Grand Ave., Racine, WI 53403; Mailing: 1509 Grand Ave., Racine, WI 53403 t) 262-637-8374 info@strichard-parish.org; jdclarke@strichard-parish.org www.strichard-parish.org Rev. Juan Manuel Camacho, Admin.; Rev. Jose Mario Nieto Restrepo (Colombia), Assoc. Pst.; Dcn. Howard J. Wirtz; John Clarke, DRE; CRP Stds.: 26

St. Rita's Congregation - 4339 Douglas Ave., Racine, WI 53402 t) 262-639-6280 (CRP); 262-639-3223 parishoffice@stritaracine.org; kroesr@stritaracine.org www.st-ritas.org/ Affiliated with St. Rita School operated by Siena Catholic Schools of Racine, Inc. Rev. Michael C. Petersen, Pst.; Rachel Kroes, DRE; CRP Stds.: 78

Sacred Heart Congregation - 2201 Northwestern Ave., Racine, WI 53404 t) 262-634-5526 shracine@shracine.org; shracineformation@gmail.com www.sacredheartracine.com Very Rev. Ricardo Martin Pinillos, Pst.; CRP Stds.: 26

RANDOM LAKE

Congregation of Our Lady of the Lakes - 230 Butler St., Random Lake, WI 53075-1710 t) 920-994-4380 ourladylakes@dsoll.org www.dsoll.org Rev. Donald H. Thimm, Supervising Priest; Rev. Stephen J. Lampe, Assisting Priest; Debbie Hamm, Dir.; Terri Riesselmann, DRE; Katherine Dimmer, Outreach Coord.; CRP Stds.: 43

REESEVILLE

Congregation of the Holy Family - 304 Prairie St., Reeseville, WI 53579-0277; Mailing: P O Box 277, Reeseville, WI 53579 t) 920-927-3102 triparish@charter.net www.triparishwi.com Also serves St. Columbkille, Elba and St. John the Baptist, Clyman. Rev. William Arnold, Admin.; Rev. Onildo Orellana Diaz, MFM (Guatemala), Assoc. Pst.; John Pryme, Youth Min.; Connie Caine, DRE; Mary Hensen, Bus. Mgr.; CRP Stds.: 26

RIPON

St. Catherine of Siena Congregation - 218 E. Blossom St., Ripon, WI 54971-1526 t) 920-748-2325 office@stcatofsiena.org; dianenowinski@stcatofsiena.org www.stcatofsiena.org Diane Nowinski, Dir.; CRP Stds.: 49

RUBICON

St. John's Congregation - W1170 Rome Rd., Rubicon, WI 53078; Mailing: 428 Forest St., Hartford, WI 53027 t) 262-673-4831 parishoffice@stkiliancong.org; billthimm@gmail.com Also serves St. Kilian, Hartford. Rev. Britto Raja Suresh, Admin.; William Thimm, DRE; CRP Stds.: 56

SHARON

St. Catherine's Congregation - 125 Pearl St., Sharon, WI 53585-0393; Mailing: PO Box 393, Sharon, WI 53585-0393 t) 262-736-4615; (262) 728-5922 x101 stewardship@saspcatholics.org Rev. Oriol Regales, Pst.; Rev. Josegerman Zapata-Ramirez, Assoc. Pst.; CRP Stds.: 15

SHEBOYGAN

St. Clement's Congregation - 707 N. 6th St., Sheboygan, WI 53081; Mailing: 807 Superior Ave., Sheboygan, WI 53081 t) 920-457-4629; 920-458-5390 (CRP); 920-458-7721 (CRP) woelfell@catholicnorth.org; torresl@catholicnorth.org www.sheboygannorthcatholicparishes.org Rev. Mark J. Brandl, Pst.; Rev. Norberto Sandoval, Assoc. Pst.; CRP Stds.: 91

Sts. Cyril and Methodius' Congregation - 822 New Jersey Ave., Sheboygan, WI 53081; Mailing: 1439 S. 12th St., Sheboygan, WI 53081 t) 920-457-1077 triparishoffice@catholicsouthside.com www.sscparishes.org Rev. Paul J. Fliss, Pst.; Rev. Subi Pootharayil Thomas, MCBS, Assoc. Pst.; Dcn. John R. Gavin; Dcn. Richard P. Gulig; Margaret Ausloos, Dir.; Rochelle Ross, Liturgy Dir.; Christine Immel, DRE; Lauren Monaghan, DRE; CRP Stds.: 8

Christ Child Academy - (Grades PreK-8) 2722 Henry St., Sheboygan, WI 53073 t) 920-459-2660 christchildacademyoffice@gmail.com www.christchildacademy.com Mark Ruedinger, Prin.; Stds.: 61; Lay Tchrs.: 5

St. Dominic Congregation - 2133 N. 22nd St., Sheboygan, WI 53081 t) 920-458-7070; 920-458-5390 (CRP); 920-458-5390 (CRP) torresl@catholicnorth.org; woelfell@catholicnorth.org www.sheboygannorthcatholicparishes.org Rev. Mark J. Brandl, Pst.; Rev. Norberto Sandoval, Assoc. Pst.; CRP Stds.: 143

Congregation of the Holy Name - 818 Huron Ave., Sheboygan, WI 53081; Mailing: 807 Superior Ave., Sheboygan, WI 53081-3442 t) 920-458-7721 x101; 920-458-5390 (CRP) zastrowd@catholicnorth.org www.sheboygannorthcatholicparishes.org Rev. Mark J. Brandl, Pst.; Rev. Norberto Sandoval, Assoc. Pst.; CRP Stds.: 127

Immaculate Conception Congregation - 1305 Humboldt Ave., Sheboygan, WI 53081; Mailing: 1439 S. 12th St., Sheboygan, WI 53081 t) 920-457-1077 triparishoffice@catholicsouthside.com www.sscparishes.org Rev. Paul J. Fliss, Pst.; Rev. Subi Pootharayil Thomas, MCBS, Assoc. Pst.; Dcn. Richard P. Gulig; Dcn. John R. Gavin; Margaret Ausloos, Dir.; Rochelle Ross, Liturgy Dir.; Lauren Monaghan, DRE; Christine Immel, DRE; CRP Stds.: 47

Christ Child Academy - (Grades PreK-8) 2722 Henry St., Sheboygan, WI 53081 t) 920-459-2660 christchildacademyoffice@gmail.com www.christchildacademy.com Mark Ruedinger, Prin.; Stds.: 89; Lay Tchrs.: 5

St. Peter Claver Congregation - 1439 S. 12th St., Sheboygan, WI 53081 t) 920-457-1077 triparishoffice@catholicsouthside.com www.sscparishes.org Rev. Paul J. Fliss, Pst.; Rev. Subi Pootharayil Thomas, MCBS, Assoc. Pst.; Dcn. Richard P. Gulig; Dcn. John R. Gavin; Margaret Ausloos, Dir.; Rochelle Ross, Liturgy Dir.; Lauren Monaghan, DRE; Christine Immel, DRE; CRP Stds.: 42

Christ Child Academy - (Grades PreK-5) 2722 Henry St., Sheboygan, WI 53081 t) 920-459-2660 christchildacademyoffice@gmail.com www.christchildacademy.com Mark Ruedinger, Prin.; Stds.: 80; Lay Tchrs.: 5

SHEBOYGAN FALLS

Blessed Trinity Congregation - 319 Giddings Ave., Sheboygan Falls, WI 53085-1598; Mailing: 115 Summer St., Sheboygan Falls, WI 53085 t) 920-467-4616; 920-467-6282 (CRP) sandy@btsje.org; lisa@btsje.org www.blessedtrinitysheboyganfalls.org Rev. Jonathon A. Schmeckel, Admin.; Lisa Gross, DRE; CRP Stds.: 91

SHOREWOOD

St. Robert's Congregation - 2200 E. Capitol Dr., Shorewood, WI 53211-2110; Mailing: 4019 N. Farwell Ave., Shorewood, WI 53211-2110 t) 414-332-1164 x3010 ddannecker@strobert.org www.strobert.org Very Rev. J. Enrique Hernandez, Pst.; Rev. Andrew Infanger, Assoc. Pst.; Donna Shriner, RCIA Coord.; Caitlin Raether, Youth Min.; Mary Grace Sanchez, Music Min.; Karen Raap, Bus. Mgr.; CRP Stds.: 143

St. Robert of Newminster School - (Grades PreK-8) t) (414) 332-1164 x3018 cward@strobert.school strobert.school/ Carol Ward, Prin.; Stds.: 306; Lay Tchrs.: 25

SLINGER

St. Peter's Congregation - 200 E. Washington St., Slinger, WI 53086; Mailing: 208 E. Washington St., Slinger, WI 53086 t) 262-644-8083 x2105 (Parish); 262-644-8083 x2209 (Asst. Pastor); 262-644-8083 x2106 (Pastor); (262) 644-8083 x2211 (Formation Office) formation@stpeterslinger.org; parishsecretary@stpeterslinger.org www.stpeterslinger.org Very Rev. Richard J. Stoffel, Pst.; Rev. Russell L. Arnett, Assoc. Pst.; CRP Stds.: 355

St. Peter School - (Grades PreK-5) 206 E. Washington St., Slinger, WI 53086 schoolsecretary@stpeterslinger.org; cheryl.jaeger@stpeterslinger.org www.spcsslinger.org Cheryl Jaeger, Prin.; Stds.: 94; Lay Tchrs.: 8

SOUTH MILWAUKEE

Divine Mercy Congregation - 800 Marquette Ave., South Milwaukee, WI 53172; Mailing: 695 College Ave., South Milwaukee, WI 53172 t) 414-762-6810 dmparish@divinemercysm.org; marywenger@divinemercysm.org divinemercysm.org Rev. Joseph Pradeep Sebastian, MCBS, Pst.; CRP Stds.: 83

Divine Mercy School - (Grades PreK-8) 695 College Ave., c/o Divine Mercy Parish, South Milwaukee, WI 53172 t) 414-764-4360 divinemercy@divinemercysm.org Loreve Rucka, Prin.; Stds.: 209; Lay Tchrs.: 15

ST. FRANCIS

Sacred Heart of Jesus Congregation - 3635 S. Kinnickinnic Ave., St. Francis, WI 53235; Mailing: 2530 S. Howell Ave., Milwaukee, WI 53207 t) 414-489-2806; 414-481-0777 x1117 (CRP) sacredheart.shj@aol.com; karen@secatholic.org sacredheartofjesus.weconnect.com affiliated with St. Thomas Aquinas Academy, Milwaukee operated by Seton Catholic Schools, Inc. Rev. Philip J. Schumaker, Pst.; Karen Bushman, DRE; Paul Weisenberger, Liturgy Dir.; Christine Stemwell, Bus. Mgr.; CRP Stds.: 6

STURTEVANT

St. Sebastian Congregation - 3050 95th St., Sturtevant, WI 53177; Mailing: 3126 95th St., Sturtevant, WI 53177 t) 262-886-4398 parishoffice@stsebracine.org www.stsebracine.org Rev. Thomas Vathappallil, M.C.B.S., Pst.; Dcn. Eric M. Sewell; Eric Antrim, Youth Min.; Sarah Amason, DRE; CRP Stds.: 6

THERESA

St. Theresa's Congregation - 102 Church St., Theresa, WI 53091; Mailing: P.O. Box 22, Mayville, WI 53050 t) 920-387-3130 jdominic@stmarymayville.org www.stsandrewmarytheresa.org Also serves St. Andrew, Leroy & St. Mary's, Mayville Rev. Joseph Dominic, S.A.C., Pst.; CRP Stds.: 13

TWIN LAKES

St. John the Evangelist Congregation - 701 N. Lake Ave., Twin Lakes, WI 53181 t) 262-877-2557 (CRP) office.staljohn@gmail.com; staljohnevdas@gmail.com www.staljohn.org Rev. Arthur W. Mattox, Admin.; CRP Stds.: 54

UNION GROVE

Congregation of St. John the Baptist - 1501 172nd Ave., Union Grove, WI 53182; Mailing: 1704 240th Ave., Kansasville, WI 53139 t) 262-878-2267 business@krcatholics.org www.krcatholics.org Dcn. Anton B. Nickolai, Parish Dir.; Kathi Andrioni, Dir., Faith Formation; Sheryl Miller, Dir., Finance; Troy J Temple, Dir., Opers.; Maria Wargolet, Dir., Liturgy & Music; CRP Stds.: 51

St. Robert Bellarmine Congregation - 3320 S. Colony Ave., Union Grove, WI 53182 t) 262-878-3476 business@krcatholics.org www.krcatholics.org Dcn. Anton B. Nickolai, Parish Dir.; Kathi Andrioni, Dir., Faith Formation; Sheryl Miller, Dir., Finance; Troy J Temple, Dir., Oper.; Maria Wargolet, Dir., Liturgy & Music; CRP Stds.: 59

WATERFORD

St. Thomas Aquinas Congregation - 305 S. First St., Waterford, WI 53185 t) 262-534-2255; 262-534-2255 x248 (CRP) starectory@saintthomaswaterford.org www.saintthomaswaterford.org Rev. Edward Tlucek, O.F.M., Pst.; Dcn. Michael Hoffman; Dcn. Jim Nickel; Blaise C Beaulier, Admin.; Nancy Hutchings, Business Admin.; CRP Stds.: 224

St. Thomas Aquinas Pre-School - (Grades PreSchool-PreK) 302 S. Second St., Waterford, WI 53185 t) 262-534-2265 stapreschool@saintthomaswaterford.org www.saintthomaswaterford.org/preschool/ Erika Rondeau, Dir.; Stds.: 15; Lay Tchrs.: 2

WAUKESHA

St. John Neumann, Catholic Community of Waukesha - 2400 W. State Hwy. 59, Waukesha, WI 53189-6323 t) 262-549-0223; 262-547-6555 (CRP) communication@ccwauk.org; eerickson@ccwauk.org ccwauk.org Rev. Matthew J. Widder, Pst.; Rev. Jorge Perez (Venezuela), Assoc. Pst.; Rev. Charles Wrobel, Assoc. Pst.; Rev. Patrick E. Heppe, Pastor Emer.; Dcn. Jorge Benavente; Dcn. Scott Campbell; Dcn. Aristeo Ortiz; Dcn. Antonio Palacios; Dcn. Gary J. Stephani; Bob Gallagher, Liturgy Dir.; Erin Erickson, DRE; CRP Stds.: 36

St. Joseph, Catholic Community of Waukesha - 818 N. East Ave., Waukesha, WI 53186 t) 262-542-2589; 262-547-6555 (CRP) communication@ccwauk.org; formation@ccwauk.org ccwauk.org Rev. Matthew J. Widder, Pst.; Rev. Jorge Perez (Venezuela), Assoc. Pst.; Rev. Charles Wrobel, Assoc. Pst.; Rev. Patrick E. Heppe, Pastor Emer.; Dcn. Jorge Benavente; Dcn. Scott Campbell; Dcn. Aristeo Ortiz; Dcn. Antonio Palacios; Dcn. Gary J. Stephani; Bob Gallagher, Liturgy Dir.; Erin Erickson, Dir., Formation; CRP Stds.: 157

St. Mary, Catholic Community of Waukesha - 225 S. Hartwell Ave., Waukesha, WI 53186-6400 t) 262-547-6555; 262-547-6555 x1350 (CRP) communication@ccwauk.org; formation@ccwauk.org ccwauk.org Rev. Matthew J. Widder, Pst.; Rev. Jorge Perez (Venezuela), Assoc. Pst.; Rev. Charles Wrobel, Assoc. Pst.; Rev. Patrick E. Heppe, Pastor Emer.; Dcn. Jorge Benavente; Dcn. Scott Campbell; Dcn. Aristeo Ortiz; Dcn. Antonio Palacios; Dcn. Gary J. Stephani; Bob Gallagher, Liturgy Dir.; CRP Stds.: 155

St. Paul's Catholic Church - S38 W31602 Wern Way (Hwy. D), Waukesha, WI 53189; Mailing: P.O. Box 95, Genesee Depot, WI 53127 t) 262-968-3865; 262-968-2276 (CRP) office@stpaulgenesee.net www.stpaulgenesee.net Karin Marcus, Admin.; Rev. Daniel P. Volkert, Admin.; Dcn. Joseph M. Senglaub; Matt Byczynski, Liturgy Dir.; CRP Stds.: 199

St. William, Catholic Community of Waukesha - 440 N. Moreland Blvd., Waukesha, WI 53188 t) 262-547-2763 communication@ccwauk.org; formation@ccwauk.org ccwauk.org Rev. Matthew J. Widder, Pst.; Rev. Jorge Perez (Venezuela), Assoc. Pst.; Rev. Charles Wrobel, Assoc. Pst.; Rev. Patrick E. Heppe, Pastor Emer.; Dcn. Jorge Benavente; Dcn. Scott Campbell; Dcn. Aristeo Ortiz; Dcn. Antonio Palacios; Dcn. Gary J. Stephani; Robert Gallagher, Liturgy Dir.; Erin Erickson, Director of Formation; CRP Stds.: 199

WAUPUN

St. Josephs Congregation - 118 W. Main St., Waupun, WI 53963 t) 920-324-5400 office@stjoeschurch.org www.stjoeschurch.org Rev. John J. Radetski, Pst.; Peter Laning, DRE; CRP Stds.: 49

WAUWATOSA

St. Bernard's Congregation - 1500 Wauwatosa Ave., Wauwatosa, WI 53213; Mailing: 7474 Harwood Ave., Wauwatosa, WI 53213 t) 414-258-4320 bulletin@stbernardparish.org; admin@stbernardparish.org www.stbernardparish.org Very Rev. Phillip A. Bogacki, Pst.; Rev. Michael J. Lawinger, Assoc. Pst.; CRP Stds.: 39

Christ King Congregation - 2604 N. Swan Blvd., Wauwatosa, WI 53226 t) 414-258-2604 brownl@christkingparish.org; bogackip@christkingparish.org www.christkingparish.org Very Rev. Phillip A. Bogacki, Pst.; Rev. Michael J. Lawinger, Assoc. Pst.; Dcn. Peter Rebholz; Sarah Daszczuks, Youth Min.; Samantha El-Azem, DRE; CRP Stds.: 282

Christ King School - (Grades PreK-8) 2646 N. Swan Blvd., Wauwatosa, WI 53226 t) 414-258-4160 principal@christkingschool.org www.christkingschool.org Grace M. Urbanski, Prin.; Stds.: 290; Sr. Tchrs.: 1; Lay Tchrs.: 22

St. Joseph Congregation - 12130 W. Center St., Wauwatosa, WI 53222-4096 t) 414-771-4626 fernandeza@stjoetosa.com; navarroe@stjoetosa.com www.stjoetosa.com Rev. Adam F. Hirudayasamy, SMA (India), Admin.; CRP Stds.: 106

St. Joseph Congregation School - (Grades PreK-8) 2750 N. 122nd St., Wauwatosa, WI 53222 taubnerl@stjosephschooltosa.com Christopher Multhauf, Prin.; Stds.: 200; Lay Tchrs.: 13

St. Jude Congregation - 734 Glenview Ave., Wauwatosa, WI 53213 t) 414-258-8821; 414-258-8821 x230 (CRP) gheun@stjudetheapostle.net; dengelhart@stjudetheapostle.net Rev. Michael J. Erwin, Pst.; Rev. Mark C. Obeten (Nigeria), In Res.; David Grunwaldt, Admin.; Michael Batcho, Dir.; Gerald Stilp, Dir.; David Heckendorf, Mgr.; Gary Heun, DRE; CRP Stds.: 149

St. Jude the Apostle School - (Grades PreK-8) 800 Glenview Ave., Wauwatosa, WI 53213 t) 414-771-1520 cladien@saintjudeschool.net Catherine LaDien, Prin.; Stds.: 388; Lay Tchrs.: 23

St. Pius Congregation - 2506 N. Wauwatosa Ave., Wauwatosa, WI 53213 t) 414-453-3875 frpaul@stpiusparish.org www.stpiusparish.org Rev. Paul Portland, S.D.S., Pst.; CRP Stds.: 25

WEST ALLIS

St. Augustine Congregation - 6768 W. Rogers St., West Allis, WI 53219-1344; Mailing: 6762 W. Rogers St., West Allis, WI 53219-1344 t) 414-541-7515 (Main Office @ St Rita); 414-541-5207 (Office, St. Augustine) barb.strita@wi.rr.com; staugwa@gmail.com staugwa.org Affiliated with Mary Queen of Saints Catholic Academy, West Allis operated by Seton Catholic Schools, Inc. Rev. Gerardo Raul Carcar, I.Sch. (Argentina), Pst.; Barbara Krieger, DRE;

Congregation of the Holy Assumption - 7109 W. Orchard St., West Allis, WI 53214; Mailing: 1526 S. 72nd St., West Allis, WI 53214 t) 414-774-3010 hacparish@gmail.com haccparish.org Affiliated with Mary Queen of Saints Catholic Academy, West Allis, operated by Seton Catholic Schools Rev. Gerardo Raul Carcar, I.Sch. (Argentina), Pst.; Rev. Matthew J. Kirk, Assoc. Pst.; CRP Stds.: 20

Mother of Perpetual Help Congregation - 1121 S. 116th St., West Allis, WI 53214 t) 414-453-5192 office@mphwa.org www.mphwa.org Affiliated with Mary Queen of Saints Catholic Academy, West Allis operated by Seton Catholic Dcn. Keith R. Marx; Rev. Mathew Perumpil, M.I., Pst.; CRP Stds.: 62

St. Rita's Congregation - 2318 S. 61st St., West Allis, WI 53219 t) 414-541-7515 stritaparishwa@wi.rr.com stritawestallis.org Affiliated with Mary Queen of Saints Catholic Academy, West Allis operated by Seton Catholic Schools, Inc. Rev. Gerardo Raul Carcar, I.Sch. (Argentina), Pst.; Rev. Matthew J. Kirk, Assoc. Pst.; Kevin Bourassa, Music Min.; CRP Stds.: 11

WEST BEND

St. Frances Cabrini Congregation - 1025 S. 7th Ave., West Bend, WI 53095 t) 262-338-2366 jrude@wbparishes.org; cchlebek@wbparishes.org www.saintfrancescabrini.com Very Rev. Nathan D. Reesman, Pst.; Rev. Kevin T. Harmon, Assoc. Pst.; Julie Braun, DRE; Chris Chlebek, Bus. Mgr.; CRP Stds.: 196

St. Frances Cabrini School - (Grades PreK-8) 529 Hawthorn Dr., West Bend, WI 53095 t) 262-334-7142 wwaech@wbparishes.org William Waech, Prin.; Stds.: 203; Lay Tchrs.: 12

Congregation of Holy Angels - 138 N. 8th Ave., West Bend, WI 53095 t) 262-334-9393 (CRP); 262-334-3038 berglandh@hawb.org; holyangelswb@gmail.com hawb.org Rev. Howard G. Haase, Pst.; Dcn. Mark Jansen; Dcn. David N. Young; Barbara VanderWielen, Bus. Mgr.; CRP Stds.: 283

Holy Angels School - (Grades PreK-8) 230 N. 8th Ave., West Bend, WI 53095 t) 262-338-1148 has@has.pvt.k12.wi.us www.has.pvt.k12.wi.us Michelle Spaeth, Prin.; Stds.: 235; Lay Tchrs.: 16

Congregation of the Immaculate Conception - 1610 Monroe St., West Bend, WI 53090; Mailing: 406 Jefferson St., West Bend, WI 53090 t) 262-338-5600 rprim@wbparishes.org; mabel@wbparishes.org www.stmaryparishwb.org Very Rev. Nathan D. Reesman, Pst.; Rev. Kevin T. Harmon, Assoc. Pst.; Elizabeth Habersetzer, Music Min.; Chris Crom, Pst. Min./Coord.; Mary Abel, DRE; Chris Chlebek, Bus. Mgr.; CRP Stds.: 106

WEST MILWAUKEE

St. Florian's Congregation - 1233 S. 45th St., West Milwaukee, WI 53214-3615; Mailing: 1210 S. 45th St., West Milwaukee, WI 53214-3614 t) 414-383-3565; (414) 774-3010 (CRP) stflorianoffice@gmail.com; stflorianpastor@gmail.com www.stflorian.org Affiliated with Mary Queen of Saints Catholic Academy, West Allis operated by Seton Catholic Schools. Very Rev. Michael Berry, OCD, Admin.; Very Rev. Elijah Martin, O.C.D., In Solidum Team Mem.; CRP Stds.: 2

WHITEFISH BAY

Holy Family Congregation - 4825 N. Wildwood Ave., Whitefish Bay, WI 53217 t) 414-332-8156 (CRP); 414-332-9220 holyfam@hfparish.org; hfreled@hfparish.org www.hfparish.org Very Rev. J. Enrique Hernandez, Pst.; Rev. Andrew Infanger, Assoc. Pst.; CRP Stds.: 153

Holy Family School - (Grades PreK-8) 4849 N. Wildwood Ave., Whitefish Bay, WI 53217 t) 414-332-8175 hfpschool@hfparishschool.org Amy Kern, Prin.; Stds.: 184; Lay Tchrs.: 17

St. Monica's Congregation - 5681 N. Santa Monica Blvd, Whitefish Bay, WI 53217 t) 414-332-1576 smoffice@stme.church; jlambrecht@stme.church www.stme.church Very Rev. Mark C. Payne, Pst.; Rev. Tonny Kizza, Assoc. Pst.; Dcn. Brian Witteman; Dcn. Robert Larkin; David Bonofiglio, Dir., Music and Liturgy; Sue Devine, Bus. Mgr.; Jeanette Lambrecht, DRE; Anne B. Rice, Dir.; Joyce Swietlik, Youth Min.; Rev. Patrick Behling, In Res.; Rev. Stephen Buting, In Res.; CRP Stds.: 182

St. Monica School - (Grades PreK-8) 5635 N. Santa Monica Blvd., Whitefish Bay, WI 53217 t) 414-332-3660 www.stmonica.school Shared With: St. Eugene, Fox Point Emily Friday, Prin.; Tim Kasprzak, Vice Prin.; Stds.: 420; Lay Tchrs.: 32

WHITEWATER

St. Patrick's Congregation - 1225 W. Main St., Whitewater, WI 53190-1620 t) 262-473-3143 stpatrickww@gmail.com stpatrickwhitewater.org Rev. Antony Primal Thomas, Pst.; Dcn. Hector Villarreal, Pst. Assoc.; Richard Rupprecht, DRE; Lisa Cronin, Liturgy Dir.; Barbara Gawlik, Bus. Mgr.; CRP Stds.: 96

WIND LAKE

St. Clare Congregation - 7616 Fritz St., Wind Lake, WI 53185 t) 262-895-2797 (CRP); 262-895-2729 bulletins@tds.net; julieboulware.stclare@gmail.com www.stclarewindlake.org Rev. Edward Tlucek, O.F.M., Admin.; Julie Boulware, Admin.; Christina Kuenzi, Music Min.; Maureen LeGros, Youth Min.; Trista Minezes, DRE; CRP Stds.: 81

SCHOOLS: PRESCHOOL THRU HIGH SCHOOL

SCHOOLS

STATE OF WISCONSIN

BURLINGTON

Burlington Catholic School, Inc. - (DIO) (Grades PreK-8) 225 W. State St., Burlington, WI 53105 t) 262-763-1515; 262-763-2848 eberg@ourbcs.org www.ourbcs.org Emily Berg, Prin.; Stds.: 423; Lay Tchrs.: 40

FOND DU LAC

St. Mary's Springs Academy of Fond du Lac, WI - (PAR) (Grades PreK-12) 255 County Rd. K, Fond du Lac, WI 54937 t) 920-924-0993; 920-921-4870 x8009 (Bus. Office) knett@smsacademy.org; info@smsacademy.org www.smsacademy.org Stacey L Akey, Pres.; Nichole Rusniaczek, Librn.; Stds.: 845; Lay Tchrs.: 60

Pre-School & Elementary - (Grades PreK-12) Steven Kelnhofer, Prin.; Stds.: 570

High School - (Grades PreK-12) Eamonn O'Keeffe, Prin.; Stds.: 275; Lay Tchrs.: 24

KENOSHA

All Saints Catholic School of Kenosha, Inc. - (DIO) (Grades PreK-8) 4400 22nd Ave., Kenosha, WI 53140 t) 262-925-4000 info@allsaintskenosha.org www.allsaintskenosha.org Kelly Neu, Prin.; Stds.: 393; Sr. Tchrs.: 1; Lay Tchrs.: 28

St. Joseph Catholic Academy, Inc. - (DIO) (Grades PreK-12) 2401 69th St., Kenosha, WI 53143 t) 262-654-8651; 262-656-7360 mrizzo@sjcawi.org; bbartholomew@sjcawi.org www.sjcawi.org Bridget Bartholomew, Prin.; Rev. Todd Belardi, Chap.; Matthew Rizzo, Pres.; Stds.: 799; Pr. Tchrs.: 1; Sr. Tchrs.: 1; Lay Tchrs.: 60

MALONE

Holyland Catholic School - (PAR) (Grades PreK-8) N9290 County Rd. W, Malone, WI 53049 t) 920-795-4222 holylandcatholic@gmail.com www.holylandcatholicschool.org Members: St. John the Baptist, Johnsburg; St. Mary, Marytown; Holy Cross Parish, Mount Calvary, St. Cloud Church, St. Cloud, St. Joseph, St. Cloud. Nicole M Klein, Prin.; Stds.: 57; Lay Tchrs.: 6

MILWAUKEE

St. Coletta Day School of Milwaukee - (PRV) (Grades 3-12) 1740 N. 55th St., Milwaukee, WI 53208 t) 414-453-1850 scdsmke@scdsmke.org www.scdsmke.org For students with intellectual and/or developmental disabilities. CindySue Nielsen, Admin.; Stds.: 27; Lay Tchrs.: 5

Messmer Catholic Schools, Inc. - (PRV) (Grades PreK-12) 742 W. Capitol Dr., Milwaukee, WI 53206 t) 414-264-5440 generalinfo@messmerschools.org www.messmerschools.org Jim Piatt, Pres.; Mike Bartels, Vice Pres.; Stds.: 1,212; Lay Tchrs.: 102

***Messmer High School** - (Grades PreK-12) t) (414) 264-5440 Shenora Staten Jordan, Prin.; Stds.: 490; Lay Tchrs.: 48

Messmer Saint Rose - (Grades PreK-12) 514 N. 31st St., Milwaukee, WI 53208 t) 414-933-6070 www.messmerschool.org Elizabeth Fritsch, Prin.; Stds.: 354; Lay Tchrs.: 21

Messmer Saint Mary - (Grades PreK-12) 3027 N. Fratney St., Milwaukee, WI 53212 t) 414-264-6070 Curtis Borry, Prin.; Stds.: 384; Lay Tchrs.: 22

Nativity Jesuit Academy, Inc. (Wisconsin Province of the Society of Jesus.) - (PRV) (Grades PreK-8) 1515 S. 29th St., Milwaukee, WI 53215-1912 t) 414-645-1060 info@nativityjesuit.org; businessoffice@nativityjesuit.org www.nativityjesuit.org Ally Beckwith, Vice Prin.; Monique Deshotels, Vice Prin.; Vanessa Solis, Pres.; Stds.: 258; Lay Tchrs.: 14

Notre Dame School of Milwaukee, Inc. - (PRV) (Grades PreSchool-8) 1418 S. Layton Blvd., Milwaukee, WI 53215; Mailing: 2604 W. Orchard St., Milwaukee, WI 53204 t) 414-671-3000 (Blessed Theresa Campus); 414-431-7950 (Mother Caroline Campus) plandry@notredamemke.org; htassone@notredamemke.org www.notredamemke.org Sponsored by: School Sisters of Notre Dame. Matthew Cashman, Prin.; David D'Anfonio, Prin.; Amy Snyder, Prin.; Patrick Landry, Pres.; Stds.: 642; Sr. Tchrs.: 1; Lay Tchrs.: 43

RACINE

Siena Catholic Schools of Racine, Inc. - (Grades PreK-12) 245 Main St., Ste. 402, Racine, WI 53403 t) 262-800-1111 info@sienacatholicschools.org www.sienacatholicschools.org System of six Catholic schools (five K-8, one high school) in Racine, WI. Brenda White, Pres.; Stds.: 1,585; Lay Tchrs.: 94

Our Lady of Grace Academy - (Grades PreK-12) 1435 Grove Ave., Racine, WI 53405 t) 262-833-7100 asmith@sienacatholicschools.org www.ologa.org Operated by Siena Catholic Schools of Racine, Inc. Ashley Smith, Prin.; Stds.: 261; Lay Tchrs.: 12

St. Joseph School - (Grades PreK-12) 1525 Erie St., Racine, WI 53402 t) 262-633-2403 hhernandez@sienacatholicschools.org www.st-joes-school.org Operated by Siena Catholic Schools of Racine, Inc. Heidi Hernandez, Prin.; Stds.: 221; Lay Tchrs.: 13

St. Lucy Catholic School - (Grades PreK-12) 3035 Drexel Ave., Racine, WI 53403 t) 262-554-1801 x211 sthostenson@sienacatholicschools.org www.stlucysschool.com Operated by Siena Catholic Schools of Racine, Inc. Sarah Thostenson, Prin.; Stds.: 194; Lay Tchrs.: 12

St. Rita School - (Grades PreK-12) 4433 Douglas Ave., Racine, WI 53402 t) 262-639-3333 ssavaglio@sienacatholicschools.org www.st-ritasschool.org Dr. Susan Savaglio-Jarvis, Prin.; Stds.: 223; Lay Tchrs.: 12

St. Catherine's High School - (Grades PreK-12) 1200 Park Ave., Racine, WI 53403 t) 262-632-2785 marendt@sienacatholicschools.org www.saintcats.org Operated by Siena Catholic Schools of Racine, Inc. Deborah Forrest, Vice Prin.; Mike Arendt, Prin.; Heather Collum, Vice Prin.; Stds.: 419; Lay Tchrs.: 27

John Paul II Academy - (Grades PreK-12) 2023 Northwestern Ave., Racine, WI 53404 t) 262-637-2012 gschumacher@sienacatholicschools.org johnpaulacademy.org Operated by Siena Catholic Schools of Racine, Inc. Gloria Schumacher, Prin.; Stds.: 217; Lay Tchrs.: 10

SHEBOYGAN

St. Elizabeth Ann Seton Catholic School, Inc. - (PAR) (Grades PreK-8) 814 Superior Ave., Sheboygan, WI 53081 t) (920) 452-1571 widmannm@sheboyganseton.org; billmeiers@sheboyganseton.org www.sheboyganseton.org School is supported by Holy Name of Jesus, St. Clement, and St. Dominic parishes, Sheboygan. Mary Widmann, Prin.; Stds.: 77; Lay Tchrs.: 14

ST. FRANCIS

Seton Catholic Schools, Inc. - (PAR) (Grades PreSchool-8) 3501 S. Lake Dr., St. Francis, WI 53235;

Mailing: P.O. Box 070912, Milwaukee, WI 53207-0912 t) 414-831-8400 setonadmin@setoncatholicschools.org www.setoncatholicschools.com Brian Couch, Pres.; Stds.: 2,531; Lay Tchrs.: 172

St. Catherine School - (Grades PreSchool-8) 2647 N. 51st St., Milwaukee, WI 53210 t) 414-445-2846 jcottrell@saintcatherine.org www.saintcatherine.org/ Ernie DiDomizio, Prin.; Stds.: 145; Lay Tchrs.: 10

St. Charles Borromeo School - (Grades PreSchool-8) 3100 W. Parnell Ave., Milwaukee, WI 53221 t) 414-282-0767 smejac@scbmil.org www.stcharlesborromeoschool.com/ Stacey P. Mejac, Prin.; Stds.: 223; Lay Tchrs.: 14

St. Margaret Mary School - (Grades PreSchool-8) 3950 N. 92nd St., Milwaukee, WI 53222-2587 t) 414-463-8760 komdahl@stmms.org www.stmms.org/ Jessica Borkowski, Prin.; Stds.: 136; Lay Tchrs.: 11

Our Lady Queen of Peace School - (Grades PreSchool-8) 2733 W. Euclid Ave., Milwaukee, WI 53215 t) 414-672-6660 jorlow@olqpstaff.org Janet Orlowski, Prin.; Stds.: 181; Lay Tchrs.: 16

Prince of Peace School - (Grades PreSchool-8) 1646 S. 22nd St., Milwaukee, WI 53204 t) 414-645-4922 vegaj@princeofpeaceschool.org www.princeofpeaceschool.org Jen Vega, Prin.; Stds.: 382; Lay Tchrs.: 24

St. Rafael the Archangel School - (Grades PreSchool-8) 2251 S. 31st St., Milwaukee, WI 53215 t) 414-645-1300 eaviles@strafael.org www.strafael.org Elizabeth Aviles, Prin.; Stds.: 308; Lay Tchrs.: 19

St. Roman School - (Grades PreSchool-8) 1810 W. Bolivar Ave., Milwaukee, WI 53221 t) 414-282-7970 sue.shawver@stromanschool.com www.stromanschool.com/ Susan Shawver, Prin.; Stds.: 342; Lay Tchrs.: 24

Catholic East Elementary - (Grades PreSchool-8) 2461 N. Murray Ave., Milwaukee, WI 53211 t) 414-964-1770 ttrzcinko@catholiceast.org catholiceast.org Timothy Trzcinko, Prin.; Stds.: 243; Lay Tchrs.: 15

Mary Queen of Saints Catholic Academy (A Seton Catholic School) - (Grades PreSchool-8) 11217 S. 116th St., West Allis, WI 53214 t) 414-476-0751 leen@mqscateacher.org mqsca.org Nicholas Lee, Prin.; Stds.: 138; Lay Tchrs.: 15

St. Thomas Aquinas Academy - (Grades PreSchool-8) 341 E. Norwich St., Milwaukee, WI 53207 t) 414-744-1214 bergmanna@staamke.org thomasaquinasacademy.com Andrea Bergmann, Prin.; Stds.: 233; Lay Tchrs.: 15

Northwest Catholic School - (Grades PreSchool-8) 7140 N. 41st St., Milwaukee, WI 53209 t) 414-352-6927 x300 loganl@nwcschool.org www.nwcschool.org Rev. Gregory J. Greiten, Admin.; Dr. Tasha Johnson, Prin.; Stds.: 200; Lay Tchrs.: 9

WAUKESHA

Waukesha Catholic School System, Inc. - (PAR) (Grades PreK-8) 221 S. Hartwell Ave., Waukesha, WI 53186 t) 262-896-2929 lkovaleski@waukeshacatholic.org www.waukeshacatholic.org Members: St. Joseph, St. Mary, St. John Neumann, St. William. Lisa Kovaleski, Prin.; Stds.: 438; Lay Tchrs.: 28

WAUWATOSA

Wauwatosa Catholic School - (PAR) (Grades PreK-8) 1500 Wauwatosa Ave., Wauwatosa, WI 53213 t) 414-258-9977 businessmgr@wauwatosacatholic.org www.wauwatosacatholic.org Nicolle R. Schroeder, Prin.; Stds.: 178; Lay Tchrs.: 10

HIGH SCHOOLS

STATE OF WISCONSIN

BURLINGTON

Catholic Central High School of Burlington, Inc. - (DIO) (Grades 9-12) 148 McHenry St., Burlington, WI 53105 t) 262-763-1510 brianshimon@cchsnet.org www.catholiccentralhs.org Officially affiliated with the School Sisters of Notre Dame Brian Shimon, Prin.; Stds.: 128; Lay Tchrs.: 16

MILWAUKEE

Cristo Rey Jesuit Milwaukee High School, Inc. - (PRV) (Grades 9-12) 1818 W. National Ave., Milwaukee, WI 53204 t) 414-436-4600 mtalavera@cristoreymilwaukee.org; astith@cristoreymilwaukee.org www.cristoreymilwaukee.org Luke Harrison, Prin.; Andrew Stith, Pres.; Stds.: 436; Lay Tchrs.: 29

Divine Savior Holy Angels High School - (PRV) (Grades 9-12) 4257 N. 100th St., Milwaukee, WI 53222 t) 414-462-3742 czosneks@dsha.info; konieczny k@dsha.info www.dsha.info (Girls) Sponsored by the Sisters of the Divine Savior Dan Quesnell, Prin.; Katie Konieczny, Pres.; Stds.: 677; Lay Tchrs.: 55

St. Joan Antida High School, Inc. - (PRV) (Grades 9-12) 1341 N. Cass St., Milwaukee, WI 53202 t) 414-272-8423 mcoryell@saintjoanantida.org; motero@saintjoanantida.org www.saintjoanantida.org (All girls high school) Marikris Coryell, Pres.; Megan Otero, Prin.; Melissa Rios, Vice Prin.; Aracelly Bonilla, Bus. Mgr.; Stds.: 189; Lay Tchrs.: 17

Marquette University High School - (PRV) (Grades 9-12) 3401 W. Wisconsin Ave., Milwaukee, WI 53208 t) 414-933-7220 info@muhs.edu www.muhs.edu Boys. Rev. Michael J. Marco, S.J., Pres.; Jeff Monday, Prin.; Stds.: 898; Pr. Tchrs.: 1; Lay Tchrs.: 81

Pius XI Catholic High School - (DIO) (Grades 9-12) 135 N. 76th St., Milwaukee, WI 53213 t) 414-290-7000 www.piusxi.org Ryan Krienke, Prin.; John Herbert, Pres.; Stds.: 699; Sr. Tchrs.: 1; Lay Tchrs.: 43

St. Thomas More High School - (DIO) (Grades 9-12) 2601 E. Morgan Ave., Milwaukee, WI 53207 t) 414-481-8370 ljanick@tmore.org; dsteffes@tmore.org www.tmore.org (Coed) John Hoch, Pres.; Stds.: 544; Lay Tchrs.: 38

WAUKESHA

***Catholic Memorial High School of Waukesha, Inc.** - (DIO) (Grades 9-12) 601 E. College Ave., Waukesha, WI 53186-5538 t) 262-542-7101 dbembenek@catholicmemorial.net www.catholicmemorial.net Donna Bembenek, Pres.; Stds.: 576; Lay Tchrs.: 44

WHITEFISH BAY

Dominican High School - (PRV) (Grades 9-12) 120 E. Silver Spring Dr., Whitefish Bay, WI 53217 t) 414-332-1170 lgiese@dominicanhighschool.com www.dominicanhighschool.com Sponsored by Sinsinawa Dominicans. Nate Friday, Campus Min.; Vincent A. Murray, Dean; Edward Foy, Prin.; Leanne M. Giese, Pres.; Stds.: 325; Lay Tchrs.: 28

INSTITUTIONS LOCATED IN DIOCESE

ASSOCIATIONS [ASN]

MILWAUKEE

National Association of Catholic Chaplains - 4915 S. Howell Ave., Ste. 501, Milwaukee, WI 53207 t) 414-483-4898 info@nacc.org www.nacc.org Erica Cohen Moore, Exec.;

NASHOTAH

The Milwaukee Guild of the Catholic Medical Association - W338 N5215 Township Rd. O, Nashotah, WI 53058 c) (262) 951-1783 franklin.smith@me.com www.mgcma.org Catholic Physicians Guild Dr. Franklin Leo Smith, Pres.;

ST. FRANCIS

Milwaukee Archdiocesan Principals' Association (MAPA) - 3501 S. Lake Dr., St. Francis, WI 53235; Mailing: P.O. Box 070912, Milwaukee, WI 53207-0912 t) (414) 758-2252 varickb@archmil.org Archdiocese of Milwaukee, Office for Schools. Bruce Varick, Assoc. Supt.;

CAMPUS MINISTRY / NEWMAN CENTERS [CAM]

MILWAUKEE

Marquette University/Campus Ministry - 1442 W. Wisconsin Ave., Campus Ministry AMU 236, Milwaukee, WI 53233; Mailing: P.O. Box 1881, Campus Ministry/AMU 236, Milwaukee, WI 53201 t) 414-288-6873 ann.hilbert@marquette.edu www.marquette.edu/cm Rev. James Voiss, S.J., Vice. Pres.; Mary Sue Callan-Farley, Dir.;

ST. FRANCIS

Milwaukee Archdiocesan Campus Ministry - 3501 S. Lake Dr., St. Francis, WI 53235; Mailing: P.O. Box 070912, Milwaukee, WI 53207-0912 t) 414-758-2219 burdsp@archmil.org brewcitycatholic.com Peter Burds, Dir.;

Catholic Campus Ministry Newman Center - U.W. Milwaukee - 3001 N. Downer Ave., Milwaukee, WI 53211 t) 414-964-6640 infangera@hfparish.org panthercatholic.com Rev. Andrew Infanger, Dir.;

Catholic Campus Ministry - U.W. Whitewater - 344 N. Prairie St., Whitewater, WI 53190 t) 262-473-5555 schuellera@archmil.org Andrew Schueller, Campus Min.;

CATHOLIC CHARITIES [CCH]

ST. FRANCIS

Catholic Charities of the Archdiocese of Milwaukee, Inc. - 3501 S. Lake Dr., St. Francis, WI 53235; Mailing: P.O. Box 070912, Milwaukee, WI 53207-0912 t) 414-769-3400 info@ccmke.org www.ccmke.org Very Rev. David H. Reith, Vicar; Asstd. Annu.: 52,500; Staff: 72

CEMETERIES [CEM]

CUDAHY

Holy Sepulcher - 3800 E. College Ave., Cudahy, WI 53110 t) 414-762-2860 (Office); 414-769-3336 (Bookkeeper) holysepcemetery@gmail.com; parishfinance@archmil.org Very Rev. Carmelo Giuffre, Mem.; Rev. Pradeep Joseph Sebastian, M.C.B.S., Mem.; Lawrence Miller, Dir.;

MEQUON

Resurrection - 9400 W. Donges Bay Rd., Mequon, WI 53092 t) 262-242-3850 mthiel@cfcsmission.org Mary Thiel, Dir.;

MILWAUKEE

St. Adalbert - 3801 S. 6th St., Milwaukee, WI 53221 t) 414-483-3663 mthiel@cfcsmission.org Mary Thiel, Dir.;

Calvary - 5503 W. Bluemound Rd., Milwaukee, WI 53208; Mailing: 7301 W. Nash St., Milwaukee, WI 53216 t) 414-438-4430 mthiel@cfcsmission.org Mary Thiel, Dir.;

Holy Cross - 7301 W. Nash St., Milwaukee, WI 53216 t) 414-438-4420 mthiel@cfcsmission.org Mary Thiel, Dir.;

Holy Trinity - 3564 S. 13th St., Milwaukee, WI 53221; Mailing: 3801 S. 6th St., Milwaukee, WI 53221 t) 414-483-3663 mthiel@cfcsmission.org Mary Thiel, Dir.;

Mount Olivet - 3801 W. Morgan Ave., Milwaukee, WI 53221 t) 414-645-0611 mthiel@cfcsmission.org Mary Thiel, Dir.;

PLEASANT PRAIRIE

All Saints - 3300 Springbrook Rd., Pleasant Prairie, WI 53158-5712 t) 262-694-2040 mthiel@cfcsmission.org Mary Thiel, Dir.;

SHEBOYGAN

Calvary Cemetery, Sheboygan, Wisconsin - 902 North Ave., Sheboygan, WI 53083; Mailing: 807 Superior Ave., Sheboygan, WI 53081 t) 920-458-7721 c) 920-946-2529 jljacobchick@gmail.com; woelfell@catholicnorth.org www.sheboygancalvarycemetery.com Lori Woelfel, Bus. Mgr.;

TAYCHEEDAH

St. Charles Cemetery - W4287 Golf Course Dr. (cor. Cty UU), Taycheedah, WI 54935; Mailing: 271 4th St. Way, Fond Du Lac, WI 54937 t) 920-921-0580 ellenk@hffdl.org Contact Holy Family Congregation, Fond du Lac, WI. Most Rev. Jerome E. Listecki, Pres.; Rev. Ryan J. Pruess, Vice. Pres.;

WAUKESHA

St. Joseph - S22 W22890 Broadway, Waukesha, WI 53186; Mailing: 3501 S. Lake Dr., St. Francis, WI 53235 t) 262-547-4927 mthiel@cfcsmission.org Mary Thiel, Dir.;

COLLEGES & UNIVERSITIES [COL]

FOND DU LAC

Marian University, Inc. - 45 S. National Ave., Fond du Lac, WI 54935 t) 920-923-7600 admissions@marianuniversity.edu www.marianuniversity.edu Sr. Edie Crews, Campus Min.; Michelle Majewski, Pres.; Dr. Kenneth Mulliken, Vice Pres., Academic Affairs; Stds.: 2,000; Lay Tchrs.: 75; Sr. Tchrs.: 1

MILWAUKEE

Alverno College - 3400 S. 43rd St., Milwaukee, WI 53234-3922; Mailing: P.O. Box 343922, Milwaukee, WI 53234-3922 t) 414-382-6000 president.ac@alverno.edu www.alverno.edu Kathy Hudson, Chair; Larry Duerr, Librn.; Stds.: 1,596; Lay Tchrs.: 99; Sr. Tchrs.: 7

Cardinal Stritch University (Sisters of St. Francis of Assisi) - 6801 N. Yates Rd., Milwaukee, WI 53217 t) 414-410-4000 president@stritch.edu; kghohl@stritch.edu www.stritch.edu Daniel Scholz, Pres.; Dr. Kate Meudt, Vice. Pres.; Rachel Nielsen, CFO; Tracy Fischer, Vice. Pres.; Donney Moroney, Vice. Pres.; Jeffrey Reinke, Vice. Pres.; Stds.: 1,365; Lay Tchrs.: 49; Sr. Tchrs.: 1

***Marquette University** - Zilber 235, Milwaukee, WI 53201-1881; Mailing: P.O. Box 1881, Milwaukee, WI 53201-1881 t) 414-288-7452 stacy.tuchel@marquette.edu www.marquette.edu Conducted under the auspices of the Society of Jesus. Michael R. Lovell, Pres.; Tim McMahon, Vice. Pres.; Joel Pogodzinski, Vice. Pres.; Rev. James Voiss, S.J., Vice. Pres.; Bill Scholl, Vice Pres. & Dir.; Lora Strigens, Vice Pres.; Stds.: 11,550; Bro. Tchrs.: 1; Lay Tchrs.: 1,238; Pr. Tchrs.: 14; Sr. Tchrs.: 2

Mount Mary University (School Sisters of Notre Dame) - 2900 N. Menomonee River Pkwy., Milwaukee, WI 53222-4597 t) 414-930-3354 mmu-president@mtmary.edu www.mtmary.edu Sr. Debra M. Sciano, SSND, Corp. Bd. Mem.; Stds.: 1,232; Lay Tchrs.: 60

CONVENTS, MONASTERIES, AND RESIDENCES FOR WOMEN [CON]

BURLINGTON

Misioneras Franciscanas de la Juventud, Inc. - 456 Kendall St., Burlington, WI 53105 t) 262-745-2733 pglg@yahoo.com Sr. Lilia G. Paredes, M.F.J., Contact; Srs.: 4

Missionary Sisters of the Holy Family - 31144 Hunters Tr., Burlington, WI 53105 t) 262-661-4074 sistersburlington@gmail.com Sr. Krystyna Kosakowska, M.S.F., Supr. Del.; Srs.: 4

CEDAR GROVE

Sacred Heart of the Lake Chalet - 6378 Sauk Tr., Cedar Grove, WI 53013; Mailing: Box 46A, Cedar Grove, WI 53013 t) 262-285-5019; 920-652-0653 sjudithmk@feliciansisters.org Recreation Home for Felician Sisters of Our Lady of Hope Province. Sr. Judith Marie Kubicki, Prov.; Srs.: 413

DELAVAN

Villa Celine - 3127 S. Shore Dr., Delavan, WI 53115; Mailing: 7260 W. Peterson Ave., E-216, Chicago, IL 60631 t) 773-792-6363 srdonna01@gmail.com Summer Rest Home for Sisters of the Resurrection. Sr. Donna Marie Wolowicki, Prov.;

FOND DU LAC

Nazareth Center-Nazareth Court - 375 Gillett St., Fond du Lac, WI 54935 t) 920-923-7993 dawn.quednow@ssmhealth.com Retirement Home of the Congregation of Sisters of St. Agnes Dawn Quednow, Admin.; Srs.: 38

St. Agnes Convent (Congregation of Sisters of St. Agnes of Fond du Lac, Wisconsin, Inc.) - 320 County Rd. K, Fond du Lac, WI 54937-8158 t) 920-907-2300 spollnow@csasisters.org www.csasisters.org Motherhouse Sr. Sharon Pollnow, CSA, Supr.; Srs.: 27

GREENFIELD

Cloistered Dominican Sisters of the Perpetual Rosary. - 3980 W. Kimberly Ave., Greenfield, WI 53221 c) 414-258-0579; 414-322-9744 mjoannahastings@gmail.com www.dsopr.org Sr. Joanna Hastings, O.P., Prioress; Srs.: 4

Our Lady of the Angels, Inc. - 3995 S. 92nd St., Greenfield, WI 53228 t) 414-810-0950 tasmith@olacommunity.org Convent for Retired School Sisters of Notre Dame and School Sisters of St. Francis Taylor Smith, Admin.; Srs.: 48

MILWAUKEE

St. Clare Convent - 3276 S. 16th St., Milwaukee, WI 53215 t) 724-384-5300 sjudithmk@feliciansisters.org www.feliciansistersna.org Felician Sisters. Srs.: 3

St. Francis Convent - 3170 S. 17th St., Milwaukee, WI 53215 t) (414) 488-9228 Felician Sisters. Sr. Mary Victoria Richardson, DSSF, Postulate Dir.; Srs.: 2

Mercedes Molina, Inc. - 1234 N. 24th Pl., Milwaukee, WI 53205 t) 414-210-4700 milwaukeemarianitas94@gmail.com Sr. Gloria Piedad Garzon, Supr.; Srs.: 3

Sacred Heart - 1545 S. Layton Blvd., Milwaukee, WI 53215 t) 414-383-9038 ckelling@sssf.org www.sssf.org/unitedstates/sacredheart/htm Sponsored by the School Sisters of St. Francis. Retirement community for religious women providing independent, assisted living and skilled nursing. Cathleen Kelling, Dir.; Srs.: 86

San Damiano Convent - 3159 S. 17th St., Milwaukee, WI 53215 t) 414-489-9195 smramona@fs-inc.net www.feliciansistersna.org Srs.: 3

The School Sisters of St. Francis of St. Joseph's Convent, Milwaukee, Wisconsin, Inc. - 1545 S. Layton Blvd., Milwaukee, WI 53215 t) 414-384-1515 info@sssf.org www.sssf.org Sr. Kathleen O'Brien, OSF, Prov.; Sr. Kathy Braun, OSF, Prov. Asst.; Sr. Mary Catherine Schneider, OSF, Prov. Asst.; Srs.: 268

School Sisters of St. Francis, Inc. - 1501 S. Layton Blvd., Milwaukee, WI 53215 t) 414-808-3779 internationalteam@sssf.org www.sssf.org Sr. Deborah Fumagalli, O.S.F., Pres.; Sr. Tresa Abraham Kizhakeparambil, 1st Vice Pres.; Sr. Matilde Maravi, O.S.F., Vice. Pres.; Sr. Jincy Vilayappillil, O.S.F., Vice. Pres.; Sr. Catherine Ryan, Treas.; Srs.: 561

Sisters of Charity of St. Joan Antida Convent (Presentation) - 1329 N. Cass St., Milwaukee, WI 53202 t) 414-276-4173 elizabeth@scsja.org Sr. Elizabeth A. Weber, S.C.S.J.A., Supr.; Srs.: 5

Sisters of Charity of St. Joan Antida Convent (St. Charles Community) - 3214 W. Parnell Ave., Milwaukee, WI 53221 t) 414-282-9627 jennifer@scsja.org Sr. Jennifer L. Daul, Supr.; Srs.: 4

Sisters of Charity of St. Joan Antida Regina Mundi Provincial House and Novitiate - 8560 N. 76th Pl., Milwaukee, WI 53223 t) 414-354-9233 sisters@scsja.org Sr. Theresa Rozga, Prov.; Srs.: 4

Sisters of the Divine Savior - 4311 N. 100th St., Milwaukee, WI 53222-1393 t) 414-466-0810 admin-offmgr@salvatoriansisters.org sistersofthedivinesavior.org Sr. Jean Schafer, SDS, Prov.; Sr. Mary Lee Grady, SDS, Vicaress; Sr. Sheila Novak, SDS, Provincial Councilor; Sr. Mary Evelyn Zimbauer, SDS, Provincial Councilor; Sr. Patrice Colletti, SDS, Provincial Councilor; Sr. Ellen Sinclair, S.D.S., Treas.; Sr. Nelda Hernandez, S.D.S., Secy.; Srs.: 45

MOUNT CALVARY

Congregation of Sister Servants of Christ the King, Inc. - N8114 County WW, Mount Calvary, WI 53057 t) 920-753-1055 nunbetterfarm@hotmail.com; boddenw@yahoo.com www.cristoreyranch.org General Motherhouse of Sister-Servants of Christ the King Sr. Stephen Bloesl, Pres.; Srs.: 3

PEWAUKEE

Carmel of the Mother of God (Discalced Carmelite Nuns of Milwaukee) - W267 N2517 Carmelite Rd., Pewaukee, WI 53072-4528 t) 262-691-0336 pewaukeecarmel@aol.com www.pewaukeecarmel.com Rev. Jude Peters, O.C.D., Chap.; Sr. Mary Agnes Kramer, Prioress; Srs.: 9

RACINE

Convent of St. Catherine of Siena - 5635 Erie St., Racine, WI 53402-1934 t) 262-639-4100 sgeertsen@racinedominicans.org; mmcmahon@racinedominicans.org www.racinedominicans.org Sr. Maryann A. McMahon, O.P., Pres.; Sr. Chris Broslavick, OP, Vice Pres.; Sr. Agnes Johnson, OP, Vice Pres.; Sr. Mary Ann Pevas, OP, Vice Pres.; Srs.: 84

St. Rita's Convent - 4014 N. Green Bay Rd., Racine, WI 53404 t) 262-639-1766 sr.angelica@sbcglobal.net sistersofstrita.org Sr. Angelica Summer, O.S.A., Supr.; Srs.: 3

SLINGER

Carmelite Hermit of the Trinity - CHT - 4270 Cedar Creek Rd., Slinger, WI 53086-9372 c) 262-388-2234 www.carmelitehermit.homestead.com Mount Carmel Hermitage (Canonical Hermit) Rev. James M. Tambornino, S.O.L.T., In Res.; Sr. Joseph Marie, C.H.T., Mem.;

ST. FRANCIS

The Sisters of St. Francis of Assisi, Inc. - St. Francis Convent, 3221 S. Lake Dr., St. Francis, WI 53235-3702 t) 414-744-1160 tergerson@lakeosfs.org www.lakeosfs.org Corporate Title: The Sisters of St. Francis of Assisi, Milwaukee, Wis. Sr. Diana De Bruin, O.S.F., Dir.; Sr. Ellen Carr, OSF, Rel. Ord. Ldr.; Sr. Kathryn Dean Strandell, OSF, Rel. Ord. Ldr.; Srs.: 128

WAUWATOSA

Notre Dame of Milwaukee (The School Sisters of Notre Dame of the Central Pacific Province) - 10700 W. Research Dr., Ste. 145, Wauwatosa, WI 53226 t) 414-644-0173 mhummert@ssndcp.org www.ssndcp.org S.S.N.D. Assisted Care, Independent Living. Sr. Debra M. Sciano, SSND, Prov.; Srs.: 85

Provincial Motherhouse of the Carmelite Sisters of the Divine Heart of Jesus (Carmelite Sisters of the Divine Heart of Jesus, Milwaukee, Wisconsin) - 1230 Kavanaugh Pl., Wauwatosa, WI 53213 t) 414-453-4040 carmeldcjnorth@gmail.com www.carmelitedcjnorth.org Sr. M. Gabriela Hilke, Supr.; Sr. Maria Giuseppe, Prov.; Sr. M. Rose Therese de Castro, Prov. Asst.; Srs.: 23

ENDOWMENTS / FOUNDATIONS / TRUSTS [EFT]

BROWN DEER

The Manna Charitable Trust - 8858 N. 60th St., Brown Deer, WI 53223 t) 414-357-8940 to help provide for the needs of the aged and infirm members of the Sisters of the Sorrowful Mother.

FOND DU LAC

***Agnesian HealthCare Foundation, Inc.** - 430 E. Division St., Fond du Lac, WI 54935; Mailing: 10101 Woodfield Ln., St. Louis, MO 63132 t) 920-926-5421 Shawn Fisher, Dir.;

***St. Mary's Springs Academy Foundation** - 255 County Rd. K, Fond du Lac, WI 54937 t) 920-322-8011 www.smsacademy.org Katie Tank, Contact;

HALES CORNERS

Congregation of the Priests of the Sacred Heart Support and Maintenance Trust - 7373 S. Lovers Lane Rd., Hales Corners, WI 53130; Mailing: P.O. Box 289, Hales Corners, WI 53130 t) 414-425-6910 provtreas@poshusa.org www.dehoniansusa.org Rev. James Walters, S.C.J.; Bro. Raymond Kozuch, S.C.J.;

MILWAUKEE

***Archdiocese of Milwaukee Catholic Community Foundation, Inc.** - 637 E. Erie St., Milwaukee, WI 53202 t) 414-431-6402 info@legaciesoffaith.org legaciesoffaith.org Mary Ellen Markowski, Pres.;

***Ascension Wisconsin Foundation, Inc.** - 2320 N. Lake Dr., Ste. 1611, Milwaukee, WI 53211 t) 414-447-2844 timothy.waldoch@ascension.org healthcare.ascension.org/donate Sponsored by Ascension Health Ministries (Ascension Sponsor), a public juridic person. Bernie Sherry, CEO; Timothy Waldoch, Chief Mission Integration Officer;

***Erica P. John Fund, Inc.** - 330 E. Kilbourn Ave., Ste. 1454, Milwaukee, WI 53202-3144 t) 414-607-6040 epjfund@epjfund.org Paula N. John, Pres.;

***St. Joan Antida High School Foundation, Ltd.** - 1341 N. Cass St., Milwaukee, WI 53202; Mailing: 8560 N. 76th Pl., Milwaukee, WI 53223 t) 414-354-9233 kathy@scsja.org Sr. Kathleen M. Lundwall, S.C.S.J.A., Contact;

Pallottine Fathers and Brothers, Inc., Disability Trust - 5424 W. Bluemound Rd., Milwaukee, WI 53208 t) 414-259-0688 pallotti.milw@pallottines.org www.pallottines.org Rev. Joseph Koyickal, S.A.C., Pres.;

Pallottine Fathers and Brothers, Inc., Educational and Apostolic Ministry Trust - 5424 W. Bluemound Rd., Milwaukee, WI 53208 t) 414-259-0688 pallotti.milw@pallottines.org www.pallottines.org Rev. Joseph Koyickal, S.A.C., Pres.;

Society of the Divine Savior Ongoing Community Support Trust - 1735 N. Hi Mount Blvd., Milwaukee, WI 53208-1720 t) 414-258-1735 sds@salvatorians.com salvatorians.com Ongoing Community Support Trust Rev. Scott Wallenfelsz, S.D.S., Treas.;

RACINE

Ascension All Saints Hospital Foundation, Inc. - 1320 Wisconsin Ave., Racine, WI 53403 t) 262-687-2239 timothy.waldoch@ascension.org healthcare.ascension.org/donate Sponsored by Ascension Health Ministries (Ascension Sponsor), a public juridic person. Bernie Sherry, CEO; Timothy Waldoch, Chief Mission Integration Officer;

ST. FRANCIS

Archdiocese of Milwaukee Cemeteries Perpetual Care Trust - 3501 S. Lake Dr., St. Francis, WI 53235; Mailing: P.O. Box 070912, Milwaukee, WI 53207-0912 t) 414-769-3325 brownc@archmil.org Most Rev. Jerome E. Listecki;

Canticle and Juniper Courts Foundation, Inc. - 3221 S. Lake Dr., St. Francis, WI 53235 t) 414-744-3150 tergerson@lakeosf.org; amy681502@gmail.com Amy Schmidt, Treas.;

Faith in Our Future Trust - 3501 S. Lake Dr., St. Francis, WI 53235; Mailing: P.O. Box 070504, Milwaukee, WI 53207-0504 t) 414-769-3334 jmarek@archmil.org www.faithinourfuture.org Most Rev. Jerome E. Listecki;

Foundation for Religious Retirement, Inc. - 3221 S. Lake Dr., St. Francis, WI 53235 t) 414-294-7324 jparrott@thefrr.org; jparrott@lakeosfs.org www.thefrr.org To raise funds to assist in supporting retired women religious in the Archdiocese of Milwaukee. Jan Parrott, Exec.;

Love One Another Trust - 3501 S. Lake Dr., St. Francis, WI 53235; Mailing: P.O. Box 070912, Milwaukee, WI 53207 t) (414) 769-3300 Most Rev. Jerome E. Listecki, Trustee;

St. Michael's Priest Fund Trust - 3501 S. Lake Dr., St. Francis, WI 53235; Mailing: P O Box 070912, Milwaukee, WI 53207-0912 t) 414-769-3300 x3326 Rev. Kevin J. Kowalske, Vice. Pres.;

WAUWATOSA

Order of St. Camillus Foundation, Inc. - 10200 W. Bluemound Rd., Wauwatosa, WI 53226 t) 414-259-8335 swatson@stcam.com stcam.com Rev. Agustin R. Orosa, M.I., Prov.; Steve Watson, Exec.;

HOSPITALS / HEALTH SERVICES [HOS]

FOND DU LAC

Agnesian Health Care, Inc. (St. Agnes Hospital) - 430 E. Division St., Fond du Lac, WI 54935; Mailing: 10101 Woodfield Ln., St. Louis, MO 63132 t) 920-929-2300 www.agnesian.com Katherine Vergos, Pres.; Bed Capacity: 146; Asstd. Annu.: 777,229; Staff: 2,379

GLENDALE

Ministry Health Care, Inc. - 400 W. River Woods Pkwy., Glendale, WI 53212 t) 414-465-3000 timothy.waldoch@ascension.org healthcare.ascension.org/ Sponsored by Ascension Health Ministries (Ascension Sponsor), a public juridic person Bernie Sherry, CEO; Timothy Waldoch, Chief Mission Integration Officer; Staff: 22

MEQUON

Columbia St. Mary's Hospital Ozaukee, Inc. - 13111 N. Port Washington Rd., Mequon, WI 53097-2416 t) 262-243-7300 timothy.waldoch@ascension.org healthcare.ascension.org/ Sponsored by Ascension Health Ministries (Ascension Sponsor) a public juridic person Bernie Sherry, CEO; Timothy Waldoch, Chief Mission Integration Officer; Bed Capacity: 121; Asstd. Annu.: 255,094; Staff: 592

MILWAUKEE

Ascension SE Wisconsin Hospital, Inc. - 5000 W. Chambers St., Milwaukee, WI 53210 t) 414-447-2000 timothy.waldoch@ascension.org healthcare.ascension.org Sponsored by Ascension Health Ministries (Ascension Sponsor), a public juridic person. Bernie Sherry, CEO; Timothy Waldoch, Chief Mission Integration Officer; Bed Capacity: 343; Asstd. Annu.: 402,921; Staff: 1,560

Ascension St. Francis Hospital, Inc. - 3237 S. 16th St., Milwaukee, WI 53215 t) 414-647-5000 timothy.waldoch@ascension.org healthcare.ascension.org Sponsored by Ascension Health Ministries (Ascension Sponsor), a public juridic person. Bernie Sherry, CEO; Timothy Waldoch, Chief Mission Integration Officer; Bed Capacity: 153; Asstd. Annu.: 136,426; Staff: 537

Columbia St. Mary's Hospital Milwaukee, Inc. - 2320 N. Lake Dr., Milwaukee, WI 53211 t) 414-291-1000 timothy.waldoch@ascension.org healthcare.ascension.org/ Sponsored by Ascension Health Ministries (Ascension Sponsor) a public juridic person Bernie Sherry, CEO; Timothy Waldoch, Chief Mission Integration Officer; Bed Capacity: 401; Asstd. Annu.: 716,905; Staff: 2,376

RACINE

Ascension All Saints Hospital, Inc. - 3801 Spring St., Racine, WI 53405 t) 262-687-4011 timothy.waldoch@ascension.org healthcare.ascension.org Sponsored by Ascension Health Ministries (Ascension Sponsor), a public juridic person. Bernie Sherry, CEO; Timothy Waldoch, Chief Mission Integration Officer; Bed Capacity: 258; Asstd. Annu.: 455,051; Staff: 1,193

SHEBOYGAN

St. Nicholas Hospital (Prevea Health) - 3100 Superior Ave., Sheboygan, WI 53081 t) 920-459-8300 mary.salm@hshs.org www.stnicholashospital.org Justin Selle, Pres.; Bed Capacity: 46; Asstd. Annu.: 88,992; Staff: 320

WAUPUN

Waupun Memorial Hospital, Inc. - 620 W. Brown St., Waupun, WI 53963; Mailing: 10101 Woodfield Ln., St. Louis, MO 63132 t) 920-324-5581 www.agnesian.com Deann Thurmer, Pres.; Bed Capacity: 25; Asstd. Annu.: 78,861; Staff: 271

MISCELLANEOUS [MIS]

BELOIT

Franciscan Sisters of Our Lady - 2110 Bootmaker Dr., Beloit, WI 53511-2318 t) 608-207-3880 Sr. Timothy Geenen, F.S.O.L., Supr.;

BROOKFIELD

Prelature of the Holy Cross and Opus Dei Layton Study Center - 12900 W. North Ave., Brookfield, WI 53005 t) 262-784-1523 info@opusdei.org Rev. Eduardo J. Castillo; Rev. John C. Kubeck;

BROWN DEER

Sisters of the Sorrowful Mother International Finance, Inc. - 8858 N. 60th St., Brown Deer, WI 53223 t) 414-357-8940 ssmgen.org Sr. Catherine Hanegan, Chair;

Sisters of the Sorrowful Mother-Generalate, Inc. - 8858 N. 60th St., Brown Deer, WI 53223 t) 414-357-8940 www.ssmgen.org Sr. Catherine Hanegan, Supr.;

BURLINGTON

General Secretariat of the Franciscan Missions, Inc. - 940 N. Browns Lake Dr., Burlington, WI 53105; Mailing: P.O. Box 130, Waterford, WI 53185 t) 262-534-5470 info@franciscanmissions.org franciscanmissions.org Bro. Andrew J. Brophy, O.F.M., Exec.; Rev. Bernardo Moya Montero, O.F.M. (Mexico), Dir.; Rev. Gil Abad Noriega Muniz, O.F.M. (Mexico), Dir.; Rev. Joy K. Devassy, O.F.M. (India), Bus. Mgr.;

CEDARBURG

Works of Mercy Ministry, Inc. - W63 N605 Hanover Ave., #468, Cedarburg, WI 53012 t) 414-305-3384 aveik@thecapuchins.org worksofmercyministry.org Religious charitable organization serving persons with intellectual and developmental disabilities. Rev. Alan D. Veik, O.F.M.Cap., Pres.; Rev. Donald H. Thimm, Secy.;

FOND DU LAC

Cold Springs Charitable Trust - 320 County Rd. K, Fond du Lac, WI 54937 t) 920-907-2301 spollnow@csasisters.org Sr. Sharon Pollnow, CSA, Trustee;

Hazotte Ministries, Inc. - 320 County Rd. K, Fond du Lac, WI 54937-8158 t) 920-907-2300 Sponsored by the Congregation of Sisters of St. Agnes. Sr. Hertha Longo, C.S.A., Pres.;

FRANKLIN

Franciscan Pilgrimage Programs, Inc. - 9230 W. Highland Park Ave., Franklin, WI 53132; Mailing: P.O. Box 321490, Franklin, WI 53132-6231 t) 414-427-0570 infofpp@thefranciscans.net; info@franciscanpilgrimages.com www.franciscanpilgrimages.com Rev. John Cella, O.F.M., Dir.;

Franciscan Sisters of Saint Clare, Inc. - 7732 S. 51st St., Franklin, WI 53132 t) 414-423-5277 Non-Cloistered Contemplative Community. Sr. Patricia Reilly, Contact;

GLENDALE

***Ascension Medical Group - Southeast Wisconsin, Inc.** - 400 W. River Woods Pkwy., Glendale, WI 53212 t) 414-465-3000 timothy.waldoch@ascension.org healthcare.ascension.org Sponsored by Ascension Health Ministries (Ascension Sponsor), a public juridic person. Bernie Sherry, CEO; Timothy Waldoch, Chief Mission Integration Officer;

***Columbia St. Mary's Inc.** - 400 W. River Woods Pkwy., Glendale, WI 53212 t) 414-447-2844 timothy.waldoch@ascension.org healthcare.ascension.org Sponsored by Ascension Health Ministries (Ascension Sponsor), a public juridic person Bernie Sherry, CEO; Timothy Waldoch, Chief Mission Integration Officer;

***Wheaton Franciscan Healthcare-Southeast Wisconsin, Inc.** - 400 W. River Woods Pkwy., Glendale, WI 53212 t) 414-465-3111 timothy.waldoch@ascension.org healthcare.ascension.org Sponsored by Ascension Health Ministries (Ascension Sponsor), a public juridic person. Bernie Sherry, CEO; Timothy Waldoch, Chief Mission Integration Officer;

GREENFIELD

***St. Vincent de Paul Society of Milwaukee** - 4476 S. 108 St., Greenfield, WI 53228; Mailing: PO Box 26537, Milwaukee, WI 53226 t) 414-462-7837 council@svdpmilw.org svdpmilw.org/home.aspx Deborah Duskey, Exec.;

HALES CORNERS

Development Office (U.S. Province of the Priests of the Sacred Heart) - 6889 S. Lovers Lane Rd., Hales Corners, WI 53130; Mailing: P.O. Box 367, Hales Corners, WI 53130 t) 414-425-3383 provtreas@usprovince.org www.poshusa.org Sacred Heart Monastery-Priests of the Sacred Heart-Reign of the Sacred Heart, Inc. Linda Church, Exec.; Dcn. David Nagel, S.C.J., Exec.;

KENOSHA

Assisi Homes - Saxony, Inc. - 1850 22nd Ave., Kenosha, WI 53140 t) 262-551-9005; 303-830-3300 mrankin@mercyhousing.org www.mercyhousing.org Independent Housing for Low Income Elderly Melissa Clayton, Contact;

Catholic Woman's Club of Kenosha - 3524 7th Ave., #127, Kenosha, WI 53140 t) (262) 484-5320 rthomas2031@wi.rr.com Sherry Thomas, Pres.;

MILWAUKEE

Adult Learning Center, Inc. - 2224 W. Kilbourn Ave., Milwaukee, WI 53233 t) 414-263-5874 info@alcmke.org alcmke.org Adult Education Classes - GED/HSED, Digital Literacy; in-person and online classes available Sr. Callista Robinson, Admin.; Jon Gilgenbach, Dir.;

Apostleship of Prayer, Pope's Worldwide Prayer Network - 1501 S. Layton Blvd., Milwaukee, WI 53215-1924 t) 414-486-1152 frlaramiesj@popesprayerusa.net www.popesprayerusa.net Rev. Joseph W. Laramie, S.J., Dir.;

Archdiocesan Marian Shrine - 114 N. 68th St., Milwaukee, WI 53213; Mailing: PO Box 070912, Milwaukee, WI 53207-0912 t) 414-769-3325 brownc@archmil.org Christopher Brown, Contact;

***Ascension Wisconsin Laboratories, Inc.** - 3237 S. 16th St., Milwaukee, WI 53215 t) 414-256-5570 timothy.waldoch@ascension.org healthcare.ascension.org Sponsored by Ascension Health Ministries (Ascension Sponsor), a public juridic person. Bernie Sherry, CEO; Timothy Waldoch, Chief Mission Integration Officer;

Capuchin Community Services - 930 W. State St., Milwaukee, WI 53233 t) 414-933-1300; 414-271-0135 ccs@thecapuchins.org www.capuchincommunityservices.org Serving the poor, hungry and homeless Rev. Michael Bertram, O.F.M.Cap, Dir.; Rev. Francis Dombrowski, O.F.M.Cap., In Res.; Rev. Jerome Schroeder, OFM Cap., In Res.; Rev. Alan D. Veik, O.F.M.Cap., In Res.; Bro. Brenton Ertel, OFM Cap., Pst. Min./Coord.; Bro. Jerome Smith, O.F.M.Cap., Social Worker/MSW;

***Christ Child Society, Inc. - Milwaukee Chapter** - 4033 W. Good Hope Rd., Milwaukee, WI 53209-2268 t) 414-540-0489 christchildmilwaukee@gmail.com www.christchildmilwaukee.org Judy Keenan, Co-President; Kathleen Semrad, Co-President;

St. Clare Management, Inc. - 1545 S. Layton Blvd., Milwaukee, WI 53215 t) 414-385-5330 christinem@stclaremgt.org; margaretk@stclaremgt.org www.stclaremgt.org A HUD housing management corporation to ensure the quality of life, safety, and independence of underserved, low income people with disabilities. Margaret E. Kidder, Exec. Dir.;

Clare Towers, Inc. - 1545 S. Layton Blvd., Milwaukee, WI 53215 t) 414-385-5330 christinem@stclaremgt.org; margaretk@stclaremgt.org www.stclaremgt.org HUD subsidized housing for the physically disabled to live independently. Sponsored by School Sisters of St. Francis. Margaret E. Kidder, Exec. Dir.;

Cristo Rey Jesuit Corporate Work Study Program, Inc. - 1818 W. National Ave., Milwaukee, WI 53204 t) 414-436-4600 mtalavera@cristoreymilwaukee.org; astith@cristoreymilwaukee.org www.cristoreymilwaukee.org Andrew Stith, Pres.;

Cursillos in Christianity - 1710 W. Bolivar Ave., Milwaukee, WI 53221 c) 414-852-1865 milwaukeecurcillos@gmail.com; carlosalbertoz@hotmail.com www.natl-cursillo.org/milwaukee Gilberto Martinez, Dir.; Rev. Carlos Alberto Zapata, Spiritual Adv./Care Srvcs.;

Dismas Ministry - 6801 N. Yates Rd., Bonventure Hall, 012, Milwaukee, WI 53217; Mailing: P.O. Box 070363, Milwaukee, WI 53207 t) 414-486-2383 dismas@dismasministry.org; tyler.curtis@dismasministry.org www.dismasministry.org A national Catholic outreach to inmates, victims, their families, those released from prison, and the community. Mary Tyler Curtis, Dir.;

Dominican Center for Women, Inc. - 2470 W. Locust St., Milwaukee, WI 53206-1134 t) 414-444-9930 maricha@dominican-center.org www.dominican-center.org/ Works with Amani residents and partners to build a better future. Maricha Harris, Dir.;

Franciscan Peacemakers, Inc., Milwaukee - 3333 W. Lisbon Ave., Milwaukee, WI 53208 t) 414-559-5761; 414-562-4780 deaconsteve@franciscanpeacemakers.org www.franciscanpeacemakers.org Dcn. Steven J. Przedpelski, Exec. Dir.; Mary Leach-Sumlin, Assoc. Dir.; Katie Coffey, Social Enterprise Dir.;

Lay Salvatorians, Inc. - 1735 N. Hi-Mount Blvd., Milwaukee, WI 53208-1720 t) 520-260-4612 jwhite45@cox.net Bobby Pantuso, Dir.;

Layton Blvd. West Neighbors, Inc. - 1545 S. Layton Blvd., Milwaukee, WI 53215 t) 414-383-9038; 414-585-8539 info@viacdc.org www.viacdc.org Community development organization JoAnna Bautch, Exec. Dir.;

Legion of Mary - 6962 N Raintree Dr., Unit D, Milwaukee, WI 53223 c) 828-280-1438 hudsoncolin@yahoo.com Colin Hudson, Pres.;

Salvatorian Advocacy for Victims of Exploitation (S.A.V.E.) - 4311 N. 100th St., Milwaukee, WI 53222-1393 t) 414-466-0810 Sr. Jean Schafer, SDS, Contact;

Salvatorian Institute of Philosophy and Theology, Inc. - 1735 N. Hi Mount Blvd., Milwaukee, WI 53208-1720 t) 414-258-1735 sds@salvatorians.com Rev. Scott Wallenfelsz, S.D.S., Dir.;

***Santa Fe Communications, Inc. (Heart of the Nation)** - 1205 S. 70th St. #701, Milwaukee, WI 53214 t) 414-475-4444 www.heartofthenation.org Catholic Television Ministry Bruno John, Pres.;

SASC, Inc. - 3800 N. 92nd St., Milwaukee, WI 53222-2589 t) 414-463-7570 jkrahn@stannescampus.org; tlipke@stannescampus.org illuminus.us/communities/st-annes Janet Krahn, CEO; Rev. Thomas Perrin, S.D.S., Dir.;

Secular Institute of the Schoenstatt Sisters of Mary - 5310 W. Wisconsin Ave., Milwaukee, WI 53208-3061 t) 414-774-3536 Sr. M. Emily Kenkel, Prov. Supr.;

***SPRED Partners, Inc.** - 6650 W. State St., Ste. 198, Milwaukee, WI 53213 c) (414) 595-7921 spredpartners1@gmail.com spredmilwaukee.org Finds funds to support SPRED, which meets the spiritual needs of those with developmental disabilities. Rev. Timothy L. Kitzke, Pres.;

Telos, Inc. (Clare Place & Clare Central) - 1545 S. Layton Blvd., Milwaukee, WI 53215 t) 414-385-5330 christinem@stclaremgt.org; margaretk@stclaremgt.org www.stclaremgt.org HUD subsidized housing for the physically disabled to live independently. Sponsored by the School Sisters of St. Francis. Margaret E. Kidder, Exec. Dir.;

St. Thomas More Lawyers Society of Wisconsin - 111 E. Kilbourn Ave. # 1900, c/o Atty. Brian Tokarz, Milwaukee, WI 53202 t) 414-273-1300 bct@mtfn.com stmls-wi.blogspot.com Rev. Brad A. Krawczyk, Chap.; John Remington, Pres.; Brian C Tokarz, Treas.;

NEOSHO

***Laudato Si Project, Inc.** - W1468 County Rd. NN, Neosho, WI 53059 t) 262-419-8558 laudatosiproject@gmail.com laudatosiproject.com/ Rob B Shelledy, Dir.;

NEW BERLIN

Milwaukee Archdiocesan Holy Name Union - 18245 W. Crabtree Ln., New Berlin, WI 53146 t) 414-750-7971 stevenandbecky@sbcglobal.net Rev. Edward Griesemer, S.C.J., Chap.; Steven R. Lazarczyk, Pres.;

RACINE

***Catherine Marian Housing, Inc. (Bethany Apartments)** - 806 Wisconsin Ave., Racine, WI 53403-1569; Mailing: 5635 Erie St., Racine, WI 53402-1934 t) 262-633-9446 regarczynski@racinedominicans.org www.bethanyapartments.org Offers survivors of domestic abuse and their families the resources needed to live, heal, and grow in a supportive, safe, and secure environment. Sr. Maryann A. McMahon, O.P., Pres.; Sr. Chris Broslavick, OP, Vice Pres.; Sr. Agnes Johnson, OP, Vice Pres.; Sr. Mary Ann Pevas, OP, Vice Pres.; Pamela Handrow, Exec. Dir.;

St. Catherine's High School of Racine, Inc. - 5635 Erie St., Racine, WI 53402-1934 t) 262-639-4100 sgeertsen@racinedominicans.org Sr. Maryann A. McMahon, O.P., Pres.; Sr. Chris Broslavick, OP, Vice Pres.; Sr. Agnes Johnson, OP, Vice Pres.; Sr. Mary Ann Pevas, OP, Vice Pres.;

Community of St. Paul, Inc. - 1505 Howard St., Racine, WI 53404 t) 262-634-2666 racine@comsp.org www.comsp.org/en Public Association of Christian Faithful, comprised of clergy and laity. Rev. Marti Colom, Pres.; Very Rev. Ricardo Martin Pinillos, Vice. Pres.; Rev. Esteve Redolad, Secy.; Rev. Juan Manuel Camacho, Treas.; Rev. Javier Guativa, Mem.; Dolors Puertolas, Mem.; Rev. Michael Wolfe, Mem.;

Dominicans at Siena on the Lake, Inc. - 5635 Erie St., Racine, WI 53402-1934 t) 262-639-4100 sgeertsen@racinedominicans.org Sr. Maryann A. McMahon, O.P., Pres.; Sr. Chris Broslavick, OP, Vice Pres.; Sr. Agnes Johnson, OP, Vice Pres.; Sr. Mary Ann Pevas, OP, Vice Pres.;

***Eco-Justice Center, Inc.** - 7133 Michna Rd., Racine, WI 53402-1049; Mailing: 5635 Erie St., Racine, WI 53402-1934 t) 262-681-8527 sgeertsen@racinedominicans.org www.ecojusticecenter.org Sr. Maryann A. McMahon, O.P., Pres.; Sr. Chris Broslavick, OP, Vice Pres.; Sr. Agnes Johnson, OP, Vice Pres.; Sr. Mary Ann Pevas, OP, Vice Pres.; MaryLynn Conter Strack, Exec. Dir.;

***HOPES Center of Racine, Inc.** - 521 6th St., Racine, WI 53403; Mailing: 5635 Erie St., Racine, WI 53402-1934 t) 262-898-2940 sgeertsen@racinedominicans.org www.hopescenter.org Provides services directly to people experiencing homelessness or who are at risk of homelessness in their journey to a stable home. Sr. Maryann A. McMahon, O.P., Pres.; Sr. Chris Broslavick, OP, Vice Pres.; Sr. Agnes Johnson, OP, Vice Pres.; Sr. Mary Ann Pevas, OP, Vice Pres.; Scott Metzel, Exec. Dir.;

M.B. Bauer Group, Inc. - 5635 Erie St., Racine, WI 53402-1934 t) 262-639-4100 sgeertsen@racinedominicans.org www.racinedominicans.org dba M.B. Bauer Group, Inc. Sr. Maryann A. McMahon, O.P., Pres.; Sr. Chris Broslavick, OP, Vice Pres.; Sr. Agnes Johnson, OP, Vice Pres.; Sr. Mary Ann Pevas, OP, Vice Pres.;

***Senior Companion Program, Inc.** - 5111 Wright Ave., Racine, WI 53406-4506; Mailing: 5635 Erie St., Racine, WI 53402-1934 t) 262-898-1941 sgeertsen@racinedominicans.org www.seniorcompanionprogram.org Sr. Maryann A. McMahon, O.P., Pres.; Sr. Chris Broslavick, OP, Vice Pres.; Sr. Agnes Johnson, OP, Vice Pres.; Sr. Mary Ann Pevas, OP, Vice Pres.; Sue Craanen, Exec. Dir.;

SHEBOYGAN

The Sheboygan County Catholic Fund, Inc. - 1439 S. 12th St., Sheboygan, WI 53081 t) 920-457-1077 frsubi@catholicsouthside.com A fund to provide youth and adult religious education programs within the county. Rev. Mark J. Brandl, Pres.; Rev. Paul J. Fliss, Vice. Pres.; Rev. Subi Poothatayil Thomas, MCBS, Treas.; Rev. Norberto Sandoval, Mem.; Rev. Jonathon A. Schmeckel, Mem.; Very Rev. Philip D. Reifenberg, Mem.;

ST. FRANCIS

The Catholic Charismatic Renewal Office of Southeastern Wisconsin, Inc. - 3501 S. Lake Dr., St. Francis, WI 53235; Mailing: P.O. Box 070637, Milwaukee, WI 53207-0637 t) 414-482-1727 ccroffice@archmil.org; liaison.815@archmil.org www.ccrmilwaukee.com Marianne Skrobiak, Liaison;

Catholic Charities Foundation, Inc. - 3501 S. Lake Dr., St. Francis, WI 53235; Mailing: P.O. Box 070912, Milwaukee, WI 53207-0912 t) 414-769-3400 rcisneros@ccmke.org; jrekowski@ccmke.org www.ccmke.org Very Rev. David H. Reith, Vicar; Ricardo Cisneros, COO;

Mareda - 3501 S. Lake Dr., Archdiocese of Milwaukee - Office of Evangelization & Catechesis, St. Francis, WI 53235; Mailing: P. O. Box 070912, Milwaukee, WI 53207-0912 t) 414-758-2242 pokornyg@archmil.org www.mareda.org/ Association of Catechetical Leaders in the Archdiocese of Milwaukee Taylor Baar, Chair;

Milwaukee Archdiocesan Council of Deacons - 3501 S. Lake Dr., St. Francis, WI 53235; Mailing: P.O. Box 070912, Milwaukee, WI 53207-0912 t) 414-769-3409 starkej@archmil.org Dcn. James J. Starke;

Milwaukee Archdiocesan Office for World Mission - 3501 S. Lake Dr., St. Francis, WI 53235; Mailing: P.O. Box 07912, Milwaukee, WI 53207-0912 t) 414-758-2280 wmo@archmil.org www.archmil.org/offices/world-mission.htm Educates and raises funds for global missionary activity in support of the archdiocesan sister parish, La Sagrada Familia in the Dominican Republic. Antoinette Mensah, Dir.;

Priests' Purgatorial Society - 3501 S. Lake Dr., St. Francis, WI 53235; Mailing: P.O. Box 070912, Milwaukee, WI 53207-0912 t) 414-769-3340 cusackb@archmil.org archmil.org Barbara Anne Cusack, Secy.;

Society for the Propagation of the Faith, Archdiocese of Milwaukee - 3501 S. Lake Dr., St. Francis, WI 53235; Mailing: P.O. Box 07912, Milwaukee, WI 53207-0912 t) 414-758-2280 wmo@archmil.org www.archmil.org/offices/world-mission.htm Serves as representative for the Archdiocese of Milwaukee on all matters related to the US Pontifical Mission Societies. Antoinette Mensah, Dir.;

Society for the Propagation of the Faith, Missionary Childhood Association - 3501 S. Lake Dr., St. Francis, WI 53235; Mailing: P.O. Box 070912, Milwaukee, WI 53207-0912 t) 414-758-2280 wmo@archmil.org www.archmil.org/offices/world-mission.htm (Pontifical Mission Societies) Antoinette Mensah, Dir.;

St. Stephen's League - 3501 S. Lake Dr., St. Francis, WI 53235; Mailing: P.O. Box 070912, Milwaukee, WI 53207-0912 t) 414-769-3409 starkej@archmil.org (of the Archdiocesan Council of Deacons) Dcn. James J. Starke;

Wisconsin Catholic Media Apostolate, Inc. - 3501 S. Lake Dr., St. Francis, WI 53235; Mailing: P.O. Box 070913, Milwaukee, WI 53207-0913 t) (414) 769-3464 catholicherald@archmil.org www.catholicherald.org Jerry Topczewski, Dir.; Larry Hanson, Managing Editor;

Wisconsin Religious Collaborative, Inc. - 3221 S. Lake Dr., St. Francis, WI 53235-3702 t) 414-744-3150 (Registered Agent); 715-539-1461 (Bd. Pres.) executivedirector@wrcollaborative.org www.wrcollaborative.org Sr. Diana DeBruin, Rel. Ord. Ldr.;

WAUKESHA

Secular Institute of Schoenstatt Fathers - W284 N746 Cherry Ln., Waukesha, WI 53188 t) 262-548-9061 mark.niehaus@schoenstatt-fathers.org schoenstatt-fathers.us Rev. Mark J. Niehaus, I.S.P., Supr.;

Schoenstatt Fathers - t) (262) 548-9061 fr.mjniehaus@gmail.com

Secular Institute of the Schoenstatt Sisters of Mary - W284 N404 Cherry Ln., Waukesha, WI 53188-9416 t) 262-522-4200 schoenstattsisters@schsrsmary.org www.schoenstattsistersofmary.us Sr. M. Emily Kenkel, Prov. Supr.; Sr. M. Gloriana Rivera, Prov. Asst.;

WAUWATOSA

St. Camillus Health System, Inc. - 10101 W. Wisconsin Ave., Wauwatosa, WI 53226 t) 414-258-1814 jorosa@stcam.com Management Corporation. Order of the Servants of the Sick (Order of St. Camillus). Rev. Agustin R. Orosa, M.I., Pres.; Rev. Leandro Blanco, M.I., Treas.; Rev. Varghese Johnson Vellachira, Secy.;

St. Camillus Ministries, Inc. - 10101 W. Wisconsin Ave., Wauwatosa, WI 53226 t) 414-258-1814 Operates under the auspices of the Order of St. Camillus and sponsors all social concerns ministry of the Order. Rev. Agustin R. Orosa, M.I., Prov. Del.; Rev. Varghese Johnson Vellachira, Secy.; Rev. Leandro Blanco, M.I., Treas.;

Carmelite Ministry of St. Teresa - 1215 Dewey Ave., Wauwatosa, WI 53213 t) 414-302-9454 c) 414-379-6489 carmeldcjnorth@gmail.com; carmeliteministrywauwatosa@gmail.com www.carmeliteministry.org Residential Apartments and Formation Enrichment Center for Persons with Intellectual & Developmental Disabilities. Sr. M. Gabriela Hilke, Supr.; Sr. M. Rose Therese de Castro, Treas.; Sr. Mary Brigid Poso, Dir.;

Friends of Calvary Cemetery, Inc. - 2515 N. 66th St., Wauwatosa, WI 53213 c) 414-322-7374 swerk@juno.com www.friendsofcalvarycemetery.org/ Raise funds for the restoration of Calvary Chapel/ Mausoleum at Calvary Cemetery, Milwaukee, WI Keith Schultz, Pres.;

MONASTERIES AND RESIDENCES FOR PRIESTS AND BROTHERS [MON]

BENET LAKE

St. Benedict's Abbey (Benedictine Monks of Wisconsin, Inc.) - 12605 224th Ave., Benet Lake, WI 53102-1000 t) 262-396-4311 macario@benetlake.org www.benetlake.org Rev. Macario J. Martinez, O.S.B., Supr.; Rt. Rev. Edmund J. Boyce, O.S.B., Treas.; Rev. Daniel Petsche, O.S.B., Retreat Master; Bro. Matthew Marie, OSB, Asst. Retreat Master; Brs.: 1; Priests: 3

BURLINGTON

Queen of Peace Friary (Franciscan Friars of the Assumption B.V.M. Province) - 2281 Browns Lake Dr., Burlington, WI 53105 t) 262-763-3241 craigofm2@yahoo.com Retirement Home for Franciscan Friars Bro. Craig Wilking, Guardian; Rev. Anthony Chojnacki, In Res.; Rev. Stan Janowski, O.F.M., In Res.; Rev. Warren Rector, OFM, In Res.; Rev. William Stout, O.F.M., In Res.; Rev. Edward Tlucek, O.F.M., In Res.; Rev. Richard Tulko, O.F.M., In Res.; Rev. Thomas Wojciechowski, O.F.M., In Res.; Bro. Andre Lemay, In Res.; Bro. Regis Howitz, In Res.; Bro. Stephen Dupuis, OFM, In Res.; Bro. Reynold Lesnar, In Res.; Bro. Patrick McCormack, In Res.; Bro. Augustine Paulik, In Res.; Bro. David Dodge, O.F.M., In Res.; Brs.: 16; Priests: 52

CUDAHY

Missionary Congregation of the Blessed Sacrament, Inc., Zion Province - 6155 S. Creekside Dr., Unit 5, Cudahy, WI 53110 t) 262-225-3357 c) 414-393-7979 kaippallymcbs@gmail.com; subimcbs@gmail.com Rev. Pradeep Joseph Sebastian, M.C.B.S., Contact; Rev. Dominic Thomas; Rev. Sujan Jacob, MCBS, Mem.; Rev. Subi Pootharayil Thomas, MCBS, Mem.; Rev. Thomas Vathappallil, M.C.B.S., Treas.; Tijo Naduviledom, Mem.; Binu Sebastian, Mem.; Priests: 8

EAST TROY

Divine Word Missionaries - N8855 Seminary Rd., East Troy, WI 53120; Mailing: P.O. Box 107, East Troy, WI 53120-0107 t) 262-642-3300 edp510@gmail.com Society of the Divine Word. Rev. Edward Peklo, S.V.D., Rector; Rev. Walter Ostrowski, S.V.D.; Rev. Jefferson Pool, SVD; Bro. Kevin Diederich, S.V.D.; Bro. Bernard Scherger, S.V.D.; Brs.: 2; Priests: 4

FRANKLIN

Dehon House (Priests of the Sacred Heart) - 10731 W. Rawson Ave., Franklin, WI 53132 t) 414-425-3768 provsec@usprovince.org www.dehoniansusa.org Dcn. David Nagel, S.C.J., Treas.;

Francis and Clare Friary - 9230 W. Highland Park Ave., Franklin, WI 53132 t) 414-525-9253 province@ofm-abvm.org; provinceofm@thefranciscans.net www.franciscan-friars.org Rev. John Cella, O.F.M., Supr.; Rev. Joel Szydlowski, O.F.M., Chap.; Rev. James Gannon, O.F.M., Prov.; Rev. Sante DeAngelis, O.F.M., Mem.; Rev. John Puodziunas, O.F.M., Mem.; Rev. Leonard Stunek, O.F.M., Mem.; Bro. Didacus Weber, O.F.M., Mem.; Bro. Paul Belco, OFM, Mem.; Brs.: 3; Priests: 5

Provincial Offices of the Franciscan Friars, Assumption BVM Province, Inc. - Rev. William Stout, O.F.M.; Rev. Edward Tlucek, O.F.M., Secy.;

St. Francis Residence - 12001 W. Woods Rd., Franklin, WI 53132 t) 414-425-6910 provsec@usprovince.org Rev. Dominic Peluse, S.C.J., Supr.; Rev. Charles Brown, S.C.J.; Bro. Matthew Miles, S.C.J., In Res.; Brs.: 1; Priests: 2

St. Joseph's at Monastery Lake (Priests of the Sacred Heart) - 7330 S. Lovers Lane Rd., Franklin, WI 53132-1849 t) 414-525-2457 provsec@usprovince.org www.dehoniansusa.org Rev. Terence Langley, S.C.J.; Bro. Frank Presto, S.C.J., Admin.; Very Rev. Vien Nguyen, S.C.J., In Res.; Rev. Wojciech Adamczyk, SCJ, In Res.; Rev. Son Thai Nguyen, SCJ, In Res.; Rev. Francis Vu Tran, SCJ, In Res.; Dcn. Henry Nguyen, S.C.J., In Res.; Brs.: 1; Priests: 5

Sacred Heart at Monastery Lake - 7330 S. Lovers Lane Rd., Franklin, WI 53132 t) 414-425-5968; 414-425-5981 provtreas@usprovince.org www.dehoniansusa.org Bro. Duane Lemke, S.C.J., Supr.; Most Rev. Joseph Potocnak, SCJ, In Res.; Rev. James D. Brackin, S.C.J.; Rev. Nicholas Brown, S.C.J.; Rev. Thomas Cassidy, S.C.J.; Rev. John Czyzynski, S.C.J.; Rev. Jan de Jong, S.C.J.; Rev. Mark Fortner, S.C.J.; Rev. Edward Griesemer, S.C.J.; Rev. Wayne Jenkins, S.C.J.; Rev. Anthony Kluckman, S.C.J.; Rev. Gary Lantz, S.C.J.; Rev. Richard J. MacDonald, S.C.J.; Rev. Anthony P. Russo, S.C.J.; Rev. James Schroeder, S.C.J.; Rev. James Walters, S.C.J.; Rev. Thomas Westhoven, S.C.J.; Rev. Charles Wonch, S.C.J.; Bro. Raymond Kozuch, S.C.J.; Bro. Peter Mankins, S.C.J.; Bro. Brian Tompkins, S.C.J.; Bro. Leonard Zaworski, S.C.J.; Bro. Clay Diaz; Bro. Andrew Lewandowski, S.C.J., In Res.; Dcn. David Nagel, S.C.J.; Brs.: 7; Priests: 18

Sacred Heart at Monastery Lake, Inc. - 7330 & 7350 S. Lovers Lane Rd., Franklin, WI 53132 t) 414-425-3383 provtreas@usprovince.org Dcn. David Nagel, S.C.J., Treas.;

FRANKSVILLE

Sacred Heart Novitiate - 8409 3 Mile Rd., Franksville, WI 53126 c) 414-779-0712 provsec@usprovince.org www.dehoniansusa.org Rev. Byron Haaland, S.C.J., Novice Master; Rev. Andrzej Sudol, SCJ, Asst. Novice Master; Rev. Joseph N. Mukuna, SCJ, In Res.; Priests: 3

HALES CORNERS

Priests of the Sacred Heart - 7373 S. Lovers Lane Rd., Hales Corners, WI 53130-0289; Mailing: P.O. Box 289, Hales Corners, WI 53130-0289 t) 414-425-6910 provsec@usprovince.org www.dehoniansusa.org Very Rev. Vien Nguyen, S.C.J., Prov.; Bro. Frank Presto, S.C.J., Secy.; Dcn. David Nagel, S.C.J., Treas.; Brs.: 1; Priests: 1

Sacred Heart Monastery - 7335 S. Lovers Ln. Rd., Hales Corners, WI 53130; Mailing: P.O. Box 566, Hales Corners, WI 53130 t) 414-425-8300 provsec@usprovince.org www.dehoniansusa.org Rev. Duy Nguyen, S.C.J., Supr.; Rev. Frank Wittouck, S.C.J.; Rev. Joseph Thien-Dinh, S.C.J., In Res.; Rev. Yvon Sheehy, S.C.J., In Res.; Rev. Edward Zemlik, S.C.J., In Res.; Rev. Zbigniew Morawiec, S.C.J., In Res.; Bro. Jacob Smith, SCJ, In Res.; Bro. Michael Wodarcxyk, SCJ, In Res.; Bro. Jonathan Nguyen-Voung, SCJ, In Res.; Phong Paul Hoang, In Res.; Brs.: 3; Priests: 6

HUBERTUS

Discalced Carmelite Friars of Holy Hill, Inc. - 1525 Carmel Rd., Hubertus, WI 53033 t) 262-628-1838 www.holyhill.com Rev. Jude Peters, O.C.D., Pst.; Rev. Mark-Joseph DeVelis, O.C.D., Prior; Rev. Phillip Thomas, O.C.D., Subprior; Rev. David Joseph Centner, O.C.D., Secy.; Rev. Ernest Unverdorben, O.C.D., Treas.; Rev. Fred Alexander, O.C.D., Mem.; Rev. Daniel Chowning, O.C.D., Mem.; Rev. Kevin Culligan, OCD, Mem.; Rev. Thomas-Mary Gilbert, O.C.D., Mem.; Rev. Cyril Guise, O.C.D., Mem.; Rev. George Mangiaracina, O.C.D., Mem.; Rev. Pier-Giorgio Pacelli, O.C.D., Mem.; Rev. Michael-Joseph Paris, O.C.D., Mem.; Rev. Celedonio Martinez Daimiel, O.C.D., Second Counselor; Priests: 14

Discalced Carmelite Friars of Holy Hill, Inc. - 1525 Carmel Rd., Hubertus, WI 53033 t) (262) 628-5286 guesthouse@holyhill.com Retreat Center

MILWAUKEE

Alexian Brothers Community - 8000 Limerick Rd., Milwaukee, WI 53223-1072; Mailing: 600 Alexian Way, Elk Grove Village, IL 60007 t) 414-371-7660 www.alexianbrothers.net Immaculate Conception Province Bro. John Howard, C.F.A., Dir.; Bro. Patrick McCabe, C.F.A., Dir.; Bro. Warren Longo, C.F.A., Volunteer; Bro. Joe Pense, Volunteer; Bro. Robert Podjarsky, Volunteer; Brs.: 5

Arrupe House Jesuit Community - 831 N. 13th St., Milwaukee, WI 53233-1706 t) 414-288-5855 Society of Jesus, Midwest Prov. Rev. R. Benjamin Osborne, S.J., Supr.; Rev. Richard P. Abert, S.J.; Rev. Thomas G. Boedy, S.J.; Rev. D. Thomas Hughson, S.J.; Rev. William T. Johnson, S.J.; Rev. Philip Sutherland, S.J.; Rev. Thomas P. Sweetser, S.J.; Rev. Nathaniel O. Lubanga, S.J., Graduate Studies; Rev. David M. Shields, S.J., Spiritual & Pst. Prog., Casa Romero Renewal Center; Priests: 15

Jesuit Community at Marquette University (Marquette Jesuit Associates, Inc.) - 1345 W. Wells St., Milwaukee, WI 53233-1714 t) 414-288-5000 obrien.jesuits@marquette.edu www.marquette.edu/jesres Rev. Thomas S. Anderson, S.J., Par. Vicar; Rev. Ronald Bieganowski, S.J., Prof.; Rev. Cathal Doherty, S.J., Prof.; Rev. Ryan Gerard Duns, S.J., Prof.; Rev. Deogratias Fikiri Kamunto, SJ, Mem.; Rev. Grant S. Garinger, S.J., Prof.; Rev. Jose Miguel Jaramillo, S.J., Mem.; Rev. Robert J. Kroll, S.J., Spiritual Adv./Care Srvcs.; Rev. James Kubicki, Mem.; Rev. Jeffrey T. LaBelle, S.J., Prof.; Rev. Joseph W. Laramie, S.J., Dir.; Rev. John D. Laurance, S.J., Mem.; Bro. Gerald E. Peltz, S.J., Dir., Opers.; Rev. James M. Pribek, S.J., Asst. Vice Pres.; Rev. Michael W. Maher, S.J., Prof.; Rev. Douglas J. Leonhardt, S.J., Mem.; Rev. Gregory Alfred Lynch, S.J., Mem.; Rev. Timothy T. Manatt, S.J., Pst.; Rev. Michael J. Marco, S.J., Pres.; Rev. D. Edward Mathie, S.J., Mem.; Rev. Thomas D. Mbatna Taiwe, S.J., Mem.; Rev. T. Michael McNulty, S.J., Mem.; Rev. Gregory J. O'Meara, S.J., Rector; Rev. Ross T. Pribyl, S.J., Teacher; Rev. Nathaniel Romano, Campus Min.; Rev. David G. Schultenover, S.J., Mem.; Rev. John A. Schwantes, S.J., Mem.; Rev. Thomas J. E. Schwarz, S.J., Prof.; Rev. John S. Thiede, S.J., Prof.; Rev. Andrew J. Thon, S.J., Prof.; Rev. Emmanuel Ugwejeh, S.J., Mem.; Rev. James Voiss, S.J., Vice. Pres.; Rev. Frederick P. Zagone, S.J., Mem.; Rev. Michael J. Zeps, S.J., Prof.; Brs.: 1; Priests: 33

Pallotti House - 5424 W. Bluemound Rd., Milwaukee, WI 53208 t) 414-258-0653 pallotti.milw@pallottines.org www.pallottines.org Residence of Fathers and Brothers and Offices of Mother of God Province of the Society of the Catholic Apostolate also, Provincial House. Rev. Thomas Varkey, SAC (India), Par. Admin.; Rev. Thomas Pulikkeel Chacko, SAC (India), Mem.; Rev. Jose Eluvathingal, S.A.C. (India), Mem.; Rev. Bruce J. Schute, S.A.C., Mem.; Rev. Gregory P. Serwa, S.A.C., Mem.; Rev. Joseph Dominic, S.A.C., Pst.; Rev. Thomas Manjaly, S.A.C., Pst.; Rev. James Palakudy, S.A.C., Pst.; Rev. Joseph Koyickal, S.A.C., Pst.; Rev. Davies Edassery, S.A.C., Prov.; Rev. Joy A. Thachil, S.A.C., Pst.; Rev. Sergio Lizama, S.A.C., Assoc. Pst.; Rev. Leon J. Martin, S.A.C., Dir.; Bro. James Scarpace, S.A.C., Admin.; Brs.: 1; Priests: 13

Washington Province of Discalced Carmelite Friars, Inc. - 1233 S. 45th St., Milwaukee, WI 53214-3693 t) 414-672-7212 provincial.ihm.ocd@gmail.com www.discalcedcarmel.org Very Rev. Michael Berry, OCD, Prov.; Very Rev. Elijah Martin, O.C.D., 1st Councilor & Vocation Dir.; Rev. Mark-Joseph DeVelis, O.C.D., Councilor; Rev. Ralph-Elias Haddix, O.C.D., Councilor; Rev. Bonaventure Lussier, O.C.D., Secy.; Rev. Arnold Boehme, O.C.D., Supr., Philippines; Rev. Thomas Martin, O.C.D., Formation Dir. Quezon City, Philippines; Rev. Alan J. Rieger, O.C.D., Davao City, Philippines; Bro. Gilbert Tovares, O.C.D., Assisted Living; Bro. Sebastian Reale, O.C.D., Biddeford, ME; Rev. Lawrence Daniels, O.C.D., Supr. Kiserian, Kenya; Rev. Dennis Geng, O.C.D., Reg Treas., Nairobi, Kenya; Brs.: 15; Priests: 30

Discalced Carmelite Friars - t) 414-383-3565

Salvatorian Provincial Offices (Society of the Divine Savior) - 1735 N. Hi Mount Blvd., Milwaukee, WI 53208-1720 t) 414-258-1735 sds@salvatorians.com salvatorians.com Very Rev. Jeffrey Wocken, S.D.S., Prov.; Rev. Peter Schuessler, S.D.S., Vicar; Rev. Michael Burns, S.D.S., Mem.; Rev. Bruce Clanton, S.D.S., Mem.; Rev. David C. Cooney, S.D.S., Mem.; Rev. Neil Durham, S.D.S., Mem.; Very Rev. Raúl Gómez-Ruiz, S.D.S., Mem.; Bro. Silas Henderson, S.D.S., Mem.; Rev. Joe Jagodensky, S.D.S., Mem.; Bro. Samuel Larson, S.D.S., Mem.; Bro. George Maufort, S.D.S., Mem.; Rev. John Tigatiga, SDS, Mem.; Rev. Simon Muema, SDS, Mem.; Bro. Sean McLaughlin, S.D.S., Mem.; Rev. Reed C. Mungovan, S.D.S., Mem.; Rev. John Vianney Muweesi, S.D.S., Mem.; Rev. Patrick Nelson, S.D.S., Mem.; Rev. Virginus Osuagwu, S.D.S., Mem.; Rev. Thomas Perrin, S.D.S., Mem.; Rev. Joseph C. Rodrigues, S.D.S., Mem.; Bro. Jeffrey St. George, S.D.S., Mem.; Rev. Octavio Trejo-Flores, S.D.S., Mem.; Rev. Thomas Tureman, S.D.S., Mem.; Rev. Scott Wallenfelsz, S.D.S., Mem.; Rev. Paul Timothy Wilken, S.D.S., Mem.; Rev. Arturo Ysmael, S.D.S., Mem.; Ricardo Rivera Gutierrez, Cl; Brs.: 14; Priests: 49

Holy Apostles House of Formation - 937 N. 37th St., Milwauke, WI 53208-3104; Mailing: 1735 N. Hi Mount Blvd., Milwaukee, WI 53208-1720 t) (414) 988-4390 Rev. Paul Portland, S.D.S., Contact; Rev. Robert Marsicek, S.D.S., Mem.; Bro. Van Todd, S.D.S., Mem.; Rev. James Weyker, S.D.S., Mem.;

Salvatorians - Jordan Hall - 7979 W. Glenbrook Rd., Milwaukee, WI 53223-1055 t) 414-357-5152 johau324@gmail.com Fathers & Brothers of the Society of the Divine Savior. Bro. John Hauenstein, S.D.S., Contact; Rev. Hugh G. Birdsall, S.D.S., Mem.; Bro. Ervan Digman, S.D.S., Mem.; Rev. Richard Driscoll, S.D.S., Mem.; Bro. Peter Farnesi, S.D.S., Mem.; Bro. Regis Fust, S.D.S., Mem.; Bro. Kilian Harrington, S.D.S., Mem.; Rev. Michael Hoffman, S.D.S., Mem.; Bro. Marvin Kluesner, S.D.S., Mem.; Rev. Donald Loskot, S.D.S., Mem.; Bro. Thomas Meyer, S.D.S., Mem.; Rev. Roman Mueller, S.D.S., Mem.; Bro. Roger Nelson, S.D.S., Mem.; Rev. Andre Papineau, S.D.S., Mem.; Rev. Michael Shay, S.D.S., Mem.; Rev. Dennis D. Thiessen, S.D.S., Mem.; Rev. Alan Wagner, S.D.S., Mem.; Rev. Robert Wicht, S.D.S., Mem.;

MOUNT CALVARY

St. Lawrence Friary - 301 Church St., Mount Calvary, WI 53057 t) 920-753-7550 c) 920-204-1548 brdave@stlawrence.edu; brdaveschwab@gmail.com stlawrence.edu Rev. Paul J. Koenig, OFM Cap, Pst.; Rev. James P. Leary, O.F.M.Cap, Assoc. Pst.; Rev. Peter Kafumu, OFM Cap., Sacr. Min.; Rev. Zoilo Garibay, O.F.M.Cap., Rector; Rev. Chrispin Shirima, O.F.M.Cap., Prof.; Rev. Larry Abler, O.F.M.Cap.; Rev. Paul Craig, O.F.M.Cap.; Rev. Ed Hagman; Rev. Elroy Pesch, O.F.M.Cap.; Rev. Jerome Higgins, O.F.M.Cap., In Res.; Rev. Thomas Zelinski, OFM Cap, In Res.; Bro. Jerome Campbell, O.F.M.Cap.; Bro. Mitchell Frantz, O.F.M.Cap.; Bro. Neal Plale, O.F.M.Cap.; Bro. David Schwab, O.F.M.Cap.; Dcn. Truong Dinh, ofm cap, Youth Min.; Dcn. Nathan Linton, ofm Cap, Youth Min.; Brs.: 6; Priests: 12

TWIN LAKES

La Salette Missionaries - 10330 336th Ave., Twin Lakes, WI 53181 t) 262-877-3111 lasaletteshrinetl@gmail.com www.lasaletteshrine.org Our Lady of La Salette Shrine Rev. Andrew Zagorski, M.S., Dir.; Rev. Lukasz Krzanowski, MS, Assoc. Dir.; Rev. Peter Stangricki, M.S., Assoc. Dir.; Priests: 3

WAUWATOSA

St. Camillus Communities, Inc. - 10101 W. Wisconsin Ave., Wauwatosa, WI 53226 t) (414) 258-1814 jorosa@stcam.com Rev. Agustin R. Orosa, M.I., Prov.; Rev. Leandro Blanco, M.I., Vicar; Rev. Anthoni Jeorge, M.I. (India), Chap.; Rev. Varghese Johnson Vellachira, Secy.; Rev. Joseph Bisoffi, M.I., Mem.; Rev. Mathai Naveen Pallurathil, M.I., Mem.; Rev. Mathew Perumpil, M.I., Mem.; Rev. Peter Pham Kim Quyen, M.I., Mem.; Rev. Peter C. Opara, M.I., Mem.; Rev. Albert Schempp, Mem.; Rev. Louis Lussier, M.I., Mem.; Rev. Reji Chacko, Mem.; Bro. Mario Crivello, Mem.; Brs.: 1; Priests: 12

St. Camillus Jesuit Community (Society of Jesus, USA Midwest Province) - 10201 W. Wisconsin Ave., Wauwatosa, WI 53226-3541 t) 414-259-6399 sosullivan@jesuits.org; gwinzenburg@jesuits.org Rev. Sean A. O'Sullivan, S.J., Minister; Rev. Charles Baumann, S.J., In Res.; Rev. Burnell B. Bisbee, S.J., In Res.; Rev. Walter E. Boehme, S.J., In Res.; Rev. Hubert G. Boschert, S.J., In Res.; Rev. Joseph Bracken, S.J., In Res.; Rev. Thaddeus J. Burch, S.J., In Res.; Rev. Patrick J. Burns, S.J., In Res.; Rev. Thomas A. Caldwell, S.J., In Res.; Rev. Anthony L. Dagelen, S.J., In Res.; Rev. James M. Dixon, S.J., In Res.; Rev. J. Patrick Donnelly, S.J., In Res.; Rev. James L. Empereur, S.J., In Res.; Rev. David H. Gau, S.J., In Res.; Rev. William Gerut, S.J., In Res.; Rev. Gerald E. Goetz, S.J., In Res.; Rev. M. Dennis Hamm, S.J., In Res.; Rev. John A. Hennessy, S.J., In Res.; Rev. Robert J. Joda, S.J., In Res.; Rev. Theodore M. Kalamaja, S.J., In Res.; Rev. Kevin Kersten, S.J., In Res.; Rev. James J. King, S.J., In Res.; Rev. Leon Klimczyk, S.J., In Res.; Rev. Michael D. Kurimay, S.J., In Res.; Rev. William S. Kurz, S.J., In Res.; Rev. Jeffrey R. Loebl, S.J., In Res.; Rev. Frank A. Majka, S.J., In Res.; Rev. Donald R. Matthys, S.J., In Res.; Rev. Patrick J. McAteer, S.J., In Res.; Rev. James J. O'Leary, S.J., In Res.; Rev. Nicholas F. Pope, S.J., In Res.; Rev. Donald Rauscher, S.J., In Res.; Rev. Luis Rodriguez, S.J., In Res.; Rev. Philip J. Rossi, S.J., In Res.; Rev. Thomas N. Schloemer, S.J., In Res.; Rev. Thomas J. Shanahan, S.J., In Res.; Rev. Peter E. Sharkey, S.J., In Res.; Rev. George R. Sullivan, S.J., In Res.; Rev. Albert R. Thelen, SJ, In Res.; Rev. James Vorwoldt, S.J., In Res.; Rev. James B. Warosh, S.J., In Res.; Rev. Robert A. Wild, S.J., In Res.; Rev. George E. Winzenburg, S.J., Supr.; Rev. M. John Wymelenberg, S.J., In Res.; Bro. James F. Heidrick, In Res.; Bro. Thomas B Arms, In Res.; Brs.: 2; Priests: 45

NURSING / REHABILITATION / CONVALESCENCE / ELDERLY CARE [NUR]

FOND DU LAC

St. Francis Home - 33 Everett St., Fond du Lac, WI 54935 t) 920-923-7980 Member of SSM Healthcare of WI Douglas Trost, Pres.; Asstd. Annu.: 142; Staff: 269

St. Clare Terrace - 31 Everett St., Fond Du Lac, WI 54935 t) 920-923-7996 Dawn Stephanie, Admin.;

St. Francis Terrace - 345 E. First St., Fond Du Lac, WI 54935 t) (920) 926-6068

GLENDALE

Ascension Wisconsin Pharmacy, Inc. - 400 W. River Woods Pkwy., Glendale, WI 53212 t) 414-465-3111 timothy.waldoch@ascension.org healthcare.ascension.org Sponsored by Ascension Health Ministries (Ascension Sponsor), a public juridic person. Bernie Sherry, CEO; Timothy Waldoch, Chief Mission Integration Officer; Staff: 52

GREENFIELD

Clement Manor Health Center - 3939 S. 92nd St., Greenfield, WI 53228 t) 414-321-1800 info@clementmanor.org www.clementmanor.com Corporate Title: Clement Manor, Inc. A skilled nursing care and short-term rehabilitation care facility. Sponsored by School Sisters of St. Francis. Dennis Ferger, CEO; Tom Brefka, Dir., Pastoral Care; Asstd. Annu.: 94; Staff: 195

Clement Manor Retirement Community - 9339 W. Howard Ave., Greenfield, WI 53228 t) 414-321-1800 info@clementmanor.com; nstrade@clementmanor.org www.clementmanor.com Includes independent living, assisted living and memory care. Sponsored by the

School Sisters of St. Francis Dennis Ferger, Pres.; Tom Brefka, Dir., Pastoral Care; Asstd. Annu.: 200; Staff: 69

KENOSHA

The Legacy at St. Joseph's Home - 9244 29th Ave., Kenosha, WI 53143 t) 262-694-0080 (Mainline) c) (414) 807-8601 asi@legacy-sj.com www.legacy-sj.org Corporate Title: St. Joseph's Home of Our Lady of Mt. Carmel, Inc. Sr. Anne Marie Cheikh, Supr.; Asstd. Annu.: 70; Staff: 60

MILWAUKEE

St. Anne's Home for the Elderly, Milwaukee, Inc. (Sisters of the Divine Savior) - 3800 N. 92nd St., Milwaukee, WI 53222-2589 t) 414-463-7570 jkrahn@stannescampus.org; tlipke@stannescampus.org illuminus.us/communities/st-annes Janet Krahn, CEO; Rev. Thomas Perrin, S.D.S., Dir.; Asstd. Annu.: 340; Staff: 215

Alexian Village of Milwaukee, Inc. - 9301 N. 76th St., Milwaukee, WI 53223 t) 314-292-9308 ahscm-mission@ascension.org www.ascensionliving.org/ Ryan Endsley, COO; Asstd. Annu.: 318; Staff: 133

***Milwaukee Catholic Home, Inc.** - 2462 N. Prospect Ave., Milwaukee, WI 53211-4462 t) 414-224-9700 lcardinale@milwaukeecatholichome.org milwaukeecatholichome.org David Fulcher, Exec.; Kara Grennier, Dir., Residential & Supportive Living; Asstd. Annu.: 700; Staff: 300

Villa St. Francis, Inc. - 1910 W. Ohio Ave., Milwaukee, WI 53215 t) 414-649-2888 rhumpal@villastfrancis.org; kkeidl@villastfrancis.org www.villastfrancis.org Assisted Living Facility for the Elderly. Sponsored by the Congregation of the Sisters of St. Felix of Cantalice of the North American Province, Inc. Rodney Humpal, CEO; Kurt Keidl, Dir., Missions; Asstd. Annu.: 70; Staff: 51

***Wheaton Franciscan Healthcare – Terrace at St. Francis, Inc.** - 3200 S. 20th St., Milwaukee, WI 53215 t) 314-292-9308 ahscm-mission@ascension.org www.ascensionliving.org/ Ryan Endsley, COO; Asstd. Annu.: 362; Staff: 48

MOUNT CALVARY

Villa Loretto Nursing Home - N8114 County WW, Mount Calvary, WI 53057; Mailing: 10101 Woodfield Ln., St. Louis, MO 63132 t) 920-753-3211 agnesian.com Corporate Title: Sister Servants of Christ the King, Inc. Member of SSM Healthcare of WI. Douglas Trost, Pres.; Asstd. Annu.: 85; Staff: 82

Villa Rosa, Inc. - N8120 County WW, Mount Calvary, WI 53057; Mailing: 10101 Woodfield Ln., St. Louis, MO 63132 t) 920-753-3015 agnesian.com member of SSM Healthcare of WI Douglas Trost, Pres.; Asstd. Annu.: 23; Staff: 11

RACINE

Ascension Living - Lakeshore at Siena, Inc. - 5643 Erie St., Racine, WI 53402; Mailing: 4600 Edmundson Rd., St. Louis, MO 63134 t) (314) 292-9308 www.ascensionliving.org Ryan Endsley, COO; Asstd. Annu.: 230; Staff: 77

St. Monica's Senior Living - 3920 N. Green Bay Rd., Racine, WI 53404 t) 262-639-5050 slichter@stmonicasseniorliving.com www.stmonicasseniorliving.com Nonprofit Corp. Stephany Lichter, Admin.; Asstd. Annu.: 146; Staff: 145

SOUTH MILWAUKEE

CHI Franciscan Villa - 3601 S. Chicago Ave., South Milwaukee, WI 53172 t) 414-764-4100 mgulock@chilivingcomm.org www.homeishere.org An operating unit of CHI Living Communities, which is a subsidiary of CommonSpirit Health Michael Gulock, Exec.; John Herbert, Mission Integration/Chaplain; Asstd. Annu.: 508; Staff: 175

ST. FRANCIS

Canticle Court, Inc. - 3201 S. Lake Dr., St. Francis, WI 53235-3708 t) 414-744-5878 tergerson@lakeosfs.org; amy681502@gmail.com www.canticlejunipercourts.org An apartment building sponsored by the Sisters of St. Francis of Assisi funded by HUD for low income elderly persons who can live independently. Amy Schmidt, Treas.; Asstd. Annu.: 48; Staff: 3

Juniper Court, Inc. - 3209 S. Lake Dr., St. Francis, WI 53235-3712 t) 414-744-3150; (414) 744-5878 tergerson@lakeosfs.org; amy681502@gmail.com www.canticlejunipercourts.org Apartments for persons of low to moderate income who can live independently. Sponsored by the Sisters of St. Francis of Assisi, St. Francis, WI Amy Schmidt, Treas.; Asstd. Annu.: 52; Staff: 3

WAUWATOSA

St. Camillus - 10200 W. Blue Mound Rd., Wauwatosa, WI 53226 t) 414-259-6300 jleveritt@stcam.com www.stcam.com Independent living facilities for older adults. Rev. Agustin R. Orosa, M.I., Pres.; Rev. Leandro Blanco, M.I., Treas.; Rev. Varghese Johnson Vellachira, Secy.; Shannon Angell, CEO; Julie Leveritt, Admin.; Asstd. Annu.: 550; Staff: 134

St. Camillus Health Center, Inc. - 10101 W. Wisconsin Ave., Wauwatosa, WI 53226 t) 414-258-1814 www.stcam.com Skilled Nursing Home, Assisted Living, Home Care & Hospice. Rev. Agustin R. Orosa, M.I., Pres.; Rev. Varghese Johnson Vellachira, Secy.; Rev. Leandro Blanco, M.I., Treas.; Shannon Angell, CEO; Asstd. Annu.: 150; Staff: 225

PRESCHOOLS / CHILDCARE CENTERS [PRE]

MILWAUKEE

St. Joseph Academy - 1600 W. Oklahoma Ave., Milwaukee, WI 53215 t) 414-645-5337 tjones@sjamilwaukee.org; srcarlotta@sjamilwaukee.org www.sjamilwaukee.org Sponsored by Congregation of the Sisters of St. Felix of Cantalice of the North American Province, Inc. (Felician Sisters). Serving children 6 wks-8th Sr. Carlotta Myszka, Mission Dir.; Scott Hanson, Prin.; Tabia Jones, Pres.; Epros Weiss, Librn.; Stds.: 512; Lay Tchrs.: 53

SOUTH MILWAUKEE

Franciscan Villa Child Day Center - 3601 S. Chicago Ave., South Milwaukee, WI 53172 t) 414-570-5410 jgrabczyk@chilivingcomm.org www.homeishere.org An operating unit of CHI Living Communities, a subsidiary of CommonSpirit Health Judy Grabczyk, Dir.; Stds.: 37; Lay Tchrs.: 7

RETREAT HOUSES / RENEWAL CENTERS [RTR]

BENET LAKE

St. Benedict's Retreat Center (Benedictine Monks of Wisconsin, Inc.) - 12605 224th Ave., Benet Lake, WI 53102-1000 t) 262-396-4311 benetlakeretreatcenter@gmail.com www.benetlake.org Tracie Young, Dir.; Rev. Macario J. Martinez, O.S.B., Retreat Master; Rev. Daniel Petsche, O.S.B., Retreat Master; Bro. Matthew Marie, OSB, Asst. Retreat Master;

BRISTOL

Mercy Retreat Center (Sisters of Mercy of the Americas) - 12009 221st Ave., Bristol, WI 53104 t) 262-624-4089 mvalenti@sistersofmercy.org Mary Jo Valenti, Mgr.;

ELKHORN

St. Vincent Pallotti Center - N. 6409 Bowers Rd., Elkhorn, WI 53121 t) 262-723-2108 retreat@pallottines.org www.pallottines.org Pallottine Fathers & Brothers, Inc., Retreat and Christian Formation Center Rev. John R. Scheer, S.A.C., Admin.; Jeffrey Johnson, Dir.;

MILWAUKEE

Casa Romero Renewal Center, Inc. - 423 W. Bruce St., Milwaukee, WI 53204 t) 414-224-7564 dcortes@casaromerocenter.org; mcoffey@casaromerocenter.org www.casaromerocenter.org Rev. David M. Shields, S.J., Chap.; Michael Coffey, Exec.;

OCONOMOWOC

Our Mother of Perpetual Help Retreat Center (The Redemptorist Retreat Center) - 1800 N. Timber Trail Ln., Oconomowoc, WI 53066-4897 t) 262-567-6900 rrc@redemptoristretreat.org www.redemptoristretreat.org Rev. Theodore Lawson, C.Ss.R., Dir.; Rev. Joseph Butz, C.Ss.R., In Res.; Bro. Bruce Davidson, C.Ss.R., Hermitages Mgr.; Bro. Michael Rhodes, C.Ss.R., Staff;

RACINE

***Siena Retreat Center, Inc.** - 5637 Erie St., Racine, WI 53402-1900 t) 262-898-2590 retreats@racinedominicans.org www.sienaretreatcenter.org/ Claire Anderson, Contact;

WAUKESHA

Schoenstatt Retreat Center - W284 N698 Cherry Ln., Waukesha, WI 53188-9402 t) 262-522-4300 intlcenter@schsrsmary.org schoenstatt-wisconsin.us/ Sr. Rita Marie Otto, Supr.; Sr. M. Faustina Yank, Dir.;

SEMINARIES [SEM]

FRANKLIN

Sacred Heart Seminary and School of Theology - 7335 S. Hwy. 100, Franklin, WI 53132; Mailing: P.O. Box 429, Hales Corners, WI 53130-0429 t) 414-425-8300 mmisey@shsst.edu www.shsst.edu Very Rev. Raúl Gómez-Ruiz, S.D.S., Pres.-Rector; Rev. John P. Mack, Vice Pres., Formation Prog.; Rev. Jose Gonzalez, Dir., Hispanic Min. Prep. Prog. & Instructor; Dcn. Steven L. Kramer, Dir., Recruitment & Homiletics & Assoc. Prof.; Julie O'Connor, Vice Pres., Student Svcs.; Stds.: 161; Lay Tchrs.: 12; Pr. Tchrs.: 4

Xaverian Missionary Fathers College Seminary - 4500 Xavier Dr., Franklin, WI 53132-9066 t) 414-421-0831 xavmissionswi@hotmail.com www.xaverianmissionaries.org Rev. Alejandro Rodriguez Gomez, S.X., Rector; Rev. Dominic Caldognetto, S.X. (Italy), Asst. Treas.; Rev. Hery Junianto, S.X.; Rev. Ignacio Torres, sx, English Student; Rev. Pablo Torres, sx, English Student; Rev. Everson L. Kloster, SX, English Student;

MOUNT CALVARY

St. Lawrence Seminary High School - 301 Church St., Mount Calvary, WI 53057 t) 920-753-7500 frzoy@stlawrence.edu www.stlawrence.edu Rev. Zoilo Garibay, O.F.M.Cap., Rector; Rev. Peter Kafumu, OFM Cap., Vice Rector; Rev. Chrispin Shirima, O.F.M.Cap., Student Supvr.; Bro. Mitchell Frantz, O.F.M.Cap., Student Supvr.; Bro. Neal Plale, O.F.M.Cap.; Bro. David Schwab, O.F.M.Cap., Bus. Mgr.; Dcn. Nathan Linton, ofm Cap, Campus Min.; Dcn. Truong Dinh, ofm cap, Student Supvr.; Timothy Schroeder, Dir. Oper.; David Bartel, Academic Dean/ Prin.; Kevin Buelow, Dean of Students; Stds.: 127; Bro. Tchrs.: 1; Lay Tchrs.: 19; Pr. Tchrs.: 1

ST. FRANCIS

Saint Francis de Sales Seminary - 3257 S. Lake Dr., St. Francis, WI 53235 t) 414-747-6400 dbrotz@sfs.edu www.sfs.edu Very Rev. Luke N. Strand, Rector; Rev. John J. Baumgardner, Vice Rector; William Hudson, Assoc. Dir., Human Formation; Agnieszka Kosmecka, Director of Liturgical Music; Rev. Justin J. Kizewski, Dir., Intellectual Formation; Rev. Brad A. Krawczyk, Dir., Liturgical Formation; Rev. Robert J. Kroll, S.J., Dir., Spiritual Formation; Rev. John Paul C. Mitchell, Formator; Rev. Glenn E. Powers, Dir., Pastoral Formation; Timothy Shininger, Pastoral Counseling; Marijo Boushon, Librn.; Mark Schrauth, Librn.; Stds.: 81; Lay Tchrs.: 2; Pr. Tchrs.: 7

SPECIAL CARE FACILITIES [SPF]

MEQUON

Sacred Heart Rehabilitation Institute, Inc. - 13111 N. Port Washington Rd, Mequon, WI 53097 t) 414-585-6750 timothy.waldoch@ascension.org healthcare.ascension.org/ Sponsored by Ascension Health Ministries (Ascension Sponsor), a juridic person. Bernie Sherry, CEO; Timothy Waldoch, Chief Mission Integration Officer; Bed Capacity: 15; Asstd. Annu.: 7,663; Staff: 43

MILWAUKEE

St. Ann Center for Intergenerational Care, Inc. - 2801 E. Morgan Ave., Milwaukee, WI 53207 t) 414-977-5000 jjansen@stanncenter.org; sbrown@stanncenter.org www.stanncenter.org Intergenerational day care center for both children and adults. Jessica Davis, Dir., Grants; Bed Capacity: 18; Asstd. Annu.: 850; Staff: 172

Eastside Senior Services - 2618 N. Hackett Ave., Milwaukee, WI 53211 t) 414-210-5881 essmilw@gmail.com www.essmilw.org Corporate Title: Eastside Senior Services, Inc. - a Neighborhood Outreach Program Melissa Meier, Dir.; Asstd. Annu.: 350; Staff: 3

MOUNT CALVARY

Cristo Rey Ranch, Inc. (Sister Servants of Christ the King) - N8114 County Rd. WW, Mount Calvary, WI 53057 t) 920-753-1053; 920-904-5033 boddenw@yahoo.com; nunbetterfarm@hotmail.com www.cristoreyranch.org Sr. Stephen Bloesl, Pres.; Staff: 14

An asterisk (*) denotes an organization that has established tax-exempt status directly with the IRS and is not covered by the USCCB Group Ruling.

Archdiocese of Mobile

(Archidioecesis Mobiliensis)

MOST REVEREND THOMAS J. RODI

Archbishop of Mobile; ordained May 20, 1978; appointed Bishop of Biloxi May 15, 2001; ordained and installed July 2, 2001; appointed Archbishop of Mobile April 2, 2008; installed June 6, 2008. Chancery Office: 400 Government St., Mobile, AL 36602. T: 251-434-1585; archbishop@mobarch.org.

Chancery Office: 400 Government St., Mobile, AL 36602. T: 251-434-1585; F: 251-434-1588. chancery@mobarch.org

Square Miles 22,969.

Established as Vicariate-Apostolic of Alabama and the Floridas, 1825; Diocese of Mobile, May 15, 1829; Name changed to Diocese of Mobile-Birmingham, July 9, 1954; Redesignated, June 28, 1969. Raised to rank of Archdiocese November 16, 1980.

Comprises the lower 28 Counties of the State of Alabama, namely: Choctaw, Clarke, Wilcox, Dallas, Autauga, Elmore, Lee, Russell, Macon, Montgomery, Lowndes, Barbour, Bullock, Pike, Crenshaw, Butler, Monroe, Conecuh, Escambia, Covington, Coffee, Geneva, Dale, Henry, Houston, Washington, Baldwin and Mobile.

For legal titles of parishes and archdiocesan institutions consult the Chancery Office.

STATISTICAL OVERVIEW

Personnel
Archbishops....1
Priests: Diocesan Active in Diocese....56
Priests: Diocesan Active Outside Diocese....2
Priests: Retired, Sick or Absent....24
Number of Diocesan Priests....82
Religious Priests in Diocese....19
Total Priests in your Diocese....101
Extern Priests in Diocese....9
Ordinations:
Transitional Deacons....1
Permanent Deacons....16
Permanent Deacons in Diocese....71
Total Brothers....4
Total Sisters....89

Parishes
Parishes....76
With Resident Pastor:
Resident Diocesan Priests....49
Resident Religious Priests....11
Without Resident Pastor:
Administered by Priests....16
Missions....7
Pastoral Centers....2

Professional Ministry Personnel:
Sisters....4
Lay Ministers....119

Welfare
Catholic Hospitals....1
Total Assisted....142,543
Homes for the Aged....1
Total Assisted....76
Day Care Centers....2
Total Assisted....71
Special Centers for Social Services....9
Total Assisted....21,726
Residential Care of Disabled....1
Total Assisted....49

Educational
Diocesan Students in Other Seminaries....13
Total Seminarians....13
Colleges and Universities....1
Total Students....1,191
High Schools, Diocesan and Parish....3
Total Students....1,454
Elementary Schools, Diocesan and Parish....14
Total Students....3,126
Elementary Schools, Private....2
Total Students....150

Catechesis / Religious Education:
High School Students....749
Elementary Students....2,098
Total Students under Catholic Instruction....8,781
Teachers in Diocese:
Priests....1
Sisters....2
Lay Teachers....467

Vital Statistics
Receptions into the Church:
Infant Baptism Totals....909
Minor Baptism Totals....88
Adult Baptism Totals....90
Received into Full Communion....160
First Communions....774
Confirmations....765
Marriages:
Catholic....182
Interfaith....98
Total Marriages....280
Deaths....610
Total Catholic Population....107,870
Total Population....1,852,080

LEADERSHIP

Vicar General and Moderator of the Curia - Rev. Msgr. William J. Skoneki (vicargeneral@mobarch.org);

Vicars Forane - Very Rev. Stephen G. Vrazel, Mobile Deanery; Rev. Msgr. Michael L. Farmer, Montgomery Deanery; Very Rev. David M. Shoemaker, Dothan Deanery;

Vicar for Priests - Very Rev. William P Saucier (wsaucier@mobarch.org);

Judicial Vicar - Rev. Msgr. James S. Kee;

Chancellor - Dcn. Ronnie A. Hathorne (rhathorne@mobarch.org);

Archdiocesan Consultors - Rev. Msgr. William J. Skoneki (vicargeneral@mobarch.org); Rev. Msgr. Michael L. Farmer; Rev. Msgr. James S. Kee;

Archdiocesan Finance Council - Michele C. Smith, Exec. Dir. (msmith@mobarch.org);

Presbyteral Council - Most Rev. Thomas J. Rodi, Pres. (archbishop@mobarch.org); Very Rev. Paul G. Zoghby, Chair; Rev. Msgr. William J. Skoneki, Secy. (vicargeneral@mobarch.org);

Elected Members - Rev. David J. Tokarz; Rev. Johnny S. Savoie; Rev. James N. Morrison;

Jesuit Representative - Rev. Robert Poirier, SJ, Mem.;

Religious Representative - Rev. Justin Isaac, H.G.N.;

Priests' Personnel Committee - pzoghby@mobarch.org Very Rev. Paul G. Zoghby, Chair;

OFFICES AND DIRECTORS

Archives Office - t) 251-415-3850 archives@mobarch.org Karen J. Horton, Archivist;

The Catholic Week - t) 251-432-3529 tcw@mobarch.org Robert W. Herbst, Editor (rherbst@mobarch.org);

Censor Librorum - Rev. Msgr. William J. Skoneki (vicargeneral@mobarch.org);

Office of Development and Stewardship - t) 251-438-9668 Shannon D. Roh, Exec. Dir. (sroh@mobarch.org);

Catholic Charities Appeal - catholiccharities@mobarch.org

Metropolitan Tribunal - t) 251-432-4609 Rev. Msgr. James S. Kee, Judicial Vicar;

Manager and Judge - Rev. Daniel F. Good;

Associate Judge - Dcn. William J. Harkins;

Defender of the Bond - Rev. Msgr. Leonardo C. Guadalquiver;

Notaries and Secretaries - Barbara Williams; Sarah K. Arendall;

Legal Services - t) 251-434-1540 Lisa B. Hansen, Gen. Counsel (lhansen@mobarch.org);

Liaison With Religious - Sisters, Nuns & Brothers - t) 251-753-4872 Sr. Deborah Kennedy, R.S.M. (dkennedy@sistersofmercy.org);

Mass for Homebound - t) 251-865-6902 wgraham@mobarch.org Dcn. William H. Graham, Contact;

Office for the Protection of Minors and Adults - t) 251-434-1559 childprotection@mobarch.org Ginger N. Koppersmith, Dir. (gkoppersmith@mobarch.org); Kathryn J. Lollis, Admin. Asst.;

Permanent Diaconate Program - t) 251-689-8141 Dcn. Ronnie A. Hathorne, Dir. (rhathorne@mobarch.org);

Vocations - t) 251-415-3871 Rev. Victor P. Ingalls, Dir. (vocations@mobarch.org);

EDUCATION

Catholic Department of Education - t) 251-438-4611 www.mobarchschools.org Gwendolyn P. Byrd, Exec. Dir. (gbyrd@mobarch.org);

Office of Catholic Schools - Gwendolyn P. Byrd, Supt.; Karen F. Abreo, Assoc. Supt. Academics; Ginger N. Koppersmith, Assoc. Supt. Student Svcs.;

Office of Evangelization and Family Life - t) 251-433-6991 www.mobarch.org/oefl Patrick J. Arensberg, Dir.; Janet M. Masline, Assoc. Dir.;

Hispanic Ministry - t) 251-690-6907 Dcn. Hector J. Donastorg, Archdiocesan Dir.;

Prison Ministry - t) 251-434-1577 Dcn. Stephen A. Tidwell, Archdiocesan Dir.;

Office of Youth and Young Adult Ministry - t) 251-433-4138 Tex Phelps, Dir.;

FINANCE

Financial Services - t) (251) 434-1548 Michele C. Smith, Exec. Dir. (msmith@mobarch.org);

Accounting Department - Gary E. Connick, Controller;

Information Systems/Technology - t) 251-434-1539 Dcn. Andrew M. Pitts, Mgr.;

Personnel Administration and Benefits - Vicki A. Stricklin, Mgr.;

Real Estate, Property/Liability Insurance & Risk Management - Lisa B. Hansen, Dir.;

Facilities Management - t) 251-434-1534 Robin M. Rockstall, Mgr.;

ORGANIZATIONS

Apostleship of Prayer - Rev. Msgr. William J. Skoneki (vicargeneral@mobarch.org);

Apostleship of the Sea - t) 251-432-7339 Dcn. John J. Archer; Rev. Lito J. Capeding, Chap. (lcapeding@mobarch.org);

Archdiocesan Council of Catholic Women (ACCW) - t) (334) 657-8862 Jessica Darrington, Pres.;

Pontifical Mission Societies of the United States - Rev. Msgr. William J. Skoneki, Dir. (vicargeneral@mobarch.org);

Vietnamese Community Council - t) 251-479-7360 Rev. Cu Minh Duong, Vicar for Vietnamese Affairs (cduong@mobarch.org);

SOCIAL SERVICES

Catholic Social Services - t) 251-434-1550 Marilyn D. King, Exec. Dir. (mdking@mobarch.org);

Adoption Services - t) 251-232-2531

Catholic Deaf Ministry - t) 251-340-0990 William F. Jones;

Clarke County Office - t) 251-246-0131 Alane B Hutchinson, Admin. Asst.;

Counseling - Buffy L. Marston, Dir.;

Disability Ministry and Services -

Disaster Preparedness/Response -

Dothan Office - t) 334-793-3601 Celeste C Kelly, Dir.;

Emergency Assistance Program - t) 251-434-1500; 251-232-2531 Caroline Duncan, Prog. Mgr.;

Montgomery Office - t) 334-288-8890 Dcn. Raymond M. Gueret, Dir.;

St. Margaret's Services - Latonya Gamble, Prog. Supvr.;

Opelika Lee County - t) (334) 363-0698 Tyler Kirsch, Dir.;

Pregnancy Services -

2-B Choices for Women - t) 251-343-4636 2bchoices@bellsouth.net Ashley Thompson;

To Be Options for Pregnant Women - t) 251-923-3305 Deborah Gomillion, Prog. Mgr.;

Refugee Resettlement - t) 251-432-2727

Robertsdale Baldwin Office - t) 251-947-2293 Angela Hickey, Dir.;

St. Teresa of Calcutta Senior Ministry - Sabrina Joshi, Prog. Mgr.;

PARISHES, MISSIONS, AND CLERGY

STATE OF ALABAMA

ANDALUSIA

Christ the King - 508 Sanford Rd., Andalusia, AL 36420 t) 334-222-4808 ctkandalusia@gmail.com Rev. Bieu Van Nguyen, Pst.; Dcn. Robert D. Bailey;

ATMORE

St. Robert Bellarmine - 600 S. Main St., Atmore, AL 36502-2825 t) 251-368-3615 strobertparish@frontiernet.net Rev. Joseph M. C. Chacko (India), Pst.;

AUBURN

St. Michael - 1100 N. College St., Auburn, AL 36830 t) 334-887-5540; (334) 887-5573 parish@stmichaelsauburn.com www.stmichaelsauburn.com Rev. Msgr. Michael L. Farmer, Pst.; Rev. Peyton Plessala, Par. Vicar; Dcn. Paul W. Brown; Dcn. Hector Donastorg;

St. Michael Catholic School - (Grades PreK-3) t) (334) 887-5540 office@stmichaelcatholicschool.com Deborah A. Brooks, Prin.;

BAY MINETTE

St. Agatha Parish, Bay Minette - 1001 Hand Ave., Bay Minette, AL 36507 t) 251-937-8600 stagathabm@gmail.com Rev. Joseph M. C. Chacko (India), Pst.;

BAYOU LA BATRE

St. Margaret Parish, Bayou La Batre - 13790 S. Wintzell Ave., Bayou La Batre, AL 36509; Mailing: P. O. Box 365, Bayou La Batre, AL 36509 t) 251-824-2415 fleetblessing@gmail.com www.stmargaretparish.org Rev. Michael Long Vu, SVD, Pst.;

BON SECOUR

Our Lady of Bon Secour Parish - 17266 County Rd. 49 S., Bon Secour, AL 36511; Mailing: 10800 Saint John's Ln., c/o St. John Parish, Foley, AL 36535 t) 251-965-7719 stjohnmagspg@gulftel.com (Mission of St. John the Baptist Parish, Magnolia Springs) Rev. Nicholas J. Napolitano, Pst.;

BREWTON

St. Maurice Parish, Brewton - 202 E. Jackson St., Brewton, AL 36427-0206; Mailing: P.O. Box 206, Brewton, AL 36427-0206 t) 251-867-5189 c) 251-769-3324 saintmauricebrewton.org Rev. Patrick J. Madden, Pst.; Dcn. Stephen A Tidwell;

BROMLEY

St. John Mission Parish, Bromley - 7488 Herman Sledge Rd., Bromley, AL 36507; Mailing: P.O. Box 1497, Daphne, AL 36526-1497 t) 251-239-8200 Rev. Lito J. Capeding, Pst.;

BUTLER

St. John the Evangelist - 401 E. Pushmataha St., Butler, AL 36904; Mailing: PO Box 70, Grove Hill, AL 36451 t) 251-275-3665 Rev. Travis J. Burnett, Pst.; CRP Stds.: 14

CAMDEN

St. Joseph Mission Parish, Camden - 302 Whiskey Run Rd., Camden, AL 36726; Mailing: 565 Whetstone St,, Monroeville, AL 36460 t) 251-575-2644 annuncat@frontiernet.net (Mission of Annunciation Parish, Monroeville) Rev. Stephen C. Hellman, Pst.;

CHASTANG

St. Peter the Apostle - 16650 Hwy. 43, Chastang, AL 36560; Mailing: P.O. Box 456, Mount Vernon, AL 36560 t) 251-829-5134 stpetertheapostle19@gmail.com Rev. Augustin Iruthayasamy, IVDei, Par. Admin.;

CHICKASAW

St. Thomas the Apostle - 251 N. Craft Hwy., Chickasaw, AL 36611 t) 251-456-7931; 251-452-9837 (Office) office@stthomastheapostlecatholicchurch.com stthomastheapostlecatholicchurch.com Very Rev. William P Saucier, Pst.; Dcn. James H. Bullock; Dcn. Charles P Groves; CRP Stds.: 22

CITRONELLE

St. Thomas Aquinas Parish, Citronelle - 8025 State St., Citronelle, AL 36522; Mailing: P.O. Box 61, Citronelle, AL 36522 t) 251-866-7505 Rev. John P. Coghlan, Pst.;

CLIO

Our Lady of Guadalupe Parish - 1022 Brundridge St., Clio, AL 36017; Mailing: 1444 Hwy. 165, Fort Mitchell, AL 36856 t) 334-855-3148 clioguadalupe@gmail.com (Mission of St. Joseph Parish, Holy Trinity) Rev. David A. Hamm, S.T., Pst.; CRP Stds.: 70

CODEN

St. Michael Parish, Heron Bay - 15872 Heron Bay Loop Rd. E., Coden, AL 36523; Mailing: 9101 Dauphin Island Pkwy., Theodore, AL 36582 t) 251-973-2096 Rev. Daniel F. Good, Pst.;

St. Rose of Lima Parish, Mon Luis Island - 2951 Durette Ave. (Mon Luis Island), Coden, AL 36523 t) 251-973-2592; 251-973-5032 stroseonmonluis@gmail.com; leocejas@yahoo.com www.stroseonmonlouis.com Rev. Msgr. Leonardo C. Guadalquiver, Pst.;

DAPHNE

Christ the King Parish, Daphne - 711 College Ave., Daphne, AL 36526 t) 251-626-5963 (CRP); 251-626-2343 office@ctkdaphne.org Rev. Matthew J. O'Connor, Pst.; Rev. Gabriel V Mills, Par. Vicar; Dcn. Walter J. Crimmins; Dcn. C. Theodore Schmidt; Dcn. G. Mathew Pope; Sam Di Benedetto, DRE;

Christ the King Parish, Daphne School - (Grades PreK-8) 1503 Main St., Daphne, AL 36526; Mailing: 708 Dryer Ave., Daphne, AL 36526 t) 251-626-1692 garlock@ctkcsdaphne.org Jacklyn M Garlock, Prin.;

Shrine of the Holy Cross Parish, Daphne - 612 Main St., Daphne, AL 36526; Mailing: P.O. Box 1497, Daphne, AL 36526 t) 251-621-9793 Rev. Lito J. Capeding, Pst.;

DAUPHIN ISLAND

St. Edmund-by-the-Sea Parish, Dauphin Island - 823 Cadillac Ave., Dauphin Island, AL 36528; Mailing: P.O. Box 6, Dauphin Island, AL 36528 t) 251-895-5454 stedmundauphin@gmail.com Rev. Msgr. Leonardo C. Guadalquiver, Pst.;

DOTHAN

St. Columba Parish, Dothan - 2700 W. Main St., Dothan, AL 36301 t) 334-792-3065 (CRP); 334-793-5802 office@stcolumbacatholic.com Rev. James E. Dane, Pst.; Rev. Jose J. Paillacho, Par. Vicar; Dcn. Joseph D. Mueller;

ELBERTA

St. Bartholomew Parish, Elberta - 12795 Illinois St., Elberta, AL 36530 t) 251-986-8142 www.stbartselberta.com Rev. Wayne M. Youngman, Pst.; Dcn. James C. Brewer; Dcn. Kenneth J. Kaiser; CRP Stds.: 22

ENTERPRISE

St. John - 123 Heath St., Enterprise, AL 36330 t) 334-347-6751 office@stjohnenterprise.org Rev. Zachary L. Greenwell, Pst.; Dcn. Cesar A. Ortega Natal; Dcn. Alfonso M. Diaz-Rivera; Dcn. Karl L. Lukas;

St. John Catholic Montessori School - t) 334-347-0413 sjcmontessori@yahoo.com saintjohnmontessori.com Sandra P. Pellissier, Dir.;

EUFAULA

Holy Redeemer Parish, Eufaula - 515 W. Broad St., Eufaula, AL 36027 t) 334-687-3716 hredeemer2015@yahoo.com Very Rev. David M. Shoemaker, Pst.;

FAIRFORD

Our Lady of Sorrow Mission Parish, Fairford - 2157 Little Chestang Rd., Fairford, AL 36553; Mailing: P.O. Box 456, Mount Vernon, AL 36560 t) 251-829-5134 stpetertheapostle19@gmail.com (Mission of St. Peter the Apostle, Chastang) Rev. Augustin Iruthayasamy, IVDei, Par. Admin.;

FAIRHOPE

St. Lawrence Parish, Fairhope - 370 S. Section St., Fairhope, AL 36532 t) 251-928-5931 office@stlawrencefairhope.com www.stlawrencefairhope.com Rev. Steven T. Williams, Pst.; Rev. Augusty Puthanpura (India), Assoc. Pst.; Dcn. Francis A. Zieman; CRP Stds.: 199

FOLEY

St. John the Baptist - 10800 Saint John's Ln., Foley, AL 36535 t) 251-965-7719 office@stjohnms.com www.stjohnms.com Rev. Nicholas J. Napolitano, Pst.; CRP Stds.: 10

St. Margaret Queen of Scotland - 601 W. Laurel Ave., Foley, AL 36535 t) 251-943-4009 stmargaretofscotlandfoley@outlook.com Very Rev. Paul G. Zoghby, Pst.;

FORT MITCHELL

St. Joseph Parish Holy Trinity - 1444 Hwy. 165, Fort Mitchell, AL 36856 t) 334-855-3148 secretrary@holytrinityal.org Rev. David A. Hamm, S.T., Pst.; Rev. Raul A. Vasquez, S.T., Par. Vicar; Rev. Victor Manuel Perez, Par. Vicar; Rev. Bertin Glennon, S.T., Par. Vicar; Bro. Senan Gallagher, S.T.; CRP Stds.: 59

Blessed John XXIII Center - 16 Sussex St., Hurtsboro, AL 36860; Mailing: P.O. Box 117, Hurtsboro, AL 36860 t) 334-667-7770 Catherine Metzler, Dir.;

St. Joseph Child Development Center - t) 334-855-4675 saintjosephcdc@gmail.com Anjeanette Lawson, Prin.;

GENEVA

St. Mary Mission Parish, Geneva - 100 S. Commerce St., Geneva, AL 36340; Mailing: 123 Heath St., Enterprise, AL 36330 t) 334-797-6920 zgreenwell@mobarch.org (Mission of St. John Parish, Enterprise) Rev. Zachary L. Greenwell, Pst.;

GRAND BAY

St. John the Baptist - 12450 Hwy. 188, Grand Bay, AL 36541; Mailing: P.O. Box 417, Grand Bay, AL 36541 t) 251-865-6902 stjohngrandbay@gmail.com Rev. Selvam Arputharaj, HGN, Pst.; Dcn. William H. Graham;

GREENVILLE

St. Elizabeth - 407 E. Walnut St., Greenville, AL 36037 t) 334-382-6203 Rev. Bieu Van Nguyen, Pst.; Dcn. Robert D. Bailey;

GROVE HILL

Sacred Heart - 19730 Hwy. 43, Grove Hill, AL 36451; Mailing: P.O. Box 70, Grove Hill, AL 36451 t) 251-275-3665 Rev. Travis J. Burnett, Pst.; CRP Stds.: 8

GULF SHORES

Our Lady of the Gulf Parish, Gulf Shores - 308 E. 22nd Ave., Gulf Shores, AL 36542 t) 251-968-7062 office@olgal.org www.olgal.org Rev. David P. Carucci, Pst.; Suzette Taylor, DRE;

LILLIAN

St. Joseph - 12688 Santa Piedro St., Lillian, AL 36549 t) 251-962-3649 office@saint-josephs.org www.saint-josephs.org Rev. Alwin P. Legaspi, Pst.;

MOBILE

Cathedral-Basilica of the Immaculate Conception Parish, Mobile - 2 S. Claiborne St., Mobile, AL 36602; Mailing: 307 Conti St., Mobile, AL 36602 t) 251-434-1565 office@mobilecathedral.org Most Rev. Thomas J. Rodi, Pst.; Rev. Msgr. William J. Skoneki, Rector; Dcn. George F. Ralph; Dcn. John J. Archer; Rev. Victor P. Ingalls, In Res.;

Cathedral & Rectory - 400 Government St., Mobile, AL 36602 t) (251) 434-1586

The Portier House - 307 Conti St., Mobile, AL 36602 t) (251) 434-1565 www.mobilecathedral.org (Historic home of first bishop of Mobile) Rev. Msgr. William J. Skoneki, Rector;

St. Catherine of Siena - 2605 Springhill Ave., Mobile, AL 36607 t) 251-473-1415 stcathmob@gmail.com Rev. Frederick G. Boni, Pst.; Dcn. Andrew M. Pitts;

Corpus Christi Parish, Mobile - 6300 McKenna Dr., Mobile, AL 36608 t) 251-342-1852 office@corpuschristiparish.com www.corpuschristiparish.com Rev. Patrick J. Arensberg, Pst.; Rev. Alexander M Crow, Par. Vicar;

Corpus Christi Parish School - (Grades PreK-8) t) 251-342-5474 school@corpuschristiparish.com www.corpuschristiparish.com/school Kristy F. Martin, Prin.; Sally S McKenna, Vice Prin.;

St. Dominic Parish, Mobile - 4156 Burma Rd., Mobile, AL 36693 t) 251-661-5130 Rev. Patrick R. Driscoll, Pst.; Dcn. Wiley J Christian; Dcn. Robert E. Kirby; Dcn. Aldon O. Ward; Rev. J. Francis Sofie, In Res.;

St. Dominic Parish, Mobile School - (Grades PreK-8) 4160 Burma Rd., Mobile, AL 36693 t) 251-661-5226 Laurie S. Michener, Prin.; Debra A. Peuschel, Vice Prin.;

Convent - 1201 Belle Chene Dr., Mobile, AL 36693 t) 251-661-3229 Sr. Anne Brady, RSM, Rel. Ord. Ldr.;

St. Francis Xavier Parish, Mobile - 2034 St. Stephens Rd., Mobile, AL 36617 t) 251-473-4975 Rev. Justin Isaac, H.G.N., Pst.;

Holy Family Parish, Mobile - 1400 Joyce Rd., Mobile, AL 36618 t) 251-344-0271 office@holyfamilymobile.com www.holyfamilymobile.com Rev. Mark I. Neske, Pst.; CRP Stds.: 6

St. Ignatius Parish, Mobile - 3704 Springhill Ave., Mobile, AL 36608 t) 251-342-9221 church@stignatius.org Rev. W. Bry Shields, Pst.; Rev. Francis Matiru, FMH, Par. Vicar; Dcn. T. Todd Martin; Dcn. William J. Harkins;

St. Ignatius Parish, Mobile School - (Grades PreK-8) 3650 Springhill Ave., Mobile, AL 36608 t) 251-342-5442 Tori Y. Miller, Prin.; Elizabeth Collins, Vice Prin.; Dorothy Beattie, Librn.;

Early Learning Center - 3650 Springhill Ave., Mobile, AL 36608 t) (251) 342-5442 Ingrid S Franklin, Dir.;

St. Joan of Arc Parish, Mobile - 1260 Elmira St., Mobile, AL 36604 t) 251-432-3505 office@stjoanofarc.net Very Rev. Stephen G. Vrazel, Pst.; Rev. Cecil R. Spotswood, Assoc. Pst.; Dcn. Douglas M. McEnery;

St. Joseph Parish, Maysville - 1703 Dublin St., Mobile, AL 36605 t) 251-473-3761 stjosephmaysville@josephite.com Rev. Bura Aloysius Koroba, S.S.J., Pst.; Dcn. Ronnie A. Hathorne;

Little Flower Parish, Mobile - 2053 Government St., Mobile, AL 36606 t) 251-478-3381 lfbulletin@littleflower.cc www.littleflowermobile.com Rev. John G. Lynes, Pst.; Dcn. Curt Crider; Dcn. Ronald Martin; Sr. Mary Joyce Bringer, C.S.J., Pst. Assoc.;

Little Flower Parish, Mobile School - (Grades PreK-8) 2103 Government St., Mobile, AL 36606 t) 251-479-5761 school@littleflower.cc Alesa Weiskopf, Prin.;

Convent - 411 Glenwood Ave., Mobile, AL 36606 t) 251-378-5761

St. Mary Parish, Mobile - 1453 Old Shell Rd., Mobile, AL 36604; Mailing: 106 Providence St., Mobile, AL 36604 t) 251-432-8678 mrnaman@stmarymobile.org; lwallace@stmarymobile.org www.stmarymobile.org Very Rev. Stephen G. Vrazel, Pst.; Rev. Cecil R. Spotswood, Par. Vicar; Dcn. Mark S. Thompson;

St. Mary Parish, Mobile School - (Grades PreK-8) 107 N. Lafayette St., Mobile, AL 36604 t) 251-433-9904 Debbie D. Ollis, Prin.; Sue Lyon, Librn.;

St. Matthew Parish, Mobile - 906 Garrity St., Mobile, AL 36605-4699 t) 251-432-4784 stmat9t@comcast.net Rev. Joseph M. Bolling, Pst.; Dcn. Joseph V. Connick;

St. Monica Parish, Mobile - 1131 Dauphin Island Pkwy., Mobile, AL 36605 t) 251-479-7360 Rev. Cu Minh Duong, Pst.;

Most Pure Heart of Mary Parish, Mobile - 304 Sengstak St., Mobile, AL 36603 t) 251-487-8891 (CRP); 251-432-3344 Rev. Bura Aloysius Koroba, S.S.J., Pst.; Dcn. James D. Bryant; Latanya Brown, DRE;

Our Lady of Lourdes Parish, Mobile - 1621 Boykin Blvd., Mobile, AL 36605 t) 251-479-9885 ollparish@att.net Rev. Prabhu Arockiasamy, HGN, Pst.; Dcn. Edward G. Connick;

Our Savior Parish, Mobile - 1801 Cody Rd. S., Mobile, AL 36695 t) 251-633-6762 office@oursaviorparish.org www.oursaviorparish.org Rev. David J. Tokarz, Pst.; Dcn. Jay F. Boyd; Dcn. Norman M. Gale; Dcn. Francis H. N. Tran;

St. Pius X Parish, Mobile - 217 S. Sage Ave., Mobile, AL 36606 t) 251-471-2449 spx@stpiustenth.com stpiustenth.com Rev. Johnny S. Savoie, Pst.; CRP Stds.: 37

St. Pius X Parish School - (Grades PreK-8) t) 251-473-5004 office@stpiusxmobile.com Lauren K. Alvarez, Prin.;

Prince of Peace Parish, Mobile - 454 Charleston St., Mobile, AL 36603 t) 251-432-2364 princeofpeace@bellsouth.net Rev. Christopher Matumbai Sialo, F.M.H., Pst.;

St. Vincent de Paul Parish, Mobile - 4980 St. Vincent Dr., Mobile, AL 36619 t) 251-661-3908 www.svdpmobile.com Rev. Msgr. James S. Kee, Pst.; Dcn. J. Douglas Sinchak; Dcn. Gary J Vrazel;

St. Vincent De Paul Daycare - t) 251-666-4066 Shauntel D Odom, Dir.;

MONROEVILLE

Annunciation - 565 Whetstone St., Monroeville, AL 36460 t) 251-575-2644 annuncat@frontiernet.net Rev. Stephen C. Hellman, Pst.;

St. Joseph - 302 Whiskey Run Rd., Camden, AL 36726 t) (251) 575-2644

MONTGOMERY

St. Andrew Kim Taegon Parish, Montgomery - 433 Clayton St., Montgomery, AL 36104 t) 334-430-6453 Rev. Dongsik Lee, Pst.;

St. Bede the Venerable Catholic Church - 3870 Atlanta Hwy., Montgomery, AL 36109 t) 334-272-3463 Rev. Alejandro E. Valladares, Pst.; Rev. Connor R. Plessala, Par. Vicar; Dcn. Michael Castanza;

Montgomery Catholic Preparatory School - St. Bede Campus - (Grades PreK-6) 3850 Atlanta Hwy., Montgomery, AL 36109 t) 334-272-3033 montgomerycatholic.org Laurie A. Gulley, Prin.;

The City of St. Jude Parish, Montgomery - 2048 W. Fairview Ave., Montgomery, AL 36108 t) 334-265-6791 parish@cityofstjude.org www.cityofstjude.org Rev. Andrew B Jones, Pst.; Dcn. Clarence E. Darrington; Dcn. Deo G. McMeans; CRP Stds.: 15

Holy Spirit Parish, Montgomery - 8570 Vaughn Rd., Montgomery, AL 36117 t) 334-277-5631 office@holyspiritmgm.org; dre@holyspiritmgm.org www.holyspiritmgm.org Rev. Sherwin C. Monteron, Pst.; Rev. Patrick J. Gilbreath, Par. Vicar; Dcn. G. David Ray; Dcn. Raymond M. Gueret; Rev. Michael J. Sreboth, In Res.;

Montgomery Catholic Preparatory School - Holy Spirit Campus - (Grades PreK-6) 8580 Vaughn Rd., Montgomery, AL 36117 t) 334-649-4404 www.montgomerycatholic.org Nancy H. Foley, Prin.;

St. John the Baptist Parish, Montgomery - 543 S. Union St., Montgomery, AL 36104; Mailing: P.O. Box 95, Montgomery, AL 36104 t) 334-288-2850 Rev. Msgr. Juan R. Celzo, Pst.;

Our Lady Queen of Mercy Parish, Montgomery - 4421 Narrow Lane Rd., Montgomery, AL 36116; Mailing: P.O. Box 95, Montgomery, AL 36101 t) 334-288-2850 Rev. Msgr. Juan R. Celzo, Pst.;

St. Peter - 219 Adams Ave., Montgomery, AL 36104 t) 334-262-7304 secretary@stpetermontgomery.com www.stpetermontgomery.net Rev. Saleth Mariadoss, Pst.; Dcn. Jerry A. Conrad; Dcn. James R. Labadie;

Resurrection Catholic Church - 2815 Forbes Rd., Montgomery, AL 36110 t) 334-263-4221 parishoffice@rcmsouth.org www.rcmsouth.org Rev. Manuel B. Williams, C.R., Pst.; CRP Stds.: 42

MOUNT VERNON

St. Cecilia Parish, Mt. Vernon - 1305 Military Rd., Mount Vernon, AL 36560; Mailing: P.O. Box 847, Mount Vernon, AL 36560 t) 251-866-7505 Rev. John P. Coghlan, Pst.;

OPELIKA

St. Mary of the Mission Parish, Opelika - 1000 Fourth Ave., Opelika, AL 36801 t) 334-749-8359 stmarysopelika@gmail.com www.stmaryopelika.org Rev. Gilbert T. Pierre, Pst.;

ORANGE BEACH

St. Thomas by the Sea - 26547 Perdido Beach Blvd., Orange Beach, AL 36561; Mailing: P.O. Box 1190, Orange Beach, AL 36561 t) 251-981-8132 parishoffice@stthomasbythesea.com www.stthomasbythesea.org Rev. Paul Vincent Ravi Iruthayasamy, HGN, Pst.; Dcn. Stephen R. Seymour;

ORRVILLE

Immaculate Conception Parish, Orrville - 13663 AL Hwy. 22 W., Orrville, AL 36767; Mailing: P.O. Box 248, Orrville, AL 36767 t) (802) 922-3777 Rev. Stephen William Hornat, S.S.E., Pst.;

OZARK

St. John the Evangelist Parish, Ozark - 475 Camilla Ave., Ozark, AL 36361; Mailing: P.O. Box 1008, Ozark, AL 36361 t) 334-774-6826 stjozark@gmail.com sjccozark.weconnect.com Rev. Christopher G. Boutin, Pst.; Dcn. Joseph L. Pattberg;

PHENIX CITY

St. Patrick Parish, Phenix City - 1502 Broad St., Phenix City, AL 36867-0147 t) 334-298-9025 stpats123@gmail.com stpatsphenixcity.org Rev. David A. Hamm, S.T., Pst.; Rev. Bertin Glennon, S.T., Par. Vicar; Rev. Victor Manuel Perez, Par. Vicar; Rev. Raul A. Vasquez, S.T., Par. Vicar;

PRATTVILLE

St. Joseph Parish, Prattville - 511 N. Memorial Dr., Prattville, AL 36067 t) 334-365-8680 x212 (CRP); 334-365-8680 www.stjosephprattville.org Rev. Michael Dennis Irwin, Pst.;

PRICHARD

St. James Major - 714 N. College St., Prichard, AL 36610 t) 251-456-6842 Rev. Godwin B Imoru, Pst.;

Our Mother of Mercy Parish, Mobile - 805 East St., Prichard, AL 36610; Mailing: PO Box 10306, Mobile, AL 36610 t) 251-473-4975 Rev. Justin Isaac, H.G.N., Pst.;

ROBERTSDALE

St. Patrick Parish, Robertsdale - 23035 State Hwy. 59 N., Robertsdale, AL 36567 t) 251-947-5054 c.pinkertspcc@gmail.com www.stpatcatholic.com Rev. James N. Morrison, Pst.; Dcn. Stephen M. Kingsmore;

St. Patrick Parish, Robertsdale School - (Grades PreK-8) 23070 State Hwy. 59 N, Robertsdale, AL 36567; Mailing: P.O. Box 609, Robertsdale, AL 36567 t) 251-947-7395 www.school.stpatcatholic.com Sr. Margaret Harte, P.B.V.M., Prin.;

SELMA

Our Lady Queen of Peace Parish, Selma - 309 Washington St., Selma, AL 36703 t) 334-874-8931 Rev. Stephen William Hornat, S.S.E., Pst.; Gabe Norton, DRE;

SEMMES

Holy Name of Jesus Parish, Semmes - 2275 Snow Rd. N., Semmes, AL 36575 t) 251-649-4794 office@hnjcatholic.com hnjcatholic.com Rev. Msgr. Stephen E. Martin, Pst.; Dcn. Charles L. Drake;

SPANISH FORT

Blessed Francis Xavier Seelos Parish, Malbis - 31122 US Hwy. 31, Spanish Fort, AL 36527 t) 251-288-4500 francisxseelos@gmail.com www.francisxseelos.org Rev. James J. Cink, Pst.; Dcn. Steven L. Nelson;

TALLASSEE

St. Vincent de Paul Parish, Tallassee - 620 Gilmer Ave., Tallassee, AL 36078 t) 334-283-2169 c) 251-599-4597 stvincent620@gmail.com stvincent-tallasssee.org Rev. Mateusz K. Rudzik, Pst.; CRP Stds.: 60

THEODORE

St. Philip Neri Parish, Belle Fontaine - 9101 Dauphin Island Pkwy., Theodore, AL 36582 t) 251-973-2096 loweralabamacatholic.com Rev. Daniel F. Good, Pst.; Dcn. James L. Scott;

TROY

St. Martin of Tours - 725 Elba Hwy., Troy, AL 36079 t) 334-566-2630 stmartintroyalabama@gmail.com Rev. Christopher G. Boutin, Pst.; Dcn. David R. Newell;

TUSKEGEE INSTITUTE

St. Joseph - 2007 W. Montgomery Rd., Tuskegee Institute, AL 36088 c) 251-599-4597 stjosephtuskegee@gmail.com stjoseph-tuskegee.org Rev. Mateusz K. Rudzik, Pst.; Dcn. Stanley B. Maxwell;

UNION SPRINGS

St. Pius X Parish - 308 Kennon St., Union Springs, AL 36089; Mailing: 515 W. Broad St., Eufaula, AL 36027 t) 334-687-3716 (Mission of Holy Redeemer Parish, Eufaula) Very Rev. David M. Shoemaker, Pst.;

WEST MOUNT VERNON

St. Theresa Parish, West Mount Vernon - 1875 Hwy. 96, West Mount Vernon, AL 36560; Mailing: P.O. Box 61, Citronelle, AL 36522 t) 251-866-7505 Rev. John P. Coghlan, Pst.;

WETUMPKA

Our Lady of Guadalupe Parish, Wetumpka - 545 White Rd., Wetumpka, AL 36092; Mailing: P.O. Box 479, Elmore, AL 36025 t) 334-567-0047 olgoffice@ologchurch.org ologchurch.org Rev. James N. Dean, Pst.; Rev. Msgr. F. Charles Troncale, In Res.;

WHISTLER

St. Bridget - 3625 W. Main St., Whistler, AL 36612 t) 251-457-6847; (251) 452-9837 office@stthomastheapostlecatholicchurch.com stthomastheapostlecatholicchurch.com Very Rev. William P Saucier, Pst.; Dcn. James H. Bullock; Dcn. Charles P Groves; Rev. Eamon Miley, In Res.;

SCHOOLS: PRESCHOOL THRU HIGH SCHOOL

SCHOOLS

STATE OF ALABAMA

ELBERTA

St. Benedict School - (DIO) (Grades PreK-8) 12786 S. Illinois St., Elberta, AL 36530 t) 251-986-8143 www.saintbenedict.net Dr. Kathy McCool, Prin.;

MONTGOMERY

Resurrection Early Childhood Center and Resurrection Catholic School - (PRV) (Grades PreK-8) 2815 Forbes Dr., Montgomery, AL 36110 t) 334-230-1970 Dr. Martha Pettway, Prin.;

HIGH SCHOOLS

STATE OF ALABAMA

FAIRHOPE

St. Michael Catholic High School - (Grades 9-12) 11732 Saint Michael Way, Fairhope, AL 36532 t) 251-459-0210 pknapstein@mobarch.org www.stmichaelchs.org Paul Thomas Knapstein, Prin.; Stds.: 353; Lay Tchrs.: 31

MOBILE

McGill-Toolen Catholic High School - (DIO) (Grades 9-12) 1501 Old Shell Rd., Mobile, AL 36604 t) 251-445-2900 shieldsb@mcgill-toolen.org www.mcgill-toolen.org Michelle T. Haas, Prin.; Rev. W. Bry Shields, Pres.;

Catholic Youth Organization - 11 N. Lafayette St., Mobile, AL 36604; Mailing: P.O. Box 6955, Mobile, AL 36660 t) 251-441-0805 David A. Weems, Dir.;

MONTGOMERY

Montgomery Catholic Preparatory School - (DIO) (Grades PreK-12) 5350 Vaughn Rd., Montgomery, AL 36116 t) 334-272-7220 jcastanza@montgomerycatholic.org montgomerycatholic.org Eileen Aaron, Prin.; Justin Castanza, Pres.; Mindy Walski, Librn.; Laura Reilly, Vice Prin., Academic Affairs; Julie Wood, MS Asst. Prin.;

High School Campus - (Grades PreK-12) t) (334) 272-7220

Middle School Campus - (Grades PreK-12) t) 334-272-2465

INSTITUTIONS LOCATED IN DIOCESE

ASSOCIATIONS [ASN]

MOBILE

Catholic High Schools Alumni Association of Mobile - 1501 Old Shell Rd., Mobile, AL 36604 t) 251-445-2913 pritchl@mcgill-toolen.org www.mcgill-toolen.org

Lauren Pritchett, Dir.;

CAMPUS MINISTRY / NEWMAN CENTERS [CAM]

AUBURN

Auburn University Campus Ministry - 115 Mitcham Ave., Auburn, AL 36830 t) 334-209-1711 rudiaucatholic@gmail.com www.aucatholic.org Rudi A. DiPrima, Campus Min.;

MOBILE

Sacred Heart of Jesus Catholic Student Center at University of South Alabama - 6051 Old Shell Rd., Catholic Student Center, Mobile, AL 36608 t) 251-343-3662 sacredheart@csajags.com www.csajags.com Rev. Norbert K. Jurek, Chap.;

Spring Hill College Campus Ministry - 4000 Dauphin St., Mobile, AL 36608-1791 t) 251-380-3495 campusministry@shc.edu kudzu.shc.edu/campusministry Colleen F. Lee, Campus Min.;

MONTGOMERY

Auburn University Montgomery Campus Ministry - 8570 Vaughn Rd., Holy Spirit Parish, Montgomery, AL 36117 t) 334-277-5631 Rev. Sherwin C. Monteron, Pst.;

SELMA

Marion Military Institute Campus Ministry - 309 Washington St., Selma, AL 36703 t) 334-874-8931 Rev. Stephen William Hornat, S.S.E., Pst.;

TROY

Mother Teresa Catholic Newman Ministry at Troy University - 725 Elba Hwy., Troy, AL 36079 t) 334-566-2630 Rev. Christopher G. Boutin, Pst.;

TUSKEGEE INSTITUTE

Tuskegee University Newman Center - 2007 Montgomery Rd., Tuskegee Institute, AL 36088 t) 334-727-2710 mrudzik@mobarch.org; stjosephtuskegee@gmail.com Rev. Mateusz K. Rudzik, Chap.;

COLLEGES & UNIVERSITIES [COL]

MOBILE

Spring Hill College - 4000 Dauphin St., Mobile, AL 36608 t) 251-380-4000 www.shc.edu Dr. Mary H. Van Brunt, Pres.;

CONVENTS, MONASTERIES, AND RESIDENCES FOR WOMEN [CON]

FORT MITCHELL

Blessed Trinity Shrine Retreat and Cenacle - 107 Holy Trinity Rd., Fort Mitchell, AL 36856 t) 334-855-4474 btsr@msbt.org www.msbt.org/btsr Elisabeth Donner, Dir.; Srs.: 3

MARBURY

Dominican Monastery of St. Jude (St. Jude Monastery) - 143 County Rd. 20 E., Marbury, AL 36051 t) 205-755-1322 stjudemonastery@aol.com; contact@marburydominicannuns.org www.marburydominicannuns.org Legal Title: Dominican Sisters of the Perpetual Rosary, Inc. Mother Mary of the Precious Blood Gracey, O.P., Prioress; Srs.: 7

MOBILE

Convent of the Sisters of Mercy of the Americas South Central Community - 101 Wimbledon Dr. W., Mobile, AL 36608 t) 251-344-1377 www.mercysistersbalt.com Sr. Mary Chabanel Finnegan, RSM, Dir.; Sr. Deborah Kennedy, RSM, In Res.; Srs.: 13

Convent of the Sisters of Mercy of the Americas South Central Community - 172 N. Lafayette St., Mobile, AL 36604 t) 251-432-3178 Sr. Elizabeth Ann Cannon, RSM, Rel. Ord. Ldr.;

Monastery of Discalced Carmelite Nuns - 716 Dauphin Island Pkwy., Mobile, AL 36606 c) 251-401-1223 bradbmb55@gmail.com; carmelmobile.viet@gmail.com www.carmelmobileal.com Mother Catherine Mary Nguyen, Prioress; Srs.: 12

Visitation Monastery and Retreat House - 2300 Spring Hill Ave., Mobile, AL 36607 t) 251-473-2321 www.visitationmonasterymobile.org Mother Margaret Mary Rumpf, VHM, Supr.; Srs.: 20

SELMA

Sisters of St. Joseph of Rochester - 2511 Summerfield Rd., Selma, AL 36701 t) 334-526-2536 knavarra@ssjrochester.org www.ssjrochester.org Srs.: 2

ENDOWMENTS / FOUNDATIONS / TRUSTS [EFT]

MOBILE

Catholic Foundation of the Archdiocese of Mobile, Inc. - 356 Government St., Mobile, AL 36602; Mailing: PO Box 230, Mobile, AL 36601 t) 251-434-1556 sroh@mobarch.org www.catholicfoundationalabama.org Shannon D Roh, Exec.;

McGill Institute Charitable Trust - 400 Government St., Mobile, AL 36602 t) 251-434-1548 Michele C. Smith, Exec.;

McGill-Toolen Foundation, Inc. - 1501 Old Shell Rd., Mobile, AL 36604 t) (251) 445-2939 woodj@mcgill-toolen.org Jenna L Wood, Dir.;

Providence Foundation - 6701 Airport Blvd. B 227, Mobile, AL 36608; Mailing: P.O. Box 850429, Mobile, AL 36608 t) 251-266-2050 don.king@ascension.org; loraine.brown@ascension.org Don King, CEO; Loraine Brown, Chief Mission Integration Officer;

HOSPITALS / HEALTH SERVICES [HOS]

MOBILE

Gulf Coast Health System - 6801 Airport Blvd., Mobile, AL 36608; Mailing: P.O. Box 850429, Mobile, AL 36608 t) 251-266-1660 don.king@ascension.org; loraine.brown@ascension.org Don King, CEO; Loraine Brown, Chief Mission Integration Officer;

Providence Hospital - 6801 Airport Blvd., Mobile, AL 36685; Mailing: P.O. Box 850429, Mobile, AL 36685 t) 251-266-1600 don.king@ascension.org; loraine.brown@ascension.org www.providencehospital.org Don King, CEO; Loraine Brown, Chief Mission Integration Officer; Bed Capacity: 302; Asstd. Annu.: 142,543; Staff: 1,131

Seton Medical Management, Inc. - 6801 Airport Blvd., Mobile, AL 36608; Mailing: P.O. Box 850429, Mobile, AL 36608 t) 251-266-2861 loraine.brown@ascension.org; don.king@ascension.org Don King, CEO; Loraine Brown, Chief Mission Integration Officer; Asstd. Annu.: 11,362; Staff: 31

MISCELLANEOUS [MIS]

ATMORE

Confraternity of Intercessors for Priests in the Heart of St. Joseph - 600 S. Main St., c/o St. Robert Bellarmine Parish, Atmore, AL 36502 t) (251) 368-3615 matthewfivesix@hotmail.com www.intercessorsforpriests.com Confraternity currently on hiatus. David Kralik, Dir.;

FAIRHOPE

***Archangel Communications** - 399 S. Section St., Fairhope, AL 36533; Mailing: P.O. Box 1526, Fairhope, AL 36533 t) 251-928-2111 office@archangelradio.org Joseph M. Roszkowski, Pres.; Ellen Taylor, Exec.;

MOBILE

Allen Memorial Home, Inc. - 400 Government St., Mobile, AL 36601; Mailing: PO Box 230, Mobile, AL 36601 t) (251) 434-1548

Camp Cullen, Inc. - 400 Government St., Mobile, AL 36602 t) 251-434-1548 msmith@mobarch.org Rev. Msgr. William J. Skoneki, Pres.; Michele C. Smith, Treas.;

Sacred Heart Chapel (Battles Wharf) - 18673 Scenic Hwy. 98, Fairhope, AL 36532; Mailing: 352 Government St., Mobile, AL 36602 t) (251) 433-4138 info@holyspirithall.org Tex Phelps, Contact;

Catholic Cemeteries, Inc. - 400 Government St., Mobile, AL 36602 t) 251-434-1557 fyoung@mobarch.org mobarchcemeteries.org Frankie M Young, Admin.; J. Tilmon Brown, Dir.; Michele C. Smith, Treas.;

Catholic Cemetery of Mobile - 1700 Dr. Martin Luther King Ave., Mobile, AL 36617; Mailing: 400 Government St., Mobile, AL 36602 t) 251-479-5305 cemeteries@mobarch.org Frankie M. Young, Admin.;

St. Margaret Cemetery - 829 Columbus St., Montgomery, AL 36104; Mailing: 400 Government St., Mobile, AL 36602 cemeteries@mobarch.org Frankie M. Young, Admin.;

Catholic Scouting - Boy Scouts - 106 Providence St., St. Mary Parish, Mobile, AL 36604 t) 251-432-8678 svrazel@mobarch.org Very Rev. Stephen G. Vrazel, Chap.;

Catholic Social Services - 188 S. Florida St., Mobile, AL 36616; Mailing: P.O. Box 161229, Mobile, AL 36616 t) 251-434-1550 mdking@mobarch.org catholicsocialservicesmobile.com Marilyn D. King, Exec.;

St. Mary's Home, Mobile - 188 S. Florida St., Mobile, AL 36606 t) 251-434-1550 Marilyn D. King, Exec.;

Men of St. Joseph - 14 Midtown Park E., Mobile, AL 36606; Mailing: P.O. Box 160583, Mobile, AL 36616 c) 972-765-1235 www.menofstjoseph.com Jack McNichol, Chair;

Mobile Provincial Conference of Bishops and Priests' Councils - 400 Government St., Mobile, AL 36602 t) 251-434-1587 archbishop@mobarch.org Most Rev. Thomas J. Rodi;

***Providence Building Corporation Inc.** - 6801 Airport Blvd., Mobile, AL 36608 t) 251-266-1600 loraine.brown@ascension.org providencehospital.org Don King, CEO; Loraine Brown, Chief Mission Integration Officer;

Saint Serra Club of Mobile - 2768 N. Barksdale Dr., Mobile, AL 36606; Mailing: P.O. Box 6731, Mobile, AL 36660 t) 251-422-9060 dbarnett31@hotmail.com Danny Barnett, Dir.;

MONTGOMERY

Catholic Housing Authority of Montgomery, Inc. - 3721 Wares Ferry Rd., Montgomery, AL 36109; Mailing: 400 Government St., Mobile, AL 36602 t) (251) 434-1548 Michele C. Smith, Treas.;

Father Purcell Memorial Exceptional Children's Center, Inc. - 2048 W. Fairview Ave., Montgomery, AL 36108 t) 334-834-5590 Brenda F. Withers, Admin.;

St. Jude Apartments Inc. - 2048 W. Fairview Ave., Montgomery, AL 36108 t) 334-265-6791 msmith@mobarch.org Marilyn D. King, Exec.; Michele C. Smith, Treas.;

Resurrection Catholic Missions - 2815 Forbes Rd., Montgomery, AL 36110 t) 334-263-4221 info@rcmsouth.org Rev. Manuel B. Williams, C.R., Dir.;

Seton Haven Management Corporation - 3721 Wares Ferry Rd., Montgomery, AL 36109 t) 334-272-4000 setonhaven@bellsouth.net Brian Bonikowski, Pres.;

PHENIX CITY

Cursillo - 3009 3rd Ave., Phenix City, AL 36867 c) 706-326-7662 Rob Wilburn, Dir.;

SELMA

Edmundite Guild - 1428 Broad St., Selma, AL 36701; Mailing: P.O. Box 2114, Selma, AL 36702-2114 t) 800-681-9773 Society of St. Edmund, Inc. Chad McEachern, Pres.;

Fathers of St. Edmund, Southern Missions, Inc. - 1428 Broad St., Selma, AL 36701; Mailing: P.O. Box 2114, Selma, AL 36702-2114 t) 334-872-2359 chadm@edmunditemissions.org www.edmunditemissions.org Chad McEachern, Pres.;

MONASTERIES AND RESIDENCES FOR PRIESTS AND BROTHERS [MON]

FORT MITCHELL

St. Joseph Cenacle - 1444 Hwy. 165, Fort Mitchell, AL 36856 t) (334) 855-3148 Rev. Bertin Glennon, S.T.; Rev. David A. Hamm, S.T.; Rev. Victor Manuel Perez; Rev. Raul A. Vasquez, S.T.; Bro. Pierre Andral, S.T.; Bro. Senan Gallagher, S.T.; Bro. Ernesto Sandoval, S.T.; Brs.: 3; Priests: 4

MOBILE

***Divine Mercy Province of Heralds of Good News, Inc.** - 1 St. Louis St., Ste. 4000, c/o Lawrence J. Seiter, Mobile,

AL 36602; Mailing: PO Box 1336, Daphne, AL 36526 c) 251-278-4900 Rev. Selvam Arputharaj, HGN, Supr.; Priests: 4

Jesuits of Mobile, Inc. - 3966 Loyola Ln., Mobile, AL 36608; Mailing: 4000 Dauphin St., Spring Hill College, Mobile, AL 36608 t) 251-460-2167 rpoirier@shc.edu kudzu.shc.edu/jesuits Rev. Robert Poirier, SJ, Supr.; Rev. Jose Luis Mesa, S.J., Hispanic Min.; Rev. Christopher J. Viscardi, S.J., Div. Chair Theology & Philosophy; Rev. Michael A. Williams, S.J., Prof. Emeritus; Bro. Ferrell Blank, SJ, Facilities Dir. Emeritus; Brs.: 1; Priests: 4

SELMA

Fathers of St. Edmund Southern Missions, Inc. - 1423-A Broad St., Edmundite Res., Selma, AL 36701 t) (334) 874-8931 Rev. Stephen William Hornat, S.S.E., Rel. Ord. Ldr.; Priests: 1

NURSING / REHABILITATION / CONVALESCENCE / ELDERLY CARE [NUR]

MOBILE

Little Sisters of the Poor, Home For the Aged, Inc. - 1655 McGill Ave., Sacred Heart Res., Mobile, AL 36604 t) 251-476-6335 msmobile@littlesistersofthepoor.org; devmobile@littlesistersofthepoor.org www.littlesistersofthepoormobile.org Rev. Antony Kadavil, Chap.; Rev. Msgr. Kenneth J. Klepac, In Res.; Sr. Judith Mary Meredith, L.S.P., Supr.;

Mercy Life of Alabama - 2900 Springhill Ave., Mobile, AL 36607 t) 251-287-8420 dianeb@mercylifeal.com www.mercylifeal.com Diane Brown, Dir.;

MONTGOMERY

Seton Haven - 3721 Wares Ferry Rd., Montgomery, AL 36109 t) 334-272-4000 setonhaven@bellsouth.net A. Ann Alosi, Admin.; Brian Bonikowski, Pres.;

RETREAT HOUSES / RENEWAL CENTERS [RTR]

FAIRHOPE

Holy Spirit Ministries, Inc. - 18673 Scenic Hwy. 98, Fairhope, AL 36532; Mailing: P.O. Box 230, Mobile, AL 36601 t) 251-433-4138 info@holyspirithall.org holyspirithall.org/ Holy Spirit Hall at Camp Cullen. Rev. Steven T. Williams, Pres.; Tex Phelps, Dir.;

An asterisk (*) denotes an organization that has established tax-exempt status directly with the IRS and is not covered by the USCCB Group Ruling.

Diocese of Monterey in California

(Montereyensis in California)

MOST REVEREND DANIEL E. GARCIA, D.D.

Bishop of Monterey; ordained May 28, 1988; appointed Titular Bishop of Capsus and Auxiliary Bishop of Austin January 21, 2015; ordained March 3, 2015; appointed Fifth Bishop of Monterey November 27, 2018; installed January 29, 2019. bishop@dioceseofmonterey.org.

Pastoral Office: 425 Church St., Monterey, CA 93940. T: 831-373-4345; F: 831-373-1175.

ESTABLISHED DECEMBER 14, 1967.

Square Miles 21,916.

Comprises the Counties of Monterey, San Benito, San Luis Obispo and Santa Cruz in the State of California.

Legal Titles: Diocese of Monterey in California; The Roman Catholic Bishop of Monterey, California, a Corporation Sole. Diocese of Monterey Parish & School Operating Corp.; The Bishop Harry A. Clinch Endowment Fund of the Diocese of Monterey; Catholic Charities of the Diocese of Monterey (Corporation); Ave Maria Convalescent Hospital, Inc.; St. Francis High School; Salesian College Preparatory; Bishop Harry A. Clinch Trust Fund; The Roman Catholic Bishop of Monterey Irrevocable Real Property Charitable Trust; The Diocese of Monterey Parish & School Operating Corporation Irrevocable Real Property Charitable Trust; Bishop Sylvester Ryan Tuition Opportunity Program Trust.

For legal titles of parishes and diocesan institutions, consult the Pastoral Office.

STATISTICAL OVERVIEW

Personnel

Bishop....1
Retired Bishops....1
Priests: Diocesan Active in Diocese....64
Priests: Diocesan Active Outside Diocese....3
Priests: Retired, Sick or Absent....31
Number of Diocesan Priests....98
Religious Priests in Diocese....31
Total Priests in your Diocese....129
Extern Priests in Diocese....11
Ordinations:
Diocesan Priests....2
Transitional Deacons....3
Permanent Deacons in Diocese....32
Total Brothers....12
Total Sisters....49

Parishes

Parishes....46
With Resident Pastor:
Resident Diocesan Priests....42
Resident Religious Priests....3
Without Resident Pastor:
Administered by Priests....1
Missions....7
Professional Ministry Personnel:
Brothers....12
Sisters....42
Lay Ministers....1

Welfare

Catholic Hospitals....1
Total Assisted....188,326
Homes for the Aged....1
Total Assisted....206
Special Centers for Social Services....8
Total Assisted....32,000

Educational

Diocesan Students in Other Seminaries....6
Total Seminarians....6
High Schools, Diocesan and Parish....2
Total Students....460
High Schools, Private....3
Total Students....892
Elementary Schools, Diocesan and Parish....9
Total Students....2,175
Elementary Schools, Private....3
Total Students....680
Catechesis/Religious Education:
High School Students....3,318
Elementary Students....5,678
Total Students under Catholic Instruction....13,209
Teachers in Diocese:
Priests....2
Brothers....1
Sisters....3
Lay Teachers....274

Vital Statistics

Receptions into the Church:
Infant Baptism Totals....4,872
Minor Baptism Totals....227
Adult Baptism Totals....75
Received into Full Communion....215
First Communions....2,480
Confirmations....1,702
Marriages:
Catholic....559
Interfaith....68
Total Marriages....627
Deaths....1,334
Total Catholic Population....371,000
Total Population....1,072,786

ADMINISTRATION

Vicar General - t) 831-373-4345 Very Rev. Miguel Angel Grajeda (mgrajeda@dioceseofmonterey.org); Nicole Wales, Exec. Asst. (nwales@dioceseofmonterey.org);
Vicar for Priests - t) (831) 373-4345 Very Rev. Fredy Calvario (fcalvario@dioceseofmonterey.org); Nicole Wales, Exec. Asst. (nwales@dioceseofmonterey.org);
Chancellor and COO - t) 831-373-4345 Dcn. Hugo Patino (hpatino@dioceseofmonterey.org); Leticia Flores-McPherson, Exec. Asst. (lmcpherson@dioceseofmonterey.org);
Vice Chancellor - t) 831-373-4345 Dcn. David R. Ford (dford@dioceseofmonterey.org);
Pastoral Office - t) 831-373-4345 Bernardine Johnson Parry, Office Mgr. (bjohnson@dioceseofmonterey.org);

OFFICES AND DIRECTORS

Archives & Records - t) 831-373-2127 Kevin J. Kiper, Archivist (kkiper@dioceseofmonterey.org);
California Missions - t) 831-373-4345 x203 Jewel Gentry, Coord. (jgentry@dioceseofmonterey.org);
Campus Ministry - t) 831-373-4345 Dcn. David R. Ford, Dir. (dford@dioceseofmonterey.org);
Catechetical Ministries - t) 831-373-1335 Tish Scargill, Dir. (tscargill@dioceseofmonterey.org); Terry Burrows, Assoc. Dir. (tburrows@dioceseofmonterey.org);
Catholic Campaign for Human Development - t) 831-645-2845 Dcn. Warren E. Hoy, Dir. (whoy@dioceseofmonterey.org);
Catholic Relief Services - t) 831-373-1335 Tish Scargill, Dir. (tscargill@dioceseofmonterey.org); Dcn. Warren E. Hoy, Dir. (whoy@dioceseofmonterey.org);
Catholic Schools Department - t) 831-373-1608 Kimberly Cheng, Supt. (kcheng@dioceseofmonterey.org); Mary Joplin, Exec. Asst. (mjoplin@dioceseofmonterey.org);
Communications & Media Relations - t) 831-373-4345
Diocese of Monterey Catholic Cemeteries - t) 831-373-4345 Berenice Rosillo, Dir. (berenicer@domcemeteries.org);
Facilities - t) (831) 373-4345 Jewel Gentry, Dir. (jgentry@dioceseofmonterey.org);
Finance & Accounting - Clancy D'Angelo, Finance Officer (cdangelo@dioceseofmonterey.org); Kathy Aldrete, Controller (kaldrete@dioceseofmonterey.org); Erika Mazzoco, Exec. Asst. (emazzoco@dioceseofmonterey.org);
Human Resources - t) 831-373-4345 Stefanie Olsen, Acting Dir. (solsen@dioceseofmonterey.org); Angelica Gordon, Exec. Asst. (agordon@dioceseofmonterey.org);
Office of Divine Worship - t) 831-423-4973 Sr. Barbara Ann Long, O.P., Dir.;
Office of Hispanic & Migrant Ministry - t) 831-645-2835 Socorro Lagarda-Quiroz, Dir. (slagarda-quiroz@dioceseofmonterey.org); Petra Robles, Admin. Asst./Migrant Ministry Coord. (probles@dioceseofmonterey.org);
Office of Legal Counsel - t) 831-373-4345 Susan A. Mayer (smayer@dioceseofmonterey.org); Angelica Gordon, Exec. Asst. (agordon@dioceseofmonterey.org);
Office of Life, Justice and Charity - t) 831-645-2845 Dcn. Warren E. Hoy, Dir. (whoy@dioceseofmonterey.org);
Office of Marriage and Family Life - t) 831-645-2845 Dcn. Warren E. Hoy, Dir. (whoy@dioceseofmonterey.org);
Office of Stewardship and Development - t) 831-373-4345 Adriana Aquino-Diaz, Coord. Stewardship & Devel. (aaquino-diaz@dioceseofmonterey.org); Rosario Robles, AMA Asst. (rrobles@dioceseofmonterey.org);
Office of Vocations - t) 831-373-4345 Rev. Robert D. Sullivan, Dir. (rsullivan@dioceseofmonterey.org);
Pastoral Response Coordinator - t) 800-321-5220 Rio Castillo (rcastillo@dioceseofmonterey.org);
Permanent Diaconate - t) 831-373-4345 Dcn. David R. Ford, Vice Chancellor (dford@dioceseofmonterey.org); Ann Ventura, Exec. Asst. (aventura@dioceseofmonterey.org);
Pontifical Mission Societies - t) 831-373-4345 Dcn. Hugo Patino, Dir. (hpatino@dioceseofmonterey.org);
Pope Francis School of Ministry for Lay Formation - t) 831-373-1335 Dcn. David R. Ford, Vice Chancellor (dford@dioceseofmonterey.org); Ann Ventura, Prog. Coord. (aventura@dioceseofmonterey.org);
Protection of Children and Young People - t) 831-373-4345 Susan A. Mayer, Dir. (smayer@dioceseofmonterey.org); Terry Burrows, Assoc. (tburrows@dioceseofmonterey.org);
Respect Life - t) 831-722-5490 Rev. Derek Hughes, Dir. (derekmhughes@mac.com);
Vicar for Religious - t) 831-373-1335 Sr. Jaise Thomas, I.M. (jthomas@dioceseofmonterey.org);
Youth & Young Adult Ministries - t) 831-373-4345 x213 Rev. Gerson Espinosa, Dir. (gespinosa@dioceseofmonterey.org);

ADVISORY BOARDS, COMMISSIONS, COMMITTEES, AND COUNCILS

Administrative Committee Priests' Pension Plan - Rev. Paul R. Valdez, Chair;
Ave Maria Board - Clancy D'Angelo, Pres. (cdangelo@dioceseofmonterey.org);
The Bishop Harry A. Clinch Endowment Fund - Clancy D'Angelo, Finance Officer (cdangelo@dioceseofmonterey.org); Robert Semas, Pres.;
Catholic Charities Board - Nanci Perocchi, Pres.; Jordan Lewis, Vice. Pres.;
Clergy Personnel Board - Very Rev. Miguel Angel Grajeda, Chair (mgrajeda@dioceseofmonterey.org);
Finance Council - Mary Hubbell, Pres.;
Priestly Life & Ministry Committee - t) (831) 637-9212 Rev. Stephen Akers, Chair (frstephen@catholichollister.org);
Safety Committee - Susan A. Mayer, Chair (smayer@dioceseofmonterey.org);
St. Francis Central Coast Catholic High School, Inc. - Most Rev. Daniel E. Garcia, Chair;

CATHOLIC CHARITIES

Catholic Charities of the Diocese of Monterey - Angela Di Novella, Exec. Dir. (adinovella@catholiccharitiesdom.org); Allen Ganaden, Oper. & IT Admin. (aganaden@catholiccharitiesdom.org);
- **Catholic Charities - Administration, Family Supportive Services and Immigration** - t) 831-393-3110
  - **Catholic Charities - Salinas Office** - t) 831-422-0602
  - **Catholic Charities - San Luis Obispo Office** - t) 805-541-9110
  - **Catholic Charities - Santa Cruz Office** - t) 831-431-6939
  - **Catholic Charities - Watsonville Office** - t) 831-722-2675

DEANERIES

Monterey Peninsula Vicariate - Very Rev. Michael Volk, Vicar Urbane;
Salinas Area Vicariate - Very Rev. Fredy Calvario, Vicar Forane (fcalvario@dioceseofmonterey.org);
Salinas Valley Vicariate - Very Rev. Enrique Herrera, Vicar Forane;
San Benito County Vicariate - Very Rev. Heibar Castaneda, Vicar Forane;
San Luis Obispo County - Southeast Vicariate -
San Luis Obispo County - Southwest Vicariate -
Santa Cruz County - Northern Vicariate -
Santa Cruz County - Southern Vicariate - Very Rev. Jason Simas, Vicar Forane (jason@ourfatherslove.net);

TRIBUNAL

Office of The Tribunal - t) 831-373-1833 Cecilia Brennan, Dir. (cbrennan@dioceseofmonterey.org); Maria Gonzalez, Marriage Case Mgr. (mgonzalez@dioceseofmonterey.org);
- **Advocate** - Dcn. Warren E. Hoy;
- **Defenders of the Bond** - Rev. Pedro Espinoza; Ashley Subler;
- **Judges** - Rev. Kenneth J. Laverone, O.F.M.; Karla Felix-Rivera;
- **Judicial Vicar** - Rev. Robert Hayes;
- **Notary** - Maria Gonzalez;
- **Promoter of Justice** - Karla Felix-Rivera;

PARISHES, MISSIONS, AND CLERGY

STATE OF CALIFORNIA

APTOS

Resurrection - 7600 Soquel Dr., Aptos, CA 95003; Mailing: PO Box 87, Aptos, CA 95001 t) 831-688-4300 pfconway@sbcglobal.net; resurrectionparish@sbcglobal.net resurrection-aptos.org/ Rev. Romeo Evangelista, Pst.; Dcn. Patrick Conway, Pst. Assoc.; CRP Stds.: 102

ARROYO GRANDE

St. Patrick - 501 Fair Oaks Ave., Arroyo Grande, CA 93420 t) 805-489-2680 www.stpatsag.org Rev. Jose Alberto Vazquez-Martinez, Pst.; Rev. David Allen, Par. Vicar; Stacy Huck, DRE; CRP Stds.: 203
- **St. Patrick School** - (Grades PreK-8) 900 W. Branch St., Arroyo Grande, CA 93420 t) 805-489-1210 mhalderman@stpatschoolag.com www.stpatschoolag.com Maureen Halderman, Prin.; Stds.: 289; Lay Tchrs.: 13
- **St. Francis of Assisi** - 1711 Beach St., Oceano, CA 93445; Mailing: 501 Fair Oaks Ave., Arroyo Grande, CA 93420
- **Shamrock Thrift Shop** - 924 Grand Ave., Grover Beach, CA 93433 t) 805-481-0612 thriftstore@stpatschoolag.com

ATASCADERO

St. William's - 6410 Santa Lucia Rd., Atascadero, CA 93422 t) 805-466-0849 office@stwilliams.org; faithformation@stwilliams.org www.stwilliams.org Rev. Edwin Limpiado, Pst.; Rev. Dennis M. Peterson, Par. Vicar; CRP Stds.: 140

BOULDER CREEK

St. Michael's - 13005 Pine St., Boulder Creek, CA 95006 t) 831-338-6112 info@stmichaelschurchbc.org www.stmichaelschurchbc.org Rev. David Anthony Ramirez, Par. Admin.; Rebecca Guerrero, DRE; CRP Stds.: 3

CAMBRIA

Santa Rosa - 1174 Main St., Cambria, CA 93428 t) 805-924-1728 (CRP); 805-927-4816 santarosa.helper@gmail.com www.santarosaparish.org Very Rev. Miguel Angel Grajeda, Pst.; CRP Stds.: 116

CAPITOLA

St. Joseph - 435 Monterey Ave., Capitola, CA 95010 t) 831-475-8211 x40 saint-josephs.church Rev. Wayne Dawson, Pst.; CRP Stds.: 91

CARMEL

San Carlos Borromeo Basilica - 3080 Rio Rd., Carmel, CA 93923 t) 831-624-1271 reception@carmelmission.org; faithformation@carmelmission.org (Carmel Mission) Rev. Paul Patrick Murphy, Pst.; Rev. Reynaldo Esquivel, Par. Vicar; Dcn. Warren E. Hoy; CRP Stds.: 47
- **St. Francis of the Redwoods** - Hwy. 1, Big Sur, CA 93920 liturgy@carmelmission.org
- **Blessed Sacrament** - liturgy@carmelmisson.org Rev. Paul P. Murphy, Pst.;

CARMEL VALLEY

Our Lady of Mt. Carmel - 9 El Caminito Rd., Carmel Valley, CA 93924 t) 831-659-2224 olmc@ourladycarmelvalley.org Rev. Jhonnatan Flórez Carmona, Pst.; CRP Stds.: 39

CASTROVILLE

Our Lady of Refuge - 11140 Preston St., Castroville, CA 95012 t) 831-633-4015 info@olorc.org; manager@olorc.org www.olorc.org Rev. Rodrigo Paredes, Par. Admin.; Sr. Lourdina D Souza, DRE; Sr. Suchita Xalxo, DRE; CRP Stds.: 437

CAYUCOS

St. Joseph - 360 Park Ave., Cayucos, CA 93430; Mailing: P.O. Box 437, Cayucos, CA 93430 t) 805-995-3243 stjosephscayucos@gmail.com www.stjosephcayucos.org Rev. Pedro Espinoza, Pst.; Rev. Msgr. Charles G. Fatooh, Pst.;

CORRALITOS

Holy Eucharist - 527 Corralitos Rd., Corralitos, CA 95076 t) 831-722-5490 maura.holyeucharistca@yahoo.com; office.holyeucharistca@yahoo.com www.holyeucharistca.com Rev. Derek Hughes, Pst.; Maura Motta, DRE; CRP Stds.: 150

DAVENPORT

St. Vincent De Paul - 123 Marine View Ave., Davenport, CA 95017; Mailing: 544 W. Cliff Dr., Santa Cruz, CA 95060 t) 831-457-1868 x3 (CRP); 831-325-0035 Rev. Chummar Chirayath, OSJ, Par. Admin.; Josephine Gilbert, DRE;

FELTON

St. John's - 120 Russell Ave., Felton, CA 95018; Mailing: P.O. Box M-1, Felton, CA 95018 t) 831-335-4657 www.stjohnsfelton.org Rev. Roy Margallo, O.S.A., Pst.; Judie D. Kolbmann, DRE; CRP Stds.: 1

GONZALES

St. Theodore - 125 S. Center St., Gonzales, CA 93926; Mailing: P.O. Drawer B, Gonzales, CA 93926 t) 831-675-2100 (CRP); 831-675-3648 sttheodripo@gmail.com Rev. Miguel Corona, Par. Admin.; Sr. Mercy Varghese, DRE; CRP Stds.: 235

Chualar Mission - Scott & Grant Sts., Chualar, CA 93925; Mailing: P.O. Box B, Gonzales, CA 93926 t) (831) 675-3648

GREENFIELD

Holy Trinity - 27 S. El Camino Real, Greenfield, CA 93927; Mailing: Box 276, 27 S. El Camino Real, Greenfield, CA 93927 t) 831-674-3695 (CRP); 831-674-5428 holytrinitychurch276@yahoo.com Very Rev. Enrique Herrera, Pst.; CRP Stds.: 594

HOLLISTER

Sacred Heart/St. Benedict Catholic Community - 680 College St., Hollister, CA 95023 t) 831-637-9212; 831-637-9213 (CRP); 831-637-8291 (CRP) info@catholichollister.org; mauricio@catholichollister.org www.catholichollister.org Rev. Stephen Akers, Pst.; Rev. Jose Miguel Aguayo, Par. Vicar; Rev. Braulio Valencia, Par. Vicar; Very Rev. Heibar Castaneda, In Res.; Maria Villegas, Faith Formation; Travis Segura, Dir., Youth Ministry; Nancy Lopez, DRE; CRP Stds.: 345

Sacred Heart/St. Benedict Catholic Community School - (Grades PreK-8) 670 College St., Hollister, CA 95023 t) 831-637-4157 rmckenna@sacredheartschool.org sacredheartschool.org Rachel McKenna, Prin.; Stds.: 239; Lay Tchrs.: 14

Saint Benedict Church - 1200 Fairview Rd, Hollister, CA 95023; Mailing: 680 College St., Hollister, CA 95023 t) (831) 637-9212

JOLON

Mission San Antonio de Padua - End of Mission Rd., Jolon, CA 93928; Mailing: P O Box 803, Jolon, CA 93928-0803 t) 831-385-4478 x10 office@missionsanantonio.net www.missionsanantonio.net Rev. Dennis M. Peterson, Sacr. Min.; Joan Steele, Admin.;

KING CITY

St. John the Baptist - 504 N. Third St., King City, CA 93930 t) 831-385-3464 (CRP); 831-385-3377 church@stjbchurch.org; msolis@stjbchurch.org Rev. German Rodriguez, Pst.; Rev. Martel Ramos, Par. Vicar; CRP Stds.: 428

St. Luke - Main St., San Lucas, CA 93954; Mailing: 504 N 3rd St., KIng City, CA 93930 stjohnscc@att.net

LOS GATOS

Christ Child - 23230 Summit Rd., Los Gatos, CA 95033 t) 408-353-2210 emedinaruiz65@yahoo.com www.christchild.org Rev. Efrain Medina Ruiz, Pst.; CRP Stds.: 26

LOS OSOS

St. Elizabeth Ann Seton - 2050 Palisades Ave., Los Osos, CA 93402 t) 805-528-5319 c) 805-235-8803 seaschurchlo@gmail.com www.seasparishlo.org Rev. Joey R. Buena, Pst.; Javier Soto Osorio, Bus. Mgr.; CRP Stds.: 23

MARINA

St. Jude Parish Community - 303 Hillcrest Ave., Marina, CA 93933-3599 t) 831-384-5434 st_jude_marina_amy@sbcglobal.net www.stjudemarina.org Rev. Jeronimo Marcelo, Pst.; CRP Stds.: 85

MONTEREY

Cathedral of San Carlos Borromeo - 500 Church St., Monterey, CA 93940 t) 831-373-2628 rmurray@sancarloscathedral.org; azepeda@sancarloscathedral.org www.sancarloscathedral.org Most Rev. Sylvester Ryan; Rev. Victor Ommar Solis, Rector; Rev. Patrick Dooling, In Res.; Rev. Ron Shirley, In Res.; Dcn. Hugo Patino; Sr. Theresita Crasta, I.M., Liturgy Dir.; CRP Stds.: 182

San Carlos School - (Grades PreK-8) 450 Church St., Monterey, CA 93940 t) 831-375-1324 principal@sancarlosschool.org www.sancarlosschool.org Teresa Bennett, Prin.; Karen McKenzie, Vice Prin.; Stds.: 285; Lay Tchrs.: 17

MORRO BAY

St. Timothy - 962 Piney Way, Morro Bay, CA 93442 t) 805-772-2840 osainttims@yahoo.com www.sttimothymorrobay.org Rev. Gabriel Okafor, Par. Admin.; Heather Hurley, DRE; CRP Stds.: 30

NIPOMO

St. Joseph - 298 S. Thompson, Nipomo, CA 93444 t) 805-929-1922 office@stjonipomo.org; secretary@stjonipomo.org www.stjonipomo.org Rev. Miguel Rodriguez, Pst.; Rev. Fiacre Fahey, Par. Vicar; Dcn. Greg Barata; CRP Stds.: 199

PACIFIC GROVE

St. Angela Merici Church - 362 Lighthouse Ave., Pacific Grove, CA 93950; Mailing: 146 8th St., Pacific Grove, CA 93950 t) 831-655-4160 www.stangelamericipacificgrove.org Rev. Peter A. Crivello, Pst.; Dcn. David Ford; Jordan Lewis, DRE; CRP Stds.: 68

St. Angela Preschool - (Grades PreK-PreK) 136 Eighth St., Pacific Grove, CA 93950 t) 831-372-3555 office@stangelaspreschool.org stangelaspreschool.org/ Heather Diaz, Dir.; Stds.: 68; Lay Tchrs.: 8

PASO ROBLES

St. Rose of Lima Church - 820 Creston Rd, Paso Robles, CA 93447; Mailing: 642 Trigo Ln., Paso Robles, CA 93446 t) 805-238-2218 strose@saintrosechurch.org www.saintrosechurch.org Rev. Rodolfo Contreras, Pst.; Rev. Jason Taganahan, Par. Vicar; Dcn. David Vargas; CRP Stds.: 335

St. Rose of Lima Church School - (Grades PreK-8) 900 Tucker Ave., Paso Robles, CA 93446 t) 805-238-0304 srsoffice@saintrosecatholicschool.org www.saintrosecatholicschool.org Trevor Knable, Prin.; Stds.: 244; Lay Tchrs.: 13

PISMO BEACH

St. Paul the Apostle - 800 Bello St., Pismo Beach, CA 93449 t) 805-773-2219 fatherthomas@stpaulspismobeach.com; admin@stpaulspismobeach.com www.stpaulspismobeach.com/ Rev. Thomas Czeck, OFM, Conv., Pst.; Rev. Alphonse Van Guilder, OFM Conv., Par. Vicar; Rev. John Farao, OFM Conv., Chap.; Christopher Thomas Garza, Bus. Mgr.; Ann Boulais, DRE; CRP Stds.: 28

ROYAL OAKS

Our Lady of the Assumption - 100 Salinas Rd., Royal Oaks, CA 95076 t) 831-722-1104 x18 (CRP); 831-722-1104 info@ladyassumptionchurch.org Rev. Victor M. Prado, Pst.; Rev. Manuel Galvez, Par. Vicar; Dcn. Salvador Lopez; Chano Figueroa III, DRE; CRP Stds.: 294

SALINAS

Christ the King - 240 Calle Cebu, Salinas, CA 93901 t) 831-422-6722 (CRP); 831-422-6543 chiwcatequesiscristorey@gmail.com; christtheking@dioceseofmonterey.org Rev. Antonio Sanchez, Pst.; Rev. Aurelio Ortiz, Par. Vicar; Patricia Chiw, DRE; CRP Stds.: 738

Madonna Del Sasso - 320 E. Laurel Dr., Salinas, CA 93906 t) 831-422-6043 (CRP); 831-422-5323 yolandai@mdschurch.org; info@mdschurch.org www.mdschurch.org Rev. Gregory Sandman, Pst.; Rev. Gerardo Barajas Valencia, Par. Vicar; Dcn. Carl Figenshow; Yolanda Irinco, DRE; CRP Stds.: 374

Madonna Del Sasso School - (Grades PreK-8) 20 Santa Teresa Way, Salinas, CA 93906 t) 831-424-7813 information@mdsschool.com; jevans@mdsschool.com James Evans, Prin.; Stds.: 226; Lay Tchrs.: 11

St. Mary of the Nativity - 424 Towt St., Salinas, CA 93905; Mailing: 1702 2nd Ave., Salinas, CA 93905 t) 831-422-9964 (CRP); 831-758-1669 admin@stmarysalinas.org; business@stmarysalinas.org www.stmarysalinas.org Very Rev. Fredy Calvario, Pst.; Rev. Louie Bellen, Par. Vicar; CRP Stds.: 639

Sacred Heart - 22 Stone St., Salinas, CA 93901-2643 t) 831-424-1959 office@shsalinas.org www.shsalinas.org Rev. Kelly M. Vandehey, J.C.L., Pst.; Rev. Ronald L. Green, Par. Vicar; Dcn. Todd Fredrickson; Dcn. David Lansford; Mary Scattini, DRE; CRP Stds.: 279

Sacred Heart School - (Grades PreK-8) 123 W. Market St., Salinas, CA 93901 t) 831-771-1310 rmeyers@shschool.com www.shschool.com Rachel Meyers, Prin.; Stds.: 345; Lay Tchrs.: 12

SAN JUAN BAUTISTA

San Juan Bautista - 406 Second St., San Juan Bautista, CA 95045; Mailing: P.O. Box 400, San Juan Bautista, CA 95045 t) 831-623-4178 (CRP); 831-623-2127 rosalba@oldmissionsjb.org; magda@oldmissionsjb.org www.oldmissionsjb.org (Old Mission) Rev. Alberto Cabrera, Pst.; CRP Stds.: 182

SAN LUIS OBISPO

Nativity of Our Lady - 221 Daly Ave., San Luis Obispo, CA 93405-1099 t) 805-544-2357 parish@nativityslo.org nativityslo.org Rev. Matthew Pennington, Pst.; Dcn. Tom O'Brien, Pst. Assoc.; CRP Stds.: 57

Old Mission Church (Mission San Luis Obispo de Tolosa) - 751 Palm St., San Luis Obispo, CA 93401 t) 805-781-8220 x13; 805-781-8220 (CRP) office@oldmissionslo.org; conato@oldmissionslo.org www.missionsanluisobispo.org Very Rev. Martin Cain, Pst.; Rev. Raphael Reniva, Assoc. Pst.; Dcn. Charles M. Roeder; CRP Stds.: 147

Old Mission Church School - (Grades PreK-8) 761 Broad St., San Luis Obispo, CA 93401 t) 805-543-6019 bjwoods@omsslo.com www.oldmissionschool.com Therese Grimes Barket, Prin.; Stds.: 281; Lay Tchrs.: 12

SAN MIGUEL

San Miguel - 775 Mission St., San Miguel, CA 93451; Mailing: P.O. Box 69, San Miguel, CA 93451 t) 805-467-2131 (Old Mission) Rev. Lucas Pantoja, Par. Admin.; CRP Stds.: 90

Our Lady of Ransom - Cattlemen Rd., San Ardo, CA 93450

Our Lady of Guadalupe - Bradley Rd., Bradley, CA 93426

SANTA CRUZ

Holy Cross - 126 High St., Santa Cruz, CA 95060; Mailing: 210 High St., Santa Cruz, CA 95060 t) 831-458-3041 (CRP); 831-423-4182

elizborgeshc@gmail.com; hcfaithformation2019@gmail.com www.holycrosssantacruz.com Rev. Manuel Recera, Pst.; Dcn. Joe DePage; Elizabeth Borges-Yee, Youth Min.; CRP Stds.: 91

Holy Cross School - (Grades PreK-8) 150 Emmet St., Santa Cruz, CA 95060 t) 831-423-4447 admin@holycsc.org www.holycsc.org Patty Patano, Prin.; Stds.: 198; Lay Tchrs.: 12

Mission Galeria - 130 Emmet St., Santa Cruz, CA 95060 t) 831-426-5686 holycrosssantacruz.com/mission-santa-cruz/ Rhonda Lieb, Contact;

Our Lady Star of the Sea - 515 Frederick St., Santa Cruz, CA 95062 t) 831-429-1018 www.ourladystar.org Rev. Robert D. Sullivan, Pst.; Rev. Tim Nondorf, Par. Vicar; Ana Rosa Herrera, DRE; Nancy Soto, Bus. Mgr.; CRP Stds.: 284

Villa Maria del Mar - 21918 E. Cliff Dr., Santa Cruz, CA 95062 t) 831-475-1236 Joanna Pollock, Exec. Dir.;

SANTA MARGARITA

Santa Margarita de Cortona - 22515 H St., Santa Margarita, CA 93453; Mailing: P.O. Box 350, Santa Margarita, CA 93453 t) 805-438-5383 decortona@aol.com Rev. Robert Travis, Pst.; Julie Smeltzer, DRE; CRP Stds.: 18

SCOTTS VALLEY

San Agustin - 257 Glenwood Dr., Scotts Valley, CA 95066 t) 831-438-3633 info@sanagustin.church www.sanagustin.church Rev. Seamus O'Brien, Pst.; CRP Stds.: 59

SEASIDE

St. Francis Xavier - 1475 La Salle Ave., Seaside, CA 93955 t) 831-394-8546 gsfxparish@aol.com www.stfxavier.org Rev. Eleazar Diaz Gaytan, Par. Admin.; Sr. Benedicta Wasonga, I.H.S.A., Admin.; Sr. Rosangela Filippini, I.M., DRE; CRP Stds.: 841

SOLEDAD

Our Lady of Solitude - 235 Main St., Soledad, CA 93960 t) 831-678-2731; 831-296-4177 (CRP) ourladyofsolitude@yahoo.com; catechethical@ladyofsolitude.org Rev. Claudio Cabrera-Carranza (Mexico), Pst.; Rev. Jose Chavez, Par. Vicar; Dcn. Jose Alcala; Dcn. Ron Panziera; Sr. Liza Raphael, I.M., DRE; CRP Stds.: 610

Nuestra Senora de la Soledad - 36641 Fort Romie Rd., Soledad, CA 93960; Mailing: Rt. 1 Box 72, Soledad, CA 93960 t) 831-678-2586

SPRECKELS

St. Joseph - Spreckels Blvd. & Railroad Ave., Spreckels, CA 93962; Mailing: P.O. Box 7158, Spreckels, CA 93962 t) 831-455-8720 (CRP); 831-455-2249 office@stjchurch.org stjchurch.org Very Rev. Michael Volk, Pst.; Rev. Tyler Harris, Par. Vicar; Dcn. Steven Brau; Sr. Jaise Thomas, I.M., DRE; CRP Stds.: 163

TRES PINOS

Immaculate Conception - 7290 Airline Hwy., Tres Pinos, CA 95075; Mailing: P.O. Box 247, Tres Pinos, CA 95075 t) 831-628-3216 office@immaculateattrespinos.org; dre@immaculateattrespinos.org www.immaculateattrespinos.org Very Rev. Heibar Castaneda, Pst.; Dianne Slykas, DRE; CRP Stds.: 84

WATSONVILLE

Our Lady Help of Christians - 2401 E. Lake Ave., Watsonville, CA 95076 t) 831-722-2392 (CRP); 831-722-2662 religioused@olhcchurch.org; info@olhcchurch.org olhcchurch.org Rev. Rafael Saiz, SDB, Pst.; Rev. Thinh Nguyen, SDB, Campus Min.; Lorena Martinez, DRE; CRP Stds.: 170

St. Patrick - 721 Main St., Watsonville, CA 95076 t) 831-740-2384 (CRP); 831-724-1317 office@spatricks.org; formation@spatricks.org spatricks.org Rev. Jason J. Simas, Pst.; Rev. Abraham Barrera, Rev, Par. Vicar; Dcn. Pedro Ramos; Silvia Pineda, DRE; Juana Uribe, Bus. Mgr.; CRP Stds.: 888

SCHOOLS: PRESCHOOL THRU HIGH SCHOOL

SCHOOLS

STATE OF CALIFORNIA

CORRALITOS

Salesian Elementary & Jr. High School: Mary Help of Christians Youth Center - (PRV) (Grades K-8) 605 Enos Ln., Corralitos, CA 95076 t) 831-728-5518 office@salesianschool.org salesianschool.org Sr. Carmen Botello, F.M.A., Prin.; Stds.: 157; Sr. Tchrs.: 3; Lay Tchrs.: 9

MONTEREY

Santa Catalina Lower School - (PRV) (Grades PreK-8) 1500 Mark Thomas Dr., Monterey, CA 93940-5291 t) 831-655-9324 christy.pollacci@santacatalina.org www.santacatalina.org (Coed) Christy Pollacci, Admin.; Dr. Barbara Ostos, Headmaster; Stds.: 255; Lay Tchrs.: 28

WATSONVILLE

Moreland Notre Dame School - (PRV) (Grades PreK-8) 133 Brennan St., Watsonville, CA 95076 t) 831-728-2051 cmottau@mndschool.org www.mndschool.org Jeannie Nunez, Admin.; Cathy Mottau, Prin.; Stds.: 268; Lay Tchrs.: 15

HIGH SCHOOLS

STATE OF CALIFORNIA

MONTEREY

Santa Catalina Upper School - (PRV) (Grades 9-12) 1500 Mark Thomas Dr., Monterey, CA 93940-5291 t) 831-655-9315 peter.myers@santacatalina.org www.santacatalina.org (Girls) Peter Myers, Admin.; Dr. Barbara Ostos, Headmaster; Stds.: 211; Lay Tchrs.: 28

SALINAS

Christian Brothers Institute of California, Inc. (Palma School) - (PRV) (Grades 6-12) 919 Iverson St., Salinas, CA 93901-1816 t) 831-422-6391 dalman@palmaschool.org www.palmaschool.org (Boys) David J. Sullivan, Prin.; Chris Dalman, Pres.; Bro. Dominic Murray, Res. Christian Brother on Campus; Stds.: 470; Bro. Tchrs.: 1; Lay Tchrs.: 28

Notre Dame High School - (DIO) (Grades 9-12) 455 Palma Dr., Salinas, CA 93901 t) 831-751-1850 businessmanager@notredamesalinas.org; kmclaughlin@notredamesalinas.org www.notredamesalinas.org Kristi E McLaughlin, Prin.; Corrie Cubillas, Bus. Mgr.; Patrick DeLorenzo, Campus Min.; Stds.: 160; Lay Tchrs.: 15

SAN LUIS OBISPO

Mission College Preparatory Catholic High School - (DIO) 682 Palm St., San Luis Obispo, CA 93401 t) 805-543-2131 msusank@missionprep.org www.missionprep.org Michael Susank, Prin.; Stds.: 300; Lay Tchrs.: 26

WATSONVILLE

St. Francis High School Salesian College Preparatory (St. Francis Central Coast Catholic High School) - (PRV) (Grades 9-12) 2400 E. Lake Ave., Watsonville, CA 95076 t) 831-724-5933 lee@stfrancishigh.net www.stfrancishigh.net Joint High School between Diocese of Monterey and Salesians of St. John Bosco. Patrick Lee, Pres.; Stds.: 211; Pr. Tchrs.: 2; Lay Tchrs.: 13

INSTITUTIONS LOCATED IN DIOCESE

CAMPUS MINISTRY / NEWMAN CENTERS [CAM]

MONTEREY

Department of Campus Ministry - 425 Church St., Monterey, CA 93940 t) 831-373-4345 dford@dioceseofmonterey.org www.dioceseofmonterey.org Dcn. David Ford, Dir.;

Cabrillo College - 285 Meder St., Santa Cruz, CA 95064 t) 760-684-2121 ucscnewmancenter@gmail.com www.ucscnewman.com Rev. Dat Nguyen, Chap.;

California State Polytechnic Institute/Cuesta College - 1472 E. Foothill Blvd., San Luis Obispo, CA 93405-1416 t) 805-543-4105 ncc@slonewman.org slonewman.org Rev. Gerald Robinson, S.J., Dir.; Jean Conde, Admin.; Andrew Souza, Campus Min.; Terry Burrows, Liturgy & Sacramental Prep.;

University of California at Santa Cruz - 285 Meder St., Santa Cruz, CA 95060 t) 760-684-2121 ucscnewmancenter@gmail.com www.ucscnewman.com Rev. Dat Nguyen, Chap.;

CEMETERIES [CEM]

HOLLISTER

Sacred Heart/Calvary Cemetery - 1100 Hillcrest Rd., Hollister, CA 95023; Mailing: P.O. Box 1166, Hollister, CA 95024 t) 831-637-0131 claudiag@domcemeteries.org www.dioceseofmonterey.org/cemeteries Claudia Garcia, Cemetery Mgr.;

MONTEREY

Diocesan Cemeteries Office - 425 Church St., Monterey, CA 93940 t) 831-645-2809 berenicer@domcemeteries.org www.dioceseofmonterey.org/ Berenice Rosillo, Dir.;

San Carlos (Monterey) - 792 Fremont Blvd., Monterey, CA 93940 t) 831-372-0327 sancarlos@domcemeteries.org Clara Suarez Pinto II, Location Mgr.;

SALINAS

Queen of Heaven Salinas - 18200 Damian Way, Salinas, CA 93907 t) 831-449-5890 daisyh@domcemeteries.org www.dioceseofmonterey.org/cemeteries Daisy Hernandez, Cemetery Mgr.;

SAN LUIS OBISPO

Old Mission San Luis Obispo - 101 Bridge St., San Luis Obispo, CA 93401; Mailing: 751 Palm St., San Luis Obispo, CA 93401 t) 805-541-0584 benm@domcemeteries.org www.dioceseofmonterey.org/cemeteries Ben Martins, Cemetery Mgr.;

Old Santa Rosa (Cambria) - 2353 Main St., San Luis Obispo, CA 93428; Mailing: P.O. Box 13428, San Luis Obispo, CA 93401 t) 805-541-0584 benm@domcemeteries.org www.dioceseofmonterey.org/cemeteries Ben Martins, Cemetery Mgr.;

SANTA CRUZ

Holy Cross Cemetery Santa Cruz - 2271 7th Ave., Santa Cruz, CA 95062 t) 831-475-3222 nhanhart@domcemeteries.org Nicholas Hanhart, Cemetery Mgr.;

CONVENTS, MONASTERIES, AND RESIDENCES FOR WOMEN [CON]

CARMEL

Sisters of Notre Dame de Namur - 27951 Hwy. 1, Carmel, CA 93923 t) 831-624-9416 Sr. Michelle Henault, S.N.D.de N., Admin.; Srs.: 2

CORRALITOS

Daughters of Mary Help of Christians - 605 Enos Ln., Corralitos, CA 95076 t) 831-728-4700 sr.carmen@salesianschool.org Sr. Carmen Botello, F.M.A., Supr.; Srs.: 6

GONZALES

Sisters of Charity of the Infant Mary Capitanio Convent - 512 Fairview Dr., Gonzales, CA 93926; Mailing: P.O. Box 178, Gonzales, CA 93926 t) 831-675-2975 sistersmb@att.net Sr. Mercy Varghese, Supr.; Srs.: 3

GROVER BEACH

Sisters of Mercy - 111 Anita Ave, Grover Beach, CA 93433 t) (805) 801-2495 mgtm1122@yahoo.com Sr. Margaret Malone, R.S.M., Contact; Srs.: 1

SALINAS

Sisters of Charity of the Infant Mary - 15785 Alto Way,

Salinas, CA 93907-9148 t) 831-663-3675 virgennina@aol.com Sr. Rosangela Filippini, I.M., Supr.; Srs.: 5

Sisters of Notre Dame de Namur - 56 Talbot St., Salinas, CA 93901 t) 831-424-4370 bmatasci@aol.com Sr. Barbara Matasci, S.N.D., Contact; Srs.: 2

SOQUEL

St. Clare's Retreat & Convent - 2381 Laurel Glen Rd., Soquel, CA 95073 t) 831-423-8093 stclaresretreatcenter@gmail.com stclaresretreat.org Sr. Mary Vincent Nguyen, Supr.; Srs.: 4

ENDOWMENTS / FOUNDATIONS / TRUSTS [EFT]

MONTEREY

Newman Institute for Historical and Religious Studies/ Domus Patris Foundation - 302 High St., Monterey, CA 93940; Mailing: P.O. Box 748, Monterey, CA 93942 t) 831-373-0476 Very Rev. Msgr. Michael Palud, C.O., Contact;

HOSPITALS / HEALTH SERVICES [HOS]

SANTA CRUZ

Dominican Hospital - 1555 Soquel Dr., Santa Cruz, CA 95065 t) 831-462-7700 pam.koerner@commonspirit.org www.dominicanhospital.org Sponsored by Catholic Health Care Federation Nanette Mickiewicz, Pres.; Bed Capacity: 222; Asstd. Annu.: 188,326; Staff: 1,700

MONASTERIES AND RESIDENCES FOR PRIESTS AND BROTHERS [MON]

ARROYO GRANDE

St. Francis of Assisi Friary & Novitiate - 1352 Dale Ave., Arroyo Grande, CA 93420-5913 t) 805-489-1012 friarjwood@gmail.com Bro. Joseph Wood, OFM Conv, Dir., Novices/Guardian; Rev. Marek Stybor, OFM Conv., In Res.; Brs.: 1; Priests: 2

BIG SUR

New Camaldoli Hermitage (Camaldolese Hermits of America) - 62475 Hwy. 1, Big Sur, CA 93920-9533 t) 831-667-2456 x105; 831-667-5126 x102 nchprior@gmail.com www.contemplation.com Rev. Cyprian Consiglio, O.S.B.Cam., Prior; Bro. Benedict Dell'Osa, OSB Cam., Mem.; Bro. Michael Harrington, OSB Cam., Mem.; Rev. Raniero Hoffman, O.S.B.Cam., Mem.; Rev. Thomas Matus, O.S.B.Conv., Mem.; Bro. David Meyers, OSB Cam., Mem.; Rev. Zacchaeus Maria Naegele, O.S.B.Cam., Mem.; Rev. Isaiah Teichert, O.S.B.Cam., Mem.; Rev. Ignatius Tully, OSB Cam., Mem.; Brs.: 4; Priests: 6

CARMEL

Carmelite Monastery of Our Lady and St. Therese - 27601 Hwy. 1, Carmel, CA 93923-9612 t) 831-624-3043 srteresitaocd@gmail.com www.carmelitesistersbythesea.org Sr. Teresita Flynn, O.C.D., Prioress; Srs.: 15

MONTEREY

Oratorian Community-Congregation of the Oratory of Pontifical Right - 302 High St., Monterey, CA 93940; Mailing: P.O. Box 1688, Monterey, CA 93942-1688 t) 831-373-0476 Very Rev. Msgr. Michael Palud, C.O., Contact;

New Pentecost Catholic Ministries - t) 831-277-3864 contactnpcm@gmail.com www.anewpentecost.com A ministerial organization of the faithful to provide spiritual gifting to the Body of Christ.

SALINAS

Congregation of Edmund Rice Christian Brothers - 263 W. Acacia St., Salinas, CA 93901 c) (808) 225-0221 samp@palmaschool.org Bro. Bernard S. Samp, CFC, In Res.; Bro. Donald Dominic Murray, C.F.C., In Res.; Brs.: 2

SAN JUAN BAUTISTA

Franciscan Friars - 549 Mission Vineyard Rd., San Juan Bautista, CA 95045-0970; Mailing: P.O. Box 970, San Juan Bautista, CA 95045 t) 831-623-4234 jdswan@stfrancisretreat.com Rev. Paul Bottehagen, OFM, Mem.; Bro. James Swan OFM, Mem.; Brs.: 1; Priests: 1

SAN LUIS OBISPO

Monastery of the Risen Christ - 2308 O'Connor Way, San Luis Obispo, CA 93405; Mailing: PO Box 3931, San Luis Obispo, CA 93403 t) 805-544-1810 monasteryrc@gmail.com mrcslo.com Private retreats available. Rev. Daniel Manger, O.S.B.Cam., Prior; Rev. Stephen G. Coffey, O.S.B. Cam., Bus. Mgr.; Priests: 2

SANTA CRUZ

Oblates of St. Joseph Provincial House and Shrine - 544 W. Cliff Dr., Santa Cruz, CA 95060 t) 831-457-1868 provincial@osjusa.org www.osjusa.org Rev. Matthew Daniel Spencer, O.S.J., Prov.; Bro. Mathew Chipp, O.S.J., Mem.; Rev. Chummar Chirayath, OSJ, Mem.; Brs.: 1; Priests: 2

Shrine of St. Joseph - t) 831-471-0442 shrinestjoseph.com/ Rev. Paul McDonnell, O.S.J., Dir.;

WATSONVILLE

Salesians of St. John Bosco - 2401 E. Lake Ave., Watsonville, CA 95076-2670 t) 831-722-2665 info@olhcchurch.org Rev. Rafael Saiz, SDB, Pst.; Rev. Thinh Nguyen, SDB, Campus Min.; Rev. Joseph M. Paradayil, S.D.B.; Bro. Khoa Luong, SDB, CEO; Brs.: 1; Priests: 4

Saint Francis Salesian Community - t) (831) 722-2665 www.donboscowest.org Rev. Thien Nguyen, SDB, Mem.; Rev. Kristian Laygo, S.D.B., Mem.;

NURSING / REHABILITATION / CONVALESCENCE / ELDERLY CARE [NUR]

SANTA CRUZ

Dominican Oaks Corporation - 3400 Paul Sweet Rd., Santa Cruz, CA 95065 t) 831-462-6257 pam.koerner@commonspirit.org www.dominicanoaks.com Sponsored by Catholic Health Care Federation Kathy Will, Admin.; Asstd. Annu.: 206; Staff: 100

RETREAT HOUSES / RENEWAL CENTERS [RTR]

APTOS

Camp St. Francis - 2320 Sumner Ave., Aptos, CA 95003 t) 831-684-1439 khoasdb@gmail.com Summer Camp for Boys 8-13. Conducted by Salesians of St. John Bro. Khoa Luong, SDB, CEO;

SAN JUAN BAUTISTA

St. Francis Retreat Center - 549 Mission Vineyard Rd., San Juan Bautista, CA 95045; Mailing: PO Box 970, San Juan Bautista, CA 95045 t) 831-623-4234 info@stfrancisretreat.com www.stfrancisretreat.com Benjamin Combs, Exec. Dir.; Bro. James D. Swan, O.F.M.; Tyler Dawn;

SANTA CRUZ

Villa Maria del Mar Retreat Center (Sisters of the Holy Names of Jesus and Mary, U.S.-Ontario Province Corp) - 21918 E. Cliff Dr., Santa Cruz, CA 95062 t) 831-475-1236 villamaria@snjmuson.org www.villamariadelmar.org Joanna Pollock, Exec. Dir.;

SOQUEL

St. Clare's Retreat House - 2381 Laurel Glen Rd., Soquel, CA 95073 t) 831-423-8093 stclaresretreatcenter@gmail.com stclaresretreat.org Sr. Mary Vincent Nguyen, Supr.;

SHRINES [SHR]

SANTA CRUZ

Shrine of St. Joseph Guardian of the Redeemer - 544 W. Cliff Dr., Santa Cruz, CA 95060-6147 t) 831-471-0442 www.shrinestjoseph.com Rev. Matthew Daniel Spencer, O.S.J., Prov.; Rev. Chummar Chirayath, OSJ, Admin.; Bro. Mathew Chipp, O.S.J., Mem.;

Guardian of the Redeemer Bookstore - guardian@osjoseph.org

An asterisk (*) denotes an organization that has established tax-exempt status directly with the IRS and is not covered by the USCCB Group Ruling.

Diocese of Nashville

(Dioecesis Nashvillensis)

MOST REVEREND J. MARK SPALDING

Bishop of Nashville; ordained August 3, 1991; appointed Bishop of Nashville November 21, 2017; installed February 2, 2018. Chancery Office, 2800 McGavock Pike, Nashville, TN 37214.

Chancery Office: 2800 McGavock Pike, Nashville, TN 37214. T: 615-383-6393
www.dioceseofnashville.com

ESTABLISHED JULY 28, 1837.

Square Miles 16,302.

Established Diocese of Nashville, comprising entire State of Tennessee, July 28, 1837; comprising Middle and East Tennessee, January 6, 1971, after the establishment of the Diocese of Memphis; comprising the following thirty-eight Counties of Middle Tennessee, September 8, 1988, after the establishment of the Diocese of Knoxville: Bedford, Cannon, Cheatham, Clay, Coffee, Davidson, DeKalb, Dickson, Franklin, Giles, Grundy, Hickman, Houston, Humphreys, Jackson, Lawrence, Lewis, Lincoln, Macon, Marshall, Maury, Montgomery, Moore, Overton, Perry, Putnam, Robertson, Rutherford, Smith, Stewart, Sumner, Trousdale, VanBuren, Warren, Wayne, White, Williamson and Wilson.

Primary Patron: St. Joseph, Spouse of the Blessed Virgin Mary.

Secondary Patroness: Our Lady of Guadalupe.

For legal titles of parishes and diocesan institutions, consult the Chancery Office.

STATISTICAL OVERVIEW

Personnel	
Bishop	1
Priests: Diocesan Active in Diocese	61
Priests: Diocesan Active Outside Diocese	1
Priests: Retired, Sick or Absent	21
Number of Diocesan Priests	83
Religious Priests in Diocese	15
Total Priests in your Diocese	98
Extern Priests in Diocese	13
Ordinations:	
Diocesan Priests	2
Transitional Deacons	2
Permanent Deacons in Diocese	89
Total Sisters	50
Parishes	
Parishes	53
With Resident Pastor:	
Resident Diocesan Priests	36
Resident Religious Priests	11
Without Resident Pastor:	
Administered by Priests	6
Missions	3
Pastoral Centers	2
New Parishes Created	1
Professional Ministry Personnel:	
Brothers	1
Sisters	31
Lay Ministers	80
Welfare	
Catholic Hospitals	4
Total Assisted	300,000
Homes for the Aged	2
Total Assisted	450
Day Care Centers	2
Total Assisted	260
Special Centers for Social Services	7
Total Assisted	860
Educational	
Diocesan Students in Other Seminaries	21
Total Seminarians	21
Colleges and Universities	1
Total Students	60
High Schools, Diocesan and Parish	2
Total Students	1,657
High Schools, Private	1
Total Students	299
Elementary Schools, Diocesan and Parish	14
Total Students	4,304
Elementary Schools, Private	2
Total Students	762
Catechesis/Religious Education:	
High School Students	1,129
Elementary Students	6,788
Total Students under Catholic Instruction	15,020
Teachers in Diocese:	
Priests	2
Sisters	40
Lay Teachers	678
Vital Statistics	
Receptions into the Church:	
Infant Baptism Totals	1,836
Minor Baptism Totals	255
Adult Baptism Totals	134
Received into Full Communion	343
First Communions	2,036
Confirmations	1,905
Marriages:	
Catholic	332
Interfaith	122
Total Marriages	454
Deaths	507
Total Catholic Population	90,390
Total Population	2,870,202

LEADERSHIP

Vicars General - Rev. Dexter S. Brewer;
Deans - Rev. Joseph V. McMahon, Central Deanery; Rev. Eric L. Fowlkes, City Deanery; Rev. Jacob Dio, M.S.F.S., Northwest Deanery;
Chancery Office - t) (615) 383-6393 https:www.dioceseofnashville.com
Chancellor - Julie Perrey, Vice Chancellor; Brian Cooper;
Vice Chancellor - Julie Perrey, Vice Chancellor;
Executive Assistant to the Bishop - Jenny Scaggs;
Accounting Systems - John Roberts, CFO (John.Roberts@dioceseofnashville.com);
Diocesan Tribunal - t) 615-783-0765
Judicial Vicar -
Adjutant Judicial Vicar - Rev. Dexter S. Brewer;
Director of Tribunal - Erin Stracener;
Defender of the Bond - Janette Buchanan;
Advocates - Rev. Rhodes Winslow Bolster; Rev. Jayd Neely; Rev. Luke Wilgenbusch;
Judges - Rev. Dexter S. Brewer; Janette Buchanan;
Formal Case Instructor - Heather Mendiola;
Secretary-Notary - Heather Mendiola;
Presbyteral Council - Rev. Dexter S. Brewer; Rev. John Hammond; Rev. Patrick J. Kibby;
Diocesan Finance Board - John Gromos, Chair; William J. Whalen, CFO; Angela M. Robinson;

OFFICES AND DIRECTORS

Archives and Records - Brent Wiebe, Archivist;
Campus Ministries - Rev. Rhodes Winslow Bolster, Assoc. Dir. (frbolster@stphilipfranklin.com); Rev. Gervan Menezes, Dir.;
Austin Peay-Clarksville - t) 931-645-6275 Dcn. Timothy F. Winters;
Fisk-Meharry-Tennessee State University Campus Ministries - t) 615-320-0695 Barbara King;
MTSU-Murfreesboro - St. Rose of Lima Church - t) 615-893-1843
Tenn. Tech-Cookeville - t) 931-526-2575 Rev. Gervan Menezes, Dir.; Clark Jameson; Martha Jameson;
Univ. of South-Sewanee - Good Shepherd Church - t) 931-967-0961 Rev. Gervan Menezes, Campus Ministry Dir.;
University Catholic - t) 615-322-0104 Rev. Rhodes Winslow Bolster, Dir. University Catholic;
Catholic Charismatic Renewal - Teresa Seibert, Assoc. Liaison;
Catholic Charities of Tennessee, Inc. - t) 615-352-3087 Judith Orr, Dir.;
Catholic Charities of Tennessee Social Services - t) 615-352-3087
Catholic Charities Refugee Services - t) 615-259-3567 Kellye Branson, Dir.;
Catholic Medical Association, Nashville Chapter - E. Wesley Ely, Pres. (nashvillecmaguild@gmail.com);
Catholic Public Policy Commission of TN - t) 615-783-0753 Rick Mussachio, Exec. Dir.; Julie Perrey, Vice Chancellor;
Catholic Relief Services - Dcn. Hans M. Toecker, Dir.;
Catholic Youth Office and Search Program - t) 615-383-6393 Shelby Conner, Dir. (shelby.conner@dioceseofnashville.com);
Cemeteries - Dcn. Mike Wilkins, Cemetery Mgr.;
Censor Librorum - Rev. Andrew Bulso;
Clergy and Pastoral Support Office - t) 615-783-0765 hans.toecker@dioceseofnashville.com Dcn. Hans M. Toecker, Dir., Clergy & Pastoral Support;
Continuing Education of Priests - Rev. Austin Gilstrap, Episcopal Vicar for Formation;
Cursillo - Gary Guinn, Dir.; Jennie Guinn, Dir.; Dcn. Martin Deschenes, Assoc. Spiritual Advisor;
Diocesan Marketing Director - Joe Cacopardo (joe.cacopardo@dioceseofnashville.com);
Diocesan Planning -
Hispanic Ministry - Rev. David Ramirez, Dir.; Anabell C. Trevino, Asst. Dir.;
Holy Childhood Association -
Korean Catholic Community - t) 615-727-1225 aionia0033@gmail.com Rev. S. Bang;
Lay Retirement Administrative Board - D. Scott Donnellan; Christopher P. Kelly; John Schneider;
Liturgical Life -
Ministry Formation - Dr. Brad Peper, Dir.;
Mission Support Office - Julie Perry, Chief;
Human Resources - Julie Perry, Dir.;
Newspaper - Andy Telli, Mng. Editor (Andy.Telli@dioceseofnashville.com);
Permanent Diaconate Personnel - Dcn. Hans M. Toecker, Dir.;
Pontifical Mission Societies - Dcn. Hans M. Toecker, Dir.;
Priest Benefit Foundation - t) 615-783-0765 Rev. Nicholas Allen; Rev. Justin N. Raines; Rev. Dexter S. Brewer;
Prison Ministry - Dcn. James Booth;
Schools Office - t) 615-383-6393 Dr. Rebecca Hammel, Supt. (Rebecca.Hammel@dioceseofnashville.com); Dr. Tony Bonta, Asst. Supt. (Tony.Bonta@dioceseofnashville.com); Kim White, Asst. Supt. (Kim.White@dioceseofnashville.com);
Stewardship and Development - Ashley Linville, Dir.;
Victim Assistance Coordinator - t) 615-783-0753 Vicki Lawson;
Vietnamese Ministry - Rev. Hung Pham;
Vocations - Rev. Luke Wilgenbusch, Dir.;

COMMUNICATIONS

Chief Marketing Officer - Gia Riney (gia.riney@dioceseofnashville.com);

MISCELLANEOUS / OTHER OFFICES

Safe Envirnoment Coordinator - Jason Liuzzi;

PARISHES, MISSIONS, AND CLERGY

STATE OF TENNESSEE

ANTIOCH

St. Ignatius of Antioch - 601 Bell Rd., Antioch, TN 37013 t) 615-367-0085 x21 mariabraswell@stignatiuscc.com stignatiuscc.com Rev. Titus Augustine, Pst.; Dcn. Roberto Ochoa; Dcn. John Calzavara, DRE; Dcn. Doug Shafer; CRP Stds.: 99
Our Lady of Guadalupe - 3112 Nolensville Pike, Antioch, TN 37211 t) 615-333-8660 olog3112@gmail.com www.nsdeguadalupe.org Rev. Fernando Lopez, Pst.; Rev. Ramon Ayala, Assoc. Pst.; Dcn. Hernan Andrade; CRP Stds.: 390

ASHLAND CITY

St. Martha - 3331 Bell St., Ashland City, TN 37015 t) 615-792-4255 www.stmarthacatholicchurch.org/ Rev. Benjamin Butler, Pst.;

BRENTWOOD

Holy Family - 9100 Crockett Rd., Brentwood, TN 37027 t) 615-373-4351 (CRP); 615-373-4696 bettylou.burnett@holyfamilycc.com www.holyfamilycc.com Rev. Joseph V. McMahon, Pst.; Rev. Mark Simpson, Assoc. Pst.; Dcn. William Hill; Betty Lou Burnett, Parish Life Coord.; Catherine Birdwell, DRE; Jane Ridlen, Bus. Mgr.; CRP Stds.: 998

CENTERVILLE

Christ the Redeemer - 1515 Woodland Dr., Centerville, TN 37033; Mailing: P.O. Box 323, Centerville, TN 37033 t) 931-796-3738; 931-729-4669 (CRP) holytrinity67477@bellsouth.net; fr.john@holytrinityhohenwald.org Holy Trinity, Hohenwald. Rev. John O'Neill, Pst.; Chrissey Delaney, DRE; CRP Stds.: 5

CLARKSVILLE

Immaculate Conception - 709 Franklin St., Clarksville, TN 37040 t) 931-645-6275 www.immaconception.org/ Rev. Jacob Dio, M.S.F.S., Pst.; Rev. Paul Nguyen, Assoc. Pst.; Dcn. Dominick Azzara; Dcn. Robert Berberich; Dcn. Manuel Martinez; Dcn. Orin Rovito; Dcn. Timothy Winters; Dcn. Juan Garza, DRE; CRP Stds.: 332
Immaculate Conception School - (Grades K-8) 1901 Madison St., Clarksville, TN 37043; Mailing: 709 Franklin St., Clarksville, TN 37040 t) 931-645-1865 icaaccounts@immaconception.org www.icschooltn.org/ Stephanie Stafford, Prin.; Rebecca Dean, Librn.; Stds.: 132; Lay Tchrs.: 14

COLUMBIA

St. Catherine - 3019 Cayce Ln., Columbia, TN 38401 t) 931-381-6784 (CRP); 931-388-3803 jsparkman@stcatherinecc.org; tbailey@stcatherinecc.org www.stcatherinecc.org Rev. Daniel J. Reehil, Pst.; Dcn. Price Keller; Dcn. Daniel McCulley; Dcn. Raymond Seibold; Jeanette Sparkman, DRE; CRP Stds.: 143

COOKEVILLE

St. Thomas Aquinas - 421 N. Washington Ave., Cookeville, TN 38501 t) 931-526-2575 (CRP); 913-526-2575 stewardship@saintrose.org; sta.religious.ed.38501@gmail.com www.saintthomasaquinaschurch.com/ Rev. Gervan Menezes, Pst.; Rev. Aby Thankickal, CMI, Pst. Assoc.; Valerie Richardson, DRE; CRP Stds.: 261

DECHERD

Good Shepherd - 2021 Decherd Blvd., Decherd, TN 37324 t) 931-967-0961 info@goodshepherdtn.com; gsoffice1@bellsouth.net Rev. Anthony Mutuku, Pst.; Dcn. Philip Johnson; Patty Davidson, DRE; CRP Stds.: 61
St. Margaret Mary - 9458 Old Alto Hwy., Alto, TN 37324 t) (931) 967-0961 David Gallagher, Contact;

DICKSON

St. Christopher - 713 W. College St., Dickson, TN 37055 t) 615-446-3927 amyschoenly@stchristophercc.com; frabraham@stchristophercc.com stchristophercc.com Rev. Abraham Panthalanickal, Pst.; Dcn. James Tucker; CRP Stds.: 126

DOVER

St. Francis of Assisi - 1489 Donelson Pkwy., Dover, TN 37058 t) 931-232-9422 stfroa@gmail.com Rev. Joseph Mundakal, C.M.I., Pst.; Linda Allen, DRE; CRP Stds.: 29

FAYETTEVILLE

St. Anthony - 1900 Huntsville Hwy., Fayetteville, TN 37334 t) 931-433-6525 stanthony@fpunet.com www.stanthonyfayetteville.org Rev. George Panthananickal, C.M.I., Pst.; CRP Stds.: 75

FRANKLIN

St. Matthew - 535 Sneed Rd. W., Franklin, TN 37069 t) 615-646-0378 info@stmatthewtn.org www.stmatthewtn.org Rev. Justin N. Raines, Pst.; Dcn. Bill Forte; Rev. Tien Tran, Assoc. Pst.; Tony Jesse, DRE; CRP Stds.: 124
St. Matthew School - (Grades PreK-8) 533 Sneed Rd. W., Franklin, TN 37069 t) 615-662-4044 Tim Forbes, Prin.; Lori Bellante, Dir.; Holly Ledieu, Dir.; Stds.: 448; Lay Tchrs.: 31
St. Philip - 113 2nd Ave. S., Franklin, TN 37064 t) 615-794-8588 office@stphilipfranklin.com www.stphilipfranklin.com Rev. Edward F. Steiner III, Pst.; Rev. Michael Baltrus, Assoc. Pst.; Dcn. Paul Brancheau; Dcn. Raphael Bougrat; Dcn. John Froning; Michaela Miller, Dir.; Susan Skinner, Dir.; Karen Williams, Dir.; Alondra Banales, Assoc. Dir.; Ana Zarraga, Pst. Assoc.; Maria Herrera, CRE; Jessica Nelson, RCIA Coord.; John Angotti, Liturgy Dir.; Kimberlie Leisinger, Bus. Mgr.; CRP Stds.: 535

GALLATIN

St. John Vianney - 449 N. Water Ave., Gallatin, TN 37066 t) 615-452-2977 sjvcatholicchurch@gmail.com www.saintjohnvianneychurch.org Rev. Richard Childress, Pst.; Dcn. James Nardini; Shirley Lafferty, DRE; CRP Stds.: 68
St. John Vianney School - (Grades PreK-8) 501 N. Water St., Gallatin, TN 37066 t) 615-230-7048

n.eskert@stjvcs.org Natalie Eskert; Stds.: 134; Lay Tchrs.: 13

HENDERSONVILLE

Our Lady of the Lake - 1729 Stop 30 Rd., Hendersonville, TN 37075 t) 615-824-3276 www.ololcconline.com Rev. Austin Gilstrap, Pst.; Rev. Thomas Kalam, C.M.I., Assoc. Pst.; Rev. Nonso Ohanaka, Assoc. Pst.; Dcn. John Lammers; Dcn. Mike Rector; CRP Stds.: 668

HOHENWALD

Holy Trinity - 610 Kimmins St., Hohenwald, TN 38462 t) 931-796-3738 holytrinity67477@bellsouth.net Rev. John O'Neill, Pst.; CRP Stds.: 5

JOELTON

St. Lawrence - 5655 Clarksville Hwy., Joelton, TN 37080 t) 615-876-2127 stlawrence@comcast.net www.stlawrencejoelton.com Rev. Joseph P. Edwidge Carre, Pst.; Dcn. Rock Hasenberg; CRP Stds.: 4

LAFAYETTE

Holy Family - 431 Old Hwy. 52, Lafayette, TN 37083 t) 615-666-6466 holyfamily@nctc.com Rev. Charles Osewe Aketch, G.H.M., Pst.; Rev. Samuel Mungai, Assoc. Pst.; Tania Delgado, DRE; CRP Stds.: 55

Divine Savior - 150 Divine Savior Rd., Celina, TN 38551 t) 931-243-2618 Dcn. Jose G. Pineda;

LAWRENCEBURG

Sacred Heart - 221 Berger St., Lawrenceburg, TN 38464; Mailing: P.O. Box 708, Lawerenceburg, TN 38464 t) 931-762-3183 parishoffice@shclb.org shclb.org Rev. Andrew Forsythe, Pst.; CRP Stds.: 40

Sacred Heart School - (Grades K-8) 220 Berger St., Lawrenceburg, TN 38464 t) 931-762-6125 amy.kostal@shslburg.com www.shslburg.com Marian Pickett, Prin.; Stds.: 84; Lay Tchrs.: 6

LEBANON

St. Frances Cabrini - 300 S. Tarver Ave., Lebanon, TN 37087 t) 615-444-0524 sec@sfctn.org www.sfctn.org Rev. James Panackal, C.M.I., Pst.; Dcn. Luis Ascencio; CRP Stds.: 254

LEWISBURG

St. John the Evangelist - 1061 S. Ellington Pkwy., Lewisburg, TN 37091 t) 931-359-5017 Rev. Regimon Augustine, MSFS, Pst.; Daniel Brindle, DRE; CRP Stds.: 80

LORETTO

Sacred Heart - 305 Church St., Loretto, TN 38469; Mailing: P.O. Box 86, Loretto, TN 38469 t) 931-853-4370 amy.sacred.heart@gmail.com shsjparishes.com Rev. Delphinus Mutajuka, Admin.; Sue Vess, DRE; CRP Stds.: 25

Sacred Heart School - (Grades PreK-8) 307 Church St., Loretto, TN 38469; Mailing: P.O. Box 277, Loretto, TN 38469 t) 931-853-4388 tleon@shsloretto.com www.shsjparishes.com/school Stds.: 73; Lay Tchrs.: 7

MADISON

St. Joseph - 1225 Gallatin Pike S., Madison, TN 37115 t) (615) 865-1071; 615-865-1071 (CRP) sjsecretary@sjsandchurch.com Rev. Jean Baptiste Kyabuta, Pst.; Dcn. Don Craighead; Dcn. Gordon W. McBride Sr.; Dcn. Theodore B. Welsh; Mike Zimmerman, DRE; Savannah Smith, DRE; CRP Stds.: 114

St. Joseph School - (Grades PreK-8) t) 615-865-1491 alavender@stjosephnashville.org Amy Lavender, Prin.; Stds.: 310; Sr. Tchrs.: 2; Lay Tchrs.: 24

MANCHESTER

St. Mark - 2941 McMinnville Hwy., Manchester, TN 37355 t) 931-455-3050 (CRP); 931-723-4107 stpaulchurch@cafes.net; saintmarkchurchmanchester@gmail.com Rev. Stephen A. Klasek, Pst.; Dcn. Ronald F. Munn; CRP Stds.: 91

MCEWEN

St. Patrick's - 175 St. Patrick's St., McEwen, TN 37101 t) 931-582-3633 stpatsfinance@bellsouth.net Rev. Zack Kirangu, Pst.; CRP Stds.: 2

St. Patrick's School - (Grades PreK-8) t) 931-582-3493 vicki.james@sps-tn.org Karen Martin, Librn.; Stds.: 161; Sr. Tchrs.: 5; Lay Tchrs.: 7

MCMINNVILLE

St. Catherine - 1024 Faulkner Spring Rd., McMinnville, TN 37110 t) 931-473-4932 balamarneni@gmail.com Rev. Bala Showraiah, OFM, Admin.; Sonia Remirez, DRE; CRP Stds.: 150

MURFREESBORO

St. Rose of Lima - 1601 N. Tennessee Blvd., Murfreesboro, TN 37130 t) 615-893-1843; 615-895-1150 (CRP) formation@saintrose.org; stewardship@saintrose.org www.saintrose.org Rev. Christiano Nunes de Silva, Pst.; Rev. Msgr. Cyriac Kurian, C.M.I., Pst. Assoc.; Dcn. John D'Amico; Dcn. Michael Plese; Dcn. Peter Semich; Dr. Benjamin Smith, Dir.; CRP Stds.: 266

St. Rose of Lima School - (Grades K-8) t) 615-898-0555 Sr. Mary Patrick, O.P., Prin.; Holly Bruser, Librn.; Stds.: 400; Sr. Tchrs.: 4; Lay Tchrs.: 31

NASHVILLE

Cathedral of the Incarnation - 2015 W. End Ave., Nashville, TN 37203 t) 615-327-2330 info@cathedralnashville.org cathedralnashville.org/ Rev. Eric L. Fowlkes, Pst.; Rev. Anh Tuan Phan, Assoc. Pst.; Dcn. Mark Faulkner; Dcn. Thales Finchum; Dcn. Joe Holzmer; Melissa Doyle, DRE; CRP Stds.: 48

St. Ann - 5101 Charlotte Ave., Nashville, TN 37209 t) 615-298-1782 churchoffice@stannnash.org saintannparish.com Rev. Michael Fye, Pst.; Dcn. Jim Holzemer; Dcn. John P. Casey; CRP Stds.: 181

St. Ann School - (Grades PreK-8) 5105 Charlotte Ave., Nashville, TN 37209 t) 615-269-0568 arumfola@stannnash.org Anna Rumfola, Prin.; Judy Graham, Librn.; Stds.: 205; Lay Tchrs.: 17

Assumption - 1227 Seventh Ave. N., Nashville, TN 37208 t) 615-256-2729 assumption1859@gmail.com www.assumptionnashville.org Rev. Bede Price, Pst.; CRP Stds.: 74

Christ the King - 3001 Belmont Blvd., Nashville, TN 37212 t) 615-292-2884 info@ctk.org ctk.org Rev. Dexter S. Brewer, Pst.; Rev. Mark Sappenfield, Assoc. Pst.; Dcn. David Lybarger; Dcn. Brian Schulz; CRP Stds.: 257

Christ the King School - (Grades PreK-8) 3105 Belmont Blvd., Nashville, TN 37212 t) 615-292-9465 Sherry Woodman, Prin.; Rai Lynn Wood, Librn.; Stds.: 252; Lay Tchrs.: 19

Holy Name Catholic Church - 521 Woodland St., Nashville, TN 37206 t) 615-254-8847 holynamechurchnashville@comcast.net www.holynamenashville.com Rev. Theophilus Ebulueme (Nigeria), Pst.; Dcn. Robert L. Mahoney; Savannah Brien, DRE; Tommy Habib, Music Min.; CRP Stds.: 20

St. Edward - 188 Thompson Ln., Nashville, TN 37211 t) 615-833-5520 shouse@stedward.org Rev. Andrew Bulso, Pst.; Rev. Brent Thayer, Assoc. Pst.; Dcn. Brian Edwards; Teresa Osborne, Dir.; Julianne Staley, DRE; CRP Stds.: 65

St. Edward School - (Grades PreK-8) 190 Thompson Ln., Nashville, TN 37211 t) 615-833-5770 Marsha Wharton, Prin.; Stds.: 191; Lay Tchrs.: 19

St. Henry - 6401 Harding Pike., Nashville, TN 37205 t) 615-352-2259 reled@sthenry.org; chale@sthenry.org www.sthenry.org Rev. Mark Beckman, Pst.; Rev. Shinto Padinjaredathu, C.M.I., Assoc. Pst.; Dcn. Michael Catalano; Dcn. Mark Deschenes; Rev. Patrick J. Kibby, In Res.; Beth Holzapfel, DRE; CRP Stds.: 139

St. Henry School - (Grades K-8) t) 615-352-1328 klong@sthenry.org Sister Mary Elizabeth, O.P., Prin.; Harriett Hudson, Librn.; Stds.: 707; Sr. Tchrs.: 4; Lay Tchrs.: 42

Holy Rosary - 192 Graylynn Dr., Nashville, TN 37214 t) 615-889-4065 cynthia@holyrosary.edu; cyndi.anderson17@gmail.com Rev. Daniel J. Steiner, Pst.; Dcn. Wayne Gregory; Dcn. Mike Wilkins; CRP Stds.: 40

Holy Rosary School - (Grades PreK-8) 190 Graylynn Dr., Nashville, TN 37214 t) 615-883-1108 halliburtonk@holyrosary.edu Kimber Halliburton, Prin.; Stds.: 352; Lay Tchrs.: 31

St. Mary of the Seven Sorrows - 328 Rep. John Lewis Way N., Nashville, TN 37219; Mailing: P.O. Box 190606, Nashville, TN 37219 t) 615-256-1704 office@stmarysdowntown.org stmarysdowntown.org Rev. Jayd Neely, Pst.; Joe Augustine, DRE; CRP Stds.: 142

St. Mary Villa Chapel - 34 White Bridge Rd., Nashville, TN 37205 t) 615-353-6181 lyndsey.gower@maryqueenofangels.com maryqueenofangels.com/ Rev. Mark Hunt, Chap.;

St. Patrick - 1219 2nd Ave. S., Nashville, TN 37210 t) 615-256-6498 secretary@stpatricksnashville.org stpatricksnashville.org Rev. John Hammond, Pst.; CRP Stds.: 3

St. Pius X - 2800 Tucker Rd., Nashville, TN 37218 t) 615-255-2049 jharper@stpiusnashville.org; tcat@stpiusnashville.org Rev. Hung Pham, Pst.; Dcn. Ken Levinson; Cynthia Catignani, DRE; CRP Stds.: 25

St. Pius X Classical Academy - (Grades PreK-8) 2750 Tucker Rd., Nashville, TN 37218 stpiusxschool@yahoo.com Samatha Kaufman, Prin.; Stds.: 75; Sr. Tchrs.: 1; Lay Tchrs.: 7

St. Vincent de Paul - 1700 Heiman St., Nashville, TN 37208 t) 615-320-0695 x100; 615-320-0695 (CRP) stvincentchurchfamily01@gmail.com www.stvincentchurchfamily.com Rev. Francis G. Appreh, Pst.; Tijvana Young, Youth Min.; Dr. Charlene Dewey, DRE; Dcn. Harry Guess; CRP Stds.: 24

NOLENSVILLE

Mother Teresa - 7668 Nolensville Rd, Nolensville, TN 37135; Mailing: P.O. Box 866, Nolensville, TN 37135 t) 615-283-3119 info@motherteresacc.com www.motherteresacc.com Rev. Anthony Stewart, Pst.; Laura Fagin, Admin.; Bridget Guarente, Bus. Mgr.; Jennifer Turner, DRE; CRP Stds.: 163

OLD HICKORY

St. Stephen - 14544 Lebanon Rd., Old Hickory, TN 37138 t) (615) 758-2424 gkarn@ssccohtn.org; abosio@ssccohtn.org www.saintstephencommunity.org Rev. Davis Chackaleckel, M.S.F.S., Pst.; Rev. Nicholas Allen, Assoc. Pst.; Dcn. Hans M. Toecker; Dcn. Fred Bourland; Dcn. Steve Molnar; Dcn. Robert A. Montini; Dcn. Tom Samoray; Dcn. Paul Taylor; Greg Karn, DRE; Scott Goudeau, RCIA Coord.; Connie Blevins, RCIC Dir.; Angie Bosio, Dir., Youth Ministry; CRP Stds.: 267

PULASKI

Immaculate Conception - 100 Chapel Rd., Pulaski, TN 38478 t) 931-363-5776 beamteam@ardmore.net Rev. George Panthananickal, C.M.I., Pst.; Dcn. W. Michael Hume; JoAnn Beam, DRE; CRP Stds.: 12

SHELBYVILLE

St. William of Montevergine - 500 S Brittain St., Shelbyville, TN 37160 t) 931-735-6004 stwilliamshelbyville.org/ Rev. Edwuin Cardona, Pst.; CRP Stds.: 300

SMITHVILLE

St. Gregory - 712 W. Main St., Smithville, TN 37166 t) 615-597-1970; 615-597-7116 (CRP) stgregorys2@dtccom.net St. Andrew, Sparta, TN Rev. Emanuel Dirichukwu, Pst.; Berenice Alamilla, DRE; CRP Stds.: 60

SMYRNA

St. Luke - 10682 Old Nashville Hwy., Smyrna, TN 37167 t) 615-459-9672 finance@stluketn.org; frontoffice@stluketn.org www.stlukesmyrnatn.com Rev. Phillip A. Halladay, Pst.; Dcn. Ernie Gartung; Dcn. Roger F. Huber; Dcn. Jose G. Pineda, DRE; CRP Stds.: 613

SPARTA

St. Andrew - 829 Valley View Dr., Sparta, TN 38583 t) 931-738-2140; 931-946-7571 (CRP) saccsec@blomand.net Rev. Emanuel Dirichukwu, Pst.; CRP Stds.: 27

SPRINGFIELD

Our Lady of Lourdes - 103 Golf Club Ln., Springfield, TN 37172 t) 615-384-6200 ollsmchurch@gmail.com www.ollsm.com Rev. Anthony Lopez, Pst.; Dcn.

Michael Morris; Jennifer Beard, DRE; CRP Stds.: 190

ST.JOSEPH

St. Joseph - 304 American Blvd, St.Joseph, TN 38481; Mailing: PO Box 86, Loretto, TN 38469 t) 931-853-4370 amy.sacred.heart@gmail.com shsjparishes.com Sacred Heart, Loretto. Rev. Delphinus Mutajuka, Admin.;

TENNESSEE RIDGE

St. Elizabeth Ann Seton - 755 State Rte. 49, Tennessee Ridge, TN 37178 t) 931-721-3769 seastnoffice@aol.com seastn.com St. Patrick, McEwen. Rev. Joseph Mundakal, C.M.I.; Valerie Brown, DRE; CRP Stds.: 7

THOMPSONS STATION

Church of the Nativity - 2793 Buckner Ln., Thompsons Station, TN 37179 t) 615-794-4004 parishoffice@nativitycatholic.net www.nativitycatholic.net Rev. Gerard Jerry Strange, Pst.; Dcn. Timothy Conley; Dcn. Philip Moore; Gina Taddeo, DRE; CRP Stds.: 350

TULLAHOMA

St. Paul the Apostle Catholic Church - 304 W. Grizzard St., Tullahoma, TN 37388 t) 931-455-3050 stpaulchurch@cafes.net www.stpaulstullahoma.com Rev. Stephen A. Klasek, Pst.; Dcn. Ronald F. Munn; Terri Daugherty, DRE; CRP Stds.: 79

WAYNESBORO

St. Cecilia - 50 Willowbrook Dr., Waynesboro, TN 38485; Mailing: 610 Kimmins St., Hohenwald, TN 38462 t) 931-796-3738 holytrinity67477@bellsouth.net Holy Trinity, Hohenwald. Rev. John O'Neill, Pst.;

SCHOOLS: PRESCHOOL THRU HIGH SCHOOL

SCHOOLS

STATE OF TENNESSEE

NASHVILLE

***Saint Bernard Academy Corporation** - (PRV) (Grades PreK-8) 2304 Bernard Ave., Nashville, TN 37212-4202 t) 615-385-0440 www.stbernardacademy.org Leigh Toomey, Prin.; Stds.: 383; Lay Tchrs.: 54

Overbrook School - (PRV) (Grades PreK-8) 4210 Harding Pike, Nashville, TN 37205 t) 615-292-5134 information@overbrook.edu www.overbrook.edu Sr. Marie Blanchette, Prin.; Stds.: 279; Sr. Tchrs.: 6; Lay Tchrs.: 35

NOLENSVILLE

St. Michael Academy, Inc. - 7668 Nolensville Rd., Nolensville, TN 37135-9458 t) (615) 430-0020 jweaver@stmichael-academy.com Shana Druffner, Prin.; JoLind Weaver, Dir.;

HIGH SCHOOLS

STATE OF TENNESSEE

HENDERSONVILLE

Pope John Paul II High School, Inc. - (DIO) (Grades 6-12) 117 Caldwell Dr., Hendersonville, TN 37075 t) 615-822-2375 info@jp2hs.org www.popeprep.org Laura Thigpen, CFO; Stds.: 775; Pr. Tchrs.: 1; Lay Tchrs.: 95

NASHVILLE

St. Cecilia Academy - (PRV) 4210 Harding Pike, Nashville, TN 37205 t) 615-298-4525 capriolic@stcecilia.edu www.stcecilia.edu Sr. Anna Laura Karp, O.P., Prin.; Cheryl Carpenter, Librn.; Stds.: 299; Sr. Tchrs.: 12; Lay Tchrs.: 28

Father Ryan High School - (DIO) (Grades 9-12) 700 Norwood Dr., Nashville, TN 37204 t) 615-383-4200 foremanc@fatherryan.org www.fatherryan.org Corporate Title: Father Ryan High School, Inc. Paul Davis, Pres.; Christy Foreman, Librn.; Stds.: 882; Lay Tchrs.: 88

Father Ryan Board of Trust - Devel. & Alumni Office, 770 Norwood Dr., Nashville, TN 37204 t) (615) 383-4200 x3244

INSTITUTIONS LOCATED IN DIOCESE

ASSOCIATIONS [ASN]

GALLATIN

Magnificat - Nashville, TN Chapter, Inc. - 1697 Foston Ln., Gallatin, TN 37066 t) (615) 598-3926 Ministry to Catholic Women.

NASHVILLE

Mid-Tennessee Rural Outreach Association (Assumption-St. Vincent North Nashville Outreach Association) - 2800 McGavock Pike, Nashville, TN 37214 t) 615-352-3087 contact@cctenn.org Judith Orr, Dir.;

CATHOLIC CHARITIES [CCH]

NASHVILLE

Ladies of Charity Welfare Agency, Inc. - 2212 State St., Nashville, TN 37203 t) 615-327-3430 info@nashvilleloc.org www.ladiesofcharitynashville.org/ Diana Miller, Dir.; Asstd. Annu.: 589; Staff: 1

CEMETERIES [CEM]

NASHVILLE

Calvary Cemetery - 1001 Lebanon Rd., Nashville, TN 37210 t) 615-256-4590 michael.wilkins@dioceseofnashville.com Dcn. Mike Wilkins, Admin.; John Roberts, CFO;

COLLEGES & UNIVERSITIES [COL]

NASHVILLE

Aquinas College - 4210 Harding Pike, Nashville, TN 37205 t) 615-297-7545 www.aquinascollege.edu Mother Anna Grace Neenan, O.P., Chair; Sr. Cecilia Anne Wanner, O.P., Pres.; Sr. Mary Edith Humphries, O.P., Vice. Pres.; Dr. Bill Smart, Dean; Sr. Marie Hannah Seiler, O.P., Dean; Stds.: 60; Lay Tchrs.: 3; Sr. Tchrs.: 6

CONVENTS, MONASTERIES, AND RESIDENCES FOR WOMEN [CON]

NASHVILLE

St. Cecilia Congregation - 801 Dominican Dr., Nashville, TN 37228-1905 t) 615-256-5486 x1312 slmsiemering@op-tn.org www.nashvilledominican.org Mother Anna Grace Neenan, O.P., Prioress; Sr. Lucia Marie Siemering, O.P., Secy.; Srs.: 313

Sisters of Mercy of Nashville, TN, Inc. - 2629 Pennington Bend Rd., Nashville, TN 37214 t) 615-885-1863 bhiggins@mercysc.org Rev. Mark Hunt, Chap.; Srs.: 21

ENDOWMENTS / FOUNDATIONS / TRUSTS [EFT]

MURFREESBORO

Saint Thomas Rutherford Foundation - 1700 Medical Center Pkwy., Murfreesboro, TN 37129; Mailing: 102 Woodmont Blvd., Ste. 800, Nashville, TN 37205 t) 615-396-4996 gpope@ascension.org www.ascension.org DBA Ascension Saint Thomas Rutherford Foundation Timothy Adams, CEO; Greg Pope, Chief Mission Officer;

NASHVILLE

Catholic Foundation - Diocese of Nashville - 2800 McGavock Pike, Nashville, TN 37214 t) 615-645-9768 ashley.linville@dioceseofnashville.com www.ccfmtn.org Ashley Linville, Dir.;

Catholic Foundation of Tennessee, Inc. - 2800 McGavock Pike, Nashville, TN 37214 john.roberts@dioceseofnashville.com Ashley Linville, Dir.;

The Catholic Diocese of Nashville Advancement of Catholic Education - 2800 McGavock Pike, Nashville, TN 37214 t) 615-383-6393 john.roberts@dioceseofnashville.com John Roberts, Bus. Mgr.;

***Visitation Hospital Foundation** - 237 Old Hickory Blvd., Ste. 201, Nashville, TN 37221 t) 615-673-3501 admin@visitationhospital.org www.visitationhospital.org Fund for medical care/clinic in rural Petite Riviere de Nippes, Haiti Theresa Patterson, Exec.;

HOSPITALS / HEALTH SERVICES [HOS]

CENTERVILLE

Saint Thomas Hickman Hospital - 135 E. Swan St., Centerville, TN 37033-1466; Mailing: 102 Woodmont Blvd., Ste. 800, Nashville, TN 37205 t) 931-729-4271 gpope@ascension.org www.ascension.org Timothy Adams, CEO; Greg Pope, Chief Mission Officer; Bed Capacity: 48; Asstd. Annu.: 27,289; Staff: 120

MURFREESBORO

Saint Thomas Rutherford Hospital (Middle Tennessee Medical Center, Inc., Ascension Saint Thomas Rutherford) - 1700 Medical Center Pkwy., Murfreesboro, TN 37129; Mailing: 102 Woodmont Blvd., Ste. 800, Nashville, TN 37205 t) 615-396-4101 gpope@ascension.org www.ascension.org Timothy Adams, CEO; Greg Pope, Chief Mission Officer; Bed Capacity: 358; Asstd. Annu.: 131,043; Staff: 1,690

NASHVILLE

Saint Thomas Health Foundations - 4220 Harding Rd., Nashville, TN 37205; Mailing: 102 Woodmont Blvd., Ste. 800, Nashville, TN 37205 t) 615-222-6800 gpope@ascension.org www.ascension.org Timothy Adams, CEO; Greg Pope, Chief Mission Officer; Asstd. Annu.: 6,806,284; Staff: 7

Saint Thomas Regional Hospitals - 4220 Harding Pike, Nashville, TN 37205; Mailing: 102 Woodmont Blvd., Ste. 800, Nashville, TN 37205 t) 844-655-2111 gpope@ascension.org www.ascension.org Timothy Adams, CEO; Greg Pope, Chief Mission Officer; Bed Capacity: 28; Asstd. Annu.: 22,876; Staff: 109

Saint Thomas West Hospital - 4220 Harding Rd., Nashville, TN 37205; Mailing: 102 Woodmont Blvd., Ste. 800, Nashville, TN 37205 t) 615-222-2111 gpope@ascension.org www.ascension.org Timothy Adams, CEO; Greg Pope, Chief Mission Integration Officer; Bed Capacity: 1,002; Asstd. Annu.: 253,856; Staff: 3,616

St. Thomas Network - ; Mailing: 102 Woodmont Blvd., Ste. 600, Nashville, TN 37205

MISCELLANEOUS [MIS]

ASHLAND CITY

Diocesan Council of Catholic Women - 3384 Bell St., Ashland City, TN 37015 t) 615-476-6244 ejbardet@comcast.net JoAnn Bardett, Contact;

NASHVILLE

Catholic Community Investment and Loan, Inc. - 2800 McGavock Pike, Nashville, TN 37214 t) 615-383-6393 teresa.coburn@dioceseofnashville.com John Roberts, CFO;

***Catholic Media Productions, Inc.** - 2800 McGavock Pike, Nashville, TN 37214 t) 615-783-0754 bill.staley@dioceseofnashville.com www.webelieveshow.org Joe Cacopardo, Contact; Gia Raney, Contact;

Diocesan Properties, Inc. (Marina Manor East Apartments) - 414 Neill Ave., Nashville, TN 37206; Mailing: 2800 McGavock Pike, Nashville, TN 37214 t) 615-383-6393

Dominican Campus - 4210 Harding Pike, Nashville, TN 37205 t) 615-383-3230 srahyacinth@dominicancampus.org Sr. Ann Hyacinth, Admin.;

FrassatiUSA Inc. (University Catholic) - 2004 Terrace Pl., Nashville, TN 37203; Mailing: P.O. Box 50571, Nashville, TN 37205 t) 615-322-0104 kathleencordell@gmail.com Rev. Rhodes Winslow Bolster, Chap.;

Hand in Hand Options, Inc. - 2800 McGavock Pike, Nashville, TN 37214 t) 615-540-1255 kathy.boles@dioceseofnashville.com Kathy Harrigan Boles, Dir.;

Ladies of Charity of Nashville, Inc. - 2216 State St., Nashville, TN 37203 t) 615-327-3453; 615-327-3430 info@ladiesofcharity.org Affiliated with the Ladies of Charity of the United States of America, LCUSA, and the Association of International Charities, AIC. Terri Puma, Admin.;

St. Mary Villa, Inc. - 1700 Heiman St., Nashville, TN 37208 t) 615-356-6336 yneal@stmaryvilla.org Alyssa Garnett, Exec.;

Parish Twinning Program of the Americas - 309 Windemere Woods Dr., Nashville, TN 37215 t) 615-298-3002 parishprogram@aol.com www.parishprogram.org Theresa Patterson, Exec.;

Priests Eucharistic League - 2800 McGavock Pike, Nashville, TN 37214 t) 615-383-6393 hans.toecker@dioceseofnashville.com Dcn. Hans M. Toecker;

NURSING / REHABILITATION / CONVALESCENCE / ELDERLY CARE [NUR]

NASHVILLE

Villa Maria Manor, Inc. - 32 White Bridge Rd., Nashville, TN 37205 t) 615-352-3084 richard.borofski@maryqueenofangels.com Richard Borofski, CEO; Asstd. Annu.: 300; Staff: 12

PRESCHOOLS / CHILDCARE CENTERS [PRE]

FAIRVIEW

Camp Marymount - 1318 Fairview Blvd., Fairview, TN 37062 t) 615-799-0410 info@campmarymount.com www.campmarymount.com Summer camp. Tommy Hagey, Dir.; Stds.: 780; Lay Tchrs.: 70

NASHVILLE

***St. Bernard After School Program** - 2020 24th Ave. S., Nashville, TN 37212 t) (615) 298-1298; (615) 385-3440 jharkey@stbernard.org Stds.: 100; Lay Tchrs.: 7

St. Mary Villa Child Development Center - 1700 Heiman St., Nashville, TN 37208 t) 615-356-6336 claire.givens@stmaryvilla.org Alyssa Garnett, Exec.; Stds.: 160; Lay Tchrs.: 30

RETREAT HOUSES / RENEWAL CENTERS [RTR]

DICKSON

Bethany Retreat House - 2002 Garners Creek Rd., Dickson, TN 37055 t) 615-446-2063; 615-878-0280 (Reservations) bethanyretreat@op-tn.org Owned and operated by St. Cecilia Congregation.

LIBERTY

Carmel Center of Spirituality - 112 Hermitage Ln., Liberty, TN 37095; Mailing: P.O. Box 117, Liberty, TN 37095 t) 615-536-5177 carmelcentertn@gmail.com; jamespanckal@gmail.com Rev. Sebastian Thekkedam, C.M.I., Pres.; Rev. James Panackal, C.M.I., Dir.; Rev. Davy Kavungal, C.M.I., Mem.; Rev. Roy Palatty, C.M.I., Bd. Mem.;

SPECIAL CARE FACILITIES [SPF]

NASHVILLE

Mary, Queen of Angels. Inc. - 34 White Bridge Rd., Nashville, TN 37205 t) 615-760-4424 richard.borofski@maryqueenofangels.com www.maryqueenofangels.com Richard Borofski, CEO; Bed Capacity: 110; Asstd. Annu.: 150; Staff: 85

An asterisk (*) denotes an organization that has established tax-exempt status directly with the IRS and is not covered by the USCCB Group Ruling.

Archdiocese of Newark

(Archidioecesis Novarcensis)

HIS EMINENCE JOSEPH CARDINAL TOBIN, C.SS.R.

Archbishop of Newark; ordained a priest of the Congregation of the Most Holy Redeemer June 1, 1978; Episcopal Ordination as Titular Archbishop of Obba October 9, 2010; installed Archbishop of Indianapolis December 3, 2012; appointed Archbishop of Newark November 7, 2016; Elevated to Cardinal November 19, 2016; installed Archbishop of Newark January 6, 2017. Office: 171 Clifton Ave., P.O. Box 9500, Newark, NJ 07104-9500.

Archdiocesan Center: 171 Clifton Ave., P.O. Box 9500, Newark, NJ 07104-9500. T: 973-497-4000; F: 973-497-4033.
www.rcan.org webmaster@rcan.org

Square Miles 513.

Diocese Established, 1853; Erected an Archdiocese, December 10, 1937.

Comprises Four Counties in the State of New Jersey, viz.: Bergen, Hudson, Essex and Union.

For legal titles of parishes and archdiocesan institutions, consult the Chancery Office.

MOST REVEREND MANUEL A. CRUZ
Auxiliary Bishop of Newark; ordained May 31, 1980; appointed Titular Bishop of Gaguari and Auxiliary Bishop of Newark May 19, 2008; Episcopal ordination September 8, 2008; installed September 8, 2008. 171 Clifton Ave., Newark, NJ 07104. T: 201-320-6367; T: 973-497-4009.

MOST REVEREND MICHAEL A. SAPORITO, D.D.
Auxiliary Bishop of Newark; ordained May 30, 1992; appointed Titular Bishop of Luperciana and Auxiliary Bishop of Newark February 27, 2020; Episcopal ordination June 30, 2020. Office: 348 N. Franklin Tpke., Ho Ho Kus, NJ 07423. T: 201-375-6438.

MOST REVEREND ELIAS E. LORENZO, O.S.B.
Auxiliary Bishop of Newark; ordained June 24, 1989; appointed Titular Bishop of Tabuda and Auxiliary Bishop of Newark February 27, 2020; Episcopal ordination and installed June 30, 2020. Office & Res.: 306 Morris Ave., Summit, NJ 07901. T: 908-273-5618; F: 908-273-5908.

MOST REVEREND GREGORY J. STUDERUS, D.D.
Auxiliary Bishop of Newark; ordained May 31, 1980; appointed Titular Bishop of Tarasa in Byzacena and Auxiliary Bishop of Newark February 27, 2020; Episcopal ordination June 30, 2020. Office: Hudson Catholic Regional High School, 790 Bergen Ave., Jersey City, NJ 07306. T: 201-332-5970, Ext. 153.

STATISTICAL OVERVIEW

Personnel	
Cardinals	1
Auxiliary Bishops	4
Retired Bishops	2
Abbots	1
Priests: Diocesan Active in Diocese	328
Priests: Diocesan Active Outside Diocese	30
Priests: Diocesan in Foreign Missions	12
Priests: Retired, Sick or Absent	206
Number of Diocesan Priests	576
Religious Priests in Diocese	151
Total Priests in your Diocese	727
Extern Priests in Diocese	47
Ordinations:	
Diocesan Priests	5
Religious Priests	4
Transitional Deacons	1
Permanent Deacons in Diocese	139
Total Brothers	61
Total Sisters	708
Parishes	
Parishes	212
With Resident Pastor:	
Resident Diocesan Priests	167
Resident Religious Priests	24
Without Resident Pastor:	
Administered by Priests	21
Professional Ministry Personnel:	
Brothers	6
Sisters	65
Lay Ministers	479
Welfare	
Catholic Hospitals	3
Total Assisted	949,770
Health Care Centers	1
Total Assisted	11,077
Homes for the Aged	4
Total Assisted	741
Day Care Centers	4
Total Assisted	566
Specialized Homes	5
Total Assisted	719
Special Centers for Social Services	23
Total Assisted	71,952
Educational	
Seminaries, Diocesan	3
Students from This Diocese	31
Total Seminarians	31
Colleges and Universities	4
Total Students	17,233
High Schools, Diocesan and Parish	13
Total Students	5,720
High Schools, Private	10
Total Students	4,495
Elementary Schools, Diocesan and Parish	45
Total Students	11,058
Elementary Schools, Private	5
Total Students	1,229
Catechesis/Religious Education:	
High School Students	4,000
Elementary Students	60,603
Total Students under Catholic Instruction	104,369
Teachers in Diocese:	
Priests	12
Brothers	6
Sisters	43
Lay Teachers	2,447
Vital Statistics	
Receptions into the Church:	
Infant Baptism Totals	8,584
Minor Baptism Totals	156
Adult Baptism Totals	154
Received into Full Communion	175
First Communions	7,033
Confirmations	6,937
Marriages:	
Catholic	1,273
Interfaith	168
Total Marriages	1,441
Deaths	7,222
Total Catholic Population	1,220,143
Total Population	3,119,659

LEADERSHIP

Archdiocesan Archbishop - His Eminence Joseph Cardinal Tobin, C.Ss.R.;
Priest Secretary to the Archbishop - Rev. Jason J. Makarow;
Chancellor - t) 973-497-4128 Sr. Donna L. Ciangio, O.P.;
Vicar General - Rev. John J. Chadwick, Vicar;
Auxiliary Bishop of Newark and Regional Bishop for Union County - Most Rev. Elias R. Lorenzo, O.S.B. (most.rev.elias.lorenzo@rcan.org);
Auxiliary Bishop of Newark and Regional Bishop for Hudson County - Most Rev. Gregory J. Studerus (most.rev.gregory.studerus@rcan.org);
Auxiliary Bishop of Newark and Regional Bishop for Bergen County - Most Rev. Michael A. Saporito (most.rev.michael.saporito@rcan.org);
Auxiliary Bishop of Newark and Regional Bishop for Essex County - Most Rev. Manuel A. Cruz (cruz.manuel@mac.com);
Chief Operating Officer - t) 973-497-4012 Lawrence Boland (lawrence.boland@rcan.org);
Delegate for Religious - t) 973-497-4582 Sr. Patricia Wormann, O.P.;
Metropolitan Judicial Vicar - t) 973-497-4145 Rev. Raphael Lee, Vicar (rev.raphael.lee@rcan.org);
Episcopal Vicar for Healthcare and Social Concerns - t) 201-444-2000 Rev. Msgr. Ronald J. Rozniak, Vicar;
Vicar for Education/Interim Superintendent of Schools - t) 973-497-4253 Rev. Msgr. Thomas J. McDade, Supt.;
Cardinal's Delegate for Canonical Affairs - t) 973-497-4292 Sr. Rosemary Smith, S.C.;
Vicar for Priests and Director of Clergy Personnel - t) 973-497-4222 Rev. Charles Pinyan, Vicar (rev.charles.pinyan@rcan.org);
Chief Financial Officer - t) 973-497-4560 Joseph C. Pescatore (pescatjo@rcan.org);
Minister for Priests - Rev. Gabriel B. Costa;
Executive Director of Human Resources - Dcn. John J. McKenna, Vice Chancellor (mckennjo@rcan.org);
Director of Vocations - t) 973-313-6190 Rev. Eugenio P. De La Rama;

OFFICES AND DIRECTORS

Advocate Publishing Corp. - t) 973-497-4190
Apostleship of the Air - t) 973-497-4218 Rev. John McCrone, Chap.;
Apostleship of the Sea - t) 973-589-7946 Rev. John F. Corbett, Dir.;
Campus Ministry - t) 973-497-4305 Rev. James N. Chern, Dir.;
Catechetical Office - t) 973-497-4285; 973-497-4291
Catholic Charities of the Archdiocese of Newark -
Administration - t) 973-596-4100 Rev. Msgr. Robert J. Fuhrman, Chair; John Westervelt, Pres.;
Bishop Francis Immigration Services - Kiera LoBreglio, Mng. Attorney; Polliann Hardeo, Staff Attorney; Michael Younker, Staff Attorney;
Catholic Charities of the Archdiocese of Newark - t) 973-596-4100 Joycelynn J. Murray, Exec. Asst. to CEO;
Catholic Charities - Programs -
Child Protective Services & In-Home Hispanic Family Services - t) 908-497-3946 Dawn Glasgow, Prog. Mgr.;
Connecting Youth - t) 908-497-3946 Dawn Glasgow, Prog. Mgr.;
DCA Housing Counseling Program - Kerri Brown, Supvr.; Emma Papiol-Izquierdo, Housing Counselor; Shirley Hill, Prog. Asst.;
Family and Adoption Services - t) 201-246-7379 Patricia Chiarello, Prog. Mgr.;
Family Resource Center - Gilma Garcia, Prog. Mgr.;
Hudson Mobile Response and Stabilization Services (MRSS) - t) 201-798-7452 Patricia Valdivia, Prog. Mgr.;
Intensive Family Support Services - t) 201-798-9925 Iskra Gomez, Prog. Mgr.;
Intensive In-Home Family Counseling - t) 201-798-9921 Susan Takvorian, Prog. Mgr.;
Partners With Parents and Families - t) 201-246-7379 Patricia Chiarello, Prog. Mgr.;
Partnership for Children - t) 973-266-7983 Shelley Steinberg, Prog. Mgr.;
Providence Place - t) 201-433-1832 Christina Acosta, Prog. Mgr.;
School Social Work Services - t) 973-266-7983 Shelley Steinberg, Prog. Mgr.;
SSVF, Bergen County - Lorena Libreros, Case Mgr.; Anna Rizzo, Case Mgr. Asst.;
SSVF, Essex County - Karolyn Mora, Case Mgr.; Brianna Williams, Case Mgr. Asst.; Adria Goldenkranz, Outreach Worker;
SSVF Hudson County - Briana Washington, Case Mgr.; Anna Rizzo, Case Mgr. Asst.;
SSVF Union County - Johnia Osias, Case Mgr.; Maricarmen Richter, Case Mgr. Asst.;
Strong Futures - t) 201-864-2290 Kathy Elias, Prog. Mgr.;
Supportive Services for Veterans Families (SSVF), Essex County - Lakisha Stewart, Prog. Supvr.;
West Side Children's Counseling Center - Suzy Takvorian, Screener;
Community Access and Volunteer Services Division - t) 973-266-7978 Susana Armas, Dir.;
Adult Protective Services - t) 908-497-3932 Susan Harrigan Fowles;
Bergen Care Management Program - Bergen Senior Center - t) 201-441-9428 Tamar Aulet, Prog. Mgr.;
City of Newark: Rapid Re-Housing - t) 973-266-7969 Melanie Daniels;
Emergency Food and Nutrition Network - t) 908-497-3903; 908-407-4012 Constanza Robledo, Dir.;
Mental Health Caregiver Program - t) 908-497-4011 Margaret McGroary, Caregiver Clinician/Project Mgr.;
New Day Community - t) 973-763-6430 Vincent McMahon, Dir.;
Parish Access Center - Essex County - t) 973-266-7991 Karen Carinha;
Parish Access Center - Hudson County - t) 201-798-9958 Yanil Mendonza;
Parish Access Center - Union County - t) 908-497-3966
Parish Access Centers - t) 800-227-7413 Pamela Graham, Exec. Sec.;
Telephone Reassurance, Home Shopping Services, Hispanic Older Adult Information and Referral, Visually Impaired Seniors Program - Gabriela Richter; Jacklyn Milonas, Secy.; Gloria Lepore, Front Desk Recep.;
Domus Corporation - t) 973-596-3984 John Westervelt, Pres.; Elizabeth A. McClendon, Vice. Pres.; Bro. Benedict LoBalbo, F.M.S., Secy.;
Education Division -
Early Childhood Programs - Susan Harbace, Dir.;
Mount Carmel Guild Cares - Dorothy Cimo, Mgr.;
Mount Carmel Guild Little Schoolhouse - t) 908-282-4610 Susan Harbace, Dir.;
Housing Division - Rose Howard, Dir.; Minerva Perez, Admin. Asst.;
Canaan House - t) 201-434-3939 Lance Kearny, Prog. Mgr.;
Franciska Residence - t) 201-653-3366 James Smith, Prog. Mgr.;
Hope House - t) 201-420-1220 Lillybeth Ramirez, Prog. Mgr.;
PATH Outreach - Homeless Street Outreach PATH Train Stations - t) 201-653-3366 Rose Howard, Dir.;
St. Bridget Residence - t) 973-799-0484 Shronica Thompson, Prog. Mgr.;
St. Jude Oasis - t) 201-656-7201 Rose Howard, Dir.;
St. Lucy Single Person Shelter - t) 201-656-7201 Laurie Cherry, Acting Prog. Mgr.;
St. Rocco Emergency Family Shelter - t) 973-286-4175 Makagbe Swaray, Prog. Mgr.;
Hudson County Jail (Men's Substance Abuse Progran & HIV Rapid Testing) -
Hudson County Prevention, Information, and Education Services for Seniors (P.I.E.S. for Seniors) - t) 908-497-3953 Alicia Boone, Prog. Mgr.;
Hudson County, Visually Impaired Socialization Program - t) 201-325-4811 Ivis L. Alvarez;
Mount Carmel Guild Behavioral Health System - John Westervelt, CEO; Elizabeth A. McClendon, Exec.;
Behavioral Health Services - Rima Patel, Outpatient & Partial Care Clinical Team Leader, Essex County; Margery A. Grimm-DeFranco, Dir.; Ahylazbeth Giannantonio, Partial Clinical Team Leader;
ICMS-Essex (Integrated Case Management Services-Essex County) - t) 973-522-2125 Rogena Navarin, Prog. Mgr.;
ICMS-Union (Integrated Case Management Services-Union County) - Cheryl Tolentino, Prog. Mgr.; Rosalva Villaronga, Admin. Specialist;
PACT (Program for Assertive Community Treatment) - t) 973-466-1348 Rashidah Jenious, Dir. PACT/ICMS;
Mount Carmel Guild Education - John Westervelt, CEO; Joycelynn J. Murray, Exec. Asst.;
Mount Carmel Guild Academy - t) 973-325-4000 James Badavas, Prin.; Catherine Cruz, Prin.; Roussel Simon, Prin.;
Patient Accounts - t) 973-596-4058 Mary Meehan-Cairns, Dir.;
Residential Services - Jennifer Quick, Dir.; Catherine Miguel, Team Leader, Union City Residential;
Union County Jail (HIV Rapid Testing & Ryan White HIV Discharge Planning) - t) 908-497-3953 Alicia Boone, Prog. Mgr.;
Workforce Development Division - t) 973-268-3162 Sandra Fils, Dir.;
SAIF: Middlesex/Union - t) 973-266-7993 Reginald Holding Jr., Prog. Mgr.; Rachid Taylor; A'Nijaah Hollaway;
Supported Employment Program - Harry Frazier, Prog. Mgr.; Michelle Bravo, Vocational Counselor;
Workforce Development - Boland Training Center - Sandra Fils; Daniella Hincapie, Prog. Mgr.; Armando Rivera, Displaced Homemaker;
Workforce Development - SAIF - Sophia Davis, Prog. Mgr.; Reginald Holding Jr., Prog. Mgr. Middlesex/Union; Ivette Davis, Admin. Asst.;
Catholic Scouting -
Boy Scouts/Girl Scouts/Catholic Committee on Scouting - t) 201-998-0088 www.newarkoym.com Rich Donovan, Assoc. Dir., Events, Camp & Scouting; Rev. Timothy G. Graff, Chap.; Rev. Eugene J. Field, Chap.;
Central Office of Catholic Cemeteries - t) 973-497-7981 www.rcancem.org Andrew P. Schafer, Exec. (schafean@rcan.org);
Archdiocesan Cemeteries -
Mausoleum Office - t) 973-497-7988 Andrew P. Schafer, Exec.;
Parochial Cemeteries -
CYO Youth Retreat Center - t) 201-998-0088 www.newarkoym.com Thomas G. Conboy, Dir. (conboyth@rcan.org);
Delegate for Religious - Sr. Patricia Wormann, O.P., Dir.; Karin Walters, Admin. Asst. (walterka@rcan.org);
Department of Social Concerns - t) 973-497-4318 Rev. Timothy G. Graff, Dir. (grafftim@rcan.org);
Director of Communications and Public Relations - t) 973-497-4186 Maria Margiotta (maria.margiotta@rcan.org);
Executive Director of Parish Business Services - Nancy F. Lystash, Vice Chancellor (lystasna@rcan.org);
Family Life Ministries - t) 973-497-4328 www.rcan.org/famlife/precana.htm Brian Caldwell, Dir.;
Hispanic Family Life Ministries - t) 973-497-4326

Yamilka Genao, Assoc. Dir.;
Ministry to the Bereaved, Separated, Divorced, Widowed - t) 973-497-4317 Brian Caldwell;
Natural Family Planning - t) 973-497-4317 Brian Caldwell;
Worldwide Marriage Encounter - t) 800-823-5683 www.wwme.org Peter Torpie; Lynne Torpie; Michael Turco;
General Counsel - t) 973-497-4299 Steven Llanes;
Hispanic Apostolate - Most Rev. Manuel A. Cruz, Vicar (cruz.manuel@mac.com); Dcn. Asterio Velasco, Coord. (velascas@rcan.org);
Italian Apostolate -
Korean Apostolate - t) 973-763-1170 Rev. Minhyun Cho, Coord.;
Liaison to the Irish Community - t) 973-325-6624 Rev. Msgr. Michael E. Kelly;
Metropolitan Tribunal - t) 973-497-4140 Rev. Raphael Lee, Vicar (rev.raphael.lee@rcan.org);
Archdiocesan Judges - Rev. John J. Cryan; Rev. Paul A. Cannariato; Rev. Frank Rose;
Defenders of the Bond - Rev. Msgr. Frank G. Del Prete, Promoter of Justice; Rev. Msgr. Mark Condon; Christina Hip-Flores;
Full-time Staff - Rev. Carmine Rizzi;
Notaries - Sandra Perrini; John Walsh;
Part-time Staff/Advocates/Procurators - Rev. Paul A. Cannariato; Rev. Robert Wolfee; Rev. Vincent D'Agostino;
Secretarial Staff - Rose Marie Fitzgerald; Nancy I. Negron;
Multicultural Affairs - t) 973-497-4013 Rev. John F. Gordon, Coord.;
Asian-Indian Apostolate - t) 201-433-8500 Rev. Theesmas Pankiraj, Coord.;
Brazilian Apostolate - t) 973-344-8322 Rev. Clement M. Krug, C.Ss.R., Coord.;
Croatian Apostolate - Rev. Giordano Belanich, Coord.;
Filipino Apostolate - Rev. Ernesto Tibay, Coord.;
Haitian Apostolate - t) 973-372-1272 Rev. Msgr. Beaubrun Ardouin, Coord.;
Liaison to the Chinese Community - t) 732-519-1372 Sr. Dong Hong Marie Zhang, C.Ss.R., Coord.;
Nigerian IBO Catholic Community - t) 973-824-6548 Rev. Erasmus Okere, Coord.;
Office for the Protection of the Faithful - t) 973-497-4254 Karen Clark, Dir. (clarkkar@rcan.org);
Office of African American, African, and Caribbean Apostolate - t) 973-497-4304 Rev. Emeka Okwuosa, Coord.;
Office of Archdiocesan Counsel - t) 973-994-1700 Steven Llanes;
Office of Banking and Investments - t) 973-497-4069 Matthew Phelan, Dir.;
Office of Clergy Personnel - t) 973-497-4220 Rev. Charles Pinyan, Dir. (rev.charles.pinyan@rcan.org); Roseann Vazquez, Senior Exec. Asst.;
Adjunct Clergy Personnel - Rev. John Stanley Gomes, Dir.; Teresa Grillo, Secy.;
Continuing Education and Formation of Priests - Rev. John M. McCrone, Dir.; Teresa Grillo, Admin. Asst.;
Ministry to Retired Priests - Rev. John Stanley Gomes; Karin Walters, Admin. Asst.;
Office of the Permanent Diaconate - Rev. James V. Teti, Dir.; Dcn. John J. McKenna, Dir.;
Office of Communications and Public Relations - t) 973-497-4186 Maria Margiotta, Dir. (maria.margiotta@rcan.org);
Office of Development & Stewardship - www.rcan.org/development Thomas Smith, Dir. (thomas.smith@rcan.org);
Office of Divine Worship - Rev. Thomas A. Dente, Dir. (dentetom@rcan.org); Rev. Joseph A. Mancini, Dir.; Rev. Armand Mantia, Dir.;
Office of Evangelization - t) 973-497-4353 Rev. John F. Gordon, Dir. (gordonjo@rcan.org);
Couples for Christ - Rev. Edgardo P. Jocson, Spiritual Adv./Care Srvcs.; Rodger Santos, Dir.;
Focolare Movement - t) 201-736-2821 www.focolare.us Rod Vega; Yvette Vega; Mariapolis Luminosa;
Marriage Preparation - t) 973-497-4328 Jennifer Ferraioli;
Office of Finance - Joseph C. Pescatore, CFO (pescatjo@rcan.org); Stephanie M. Alcuino, Controller (alcuinst@rcan.org); Josue Philistin, Asst. Controller;
Office of Human Resources - Dcn. John J. McKenna, Exec. (mckennjo@rcan.org); Dennis Miller, Dir. (dennis.miller@rcan.org); Maria Joyner, Dir. (joynerma@rcan.org);
Office of Information Technology Services - t) 973-497-4161 Robert J. Kennelly, Chief Technology Officer;
Office of Parish Internal Audit - t) 973-497-4073 Therese A. Kropp, Asst. Dir.;
Office of Property Management Administration - Steven Belloise, Exec. (belloist@rcan.org); Nassar Shabo, Dir. (shabonas@rcan.org); Kevin Comp, Dir. (compkevi@rcan.org);
Office of Research and Planning - t) 973-497-4024 Mark Howard, Dir. (howard@rcan.org);
Office of School Business Services - Donna Quinn, Dir.; Julian Ferreira, Coord. School Business Svcs.; Heidi Kopala, Sr. Auditor Regl. & Parish High School Finances;
Office of the Archbishop -
Assistant to the Archbishop for Public Affairs - t) 973-497-4107 Rev. Msgr. Christopher J. Hynes;
Chancellor - t) 973-497-4128 Sr. Donna L. Ciangio, O.P.;
Priest Secretary to the Archbishop - t) 973-497-4005 Rev. Jason J. Makarow;
Office of the Vicar General - t) 973-497-4002 Rev. John J. Chadwick;
Cardinal's Delegate for Canonical Affairs - Sr. Rosemary Smith, S.C.;
Chief Operating Officer - t) 973-497-4012 Lawrence Boland;
Executive Assistant to the Vicar General (Vacant) - t) 973-497-4003
Office Services/Mailroom - t) 973-497-4035 Lucia Lopez, Oper. Supvr. (lopezluc@rcan.org);
Parish Business Services - Nancy F. Lystash, Exec. (lystasna@rcan.org); Arlene Wisniowski, Business Systems Analyst (wisnioar@rcan.org);
Pastoral Ministries with Persons with Disabilities - t) 973-497-4309 Anne Masters, Dir. (anne.masters.@rcan.org);
Pastoral Ministry with the Deaf - t) 973-552-2210 Rev. Thomas Coughlin, Dir.;
Polish/Slavic Apostolate - t) 973-344-2743 Rev. Andrzej Ostaszewski, Coord.;
Portuguese Apostolate - t) 908-355-3810 Rev. Joseph E.S. Dos Santos, Coord.;
Public Policy Committee of the New Jersey Catholic Conference - Rev. Timothy G. Graff, Social Concerns Rep. (grafftim@rcan.org);
Respect Life Office - t) 973-497-4350 Cheryl Riley, Dir. (rileyche@rcan.org);
The Mercy House - t) 973-643-8000 mercyhouseinfo@rcan.org Cheryl Riley;
Risk Management, Insurance Services and Business Administration - Donna M. Wrobel, Dir. (wrobeldo@rcan.org); Diannah P. Hedgebeth, Account Svc. Mgr.;
Vicar for Education/Interim Superintendent of Schools - t) 973-497-4253 Rev. Msgr. Thomas J. McDade, Supt.; Sr. Patricia Butler, S.C., Dir.; Mary McElroy, Dir.;
Assistant Superintendent of Curriculum, Instruction and Assessment - Barbara Dolan; June Butchko, Prog. Asst., Curriculum & Assessment;
Assistant Superintendents for Elementary Schools - Sr. Marie Gagliano, M.P.F., Asst. Supt.;
Assistant Superintendents for Secondary Schools -
Victims Assistance Coordinator - t) 201-407-3256 Wendy Pierson;
Vietnamese Apostolate - t) 201-434-8500 Rev. Joseph Minh Nguyen, Coord.;
Vocations Office - t) 973-313-6190 www.newpriestnj.org Rev. Eugenio P. De La Rama, Dir.; Matthew Higgins, Assoc. Dir. (higginma@rcan.org);
Vocations Board - Rev. Eugenio P. De La Rama; Rev. John J. Chadwick; Rev. Sean A. Manson;
Youth and Young Adult Ministries - t) 201-998-0088 www.newarkoym.com Thomas G. Conboy, Dir. (conboyth@rcan.org); Rev. Timothy G. Graff, Chap. (grafftim@rcan.org); Geraldine Ricci-Menegolla, Office Mgr. & Exec. Sec. (ricciger@rcan.org);

ADVISORY BOARDS, COMMISSIONS, COMMITTEES, AND COUNCILS

Archdiocesan Finance Council - Rev. John J. Chadwick, Vicar Gen.; Henry J. Amoroso, Vice Chm.; Charles C. Carella;
College of Consultors - His Eminence Joseph Cardinal Tobin, C.Ss.R.; Rev. John J. Chadwick, Vicar; Most Rev. Michael A. Saporito, Regl. Bishop for Bergen County (most.rev.michael.saporito@rcan.org);
Council of Priests - His Eminence Joseph Cardinal Tobin, C.Ss.R., Pres.; Most Rev. Manuel A. Cruz, Episcopal Vicar of Essex County (cruz.manuel@mac.com); Most Rev. John W. Flesey, Retired Auxiliary Bishop of Bergen County (jflesey@mbschurchnj.org);
Appointed - Rev. Yuvan A. Alvarez, Pst.; Rev. Michael A. Hanly; Rev. Esterminio Chica, Pst.;
Elected - Rev. John R. Job; Rev. Joseph A. Scarangella; Rev. Paul A. Cannariato;
Diaconate Executive Committee - Dcn. Joseph Yandoli, Chair;
New Energies - Implementation Team (New Energies Parish Transition Project) - t) 973-497-4318 Rev. Timothy G. Graff, Chair (grafftim@rcan.org);
Priest Personnel Policy Board - Rev. Joseph A. D'Amico; Rev. Timothy G. Graff (grafftim@rcan.org); Rev. Charles Pinyan, Chair (rev.charles.pinyan@rcan.org);

DEANERIES

Regional Bishops & Deans - Most Rev. Manuel A. Cruz, Regl. Bishop for Essex County (cruz.manuel@mac.com); Most Rev. Elias R. Lorenzo, O.S.B., Regl. Bishop for Union County (most.rev.elias.lorenzo@rcan.org); Rev. Msgr. Gregory J. Studerus, Regl. Bishop for Hudson County;

ORGANIZATIONS

Affirmative Action - t) 973-994-1700 Charles M. Carella, Counselor at Law;
Archdiocesan Commission for Interreligious Affairs - t) 201-935-6492 Rev. Philip F. A. Latronico, Chair;
Archdiocesan Commission of Christian Unity - Rev. Luke A. Edelen, O.S.B., Chair; Rev. Philip F. A. Latronico, Exec. Sec.;
Archdiocesan Commission on Justice and Peace - t) 973-497-4341 Rev. Timothy G. Graff, Exec. Sec. (grafftim@rcan.org);
Archdiocesan Council of Catholic Women (N.C.C.W.) - t) 973-497-4356 D. Jean Schneider, Pres. (d.jeansch@juno.com); Florence Horgan, Vice. Pres.; Margaret Henderson, Vice. Pres.;
Archdiocesan Liturgical Commission -
Archdiocesan Liturgies for the Archdiocese of Newark - Rev. Joseph A. Mancini, Dir.;
Archdiocesan Pro-Life Commission - James Sondey, Chair;
Archdiocesan/University Archives - Seton Hall University, Walsh Library - t) 973-761-9476 Brianna Losardo, Archivist (briana.losardo@rcan.org); Alan Delozier, University Archivist (alan.delozier@shu.edu);
Archdiocesan Women's Commission - t) 973-497-4137
Bukas-Loob Sa Diyos Community (BLD) (Open to the Spirit of God) - t) 973-856-8222 secretariat@bldnewark.com www.bldnewark.com Rev. Joseph R. Meagher, Spiritual Adv./Care Srvcs. (saintantoninuschurch@gmail.com); Jovy Lucero; Fil Flores, Evangelization;

Buklod Ng Pag-Ibig Foundation, USA, Inc. (Bond of Love) - t) 201-521-1019 Rev. Christopher M. Panlilo; Rev. Joemarie M. Parcon; Pantaleon Escober Jr.;
Cathedral Affiliated Group at Orange, Inc. - t) 973-690-3606
Censores Librorum - Rev. Msgr. Robert F. Coleman, Chair; Rev. John J. Chadwick; Rev. Hong-Ray Peter Cho;
Charismatic Renewal - t) 973-497-4353 Rev. John F. Gordon (gordonjo@rcan.org);
Commission for the Men's Apostolate - John D'Alessio, Chair; Dcn. Asterio Velasco, Chair (velascas@rcan.org);
The Community of God's Love - Doreen Cevasco, Dir.; Rev. Philip F. A. Latronico, Chap.;
Cursillo Movement - Rev. Thomas P. Lipnicki, Dir.; Anne Ventola, Dir.; Joanne Rinkus, Secy.;
Holy Name Federation - t) 908-486-6363 Norman S. Karf, Dir.;
Legion of Mary -
Archdiocese of Newark Commitium - t) 973-674-0110 Rev. Jose M. Parcon, Spiritual Dir.;
Foundation of Mercy Curia - t) 201-803-7557 Rev. Paul Kyung Lee, Dir.;
Hispanic Curia of Essex and Union Counties - t) 973-372-1272 Rev. Carlos M. Viego, Dir.;
Hispanic Curia of Hudson County - t) 201-945-4865 Rev. Joseph D. Girone, Dir.;
Maria Immaculata Curia of Hudson County (Vacant) -
Mary Most Humble Curia (Korean) - t) 201-767-1954 Rev. Didaco Yung Soo Kim, Spiritual Dir.;
Our Lady Gate of Heaven Curia - t) 973-763-1170 Rev. Min (Joseph) Hyun Cho, Dir.;
Our Lady Mother of God Curia (Korean) - t) 201-703-0080 Rev. Hongshik Don Bosco Park, Spiritual Dir.;
Our Lady of Love Curia - t) 201-803-7557 Rev. Paul Kyung Lee, Dir.;
Our Lady of the Most Holy Eucharist Curia of Bergen County - t) 973-617-6407 Rev. John T. Michalczak, Dir.;
Throne of God's Wisdom Curia - t) 201-767-1954 Rev. Didaco Yung Soo Kim, Dir.;
New Jersey Historical Records Commission - Seton Hall University - t) 973-275-2773 Alan Delozier, Exec. (alan.delozier@shu.edu);
Our Lady of Fatima First Saturday Family - Rev. Msgr. Paul L. Bochicchio, Chap.; Rev. Kevin E. Carter, Chap.;
Pastoral Association for Music & Liturgy - Andrew Cyr, Pst. Assoc.;
Pastoral Services Team - Rev. Jeremiah Browne; Rev. Alejandro Lopez-Cardinale; Sr. Maureen Colleary, F.S.P.;
Pontifical Mission Societies -
Propagation of the Faith; Society of St. Peter the Apostle; Missionary Childhood Association; Missionary Union of Priests & Religious - t) 973-497-4372 Rev. Msgr. Robert J. Fuhrman, Dir.;
RENEW International - t) 908-769-5400 renew@renewintl.org www.renewtot.org Greg Tobin, Pres.; Dcn. Peter Fiore, Exec. Dir.; Dcn. Charles Paolino, Mng. Editor;
The Scholarship Fund for Inner City Children - Michelle L. Hartman, CEO (dr.michelle.hartman@rcan.org); Hope C. Rhodes, Office Mgr. (hope.rhodes@rcan.org); Jasmin Roman, Scholarship Prog. Mgr. (jasmin.roman@rcan.org);
Serra Clubs - t) 201-954-1990 Joseph Pagano, Governor, District 22; Paul C. Tully, Past District Governor; Rose Marie Deehan, Secy.;
Serra Club of Bergen County - t) 201-998-9710 Mary Norton, Pres.; Rev. Joseph M. Quinlan Jr., Chap.;
Serra Club of Hudson County - t) 201-436-0263 Michael Bruzzio, Pres.; Rev. Philip A. Sanders, Chap.;
Serra Club of North Essex - t) 973-227-4689 Neil Pagano, Pres.; Rev. James M. Manos, Chap.;
Serra Club of the Oranges - Charlie Cameron, Pres.; Rev. Msgr. Thomas P. Nydegger, Chap.;
Serra Club of Union County West - t) 908-464-4058
Serra Club of West Essex - t) 973-669-8001 Theresa O'Boyle, Pres.; Rev. Daniel Danik, Chap.;
University Heights Property Co., Inc. - t) 973-690-3606

PARISHES, MISSIONS, AND CLERGY

STATE OF NEW JERSEY

ALLENDALE

Guardian Angel - 320 Franklin Tpke., Allendale, NJ 07401 t) 201-327-0352 (CRP); 201-327-4359 gachurch@guardianangelchurch.org; fferraro@guardianangelchurch.org www.guardianangelchurch.org Rev. Tadeusz Jank, Pst.; Dcn. Reynaldo Escalon; Frances Ferraro, DRE; Jennifer Kavanagh, Youth Min.; Klajdi Cerriku, Music Min.; CRP Stds.: 226

BAYONNE

St. Henry - 645 Ave. C, Bayonne, NJ 07002; Mailing: 82 W. 29th St., Bayonne, NJ 07002 t) 201-436-0857 sthenryrc@optonline.net www.sthenryrc.org Rev. Raul R. Gaviola, Pst.; Rev. Alfie A. Pangilinan, Assoc. Pst.;
Saint John Paul II Church - 39 E. 22nd St., Bayonne, NJ 07002 Rev. Zenon Boczek, S.D.S., Pst.; Rev. Andrzej Kujawa, S.D.S., Assoc. Pst.; Debra Czerwienski, DRE;
The Parish of Blessed Miriam Teresa Demjanovich Church - 326 Ave. C, Bayonne, NJ 07002 t) 201-437-4090 ccd@bmtparish.org; secretary@bmtparish.org bmtparish.org Rev. Philip A. Sanders, Pst.; Rev. Johan D. Betancourt, Par. Vicar; Philomena Coco, DRE; CRP Stds.: 148
All Saints Catholic Academy - (Grades PreK-8) 19 W. 13th St., Bayonne, NJ 07002 t) 201-443-8384 rfritzen@ascabayonne.org Sr. Rita M. Fritzen, Prin.;
St. Mary, Star of the Sea Church - t) 201-473-4090
St. Andrew the Apostle Church - 10 W. 4th St., Bayonne, NJ 07002
St. Vincent de Paul - 979 Ave. C, Bayonne, NJ 07002 t) 201-823-0184 Dcn. Michael P. Missaggia; Rev. Sergio O. Nadres (Philippines), Pst.; Rev. Hermes Diaz, Assoc. Pst.; Rev. Carl J. Arico, In Res.; Rev. David Buckles, In Res.; Christina Smith, DRE;

BELLEVILLE

St. Peter - 155 William St., Belleville, NJ 07109 t) 973-751-4290 (CRP); 973-751-2002 parish@spbnj.org www.spbnj.org Rev. Ivan Sciberras, Pst.; Rev. Darren Santo Tomas, Vicar; Dcn. Rodrigo Soriano; Lisa Melillo, DRE;
St. Peter School - (Grades PreK-8) 152 William St., Belleville, NJ 07109 t) 973-759-3143 Phyllis A. Sisco, Prin.;
Retreat Center - 149 William St., Belleville, NJ 07109

BERGENFIELD

St. John the Evangelist - 29 N. Washington Ave., Bergenfield, NJ 07621 t) 201-384-0101 pastor@sjrc.org www.sjrc.org Rev. Msgr. Richard J. Arnhols, Pst.; Rev. Cesar A. Infante, Par. Vicar; Rev. Oliver D. Nilo, Par. Vicar; Rev. Ashton I.F. Wong, Par. Vicar; Dcn. James Detura; Dcn. Airan Negrin; CRP Stds.: 497

BERKELEY HEIGHTS

Church of the Little Flower - 310 Plainfield Ave., Berkeley Heights, NJ 07922; Mailing: 290 Plainfield Ave., Berkeley Heights, NJ 07922 t) 908-464-1585 officemgr.lf@gmail.com www.littleflowerbh.org/ Rev. Andrew M. Prachar, Pst.; Rev. Matthew R. Dooley, Assoc. Pst.; Liz Mancinelli, Music Min.; Sabina Opechowski, Bus. Mgr.;

BLOOMFIELD

Church of St. Thomas the Apostle - 60 Byrd Ave., Bloomfield, NJ 07003 t) 973-338-7400 (CRP); 973-338-9190 rclan1@verizon.net; registration@stachurchbloomfield.com Rev. Lawrence J. Fama, Pst.; Rev. Lukasz Stanislaw Rokita, Par. Vicar; Dcn. Thomas J. Coyle; Dcn. Brian Murphy; Dcn. Michael Pasquale; Rev. Charles Pinyan, In Res.; Dr. Patricio Molina, Music Min.; Tracey K. Hann, DRE; Dr. Robert Miller, RCIA Coord.;
Church of St. Thomas the Apostle School - (Grades PreK-8) 50 Byrd Ave., Bloomfield, NJ 07003 t) 973-338-8505 mpetrillo@stthomastheapostlenj.com Michael Petrillo, Prin.; Ann Bialkowski, Librn.;
Sacred Heart - 76 Broad St., Bloomfield, NJ 07003 t) 973-743-4061 (CRP); 973-748-1800 nancy@shcbloomfield.org; info@shcbloomfield.org Rev. Gerald F. Greaves; Rev. James T. Brown, Pst.; Rev. Lukasz Stanislaw Rokita, Par. Vicar; Dcn. Guy W. Mier; Dcn. Jerry S. Rossi; Nancy Plate, DRE;
St. Valentine - 125 N. Spring St., Bloomfield, NJ 07003 t) 973-743-0220 stvalentine@yahoo.com Rev. Nnaemeka A. Onyemaobi, Admin.; Marta Girilli-Kuebler, DRE;

BOGOTA

St. Joseph - 115 E. Fort Lee Rd., Bogota, NJ 07603-1301 t) 201-343-4316 Rev. Timothy G. Graff, Pst.; Rev. Luis F. Diaz, Assoc. Pst.; Patricia Rodriguez, DRE;

CALDWELL

St. Aloysius - 219 Bloomfield Ave., Caldwell, NJ 07006 t) 973-226-0221 www.stalscaldwell.org Rev. Msgr. Robert E. Emery, Pst.; Rev. Lynx Soliman, Par. Vicar; Rev. Thomas F. Blind, In Res.; Rev. John J. Cryan, In Res.; Joseph T. Wozniak, Music Min.; Cathy Gibbons, Pst. Assoc.; Jacqueline A. Alworth, DRE; Sr. Alice Uhl, O.P., RCIA Coord.;

CEDAR GROVE

St. Catherine of Siena - 339 Pompton Ave., Cedar Grove, NJ 07009 t) 973-239-3332 Rev. Msgr. Robert H. Slipe, Pst.; Rev. Stephen A. Kopacz, Assoc. Pst.; Rev. Daniel Raymond Peterson, Assoc. Pst.; Rev. Msgr. Charles W. Gusmer, Pastor Emer.; Carol Orlando, Pst. Assoc.; Rosemary Couillou, DRE;
St. Catherine of Siena School - 39 E. Bradford Ave., Cedar Grove, NJ 07009 t) 973-239-6968 c.kerwin@scs-school-cedargrovenj.org Celine Kerwin, Prin.;

CLARK

St. Agnes - 332 Madison Hill Rd., Clark, NJ 07066 t) 732-388-2560 (CRP); 732-388-7852 cff@stagnesparish.com; stagneschurch@comcast.net www.stagnesparish.com Rev. William P. Sheridan, Pst.; Rev. Andrew De Silva, Par. Vicar; Joseph Rendeiro, DRE;

CLIFFSIDE PARK

Epiphany - 247 Knox Ave., Cliffside Park, NJ 07010 t) 201-943-7320 epiphanycp@juno.com Rev. Bruce E. Harger, Pst.; Rev. Boniface Anusiem, Par. Vicar; Donna Murtagh, DRE;
Sacred Heart - ; Mailing: 246 Hudson Place, Cliffside Park, NJ 07010 t) 201-943-0305 info@shpnb.com www.sacredheartnorthbergen.com Rev. Kevin J. Schott, Pst.;

CLOSTER

St. Mary - 20 Legion Pl., Closter, NJ 07624 t) 201-767-8247 Dcn. James P. Tobin; Rev. Paul A. Cannariato, Pst.; Rev. Richard J. Mroz, In Res.; Mary Jo Armen, DRE;

CRANFORD

St. Michael - 40 Alden St., Cranford, NJ 07016 t) 908-276-0360 (CRP); 908-276-2050 parishcenter@stmichaelscranford.org; msilva@stmichaelcranfordre.org www.stmichaelcranford.org Rev. Msgr. Timothy J. Shugrue, Pst.; Rev. Sebastian Valencia Obando, Par. Vicar; Margaret Silva, DRE; CRP Stds.: 700
St. Michael School - (Grades PreK-8) 100 Alden St., Cranford, NJ 07016 t) 908-276-9425 saint.michael@verizon.net www.smscranford.com Sandy Miragliotta, Prin.; Maria Singer, Librn.; Stds.: 300; Lay Tchrs.: 18

CRESSKILL

St. Therese of Lisieux - 120 Monroe Ave., Cresskill, NJ 07626; Mailing: 200 Jefferson Ave., Cresskill, NJ 07626

t) 201-567-4781 (CRP); 201-567-2528 sttherese@sttheresecresskill.org www.sttheresecresskill.org Rev. Samuel Citero, O.Carm., Pst.; Rev. Michael Joyce, O. Carm., Par. Vicar; Dcn. Anthony Porcaro, T.O. Carm; CRP Stds.: 166

DEMAREST

Parish of St. Joseph - 573 Piermont Rd., Demarest, NJ 07627 t) 201-768-2371; 201-767-3115 (Korean) stjosephdemarest@gmail.com; info@sjdnj.org www.stjosephdemarest.com English and Korean Rev. Don Bosco Park, Pst.; Rev. James Cho, Par. Vicar;

DUMONT

St. Mary - 280 Washington Ave., Dumont, NJ 07628 t) 201-384-0557 info@stmarysdumont.org; religioused@stmarysdumont.org Rev. Stephen A. Carey, Pst.; Rev. Patrick W. Donohue, In Res.; Dcn. John Sylvester; William J. Mascitello, DRE; CRP Stds.: 355

EAST ORANGE

Holy Name of Jesus - 184 Midland Ave., East Orange, NJ 07017 t) 973-675-4444 info@hnjeo.org www.hnjeo.org Dcn. Leo Woodruff; Rev. Frederick Pfeifer, Pst.;

Parish Center - 200 Midland Ave., East Orange, NJ 07017-1855

Holy Spirit-Our Lady Help of Christians - 17 N. Clinton St., East Orange, NJ 07017 t) 973-673-1077 Rev. Jean Max Osias, Pst.; Anita Hernandez, DRE;

Saint Joseph Parish - 110 Telford St., East Orange, NJ 07018 t) 973-678-4030 st.josepheo@verizon.net Dcn. Jerry Romero; Rev. Jose Manuel Abalon, Pst.; Rev. Julius M. Eyyazo, In Res.; Rev. Didam David Kazzahchiyang, In Res.; Rev. John Opara, In Res.; Rev. Anthony Uwandu, In Res.;

Saint Joseph School - 115 Telford St., East Orange, NJ 07018 t) 973-674-2326 kcavaness@stjosepheo.com Karen Cavaness, Prin.;

EAST RUTHERFORD

St. Joseph - 120 Hoboken Rd., East Rutherford, NJ 07073 t) 201-939-0457 stjosepher@aol.com Rev. Joseph J. Astarita, Pst.; Rev. Arokiadoss Raji, Par. Vicar;

EDGEWATER

Holy Rosary - 365 Undercliff Ave., Edgewater, NJ 07020 Dcn. Michael A. Lydon; Dcn. Robert E. Thomson; Rev. George Ruane, Pst.; Linda Corona, DRE;

ELIZABETH

Saint Adalbert and Saints Peter & Paul - 250 E. Jersey St., Elizabeth, NJ 07206 t) 908-352-2791 office@stadalbert.us www.stadalbert.us Rev. Krzysztof Szczotka (Poland), Pst.;

St. Anthony of Padua - 853 Third Ave., Elizabeth, NJ 07202 Rev. Oscar Martin, Pst.; Sr. M. Charitina Frabizio, S.C., DRE;

Convent - t) 908-354-0825

Blessed Sacrament - 1096 North Ave., Elizabeth, NJ 07201 t) 908-352-0338 bseliz@optonline.net Rev. Gerardo D. Gallo, Pst.; Rev. Fredy Sanchez, Assoc. Pst.; Rev. Alejandro Lopez-Cardinale, In Res.; Susan Hernandez, DRE; Lucia Solis, DRE;

St. Genevieve - 200 Monmouth Rd., Elizabeth, NJ 07208 t) 908-351-4444 stgens@optonline.net www.stgensrcc.com Dcn. Joseph Caporaso; Rev. Armand Mantia, Pst.; Rev. Miroslaw Kusibab, Par. Vicar;

Convent -

St. Hedwig - 716 Clarkson Ave., Elizabeth, NJ 07202; Mailing: 717 Polonia Ave., Elizabeth, NJ 07202 t) (908) 352-1448 office@sainthedwignj.org Rev. Maciej Jan Zajac, Pst.; CRP Stds.: 24

Religious Education Center - 717 Polonia Ave., Elizabeth, NJ 07202 Michele Yamakaitis, DRE;

Immaculate Conception - 425 Union Ave., Elizabeth, NJ 07208; Mailing: 417 Union Ave. - Parish Center, Elizabeth, NJ 07208 t) 908-352-6662 info@iconceptionparish.org iconceptionparish.org Rev. Duverney Bermudez, Pst.; Rev. Juan Pablo Esteban, In Res.; Rev. Brendan Quinn, In Res.;

Immaculate Heart of Mary and Saint Patrick - 215 Court St., Elizabeth, NJ 07206 Dcn. Nestor Charriez;

St. Mary of the Assumption - 155 Washington Ave., Elizabeth, NJ 07202 t) 908-352-5154 stmaryoftheassumption@gmail.com Rev. Manuel D. Rios, Pst.; Rev. Thomas P. THE Quinn, Par. Vicar; Rev. Msgr. Jeremias R. Rebanal, In Res.;

Our Lady of Fatima - 403 Spring St., Elizabeth, NJ 07201 t) 908-352-9713 Dcn. Manuel Almeida; Rev. Antonio Nuno Rocha, Pst.; Rev. Adauto Alves, Assoc. Pst.; Margaret De Jesus, Music Min.; Christina Simoes, DRE;

Our Lady of Most Holy Rosary/St. Michael - 52 Smith St., Elizabeth, NJ 07201 Dcn. Wilbert Alexandre; Rev. Jose Amante M. Abalon, Pst.;

ELMWOOD PARK

St. Leo - 324 Market St., Elmwood Park, NJ 07407 Rev. Reinerio Agaloos, Pst.; William Schulenburg, DRE;

St. Leo School - (Grades PreK-8) 300 Market St., Elmwood Park, NJ 07407 t) 201-796-5156 www.stleosschool.org Elizabeth Ventola, Prin.;

Convent - 305 Miller Ave., Elmwood Park, NJ 07407 t) 201-797-6993

EMERSON

Assumption - 29 Jefferson Ave., Emerson, NJ 07630 t) 201-986-0970 (CRP); 201-262-1122 church@assumptionacad.org www.assumption-emerson.org Dcn. John E. Hogan; Dcn. Joseph J. Paulillo; Rev. Paul A. Cannariato, Pst.; Rev. Charles M. Kelly, Par. Vicar; Rev. Eugene Joseph Bettinger, O.Carm., In Res.; Judi Agnew, DRE;

ENGLEWOOD

St. Cecilia - 55 W. Demarest Ave., Englewood, NJ 07631 t) 201-568-7882 (CRP); 201-568-0364 st.cecilia55d@aol.com www.stceciliachurch.com Rev. Herman Kinzler, O.Carm., Pst.; Rev. Agung Wahyudianto, Par. Vicar; Rev. Emilio Rodriguez, O. Carm., Director of Hispanic Ministry; Rev. Joseph P. O'Brien, O.Carm., Director Carmelite Missions; Rev. Hilary Milton, O.Carm., In Res.; Rev. Nelson Belizario, In Res.; Michael Mulhall, O. Carm., Other; Esther Lara, DRE; Rev. Ashley J. Harrington, O.Carm., In Res.; Rev. Daniel O'Neill, O.Carm., Prior; CRP Stds.: 165

Office of Concern - 85 W. Demarest Ave., (rear), Englewood, NJ 07631 t) 201-568-1465 officeofconcern@verizon.net www.officeofconcern.com Food Pantry Donald Wuertz, Dir.;

FAIR LAWN

St. Anne - 15-05 Saint Anne St., Fair Lawn, NJ 07410 Dcn. Richard M. McGarry; Rev. Joseph C. Doyle, Pst.; Rev. Colin Adrian Kay, Assoc. Pst.; Donna Stickna, DRE;

FAIRFIELD

St. Thomas More - 12 Hollywood Ave., Fairfield, NJ 07004; Mailing: 210 Horseneck Rd., Fairfield, NJ 07004 t) 973-227-0055 stmparishoffice@gmail.com Dcn. P. Aidan King; Rev. Marek Chachlowski (Poland), Pst.; Rev. Roberto A. Lamirez, Par. Vicar; Dcn. Michael Pontoriero;

FAIRVIEW

St. John the Baptist - 239 Anderson Ave., Fairview, NJ 07022 t) 201-945-4865 sjbhope2@verizon.net Rev. Fernando Diaz, Par. Vicar; Rev. Herman Kinzler, O.Carm., Admin.;

Our Lady of Grace - 395 Delano Pl., Fairview, NJ 07022 t) 201-945-1201 (CRP); 201-943-0904 frpeter@nj.rr.com Rev. Peter T. Sticco, S.A.C., Pst.; Rev. Luiz Quaini, S.A.C., Assoc. Pst.;

Our Lady of Grace School - (Grades PreSchool-8) 400 Kamena St., Fairview, NJ 07022 t) 201-945-8300 olgschool@olgfairview.org www.olgfairview.org (plus 2 & 3 yr. old program) Filomena D'Amico, Prin.;

St. Vincent Pallotti - 545 Victory Ave., Ridgefield, NJ 07657

FORT LEE

Holy Trinity - 2367 Lemoine Ave., Fort Lee, NJ 07024-6269 t) 201-947-1216 Rev. Richard E. Cabezas, Pst.; Rev. Edmundo Sombilon, Assoc. Pst.; Peter Baratta Jr., Music Min.; Rosemarie Flood, DRE;

Christ the Teacher Interparochial School - (Grades PreK-8) t) 201-944-0421 Co-Sponsored. (See Madonna Parish, Fort Lee). Katherine Murphy, Prin.;

Convent -

Madonna - 340 Main St., Fort Lee, NJ 07024 t) 201-944-2727; 201-803-7557 info@madonnachurch.org www.madonnachurch.org Rev. Jungsoo Kim, Pst.; Rev. William F. Benedetto, Par. Vicar; Rev. Steve Chun, Par. Vicar; CRP Stds.: 240

Christ the Teacher Interparochial School - (Grades PreK-8) 359 Whiteman St., Fort Lee, NJ 07024 t) 201-944-0421 Cynthia Schirm, Prin.;

FRANKLIN LAKES

Most Blessed Sacrament - 787 Franklin Lake Rd., Franklin Lakes, NJ 07417 t) 201-891-4200 (CRP); 201-891-4200 x280 kpastor@mbschurchnj.org; jjob@mbschurchnj.org www.mostblessedsacrament.ws Rev. John R. Job, Pst.; Most Rev. John W. Flesey, In Res.; Sr. Rose Marie Kean, S.S.J., Pst. Assoc.; Krista Pastor, DRE; CRP Stds.: 402

Academy of the Most Blessed Sacrament - (Grades PreK-8) 785 Franklin Lake Rd., Franklin Lakes, NJ 07417 t) 201-891-4250 rmanzo@rcmbs.org www.ambs.org Alycia Manzo, Prin.; Stds.: 82; Lay Tchrs.: 12

Convent - 782 Franklin Lake Rd., Franklin Lakes, NJ 07417 t) 201-891-1836 rkean@mbschurchnj.org

Residence - 835 High Mountain Rd., Franklin Lakes, NJ 07417 t) 201-485-7865

GARFIELD

Most Holy Name - 99 Marsellus Pl., Garfield, NJ 07026 Rev. Msgr. William J. Reilly, Pst.; Maricela Quintana, Pst. Assoc.; Dalia Serrano, Pst. Assoc.;

Our Lady of Mt. Virgin - 188 MacArthur Ave., Garfield, NJ 07026 Rev. Peter J. Palmisano, Pst.; Rev. George M. Reilly, In Res.; Rose Todaro, DRE;

St. Stanislaus Kostka - 184 Ray St., Garfield, NJ 07026 t) 973-772-7222 ststankostka@optonline.net www.ststangarfield.org Rev. Piotr Haldas, SDS, Pst.; Rev. Dawid Adamczak, S.D.S., Par. Vicar; Rev. Andrzej Kujawa, S.D.S., Par. Vicar; CRP Stds.: 200

GARWOOD

St. Anne - 325 Second Ave., Garwood, NJ 07027 t) 908-789-0280 x10 stannereled@comcast.net Rev. Msgr. Ronald J. Marczewski, Pst.;

GLEN ROCK

St. Catharine - 905 S. Maple Ave., Glen Rock, NJ 07452 t) 201-444-5690 (CRP); 201-445-3703 religiouseducation@stcatharinechurch.org; maryann@stcatharinechurch.org www.stcatharinechurch.org Rev. Thomas S. Wisniewski, Pst.; Rev. Bogumil Misiuk, Par. Vicar; Sally Trahan, Music Min.; Dcn. George Carbone, Pst. Assoc.; Dcn. Joseph Castoro, Pst. Assoc.; Dcn. Leonard A. Minichino, Pst. Assoc.; Dcn. James A. Mueller, Pst. Assoc.; Dcn. John A. Sarno, Pst. Assoc.; Megan Breitenbach, Youth Min.; Maryann Facciolo, DRE; Michelle Torpey, DRE;

Academy of Our Lady - (Grades PreK-8) 180 Rodney St., Glen Rock, NJ 07452 t) 201-445-0622 jnewman@academyofourlady.org www.academyofourlady.org Carol LaSalle, Prin.;

HACKENSACK

St. Francis of Assisi - 50 Lodi St., Hackensack, NJ 07601 t) 201-488-2614 (CRP); 201-343-6243 st.francisrcchurch@gmail.com stfrancisofassisihackensack.com/ Dcn. Douglas Christmann; Dcn. Angel Hernandez; Dcn. Alejandro Polanco; Friar Martin Schratz, O.F.M.Cap., Pst.; Rev. Tulasi Babu Garapati, O.F.M. Cap., Par. Vicar; Alex Collantes, DRE;

Holy Trinity - Sr. Emily's Way, 34 Maple Ave., Hackensack, NJ 07601 t) 201-343-5170 churchholytrinity@yahoo.com www.holytrinity1861.org Rev. Paul Prevosto, Pst.; Rev. Octavio Gonzalez, Par. Vicar; Rev. Armando S. Crisostomo Jr., Chap.; Lynn Berhalter, Pst. Assoc.; Julian Garcia, DRE;

Immaculate Conception (St. Mary's) - 49 Vreeland Ave.,

Hackensack, NJ 07601 t) 201-440-2798 immcon@verizon.net www.icchackensack.com Rev. Michael S. P. Trainor, Pst.; CRP Stds.: 27

St. Joseph - 460 Hudson St., Hackensack, NJ 07601 Rev. Wlodzimierz R. Las, S.D.S., Pst.; Marzanna Kopacz, DRE;

HARRINGTON PARK

Our Lady of Victories - 81 Lynn St., Harrington Park, NJ 07640-1831 t) 201-768-1400 (CRP); 201-768-1706 Dcn. Tom Lagatol; Dcn. Al McLaughlin; Rev. Wojciech B. Jaskowiak, Pst.; Rev. Edmond P Ilg, Par. Vicar; Curtis Stella, Youth Min.;

Convent - 145 The Parkway, Harrington Park, NJ 07640-1820

HARRISON

Holy Cross - 323 Harrison Ave., Harrison, NJ 07029; Mailing: 16 Church Sq., Harrison, NJ 07029 t) 973-484-5678 holycrossharrison@verizon.net Rev. John C. DeSousa, Pst.; Rev. Jose De Jesus Rodriguez-Reyes, Par. Vicar;

Convent - 324 Jersey St., Harrison, NJ 07029 t) 973-485-7233

Our Lady of Czestochowa - 115 S. Third St., Harrison, NJ 07029 Rev. Pawel Molewski, Pst.; Rev. Msgr. Joseph P. Plunkett, In Res.; Marzena Zmude-Dudek, DRE;

HASBROUCK HEIGHTS

Corpus Christi - 218 Washington Pl., Hasbrouck Heights, NJ 07604 t) 201-288-4844 x142 Dcn. Paul Carris; Dcn. Vincent J. DeFedele; Rev. Patrick M. Mulewski, Pst.; Rev. Juan Camilo Restrepo, Assoc. Pst.; Joanna Kowalska, Music Min.; Verna Paiotti, DRE;

Corpus Christi School - (Grades PreK-8) 215 Kipp Ave., Hasbrouck Heights, NJ 07604 t) 201-288-0614 epinto@corpuschristischool.net Jason Feliciano, Prin.;

HAWORTH

Sacred Heart - 102 Park St., Haworth, NJ 07641 t) 201-387-0080 shhaw@aol.com www.sacredhearthaworth.com Rev. Robert Wolfee, Pst.; Rev. John R. O'Connell, In Res.; Rev. Ashley J. Harrington, O.Carm., Weekend Assistant; Sr. Joanne Picciurro, Pst. Assoc.; Linda Corona, DRE; Corinn Somers, Music Min.; CRP Stds.: 125

HILLSDALE

St. John the Baptist - 69 Valley St., Hillsdale, NJ 07642 t) 201-664-3131 www.stjohnhillsdale.org Dcn. Albert J. Ganter; Dcn. John A. Gray Jr.; Rev. Msgr. Peter Smutelovic, Pst.; Rev. Msgr. Philip D. Morris, Pastor Emer.; Roberto Sabastiani, Music Min.; Catherine Wollyung, Pst. Assoc.; Jennifer Cannon, Bus. Mgr.;

St. John Academy Interparochial - (Grades PreK-8) 460 Hillsdale Ave., Hillsdale, NJ 07642 t) 201-664-6364 ssocha@sja-hillsdale.org; info@sja-hillsdale.org sjahillsdale.org/ Suzanne Socha, Prin.;

HILLSIDE

St. Catherine of Siena - 19 King St., Hillside, NJ 07205 Rev. Aurelio Yanez Gomez (Colombia), Pst.; Rev. Marco Hurtado-Olazo, Assoc. Pst.;

Christ the King - 411 Rutgers Ave., Hillside, NJ 07205 ginabejar@yahoo.com; mcconloguejm@aol.com Rev. Andrew J. Njoku (Nigeria); Rev. Luke Duc Tran, Pst.; Gina Bejar, DRE; Jane McConlogue, DRE;

HO HO KUS

St. Luke - 340 N. Franklin Tpke., Ho Ho Kus, NJ 07423 t) 201-447-2779 ccd@churchofstluke.org Dcn. John McKeon; Dcn. Andrew E. Saunders; Rev. James M. Manos, Pst.; Bridget Sarkowicz, DRE; Barbara Weiss, Bus. Mgr.;

HOBOKEN

St. Ann - 704 Jefferson St., Hoboken, NJ 07030 t) 201-659-1114 parishoffice@stannhoboken.com stannhoboken.com/ Rev. Remo DiSalvatore, O.F.M.Cap., Pst.; Rev. Vincent Fortunato, O.F.M. Cap., Par. Vicar; Rev. Charles Hanley, O.F.M. Cap., Par. Vicar; Lisa DelValle, DRE; Cheryl James, RCIA Coord.;

Hoboken Catholic Academy - (Grades PreK-8) 555 Seventh St., Hoboken, NJ 07030 t) 201-963-9535 jcordova@hobokencatholic.org www.hobokencatholic.org Sr. Lisa Perez, Prin.;

St. Francis of Assisi - 308 Jefferson St., Hoboken, NJ 07030 t) 201-659-1772 stfrancis308@gmail.com stfrancishoboken.net Rev. Christopher Panlilio, Pst.; Rev. Msgr. Paul L. Bochicchio, In Res.; Eileen Carvalho, DRE;

Our Lady of Grace and Saint Joseph Parish - 400 Willow Ave., Hoboken, NJ 07030 t) 201-659-0369 olgrace@optonline.net www.olghoboken.com Rev. Alexander M. Santora, Pst.; Rev. Philip Micele, Par. Vicar; Kathleen McNally, Music Min.; Andrew Fellows, Pst. Assoc.; Angela Maffei, Pst. Assoc.;

Ss. Peter and Paul - 404 Hudson St., Hoboken, NJ 07030 t) (201) 659-2276 Rev. Msgr. Michael A. Andreano, Pst.;

IRVINGTON

Good Shepherd - 954 Stuyvesant Ave., Irvington, NJ 07111 t) 908-296-3511 (CRP); 973-375-8568 perryden@verizon.net; gsirvington@comcast.net Rev. Frank J. Rocchi, Pst.; Denise Perry, DRE;

St. Leo - 103 Myrtle Ave., Irvington, NJ 07111 Dcn. Nelson Ramirez; Rev. Msgr. Beaubrun Ardouin, Pst.; Rev. Carlos M. Viego, Assoc. Pst.; Rev. Stephen Aribe, In Res.; Christian Nunes, DRE;

Sacred Heart of Jesus - 537 Grove St., Irvington, NJ 07111 t) 973-373-2232 sacredheart07111@gmail.com Rev. Tadeusz Trela, Pst.; Anna Skiba, CRE; CRP Stds.: 70

JERSEY CITY

St. Aedan - 800 Bergen Ave., Jersey City, NJ 07306 t) 201-433-6800 saintaedanjc@gmail.com staedans.org Rev. Rocco C. Danzi, S.J., Admin.; Rev. John R. Hyatt, S.J., Assistant; CRP Stds.: 115

St. Aloysius - 691 West Side Ave., Jersey City, NJ 07304 t) 201-433-6365 saintaloysius@verizon.net staloysiuschurch.com Rev. Juancho D. De Leon, Pst.; Rev. Gustavo A. Alfaro, Par. Vicar;

St. Aloysius School - (Grades PreK-8) 721 West Side Ave., Jersey City, NJ 07306 t) 201-433-4270 hoconnell@stalselem.org www.stalselm.org Jorge Rivera, Prin.;

St. Ann - 291 St. Pauls Ave., Jersey City, NJ 07306-5008 Dcn. John J. Karal; Rev. Kazimierz Kuczynski, Pst.;

Mission - t) 201-656-0405

St. Anne - 3545 John F. Kennedy Blvd., Jersey City, NJ 07307 Rev. Nigel R. Mohammed, Pst.;

St. Anthony of Padua - 330 Sixth St., Jersey City, NJ 07302 Rev. Joseph Urban, Pst.;

Christ, the King - 768 Ocean Ave., Jersey City, NJ 07304 t) 201-333-4862 ctkjerseycity@gmail.com www.christthekingjerseycity.org Rev. Esterminio Chica, Admin.; Rev. Robert E. Tooman, In Res.; Henry Rawls, Music Min.; Ann Marie Warren, DRE & Bus. Mgr.;

Holy Rosary - 344 Sixth St., Jersey City, NJ 07302 t) 201-795-0120 holyrosarychurch@gmail.com www.holyrosarychurch.com Rev. Jerzy R. Zaslona, Pst.; Melissa Szpala, DRE; CRP Stds.: 25

St. John the Baptist - 3026 John F. Kennedy Blvd., Jersey City, NJ 07306 t) 201-653-8814 johns3026@comcast.net stjohnbjc.org/ Rev. John Berchmans Antony (India), Pst.;

St. Joseph - 511 Pavonia Ave., Jersey City, NJ 07306 t) 201-653-0392 stjosephjc@yahoo.com stjosephjc.com Rev. James Raphel, CMF, Pst.; Rev. Rohan Dominic, C.M.F., In Res.; Rev. Henry Ramirez Soler, C.M.F., In Res.; Robert P De Tagle, Admin.; Rossana McLaughlin, Music Min.;

St. Joseph School - (Grades PreK-8) 509 Pavonia Ave., Jersey City, NJ 07306 t) 201-653-0128 stjosephgrasch@yahoo.com John Richards, Prin.;

St. Mary Parish - 209 Third St., Jersey City, NJ 07302 t) 201-434-8500 Rev. Jose Helber Victoria, Pst.;

St. Michael Parish - 252 Ninth St., Jersey City, NJ 07302 t) 201-653-7328 st.michael.jerseycity@gmail.com Dcn. Ralph M. Savo; Rev. Thomas Patrick Quinn, Pst.; Rev. Joseph Minh Nguyen, In Res.; Linda Reagan, DRE;

St. Nicholas - 122 Ferry St., Jersey City, NJ 07307 t) 201-659-5354 www.saintnicholasparishjcnj.org Dcn. Robert A. Baker Sr.; Dcn. Wilson Cordero; Dcn. Clodualdo M. Leonida; Rev. Ordanico De La Pena, Pst.; Rev. Jose deJesus Rodriguez, Assoc. Pst.; Rev. Alexander Ver (Philippines), Assoc. Pst.; Debra Baker, DRE; Clarice Perdono, DRE;

St. Nicholas School - (Grades PreK-8) 118 Ferry St., Jersey City, NJ 07307 t) 201-659-5948 principal@snsjc.com www.snsjc.com Bernadette Miglin, Prin.;

Convent - t) 201-659-5644

Our Lady of Czestochowa - 120 Sussex St., Jersey City, NJ 07302 t) 201-434-0798 www.olcjc.org Rev. Bryan E. Page, Pst.; Rev. Thomas J. Ciba, Pastor Emer.; Dr. Thomas Juneau, Music Min.;

Our Lady of Czestochowa School - (Grades PreK-8) 248 Marin Blvd., Jersey City, NJ 07302 t) 201-434-2405 office@olcschool.org www.olcschool.org Madeline Martineau, Vice Prin.;

Our Lady of Mercy - 40 Sullivan Dr., Jersey City, NJ 07305 t) 201-434-7500 olmparish@olmnj.org olmnj.org Rev. Marty Borbon Jacinto, Pst.; Rev. Chung Yeol Jung, Par. Vicar; Dcn. Edwin Dava; Dcn. Meynardo Espeleta; Regina Matias-Villa, DRE;

Our Lady of Mt. Carmel - 99 Broadway, Jersey City, NJ 07306 Rev. Pedro Repollet, Assoc. Pst.; JoAnne Oziemblo, DRE;

Our Lady of Sorrows - 93 Clerk St., Jersey City, NJ 07305-4323 t) 201-433-0626 ols9395@comcast.net olsjc.com Rev. Marty Borbon Jacinto, Admin.; Sr. Alice McCoy, O.P., Pst. Assoc.; Sr. Elise Redmerski, O.P., Pst. Assoc.;

Mary House Peace Center and Food Pantry - t) 201-434-3175

Our Lady of Victories - 2217 John F. Kennedy Blvd., Jersey City, NJ 07304-1416 t) 201-433-4152 contactus@olvjc.org; pastor@olvjc.org olvjc.org Rev. Ralph D. Siendo, Pst.; Rev. Michael E. Gubernat, Vicar; CRP Stds.: 39

St. Patrick and Assumption/All Saints Church - 492 Bramhall Ave., Jersey City, NJ 07304 Dcn. Jesus Reyes; Rev. Marc-Arthur Francois (Haiti), Pst.; Ann Marie Padilla, DRE;

Convent - 344 Pacific Ave., Jersey City, NJ 07304 t) 201-451-2765

St. Paul of the Cross - 156 Hancock Ave., Jersey City, NJ 07307 Dcn. Arnulfo Cuesta; Rev. George Joseph, Pst.; Rev. Donato Cabardo, Assoc. Pst.;

Saint Paul the Apostle - 14 Greenville Ave., Jersey City, NJ 07305 t) 201-433-8500; 201-435-8204 (CRP) stpauljc@aol.com Rev. Thomas Thottungal, Pst.; Rev. Richard Thaddeus De Brasi, Assoc. Pst.; Virginia San Lorenzo, DRE;

KEARNY

St. Cecilia - 120 Kearny Ave., Kearny, NJ 07032 t) 201-991-1116 jwassell@stceciliakearny.org; stcecilia@stceciliakearny.org www.stceciliakearny.org Rev. John E. Wassell, Pst.; Rev. Juan Carlos Velasquez-Ducayin, Assoc. Pst.; Dcn. Justo Aliaga; Dcn. Arcadio Cordova; Rev. Richard J. Mroz, In Res.; Leonidas Aliaga, Pst. Assoc.; CRP Stds.: 240

Our Lady of Sorrows - 136 Davis Ave., Kearny, NJ 07032 t) 201-998-4616 dcalcado@olskearny.org; office@olskearny.org Rev. John E. Wassell, Admin.; Rev. Juan Carlos Velasquez-Ducayin, Par. Vicar; Dcn. John P. Sarnas; Rev. Patrick R.C. Wilhelm, In Res.; Lucille Muldoon, DRE; CRP Stds.: 38

St. Stephen - 141 Washington Ave., Kearny, NJ 07032 t) 201-998-3314 x338 (CRP); 201-998-3314 marthalanedre@gmail.com; thechurchofsaintstephen@gmail.com www.ststephenkearny.com Rev. Joseph A. Mancini, Pst.; Rev. Luis Carlos Rodrigues deAraujo, Par. Vicar; Dcn. Douglas Christmann; Dcn. Earl W. White; Robert Maidhof, Music Min.; Martha Lane, DRE; CRP Stds.: 195

KENILWORTH

St. Theresa - 541 Washington Ave., Kenilworth, NJ 07033 t) 908-276-4881 Dcn. Gino de la Rama; Rev. Joseph J. Bejgrowicz, Pst.; Rev. Vincent D'Agostino, Assoc. Pst.; Rev. Michele Mario Pedroni, Assoc. Pst.;

Rev. Msgr. Venantius M. Fernando, In Res.; Richard Donovan, Youth Min.; Sr. Monique Huarte, F.M.A., DRE;

St. Theresa School - (Grades PreK-8) 540 Washington Ave., Kenilworth, NJ 07033 t) 908-276-7220 lcaporaso@mysts.org Sr. Louise A. Fantauzza, FMA, Prin.;

Convent - 112 W 23rd St., Kenilworth, NJ 07033 t) 908-276-5028

LEONIA

St. John the Evangelist - 470 Broad Ave., Leonia, NJ 07605; Mailing: 235 Harrison St., Leonia, NJ 07605 t) 201-944-4346 (CRP); 201-947-4545 religiouseducation@stjohnleonia.org; parishoffice@stjohnleonia.org www.stjohnleonia.org Rev. Bryan F.J. Adamcik, Pst.; Rev. Richard P. Kwiatkowski, Pastor Emer.; Dcn. Brian Burke; Mirela Tarabokija, DRE;

LINDEN

St. Elizabeth of Hungary - 220 E. Blancke St., Linden, NJ 07036; Mailing: 179 Hussa St., Linden, NJ 07036 t) 908-486-2514 c) 908-403-1513 office@sehplinden.org; religiouseducation@sehplinden.org www.sehlplinden.org Rev. Edgardo P. Jocson, Pst.; Tanya Grissett, DRE; Dcn. John P. Bejgrowicz;

Holy Family - 210 Monroe St., Linden, NJ 07036 Rev. Jozef Krajnak, Pst.; Anita Garcia, DRE;

St. John the Apostle - 1805 Penbrook Ter., Linden, NJ 07036 t) 732-388-1253 (CRP); 908-486-6363 parish@sjanj.net; myork@sjanj.net www.sjanj.net Rev. Mauro Primavera, Pst.; Rev. Gabriel Camacho, Par. Vicar; Rev. Peter Volz, Par. Vicar; Dcn. Michael D. York; CRP Stds.: 335

St. John the Apostle School - (Grades PreK-8) Valley Rd., Clark, NJ 07066 t) 732-388-1360 degan@sjanj.org www.sjanj.org Deborah Egan, Prin.;

St. Theresa of the Child Jesus - 122 Liberty St., Linden, NJ 07036 t) 908-862-7551 sirene0713@hotmail.com (Archdiocesan Shrine of St. John Paul II) Rev. Ireneusz Pierzchala, Pst.; Rev. Tomasz Koszalka, Assoc. Pst.; Rev. Tadeusz Mierzwa, Assoc. Pst.; Rev. Zachary Swantek, Assoc. Pst.; Sr. Irene Lisowska, L.S.I.C., DRE;

LITTLE FERRY

St. Margaret of Cortona - 31 Chamberlain Ave., Little Ferry, NJ 07643-1898 t) 201-641-3937 (CRP); 201-641-2988 smcortona1912@aol.com stmargaretlfnj.org Rev. Kevin E. Carter, Pst.; Rev. Onyedika Michael Otuwurunne, In Res.; Sr. Dorothy A. Donovan, S.S.J., Pst. Assoc.;

LIVINGSTON

St. Philomena - 386 S. Livingston Ave., Livingston, NJ 07039 t) 973-992-4466 (CRP); 973-992-0994 staff@stphilomena.org; gruth2@verizon.net www.stphilomena.org Dcn. John F. Smith; Rev. Msgr. Robert J. Fuhrman, Pst.; Rev. Francisco Maria Cordeiro Mendonca, Assoc. Pst.; Rev. Jacek J. Napora, Assoc. Pst.; Rev. Mathew Eraly (India), In Res.; Gary Ruth, DRE;

Aquinas Academy - (Grades PreK-8) 388 S. Livingston Ave., Livingston, NJ 07039 t) 973-992-1587 jcohrs@aquinasacademynj.org Eileen O'Neill, Prin.;

Aquinas Academy Pre-School - t) 973-992-5181 Gloria Castucci, Dir.;

Convent - 392 S. Livingston Ave., Livingston, NJ 07039 t) 973-992-1581

St. Raphael - 346 E. Mt. Pleasant Ave., Livingston, NJ 07039 t) 973-992-9490 straphaelrcc@comcast.net www.straphaelnj.org Rev. Jose Erlito Ebron (Philippines), Pst.; Rev. Gerald F. Greaves, Pastor Emer.; Rev. Joseph J. Bejgrowicz, In Res.; Kevin McCarthy, Youth Min.;

LODI

St. Francis de Sales Church - 125 Union St., Lodi, NJ 07644 t) 973-779-4330; 973-779-3949 (CRP) francisdesales@hotmail.com saintfrancisdesaleslodinj.org Very Rev. Francisco J. Rodriguez, Pst.; Rev. Preston D. Perez, Par. Vicar; Sr. Lois Parente, CSSF, Bus. Mgr.; Sr. Martine Pijanowski, CSSF, Pst. Assoc.; Maria Victoria Maldonado, Parish Life Coord.; Judith Santlofer, DRE; Joseny Sanchez, Youth Min.; Rosa Maria De Leon, RCIA Coord.; Paul Weiner, Music Min.; Francia Polanco, Music Min.; CRP Stds.: 164

Convent - t) 973-773-4366

St. Joseph Church - 40 Spring St., Lodi, NJ 07644 t) 973-779-0643 stjosephparishlodi@gmail.com stjosephchurchlodi.org/ Rev. Shijomon Kurian, Admin.; Dcn. Jorge E. Ochoa; Maria Cristina DeGuzman, Pst. Assoc.; Jennifer DeCaux, DRE; CRP Stds.: 130

LYNDHURST

St. Michael the Archangel - 624 Page Ave., Lyndhurst, NJ 07071 t) 201-939-1161 stmichaellyndhurst@gmail.com; stmichaellyndhurstccd@gmail.com www.stmichaellyndhurst.org Rev. Marek B. Wysocki, Pst.; CRP Stds.: 70

Our Lady of Mount Carmel - 197 Kingsland Ave., Lyndhurst, NJ 07071 Rev. Nazareno Orlandi, Pst.;

Sacred Heart - 324 Ridge Rd., Lyndhurst, NJ 07071 t) 201-935-3094 (CRP); 201-438-1147 www.sacredheartlynd.org Rev. Theesmas Pankiraj, Pst.; Rev. Cesar Chen, Par. Vicar;

Sacred Heart School - (Grades PreK-8) 620 Valley Brook Ave., Lyndhurst, NJ 07071 t) 201-939-4277 sacredheartlynd@hotmail.com sacredheartlynd.org Linda Durocher, Prin.; Joann Hessian, Librn.;

MAHWAH

Immaculate Conception - 900 Darlington Ave., Mahwah, NJ 07430 t) 201-825-0333 (CRP); 201-327-1276 info@iccmahwah.org Rev. Manolo Punzalan (Philippines), Pst.; Patrice Hess, DRE;

Immaculate Heart of Mary - 47 Island Rd., Mahwah, NJ 07430 t) 201-529-2294 (CRP); 201-529-3517 religiouseducation@ihmcmahwah.org; pastor@ihmcmahwah.org www.ihmcmahwah.org Rev. Jacek Marchewka, Pst.; Rev. Marcin Fuks, Assoc. Pst.; Anne Laura, DRE;

MAPLEWOOD

St. Andrew Kim - 280 Parker Ave., Maplewood, NJ 07040 Rev. Paul Kyung Lee, Pst.; Rev. Sangkyun Kim, Assoc. Pst.; Inhyon Park, Pst. Assoc.; Kwang Oh Chi, DRE; Matthew Park, DRE;

Convent - t) 973-762-1297 maplewoodsisters@gmail.com

St. Joseph - 767 Prospect St., Maplewood, NJ 07040 www.stjosephmaplewood.org Dcn. John J. Florio; Rev. James Worth, Pst.; Rev. Thomas A. Dente, In Res.; Rev. Matthew R. Dooley, In Res.; Darlene Wade, DRE; Leslie Frost, Dir.;

MAYWOOD

Our Lady Queen of Peace - 400 Maywood Ave., Maywood, NJ 07607 t) 201-845-9566 x117 (CRP); 201-845-9566 reed@olqp.org; parish@olqp.org www.olqp.org Rev. Antonio L. Ricarte, Pst.; Dcn. Joseph L. Mantineo; Janue Vargas, Music Min.; Justine Garcia, DRE; Julius Pulmano, Bus. Mgr.; CRP Stds.: 165

MIDLAND PARK

Church of the Nativity - 315 Prospect St., Midland Park, NJ 07432 t) 201-447-1776 Rev. Edward George Klybus, Pst.; Rev. Msgr. James A. Burke, In Res.; Olivia Harrington, DRE;

MONTCLAIR

St. Peter Claver - 56 Elmwood Ave., Montclair, NJ 07042 Rev. Zephyrin Kabengele Katompa, Pst.; Sharon Huebner, DRE;

Saint Teresa of Calcutta Parish - 1 Munn St., Montclair, NJ 07042 t) 973-744-5650; 973-744-5650 x118 (CRP) parish@montclaircatholics.org montclaircatholics.org Rev. Amilcar B. Prado, Pst.; CRP Stds.: 134

Immaculate Conception Cemetery & Mausoleum - 712 Grove St., Upper Montclair, NJ 07043 t) 973-744-5939

Immaculate Conception Church - 30 N. Fullerton Ave., Montclair, NJ 07042 t) (973) 744-5650

Our Lady of Mt. Carmel Oratory - 94 Pine St., Montclair, NJ 07042 t) (862) 243-3176 olmcmontclair.org Rev. Giandomenico M. Flora;

MOUNTAINSIDE

Our Lady of Lourdes - 300 Central Ave., Mountainside, NJ 07092 t) 908-233-1777 (CRP); 908-232-1162 office@ollmountainside.org www.ollmountainside.org Dcn. Michael DeRoberts; Rev. Richard J. Carrington, Pst.; Rev. William F. Benedetto, Assoc. Pst.; Kevin Donahue, Youth Min.; Fran Michetti, DRE;

NEW MILFORD

Ascension - 256 Azalea Dr., New Milford, NJ 07646 t) 201-836-8961 ascension@optonline.net Rev. James T. Brown, Pst.; Serina Sharkey, Bus. Mgr.; Theresa Carbone, CRE;

St. Joseph - 105 Harrison St., New Milford, NJ 07646 t) 201-261-1144 (CRP); 201-261-0146 office@sjcnj.org Dcn. Jorge A. Montalvo; Rev. Msgr. David C. Hubba, Pst.; Rev. John Z. Radwan, Assoc. Pst.; Rev. Christian Scalo, Par. Vicar; Thomas Meli, Dir.; CRP Stds.: 276

St. Joseph School - (Grades PreK-8) 305 Elm St., Oradell, NJ 07649 t) 201-261-2388 valentip@sjsusa.org Paula Valenti, Prin.;

NEW PROVIDENCE

Our Lady of Peace - 111 South St., New Providence, NJ 07974 t) 908-464-7600 (Office); 908-464-8156 (CRP) catoff@olpnp.com; secretary@olpnp.com www.olpnp.com Rev. Francisco Maria Cordeiro Mendonca, Pst.; Gloria Alves, DRE; CRP Stds.: 188

The Academy of Our Lady of Peace - (Grades PreK-8) 99 South St., New Providence, NJ 07974 t) 908-464-8657 khart@theacademyolp.org www.theacademyolp.org Dr. Kelly Hart, Prin.;

Convent -

NEWARK

Cathedral Basilica of the Sacred Heart - 89 Ridge St., Newark, NJ 07104 Dcn. Thomas DeBenedictis; Rev. Joseph A. Mancini; Dcn. Guy W. Mier; Rev. Joseph A. Scarangella; Dcn. Craig Stewart; Most Rev. Manuel A. Cruz, Rector; Rev. Msgr. Michael A. Andreano, In Res.; Most Rev. John J. Myers, In Res.; Sr. Josefa Gonzalez, H.S.C.J., DRE; John J. Miller, Dir.;

Sacred Heart Convent - 109 Parker St., Newark, NJ 07104 t) 973-484-1516

St. Aloysius - 66 Fleming Ave., Newark, NJ 07105 t) 973-344-4736 aloysiuschurch@gmail.com saintaloysiusnewark.com/ Rev. Elky Reyes, Pst.; Paula Correia, DRE; CRP Stds.: 130

St. Anthony of Padua - 750 N. Seventh St., Newark, NJ 07107 Dcn. Louis Acocella; Rev. Dave Thomas N. Sison, Pst.; Rev. Robert S. Gajewski, Assoc. Pst.;

St. Antoninus - 337 South Orange Ave., Newark, NJ 07103 Rev. Joseph R. Meagher, Pst.; Gerard Cleffi, Pst. Assoc.;

St. Augustine - ; Mailing: P.O. Box 7126, Newark, NJ 07107 Rev. Andres Codoner-Contell, Pst.;

Sisters Missionaries of Charity - 168 Sussex Ave., Newark, NJ 07103 t) 973-483-0165 Sr. M. Regi Paul, M.C., Supr.;

Soup Kitchen and Women's Shelter Queen of Peace - 170 Sussex Ave., Newark, NJ 07103 t) 973-481-9056

St. Benedict - 65 Barbara St., Newark, NJ 07105 t) 973-589-7930 saintbenedictnewark@gmail.com saintbenedictnewark.com/ Rev. Elky Reyes, Pst.; Rev. Jose Arturo Ortiz, Vicar; Ronald Ronald Livingston, Music Min.; Marina Galindez, DRE; Paulo Correia, Bus. Mgr.; CRP Stds.: 101

Blessed Sacrament-St. Charles Borromeo - 15 Van Ness Pl., Newark, NJ 07108 bsscbchurch@yahoo.com Dcn. Emeruwa Anyanwu; Rev. Msgr. Anselm I. Nwaorgu, Pst.; Rev. Erasmus Okere, Assoc. Pst.; Rev. Longinus N. Ugwuegbulem, Assoc. Pst.; Rev. Albert Nzeh, Admin.;

St. Casimir - 164 Nichols St., Newark, NJ 07105-2596 t) 973-344-2743 stcasimirnewark@gmail.com www.stcnewark.com Rev. Andrzej Ostaszewski, Pst.;

St. Columba - 25 Thomas St., Newark, NJ 07114 Rev. Andres Codoner-Contell, Pst.; Rev. Jose Carlos Garzon-Pastrana, Assoc. Pst.; Rev. Hector Larrea, In Res.; Irma Garcia, DRE;

Convent - 7 South St., Newark, NJ 07102

t) 973-622-7325 Sisters of Charity
Holy Trinity - Epiphany - 207 Adams St., Newark, NJ 07105 Rev. Ezio Antunes, Pst.;
Immaculate Conception - 372 Woodside Ave, Newark, NJ 07104; Mailing: 654 Summer Ave., Newark, NJ 07104 t) 973-482-0619 parish@gcicnewark.org www.gcic.newark.org Very Rev. Jorge E. Acosta Pena (Nicaragua), Pst.; Rev. Marcos Sequeira (Costa Rica), Assoc. Pst.;
Immaculate Heart of Mary - 202 Lafayette St., Newark, NJ 07105 Dcn. Miguel Loperena; Rev. Luis A. Vargas, T.O.R. (Peru), Pst.; Rev. Lucio M. Nontol, T.O.R. (Peru), Assoc. Pst.;
St. James - 142 Jefferson St., Newark, NJ 07105 t) 973-344-8322 saintjamesrc@outlook.com stjameschurchrc.com Rev. Celso Martins Jr., C.Ss.R., Pst.; Rev. Clement M. Krug, C.Ss.R., Assoc. Pst.; Rev. Gerard Oberle, C.Ss.R., Assoc. Pst.; Sr. Luiza Dal Moro, MSCS, DRE; Sr. Hilaria de Oliveira, O.S.F., DRE;
St. John - 22 Mulberry St., Newark, NJ 07102; Mailing: P.O. Box 200147, Newark, NJ 07102 t) 973-623-0822 info@njsoupkitchen.org njsoupkitchen.org Soup Kitchen and Health Center. Rev. Camilo E. Cruz, Pst.; Rev. Juan Alexander Ortiz, Par. Vicar; Dcn. Thomas M. Smith;
St. Lucy - 118 Seventh Ave., Newark, NJ 07104 t) 973-803-4207 (CRP); 973-803-4200 stlucysnwk@yahoo.com Dcn. Simplice Ahoua; Dcn. Dennis F. LaScala; Rev. Paul Donohue, M.C.C.J., Pst.; Rev. Msgr. Joseph J. Granato, Pastor Emer.; Omar Navarro, DRE;
Comboni Missionaries of the Heart of Jesus (Verona Fathers) -
St. Mary of the Immaculate Conception - 528 Martin Luther King, Jr. Blvd., Newark, NJ 07102 t) 973-792-5790 pwaters@sbp.org; lklaiss@sbp.org www.smcnewark.org (Newark Abbey Church) Rt. Rev. Augustine J. Curley, O.S.B., Abbot; Rev. Philip J. Waters, O.S.B., Rector; Sr. Linda Klaiss, S.S.J., Pst. Assoc.; Ambrose Amoakoh, Pastoral Min.; Rev. Linus V. Edogwo (Nigeria), In Res.; CRP Stds.: 60
St. Michael - 172 Broadway, Newark, NJ 07104 t) 973-484-7100; 973-482-1109 (CRP) smc172broadway@yahoo.com www.saintmichaelparish.com Dcn. Miguel Figueroa; Bro. Harold Hernandez, S.D.V.; Dcn. Jose A. Negron; Dcn. Cecilio S. Polanco; Dcn. Restituto Quintana; Dcn. Daniel Ravelo; Rev. Michael Reardon, S.D.V., Pst.; Rev. Robinson Gonzalez Herrera, S.V.D., Assoc. Pst.; Rev. Eric I. Ugochukwu, S.D.V. (Nigeria), Assoc. Pst.;
St. Michael School - (Grades K-8) 27 Crittenden St., Newark, NJ 07104 t) 973-482-7400 lindacerino@yahoo.com www.stmichaelnwkpenguins.com Linda C. Cerino, Prin.;
Perpetual Help Day Nursery - 170 Broad St., Newark, NJ 07104 t) 973-484-3535
Our Lady of Fatima - 82 Congress St., Newark, NJ 07105 t) 973-589-8433 x20 fatimachurchnewark@gmail.com fatimachurchnewark.com Dcn. Albino P. Marques; Rev. Antonio F. da Silva, Pst.; Rev. Joseph E.S. Dos Santos, Assoc. Pst.; Laura Martins, DRE;
Our Lady of Good Counsel - 654 Summer Ave, Newark, NJ 07104 t) 973-482-1274 parish@gcicnewark.org www.gcic.newark.org Rev. Marcos Sequeira (Costa Rica), Assoc. Pst.; Very Rev. Jorge E. Acosta Pena (Nicaragua), Pst.; CRP Stds.: 150
Our Lady of Mt. Carmel - 259 Oliver St., Newark, NJ 07105 t) 973-589-2090 mtcarmel259@verizon.net mountcarmelnewark.com/ Rev. Danny Santos Rodrigues, Admin.; Isabel Jacinto, DRE; Eric Lavin, Bus. Mgr.;
Parish of the Transfiguration - 103 16th Ave., Newark, NJ 07103 t) 973-642-4217; 973-824-1652 trnsfiguration@optonline.net; elaramirez4142@gmail.com Rev. Josephat Kato Kalema (Uganda), Pst.; Rev. Jose Wilson Bello, Assoc. Pst.; Dcn. Justo Rodriguez; Ela Ramirez, DRE;
St. Anne - (Worship Site)
St. Patrick Pro-Cathedral - 91 Washington St., Newark, NJ 07102 t) 973-623-0497 info@stppcnewark.org spnewark.com Rev. Camilo E Cruz, Pst.; Rev. Juan Alexander Ortega, Par. Vicar;
St. Rose of Lima - 11 Gray St., Newark, NJ 07107 t) 973-482-0682 fatherjoestrose@gmail.com Dcn. Pedro Herrera; Rev. Joseph Kwiatkowski, Pst.; Rev. Marco Hurtado-Olazo, Assoc. Pst.; Sr. Monica Alvarado, H.S.C.J., Pst. Assoc.; CRP Stds.: 220
Shrine of Divine Mercy St. Francis Xavier - 243 Abington Ave., Newark, NJ 07107-2598 Rev. Dieuseul Adain (Haiti); Rev. Cayetano Moncada Laguado, Pst.; Rev. Jan Sasin, Assoc. Pst.;
St. Stanislaus - 146 Irvine Turner Blvd., Newark, NJ 07103 Rev. Marian Spanier, Pst.; Rev. Bogumil Chrusciel, Assoc. Pst.;

NORTH ARLINGTON

Queen of Peace - 10 Franklin Pl., North Arlington, NJ 07031 t) 201-998-0901 www.qpgs.org/church.htm Dcn. William H. Myers; Rev. Edward M. Donovan, Pst.; Rev. Scott Attanasio, Assoc. Pst.; Rev. Jeivi Miguel Hercules, Assoc. Pst.; Rev. Msgr. Thomas G. Madden, Pastor Emer.; Bro. Francis M. Farrell, F.M.S., Pst. Assoc.; Sr. Anita Maria O'Dwyer, S.S.J., Pst. Assoc.; Dcn. William R. Benedetto, DRE;
Queen of Peace School - (Grades PreK-8) 21 Church Pl., North Arlington, NJ 07031 t) 201-998-8222 enaughton@qpgs.org www.qpgs.org Ellen Naughton, Prin.;
Convent - t) 201-997-2141; 201-991-0235 (La Salle Parish Center)
Queen of Peace High School - 191 Rutherford Pl., North Arlington, NJ 07031 t) 201-998-8227 info@qphs.org www.qphs.org John Tonero, Prin.; Don DePascale, Assistant Principle;

NORTH BERGEN

Our Lady of Fatima - 8016 Kennedy Blvd., North Bergen, NJ 07047 t) 201-869-0506 (CRP); 201-869-7244 Rev. Yuvan A. Alvarez, Pst.; Silvia Velasquez, DRE;

NORTH CALDWELL

Notre Dame - 359 Central Ave., North Caldwell, NJ 07006 t) 973-226-0979 info@ndparishnc.com www.ndparishnc.com Rev. Thomas A. Dente, Pst.; Rev. Marcin Kuperski, Par. Vicar; Dcn. Matthew DeVoti; Rev. George Ruane, In Res.; Joy McDonald, DRE;

NORTHVALE

St. Anthony - 199 Walnut St., Northvale, NJ 07647 t) 201-768-5945 Rev. Gerald T. Hahn, Pst.; Debbie Pumilia, DRE;

NORWOOD

Immaculate Conception - 211 Summit St., Norwood, NJ 07648 t) 201-768-1771 (CRP); 201-768-1600 immaculateconception@iccnorwood.org iccnorwood.org Rev. Leo J. Butler, Pst.; Christian Liguori, Music Min.; Christina Benaquista, DRE; Sr. Susanne Reynolds, S.S.J., DRE; Sr. Elizabeth Holler, S.C., Pastoral Min. to the Homebound & Infirm;

NUTLEY

Holy Family - 28 Brookline Ave., Nutley, NJ 07110 t) 973-667-6018 Rev. Joseph A. Ferraro, Pst.; Rev. Francesco Donnarumma, Assoc. Pst.; Rev. Mauro Primavera, Assoc. Pst.; Sr. Eileen Hubbert, S.S.J., Pst. Assoc.; Sr. Ella Mae McDonald, M.P.F., DRE;
Convent - t) 973-667-2050
Good Shepherd Academy - 24 Brookline Ave., Nutley, NJ 07110 t) 973-667-2049 principal@gsanutley.org Elementary Jaclyn Pilat, Prin.;
St. Mary - 17 Msgr. Owens Pl., Nutley, NJ 07110 t) 973-667-8239 Rev. Richard J. Berbary, Pst.; Rev. Thomas D. Nicastro Jr., Assoc. Pst.; Anthony Armando, DRE;
Our Lady of Mount Carmel - 120 Prospect St., Nutley, NJ 07110 t) 973-667-2580 olmc.religion@optimum.net; olmcnutley@optimum.net Rev. Paciano A. Barbieto, Pst.; Dcn. Aldo P. Antola; Rev. Peter M. Aquino, In Res.; Sr. Mary Rose Conforto, M.P.F., DRE;
Convent - 60 Harrison St., Nutley, NJ 07110 t) 973-667-2050

OAKLAND

Our Lady of Perpetual Help - 25 Purdue Ave., Oakland, NJ 07436 t) 201-337-7596; 201-337-5537 parish@olphoakland.org; reled@olphoakland.org www.olphoakland.org Rev. Thomas P. Lipnicki, Pst.; Joel Peters, Pst. Assoc.; Kristen Porcaro, Youth Min.; Michael Wada, Music Min.; Darlene DiPentima, Bus. Mgr.; CRP Stds.: 200

OLD TAPPAN

St. Pius X - 268 Old Tappan Rd., Old Tappan, NJ 07675 t) 201-664-0927 spxpcl@optonline.net Dcn. John J. McKenna; Rev. Marek B. Wysocki, Pst.; Agnes Kalinowski, Music Min.; Maria C. Charowsky, DRE;

ORANGE

St. John - 94 Ridge St., Orange, NJ 07050 Rev. George Faour, Pst.; Rev. Peter West, Assoc. Pst.; Rev. Msgr. Ricardo Gonzalez, Pastor Emer.; Saadatu Lynch, DRE; Estela Rodas, DRE; Carlos Sposate, DRE;
Convent - t) 973-677-0379
Daughters of Divine Love - 70 Ridge St., Orange, NJ 07050 t) 973-673-1263
Our Lady of Mt. Carmel - 103 S. Center St., Orange, NJ 07050 t) 973-674-2052 secolmc@gmail.com www.olmcorange.com Rev. Bernard Marie Guerin-Boutaud, C.S.J., Pst.; Rev. Jesus Rodriguez, C.S.J., Assoc. Pst.; Rev. Philippe-Joseph LeGallic, C.S.J., Campus Min.;
Our Lady of the Valley - 510 Valley St., Orange, NJ 07050 t) 973-674-4272 (CRP); 973-674-7500 olvgeneral@olvsalesianchurch.org www.olvsalesianchurch.org Rev. Miguel Angel Suarez, S.B.D., Pst.; CRP Stds.: 151

PALISADES PARK

St. Michael - 19 E. Central Blvd., Palisades Park, NJ 07650 t) 201-944-1061 stmichaelpp@gmail.com www.stmichael-catholic.org Rev. Minhyun Cho, Pst.; Dcn. David Yoon; Rev. Stanley M. Lobo, In Res.; Sr. Miseongemma Kim, Pst. Assoc.; Toni Fordyce, DRE;
Notre Dame Academy - (Grades PreK-8) 312 First St., Palisades Park, NJ 07650 t) 201-947-5262 Mark Valvano, Prin.;
St. Nicholas - 442 E. Brinkerhoff Ave., Palisades Park, NJ 07650 t) 201-944-1138 Dcn. Thomas La Russa; Rev. Christogonus Iwunze, S.D.V., Pst.; Rev. Louis Caputo, S.D.V., Assoc. Pst.; Rev. Roberto da Silva, S.D.V., Assoc. Pst.;

PARAMUS

Annunciation - 49 Demarest Rd., Paramus, NJ 07652-2109 t) 201-261-4119 annunciationchurch.org Dcn. William D. Joyce; Rev. James V. Teti, Pst.; Rev. Msgr. Richard F. Groncki, In Res.; Rev. Donald K. Hummel, In Res.; Gladys Pozza, DRE;
Our Lady of the Visitation - 234 Farview Ave., Paramus, NJ 07652 t) 201-265-3812 Dcn. Peter R. Emr; Dcn. Todd Rushing; Rev. Eugene J. Field, Pst.; Rev. Jose Monte De Oca, Assoc. Pst.; Rev. Msgr. Paul D. Schetelick, In Res.; Robert Leichte, Youth Min.; Barbara D'Arrigo, DRE;
Visitation Academy - (Grades PreK-8) 222 Farview Ave., Paramus, NJ 07652 t) 201-262-6067 principal@visitationacademyparamus.org www.visitationacademyparamus.org Co-Sponsored. Karen Mirro-Drew, Prin.;

PARK RIDGE

Our Lady of Mercy - 2 Fremont Ave., Park Ridge, NJ 07656 t) 201-391-5315 olm.church@gmail.com www.urolm.org Dcn. Joseph S. Romano; Rev. Joseph Chapel, Pst.; Rev. Patrick J. Seo, Assoc. Pst.; Rev. Robert T. Ulak, Assoc. Pst.; John Rokoszak, Pst. Assoc.;
Our Lady of Mercy Academy - (Grades PreK-8) 25 Fremont Ave., Park Ridge, NJ 07656 t) 201-391-3838 lmeehan@olmacademy.org www.olmacademy.org/ Michelle Powrie, Prin.;

PLAINFIELD

St. Bernard of Clairvaux and St. Stanislaus Kostka - 1235 George St., Plainfield, NJ 07062; Mailing: 368 Sumner Ave., Plainfield, NJ 07062 t) 908-756-3393 office@bestchurch.net Rev. Frank Rose, Pst.; Rev. Jan Krzystof Lebdowicz (Poland), Assoc. Pst.; Karole Lechowski, Youth Min.; Linda Knowles-Mayers, DRE;

St. Mary - 516 W. Sixth St., Plainfield, NJ 07060 t) 908-756-0085 Dcn. Pedro Nieves; Rev. Manoel J. Oliveira, Pst.; Rev. Francesco Carraro, Assoc. Pst.; Rev. Pablo A. Martinez, Assoc. Pst.; Rev. Jose A. Ortiz, Assoc. Pst.; Rev. Marco Pacciana (Italy), Assoc. Pst.; Rev. Michael J. Feketie, In Res.;

Missionaries of Charity, (Contemplative) - 513 Liberty St., Plainfield, NJ 07060 t) 908-754-1978

Cemetery - 300 Berckman St., Plainfield, NJ 07060

RAHWAY

Divine Mercy Parish - 232 Central Ave., Rahway, NJ 07065 t) 732-382-0004 (CRP); 732-388-0082; 732-388-0083 office@divinemercyrahway.church; ccd@divinemercyrahway.church divinemercyrahway.church/ Merged with St. Mary's and St. Mark's Church Rev. Alexander Cruz, Pst.; Rev. Jozef Krajnak, In Res.; Eleanor Atienza, DRE; CRP Stds.: 130

RAMSEY

Church of St. Paul - 193 Wyckoff Ave., Ramsey, NJ 07446 t) 201-327-8010 Dcn. Thomas Patrick Flanagan; Rev. John D. Gabriel, Pst.; Rev. Sung Gye Hong, Assoc. Pst.; Rev. Paul C. Houlis, Assoc. Pst.; Kristin Dabaghian, Music Min.; John Nunziata, Pst. Assoc.; Eric Erler, Youth Min.; Colleen Jagde, DRE; John Weiss, Bus. Mgr.; Donna Schifano, Dir.;

Academy of St. Paul - (Grades PreK-8) 187 Wyckoff Ave., Ramsey, NJ 07446 t) 201-327-1108 gritchie@academyofstpaul.org Tracy Graham, Prin.;

RIDGEFIELD

St. Matthew - 555 Prospect Ave., Ridgefield, NJ 07657 t) 201-945-3500 stmatthewridgefield.org Dcn. Joseph A. Dickson; Rev. Steven Conner, Pst.; Rev. Gerard J. Graziano, In Res.; Rev. George F. Sharp, In Res.;

Notre Dame Academy - (Grades PreK-8) 312 First St., Palisades Park, NJ 07650 t) 201-947-5262 mvalvano@notredameint.org www.notredameint.org Mark Valvano, Prin.;

RIDGEFIELD PARK

St. Francis of Assisi - 114 Mt. Vernon St., Ridgefield Park, NJ 07660 t) 201-641-6464 pacosta@stfrancisrp.org Rev. Larry Evans II, Pst.; Rev. Bartley Baker, Assoc. Pst.; Rev. Fernando E. Guillen, Assoc. Pst.; Celeste Farrell, DRE;

RIDGEWOOD

Our Lady of Mount Carmel - 1 Passaic St., Ridgewood, NJ 07450-4309 t) 201-444-0211 (CRP); 201-444-2000 x205 pfrazza@olmcridgewood.com www.olmcridgewood.com Dcn. Nicholas De Lucca; Dcn. Roberto F. Liwanag; Dcn. Robert V. Thomann; Rev. Msgr. Ronald J. Rozniak, Pst.; Rev. Frank J. Fano, Par. Vicar; Rev. Anthony Palombo, Par. Vicar; Rev. Stephen J. Toth, Chap.; Peter Sicko, Music Min.; Peter Denio, Pst. Assoc.; Sr. Mary Spano, Pst. Assoc.; Giana Castelli, Youth Min.; Glen McCall, Youth Min.; Cathy Hunt, DRE; Rev. Mert Cordero, Chap.; CRP Stds.: 1,118

Academy of Our Lady - (Grades PreK-8) 180 Rodney St., Glen Rock, NJ 07452 t) 201-445-0622 jnewman@academyofourlady.org www.academyofourlady.org James Newman, Prin.;

RIVER EDGE

St. Peter the Apostle - 445 Fifth Ave., River Edge, NJ 07661 t) 201-265-6019 (CRP); (201) 261-3366 (CRP) faithformation@saint-peter.org; cinnis@spare.org www.saint-peter.org Dcn. Edward Bowen; Dcn. Andrew J. Golden; Dcn. Paul Kazanecki; Rev. Michael J. Sheehan, Pst.; Rev. Andrew De Silva, Par. Vicar; Eileen Hanrahan, DRE;

St. Peter Academy - (Grades PreK-8) 431 Fifth Ave., River Edge, NJ 07661 t) 201-261-3468 www.spare.org Glenn Clark, Prin.;

ROCHELLE PARK

Sacred Heart - 12 Terrace Ave., Rochelle Park, NJ 07662; Mailing: 15 Forest Place, Rochelle Park, NJ 07662 t) 201-843-1722 faithform@wearesacredheart.org; jbecht@wearesacredheart.org www.wearesacredheart.org Rev. Richard J. Kelly, Pst.; CRP Stds.: 182

ROSELAND

Our Lady of the Blessed Sacrament - 28 Livingston Ave., Roseland, NJ 07068 t) 973-226-5251 (CRP); 973-226-7288 parishinfo@olbs.org Rev. Robert G. Laferrera, Pst.; Rev. Sung Gye Hong, Par. Vicar; Donald Pennell, Music Min.; Catherine Gibbons, DRE;

ROSELLE

St. Joseph the Carpenter (Sisters of St. Joseph, Chestnut Hill) - 157 E. Fourth Ave., Roselle, NJ 07203 Rev. Krzysztof K. Maslowski, Pst.; Rev. Luis Mario Garcia, Assoc. Pst.;

St. Joseph the Carpenter School - (Grades PreK-8) 140 E. Third Ave., Roselle, NJ 07203 t) 908-245-6560 mullen@stjosephroselleschool.org www.stjosephsroselleschool.org Patricia Cymbaluk, Prin.;

Convent - 135 E. Fourth Ave., Roselle, NJ 07203 t) 908-245-1594

ROSELLE PARK

Assumption - 113 Chiego Pl., Roselle Park, NJ 07204 t) 908-245-6572 (CRP); 908-245-1107 assumptionrp@yahoo.com www.assumptionrp.com Rev. James F. Spera, Pst.; Dcn. David Farrell, Pst. Assoc.; Ruth Anne Munroe, DRE;

RUTHERFORD

St. Mary - 91 Home Ave., Rutherford, NJ 07070 t) 201-438-2476 rcansmr@aol.com www.stmaryrutherford.org Dcn. James J. Guida; Rev. Michael J. Kreder, Pst.; Rev. Piotr Koziolkiewicz, Assoc. Pst.; Betty Hatler, DRE;

St. Mary High School - 64 Chestnut St., Rutherford, NJ 07070 t) 201-933-5220 tbrunt@stmaryhs.org www.stmaryhs.org Dennis Hulse, Dean; Tara Brunt, Prin.; Marci Schrank, Prin.; Virginia Mitchell, Librn.;

SADDLE BROOK

Church of Korean Martyrs - 585 Saddle River Rd., Saddle Brook, NJ 07663 t) 201-703-0002 martyrsnj@yahoo.com www.rcckm.org/ Dcn. Francisco E. Noh; Rev. Andrew J. Park, Pst.; Rev. Raphael Lee, In Res.;

St. Philip the Apostle - 488 Saddle River Rd., Saddle Brook, NJ 07663 t) 201-843-2240 (CRP); 201-843-1888 reled@stphilipsb.org www.stphilipsb.org Rev. Bruce G. Janiga, Pst.; Rev. Marek Bokota, Par. Vicar; Peter O'Brien, DRE; CRP Stds.: 183

SADDLE RIVER

St. Gabriel the Archangel - 88 E. Saddle River Rd., Saddle River, NJ 07458; Mailing: 3 W. Church Rd., Saddle River, NJ 07458 t) 201-327-5663 (CRP); 201-327-5663 x301 office@stgabrielsr.org; office@stgabriel.org Rev. Msgr. Frank G. Del Prete, Pst.; Patricia Pula, DRE;

SCOTCH PLAINS

St. Bartholomew - 2032 Westfield Ave., Scotch Plains, NJ 07076 t) 908-322-2359 Rev. John J. Paladino, Pst.; Rev. David C. Santos, Assoc. Pst.; Rev. Msgr. Donald E. Guenther, In Res.; Rev. Michael A. Hanly, In Res.; Dcn. Don Hessemer; Dcn. Robert Gurske; Paul Milan, Music Min.; Connie Boruch, DRE; Patricia Krema, DRE; Jennifer Ryan, DRE;

St. Bartholomew Academy - (Grades PreK-8) t) 908-322-4265 principal@stbacademy.org Kimberly A. Harrigan, Prin.;

Convent - t) 908-322-5619

Immaculate Heart of Mary - 1571 S. Martine Ave., Scotch Plains, NJ 07076 t) 908-889-2100 www.ihmparish.net Rev. Michael G. Ward, Pst.; Rev. Valentine C. Ugwuanya, Assoc. Pst.; John McGuire, Pst. Assoc.; CRP Stds.: 206

SECAUCUS

Immaculate Conception - 1219 Paterson Plank Rd., Secaucus, NJ 07094 t) 201-520-0482 (CRP); 201-863-4840 iccdre@gmail.com; iccofficemail@gmail.com Dcn. Earle S. Connelly Jr.; Rev. Victor P. Kennedy, Pst.; Rev. Rolando R. Yadao, Assoc. Pst.; Linda Meyer, DRE;

SHORT HILLS

St. Rose of Lima - 50 Short Hills Ave., Short Hills, NJ 07078 t) 973-376-1960 (CRP); 973-379-3912 x3501 ksoccodato@stroseshorthills.org www.stroseshorthills.org Dcn. David J. Hughes; Rev. Msgr. Robert E. Harahan, Pst.; Rev. M. Christen Beirne, Assoc. Pst.; Michael Wojcik, DRE;

St. Rose of Lima School - (Grades PreK-8) 52 Short Hills Ave., Short Hills, NJ 07078 t) 973-379-3973 principal@srlacademy.org Tina Underwood, Prin.;

SOUTH ORANGE

Our Lady of Sorrows - 217 Prospect St., South Orange, NJ 07079 t) 973-763-5454 x235 (CRP); 973-763-5454 sorrowschurch@gmail.com Rev. Brian X. Needles, Pst.; Dcn. Walter Wiggins; Sr. Mary Selena McHugh, S.C.C., Pst. Assoc.; Christopher Kaiser, Youth Min.; CRP Stds.: 200

Our Lady of Sorrows School - (Grades PreK-8) 172 Academy St., South Orange, NJ 07079 t) 973-763-5169 principal@ourladyofsorrowsschool.org www.ourladyofsorrowsschool.org Judy Foley, Prin.; Barbara McArthy, Librn.;

Day Care Nursery - t) 973-763-4040 karlene@thenurseryatols.org Karlene Snipe, Dir.;

SPRINGFIELD

St. James - 45 S. Springfield Ave., Springfield, NJ 07081 t) 973-376-2061 (CRP); 973-375-6304 frsantos@saintjamesparish.org www.saintjamesparish.org Dcn. Jerry Bongiovanni; Rev. Joseph F. Barbone, Pst.; Ann Marie Gesualdo, Youth Min.; Nancy Caputo, DRE;

SUMMIT

Saint Teresa of Avila - 306 Morris Ave., Summit, NJ 07901 t) 908-277-3700 office@stteresaavila.org www.st-teresa.org Rev. Msgr. Robert S. Meyer, Pst.;

St. Teresa Early Childhood Center - (Grades PreK-K) t) 908-277-6043 christinem@stteresaavila.org www.stteresaofavilaschool.org Christine Monaco, Prin.;

Cemetery & Mausoleum - 136 Passaic Ave, Summit, NJ 07901 t) 908-598-9426 (Cemetery); 908-277-3741 (Mausoleum) markm@stteresaavila.org Mark Maher, Supt.;

TEANECK

St. Anastasia - 1095 Teaneck Rd., Teaneck, NJ 07666 t) 201-837-3356 (CRP); 201-837-3354 secretary@saintanastasia.org; stasfaithform@gmail.com www.saintanastasia.org Rev. Joseph A. D'Amico, Pst.; Rev. Danny Alexis Pabon, Par. Vicar; Dcn. Larry Bonnemere; Dcn. Kevin J. Regan; CRP Stds.: 140

Carmelite Chapel of St. Therese - 1095 Teaneck Rd., Teaneck, NJ 07666 Rev. Eugene Joseph Bettinger, O.Carm., Dir.;

Chapel - Bergen Town Center, Chapel Doors #7 & #8, Rte. 4 E., Paramus, NJ 07652 t) 201-845-6115

TENAFLY

Our Lady of Mount Carmel - 10 County Rd., Tenafly, NJ 07670 t) 201-871-4662 (CRP); 201-568-0545 reled@olmc.us; rectory@olmc.us www.olmc.us Rev. Richard A Supple, O. Carm., Pst.; Dcn. Lex Ferrauiola; Dcn. Michael Anthony Giuliano; Rev. Emmett Gavin, O.Carm., In Res.; Sr. Regina Chassar, S.S.J., DRE; CRP Stds.: 252

Our Lady of Mount Carmel School - (Grades PreK-8) t) 201-567-6491 kkoval@academyolmc.org www.academyolmc.org Verdonck Barbara, Prin.;

UNION

Holy Spirit - 984 Suburban Rd., Union, NJ 07083 t) 908-687-3327 holyspiritchurch@comcast.net Dcn. Joseph J. Carlo; Dcn. Kurt Landeck; Rev. Armand Mantia, Pst.; Rev. Jose R. Valencia, Assoc. Pst.;

Holy Spirit School - (Grades PreK-8) 970 Suburban Rd., Union, NJ 07083 t) 908-687-8415 alaberti@holyspiritunionnj.org Armand Lamberti, Prin.;

Saint Michael the Archangel - 1212 Kelly St., Union, NJ 07083 t) 908-964-0965 (CRP); 908-688-1063 rscicolone@smsunion.org Rev. Robert Wolfee, Pst.; Rev. Emmanuel O. Agu, Assoc. Pst.; Rev. Camilo Lopez, Assoc. Pst.; Rev. Charles B. McDermott, Pastor Emer.; Philip Matrale, Youth Min.; Marilynn Dragone, DRE;

Saint Michael the Archangel School - (Grades PreK-8) ttelle@smsunion.org Rebekah Scicolone, Prin.;

UNION CITY

St. Anthony of Padua - 615 Eighth St., Union City, NJ 07087 Rev. Jose Manuel de la Pena, Pst.; Rev. Yunior Almonte, Assoc. Pst.; Rev. Trinidad Jose Cuevas, Assoc. Pst.; Luis Tobar, DRE;

St. Augustine - 3900 New York Ave., Union City, NJ 07087 t) 201-863-0233 Dcn. Edward Donosso; Rev. Thomas J. Devine, O.A.R., Pst.; Rev. Jose Antonio Ciordia, Assoc. Pst.; Rev. Tonatiuh Espinosa, O.A.R., Assoc. Pst.; Rev. Blas Montenegro, O.A.R., Assoc. Pst.; Elkin Bustamente, DRE; David Pressey Waldburg, DRE;

Convent - 342 39th St., Union City, NJ 07087 t) 201-348-0527

Holy Family - 530 35th St., Union City, NJ 07087 Rev. Thomas J. Devine, O.A.R., Pst.; Rev. Dionisio Gutierrez, O.A.R. (Spain), Assoc. Pst.; Juana Alvarado, DRE; Milagros Villarreal, DRE;

SS. Joseph and Michael - 1314 Central Ave., Union City, NJ 07087 t) 201-863-8145 Dcn. Ricardo L. Flores; Dcn. Asterio Velasco; Rev. Aro Nathan, Pst.; Rev. Guillermo Mora (Colombia), Assoc. Pst.;

Saint Rocco/Saint Brigid - 4206 Kennedy Blvd., Union City, NJ 07087 t) 201-863-1427; 201-863-0160 stroccounioncity@gmail.com Rev. Joseph D. Girone, Pst.; Teresita Ghabrial, DRE; Rita Mendez, RCIA Coord.; Luz Veronica Orejuela, Bus. Mgr.; Carolyn Angelosante, Trustee; Keith Crichlow, Trustee; CRP Stds.: 93

UPPER MONTCLAIR

St. Cassian - 187 Bellevue Ave., Upper Montclair, NJ 07043 t) 973-744-2850 rasammon@stcassianchurch.org www.stcassianchurch.org Rev. Marc A. Vicari, Pst.; Regina Sammon, DRE;

St. Cassian School - (Grades PreK-8) 190 Lorraine Ave., Upper Montclair, NJ 07043 t) 973-746-1636 info@stcassianschool.org www.stcassianschool.org Maria A. Llanes, Prin.;

UPPER SADDLE RIVER

Church of the Presentation - 271 W. Saddle River Rd., Upper Saddle River, NJ 07458 Rev. Robert B. Stagg, Pst.; Rev. Jesus Carlo Leonardo Merino, Assoc. Pst.; Rev. Msgr. Edward J. Ciuba, In Res.;

VERONA

Our Lady of the Lake - 32 Lakeside Ave., Verona, NJ 07044; Mailing: 22 Lakeside Ave., Verona, NJ 07044 t) 973-239-5696 rectory@ollverona.org; pastor@ollverona.org www.ollverona.org Dcn. Paul Hui Ra-Se Pak; Dcn. Ralph F. Powell; Rev. Peter G. Wehrle, Pst.; Rev. Jerome S. Arthasseril, In Res.; CRP Stds.: 575

Our Lady of the Lake School - (Grades PreK-8) 26 Lakeside Ave., Verona, NJ 07044 t) 973-239-1160 info@myoll.org www.myoll.org Benjamin Ronquillo, Prin.;

Fr. Michael Hanly Pastoral Center - 22 Lakeside Ave., Verona, NJ 07044

WALLINGTON

Most Sacred Heart of Jesus - 127 Paterson Ave., Wallington, NJ 07057 t) 973-777-9505 (CRP); 973-778-7405 mostsacredheart@verizon.net Dcn. Domenick DiBernardo; Rev. Canon Felix R. Marciniak, Pst.; Rev. Steven D. D'Andrea, Assoc. Pst.; Rev. Marcin Kuperski, Assoc. Pst.; Sr. Lisa Marie DiSabatino, C.S.S.F., Pst. Assoc.; Sr. Emilia Zdeb, S.S.N.D., Pst. Assoc.; Sr. Marie Victoria Bartkowski, DRE;

Convent - 27 Dankhoff Ave., Wallington, NJ 07057 t) 973-777-5124

WASHINGTON

Our Lady of Good Counsel - 668 Ridgewood Rd., Washington, NJ 07676 t) 201-664-1679 (CRP); 201-664-6624 olgcwt@aol.com; olgcreligioused@gmail.com www.olgcwt.org Dcn. Robert Glasner; Rev. Raymond E. Rodrigue, Admin.; CRP Stds.: 205

WEEHAWKEN

St. Lawrence - 22 Hackensack Ave., Weehawken, NJ 07086 t) 201-863-6464 coordinator@stlweehawken.com Rev. Eric W. Fuchs, Admin.;

WEST NEW YORK

Holy Redeemer - 569-65th St., West New York, NJ 07093 t) (201) 868-9444 Dcn. Jesus D. Aristy; Rev. Angelo Pochelti (Italy); Rev. Carlo Fortunio (Italy), Pst.; Ed Mendoza, Bus. Mgr.; Jaime Trelles, DRE; Rosa Trelles, DRE;

Our Lady Help of Christians/St. Mary Church - (Worship Site)

Our Lady of Libera Church - (Worship Site)

St. John Nepomucene Church - (Worship Site)

St. Joseph of the Palisades - 6401 Palisade Ave., West New York, NJ 07093 t) 201-854-7006 info@saintjosephpalisades.com saintjosephpalisades.com/ Rev. Jose Helber Victoria, Pst.; Rev. Cesar A. Infante, Assoc. Pst.; Rev. Nelson Oyola, Assoc. Pst.; Rev. Ernesto Tibay, Assoc. Pst.; Marco Guerrero, DRE;

Academy of St. Joseph of the Palisades - (Grades PreK-8) 6408 Palisade Ave., West New York, NJ 07093 t) 201-861-3227 info@stjosephpalisadeselem.com www.stjosephpalisadeselem.com Lauren Lytle, Prin.;

Immaculate Heart of Mary - 7615 Broadway, North Bergen, NJ 07047

WEST ORANGE

St. Joseph - 44 Benvenue Ave., West Orange, NJ 07052 t) 973-669-3221; 973-669-8331 (CRP) www.stjoeswestorange.com Dcn. Richard O'Hara; Rev. James R. White; Rev. Dominick J. Lenoci, Pst.; Pauline Alger, Pst. Assoc.;

St. Mary - 425 Northfield Ave., #19, West Orange, NJ 07052 frdennismary@gmail.com Rev. Dennis Culic, Pst.;

St. Mary Academy - Irene Manning, Prin.;

Our Lady of Lourdes - 1 Eagle Rock Ave., West Orange, NJ 07052 t) 973-325-0029 Rev. James P. Ferry, Pst.;

Convent - t) 973-325-0318

WESTFIELD

St. Helen - 1600 Rahway Ave., Westfield, NJ 07090 t) 908-232-1214 sthelen@sainthelen.org sainthelen.org Rev. Msgr. Thomas P. Nydegger, Pst.; Rev. Juan Gabriel Rojas-Hernandez, Par. Vicar; Marilyn Ryan, Pst. Assoc.; Adrian Soltys, Music Min.; Patricia Gardner, Youth Min.; Michael Fusco, DRE; Nicole E. Murphy, DRE; Tracey Sowa, Pst. Min./Coord.; Christopher Steiner, Facilities Manager; Carolyn Colonna, Bus. Mgr.; CRP Stds.: 1,164

Holy Trinity - 506 Westfield Ave., Westfield, NJ 07090; Mailing: 315 First St., Westfield, NJ 07090 t) 908-232-8137; 908-233-7455 (CRP) secretary@htrcc.org; mlizzo@htrcc.org www.htrcc.org Dcn. Keith Gibbons; Dcn. Thomas A. Pluta; Rev. Anthony J. Randazzo, Pst.; Patricia Martin, Youth Min.; Marguerite Lizzo, DRE;

Holy Trinity School - (Grades PreK-8) 336 First St., Westfield, NJ 07090 t) 908-233-0484 office@holytrinityschool.org www.holytrinityschool.org Dr. Adele Ellis, Prin.;

WESTWOOD

St. Andrew - 120 Washington Ave., Westwood, NJ 07675 t) (201) 669-3900 parishinfo@standrewcc.com Dcn. Robert S. Pontillo; Rev. Msgr. Joseph Chapel, Pst.; Rev. Diego Arce, Par. Vicar; Dcn. Paul Zeller; Irina Robinson, Music Min.; Jessica Giglio, Pst. Assoc.; Maura Roem, Pst. Assoc.; James Kenny, Bus. Mgr.; CRP Stds.: 425

WOOD RIDGE

Assumption of Our Blessed Lady - 143 First St., Wood Ridge, NJ 07075 t) 201-933-6118 arewrnj@yahoo.com www.assumption-parish.org Dcn. Francis P. Materia; Rev. Richard J. Mucowski, O.F.M., Pst.; Rev. Paul Keenan, O.F.M., Assoc. Pst.; Rev. Robert Norton, O.F.M., Assoc. Pst.; Bro. Gary J. Maciag, O.F.M., In Res.; Kristen Dziuba, Youth Min.; Donna Ryan, DRE;

Convent - 450 Main Ave., Wood Ridge, NJ 07075

Hayes Center - 142 Second St., Wood Ridge, NJ 07075

WOODCLIFF LAKE

Our Lady Mother of the Church - 209 Woodcliff Ave., Woodcliff Lake, NJ 07677 t) 201-391-2826; 201-391-7400 (CRP) info@motherofthechurch.com www.motherofthechurch.org Dcn. Stanley F. Fedison; Rev. Sean A. Manson, Pst.; Rev. Siffredus B. Rwechungura, Assoc. Pst.; Rev. Msgr. Cajetan P. Salemi, Pastor Emer.; Patricia Keenaghan, DRE;

WYCKOFF

St. Elizabeth - 700 Wyckoff Ave., Wyckoff, NJ 07481 t) 201-891-3262 (CRP); 201-891-1122 rectory@saintelizabeths.org www.saintelizabeths.org Rev. Stephen J. Fichter, Pst.; Rev. Francis Perry Azah (Ghana), Par. Vicar; Rev. Jae Joo, Par. Vicar; Dcn. Andrew E. Saunders; Dcn. John LaDuca, DRE; CRP Stds.: 862

St. Elizabeth School - (Grades PreK-8) t) 201-891-1481 admin@sainte-school.org www.sainte-school.org Karen Lewis, Prin.;

SCHOOLS: PRESCHOOL THRU HIGH SCHOOL

SCHOOLS

STATE OF NEW JERSEY

JERSEY CITY

St. Joseph's School for the Blind - (PRV) (Grades PreK-12) 761 Summit Ave., Jersey City, NJ 07307 t) 201-876-5432 info@schoolfortheblind.org schoolfortheblind.org Pre-k to 12th Non-graded, visually Impaired, multi-disabled students; Early Intervention Program; Self-directed Program for adults with special needs. Katie Hardgrove, Prin.; David Feinhals, Exec.; Stds.: 155; Lay Tchrs.: 18

LODI

The Felician School for Exceptional Children - (PRV) 260 S. Main St., Lodi, NJ 07644 t) 973-777-5355 fsecinlodi@aol.com www.fsec.org Patricia Urgo, Prin.; Sr. Rosemarie Smiglewski, C.S.S.F., Dir.;

Day Program -

SUMMIT

Oak Knoll School of The Holy Child, Lower School - (PRV) (Grades K-6) 44 Blackburn Rd., Summit, NJ 07901 t) 908-522-8120; 908-522-8100 (Main) timothy.saburn@oakknoll.org www.oakknoll.org (Coed) Christine Spies, Prin.; Megan Watkins, Dir.; Elinor Takenaga, Librn.;

UNION CITY

St. Francis Academy (Missionary Franciscan Sisters of the Immaculate Conception) - (PRV) 1601 Central Ave., Union City, NJ 07087 t) 201-863-4112 lucy@stfrancisacademy.com www.stfrancisacademy.com Deborah Savage, Prin.; Sr. Mary Dora Sartino, O.S.F., Pres.; Rose Farinola, Librn.;

HIGH SCHOOLS

STATE OF NEW JERSEY

CALDWELL

Mount St. Dominic Academy - (PRV) 3 Ryerson Ave., Caldwell, NJ 07006-6196 t) 973-226-0660 mainoffice@msdacademy.org www.msdacademy.org (Girls) Linda Arndt, Dean; Pauline Condon, Dir.; Irena

Telyan, Librn.;

CLARK

Mother Seton (Girls) Regional High School - (DIO) One Valley Rd., Clark, NJ 07066 t) 732-382-1952 missbarron@motherseton.org www.motherseton.org Sr. Mary Anne Katlack, S.C., Campus Min.; Sr. Jacquelyn Balasia, S.C., Prin.; Maureen Connell, Prin.; Joan Barron, Dir.; Marge Barkan, Librn.;

DEMAREST

Academy of the Holy Angels - (PRV) (Grades 6-12) 315 Hillside Ave., Demarest, NJ 07627 t) 201-768-7822 jmiller@holyangels.org www.holyangels.org (Girls) Jean Miller, Prin.; Melinda Hanlon, Pres.; Catherine Korvin, Librn.;

JERSEY CITY

St. Dominic Academy - (PRV) 2572 John F. Kennedy Blvd., Jersey City, NJ 07304 t) 201-434-5938 sdegnan@stdominicacad.com www.stdominicacad.com (Girls) Sr. MaryLou Bauman, Dean; M. Guendolyn Farrales, Dean; Sarah Degnan-Moje, Headmaster; Andrea Apruzzese, Dir.; Sharon Buge, Dir.;

Hudson Catholic Regional High School - (DIO) 790 Bergen Ave., Jersey City, NJ 07306 t) 201-332-5970 rgaribell@hudsoncatholic.org www.hudsoncatholic.org Richard Garibell, Pres.;

St. Peter Preparatory School - (PRV) 144 Grand St., Jersey City, NJ 07302 t) 201-547-6400 principal@spprep.org www.spprep.org John Morris, Dean; James C. DeAngelo, Prin.; Philip F. McGovern Jr., Chair; Dr. Michael Gomez, Pres.;

Jesuit Community - 50 Glenwood Ave., Jersey City, NJ 07302 Rev. Anthony J. Azzarto, S.J.; Rev. Matthew J. Cassidy, S.J.; Rev. John A. Mullin, S.J.; Rev. Claudio Burgaleta, S.J., Rector; Rev. Robert V. O'Hare, S.J., Dir.; William Reese, Librn.;

LODI

Immaculate Conception High School - (PRV) 258 S. Main St., Lodi, NJ 07644 t) 973-773-2400 jazzolino@ichslodi.org; dlaverty@ichslodi.org www.ichslodi.org Jessica Fava-Cutrona, Dean; Joseph R. Azzolino, Pres.;

MONTCLAIR

Immaculate Conception High School - (PRV) 33 Cottage Pl., Montclair, NJ 07042 t) 973-744-7445 mseeback@ichspride.org www.ichspride.org (Coed) Michele Neves, Prin.; Caridad Rigo, Pres.; Sr. Ann Fay, S.C., Librn.;

MONTVALE

St. Joseph Regional High School - (DIO) (Grades 9-12) 40 Chestnut Ridge Rd., Montvale, NJ 07645 t) 201-391-3300 brunom@sjrnj.org www.saintjosephregional.org/ (Boys). Michael Bruno, Prin.; Margaret Sullivan, Librn.; Stds.: 447; Lay Tchrs.: 39

NEWARK

Saint Benedict Preparatory School - (PRV) (Grades K-12) 520 Dr. Martin Luther King Jr. Blvd., Newark, NJ 07102-1314 t) 973-792-5700 graybee@sbp.org www.sbp.org Rev. Edwin D. Leahy, O.S.B., Headmaster; Michelle Tuorto, Associate Headmaster; Dr. Ivan Lamourt, Associate Headmaster; James Duffy, Dean of the Middle Division; Sr. Ann Marie Gass, S.S.J., Dean of the Elementary Division; Stds.: 964; Lay Tchrs.: 51

St. Vincent Academy - (PRV) 228 W. Market St., Newark, NJ 07103 t) 973-622-1613 jfavata@svanj.org www.svanj.org (Girls) Joan Tyburczy, Prin.; Sr. June Favata, Pres.; Sr. Margaret Killough, Dir.; Mary F. Nolan, Dir.; Elizabeth Lyman, Librn.;

ORADELL

Bergen Catholic High School - (PRV) 1040 Oradell Ave., Oradell, NJ 07649 t) 201-261-1844 drmahoney@bergencatholic.org www.bergencatholic.org (Boys) Rev. Colin Adrian Kay, Chap.; Timothy J. McElhinney, Prin.; Brian S Mahoney, Pres.;

PARAMUS

Paramus Catholic High School - (DIO) 425 Paramus Rd., Paramus, NJ 07652 t) 201-445-4466 jvail@paramus-catholic.org www.paramuscatholic.org (Coed) Rev. Donald K. Hummel, Chap.; Rev. Doroteo B. Layosa II, Chap.; Stephanie Macaluso, Prin.; Danielle Moore, Prin.; Jean Cousins, Librn.; Declan Lynch, Vice Pres., Finance;

RAMSEY

Don Bosco Preparatory High School (Salesians of St. John Bosco) - (PRV) 492 N. Franklin Tpke., Ramsey, NJ 07446 t) 201-327-8003 rfazio@donboscoprep.org www.donboscoprep.org Rev. Louis Konopelski, S.D.B., Vicar; Rev. Sasika Lokuhettige, S.B.D., Campus Min.; Thomas DeLucci, Admin.; Bro. Thomas Dion, S.D.B., Admin.; Ermanno Morelli, Prin.; Robert Fazio, Pres.; Michael Pender, Treas.; Rev. James Heuser, S.D.B., Dir.; Bro. Alfred Flatoff, S.D.B., Staff; Rev. James Mulloy, S.D.B., Teacher;

ROSELLE

Roselle Catholic High School - (DIO) 350 Raritan Rd., Roselle, NJ 07203 t) 908-245-2350 info@rosellecatholic.org www.rosellecatholic.org (Coed) Thomas C. Berrios, Prin.;

SCOTCH PLAINS

Union Catholic Regional High School - (DIO) (Grades 9-12) 1600 Martine Ave., Scotch Plains, NJ 07076 t) 908-889-1600 mainoffice@unioncatholic.org www.unioncatholic.org (Coed) Sr. Percylee Hart, R.S.M., Prin.; David Luciano, Dir.; Karen Piasecki, Assoc. Prin.; Noreen Andrews, Asst. Prin.; James Reagan Jr., Asst. Prin.;

SUMMIT

Oak Knoll School of the Holy Child Upper School - (PRV) (Grades 7-12) 44 Blackburn Rd., Summit, NJ 07901 t) 908-522-8130 timothy.saburn@oakknoll.org www.oakknoll.org (Girls) Mary Hoskins-Clark, Librn.;

Oratory Preparatory School - (PRV) (Grades 7-12) 1 Beverly Rd., Summit, NJ 07901; Mailing: 425 Morris Ave., Summit, NJ 07901 t) 908-273-1084 jmoran@oratoryprep.org; csilletti@oratoryprep.org www.oratoryprep.org Rev. Matthew R. Dooley, Chap.; Elizabeth Acquardo, Dean; Robert Costello, Headmaster; Owen McGowan, Associate Head of School; Stds.: 396

UPPER MONTCLAIR

Lacordaire Academy - (PRV) (Grades PreK-12) 155 Lorraine Ave., Upper Montclair, NJ 07043 t) 973-744-1156 mmannato@lacordaire.net www.lacordaireacademy.com Megan Mannato, Headmaster;

WASHINGTON

Immaculate Heart Academy - (DIO) (Grades 9-12) 500 Van Emburgh Ave., Washington, NJ 07676 t) 201-445-6800 jschlereth@ihanj.com; kcarroll@ihanj.com www.ihanj.com All-Girls, College-Prep High School Kerry Carroll, Prin.; Jason Schlereth, Pres.;

WEST ORANGE

Seton Hall Preparatory School - (PRV) (Grades 9-12) 120 Northfield Ave., West Orange, NJ 07052 t) 973-325-6624 mkelly@shp.org www.shp.org Rev. Bogumil Misiuk, Chap.; Rev. James R. White, Chap.; Michael Gallo, Headmaster; Rev. Msgr. Michael E. Kelly, Pres.; Mary Ann DeTrolio, Librn.; Rev. William J. Melillo, Campus Min.; Sharon Rondinella, Campus Min.; Stds.: 970; Pr. Tchrs.: 3; Lay Tchrs.: 74

INSTITUTIONS LOCATED IN DIOCESE

ASSOCIATIONS [ASN]

HILLSIDE

Association of St. Philomena Helpers and Servants to the Suffering & the Poor - 1293 Myrtle St., Hillside, NJ 07205 t) 973-926-0137 Dcn. Stanley Kwiatek Jr.;

LODI

Association of Franciscan Colleges and Universities, Inc. - Felician University, 262 S. Main St., Lodi, NJ 07644 t) 973-778-4517 afcu@felician.edu www.franciscancollegesuniversities.org Bro. Gary J. Maciag, O.F.M., Exec.;

SUMMIT

North American Association of Dominican Monasteries, Inc. - 543 Springfield Ave., Summit, NJ 07901-4400 t) 650-322-1801 x17 prioress@summitdominicans.org; christinemenlo@comcast.net Sr. Maria Christine Behlow, O.P., Pres.; Sr. Mary Rose Carlin, O.P., Secy.; Sr. Denise Marie Atkins, O.P., Treas.; Sr. Mary Catharine Perry, O.P., Vice Pres.;

CAMPUS MINISTRY / NEWMAN CENTERS [CAM]

HOBOKEN

Stevens Institute of Technology - Castle Point on Hudson, Hoboken, NJ 07030-5991 t) 201-216-5000 Laurence Laurente, Campus Min.;

JERSEY CITY

New Jersey City University, Gilligan Student Union - 2039 Kennedy Blvd., GSUB Rm. 316, Jersey City, NJ 07305-1597 t) 201-200-2565 (Office); 973-792-5710 (Residence) www.catholiccampusministry.org Laurence Laurente, Campus Min.;

MAHWAH

Ramapo College - 505 Ramapo Valley Rd., Room SC207, Mahwah, NJ 07430 t) 201-684-7251 www.ramapo.edu Rev. Kevin Gugliotta, Chap.;

NEWARK

The Newman Catholic Center at University Heights (Rutgers-Newark/NJIT/Essex) - 91 Washington St., Newark, NJ 07102 t) 973-624-1301 newmancenter@optonline.net www.newmanclubnewark.org Serving Essex County College, Rutgers University-Newark Campus, New Jersey Institute of Technology Joselina Castillo, Campus Min.; Rev. Pedro Bismarck Chau, Dir.;

TEANECK

Fairleigh Dickinson Univ.-Teaneck Campus - 1000 River Rd., Teaneck, NJ 07666 t) 201-692-2570 Breanna Silva, Campus Min.;

UNION

Kean University - Catholic Campus Ministry, 1000 Morris Ave., Downs Hall 130, Union, NJ 07083-7131 t) 908-737-4835 Jackie Oesmann, Campus Min.; Rev. William P. Sheridan, Dir.;

UPPER MONTCLAIR

Newman Catholic Center at Montclair State University - 894 Valley Rd., Upper Montclair, NJ 07043-2116 t) 973-746-2323 chernjam@comcast.net www.msunewman.com Sean Grealy, Campus Min.; Mary Kominsky, Pst. Assoc.; Rev. James N. Chern, Dir.;

CATHOLIC CHARITIES [CCH]

ELIZABETH

St. Joseph Social Service Center - 118 Division St., Elizabeth, NJ 07201 t) 908-354-5456 bmurphy@sjeliz.org www.sjeliz.org Rev. Anthony J. Randazzo, Chap.; Bernadette Murphy, Dir.; Asstd. Annu.: 5,000; Staff: 14

CEMETERIES [CEM]

BELLEVILLE

St. Peter -

BLOOMFIELD

Mount Olivet -

CLARK

St. Mary -

COLONIA

St. Gertrude -

EAST HANOVER

Gate of Heaven -

EAST ORANGE

Holy Sepulchre -

St. Mary -

FORT LEE
Madonna -
FRANKLIN LAKES
Christ the King -
HACKENSACK
St. Joseph -
HO HO KUS
St. Luke -
JERSEY CITY
Holy Name -
Saint Peter -
LINDEN
Mount Calvary -
LYNDHURST
St. Joseph -
MAHWAH
Maryrest -
NEWARK
Mount Olivet -
Office of Catholic Cemeteries - 171 Clifton Ave., Newark, NJ 07104 t) 973-497-7981; 973-497-7988 (Mausoleum Office) www.rcancem.org Andrew P. Schafer, Exec.;
NORTH ARLINGTON
Holy Cross -
ORANGE
St. John -
PLAINFIELD
St. Mary -
RIVER VALE
St. Andrew -
SHORT HILLS
St. Rose of Lima -
SUMMIT
St. Teresa -
TENAFLY
Mount Carmel -
UPPER MONTCLAIR
Immaculate Conception -

COLLEGES & UNIVERSITIES [COL]

CALDWELL
Caldwell University - 120 Bloomfield Ave., Caldwell, NJ 07006 t) 973-618-3000 admissions@caldwell.edu www.caldwell.edu Incorporated under the laws of the State of New Jersey with full power to confer degrees. Nancy H. Blattner, Pres.; Nancy Becker, Dir.; Barbara Chesler, Vice Pres., Academic Affairs;
JERSEY CITY
Saint Peter University - 2641 Kennedy Blvd., Jersey City, NJ 07306-5997 t) 201-761-6000 jconstantino@jesuits.org www.saintpeters.edu Eugene Cornacchia, Pres.; Rev. Rocco C. Danzi, S.J., Admin., St. Aedan's Church; Rev. Andrew Downing, Vice Pres., Mission & Ministry;
St. Aedan: St. Peter University Church - 800 Bergen Ave., Jersey City, NJ 07306 t) 201-433-6800 saintaedanjc@gmail.com Rev. John R. Hyatt, S.J., Admin.;
St. Peter University Jesuit Community - Gothic Towers, 50 Glenwood Ave., Jersey City, NJ 07306-4606 Rev. Claudio Burgaleta, S.J.; Rev. John R. Hyatt, S.J.;
LODI
Felician University, A N.J. Nonprofit Corp. - t) 201-559-6000 martink@felician.edu; cachezs@felician.edu www.felician.edu
Lodi Campus - 262 Main St., Lodi, NJ 07644 Edward H. Ogle, Pres.; Anne M. Prisco, Pres.; Rev. Richard J. Kelly, Dir.;
SOUTH ORANGE
Seton Hall University - 400 South Orange Ave., South Orange, NJ 07079 t) 973-761-9000 www.shu.edu Rev. Renato J. Bautista; Rev. Donald E. Blumenfeld; Rev. Ian Boyd; Rev. W. Jerome Bracken, C.P.; Rev. Gerald J. Buonopane; Rev. Alfred V. Celiano; Rev. John J. Chadwick; Rev. Hong-Ray Peter Cho; Rev. Christopher M. Ciccarino; Rev. Gabriel B. Costa; Rev. John D. Dennehy; Rev. Nicholas G. Figurelli; Rev. Lawrence E. Frizzell; Rev. Pablo T. Gadenz; Rev. Nicholas S. Gengaro; Rev. Msgr. Thomas G. Guarino; Rev. Msgr. Anthony J. Kulig; Rev. Joseph R. Laracy; Rev. Msgr. Richard M. Liddy; Rev. Msgr. Dennis Mahon; Rev. Msgr. Gerard H. McCarren; Rev. William McDonald; Rev. Frederick L. Miller; Rev. Brian Keenan Muzas; Rev. Robert P. Nestor; Rev. Lawrence B. Porter; Rev. Msgr. John A. Radano; Rev. John J. Ranieri; Rev. Msgr. Joseph R. Reilly; Rev. Msgr. Robert T. Sheeran; Rev. Robert K. Suszko; Rev. Msgr. James C. Turro; Rev. Msgr. Robert J. Wister; Rev. Msgr. C. Anthony Ziccardi; Rev. Msgr. Christopher J. Hynes, Prof.; Rev. Msgr. Thomas P. Nydegger, Prof.; Rev. Duverney Bermudez, Vice Rector, St. Andrew College Seminary; Rev. Msgr. Robert F. Coleman, Assoc. Vice Provost & Minister Comm.; Rev. Paul A. Holmes, Vice Pres. & Interim Dean; Rev. Brian X. Needles, Dir. Campus Min.;
College of Arts and Sciences - Peter W. Shoemaker, Dean;
College of Education and Human Services - Maureen Gilette, Dean;
College of Nursing - Marie C. Foley, Dean;
School of Business - Joyce Strawser, Dean;
School of Diplomacy and Intl. Rels. - Andrea Bartoli, Dean;
School of Health and Medical Science - Brian B. Shulman, Dean;
School of Law - One Newark Center, Newark, NJ 07102 t) 973-642-8750 Kathleen M. Boozang, Dean;
School of Theology -

CONVENTS, MONASTERIES, AND RESIDENCES FOR WOMEN [CON]

CALDWELL
Motherhouse of Sisters of St. Dominic - 1 Ryerson Ave., Caldwell, NJ 07006 t) 973-403-3331 www.caldwellop.org Sr. Luella Ramm, O.P., Prioress; Srs.: 85
DEMAREST
Missionary Benedictine Sisters of Tutzing - 274 County Rd., Demarest, NJ 07627 t) 201-767-3114 Sr. Ottilia Kim, O.S.B., Supr.;
ELIZABETH
Holy Family Sisters of the Needy - 1017-1019 Julia St., Elizabeth, NJ 07201 t) 908-662-0996 c) 908-209-7436 hfsnbeth2014@outlook.com; paschalineu2004@yahoo.com holyfamilysistersoftheneedy.org Mother Mary Michael Okafor, H.F.S.N., Supr.; Sr. Paschaline Uzochukwu, H.F.S.N., Supr.; Sr. Damian Ogonna Nwafor, Secy.; Sr. Maria Benigna Osinakachukwu Chilaka, Treas.;
ENGLEWOOD CLIFFS
St. Michael Villa (Sisters of St. Joseph of Peace) - 399 Hudson Ter., Englewood Cliffs, NJ 07632 t) 201-871-1620 klapara@csjp.org Senior Sisters Residence and Infirmary for Eastern Region. Rev. James R. McDonald, C.Ss.R., Chap.; Karen LaPara, Admin.; Srs.: 34
Congregation of Sisters of St. Joseph of Peace. - 399 Hudson Terrace, Englewood Cliffs, NJ 07632 t) 201-568-6348 pweidner@csjp.org www.csjp.org/sjp Sr. Margie Fort, CSJP, Congregation Councillor; Sr. Susan Francois, CSJP, Asst. Congregation Leader; Sr. Sheena George, CSJP, Congregation Councillor; Sr. Andrea Nenzel, CSJP, Congregation Leader; Sr. Kathleen Pruitt, CSJP, Congregation Councillor; Srs.: 46
St. Ann Day Care (Peace Care St. Ann's) - 198 Old Bergen Rd., Jersey City, NJ 07305 t) 201-433-0950 x561 hdejesus@peacecarenj.org Hector DeJesus, Program Manager;
St. Ann Home for the Aged (Peace Care St. Ann's) - 198 Old Bergen Rd., Jersey City, NJ 07305 t) 201-433-0950 rreyes@peacecarenj.org www.peacecarenj.org Robert J Reyes, Admin.;
Holy Name Medical Center - 718 Teaneck Rd., Teaneck, NJ 07666 t) 201-833-3000 mmaron@holyname.org www.holyname.org Michael Maron, CEO;
St. Joseph Home - 81 York St., Jersey City, NJ 07302 t) 201-451-9838 gacosta@yorkstreetproject.org www.yorkstreetproject.org Gloria Acosta, Dir.;
St. Joseph Home for the Blind - Sisters of St. Joseph of Peace - Shalom Center - 399 Hudson Terr., Englewood Cliffs, NJ 07632 t) (201) 608-5401 andrean@csjp.org Sisters of St. Joseph of Peace
St. Joseph School for the Blind: A New Jersey Non-profit Corp. - 761 Summit Ave., Jersey City, NJ 07307 t) 201-876-5432 dfeinhals@schoolfortheblind.org schoolfortheblind.org David Feinhals, Exec. Dir.;
Margaret Anna Cusack Care Center, Inc. (Peace Care St. Joseph's) - 537 Pavonia Ave., Jersey City, NJ 07306 t) 201-653-8300 tsheehy@peacecarenj.org www.peacecarenj.org Skilled Nursing Facility providing post acute and long term care for Men & Women Thomas P. Sheehy, Admin.;
St. Mary Residence - 240 Washington St., Jersey City, NJ 07302 t) 201-451-9838 gacosta@yorkstreetproject.org www.yorkstreetproject.org Gloria Acosta, Dir.;
St. Michael Villa - 399 Hudson Terr., Englewood Cliffs, NJ 07632 t) 201-871-1620 klapara@csjp.org Karen LaPara, Admin.;
Nurturing Place Day Care - 81 York St., Jersey City, NJ 07302 t) 201-451-9838 vhayes@yorkstreetproject.org www.yorkstreetproject.org Child Development Center Victoria Hayes, Dir.;
***Peace Care, Inc.** - 537 Pavonia Ave., Jersey City, NJ 07306 t) 201-653-8300 x2154 khreben@peacecarenj.org www.peacecarenj.org Kyle Hreben, COO;
Peace Ministries, Inc. - 399 Hudson Terr., Englewood Cliffs, NJ 07632 t) 201-731-3325 mdonohue@csjp.org csjp.org/peaceministries Maureen Donohue, Exec. Dir.;
Retirement Trust Fund for St. Joseph Province of the Sisters of St. Joseph of Peace - 399 Hudson Terr., Englewood Cliffs, NJ 07632 t) (201) 568-6348 x11 Sr. Sondra Perrotta, C.S.J.P., Vice. Pres.; Sr. Teresa Donohue, C.S.J.P., Trustee; Sr. Kathleen Doyle, C.S.J.P., Trustee; Sr. Agnes Fox, C.S.J.P., Trustee; Sr. Joanne Rusch, C.S.J.P., Trustee;
Stella Maris Retreat Center - 399 Hudson Terr., Englewood Cliffs, NJ 07632 t) (201) 608-5401 andrean@csjp.org
WATERSPIRIT Ministry - 4 E. River Rd., Rumson, NJ 07760 t) 732-923-9788 water@waterspirit.org waterspirit.org Blair Nelsen, Exec. Dir.;
The York Street Project - 89 York St., Jersey City, NJ 07302 t) 201-451-9838 sbyrne@yorkstreetproject.org yorkstreetproject.org Susanne Byrne, Exec. Dir.;
FORT LEE
Holy Trinity Convent (Inter Community) - 199 Myrtle Ave., Fort Lee, NJ 07024 t) 201-944-2911
IRVINGTON
Immaculate Conception Convent - 121 Myrtle Ave., Irvington, NJ 07111 t) 973-757-2432
JERSEY CITY
St. Nicholas Convent - 115 Ferry St., Jersey City, NJ 07307 t) 201-659-5644 sjmaumand@yahoo.com Sr. Joann Marie Aumand, S.C.C., Supr.;
LODI
Immaculate Conception Convent (Congregation of the Sisters of Saint Felix Convent and Healthcare Center of the Felician Sisters) - 260 S. Main St., Lodi, NJ 07644-2196 t) 973-473-7447 sjudithmk@feliciansisters.org www.feliciansistersna.org Convent of the Felician Sisters. Sr. Judith Marie Kubicki, Prov.; Srs.: 63
NEWARK
Daughters of Mary Mother of Mercy (DMMM) - 44 Monticello Ave., Newark, NJ 07106 t) 862-902-7029
Hermanas Misioneras del Corazon de Jesus (HMCJ) - Sacred Heart Convent, 109 Parker St., Newark, NJ 07104 t) 973-484-1516 misionerascj@aol.com Parish Ministry. Sr. Josefa Gonzalez, H.S.C.J., Supr.;
Missionaries of Charity - St. Augustine Convent - 168

Sussex Ave., Newark, NJ 07103 t) 973-483-0165 Sr. M. Assisi Jimenez, M.C., Supr.;

Missionary Sisters of the Most Blessed Sacrament and Mary Immaculate - 121 Congress St., Newark, NJ 07105 t) 973-589-5794 stisbeldehungria@yahoo.com; nepo867@msn.com Day Care Center. Rev. Lucio M. Nontol, T.O.R. (Peru), Dir.;

Sisters of St. Joseph of Chestnut Hill, Thea House - 39 Bleeker St., Newark, NJ 07102-1913 t) 973-622-7056 ssjthea@gmail.com

Vocationist Sisters - 170 Broad St., Newark, NJ 07104 t) 973-484-3535 perhelp@yahoo.com (Our Lady of Perpetual Help Center). Perpetual Help Day Nursery.

PLAINFIELD

Contemplative Convent of the Missionaries of Charity - 513 Liberty St., Plainfield, NJ 07060 t) 908-754-1978 Sr. Mary Nazarene, M.C., Supr.;

RIDGEFIELD

Pallottine Sisters - St. Vincent Pallotti Convent - 545 Victory Ave., Ridgefield, NJ 07657 t) 201-941-4552 sralicemarie@gmail.com

SADDLE BROOK

Miyazaki Caritas Sisters (Korea) - Caritas Sisters Convent - 9 Jamros Ter., Saddle Brook, NJ 07663 t) 201-703-0002

SCOTCH PLAINS

Union Catholic Convent - 1600 Martine Ave., Scotch Plains, NJ 07076 t) 908-889-1600 mainoffice@unioncatholic.org Sr. Percylee Hart, R.S.M., Supr.;

SUMMIT

Monastery of Our Lady of the Rosary - 543 Springfield Ave., Summit, NJ 07901 t) 908-273-1228 info@summitdominicans.org www.nunsopsummit.org Rev. Gregory Salomone, O.P., Chap.; Sr. Mary Martin Jacobs, O.P., Prioress; Srs.: 18

TENAFLY

Convent of Our Lady of the Angels (Missionary Franciscan Sisters of the Immaculate Conception) - 253 Knickerbocker Rd., Tenafly, NJ 07670 t) 201-568-2171 www.mficusa.org

UNION

Sisters of St. Francis of the Providence of God - 1137 Burnet Ave., Union, NJ 07083 t) 908-206-1136

UNION CITY

Holy Rosary Convent (Sisters of the Catholic Apostolate (Pallottines)) - 1514 Central Ave., Union City, NJ 07087 t) 201-617-4638 holyrosaryconvent@verizon.net

ENDOWMENTS / FOUNDATIONS / TRUSTS [EFT]

JERSEY CITY

St. Patrick and Assumption All Saints Foundation - 511 Bramhall Ave., Jersey City, NJ 07304 t) 201-521-0200 jcfran@bellatlantic.net Rev. Francis E. Schiller, Contact;

NEWARK

Deacon St. Lawrence Welfare Fund - 171 Clifton Ave., Newark, NJ 07104-9500; Mailing: P.O. Box 9500, Newark, NJ 07104-9500 t) 973-497-4125 mckennjo@rcan.org Dcn. John J. McKenna;

St. Michael Foundation, Inc. - 111 Central Ave., Newark, NJ 07102 t) 973-690-3606 Subsidiary of Saint Michael Medical Center. David A. Ricci, Pres.;

HOSPITALS / HEALTH SERVICES [HOS]

ELIZABETH

Trinitas Regional Medical Center (Sisters of Charity of Saint Elizabeth and Elizabethtown Healthcare Foundation) - 225 Williamson St., Elizabeth, NJ 07207 t) 908-994-5754 www.trinitasrmc.com Rev. Stephen Aribe, Chap.; Rev. John T. Michalczak, Chap.; Rev. Brendan Quinn, Chap.; Sr. Mary Corrigan, S.C., Pres.; Gary S. Horan, Pres.; William McHugh, Dir.;

***Marillac Corp.** - 240 Williamson St., Elizabeth, NJ 07207 t) 908-994-5794

Trinitas Regional Medical Center -

Trinitas Regional Medical Center - New Point Campus, 655 E. Jersey St., Elizabeth, NJ 07206 t) 908-994-5000

NEWARK

St. James Campus of Saint Michael Medical Center, Newark - 155 Jefferson St., Newark, NJ 07105 t) 973-589-1300 www.cathedralhealth.org Parent Corporation: Saint Michael's Medical Center, Inc., A member of Catholic Health East.

Saint Michael Medical Center - 111 Central Ave., Newark, NJ 07102-9880 t) 973-877-5000 Parent Corporation: Catholic Health East., A member of Catholic Health East. Rev. David S. McLaughlin, Chap.; Claudia Komer, Pres.; David A. Ricci, Pres.;

Mount Carmel Guild Behavioral Health System, Inc. - 590 N. 7th St., Newark, NJ 07107 t) 973-266-7992 www.ccannj.org Behavioral Health Services in 3 counties. John Westervelt, CEO; Elizabeth A. McClendon, Dir.;

TEANECK

Holy Name Medical Center (Peace Ministries, Inc.) - 718 Teaneck Rd., Teaneck, NJ 07666 t) 201-833-3000 nbischoff@holyname.org www.holyname.org Maureen Morosco, Chap.; Rev. John Opara, Chap.; Rev. Edwardo Veluz, Chap.; Michael Maron, Pres.; Bed Capacity: 361; Asstd. Annu.: 113,928; Staff: 3,441

Holy Name EMS - t) 201-833-3248

Holy Name Medical Center Foundation, Inc. - 718 Teaneck Rd., Teaneck, NJ 07666 t) 201-833-3014 foundation@mail.holyname.org; cdavey@holyname.org Cathleen Davey, Pres.;

School of Nursing - t) 201-833-3002 Rev. Maciej Jan Zajac, Chap.;

MISCELLANEOUS [MIS]

ELIZABETH

Josephine's Place, Inc. - 622 Elizabeth Ave., Elizabeth, NJ 07206

ENGLEWOOD

Carmelite Missions - 55 W. Demarest Ave., Englewood, NJ 07631 t) 201-568-0364 x25 carmelitemissions@carmelitemissions.org www.carmelitemissions.org Rev. Joseph P. O'Brien, O.Carm., Dir.;

FAIRVIEW

Pallottine Intra-Community Operating Corporation - 395 Delano Pl., Fairview, NJ 07022; Mailing: P.O. Box 979, South Orange, NJ 07079 t) 973-762-2926; 201-943-0972 Rev. Frank Donio, S.A.C.;

JERSEY CITY

Ignatius Hall Development, Inc. - c/o St. Peter's University, 2641 John F. Kennedy Blvd., Jersey City, NJ 07306

Kenmare School - 89 York St., Jersey City, NJ 07302 t) 201-451-9838 vhayes@yorkstreetproject.org www.yorkstreetproject.org Victoria Hayes, Dir.;

St. Patrick Housing Corp. - 492 Bramhall Ave., Jersey City, NJ 07304 t) 201-401-4306 Rev. Eugene P. Squeo, Pres.;

KEARNY

Family of Nazareth, Inc. - 672 Passaic Ave., Kearny, NJ 07032 t) 201-997-3220 fnazareth@rmnewark.org A foundation to support the work of the Redemptoris Mater Missionary Seminary and for the new evangelization. Luis Abarca, Pres.;

LINDEN

Friends of St. John Paul II Be Not Afraid Center, Inc. - 122 Liberty Ave., Linden, NJ 07036 t) 908-862-1116

MAHWAH

Paulist Press - 997 MacArthur Blvd., Mahwah, NJ 07430 t) 201-825-7300 info@paulistpress.com; bbyrns@paulistpress.com www.paulistpress.com Rev. Mark-David Janus, C.S.P., Pres.;

MONTCLAIR

Investor Advocates for Social Justice, Inc. - 40 S. Fullerton Ave., Montclair, NJ 07042 t) 973-509-8800 iasj.org/ Courtney Wicks, Dir.;

Tri-State Coalition for Responsible Investment - 40 S. Fullerton Ave., Montclair, NJ 07042 t) 973-509-8800 mbgallagher@tricri.org www.tricri.org Mary Beth Gallagher, Dir.;

NEWARK

CatholiCare, Inc. - 171 Clifton Ave., Newark, NJ 07104-0500; Mailing: P.O. Box 9500, Newark, NJ 07104-0500 t) 973-497-4002

Diaconate Executive Committee - 171 Clifton Ave., Newark, NJ 07104-9500; Mailing: P.O. Box 9500, Newark, NJ 07104-9500 t) 973-497-4125 mckennjo@rcan.org Dcn. John J. McKenna;

Saint James Care, Inc. - 155 Jefferson St., Newark, NJ 07107 A member of Catholic Health East. Alexander J. Hatala, Pres.;

Life at Saint Michael, Inc. - 111 Central Ave., Newark, NJ 07102-9880 t) 973-877-5350 David A. Ricci, Pres.;

St. Mary Senior Residence, Inc. - 590 N. 7th St., Newark, NJ 07107 t) 973-596-3984 John Westervelt, Pres.;

Missionaries of Charity, Queen of Peace Women's Shelter & Soup Kitchen - 168 Sussex Ave., Newark, NJ 07103 t) 973-481-9056; 973-483-0165

New Jersey Caritas Corporation, Inc. - 171 Clifton Ave., Newark, NJ 07104 t) 973-497-4002 Rev. Msgr. Thomas G. Madden, Mem.; Sr. Donna L Ciangio, O.P., Trustee; Rev. Msgr. Thomas P. Nydegger, Trustee; His Eminence Joseph Cardinal Tobin, C.Ss.R., Trustee;

Canaan House, Inc. - 494 Broad St., Newark, NJ 07102 t) 973-596-5115

Carmel House of Jersey City, Inc. - 494 Broad St., Newark, NJ 07102 t) 973-596-5115

Domus Corporation, Inc. - 590 N. 7th St., Newark, NJ 07107 t) 973-596-3984

Myers Senior Residence, Inc. - 590 N. 7th St., Newark, NJ 07107 t) 973-596-3984

River Vale Senior Residence, Inc. - 590 N. 7th St., Newark, NJ 07107 t) 973-596-3984

Sunrise House - 185 Parkhurst St., Newark, NJ 07114 t) 973-624-9478

University Heights Property Company, Inc. - 111 Central Ave., Newark, NJ 07102 t) 973-690-3514 Roosevel N. Nesmith, Chair; David A. Ricci, Pres.; Ronald J. Napiorski, Vice Pres. Finance;

NUTLEY

The Saint Gerard Society in Memorium Mary Grace Bellotti - 17 Monsignior Owens Pl., Nutley, NJ 07110

OLD TAPPAN

***Array of Hope, Inc.** - 180 Old Tappan Rd., Bldg. 2, Ste. 2, Old Tappan, NJ 07675 t) 201-261-3372 mario@arrayofhope.net www.arrayofhope.net Mario Costabile, Exec.;

ORANGE

Congregation of St. John, Inc. - 103 S. Center St., Orange, NJ 07050 t) 973-674-2052 fr.bm@stjean.com

Mee Joo Catholic Inc. - 18 Cleveland St., Orange, NJ 07050 t) 973-919-7124 augpark@yahoo.com

PLAINFIELD

***The Koinonia Academy** - 1040 Plainfield Ave., Plainfield, NJ 07060 t) 908-668-9002 office@koinoniaacademy.org koinoniaacademy.org PreK-12 Private Catholic Liberal Arts Academy Patricia Kinney, Prin.;

***The People of Hope** - 1040 Plainfield Ave., St. Francis Bldg., Plainfield, NJ 07060 t) 908-222-9722 www.peopleofhope.net David Touhill, Sr. Coord.;

RENEW International - 1232 George St., Plainfield, NJ 07062-1717 t) 908-769-5400 renew@renewintl.org www.renewintl.org Sr. Theresa Rickard, O.P., Pres.; Rev. Jeremiah Browne, RENEW Africa Office; Dcn. Peter Fiore, Director of Sales and Marketing; Rev. Msgr. Thomas A. Kleissler, President Emeritus; Dcn. Charles Paolino, Managing Editor;

RAMSEY

Don Bosco Preparatory High School, Inc. - 492 N. Franklin Turnpike, Ramsey, NJ 07446 t) 201-327-8003 www.donboscoprep.org Robert Fazio, Pres.; Rev. James Heuser, S.D.B., Dir.;

RUTHERFORD

The Community of God's Love - 70 W. Passaic Ave., Rutherford, NJ 07070 t) 201-935-0344 thecgl@aol.com thecgl.org Catholic Charismatic Community Rev. Philip F. A. Latronico, Chap.; Doreen Cevasco, Dir.;

SHORT HILLS

Friends of the Newark Monastery, Inc. - 9 Grosvenor Rd., Short Hills, NJ 07078 aluzarraga@shearman.com Alberto Luzarraga, Pres.;

SOUTH ORANGE

The Pallottines of South Orange, Inc. - 204 Raymond Ave., South Orange, NJ 07079-2305 t) 973-763-5591 Rev. Peter T. Sticco, S.A.C., Supr.;

Salesians of Don Bosco - Salesians House, 315 Self Pl., South Orange, NJ 07079 t) 973-761-0201 ym@salesianym.com www.salesianym.com Rev. P. Francis Pinto, S.D.B.; Rev. Dennis Donovan, S.D.B., Treas.; Rev. Steve Ryan, S.D.B., Dir.;

SUMMIT

Christ Child Society of Summit, New Jersey, Inc. - ; Mailing: P.O. Box 125, Summit, NJ 07902-0125 t) 908-578-9862 ccssummit@gmail.com Christine L. Murray, Pres.;

TEANECK

Holy Name Health, Inc. (Peace Ministries, Inc.) - 718 Teaneck Rd., Teaneck, NJ 07666 t) 201-833-3000 nbischoff@holyname.org www.holyname.org Michael Maron, CEO;

UNION CITY

Cofradia Arquidiocesana de la Virgen de la Caridad del Cobre, Inc. - 909 20th St., Union City, NJ 07087; Mailing: P.O. Box 682, Union City, NJ 07087 t) 201-330-1352 Ana Theresa Serrand, Treas.;

***New Jersey Friends of Mandeville, Inc.** - 526 Monastery Pl., Union City, NJ 07087

MONASTERIES AND RESIDENCES FOR PRIESTS AND BROTHERS [MON]

CALDWELL

The Rev. Msgr. James F. Kelley Residence for Retired Priests - 247 Bloomfield Ave., Caldwell, NJ 07006 t) 973-364-1121 Rev. Eugene Diurczak; Rev. Leo O. Farley; Rev. Dominic J. Fiorino; Rev. Msgr. Kenneth J. Herbster; Rev. John B. Martin; Rev. Francis J. McNulty; Rev. Ward P. Moore; Rev. John A. Quill; Joan Stevens, Admin.; Rev. James F. Benedetto, Dir.;

ELIZABETH

Benedictine Sisters of Elizabeth, NJ - 851 N. Broad St., Elizabeth, NJ 07208 t) 908-352-4278 benedictinesisters@bensisnj.org www.bensisnj.org Sr. Mariette Thérèse Bernier, OSB, Prioress; Srs.: 22

JERSEY CITY

Brothers of the Christian Schools - 790 Bergen Ave., Jersey City, NJ 07306-4535 t) 201-332-5970; 201-332-0971 (House) Hudson Catholic Brothers' Residence

Jesuits of Saint Peter College, Inc. - 50 Glenwood Ave., Apt 105, Jersey City, NJ 07306-4606 c) (718) 755-3670 Rev. Joseph S. Costantino, S.J., Supr.; Rev. Claudio Burgaleta, S.J., In Res.; Rev. Rocco C. Danzi, S.J., Admin., St. Aedan's Church; Rev. Andrew Downing, VP for Mission & Min., St. Peter's Univ.; Rev. John R. Hyatt, S.J., Asst., St. Aedan's Church; Rev. Edmund W. Majewski, S.J., Prof., St. Peter's Univ.; Rev. Walter F. Modrys, S.J., Treas.; Rev. John A. Mullin, S.J., Guidance Counselor, St. Peter's Prep; Rev. Robert V. O'Hare, S.J., Teacher-St. Peter's Prep; Priests: 10

MAHWAH

Paulist Fathers - Paulist Press - 997 MacArthur Blvd., Mahwah, NJ 07430 t) 201-825-7300 info@paulistpress.com www.paulistpress.com Rev. Mark-David Janus, C.S.P., Pres.;

NEWARK

Comboni Missionaries of the Heart of Jesus (Verona Fathers) - 118 7th Ave., Newark, NJ 07104 t) 973-744-8080 luigizb@yahoo.com Rev. John Michael Converset, M.C.C.J.; Rev. Provvido Crozzoletto, M.C.C.J.; Rev. Paul Donohue, M.C.C.J.; Rev. John Paolo Pezzi, M.C.C.J.; Rev. Luigi Zanotto, M.C.C.J., Supr.;

Franciscan Friars of the Renewal (Most Blessed Sacrament Friary) - 375 13th Ave., Newark, NJ 07103 t) 973-622-6622 cfrgensec@franciscanfriars.com www.newarkfriary.org Rev. Stephen Marie Dufrene, C.F.R., Supr.; Rev. Francis Mary Roaldi, C.F.R., Vicar; Rev. Raphael Jacques Chilou, C.F.R., Pst. Assoc.; Rev. Sebastian Kajko, Pst. Assoc.; Bro. Andre Manders, C.F.R., Mem.; Bro. Zachary John Indovino, CFR, Friar; Bro. Simeon Synoski, CFR, Mem.;

Benedictine Abbey of Newark - 528 Dr. Martin Luther King, Jr. Blvd., Newark, NJ 07102; Mailing: 520 Dr. Martin Luther King, Jr. Blvd., Newark, NJ 07102 t) 973-792-5700 www.newarkabbey.org Rt. Rev. Augustine J. Curley, O.S.B., Abbot; Rt. Rev. Melvin J. Valvano, O.S.B., Resigned Abbot; Rev. Albert T. Holtz, O.S.B., Prior; Bro. Patrick Winbush, O.S.B., Subprior; Rev. Maximillian Buonocore, O.S.B., Mem.; Bro. Simon Clayton, Mem.; Rev. Luke A. Edelen, O.S.B., Mem.; Rev. Francis Flood, O.S.B., Mem.; Bro. Thomas Aquinas Hall, O.S.B., Mem.; Bro. Robert Moises Islas, O.S.B., Mem.; Rev. Mark Dilone, Mem.; Rev. Maynard G. Nagengast, O.S.B., Mem.; Rev. Asiel Rodriguez, Mem.; Rev. Edwin D. Leahy, O.S.B., Mem.; Bro. Bruno Mello, Mem.; Rev. Philip J. Waters, O.S.B., Mem.; Bro. Francis M. Woodruff, O.S.B., Mem.; Brs.: 4; Priests: 11

ORADELL

Congregation of Christian Brothers - Bergen Catholic Brothers' Residence, 1040 Oradell Ave., Oradell, NJ 07649 t) 201-261-1844 president@bergencatholic.org Bro. Brian M. Walsh, C.F.C., Contact;

ORANGE

The Salesian Community - Don Bosco Residence, 518-B Valley St., Orange, NJ 07050 t) 973-674-2400 Rev. Javier Aracil, S.D.B.; Rev. James Berning, S.D.B.; Bro. Jhoni Chamorro, S.D.B.; Bro. Ronald Chauca, S.D.B.; Bro. Paul Garcia, S.D.B.; Bro. Branden Gordon, S.B.D.; Bro. Benito Guerrero, S.D.B.; Bro. Travis Gunther, S.D.B.; Rev. Dennis Hartigan, S.D.B.; Bro. James Nguyen, S.B.D.; Rev. Vincent Paczkowski, S.D.B.; Bro. Wilgintz Polynice, S.D.B.; Bro. Juan Pablo Rubio, S.D.B.; Bro. Joshua Sciullo, S.B.D.; Bro. Simon Song; Rev. Derek Van Daniker, S.D.B.; Bro. Raphael Vargas, S.D.B.; Rev. Steven Dumais, S.D.B., Pst.; Rev. Dominic Tran, S.D.B., Dir.;

RAMSEY

Adorno Fathers - 575 Darlington Ave., Ramsey, NJ 07446 t) 201-327-7375

Don Bosco Prep Salesian Residence - 492 N. Franklin Tpke., Ramsey, NJ 07446-2811 t) 201-327-8100 Rev. James Cerbone, S.D.B.; Bro. Alfred Flatoff, S.D.B.; Rev. Louis Konopelski, S.D.B.; Rev. Sasika Lokuhettige, S.B.D.; Rev. James Mulloy, S.D.B.; Bro. James Wiegand, S.D.B.; Rev. James Heuser, S.D.B., Pres.;

ROSELLE

Marist Brothers Residence - 376 Raritan Rd., Roselle, NJ 07203 t) 908-245-3574

RUTHERFORD

St. John Vianney Residence for Retired Priests - 60 Home Ave., Rutherford, NJ 07070 t) 201-933-5155 Rev. Msgr. Peter A. Cheplic, In Res.; Rev. Msgr. Joseph Chiang, In Res.; Rev. Joseph F. Coda, In Res.; Rev. Neil J. Collins, In Res.; Rev. Msgr. Edward J. Eilert, In Res.; Rev. Michael J. German, In Res.; Rev. John Stanley Gomes, In Res.; Rev. Alan F. Guglielmo, In Res.; Rev. Sebastian Kunnath, In Res.; Rev. Msgr. Thomas G. Madden, In Res.; Rev. James J. Reilly, In Res.; Rev. Jose C. Saltarin, In Res.; Rev. Msgr. Richard T. Strelecki, In Res.; Rev. Rudolf Zubik, In Res.; Carol Hubba, Admin.;

SOUTH ORANGE

Pallottine Fathers & Brothers - 204 Raymond Ave., South Orange, NJ 07079-0979; Mailing: P.O. Box 979, South Orange, NJ 07079-0979 t) 201-943-0972 Rev. Peter T. Sticco, S.A.C., Prov.;

TENAFLY

Society of African Missions, Provincialate, S.M.A. Fathers - 23 Bliss Ave., Tenafly, NJ 07670 t) 201-567-0450 x200; 201-567-0450 x244 (Museum) tenafly-superior@smafathers.org; provincial@smafathers.org www.smafathers.org Very Rev. Ranees Anbukumar Rayappan, SMA (India), Prov.; Rev. Dermot Roache, SMA, Vice-Provincial; Rev. Richard A Mwisheni, SMA (Kenya), Councilor; Rev. Frank Wright, SMA, Supr.; Rev. Michael Adebote, SMA (Nigeria), Chap.; Rev. Simon Assogba, SMA (Benin), Par. Vicar; Rev. Michael Bova, SMA, Overseas Assignment; Rev. John P. Brennan, SMA, Mem.; Rev. Gustavo Buccilli (Argentina), Assoc. Priest; Rev. Matthew Cole, SMA, Par. Vicar; Rev. Albert Cooney, SMA, In Res.; Rev. Julien Esse, SMA (Togo), In Res.; Rev. Edward Galvin, SMA, In Res.; Rev. James Gessler, SMA, Mem.; Rev. Adam F. Hirudayasamy, SMA (India), Pst.; Rev. Ghislain Inai, SMA (Ivory Coast), Par. Vicar; Rev. Anthony Korir, SMA (Kenya), Par. Vicar; Rev. Patrick Machayi, SMA (Zambia), Mem.; Rev. Joseph Chacha Marwa, SMA (Tanzania), Pst.; Rev. James J. McConnell, SMA, In Res.; Rev. Michael P. Moran, SMA, Pst.; Rev. Marc Nkulu, SMA (Congo), Mem.; Rev. Austin Charles Ochu, S.M.A. (Nigeria), Chap.; Rev. Eliecer Sandoval, SMA (Panama), Mem.; Theresa Hicks, S.M.A., Lay Assoc.; Priests: 25

UNION CITY

Augustinian Recollects, St. Nicholas of Tolentine Monastery - 3201 Central Ave., Union City, NJ 07087 t) 201-433-7550 nicholas@agustinosrecoletos.org Prov. of St. Nicholas of Tolentine Rev. Francisco Sigulenza, O.A.R., Supr.;

Capuchin Friars - Province of the Sacred Stigmata of St. Francis - 319 36th St., Union City, NJ 07087; Mailing: P.O. Box 809, Union City, NJ 07087 t) 201-865-0611; (201) 865-6107 stigmataprovince@capuchinfriars.org capuchinfriars.org Rev. Robert Williams, O.F.M.Cap., Vicar; Rev. Remo DiSalvatore, O.F.M.Cap., Prov.; Bro. Rudolph Pieretti, O.F.M. Cap., Secy.; Friar Martiz Schratz, OFM Cap., Mem.; Rev. Francisco Arredondo, Councilor; Rev. Robert Perez, Councilor; Brs.: 14; Priests: 24

VERONA

The Salvatorian Fathers - 23 Crestmont Rd., Verona, NJ 07044 t) 973-746-8770; 973-433-7626 veronasds@gmail.com www.veronasds.com (Polish Mission House) Rev. Pawel Dolinski, S.D.S.; Rev. Andrzej Kielkowski, S.D.S.; Bro. Marek Miazga; Rev. Jan J. Mysliwiec, S.D.S.; Rev. Damian Tomiczek, S.D.S.; Rev. Strzadala Wieslaw, S.D.S.; Rev. Zenon Boczek, S.D.S., Supr.;

WEST ORANGE

Augustinian Recollects - 29 Ridgeway Ave., West Orange, NJ 07052 t) 973-731-0616 x12 saprovince@oar.cc www.augustinianrecollects.us Prov. Res., Monastery of St. Cloud

NURSING / REHABILITATION / CONVALESCENCE / ELDERLY CARE [NUR]

CALDWELL

St. Catherine of Siena, Inc. - 7 Ryerson Ave., Caldwell, NJ 07006 t) 973-226-1577 dradtke@caldwellop.org www.caldwellop.org Sr. Luella Ramm, O.P., Vicar; Deirdre Radtke, Admin.; Sr. Arlene Antczak, O.P., Prioress; Sr. Patricia Stringer, O.P., Secy.;

CEDAR GROVE

St. Vincent Nursing Home - 315 E. Lindsley Rd., Cedar Grove, NJ 07009 t) 973-754-4800 (Div. of St. Joseph's Regional Medical Center) Sr. Elizabeth Noonan, Chap.; Deborah Quinn Martone, Admin.;

JERSEY CITY

St. Ann Home for the Aged (Peace Care St. Ann's) - 198 Old Bergen Rd., Jersey City, NJ 07305 t) 201-433-0950 rreyes@peacecarenj.org www.peacecarenj.org Robert J Reyes, Admin.; Asstd. Annu.: 354; Staff: 187

PRESCHOOLS / CHILDCARE CENTERS [PRE]

JERSEY CITY

St. Elizabeth School & Child Care Center, Inc. - 129 Garrison Ave., Jersey City, NJ 07306 t) 201-795-1443 st.stelizabethfsse@yahoo.com Sr. Shelcy Catherine Kulangara, Prin.; Sr. Anne Mankuzha, Supr.;

Trinity Child Care Center - 509 Bramhall Ave., Jersey City, NJ 07304 t) 201-433-2701 sgarlin@trinityccc.org www.trinityccc.org Sonja Garlin, Dir.;

NEWARK

Perpetual Help Day Nursery - 170 Broad St., Newark, NJ 07104 t) 973-484-3535 srmcriscinasdv@yahoo.com; srmcriscina@yahoo.com Sr. Christina Peteros, Prin.;

NUTLEY

Holy Family Day Nursery and Convent - 174 Franklin Ave., Nutley, NJ 07110 t) 973-235-1170 holyfamilydns@yahoo.com www.holyfamilydaynurseryschool.com Sr. Cathy Lynn Cummings, F.S.S.E., Prin & Supr.; Stds.: 60; Lay Tchrs.: 2

RAMSEY

St. Joseph Pre-School - 372 Wyckoff Ave., Ramsey, NJ 07446 t) 201-825-8386 Sr. Clare Arangassery, Supr.;

RETREAT HOUSES / RENEWAL CENTERS [RTR]

KEARNY

Saint John Paul II Youth Retreat Center - 499 Belgrove Dr., Kearny, NJ 07032 t) 201-998-0088 tom.conboy@rcan.org www.newarkoym.com Thomas G. Conboy, Dir.;

SEMINARIES [SEM]

KEARNY

Redemptoris Mater Archdiocesan Missionary Seminary - 672 Passaic Ave., Kearny, NJ 07032 t) 201-997-3220 rmnewark@gmail.com www.rmnewark.org Rev. Msgr. Renato Grasselli, Rector; Rev. Manuel Duenas, Vice Rector; Rev. Justino Cornejo-Castillero, Spiritual Director; Rev. Zbigniew Kukielka, Prefect of Studies; Stds.: 35

SOUTH ORANGE

College Seminary of the Immaculate Conception (Saint Andrew's Hall) - Seton Hall University, 400 S. Orange Ave., South Orange, NJ 07079 t) 973-761-9420 www.collegeseminary.shu.edu Rev. Duverney Bermudez, Rector; Rev. Hong-Ray Peter Cho, Rector; Rev. Frederick L. Miller, Dir.;

Immaculate Conception Seminary School of Theology - Seton Hall University, 400 S. Orange Ave., South Orange, NJ 07079 t) 973-761-9575 theology@shu.edu theology.shu.edu Rev. Douglas J. Milewski, Prof.; Rev. James P. Platania, Prof.; Rev. Pawel Tomczyk, Prof.; Rev. Msgr. C. Anthony Ziccardi, Prof.; Stella F. Wilkins, Librn.; Rev. Robert K. Suszko, Vice Rector; Rev. Msgr. Gerard H. McCarren, Rector; Rev. Renato J. Bautista, Dir. Formation; Dcn. Andrew E. Saunders, Dir. Diaconal Formation; Rev. Roberto Ortiz, Prof.; Rev. Christopher M. Ciccarino, Assoc Dean; Rev. Mariusz Koch, C.F.R., Spiritual Dir.; Dr. Dianne M. Traflet, Assoc Dean;

SHRINES [SHR]

KEARNY

Eucharistic Shrine of the Adorable Face of Jesus - 672 Passaic Ave., Kearny, NJ 07032-1305 t) 201-997-1270 eushrine@gmail.com Rev. Msgr. Renato Grasselli, Dir.;

SPECIAL CARE FACILITIES [SPF]

HOBOKEN

Good Counsel, Inc. - 411 Clinton St., Hoboken, NJ 07030 t) 201-798-9059; 201-795-0637; 800-723-8331 (Hotline) cbell@goodcounselhomes.org www.postabortionhelp.org Mark Swartzberg, Chair; Christopher R. Bell, Pres.;

Good Counsel, Inc. - ; Mailing: P.O. Box 6068, Hoboken, NJ 07030 Residences for single mothers and children. Post-abortion counseling and referrals through the Lumina Program.

JERSEY CITY

St. Joseph Home - 81 York St., Jersey City, NJ 07302 t) 201-451-9838 gacosta@yorkstreetproject.org www.yorkstreetproject.org Transitional housing for homeless women and children. Gloria E. Acosta, Dir.; Bed Capacity: 60; Asstd. Annu.: 290; Staff: 21

The Nurturing Place - 81 York St., Jersey City, NJ 07302 vhayes@yorkstreetproject.org A developmental child care center for disadvantaged youngsters; homeless & economically deprived. Victoria Hayes, Dir.;

Margaret Anna Cusack Care Center, Inc. (Peace Care St. Joseph's) - 537 Pavonia Ave., Jersey City, NJ 07306 t) 201-653-8300 tsheehy@peacecarenj.org www.peacecarenj.org Skilled Nursing Facility providing post acute and long-term care for Men & Women. Thomas P. Sheehy, Admin.; Bed Capacity: 139; Asstd. Annu.: 350; Staff: 160

St. Mary Residence - 240 Washington St., Jersey City, NJ 07302-3806 t) 201-451-9838 gacosta@yorkstreetproject.org www.yorkstreetproject.org Serves single working women of low income; no children. Gloria E. Acosta, Dir.; Bed Capacity: 44; Asstd. Annu.: 47; Staff: 10

LODI

***The Promise Outreach, Inc.** - 260 S. Main St., Lodi, NJ 07644 t) 973-460-3229 smantonelle@feliciansisters.org home.catholicweb.com/thepromiseoutreachinc Sr. Antonelle Chunka, C.S.S.F., Dir.; Bro. Thomas Corey, B.S.C.D., Dir.;

An asterisk (*) denotes an organization that has established tax-exempt status directly with the IRS and is not covered by the USCCB Group Ruling.

Archdiocese of New Orleans

(Archidioecesis Novae Aureliae)

MOST REVEREND GREGORY M. AYMOND, D.D.

Archbishop of New Orleans; ordained May 10, 1975; ordained Auxiliary Bishop of New Orleans January 10, 1997; appointed Coadjutor Bishop of Austin June 2, 2000; installed Bishop of Austin August 3, 2000; appointed Archbishop of New Orleans June 12, 2009; Pallium conferred by Pope Benedict XVI at the Vatican June 29, 2009; installed Archbishop of New Orleans August 20, 2009. Archdiocesan Administration Building: 7887 Walmsley Ave., New Orleans, LA 70125-3496. T: 504-861-9521.

Archdiocesan Administration Building: 7887 Walmsley Ave., New Orleans, LA 70125-3496. T: 504-861-9521; F: 504-866-2906.
www.archdiocese-no.org

Square Miles 4,208.

Established April 25, 1793; Archdiocese July 19, 1850.

Comprises the following Parishes of Louisiana: Orleans, St. Bernard, Plaquemines, Jefferson, St. Charles, St. John the Baptist, St. Tammany and Washington.

For legal titles of parishes and archdiocesan institutions, consult the Chancery Office.

Most Reverend Fernand J. Cheri, III, O.F.M.
Auxiliary Bishop of New Orleans; ordained May 20, 1978; appointed Titular Bishop of Membressa and Auxiliary Bishop of New Orleans January 12, 2015; ordained March 23, 2015. Office: 7887 Walmsley Ave., New Orleans, LA 70125-3496.

STATISTICAL OVERVIEW

Personnel
Archbishops....1
Retired Archbishops....1
Auxiliary Bishops....1
Abbots....1
Priests: Diocesan Active in Diocese....147
Priests: Diocesan Active Outside Diocese....2
Priests: Diocesan in Foreign Missions....1
Priests: Retired, Sick or Absent....54
Number of Diocesan Priests....204
Religious Priests in Diocese....97
Total Priests in your Diocese....301
Extern Priests in Diocese....25
Ordinations:
Diocesan Priests....6
Religious Priests....3
Transitional Deacons....4
Permanent Deacons....16
Permanent Deacons in Diocese....221
Total Brothers....57
Total Sisters....295

Parishes
Parishes....112
With Resident Pastor:
Resident Diocesan Priests....88
Resident Religious Priests....20
Without Resident Pastor:
Administered by Priests....4
Missions....6
Pastoral Centers....2

Welfare
Catholic Hospitals....1
Total Assisted....140,000
Health Care Centers....3
Total Assisted....202
Homes for the Aged....25
Total Assisted....2,800
Day Care Centers....8
Total Assisted....478
Specialized Homes....6
Total Assisted....238
Special Centers for Social Services....372
Total Assisted....61,908
Residential Care of Disabled....3
Total Assisted....45
Other Institutions....10
Total Assisted....1,904

Educational
Seminaries, Diocesan....1
Students from This Diocese....25
Students from Other Dioceses....104
Diocesan Students in Other Seminaries....5
Seminaries, Religious....1
Total Seminarians....30
Colleges and Universities....3
Total Students....9,327
High Schools, Diocesan and Parish....8
Total Students....4,194
High Schools, Private....13
Total Students....8,168
Elementary Schools, Diocesan and Parish....40
Total Students....16,475
Elementary Schools, Private....8
Total Students....2,890
Non-residential Schools for the Disabled....2
Total Students....433
Catechesis/Religious Education:
High School Students....1,968
Elementary Students....5,186
Total Students under Catholic Instruction....48,671
Teachers in Diocese:
Priests....29
Brothers....10
Sisters....19
Lay Teachers....2,637

Vital Statistics
Receptions into the Church:
Infant Baptism Totals....2,769
Minor Baptism Totals....201
Adult Baptism Totals....128
Received into Full Communion....676
First Communions....2,619
Confirmations....4,325
Marriages:
Catholic....928
Interfaith....216
Total Marriages....1,144
Deaths....3,610
Total Catholic Population....514,847
Total Population....1,287,117

LEADERSHIP

Vicars General - Most Rev. Fernand J. Cheri III, O.F.M.; Very Rev. Patrick J. Williams (pwilliams@archdiocese-no.org);
Moderator of the Curia (Vacant) -
Chancellor and Special Delegate for Dispensations and Permissions - t) 504-861-6256 Very Rev. Peter O. Akpoghiran (tribunal@archdiocese-no.org);
Vice Chancellor and Special Delegate for Dispensations and Permissions - Rev. Vinh Dinh Luu;
Archdiocesan Administration Building - t) 504-861-9521
Archdiocesan Consultors - Most Rev. Fernand J. Cheri III, O.F.M., Mem.; Very Rev. Peter O. Akpoghiran, Mem. (tribunal@archdiocese-no.org); Rev. James A. Wehner, Mem.;
Deans -
Deanery I (Cathedral Deanery) - Very Rev. Henry J. Davis, S.S.J.;
Deanery II (City Park-Gentilly) - Very Rev. Jonathan P. Hemelt, Dean;
Deanery III (Uptown) - Very Rev. Michael J. Schneller;
Deanery IV (East Jefferson) - Very Rev. Luis F. Rodriguez, Dean;
Deanery V (St. John-St. Charles) - Very Rev. Stephen Dardis;
Deanery VI (West Bank) - Rev. Colin V. Braud, Dean;
Deanery VII (Algiers-Plaquemines) - Rev. Eugene F. Jacques;
Deanery VIII (St. Bernard) - Very Rev. Marlon Mangubat;
Deanery IX (West St. Tammany-Washington) - Rev. Charles Benoit, O.S.B.;
Deanery X (East St. Tammany-Washington) - Very Rev. Gerald L. Seiler Jr., Dean;
Archdiocesan Administrative Council - Most Rev. Gregory M. Aymond, Chair (archbishop@arch-no.org); Most Rev. Fernand J. Cheri III, O.F.M.; Very Rev. Patrick J. Williams (pwilliams@archdiocese-no.org);
Presbyteral Council of the Archdiocese of New Orleans - Most Rev. Gregory M. Aymond, Chair (archbishop@arch-no.org);
Archdiocesan Finance Council - Most Rev. Gregory M. Aymond, Chair (archbishop@arch-no.org);
Archdiocesan Development Council - Cory J. Howat, Chair (info@ccfnola.org);
Chancellor - Very Rev. Peter O. Akpoghiran (tribunal@archdiocese-no.org);
Ministerial Council -
Archbishop - Most Rev. Gregory M. Aymond;
Vicars General - Most Rev. Fernand J. Cheri III, O.F.M.; Very Rev. Patrick J. Williams;
Chairman - Very Rev. Patrick J. Williams;
Censores Librorum - Very Rev. Jose I. Lavastida, Mem.; Rev. Dennis J. Hayes III, Mem.; Very Rev. Patrick J. Williams, Mem.;
Louisiana Conference of Catholic Bishops - t) 225-344-7120 Thomas M. Costanza, Exec. Dir.;

OFFICES AND DIRECTORS

Archdiocesan Administration Accounting - t) 504-861-6236 Christopher Countiss, Dir.;
Parish Accounting - Colette Theriot, Dir. Compliance & Parish Accounting (ctheriot@arch-no.org);
Archives and Records (Archdiocesan) - t) 504-861-6241 archives@arch-no.org Kimberly Johnson, Archivist;
Compliance and Accounting - Colette Theriot, Contact (ctheriot@arch-no.org);
Black Catholic Ministries - t) 504-861-9521; 504-861-6207 bcatholics@arch-no.org Dr. Ansel Augustine, Dir.;
Building Office - t) 504-861-6210 Ken Zito, Dir.;
Campus Ministry - yam@arch-no.org James Behan Jr., Archdiocesan Coord.;
Catholic Counseling Service - t) 504-861-6245 ccs@arch-no.org Dr. Joey Pistorius, Dir.;
Catholic Cultural Heritage Center/Old Ursuline Convent - t) 504-525-9585 x135 cathedral@arch-no.org Very Rev. Philip G. Landry, Dir.;
Catholic Education and Faith Formation - t) 504-866-7916 superintendent@archdiocese.no.org nolacatholicschools.org Dr. RaeNell Billiot Houston, Supt.;
Deputy Superintendent, Catholic Schools - Martha M. Mundine;
Deputy Superintendent, Faith Formation - Dcn. Michael Whitehouse;
Associate Superintendent, Academic Excellence - Kasey Webb;
Associate Superintendent, Academic Formation & Accessibility - Katherine Shea;
Associate Superintendent, Elementary Schools - Michael Buras II, Associate Superintendent of Elementary Schools;
Associate Superintendent, Network Schools - Ingrid R. Fields;
Associate Superintendent, Secondary Schools - Dcn. Lawrence C. Houston, Assoc. Dir.;
Coordinator of Parish Schools - Barbara McAtee, Assoc. Dir. Faith Formation;
Instructional Coach - Tamika Duroncelay;
Center of Jesus the Lord - t) 504-529-1636 office@centerofjesusthelord.org
Charismatic Renewal - Timmy McCaffery, Exec. Dir. (tmccaffery@arch-no.org);
Clergy - t) 504-861-6268 Very Rev. Patrick J. Williams, Exec. (pwilliams@archdiocese-no.org);
Communications - t) 504-596-3023 Sarah Comiskey McDonald, Dir. (communications@arch-no.org);
Cultural Heritage Office - t) 504-527-5781 archives@archdiocese-no.org Kimberly Johnson, Dir.;
CYO - Youth and Young Adult Ministry Office - t) 504-836-0551 Adrian Jackson, Dir. (ajackson@arch-no.org);
Camp Abbey Retreat Center and Camp Abbey Summer Program - cyo-no.org Adrian Jackson, Dir.; Denise Emmons, Admin.; William O'Regan IV, Camp Abbey Prog. Coord.;
Deaf Apostolate - Arthine Vicks Powers, Dir.;
Ecumenical Officer - t) 504-341-9522 Rev. Emile G. (Buddy) Noel (frbuddy@olps.nocoxmail.com);
Commission for Persons with Disabilities - t) 504-861-6294 vicargeneral@arch-no.org
Filipino Catholic Ministry - t) 504-280-7370 Very Rev. Marlon Mangubat, Spiritual Advisor; Adlai DePano, Coord.;
Financial and Administrative Services - Dirk Wild, CFO; Rev. Patrick Carr, Vicar of Finance (fr.patrick@stangela.org);
Hispanic Apostolate - t) 504-467-2550 Rev. Sergio Serrano, O.P., Dir.;
Human Resources - t) 504-310-8792 Dr. Chalana Alexander Landry, Dir. (clandry@arch-no.org);
Information Technology - t) 504-596-3064 it@arch-no.org David John, Dir.;
Risk Management Office - t) 504-206-4881 (Insurance Certificates, Insurance Changes, Property Claims); 855-902-5818 (Claims - Liability, Workers' Comp); 504-302-8633 (Contract Review) Susan Anderson Zeringue, Contract Review (szeringue@arch-no.org);
Legal Services - Susan Anderson Zeringue, Archdiocesan Legal Counsel (szeringue@arch-no.org); Charles I. Denechaud III; Otto Schoenfeld;
Marriage and Family Life - t) 504-861-6243 mfl@arch-no.org Christopher O'Neill, Dir.; James Behan Jr., Assoc. Dir.;
Metropolitan Tribunal - t) 504-861-6291 Very Rev. Peter O. Akpoghiran, Vicar (tribunal@archdiocese-no.org);
Court of First Instance -
Court of Second Instance -
Defenders of the Bond - Rev. Matthew D. Johnston; Rev. Timothy D. Hedrick; Geri M. Woodward;
Ecclesiastical Notaries - Janice Buhler; Olivia George; Janet Urrutia;
Judges - Very Rev. Peter O. Akpoghiran; Rev. Vinh Dinh Luu; Very Rev. Gerald L. Seiler Jr.;
Procurators and Advocates -
Promoter of Justice - Very Rev. Jonathan P. Hemelt, Promoter of Justice;
Northshore Catholic Center - t) 985-605-5840 Stephanie Dupepe, CCANO Coord., Northshore Svcs.;
Permanent Diaconate - t) 504-861-6329 Dcn. Raphael Duplechain Jr., Dir.;
Pontifical Mission Societies - t) 504-527-5771
Missionary Childhood Association -
Missionary Union -
Society of St. Peter the Apostle -
Society of the Propagation of the Faith -
Priestly Life and Ministry Committee - t) 504-861-6269 Rev. Kenneth Allen, Dir.;
Property and Building Management - t) 504-596-3070 Elizabeth F. Lacombe, Dir. (llacombe@archdiocese-no.org);
Religious - Sr. Elizabeth Fitzpatrick, O.Carm., Exec. Dir. (rpersonnel@archdiocese-no.org);
Respect Life Office - t) 504-286-1119 respectlife@arch-no.org www.respectlife.arch-no.org Michelle Black, Dir.;
Safe Environment Coordinator - t) 504-861-6278 Sr. Mary Ellen Wheelahan, O.Carm., Coord. (srmwheelahan@arch-no.org);
Victims Assistance Coordinator - Dr. Joey Pistorius, Coord.;
Vicars General - t) 504-861-6262 Most Rev. Fernand J. Cheri III, O.F.M.; Very Rev. Patrick J. Williams (pwilliams@archdiocese-no.org);
Vietnamese Catholics Office - Rev. Nghiem Van Nguyen, Liaison for the Vietnamese Community;
Liaisons for the Vietnamese Community - Rev. Nghiem Van Nguyen; Rev. John-Nhan Tran;
Vocation Office - t) 504-861-6298 Rev. Colm Cahill, Dir.;
Worship Office - t) 504-861-6300 worship@archdiocese-no.org Rev. Nile C. Gross, Dir.; Betty-Ann Hickey, Assoc. Dir.;
Liturgical Commission - Rev. Nile C. Gross, Coord.;

CATHOLIC CHARITIES

Catholic Charities Archdiocese of New Orleans - t) 504-523-3755 ccano@ccano.org www.ccano.org Sr. Marjorie A. Hebert, M.S.C., Pres.; Dcn. Martin Gutierrez, COO; Cheryl D. LaBorde, CFO;
Catholic Charities School-Based Counseling (CCSBC) - t) 985-307-6882 Susan Fendlason, Admin.;
Ciara Independent Living - t) 504-524-8394 Brittany Simmons, Prog. Coord.;
Cornerstone Builders - t) 504-310-8772 Stephanie Mills, Re-entry Prog. Dir.;
Counseling Solutions - t) 985-785-2113 Lisa Surrency, Dir.;
ESL Services - t) 504-861-6348 Alison Hanson, Prog. Dir.;
Food for Seniors - t) 504-245-7207
Foster Grandparents - t) 504-310-6882 Brian Broussard, Dir.;
Head Start Centers - t) 504-861-6359 Rhonda Taylor, Dir.;
Incarnate Word Head Start/Early Head Start -
St. John the Baptist Head Start -
St. Mary of the Angels Head Start/Early Head Start -
St. Paul the Apostle Head Start/Early Head Start -
Health Guardians - t) 504-310-6911 Khyati Patel, Prog. Dir.;
Homeless Services - t) 504-310-8788
Bethlehem Housing Services - t) 504-236-8325 Trinna Stanford, Dir.;
Bridges to Self-Sufficiency - t) 504-310-8788 Johnell Williams, Case Mgr.;
Immigration Services - t) 504-457-3462 Shaula Lovera, Prog. Admin., Immigration & Refugee Svcs.;
North Shore Branch Office - t) 985-605-5847 Stephanie Dupepe, Coord. North Shore Svcs.;
Office of Institutional Advancement - t) 504-592-5688 Lauren Combel, Communications Mgr.;
Archbishop Hannan Community Appeal (AHCA) - t) 504-592-5688

Office of Justice and Peace - t) 504-592-5692 Kevin Fitzpatrick, Dir.;
Catholic Campaign for Human Development (CCHD) - Kevin Fitzpatrick, Dir.;
Catholic Relief Services (CRS) -
Prison Ministry - t) 504-267-9727 John Messenheimer, Coord.;
PACE Greater New Orleans - t) 504-227-3491 Kurt Wootan, Interim Exec. Dir.;
Hope Haven St. John Bosco PACE Center -
Shirley Landry Benson PACE Center -
Padua Community Services - t) 504-392-0502 Tanna Barthelemy, Admin.;
Padua Community Homes -
Padua House -
Parish & Community Ministries - t) 504-451-1889 Stephanie Dupepe, Admin.;
PHILMAT, Inc. - t) 504-596-3099 Sr. Marjorie A. Hebert, M.S.C., Pres.;
Pregnancy and Adoption Services (formerly ACCESS) - t) 504-885-1141 Michelle Black, Dir.;
Adoption Services - t) 504-885-1141 Danna P. Cousins, Dir.;
St. Vincent Maternity Clinic - t) 504-837-6346 Michelle Black, Dir.;
Project SAVE - t) 504-310-6871 Allyson Tuttle, Admin.;
Refugee Services - t) 504-457-3462 Janet Lopez, Assoc. Dir., Refugee & Resettlement;
Sacred Heart Apartments - t) 504-821-1786 Shayla Kaywood, Prog. Dir.;
Spirit of Hope Disaster Response - t) 504-596-3097 Stephanie Dupepe, Prog. Admin.;
Therapeutic Family Services - t) 504-310-6939 Shacidy Hadley-Bush, Admin.;
Volunteer Department - t) 504-310-6962 Cindy Self, Assoc. Dir.;

CLERGY AND RELIGIOUS SERVICES

St. Gertrude's Retirement Center -

ORGANIZATIONS

Apostleship of the Sea - t) 985-307-0601 Dcn. Wayne A. Lobell, Dir.;
Archdiocese of New Orleans Indemnity, Inc. - t) 802-922-9457 Dirk Wild, CFO;
Bernard A. Grehan Trust - t) 504-861-9521
Catholic Charities Children's Day Care Centers Inc. -
Catholic Community Foundation for the Archdiocese of New Orleans, Inc. - t) 504-596-3045 Cory J. Howat, Exec. (info@ccfnola.org);
Christopher Homes, Inc. - t) 504-596-3460 Dcn. Dennis Adams, Dir. (dfadams@chi-ano.org);
Christopher Inn -
Clarion Herald Newspaper - t) 504-596-3035 Peter P. Finney Jr., Exec. Editor/Gen. Mgr. (clarionherald@clarionherald.orgald.org);
Hanmaum Korean Catholic Chapel - t) 504-888-8772 Rev. Byoung-Ok Park (Korea), Chap.;
Mental Health Association Development Corporation - t) 504-861-9521
New Orleans Archdiocesan Cemeteries and New Orleans Cemeteries Trust - t) 504-596-3050 Sherri Peppo, Dir. (speppo@archdiocese-no.org);
Notre Dame Health System - Dcn. Jeffrey R. Tully, Pres./CEO (jtully@arch-no.org); Ryan Caruso, Senior Vice Pres. Finance; Sherri Guidry, Senior Vice Pres. Oper.;
President/CEO - Dcn. Jeffrey R. Tully, Pres.;
Chateau de Notre Dame Apartments - t) 504-866-2741 www.notredamehealth.org Anita Burns, Admin.;
Chateau de Notre Dame Nursing Home - t) 504-866-2741 www.notredamehealth.org Patricia Taylor, Admin.;
Our Lady of Wisdom Healthcare Center - t) 504-394-5991 www.notredamehealth.org Lisa Heisser, Admin.;
Wynhoven Health Care Center - t) 504-347-0777 www.notredamehealth.org Michelle Matthew, Admin.;
Chateau de Notre Dame Facilities Corporation -
Our Lady of Wisdom Facility Corporation -
Project Lazarus - t) 504-949-3609 info@projectlazarus.net www.projectlazarus.net Susanne B Dietzel, Interim Exec. Dir. (sdietzel@projectlazarus.net); Liv Ferrick, Devel. Mgr.;
St. Elizabeth's Guild - Kathleen Robert, Pres.;
St. Mary's Catholic Orphan Boys' Asylum Board -
St. Michael Special School - t) 504-524-7285 www.archdiocese-no.org/stmichael
St. Vincent's Infant and Maternity Home Guild - Marcy Mayeaux;
School Food and Nutrition Services of New Orleans Inc. - t) 504-596-3434 egauthreaux@schoolcafe.org Ellen Gauthreaux, Exec.;
***Second Harvest Food Bank of Greater New Orleans and Acadiana** - t) 504-734-1322 www.no-hunger.org Natalie Jayroe, Pres./CEO;

MISCELLANEOUS / OTHER OFFICES

7887 Walmsley, Inc. - t) 802-922-9457 Jeffrey J. Entwisle, Dir.;
Archconfraternity of St. Ann -
Beginning Experience - Melanie Trimarco, Pres.;
Blue Army of Our Lady of Fatima - t) 504-529-1636 Rev. Denzil M. Perera, Dir.;
The Christ in Christmas Committee of New Orleans - t) 504-615-1303 kcicno@bellsouth.net Stephen F. Hart, Chair;
Confraternity of the Holy Face -
Council of Catholic School Cooperative Clubs - www.ccscc.catholicweb.com Roxanne Valenti, Pres. (roxannevalenti@gmail.com);
The Cursillo Movement - t) 504-464-0181 Billy App, Lay Dir.; Rev. Michael Mitchell, Spiritual Dir. (frmikemj@bellsouth.net);
Engaged Encounter - Stacey Hebert, Exec. Couple; Chris Hebert, Exec. Couple;
Holy Name Societies - t) 504-481-3407 Vince Petreikis, Pres.; Anthony Smith, Secy.;
Ladies of Charity of the Archdiocese - t) 504-810-1733 Tanya Cenac, Pres.; Sr. Suzanne Anglim, D.C., Spiritual Adv./Care Srvcs.;
Lay Carmelites of Our Lady of Mount Carmel -
Legatus of New Orleans - t) 504-343-2478 neworleans@legatus.org www.legatus.org Louis Rodriguez, Pres.;
Legion of Mary - t) 504-975-6930 lalegionofmary@att.net Richard E. Launey, Pres.;
Magnificat Chapters - Cindy Delger, Coord. (cindythree@att.net);
Metairie Chapter - t) (504) 888-0655 Lisa Winter;
Slidell Chapter - t) 985-502-0349 Deborah Callens;
West Bank Chapter - Rev. Msgr. Lanaux J. Rareshide, Spiritual Adv./Care Srvcs.; Cindy Delger, Coord.;
West St. Tammany Chapter - t) 985-635-9665 Nicole Johnson, Coord.; Rev. Robert C. Cavalier, Spiritual Adv./Care Srvcs.;
Magnificat, Ministry to Catholic Women - t) 504-828-6279 magnificatcst@aol.com www.magnificat-ministry.org Rev. Msgr. David Toups, Spiritual Adv./Care Srvcs.; Donna Ross, Coord. Central Svc. Team;
Marians of New Orleans - t) 504-466-2295 Bobbie Fazende, Pres. (office@sleoh.com);
Mary's Children - t) 504-218-8739 Nora Lambert, Pres.;
Mary's Helpers - t) 800-573-4130; 504-348-7729 Brenda Ourso, Admin.;
MIR Group - t) 504-849-2570 Robert Hale, Pres.;
Missionaries of St. Therese - t) 504-527-5771 Lynn Schonberg, Pres.;
Naim Conference - Joan Mascaro, Pres. (mfl@arch-no.org);
National Council of Catholic Men -
National Council of Catholic Women (Vacant) -
***National T.E.C. Conference** -
Pax Christi New Orleans - paxchristiusa.org Kevin Cahalan, Chair; Ben Gordon, Chair;
People Program - t) 504-284-7678 info@peopleprogram.org www.peopleprogram.org Scott Wallace, Exec. Dir.;
Westbank Program - t) 504-394-5433
Priests for Life -
Retrouvaille/Rediscovery - t) 504-861-6243 mfl@arch-no.org www.helpyourmarriage.org
Rosary Congress Committee - t) 504-482-4156 www.rosarycongress.org Rev. Steven V. Bruno, Spiritual Dir.;
St. Thomas More Catholic Lawyers Association - t) 504-834-0340 Rev. Joseph S. Palermo Jr.;
St. Vincent de Paul Society - t) 504-940-5031 Michael Bourg, Exec. Dir.; Michael Champagne, Pres.;
St. Vincent's Infant and Maternity Guild - Cindy Wooderson, Pres.;
Scouting -
Archdiocesan Liaison - Adrian Jackson;
Catholic Committee on Boy Scouting - t) 504-737-8370 Dcn. Daniel Flynn, Pst. Min./Coord.; Susan Guidry, Chair;
Catholic Committee on Girl Scouting - t) 504-885-3780 Dcn. Richard Brady, Pst. Min./Coord.; Gloria St. Pierre, Chair;
Serra Clubs -
Serra Club of East Jefferson - t) 504-888-3958 Rev. Msgr. Robert D. Massett, Chap.; Joe Dicharry, District Governor;
Serra Club of East St. Tammany - t) 504-774-6923
Serra Club of New Orleans - t) 504-861-6298 Rev. Joseph M. Krafft, Chap.;
Serra Club of River Parishes - t) 504-774-1863 Rev. David Ducote, Chap.;
The Theresians International - t) 504-288-1897 Sally Duplantier, Pres.;
Woman's New Life Center - t) 504-831-3117 info@womansnewlife.com www.womansnewlife.com Allison Millet, CEO;

PARISHES, MISSIONS, AND CLERGY

STATE OF LOUISIANA

ABITA SPRINGS

St. Jane de Chantal Roman Catholic Church, Abita Springs, Louisiana - 72040 Maple St., Abita Springs, LA 70420; Mailing: P.O. Box 1870, Abita Springs, LA 70420-1870 t) 985-892-1439; 985-893-3914 (CRP) saintjanedechantal.com Rev. Kenneth Allen, Pst.; Rev. Alexander Guzman, In Res.; Dcn. Mark C. Coudrain; Dcn. Michael J. Talbot; Christina Uhlich, DRE;
St. Michael the Archangel - 81349 Hwy. 41, Bush, LA 70431; Mailing: P O Box 1870, Abita Springs, LA 70420 t) 985-886-1015

AMA

St. Mark Roman Catholic Church, Ama, Louisiana - 10773 River Rd., Ama, LA 70031 t) 504-289-2900 (CRP); 504-431-8505 restmarkama@arch-no.org; stmarkama@arch-no.org www.stmarkama.com Rev. Peter O. Akpoghiran, Pst.; Mary Loup, DRE;

AVONDALE

Assumption of Mary Roman Catholic Church, Avondale, Louisiana - 172 Andre Dung Lac Dr., Avondale, LA 70094; Mailing: 533 S. Jamie Blvd., Avondale, LA 70094 t) 504-304-6698 assumptionofmary@archdiocese-no.org Rev. Peter Hoai T. Nguyen, Pst.;
St. Bonaventure Roman Catholic Church, Avondale, Louisiana - 329 S. Jamie Blvd., Avondale, LA 70094-2821 t) 504-436-1279 Rev. Francis Offia, Pst.; Miranda Enclade, DRE;

BELLE CHASSE

Our Lady of Perpetual Help - 8968 Hwy. 23, Belle

Chasse, LA 70037-2296 t) 504-394-0314 cre@olphbc.org; churchoffice@olphbc.org olphbc.org Dcn. George E. Merritt Jr.; Rev. Kyle V. Dave, Pst.; Cecilia Merritt, DRE;

Our Lady of Perpetual Help School - 8970 Hwy. 23, Belle Chasse, LA 70037-2297 t) 504-394-0757 olphschool@olphbc.org www.school.olphbc.org Brittany Breaux, Prin.;

BOGALUSA

Annunciation Catholic Church - 517 Ave. B, Bogalusa, LA 70427-3711 t) 985-732-4280 annchurch@att.net Rev. Daniel E. Brouillette, Pst.; Dcn. Edward Francis Kelley;

Annunciation Catholic Church School - 511 Ave. C, Bogalusa, LA 70427-3797 t) 985-735-6643 annunciationsch@archdiocese-no.org www.acsbogalusa.org Rev. Angel Antonio Diaz-Perez, O.P., Prin.;

CHALMETTE

Our Lady of Prompt Succor - 2320 Paris Rd., Chalmette, LA 70043-5098 t) 504-271-1217; 504-271-3441 info@olps-chalmette.org www.olps-chalmette.org Parish assumed territory of Prince of Peace, Chalmette, St. Bernard Parish; St. Louise de Marillac, Arabi, St. Bernard Parish; St. Mark, Chalmette. Rev. Andy Gonzalez, Par. Vicar; Dcn. Lino G. Parulan; Very Rev. Marlon Mangubat, Pst.; Terri Smith, DRE;

Our Lady of Prompt Succor School - 2305 Fenelon St., Chalmette, LA 70043-4951 t) 504-271-2953 scoll8312@aol.com www.olpsschool.org Charol Armand, Prin.;

COVINGTON

St. Benedict Roman Catholic Church, Covington, Louisiana - 20370 Smith Rd., Covington, LA 70435 t) 985-892-5202 office@stbencov.org www.stbenedictchurchcovington.com/ Rev. Charles Benoit, O.S.B., Pst.; Dcn. Ellis Iverson; Dcn. Daniel P. Musso; CRP Stds.: 119

Most Holy Trinity Roman Catholic Church, Louisiana - 501 Holy Trinity Dr., Covington, LA 70433 t) 985-892-0642 office@mhtcc.net; cgamundi@mhtcc.net Rev. Daniel L. Dashner, Par. Vicar; Dcn. Robert M. Rivault; Rev. Rodney P. Bourg, Pst.; Dcn. Thomas E. Caffery Jr.; Dcn. Stephen W. Sperier; Dcn. Charles R. Swift; Eric Wilkes, CRE; CRP Stds.: 125

St. Peter - 125 E. 19th Ave., Covington, LA 70433-3195 t) 985-892-2422 bookkeeper@stpeterparish.com www.stpeterparish.com St. Peter Roman Catholic Church Dcn. Victor Bonnaffee III; Dcn. Francisco J. Rodriguez; Rev. Chinedu Daniel Okafor, Par. Vicar; Dcn. Dennis F. Adams; Rev. Daniel E. Brouillette, Pst.; Dcn. Brian M. McKnight Sr.;

St. Peter School - (Grades PreSchool-7) 130 E Temperance St, Covington, LA 70433 t) 985-892-1831 stpetercov@stpetercov.org stpetercov.org/ Michael Kraus, Prin.; Stds.: 827; Lay Tchrs.: 45

DES ALLEMANDS

St. Gertrude - 17292 LA Hwy. 631, Des Allemands, LA 70030 t) 985-758-1332 (CRP); 985-758-7542 office@stgertrude.nocoxmail.com; ccd@stgertrude.nocoxmail.com Rev. Ray A. Hymel, Pst.; Betty Hogan, DRE;

DESTREHAN

St. Charles Borromeo - 13396 River Rd., Destrehan, LA 70047; Mailing: P O Box 428, Destrehan, LA 70047-0428 t) 985-764-6383 rrodrigue@scbhumilitas.org www.scblittleredchurch.org Rev. Dominic Arcuri, Pst.; Dcn. Paul J. Ory; Dcn. Harry Schexnayder; Dcn. Michael Stohlman; Dcn. Bruce S. Trigo; Dcn. Jeffrey R. Tully; Rev. John Yike, Par. Vicar;

St. Charles Borromeo School - t) 985-764-9232 Rachel Levet Hafford, Prin.;

EDGARD

St. John the Baptist - 2361 Hwy. 18, Edgard, LA 70049-9101 t) 985-497-3412 stjohnedgard@arch-no.org Rev. Robustiano D. Morgia, Pst.;

FOLSOM

St. John the Baptist - 11345 St. John Church Rd., Folsom, LA 70437-7155 t) 985-796-3806; 985-796-5507 (CRP) stjohnthebaptistfolsom@yahoo.com stjohnbaptistfolsom.org Rev. Vincent Phan, Pst.; Dcn. Jeffrey J. Stein; Dcn. Julius T. Zimmer; Theresa Wilfert, DRE;

FRANKLINTON

Holy Family Roman Catholic Church, Franklinton, Louisiana - 1220 14th Ave., Franklinton, LA 70438 t) 985-839-4040 holyfamilyfranklinton@arch-no.org www.holyfamilyfranklinton.org Rev. Kyle J. Sanders, Pst.; CRP Stds.: 43

GARYVILLE

St. Hubert - 176 Anthony Monica St., Garyville, LA 70051-0851; Mailing: 541 S. Church St., Garyville, LA 70051 t) 985-535-3312 sthubert@rtconline.com Rev. Joel P. Cantones, Pst.; Dcn. Garland J. Roussel Jr.;

GRETNA

St. Anthony - 924 Monroe St., Gretna, LA 70053-2299 t) 504-368-6161; 504-368-1313 (Pastor, St Joseph, Gretna) c) 504-485-3164 stjosephgretna@bellsouth.net; stanthonygretna@arch-no.org www.stjosephgretna.com Rev. Gary P. Copping, Pst.; Dcn. Oscar D. Alegria; Dcn. Leonard E. Enger II; Rev. Msgr. Lanaux J. Rareshide, In Res.;

St. Anthony School - 900 Franklin Ave., Gretna, LA 70053-2224 t) 504-367-0689 pwaddell@stanthonygretna.org Patti Waddell, Prin.;

St. Cletus Roman Catholic Church, Gretna, Louisiana - 3600 Claire Ave., Gretna, LA 70053-7699 t) 504-367-7951 stcletuschurch@arch-no.org stcletuschurch.com Rev. Christopher P. Zavackis, Pst.; Dcn. Patrick L. Dempsey;

St. Cletus School - (Grades PreK-7) 3610 Claire Ave., Gretna, LA 70053-7699 t) 504-366-3538 stcletus@arch-no.org; jgrabert@stcletuscolts.com stcletus.com Jill Grabert, Prin.;

St. Joseph Church and Shrine on the Westbank - 610 Sixth St., Gretna, LA 70053-6098 t) 504-368-1313 c) 504-485-3164 stjosephgretna@arch-no.org www.stjosephgretna.com Rev. Gary P. Copping, Pst.; Rev. Msgr. Lanaux J. Rareshide, Contact; Dcn. Oscar D. Alegria; Dcn. Leonard E. Enger II; Dcn. Gerard L. Labadot; Diane Crawford, DRE; Kristen Albarado, Music Min.; Paul Coles, Pst. Min./Coord.;

HAHNVILLE

Our Lady of the Holy Rosary - 1 Rectory Ln., Hahnville, LA 70057 t) 985-783-1199 olrhahn@arch-no.org olrhahnville.org Rev. Paul Clark, Pst.; Therese Faucheux, CRE; LaSandra Gordon, CRE;

HARAHAN

St. Rita - 7100 Jefferson Hwy., Harahan, LA 70123-4928 parish@stritaharahan.com; emaffe@arch-no.org Rev. Steven V. Bruno, Pst.; Rev. Sylvester Agoda, Par. Vicar; Rev. David Frank, Par. Vicar; Dcn. Gary J. Borne; Dcn. Greg A. Flores; Dcn. Danny Flynn;

St. Rita School - 194 Ravan Ave., Harahan, LA 70123-4999 t) 504-737-0744 stritahar@archdiocese-no.org Miriam Daniel, Prin.;

HARVEY

St. John Bosco Roman Catholic Church, Harvey, Louisiana - 2114 Oakmere Dr., Harvey, LA 70058-2275 t) 504-340-0444 office@saintjohnboscochurch.org Rev. Mark Hyde, S.D.B., Pst.; Rev. George Hanna, S.D.B., Par. Vicar; Rev. Wilgintz Polynice, S.D.B., Par. Vicar; Dcn. Kevin M. Steel; Sarah Bui, Youth Min.; Paul G. Haddican Jr., Youth Min.; Caroline Vuong, Youth Min.;

St. Martha Roman Catholic Church, Harvey, Louisiana - 2555 Apollo Dr., Harvey, LA 70058-5813 t) 504-366-4142 (CRP); 504-366-1604 stmartha@arch-no.org stmarthaharvey.com/ Rev. Lich Van Nguyen, Pst.; Dcn. Tyrell Manieri; Dcn. Larry Murphy; Dcn. Brian P. Soileau Sr.;

Infant Jesus of Prague - 700 Maple St., Harvey, LA 70058-4008 t) 504-368-1397

St. Rosalie - 601 2nd Ave., Harvey, LA 70058-2728; Mailing: 600 2nd Ave., Harvey, LA 70058-2728 t) 504-340-1962 strosalieparish.com Rev. Mark Hyde, S.D.B., Pst.; Rev. George Hanna, S.D.B., Assoc. Pst.; Guyann Murphy, DRE;

JEFFERSON

St. Agnes - 3310 Jefferson Hwy., Jefferson, LA 70121-2699 t) 504-833-3366; 504-833-4118 parish@stagnesjefferson.org www.stagnesjefferson.org Rev. Bac-Hai Viet Tran, Pst.; Rev. Vinh Dinh Luu, In Res.; Rev. Thomas M. McCann III, In Res.; Dcn. Piero Caserta; Dcn. Frank G. DiFulco; Brenda Miller, DRE; CRP Stds.: 16

KENNER

Divine Mercy Roman Catholic Church, Kenner, Louisiana - 4337 Sal Lentini Pkwy., Kenner, LA 70065 t) 504-466-5016 office@divinemercyparish.org www.divinemercyparish.org Rev. Robert T. Cooper, Pst.; Rev. Luis Duarte, Par. Vicar; Dcn. David Caldero; Dcn. Andrea Capaci; Dcn. Noel W. Martinsen; Dcn. Larry D. Oney;

St. Elizabeth Ann Seton - 4335 Sal Lentini Parkway, Kenner, LA 70065 t) 504-468-3524 elizabeth@arch-no.org www.seasparish.com/school Joan Kathmann, Prin.;

St. Jerome Roman Catholic Church, Kenner, Louisiana - 2400 33rd St., Kenner, LA 70065-3899; Mailing: 2402 33rd St., Kenner, LA 70065-3899 t) 504-443-3174 stjeromepsh@archdiocese-no.org stjeromecatholic.org Rev. David W. Dufour, Pst.; Dcn. Leo Tran; Gail Bordelon, DRE;

Our Lady of Perpetual Help - 1908 Short St., Kenner, LA 70062-7599 t) 504-464-0361 www.olphla.net Rev. Charles W. Dussouy, Pst.; Dcn. Greg A. Gross;

Our Lady of Perpetual Help School - 530 Minor St., Kenner, LA 70062-7598; Mailing: 531 Williams Blvd., Kenner, LA 70062 t) 504-464-0531 olph@olphla.org www.olphla.org Jacob Owens, Prin.;

LA PLACE

Ascension of Our Lord Roman Catholic Church, LaPlace, Louisiana - 799 Fairway Dr., La Place, LA 70068-2007 t) 985-652-2615 andreemgurdian@gmail.com; aolparishoffice@gmail.com www.aolparish.org Rev. Cyril Buyeera, Pst.; Dcn. Julius A. Laurent; Dcn. Thomas J. St. Pierre; Andree Gurdian, DRE; CRP Stds.: 44

Ascension of Our Lord Roman Catholic Church, LaPlace, Louisiana School - (Grades PreK-7) 1809 Greenwood Dr., La Place, LA 70068-2098 t) 985-652-4532 office@aolcrusaders.org www.aolcrusaders.org/ Douglas V Triche, Prin.; Stds.: 140; Lay Tchrs.: 14

St. Joan of Arc - 529 W. 5th St., La Place, LA 70068 t) 985-652-9100 dre@sjachurch.com; office@sjachurch.com sjachurch.com Rev. David Ducote, Pst.; Dcn. Maurice V. Casadaban; Dcn. Daniel F. Reynolds;

St. Joan of Arc School - 412 Fir St., La Place, LA 70068-4310 t) 985-652-6310 www.sja-school.com Jennifer Poulos, Prin.;

Daughters of Divine Providence - 386 Fir St., La Place, LA 70068-3941 t) 985-359-3163

LACOMBE

St. John of the Cross Roman Catholic Church, Lacombe, Louisiana - 61030 Brier Lake Dr., Lacombe, LA 70445-2911 t) 985-882-6625 (CRP); 985-882-3779 sjc1286@bellsouth.net; sjc@arch-no.org www.stjohnofthecrosslacombe.org Rev. Tuan Anh Pham, Pst.; Dcn. Francis W. Drake; Dcn. Donald St. Germain; Dcn. Ricky J. Suprean; Dcn. Eugene P. Templet; Lynn Suprean, DRE;

Community Center - 61038 Brier Lake Dr., Lacombe, LA 70445-2911

Sacred Heart - 28029 Main St., Lacombe, LA 70445; Mailing: P.O. Box 1080, Lacombe, LA 70445-1080 t) 985-882-8041 (CRP); 985-882-5229 shcadm@arch-no.org Rev. Thomas Kilisara, Pst.; Dcn. William P. Curry Jr.; Dcn. Steven L. Ferran;

LAFITTE

St. Anthony - 2653 Jean Lafitte Blvd., Lafitte, LA 70067 t) 504-689-0069 (CRP); 504-689-4101 stanthony@arch-no.org stanthonylafitte.org Assumed parish territory of St. Pius X, Crown Point which became a mission of the parish. Rev. Luke H. Nguyen, Pst.; Dcn. Edward J. Cain Jr.; Wendy M. Houin, DRE; Paula Martin, DRE;

St. Pius X - 8151 Barataria Blvd., Crown Point, LA 70072-9704

LULING

St. Anthony of Padua - 234 Angus Dr., Luling, LA 70070-4427 t) 504-785-0050 (CRP); 985-785-8885 stanthonyluling@arch-no.org Rev. Anthony Odiong, Pst.; Dcn. Michael A. Fabre Sr.; Dcn. Kevin M. Robicheaux; Melanie Saunee, DRE;

Holy Family Roman Catholic Church, Luling, Louisiana - 155 Holy Family Ln., Luling, LA 70070-6103 t) 985-331-9100 (CRP); 985-785-8585 hfcstaff@holyfamilyluling.org Very Rev. Stephen Dardis, Pst.; Dcn. Coy Landry; Dcn. Jason A. Binet; CRP Stds.: 336

Holy Family Pre-School - (Grades PreK-PreK) t) 985-785-9244 holyfamilypreschoolluling@gmail.com Yvonne Pertuit, Dir.;

MADISONVILLE

St. Anselm - 306 St. Mary St., Madisonville, LA 70447 t) 985-845-7342 www.stanselmparish.org Rev. Msgr. Frank J. Giroir, Pst.; Rev. Pedro Prada, Par. Vicar; Dcn. Edward R. Morris; Dcn. Dennis J. Hickey; Dcn. Henry P. Wellmeyer; Tammy Frank Morris, DRE;

MANDEVILLE

Mary, Queen of Peace Roman Catholic Church, Mandeville, Louisiana - 1501 W. Causeway Approach, Mandeville, LA 70471-3047 t) 985-674-9794 (CRP); 985-626-6977 mqop@maryqueenofpeace.org www.maryqueenofpeace.org/ Rev. Msgr. Henry J. Bugler, Admin.; Dcn. Edward Beckendorf; Dcn. Timothy R. Jackson; Rev. Edward Kofi Owusu-Ansah, Par. Vicar; Jewell Bayhi, DRE;

Mary, Queen of Peace Roman Catholic Church, Mandeville, Louisiana School - (Grades PreK-7) 1515 W. Causeway Approach, Mandeville, LA 70471 t) 985-674-2466 school@maryqueenofpeace.org www.mqpcs.org Sybil Skansi, Prin.;

Our Lady of the Lake Roman Catholic Church - 312 Lafitte St., Mandeville, LA 70448-5827 t) 985-626-5671 bonnie@ollparish.info Rev. Douglas Busch, Pst.; Rev. Vincent Nguyen, Par. Vicar; Dcn. Steven R. Cohan; Dcn. Owen Francis; Dcn. Andrew P. Raspino Sr.; Dcn. Jay C. Frantz; CRP Stds.: 210

Our Lady of the Lake Roman Catholic Church School - 316 Lafitte St., Mandeville, LA 70448-5827 t) 985-626-5678 pjohnson@ourladyofthelakeschool.org www.ourladyofthelakeschool.org Frank Smith, Prin.;

MARRERO

St. Agnes Le Thi Thanh Roman Catholic Church, Marrero, Louisiana - 6851 St. Le Thi Thanh St., Marrero, LA 70072-2556; Mailing: 1000 Westwood Dr., Marrero, LA 70072-2415 t) 504-347-4725 stagnesltt@archdiocese-no.org (Personal Parish for Southeast Asians) Rev. Peter Nam Van Tran, Pst.;

Immaculate Conception - 4401 7th St., Marrero, LA 70072-2099 t) 504-341-9516 raaucoin@gmail.com iccmarrero.org Rev. Stephen Leake, S.D.B., Temp. Admin.; Dcn. James H. Simmons; Dcn. Oscar D. Alegria; Rhoda Aucoin, DRE; Janel Ockman, Music Min.;

Immaculate Conception School - 4520 6th St., Marrero, LA 70072-2098 t) 504-347-4409 iconception@archdiocese-no.org icschargers.org Kim DiMarco, Prin.;

St. Joachim Roman Catholic Church, Marrero, Louisiana - 5505 Barataria Blvd., Marrero, LA 70072-6660 t) 504-341-9226 stjoachim@arch-no.org www.stjoachimmarrero.org Rev. Stephen Leake, S.D.B., Temp. Admin.;

St. Joseph the Worker - 455 Ames Blvd., Marrero, LA 70072-1599 t) 504-347-8438 frgene@archdiocese-no.org Rev. Sidney Speaks, Pst.; Dcn. Charles E. Allen;

The Visitation of Our Lady Roman Catholic Church, Marrero, Louisiana - 3500 Ames Blvd., Marrero, LA 70072-5699 t) 504-341-8477 (CRP); 504-347-2203 volchurch@vol.org Rev. Colin V. Braud, Pst.; Rev. Jude O. Emunemu, Par. Vicar; Dcn. James P. Rooney Jr.; Dcn. James A. Venturella; Jenny Doskey, DRE;

The Visitation of Our Lady Roman Catholic Church, Marrero, Louisiana School - 3520 Ames Blvd., Marrero, LA 70072-5698 t) 504-347-3377 volschool@vol.org Carolyn Levet, Prin.;

METAIRIE

St. Angela Merici Roman Catholic Church, Metairie, Louisiana - 835 Melody Dr., Metairie, LA 70002; Mailing: 901 Beverly Garden Dr., Metairie, LA 70002 t) 504-835-0324 parish@stangela.org www.stangela.org Rev. Clayton J. Charbonnet III, Pst.; Rev. Lawrence Murori, Par. Vicar; Dcn. David P. Aaron; Dcn. Nicholas Chetta; Dcn. Raymond E. Heap; Dcn. Thomas M. Kratochvil; Dcn. Gilbert R. Schmidt; Audrey Huck, DRE; CRP Stds.: 59

St. Angela Merici Roman Catholic Church, Metairie, Louisiana School - (Grades PreK-7) t) 504-835-8491 pbennett@stangelaschool.org www.stangelaschool.org Paige Bennett, Prin.; Stds.: 384; Lay Tchrs.: 26

St. Ann Roman Catholic Church and Shrine, Metairie, Louisiana - 3601 Transcontinental, Metairie, LA 70006-4040; Mailing: 4940 Meadowdale St., Metairie, LA 70006-4040 t) 505-455-7071 contact@stannchurchandshrine.org stannchurchandshrine.org Rev. William O'Riordan, Pst.; Rev. Michael Lamy, Par. Vicar; Dcn. Thomas H. Fox; Dcn. W. Gerard Gautrau; David Wilson, DRE;

St. Ann Roman Catholic Church and Shrine, Metairie, Louisiana School - (Grades PreK-7) 4921 Meadowdale St., Metairie, LA 70006-4098 t) 504-455-8383 stann@stannschool.org www.stannschool.org Lindsay Guidry, Prin.;

St. Benilde Roman Catholic Church, Metairie, Louisiana - 1901 Division St., Metairie, LA 70001-2798 t) 504-834-4980 stbenildechurch@cox.net www.stbenilde.org Rev. Matthew D. Johnston, Pst.; Dcn. Biaggio DiGiovanni; Dcn. Stephen J. Gordon; Dcn. Michael J. Sorensen; Dcn. Clifford S. Wright; Natalie Bostick, DRE;

St. Benilde Roman Catholic Church, Metairie, Louisiana School - 1801 Division St., Metairie, LA 70001-2799 t) 504-833-9894 stbenilde@stbenilde.com www.stbenilde.com Thomas Huck, Prin.;

St. Catherine of Siena - 105 Bonnabel Blvd., Metairie, LA 70005-3736 t) 504-835-9343 michelle@scschurch.com; info@scschurch.com www.scschurch.com Rev. Timothy D. Hedrick, Pst.; Rev. Andrew Gutierrez, Par. Vicar; Dcn. Michael Coney; Dcn. Paul G. Hauck; Dcn. Don M. Richard; Dcn. A. David Warriner Jr.;

St. Catherine of Siena School - 400 Codifer Blvd., Metairie, LA 70005-3797 t) 504-831-1166 www.scsgators.org Maria Mateu Ward, Prin.;

St. Christopher the Martyr - 309 Manson Ave., Metairie, LA 70001-4898 t) 504-837-8214 pastor@stchristopherano.com www.stchristopherano.com Rev. Raymond Igbogidi, Pst.; Dcn. Michael A. Cardella Jr.; Dcn. Philip C. McManamon; CRP Stds.: 22

St. Christopher the Martyr School - (Grades PreSchool-8) 3900 Derbigny St., Metairie, LA 70001-4999 t) 504-837-6871; 504-837-5929 arnochrist@archdiocese-no.org www.stchristopherschool.org

St. Clement of Rome Roman Catholic Church, Metairie, Louisiana - 4317 Richland Ave., Metairie, LA 70002-3097 t) 504-887-7821 stclement@scrparish.org Dcn. Rogelio Ibarra; Very Rev. Luis F. Rodriguez, Pst.; Rev. Andrew Rudmann, Par. Vicar; Dcn. Martin Gutierrez; Dcn. Carlo Maniglia; Dcn. Robert E. Pendzimaz;

St. Clement of Rome Roman Catholic Church, Metairie, Louisiana School - -7) 3978 W. Esplanade Ave., Metairie, LA 70002-3099 t) 504-888-0386 pspeeg@scrschool.org Kimberly Downes, Prin.;

St. Edward the Confessor Roman Catholic Church, Metairie, Louisiana - 4921 W. Metairie Ave., Metairie, LA 70001-4466 t) 504-888-0703 Rev. Joseph Man Tran, Pst.; Rev. Cletus Orji, Assoc. Pst.; Dcn. Steven J. Koehler; Dcn. Timothy G. Meaut; CRP Stds.: 20

St. Edward the Confessor School - (Grades PreK-7) t) 504-888-6353 Thomas Becker, Prin.; Stds.: 375; Sr. Tchrs.: 4; Lay Tchrs.: 28

Hanmaum Korean Catholic Chapel - 4812 W. Napoleon Ave., Metairie, LA 70001-2364 t) 504-888-8772

St. Francis Xavier - 444 Metairie Rd., Metairie, LA 70005-4307 t) 504-834-0340; 504-834-0348 (CRP) rgriffin@stfrancisxavier.com; ctodaro@stfrancisxavier.com church.stfrancisxavier.com Rev. Joseph S. Palermo Jr., Pst.; Dcn. Kevin J. Darrah; Dcn. Robert D. Normand;

St. Francis Xavier School - 215 Betz Pl., Metairie, LA 70005-4167 t) 504-833-1471 school.stfrancisxavier.com Jessica Dwyer, Prin.;

Hanmaum Korean Catholic Chapel - 4812 W. Napoleon Ave., Metairie, LA 70001-2364 t) 504-888-2366 Rev. Byoung-Ok Park (Korea), Chap.;

St. Louis King of France - 1609 Carrollton Ave., Metairie, LA 70005-1498 t) 504-834-9977 stlouisrectory@aol.com Rev. Mark S. Raphael, Pst.; Rev. Suvakin Arulandu, Par. Vicar; Dcn. J. Glen Casanova;

St. Louis King of France School - 1600 Lake Ave., Metairie, LA 70005-1499 t) 504-833-8224 info@slkfschool.com www.slkfschool.com Pamela Schott, Prin.;

St. Mary Magdalen - 6425 W. Metairie Ave., Metairie, LA 70003-4327 t) 504-733-0922; 504-733-0923 smmchurch@arch-no.org www.stmarymagdalenchurch.com Rev. Christian W. DeLerno Jr., Pst.; Dcn. James Heneghan; Dcn. James C. LeBlanc; Rev. Kenneth Smith, In Res.; Maria Steen, DRE; Debbie Curole, Bus. Mgr.;

Our Lady of Divine Providence Roman Catholic Church, Metairie, Louisiana - 1000 N. Starrett Rd., Metairie, LA 70003-5899 t) 504-466-4511 oldpparish@archdiocese-no.org www.oldp.org Assumed parish territory of St. Lawrence the Martyr, Metairie. Rev. Michael Mitchell, Pst.; Dcn. Roberto Angeli; Dcn. Daniel J. Cordes; Dcn. Roberto Garcia; Earl Gervais, DRE; Deborah Federer, Music Min.;

St. Philip Neri - 6500 Kawanee Ave., Metairie, LA 70003-3298 t) 504-887-5535; 504-887-5561 sgelpi@spnparish.net; frandrew@spnparish.net spnparish.net Rev. Andrew Rudmann, Pst.; Rev. Edward Owusu-Ansah, Par. Vicar; Ruby Kirsch, DRE; Dcn. Thomas P. Lotz; Staci Gelpi, Bus. Mgr.; CRP Stds.: 57

St. Philip Neri School - (Grades PreSchool-7) 6600 Kawanee Ave., Metairie, LA 70003-3199 t) 504-887-5600 rhill@stphilipneri.org www.stphilipneri.org Richard D. Hill Jr., Prin.; Stds.: 596; Lay Tchrs.: 49

St. Philip Neri Learning Center - 6500 Kawanee Avenue, Metairie, LA 70003 t) 504-887-2322 lrobinette@stphilipneri.org (6 weeks to 2 yrs.) Lori Robinette, Dir.;

NEW ORLEANS

Cathedral - Basilica of St. Louis King of France - 615 Pere Antoine Alley, New Orleans, LA 70116-3291 t) 504-525-9585 www.stlouiscathedral.org (A Minor Basilica). Most Rev. Gregory M. Aymond, Pst.; Very Rev. Philip G. Landry, Rector; Dcn. Richard Brady; Dcn. Ronald Guidry; Dcn. Eduardo Melendreras;

St. Mary's Roman Catholic Church, New Orleans, Louisiana - 1116 Chartres St., New Orleans, LA 70116 t) (504) 525-9585 x5341

All Saints - 1441 Teche St., New Orleans, LA 70114-5899 t) 504-361-8835; 504-361-9931 (Rectory) allsaint.church@att.net allsaintschurchnola.org Rev. Fred Kaddu, S.S.J., Admin.;

St. Alphonsus - 2030 Constance St., New Orleans, LA 70130-5099 t) 504-522-6748 stalphonsusoffice@stalphonsusno.com www.stalphonsusno.com Rev. Allen Weinert, C.Ss.R., Pst.; Rev. Dominic Bao Quoc Tran, C.Ss.R., Assoc. Pst.; Rev. Gilbert Enderle, C.Ss.R., Vice Postulator, Blessed Seelos; Rev. Richard Boever, C.Ss.R., Dir., Blessed Seelos Ctr.; Rev. Maurice J. Nutt, C.Ss.R., In Res.; Dcn. Thien Hoang, C.Ss.R.;

St. Alphonsus School - 2001 Constance St., New Orleans, LA 70130-5094 t) 504-523-6594 stalphonsus@archdiocese-no.org Sr. Monica Ellerbusch, R.S.M., Prin.;

St. Andrew the Apostle - 3101 Eton St., New Orleans, LA 70131-5399 t) 504-393-2334 info@standrewparish.net www.standrewparish.net Rev. John F. Talamo, Pst.; Dcn. Thomas S. Beyer; Dcn. Edward S. Rapier Jr.; Francis Harrison, DRE; CRP Stds.: 37

St. Andrew the Apostle School - 3131 Eton St., New Orleans, LA 70131 t) 504-394-4171 info@sasno.org Katherine Houin, Prin.; Elizabeth Konecni, Headmaster;

St. Anthony of Padua - 4640 Canal St., New Orleans, LA 70119-5808 t) 504-488-2651 church@sapparish.org www.sapparish.org Assumed parish territory of Sacred Heart of Jesus, New Orleans. Rev. Augustine DeArmond, O.P., Pst.; Rev. Victor Laroche, O.P., Prior; Bro. Herman D. Johnson, O.P., Subprior; Rev. Justin Kauchak, O.P., In Res.; Rev. David K. Seid, O.P., In Res.; Dcn. Joseph M. Dardis;

St. Augustine - 1210 Gov. Nicholls St., New Orleans, LA 70116-2324 t) 504-525-5934 staugustine@archdiocese-no.org staugchurch.org Rev. Emmanuel Mulenga, O.M.I., Pst.; Willie Glaze, DRE;

Blessed Francis Xavier Seelos - 3037 Dauphine St., New Orleans, LA 70117-6794 t) 504-943-5566 pastor@bfs.nocoxmail.com; gerarddeaf@arch-no.org Dcn. Jesse A. Watley; Very Rev. Jose I. Lavastida, Pst.; Arthine T. Vicks, DRE;

Blessed Sacrament-St. Joan of Arc - 8321 Burthe St., New Orleans, LA 70118-1195 t) 504-866-7330 bssjaparish@arch-no.org bssjaparish.com Rev. Charles Andrus, S.S.J., Pst.;

St. Joan of Arc School - 919 Cambronne St., New Orleans, LA 70118-1199 t) 504-861-2887 stjoanno@archdiocese-no.org Sean Goodwin, Prin.; David Delio, DRE;

Blessed Trinity - 4230 S. Broad St., New Orleans, LA 70125-3699; Mailing: 8321 Burthe St., New Orleans, LA 70118-1198 t) 504-822-3394 boss@josephite.com Dcn. Michael J. Taylor; Sadie White, DRE; Rev. Bartholomew Chukwuma, Pst.;

Corpus Christi-Epiphany - 2022 St. Bernard Ave., New Orleans, LA 70116-1388 t) 504-945-8931 corpuschristiepiphanychurch@ccecno.org www.ccecno.org Rev. Kingsley Ogbuji, S.S.J., Admin.; Very Rev. Henry J. Davis, S.S.J., Pst.; Dcn. Larry L. Calvin; CRP Stds.: 24

St. David - 5617 St. Claude Ave., New Orleans, LA 70117-2533 t) 504-947-2853 stdavid@arch-no.org stdavidnola.com Assumed territory of St. Maurice, New Orleans. Rev. Oswald Pierre-Jules Jr., S.S.J., Pst.;

St. Dominic - 775 Harrison Ave., New Orleans, LA 70124-3192 t) 504-482-4156; 504-486-9731 (CRP) www.stdominicparish.com Rev. Wayne C. Paysse, Pst.; Rev. Jeffrey Merritt, Par. Vicar; Dcn. Bryan E. McCauley; Dcn. Jody J. Fortunato; Dcn. John Pippenger; CRP Stds.: 53

St. Dominic School - (Grades PreSchool-7) 6326 Memphis St., New Orleans, LA 70124 t) 504-482-4123 Dr. Ashley Lynn Ogden, Prin.; Stds.: 750; Lay Tchrs.: 59

St. Francis of Assisi - 631 State St., New Orleans, LA 70118-5899; Mailing: 611 State St., New Orleans, LA 70118 t) 504-891-4479 sfa@stfrancisuptown.com www.stfrancisuptown.com Dcn. Timothy O. Kettenring; Very Rev. Michael J. Schneller, Pst.;

St. Gabriel the Archangel - 4700 Pineda St., New Orleans, LA 70126-3599 t) 504-282-0296 stgabriel@arch-no.org www.stgabe.net Rev. Rodney Anthony Ricard, Pst.; Dcn. Uriel Andrew Durr; Cheryllyn Branche-Baker, Diocesan CRE;

Good Shepherd Roman Catholic Church, New Orleans, Louisiana - 1025 Napoleon Ave., New Orleans, LA 70115-2898 t) 504-899-1378 ststephenpar@archdiocese-no.org goodshepherdparishnola.com Including St. Stephen, St. Henry and Our Lady of Good Council Churches Rev. Msgr. Christopher Nalty, Pst.; Dcn. Richard B. Eason; Rev. Douglas C. Brougher, In Res.; Phillip Bellini, DRE;

St. Stephen Catholic School - (Grades PreK-7) 1027 Napoleon Ave., New Orleans, LA 70115-2899 t) 504-891-1927 ststephen@archdiocese-no.org; rkendrick@sscschool.org Rosie Kendrick, Prin.;

Holy Name of Jesus - 6367 St. Charles Ave., New Orleans, LA 70118-6236; Mailing: 6220 La Salle Pl., New Orleans, LA 70118 t) 504-865-7430 holyname@hnjchurch.org www.hnjchurch.org Assumed parish territory of St. Thomas More, New Orleans. Rev. Mark Edward Thibodeaux, S.J., Pst.; Rev. Edwin L. Gros, S.J., Par. Vicar; Rev. Stephen C. Rowntree, S.J., Assoc. Pst.; Diane Blair, Parish Life Coord.; CRP Stds.: 65

Holy Name of Jesus School - 6325 Cromwell Pl., New Orleans, LA 70118-6299 t) 504-861-1466 hnjschool@hnjschool.org Kirsch Wilberg, Prin.; Stds.: 523; Lay Tchrs.: 60

Holy Name of Mary (Algiers) - 400 Verret St., New Orleans, LA 70114-1098; Mailing: 500 Eliza St., New Orleans, LA 70114-1098 t) 504-362-5511 hnmary@arch-no.org holynameofmarynola.org Rev. Eugene F. Jacques, Pst.; CRP Stds.: 6

Holy Spirit Roman Catholic Church, New Orleans, Louisiana - 6201 Stratford Pl., New Orleans, LA 70131-7397 t) 504-394-5492 holyspirit@archdiocese-no.org Rev. Patrick Collum, Pst.; Pam Kamphuis, Music Min.; Jane Mix, DRE;

Immaculate Conception - 130 Baronne St., New Orleans, LA 70112-2304 t) 504-529-1477 icjc@arch-no.org www.jesuitchurch.net Rev. Anthony F. McGinn, S.J., Pst.; Rev. Stephen Alphonsus Kramer, S.J., Par. Vicar;

St. James Major - 3736 Gentilly Blvd., New Orleans, LA 70122-6199 t) 504-304-6750 stjamesmajor@sjmc.nocoxmail.com; stjamesmajor@arch-no.org saintjamesmajor.org Rev. Michael M. Labre, Pst.; Dcn. Glenn J. Wiltz; Jancinta Hawkins, DRE; Evangeline Richard, DRE;

St. John the Baptist - 1139 Oretha Castle Haley Blvd., New Orleans, LA 70130-3757; Mailing: 724 Camp St., New Orleans, LA 70130-3757 t) 504-525-4413 stpatricksnola.rectory@gmail.com goldensteeple.com Church under care of pastor of St. Patrick, New Orleans. Dcn. Chris J. DiGrado; Rev. Garrett M. O'Brien, Pst.; Joseph Meisch, DRE;

St. Joseph Roman Catholic - 1802 Tulane Ave., New Orleans, LA 70112-2246 t) 504-522-3186 x141 stjoseph@bellsouth.net Rev. Thomas J. Stehlik, C.M., Pst.;

St. Joseph Roman Catholic Church, Algiers, Louisiana - 6450 Kathy Ct., New Orleans, LA 70131-7515; Mailing: 4410 Fields St., New Orleans, LA 70131 t) 504-347-4725 stjosephalgiers@archdiocese-no.org Rev. Joseph Thang Dinh Tran, Pst.;

St. Katharine Drexel - 2001 Louisiana Ave., New Orleans, LA 70115; Mailing: Office: 3325 Danneel St., New Orleans, LA 70115 t) 504-891-3172 stkatherine@arch-no.org Rev. Lambert Lien, S.V.D., Pst.; Grace Lemieux, DRE;

St. Maria Goretti - 7300 Crowder Blvd., New Orleans, LA 70127-1599 t) 504-242-7554 stmariagoretti@smgnola.com Assumed parish territory of Immaculate Heart of Mary & St. Simon Peter, New Orleans. Rev. Daniel H. Green, Pst.; Rev. Raphael Mbotela Kasele, F.M.H., Par. Vicar; Dcn. Terrel J. Broussard;

St. Maria Goretti School - t) 504-242-1313

St. Mary of the Angels - 3501 N. Miro St., New Orleans, LA 70117-5899 t) 504-945-3186 frjoe@smaneworleans.org smaneworleans.org Rev. Joseph Hund, O.F.M., Pst.; Friar Michael Martin Haney, O.F.M., Par. Vicar; Friar Daniel Barrett, OFM, Pst. Assoc.; Vanessa Matthews, DRE; Jeoffre Duplessis, Music Min.;

Mary, Queen of Vietnam Roman Catholic Church, New Orleans, Louisiana - 5069 Willowbrook Dr., New Orleans, LA 70129; Mailing: P.O. Box 870607, New Orleans, LA 70187 t) 504-254-5247 (CRP); 504-254-5660 maryqueenvn.org/ Assumed St. Nicholas of Myra & St. Brigid, New Orleans. Rev. Thien Nguyen, Par. Vicar; Rev. Nghiem Van Nguyen, Pst.; Dcn. Vinh V. Tran; CRP Stds.: 620

Vietnamese Martyrs - 14400 Peltier Dr., New Orleans East, LA 70129-1713

Vietnamese Martyrs Shrine of the Archdiocese of New Orleans -

St. Mary's Assumption - 2030 Constance St., New Orleans, LA 70130-5004 t) 504-522-6748 stalphonsusoffice@stalphonsusno.com Rev. Allen Weinert, C.Ss.R., Pst.; Rev. Dominic Bao Quoc Tran, C.Ss.R., Assoc. Pst.; Dcn. Thien Hoang, C.Ss.R.;

Mater Dolorosa - 8128 Plum St., New Orleans, LA 70118-2012 t) 504-866-3669 materdolorosa@arch-no.org; materdolorosa@archdiocese-no.org mdolorosa.com Assumed Incarnate Word, New Orleans & St. Theresa of the Child Jesus, also known as St. Theresa of the Little Flower. Rev. Francis Ferrie; Rev. Herbert J. Kiff Jr., Pst.; Maria Oppliger, DRE;

National Shrine of Our Lady of Prompt Succor - 2701 State St., New Orleans, LA 70118; Mailing: 2734 Nashville Ave., New Orleans, LA 70115 t) 504-866-0200 (Sacristy); 504-866-0216 (Bus. Office) shrineolps@gmail.com www.shrineolps.com Sr. Carolyn Marie Brockland, OSU, Dir.;

St. Nicholas of Myra Byzantine Catholic Mission - 2435 S. Carrollton Ave., New Orleans, LA 70118; Mailing: 4680 W. Main St., Houma, LA 70360-4916 t) 504-861-0806 c) (985) 232-6841 (May send Text Messages.) stnicholasnola@yahoo.com www.archpitt.org/place/neworleansla-2/ Ruthenian Rite Church Jurisdiction. Dcn. Gregory A. Haddad, Admin.; Rev. Nile C. Gross, Assoc. Pst.; Rev. John Mefrige, Assoc. Pst.;

Our Lady of Guadalupe/International Shrine of St. Jude - 411 N. Rampart St., New Orleans, LA 70112 t) 504-522-8546 (CRP); 504-525-1551 judeshrine@aol.com Rev. Anthony Rigoli, O.M.I., Pst.; Rev. Emmanuel Mulenga, O.M.I., Par. Vicar; Rev. Donald McMahon, O.M.I., In Res.;

St. Jude Community Center - 400 N. Rampart St., New Orleans, LA 70112-3594 t) 504-553-5790 Sr. Beth Mouch, M.S.C., Dir.;

Our Lady of Lavang Roman Catholic Church, New Orleans, Louisiana - 6054 Vermillion Blvd., New Orleans, LA 70122 t) (504) 283-0559 lavangoffice@gmail.com Rev. Francis Nguyen, S.D.D., Pst.;

Our Lady of the Rosary - 3368 Esplanade Ave., New Orleans, LA 70119-3132; Mailing: 1322 Moss St., New Orleans, LA 70119 t) 504-488-2659 www.olr-nola.org Very Rev. Jonathan P. Hemelt, Pst.; Rev. Colm Cahill, In Res.; Dcn. Ronald J. Drez Jr.; Dcn. James A. Bialas;

Our Lady Star of the Sea - 1835 St. Roch Ave., New Orleans, LA 70117-8199 t) 504-944-0166 olssno@arch-no.org Rev. Emanuel Tanu, S.V.D., Pst.;

St. Patrick - 724 Camp St., New Orleans, LA 70130-3757 t) 504-525-4413 oldstpatricks.org Assumed St. John the Baptist, New Orleans. Rev. Garrett M. O'Brien, Pst.; Dcn. Chris J. DiGrado; Dcn. Kenneth Ulrich Jr.;

St. Paul the Apostle - 6828 Chef Menteur Hwy., New Orleans, LA 70126-5297 t) 504-242-8820 charityjoy4725@att.net Rev. Charles Ndumbi, S.V.D., Pst.; Dcn. Duane E. Cruse Sr.; Jacqueline E. Mayo, DRE;

St. Peter Claver - 1923 St. Philip St., New Orleans, LA 70116-2199 t) 504-822-8059 pastor@spclaverchurch.org; ereed@spclaverchurch.org www.stpeterclaverneworleans.org Rev. Ajani K. Gibson, Admin.; Dcn. Lawrence C. Houston; Dcn. Allen Stevens; Alena Boucree, DRE; Marinda Lee-Houston,

Youth Min.;

St. Pius X - 6666 Spanish Fort Blvd., New Orleans, LA 70124-4324 t) 504-282-3332 spxparish@arch-no.org Very Rev. Patrick J. Williams, Pst.; Dcn. Christopher A. Bertucci; Dcn. Gary T. Levy;

St. Pius X School - 6600 Spanish Fort Blvd., New Orleans, LA 70124-4399 t) 504-282-2811 spxsch@archdiocese-no.org Deirdre D. Macnamara, Prin.;

St. Raymond-St. Leo the Great - 2916 Paris Ave., New Orleans, LA 70119 t) 504-945-8750 crivera@archdiocese-no.org Rev. Stanley Ihuoma, S.S.J., Pst.; Rev. Victor H. Cohea, In Res.; Dcn. Royal C. Shelton, Pst. Assoc.; Dcn. Troy Anthony Smith; Marlene Wilson, DRE;

St. Leo the Great School - 1501 Abundance St., New Orleans, LA 70119-2098 t) 504-943-1482 cmire@archdiocese-no.org Carmel Mire, Prin.;

Resurrection of Our Lord Roman Catholic Church, New Orleans, Louisiana (St. Nicholas of Myra Mission) - 9701 Hammond St., New Orleans, LA 70127-3519 t) 504-242-8669 resurrectionchurch@archdiocese-no.org www.resurrectionofourlord.org Rev. Geoffrey Omondi Muga, F.M.H., Pst.;

Resurrection of Our Lord School - 4861 Rosalia Dr., New Orleans, LA 70127-3598 t) 504-243-2257 resurrection@archdiocese-no.org Vickie Helmstetter, Prin.;

St. Nicholas of Myra - 21420 Chef Menteur Hwy., New Orleans, LA 70129 t) 504-848-8669

St. Rita Catholic Church - 2729 Lowerline St., New Orleans, LA 70125-3599 t) 504-866-3621 stritachurchno@archdiocese-no.org Rev. Patrick Carr, Pst.; Rev. Paul Van Tung Nguyen, In Res.;

St. Theresa of Avila - 1404 Erato St., New Orleans, LA 70130-4387 t) 504-525-4226 www.sttheresanola.org Special care to the Hispanic Community. Rev. Lance Campo, Admin.;

Transfiguration of the Lord - 2212 Prentiss Ave., New Orleans, LA 70122 t) 504-302-7931 transfiguration@arch-no.org transfigurationnola.org Rev. Msgr. Kenneth J. Hedrick, Admin.; Dcn. Lloyd E. Huck; Dcn. Peter C. Rizzo; Dcn. Kerry J. Winder Jr.;

NORCO

Sacred Heart of Jesus - 401 Spruce St., Norco, LA 70079-2137 t) 985-764-6503 c.s.larosa@gmail.com; shn@archdiocese-no.org Rev. Edmund Akordor, Pst.; Cristina Larosa, DRE;

PARADIS

St. John the Baptist - 15405 Hwy. 90, Paradis, LA 70080-1498; Mailing: P.O. Box 1498, Paradis, LA 70080 t) 985-758-1593 (CRP); 985-758-2668 stjohnch@nocoxmail.com; stjohnch@arch-no.org www.stjohnparadis.org Rev. Joseph Duc Dzien, Pst.; Danielle Babin, CRE;

PEARL RIVER

SS. Peter and Paul Roman Catholic Church, Pearl River, Louisiana - 66192 St. Mary Dr., Pearl River, LA 70452-5705 t) 985-863-7935 info@sppcprla.com www.sppcprla.com Rev. Kevin T. DeLerno, Pst.; CRP Stds.: 70

POINTE-A-LA-HACHE

St. Thomas - 17605 Hwy. 15, Pointe-A-La-Hache, LA 70082; Mailing: 6951 Hwy. 39, Braithwaite, LA 70040 t) 504-682-5607; 504-278-4008 myparishstthomas.org Rev. Sampson Abdulai, Pst.;

Assumption of the Blessed Virgin Mary Roman Catholic Church, Braithwaite, Louisiana - 6951 Hwy 39, Braithwaite, LA 70040

PORT SULPHUR

St. Patrick - 28698 Hwy. 23, Port Sulphur, LA 70083-9623 t) 504-564-6792 stpatrickps@aol.com; stpatrickchurch@arch-no.org www.stpatrickportsulphur.com Assumed St. Jude, Diamond and Our Lady of Good Harbor, Buras and its missions, St. Ann, Empire and St. Anthony, Boothville-Venice. Rev. Gerard P. Stapleton, Pst.;

St. Ann -

RESERVE

Our Lady of Grace Roman Catholic Church - 780 Hwy. 44, Reserve, LA 70084; Mailing: P.O. Box 464, Reserve, LA 70084-0464 t) 985-536-2613 olgchurch@arch-no.org olgcommunity.com Rev. Godwin Ani, S.S.J., Pst.; Myrtle Ann Lucas, DRE;

St. Peter - 1550 Hwy. 44, Reserve, LA 70084; Mailing: P.O. Box 435, Reserve, LA 70084-0435 t) 985-536-2886 (CRP); 985-536-2887 petesec@rtconline.com Dcn. Richard S. Abbondante; Rev. John J. Marse, Pst.;

St. Peter School - t) 985-536-4296 Marie Comeaux, Prin.;

RIVER RIDGE

St. Matthew the Apostle - 10021 Jefferson Hwy., River Ridge, LA 70123-2498 t) 504-737-4537; 504-737-2662 stmatthewchurch@arch-no.org stmatthewtheapostle.net Rev. Leon Poche Jr., Pst.; Rev. Truong Pham, Par. Vicar; Dcn. Jerry B. Clark Sr.; Dcn. Wayne A. Lobell; Dcn. Nathan F. Simoneaux Jr.;

St. Matthew the Apostle School - t) 504-737-4604 www.smaschool.net Tony Bonura, Prin.;

SLIDELL

St. Genevieve Roman Catholic Church, Slidell, Louisiana - 58203 Hwy. 433, Slidell, LA 70460; Mailing: 58025 St. Genevieve Ln., Slidell, LA 70460 t) 985-643-3832; 985-285-1341 (CRP) stgenevieve@stgenevieve.us www.stgenevieve.us Very Rev. Gerald L. Seiler Jr., Pst.; Dcn. Daniel B. Haggerty; Dcn. Reginald J. Seymour; Ona New, DRE;

St. Luke the Evangelist Roman Catholic Church, Slidell, Louisiana - 910 Cross Gates Blvd., Slidell, LA 70461-8414 t) 985-641-2570 (CRP); 985-641-6429 office@stlukeslidell.org Rev. Jared Rodrigue, Pst.; Rev. Warren L. Cooper, Sacramental Asst.; Dcn. Harold J. Burke; Dcn. William Faustermann Jr.; Dcn. Ronald C. LeBlanc; Dcn. Mark A. Pennington;

St. Margaret Mary Roman Catholic Church, Slidell, Louisiana - 1050B Robert Blvd., Slidell, LA 70458-2098 t) 985-649-3055 (CRP); 985-643-6124 stmargaretmary@saintmm.org saintmmchurch.org Rev. Daniel Darmanin, Par. Vicar; Dcn. Louis F. Bauer; Dcn. Gilbert F. Ganucheau Jr.; Dcn. Christopher M. Schneider Sr.; Dcn. Roberto L. Zambrano;

St. Margaret Mary School - t) 985-643-4612 saintmm.org Christopher Collins, Prin.;

Our Lady of Lourdes - 400 Westchester Blvd., Slidell, LA 70458; Mailing: 3924 Berkley St., Slidell, LA 70458-5143 t) 985-643-4137 jstains@ollourdes.org; mguidry@ollourdes.org ollparishslidell.com Rev. Christopher P. Zavackis, Pst.; Dcn. Warren L. Berault; Dcn. Charles B. Faler Jr.; Dcn. Peter J. Miranda; Dcn. Michael Whitehouse; Janet Stains, DRE; CRP Stds.: 47

Our Lady of Lourdes School - 345 Westchester Pl., Slidell, LA 70458-5299 t) 985-643-3230 info@ollourdes.org Roy H. Delaney Sr., Prin.; Stds.: 420; Lay Tchrs.: 49

ST. BERNARD

St. Bernard - 2805 Bayou Rd., St. Bernard, LA 70085 t) 504-281-2267 stbernard@arch-no.org www.stbernard-stbla.com Assumed parish territory of San Pedro Pescador, Florissant. Rev. Hoang Minh Tuong, Pst.; Dcn. Norbert P. Billiot Jr.; Sr. Anne Marie Khuong, F.M.S.R., DRE;

TERRYTOWN

Christ the King - 535 Deerfield Rd., Terrytown, LA 70056-2899 t) 504-361-1500 ckchurch@bellsouth.net www.christkingterrytown.com Rev. Michael Nam Hoang Nguyen, Pst.; Rev. Stephen Leake, S.D.B., Hispanic Min.; Dcn. Walfredo Corral; Dcn. William B. Jarrell; Dcn. John Walker IV; CRP Stds.: 61

VIOLET

Our Lady of Lourdes Roman Catholic Church, Violet, Louisiana - 2621 Colonial Blvd., Violet, LA 70092 t) 504-682-7070 oll@arch-no.org www.olol-church.com Rev. Kenneth Smith, Pst.; Dcn. Craig P. Taffaro Jr.; Debbie Taffaro, DRE;

WAGGAMAN

Our Lady of the Angels Roman Catholic Church, Waggaman, Louisiana - 6851 River Rd., Waggaman, LA 70094-2404 t) 504-436-4459 office@oloa.nocoxmail.com www.oloacatholicchurch.org Rev. John M. Perino, Pst.; Dcn. Ozema J. Prestenbach; CRP Stds.: 18

WESTWEGO

Our Lady of Prompt Succor Church - 146 Fourth St., Westwego, LA 70094-4297 t) 504-341-9522 smsyrri@aol.com; mclements@arch-no.org www.olpsw.org Rev. Emile G. (Buddy) Noel, Pst.; Dcn. Quinsiniano Ortega; Greg Smith, DRE;

Our Lady of Prompt Succor School - 531 Ave. A, Westwego, LA 70094-4294 t) 504-341-9505 olpswestwego@archdiocese-no.org Sr. Anna Bui, Prin.;

Holy Guardian Angels Mission - 1701 Bridge City Ave., Bridge City, LA 70094 www.hgaparish.org

SCHOOLS: PRESCHOOL THRU HIGH SCHOOL

SCHOOLS

STATE OF LOUISIANA

METAIRIE

St. Therese Catholic Academy - (DIO) (Grades PreSchool-12) 6421 W. Metairie Ave., Metairie, LA 70003-5898 t) 504-513-4400 sbland@sttheresenola.org sttheresenola Shannon Bland, Admin.; Stds.: 210; Lay Tchrs.: 40

NEW ORLEANS

Academy of the Sacred Heart - (PRV) (Grades PreSchool-12) 4521 St. Charles Ave., New Orleans, LA 70115-4831 t) 504-891-1943 communications@ashrosary.org www.ashrosary.org Micheline Dutil, Head of School;

St. Benedict the Moor School - (PRV) (Grades PreK-4) 5010 Piety Dr., New Orleans, LA 70126 t) 504-288-2745 stbenmoor@archdiocese-no.org sbmschool.org Vanessa Johnson Chavis, Prin.;

Christian Brothers School, Canal Street Campus - (PRV) (Grades PreK-7) 4600 Canal St., New Orleans, LA 70119-5893 t) 504-488-4426 school@cbs-no.org www.cbs-no.org Richard Neider, Prin.; Michael Prat, Prin.; Joey M. Scaffidi, Pres.; Stds.: 810; Lay Tchrs.: 67

Christian Brothers School - (Grades PreK-7) #8 Friedrichs Ave., City Park, New Orleans, LA 70119-5893 t) 504-486-6770

Good Shepherd Nativity School - (PAR) 1839 Agriculture St., New Orleans, LA 70119 t) 504-598-9399 tmoran@thegoodshepherdschool.org www.thegoodshepherdschool.org Don Boucree, Dean; Kelli Ramon, Prin.; Thomas G. Moran, Pres.; Luellen Howard, Librn.;

Holy Cross School - (PRV) (Grades PreK-4) 5601 Elysian Fields Ave., New Orleans, LA 70122 t) 504-942-1850 contacthc@holycrosstigers.com www.holycrosstigers.com (Primary Campus) Rev. Joseph M. Moyer, C.S.C., Chap.; Eric DesOrmeaux, Prin.;

St. Mary's Academy - (PRV) (Grades PreK-12) 6905 Chef Menteur Blvd., New Orleans, LA 70126 t) 504-245-0200 smaoffice@archdiocese-no.org www.smaneworleans.com Founded in 1867. Pamela Rogers, Pres.; Aisha Jones, Vice Prin.; Stds.: 465; Sr. Tchrs.: 4; Lay Tchrs.: 60

St. Michael Special School - 1522 Chippewa St., New Orleans, LA 70130 t) 504-524-7285 stmichspecial@archdiocese-no.org www.stmichaelspecialschool.com Cissy LaForge, Head of School; Laurel Alonzo, Assoc. Head of School;

Stuart Hall School for Boys - (PRV) 2032 S. Carrollton Ave., New Orleans, LA 70118 t) 504-861-1954 bhagan@stuarthall.org www.stuarthall.org Dr. Tim Burns, Interim Head of School; Kellie Maurin, Assoc.

Head of School; Nancy Dunphy, Librn.;
Ursuline Academy of New Orleans - (PRV) (Grades PreSchool-12) 2635 State St., New Orleans, LA 70118-6399 t) 504-861-9150 admissions@uanola.org; info@uanola.org go.uanola.org Sue Heidel, Prin.; Dr. Karen G. Jakuback, Pres.; Stds.: 538

HIGH SCHOOLS

STATE OF LOUISIANA

COVINGTON

Archbishop Hannan High School - (DIO) 71324 Hwy. 1077, Covington, LA 70433 t) 985-249-6363 communications@hannanhigh.org www.hannanhigh.org Chad Barwick, Head of School; Nancy Baird, Assoc. Head of School; Joe Hines, Admin.; Denis Schexnaydre, Admin.; Steven Shepherd, Admin.;
The St. Paul's School - (PRV) (Grades 8-12) 917 S. Jahncke Ave., Covington, LA 70433; Mailing: P.O. Box 928, Covington, LA 70434-0928 t) 985-892-3200 stpauls@stpauls.com www.stpauls.com Day school for young men. Trevor Watkins, Prin.; Bro. Raymond Bulliard, F.S.C., Pres.;
St. Scholastica Academy - (DIO) 122 S. Massachusetts St., Covington, LA 70433 t) 985-892-2540 sgillio@ssacad.org www.ssacad.org Sheri H Gillio, Prin.;

LA PLACE

St. Charles Catholic High School - (DIO) (Grades 8-12) 100 Dominican Dr., La Place, LA 70068-3499 t) 985-652-3809 creppel.christine@stcharlescatholic.org; hotard.rachel@stcharlescatholic.org www.stcharlescatholic.org Dr. Courtney Millet, Prin.; Christine Creppel, Admin.; Stds.: 412; Lay Tchrs.: 38

MARRERO

Academy of Our Lady - (DIO) (Grades 8-12) 5501 Westbank Exprwy., Marrero, LA 70072-2934 t) 504-341-6217 ourlady@theacademyofourlady.org www.theacademyofourlady.org Sr. Michelle Geiger, F.M.A., Prin.; Donna Blanchard, Vice Prin.; Amy Danos, Vice Prin.; Michelle Maher, Librn.; Stds.: 481; Sr. Tchrs.: 4; Lay Tchrs.: 34
Archbishop Shaw High School (Salesians of St. John Bosco) - (DIO) (Grades 8-12) 1000 Salesian Ln., Marrero, LA 70072 t) 504-340-6727 shawdir@arch-no.org www.archbishopshaw.org Rev. Stephen C. Ryan, S.D.B., Head of School; Nicholas Marchese, Assoc. Head of School; Rev. John Langan, S.D.B., Campus Min.; Rev. Wilgintz Polynice, S.D.B., In Res.; Bro. Thomas Junis, SDB, In Res.; Warren Gabriel, Librn.;

METAIRIE

Archbishop Chapelle High School - (DIO) 8800 Veterans Memorial Blvd., Metairie, LA 70003-5235 t) 504-467-3105 info@archbishopchapelle.org www.archbishopchapelle.org Connie Dantagnan, Prin.; Susan Panzavecchia, Vice Prin.;
Archbishop Rummel High School - (DIO) 1901 Severn Ave., Metairie, LA 70001 t) 504-834-5592 info@rummelraiders.com www.rummelraiders.com Marc Milano, Prin.; Douglas Neill, Vice Prin.;
Archbishop Rummel Alumni Association - Douglas Tillman, Pres.;
St. Therese Academy - 917 N. Atlanta St., Metairie, LA 70003-5898 t) 504-513-4400 office@sttheresenola.org sttheresenola.org Shannon Bland, Head of School;

NEW ORLEANS

Academy of the Sacred Heart "The Rosary" - (PRV) 4521 St. Charles Ave., New Orleans, LA 70115-9990 t) 504-891-1943 ash@ashrosary.org www.ashrosary.org Micheline Dutil, Head of School; Julie Boyd, Head of Upper School; Josephine Schloegel, Librn.;
St. Augustine High School - (PRV) (Grades 6-12) 2600 A.P. Tureaud Ave., New Orleans, LA 70119-1299 t) 504-944-2424 staug@purpleknights.com www.staugnola.org Gerald DeBose, Prin.; Aulston Taylor, Pres.; Rev. Roderick Coates, S.S.J., Chief Religious Officer;
Brother Martin High School - (PRV) (Grades 8-12) 4401 Elysian Fields Ave., New Orleans, LA 70122-3898 t) 504-283-1561 gmrando@cox.net; lgreco@brothermartin.com brothermartin.com Amanda Gason, Librn.; Ryan Gallagher, Prin.; Gregory Rando, Pres.; Stds.: 1,083; Lay Tchrs.: 82
Cabrini High School - (PRV) (Grades 8-12) 1400 Moss St., New Orleans, LA 70119 t) 504-482-1193 jtruxillo@cabrinihigh.com www.cabrinihigh.com Sheri Salvagio, President & CEO; Cristen Watters, Dean; Yvonne L. Hrapmann, Prin.; Vivian Coutin, Vice Prin.;
Cabrini High School, Inc. - (Grades 8-12) cabrinihigh.com Sandra Granier, Librn.;
De La Salle High School - (PRV) (Grades 8-12) 5300 St. Charles Ave., New Orleans, LA 70115-4999 t) 504-895-5717 pkelly@delasallenola.com www.delasallenola.com (Coed) Perry Rogers, Prin.; Paul Kelly, Pres.;
Holy Cross School - (PRV) (Grades 5-12) 5500 Paris Ave., New Orleans, LA 70122-2659 t) 504-942-3100 contacthc@holycrosstigers.com www.holycrosstigers.com William J. Gallagher, Headmaster; Rev. Joseph M. Moyer, C.S.C., Chap.; Eric DesOrmeaux, Prin.;
Jesuit High School - (PRV) 4133 Banks St., New Orleans, LA 70119-6883 t) 504-486-6631 principal@jesuitnola.org www.jesuitnola.org (Boys) Rev. Kevin B. Dyer, S.J., Chap.; Peter S. Kernion, Prin.; Rev. John Brown, S.J., Pres.;
St. Mary's Academy of the Holy Family - (PRV) (Grades PreK-12) 6905 Chef Menteur Blvd., New Orleans, LA 70126-5215 t) (504) 245-0200 smaoffice@archdiocese-no.org www.smaneworleans.com Pamela Rogers, Pres.; Aisha Jones, Vice Prin.; Stds.: 495; Sr. Tchrs.: 4; Lay Tchrs.: 60
St. Mary's Dominican High School - (PRV) 7701 Walmsley Ave., New Orleans, LA 70125-3494 t) 504-865-9401 cthomas@stmdhs.org www.stmarysdominican.org Carolyn Favre, Prin.; Cynthia A. Thomas, Pres.; Kathleen Fasold, Librn.; Stds.: 835; Sr. Tchrs.: 1; Lay Tchrs.: 73
Mount Carmel Academy - (PRV) (Grades 8-12) 7027 Milne Blvd., New Orleans, LA 70124-2395 t) 504-288-7626 mca@mcacubs.org; admissions@mcacubs.org www.mcacubs.com Beth Ann Simno, Prin.; Sr. Camille Anne Campbell, O.Carm., Pres.; Stds.: 1,200; Lay Tchrs.: 142
Ursuline Academy - (PRV) (Grades PreSchool-12) 2635 State St., New Orleans, LA 70118-6399 t) 504-861-9150 admissions@uanola.org; info@uanola.org go.uanola.org Sue Heidel, Prin.; Dr. Karen G. Jakuback, Pres.; Stds.: 535

SLIDELL

Pope John Paul II Catholic High School - (DIO) (Grades 8-12) 1901 Jaguar Dr., Slidell, LA 70461-9098 t) 985-649-0914 info@pjp.org www.pjp.org Ryan Cosse, Campus Min.; Kimberly Kilroy, Prin.;

INSTITUTIONS LOCATED IN DIOCESE

CEMETERIES [CEM]

NEW ORLEANS

St. Tammany Catholic Cemetery - 7887 Walmsley Ave., New Orleans, LA 70125 t) 504-861-6200 Dirk Wild, CFO;

COLLEGES & UNIVERSITIES [COL]

NEW ORLEANS

Loyola University New Orleans - 6363 St. Charles Ave., New Orleans, LA 70118-6195 t) (504) 865-3240 (Admissions Office); (504) 865-3847 (President's Office) pres@loyno.edu www.loyno.edu Rev. Justin Daffron, S.J., Pres.; Dr. Tanuja Singh, Vice. Pres.; Carol Markowitz, COO; Rev. Gregory S. Waldrop, S.J., Rector; Rev. Gregg Grovenburg, S.J., Campus Min.; Rev. W. Penn Dawson III, S.J., Prof.; Rev. Lawrence Moore, S.J., Prof.; Rev. Mark S. Mossa, S.J., Prof.; Rev. Nathan O'Halloran, S.J., Prof.; Rev. Edward Vacek, S.J., Prof.; Joshua Hinchie, S.J., Prof.; Jordan Jones, S.J., Prof.; Stds.: 4,436; Lay Tchrs.: 268; Pr. Tchrs.: 7; Sr. Tchrs.: 1; Scholastics: 2
University of Holy Cross (Our Lady of Holy Cross College) - 4123 Woodland Dr., New Orleans, LA 70131-7399 t) 504-394-7744 communications@uhcno.edu; jpierce@uhcno.edu uhcno.edu Angie Ruiz, Campus Min.; Stanton F. McNeely III, Pres.; Ken Tedesco, Exec.; Diana Schaubhut, Librn.;
Xavier University of Louisiana - One Drexel Dr., New Orleans, LA 70125-1098 t) 504-520-7411 apply@xula.edu www.xula.edu (Coed) C. Reynold Verret, Pres.; Lisa Lewis McClain, Dir.;

CONVENTS, MONASTERIES, AND RESIDENCES FOR WOMEN [CON]

ABITA SPRINGS

Sisters of Benedict of Colorado, Inc. - 102 Maria Ave., Abita Springs, LA 70420 t) 303-916-1991 sean.conrad.osb@gmail.com Sr. Shawn Conrad, O.S.B., Pres.; Srs.: 2

COVINGTON

Carmelite Nuns, Discalced, O.C.D., Monastery of St. Joseph and St. Teresa - 73530 River Rd., Covington, LA 70435-2206 t) 985-898-0923 covingtoncarmel@yahoo.com www.covingtoncarmel.org Sr. Edith Turpin, Prioress; Srs.: 9
Congregation of the Marianites of Holy Cross - 75520 Hwy.1081, Covington, LA 70435-6349; Mailing: 21388 Smith Rd., Covington, LA 70435-6349 t) 985-893-5201 c) 985-373-9180 jimcpa@marianites.org www.marianites.org Jim E. Durbin Jr., CEO; Sr. Ann Lacour, M.S.C., Rel. Ord. Ldr.; Srs.: 74
Daughters of Divine Providence, F.D.P. - 74684 Airport Rd., Covington, LA 70435-5621 t) 985-809-8854 daughtersofdivineprovidence@gmail.com daughtersofdivineprovidenceusa.org Sr. Barbara Dichiara, Treas.; Srs.: 3
Teresian Sisters (Society of St. Teresa of Jesus), S.T.J. - Provincial Office,18080 St. Joseph's Way, Covington, LA 70435-5623 t) 985-893-1470 cecilia.castillo@stjteresianas.org; clarice.suchy@stjteresianas.org www.teresiansisters.org Sr. Clarice Suchy, S.T.J., Councilor Del. in the U.S.; Sr. Gina Geraci, S.T.J., Local Coord.; Srs.: 22

HARVEY

Salesian Sisters (Daughters of Mary Help of Christians) F.M.A. - 608 1st Ave., Harvey, LA 70058-5980 t) 504-325-5980 secharveyic19@gmail.com www.salesiansisters.org Srs.: 4

LACOMBE

Congregation of Our Lady of Mount Carmel, O.Carm. - 62284 Fish Hatchery Rd., Lacombe, LA 70445-0476; Mailing: P.O. Box 476, Lacombe, LA 70445-0476 t) 985-882-7577; 504-524-2398 admin@sistersofmountcarmel.org; finance@sistersofmountcarmel.org www.sistersofmountcarmel.org/ Sr. Lawrence Habetz, O.Carm., Pres.; Sr. Maria Sheila Undang, O.Carm., Vice. Pres.; Srs.: 64
Carmelite Ministries, Inc./Cub Corner Preschool - 420 Allen Toussaint Blvd, New Orleans, LA 70124 t) 504-286-8673 Sr. Gwen Grillot, O.Carm., Exec.;
Carmelite NGO - 1725 General Taylor St., New Orleans, LA 70115 t) 504-458-3029 jfremson@gmail.com carmelitengo.org
Mount Carmel Development Office - development@sistersofmountcarmel.org

METAIRIE

Daughters of St. Paul Convent, F.S.P. - Pauline Book & Media Center, 4403 Veterans Memorial Blvd., Metairie, LA 70006-5321 t) 504-887-7631 metairie@paulinemedia.com Sr. Mary Martha Moss,

F.S.P., Supr.; Srs.: 4
Sisters of the Living Word, S.L.W. - 4901 W. Metairie Ave., Metairie, LA 70001 t) 504-455-5905 srstump@steddy.org www.slw.org Sr. Julia Stump, Contact; Srs.: 2
NEW ORLEANS
Congregation of St. Joseph, C.S.J. - 4030 Delgado Dr., New Orleans, LA 70119-3807; Mailing: 3020 Nashville Ave., New Orleans, LA 70125 pwarbritton@csjoseph.org www.csjoseph.org Sr. Barbara Hughes, Contact; Srs.: 2
Congregation of St. Joseph Ministry Against the Death Penalty - 3009 Grand Rte. St. John, #6, New Orleans, LA 70119 t) 504-948-6557 hprejean@sisterhelen.org www.sisterhelen.org Elizabeth Ryan, Dir.;
Congregation of the Sisters of the Holy Faith, C.H.F. - 1063 Moss St., New Orleans, LA 70119 t) 504-905-6295 www.holyfaithsisters.net
Daughters of Charity of St. Vincent de Paul, D.C. - 7817 S. Claiborne Ave., New Orleans, LA 70125; Mailing: 2820 Burdette St., Apt. 314, New Orleans, LA 70125 Sr. Suzanne Anglim, D.C., Contact; Srs.: 9
Daughters of Our Lady of the Holy Rosary - 1492 Moss St., New Orleans, LA 70119-2904 t) 504-486-0039 fmsrusa@gmail.com www.dongmancoi.org Sr. Thu Mai Thi Nguyen, F.M.S.R., Prov.; Srs.: 65
Dominican Sisters (Cabra, Ireland) O.P. - 916 St. Andrew St., New Orleans, LA 70130; Mailing: 718 Josephine St., New Orleans, LA 70130 t) 504-522-5974 tlenehanop@gmail.com www.dominicansisters.com Srs.: 1
Dominican Sisters of Peace - 5660 Bancroft Dr., New Orleans, LA 70122 t) 504-283-1122 srkatop@aol.com Sr. Kathy Broussard, Coord.; Srs.: 12
Franciscan Poor Clares - 720 Henry Clay Ave., New Orleans, LA 70118-5891 t) 504-895-2019 sisterct2@gmail.com www.poorclarenuns.com Sr. Charlene Theresa Toups, Abbess; Srs.: 6
Presentation Sisters of the Blessed Virgin Mary (Union of Sisters of the Presentation of the Blessed Virgin Mary (United States Prov.)) - 1706 S. Saratoga St., New Orleans, LA 70113 t) 504-715-9798 marylou@dubuquepresentations.org www.dubuquepresentations.org Srs.: 2
Society of the Sacred Heart - 1719 Napoleon Ave., New Orleans, LA 70115-4809; Mailing: 4525 Baronne St., New Orleans, LA 70115 t) 337-945-6264 bkearney@rscj.org www.rscj.org Sr. Bonnie K., Dir.; Srs.: 7
Carondelet Community - 4600 Carondelet St., New Orleans, LA 70115 t) 504-891-0412; 504-382-0782 llieux@rscj.org
Shannon House - 1500 State St., New Orleans, LA 70118 t) 504-510-4543 mguste@rscj.org; gparizek@rscj.org
Sophie Barat House - t) 504-899-6027 jmckinlay@rscj.org; mchicoine@rscj.org Sr. Jane McKinlay, R.S.C.J., Dir.;
Servants of Mary, Ministers to the Sick - 5001 Perlita St., New Orleans, LA 70122-1999 t) 504-282-5549 ssm2@cox.net sisterservantsofmary.com Sr. Angelica Ramos, S.deM., Supr.; Srs.: 8
Sisters of Mercy of the Americas, South Central Community, Inc. - 6024 Freret St., New Orleans, LA 70118 t) 504-343-9474 tbednarz@oppeace.org www.mercysc.org Srs.: 9
Sisters of the Blessed Sacrament, S.B.S. - 4921 Dixon St., New Orleans, LA 70125 t) 225-751-7161
Raphael Convent -
Trinity House -
Umoja -
Sisters of the Holy Family Motherhouse, S.S.F. - 6901 Chef Menteur Hwy., New Orleans, LA 70126-5215; Mailing: 6901 Chef Menteur Hwy, New Orleans, LA 70126-5215 t) 504-241-3088 x102 aliciacosta14@gmail.com www.sistersoftheholyfamily.com Founded in 1842 by Venerable Henriette Delille Sr. Alicia Christina Costa, S.S.F., Rel. Ord. Ldr.; Srs.: 65
Ursuline Sisters of the Roman Union, O.S.U. - 2734 Nashville Ave., New Orleans, LA 70115 t) 504-891-3665; 504-861-4686 annb@osucentral.org Sr. Ann Barrett, O.S.U., Prioress; Srs.: 5

ENDOWMENTS / FOUNDATIONS / TRUSTS [EFT]

METAIRIE
Catholic Community Foundation Archdiocese of New Orleans, Inc. - 3330 N. Causeway Blvd., Ste. 361, Metairie, LA 70005; Mailing: 7887 Walmsley Ave., New Orleans, LA 70125 t) 504-596-3045 info@ccfnola.org ccfnola.org Cory J. Howat, Exec. Dir.;
International Dominican Foundation, U.S.A. - One Galleria Blvd., Ste. 710-B, Metairie, LA 70001 t) 504-836-8180 info@intldom.org www.internationaldominicanfoundation.org Rev. Allen B. Moran, O.P., Pres.;
MONTZ
***Lyke Foundation** - 102 Ann Ct., Montz, LA 70068-8980 t) 985-287-0161 www.lykefoundation.org Andrew Lyke, Secy.; Most Rev. Fernand Cheri, O.F.M., Treas.; Kathleen Kennedy, Pres.; Richard Cheri, Exec.;
NEW ORLEANS
Archbishop Francis B. Schulte Testamentary Trust - 7887 Walmsley Ave., New Orleans, LA 70125
Christian Brothers Foundation - 8 Friederichs Ave., New Orleans, LA 70124-4602 t) 504-488-2802 foundation@cbs-no.org Carol Couvillion, Opers. Exec.;
Jesuit Seminary and Mission Fund - 909 Poydras, Suite 2500, New Orleans, LA 70112 t) 314-361-7765 ucsprov@jesuits.org www.jesuitscentralsouthern.org Rev. J. Daniel Daly, Treas.;
MCA Foundation - 7027 Milne Blvd., New Orleans, LA 70124 t) 504-288-7626 x137 mca@mcacubs.org www.mcacubs.com Sr. Camille Anne Campbell, O.Carm., Pres.;
Pierre Toussaint Foundation of New Orleans, Inc. - 2600 A.P. Tureaud Ave., New Orleans, LA 70119-1299 t) 504-944-2424 Aulston Taylor, Pres.;
Stella Roman Foundation, Inc. - 201 St. Charles Ave., Ste. 3920, New Orleans, LA 70170 t) 504-522-4756 rbordelon@denechaudlaw.com Most Rev. Gregory M. Aymond;
***WLAE-TV, Educational Broadcasting Foundation, Inc.** - 3900 Howard Ave., New Orleans, LA 70125; Mailing: P.O. Box 792497, New Orleans, LA 70179-2497 t) 504-830-3700 info@wlae.com www.wlae.com Ron Yager, Pres.;

HOSPITALS / HEALTH SERVICES [HOS]

BOGALUSA
Our Lady of the Angels Hospital, Inc. - 433 Plaza St., Bogalusa, LA 70427 t) 985-730-6706 c.bryanmiller@fmolhs.org www.oloah.org Dr. C. Bryan Miller, Pres.; Bed Capacity: 92; Asstd. Annu.: 141,827; Staff: 398

MISCELLANEOUS [MIS]

ABITA SPRINGS
The Christ in Christmas Committee of New Orleans - 123 Iroquois Dr., Abita Springs, LA 70420 c) 504-615-1303 kcicno@bellsouth.net keepchristinchristmasnola.org Stephen F. Hart, Chair;
COVINGTON
Caritas - 601 Holy Trinity Dr., Covington, LA 70433 t) 985-892-4345 caritas11r@aol.com Barbara Bahlinger, Contact;
Magnolia Lafayette, Inc. - 104 W. 11th Ave., Covington, LA 70433 t) 985-892-2004 ngonzalez@dlsi.org Bro. Nick Gonzalez, F.S.C., Prov.; Bro. Christopher Brady, F.S.C., Prov. Asst.;
MANDEVILLE
St. Dymphna Catholic Center and Chapel - 23515 Hwy. 190, Mandeville, LA 70470-3850 t) (504) 227-3606
METAIRIE
Equestrian Order of the Holy Sepulchre of Jerusalem - 2955 Ridgelake Dr., Ste. 205, Metairie, LA 70002 t) 504-832-0892 office@sleohs.com; lieutenant@sleohs.com (Southeastern Lieutenancy of the U.S.). Joseph A. Marino Sr., Lieutenant;
NEW ORLEANS
Archdiocese of New Orleans Indemnity, Inc. - 7887 Walmsley Ave., New Orleans, LA 70125
Aspiring Scholars - 1000 Howard Ave., Ste. 800, New Orleans, LA 70113; Mailing: 7887 Walmsley Ave., New Orleans, LA 70125 t) 504-596-3045 chowat@ccfnola.org Cory Howat, Pres.;
Catholic Charities Archdiocese of New Orleans - 1000 Howard Ave., Ste. 200, New Orleans, LA 70113; Mailing: 7887 Walmsley Avenue, New Orleans, LA 70125 t) 504-523-3755 ccano@ccano.org www.ccano.org Sr. Marjorie A. Hebert, M.S.C., CEO; Dcn. Martin Gutierrez, COO; Cindy Distefano, Div. Dir.; Shaula Lovera, Div. Dir.; Cheryl D. LaBorde, CFO; Maria Pardo Huete, Dir., Institutional Advancement;
Catholic Cultural Heritage Center St. Mary Chapel - 1100 Chartres St., New Orleans, LA 70116-2596 t) 504-525-9585 (Shrine of St. Lazarus of Jerusalem) Very Rev. Philip G. Landry, Rector;
Chapel of the Vietnamese Martyrs - 5069 Willowbrook Dr., New Orleans, LA 70129; Mailing: P.O. Box 870607, New Orleans, LA 70187-0607 t) 504-254-5660 Rev. Nghiem Van Nguyen; Rev. Joseph Nguyen Van Nguyen, In Res.;
Chateau de Notre Dame Facilities Corporation - 7887 Walmsley Ave., New Orleans, LA 70125 t) 504-861-2906
Christopher Homes, Inc. - 1000 Howard Ave., Ste. 100, New Orleans, LA 70113 t) 504-596-3460 Dcn. Dennis Adams, Dir.;
Congar Institute for Ministry Development - 1611 Mirabeau Ave., New Orleans, LA 70122; Mailing: PO Box 8129, New Orleans, LA 70182 t) 210-341-1366 x271 wcavalier@ost.edu; congarinstitute@ost.edu www.congarinstitute.org Full-service bilingual consulting ministry to prepare lay women and men for pastoral leadership in the Church. Rev. Wayne A. Cavalier, O.P., Dir.;
Domus Dei Clerical Society of Apostolic Life, U.S.A., Inc. - 13401 N. Lemans St., New Orleans, LA 70129 c) (503) 473-7987 domusdeiusa@gmail.com www.nhachua.org Very Rev. Joseph Dang Vu, S.D.D., Pres.; Rev. Dat Huu Pham, S.D.D., Vice. Pres.; Rev. David Kim, S.D.D., Supr.; Rev. Thang Thiet Nguyen, S.D.D., Secy.; Rev. Thanh Dinh Vo, S.D.D., Treas.; Rev. Binh The Cao, S.D.D., Mem.; Rev. Vinh Van Nguyen, S.D.D., Mem.; Rev. Bernardo Son Pham, S.D.D., Mem.; Rev. Tung Duc Vu, S.D.D., Mem.; Bro. Khoi Trong Le, S.D.D., Mem.; Bro. Hien Vinh Nguyen, S.D.D., Mem.; Bro. Manh Xuan Nguyen, S.D.D., Mem.; Bro. Thai Hoang Nguyen, S.D.D., Mem.; Bro. Andrew Tran Pham, S.D.D., Mem.; Bro. Minh Tam Tran, S.D.D., Mem.; Bro. Nhiem Van Tran, S.D.D., Mem.; Bro. Paul Thanh Tran, S.D.D., Mem.; Bro. Phuong Kim Tran, S.D.D., Mem.;
Holy Trinity Drive Land Corporation - 7887 Walmsley Ave., New Orleans, LA 70125 Dirk Wild, Contact;
Hope Revitalization Corporation - 1 Drexel Dr., New Orleans, LA 70125
#iGIVECATHOLIC - 7887 Walmsley Ave., New Orleans, LA 70125 t) (504) 527-5788 igivecatholic.org Ronan Canuto, Contact;
St. Joseph Chapel - St. Joseph Cemetery, 2220 Washington Ave., New Orleans, LA 70113-2647; Mailing: 1000 Howard Ave, Ste. 500, New Orleans, LA 70113-1903 t) 504-488-4989; 504-596-3050; 504-488-5200 nolacatholiccem@arch-no.org
***Lord, Teach Me To Pray, Inc.** - 11 Warbler St., New Orleans, LA 70124-4401 t) 504-439-5933 (Dir.) c) (832) 837-9091 (Rev. William Farge SJ) carolweiler@cox.net www.lordteachmetopray.com Carol Weiler, Dir.;
St. Mary's Chapel - 1516 Jackson Ave., New Orleans, LA 70130 t) 504-522-6748 Rev. Allen Weinert, C.Ss.R., Pst.; Rev. Dominic Bao Quoc Tran, C.Ss.R., Assoc. Pst.; Dcn. Thien Hoang, C.Ss.R.;
St. Marys Dominican Education New Orleans

Corporation - 7701 Walmsley Ave., New Orleans, LA 70125

***National T.E.C. Conference** - 2241 Mendez St., New Orleans, LA 70122 t) 504-227-3233 office@tecconference.org; billy@tecconference.org www.tecconference.org William O'Regan IV, Dir.;

124 Airline Drive, Inc. - 4133 Banks St., New Orleans, LA 70119-6883 t) 504-486-6631 Rev. John Brown, S.J., Pres.;

Our Lady of Wisdom Facility Corporation - 7887 Walmsley Ave., New Orleans, LA 70125 t) 504-861-2906 jentwisle@archdiocese-no.org

PACE Greater New Orleans - 1000 Howard Ave., Ste. 200, New Orleans, LA 70113 t) 504-941-6050 pbriceno-figueredo@ccano.org; kwootan@ccano.org Elderly care. Kurt Wootan, Exec. Dir.; Sr. Marjorie A. Hebert, M.S.C., Pres.;

The Patrons of the Vatican Museums in the South, Inc. - 1137 Jefferson Ave., New Orleans, LA 70115 t) 504-895-6822 fesmd2@gmail.com Frank Schmidt, Pres.;

Peace Center - 2837 Broadway St., New Orleans, LA 70125-2655 t) 504-267-3342 srsueop@aol.com Sr. Suzanne Brauer, Dir.;

Philmat, Inc. - 1000 Howard Ave., Ste. 200, New Orleans, LA 70113 t) 504-227-3491 pbriceno-figueredo@ccano.org Sr. Marjorie A. Hebert, M.S.C., Pres.;

St. Roch Chapel - St. Roch Cemetery, 1725 St. Roch Ave., New Orleans, LA 70117-8223; Mailing: c/o Archdiocesan Cemeteries Office, 1000 Howard Ave., Ste. 500, New Orleans, LA 70113 t) 504-304-0576; 504-482-5065; 504-596-3050 nolacatholiccem@arch-no.org nolacatholiccemeteries.org

School Food and Nutrition Services of New Orleans, Inc. - 7887 Walmsley Ave., New Orleans, LA 70125 t) 504-596-3434 egauthreaux@schoolcafe.org www.schoolcafe.org Ellen Gauthreaux, Exec. Dir.;

***Second Harvest Food Bank of Greater New Orleans and Acadiana** - 700 Edwards Ave., New Orleans, LA 70123-2236 t) 504-734-1322 help@secondharvest.org www.no-hunger.org Natalie Jayroe, Pres. & CEO;

7887 Walmsley, Inc. - 7887 Walmsley Ave., New Orleans, LA 70125

Southern Dominican Global Missions - 4640 Canal St., New Orleans, LA 70119 t) 504-488-2652 hjohnson@xula.edu Bro. Herman D. Johnson, O.P., Exec. Dir.;

***Willwoods Community** - 3900 Howard Ave., New Orleans, LA 70125 t) 504-830-3700 willwoods@willwoods.org www.willwoods.org Ministries of affordable housing, faith & marriage and digital media/broadcast TV. Ron Yager, Exec. Dir.;

MONASTERIES AND RESIDENCES FOR PRIESTS AND BROTHERS [MON]

COVINGTON

De La Salle Christian Brothers (NOSF, Inc.) - 104 W. 11th Ave., Covington, LA 70433 t) 985-892-2004 ngonzalez@dlsi.org Bro. Nick Gonzalez, F.S.C., Prov.; Bro. Christopher Brady, F.S.C., Prov. Asst.;

Brothers of the Christian Schools of Lafayette - Retirement Trust - 104 W. 11th Ave., Covington, LA 70433 t) (985) 892-2004 jlaporte@ericksenkrentel.com James LaPorte, Chair;

St. La Salle Auxiliary - 104 W. 11th Ave., Covington, LA 70433 t) (707) 252-3861 c) (504) 606-1151 bgale@dlsi.org Development project of "De La Salle Christian Brothers," a nonprofit organization. Bro. Gale Condit, Dir.;

NEW ORLEANS

Brothers of the Sacred Heart of New Orleans, Inc. - 4600 Elysian Fields Ave., New Orleans, LA 70122-3826 t) 504-301-4758 unitedstatesprovince@gmail.com Bro. James Burns, S.C., In Res.; Bro. Bernard Couvillion, S.C., In Res.; Bro. Chris Sweeney, S.C., In Res.; Bro. Neri Falgout, S.C., In Res.; Bro. Neal Golden, S.C., In Res.; Bro. Ivy LeBlanc, S.C., Treas.; Bro. Ronald Hingle, S.C., Prov.; Bro. William Boyles, S.C., In Res.; Bro. Leo Labbe, S.C., In Res.; Brs.: 9

Brothers of the Sacred Heart Foundation, Inc. - 4600 Elysian Fields Ave., New Orleans, LA 70122 t) (504) 301-4758 bileblancsc@gmail.com

Congregation of the Mission Western Province (Vincentians) (DePaul Residence) - 812 Constantinople St., New Orleans, LA 70115-2726 c) 504-413-7413 frtjscm@aol.com Rev. Louis Arceneaux, C.M.; Rev. Thomas J. Stehlik, C.M., Supr.;

Dominican Friars, Southern Dominican Province of St. Martin de Porres - 1611 Mirabeau Ave., New Orleans, LA 70122; Mailing: PO Box 8129, New Orleans, LA 70182 t) 504-837-2129 provincial@opsouth.org www.opsouth.org Very Rev. Jorge Rativá, O.P., Vicar; Rev. Roberto Merced, O.P., Prov.; Rev. Augustine DeArmond, O.P., Treas.; Friar Carl Paustian, O.P., Dir.; Brs.: 3; Priests: 66

Dominican Vocation Sponsors - ; Mailing: Post Office Box 8129, New Orleans, LA 70182 t) (504) 837-2129

Southern Dominican Global Missions - 4640 Canal St., New Orleans, LA 70119 t) 504-488-2652 Bro. Herman D. Johnson, O.P., Dir.;

Jesuit Provincial Office (Catholic Society of Religious and Literary Education) - 909 Poydras, Suite 2500, New Orleans, LA 70112 t) 314-361-7765 ucsprov@jesuits.org U.S. Central and Southern Province, Society of Jesus Rev. Thomas P. Greene, S.J., Prov.; Rev. David A. Brown, S.J.; Rev. Joseph A. Carola, S.J.; Rev. Mark Lewis, S.J.; Rev. Jesus Rodriguez, S.J.; Rev. J. Daniel Daly, Treas.; Rev. Francis W. Huete, S.J., Prov. Asst.; Rev. John F. Armstrong, S.J., Prov. Asst.; Priests: 10

Josephite Fathers and Brothers - 2600 A.P. Tureaud, New Orleans, LA 70119 t) 504-944-2424

The Josephite Faculty House of St. Augustine High School - Rev. Howard W. Byrd, S.S.J.; Rev. Anthony Okum, S.S.J.; Bro. Laurence E. Price, S.S.J.;

Loyola Jesuit Community - 1575 Calhoun St., New Orleans, LA 70118-6153 t) 504-865-3866; 504-865-3875 gwaldrop@jesuits.org; ggrovenburg@jesuits.org Rev. John Brown, S.J., Pres., Jesuit HS; Rev. Richard Buhler, S.J., Spiritual Dir., Manresa House of Retreats; Rev. Justin Daffron, S.J., Interim Pres., Loyola Univ. New Orleans; Rev. W. Penn Dawson III, S.J., Prof.; Rev. William J. Farge, S.J., Spiritual Dir., JHS & Notre Dame Sem.; Rev. Edwin L. Gros, S.J., Par. Vicar; Rev. Gregg Grovenburg, S.J., Campus Min.; Bro. Lawrence J. Huck, S.J., Dir., Manresa House of Retreats; Rev. Steven E. Kimmons, S.J., Spiritual Dir., Manresa House of Retreats; Rev. Stephen Alphonsus Kramer, S.J., Teacher, JHS; Rev. Anthony F. McGinn, S.J., Pst.; Rev. Lawrence Moore, S.J., Prof.; Rev. Mark S. Mossa, S.J., Prof.; Rev. Earl C. Muller, S.J., Spiritual Dir., Notre Dame Sem.; Rev. Nathan O'Halloran, S.J., Prof.; Rev. Jonathon Polce, S.J., Chap.; Rev. Stephen C. Rowntree, S.J., In Res.; Rev. Mark Edward Thibodeaux, S.J., Pst.; Rev. Edward Vacek, S.J., Prof.; Rev. Gregory S. Waldrop, S.J., Rector; Nicholas Blair, S.J., Teacher, JHS; Joshua Hinchie, S.J., Prof.; Jordan Jones, S.J., Prof.; Jeff Ryan Miraflor, S.J., Teacher, JHS; Brs.: 1; Priests: 21

ST. BENEDICT

St. Joseph Abbey - 75376 River Rd., St. Benedict, LA 70457 t) 985-892-1800 abbotsecretary@sjasc.edu www.saintjosephabbey.com Rt. Rev. Justin Brown, O.S.B., Abbot; Bro. Brian Harrington, O.S.B., Prior; Rev. Augustine E. Foley, O.S.B., Subprior; Rev. Peter E. Hammett, O.S.B.; Rev. Aelred Kavanagh, O.S.B.; Rev. Scott J. Underwood, O.S.B.; Rev. Jonathan M. DeFrange, O.S.B.; Rev. Timothy J. Burnett, O.S.B.; Rev. Matthew R. Clark, O.S.B.; Rev. Gregory M. Boquet, O.S.B.; Rev. Sean B. Duggan, O.S.B.; Rev. Charles Benoit, O.S.B.; Rev. Killian Tolg, O.S.B.; Rev. Jude Israel, O.S.B.; Brs.: 14; Priests: 14

NURSING / REHABILITATION / CONVALESCENCE / ELDERLY CARE [NUR]

COVINGTON

St. Anthony's Gardens - 601 Holy Trinity Dr., Covington, LA 70433 t) 985-605-5950 iblundell@stag-ano.org www.stanthonysgardens.org Adult retirement community with independent and assisted living and memory care. Dr. Tracy Brown, Mng. Dir.; Iris Blundell, Dir.;

LAPLACE

Dubourg Home - 201 Rue Dubourg, LaPlace, LA 70068; Mailing: 2729 Lowerline St., New Orleans, LA 70125 t) 985-652-1981; 504-596-3460 rdubroc@chi-ano.org Elderly Affordable Housing. Dcn. Dennis Adams, Exec. Dir.; Ramona Dubroc, Community Mgr.; Asstd. Annu.: 143; Staff: 6

MANDEVILLE

Rouquette III - 4300 Hwy. 22, Mandeville, LA 70471; Mailing: 1000 Howard Ave., Ste. 100, New Orleans, LA 70113 t) 985-635-0305; 504-596-3460 edoran@chi-ano.org Elderly Affordable Housing Dcn. Dennis Adams, Exec. Dir.; Elizabeth Doran, Community Mgr.; Asstd. Annu.: 87; Staff: 4

St. Bernard III/Rouquette IV - 4310 Hwy. 22, Mandeville, LA 70471; Mailing: 2729 Lowerline St., New Orleans, LA 70125 t) 985-635-0305; 504-596-3460 edoran@chi-ano.org Elderly Affordable Housing Dcn. Dennis Adams, Exec. Dir.; Elizabeth Doran, Community Mgr.; Asstd. Annu.: 76; Staff: 2

St. Tammany Manor/Rouquette Lodge - 4300 Hwy. 22, Mandeville, LA 70471; Mailing: 2729 Lowerline St., New Orleans, LA 70125 t) 985-626-5217; 504-596-3460 pfulkerson@chi-ano.org Elderly Affordable Housing. Dcn. Dennis Adams, Exec. Dir.; Patricia Fulkerson, Dir., Opers.; Asstd. Annu.: 199; Staff: 12

MARRERO

Monsignor Wynhoven Apartments, Inc. - 4600-10th St., Marrero, LA 70072; Mailing: 2729 Lowerline St., New Orleans, LA 70125 t) 504-347-8442; 504-596-3460 tpoche@chi-ano.org Elderly Affordable Housing Dcn. Dennis Adams, Exec. Dir.; Teresa Poche, Lead Mgr.; Asstd. Annu.: 376; Staff: 15

Wynhoven Health Care Center - 1050 Medical Center Blvd., Marrero, LA 70072-3170 t) 504-347-0777 www.wynhoven.org Dcn. Jeffrey R. Tully, CEO; Michelle Matthew, Admin.;

MERAUX

St. Bernard Manor - 2400 Archbishop Hannan Blvd., Meraux, LA 70075; Mailing: 2729 Lowerline St., New Orleans, LA 70125 t) 504-596-3460; 504-227-3380 wrobertson@chi-ano.org Elderly Affordable Housing Dcn. Dennis Adams, Exec. Dir.; Wanda Robertson, Community Mgr.; Asstd. Annu.: 90; Staff: 4

METAIRIE

St. Bernard II (Metairie IV) - 4937 York St., Metairie, LA 70001; Mailing: 2729 Lowerline St., New Orleans, LA 70125 t) 504-267-9067; 504-596-3460 droyes@chi-ano.org Elderly Affordable Housing Dcn. Dennis Adams, Exec. Dir.; Dawn Royes, Community Mgr.; Asstd. Annu.: 84; Staff: 4

Metairie Manor - 4929 York St., Metairie, LA 70001; Mailing: 2729 Lowerline St., New Orleans, LA 70125 t) 504-596-3460; 504-456-1467 droyes@chi-ano.org Elderly Affordable Housing Dcn. Dennis Adams, Exec. Dir.; Dawn Royes, Community Mgr.; Asstd. Annu.: 318; Staff: 16

Metairie III - 4929 York St., Metairie, LA 70001; Mailing: 2729 Lowerline St., New Orleans, LA 70125 t) 504-456-1467; 504-596-3460 droyes@chi-ano.org Elderly Affordable Housing Dcn. Dennis Adams, Exec. Dir.; Dawn Royes, Community Mgr.; Asstd. Annu.: 89; Staff: 3

NEW ORLEANS

Annunciation Inn, Inc. - 1220 Spain St., New Orleans, LA 70117; Mailing: 2729 Lowerline St., New Orleans, LA 70125 t) 504-596-3460; 504-944-0512 dhicks@chi-ano.org Elderly Affordable Housing Dcn. Dennis F. Adams, Exec. Dir.; Dechaun Hicks, Asst. Dir., Opers.; Asstd. Annu.: 113; Staff: 6

The Apartments at Mater Dolorosa - 1226 S. Carrollton Ave., New Orleans, LA 70118; Mailing: 2729 Lowerline St., New Orleans, LA 70125 t) 504-596-3460; 504-865-7222 dpertuit@chi-ano.org Elderly Affordable Housing Dcn. Dennis F. Adams, Exec. Dir.; Dagianna

Pertuit, Community Mgr.; Asstd. Annu.: 79; Staff: 4

Christopher Inn - 2110 Royal St., New Orleans, LA 70116; Mailing: 2729 Lowerline St., New Orleans, LA 70125 t) 504-596-3460; 504-949-0312 fhanagan@chi-ano.org Elderly Affordable Housing Dcn. Dennis Adams, Exec. Dir.; Frances Hanagan, Community Mgr.; Asstd. Annu.: 144; Staff: 5

DeLille Inn - 6924 Chef Menteur Hwy., New Orleans, LA 70126; Mailing: 2729 Lowerline St., New Orleans, LA 70125 t) 504-245-8660; 504-596-3460 asampia@chi-ano.org Elderly Affordable Housing Dcn. Dennis F. Adams, Exec. Dir.; Sr. Agnes Sampia, Community Mgr.; Asstd. Annu.: 55; Staff: 2

St. John Berchman's Manor - 3400 St. Anthony Ave., New Orleans, LA 70122; Mailing: 2729 Lowerline St., New Orleans, LA 70125 t) 504-596-3460; 504-943-9331 dhicks@chi-ano.org Elderly Affordable Housing Dcn. Dennis F. Adams, Exec. Dir.; Dechaun Hicks, Asst. Dir., Opers.; Asstd. Annu.: 162; Staff: 5

Lafon Nursing Facility of the Holy Family (Sisters of the Holy Family) - 6900 Chef Menteur Hwy., New Orleans, LA 70126-5216 t) 504-241-6285 aliciacosta14@gmail.com; awatkins@lafonnursing.org www.lafonnursingfacility.com Anieze Watkins, Dir.; Sonya Berry, Admin.; Sr. Alicia Christina Costa, S.S.F., Rel. Ord. Ldr.; Asstd. Annu.: 90; Staff: 146

St. Martin's Manor - 1501 N. Johnson St., New Orleans, LA 70116; Mailing: 2729 Lowerline St., New Orleans, LA 70125 t) 504-227-3390; 504-596-3460 tgoodman@chi-ano.org Elderly Affordable Housing Dcn. Dennis Adams, Exec. Dir.; Tanisha Goodman, Community Mgr.; Asstd. Annu.: 154; Staff: 7

The Mental Health Association Development Corporation (St. Martin House) - 1540 N. Johnson St., New Orleans, LA 70116-1721; Mailing: 2729 Lowerline St., New Orleans, LA 70125 t) 504-596-3460; 504-227-3390 tgoodman@chi-ano.org Affordable Housing for the Mentally Ill Dcn. Dennis Adams, Exec. Dir.; Tanisha Goodman, Community Mgr.; Asstd. Annu.: 14; Staff: 1

Nazareth II - 9640 Hayne Blvd., New Orleans, LA 70127; Mailing: 2729 Lowerline St., New Orleans, LA 70125 t) 504-596-3460; 504-246-9640 tpoche@chi-ano.org Elderly Affordable Housing Dcn. Dennis F. Adams, Exec. Dir.; Teresa Poche, Community Mgr.; Asstd. Annu.: 134; Staff: 2

Nazareth Manor - 9630 Hayne Blvd., New Orleans, LA 70127; Mailing: 2729 Lowerline St., New Orleans, LA 70125 t) 504-596-3460; 504-246-9630 tpoche@chi-ano.org Elderly Affordable Housing. Dcn. Dennis F. Adams, Exec. Dir.; Teresa Poche, Community Mgr.; Asstd. Annu.: 172; Staff: 7

Notre Dame Health System - 2832 Burdette St., New Orleans, LA 70125-2596; Mailing: 1000 Howard Ave. 10th Fl., New Orleans, LA 70113 t) 504-866-2741 wplaisance@archdiocese-no.org cdnd.org Residence and Nursing Home Dcn. Jeffrey R. Tully, Pres. & CEO;

Our Lady of Wisdom Healthcare Center - 5600 Gen. de Gaulle Dr., New Orleans, LA 70131 t) 504-394-5991 lheisser@arch-no.org www.olwhealth.org Inter-community healthcare facility for Archdiocesan clergy and Religious Men & Women. Lisa Heisser, Admin.;

Villa St. Maurice, Inc. - 500 St. Maurice Ave., New Orleans, LA 70117; Mailing: 2729 Lowerline St., New Orleans, LA 70125 t) 504-596-3460; 504-267-9640 tgoodman@chi-ano.org Elderly Affordable Housing Dcn. Dennis Adams, Exec. Dir.; Tanisha Goodman, Community Mgr.; Asstd. Annu.: 94; Staff: 4

SLIDELL

Villa Additions - 1938 Gause Blvd. W., Slidell, LA 70460; Mailing: 2729 Lowerline St., New Orleans, LA 70125 t) 504-596-3460; 985-605-5940 sobrien@chi-ano.org Elderly Affordable Housing Dcn. Dennis Adams, Exec. Dir.; Sharline O'Brien, Community Mgr.; Asstd. Annu.: 87; Staff: 1

PRESCHOOLS / CHILDCARE CENTERS [PRE]

NEW ORLEANS

Carmelite Ministries, Inc. Cub Corner Preschool - 420 Allen Toussaint Blvd., New Orleans, LA 70124 t) 504-286-8673 cubcornerpreschoolwaitinglist@yahoo.com www.home.bellsouth.net/p/pwp-mountcarmel Sr. Gwen Grillot, O.Carm., Exec.; Elizabeth Coe, Dir.;

***Covenant House New Orleans** - 611 N. Rampart St., New Orleans, LA 70112-3540 t) 504-584-1102 jkelly@covenanthouse.org covenanthouseno.org Home for runaway, abused & homeless youth aged 16-21. Rheneisha Robertson, Exec. Dir.;

St. John Berchmans Child Development Center - 2710 Gentilly Blvd., New Orleans, LA 70122-3098 t) 504-309-8125 stjohnberchmans1@gmail.com stjohnberchmansecdc.weebly.com/ Sr. Andria Donald, S.S.F., Prin.; Stds.: 70; Lay Tchrs.: 10

Rosary Child Development Center - 5100 Willowbrook Dr., New Orleans, LA 70129-1047 t) 504-254-1528 rosarycdc@yahoo.com Sr. M. Jacynta Minh-Tuyet Nguyen, F.M.S.R., Dir.;

RETREAT HOUSES / RENEWAL CENTERS [RTR]

COVINGTON

Camp Abbey Retreat Center - 77002 KC Camp Rd., Covington, LA 70435 t) 985-327-7240 campabbey@arch-no.org Denise Emmons, Contact; William O'Regan IV, Contact;

METAIRIE

Archdiocesan Spirituality Center - 2501 Maine Ave., Metairie, LA 70003-5446 t) 504-861-3254 archspirctr@archdiocese-no.org Sr. Dorothy Trosclair, O.P., Exec.;

Archdiocese of New Orleans Retreat Center - 5500 St. Mary St., Metairie, LA 70006 t) 504-887-1420 retreats@arch-no.org Dedicated to Our Lady of the Cenacle. Aline Harbison, Exec. Dir.;

NEW ORLEANS

Center of Jesus the Lord - 1307 Louisiana Ave, New Orleans, LA 70115 t) 504-529-1636 glicata@centerofjesusthelord.org www.centerofjesusthelord-nola.org Rev. Lance Campo, Dir.;

ST. BENEDICT

St. Joseph Abbey Retreat Center - 75376 River Rd., St. Benedict, LA 70457-9900 t) 985-892-3473 clc@sjasc.edu www.saintjosephabbey.com/retreat-center Conducted by Benedictine Monks. Dcn. Steven L. Ferran, Dir.;

SEMINARIES [SEM]

METAIRIE

Congregation of the Mother Coredemptrix Formation House - 112 Lilac St., Metairie, LA 70005-1817 t) 504-835-9746

NEW ORLEANS

Notre Dame Seminary Graduate School of Theology - 2901 S. Carrollton Ave., New Orleans, LA 70118-4391 t) 504-866-7426 jhattier@nds.edu www.nds.edu Very Rev. Joshua J. Rodrigue, Rector & Pres.; Rev. Deogratias O. Ekisa, Vice-Rector, Configuration Form.; Rev. Joseph M. Krafft, Vice-Rector., Pastoral Synthesis; Rev. Minh Phan, Vice-Rector, Discipleship Form.; Rev. Kurt Young, Vice-Rector, Propaedeutic Form.; Rev. Nile C. Gross, Coord., Intellectual/Liturgical Form.; Rev. Joshua M. Neu, Coord., Spiritual Form.; Rev. Jeffrey A. Montz, Spiritual Dir.; Rev. Luke D. Buckles, O.P., Faculty; Rev. Michael Champagne, C.J.C., Faculty; Rev. Timothy D. Hedrick, Faculty; Most Rev. Alfred C. Hughes, Faculty; Rev. David Kelly, Faculty; Rev. Earl C. Muller, S.J., Faculty; Rev. Msgr. Christopher Nalty, Faculty; Rev. Mark S. Raphael, Faculty; Rev. Bryce Sibley, Faculty; Stds.: 134; Bro. Tchrs.: 1; Lay Tchrs.: 12; Pr. Tchrs.: 14

SAINT BENEDICT

Saint Joseph Seminary College - 75376 River Rd., Saint Benedict, LA 70457-9999 t) 985-867-2263 rectorsec@sjasc.edu www.sjasc.edu Rt. Rev. Justin Brown, O.S.B., Abbot; Rev. Gregory M. Boquet, O.S.B., Rector; Rev. Matthew R. Clark, O.S.B., Vice Rector; Rev. Jerome Aubert, O.S.B., Dean, Students; Rev. Msgr. J. Douglas Courville, Propaedeutic Prog. Dir.; Rev. Kenneth G. Davis, O.F.M., Spiritual Adv./Care Srvcs.; Rev. Msgr. D. Bruce Miller, Spiritual Adv./Care Srvcs.; Rev. Michael Chukwu (Nigeria), Prof.; Rev. Don Bosco Darsi (India), Prof.; Rev. Augustine E. Foley, O.S.B., Prof.; Rev. Damian Hinojosa, Prof.; Rev. Jude Israel, O.S.B., Prof.; Rev. Higinio Rosolen, I.V.E. (Argentina), Prof.; Rev. David K. Seid, O.P., Prof.; Stds.: 104; Lay Tchrs.: 16; Pr. Tchrs.: 10

SHRINES [SHR]

METAIRIE

St. Ann National Shrine - 3601 Transcontinental Dr., Metairie, LA 70006; Mailing: 4940 Meadowdale St., Metairie, LA 70006-4040 t) 504-455-7071 Rev. William O'Riordan, Pst.;

NEW ORLEANS

National Shrine of Blessed Francis Xavier Seelos - 919 Josephine St., New Orleans, LA 70130-5071 t) 504-525-2495 www.seelos.org Rev. Richard Boever, C.Ss.R., Dir.; Rev. Gilbert Enderle, C.Ss.R., Vice Postulator;

National Shrine of Our Lady of Prompt Succor - 2701 State St., New Orleans, LA 70118; Mailing: 2734 Nashville Ave., New Orleans, LA 70115 t) 504-866-0216 (Bus. Office); 504-866-0200 (Sacristy) shrineolps@gmail.com www.shrineolps.com Sr. Carolyn Brockland, O.S.U., Dir.;

Ursuline Nuns of the Parish of Orleans - 2734 Nashville Ave., Business Office, New Orleans, LA 70115 t) (504) 891-3665 c) (314) 601-4087 annb@osucentral.org usaromanunionursulines.org Sr. Ann Barrett, O.S.U., Prioress;

Shrine of St. Jude Thaddeus - 411 N. Rampart St., New Orleans, LA 70112-3594 t) 504-525-1551; 504-522-8546 (CRP) judeshrine@aol.com Rev. Anthony Rigoli, O.M.I., Pst.;

Shrine of St. Lazarus of Jerusalem - 1100 Chartres St., New Orleans, LA 70116-2596 t) 504-529-3040 Very Rev. Philip G. Landry, Rector;

SPECIAL CARE FACILITIES [SPF]

METAIRIE

Mercy - 110 Veterans Memorial Blvd., Ste. 425, Metairie, LA 70005 t) 504-838-8283 marynell.ploch@mercy.net Mercy Family Center Rex Menasco, Pres. & Exec. Dir.; Philip Wheeler, Pres.;

Mercy - 1445 W. Causeway Approach, Mandeville, LA 70471 t) 985-727-7993 douglas.walker@mercy.net Elaine Moore, Pres.;

NEW ORLEANS

Boys Hope Girls Hope - 4128 Baudin St., New Orleans, LA 70119; Mailing: P.O. Box 19307, New Orleans, LA 70179 t) 504-484-7744 www.bhghnola.org Group homes for boys and girls. Chuck Roth, Exec.;

Ascension DePaul Services - 3201 S. Carrollton Ave., New Orleans, LA 70118-4307 t) (504) 482-2080 john.tersigni@ascension.org www.dcsno.org Michael G. Griffin, CEO; John Tersigni, Chief Mission Integration Officer; Asstd. Annu.: 45,096; Staff: 404

Ascension DePaul Foundation of New Orleans, LLC - 3201 S. Carrollton Ave., New Orleans, LA 70118-4307; Mailing: P.O. Box 850258, New Orleans, LA 70185-0528

DePaul Community Health Centers - Gentilly - 100 Warrington Dr., New Orleans, LA 70122 t) (504) 282-0089 www.depaulcommunityhealthcenters.org

Daughters of Charity Neighborhood Health Partnership - 3201 S. Carrollton Ave., New Orleans, LA 70118-4307 t) 504-482-2080 john.tersigni@ascension.org

Daughters of Charity Services of New Orleans Foundation - 3201 S. Carrollton Ave., New Orleans, LA 70118-4307 t) 504-482-2080

Daughters of Charity Services of New Orleans East - 3201 S. Carrollton Ave., New Orleans, LA 70118 t) 504-212-9568 john.tersigni@ascension.org www.dcsno.org Michael G. Griffin, CEO; John Tersigni,

Chief Mission Integration Officer;

***Marillac Community Health Centers (DePaul Community Health Centers)** - 3201 S. Carrollton Ave., New Orleans, LA 70118-4307 t) 504-207-3060 x2205 john.tersigni@ascension.org Michael G. Griffin, CEO; John Tersigni, Chief Mission Integration Officer;

DePaul Community Health Centers - Bywater/St. Cecilia - 1030 Lesseps St., New Orleans, LA 70117 t) 504-941-6041

DePaul Community Health Centers - Metairie - 111 N. Causeway Blvd., Metairie, LA 70001 t) 504-482-0084 www.depaulcommunityhealthcenters.org

DePaul Community Health Centers - Carrollton - 3201 S. Carrollton Ave., New Orleans, LA 70118 t) 314-733-8000

DePaul Community Health Centers - New Orleans East - 5630 Read Blvd., New Orleans, LA 70127 t) 504-248-5357; 314-733-8000 www.depaulcommunityhealthcenters.org

Ozanam Inn - 843 Camp St., New Orleans, LA 70130-3751; Mailing: P O Box 30565, New Orleans, LA 70190 t) 504-523-1184 admin@ozanaminn.org www.ozanaminn.org Multi-purpose shelter for men, women and children. Sponsored by Society of St. Vincent de Paul. Clarence Adams, CEO;

Project Lazarus - 2824 Dauphine St, New Orleans, LA 70117; Mailing: P.O. Box 3906, New Orleans, LA 70177-3906 t) 504-949-3609 info@projectlazarus.net www.projectlazarus.net Residential program for persons with HIV/AIDS. Susanne B Dietzel, Exec. Dir.; Bed Capacity: 13; Asstd. Annu.: 35; Staff: 12

An asterisk (*) denotes an organization that has established tax-exempt status directly with the IRS and is not covered by the USCCB Group Ruling.

Diocese of New Ulm

(Dioecesis Novae Ulmae)

MOST REVEREND CHAD W. ZIELINSKI

Bishop of New Ulm; ordained June 8, 1996; appointed Bishop of Fairbanks, November 8, 2014; Episcopal ordination December 15, 2014; appointed Bishop of New Ulm July 12, 2022; installed September 27, 2022.
Office: 1421 Sixth St., N., New Ulm, MN 56073-2071

Diocesan Pastoral Center: 1421 Sixth St. N., New Ulm, MN 56073-2071. T: 507-359-2966; F: 507-354-0268.
www.dnu.org
dnu@dnu.org

ESTABLISHED NOVEMBER 18, 1957.

Square Miles 9,863.

Comprises the Counties of Big Stone, Brown, Chippewa, Kandiyohi, Lac Qui Parle, Lincoln, Lyon, McLeod, Meeker, Nicollet, Redwood, Renville, Sibley, Swift, and Yellow Medicine in the State of Minnesota.

For legal titles of parishes and diocesan institutions, consult the Diocesan Pastoral Center.

STATISTICAL OVERVIEW

Personnel

Bishop	1
Retired Bishops	1
Priests: Diocesan Active in Diocese	34
Priests: Diocesan in Foreign Missions	1
Priests: Retired, Sick or Absent	20
Number of Diocesan Priests	55
Religious Priests in Diocese	2
Total Priests in your Diocese	57
Extern Priests in Diocese	2
Ordinations:	
Diocesan Priests	3
Permanent Deacons in Diocese	18
Total Sisters	33

Parishes

Parishes	59
With Resident Pastor:	
Resident Diocesan Priests	19
Resident Religious Priests	1
Without Resident Pastor:	
Administered by Priests	39
Pastoral Centers	1

Welfare

Catholic Hospitals	1
Homes for the Aged	8
Special Centers for Social Services	1
Total Assisted	596

Educational

Diocesan Students in Other Seminaries	5
Total Seminarians	5
High Schools, Diocesan and Parish	3
Total Students	243
Elementary Schools, Diocesan and Parish	13
Total Students	1,384
Catechesis/Religious Education:	
High School Students	1,523
Elementary Students	2,738
Total Students under Catholic Instruction	5,893
Teachers in Diocese:	
Priests	1
Sisters	3
Lay Teachers	188

Vital Statistics

Receptions into the Church:	
Infant Baptism Totals	583
Minor Baptism Totals	21
Adult Baptism Totals	7
Received into Full Communion	24
First Communions	598
Confirmations	595
Marriages:	
Catholic	87
Interfaith	46
Total Marriages	133
Deaths	730
Total Catholic Population	47,417
Total Population	283,068

LEADERSHIP

Diocesan Pastoral Center - t) 507-359-2966

Diocesan Administrator - t) 507-359-2966 Rev. Msgr. Douglas L. Grams;

College of Consultors - Rev. Msgr. Douglas L. Grams; Rev. Msgr. Eugene L. Lozinski; Rev. Steven J. Verhelst;

Chancellor - t) 507-359-2966 x5315 elozinski@dnu.org Rev. Msgr. Eugene L. Lozinski;

Corporate Board - Rev. Msgr. Eugene L. Lozinski; Rev. Msgr. Douglas L. Grams; Michael H. Boyle;

Vicar General (Vacant due to Vacant See) - t) 507-359-2966

Priests' Council (Inactive due to Vacant See) - Rev. Msgr. Douglas L. Grams; Rev. Msgr. Eugene L. Lozinski; Rev. Jeremy G. Kucera;

Human Resources Consultant - t) 320-441-2931 nmiller@vinnahumanresources.com Nancy Miller;

Diocesan Tribunal - t) 507-359-2966 x5329 tribunal@dnu.org www.dnu.org/tribunal Aldean B. Hendrickson, Dir. (ahendrickson@dnu.org);

Judicial Vicar (Officialis) - Rev. Mark S. Steffl;

Director - ahendrickson@dnu.org Aldean B. Hendrickson;

Associate Judges - Rev. Msgr. Eugene L. Lozinski; Rev. Paul L. Wolf; Rev. Msgr. Douglas L. Grams;

Defenders of the Bond - Rev. Mark S. Mallak; Heather Eichholz;

Promoter of Justice - Rev. Mark S. Mallak;

Notary - Penny Forst;

OFFICES AND DIRECTORS

Office of Adult Faith Formation - t) 507-359-2966 x5310 mmckeown@dnu.org www.dnu.org/re-aff Dcn. Mike McKeown, Dir.;

Bishop's Delegate for the Permanent Diaconate - Rev. Matthew J. Wiering (fatherwiering@gmail.com);

Bishop's Delegate in Matters Pertaining to Sexual Misconduct - Rev. Msgr. Douglas L. Grams;

Safe Environment Coordinator - t) 507-359-2966 x5329 www.dnu.org/safeenvironment Aldean B. Hendrickson;

Victim Assistance Coordinator - t) 507-359-2966 x5313 Sr. Candace Fier, I.S.S.M.;

Office of Communications - t) 507-359-2966 x5332 dnu@dnu.org www.dnu.org/communications Christine Clancy, Communications Specialist (cclancy@dnu.org);

The "Prairie Catholic" - Christine Clancy, Editor;

Office of Continuing Education of Clergy - t) 507-359-2966 x5323 mkramer@dnu.org Michelle Kramer, Dir.;

Office of Development - t) 507-359-2966 x5310 mmckeown@dnu.org www.dnu.org/development Dcn. Mike McKeown, Dir.;

Office of Family Life - t) 507-359-2966 x5329 www.dnu.org/familylife Sr. Candace Fier, I.S.S.M., Dir.;

Retrouvaille - t) 800-470-2230

Office of Hispanic Ministry (Vacant) - www.dnu.org/hispanic-ministry

Office of Catholic Charities - t) 507-359-2966 x339; 507-233-5339; 866-670-5163 www.dnu.org/catholiccharities Sr. Lois L. Byrne, P.B.V.M., Dir. (willois@dnu.org);

Hutchinson Regional Office - Sandra Sam Rickertsen;

Marshall Regional Office - Tami Behnke;

New Ulm Diocesan Office - Dr. Dorine Reiter, Psychologist;

Willmar Regional Office - Sr. Lois L. Byrne, P.B.V.M.;

Office of Finance - t) 507-359-2966 x5309 www.dnu.org/finance Dcn. Richard J. Christiansen, Interim Dir.; Carol Hacker, Finance Office Mgr. (clhacker@dnu.org);

Finance Council - Dcn. Richard J. Christiansen, Staff Liaison; Rev. Mark S. Steffl; Mary Nordstrom;

Board of Trustees for Pension Plan for Priests - Rev. Msgr. Douglas L. Grams; Rev. Msgr. Eugene L. Lozinski; Rev. Zachary D. Peterson;

Office of Social Concerns - www.dnu.org/socialconcerns Dcn. Timothy P. Dolan, Dir.;

Social Concerns Committee - t) 507-359-2966 x5326 Dcn. Timothy P. Dolan, Dir.; Paul Hayden; Judy Hoffer;

Office of Worship - t) 507-359-2966 x320; 507-233-5320 www.dnu.org/worship Rev. Aaron T. Johanneck, Dir.;

Ecumenism and Interreligious Affairs - t) 507-359-2966 x5320 Rev. Aaron T. Johanneck;

Worship Committee - t) 507-359-2966 x5320 worship@dnu.org Rev. Aaron T. Johanneck, Staff Liaison; Rev. Paul D. Timmerman; John Rabaey, Mem. At-Large;

Office of Pastoral Planning (Vacant) - t) 507-359-2966 www.dnu.org/pastoral-planning

Committee on Parishes - Dcn. Ken Noyes, Chair; Rev. Msgr. Douglas L. Grams; Rev. Anthony J. Stubeda;

Office of Priest Personnel - Rev. Steven J. Verhelst, Dir.;

Priest Personnel Board - Rev. Steven J. Verhelst, Exec.; Rev. Msgr. Douglas L. Grams; Rev. Dennis C. Labat;

Office of Propagation of the Faith/Holy Childhood Association - t) 507-359-2966 x5308 Rev. Philip M. Schotzko;

Office of Religious Education - t) 507-359-2966 x5327 www.dnu.org/re-aff Kevin Losleben, DRE;

Office of Catholic Schools - t) 507-359-2966 x5323 mkramer@dnu.org www.dnu.org/schools Michelle Kramer, Dir.;

Office of Vocations - t) 507-359-2966 www.dnu.org/vocations Rev. Garrett Ahlers, Dir.; Rev. Craig A. Timmerman, Asst. Dir. (fathercraig@gmail.com);

Vocations Team - Rev. Garrett Ahlers; Rev. Msgr. Douglas L. Grams; Rev. Craig A. Timmerman;

Office of Youth and Young Adult Ministry - t) 507-359-2966 x5327 klosleben@dnu.org www.dnu.org/youth Kevin Losleben, Dir.;

ADVISORY BOARDS, COMMISSIONS, COMMITTEES, AND COUNCILS

Building Committee - t) 320-365-3593 Rev. George V. Schmit Jr., Chair; Rev. Aaron T. Johanneck; Richard Greene;

Diocesan Pastoral Council (Inactive due to Vacant See) - Brent Sundve, Chair; Julie Treinen; Randy Krzmarzick;

ORGANIZATIONS

Boy Scouts - t) 507-629-4075 Rev. Andrew J. Michels, Chap.;

Catholic Medical Association - t) 507-276-3070 Frani Knowles;

Diocesan Council of Catholic Women - Barbara Mathiowetz, Pres.; Betty Thooft, Immediate Past Pres.; Rev. Msgr. Eugene L. Lozinski, Spiritual Advisor;

Girl Scouts - t) 320-235-3471 Mary Reitsma;

Marriage Encounter - t) 507-829-8869 Craig Wetter, Contact; Barb Wetter, Contact;

PARISHES, MISSIONS, AND CLERGY

STATE OF MINNESOTA

APPLETON

St. John - 350 S Edquist St, Appleton, MN 56208-1516; Mailing: 349 E. Reuss Ave., Appleton, MN 56208-1516 t) 320-289-1146; 320-842-4271 stjccao@gmail.com stisidorethefarmerafc.org (St. Isidore the Farmer Area Faith Community with Benson; DeGraff; Murdock; Clontarf; & Danvers). Rev. Jeremy G. Kucera, Pst.; CRP Stds.: 13

ARLINGTON

St. Mary - 504 7th Ave., N.W., Arlington, MN 55307-0392; Mailing: P.O. Box 392, Arlington, MN 55307-0392 t) 507-964-5413 stmararl@frontiernet.net; bethwalters06@gmail.com corpuschristiafc.org (Area Faith Community with Gaylord; Henderson; & St John - Assumption). Dcn. Timothy P. Dolan; Rev. Msgr. Eugene L. Lozinski, Pst.; CRP Stds.: 117

BELLE PLAINE

St. John-Assumption - 26523 200th St., Belle Plaine, MN 56011; Mailing: P.O. Box 427, Henderson, MN 56044 t) 507-248-3550 stjos@frontiernet.net (Corpus Christi AFC with St. Mary, Arlington, St. Michael, Gaylord, & St. Thomas, Jessenland, St. Brendan, Green Isle & St. Joseph, Henderson). Rev. Msgr. Eugene L. Lozinski, Pst.; CRP Stds.: 34

BELLINGHAM

St. Joseph - 1741 340th St., Bellingham, MN 56212; Mailing: 421 Madison Ave., Ortonville, MN 56278-2713 t) 320-839-2772 www.spiritoflifeafc.org (Spirit of Life Area Faith Community with Ortonville, Graceville & Madison). Rev. Brian W. Oestreich, Pst.; CRP Stds.: 17

BENSON

St. Francis - 508 13th St. N., Benson, MN 56215-1228 t) 320-842-4271 stisidorethefarmerafc.org (St. Isidore the Farmer Area Faith Community with Clontarf; Danvers; De Graff; Murdock; & Appleton). Rev. Jeremy G. Kucera, Pst.; CRP Stds.: 31

BIRD ISLAND

St. Mary - 220 S. 10th St., Bird Island, MN 55310-0500; Mailing: 302 S. 10th St., Olivia, MN 56277 t) 320-365-3593; 320-365-3593 x251 (CRP); 320-523-2030 stmary@heartofjesusafc.org; michellep@heartofjesusafc.org www.heartofjesusafc.org.com (Heart of Jesus Area Faith Community with Hector; Olivia; & Renville.) Rev. Zachary D. Peterson, Assoc. Pst.; Rev. Joseph A. Steinbeisser, Pst.; Rev. George V. Schmit Jr., Assoc. Pst.;

St. Mary School - (Grades PreK-8) 140 S. 10th St., Bird Island, MN 55310-0500 t) 320-365-3693 www.stmarysschoolbirdisland.com Tracy Bertrand Sigurdson, Prin.; Julie Elfering, Librn.; Stds.: 145

CANBY

St. Peter - 307 W. 4th St., Canby, MN 56220-1211 t) 507-223-7304 christthekingafc.com Christ the King Area Faith Community with St. Leo; Lake Benton; Ivanhoe; Tyler; Wilno). Rev. Ronald V. Huberty, Pst.; Rev. Michael M. Doyle, Assoc. Pst.; Rev. Keith R. Salisbury, Assoc. Pst.; CRP Stds.: 119

St. Peter School - (Grades PreK-6) 410 Ring Ave. N., Canby, MN 56220-1237 t) 507-223-7729 lori.rangaard@schoolofstpeter.com www.schoolofstpeter.com Lori Rangaard, Prin.;

CLARA CITY

St. Clara - 414 N. Main St., Clara City, MN 56222-0310; Mailing: 713 12th St SW, Willmar, MN 56201 t) 320-235-0118 afcoffice@ourlivingwater.org www.ourlivingwater.org (Jesus Our Living Water Area Faith Community with Willmar & Spicer). Rev. Steven J. Verhelst, Pst.; Rev. Christian Adike, Assoc. Pst.; CRP Stds.: 36

CLONTARF

St. Malachy - 300 Armagh St. SW, Clontarf, MN 56226; Mailing: 508 13th St. N., Benson, MN 56215 t) 320-842-4271 stisidorethefarmerafc.org (St. Isidore the Farmer Area Faith Community with Benson; Danvers; DeGraff; Murdock & Appleton). Rev. Jeremy G. Kucera, Pst.; CRP Stds.: 6

COMFREY

St. Paul - 209 Field St N, Comfrey, MN 56019; Mailing: PO Box 277, Comfrey, MN 56019-0277 t) 507-877-2361 stpcomfrey@yahoo.com (Divine Mercy Area Faith Community with Morgan, Leavenworth & Sleepy Eye). Rev. Tanner Thooft; Rev. Mark S. Steffl, Pst.; Rev. Samuel F. Perez, Assoc. Pst.; CRP Stds.: 17

COTTONWOOD

St. Mary - 255 W. 4th St. S., Cottonwood, MN 56229-0228; Mailing: P.O. Box 228, Cottonwood, MN 56229-0228 t) 507-423-5220 stmarys.cottonwood@yahoo.com www.holyredeemer.com (Bread of Life Area Faith Community with Marshall). Rev. Anthony J. Stubeda, Pst.; Rev. Dennis C. Labat, Assoc. Pst.; Rev. Andrew J. Michels, Assoc. Pst.; CRP Stds.: 100

DANVERS

Church of the Visitation (Oratory) - 201 County Rd. 14, Danvers, MN 56231; Mailing: 508 13th St. N., Benson, MN 56215 t) 320-842-4271 stisidorethefarmerafc.org (St. Isidore the Farmer Area Faith Community with Benson; Clontarf; De Graff; Murdock & Appleton). Rev. Jeremy G. Kucera, Pst.;

DARWIN

St. John - 106 N. 4th St., Darwin, MN 55324-6016 t) 320-275-2915; 320-693-9496; 320-286-2800 (CRP) dcnjohnhansen@gmail.com; jschmitz@shepherdofsouls.org www.shepherdofsouls.org (Shepherd of Souls Area Faith Community with Forest City; Litchfield; & Manannah). Rev. Jeffrey P. Horejsi, Pst.; Rev. Brian L. Mandel, Assoc. Pst.; Dcn. John A. Hansen, CRE; CRP Stds.: 55

DAWSON

St. James - 1012 Locust St., Dawson, MN 56232; Mailing: 512 Black Oak Ave., Montevideo, MN 56265 t) 320-269-5954 www.holyfamilyarea.org (Holy Family Area Catholic Community with Montevideo; & Granite Falls). Rev. Paul D. Timmerman, Pst.; CRP Stds.: 43

DEGRAFF

St. Bridget - 501 3rd St. S., DeGraff, MN 56271; Mailing: 508 13th St. N., Benson, MN 56215-1228 t) 320-842-4271 www.stisidorethefarmerafc.org (St. Isidore the Farmer Area Faith Community with Benson; Clontarf; Danvers; Murdock & Appleton). Rev. Jeremy G. Kucera, Pst.; CRP Stds.: 6

FAIRFAX

St. Andrew - 15 S.E. First St., Fairfax, MN 55332-0903; Mailing: P.O. Box C, Fairfax, MN 55332-0903 t) 507-426-7739; 507-426-7742 (CRP) allsaints7739@gmail.com www.allsaintsafc.org (All Saints Area Faith Community with Gibbon; & Winthrop). Rev. Bruno Santiago, Pst.; CRP Stds.: 55

GAYLORD

St. Michael - 362 - 5th St, Gaylord, MN 55334; Mailing: P.O. Box 392, Arlington, MN 55307-0392 t) 507-964-5413 stmararl@frontiernet.net corpuschristiafc.org (Corpus Christi Area Faith Community with Arlington; Henderson; & St. John Assumption). Rev. Msgr. Eugene L. Lozinski, Pst.;

GHENT

St. Eloi - 306 W. McQuestion, Ghent, MN 56239-9750; Mailing: 408 N Washington, Minneota, MN 56264 t) 507-428-3285 (Good Teacher Area Faith Community with Minneota). Rev. Todd J. Petersen, Pst.; CRP Stds.: 11

GIBBON

St. Willibrord - 1032 Ash Ave., Gibbon, MN 55335-0436; Mailing: P.O. Box 436, Gibbon, MN 55335-0436 t) 507-426-7739 allsaints7739@gmail.com www.allsaintsafc.org (All Saints Area Faith Community with Fairfax; & Winthrop). Rev. Bruno Santiago, Pst.; CRP Stds.: 45

GLENCOE

St. Pius X - 1014 Knight Ave. N., Glencoe, MN 55336-2300 t) 320-864-5162 businessadmin@stpiusxglencoe.org www.stpiusxglencoe.org (Saint John Paul II Area Faith Community with Silver Lake; & Winsted). Rev. Matthew J. Wiering, Pst.; Rev. John Hayes, Par. Vicar; CRP Stds.: 85

GRACEVILLE

Holy Rosary - 511 Studdart Ave., Graceville, MN 56240-0007; Mailing: 421 Madison Ave, Ortonville, MN 56278-1327 t) 320-748-7313 holygraceville@gmail.com www.spiritoflifeafc.org (Spirit of Life Area Faith Community with Ortonville; Rosen; & Madison). Dcn. Art D. Abel; Rev. Brian W. Oestreich, Pst.; CRP Stds.: 79

GRANITE FALLS

St. Andrew - 1094 Granite St., Granite Falls, MN 56241-1355; Mailing: 512 Black Oak Ave., Montevideo, MN 56265 t) 320-269-5954 www.holyfamilyarea.org (Holy Family Area Faith Community with Montevideo; & Dawson). Rev. Paul D. Timmerman, Pst.; CRP Stds.: 37

GREEN ISLE

St. Brendan - 221 McGrann St. S., Green Isle, MN 55338-0085; Mailing: 34664 Jessenland Rd, Henderson, MN 56044 c) (763) 772-8386 stbrendan@frontiernet.net (Corpus Christi Area Faith Community with Arlington; Gaylord; Henderson; Belle Plaine; & Green Isle). Rev. Msgr. Eugene L. Lozinski, Pst.;

GROVE CITY

Church of Our Lady - 57482 CSAH 3, Grove City, MN 56243-9786 t) 320-693-8900 sknisley@shepherdofsouls.org; jschmitz@shepherdofsouls.org www.shepherdofsouls.org (Shepherd of Souls Area Faith Community with Litchfield; Darwin; & Forest City). Rev. Jeffrey P. Horejsi, Pst.; Rev. Brian L. Mandel, Assoc. Pst.; CRP Stds.: 73

HENDERSON

St. Joseph - 213 S. 6th St., Henderson, MN 56044-0427; Mailing: P.O. Box 427, Henderson, MN 56044-0427 t) 507-248-3550 stjos@frontiernet.net (Corpus Christi Area Faith Community with St. Mary, Arlington; St. Michael, Gaylord; St. John-Assumption; St. Brendan). Rev. Msgr. Eugene L. Lozinski, Pst.; CRP Stds.: 36

St. Thomas (Oratory) - 31624 Scenic Byway Rd, Henderson, MN 56044-0427; Mailing: P.O. Box 427, Henderson, MN 56044 t) 507-248-3550 stjos@frontiernet.net Rev. Msgr. Eugene L. Lozinski, Pst.;

HUTCHINSON

Church of St. Anastasia - 460 Lake St., S.W., Hutchinson, MN 55350-2349 t) 320-587-6507; 320-587-2490 (CRP) religioused@stanastasia.net www.stanastasia.net (Area Faith Community with Stewart). Rev. Paul L. Wolf, Pst.; CRP Stds.: 145

Church of St. Anastasia School - (Grades PreK-6) 400 Lake St., S.W., Hutchinson, MN 55350 principal@stanastasia.net Julie Shelby, Prin.;

IVANHOE

St. John Cantius - 3069 Kowno St., Ivanhoe, MN 56142-0049; Mailing: P.O. Box 49, Ivanhoe, MN 56142-0049 t) 507-694-1402; 507-247-3464 (CRP) (Christ the King Area Faith Community with Ivanhoe; Lake Benton; & Tyler). Rev. Ronald V. Huberty, Pst.; CRP Stds.: 84

SS. Peter & Paul - 111 N. Sherwood St., Ivanhoe, MN 56142; Mailing: P.O. Box 49, Ivanhoe, MN 56142-0049 t) 507-694-1402; 507-247-3464 (CRP) christthekingafc.org (Christ the King Area Faith Community with Lake Benton; Tyler; & Wilno.) Rev. Ronald V. Huberty, Pst.; CRP Stds.: 47

LAFAYETTE

St. Gregory the Great - 440 6th St., Lafayette, MN 56054; Mailing: PO Box 5, Lafayette, MN 56054-0005 t) 507-354-4158 stgregory@holycrossafc.org www.holycrossafc.org (Holy Cross Area Faith Community with Cathedral & St. Mary's, New Ulm; St. John's, Searles; & St. George, West Newton). Rev. Msgr. Douglas L. Grams;

LAKE BENTON

St. Genevieve - 111 S. Sherman St., Lake Benton, MN 56149; Mailing: P.O. Box 310, Tyler, MN 56178 t) 507-247-3464 rhuberty@dnu.org; bev.jerzak@gmail.com www.christthekingafc.com (Christ the King Area Faith Community with Ivanhoe; Tyler; Canby; St. Leo; & Wilno). Rev. Ronald V. Huberty, Pst.; CRP Stds.: 21

LAMBERTON

St. Joseph - 400 W. 2nd Ave., Lamberton, MN 56152-0458; Mailing: P.O. Box 458, Lamberton, MN 56152-0458 t) 507-752-7269; 507-752-2769 (CRP) stjoseph@centurylink.net (Area Faith Community with Sanborn; & Springfield). Rev. Garrett Ahlers, Pst.;

St. Thomas - 301 E. Winona St., Sanborn, MN 56083 t) 507-648-3754

LITCHFIELD

St. Philip - 821 E. 5th St., Litchfield, MN 55355-2223 t) 320-693-3313 stphilip@hutchtel.net www.shepherdofsouls.org (Shepherd of Souls Area Faith Community with Manannah; Forest City; & Darwin). Rev. Jeffrey P. Horejsi, Pst.; Rev. Brian L. Mandel, Assoc. Pst.; CRP Stds.: 180

St. Philip School - (Grades PreK-5) 225 E. 3rd St., Litchfield, MN 55355 t) 320-693-6283 mkramer@thechurchofstphilip.org Michelle Kramer, Prin.;

LUCAN

Our Lady of Victory - ; Mailing: P.O. Box 96, Lucan, MN 56255-0096 t) 507-747-2231; 507-342-5190 (CRP) www.lowafc.org (Light of the World Area Faith Community with Seaforth; Wabasso; & Wanda). Rev. Anthony R. Hesse, Pst.; Sherry Plaetz, DRE;

MADISON

St. Michael - 412 3rd St. W., Madison, MN 56256-1494 t) 320-598-3690 stmichael1891@gmail.com spiritoflifeafc.org (Spirit of Life Area Faith Community with Graceville; Ortonville; & Rosen). Rev. Brian W. Oestreich, Pst.; CRP Stds.: 42

MARSHALL

St. Clotilde - 3272 270th Ave., Marshall, MN 56258 t) 507-531-7970 www.stclotilde.com (Bread of Life Area Faith Community with Cottonwood; & Marshall). Rev. Anthony J. Stubeda, Pst.;

Holy Redeemer - 503 W. Lyon St., Marshall, MN 56258-1311 t) 507-532-5711 lnelson@holy-redeemer.com; beckij@holy-redeemer.com www.holy-redeemer.com (Bread of Life Area Faith Community with Cottonwood; & Green Valley). Rev. Anthony J. Stubeda, Pst.; Rev. Dennis C. Labat, Assoc. Pst.; Rev. Andrew J. Michels, Assoc. Pst.; CRP Stds.: 223

Holy Redeemer School - (Grades PreSchool-8) 501 S. Whitney, Marshall, MN 56258-1995 t) 507-532-6642 ahonetschlager@holy-redeemer.com; sdonner@holy-redeemer.com Ashley Honetschlager, Prin.; Stds.: 243; Lay Tchrs.: 27

MILROY

St. Michael - 200 Euclid Ave., Milroy, MN 56263 t) 507-336-2505 www.ourladyoftheprairie-afc.org (Our Lady of the Prairie Area Faith Community with Tracy; St. Mary; and shares priests with Marshall). Rev. Anthony J. Stubeda, Pst.; Rev. Dennis C. Labat, Assoc. Pst.; Rev. Andrew J. Michels, Par. Vicar; CRP Stds.: 52

MINNEOTA

St. Edward - 408 N Washington, Minneota, MN 56264 t) 507-872-6346 www.goodteacherafc.com (Good Teacher Area Faith Community with Ghent). Rev. Todd J. Petersen, Pst.; CRP Stds.: 126

St. Edward School - (Grades PreK-8) 210 W. 4th St., Minneota, MN 56264 t) 507-872-6391 jgarvey@stedscatholicschool.com stedwardcatholicschool.com Jaci Garvy, Prin.; Stds.: 51; Lay Tchrs.: 6

MONTEVIDEO

St. Joseph - 512 Black Oak Ave., Montevideo, MN 56265-1874 t) 320-269-5954 www.holyfamilyarea.org (Holy Family Area Faith Community with Granite Falls; & Dawson). Rev. Paul D. Timmerman, Pst.; CRP Stds.: 63

MORGAN

St. Michael - 510 W. 3rd St., Morgan, MN 56266; Mailing: P.O. Box 459, Morgan, MN 56266-0459 t) 507-249-3192 churchofstmichaelmorgan@gmail.com www.divinemercyafc.org (Divine Mercy Area Faith Community with Clements; Comfrey; Leavenworth; & Sleepy Eye.) Rev. Mark S. Steffl, Pst.; Rev. Samuel F. Perez, Assoc. Pst.; CRP Stds.: 48

MURDOCK

Church of the Sacred Heart - 201 Orleans, Murdock, MN 56271; Mailing: PO Box 9, Murdock, MN 56271 t) 320-875-2451; 320-842-4271 sacredheart@stisidorethefarmerafc.org www.stisidorethefarmerafc.org (St. Isidore the Farmer Area Faith Community with Benson; Clontarf; Danvers; De Graff; & Appleton). Rev. Jeremy G. Kucera, Pst.;

CRP Stds.: 45

NEW ULM

Cathedral of the Holy Trinity - 605 N. State St., New Ulm, MN 56073-1898 t) 507-354-4158 cathedral@holycrossafc.org www.holycrossafc.org (Holy Cross Area Faith Community with St. George, West Newton; St. John the Baptist, Searles; & St. Mary's, New Ulm). Rev. Msgr. Douglas L. Grams, Rector; Rev. Joshua Bot, Par. Vicar; Rev. Nathan Hansen, Par. Vicar; Rev. Gerald Stanley Meidl, Par. Vicar; Dcn. Richard J. Christiansen; CRP Stds.: 137

St. George - 63105 Fort Rd., New Ulm, MN 56073; Mailing: 63128 388th Ln., New Ulm, MN 56073 t) 507-276-5461 stgeorge@holycrossafc.org www.holycrossafc.org/church-of-st-george (Holy Cross Area Faith Community with Cathedral & St. Mary's, New Ulm; & Searles). Rev. Msgr. Douglas L. Grams, Pst.; Rev. Gerald Meidl, Par. Vicar; Rev. Joshua Bot, Par. Vicar; Rev. Nathan Hansen, Par. Vicar; CRP Stds.: 21

St. John the Baptist - 18241 First Ave., New Ulm, MN 56073-5171 t) 507-359-4244 stjohn@holycrossafc.org holycrossafc.org (Holy Cross Area Faith Community with Cathedral & St. Mary's, New Ulm; Lafayette; & West Newton). Rev. Msgr. Douglas L. Grams, Pst.; Rev. Joshua Bot, Assoc. Pst.; Rev. Gerald Meidl, Assoc. Pst.; Rev. Nathan Hansen, Assoc. Pst.; CRP Stds.: 11

St. Mary - 417 S. Minnesota St., New Ulm, MN 56073-2120 t) 507-233-9500 stmary@holycrossafc.org; faithformation@holycrossafc.org www.holycrossafc.org/church-of-st-mary.html (Holy Cross Area Faith Community with Cathedral of Holy Trinity, New Ulm; St. John the Baptist, Searles and St. George, West Newton Township) Rev. Msgr. Douglas L. Grams, Pst.; Rev. Nathan Hansen, Par. Vicar; Rev. Gerald Meidl, Par. Vicar; Rev. Joshua Bot, Par. Vicar; CRP Stds.: 168

NICOLLET

St. Paul - 410 5th St., Nicollet, MN 56074-0248; Mailing: P.O. Box 248, Nicollet, MN 56074-0248 t) 507-232-3857 stpaulccnicollet@gmail.com (Apostles Peter & Paul Area Faith Community with St. Peter). Rev. Craig A. Timmerman, Pst.;

NORTH MANKATO

Holy Rosary - 525 Grant Ave., North Mankato, MN 56003-2939 t) 507-387-6501 hros2@hickorytech.net www.holyrosarynorthmankato.com Rev. Paul H. van de Crommert, Pst.; CRP Stds.: 229

OLIVIA

St. Aloysius - 302 S. 10th St., Olivia, MN 56277-1288 t) 320-523-2030 staloysius@heartofjesusafc.org www.heartofjesusafc.org (Heart of Jesus Area Faith Community with Renville; Hector; & Bird Island). Rev. Zachary D. Peterson, Assoc. Pst.; Rev. Joseph A. Steinbeisser, Pst.; Rev. George V. Schmit Jr., Assoc. Pst.; CRP Stds.: 91

ORTONVILLE

St. John - 421 Madison Ave., Ortonville, MN 56278-2713 t) 320-839-2772 www.spiritoflifeafc.org (Spirit of Life Area Faith Community with Madison; Rosen; & Graceville). Rev. Brian W. Oestreich, Pst.; Dcn. Paul W. Treinen; CRP Stds.: 57

REDWOOD FALLS

St. Catherine - 900 E. Flynn St., Redwood Falls, MN 56283-0383; Mailing: P.O. Box 383, Redwood Falls, MN 56283-0383 t) 507-644-2278 kris@mystcatherines.org www.mystcatherines.org (Area Faith Community with St. Anne, Wabasso). Rev. Anthony R. Hesse, Pst.; Rev. Cornelius Ezeiloaku; CRP Stds.: 187

RENVILLE

Holy Redeemer - 106 3rd St., S.E., Renville, MN 56284; Mailing: 302 S. 10th St., Olivia, MN 56277 t) 320-523-2030 staloysius@heartofjesusafc.org; holyredeemer@heartofjesusafc.org www.heartofjesusafc.org (Heart of Jesus Area Faith Community with Olivia; Bird Island; & Hector). Rev. Zachary D. Peterson, Assoc. Pst.; Rev. Joseph A. Steinbeisser, Pst.; Rev. George V. Schmit Jr., Assoc. Pst.; CRP Stds.: 69

SANBORN

St. Thomas (Oratory) - 301 E. Winona St., Sanborn, MN 56083-0176; Mailing: P.O. Box 176, Sanborn, MN 56083-0176 t) 507-752-7269 stjoseph@centurylink.net (Vine and Branches Area Faith Community with Springfield; & Lamberton). Rev. Garrett Ahlers, Pst.;

SILVER LAKE

Church of the Holy Family - 720 Main St. W., Silver Lake, MN 55381-0326; Mailing: 700 Main St. W., Silver Lake, MN 55381 t) 320-327-2356; 320-327-2931 (CRP) businessadmin@stpiusxglencoe.org www.holyfamilysilverlake.org (St. John Paul II Area Faith Community with Glencoe; & Winsted). Rev. Matthew J. Wiering, Pst.; Rev. John Hayes, Par. Vicar; CRP Stds.: 70

SLEEPY EYE

Church of the Japanese Martyrs - 30881 County Rd. 24, Sleepy Eye, MN 56085-4361 t) 507-794-6974 jmartyrs@sleepyeyetel.net (Divine Mercy Area Faith Community with Comfrey; Morgan; & Sleepy Eye). Rev. Mark S. Steffl, Pst.;

St. Mary - 636 First Ave. N., Sleepy Eye, MN 56085-1004 t) 507-794-4171; 507-794-4121 (CRP) saintmaryse@sleepyeyetel.net www.divinemercyafc.org (Divine Mercy Area Faith Community with Comfrey; Leavenworth; & Morgan). Rev. Mark S. Steffl, Pst.; Rev. Samuel F. Perez, Assoc. Pst.; Rev. Tanner Thooft, Assoc. Pst.; Dcn. Mark D. Kober; Dcn. Mike McKeown; CRP Stds.: 61

St. Mary High School - (Grades 7-12) 104 St. Mary's St., N.W., Sleepy Eye, MN 56085 www.sesmschool.com Peter Roufs, Prin.;

St. Mary Elementary School - 104 St. Mary's St NW, Sleepy Eye, MN 56085 t) 507-794-6141 www.sesmschool.com Mary Gangelhoff, Prin.;

SPICER

Our Lady of the Lakes - 6680-153rd Ave., N.E., Spicer, MN 56288-9659 t) 320-796-5664 afcoffice@ourlivingwater.org www.ourlivingwater.org (Jesus Our Living Water Area Faith Community with Willmar; & Clara City). Rev. Steven J. Verhelst, Pst.; Rev. Christian Adike, Assoc. Pst.; CRP Stds.: 127

SPRINGFIELD

St. Raphael - 112 W. Van Dusen St., Springfield, MN 56087-1396; Mailing: 20 W Van Dusen St, Springfield, MN 56087 t) 507-723-4137 straphael@newulmtel.net www.vineandbranchesafc.org (Vine & Branches Area Faith Community with Lamberton; & Sanborn). Rev. Garrett Ahlers, Pst.; CRP Stds.: 120

St. Raphael School - (Grades PreK-6) 20 W. Van Dusen St., Springfield, MN 56087 t) 507-723-4135 straysschooloffice@newulmtel.net; straysprincipal@newulmtel.net vineandbranchesafc.org Jennifer Fischer, Prin.;

ST. LEO

St. Leo - 202 W. Church St., St. Leo, MN 56264; Mailing: 307 4th St. W., Canby, MN 56220 t) 507-223-7304 (Christ the King Area Faith Community with Canby; Ivanhoe; Wilno; Tyler & Lake Benton) Rev. Ronald V. Huberty, Pst.; Rev. Michael M. Doyle, Assoc. Pst.; Rev. Keith R. Salisbury, Assoc. Pst.; CRP Stds.: 6

ST. PETER

Church of St. Peter - 1801 W. Broadway, St. Peter, MN 56082 t) 507-931-1628 office@churchofstpeter.org www.churchofstpeter.org (Apostles Peter & Paul Area Faith Community with Nicollet). Rev. Craig A. Timmerman, Pst.; CRP Stds.: 189

John Ireland School - (Grades K-6) t) 507-931-2810 colleen.wenner@johnirelandschool.org

STEWART

Church of St. Boniface - 551 Main St., Stewart, MN 55385-0202; Mailing: P.O. Box 202, Stewart, MN 55385-0202 t) 320-562-2344; 320-833-6020 (CRP) mmaiers84@gmail.com (Area Faith Community with Hutchinson). Rev. Paul L. Wolf, Pst.; CRP Stds.: 37

TRACY

St. Mary - 249 6th St., Tracy, MN 56175-1114 t) 507-629-4075 www.ourladyoftheprairie-afc.org (Our Lady of the Prairie Area Faith Community with Walnut Grove; & Milroy). Rev. Shawn Polman, Assoc. Pst.; Rev. Anthony J. Stubeda, Pst.; Rev. Dennis C. Labat, Assoc. Pst.; Rev. Andrew J. Michels, Assoc. Pst.; CRP Stds.: 59

St. Mary School - (Grades PreK-6) 225 6th. St., Tracy, MN 56175 t) 507-629-3270 lisa.dieter.sms@gmail.com stmarysschooltracy.org Lisa Dieter, Prin.; Stds.: 66; Lay Tchrs.: 5

TYLER

St. Dionysius - 213 Linwood St, Tyler, MN 56178-0310; Mailing: P.O. Box 310, Tyler, MN 56178-0310 t) 507-247-3464 bev.jerzak@gmail.com christthekingafc.com (Christ the King Area Faith Community with Ivanhoe; Lake Benton; & Wilno). Rev. Ronald V. Huberty, Pst.; CRP Stds.: 53

WABASSO

St. Anne - 1052 Cedar St., Wabasso, MN 56293-0239; Mailing: P.O. Box 239, Wabasso, MN 56293-0239 t) 507-342-5190 lowafc.org (Light of the World Area Faith Community with Lucan; Wanda; & Seaforth). Rev. Anthony R. Hesse, Pst.; Rev. Cornelius Ezeiloaku; CRP Stds.: 45

St. Anne School - (Grades PreSchool-6) 1054 Cedar St., Wabasso, MN 56293-0239 t) 507-342-5389 stannesschool@wabassostanneschool.com wabassostannesschool.com Mary Franta, Prin.;

St. Mary - ; Mailing: P.O. Box 239, Wabasso, MN 56293-0239 t) 507-342-5190 lowafc.org (Light of the World Area Faith Community with Wabasso; Lucan; & Wanda). Rev. Anthony R. Hesse, Pst.;

St. Mathias - ; Mailing: P.O. Box 239, Wabasso, MN 56293-0239 t) 507-342-5190 lowafc.org (Light of the World Area Faith Community with Seaforth; Lucan; & Wabasso). Rev. Anthony R. Hesse, Pst.;

WATKINS

Church of St. Anthony - 201 Central Ave. S., Watkins, MN 55389-0409; Mailing: P.O. Box 409, Watkins, MN 55389-0409 t) 320-764-2755 stanthony@meltel.net www.stanthonywatkins.com Rev. Aaron Nett, Pst.; CRP Stds.: 132

WILLMAR

St. Mary - 713 12th St., S.W., Willmar, MN 56201-3099 t) 320-235-0118 afcoffice@ourlivingwater.org www.ourlivingwater.org (Jesus Our Living Water Area Faith Community with Spicer; and Clara City). Rev. Steven J. Verhelst, Pst.; Rev. Christian Adike, Assoc. Pst.; CRP Stds.: 257

WINSTED

Holy Trinity - 111 Winsted Ave. W., Winsted, MN 55395-0009; Mailing: P.O. Box 9, Winsted, MN 55395-0009 t) 320-485-5651; 320-485-2182 x5633 (CRP) htparish@htwinsted.org; lpenas@htwinsted.org www.winstedholytrinity.org (Blessed John Paul II Area Faith Community with Glencoe; & Silver Lake). Rev. Matthew J. Wiering, Pst.; Rev. John Hayes, Assoc. Pst.; CRP Stds.: 89

Holy Trinity School - (Grades PreSchool-12) 110 Winsted Ave., Winsted, MN 55395-0038; Mailing: P.O. Box 38, Winsted, MN 55395-0038 info@winstedholytrinity.org Anthony Biese, Prin.;

WINTHROP

St. Francis de Sales - 510 N. Brown St., Winthrop, MN 55396-0447; Mailing: P.O. Box 447, Winthrop, MN 55396-0447 t) 507-426-7739 allsaints7739@gmail.com www.allsaintsafc.org (All Saints Area Faith Community with Fairfax; & Gibbon). Rev. Bruno Santiago, Pst.; CRP Stds.: 27

SCHOOLS: PRESCHOOL THRU HIGH SCHOOL

SCHOOLS

STATE OF MINNESOTA

NEW ULM

New Ulm Area Catholic Schools - (PAR) (Grades PreSchool-12) 514 N. Washington St., New Ulm, MN 56073-1897 t) 507-354-2719 www.nuacs.com Rev. Msgr. Douglas L. Grams, Bd. Delegate & Canonical Admin.; Stds.: 410; Sr. Tchrs.: 1; Lay Tchrs.: 28

St. Anthony Elementary School - (Grades PreSchool-12) 514 N. Washington St., New Ulm, MN 56073-1897 t) 507-354-2928 karen.schulte@nuacs.com Stds.: 229; Sr. Tchrs.: 1; Lay Tchrs.: 14

Cathedral High School - (Grades PreSchool-12) 600 N. Washington St., New Ulm, MN 56073-1897 t) 507-354-4511 sjulie.brandt@nuacs.com; erica.devries@nuacs.com Stds.: 181; Lay Tchrs.: 14

INSTITUTIONS LOCATED IN DIOCESE

HOSPITALS / HEALTH SERVICES [HOS]

GRACEVILLE

Graceville Health Center - 115 W. 2nd St., Graceville, MN 56240-0157; Mailing: P.O. Box 157, Graceville, MN 56240-0157 t) 320-748-8203 julie.rosenberg@essentiahealth.org

Graceville Health Center - 101 S. Main St., Chokio, MN 56221 t) 320-324-7500 kevin.gish@essentiahealth.org

MARSHALL

***Avera Marshall** - 300 S. Bruce St., Marshall, MN 56258-1934 t) 507-532-9661 debbie.streier@avera.org www.avera.org Sponsored by the Sisters of the Presentation of the BVM of Aberdeen, South Dakota, and the Benedictine Sisters of Sacred Heart Monastery, Yankton, SD. Debbie Streier, Pres.; Bed Capacity: 111; Asstd. Annu.: 196,717; Staff: 511

MISCELLANEOUS [MIS]

EAGAN

Friends of San Lucas - 3459 Washington Dr., Suite 207, Eagan, MN 55122 c) 651-508-1848; 651-208-1693 bill.peterson@sanlucasmission.org www.sanlucasmission.org Bill Peterson, Dir.;

GHENT

Sisters of Maria Stella Matutina - 318 W. McQuestion St., Ghent, MN 56239 t) 507-428-3919 www.mariastellamatutina.org Sr. Aude Renard, Prioress; Sr. Mary Thomas Leary, Prov.;

IVANHOE

Divine Providence Apartments - 312 E. George St., Ivanhoe, MN 56142 t) 507-694-1414 allen.anderson@avera.org Margaret Schmidt, Admin.;

NEW ULM

Handmaids of the Heart of Jesus (ACJ) - 515 N. State St., New Ulm, MN 56073 t) 507-276-9128 www.handmaidsoftheheartofjesus.com Mother Mary Clare Roufs, Supr.;

NURSING / REHABILITATION / CONVALESCENCE / ELDERLY CARE [NUR]

GRACEVILLE

Graceville Health Center - 116 W. 2nd St., Graceville, MN 56240; Mailing: P.O. Box 638, Graceville, MN 56240 t) 320-748-7261 julie.rosenberg@essentiahealth.org

SLEEPY EYE

Divine Providence Community Home & Lake Villa Maria Senior Apts (Daughters of St. Mary of Providence) - 700 3rd Ave., N.W., Sleepy Eye, MN 56085-1099 t) 507-794-3011; 507-794-5333 (Lake Villa) jgroebner@dpch.net divineprovidencehome.org Sr. Sharon Williams, Supr.; Jayna Groebner, Admin.; Asstd. Annu.: 92; Staff: 79

ST. PETER

Benedictine Living Community - St. Peter - 1907 Klein St., St. Peter, MN 56082 t) 507-934-8273 teresa.hildebrandt@benedictineliving.org www.benedictineliving.org/st-peter-mn/ Teresa Hildebrandt, Exec. Dir.; Asstd. Annu.: 400; Staff: 91

Benedictine Senior Living Community of St. Peter - 1906 N. Sunrise Dr., St. Peter, MN 56082 t) 507-934-8817 www.benedictineliving.org/st-peter-mn/ dba Benedictine Heritage Meadows Teresa Hildebrandt, Exec. Dir.; Asstd. Annu.: 66; Staff: 12

RETREAT HOUSES / RENEWAL CENTERS [RTR]

SLEEPY EYE

Schoenstatt Sisters of Mary (Secular Institute) - 27762 County Rd. 27, Sleepy Eye, MN 56085-9801 t) 507-794-7727 schoenstattonthelake@schsrsmary.org schoenstattmn.com/ Sr. Marcia Vinje, Supr.; Sr. Marie Day, Movement Coordinator;

An asterisk (*) denotes an organization that has established tax-exempt status directly with the IRS and is not covered by the USCCB Group Ruling.

Archdiocese of New York

(Archidioecesis Neo-Eboracensis)

HIS EMINENCE TIMOTHY MICHAEL CARDINAL DOLAN, D.D., PH.D.

Archbishop of New York; ordained June 19, 1976; appointed Auxiliary Bishop of St. Louis June 19, 2001; received Episcopal consecration August 15, 2001; appointed Archbishop of Milwaukee June 25, 2002; installed as Tenth Archbishop August 28, 2002; appointed Archbishop of New York February 23, 2009; installed April 15, 2009; elevated to College of Cardinals February 18, 2012. Office: 1011 First Ave., New York, NY 10022.

Catholic Center: 1011 First Ave., New York, NY 10022. T: 212-371-1000; F: 212-813-9538.
www.archny.org

SEE ERECTED APRIL 8, 1808.

Square Miles 4,683.

Created an Archdiocese July 19, 1850.

Comprises the Boroughs of Bronx, Manhattan and Richmond of the City of New York, and the Counties of Dutchess, Orange, Putnam, Rockland, Sullivan, Ulster and Westchester in the State of New York.

Legal Title: Archdiocese of New York.

MOST REVEREND PETER J. BYRNE, D.D.
Auxiliary Bishop of New York; ordained December 1, 1984; appointed Titular Bishop of Cluain Iraird and Auxiliary Bishop of New York June 14, 2014; received Episcopal consecration August 4, 2014. Res: Church of the Blessed Sacrament, 30 Manor Rd., Staten Island, NY 10310.

MOST REVEREND GERARDO J. COLACICCO, D.D., S.T.L.
Auxiliary Bishop of New York; ordained November 6, 1982; appointed Titular Bishop of Erdonia and Auxiliary Bishop of New York October 10, 2019; received Episcopal consecration December 10, 2019. Res: Church of St. Mary, 11 Clinton St., Wappingers Falls, NY 12590.

MOST REVEREND EDMUND J. WHALEN, D.D., S.T.D.
Auxiliary Bishop of New York; ordained June 23, 1984; appointed Titular Bishop of Cemerinianus and Auxiliary Bishop of New York October 10, 2019; received Episcopal consecration December 10, 2019. Office: 1011 First Avenue, New York, NY 10022.

MOST REVEREND JOHN S. BONNICI, D.D., S.T.D.
Auxiliary Bishop of New York; ordained June 22, 1991; appointed Titular Bishop of Arindela and Auxiliary Bishop of New York January 25, 2022; received Episcopal consecration March 1, 2022. Res: Sts. John and Paul; 280 Weaver St., Larchmont, NY 10538.

THE MOST REVEREND JOSEPH A. ESPAILLAT, D.D.
Auxiliary Bishop of New York; ordained on May 17, 2003; appointed Titular Bishop of Tagarbala and Auxiliary Bishop of New York on January 25, 2022; received Episcopal consecration March 1, 2022. Res: Church of St. Anthony of Padua; 832 East 166th St., Bronx, NY 10459.

STATISTICAL OVERVIEW

Personnel

Cardinals	1
Auxiliary Bishops	5
Retired Bishops	5
Priests: Diocesan Active in Diocese	330
Priests: Diocesan Active Outside Diocese	9
Priests: Retired, Sick or Absent	160
Number of Diocesan Priests	499
Religious Priests in Diocese	624
Total Priests in your Diocese	1,123
Extern Priests in Diocese	163
Ordinations:	
Religious Priests	9
Transitional Deacons	3
Permanent Deacons	10
Permanent Deacons in Diocese	310
Total Brothers	129
Total Sisters	1,696

Parishes

Parishes	282
With Resident Pastor:	
Resident Diocesan Priests	224
Resident Religious Priests	58
Missions	32
Closed Parishes	1
Professional Ministry Personnel:	
Brothers	43
Sisters	516
Lay Ministers	330

Welfare

Catholic Hospitals	6
Total Assisted	35,300
Health Care Centers	7
Total Assisted	6,800
Homes for the Aged	11
Total Assisted	10,000
Residential Care of Children	32
Total Assisted	957
Day Care Centers	346
Total Assisted	4,307
Specialized Homes	29
Total Assisted	1,136
Special Centers for Social Services	101
Total Assisted	325,919
Residential Care of Disabled	111
Total Assisted	2,451
Other Institutions	2,134
Total Assisted	20,592

Educational

Seminaries, Diocesan	1
Students from This Diocese	14
Students from Other Dioceses	33
Diocesan Students in Other Seminaries	10
Seminaries, Religious	6
Students, Religious	18
Total Seminarians	42
Colleges and Universities	9
Total Students	41,498
High Schools, Diocesan and Parish	8
Total Students	2,738
High Schools, Private	35
Total Students	18,088
Elementary Schools, Diocesan and Parish	105
Total Students	29,394
Elementary Schools, Private	14
Total Students	3,238
Non-residential Schools for the Disabled	1
Total Students	49
Catechesis / Religious Education:	
High School Students	3,770
Elementary Students	62,935
Total Students under Catholic Instruction	161,752
Teachers in Diocese:	
Priests	8
Brothers	9
Sisters	19
Lay Teachers	3,109

Vital Statistics

Receptions into the Church:	
Infant Baptism Totals	13,069
Minor Baptism Totals	1,144
Adult Baptism Totals	493
Received into Full Communion	906
First Communions	10,888
Confirmations	11,555
Marriages:	
Catholic	2,345
Interfaith	331
Total Marriages	2,676
Deaths	11,118
Total Catholic Population	3,194,596
Total Population	7,961,862

LEADERSHIP

Archbishop of New York - His Eminence Timothy M. Dolan;
Secretary to the Archbishop - Rev. Stephen Ries;
Vicar General and Moderator of the Curia - Rev. Msgr. Joseph P. LaMorte;
Auxiliary Bishops - Rev. John S. Bonnici; Most Rev. Peter J. Byrne; Most Rev. Gerardo J. Colacicco;
Bishops Emeriti - Most Rev. Gerald T. Walsh; Most Rev. John J. Jenik; Most Rev. Dominick J. Lagonegro;
Deans -
Bronx East - t) 718-792-5500 Rev. Msgr. John K. Graham, Dean;
Bronx West - t) (718) 295-3770 Very Rev. Jose Felix Ortega de la Fuente, Dean;
Dutchess and Putnam - t) 845-635-1700 Very Rev. Joseph M. McLafferty, Dean;
Manhattan North - t) 212-568-0091 Very Rev. Peter Mushi, A.J., Dean;
Manhattan South - t) 212-254-0200 Rev. Msgr. Kevin J. Nelan, Dean;
Orange County - t) 845-343-6013 Very Rev. Dennis A. Nikolic, Dean;
Rockland County - t) 845-735-7405 Rev. Msgr. Emmet R. Nevin, Dean;
Staten Island - t) 718-442-5412 Rev. Msgr. William J. Belford, Dean;
Sullivan County - t) 845-439-5625 Very Rev. Edward Bader, Dean;
Ulster County - t) 845-338-1554 Rev. Msgr. Desmond O'Connor, Dean;
Westchester North - t) 914-962-5050 Rev. Msgr. Joseph R. Giandurco, Dean;
Westchester South - t) 914-967-0142 Rev. Msgr. Donald M. Dwyer, Dean;
Chancellor - John P. Cahill;
Vice-Chancellors - Rev. Msgr. Douglas J. Mathers; Rev. Stephen Ries; Eileen Mulcahy;
Vicar for Clergy - Most Rev. Edmund J. Whalen;
Vicar for Religious - Sr. Joan Curtin, C.N.D.;
Chief Financial Officer - William E. Whiston;
Chief Administrative Officer - Frank Napolitano;
Deputy Chief Financial Officer - Aniello Forcellati;
Canon 1742 Panel of Pastors - Rev. Msgr. Francis J. McAree; Rev. Msgr. Joseph R. Giandurco; Rev. Msgr. John K. Graham;
College of Consultors - Rev. Msgr. Joseph P. LaMorte; Most Rev. Peter J. Byrne; Most Rev. Gerardo J. Colacicco;
Metropolitan Tribunal - t) 646-794-3200 tribunal@archny.org
Judicial Vicar - Rev. Msgr. Robert Hospodar;
Associate Judicial Vicar - Rev. Anthony O. Omenihu;
Judges - Rev. Msgr. Robert Hospodar; Rev. Nicholas E. Callaghan; Rev. Anthony O. Omenihu;
Defenders of the Bond - Rev. Michael T. Martine; Rev. Jayaraj Putti;
Promoter of Justice - Rev. Michael T. Martine;
Auditors - Rev. Jayaraj Putti; Maria Belardo; Ingrid Pena;
Moderator of the Tribunal Chancery - Jane Ann Sargia;
Office Finance Administrator - Catherine Campisi;
Advocates - Kimberly Baez; Maria Belardo; Ingrid Pena;
Notaries - Gabriela Arechiga; Kayla Beiter; Angela Epps;
Censors Librorum - Rev. Matthew S. Ernest; Rev. Peter Andrew Heasley; Rev. Richard G. Smith;
Archbishop's Delegate for Healthcare - Dr. Walid Michelen;

OFFICES AND DIRECTORS

Adult Faith Formation - Elizabeth Guevara de Gonzalez, Dir.;
Archbishopric of New York -
ArchCare - Francis J. Serbaroli, Chair; Scott LaRue, Pres.;
Archives - Kate Feighery, Dir.; John Joseph Jackson, Records, Mgr.; Caitlin Monaco, Asst. Archivist;
Benefits Office - Mary Collins, Assoc. Dir.;
Black Ministry, Office of - Bro. Tyrone Davis, C.F.C., Dir.;
Building Commission - t) 914-476-1058 Ron Angelo;
Consultant - Jane Schwedfeger;
Catholic Charities - Rev. Msgr. Kevin L. Sullivan, Exec.; Rev. Eric Cruz, Regl. Coord. CC Bronx Svcs.;
Catholic Health Care Foundation of the Archdiocese of New York, Inc. - t) 646-633-4700 Scott LaRue, Chair;
Catholic High School Association - t) 646-794-2707 Frank Napolitano, Treas.;
Cemeteries - t) 212-753-4883 Mary Ellen Gerrity, Dir.;
Central Services - t) 212-371-1000
Communications Office - t) 646-794-2997 Joseph Zwilling, Dir.;
Data Systems Center and Telecommunication Office - Andrew J. Donnelly, Dir.;
Development Office - t) 646-794-3300 Susan George, Chief Advancement & Stewardship Officer;
Alfred E. Smith Memorial Foundation - t) (646) 794-2294 Kathleen McGowan, Exec. Dir.;
Parish Development - t) 646-794-2104 Kelvin Gentles, Exec. Dir.;
Cardinal's Appeal - t) (646) 794-3234 Justine Carroll, Dir.;
Ecclesiastical Assistance Corporation - t) 212-371-1000
Ecclesiastical Communications Corp. - t) 212-371-1000
Ecclesiastical Maintenance Services, Inc. -
Ecclesiastical Properties Corporation - t) 212-371-1011 x2069 Nicholas Canepa;
Education, Department of - t) 212-371-1000 x2802
Educational Services of the Archdiocese of New York, Inc. -
Family Life - t) (646) 794-3186 Theodore Musco, Dir.;
Hispanic Charismatic Catholic Center - Most Rev. Joseph Espaillat II, Dir.; Juan De La Rosa, Dir.;
Hispanic Ministry, Office of - t) 212-371-1000 x2994 Most Rev. Peter J. Byrne; Most Rev. Joseph Espaillat II; Wanda F. Vasquez, Dir.;
Hospital Apostolate, Office of the - John Schultz, Dir.;
Human Resources - Ella O'Sullivan, Exec. Dir.;
Information, Bureau of and Radio-T.V. Communications -
Inner City Scholarship Fund, Inc. - t) 212-753-8583 Jill Lloyd, Exec. Dir.;
Institutional Commodity Services Corporation - t) 646-794-2735 Theresa Cullen-Seidel, Exec. Dir.;
Inter-Parish Finance, Commission for - t) 212-371-1000 Rev. Joy Mampill, Chair;
Internal Audit, Office of - Luana Darson, Dir.;
Italian Apostolate, Office of the - Rev. Msgr. Thomas P. Sandi;
Justice and Peace, Archdiocesan Office of - George Horton, Dir.;
Legal Affairs, Office of - Roderick J. Cassidy, General Counsel;
Office of Ecumenical and Interreligious Activities - Rev. Brian E. McWeeney;
Office of Liturgy - t) 914-968-6200 Rev. Matthew S. Ernest;
Parish Assistance Corporation - t) 646-794-3381 Rev. Msgr. Joseph P. LaMorte, Pres.; Denise Magyer, Dir.;
Parish Planning, Office of - Eileen Mulcahy, Dir.;
Partnership for Quality Education - t) (646) 794-3322 Margaret Ukrop, Senior Mgr., Donor Rels. & School Prog.;
Partnership Schools - t) 646-794-3338 Jill Kafka, Exec.;
Pension Office - t) 212-371-1000 x3062 Dorene Conlon, Dir.;
Permanent Diaconate Office - t) 914-367-8269 Dcn. Jaime A. Bello, Dir.; Dcn. Francis B. Orlando, Dir.;
Presbyteral Council of the Archdiocese of New York - His Eminence Timothy M. Dolan, Pres.; Rev. Arthur Mastrolia, Chair; Marc Villancourt, Vice Chm.;
Priest Personnel Board - Most Rev. Edmund J. Whalen;
Priest Personnel, Office of - t) 212-371-1000 x2930 Most Rev. Edmund J. Whalen, Dir.;
Adjunct and International Clergy Office - t) 914-968-6200 x8122 Theresa Jenson, Admin. Asst.;
Priest Retiree Affairs - t) 914-968-1252 Mary B. Lynch;
Priest Wellness Office - t) 914-367-8245 Dcn. Steven DeMartino, Dir.;
Prison Apostolate - t) 212-371-1000 x3065 Rev. Msgr. Marc J. Filacchione, Dir.;
Respect Life - t) 646-689-2613; 646-476-0931 Sr. Virginia Joy, S.V., Dir.;
Risk Management and Insurance Services - Louise Zacher, Dir.;
Safe Environment Office - t) 646-794-2807 Edward Mechmann, Dir.;
Schools, Superintendent of - Michael Deegan;
The Good News Room - t) (646) 794-3536 Rachel Sheehan, Dir.;
Trustees of St. Patrick's Cathedral in the City of New York, Inc. - Rev. Msgr. Dennis P. Keane, Exec. Dir.;
Victim Assistance Coordinator - t) 646-794-2949 victimsassistance@archny.org Eileen Mulcahy, Dir.;
Vocations, Archdiocesan Office for - t) 914-968-1340 Rev. George Sears, Dir.;
Young Adult Outreach - t) 646-794-3159 Colin Nykaza, Dir.;
Youth Faith Formation - t) 212-371-1000 x2821 Ela Milewska, Exec.;
Youth Ministry, Office of - t) 646-794-2853

PARISHES, MISSIONS, AND CLERGY

STATE OF NEW YORK

AMENIA

Parish of Immaculate Conception and St. Anthony - 4 Lavelle Rd., Amenia, NY 12501; Mailing: Box 109, Amenia, NY 12501 t) 845-373-8193 icspamen@optonline.net Rev. Robert K. Wilson, Pst.; Dcn. David Weinstein;

ARDSLEY

Our Lady of Perpetual Help - 535 Ashford Ave., Ardsley, NY 10502; Mailing: 616 Warburton Ave., Hastings on Hudson, NY 10706 t) 914-478-2822 office@stmolph.com www.stmolph.com Administered from Parish of St. Matthew and Our Lady of Perpetual Help, 616 Warburton Ave., Hastings-on-Hudson. Rev. Robert P. Henry, Pst.;

ARMONK

St. Patrick - 29 Cox Ave., Armonk, NY 10504; Mailing: P.O. Box 6, Armonk, NY 10504 t) 914-273-8226 (CRP); 914-273-9724 reled@stpatrickinarmonk.org; churchofstpat@optonline.net Rev. Thadeus Aravindathu, Pst.; Allanna Hasselgren, DRE;

BEACON

St. Joachim - St. John the Evangelist - 2 Oak St., Beacon, NY 12508 t) 845-831-6550 (CRP); 845-838-0915 parish@stjoachim-stjohn.org www.stjoachimstjohn.org Rev. Richard G. Smith, Pst.; Rev. Innocent Nwachukwu (Nigeria), Par. Vicar; Dcn. Oscar Cifuentes; Dcn. Martin Mayeski; Catherine Crocco, Music Min.; Sr. Kathleen Marie, O.S.F., Pst. Assoc.; Albert Griffith, DRE;

BEDFORD

St. Patrick - 7 Pound Ridge Rd., Bedford, NY 10506; Mailing: Box 303, Bedford, NY 10506 t) 914-234-3775 patrick485@optonline.net stpatricksbedford.org/ Rev. Msgr. John T. Ferry, Pst.; Rev. Joseph Domfeh-Boateng (Ghana), Assoc. Pst.; Donna Marino, DRE; Karen Schmidt, DRE;

BLAUVELT

St. Catharine - 523 Western Hwy., Blauvelt, NY 10913 t) 845-359-0542; 845-359-4014 saintcatharineschurch@gmail.com; stcatharineprep1@gmail.com www.saintcatharines.org

Rev. Msgr. Francis J. McAree, Pst.; Rev. Abraham Vallayil, C.M.I., Assoc. Pst.; Dcn. John Jurasek; Dcn. John C. Kelleher; Bernadette Kowalchuk, DRE; CRP Stds.: 375

BREWSTER

St. Lawrence O'Toole - 31 Prospect St., Brewster, NY 10509 t) 845-279-6098 (CRP); 845-279-2021 stlotoole@comcast.net www.stlawrenceotoole.org Rev. Richard Gill, Pst.; Dcn. Gregory Miller; Dcn. Mark Shkreli; Theresa Scorca, DRE;

BRIARCLIFF MANOR

St. Theresa - 1394 Pleasantville Rd., Briarcliff Manor, NY 10510 t) (914) 941-1646; (914) 941-2582 stchurch@optonline.net Rev. Paul M. Waddell, Pst.; Rev. John T. McLoughlin, Pastor Emer.;

Our Lady of the Wayside - 219 Saw Mill River Rd., Millwood, NY 10546

BRONX

St. Angela Merici - 917 Morris Ave., Bronx, NY 10451 t) 718-293-0984 nagirembabazi@yahoo.com; saintangelamerici@yahoo.com saintangelamericichurch.org (Apostles of Jesus) Rev. Nestorio Agirembabazi, A.J., Pst.; Dcn. Felipe Sin; CRP Stds.: 110

St. Ann - 3519 Bainbridge Ave., Bronx, NY 10467 All records at Parish of St. Brendan and St. Ann, Bronx. Rev. Raul G. Miguez (Cuba), Pst.; Rev. Francis P. Scanlon, Assoc. Pst.; Rev. Misael Bacleon (Philippines), In Res.; Rev. Andrew Ovienloba (Nigeria), In Res.;

Parish of St. Anselm and St. Roch - 685 Tinton Ave., Bronx, NY 10455 t) 718-585-8542 (Augustinian Recollects) Rev. Michael Eguino, Pst.; Rev. Jose Antonio Rodrigalvarez, O.A.R., Assoc. Pst.;

St. Anthony - 1496 Commonwealth Ave., Bronx, NY 10460 t) (718) 931-4040 stanthonybronx.org Rev. Jose A. Serrano, Admin.; CRP Stds.: 92

St. Anthony - 4307 Barnes Ave., Bronx, NY 10466 Records at Parish of St. Frances of Rome, St. Francis of Assisi, St. Anthony, and Our Lady of Grace, 4307 Barnes Ave., Bronx. Rev. Georginus Esiofor Ugwu, M.S.P., Pst.;

St. Anthony of Padua - 832 E. 166th St., Bronx, NY 10459 Most Rev. Joseph Espaillat II, Pst.; Rev. Eduardo Gomez-Rivera, Assoc. Pst.; Rev. Shane Johnson, L.C., Assoc. Pst.; Dcn. Nelson Duran; Dcn. Luis J. Feliz;

St. Athanasius - 878 Tiffany St., Bronx, NY 10459 t) 718-328-2558 stathanasiuschurchbx@gmail.com www.stathanasiusbx.org Rev. Jose Rivas, Pst.; Juan A. Sotomayor Jr., DRE; CRP Stds.: 109

St. Augustine Our Lady of Victory - 1512 Webster Ave., Bronx, NY 10457 t) 718-583-4044 Rev. George R. Stewart, Pst.; Rev. Luke Ibeh, In Res.; Sr. Dorothy Hall, O.P., Pst. Assoc.; Maria Peguero, Pst. Assoc.; W. Giles Naedler, DRE; Lourdes Reyes, DRE;

St. Augustine Chapel - 1168 Franklin Ave., Bronx, NY 10456 t) 718-617-7581

St. Barnabas - 409 E. 241st St., Bronx, NY 10470 t) 718-324-0865 (CRP); 718-324-1478 stbarnabasbronx@aol.com www.stbarnabasbronx.org Very Rev. Brendan A. Fitzgerald, Pst.; Rev. Joseph Zkunaeziri, Assoc. Pst.; Dcn. Salvatore Mazzella; Dcn. Eymard Smith; Rev. John Smart, In Res.;

St. Barnabas High School Chapel -

St. Benedict - 2969 Otis Ave., Bronx, NY 10465-2198 t) 718-829-1200 (CRP); 718-828-3403 Rev. Nikolin Pergjini, Pst.; Rev. Christian Amah, Par. Vicar;

Blessed Sacrament - 1170 Beach Ave., Bronx, NY 10472 t) (718) 892-3214 blessedsacramentbx.org Administered from Parish of Holy Family, Blessed Sacrament, and St. John Vianney, 2158 Watson Ave., Bronx. Rev. Stephen Mallanga, Pst.;

Parish of St. Brendan and St. Ann - 333 E. 206th St., Bronx, NY 10467 t) 718-654-6424 Rev. Raul G. Miguez (Cuba), Pst.; Rev. Msgr. Joachim B. Beaumont, Assoc. Pst.; Rev. Sancho Garrote, Assoc. Pst.; Rev. Ambrose Madu, Assoc. Pst.; Rev. Sunny Mathew (India), Assoc. Pst.; Dcn. Paul Hveem; Judith Cordero, DRE;

Christ the King - 141 Marcy Pl., Bronx, NY 10452 Rev. Ambrose Madu, Pst.; Dcn. Rafael Carvajal;

Church of Our Saviour - 2317 Washington Ave., Bronx, NY 10458 t) 718-295-9600 oursavior4@hotmail.com churchoursaviour.org (Yarumal Missionaries) Rev. Jorge Ivan Fernandez, mxy, Pst.; Rev. Tulio E. Ramirez, M.X.Y., Par. Vicar;

St. Clare of Assisi - 1918 Paulding Ave., Bronx, NY 10462 t) 718-829-9624 Rev. Salvatore DeStefano, Pst.; Sr. Linda Giovanelly, P.V.M.I., DRE;

St. Dominic - 1739 Unionport Rd., Bronx, NY 10462; Mailing: 731 Morris park Ave, Bronx, NY 10462 t) 718-863-3282 ols.sd.faith.formation@gmail.com; ols731@optimum.net Dcn. Reynaldo Rosado; Rev. Robert P. Badillo, M.Id, Pst.; Rev. Emmanuel Sebamalai, Par. Vicar;

St. Frances de Chantal - 190 Hollywood Ave., Bronx, NY 10465 t) 718-792-5500; 718-792-5500 x210 (CRP) sfdchantal@gmail.com www.sfdchantal.org/ Rev. Msgr. John K. Graham, Pst.; Rev. Ricardo Garcia, Par. Vicar; Rev. Robert Mensah, Par. Vicar; Dcn. Fernando Vazquez; Christi Chiapetti, CRE; CRP Stds.: 62

Convent of Sisters of Life - 198 Hollywood Ave., Bronx, NY 10465 t) 718-863-2264 evangelization@sistersoflife.org; vocations@sistersoflife.org sistersoflife.org Sr. Maria Regina Williams, S.V., Vocations Dir.; Sr. Mariae Agnus Dei Yates, S.V., Postulant Dir.;

Parish of St. Frances of Rome, St. Francis of Assisi, St. Anthony, and Our Lady of Grace - 4307 Barnes Ave., Bronx, NY 10466 t) 718-324-5340 Rev. Georginus Esiofor Ugwu, M.S.P., Pst.; Rev. Francis A. Oroffa, Assoc. Pst.; Dcn. John Maulucci; Dcn. Jose Ojeda; Bro. Lucian Knaap, C.F.C., DRE;

St. Anthony - 4505 Richardson Ave., Bronx, NY 10470

St. Francis of Assisi - 4330 Baychester Ave., Bronx, NY 10466

St. Francis of Assisi - 1544 Shakespeare Ave., Bronx, NY 10452; Mailing: P.O. Box 520013, Bronx, NY 10452 t) 718-731-6840; 718-731-6841 Mission of Sacred Heart. Records at Sacred Heart, Bronx.

St. Francis of Assisi - 4307 Barnes Ave., Bronx, NY 10466 Administered from Parish of St. Frances of Rome, St. Francis of Assisi, St. Anthony, and Our Lady of Grace, Bronx. Rev. Georginus Esiofor Ugwu, M.S.P., Pst.;

St. Francis Xavier - 1703 Lurting Ave., Bronx, NY 10461 Rev. Salvatore DeStefano, Pst.; Rev. Matthew W. Reiman, Assoc. Pst.; Dcn. Peter Genares; Rev. Hippolytus Duru, In Res.;

St. Francis Xavier Convent - 1661 Haight Ave., Bronx, NY 10461 t) 718-892-9466 (San Damiano Convent Franciscan Sisters of the Renewal)

St. Gabriel - 3250 Arlington Ave., Bronx, NY 10463 t) 718-548-6585 Administered from Parish of St. Margaret of Cortona and St. Gabriel, 6000 Riverdale Ave., Bronx. Very Rev. Brian P. McCarthy, Pst.; Marie-Jeanne Gwertzman, DRE;

St. Helena - 1315 Olmstead Ave., Bronx, NY 10462 t) 718-892-3233 Rev. David B. Powers, Sch.P., Pst.; Rev. Richard S. Wyzykiewicz, Sch.P., Assoc. Pst.;

Holy Cross - 620 Thieriot Ave., Bronx, NY 10473 t) 718-893-5550 holycrossbronx.org Rev. John J. Higgins, Pst.; Rev. Vincent J. Druding III, Vicar; Dcn. Jaime A. Bello, DRE; Dcn. Valentin Acabeo; Dcn. Luis J. Torres;

Parish of Holy Family, Blessed Sacrament, and St. John Vianney - 2158 Watson Ave., Bronx, NY 10472 t) 718-822-8030 Rev. Stephen Mallanga, Pst.; Rev. Michael Mburu, Assoc. Pst.; Dcn. Edwin J. Cruz;

Holy Family - 2155 Blackrock Ave., Bronx, NY 10472 Dcn. Carlos M. Porcell; Dcn. Epimegnio Portalatin;

Parish of Holy Rosary and Nativity of Our Blessed Lady - 1510 Adee Ave., Bronx, NY 10469 t) 718-654-9381 Rev. Dennis T. Williams, Pst.; Rev. Sebastian Pandarathikudiyil, V.C. (India), Assoc. Pst.; Rev. Anthony J. Pleho, Chap.;

Holy Spirit - 1940 University Ave., Bronx, NY 10453 Rev. Jose Gabriel Piedrahita, Pst.; Rev. Damian Ekete (Nigeria), Assoc. Pst.;

Immaculate Conception - 389 E. 150th St., Bronx, NY 10455 t) 718-292-6970 x15 (CRP); 718-292-6970 garzamps@yahoo.com; immaculateconception389@gmail.com (Redemptorist) Rev. Sean J. McGillicuddy, C.Ss.R., Pst.; Rev. Charles Hergenroeder, Par. Vicar; Rev. Gary Lauenstein, C.Ss.R., Par. Vicar; Sr. Consuelo Morales, Pst. Assoc.; Rev. Joseph Thong Ngo, C.Ss.R.; Rev. Robert Wojtek, C.Ss.R.; Bro. Augustus Riviere, In Res.; Rev. Mathee Srivokoral, In Res.; Rev. Ciya Thomas, C.Ss.R., In Res.; Sr. Melissa Garza, DRE; Bro. Eugene Patin, C.Ss.R., Treas.; CRP Stds.: 183

Sisters of Christian Charity - 365 E. 150th St., Bronx, NY 10455 t) 718-585-8981

Immaculate Conception - 754 E. Gun Hill Rd., Bronx, NY 10467 t) 718-653-2200 x141 kevinp1958@gmail.com (Capuchin) Rev. Luis Saldana, Pst.; Rev. Louis Jacques Fleurimond, OFM Cap., Par. Vicar; Rev. Dasu Prathipati, OFM Cap., Par. Vicar; Bro. Walter Fitzpatrick, O.F.M.Cap., Pst. Assoc.; Bro. Jesu Perez, O.F.M.Cap., Pst. Assoc.; Roberta Lener, DRE; Bro. Kevin O'Loughlin, O.F.M.Cap., Bus. Mgr.;

St. Jerome's - 230 Alexander Ave., Bronx, NY 10454 Rev. Javier Correa-Llano, I.V.E., Pst.;

St. Joan of Arc - 1372 Stratford Ave., Bronx, NY 10472 t) 718-842-2233 pastorstjoanofarc@gmail.com Rev. Paul J. LeBlanc, Pst.; Dcn. Angel Alvarez; Dcn. Ismael Camacho; CRP Stds.: 365

Parish of St. John and Visitation - 3021 Kingsbridge Ave., Bronx, NY 10463 t) 718-548-1221 stjohnvisitation@yahoo.com www.stjohnvisitationparish.org Rev. Michael Kerrigan, Pst.; Rev. Asdruval Antonio Astudillo Montalvan (Ecuador), Assoc. Pst.; Jeanette Guzman, DRE; CRP Stds.: 193

St. John Chrysostom - 985 E. 167th St., Bronx, NY 10459 t) 718-328-7723 (CRP); 718-542-6164 stjohnchry@gmail.com sjcbronx.org Rev. Richard Marrano, Pst.;

St John Nam - 3663 White Plains Rd., Bronx, NY 10467 Rev. Michael C. Moon, Pst.; Rev. Andrew H. Lee (Korea), Assoc. Pst.;

St. John Vianney, Cure of Ars - 725 Castle Hill Ave., Bronx, NY 10473 Records at Parish of Holy Family, Blessed Sacrament, and St. John Vianney, 2158 Watson Ave., Bronx. Very Rev. Peter Mushi, A.J., Pst.;

St. Joseph - 1949 Bathgate Ave., Bronx, NY 10457 Records at Parish of St. Simon Stock and St. Joseph, 2191 Valentine Ave., Bronx. Rev. Nelson Belizario, O.Carm., Pst.; Rev. Christopher J. Iannizzotto, O.Carm., Assoc. Pst.;

St. Lucy - 833 Mace Ave., Bronx, NY 10467 t) 718-882-0710 stlucybronx@gmail.com stlucybronx.org Rev. Robert Rodriguez, Pst.; Rev. Peter R. Pilsner, In Res.; Dcn. Santos Arroyo; CRP Stds.: 252

St. Luke - 623 E. 138th St., Bronx, NY 10454 t) 718-801-5512 Rev. Eric Cruz, Pst.; Dcn. Martin Asiamah; Rev. Osiris Salcedo, S.D.B. (Dominican Republic);

St. Luke Convent - 621 E. 138th St., Bronx, NY 10454 t) 718-292-3016

St. Margaret Mary - 1914 Morris Ave., Bronx, NY 10453-5904 t) 718-299-4233 Rev. Rudolph Francis Gonzalez, Pst.; Rev. Msgr. Joachim Beaumont, Assoc. Pst.; Yolanda Santiago, DRE;

Parish of St. Margaret of Cortona and St. Gabriel - 6000 Riverdale Ave., Bronx, NY 10471 t) 718-884-9777 (CRP); 718-549-8053 smcchurch@optonline.net 6599.sites.ecatholic.com/ Very Rev. Brian P. McCarthy, Pst.; Rev. Timothy Boman, Par. Vicar; Rev. Sandro Leyton-Rodriguez, Par. Vicar; Rev. George C. Lodi, Par. Vicar; Dcn. Joaquim Pereira; Dcn. George Pitula; Dcn. Donald M. Quigley;

St. Gabriel School - (Grades PreK-8) 590 W. 235 St., Bronx, NY 10463 t) 718-548-0444 stgabrielsinthebronx.org (Regional) Anthony Naccari, Prin.; Stds.: 208; Lay Tchrs.: 13

St. Martin of Tours - 664 Grote St., Bronx, NY 10457 Rev. Cosme S. Fernandes, Pst.; Rev. Francis

Nampiaparambil Luke, Assoc. Pst.; Dcn. Luis Velasquez; Sr. Georgina Maria, DRE;

St. Mary - White Plains Rd., Bronx, NY 10466-3932 t) 718-231-2569 Records at: Our Lady of Grace, Bronx, NY 10466 (718-652-4817).

Convent - 3961 Carpenter Ave., Bronx, NY 10466 t) 718-652-2873

School Chapel - E. 224th St., Bronx, NY 10466

St. Mary Star of the Sea - 595 Minneford Ave., Bronx, NY 10464-1118 t) 718-885-1440 stmssci@gmail.com Administered from Parish of Our Lady of the Assumption and St. Mary Star of the Sea, 1634 Mahan Ave., Bronx. Rev. John M. Knapp, Pst.; Rev. Augustus Onwubiko (Nigeria), In Res.; Sr. Bernadette Hannaway, O.S.U., DRE;

Ursuline Community - 596 Minnieford Ave., Bronx, NY 10464 t) 718-885-2139

Daughters of Mary Convent - 176 Kilroe St., Bronx, NY 10464 t) 718-885-1842

St. Michael - 765 Co-Op City Blvd., Bronx, NY 10475-1601 t) 718-671-8050 office@saintmichaels-cc.org Rev. Kareem R. Smith, Pst.; Rev. Benedict Paul, Assoc. Pst.; Dcn. Candido Padro Jr.; Dcn. Thomas R. Tortorella;

Nativity of Our Blessed Lady - 1531 E. 233rd St., Bronx, NY 10466 Records at Parish of Holy Rosary and Nativity of Our Blessed Lady, 1510 Adee Ave., Bronx. Rev. Dennis T. Williams, Pst.;

Convent - 1534 E. 233rd St., Bronx, NY 10466 t) 718-325-5355

St. Nicholas of Tolentine - 2345 University Ave., Bronx, NY 10468 t) 718-295-6800 pastor@stnicholasoftolentinebronx.org www.stnicholasoftolentinebronx.org (Augustinian) Rev. Luis A. Vera, O.S.A., Pst.; Rev. Joseph Tran, Assoc. Pst.; Rev. Carlos Urbina, O.S.A., Assoc. Pst.; Rev. Joseph Aloysius Murray, O.S.A., In Res.; Bro. Bienvenido Rodriguez, OSA, In Res.; Rev. William J. Wallace, O.S.A., In Res.; Jesus de La Rosa, DRE;

Convent of St. Nicholas of Tolentine - 2341 University Ave., Bronx, NY 10468 t) 718-367-3102

Our Lady of Angels - 2860 Webb Ave., Bronx, NY 10468 t) 646-508-3699 ourladyofangels/ religioused@hotmail.com Rev. Joseph E. Franco, Pst.; Rev. Ricardo Garcia, Assoc. Pst.; Sr. Lorena Pallares, P.C., DRE; Rev. Steven Gonzalez, Par. Vicar; Dcn. Carlos Sanchez; Dcn. Wilson Martinez;

Our Lady of Grace - 3985 Bronxwood Ave., Bronx, NY 10466 Records at St. Frances of Rome, St. Francis of Assisi, St. Anthony and Our Lady of Grace, 4307 Barnes Ave., Bronx. Dcn. W. Joseph Mulryan; Rev. Georginus Esiofor Ugwu, M.S.P., Pst.; Rev. Felix Gonzalez, Assoc. Pst.; Rev. Charles Udokang, In Res.;

Our Lady of Mercy - 2496 Marion Ave., Bronx, NY 10458 Rev. Jose Ambooken, Pst.; Sr. Reyna Huerta, H.M.S.P., DRE;

Our Lady of Mt. Carmel - 627 E. 187th St., Bronx, NY 10458 t) 718-295-3770 info@ourladymtcarmelbx.org www.ourladymtcarmelbx.org/ Rev. Jose Felix Ortega, Pst.; CRP Stds.: 305

Our Lady of Refuge - 290 E. 196th St., Bronx, NY 10458 t) 718-367-3384 Rev. Patric D'Arcy, Pst.;

Our Lady of Solace - 731 Morris Park Ave., Bronx, NY 10462 t) 718-239-6926 (CRP); 718-863-3282 ols.sd.faith.formation@gmail.com; ols731@optimum.net Rev. Robert P. Badillo, M.Id, Pst.; Rev. Emmanuel Sebamalai, Par. Vicar; Heidy Olivo, DRE;

Parish of Our Lady of the Assumption - St. Mary Star of the Sea - 1634 Mahan Ave., Bronx, NY 10461 t) 718-904-8464 (CRP); 718-824-5454 olareled@verizon.net olasmss.com Rev. John M. Knapp, Pst.; Rev. Geomon Kalladanthiyil, Par. Vicar; Rev. Augustus Onwubiko (Nigeria), Par. Vicar; Dcn. William J. Mueller; Diana Liccese, DRE; CRP Stds.: 110

Convent - 1639 Parkview Ave., Bronx, NY 10461 t) 718-829-7980

St. Peter and St. Paul - 833 St. Ann's Ave., Bronx, NY 10456 Rev. Richard Mederich Marcelino Cisneros, Pst.; Dcn. James Francis;

SS. Philip and James - 1160 E. 213th St., Bronx, NY 10469 Rev. Steven Masinde, Pst.;

Chapel - 1180 E. 214th St., Bronx, NY 10469

St. Philip Neri - 3025 Grand Concourse, Bronx, NY 10468 Rev. Daniel O'Reilly, Pst.; Rev. Marco Antonio Ortega (Peru), Assoc. Pst.; Dcn. Angel Filpo;

St. Pius V - 448 College Ave., Bronx, NY 10451 Records at Parish of St. Rita of Cascia and St. Pius V, 448 College Ave., Bronx. Rev. Pablo Gonzalez, Pst.;

St. Raymond - 1759 Castle Hill Ave., Bronx, NY 10462 t) 718-792-4044 x238 Rev. James A. Cruz, Pst.; Rev. Luis Silva Cervantes, Par. Vicar; Rev. Patrick K. Agbeko, In Res.; Rev. Raphael Boansi, In Res.; Rev. William Brogan, In Res.; Rev. Joseph Darbouze, In Res.; Rev. Elvin Rivera, In Res.; Sr. Adelina Garcia, P.C.I., DRE;

Brothers Residence - 1754 Castle Hill Ave., Bronx, NY 10462 t) 718-829-1417

Parish of St. Rita of Cascia and St. Pius V - 448 College Ave, Bronx, NY 10451 t) 718-585-5900 santaritabronx@gmail.com www.santaritabronx.com Rev. Pablo Gonzalez, Admin.;

St. Roch - 525 Wales Ave., Bronx, NY 10455 Records at Parish of St. Anselm and St. Roch, 685 Tinton Ave., Bronx. (Augustinian Recollects) Rev. Antonio Palacios, O.A.R., Pst.;

Sacred Heart - 1253 Shakespeare Ave., Bronx, NY 10452 t) 718-293-2766 redirector@bronxaltar.org; receptionist@bronxaltar.org www.bronxaltar.org Rev. Jose Cruz Alverez, Pst.; Dcn. Juan Chaparro; Dcn. Alfonso Ramos; Dcn. Ralph Rios; Rev. Isaac Mensah, In Res.; Rev. Msgr. Kevin P. O'Brien, In Res.; Vera V. Galeas, DRE; CRP Stds.: 200

Santa Maria - 2352 St. Raymond Ave., Bronx, NY 10462 (Idente Missionaries) Rev. Cristobal Martin Flores, M.Id, Pst.; Dcn. Vincent Verlezza, DRE;

Santa Maria Convent - 1460 Zerega Ave., Bronx, NY 10462

Parish of St. Simon Stock and St. Joseph - 2191 Valentine Ave., Bronx, NY 10457 t) 718-367-1251 stsimonstockchurch@gmail.com; victorialourdes721@gmail.com (Carmelite) Rev. Michael Kissane, O.Carm., Pst.; Rev. Emiel Abalahin, O.Carm., Prior; Bro. Robert Chiulli, O.Carm., In Res.; Lourdes Victoria, DRE;

St. Theresa of the Infant Jesus - 2855 St. Theresa Ave., Bronx, NY 10461 t) 718-892-1900 rectorystc@aol.com www.sttheresachurchbronx.org Rev. Msgr. Thomas B. Derivan, Pst.; Rev. Joseph Ligory, Assoc. Pst.; Rev. Edmundo Gomez, In Res.; Marie McCarrick, DRE; CRP Stds.: 101

St. Thomas Aquinas - 1900 Crotona Pkwy., Bronx, NY 10460 t) 718-861-3638 Rev. Miguel Zavala, I.V.E, Pst.; Rev. Jeffrey Obniski, I.V.E., Assoc. Pst.;

Visitation - 160 Van Cortlandt Park S., Bronx, NY 10463 Records at Parish of St. John and Visitation, Bronx. Rev. Michael Kerrigan, Pst.;

BRONXVILLE

St. Joseph - 15 Cedar St., Bronxville, NY 10708 t) 914-337-6383 (CRP); 914-337-1660 saintjosephsbronxville@gmail.com saintjosephsbronxville.org/ Rev. Peter McGeory, Pst.; Dcn. Bernard Moran; Rev. Dawson Ambosta (India), In Res.; Rev. Msgr. Seth Agyemang (Ghana), Pst. Assoc.; Antoinette Gilligan, DRE;

BUCHANAN

Parish of St. Christopher and St. Patrick - 3094 Albany Post Rd., Buchanan, NY 10511 t) 914-737-1437 lisaduffyquist@gmail.com Rev. George Oonnoonny, Pst.; Rev. Regimon Cherian (India), Assoc. Pst.; Dcn. Vincent Astarita; Rev. Matthew Ugwoji, In Res.; Lisa Quist, DRE;

CALLICOON

Holy Cross - 9719 State Rte. 97, Callicoon, NY 12723; Mailing: P.O. Box 246, Callicoon, NY 12723 Rev. John Kennady Arvlanandu, MMI, Pst.; Dcn. John Lyttle;

St. Patrick, -

Callicoon, Holy Cross Rectory -

CARMEL

St. James the Apostle - 14 Gleneida Ave., Carmel, NY 10512 t) 845-225-6504 Rev. Szymon Kurpios, Sch.P. (Poland), Admin.; Rev. Msgr. Joseph Martin, Assoc. Pst.; Dcn. Scott Bierbaum; Dcn. Charles T. Borsavage; Dcn. Anthony Gruerio; Dcn. John Scott; Dcn. Arthur Weiner;

Our Lady of the Lake/Mt. Carmel - 1 Doherty Dr., Lake Carmel, NY 10512 t) 845-228-1235

Chapel of Life, Carmel -

CHAPPAQUA

St. John and St. Mary - 15 St. John's Pl., Chappaqua, NY 10514 t) 914-238-3696 kidsrelig@optimum.net Rev. Edward P. O'Halloran, Pst.; Dcn. Anthony Reino; Dcn. Charles Devlin; Joan Corso Ferroni, Pst. Assoc.;

CHESTER

St. Columba - 27 High St., Chester, NY 10918 t) 845-469-9503 Rev. Christopher Argano, Pst.; Dcn. Peter E. Reynolds; Rev. John S. Bonnici;

COLD SPRING

Our Lady of Loretto - 24 Fair St., Cold Spring, NY 10516 t) 845-265-2594 (CRP); 845-265-3718 ollfaithformation@gmail.com; lorettochurch@gmail.com Rev. Thomas P. Lutz, Pst.; Rev. Anthony Yorke (Ghana), Assoc. Pst.;

St. Joseph's Chapel -

CONGERS

St. Ann - 82 Lake Rd., Congers, NY 10920 t) 845-358-3758 julielepore@verizon.net Administered from Parish of St. Paul and St. Ann, Congers. Rev. Vladimir Chripko, C.O., Pst.; Rev. Fidelis Enzeani (Nigeria), Assoc. Pst.; Rev. Simon Gyanobeng, Assoc. Pst.; Dcn. Thomas Luke Conroy; Julie LePore, DRE;

Convent - 150 Third Ave., Nyack, NY 10960

Parish of St. Paul and St. Ann - 82 Lake Rd. W., Congers, NY 10920 t) 845-268-5442 Rev. Vladimir Chripko, C.O., Pst.; Rev. Peter Bujdos, Assoc. Pst.; Rev. Roman Dominic Palecko, C.O., Assoc. Pst.; Rev. Arogya Raju, Assoc. Pst.; Dcn. Dominic Buonocore; Marianna Dalsass, DRE; Dcn. Luke Conroy, Sacr. Min.; Dcn. Gerald Fenton, Sacr. Min.;

Sisters' Convent and School, Valley Cottage -

CORNWALL-ON-HUDSON

St. Marianne Cope - 340 Hudson St., Cornwall-on-Hudson, NY 12520 t) 845-534-2547 faithformation@stmariannecope.com; office@stmariannecope.com stmariannecope.com Formerly St. Thomas of Canterbury and St. Joseph. Rev. Rees W. Doughty, Pst.; Dcn. Leonard Farmer; Dcn. Anthony P. Ferraiuolo; Dcn. Joseph Lieby; Dcn. John V. Pelella; Vincent Mateo, Music Min.; Mary Ellen Tiernan, DRE; Nataly Flores, Bus. Mgr.; CRP Stds.: 358

CORTLANDT MANOR

St. Columbanus - 122 Oregon Rd., Cortlandt Manor, NY 10567 t) 914-739-2441 Rev. Francis Samoylo, Pst.; Rev. Msgr. Patrick J. Keenan, Pastor Emer.; Dcn. Christopher Mendoza; Isabel Arroyo, DRE;

North American Martyrs - 55 Oscawana Lake Rd., Putnam Valley, NY 10579

Holy Spirit - 1969 Crompond Rd., Cortlandt Manor, NY 10567-4113 t) 914-734-9243 (CRP); 914-737-2316 re_holyspiritchurch1969@verizon.net; holyspiritchurch1969@verizon.net www.holyspirit-cortlandtmanor.org Rev. John A. DeBellis, Pst.; Rev. Vernon P. Wickrematunge (Sri Lanka), Par. Vicar; Dcn. Lawrence Candarelli; Dcn. A. Michael Salvatorelli; Elizabeth Kogler, DRE; CRP Stds.: 497

CRESTWOOD

Parish of Annunciation-Our Lady of Fatima - 470 Westchester Ave., Crestwood, NY 10707 t) 914-779-2374 Dcn. Michael J. Fox; Very Rev. Robert F. Grippo, Pst.; Rev. Livinus Anweting, Assoc. Pst.; Rev. Salvatore Riccardi, C.P., Assoc. Pst.; Rev. Christopher Argano, In Res.; Mary Rose, DRE; Rev. Robert Carolan, Par. Vicar;

CROTON-ON-HUDSON

Holy Name of Mary - 114 Grand St., Croton-on-

Hudson, NY 10520 t) 914-271-4254 Rev. Nelson Couto (India), Pst.;

Chapel of the Good Shepherd - Benedict Blvd. and Young Ave., Harmon, NY 10520

DOBBS FERRY

Parish of Sacred Heart and Our Lady of Pompeii - 18 Bellewood Ave., Dobbs Ferry, NY 10522 t) 914-479-1045 (CRP); 914-693-0119 x200 reled@sh-olp.com; info@sh-olp.com sh-olp.com Rev. Christopher W. Monturo, Pst.; Rev. Fidelis H. Oppong, S.T.D., Pst. Assoc.; Rev. Siby Thomas, CMI, Pst. Assoc.; CRP Stds.: 250

Sacred Heart - 417 Broadway (corner Broadway & Ashford Ave.), Dobbs Ferry, NY 10522 t) 914-693-5541 shrectory@aol.com

Our Lady of Pompeii - 95 Palisade St., Dobbs Ferry, NY 10522; Mailing: 18 Bellewood Ave., Dobbs Ferry, NY 10522

ELLENVILLE

St. Mary and St. Andrew - 137 S. Main St., Ellenville, NY 12428 Rev. Kenneth Riello, Pst.; Rev. Y. Vijaya Shekar, Assoc. Pst.; Bruce Santiago, DRE;

Our Lady of Lourdes -

ELMSFORD

Our Lady of Mt. Carmel - 59 E. Main St., Elmsford, NY 10523 t) 914-592-4280 (CRP); 914-592-6789 secraolmc@gmail.com olmcchurchelmsford.com/ Rev. Robert J. Norris, Pst.; Rev. Augustine Dada, Vicar; Dcn. Daniel Moliterno; Dcn. Jorge Montealegre; CRP Stds.: 210

FISHKILL

Church of St. Mary, Mother of the Church - 103 Jackson St., Fishkill, NY 12524-0499; Mailing: P.O. Box 780, Fishkill, NY 12524-0499 t) 845-896-6430 Rev. Joseph A. Blenkle, Pst.; Rev. Thomas Colucci, Assoc. Pst.; Rev. Adolfo Occeno (Philippines), Assoc. Pst.; Rev. Carmine Caruso, Par. Vicar; Kathy Hamilton, DRE; Dcn. Michael Decker; Dcn. Joseph R. Hafeman; Dcn. Rommel Pampolina; Dcn. Paul L. Smith;

FLORIDA

St. Joseph - 14 Glenmere Ave., Florida, NY 10921 t) 845-651-7792 saintjoseph@optonline.net stjosephfloridany.org Rev. Jack Arlotta, Admin.; CRP Stds.: 146

St. Stanislaus - 17 Pulaski Hwy., Pine Island, NY 10969 t) 845-258-4426

FORESTBURGH

St. Thomas Aquinas - One Forestburgh Rd., Forestburgh, NY 12777 Records at Parish of St. Anthony of Padua and St. Thomas Aquinas, 25 Beaver Brook Rd., Yulan. Rev. Joselin Pens Berkmans, M.M.I., Pst.;

GARDINER

St. Charles Borromeo - 2212 Rte. 44/55, Gardiner, NY 12525 t) 845-255-1374 borromeogardiner@aol.com Rev. Matthew Yatkauskas, Pst.;

GARNERVILLE

St. Gregory Barbarigo - 21 Cinder Rd., Garnerville, NY 10923 t) (845) 429-2775; 845-947-1873 sgbreled@gmail.com; sgbdeirdre@gmail.com www.stgregorybarbarigo.org Rev. Joseph Fallon, Pst.; Dcn. George M. Albin Jr.; Dcn. John J. Kelly; Donald A. Ruzzi, DRE;

GOSHEN

St. John the Evangelist - 71 Murray Ave., Goshen, NY 10924 t) 845-294-6947 (CRP); 845-294-5328 religed@hotmail.com www.sjegoshen.org Rev. George Hafemann, Pst.; Rev. Anthony A. Amponsah, Assoc. Pst.; Rev. Anthony Giacona, Assoc. Pst.; Dcn. William Castellane; Dcn. James Faulkner; Cathy Fife, DRE;

Valley View Nursing and Rehabilitation Center - t) 845-294-7971

Campbell Hall Nursing Facility - t) 845-294-8154

GREENWOOD LAKE

Holy Rosary - 41 Windermere Ave., Greenwood Lake, NY 10925-2105 t) 845-477-8378 holy_rosary_gwl@yahoo.com www.holyrosary-ny.org Rev. T. Augustine Badgley, Admin.; Jane E Kubenik, DRE; CRP Stds.: 82

HARRIMAN

St. Anastasia - 21 N. Main St., Harriman, NY 10926 t) 845-782-5099; (845) 238-3844 Rev. Michael F. Keane, Pst.; Dcn. Eugene E. Bormann; Dcn. Lucas Garcia; Dcn. Brian O'Neill; CRP Stds.: 200

HARRISON

St. Gregory the Great - 215 Halstead Ave., Harrison, NY 10528 t) 914-835-3685 (CRP); 914-835-0677 stgreggreat@aol.com stgregorythegreatharrison.com Rev. Joseph P. Tierney, Pst.; Rev. Soosairaj Michael, Assoc. Pst.; CRP Stds.: 398

HARTSDALE

Church of Our Lady of Shkodra - 361 W. Hartsdale Ave., Hartsdale, NY 10530 Rev. Peter Popovich, Pst.;

Sacred Heart - 10 Lawton Ave., Hartsdale, NY 10530 t) 914-428-5043 (CRP); 914-949-0028; 914-949-0029 sacredheart.re@aol.com; shchartsdale@gmail.com Rev. Michael C. Moon, Pst.;

Convent - 11 Lawton Ave., Hartsdale, NY 10530 t) 914-946-2581

HASTINGS-ON-HUDSON

Parish of St. Matthew and Our Lady of Perpetual Help - 616 Warburton Ave., Hastings-on-Hudson, NY 10706 t) 914-478-2822 office@stmolph.com www.stmolph.com Rev. Douglas Y. Crawford, Pst.;

Our Lady of Perpetual Help - 535 Ashford Ave., Ardsley, NY 10502 Worship Site

HAVERSTRAW

St. Mary of the Assumption - 115 Broadway, Haverstraw, NY 10927 t) 845-429-2196 Rev. Thomas F. Madden, Pst.;

Parish of St. Peter and St. Mary of the Assumption - 115 Broadway, Haverstraw, NY 10927 t) 845-429-2196 pastor@stpeterstmary.us www.stpeterstmary.us Rev. Thomas F. Madden, Admin.; Rev. Osvaldo Hernandez, Assoc. Pst.; Dcn. Jorge Estela; Dcn. Eugene R. Hamilton; Dcn. Paul Stolz; Milagros Cobb, DRE; CRP Stds.: 611

Green Hills Home - t) 914-429-8411

Northern Riverview Health Care Center - t) 914-429-5381

HAWTHORNE

Holy Rosary - 170 Bradhurst Ave., Hawthorne, NY 10532 t) 914-769-0030 x23 (CRP); 914-769-0030 hrc10532@gmail.com www.holyrosaryhawthorne.org Rev. Sebastian Panadarathikudiyil, Pst.; Dcn. Richard McLaughlin;

HIGHLAND

St. Augustine - 55 Main St., Highland, NY 12528 Rev. John W. Lynch, Pst.; Rev. Joseph Peh Akomeah (Ghana), Assoc. Pst.; Dcn. Marc Fanelli; Dcn. Frank S. Ottaviano;

HIGHLAND FALLS

Sacred Heart of Jesus - 353 Main St., Highland Falls, NY 10928 t) 845-446-2674 Rev. Joseph M. Tokarczyk, Pst.; Maryann Brigham, DRE;

Blessed Sacrament - 794 Rte 9W, Fort Montgomery, NY 10922

HIGHLAND MILLS

St. Patrick - 26 Hunter St., Highland Mills, NY 10930 t) 845-928-6027 (Office); 845-928-6688 (CRP) margie.lynch@stpatrickny.org www.stpatrickny.org Rev. Joseph J. Tyrrell, Pst.; Dcn. Paul J. Weireter; Jennie Dabney, DRE;

HOPEWELL JUNCTION

St. Columba - 835 Main St., Hopewell Junction, NY 12533; Mailing: PO Box 428, Hopewell Junction, NY 12533 t) 845-221-4900 (CRP); 845-227-8380 stcolumbareled@gmail.com; rectory@stcolumbaonline.org www.stcolumbaonline.org Rev. Michael P. McLoughlin, Pst.; Rev. Walter Genito Jr., Par. Vicar; Dcn. Stephen Broussard; Dcn. Dennis McCormack; Dcn. Christopher Merenda; CRP Stds.: 577

St. Denis - 602 Beekman Rd., Hopewell Junction, NY 12533; Mailing: PO Box 10, Hopewell Junction, NY 12533 t) 845-227-8382 rectory@stdenischurch.org stdenischurch.org Rev. Andrew P. Carrozza, Pst.; Dcn. Walter Dauerer; Dcn. Enrico Messina; Dcn. Frank Munoz; Dcn. Robert Pelech; Dcn. John McCormack; CRP Stds.: 265

The Ark and The Dove Preschool - 604 Beekman Rd., Hopewell Junction, NY 12533; Mailing: P.O. Box 1139, Hopewell Junction, NY 12533 t) 845-227-5232 noah1@stdenischurch.org

HYDE PARK

Regina Coeli - 2 Harvey St., Hyde Park, NY 12538 t) 845-229-9139 Rev. Michael Morris, Pst.; Rev. Joseph A. Gaspar, Assoc. Pst.; Dcn. Peter Dalmer; Dcn. Frank Gohl; Dcn. James R. Hayes; Dcn. Gerard Lindley; Dcn. Mark O'Sullivan;

St. Paul - Mulford Ave., Staatsburg, NY 12580

IRVINGTON

Immaculate Conception - 16 N. Broadway, Irvington, NY 10533 t) 914-591-7740 ccdicc@optonline.net Rev. Robert Ashman, Pst.; Rev. Roy Chettaniyil (India), Assoc. Pst.;

JEFFERSONVILLE

St. George-St. Francis - 97 Schoolhouse Hill Rd., Jeffersonville, NY 12748; Mailing: P.O. Box 672, Jeffersonville, NY 12748 t) 845-482-4640 stgeorgestfrancis.org/ Rev. Roland Antony Raj, M.M.I. (India), Pst.; CRP Stds.: 43

St. Francis of Assisi - 4020 State Rte. 52, Youngsville, NY 12791 t) (845) 482-4640

KATONAH

St. Mary of the Assumption - 117 Valley Rd., Katonah, NY 10536 t) 914-232-4648 (CRP); 914-232-3356 stmarysparish@yahoo.com Rev. Mark G. Vaillancourt, Pst.; Rev. Vincent Paul, Par. Vicar; Rev. Aloysius Thumma (India), Par. Vicar; Dcn. George Chiu; Dcn. Stephen DiGangi;

St. Matthias - 107 Babbitt Rd., Bedford Hills, NY 10507

KINGSTON

Immaculate Conception - 467 Delaware Ave., Kingston, NY 12401 t) 845-331-7352 Rev. Miroslaw Pawlaczyk (Poland), Admin.;

St. Joseph - 242 Wall St., Kingston, NY 12401 t) 845-339-4391 Rev. Msgr. Desmond O'Connor, Pst.; Rev. George K. Nedumaruthumchalil (India), Assoc. Pst.; Dcn. Joseph Doherty; Dcn. Richard Frohmiller;

Msgr. O'Reilly Chapel - Zandhoeck Rd., Hurley, NY 12443

Parish of St. Mary/Holy Name of Jesus and St. Peter - 160 Broadway, Kingston, NY 12401 t) (845) 331-0301 Rev. William A. Scafidi, M.Ss.A., Pst.; Dcn. John Carr; Rev. Daniel Machiki (Nigeria), In Res.;

Saint Peter the Apostle - 93 Wurts St., Kingston, NY 12401-6328 Records at Parish of St. Mary/Holy Name of Jesus and St. Peter, 160 Broadway, Kingston. Rev. Robert J. Bubel, Pst.;

LAGRANGEVILLE

Saint Kateri Tekakwitha - 1925 Rte. 82, LaGrangeville, NY 12540 t) 845-227-1710 x3 saintkateri@optonline.net Very Rev. Joseph M. McLafferty, Pst.; Rev. John Wilson, Par. Vicar; Dcn. Anthony Cirone; Sr. Cherree Ann Power, C.R., DRE; CRP Stds.: 455

LAKE KATRINE

Roman Catholic Church of St. Catherine Laboure and St. Colman - 200 Tuytenbridge Rd., Lake Katrine, NY 12449; Mailing: P.O. Box 271, Lake Katrine, NY 12449 t) 845-382-1133 parish383ny@gmail.com www.parish383ny.com Rev. Slawomir Ciszkowski (Poland), Pst.; CRP Stds.: 24

LARCHMONT

St. Augustine - 18 Cherry Ave., Larchmont, NY 10538 t) 914-834-1220; 914-834-9523 abetkowski@staugustineny.org Rev. John S. Bonnici, Pst.; Rev. Louis Masi, Par. Vicar; Dcn. Robert Gontcharuk; Rev. James Rebeta, In Res.; Sr. Suzanne Duzen, SS.C.M., DRE;

SS. John and Paul - 280 Weaver St., Larchmont, NY 10538 t) 914-834-5458 office@sjpparish.org Rev. John S. Bonnici, Pst.; Rev. Louis P Masi, Par. Vicar; Dcn. James A. Brown; Dcn. John Shea;

LIBERTY

St. Peter - 264 N. Main St., Liberty, NY 12754

t) 845-292-4525 srectory1@hvc.rr.com www.stpetersliberty.com Very Rev. Edward Bader, Pst.; Dcn. Donald Prendergast;

LIVINGSTON MANOR

St. Aloysius - 22 Church St., Livingston Manor, NY 12758; Mailing: Box 206, Livingston Manor, NY 12758 Very Rev. Edward Bader, Pst.;

Sacred Heart - ; Mailing: P.O. Box 206, De Bruce, NY 12758

Gate of Heaven - Highland Ave., Roscoe, NY 12776

MAHOPAC

St. John the Evangelist - 221 E. Lake Blvd., Mahopac, NY 10541 Rev. Philip J. Caruso, Admin.; Rev. Patrick J. McCarthy, Assoc. Pst.; Rev. Maximo Villanueva (Philippines), Assoc. Pst.; Dcn. John Scarfi;

Convent of Religious of the Divine Compassion - t) 914-628-6497

MAMARONECK

Most Holy Trinity - 320 E. Boston Post Rd., Mamaroneck, NY 10543 Records at Parish of St. Vito and Most Holy Trinity, 816 Underhill Ave., Mamaroneck. Dcn. Augustine DiFiore; Rev. Robert P. Henry, Assoc. Pst.; Rev. Joseph Kahumburu (Kenya), Assoc. Pst.;

Parish of St. Vito and Most Holy Trinity - 816 Underhill Ave., Mamaroneck, NY 10543 t) 914-698-2648 stvitochurch@optonline.net www.stvitomhtchurch.com Rev. Joseph P. Tierney, Admin.; Dcn. Juan Martinez;

MARLBORO

Parish of St. Mary and St. James - 71 Grand St., Marlboro, NY 12542; Mailing: P.O. Box 730, Marlboro, NY 12542 t) (845) 236-4340 stmarysmarlboro@gmail.com stmarys-marlboro.com Rev. Thomas Dicks, Pst.; Dcn. Vincent Porcelli; Tonia Borchert, Admin.; CRP Stds.: 165

Our Lady of Mercy - 977 River Rd., Newburgh, NY 12550

MAYBROOK

Church of the Assumption - 211 Homestead Ave., Maybrook, NY 12543; Mailing: P.O. Box 320, Maybrook, NY 12543 t) 845-427-5318 Administered from Parish of Holy Name of Mary and Assumption, 89 Union St., Montgomery, NY. Rev. Daniel M. O'Hare, Pst.;

MIDDLETOWN

Holy Cross - 626 County Rte. 22, Middletown, NY 10940 t) 845-355-6255 (CRP); 845-355-4439 hnojotisville@frontiernet.net; riley022760@frontier.com holycrosscatholicparish.com Rev. Michael L. Palazzo, Admin.; Dcn. Robert Leavy; CRP Stds.: 252

St. Joseph - 149 Cottage St., Middletown, NY 10940 t) 845-343-6013; 845-343-4415 parish@sjchurch.com www.sjchurch.com Very Rev. Dennis A. Nikolic, Pst.; Rev. Kevin E. Panameno, Par. Vicar; Rev. Simon Nwachukwu, Chap.; Dcn. Alexander Gapay; Dcn. Edmund Lazzari, RCIA Coord.; Dcn. Richard Trapani; Linda Byrons, DRE; CRP Stds.: 489

Our Lady of Mt. Carmel - 90 Euclid Ave., Middletown, NY 10940; Mailing: P.O. Box 883, Middletown, NY 10940 t) 845-342-1510 (CRP); 845-343-4121 olmcre90@gmail.com; ourladyofmtcarmel883@hotmail.com www.olmcmiddletown.org Rev. Paul Denault, O.Carm., Pst.; Rev. Sean R. Harlow, O.Carm., Par. Vicar; Rev. Leonard Paul Richmond, O. Carm., Par. Vicar; Dcn. Carl Locatelli; Dcn. Edward J. Woods; Dcn. Michael G. McCabe; Kim Gatto, CRE; CRP Stds.: 135

Our Lady of the Assumption - 17 High Street, Bloomingburg, NY 12721; Mailing: P.O. Box 527, Bloomingburg, NY 12721-0527 t) 845-733-1477 assumptionchurch@frontiernet.net

St. Paul - Rte. 17K, Bullville, NY 10915; Mailing: P.O. Box 222, Bullville, NY 10915 t) 845-361-3107

MILLBROOK

Parish of St. Joseph and Immaculate Conception - 15 North Ave., Millbrook, NY 12545; Mailing: P.O. Box 439, Millbrook, NY 12545 t) 845-677-3273 (CRP); 845-677-3422 ccdstjosephmillbrook@gmail.com; stjosephmillbrook@gmail.com www.stjosephmillbrookny.org Rev. Hartley Bancroft, Pst.; Melissa Paglia, DRE; CRP Stds.: 112

Green Briar Home - t) 845-677-9997

The Fountains - t) 845-677-8550

MONROE

Sacred Heart Church - 26 Still Rd., Monroe, NY 10950 t) 845-782-7420 Rev. David Rider, Pst.; Rev. Anthony A. Amponsah, Assoc. Pst.; Rev. Raymond Nwegede, Assoc. Pst.; Dcn. Peter Brockmann; Dcn. Angelo Corsaro; Dcn. Robert Duncan; Sr. Rose O'Rourke, DRE;

Convent - Still Rd., Monroe, NY 10950

Sacred Heart Chapel - 151 Stage Rd., Monroe, NY 10950

MONTGOMERY

Parish of Holy Name of Mary - Assumption - 89 Union St., Montgomery, NY 12549 t) 845-457-1738 Rev. Matthew W. Reiman, Pst.; Dcn. Edward Grosso;

Assumption - 211 Homestead Ave., Maybrook, NY 12543 t) (845) 457-5276 www.holynameofmary-assumption.org (Worship Site)

MONTICELLO

St. Peter - 10 Liberty St., Monticello, NY 12701 t) (845) 794-5577 stpetersmonticello.org Rev. Robert D. Porpora, Pst.; Rev. John P. Sheehan, Assoc. Pst.; Rev. Stanislaus Ogbonna, C.S.Sp. (Nigeria), In Res.; CRP Stds.: 160

St. Joseph -

St. Anne -

MOUNT VERNON

Parish of St. Mary-Our Lady of Mt. Carmel - 23 S. High St., Mount Vernon, NY 10550 t) 914-664-5855 stmarymv@yahoo.com www.stmarys-ny.com/ Rev. Francis P. Scanlon, Pst.; Dcn. William L. Battersby; Dcn. Joseph Patrona; CRP Stds.: 96

Parish of Our Lady of Victory and Sacred Heart - 28 W. Sidney Ave., Mount Vernon, NY 10550 Rev. Joseph Akunaeziri, Pst.;

Parish of Sts. Peter and Paul and St. Ursula - 129 Birch St., Mount Vernon, NY 10552 t) 914-668-9880 rectory@stspeterpaulandstursula.org www.stspeterpaulandstursula.org Rev. John F. Lauri, Pst.; Dcn. Richard Ellison; Rev. Robert Barnabass, In Res.; CRP Stds.: 50

Sacred Heart - 115 S. Fifth Ave., Mount Vernon, NY 10550 Records at Parish of Our Lady of Victory and Sacred Heart, 28 W. Sidney Ave., Mount Vernon. Very Rev. Alfredo Monteiro, Pst.; Rev. Andrew Florez, Assoc. Pst.;

St. Ursula - 214 E. Lincoln Ave., Mount Vernon, NY 10552 t) 914-699-7964 Records at Parish of Sts. Peter and Paul and St. Ursula, 129 Birch St., Mount Vernon. Rev. John F. Lauri, Pst.; Rev. Francis Michaelsamy (India), Assoc. Pst.; Mona Parkinson, DRE;

MT. KISCO

St. Francis of Assisi - 2 Green St., Mt. Kisco, NY 10549 t) (914) 666-5986 sfamountkisco.org Rev. Steven E. Clarke, Pst.; Dcn. Isaac Marquez, Pst. Assoc.; Dcn. Harold Hochstein; Dcn. Jose Marquez; Rev. Msgr. John J. Budwick, In Res.; CRP Stds.: 253

NANUET

St. Anthony - 36 W. Nyack Rd., Nanuet, NY 10954 t) 845-623-2138; 845-624-2230 stanthony.accounting@verizon.net; stanthony.prep@gmail.com thechurchofstanthony.com Rev. Joseph J. Deponai, Pst.; Rev. Cresus Fernando, Assoc. Pst.; Rev. Antonio Ferrer, Assoc. Pst.; Dcn. Raymundo Masbad; Ursula Magee, DRE; CRP Stds.: 370

St. Anthony Shrine Church -

NARROWSBURG

St. Francis Xavier - 151 Bridge St., Narrowsburg, NY 12764 (Franciscan) Rev. Dennis M. Dinan, Pst.;

Our Lady of the Lake - Rte. 52, Lake Huntington, NY 12752 www.ollhuntington.com

NEW CITY

St. Augustine - 140 Maple Ave., New City, NY 10956 t) 845-634-8462 staugustinereo@gmail.com Rev. William B. Cosgrove, Pst.; Dcn. Joseph Crothers; Dcn. Samir Mobarek; Dcn. James Suchy;

NEW PALTZ

St. Joseph - 34 S. Chestnut St., New Paltz, NY 12561 t) 845-255-0237 (Capuchin Franciscans) Rev. Salvatore Cordaro, O.F.M.Cap., Pst.; Rev. John Koelle, O.F.M. Cap., Par. Vicar; Sr. Philomena Fleck, O.S.B., DRE;

NEW ROCHELLE

Blessed Sacrament - 15 Shea Pl., New Rochelle, NY 10801 t) 914-632-3700 rectory@blessedsacramentnr.com blessedsacramentnr.com Rev. William J. Luciano, Pst.; Rev. George Obeng-Yeboah-Asuamah, Assoc. Pst.; Rev. Biju Peter, C.M.I., Assoc. Pst.; Dcn. Rudy Babor; CRP Stds.: 114

Parish of St. Gabriel and St. Joseph - 120 Division St., New Rochelle, NY 10801 Rev. Cruz Sanchez Mares, Pst.; Maria Elena Marquez, DRE;

Holy Family - 83 Clove Rd., New Rochelle, NY 10801 t) 914-632-0673; 914-636-6758 holy-family-church.com Rev. Msgr. Dennis P. Keane, Pst.; Rev. Patrick N. Nsionu (Nigeria), Par. Vicar; Dcn. Donald Gray; Dcn. Raymond Hall; Rev. John J. Duff, In Res.; CRP Stds.: 300

Ursuline Sisters - 1352 N. Ave., New Rochelle, NY 10804 t) 914-636-3456

Iona Grammar and Preparatory Schools - 173 Stratton Rd., New Rochelle, NY 10804 t) 914-633-7744; 914-632-2727

Iona College - 715 N. Ave., New Rochelle, NY 10801 t) 914-633-2000

St. Joseph's Residence, St. Patrick Prov. - 30 Montgomery Circle, New Rochelle, NY 10801 t) 914-633-6851 Bro. James B. Moffett, C.F.C., Admin.;

Edmond Rice Hall - 33 Pryer Ter., New Rochelle, NY 10804 t) 914-636-6194

Opus Dei - 99 Overlook Cir., New Rochelle, NY 10804 t) 914-235-1201

Holy Name of Jesus - 75 Lispenard Ave., New Rochelle, NY 10801 t) 914-576-6038 Rev. Michael F. Challinor, Pst.; Rev. Francis Maurice, Assoc. Pst.; Dcn. Carmine DeMarco;

Sisters of Charity Convent - 78 Petersville Rd., New Rochelle, NY 10801 t) 914-636-4354

Salesian HS Chapel - 148 Main St., New Rochelle, NY 10801 t) 914-632-0248

Salesian Provincial House Chapel - t) 914-636-4225

St. Joseph - 280 Washington Ave., New Rochelle, NY 10801 t) 914-632-0675 stjoenr@aol.com Administered from Parish of St. Gabriel and St. Joseph, 120 Division St., New Rochelle. Rev. Edward P. O'Halloran, Pst.; Antoinette Rossetti, DRE;

St. Joseph School of Religion - 53 Sixth St., New Rochelle, NY 10801 t) 914-632-3458

NEW WINDSOR

St. Joseph - 4 St. Joseph Pl., New Windsor, NY 12553 Administered from Parish of St. Thomas of Canterbury and St. Joseph, 10 Second St., Cornwell-on-Hudson. Rev. Rees W. Doughty, Pst.;

NEW YORK

Cathedral of St. Patrick - 50-51 St. and Fifth Ave., New York, NY 10022; Mailing: 460 Madison Ave., New York, NY 10022 t) 212-753-2261 saintpatrickscathedral.org Very Rev. Enrique Salvo, Rector; Rev. Edward M. Dougherty, M.M., Assoc. Pst.; Rev. Arthur A. Golino, Assoc. Pst.; Rev. Donald Haggerty, Assoc. Pst.; Rev. Andrew King, Assoc. Pst.; Dcn. Anthony Gostkowski; Dcn. Edmundo A. Ramos; Dcn. Jeffrey Trexler;

St. Agnes - 143 E. 43rd St., New York, NY 10017 t) 212-682-5722 church@stagneschurchnyc.org (Opus Dei) Rev. Michael Barrett, Pst.; Rev. Robert A. Brisson, Assoc. Pst.; Most Rev. John J. O'Hara, In Res.; Heitor A. Caballero, Music Min.;

All Saints - 47 E. 129th St., New York, NY 10035 t) 212-534-3535 Records at Parish of St. Charles Borromeo and All Saints, 211 W. 141st St., New York. Rev. Gregory Chisholm, S.J., Pst.; Rev. Evariste Ouedraogo, In Res.;

St. Aloysius - 219 W. 132nd St., New York, NY 10027 t) 917-261-6507 (Jesuit) Rev. Victor O. Emumwen, Pst.; Rev. Frederick J. Pellegrini, S.J., Pst.; Rev. Thomas P. Green, S.J., Assoc. Pst.;

St. Andrew - 20 Cardinal Hayes Pl., New York, NY 10007 Administered from Parish of Our Lady of Victory and St. Andrew, 60 William St., New York. Rev. Myles P. Murphy, Pst.;

New York Presbyterian Lower Manhattan Hospital - 170 William St., New York, NY 10007 t) 212-312-5000

St. Margaret's House - 49 Fulton St., New York, NY 10007 t) 212-766-8122

Parish of St. Ann and St. Lucy - 312 E. 110th St., New York, NY 10029 (PIME Missionaries) Rev. Vijay Marneni, PIME, Pst.;

St. Ann's Convent - 319 E. 109 St., New York, NY 10029

St. Ann's Roman Catholic Church - 110 E. 12th St., New York, NY 10003; Mailing: 414 E. 14th St., New York, NY 10009 Administered from and records located at Immaculate Conception, 414 E. 14th St., New York, NY 10009. Tel: 212-254-0200.

Annunciation - 88 Convent Ave., New York, NY 10027 t) 212-234-1919 office@theannunciation.net www.theannunciation.net (Piarist Fathers) Rev. Orlando J. Rodriguez, Sch.P., Pst.; Rev. Jose M. Clavero, Sch.P. (Spain), Par. Vicar; Rev. Felix Ganuza, Sch.P. (Spain), Par. Vicar;

St. Anthony of Padua - 154 Sullivan St., New York, NY 10012 t) 212-777-2755 stanthonynyc.org (Franciscan) Rev. Mario Julian, O.F.M., Pst.; Bro. Charles Trebino, O.F.M., Pst. Min./Coord.; CRP Stds.: 55

Ascension - 221 W. 107th St., New York, NY 10025 t) 212-749-5938 (CRP); 212-222-0666 faithformation@ascensionchurchnyc.org; frkearney@ascensionchurchnyc.org www.ascensionchurchnyc.org Rev. Daniel S. Kearney, Pst.; Dcn. Escolastico Daniel Corniel Tejada; Dcn. Nelson Falcon; Rev. Daniel LeBlanc, O.M.I., In Res.; CRP Stds.: 98

Riverside Study Center - 330 Riverside Dr., New York, NY 10025 t) 212-222-3285 (Opus Dei)

St. Benedict the Moor - 457 W. 51st St., New York, NY 10019 Sacred Heart of Jesus, New York Rev. Msgr. Kevin J. Nelan, Pst.;

Blessed Sacrament - 152 W. 71st St., New York, NY 10023 t) 212-877-3111 Rev. David E. Nolan, Pst.;

Convent of Blessed Sacrament - 133 W. 70th St., New York, NY 10023

St. Agnes' Home - 237 W. 74th St., New York, NY 10023 t) 212-874-9203

St. Brigid - 119 Ave. B, New York, NY 10009 Rev. Sean Connolly, Pst.;

St. Catherine of Genoa - 506 W. 153rd St., New York, NY 10031 t) 212-862-6130 Rev. Evaristus C. Ohuche, Pst.; Rev. Dessier Predelus (Haiti), Assoc. Pst.; Dcn. Jose Abreu;

St. Catherine of Siena - c/o St. Vincent Ferrer, 869 Lexington Ave., New York, NY 10065-6648 Administered from Parish of St. Vincent Ferrer and St. Catherine of Siena, 869 Lexington Ave, New York. Rev. Walter Cornelius Wagner, O.P., Pst.; Rev. Joseph Allen, O.P., Assoc. Pst.; Rev. Jonah F. Pollock, O.P., Assoc. Pst.; Rev. Philip Innocent Smith, O.P., Assoc. Pst.; Bro. Thomas Aquinas Dolan, O.P., In Res.; Rev. John Aquinas Farren, O.P., In Res.; Rev. John Patrick McGuire, O.P., In Res.; Sr. Margaret T. Oettinger, O.P., Chap.;

Parish of St. Cecilia and Holy Agony - 125 E. 105th St., New York, NY 10029 t) 212-534-1350 (Apostles of Jesus) Dcn. Jose M. Hernandez; Very Rev. Peter Mushi, A.J., Pst.; Rev. Godfrey Awobi, A.J., In Res.;

Chapel of the Resurrection - 276 W. 151st St., New York, NY 10039 Mission of St. Charles Borromeo. Records at St. Charles Borromeo, 211 W. 141st St., New York, NY 10030 (212-281-2100). Francis Mendez, DRE; Yolanda Torres, DRE;

Chapel of the Resurrection - t) 212-281-2100 scbharlem211@gmail.com scbrchurch.org All sacraments are administered through St. Charles Church.

Chapel of the Sacred Hearts of Jesus and Mary - 142 E. 29th St., New York, NY 10016 Administered from Parish of Our Saviour and St. Stephen/Our Lady of the Scapular, 59 Park Ave., New York. Rev. Robert J. Robbins, Admin.;

Parish of St. Charles Borromeo and All Saints - 211 W. 141st St., New York, NY 10030 t) 212-281-2100 Rev. Wilhelmus J Klaver, M.H.M, Pst.; Rev. Thomas B. Fenlon, Assoc. Pst.; Dcn. Rodney Beckford; Dcn. Michel Hodge; Dcn. Kenneth L. Radcliffe; CRP Stds.: 23

Resurrection - 276 W. 151st St., New York, NY 10039 t) 212-690-7555

St. Columba - 343 W. 25th St., New York, NY 10001 t) 212-807-8876 Administered from Parish of Guardian Angel and St. Columba, 193 Tenth Ave., New York. Rev. James H. Hauver, Pst.; Rev. Msgr. Walter J. Niebrzydowski, Assoc. Pst.; Rev. Tomas DelValle, In Res.; Rev. Chrisanth Mugasha, A.J., In Res.; Rev. Francis Okoli, In Res.; David Strickland, Music Min.; Elizabeth Foley, RCIA Coord.;

Sisters of Congregation of Notre Dame - 329 W. 25th St., New York, NY 10001 t) 212-243-1760

Corpus Christi - 529 W. 121st St., New York, NY 10027 t) 212-666-9350 Rev. Peter Andrew Heasley, Pst.; Rev. Michael K. Holleran, Assoc. Pst.; CRP Stds.: 10

St. Cyril - 62 St. Marks Pl., New York, NY 10003; Mailing: 151 First Ave, #185, New York, NY 10003 t) 212-674-3442 krizolog@yahoo.com (Franciscan) Rev. Krizolog Cimerman, O.F.M., Pst.;

SS. Cyril and Methodius - St. Raphael - 502 W. 41st St., New York, NY 10036 t) 212-563-3395 (Franciscan) Rev. Nikola Pasalic, O.F.M., Pst.; Rev. Zegko Barbaric, O.F.M., Assoc. Pst.; Rev. Iliya Puyic, O.F.M., Assoc. Pst.;

St. Elizabeth - 268 Wadsworth Ave., New York, NY 10033 t) 212-923-4900 (CRP); 212-568-8803 Rev. Ambiorix Rodriguez, Pst.; Rev. Lorenzo Laboy, Assoc. Pst.;

Sisters Residence - 612 W. 187th St., New York, NY 10033

Cabrini Chapel - 701 Ft. Washington Ave., New York, NY 10040 t) 212-923-3536 st.francescabrinishrine@verizon.net

Isabella Geriatric Center - 515 Audubon Ave., New York, NY 10040 t) 212-342-9245

St. Elizabeth of Hungary - 211 E. 83rd St., New York, NY 10028-2854 t) 212-734-5747 Records at Parish of St. Monica, St. Elizabeth of Hungary, and St. Stephen of Hungary, 413 E. 79th St., New York. Very Rev. Donald C. Baker, Pst.; Rev. Msgr. Patrick P. McCahill, Assoc. Pst.; Rev. James C. Sheehan, In Res.;

St. Emeric - 185 Ave. D, New York, NY 10009 Records at St. Brigid, 119 Ave. B, New York. Rev. Lorenzo Ato, Admin.;

Epiphany - 239 E. 21st St., New York, NY 10010 t) 212-475-1966 Rev. Austin E. Titus, Pst.; Rev. James Mayzik, Par. Vicar;

St. Frances Cabrini - 411 E. 66th St., New York, NY 10065 t) 212-734-4613 parishoffice@eastrivercatholics.org www.eastrivercatholics.org Administered from Parish of St. John Nepomucene, St. Frances Cabrini, and St. John the Martyr, 411 E. 66th St., New York. Rev. Stefan Chanas, Pst.; Rev. Ronelo Anung, Par. Vicar; Rev. Martin Kertys, Par. Vicar;

St. Francis de Sales - 135 E. 96th St., New York, NY 10128 t) 212-289-0425 fatherkelly@sfdsnyc.org stfrancis96.org Rev. Philip J. Kelly, Pst.; Jayne Porcell, DRE; CRP Stds.: 67

St. Francis of Assisi - 135 W. 31st St., New York, NY 10001 t) 212-736-8500 Rev. Thomas Gallagher, OFM, Pst.; Rev. Michael Carnevale, O.F.M., Pst. Assoc.; Rev. Julian Jagudilla, O.F.M., Assoc. Pst.; Rev. Jinyeol Kim, OFM, Assoc. Pst.; Rev. Barry James Langley, OFM, Assoc. Pst.; Rev. Steven Patti, OFM, Pst. Assoc.;

St. Francis Xavier - 46 W. 16th St., New York, NY 10011; Mailing: 55 W. 15th St., New York, NY 10011 t) 212-627-2100 stfrancisxavier@sfxavier.org www.sfxavier.org (Jesuit) Rev. Kenneth Boller, SJ, Pst.; Rev. James J. Miracky, S.J., Assoc. Pst.; John Uehlein, Music Min.; Luz Marina Diaz, DRE; CRP Stds.: 110

Good Shepherd - 608 Isham St., New York, NY 10034 (Capuchin Franciscans) Rev. Thomas Faiola, O.F.M.Cap., Pst.; Rev. Michael Ramos, O.F.M.Cap., Par. Vicar; Dcn. Antonio Guzman; Dcn. Rafael Then; Rev. Royston Menolickal, OFM Cap., In Res.;

Chapel - 630 Isham St., New York, NY 10034 t) 212-567-1600 (Private)

St. Gregory - 144 W. 90th St., New York, NY 10024 stgregnyc@aol.com Administered from Parish of Holy Name of Jesus and St. Gregory the Great, 207 W. 96th St., New York. Rev. Lawrence D. Ford, O.F.M., Pst.; Rev. Msgr. Michael Crimmins, Assoc. Pst.; Rev. Luis Pulido, Assoc. Pst.;

Parish of Guardian Angel and St. Columba - 193 Tenth Ave., New York, NY 10011-4709 t) (212) 929-5966 c) (917) 439-2328 parish@guardianangelstcolumba.org guardianangelstcolumba.org Rev. Pancrose Kalist, Pst.;

Holy Agony - 1834 Third Ave., New York, NY 10029 Records at Parish of St. Cecilia and Holy Agony, 125 W. 105th St., New York. (Vincentian) Very Rev. Peter Mushi, A.J., Pst.; Rev. Jesus Arellano, C.M., Assoc. Pst.; Rev. Godfrey Awobi, A.J., Assoc. Pst.;

Parish of Holy Cross and St. John the Baptist - 329 W. 42nd St., New York, NY 10036 t) 212-246-4732 t.tracy@christinthecity.nyc Rev. Francis Gasparik, O.F.M.Cap., Pst.; Rev. John B. Riordan, O.F.M.Cap., Assoc. Pst.; Rev. Thomas Franks, O.F.M.Cap., Guardian; Rev. Michael Marigliano, O.F.M.Cap., Priest;

Holy Family - 315 E 47th St., New York, NY 10017-2313 t) 212-753-3401 e.rivera@churchholyfamily.org; info@churchholyfamily.org www.churchholyfamily.org Rev. Gerald E. Murray, Pst.; Rev. Joseph T. Chacko, Assoc. Pst.; Elizabeth Rivera, DRE; CRP Stds.: 80

Holy Innocents - 128 W. 37th St., New York, NY 10018 Rev. James L. Miara, Pst.; Rev. Louis M. Van Thanh, Assoc. Pst.; Rev. Oliver Chanama (Nigeria), In Res.;

Parish of Holy Name of Jesus and St. Gregory the Great - 207 W. 96th St., New York, NY 10025 t) 212-749-0276 x116 (Franciscan) Rev. George Sears, Pst.; Rev. Lawrence Hayes, O.F.M., Assoc. Pst.; Rev. Michael McDonnell, O.F.M., Assoc. Pst.; Rev. Kevin Tortorelli, O.F.M., Assoc. Pst.; Dcn. Andre Alexandre, In Res.; Rev. John J. Coughlin, O.F.M., In Res.; Rev. Matthew A. Pravetz, O.F.M., In Res.; Rev. Wesbee Victor, Par. Vicar;

Holy Rosary - 444 E. 119th St., New York, NY 10035 Records at Parish of St. Paul and Holy Rosary, 113 E. 117th St., New York. (Augustinian) Rev. Pablo Waldmann, I.V.E. (Argentina), Pst.; Rev. Basilio S. Alava, O.S.A., Assoc. Pst.; Rev. Abel Alvarez, O.S.A., Assoc. Pst.; Rev. Gilbert Luis R. Centina III, O.S.A., Assoc. Pst.;

Holy Trinity - 213 W. 82nd St., New York, NY 10024 Rev. Msgr. Thomas P. Sandi, Pst.; Rev. Stephen M. Koeth, C.S.C., In Res.; Rev. Gary M. Mead, In Res.;

St. Ignatius Loyola - 980 Park Ave., New York, NY 10028 t) 212-288-3588 church@saintignatiusloyola.org www.ignatius.nyc (Jesuit) Rev. Dennis J. Yesalonia, S.J., Pst.; Rev. Mark Hallinan, S.J., Assoc. Pst.; Rev. Michael P. Hilbert, S.J., Assoc. Pst.; Jean Santopatre, Pst. Assoc.; Kate Noonan, DRE; Rev. William J. Bergen, S.J., Senior Priest; CRP Stds.: 221

Loyola School - (Grades 9-12) t) 212-288-3522 loyolaprincipal@adnyeducation.org www.loyolanyc.org/ (Independent Catholic) James Lyness, Prin.; Tony Oroszlany, Pres.; Stds.: 219; Lay Tchrs.: 23

Immaculate Conception - 414 E. 14th St., New York, NY 10009 t) (212) 254-0200 iccboss@aol.com immaculateconception-nyc.org Rev. Msgr. Kevin J. Nelan, Pst.; Rev. Lorenzo Laboy, Par. Vicar; Dcn. Rene

Garcia; CRP Stds.: 50

Incarnation - 1290 St. Nicholas Ave., New York, NY 10033 t) 212-927-7474 incarnationchurchnyc@gmail.com Very Rev. Edward K. Russell, Pst.; Rev. Edwin Bonifacio, Par. Vicar; Rev. Francisco Tejada, Par. Vicar; Rafael Aledo, DRE;

St. James - 23 Oliver St., New York, NY 10038 Records at Parish of Transfiguration and St. James/St. Joseph, 29 Mott St., New York. Rev. Raymond J. Nobiletti, M.M., Pst.; Elba Feliciano, DRE;

St. Jean Baptiste - 184 E. 76th St., New York, NY 10021 t) 212-288-5082 x30 (CRP); 212-288-5082 x10 robinscott@yahoo.com; sjbrcc@yahoo.com (Blessed Sacrament Fathers & Brothers) Rev. John A. Kamas, S.S.S., Pst.; Rev. Bernard J. Camire, S.S.S., Assoc. Pst.; Rev. Ernest R. Falardeau, S.S.S., Assoc. Pst.; Rev. Jude Gregory Fernando, S.S.S., Assoc. Pst.; Rev. James Hayes, S.S.S., Assoc. Pst.; Rev. Norman Pelletier, S.S.S., Assoc. Pst.; Joan Prenty, DRE;

Sisters' Convent - t) 212-472-1230 (Apt. A); 212-472-8821 (Apt. B) www.cnd-m.com

Parish of St. John Nepomucene, St. Frances Cabrini, and St. John the Martyr - 411 E. 66th St., New York, NY 10065 t) 212-734-4613 parishoffice@eastrivercatholics.org www.eastrivercatholics.org (Slovak) Rev. Stefan Chanas, Pst.; Rev. Ronelo Anung, Par. Vicar; Rev. Martin Kertys, Par. Vicar; CRP Stds.: 37

Sisters' Convent - 320 E. 66th St., New York, NY 10065 t) 212-737-0221

St. John the Baptist - 213 W. 30th St., New York, NY 10001 Administered from Parish of Holy Cross and St. John the Baptist, 329 W. 42nd St., New York. (Capuchin) Rev. Thomas Franks, O.F.M.Cap., Pst.; Rev. John B. Riordan, O.F.M.Cap., Assoc. Pst.; Bro. George McCloskey, O.F.M.Cap., In Res.;

Parish of St. John the Evangelist and Our Lady of Peace - 348 E. 55th St., New York, NY 10022 t) 212-753-8418 churchofstjohn@cs.com stjohnevannyc.com/ Rev. Msgr. Douglas J. Mathers, Pst.; Rev. Bernal Stainwall, Par. Vicar;

St. John the Martyr - 259 E. 71st St., New York, NY 10021 t) 212-734-4613 parishoffice@eastrivercatholics.org Records at Parish of St. John Nepomucene, St. Frances Cabrini, and St. John the Martyr, 411 E. 66th St., New York. Rev. Stefan Chanas, Pst.;

St. Joseph - 371 Sixth Ave., New York, NY 10014 t) 212-741-1274 office@stjosephgv.nyc www.stjosephgv.nyc (Dominican) Rev. Boniface Endorf, Pst.; Rev. Clement Dickie, O.P., Vicar; Rev. Isaiah Beiter, OP, Chap.; Nicole Michell-Bogatz, DRE;

St. Joseph - 5 Monroe St., New York, NY 10002 Records at Parish of Transfiguration and St. James/St. Joseph, 29 Mott St., New York. (Scalabrinian) Rev. Raymond J. Nobiletti, M.M., Pst.;

Convent - 83 Madison St., New York, NY 10002 t) 212-233-5670

St. Joseph Church - Yorkville - 404 E. 87th St., New York, NY 10128 t) (212) 289-6030 www.stjosephsyorkville.org Rev. James Boniface Ramsey, Pst.; Rev. Elias Mallon, S.A., In Res.;

St. Joseph of the Holy Family - 405 W. 125th St., New York, NY 10027 Rev. Joseph Kinda, Pst.; Rev. Ransford Clarke, Assoc. Pst.; Rev. Neil J. O'Connell, O.F.M., Assoc. Pst.;

Convent - 400 W. 126th St., New York, NY 10027

St. Jude - 439 W. 204th St., New York, NY 10034 t) 212-569-3002 Rev. Felix Antonio Reyes Alba, C.R.L., Pst.; Dcn. Porfirio Rodriguez; Dcn. Rafael Taveras;

St. Lucy - 344 E. 104th St., New York, NY 10029 Administered from Parish of St. Ann and St. Lucy, New York. Rev. Vijay Marneni, PIME, Admin.;

St. Malachy's - 239 W. 49th St., New York, NY 10019 t) 212-489-1340 parishoffice@actorschapel.org www.actorschapel.org (The Actors' Chapel) Rev. John Fraser, Pst.; Rev. Msgr. Oscar A. Aquino, In Res.; CRP Stds.: 30

Encore Community Services - t) 646-726-4299 www.encorecommunityservices.org Sr. Elizabeth Hasselt, O.P., Exec.; Peggy Gearity, Dir.; Sr. Lillian McNamara, O.P., Dir.;

Encore Community Center & Programs - t) 212-581-2910

St. Mark the Evangelist - 65 W. 138th St., New York, NY 10037 (Holy Spirit Fathers) Rev. Jean Pierre Kapumet Tambwe, C.S.Sp., Pst.;

St. Mark Convent - t) 212-283-5306

St. Mary - 28 Attorney St., New York, NY 10002 Rev. Andrew O'Connor, Admin.;

Mary Help of Christians - 440 E. 12th St., New York, NY 10009 (Salesian), Records at: Immaculate Conception, 414 E. 14th St., New York, NY 10009 (212-254-0200)

St. Michael - 424 W. 34th St., New York, NY 10001 t) 212-563-2575 stmichaelc091@gmail.com stmichaelnyc.org Rev. Msgr. Marc J. Filacchione, Admin.; CRP Stds.: 6

St. Michael Chapel - 266 Mulberry St., New York, NY 10012 t) 212-226-2644 ligreci@msn.com Protodeacon Christopher LiGreci; Rev. Volodymyr Sibirnyy, Pst.;

Parish of St. Monica, St. Elizabeth of Hungary, and St. Stephen of Hungary - 413 E. 79th St., New York, NY 10075 Very Rev. Donald C. Baker, Pst.; Rev. Joseph A. Francis, Assoc. Pst.;

Most Holy Crucifix - 378 Broome St., New York, NY 10013 Records at Basilica of St. Patrick's Old Cathedral, 263 Mulberry St., New York, NY 10012. Tel: 212-226-8075.

Parish of Most Holy Redeemer and Nativity - 173 E. Third St., New York, NY 10009 t) 212-673-4224 (Redemptorist) Rev. Sean Connolly, Pst.; Rev. James R. Cascione, C.Ss.R., Assoc. Pst.; Rev. Charles Coury, C.Ss.R., In Res.; Rev. Adam M. Koncik, C.Ss.R., In Res.; Rev. Robert M. Pagliari, C.Ss.R., In Res.;

Most Precious Blood - 109 Mulberry St., New York, NY 10013 Administered from Parish of St. Patrick's Old Cathedral and Most Precious Blood, 263 Mulberry St., New York. (Franciscan) Rev. Msgr. Donald Sakano, Pst.;

Nativity - 141 Henry St., New York, NY 10002 Records at Parish of Most Holy Redeemer and Nativity, 173 Third St., New York. Rev. Sean J. McGillicuddy, C.Ss.R., Pst.;

Nativity Mission Center - 204 Forsyth St., New York, NY 10002 t) 212-477-2472

Notre Dame - 405 W. 114th St., New York, NY 10025 t) (212) 866-1500 ndparish.org Rev. Peter Andrew Heasley, Pst.; Rev. Michael K. Holleran, Assoc. Pst.; CRP Stds.: 15

St. Luke's Hospital - t) 212-523-4000

Amsterdam Nursing Home - 1060 Amsterdam Avenue, New York, NY 10025 t) 212-316-7700 www.amsterdamcares.org Moshe Blackstein, Admin.;

Our Lady of Esperanza - 624 W. 156th St., New York, NY 10032 Rev. Ramon A. Lopez, Pst.;

Parish of Our Lady of Good Counsel and St. Thomas More - 230 E. 90th St., New York, NY 10128 Rev. Kevin V. Madigan, Pst.; Rev. Msgr. Patrick P. McCahill, In Res.; Marcelle Devine, DRE;

Our Lady of Guadalupe at St. Bernard's - 328 W. 14th St., New York, NY 10014 Rev. Jesus Ledezma, Pst.;

St. Veronica - 149 Christopher St., New York, NY 10014

Our Lady of Lourdes - 472 W. 142nd St., New York, NY 10031 Rev. Gilberto Angel-Neri, Pst.; Dcn. Pedro O'Brien-Lambert; Hector Martinez, Music Min.; Pablo Ortega, DRE;

Convent of Our Lady of Lourdes - 463 W. 142nd St., New York, NY 10031 t) 212-862-4380

Our Lady of Mt. Carmel - 448 E. 116th St., New York, NY 10029-0614 (Pallottine) Rev. Marian Wierzchowski, S.A.C., Pst.;

Convent - 456 E. 116th St., New York, NY 10029-0614 t) 212-427-2381

Our Lady of Peace - 348 E. 55th St., New York, NY 10065 Records at Parish of St. John the Evangelist and Our Lady of Peace, 348 E. 55th St., New York. Dcn. G. Thomas Harenchar; Rev. Msgr. Douglas J. Mathers, Pst.; Rev. Andrew Bielak (Poland), In Res.;

Our Lady of Pompeii - 25 Carmine St., New York, NY 10014 t) (212) 989-6805 olpnyc.org (Scalabrinian) Rev. Angelo Plodari, C.S., Admin.; Rev. Andrei Zanon, C.S., Vicar; Rev. Jairo Francisco Guidini, C.S., Vicar; Rev. Ezio Marchetto, C.S., Vicar;

Our Lady of Sorrows - 213 Stanton St, New York, NY 10002-1898 t) 212-673-0900 x301 oloschurch@yahoo.com www.ols.weconnect.com (Capuchin) Rev. Thomas McNamara, O.F.M.Cap., Pst.; Bro. Robert Gerdin, O.F.M.Cap., Pst. Assoc.; Rev. Arlen Harris, O.F.M.Cap., Par. Vicar; Yvette Rivera, DRE; Friar Benedict Ayodi, OFM Cap, In Res.; Rev. Paul Bielecki, OFM Cap., In Res.;

Our Lady of the Rosary - 7 State St., New York, NY 10004 Administered from Parish of St. Peter and Our Lady of the Rosary, 18 Vesey St., New York. Shrine of St. Elizabeth Ann Seton. Rev. Jarlath Quinn, Pst.; Rev. Msgr. Leslie Ivers, In Res.; Rev. Robert A. Jeffers, In Res.; Maiwenn Jeffers-Bell, DRE;

Parish of Our Lady of Victory and St. Andrew - 60 William St., New York, NY 10005 t) 212-422-5535 parishmail@olvsta.org www.olvsta.org Rev. Myles P. Murphy, Pst.; Rev. Edwin Ezeokeke, Par. Vicar; Rev. Lino Gonsalves, In Res.;

Our Lady Queen of Martyrs - 91 Arden St., New York, NY 10040 Rev. Felix Antonio Reyes Alba, C.R.L., Pst.; Rev. Edison Navarro, C.R.L., Par. Vicar; Dcn. Narcisco Hernandez; Dcn. Delio Fernandez; Dcn. Bienvenido Valdez;

Parish of Our Saviour and St. Stephen/Our Lady of the Scapular - 59 Park Ave., New York, NY 10016 Rev. Msgr. Kevin L. Sullivan, Admin.; Rev. Robert J. Robbins, Pst.; Rev. Andrew E. Kurzyna, Assoc. Pst.;

St. Stephen and Our Lady of the Scapular - 142 E. 29th St., New York, NY 10016

Chapel of the Sacred Hearts of Jesus and Mary - 325 E. 33rd St., New York, NY 10016 t) 212-213-6027

Parish of St. Patrick's Old Cathedral and Most Precious Blood - 263 Mulberry St., New York, NY 10012 Rev. Msgr. Kevin J. Nelan, Pst.; Rev. Andrew Thi, Assoc. Pst.; Dcn. Paul Vitale;

St. Michael - 266 Mulberry St., New York, NY 10012 t) 212-226-2644

Parish of St. Paul and Holy Rosary - 113 E. 117th St., New York, NY 10035 t) 212-534-4422 x19 ccdstpaul@servidoras.org (Institute of the Incarnate Word) Rev. Pablo Waldmann, I.V.E. (Argentina), Pst.; Bro. Pablo Torre, I.V.E., Assoc. Pst.;

Convent - St. Paul Convent, 149 E. 117th St., New York, NY 10035 t) 917-492-3668 c.roseduchesne@servidoras.org www.ssvmusa.org (Sisters of The Servants of the Lord and The Virgin of Matara)

St. Paul the Apostle - 405 W. 59th St., New York, NY 10019 t) 212-265-3495 contact@stpaultheapostle.org www.stpaultheapostle.org (Paulist. See also Paulist Fathers' Motherhouse under Monasteries located in the Institution section.) Rev. Broderick Matthew Walsh, CSP, Pst.; Rev. Paul S Rospond, CSP, Assoc. Pst.; Dcn. Waldemar Sandoval;

Parish of Saint Peter and Our Lady of the Rosary - 22 Barclay St., New York, NY 10007 t) 212-233-8355 info@spcolr.org www.spcolr.org Rev. Jarlath Quinn, Pst.; Rev. Edwin Ezeokeke, Pst. Assoc.; Maiwenn Jeffres-Bell, DRE; CRP Stds.: 250

St. Rose of Lima - 510 W. 165th St., New York, NY 10032 Rev. Ramon A. Lopez, Pst.; Rev. Jesus Ledezma, Assoc. Pst.; Rev. Richard Marrano, Assoc. Pst.; Rev. Melchor Ferrer, S.D.B., In Res.; Sr. Ramona Liriano, DRE;

St. Rose of Lima Convent - 509 W. 164th St., New York, NY 10032

Sacred Heart of Jesus - 457 W. 51st, New York, NY 10019 t) 212-265-5020 x16 Rev. Lorenzo Ato, Pst.;

Centro Maria - 539 W. 54th St., New York, NY 10019 t) 212-757-6989

Convent of the Sisters of Life - 450 W. 51st St., New York, NY 10019 t) 212-397-1396 sistersoflife.org Sr. Faustina Maria Pia Bianchi, S.V., Local Sup.;

St. Stanislaus Bishop and Martyr - 101 E. Seventh St., New York, NY 10009 (Pauline Fathers) Rev. Michal Czyzewski, OSPPE, Pst.; Rev. Piotr D. Bednarski, O.S.P.P.E., Assoc. Pst.;

St. Stephen and Our Lady of the Scapular - 142 E. 29th St., New York, NY 10016 Administered from Parish of Our Saviour and St. Stephen/Our Lady of the Scapular, 59 Park Ave., New York. Rev. Robert J. Robbins, Admin.;

Chapel of the Sacred Hearts of Jesus and Mary - 325 E. 33rd St., New York, NY 10016 t) 212-213-6027

St. Stephen of Hungary - 414 E. 82nd St., New York, NY 10028 Records at Parish of St. Monica, St. Elizabeth of Hungary, and St. Stephen of Hungary, 413 E. 79th St., New York. (Franciscan) Very Rev. Donald C. Baker, Pst.;

Dewitt Nursing Home - 211 E. 79th St., New York, NY 10021 t) 212-879-1600

St. Teresa - 141 Henry St., New York, NY 10002 Rev. Alexis Bastidas (Venezuela), Pst.; Rev. Joseph Guo Zhang Ruan, Assoc. Pst.;

Church of the Nativity - 44 - 2nd Ave., New York, NY 10003 t) 212-674-8590

St. Thomas More - 65 E. 89th St., New York, NY 10128 Administered from Parish of Our Lady of Good Counsel and St. Thomas More, 230 E. 90th St., New York. Rev. Kevin V. Madigan, Pst.;

St. Thomas the Apostle - 262 W. 118th St., New York, NY 10026 Records at St. Joseph of the Holy Family, New York, NY.

Parish of Transfiguration and St. James/St. Joseph - 29 Mott St., New York, NY 10013-5006 Rev. Roger Kwan, Pst.; Rev. Raymond J. Nobiletti, M.M.; Dcn. Patrick So;

Early Childhood Campus - (Grades PreK- 10 Confucius Pl., New York, NY 10002 t) 212-431-8769 earlychildhood@transfigurationschoolnyc.org; emily.tran@adnyeducation.org Emily Eng, Prin.;

Parish of St. Vincent Ferrer and St. Catherine of Siena - 869 Lexington Ave., New York, NY 10065-6648 t) 212-744-2080 parish@svsc.info www.svsc.info (Dominican) Rev. Peter Martyr Yungwirth, OP, Pst.; Rev. Joseph Allen, O.P., Par. Vicar; Rev. Reginald Hoefer, Par. Vicar; Rev. Francis Belanger, Par. Vicar; Dcn. John Powers; Bro. John Damian McCarthy, O.P.;

Dominican Sisters of Our Lady of the Springs - 152 E. 66th St., New York, NY 10065 t) 212-744-2375

Dominican Academy - 44 E. 68th St., New York, NY 10065 t) 212-744-0195

NEWBURGH

St. Mary - 180 South St., Newburgh, NY 12550 Records at Parish of St. Patrick and St. Mary, Newburgh. Rev. Fernando A. Hernandez, Pst.;

Parish of St. Patrick and St. Mary - 55 Grand St., Newburgh, NY 12550 t) 914-561-6470 Rev. Fernando A. Hernandez, Pst.; Rev. Patrick Bonner, Assoc. Pst.; Rev. Bladi J. Socualaya, Assoc. Pst.; Dcn. Thomas Neppl; Dcn. Donald Halter; Dcn. Dennis White;

Our Lady of the Lake - Lakeside & Rte. 52, Orange Lake, NY 12550 t) 914-561-9537

Roman Catholic Church of Sacred Heart and Saint Francis of Assisi - 301 Ann St., Newburgh, NY 12550 t) 845-561-2589 (CRP); 845-561-2264 sacredheart.newburgh@verizon.net; saintfrancisnewburgh@gmail.com www.stmotherteresanewburgh.com Rev. Fernando A. Hernandez, Pst.; Rev. John Francis Antony, Par. Vicar; Rev. Joseph J. Tyrrell, Par. Vicar; Dcn. Peter R. Haight;

OBERNBURG

St. Mary - 386 Country Route 95, Obernburg, NY 12767; Mailing: P.O. Box 1, Obernburg, NY 12767 Rev. George E. Baker, Admin.; Dcn. Lawrence F. Knack;

OSSINING

St. Ann - 25 Eastern Ave., Ossining, NY 10562 t) 914-941-2420 (CRP); 914-941-2556 info@stannsoss.com Rev. Elvin Rivera, Pst.; Rev. Jorge Luis Cleto, O.S.A., Par. Vicar; Dcn. Jose L. De Jesus;

St. Augustine - 381 N. Highland Ave., Ossining, NY 10562 t) 914-941-0067 joan.pires@staugny.org Rev. Brian T. McSweeney, Pst.; Dcn. Clifford Calanni; Dcn. John Barbera; Dcn. Steven DeMartino; Rev. John Figueroa; CRP Stds.: 158

OTISVILLE

Holy Name of Jesus - 45 Highland Ave., Otisville, NY 10963-0597; Mailing: P.O. Box 597, Otisville, NY 10963-0597 t) 845-386-2327 (CRP); 845-386-1320 hnojre@yahoo.com; hnojotisville@frontiernet.net www.hnojotisville.com Rev. Michael L. Palazzo, Pst.; Dcn. Robert Leavy; Sr. Nancy Elizabeth Doran, S.S.C., DRE; CRP Stds.: 89

PATTERSON

Sacred Heart - 414 Haviland Dr., Patterson, NY 12563 www.sacredheartpattersonny.org Rev. Richard Gill, Pst.; Margaret Cairney, DRE;

PAWLING

St. John the Evangelist, St. Charles Borromeo - 39 E. Main St., Pawling, NY 12564 t) 845-855-9408 (CRP); 845-855-5488 scbsje@gmail.com Rev. John F. Palatucci, Pst.; Rev. Sibi Thomas, Assoc. Pst.; Dcn. Gerard Cartwright; Dcn. Adhur Lekovic;

PEARL RIVER

St. Aedan - 23 Reld Dr., Pearl River, NY 10965 t) 845-735-2036 staedan3@verizon.net Rev. Msgr. Emmet R. Nevin, Pst.; Rev. John F. Palatucci, Assoc. Pst.; Dcn. James F. Maher;

St. Margaret of Antioch - 33 N. Magnolia St., Pearl River, NY 10965 t) 845-735-5489 (CRP); 845-735-4746 smparish.com Rev. Eric P. Raaser, Pst.; Rev. Ransford Clarke, Par. Vicar; Brenda Lattuca, DRE;

PEEKSKILL

Church of the Assumption - 131 Union Ave., Peekskill, NY 10566 t) 914-737-2231 (CRP); 914-737-2071 info@assumptionpeekskill.org; pastor@assumptionpeekskill.org assumptionpeekskill.org/ Rev. Esteban Sanchez Guanga, Pst.; Rev. Carlos Limongi, Par. Vicar; Dcn. Carlos H. Campoverde; Catherine Bischoff, DRE;

PELHAM

St. Catharine - 25 Second Ave., Pelham, NY 10803 t) 914-738-1332 Administered from Parish of Our Lady of Perpetual Help and St. Catharine, Pelham Manor. Rev. Robert J. DeJulio, Pst.; Rev. Trevor Nicholls, Assoc. Pst.;

PELHAM MANOR

Parish of Our Lady of Perpetual Help and St. Catharine - 559 Pelham Manor Rd., Pelham Manor, NY 10803 t) 914-738-0670 (CRP); 914-738-1449 olph10803@msn.com; olphccd0670@optonline.net www.olph-pelhammanor.org Rev. Msgr. Thomas F. Petrillo, Pst.; Rev. Ernest Frimpong, Assoc. Pst.; Rev. Ferdinand Madaki, Assoc. Pst.; Rev. Oliver Offor, Assoc. Pst.; Dcn. Paul Brisson; Dcn. John Catalano;

St. Catherine - 25 Second Ave., Pelham, NY 10803 t) 914-738-1491

PHOENICIA

St. Francis de Sales - 109 Main St., Phoenicia, NY 12464; Mailing: P.O. Box 25, Phoenicia, NY 12464 t) 845-688-5617 sfdchurch@hvc.rr.com Rev. Raphael Iannone, O.F.M.Cap., In Res.; Gerry Nilsen, DRE;

PINE BUSH

The Infant Saviour - 22 Holland Ave., Pine Bush, NY 12566 t) 845-744-9944 (CRP); 845-744-2391 shintydre@gmail.com; infsavpb@hvc.rr.com infantsaviour.org Rev. Niranjan Rodrigo, Pst.; Dcn. Francis Rose; Sr. Shinty Antony, DRE; CRP Stds.: 165

Our Lady of the Valley -

PINE ISLAND

St. Stanislaus Mission - 17 Pulaski Hwy., Pine Island, NY 10969 Mission of St. Joseph. Records at St. Joseph, 14 Glenmare Ave., Florida, NY 10921. Rev. Frank Borkowski, Pst.;

PINE PLAINS

St. Anthony - 68 Poplar Ave., Pine Plains, NY 12567 t) 845-373-8193 icspamen@optonline.net Administered from Parish of Immaculate Conception and St. Anthony, 4 Lavelle Rd., Box 109, Amenia. Rev. Robert K. Wilson, Pst.;

PLATTEKILL

Our Lady of Fatima - 1250 State Rt. 32, Plattekill, NY 12568; Mailing: P.O. Box 700, Plattekill, NY 12568 Rev. Michael Omachi, Pst.;

PLEASANT VALLEY

St. Stanislaus Kostka - 1590 Main St., Pleasant Valley, NY 12569; Mailing: P.O. Box 558, Pleasant Valley, NY 12569 t) 845-635-1700 www.saintstanislaus.net Rev. John J. Backes, Pst.; Dcn. Richard Aglietti; Dcn. John J. Nash; CRP Stds.: 103

PLEASANTVILLE

Church of the Holy Innocents - 431 Bedford Rd., Pleasantville, NY 10570 t) 914-769-0025 office@hiparish.org; lukehoyt@hiparish.org www.hiparish.org (Dominican Friars) Friar Luke Hoyt, OP, Pst.; Friar Leo Camurati, OP, Assoc. Pst.; Rev. Daniel G. Doherty, O.P., In Res.; Rev. Frank I. Sutman, O.P., In Res.;

Our Lady of Pompeii - Saratoga and Garrigan, Pleasantville, NY 10570

PORT CHESTER

Parish of St. John Bosco - 260 Westchester Ave., Port Chester, NY 10573 Rev. Patrick Angelucci, S.D.B., Pst.; Rev. Tarcisio Dos Santos, S.D.B. (Brazil), Assoc. Pst.; Rev. Peter Granzotto, S.D.B., Assoc. Pst.; Rev. Joseph Vien Hoang, S.D.B., Assoc. Pst.; Dcn. William N. Vaccaro; Rev. John Grinsell, S.D.B., In Res.; Rev. David Moreno, S.D.B., In Res.; Rev. Lawrence (Subroto) Naskar (India), In Res.; Rev. Jorge Rodriguez, S.D.B., In Res.; Sr. Ana Maria Causa, S.A., Pst. Assoc.; Irma Austin, DRE; Dcn. Ivan Gemio; Dcn. Michael Gizzo;

Adoration Chapel - 23 Nicola Pl., Port Chester, NY 10573

Sacred Heart of Jesus - 229 Willett Ave., Port Chester, NY 10573 t) 914-939-1497 Administered from Parish of Saint John Bosco, Port Chester. Rev. Michael F. Challinor, Pst.;

PORT EWEN

Parish of Presentation of the Blessed Virgin Mary and Sacred Heart - 209 Hoyt St., Port Ewen, NY 12466; Mailing: P O Box 904, Port Ewen, NY 12466 t) 845-331-0053; 845-384-6828 secyportewen@presentationsacredheart.org www.presentationsacredheart.org Extraordinary Form Mass on Sundays and Certain Feasts. Confessions in Spanish available. Rev. Arthur F. Rojas, Admin.; Dcn. Timothy Dean; Dcn. John J. Larkin; Michelle Metelski, CRE; CRP Stds.: 17

Presentation of the Blessed Virgin Mary - Sacred Heart Church, Esopus, NY. Rev. Arthur Fernando Rojas, Admin.;

Sacred Heart - 1055 Broadway, Esopus, NY 12429; Mailing: Box 200, Esopus, NY 12429 genejgrohe@aol.com www.sacredheartesopus.org

PORT JERVIS

Immaculate Conception - 50 Ball St., Port Jervis, NY 12771; Mailing: P.O. Box 712, Port Jervis, NY 12771 t) 845-858-4208 (CRP); 845-856-8212 st-marys-rectory@hvc.rr.com stmarysportjervis.com Rev. Anthony Giacona, Admin.; Dcn. Richard Marino; Teresa Lothian, DRE; Rev. Ivan L. Csete, Senior Priest in Residence; CRP Stds.: 76

Most Sacred Heart - 12 McAllister St., Port Jervis, NY 12771-0712; Mailing: P.O. Box 712, Port Jervis, NY 12771-0712 office@stmarysportjervis.com stmarysportjervis.com Records at: Immaculate Conception, P.O. Box 712, 50 Ball St., Port Jervis, NY 12771 (845-856-8212/5924)

POUGHKEEPSIE

Holy Trinity - 775 Main St., Poughkeepsie, NY 12603 t) 845-452-1863; 845-471-5838 (CRP) htparishrectory@gmail.com; dre@holytrinitypoughkeepsie.org www.holytrinitypoughkeepsie.com Rev. Anthony Mizzi-Gill, Pst.; Rev. Ajith Wellington, Vicar; Dcn. Shaun

Boyce; Rev. Gamini E. Fernando (Sri Lanka), In Res.; CRP Stds.: 128

St. Martin de Porres - 118 Cedar Valley Rd., Poughkeepsie, NY 12603 t) 845-473-4222 smdpnorman@gmail.com stmartindeporres.org Rev. Matthew J. Furey, Pst.; Rev. Charles Achi, Par. Vicar; Rev. Michael Connolly, Par. Vicar; Dcn. Michael Correale, Pst. Assoc.; Dcn. James Fiorio, Pst. Assoc.; Dcn. Kevin McGuirk, Pst. Assoc.; Dcn. David Nash, Pst. Assoc.; Dcn. Victor Salamone, Pst. Assoc.; Kimberly Papineau, DRE;

Parish of St. Mary-St. Joseph and Our Lady of Mount Carmel - 231 Church St., Poughkeepsie, NY 12601-4200 t) 845-471-4747 (CRP); 845-452-8250 d526@archny.org Rev. Ronald P. Perez, Pst.; Rev. Charles Heston Joseph, Assoc. Pst.; Dcn. Robert Horton; Sally Bellacicco, DRE;

St. Peter - 6 Father Cody Plaza, Poughkeepsie, NY 12601 t) 845-452-8580 x1 stpetersparishny.com/ Rev. Ajith Kirialdeniyage, OMI, Pst.; CRP Stds.: 119

Poughkeepsie, Convent of St. Peter -

Hyde Park, P.J. Kenedy Memorial Chapel of Our Lady of the Way - Albany Post Rd., Hyde Park, NY 12538 Rev. Marc K. Oliver, Chap.;

Our Lady of the Rosary Chapel - 99 Inwood Ave., Poughkeepsie, NY 12601

Our Lady of the Holy Souls - 171 Salt Pt. Tpk., Poughkeepsie, NY 12603

RED HOOK

Parish of St. Christopher and St. Sylvia - 7411 S. Broadway, Red Hook, NY 12571 t) 845-758-5506 (CRP); 845-758-3732 (Office) rectory@stchrisredhook.org www.stchrisredhook.org Rev. Jeffrey J. Maurer, Pst.; Dcn. Raymond Ricci; Dcn. Keith White; Ellen Farina, DRE;

RHINEBECK

Church of the Good Shepherd - 3 Mulberry St., Rhinebeck, NY 12572 t) 845-876-4583 goodshep1@frontiernet.net Rev. Jeffrey J. Maurer, Pst.;

St. Joseph - Church St., Rhinecliff, NY 12574

Rhinebeck, Ferncliff Nursing Home - t) 845-876-2011

ROSENDALE

St. Peter - 1017 Keator Ave., Rosendale, NY 12472; Mailing: P.O. Box 471, Rosendale, NY 12472 t) 845-658-8911 stpeterrosendale.org Rev. Kevin M. Malick, Pst.; CRP Stds.: 44

RYE

Resurrection - 910 Boston Post Rd., Rye, NY 10580 t) 914-925-2754 resprep@optonline.net Rev. Msgr. Donald M. Dwyer, Pst.; Rev. Epifanio Marcaida (Philippines), Assoc. Pst.; Rev. Jon Tviet, Assoc. Pst.;

SAUGERTIES

Parish of St. Mary of the Snow/St. Joseph/St. John the Evangelist - 36 Cedar St., Saugerties, NY 12477 t) (845) 246-4913; (845) 217-3333 (CRP) u533@archny.org stmaryofthesnow.org/ Rev. Christopher H. Berean, Pst.; Dcn. Robert Cranston; Dcn. Arnie Hyland; Dcn. Karl Pietkiewicz; Dcn. Henry Smith; Dcn. Donald F. Trees; Dcn. Michael Sweeney, Music Min.; Alison Belfance, CRE;

Saugerties, Parish Center -

SCARSDALE

Immaculate Heart of Mary - 8 Carman Rd., Scarsdale, NY 10583 t) (914) 723-0276; (914) 723-0281 ihmchurch@ihmscarsdale.org ihm-parish.org Rev. Msgr. Luke M. Sweeney, Pst.; Rev. Rayappa Reddy Thumma (India), Assoc. Pst.; Tracy Keelin, Prin.; Laura Covais, CRE; Liz Reyes, Bus. Mgr.; CRP Stds.: 675

St. Pius X - 91 Secor Rd., Scarsdale, NY 10583 t) 914-472-5594 stpiusxreled@yahoo.com Rev. Francisco Sebastian Bacatan, A.M. (Philippines), Pst.; Rev. Romeo Ascan, A.M. (Philippines), Assoc. Pst.; Rev. Jose C. Ramos, A.M. (Philippines), Assoc. Pst.;

SHRUB OAK

Saint Elizabeth Ann Seton - 1377 E. Main St., Shrub Oak, NY 10588 t) 914-528-3547 seton@seton-parish.org www.seton-parish.org Rev. Robert A. Quarato, Pst.; Rev. Kareem R. Smith, Par. Vicar; Dcn. Walter Lopez; Dcn. John Trembley; Lavoie Jennifer, Music Min.; Donna S. Vallario, DRE; Dcn. Michael F. Wilson;

SLEEPY HOLLOW

Immaculate Conception - 199 N. Broadway, Sleepy Hollow, NY 10591 t) 914-631-0446 jpiimc.ny@gmail.com Rev. Dany Abi Akar, Pst.;

The Magdalene - 525 Bedford Rd., Pocantico Hills, Sleepy Hollow, NY 10591-1216 Rev. Timothy Wiggins, Pst.;

St. Teresa of Avila - 130 Beekman Ave., Sleepy Hollow, NY 10591 t) 914-631-1831 Rev. Rumando Peralta Genao, C.R.L., Pst.; Rev. Edison Navarro, C.R.L., Assoc. Pst.; Rev. Felix Reyes, C.R.L., Assoc. Pst.;

SLOATSBURG

Parish of St. Joan of Arc-Our Lady of Mount Carmel - 32 Eagle Valley Rd., Sloatsburg, NY 10974 t) 845-753-5193 Rev. Joseph A. Emmanuel, Pst.;

SOMERS

St. Joseph - 95 Plum Brook Rd., Somers, NY 10589 t) 914-276-1067 Rev. John M. Lagiovane, Pst.; Rev. Jude Aguwa (Nigeria), Assoc. Pst.; Rev. Matthew MacDonald, Assoc. Pst.; Rev. Matthew Breslin, Par. Vicar;

SPRING VALLEY

Parish of Saint Joseph/Saint Boniface - 245 N. Main St., Spring Valley, NY 10977; Mailing: 333 Sneden Pl. W., Spring Valley, NY 10977 t) 845-356-0054 (CRP); 845-356-0311 stjosephspringvalley.org/ Rev. Levelt Germain, Pst.; Rev. Patrick Adekola (Nigeria), Assoc. Pst.; Rev. Jaccius Jean-Pierre, Par. Vicar; Rev. Adaly Rosado, Par. Vicar; Dcn. Jose Pena; Maureen Foley, DRE;

STATEN ISLAND

Parish of St. Adalbert and St. Roch - 602 Port Richmond Ave., Staten Island, NY 10302 t) 718-442-4755 stastr602@gmail.com Rev. Albin Roby, Pst.; CRP Stds.: 160

St. Ann - 101 Cromwell Ave., Staten Island, NY 10304 t) 718-351-0270 stannschurch@verizon.net www.stannschurchstatenisland.org Rev. Jacob Thumma (India), Pst.; Kathleen Daly, DRE;

St. Anthony of Padua - 24 Shelly Ave., Staten Island, NY 10314 Administered from Parish of Our Lady of Pity and St. Anthony of Padua, 1616 Richmond Ave., Staten Island. Rev. John J. Wroblewski, Pst.;

Assumption/St. Paul - 53 St. Mark's Pl., Staten Island, NY 10301 t) (718) 727-2672 www.assumptionstpaulsi.com Records at Parish of Sts. Peter and Paul and Assumption, 53 St. Mark's Pl., Staten Island. Rev. Louis R. Jerome, Pst.; Rev. Matthew Takyi-Asante, Par. Vicar;

Blessed Sacrament - 30 Manor Rd., Staten Island, NY 10310 t) 718-448-0378 (CRP); 718-442-1581 blessedsacramentchurchsi.org Most Rev. Peter J. Byrne, Pst.; Rev. Francisco Lanzaderas, Assoc. Pst.; Rev. Roland Antony Raj, M.M.I. (India), Assoc. Pst.; Dcn. Christopher Wodzinski;

St. Charles - 644 Clawson St., Staten Island, NY 10306 t) 718-987-2670 secretary@stcharlessi.org; stcharlesccd@stcharlessi.org Rev. Patrick F. Buckley, Pst.; Rev. Ruwandana Mendis, Par. Vicar; Rev. Jeffrey Pomeisl, Par. Vicar; Dcn. Lawrence Droge Sr.; Dcn. Stephen Tobon; CRP Stds.: 328

St. Christopher and St. Margaret Mary - 130 Midland Ave., Staten Island, NY 10306 t) 718-351-2452 mmaryrectoryreled1@verizon.net; i315@archnewyork.org scsmmsi.org/ Rev. Michael W Cichon, Pst.; Rev. Adaly Rosado, Par. Vicar; Dcn. Patrick Graham; Rev. Edgar Devina, In Res.; Barbara Regan, DRE; CRP Stds.: 69

St. Clare - 110 Nelson Ave., Staten Island, NY 10308 t) 718-948-4829 (CRP); 718-984-7873 rectory@stclaresi.com www.stclaresi.com Rev. Arthur Mastrolia, Pst.; Rev. Joseph Harrison, Assoc. Pst.; Rev. Brendan Gormley, Assoc. Pst.; Rev. Jacob Thomas, Pst. Assoc.; Dcn. Richard Mitchell; Dcn. Richard Salhany; Marie Ferro, DRE; CRP Stds.: 660

St. Clement - 207 Harbor Rd., Staten Island, NY 10303 t) 718-727-6442 Rev. Jean-Paul Soler, Pst.;

Holy Child - 4747 Amboy Rd., Staten Island, NY 10312 t) 718-356-5277 Rev. Edwin H. Cipot, Pst.; Rev. Wilfred Y. Dodo, Assoc. Pst.; Sandra Pace, Music Min.; Marie Ferro, DRE;

Holy Family - 366 Watchogue Rd., Staten Island, NY 10314 t) 718-761-6671 holyfamily@si.rr.com Rev. Angelo J. Micciulla, Pst.; Rev. Anthony Enyinmful (Ghana), Assoc. Pst.; Dcn. Joseph Schiavone;

Holy Rosary - 80 Jerome Ave., Staten Island, NY 10305 t) 718-273-6695 (CRP); 718-727-3360 www.hrosary.com Rev. Michael T. Martine, Pst.; Rev. Rizalino P. Garcia, C.M., Assoc. Pst.; Rev. Bernal Stainwall, Assoc. Pst.; Rev. Patrick Anthony (Pakistan), Chap.; Jennifer Rizzuto, DRE;

Immaculate Conception - 128 Targee St., Staten Island, NY 10305 Administered from Parish of St. Joseph, Immaculate Conception and St. Mary, Staten Island. Dcn. Hector Espinal; Rev. Fredy Patino Montoya, Pst.;

St. John Neumann - 1380 Arthur Kill Rd., Staten Island, NY 10312 t) 718-966-7327 Rev. Patrick Anthony (Pakistan); Rev. Robert W. Dillon, Assoc. Pst.;

St. John the Baptist de La Salle - 463 Tompkins Ave., Staten Island, NY 10305 Records at: Immaculate Conception, 463 Tompkins Ave., Staten Island, NY 10305. Tel: 718-816-0047.

Korean Catholic Apostolate of Staten Island - 76 Jackson St., Staten Island, NY 10304 t) 718-273-3311 kcasi08@hanmail.net Rev. Hyunsang Sung, Pst.;

Saint Joseph and Saint Mary Immaculate - 466 Tompkins Ave., Staten Island, NY 10305; Mailing: 463 Tompkins Ave., Staten Island, NY 10305-1722 t) 718-816-0047 reled463@gmail.com; secretary@sjsmiparish.org jmi.life Rev. Carlos Limongi, Admin.; Rev. Ariel Trujillo, Vicar; Dcn. Hector Espinal; Dcn. Paul Kosinski; B. Nelly Corona, DRE; Terry Ann Venturini, DRE;

St. Joseph-St. Thomas St. John Neumann Parish - 6097 Amboy Rd., Staten Island, NY 10309 t) 718-356-0294; 718-984-1156 (CRP) Rev. Eric Rapaglia, Pst.; Rev. Rizalino P. Garcia, C.M., Assoc. Pst.; Rev. Neil A. Kelly, Assoc. Pst.; Rev. Evangelio R. Suaybaguio, Assoc. Pst.; Dcn. Engracio G. Villanueva; Elizabeth Brim, DRE;

St. Margaret Mary - 560 Lincoln Ave., Staten Island, NY 10306 Administered from Parish of St. Christopher and St. Margaret Mary, 130 Midland Ave., Staten Island. Dcn. Patrick Graham; Very Rev. Joseph M. McLafferty, Admin.;

St. Mary of the Assumption - 1265 Castleton Ave., Staten Island, NY 10310 Records are now at Parish of Our Lady of Mount Carmel-St. Benedicta and St. Mary of the Assumption, 1265 Castleton Ave., Staten Island. (Jesuit) Dcn. James Stahlnecker; Rev. Hernan Paredes Carrera, S.J., Pst.;

St. Michael - 207 Harbor Rd., Staten Island, NY 10303 t) 718-727-6442 Rev. Richard Alejunas, S.D.B., Pst.;

Our Lady Help of Christians - 7396 Amboy Rd., Staten Island, NY 10307 t) 718-317-9772 fr.james.ferreira@olhcparish.org www.olhcparish.org Rev. James Ferreira, Pst.; Dcn. John A. Singler;

Our Lady of Good Counsel - 10 Austin Pl., Staten Island, NY 10304 (Augustinian) Rev. Louis R. Jerome, Pst.; Rev. Anthony Sebamalai (Sri Lanka), Assoc. Pst.; Linda Affatato, DRE;

Parish of Our Lady of Mount Carmel-St. Benedicta and St. Mary of the Assumption - 1265 Castleton Ave., Staten Island, NY 10310 Rev. Hernan Paredes Carrera, S.J., Pst.; Rev. Marc J. Roselli, S.J., Assoc. Pst.;

Parish of Our Lady of Pity and St. Anthony of Padua - 1616 Richmond Ave., Staten Island, NY 10314 t) 718-761-5421; 718-494-0308 (CRP) i308@archny.org; religiouseducation@olpsare.com ourladyofpity-stanthony.org Rev. John J. Wroblewski, Pst.; Dcn. Michael Venditto; Dcn. Joseph Rentkowski; Diane Becker, DRE; Frank A Marchese, DRE;

Our Lady Star of the Sea - 5411 Amboy Rd., Huguenot Park, Staten Island, NY 10312; Mailing: 5371 Amboy Rd., Staten Island, NY 10312 t) 718-984-0593 olssparish@si.rr.com olssparish.org Rev. Joy Mampilly, Pst.; Dcn. James Quadrino, DRE; Debra Emigholz,

Office Administrator; CRP Stds.: 605

Our Lady, Queen of Peace - 90 Third St., Staten Island, NY 10306; Mailing: 737 Ilyssa Way, Staten Island, NY 10312 t) 718-979-0989 (CRP); 718-351-1093 olqpchurch@verizon.net olqpchurch.org Rev. Dominic Thomas, Pst.; Rev. Sujan Joseph, Pst.; Dcn. Thomas Finnerty; Dcn. Dennis Hogan; CRP Stds.: 108

Our Lady of Lourdes - 130 Cedar Grove Ave., New Dorp Beach, NY 10306

St. Patrick - 53 St. Patrick's Pl., Staten Island, NY 10306 t) 718-979-4227 (Office); 718-979-1272 (CRP); 718-351-0044 (Rectory) religioused@stpatrickssi.org; parishadmin@stpatrickssi.org stpatrickssi.org Rev. Robert W. Dillon, Pst.; Rev. Joseph Victor Maynigo-Arenas (Philippines), In Res.; Maria Giura, DRE; Rev. Tony Bautista, Sunday Associate; CRP Stds.: 153

St. Paul - 53 St. Mark's Pl., Staten Island, NY 10301 t) 718-727-2672 assumptionstpaulsi@gmail.com Records at Parish of Sts. Peter and Paul and Assumption, 53 St. Mark's Pl., Staten Island. Rev. Michael W. Cichon, Pst.;

Christian Brothers Residence - 148 Cassidy Pl., Staten Island, NY 10301

Parish of Sts. Peter and Paul and Assumption - 53 St. Mark's Pl., Staten Island, NY 10301 t) 718-447-1290 (CRP); 718-727-2672 mcmalena068@gmail.com; assumptionstpaulsi@gmail.com stpetersi.com Rev. Michael W. Cichon, Pst.; Rev. Matthew Takyi-Asante, Assoc. Pst.; Dcn. Charles J. Carroll; Maria Magdalena Centeno, DRE;

St. Rita - 281 Bradley Ave., Staten Island, NY 10314 t) 718-982-6948 (CRP); 718-698-3746 mgillespie@stritachurch.net www.stritachurch.net Rev. Eugene J. Carrella, Pst.; Rev. Anthony Gonzales, Assoc. Pst.; Rev. Stephen G. Challman, In Res.; Mary Gillespie, DRE;

Dominican Sisters - 61 Wellbrook Ave., Staten Island, NY 10314 t) 718-761-1171 (Roman Congregation of St. Dominic)

Sacred Heart - 981 Castleton Ave., Staten Island, NY 10310 t) 718-448-1536 Rev. Rizalino P. Garcia, C.M., Pst.; Dcn. James Cowan;

St. Stanislaus Kostka - 109 York Ave., Staten Island, NY 10301 t) 718-447-3937 parish@stanislawkostkasi.org www.stanislawkostkasi.org Polish Rev. Jacek Wozny, Pst.;

St. Sylvester - 854 Targee St., Staten Island, NY 10304-4517 t) 718-420-1374 Rev. Jacob Thumma (India), Pst.;

St. Teresa - 1634 Victory Blvd., Staten Island, NY 10314 t) 718-442-5412 rectory@stteresasi.org www.saintteresasi.org Rev. Msgr. William J. Belford, Pst.; Rev. John Kallattil, V.C., Assoc. Pst.; Dcn. Jonathan Reyes; CRP Stds.: 265

St. Nicholas - La Bau Ave. & Northern Blvd., Staten Island, NY 10301

STONY POINT

Immaculate Conception - 26 John St., Stony Point, NY 10980 t) 845-786-2742; 845-786-5298 (CRP) r547@archny.org; immaculateprep@yahoo.com Rev. Herbert T. DeGaris, Pst.; Dcn. Daniel Condon; Dcn. Philip A. Marino; Dcn. John Sadowski; Ughetta Jilleba, DRE; CRP Stds.: 180

SUFFERN

Sacred Heart - 129 Lafayette Ave., Suffern, NY 10901 t) 845-357-6044 (CRP); 845-357-0035 sacredheartreligiouseducation@yahoo.com; shsuff@gmail.com www.sacredheartparish.org Rev. John Michael Rafferty, OAR, Pst.; Rev. Eric Crelencia, OAR, Par. Vicar; Rev. John Gruben, O.A.R., Pst. Assoc.; Janis Batewell, DRE;

Good Samaritan Hospital - 255 Lafayette Ave., Suffern, NY 10901 t) 845-368-5000

Tagaste Monastery - 220 Lafayette Ave., Suffern, NY 10901 t) 845-357-0067

TAPPAN

St. John Henry Newman - 120 King's Hwy., Tappan, NY 10983 t) (845) 359-1230 admin@stjohnnewman.org stjohnnewman.org Rev. Thomas Kunnel, C.O., Pst.; Dcn. Robert Pang;

TARRYTOWN

Transfiguration - 268 S. Broadway, Tarrytown, NY 10591 t) 914-631-2380 (CRP); 914-631-1672 pastortransfig10591@gmail.com; transfigsec@gmail.com www.transfiguration-tarrytown.org (Carmelite) Rev. Francis Amodio, O.Carm., Pst.; Rev. Justin Cinnante, O. Carm., In Res.; Rev. Huy Tran, O. Carm., Par. Vicar;

TIVOLI

St. Sylvia - 104 Broadway, Tivoli, NY 12583-0095; Mailing: P.O. Box 95, Tivoli, NY 12583-0095 Records at Parish of St. Christopher and St. Sylvia, 7411 S. Broadway, Red Hook. Rev. Patrick F. Buckley, Pst.;

TUCKAHOE

Annunciation-Our Lady of Fatima - 470 Westchester Ave., Tuckahoe, NY 10707 t) (914) 779-7345 www.annunciation-fatima.com Administered from Parish of Annunciation and Our Lady of Fatima, 470 Westchester Ave., Crestwood. Very Rev. Robert F. Grippo, Pst.; Dcn. Albert Messana;

Assumption - 53 Winterhill Rd., Tuckahoe, NY 10707 t) (914) 961-3643 www.icaparish.org Administered from Parish of Immaculate Conception and Assumption, 53 Winter Hill Rd., Tuckahoe. Rev. Anthony D. Sorgie, Pst.;

Parish of Immaculate Conception and Assumption - 53 Winterhill Rd., Tuckahoe, NY 10707 t) 914-961-1076 ica.prep.office@gmail.com Rev. Anthony D. Sorgie, Pst.; Rev. Sean Connolly, Assoc. Pst.; Rev. Paul M. Waddell, Assoc. Pst.; Sr. Cora Lombardo, DRE; Dcn. Carl Degenhardt; Dcn. Francis B. Orlando; Dcn. Paul Reisman; Dcn. Anthony Viola;

TUXEDO

Our Lady of Mount Carmel - 5 Tobin Way, Tuxedo, NY 10987; Mailing: P.O. Box 697, Tuxedo, NY 10987 Administered from Parish of St. Joan of Arc and Our Lady of Mount Carmel, 32 Eagle Valley Rd., Sloatsburg. Rev. Joseph A. Emmanuel, Pst.;

VALHALLA

Holy Name of Jesus - Two Broadway, Valhalla, NY 10595 t) 914-949-1422 hnjre@aol.com Rev. Abraham A. Berko (Ghana), Pst.; Dcn. Thomas J. Abbamont;

VERPLANCK

St. Patrick - 240 11th St., Verplanck, NY 10596; Mailing: P.O. Box 609, Verplanck, NY 10596 Administered from Parish of St. Christopher and St. Patrick, 3094 Albany Post Rd., Buchanan. Rev. George Oonnoonny, Pst.;

WALDEN

Most Precious Blood - 42 Walnut St., Walden, NY 12586 t) 845-778-7081 mpbreled@aol.com Rev. Thomas Colucci, Pst.;

St. Benedict -

WAPPINGERS FALLS

St. Mary - 11 Clinton St., Wappingers Falls, NY 12590 t) 845-297-7586 (CRP); 845-297-6261 churchstmaryswf@gmail.com stmarywappingers.org/ Most Rev. Gerardo J. Colacicco, Pst.; Dcn. Mark Wisniewski; Rev. Michael Connolly, In Res.; Rev. Jon Tveit, Admin.; CRP Stds.: 174

WARWICK

St. Stephen - 75 Sanfordville Rd., Warwick, NY 10990 t) 845-986-2231 reledoffice@gmail.com Rev. Jack Arlotta, Pst.; Rev. Richard Marrano, Assoc. Pst.; Dcn. Daniel Byrne; Dcn. Thomas MacDougall; Dcn. Emmet Noonan; Dcn. John Tomasicchio; Lydia vanDuynhoven, DRE;

WASHINGTONVILLE

St. Mary - 42 Goshen Ave, Washingtonville, NY 10992 t) 845-496-3730 stmaryswashingtonville@gmail.com saintmaryswashingtonville.com/ Rev. Christopher Argano, Pst.; Rev. Matthew MacDonald, Assoc. Pst.; Dcn. Timothy D. Curran; Dcn. Bernard Kahn; Rev. Innocent Madu, In Res.;

WEST HARRISON

St. Anthony of Padua - 85 Harrison St., West Harrison, NY 10604 t) 914-949-0212 (CRP); 914-948-1480 stanthonyreled@optonline.net; admin@saintanthonyofpaduawh.org www.sapwh.org Rev. Thomas J. Byrnes, Pst.; Rev. Rubenus Cammayo (Philippines), Par. Vicar; Rev. George Kanshamba (Zambia), Par. Vicar; Dcn. Thomas A. Vargas; Jean Jackson, DRE;

WEST NYACK

St. Francis of Assisi - 128 Parrott Rd., West Nyack, NY 10994 t) 845-638-4215 (CRP); 845-634-4957 stfrancisprepoffice@gmail.com; stfrancisassisiparish@gmail.com www.stfrancis-assisi.org Rev. Robert F. McKeon, Pst.; Rev. Richard Baker, Par. Vicar; Dcn. Thomas Bennett; Sr. Patricia Hogan, O.P., Pst. Assoc.; Catherine Saladino, DRE; James Russell, Youth Min.; Tom Snowden, Music Min.; CRP Stds.: 832

WEST POINT

Catholic Chapel of the Most Holy Trinity - 699 Washington Rd., West Point, NY 10996 t) 845-938-8760; 845-938-8761 (CRP) Rev. Kenneth W. Nielson, Pst.; Joseph L. Lynch, DRE;

WHITE PLAINS

St. Bernard - 51 Prospect St., White Plains, NY 10606 t) 914-949-2111 stbernardswp.com/ Rev. Robert J. Morris, Pst.; Dcn. Fernando Cortes; CRP Stds.: 300

Parish of St. John the Evangelist and Our Lady of Mount Carmel - 148 Hamilton Ave., White Plains, NY 10601 t) 914-437-5144 (CRP); 914-949-0439; 914-948-5909 info@sjeolmc.org www.sjeolmc.org Rev. Domingo Pon-an Arnaiz, MHM, Admin.; Rev. Richard Githang'a Njoroge, MHM, Par. Vicar; Rev. Chellan Joseph, In Res.; CRP Stds.: 249

Our Lady of Mount Carmel - 92 S. Lexington Ave., White Plains, NY 10606; Mailing: 148 Hamilton Ave., White Plains, NY 10601 t) 914-948-5909; 914-949-0439; 914-437-5144 (CRP) info@sjeolmc.org www.sjeolmc.org Administered from Parish of St. John the Evangelist and Our Lady of Mount Carmel, 148 Hamilton Ave., White Plains. Rev. Domingo Pon-an Arnaiz, MHM, Admin.; Rev. Richard Githang'a Njoroge, MHM, Par. Vicar; Rev. Chellan Joseph, In Res.; CRP Stds.: 249

Our Lady of Sorrows - 920 Mamaroneck Ave., White Plains, NY 10605 t) (914) 949-9819 www.olscc.com Rev. Thomas E. Collins, Pst.; Dcn. Paul Brisson; Jennifer DeMilio, DRE;

WOODBOURNE

Immaculate Conception - 6317 State Rte. 42, Woodbourne, NY 12788; Mailing: P.O. Box 66, Woodbourne, NY 12788 t) 845-436-7370 Rev. Ignas Maria Dhason, MMI, Admin.;

WOODSTOCK

St. John - 12 Holly Hills Dr., Woodstock, NY 12498 t) 914-679-2869 Rev. Thomas P. Kiely, Pst.;

St. Augustine - Watson Hollow Rd., West Shokan, NY 12494 t) 914-657-2190

WURTSBORO

St. Joseph - 180 Sullivan St., Wurtsboro, NY 12790; Mailing: P.O. Box 277, Wurtsboro, NY 12790 t) (845) 888-4522 Rev. Peter J. Madori, Pst.; Rev. Matthias Ndulaka, In Res.;

YONKERS

St. Ann - 854 Midland Ave., Yonkers, NY 10704 t) 914-965-1555 michael.vicario@archny.org; stannsparishyonkers@gmail.com stannsyonkers.org Rev. Stephen P. Norton, Pst.; Rev. James K. Annor-Ohene (Ghana), Assoc. Pst.; Michael Vicario, DRE;

St. Anthony - 10 Squire Ave., Yonkers, NY 10703 t) 914-965-5535 Rev. Daniel Tuite, Pst.;

St. Bartholomew - 15 Palmer Rd., Yonkers, NY 10701 t) (914) 965-0566 (Parish Office); (914) 476-6676 (Religious Ed) www.saintbartsparish.org (Missionaries of St. Paul of Nigeria) Rev. Raphael Ezeh, M.S.P., Pst.; Rev. Victor Ameh, Par. Vicar; CRP Stds.: 120

St. Casimir - 239 Nepperhan Ave., Yonkers, NY 10701 Rev. Marek Rudecki, S.A.C., Pst.; Rev. Mark Kreis, O.S.P.P.E., Assoc. Pst.;

Christ the King - 740 N. Broadway, Yonkers, NY 10701 t) 914-963-7474 ctkyonkers@gmail.com;

ctkreledyonkers@gmail.com ctkyonkers.org Rev. Robert J. Robbins, Pst.; Rev. Sebastian Mathew, C.M.I., Assoc. Pst.; Rev. Robert J. Staar, Pastor Emer.; Zachary Paul, Religious Education Coordinator;

St. Denis - 470 Van Cortlandt Park Ave., Yonkers, NY 10705 Records at Parish of St. Peter and St. Denis, Yonkers. Rev. Donald Kaufman, L.C., Pst.; Dcn. Jose Camacho;

St. Eugene - 707 Tuckahoe Rd., Yonkers, NY 10710; Mailing: 31 Massitoa Rd., Yonkers, NY 10710 t) 914-961-2590 fatherfernan@csey.org; ginamastrangelo@csey.org www.csey.org Rev. Matthew F. Fernan, Pst.; Rev. Anthony Gyamerah, Assoc. Pst.; Dcn. John Duffy; Gina Mastrangelo, DRE & Bus. Mgr.;

Immaculate Conception - 103 S. Broadway, Yonkers, NY 10701 t) 914-963-1053 Rev. Anthony Ekanem, M.S.P., Pst.; Rev. Fares Hattar (Jordan), Assoc. Pst.; Rev. Felino Reyes (Dominican Republic), Assoc. Pst.;

Good Shepherd Arabic Community of St. Mary - Parish of St. John the Baptist and Most Holy Trinity - 670 Yonkers Ave., Yonkers, NY 10704 t) 914-963-1486 stjohnsp@optonline.net www.sjbyonkers.org Rev. Stephen P. Norton, Pst.; Rev. Joseph Mathew (India), Assoc. Pst.; Rev. Daniel Ulloa, O.P. (Mexico), Assoc. Pst.; Dcn. Martin J. Olivieri; Dcn. Nicholas Ramoni; Angela Minchilli, DRE; CRP Stds.: 138

St. Joseph Parish - 141 Ashburton Ave., Yonkers, NY 10701 Rev. Joseph A. Francis, Pst.; Dcn. Jose Luis Velasquez;

St. Margaret of Hungary - 141 Ashburton Ave., Yonkers, NY 10701 Records at St. Joseph, Yonkers.

Our Lady of Fatima Portuguese Roman Catholic Church - 355 S. Broadway, Yonkers, NY 10705 Rev. Osvaldo Franklin, Pst.; Angelina Tome, DRE;

Our Lady of Mt. Carmel - 70 Park Hill Ave., Yonkers, NY 10701 (Pallottine) Rev. Marek Rudecki, S.A.C., Pst.; Dcn. Alfred R. Impallomeni; Dcn. Nicholas A. Mazzei;

St. Paul the Apostle - 602 McLean Ave., Yonkers, NY 10705 t) 914-963-7330 stpaulyonkers@gmail.com stpaulyonkers.org Rev. Leonard F. Villa, Pst.; Rev. Michael D. Morrow, Par. Vicar; Rev. George Valliamthadathil, M.S.F.S., Par. Vicar; Dcn. Thomas J. Barbagallo; Dcn. Rudolfo Teng; Sr. Eileen Treanor, P.B.V.M., DRE;

Parish of St. Peter and St. Denis - 91 Ludlow St., Yonkers, NY 10705 t) 914-969-3813 Rev. Donald Kaufman, L.C., Pst.; Rev. Jose Helio Cantu, L.C., Assoc. Pst.; Dcn. Pedro Irizarry; Rev. Eric Nielsen, Youth Min.;

Roman Catholic Church of the Sacred Heart - 110 Shonnard Pl., Yonkers, NY 10703; Mailing: 40 Convent Ave., Yonkers, NY 10703 t) 914-963-4205 sacredheartyonkers@gmail.com sacredheartyonkers.org (Capuchin) Rev. Robert J. Abbatiello, O.F.M.Cap., Pst.; Rev. John McHugh, O.F.M.Cap., Assoc. Pst.; Bro. Roger Deguire, O.F.M.Cap., Pst. Assoc.; Dcn. Gianni DiPaolo; Deanne May, DRE; Rev. John Gallagher, OFM Cap., In Res.; Bro. John Shento, O.F.M.Cap., In Res.; CRP Stds.: 140

Convent - 27 Convent Ave., Yonkers, NY 10703 t) (914) 963-4205

YORKTOWN HEIGHTS

St. Patrick - 137 Moseman Rd., Yorktown Heights, NY 10598 t) 914-962-5586 (CRP); 914-962-5050 stpatsyorktown@optonline.net stpatricks-yorktown.org Rev. Msgr. Joseph R. Giandurco, Pst.; Rev. Ryan Muldoon, Par. Vicar; Dcn. Douglas Fitzmorris; Dcn. Steven Morgante; Dcn. Richard Scheibe;

YULAN

Parish of St. Anthony of Padua and St. Thomas Aquinas - 25 Beaver Brook Rd., Yulan, NY 12792 t) (845) 456-0404 (Franciscan) Rev. Richard Bretone, Admin.;

Sacred Heart - Berme Church Rd., Pond Eddy, NY 12770

SCHOOLS: PRESCHOOL THRU HIGH SCHOOL

SCHOOLS

STATE OF NEW YORK

BEACON

Catholic School Region of Dutchess - 60 Liberty St., Beacon, NY 12508 t) 845-831-3073 maryjane.daley@archny.org Mary Jane Daley, Supt.;

St. Mary, Mother of the Church School - 106 Jackson St., Fishkill, NY 12524-0499; Mailing: P.O. Box 780, Fishkill, NY 12524-0499 t) 845-896-9561 d428@adnyeducation.org www.stmaryfishkill.org (Regional) Thomas J. Hamilton, Prin.; Stds.: 235; Lay Tchrs.: 11

The Ark and the Dove School - ; Mailing: P.O. Box 1139, Hopewell Junction, NY 12533 t) 845-227-5232 arkdove@adnyeducation.org; noah1@stdenischurch.org Early Childhood Jennifer Corsano, Dir.; Stds.: 73

St. Denis - St. Columba School - 849 Rte. 82, Hopewell Junction, NY 12533; Mailing: P.O. Box 368, Hopewell Junction, NY 12533 t) 845-227-7777 d392@adnyeducation.org Sr. Kathleen Marie Gerritse, Prin.; Stds.: 266; Lay Tchrs.: 9

Holy Trinity School - 20 Springside Ave., Poughkeepsie, NY 12603 t) 845-471-0520 d520@adnyschools.org www.holy-trinity-school.com (Regional) Kathleen Spina, Prin.; Stds.: 478; Lay Tchrs.: 23

St. Martin de Porres School - 122 Cedar Valley Rd., Poughkeepsie, NY 12603 t) 845-452-4428 d525@adnyeducation.org www.smdpschool.net Grregory Viceroy, Prin.; Stds.: 405; Lay Tchrs.: 12

Catholic School Region of Northern Westchester-Putnam - 60 Liberty St., Beacon, NY 12508 t) 845-831-3073

St. James the Apostle School - 12 Gleneida Ave., Carmel, NY 10512 t) 845-225-9365 p610@adnyeducation.org www.edline.net/pages/st_james_the_school Maura Crawford, Prin.; Stds.: 136; Lay Tchrs.: 9

St. Columbanus School - 122 Oregon Rd., Cortlandt Manor, NY 10567 t) 914-739-1200 w552@adnyeducation.org www.st-columbanus.com (Regional) Carole Arbolino, Prin.; Stds.: 167; Lay Tchrs.: 10

St. Augustine School - Eagle Park, 381 N. Highland Ave., Ossining, NY 10562 t) 914-941-3849 w496@adnyeducation.org www.staugny.org Sr. Mary Elizabeth Donoghue, Prin.; Stds.: 415; Lay Tchrs.: 19

St. Ann's Peas & Karrots Program - 16 Elizabeth St., Ossining, NY 10562 t) 914-941-0312 Early Childhood Education Cookie Colucci, Dir.;

St. Patrick School - 117 Moseman Rd., Yorktown Heights, NY 10598 t) 914-962-2211 w583@adnyeducation.org www.stpatricks-yorktown.org (Regional) John Amelio, Prin.; Stds.: 218; Lay Tchrs.: 11

BRONX

Catholic School Region of Northeast-East Bronx - 2962 Harding Ave., Ste. 401, Bronx, NY 10465 t) 718-892-5359 linda.doughty@archny.org Linda Dougherty, Supt.;

St. Benedict School - 1016 Edison Ave., Bronx, NY 10465 t) 718-829-9557 b230@adnyeducation.org www.stbenedictschoolbx.org/ (Regional) Mary Sheer, Prin.; Stds.: 321; Lay Tchrs.: 13

St. Clare of Assisi School - 1911 Hone Ave., Bronx, NY 10461 t) 718-892-4080 b232@adnyschools.org www.stclareassisischool.org (Regional) Theresa Bivona, Prin.; Stds.: 359; Lay Tchrs.: 19

St. Francis of Assisi School - 4300 Baychester Ave., Bronx, NY 10466 t) 718-994-4650 b268@adnyeducation.org www.sfabx.com (Regional) Mark Silva, Prin.; Stds.: 404; Lay Tchrs.: 18

St. Frances de Chantal School - 2962 Harding Ave., Bronx, NY 10465 b235@adnyeducation.org www.sfdchantal.org (Regional) Sr. Patricia Brito, R.J.M., Prin.; Stds.: 358; Lay Tchrs.: 19

St. Francis Xavier School - 1711 Haight Ave., Bronx, NY 10461 t) 718-863-0531 b237@adnyeducation.org www.stfrancisxavierbx.com (Regional) Marie O'Shea, Prin.; Stds.: 247; Lay Tchrs.: 16

St. Helena School - 2050 Benedict Ave., Bronx, NY 10462 t) 718-892-3234 b239@adnyeducation.org www.sthelenaelementary.com Richard Meller, Prin.; Stds.: 294; Lay Tchrs.: 17

Holy Cross School - 1846 Randall Ave., Bronx, NY 10473 t) 718-842-4492 b202@adnyeducation.org www.holycrossbx.org Ernie Zalamea, Prin.; Stds.: 261; Lay Tchrs.: 14

Holy Family School - 2169 Blackrock Ave., Bronx, NY 10472 t) 718-863-7280 b203@adnyeducation.org www.hfsny.org (Regional) David Ojeda, Prin.; Stds.: 197; Lay Tchrs.: 12

Holy Rosary School - 1500 Arnow Ave., Bronx, NY 10469 t) 718-652-1838 b204@adnyeducation.org www.holyrosaryschoolbronx.org (Regional) Maryann Fusco, Prin.; Stds.: 360; Lay Tchrs.: 13

Immaculate Conception School - 760 E. Gun Hill Rd., Bronx, NY 10467 t) 718-547-3346 b207@adnyeducation.org www.schoolofimmaculateconception.org (Regional) Amy Rodriguez, Prin.; Stds.: 282; Lay Tchrs.: 16

St. Lucy School - 830 Mace Ave., Bronx, NY 10467 t) 718-882-2203 b246@adnyeducation.org www.stlucys.org (Regional) Jane Stefanini, Prin.; Stds.: 369; Lay Tchrs.: 20

Our Lady of Grace School - 3981 Bronxwood Ave., Bronx, NY 10466 t) 718-547-9918 b211@adnyeducation.org www.olgschoolbronx.com (Regional) Richard Helmrich, Prin.; Stds.: 328; Lay Tchrs.: 15

Santa Maria School - 1510 Zerega Ave., Bronx, NY 10462 t) 718-823-3636 b265@adnyeducation.org santamariabronx.org/ (Regional) Sr. Christine Hoffner, Prin.; Stds.: 291; Lay Tchrs.: 18

St. Raymond School - 2380 E. Tremont Ave., Bronx, NY 10462 t) 718-597-3232 b258@adnyeducation.org www.straymondelementary.org Eugene Scanlon, Prin.; Stds.: 574; Sr. Tchrs.: 1; Lay Tchrs.: 28

St. Theresa School - 2872 St. Theresa Ave., Bronx, NY 10461 t) 718-792-3688 b262@adnyeducation.org www.sttheresaschoolbronx.org Josephine Fanelli, Prin.; Stds.: 352; Lay Tchrs.: 15

Villa Maria Academy - 3335 Country Club Rd., Bronx, NY 10465 t) 718-824-3260 villa@archny.org www.vma-ny.org Janice Mastropietro, Prin.; Stds.: 305; Lay Tchrs.: 19

Catholic School Region of the Northwest and South Bronx - 2962 Harding Ave., Bronx, NY 10465 t) 718-597-3134 claudia.cabelloglass@archny.org; jr@archny.org catholicschoolsny.org John Riley, Supt.; Pr. Tchrs.: 1; Lay Tchrs.: 9

St. Angela Merici School - 266 E. 163rd St., Bronx, NY 10451 t) 718-293-3365 b221@adnyeducation.org www.saintangelamericischool.org (Regional) Yesenia Teron, Prin.; Stds.: 238; Lay Tchrs.: 12

Preschool - 838 Brook Ave., Bronx, NY 10456 t) 718-665-2056 (Regional), PreK3-PreK4.

St. Anselm School - 685 Tinton Ave., Bronx, NY 10455 t) 718-993-9464 b223@adnyeducation.org www.stanselmbx.org Theresa LoPuzzo, Prin.; Stds.: 217; Lay Tchrs.: 10

St. Athanasius School - 830 Southern Blvd., Bronx, NY 10459 t) 718-542-5161 b227@adnyschools.org www.stathanasiusbronx.org/ (Partnership) Jessica Aybar, Prin.; Stds.: 422; Lay Tchrs.: 18

St. Brendan School - 268 E. 207th St., Bronx, NY 10467 t) 718-653-2292 b231@adnyeducation.org www.stbrendanschoolbronx.org (Regional) Michele Pasquale, Prin.; Stds.: 241; Lay Tchrs.: 12

Christ the King School - 1345 Grand Concourse, Bronx, NY 10452 t) 718-538-5959 b201@adnyeducation.org christthekingbronx.org (Regional) Steven Iuso, Prin.; Stds.: 264; Lay Tchrs.: 14

St. Gabriel School - 590 W. 235th St., Bronx, NY 10463 t) 718-548-0444 b23@adnyeducation.org www.saintgabrieldschoolbronx.org (Regional) Anthony Naccari, Prin.; Stds.: 208; Lay Tchrs.: 13

Immaculate Conception School - 378 E. 151st St., Bronx, NY 10455 t) 718-585-4843 b206@adnyeducation.org www.icsfamily.org (Partnership) Alexandra Benjamin, Prin.; Stds.: 385; Lay Tchrs.: 19

St. John Chrysostom School - 1144 Hoe Ave., Bronx, NY 10459 t) 718-328-7226 b243@adnyeducation.org www.sjcbronx.org Sr. Mary Elizabeth Mooney, O.P., Prin.; Stds.: 212; Lay Tchrs.: 12

St. Margaret of Cortona School - 452 W. 260th St., Bronx, NY 10471 t) 718-549-8580 b248@adnyeducation.org www.smcsriverdale.org (Regional) Hugh Keenan, Prin.; Stds.: 244; Lay Tchrs.: 14

St. Margaret Mary School - 121 E. 177th St., Bronx, NY 10453-5901 t) 718-731-5905 b249@adnyeducation.org www.stmargaretmaryschool.net Melissa Moore, Prin.; Stds.: 138; Lay Tchrs.: 10

Our Lady of Mt. Carmel School - 2465 Bathgate Ave., Bronx, NY 10458 t) 718-295-6080 b213@adnyeducation.org wwwmtcarmelschoolbronx.org (Regional) John Musto, Prin.; Stds.: 257; Lay Tchrs.: 15

Our Lady of Refuge School - 2708 Briggs Ave., Bronx, NY 10458 t) 718-367-3081 b215@adnyeducation.org www.olrbronx.com (Regional) Robert W. Billings, Prin.; Stds.: 177; Lay Tchrs.: 9

St. Philip Neri School - 3031 Grand Concourse, Bronx, NY 10468 t) 718-365-8806 b256@adnyeducation.org www.school.stphilipneribronx.org (Regional) Ajeia Brown-Beebe, Prin.; Stds.: 293; Lay Tchrs.: 15

Sacred Heart School - 95 W. 168th St., Bronx, NY 10452 t) 718-293-4288 b219@adnyeducation.org www.shhighbridge.org (Partnership) Abigail Akano, Prin.; Stds.: 445; Lay Tchrs.: 19

St. Simon Stock School - 2195 Valentine Ave., Bronx, NY 10457 t) 718-367-0453 tbraswell@stsimonstockschool.org www.stsimonstockschool.org (Regional) Tara Braswell, Prin.; Stds.: 168; Lay Tchrs.: 11

Saint Ignatius School - 740 Manida St., Bronx, NY 10474-5420 t) 718-861-9084 info@sis-nativity.org www.sis-nativity.org Co-ed, Jesuit-sponsored and scholarship middle school Richard Darrell, Headmaster; Stds.: 70; Pr. Tchrs.: 1; Lay Tchrs.: 9

St. Joseph's School for the Deaf - 1000 Hutchinson River Pkwy., Bronx, NY 10465 t) 718-828-9000 darles@sjsdny.org Debra Arles, Exec.;

CAMPBELL HALL

***Saint Therese Classical Learning Center Inc.** - (PRV) 3348 State Rte. 208, Bldg. 2, Campbell Hall, NY 10918 t) (845) 610-5288 stcacademy.org Terri Raciti, Headmistress;

FLORIDA

Catholic School Region of Ulster-Sullivan-Orange - 19 Glenmere Ave., Florida, NY 10921 t) 845-508-6628 cathleen.cassel@archny.org

St. John School - 77 Murray Ave., Goshen, NY 10924 t) 845-294-6434 sjsoffice@saintjohngoshen.org; or433@adnyeducation.org www.saintjohngoshen.org (Regional) Joseph DeBona, Prin.; Stds.: 167; Lay Tchrs.: 7

Kingston Catholic School - 159 Broadway, Kingston, NY 12401 t) 845-331-9318 ul452@adnyeducation.org kingstoncatholicschool.com (Regional) Jill Albert, Pres.;

Kingston Catholic Elementary School - 159 Broadway, Kingston, NY 12401 t) (845) 331-9318 www.kingstoncatholic.org Stds.: 176; Lay Tchrs.: 10

Our Lady of Mt. Carmel School - 205 Wawayanda Ave., Middletown, NY 10940 t) 845-343-8836 or465@archny.org www.mtcarmelschoolmiddletown.org (Regional) Jennifer Langford, Prin.; Stds.: 167; Lay Tchrs.: 11

Most Precious Blood School - 180 Ulster Ave., Walden, NY 12586 t) 845-778-3028 or554@adnyeducation.org www.mpbschool.org (Regional) Patricia Luzar, Prin.; Stds.: 166; Lay Tchrs.: 11

Bishop Dunn Memorial School (Dominican Sisters of Hope) - 50 Gidney Ave., Newburgh, NY 12550 t) 845-569-3494 bishdunn@adnyeducation.org www.bdms.org Stds.: 207; Lay Tchrs.: 13

Nora Cronin Presentation Academy - 69 Bay View Terr., Newburgh, NY 12550-6004 t) 845-567-0708 presentationacad@ncpany.org; ncpa@adnyeducation.org www.noracroninpresentationacademy.org Dr. Tammy Barnett, Prin.; Stds.: 49; Lay Tchrs.: 4

IRVINGTON

John Cardinal O'Connor School - (Grades 2-8) 16 N. Broadway, Irvington, NY 10533 t) 914-591-9330 jcoconnor@adnyeducation.org www.johncardinaloconnorschool.org Sr. Jeam Marie Humphries, Prin.; Stds.: 53; Lay Tchrs.: 6

NANUET

Catholic School Region of Rockland - 32 W. Nyack Rd., Nanuet, NY 10954 t) 845-623-3504 cathleen.cassel@archny.org Cathleen Cassel, District Superintendent;

St. Anthony-St. Paul School - 365 Kings Hwy., Valley Cottage, NY 10989 t) 914-268-6506 rk417@adnyeducation.org www.saintpaulschoolvc.org (Regional) Dr. Anna Ramirez-Adam, Prin.; Stds.: 332; Lay Tchrs.: 19

St. Gregory Barbarigo School - 29 Cinder Rd., Garnerville, NY 10923 t) 845-947-1330 rk431@adnyeducation.org www.stgregorybarbarigoschool.org (Regional) Dana Spicer, Prin.; Stds.: 270; Sr. Tchrs.: 1; Lay Tchrs.: 14

St. Anthony-St. Paul School - 34 W. Nyack Rd., Nanuet, NY 10954 t) 845-623-2311 rk480@adnyeducation.org www.stanthonyschoolnanuet.org (Regional) Dr. Anna Ramirez-Adam, Prin.; Stds.: 332; Lay Tchrs.: 19

St. Margaret School - 34 N. Magnolia St., Pearl River, NY 10965 t) 845-735-2855 rk499@adnyschools.org www.saintmargaretschool.com (Regional) Patricia Maldonado, Prin.; Stds.: 253; Lay Tchrs.: 12

NEW ROCHELLE

Catholic School Region of Central Westchester - 86 Mayflower Ave., New Rochelle, NY 10801 t) 914-481-5993 noel.beale@archny.org Noelle Beale, Supt.;

St. Barnabas School - 413 E. 241st St., Bronx, NY 10470 t) 718-324-1088 b229@adnyeducation.org www.stbarnabasschool.org (Regional) Lauren Iorio, Prin.; Stds.: 478; Lay Tchrs.: 27

St. Joseph School - 30 Meadow Ave., Bronxville, NY 10708 t) 914-337-0261 w410@adnyeducation.org www.saintjosephbronxville.org Karen Valenti, Prin.; Stds.: 260; Lay Tchrs.: 13

Annunciation School - 465 Westchester Ave., Crestwood, NY 10707 t) 914-337-8760 w419@adnyeducation.org www.school.annunciationcrestwood.com Caitlin Gerahty, Prin.; Stds.: 415; Lay Tchrs.: 20

Our Lady of Mt. Carmel School - 59 E. Main St., Elmsford, NY 10523 t) 914-592-7575 w427@adnyeducation.org www.olmcelmsford.com Sr. Mary Healy, Prin.; Stds.: 130; Lay Tchrs.: 10

Sacred Heart School - 59 Wilson St., Hartsdale, NY 10530 t) 914-946-7242 w437@adnyeducation.org www.shshartsdale.org (Regional) Adam Perez, Prin.; Stds.: 162; Lay Tchrs.: 9

SS. John and Paul School - 280 Weaver St., Larchmont, NY 10538 t) 914-834-6332 w457@adnyeducation.org www.sjpschool.org Fatima Carvalho-Gianni, Prin.; Stds.: 391; Lay Tchrs.: 20

Our Lady of Victory School - 38 N. Fifth Ave., Mount Vernon, NY 10550 t) 914-667-4063 w475@adnyeducation.org www.ourladyofvictoryschool.org (Regional) Helena Castilla-Byrne, Prin.; Stds.: 325; Lay Tchrs.: 16

Corpus Christi - Holy Rosary School - 135 S. Regent St., Port Chester, NY 10573 t) 914-937-4407 w513m@adnyeducation.org www.cchrs.org (Regional) Deirdre McDermott, Prin.; Stds.: 405; Lay Tchrs.: 20

Resurrection Grammar School - 116 Milton Rd., Rye, NY 10580 t) 914-967-1218 w532@adnyeducation.org www.resurrectionschool.com Gina Marie Fonte, Prin.; Stds.: 422; Lay Tchrs.: 25

Immaculate Heart of Mary School - 201 Boulevard, Scarsdale, NY 10583 t) 914-723-5608 w534@adnyeducation.org www.ihmscarsdale.org Tracy Keelin, Prin.; Stds.: 263; Lay Tchrs.: 16

Transfiguration School - 40 Prospect Ave., Tarrytown, NY 10591 t) 914-631-3737 w545@adnyeducatio.org www.transfigurationschool.org (Regional) Margaret Kazan, Prin.; Stds.: 130; Lay Tchrs.: 9

Immaculate Conception School - 53 Winterhill Rd., Tuckahoe, NY 10707 t) 914-961-3785 w549@adnyeducation.org www.icschoolonline.org (Regional) Maureen J. Harten, Prin.; Stds.: 245; Lay Tchrs.: 12

Our Lady of Sorrows School - 888 Mamaroneck Ave., White Plains, NY 10605 t) 914-761-0124 w561@adnyeducation.org www.olsschoolwp.com (Regional) Sr. Marie Cecile, R.D.C., Prin.; Stds.: 186; Lay Tchrs.: 11

St. Anthony School - 1395 Nepperhan Ave., Yonkers, NY 10703 t) 914-476-8489 w482@adnyeducation.org www.stanthonyschoolyonkers.org (Regional) Sharyn O'Leary, Prin.; Stds.: 179; Lay Tchrs.: 12

St. John the Baptist School - 670 Yonkers Ave., Yonkers, NY 10704 t) 914-965-2356 w578@adnyeducation.org www.sjbyonkers.org/sjbschool Sr. Maryalice Reamer, Prin.; Stds.: 246; Lay Tchrs.: 10

St. Peter School - 204 Hawthorne Ave., Yonkers, NY 10705 t) 914-963-2314 w582@adnyeducation.org www.stpetersny.com (Regional) Sheila Alagia, Prin.; Stds.: 169; Lay Tchrs.: 14

Sacred Heart Grade School - 34 Convent Ave., Yonkers, NY 10703 t) 914-963-5318 w571@adnyeducation.org www.shgsyonkers.org (Regional) Tracy Strub, Prin.; Stds.: 178; Lay Tchrs.: 11

Holy Name of Mary Montessori School - 110 Grand St., Croton-on-Hudson, NY 10520 t) 914-271-5182 hnom@adnyeducation.org Early Childhood Feliz Quinlan, Dir.; Stds.: 26; Lay Tchrs.: 2

The Little Disciple Learning Center, Inc. - 348 S. Lexington Ave., White Plains, NY 10606 t) 914-949-2111 littledisciple@adnyeducation.org Jennifer Frias, Dir.;

Iona Grammar School - 173 Stratton Rd., New Rochelle, NY 10804 t) 914-633-7744 ionagram@adnyeducation.org www.ionagrammar.com Deirdre Mone, Prin.; Stds.: 225; Lay Tchrs.: 12

St. Eugene School - 707 Tuckahoe Rd., Yonkers, NY 10710 t) 914-779-2956 w577@adnyeducation.org Joan Fox, Prin.; Stds.: 250; Lay Tchrs.: 13

School of the Holy Child - 2225 Westchester Ave., Rye, NY 10580 t) 914-967-5622 holychild@adnyeducation.org Colleen Pettus, Headmaster; Stds.: 123; Lay Tchrs.: 9

NEW YORK

Catholic School Region of Manhattan - 1011 First Ave., 12th Fl., New York, NY 10022 t) 212-371-1000 x2006 info@transfigurationschoolnyc.org Peter Lo Chi Yuan,

Admin.;

Ascension School - 220 W. 108th St., New York, NY 10025 t) 212-222-5161 m003@adnyeducation.org www.ascensionschoolnyc.org (Regional) Jacquelyn Alvarez, Prin.; Stds.: 163; Lay Tchrs.: 12

Blessed Sacrament School - 147 W. 70th St., New York, NY 10023 t) 212-724-7561 m010@adnyeducation.org www.blessedsacramentnyc.org (Regional) Megan Gonzalez, Prin.;

St. Charles Borromeo School - 214 W. 142 St., New York, NY 10030 t) 212-368-6666 m059@adnyeducation.org www.stcharlesborromeoschool.org (Partnership as of September, 2019) Natalia Rodrigo, Prin.; Stds.: 375; Lay Tchrs.: 18

St. Elizabeth School - 612 W. 187th St., New York, NY 10033 t) 212-568-7291 m064@adnyeducation.org www.saintelizabethschool.org (Regional) Matthew Stark, Prin.; Stds.: 280; Lay Tchrs.: 16

The Epiphany School - 234 E. 22nd St., New York, NY 10010 t) 212-473-4128 m005@adnyeducation.org www.theepiphanyschool.org Kate McHugh, Prin.; Stds.: 411; Lay Tchrs.: 21

Good Shepherd School - 620 Isham St., New York, NY 10034 t) 212-567-5800 m006@adnyeducation.org www.gsschoolnyc.org Margaret Lee, Prin.; Stds.: 213; Lay Tchrs.: 13

Guardian Angel School - 193 10th Ave., New York, NY 10011-4709 t) 212-989-8280 m007@adnyeducation.org www.guardianangels.org (Regional) Christie Acosta-Perez, Prin.; Stds.: 170; Lay Tchrs.: 11

St. Ignatius Loyola School - 48 E. 84th St., New York, NY 10028 t) 212-861-3820 m074@adnyeducation.org www.stignatiusloyola.org Mary Larkin, Prin.; Stds.: 535; Lay Tchrs.: 27

St. Ignatius Loyola Day Nursery - 240 E. 84th St., New York, NY 10028 t) 212-734-6427 yesaloniad@saintignatiusloyola.org Early Childhood School Joy Blom, Prin.;

Marymount School of New York - 1026 Fifth Ave., New York, NY 10028 t) 212-744-4486 marymtes@adnyeducation.org (Independent Catholic) Concepcion Alvar, Headmaster; Stds.: 496; Lay Tchrs.: 49

Immaculate Conception School - 419 E. 13th St., New York, NY 10009 t) 212-475-2590 m016@adnyeducation.org www.immaculateconceptionschoolnyc.org Mary Barry, Prin.; Stds.: 158; Lay Tchrs.: 10

Incarnation School - 570 W. 175th St., New York, NY 10033 t) 212-795-1030 m017@adnyeducation.org www.incarnationnyc.org (Regional) Stds.: 266; Lay Tchrs.: 15

St. Joseph Church - Yorkville School - 420 E. 87th St., New York, NY 10128 t) 212-289-3057 m082@adnyeducation.org www.sjyorkville.org Theresa Bernero, Prin.; Stds.: 303; Lay Tchrs.: 16

St. Mark the Evangelist School - 55 W. 138th St., New York, NY 10037 t) 212-283-4848 m088@adnyeducation.org www.saintmarkschool.org (Partnership) Chinique Pressley, Prin.; Stds.: 251; Lay Tchrs.: 11

Our Lady of Lourdes School - 468 W. 143rd St., New York, NY 10031 t) 212-926-5820 m029@adnyeducation.org www.ollnyc.org (Regional) Suzanne Kaszynksi, Prin.; Stds.: 204; Lay Tchrs.: 10

Mt. Carmel - Holy Rosary School - 371 Pleasant Ave., New York, NY 10035 t) 212-876-7555 m014@adnyeducation.org www.mtcarmelholyrosary.org (Partnership School) Trista Rivera, Prin.; Stds.: 177; Lay Tchrs.: 11

Our Lady Queen of Martyrs School - 71 Arden St., New York, NY 10040 t) 212-567-3190 m035@adnyeducation.org www.olqmnyc.org (Regional) Andrew Woods, Prin.; Stds.: 247; Lay Tchrs.: 16

Academy of St. Paul - St. Ann - 114 E. 118th St., New York, NY 10035 t) 212-534-0619 m095@adnyeducation.org www.stpaulschool.us (Regional) John-Paul Barnaba, Prin.; Stds.: 215; Lay Tchrs.: 13

St. Stephen of Hungary School - 408 E. 82nd St., New York, NY 10028 t) 212-288-1989 m103@adnyeducation.org www.saintstephenschool.org Allyson Genova Hall, Prin.; Stds.: 335; Lay Tchrs.: 19

Convent of the Sacred Heart - 1 E. 91st St., New York, NY 10128 t) 212-722-4745 coshes@adnyeducation.org cshnyc.org (Girls) Joseph J. Ciancaglini, Headmaster; Stds.: 462; Lay Tchrs.: 126

Academy of St. Joseph - 111 Washington Pl., New York, NY 10014 t) 212-243-5420 josephvillage@adnyeducation.org www.academyofsaintjoseph.org Angela M. Coombs, Prin.; Stds.: 109; Lay Tchrs.: 10

Transfiguration School - Lower School - 29 Mott St., New York, NY 10013-5006 t) 212-964-8965 m110@adnyeducation.org www.transfigurationschoolnyc.org Michael Lenahan, Prin.; Stds.: 283; Lay Tchrs.: 19

Transfiguration School - Upper School - 37 St. James Pl., New York, NY 10038 t) 212-267-9289 m110@adnyeducation.org Michael Lenahan, Prin.;

Our Lady Queen of Angels School - 232 E. 112th St., New York, NY 10029 t) 212-722-9277 m024@adnyeducation.org www.olqaeastharlem.org (Partnership) Elizabeth Nuzzolese, Prin.; Stds.: 263; Lay Tchrs.: 12

Cornelia Connelly Center for Education//Middle School of the Holy Child - 220 E. 4th St., New York, NY 10128 t) 212-982-2287 holchimd@adnyeducation.org www.connellycenter.org Shalonda Gutierrez-Neeley, Prin.; Stds.: 85; Lay Tchrs.: 10

STATEN ISLAND

Catholic School Region of Staten Island - 2820 Amboy Rd., Staten Island, NY 10306 t) 718-667-5350 x1006 zoilita.herrera@archny.org Zoilita Herrera, District Superintendent;

St. Ann School - 125 Cromwell Ave., Staten Island, NY 10304 t) 718-351-4343 si312@adnyeducation.org www.stannschoolstatenisland.com (Regional) Bernadette Ficchi, Prin.; Stds.: 259; Lay Tchrs.: 11

Blessed Sacrament School - 830 Delafield Ave., Staten Island, NY 10310 t) 718-442-3090 si301@adnyeducation.org www.blessedsacramentsi.com (Regional) Joseph Cocozello, Prin.; Stds.: 557; Lay Tchrs.: 21

St. Charles School - 200 Penn Ave., Staten Island, NY 10306 t) 718-987-0200 si314@adnyschools.org www.saintcharlesschoolsi.org (Regional) John Kiernan, Prin.; Stds.: 473; Lay Tchrs.: 23

St. Christopher School - 15 Lisbon Pl., Staten Island, NY 10306 t) 718-351-0902 si315@adnyeducation.org www.stchristophersi.com (Regional) Catherine Falabella, Prin.; Stds.: 241; Lay Tchrs.: 13

St. Clare School - 151 Lindenwood Rd., Staten Island, NY 10308 t) 718-984-7091 si316@adnyeducation.org www.stclaresi.com Denise Olsen, Prin.; Stds.: 608; Lay Tchrs.: 22

Holy Child Pre-School - 4747 Amboy Rd., Staten Island, NY 10312 t) 718-356-5159 www.holychildsi.com Elizabeth Esposito, Prin.; Stds.: 219

Father Vincent Capodanno Catholic Academy - 100 Jerome Ave., Staten Island, NY 10305 t) 718-447-1195 si302@adnyeducation.org frcapodannocatholicacademy.org (Regional) Diane Hesterhagen, Prin.; Stds.: 326; Lay Tchrs.: 18

Our Lady of Good Counsel School - 42 Austin Pl., Staten Island, NY 10304 t) 718-447-7260 si304@adnyschools.org www.goodcounselsch.org Tara Hynes, Prin.; Stds.: 310; Lay Tchrs.: 11

Our Lady, Queen of Peace School - 22 Steele Ave., Staten Island, NY 10306 t) 718-351-0370 si307@adnyeducation.org www.olqpsi.com (Regional) Margaret O'Connor, Prin.; Stds.: 365; Lay Tchrs.: 17

Our Lady Star of the Sea School - 5411 Amboy Rd., Staten Island, NY 10312 t) 718-984-5750 si309@adnyeducation.org www.oss-si.org Jeanine Roland, Prin.; Stds.: 620; Lay Tchrs.: 22

St. Patrick School - 3560 Richmond RD., Staten Island, NY 10306 t) 718-979-8815 si325@adnyeducation.org www.school.stpatrickssi.org Vincent Sadowski, Prin.; Stds.: 384; Lay Tchrs.: 15

Sacred Heart School - 301 N. Burgher Ave., Staten Island, NY 10310 t) 718-442-0347 si310@adnyeducation.org sacredheartschoolsi.org (Regional) Celeste Catalano, Prin.; Stds.: 313; Lay Tchrs.: 15

St. Teresa - St. Rita STREAM Academy - 1632 Victory Blvd., Staten Island, NY 10314 t) 718-448-9650; 718-447-6426 si332@education.org stsrstreamacademy.com (Regional) Nicole C. Garelick-Fresca, Prin.; Stds.: 334; Lay Tchrs.: 15

Academy of St. Dorothy - 1305 Hylan Blvd., Staten Island, NY 10305 t) 718-351-0939 dorothy@adnyeducation.org; srsharon@adnyeducation.org www.ny02224597.schoolswire.net Sr. Sharon A. McCarthy, S.S.D., Prin.; Stds.: 189; Sr. Tchrs.: 1; Lay Tchrs.: 10

Notre Dame Academy - Elementary School - 78 Howard Ave., Staten Island, NY 10301 t) 718-273-9096 ntdames@adnyeducation.org www.notredameacademy.org Rebecca Giaccio, Prin.; Stds.: 224; Lay Tchrs.: 11

St. Joseph Hill Academy Elementary School - 850 Hylan Blvd., Staten Island, NY 10305 t) 718-981-1187 joshiles@adnyschools.org www.stjosephhill.org Lawrence Hansen, Prin.; Stds.: 616; Lay Tchrs.: 17

Seton Foundation for Learning, Inc. - 315 Arlene St., Staten Island, NY 10314 t) 718-982-5084 mhughes@sflschools.org www.sflschools.org Mary D. Hughes, Exec.; Donna Jennings, Dir.; Diane Taranto, Dir.; Stds.: 89; Lay Tchrs.: 14

Bishop Patrick V. Ahern High School - Mother Franciska Elementary School - 850 Hyland Blvd., Staten Island, NY 10305 t) 718-876-0939

Joan Ann Kennedy Memorial Preschool - 850 Hylan Blvd., Staten Island, NY 10305 t) 718-876-0939

HIGH SCHOOLS

STATE OF NEW YORK

BARDONIA

Albertus Magnus - (PRV) 798 Rte. 304, Bardonia, NY 10954 t) 845-623-8842 albertus@adnyeducation.org www.albertus.edu Christopher Power, Prin.; Joseph Tweed, Pres.;

BRONX

Academy of Mount St. Ursula - (PRV) (Grades 9-12) 330 Bedford Park Blvd., Bronx, NY 10458 t) 718-364-5353 www.amsu.org Girls High School Barbara Bunten, Director of Finance; Jeannie DiBendetto, Director of Student Life & Ministries; Leydi Imam, Director of Admissions & Recruitment; Penny Kapanika, Interim Principal; Ellen Manger, Exec Director Alumnae Relations, Development & External Affairs;

All Hallows Institute - (PRV) 111 E. 164th St., Bronx, NY 10452 t) 718-293-4545 hallows@adnyeducation.org www.allhallows.org (Boys) Susan Natale, Prin.; Ronald Schutte, Pres.;

Aquinas High School - (PRV) 685 E. 182nd St., Bronx, NY 10457 t) 718-367-2113 info@aquinashs.org www.aquinashs.org (Girls) Sr. Grace Hogan, Rel. Ord. Ldr.;

St. Barnabas High School - 425 E. 240th St., Bronx, NY 10470 t) 718-325-8820 barnabas@adnyeducation.org www.stbarnabashigh.com Theresa Napoli, Prin.;

Cardinal Hayes High School - (DIO) 650 Grand Concourse, Bronx, NY 10451 t) 718-292-6100 hayes@adnyeducation.org www.cardinalhayes.org (Boys). Bro. Tyrone Davis, C.F.C., In Res.; Rev. Thomas Mestriparampil, In Res.; Rev. Emmanuel Okpalauwaekwe, In Res.; Rev. James Sheehan, In Res.; Bro. William Sherlog, C.F.C., In Res.; William D. Lessa, Prin.; Rev. Joseph P. Tierney, Pres.;

Cardinal Spellman High School - One Cardinal Spellman Pl., Bronx, NY 10466 t) 718-881-8000 dokeefe@cardinalspellman.org; ehealy@cardinalspellman.org www.cardinalspellman.org Rev. John R. Kraljic; Rev. James J. O'Shaughnessy; Rev. Peter R. Pilsner; Daniel O'Keefe, Prin.; Maria Piri, Prin.; Kathy Steves, Librn.;

St. Catharine Academy - (PRV) (Grades 9-12) 2250 Williamsbridge Rd., Bronx, NY 10469-4891 t) 718-882-2882 stcatharine@scahs.org www.scahs.org (Girls) Sr. Ann M. Welch, R.S.M., Prin.; Sr. Patricia Wolf, R.S.M., Pres.; Stds.: 302; Sr. Tchrs.: 3; Lay Tchrs.: 23

Fordham Preparatory School - (PRV) (Grades 9-12) 441 E. Fordham Rd., Bronx, NY 10458 t) 718-367-7500 fordhamprep@adnyeducation.org www.fordhamprep.org (Boys) Rev. Stanley J. O'Konsky, S.J.; Steven Pettus, Dean; Joseph Petriello, Prin.; Rev. Christopher Devron, S.J., Pres.; Michael Higgins, Treas.; Brian Carney, Vice Pres. Mission & Identity;

Mount St. Michael Academy - (PRV) (Grades 6-12) 4300 Murdock Ave., Bronx, NY 10466 t) 718-515-6400 mount@adnyschools.org www.mountstmichael.org (Boys) Nina Lokar, Campus Min.; Bro. Brian Poulin, F.M.S., Campus Min.; Bro. Stephen Schlitte, F.M.S., Prin.; Peter Corritori, Pres.; Sr. Joan Whittle, O.P., Librn.;

Msgr. Scanlan High School - 915 Hutchinson River Pkwy., Bronx, NY 10465 t) 718-430-0100 scanlan@adnyeducation.org www.scanlanhs.edu (Coed) (Independent) Peter Doran, Prin.;

Preston High School - (PRV) 2780 Schurz Ave., Bronx, NY 10465 t) 718-863-9134 preston@adnyeducation.org www.prestonhs.org (Girls) Jennifer R. Connolly, Prin.; Edgar Martinez, Vice Prin.; Craig Youngren, Vice Prin.; Kathleen Welton, Librn.; Stds.: 368

St. Raymond High School - (PAR) 1725 Castle Hill Ave., Bronx, NY 10462 t) 718-824-4220 rayacad@adnyschools.org www.saintraymondacademy.org (Girls) Sr. Mary Ann D'Antonio, S.C., Prin.;

St. Raymond High School for Boys - (PAR) 2151 St. Raymond Ave., Bronx, NY 10462 t) 718-824-5050 rayhsboy@adnyeducation.org www.straymondhighschool.org (Boys) Judy Carew, Prin.;

GOSHEN

John S. Burke Catholic High School - 80 Fletcher St., Goshen, NY 10924 t) 845-294-5481 jdolan@burkecatholic.org; burke@adnyeducation.org www.burkecatholic.org Audrey Clarke, Prin.;

HARTSDALE

Maria Regina High School (Sisters of the Resurrection) - (DIO) 500 W. Hartsdale Ave., Hartsdale, NY 10530 t) 914-761-3300 mariareg@adnyeducation.org www.mariaregina.org Rosemarie Decker, Prin.; Sr. Mary Krystyna Kobielus, C.R., Librn.;

HURLEY

John A. Coleman Catholic High School - (DIO) 430 Hurley Ave., Hurley, NY 12443 t) 845-338-2750 office@colemancatholic.net; coleman@adnyeducation.org www.colemancatholic.net James Lyons, Prin.; Susan Bannon, Librn.;

MOUNT VERNON

***The Montfort Academy** - (PRV) 125 E. Birch St., Mount Vernon, NY 10552 t) 914-699-7090 montfort@adnyeducation.org; office@themontfortacademy.org www.themontfortacademy.org David Petrillo, Headmaster;

NEW ROCHELLE

Iona Preparatory School (Edmund Rice Christian Brothers North America) - (PRV) (Grades K-12) 255 Wilmot Rd., New Rochelle, NY 10804 t) 914-632-0714; 914-633-7744 ionaprep2@adnyeducation.org www.ionaprep.org (All Boys) Bro. Michael Binkley, C.F.C.; Bro. John H. Greenan, C.F.C.; Bro. William R. Harris, C.F.C.; Bro. Kevin J. Kiernan, C.F.C.; Bro. Lucian Knaap, C.F.C.; Bro. Gerard Menezes, C.F.C.; Bro. Andrew Prendergast, C.F.C.; Bro. Anthony Reynolds, C.F.C.; Kiernan Daly, Prin.; Bro. Thomas R. Leto, C.F.C., Pres.;

Salesian High School - (PRV) 148 Main St., New Rochelle, NY 10801 t) 914-632-0248 info@salesianhigh.org www.salesianhigh.org Rev. Timothy Ploch, SDB, Dir.; Rev. James Heuser, S.D.B., Pres.; Devin Chisholm, Prin.; Cynthia Chambers, Vice Prin.; Christopher Fraticelli, Dean; Stds.: 330; Pr. Tchrs.: 2; Bro. Tchrs.: 2; Lay Tchrs.: 21

The Ursuline School - (PRV) (Grades 6-12) 1354 North Ave., New Rochelle, NY 10804 t) 914-636-3950 melnykc@ursulinenewrochelle.org www.ursulinenewrochelle.org Rosemary Beirne, Prin.; Dr. Colleen Melnyk, Pres.; James Phelan, Treas.;

NEW YORK

Cathedral High School - (DIO) 350 E. 56th St., New York, NY 10022 t) 212-688-1545 cathedhs@adnyeducation.org www.cathedralhs.org (Girls) Maria Spagnuolo, Prin.;

Convent of the Sacred Heart (Religious of the Sacred Heart) - (PRV) One E. 91st St., New York, NY 10128-0689 t) 212-722-4745 coshhs@adnyeducation.org www.cshnyc.org (Girls) Angela Carstensen, Librn.;

Cristo Rey New York Corporate Work Study Program, Inc. - (PRV) 112 E. 106th St., New York, NY 10029 t) 212-996-7000 wporcaro@cristoreyny.org www.cristoreyny.org Catalina Gutierrez, Dir.;

***Cristo Rey New York High School, Inc.** - (PRV) 112 E. 106th St., New York, NY 10029 t) 212-996-7000 cristorey@adnyeducation.org www.cristoreyny.org William P. Ford III, Prin.; Rev. Joseph P. Parkes, S.J., Pres.; Catalina Gutierrez, Dir.;

Dominican Academy - (PRV) 44 E. 68th St., New York, NY 10065 t) 212-744-0195 dominica@adnyeducation.org www.dominicanacademy.org (Girls) Dr. Alexandria Egler, Pres.; Dr. Leslie Poole Petit, Prin.; Murielle Louis, Librn.;

La Salle Academy (Brothers of the Christian Schools) - (PRV) (Grades 9-12) 215 E. 6th St., New York, NY 10003 t) 212-475-8940 info@lasalleacademy.org www.lasalleacademy.org (Boys) Bro. Richard Galvin, F.S.C., In Res.; Bro. William Johnson, In Res.; Kerry Conroy, Prin.; Bro. Thomas P. Casey, Pres.;

Loyola School - (PRV) (Grades 9-12) 980 Park Ave., New York, NY 10028 t) 212-288-3522 info@loyolanyc.org www.loyolanyc.org (Coed) Rev. James Carr, Chap.; James Lyness, Prin.; Mary Claire Lagno, Chair; Tony Oroszlany, Pres.;

Marymount School (Religious of the Sacred Heart of Mary) - (PRV) (Grades 9-12) 1026 Fifth Ave., New York, NY 10028 t) 212-744-4486 marymths@adnyeducation.org www.marymountnyc.org Concepcion Alvar, Headmaster; Carolyn Booth, Dir.; Alexis Bradford, Dir.; Nora Gibson, Dir.; Annah Jones, Librn.;

Notre Dame School of Manhattan - (PRV) 327 W. 13th St., New York, NY 10014 t) 212-620-5575 ntdamehs@adnyeducation.org www.cheznous.org (Girls) Jaclyn Brilliant, Prin.; Sr. Virginia O'Brien, Pres.; Andrea Catenaccio, Librn.;

Regis High School - (PRV) (Grades 9-12) 55 E. 84th St., New York, NY 10028 t) 212-288-1100 regishs@adnyeducation.org www.regis.org (Boys). Rev. Christopher Devron, S.J., Pres.; Rev. Arthur C. Bender, S.J., Faculty; Rev. James P. Ferus, SJ, Director of Mission and Identity; Stds.: 528; Pr. Tchrs.: 2; Lay Tchrs.: 60

Residence - 53 E. 83rd St., New York, NY 10028 fpellegrini@jesuits.org

St. Jean Baptiste High School - (PAR) 173 E. 75th St., New York, NY 10021 t) 212-288-1645 bapt@adnyeducation.org www.stjean.org Girls. Sr. Maria Cassano, C.N.D., Prin.;

St. Vincent Ferrer High School - (PAR) 151 E. 65th St., New York, NY 10065-6607 t) 212-535-4680 vincferr@adnyeducation.org www.saintvincentferrer.com Sr. Gail Morgan, O.P., Prin.;

Xavier High School - (PRV) 30 W. 16th St., New York, NY 10011 t) 212-924-7900 xavierhs@adnyeducation.org www.xavierhs.org Boys. Rev. Louis T. Garaventa, S.J.; Rev. James J. Hederman, S.J.; Rev. John Replogle, S.J.; Rev. Ralph Rivera, S.J., Chap.; John R. Raslowsky II, Pres.; Rev. Vincent L. Biagi, S.J., Dir.; Tracy Tong, Librn.;

POUGHKEEPSIE

Our Lady of Lourdes High School - (PRV) 131 Boardman Rd., Poughkeepsie, NY 12603 t) 845-463-0400 lourdes@adnyeducation.org www.ollchs.org Charles Junjulas Jr., Campus Min.; Michael Krieger, Prin.; Catherine B. Merryman, Prin.;

RYE

School of the Holy Child - (PRV) (Grades 5-12) 2225 Westchester Ave., Rye, NY 10580 t) 914-967-5622 admission@holychildrye.org www.holychildrye.org (Girls) Colleen Pettus, Prin.; Donald Devine II, Bus. Mgr.;

SOMERS

John F. Kennedy Catholic High School (Diocesan Priests, Sisters of the Divine Compassion) - (DIO) 54 Rte. 138, Somers, NY 10589 t) 914-232-5061 jfkhs@adnyeducation.org www.kennedycatholic.org Rev. Mark G. Vaillancourt, Pres.; Sr. Barbara Heil, R.D.C., Dir.;

STATEN ISLAND

St. Joseph by the Sea, High School - (PRV) 5150 Hylan Blvd., Staten Island, NY 10312 t) 718-984-6500 josbysea@adnyeducation.org (Coed) Rev. Michael P. Reilly, Prin.;

St. Joseph Hill Academy - (PRV) 850 Hylan Blvd., Staten Island, NY 10305-2095 t) 718-447-1374 inquiry@stjhill.org; joshill@adnyeducation.org www.stjosephhillacademy.com (Girls) Maria Molluzzo, Prin.; Stds.: 383; Sr. Tchrs.: 1; Lay Tchrs.: 37

Monsignor Farrell High School - (DIO) 2900 Amboy Rd., Staten Island, NY 10306 t) 718-987-2900 mainoffice@msgrfarrellhs.org; farrell@adnyeducation.org www.msgrfarrellhs.org Most Rev. Edmund J. Whalen, Prin.; Kathleen Sparnroft, Librn.;

Moore Catholic High School - (DIO) 100 Merrill Ave., Staten Island, NY 10314 t) 718-761-9200 moorecats@adnyeducation.org www.moorechs.org Gina De Santis, Prin.; Marie DeAngelo, Librn.;

Notre Dame Academy High School - (PRV) 134 Howard Ave., Staten Island, NY 10301 t) 718-447-8878 kjaenicke@notredameacademy.org; ntdameac@adnyeducation.org www.hs.notredameacademy.org Kathryn Jaenicke, Prin.; Sr. Patricia Corley, C.N.D., Pres.; Christine Gullo, Librn.;

St. Peter's Boys High School - (PAR) 200 Clinton Ave., Staten Island, NY 10301 t) 718-447-1676 mcosentino@stpetersboyshs.org; stpeterb@adnyeducation.org www.stpetersboyshs.org Michael Consentino, Prin.;

WHITE PLAINS

Archbishop Stepinac High School - 950 Mamaroneck Ave., White Plains, NY 10605 t) 914-946-4800 stepinac@adnyeducation.org www.stepinac.org Paul Carty, Prin.; Rev. Thomas E. Collins, Pres.; Patrick Duffy, Librn.;

YONKERS

Sacred Heart High School - (PAR) (Grades 9-12) 34 Convent Ave., Yonkers, NY 10703 t) 914-965-3114 www.sacredhearths.org Kyle O'Donnell, Prin.; Rev. Robert J. Abbatiello, O.F.M.Cap., Pres.; Stds.: 240; Lay Tchrs.: 18

INSTITUTIONS LOCATED IN DIOCESE

ASSOCIATIONS [ASN]

BRONX

Catholic High Schools' Athletic Association of the Archdiocese of New York - 441 E. Fordham Rd., Bronx, NY 10458-5175 t) 347-334-1243 pigottk@fordhamprep.org Bro. Paul Hannon, Secy.; Chris Beal, Treas.; Kevin Cullen, Pres.; Kevin Pigott, Pres.;

Catholic High Schools' Athletic Association of the Archdiocese of New York - 4300 Murdock Ave., Bronx, NY 10466 t) 718-325-6423

HAVERSTRAW

Ladycliff College Alumnae Association, Inc. - 20 Ridge St., Haverstraw, NY 10927-1198 t) (973) 962-7221 www.ladycliffcollege.org Marion Tuttle, Pres.;

MARYKNOLL

Maryknoll Mission Association of the Faithful - ; Mailing: P.O. Box 307, Maryknoll, NY 10545-0307 t) 914-762-6364 info@mklm.org www.mklm.org Ted Miles, Exec.; Marj Humphrey, Dir.;

Maryknoll Lay Missioners Foundation - mboyle@mklm.org

NEW YORK

Association of New York Catholic Homes, Inc. - 1011 First Ave., New York, NY 10022 t) 212-371-1000 x2939 william.whiston@archny.org William E. Whiston, Treas.;

Brooklyn Prep Alumni Association - 30 W. 16th St., New York, NY 10011-6302 t) 212-924-7900 brooklynprep@gmail.com www.brooklynprep.org Rev. Daniel J. Fitzpatrick, S.J., Contact;

The Catholic Camp Association Inc. - 1011 First Ave., New York, NY 10022 t) 212-371-1000

Hill Camp -

John V. Mara CYO Camps -

Valley Camp -

Catholic Elementary School Association of New York - 1011 First Ave., 19th Fl., New York, NY 10022 t) 212-371-1000 superintendent@archny.org www.archny.org

Catholic High School Association of New York - 1011 First Ave., 19th Fl., New York, NY 10022 t) 212-371-1000 superintendent@archny.org www.archny.org

Lay Women's Association/Secular Institute of the Missionaries of the Kingship of Christ - 33 W. 60th St., Ste. 1127, New York, NY 10023 c) 917-327-0255 www.simkc.org Rev. Dominic Monti, OFM;

Missionary Childhood Association - 1011 First Ave., New York, NY 10022 t) 212-371-1000 x2700 msgr.marc.filacchione@archny.org (Holy Child Association) Rev. Msgr. Marc J. Filacchione;

CAMPUS MINISTRY / NEWMAN CENTERS [CAM]

NEW YORK

University Apostolate - 1011 First Ave., Fl. 7, New York, NY 10022 t) 646-794-3168 vincent.dasilva@archny.org Vincent DaSilva, Dir.;

Baruch College - 55 Lexington Ave., New York, NY 10010 t) 646-312-4762 www.baruch.cuny.edu Sr. Kathleen Logan, O.P., Campus Min.;

Bronx Community College - Loew Hall-Room 422, University Ave. & W. 181st St., Bronx, NY 10453 t) 718-289-5954 www.bcc.cuny.edu Sr. Barbara Ann Mueller, O.P., Campus Min.;

City College of New York - Baskerville, 204, 137th St. & Convent Ave., New York, NY 10031 t) 212-650-5866 www.ccny.cuny.edu Sr. Barbara Ann Mueller, O.P., Campus Min.;

College of Mt. St. Vincent - 6301 Riverdale Ave., Riverdale, NY 10471 t) 718-405-3200; 718-405-3215; 718-405-3216 www.cmsv.edu

College of New Rochelle - 29 Castle Pl., New Rochelle, NY 10805 t) 914-654-5052; 914-654-5867 hwolf@cnr.edu www.cnr.edu Rev. John Joseph Flynn, O.F.M.Cap., Chap.; Helen Wolf, Dir.;

Columbia University - 110 Earl Hall, New York, NY 10027 t) 212-854-5110 www.columbia.edu Rev. Jonathan Morris, Campus Min.; Rev. Daniel O'Reilly, Campus Min.;

Culinary Institute of America - 93 Wurts St., Kingston, NY 12401 t) 845-331-0436 chaplainua@gmail.com www.ciachef.edu Rev. Marc K. Oliver, Campus Min.;

Dominican College - 470 Western Hwy., Orangeburg, NY 10962 t) 845-848-7800 henrietta.malzacher@dc.edu dc.edu Sr. Barbara McEneany, O.P., Dir.;

Dutchess Community College - 93 Wurts St., Kingston, NY 12401-4509 t) 845-331-0436 www.cunydutchess.edu Rev. Marc K. Oliver, Campus Min.;

Fordham Lincoln Center - 113 W. 60th St., Lowenstein 217, New York, NY 10023 t) 212-636-6267; 212-636-6268 Joan Cavanagh, Dir.;

Fordham University at Rosehill - 441 E. Fordham Rd., Bronx, NY 10458 t) 718-817-4500 currie@fordham.edu www.fordham.edu/cm Rev. Philip A. Florio, S.J.; Sr. Regina DeVitto, C.N.D., DRE; Robert Minotti, Dir.; Lisandro Pena, Liturgy Coord.;

Herbert H. Lehman College - Student Life Bldg., 250 Bedford Park Blvd. W. (222E), Bronx, NY 10468 t) 718-960-4979 www.lehman.cuny.edu Sr. Barbara Ann Mueller, O.P., Campus Min.;

Hostos Community College - 475 Grand Concourse (Rm. C371), Bronx, NY 10451 t) 718-518-6873 www.hostos.cuny.edu Sr. Barbara Ann Mueller, O.P., Campus Min.;

Hunter College - Newman Catholic Center, 695 Park Ave., Rm. 1317 E. Bldg., New York, NY 10021 t) 212-772-4752 www.hunter.cuny.edu Sr. Barbara Ann Mueller, O.P., Campus Min.;

Iona College - 715 North Ave., New Rochelle, NY 10801 t) 914-633-2632 www.iona.edu Tiffany Di Nomi, Campus Min.; Rev. Francis F. Dixon, O.Carm., Campus Min.; Jeanne McDermott, Campus Min.; Carl Procario-Foley, Dir.;

St. John's University - 300 Howard Ave., Rm. B9, Staten Island, NY 10301 t) 718-390-4473 www.stjohns.edu James Behan Jr., Campus Min.; Melissa Gibilaro, Campus Min.; Stephen DeBlasio, Dir.;

Manhattan College - 4513 Manhattan College Pkwy., Bronx, NY 10471 t) 718-862-7972 lois.harr@manhattan.edu www.manhattan.edu Rev. George H. Hill, Chap.; Jennifer Edwards, Campus Min.; Kevin McCloskey, Campus Min.; Lois Harr, Dir.;

Manhattanville College - 2900 Purchase St., Purchase, NY 10577 t) 914-323-5150 x447 Rev. William Tyrrell, S.A., Campus Min.;

Marist College - 3399 North Rd., Poughkeepsie, NY 12601 t) 845-575-3130; 845-575-3000 x2275 francis.kelly@marist.edu Rev. Richard LaMorte, Chap.; Bro. Frank Kelly, F.M.S., Campus Min.;

Mt. St. Mary College - 330 Powell Ave., Newburg, NY 12550 t) 845-569-3517 www.msmc.edu Rev. Gregoire Fluet, Chap.;

New York Maritime College - 6 Pennyfield Ave., Fort Schuyler, Bronx, NY 10465-4198 t) 718-409-7200 www.sunymaritime.edu Mary Ellen Keefe, Campus Min.;

New York University - Catholic Center at NYU, 238 Thompson St., New York, NY 10012 t) 212-995-3990 contact@catholiccenternyu.org catholiccenternyu.org Rev. Sebastian White, O.P., Chap.;

New York University - 371 - 6th Ave., New York, NY 10014 t) 212-741-1274

Pace University - One Pace Plaza, 20 Cardinal Hayes Pl., New York, NY 10038 t) 212-962-3972 www.pace.edu Rev. John McGuire, O.P., Campus Min.;

Rockland Community College - 145 College Rd., Suffern, NY 10901 t) 845-574-4531 www.sunyrockland.edu Michael Ver'Schneider, Campus Min.;

SUNY Maritime - University Apostolate - 6 Pennyfield Ave., Bronx, NY 10465 t) 718-409-7200 Peter St. Lawrence, Campus Min.;

SUNY Purchase - Campus Ministry Program - 35 Anderson Hill Rd., Purchase, NY 10577 Peter St. Lawrence, Campus Min.;

SUNY/New Paltz - 75 S. Manheim Blvd., New Paltz, NY 12561 t) 845-691-7151 www.newpaltz.edu Henry Grimsland, Campus Min.;

St. Thomas Aquinas - 125 Rte. 340, Sparkill, NY 10976 t) 845-398-4062 www.stac.edu Sr. Madeleine Murphy, O.P., Campus Min.;

Vassar College - St. Raymond Ave., Poughkeepsie, NY 12604 t) 845-437-7000 www.vassar.edu Linda Tuttle, Campus Min.;

Wagner College & The College of Staten Island - One Campus Rd., Staten Island, NY 10301 t) 718-390-3461 (Wagner); 718-982-2652 (College of Staten Island) www.csi.cuny.edu Sr. Kathleen Logan, O.P., Campus Min.;

CATHOLIC CHARITIES [CCH]

BRONX

Casita Maria Inc. - 928 Simpson St., 6th Fl., Bronx, NY 10459 t) 718-589-2230 info@casitamaria.org www.casitamaria.org Jacqueline Weld, Chair; Haydee Morales, Exec.;

Casita Maria Inc. - 928 Simpson St., Bronx, NY 10459

GOSHEN

Catholic Charities of Orange, Sullivan and Ulster - 27 Mathews St., Goshen, NY 10924 t) 845-294-5124 Dean Scher, Dir.;

Chemical Dependency Clinic - t) 845-294-5888

Chemical Dependency Clinic - 305 North St., Middletown, NY 10940 t) 845-343-7675

Chemical Dependency Clinic - 101 Carpenter Pl., Monroe, NY 10950 t) 845-782-0295

Chemical Dependency Clinic - 280 Broadway, Newburgh, NY 12550 t) 845-562-8255; 845-569-0034

Chemical Dependency Clinic - 17 Sussex St., Port Jervis, NY 12771 t) 845-856-6344

Chemical Dependency Clinic - 8 Scofield St., Walden, NY 12586 t) 845-778-5628

Community Outreach Services - Immigration Services - 305 North St., Middletown, NY 10940 t) 845-341-1978

Community Outreach Services - Social Services - 305 North St., Middletown, NY 10940 t) 845-344-4242

Community Outreach Services - Social Services - 78 Mathews St., Goshen, NY 10924

Employee Assistance Program - 305 North St., Middletown, NY 10940 t) 845-344-5565

Housing Resource Center - 280 Broadway, Newburgh, NY 12550 t) 845-561-1665 Provides eviction prevention services.

Student Assistance Services - 305 North St., Middletown, NY 10940 t) 845-344-5565 Chemical dependency awareness, prevention, life skills education; Counseling, assessment, & referral services for students.

HAVERSTRAW

Catholic Charities Community Services of Rockland, Inc. - 78 Hudson Ave., Haverstraw, NY 10927 t) 845-942-5791 martha.robles@archny.org Emergency services. Martha Robles, Dir.;

NEW YORK

Catholic Charities Alliance - 1011 First Ave., New York, NY 10022 t) 212-371-1011 x2400 msgr.kevin.sullivan@archny.org Rev. Msgr. Kevin L.

Sullivan, Pres.;

Catholic Charities Community Services, Beacon of Hope - 1011 First Ave., 6th Fl., New York, NY 10022 t) 212-371-1000 x3608 denise.bauer@archny.org www.catholiccharitiesny.org Denise Bauer, Dir.;

Catholic Charities Community Services, Community Outreach Services Division - 1011 First Ave., New York, NY 10022 t) 212-371-1000 x2010

Catholic Charities Community Services Hudson Valley Regional Services - Putnam Catholic Center, 175 Main St., Brewster, NY 10509 t) 845-279-5276 Mary Ellen Ros, Dir.;

Central Harlem - Lt. Joseph P. Kennedy Jr. Memorial Center, 34 W. 134th St., New York, NY 10037 t) 212-862-6401

Central Office - t) 888-744-7900

Dutchess County - Poughkeepsie Catholic Center, 218 Church St., Poughkeepsie, NY 12601 t) 845-454-3855 Mary Marshall, Contact;

East Manhattan - St. Cecilia's Church, 125 E. 105th St., New York, NY 10029 t) 212-348-0488

Emergency Food Services - 34 W. 134th St., New York, NY 10030 t) 212-862-6401

Homelessness Prevention Services - 34 W. 134th St., New York, NY 10030 t) 212-862-6401

Homelessness Prevention Services - 4377 Bronx Blvd., 3rd Fl., Bronx, NY 10472 t) 347-414-1050

Homelessness Prevention Services - 2155 Blackrock Ave., Bronx, NY 10472 t) 718-414-1050

Lower Manhattan - Our Lady of Sorrows, 213 Stanton St., New York, NY 10002 t) 212-673-0900

Putnam County - 175 Main St., Brewster, NY 10509 t) 845-279-5276 lakisha.morris@archny.org Frank Kortright, Dir.; John Scarfi, Parish Social Min.;

Rockland County - 78 Hudson Ave., Haverstraw, NY 10927 t) 845-942-5791

South Bronx - 402 E. 152nd St., Bronx, NY 10455 t) 718-292-1485

Staten Island - 120 Anderson Ave., Staten Island, NY 10302 t) 718-448-5757

Sullivan County - 59 North St., Monticello, NY 12701 t) 845-791-6023 Rhetta Eason, Admin.;

Ulster County - 6 Adams St., Kingston, NY 12401 t) 845-340-9170 Thomas Kelly, Admin.;

Washington Hts. - 4111 Broadway, New York, NY 10033 t) 212-795-6860

Westchester County/Peekskill - Our Lady of the Rosary, 22 Don Bosco Pl., Port Chester, NY 10573 t) 914-939-0547

Westchester County/Yonkers - 204 Hawthorne Ave., Yonkers, NY 10701 t) 914-476-2700

Catholic Charities Department of Social and Community Development - 1011 First Ave., Room 787, New York, NY 10022 t) 212-371-1000 x2480 George B. Horton, Dir.;

Association of New York Catholic Homes - 80 Maiden Ln., 13th Fl., New York, NY 10038 t) (646) 794-3167 susan.albrecht@archny.org catholichomesny.org Susan Albrecht, Dir.;

Deaf Apostolate - Rev. Msgr. Patrick P. McCahill, Dir.;

Education Outreach Program - Alison Hughes-Kelsick, Dir.;

The Guild for Dorothy Day -

Institute for Human Development - 80 Maiden Ln., 13th Fl., New York, NY 10038 Melissa Pavone, Dir.;

Justice and Peace Ministry -

Catholic Charities Immigrant Legal Services - 80 Maiden Ln., 13th Fl., New York, NY 10038 t) 212-419-3700 immigration.services@archny.org www.catholiccharitiesny.org Raluca Oncioiu, Dir.; C. Mario Rusell, Dir.;

New York State New American Hotline - t) 212-419-3737; 800-566-7636 newamericans.hotline@archny.org Stephanie Ortiz, Contact;

Project Irish Outreach - 990 McLean Ave., Yonkers, NY 10704 t) 914-237-5098

Refugee Resettlement - t) 212-419-3726 Kelly Agnew, Dir.;

The Catholic Charities of the Archdiocese of New York - 1011 First Ave., New York, NY 10022 t) 212-371-1000 marion.boteju@archny.org wwwcatholiccharitiesny.org Rev. Msgr. Kevin L. Sullivan, CEO; Philip Dorian, Dir.; William Gentles, Dir.; George B. Horton, Dir.; Talia Lockspeiser, Dir.; Luz Taverez-Salazar, Dir.; Marion Boteju, Corporate Secretary and Chief of Staff; Kenneth Dempsey, Treasurer and Chief Financial Officer;

Catholic Charities Community Services, Archdiocese of New York - Beatriz Diaz, Exec.; Joy Jasper, Dir.; Dianna Johnson, Dir.; Harrold Moss, Dir.; C. Mario Russell, Dir.; Eddie Silvero, Dir.;

Holy Name Centre for Homeless Men, Inc. - 101 First Ave., New York, NY 10022 t) 466-794-2492

The Ladies of Charity of the Catholic Charities of the Archdiocese of New York - loc@archny.org Mary Buckley Teatum, Pres.;

Providence Health Services - 1249 Fifth Ave., New York, NY 10029 Karl Adler, Pres.;

Roman Catholic Fund for Children and Other Purposes -

St. Joseph's Immigrant Home - 425 W. 44th St., New York, NY 10036-4402 t) 212-246-5363 For students and working women. Sr. Mary Celine, D.M., Admin.;

Life Experience and Faith Sharing Associates - 1991A Lexington Ave., New York, NY 10035 t) 212-987-0959 jaddison@scny-lefsa.com; cpetrus@scny-lefsa.com www.scny-lefsa.org James Addison, Operations Manager;

St. Michael's Home - c/o The Catholic Charities of the Archdiocese of New York, 1011 First Ave., New York, NY 10022 t) 212-371-1000 cathwww.org Bernard E. Reidey, Vice Pres.;

OSSINING

The Cardinal McCloskey Emergency Residential School - 155 N. Highland Ave., Ossining, NY 10562 t) 914-762-5302 jfedele@cardinalmccloskey.org

POUGHKEEPSIE

Catholic Charities Community Services of Dutchess, Inc. - 218 Church St., Poughkeepsie, NY 12601 t) 845-452-1400 Julie West, Exec.;

RYE

Catholic World Mission, Inc. - 815 Boston Post Rd., Rye, NY 10580 t) 770-828-4966 eramirez@arcol.org www.catholicworldmission.org Rev. Daniel Brandenburg, LC, Pres.; Asstd. Annu.: 100,000; Staff: 8

CEMETERIES [CEM]

AIRMONT

Ascension Cemetery - 650 Saddle River Rd., Airmont, NY 10952 t) (845) 352-7220 www.alliedcemeteries.com/ascension-cemetery/

HAWTHORNE

Gate of Heaven Cemetery -

STATEN ISLAND

Resurrection Cemetery - 361 Sharrott Ave., Staten Island, NY 10309 t) (718) 356-7738 www.calvaryandalliedcemeteries.com

WOODSIDE

Calvary Cemetery - 49-02 Laurel Hill Boulevard, Woodside, NY 11377 t) (718) 786-8000 calbaryandalliedcemeteries.com/calvary-cemetery

COLLEGES & UNIVERSITIES [COL]

BRONX

***Fordham University** - 441 E. Fordham Rd., Bronx, NY 10458 t) 718-817-1000 president@fordham.edu www.fordham.edu Tania Tetlow, Pres.; Rev. John J. Cecero, S.J., Vice. Pres.; Martha Hirst, Sr. Vice Pres., CFO & Treas.; Stds.: 17,624; Lay Tchrs.: 753; Pr. Tchrs.: 23

NEW ROCHELLE

Iona University - 715 North Ave., New Rochelle, NY 10801 t) 914-633-2000 webmaster@iona.edu www.iona.edu Dr. Seamus Carey, Pres.; Richard Palladino, Dir., Libraries;

NEW YORK

College of Mount Saint Vincent - 6301 Riverdale Ave., New York, NY 10471-1093 t) 718-405-3200 dan.regan@mountsaintvincent.edu; president@mountsaintvincent.edu www.mountsaintvincent.edu Dr. Susan R. Burns, Pres.; Joseph Levis, Librn.; Lynne Bongiovanni, Provost and Dean of the College; Madeline Melkonian, Sr. Vice Pres., Inst. Advancement and College Rels.;

Marymount Manhattan College - 221 E. 71st St., New York, NY 10021 t) 212-517-0400 vdorgan@mmm.edu www.mmm.edu Sr. Virginia Dorgan, R.S.H.M., Campus Min.; Judson Shaver, Pres.;

NEWBURGH

Mt. St. Mary College - 330 Powell Ave., Newburgh, NY 12550 t) 845-561-0800 ryan.williams@msmc.edu www.msmc.edu Divisions: Arts & Letters; Education; Natural Sciences; Mathematics & IT; Philosophy & Religious Studies; Social Sciences. Schools: Business & Nursing Rev. Gregoire Fluet, Chap.; Jannelle Haug, Registrar; Jason Adsit, Pres.; George Abaunza, Vice. Pres.; Vivian Milczarski, Dir.; Stds.: 2,320; Lay Tchrs.: 76

ORANGEBURG

Dominican University New York - 470 Western Hwy., Orangeburg, NY 10962 t) 845-848-7800 admissions@dc.edu www.dc.edu Chartered by University of the State of New York. Sr. Kathleen Sullivan, O.P., Chancellor; Sr. Barbara McEneany, O.P., Campus Min.; Sr. Mary Eileen O'Brien, O.P., Pres.;

RIVERDALE

Manhattan College - 4513 Manhattan College Pkwy., Riverdale, NY 10471 t) 718-862-7200; 800-622-9235 admit@manhattan.edu www.manhattan.edu Brennan O'Donnell, Pres.; William H. Walters, Librn.; William Clyde, Provost & Exec. Vice Pres., Academic Affairs;

SPARKILL

St. Thomas Aquinas College - 125 Rte. 340, Sparkill, NY 10976 t) 845-398-4000 news@stac.edu www.stac.edu Kenneth D. Daly, Pres.; Dr. Robert D Murray, Vice. Pres.;

STATEN ISLAND

St. John's University Staten Island Campus - 300 Howard Ave., Staten Island, NY 10301 t) 718-390-4545 admhelp@stjohns.edu www.stjohns.edu Sponsored by the Vincentian Priests and Brothers Eastern Province of the Congregation of the Mission. Rev. Brian J Shanley, O.P., Pres.; Rev. Aidan R Rooney, C.M., Executive Vice President for Mission; Dr. Simon Moller, Provost & VP for Academic Affairs; Sharon Hewitt Watkins, Vice Pres. Business Affairs, CFO & Treas.; Joseph Oliva, VP for Admin., Secy & Gen. Counsel; Dr. Christian Vaupel, Vice Pres., Advancement & University Rels; Dr. Rachel Pereira, Vice President of Equity and Inclusion; Nunziatina A Manuli, Vice President and Chief of Staff to the President; Sarah Jean Kelly, Vice President for Student Success and Retention Strategy; David N Gachigo, Interim Vice Provost, Staten Island; Stds.: 2,263; Lay Tchrs.: 615; Pr. Tchrs.: 4

VALHALLA

***New York Medical College** - 40 Sunshine Cottage Rd., Valhalla, NY 10595 t) 914-594-4600 www.nymc.edu

CONVENTS, MONASTERIES, AND RESIDENCES FOR WOMEN [CON]

BEACON

Carmelite Monastery - 89 Hiddenbrooke Dr., Beacon, NY 12508-2230 t) 845-831-5572 carmelitesbeacon@gmail.com www.carmelitesbeacon.org Sr. Marjorie Robinson, O.C.D., Prioress; Srs.: 13

Redemptoristine Nuns of NY, Inc. - 89 Hiddenbrooke Dr., Beacon, NY 12508-2230 t) 845-831-3132 rednunsny@gmail.com www.rednunsny.org Sr. Moira Quinn, O.SS.R., Prioress; Srs.: 5

BLAUVELT

Congregation of Sisters of St. Dominic of Blauvelt - 496 Western Hwy., Blauvelt, NY 10913 t) 845-359-5600 mconnolly@opblauvelt.org www.opblauvelt.org Sr. Michaela Connolly, O.P., Prioress;

BRONX

Franciscan Missionaries of Mary - 3305 Wallace Ave., Bronx, NY 10467-6519 t) 718-547-4604 nmfmm@aol.com www.fmmusa.org Sr. Noreen Murray, Prov.;

FMM Provincialate - t) 718-547-4693

Our Lady of Millbrook Convent - ; Mailing: Box K, Millbrook, NY 12545 t) 845-677-6739 fmmch@aol.com

Franciscan Sisters of the Renewal - 1661 Haight Ave., Bronx, NY 10461 t) 718-863-8040; 718-829-9466 www.franciscansisterscfr.com (Motherhouse, Novitiate House, Convent of Damiano)

Franciscan Sisters of the Renewal - 3537 Bainbridge Ave., Bronx, NY 10467 t) 718-547-9840; 718-828-4104 www.franciscansisterscfr.com (Franciscans Sisters of the Renewal) Sr. Clare Marie Matthiass, C.F.R., Dir.;

Missionaries of Charity, Inc. - 335 E 145th St., Bronx, NY 10451 t) 718-292-0019 santaritabronx@gmail.com Sr. Maria Agnes, M.C., Supr.; Sr. M. Regi Paul, M.C., Supr.;

Missionaries of Charity - 406 W. 127th St., New York, NY 10027 t) 212-222-7229 Sr. Marie Joel, M.C,, Supr.;

Missionaries of Charity - 657 Washington St., New York, NY 10014 t) 212-645-0587 Sr. M. Eva Shalini, MC, Supr.;

Missionary Sisters of Our Lady of Perpetual Help, Inc. - 389 E. 150th St., Bronx, NY 10455 t) 718-801-2461 garzamps@yahoo.com Sr. Melissa Garza, Supr.;

Missionary Sisters of the Immaculate Heart of Mary - 2550 Webb Ave., Apt. 7E, Bronx, NY 10468 District House Sr. Kathryn Vercelline, I.C.M., Treas.;

Parish Visitors of Mary Immaculate - 2151 Watson Ave., Bronx, NY 10472-5401 t) 718-823-0350 bronxpvmi@gmail.com Sr. Mylene Rosemarie Lindo, Supr.;

Sisters of Charity Novitiate - Mount Saint Vincent, Rosary Hall, Bronx, NY 10471 t) 718-549-9200 mmccormick@scny.org Sr. Mary McCormick, Dir.;

Sisters of St. John the Baptist - Provincial Residence, 3308 Campbell Dr., Bronx, NY 10465-1358 t) 718-518-7820 provsecretary@baptistines.org baptistines.org Sr. Claudette Jasczynski Sr., CSJB, Prov.; Srs.: 55

Mt. St. John Convent - 150 Anderson Hill Rd., Purchase, NY 10577 t) 914-761-7965 jpmand1215@aol.com (Retired Sisters' Residence) Sr. Joseph Paul Manderine, CSJB, Supr.;

Society of Helpers - 385 W. 263rd St., Bronx, NY 10471 t) 718-884-3100 nyhelper@verizon.net www.helpers.org Sr. Geraldine Finan, Supr.;

GARRISON

Franciscan Sisters of the Atonement, Inc. - 41 Old Highland Tpke., Garrison, NY 10524 t) 845-424-3625; 845-230-8235 (Secy. Gen.) www.graymoor.org Sr. Diane Bernier, S.A., Supr.; Sr. Nancy Conboy, S.A., Secy.; Srs.: 74

Mother Lurana House of Graymoor (Franciscan Sisters of the Atonement) - 166 Old W. Point Rd. E., Garrison, NY 10524 t) 845-424-3184 www.graymoor.org Sr. Loretta Bezner, S.A., Admin.;

Our Lady of the Atonement Retreat House (Franciscan Sisters of the Atonement, Graymoor) - 41 Old Highland Tpke., Garrison, NY 10524 t) 845-424-3300 retreathouse@graymoor.org www.graymoor.org Sr. Eleanor White, S.A., Dir.;

HARTSDALE

Institute of the Sisters of Mercy of the Americas, Mid-Atlantic Community (The Sisters of Mercy, Inc., Sisters of Mercy) - 150 Ridge Rd., Hartsdale, NY 10530-2205 t) 914-328-3200 www.mercymidatlantic.org Sr. Patricia Vetrano, R.S.M., Pres.;

HAVERSTRAW

Sisters of St. Francis of Peace - 20 Ridge St., Haverstraw, NY 10927-1198 t) 845-942-2527 hwacker@fspnet.org www.fspnet.org Srs.: 37

HAWTHORNE

Motherhouse & Novitiate of the Sisters of St. Dominic, Congregation of St. Rose of Lima - 600 Linda Ave, Hawthorne, NY 10532 t) 914-769-5628 superiorgeneral@hawthorne-dominicans.org www.hawthorne-dominicans.org Friar Jacob Restrick, OP, Chap.; Mother Marie Edward Deutsch, OP, Supr.; Srs.: 46

HIGHLAND MILLS

Correct Convent of Jesus & Mary of Highland Mills, New York, Inc. - 15 Bethany Dr., Highland Mills, NY 10930-1003; Mailing: 821 Varnum St., NE, Washington, DC 20017-2144 t) 202-526-3203 jstolba@rjmusa.org Sr. Janet Stolba, Secy.; Srs.: 2

HOPEWELL JUNCTION

Oblates to the Blessed Trinity, St. Aloysius Novitiate - 306 Beekman Rd., Hopewell Junction, NY 12533; Mailing: P.O. Box 98, Hopewell Junction, NY 12533 t) 845-226-5671 jstab35097@aol.com www.oblatestotheblessedtrinity.org Sr. Gloria Castro, Supr.;

LIBERTY

Blessed Kateri Tekakwitha Religious Education Center - 16 Frankie Ln., Liberty, NY 12754; Mailing: Box 1011, Liberty, NY 12754 t) 845-292-9100 bkt4@verizon.net Kevin John Shields, O.P., DRE;

LIVINGSTON MANOR

Monastic Sisters of Bethlehem and of the Assumption of the Virgin - 393 Our Lady of Lourdes Camp Rd., Livingston Manor, NY 12758 t) 845-439-4300 monasterybethlehem@gmail.com Sr. Rafqa Saad, Prioress; Srs.: 10

MARYKNOLL

Maryknoll Communities, Inc. - 77 Ryder Rd., Maryknoll, NY 10545-0133; Mailing: P.O. Box 133, Maryknoll, NY 10545-0133 t) 914-941-7590 msnyder@maryknoll.org Rev. Michael J. Snyder, M.M., Chair;

Maryknoll Residential Care - Maryknoll Sisters Center, Maryknoll, NY 10545-0311 t) 914-941-9230 swaldstein@mksisters.org www.maryknoll.org Skilled Nursing home for the Maryknoll sisters only. Sr. Patricia Edmiston, M.M., Admin.;

Maryknoll Sisters Charitable Trust - 77 Ryder Rd., Maryknoll, NY 10545-0603; Mailing: P.O. Box 306, Maryknoll, NY 10545-0306 t) 914-941-7590 Rev. J. Edward Szendrey, M.M., Chair;

Maryknoll Sisters Contemplative Community - ; Mailing: P.O. Box 311, Maryknoll, NY 10545-0311 t) 914-941-7575 mkcontemplative@optimum.net

Maryknoll Sisters of St. Dominic Inc. - ; Mailing: P.O. Box 311, Maryknoll, NY 10545-0311 t) 914-941-7575 secretariat@mksisters.org www.maryknollsisters.org

MILLBROOK

Franciscan Missionaries of Mary - ; Mailing: P.O. Box K, Millbrook, NY 12545 t) 845-677-6739 fmmch@aol.com fmmusa.org

MONROE

Parish Visitors of Mary Immaculate, Inc. - 164 Quaker Hill Rd., Marycrest, Monroe, NY 10950; Mailing: P.O. Box 658, Marycrest, Monroe, NY 10949-0658 t) 845-783-2251 marycrest@frontiernet.net parishvisitorsisters.org Mother Maria Iannotti, Supr.; Sr. Mary Beata Im, Dir.; Srs.: 62

Queen of Apostles Convent - 98 Harriman Heights Rd., Monroe, NY 10950 t) 845-492-5000 qoaconvent@hotmail.com www.pallottinesisters.org Provincial Retirement Home and Provincialate of the Sisters of the Catholic Apostolate (Pallottine). Rev. Michael F. Keane, Chap.; Sr. Angela Marie Verdi, C.S.A.C., Supr.; Sr. Ann Joachim Firneno, C.S.A.C., Prov.;

MONSEY

St. Zita's Villa - 50 Saddle River Rd., N., Monsey, NY 10952 t) 845-356-2011 Motherhouse and Novitiate of Sisters of Reparation of the Congregation of Mary. Sr. Maureen Francis, S.R.C.M., Supr.;

NEW ROCHELLE

Franciscan Sisters of the Immaculate Heart of Mary United States Mission, Inc. - 42 Fifth Ave., New Rochelle, NY 10801

Ursuline Bedford Park Convent - 1338 North Ave., New Rochelle, NY 10804 t) 914-712-0060 osueast.org Sr. Kathleen Finnerty, osu, Pres.;

Ursuline Communities, Inc. - 1338 North Ave., New Rochelle, NY 10804 t) 914-712-0060 maureen.welch@osueast.org osueast.org Sr. Maureen Welch, Pres.;

Ursuline Convent of St. Teresa's, New York - 39 Willow Dr., New Rochelle, NY 10805 t) 914-632-1199 msosu@aol.com Sr. Mary Sullivan, Pres.;

Ursuline Provincialate Eastern Province of the United States, Inc. - 1338 North Ave., New Rochelle, NY 10804-2121 t) 914-712-0060 osueast.org Sr. Maureen Welch, Prov.;

Ursuline Residence, Inc. - 1338 North Ave., New Rochelle, NY 10804 t) 914-712-0060 maureen.welch@osueast.org osueast.org Sr. Maureen Welch, Pres.;

NEW WINDSOR

Sisters of the Presentation of the Blessed Virgin Mary, Inc. - 84 Presentation Way, New Windsor, NY 12553 t) 845-564-0513 pbvmadministration@hvc.rr.com sistersofthepresentation.org Sr. Patricia Anastasio, P.B.V.M., Pres.;

NEW YORK

Convent of Our Lady of the Presentation - 419 Woodrow Rd., New York, NY 10312 t) 718-356-2121 lorraine.hale1@verizon.net Motherhouse and Novitiate of the Sisters of the Presentation.

Corpus Christi Monastery - 1230 Lafayette Ave., New York, NY 10474-5399 t) 718-328-6996 dominicannunsny@verizon.net Sr. Maria Pia, Prioress;

Franciscan Sisters of the Poor - 505 8th Ave., Ste. 900, New York, NY 10018 t) 718-643-1945 sfp@franciscansisters.org www.franciscansisters.org Srs.: 102

Franciscan Sisters of the Poor Foundation, Inc. - 505 8th Ave., Ste. 900, New York, NY 10018 t) 212-818-1987 akearns@franciscanfoundation.org www.franciscanfoundation.org Sr. Licia Mazzia, S.F.P., Pres.;

International Presentation Association of the Sisters of the Presentation of the Blessed Virgin Mary - 1011 First Ave., #1313, New York, NY 10022 t) 646-794-3093 ipa.ngo.rep@gmail.com globalpres.org Despoina Afroditi Milaki, NGO Representative at the UN; Srs.: 1,410

Little Sisters of the Assumption - 475 E. 115th St., 1st Fl., New York, NY 10029 t) 212-289-4014 lsaterritory@gmail.com www.littlesisters.org Srs.: 7

Little Sisters of the Assumption - 475 E. 115th St., New York, NY 10029 t) 212-369-2097

Sisters of Charity Center (The Sisters of Charity of Saint Vincent de Paul of New York, Sisters of Charity Center, Mount Saint Vincent on Hudson) - 6301 Riverdale Ave., New York, NY 10471-1093 t) 718-549-9200 megan@scny.org www.scny.org Sr. Donna Dodge, S.C., Pres.; Srs.: 158

Sisters of the Good Shepherd - 337 E. 17th St., New York, NY 10003-3804 t) 212-475-4245 Srs.: 2

Society of the Sacred Heart, R.S.C.J. - 501 W. 52nd St., #4E, New York, NY 10019 t) 212-581-3894 Sr. Lydia Cho, Supr.;

Society of the Sacred Heart, R.S.C.J. - 310 E. 120th St., New York, NY 10035 t) 212-876-2895

NEWBURGH

Daughters of Mary Immaculate - 15 Stori Rd., Newburgh, NY 12550 t) 845-565-5034 Sr. Alba Danese, F.M.I., Supr.;

NYACK

Sisters of Our Lady of Christian Doctrine - 110 Larchdale Ave., Nyack, NY 10960 t) 845-512-8669 rcdsisters@gmail.com www.sistersrcd.org Visitation House Sr. Mary Murray, O.P., Pres.;

OSSINING

Dominican Sisters of Hope, Inc. - 299 N. Highland Ave., Bldg. 5, Ossining, NY 10562-2327 t) 914-941-4420 cmcdonnell@ophope.org; mkisob@ophope.org www.ophope.org Sr. Catherine McDonnell, OP,

Prioress; Srs.: 110

Sisters of St. Dominic Charitable Trust - 299 N. Highland Ave., Bldg. 5, Ossining, NY 10562 t) 914-941-4455 hdowney@ophope.org

PEEKSKILL

Mt. St. Francis, Motherhouse & Infirm of Franciscan Missionary Sisters of Sacred Heart - 250 South St., Peekskill, NY 10566 t) 914-737-5409 slmfmsc@mail.com fmscusa.org Canonical Name: Franciscan Missionary Sisters of the Sacred Heart. Sr. Laura Morgan, F.M.S.C., Prov.;

SCARSDALE

Blessed Sacrament Monastery (Sacramentine Nuns) - 86 Dromore Rd., Scarsdale, NY 10583-1706 t) 914-722-1657 obsny@optonline.net www.catholic.org/macc Sr. Mary Francis Blackmore, O.S.S., Prioress;

SLOATSBURG

St. Mary's Villa, Spiritual & Educational Center - 150 Sisters Servants Ln., Sloatsburg, NY 10974-0009; Mailing: P.O. Box 9, Sloatsburg, NY 10974-0009 t) 845-753-5100 ssminy@aol.com Sr. Kathleen Hutsko, S.S.M.I., Prov.;

SPARKILL

Dominican Convent of Our Lady of the Rosary - 175 Rte. 340, Sparkill, NY 10976-1047 t) 845-359-6400 ghogan@sparkill.org www.sparkill.org Motherhouse and General Novitiate of Dominican Sisters of Congregation of Our Lady of the Rosary. Sr. Irene Ellis, O.P., Prioress; Rev. Vladimir Chripko, C.O., Prov.; Srs.: 209

STATEN ISLAND

Academy of St. Dorothy (Sisters of St. Dorothy) - 1305 Hylan Blvd., Staten Island, NY 10305; Mailing: 1305 Hyland Blvd, Staten Island, NY 10305 t) 718-987-0677; 718-351-0939 dorothy@adnyeducation.org; cportu@gmail.com

Daughters of St. Paul, Pious Society (Missionary Sisters of the Communications Media) - 236 Richmond Ter., Staten Island, NY 10301 t) 718-447-5071 statenisland@pauline.org www.pauline.org Sr. Sean Marie David Mayer, Supr.;

Franciscan Handmaids of the Most Pure Heart of Mary - 63 Bayside Ln., Staten Island, NY 10309; Mailing: 1175 E. 223 St., Bronx, NY 10466 t) 718-227-5575; 212-289-5655 handmaidsofmary@aol.com www.passionforsocialjustice.com Generalate of the Franciscan Handmaids of Mary. Sr. Chala Marie Hill, F.H.M., Vicar; Srs.: 31

St. Edward Food Pantry - 6581 Hylan Blvd., Staten Island, NY 10309 t) 718-984-1625 st.edwardfoodpantry@gmail.com Sr. Precilia Nkezi Takuh, F.H.M., Dir.;

Handmaids of Mary Altar Bread Distribution Service - 6581 Hylan Blvd., Staten Island, NY 10309 t) 718-984-1625 st.edwardfoodpantry@gmail.com

Most Pure Heart of Mary Convent - Sr. Precilia Nkezi Takuh, F.H.M., Food Pantry Director;

Holy Family Provincialate - 850 Hylan Blvd., Staten Island, NY 10305 t) 718-727-5700 smcoffeltfdc@hotmail.com; rgegic@aol.com www.daughtersofdivinecharity.org Provincialate of the Daughters of Divine Charity (Holy Family Province). Sr. Mary Coffelt, F.D.C., Prov.; Srs.: 31

Pious Disciples of the Divine Master - 60 Sunset Ave., Staten Island, NY 10314 t) 718-761-2323; 718-494-8597 www.pddm.us Sr. M. Josephine Fallon, P.D.D.M., Supr.;

SUFFERN

Sisters of Life - Annunciation, 38 Montebello Rd., Suffern, NY 10901 t) 845-357-3547 sistersoflife@sistersoflife.org; vocations@sistersoflife.org sistersoflife.org Mother Agnes Mary Donovan, S.V., General Superior; Sr. Faith Marie Zerwic, Local Superior; Sr. Grace Dominic Gomes, S.V., Novice Director; Sr. Veronica Mary Sullivan, Local Superior, Asst. to Sup. Gen. for Health Care; Srs.: 126

St. Frances de Chantal (Sisters of Life) - 198 Hollywood Ave., Bronx, NY 10465 t) 718-863-2264 evangelization@sistersoflife.org sistersoflife@sistersoflife.org Formation; Vocations Sr. Mariae Agnus Dei Yates, S.V., Postulant Dir./Local Supr.; Sr. Maria Regina Williams, S.V., Vocations Dir.;

St. Paul the Apostle (Sisters of Life) - 586 McLean Ave., Yonkers, NY 10705 t) 914-968-8094 hopeandhealing@sistersoflife.org Sr. Mariana Benedict Uribe, S.V., Supr.;

Sacred Heart of Jesus (Sisters of Life) - 450 W. 51st St., New York, NY 10019 t) 212-397-1396 Sr. Faustina Maria Pia Bianchi, S.V., Supr.; Sr. Virginia Joy Cotter, S.V., Director of Respect Life Office;

Sisters of Life Center (Mission to Serve Pregnant Women) - 20 Cardinal Hayes Pl., New York, NY 10007 t) 877-777-1277 (Pregnancy assistance); 212-737-0221 visitation@sistersoflife.org; coworkers@sistersoflife.org visitationcenterus.org Sr. Mary Concepta Yates, SV, Dir.; Sr. Amata Filia Dierschke, S.V., CoWorker Mission Coordinator;

Visitation Convent - 320 E. 66th St., New York, NY 10065 t) 212-737-0221 visitation@sistersoflife.org (Sisters of Life) Sr. Mary Concepta Yates, SV, Supr.; Sr. Magdalene Teresa Herbert, S.V., Ast. to Sup. Gen. for Missions: Services to Women;

TARRYTOWN

Provincial Center, Religious Sacred Heart of Mary - 50 Wilson Park Dr., Tarrytown, NY 10591-3023 t) 914-631-8872 cvincie@rshmeap.org; susanrshm@gmail.com www.rshm-east.org Sr. Rosamond Blanchet, RSHM, Eastern American Area Leader; Sr. Susan Gardella, RSHM, Eastern American Area Councilor; Sr. Catherine Vincie, R.S.H.M., Eastern American Area Councilor; Catherine Wilkins, Director of Advancement and Communications; Srs.: 96

WAPPINGERS FALLS

Monastery of St. Clare - Franciscan Poor Clare Nuns - 70 Nelson Ave., Wappingers Falls, NY 12590-1121 t) 845-297-1685 claresny@gmail.com www.poorclaresny.com Sr. Mary Michael Boisseau, O.S.C., Abbess;

WARWICK

Mt. Alverno Center, Bon Secours Charity Health System - 20 Grand St., Warwick, NY 10990 t) 845-986-2267 bschs.bonsecours.com St. Francis Center at the Knolls. Clare Brady, Senior Vice Pres. Mission; Jeff Reilly, Senior Vice Pres. & Admin.;

WHITE PLAINS

Convent of Our Lady of Good Counsel - 52 N. Broadway, White Plains, NY 10603 t) 914-798-1300 ldonovan@divinecompassion.org divinecompassion.org Administrative Offices of the Sisters of the Divine Compassion Sr. Laura Donovan, R.D.C., Pres.; Srs.: 54

YONKERS

The Congregation of The Daughters of Mary, Inc. - 15 Trinity St., Yonkers, NY 10701 t) 914-207-6854 dmcityisland@optimum.net Sr. Agnes Jose, D.M., Secy.;

ENDOWMENTS / FOUNDATIONS / TRUSTS [EFT]

BRONX

Calvary Fund, Inc. - 1740 Eastchester Rd., Bronx, NY 10461 t) 718-518-2077 webmaster@calvaryhospital.org calvaryhospital.org Carlos M. Hernandez, Chair; Frank A. Calamari, Pres.;

Fordham Prep Formation Foundation Trust - 441 E. Fordham Rd., C/O Fordham Prep, Bronx, NY 10458 t) 718-367-7500 x267 higginsm@fordhamprep.org Rev. Joseph P. Parkes, S.J., Trustee;

Foundation of Christ the Redeemer - 2352 St. Raymond Ave., Bronx, NY 10462 t) 718-828-2380 rpbadillo@gmail.com Institute Id of Christ the Redeemer, Idente Missionaries. Rev. Francisco Sanchez, M.Id, Rector; Rev. Robert P. Badillo, M.Id, Prov.;

St. Joseph's School for the Deaf Childrens Fund, Inc. - 1000 Hutchinson River Pkwy., Bronx, NY 10465 t) 718-828-9000 darles@sjsdny.org

Saint Jutta Foundation, Inc. - 515 E. Fordham Rd., Bronx, NY 10458-5029 t) 718-817-3671 hegyi@fordham.edu

The Land Trust of the Sisters of Charity at Mount St. Vincent - 6301 Riverdale Ave., Bronx, NY 10471-1093

Sisters of Charity of New York Charitable Trust - 6301 Riverdale Ave., Bronx, NY 10471-1093 t) 718-549-9200 megan@scny.org www.scny.org Sr. Margaret Egan, SC, Secy.;

Sisters of Charity Center - emcgrory@scny.org Sr. Eileen McGrory, Secy.;

MARYKNOLL

Maryknoll Fathers and Brothers Apostolic Trust - 77 Ryder Rd., Maryknoll, NY 10545-0603; Mailing: P.O. Box 306, Maryknoll, NY 10545-0306 t) 914-941-7590 Rev. Edward J. Phillips, M.M., Chair;

Maryknoll Missionary Education Trust - 77 Ryder Rd., Maryknoll, NY 10545-0603; Mailing: P.O. Box 306, Maryknoll, NY 10545 t) 914-941-7590 Rev. Alfonso Kim, M.M., Chair;

NEW ROCHELLE

Edmund Rice Christian Brothers Foundation - 260 Wilmot Rd., New Rochelle, NY 10804 t) 914-636-1035 gmd@cbinstitute.org; kbrewer@cbfoundation.org www.ercbna.org Bro. Peter E. Zawot, C.F.C, Pres.;

Marian Residence Trust Fund - 1338 North Ave., New Rochelle, NY 10804 t) 914-712-0060 maureen.welch@osueast.org osueast.org Sr. Maureen Welch, Prov.;

OSU Charitable Trust - 1338 North Ave., New Rochelle, NY 10804 t) 914-712-0060 maureen.welch@osueast.org osueast.org Sr. Maureen Welch, Prov.;

NEW YORK

Aged and Infirm Trust - 39 E. 83rd St., New York, NY 10028 t) 212-774-5500 unesocius@jesuits.org Rev. John J. Cecero, S.J., Prov.;

Alfred E. Smith Memorial Foundation, Inc., The - 1011 First Ave., Ste. 1400, New York, NY 10022-4134 t) 646-794-3331 juliette.picciano@archny.org Juliette Picciano, Contact;

Apostolic Works Trust - 39 E. 83rd St., New York, NY 10028 t) 212-774-5500 uneprovincial@jesuits.org Rev. John J. Cecero, S.J., Prov.;

Benefit Trust for the Care & Support Plan for Dominican Friars, Province of St. Joseph - 141 E. 65th St., New York, NY 10065 t) 212-737-5757 Bro. Martin Davis, OP, Chair;

Cabrini Housing Development Fund Corporation - 220 E. 19th St., New York, NY 10003; Mailing: c/o of St. Cabrini Nursing Home, Inc., 115 Broadway, Dobbs Ferry, NY 10522 t) 914-693-6800 pkrasnausky@cabrini-eldercare.org www.cabrini-eldercare.org Patricia Krasnausky, Pres.;

Cardinal Cooke Memorial Foundation - 1011 First Ave., Rm. 1940, New York, NY 10022 t) 212-371-1000

The Cardinal Spellman Memorial Foundation - 1011 First Ave., New York, NY 10022

Cardinal's Fund for Children - 1011 First Ave., Rm. 1130, New York, NY 10022

Carmel Housing Development Fund Co., Inc. - 1011 First Ave., New York, NY 10022 t) 212-371-1000 Rev. Msgr. Kevin L. Sullivan, Pres.;

Catholic Health Care Foundation of the Archdiocese of New York, Inc. - 205 Lexington Ave., 3rd Fl., New York, NY 10016 t) 212-752-4735 poconnor@archcare.org www.archcare.org Patricia O'Connor, Contact;

Cor Mariae Development Fund Corporation - 1011 First Ave., New York, NY 10022 Rev. Msgr. Kevin L. Sullivan, Pres.;

Cor Mariae Housing Development Fund, Inc. - 1011 First Ave., New York, NY 10022 t) 212-371-1000 x2400 Rev. Msgr. Kevin L. Sullivan, Pres.;

The Dominican Foundation of Dominican Friars, Province of St. Joseph, Inc. - 141 E. 65th St., New York, NY 10065 t) 212-535-3664 df@dominicanfriars.org www.dominicanfriars.org Rev. John Paul Kern, O.P., Exec. Dir.;

Dominican Mission Secretariat - Rev. David Adiletta,

O.P., Exec.;
***The Elizabeth Seton Housing Development Fund Corporation** - 1991 Lexington Ave., New York, NY 10035; Mailing: Sisters of Charity Housing, 150 Brielle Ave., Staten Island, NY 10314 t) (718) 477-6803 ceo@schousinyny.org www.schdcorp.org
Felix Varela Foundation, Inc., The - 1011 First Ave., New York, NY 10022 t) 718-229-8001 x677; 718-281-9677 Most Rev. Octavio Cisneros, Pres.;
Formation Trust - 39 E. 83rd St., New York, NY 10028 t) 212-774-5500 unesocius@jesuits.org Rev. John J. Cecero, S.J., Prov.;
Foundation of the Order of Friars Minor of the Province of the Most Holy Name - 129 W. 31st St., 2nd Fl., New York, NY 10001-3403 t) 646-473-0265 mharlan@hnp.org Rev. Kevin Mullen, O.F.M., Pres.;
Foundation Trust - 39 E. 83rd St., New York, NY 10028 t) 212-774-5500 unesocius@jesuits.org Rev. John J. Cecero, S.J., Prov.;
Franciscan Sisters of the Poor Charitable Trust - 505 8th Ave., Ste. 900, New York, NY 10018 t) 718-643-1945 sfp@franciscansisters.org www.franciscansisters.org
Franciscans of Holy Name Province Benevolence Trust, Inc. - 129 W. 31st St., 2nd Fl., New York, NY 10001-3403 t) 646-473-0265 mharlan@hnp.org hnp.org Rev. Kevin Mullen, O.F.M., Pres.;
Franciscans of Holy Name Province Education and Formation Trust - 129 W. 31st St., 2nd Fl., New York, NY 10001-3403 t) 646-473-0265 mharlan@hnp.org www.hnp.org Bro. Michael Joseph Harlan, OFM, Secy.;
Franciscans of Holy Name Province Sick, Aged and Retired Trust - 129 W. 31st St., 2nd Fl., New York, NY 10001-3403 t) 646-473-0265 mharlan@hnp.org Rev. Kevin Mullen, O.F.M., Pres.;
The Housing Fund of the Archdiocese of New York - 1011 First Ave., New York, NY 10022 t) 212-371-1000 Rev. Msgr. Kevin L. Sullivan, Vice. Pres.;
Incarnation Children's Center Fund, Inc. - 142 Audubon Ave., New York, NY 10032 t) 212-928-2590 ccastro@incarnationchildrenscenter.org www.incarnationchildrenscenter.org Carolyn Castro, Exec.;
Inner City Scholarship Fund, Inc. - 1011 First Ave., New York, NY 10022
Joint Perpetual Care Fund, Inc. - 1011 First Ave., New York, NY 10022
***The Malta Human Services Foundation** - 1011 First Ave., Rm. 1350, New York, NY 10022 t) 212-371-1522 Dcn. Jeffrey Trexler, Exec.;
NAC Janiculum Hill Foundation - c/o Cardinal's Office - 20th Floor (Attn: JM Crowley), Archdiocese of New York - 1011 First Ave., New York, NY 10022-4112 t) 215-327-7788 jmcrowley@msn.com Most Rev. James F. Checchio, Pres.; Most Rev. William Francis Murphy, Treas.; Most Rev. Paul S. Loverde, Secy.;
New York Catholic Foundation, Inc. - 1011 First Ave., 19th Floor, New York, NY 10022 t) 646-794-3289 susan.george@archny.org archny.org Rev. Msgr. Kevin P. O'Brien, Contact;
New York Society of the John Paul II Foundation, Inc. - 101 E. 7th St., New York, NY 10009 t) 718-383-9587 polstarshop1@gmail.com Michael Pajak, Pres.;
St. Patrick's Cathedral Landmark Foundation, Inc. - 1011 1st Ave., 17th Fl., New York, NY 10022 t) 646-794-2790 www.saintpatrickscathedral.org
Paulist Religious Property Trust - 415 W. 59th St., New York, NY 10019 t) 212-757-8072 admingenoffice@paulist.org Rev. Frank Desiderio, C.S.P.;
Regis Fund Trust - 55 E. 84th St., New York, NY 10028
Regis High School Property Trust - 55 E. 84th St., New York, NY 10028
Religious Property Trust - 39 E. 83rd St., New York, NY 10028 t) 212-774-5500 unesocius@jesuits.org Rev. John J. Cecero, S.J., Prov.;
St. Thomas Aquinas Foundation of the Dominican Fathers of the United States (STAF) - 141 E. 65th St., New York, NY 10065 t) 212-737-5757 www.opeast.org National Headquarters (Order of Preachers, St. Joseph Prov.) Very Rev. Christopher Fadok, O.P.; Rev. Roberto Merced, O.P.; Rev. Albert Duggan, O.P., Chair; Bro. Martin Davis, OP, Treas.; Rev. James Marchionda, O.P.;
Trust for the Center for Migration Studies in New York - 307 E. 60th St., 4th Fl., New York, NY 10022; Mailing: 27 Carmine St., New York, NY 10014 t) 212-675-3993 scbprovince@gmail.com www.cmsny.org Rev. Angelo Plodari, C.S., Pres.;

NYACK

The Mother Marianne Gurney Charitable Trust - 110 Larchdale Ave., Nyack, NY 10960

RHINEBECK

***The Children's Foundation of Astor** - 6339 Mill St., Rhinebeck, NY 12572-5005; Mailing: P.O. Box 5005, Rhinebeck, NY 12572-5005 t) 845-871-1117 smoorhead@astorservices.org www.astorservices.org Sonia Barnes-Moorhead, Exec.;

RIVERDALE

Holy Innocents Foundation - 5272 Post Rd., Riverdale, NY 10471 ktoreilly@hotmail.com Kevin T. O'Reilly, Pres.;

RYE

Legion of Christ and Consecrated Regnum Christi Members Assistance Foundation - 815 Boston Post Rd., Rye, NY 10580 t) 770-828-4950 fformolo@legionaries.org Rev. Frank Formolo, Contact;
The Resurrection School Foundation, Inc. - 910 Boston Post Rd., Rye, NY 10580 t) 914-925-2731 admin.foundation@resurrectionschool.com www.resurrectionschool.com Kathleen Callahan, Dir.;

SLOATSBURG

The Blessed Josaphata Fund - 9 Emmanuel Dr., Sloatsburg, NY 10974-0009; Mailing: P.O. Box 9, Sloatsburg, NY 10974-0009 t) 845-753-2840 rmulcahey@sbcq.com; ssminy@aol.com Richard T. Mulcahey, Contact; Sr. Kathleen Hutsko, S.S.M.I., Prov.;

SPARKILL

Sisters of St. Dominic of Sparkill Charitable Trust - 175 Rte. 340, Sparkill, NY 10976-1047 t) 845-359-6400 www.sparkill.org Sr. Irene Ellis, O.P., Prioress;

SUFFERN

Good Samaritan Foundation for Better Health, Inc. - 255 Lafayette Ave., Suffern, NY 10901-4869 t) 845-368-5151 stacey_kirschenbaum@bshsi.org www.bschsf.org Fundraising arm of Good Samaritan Hospital, Suffern, NY. Sr. Mary Louise Moran, S.C., Pres.; Stacey Kirschenbaum, Dir.;

TARRYTOWN

***The Crotona Thorpe Housing Development Fund Corporation** - 48 Wilson Park Dr., Tarrytown, NY 10591 t) 845-359-6400 Sr. Irene Ellis, O.P., Pres.;
Leviticus 25:23 Alternative Fund, Inc. - 220 While Plains Rd., Ste. 125, Tarrytown, NY 10591 t) 914-909-4381 info@leviticusfund.org www.leviticusfund.org Gregory Maher, Exec.;
Religious of the Sacred Heart of Mary Charitable Trust - 50 Wilson Park Dr., Tarrytown, NY 10591 t) 914-631-2979 bkenny1@mindspring.com Sr. Bernadette Kenny, Contact;

WHITE PLAINS

Capuchin Friars International, Inc. - 30 Gedney Park Dr., White Plains, NY 10605-3599; Mailing: 3613 Wyandot St., Denver, CO 80211 c) 303-358-0312 capuchinfriarsintl@outlook.com www.ofmcap.org Bro. Celestino Arias, O.F.M.Cap., Pres.; Bro. Justino Sanchez Duran, O.F.M.Cap., Treas.; Rev. Victorius Pictorius, O.F.M.Cap., Vice Pres.; Bro. Mark Schenk, O.F.M.Cap., Secy.;
St. Francis of Assisi Foundation - St. Conrad Friary, 30 Gedney Park Dr., White Plains, NY 10605-3599; Mailing: 3613 Wyandot St., Denver, CO 80211 c) 303-358-0312 stfrancisfdtn@outlook.com Rev. Giampiero Gambaro, O.F.M.Cap. (Italy), Pres.; Bro. Justino Sanchez Duran, O.F.M.Cap., Treas.; Bro. Mark Schenk, O.F.M.Cap., Asst. Secy.;
Religious of Divine Compassion Charitable Trust - 52 N. Broadway, White Plains, NY 10603 t) 914-798-1300 ldonovan@divinecompassion.org divinecompassion.org Sr. Laura Donovan, R.D.C., Pres.;

YONKERS

St. Elizabeth Seton Children's Foundation Ltd. (Elizabeth Seton Children's Foundation) - 300 Corporate Blvd. S., Yonkers, NY 10701 t) 914-294-6301 ptursi@setonchildrens.org www.setonchildrens.org Sponsored by the Sisters of Charity Ministry Network Patricia A. Tursi, Exec.;
Magnificat Foundation, Inc. - ; Mailing: P.O. Box 845, Yonkers, NY 10702 t) 914-502-1859 www.magnificatfoundation.org

HOSPITALS / HEALTH SERVICES [HOS]

BRONX

Calvary Hospital - 1740 Eastchester Rd., Bronx, NY 10461 t) 718-863-6900 sgarry@calvaryhospital.org www.calvaryhospital.org For advanced cancer patients. Frank A. Calamari, Pres.; Rev. Chux Okochi, Dir.;

HARRISON

St. Vincent's Hospital Westchester, a Division of Saint Joseph's Medical Center - 275 North St., Harrison, NY 10528 t) 914-967-6500 www.svcmc.org

KINGSTON

Benedictine Hospital - 105 Mary's Ave., Kingston, NY 12401 t) 845-338-2500 www.hahv.org Sr. Mary Dorothy Huggard, O.S.B., Dir.; Sr. Mary Feehan, O.S.B., Senior Vice Pres., Mission Effectiveness;

NANUET

St. Agatha Home of the New York Foundling Hospital - 135 Convent Rd., Nanuet, NY 10954 t) 845-623-3461

NEW YORK

Terence Cardinal Cooke Health Care Center - 1249 Fifth Ave., New York, NY 10029 t) 212-360-1000 npollack@archcare.org www.archcare.org Neil Pollack, Admin.;
Developmental Disabilities Clinic - t) 212-360-3703 Comprehensive Outpatient medical, therapeutic and educational services. On site and off site OMRDD Article 16 services.
Saint Vincent Catholic Medical Centers of New York - 5 Penn Plaza, 9th Fl., New York, NY 10001 t) (212) 356-5962 (CEO) jcoffey@svcmcny.org; skorf@svcmcny.org svcmc.org Steven Korf, CEO; Asstd. Annu.: 12,000; Staff: 80
Bayley Seton Campus - 75 Vanderbilt Ave., Staten Island, NY 10304 t) 212-356-4792

PORT JERVIS

Bon Secours Community Hospital - 160 E. Main St., Port Jervis, NY 12771 t) 845-858-7000 jeff_reilly@bshsi.org bschs.bonsecours.com Part of Bon Secours Charity Health System Jeff Reilly, Sr. Vice Pres. Opers.;

SUFFERN

Good Samaritan Hospital - 255 Lafayette Ave., Suffern, NY 10901 t) 845-368-5000 bsch.bonsecours.com Part of Bon Secours Charity Health System Mary P. Leahy, CEO; Sr. Susan Evelyn, R.S.M., Sr. Vice Pres. Mission;

WARWICK

St. Anthony Community Hospital - 15-19 Maple Ave., Warwick, NY 10990 t) 845-986-2276 bschs.bonsecours.com Part of Bon Secours Charity Health System Jeff Reilly, Senior Vice Pres. & Admin.;

YONKERS

***Elizabeth Seton Pediatric Center** - 300 Corporate Blvd. S., Yonkers, NY 10701 t) 914-294-6301 ptursi@setonchildrens.org www.setonchildrens.org Sponsored by the Sisters of Charity Ministry Network Patricia A. Tursi, CEO; Bed Capacity: 169; Asstd. Annu.: 185; Staff: 803
St. Joseph's Medical Center - 127 S. Broadway, Yonkers, NY 10701 t) 914-378-7000 public.relations@saintjosephs.org saintjosephs.org Rev. Thomas Murphy, O.F.M.Cap.; Michael J. Spicer, Pres.; Sr. Dolores Doyle, P.B.V.M., Dir.;

MISCELLANEOUS [MIS]

BARRYVILLE

New Hope Manor, Inc. - 35 Hillside Rd., Barryville, NY 12719 t) 845-557-8353 bgardner@newhopemanor.org www.newhopemanor.org Rev. Daniel Callahan, Chair; Sarah Eilbacher, Dir.;

BEACON

Carmelite Communion, Inc. - 89 Hiddenbrooke Dr., Beacon, NY 12508-2230 t) 845-831-5572 carmelitesbeacon@gmail.com www.carmelitesbeacon.org Sr. Marjorie Robinson, O.C.D., Prioress;

BRONX

Abraham House, Inc. - 340 Willis Ave., Bronx, NY 10454; Mailing: P.O. Box 305, Bronx, NY 10454 t) 718-292-9321 abrooks@abrahamhouse.org Robert Murphy, Pres.;

American St. Boniface Society, Incorporated - 4011 Wickham Ave., Bronx, NY 10466-1352 t) 914-281-1371 Teri Powers, Exec.;

St. Anthony Shelter for Renewal - 410 E. 156th St., Bronx, NY 10455 t) 718-993-5161 stanthonyshelter.org/ Rev. Ignatius Mary Shin, C.F.R., Dir.;

Apostles of the Sacred Heart of Jesus of New York, Inc. - 1651 Zerega Ave., Bronx, NY 10462 t) 718-863-5047 choffner@ascjus.org Sr. Maureen Flynn, ASCJ, Pres.; Sr. Christine Hoffner, Vice. Pres.;

Calvary Holding Company, Inc. - 1740 Eastchester Rd., Bronx, NY 10461 t) 718-518-2251 fcalamari@calvaryhospital.org Thomas J. Fahey Jr., Chair; Frank A. Calamari, Pres.;

Catholic Charismatic Center (Centro Carismatico Catolico) - 826 166th St., Bronx, NY 10460 t) 212-378-1734 Most Rev. Joseph Espaillat II, Dir.;

Centro Carismatico Catolico Hispano De La Arquidiocesis De Nueva York - 826 E. 166th St., Bronx, NY 10459 t) 718-378-1734 centro826@aol.com www.centrocatolicocarismatico.com Most Rev. Joseph Espaillat II, Dir.;

Church of St. Philip Neri Holding Corp. - 3025 Grand Concourse, Bronx, NY 10468

Ciszek Hall Jesuit Residential College - 2502 Belmont Ave., Bronx, NY 10458-6282 t) 718-817-9100 jccuciszekrector@jesuits.org www.jesuits.org/our-work/ciszekhall/ Rev. William T. Sheahan, S.J., Rector;

Corazon Puro - 420 E. 156th St., Bronx, NY 10455; Mailing: P.O. Box 946, Bronx, NY 10455 c) (718) 912-1861 info@corazonpuro.org www.corazonpuro.org Formation for young adults, and families in vulnerable communities in English and Spanish Luis Cifuentes, Bus. Mgr.; Ana Tokeshi, Assoc. Dir.; Rev. Agustino Miguel Torres, C.F.R., Pres.; Odelis Bisono, Mem.;

Emmanuel School of Mission, Inc. - 371 E. 150 St., Bronx, NY 10455; Mailing: 559 Pelham Manor Rd, Pelham, NY 10803 t) 347-862-2690 esm-nyc.com Rev. Philippe Bernard Marie Vigneron, EC (France), Dir.;

Focolare Movement, Women's Branch (New York) - 179 Robinson Ave., Bronx, NY 10465 t) 718-828-1969 c) 718-594-6242 focfny@gmail.com www.focolare.us A Gospel-based ecclesial movement for spiritual & social renewal.It's spirituality of unity has become a lifestyle for people of all ages & background Endy Moraes, Dir.;

Focolare Movement Formation Fund - 179 Robinson Ave., Bronx, NY 10465 c) 718-594-6242 na-zonecenters-red@focolare.us www.focolare.us John Chesser, Pres.;

***Francesco Productions Inc.** - 420 E. 156th St., Bronx, NY 10455 t) 718-401-1589 www.francescoproductions.com Rev. Stanley Fortuna, C.F.R.; Kim Yu, Dir.;

Franciscan Mission Outreach, Inc. - 420 E. 156th St., Bronx, NY 10455 t) 718-402-8255 franciscan.mission@gmail.com www.franciscanmissionoutreach.org/ Rev. Herald Joseph Brock, C.F.R., Dir.;

Franciscan Renewal Ministries, Inc. - 421 E. 155th St., Bronx, NY 10455 t) 718-402-8255 x5 cfrgenalm@franciscanfriars.com Bro. Peter Marie Westall, C.F.R., Dir.;

Hispanic Catholic Charismatic Center of the Archdiocese of New York - 826 E. 166th St., Bronx, NY 10459 t) 718-378-1734 centro826@aol.com wwwcentrocatolicocarismatico.com Most Rev. Joseph Espaillat II;

Institute of the Helpers - 385 W. 263rd St., Bronx, NY 10471 t) 718-884-3100 nyhelper@verizon.net

St. Joseph's Center - 275 W. 230th St., Bronx, NY 10463 t) 718-796-4340 For the development of Lay Leaders, Cursillo Center, Marriage Encounter. (Spanish) Rev. Jose Luis Martinez, O.A.R., Dir.;

LAMP Ministries, Inc. - 2704 Schurz Ave., Bronx, NY 10465 t) 718-409-5062 tscheuring@lampministries.org www.lampministries.org Tom Scheuring, Dir.;

***Mercy Center, Inc.** - 377 E. 145th St., Bronx, NY 10454-1006 t) 718-993-2789 administration@mercycenterbronx.org www.mercycenterbronx.org Parenting skills courses, business training, support groups, spirituality groups, & ESL. Stephen J. Stritch III, Dir.;

Metro New York Christian Life Communities, Inc. - 2540 Hughes Ave., Bronx, NY 10458 t) 718-817-5454 metronyclc@yahoo.com www.fordham.edu/clc Sr. Eileen Schulenburg, S.C., Contact;

Nativity Mission Center, Inc. - 740 Manida St., Bronx, NY 10474 t) 718-861-9084 info@sis-nativity.org www.sis-nativity.org Eavan O'Driscoll, Pres.;

The Saint Padre Pio Shelter Corporation - 427 E. 155th St., Bronx, NY 10455 t) 718-292-3713 Rev. Bonaventure Rummell, C.F.R., Dir.;

Park Avenue Thorpe, HDFC - 406 E. 184th St., Bronx, NY 10458 t) 718-295-2550

Preston Center of Compassion, Inc. - 2780 Schurz Ave., Bronx, NY 10465 t) 718-892-8977 operations@prestoncenterofcompassion.org www.prestoncenterofcompassion.org/ Michael J Fahey, Pres.; Sr. Patricia Warner, R.D.C., Exec. Dir.;

Rosalie Hall Maternity Services Division of Catholic Guardian Society & Home Bureau - 420 Howe Ave., Bronx, NY 10473 t) 718-684-3855 clongley@catholicguardian.org Craig Longley, Dir.;

St. Joseph's Cursillo Center - 620 Thieriot Ave., Bronx, NY 10473 Rev. Ramon A. Lopez, Dir.;

Siervas De Cristo Resucitado, Inc. - 832 E. 166th St., Bronx, NY 10459; Mailing: 826 E. 166th St., Bronx, NY 10459 t) 718-542-7293 x27 siervas.scrny826@gmail.com Sr. Alexandra Rosa, SCR, Dir.;

Sisters of Charity Federation, Inc. - 6301 Riverdale Ave., Bronx, NY 10471 c) (724) 454-5571 ghartzog@sistersofcharityfederation.org sistersofcharityfederation.org Sr. Grace Hartzog, S.C., Dir.;

***Sisters of Charity Ministry Network Inc.** - 6301 Riverdale Ave., Bronx, NY 10471 t) (718) 549-9200 www.sistersofcharityministrynetwork.org Sr. Donna Dodge, S.C., Chair;

Sisters, Servants of Mary, Ministers to the Sick - 3305 Country Club Rd., Bronx, NY 10465 t) 718-829-0428 superiorany@gmail.com sistersservantsofmary.org Home nursing. Mother Silvia Juarez, S. de M., Supr.;

Thorpe Family Residence, Inc. - 2252 Crotona Ave., Bronx, NY 10457 t) 212-982-7571

***Tolentine-Zeiser Community Life Center, Inc.** - 2345 University Ave., Bronx, NY 10468 t) 718-933-6935

BRONXVILLE

Polish Knights of Malta, Inc. - 3 Stoneleigh Plaza, #4-E, Bronxville, NY 10708 t) 914-793-4596 witoldsulimirski@cs.com Witold S. Sulimirski, Pres.;

DOVER PLAINS

RDC Loaves and Fishes, Inc. - 52 Mill St., Dover Plains, NY 12522; Mailing: P.O. Box 665, Dover Plains, NY 12522 t) 845-877-9076 roccenterofcompassion.org Lori Vincent, Dir.;

ESOPUS

MBCE Mid Hudson Valley Camp, Inc. - 1455 Broadway, Rte. 9W, Esopus, NY 12429; Mailing: P.O. Box 197, Esopus, NY 12429

GARNERVILLE

1011 First Avenue, Inc. - 29 Cinder Rd., Garnerville, NY 10923 t) 458-947-1330 sgbs29@aol.com www.stgregorybarbarigoschool.org/ Dana Spicer, Prin.;

HARTSDALE

Marian Woods, Inc. - 152 Ridge Rd., Hartsdale, NY 10530 t) 914-750-6000 adonovan@marianwoods.org www.marianwoods.org Sr. Aileen Donovan, O.P., Exec.;

Mercy Education Support Fund, Inc. - 150 Ridge Rd., Hartsdale, NY 10530 t) 914-882-2882 x128 srpwolf@optonline.net Sr. Patricia Wolf, R.S.M., Pres.;

HAVERSTRAW

Franciscan Sisters of Peace - 20 Ridge St., Haverstraw, NY 10927-1198 t) 845-942-2527 hwacker@fspnet.org www.fspnet.org Sr. Dorothy DeYoung, Contact;

HAWTHORNE

Blessed Margaret's Cancer Relief Fund, Inc. - 600 Linda Ave., Hawthorne, NY 10532 t) 914-769-0923 sistermaryjoseph@hawthorne-dominicans.org Mother Marie Edward, Pres.;

The Rose Hawthorne Guild - 600 Linda Ave., Hawthorne, NY 10532 t) 914-769-0114 srmjoseph@gmail.com www.hawthorne-dominicans.org Mother Marie Edward, Pres.;

HOPEWELL JUNCTION

Camp Veritas - 67 Winter Park Dr., Hopewell Junction, NY 12533 t) 845-266-5784 ryan1@campveritas.com www.campveritas.com

HYDE PARK

Focolare Movement (Men's Branch) - National Center - 7 Intellect Way, Hyde Park, NY 12538 c) 718-594-6242 www.focolare.us An ecclesial movement founded in Italy in 1943 by Chiara Lubich, reached 183 countries. Inspired by Jesus' prayer: "May they all be one" (Jn 17:21). Ana Dias, Contact;

Focolare Movement, (Women's Branch) - National Center - 200 Cardinal Rd., Hyde Park, NY 12538 c) 718-594-6242 www.focolare.us An ecclesial movement founded in Italy in 1943 by Chiara Lubich, reached 183 countries. Inspired by Jesus' prayer: "May they all be one" (Jn 17:21). Ana Dias, Contact;

Focolare Movement, Mariapolis Luminosa - 200 Cardinal Rd., Hyde Park, NY 12538; Mailing: 5506 Jackson St., Pittsburgh, PA 15206 t) 845-229-0230 c) 718-594-6242 luminosa@focolare.us; na-zonecenters-red@focolare.us luminosa.focolare.us/ M. Luminosa wants to be an example of a society renewed by the Gospel message of unity. An ideal place for family vacation, spiritual retreat, outings Margaret Kelly, Dir.; Attilio Polsoni, Dir.;

Focolare Movement, Women's Branch (East Coast) - 257 Peace Ave., Hyde Park, NY 12538 c) 718-594-6242 na.red@focolare.us www.focolare.us A Gospel-based ecclesial movement for spiritual & social renewal.It's spirituality of unity has become a lifestyle for people of all ages & background Maria Teresa Fronza, Pres.;

Focolare Movement, Men's Branch (New York) - 7 Intellect Way, Hyde Park, NY 12538 c) 718-594-6242 www.focolare.us A Gospel-based ecclesial movement for spiritual & social renewal.It's spirituality of unity has become a lifestyle for people of all ages & background Domenico Casella, Pres.;

Living City of the Focolare Movement, Inc. - 202 Comforter Blvd., Hyde Park, NY 12538 c) 718-594-6242 Matteo Pota, CEO;

New City Press of the Focolare Movement, Inc. - 202 Comforter Blvd., Hyde Park, NY 12538 t) 845-229-0335 x103 matteo.pota@focolaremedia.com www.youtube.com/@focolaremedia Content to grow spiritually,improve relationships,engage in dialogue,foster collaboration in the Church and throughout society. Includes NCP and LC. Matteo Pota, Exec. Dir.;

LARCHMONT

Spiritual Development Office - 1 Pryer Manor Rd., Larchmont, NY 10538 t) 914-235-6939 Rev. Eugene J. Fulton, Dir.;

LIVINGSTON MANOR

The Monastic Family of Bethlehem - 393 Our Lady of Lourdes Camp Rd., Livingston Manor, NY 12758 t) 845-439-4300 monasterybethlehem@gmail.com monasteryofbethlehemnewyork.com Sr. Rafqa Saad,

Prioress;

MARYKNOLL

The Field Afar Initiative, Inc. - 77 Ryder Rd., Maryknoll, NY 10545

MOUNT VERNON

St. Dymphna Devotion (Province of the Immaculate Conception) - 274-280 W. Lincoln Ave., Mount Vernon, NY 10551-0598; Mailing: P.O. Box 598, Mount Vernon, NY 10551-0598 t) 914-664-5604 mbonnici@franciscanmissionassoc.org Rev. Robert M. Campagna, O.F.M., Prov.; Madeline Bonnici, Exec.;

NANUET

Catholic School Region of Rockland Co. - 32 W. Nyack Rd., Nanuet, NY 10954 t) 845-623-3504

NEW ROCHELLE

Salesian Missions, Inc. - 2 Lefevre Ln., New Rochelle, NY 10801 t) 914-633-8344 joanno@salesianmissions.org www.salesianmissions.org Rev. Timothy Zak, S.D.B.;

Salesian Office of Vocations - 148 E. Main St., New Rochelle, NY 10802-0639; Mailing: Box 639, New Rochelle, NY 10802-0639 t) 914-636-4225 info@salesiansofdonbosco.org Rev. Dominic Dahn Cong Tran, S.D.B.;

Songcatchers, Inc. - 50 Washington Ave., New Rochelle, NY 10801; Mailing: 2005 Palmer Ave. #252, Larchmont, NY 10801 t) 914-654-1178 info@songcatchers.org www.songcatchers.org Karenann Carty, Pres.; Angela Belsole, Dir.; Kathleen McEntee, Dir.;

NEW YORK

America Media - 1212 Ave. of the Americas, 11th Fl., New York, NY 10036 t) 212-581-4640 america@americamedia.org www.americamedia.org William R. Kunkel, Chair; Rev. Matthew F. Malone, S.J., Pres.;

American Committee on Italian Migration, Inc. - 25 Carmine St., New York, NY 10014 t) 212-247-7373 acimny@aol.com www.aciminnigra.org Rev. Matthew Didone, C.S.;

St. Ansgar Scandinavian Catholic League - 430 E. 20th St., Apt. MB, New York, NY 10009 t) 212-675-0400 viggor@rambusch.com www.saintansgars.org Rev. Philip Sandstrom, Chap.; Viggo B. Rambusch, Treas.; Lennard Rambusch, Pres.; Catha Rambusch, Vice Pres. & Sec.;

Apostleship of the Sea - Pier 52, New York, NY 10019 t) 212-265-5020 Rev. Msgr. Kevin J. Nelan, Dir.;

Archbishop Fulton J. Sheen Center, Inc. - 18 Bleecker St., New York, NY 10012 t) 212-219-3132 www.sheencenter.org David DiCerto, Exec. Dir.;

ArchCare Community Services - 205 Lexington Ave., 3rd Fl., New York, NY 10016 t) 646-633-4700 info@archcare.org www.archcare.org Scott LaRue, CEO;

Benefice Advantage - 205 Lexington Ave., 3rd Fl., New York, NY 10016 t) 646-633-4422 hpizarro@archcare.org; mbryanmaher@archcare.org

Cabrini Immigrant Services of New York City, Inc. - 139 Henry St., New York, NY 10002 t) 212-791-4590 info@cis-nyc.org cis-nyc.org/ Javier Ramirez-Baron, Contact;

Catholic Alumni Club of the Archdiocese of New York - 83 Christopher St., New York, NY 10014 t) 212-243-6513 marydplaza@yahoo.com www.caci.org/cac/newyorkcac.html Marguerite Cronin, Pres.;

Catholic Alumni Partnership - 1011 First Ave., 14th Fl., New York, NY 10022 t) 646-794-3376

Catholic Big Sisters and Big Brothers - 137 E. 2nd St., 2nd Fl., New York, NY 10009 t) 212-475-3291 director@cbsbb.org www.cbsbb.org

Catholic Daughters of the Americas and All its Courts - 10 W. 71st St., New York, NY 10023 t) 212-877-3041 cdofanatl1@aol.com www.catholicdaughters.org Martha Hamboussi, Dir.;

Catholic Health Care System - 205 Lexington Ave., 3rd Fl., New York, NY 10016 t) 212-752-4735; 646-475-4839 slarue@archcare.org; mbryanmaher@archcare.org www.archcare.org d/b/a ArchCare Scott LaRue, CEO;

Catholic Indemnity Insurance Company - c/o 1011 First Ave., New York, NY 10022 t) 212-371-1000 frank.napolitano@archny.org

Catholic Interracial Council of N.Y., The - 899 10th Ave., New York, NY 10019 t) 212-237-8600 Gerard W. Lynch, Pres.;

***Catholic League for Religious and Civil Rights** - 450 Seventh Ave., 34th Fl., New York, NY 10123 t) 212-371-3191 cl@catholicleague.org www.catholicleague.org William A. Donohue, Pres.; Bernadette Brady-Egan, Vice Pres.;

Catholic Medical Mission Board, Inc. - 10 W. 17th St., New York, NY 10011-5765 t) 212-242-7757 info@cmmb.org www.cmmb.org Rev. J. Peter Schineller, S.J.; Most Rev. Joseph M. Sullivan; Bruce Wilkinson, Pres.;

Catholic Near East Welfare Association (CNEWA) - 1011 First Ave., New York, NY 10022 t) 212-826-1480 cnewa@cnewa.org www.cnewa.org His Eminence Timothy M. Dolan, Chair; Rev. Msgr. Peter I. Vaccari, Pres.;

Catholic Resources, Inc. - 1339 York Ave., New York, NY 10021 t) 646-475-4835 kmcguire@chcsnet.org Kathryn McGuire, Sr. Vice Pres.;

Catholic Spiritual Family, The Work, Inc. - 419 E. 13th St., New York, NY 10009 t) 212-677-5680 inc@theworkfso.org www.thework-fso.org Sr. Maria Hugens, F.S.O., Treas.;

***Catholic Voices USA** - 1011 First Ave., New York, NY 10022

The Catholic World Wide Web Corporation - 1011 First Ave., New York, NY 10022 t) 212-371-1000 bernard.reidy@archny.org www.archny.org

Centro Altagracia de Fe y Justicia, Inc. (Altagracia Center of Faith and Justice, Inc.) - 39 E. 83rd St., New York, NY 10028 t) 127-774-5505 unesocius@jesuits.org www.jesuitseast.org Rev. John J. Cecero, S.J., Prov.;

Chapel San Lorenzo Ruiz (Philippine Pastoral Center) - 378 Broome St., New York, NY 10013 t) 212-966-1019 chapelofsanlorenzoruiz@gmail.com www.chapelofsanlorenzo.com Rev. Erno Diaz, Dir.;

Chemin Neuf Community Corporation - 1047 Amsterdam Ave., New York, NY 10025

Chinese Catholic Information Center - 86 Riverside Dr., New York, NY 10024; Mailing: 54-17 90th St., Elmhurst, NY 11373 t) 212-787-6969 brotherli2000@yahoo.com Bro. Peter Li, C. S. J. B., Secy.; Rev. Phi Phu Ho, C.S.J.B. (Taiwan), Dir.;

The Christophers - 5 Hanover Sq., 22nd Fl., New York, NY 10004 t) (212) 759-4050 x241 mail@christophers.org www.christophers.org Mary Ellen Robinson, Pres.; Tony Rossi, Editor;

CIF Catholic Corp. - 1011 First Ave., New York, NY 10022

Committee for Mission Responsibility Society, Inc. - 1011 First Ave., New York, NY 10022 t) 212-371-1000 x2700 pchirchirillo@aol.com

Community of St. Egidio, U.S.A., Inc. - 380 Lenox Ave., 6H, New York, NY 10027 t) 212-663-1483 c) 646-765-3899 santegidiousa@gmail.com www.santegidio.org Charitable work with people in need and peace Paola Piscitelli, Pres.;

Courage International, Incorporated - 415 W, 59th St., New York, NY 10019 t) 212-265-3495 x291 nycourage@aol.com www.couragerc.org Rev. James B. Lloyd, C.S.P.;

Deaf Catholic Center - 1011 First Ave., New York, NY 10022 t) 212-988-8563 Rev. Msgr. Patrick P. McCahill, Dir.;

Department of Education, Superintendent of Schools Office - 1011 First Ave., New York, NY 10022 t) 212-371-1000 x2800 dr.timothy.mcniff@archny.org www.buildboldfutures.org Lucia DiJusto, Admin.; Noelle Beale, Supt.; Cathleen Cassel, Supt.; Michael Coppotelli, Supt.; Mary Jane Daley, Supt.; Michael Deegan, Supt.; Linda Dougherty, Supt.; Damian Hermann, Supt.; Zoilita Herrera, Supt.; Timothy J. McNiff, Supt.; John Riley, Supt.; Paige Sanchez, Supt.; Steven Virgadamo, Supt.; Frank Viteritti, Supt.;

Archdiocesan Catechetical Office - 1011 First Ave., New York, NY 10022 sr.joan.curtin@archny.org Sr. Zelide M. Ceccagno, M.S.C.S., Dir.; Sr. Joan Curtin, C.N.D., Dir.; Sr. Teresita Morse, R.J.M., Dir.; Sr. Mary Crucifix Pandullo, C.S.J.B., Dir.; Sr. Kevin John Shields, O.P., Dir.;

Archdiocesan Drug Abuse Prevention Program - 2789 Schurz Ave., New York, NY 10465 t) 718-904-1333 info@adapp.org www.adapp.org Christine Cavallucci, Dir.;

Center for Spiritual Development -

Department of Education Archdiocese of NY Child Nutrition Program - Thomas Smith, Dir.;

Family Life/Respect Life Office - Kathleen Wither, Dir.;

Instructional Television - 215 Seminary Ave., Yonkers, NY 10704 t) 914-968-7800 Rev. Gary M. Mead, Dir.;

Office of Finance - t) 212-371-1011 x2707 Frank Napolitano, Exec.;

University Apostolate - Campus Ministry - 1011 First Ave., 7th Flr., New York, NY 10022 t) 646-794-3168 Christopher Oravetz, Dir.;

Descubriendo El Siglo XXI, Inc. (Discovering XXI Century Inc.) - 329 W. 42nd St., New York, NY 10036; Mailing: P.O. Box 1170, New York, NY 10018 t) 212-244-4778 radiosigloxxi@aol.com www.descubriendoelsiglo21.com Rev. Tomas Del Valle-Reyes, Pres.;

Dominican Friars' Guilds - 141 E. 65th St., New York, NY 10065 t) 212-535-3664 df@dominicanfriars.org Rev. John Paul Kern, O.P., Exec. Dir.;

Deserving Poor Boys Priesthood Association -

Dominican Rosary Apostolate -

St. Jude Dominican Missions - 141 E. 65th St., New York, NY 10065 t) (212) 744-2410

St. Martin de Porres Guild -

Dominican Friars Health Care Ministry of New York, Inc. - 411 E. 68th St., New York, NY 10065-6305 t) 212-988-8303 info@dfhcmny.org www.healthcareministry.org/ Rev. Hyacinth Grubb, O.P., Exec. Dir.;

Dominican Shrine of St. Jude, Inc. - St. Catherine of Siena Priory, 411 E. 68th St., New York, NY 10065-6305 t) 212-249-6067 kfrancekelly@dominicanshrineofsaintjude.org www.dominicanshrineofsaintjude.org Rev. John Aquinas Farren, O.P., Dir.;

Droste Mental Health Services, Inc. - 171 Madison Ave., Ste. 400, New York, NY 10016-5153 t) 212-889-4042 j.deluca@drostemhservices.org www.drostemhservices.org Sarah Strole, Exec. Dir.;

Ecclesiastical Communications Corp. - 1011 First Ave., New York, NY 10022

Ecclesiastical Maintenance Services, Inc. - 1011 First Ave., New York, NY 10022

Educational Services of the Archdiocese of New York, Inc. - 1011 First Ave., New York, NY 10022

Franciscan Bread for the Poor, Inc. - 129 W. 31st St., 2nd Fl., New York, NY 10001-3439 t) 646-473-0265 mharlan@hnp.org Bro. Michael Joseph Harlan, OFM, Secy.;

Franciscan Missionary Charities, Inc. - 2101 Fifth Ave., Unit 1S, New York, NY 10035 t) 917-797-8890 Rev. Ronald P. Stark, O.F.M., Pres.; Rev. Francis K. Kim, O.F.M., Exec.;

Franciscan Missionary Union, Province of the Most Holy Name - 144 W. 32nd St., New York, NY 10001-3202 t) 212-564-8799 info@fmu.org www.fmunion.org Bro. Michael Joseph Harlan, OFM, Secy.;

Franciscan Sisters of the Poor Communities, Inc. - 505 8th Ave., Ste. 900, New York, NY 10018 t) 718-643-1945 sfp@franciscansisters.org www.franciscansisters.org Sr. Licia Mazzia, S.F.P., Pres.;

Franciscans International, Inc. - 246 E. 46th St., #1F, New York, NY 10017 t) 917-675-1075 newyork@fiop.org www.franciscansinternational.org Rev. Markus Heinze, O.F.M., Exec.; Friar Benedict

Ayodi, OFM Cap, Mem.;
The Fratecelli Corporation - 129 W. 31st St., 2nd Fl., New York, NY 10001-3403 t) 646-473-0265 mharlan@hnp.org Bro. Michael Joseph Harlan, OFM, Secy.;
Friends of American Art in Religion, Inc., Vacant, Pres. - 143 E. 43rd St., New York, NY 10017 t) 212-682-5722
The Good Shepherd Volunteers, Inc. - 337 E. 17th St., New York, NY 10003 t) 212-475-4245 x718 gsv@goodshepherds.org www.gsvolunteers.org Michele G. Gilfillan, Dir.;
Guild of Catholic Lawyers, The - c/o Kelley Drye & Warren LLP, Attn: Neil Merkl, 3 World Trade Center, 175 Greenwich St., New York, NY 10007 t) 212-808-7811 nmerkl@kelleydrye.com Neil M Merkl, Pres.;
Holy Name Society Archdiocesan Union of New York - 1011 First Ave., New York, NY 10022-4112; Mailing: 1905 Tenbroeck Ave., Bronx, NY 10461-1833 t) 718-931-9239 ajm1905@aol.com Dcn. Thomas R. Tortorella, Associate Spiritual Director;
The Human Adventure Corp. - 125 Maiden Ln., 15th Fl., New York, NY 10038 t) 212-337-3580 cladministration@clhac.com www.clonline.us Rev. Jose Medina, Exec.;
Hungarian Catholic League of America, Inc. - 414 E. 82 St., New York, NY 10028 t) 212-327-2959
***The Jesuit Collaborative** - 39 E. 83rd St., New York, NY 10028-0810 t) 212-774-5505 ueasocius@jesuits.org Very Rev. Joseph O'Keefe, S.J.;
Jesuit Seminary and Mission Bureau, Inc. - 39 E. 83rd St., New York, NY 10028 t) 212-774-5500 ueasocius@jesuits.org See USA East Province of the Society of Jesus. Very Rev. Joseph O'Keefe, S.J., Prov.;
Language Institute - 1011 First Ave., New York, NY 10022 t) 212-371-1000 x2982
LaSalle New York City, Inc. - 215 E. 6th St., New York, NY 10003; Mailing: 444A Rte. 35 S., Eatontown, NJ 07724 t) 732-380-7926 x103 juliano@fscdena.org www.lasalleacademy.org Bro. Joseph Juliano, F.S.C., Secy.;
The Lay Fraternity of St. Dominic, Inc. - 141 E. 65th St., New York, NY 10021-6618 t) 212-737-5757 laydominicans.org/ Cosette Heimann, Pres.;
Legion of Mary, Office - 1011 First Ave., New York, NY 10022 t) 212-752-7966 ny.senatus@verizon.net legion-of-mary-ny.org John Kinney, Pres.;
***Life Athletes, Inc.** - 1011 First Ave., New York, NY 10022 t) 574-237-9000 chris@lifeathletes.org www.lifeathletes.org Christopher J. Godfrey, Pres.;
Light and Life Evangelization Program - 523 W. 142nd St., New York, NY 10031 t) 212-926-7433
Little Sisters of the Assumption Family In Mission, Inc. - 475 E. 115th St., 1st. Fl., New York, NY 10029 t) 212-289-4014 coordinator@lsafim.org www.lsafim.org Sr. Annette Allain, L.S.A., Exec.;
Lumen Dei - 340 W. 53rd St., New York, NY 10019 t) 212-586-4447 newyorkfem2@gmail.com www.lumendei.org Rev. Wilberto Reyes-Garced, L.D., Supr.;
The Migrant Center of New York, Inc. - 135 W. 31st St., New York, NY 10001 t) 212-736-8500 Rev. Dennis M. Wilson, O.F.M., CFO;
The Missionary Society of St. Paul the Apostle in the State of California - 415 W. 59th St., New York, NY 10019 t) 212-757-8072 admingenoffice@paulist.org Rev. Gilbert S. Martinez, C.S.P., Pres.;
***Monsignor Robert Fox Memorial Shelter Housing Development, Inc.** - Fox House, 111 E. 117th St., New York, NY 10035 t) 212-534-6634; (718) 477-6803 www.schdcorp.org
National Federation for Life - 1011 First Ave., Rm. 1417, New York, NY 10022
National Office of the Devotees of Padre Pio, Inc. - 1154 1st Ave., New York, NY 10065 t) 212-838-6549 Mario Bruscki, Dir.;
The National Shrines of St. Anthony and St. Jude, Inc. - 144 W. 32nd St., New York, NY 10001-3202 t) 212-564-8799; 646-473-0265 mharlan@hnp.org Bro. Michael Joseph Harlan, OFM, Secy.;
***Nazareth Housing, Inc.** - 519 E. 11th St., New York, NY 10009 t) 212-777-1010 www.nazarethhousingnyc.org
New York Catholic Continuum Care, Inc. (NYCCC) - 1011 First Ave., 11th Fl., New York, NY 10022 t) 212-371-1011 x2462 Doug Sansted, Contact;
The New York Foundling - 590 Ave. of the Americas, New York, NY 10011 t) 212-633-9300 development@nyfoundling.org www.nyfoundling.org Melanie Hartzog, Pres.; Asstd. Annu.: 30,000; Staff: 2,700
Northeast Hispanic Catholic Center - 1011 First Ave., New York, NY 10022 t) 212-751-7045 nhcc1011@aol.com Doris N. Valentin, Exec.;
Order of Malta Worldwide Relief Malteser International Americas, Inc. - 1011 First Ave., Ste. 1322, New York, NY 10022 t) (646) 794-3457 orderofmaltarelief.org John E. McInerney III, Pres. & Chmn.;
***Paideia, Inc./New York Encounter** - 42 Broadway, Suite 12-300, New York, NY 10004 c) 914-548-1275 odanese@newyorkencounter.org www.newyorkencounter.org Olivetta Danese, Treas.;
Parish Assistance Corporation - 1011 First Ave., New York, NY 10022 t) 646-794-3394 paul.kefer@archny.org Paul Kefer, Dir.;
Partnership Schools - 1011 First Ave., Ste. 1800, New York, NY 10022 t) 646-794-3338 jill.kafka@partnershipnyc.org thepartnershipschools.org/ Jill Kafka, Exec.;
Partnership for Quality Education, Inc. - 1011 First Ave., 18th Fl., New York, NY 10022 t) 646-794-3670
St. Patrick's International Inc. - c/o Cullen & Dykman,, One Battery Park Plaza, 34th Floor, New York, NY 10004; Mailing: St Patrick's, 8422 W. Windsor Ave., Chicago, IL 60656-4252 t) (773) 973-3737 burgeneral@spms.ie www.spms.org Rev. Richard Filima, SPS (Nigeria), Pres.;
Patrons of the Arts in Vatican Museums - 1011 First Ave., New York, NY 10022 t) 929-290-0330 fr.richard.veras@archny.org www.patronsvaticanmuseum.org Rev. Richard Veras, Dir.;
Pauline Books & Media - 115 E 29th St., New York, NY 10016 t) 212-754-1110 manhattan@paulinemedia.com www.pauline.org Sr. Sean Marie David Mayer, Supr.; Sr. Neville Forchap, Bus. Mgr.;
St. Paul's Guild, Inc. - 1011 First Ave., Rm. 1940, New York, NY 10022 t) 212-371-1000
Pax Christi Metro New York - 135 W. 31st St., New York, NY 10001 t) 212-420-0250 info@nypaxchristi.org www.nypaxchristi.org Elda Luisi, Admin.;
Pontifical Mission Society Propagation of the Faith - 1011 First Ave., New York, NY 10022 t) 212-371-1000 x2700 propagation@archny.org Rev. Msgr. Marc J. Filacchione, Dir.;
Prelature of the Holy Cross and Opus Dei - 139 E. 34th St., New York, NY 10016 t) 646-742-2700 newyork@opusdei.org www.opusdei.org Rev. John C. Agnew; Rev. James W. Albrecht; Rev. Jichael J. Barret; Rev. Robert A. Brisson; Rev. Msgr. Javier Garcia de Cardenas; Rev. Jeffrey J. Langan; Rev. Timothy J. Uhen; Rev. Msgr. Thomas G. Bohlin, Vicar;
Personal Prelature - t) 914-235-0199 Rev. Bradley K. Arturi; Rev. Thomas J. Lamb; Rev. Michael J. Manz;
Personal Prelature - 139 E. 34th St., New York, NY 10016-4704 t) 212-222-3285 info.us@opusdei.org www.opusdei.org Rev. Msgr. Thomas G. Bohlin, Vicar;
Personal Prelature - 99 Overlook Cir., New Rochelle, NY 10804 t) 914-235-6128 Rev. Orestes Gonzalez, Other; Rev. Malcolm M. Kennedy, Other;
Propagation of the Faith National Office - 70 W. 36th St., New York, NY 10018 t) 212-563-8700 Rev. Andrew Small, O.M.I., Dir.;
Regina Coeli Society - ; Mailing: P.O. Box 939, New York, NY 10272-0604 t) 646-610-6169 Det. Gloria Felix, Pres.;
St. Rose's Settlement - 1011 First Ave., Rm. 1940, New York, NY 10022 t) 212-371-1000
Sacred Heart Residence (Congregation of Mothers of the Helpless) - 432 W. 20th St., New York, NY 10011 t) 212-929-5790 sacredheartresidence@hotmail.com www.sacredheartresidence.com Sr. Josefina Jimenez, Supr.; Bed Capacity: 35; Staff: 3
Scalabrini International Migration Network - 307 E. 60th St., New York, NY 10022-1505 t) 212-913-0207 contact@simn-global.org www.simn-global.org Rev. Sergio Dall'Agnese, C.S., Pres.; Rev. Jairo Francisco Guidini, C.S., Dir.;
The Society of St. Stephen USA - 125 Maiden Ln., Ste. 15E, New York, NY 10038
***Sovereign Military Hospitaller Order of Saint John of Jerusalem of Rhodes and of Malta** - 1011 First Ave., Suite. 1350, New York, NY 10022 t) 212-371-1522 www.orderofmaltaamerican.org American Association, U.S.A. Dcn. Jeffrey Trexler, Exec.;
The Thomas Merton Institute for Catholic Life - 405 W. 114th St., New York, NY 10025
***Thrive For Life Prison Project** - 30 W. 16th St., New York, NY 10011 t) (212) 337-7544 thriveforlife.org Rev. Zachariah Presutti, S.J., Exec. Dir.;
Trustees of St. Patrick's Cathedral in the City of New York, Inc. - 1011 First Ave., New York, NY 10022
Voluntas Dei USA - 244 Fifth Ave., Ste. P250, New York, NY 10001 t) 212-726-2286 anthonyciorra@gmail.com Rev. Anthony J. Ciorra, Dir.;
***WorldPriest, Inc.** - 600 Third Ave., 2nd Fl., New York, NY 10016 t) 646-355-4106 info.worldpriest@gmail.com www.worldpriest.com Marian Mulhall, CEO;
***Xavier Mission, Inc.** - 55 W. 15th St., New York, NY 10011 t) 212-627-2100 cagredo@xaviermission.org; info@xaviermission.org www.xaviermission.org Rev. Kenneth Boller, SJ, Pres.; Cassandra Agredo, Exec.;
Xavier Society for the Blind - 248 W 35th St Ste 1502, New York, NY 10001 t) 212-473-7800 info@xaviersocietyfortheblind.org www.xaviersocietyfortheblind.org Malachy Fallon Jr., Dir.;

NEWBURGH

***Newburgh Ministry** - 9 Johnston St., Newburgh, NY 12551; Mailing: P.O. Box 1449, Newburgh, NY 12551 t) 845-561-0070 Colin Jarvis, Exec.; Michele McKeon, Chairperson, Bd. Dir.;
Newburgh San Miguel Program - 245 Renwick St., Newburgh, NY 12550; Mailing: P.O. Box 284, Chappaqua, NY 10514 t) 845-561-2822 connell.sanmiguel@gmail.com; fsnyder@sanmiguelacademy.org newburghsanmiguel.org/ Rev. Mark J. Connell, Pres.;
Our Lady of Comfort Women's Center - 91 Ann St., Newburgh, NY 12550 t) 845-561-6267 Shelter for Women & Children. Nina Faulkner, Treas.;

NYACK

Marydell Faith and Life Center - 640 N. Midland Ave., Nyack, NY 10960 t) 845-358-5399 marydellflc@gmail.com www.marydellsisters.com Maria Joy, Dir.;

OSSINING

Dominicare, Inc. - Office of Pres, 299 N. Highland Ave., Bldg. 5, Ossining, NY 10562-2327 t) 914-941-4420 lelcock@ophope.org www.ophope.org Sr. Lorelle Elcock, O.P., Pres.;

PELHAM MANOR

American Compassion Services, Inc. (Fidesco USA) - 559 Pelham Manor Rd, Pelham Manor, NY 10803 t) 703-260-1904 c) 484-619-3824 dleblond@fidescousa.org www.fidescousa.org/ Rosemary Leblond, Exec.;
Emmanuel Community Inc. - 559 Pelham Manor Rd, Pelham Manor, NY 10803 c) (314) 810-2433 tithe@emmanuelcommunity.com www.emmanuelcommunity.com

PORT CHESTER

***Caritas of Port Chester, Inc.** - 19 Smith St., Port Chester, NY 10573; Mailing: P.O. Box 682, Port Chester, NY 10573 t) 914-305-3967 caritaspc@hotmail.com caritaspc.org Patricia Walsh Hart, Pres.;

Don Bosco Community Center of Port Chester, Inc. - Office of the Pres., 22 Don Bosco Pl., Port Chester, NY 10573 t) 914-939-0323 x11 dbccportchester@yahoo.com www.donboscocenter.com

Don Bosco Workers, Inc. - 22 Don Bosco Pl., Port Chester, NY 10573 t) 914-433-6666 Ann Heekin, Pres.;

RYE

Alpha Omega Family Center, Inc. - 815 Boston Post Rd., Rye, NY 10580 t) 770-828-4950 eramirez@arcol.org Rev. Frank Formolo, Secy.;

Arke, Inc. - 815 Boston Post Rd., Rye, NY 10580 t) 770-828-4950 fformolo@legionaries.org Rev. Frank Formolo, Contact;

Catholic Net, Inc. - 815 Boston Post Rd., Rye, NY 10580 t) (770) 828-4950 eramirez@arcol.org Rev. Frank Formolo, Contact;

Consolidated Catholic Administrative Services, Inc. - 815 Boston Post Rd., Rye, NY 10580 t) 770-828-4950 eramirez@arcol.org Rev. Frank Formolo, Pres.;

Helping Hands Medical Missions, Inc. - 815 Boston Post Rd., Rye, NY 10580 t) 972-253-1800 eramirez@arcol.org hhmm.org/ Rev. Frank Formolo, Secy.;

Legion of Christ North America, Inc. - 815 Boston Post Rd., Rye, NY 10580 t) 770-828-4950 Rev. Frank Formolo, Contact;

Legion of Christ, Incorporated - 815 Boston Post Rd., Rye, NY 10580 t) 770-828-4950 eramirez@arcol.org Rev. Frank Formolo, Secy.;

The Legion of Christ, Incorporated - 815 Boston Post Rd., Rye, NY 10580 t) 770-828-4950 fformolo@legionaries.org legionariesofchrist.org Rev. Frank Formolo, Admin.;

Logos, Inc. - 815 Boston Post Rd., Rye, NY 10580 t) 770-828-4950 eramirez@arcol.org Rev. Frank Formolo, Secy.;

Mission Network Programs USA, Inc. - 815 Boston Post Rd., Rye, NY 10580 t) 855-556-6872 tbrechbill@rcactivities.com

Nueva Primavera Inc. - 815 Boston Post Rd., Rye, NY 10580 t) 770-828-4950 Rev. Frank Formolo, Contact;

Pastoral Support Services, Inc. - 815 Boston Post Rd., Rye, NY 10580 t) 770-828-4950 sbaldwin@regnumchristi.net

Regina Apostolorum, Inc. - 815 Boston Post Rd., Rye, NY 10580 t) 770-828-4950 Rev. Frank Formolo, Contact;

Rossotto, Inc. - 815 Boston Post Rd., Rye, NY 10580 t) 770-828-4950 eramirez@arcol.org Rev. Frank Formolo, Secy.;

RYE BROOK

***New Jersey Friends of Mandeville Inc.** - 111 S. Ridge St., Ste. 302, Rye Brook, NY 10573 t) 914-908-6737 Rev. James Price, C.P., Secy.; Rev. William Murphy, C.P., Assistant Secretary and Assistant Treasurer; Rev. James O'Shea, C.P., Pres.; Rev. David Monaco, C.P., Treas.; Most Rev. Neil E. Tiedemann, C.P., Vice Pres.;

Passionist Communications, Inc. - 111 S. Ridge St., Ste. 303, Rye Brook, NY 10573; Mailing: PO Box 111, Rye Brook, NY 10573 t) 914-738-3344 contact@thesundaymass.org www.thesundaymass.org Rev. Paul R. Fagan, C.P.; Shahib Narine, Staff; Kathy Rego, Staff;

SCARSDALE

Catholic Charismatic Renewal Office - 194 Gaylor Rd., Scarsdale, NY 10583 t) 914-725-1773 charismny@optonline.net www.catholiccharismaticny.org Rev. William B. Cosgrove, Liaison;

Charismatic Renewal Office - 194 Gaylor Rd., Scarsdale, NY 10583 t) 914-925-1973 Rev. William B. Cosgrove;

SLEEPY HOLLOW

RSHM Life Center, Inc. (Sacred Heart of Mary) - 32-34 Beekman Ave., Sleepy Hollow, NY 10591 t) 914-366-9710 susan@rshmlifecenter.org www.rshmlifecenter.org Sr. Susan Gardella, RSHM, Dir.;

SLOATSBURG

St. Mary's Villa, Inc. - 150 Sisters Servants Ln., Sloatsburg, NY 10974-0009; Mailing: P.O. Box 9, Sloatsburg, NY 10974-0009 t) 845-753-5100 ssminy@aol.com Sr. Cecelia Sworin, S.S.M.I., Secy.; Sr. Kathleen Hutsko, S.S.M.I., Pres.;

SPARKILL

Hallel Institute - 175 Rte. 340, Sparkill, NY 10976-1047 t) 845-365-2277 hallel@hallel.net hallel.net Rev. George J. Torok, C.O., Pres.;

New York Oratory of St. Philip Neri, Inc. - 175 Rte. 340, Sparkill, NY 10976 t) 845-365-2277 nyoratory@yahoo.com Rev. Vladimir Chripko, C.O.; Rev. Martin Kertys; Rev. Thomas Kunnel, C.O.; Rev. Roman Dominic Palecko, C.O.; Rev. George J. Torok, C.O.; Rev. Frantisek Conka, C.O., Secy.;

One to One Learning, Inc. - Office of Pres, 175 Rte. 340, Sparkill, NY 10976 t) 845-512-8176 clpangel59@gmail.com Sr. Cecilia LaPietra, O.P., Exec.;

STATEN ISLAND

***Catholic High School Football League of Metropolitan N.Y.** - 200 Clinton Ave., Staten Island, NY 10301 t) 718-447-1676 John Fodera, Prin.;

Catholic School Region of Staten Island - 139 Windsor Rd., Staten Island, NY 10314 t) 718-447-1034

Indian Knanaya Catholic Community of Greater NY, Inc. - 94 Wilcox St., Staten Island, NY 10303 t) 914-494-7571 ikcc@hotmail.com Jose Chummar, Pres.;

St. Joseph's Union of Staten Island, New York Inc. - 108 Bedell St., Staten Island, NY 10309 t) 718-984-9296

Korean Catholic Apostolate of Staten Island, Inc. - 76 Jackson St., Staten Island, NY 10304 t) 718-273-3311 kcasi08@hanmail.net Rev. Hyunwoung Park, Contact;

North American College of Rome, Alumni Assoc. of - 2900 Amboy Rd., Staten Island, NY 10306 t) 718-987-2900 Most Rev. Edmund J. Whalen;

Schoenstatt Sisters of Mary, Secular Institute - 337 Cary Ave., Staten Island, NY 10310-2041 t) 718-727-8005 shrineny@schsrsmary.org Sr. M. Verónica Muniz, Supr.;

***Sisters of Charity Housing Development, Corp.** - 150 Brielle Ave., Staten Island, NY 10314-6400 t) 718-477-6803 mjaneczko@schousingny.org; vreilly@schousingny.org www.sistersofcharityhousing.org Matthew Janeczko, CEO;

SUFFERN

The Given Institute - 38 Montebello Rd., Suffern, NY 10901

TUCKAHOE

***Peace Through Divine Mercy, Inc.** - 70 Lime Kiln Rd. #2F, Tuckahoe, NY 10707 t) 914-771-7717 reginacleri@aol.com; mjkm67@gmail.com Apostolate for priestly and family renewal. Kathleen Keefe, Contact;

WEST PARK

Sacred Heart Center for New Americans, Inc. - 2085 Rt. 9W, West Park, NY 12493-0244; Mailing: 222 E. 19th St., Ste. 5B, New York, NY 10003 t) (212) 375-0752 inquiries@msshnyc.org Sr. Diane Olmstead, MSC, Chair;

WHITE PLAINS

Company of St. Paul - 52 Davis Ave., White Plains, NY 10605 t) 914-946-1019 jssandberg@optonline.net Rev. Stuart Sandberg, Pres.;

Concerts at the Chapel, Inc. - 52 N. Broadway, White Plains, NY 10603 t) 914-798-1201 www.divinecompassion.org

Deutschsprachige Katholische Gemeinde New York-German Speaking Catholic Congregation New York - 106 Greenacres Ave., White Plains, NY 10606 t) 914-831-3165 Rev. Peter Bleeser, Contact;

Children's Rehabilitation Center, Inc. - 317 North St., White Plains, NY 10605; Mailing: 300 Corporate Blvd. S., Yonkers, NY 10701 t) 914-294-6128 cperruccio@setonchildrens.org www.setonchildrens.org Sponsored by the Sisters of Charity Ministry Network Carla Perruccio, CFO;

YONKERS

Casa Juan Diego, Inc. - 97 Yonkers Ave., Yonkers, NY 10701 t) 914-963-0250 Services to the needy; especially Spanish Speaking immigrants, day laborers. Rev. Agustino Miguel Torres, C.F.R., Exec.; Bro. Philip Allen, C.F.R., Dir.;

Finian Sullivan Corporation - One Father Finian Sullivan Dr., Yonkers, NY 10703 t) 914-969-6159 scorbett@hhmgmt.com Peter Bassano, Contact;

Instructional T.V. Communications Center - 201 Seminary Ave., Yonkers, NY 10704 t) 914-968-7800 www.itvny.org

Jesus Caritas Fraternity, Inc. - 4 Curran Ct., 1R, Yonkers, NY 10710 t) 914-961-0050 margebaker@secularinstitutes.org

Sisters of Mary Reparatrix - 287 Hayward St., Yonkers, NY 10704 t) 914-376-3245 kasparek@comcast.net

YORKTOWN HEIGHTS

The Cardinal Cooke Guild - 137 Moseman Rd., Yorktown Heights, NY 10598 t) 914-962-5050 cardinal.cookeguild@archny.org www.terencecardinalcooke.org Avv. Andrea Ambrosi, Roman Postulator; Rev. Msgr. Joseph R. Giandurco, Vice Postulator Coord.;

MONASTERIES AND RESIDENCES FOR PRIESTS AND BROTHERS [MON]

BRONX

Brothers of the Christian Schools of Manhattan College, Inc. - 4415 Post Rd., Bronx, NY 10471 t) 718-884-0613 rbimonte01@manhattan.edu Bro. Robert Bimonte, FSC, Pres.; Bro. William Man, Treas.; Brs.: 23

St. Crispin Friary - 420 E. 156th St., Bronx, NY 10455 t) 718-665-2441 cfrgensec@franciscanfriars.com www.franciscanfriars.com Rev. Ignatius Mary Shin, C.F.R., Vicar; Rev. James Mary Atkins, C.F.R., Pst. Assoc.; Rev. Giles Barrie, CFR, Pst. Assoc.; Rev. Malachy Napier, C.F.R., Pst. Assoc.; Rev. John Anthony Boughton, C.F.R., Rel. Ord. Ldr.; Rev. John Paul Ouellette, C.F.R., Rel. Ord. Ldr.; Bro. Damien Joseph Novak, CFR, Mem.; Bro. Jan Cyril Vanek, CFR, Mem.; Brs.: 2; Priests: 6

Franciscan Friars of the Renewal - 421 E. 155th St., Bronx, NY 10455 t) 718-402-8255 Rev. John Paul Ouellette, Supr.; Rev. Fidelis Moscinski, C.F.R., Admin.; Bro. Peter Westall, C.F.R., Treas.; Bro. Maximilian Stelmachowski, Secy.;

Idente Missionaries - Santa Maria Residence - 2352 St. Raymond Ave., Bronx, NY 10462 t) 718-828-2380 rpbadillo@gmail.com Rev. Francisco Sanchez, M.Id, Rector; Rev. Robert P. Badillo, M.Id, Supr.;

John Cardinal O'Connor Residence - 5655 Arlington Ave., Bronx, NY 10471 t) 718-581-0070 mail@jmcpllc.com Rev. Christopher H. Daly; Rev. Msgr. Peter C. O'Donnell;

Marist Brothers Champagnat Hall Community - 2115 Pitman Ave., Bronx, NY 10466-1928 t) 718-994-4227 x34; 917-292-2671 provincefinance@gmail.com Bro. Gerard Cormier, F.M.S.; Bro. Thomas Delaney, F.M.S.; Bro. Gerald Doherty, F.M.S.; Bro. Francis Klug, F.M.S.; Bro. Augustine Landry, F.M.S.; Bro. Joseph McAlister, F.M.S.; Bro. Luke Reddington, F.M.S.; Bro. Julian Roy, F.M.S.; Bro. Joseph Scanlon, F.M.S.; Bro. Joseph Teston, F.M.S.; Bro. James Adams, F.M.S., Dir.;

Marist Brothers-St. Benedict Community - 1082 Edison Ave., Bronx, NY 10465 t) 718-931-3744 Bro. Eugene Birmingham; Bro. Armand Lamagna, F.M.S.; Bro. Thomas Schady, F.M.S.; Bro. Gerald Doherty, F.M.S., Dir.; Bro. Frederick Sambor, F.M.S., Dir.;

Murray-Weigel Hall (A Jesuit Community at Murray-Weigel Hall and Kohlmann Hall) - 515 E. Fordham Rd., Bronx, NY 10458-5004 t) 718-430-4900 Rev. Anthony Azzarto, Other; Rev. George H. Belgarde, S.J., Other; Rev. Joseph E. Billotti, S.J., Other; Rev. James Bowes, S.J., Other; Rev. Pierce A. Brennan, S.J., Other; Rev. Raymond A. Bucko, S.J., Other; Rev. David J. Casey, S.J., Other; Bro. Ralph Cilia, S.J., Other; Rev. John M.

Costello, S.J., Other; Rev. Brian Daley, S.J., Other; Rev. Leo Daly, S.J., Other; Rev. Edward T. Dowling, S.J., Other; Rev. Daniel J. Fitzpatrick, S.J., Other; Rev. Gerald P. Fogarty, S.J., Other; Rev. Francois Gick, S.J., Other; Rev. Pasquale T. Giordano, S.J., Other; Rev. Robert R. Grimes, S.J., Other; Rev. Damian Halligan, S.J., Other; Rev. James F. Joyce, S.J., Other; Rev. John R. Keating, S.J., Other; Rev. Robert E. Kennedy, S.J., Other; Rev. Joseph W. Lux, S.J., Other; Rev. Donal MacVeigh, S.J., Other; Rev. Oscar Magnan, S.J., Other; Rev. Leo M. Manglaviti, S.J., Other; Rev. Robert McCarty, S.J., Other; Rev. Vincent McDonough, S.J., Other; Bro. Jerome P. Menkhaus, S.J., Other; Rev. Daniel J. Mulhauser, S.J., Other; Rev. Ugo R. Nacciarone, S.J., Other; Rev. Leo J. O'Donovan, S.J., Other; Rev. Joseph J. Papaj, S.J., Other; Rev. Frederick J. Pellegrini, S.J., Supr.; Rev. Thomas S. Prout, S.J., Other; Rev. John F. Replogle, S.J., Other; Rev. Vincent J. Ritchie, S.J., Other; Rev. Matthew F Roche, SJ, Other; Rev. J. Peter Schineller, S.J., Other; Rev. Brendan T. Scott, S.J., Other; Bro. Edward P. Sheehy, S.J., Other; Rev. Thomas E. Smith, S.J., Other; Rev. Patrick J. Sullivan, S.J., Other; Rev. Andrew Szebenyi, S.J., Other; Bro. Francis W. Turnbull, S.J., Other; Rev. James J. Yannarell, S.J., Other; Brs.: 4; Priests: 46

Kolhmann Hall Jesuit Community - 515 E. Fordham Rd., Bronx, NY 10458 t) (718) 430-4900 Formerly part of the Fordham Jesuit Community. It is now attached to Murray-Weigel Hall. Rev. Daniel J. Gatti, S.J., Other; Rev. Richard D. Hunt, S.J., Other; Rev. David X. Stump, S.J., Other; Rev. Robert D. Wiesenbaugh, S.J., Other;

Murray-Weigel Hall Jesuit Community - 515 E. Fordham Rd., Bronx, NY 10458-5004 t) (718) 430-4900

Our Lady of Consolation Residence - 3103 Arlington Ave., Bronx, NY 10463 t) 718-548-0888 Rev. Edward J. O'Neill, Contact;

Our Lady of the Angels Friary - 427 E. 155th St., Bronx, NY 10455 t) 718-993-3405 cfrgensec@franciscanfriars.com www.franciscanfriars.com (Franciscan Friars of the Renewal) Rev. Pierre Toussaint Guiteau, CFR, Supr.; Rev. Seraphim Pio Baalbaki, C.F.R., Vicar; Rev. Stanley Fortuna, C.F.R., Pst. Assoc.; Rev. Pio Maria Hoffman, C.F.R., Pst. Assoc.; Bro. Maximilian Mary Stelmachowski, C.F.R., Secy.; Bro. John Francis Thomson, CFR, Mem.; Bro. Joseph Pio Young, CFR, Friar; Bro. Francis Xavier Marie Danos, CFR, Friar; Brs.: 4; Priests: 4

Passionist Residence Riverdale - 5801 Palisade Ave. Ste 300, Bronx, NY 10471; Mailing: Passionist Province Pastoral Center, 111 S. Ridge St., Ste. 302, Rye Brook, NY 10573 t) 929-419-7500 provincialstpaul@cpprov.org www.thepassionists.org Rev. James O'Shea, C.P., Exec.;

Yarumal Mission Society, Inc. - 2317 Washington Ave., Bronx, NY 10458 t) 718-561-8248 imeyusa@aol.com www.semisiones.org/ Foreign mission society from Colombia, South America. Rev. Tulio E. Ramirez, M.X.Y., Pres.; Rev. Jorge Ivan Fernandez, mxy, Secy.; Brs.: 5; Priests: 170

CORNWALL

Jogues Retreat Center - ; Mailing: P.O. Box 522, Cornwall, NY 12518-0522 t) 845-534-7570 conroyp48@hotmail.com Rev. Michael R. Hoag, S.J., Supr.;

FOREST HILLS

Marist Brothers F.M.S. (Province of U.S.A.) - 70-20 Juno St., Forest Hills, NY 11375 t) (718) 480-1306 brdano@hotmail.com Bro. Daniel O'Riordan, F.M.S., Prov; Bro. Owen Ormsby, F.M.S., Prov. Asst.; Frank Pellegrino, CFO; Paulette Karas, Assoc. Dir.; Brs.: 109

GARRISON

St. Christopher's Inn Friary - 21 Franciscan Way, Garrison, NY 10524-0150; Mailing: Box 150, Garrison, NY 10524-0150 t) 845-335-1000 www.stchristophersinn-graymoor.org Rev. John W. Coppinger, S.A.; Rev. William Drobach, S.A.; Bro. Charles Kenney, S.A.; Rev. John F. Kiesling, S.A.; Bro. Joseph O'Gara, S.A.; Bro. John O'Hara, S.A.; Bro. Benedict Terasawa, S.A.; Rev. Robert Warren, S.A.;

Franciscan Friars of the Atonement - Graymoor, 40 Franciscan Way, Garrison, NY 10524-0300; Mailing: P.O. Box 300, Garrison, NY 10524-0300 t) 845-424-3671; 845-424-3672; 845-424-3673 csharon@atonementfriars.org www.atonementfriars.org Rev. Emil Tomaskovic, S.A., Dir.; Rev. Robert Warren, S.A., Spiritual Dir.; Rev. Martin Carter, S.A.; Rev. Francis Eldridge, S.A.; Rev. David Fitzgerald, S.A.; Bro. Daniel Houde, S.A.; Bro. Hugh MacIsaac, S.A.; Bro. Dominic McDonnell, S.A.; Bro. Joseph O'Gara, S.A.; Bro. John O'Hara, S.A.; Rev. Thomas Orians, S.A.; Bro. DePorres Poncia, S.A.;

St. Christopher's Inn - Graymoor, Garrison, NY 10524-0150; Mailing: P.O. Box 150, Garrison, NY 10524-0150 t) 845-424-3616 Bro. Charles Kenney, S.A.; Rev. Dennis Polanco, S.A., Pres.; Rev. William Drobach, S.A., Other;

St. Francis of Assisi Novitiate - Rev. Charles J. Sharon, S.A., Other;

Graymoor Ecumenical and Interreligious Institute - 475 Riverside Dr., Rm. 1960, New York, NY 10115-1999 t) 212-870-2330 Rev. James L. Loughran, S.A., Dir.;

Atonement Friars - 138 Waverly Pl., New York, NY 10014 t) 212-243-4692 Rev. Francis Eldridge, S.A., Pst.; Rev. David Fitzgerald, S.A., Pst.; Bro. Gerard Hand, S.A., In Res.;

Franciscan Friars of the Atonement, Minister General Office - Graymoor, 40 Franciscan Way, Garrison, NY 10524-0300; Mailing: P.O. Box 300, Garrison, NY 10524-0300 t) 845-424-2113 ministergen@atonementfriars.org www.atonementfriars.org Rev. Daniel Callahan, S.A., Gen. Councilor; Rev. Martin Carter, S.A.; Rev. Kenneth Cienik, S.A.; Rev. Patrick Cogan, S.A.; Rev. Francis Eldridge, S.A.; Rev. David Fitzgerald, S.A.; Rev. James Gardiner, S.A., Dir.; Rev. Arthur Gouthro, S.A.; Rev. Joseph Hiramatsu, S.A (Japan), Regional Min.; Rev. John Keane, S.A.; Rev. Robert Langone, S.A., Gen. Councilor; Rev. James L. Loughran, S.A., Vicar; Rev. Timothy I. MacDonald, S.A., Gen. Councilor; Rev. Damian MacPherson, S.A. (Canada), Dir.; Rev. Elias D. Mallon, S.A.; Rev. Robert Mercer, S.A.; Rev. Thomas Orians, S.A., Dir.; Rev. Bernard Palka, S.A.; Rev. David Poirier, S.A.; Rev. Dennis Polanco, S.A., Dir.; Rev. James F. Puglisi, S.A.; Rev. Michael Seed, S.A. (England); Rev. Charles J. Sharon, S.A., Treas.; Rev. Brian F. Terry, S.A., Supr.; Rev. Emil Tomaskovic, S.A., Dir.; Rev. Robert Warren, S.A., Spiritual Dir.; Bro. Thomas Banacki, S.A.; Bro. Denis Burgelin, S.A.; Bro. Gerard Hand, S.A.; Bro. Daniel Houde, S.A.; Bro. Charles Kenney, S.A.; Bro. Ignatius Kobayashi, S.A.; Bro. Alan LeMay, S.A.; Bro. Timothy MacDonald, S.A.; Bro. Hugh MacIsaac, S.A.; Bro. Louis Marek, S.A.; Bro. William Martyn, S.A.; Bro. Dominic McDonnell, S.A.; Bro. Paolo Salvatore Nicosia, SA; Bro. Joseph O'Gara, S.A.; Bro. John O'Hara, S.A.; Bro. DePorres Poncia, S.A.;

Graymoor Ecumenical & Interreligious Institute - 475 Riverside Dr., Rm. 1960, New York, NY 10115-1999 t) 212-870-2330 lmnygeii@aol.com www.geii.org

HARTSDALE

Mill Hill Fathers Residence - 222 W. Hartsdale Ave., Hartsdale, NY 10530-1667 t) 914-682-0645 mhmna1866@aol.com www.millhillmissionaries.com Rev. Robert J. O'Neil, M.H.M., Admin.; Rev. Domingo Pon-an Arnaiz, MHM, Mem.; Rev. Lester Lonergan, M.H.M., Mem.; Rev. Peter Major, M.H.M., Mem.; Rev. Richard Githang'a Njoroge, MHM, Mem.; Rev. Benedict Oduor Ohanga, MHM, Mem.; Rev. Wilhelmus J Klaver, M.H.M, Society Representative; Priests: 7

JAMAICA

The Congregation of the Passion - St. Paul of the Cross Province - 86-45 Edgerton Blvd, Jamaica, NY 11432; Mailing: 86-45 Edgerton Blvd., Jamaica, NY 11432 t) 929-419-7500 contact@thepassionists.org www.thepassionists.org Rev. James O'Shea, C.P., Prov.; Rev. Salvatore Enzo Del Brocco, C.P., Vice Prov.; Rev. James Price, C.P., 2nd Consultor; Rev. William Murphy, C.P., 3rd Consultor; Rev. Hugo Esparza-Perez, C.P., 4th Consultor; Rev. Javier Montalvo Aviles Mercado, C.P., Mem.; Rev. Richard Award, C.P., Mem.; Rev. James Barry, C.P., Mem.; Rev. Edward L. Beck, C.P., Mem.; Rev. Thomas Bonacci, C.P., Mem.; Rev. Vincent Boney, C.P., Mem.; Rev. Jerome Bracken, C.P., Mem.; Rev. Thomas Brislin, C.P., Mem.; Rev. Richard Burke, C.P., Mem.; Rev. Alberto Cabrera, C.P., Mem.; Rev. Rob Carbonneau, C.P., Mem.; Rev. John Cashman, C.P., Mem.; Rev. Paul Chenot, C.P., Mem.; Rev. David Cinquegrani, C.P., Mem.; Rev. Lucian Clark, C.P., Mem.; Rev. Christopher Cleary, C.P., Mem.; Rev. Theophane Cooney, C.P., Mem.; Rev. Patrick Daugherty, C.P., Mem.; Rev. Charles Dougherty, C.P., Mem.; Rev. Stephen Dunn, C.P., Mem.; Rev. Jesus Echeandia, C.P., Mem.; Rev. Paul R. Fagan, C.P., Mem.; Rev. Francis Finnigan, C.P., Mem.; Rev. Richard Frechette, C.P., Mem.; Rev. Evans Fwamba, C.P., Mem.; Rev. Patrick Geinzer, C.P., Mem.; Rev. James Gillette, C.P., In Res.; Rev. Peter Grace, C.P., Mem.; Rev. Michael Greene, C.P., Mem.; Rev. Lee Havey, C.P., Mem.; Rev. Victor Hoagland, C.P., Mem.; Rev. Robert H. Joerger, C.P., Mem.; Rev. Joseph R. Jones, C.P., Mem.; Rev. Earl Keating, C.P., Mem.; Rev. Justin Kerber, C.P., Mem.; Rev. Curtis Kiddy, C.P., Mem.; Rev. Terence Kristofak, C.P., Mem.; Rev. Gerald Laba, C.P., Mem.; Rev. Francis Landry, C.P., Mem.; Rev. John Michael Lee, C.P., Mem.; Rev. Luis Alfredo Lopez Galarza, C.P., Mem.; Rev. William Maguire, C.P., Mem.; Rev. Thomas McCann, C.P., Mem.; Rev. Bernard McEachern, C.P., Mem.; Rev. Jerome McKenna, C.P., Mem.; Rev. John McMillan, C.P., Mem.; Rev. David Monaco, C.P., Mem.; Rev. Jose Ramon Montanez Lopez, C.P., In Res.; Rev. Edwin Moran, C.P., Mem.; Rev. John Muthengi, C.P., Mem.; Rev. Richard Nalepa, C.P., Mem.; Rev. Gaston Nsongolo, C.P., Mem.; Rev. Gilbert Otieno Omolo, C.P., Mem.; Rev. Lionel Pacheco, C.P., Mem.; Rev. Sibi Padinjaredath, C.P., Mem.; Rev. Kenan Peters, C.P., Mem.; Rev. Claudio Piccinini, C.P., Mem.; Rev. John Powers, C.P., Mem.; Rev. Brando Recana, C.P., Mem.; Rev. Salvatore Riccardi, C.P., Mem.; Rev. Anibal Rodriguez, C.P., Mem.; Rev. Carlos Luis Rodriguez Hernandez, C.P., Mem.; Rev. Michael Rowe, C.P., Mem.; Rev. Paul Ruttle, C.P., Mem.; Rev. Robin Ryan, C.P., Mem.; Rev. Lawrence Rywalt, C.P., Mem.; Rev. Michael J. Salvagna, C.P., Mem.; Rev. Joseph Sedley, C.P., Mem.; Rev. Melvin Shorter, C.P., Mem.; Rev. Terence Skorka, C.P., Mem.; Rev. Jed Sumampong, C.P., Mem.; Rev. Paul Vaeth, C.P., Mem.; Rev. Theodore Vitali, C.P., Mem.; Rev. Mark Ward, C.P., Mem.; Rev. Mark G. Ward, C.P., Mem.; Rev. Donald Ware, C.P., Mem.; Rev. Paul Wierichs, C.P., Mem.; Rev. Edward Wolanski, C.P., Mem.; Rev. Vincent Youngberg, C.P., Mem.; Bro. Leo DiFiore, C.P., Mem.; Bro. Luis Daniel Guivas Gerena, C.P., Mem.; Bro. Edward Hall, C.P., Mem.; Bro. Augustine Lowe, C.P., Mem.; Bro. Cristian Joel Martinez Montalvo, C.P., Mem.; Bro. Andre Mathieu, C.P., Mem.; Bro. Robert McKenna, C.P., Mem.; Bro. Michael Moran, C.P., Mem.; Bro. Jonathan Emanuel Pabon Tirado, C.P., Mem.; Bro. August Parlavechio, C.P., Mem.; Bro. Joseph Rogers, C.P., Mem.; Bro. Terrence Scanlon, C.P., Mem.; Bro. Michael Stomber, C.P., Mem.; Bro. Daniel Turner, C.P., Mem.; Brs.: 14; Priests: 84

Passionist Volunteers International - 111 S. Ridge St., Ste 302, Rye Brook, NY 10573 t) 202-210-5175 passionistvolunteers.org Ross Boyle, Dir.;

MARYKNOLL

M.M.A.F. Charitable Trust - ; Mailing: P.O. Box 306, Maryknoll, NY 10545-0306 t) 914-941-7590 rcallahan@maryknoll.org Rev. Richard B. Callahan, M.M., Contact;

Maryknoll Fathers and Brothers Charitable Trust - 77 Ryder Rd., Maryknoll, NY 10545-0603; Mailing: P.O. Box 306, Maryknoll, NY 10545-0306 t) 914-941-7590 Rev. Francis J. Breen, M.M., Chair;

MIDDLETOWN

St. Albert's Priory - 50 Waverly Place, Middletown, NY 10940-0908; Mailing: P.O. Box 908, Middletown, NY 10940-0908 t) 845-344-2220 Rev. Maurice Cummings, O.Carm., Prior; Rev. Thomas Zalewski, O.Carm., Treas.; Rev. Marlon Ricardo Beharry, O. Carm, Chap.; Rev. Lucian Beltzner, O.Carm., In Res.; Rev. Francis F. Dixon, O.Carm., In Res.; Bro. Michael Garraghan, O.Carm., In Res.; Rev. Augustine Graap, O.Carm., In Res.; Rev. Roberto Perez, O.F.M. Cap., In Res.; Brs.: 2; Priests: 7

The National Shrine of Our Lady of Mount Carmel - 70 Carmelite Dr., Middletown, NY 10940-2163; Mailing: P.O. Box 2163, Middletown, NY 10940-2163 t) 845-343-1879

Brandsma Priory (Carmelite Friars (North American Prov. of St. Elias and Most Pure Heart of Mary Province)) - 1 Carmelite Dr., Middletown, NY 10940-0439; Mailing: P.O. Box 2127, Middletown, NY 10940-0439 t) 845-343-2959 brandsmapriory@gmail.com Rev. Quinn Conners, O.Carm., Dir.; Rev. Timothy Ennis, O.Carm., Dir.; Brs.: 4; Priests: 2

Carmelite Friars (North American Province of St. Elias) - 68 Carmelite Dr., Middletown, NY 10940-0890; Mailing: P.O. Box 3079, Middletown, NY 10940 t) 845-344-2223; 845-344-2225 (Vocation); 845-344-2474; 845-344-2224 (Procurator) selsecretary@carmelites.com; vocations@carmelites.com www.carmelites.com Rev. Mario Esposito, O.Carm., Prov.; Rev. Mark Zittle, O.Carm, Treas.; Rev. Francis Amodio, O.Carm., Dir.; Brs.: 6; Priests: 59

Office of Lay Carmelites - ; Mailing: P.O. Box 3079, Middletown, NY 10940-0890

MOUNT VERNON

St. Bernardine of Siena Friary (Franciscan Friars, Province of Immaculate Conception) - 25 Laurel Ave., Mount Vernon, NY 10552-1018 t) 914-699-1221 Rev. Andre Cirino, O.F.M., In Res.; Rev. James Villa, O.F.M., Admin.;

Franciscan Mission Associates (Province of the Immaculate Conception) - 274-280 W. Lincoln Ave., Mount Vernon, NY 10550; Mailing: P.O. Box 598, Mount Vernon, NY 10550 t) 914-664-5604 mbonnici@franciscanmissionassoc.org www.franciscanmissionassoc.org Rev. Robert M. Campagna, O.F.M., Prov.; Madeline Bonnici, Exec.; Rev. Jose Alvin Te, OFM, Dir.; Brs.: 1; Priests: 1

Kolbe Friary (Franciscan Friars, Province of the Immaculate Conception) - 274-280 W. Lincoln Ave., Mount Vernon, NY 10550 t) 914-664-7169 Bro. Angelo Monti, O.F.M.;

NEW PALTZ

St. Joseph Friary (Capuchin Franciscans, Province of St. Mary) - 34 S. Chestnut St., New Paltz, NY 12561 t) 914-255-5635 Bro. Timothy Aller, O.F.M.Cap.; Rev. Salvatore Cordaro, O.F.M.Cap.; Rev. Raphael Iannone, O.F.M.Cap.; Rev. Michael Ramos, O.F.M.Cap.;

NEW ROCHELLE

Edmund Rice Christian Brothers North America Congregation of Christian Brothers - 260 Wilmot Rd., New Rochelle, NY 10804 t) 914-636-6194 gmd@cbinstitute.org; gguarente@cbinstitute.org www.ercbna.org Bro. Peter E. Zawot, C.F.C, Prov.; Georganne Dotto, Treas.; Brs.: 150

Saint Joseph Residence, Inc. - 30 Montgomery Cir., New Rochelle, NY 10804 t) 914-633-6851 Limited care facility for male religious. Bro. Vincent McNally, C.F.C.;

Saint Joseph Residence, Inc. - 30 Montgomery Cir., New Rochelle, NY 10804-4413 t) 914-633-6851 crhaynes@hotmail.com A facility of limited care for male religious. Bro. Peter E. Zawot, C.F.C; Bro. Thomas C. Higgins, Secy.; Bro. Charles Haynes, Vice Pres. Finance; Bro. James B. Moffett, C.F.C., Vice Pres. Admin.; Brs.: 20

Salesian Cooperators of St. John Bosco - 148 E. Main St., New Rochelle, NY 10802-0639; Mailing: P.O. Box 639, New Rochelle, NY 10802-0639 t) 914-636-4225 mjhahn@hahneng.com Rev. Thomas Dunne, S.D.B.;

Salesian Office of Youth & Young Adult Ministry - 148 E. Main St., New Rochelle, NY 10801; Mailing: PO Box 639, New Rochelle, NY 10802-0639 t) 914-636-4225 ym@salesianym.com www.salesianym.com Rev. Abraham Feliciano, S.D.B.;

Salesian Provincial House - 148 Main St., New Rochelle, NY 10802-0639; Mailing: P.O. Box 639, New Rochelle, NY 10802-0639 t) 914-636-4225 sdbsue@aol.com www.salesians.org Rev. Dominic Dahn Cong Tran, S.D.B., Vicar; Rev. Louis Molinelli, Youth Min.; Rev. Michael Mendl, SDB, Archivist; Rev. David Moreno, SDB, Secy.; Rev. Michael Conway, S.D.B., Treas.; Rev. Timothy Zak, S.D.B., Prov.; Brs.: 3; Priests: 13

NEW YORK

All Saints Friary - 47 E. 129th St., New York, NY 10035 t) 212-534-3535

America; Residence and Publication Office of the America Press - 120 W. 60th St., New York, NY 10023 t) 917-444-5313 americahouseguest@gmail.com Rev. Robert C. Collins, S.J.; Rev. Vincent P. DeCola, S.J.; Rev. Daniel J. Gatti, S.J.; Rev. Roger D. Haight, S.J.; Rev. John J. Hanwell, S.J.; Rev. James J. Martin, S.J.; Rev. James J. Miracky, S.J.; Rev. Damian O'Connell, S.J.; Rev. Leo J. O'Donovan, S.J.; Rev. Joseph P. Parkes, S.J.; Rev. Samuel Sawyer; Rev. Edward W. Schmidt, S.J.; Rev. Michael E. Sehler, S.J.; Rev. Jeremy Zipple; Rev. Philip G. Judge, S.J., Supr.; Rev. Matthew F. Malone, S.J., Editor;

Atonement Friars - 138 Waverly Pl., New York, NY 10014-3845 t) 212-243-4692 www.atonementfriars.org Rev. James L. Loughran, S.A., Vicar; Bro. Gerard Hand, S.A., In Res.; Rev. Charles J. Sharon, S.A., Secretary General, Treasurer; Rev. Brian F. Terry, S.A., Minister General;

Calasanzian Fathers (Piarists) - 88 Convent Ave., New York, NY 10027 t) 212-234-1919 annunciationchurchnyc@yahoo.com Rev. Baltazar Sanchez, Sch.P. (Mexico), Pst.; Rev. Jose M. Clavero, Sch.P. (Spain), Assoc. Pst.; Rev. Felix Ganuza, Sch.P. (Spain), Assoc. Pst.; Rev. Szymon Kurpios, Sch.P. (Poland), Assoc. Pst.;

St. Catherine of Siena Priory - 411 E. 68th St., New York, NY 10021 t) 212-988-8300 info@stcatherinenyc.org Bro. Thomas Aquinas Dolan, O.P.; Rev. Joseph Allen, O.P., Par. Vicar; Rev. Jonah F. Pollock, O.P., Chap.; Rev. David Adiletta, O.P., Secy.; Rev. Walter Cornelius Wagner, O.P., Prior; Bro. Ignatius Perkins, O.P., Dir.;

Franciscan Ministries, Inc. - 129 W. 31st St., 2nd Fl., New York, NY 10001-3403 t) 646-473-0265 mharlan@hnp.org Bro. Michael Joseph Harlan, OFM, Secy.;

Franciscan Friars, Holy Name Province (The Order of Friars Minor of the Province of the Most Holy Name) - 129 W. 31st St., 2nd Fl., New York, NY 10001-3403 t) 646-473-0265 hnp@hnp.org www.hnp.org Rev. Lawrence Hayes, O.F.M., Vicar; Rev. Canon Kevin J. Mullen, O.F.M., Pres.; Bro. Michael Harlan, OFM, Secy.; Rev. Dennis Wilson, OFM, Treas.; Brs.: 47; Priests: 184

Franciscan Province of the Immaculate Conception - 125 Thompson St., New York, NY 10012 t) 212-674-4388 internos@icprovince.org; jolorenzo1@me.com www.icprovince.org Rev. Celestino Canzio, O.F.M.; Rev. Michael D'Cruz, O.F.M.; Rev. Ciro Iodice, O.F.M.; Rev. Giacomo LaSelva, O.F.M.; Rev. Rohwin Pais, O.F.M.; Rev. Charles Soto, O.F.M.; Rev. Michael Travaglione, O.F.M.; Rev. James Wells, O.F.M.; Rev. Jimmy Zammit, O.F.M.; Rev. Patrick Boyle, O.F.M., Vicar; Rev. Robert M. Campagna, O.F.M., Prov.; Bro. Gabriel Aceto, OFM, Prov. Asst.; Bro. Vincent de Paul Ciaravino, O.F.M., Prov. Asst.; Rev. Antonio Riccio, O.F.M., Prov. Asst.; Rev. Joseph Lorenzo, O.F.M., Secy.; Rev. Jose Alvin Te, O.F.M. (Canada), Exec.; Rev. Brennan Egan, O.F.M., Residential Housing; Rev. Albin Fusco, O.F.M., Nursing Home; Rev. Regis Gallo, O.F.M., Nursing Home; Rev. Antonio Nardoianni, O.F.M./I.C., Canadian Ministry; Rev. Richard Martignetti, O.F.M., Campus Min.; Brs.: 22; Priests: 78

Franciscan Mission Associates - 274-280 W. Lincoln Ave., Mount Vernon, NY 10550 t) 914-664-5604 mbonnici@franciscanmissionassoc.org Rev. Pierre John Farrugia, O.F.M.; Madeline Bonnici, Exec.;

The Franciscan Vocation Ministry of Holy Name Province - 129 W. 31st St., 2nd Fl., New York, NY 10001-3403 t) 646-473-0265; 800-677-7788 vocations@hnp.org www.vocation.org Bro. Basil John Valente, OFM, Dir.; Brs.: 1

St. Ignatius Loyola Residence - 53 E. 83rd St., New York, NY 10028 t) 212-606-3420 jcarr@jesuits.org Rev. Arthur C. Bender, S.J.; Rev. William J. Bergen, S.J.; Rev. James Carr; Rev. James A Casciotti, S.J.; Bro. Christopher Derby, S.J.; Rev. Christopher Devron, S.J.; Rev. James P. Ferus, SJ; Rev. Philip A. Florio, S.J.; Rev. Mark Hallinan, S.J.; Rev. Michael P. Hilbert, S.J.; Rev. Stephen N Katsouros, S.J.; Rev. Richard A McGowan, S.J.; Rev. Daniel G. O'Hare, S.J.; Very Rev. Joseph O'Keefe, S.J.; Rev. Michael J. Sala, S.J.; Rev. John W Swope, S.J.; Rev. Michael F Tunney, S.J.; Rev. Dennis J. Yesalonia, S.J.; Brs.: 1; Priests: 17

Immaculate Conception Friary (Capuchin Friars of the Province of the Stigmata of St. Francis) - 754 E. Gun Hill Rd., New York, NY 10467 t) 212-653-2200 Rev. John Aurilia, O.F.M.Cap.;

Institute of the Incarnate Word, Inc. - 113 E. 117th St., New York, NY 10035 t) 301-853-2789 prov.immaculate.conception@ive.org www.iveamerica.org Rev. Alberto Barattero, I.V.E., Pres.;

Jesuit Community at Fordham University - 441 E. Fordham Rd., Spellman Hall, New York, NY 10458 t) 718-817-5350 rotton@fordham.edu Rev. Thomas Regan, S.J., Supr.; Rev. Nicholas D Lombardi, S.J., Rector; Rev. R. Bentley Anderson, S.J.; Rev. Mark Burke; Rev. Johnathan Castelblanco, SJ (Colombia); Rev. John J. Cecero, S.J.; Rev. James K. Coughlin, S.J.; Rev. Christopher Cullen, S.J.; Rev. John D. Cunningham, S.J.; Rev. George W. Drance, S.J.; Rev. John T. Dzieglewicz, S.J.; Rev. Brendan Horan, S.J.; Rev. Joseph T. Lienhard, S.J.; Rev. David P. Marcotte, S.J.; Rev. Thomas J. Massaro; Rev. Francis X. McAloon, S.J.; Rev. Paul D. McNelis, S.J.; Rev. Collins Obidiagha, SJ (Nigeria); Rev. Stanley J. O'Konsky, S.J.; Rev. Jose Luis S. Salazar, S.J.; Rev. Stephen Schloesser, S.J.; Rev. Thomas J. Scirghi, S.J.; Rev. John J. Shea, S.J.; Rev. Kevin Spinale, SJ; Rev. Thomas Worcester, SJ; Rev. Taiju Yamanaka, SJ (Japan); Priests: 28

Cardinal Spellman Hall, Jesuit Community - 441 E. Fordham Rd., Bronx, NY 10458 tregan@jesuits.org Rev. Douglas Jones, S.J., Regent; Rev. Christopher J. Devron, S.J., Pres.; Rev. Joseph M. McShane, S.J., Pres.; Rev. John Bentz, S.J., Priest; Rev. Christopher M. Cullen, S.J., Priest; Rev. Joseph W. Koterski, S.J., Priest; Rev. Michael C. McCarthy, S.J., Priest; Rev. Patrick J. Ryan, S.J., Priest; Rev. Michael F. Suarez, S.J., Priest; Rev. Raymond M. Sweitzer, S.J., Priest;

St. Joseph's Friary - 523 W. 142nd St., New York, NY 10031 t) 212-234-9089; 212-281-4355 (Vocations Office) cfrgensec@franciscanfriars.com www.franciscanfriars.com (Franciscan Friars of the Renewal), (Postulancy) Rev. Gabriel Monahan, C.F.R., Vicar; Rev. Mark Ames, CFR, Pst. Assoc.; Rev. Gabriel Mary Bakkar, C.F.R., Pst. Assoc.; Rev. Angelus Immaculata Montgomery, C.F.R., Pst. Assoc.; Rev. Innocent Mariae Montgomery, C.F.R., Supr.; Rev. Glenn Sudano, C.F.R., Rel. Ord. Ldr.; Bro. Peter Marie Westall, C.F.R., Treas.; Bro. Angelo Marie LeFever, C.F.R, Friar; Bro. Kolbe Immaculata Blashock, C.F.R., Mem.; Bro. Mariano Ravazzano, CFR, Mem.; Bro. Paul Joseph Jones, CFR, Friar; Brs.: 5; Priests: 5

Marist Residence - 226 E. 113th St., New York, NY 10029 t) 212-348-2702 Bro. Santos Garcia Garcia, F.M.S.; Bro. James McKnight, F.M.S.; Bro. Luis Vega, F.M.S.;

Maryknoll House (Catholic Foreign Mission Society of America, Inc.) - 121 E. 39th St., New York, NY 10016

t) 212-697-4470 mklnyc@aol.com www.maryknollsociety.org Rev. Francis T. McGourn, M.M., Dir.; Bro. Wm. Timothy Raible, M.M., Dir.; Brs.: 1; Priests: 1

Padua Friary - 151 Thompson St., New York, NY 10012-3110 t) 212-254-9553 x1100 jolorenzo1@me.com; jlorenzo@icprovince.org Rev. Romano S. Almagno, O.F.M.; Bro. Ronald Bolfeta, O.F.M.; Bro. Paschal De Mattia, O.F.M.; Rev. Louis Troiano, O.F.M.; Bro. Dominic Poirier, O.F.M., Vicar; Rev. Simeon C. Distefano, O.F.M., In Res.; Rev. Joseph Lorenzo, O.F.M., Supr.; Bro. Vincent de Paul Ciaravino, O.F.M., Health Care Director; Bro. Courtland Campbell, Health Care Director; Brs.: 5; Priests: 4

Pallottine Fathers - Society of the Catholic Apostolate, 448 E. 116th St., New York, NY 10029 t) 212-534-0681 Rev. Christopher Salvatori, S.A.C., Admin.; Rev. Terzo Vinci, S.A.C., Admin.;

Paulist Fathers - Generalate - 415 W. 59th St., New York, NY 10019 t) 212-757-8072 admingenoffice@paulist.org www.paulist.org Rev. Frank Desiderio, C.S.P., Vice President; Rev. David P. Dwyer, C.S.P., First Consultor/Dir. Busted Halo; Rev. Steven Bell, CSP; Rev. Matthew J Berrios, CSP, Grad. Student; Rev. James A. Haley, C.S.P.; Rev. Thomas P. Hall, C.S.P.; Rev. James M. Kolb, C.S.P.; Rev. Vincent W. McKiernan, C.S.P.; Rev. Steven J. Petroff, C.S.P., Rector; Rev. Larry Rice, C.S.P., Campus Min.;

Paulist Fathers' Motherhouse - 415 W. 59th St., New York, NY 10019; Mailing: 405 W. 59th St., New York, NY 10019 t) 212-265-3209 johnbehenke@aol.com; pfmotherhouse@aol.com www.paulist.org See also St. Paul the Apostle Parish Rev. Frank Desiderio, C.S.P., Vice President; Rev. David P. Dwyer, C.S.P., First Consultor/Dir. Busted Halo; Rev. John J. Behnke, C.S.P., Superior/Dir. Archives; Rev. Eric P. Andrews, C.S.P., In Res.; Rev. Vincent P. Manalo, C.S.P., Composer/Theologian/Missionary; Rev. Charles Brunick, C.S.P., In Res.; Rev. Bernard J. Campbell, C.S.P., In Res.; Rev. Donald Campbell, C.S.P., In Res.; Rev. Joseph Anthony Ciccone, CSP, In Res.; Rev. John E. Collins, C.S.P., In Res.; Rev. Evan Cummings, CSP, Assoc. Pst./Assoc. Dir. Busted Halo; Rev. John F. Duffy, C.S.P., In Res.; Rev. James M. DiLuzio, C.S.P., Preaching Apostolate/Ecumenical & Multi-Faith Relations; Rev. Frank Sabbatte, C.S.P., Cultural Outreach; Rev. Mark-David Janus, C.S.P., Pres. Paulist Press; Rev. Ronald A. Franco, C.S.P., In Res.; Rev. John J. Foley, C.S.P., Asst. Archivist; Rev. Thomas J. Holahan, C.S.P., In Res.; Rev. Thomas Anthony Kane, C.S.P., In Res.; Rev. James B. Lloyd, C.S.P., In Res.; Rev. James F. McQuade, C.S.P., In Res.; Rev. Edward S. Pietrucha, C.S.P., In Res.; Rev. Paul Robinchaud, In Res.; Rev. Paul S. Rospond, C.S.P., Assoc. Pst.; Rev. Timothy P. Tighe, C.S.P., In Res.; Rev. Broderick Matthew Walsh, CSP, Pst.;

Redemptorist Priests and Brothers, C.Ss.R. - Redemptorist Residence, 323 E. 61st St., New York, NY 10065-8204 t) 212-838-1324 (Prov. of Baltimore)

Scalabrinian Missionaries (The Pious Society of the Missionaries of St. Charles Boromeo, Inc.) - 27 Carmine St., New York, NY 10014 t) 212-675-3993 scbprovince@gmail.com www.scalabrinisaintcharles.org Rev. Angelo Plodari, C.S., Prov.; Rev. Jesus Erasmo Salinas Hernandez, C.S., Vicar; Rev. Ezio Marchetto, C.S., Treas.; Rev. Edison Adolfo Osorio Agudelo, C.S., Dir.; Rev. Rubens Sylvain, CS, Dir.; Brs.: 19; Priests: 92

The Society of Jesus of New England - 39 E. 83rd St., New York, NY 10028 t) 212-774-5500 See the USA East Province of the Society of Jesus. Very Rev. Joseph O'Keefe, S.J., Prov.;

Society of Jesus, New York Province - 39 E. 83rd St., New York, NY 10028-0810 t) 212-774-5500 a.k.a. Jesuit Seminary and Mission Bureau, Inc. and USA Northeast Province of the Society of Jesus. See USA East Province of the Society of Jesus. Very Rev. Joseph O'Keefe, S.J., Prov.;

USA East Province of the Society of Jesus, Inc. - 39 E. 83rd St., New York, NY 10028 t) 212-774-5500 ueaprovincial@jesuits.org www.jesuitseast.org Very Rev. Joseph O'Keefe, S.J., Prov.; Brs.: 21; Priests: 535

USA Northeast Province of the Society of Jesus, Inc. - 39 E. 83rd St., New York, NY 10028 t) 212-774-5500 ueaprovincial@jesuits.org www.jesuitseast.org See USA East Province of the Society of Jesus. Very Rev. Joseph O'Keefe, S.J., Prov.;

Jesuit Provincial's Office - See USA East Province of the Society of Jesus.

St. Vincent de Paul Residence - 900 Intervale Ave., New York, NY 10459 t) 718-589-6965 svdpres@chcn.org www.svdpres.org

St. Vincent Ferrer Priory - 869 Lexington Ave., New York, NY 10065-6648 t) 212-744-2080 Dominican Friars Provincial House (Province of St. Joseph). Friar Jacob Restrick, OP; Friar Peter Martyr Yungwirth, O.P., Pst.; Rev. Reginald Hoefer, Par. Vicar; Rev. John Chrysostom Kozlowski, O.P., Prov. Asst.; Bro. Martin Davis, OP, Mem.; Rev. John Paul Kern, O.P., Mem.; Rev. Ronald Eugene Henery, O.P; Bro. John Damian McCarthy, O.P.; Rev. Matthew Paul Carroll, OP, Mem.; Rev. J. Albert Paretsky, O.P., Subprior; Rev. Athanasius Murphy, O.P., In Res.; Rev. Hyacinth Grubb, O.P., Chap.; Rev. Albert Duggan, O.P., Prior; Rev. James Ritch, O.P., Treas.; Rev. William Alexander Holt, OP, Mem.; Brs.: 2; Priests: 12

Vincentian Fathers (Padres Paules Community (Vincentians) Inc.) - 1834 Third Ave., New York, NY 10029 t) 212-289-5589 milagha2@verizon.net Rev. Candido Arrizurieta, C.M.; Rev. Jesus Arellano, C.M., Vicar; Rev. Victor Elia, C.M., Supr.;

Xavier Jesuit Community - 30 W. 16th St., New York, NY 10011 t) 917-409-5580 thfs@hotmail.com www.xavierhs.org (For list of faculty see the high school listing for Xavier High School) Rev. Kenneth Boller, SJ, Pst.; Rev. Ricardo da Silva, SJ, Assoc. Pst.; Rev. John Fagan, Assoc. Pst.; Rev. James J. Miracky, S.J., Assoc. Pst.; Rev. Brian F. Linnane, S.J., Prof.; Rev. Thomas H. Feely, S.J., Supr.; Rev. Zachariah Presutti, S.J., Dir.; Rev. James McDermott, S.J., Writer; John Pignone, SJ, Teacher; Rev. Louis T. Garaventa, S.J., Admin.; Rev. James J. Hederman, S.J., Teacher; Rev. James L. Pierce, S.J., Sacr. Min.; Rev. John Wronski, Province Staff; Rev. James Mayzik, Vicar; Rev. James F. Keenan, S.J., Admin.; Priests: 15

<u>OSSINING</u>

Maryknoll Fathers and Brothers (Catholic Foreign Mission Society of America, Inc.) - 55 Ryder Rd., Ossining, NY 10562; Mailing: P. O. Box 303, Maryknoll, NY 10545-0303 t) 914-941-7590 mklcouncil@maryknoll.org www.maryknollsociety.org Rev. Lance P. Nadeau, M.M., Superior General & President; Rev. James M. Lynch, M.M., Vicar General & Vice President; Rev. Juan M. Zuñiga, M.M., Secretary General; Rev. Timothy O. Kilkelly, M.M., Assistant General; Rev. Edward J. Phillips, M.M., Treas.; Rev. Alfonso Kim, M.M., Supr.; Rev. John J. McAuley, M.M., Supr.; Rev. Rodrigo Ulloa-Chavarry, M.M., Vocation Director; Rev. Richard Albertine, M.M., Mem.; Bro. John E. Argauer, M.M., Mem.; Rev. Richard Aylward, M.M., Mem.; Rev. Richard M. Baker, M.M., Mem.; Rev. Dale F. Barron, M.M., Mem.; Rev. Brian Barrons, M.M., Mem.; Rev. Peter J. Barry, M.M., Mem.; Rev. Richard W. Bauer, M.M., Mem.; Rev. Paul D. Belliveau, M.M., Mem.; Rev. Francis H. Beninati, M.M., Mem.; Bro. John J. Blazo, M.M., Mem.; Rev. Leslie F. Blowers, M.M., Mem.; Rev. Francis J. Breen, M.M., Mem.; Rev. John T. Brinkman, Mem.; Rev. Jeremiah R. Burr, M.M., Mem.; Bro. Robert A. Butsch, M.M., Mem.; Rev. Curtis R. Cadorette, M.M., Mem.; Rev. Michael G. Callanan, M.M., Mem.; Rev. Robert J. Carleton, M.M., Mem.; Bro. Eugene E. Casper, M.M., Mem.; Rev. Peter L. Chabot, M.M., Mem.; Rev. John Cioppa, M.M., Mem.; Rev. Vincent P. Cole, M.M., Mem.; Rev. Edward L. Cookson, M.M., Mem.; Rev. Vincent F. Corbelli, M.M., Mem.; Bro. Brendan J. Corkery, M.M., Mem.; Rev. Robert F. Crawford, M.M., Mem.; Rev. Edward O. Custer, M.M., Mem.; Bro. Kevin F. Dargan, M.M., Mem.; Rev. Rafael R. Davila, M.M., Mem.; Rev. Edward V. Davis, M.M., Mem.; Rev. Marvin F. Deutsch, M.M., Mem.; Rev. William Donnelly, M.M., Mem.; Rev. Joseph J. Donovan, M.M., Mem.; Rev. Edward M. Dougherty, M.M., Mem.; Rev. Paul J. Duffy, M.M., Mem.; Rev. Michael A. Duggan, M.M., Mem.; Rev. Emile E. Dumas, M.M., Mem.; Rev. Thomas Dunleavy, M.M., Mem.; Rev. Thomas R. Egan, M.M., Mem.; Rev. Philip N. Erbland, M.M., Mem.; Rev. John F. Felago, M.M., Mem.; Rev. Francis J. Felter, M.M., Mem.; Rev. Raymond J. Finch, M.M., Mem.; Bro. Wayne J. Fitzpatrick, M.M., Mem.; Bro. Vianney R. Flick, M.M., Mem.; Rev. Herbert T. Gappa, M.M., Mem.; Rev. Regis Ging, M.M., Mem.; Rev. Donald F. Glover, M.M., Mem.; Rev. John F. Gorski, M.M., Mem.; Rev. Fernand L. Gosselin, M.M., Mem.; Rev. Kevin J. Hanlon, M.M., Mem.; Rev. Scott T. Harris, M.M., Mem.; Rev. Joseph G. Healey, M.M., Mem.; Rev. Joseph A. Heim, M.M., Mem.; Rev. James L. Hilgeman, M.M., Mem.; Rev. Lam M. Hua, M.M., Mem.; Rev. Delos A. Humphrey Jr., M.M., Mem.; Rev. James H. Huvane, M.M., Mem.; Rev. John M. Kaserow, M.M., Mem.; Rev. John E. Keegan, M.M., Mem.; Bro. Lawrence E. Kenning, M.M., Mem.; Rev. Michael C. Kirwen, M.M., Mem.; Rev. James W. Kofski, M.M., Mem.; Rev. James H. Kroeger, M.M., Mem.; Rev. Ralph S. Kroes, M.M., Mem.; Rev. David E. La Buda, M.M., Mem.; Rev. Joseph P. LaMar, M.M., Mem.; Rev. John J. Lange, M.M., Mem.; Rev. Peter M. Le Jacq, M.M., Mem.; Rev. Francis J. Leong, M.M., Mem.; Rev. Lawrence J. Lewis, M.M., Mem.; Rev. Robert J. Lloyd, M.M., Mem.; Bro. Anthony Lopez, M.M., Mem.; Rev. Martin J. Lowery, M.M., Mem.; Rev. William T. Madden, M.M., Mem.; Bro. Andrew E. Marsolek, M.M., Mem.; Rev. Thomas J. Marti, M.M., Mem.; Rev. John P. Martin, M.M., Mem.; Rev. Douglas E. May, M.M., Mem.; Rev. James D. McAuley, M.M., Mem.; Rev. Joseph V. McCabe, M.M., Mem.; Rev. William E. McCarthy, M.M., Mem.; Rev. Lawrence F. McCulloch, M.M., Mem.; Rev. William J. McIntire, M.M., Mem.; Bro. David E. McKenna, M.M., Mem.; Rev. Francis S. Meccia, M.M., Mem.; Rev. Carl P. Meulemans, M.M., Mem.; Rev. Kenneth J. Moody, M.M., Mem.; Rev. John J. Moran, M.M., Mem.; Rev. John C. Moynihan, M.M., Mem.; Rev. James J. Mylet, M.M., Mem.; Rev. James Najmowski, M.M., Mem.; Rev. Robert V. Nehrig, M.M., Mem.; Rev. Cuong H. Nguyen, M.M., Mem.; Rev. Bryce T. Nishimura, M.M., Mem.; Bro. Frank J. Norris, M.M., Mem.; Rev. Thomas J. O'Brien, M.M., Mem.; Rev. Daniel Ohmann, M.M., Mem.; Rev. Norbert a. Pacheco, M.M., Mem.; Bro. Albert F. Patrick, M.M., Mem.; Rev. Richard E. Paulissen, M.M., Mem.; Rev. Gerald J. Persha, M.M., Mem.; Rev. Thomas E. Pesaresi, M.M., Mem.; Rev. Thomas A. Peyton, M.M., Mem.; Rev. David L. Pfeiffer, M.M., Mem.; Rev. Clyde Phillips, M.M., Mem.; Rev. Raymond G. Pierini, M.M., Mem.; Rev. Lawrence D. Radice, M.M., Mem.; Rev. Robert J. Reiley, M.M., Mem.; Rev. John A. Rich, M.M., Mem.; Rev. Richard S. Rolewicz, M.M., Mem.; Rev. James R. Roy, M.M., Mem.; Bro. Venard F. Ruane, M.M., Mem.; Rev. Peter L. Ruggere, M.M., Mem.; Rev. Steven S. Scherrer, M.M., Mem.; Rev. Leo B. Shea, M.M., Mem.; Bro. Martin J. Shea, M.M., Mem.; Bro. Leo V. Shedy, M.M., Mem.; Rev. John C. Sivalon, M.M., Mem.; Rev. Joseph Slaby, M.M., Mem.; Rev. David A. Smith, M.M., Mem.; Rev. Richard P. Smith, M.M., Mem.; Rev. Michael J. Snyder, M.M., Mem.; Rev. Romane St. Vil, M.M., Mem.; Bro. DePorres Stilp, M.M., Mem.; Rev. Kenneth J. Sullivan, M.M., Mem.; Rev. J. Edward Szendrey, M.M., Mem.; Bro. Frank Tenhoopen, M.M., Mem.; Bro. Raymond C. Tetrault, M.M., Mem.; Rev. Joseph L. Thaler, M.M., Mem.; Rev. Eugene W. Toland, M.M., Mem.; Rev. Joseph W. Towle, M.M., Mem.; Rev. Joseph R. Veneroso, M.M., Mem.; Rev. Robert W. Vujs, M.M., Mem.; Bro. Alexander J. Walsh, M.M., Mem.; Rev. Michael P. Walsh, M.M., Mem.; Most Rev. J. Quinn

Weitzel, M.M., Mem.; Rev. Edward J. Whelan, M.M., Mem.; Rev. Gerald M. Wickenhauser, M.M., Mem.; Rev. Robert F. Wynne, M.M., Mem.; Bro. Goretti A. Zilli, M.M., Mem.; Brs.: 28; Priests: 187

PELHAM

Marist Brothers Community - 26 First Ave., Pelham, NY 10803 t) 914-738-1218 Bro. John Klein, FMS, Dir.;

PELHAM MANOR

St. Vincent Strambi Residence (The Passionists) - 190 Mount Tom Rd., Pelham Manor, NY 10803-3309 t) 914-738-6138 pfagan@cpprov.org; edwardlbeck@aol.com Rev. Paul R. Fagan, C.P., Supr.; Rev. James O'Shea, C.P., Prov.; Rev. Edward L. Beck, C.P., Mem.; Rev. Robert H. Joerger, C.P., Mem.; Rev. Salvatore Enzo Del Brocco, C.P., 1st Consultor; Priests: 4

POUGHKEEPSIE

Marist Brothers - 2 Eden Ter., Poughkeepsie, NY 12601-4803 t) 845-471-8354 Bro. Kenneth V. Hogan, F.M.S.; Bro. John Nash, F.M.S.; Bro. John Malich, F.M.S., Dir.;

RYE

Legionaries of Christ - 815 Boston Post Rd., Rye, NY 10580 t) 301-580-3040 dray@legionaries.org www.legionofchrist.org Rev. Donald Kaufman, L.C., Pst.; Rev. Jose Helio Cantu, L.C., Par. Vicar; Rev. Stephen Howe, Par. Vicar; Rev. Mark Haydu, L.C., Chap.; Rev. Eric Nielsen, Chap.; Rev. Jorge Obregon, L.C., Chap.; Rev. Daniel Ray, L.C., Supr.; Priests: 7

STATEN ISLAND

St. Francis Friary - 500 Todt Hill Rd., Staten Island, NY 10304 t) 718-981-3131 bjfarleo@aol.com Rev. Edward Costello, O.F.M.Conv.; Rev. Brennan-Joseph Farleo, O.F.M.Conv.; Rev. George Sabol, O.F.M. Conv.; Bro. Joseph Freitag, In Res.; Rev. Philip Blaine, O.F.M.Conv., Dir.;

Friars Minor Conventual Immaculate Conception Province Charitable Trust -

WEST PARK

Congregation of Christian Brothers - Santa Maria-on-Hudson, West Park, NY 12493; Mailing: P.O. Box 39, West Park, NY 12493 t) 845-384-3006 Bro. John B. Chaney, C.F.C.; Bro. D. D. Crimmins, C.F.C.; Bro. J. Laurence Heathwood, C.F.C.; Bro. R.J. Lasik, C.F.C.; Bro. Richard E. Pigott, C.F.C.; Bro. Anthony Alex Cannon, C.F.C., Contact;

WHITE PLAINS

Capuchin Friars of North America (NAPCC/North America Pacific Capuchin Conference) - 30 Gedney Park Dr., White Plains, NY 10605-3599; Mailing: 158 Aberdeen Dr., Cranberry Township, PA 16066 t) 914-761-3008 c) 724-272-9394 tomgrayjr01@gmail.com San Lorenzo Novitiate Seminary Bro. Mark Schenk, O.F.M.Cap., Pres.; Rev. Michael Greco, OFM Cap, Vice. Pres.; Thomas Gray Jr., Treas.; Brs.: 564; Priests: 520

The Province of St. Mary of the Capuchin Order - 30 Gedney Park Dr., White Plains, NY 10605-3599 t) 914-761-3008 treasurer@capuchin.org www.capuchin.org Rev. Robert J. Abbatiello, O.F.M.Cap., Vicar; Rev. Joseph Flynn, O.F.M.Cap., In Res.; Bro. Timothy Jones, OFMCap, In Res.; Rev. Fred Nickle, O.F.M.Cap., In Res.; Rev. Gregory Reisert, OFMCap, In Res.; Rev. John Rathschmidt, O.F.M.Cap., Sacr. Min.; Rev. Michael Greco, OFM Cap, Prov.; Bro. Roger Deguire, O.F.M.Cap., Archivist; Rev. Charles Sammons, OFMCap, Secy.; Bro. Joseph S Yakimovich, OFMCap, Treas.; Diane Cassidy, Bus. Mgr.; Brs.: 30; Priests: 91

YONKERS

St. Clare Friary (Capuchin Franciscan Friars, Province of St. Mary) - 110 Shonnard Pl., Yonkers, NY 10703 t) 914-423-2392 Residence for Senior Friars. Rev. Gordon Combs, O.F.M.Cap., In Res.; Rev. Michael Connolly, In Res.; Rev. Theodosius Corley, O.F.M.Cap., In Res.; Bro. Paul Crawford, OFM Cap, In Res.; Rev. Don Bosco Duquette, OFM Cap, In Res.; Dcn. Salvatore Patricola, O.F.M. Cap.; Bro. Carmine Funaro, OFM Cap, In Res.; Rev. Patrick Glavin, OFM Cap, In Res.; Rev. Joseph Gurdak, OFM Cap, In Res.; Rev. Thomas Houle, OFM Cap, In Res.; Rev. Eugene O'Hara, OFM Cap, In Res.; Rev. Philip Romano, O.F.M. Cap., In Res.; Rev. Eugene Sheehan, OFM Cap, In Res.; Rev. Raynold Thibodeau, OFM Cap, In Res.; Rev. William Winters, OFM Cap., In Res.; Bro. Timothy Aller, O.F.M.Cap., Guardian; Rev. Michael Banks, OFM Cap., Fraternal Vicar; Bro. Roger Deguire, O.F.M.Cap., Provincial Archivist; Rev. Gabriel Massaro, OFM Cap, Senior Care Team; Rev. Andrew Nowak, OFM Cap, Senior Care Assistant; Rev. Senan Taylor, O.F.M.Cap., Senior Care Team;

St. Leopold's Friary - 259 Nepperhan Ave., Yonkers, NY 10701-3461 t) 914-965-8143 cfrgensec@franciscanfriars.com www.franciscanfriars.com (Franciscan Friars of the Renewal), (House of Studies) Rev. John-Mary Johannssen, Supr.; Rev. Joseph Michael Fino, C.F.R., Vicar; Rev. Conrad Osterhout, CFR, Pst. Assoc.; Rev. Fidelis Moscinski, C.F.R., Pst. Assoc.; Rev. Luke Mary Fletcher, C.F.R., Pst. Assoc.; Rev. Lawrence Schroedel, CFR, Pst. Assoc.; Bro. Pius Gagne, C.F.R., Mem.; Bro. Michelangelo Best, CFR, Seminarian; Bro. Francois Marie Fontanie, CFR, Seminarian; Bro. Lawrence Johnson, CFR, Seminarian; Brs.: 4; Priests: 6

NURSING / REHABILITATION / CONVALESCENCE / ELDERLY CARE [NUR]

BRONX

Bon Secours New York Health System, Inc. (Frances Schervier Home and Hospital, Frances Schervier Housing Development Fund Corporation) - 2975 Independence Ave., Bronx, NY 10463-4699 t) 718-548-1700 sdschitter1@mercy.com www.scherviercares.org Travis Crum, Trustee;

Jeanne Jugan Residence - 2999 Schurz Ave., Bronx, NY 10465 t) 347-329-1800 bxmothersuperior@littlesistersofthepoor.org www.littlesistersofthepoorbronx.org Sr. Gertrude Maiorino, Pres.; Asstd. Annu.: 47; Staff: 9

St. Patrick's Home for the Aged and Infirm (Carmelite Sisters for the Aged and Infirm) - 66 Van Cortlandt Park S., Bronx, NY 10463 t) 718-519-2800 admissions@stpatrickshome.org www.stpatrickshome.org/ The Carmelite System Sr. M. Kevin Patricia, O.Carm., Admin.; Asstd. Annu.: 542; Staff: 237

Providence Rest - 3304 Waterbury Ave., Bronx, NY 10465 t) 718-931-3000 prnh@providencerest.org www.providencerest.org Richard Biscotti, Admin.;

St. Vincent de Paul Residence - 900 Intervale Ave., Bronx, NY 10459 t) 917-645-9200 www.archcare.org/san-vicente-de-paul Richard Biscotti, Admin.;

DOBBS FERRY

Cabrini of Westchester - 115 Broadway, Dobbs Ferry, NY 10522 t) 914-693-6800 www.cabrini-eldercare.org Patricia Krasnausky, Pres.; Rev. Thomas John Vadakemuriyil, CMI (India), Dir.;

MIDDLETOWN

St. Teresa's Nursing Home - 120 Highland Ave., Middletown, NY 10940 t) 845-342-1033 mchaiken@chcsnet.org

NEW YORK

Kateri Residence - 150 Riverside Dr., New York, NY 10024-2201 t) 646-633-4700 www.archcare.org Skilled Nursing Care/Residential Health Care Facility for the Elderly.

Mary Manning Walsh Home (Carmelite Sisters for the Aged and Infirm) - 1339 York Ave., New York, NY 10021 t) 212-628-2800 www.archcare.org/mary-manning-walsh Michael Monahan, Admin.;

Terence Cardinal Cooke Health Care Center - 1249 Fifth Ave., New York, NY 10029 t) 212-360-1000 www.archcare.org/terence-cardinal-cooke Rosalie Bernard, Admin.;

RHINEBECK

Ferncliff Nursing Home - 21 Ferncliff Dr., Rhinebeck, NY 12572 t) 845-876-2011 www.archcare.org/ferncliff Member: Catholic Health Care System. Michael Deyo, Admin.;

STATEN ISLAND

Carmel Richmond Healthcare and Rehabilitation Center (Carmelite Sisters for the Aged and Infirm) - 88 Old Town Rd., Staten Island, NY 10304-4299 t) 718-979-5000 www.archcare.org/carmel-richmond Sr. Maureen T. Murray, O.Carm., Pres.;

Friends of Carmel Richmond, Inc. - Adult Daycare Program.

WARWICK

Schervier Pavilion (Sisters of Charity of St. Elizabeth, Sisters of Bon Secours) - 22 Van Duzer Pl., Warwick, NY 10990 t) 845-987-5717 bschs.bonsecours.com Part of Bon Secours Charity Health System. Clare Brady, Senior Vice Pres. Mission; Jeff Reilly, Senior Vice Pres. & Admin.;

PRESCHOOLS / CHILDCARE CENTERS [PRE]

BRONX

St. Francis Youth Center, Inc. - 427 E. 155th St., Bronx, NY 10455 t) 718-402-6235 Yvette Torres, Admin.; Rev. Bonaventure Rummell, C.F.R., Dir.;

Little Angels Head Start Program - 529 Courtlandt Ave., Bronx, NY 10451; Mailing: 115 Stevens Ave., Ste. LL5, Valhalla, NY 10595 t) 718-402-0081 rgershenlowy@cmcs.org www.littleangelsheadstart.org Beth Finnerty, Pres.;

Youth Ministries for Peace & Justice, Inc. - 1384 Stratford Ave., Bronx, NY 10472 t) 718-328-5622 dshuffler@ympj.org www.ympj.org

GARRISON

Capuchin Youth and Family Ministries - ; Mailing: PO Box 268, Garrison, NY 10524 t) 845-424-3609 cyfm@cyfm.org www.cyfm.org A ministry of the Capuchin Franciscan Province of St. Mary. Rev. Erik Lenhart, Chap.; Rev. Fred Nickle, O.F.M.Cap., Chap.;

HIGHLAND MILLS

Thevenet Montessori School (Religious of Jesus and Mary) - 21 Bethany Dr., Highland Mills, NY 10930 t) 845-928-6981 thevenet02@optimum.net Sr. Joan Faraone, R.J.M., Dir.; Stds.: 115; Lay Tchrs.: 10

LINCOLNDALE

Lincoln Hall - ; Mailing: P.O. Box 600, Lincolndale, NY 10540 t) 914-248-7474 info@lincolnhall.org Jack Flavin, Exec.;

MILLBROOK

Cardinal Hayes Home for Children (Cardinal Hayes Home for Children at Millbrook New York) - 60 St. Joseph Dr., Millbrook, NY 12545; Mailing: P.O. Box CH, Millbrook, NY 12545 t) 845-677-6363 msontheimer@cardinalhayeshome.org; mbroe@cardinalhayeshome.org www.cardinalhayeshome.org Residential care for developmentally disabled children and young adults. Mary Sontheimer, CEO; Stds.: 119

Cardinal Hayes School for Special Children - 3374 Franklin Ave., Millbrook, NY 12545; Mailing: P.O. Box CH, Millbrook, NY 12545 t) 845-677-3251 mschipani@cardinalhayeshome.org www.hayesdayschool.org Mary Sontheimer, CEO; Stds.: 55; Lay Tchrs.: 10

NEW YORK

St. Benedict's Day Nursery, Day Care Center - 21 W. 124th St., New York, NY 10027 t) 212-423-5715 st.benedictdaynursery@yahoo.com Doris Moore, Admin.; Sr. Mary Ann Baichan, F.H.M., Prin.;

Cardinal Spellman Center, Inc. - 137 E. Second St., New York, NY 10009 t) 212-677-6600 Community Centers foster and promote the positive development of children, youth, their families.

Catholic Guardian Services - 1011 First Ave., 10th Fl., New York, NY 10022 t) 212-371-1000 x2300 clongley@catholicguardian.org www.catholicguardian.org Craig Longley, Exec.;

Catholic Youth Organization of the Archdiocese of New York Inc. - Executive Office, 1011 First Ave., New York, NY 10022-4187 t) 212-371-1000 Chris Gallagher, Pres.; Edwin Broderick, Exec.;

Archdiocesan Committee on Scouting - t) 845-340-9170 Anthony Badger, Dir.; Seth Peloso, Dir.;
CYO Bronx County - CYO New York County - 1011 First Ave., New York, NY 10022 Anthony D'Angelo, Dir.;
CYO Dutchess Office - Catholic Center, 218 Church St., Poughkeepsie, NY 12601 t) 845-452-1400 Jill Dennin, Dir.;
CYO Orange Office - ; Mailing: P.O. Box 234, Highland Mills, NY 10930 t) 845-534-7700 John Smith, Dir.;
CYO Rockland Office - 34 Graney Ct., Pearl River, NY 10965 t) 845-620-1662 Thomas F. Collins, Dir.;
CYO Staten Island County - 120 Anderson Ave., Staten Island, NY 10302 t) 718-448-4949; 718-448-4950 Michael Neely, Dir.;
CYO Ulster - 59 Pearl St., Kingston, NY 12401 t) 845-340-9170 Walter Gaceta, Dir.;
CYO Westchester/Putnam Offices - 9 Brookview Blvd., Chestnut Ridge, NY 10977 t) 845-623-2785 Frank Magaletta, Dir.;
Drew-Hamilton CYO Center - 220 W. 143rd St., New York, NY 10030 Serves Central Harlem.
***Good Shepherd Services** - 305 7th Ave., 9th Fl., New York, NY 10001 t) 212-243-7070 michelle_yanche@goodshepherds.org www.goodshepherds.org Sr. Maureen McGowan, Trustee;
Kennedy Children's Center - 2212 Third Ave., 2nd Fl., New York, NY 10035 t) 212-988-9500 info@kenchild.org www.kenchild.org Jeanne Alter, Exec.; Stds.: 362; Lay Tchrs.: 39
Bronx Site - 1028 E. 179th St., Bronx, NY 10460 t) 718-842-0200
Lieut. Joseph P. Kennedy, Jr. Memorial Community Center - 34 W. 134th St., New York, NY 10037 t) 212-862-6401 x410 Dcn. Rodney Beckford;
Providence Rest Child Day Care Center, Inc. - 3310 Campbell Dr., New York, NY 10465 t) 718-823-3588 (UPK District 8) Sr. Theresa Ann D'Onofrio, C.S.JB., Dir.;
San Jose Day Nursery - 430 W. 20th St., New York, NY 10011; Mailing: 432 W 20th St., New York, NY 10011 t) 212-929-0839 sanjosenursery430@gmail.com www.sanjosedaynursery.com Sr. Josefina Jimenez, Supr.; Sr. Irene Catherine Sheehan, Dir.; Stds.: 42; Lay Tchrs.: 10
Vincent J. Fontana Center for Child Protection - 590 Ave. of the Americas, New York, NY 10011 t) 212-660-1323
RHINEBECK
Astor Learning Center, The - 6339 Mill St., Rhinebeck, NY 12572 t) 845-871-1032 john.kegan@astorlearning.org www.astorservices.org School-based treatment program operated by Astor Services for Children & Families. John J. Kegan, Prin.;
Astor Services for Children & Families - 6339 Mill St., Rhinebeck, NY 12572 t) 845-871-1000 ybairan@astorservices.org www.astorservices.org Residential Treatment Facility for severe emotionally disturbed-mentally ill boys and girls, ages 5-12. Bairan Yvette, CEO;
Astor Family Services Program, Bronx - (Ages birth-18)
Counseling Centers: Poughkeepsie, Beacon, Bronx, Dover, Hyde Park, Ulster County - Kingston, Ellenville, New Paltz - (Ages birth-18)
Day Care Centers: Beacon, Wingdale -
Day Treatment Programs - (Ages 3-12)
Early Head Start -
Head Start-Day Care Centers: Poughkeepsie, Beacon, Millerton, Wingdale, Wappingers Falls, Red Hook, Hyde Park -
Residential Treatment Center (Rhinebeck) -
Special Class Integrated Services - (Ages 3-5)
RYE
RC Activities, Inc. - 815 Boston Post Rd., Rye, NY 10580 t) 855-556-6872 tbrechbill@rcactivities.com Stds.: 2,000
STATEN ISLAND
Catholic Charities of Staten Island - 6581 Hylan Blvd., Staten Island, NY 10309 t) 718-317-2803; 718-984-1500 info@mountloretto.org www.mountloretto.org Vincent Ignizio, CEO;
Day Care Center & Universal Pre-K - t) 718-317-2849
Day Habilitation Program - t) 718-317-2825
Individual Residential Alternatives (I.R.A.) - t) 718-317-2825
Intermediate Care Facility - t) 718-317-2825
Residential & Day Care - t) 718-317-2825
Staten Island CYO Center - 120 Anderson Ave., Port Richmond, Staten Island, NY 10302 t) 718-273-8361
THORNWOOD
Youth and Family Encounter, Inc. - 590 Columbus Ave., Thornwood, NY 10594 t) 914-773-1368 Rev. Jose Felix Ortega, Contact;
YONKERS
Queen's Daughters Day Care Center, Inc. - 73 Buena Vista Ave., Yonkers, NY 10701 t) 914-969-4491 qddcc@excite.com Barbara Berrios, Dir.;

RETREAT HOUSES / RENEWAL CENTERS [RTR]

BEACON
St. Lawrence of Brindisi Friary - 180 Sargent Ave., Beacon, NY 12508-3993 t) 845-831-0394 stlawrenceretreat@gmail.com stlawrenceretreatcenter.org Bro. Rudolph Pieretti, O.F.M. Cap, Vicar; Bro. Carlos Hernandez, O.F.M.Cap., Supr.;
BRONX
St. Joseph's Center - 275 W. 230th St., Bronx, NY 10463 t) 718-796-4340 (Spanish Cursillo Center) Bro. Mario Alvarez, O.A.R., Admin.; Rev. Jose Luis Martinez, O.A.R., Dir.;
ESOPUS
Marist Brothers of Ulster County - ; Mailing: P.O. Box 197, Esopus, NY 12429 t) 845-384-6620 maristbce@gmail.com www.maristretreathouse.com Tomas O'Riordan, Exec. Dir.; Tim Hagan, Dir.;
HIGHLAND MILLS
Bethany Spirituality Center, Inc. (Religious of Jesus and Mary) - 15 Bethany Dr., Highland Mills, NY 10930; Mailing: 821 Varnum St., NE, Washington, DC 20017-2144 t) 202-526-3203 Mary C. Spanos, Admin.;
LARCHMONT
St. Francis Retreat, Inc. - 1 Pryer Manor Rd., Larchmont, NY 10538 t) 718-402-8255 Bro. Patrick Crowley, CFR, Dir.;
Trinity Retreat - 1 Pryer Manor Rd., Larchmont, NY 10538 t) 914-235-6839 trinityret@aol.com (Retreat Center for Clergy) Rev. Eugene J. Fulton, Dir.;
MIDDLETOWN
National Shrine of Our Lady of Mount Carmel - 70 Carmelite Dr., Middletown, NY 10940-2163; Mailing: P.O. Box 2163, Middletown, NY 10940-2163 t) 845-343-1879 cbezak@carmelites.com www.ourladyofmtcarmelshrine.com Rev. Marlon Ricardo Beharry, O. Carm, Chap.; Carol Bezak, Dir.;
RHINEBECK
Convent of St. Ursula - Sisters Residence at Linwood - 50 Linwood Rd., Rhinebeck, NY 12572-2507 t) 845-876-2341 lditolla@earthlink.net www.societyofstursula.org Legal Title: Sisters of St. Ursula of the Blessed Virgin of New York Sr. Elizabeth DiTolla, SU, Supr.; Srs.: 20
Linwood Spiritual Center - 50 Linwood Rd., Rhinebeck, NY 12572 t) (845) 876-4178 www.linwoodspiritual.com Sponsored Ministry of the Sisters of St. Ursula Terence McCorry, Dir.;
SLOATSBURG
St. Mary's Villa (Sisters Servants of Mary Immaculate) - 150 Sisters Servants Ln., Sloatsburg, NY 10974-0009; Mailing: P.O. Box 9, Sloatsburg, NY 10974-0009 t) 845-753-5100 ssminy@aol.com Spiritual and Educational Center. (Retreats) Sr. Kathleen Hutsko, S.S.M.I., Prov.;
STATEN ISLAND
***Mount Manresa Jesuit Retreat House (Society of Jesus)** - 239 Fingerboard Rd., Staten Island, NY 10305 t) 718-727-3844 info@mountmanresa.org www.mountmanresa.org Rev. Thomas M. Gavin, S.J.; Rev. Matthew F. Roche, S.J.; Arlene Volsario, Admin.; Fred Herron, Dir.;
STONY POINT
Don Bosco Retreat Center and Marian Shrine - 174 Filors Ln., Stony Point, NY 10980-2620 t) 845-947-2200 directorssecretary@yahoo.com www.marianshrine.org Rev. Richard J. Putnam, S.D.B., Vicar; Rev. Javier Aracil, S.D.B., In Res.; Rev. William Ferruzzi, S.D.B., In Res.; Rev. Manuel Gallò, In Res.; Rev. Sasika Lokuhettige, S.B.D., In Res.; Bro. Richard Pasiak, S.D.B., In Res.; Rev. Steve Shafran, In Res.; Rev. Kenneth Shaw, S.D.B., In Res.; Rev. Waclaw Swierzbiolek, S.D.B., In Res.; Bro. Charles Thenier, In Res.; Bro. Henry Vandervelden, In Res.; Ann Cenname, Admin.; Laura Piranio, Treas.; Rev. Dennis Donovan, S.D.B., Dir.;
Marian Shrine - 174 Filors Ln., Stony Point, NY 10980-2620 t) 845-947-2200 www.marianshrine.org Rev. Richard J. Putnam, S.D.B., Vicar; Bro. Joseph Ackroyd, In Res.; Rev. Javier Aracil, S.D.B., In Res.; Rev. William Ferruzzi, S.D.B., In Res.; Rev. Manuel Gallo, In Res.; Rev. Sasika Lokuhettige, S.B.D., In Res.; Bro. Richard Pasaik, S.D.B., In Res.; Rev. Steve Shafran, In Res.; Rev. Kenneth Shaw, S.D.B., In Res.; Rev. Waclaw Swierzbiolek, S.D.B., In Res.; Bro. Charles Thenier, In Res.; Bro. Henry Vandervelden, In Res.; Ann Cenname, Admin.; Laura Piranio, Treas.; Rev. Dennis Donovan, S.D.B., Dir.;
ULSTER PARK
Redemptorist Community at Esopus (Redemptorist Fathers and Brothers) - 32 Peters Ln., Ulster Park, NY 12487 t) 845-340-1732 Rev. Thomas (Martin) Deely, C.Ss.R.; Rev. Eugene J. Grohe, C.Ss.R.; Rev. Thomas J. Travers, C.Ss.R.;
WAPPINGERS FALLS
Mt. Alvernia Retreat House - 158 Delavergne Ave., Wappingers Falls, NY 12590; Mailing: PO Box 858, Wappingers Falls, NY 12590 t) 845-297-5706 mtalverniaretreat@gmail.com www.mtalvernia.org Rev. Paul Guido, O.F.M., In Res.; Rev. Mario Julian, O.F.M., Dir.; Rev. Thomas Garone, O.F.M., In Res.; Rev. Armand Padula, O.F.M., In Res.;

SEMINARIES [SEM]

BEACON
St. Lawrence of Brindisi Friary - 180 Sargent Ave., Beacon, NY 12508-3993 t) 845-831-0394 stlfriary@gmail.com Bro. Rudolph Pieretti, O.F.M. Cap, Vicar; Bro. Carlos Hernandez, O.F.M.Cap., Supr.;
STATEN ISLAND
Society of St. Paul - 2187 Victory Blvd., Staten Island, NY 10314 t) 718-761-0047 c) 917-515-8798 provincialoffice@stpauls.us www.stpaulsusa.com Rev. Matthew Roehrig, S.S.P., Supr.; Bro. Tim Joshua Seidl Douglas, Supr.; Rev. Tony Bautista, Prov.; Marco Bulgarelli, Sec. & Treas.; Bro. Donald Dominic Calabro, CTNY Production Assistant;
SUFFERN
Tagaste Monastery - 220 Lafayette Ave., Suffern, NY 10901 t) 845-357-0067 tagastesuffern@gmail.com www.tagastemonastery.org Major Seminary of the Province of St. Augustine of the Augustinian Recollect Fathers & Brothers Rev. Fidel Hernandez, O.A.R., In Res.; Rev. John Oldfield, O.A.R., In Res.; Rev. John Gruben, O.A.R., Prior; Rev. Michael Rafferty, Prior;
YONKERS
Cathedral Prep Program - 201 Seminary Ave., Yonkers, NY 10704 t) 914-968-1340 cprep@archny.org www.nypriest.com Rev. Christopher Argano, Dir.;
St. Joseph's Seminary - 201 Seminary Ave., Yonkers, NY 10704-1896 t) 914-968-6200 sjs@archny.org dunwoodie.edu Most Rev. James Massa, Rector; Rev. William Cleary, Vice Rector; Rev. Michael Bruno, Dean of Seminarians; Rev. Matthew S. Ernest, Academic

Dean; Rev. Msgr. Steven J. Aguggia, Adjunct Professor; Rev. Thomas V. Berg, Prof.; Rev. Seraphim Pio Baalbaki, C.F.R., Adjunct Professor; Rev. Charles Caccavale, Director of Spiritual Formation (Acting); Rev. Christopher Cullen, S.J., Adjunct Professor; Rev. John P. Cush, Prof.; Rev. William S. Elder, Prof.; Very Rev. Joseph R. Gibino, Adjunct Professor; Rev. Msgr. Donald A. Guglielmi, Adjunct Professor; Rev. Peter Andrew Heasley, Adjunct Professor; Rev. David Monaco, C.P., Prof.; Rev. Ryan Muldoon, Adjunct Professor; Rev. John O'Neill, Adjunct Professor; Dcn. Thomas Rich, Adjunct Professor; Bro. Owen Sadlier, O.S.F., Prof.; Rev. Luis Saldana, Adjunct Professor; Rev. Msgr. Robert J. Sarno, Prof.; Rev. Timothy J. Scannell, Adjunct Professor; Rev. Richard G. Smith, Adjunct Professor; Rev. Msgr. Robert Thelen, Adjunct Professor; Rev. Mark G. Vaillancourt, Adjunct Professor; Rev. Carlos C. Velasquez, Adjunct Professor; Rev. Richard Veras, Director of Pastoral Formation; Stds.: 62; Bro. Tchrs.: 1; Lay Tchrs.: 7; Pr. Tchrs.: 11

SHRINES [SHR]

NEW YORK

St. Frances X. Cabrini Shrine - 701 Fort Washington Ave., New York, NY 10040 t) 212-923-3536 jattaway@cabrinishrinenyc.org cabrinishrinenyc.com Julia Attaway, Exec. Dir.;

SPECIAL CARE FACILITIES [SPF]

BARRYVILLE

New Hope Manor - 35 Hillside Rd., Barryville, NY 12719 t) 845-557-8353 newhopemnr@aol.com www.newhopemanor.org Sr. Maureen Conway, O.P., Dir.; Barrie Jacobsen, Dir.; Bro. Charles Kinney, S.A., Dir.; Sr. Margaret Murphy, O.P., Dir.;

BEACON

Metropolitan Association of Contemplative Communities, Inc. - 89 Hiddenbrooke Dr., Beacon, NY 12508 t) 845-831-5572 macc.catholic.org Sr. Michaelene Devine, O.C.D., Contact;

Metropolitan Association of Contemplative Communities, Inc. - 89 Hiddenbrooke Dr., Beacon, NY 12508 t) 845-831-3132 rednunsny@gmail.com macc.catholic.org Sr. Moira Quinn, O.SS.R., Contact;

BLAUVELT

St. Dominic's Family Services, St. Dominic's Home - 500 Western Hwy., Blauvelt, NY 10913 t) 845-359-3400 jkydon@sdomhome.org www.stdominicshome.org Judith D. Kydon, Pres.;

Community Based Services/Waiver - 1 Fordham Plaza, Ste. 901, Bronx, NY 10458 t) 718-295-9112

Community residences for developmentally disabled -

Community residences for mentally ill -

St. Dominic's School - Serves children and adolescents with emotional disabilities, K-12th.

Foster Care - 853 Longwood Ave., Ste. 202, Bronx, NY 10459 t) 917-645-9100

Friends of St. Dominic's Inc. - smflood@sdfs.org Sr. Margaret Flood, O.P., Pres.;

Torch Annex - 2195 Valentine Ave., Bronx, NY 10457

TORCH (To Reach Children) - 2340 Andrews Ave., Bronx, NY 10468 t) 718-365-7238

BRONX

Centro Maria, Inc. - 3103 Arlington Ave, Bronx, NY 10463 t) (718) 708-4661 c) (347) 499-7169 cmarianewyork@gmail.com; centromaria.ny.residence@gmail.com www.religiosasmariainmaculada.org Dormitory for young women (18-29 years old). Sr. Clara Nayade Echeverria Romero, RMI, Supr.; Bed Capacity: 25; Asstd. Annu.: 25; Staff: 6

Saint Dominic's Home - Prevention Program (ASTAAN) - 2345 University Ave., Bronx, NY 10468 t) 718-584-4407 kthompson@sdomhome.org www.stdominicshome.org/friends Parent Aide Counseling Advocacy Information and Referral.

St. Eleanora's Home for Convalescents - Sisters of Charity Center, 6301 Riverdale Ave., Bronx, NY 10471-1046 t) 718-549-9200 mobrien@scny.org scny.org Sr. Margaret M. O'Brien, Treas.; Asstd. Annu.: 25; Staff: 7

Kolping-on-Concourse - 2916 Grand Concourse, Bronx, NY 10458 t) 718-733-6119 kolpingconcourse@yahoo.com www.kolpingny.org Catholic Kolping Society New York, Inc. Residence for working Catholics and students Katrina Dengler, Vice. Pres.; Kelly Moeller, Bus. Mgr.;

Lavelle School for the Blind - 3830 Paulding Ave., Bronx, NY 10469 t) 718-882-1212 info@lavelleschool.org www.lavelleschool.org Sisters of St. Dominic of Blauvelt Dr. Rebecca Renshaw, Dir.; Staff: 115

GARRISON

St. Christopher's Inn (Atonement Friars) - 21 Franciscan Way, Garrison, NY 10524-0150; Mailing: P.O. Box 150, Garrison, NY 10524-0150 t) 845-335-1000 dpolanco@atonementfriars.org www.stchristophersinn-graymoor.org Rev. Dennis Polanco, S.A., Pres.;

HAWTHORNE

Rosary Hill Home (The Servants of Relief for Incurable Cancer) - 600 Linda Ave, Hawthorne, NY 10532 t) 914-769-0114 sisterdamien@gmail.com www.rosaryhillhome.org Sr. Stella Mary Morales, Admin.; Sr. Mary Damien, Supr.; Bed Capacity: 54; Asstd. Annu.: 73; Staff: 39

MONTROSE

Kolping-on-Hudson - 95 Montrose Point Rd., Montrose, NY 10548 t) 914-736-0117 kohmanager95@gmail.com www.kolpingny.org Catholic Kolping Society New York, Inc. Gerhard A. Schmitt, Pres.; Katrina Dengler, Vice. Pres.;

MOUNT VERNON

St. Theresa's Residence - 30 S. 10th Ave., Mount Vernon, NY 10550 t) 914-664-5900 John Schroeder, Exec.;

NEW YORK

St. Agnes' Residence - 237 W. 74th St., New York, NY 10023 t) 212-874-1361 For students and working women. Nancy Clifford, Admin.;

Catholic Charities Community Services Beacon of Hope House Division - 1011 First Ave., New York, NY 10022 t) 212-371-1000 denise.bauer@archny.org www.archny.org Joy Jasper, Dir.; Michele Miller, Dir.; Harold Moss, Dir.; Deborah Neal, Dir.; Seth Poloso, Dir.; Dennis Scimone, Dir.;

Beacon of Hope House Bronx Congregate Services - 1400 Waters Pl., Bronx, NY 10461 t) 718-892-3494 Jacqueline Rosario-Perez, Dir.;

Beacon of Hope House Staten Island Supervised Programs - 777 Seaview Ave., Bldg. D, 2nd Fl., Staten Island, NY 10305 t) 718-980-1072

Bronx Supported Housing - 2510 Westchester Ave., Ste. 210, Bronx, NY 10461 t) 718-239-5206 Michael Harris, Dir.;

Highbridge Neighborhood Supported Housing Program - 1484 Nelson Ave., Ste. A, Bronx, NY 10452 t) 718-503-8106

Kingsborough Intensive Supported Apartment Program - 647 Vanderbilt Ave., Brooklyn, NY 11238 t) 718-398-4556

Staten Island Apartment Programs - 90-92 Hancock St., Staten Island, NY 10305 t) 718-979-6241

Terence Cardinal Cooke Residence - 2467 Bathgate Ave., Bronx, NY 10458 t) 718-367-6990; 718-367-5405 (TTY)

Catholic Charities Department of Housing, Housing Development Institute, Inc. - 1011 First Ave., New York, NY 10022 t) 212-371-1000 Rev. Msgr. Kevin L. Sullivan, Pres.;

Cor Mariae - c/o 1011 First Ave., Rm. 1130, New York, NY 10022 t) 212-371-1000 x2435 Residence for formerly homeless senior women.

Covenant House Under 21 - 550 10th Avenue, New York, NY 10018 t) 212-613-0300 info@covenanthouse.org ny.covenanthouse.org/ Sr. Nancy Downing, Exec.;

Crisis Center - Emergency Shelter.

Rights of Passage - Transition Housing.

The Dwelling Place of NY, Inc. (Franciscan Sisters of Allegany, Inc.) - 409 W. 40th St., New York, NY 10018 t) 212-564-7887 admin@thedwellingplaceofny.org www.thedwellingplaceofny.org Deborah Pollock, Admin.; Bed Capacity: 14; Asstd. Annu.: 2,000; Staff: 5

El Carmelo Residence - 249 W. 14th St., New York, NY 10011 t) 212-242-8224 Sr. Modesta Perez, Supr.;

St. Francis Counseling Center, Inc. - 135 W. 31st St., New York, NY 10001 t) 212-736-8500 www.stfrancisnyc.org Rev. Joseph F. Cavoto, OFM, Chap.;

Grace Institute - 40 Rector St., 14th Fl., New York, NY 10006 t) 212-832-7605 info@graceinstitute.org www.graceinstitute.org

The Jeanne d'Arc Residence - 253 W. 24th St., New York, NY 10011 t) 212-989-5952 jdaresidence@gmail.com Women. Eileen C. Piazza, Admin.;

Kolping Society of New York Residence (Catholic Kolping Society New York, Inc.) - 165 E. 88th St., New York, NY 10128 t) 212-369-6647 residence@kolpingny.org; kolpingny@gmail.com www.kolpingny.org Gerhard A. Schmitt, Pres.; Katrina Dengler, Vice. Pres.; Rev. Richard Bretone, Admin.;

The Leo House - 332 W. 23rd St., New York, NY 10011 t) 212-929-1010 ihreservations@332west23nyc.org www.leohousenyc.org Guesthouse Ashley Bryant, Exec.; Bed Capacity: 81; Asstd. Annu.: 38,204; Staff: 36

Little Sisters of the Assumption Family Health Service, Inc. - 333 E. 115th St., New York, NY 10029 t) 646-672-5200 info@lsafhs.org Reada Edelstein, CEO;

St. Mary's Residence - 225 E. 72nd St., New York, NY 10021 t) 212-249-6850 st.marysres72@aol.com; britofdc@aol.com www.stmarysresidence.org For students and working women. Sr. Almaisa Brito, F.D.C., Admin.; Lisa Rodriguez, Dir.; Bed Capacity: 152; Asstd. Annu.: 145; Staff: 11

New York Catholic Deaf Center - 65 E. 89th St., New York, NY 10128 t) 212-988-8563; 646-755-3086 (Video Phone) msgr.patrick.mccahill@archny.org www.deafcathnyc.org Rev. Msgr. Patrick P. McCahill, Dir.;

New York Foundling Charitable Corp. - 590 Avenue of the Americas, New York, NY 10011 t) 212-633-9300 www.nyfoundling.org William Baccaglini, Treas.;

Thorpe Family Residence, Inc. - 2252 Crotona Ave., New York, NY 10457 t) 718-933-7312 mcallaghan@nazarethhousingnyc.org thorpeonline.org Bernard Carr, Exec.;

OSSINING

Cardinal McCloskey Emergency Residential School - 155 N. Highland Ave., Ossining, NY 10562; Mailing: 115 Stevens Avenue, Suite LL5, Valhalla, NY 10595 t) 914-762-5302 bfinnerty@cmcs.org Beth Finnerty, Pres.;

SPRING VALLEY

Good Counsel, Inc. - 22 Linden Ave., Spring Valley, NY 10977 t) 845-356-0517; 800-723-8331 (Info & Referrals) www.postabortionhelp.org (Homes for Women) Mark Swartzberg, Chair; Christopher Bell, Pres.;

Good Counsel, Inc. - 38 Wiman Pl., Staten Island, NY 10305 t) 718-650-6994

Good Counsel, Inc. - 1157 Fulton Ave., Bronx, NY 10456 t) 718-312-3980 x10 www.goodcounselhomes.org

Good Counsel/Daystar Program - 205 E. Prospect Ave., Mount Vernon, NY 10550 t) 914-925-9834

VALHALLA

Cardinal McCloskey Community Services - 115 Stevens Ave., Valhalla, NY 10595 t) 914-997-8000 bfinnerty@cmcs.org www.cardinalmccloskeycommunityservices.org Beth Finnerty, Pres.; Asstd. Annu.: 3,632; Staff: 720

***Dominican Sisters Family Health Service, Inc. (DSFHS) (Corporate Office/Administration)** - 115 E. Stevens Ave., Valhalla, NY 10595 t) 914-810-2601 rscanga@dsfhs.org www.archcare.org/home-care Joint Commission Accredited Certified Home Health Agency. Tami Siedler, Vice. Pres.;

***Family Home Health Care, Inc.** - 65 S. Broadway,

Tarrytown, NY 10591 t) 914-631-7200 sniman@dsfhs.org (Licensed Home Health Care Affiliate) (LHCSA) Sharon Niman, Vice Pres. LCHSA Svcs.;

Family Home Health Care, Inc. - 3237 Rte. 112, Bldg. 6, Medford, NY 11763 t) 631-289-9560 sniman@dsfhs.org (Licensed Home Health Care Affiliate) (LHCSA) Sharon Niman, Vice Pres. LCHSA Svcs.;

Hudson Valley Offices - 299 N. Highland Ave., Bldg. 4, Ossining, NY 10562 t) 914-941-1710 acrane@dsfhs.org Ann Crane, Admin.;

New York City Offices - 279 Alexander Ave., Bronx, NY 10454 t) 718-665-6557 Mary Lou Harren-Matamoras, Admin.;

Suffolk County Office - 3237 Rte. 112, Bldg. 6, Medford, NY 11763 t) 631-736-1527

Suffolk County Office - 103-6 W. Montauk Hwy., Hampton Bays, NY 11946 t) 631-728-0181 ptobin@dsfhs.org www.dsfhs.org Patricia Tobin, Admin.;

WEST PARK

St. Cabrini Home - Rte. 9W, West Park, NY 12493; Mailing: P.O. Box 69, West Park, NY 12493 t) 212-375-0752; 732-547-5452 mlefante@msshnyc.org

YONKERS

Contemplative Outreach, Ltd. - 1 David Ln., Apt. 7H, Yonkers, NY 10701 t) 914-423-4888 office@coutreach.org www.contemplativeoutreach.org Patricia Johnson, Admin.; Rt. Rev. Thomas Keating, O.C.S.O., Dir.;

John A. Coleman School (Elizabeth Seton Children's School) - 300 Corporate Blvd. S., Yonkers, NY 10701 t) 914-294-6200 mtomkiel@setonchildrens.org; sherl@setonchildrens.org www.setonchildrens.org Sponsored by the Sisters of Charity Ministry Network Sharon Herl, Prin.; Maureen Tomkiel, Exec.; Bed Capacity: 216; Asstd. Annu.: 900; Staff: 262

An asterisk (*) denotes an organization that has established tax-exempt status directly with the IRS and is not covered by the USCCB Group Ruling.

Diocese of Norwich

(Dioecesis Norvicensis)

MOST REVEREND MICHAEL R. COTE, D.D.

Bishop of Norwich; ordained June 29, 1975; appointed Titular Bishop of Cebarades and Auxiliary Bishop of Portland May 9, 1995; ordained July 27, 1995; appointed Bishop of Norwich March 11, 2003; installed May 14, 2003. Res.: 274 Broadway, Norwich, CT 06360.

Chancery: 201 Broadway, Norwich, CT 06360. T: 860-887-9294; F: 860-886-1670.
www.norwichdiocese.org

ESTABLISHED AUGUST 6, 1953.

Square Miles 1,978.

Corporate Title: The Norwich Roman Catholic Diocesan Corporation.

Comprises the Counties of Middlesex, New London, Tolland and Windham in the State of Connecticut and Fishers Island, a portion of Suffolk County in the State of New York.

For legal titles of parishes and diocesan institutions, consult the Chancery Office.

STATISTICAL OVERVIEW

Personnel
Bishop....1
Priests: Diocesan Active in Diocese....56
Priests: Diocesan Active Outside Diocese....2
Priests: Diocesan in Foreign Missions....3
Priests: Retired, Sick or Absent....17
Number of Diocesan Priests....78
Religious Priests in Diocese....32
Total Priests in your Diocese....110
Extern Priests in Diocese....4
Ordinations:
Diocesan Priests....1
Permanent Deacons in Diocese....55
Total Brothers....11
Total Sisters....118

Parishes
Parishes....51
With Resident Pastor:
Resident Diocesan Priests....47
Resident Religious Priests....2
Without Resident Pastor:
Administered by Priests....2
Missions....2
Pastoral Centers....7

Professional Ministry Personnel:
Brothers....2
Sisters....17
Lay Ministers....7

Welfare
Homes for the Aged....2
Total Assisted....442
Special Centers for Social Services....6
Total Assisted....23,185

Educational
Students from Other Dioceses....2
Diocesan Students in Other Seminaries....4
Seminaries, Religious....1
Students, Religious....26
Total Seminarians....30
Colleges and Universities....1
High Schools, Diocesan and Parish....3
Total Students....1,251
High Schools, Private....1
Total Students....28
Elementary Schools, Diocesan and Parish....9
Total Students....1,304
Catechesis/Religious Education:
High School Students....446
Elementary Students....2,630
Total Students under Catholic Instruction....5,689
Teachers in Diocese:
Priests....2
Sisters....9
Lay Teachers....149

Vital Statistics
Receptions into the Church:
Infant Baptism Totals....811
Minor Baptism Totals....39
Adult Baptism Totals....25
Received into Full Communion....51
First Communions....725
Confirmations....926
Marriages:
Catholic....186
Interfaith....34
Total Marriages....220
Deaths....1,602
Total Catholic Population....228,520
Total Population....710,975

LEADERSHIP

Office of the Bishop - Most Rev. Michael R. Cote (bpcote@norwichdiocese.net); Dcn. Jorge Escalona, Master of Ceremonies; Alice Pelletier, Admin. Asst. (alice@norwichdiocese.net);
Chancery - t) 860-887-9294
Vicar General - Rev. Msgr. Leszek T. Janik (vicargeneral@norwichdiocese.net); Terri Zampini, Secy. (financeterriz@norwichdiocese.net);
Chancellor - Rev. Peter J. Langevin, Chancellor; Becky Cady, Secy. (becky@norwichdiocese.net);
Vice Chancellor - Rev. Brian J. Romanowski (ajudicialvicar@norwichdiocese.net);
Vicar for Clergy - Rev. Dennis M. Perkins (vicarclergy@norwichdiocese.net); Alice Pelletier, Sec. (alice@norwichdiocese.net);
Diaconate: Office of Permanent Deacon Personnel - www.norwichdeacons.org Dcn. Douglas A. Hoffman;
Diocesan Attorney - t) 860-889-3321 Michael E. Driscoll;
Diocesan Finance Office - t) 860-887-9294 Karen Huffer, Diocesan Finance Officer; Janet West, Finance Analyst; Alec Ogborne, Benefits Admin.;
College of Consultors - Rev. Peter J. Langevin; Rev. Michael L. Phillippino; Rev. Brian J. Romanowski (ajudicialvicar@norwichdiocese.net);
Presbyteral Council - Rev. Michael Castiblanco; Rev. Roland C. Cloutier; Rev. Anthony J. DiMarco;
Deans - Rev. Msgr. Leszek T. Janik, Norwich (vicargeneral@norwichdiocese.net); Rev. Laurence A.M. LaPointe, Willimantic; Rev. Richard J. Ricard, Vernon;
Diocesan Pastoral Council - Most Rev. Michael R. Cote, Chair (bpcote@norwichdiocese.net); Rev. Msgr. Leszek T. Janik (vicargeneral@norwichdiocese.net); Rev. Ted F. Tumicki;
Diocesan Historian - t) 845-869-3154 Rev. Gregoire J. Fluet, Archivist;

OFFICES AND DIRECTORS

Annual Catholic Appeal (ACA) -
Bishop's Delegate for Safe Environments - Rev. Brian J. Romanowski (ajudicialvicar@norwichdiocese.net);
Bishop's Liaison with Retired Clergy - t) 860-887-9294 Rev. Roland C. Cloutier;
Board of Conciliation and Arbitration - Rev. Brian J. Romanowski, Exec. (ajudicialvicar@norwichdiocese.net);
Campaigns -
  Campaign for Human Development - t) 860-887-9294 x234 Alice Pelletier;
  Catholic Relief Services - Rev. Peter J. Langevin, Dir.; Becky Cady;
Campus Ministry - t) 860-423-0856 Rev. Laurence A.M. LaPointe, Dir.;
  Middletown - Wesleyan University -
  New London - Connecticut College, Harkness Chapel - t) 860-439-2450
  Storrs - St. Thomas Aquinas Chapel - t) 860-429-6436
  Willimantic - Eastern Connecticut State University - Rev. Laurence A.M. LaPointe, Campus Min.;
Catechetical Ministry -
Catholic Charities, Diocese of Norwich, Inc. - Keyla Santos (keylasantos@ccfsn.org); Susan Connelly, COO;
  Adoption Services - t) 860-889-8346 terrifontaine@ccfsn.org Terri Fontaine;
  Chief Operations Office - t) (860) 889-1022 Susan Connelly;
  Intensive Case Management/Emergency Basic Needs - t) 860-443-5328; 860-423-7065; 860-889-8346; (860) 823-0109
  Pregnancy Services & Education - t) (860) 823-1014 Terri Fontaine;
The Catholic Foundation - t) 860-886-1928 Mary Ellen Mahoney, Dir. (memahoney@norwichdiocese.net);
Catholic Mutual Relief Society - Robin Holtsclaw, Claims/Risk Mgr. (rholtsclaw@catholicmutual.org);
Catholic Youth Organization (CYO) -
Cemetery Corporation and Subsidiaries, Diocesan Cemeteries - t) 860-887-1019 Melissa Egbert, Contact (melissae@norwichdiocese.net); Joseph M. Muscarella, Dir.;
  Moosup -
  New London - t) 860-887-1019
  Norwich - t) (860) 887-1019 Joseph M. Muscarella, Dir.;
  Taftville -
  Uncasville -
  Wauregan -
  Westbrook - t) 860-887-1019
Censor of Books - t) 860-423-8439 Rev. Laurence A.M. LaPointe;
Chaplain and Director of Twinning in Haiti - Rev. Francis Rouleau;
Communications, Office of - t) 860-887-3933 Wayne Gignac; Dcn. Benedict LoCasto, Mktg./Production Mgr.; Ryan Blessing, Sr. Writer & Social Media;
  Four County Catholic Magazine - t) 860-886-1281; (860) 887-3933 Wayne Gignac, Editor; Most Rev. Michael R. Cote, Publisher; Rev. Ted F. Tumicki, Theological Advisor;
    Publisher - Most Rev. Michael R. Cote, Bishop of Norwich;
    Theological Advisor - Rev. Ted F. Tumicki;
Community Ministries -
  St. Vincent de Paul Middletown - t) 860-344-0097 Maryellen Shuckerow, Exec.; Terry Carbone, Dir.;
  St. Vincent de Paul - t) 860-889-7374 Jillian Corbin, Exec.;
Connecticut Catholic Conference - t) 860-524-7882 Christopher Healy, Exec.; Dcn. David Reynolds, Legislative Liaison (ccc@ctcatholic.org);
Continuing Education and Formation Commission for the Clergy - Rev. Grzegorz P. Brozonowicz; Rev. David P. Choquette; Rev. Peter B. Liszewski;
Council of Catholic Women - t) 860-887-1565 Rev. Michael L. Phillippino, Willimantic Deanery; Rev. Brian Maxwell, Diocesan Spiritual Advisor; Rev. Stephen S. Gulino, Norwich Deanery;
Delegate for Internal Investigations - Richard Wheeler;
Development, Diocesan Office of (DOD) - t) 860-886-1928 Mary Ellen Mahoney, Exec. (memahoney@norwichdiocese.net); Heather Harris, Campaign Mgr.; Rosela Precopio, Office Admin.;
Diocesan Finance Council - William J. Russell; Most Rev. Michael R. Cote, Chair (bpcote@norwichdiocese.net); Rev. Msgr. Leszek T. Janik (vicargeneral@norwichdiocese.net);
Diocesan Panel of Pastors, Canon 1742 - Rev. Msgr. Anthony S. Rosaforte; Rev. Dennis M. Perkins (vicarclergy@norwichdiocese.net); Rev. Richard J. Ricard;
Diocesan Pastoral Council - Most Rev. Michael R. Cote, Chair (bpcote@norwichdiocese.net); Rev. Msgr. Leszek T. Janik; Rev. Ted F. Tumicki;
Ecumenism -
  Ecumenical and Interreligious Affairs, Office of (Vacant) - t) 860-887-9294 x100
Evangelization & Catechumenate (RCIA), Office of -
Faith Events, Office of - t) 860-848-2237 x203 faithevents@norwichdiocese.net Andrea Hoisl, Dir.; Liza Roach, Youth Min.; Marianne Nicholas, Admin. Asst. (manicholas@norwichdiocese.net);
  Catholic Family Services - Mary-Jo McLaughlin, Coord.;
  Deaf Ministry - Andrea Hoisl, Coord.;
  Diocesan Catholic Scouting - scouting@norwichdiocese.net Pam Plasse, Chair;
  One Heart Ministry - Andrea Hoisl, Dir.;
Faith Formation, Office for -
Haiti, Diocese of Norwich Outreach to, Inc. - t) 860-800-3601 Susan Wallace, Exec.;
Hispanic Ministry - t) 860-456-3349 Mother Mary Jude Lazarus, S.C.M.C., Dir. (aposthispano@gmail.com);
  Clinton - t) (860) 669-8512 Sr. Gloria Saldarriaga, R.O.D.A.;
    St. Mary of the Visitation Church - Spanish Apostolate - t) 860-669-8512 Sr. Gloria Saldarriaga, R.O.D.A., Pst. Assoc.; Rev. Juan Angel Aguirre Palacio;
  Middletown -
    St. Francis of Assisi Church - Spanish Apostolate - t) 860-347-4684 Rev. Russell F. Kennedy, Pst.; Dcn. Octavio Flores; Sr. Gloria Saldarriaga, R.O.D.A., Pst. Assoc.;
  New London -
    St. Mary, Star of the Sea Church - Spanish Apostolate - t) 860-447-1431 stmarysnl@aol.com Rev. Mark D. O'Donnell, Pst.; Dcn. Jesus A. Diez-Canseco; Sr. Estela Moya Solano, R.O.D.A., Pst. Assoc.;
  Norwich -
    St. Mary Church - Spanish Apostolate - t) 860-887-2565 c) 860-694-9474 Rev. Robert Washabaugh; Sr. Leidy Castillo, R.O.D.A., Pst. Assoc.;
  Windham -
    Iglesia del Sagrado Corazon de Jesus - t) 860-423-8617 Rev. Laurence A.M. LaPointe, Pst.; Dcn. Felipe Silva, Pst. Assoc.; Sr. Leidy Castillo, R.O.D.A., Pst. Assoc.;
Holy Childhood -
Holy Name Societies - t) 860-887-9294
Insurance -
Justice & Peace -
Lawyers, Guild of Catholic - t) 860-887-9294 Michael E. Driscoll, Pres.; Terri Zampini, Sec. (financeterriz@norwichdiocese.net);
Legion of Mary - t) 860-447-1431 Rev. Victor Chaker, Spiritual Adv./Care Srvcs.;
Marriage Encounter/Catholic Family Services - t) (860) 848-2237 x312 Mary-Jo McLaughlin;
Mercy Xavier Fund - t) 860-346-7735 David Eustis, Headmaster;
Office of Diocesan Properties & Cemeteries - t) 860-887-1019 Joseph M. Muscarella, Dir.;
Office of Internal Affairs - t) 860-889-4455; 800-624-7407 Richard Wheeler, Bishop's Delegate for Internal Investigations; Dcn. Benedict LoCasto, Assistance Coord.;
People with Disabilities -
Planned Giving - Mary Ellen Mahoney (memahoney@norwichdiocese.net);
Planned Giving Office - Mary Ellen Mahoney (memahoney@norwichdiocese.net);
Pontifical Association of the Holy Childhood - t) 860-887-9294 Rev. P. Grzegorz Jednaki;
Pontifical Society for the Propagation of the Faith - t) 860-564-3313 standrebparish@gmail.com Rev. P. Grzegorz Jednaki, Dir.;
Prison Ministry for Diocese of Norwich - t) 860-848-2237 x211 prison@norwichdiocese.net
  Niantic -
    York Correctional Institution - t) 860-691-6529 Dcn. William Dziatko, Chap.;
  Somers -
    Northern Correctional Institution - t) 860-763-8686 Dcn. Ramon Rosado, Chap.; Dcn. Michael Torres, Chap.;
    Osborn Correctional Institution - t) 860-749-8391 x5476 Rev. Robert Vujs, M.M., Chap.; Dcn. Ramon Rosado, Chap.;
    Willard-Cybulski Correctional Institution - t) 860-763-6599 Dcn. Michael Torres;
  Uncasville -
    Corrigan-Radgowski Correctional Institution - t) 860-848-5034
Pro-Life Activities - t) 860-434-1669 Rev. Walter M. Nagle, Dir.;
Property and Assets Committee - Karen Huffer; Joseph M. Muscarella; Rev. Peter J. Langevin;
RCIA -
Religious -
Retirement -
  Priests' Retirement Plan Board - Most Rev. Michael R. Cote; Rev. Dennis M. Perkins; Rev. Msgr. Leszek T. Janik;
Safe Environments, Office of - t) 860-848-2237

ose@norwichdiocese.net Rev. Brian J. Romanowski, Bishop's Delegate (ajudicialvicar@norwichdiocese.net); Kathy D'Amelio, Dir.;
School Office, Diocesan - t) 860-445-0611 superintendentdso@norwichdiocese.net www.norwichdso.org Gail Kingston, Supt.;
Scouting -
Sick, Ministry to the - t) 860-889-8331 x2298
Soup Kitchen - svdpp@sbcglobal.net Jillian Corbin (jcsvdpp@gmail.com);
Spanish Speaking Apostolate -
Spiritual Renewal Services - t) (860) 848-2237 x210 srs1223@sbcglobal.net Rev. Raymond D. Intovigne, Chap.;
Stewardship - Gina Foster;
Vicar for Consecrated Life - t) 860-635-5590 Friar Mark L. Curesky, O.F.M.Conv.;
Victim Assistance Coordinator - t) 800-624-7407 Dcn. Benedict LoCasto;
Vocation - t) 860-887-9294 Rev. Jonathan J. Ficara, Dir.; Terri Zampini, Secy. (financeterriz@norwichdiocese.net);
Seminarian Advisory Board - Rev. Brian J. Converse; Rev. Mark D. O'Donnell; Rev. Dennis M. Perkins;
Worship, Office of - t) 860-848-2237 x203

TRIBUNAL

Diocesan Tribunal - t) 860-887-9294
Adjutant Judicial Vicar - Rev. Brian J. Romanowski, Vicar;
Administrative Assistant of the Tribunal - David Ostafin;
Advocate - Jacqueline M. Keller;
Auditor/Assessors - Sr. Elissa Rinere, C.P.; Jacqueline M. Keller;
Defender of the Bond - Sr. Elissa Rinere, C.P.; Rev. Jeffrey R. Ellis;
Judges - Rev. Msgr. Leszek T. Janik; Rev. George J. Richards Jr.; Rev. Brian J. Romanowski;
Judicial Vicar - Rev. Ted F. Tumicki;
Notaries - Alice Pelletier; David Ostafin;

PARISHES, MISSIONS, AND CLERGY

STATE OF CONNECTICUT

ASHFORD

St. Philip the Apostle - 64 Pompey Hollow Rd., Ashford, CT 06278-1540 t) 860-429-2860 saintphilipct.com Rev. Michael C. Giannitelli, Pst.; CRP Stds.: 26

BALTIC

St. Mary of the Immaculate Conception - 70 W. Main St., Baltic, CT 06330-1348 t) 860-822-6378 saintjosephschool@att.net Yoked with St. Joseph, Occum and Sacred Heart, Taftville Rev. Joseph Tito, Pst.; Rev. Christopher J. Zmuda, Assoc. Pst.; CRP Stds.: 40
St. Joseph - 10 School Hill Rd., Baltic, CT 06330 t) 860-822-6141 st33@snet.net Sr. Mary Patrick Mulready, S.C.M.C., Prin.;

BOLTON

St. Maurice - 32 Hebron Rd., Bolton, CT 06043-7606 t) 860-643-4466 saintmauricechurchbolton@gmail.com Rev. William J. Olesik, Pst.;

BROOKLYN

Our Lady of La Salette - 21 Providence Rd., Brooklyn, CT 06234-0211; Mailing: P.O. Box 211, Brooklyn, CT 06234-0211 t) 860-774-6275 ourladybrooklyn@gmail.com Rev. Ben Vinjoe, Admin.; Manon Meunier, DRE; CRP Stds.: 25
Our Lady of Lourdes - 41 Cedar Swamp Rd., Hampton, CT 06247

CLINTON

St. Mary Church of the Visitation - 54 Grove St., Clinton, CT 06413-1999 t) 860-669-7375 (CRP); 860-669-8512 godsquad@stmarysclinton.org stmarysclinton.com Margo Burke, Youth Min.; Peggy Abbott, DRE; Rev. Daniel Long, Pst.; Rev. Juan Angel Aguirre Palacio, Par. Vicar; CRP Stds.: 190

COLCHESTER

Guardian Angels Parish - 128 Norwich Ave., Colchester, CT 06415-1269 t) 860-537-2355 parishoffice@guardianangelsparishofcolchester.org www.guardianangelsparishofcolchester.org/ Rev. Marek Masnicki, Pst.; Rev. Richard D. Breton, Assoc. Pst.; Ron Kristofik, DRE; CRP Stds.: 181

COLUMBIA

Good Shepherd Parish (Church of the Holy Family of Hebron, Incorporated) - 328 Junction Rts. 66 and 87, Columbia, CT 06237-0146; Mailing: P.O. Box 146, Columbia, CT 06237-0146 t) 860-228-3727 sec.stcolumba@sbcglobal.net Rev. Michael L. Phillippino, Pst.; CRP Stds.: 123

COVENTRY

Our Lady Queen of Peace Parish - 1600 Main St., Coventry, CT 06238-0250 t) 860-742-0681 (St Mary Coventry); 860-742-1092 (CRP); 860-429-6436 (St Thomas Aquinas Storrs) info@olqop.com; olqopreligioused@gmail.com www.olqop.com Rev. Gregory P. Galvin, Pst.; Dcn. Kim Thompson; Rebecca Holmes, DRE; CRP Stds.: 83

CROMWELL

St. John - 5 St. Johns Court, Cromwell, CT 06416-2118 t) 860-635-5590 (CRP); 860-635-5156 sjcffdre@gmail.com; pastormarkc@yahoo.com www.saintjohn-cromwell.org Friar Mark L. Curesky, O.F.M.Conv., Pst.; Karen Romegialli, DRE; CRP Stds.: 285

DANIELSON

St. James - 12 Franklin St., Danielson, CT 06239 t) 860-774-8459 (CRP); 860-774-3900 stjames_parish@yahoo.com Dcn. Rene N. Barbeau Jr.; Rev. Thomas Sickler, M.S., Assoc. Pst.; Rev. John E. Welch, M.S., In Res.; Rev. Roy Parayill, M.S., Pst.; CRP Stds.: 90
St. James School - (Grades PreK-8) 120 Water St., Danielson, CT 06239 t) 860-774-3281 c.benoit@stjamesdanielson.org; l.joyal@stjamesdanielson.org www.stjamesdanielson.org Linda Joyal, Prin.;

DURHAM

Our Lady of Mercy Parish - 272 Main St., Durham, CT 06422-1611 t) 860-349-3058; 860-349-3059 (CRP) scndchurches@comcast.net; scndfaith@gmail.com ourladyofmercyparish.org Rev. Jan Swiderski, Pst.; Diana Cathcart, CRE; CRP Stds.: 234

EAST HAMPTON

St. John Paul II - 47 W. High St., East Hampton, CT 06424 t) 860-267-6644 stpatrick47@sbcglobal.net Rev. Dariusz K. Dudzik, J.C.L., Pst.; Sr. Dominic Joseph Valla, A.S.C.J., Pst. Assoc.; Dcn. Dan D'Amelio;

EAST LYME

Saint Matthias Church Corporation - 317 Chesterfield Rd., East Lyme, CT 06333; Mailing: 22 Haigh Ave., Niantic, CT 06357 t) 860-739-9722 office.stjohn23@gmail.com; dre.agnesmatthias@gmail.com www.saintagnescatholicchurch.com Yoked with Saint Agnes, Niantic Rev. Gregory C. Mullaney, Pst.; Meghan Cambridge, DRE;

ELLINGTON

St. Luke - 141 Maple St., Ellington, CT 06029-0246; Mailing: P.O. Box 246, Ellington, CT 06029-0246 t) 860-875-4951 (CRP); 860-875-8552 stlukedre@comcast.net; stluke_ellington@comcast.net Dcn. Frank Hann; Rev. Bijoy Joseph, CFT, Par. Vicar; Rev. George Villamthanam, C.S.T., Admin.; Kim Bocchino, DRE;

ESSEX

Saint Teresa of Calcutta Parish - 14 Prospect St., Essex, CT 06426-1049 t) 860-767-1284; 860-767-1074 (CRP) officeolos@comcast.net Rev. Arul Rajan Peter, Pst.; Dcn. William Kaiser Jr.; Dcn. Lawrence Moneypenny; CRP Stds.: 73

GALES FERRY

Our Lady of Lourdes - 1650 Rte. 12, Gales Ferry, CT 06335-1534 t) 860-464-7251 www.ololgf.org Rev. Brian J. Converse, Pst.; Dcn. Douglas A. Hoffman; Debbie Sijkowicz, Bus. Mgr.; Josephine Cometa, DRE; CRP Stds.: 91

GROTON

St. Mary Mother of the Redeemer - 69 Groton Long Point Rd., Groton, CT 06340 t) 860-445-1446 office@stmarysgroton.org stmarysgroton.org Yoked with Sacred Heart Church, Groton and Our Lady of Lourdes, Gales Ferry, CT Rev. Brian J. Converse, Pst.; Rev. Brian Maxwell, Par. Vicar; Dcn. Douglas A. Hoffman; Catherine A Hoffman, DRE;
Sacred Heart - 56 Sacred Heart Dr., Groton, CT 06340-4431 t) (860) 445-1446 x12; (896) 445-1446 dre@sacredheartgroton.org; secretary@sacredheartgroton.org sacredheartgroton.org Yoked with St. Mary Mother of the Redeemer Church, Groton, CT and Our Lady of Lourdes, Gales Ferry, CT. Rev. Brian J. Converse, Pst.; Rev. Brian Maxwell, Par. Vicar; Dcn. Douglas A. Hoffman; Catherine A Hoffman, DRE; CRP Stds.: 129
Sacred Heart School - (Grades PreK-8) 50 Sacred Heart Dr., Groton, CT 06340-4431 t) 460-445-0611 principal@sacredheartgroton.org Gail Kingston, Prin.;

HIGGANUM

St. Peter - 30 St. Peter Ln., Higganum, CT 06441-0707; Mailing: P.O. Box 707, Higganum, CT 06441-0707 t) 860-345-8018 stpeterhigganum@yahoo.com www.stpeterhigganum.com/ Yoked with St. Lawrence, Killingworth Rev. Joseph F. DeCosta, Pst.; Rev. Martin J.W. Jones, Par. Vicar; CRP Stds.: 88

JEWETT CITY

St. Mary - 34 N. Main St., Jewett City, CT 06351-2012 t) 860-376-2044 Yoked with St. Catherine of Siena, Preston & SS. Thomas & Anne, Voluntown. Rev. Ted F. Tumicki, Pst.; Rev. Thomas Griffin, Par. Vicar; Dcn. Bryan Jones;

KILLINGWORTH

St. Lawrence - 7 Hemlock Dr., Killingworth, CT 06419-2227 t) 860-663-2576 www.stlawrencechurch.com Yoked with St. Peter, Higganum Rev. Joseph F. DeCosta, Pst.; Rev. Martin J.W. Jones, Par. Vicar; Dcn. John A. Balchus; Dcn. Robert Ferraro; Eileen S. Boulay, Admin.; CRP Stds.: 84

MIDDLETOWN

St. Francis of Assisi - 10 Elm St., Middletown, CT 06457-4427 t) 860-347-4684 office@stfrancisct.org www.stfrancisct.com Rev. Russell F. Kennedy, Pst.; Dcn. Octavio Flores; CRP Stds.: 47
St. John - 19 John's Sq., Middletown, CT 06457-2201 t) 860-347-5626 stjohnsecretary@comcast.net www.saintjohnmiddletownct.weebly.com Yoked with Saint Sebastian, Middletown Rev. James Thaikoottathil, Pst.; Kathryn Connelly, DRE; Sr. Ann Mack, R.S.M., DRE; Rev. George Richards, Par. Vicar;
St. Mary of Czestochowa - 79 S. Main St., Middletown, CT 06457-3606 t) 860-347-2365 faithformation@stmarymiddletown.com; office@stmarymiddletown.com www.stmarymiddletown.com Erin Da Costa, D.R.E, DRE; Rev. Richard Sliwinski, Pst.; CRP Stds.: 50
St. Pius X - 310 Westfield St., Middletown, CT 06457-2080 t) 860-346-9100 (CRP); 860-347-4441 c.butler@saintpius.org; office@saintpius.org www.saintpius.org Rev. Martin Curtin, O.F.M., Cap., Pst.; Rev. Ernest Bedard, O.F.M., Cap., Par. Vicar; Bro. Brian Champoux, O.F.M., Cap., In Res.; Carol Butler, DRE; Natalia Nawrot, DRE; Rev. Matthias Wesnofske, O.F.M., Cap., In Res.; CRP Stds.: 238
St. Sebastian - 155 Washington St., Middletown, CT 06457-2800 t) 860-347-2638 church6892@att.net; pastor.st.sebastian@gmail.com stsebastianmiddletownct.weebley.com Yoked with St. John, Middletown Rev. James Thaikoottathil, Pst.;

MYSTIC

St. Patrick - 32 E. Main St., Mystic, CT 06355 t) 860-536-6808 (CRP); 860-536-1800 secretary@saintpatrickmystic.org stpatrickmystic.org Rev. Kevin M. Reilly, Pst.; Kate Kappes, DRE;

NEW LONDON

St. Brendan the Navigator Parish - 149 Montauk Ave., New London, CT 06320; Mailing: 37 Squire St., New London, CT 06320 t) 860-443-5393 www.saintjosephcatholicchurch.org. St. Brendan the Navigator Parish Rev. Mark D. O'Donnell, Pst.; Rev. Henry Agudelo, Assoc. Pst.; Rev. Anthony J. DiMarco, Assoc. Pst.;

St. Joseph School - (Grades K-8) 25 Squire St., New London, CT 06320 t) 860-442-1720 principal@sjsnl.org sjsnl.com

Our Lady of Grace - 37 Squire St., New London, CT 06320; Mailing: Alpine Ave., P.O. Box 425, Fishers Island, NY 06390 t) 631-788-7353 olog@fishersisland.net Yoked with St. Joseph Church, New London, CT, St. Mary Star of the Sea, New London, CT and St. Paul, Waterford, CT. Rev. Mark D. O'Donnell, Pst.; Rev. Henry Agudelo, Assoc. Pst.; Rev. Anthony J. DiMarco, Assoc. Pst.;

NIANTIC

St. Agnes - 22 Haigh Ave., Niantic, CT 06357-3129 t) 860-739-9722 office.stjohn23@gmail.com; dre.agnesmatthias@gmail.com saintagnescatholicchurch.com Yoked with St. Matthias, East Lyme Rev. Gregory C. Mullaney, Pst.; Meghan Cambridge, DRE;

Crescent Beach, St. Francis Chapel (Summer) -

NORWICH

St. Patrick Cathedral - 213 Broadway, Norwich, CT 06360-4307 t) 860-889-8441 stpatricknorwich@sbcglobal.net stpatsnorwich.org Rev. Msgr. Anthony S. Rosaforte, Rector; Rev. Peter J. Langevin, In Res.; Rev. Brian J. Romanowski, In Res.; Rev. Michael Bovino, Par. Vicar; CRP Stds.: 93

St. Patrick Cathedral School - 211 Broadway, Norwich, CT 06360 t) 860-889-4174 info@st-patrickschoolnorwich.org www.st-patrickschoolnorwich.org Catherine Reed, Prin.;

St. Joseph - 120 Cliff St., Norwich, CT 06360-5134 t) 860-887-4565 (CRP); 860-887-1565 stjosephnorwich@yahoo.com jnccfaith.org Yoked with Sacred Heart Church, Norwichtown Rev. Msgr. Leszek T. Janik, Pst.; Rev. James. J. Sucholet, Pst. Assoc.; CRP Stds.: 6

St. Mary - 70 Central Ave., Norwich, CT 06360-4794 t) 860-204-9875 (CRP); 860-887-2565 secretary@stmarys1845.org Yoked with SS Peter & Paul, Norwich Rev. Robert J. Washabaugh, Pst.; Sr. Leidy Castillo, R.O.D.A., Pst. Assoc.; Sr. Yannick Saieh, Pst. Assoc.; Maria Junco, DRE; CRP Stds.: 81

SS. Peter and Paul - 181 Elizabeth St., Norwich, CT 06360-6199 t) 860-887-9857 ssppnorwich@yahoo.com jnccfaith.org Cluster with St. Mary, Norwich, CT. Rev. Robert Washabaugh, Pst.; CRP Stds.: 14

NORWICHTOWN

Sacred Heart - 52 W. Town St., Norwichtown, CT 06360-2296 t) 860-887-1715 (CRP); 860-887-1030 sacredheart06360@gmail.com sacredheartnorwichct.org Yoked with St. Joseph Church, Norwich Rev. Msgr. Leszek T. Janik, Pst.; CRP Stds.: 13

St. John - 190 Fitchville Rd., Bozrah, CT 06334

OLD LYME

Christ the King - 1 McCurdy Rd., Old Lyme, CT 06371-1629 t) 860-434-1669; 860-434-9873 ctkoldlyme@aol.com; lyctkoldlyme@aol.com Rev. Joseph C. Ashe, Pst.; Rev. Walter M. Nagle, Par. Vicar; Louise Young, DRE; CRP Stds.: 135

OLD SAYBROOK

Saint Pio Parish - 161 Main St., Old Saybrook, CT 06475-2367 t) 860-388-3787 office@saintpioct.org www.saintpioct.org Rev. Grzegorz P. Brozonowicz, Pst.; Rev. Martin S. Noe, Assoc. Pst.; Dcn. Nicholas J. Iassogna Jr.; Dcn. Thomas E. Rymut; CRP Stds.: 146

PAWCATUCK

St. Michael's Church, Pawcatuck Parish - 60 Liberty St., Pawcatuck, CT 06379 t) 860-599-5580 akapolowicz@stmichaelpawcatuck.com www.stmichaelpawcatuck.com Rev. Dennis M. Perkins, Pst.; CRP Stds.: 143

PLAINFIELD

Saint Andre Bessette Parish (St. John the Apostle Church) - 15 Railroad Ave., Plainfield, CT 06374-1215; Mailing: 10 Railroad Ave., Plainfield, CT 06374 t) 860-564-3313 standrebparish@gmail.com standrebparish.wixsite.com/standrebessetteparis St. Andre Bessette Parish consists of: St. John the Apostle Church in Plainfield, All Hallows Church in Moosup, and St. Augustine in Canterbury. Rev. P. Grzegorz Jednaki, Pst.; CRP Stds.: 35

PORTLAND

St. Mary - 45 Freestone Ave., Portland, CT 06480; Mailing: P.O. Box 307, Portland, CT 06480-0307 t) 860-342-2308 (CRP); 860-342-2328 stmarydre@gmail.com; stmaryportlandoffice@gmail.com Rev. John N. Antonelle, Pst.; Susan Ferriauolo, DRE;

PRESTON

St. Catherine of Siena - 243 Rte. 164, Preston, CT 06365-8726; Mailing: 34 N. Main St., Jewett City, CT 06351 t) 860-376-2044 nancy.stc@sbcglobal.net; stcatherine.secretary@yahoo.com Yoked with St. Mary, Jewett City & St. Thomas the Apostle, Voluntown. Dcn. Jorge Escalona; Rev. Ted F. Tumicki, Pst.; Rev. Thomas Griffin, Par. Vicar; Dcn. Bryan Jones;

PUTNAM

St. Therese of Lisieux Parish - 218 Providence St., Putnam, CT 06260-1514; Mailing: P.O. Box 665, Putnam, CT 06260 t) 860-928-6535 sttheresеputnam@gmail.com sttheresеputnam.org Rev. David P. Choquette, Pst.; Dcn. Pierre M. Desilets; Dcn. Wayne Sinclair; Rev. George Busto, C.O., Par. Vicar; CRP Stds.: 94

ROCKVILLE

Blessed Sacrament Parish - 25 St. Bernard's Terr., Rockville, CT 06066-3217 t) 860-875-0753 rectory@cath-comm.org www.blessedsacramentct.org Rev. Richard J. Ricard, Pst.; Dcn. Michael Berstene; Dcn. Ronald Freedman; Brian Kenny, Bus. Mgr.; CRP Stds.: 403

St. Joseph - 33 West St., Rockville, CT 06066-6154 t) 860-871-1970 info@stjosephct.org Rev. Tadeusz Zadorozny (Poland), Pst.;

SOMERSVILLE

All Saints - 25 School St., Somersville, CT 06072-0913; Mailing: P.O. Box M, Somersville, CT 06072-0913 t) 860-749-8625 alstchurch@yahoo.com somersallsaints.church Rev. Gerald S. Kirby, Pst.; CRP Stds.: 51

STAFFORD SPRINGS

St. Edward - 27 Church St., Stafford Springs, CT 06076 t) 860-684-2705 stedwardparish@stedward-stafford.org www.stedward-stafford.org Rev. Peter B. Liszewski, Pst.; CRP Stds.: 80

TAFTVILLE

Sacred Heart - 156 Providence St., Taftville, CT 06380; Mailing: P.O. Box 208, Taftville, CT 06380 t) 860-887-3072 sacredhearttaftville@yahoo.com Yoked with St. Mary, Baltic and St. Joseph, Occum Rev. Joseph Tito, Pst.; Rev. Christopher J. Zmuda, Pst.; Rev. Raymond Introvigne, In Res.; CRP Stds.: 9

Sacred Heart School - -8) 15 Hunters Ave., Taftville, CT 06380-0208 t) 860-887-1757 principal@sacredhearttaftville.org www.sacredhearttaftville.org Sr. Mary Christina Van Beck, S.C.M.C., Prin.;

UNCASVILLE

Divine Mercy Parish - 22 Maple Ave., Uncasville, CT 06382-2327 t) 860-848-1257 office@divinemercyparish.net www.divinemercyfaithcommunity.org Rev. Robert F. Buongirno, Pst.; Rev. Francis Gilbert, Par. Vicar; Dcn. William T. Herrmann; CRP Stds.: 79

VERSAILLES

St. Joseph - 11 Baltic Rd., Versailles, CT 06383; Mailing: P.O. Box 208, Taftville, CT 06380 t) 860-887-3072 sacredhearttaftville@yahoo.com Yoked with St. Mary, Baltic and Sacred Heart, Taftville Rev. Joseph Tito, Pst.; Rev. Christopher J. Zmuda, Pst. Assoc.;

Saint Society Church - (Corporate Title: St. Joseph Church Society of Occum, CT, Inc.)

VOLUNTOWN

St. Thomas the Apostle - 61 Preston City Rd., Voluntown, CT 06384; Mailing: 34 N. Main St., Jewett City, CT 06351 t) 860-376-2044 Yoked with St. Mary, Jewett City & St. Catherine of Siena, Preston. Rev. Ted F. Tumicki, Pst.; Rev. Thomas Griffin, Par. Vicar; Dcn. Bryan Jones; Cathy Becotte, DRE;

WILLIMANTIC

Corpus Christi Catholic Parish - 99 Jackson St., Willimantic, CT 06226-3077 t) 860-423-8439; 860-423-5835 catholicwindham@gmail.com; catholicwindham.business@gmail.com www.catholicwindham.org Rev. Laurence A.M. LaPointe, Pst.; Rev. Michael Castiblanco, Par. Vicar; Dcn. Lawrence Goodwin; Dcn. Felipe Silva; CRP Stds.: 220

SCHOOLS: PRESCHOOL THRU HIGH SCHOOL

SCHOOLS

STATE OF CONNECTICUT

MIDDLETOWN

Saint John Paul II Regional School - (DIO) (Grades PreK-8) 87 S. Main St., Middletown, CT 06457-3606 t) 860-347-2978 office@jpii.org; principal@jpii.org jpii.org Tiffany Ruvolo, Prin.; Stds.: 205; Lay Tchrs.: 14

HIGH SCHOOLS

STATE OF CONNECTICUT

BALTIC

Academy of the Holy Family - (PRV) (Grades 9-12) 54 W. Main St., Baltic, CT 06330-0691; Mailing: P.O. Box 691, Baltic, CT 06330-0691 t) 860-822-9272 mothermdavid@gmail.com www.ahfbaltic.org Henry Fiore Jr., Prin.; Mother Mary David Riquier, SCMC, Dir.; Stds.: 37; Sr. Tchrs.: 5; Lay Tchrs.: 4

MIDDLETOWN

Mercy High School - (DIO) (Grades 9-12) 1740 Randolph Rd., Middletown, CT 06457-5155 t) 860-346-6659 info@mercyhigh.com; finance@mercyhigh.com www.mercyhigh.com Alissa DeJonge, Pres.; Melissa Bullock, Prin.; Ann Drewry, Prin.; Ann Derbacher, Campus Min.; Jennifer Crutchfield, Librn.; Stds.: 392; Lay Tchrs.: 39

Xavier High School Corporation of Middletown (Brothers of St. Francis Xavier and Diocese of Norwich) - (PRV) (Grades 9-12) 181 Randolph Rd., Middletown, CT 06457-5635 t) 860-346-7735 deustis@xavierhighschool.org; djaskot@xavierhighschool.org www.xavierhighschool.org David Eustis, Headmaster; Brendan Donohue, Prin.; Stds.: 593; Bro. Tchrs.: 3; Lay Tchrs.: 49

THOMPSON

Marianapolis Preparatory School - (PRV) 26 Chase Rd., Thompson, CT 06277-0304; Mailing: P.O. Box 304, Thompson, CT 06277-0304 t) 860-923-9565 ddaniels@marianapolis.org www.marianapolis.org Rev. Timothy Roth, M.I.C., Chap.; Joseph C. Hanrahan, Headmaster;

Congregation of Marian Fathers of the Immaculate Conception of the B.V.M. - 206 Chase Rd., .,

Thompson, CT 06277-0368; Mailing: P.O. Box 368, Thompson, CT 06277-0368 t) 860-923-2220 aragon1948@yahoo.com; troth@marianapolis.org Rev. Allen Alexander, M.I.C., Supr.; Bro. Brian Manian, M.I.C., Treas.; Rev. Daniel Cambra, M.I.C., Mem.; Rev. Timothy J. Roth, M.I.C., Secy.;

UNCASVILLE

Saint Bernard School - (DIO) (Grades 6-12) 1593 Norwich-New London Tpke., Uncasville, CT 06382-1399 t) 860-848-1271 advancement@saint-bernard.com; headmaster@saint-bernard.com www.saintbernardschool.org Donald Macrino, Headmaster; Stds.: 400; Lay Tchrs.: 32

Grades 6-12 School - (Grades 6-12) info@saint-bernard.com

INSTITUTIONS LOCATED IN DIOCESE

CAMPUS MINISTRY / NEWMAN CENTERS [CAM]

WILLIMANTIC

Campus Ministry - 290 Prospect St., Willimantic, CT 06226 t) 860-423-0856 lapointel@easternct.edu www.norwichdiocese.org Rev. Laurence A.M. LaPointe, Dir.;

Connecticut College - Harkness Chapel, 270 Mohegan Ave., New London, CT 06320-4196 t) 860-439-2450 rwashaba@conncoll.edu www.conncoll.edu Rev. Jonathan J. Ficara, Chap.; Rev. Robert Washabaugh, Chap.;

University of Connecticut - St. Thomas Aquinas Chapel, 46 N. Eagleville Rd., Storrs, CT 06268-1710 t) 860-429-6436 frjohnantonellesta@gmail.com www.stmary-stthomas.community Rev. John N. Antonelle, Chap.;

Wesleyan University-The University Ministry - University Catholic Chaplain, Wesleyan University, 171 Church St., Middletown, CT 06459-0029; Mailing: Office of Religious & Spiritual Life, Wesleyan University, 171 Church St., Middletown, CT 06459-0029 t) 860-685-2285 wwallace@wesleyan.edu www.wesleyan.edu/chaplains Rev. William Wallace, O.S.A., Chap.;

CONVENTS, MONASTERIES, AND RESIDENCES FOR WOMEN [CON]

BALTIC

Sisters of Charity of Our Lady, Mother of the Church - 54 W. Main St., Baltic, CT 06330-0691; Mailing: P.O. Box 691, Baltic, CT 06330-0691 t) 860-822-8241 sistermariejulie@gmail.com; mothermdavid@gmail.com www.sistersofcharity.com Mother Marie Julie Saegaert, S.C.M.C., Supr.; Srs.: 46

HIGGANUM

Apostles of the Sacred Heart of Jesus - Sacred Heart on the Lake, 529 Brainard Hill Rd., Higganum, CT 06441-4010 t) 860-345-4653 ljsmith@ascjus.org sacredheartonthelake.org Sr. Lany Jo Smith, ASCJ, Superior/Director; Srs.: 3

MIDDLETOWN

Daughters of Our Lady of the Garden - 67 Round Hill Rd., Middletown, CT 06457-6119 t) 860-346-5765; 860-740-5169 (School) juana.olmedo.fmh@gmail.com www.gianelliselc.org/ Convent and Nursery School. Sr. Juana Olmedo, F.M.H., Supr.; Srs.: 5

Sisters of Mercy of the Americas, Northeast Community - 34 West St., 2nd Fl., Middletown, CT 06457 t) (860) 346-0328 mconkel7@gmail.com Srs.: 2

MOOSUP

All Hallows Convent - 130 Prospect St., Moosup, CT 06354 t) 860-564-5409 tvanassedhs@att.net Sr. Therese Vanasse, Contact; Srs.: 5

PUTNAM

Daughters of the Holy Spirit Administrative Offices - 508B Pomfret St, Putnam, CT 06260; Mailing: P.O. Box 419, Putnam, CT 06260 t) 860-928-0891 dhsprovsec@gmail.com daughtersoftheholyspirit.org/ Sr. Gertrude Lanouette, D.H.S., Prov.;

Immaculate Conception Convent - 600 Liberty Hwy., Putnam, CT 06260-2503 t) 860-928-7955 sesigne@gmail.com; eugenia.luko@gmail.com immaculateconceptioncenter.org Sr. Igne Marijosius, M.V.S., Prov.; Srs.: 8

Provincialate Community of the Daughters of the Holy Spirit - 31 Ravine St., Putnam, CT 06260-1817 c) (860) 716-3620 trudidhs@gmail.com; dhsprovsec@gmail.com www.daughtersoftheholyspirit.org Sr. Gertrude Lanouette, D.H.S., Prov.; Srs.: 2

WILLIMANTIC

Sisters of Charity of Our Lady, Mother of the Church - St. Joseph Convent, 88 Jackson St., Willimantic, CT 06226 t) 860-423-5122 aposthispano@gmail.com Mother Mary Jude Lazarus, S.C.M.C., Supr.; Srs.: 3

ENDOWMENTS / FOUNDATIONS / TRUSTS [EFT]

MIDDLETOWN

Mercy-Xavier Fund Corporation - 1740 Randolph Rd, Mercy High School, Middletown, CT 06457 t) 860-346-6659 (Mercy High School); (860) 343-5989 (Finance Office) deustis@xavierhighschool.org; finance@mercyhigh.com Lori Flynn, Admin.; David Eustis, Headmaster; Alissa DeJonge, Pres.;

NORWICH

The Catholic Foundation of the Diocese of Norwich, Inc. - 197 Broadway, Norwich, CT 06360 t) 860-886-1928 memahoney@norwichdiocese.net; dodadm@norwichdiocese.net www.norwichdiocesedevelopment.org Mary Ellen Mahoney, Dir.;

The Donor Advised Funds of the Diocese of Norwich, Inc. - 201 Broadway, Norwich, CT 06360 t) 860-887-9294 financekarenh@norwichdiocese.net Rev. Peter J. Langevin, Chancellor;

PUTNAM

The Daughters of the Holy Spirit Charitable Trust - 508 B Pomfret St., Putnam, CT 06260; Mailing: P.O. Box 419, Putnam, CT 06260 t) 860-928-0891 srbonniemorrow@gmail.com; dhsprovsec@gmail.com daughtersoftheholyspirit.org Sr. Bonnie Morrow, Contact;

MISCELLANEOUS [MIS]

MIDDLETOWN

Office of Advancement - 1740 Randolph Rd., Middletown, CT 06457 t) 860-347-8957; 860-346-6659 advancement@mercyhigh.com; finance@mercyhigh.com www.mercyhigh.com Marie Kalita, Constituent Relations Liaison; Alissa DeJonge, Pres.;

Xavier Advancement Office - 181 Randolph Rd., Middletown, CT 06457 t) 860-346-7735 advancement@xavierhighschool.org www.xavierhighschool.org Liz Whitty, Dir.; Greg Jaskot, Assoc. Dir.;

NORWICH

The Annual Catholic Appeal of the Diocese of Norwich, Inc. - 197 Broadway, Norwich, CT 06360 t) 860-886-1928 memahoney@norwichdiocese.net; dodadm@norwichdiocese.net www.norwichdiocesedevelopment.org Rosela Precopio, Admin.; Mary Ellen Mahoney, Exec.; Heather Harris, Campaign Manager;

Marian Housing Corporation - 201 Broadway, Norwich, CT 06360-4328 t) 860-632-1688 manager.rookretirement@barkanmangement.com Elizabeth Wytas, Contact;

PLAINFIELD

Secular Branch of the Daughters of the Holy Spirit - 5 Third St. Ext., Plainfield, CT 06374-1154 t) (860) 564-0758 conssecdhs@aol.com

WINDHAM

Sagrado Corazon de Jesus, Inc. of Windham - 61 Club Rd., Windham, CT 06280 t) 860-423-8617 sagradocor@sbcglobal.net Rev. Laurence A.M. LaPointe;

MONASTERIES AND RESIDENCES FOR PRIESTS AND BROTHERS [MON]

CROMWELL

Society of the Missionaries of the Holy Apostles - 22 Prospect Hill Rd., Cromwell, CT 06416-2005 t) 860-316-5926 c) (860) 466-0329 provincial@msa-usa.org; mrooney@msa-usa.org www.msa-usa.org Very Rev. Luis Luna-Barrera, M.S.A., General Animator; Very Rev. Martin Rooney, M.S.A., Provincial Animator; Rev. Edward Przygocki, M.S.A., Treas.; Rev. Charles Bak, M.S.A., Cromwell Local Animator; Very Rev. Peter Kucer, M.S.A., President-Rector HAC&S; Rev. James Anderson, M.S.A.; Rev. Robert Anello, M.S.A.; Rev. Patrick Biegler, M.S.A.; Rev. J. Patrick Boyhan, M.S.A.; Rev. William Broome, M.S.A.; Rev. Dennis P. Connell, M.S.A.; Rev. James Downs, M.S.A.; Rev. Harold Dunn, M.S.A.; Rev. Stanley Grove, M.S.A.; Rev. Addison Hallock, M.S.A.; Rev. Richard Hite, M.S.A.; Rev. Vincent Kilidjian, M.S.A.; Rev. Edard Reiter, M.S.A.; Rev. Vincent Salamoni, M.S.A.; Rev. Robert Sickler, M.S.A.; Rev. Thomas Simon, M.S.A.; Rev. Jeffrey Thompson, M.S.A.; Rev. David Zercie, M.S.A.; Bro. Jerome McCallum, Brother; Bro. Robert Whitton, M.S.A., Librn.; Bro. Jeffrey Herrmann; Bro. Daniel Valente, M.S.A.; Bro. James Lonon, M.S.A.; Brs.: 5; Priests: 23

GRISWOLD

Marian Friary of Our Lady of Guadalupe - 199 Colonel Brown Rd., Griswold, CT 06351 t) 860-376-6840 ffi.griswold@gmail.com www.figuadalupe.com Friar John Astillero, Lay Brother; Rev. Josemaria Barbin, Guardian; Rev. Ignatius Manfredonia, Regional Delegate Superior; Bro. Jude McFeeley, F.I., Resident; Rev. Dominic Savio Mary Murphy, F.I., Vicar; Bro. Friar Pasquale Gilbert, Secy.; Rev. Elias Mills, Treas.; Brs.: 3; Priests: 4

MIDDLETOWN

Congregation of the Brothers of St. Francis Xavier - 181 Randolph Rd., Middletown, CT 06457-5635 t) 860-346-8585 deustis@xavierhighschool.org Bro. Philip Revell, C.F.X.; Bro. Thomas Ryan, C.F.X.; Bro. John Sullivan, C.F.X.; Bro. Brian Davis, C.F.X., Dir.; Brs.: 4

MYSTIC

St. Edmund's of Connecticut, Inc. - 1 Enders Island, Mystic, CT 06355-0399; Mailing: P.O. Box 399, Mystic, CT 06355-0399 t) 860-536-0565 cstclair@endersisland.org www.endersisland.com Most Rev. Thomas Tobin; David Cray, SSE, Supr.; Most Rev. Michael R. Cote, Pres.; Rev. Thomas F.X. Hoar, S.S.E., Secy.; Priests: 2

THOMPSON

Marians of the Immaculate Conception of the B.V.M. - 206 Thompson Rd., Thompson, CT 06277-0368; Mailing: P.O. Box 368, Thompson, CT 06277 t) 860-923-2220 c) 860-382-3126 aragon1948@yahoo.com; troth@marianapolis.org Rev. Allen Alexander, M.I.C., Supr.; Rev. Timothy Roth, M.I.C., Secy.; Bro. Brian Manian, M.I.C., Treas.; Rev. Daniel Cambra, M.I.C., Mem.; Brs.: 1; Priests: 3

NURSING / REHABILITATION / CONVALESCENCE / ELDERLY CARE [NUR]

PUTNAM

Matulaitis Nursing Home Inc. - 10 Thurber Rd., Putnam, CT 06260-2518 t) 860-928-7976 ochalifoux@matulaitisnh.org matulaitisnh.org Olivia Rose Chalifoux, Spiritual Adv./Care Srvcs.; Rev. Izydor Sadowski, S.D.B., Chap.; Lisa Ryan, Admin.; Srs.: 1; Asstd. Annu.: 222; Staff: 128

WILLIMANTIC

Saint Joseph Home for the Aged, Inc. - 88 Jackson St., Willimantic, CT 06226 t) 860-887-9294

financekarenh@norwichdiocese.net Karen Huffer, Contact;

WINDHAM

St. Joseph Living Center - 14 Club Rd., Windham, CT 06280-1000 t) 860-456-1107 info@sjlcct.org sjlivingcenter.org Ginny Person, Admin.; Asstd. Annu.: 220; Staff: 195

RETREAT HOUSES / RENEWAL CENTERS [RTR]

MYSTIC

St. Edmund's Retreat, Inc. - 1 Enders Island, Mystic, CT 06355-0399; Mailing: P.O. Box 399, Mystic, CT 06355-0399 t) 860-536-0565 cstclair@endersisland.org www.endersisland.org Rev. Thomas F.X. Hoar, S.S.E., Pres.; Mary Kathleen Careb, Chair; Frank Durst, Vice Chair; Lynne Wilson, Treas.;

SEMINARIES [SEM]

CROMWELL

Holy Apostles College and Seminary - 33 Prospect Hill Rd., Cromwell, CT 06416-2005 t) 860-632-3010; 860-632-3012 (Admissions) rector@holyapostles.edu www.holyapostles.edu Very Rev. Peter Kucer, M.S.A., Pres.; Rev. Danh Nguyen, M.S.A., Vice Rector; Rev. Charles Bak, M.S.A., Spiritual Dir.; Rev. Richard D. Breton, Spiritual Advisor; Rev. Robert Sickler, M.S.A., Spiritual Adv./Care Srvcs.; Rev. Tuan Mai, Spiritual Advisor; Rebecca Davis, Registrar; Clare Adamo, Librn.; William J. Russell, CFO; Dr. Lesley DeNardis, Vice Pres., Academic Affairs & Chief Academic Officer; Stds.: 654; Lay Tchrs.: 6

SPECIAL CARE FACILITIES [SPF]

WILLIMANTIC

Holy Family Home and Shelter, Inc. - 88 Jackson St., Willimantic, CT 06226-0884; Mailing: P.O. Box 884, Willimantic, CT 06226 t) 860-423-7719 ryan@hfhscommunity.org www.holyfamilywillimantic.org Ryan Fitzgibbons, Dir.; Bed Capacity: 34; Asstd. Annu.: 84; Staff: 12

An asterisk (*) denotes an organization that has established tax-exempt status directly with the IRS and is not covered by the USCCB Group Ruling.

Diocese of Oakland

(Dioecesis Quercopolitana)

MOST REVEREND MICHAEL C. BARBER, S.J.

Bishop of Oakland; ordained June 8, 1985; appointed Bishop of Oakland May 3, 2013; ordained and installed May 25, 2013. Office: 2121 Harrison St., Ste. 100, Oakland, CA 94612-3788. T: 510-267-8316; F: 510-839-6770.

Chancery Office: 2121 Harrison St., Ste. 100, Oakland, CA 94612-3788. T: 510-893-4711; F: 510-893-0945.
chancellor@oakdiocese.org
www.oakdiocese.org

ESTABLISHED JANUARY 13, 1962.

Square Miles 1,467.

Comprises two Counties in the State of California–viz., Alameda and Contra Costa.

Legal Title: The Roman Catholic Bishop of Oakland, a Corporation Sole.

For legal titles of parishes and diocesan institutions, consult the Chancery Office.

STATISTICAL OVERVIEW

Personnel	
Bishop	1
Retired Bishops	1
Priests: Diocesan Active in Diocese	145
Priests: Diocesan Active Outside Diocese	3
Priests: Retired, Sick or Absent	67
Number of Diocesan Priests	215
Religious Priests in Diocese	160
Total Priests in your Diocese	375
Extern Priests in Diocese	35
Ordinations:	
Diocesan Priests	1
Transitional Deacons	1
Permanent Deacons	1
Permanent Deacons in Diocese	114
Total Brothers	98
Total Sisters	366
Parishes	
Parishes	82
With Resident Pastor:	
Resident Diocesan Priests	44
Resident Religious Priests	9
Without Resident Pastor:	
Administered by Priests	30
Administered by Deacons	1
Missions	1
Pastoral Centers	10
Professional Ministry Personnel:	
Brothers	4
Sisters	29
Lay Ministers	118
Welfare	
Health Care Centers	1
Total Assisted	4,344
Homes for the Aged	2
Total Assisted	280
Day Care Centers	1
Total Assisted	216
Specialized Homes	3
Total Assisted	3,404
Special Centers for Social Services	4
Total Assisted	249,875
Residential Care of Disabled	1
Total Assisted	900
Educational	
Diocesan Students in Other Seminaries	12
Total Seminarians	12
Colleges and Universities	1
Total Students	943
High Schools, Diocesan and Parish	2
Total Students	1,667
High Schools, Private	7
Total Students	4,133
Elementary Schools, Diocesan and Parish	38
Total Students	9,318
Elementary Schools, Private	1
Total Students	38
Catechesis/Religious Education:	
High School Students	5,047
Elementary Students	10,577
Total Students under Catholic Instruction	31,735
Teachers in Diocese:	
Priests	7
Brothers	5
Sisters	6
Lay Teachers	1,304
Vital Statistics	
Receptions into the Church:	
Infant Baptism Totals	4,876
Minor Baptism Totals	338
Adult Baptism Totals	183
Received into Full Communion	502
First Communions	3,684
Confirmations	3,199
Marriages:	
Catholic	611
Interfaith	80
Total Marriages	691
Deaths	2,031
Total Catholic Population	367,389
Total Population	2,848,280

LEADERSHIP

Chancery Office - t) 510-893-4711

Office of the Bishop - t) 510-267-8316 Most Rev. Michael C. Barber, S.J., Bishop; Veronica Rosas, Exec.;

Vicar General - t) (510) 893-4711 Very Rev. Lawrence C. D'Anjou, Vicar; Teresa Pena, Exec.;

Chancellor - t) 510-267-8306 chancellor@oakdiocese.org Rick A. Medeiros, Chancellor (rmedeiros@oakdiocese.org); Marissa Ortega Smith, Exec.;

Chief Financial Officer - t) (510) 893-4711 Paul Bongiovanni (pbongiovanni@oakdiocese.org);

Judicial Vicar - Rev. Bich N. Nguyen (BNguyen@oakdiocese.org);

Interim Director of Communications and Community Relations - t) (510) 271-1931 Helen Osman;

Catholic Cathedral Corporation of the East Bay (CCCEB) - t) (510) 893-4711 Very Rev. Brandon Macadaeg, Pres./Contact (bmacadaeg@oakdiocese.org); Paul Bongiovanni, Treas. (pbongiovanni@oakdiocese.org);

Christ the Light Cathedral Corporation - t) (510) 893-4711 Most Rev. Michael C. Barber, S.J., Pres.; Very Rev. Brandon Macadaeg, Contact (bmacadaeg@oakdiocese.org); Paul Bongiovanni, Treas. (pbongiovanni@oakdiocese.org);

The Roman Catholic Welfare Corporation of Oakland - t) 510-893-4711 Rev. Larry E. Young, Pres.; Paul Bongiovanni, Secy. (pbongiovanni@oakdiocese.org);

Diocesan Consultors - Rev. Joy Kumarthusseril, M.F. (India); Rev. Paul Coleman; Rev. George E. Mockel;

Diocesan Finance Council - William Utic, Chair; David L. Ash; Frank Balestreri;

Diocesan Review Board - Rick A. Medeiros, Chancellor (rmedeiros@oakdiocese.org); Very Rev. Lawrence C. D'Anjou, Adult Review Bd.; Very Rev. Mark Richards, Minor Review Bd.;

Presbyteral Council - Rev. Paul R. Vassar, Vice Chairperson; Rev. Kevin Schindler-McGraw, O.F.M.Conv., Secy.; Rev. Sergio Mora;

Ex Officio - Very Rev. Lawrence C. D'Anjou;

Deans - t) (510) 893-4711 Very Rev. Brandon Macadaeg, Deanery 1 (bmacadaeg@oakdiocese.org); Rev. Kenneth Nobrega, Deanery 2 (fatherkennethnobrega@icloud.com); Rev. Glenn A. Naguit, Deanery 3 (gnaguit@stmargaretm.org);

OFFICES AND DIRECTORS

Archivist/Records Management - t) 510-267-8318 Rick A. Medeiros, Chancellor (rmedeiros@oakdiocese.org);

Bishop's Representative for the Eastern Catholic Churches - c) (510) 536-2907 Rev. David Link;

Canon Law Department-Marriage Tribunal - t) (510) 267-8330 tribunal@oakdiocese.org Mary O'Sullivan (mosullivan@oakdicoese.org);

Adjutant Judicial Vicar - t) (510) 267-8330 Mary O'Sullivan, Contact; Rev. David E. Staal, Vicar;

Auditors - Dcn. John Kortuem; Dcn. Loc H. Nguyen; Marco Pozo;

Censor - t) (510) 267-8330 Rev. David E. Staal;

Court of Second Instance - t) (510) 267-8330 Rev. Bich N. Nguyen; Mary O'Sullivan, Notary;

Defenders of the Bond - t) (510) 267-8330 Rev. David K. O'Rourke, O.P.; Rev. Timothy T. Ferguson;

Ecclesiastical Notaries - t) (510) 267-8332 Nina M. Woodcock; Mary O'Sullivan;

Judges - Rev. Bich N. Nguyen; Rev. David E. Staal; Rev. Sergio Lopez;

Judicial Vicar & Director - Rev. Bich N. Nguyen;

Promoter of Justice - Rev. Salvador Macias;

Catholic Funeral and Cemetery Services - t) 925-946-1440 Robert W. Seelig, Pres.; Rev. George E. Mockel, Vice. Pres.; Paul Bongiovanni, Secy. (pbongiovanni@oakdiocese.org);

Catholic Youth Organization and Catholic Scouting - t) 510-893-5154 Bill Ford, Dir.;

Diocesan Chaplain for Catholic Scouting - t) (510) 917-0125 Rev. Jayson J. Landeza;

Clergy Services - t) 510-267-8307 Rev. Michael T. Castori, S.J., Vicar for Priests;

Apostleship of the Sea - t) 510-444-7885 Rev. Joseph Duong Phan, Chap.;

Diaconate - t) 510-267-8305 Dcn. Timothy L. Moore, Bishop's Rep. to Diaconate & Dir. Deacon Personnel;

Office of Permanent Deacon Formation - t) 510-267-8356 Dcn. Timothy L. Moore, Dir.;

Ongoing Formation of Priests - t) 510-267-8364 Rev. Kevin Schindler-McGraw, O.F.M.Conv., Dir.;

Priest Personnel Board - Very Rev. Lawrence C. D'Anjou; Rev. George E. Mockel; Rev. Carl Tacuyan Arcosa;

Vocations - t) 510-267-8356 Rev. Carl Tacuyan Arcosa, Dir.;

Department of Diocesan Worship - t) (510) 893-4711 John Renke;

Department of Faith Formation and Evangelization - t) (510) 267-8340 Rev. Jimmy Macalinao, Dir.;

Catechetical Formation and RCIA - c) (510) 267-8370 Scarlett Salaverria, Dir.;

Latino Ministry - Hector D. Medina, Coord.;

Life and Justice Ministry - Cristina Hernandez, Coord.;

Marriage and Family Life Ministry - Mimi Streett, Coord.;

St. Joseph Center for the Deaf Catechetical and Faith Formation - www.oakdiocese.org

Special Religious Education (SPRED) - t) (510) 893-4711 www.oakdiocese.org/education/spred Michelle Martinez-Kilty, Coord.;

Youth and Young Adult Ministry - t) (510) 893-4711 Joseph Nufable, Coord.;

Diocesan Vicar for Religious - Rev. Bich N. Nguyen (BNguyen@oakdiocese.org);

Ethnic Pastoral and Cultural Centers -

African American Community - t) (510) 913-5695 Jo Ann Evans;

Asian/Indian Community - t) 510-357-0940 Bella Comelo;

Brazilian Community - t) 510-232-4328 Jose Freitas;

Chinese Pastoral Center - t) (925) 706-1647 Dcn. Danny Wong;

Eritrean Community - t) 510-547-5948 Rev. Ghebriel Woldai, Dir.;

Ethiopian Community in Formation - t) 510-620-0594 Elizabeth Gabre-Kristos;

Fijian Community - t) 510-329-8621 Sam Deo;

Filipino Catholic Community -

Indonesian Community - t) 408-824-0052 Irwan Sie;

Kenyan Community - Bernard Wango; David Mwangi;

Kmhmu/Laotian Pastoral Center - t) 510-610-4466 Kan Souriya;

Korean Pastoral Center - t) 925-600-0177 office@tvkcc.org Simon Peter Lee, Contact; Augustine Sung, Contact; Rev. John Hyun Guk Kim, Pst.;

Nigerian-Igbo Community - Rev. Modestus Mgbaramuko;

Polish Pastoral Center - t) 925-779-1027 Dcn. Witold Cichon, Dir.;

Tongan Community - t) 925-727-8239 Nativi Halafihi;

Vietnamese Pastoral Center - t) 510-628-2153 Sr. Rosaline Nguyen, L.H.C.;

Facilities, Planning and Services - t) 510-267-8355 Sylvia Martinez, Assoc. Dir. (sjmartinez@oakdiocese.org);

Design Review Board - t) (510) 893-4711 Rev. Fred A. Riccio; Rev. Larry E. Young; Paul Bongiovanni, Finance;

Financial Services - t) (510) 893-4711 Paul Bongiovanni, CFO (pbongiovanni@oakdiocese.org); Janet Ang, Contact;

Human Resources - t) 510-267-8359 Gloria Espinoza, Dir. (gespinoza@oakdiocese.org);

Safe Environment for Children - t) 510-267-8315 Diana Bitz, Prog. Coord.;

Newspaper: "The Catholic Voice" - t) 510-419-1073 www.catholicvoiceoakland.org Michele Jurich, Editor;

El Heraldo Catolico - t) (510) 419-1075 www.elheraldocatolico.org Michele Jurich, Editor;

Office for Mission Advancement - Giles Miller, Dir. Major Gifts & Campaigns (gmiller@oakdiocese.org); Terri Porter, Dir. Family Aid-Catholic Educ. (tporter@oakdiocese.org); Angela Chang, Oper. & Data Support Asst.;

Organizations and Services -

Catholic Campaign for Human Development - t) 510-768-3176 Marc McKimmey, Coord.;

Catholic Charismatic Renewal - t) 925-757-4020 Rev. Olman Solis, Dir.; Rev. Robert Mendonca, Dir.;

Catholic Relief Services - t) 510-768-3176 Marc McKimmey, Coord.;

Confraternity of Eucharistic Devotion (CEDDO) - t) (510) 893-4711 Very Rev. Brandon Macadaeg, Chap.; Glenda Dubsky, Mod.; Rico Banson, Asst. Mod.;

Courage - Oakland Chapter - t) 510-893-4711; (650) 450-2286 Rev. John Direen, Chap.; Rev. Francisco Figueroa-Esquer, Chap.;

Cursillo Movement - t) 510-530-4343; 925-687-8095 Rev. Leo J. Edgerly Jr., Diocesan Spiritual Dir.; Dcn. Rey Encarnacion, Spiritual Dir., Filipino Cursillo Community;

Exorcist - t) (510) 522-8933 Rev. Kenneth Nobrega;

Pontifical Association of the Holy Childhood - Very Rev. Lawrence C. D'Anjou, Dir.;

St. Peter the Apostle Society - t) (510) 848-7812 Very Rev. Lawrence C. D'Anjou, Dir.;

St. Vincent de Paul Society - t) (510) 638-7600 Blase Bova, Alameda County, Exec. Dir.; Claudia Ramirez, Contra Costa County, Exec. Dir.;

Pastoral Planning - Very Rev. Lawrence C. D'Anjou;

Propagation of the Faith - t) (510) 267-8317 Very Rev. Lawrence C. D'Anjou, Dir.;

Schools - t) 510-628-2151 Dr. Andrew Currier, Supt. (acurrier@oakdiocese.org);

PARISHES, MISSIONS, AND CLERGY

STATE OF CALIFORNIA

ALAMEDA

St. Barnabas - 1427 Sixth St., Alameda, CA 94501-3760 t) 510-522-8933 sbarnabas.weebly.com/ Rev. Kenneth Nobrega, Par. Admin.; Agatha Leong, DRE; Maria Tiangha, Confirmation Coordinator; CRP Stds.: 24

St. Joseph Basilica - 1109 Chestnut St., Alameda, CA 94501-4212 t) 510-995-9409 (CRP); 510-522-0181 (Main Line) afourre@sjbalameda.org; parish@sjbalameda.org www.sjbalameda.org Rev. Mario Rizzo, Admin.; Rev. Sunil Orathel, SDB, In Res.; Anne Marie Fourre, DRE; CRP Stds.: 156

St. Philip Neri-St. Albert the Great - 3100 Van Buren St. (St. Philip Neri Church), Alameda, CA 94501-4840; Mailing: 3101 Van Buren St., Alameda, CA 94501-4840 t) 510-373-5200 secretary@spnsa.org www.spnsa.org 1022 Holly St. (St. Albert the Great Church), Alameda, CA. Rev. Joseph Pathiyil, M.F. (India), Pst.; Rev. Paul Kannampilly, Par. Vicar; Rev. James B. Pickett, In Res.; Rev. Paul J. Schmidt, In Res.; Diane Bustos, DRE; Catherine Morales, DRE; CRP Stds.: 83

St. Philip Neri-St. Albert the Great School - (Grades K-8) 1335 High St., Alameda, CA 94501-3165 t) 510-521-0787 juthomas@csdo.org www.spnalameda.org Julie Thomas, Prin.;

ANTIOCH

St. Ignatius of Antioch - 3351 Contra Loma Blvd., Antioch, CA 94509-5468 t) 925-778-0768 st.ignatius@sbcglobal.net www.stignatiusofantioch.org Rev. Robert K. Rien, Pst.; Dcn. Gary Hack; CRP Stds.:

40

Most Holy Rosary - 1313 A St., Antioch, CA 94509-2328; Mailing: 21 E. 15th St., Antioch, CA 94509 t) 925-757-9515 (CRP); 925-757-4020 x10 office@holyrosaryantioch.org www.holyrosaryantioch.org Rev. Ramiro Flores, Pst.; Rev. Olman Solis, Par. Vicar; Rev. Kevin Ezeh, In Res.; Dcn. Jorge Aragon; CRP Stds.: 365

Most Holy Rosary School - (Grades PreK-8) 25 E. 15th St., Antioch, CA 94509 t) 925-757-1270 administration@holyrosarycatholicschool.org www.holyrosarycatholicschool.org Fely Fajardo, Prin.;

BAY POINT

Our Lady, Queen of the World - 3155 Winterbrook Dr., Bay Point, CA 94565-3264 t) 925-458-4574 (CRP); 925-458-4718 director@olqwre.com; rectory@olqw.org www.olqw.org Rev. Thomas Khue, Admin.; Dcn. Loc H. Nguyen; Rene Asuncion, DRE; CRP Stds.: 153

BERKELEY

St. Ambrose - 1145 Gilman St., Berkeley, CA 94706-2252 t) 510-525-2620 stambrosechurch@comcast.net www.saintambroseberkeley.org Rev. John Prochaska, Admin.; Dcn. Ralph Nagel; Ana Perez, DRE;

Holy Spirit Parish/Newman Hall - 2700 Dwight Way, Berkeley, CA 94704-3113 t) 510-848-7812 info@calnewman.org; pastor@calnewman.org www.calnewman.org (Newman Center 1899). Campus Ministry to UC Berkeley Rev. Ryan P Casey, C.S.P., Par. Vicar; Rev. Ivan Tou, C.S.P., Pst.; Rev. Kenneth Boyack, In Res.; CRP Stds.: 47

St. Joseph the Worker - 1640 Addison St., Berkeley, CA 94703-1404 t) 510-843-2244 info@stjosephtheworkerchurch.org www.stjosephtheworkerchurch.org Rev. John Prochaska, Pst.; Rev. Alberto A. Perez, In Res.;

St. Mary Magdalen - 2005 Berryman St., Berkeley, CA 94709-1920 t) 510-526-4811 parish@marymagdalen.org; pastor@marymagdalen.org marymagdalen.org Rev. Nicholas Glisson, Pst.; Rev. Ioane Ono, In Res.; CRP Stds.: 294

School of the Madeleine - (Grades K-8) 1225 Milvia St., Berkeley, CA 94709-1932 t) 510-526-4744 mschweska@themadeleine.com www.themadeleine.com Joseph Nagel, Prin.;

BRENTWOOD

Immaculate Heart of Mary - 500 Fairview Ave., Brentwood, CA 94513-1742 t) 925-634-4154 x106; 925-634-4154 x117 (CRP) lkortuem@ihmbrentwood.com; ihmchurch@ihmbrentwood.com www.ihmbrentwood.com Rev. Quang Minh Dong, Pst.; Rev. Mark S. Ruiz, Par. Vicar; Dcn. Paul Abenoja; Dcn. Leland DeFrates; Dcn. John Kortuem; Linda Kortuem, DRE; CRP Stds.: 553

BYRON

St. Anne - 2800 Camino Diablo Rd., Byron, CA 94514; Mailing: P.O. Box 476, Byron, CA 94514-0476 t) 925-634-6625; 925-634-6625 x224 (CRP) office@anne.church; faithformation@anne.church Rev. Ronald G. Schmit, Pst.; Sr. Barbara Nixon, S.N.J.M., DRE; CRP Stds.: 270

CASTRO VALLEY

Our Lady of Grace - 3433 Somerset Ave., Castro Valley, CA 94546-3354 t) 510-582-9266 (CRP); 510-537-0806 olgcv@sbcglobal.net; parish@olgcv.org www.olgcv.org Rev. Raymond Mallett, OFM Conv., Par. Admin.; Rev. James Phan, Par. Vicar; Rev. Francisco Nahoe, O.F.M.Conv., In Res.; Rev. Paul Fazio, O.F.M. Conv, In Res.; CRP Stds.: 112

Our Lady of Grace School - (Grades K-8) 19920 Anita Ave., Castro Valley, CA 94546 t) 510-581-3155 kgannon-briggs@csdo.org www.olgschool.org Kathy Gannon-Briggs, Prin.;

Transfiguration - 4000 E. Castro Valley Blvd., Castro Valley, CA 94552-4908 t) (510) 538-7941 transfig_office@sbcglobal.net www.transfigchurch.com Dcn. Timothy L. Moore; Rev. Mario L. Borges, Pst.; Dcn. John Mignano; Dcn. Martin J Leach; Wendy R Estrada Estrella, DRE; CRP Stds.: 129

CONCORD

St. Agnes - 3966 Chestnut Ave., Concord, CA 94519-1955 t) 925-689-0838 chemans@gmail.com; david.staganesparish@gmail.com www.stagnesparish.net Rev. Johnson C. Abraham (India), Pst.; Dcn. Sumner Peery; CRP Stds.: 68

St. Agnes School - (Grades PreK-8) 3886 Chestnut Ave., Concord, CA 94519-1907 t) 925-689-3990 jlucia@csdo.org www.stagnesconcord.com Jill Lucia, Prin.;

St. Bonaventure - 5562 Clayton Rd., Concord, CA 94521 t) 925-672-5800 cfairfield@stbonaventure.net; mgugliemo@stbonaventure.net www.stbonaventure.net Rev. Ramon Urbina, Par. Vicar; Anastasia Harkevich, Youth Min.; Very Rev. Lawrence C. D'Anjou, Pst.; Dcn. William Gall; Dcn. Peter Nixon; Dcn. Dominic Tarantino; Anthony Arteaga, Liturgy Dir.; Eileen Limberg, DRE; Christa L. Fairfield, Dir.; Rev. David Lawrence, S.J., Priest In Residence; Dcn. Mariano Preza; CRP Stds.: 557

St. Francis of Assisi - 860 Oak Grove Rd., Concord, CA 94518-3461 t) 925-682-5447 church@sfaconcord.org; parish-office@sfaconcord.org www.sfaconcord.com Dcn. John Mazibrook; Dcn. Charles Palomares; Rev. Ismael Gutierrez, Pst.; Rev. Joseph Tuan Anh Le, Par. Vicar; Rev. Fernando Rubio-Boitel, In Res.; Scarlett Salaverria, DRE; Janet Bina Money, Bus. Mgr.; CRP Stds.: 135

St. Francis of Assisi School - (Grades PreK-8) 866 Oak Grove Rd., Concord, CA 94518-3461 t) 925-682-5414 clauer@csdo.org www.sfaconcord.org Cathy VanderKlught, Prin.; Stds.: 450; Lay Tchrs.: 15

Queen of All Saints - 2390 Grant St., Concord, CA 94520 t) 925-685-8707 (Faith Formation Office); 925-825-0350 qassecretary@gmail.com www.qaschurch.org Rev. Neal C. Clemens, Pst.; Rev. Rafael L. Chavez, Par. Vicar; Nancy Tomsic, DRE; Rev. Paul Feng Chen, Chap.; CRP Stds.: 434

Queen of All Saints School - (Grades K-8) 2391 Grant St., Concord, CA 94520-2244 t) 925-685-8700 aboatman@csdo.org; pfrancisco@csdo.org www.qasconcord.org Lucia Prince, Prin.;

CROCKETT

St. Rose of Lima - 555 Third Ave., Crockett, CA 94525-1114 t) 510-787-2052 strosecrockett@comcast.net stroseoflimacrockettca.org/ Rev. Leonardo Asuncion (Philippines), Admin.; Trudi Jensen, DRE; CRP Stds.: 16

St. Patrick - Prospect & Lake Canyon Rd., Port Costa, CA 94569

DANVILLE

St. Isidore - 445 La Gonda Way, Danville, CA 94526-2562; Mailing: 440 La Gonda Way, Danville, CA 94526-2562 t) 925-362-1900 (Faith Formation Office); 925-837-2122 (Parish Office) office@sichurch.com www.sichurch.com Rev. Candelario Jimenez, Par. Vicar; Rev. Matthew Murray, Pst.; CRP Stds.: 530

St. Isidore School - (Grades K-8) 435 La Gonda Way, Danville, CA 94526 t) 925-837-2977 mward@stisidore.org www.stisidore.org Carol Bender, Prin.;

DUBLIN

St. Raymond - 11555 Shannon Ave., Dublin, CA 94568-1376 t) 925-828-2460 info@srcdublin.org www.srcdublin.org Rev. John Erick Villa, Admin.; Rev. Mark Hoc, Par. Vicar; Dcn. Robert Falco; Maggie Ringle, DRE; CRP Stds.: 363

St. Raymond School - (Grades K-8) 11557 Shannon Ave., Dublin, CA 94568 t) 925-828-4064 gpeterson@csdo.org straymondschool.org Greg Peterson, Prin.;

EL CERRITO

St. Jerome Church - 308 Carmel Ave., El Cerrito, CA 94530 t) 510-525-0876 churchsaintjerome@gmail.com www.stjeromeec.org Rev. Michael Pham, Admin.; Elizabeth Oisha, DRE; CRP Stds.: 62

St. John the Baptist - 11150 San Pablo Ave., El Cerrito, CA 94530-2131 t) 510-232-5659 richard@sjtbc.us; youthministry@sjtbc.us www.sjtbc.us Rev. Thuong Hoai Nguyen, Pst.; Gina de la Torre, Youth Min.; Rev. Joseph Tran, In Res.; Christine Hickey, RCIA Coord.; Dcn. Loch Sekona, Baptism & Ministry Leader; CRP Stds.: 19

St. John the Baptist School - (Grades K-8) 11156 San Pablo Ave., El Cerrito, CA 94530-2131 t) 510-234-2244 info@stjohnec.org www.stjohnec.org Dina Trombettas, Prin.;

EL SOBRANTE

St. Callistus - 3580 San Pablo Dam Rd., El Sobrante, CA 94803 t) 510-222-0432 (CRP); 510-223-1153 aan.stcal@gmail.com; st.callistus@sbcglobal.net Rev. Dante Tamayo, Admin.; Sr. Anitha Antony, DRE; CRP Stds.: 53

FREMONT

Corpus Christi - 37891 Second St, Fremont, CA 94536; Mailing: 37968 Third St, Fremont, CA 94536 t) 510-790-3207 office@corpuschristifremont.org corpuschristifremont.org Rev. Luis Lopez, In Res.; Dcn. Alfonso Perez, Admin.; CRP Stds.: 42

Holy Spirit - 37588 Fremont Blvd., Fremont, CA 94536-3707 t) 510-366-4444 (CRP); 510-797-1660 dcnrigo@gmail.com; info@holyspiritfremont.org www.holyspiritfremont.org Dcn. Charles Glover; Dcn. Stephen Lewellyn; Rev. Kenneth L. Sales, Pst.; Rev. Edilberto S. Castanas, Par. Vicar; Rev. Peter Lawongkerd, Par. Vicar; Friar Bernard Liwanag; Rev. Frank Kuwornu, In Res.; Dcn. Rigoberto Cabezas, DRE; CRP Stds.: 468

Holy Spirit School - (Grades PreK-8) 3930 Parish Ave., Fremont, CA 94536 t) 510-793-3553 hmarsh@csdo.org www.holyspiritfmt.com Holly Marsh, Prin.;

St. James the Apostle - 34700 Fremont Blvd., Fremont, CA 94555 t) 510-792-1962 stjamesapostle@att.net Rev. Anthony Vazhappilly, Pst.; Dcn. Ernesto Dandan; Sheila Reduta, DRE; CRP Stds.: 65

St. Joseph (Old Mission San Jose) - 43148 Mission Blvd., Fremont, CA 94539; Mailing: P.O. Box 3276, Fremont, CA 94539 t) 510-657-0905 (CRP); 510-656-2364 parish@saintjosephmsj.org saintjosephmsj.org Rev. Anthony Hong Van Le, Pst.; Rev. Msgr. Manuel C. Simas, Pastor Emer.; Dcn. Richard Bayless; Dcn. Benjamin Lai; Rowena Raddich, DRE; CRP Stds.: 126

St. Joseph (Old Mission San Jose) School - (Grades K-8) 43222 Mission Blvd., Fremont, CA 94539-5827 t) 510-656-6525 pcalton@csdo.org www.stjosephschoolfremont.org

Our Lady of Guadalupe - 41933 Blacow Rd., Fremont, CA 94538-3365 t) 510-651-4966 (CRP); 510-657-4043 (Office) ologff@olog.church; secretary@olog.church www.olog.church Rev. Hai Du Truong Nguyen, MF, Chap.; Rev. Joy Kumarthusseril, M.F. (India), Pst.; Rev. Gabriel Selvanathan Augustine, M.F. (India), Par. Vicar; Dcn. Laurento Aseo; Dcn. Steven Budnik Sr.; Juan Jose Suarez, DRE; Jean Hui, Bus. Mgr.; CRP Stds.: 320

Our Lady of Guadalupe School - (Grades PreK-8) 40374 Fremont Blvd., Fremont, CA 94538-3409 t) 510-657-1674 sjtwellington@csdo.org olgweb.org/ Sr. Janice Therese Wellington, Prin.;

HAYWARD

All Saints - 22824 Second St., Hayward, CA 94541-5217 t) 510-581-2570 myallsaintshwd@yahoo.com; allsaintshwd@gmail.com Rev. Ramon Gomez, Pst.; Rev. Michael T. Castori, S.J., Par. Vicar; Dcn. Jorge Angel; Dcn. Juan Carlos Bermudez; Rev. Marcelino Cortez, In Res.; Gean Easterly, DRE; CRP Stds.: 230

All Saints School - (Grades K-8) 22870 Second St., Hayward, CA 94541 t) 510-582-1910 jdiaz@csdo.org www.ascshayward.org Jennifer Diaz, Prin.;

St. Bede - 26950 Patrick Ave., Hayward, CA 94544-3851 t) 510-782-4292 (CRP); 510-782-2171 st.bedechurch@yahoo.com www.stbedechurchhay.org Rev. Seamus J. Farrell, Pst.; Michael Verceles, DRE; CRP Stds.: 402

St. Bede School - (Grades K-8) 26910 Patrick Ave., Hayward, CA 94544-3851 t) 510-782-3444

info@stbedeparish.org www.mystbede.com Janine Durana, Prin.;

St. Clement - 738 Calhoun St., Hayward, CA 94544-4202; Mailing: 750 Calhoun St., Hayward, CA 94544-4202 t) 510-582-7282 saintclementhayward@gmail.com; vanessastclement@gmail.com Rev. Juan Franco, Par. Admin.; Rev. James Sullivan, In Res.; Angelica Castillo, DRE; CRP Stds.: 296

St. Clement School - (Grades K-8) 790 Calhoun St., Hayward, CA 94544-4202 t) 510-538-5885 vhernandez@csdo.org www.sclement.org Veronica Hernandez, Prin.;

St. Joachim - 21250 Hesperian Blvd., Hayward, CA 94541-5809 t) 510-785-1818 (CRP); 510-783-2766 stjoachimoffice@gmail.com stjoachim.net Rev. Henryk Noga, S.V.D., Pst.; Rev. Emilio Reyes, S.V.D., Par. Vicar; CRP Stds.: 308

St. Joachim School - (Grades PreK-8) t) 510-783-3177 aseishas@csdo.org www.stjoachimschool.org Armond Seishas, Prin.;

LAFAYETTE

St. Perpetua - 3454 Hamlin Rd., Lafayette, CA 94549-5019 t) 925-283-0272 wlevich@stperpetua.org; office@stperpetua.org www.stperpetua.org Rev. Jimmy Macalinao, Par. Admin.; Kim Anderson, DRE; Wendy Levich, Bus. Mgr.; CRP Stds.: 350

St. Perpetua School - (Grades K-8) 3445 Hamlin Rd., Lafayette, CA 94549-5018 t) 925-284-1640 kgoodshaw@csdo.org Karen Goodshaw, Prin.;

LIVERMORE

St. Charles Borromeo - 1315 Lomitas Ave., Livermore, CA 94550-6441 t) 925-447-4549 office@stcharlesborromeo.org www.stcharleslivermore.org Dcn. David Cloyne; Dcn. Gilbert Pesqueira; CRP Stds.: 174

St. Michael - 458 Maple St., Livermore, CA 94550-3238 t) 925-447-1585 office@stmichaellivermore.com www.stmichaellivermore.com Rev. Carl Tacuyan Arcosa, Pst.; Rev. John Pietruszka, Par. Vicar; Rev. David E. Staal, Weekend Associate; Dcn. William Archer; Dcn. Robert Federle; Dcn. David Rezendes; Dcn. Eric Simontis; Janet Hancock, Music Min.; Glenda Aragon, Pst. Assoc.; Mercedes Acosta, Bus. Mgr.; Rev. Theodbriel Villariza, In Res.; Rev. Ryan Salvador Dellota, In Res.; CRP Stds.: 285

St. Michael School - (Grades K-8) 345 Church St., Livermore, CA 94550-3205 t) 925-447-1888 awilkie@csdo.org www.smsliv.org Alison Wilkie, Prin.;

MARTINEZ

St. Catherine of Siena - 606 Mellus St., Martinez, CA 94553; Mailing: 1125 Ferry St., Martinez, CA 94553 t) 925-228-2230 (CRP); 925-228-2230 x1 stcathmtz@yahoo.com www.stcathmtz.org Dcn. Alberto Dizon; Dcn. David Holland; Rev. Michael Figura Nufable, Admin.; CRP Stds.: 62

St. Catherine of Siena School - (Grades PreK-8) 604 Mellus St., Martinez, CA 94553-1639 t) 925-228-4140 jgriswold@csdo.org www.stcath.net Jessica Griswold, Prin.;

Pre-School and Transitional Kindergarten - 1125 Ferry St., Martinez, CA 94553 t) 925-229-2255 dshapiro@csdo.org www.stcatherinemartinez.com

MORAGA

St. Monica - 1001 Camino Pablo, Moraga, CA 94556-1831 t) 925-376-6900 office@stmonicamoraga.com www.stmonicamoraga.com Rev. Paul Coleman, Admin.; CRP Stds.: 75

NEWARK

St. Edward - 5788 Thornton Ave., Newark, CA 94560-3826 t) 510-797-5588 (CRP); 510-797-0241 parishoffice@stedwardcatholic.church www.stedwardcatholic.com Rev. Mark C. Amaral, Pst.; Rev. Alfonso Borgen, O.F.M.Conv., Par. Vicar; Dcn. Alexander Ebarle; Dcn. Roger Wedl; Rev. Robert McTeigue, S.J, In Res.; Mirian Lopez, DRE; CRP Stds.: 174

St. Edward School - (Grades PreK-8) t) 510-793-7242 kmccall@csdo.org stedcs.org Tina Cruz, Prin.;

OAKLAND

Cathedral Parish of Christ the Light - 2121 Harrison St., Ste. 130, Oakland, CA 94612 t) 510-832-5057 cathedral@oakdiocese.org ctlcathedral.org Rev. Brandon E. Macadaeg, Rector; Dcn. Timothy Roberto; Dcn. Tony Santos; Rev. Dennis McManus, Par. Vicar; Rev. Bich N. Nguyen, Vice Rector; CRP Stds.: 13

St. Anthony-Mary Help of Christians - 1610 E. 15th St., Oakland, CA 94606; Mailing: 1535 16th Ave., Oakland, CA 94606 t) 510-534-2117 office@stanthony-maryhelp.org Rev. Huong Dinh, Par. Vicar; Rev. Ghebriel Woldai, Admin.; Carmen Hernandez, DRE; Diana Mariscal, DRE; Tuan Nguyen, DRE; Uyen Nguyen, DRE; CRP Stds.: 301

St. Anthony School - (Grades K-8) 1500 E. 15th St., Oakland, CA 94606 t) 510-534-3334 mpreciado@csdo.org stanthony-oakland.org Marisol Preciado, Prin.;

St. Augustine - 400 Alcatraz Ave., Oakland, CA 94609-1106 t) 510-653-8631 staugustinefrontdesk@gmail.com; april.mcneely@gmail.com Rev. Augustine Joseph, Admin.; April McNeely, DRE; CRP Stds.: 20

St. Benedict - 2245 82nd Ave., Oakland, CA 94605-3407 t) 510-632-1847; 510-610-2465 owanzo@yahoo.com; saintbenedictcrh@aol.com www.saintbenedictoakland.com Rev. Jayson J. Landeza, Pst.; Dcn. Ronald Tutson; Rev. Vincent Cotter, In Res.; Ofelia Wanzo, DRE; CRP Stds.: 9

St. Bernard - 1620-62nd Ave., Oakland, CA 94621-4221 t) 510-632-3013 st.bernard.church@sbcglobal.net Dcn. Javier Fuentes; Rev. Stephen Ayisu, S.V.D., Pst.; CRP Stds.: 164

St. Columba - 6401 San Pablo Ave., Oakland, CA 94608-1233 t) 510-654-7600 parish@stcolumba-oak.com www.stcolumba-oak.com Rev. Aidan McAleenan, Pst.; Margaret Roncalli, Pst. Assoc.; CRP Stds.: 30

Divine Mercy Parish - 3725 High St., Oakland, CA 94619 t) 510-530-0761 info@divinemercyoak.org www.divinemercyoak.org Rev. Jayson J. Landeza, Pst.; Rev. Joseph Duong Phan, In Res.; CRP Stds.: 121

St. Paschal Baylon Church - 3700 Dorisa Ave., Oakland, CA 94605

St. Lawrence O'Toole Church -

St. Elizabeth - 1500 34th Ave., Oakland, CA 94601-3024 t) 510-536-1266 stelizabethchurch@yahoo.com www.saintelizabethoak.org Rev. Antonio Galindo Carreon, OFM, Pst.; Rev. Jose Luis Barrios Delgado, OFM, Admin.; CRP Stds.: 258

St. Elizabeth - 1516 - 33rd Ave., Oakland, CA 94601-3024 t) 510-532-7392 lmullen@csdo.org Lynne Mullen, Prin.;

St. Jarlath - 2620 Pleasant St., Oakland, CA 94602-2125 t) 510-532-2068 raquesemail@gmail.com www.stjarlath.org Rev. Hai Ho, O.F.M.Cap., Pst.; Rev. Anson Antony, Par. Vicar; Rev. Joseph Seraphin Dederick, In Res.; Bro. Nikolas Barth, In Res.; Bro. Austin Cambon, In Res.; Raquel Vasquez, DRE; CRP Stds.: 170

St. Leo the Great - 176 Ridgeway Ave., Oakland, CA 94611-5122 t) 510-654-6177 stleo@pacbell.net www.churchofstleothegreat.org Dcn. Dac Cao; Rev. John Direen, In Res.; Rev. Joseph T. Nguyen, Admin.; CRP Stds.: 10

St. Leo the Great School - (Grades PreK-8) 4238 Howe St., Oakland, CA 94611-4705 t) 510-654-7828 ssimril@csdo.org www.stleothegreat.org Sonya Simril, Prin.;

St. Louis Bertrand - 1410-100th Ave., Oakland, CA 94603-2506 t) 510-568-1080 parishslb@gmail.com www.slboakland.com Rev. Enrique Ballesteros, Par. Admin.; Dcn. Earl Johson; Dcn. Noe Alfaro Gonzalez; Sr. Silvia Enriquez, DRE; CRP Stds.: 204

St. Margaret Mary - 1219 Excelsior Ave., Oakland, CA 94610 t) 510-482-0596 parishoffice@stmargaretm.org www.stmargaretmaryoak.org Rev. Glenn A. Naguit, Pst.; Rev. Canon Benjamin Norman, Institute of Christ the King Sovereign Priest; CRP Stds.: 73

Our Lady of Lourdes - 2808 Lakeshore Ave., Oakland, CA 94610 t) 510-451-1790 lourdesoakland@icloud.com www.lourdesoakland.com Very Rev. Brandon Macadaeg, Admin.; Lael Carlson, Music Min.; Rev. James Schexnayder, Pst. Min./Coord.; Keith Maczkiewicz, S.J., DRE; Gwen Eyike, Office Manager; Rev. Andres M. Emmanuelli, In Res.; CRP Stds.: 7

St. Patrick - 1005 Peralta St., Oakland, CA 94607-1927; Mailing: 1023 Peralta St., Oakland, CA 94607 t) 510-444-1081 stpatricksecy@gmail.com www.stpatrickwo.org Dcn. Rigoberto Cabezas, Admin.; CRP Stds.: 59

Sacred Heart - 4025 Martin Luther King Jr. Way, Oakland, CA 94609-2317 t) 510-655-9209 shoakland@comcast.net www.sacredheartoak.com Rev. John Mark Ettensohn, OMI, Pst.; Rev. John-Raymond Lau, Par. Vicar; Rev. Scott Hill, O.M.I., In Res.; Rev. Philip Singarayar, O.M.I., In Res.; CRP Stds.: 4

St. Theresa of the Infant Jesus (The Little Flower) - 30 Mandalay Rd., Oakland, CA 94618 t) 510-547-2777 x120 (CRP); 510-547-2777 admin@sttheresaoakland.org; melody@sttheresaoakland.org www.sttheresaoakland.org Rev. Robert J. McCann, Pst.; Rev. Abraham Markos Addam, IMC, In Res.; Rev. Wilson E Ngema, In Res.; CRP Stds.: 71

St. Theresa of the Infant Jesus School - (Grades K-8) 4850 Clarewood Dr., Oakland, CA 94618 t) 510-547-3146 aortegon@csdo.org www.sttheresaschool.org Alicia Ortegon, Prin.;

OAKLEY

St. Anthony - 971 O'Hara Ave., Oakley, CA 94561-5785 t) 925-625-2048 parish@stanthonyoakley.com www.stanthonyoakley.com Rev. Rafael Hinojosa, Admin.; Rev. Benjamin Mac Lingo, Par. Vicar; Dcn. Alberto Cruz; Emma Arcayena, Moderator; Lizette Avalos, Moderator; Michael Maeda, RCIA Coord.; Gallardo Jajahira, Moderator; CRP Stds.: 170

ORINDA

Santa Maria - 40 Santa Maria Way, Orinda, CA 94563-2605 t) 925-254-2426 office@santamariaorinda.com www.santamariaparish.org Dcn. James Pearce; Rev. George E. Mockel, Pst.; Dcn. Rey Encarnacion, Sacr. Min.; CRP Stds.: 92

Convent - 50 Santa Maria Way, Orinda, CA 94563-2605

PIEDMONT

Corpus Christi - 322 St. James Dr., Piedmont, CA 94611-3627 t) 510-530-4343 (CRP); 510-530-4344 office@cc-parish.org www.corpuschristipiedmont.org Rev. Leo J. Edgerly Jr., Pst.; Rev. Basil DePinto, In Res.; Joseph Hebert, Music Min.; Rebeccah Pelle, DRE; Judith Hilgert, Bus. Mgr.; CRP Stds.: 131

Corpus Christi School - (Grades K-8) One Estates Dr., Piedmont, CA 94611-3341 t) 510-530-4056 officesecretary@corpuschristischool.com www.corpuschristischool.com Michael Sahlman, Prin.;

PINOLE

St. Joseph - 837 Tennent Ave., Pinole, CA 94564-1711; Mailing: 2100 Pear St., Pinole, CA 94564 t) 510-741-4900; 510-741-4900 (CRP) contact.sjcpinole@gmail.com www.sjcpinole.org Rev. Geoffrey Baraan, Pst.; Rev. Rafal P. Duda, Par. Vicar; Rev. Francisco Figueroa-Esquer, In Res.; Christine Suarez, DRE; Dcn. Benjamin Agustin; Aura Mendieta, Bus. Mgr.; CRP Stds.: 179

St. Joseph School - (Grades K-8) 1961 Plum St., Pinole, CA 94564 t) 510-724-0242 nlenz-acuna@csdo.org www.stjosephpinole.com Natalie Lenz-Acuna, Prin.;

PITTSBURG

Good Shepherd - 3200 Harbor St., Pittsburg, CA 94565-5444 t) 925-432-6404 x19 (CRP); 925-432-6404 office@goodshepherdpittsburg.org; dina@goodshepherdpittsburg.org www.goodshepherdpittsburg.org Rev. Arn Cabroas, In

Res.; Rev. Thi Van Hoang, Par. Admin.; CRP Stds.: 485

St. Peter, Martyr of Verona - 740 Black Diamond St., Pittsburg, CA 94565-2148 t) 925-432-7200 (CRP); 925-432-4771 stpetermartyr@yahoo.com Rev. Jesus Hernandez Vidal, Pst.; Rev. Salvador Quiroz, Par. Vicar; Emma OJeda, DRE; CRP Stds.: 276

St. Peter, Martyr of Verona School - (Grades PreK-8) 425 W. 4th St., Pittsburg, CA 94565-1968 t) 925-439-1014 kwilson@csdo.org www.stpetermartyrschool.org Katie Wilson, Prin.;

PLEASANT HILL

Christ the King - 195A Brandon Rd., Pleasant Hill, CA 94523-3220 t) 925-682-2486 office@ctkph.org; faithformation@ctkph.org www.ctkph.org Rev. Paulson Mundanmani, Pst.; Rev. Weersak (Lee) Chompoochan, Par. Vicar; Rev. Brian Timoney, In Res.; Dcn. John Ashmore, DRE; Rev. Gerard K. Moran, In Res.; CRP Stds.: 190

Christ the King School - (Grades K-8) 195- B Brandon Rd., Pleasant Hill, CA 94523 t) 925-685-1109 info@ctkschool.org www.ctkschool.org Joe Silveira, Prin.;

PLEASANTON

The Catholic Community of Pleasanton - 3999 Bernal Ave., Pleasanton, CA 94566-7264 t) 925-846-4489 x2766 omorineau@catholicsofpleasanton.org www.catholicsofpleasanton.org Rev. Mark Wiesner, Pst.; Rev. Filiberto Barrera, Par. Vicar; Rev. Luke Ssemakula (Uganda), Par. Vicar; Dcn. Joseph Gourley; Dcn. Gary Wortham; Dcn. Richard Denoix; CRP Stds.: 493

POINT RICHMOND

Our Lady of Mercy - 301 W. Richmond Ave., Point Richmond, CA 94801-3862 t) 510-232-1843 david@davidkorourke.com; svdpatolm@gmail.com www.pointrichmondcatholic.org Rev. David K. O'Rourke, O.P., Admin.;

RICHMOND

St. Cornelius - 205 28th St., Richmond, CA 94804-3001 t) 510-233-5901 st.cornelius33@yahoo.com Rev. Sergio Mora, Pst.; Rev. Javier Ramirez, Par. Vicar; Rev. Raymond Ogbemure (Nigeria), In Res.; Rev. Msgr. Antonio Valdivia, In Res.; Patricia Ramirez, DRE; CRP Stds.: 220

St. David of Wales - 5641 Esmond Ave., Richmond, CA 94805-1112 t) 510-237-1531 davidofwales@gmail.com; plynch1951@gmail.com www.stdavidofwales.com Rev. Benedict Wonganant, Admin.; Rev. Augusto Tana Acob (Philippines), In Res.; Patty Lynch, DRE; CRP Stds.: 81

St. David of Wales School - (Grades PreK-8) 871 Sonoma St., Richmond, CA 94805-1122 t) 510-232-2283 kfarr@csdo.org www.stdavidschool.org Kenneth Farr, Prin.; Stds.: 169; Lay Tchrs.: 5

St. Mark - 159 Harbour Way, Richmond, CA 94801-3553 t) 510-234-5886 parishoffice@stmarkrichmond.org www.stmarkrichmond.org Rev. Ruben Morales-Morfin, Admin.; CRP Stds.: 556

RODEO

St. Patrick - 825 Seventh St., Rodeo, CA 94572-1549 t) 510-799-4406 parishoffice@stpatrickrodeo.org; kpruett@stpatrickrodeo.org www.stpatrickrodeo.org Rev. Larry E. Young, Pst.; Rev. Rosendo R. Manalo Jr., Par. Vicar; CRP Stds.: 225

St. Patrick School - (Grades PreK-8) 907 Seventh St., Rodeo, CA 94572-1549 t) 510-799-2506 kstevens@csdo.org www.stpatrickschoolrodeo.org Kelly Stevens, Prin.;

SAN LEANDRO

Assumption of the Blessed Virgin Mary - 1100 Fulton Ave., San Leandro, CA 94577-6210 t) 510-352-1537 info@assumptionsanleandro.org www.assumptionsanleandro.org Rev. John Carillo, Admin.; Mary Schirmer, DRE; CRP Stds.: 60

Assumption of the Blessed Virgin Mary School - (Grades PreK-8) 1851 136th Ave., San Leandro, CA 94578-1661 t) 510-357-8772 lrocheford@csdo.org www.assumptionschool-sl.org Lana Rocheford, Prin.;

St. Felicitas - 1662 Manor Blvd., San Leandro, CA 94579-1509 t) 510-347-1282 (CRP); 510-351-5244 stfelicitaschurch@comcast.net www.stfelicitassl.org Vietnamese Mass Rev. Peter Dung Duc Ngo, Pst.; Dcn. Timothy Myers; Sandi Walton, DRE; CRP Stds.: 288

St. Felicitas School - (Grades PreK-8) 1650 Manor Blvd., San Leandro, CA 94579-1509 t) 510-357-2530 mjorgensen@csdo.org; lzipp@csdo.org www.stfelicitas-school.org Sr. Faustina Pham, Prin.;

St. Leander - 550 W. Estudillo Ave., San Leandro, CA 94577-3610; Mailing: 474 W. Estudillo Ave., San Leandro, CA 94577 t) 510-895-5631 stleander@sbcglobal.net www.stleanderchurch.org Rev. Fabio Correa Correa, Par. Vicar; Evelyn Gonzalez, DRE; Dcn. Victor Silveira; Rev. Michael Lacey, In Res.; Rev. Hugo Franca, Admin.; CRP Stds.: 275

St. Leander School - (Grades PreK-8) 451 Davis St., San Leandro, CA 94577 t) 510-351-4144 across@csdo.org www.stleanderschool.org Amy Cross, Prin.;

Our Lady of Good Counsel - 2500 Bermuda Ave., San Leandro, CA 94577-6402; Mailing: 14112 Azores Pl., San Leandro, CA 94577-6402 t) 510-969-7013 (Rectory) olgc.finance@gmail.com www.olgcsanleandro.com Rev. Jan Rudzewicz, Pst.; Evelyn Bonito, Bus. Mgr.; Nadine Ramos, DRE; CRP Stds.: 33

SAN LORENZO

St. John the Baptist - 264 E. Lewelling Blvd., San Lorenzo, CA 94580-1736; Mailing: 16642 Ashland Ave., San Lorenzo, CA 94580 t) 510-351-5050 x16 (CRP); 510-351-5050 stjohnsrectory@gmail.com www.stjohnsparishslz.org Rev. Sergio Lopez, Pst.; CRP Stds.: 349

St. John the Baptist School - (Grades PreK-8) 270 E. Lewelling Blvd., San Lorenzo, CA 94580-1736 t) 510-276-6632 stjohncatholicschool@gmail.com stjohncatholicschool.org Paige Child, Prin.;

SAN PABLO

St. Paul - 1845 Church Ln., San Pablo, CA 94806-3705 t) 510-672-4018 (CRP); 510-232-5931 carmennavarroccd@gmail.com; info@stpaulchurchsanpablo.org Rev. Lazaro Sandoval, O.F.M.Conv., Pst.; Rev. Anthony Howard, O.F.M.Conv., Par. Vicar; Rev. Tuan Nguyen, O.F.M.Conv., Par. Vicar; Bro. George Cherrie, O.F.M.Conv., Bus. Mgr.; Dcn. Arturo Jimenez; Carmen Navarro, DRE; CRP Stds.: 254

St. Paul School - (Grades K-8) 1825 Church Ln., San Pablo, CA 94806 t) 510-233-3080 eflores@csdo.org www.st-paulschool.org Erma Flores, Prin.;

SAN RAMON

St. Joan of Arc - 2601 San Ramon Valley Blvd., San Ramon, CA 94583-1630 t) 925-830-0600 parishoffice@sjasr.org www.sjasr.org Rev. Raymond Sacca, Pst.; Dcn. John Durden Jr.; Dcn. Fred Seril; Mary Machi, DRE; CRP Stds.: 418

UNION CITY

St. Anne - 32223 Cabello St., Union City, CA 94587-0292 t) 510-471-7766 office@saintannecatholic.org www.saintannecatholic.org Rev. Gerald Pedrera, Par. Vicar; Rev. Rolando Bartolay, Pst.; Dcn. Arsenio Reyes;

Our Lady of the Rosary - 703 C St., Union City, CA 94587-2195 t) 510-471-2609 dmarquez@olrchurch.org; admin@olrchurch.org www.olrchurch.org Rev. Jesus Nieto-Ruiz, Pst.; Donald Marquez, DRE; Robert Lee Clark Jr., Bus. Mgr.; CRP Stds.: 335

WALNUT CREEK

St. Anne - 1600 Rossmoor Pkwy., Walnut Creek, CA 94595-2507 t) 925-932-2324 st_annes@comcast.net; info@stanneswc.org www.stanneswc.org/ Rev. Leonard Marrujo, Pst.; Rev. George Da Roza, S.S.C., In Res.;

St. John Vianney - 1650 Ygnacio Valley Rd., Walnut Creek, CA 94598-3123 t) 925-939-7911 staff@sjvianney.org www.sjvianney.org Rev. William D. Rosario (India), Pst.; Rev. Christopher Berbena, In Res.; Elizabeth Rogers, DRE; CRP Stds.: 228

St. Mary - 2051 Mt. Diablo Blvd., Walnut Creek, CA 94596 t) 925-891-8900 info@stmary-wc.org www.stmary-wc.org Rev. Fred Riccio, Pst.; Maureen Tiffany, DRE; CRP Stds.: 128

St. Mary School - (Grades PreK-8) 1158 Bont Ln., Walnut Creek, CA 94596 t) 925-935-5054 stmary@st-mary.net www.st-mary.net Garrett Padia, Prin.;

St. Stephen - 1101 Keaveny Ct., Walnut Creek, CA 94597-2465 t) 925-274-1341 saintstephenwc@gmail.com saintstephenparish.org Rev. Paulson Mundanmani, Admin.;

SCHOOLS: PRESCHOOL THRU HIGH SCHOOL

SCHOOLS

STATE OF CALIFORNIA

CONCORD

De La Salle Academy - (DIO) (Grades 5-8) 1380 Galaxy Way, Suite A, Concord, CA 94520 t) 925-471-8160 giangregorioc@dls-academy.org dls-academy.org/ Christopher Giangregorio, Pres.; Stds.: 72

***Wood Rose Academy** - (PRV) (Grades PreK-8) 4347 Cowell Rd., Concord, CA 94518-1807 t) 925-825-4644 woodroseacad@sbcglobal.net; aralday@woodroseacademy.org www.woodroseacademy.org Aracely R Iniguez, Prin.; Stds.: 183; Lay Tchrs.: 16

OAKLAND

Lumen Christi Academies of the Roman Catholic Diocese of Oakland - (DIO) (Grades PreSchool-8) 2121 Harrison St., Ste. 100, Oakland, CA 94612 t) 510-590-8458 rpierre-antoine@lcacademies.org lumenchristiacademies.org/ Network of 6 schools holistically forming students and adults through a collaborative experience that is dynamic, innovative, and accessible to all. Rodney Pierre-Antoine, Exec. Dir.; Stds.: 1,010; Sr. Tchrs.: 1; Lay Tchrs.: 65

HIGH SCHOOLS

STATE OF CALIFORNIA

ALAMEDA

Saint Joseph Notre Dame High School - (PAR) (Grades 9-12) 1011 Chestnut St., Alameda, CA 94501-4315 t) 510-523-1526 dlozano@sjnd.org; mgarcen@sjnd.org www.sjnd.org Julianne Guevara, Prin.; Elizabeth Rochlin, Registrar; Mallory Cornett, Librn.; Stds.: 411; Lay Tchrs.: 41

BERKELEY

Saint Mary's College High School (Brothers of the Christian Schools) - (PRV) (Grades 9-12) Peralta Park, 1294 Albina Ave., Berkeley, CA 94706-2599 t) 510-526-9242 kwendt@stmchs.org www.saintmaryschs.org Dr. Peter Imperial, Prin.; Lawrence C. Puck, Pres.; Brian Thomas, Librn.; Stds.: 630; Bro. Tchrs.: 1; Lay Tchrs.: 48

CONCORD

Carondelet High School (Sisters of St Joseph of Carondelet) - (PRV) (Grades 9-12) 1133 Winton Dr., Concord, CA 94518-3527 t) 925-686-5353 chs@carondeleths.org www.carondeleths.org Jessica Mix, Pres.; Stds.: 800

De La Salle High School of Concord, Inc. (Brothers of the Christian Schools) - (PRV) (Grades 9-12) 1130 Winton Dr., Concord, CA 94518-3528 t) 925-288-8100 www.dlshs.org Boys. David J. Holquin, Pres.; Joe Aliotti, Dean of Students; Heather Alumbaugh, Prin.; Stds.: 1,020; Scholastics: 79; Pr. Tchrs.: 1

HAYWARD

Moreau Catholic High School - (PRV) (Grades 9-12)

27170 Mission Blvd., Hayward, CA 94544 t) 510-881-4300 eguneratne@moreaucatholic.org www.moreaucatholic.org Rev. Bruce Cecil, C.S.C, Chap.; Colleen Galloway, Prin.; Dr. Elizabeth Guneratne, Pres.; Matthew Duke, Bus. Mgr.; Jessica Simons, Librn.;

OAKLAND

Bishop O'Dowd High School - (DIO) (Grades 9-12) 9500 Stearns Ave., Oakland, CA 94605-4720 t) 510-577-9100 devans@bishopodowd.org www.bishopodowd.org Doug Evans, Prin.; Rev. James Sullivan, Chap.; James D. Childs, Pres.; Annette Counts, Librn.; Stds.: 1,250; Pr. Tchrs.: 2; Lay Tchrs.: 107

Cristo Rey De La Salle East Bay High School, Inc. (Brothers of the Christian Schools) - (PRV) (Grades 9-12) 1530 34th Ave., Oakland, CA 94601 t) 510-532-8947 info@cristoreydelasalle.org www.cristoreydelasalle.org (St. Elizabeth Campus) Maria Cortez Garcia, Director of Admission; Stephen M Murphy, Pres.; Ann Nguyen, Vice President Corporate Work Study Program; Jolanta Zakrzewski, Director - Finance; Jessica Murray, Prin.; Stds.: 309; Lay Tchrs.: 24

Holy Names High School (Sisters of the Holy Names of Jesus and Mary) - (PRV) 4660 Harbord Dr., Oakland, CA 94618-2211 t) 510-450-1110 chubbard@hnhsoakland.org; jcasella@hnhsoakland.org www.hnhsoakland.org Dr. Adams Jamie, Prin.; Constance Hubbard, Pres.; Stds.: 140; Lay Tchrs.: 30

RICHMOND

Salesian College Preparatory (Salesians of St. John Bosco) - (PRV) (Grades 9-12) 2851 Salesian Ave., Richmond, CA 94804 t) 510-234-4433 mflannery@salesian.com www.salesian.com Bro. Leo Imbert, In Res.; Bro. Patrick Maloney, S.D.B., In Res.; Rev. Joe Nguyen, SDB, In Res.; Rev. John Puntino, In Res.; Marylou Flannery, Prin.; Stephen Pezzola, Pres.; Rev. John Itzaina, SDB, Dir.; Stds.: 405; Bro. Tchrs.: 1; Lay Tchrs.: 32

INSTITUTIONS LOCATED IN DIOCESE

ASSOCIATIONS [ASN]

BERKELEY

Inter-Friendship House Association, Friendship Center - 1646 Addison St., Berkeley, CA 94703-1404; Mailing: 4270 Pomona Ave., Palo Alto, CA 94306 t) 415-308-2647 ujeanlee@gmail.com www.fuyou-berkeley.org Eugene Lee, Chair;

US-China Catholic Association - 1646 Addison St., Berkeley, CA 94703 t) 510-900-2015 director@uscatholicchina.org; admin@uscatholicchina.org www.uscatholicchina.org (Formerly: the United States Catholic China Bureau) Xin Chen, Bus. Mgr.; Rev. Michael Agliardo, Exec. Dir.;

CAMPUS MINISTRY / NEWMAN CENTERS [CAM]

MORAGA

St. Mary's College Mission and Ministry Center - 1928 Saint Marys Rd., Moraga, CA 94575-4777; Mailing: P.O. Box 4777, Moraga, CA 94575-4777 t) 925-631-4366 cao6@stmarys-ca.edu www.stmarys-ca.edu/mission-ministry-center Bro. Camillus Chavez, F.S.C.; Rev. Hai Ho, O.F.M.Cap., Chap.; Karin L. McClelland, Dir.; Bro. Christopher Brady, F.S.C., Chaplain to the Athletes; Colleen O'Healy Da Silva, Chapel Coordinator and Adminisrative Assistant; Carrie Davis, Asst. Dir.; Quang Luu, Assistant Director; Nick van Santen, Assistant Director;

OAKLAND

Holy Names University Campus Ministry - 3500 Mountain Blvd., Oakland, CA 94619-1627 t) 510-436-1002 ragusa@hnu.edu www.hnu.edu Jenny Girard Malley, Dir.; Rev. Salvatore Ragusa, S.D.S., Dir.;

CATHOLIC CHARITIES [CCH]

OAKLAND

Catholic Charities of the Diocese of Oakland - 433 Jefferson St., Oakland, CA 94607-3539 t) 510-768-3100 info@cceb.org; mkuhn@cceb.org www.cceb.org Margaret Peterson, CEO; Most Rev. Michael C. Barber, S.J., President, Board of Directors; James Jones, Chair of the Board; James Fiedler, Vice Chair of Board; Rick A. Medeiros, Bishop's Representative to the Board; Jairo Rene Leiva, Chief of Staff; Lori Wernsing, Interim Chief Financial Officer; Mounir Tyler, Chief Program Officer; Mary Kuhn, Deputy Chief of Communication/ Interim Development Leader; Asstd. Annu.: 22,756; Staff: 75

Concord Service Center - 2120 Diamond Blvd. Suite 220, Concord, CA 94520; Mailing: 433 Jefferson St., Oakland, CA 94607 t) (510) 768-3100

Oakland Service Center - 433 Jefferson St., Oakland, CA 94607-3539 t) (510) 768-3100

West County Service Center - 217 Harbour Way, Richmond, CA 94801; Mailing: 433 Jefferson St., Oakland, CA 94607 t) (510) 768-3100

COLLEGES & UNIVERSITIES [COL]

MORAGA

Saint Mary's College of California (Saint Mary's College of California, Brothers of the Christian Schools, District of San Francisco) - 1928 St. Mary's Rd., PMB 3005, Moraga, CA 94575-3005 t) 925-631-4000 president@stmarys-ca.edu www.stmarys-ca.edu Bro. Michael S. Avila, F.S.C., Prof.; Bro. Glenn Bolton, F.S.C., In Res.; Bro. Christopher Brady, F.S.C., In Res.; Bro. Kenneth W. Cardwell, F.S.C., Prof.; Bro. Camillus Chavez, F.S.C., Prof.; Bro. Ronald Gallagher, F.S.C., President Emeritus; Bro. Charles Hilken, F.S.C., Prof.; Bro. Thomas Jones, F.S.C., Dir.; Bro. Richard Lemberg, F.S.C., Librn.; Bro. Bernard LoCoco, F.S.C., In Res.; Bro. Brenden Madden, F.S.C., In Res.; Rev. Thomas McElligott, Campus Min.; Bro. Chris Donnelly, F.S.C., Facilities; Bro. Michael Meister, F.S.C., Prof.; Bro. Patrick Moore, In Res.; Rev. John Morris, O.P., Campus Min.; Bro. Michael Murphy, Prof.; Stds.: 3,169; Bro. Tchrs.: 1; Lay Tchrs.: 205

OAKLAND

Holy Names University (Sisters of the Holy Names of Jesus and Mary, A Corporation, Holy Names University, A Corporation, Sisters of the Holy Names of Jesus and Mary) - 3500 Mountain Blvd., Oakland, CA 94619-1627 t) 510-436-1000 tom@hnu.edu www.hnu.edu Rev. Salvatore Ragusa, S.D.S., Campus Min.; Michael Groener, Pres.; Sylvia Contreras, Librn.; Stds.: 973; Lay Tchrs.: 31; Sr. Tchrs.: 1

CONVENTS, MONASTERIES, AND RESIDENCES FOR WOMEN [CON]

BERKELEY

Franciscan Sisters of Little Falls, MN - 2341 Prince St., Berkeley, CA 94705-1938 t) 510-848-5721 akroll@fslf.org

BRENTWOOD

Religious Missionary Sisters of the Blessed Sacrament and Mary Immaculate - 636 - 3rd St., Brentwood, CA 94513-1357 t) 925-513-8154 grande815@msn.com; januariab@gmail.com Sr. Guadalupe Grande, M.S.S., Supr.;

CONCORD

Quinhon Missionary Sisters of the Holy Cross - 1685 Humphrey Dr., Concord, CA 94519-1810 t) 925-674-9639 catherinepdang@yahoo.com mtgqn.org Sr. Catherine Phuong Dang, L.H.C., Prov.; Srs.: 28

Aspirant House - 50 Santa Maria Way, Orinda, CA 94563-2605 t) 925-253-0831 bandieuhanh.qntshk@gmail.com Sr. Mary Margaret Phan, LHC, Dir.;

Concord Convent - 1727 Humphrey Dr., Concord, CA 94519 t) 925-676-9320 rnguyen@oakdiocese.org Sr. Rosaline Lieu Nguyen, L.H.C., Supr.;

St. Felicitas Convent - 1604 Manor Dr., San Leandro, CA 94579 t) 510-351-5577 plhhoang@yahoo.com Sr. Paulina Hang Hoang, L.H.C., Supr.;

Sisters of St. Joseph of the Third Order of St. Francis - 2301 Mt. Diablo St., Concord, CA 94520-2213 t) 925-825-2091 marygrace@eastbayservicesdd.org Sr. Marygrace Puchac, Contact;

EL CERRITO

Sisters of Sacred Hearts of Jesus and Mary - 1607 Liberty St., El Cerrito, CA 94530 t) 510-686-0615 kathleenlavertyshjm@gmail.com sacredheartsjm.org Sr. Kathleen Laverty, Contact; Srs.: 1

EMERYVILLE

Sisters of St. Francis of Penance and Christian Charity - 1231 40th St., Apt. 332, Emeryville, CA 94608 t) 510-601-8132; 510-614-2224; 510-532-2207 mariaelena10@juno.com; marylitell@franciscanway.org www.franciscanway.org Sr. Maria Elena Martinez, Contact;

Sisters of the Presentation of the Blessed Virgin Mary - 1055 47th St., Emeryville, CA 94608 t) 510-655-8132 marilynmedau026@gmail.com

FREMONT

Congregation of the Queen of the Holy Rosary (Dominican Sisters of Mission San Jose) - 43326 Mission Cir., Fremont, CA 94539-5898 t) 510-657-2468 pauline@msjdominicans.org; celeste@msjdominicans.org www.msjdominicans.org Sr. Celeste Marie Botello, OP, Prioress; Srs.: 134

St. Elizabeth Convent - 1555-34th Ave., Oakland, CA 94601-3062 t) 510-532-8344 Sr. Karen Elizabeth Zavitz, Prioress;

St. Martin Community - Sr. Mary Kidder, OP, Prioress;

Our Lady of the Angels Community - Sr. Eva Beehner, O.P., Prioress;

Queen of Peace Community - Sr. Mary Liam Brock, O.P., Prioress;

Sisters of the Holy Family - 43543 Mission Blvd., Fremont, CA 94539-5831; Mailing: P.O. Box 3248, Fremont, CA 94539-5831 t) 510-624-4596 congsecy@holyfamilysisters.org www.holyfamilysisters.org Sr. Gladys Guenther, Pres.; Srs.: 39

HAYWARD

Dominican Sisters of Oakford - 22320 Foothill Boulevard, Suite 322, Hayward, CA 94541-2719 t) 510-398-8112 oakfordusa@hotmail.com www.oakforddomnicans.org Ministries in teaching, counseling; spiritual direction, parish adult education; Migrant advocacy, social work, chaplaincy, campus ministry. Sr. Mary de Crus Nolan, O.P., Prioress; Srs.: 14

HERCULES

Congregation of the Mother of Carmel - 142 Weiss Ct., Hercules, CA 94547-3750 t) 510-724-4178; 510-965-2149 weisscarmel@gmail.com Sr. Ranit Nellissery, Contact; Srs.: 4

KENSINGTON

Carmel of Jesus, Mary and Joseph of Kensington, California - 68 Rincon Rd., Kensington, CA 94707 t) 510-267-8330 chancellor@oakdiocese.org www.carmelofkensington.org Mother Sylvia Gemma, O.C.D., Prioress; Srs.: 6

NEWARK

Congregation of the Queen of the Holy Rosary (Dominican Sisters of Mission San Jose) - 37088 Arden St., Newark, CA 94560-3702 t) (510) 933-6386 Sr. Celeste Marie Botello, OP, Prioress; Sr. Pauline Bouton, OP, Secy.;

OAKLAND

Adrian Dominican Sisters (Congregation of the Most Holy Rosary) - 3693 High St., Oakland, CA 94619-2105 t) 510-530-2621 mejcastot@gmail.com Sr. Marian Casteluccio, Contact;

Congregation of the Queen of the Holy Rosary (Dominican Sisters of Mission San Jose) - 1555-34th Ave., Oakland, CA 94601-3062 t) 510-532-8344 www.msjdominicans.org Sr. Karen Elizabeth Zavitz, Prioress;

Sisters of Mercy of the Americas (West Midwest Community) - 3431 Foothill Blvd., Oakland, CA 94601-3129 t) 402-881-4931 pat@sistersofmercy.org; sdeitchler@mercywmw.org www.mercyretirementcenter.org Sr. Pat McDermott, Pres.;

SAN LEANDRO

Missionary Sisters of the Society of Mary - 1515 Boxwood Ave., San Leandro, CA 94579-1303 t) 510-357-7816 johnpaul01@aol.com www.maristsmsm.org Sr. John Paul Chao, SMSM, Contact;

WALNUT CREEK

Sisters of St. Joseph of Carondelet - 720 N. Gate Rd., Walnut Creek, CA 94598 t) 310-889-2100 aosullivan@csjla.org Sr. Patricia Nelson, CSJ, Supr.; Sr. Adele O'Sullivan, Prov.;

St. Anthony Community - 2809 Bayview Dr., Alameda, CA 94501-6347 jawright@csjla.org

Christ the King Community - 3095 Diablo View Rd., Pleasant Hill, CA 94523-4535 t) 925-280-1562 jcgallagher@csjla.org

Kwanza House - 2203 Colonial Ct., Walnut Creek, CA 94598-1125 jawright@csjla.org

Via del Sol Community - t) 925-287-9611 aboshea442@gmail.com

ENDOWMENTS / FOUNDATIONS / TRUSTS [EFT]

FREMONT

Dominican Sisters of Mission San Jose Foundation (A Nonprofit Corp.) - 43326 Mission Cir., Fremont, CA 94539-5898 t) 510-933-6386 pauline@msjdominicans.org www.msjdominicans.org Sr. Pauline Bouton, OP, Admin.; Ana Regalia, Treas.;

Pia Backes Support Trust - 43326 Mission Ciir., Fremont, CA 94539-5898 t) 510-657-2468 tan@msjdominicans.org Sr. Mary Liam Brock, O.P., Pres.;

OAKLAND

The Benilde Religious & Charitable Trust - 1631 Telegraph Ave., Oakland, CA 94612 t) 510-899-6100 ecannon@plagemanlund.com www.plagemanlund.com Charitable trust fund to benefit the educational activities of the Brothers of the Christian Schools of San Francisco. Elizabeth Cannon, Contact;

Dominican Community Support Charitable Trust - 5877 Birch Ct., Oakland, CA 94618-1626 t) 510-658-8722 pvilla@opwest.org Very Rev. Michael Fones, OP, Socius; Very Rev. Christopher Fadok, O.P., Prof.;

The Oakland Parochial Fund, Inc. - 2121 Harrison St., Ste. 100, Oakland, CA 94612-3788

Province of Saint Barbara Fraternal Care Trust - 1500 34th Ave., Oakland, CA 94601 t) 510-536-3722 fct@sbofm.org Rev. John Hardin, O.F.M.; Rev. David Gaa, O.F.M., Prov.; Rev. Melvin A. Jurisich, O.F.M., Pres.;

MISCELLANEOUS [MIS]

ANTIOCH

***Pan De Vida Retreat** - 3836 Warbler Dr., Antioch, CA 94509 t) 925-297-7282 pandevidaretreat@gmail.com www.pandevidaretreat.com Peggy Murray, Dir.; Joe Murray, Retreat Coordinator;

BERKELEY

Multicultural Institute - 1920 Seventh St., Berkeley, CA 94710-2011 t) 510-848-4075 mirna@mionline.org www.mionline.org Victor Weisser, Pres.; Jacqueline De Anda, Vice Pres.; Rev. Rigoberto Caloca-Rivas, O.F.M., Exec.;

Opus Dei - 1827 Oxford St., Berkeley, CA 94709-1800 t) 510-549-9804 msgr.james.kelly@gmail.com Prelature of the Holy Cross and Opus Dei Rev. Javier Bujalance, Chap.; Rev. Msgr. James A. Kelly, Chap.;

CONCORD

East Bay Services to the Developmentally Disabled - 1870 Adobe St., Concord, CA 94520 t) 925-825-2091 marygrace@eastbayservicesdd.org Sr. Marygrace Puchac, Exec.;

DANVILLE

Catholic Professional & Business Breakfast Club of the Diocese of Oakland - 440 LaGonda Way, Danville, CA 94526; Mailing: 2485 Holly Oak Dr., Danville, CA 94506-2043 t) 925-525-0272 info@catholicsatwork.com www.catholicsatwork.com Rev. Paulson Mundanmani, Chap.; Rob Aceto, Treas.; Thomas Loarie, Chair; David Manion, Pres.;

OAKLAND

Adventus, a California nonprofit public benefit corporation - 2121 Harrison St., Ste. 100, Oakland, CA 94612-3788 t) 510-267-8321 pbongiovanni@oakdiocese.org Purpose: To support the mission of the Roman Catholic Diocese of Oakland. Paul Bongiovanni, Pres.; James H. McCann, Vice Pres.;

Cristo Rey De La Salle East Bay Work Study Program - 1530 34th Ave., Oakland, CA 94601 t) 510-532-8947 info@cristoreydelasalle.org www.cristoreydelasalle.org Stephen M Murphy, Pres.; Ann Nguyen, Vice President of Corporate Work Study Program;

Dominican Sisters Vision of Hope - 1555 34th Ave., Oakland, CA 94601-3062 t) 510-533-5768 amagovern@msjdominicans.org; yyildirim@msjdominicans.org www.visionofhope.org Ann Magovern, Exec.;

***Faith in Action** - 171 Santa Rosa Ave., Oakland, CA 94610-1316 t) 510-655-2801 jbaumann@faithinaction.org www.faithinaction.org Ronald White, Chair; Rev. John A. Baumann, S.J., Founder;

Franciscan Charities, Inc. - 1500 34th Ave., Oakland, CA 94601-3024 t) 510-536-3772 main@sbofm.com Rev. David Gaa, O.F.M., Pres.;

Italian Catholic Federation - 8393 Capwell Dr., Ste. 110, Oakland, CA 94621-2117 t) 510-633-9058; 888-423-1924 info@icf.org www.icf.org Rev. Christopher Bennett, Chap.;

***Next Step Learning Center, Inc.** - 2222 Curtis St., Oakland, CA 94607 t) 510-251-1731 lstringer@nextsteplc.org www.nextsteplc.org Education and tutoring center for youth and adults 17 yrs. and older. Evelyn Ashcroft, Pres.; Lisa Stringer, Exec. Dir.;

***Oakland Elizabeth House** - 6423 Colby St., Oakland, CA 94618-1309 t) 510-658-1380 www.oakehouse.org Purpose: 24-month transitional housing program for women and children. Jackie Yancy, Exec. Dir.;

***Providence House, LP** - 540 - 23rd St., Oakland, CA 94612-1718 t) 510-444-0839 jennifer.bachhuber@providence.org www.providencesupportivehousing.org Rent-subsidized housing for persons with physical disabilities including persons with AIDS. Jennifer Bachhuber, Dir.;

Redemptorist Vice Province Initiative - 8945 Golf Links Rd., Oakland, CA 94605; Mailing: c/o The Redemptorists/Denver Province, 1633 N. Cleveland Ave., Chicago, IL 60614 t) 312-248-8894 x105 Rev. Gregory May, C.Ss.R., Treas.;

PITTSBURG

***District Council of Contra Costa County Society of St. Vincent de Paul** - 2210 Gladstone Dr., Pittsburg, CA 94565 t) 925-439-5060 info@svdp-cc.org info@svdp-cc.org Bob Liles, Pres.; Claudia Ramirez, Exec. Dir.;

PLEASANTON

***Catholic Management Services (CMS)** - 4750 Willow Rd., Ste. 200, Pleasanton, CA 94588 t) 925-946-1440 ambaatz@cfcsmission.org Robert W. Seelig, CEO; Paul Bongiovanni, Bd. Dirs.; Ronald Gies, Bd. Dirs.; Rev. George E. Mockel, Bd. Dirs.;

WALNUT CREEK

Magnificat S.O.T.I. - Walnut Creek Chapter - ; Mailing: P.O. Box 4626, Walnut Creek, CA 94596 t) 925-788-7762 www.magnificat-ministry.net/ca-walnut-creek Maribel Serrano, Coordinator;

MONASTERIES AND RESIDENCES FOR PRIESTS AND BROTHERS [MON]

BERKELEY

Capuchin Franciscan Friars - 1534 Arch St., Berkeley, CA 94708-1829 t) 510-841-2229 friarhung@yahoo.com www.olcapuchins.org Rev. Hung Nguyen, OFM Cap, Supr.; Rev. Donal Burke, O.F.M.Cap., In Res.; Rev. James Johnson, O.F.M. Cap., In Res.; Rev. Alan Wilson, O.F.M.Cap, In Res.; Bro. Nikolas Barth, In Res.; Bro. Austin Cambon, In Res.; Rev. Martin Haggins, In Res.; Rev. Ron Talbott, In Res.; Brs.: 8; Priests: 6

Saint Conrad Friary -

Incarnation Monastery, Camaldolese Benedictines - 1369 La Loma Ave., Berkeley, CA 94708-2031 t) 510-845-0601 berkeleymonks@gmail.com; bedejhealey@gmail.com www.incarnationmonastery.org Bro. Thomas Mazzocco, OSB Cam, In Res.; Bro. Ivan Nicoletto, O.S.B.Cam., In Res.; Rev. Arthur Poulin, O.S.B.Cam., In Res.; Very Rev. Bede Healey, OSB Cam, Prior; Brs.: 2; Priests: 2

Jesuit Fathers and Brothers - 1756 LeRoy Ave., Berkeley, CA 94709-1157 t) 510-225-6200 jstrector@scu.edu; jstminister@scu.edu www.jstjesuits.org Bro. Sean Barry, SJ, Student; Rev. Martin T Connell, SJ, Rector; Rev. Javier Diaz y Diaz, S.J., Pst. Assoc.; Rev. Michael Tyrrell, Treas.; Rev. Joseph Mueller, SJ, Dean; Rev. Eduardo C. Fernandez, S.J., Prof.; Rev. George E. Griener, S.J., Prof.; Rev. Christopher Hadley, S.J., Prof.; Rev. Paul A. Janowiak, S.J., Prof.; Rev. Anh Q. Tran, S.J., Prof.; Rev. Rossano Zas Friz de Col, SJ, Prof.; Rev. George R. Murphy, S.J., Dir.; Rev. Nana Kofi Agyapong, SJ, Student; Rev. Augustin N'guessan Kouacou Koffi, SJ, Student; Rev. Egide Ndayisenga, SJ, Student; Rev. T. Basile Ouedraogo, SJ, Student; Rev. Manuel Santamaria Belda, SJ, Student; Very Rev. Wossoyam Elie Yoda, SJ, Student; Rev. Chikere A Agbo, SJ, Student; Rev. Jayaraju Ghattamaneni, SJ, Student; Rev. Jean Claude Havyarimana, SJ, Student; Rev. Aloysius Ming-te Hsu, SJ, Student; Rev. Jeremie Kinzamba, SJ, Student; Rev. Marco Tulio Martinez, SJ, Student; Rev. Patrick Ng'ang'a, SJ, Student; Rev. Minh Trieu Nguyen, SJ, Student; Rev. Mark Ngwenya, SJ, Student; Rev. Boyd Kapyunga Nyirenda, SJ, Student; Bro. Hugo Xicohtencatl, SJ, Student; Brs.: 2; Priests: 27

Priests of the Congregation of Holy Cross - 2597 Virginia St., Berkeley, CA 94709-1108 t) 510-548-8515 x17 Rev. Bruce Cecil, C.S.C; Priests: 1

Salesians of Don Bosco - Don Bosco Hall, 1831 Arch St., Berkeley, CA 94709-1309 t) 510-204-0800; 510-220-8064 (Supr.) jobonz@gmail.com Religious house of formation Rev. Alejandro Rodriguez, SDB, Vicar; Rev. Joseph Boenzi, S.D.B., Dir.; Rev. John Gibson, S.D.B., In Res.; Bro. Damien Ho, Student; Dang Khoa Pham, Student; Rev. Gilbert Jeyaraj, In Res.; Brs.: 1; Priests: 8

Society of the Precious Blood - 2800 Milvia St., Berkeley, CA 94703-2209 t) 816-522-9420 dmatzcpps@gmail.com Rev. Joseph Nassal, C.PP.S., In Res.; Rev. James Smith, C.PP.S., In Res.; Rev. David Matz, C.PP.S., Dir.; Priests: 3

CASTRO VALLEY

Conventual Franciscans (Province of St. Joseph of Cupertino) - St. Joseph of Cupertino Friary, 19697 Redwood Rd., Castro Valley, CA 94546-3456 t) 510-582-7333 x4 jreiter822@gmail.com Bro. James Reiter, O.F.M.Conv., Supr.; Rev. Victor P. Abegg, O.F.M.Conv., Prov.; Rev. Kevin Schindler-McGraw, O.F.M.Conv., Resident; Bro. Francisco Cabral, O.F.M.Conv., Resident; Rev. John Heinz, O.F.M.Conv., Treas.; Rev. Tammylee Ngo, Resident; Bro. Patrick Lytell, O.F.M.Conv., Resident; Bro. Christopher Saindon, O.F.M.Conv., Resident; Rev. James Phan, Resident; Bro. Michael Paul, O.F.M.Conv., Resident; Friar Joseph Martin Hoang, Resident; Bro. Christopher Garcia, Resident; Brs.: 7; Priests: 3

Conventual Franciscans (Province of St. Joseph

Cupertino) Provincial Center - St. Joseph of Cupertino Friary, 19697 Redwood Rd., Castro Valley, CA 94546-3456 t) 510-582-7333 jreiter822@gmail.com; vpabegg@gmail.com Rev. Victor P. Abegg, O.F.M.Conv., Prov.; Bro. James Reiter, O.F.M.Conv., Vicar; Rev. John Heinz, O.F.M.Conv., Treas.; Rev. Carlos Morales, O.F.M.Conv., Trustee; Rev. Paul T. Gawlowski, O.F.M.Conv., Trustee; Rev. Tammylee Ngo, Trustee; Brs.: 1; Priests: 5

FREMONT

***Missionaries of Faith-India Inc.** - 41933 Blacow Rd., Fremont, CA 94538 t) 510-315-7001; 510-220-0461 kmfrjoy@gmail.com Rev. Gabriel Selvanathan Augustine, M.F. (India), Par. Vicar; Rev. Poulose K. Chakkappan, M.F., Par. Vicar; Rev. Robert K. Chinnapan, M.F., Pst.; Rev. Joy Kumarthusseril, M.F. (India), Supr.; Rev. Lourdu R. Madanu, M.F., Par. Admin.; Rev. Krishnarao Mekala, M.F., Par. Vicar; Rev. Chacko Muthoottil, M.F., Pst.; Rev. Kuriakose Nadooparambil, M.F., Pst.; Rev. Du Truong Hai Nguyen, M.F. (Vietnam), Chap.; Rev. Joseph Pathiyil, M.F. (India), Pst.; Rev. Jojo Puthussery, M.F. (India), Pst.; Priests: 11

OAKLAND

Franciscan Friars of California (Province of St. Barbara) - 1500 34th Ave., Oakland, CA 94601-3091 t) (510) 536-3722 main@sbofm.org www.sbfranciscans.org Rev. Rigoberto Caloca-Rivas, O.F.M.; Bro. Didacus Clavel, O.F.M.; Bro. David Cobian, O.F.M.; Bro. Anthony Lavorin, O.F.M.; Rev. Richard McManus, O.F.M.; Rev. Nghia Phan, O.F.M.; Bro. Freddy Rodriguez; Bro. Robert Valentine, O.F.M.; Bro. Victor Vega, O.F.M.; Rev. Louis Vitale, O.F.M.; Rev. Ignatius DeGroot, OFM, In Res.; Rev. Antonio Galindo Carreon, OFM, In Res.; Bro. Christopher Best; Bro. John Summers; Rev. Jose Luis Barrios Delgado, OFM, Par. Admin.; Friar William Shaughnessy, O.F.M., In Res.; Rev. Philip Garcia, OFM, In Res.; Friar Ray Bucher, In Res.; Rev. Armando Lopez, OFM, In Res.; Rev. Melvin A. Jurisich, O.F.M., In Res.;

Franciscan Friars of California (Province of St. Barbara) - 1500-34th Ave., Oakland, CA 94601-3092 t) 510-536-3722 main@sbofm.org www.sbfranciscans.org Rev. David Gaa, O.F.M., Prov.; Rev. Martin Ibarra, O.F.M., Vicar Prov.; Rev. Thomas West, O.F.M., Prov. Secy.; Rev. Melvin A. Jurisich, O.F.M., Treas.; Stanley Raggio, Chief Opers. Officer; Bro. Brian Trawick, Admin.; Bro. Hajime Okuhara, O.F.M., Office Asst.; Bro. Eric Pilarcik, O.F.M., Dir., Vocations; Bro. Mark Schroeder, O.F.M., Dir., Franciscans for Justice;

Jesuit Fathers and Brothers - 171 Santa Rosa Ave., Oakland, CA 94610-1316 t) 510-459-6818 tweston@jesuits.org Rev. Ike Udoh, S.J., Pst. Assoc.; Rev. John A. Baumann, S.J., Spiritual Adv./Care Srvcs.; Rev. James Michael Harbaugh, S.J., Spiritual Adv./Care Srvcs.; Rev. Stephen M. Kelly, S.J., Spiritual Adv./Care Srvcs.; Rev. Thomas C. Weston, S.J., Supr.; Rev. Lester E. Love, S.J., Mem.; Brs.: 6; Priests: 6

Missionary Oblates of Mary Immaculate Western - 290 Lenox Ave., Oakland, CA 94610-4625 t) 510-452-1550 lenoxhouse@omiusa.org lenox.house Rev. Raymond John Marek Jr., OMI, Director and Superior; Rev. Donald Arel, OMI, In Res.; Priests: 2

Order of Preachers (Province of the Most Holy Name of Jesus - Western Dominican Province) - 5877 Birch Ct., Oakland, CA 94618-1626 t) 510-658-8722 info@opwest.org www.opwest.org Very Rev. Christopher Fadok, O.P., Prior Provincial; Very Rev. Michael Fones, OP, Prov. Asst.; Rev. Stephen Maria Lopez, O.P., Treas.; Brs.: 27; Priests: 110

Order of Preachers (Province of the Most Holy Name of Jesus - Western Dominican Province) - St. Albert Priory, 5890 Birch Ct., Oakland, CA 94618-1627 t) 510-596-1800 sapprior@opwest.org www.op.org/opwest/sap Very Rev. James D Thompson, O.P., Prior; Rev. Bryan Kromholtz, O.P., Subprior; Rev. Gregory T. Tatum, O.P.; Bro. John Peter Anderson, OP, In Res.; Bro. Jose Maria Barrero, O.P., In Res.; Bro. Benedict Mary Bartsch, O.P., In Res.; Rev. Luke D. Buckles, O.P., In Res.; Bro. Antony Augustine Cherian, OP, In Res.; Rev. Paul Conner, In Res.; Very Rev. Christopher Paul Fadok, O.P., Prov.; Rev. Dominic DeDomenico, O.P., In Res.; Rev. Dominic DeMaio, OP, In Res.; Bro. Elias Guadalupe Ford, OP, In Res.; Bro. Philip Neri Gerlomes, O.P., In Res.; Bro. Columban Mary Hall, O.P., In Res.; Rev. LaSalle Hallissey, O.P., In Res.; Rev. Bartholomew J. Hutcherson, O.P., In Res.; Bro. Andrew Kang, In Res.; Rev. Dennis Klein, O.P., In Res.; Bro. Luke Maria Lee, O.P., In Res.; Bro. Anselm Dominic LeFave, In Res.; Rev. Hilary Martin, O.P., In Res.; Bro. Jordan Martin, In Res.; Bro. Nathaniel Maria Mayne, OP, In Res.; Rev. Brendan McAnerney, O.P., In Res.; Rev. John Thomas Mellein, O.P., In Res.; Rev. Sergius Propst, O.P., In Res.; Bro. Patrick Rooney, O.P., In Res.; Bro. John Vianney Russell, In Res.; Rev. Ambrose Sigman, O.P., In Res.; Rev. Eugene Sousa, O.P., In Res.; Rev. Michael Sweeney, O.P., In Res.; Rev. John Marie Bingham, O.P., Promotor of Vocations; Bro. Peter Pius Chu, Vietnamese Vicariate; Bro. Peter Augustine Hoang, Vietnamese Vicariate; Rev. Joseph Quoc Quang Le, OP, Vietnamese Vicariate; Rev. Stephen Maria Lopez, O.P., Master of Students and Treasurer/Syndic of the Province; Bro. Francis Dominic Nguyen, O.P., Vietnamese Vicariate; Bro. Phong Hoang Nguyen, OP, Vietnamese Vicariate; Rev. Lawrence Tu Toan Ninh, OP, Vietnamese Vicariate; Brs.: 17; Priests: 25

Order of Preachers (Province of the Most Holy Name of Jesus - Western Dominican Province) - Siena House, 5730 Presley Way, Oakland, CA 94618-1633 wdp@opwest.org Very Rev. Michael Fones, OP; Rev. Michael J. Dodds, O.P.; Rev. Cassian Lewinski; Rev. David K. O'Rourke, O.P.; Rev. Christopher J. Renz, O.P.;

NURSING / REHABILITATION / CONVALESCENCE / ELDERLY CARE [NUR]

OAKLAND

Bishop Begin Villa - 3418 E. 18th St., Oakland, CA 94601-3004 t) 510-536-0719 (Retired Priests) Rev. David Link, In Res.; Rev. George E. Crespin, In Res.; Rev. John R. Blaker, In Res.;

Mercy Retirement and Care Center - 3431 Foothill Blvd., Oakland, CA 94601-3129 t) 510-534-8540 www.mercyretirementcenter.org Senior Residential Care, Assisted Living and Skilled Nursing. Low-Income Senior Food Distribution. Affiliated with Elder Care Alliance. Rev. Alan Wilson, O.F.M.Cap., In Res.; Rev. Owen Carroll, In Res.; Bro. Didacus Clavel, O.F.M., In Res.; Most Rev. John Cummins, In Res.; Rev. William Delaney, In Res.; Rev. Patrick Evard, OFM, In Res.; Rev. Thomas Frost, OFM, In Res.; Rev. Martin Haggins, In Res.; Rev. Evan Arthur Howard, O.F.M., In Res.; Rev. Robert LaBarbera, In Res.; Rev. Alexander Snyder, In Res.; Rev. Ron Talbott, In Res.; Rev. Louis Vitale, O.F.M., In Res.; Asstd. Annu.: 242; Staff: 165

Bishop Begin Villa, Retirement Facility for Priests in the Oakland Diocese - Rev. George E. Crespin, In Res.; Rev. David Link, In Res.;

Convalescent Hospital - Skilled Nursing Facility -

PRESCHOOLS / CHILDCARE CENTERS [PRE]

OAKLAND

***Saint Vincent's Day Home, Inc.** - 1086 Eighth St., Oakland, CA 94607-2616 t) 510-832-8324 info@svdh.org www.svdh.org

RETREAT HOUSES / RENEWAL CENTERS [RTR]

DANVILLE

San Damiano Retreat - 710 Highland Dr., Danville, CA 94526-3704 t) 925-837-9141 lisab@sandamiano.org; info@sandamiano.org www.sandamiano.org Provides a hospitable place of spiritual renewal for people of all faiths in the tradition of Sts. Francis and Clare Friar Ray Bucher, In Res.; Friar Philip Garcia, OP, In Res.; Rev. Melvin A. Jurisich, O.F.M., In Res.; Friar William Shaughnessy, O.F.M., In Res.;

LAFAYETTE

Diocesan Youth Retreat Center - 1977 Reliez Valley Rd., Lafayette, CA 94549; Mailing: 2121 Harrison St., Ste. 100, Oakland, CA 94612-3788 t) 925-934-5802 youthretreat12@gmail.com www.oakdiocese.org Tim O'Hara, Bus. Mgr.;

SEMINARIES [SEM]

BERKELEY

Dominican School of Philosophy and Theology - 2301 Vine St., Berkeley, CA 94708-1816 t) 510-849-2030 info@dspt.edu www.dspt.edu (St. Albert's College) Very Rev. Christopher Paul Fadok, O.P., Chancellor; Rev. Justin C. Gable, O.P., Vice Chancellor; Rev. Bryan Kromholtz, O.P., Dean; Rev. Joseph Boenzi, S.D.B., Prof.; Rev. Michael J. Dodds, O.P., Prof.; Sr. Marianne Farina, C.S.C., Prof.; Dr. Michael Glowasky, Prof.; Dr. James Kintz, Prof.; Rev. Dennis Klein, O.P., Prof.; Rev. Edward Krasevac, O.P., Prof.; Rev. Anselm Ramelow, O.P., Prof.; Rev. Christopher J. Renz, O.P., Prof.; Rev. Ambrose Sigman, O.P., Prof.; Dr. Matthew Thomas, Prof.; Dr. Margarita Vega, Prof.; Stds.: 46; Lay Tchrs.: 4; Pr. Tchrs.: 9; Sr. Tchrs.: 1

Jesuit School of Theology of Santa Clara University (Berkeley, California Campus) - 1735 LeRoy Ave., Berkeley, CA 94709-1115 t) 510-549-5000 jblattler@scu.edu www.scu.edu/jst Rev. Joseph Mueller, SJ, Dean; Rev. Rossano Zas-Friz, S.J., Prof.; Rev. Eduardo C. Fernandez, S.J., Prof.; Rev. Christopher Hadley, S.J., Prof.; Rev. Paul A. Janowiak, S.J., Prof.; Rev. Anh Q. Tran, S.J., Prof.; Rev. George E. Griener, S.J., Faculty Emeriti; Rev. Robert J. McCann, Adjunct Faculty; Rev. George R. Murphy, S.J., Faculty Emeriti; Rev. William R. O'Neill, S.J., Faculty Emeriti; Rev. George Williams, S.J., Adjunct Faculty; Stds.: 112; Lay Tchrs.: 9; Pr. Tchrs.: 5

SPECIAL CARE FACILITIES [SPF]

FREMONT

St. Joseph's Center for Deaf and Hard of Hearing (St. Joseph's Center for the Deaf and Hard of Hearing, A Corporation) - 40374 Fremont Blvd., Fremont, CA 94538; Mailing: 2121 Harrison St., Ste. 100, Oakland, CA 94612-3788 t) 510-267-8348; 510-250-2060 lyoung@oakdiocese.org www.oakdiocese.org/sjcd Rev. Larry E. Young, Contact;

Diocese of Ogdensburg

(Dioecesis Ogdensburgensis)

MOST REVEREND TERRY R. LAVALLEY

Bishop of Ogdensburg; ordained September 24, 1988; appointed Bishop of Ogdensburg February 23, 2010; ordained and installed April 30, 2010. Mailing Address: P.O. Box 369, Ogdensburg, NY 13669.

Chancery Office: P.O. Box 369, Ogdensburg, NY 13669. T: 315-393-2920; F: 866-314-7296.
www.rcdony.org

Square Miles 12,036.

Erected by His Holiness Pius IX, February 16, 1872.

Incorporated by a special act of the Legislature of the State of New York, April 10, 1945, with the title: The Roman Catholic Diocese of Ogdensburg, New York.

Comprises that part of Herkimer and Hamilton Counties north of the northern line of the townships of Ohio and Russia as existing in 1872 with the entire Counties of Lewis, Jefferson, St. Lawrence, Franklin, Clinton and Essex in the State of New York.

For legal titles of parishes and diocesan institutions, consult the Chancery Office.

STATISTICAL OVERVIEW

Personnel

Bishop	1
Priests: Diocesan Active in Diocese	43
Priests: Retired, Sick or Absent	36
Number of Diocesan Priests	79
Religious Priests in Diocese	9
Total Priests in your Diocese	88
Extern Priests in Diocese	4
Ordinations:	
Diocesan Priests	1
Transitional Deacons	1
Permanent Deacons in Diocese	93
Total Sisters	60

Parishes

Parishes	80
With Resident Pastor:	
Resident Diocesan Priests	67
Resident Religious Priests	8
Without Resident Pastor:	
Administered by Deacons	5
Missions	3
Pastoral Centers	1
Closed Parishes	1
Professional Ministry Personnel:	
Sisters	18
Lay Ministers	19

Welfare

Homes for the Aged	1
Total Assisted	147
Special Centers for Social Services	14
Total Assisted	28,000

Educational

Diocesan Students in Other Seminaries	9
Total Seminarians	9
High Schools, Diocesan and Parish	2
Total Students	205
Elementary Schools, Diocesan and Parish	8
Total Students	1,040
Catechesis/Religious Education:	
High School Students	494
Elementary Students	1,762
Total Students under Catholic Instruction	3,510
Teachers in Diocese:	
Sisters	3
Lay Teachers	152

Vital Statistics

Receptions into the Church:	
Infant Baptism Totals	455
Minor Baptism Totals	22
Adult Baptism Totals	21
Received into Full Communion	22
First Communions	433
Confirmations	368
Marriages:	
Catholic	94
Interfaith	33
Total Marriages	127
Deaths	1,448
Total Catholic Population	71,315
Total Population	423,326

LEADERSHIP

Office of the Bishop - Most Rev. Terry R. LaValley;

Bishop's Office Secretary - Renee Grizzuto;

Vicar General - t) 315-393-3930 Rev. Joseph A. Morgan;

ADMINISTRATION

Diocesan Receptionist/Administrative Assistant - Mary Jo Rocker;

Episcopal Vicar for Pastoral Services and Moderator of the Curia - Rev. Kevin J. O'Brien;

Chancellor - Dcn. James D. Crowley;

Diocesan Archivist -

Office of Cemeteries -

Prison Chaplains -

Office of Public Information -

Development Office and Planned Giving - Scott Lalone, Exec. Dir.; Valerie Mathews, Asst. Dir.;

Bishops' Fund Appeal & Stewardship Office - Valerie Mathews, Dir.;

Fiscal Office - Mark T. Mashaw, CFO;

Insurance Claims and Risk Management Department - James Morrison, Mgr.; Rita Reynolds, Claims Svc. Rep.;

Human Resources Director - Kimberly Snover;

Parish Administrative Services Coordinator - Kathleen Donaldson;

Information Technology - Ian Fawcett, Coord.;

Living Stones Planning Committee - Gary West, Chairperson;

Department of Worship - Rev. Bryan D. Stitt, Dir.;

OFFICES AND DIRECTORS

Episcopal Vicar for Clergy - Rev. Christopher C. Carrara;

Bishop's Delegate to Pastoral Ministers - Dcn. James D. Crowley;

Permanent Deacons - Dcn. Kevin T. Mastellon, Dir.;

Deacon Formation - Rev. Msgr. Robert H. Aucoin;

Bishop's Delegate for Religious - Sr. Bernadette Marie Collins, S.S.J.;

Safe Environment and Charter Compliance - John Morrison, Dir.;

Vocations Office - Rev. Christopher C. Carrara, Dir.; Rev. Matthew Conger, Assoc. Dir.; Sr. Mary Eamon Lyng, S.S.J., Diocesan Vocations Coord.;

Episcopal Vicar for Education and the New Evangelization - Rev. Msgr. Robert H. Aucoin;

Department of Education - Sr. Ellen Rose Coughlin, S.S.J., Supt.; Karen Donahue, Asst. Supt.;

Department of Faith Formation - Sr. Ellen Rose Coughlin, S.S.J., Dir.;

Eastern Regional Center - t) 518-310-3669 Anita Soltero, Dir.;

Western Regional Center - Catherine Russell, Dir.;

Formation for Ministry - Catherine Russell, Dir.;

Office of Youth Ministry -

Catholic Scouting - Rev. Bryan D. Stitt, Chap.;

Office of New Evangelization - Marika Donders, Dir.;

Hispanic Ministry - Rev. Robert L. Decker, Dir.;

Campus Ministry - Conner Cummings, Campus Min.; Desiree M Kirk, Campus Min.; Sr. Juliana Raymond, S.S.J., Campus Min.;

Young Adult Ministry - Marika Donders, Dir.;

Office for Ecumenism - Dcn. Thomas J. Yousey, Dir.;

Office of Communications - Darcy Fargo, Dir.;

The North Country Catholic - www.northcountrycatholic.org Darcy Fargo, Editor; Christine Ward, Editorial Asst.;

Family Life Office - Stephen Tartaglia, Dir.;

Natural Family Planning Services - t) 518-483-0459 Suzanne Pietropaoli; Angelo Pietropaoli;

Respect Life Office - t) 518-524-0774 Colleen Miner; John Miner;

CANONICAL SERVICES

Judicial Vicar - Rev. Garry B. Giroux;

Adjutant Judicial Vicars - Rev. Joseph W. Giroux;

Office Manager for the Tribunal - Molly M. Ryan;

Advocates - Mary Jo Rocker; Stephen Tartaglia; Rev. Douglas A. Decker;

Defenders of the Bond - Rev. Raymond J. Moreau; Rev. Joseph A. Morgan; Rev. Alan D. Shnob;

Judges - Catherine J. Friederichs; Rev. L. William Gordon; Rev. Philip T. Allen;

Notaries - Dcn. James D. Crowley; Gidget L. Kimble;

Promoter of Justice - Rev. Msgr. John R. Murphy;

CONSULTATIVE BODIES

Vicars Foraine -

Adirondack-Franklin Deanery - Rev. John R. Yonkovig;

Clinton Deanery - Rev. Msgr. Dennis J. Duprey;

Essex Deanery - Rev. Albert J. Hauser;

Hamilton-Herkimer Deanery - Rev. Sony G. Pulickal;

Jefferson-Lewis Deanery - Rev. Arthur J. LaBaff;

St. Lawrence Deanery - Rev. Mark R. Reilly;

Diocesan Consultors - Rev. Joseph A. Morgan, Secy.; Rev. Msgr. Dennis J. Duprey; Rev. Msgr. Robert H. Aucoin;

Council of Consecrated Life - Sr. Cindy Sullivan, B.V.M., Pres.; Sr. Norma Bryant, S.S.J., Secy.; Sr. Elizabeth Menard, O.P., Treas.;

Committee for the Continuing Education of Clergy - Rev. Raymond J. Moreau, Chair; Rev. Martin E. Cline; Rev. Alan J. Lamica;

Committee on Assignments - Rev. Joseph A. Morgan; Rev. Christopher C. Carrara; Dcn. James D. Crowley;

FACILITIES

Spratt Memorial Building -

Bishop Stanislaus J. Brzana Diocesan Pastoral Center -

Bishop Paul S. Loverde Center for Education and Formation -

ORGANIZATIONS

The Foundation of the Roman Catholic Diocese of Ogdensburg, New York - Scott Lalone, Exec. Dir.;

Pontifical Mission Societies - Sr. Mary Ellen Brett, S.S.J., Dir.;

SOCIAL SERVICES

Catholic Charities - t) 315-393-2255 www.cathcharities.org Dcn. Patrick J. Donahue, CEO / Exec. Dir.; Johanna Cubi, Deputy Dir.; Jillian McNaughton, Bus. Mgr.;

Clinton / Essex County Regional Office - t) (518) 300-0272 Claudine Dailey;

Franklin County Regional Office - t) (518) 483-1460 Joelle Lamica;

Jefferson / Lewis County Regional Office - t) (315) 788-4330 Cathy Ferran;

St. Lawrence Regional Office - t) (315) 393-2660 Matthew Stiles;

Foster Grandparent Program - t) (518) 624-6788

RSVP - t) (518) 566-0944

Enhance Multi-Disciplinary Team (EMDT) - t) (518) 926-0710

Justice and Law Center - t) (315) 769-2500

Seaway House - t) 315-393-3133

Catholic Relief Services - t) (315) 393-2255 Dcn. Patrick J. Donahue;

MISCELLANEOUS / OTHER OFFICES

Apostleship of Prayer - Rev. Albert J. Hauser, Dir.;

Priests' Eucharistic League - t) 518-846-7254 Rev. Albert J. Hauser, Dir.;

PARISHES, MISSIONS, AND CLERGY

STATE OF NEW YORK

ADAMS

St. Cecilia's Church, Adams, NY - 17 Grove St., Adams, NY 13605 t) 315-232-2392 adamssec@rcdony.org www.stceciliaandqoh.org Rev. Robert L. Decker, Pst.; Dcn. Lawrence R. Ambeau; CRP Stds.: 60

Queen of Heaven - 8900 NYS Rte. 3, Henderson, NY 13650; Mailing: 17 Grove St, Adams, NY 13605

ALEXANDRIA BAY

Roman Catholic Community of Alexandria - 17 Rock St., Alexandria Bay, NY 13607; Mailing: 521 James St., Clayton, NY 13624 t) 315-482-2670 c) 315-405-6910 www.stcyrils.org Rev. Douglas G. Comstock, Pastor Emer.; Dcn. Bruce Wayne Daugherty; Dcn. Gary A. Frank; Dcn. Neil J. Fuller, Parish Life Coord.; Trina Henry, DRE; Dcn. Bernard E. Slate; Dcn. Joel E. Walentuk; Rev. Arthur J. LaBaff, Sacr. Min.; CRP Stds.: 11

St. Cyril Church - 28 Walton St., Alexandria Bay, NY 13607; Mailing: 17 Rock St., Alexandria Bay, NY 13607 stcyrils.org (Worship Site)

St. Francis Xavier Church - 28685 Butterfield Lake Rd., Redwood, NY 13679; Mailing: 17 Rock St., Alexandria Bay, NY 13607 (Worship Site)

ALTONA

Holy Angels Church, Altona, N.Y. - 522 Devils Den Rd., Altona, NY 12910; Mailing: 24 Town Hall Rd., Mooers Forks, NY 12959 t) 518-236-5632 annandangels@gmail.com www.annandangels.org Dcn. Dennis Monty, DRE; Rev. Pedro Edgardo N de la Rosa, Pst.;

AU SABLE FORKS

Catholic Community of Holy Name and St. Matthew's - 10 Church Ln., Au Sable Forks, NY 12912; Mailing: P.O. Box 719, Au Sable Forks, NY 12912 t) 518-647-8225; 518-647-8444 (CRP) ccofhnandsm@gmail.com; hnandsmreligion@gmail.com Rev. Kris C. Lauzon, Pst.; Dcn. Jack M. Lukasiewicz; CRP Stds.: 12

St. Margaret - 5789 NYS Rte. 86, Wilmington, NY 12912

Church of the Holy Name - 14203 Rte. 9N, Au Sable Forks, NY 12912 (Worship Site)

BLACK RIVER

St. Paul's Church - 210 LeRay St., Black River, NY 13612; Mailing: 8422 S. Main St., Evans Mills, NY 13637 t) (315) 629-4678 evansmillssec@rcdony.org www.rivercatholics.org Rev. Frank Natale, M.S.C., Pst.; Rev. Joseph Kanimea, M.S.C., Par. Vicar; Dcn. Daniel G. LeRoy; Dcn. Noel Voos; CRP Stds.: 12

BRASHER FALLS

St. Patrick - 836 State Hwy. 11C, Brasher Falls, NY 13613-0208; Mailing: PO Box 208, Brasher Falls, NY 13613 t) 315-389-5401 Rev. Shane M. Lynch, Pst.; Dcn. John A. Levison; Dcn. Philip J. Regan; Christine Leahy, DRE; Lynda Lemieux, Lay Minister; CRP Stds.: 35

BROWNVILLE

The Roman Catholic Community of Brownville and Dexter - 119 W. Main St., Brownville, NY 13615; Mailing: P.O. Box 99, Brownville, NY 13615 t) 315-788-7240 (CRP); 315-782-1143 brownvillesec@rcdony.org Rev. Donald A. Robinson, Pst.; Dcn. Gerald F. Bouchard; Christina M. Corey, DRE; CRP Stds.: 43

Immaculate Conception - 214 W. Main St., Brownville, NY 13615 (Worship Site)

BRUSHTON

St. Mary's Church - 1347 State Rte. 11, Brushton, NY 12916-0249 t) 518-529-7433 www.staugustinesandstmarys.org Rev. Raymond J. Moreau, Pst.; Dcn. Lee M. Trudeau; CRP Stds.: 22

CADYVILLE

St. James Church, Cadyville, NY - 23 Church Rd., Cadyville, NY 12918; Mailing: PO Box 159, Morrisonville, NY 12962 t) 518-561-5039 morrisonvillebk@rcdony.org www.stalexanders.org/ Rev. Scott R. Seymour, Pst.; Rev. Leagon Carlin, Par. Vicar; Sr. Deepali Bankar, S.C.C., DRE; Dcn. Michael J. Howley; CRP Stds.: 23

CANTON

The Roman Catholic Church of St. Mary in Canton, NY - 66 Court St., Canton, NY 13617; Mailing: 68 Court St., Canton, NY 13617 t) 315-386-2543 office@cantoncatholics.com www.cantoncatholics.com Rev. Bryan D. Stitt, Pst.; Dcn. James M. Snell; Paul J. Schrems, Pst. Assoc.; CRP Stds.: 40

CAPE VINCENT

The Roman Catholic Community of Cape Vincent, Rosiere and Chaumont - 139 N. Kanady St., Cape Vincent, NY 13618; Mailing: PO Box 288, Cape Vincent, NY 13618 t) 315-654-2662 capevincentsec@rcdony.org www.cvrchparish.org Rev. Raymond Diesbourg, M.S.C., Pst.; Rev. Pierre Aubin, M.S.C., Pastor Emer.; Dcn. Patrick J. Donahue; Julie Sharlow, DRE; CRP Stds.: 34

All Saints Church - 27420 Madison St., Chaumont, NY 13622 t) 315-300-4233 (Worship Site)

St. Vincent de Paul Church - 31399 County Rte. 4, Rosiere, NY 13618 t) (315) 654-2662 (Worship Site)

St. Vincent of Paul Church - 1626 Kanady St., Cape Vincent, NY 13618 t) (315) 654-2662 (Worship Site)

CARTHAGE

The Society of St. Jame's Church Carthage - 327 West St., Carthage, NY 13619 t) 315-493-3224 carthagesec@rcdony.org www.sj-sm.org Rev. Todd E. Thibault, Pst.; Sr. Annunciata Collins, S.S.J., Pst. Assoc.; Dcn. Richard J. Staab, Pst. Assoc.; CRP Stds.: 44

Augustinian Academy - (Grades PreK-8) 317 West St., Carthage, NY 13619 t) 315-493-1301 mmargrey@augustinianacademy.org www.c-augustinian.org Mary Ann Margrey, Prin.; Stds.: 137; Lay Tchrs.: 11

Convent - 317 West St., Carthage, NY 13619 t) 315-493-1672 smacollinsssj@yahoo.com Sr. Constance Marie Sylver, S.S.J., Resident;

CHAMPLAIN

The Church of Saint Mary of Champlain - 90 Church St., Champlain, NY 12919; Mailing: P.O. Box 368, 86 Church St., Champlain, NY 12919 t) 518-298-8244; (518) 298-8614 (CRP) churchofstmary@yahoo.com www.stmaryschamplain.org Rev. Clyde A. Lewis, Pst.; Rev. Alan D. Shnob, In Res.; Sr. Rani Selvaraj, Pst. Assoc.; Patricia Gladd, DRE; CRP Stds.: 8

CHATEAUGAY

Catholic Community of Burke and Chateaugay - 132 W. Main St., Chateaugay, NY 12920-0908; Mailing: P.O. Box 908, Chateaugay, NY 12920-0908 t) 518-497-6673 chateaugaysec@rcdony.org ccfcatholics.com Dcn. Brian T. Dwyer, Pst. Assoc.; Rev. Medenel Angrand, Sacr. Min.; CRP Stds.: 40

St. Patrick's Church - (Worship Site)

CHAZY

The Sacred Heart Church of Chazy, NY - 31 Church St., Chazy, NY 12921; Mailing: PO Box 459, Chazy, NY 12921 t) 518-846-7650 sacredheart@westelcom.com Rev. Theodore A. Crosby, Pst.; Dcn. Mark T. Webster; Susan Barriere, DRE; Noreen N. Barcomb, Bus. Mgr.; CRP Stds.: 45

CLAYTON

St. Mary's of Clayton - 521 James St., Clayton, NY 13624 t) 315-686-2638 (CRP); 315-686-3398 (Parish Office) claytonsec@rcdony.org; claytondre@rcdony.org www.stmarysclayton.org Dcn. Bruce Wayne Daugherty; Dcn. Gary A. Frank; Dcn. Neil J. Fuller, Parish Life Coord.; Rev. Arthur J. LaBaff, Sacr. Min.; CRP Stds.: 36

St. John the Evangelist Oratory - 35923 NYS Rte. 180, Lafargeville, NY 13656

Saint Mary's Church - (Worship Site)

COLTON

Saint Patrick's Church, Colton, NY - 4897 State Hwy. 56, Colton, NY 13625; Mailing: PO Box 315, Colton, NY 13625 t) 315-262-2871 x2 coltonbk@rcdony.org; formationstp@gmail.com www.stmarystpatrick.net Rev. Joseph W. Giroux, Pst.; Dcn. Richard L. Burns; Conner Cummings, Pst. Assoc.; Elizabeth Tarbox, DRE; CRP Stds.: 13

St. Paul Oratory - 3871 State Hwy. 56, South Colton, NY 13687; Mailing: P.O. Box 315, Colton, NY 13625

CONSTABLE

The Catholic Community of Constable, Westville and Trout River - 5 Poplar St., Constable, NY 12926; Mailing: P.O. Box 78, Constable, NY 12926 t) 518-483-0486 officecwtr@gmail.com www.ccfcatholics.com Rev. Medenel Angrand, Sacr. Min.; Dcn. Brian T. Dwyer, Parish Life Coord.; CRP Stds.: 28

St. Francis of Assisi Church - t) (518) 483-0486 (Worship Site)

CONSTABLEVILLE

St. Mary's Catholic Church, Constableville - 5905 James St., Constableville, NY 13325; Mailing: P.O. Box 382, Constableville, NY 13325 t) 315-397-2556 stmarys1@frontier.com catholicparishesofslc.weebly.com Rev. Lawrence E. Marullo, Pst.; Dcn. James W. Chaufty; Dcn. Michael Lieber; CRP Stds.: 8

COPENHAGEN

St. Mary's Church, Copenhagen, NY - 9790 NYS Rte. 12, Copenhagen, NY 13626-0012; Mailing: P.O. Box 12, Copenhagen, NY 13626 t) 315-688-2683 copenhagenpa@rcdony.org www.sj-sm.org Dcn. Richard J. Staab; Rev. Todd E. Thibault, Pst.; Sr. Mary Ellen Brett, S.S.J., Pst. Assoc.; CRP Stds.: 15

CROGHAN

St. Stephen's Church, Croghan, NY - 9748 State Rte. 812, Croghan, NY 13327-0038; Mailing: P.O. Box 38, Croghan, NY 13327-0038 t) 315-346-6963 (CRP); 315-346-6958 croghanbk@rcdony.org www.ststephenscroghan.rcdony.org Rev. Donald J. Manfred, Pst.; Dcn. Peter Woolschlager; CRP Stds.: 70

St. Vincent de Paul Oratory - 9551 Erie Canal Rd., Belfort, NY 13327

St. Peter Oratory - 6466 Tillman Rd., New Bremen, NY 13367

CROWN POINT

Church of the Sacred Heart of Jesus - 2673 Main St., Crown Point, NY 12928; Mailing: P.O. Box 479, Crown Point, NY 12928 t) 518-546-7254 stpats12974@gmail.com www.catholiccommunityofmoriah.com/ Rev. Albert J. Hauser, Pst.; CRP Stds.: 8

DANNEMORA

Saint Joseph's Church, Dannemora - 179 Smith St., Dannemora, NY 12929-0418; Mailing: 78 Clinton St., Redford, NY 12978 t) 518-293-5168 carousel1850@assumptionredford.com Rev. Michael Jablonski, Pst.; Alice Mattoon, DRE; CRP Stds.: 29

EDWARDS

The Sacred Heart Church of Edwards, NY - Merged Aug 2022 Merged with St. James Church, Gouverneur.

ELIZABETHTOWN

The St. Elizabeth Roman Catholic Church - 7478 Court St, Elizabethtown, NY 12932; Mailing: PO Box 368, 8434 NYS RTE 9N, Elizabethtown, NY 12932 t) 518-873-6760 rccowe@gmail.com www.wewe4.org/ Rev. Justin Thomas, H.G.N., Pst.; Dcn. Paul M. White;

ELLENBURG CENTER

St. Bernard's and St. Edmund's Parish - 5526 State Rte. 11, Ellenburg Center, NY 12934 t) 518-594-3907 cathcommsbse@gmail.com www.cathcommsbse.org Rev. Tojo Chacko, H.G.N., Pst.; Dcn. Kenneth L. Lushia; Myndi Leah Almodovar, DRE; Izabelle Jeanette Almodovar, Bus. Mgr.; CRP Stds.: 66

St. Bernard's Church - 10 Church Pond Rd., Lyon Mountain, NY 12934 (Worship Site)

St. Edmund's Church - 5526 Rte. 11, Ellenburg Center, NY 12934 (Worship Site)

EVANS MILLS

St. Mary's Roman Catholic Church of Evans Mills, NY - 8422 S. Main St., Evans Mills, NY 13637 t) 315-629-4678 rivercatholics.org Rev. Frank Natale, M.S.C., Pst.; Rev. Joseph Kanimea, M.S.C., Par. Vicar; Dcn. Daniel G. LeRoy; Dcn. Noel Voos; CRP Stds.: 9

FORT COVINGTON

St. Mary's of the Fort, Fort Covington, NY - 2549 Chateaugay St., Fort Covington, NY 12937; Mailing: P.O. Box 499, 3 Burns-Holden Rd., Fort Covington, NY 12937 t) 518-358-2500 smsjoffice@gmail.com www.ccfcatholics.com Dcn. Garry N. Burnell; Dcn. Brian T. Dwyer, Parish Life Coord.; Rev. Medenel Angrand, Sacr. Min.; Jocelyn Kelly, DRE; CRP Stds.: 25

GOUVERNEUR

Saint James Church of Gouverneur - 164 E. Main St., Gouverneur, NY 13642 t) 315-287-0114 gouverneursec@rcdony.org oswegatchiecatholics.org Rev. James W. Seymour, Pst.; Dcn. Philip F. Giardino; Dcn. Henry J. Leader; Dayna Leader, DRE; CRP Stds.: 22

St. James School - (Grades PreK-6) 20 S. Gordon St., Gouverneur, NY 13642 t) 315-287-0130 principal@stjamesk-6.org www.stjamesk-6.org Bridgette LaPierre, Prin.; Stds.: 117; Lay Tchrs.: 7

Sacred Heart Church - 20 Trout Lake St., Edwards, NY 13635; Mailing: 164 E. Main St., Gouverneur, NY 13642 t) (315) 287-0014

HARRISVILLE

St. Francis Solanus Church, Harrisville, New York - 14361 Maple St., Harrisville, NY 13648; Mailing: P.O. Box 208, 14355 Maple St., Harrisville, NY 13648 t) 315-543-2421 solanus@verizon.net Rev. Donald J. Manfred, Pst.; Dcn. Michael J. Allan; Dcn. Peter Woolschlager; CRP Stds.: 18

HEUVELTON

St. Raphael's - 3 Clinton St., Heuvelton, NY 13654; Mailing: 5 Clinton St., P.O. Box 377, Heuvelton, NY 13654 t) 315-344-2383 saintraphael@twcny.rr.com Dcn. Richard L. Van Kirk; Rev. Kevin J. O'Brien, Pst.; Carolyn Pierce, DRE; CRP Stds.: 24

HOGANSBURG

St. Regis Mission - 597 State Rte. 37, Hogansburg, NY 13655; Mailing: PO Box 429, Hogansburg, NY 13655 t) 613-575-2753 jeromebpastores@hotmail.com; stregischurchakwesasnc@outlook.com stregismission.org/ (Akwesasne), Reservation and parish on both sides of U.S.-Canadian border Rev. Jerome Bose Pastores, Pst.; Dr. Rose-Alma McDonald, DRE;

Roman Catholic Community Center, Inc. (Kateri Tekakwitha Center) - 597 State Rte. 37, Hogansburg, NY 13655; Mailing: PO Box 429, Hogansburg, NY 13655 t) (613) 575-2753

HOPKINTON

The Church of the Holy Cross of Hopkinton, NY - 2807 State Hwy. 11B, Hopkinton, NY 12965; Mailing: P.O. Box 288, St. Regis Falls, NY 12980 t) 518-856-9456 ahfish20@gmail.com Rev. Alfred H. Fish, Pst.;

INDIAN LAKE

St. Mary's and St. Paul's Parish - 6335 NYS Rte. 30, Indian Lake, NY 12842; Mailing: P.O. Box 332, Indian Lake, NY 12842 t) 518-648-5422 smil@frontiernet.net Rev. Philip T. Allen, Pst.; Jennifer Zahray, DRE; CRP Stds.: 6

St. Mary's Church - (Worship Site)

St. Paul's Church - 3426 NYS Rte. 28, Blue Mountain Lake, NY 12812 (Worship Site)

INLET

St. Anthony of Padua Parish of Inlet and Raquette Lake - 183 N. Rte. 28, Inlet, NY 13360; Mailing: P.O. Box 236, Old Forge, NY 13420 t) 315-369-3554 stbartholomews@frontier.com fultonchaincatholic.rcdony.org Rev. Thomas E. Kornmeyer, Pst.; Dcn. Timothy D. Foley;

St. William Oratory - County Rte. 2, Raquette Lake, NY 13436 Seasonal Chapel

KEENE

Saint Brendan's Roman Catholic Church - 25 Church St., Keene, NY 12942; Mailing: 169 Hillcrest Ave., Lake Placid, NY 12946 t) 518-523-2200 stagneschurch@stagneslp.org www.stagneslakeplacid.com Rev. John R. Yonkovig, Pst.;

KEESEVILLE

The Roman Catholic Community of Keeseville - 1804 Main St., Keeseville, NY 12944-3745; Mailing: P.O. Box 719, Au Sable Forks, NY 12912 t) (518) 674-8225 Rev. Kris C. Lauzon, Pst.; Dcn. Jack M. Lukasiewicz; CRP Stds.: 5

Church of the Immaculate Conception - 1660 Front St.,

Keeseville, NY 12944 t) (518) 647-8225

St. John the Baptist Church - 1803 Main St., Rte. 22, Keeseville, NY 12944 t) (518) 647-8225

LAKE PLACID

Saint Agnes Church, Lake Placid, NY - 2338 Saranac Ave., Lake Placid, NY 12946; Mailing: 169 Hillcrest Ave., Lake Placid, NY 12946 t) 518-523-2200 lakeplacidsec@rcdony.org www.stagneslakeplacid.com Rev. John R. Yonkovig, Pst.; Marcia Bugbee, DRE; CRP Stds.: 69

St. Agnes School - (Grades PreK-3) 2322 Saranac Ave., Lake Placid, NY 12946 t) 518-523-3771 admin@stagneslp.org; info@stagneslp.org www.stagneslp.org Catherine Bemis, Prin.; Stds.: 115; Lay Tchrs.: 12

LAKE PLEASANT

Church of St. James Major, Lake Pleasant, Hamilton County - 2567 State Rte. 8, Lake Pleasant, NY 12108; Mailing: 2781 State Rte. 8, P.O. Box 214, Speculator, NY 12164 t) 518-548-6275 sjcsac@frontiernet.net Rev. Sony G. Pulickal, Pst.;

LISBON

SS. Philip and James - 6892 County Rt. 10, Lisbon, NY 13658; Mailing: P.O. Box 377, Heuvelton, NY 13654 t) 315-344-2383 saintraphael@twcny.rr.com Dcn. Richard L. Van Kirk; Rev. Kevin J. O'Brien, Pst.; Christine Ward, DRE; CRP Stds.: 18

LONG LAKE

St. Henry - 1187 Main St., Long Lake, NY 12847; Mailing: 18 Adams Ln., Newcomb, NY 12852 t) 518-582-3671 (St Therese) stetheresechurch@gmail.com tupperlakecatholics.org/ Rev. James V. Teti, Pst.; Rev. Clement Rimonds, H.G.N. (India), Par. Vicar; Dcn. James T. Ellis; Dcn. Gerald H. Savage;

LOWVILLE

Catholic Community of St. Peter and St. Mary and St. Hedwig - 5449 Shady Ave., Lowville, NY 13367; Mailing: 5457 Shady Ave., Lowville, NY 13367 t) 315-376-6662; 315-376-6662 x226 (CRP) lturck@stpeterslowville.com; dmullin75@yahoo.com spsmshcatholic.org formerly St. Peters Church of Lowville Rev. Douglas A. Decker, Pst.; Dcn. Ronald J. Pominville; Dcn. Kenneth A. Seymour; Dcn. Robert S. Uttendorfsky; Dcn. Thomas J. Yousey; Dcn. Ron Gingerich, Youth Min.; Deborah Mullin, DRE; CRP Stds.: 66

St. Hedwig's Church - 5432 State Rte. 26, Houseville, NY 13473 (Worship Site)

St. Mary's Church - 6106 Blue St., Glenfield, NY 13343 (Worship Site)

St. Peter's Church - 5457 Shady Ave, Lowville, NY 13367 (Worship Site)

MADRID

Church of St. John the Baptist Madrid - 29 North St., Madrid, NY 13660; Mailing: P.O. Box 187, c/o St. Mary's Parish, Waddington, NY 13694 t) 315-388-4466 ggiroux@rcdony.org mwcatholics.org Linked with St. Mary in Waddington, NY Rev. Garry B. Giroux, Pst.; CRP Stds.: 7

MALONE

Saint Andre Bessette Roman Catholic Parish, Malone, NY - 12 Homestead Pk., Malone, NY 12953; Mailing: P.O. Box 547, Malone, NY 12953 t) 518-483-1300 office@standres.org www.standres.org Rev. Steven M. Murray, Pst.; Rev. Fernando V. Solomon Jr., Par. Vicar; Dcn. Bryan J. Bashaw; Dcn. Brent A. Charland; Dcn. Nicholas J. Haas; CRP Stds.: 41

Notre Dame Church - 11 Church Pl., Malone, NY 12953 (Worship Site)

St. Helen Church - 755 County Hwy. 41, Malone, NY 12953 (Worship Site)

MASSENA

St. Peter's Parish - 212 Main St., Massena, NY 13662; Mailing: PO Box 329, Massena, NY 13662 t) 315-769-2469 (Office); 315-764-0239 (Rectory) pastor@massenacatholics.com massenacatholics.com See Miscellaneous regarding St. Peter's Outreach Ministry, Inc. Rev. Mark R. Reilly, Pst.; Rev. Severinus Torwoe, Par. Vicar; Rev. Nicholas J. Revilla (Philippines), Par. Vicar; Dcn. Randy Besio; Dcn. Thomas E. Proulx; Julia LaShomb, Pst. Assoc.; John Schneider, Director of Evangelization and Christian Formation; CRP Stds.: 55

Trinity Catholic School - (Grades PreK-6) 188 Main St., Massena, NY 13662 t) 315-769-5911 principal@trinitycatholicschool.net www.trinitycatholicschool.net Joyce Giroux, Prin.; Stds.: 154; Lay Tchrs.: 16

St. Mary's Church - 9 Sycamore St., Massena, NY 13662; Mailing: P.O. Box 609, Massena, NY 13662

St. Lawrence's Church - 30 Willard Rd., Massena, NY 13662

Sacred Heart Church -

St. Joseph Oratory - 22 Bayley Rd., Massena, NY 13662

MOOERS FORKS

St. Ann - 3066 Rte. 11, Mooers Forks, NY 12959; Mailing: 24 Town Hall Rd., Mooers Forks, NY 12959 t) 518-236-5632 annandangels@gmail.com annandangels.org/ Rev. Pedro Edgardo N de la Rosa, Pst.; Dcn. Dennis Monty; CRP Stds.: 16

MORRISONVILLE

The Roman Catholic Community of St. Alexander and St. Joseph - 1 Church St., Morrisonville, NY 12962; Mailing: PO Box 159, Morrisonville, NY 12962 t) 518-561-5039 morrisonvillebk@rcdony.org stalexanders.org Rev. Scott R. Seymour, Pst.; Rev. Leagon Carlin, Par. Vicar; Dcn. Michael J. Howley; Rev. L. William Gordon, In Res.; Sr. Deepali Bankar, S.C.C., DRE; CRP Stds.: 55

MORRISTOWN

Our Lady of Grace Parish - 500 Morris St., Morristown, NY 13664; Mailing: P.O. Box 216, Morristown, NY 13664 t) 315-375-6571 morristownpa@rcdony.org stjohnpeterpatrick.com Rev. Christopher C. Carrara, Pst.; Dcn. David D. Demers; Shelley Rogers Rosteck, Pst. Assoc.; CRP Stds.: 26

St. Peter's Church - 47 Main St., Hammond, NY 13646 Hammond, NY

St. Patrick's Church - 1219 County Route 3, Hammond, NY 13646; Mailing: PO Box 126, Morristown, NY 13664 Rossie, NY

St. John the Evangelist Church - 506 Gouverneur St., Morristown, NY 13664; Mailing: PO Box 216, Morristown, NY 13664

NEWCOMB

St. Therese Church, Newcomb, NY - 14 Adams Ln., Newcomb, NY 12852-1701; Mailing: 18 Adams Ln., Newcomb, NY 12852 t) 518-582-3671 stetheresechurch@gmail.com tupperlakecatholics.org Rev. James V. Teti, Pst.; Rev. Clement Rimonds, H.G.N. (India), Par. Vicar; Dcn. James T. Ellis; Dcn. Gerald H. Savage;

NORFOLK

The Parish of the Visitation and St. Raymond - 1 Morris St., Norfolk, NY 13667; Mailing: PO Box 637, 3 Morris St., Norfolk, NY 13667 t) 315-384-4242; 315-384-3575 pvsrsasec@gmail.com norfolknorwoodraymondville.org Rev. Shane M. Lynch, Pst.; Dcn. Philip J. Regan; Rev. Andrew J. Amyot, In Res.; Rev. John L. Downs, In Res.; Carol O'B. Gonthier, DRE; Dcn. John A. Levison; CRP Stds.: 26

Church of the Visitation - t) (315) 384-4242

NORTH BANGOR

The Roman Catholic Church of St. Augustine in North Bangor, NY - 2472 State Rte. 11, North Bangor, NY 12966 t) 518-483-6674 staugustinesandstmarys.org/ Rev. Raymond J. Moreau, Pst.; Dcn. Lee M. Trudeau; Rev. Daniel L. Chapin, In Res.; Rev. Alan J. Lamica, In Res.; CRP Stds.: 40

NORWOOD

Saint Andrew's Church, Norwood - 4 Park Ave., Norwood, NY 13668; Mailing: P.O. Box 637, Norfolk, NY 13667 t) 315-384-4242 (Office); 315-353-5013 (Saint Andrew's rectory) pvsrsasec@gmail.com norfolknorwoodraymondville.org Rev. Shane M. Lynch, Pst.; Dcn. John A. Levison; Dcn. Philip J. Regan;

OGDENSBURG

St. Mary's Church, Ogdensburg - 401 Hamilton St., Ogdensburg, NY 13669; Mailing: 125 Ford Ave., Ogdensburg, NY 13669 t) 315-393-3930; 315-393-5050 ogdensburgsec@rcdony.org ogdensburgcatholics.org Rev. Joseph A. Morgan, Rector; Rev. Jude Nnadibuagha, Par. Vicar; Rev. F. James Shurtleff, Pastor Emer.; Rev. Msgr. Robert H. Aucoin, In Res.; Dcn. James D. Crowley; Dcn. William P. O'Brien; Dcn. Anthony J. Pastizzo; Dcn. Roderic Roca; Sr. Bernadette Marie Collins, S.S.J., Pst. Assoc.; CRP Stds.: 115

Outreach Center - 214 Morris St., Ogdensburg, NY 13669-1714 t) 315-393-6579

Notre Dame Church - 119 Ford Ave., Ogdensburg, NY 13669 (Worship Site)

OLD FORGE

St. Bartholomew's Church of Old Forge - 103 Crosby Blvd., Old Forge, NY 13420; Mailing: P.O. Box 236, Old Forge, NY 13420 t) 315-369-3554 stbartholomews@frontier.com fultonchaincatholics.org/ Rev. Thomas E. Kornmeyer, Pst.; Dcn. Timothy D. Foley; CRP Stds.: 16

OLMSTEDVILLE

Saint Joseph's Church, Minerva - 635 Church Rd., Olmstedville, NY 12857; Mailing: P.O. Box 332, Indian Lake, NY 12842 t) 518-251-2565; 518-648-5422 smil@frontiernet.net www.stjosephsolmstedville.org Rev. Philip T. Allen, Pst.; Diane McNally, DRE; CRP Stds.: 4

St. Mary Oratory - 479 O'Neil Rd., Olmstedville, NY 12857

PERU

Saint Augustine's Church, Peru, NY - 3029 Main St., Peru, NY 12972; Mailing: P.O. Box 159, Morrisonville, NY 12962 t) (518) 561-5039 www.peruparish.org Rev. Scott R. Seymour, Pst.; Rev. Leagon Carlin, Par. Vicar; Dcn. Michael J. Howley; Rev. Msgr. Dennis J. Duprey, In Res.; Rev. Francis J. Flynn, In Res.; CRP Stds.: 19

St. Patrick Oratory - 51 Patent Rd., West Peru, NY 12972

PLATTSBURGH

Holy Cross Parish - 7 Margaret St., Plattsburgh, NY 12901 t) 518-563-0730 plattsburghoffice@rcdony.org holycrosspbg.org Rev. Kevin D. McEwan, Pst.; Rev. Michael Marzan, Par. Vicar; Rev. John Kennedy Ojuok, Par. Vicar; Rev. Norman C. Cote, In Res.; Dcn. Mark Bennett; Dcn. Frank A. Bushey Jr.; Dcn. James Carlin; Dcn. John A. Cogan; Dcn. Brent Davison; Dcn. John J. Drollette; Dcn. Brian D. Neureuther; Dcn. Leonard L. Patrie; Dcn. Tyrone A. Rabideau; Dcn. Randal J. Smith; Sr. Jackie Sellappan, Pst. Assoc.; CRP Stds.: 252

St. John the Baptist Church - 18 Broad St., Plattsburgh, NY 12901 (Worship Site)

St. John XXIII Newman Center Campus Ministry - 90 Broad St., Plattsburgh, NY 12901; Mailing: 7 Margaret St., Plattsburgh, NY 12901 (Worship Site)

Our Lady of Victory Church - 4915 S. Catherine St., Plattsburgh, NY 12901 (Worship Site)

St. Peter's Church - 114 Cornelia St., Plattsburgh, NY 12901 (Worship Site)

PORT HENRY

Catholic Community of Moriah - 12 St. Patrick's Pl., Port Henry, NY 12974 t) 518-546-7254 stpats12974@gmail.com www.catholiccommunityofmoriah.com/ Rev. Albert J. Hauser, Pst.; CRP Stds.: 27

Church of All Saints - 23 Bartlett Pond Rd., Mineville, NY 12956; Mailing: 12 St. Patrick's Place, Port Henry, NY 12974

St. Patrick's Church -

PORT LEYDEN

St. Martin - 7108 North St., Port Leyden, NY 13433; Mailing: P.O. Box 431, Port Leyden, NY 13433 t) 315-348-6104; 315-397-2556 catholicparishesofslc.weebly.com Rev. Lawrence E. Marullo, Pst.; Dcn. James W. Chaufty; Dcn. Michael Lieber; Joseph Scheve, DRE; CRP Stds.: 8

St. John's Church - 5838 McAlpine St., Lyons Falls, NY 13368; Mailing: PO Box 431, Port Leyden, NY 13433

POTSDAM

The Roman Catholic Church of Saint Mary in Potsdam, NY - 20 Lawrence Ave., Potsdam, NY 13676; Mailing: 17 Lawrence Ave., Potsdam, NY 13676 t) 315-265-9680 potsdamsec@rcdony.org; formationstp@gmail.com stmarystpatrick.net Rev. Joseph W. Giroux, Pst.; Dcn. Richard L. Burns; Conner Cummings, Campus Ministry; Elizabeth Tarbox, DRE; CRP Stds.: 37

REDFORD

The Church of the Assumption, Redford - 78 Clinton St., Redford, NY 12978 t) 518-293-5168 carousel1850@assumptionredford.com Rev. Michael Jablonski, Pst.; Bonnie Allen, DRE; CRP Stds.: 22

ROUSES POINT

Saint Patrick's Church, Rouses Point - 140 Lake St., Rouses Point, NY 12979; Mailing: P.O. Box 217, 138 Lake St., Rouses Point, NY 12979 t) 518-297-7361 stpats@twcny.rr.com www.stpatricksrpny.org Rev. Clyde A. Lewis, Pst.; Dcn. Noel A. Hinerth; Sr. Rani Selvaraj, Pst. Assoc.; Sue Lefebvre, DRE; Jo Anne Ryan, Bus. Mgr.; CRP Stds.: 45

St. Joseph Oratory - 74 Mason Rd., Champlain, NY 12919 t) (518) 297-7361

SACKETS HARBOR

Saint Andrew's Church, Sackets Harbor - 101 Woolsey St., Sackets Harbor, NY 13685; Mailing: P.O. Box 99, 119 W. Main St., Brownville, NY 13615 t) 315-782-1143 brownvillesec@rcdony.org Rev. Donald A. Robinson, Pst.; Dcn. Gerald F. Bouchard; CRP Stds.: 21

SARANAC LAKE

Saint Bernard's Church, Saranac Lake - 27 St. Bernard St., Saranac Lake, NY 12983 t) 518-891-4616 saranaclakemgr@rcdony.org stbernards.church/ Rev. Martin E. Cline, Pst.; Dcn. Joseph Szwed; Dcn. John A. Fehlner; CRP Stds.: 29

St. Bernard School - (Grades K-5) 63 River St., Saranac Lake, NY 12983 t) 518-891-2830 principal@stbernardsschool.org www.stbernards.org Andrea Kilbourne-Hill, Prin.; Stds.: 78; Lay Tchrs.: 6

Church of the Assumption - 826 State Rte. 86, Gabriels, NY 12939; Mailing: 27 St. Bernard St., Saranac Lake, NY 12983

St. Paul Oratory - 1640 State Rte. 3, Bloomingdale, NY 12913

SCHROON LAKE

Our Lady of Lourdes Church, Schroon Lake, NY - 1114 U.S. Rte. 9, Schroon Lake, NY 12870; Mailing: P.O. Box 368, Schroon Lake, NY 12870 t) 518-532-7100 ollsjcoffice@verizon.net www.route74catholics.org Rev. Christopher J. Looby, Pst.; Linda Lowe, DRE; CRP Stds.: 7

Holy Names of Jesus and Mary Oratory - 3008 U.S. Rte. 9, North Hudson, NY 12855

ST. REGIS FALLS

St. Ann's Church, St. Regis Falls, NY - 73 N. Main St., St. Regis Falls, NY 12980; Mailing: 77 N. Main St., P.O. Box 288, St. Regis Falls, NY 12980 t) 518-856-9456 ahfish20@gmail.com Rev. Alfred H. Fish, Pst.; Nicole Meacham, First Communion Teacher;

St. Peter Oratory - NYS Rte. 458 & Center St., St. Regis Falls, NY 12980

STAR LAKE

The Roman Catholic Church of Saint Hubert in Star Lake, NY - 1046 Oswegatchie Trail Rd., Star Lake, NY 13690 t) 315-848-3612 starlakesec@rcdony.org www.oswegatchiecatholics.org/ Rev. James W. Seymour, Pst.; Dcn. Philip F. Giardino; Dcn. Henry J. Leader; CRP Stds.: 2

TICONDEROGA

St. Mary's Church, Ticonderoga, NY - 18 Father Jogues Pl., Ticonderoga, NY 12883; Mailing: 22 Father Jogues Pl., Ticonderoga, NY 12883 t) 518-597-3924 (CRP); 518-585-7144 stmarysti@bridgepoint1.com www.route74catholics.org/ Rev. Christopher J. Looby, Pst.; CRP Stds.: 9

St. Mary School - (Grades PreK-8) 64 Amherst Ave., Ticonderoga, NY 12883 t) 518-585-7433 office@stmarysschoolticonderoga.org stmarysschoolticonderoga.org Sr. Sharon Anne Dalton, S.S.J., Prin.; Stds.: 63; Sr. Tchrs.: 1; Lay Tchrs.: 9

TUPPER LAKE

St. Alphonsus - Holy Name of Jesus - 40 Marion St., Tupper Lake, NY 12986 t) 518-359-3405 office@tupperlakecatholics.org www.tupperlakecatholics.org Rev. James V. Teti, Pst.; Rev. Clement Rimonds, H.G.N. (India), Par. Vicar; Dcn. James T. Ellis; Dcn. Gerald H. Savage; CRP Stds.: 57

St. Alphonsus Church - 48 Wawbeek Ave, Tupper Lake, NY 12986

WADDINGTON

St. Mary's, Waddington - 34 Oak St., Waddington, NY 13694; Mailing: P.O. Box 187, Waddington, NY 13694 t) 315-388-4466 ggiroux@rcdony.org mwcatholics.org Linked with St. John the Baptist, Madrid, NY Rev. Garry B. Giroux, Pst.; CRP Stds.: 9

Msgr. Arquett Parish Center - 36 Oak St., Waddington, NY 13694 t) 315-388-4423

WATERTOWN

Saint Anthony's Church - 850 Arsenal St., Watertown, NY 13601; Mailing: Pastoral Center, 123 S. Massey, Watertown, NY 13601 t) 315-782-1190 x1 info@sawatn.org; watertownsec@rcdony.org catholicwatertown.org/ Rev. John M. Demo, Pst.; Rev. Matthew Conger, Par. Vicar; Dcn. Guy Javarone; Dcn. Michael J. Allan; Dcn. Kevin T. Mastellon; Dcn. Edward R. Miller; Dcn. Donald Wilder; Sr. Angelica Rebello, S.C.C., Pst. Assoc.; Patrick J. Bates, Pst. Assoc.; Sr. Maria Flavia D'Costa, S.C.C., Pst. Assoc.; CRP Stds.: 18

The Church of the Holy Family - 123 Winthrop St., Watertown, NY 13601; Mailing: 129 Winthrop St., Watertown, NY 13601 t) 315-782-2468; 315-782-1190 holyfamilyre@yahoo.com; hfchurch@twcny.rr.com www.catholicwatertown.org Rev. John M. Demo, Pst.; Rev. Matthew Conger, Par. Vicar; Dcn. Guy Javarone; Dcn. Kevin T. Mastellon; Dcn. Edward R. Miller; Dcn. Donald Wilder; Rev. Msgr. Paul E. Whitmore, In Res.; Rev. Leo A. Wiley, In Res.; Patrick J. Bates, Pst. Assoc.; Sr. Maria Flavia D'Costa, S.C.C., Pst. Assoc.; Sr. Angelica Rebello, S.C.C., Pst. Assoc.; Dcn. Michael J. Allan; CRP Stds.: 132

Our Lady of the Sacred Heart - 320 W. Lynde St., Watertown, NY 13601 t) 315-782-1474 olshparish13601@gmail.com www.olshparish.org/ Rev. Frank Natale, M.S.C., Pst.; Rev. Joseph Kanimea, M.S.C., Par. Vicar; Dcn. William Michael Johnston; Dcn. John J. Trombly; Sr. Constance Marie Sylver, S.S.J., DRE; CRP Stds.: 23

The Society of St. Patrick's Church - 123 S. Massey St., Watertown, NY 13601-3201 t) 315-782-1190 x1 info@spwatn.org; watertownsec@rcdony.org catholicwatertown.org Rev. John M. Demo, Pst.; Rev. Matthew Conger, Par. Vicar; Dcn. Guy Javarone; Dcn. Kevin T. Mastellon; Dcn. Donald Wilder;

WELLS

St. Ann's - 1303 State Rte. 30, Wells, NY 12190; Mailing: P.O. Box 214, Speculator, NY 12164 t) 518-548-6275 sjcsac@frontiernet.net Rev. Sony G. Pulickal, Pst.; CRP Stds.: 13

WEST CHAZY

Saint Joseph's Church, West Chazy, NY - 56 W. Church St., West Chazy, NY 12992; Mailing: P.O. Box 224, West Chazy, NY 12992 t) 518-493-4521 stjosephsfaithformation101@gmail.com; stjosephs@westelcom.com Rev. Theodore A. Crosby, Pst.; Dcn. Mark T. Webster; Susan M. Corneau, DRE; CRP Stds.: 21

WEST LEYDEN

Church of the Nativity, B.M.V - 1183 State Rte. 26, West Leyden, NY 13489; Mailing: P. O. Box 382, Constableville, NY 13325 t) 315-397-2556 stmarys1@frontier.com catholicparishesofslc.weebly.com Dcn. James W. Chaufty; Rev. Lawrence E. Marullo, Pst.; Dcn. Michael Lieber; CRP Stds.: 5

SS. Peter & Paul Oratory - 2056 Fish Creek Rd., West Leyden, NY 13489; Mailing: P.O. Box 382, Constableville, NY 13325

WESTPORT

The St. Philip of Neri Roman Catholic Church, at Westport, NY - 6603 Main St., Westport, NY 12993; Mailing: P.O. Box 368, Elizabethtown, NY 12932 t) 518-873-6760 rccowe@gmail.com www.wewe4.org/ Rev. Justin Thomas, H.G.N., Pst.; Dcn. Paul M. White;

WILLSBORO

Catholic Community of St. Philip of Jesus and St. Joseph of Willsboro, New York - 3748 Main St., Willsboro, NY 12996; Mailing: P.O. Box 607, Willsboro, NY 12996 t) 518-536-2642 (CRP); 518-963-4524 rccowe@gmail.com www.wewe4.org/ Rev. Justin Thomas, H.G.N., Pst.; Dcn. Paul M. White;

St. Joseph Church - 2891 Essex Rd., Essex, NY 12996 (Worship Site)

St. Philip of Jesus Church - (Worship Site)

SCHOOLS: PRESCHOOL THRU HIGH SCHOOL

SCHOOLS

STATE OF NEW YORK

PLATTSBURGH

Seton Catholic School - (PAR) (Grades PreK-12) 206 New York Rd., Plattsburgh, NY 12903 t) 518-561-4031 mforbes@setonknights.org; mspilman@setonknights.org www.setonknights.org Mary Forbes, Prin.; Sharon Bainbridge, Librn.; Stds.: 230; Lay Tchrs.: 25

WATERTOWN

Immaculate Heart Central School - (PAR) (Grades PreK-12) 1316 Ives St., Watertown, NY 13601 t) 315-788-4670 daniel.charlebois@ihcschool.org; amy.mitchell@ihcschool.org www.ihcschool.org Daniel Charlebois, Prin.; Amy Mitchell, Vice Prin.; Teresa Lucas, Bus. Mgr.; Stds.: 397; Lay Tchrs.: 31

Immaculate Heart Central Primary Campus - (Grades PreK-12) 122 Winthrop St., Watertown, NY 13601 ihcschool.org Stds.: 205; Lay Tchrs.: 16

Immaculate Heart Central Junior / Senior High Campus - (Grades PreK-12) 1316 Ives St., Watertown, NY 13601 t) (315) 788-4670 daniel.charlebois@ihcschool.org Stds.: 192; Lay Tchrs.: 15

INSTITUTIONS LOCATED IN DIOCESE

CATHOLIC CHARITIES [CCH]

OGDENSBURG

Catholic Charities of the Diocese of Ogdensburg - 214 Caroline St., Ogdensburg, NY 13669 t) 315-393-2255 c) 315-264-9256 pdonahue@cathcharities.org www.cathcharities.org Dcn. Patrick J. Donahue, CEO; Asstd. Annu.: 28,865; Staff: 47

CEMETERIES [CEM]

BRASHER FALLS

St. Patrick's Cemetery Association of Brasher Falls, N.Y. - County Rte. 50, Brasher Falls, NY 13613; Mailing: PO Box 208, Brasher Falls, NY 13613 t) 315-389-5401 Michael Hoag, Contact;

CARTHAGE

St. James Cemetery Corporation - 500-576 S James St, Carthage, NY 13619; Mailing: 327 West St., Carthage, NY 13619 t) 315-493-3224 carthagesec@rcdony.org Rev. Todd E. Thibault, Pst.;

CROGHAN

St. Stephen's Cemetery Association, Inc. - 6979 Belfort Rd., Croghan, NY 13327; Mailing: PO Box 38, Croghan, NY 13327 t) 315-346-6958 fststephens@twcny.rr.com Rev. Donald J. Manfred, Contact;

MALONE

St. Joseph's Cemetery of Malone, N.Y., Inc. - Fort Covington St., Malone, NY 12953; Mailing: P.O. Box 547, Malone, NY 12953 t) 518-483-1300 office@standres.org www.standres.org Rev. Steven M. Murray, Pst.; Dcn. Brent A. Charland;

Notre Dame Cemetery of Malone, N.Y., Inc. - Andrus St., Malone, NY 12953; Mailing: P.O. Box 547, Malone, NY 12953 t) 518-483-1300 office@standres.org www.standres.org Rev. Steven M. Murray, Pst.; Dcn. Brent A. Charland;

PLATTSBURGH

Mount Carmel Cemetery - 1202-1204 Cumberland Head Rd, Plattsburgh, NY 12901; Mailing: Holy Cross Parish, 7 Margaret St., Plattsburgh, NY 12901 t) 518-563-0730 office@holycrosspbg.org Rev. Kevin D. McEwan, Pst.;

WATERTOWN

Calvary Cemetery Association of Watertown, N.Y. - 320 W. Lynde St., Watertown, NY 13601 t) 315-782-1474 olshparish13601@gmail.com www.olshparish.org/ Rev. Frank Natale, M.S.C., Pst.;

CONVENTS, MONASTERIES, AND RESIDENCES FOR WOMEN [CON]

CARTHAGE

St. James Convent, Sisters of St. Joseph - Sisters of St. Joseph, 317 West St., Carthage, NY 13619 t) 315-493-1672 smacollinsssj@yahoo.com Sr. Annunciata Collins, S.S.J., Pst. Assoc.; Srs.: 2

LAKE PLACID

St. Margaret Convent (Sisters of Mercy) - 185 Old Military Rd., Lake Placid, NY 12946 t) 518-523-2929 mokeefe@sistersofmercy.org Sr. M. Camillus O'Keefe, R.S.M., Supr.; Srs.: 4

MASSENA

Sacred Heart Convent - 212 Main St., Massena, NY 13662; Mailing: P.O. Box 91, Massena, NY 13662 c) 315-705-8509 madrecindy1@gmail.com Sr. Cindy Sullivan, BVM, Director, Meals on Wheels; Srs.: 1

OGDENSBURG

Sisters of St. Joseph - 251 Proctor Ave., Ogdensburg, NY 13669 t) 315-393-6511 Sr. Bernadette Marie Collins, S.S.J., Rel. Ord. Ldr.; Sr. Mary Eamon Lyng, S.S.J., Diocesan Vocations Coordinator; Srs.: 2

PLATTSBURGH

Dominican Sisters of Hope, Ossining - 21 Bushey Blvd., Plattsburgh, NY 12901 t) 518-561-8252 elizmenard40@gmail.com Sr. Elizabeth Menard, O.P., Contact; Srs.: 4

Sisters of Charity of St. Louis - 4907 S. Catherine St., Apt. 107, Plattsburgh, NY 12901 t) 518-802-0331 srbernadetted@gmail.com Sr. Bernadette Ducharme, S.C.S.L., Supr.; Srs.: 3

Sisters of Mercy - 101 Bea's Way, Apt. 102, Plattsburgh, NY 12901 t) 518-561-9689 blatour@sistersofmercy.org Sisters of Mercy Srs.: 1

SARANAC LAKE

Sisters of Mercy of the Americas - 35 Trudeau Rd., Saranac Lake, NY 12983-5635 t) 518-891-3234 srmcarolyn@roadrunner.com Srs.: 1

TICONDEROGA

St. Mary's Convent, Sisters of St. Joseph - 145 Lake George Ave., Ticonderoga, NY 12883 t) 518-585-6547 office@stmarysschoolticonderoga.org Sr. Sharon Anne Dalton, S.S.J., Contact; Srs.: 2

WATERTOWN

Precious Blood Monastery, Sister Adorers of the Precious Blood - 400 Pratt St., Watertown, NY 13601 t) 315-788-1669 srm1@twcny.rr.com; tenthiet@gmail.com sisterspreciousblood.org Sr. Rose Mary Rossi, APB, Supr.; Srs.: 4

Sisters of St. Joseph Motherhouse - 1425 Washington St., Watertown, NY 13601-4533 t) 315-782-3460 ssjcongr@rcdony.org www.ssjwatertown.org Sr. Shirley Anne Brown, S.S.J., Supr.; Srs.: 27

ENDOWMENTS / FOUNDATIONS / TRUSTS [EFT]

OGDENSBURG

St. Joseph's Foundation, Inc. - 950 Linden St., Ogdensburg, NY 13669 t) (315) 393-3780 x1012 csteele@stjh.org; dluckie@stjh.org www.stjh.org Colleen Steele, Admin.;

WATERTOWN

Sacred Heart Foundation - 320 W. Lynde St., Watertown, NY 13601 t) 315-782-3344 mail@sacredheartfoundation.com www.sacredheartfoundation.com Sabrina Rizzo, Bus. Mgr.;

MISCELLANEOUS [MIS]

CHAUMONT

Mission Project Service - 27396 Madison St., Chaumont, NY 13622; Mailing: P.O. Box 100, Chaumont, NY 13622 t) 315-300-4233 misprojser2@gmail.com www.missionprojectservice.org Rev. Pierre Aubin, M.S.C., Dir.;

LAKE PLACID

Mercy Care for the Adirondacks, Inc. - 185 Old Military Rd., Lake Placid, NY 12946 t) 518-523-5580; 518-523-5581 dbeal@adkmercy.org www.adkmercy.org Donna Beal, Exec.;

MASSENA

St. Peter's Outreach Ministry, Inc. - 124 Main St., 128 Main St, Massena, NY 13662; Mailing: 128 Main St., Massena, NY 13662 t) 315-769-1200 svdp128@gmail.com Alice Felix, Program Manager;

OGDENSBURG

The Pontifical Mission Societies of the Diocese of Ogdensburg, New York, Inc. - 622 Washington St., Ogdensburg, NY 13669; Mailing: P.O. Box 369, Ogdensburg, NY 13669 t) 315-393-2920 www.rcdony.org/mission.html Sr. Mary Ellen Brett, S.S.J., Dir.;

SARANAC LAKE

Guggenheim Center for Religious Programs - 1468 County Rte. 18, Saranac Lake, NY 12983; Mailing: P.O. Box 664, Saranac Lake, NY 12983 t) 518-891-0809 (Lodge); 518-891-3323 (Dorm) bennett5@roadrunner.com Ralph Bennett, Dir.;

WATERTOWN

The Federation of Sisters of the Precious Blood, Inc. - 400 Pratt St., Watertown, NY 13601 t) 315-788-1669 srm1@twcny.rr.com; smarilyn@twcny.rr.com Sr. Rose Mary Rossi, APB, Supr.; Sr. Joan Milot, A.P.B., Pres.;

MONASTERIES AND RESIDENCES FOR PRIESTS AND BROTHERS [MON]

WATERTOWN

Missionaries of the Sacred Heart - 668 Thompson St., Watertown, NY 13601 t) 315-782-3480 cvrch219@gmail.com www.misacor-usa.org Rev. Raymond Diesbourg, M.S.C., Supr.; Rev. Frank Natale, M.S.C., Pst.; Rev. Corneille Boyeye, M.S.C., Chap.; Rev. Joseph Kanimea, M.S.C., Par. Vicar; Rev. Pierre Aubin, M.S.C., Pastor Emer.; Rev. David DeLuca, M.S.C., In Res.; Priests: 6

NURSING / REHABILITATION / CONVALESCENCE / ELDERLY CARE [NUR]

OGDENSBURG

St. Joseph's Home - 950 Linden St, Ogdensburg, NY 13669 t) 315-393-3780 csteele@stjh.org www.stjh.org Certified long term care. Colleen Steele, Admin.; Asstd. Annu.: 200; Staff: 102

RETREAT HOUSES / RENEWAL CENTERS [RTR]

ELLENBURG CENTER

Our Lady of the Adirondacks Inc. House of Prayer - 7270 Star Rd., Rte. 190, Ellenburg Center, NY 12934-2501 t) 518-594-3253 olaprayerhouse@gmail.com www.ourladyoftheadirondacks.com Rev. (Bill) Guy F. Edwards, Spiritual Adv./Care Srvcs.;

Our Lady of the Adirondacks Community -

Our Lady of the Adirondacks Prayer Association -

OGDENSBURG

Wadhams Hall - 6866 State Hwy. 37, Ogdensburg, NY 13669-4420 t) 315-393-4231 admin@wadhams.edu www.wadhams.org William Seymour, Dir.;

An asterisk (*) denotes an organization that has established tax-exempt status directly with the IRS and is not covered by the USCCB Group Ruling.

Archdiocese of Oklahoma City

(Archidioecesis Oklahomapolitana)

MOST REVEREND PAUL S. COAKLEY

Archbishop of Oklahoma City; ordained May 21, 1983; appointed Bishop of Salina October 21, 2004; installed December 28, 2004; appointed Archbishop of Oklahoma City December 16, 2010; installed February 11, 2011. Catholic Pastoral Center: 7501 Northwest Expwy., P.O. Box 32180, Oklahoma City, OK 73123.

Catholic Pastoral Center: 7501 Northwest Expwy., P.O. Box 32180, Oklahoma City, OK 73123. T: 405-721-5651; F: 405-721-5210.

ESTABLISHED FEBRUARY 6, 1973.

Square Miles 42,470.

Erected into a Vicariate Apostolic by Brief of May 29, 1891. Erected into the Diocese of Oklahoma with the See in Oklahoma City by a Brief of Pope Pius X, August 17, 1905. Name changed to Diocese of Oklahoma City and Tulsa by Bull of Pope Pius XI, November 14, 1930. Erected into Archdiocese of Oklahoma City by a Bull of Pope Paul VI, December 13, 1972. The Province includes the Dioceses of Tulsa and Little Rock.

Comprises the following 46 Counties: Alfalfa, Beaver, Beckham, Blaine, Caddo, Canadian, Carter, Cimarron, Cleveland, Comanche, Cotton, Custer, Dewey, Ellis, Garfield, Garvin, Grady, Grant, Greer, Harmon, Harper, Jackson, Jefferson, Johnston, Kay, Kingfisher, Kiowa, Lincoln, Logan, Love, McClain, Major, Marshall, Murray, Noble, Oklahoma, Pontotoc, Pottawatomie, Roger Mills, Seminole, Stephens, Texas, Tillman, Washita, Woods and Woodward.

For legal titles of parishes and archdiocesan institutions, consult the Secretariat for Administration.

STATISTICAL OVERVIEW

Personnel

Archbishops	1
Retired Archbishops	1
Abbots	1
Retired Abbots	2
Priests: Diocesan Active in Diocese	57
Priests: Retired, Sick or Absent	12
Number of Diocesan Priests	69
Religious Priests in Diocese	7
Total Priests in your Diocese	76
Extern Priests in Diocese	34
Ordinations:	
Diocesan Priests	1
Permanent Deacons in Diocese	112
Total Brothers	7
Total Sisters	51

Parishes

Parishes	67
With Resident Pastor:	
Resident Diocesan Priests	64
Resident Religious Priests	3
Missions	46
Professional Ministry Personnel:	
Brothers	7
Sisters	45
Lay Ministers	91

Welfare

Catholic Hospitals	12
Total Assisted	1,188,938
Homes for the Aged	6
Total Assisted	723
Special Centers for Social Services	2
Total Assisted	9,057
Residential Care of Disabled	1
Total Assisted	130

Educational

Diocesan Students in Other Seminaries	14
Total Seminarians	14
High Schools, Diocesan and Parish	3
Total Students	1,375
Elementary Schools, Diocesan and Parish	15
Total Students	3,500
Non-residential Schools for the Disabled	1
Total Students	24
Catechesis/Religious Education:	
High School Students	3,500
Elementary Students	7,000
Total Students under Catholic Instruction	15,413
Teachers in Diocese:	
Sisters	1
Lay Teachers	448

Vital Statistics

Receptions into the Church:	
Infant Baptism Totals	1,777
Minor Baptism Totals	255
Adult Baptism Totals	127
Received into Full Communion	445
First Communions	2,339
Confirmations	2,706
Marriages:	
Catholic	416
Interfaith	118
Total Marriages	534
Deaths	1,015
Total Catholic Population	222,674
Total Population	2,226,742

LEADERSHIP

Moderator of the Curia and Vicar General - t) 405-721-1811 Very Rev. William L. Novak (wnovak@archokc.org);

Chancellor - t) 405-721-1811 Michael A. Scaperlanda, Chancellor (mscaperlanda@archokc.org);

ADMINISTRATION

Secretariat for Administration - t) 405-721-1811

Archives - t) 405-721-5651 x141 George Rigazzi, Archivist;

Finance - David J. Johnson, CFO;

Priests' Medical Fund - Very Rev. William L. Novak, Moderator of the Curia & Vicar Gen.;

Priests' Retirement Trust Fund - David J. Johnson;

Letters of Suitability - t) (405) 721-1416 chancellorsoffice@archokc.org

Human Resources - Rhonda McMillin, Dir.;

Propagation of the Faith, Holy Childhood Assoc., Missionary Cooperation Plan - t) 405-721-5651 David J. Johnson;

Safe Environment Coordinator - t) 405-709-2748 Page Houser;

Victim Assistance Coordinator - t) 405-720-9878 Jennifer Goodrich;

ADVISORY BOARDS, COMMISSIONS, COMMITTEES, AND COUNCILS

Archdiocesan Finance Council - djohnson@archokc.org Michael Milligan, Chair; Steve Brown; Joe Fleckinger;

Building and Real Estate Committee - Very Rev. William L. Novak, Pres. (wnovak@archokc.org); Steve Cooper, Chair (scooper@archokc.org); John Ward, Secy.;

CLERGY AND RELIGIOUS SERVICES

Secretariat for Clergy and Consecrated Life and Vocations - t) 405-721-9351

Blessed Stanley Rother Cause - Dcn. Norman Mejstrik, Dir.;

Clergy Education - Rev. Joseph M. Irwin, Coord.;

Master of Ceremonies - Rev. Zachary Boazman, Dir.; Rev. Stephen V. Hamilton, Asst.; Rev. Cory D. Stanley, Asst.;

Priests' Nurse - t) 405-709-2731 Suzanne Clem;

Permanent Diaconate - Dcn. Norman Mejstrik, Dir.;

Vicar for Priests - Rev. Joseph M. Irwin;

Vocations and Seminarians - Rev. Brian E. Buettner, Dir.; Rev. John D. Herrera, Assoc. Dir.; Rev. John Paul Lewis, Assoc. Dir.;

COMMUNICATIONS

Communications - t) 405-721-1810 Avery Holt, Dir.;

Sooner Catholic Newspaper - t) (405) 721-1810 archokc.org/sooner-catholic

CONSULTATIVE BODIES

Archdiocesan Consultors - Very Rev. William L. Novak (wnovak@archokc.org); Rev. Raymond K. Ackerman (raymond.ackerman@archokc.org); Rev. Stephen J. Bird (sbird@archokc.org);

Presbyteral Council - Very Rev. Christopher T. Brashears, Chair (cbrashears@archokc.org); Rev. Jerome Krug, Vice-Chairman (fr.jerome@steugenes.org); Rev. Joseph M. Irwin, Vicar for Priests, Ex Officio;

Priests' Personnel Board - Rev. Joseph M. Irwin; Rev. Timothy D. Luschen; Rev. John R. Metzinger;

Vocations Board - t) 405-721-9351 bbuettner@archokc.org Sr. Maria of the Trinity Faulkner (srmaria@gospeloflifedisciples.org); Dr. Laura Webb; Luis Soto;

DEANERIES

Central North Deanery - Rev. Stephen J. Bird (sbird@archokc.org);

Central South Deanery - Rev. Timothy M. Fuller;

Northwest Deanery - Very Rev. Christopher T. Brashears (cbrashears@archokc.org);

Northeast Deanery - Rev. Carson Krittenbrink (carson.krittenbrink@archokc.org);

Southwest Deanery - Rev. Philip M. Seeton (philip.seeton@archokc.org);

Southeast Deanery - Rev. Kevin J. Ratterman (Kevin.Ratterman@archokc.org);

EVANGELIZATION

Secretariat for Evangelization and Catechesis - t) 405-721-5651 x201

American Indian Catholic Outreach - t) 918-822-3255 nativeamerican@archokc.org Dcn. Roy Don Callison, Coord.;

Blessed Stanley Rother Institute - t) (405) 709-2718 Dr. Jason Fugikawa, Dir.;

Catholic Education - t) 405-709-2701 Dr. Lara Schuler, Dir.;

Children's Evangelization and Discipleship - Katie Murphree, Assoc. Dir.;

Ecumenical and Interreligious Affairs - Rev. James A. Goins;

Hispanic Leadership Development - Connie Jackson;

Marriage and Family Life Ministry - Dr. Alex Schimpf, Dir.;

Family Enrichment / Disability Ministries -

Respect Life Coordinator - Dcn. Joe Vandervort;

Parish Leadership Engagement - Dr. Larann Wilson, Dir.;

Prison Ministry - Dcn. James E. Smith, Coord.;

Youth, Young Adult and Campus Evangelization and Discipleship - t) (405) 709-2783 Jayce Palmer, Dir.; Kendra Mann, Coord.;

OLOG Camp - t) (405) 709-2783 campolog.org

Scouting - Chad Goodman; Janie Goodman, Catholic Scouts Outside of Parishes; Matt Jackson, Scouting in Parishes;

Youth Evangelization and Summer Camp - t) (405) 709-2715 Caden Bennett;

FACILITIES

Catholic Pastoral Center - t) 405-721-5651 x104 Shari Conrady, Assoc. Dir. (sconrady@archokc.org);

St. Francis de Sales Seminary - Most Rev. Paul S. Coakley; David Johnson, Treas.;

ORGANIZATIONS

Catholic Lawyers Guild - t) 405-721-5651 Miguel Garcia;

Catholic Physicians Guild - t) 405-942-4084 Rev. Richard D. Stansberry Jr., Chap. (rstansberry@archokc.org);

Archdiocesan Council of Catholic Women - Rev. Bill H. Pruett (bpruett@archokc.org);

SPIRITUAL LIFE

Secretariat for Divine Worship - t) 405-721-5651 x451 Rev. Stephen J. Bird, Dir. (sbird@archokc.org); Rev. Zachary Boazman, Assoc. Dir. (Zachary.Boazman@archokc.org);

STEWARDSHIP

Secretariat for Stewardship and Development - t) 405-709-2745 stewardship@archokc.org Peter de Keratry, Exec. Dir. (pdekeratry@archokc.org);

Assembly of Catholic Professionals -

TRIBUNAL

Metropolitan Tribunal of Oklahoma - t) 405-721-5651 x401

Judicial Vicar - Rev. Richard D. Stansberry Jr.;

Adjunct Judicial Vicar - Rev. Bill H. Pruett;

Collegiate Judges - Very Rev. Christopher T. Brashears; Rev. William Banowsky; Matthew Robinson;

Defender of the Bond - Rev. Francis T. Nguyen;

Notaries - Edith Miranda; Ana Romero; Carol Davito;

PARISHES, MISSIONS, AND CLERGY

STATE OF OKLAHOMA

ADA

St. Joseph - 1300 E. Beverly St., Ada, OK 74820; Mailing: P.O. Box 1585, Ada, OK 74820 t) 580-332-4811 pom.stjosephada@gmail.com www.stjosephada.com Rev. Aaron J. Foshee, Pst.; Dcn. Dennis D. Fine; CRP Stds.: 49

St. Francis Xavier - 700 E. Oklahoma, Sulphur, OK 73086; Mailing: 1313 E. 7th St., Sulphur, OK 73086 t) 580-622-3070 altarsociety@yahoo.com Rosalina Aglialoro-Hoyle, Parish Life Coord.;

ALTUS

Prince of Peace - 1500 Falcon Rd., Altus, OK 73521 t) 580-482-3363 secretary@popaltus.org www.princeofpeacealtus.org Rev. Joseph David, Pst.; Dcn. Eulis Mobley; Judy Cosway, Music Min.; CRP Stds.: 162

St. Helen Church - 507 E. Highview, Frederick, OK 73542; Mailing: PO BOX 608, Frederick, OK 73542 t) (580) 335-3953 www.sthelenok.org

ALVA

Sacred Heart - 627 12th St., Alva, OK 73717 t) 580-327-0339 office@sacredheartalva.org sacredheartalva.org/ Rev. Balraj Sagili Jesudas, Pst.; CRP Stds.: 48

Our Mother of Mercy - 1325 Main St., Waynoka, OK 73860; Mailing: 627 12 St, Alva, OK 73717 t) (580) 327-0339

St. Cornelius - 404 S. Massachusetts, Cherokee, OK 73728; Mailing: 627 12 St., Alva, OK 73717 t) (580) 327-0339

ANADARKO

St. Patrick's - 1101 W. Petree Rd., Anadarko, OK 73005; Mailing: Po Box 628, Anadarko, OK 73005 t) 405-247-5255 st.pats1889@gmail.com www.stpatrickanadarko.org/ Rev. Vuong "Vic" Luong; CRP Stds.: 71

Our Lady of the Most Holy Rosary - Hwy. 152, Binger, OK 73009; Mailing: P.O. Box 628, Anadarko, OK 73005 t) (405) 247-5255

St. Richard - 427 S. Highland St., Carnegie, OK 73015 t) (405) 247-5255 Rev. Vuong "Vic" Luong, Pst.;

ARDMORE

St. Mary - 101 E St., S.W., Ardmore, OK 73401 t) 580-223-0231 stmaryardmore@hotmail.com www.stmaryardmore.org Rev. Kevin J. Ratterman, Pst.; Dcn. Robert Highsmith; Dcn. Juan Jimenez, Dir., Hispanic Min & Parish Life; CRP Stds.: 154

BLACKWELL

St. Joseph's - 324 W. Bridge, Blackwell, OK 74631; Mailing: PO Box 578, Blackwell, OK 74631 t) 580-363-0441 Rev. Balaswamy Bathini, Pst.; Mistie Jackson, DRE; CRP Stds.: 5

CHANDLER

Our Lady of Sorrows - 409 Price Ave., Chandler, OK 74834; Mailing: P.O. Box 543, Chandler, OK 74834 t) 405-258-1239 olschandler@att.net www.ourladyofsorrowschandler.org Rev. Timothy Ruckel, Pst.; Dcn. B.D. Tidmore; CRP Stds.: 25

St. Louis - Hwy. 99 & Eighth Ave., Stroud, OK 74079; Mailing: PO Box 543, Chndler, OK 74834 t) (405) 258-1239

CHICKASHA

Holy Name of Jesus Catholic Church - 210 S. 7th St., Chickasha, OK 73018; Mailing: PO Box 748, Chickasha, OK 73023 t) 405-224-6068 secretary@holynamechickasha.org www.holynamechickasha.org Rev. Michael Wheelahan, Pst.; Dcn. Louis Nix; Rosa Munoz, DRE; CRP Stds.: 185

St. Peter Church - E. Second & Quapah, Lindsay, OK 73052 t) (405) 224-6068 holynamechickasha.org

CLINTON

St. Mary's - 1218 Knox Ave., Clinton, OK 73601; Mailing: P.O. Box 1295, Clinton, OK 73601 t) 580-323-0345 k.hubbard@stmarysclintonok.org www.stmarysclintonok.org Rev. Balaswamy Mandagiri, Pst.; Dcn. Hector Hernandez; Kristine Moreno, DRE; Kimber Hubbard, Office Manager; CRP Stds.: 250

St. Anne - 522 E. 3rd, Cordell, OK 73632 t) (580) 323-0345 Josh Ferrero, DRE;

DEL CITY

St. Paul, Apostle - 3901 S. Sunnylane Rd., Del City, OK 73115 t) 405-677-4873 stpaulch@coxinet.net stpaulscatholic.org Rev. Joseph Sundar Raju Pudota, Pst.; Dcn. John J. Page; Michelle Hill, Music Min.; Kristen Danner, DRE;

DUNCAN

Assumption - 711 W. Hickory Ave., Duncan, OK 73533 t) 580-255-0590 pneal@assumptionduncanok.com; rev.p.jandaczek@gmail.com www.assumptionduncanok.com Rev. Peter Jandaczek, Pst.; Dcn. James Conway; Dcn. Manuel G. Garcia; Dcn. Mark Gildon; Maria Martinez, DRE; CRP Stds.: 70

Immaculate Conception - 307 N 4th St, Marlow, OK 73055; Mailing: PO Box 328, Marlow, OK 73055 t) 580-658-2365

EDMOND

St. Damien of Molokai Church - 8455 N.W. 234th St., Sorghum Mill, Edmond, OK 73025 t) 405-330-9968 leperpriestokc@gmail.com www.stdamiens.com Latin Mass Apostolate of the Priestly Fraternity of Saint Peter Rev. Simon Zurita, F.S.S.P., Pst.; CRP Stds.: 153

St. John the Baptist - 900 S. Littler Ave., Edmond, OK 73013; Mailing: PO Box 510, Edmond, OK 73083-0510 t) 405-340-9871 (CRP); 405-340-0691 parish_office@stjohn-catholic.org www.stjohn-catholic.org Rev. Raymond K. Ackerman, Pst.; Rev. Alexander Kroll, Assoc. Pst.; Dcn. David Ashton; Dcn. Robert Dunlap; Dcn. Randy Hearn; Dcn. Zsolt Nagykaldi; Dcn. Richard Rosencrans; Jennifer Dolf, Bus. Mgr.; CRP Stds.: 604

St. Elizabeth Ann Seton School - -8) 925 South Blvd., Edmond, OK 73034-4710 t) 405-348-5364 seas@stjohn-catholic.org www.stelizabethedmond.org Nicole De Longe, Prin.; Stds.: 420; Lay Tchrs.: 31

St. Monica - 2001 N. Western, Edmond, OK 73012 t) 405-359-2700; 405-350-2700 (CRP) www.stmonica-edmond.org Rev. Stephen V. Hamilton, Pst.; Rev. Balireddy Ponnapati, Assoc. Pst.; Dcn. Jorge Pereira; Dcn. Edward Donosso; CRP Stds.: 338

EL RENO

Sacred Heart - 208 S. Evans Ave., El Reno, OK 73036-3636 t) 405-262-1405 pastor@sacredheartelreno.com www.sacredheartelreno.com Rev. Lance A. Warren, Pst.; CRP Stds.: 140

Sacred Heart School - (Grades PreK-8) 210 S. Evans, El Reno, OK 73036 t) 405-262-2284 sacredheart@coxinet.net Shannon Statton, Prin.; Stds.: 98; Lay Tchrs.: 8

ELGIN

St. Ann - 8492 State Hwy. 17, Elgin, OK 73538; Mailing: P.O. Box 10, Elgin, OK 73538 t) 580-492-5914 stann@tds.net www.triparishok.org Rev. Rayanna Narisetti, Pst.; Dcn. Thomas E. Biles, DRE; CRP Stds.: 50

Our Lady of Perpetual Help - 220 N. A St., Sterling, OK 73567; Mailing: PO Box 10, Elgin, OK 73538 t) (580) 492-5914 triparishok.org

Mother of Sorrows - 521 E. Wallace, Apache, OK 73006; Mailing: PO BOX 10, Elgin, OK 73538 t) (580) 492-5914

ELK CITY

St. Matthew's - 3001 E. Hwy. 66, Elk City, OK 73644-9607 t) 580-225-0066 stmatthewre@outlook.com; dgrover2010@gmail.com www.stmatthew.weconnect.com Rev. Daniel G. Grover, Pst.; Kathy Noble, Music Min.; Katie Bartlett, DRE; CRP Stds.: 191

Queen of All Saints - 914 N. 5th St., Sayre, OK 73662; Mailing: 131 Killian Ln., Sayre, OK 73644 t) (580) 225-0066

ENID

St. Francis Xavier - 110 N. Madison St., Enid, OK 73701; Mailing: P.O. Box 3527, Enid, OK 73702-3527 t) 580-237-0812 xavier_enid@yahoo.com www.stfrancisenid.com Rev. Mark E. Mason, Pst.; Rev. John D. Herrera, Pst. Assoc.; Dcn. Anthony Crispo; Dcn. Val Ross; CRP Stds.: 438

St. Joseph Catholic School - (Grades PreK-5) 110 N. Madison, ENid, OK 73701 t) 580-242-4449 school@stjosephschoolenid.com stjosephschoolenid.com George Fred Martin, Prin.; Stds.: 113; Lay Tchrs.: 10

St. Michael - 100 E Main St., Goltry, OK 73739; Mailing: 1924 W. Willow Rd, Enid, OK 73703 t) (580) 233-4589

St. Gregory the Great - 1924 W. Willow Rd., Enid, OK 73703 t) 580-233-4589 stgregorys@sbcglobal.net stfrancisenid@yahoo.com

GUTHRIE

St. Mary - 411 N. Elm, Guthrie, OK 73044; Mailing: PO Box 1556, Guthrie, OK 73044 t) 405-282-4239 x4 office@stmaryguthrie.com www.stmaryguthrie.com Rev. James A. Wickersham, Pst.; Dcn. James S. Fourcade; CRP Stds.: 64

St. Margaret Mary - 700 N. Grand, Crescent, OK 73028; Mailing: PO Box 632, Crescent, OK 73028 t) (405) 282-4239

GUYMON

St. Peter's - 1220 N. Quinn St., Guymon, OK 73942 t) (806) 340-0012 sec@panhandlecatholic.org www.panhandlecatholic.org Very Rev. Christopher T. Brashears, Pst.; Dcn. Joseph M. Cruz; Dcn. Luis De La Garza; Dcn. Emilio Rodriguez; Dcn. Joel Salcedo; CRP Stds.: 224

Sacred Heart - 106 N. Albright, Hooker, OK 73945; Mailing: P.O. Box 468, Hooker, OK 73945 t) (580) 652-2320 www.panhanhandlecatholic,org

Good Shepherd - S. Ellis at Second, Boise City, OK 73933; Mailing: P.O. Box 966, Boise City, OK 73933 t) (580) 544-3443

St. Frances Cabrini - 101 Ave. C, Beaver, OK 73932 t) (580) 338-7212

HARRAH

St. Teresa of Avila - 1576 Tim Holt Dr., Harrah, OK 73045 t) 405-454-2819; 405-454-9440 (CRP) staharrah@gmail.com www.stteresaharrah.org Rev. Deva Undralla, Pst.; CRP Stds.: 110

Saint Vincent de Paul Church - 123 S. 9th St., McLoud, OK 74851; Mailing: P.O. Box 585, Mcloud, OK 74851 t) (405) 964-5606 stvincentmcloud@gmail.com stteresaharrah.org

HENNESSEY

St. Joseph's - 211 N. Cherokee St., Hennessey, OK 73742 t) 405-853-2158 stjoseph@pldi.net Rev. Edward T. Menasco, Pst.; Dcn. Jeffrey Kelly; CRP Stds.: 134

St. Joseph - 101 First St., Bison, OK 73720; Mailing: 211 N. Cherokee St., Hennessey, OK 73742 t) (580) 758-3482 stjosephhennesseyok.com

KINGFISHER

SS. Peter and Paul - 309 S. Main, Kingfisher, OK 73750 t) 405-375-4581 secretary@stspeterandpaul.org www.stspeterandpaul.org Rev. Benjamin Lwin, Pst.; Dcn. Terrence R. Rice; Sandy Murray, DRE; CRP Stds.: 165

St. Rose of Lima - 900 N. Clarence Nash Blvd., Watonga, OK 73772; Mailing: 309 S. Main, Kingfisher, OK 73750 t) (405) 375-4581

KONAWA

Sacred Heart - 47943 Abbey Rd., Konawa, OK 74849 t) 580-925-2145 sacredheartok@gmail.com; sacredheartok@gmail.com Rev. Joseph Reddy Duggempudi, Admin.; CRP Stds.: 13

St. Mary - 3rd and Miller, Wanette, OK 74878; Mailing: 4793 Abbey Rd., Konawa, OK 74849 t) (580) 925-2145

LAWTON

Blessed Sacrament - 12 S.W. 7th St., Lawton, OK 73501; Mailing: P.O. Box 2546, Lawton, OK 73502 t) 580-355-2054 re@lawtoncatholic.com; office@lawtoncatholic.com www.lawtoncatholic.com Rev. John Paul Lewis, Pst.; Dcn. Howard Dale Harper; Dcn. Robert L. Quinnett Jr.;

St. Patrick Church - 202 E. Ohio St., Walters, OK 73572; Mailing: PO Box 2546, Lawton, OK 73502 t) (580) 355-2054

Holy Family - 1010 N.W. 82nd St., Lawton, OK 73505 t) 580-536-6355 (CRP); 580-536-6351 (Office) vgable@holyfamilylawton.org; mromaka@holyfamilylawton.org www.holyfamilylawton.org (Formerly St. Barbara) Rev. Philip M. Seeton, Pst.; Dcn. James Cerrone; Dcn. James Coe; Vicki Gable, DRE; Dcn. David B. Bunch; Dcn. Wuse Cara; Dcn. Anthony Layton; Dcn. Michael J. Romaka, Bus. Mgr.; CRP Stds.: 111

MADILL

Holy Cross Church - 14 W. Francis St., 1010 S. 5th, Madill, OK 73446-3234; Mailing: P.O. Box 791, Madill, OK 73446-0791 t) 580-795-3721; 903-312-5956 (CRP) hcccmadill@hotmail.com; robbieroberts0123@gmail.com Rev. Oby J. Zunmas, Pst.; Dcn. Gus Orellana; Roberta Roberts, DRE; Carol Steinbock, DRE; CRP Stds.: 190

Good Shepherd - 200 N.W. 8th, Marietta, OK 73448; Mailing: P.O. Box 127, Marietta, OK 73448 t) 580-276-9604 Rev. Raul Sanchez, Pst.;

MANGUM

Sacred Heart - 409 N. Byers, Mangum, OK 73554; Mailing: P.O. Box 310, Mangum, OK 73554 t) 580-450-8451 c) 580-471-9918 kgelnar@yahoo.com; choo.choo@sbcglobal.net Rev. Arokiasamy Andarias, Pst.; Kathy Gelnar, DRE; CRP Stds.: 80

Sts. Peter and Paul - 328 S. Randlett St., Hobart, OK 73651 t) 580-682-3011; 580-682-4006 arudkins8@gmail.com www.stspeter-paul.com Amy Rudkins, Contact;

Our Lady of Guadalupe - 524 E. Chestnut, Hollis, OK 73550 c) 580-381-0480 (DRE); 580-471-5248 (Secy) emin_flores@yahoo.com; olghollisokc@gmail.com Ester Flores, DRE;

MEDFORD

St. Mary's - 214 W. Cherokee, Medford, OK 73759-0360; Mailing: Box 360, Medford, OK 73759-0360 t) 580-395-2148 c) (580) 761-3866 (Contact); (580) 395-0184 (RE) Rev. Joseph Nettem, Pst.; CRP Stds.: 30

St. Mary's Assumption - 1938 Main St., Wakita, OK 73771; Mailing: PO Box 360, Medford, OK 73759 t) (580) 395-2148

St. Joseph's - S. Hwy. 81, Pond Creek, OK 73766 t) (580) 395-2148 joseph.netterm@archokc.org

MIDWEST CITY

St. Philip Neri - 1107 Felix Pl., Midwest City, OK 73110-5331 t) 405-737-4476 x102 (CRP); 405-737-4476 x100 dre@stphilipnerimwc.org; sec@spnmwc.org www.spnmwc.org Rev. Robert T. Wood, Pst.; Dcn. Norman Mejstrik; Dcn. Javier Solis; Dcn. James Tucker; Dcn. Richard Painter; CRP Stds.: 112

St. Philip Neri School - (Grades PreK-8) 1121 Felix Pl., Midwest City, OK 73110-5331 t) 405-737-4496 btener@spok.org www.stphilipnerischool.com/ Brenda Tener, Prin.; Stds.: 169; Lay Tchrs.: 15

MOORE

St. Andrew the Apostle Catholic Church - 800 N.W. Fifth St., Moore, OK 73160 t) 405-799-3334 ttran@standrewmoore.com; agrover@standrewmoore.com www.standrewmoore.com Rev. Francis T. Nguyen, Pst.; Dcn. George Fombe; Dcn. Thai Pham; Tomasita Tran, DRE; CRP Stds.: 181

MUSTANG

Holy Spirit Catholic Church - 1100 N. Sara Rd., Mustang, OK 73064; Mailing: P.O. Box 246, Mustang, OK 73064 t) 405-376-5633 (CRP); 405-376-9435 parish@holyspiritmustang.org www.holyspiritmustang.org Rev. Joseph A. Jacobi, Pst.; Dcn. William A. Hough; Dcn. Paul D. Lewis, Pst. Assoc.; CRP Stds.: 145

NORMAN

St. Joseph's - 421 E. Acres St., Norman, Norman, OK 73071; Mailing: PO Box 1227, Norman, OK 73070 t) 405-321-8080 brad.forshee@stjosephsok.org www.stjosephsok.org Dcn. Richard Montedoro; Dcn. Larry Sousa; Rev. Joseph M. Irwin, Pst.; Dcn. Steve Lewis; CRP Stds.: 99

St. Mark the Evangelist - 3939 W. Tecumseh Rd., Norman, OK 73072-1708 t) 405-366-7676 kristin@saintmarknorman.org www.saintmarknorman.org Rev. Timothy M. Fuller, Pst.; Dcn. Charles L. Allen; Dcn. Joe Vandervort; CRP Stds.: 210

St. Thomas More University Parish - 1535 Jenkins Ave., Norman, OK 73072; Mailing: 100 Stinson St., Norman, OK 73072 t) 405-321-0990 brigid@stm-ou.org stm-ou.org Rev. Brian E. Buettner, Pst.; Dcn. John D. Pigott; Brigid Brink, Bus. Mgr.; Alex Sanchez, Campus Min.; David R. Lawrie, Music Min.; Casey Partridge, Parish Life Coord.; Cathy Irwin, DRE; CRP Stds.: 150

OKARCHE

Holy Trinity - 211 W. Missouri, Okarche, OK 73762-0185; Mailing: P. O. Box 185, Okarche, OK 73762-0185 t) 405-263-7930 info@holytrinityok.org www.holytrinityok.org Rev. Cory D. Stanley, Pst.; Dcn. Charles Krumsiek; Dcn. Max Schwarz; CRP Stds.: 143

Holy Trinity School - (Grades PreK-8) 2nd and Missouri, Okarche, OK 73762; Mailing: P. O. Box 485, Okarche, OK 73762 t) 405-263-4422 anewman@holytrinityok.org holytrinityok.org/school Alice Newman, Prin.; Stds.: 105; Lay Tchrs.: 15

Immaculate Heart of Mary - 107 Freehome, Calumet, OK 73014 t) (405) 263-7930 frstanlely@holytrinityok.org

OKEENE

St. Anthony's - 211 S. 5th, Okeene, OK 73763; Mailing: P.O. Box 767, Okeene, OK 73763 t) 580-822-3544; 580-822-3511 (Rectory) stanthony@pldi.net Rev. Jaroslaw P. Topolewski, Pst.; Dcn. Michael Buchanan; Dcn. Paul Reinart; CRP Stds.: 40

St. Ann - 424 S. 6th, Fairview, OK 73737 t) (580) 822-3544

St. Thomas - 105 W. McAlester, Seiling, OK 73663 t) 580-922-4376

OKLAHOMA CITY

Cathedral of Our Lady of Perpetual Help - 3214 Lake Ave, 3214 N Lake Ave, Oklahoma City, OK 73118 t) 405-525-2349 mail@cathedralokc.org www.cathedralokc.org Dcn. De Forest W. Hearn; Rev. Richard D. Stansberry Jr., Rector; Rev. Thanh Van Nguyen, Assoc. Pst.; Dcn. Hans Nguyen; Dcn. Jacob Nguyen; CRP Stds.: 226

Bishop John Carroll Cathedral School - (Grades PreK-8) 1101 N.W. 31, Oklahoma City, OK 73118; Mailing: 1100 N.W. 32, Oklahoma City, OK 73118 t) 405-525-0956 principal@bjccs.org www.bjccs.org Helen Treacy, Prin.; Stds.: 229; Lay Tchrs.: 17

St. Andrew Dung-Lac - 3115 S. W. 59th St., Oklahoma City, OK 73119; Mailing: P.O. Box 891584, Oklahoma City, OK 73189 t) 405-681-2665 vietgreg@gmail.com; huenguyen2001@msn.com www.saintandrewdunglacokc.org Rev. Gregory Nguyen, Pst.; Dcn. Kha Nguyen; Dcn. Ty Van Nguyen; Dcn. Cuu Nguyen; CRP Stds.: 432

St. Charles Borromeo - 5024 N. Grove Ave., Oklahoma City, OK 73122 t) 405-789-2595 secretary@stcharlesokc.org www.stcharlesokc.org Rev. Timothy D. Luschen, Pst.; Rev. William Banowsky, Par. Vicar; Dcn. William King; Dcn. Thomas Phan; CRP Stds.: 700

St. Charles Borromeo School - (Grades PreK-8) 5650 NW 50th St, Oklahoma City, OK 73122 t) 405-789-0224 office@scbokc.org scbokc.org Todd Gungoll, Prin.; Stds.: 153; Lay Tchrs.: 15

Christ the King - 8005 Dorset Dr., Oklahoma City, OK 73120-4713; Mailing: P.O. Box 20508, Oklahoma City, OK 73156-0508 t) 405-842-1481 jenni@ckokc.org; jayne@ckokc.org www.ckokc.org Rev. Rex A. Arnold, Pst.; Rev. Prabhakar Kalivela, Par. Vicar; Dcn. Philip Bodman; Dcn. Richard L. Boothe III; Dcn. James E. Smith; Antonio Guzman, Youth Min.; Margaret Tunell, Children's Formation Coordinator; Jennifer Butch, Director of Discipleship & Evangelization; CRP Stds.: 236

Christ the King School - (Grades PreK-8) 1905 Elmhurst, Oklahoma City, OK 73120-4719 t) 405-843-3909 spiper@ckschool.com www.ckschool.com Amy Feighny, Prin.; Katelyn Bright, Vice Prin.; Dr. Jenny Richard, Vice Prin.; Stds.: 523; Lay Tchrs.: 39

Church of the Epiphany of the Lord - 7336 W. Britton Rd., Oklahoma City, OK 73132 t) 405-722-0051 (CRP); 405-722-2110 redirector@epiphanyokc.com; epiphany@epiphanyokc.com www.epiphanyokc.com Rev. Stephen J. Bird, Pst.; Rev. Zachary Boazman, Assoc. Pst.; Dcn. Frank Alexander; Dcn. Robert Heskamp; Dcn. Richard Fahy; Marianne Kokojan, Music Min.; Jenny Fenner, Pst. Assoc.; Mandy Brown, DRE; Sarah Holt, Youth Min.; CRP Stds.: 130

Corpus Christi - 1616 N. Kelley Ave., Oklahoma City, OK 73117; Mailing: 1005 N.E. 15th St., Oklahoma City, OK 73117 t) 405-236-4301 corpuschristichurchokc@gmail.com corpuschristichurchok.org Dcn. Dunn Cumby; Dcn. J. Bernie Hollier; Rev. Tang Titus Pau, Admin.; Benton Jones, Bus. Mgr.; CRP Stds.: 44

St. Robert Bellarmine - 121 N.W. 1st St., Jones, OK 73049; Mailing: P.O. Box 280, Jones, OK 73049 t) 405-399-1727 strobertjones.org/

St. Eugene's - 2400 W. Hefner Rd., Oklahoma City, OK 73120 t) 405-751-7115 manager@steugenes.org www.steugenes.org Rev. James A. Goins, Pst.; Rev. Jerome Krug, Par. Vicar; Dcn. Adolfo Aleman; Dcn. Robert Blakely; Dcn. Terrence Givens; Dcn. Thomas O. Goldsworthy; Dcn. Patrick Gaffney; Dcn. Mickey Reeves; CRP Stds.: 385

St. Eugene's School - (Grades PreK-8) t) 405-751-0067 principal@steugeneschool.org www.steugeneschool.org Molly Goldsworthy, Prin.; Stds.: 324; Lay Tchrs.: 40

St. Francis of Assisi - 1901 N.W. 18th St., Oklahoma City, OK 73106 t) 405-528-0485 teresa-schumacher@att.net; secretary@stfrancisokc.com www.stfrancisokc.com Very Rev. William L. Novak, Pst.; Rev. Linh N. Bui, Par. Vicar; Dcn. John Harned; Teresa Schumacher, DRE; Alvez Barkoskie IV, Music Min.; CRP Stds.: 110

Rosary Catholic School - -8) 1919 N.W. 18th St., Oklahoma City, OK 73106 t) 405-525-9272 principal@rosaryschool.com www.rosaryschool.com Christy Harris, Prin.; Stds.: 253; Lay Tchrs.: 16

Holy Angels - 317 N. Blackwelder St., Oklahoma City, OK 73106 t) 405-232-6572 parish_office@holyangelsokc.org www.holyangelsokc.org Rev. Russell L. Hewes, Pst.; Dcn. Sergio Vera-Silva; Jose M Marull, Bus. Mgr.; CRP Stds.: 300

St. James the Greater - 4201 S. McKinley, Oklahoma City, OK 73109 t) 405-636-6840 (CRP); 405-636-6800 office@stjamesokc.com; rcia@stjamesokc.com www.stjames-catholic.org Rev. Bill H. Pruett, Pst.; Rev. Scott A. Boeckman, Assoc. Pst.; Dcn. Marti Gulikers; Dcn. Fernando Hernandez; Dcn. Long Luong; Dcn. Arnoldo Moreno; Angelicia Nizza, DRE; CRP Stds.: 541

St. James the Greater School - (Grades PreSchool-8) 1224 S.W. 41st St., Oklahoma City, OK 73109 t) 405-636-6810 avazquez@stjames-catholic.org Alicia Vazquez, Prin.; Stds.: 177; Lay Tchrs.: 15

St. Joseph Old Cathedral - 307 NW 4th St., Oklahoma City, OK 73102; Mailing: P.O. Box 408, Oklahoma, OK 73101 t) 405-235-4565 office@sjocokc.org www.sjocokc.org Rev. Brian E. Buettner, Pst.; Rev. Miguel Eli Ayuso, Assoc. Pst.; Dcn. Paul Albert; Dcn. David Ashton; Dcn. Herbert Reeves Vance; CRP Stds.: 80

Korean Martyrs - 2600 S.W. 74th St., Oklahoma City, OK 73159 t) 405-681-6464 kmcc7517@gmail.com Rev. Rakkun Park, STM, Pst.;

Our Lady of Mount Carmel and St. Therese Little Flower - 1125 S. Walker Ave., Oklahoma City, OK 73109-1341 t) 405-235-2037 lfcokc@gmail.com littleflowerparishokc.org/ Little Flower Clinic: Free medical service for the poor. Rev. Luis Gerardo Belmonte-Luna, O.C.D., Pst.; Rev. Jesus Sancho, O.C.D., Par. Vicar; Sr. Maria Carolina Ceja, M.E.S.T., DRE;

Eucharistic Missionaries of St. Theresa - 526 S.W. 10th St., Oklahoma City, OK 73109

St. Patrick Church - 2121 N. Portland, Oklahoma City, OK 73107 t) 405-946-4441 info@stpatrickokc.com www.stpatrickokc.com Rev. Joseph H. Arledge, Pst.; Dcn. Duane Fischer; CRP Stds.: 562

Sacred Heart - 2706 S. Shartel Ave., Oklahoma City, OK 73109 t) 405-634-2458 re-yamil@sacredheartokc.org sacredheartokc.org Rev. Donald J. Wolf, Pst.; Rev. Russell L. Hewes, Par. Vicar; Rev. Brannon Lepak, Par. Vicar; Dcn. Fernando Hernandez; Dcn. Alejandro Randolph; Liliana Duron, DRE; CRP Stds.: 820

Sacred Heart School - 2700 S. Shartel Ave., Oklahoma City, OK 73109 t) 405-634-5673 principal@sacredheartokc.org www.sacredheartokc.org Tera Albert, Prin.; Stds.: 136; Lay Tchrs.: 12

PAULS VALLEY

St. Catherine of Siena - 205 W. Bert St., Pauls Valley, OK 73075 t) 405-238-3741 st.catofsiena@att.net www.stcatherineofsienacatholicpv.com/ Rev. Nerio A. Espinoza, Pst.; Dcn. Juan Frausto; Dcn. Adrian Meave; CRP Stds.: 68

PERRY

St. Rose of Lima - 421 9th St., Perry, OK 73077; Mailing: PO Box 603, Perry, OK 73077 t) 580-336-9300 c) 580-786-8283 stroseperry@sbcglobal.net www.stroseperry.com Rev. Bala Raju Pudota, Pst.; CRP Stds.: 28

Sacred Heart - Broadway & Lowe, Billings, OK 74630 t) (580) 336-9300 stroseperry.com

PONCA CITY

St. Mary's Catholic Church - 707 E. Ponca Ave., Ponca City, OK 74601; Mailing: 408 S. 8th St., Ponca City, OK 74601-5551 t) 580-382-6010 (CRP); 580-765-7794 drestmarys@gmail.com; office@stmarypc.com www.stmarypc.com Rev. Carson Krittenbrink, Pst.; Dcn. Richard Robinson; Bridgit Coleman, DRE; CRP Stds.: 71

St. Mary - (Grades PreK-8) 415 S. 7th, Ponca City, OK 74601 t) 580-765-4387 info@smsponcacity.org www.stmaryspsok.com Wade Laffey, Prin.; Stds.: 105; Pr. Tchrs.: 1; Lay Tchrs.: 11

St. Francis of Assisi - 610 W 9 St, Newkirk, OK 74647; Mailing: P.O. Box 11, Newkirk, OK 74647 t) (580) 362-3320 sfcnewkirk@sbcglobal.net Dcn. William Horinek;

PRAGUE

St. Wenceslaus, National Shrine of the Infant Jesus of Prague - 304 Jim Thorpe Blvd., Prague, OK 74864; Mailing: Box 488, Prague, OK 74864 t) 405-567-3080 infantofpragueshrine@gmail.com www.shrineofinfantjesus.com Rev. Long N. Phan, Pst.; Cecilia Hecker, DRE;

St. Michael - 217 S. Koonce, Meeker, OK 74855; Mailing: P.O. Box 488, Prague, OK 74864 t) (580) 395-8214

PURCELL

Our Lady of Victory - 307 W. Jefferson St., Purcell, OK 73080; Mailing: P O Box 1280, Purcell, OK 73080 t) 405-527-3077 infoolvpurcell@gmail.com olvpurcell.org Rev. John Peter Swaminathan, Pst.; Dcn. Jose Ortiz; Dcn. John Warren; CRP Stds.: 109

SHAWNEE

St. Benedict - 632 N. Kickapoo, Shawnee, OK 74801

t) 405-275-5399 (CRP); 405-275-0001 www.stbenedictchurch.net Rev. Joseph Patrick Schwarz, Pst.; Rev. Lawrence Damian, Assoc. Pst.; Dcn. David Schrupp; Dcn. William T. Thurman; CRP Stds.: 90

St. Joseph Chapel - 702 S. Seminole, Wewoka, OK 74884; Mailing: 632 N. Kickapoo, Shawnee, OK 74801 t) (405) 382-3602

Immaculate Conception - 811 W. Wrangler Blvd., Seminole, OK 74818-0164; Mailing: P.O. Box 164, Seminole, OK 74818-0164 t) 405-382-3602 stbenedictchurch.net

TONKAWA

St. Joseph's - 320 W. North St., Tonkawa, OK 74653; Mailing: P.O. Box 525, Tonkawa, OK 74653 t) 580-628-2416 c) 580-761-6937 stjosephtonkawa@att.net www.stjosephtonkawa.org Rev. Balaswamy Bathini, Pst.; CRP Stds.: 37

UNION CITY

St. Joseph's - 403 N. Kate Boevers St., Union City, OK 73090; Mailing: P.O. Box 100, Union City, OK 73090 t) 405-483-5329; 405-274-2042 (CRP) pastor@stjosephuc.com www.stjosephuc.com Rev. Lance A. Warren, Pst.; Dcn. Lloyd Menz; Deana Kappus, Contact; CRP Stds.: 23

WEATHERFORD

St. Eugene's - 704 N. Bryan, Weatherford, OK 73096 t) 580-772-3209 ste_secretary@att.net Rev. Kelly L. Edwards, Pst.; CRP Stds.: 15

Blessed Sacrament - 520 N. Oklahoma, Thomas, OK 73669; Mailing: 704 N. Bryan St., Weatherford, OK 73096 t) (580) 772-3209

Sacred Heart - 204 N. Clark Ave., Hinton, OK 73047; Mailing: 704 N Bryan St., Weatherford, OK 73096 t) (580) 772-3209

WOODWARD

St. Peter's - 2020 Oklahoma Ave., Woodward, OK 73801 t) 580-256-2966 (CRP); 580-256-5305 stpsongbird@sbcglobal.net; stpeterdre@sbcglobal.net stpeternwok.org Rev. Cristobal De Loera, Pst.; Rev. Christuraj Maddhichetty, Assoc. Pst.; Dcn. Santiago Ontiveros; CRP Stds.: 188

Sacred Heart - 301 N. Main, Mooreland, OK 73852; Mailing: 2020 Oklahoma Ave., Woodward, OK 73801 t) (580) 256-5305

Holy Name - 600 S. Main, Shattuck, OK 73858; Mailing: 2020 Oklahoma Ave., Woodward, OK 73801 t) (580) 256-5305

St. Joseph - 325 S.W. 2nd, Buffalo, OK 73834; Mailing: 2020 Oklahoma Ave., Woodward, OK 73801 t) (580) 256-5305

St. Jose Luis Sanchez del Rio - 123 S. Ohio, Laverne, OK 73848; Mailing: 2020 Oklahoma Ave., Woodward, OK 73801

YUKON

St. John Nepomuk - 600 Garth Brooks Blvd, Yukon, OK 73099; Mailing: PO Box 850249, Yukon, OK 73085-0249 t) 405-354-2743 dre@sjnok.org; achernak@sjnok.org www.sjnok.org Rev. John R. Metzinger, Pst.; Dcn. Clifford W. Fitzmorris; Dcn. Larry Germann; Dcn. John Teague; Robert Noble, Liturgy Dir.; Art Chernak, Parish Life Coord.; Jo Anna Bannister, Youth Min.; Mariavis Fitzmorris, DRE; CRP Stds.: 365

St. John Nepomuk School - (Grades PreK-8) 600 S. Garh Brooks Blvd., Yukon, OK 73099-3504 t) 405-354-2509 principal@sjnok.org www.sjnok.org/school Janet Edgar, Prin.; Stds.: 206; Lay Tchrs.: 22

SCHOOLS: PRESCHOOL THRU HIGH SCHOOL

SCHOOLS

STATE OF OKLAHOMA

NORMAN

All Saints Catholic School, Inc. - (PAR) (Grades PreK-8) 4001 36th Ave., N.W., Norman, OK 73072 t) 405-447-4600 info@allsaintsnorman.org www.allsaintsnorman.org Lou Ann Wood, Prin.; Teryle Dionisio, Librn.; Stds.: 373; Lay Tchrs.: 29

OKLAHOMA CITY

Good Shepherd Catholic School - (DIO) -3) 13404 N. Meridian, Oklahoma City, OK 73120 t) 405-752-2264 gscs@goodshepherdcs.org goodshepherdcs.org Special needs. Patricia Filer, Dir.; Stds.: 31; Lay Tchrs.: 5

HIGH SCHOOLS

STATE OF OKLAHOMA

OKLAHOMA CITY

Bishop McGuinness Catholic High School - (DIO) (Grades 9-12) 801 N.W. 50th St., Oklahoma City, OK 73118 t) 405-842-6638 advancement@bmchs.org bmchs.org (Coed) Rev. William Banowsky, Chap.; Kelly Allen, Campus Min.; Robert Epps Jr., Admin.; Anne Hathcoat, Admin.; Andrew Worthington, Admin.; David Morton, Pres.; Stds.: 723; Lay Tchrs.: 94

Cristo Rey Oklahoma City Catholic High School - (PRV) (Grades 9-12) 900 N. Portland Ave, Oklahoma City, OK 73107 t) 405-945-9100 info@cristoreyokc.org; admissions@cristoreyokc.org www.cristoreyokc.org Rev. Linh N. Bui, Chap.; Kelsey Herman, Prin.; Chip Carter, President/CEO; Stds.: 237; Lay Tchrs.: 17

Mount St. Mary High School (Sisters of Mercy of the Americas, Archdiocese of Oklahoma City) - (DIO) (Grades 9-12) 2801 S. Shartel Ave., Oklahoma City, OK 73109 t) 405-631-8865 bbasler@mountstmary.org mountstmary.org (Coed) Stds.: 367; Lay Tchrs.: 32

INSTITUTIONS LOCATED IN DIOCESE

ASSOCIATIONS [ASN]

CASTLE ROCK

The Catholic Benefits Association - 695 Jerry St., Ste. 306, Castle Rock, CO 80104 t) 303-688-3822 dougwilson@catholicbenefitsassociation.org; mandycox@catholicbenefitsassociation.org www.catholicbenefitsassociation.com Douglas G. Wilson Jr., CEO; Mandy Rose Cox, Dir.;

MOORE

***Gospel of Life Association (Gospel of Life Disciples + Dwellings)** - 4113 S. Eastern Ave., Moore, OK 73160 t) 405-378-2436 srmaria@gospeloflifedisciples.org www.gospeloflifedisciples.org Elijah Weaver, Exec.; Sr. Maria of the Trinity Faulkner, Contact;

CAMPUS MINISTRY / NEWMAN CENTERS [CAM]

OKLAHOMA CITY

Campus Ministry for the Archdiocese of Oklahoma City - 7501 Nw Expy, 7501 Nw Expy, Oklahoma City, OK 73132 t) 405-709-2783 jpalmer@archokc.org Jayce Palmer, Pst. Min./Coord.;

Cameron University - 1010 N.W. 82nd, Lawton, OK 73506 t) 580-536-6351 pseeton@holyfamilylawton.org holyfamilylawtonoffice.org Rev. Philip M. Seeton;

East Central State University - 1300 E. Beverly St., Ada, OK 74820; Mailing: P.O. Box 1585, Ada, OK 74820 t) 580-332-4811 pom.stjosephada@gmail.com stjosephada.com/ Rev. Aaron J. Foshee, Pst.;

Northern Oklahoma College - 320 W. North St., Tonkawa, OK 74653; Mailing: P.O. Box 525, Tonkawa, OK 74653 t) 580-765-7794 c) 419-203-7964 father.krittenbrink@yahoo.com Rev. Carson Krittenbrink, Pst.;

Northwestern Oklahoma State College - 627 12th St., Alva, OK 73717 t) 580-327-0339 office@sacredheartalva.org sacredheartalva.org/ Rev. Balraj Sagili Jesudas, Pst.;

Oklahoma Panhandle State University - 505 W. 2nd St., Goodwell, OK 73942; Mailing: P.O. Box 277, Goodwell, OK 73942 t) 580-338-7212 sec@panhandlecatholic.org www.panhandlecatholic.org/home Very Rev. Christopher T. Brashears, Pst.;

Southwestern Oklahoma State University - 704 N. Bryan St., Weatherford, OK 73096; Mailing: P.O. Box 407, Weatherford, OK 73096 t) 580-772-3209 ste_secretary@att.net steugenewf.com/ Rev. Kelly L. Edwards, Pst.; Miranda McGoffin, Campus Min.;

University of Central Oklahoma - 321 E. Clegern, Edmond, OK 73034 c) 845-536-1418 catholicstudentctr@stjohn-catholic.org Rev. Raymond K. Ackerman; Rev. Alexander Kroll, Chap.; Rachael Smith, Campus Min.;

University of Science & Arts of Oklahoma - 210 S. 7th St., Chickasha, OK 73018 t) 405-224-6068 secretary@holynamechickasha.org holynamechickasha.org/ Rev. Michael Wheelahan, Pst.; Rosa Munoz, Dir.;

CATHOLIC CHARITIES [CCH]

OKLAHOMA CITY

Catholic Charities of the Archdiocese of Oklahoma City, Inc. - 1232 N. Classen Blvd., Oklahoma City, OK 73106 t) (405) 582-3300 catholiccharitiesok.org Patrick J. Raglow, Exec. Dir.; Asstd. Annu.: 9,057; Staff: 89

CEMETERIES [CEM]

OKLAHOMA CITY

Resurrection Memorial Cemetery, Inc. - 7500 W. Britton Rd., Oklahoma City, OK 73132 t) 405-721-4191 resmemcem@gmail.com www.resurrectionmemorialcemetery.com Branden Seid, Dir.;

CONVENTS, MONASTERIES, AND RESIDENCES FOR WOMEN [CON]

OKLAHOMA CITY

Carmelite Sisters of St. Therese of the Infant Jesus Motherhouse - 7501 W. Britton Rd., #140, Oklahoma City, OK 73132 t) 405-837-7068 srbarbarajoseph@gmail.com www.oksister.com Sr. Barbara Joseph Foley, C.S.T., Supr.; Srs.: 9

Medical Sisters of St. Joseph - c/o 7217 N.W. 121st. St., Oklahoma City, OK 73162 t) 405-721-4390 oklittleflower@yahoo.com Sr. Rosemilla Michael, Supr.; Srs.: 4

Sisters of Mercy of the Americas - Mercy Health Center Convent, 4300 W. Memorial Rd., Oklahoma City, OK 73120-8304 t) 405-755-1515 plindgren@sistersofmercy.org www.mercy.net Retirement Center for Sisters of Mercy of Oklahoma. Srs.: 5

PIEDMONT

Carmel of St. Joseph (Discalced Carmelite Nuns (Cloistered)) - 2370 Morgan Rd. N.E., Piedmont, OK 73078-9123 t) 405-373-1735; 405-373-1726 dcn@okcarmel.org www.okcarmel.org Sr. Donna Ross, O.C.D., Prioress; Srs.: 6

ENDOWMENTS / FOUNDATIONS / TRUSTS [EFT]

ADA

Mercy Health Foundation Ada - 430 N. Monte Vista St., Ada, OK 74820 t) 314-628-3608 marynell.ploch@mercy.net Jacquelynn K. Richmond, Deputy General Counsel;

ARDMORE

Mercy Health Foundation, Ardmore - 1011 Fourteenth Ave., N.W., Ardmore, OK 73401 t) 580-220-6712; 314-628-3608 marynell.ploch@mercy.net Jacquelynn K. Richmond, Deputy General Counsel;

OKLAHOMA CITY

St. Anthony Hospital Foundation, Inc., Oklahoma City,

Oklahoma - 601 N.W. 11th St., Oklahoma City, OK 73103 t) 405-272-7070 saintsfoundation@ssmhc.com www.givetosaints.com Member of SSM Health Sherry Rhodes, Vice. Pres.;

Catholic Foundation of Oklahoma, Inc. - 7501 Northwest Expressway, Oklahoma City, OK 73132 t) (405) 721-4115 cfo@cfook.org cfook.org/ Peter de Keratry, Exec. Dir.; Owen Canfield, Assoc. Dir.; Stefanie Hale, Grant Program Coord.; Cyndi Mireles, Constituent Svcs. Coord.;

Catholic Schools Opportunity Scholarship Fund, Inc. - Tax Credit Scholarship Program, 7501 Northwest Expy, Oklahoma City, OK 73132; Mailing: PO Box 32180, Oklahoma City, OK 73123 t) 405-709-2745 info@tcsok.org www.tcsok.org Peter Luis de Keratry, Exec.;

Mercy Health Foundation of Oklahoma - 13321 N. Meridian Rd., Ste. 206, Oklahoma City, OK 73120 t) 405-486-8773; 314-628-3608 marynell.ploch@mercy.net Jacquelynn K. Richmond, Deputy General Counsel;

Mercy Health Foundation Oklahoma City - 13321 N. Meridian Rd., Ste. 206, Oklahoma City, OK 73120 t) 405-486-8773; 314-628-3608 marynell.ploch@mercy.net Jacquelynn K. Richmond, Deputy General Counsel;

HOSPITALS / HEALTH SERVICES [HOS]

ADA

Mercy Hospital Ada, Inc. - 430 N. Monte Vista St., Ada, OK 74820 t) 580-332-2323 marynell.ploch@mercy.net Jacquelynn K. Richmond, Deputy General Counsel;

ARDMORE

Mercy Hospital Ardmore, Inc. - 1011 14th Ave., N.W., Ardmore, OK 73401 t) 580-220-6611 marynell.ploch@mercy.net www.mercy.net Jacquelynn K. Richmond, Deputy General Counsel; Bed Capacity: 190; Asstd. Annu.: 118,887; Staff: 810

GUTHRIE

Mercy Hospital Logan County, Inc. - 200 S. Academy, Guthrie, OK 73044 t) 405-282-6700 marynell.ploch@mercy.net www.mercy.net Jacquelynn K. Richmond, Deputy General Counsel; Bed Capacity: 25; Asstd. Annu.: 2,451; Staff: 131

HEALDTON

Mercy Hospital Healdton, Inc. - 3462 Hospital Rd., Healdton, OK 73438 t) 580-229-0701 marynell.ploch@mercy.net Jacquelynn K. Richmond, Contact; Bed Capacity: 22; Asstd. Annu.: 934; Staff: 49

KINGFISHER

Mercy Hospital Kingfisher, Inc. - 1000 Kingfisher Hospital Dr., Kingfisher, OK 73750 t) 405-375-3141 marynell.ploch@mercy.net www.mercy.net Jacquelynn K. Richmond, Deputy General Counsel;

OKLAHOMA CITY

St. Anthony Hospital - 1000 N. Lee St., Oklahoma City, OK 73101; Mailing: P.O. Box 205, Oklahoma City, OK 73101 t) 405-272-7000 www.saintsok.com A member of SSM Health Care. Tammy Powell, Pres.; Bed Capacity: 688; Asstd. Annu.: 336,802; Staff: 3,592

Bone and Joint Hospital at St. Anthony - 1111 N. Dewey, Oklahoma City, OK 73101; Mailing: P.O. Box 205, Oklahoma City, OK 73101 t) 405-979-8000 A member of SSM Health Care. Bed Capacity: 85; Asstd. Annu.: 7,881; Staff: 231

Saint Anthony South Hospital - 2129 SW 59th St., Oklahoma City, OK 73119; Mailing: P.O. Box 205, Oklahoma City, OK 73101 t) 405-713-5751 A member of SSM Health Care. Tammy Powell, Pres.; Bed Capacity: 85; Asstd. Annu.: 116,985; Staff: 231

Mercy Hospital Oklahoma City, Inc. - 4300 W. Memorial Rd., Oklahoma City, OK 73120 t) 405-755-1515 marynell.ploch@mercy.net www.mercy.net Owned and operated by Mercy Health Oklahoma Communities, Inc. Jacquelynn K. Richmond, Deputy General Counsel; Bed Capacity: 369; Asstd. Annu.: 373,145; Staff: 2,165

SSM Health Care of Oklahoma, Inc. - 1000 N. Lee St., Oklahoma City, OK 73102; Mailing: P.O. Box 205, Oklahoma City, OK 73101 t) 405-272-7000 Joe Hodges, Pres.;

SHAWNEE

St. Anthony Shawnee Hospital - 1102 W. MacArthur St., Shawnee, OK 74804-1743 t) 405-878-8110 Angi Mohr, Pres.; Bed Capacity: 96; Asstd. Annu.: 116,985; Staff: 498

TISHOMINGO

Mercy Hospital Tishomingo, Inc. - 1000 S. Byrd St., Tishomingo, OK 73460 t) 580-371-2327 marynell.ploch@mercy.net Jacquelynn K. Richmond, Deputy General Counsel; Bed Capacity: 25; Asstd. Annu.: 787; Staff: 60

WATONGA

Mercy Hospital Watonga, Inc. - 500 N. Clarence Nash Blvd., Watonga, OK 73772 t) 580-623-7211 marynell.ploch@mercy.net www.mercy.net Jacquelynn K. Richmond, Deputy General Counsel; Bed Capacity: 25; Asstd. Annu.: 814; Staff: 50

MISCELLANEOUS [MIS]

OKLAHOMA CITY

Catholic Conference of Oklahoma - 208 NW 13th St., Ste. # 12, Oklahoma City, OK 73103 t) 888-514-1135 brett@okcatholic.org www.okcatholic.org Brett Farley, Exec.;

Catholic Pastoral Center - 7501 Northwest Expwy., Oklahoma City, OK 73132; Mailing: PO Box 32180, Oklahoma City, OK 73123 t) 405-721-5651 sconrady@archokc.org www.archokc.org Shari Conrady, Dir.;

Sister BJ's Pantry, Inc. - 819 NW 4th St., Oklahoma City, OK 73106; Mailing: 7501 W. Britton Rd., #140, Oklahoma City, OK 73132 t) 405-837-7068 srbarbarajoseph@gmail.com srbjpantry.org An apostolate of the Oklahoma Carmelite Sisters of St. Therese of the Infant Jesus, Oklahoma City, OK. Sr. Barbara Joseph Foley, C.S.T., Pres.;

MONASTERIES AND RESIDENCES FOR PRIESTS AND BROTHERS [MON]

OKLAHOMA CITY

Monastery of Our Lady of Mount Carmel and Little Flower - 1125 S. Walker Ave., Oklahoma City, OK 73109 t) 405-235-2037 executivedirector@carmelitefriarsocd.com; lfcokc@gmail.com www.carmelitefriarsocd.org/ Rev. Luis Gerardo Belmonte-Luna, O.C.D., Supr.; Rev. Jesus Sancho, O.C.D., Mem.; Priests: 2

SHAWNEE

St. Gregory's Abbey (Benedictine Fathers of Sacred Heart Mission, Inc.) - 1900 W. MacArthur Dr., Shawnee, OK 74804 t) 405-878-5491 abbot@monksok.org; retreats@monksok.org www.monksok.org Order of St. Benedict, including Novitiate, Conference Center and the Mabee-Gerrer Museum of Art. Rt. Rev. Lawrence R. Stasyszen, O.S.B., Abbot; Rev. Boniface T. Copelin, O.S.B., Prior; Rev. Simeon Z. Spitz, O.S.B., Sub-Prior, Vocation Director; Rev. Adrian R. Vorderlandwehr, O.S.B., Treas.; Rt. Rev. Martin Lugo, O.S.B., In Res.; Rev. Paul J. Zahler, O.S.B., In Res.; Rev. Brendan J. Helbing, O.S.B., Hospital Chaplain; Rev. Charles J. Buckley, O.S.B., In Res.; Rev. Manuel Magallanes, O.S.B., In Res.; Bro. Damian S. Whalen, O.S.B., In Res.; Bro. Dominic J. Ramirez, O.S.B., In Res.; Bro. Isidore D. Harden, O.S.B., In Res.; Bro. Benet S. Exton, O.S.B., In Res.; Rev. Nicholas K. Ast, O.S.B., In Res.; Bro. George A. Hubl, O.S.B., In Res.; Bro. Peter M. Shults, O.S.B., Theological Studies; Bro. John Michael F. Nguyen, O.S.B., In Res.; Brs.: 7; Priests: 11

Saint Gregory's Abbey Benefit Trust - 1900 W MacArthur St., Shawnee, OK 74804 t) (405) 878-5491 monksok.org

NURSING / REHABILITATION / CONVALESCENCE / ELDERLY CARE [NUR]

EL RENO

Saint Katharine Drexel Retirement Center, Inc. - 301 W. Wade, El Reno, OK 73036 t) 405-262-2920 director@skdelreno.org skdelreno.org Kim Bowles, Exec.; Asstd. Annu.: 83; Staff: 62

OKLAHOMA CITY

Saint Ann Retirement Center, Inc. - 7501 W. Britton Rd., Oklahoma City, OK 73132 t) 405-721-0747 joyce@saintannretirementcenter.com www.saintannretirementcenter.com Assisted and Independent Living Joyce Clark, Dir.; Asstd. Annu.: 300; Staff: 47

Columbia Square, Inc. (Villanova Apartments) - 1232 N. Classen Blvd., Oklahoma City, OK 73106 t) 405-523-3000 praglow@ccaokc.org; jmoon@ccaokc.org ccaokc.org Asstd. Annu.: 91; Staff: 2

Villanova Apartments - 305 NW 4th St, Lawton, OK 73507 t) 580-248-2550

Trinity Gardens Apartments - 3825 NW 19th St, Oklahoma City, OK 73107; Mailing: 1232 N. Classen Blvd., Oklahoma City, OK 73106 t) 405-523-3000 praglow@ccaokc.org; jmoon@ccaokc.org 58 independent-living apartments for low-income senior citizens. Asstd. Annu.: 65; Staff: 3

Villa Isenbart, Inc. - 3801 N.W. 19th St., Oklahoma City, OK 73107; Mailing: 1232 N. Classen Blvd., Oklahoma City, OK 73106 t) 405-523-3000 praglow@ccaokc.org; jmoon@ccaokc.org ccaokc.org 40 Independent-Living Apartments for Low-Income Elderly. Asstd. Annu.: 46; Staff: 3

PONCA CITY

St. Mary's Housing Foundation - 408 S. 8th St., Ponca City, OK 74602 t) 580-765-7794 office@stmarypc.com Rev. Carson Krittenbrink, Pres.; Asstd. Annu.: 6

Via Christi Village Ponca City, Inc. (Ascension Living Via Christi Village Ponca City) - 1601 Academy Rd., Ponca City, OK 74604 t) 314-292-9308 ahscm-mission@ascension.org www.ascensionliving.org/ Ryan Endsley, COO; Asstd. Annu.: 232; Staff: 89

SHRINES [SHR]

OKLAHOMA CITY

Blessed Stanley Rother Shrine, Inc. - 700 SE 89th St., Oklahoma City, OK 73149; Mailing: P.O. Box 32180, Oklahoma City, OK 73123 t) 405-438-0302 larvidson@archokc.org www.rothershrine.org Leif Arvidson, Exec.;

PRAGUE

National Shrine of the Infant Jesus of Prague - 304 Jim Thorpe Blvd., Prague, OK 74864; Mailing: P.O. Box 488, Prague, OK 74864 t) 405-567-3080 infantofpragueshrine@gmail.com www.shrineofinfantjesus.com Rev. Long N. Phan, Admin.;

SPECIAL CARE FACILITIES [SPF]

OKARCHE

***Center of Family Love** - 635 W. Texas, P.O. 245, Okarche, OK 73762 t) 405-263-4658 info@cflinc.org centeroffamilylove.org Debbie Espinosa, Dir.;

An asterisk (*) denotes an organization that has established tax-exempt status directly with the IRS and is not covered by the USCCB Group Ruling.

Archdiocese of Omaha

(Archidioecesis Omahensis)

MOST REVEREND GEORGE J. LUCAS

Archbishop of Omaha; ordained on May 24, 1975; appointed Bishop of the Diocese of Springfield in Illinois on October 19, 1999; ordained a Bishop and installed December 14, 1999; appointed Archbishop of Omaha June 3, 2009; installed July 22, 2009. Chancery Office: 2222 N. 111th St., Omaha, NE 68164-3817.

Chancery Office: 2222 N. 111th St., Omaha, NE 68164-3817. T: 402-558-3100; F: 402-558-3026.
www.archomaha.org
contact@archomaha.org

ESTABLISHED AS A VICARIATE-APOSTOLIC JANUARY 6, 1857.

Square Miles 14,051.

Erected a Diocese October 2, 1885; Archdiocese October 10, 1945.

Comprises the Counties of Boyd, Holt, Merrick, Nance, Boone, Antelope, Knox, Pierce, Madison, Platte, Colfax, Stanton, Wayne, Cedar, Dixon, Dakota, Thurston, Cuming, Dodge, Burt, Washington, Douglas and Sarpy in the State of Nebraska.

For legal titles of parishes and archdiocesan institutions, consult the Chancery Office.

STATISTICAL OVERVIEW

Personnel
Archbishops....1
Retired Archbishops....1
Abbots....1
Retired Abbots....1
Priests: Diocesan Active in Diocese....105
Priests: Diocesan Active Outside Diocese....6
Priests: Retired, Sick or Absent....54
Number of Diocesan Priests....165
Religious Priests in Diocese....55
Total Priests in your Diocese....220
Extern Priests in Diocese....13
Ordinations:
Diocesan Priests....2
Permanent Deacons in Diocese....215
Total Brothers....13
Total Sisters....167

Parishes
Parishes....122
With Resident Pastor:
Resident Diocesan Priests....76
Resident Religious Priests....2
Without Resident Pastor:
Administered by Priests....44
Missions....14
Closed Parishes....1
Professional Ministry Personnel:
Brothers....2
Sisters....6
Lay Ministers....85

Welfare
Catholic Hospitals....6
Total Assisted....323,153
Homes for the Aged....5
Total Assisted....10,487
Day Care Centers....15
Total Assisted....1,004
Specialized Homes....3
Total Assisted....1,435
Special Centers for Social Services....5
Total Assisted....315,965

Educational
Diocesan Students in Other Seminaries....22
Total Seminarians....22
Colleges and Universities....2
Total Students....9,253
High Schools, Diocesan and Parish....12
Total Students....2,676
High Schools, Private....5
Total Students....2,444
Elementary Schools, Diocesan and Parish....42
Total Students....13,261
Elementary Schools, Private....7
Total Students....3,506
Non-residential Schools for the Disabled....3
Total Students....23
Catechesis/Religious Education:
High School Students....2,095
Elementary Students....11,441
Total Students under Catholic Instruction....44,721
Teachers in Diocese:
Priests....5
Scholastics....2
Brothers....1
Sisters....7
Lay Teachers....1,509

Vital Statistics
Receptions into the Church:
Infant Baptism Totals....2,971
Minor Baptism Totals....271
Adult Baptism Totals....129
Received into Full Communion....383
First Communions....3,210
Confirmations....3,019
Marriages:
Catholic....585
Interfaith....224
Total Marriages....809
Deaths....1,854
Total Catholic Population....238,731
Total Population....1,047,607

LEADERSHIP

Vicar General - Rev. Michael W. Grewe;

Chancery Office - t) 402-558-3100 contact@archomaha.org

Chancellor - Dcn. Timothy F. McNeil;

Vice Chancellor - Elizabeth A. Sondag;

Finance Director (canonical) - James J. Stolze, CFO;

Metropolitan Tribunal -

Judicial Vicar and Vicar for Clergy - Rev. Scott A. Hastings;

Judges - Rev. James R. de Anda; Dcn. Ronald R. Ryan; Elizabeth A. Sondag;

Promoter of Justice - Dcn. Timothy F. McNeil;

Defenders of the Bond - Rev. Raymond Bueno, O.C.D.;

Appeal Court - Dcn. Ronald R. Ryan; Rev. James R. de Anda; Rev. Scott A. Hastings;

College of Consultors - Rev. Michael W. Grewe; Rev. Scott A. Hastings; Rev. Daniel R. Andrews;

Deans - Rev. David D. Belt, Dean (d.belt@stephen.org); Rev. Owen W. Korte, Dean (owkorte@archomaha.org); Rev. Walter L. Nolte, Dean;

Finance Council - Most Rev. George J. Lucas; Rev. Michael W. Grewe; James J. Stolze;

OFFICES AND DIRECTORS

Administrative Services Office - James J. Stolze, Dir.;

Catholic Schools Office - Vicki Kauffold, Supt.;

Cemeteries - Rev. Michael W. Grewe, Dir.;

Censors Librorum - Rev. Matthew J. Gutowski;

Communications - Dcn. Timothy F. McNeil;

Council of Catholic Women, Archdiocesan - Rev. Andrew L. Sohm, Spiritual Advisor;

Diaconate Formation Program - Dcn. Timothy F. McNeil;

Ecumenical Officer - Rev. Ryan P. Lewis;

Evangelization and Family Life Office - Jodi Philips, Assoc. Dir.;

Human Resources - Christine M. Sommers, Dir.;

Information Technology Office - Shawn M. Baas, CIO;

Omaha. Archdiocesan Deposit and Loan Fund, Inc. - James J. Stolze, Dir.;

Omaha Priests Retirement Plan and Trust, The - Most Rev. George J. Lucas; Rev. Harold J. Buse; Rev. Dennis A. Hanneman;

Pastoral Services - James M. Jansen, Dir.;

Priests' Council -

Deans - Rev. Owen W. Korte; Rev. Walter L. Nolte; Rev. Damian Zuerlein;

Ex Officio - Rev. Gerald A. Connealy; Rev. Michael W. Grewe, Vicar; Rev. Scott A. Hastings, Vicar for Clergy;

Officers - Rev. Jeffery S. Loseke, Pres.; Rev. Walter L. Nolte, Vice. Pres.; Rev. Ralph B. O'Donnell, Treas.;

Religious Order Representative - Rev. Thomas Aquinas Leitner, O.S.B.;

Special Group Representatives - Rev. Vincent Sunguti; Rev. Tobias Letak; Rev. David F. Liewer;

Propagation of the Faith - Dcn. Omar Gutierrez, Mgr.;

St. Cecilia Institute for Sacred Liturgy, Music and the Arts - Marie Rubis Bauer, Dir.;

Servant Minister - Rev. Gerald A. Connealy (jconnealy@stanton.net);

Stewardship & Development Office - Shannan Brommer, Dir.;

Victim Outreach and Prevention - Mary Beth Hanus, Dir. (mbhanus@archomaha.org);

Vocations Office - Rev. Scott A. Schilmoeller, Dir. (saschilmoeller@archomaha.org);

Worship Office - Marie Rubis Bauer, Dir.; Michael Emmerich, Dir.;

PARISHES, MISSIONS, AND CLERGY

STATE OF NEBRASKA

ALBION

St. Michael - 524 W. Church St., Albion, NE 68620 t) 402-395-2332 Rev. Mark A. Tomasiewicz, Pst.; Lisa Wagner, DRE; CRP Stds.: 146

St. Michael School - (Grades PreK-8) 520 W. Church St., Albion, NE 68620 t) 402-395-2926 tblecher@stmichael.esu7.org www.stmichael.esu7.org Tina Thiele-Blecher, Prin.; Stds.: 127; Lay Tchrs.: 8

ATKINSON

St. Joseph - 104 S. Tuller St., Atkinson, NE 68713; Mailing: P.O. Box 220, Atkinson, NE 68713 t) 402-925-2122 stjosephatkinson.org/ Rev. Bernard G. Starman, Pst.; Rev. Ross C. Burkhalter, Assoc. Pst.; Dcn. Roger Filips; Dcn. Maurice Kersenbrock; CRP Stds.: 85

St. Joseph School - (Grades PreK-8) 102 N. Tuller, Atkinson, NE 68713 t) 402-925-2104 stjosephatkinson.org/school Andrea Borer, Prin.; Stds.: 65; Lay Tchrs.: 5

BANCROFT

Holy Cross - 100 Park St., Bancroft, NE 68004; Mailing: 1323 R St., Tekamah, NE 68061-1542 t) 402-687-2102; (402) 374-1692 www.stpats@abbnebraska.com Rev. Kevin J. Joyce, Admin.; Charlee Weborg, DRE; CRP Stds.: 15

BATTLE CREEK

St. Patrick's - 107 N. Third St., Battle Creek, NE 68715; Mailing: PO Box 40, Battle Creek, NE 68715 t) 402-675-6345 Dcn. Tom Hughes; Dcn. Melvin Schaecher; Rev. Patrick A. McLaughlin, Pst.; Rev. Gregory P. Carl, Par. Vicar; Rev. Brett Jamrog, Par. Vicar; Teresa Wilkinson, DRE; CRP Stds.: 138

BEEMER

Holy Cross - 517 Fraisier St. N., Beemer, NE 68716; Mailing: P.O. Box 212, Beemer, NE 68716 t) 402-528-3475 Rev. Vincent Sunguti, Pst.; Renae Carlson, DRE; CRP Stds.: 4

BELLEVUE

St. Bernadette - 7600 S. 42nd St., Bellevue, NE 68147 t) 402-731-4694 x305 (CRP); 402-731-4694 Rev. Jeffrey J. Mollner, Pst.; Dcn. Ron Casart; Dcn. Pete Digilio; Dcn. Sebastian Enzolera; Dcn. Gary Krupa; CRP Stds.: 46

St. Mary - 2302 Crawford St., Bellevue, NE 68005; Mailing: 811 W. 23rd Ave., Bellevue, NE 68005 t) 402-291-1350 rectory@stmarysbellevue.com www.stmarysbellevue.com Dcn. Gary Bash; Dcn. Jeff Braxton; Dcn. Chuck L'Archevesque; Dcn. Lee Mayhan; Dcn. Ted Menzel; Dcn. John Wacha; Rev. James R. de Anda, Assoc. Pst.; Elizabeth Tomaso, DRE; Rev. Lydell T. Lape, Pst.; CRP Stds.: 92

St. Mary School - (Grades PreK-8) 903 W. Mission Ave., Bellevue, NE 68005 t) 402-291-1694 trish.wallinger@stmarysbellevue.com www.stmarysschoolbellevue.com Trish Wallinger, Prin.;

St. Matthew the Evangelist Church of Bellevue - 12330 S. 36th St., Bellevue, NE 68123 t) 402-292-7418; 402-292-7928 (CRP) mhwhite@archomaha.org; plbanks@archomaha.org stmatthewbellevue.org Rev. Leo A. Rigatuso, Pst.; Dcn. Edward J. Bevan; Dcn. Tom Deall; Dcn. Mark White, DRE; CRP Stds.: 73

St. Matthew School - (Grades PreSchool-8) 12210 S. 36th St., Ste. B, Bellevue, NE 68123 t) 402-291-2030 staff@stmattschool.com www.stmatthew.bel@archomaha.org Angie Palmer, Prin.; Stds.: 184; Sr. Tchrs.: 1; Lay Tchrs.: 10

BLAIR

St. Francis Borgia - 2005 Davis Dr., Blair, NE 68008 t) 402-426-3823 stfrancisborgia.org Rev. Damien Wee, Pst.; Rebecca A. Crotty, Bus. Mgr.; CRP Stds.: 166

BLOOMFIELD

St. Andrew - 305 S. McNamara St., Bloomfield, NE 68718; Mailing: PO Box 9, Verdigre, NE 68783 t) 402-373-2696 (CRP); 402-668-2331 stwencoffice@gpcom.net www.saintsww.org Tanya DeWald, DRE; Rev. Jeremy J. Hans, Admin.; CRP Stds.: 43

BOYS TOWN

Immaculate Conception B.V.M. - 13943 Dowd Dr., Boys Town, NE 68010 t) 531-355-1037; 531-355-1114 denise.wharton@boystown.org; cathy.keisling@boystown.org boystown.org Rev. Steven Boes, Pst.; Rev. Msgr. James E. Gilg, In Res.; Rev. Dennis A. Hanneman, In Res.; Cathy Keisling, Dir.; Denise Wharton, Catholic Ministry Coordinator;

BUTTE

Sacred Heart Parish of Boyd County - 921 Gale St., Butte, NE 68722; Mailing: PO Box 8, Buttte, NE 68722 t) 402-775-0067 bgstarman@archomaha.org Rev. Bernard G. Starman, Pst.; Rev. Ross C. Burkhalter, Assoc. Pst.; Dcn. Roger Filips; Dcn. Maurice Kersenbrock; Charlotte Mitchell, DRE; CRP Stds.: 58

Ss. Peter and Paul Church - www.holtboydcatholic.org

Assumption BVM Church - 417 S. 4th St., Lynch, NE 68746 www.holtboydcatholic.org

St. Mary Church - 304 E. South St., Spencer, NE 68777 www.holtboydcatholic.org

CEDAR RAPIDS

St. Anthony - 508 W. Main St., Cedar Rapids, NE 68627; Mailing: P.O. Box 56, Cedar Rapids, NE 68627 t) 308-358-0773 Rev. Mark A. Tomasiewicz, Pst.; CRP Stds.: 42

CENTRAL CITY

St. Michael - 2402 20th Ave., Central City, NE 68826 t) 308-946-2855 c) 402-659-8132 dlfulton@archomaha.org Rev. David L. Fulton, Pst.; Dcn. Richard Larson; Dcn. Donald Placke; Dcn. Patrick Benson; CRP Stds.: 15

CLARKS

St. Peter - 302 N. Dixon St., Clarks, NE 68628; Mailing: 315 N. Esther St., PO Box 368, Fullerton, NE 68638 t) 308-548-2745 (CRP) Rev. David L. Fulton, Pst.; CRP Stds.: 21

CLARKSON

SS. Cyril and Methodius - 120 Cherry St., Clarkson, NE 68629; Mailing: P.O. Box 457, Clarkson, NE 68629 t) 402-892-3464 sites.google.com/site/sscyrilmethodiusclarkson/ Rev. Matthew J. Gutowski, Pst.; Anita Steffensmeier, DRE; Kaitlin Reick, DRE; CRP Stds.: 42

St. John Neumann - 420 Cherry St., Clarkson, NE 68629 t) 402-892-3474 Ann Prokopec, Contact;

Holy Trinity - 1733 Rd. 12, Clarkson, NE 68629 c) 402-615-1381 cmyosten@archomaha.org; cyosten@hughes.net Rev. Stanley T. Schmit, Pst.;

CLEARWATER

St. John the Baptist - 50898 848 Rd, (Deloit Twp.), Clearwater, NE 68726; Mailing: PO Box 37, Ewing, NE 68735 t) 402-626-7605 cppnebraska.org Rev. Joseph R. Sund, Assoc. Pst.; Rev. John M. Norman, Pst.; CRP Stds.: 11

COLERIDGE

St. Michael - 315 S. Madison, Coleridge, NE 68727; Mailing: PO Box 278, Hartington, NE 68739 t) 402-254-6559 Rev. Owen W. Korte, Pst.;

COLUMBUS

St. Anthony - 562 17th Ave., Columbus, NE 68601 t) 402-564-3313 pcharrison@archomaha.org stanthonycolumbusne.org Rev. Patrick C. Harrison, Pst.; Dcn. Mark Boeding; Dcn. Kelly McGowan; Lori Olson, DRE; Kathy Steiner, Bus. Mgr.; CRP Stds.: 88

St. Anthony School - (Grades PreK-6) 1719 6th St., Columbus, NE 68601 t) 402-564-4767 asokol@sta.esu7.org sta.esu7.org/ Amy Sokol, Prin.; Stds.: 112; Lay Tchrs.: 12

St. Bonaventure - 1565 18th Ave., Columbus, NE 68601 t) 402-564-7151 www.stboncc.com Dcn. Daniel Keiter; Dcn. Lawrence Mielak; Dcn. James Naughtin; Dcn. Arthur Spenner; Rev. Patrick C. Harrison, Admin.; Cheryl Rambour, DRE; CRP Stds.: 274

St. Bonaventure School - (Grades PreSchool-6) t) 402-564-7153 czoucha@stb.esu7.org school.stboncc.com/ Cheryl Zoucha, Prin.;

St. Isidore - 3921 20th St., Columbus, NE 68601 t) 402-564-8993 isidore@sti.esu7.org saintisidorechurch.com Mary Throener, DRE; Cherie VanDyke, CRE; Rev. Joseph A. Miksch, Pst.; CRP Stds.: 103

St. Isidore School - (Grades PreSchool-6) 3821 20th St., Columbus, NE 68601 t) 402-564-2604 akuhl@sti.esu7.org Amy Evans, Prin.; Stds.: 290; Lay Tchrs.: 15

CREIGHTON

St. Ludger - 410 Bryant Ave., Creighton, NE 68729 t) 402-358-3501 ludgercatholic.org Sarah Fanta, Contact; Rev. Jeremy J. Hans, Pst.; CRP Stds.: 70

St. Ludger School - (Grades PreSchool-6) 410 Bryant Ave, Creighton, NE 68729 t) (402) 358-3501 Miranda Hornback, Contact; Stds.: 55; Lay Tchrs.: 5

St. Ignatius Mission of Creighton - 407 S. Franklin St., Brunswick, NE 68720 t) (402) 358-3501

CROFTON

St. Rose of Lima - 1314 W. 5th St., Crofton, NE 68730; Mailing: PO Box 176, Crofton, NE 68730 t) 402-388-4814 ourcatholicfamily.org Dcn. Frank Fillaus; Rev. James E. Keiter, Pst.; Rev. Andy Phan, Assoc. Pst.; Terry Mueller, DRE; CRP Stds.: 115

St. Rose School - (Grades PreK-8) 1302 W. 5th St., Crofton, NE 68730 t) 402-388-4393 jdfiscus@schools.archomaha.org stroseoflimaschoolcrofton.weebly.com Jennifer Fiscus, Prin.; Stds.: 121; Lay Tchrs.: 8

DODGE

St. Wenceslaus - 743 Second St., Dodge, NE 68633 t) 402-693-2235 clortmeier@archomaha.org www.stwenc.org Rev. Matthew J. Gutowski, Pst.; CRP Stds.: 43

St. Wenceslaus School - (Grades PreK-6) 212 N. Linden St., Dodge, NE 68633 t) 402-693-2819 stwschool@gpcom.net Danielle Klosen, Headmaster; Stds.: 21; Lay Tchrs.: 4

Sacred Heart Mission of Dodge - County Rd. 17, Olean, NE 68633; Mailing: 743 E. 2nd St., Dodge, NE 68633 t) (402) 693-2235 rudynovak@hotmail.com

DUNCAN

St. Stanislaus - 1120 8th St., Duncan, NE 68634; Mailing: PO Box 155, Platte Center, NE 68653-0155 t) 402-246-2255 Rev. Walter Jong-A-Kiem, Pst.; Theresa Wenske, DRE; CRP Stds.: 15

ELGIN

St. Boniface Church of Elgin (Nebraska Non-Profit Corporation) - 301 S. 2nd St., Elgin, NE 68636-0433; Mailing: P.O. Box B, Elgin, NE 68636-0433 t) 402-843-2345 parish@cppnebraska.org cppnebraska.org Dcn. Bill Camp; Dcn. Dennis Wiehn; Rev. John M. Norman, Pst.; Rev. Joseph R. Sund, Assoc. Pst.; Becky Kerkman, DRE; Michele Reicks, Bus. Mgr.; Ann Kurpgeweit, Safe Environment Coordinator; CRP Stds.: 16

St. Boniface School - (Grades PreK-6) 303 Remington St., Elgin, NE 68636-0433 t) 402-843-5325 lschumacher@pjcrusaders.org Lisa Schumacher, Prin.; Stds.: 69; Lay Tchrs.: 7

ELKHORN

St. Patrick (Elkhorn) - 20500 W. Maple Rd., Elkhorn, NE 68022 t) 402-289-4289; 402-289-4947 (CRP) parish@stpatselkhorn.org; ehansen@stpatselkhorn.org www.stpatselkhorn.org Rev. Thomas M. Fangman, Pst.; Rev. Padraic Stack, Assoc. Pst.; Dcn. Joseph Hartnett; Dcn. Daniel E. Perchal; Dcn. James Ricketts; Dcn. Jay D Wingler; Anna Kolterman, Liturgy Dir.; Elizabeth Hansen, DRE; Erin Keller, Dir.; Rev. Gary L. Ostrander, Senior Resident; Vicki F Payton, Dir.; CRP Stds.: 563

St. Patrick School - (Grades PreK-8) t) 402-289-5407 klandenberger@stpatselkhorn.org school.stpatselkhorn.org Kami Landenberger, Prin.; Tawnya Mann, Vice Prin.; Candace Thompson, Vice Prin.; Stds.: 723; Lay Tchrs.: 35

EMERSON

Sacred Heart - 601 N. Main St., Emerson, NE 68733; Mailing: P.O. Box 250, Emerson, NE 68733 t) 402-695-2342 stjohnthebaptistcatholicpender@gmail.com Rev. Gerald Leise Jr., Pst.; Melissa Twohig, DRE; CRP Stds.: 74

St. Mary Mission of Emerson - 211 Iowa St., Hubbard, NE 68741; Mailing: 600 N. Main St., Emerson, NE 68733

EWING

St. Peter de Alcantara - 220 W. U.S. Hwy. 275, Ewing, NE 68735-2019; Mailing: P.O. Box 37, Ewing, NE 68735-0037 t) 402-626-7605 cppnebraska.org Rev. John M. Norman, Pst.; Rev. Joseph R. Sund, Assoc. Pst.; CRP Stds.: 44

St. Theresa's Church of Clearwater (Nebraska Non-Profit Corporation) - 509 Nebraska St, Clearwater, NE 68726; Mailing: PO Box 37, Ewing, NE 68735 t) (402) 626-7605

FORDYCE

All Saints Church of Northeast Nebraska - 311 Omaha St., Fordyce, NE 68736; Mailing: P.O. Box 170, Fordyce, NE 68736 t) 402-357-3506 jekeiter@archomaha.org www.ourcatholicfamily.org Rev. James E. Keiter, Pst.; Rev. Andy Phan, Assoc. Pst.; Dcn. Brian Heine; Dcn. Marcus Potts; Dcn. Rodney Wiebelhaus; CRP Stds.: 89

St. Joseph Church - 88870 554 Ave, Constance, NE 68730; Mailing: PO Box 170, Fordyce, NE 68736

St. John the Baptist Church -

St. Boniface Church - 55768 894 Rd., Menominee, NE 68736; Mailing: PO Box 170, Fordyce, NE 68736

Holy Family Parish of Cedar County - 303 Omaha St., Fordyce, NE 68736; Mailing: P.O. Box 170, Fordyce, NE 68736 t) 402-254-3311; 402-357-2465; (402) 357-3506 Rev. James E. Keiter, Pst.; Rev. Andy Phan, Assoc. Pst.; Dcn. Shane Kleinschmitt, DRE; CRP Stds.: 131

Immaculate Conception Church - St. Helena & 9th Sts, St. Helena, NE 68774; Mailing: P.O. Box 65, Wynot, NE 68792-0065 Rev. Eric S. Olsen, Pst.;

Sacred Heart Church - W. 8th St & Emerson Ave., Wynot, NE 68792; Mailing: P.O. Box 65, Wynot, NE 68792-0065 Rev. Eric S. Olsen, Pst.;

Ss. Peter and Paul Church - Paul St. & Valley View Dr., Bow Valley, NE 68739; Mailing: P.O. Box 65, Wynot, NE 68792-0065 Rev. Eric S. Olsen, Pst.;

FORT CALHOUN

St. John the Baptist - 215 N. 13th St., Fort Calhoun, NE 68023; Mailing: P.O. Box 148, Fort Calhoun, NE 68023 t) 402-468-5659 (CRP); 402-468-5348 deaconpaulc@gmail.com; sjcc@abbnebraska.com Rev. Stephen J. Gutgsell, Admin.; Dcn. Gerald Mapes; Dcn. Paul M. Cerio, DRE; CRP Stds.: 102

FREMONT

St. Patrick - 3400 E. 16th St., Fremont, NE 68025; Mailing: 422 E. 4th St., Fremont, NE 68025 t) 402-721-6611 stpats@stpatsfremont.org www.stpatsfremont.org Rev. Walter L. Nolte, Pst.; Rev. Bill Cremers, Assoc. Pst.; Rev. Minh Tran, Assoc. Pst.; Dcn. Edward Gentrup; Dcn. Vic Henry; Dcn. Mark Hoyle; Dcn. Alberto Martinez; Dcn. Dan Mueller; Dcn. David A. Probst; Dcn. Thomas Silva; Dcn. Gilbert Snodgrass; Dcn. Craig Steel; Dcn. Joe Uhlik; CRP Stds.: 150

Archbishop Bergan High School - 545 E. 4th St., Fremont, NE 68025 t) 402-721-9683 dan.koenig@berganknights.org www.berganknights.org Dan Koenig, Prin.; Stds.: 187; Lay Tchrs.: 17

Archbishop Bergan Middle School - (Grades 7-8) 545 E. 4th St., Fremont, NE 68025 t) 402-721-9683 www.berganknights.org Dan Koenig, Prin.;

Archbishop Bergan Elementary School - (Grades PreK-6) 1515 N. Johnson Rd., Fremont, NE 68025 t) 402-721-9766 dan.koenig@berganknights.org Dan Koenig, Prin.; Stds.: 254; Lay Tchrs.: 15

Early Childhood Education Center - 450 E. 4th, Fremont, NE 68025 t) 402-721-9710 john.faulkner@berganknights.org John Faulkner, Dir.;

FULLERTON

St. Peter - 315 N. Esther, Fullerton, NE 68638; Mailing: P.O. Box 368, Fullerton, NE 68638 t) 402-659-8132 Rev. David L. Fulton, Pst.; CRP Stds.: 52

GENOA

SS. Peter and Paul - 52121 S. 380 Ave., Genoa, NE 68640; Mailing: PO Box 490, Genoa, NE 68640 t) 308-773-2282 Rev. William D. L'Heureux, Pst.; CRP Stds.: 24

St. Rose of Lima - 116 N. Elm St., Genoa, NE 68640-0490; Mailing: P.O. Box 490, Genoa, NE 68640 t) 308-773-2282 Rev. William D. L'Heureux, Pst.; CRP Stds.: 73

GRETNA

St. Charles Borromeo - 7790 S. 192nd St., Gretna, NE 68028 t) 402-916-9730 parish@scbcomaha.org www.stcharlesomaha.org Rev. Jeffery S. Loseke, Pst.; Jackie Schuler, DRE; CRP Stds.: 234

St. Patrick Catholic Church of Gretna - 508 W. Angus St., Gretna, NE 68028 t) 402-332-4444 stpatrick.gre@archomaha.org stpatricksgretna.org Rev. Gregory P. Baxter, Pst.; Dcn. Ken Broz; Dcn. Larry Heck; CRP Stds.: 742

HARTINGTON

Holy Trinity - 404 S Broadway Ave, Hartington, NE 68739; Mailing: PO Box 278, Hartington, NE 68739 t) 402-254-6559 www.holytrinityhartington.com Rev. Owen W. Korte, Pst.; CRP Stds.: 382

Holy Trinity School - (Grades PreK-6) 502 S Broadway Ave, Hartington, NE 68739 t) 402-254-6496 Christopher Uttecht, Prin.;

HOOPER

St. Rose of Lima - 405 Elk St., Hooper, NE 68031; Mailing: 422 E. 4th St., Fremont, NE 68025 t) 402-721-6611 Rev. Walter L. Nolte, Pst.; Rev. William Cremers, Assoc. Pst.; Rev. Nicholas A. Mishek, Assoc. Pst.; CRP Stds.: 29

St. Lawrence Mission of Hooper - 910 Grant St., Scribner, NE 68057

HOWELLS

St. John Nepomucene - 320 S. 2nd St., Howells, NE 68641; Mailing: 614 Center St., Howells, NE 68641 t) 402-986-1653 Rev. Stanley T. Schmit, Pst.; Renae Vogel, DRE; CRP Stds.: 27

SS. Peter and Paul - 112 N. 6th St., Howells, NE 68641; Mailing: 614 Center St., Howells, NE 68641 t) 402-986-1653 Rev. Stanley T. Schmit, Pst.; Renae Vogel, DRE; CRP Stds.: 48

HUMPHREY

St. Francis - 203 S. 5th, Humphrey, NE 68642; Mailing: P.O. Box 116, Humphrey, NE 68642 t) 402-923-0913 esolsen@archomaha.org; fr.steve@hsfschool.org humphreystfrancis.com Rev. Eric S. Olson, Rev., Pst.; Rev. Steven Emanuel, Assoc. Pst.; Lori Classen, DRE; CRP Stds.: 22

St. Francis School - (Grades PreK-12) 300 S. 7th St., Humphrey, NE 68642; Mailing: P.O. Box 277, Humphrey, NE 68642 t) 402-923-0611 jdunn@hsfschool.org www.humphreystfrancis.com Jennifer Dunn, Prin.; Stds.: 239; Lay Tchrs.: 9

JACKSON

St. Patrick - 203 E. Elk St., Jackson, NE 68743; Mailing: P.O. Box 898, Ponca, NE 68770 t) 402-755-2773 cstwohig@archomaha.org; pwendte@archomaha.org Rev. Andrew L. Sohm, Pst.; Paula Wendte, DRE; CRP Stds.: 42

LAUREL

St. Mary - 406 Elm St., Laurel, NE 68745; Mailing: P.O. Box 828, Laurel, NE 68745 t) 402-256-3303 (Rectory); 402-256-3019 (Office) stmam3303@yahoo.com Rev. Mathew Capadano, Pst.; Donna Kraft, DRE; Rev. Gerald A. Connealy, Assoc. Pst.; CRP Stds.: 49

St. Anne Mission of Laurel - 510 Browning St., Dixon, NE 68732; Mailing: PO Box 828, Laurel, NE 68745

LEIGH

St. Mary - 220 W. Third St., Leigh, NE 68643; Mailing: P.O. Box 385, Leigh, NE 68643 t) 402-923-0913 stmaryleigh@gmail.com sites.google.com/site/stmaryleigh Rev. Eric S. Olsen, Pst.; CRP Stds.: 53

LINDSAY

Holy Family - 103 E. 3rd St., Lindsay, NE 68644; Mailing: PO Box 68, Lindsay, NE 68644 t) 402-428-2455 Rev. Eric S. Olsen, Pst.; CRP Stds.: 27

Holy Family School - (Grades PreK-8) 301 Pine St., Lindsay, NE 68644; Mailing: P.O. Box 158, Lindsay, NE 68644 t) 402-428-3455 Andy Bishop, Prin.;

Holy Family High School - (Grades 9-12) 301 Pine St., Lindsay, NE 68644; Mailing: P.O. Box 158, Lindsay, NE 68644 t) 402-428-3215 Andy Bishop, Prin.; Stds.: 18; Lay Tchrs.: 14; Pr. Tchrs.: 1

LYONS

St. Joseph - 430 Lincoln St., Lyons, NE 68038; Mailing: 1323 R St., Tekamah, NE 68061-1542 t) 402-687-2102; (402) 374-1692 www.stpatstekamah.com Rev. Kevin J. Joyce, Admin.; Jill Carl, DRE; CRP Stds.: 47

MADISON

St. Leonard of Port Maurice - 504 S. Nebraska St., Madison, NE 68748; Mailing: PO Box 367, Madison, NE 68748 t) 402-454-3529 jmjurgens@archomaha.org; stleonardparish@gmail.com Rev. Patrick A. McLaughlin, Pst.; Lisa` Jackson, Youth Min.; Erin Reeves, DRE; CRP Stds.: 30

St. Leonard of Port Maurice School - (Grades PreK-6) c/o St. Leonard of Port Maurice Parish, 504 S. Nebraska St., Madison, NE 68748 t) 402-454-3525

MONTEREY

St. Boniface - 450 12th Rd., Monterey, NE 68788; Mailing: 343 N. Monitor St., West Point, NE 68788 t) 402-372-2188 wpstmary@yahoo.com wpstmary.com Rev. Matthew J. Niggemeyer, Assoc. Pst.; Rev. James M. Weeder, Admin.;

NELIGH

St. Francis of Assisi Catholic Church - 702 W. 11th St., Neligh, NE 68756; Mailing: P.O. Box 259, Neligh, NE 68756 t) 402-887-4521 www.stfranciscc.org Rev. Patrick Nields, Pst.; Amy Baker, DRE; CRP Stds.: 83

NEWCASTLE

St. Peter - 403 Annie St., Newcastle, NE 68757; Mailing: P.O. Box 898, Ponca, NE 68770 t) 402-755-2273 (CRP) cstwohig@archomaha.org Dcn. Dennis Knudsen; Rev. Andrew L. Sohm, Pst.; Denise Kneifl, DRE; CRP Stds.: 35

NORFOLK

Sacred Heart Church of Norfolk - 204 S. 5th St., Norfolk, NE 68701 t) 402-371-2621 parishoffice@sacredheartnorfolk.com www.sacredheartnorfolk.com Rev. Patrick A. McLaughlin, Pst.; Rev. Gregory P. Carl, Par. Vicar; Rev. Brett Jamrog, Par. Vicar; Dcn. Theodore Coler; Dcn. Jim Doolittle; Dcn. Leon Gentrup; Dcn. Terry Price; Dcn. Patrick Roche; Dcn. Robert Viergutz; Ana Hernandez, DRE; Ellen Wagner, DRE; Philip Zimmerman, RCIA Coord.; CRP Stds.: 410

Norfolk Catholic Elementary School - (Grades PreK-6) 2301 W. Madison Ave., Norfolk, NE 68701; Mailing: 204 S. 5th St., Norfolk, NE 68701 t) 402-371-4584 William Lafleur, Prin.; Renee Gilsdorf, Librn.; Stds.: 387; Lay Tchrs.: 22

Norfolk Catholic High School - (Grades 7-12) 2300 W. Madison Ave., Norfolk, NE 68701; Mailing: 204 S. 5th St., Norfolk, NE 68701 t) 402-371-2784 Amy Wattier, Prin.; Stds.: 143; Lay Tchrs.: 23

St. Mary's Catholic Church - 2300 W. Madison Ave., Norfolk, NE 68701; Mailing: 204 So. 5th St, Norfolk, NE 68701 sacredheartnorfolk.com

Sacred Heart Church - 200 S. 5th St., Norfolk, NE 68701; Mailing: 204 S. 5th St., Norfolk, NE 68701 t) (402) 371-2621

NORTH BEND

St. Charles Borromeo - 831 Locust St., North Bend, NE 68649; Mailing: P.O. Box 457, North Bend, NE 68649 t) 402-652-8437 (CRP); 402-652-8484 pastor.stcharles.neb@archomaha.org; pastor.stcharles.nbe@archomaha.org www.parishesonline.com Rev. Keith D. Rezac, Pst.; Kelli Emmanuel, DRE; Jenni Peters, DRE; CRP Stds.: 129

OMAHA

St. Cecilia Cathedral - 701 N 40th St, Omaha, NE 68131-1826 t) 402-551-2313 stceciliacathedral@stceciliacathedral.org; mwgrewe@archomaha.org stceciliacathedral.org Rev. Michael W. Grewe, Pst.; Rev. James M. Buckley, Assoc. Pst.; Dcn. Jim Tardy, DRE; CRP Stds.: 92

St. Cecilia Cathedral School - (Grades PreK-8) 3869 Webster St, Omaha, NE 68131-1826 t) 402-556-6655 admin@stcecilia.net stcecilia.net Julia Pick, Prin.;

St. Andrew Kim Taegon Catholic Community - 2617 S. 31st St., Omaha, NE 68105 t) 402-346-0900 c) 402-707-5756 fadavita@gmail.com; saewoh@yahoo.com Rev. Vitalis E. Anyanike, Pst.; Rev. Paul Saewan Oh, In Res.;

Assumption of the Blessed Virgin Mary-Our Lady of Guadalupe Church of Omaha - 4930 S. 23rd St., Omaha, NE 68107 t) 402-731-2196 office@assumptionguadalupechurch.org; bulletin@assumptionguadalupechurch.org assumptionguadalupechurch.org Rev. William D. Bond, Pst.; Rev. Frank E. Jindra, Assoc. Pst.; Rev. Mauricio M Tovar, Assoc. Pst.; Dcn. Ramon Contreras; Marcela Cervantes, DRE; CRP Stds.: 500

St. Benedict the Moor - 2423 Grant St., Omaha, NE 68111 t) 402-672-8884 (CRP); 402-348-0631 willamidder@yahoo.com; stbenedictomaha@gmail.com Rev. Michael B. Voithofer, Pst.; Dcn. Randy Park; Dcn. Ernie Spicer; Willa Midder, DRE; Patricia Bass, Bus. Mgr.; CRP Stds.: 22

St. Bernard - 3601 N. 65 St., Omaha, NE 68104 t) 402-551-0269 stbernardchurch@hotmail.com Rev. Daniel L. Wittrock, Pst.; Dcn. Paul Dreismeier; Dcn. Timothy F. McNeil; Dcn. Charles Sheik, DRE; CRP Stds.: 57

St. Bernard School - (Grades PreK-8) 3604 N. 65th St., Omaha, NE 68104 t) 402-553-4993 www.stbernardomahaschool.org Emily Finley, Prin.; Stds.: 174; Lay Tchrs.: 16

St. Bridget-St. Rose Church of Omaha - 4112 S. 26th St., Omaha, NE 68107 t) 402-672-6216 (CRP); 402-733-8811 2southoparishes@gmail.com; 2catholic.parishes@gmail.com Rev. William J. Safranek, Pst.; CRP Stds.: 77

Christ the King - 654 S. 86th St., Omaha, NE 68114 t) 402-391-3606 jlpietramale@archomaha.org www.ctkomaha.org/ Rev. John L. Pietramale, Pst.; Rev. Stephen Hilgendorf, Assoc. Pst.; CRP Stds.: 43

Christ the King School - (Grades PreSchool-8) 831 S. 88th St., Omaha, NE 68114 t) 402-391-0977 ctkschool@ctkomaha.org Christopher Segrell, Prin.; Jeanne Stover, Vice Prin.; Stds.: 289; Lay Tchrs.: 26

St. Elizabeth Ann - 5419 N. 114th St., Omaha, NE 68164 t) 402-572-0369 (CRP); 402-493-2186 dewillis@archomaha.org; jkusek@sjsomaha.org www.stelizabethann.org/ Dcn. Dennis Connor; Dcn. Martin Crowley; Dcn. John Dagerman; Dcn. Duane Karmazin; Dcn. David Klein; Dcn. Richard Niedergeses; Rev. Ryan P. Lewis, Pst.; Jo Kusek, DRE; CRP Stds.: 154

St. Frances Cabrini - 1248 S. 10th St., Omaha, NE 68108 t) 402-934-7706 stfrancescabrinicatholicchurch@gmail.com; djzuerlein@archomaha.org stcabriniomaha.org Rev. Damian Zuerlein, Pst.; Dcn. Doug Lenz; Karen Avila, DRE; CRP Stds.: 44

St. Francis Assisi - 4521 S. 32 St., Omaha, NE 68107; Mailing: 4112 S. 26th St., Omaha, NE 68107 t) 402-733-8811 st.roseomaha@cox.net; 2catholic.parishes@gmail.com Rev. William J. Safranek, Pst.; CRP Stds.: 100

Holy Cross - 4810 Woolworth Ave, Omaha, NE 68106; Mailing: 4803 William St., Omaha, NE 68106 t) 402-553-7500 admin@holycrossomaha.org www.holycrossomaha.org Dcn. Thomas Burton; Dcn. George Elster; Dcn. Timothy A. Mulcahy; Dcn. Nickolas Rasmussen; Rev. Carl A. Salanitro, Pst.; Rev. Anthony Ike, In Res.; Theresa McClaury, Pst. Min./Coord.; Andrea Ramsey, Bus. Mgr.; CRP Stds.: 30

Holy Ghost - 5219 S. 53rd St., Omaha, NE 68117 t) 402-731-3176; 402-731-3176 x102 (CRP) parishsecretary@holyghostomaha.org holyghostomaha.org Dcn. Al Aulner; Dcn. Paul Eubanks; Dcn. Tom Schulte; Rev. William E. Sanderson, Pst.; Rev. Phil Flott, In Res.; CRP Stds.: 20

Holy Name - 2901 Fontenelle Blvd, Omaha, NE 68104; Mailing: 3014 N 45th St, Omaha, NE 68104 t) 402-451-6622 x206; 402-451-6622 x203 (CRP) parish@holynameomaha.org; businessmgr@holynameomaha.org www.holynameomaha.org Rev. Carl J. Zoucha, Pst.; CRP Stds.: 121

Immaculate Conception, B.V.M. - 2708 S. 24th St., Omaha, NE 68108 t) 402-342-1074 office@latinmassomaha.org; pastor@latinmassomaha.org www.latinmassomaha.org Rev. John Marcus Berg, FSSP, Pst.; Rev. John Paul Audino, FSSP, Assoc. Pst.; CRP Stds.: 95

St. James - 9025 Larimore Ave., Omaha, NE 68134 t) 402-572-0499; 402-572-0369 (CRP) jkusek9212@yahoo.com; dklein@stjamescatholicchurch.org Rev. Thomas W. Weisbecker, Pst.; Rev. Benjamin Boyd, Assoc. Pst.; Dcn. Gregg Drvol; Dcn. Randy Grosse; Dcn. Richard Hopkins; Dcn. Peter Kennedy; Dcn. Stan Kurtz; Dcn. Pat Lenz; Dcn. Steven Nelson; Jo Kusek, DRE; CRP Stds.: 114

St. Joan of Arc - 3122 S. 74th St., Omaha, NE 68124 t) 402-556-1456 office@midtowncatholic.church www.midtowncatholic.church Rev. Frank E. Jindra, Pst.; Rev. Frank J. Baumert, Assoc. Pst.; Dcn. Ronald R. Ryan; Dcn. Tim Leininger; CRP Stds.: 7

St. Joan of Arc School - (Grades 1-8) 7430 Hascall St., Omaha, NE 68124 t) 402-393-2314 office@sjaomaha.org Kayleen Wallace, Prin.; Stds.: 65; Lay Tchrs.: 5

St. John Paul II Newman Center, Inc. - 1221 S. 71st St., Omaha, NE 68106 t) 402-557-5575 info@jpiiomaha.org jpiiomaha.org Rev. Scott A. Schilmoeller, In Res.; Rev. Daniel R. Andrews, Pst.; Renee Hendricks, Bus. Mgr.; Katie Winkler, Campus Min.;

St. John Vianney - 5801 Oak Hills Dr., Omaha, NE 68137 t) 402-895-0896 (CRP); 402-895-0808 www.sjvomaha.org Dcn. Joseph Choi; Dcn. Thomas H. Frankenfield; Dcn. Chris Hanson; Dcn. Ron Horner; Dcn. Harold Sawtelle; Dcn. Frank Telich; Rev. Richard J. Reiser, Pst.; CRP Stds.: 196

St. John's at Creighton University Parish - Omaha - 2500 California Pl., Omaha, NE 68178 t) 402-280-3031 www.stjohns-creighton.org Rev. Matthew S. Walsh, S.J., Pst.; CRP Stds.: 59

St. Joseph - 1723 S. 17th St., Omaha, NE 68108 t) 402-342-1618 rrmajano@archomaha.org Rev. Rafael R. Majano, Pst.; CRP Stds.: 400

St. Leo - 1920 N. 102nd St., Omaha, NE 68114 t) 402-397-0407; 402-397-0407 x208 (CRP) dina@stleo.net; jen@stleo.net www.stleo.net Rev. Craig J. Loecker, Pst.; Rev. Michael J. Swanton, Assoc. Pst.; Dcn. Kevin Fuller; Dcn. Randy Landenberger; Dcn. Trung Nguyen; Dcn. James Shipman; Dcn. Norman Tierney; Jennifer Fuller, DRE; CRP Stds.: 103

St. Margaret Mary - 6116 Dodge St., Omaha, NE 68132-2199 t) 402-558-2255 mkelly@smmomaha.org www.smmomaha.org Rev. Ralph B. O'Donnell, Pst.; Rev. Tobias Letak, Assoc. Pst.; Rev. Brian Welter, In Res.; Alyssa Morgan Beasley, DRE; Jenni Vankat, Pst. Min./Coord.; Peg Lacy, Music Min.; Wilma Ernesti, Bus. Mgr.; CRP Stds.: 50

St. Margaret Mary School - (Grades K-8) 123 N. 61st St., Omaha, NE 68132 t) 402-551-6663 mberg@smmomaha.org; msimerly@smmomaha.org www.smmomaha.org/school Maureen Berg, Prin.; Mary Simerly, Vice Prin.; Stds.: 522; Lay Tchrs.: 30

St. Mary - 3529 Q St., Omaha, NE 68107; Mailing: 5912 S 36th St., Omaha, NE 68107 t) 402-731-0204 Rev. William D. Bond, Pst.; Rev. Frank E. Jindra, Assoc. Pst.; Rev. Mauricio M Tovar, Par. Vicar;

St. Mary Magdalene - 109 S. 19th St., Omaha, NE 68102 t) 402-342-4807 rtadams@archomaha.org; kmhall@archomaha.org stmarymagdaleneomaha.org/ Rev. Rodney T. Adams, Pst.; Rev. Andrew E. Ekpenyong, In Res.;

Mary Our Queen - 3535 S. 119th St., Omaha, NE 68144 t) 402-333-8662 moq@moqchurch.org www.moqchurch.org Rev. Marc Lim, Pst.; Dcn. Steve Floersch; Dcn. Thomas H. Frankenfield; Dcn. Robert Hamilton; Dcn. David Medeiros; CRP Stds.: 136

Mary Our Queen School - (Grades PreSchool-8) 3405 S. 119th St., Omaha, NE 68144 t) 402-333-8663 www.moqschool.org Maureen Hoy, Prin.; Stds.: 609; Lay Tchrs.: 37

Mother of Perpetual Help - 5215 Seward St., Omaha, NE 68104 t) 402-558-3100 tfmcneil@archomaha.org (Church of the Deaf) Dcn. Timothy F. McNeil, Pastoral Coord.;

Our Lady of Fatima Catholic Community - 709 S. 28th St., Omaha, NE 68105-1511 c) 515-822-6743 tamnangcmc@yahoo.com Rev. Tam V. Nguyen, CMR, Pst.; CRP Stds.: 141

Our Lady of Lourdes-St. Adalbert Parish - 2110 S. 32nd Ave., Omaha, NE 68105 t) 402-346-0900 fadavita@gmail.com ollomaha.com Rev. Vitalis E. Anyanike, Pst.; Dcn. Frank Hilt; Sr. Symphorosa Imbori, DRE; CRP Stds.: 17

St. Peter - 709 S. 28th St., Omaha, NE 68105-1511 t) 402-341-4560 secretary@stpeterchurch.net www.stpeterchurch.net Rev. John P. Broheimer, Pst.; Dcn. Gregorio Elizalde; Dcn. John Zak; CRP Stds.: 312

Sts. Peter and Paul Church of Omaha - 5912 S. 36th St., Omaha, NE 68107 t) 402-731-4578 dlrodriguez@archomaha.org Rev. William D. Bond, Pst.; Rev. Frank E. Jindra, Assoc. Pst.; Rev. Mauricio M Tovar, Par. Vicar; Denise Rodriguez, DRE; CRP Stds.: 251

St. Philip Neri-Blessed Sacrament Parish of Omaha - 8200 N. 30th St., Omaha, NE 68112 t) 402-455-1289 emilybazer@gmail.com; marieatspn@yahoo.com saintphilipneriblessedsacrament.org/ Rev. Damien J. Cook, Pst.; Dcn. Brendan Kelly; Emily Bazer, DRE; CRP Stds.: 10

St. Philip Neri-Blessed Sacrament Parish of Omaha School - (Grades PreK-8) 8202 N. 31st St., Omaha, NE 68112 t) 402-315-3500 aijensen@schools.archomaha.org; dmsmith@schools.archomaha.org Jensen I. Anne, Prin.; Christine Clayton, Librn.; Stds.: 147; Lay Tchrs.: 14

St. Pius X - 6905 Blondo St., Omaha, NE 68104 t) 402-558-1898 (CRP); 402-558-8446 rectory@stpiusxomaha.org www.stpiusxomaha.org Rev. Joseph M. Wray, Pst.; Rev. Michael Ahmadu, Assoc. Pst.; Colleen Ciciulla, DRE; CRP Stds.: 36

St. Robert Bellarmine - 11802 Pacific St., Omaha, NE 68154 t) 402-333-1959 (Religious Ed); 402-333-8989 (Church) kvazquez@stroberts.com www.stroberts.com Rev. David G. Reeson, Pst.; Rev. Mark J. McKercher, Assoc. Pst.; Rev. Harold J. Buse, In Res.; Dcn. Michael Fletcher; Dcn. Joseph Laird; Dcn. Richard Petersen; CRP Stds.: 75

St. Robert Bellarmine School - (Grades K-8) 11900 Pacific St., Omaha, NE 68154 t) 402-334-1929 jreinhart@stroberts.com

Sacred Heart - 2204 Binney St., Omaha, NE 68110; Mailing: 2207 Wirt St., Omaha, NE 68110 t) 402-451-5755 info@sacredheartchurchomaha.org; plgolka@archomaha.org sacredheartchurchomaha.org Dcn. James Chambers; Dcn. Richard Crotty; Dcn. John Vrbka; Rev. David M. Korth, Pst.; Sue Vavak, DRE; CRP Stds.: 53

St. Stanislaus - 4002 J St., Omaha, NE 68107 t) 402-731-4152 prvasquez@archomaha.org www.ststansomaha.org Dcn. Daniel Saniuk; Dcn. James Staroski; Rev. William E. Sanderson, Pst.; Patricia Vasquez, Bus. Mgr.;

St. Stephen the Martyr - 16701 S St., Omaha, NE 68135 t) 402-896-9675; 402-896-5683 (CRP) m.kane@stephen.org; c.young@stephen.org www.stephen.org Rev. David D. Belt, Pst.; Rev. Zachary T. Tucker, Assoc. Pst.; Dcn. Ernest Abbott Jr.; Dcn. Chuck Botdorf; Dcn. Jerry Kozney; Dcn. C. Martin Warwick; Chelsey Young, DRE; Dcn. Dennis Dethlefs, Pst. Min./Coord.; CRP Stds.: 601

St. Stephen the Martyr School - (Grades PreSchool-8) t) 402-896-0754 Julie Perrault, Prin.; Greg Verraneault, Vice Prin.; Stds.: 704; Lay Tchrs.: 40

St. Thomas More - 4804 Grover St., Omaha, NE 68106 t) 402-556-1456 fejindra@midtowncatholic.church www.midtowncatholic.church Rev. Frank E. Jindra, Pst.; Rev. Frank J. Baumert, Assoc. Pst.; Rachel Bielstein, DRE; CRP Stds.: 22

St. Vincent de Paul - 14330 Eagle Run Dr., Omaha, NE 68164 t) 402-496-7988; 402-493-1642 (CRP) parishoffice@svdpomaha.org; mcmahanj@svdpomaha.org www.svdpomaha.org Rev. Daniel J. Kampschneider, Pst.; Rev. Andrew J. Roza, Assoc. Pst.; Dcn. Donald Clausen; Dcn. Gary J. Hennessey; Dcn. Kevin Joyce; Dcn. Jay Reilly; Dcn. Bart Zavaletta; Kathy Mayer, Liturgy Dir.; Dcn. David Bang, Pst. Min./Coord.; Nicole Florez, Pst. Min./Coord.; Hannah Keisling, Youth Min.; Jennifer McMahan, DRE; Stan Isham, Dir.; CRP Stds.: 436

St. Vincent de Paul School - (Grades PreSchool-8) 14330 Eagle Run Dr, Omaha, NE 68164 t) 402-492-2111 schooladminstaff@svdpomaha.org www.svdp-omaha.org Barbara Marchese, Prin.; Diane Warneke, Assistant Principal; Stds.: 828; Lay Tchrs.: 42

St. Wenceslaus - 15353 Pacific St., Omaha, NE 68154 t) 402-330-0304 www.stwenceslaus.org Rev. Michael P. Eckley, Pst.; Rev. Taylor Leffler, Assoc. Pst.; Rev. Timothy Podraza, Assoc. Pst.; Dcn. Mark Capoun; Dcn. William Carter Jr.; Dcn. Michael J. DeSelm; Dcn. Joe Kulus; Dcn. Jack Miller; Dcn. Bradford Schaefer; Cindy Brown, Liturgy Dir.; Dcn. Donald Cowles; Brian Corey, Pst. Min./Coord.; Julie Lukasiewicz, DRE; CRP Stds.: 317

St. Wenceslaus School - (Grades PreK-8) t) 402-330-4356 hubenw@stwenceslaus.org www.stwenceslaus.org/school William Huben, Prin.; Stds.: 878; Lay Tchrs.: 43

West Papillion Catholic Community - 2222 N. 111 St., Omaha, NE 68164 t) 402-558-3100 James J. Stolze, Contact;

O'NEILL

St. Patrick - 330 E. Benton, O'Neill, NE 68763; Mailing: 301 E. Adams St., O'Neill, NE 68763 t) 402-336-1602 www.stpatoneill.org Rev. Bernard G. Starman, Pst.; Rev. Ross C. Burkhalter, Assoc. Pst.; Dcn. Maurice Kersenbrock; Dcn. Roger Filips; Cheleigh R Sholes, Bus. Mgr.; CRP Stds.: 96

St. Mary's Catholic School of O'Neill - (Grades PreK-12) 300 N. 4th St., O'Neill, NE 68763 t) 402-336-4455; 402-336-2664 jschneider@smcards.org; patkeson@smcards.org www.stmarysoneill.org Paula Atkeson, Prin.; Jennie Schneider, Prin.; Stds.: 220; Lay Tchrs.: 20

St. Joseph Mission of O'Neill - 85632 Ivy Ave., Amelia, NE 68711; Mailing: 301 E Adams St., O'Neill, NE 68763 t) 402-482-5283 (Church Phone); (402) 336-1602 (Office Phone)

OSMOND

St. Mary of the Seven Dolors - 208 E. 5th St., Osmond, NE 68765; Mailing: P.O. Box 397, Osmond, NE 68765 t) 402-748-3433 lisaharder06@gmail.com; sevendolorsoffice@gmail.com stmaryofthesevendolors.com Lisa Harder, DRE; Rev. Kevin W. Vogel, Admin.; CRP Stds.: 47

St. Mary of the Seven Dolors School - (Grades PreK-8) 302 E. 5th St., Osmond, NE 68765; Mailing: P.O. Box 427, Osmond, NE 68765 t) (402) 748-3433 Stds.: 48; Lay Tchrs.: 5

PAPILLION

St. Columbkille - 200 E. Sixth St., Papillion, NE 68046 t) 402-339-3285 cmmcartney@saincolumbkille.org saintcolumbkille.org Suzanne Brown, DRE; Rev. Thomas A. Greisen, Pst.; Rev. Patrick E. Moser, Assoc. Pst.; Dcn. David Graef; Dcn. William Hill; Dcn. Steve Jordan; Dcn. Eldon Lauber; Dcn. Frank Mascarello; Dcn. Jerry Overkamp; Dcn. Russ Perry; Dcn. Bob Stier; Dcn. Bud Tharp; Dcn. Brian Thomas; Dcn. Eric VandeBerg; Dcn. Robert Kellar; Dcn. David Krueger; Dcn. Tracy Ortgies; David Batter, Liturgy Dir.; Nicole Cook, Pst. Min./Coord.; Emily Stuever, Bus. Mgr.; CRP Stds.: 387

St. Columbkille School - (Grades PreSchool-8) 224 E. 5th St., Papillion, NE 68046 t) 402-339-8706 bredburn@saintcolumbkilleschool.org Brandi Redburn, Prin.; Sarah Foreman, Assistant Principal; Stds.: 574; Lay Tchrs.: 25

PENDER

St. John - 108 N. 5th St., Pender, NE 68047; Mailing: P.O. Box 96, Pender, NE 68047 t) 402-385-3258 stjohnthebaptistcatholicpender@gmail.com Rev. Gerald Leise Jr., Pst.; Joanne Puckett, DRE; CRP Stds.: 64

PETERSBURG

St. John the Baptists' Church of Petersburg (Nebraska Non-Profit Corporation) - 201 N. 4th St., Petersburg, NE 68652; Mailing: P.O. Box 608, Petersburg, NE 68652-0608 t) 402-386-5580 parish@cppnebraska.org cppnebraska.org Rev. John M. Norman, Pst.; Rev. Joseph R. Sund, Assoc. Pst.; Dcn. John Starman; Lisa Wagner, DRE; Jaci Hoefer, Bus. Mgr.; CRP Stds.: 22

PIERCE

St. Joseph - 118 W. Willow St., Pierce, NE 68767 t) 402-329-4200 parishoffice@stjosephpierce.org sites.google.com/stjosephpierce.org/main/ Rev. Kevin W. Vogel, Admin.; CRP Stds.: 106

PLAINVIEW

St. Paul - 203 E. Park Ave., Plainview, NE 68769; Mailing: 410 Bryant Ave, Creighton, NE 68729 t) 402-358-3501 Rev. Jeremy J. Hans, Pst.; CRP Stds.: 47

PLATTE CENTER

St. Joseph - 155 A St., Platte Center, NE 68653-0155; Mailing: P.O. Box 155, Platte Center, NE 68653-0155 t) 402-246-2255; 402-246-5700 (Parish Hall) Rev. Walter Jong-A-Kiem, Pst.; CRP Stds.: 33

PONCA

St. Joseph - 420 W 2nd St., Ponca, NE 68770; Mailing: P.O. Box 898, Ponca, NE 68770 t) 402-755-2773 cstwohig@archomaha.org stjosephsponca.org Rev. Andrew L. Sohm, Pst.; CRP Stds.: 55

RAEVILLE

St. Bonaventure's Church of Raeville (Nebraska Non-Profit Corporation) - 2305 S R Rd., Raeville, NE 68652; Mailing: PO Box B, Elgin, NE 68636 t) 402-843-2345 parish@cppnebraska.org cppnebraska.org Rev. John M. Norman, Pst.; Rev. Joseph R. Sund, Assoc. Pst.; CRP Stds.: 4

RALSTON

St. Gerald - 9602 Q St, Ralston, NE 68127; Mailing: 7859 Lakeview St., Ralston, NE 68127 t) 402-331-1955 office@stgerald.org www.stgerald.org Rev. Mark J. Nolte, Pst.; Rev. Marcus E. Knecht, Assoc. Pst.; CRP Stds.: 83

St. Gerald School - (Grades PreK-8) c/o St. Gerald Parish, 7859 Lakeview St., Ralston, NE 68127 t) 402-331-4223 ckeenan@stgerald.org Christy Keenan, Prin.; Stds.: 291; Lay Tchrs.: 22

RANDOLPH

St. Jane Frances de Chantal - 403 N. Bridge St., Randolph, NE 68771; Mailing: 402 N. Bridge St., Randolph, NE 68771 t) 402-337-0341 (CRP); 402-337-0644 (Rectory) www.saintjanefrances.com Dcn. Doug Tunink; Rev. Kevin W. Vogel, Admin.; Sandy Thies, DRE; CRP Stds.: 82

SCHUYLER

Divine Mercy - 308 W. 10 St., Schuyler, NE 68661 t) 402-352-2149 (CRP); 402-352-3540 divinemercyschuyler@gmail.com; jairocongote@gmail.com divinemercyschuyler.com Rev. Jairo E. Congote, Pst.; Dcn. Paul Doerneman; Dcn. Librado Felipe Maiz; Dcn. Pablo Tovar; Renee Blum, DRE; Dcn. Danny Hastings; CRP Stds.: 452

SILVER CREEK

St. Lawrence - 407 Vine St., Silver Creek, NE 68663; Mailing: PO Box 332, Silver Creek, NE 68663 t) 308-773-2282 Rev. William D. L'Heureux, Pst.; CRP Stds.: 21

SNYDER

St. Leo - 304 Ash St., Snyder, NE 68664; Mailing: P.O. Box 188, Snyder, NE 68664 t) 402-652-8484 stleo.sny@archomaha.org www.parishesonline.com Rev. Keith D. Rezac, Pst.;

SOUTH SIOUX CITY

St. Michael - 1405 1st Ave, South Sioux City, NE 68776; Mailing: 1315 First Ave, South Sioux City, NE 68776 t) 402-494-5423 stmichaelsschool.schoolinsites.com/ Rev. S. Anthony Weidner, Pst.; Rev. Michael Keating, Assoc. Pst.; Maria Gomez, DRE; Sr. Blanca Trinanes, DRE; Jeannie Mahaney, Bus. Mgr.; CRP Stds.: 491

St. Michael School - (Grades PreK-8) 1315 1st Ave., South Sioux City, NE 68776 t) 402-494-1526 dnswilli2632@smcsssc.com; jeannie.mahaney@smcsssc.com

SPRINGFIELD

St. Joseph - 102 S. Ninth St., Springfield, NE 68059 t) 402-253-2949 shuntwork@msn.com; secretary68059@gmail.com stjosephspringfield.org/ Sherry Huntwork, DRE; Rev. Scott A. Hastings, Pst.; CRP Stds.: 117

ST. CHARLES

St. Anthony - 449 15th Rd., Lot #1, St. Charles, NE 68788; Mailing: 343 N. Monitor St., West Point, NE 68788 t) 402-372-2188 wpstmary@yahoo.com wpstmary.com Rev. James M. Weeder, Pst.; Rev. Matthew J. Niggemeyer, Assoc. Pst.;

ST. EDWARD

St. Edward - 805 Washington St., St. Edward, NE 68660; Mailing: PO Box A, St. Edward, NE 68660 t) 308-773-2282 saintslppr@gmail.com Dcn. Harlan Long; Rev. William D. L'Heureux, Pst.; CRP Stds.: 47

STANTON

St. Peter - 1504 Ivy St., Stanton, NE 68779; Mailing: PO Box 557, Stanton, NE 68779 t) 402-439-2147 (CRP); 402-439-2149 (CRP); 402-371-2621 www.stpetersstanton.org Rev. Patrick A. McLaughlin, Pst.; Gretchen Hupp, DRE; CRP Stds.: 74

STUART

St. Boniface - 106 E. Fourth, Stuart, NE 68780; Mailing: P.O. Box 190, Stuart, NE 68780 t) 402-924-3262 www.stbonifacestuart.com Rev. Bernard G. Starman, Pst.; Rev. Ross C. Burkhalter, Assoc. Pst.; Rev. Joseph R. Sund, Assoc. Pst.; Dcn. Maurice Kersenbrock; Jan Kunz, DRE; CRP Stds.: 80

TARNOV

St. Michael - 309 3rd St., Tarnov, NE 68642; Mailing: P.O. Box 162, Humphrey, NE 68642 t) 402-923-0913; 402-923-1308 (CRP) rbrand1@megavision.com Rev. Eric S. Olsen, Pst.; Michelle Brandl, DRE; CRP Stds.: 48

TEKAMAH

St. Patrick - 1323 R St., Tekamah, NE 68061-1542 t) 402-374-1692; (402) 307-0296 (CRP) www.stpatstekamah.com Rev. Kevin J. Joyce, Pst.; Rachel Olson, DRE; CRP Stds.: 92

Holy Family - 703 Fourth Ave., Decatur, NE 68020; Mailing: 1323 R St., Tekamah, NE 68061

TILDEN

Our Lady of Mt. Carmel - 300 E. 2nd St., Tilden, NE 68781; Mailing: P.O. Box 458, Tilden, NE 68781 t) 402-368-7710 olmctilden@frontiernet.net www.olmctilden.org Rev. Patrick K. Nields, Pst.; Corinne Frey, DRE; CRP Stds.: 54

VALLEY

St. John - 307 E. Meigs, Valley, NE 68064 t) 402-359-5783 molly@stjohnvalleyne.com; businessmanager@stjohnvalleyne.com www.stjohnvalleyne.com Rev. Timothy W. Forget, Pst.; Dcn. Thomas Manhart; Molly Zach, DRE; CRP Stds.: 190

VERDIGRE

St. Wenceslaus - 211 4th Ave., Verdigre, NE 68783-0009; Mailing: 409 S. Third St., P.O. Box 9, Verdigre, NE 68783-0009 t) 402-668-2331 stwencoffice@gpcom.net www.saintsww.org Zoe Vakoc, DRE; Dcn. Keith Pavlik; Rev. Jeremy J. Hans, Admin.; CRP Stds.: 37

St. William Mission of Verdigre - 262 Buckeye Rd., Niobrara, NE 68760; Mailing: PO Box 9, Verdigre, NE 68783

WALTHILL

St. Joseph - 501 Main St., Walthill, NE 68067; Mailing: P.O. Box 766, Winnebago, NE 68071-0766 t) 402-878-2402 newsstaugustine@archomaha.org staugustinemission.org Rev. Mark T. Beran, Assoc. Pst.; Rev. Mark M. Bridgman, Assoc. Pst.; Dcn. Donald Blackbird Jr.;

Our Lady of Fatima Mission of Walthill - Elk St., Macy, NE 68039 staugustine.org

WAYNE

St. Mary - 412 E. 8th St., Wayne, NE 68787 t) 402-375-2000 Rev. Matthew Capadano, Pst.; Rev. Gerald A. Connealy, Assoc. Pst.; CRP Stds.: 139

St. Mary's Catholic School - (Grades PreK-6) 420 E. 7th St., Wayne, NE 68787 t) 402-375-2337 stmarys@stmaryswayne.org Stds.; 43; Lay Tchrs.: 5

WEST POINT

St. Aloysius - 700 Hwy 32, West Point, NE 68788; Mailing: 343 N Monitor St, West Point, NE 68788 t) 402-372-2188 wpstmary@gmail.com wpstmary.com Rev. James M. Weeder, Pst.; Rev. Matthew J. Niggemeyer, Assoc. Pst.;

Assumption B.V.M. - 343 N. Monitor St., West Point, NE 68788 t) 402-372-2188 wpstmary@yahoo.com wpstmary.com Rev. James M. Weeder, Pst.; Rev. Matthew J. Niggemeyer, Assoc. Pst.; Alicia Lewis, DRE; Dcn. David Baumert; Dcn. Francis Meiergerd; CRP Stds.: 73

Guardian Angel Central Catholic - (Grades PreK-12) 408 E. Walnut St., West Point, NE 68788 t) 402-372-5328 (elementary school); (402) 372-5326 (high school) dwieneke@gaccbluejays.org; teresa.hasenkamp@gaccbluejays.org www.gaccbluejays.org John McAndrews, Prin.; Paula Peatrowsky, Prin.; Stds.: 427; Lay Tchrs.: 30

WINNEBAGO

St. Augustine Catholic Church - 705 S. Mission Dr., Winnebago, NE 68071; Mailing: P.O. Box 766, Winnebago, NE 68071 t) 402-878-2402; 402-878-2291 (CRP) newsstaugustine@archomaha.org staugustinemission.org (Indian Mission) Rev. Mark T. Beran, Pst.; Rev. Mark M. Bridgman, Assoc. Pst.; CRP Stds.: 3

St. Cornelius Mission of Winnebago - 410 N. Third St., Homer, NE 68030

St. Augustine Indian Mission School - (Grades K-8) dnblackbird@archomaha.org Dcn. Donald Blackbird Jr., Prin.;

WISNER

St. Joseph - 1308 Ave. G, Wisner, NE 68791; Mailing: P.O. Box 623, Wisner, NE 68791 t) 402-529-3891 stjosephwisner.org/ Rev. Vincent Sunguti, Admin.; Capri McGuire, DRE; CRP Stds.: 85

SCHOOLS: PRESCHOOL THRU HIGH SCHOOL

SCHOOLS

STATE OF NEBRASKA

HARTINGTON

East and West Catholic Elementary School of Cedar County - (PRV) (Grades PreK-6) 108 W. 889th Rd., Hartington, NE 68739-6079 t) 402-254-2146 smschroeder@schools.archomaha.org; mvpinkelman@schools.archomaha.org eastwestcatholicschools.org Serving parishes in Bow Valley, St. Helena, Wynot, Fordyce, Menominee, & Constance Sonya Schroeder, Prin.; Stds.: 65; Lay Tchrs.: 5

HOWELLS

Howells Community Catholic School - (PAR) (Grades K-6) 114 N. 6th St., Howells, NE 68641 t) 402-986-1689 office@hccs.esu7.org; sritzdorf@hccs.esu7.org www.sites.google.com/hccs.esu7.org/hccs Serving parishes in Howells, Heun Sally Ritzdorf, Admin.; Stds.: 40; Lay Tchrs.: 5

OMAHA

CUES School System - (DIO) (Grades PreK-8) 2207 Wirt St., Omaha, NE 68110 t) 402-451-5755 dmkorth@archomaha.org www.cuesschools.org/ Rev. David M. Korth, Pres.; Stds.: 547; Lay Tchrs.: 66

Holy Name School - (Grades PreK-8) 2901 Fontenelle Blvd., Omaha, NE 68104 t) 402-451-5403 tmurray@hnsomaha.org holynameschoolomaha.org Tanya Santos, Prin.; Stds.: 256; Lay Tchrs.: 21

Sacred Heart School - (Grades PreK-8) 2205 Binney, Omaha, NE 68110 t) 402-455-5858 mjensen@shsomaha.org Mike Jensen, Prin.; Stds.: 137; Lay Tchrs.: 15

All Saints School - (Grades PreK-8) 1335 S. 10th, Omaha, NE 68108 t) 402-346-4747 terri@allsaintscs.org allsaintscs.org/ Angela Whitfield, Prin.; Stds.: 154; Lay Tchrs.: 30

St. James-Seton School - (PAR) (Grades PreK-8) 4720 N. 90th St., Omaha, NE 68134 t) 402-572-0339 wkelly@sjsomaha.org sjsomaha.org William Kelly, Prin.; Stds.: 444; Lay Tchrs.: 30

Jesuit Academy - (PRV) (Grades 4-8) 2311 N. 22nd St., Omaha, NE 68110 t) 402-346-4464; (402) 346-4464 kkunkel@jesuitacademy.org www.jesuitacademy.org Mike Masek, Pres.; Stds.: 73; Lay Tchrs.: 8

Madonna School & Community-Based Services - (PAR) (Grades PreK-12) 6402 N. 71st Plaza, Omaha, NE 68104 t) 402-556-1883 jburt@madonnaschool.org www.madonnaschool.org Serving individuals with Intellectual and Developmental Disabilities and their families from Pre-K through Adulthood Jonathan Burt, Pres.; Stds.: 23; Lay Tchrs.: 8

Madonna Employment Services - (Grades PreK-12)

Life Skills Transition Program - (Grades PreK-12) Transition program for young adults 18-21 with a focus on developing essential career & life skills

Omaha Catholic School Consortium - (PRV) (Grades PreK-8) 4501 S 41 St., Omaha, NE 68107 t) 402-590-2810 www.omahacsc.org Michael Goetz, Exec.; Stds.: 1,657; Lay Tchrs.: 115

Holy Cross School Building - (Grades PreK-8) 1502 S. 48th St., Omaha, NE 68106-2599 t) 402-551-3773 cmnelson@archomaha.org www.holycrossomaha.com Chris Nelson, Prin.; Stds.: 307; Lay Tchrs.: 34

Our Lady of Lourdes School Building - (Grades PreK-8) 2124 S. 32nd Ave., Omaha, NE 68105-3198 t) 402-341-5604 llinquist@omahacsc.org www.ollomaha.com Lisa Linquist, Prin.; Stds.: 241; Lay Tchrs.: 13

St. Bernadette School - (Grades PreK-8) 7600 S. 42nd St., Omaha, NE 68147-1702 t) 402-731-3033 lschultz@stbernadetteschool.net www.stbernadetteschool.net Lynn Schultz, Prin.; Stds.: 237; Lay Tchrs.: 12

Ss. Peter & Paul Building - (Grades PreK-8) 3619 X St., Omaha, NE 68107-3247 t) 402-731-4713 abauer@sppsaints.org www.sppomaha.org Andrew Bauer, Prin.; Stds.: 278; Lay Tchrs.: 18

St. Thomas More School Building - (Grades PreK-8) 3515 S. 48th Ave., Omaha, NE 68106-4532 t) 402-551-9504 gdavis@omahacsc.org www.stmbengals.org Gary Davis, Prin.; Stds.: 405; Lay Tchrs.: 26

Dual Language Academy Building - (Grades PreK-8) 7430 Hascall St, Omaha, NE 68124 t) 402-991-3400 Angie Smith, Prin.; Stds.: 189; Lay Tchrs.: 12

St. Pius X-St. Leo School - (PAR) (Grades PreK-8) 6905 Blondo St., Omaha, NE 68104 t) 402-551-6667 cory.sepich@spsl.net www.spsl.net Cory Sepich, Prin.; Christy Vogel, Librn.; Stds.: 680; Lay Tchrs.: 45

HIGH SCHOOLS

STATE OF NEBRASKA

BELLEVUE

Daniel J. Gross Catholic High School - (DIO) (Grades 9-12) 7700 S. 43rd St., Bellevue, NE 68147 t) 402-734-2000 curry@gcgmail.org www.grosscatholic.org Dr. Tom Curry, Pres.; Stds.: 382; Lay Tchrs.: 31

COLUMBUS

Scotus Central Catholic High School (Scotus Central Catholic Secondary School of Columbus) - (DIO) (Grades 7-12) 1554 18th Ave., Columbus, NE 68601-5132 t) 402-564-7165 johnoutka@scotuscc.org; jschueth@scotuscc.org www.scotuscc.org Merlin Lahm, Vice Prin.; Brady Vancura, Vice Prin.; Jeff Ohnoutka, Pres.; Cathy Podliska, Librn.; Stds.: 373; Lay Tchrs.: 31

ELGIN

Pope John XXIII Central Catholic High School at Elgin - (DIO) (Grades 7-12) 303 Remington St., Elgin, NE 68636; Mailing: P.O. Box 179, Elgin, NE 68636 t) 402-843-5325 lschumacher@pjcrusaders.org Lisa Schumacher, Prin.; Rev. John M. Norman, Pres.; Lauren Borer, Librn.; Stds.: 52; Lay Tchrs.: 9

ELKHORN

Mount Michael Benedictine School - (PRV) (Grades 9-12) 22520 Mt. Michael Rd., Elkhorn, NE 68022-3400 t) 402-289-2541 dpeters@mountmichael.org www.mountmichael.com Rt. Rev. Michael Liebl, O.S.B., Abbot; David Peters, Head of School; Bro. Luke Clinton, O.S.B., Librn.; Rev. John Hagemann, O.S.B., Campus Min.; Rev. Daniel Lenz, O.S.B., Instructor; Bro. Roger Mangels, O.S.B., Instructor; Rev. Stephen J. Plank, O.S.B., Instructor; Bro. August Schaefer, O.S.B., Instructor; Rev. Louis L. Sojka, O.S.B., Bus. Mgr.; Stds.: 238; Pr. Tchrs.: 2; Bro. Tchrs.: 1; Sr. Tchrs.: 1; Lay Tchrs.: 24

HARTINGTON

Cedar Catholic High School - (DIO) (Grades 7-12) 401 S Broadway Ave, Hartington, NE 68739; Mailing: PO Box 15, Hartington, NE 68739 t) 402-254-3906 cuttecht@cedarcatholic.org www.cedarcatholic.org Christopher Uttecht, Prin.; Rev. Owen W. Korte, Pres.; Stds.: 182; Lay Tchrs.: 16

OMAHA

Creighton Preparatory School - (PRV) (Grades 9-12) 7400 Western Ave., Omaha, NE 68114 t) 402-393-1190 hso@creightonprep.org www.creightonprep.org Rev. Robert J. Tillman, S.J.; Rev. Matthew Spotts, S.J., Pres.; Diane Sands, Librn.; Stds.: 963; Scholastics: 2; Pr. Tchrs.: 1; Lay Tchrs.: 75

Duchesne Academy of the Sacred Heart - (PRV) (Grades PreSchool-12) 3601 Burt St., Omaha, NE 68131 t) 402-558-3800 mbrudney@duchesneacademy.org; kdagostino@duchesneacademy.org www.duchesneacademy.org Meg Brudney, Head of School; Laura Hickman, Prin.; Stds.: 340; Lay Tchrs.: 35

Marian High School (Servants of Mary) - (PRV) 7400 Military Ave., Omaha, NE 68134 t) 402-571-2618 x1212 mernst@omahamarian.org marianhighschool.net Michele Ernst, Pres.; Susie Sullivan, Prin.; Jennifer Christen, Vice Prin.; Rochelle Rohlfs, Asst Principal/ Athletic Dir; Dcn. Kevin Fuller, Campus Min.; Stds.: 612; Lay Tchrs.: 42

Marian High School Scholarship Endowment Trust - t) 402-934-1053 jbecker@omahamarian.org Joan Becker, Vice. Pres.;

Marian High School Endowment Trust - t) (402) 571-2618 x1116

Mercy High School - (PRV) (Grades 9-12) 1501 S. 48th St., Omaha, NE 68106 t) 402-553-9424 hannond@mercyhigh.org www.mercyhigh.org Kristi A Wessling, Prin.; Sr. Delores Hannon, R.S.M., Pres.; Stds.: 291; Sr. Tchrs.: 1; Lay Tchrs.: 30

Roncalli Catholic High School of Omaha - (DIO) (Grades 9-12) 6401 Sorensen Pkwy., Omaha, NE 68152 t) 402-571-7670 businessoffice@roncallicatholic.org; skeisling@roncallicatholic.org www.roncallicatholic.org Rev. Lloyd A. Gnirk, Pastor Emer.; Jerome Stoffel, Prin.; Sean Keisling, Pres.; James Meister, Assistant Principal; Stds.: 348; Lay Tchrs.: 25

V.J. & Angela Skutt Catholic High School - (DIO) 3131 S. 156th St., Omaha, NE 68130-1907 t) 402-333-0818 jeremymoore@skuttcatholic.com www.skuttcatholic.com Michael Bailey, Admin.; Rob Meyers, Prin.; Jeremy Moore, Pres.; Stds.: 730; Pr. Tchrs.: 1; Lay Tchrs.: 58

WEST POINT

Guardian Angels Central Catholic - (DIO) 419 E. Decatur, West Point, NE 68788 t) 402-372-5326 dmeister@gaccbluejays.org www.gaccbluejays.org Kate Hageman, Prin.; Paula Peatrowsky, Prin.; Rev. James M. Weeder, Pres.; Stds.: 153; Lay Tchrs.: 12

INSTITUTIONS LOCATED IN DIOCESE

CAMPUS MINISTRY / NEWMAN CENTERS [CAM]

OMAHA

St. John Paul II Newman Center, Inc. - 1221 S. 71st St., Omaha, NE 68106 t) 402-557-5575 x3028 info@jpiiomaha.org www.jpiiomaha.org Rev. Daniel R. Andrews, Pst.; Katie Winkler, Campus Min.; Renee Hendricks, Bus. Mgr.; Susan Gnann, Dir., Advancement; Lauren Hankes, Resident Mgr.; Amanda Pohlman, Outreach & Mktg.;

WAYNE

Wayne State College Newman Center - 412 E. 8th St., Wayne, NE 68787 t) 402-375-2000 parish@stmaryswayne.org www.stmaryswayne.org/wsc-newman-center Rev. Matthew Capadano, Chap.; Maddy Hoff, Campus Min.;

CATHOLIC CHARITIES [CCH]

OMAHA

Catholic Charities - 9223 Bedford Ave., Omaha, NE 68134 t) 402-554-0520 catholiccharities@ccomaha.org www.ccomaha.org Denise Bartels, Exec. Dir.; Asstd. Annu.: 300,000; Staff: 60

***Catholic Charities Foundation** - 9223 Bedford Ave., Omaha, NE 68134 t) 402-554-0520 catholiccharities@ccomaha.org www.ccomaha.org Denise Bartels, Exec. Dir.; Asstd. Annu.: 300,000; Staff: 60

Domestic Violence Services - The Shelter - c/o 9223 Bedford Ave., Omaha, NE 68134 t) 402-558-5700 melissas@ccomaha.org ccomaha.org Melissa Socha, Dir.; Asstd. Annu.: 1,075; Staff: 10

Juan Diego Center - 5211 S. 31st St., Omaha, NE 68107 t) 402-731-5413 catholiccharities@ccomaha.org ccomaha.org Services include a Microbusiness & Asset Development Program, Emergency & Supportive Food Services, and an Immigration Legal Services Program. Erin Fichter, Dir.; Mikaela Schuele, Dir.; Asstd. Annu.: 297,000; Staff: 24

Sheehan Center - 9223 Bedford Ave., Omaha, NE 68134 t) 402-554-0520 catholiccharities@ccomaha.org ccomaha.org Denise Bartels, Exec. Dir.; Dave Vankat, Exec.; Asstd. Annu.: 4,300; Staff: 30

St. Martin DePorres Center - 2111 Emmet St., Omaha, NE 68110 t) 402-453-6363 catholiccharities@ccomaha.org ccomaha.org Christine Merrell, Dir.; Mikaela Schuele, Dir.; Asstd. Annu.: 9,730; Staff: 2

SCHUYLER

El Puente Immigration Legal Services - 1123 Rd. I, Schuyler, NE 68661; Mailing: P.O. Box 528, Schuyler, NE 68661-0528 t) 402-352-3644 www.ccomaha.org Erin Fichter, Dir.; Asstd. Annu.: 105; Staff: 1

CEMETERIES [CEM]

OMAHA

Calvary - 7710 W. Center Rd., Omaha, NE 68124 t) 402-391-3711 Dcn. Steven Hill, Dir.; Rev. Michael W. Grewe, Exec. Dir.;

Catholic Cemeteries of the Archdiocese of Omaha - 7710 W. Center Rd., Omaha, NE 68124-3199 t) 402-391-3711 smhill@catholiccem.com www.catholiccem.com Rev. Michael W. Grewe, Exec.; Dcn. Steven Hill, Dir.;

Holy Sepulchre - 4912 Leavenworth St., Omaha, NE 68106; Mailing: Catholic Cemeteries of the Archdiocese of Omaha, 7710 W. Center Rd., Omaha, NE 68124 t) 402-391-3711 Dcn. Steven Hill, Dir.; Rev. Michael W. Grewe, Exec. Dir.;

St. Mary - 3353 Q St., Omaha, NE 68107; Mailing: Catholic Cemeteries of the Archdiocese of Omaha, 7710 W. Center Rd., Omaha, NE 68124 t) 402-391-3711 Dcn. Steven Hill, Dir.; Rev. Michael W. Grewe, Exec. Dir.;

St. Mary Magdalene - 5226 S. 46 St., Omaha, NE 68117; Mailing: Catholic Cemeteries of the Archdiocese of Omaha, 7710 W. Center Rd., Omaha, NE 68124 t) 402-391-3711 Dcn. Steven Hill, Dir.; Rev. Michael W. Grewe, Exec. Dir.;

Resurrection - 7800 W. Center Rd., Omaha, NE 68114; Mailing: Catholic Cemeteries of the Archdiocese of Omaha, 7710 W. Center Rd., Omaha, NE 68124 t) 402-391-3711 Dcn. Steven Hill, Dir.; Rev. Michael W. Grewe, Exec. Dir.;

COLLEGES & UNIVERSITIES [COL]

OMAHA

College of Saint Mary - 7000 Mercy Rd., Omaha, NE 68106 t) 402-399-2400 enroll@csm.edu www.csm.edu Sr. Maryanne Stevens, Pres.; Terri Campbell, Vice Pres., Alumnae & Donor Rels.; Nate Neufind, Vice Pres., Athletics, Mktg. & Tech.; Brigdette Renbarger, Vice Pres., Fin. & Admin. Srvcs.; Dr. Kimberly Allen, Vice Pres., Academic & Student Affairs; Stds.: 856; Lay Tchrs.: 83

***Creighton University** - 2500 California Plz., Omaha, NE 68178 t) 402-280-2770 www.creighton.edu Rev. Daniel S. Hendrickson, S.J., Pres.; Stds.: 8,397; Lay Tchrs.: 656; Pr. Tchrs.: 18; Sr. Tchrs.: 2; Scholastics: 2

College of Arts and Sciences - t) (402) 280-2431 Bridget Keegan, Dean;

Graduate School and College of Professional Studies - t) 402-280-2424; 402-280-2870 Gail Jensen, Dean;

Heider College of Business - t) 402-280-2852 Anthony Hendrickson, Dean;

School of Dentistry - t) 402-280-5061 Mark A. Latta, Dean;

School of Law - t) 402-280-2874 Joshua P. Fershee, Dean;

School of Medicine - t) 402-280-2600 Robert Dunlay, Dean;

College of Nursing - t) 402-280-2004 Catherine Todero, Dean;

School of Pharmacy and Health Professions - t) 402-280-1828 Evan T. Robinson, Dean;

CONVENTS, MONASTERIES, AND RESIDENCES FOR WOMEN [CON]

NORFOLK

Immaculata Monastery (Missionary Benedictine Sisters) - 300 N. 18th St., Norfolk, NE 68701-3622 t) 402-371-3438 rtoffosb@gmail.com www.mbsmissionaries.org Sr. Roseann Ocken, Prioress; Srs.: 30

OMAHA

Daughters of Mary, Inc. - 2117 S. 33rd St., Omaha, NE 68105 c) 402-660-3148 Sr. Theresia Hhayuma, Supr.; Srs.: 3

Franciscan Monastery of St. Clare (Poor Clare Nuns (Second Order of St. Francis)) - 22625 Edgewater Rd., Omaha, NE 68022-3504 t) 402-558-4916

c) 402-990-5970 www.omahapoorclare.org Sr. Kathleen of the Good Shepherd Hawkins, OSC, Supr.; Srs.: 7

Motherhouse of the Servants of Mary - 7400 Military Ave., Omaha, NE 68134-3398 t) 402-571-2547 sdeebyosm@gmail.com www.osms.org Sr. Jackie Ryan, O.S.M., Prioress; Srs.: 54

Provincial Motherhouse and Novitiate of the Notre Dame Sisters - 3501 State St., Omaha, NE 68112 t) 402-455-2994 notredamesisters@notredamesisters.org www.notredamesisters.org Sr. Rita Ostry, ND, Prov.; Srs.: 30

Sisters of Mercy of the Americas West Midwest Community, Inc. - 7262 Mercy Rd., Omaha, NE 68124-2389 t) 402-393-8225 Sr. Aine O'Connor, RSM, Pres.; Srs.: 417

ENDOWMENTS / FOUNDATIONS / TRUSTS [EFT]

ELGIN

St. Bonaventure's Church of Raeville Cemetery Endowment Trust Fund - 301 S. 2nd St., Elgin, NE 68636; Mailing: P.O. Box B, Elgin, NE 68636 t) 402-843-2345 stbonaventure.rae@archomaha.org Rev. John M. Norman, Contact;

ELKHORN

Mount Michael Foundation - 22520 Mount Michael Rd., Elkhorn, NE 68022-3400 t) 402-289-2541 business@mountmichael.org Rt. Rev. Michael Liebl, O.S.B., Abbot; Rev. John Hagemann, O.S.B., Mem.; Bro. Jerome Kmiecik, O.S.B., Mem.; Rev. Louis L. Sojka, O.S.B., Bus. Mgr.;

Saint Patrick's Parish Foundation - 20500 W. Maple Rd., Elkhorn, NE 68022 t) (402) 289-4289 Rev. Thomas M. Fangman, Contact;

FORDYCE

Cemetery Endowment for St. Boniface Church - 311 Omaha St., Fordyce, NE 68736; Mailing: Box 170, Fordyce, NE 68736 t) 402-357-3506 jekeiter@archomaha.org www.stbonifaceparish.org Rev. James E. Keiter, Contact;

GRETNA

St. Patrick's Church of Gretna Cemetery Endowment Trust Fund - 508 W. Angus St., Gretna, NE 68028 t) 402-332-4444 gpbaxter@archomaha.org Rev. Gregory P. Baxter, Contact;

NORFOLK

Missionary Benedictine Sisters Foundation - 300 N. 18th St., Norfolk, NE 68701-3622 t) 402-371-3438 rtoffosb@gmail.com Sr. Rita Marie Tofflemire, Contact;

OMAHA

Catholic Futures Foundation of Northeast Nebraska - 2222 N. 111 St., Omaha, NE 68164 t) 402-827-3737 Most Rev. George J. Lucas, Pres.;

The Office of Stewardship and Development - t) 402-557-5650 smbrommer@archomaha.org Omaha. Shannan Brommer, Dir.;

St. Adalbert Parish Endowment Trust - Omaha.

All Saints Catholic School Educational Endowment Trust - Omaha.

St. Aloysius Parish Educational Endowment Trust - Aloys, NE.

St. Aloysius Parish Endowment Trust - Aloys, NE.

St. Andrew Parish Educational Endowment Trust - Bloomfield, NE.

St. Andrew Parish Endowment Trust - Bloomfield, NE.

St. Anne Church of Dixon Cemetery Endowment Trust Fund - Laurel, NE.

St. Anne Church of Dixon Cemetery Endowment Trust Fund - Dixon, NE.

St. Anne Parish Educational Endowment Trust - Dixon, NE.

St. Anne Parish Endowment Trust - Dixon, NE.

St. Anthony Elementary School Endowment Trust - Columbus, NE.

St. Anthony Parish Educational Endowment Trust - Cedar Rapids, NE.

St. Anthony Parish Educational Endowment Trust - Columbus, NE.

St. Anthony Parish Educational Endowment Trust - St. Charles, NE.

St. Anthony Parish Endowment Trust - Cedar Rapids, NE.

St. Anthony Parish Endowment Trust - Columbus, NE.

St. Anthony Parish Endowment Trust - Omaha.

St. Anthony Parish Endowment Trust - St. Charles, NE.

Archbishop Bergan Jr./Sr. Catholic High School Educational Endowment Trust - Fremont, NE.

Archbishop Sheehan Adult Education Endowment Trust - Omaha.

Assumption Parish Cemetery Endowment Trust - Lynch, NE.

Assumption Parish Educational Endowment Trust - Lynch, NE.

Assumption Parish Endowment Trust - Lynch, NE.

St. Augustine Indian Mission Educational Endowment Trust - Winnebago, NE.

St. Augustine Indian Mission Endowment Trust - Winnebago, NE.

St. Augustine Indian Mission Tuition Relief Educational Endowment Trust - Winnebago, NE.

St. Augustine Parish Educational Endowment Trust - Schuyler, NE.

St. Augustine Parish Endowment Trust - Schuyler, NE.

St. Benedict Parish Educational Endowment Trust - Omaha.

St. Benedict Parish Endowment Trust - Omaha.

St. Bernadette Parish Educational Endowment Trust - Omaha.

St. Bernadette Parish Endowment Trust - Omaha.

St. Bernard Parish Memorial Endowment Trust - Omaha.

St. Bernard Parish Religious Education Endowment Trust - Omaha.

Black Students Catholic Educational Endowment Trust - Omaha.

Black Students Catholic Scholarship Trust Fund - Omaha.

Blessed Sacrament Parish Endowment Trust - Omaha.

Blessed Sacrament School Educational Endowment Trust - Omaha.

St. Bonaventure Church Endowment Trust - Columbus, NE.

St. Bonaventure Parish Endowment Trust - Raeville, NE.

St. Boniface Elementary School Endowment Trust - Stuart, NE.

St. Boniface Parish Educational Endowment Trust - Elgin, NE.

St. Boniface Parish Educational Endowment Trust - Menominee, NE.

St. Boniface Parish Educational Endowment Trust - Monterey, NE.

St. Boniface Parish Endowment Trust - Elgin, NE.

St. Boniface Parish Endowment Trust - Menominee, NE.

St. Boniface Parish Endowment Trust - Monterey, NE.

St. Boniface Parish Endowment Trust - Stuart, NE.

St. Boniface School Endowment Trust - Elgin, NE.

St. Bonaventure Parish/Pope John XXIII High School Educational Endowment Trust - Raeville, NE.

St. Bridget Parish Educational Endowment Trust - Omaha.

St. Bridget Parish Endowment Trust - Omaha.

The Catholic Voice Educational Endowment Trust - Omaha.

St. Cecilia Cathedral Endowment Trust - Omaha.

Cedar Catholic High School Educational Endowment Trust - Hartington, NE.

St. Charles Borromeo Parish Educational Endowment Trust - North Bend, NE.

St. Charles Borromeo Parish Endowment Trust - North Bend, NE.

Christ the King Educational Endowment Trust - Omaha.

Christ the King Parish Endowment Trust - Omaha.

Church of the Assumption Endowment Trust - Omaha.

Church of the Assumption of the B.V.M. Parish Educational Endowment Trust - West Point, NE.

Church of the Assumption of the B.V.M. Parish Endowment Trust - West Point, NE.

St. Columbkille Educational Endowment Trust - Papillion, NE.

St. Columbkille Parish Endowment Trust - Papillion, NE.

St. Cornelius Parish Educational Endowment Trust - Homer, NE.

St. Cornelius Parish Endowment Trust - Homer, NE.

SS. Cyril and Methodius Parish Educational Endowment Trust - Clarkson, NE.

SS. Cyril and Methodius Parish Endowment Trust - Clarkson, NE.

East Catholic Elementary School Educational Endowment Trust - Bow Valley, NE.

St. Edward Parish Educational Endowment Trust - St. Edward, NE.

St. Edward Parish Endowment Trust - St. Edward, NE.

St. Edward's Church of St. Edward Cemetery Endowment Trust Fund - St. Edward, NE.

St. Elizabeth Ann Parish Educational Endowment Trust - Omaha.

St. Elizabeth Ann Parish Endowment Trust - Omaha.

FEATHERS - Winnebago, NE.

St. Frances Cabrini Parish Educational Endowment Trust - Omaha.

St. Frances Cabrini Parish Endowment Trust - Omaha.

St. Frances de Chantal of Randolph Cemetery Endowment Trust Fund - Randolph, NE.

St. Frances de Chantal Parish Educational Endowment Trust - Randolph, NE.

St. Frances de Chantal Parish Endowment Trust - Randolph, NE.

St. Francis Borgia Parish Educational Endowment Trust - Blair, NE.

St. Francis Borgia Parish Endowment Trust - Blair, NE.

St. Francis Church of Humphrey Cemetery Endowment Trust Fund - Humphrey, NE.

St. Francis of Assisi Church of South Omaha Educational Endowment Trust - Omaha.

St. Francis of Assisi Church of South Omaha Endowment Trust - Omaha.

St. Francis of Assisi Parish Educational Endowment Trust - Neligh, NE.

St. Francis of Assisi Parish Endowment Trust - Neligh, NE.

St. Francis Parish Educational Endowment Trust - Humphrey, NE.

St. Francis Parish Endowment Trust - Humphrey, NE.

St. Gerald Parish Educational Endowment Trust - Ralston, NE.

St. Gerald Parish Endowment Trust - Ralston, NE.

St. Gerald School Educational Endowment Trust - Ralston, NE.

Guardian Angels Grade School Educational Endowment Trust - West Point, NE.

Holy Cross Parish Educational Endowment Trust - Bancroft, NE.

Holy Cross Parish Educational Endowment Trust - Beemer, NE.

Holy Cross Parish Endowment Trust - Bancroft, NE.

Holy Cross Parish Endowment Trust - Beemer, NE.

Holy Cross Parish Endowment Trust - Omaha.

Holy Family Parish Educational Endowment Trust - Decatur, NE.

Holy Family Parish Educational Endowment Trust - Lindsay, NE.

Holy Family Parish Educational Trust - Omaha.

Holy Family Parish Endowment Trust - Decatur, NE.

Holy Family Parish Endowment Trust - Lindsay, NE.
Holy Family Parish Endowment Trust - Omaha.
Holy Ghost Parish Educational Endowment Trust - Omaha.
Holy Ghost Parish Endowment Trust - Omaha.
Holy Name Parish Educational Endowment Trust - Omaha.
Holy Name Parish Endowment Trust - Omaha.
Holy Trinity Church of Colfax, County Parish and Cemetery Endowment Trust Fund - Clarkson, NE.
Holy Trinity Grade School Endowment Trust -
Holy Trinity Parish Educational Endowment Trust - Hartington, NE.
Holy Trinity Parish Educational Endowment Trust - Heun, NE.
Holy Trinity Parish Endowment Trust - Hartington, NE.
Holy Trinity Parish Endowment Trust - Heun, NE.
Holy Trinity Parish of Colfax County Parish and Cemetery Endowment Trust Fund - Heun, NE.
St. Ignatius Parish Educational Endowment Trust - Brunswick, NE.
St. Ignatius Parish Endowment Trust - Brunswick, NE.

Immaculate Conception Parish Educational Endowment Trust - Omaha.
Immaculate Conception Parish Educational Endowment Trust - St. Helena, NE.
Immaculate Conception Parish Endowment Trust - Omaha.
Immaculate Conception Parish Endowment Trust - St. Helena, NE.
St. Isidore Church Endowment Trust - Columbus, NE.
St. Isidore Elementary School Endowment Trust - Columbus, NE.
St. Isidore Parish Educational Endowment Trust - Columbus, NE.
St. James Parish Educational Endowment Trust - Omaha.
St. James Parish Endowment Trust - Omaha.
St. James/Seton School Educational Endowment Fund - Omaha.
St. Joan of Arc Grade School Educational Endowment Trust - Omaha.
St. Joan of Arc Parish Educational Endowment Trust - Omaha.
St. Joan of Arc Parish Endowment Trust - Omaha.
St. John Nepomucene Parish Educational Endowment Trust - Howells, NE.
St. John Nepomucene Parish Endowment Trust - Howells, NE.
St. John Parish Educational Endowment Trust - Omaha.
St. John Parish Endowment Trust - St. John, NE.
St. John Parish Endowment Trust - Omaha.
St. John the Baptist Church Educational Endowment Trust - Fort Calhoun, NE.
St. John the Baptist Church of Petersburg Cemetery Endowment Trust - Petersburg, NE.
St. John the Baptist Parish Educational Endowment Trust - Fordyce, NE.
St. John the Baptist Parish Educational Endowment Trust - Pender, NE.
St. John the Baptist Parish Endowment Trust - Fordyce, NE.
St. John the Baptist Parish Endowment Trust - Fort Calhoun, NE.
St. John the Baptist Parish Endowment Trust - Pender, NE.
St. John the Baptist Parish Endowment Trust - Petersburg, NE.
St. John the Evangelist Parish Educational Endowment Trust - Valley, NE.
St. John the Evangelist Parish Endowment Trust - Valley, NE.
St. John Vianney Church of Millard Parish Endowment Trust - Omaha.
St. John Vianney Parish Educational Endowment Trust - Omaha.
St. Joseph Church Educational Endowment Trust - Atkinson, NE.
St. Joseph Church of Constance Endowment Trust Fund - Crofton, NE.
St. Joseph Parish Educational Endowment Trust - Amelia, NE.
St. Joseph Parish Educational Endowment Trust - Constance, NE.
St. Joseph Parish Educational Endowment Trust - Lyons, NE.
St. Joseph Parish Educational Endowment Trust - Omaha.
St. Joseph Parish Educational Endowment Trust - Pierce, NE.
St. Joseph Parish Educational Endowment Trust - Platte Center, NE.
St. Joseph Parish Educational Endowment Trust - Ponca, NE.
St. Joseph Parish Educational Endowment Trust - Springfield, NE.
St. Joseph Parish Educational Endowment Trust - Walthill, NE.
St. Joseph Parish Educational Endowment Trust - Wisner, NE.
St. Joseph Parish Endowment Trust - Amelia, NE.
St. Joseph Parish Endowment Trust - Atkinson, NE.
St. Joseph Parish Endowment Trust - Constance, NE.
St. Joseph Parish Endowment Trust - Lyons, NE.
St. Joseph Parish Endowment Trust - Omaha.
St. Joseph Parish Endowment Trust - Pierce, NE.
St. Joseph Parish Endowment Trust - Platte Center, NE.
St. Joseph Parish Endowment Trust - Ponca, NE.
St. Joseph Parish Endowment Trust - Springfield, NE.
St. Joseph Parish Endowment Trust - Walthill, NE.
St. Joseph Parish Endowment Trust - Wisner, NE.
St. Lawrence Church of Silver Creek Cemetery Endowment Trust Fund - Silver Creek, NE.
St. Lawrence Parish Educational Endowment Trust - Scribner, NE.
St. Lawrence Parish Educational Endowment Trust - Silver Creek, NE.
St. Lawrence Parish Endowment Trust - Scribner, NE.
St. Lawrence Parish Endowment Trust - Silver Creek, NE.
St. Leo Parish Educational Endowment Trust - Omaha.
St. Leo Parish Educational Endowment Trust - Snyder, NE.
St. Leo Parish Endowment Trust - Omaha.
St. Leo Parish Endowment Trust - Snyder, NE.
St. Leonard Parish Educational Endowment Trust - Madison, NE.
St. Leonard Parish Endowment Trust - Madison, NE.
St. Ludger Parish Educational Endowment Trust - Creighton, NE.
St. Ludger Parish Endowment Trust - Creighton, NE.
St. Margaret Mary Parish Educational Endowment Trust - Omaha.
St. Margaret Mary Parish Endowment Trust - Omaha.

St. Mary Catholic Church Endowment Trust - Spencer, NE.
St. Mary Cemetery Endowment Trust - Spencer, NE.
St. Mary Church Educational Endowment Trust - Bellevue, NE.
St. Mary Church Endowment Trust - Bellevue, NE.
St. Mary Elementary School Endowment Trust - Omaha.
St. Mary of the Seven Dolors Parish Endowment Trust - Osmond, NE.
Mary Our Queen Educational Endowment Trust - Omaha.
Mary Our Queen Parish Endowment Trust - Omaha.
St. Mary Parish Cemetery Endowment Trust - Leigh, NE.
St. Mary Parish Educational Endowment Trust - Hubbard, NE.
St. Mary Parish Educational Endowment Trust - Laurel, NE.
St. Mary Parish Educational Endowment Trust - Omaha.
St. Mary Parish Educational Endowment Trust - Primrose, NE.
St. Mary Parish Educational Endowment Trust - Schuyler, NE.
St. Mary Parish Educational Endowment Trust - Spencer, NE.
St. Mary Parish Educational Endowment Trust - Tabor, NE.
St. Mary Parish Educational Endowment Trust - Wayne, NE.
St. Mary Parish Endowment Trust - Hubbard, NE.
St. Mary Parish Endowment Trust - Laurel, NE.
St. Mary Parish Endowment Trust - Leigh, NE.
St. Mary Parish Endowment Trust - Omaha.
St. Mary Parish Endowment Trust - Primrose, NE.
St. Mary Parish Endowment Trust - Schuyler, NE.
St. Mary Parish Endowment Trust - Tabor, NE.
St. Mary Parish Endowment Trust - Wayne, NE.
St. Mary School Foundation, Inc. - O'Neill, NE.
St. Mary's Church of Tabor Parish and Cemetery Endowment Trust Fund - Dodge, NE.
St. Matthew the Evangelist Parish Endowment Trust - Bellevue, NE.
St. Michael Catholic Church Parish Endowment Trust - Central City, NE.
St. Michael Church Educational Endowment Trust - Albion, NE.
St. Michael Church Endowment Trust - Albion, NE.
St. Michael Educational Endowment Trust - South Sioux City, NE.
St. Michael Parish Educational Endowment Trust - Central City, NE.
St. Michael Parish Educational Endowment Trust - Coleridge, NE.
St. Michael Parish Educational Endowment Trust - Tarnov, NE.
St. Michael Parish Endowment Trust - Coleridge, NE.
St. Michael Parish Endowment Trust - South Sioux City, NE.
St. Michael Parish Endowment Trust - Tarnov, NE.
Mother of Perpetual Help Parish Educational Endowment Trust - Omaha.
Mother of Perpetual Help Parish Endowment Trust - Omaha.
Mt. Michael Foundation, Inc. - Elkhorn, NE.
Music in Catholic Schools Endowment Trust - Omaha.
Norfolk Catholic High School Educational Endowment Trust - Norfolk, NE.
Our Lady of Fatima Parish Educational Endowment Trust - Macy, NE.
Our Lady of Fatima Parish Educational Endowment Trust - Omaha.
Our Lady of Fatima Parish Endowment Trust - Macy, NE.
Our Lady of Fatima Parish Endowment Trust - Omaha.
Our Lady of Guadalupe Educational Endowment Trust - Omaha.
Our Lady of Guadalupe Parish Endowment Trust - Omaha.
Our Lady of Lourdes Parish Educational Endowment Trust - Omaha.
Our Lady of Lourdes Parish Endowment Trust - Omaha.
Our Lady of Lourdes School Educational Endowment Trust - Omaha.
Our Lady of Mt. Carmel Parish Educational Endowment Trust - Tilden, NE.
Our Lady of Mt. Carmel Parish Endowment Trust - Tilden, NE.
St. Patrick Catholic Church Endowment Trust - Fremont, NE.
St. Patrick Foundation, Inc. - O'Neill, NE.
St. Patrick Parish Educational Endowment Trust - Battle Creek, NE.
St. Patrick Parish Educational Endowment Trust -

Fremont, NE.
St. Patrick Parish Educational Endowment Trust - Gretna, NE.
St. Patrick Parish Educational Endowment Trust - Jackson, NE.
St. Patrick Parish Educational Endowment Trust - Tekamah, NE.
St. Patrick Parish Endowment Trust - Battle Creek, NE.
St. Patrick Parish Endowment Trust - Elkhorn, NE.
St. Patrick Parish Endowment Trust - Gretna, NE.
St. Patrick Parish Endowment Trust - Jackson, NE.
St. Patrick Parish Endowment Trust - Omaha.
St. Patrick Parish Endowment Trust - Tekamah, NE.
St. Patrick School Endowment Trust - Elkhorn, NE.
St. Patrick School Tuition Assistance Endowment Trust - Elkhorn, NE.
St. Patrick's Church of Elkhorn Cemetery Endowment Trust Fund - Elkhorn, NE.
St. Paul Parish Educational Endowment Trust - Plainview, NE.
St. Paul Parish Endowment Trust - Plainview, NE.
SS. Peter and Paul Catholic Church Endowment for Howells Community Catholic School - Howells, NE.
SS. Peter and Paul Church Endowment Trust - Omaha.
SS. Peter and Paul Elementary School Educational Endowment Trust - Omaha.
SS. Peter and Paul Parish Educational Endowment Trust - Bow Valley, NE.
SS. Peter and Paul Parish Educational Endowment Trust - Butte, NE.
SS. Peter and Paul Parish Educational Endowment Trust - Howells, NE.
SS. Peter and Paul Parish Educational Endowment Trust - Krakow, NE.
SS. Peter and Paul Parish Educational Endowment Trust - Omaha.
SS. Peter and Paul Parish Endowment Trust - Bow Valley, NE.
SS. Peter and Paul Parish Endowment Trust - Butte, NE.
SS. Peter and Paul Parish Endowment Trust - Howells, NE.
SS. Peter and Paul Parish Endowment Trust - Krakow, NE.
St. Peter Catholic Church Endowment Trust - Fullerton, NE.
St. Peter de Alcantara Parish Educational Endowment Trust - Ewing, NE.
St. Peter de Alcantara Parish Endowment Trust - Ewing, NE.
St. Peter Parish Educational Endowment Trust - Clarks, NE.
St. Peter Parish Educational Endowment Trust - Fullerton, NE.
St. Peter Parish Educational Endowment Trust - Newcastle, NE.
St. Peter Parish Educational Endowment Trust - Omaha.
St. Peter Parish Educational Endowment Trust - Stanton, NE.
St. Peter Parish Endowment Trust - Clarks, NE.
St. Peter Parish Endowment Trust - Newcastle, NE.
St. Peter Parish Endowment Trust - Omaha.
St. Peter Parish Endowment Trust - Stanton, NE.
SS. Philip and James Parish Educational Endowment Trust - St. James, NE.
SS. Philip and James Parish Endowment Trust - St. James, NE.
St. Philip Neri Church Endowment Trust - Omaha.
St. Philip Neri Parish Educational Endowment Trust - Omaha.
St. Pius X Parish Educational Endowment Trust - Omaha.
St. Pius X Parish Endowment Trust - Omaha.
St. Pius X/St. Leo School Educational Endowment Trust - Omaha.
Pope John XXIII Central Catholic High School Endowment Trust - Elgin, NE.
Religious Education Evangelization Commission Endowment Trust - Omaha.
St. Robert Bellarmine Parish Endowment Trust - Omaha.
Roncalli Catholic High School Educational Endowment Trust - Omaha.
Roncalli Catholic High School Scholarship Endowment Trust - Omaha.
St. Rose Church Cemetery Endowment Trust Fund - Crofton, NE.
St. Rose of Lima Parish Educational Endowment Trust - Crofton, NE.
St. Rose of Lima Parish Educational Endowment Trust - Genoa, NE.
St. Rose of Lima Parish Educational Endowment Trust - Hooper, NE.
St. Rose of Lima Parish Endowment Trust - Crofton, NE.
St. Rose of Lima Parish Endowment Trust - Genoa, NE.
St. Rose of Lima Parish Endowment Trust - Hooper, NE.
St. Rose Parish Educational Endowment Trust - Omaha.
St. Rose Parish Endowment Trust - Omaha.
Sacred Heart Elementary School Educational Endowment Trust - Norfolk, NE.
Sacred Heart Parish Educational Endowment Trust - Emerson, NE.
Sacred Heart Parish Educational Endowment Trust - Naper, NE.
Sacred Heart Parish Educational Endowment Trust - Omaha.
Sacred Heart Parish Educational Endowment Trust - Wynot, NE.
Sacred Heart Parish Endowment Trust - Emerson, NE.
Sacred Heart Parish Endowment Trust - Naper, NE.
Sacred Heart Parish Endowment Trust - Norfolk, NE.
Sacred Heart Parish Endowment Trust - Olean, NE.
Sacred Heart Parish Endowment Trust - Omaha.
Sacred Heart Parish Endowment Trust - Wynot, NE.
Sacred Heart Parish Religious Education Endowment Trust - Norfolk, NE.
Sacred Parish Educational Endowment Trust - Olean, NE.
St. Boniface's Church Cemetery Endowment Fund - Menominee, NE.
St. Margaret Mary School Educational Endowment Trust - Omaha.
Scotus Central Catholic High School Endowment Trust - Columbus, NE.
St. John the Baptist Center Maintenance Endowment Trust - Petersburg, NE.
St. John the Baptist Parish Educational Endowment Trust - Petersburg, NE.
St. Patrick Parish Educational Endowment Trust - O'Neill, NE.
St. Theresa of Avila Parish Educational Endowment Trust - Clearwater, NE.
St. Stanislaus Parish Educational Endowment Trust - Duncan, NE.
St. Stanislaus Parish Educational Endowment Trust - Omaha.
St. Stanislaus Parish Endowment Trust - Duncan, NE.
St. Stanislaus Parish Endowment Trust - Omaha.
St. Stephen the Martyr Elementary School Educational Endowment Trust - Omaha.
St. Stephen the Martyr Parish Educational Endowment Trust - Omaha.
St. Stephen the Martyr Parish Endowment Trust - Omaha.
Teachers' Salary Endowment Trust Fund of St. Stephen Church of Omaha - Omaha.
St. Theresa Church of Clearwater Cemetery Endowment Trust Fund - Ewing, NE.
St. Theresa Church of Clearwater Cemetery Endowment Trust Fund - Clearwater, NE.
St. Theresa of Avila Parish Endowment Trust - Clearwater, NE.
St. Thomas More Parish Educational Endowment Trust - Omaha.
St. Thomas More Parish Endowment Trust - Omaha.
St. Thomas More School Educational Endowment Trust - Omaha.
St. Vincent de Paul Parish Educational Endowment Trust - Omaha.
St. Vincent de Paul Parish Endowment Trust - Omaha.
St. Wenceslaus Church Educational Endowment Trust - Dodge, NE.
St. Wenceslaus Church Parish Endowment Trust - Verdigre, NE.
St. Wenceslaus Parish Educational Endowment Trust - Omaha.
St. Wenceslaus Parish Educational Endowment Trust - Verdigre, NE.
St. Wenceslaus Parish Endowment Trust - Dodge, NE.
St. Wenceslaus Parish Endowment Trust - Omaha.
West Catholic Educational Endowment Trust - Fordyce, NE.
West Point Central Catholic High School Activity Center Endowment Trust - West Point, NE.
West Point Central Catholic High School Educational Endowment Trust - West Point, NE.
St. William Parish Educational Endowment Trust - Niobrara, NE.
St. William Parish Endowment Trust - Niobrara, NE.
Institute for Priestly Formation Foundation - 11626 Nicholas St., Omaha, NE 68154 t) (531) 272-8472 mbuttell@priestlyformation.org Mary Buttell, Pres.;
Latino Catholic Scholarship Fund of Omaha - 2222 N. 111 St, Omaha, NE 68164 t) 402-557-5650 smbrommer@archomaha.org www.archomaha.com Shannan M. Brommer, Contact;
Marian High School Endowment Trust - 7400 Military Ave., Omaha, NE 68134 t) 402-571-2618 mhiggins@omahamarian.org Susie Sullivan, Prin.; Mary Higgins, Pres.;
Marian High School Scholarship Endowment Trust - 7400 Military Ave., Omaha, NE 68134 t) 402-571-2618 mhiggins@omahamarian.org Susie Sullivan, Prin.; Mary Higgins, Pres.;
New Cassel Foundation - 900 N. 90th St., #100, Omaha, NE 68114-2704 t) 402-390-5317 cpetrich@newcassel.org; dcoleman@newcassel.org www.newcassel.org Cindy Petrich, Pres.;
Perpetual Care Endowment Trust Fund of Catholic Cemeteries of the Archdiocese of Omaha - 7710 W. Center Rd., Omaha, NE 68124-3199 t) 402-391-3711 dgkeller@catholiccom.com www.catholiccem.com Dcn. Daniel G. Keller, Dir.;
Saint Robert Bellarmine Parish Foundation - 11802 Pacific St., Omaha, NE 68154 t) 402-333-8989 Rev. David G. Reeson, Pst.;

PONCA

St. Joseph's Church of Ponca South Creek Cemetery Endowment Fund - 421 W. 2nd St., Ponca, NE 68770; Mailing: P.O. Box 898, Ponca, NE 68770 t) 402-755-2773 cstwohig@archomaha.org Rev. Andrew L. Sohm, Contact;

SCHUYLER

St. Benedict Center Endowment Fund - 1126 Rd. I, Schuyler, NE 68661; Mailing: P.O. Box 528, Schuyler, NE 68661-0528 t) 402-352-8819 retreats@stbenedictcenter.com www.stbenedictcenter.com Rev. Joel Macul, O.S.B., Prior;
Benedictine Mission House Endowment Trust - 1123 Rd. I, Schuyler, NE 68661; Mailing: P.O. Box 528, Schuyler, NE 68661-0528 t) 402-352-2177 monastery@missionmonks.org www.missionmonks.org Bro. Tobias Dammert, O.S.B., Contact;

ST. COLUMBANS

Columban Fathers Regional Administration - 1902 N. Calhoun St., St. Columbans, NE 68056-0010

t) 402-291-1920 www.columban.org Dan Eminger, Treas.;

St. Columban's Burse Estate Trust -

St. Columban's Central Administration - ; Mailing: P.O. Box 10, St. Columbans, NE 68056-0010 columban.org

St. Columban's Donors/Personal Trust -

St. Columban's Education Trust -

St. Columban's Gift Annuity Trust -

St. Columban's Gift Annuity Trust California -

St. Columban's Masses in Trust -

St. Columban's Medical and Retirement -

St. Columban's Priests Health Program Trust -

St. Columban's Regional Trust -

St. Columban's Retirement Fund Trust -

HOSPITALS / HEALTH SERVICES [HOS]

OMAHA

***Alegent Creighton Health** - 12809 W. Dodge Rd., Omaha, NE 68154 t) (402) 343-4611 missionintegrationmidwest@commonspirit.org www.chihealth.com Includes CHI Health Lakeside Hospital, CHI Health Midlands Hospital & CHI Health Plainview Hospital. E.J. Kuiper, CEO; Andrew J. Santos III, SVP, Mission Integration; Bed Capacity: 400; Asstd. Annu.: 64,000; Staff: 1,000

***Alegent Health - Bergan Mercy Health System** - 7500 Mercy Rd., Omaha, NE 68124; Mailing: c/o McAuley Fogelstrom Center, 12809 W. Dodge Rd., Omaha, NE 68154 t) 402-398-6060 missionintegrationmidwest@commonspirit.org www.chihealth.com Affiliate of Catholic Health Initiatives. Jayleen Casano, Pres.; Andrew J. Santos III, SVP, Mission Integration; Andrew Santos; Bed Capacity: 335; Asstd. Annu.: 70,000; Staff: 2,000

***CHI Health Foundation** - 12809 W. Dodge Rd., Omaha, NE 68154 t) 402-343-4550

***Alegent Health - Immanuel Medical Center** - 6901 N. 72nd St., Omaha, NE 68122 t) 402-572-2121 missionintegration@alegent.org www.chihealth.com Ann Schumacher, Pres.; Andrew J. Santos III, SVP, Mission Integration; Andrew Santos; Bed Capacity: 262; Asstd. Annu.: 38,000; Staff: 1,100

O'NEILL

Avera St. Anthony's Hospital - 300 N. 2nd St., O'Neill, NE 68763; Mailing: PO Box 270, O'Neill, NE 68763 t) 402-336-5131 shannon.miller@avera.org www.avera.org/st-anthonys Sponsored by Sisters of the Presentation of the B.V.M. of Aberdeen, SD & Benedictine Sisters of Sacred Heart Monastery. Shannon Miller, Bus. Mgr.; Bed Capacity: 25; Asstd. Annu.: 67,427; Staff: 203

SCHUYLER

***Alegent Health - Memorial Hospital, Schuyler** - 104 W. 17th St., Schuyler, NE 68661 t) (402) 352-8750 missionintegrationmidwest@commonspirit.org www.chihealth.com Connie Peters, Pres.; Andrew J. Santos III, SVP, Mission Integration; Andrew Santos; Bed Capacity: 10; Asstd. Annu.: 2,700; Staff: 50

WEST POINT

Franciscan Care Services, Inc. - 430 N. Monitor St., West Point, NE 68788-1595 t) 402-372-2404 mhaase@franhealth.org www.franhealth.org Tyler Toline, Admin.; Alisa Brunsing, Contact; Melissa Susan Haase, Contact; Bed Capacity: 25; Asstd. Annu.: 81,026; Staff: 292

MISCELLANEOUS [MIS]

BELLEVUE

Father Edward J. Flanagan Guild - 11909 S. 47th St., Bellevue, NE 68133 c) (402) 650-9404 omahacma.cathmed.org Guild of the Catholic Medical Association. Inspiring medical professionals to imitate Jesus Christ, the Divine Physician. Dr. Michael McCarthy, Contact;

BOYS TOWN

***Father Flanagan League Society of Devotion** - 14057 Flanagan Blvd., Boys Town, NE 68010 t) 402-513-8090 president@fatherflanagan.org www.fatherflanagan.org Steven R. Wolf, Pres.;

CENTRAL CITY

Seraphic Sisters of the Eucharist - 1826 Jackson St., Central City, NE 68826 t) 402-346-6845 hermanasseraficas@gmail.com Sr. Clara Maria Acosta-Millan, S.S.E., Supr.;

ELKHORN

The Institute of the Apostolic Oblates, Inc. (Pro Sanctity Movement) - 11002 N. 204th St., Elkhorn, NE 68022 t) 402-289-1938 prosanctity@prosanctity.org www.prosanctity.org Jessica L. Kary, Dir.;

LA VISTA

***Mercy Housing Midwest** - 7241 Edna Ct., La Vista, NE 68128; Mailing: 1600 Broadway, Ste. 2000, Denver, CO 80202 t) 303-830-3300 Joe Rosenblum, Secy.;

OMAHA

Bethlehem House - 2301 S. 15th St., Omaha, NE 68108 t) (402) 502-9224 director@bethlehemhouseomaha.org www.bethlehemhouseomaha.org We are a maternity home, serving pregnant and parenting women in crisis. TJ Ernst, Exec.;

C.M.G. Agency, Inc. - 10843 Old Mill Rd., Omaha, NE 68154-2600 t) 402-514-2400 ppeterson@catholicmutual.org Paul Peterson, Contact;

Cathedral Arts Project, Inc. - 3900 Webster St., Omaha, NE 68132 t) 402-551-4888 cakrampe@archomaha.org www.cathedralartsproject.org Chris Krampe, Exec. Dir.;

Catholic Jail and Prison Ministry - 2222 N. 111th St., Omaha, NE 68164 t) 402-342-7142 jpmcord@archomaha.org Dcn. Albert W. Aulner Jr., Coordinator;

Catholic Mutual of Canada - 10843 Old Mill Rd., Omaha, NE 68154-2600 t) 402-514-2402 mintrieri@catholicmutual.org Michael A. Intrieri, Contact;

Catholic Relief Insurance Company II - 10843 Old Mill Rd., Omaha, NE 68154 t) 402-514-2400 ppeterson@catholicmutual.org www.catholicmutual.org Paul Peterson, Secy.;

Catholic Umbrella Pool - 10843 Old Mill Rd., Omaha, NE 68154-2600 t) 402-514-2402 mintrieri@catholicmutual.org Michael A. Intrieri, Admin.;

Christ Child Society of Omaha - 1248 S. 10th St., Omaha, NE 68108 t) 402-342-4566 president@christchildsocietyomaha.org www.christchildomaha.org Abby Blair, Admin.; Rev. James E. Keiter, Pres.; Denise Snodgrass, Pres.;

Christian Family Movement (CFM) - 15025 Hawthorne Cir., Omaha, NE 68154 c) 402-212-6409 stevemccullough0@gmail.com www.cfm.org Steve Ray McCullough, Contact;

Christian Life Community-North Central Region (CLC) - 2500 California Plaza, Omaha, NE 68178 t) 402-301-3417 (Rouse); 402-215-4773 (Berry) mbr614@cox.net; jgbclc4221@gmail.com

Christians Encounter Christ - 13324 Meredith Ave., Omaha, NE 68164; Mailing: P.O. Box 27581, Omaha, NE 68127 t) 402-960-1020 corathelen@gmail.com www.cecomaha.org/home.html Cora Thelen, Contact;

The Community of IPF Priests, Inc. - 3833 Webster St., Omaha, NE 68131 t) 402-546-6384 rgabuzda@priestlyformation.org www.priestlyformation.org Clerical Public Association of Priests Rev. Richard J. Gabuzda, Moderator;

Cor Unum Family Inc. - 7323 Shirley St., #101, Omaha, NE 68124 t) 402-933-9812 bwhelan333@gmail.com Rev. Msgr. Bill S. Whelan, Contact;

CUP Re, Inc. - 10843 Old Mill Rd., Omaha, NE 68154 t) 405-514-2402 mintrieri@catholicmutual.org www.catholicumbrellapool.org Michael A. Intrieri, Admin.;

Daughters of the Eternal Father - 5215 Pine St., Omaha, NE 68106-2346 t) 402-342-1032 smafomaha@gmail.com www.omahadef.org Sr. Maryann Frances Polson, DEF, Supr.;

***Discerning Hearts** - 2117 S. 166th St., Omaha, NE 68130; Mailing: P.O. Box 45923, Omaha, NE 68144 t) 402-215-5288 kris@discerninghearts.com www.discerninghearts.com Kris McGregor, Dir.;

Equestrian Order of the Holy Sepulchre of Jerusalem, Northern Lieutenancy - ; Mailing: P.O. Box 540004, Omaha, NE 68154 t) 402-681-3430 info@eohsjnorthern.com eohsjnorthern.com Shawn T. Cleary, Lieutenant;

FOCCUS, Inc. USA (FOCCUS Marriage Ministries) - 2222 N. 111 St., Omaha, NE 68164-3817 t) (877) 883-5422 (Customer Service); (800) 383-0460 (Sales & Product Dev.) foccus@foccusinc.com www.foccusinc.com Pre-Marriage/Marriage Enrichment Inventories Mike Koley, Exec.; Sheila J Simpson, Dir.; Max R Allen, Contact;

Heart of Mary Publishing Company, Incorporated - 5215 Pine St., Omaha, NE 68106-2346 t) 402-342-9265; 402-342-1032 smafomaha@gmail.com www.heartofmaryministry.com Sr. Maryann Frances Polson, DEF, Pres.;

Institute for Priestly Formation - 11626 Nicholas St., Omaha, NE 68154 t) 402-546-6384 ipf@priestlyformation.org www.priestlyformation.org Rev. Brian T. Welter, Dir.;

IXIM, Spirit of Solidarity - 1248 S. 10th St., Omaha, NE 68108 t) 402-934-7706 cpetro@archomaha.org; djzuerlein@archomaha.org archomaha.org/ministries/missions/ixim Rev. Damian J. Zuerlein, Contact;

Legion of Mary - 709 S. 28th St., Omaha, NE 68105 t) 402-341-4560 fatherbroheimer@gmail.com Rev. John P. Broheimer, Dir.;

Magnificat-Omaha N.E. Chapter, Inc. - 1420 S. 126th St., Omaha, NE 68144 t) 402-333-7704 magnificatomaha@gmail.com; kdwyer1111@gmail.com www.magnificatomaha.org Magnificat-Omaha is an archdiocesan-wide Catholic women's organization focused on evangelization. Karen Dwyer, Pres.;

***Maria Regina Cleri** - ; Mailing: P.O. Box 540657, Omaha, NE 68154 t) 402-672-8624 vicherout@gmail.com www.prayingforourpriests.org Vicki Herout, Contact;

***Marianna, Inc.** - 2222 N. 111th St., Omaha, NE 68164; Mailing: 6111 Morrill Ave., Lincoln, NE 68507 t) (402) 466-2752 Rev. Troy J. Schweiger, Pres.; Rev. Daniel R. Andrews, Vice. Pres.; Rev. Christopher K. Kubat, Treas.; Rev. Msgr. Timothy J. Thorburn, Secy.;

The Most AMYable Roman Catholic Lending Library, Inc. - 5404 William St., Omaha, NE 68106-2355 t) 402-553-1837 rogjud@yahoo.com Roger Elliott, Pres.; Judy Elliott, Vice Pres.;

***Notre Dame Housing, Inc.** - 3439 State St., Omaha, NE 68112-1709 t) 402-451-4477 jconnealy@notredamesisters.org www.ndhinc.org Sr. Joy Connealy, ND, Contact;

Notre Dame Living Center, Inc. - 3501 State St., Omaha, NE 68112-1709 t) 402-455-2994 jconnealy@notredamesisters.org www.ndhinc.org Purpose: Provides affordable housing to the elderly, particularly those of low-income status. Sr. Joy Connealy, ND, Contact;

OLG Center for Spirituality and Divine Mercy, Inc. - 1715 N. 102 St., Omaha, NE 68114 c) 402-639-4923 P. Thomas Pogge, Contact;

One Heart One Fire Ministries, Inc. - 5525 L St., Ste. 103, Omaha, NE 68117 c) 402-750-2474 ohofministries@gmail.com; sullivan.kims@gmail.com www.oneheartonefire.org Erin Keller, Pres.;

Saint Paul VI Institute for the Study of Human Reproduction - 6901 Mercy Rd., Omaha, NE 68106 t) 402-390-6600 thomaswhilgersmd@popepaulvi.com www.popepaulvi.com Thomas W. Hilgers, Dir.;

***Sancta Familia Medical Associates Inc.** - 10506 Burt Cir., Omaha, NE 68114-2094 t) 402-991-3393 omahacatholicdoctors.org/ Dr. Peter DeMarco, Mem.; Dr. Michael Dulac, Mem.; Angelina Giles, Mem.; Teresa Kenney, Mem.; Dr. Lloyd Pierre Jr., Mem.; Jordan Radel, Mem.;

Virtus et Veritas Ministries - 356 N. 76th St., Omaha, NE 68114 t) 402-915-0482 info@v2ministries.org v2ministries.org/ Adventure experiences and formation to develop Christlike leaders Toby Korensky, Chair;

PAPILLION

***LIFE Runners** - 12080 S. 78th St., Papillion, NE 68046; Mailing: P.O. Box 460651, Papillion, NE 68046 c) 618-616-0555 exec@liferunners.org www.liferunners.org Pro-Life student organization. Dr. Pat Castle, Pres.;

PLATTE CENTER

Servants of the Heart of the Father - 408 1st St., Platte Center, NE 68653; Mailing: P.O. Box 218, Platte Center, NE 68653 t) 402-910-7111 sothotf1@aol.com www.sothotf.wildapricot.org Rev. Rodney V. Kneifl, Contact;

SPRINGFIELD

Ablaze Ministries, Inc. - 11501 Fairview Rd., Springfield, NE 68059 t) 402-301-3226 ablazeworshipministry@gmail.com; 3persons1god@gmail.com www.ablazeworship.org Rev. Michael B. Voithofer, Pres.;

TEKAMAH

His Global Love, Inc. - 1323 R St., Tekamah, NE 68061-1542 t) 402-374-1692 hisglobalove3@gmail.com Rev. Kevin J. Joyce, Pres.;

MONASTERIES AND RESIDENCES FOR PRIESTS AND BROTHERS [MON]

ELKHORN

Mount Michael Benedictine Abbey - 22520 Mount Michael Rd., Elkhorn, NE 68022-3400 t) 402-289-2541 mliebl@mountmichael.org www.mountmichael.org Rt. Rev. Michael Liebl, O.S.B., Abbot; Bro. Mark Bern, O.S.B., Mem.; Bro. Luke Clinton, O.S.B., Mem.; Bro. William Dokulil, O.S.B., Mem.; Rev. Nathanael Foshage, O.S.B., Pst.; Rev. John Hagemann, O.S.B., Mem.; Bro. Jerome Kmiecik, O.S.B., Mem.; Rev. Daniel Lenz, O.S.B., Mem.; Bro. Roger Mangels, O.S.B., Mem.; Bro. Benedict Mary Ober, O.S.B., Mem.; Rev. Stephen J. Plank, O.S.B., Mem.; Bro. August Schaefer, O.S.B., Mem.; Rev. Louis L. Sojka, O.S.B., Contact; Rt. Rev. Theodore Wolff, O.S.B., Mem.; Brs.: 7; Priests: 7

OMAHA

Jesuit Community at Creighton University - 2500 California Plaza, Omaha, NE 68178 t) 402-280-2776 umiomaha-rector@jesuits.org Rev. Andrew Alexander, S.J., Dir., Online Ministries; Rev. Kent Beausoleil, S.J., Dir., Mission, CHI Health; Rev. Gregory I. Carlson, S.J., Prof.; Arturo Carrillo, SJ, Campus Min.; Rev. James F. Clifton, S.J., Assoc. Dean; Rev. Donald A. Doll, S.J., Prof. Emer.; Bro. Patrick J. Douglas, S.J., Sabbatical; Rev. Amit D'Souza, S.J., Admin.; Rev. Robert J. Dufford, S.J., Spiritual Adv./Care Srvcs.; Rev. Kevin Embach, S.J., Prof.; Rev. Kevin FitzGerald, S.J., Prof.; Rev. Michael Flecky, S.J., Prof.; Rev. Emmanuel Foro, S.J., Prof.; Rev. Lawrence D. Gillick, S.J., Spiritual Adv./Care Srvcs.; Rev. Daniel S. Hendrickson, S.J., Pres.; Rev. Eric Immel, S.J., Admin.; Erin Kast, S.J., Prof.; Rev. Charles T. Kestermeier, S.J., Mem.; Rev. Christopher J Krall, S.J., Prof.; Rev. Jacob Martin, SJ, Prof.; Rev. David Matzko, S.J., Spiritual Adv./Care Srvcs.; Rev. Dennis McNeilly, S.J., Campus Min.; Rev. Thomas Merkel, S.J., Vice Pres., Advancement; Rev. Mahesh Nayak, S.J., Prof.; Rev. Peter P. Nguyen, S.J., Prof.; Josef Raoul Rodriguez, S.J., Prof.; Rev. Martin Renzo Rosales, S.J., Prof.; Patrick Saint-Jean, S.J., Prof.; Rev. Nicholas J. Santos, S.J., Rector; Rev. Kevin C. Schneider, S.J., Spiritual Adv./Care Srvcs.; Rev. John F. Shea, S.J., Prof.; Rev. Thomas A. Simonds, S.J., Prof.; Rev. Matthew Spotts, S.J., Pres.; Rev. Jeffrey Sullivan, S.J., Campus Min.; Rev. Robert J. Tillman, S.J., Counselor; Rev. Matthew S. Walsh, S.J., Assoc. Pst.; Brs.: 1; Priests: 32

Jesuit Residence at Creighton Prep - 7400 Western Ave., Omaha, NE 68114-1878 t) 402-393-1190 Rev. Dennis P. McNeilly, S.J., Vice. Pres.;

SCHUYLER

Benedictine Mission House - Christ the King Priory - 1123 Rd. I, Schuyler, NE 68661; Mailing: P.O. Box 528, Schuyler, NE 68661-0528 t) 402-352-2177 monastery@missionmonks.org www.missionmonks.org Rev. Joel Macul, O.S.B., Prior; Rev. Adam Patras, O.S.B., Subprior; Rev. Thomas Andrew Hillenbrand, O.S.B.; Rev. Volker Futter, O.S.B.; Rev. Thomas Aquinas Leitner, O.S.B.; Rev. Anastasius Reiser, osb; Rev. Paul L. Kasun, O.S.B.; Rev. Jacques A. Missihoun, O.S.B.; Brs.: 3; Priests: 8

ST. COLUMBANS

Missionary Society of St. Columban - 1902 N. Calhoun St., St. Columbans, NE 68056 t) 402-291-1920 directorusa@columban.org; usregionaloffice@columban.org www.columban.org Regional Headquarters and Administration Offices of the Columban Fathers in the United States Rev. Gerald Saenz, S.S.C., U.S. Regional Director; Rev. William Morton, S.S.C., U.S. Regional Vice Director; Rev. John Brannigan, S.S.C., Regional Councilor; Rev. Albert Utzig, S.S.C., Regional Councilor; Rev. Arturo Aguilar, S.S.C., Priest; Rosalia Basada, Lay Missionary; Rev. William Brunner, S.S.C., Priest; Rev. John Buckley, S.S.C., Priest; Rev. John Burger, S.S.C., Priest; Rev. Diego Cabrera, S.S.C., Priest; Rev. Francis Carroll, S.S.C., Priest; Rev. David Clay, S.S.C ., Priest; Rev. John Comiskey, S.S.C., Priest; Rev. Thomas Cusack, S.S.C., Priest; Rev. George DaRoza, S.S.C., Priest; Rev. Michael Donnelly, S.S.C., Priest; Rev. Gerard Dunne, S.S.C., Priest; Rev. James Dwyer, S.S.C., Priest; Rev. Victor Gaboury, S.S.C., Priest; Rev. Thomas Glennon, S.S.C., Priest; Rev. Donald Kelley, S.S.C., Priest; Rev. Ronald Kelso, S.S.C., Priest; Rev. Donald H Kill, S.S.C., Priest; Rev. Charles Lintz, S.S.C., Priest; Rev. John Marley, S.S.C., Priest; Rev. Vincent McCarthy, S.S.C., Priest; Rev. Mark Mengel, S.S.C., Priest; Rev. Robert Mosher, S.S.C., Priest; Rev. Kevin Mullins, S.S.C., Priest; Rev. Dennis O'Mara, S.S.C., Priest; Rev. Gerard O'Shaughnessy, S.S.C., Priest; Rev. Brendan O'Sullivan, S.S.C., Priest; Rev. Richard Pankratz, S.S.C., Priest; Rev. Thomas Reynolds, S.S.C., Priest; Rev. Thomas Shaughnessy, S.S.C., Priest; Rev. James Colm Stanley, S.S.C., Priest; Rev. William Sweeney, S.S.C., Priest; Rev. John Wanaurny, S.S.C., Priest; Priests: 37

NURSING / REHABILITATION / CONVALESCENCE / ELDERLY CARE [NUR]

OMAHA

Mercy Villa - 1845 S. 72nd St., Omaha, NE 68124 t) 402-391-6224 mhilton@sistersofmercy.org Retirement Home for the Sisters of Mercy of the Americas for the West Midwest Community. Sr. Susan Sanders, R.S.M., Vice. Pres.;

New Cassel Retirement Center (School Sisters of St. Francis) - 900 N. 90th St., Omaha, NE 68114 t) 402-393-2277 info@newcassel.org www.newcassel.org Tracy Lichti, Pres.; Asstd. Annu.: 350; Staff: 135

WEST POINT

St. Joseph's Elder Services, Inc. - 540 E. Washington St., West Point, NE 68788 t) 402-372-1118 x520 tloch@fsccm.org; sprokopec@sjeswp.org www.sjeswp.org/ Sr. Louise Hembrecht, Sacr. Min.; Samual Prokopec, Exec.; Asstd. Annu.: 10,060; Staff: 108

St. Joseph's Hillside Villa - 540 E Washington St, West Point, NE 68788 t) (402) 372-1118 sjeswp.org

St. Joseph's Retirement Community - 320 E. Decatur, West Point, NE 68788 t) (402) 372-1118 lhembrecht@sjeswp.org www.sjeswp.org

RETREAT HOUSES / RENEWAL CENTERS [RTR]

LYNCH

Niobrara Valley House of Renewal - 515 S. Fourth St, Lynch, NE 68746 t) 402-569-3433 henderson@threeriver.net Rev. Bernard G Starman, Pst.;

OAKDALE

Tintern Retreat and Resource Center - 52619 843 Rd., Oakdale, NE 68761 t) 402-776-2188 tintern670@gmail.com www.tinternretreatcenter.com Cheryl Veik, Contact;

SCHUYLER

***Saint Benedict Center** - 1126 Rd. I, Schuyler, NE 68661; Mailing: P.O. Box 528, Schuyler, NE 68661-0528 t) 402-352-8819 retreats@stbenedictcenter.com www.stbenedictcenter.com Rev. Thomas Aquinas Leitner, O.S.B., Admin.;

SHRINES [SHR]

GRETNA

Holy Family Shrine - 23132 Pflug Rd., Gretna, NE 68028; Mailing: PO Box 507, Gretna, NE 68028 t) 402-332-4565 www.holyfamilyshrine.com Bridget Chatterson, Office Manager; Matthew Sakowski, Caretaker;

An asterisk (*) denotes an organization that has established tax-exempt status directly with the IRS and is not covered by the USCCB Group Ruling.

Diocese of Orange in California

(Arausicanae in California)

MOST REVEREND KEVIN WILLIAM VANN, J.C.D., D.D.

Bishop of Orange; ordained May 30, 1981; appointed Coadjutor Bishop of Fort Worth May 17, 2005; succeeded July 12, 2005; ordained July 13, 2005; appointed Bishop of Orange September 21, 2012; installed December 10, 2012. Office: Pastoral Center, 13280 Chapman Ave., Garden Grove, CA 92840.

Chancellor's Office: 13280 Chapman Ave., Garden Grove, CA 92840. T: 714-282-3000; F: 714-282-4202.
www.rcbo.org
gdenomie@rcbo.org

ESTABLISHED JUNE 18, 1976.

Square Miles 782.

Comprises the County of Orange in the State of California.

Diocesan Patron: Our Lady of Guadalupe.

Legal Titles: (Prot. No. CD 528-76)

The Roman Catholic Bishop of Orange, a Corporation Sole.

For legal titles of parishes and diocesan institutions, consult the Diocesan Pastoral Service Office.

Most Reverend Timothy Edward Freyer, D.D.
Auxiliary Bishop of Orange; ordained June 10, 1989; appointed Auxiliary Bishop of Orange and Titular Bishop of Strathearn November 23, 2016; consecrated January 17, 2017. Office: Pastoral Center, 13280 Chapman Ave., Garden Grove, CA 92840.

Most Reverend Thanh Thai Nguyen, D.D.
Auxiliary Bishop of Orange; ordained May 11, 1991; appointed Auxiliary Bishop of Orange and Titular Bishop of Acalissus October 6, 2017; consecrated December 19, 2017. Office: Pastoral Center, 13280 Chapman Ave., Garden Grove, CA 92840.

STATISTICAL OVERVIEW

Personnel
Bishop....1
Auxiliary Bishops....2
Retired Bishops....1
Abbots....1
Priests: Diocesan Active in Diocese....127
Priests: Diocesan Active Outside Diocese....5
Priests: Retired, Sick or Absent....52
Number of Diocesan Priests....184
Religious Priests in Diocese....64
Total Priests in your Diocese....248
Extern Priests in Diocese....23
Ordinations:
Religious Priests....2
Transitional Deacons....3
Permanent Deacons in Diocese....153
Total Brothers....5
Total Sisters....289

Parishes
Parishes....57
With Resident Pastor:
Resident Diocesan Priests....47
Resident Religious Priests....5
Without Resident Pastor:
Administered by Priests....5
Missions....5
Pastoral Centers....5

Professional Ministry Personnel:
Brothers....4
Sisters....30
Lay Ministers....194

Welfare
Catholic Hospitals....3
Total Assisted....1,000,000
Health Care Centers....5
Total Assisted....65,021
Homes for the Aged....1
Total Assisted....63
Day Care Centers....2
Total Assisted....459
Specialized Homes....5
Total Assisted....981
Special Centers for Social Services....11
Total Assisted....3,989,795
Other Institutions....2
Total Assisted....191

Educational
Diocesan Students in Other Seminaries....23
Total Seminarians....23
High Schools, Diocesan and Parish....3
Total Students....4,233
High Schools, Private....2
Total Students....2,095
Elementary Schools, Diocesan and Parish....27
Total Students....9,763
Elementary Schools, Private....3
Total Students....1,135
Catechesis / Religious Education:
High School Students....2,891
Elementary Students....7,126
Total Students under Catholic Instruction....27,266
Teachers in Diocese:
Priests....6
Sisters....30
Lay Teachers....1,510

Vital Statistics
Receptions into the Church:
Infant Baptism Totals....8,410
Minor Baptism Totals....386
Adult Baptism Totals....518
Received into Full Communion....856
First Communions....6,547
Confirmations....5,367
Marriages:
Catholic....1,644
Interfaith....269
Total Marriages....1,913
Deaths....3,519
Total Catholic Population....1,360,598
Total Population....3,186,989

LEADERSHIP

Vicar General - t) 714-282-3110 asebastian@rcbo.org Very Rev. Msgr. Stephen S. Doktorczyk, Vicar General for Legal & Canonical Affairs; Rev. Angelos Sebastian, Vicar General & Moderator of the Curia;
Chancellor - t) 714-282-4212 savila@rcbo.org Rev. Daniel B. Reader, Chancellor;
Moderator of the Curia - t) 714-282-3110 Rev. Angelos Sebastian, Vicar General & Moderator of the Curia;
Master of Ceremonies - t) 714-282-3108 mkhong@rcbo.org Rev. Michael Tuan Khong;
Secretary to the Bishop - t) 714-282-3108 mkhong@rcbo.org Rev. Michael Tuan Khong;
Director of Priests' Personnel - t) 714-282-4212 savila@rcbo.org Rev. Daniel B. Reader; Avila Santiago;
Delegate for Consecrated Life - t) 714-282-3068 jpatten@rcbo.org www.rcbo.org/ocvocations/ Joan Patten, A.O., Dir.;
Episcopal Vicar/Rector of Christ Cathedral - t) (714) 282-7860 Rev. Bao Q. Thai (bthai@stceciliak8.org);
Episcopal Vicar for Priests/Ministry to Priest - t) 714-282-3053 bpatterson@rcbo.org Rev. Bruce A. Patterson, Vicar;
Episcopal Vicar for Special Projects - t) 714-282-3000 msgr.mheher@rcbo.org Rev. Msgr. Michael Heher; Rev. Christopher H. Smith;
Office of Evangelization & Faith Formation - t) 714-282-3051; 714-282-3062 kdawson@rcbo.org; sgreco@rcbo.org Dcn. Steve Greco, Dir., Evangelization & Faith Formation (steve@seasirvine.org); Katie Dawson, Dir., Parish Faith Formation;
Diocesan Pastoral Service Office - t) 714-282-6075; 714-282-3043 barmas@rcbo.org Bryan Armas, Coord.;
Tribunal and Office of Canonical Services - t) 714-282-3149 marriagetribunal@rcbo.org Rev. E. Scott Borgman (France), Dir.; Susan Stankis, Moderator;
Judicial Vicar - t) 714-282-3089 sborgman@rcbo.org Rev. E. Scott Borgman (France), Vicar;
Adjutant Judicial Vicars - t) 714-282-3080 Rev. Viet Peter Ho; Rev. Msgr. Douglas J. Cook;
Promoter of Justice - t) 714-282-3081 revj.caronan@rcbo.org Rev. John E. Caronan, O.Praem.; Rev. Sy Uy Nguyen;
Judges - t) 714-282-3080 marriagetribunal@rcbo.org www.rcbo.org/group/canonical-services/ Very Rev. Msgr. Stephen S. Doktorczyk; Rev. Msgr. Douglas J. Cook; Rev. Msgr. Tuan Joseph Pham;
Defenders of the Bond - t) 714-282-3080 Rev. Michael Duc Nguyen, Admin. (mdnguyen@rcbo.org); Rev. John Caronan, O.Praem.; Rev. Sy Uy Nguyen;
Diocesan Tribunal Advocates - t) 714-282-3080 marriagetribunal@rcbo.org www.rcbo.org/group/canonical-services/ Dcn. Thomas McGuine; Dcn. Carl Swanson; Susan Stankis;
Ecclesiastical Notaries - t) 714-282-3080 Susan Stankis, Moderator; Paula Lynn; Stephen Shon;
Archivist - t) (714) 282-6039 Rev. Daniel B. Reader, Chancellor;
Newman Apostolate - t) 949-856-0211 Rev. John Francis Vu, S.J., UCI; Rev. Andres Rafael J. Luevano Jr., Chapman Univ.; Rev. Peter Lavin, A.M., Cal State Fullerton;
Parish Councils and Parish Development - Rev. Daniel B. Reader, Chancellor;
Diaconate - t) 714-282-3037 tsaenz@rcbo.org www.rcbo.org/directory/diaconate/ Dcn. Thomas Saenz, Dir.;
Priests' Personnel Board - t) 714-282-4212 savila@rcbo.org Very Rev. Msgr. Stephen S. Doktorczyk; Rev. Enrique Sera, Chair; Rev. Daniel B. Reader, Ex-Officio;
Oversight Review Board - t) 714-282-3132 mbungcag@rcbo.org James Burns, Chair; Rev. Angelos Sebastian; Very Rev. Msgr. Stephen S. Doktorczyk;
Communications - t) 714-282-3075 www.rcbo.org Jarryd Gonzales, Dir. (jgonzales@rcbo.org); Bradley Zint, Asst. Dir.;
Orange Diocesan Council of Catholic Women - t) 949-345-9130; 949-892-6267 info@odccw.org; mraymond@rcbo.org www.odccw.org Janine Meckler, Pres.; Rev. Christopher Raymond Heath, Spiritual Advisor;
Primary Counsel - t) 714-282-3000 Andrew B. Breidenbach (abreidenbach@tocounsel.com); Alan Martin;
Council of Priests - t) 714-282-3000; 714-282-3132 mbungcag@rcbo.org Most Rev. Kevin W. Vann; Most Rev. Timothy E. Freyer; Most Rev. Thomas Thanh Thai Nguyen;
Observer - t) 714-282-3051; 714-282-3037 frabaca@rcbo.org Rev. Bruce A. Patterson; Dcn. Thomas Saenz; Rev. Alfred S. Baca;
College of Consultors - t) 714-282-3000 mbungcag@rcbo.org Rev. Kevin Sweeney, Pst.; Rev. Martin Hiep Nguyen, Pst.; Rev. Angelos Sebastian, Vicar General and Moderator of the Curia;
Safe Environment - t) 714-282-3125; 714-282-3069 naguero@rcbo.org; eramirez@rcbo.org Norma Aguero, Dir.; Esther Ramirez;
Child & Youth Protection Office - t) 714-282-3125; 714-282-3069 naquero@rcbo.org; eramirez@rcbo.org www.rcbo.org Norma Aguero, Dir.; Esther Ramirez, Prog. Asst./Custodian of Records;
Victim Assistance Coordinator - t) 800-364-3064 Sylvia Palda (palda.sylvia@gmail.com);
Pastoral Care - t) 714-282-4203; 714-282-3040 lji@rcbo.org Linda Ji, Dir.;
Propagation of the Faith - t) 714-282-3058 gwalgenbach@rcbo.org Greg Walgenbach, Dir.;
Council for Consecrated Life - t) 714-282-3068 jpatten@rcbo.org www.rcbo.org/ocvocations/consecrated-life/ Joan Patten, A.O., Dir.; Sr. Rosemary Hoang Nguyen, Mem.; Anne Guadalupe Doan, F.M.V., Mem.;
Diocesan Consultative Schools Board - t) 714-282-3077 ebarisano@rcbo.org Most Rev. Thanh Thai Nguyen; Most Rev. Kevin W. Vann; Dr. Erin Barisano;
Vocations Office - t) 714-282-3046 ocvocations@rcbo.org www.rcbo.org Rev. Brandon Dang, Dir.;
Catholic Campaign for Human Development - t) 714-970-2771 nicks@smdpyl.org Dcn. Nick Sherg, Coord.; Dcn. Phong Nguyen, Mem.; Diane Valenzuela, Mem.;

OFFICES AND DIRECTORS

Archivist - t) 714-282-4257 cheath@rcbo.org; archives@rcbo.org Rev. Christopher Raymond Heath, Dir.; Rev. William F. Krekelberg, Archivist Emeritus;
Boy Scouts/Girl Scouts - t) 714-970-2771 Dcn. Nick Sherg, Chap.; Armando Cervantes, Contact;
Catecumenate - t) 714-282-3041; 714-282-3040 worship.rcbo.org Dcn. Modesto Cordero, Dir.; Ismael Arbizo, Project Coord.;
Catholic Charities of Orange - t) 714-347-9605; 714-347-9680 eroy@ccoc.org ccoc.org/ Ellen Roy, Exec.;
Catholic Deaf Center - t) 714-282-3000 occatholicdeaf.org/ Rev. Steven Correz, Dir.;
Catholic Relief Services - t) 714-282-3058 gwalgenbach@rcbo.org www.rcbo.org Greg Walgenbach, Dir.;
Cemeteries - t) 714-282-3101 mwesner@rcbo.org www.rcbo.org/directories/cemeteries/ Michael Wesner, Dir.;
Cursillo Movement - t) 714-974-1416 Dcn. Doug Cook, Exec.; Dcn. Ramon Leon, Dir.; Rev. Thanh-Tai P. Nguyen, Spiritual Adv./Care Srvcs.;
Design and Renovation Committee - t) 714-282-3041 www.rcbo.org Rev. Timothy Freyer; Dcn. Modesto Cordero, Chair; Rev. Cheeyoon Chun (fr.cheeyoon@hforange.org);
Detention Ministry/Restorative Justice - t) 714-282-4261 flapuzza@rcbo.org www.rcbo.org Fred LaPuzza, Dir.;
Diocesan Finance Council - t) 714-282-6037 oruvalcaba@rcbo.org Tom Croal, Chair; Thomas Greeley, Vice Chair; Steve Pellegrini, Chief Financial & Admin. Officer (spellegrini@rcbo.org);
Director of Finance - t) 714-282-6037 oruvalcaba@rcbo.org Steve Pellegrini, Chief Financial & Admin. Officer (spellegrini@rcbo.org); Oralia Ruvalcaba;
Ecumenical and Interreligious Affairs - t) 714-282-3079 ebecker@rcbo.org Rev. Edward Becker, Episcopal Vicar; Anthony Vultaggio, Chair; Michelle O'Donoghue, Secy.;
Engaged Encounter - t) 714-455-9175 registration@eeweekend.org Jerry DeSantos; Eloise DeSantos;
The Family of Nazareth - t) 714-538-5161 John Mung Le; Marie Lan Le (johnle11@cox.net);
Holy Childhood - t) 714-282-3058 gwalgenbach@rcbo.org Greg Walgenbach, Dir.;
Legion of Mary - Tony Cheng, Pres. (tony_+_cheng@yahoo.com); Paul Yung, Vice. Pres. (yungpaul180@gmail.com);
English - Gudulia Salas Flores, Pres.; Natalie Tung, Pres.; Eugenia Ukpo, Pres.;
Korean - Ku (Gabriel) Hak Yon, Pres.; Sukok (Rosa) Park, Pres.; Francisco Woo, Pres.;
Vietnamese - Michael Thuc Vu, Pres.;
Life, Justice and Peace - t) 714-282-3058 gwalgenbach@rcbo.org Greg Walgenbach, Dir.;
Liturgical Commission - t) 714-282-3041 Dcn. Tom Saenz, Ex-Officio; Dcn. Modesto Cordero, Ex-Officio; Most Rev. Timothy E. Freyer, Ex-Officio;
Marriage Encounter - English - t) 714-873-5136 Joe Cruz; Teri Cruz (cruzclan2@cox.net);
Marriage Encounter - Spanish - Encuentro Matrimonial Mundial - t) 714-604-7938 Alfonso Cedillo; Enedina Cedillo (acedillofam@yahoo.com);
Mental Health Ministry - t) 714-620-8810 Louise Dunn, Dir. (ldunn@newhopenow.org);
Natural Family Planning - t) 714-282-4203 lji@rcbo.org Linda Ji, Dir.;
Office of Hispanic Ministry - t) 714-282-3066 acervantes@rcbo.org Armando Cervantes, Dir.;
Real Estate & Asset Management Advisory Sub-Committee to Diocesan Finance Council - t) 714-282-3032 ahoover@rcbo.org Andrew Hoover; Tim Psomas, Chair; Randy Sperry, Vice Chair;
Retrouvaille - English - t) 949-510-4646 Brad Griffiths; Dawn Griffiths (dawngriffiths@cox.net);
Risk Management and Insurance Services - t) 714-282-3092 amorales@rcbo.org Amber Morales, Mgr.;
Vietnamese Community Couples Retreat - t) 714-538-5161 John Mung Le; Marie Lan Le (johnle11@cox.net);
Worship - t) 714-282-3041 www.rcbo.org/group/office-for-worship/ Dcn. Modesto Cordero, Dir.;

PARISHES, MISSIONS, AND CLERGY

STATE OF CALIFORNIA

ALISO VIEJO

Corpus Christi - 27231 Aliso Viejo Pkwy., Aliso Viejo, CA 92656 t) 949-389-9008 corpuschristi@corpuschristialisoviejo.org www.avcatholics.org Rev. Timothy Ramaekers, Pst.; CRP Stds.: 92

ANAHEIM

St. Anthony Claret - 1450 E. La Palma Ave., Anaheim, CA 92805 t) 714-776-0270; 714-778-1399 (CRP) sac@stanthonymaryclaret.org www.stanthonymaryclaret.org Marisela Cabrera, DRE; Dcn. August Mones; Dcn. Salvador Sanchez; Rev. Bill T. Cao, Pst.; Dcn. Carlos Lozada; Socorro Valles, OCIA Coord.; Rev. Jaime Hernandez, Par. Vicar; CRP Stds.:

425

St. Boniface - 120 N. Janss St., Anaheim, CA 92805 t) 714-956-3110; 714-772-3060 (CRP) fguzman@saint-boniface.org stbonifaceonline.org Rev. Edward L. Poettgen Jr., Pst.; Rev. Salvador Landa, Par. Vicar; Rev. Joseph Ngu Cong Truong, Par. Vicar; Fortunato M Guzman, DRE; CRP Stds.: 563

St. Justin Martyr - 2050 W. Ball Rd., Anaheim, CA 92804 t) 714-774-2595; 714-535-6111 (CRP) info@saintjustin.org www.saintjustin.org/ Rev. Sergio Ramos, Pst.; Rev. Venancio Amidar, Par. Vicar; Rev. Alejandro Nicolat Herrera, Par. Vicar; Rev. Msgr. Kerry Beaulieu, In Res.; Rev. John Monestero, In Res.; Dcn. Jose Ferreras; Dcn. Kalini Folau; Dcn. Carlos Navarro; Dcn. Ramon Leon; CRP Stds.: 657

St. Justin Martyr School - (Grades PreK-8) 2030 W. Ball Rd., Anaheim, CA 92804 t) 714-772-4902 info@sjm-k8.com www.sjm-k8.com Elva Pelayo, Prin.;

Sacred Heart - 10852 Harcourt Ave., Anaheim, CA 92804

San Antonio de Padua Del Canon Church - 5800 E. Santa Ana Canyon Rd., Anaheim, CA 92807 t) 714-974-1416 admin@sanantoniochurch.org sanantoniochurch.org Rev. John Neneman, Pst.; Rev. Tuan John Nguyen, Par. Vicar; Dcn. Doug Cook; Dcn. Kevin Durkin; Dcn. Russell Millspaugh; CRP Stds.: 352

BREA

St. Angela Merici - 585 Walnut St., Brea, CA 92821 t) 714-529-8121 susan.degrasse@stangelabreachurch.org stangelabreachurch.org Dcn. Benjamin Flores; Rev. Francis Ng, Par. Vicar; Rev. Bruce A. Patterson, In Res.; Rev. Randy Guillen, Admin.; CRP Stds.: 454

St. Angela Merici School - (Grades PreK-8) 575 S. Walnut Ave., Brea, CA 92821 t) 714-529-6372 Nancy Windisch, Prin.;

BUENA PARK

St. Pius V - 7691 Orangethorpe Ave., Buena Park, CA 90621 t) 714-522-2193; 714-522-3971 (CRP) sre@stpius5.org www.stpiusvbp.org Rev. Martin Duc Tran, Par. Vicar; Rev. Eric Viray, Par. Vicar; Rev. Paw Lwin, Pst.; Dcn. Fidel Rodriguez; Dcn. Rick Torres; CRP Stds.: 401

St. Pius V School - (Grades PreK-8) 7681 Orangethorpe Ave., Buena Park, CA 90621 t) 714-522-5313 stpius5school.net Sandy Lewis, Prin.;

CAPISTRANO BEACH

San Felipe de Jesus - 26010 Domingo Ave., Capistrano Beach, CA 92624 See St. Edward the Confessor, Dana Point.

COSTA MESA

St. Joachim - 1964 Orange Ave., Costa Mesa, CA 92627 t) 949-574-7400 www.stjccm.org Rev. Michael P. Hanifin, Pst.; Rev. Miguel Angel Carabez, Par. Vicar; Dcn. Francisco Javier Martin; Dcn. Martin Ruiz; Dcn. Bob Ward; CRP Stds.: 349

St. Joachim School - (Grades PreSchool-8) t) 949-574-7411 Lisa Gilbert, Prin.;

St. John the Baptist - 1015 Baker St., Costa Mesa, CA 92626 t) 714-540-2214; 714-546-4102 (CRP) www.sjboc.org Rev. Pascal B. Nguyen, O.Praem., Pst.; Rev. Benedict Solomon, O.Praem., In Res.; Rev. Godfrey E. Bushmaker, O.Praem., Par. Vicar; Rev. Brendan Hankins, O.Praem., Par. Vicar; Rev. Damien V. Giap, O.Praem., Rector; Rev. Andrew P. Tran, O.Praem., Par. Vicar; Brandon Tait, Youth Min.; Christina Ford, DRE; Sr. Faustina Nguyen, DRE; Sr. Bertha Rafael, M.C., DRE; CRP Stds.: 300

St. John the Baptist School - (Grades PreK-8) 1021 Baker St., Costa Mesa, CA 92626 t) 714-557-5060 www.sjbschool.net Paula Viles, Prin.; Jeff Urbaniec, Vice Prin.;

CYPRESS

St. Irenaeus - 5201 Evergreen Ave., Cypress, CA 90630 t) 714-826-0760; 714-826-1140 (CRP) parish@sticypress.org www.sticypress.org Rev. Binh T. Nguyen, Pst.; Rev. Aaron Galvizo, Par. Vicar; Rev. Mauro Trujillo, Par. Vicar; Dcn. Jose Campos; Dcn. Del Davis; Dcn. Jose Pulido; Dcn. Jerry Pyne; Cassandra Locano, RCIA Coord.; CRP Stds.: 321

St. Irenaeus School - (Grades PreK-8) 9201 Grindlay St., Cypress, CA 90630 t) 714-827-4500 office@stischoolcypress.org www.stischoolcypress.org Stella Costello, Prin.;

DANA POINT

St. Edward the Confessor - 33926 Calle La Primavera, Dana Point, CA 92629 t) 949-496-1307; 949-496-6011 (CRP) stedward.com Rev. Philip T. Smith, Pst.; Rev. Marco Hernandez Quintanilla, O.F.M., Par. Vicar; Rev. Joseph Vincent Squillacioti, Par. Vicar; Dcn. Juan Carlos Castro; Dcn. Victor Samano; Dcn. Michael Stock; CRP Stds.: 800

St. Edward the Confessor School - (Grades PreSchool-8) 33866 Calle La Primavera, Dana Point, CA 92629 t) 949-496-1241 Catherine Muzzy, Prin.;

San Felipe de Jesus - 26010 Domingo Ave., Capistrano Beach, CA 92624

FOUNTAIN VALLEY

Holy Spirit - 17270 Ward St., Fountain Valley, CA 92708 t) 714-963-1811; 714-963-7871 (CRP) office@holyspiritfv.org; faithformation@holyspiritfv.org holyspiritfv.org Rev. Joseph Thuong Tran, Pst.; Rev. Wayne Adajar, Par. Vicar; Rev. John Duy Nguyen, Par. Vicar; Dcn. Paul Manh Van Mai;

FULLERTON

St. Juliana Falconieri - 1316 N. Acacia Ave., Fullerton, CA 92831 t) 714-879-1965 info@stjulianachurch.org www.stjulianachurch.org Dcn. Darrell Miller; Dcn. Tom Saenz; Rev. Michael M. Pontarelli, O.S.M., Pst.; Gerrick Gamboa, Youth Min.; James Abowd, Dir.; CRP Stds.: 430

St. Juliana Falconieri School - (Grades PreK-8) 1320 N. Acacia Ave., Fullerton, CA 92831 t) 714-871-2829 info@stjulianaschool.org www.stjulianaschool.org Manuel Gonzalez, Prin.;

St. Mary's - 400 W. Commonwealth Ave., Fullerton, CA 92832 t) 714-525-2500 secretary@saintmarysfullerton.org www.saintmarysfullerton.org Rev. Steven Correz, Pst.; Rev. David Otto, Par. Vicar; Rev. Hector Bedoya, Par. Vicar; Rev. Enrique J. Sera, Pastor Emer.; Dcn. Carlos Gonzalez; Dcn. Tony Mercado; CRP Stds.: 433

St. Philip Benizi - 235 S. Pine Dr., Fullerton, CA 92833 t) 714-871-3610; 714-870-0561 (CRP) spbenizi@gmail.com www.benizi.us Rev. Dennis Kriz, O.S.M., Pst.; Rev. David D Gallegos, OSM, Par. Vicar; Rev. Sebastian Mulu, OSM, Par. Vicar; Dcn. Richard Doubledee; Dcn. Richard Glaudini; Dcn. Antonio Luna; Rev. Gerald M. Horan, O.S.M., In Res.; CRP Stds.: 197

GARDEN GROVE

Christ Cathedral Parish - 13280 Chapman Ave., Tower of Hope Bldg, Garden Grove, CA 92840; Mailing: 12141 S. Lewis St., Tower Of Hope Bldg, Garden Grove, CA 92840 t) 714-971-2141; 714-971-2091 (CRP) christcathedralca.org/ Rev. Bao Q. Thai, Rector; Rev. Juan Navarro-Sanchez, Par. Vicar; Dcn. Frank Chavez; Dcn. Modesto Cordero; Dcn. Cruz Pleitez; Rev. Quyen Truong, Par. Vicar; Dcn. Joseph Khiet Nguyen; Rev. Daniel B. Reader, In Res.; Gemma Thomsen, Bus. Mgr.; CRP Stds.: 573

St. Columban - 10801 Stanford Ave., Garden Grove, CA 92840 t) 714-534-1174 bphillips@saintcolumbanchurch.org saintcolumbanchurch.org Rev. Benjamin Diep Hoang, Par. Vicar; Rev. Paul Hoa Duy Vu, Par. Vicar; Rev. Msgr. Tuan Joseph Pham, Pst.; Bridget Phillips, Bus. Mgr.; CRP Stds.: 782

St. Columban School - (Grades PreSchool-8) 10855 Stanford Ave., Garden Grove, CA 92840 t) 714-534-3947 office@saintcolumbanschool.com www.saintcolumbanschool.com Barbara Barreda, Prin.; Stds.: 351; Sr. Tchrs.: 2; Scholastics: 1; Lay Tchrs.: 13

HUNTINGTON BEACH

St. Bonaventure - 16400 Springdale St., Huntington Beach, CA 92649 t) 714-846-3359; 714-846-1187 (CRP) phyllis@stbonaventure.org; debbie@stbonaventure.org www.stbonaventure.org Rev. Joseph Knerr, Pst.; Rev. Ruben Ruiz, Par. Vicar; Rev. Hoa Tran, Par. Vicar; Dcn. John Davies; Dcn. Joseph Sullivan; Dcn. Vincent Tran; Dcn. Bill Beam; Debbie Doke, DRE; CRP Stds.: 479

St. Bonaventure School - (Grades PreK-8) 16390 Springdale St., Huntington Beach, CA 92649; Mailing: 16377 Bradbury Ln., Huntington Beach, CA 92647 t) 714-846-2472 office@stbonaventureschool.org www.stbonaventureschool.org Janice Callender, Prin.; Kim White, Prin.; Cathy Smith, Registrar; Colleen Hoffmann, Bus. Mgr.; Kathi Vogel, Librn.;

St. Mary's by the Sea - 321 10th St., Huntington Beach, CA 92648 t) 714-536-6913 officesmbs@gmail.com www.stmarysbythesea.net/ Sr. Catherine Nguyen, LHC, DRE; Rev. Quang Vinh Chu, Pst.; CRP Stds.: 30

Sts. Simon & Jude - 20444 Magnolia St., Huntington Beach, CA 92646 t) 714-962-3333 Rev. Reynold Furrell, Pst.; Rev. Michael Rizzo, Par. Vicar; Dcn. Matt Calabrese; Andrew Watson, Youth Min.; CRP Stds.: 453

Sts. Simon & Jude School - (Grades PreK-8) 20400 Magnolia St., Huntington Beach, CA 92646 t) 714-962-4451 school@ssjschool.org www.ssj.org/school/ Denise Grant, Prin.;

St. Vincent de Paul - 8345 Talbert Ave., Huntington Beach, CA 92646 t) 714-842-3000 svdp@svdphb.org; reled@svdphb.org www.svdphb.org Rev. Kevin Sweeney, Pst.; Rev. William Brewer Goldin, Vicar; Rev. Jerome T. Karcher, Pastor Emer.; Dcn. Angelo Giambrone; Dcn. Gerard Wallace;

IRVINE

St. Elizabeth Ann Seton - 9 Hillgate, Irvine, CA 92612-3265 t) 949-854-1000 x221 www.seasirvine.org Dcn. Steve Greco; Rev. Brandon Dang, In Res.; Rev. Paul Trinh, Pst.; Rev. Robert L. Stone, Par. Vicar; Dcn. Dave Tiemeier, RCIA Coord.;

Queen of Life Chapel - 2532 Dupont Dr., Irvine, CA 92612 t) 949-474-7368 tbush@bushfirm.com

St. John Neumann - 5101 Alton Pkwy., Irvine, CA 92604-8605 t) 949-559-4006 parishoffice@sjnirvine.org www.sjnirvine.org Rev. Michael Fitzpatrick, Par. Vicar; Rev. Jeffrey A. Droessler, Pst.; Dcn. John Erdag; Dcn. Alexander Menez; Miles Vose, Youth Min.; Rhiannon Jensen, DRE; Jocelyn Lacson, Bus. Mgr.; CRP Stds.: 209

St. Thomas More - 51 Marketplace, Irvine, CA 92602 t) 949-551-8601 stephanie@stmirvine.org www.stmirvine.org Rev. Eugene Lee, Pst.; Rev. Kiet A. Ta, Par. Vicar; Dcn. Tin Nguyen; Dcn. Bernardo Ocampo; Dcn. Tony Patronite; Dcn. Leonard Sun; Barbara Catiller, DRE; Stephanie Miller, Bus. Mgr.;

LA HABRA

Our Lady of Guadalupe - 900 W. La Habra Blvd., La Habra, CA 90631 t) 562-691-0533 nhuerta@olglahabra.org; ebecker@olglahabra.org www.olglahabra.org Rev. Edward Becker, Pst.; Rev. Jakub Mackowicz, Par. Vicar; Rev. Leonel M. Vargas, Par. Vicar; Dcn. Jose Manuel Chavez; Dcn. Chuck Doidge; CRP Stds.: 202

Our Lady of Guadalupe School - (Grades PreK-8) 920 W. La Habra Blvd, La Habra, CA 90631 t) (562) 691-0533

LADERA RANCH

Holy Trinity - 1600 Corporate Dr., Ladera Ranch, CA 92694 t) 949-218-3131 reception@holytrinityladera.org www.holytrinityladera.org Rev. Michael St. Paul, Pst.; Rev. Charles Tran, Par. Vicar; Dcn. Anthony Palazzolo; Dcn. Frank Chavez; Dcn. Randall McMahon; Lyssa Rollolazo, Director of Parish Life & Faith Formation; Emmanuel Perez, Youth Min.; Karina Lopez, Faith Formation Coordinator; Annadelia G Moreno, Receptionist; Joanne M Singer, Part-Time Receptionist; Daniel Catania, Bus. Mgr.; CRP Stds.: 500

LAGUNA BEACH

St. Catherine of Siena - 1042 Temple Ter., Laguna

Beach, CA 92651 t) 949-494-9701 www.stcathchurch.org Rev. Patrick N. Rudolph, Pst.; CRP Stds.: 22

LAGUNA NIGUEL

St. Timothy - 29102 Crown Valley Pkwy., Laguna Niguel, CA 92677 t) 949-249-4091 www.st-timsrc.org Rev. Patrick A. Moses, Pst.; Dcn. Kenneth Hobbs; Rev. Msgr. John Urell, Pastor Emer.;

LAGUNA WOODS

St. Nicholas - 24252 El Toro Rd., Laguna Woods, CA 92637 t) 949-837-1090; 949-837-7676 (CRP) frgblais@st-nicholaschurch.org st-nicholaschurch.org Rev. Martin Phuoc Bui, Par. Vicar; Rev. Phuong Nguyen, Par. Vicar; Rev. George P. Blais, Pst.; Dcn. Carlos Pineda; Dcn. Gerardo DeSantos; Dcn. Chau Tran; Most Rev. Thanh Thai Nguyen, In Res.; CRP Stds.: 155

LAKE FOREST

Santiago de Compostela - 21682 Lake Forest Dr., Lake Forest, CA 92630 t) 949-951-8599 www.sdccatholic.org Rev. Thomas Paul K. Naval, Pst.; Rev. Martin Vu, Par. Vicar; Dcn. Daniel Diesel; Gloria Fetta, DRE; Lyanamar Medina, DRE; Tom Haas, RCIA Coord.; Dcn. Manuel Espitia;

LOS ALAMITOS

St. Hedwig - 11482 Los Alamitos Blvd., Los Alamitos, CA 90720 t) 562-296-9000 info@sainthedwig.org www.sainthedwig.org Rev. Quan Dinh Tran, Admin.; Rev. David Klunk, Par. Vicar; Dcn. Henry Eagar; Dcn. Gary Mucho; Dcn. Larry Hurst; CRP Stds.: 256

St. Hedwig School - (Grades K-8) 3591 Orangewood Ave., Los Alamitos, CA 90720 t) 562-296-9060 Erin Rucker, Prin.;

MISSION VIEJO

St. Kilian - 26872 Estanciero Dr., Mission Viejo, CA 92691 t) 949-586-4440; 949-586-4550 (CRP) office@stkilianchurch.org; skre@stkilianchurch.org stkilianmissionviejo.org Rev. Brandon Robert Lopez, Par. Vicar; Rev. Angelos Sebastian, Pst.; Rev. Tuan Joseph Pham, Par. Vicar; Dcn. Bob Kelleher; Dcn. Mark Martin; Dcn. John Silberstein; CRP Stds.: 555

NEWPORT BEACH

Our Lady of Mount Carmel - 1441 W. Balboa Blvd., Newport Beach, CA 92661-1163 t) 949-673-3775; 949-673-2719 (CRP) rhallas@olmc.net olmc.net Rev. Msgr. Douglas J. Cook, Pst.; Dcn. Stephen Mutz; Rev. Sean Condon (Ireland), In Res.; Rev. Kenneth A. Schmit, In Res.; John Bruscia, DRE; Greg Kelley, DRE; CRP Stds.: 203

St. John Vianney - 314 Marine Ave., Balboa Island, CA 92662-1206 jshaw@olmc.net

Our Lady Queen of Angels - 2046 Mar Vista Dr., Newport Beach, CA 92660 t) 949-644-0200; 949-219-1411 (CRP) inquiry@olqa.org www.olqa.org Rev. Steven Sallot, Pst.; Rev. Thomas Tran, S.V.D., Par. Vicar; Monique Lai, Dir.; Rev. Tony Key Park, Par. Vicar; Dcn. Charles Boyer; Dcn. Jorge Sanchez; Rev. Msgr. Wilbur Davis, In Res.; CRP Stds.: 317

Our Lady Queen of Angels School - (Grades PreK-8) t) 949-644-1166 jtipton@olqa.org www.olqaschool.org Dr. Julie Tipton, Prin.; Stds.: 463; Lay Tchrs.: 34

ORANGE

Holy Family Catholic Church - 566 S. Glassell St., Orange, CA 92866 t) 714-639-2900; 714-639-2900 x235 (CRP) parish@hforange.org www.hforange.org Rev. Sy Uy Nguyen, Pst.; Rev. Cheeyoon Chun, Par. Vicar; Rev. Rudolph Alumam, Par. Vicar; Dcn. Pedro Cardenas; Dcn. David Hernandez; Dcn. Gerhard P. Stadel; CRP Stds.: 295

Cathedral of the Holy Family School - (Grades PreSchool-8) 530 S. Glassell St., Orange, CA 92866 t) 714-538-6012 www.holyfamilyk8.org/ Marie Ubl, Prin.; Elena Castillo, Librn.;

La Purisima - 11712 N. Hewes St., Orange, CA 92869 t) 714-633-5800; 714-633-5344 (CRP) Rev. Gaston Mendiola Arroyo, Par. Vicar; Dcn. Ricardo Barraza; Areli Espinoza, Faith Formation Coordinator; Alondra Larios Jimenez, Office Manager; Luis Zuniga, Confirmation Coordinator; Rev. Thomas De Nguyen, Par. Vicar; Dcn. Timothy O'Donoghue; Rev. Martin Hiep Nguyen, Pst.; Dcn. David Tran; Rev. Ismael Silva, In Res.; CRP Stds.: 658

La Purisima School - (Grades PreK-8) t) 714-633-5411 rramirez@lpcs.net; vserrano@lpcs.net www.lpcs.net Rosa Ramirez, Prin.; Viridiana Serrano, Bus. Mgr.; Sandra Ramirez, Office Manager;

St. Norbert - 300 E. Taft Ave., Orange, CA 92865 t) 714-637-4360 info@stnorbertchurch.org www.stnorbertchurch.org Rev. John W. Moneypenny, Pst.; Rev. Nam Doan, Par. Vicar; Dcn. Juan Espinoza; Dcn. Carlos Munoz; Dcn. Richard Purpura; CRP Stds.: 350

St. Norbert School - (Grades PreSchool-8) t) 714-637-6822 jciccoianni@saintnorbertschool.org www.saintnorbertschool.org Joseph Ciccoianni, Prin.;

PLACENTIA

St. Joseph - 717 N. Bradford Ave., Placentia, CA 92870-4514 t) 714-528-1487 stjosephplacentia.org Rev. Miguel A. Hernandez, Pst.; Rev. Martin Phuoc Bui, Par. Vicar; Rev. Msgr. Donald Romito, In Res.; Rev. Eamon O'Gorman, In Res.; Dcn. Ken Kleckner; Dcn. Jim Merle; Dcn. Victor Valenzuela; Dcn. Jorge Ramirez; Summer Pongetti, DRE;

St. Joseph School - (Grades PreSchool-8) 801 N. Bradford Ave., Placentia, CA 92870-4515 t) 714-528-1794 www.sjsplacentia.org Jo Ann Telles, Prin.;

RANCHO SANTA MARGARITA

San Francisco Solano Catholic Church - 22082 Antonio Pkwy., Rancho Santa Margarita, CA 92688-1993 t) 949-589-7767 info@sfsolano.org www.solanocatholic.org Dcn. Jeffery Kosidowski; Rev. Duy T. Le, Pst.; Rev. Aristotle Quan, Par. Vicar; Dcn. Carl Swanson; CRP Stds.: 567

SAN CLEMENTE

Our Lady of Fatima - 105 N. La Esperanza, San Clemente, CA 92672 t) 949-492-4101 fatima@olfchurch.net www.olfchurch.net Rev. Antonio Lopez-Flores, Pst.; Rev. Benjamin Tran, Par. Vicar; Dcn. Victor Samano; Dcn. Albert Scaduto; Rosa Rama, DRE; Dcn. Carl Swanson, Bus. Mgr.;

Our Lady of Fatima School - (Grades PreK-8) t) 949-492-7320 egosnell@olfschool.net www.olfschool.net Brett Minter, Prin.;

SAN JUAN CAPISTRANO

Mission Basilica - San Juan Capistrano - 31520 Camino Capistrano, San Juan Capistrano, CA 92675 t) 949-234-1360 www.missionparish.org The Parish includes Historic Mission San Juan Capistrano Dcn. Humberto Ramirez; Rev. Msgr. J. Michael McKiernan, Pst.; Rev. Manuel Lopez, Par. Vicar; Dcn. Gary Griffin; Rev. Msgr. Arthur Holquin, In Res.; Matthew Cereghino, Youth Min.; Martha Arenas, DRE; CRP Stds.: 180

Mission Basilica - San Juan Capistrano School - (Grades PreSchool-8) 31641 El Camino Real, San Juan Capistrano, CA 92675 t) 949-234-1385 ddauria@mbssjc.org www.missionbasilicaschool.org Alycia Beresford, Prin.;

SANTA ANA

St. Anne - 1344 S. Main St., Santa Ana, CA 92707; Mailing: 109 W. Borchard Ave., P.O. Box 2425, Santa Ana, CA 92707 t) 714-835-7434; 714-835-7435; 714-542-1213 (CRP) stannecc@gmail.com www.saparish.org Rev. Mario Juarez, Admin.; Rev. Jose Suarez (Mexico), Par. Vicar; Dcn. Francisco Martinez; Dcn. Michael Mendiola; Dcn. Salvador Del Real; Monica Aguilar, Bus. Mgr.; Angelica Gutierrez, DRE; CRP Stds.: 182

St. Anne School - (Grades PreSchool-8) 1324 S. Main St., Santa Ana, CA 92707 t) 714-542-9328 Sr. Teresa Lynch, C.S.J., Prin.;

St. Barbara Catholic Church - 730 S. Euclid St., Santa Ana, CA 92704 t) 714-775-7733; 714-775-9464; 714-775-9475 (CRP) www.saintbarbarachurch.org Rev. Danh Ngoc Trinh, Par. Vicar; Rev. Anthony Hien Vu, Par. Vicar; Dcn. Hao Nguyen, DRE; Rev. Joseph Tuan Pham, Pst.; Rev. Ramon Cisneros, Par. Vicar;

St. Barbara Catholic School - (Grades PreK-8) 5306 W. McFadden Ave., Santa Ana, CA 92704 t) 714-775-9477 sbs@stbarbara.com www.stbarbara.com Melissa Baroldi, Prin.;

Christ Our Savior Catholic Parish - 2002 W. Alton Ave, Santa Ana, CA 92704 t) 714-444-1500 parishoffice@coscp.org www.coscp.org Dcn. Luis Gallardo; Dcn. Joe Garza; Rev. Joseph Robillard, Pst.; Rev. Thanh-Tai P. Nguyen, Vicar; Dcn. Thomas Concitis; Rev. Rudolph J. Preciado, In Res.; Luis Ramirez, Dir.; CRP Stds.: 218

St. George (Chaldean Catholic) - 4807 W. McFadden, Santa Ana, CA 92704 t) 714-531-7760 Rev. Zuhair G. Toma, Pst.;

Immaculate Heart of Mary - 1100 S. Center St., Santa Ana, CA 92704 t) 714-751-5335; 714-546-5186 (CRP) ihminfo@ihmsantaana.org; ihmffinfo@ihmsantaana.org www.ihmsantaana.org Rev. Gregory Pablo Marquez, Pst.; Rev. Joseph Luan Nguyen, Par. Vicar; Rev. Armando Virrey, Par. Vicar; Dcn. Biviano Cordero; Dcn. Rigoberto Maldonado; Dcn. Adolfo Ramirez; Rev. Ignatius Lau, In Res.; Yarette Macedo, Dir.;

St. Joseph - 727 N. Minter St., Santa Ana, CA 92701 t) 714-542-4411; 714-550-8096 (CRP) Rev. Thanh-Tai P. Nguyen, Par. Vicar; Dcn. Guillermo Torres; Dcn. Alfredo Rios; Delfina Diaz, DRE; Rev. Saul Alba-Infante, Admin.;

St. Joseph School - (Grades PreK-8) 608 Civic Center Dr. E., Santa Ana, CA 92701 t) 714-542-2704 stjoeprincipal@gmail.com www.stjoesa.org Dr. Brad Snyder, Prin.;

Our Lady of Guadalupe - 1322 E. Third St., Santa Ana, CA 92701 t) 714-836-4142 olguadalupe@olgsna.org guadalupesna.com Rev. Jose Felix Troncoso Martin, OAR, Pst.; Rev. Alberto Fuentes, OAR, Par. Vicar; Dcn. Domingo Garza; Dcn. Miguel Gonzalez; Imelda Bernal, DRE; CRP Stds.: 728

Our Lady of Guadalupe, Delhi - 541 E. Central Ave., Santa Ana, CA 92707 t) 714-540-0902 Rev. Domingo Romero, O.F.M., Pst.; Dcn. Leopoldo Arana; CRP Stds.: 487

Our Lady of La Vang - 288 S. Harbor Blvd., Santa Ana, CA 92704 t) 714-775-6200 parish@ourladyoflavang.org www.ourladyoflavang.org Rev. Joseph Luan Nguyen, Pst.; Rev. Joseph Thai Nguyen, Par. Vicar; Dcn. David Phan; Dcn. Adolfo Villalpando; CRP Stds.: 417

Our Lady of the Pillar - 1622 W. 6th St., Santa Ana, CA 92703 t) 714-543-1700; 714-542-4684 (CRP) Rev. Francisco Sandval, OAR, Pst.; Rev. Thomas Devine, O.A.R, Par. Vicar; Rev. Frank Wilder, O.A.R, Par. Vicar; Dcn. Ulyses Feliciano; Dcn. Luis Gallardo; Rev. Jose Antonio Arias, O.A.R., In Res.;

SEAL BEACH

St. Anne Church - 340 Tenth St., Seal Beach, CA 90740 t) 562-431-0721; 562-431-0721 x16 (CRP) www.stannesealbeach.org Rev. John M. Shimotsu, Pst.; Dcn. Steve Byars; Michele Ballestero, DRE; Rev. Alfred S. Baca, Senior Priest; Rev. Robert S. Vidal, Pastor Emer.; Rev. Msgr. Michael Heher, Pastor Emer.;

Holy Family - 13900 Church Pl., Seal Beach, CA 90740 t) 562-430-8170 www.holyfamilysb.com Rev. Juan Caboboy, Pastor Emer.; Rev. James Hartnett, Pastor Emer.; Rev. Joseph Son Thai Nguyen, Pst.; Dcn. Jerry Dao;

STANTON

St. Polycarp - 8100 Chapman Ave., Stanton, CA 90680 t) 714-893-2766 info@stpolycarp.org www.stpolycarp.org Rev. Viet Peter Ho, Pst.; Rev. Luis G. Segura, O.F.M., Par. Vicar; Dcn. Tri Kim Do; Dcn. Larry Leone; Rev. Nicolas Toan Nguyen, Par. Vicar; Dcn. Ramiro Lopez; Tom Ma, Bus. Mgr.;

TUSTIN

St. Cecilia - 1301 Sycamore Ave., Tustin, CA 92780 t) 714-544-3250 bthai@stceciliak8.org Rev. Khoi Tan Phan, Admin.; Rev. Michael Duc Nguyen, Par. Vicar; Rev. Erialdo Ramirez, Par. Vicar; Dcn. Guerrero

Andres; Dcn. Don Ngo; Dcn. William Weeks; CRP Stds.: 400

St. Cecilia School - (Grades PreSchool-8) 1311 Sycamore, Tustin, CA 92780 t) 714-544-1533 school@stceciliak8.org morethanschool.org Mary Alvarado, Prin.; Diane Smit, Librn.;

WESTMINSTER

Blessed Sacrament - 14072 S. Olive St., Westminster, CA 92683 t) 714-892-4489; 714-897-2142 (Faith Formation) office@bsc-od.org; faithformation@bsc-od.org bsc-od.org Rev. Tuyen Van Nguyen, Pst.; Rev. Douglas Zavala, Par. Vicar; Rev. Christopher Pham, Par. Vicar; Dcn. Arturo Gimenez; Dcn. Stan Necikowski; Dcn. Phong Nguyen; Dcn. Miguel Sanchez, Spanish RCIA; Sr. Cecilia Trang Pham, L.H.C., DRE; Sr. Velasco Cinthya, LHC, English/Spanish Faith Formation Coordinator; Lupe Burciaga, Bus. Mgr.; CRP Stds.: 954

Blessed Sacrament School - (Grades PreK-8) 14146 S. Olive St., Westminster, CA 92683 t) 714-893-7701 info@bsscatholic.org www.bsscatholic.org Dr. Gloria Castillo, Prin.; Stds.: 262; Sr. Tchrs.: 1; Lay Tchrs.: 12

YORBA LINDA

St. Martin de Porres - 19767 Yorba Linda Blvd., Yorba Linda, CA 92886 t) 714-970-2771 stmartin@smdpyl.org www.smdpyl.org Very Rev. Msgr. Stephen S. Doktorczyk, Pst.; Rev. Nicolaus Duy Thai, Par. Vicar; Dcn. Denis F. Zaun, Dir.; Dcn. Nick Sherg; Dcn. Mark Murphy; CRP Stds.: 397

Santa Clara de Asis - 22005 Avenida de la Paz, Yorba Linda, CA 92887 t) 714-970-7885 www.scdayl.org Rev. Fred K. Bailey, Pst.; Dcn. Eric Summerfield; Paul Nguyen, Music Min.; Michelle Mowen, Youth Min.; Emily Bent, DRE; Mary Chavez, RCIA Coord.; CRP Stds.: 195

SCHOOLS: PRESCHOOL THRU HIGH SCHOOL

SCHOOLS

STATE OF CALIFORNIA

ANAHEIM

St. Catherine's Academy (St. Catherine's Military Academy, a Corp.) - (PRV) (Grades K-8) 215 N. Harbor Blvd., Anaheim, CA 92805 t) 714-772-1363 admissions@stcatherinesacademy.org stcatherinesacademy.org Sr. Johnellen Turner, O.P., Prin.;

GARDEN GROVE

Christ Cathedral Academy - (DIO) (Grades PreSchool-8) 13280 Chapman Ave., Garden Grove, CA 92840 t) 714-663-2330 jtapia@ccaorange.com; jmarshall@ccaorange.com christcathedralacademy.org/ Julianna Tapia, Prin.; Stds.: 355; Sr. Tchrs.: 1; Lay Tchrs.: 18

RANCHO SANTA MARGARITA

St. Junipero Serra Catholic School - (PAR) (Grades PreSchool-8) 23652 Antonio Pkwy., Rancho Santa Margarita, CA 92688-1993 t) 949-888-1990 serra@serraschool.org; communications@serraschool.org www.serraschool.org (Parishes: Holy Trinity, St. Kilian, San Francisco Solano & Santiago de Compostela) Julie Radzai, Prin.; Carol Reiss, Prin.; Tim Tolzda, Prin.;

TUSTIN

Saint Jeanne de Lestonnac School - (PRV) (Grades PreSchool-8) 16791 E. Main St., Tustin, CA 92780 t) 714-542-4271 srcduran@sjdlschool.com www.sjdlschool.com Sr. Cecilia Duran, O.D.N., Prin.; Catherine Zimmerman, Librn.; Stds.: 364; Sr. Tchrs.: 5; Lay Tchrs.: 25

YORBA LINDA

St. Francis of Assisi Catholic School - (PAR) (Grades PreK-8) 5330 E. Side Cir., Yorba Linda, CA 92887 t) 714-695-3700 office@sfayl.org www.sfayl.org (Parishes: Santa Clara de Asis, San Antonio de Padua & St. Martin) Jeannette C. Lambert, Prin.;

HIGH SCHOOLS

STATE OF CALIFORNIA

ANAHEIM

Servite High School, A California Corporation - (PRV) (Grades 9-12) 1952 W. La Palma, Anaheim, CA 92801 t) 714-774-7575 administration@servitehs.org www.servitehs.org Christopher Weir, Pres.; Stephen Walswick, Prin.; Nancy Windisch, Vice Prin.; Rev. Dennis Kriz, O.S.M., Chap.; Stds.: 793; Scholastics: 1; Lay Tchrs.: 46

FULLERTON

Rosary Academy - (DIO) (Grades 9-12) 1340 N. Acacia Ave., Fullerton, CA 92831 t) 714-879-6302 admissions@rosaryacademy.org; finance@rosaryacademy.org www.rosaryacademy.org All Girls Sean Basford, Prin.; Shawna Pautsch, Head of School; Stds.: 445; Scholastics: 1; Lay Tchrs.: 38

RANCHO SANTA MARGARITA

Santa Margarita Catholic High School - (DIO) 22062 Antonio Pkwy., Rancho Santa Margarita, CA 92688 t) 949-766-6000 information@smhs.org; pr@smhs.org www.smhs.org Rev. Tim Donovan, Chap.; Cheri L Wood, Prin.; J. Andrew Sulick, Pres.; Rev. Craig M. Butters, English Teacher;

SAN JUAN CAPISTRANO

JSerra Catholic High School - (PRV) 26351 Junipero Serra Rd., San Juan Capistrano, CA 92675 t) 949-493-9307 info@jserra.org www.jserra.org Eric Stroupe, Admin.; Richard Meyer, Headmaster; Jeanne Swedo, Librn.;

SANTA ANA

Mater Dei High School - (DIO) (Grades 9-12) 1202 W. Edinger Ave., Santa Ana, CA 92707-2191 t) 714-754-7711 admissions@materdei.org www.materdei.org (Coed) Frances Clare, Prin.; Stds.: 2,039; Bro. Tchrs.: 1; Lay Tchrs.: 100

SILVERADO

Archangel Institute (St. Michael's Preparatory School) - (PRV) (Grades 9-12) 27977 Silverado Canyon Rd., Silverado, CA 92676 t) 657-314-9071 admin@stmichaelsabbey.com www.stmichaelsabbey.com Rev. Vianney Ceja, Admin.; Rev. Joachim Aldaba, O.Praem., Admin.; Rev. David Gonzalez, O.Praem., Instructor; Rev. Frederick Schmit, O.Praem., Instructor; Rev. Louis L Hager, O.Praem., Instructor; Rev. Hildebrand J. Garceau, O.Praem., Instructor; Rev. Basil Harnish, O.Praem., Instructor; Stds.: 85

INSTITUTIONS LOCATED IN DIOCESE

ASSOCIATIONS [ASN]

PLACENTIA

Western Catholic Educational Association - 101 Kraemer Blvd., Ste. 115, Placentia, CA 92870 t) 714-447-9834 jdritschel@westwcea.org westwcea.org Nancy Coonis, Exec.;

CAMPUS MINISTRY / NEWMAN CENTERS [CAM]

FULLERTON

California State University Fullerton, Titan Catholic Newman Club - St. Juliana Falconieri, 1316 N. Acacia Ave., Fullerton, CA 92831-1202 t) 714-353-5001 csufcatholicnewman@gmail.com Rev. Floi Moren, AM, Chap.;

IRVINE

University Catholic Community at UCI - 9 Hillgate, Irvine, CA 92612; Mailing: P.O. Box 523, Garden Grove, CA 92842 t) 949-861-3445 francisttvu@gmail.com catholiccommunityatuci.weebly.com/ Rev. John Francis Vu, S.J., Chap.;

ORANGE

Chapman University - 1 University Dr., Orange, CA 92866 t) 714-532-6098 frluevano@oc.rcbo.org Rev. Andres Rafael J. Luevano Jr., Chap.;

CATHOLIC CHARITIES [CCH]

ANAHEIM

St. Thomas Korean Catholic Center - 412 N. Crescent Way, Anaheim, CA 92801 t) 714-772-3995 stthomas@stkcc.org www.stkcc.org Dcn. Peter Chung; Dcn. Thomas Song; Rev. Alex H. Ha, Dir.;

SANTA ANA

Catholic Charities of Orange County, Inc. - 1820 E. 16th St., Santa Ana, CA 92701 t) 714-347-9602 eroy@ccoc.org; mgarorti@ccoc.org www.ccoc.org Ellen Roy, CEO;

Cantlay Food Center - 3631 W. Warner St., Santa Ana, CA 92704 t) 714-668-1130

Counseling Services - 1800 E. 17th St., Santa Ana, CA 92701 t) 714-347-9674 Sharon St. Pierre, Dir.;

Immigration Services - t) 714-347-9664 Frank Murphy, Dir.;

Re-creation Camp (Special Needs) - t) 714-347-9627 mdibb@ccoc.org www.recreationcampoc.com Orange, CA., Weekend getaway and ACE camp. Mattie Dibb, Dir.;

Vietnamese Catholic Center - 1538 N. Century Blvd., Santa Ana, CA 92703 t) 714-554-4211; 714-554-5565 hiepthong2013@gmail.com www.vncatholic.net Rev. Kiem Van Tran;

WESTMINSTER

Korean Martyrs Catholic Center - 7655 Trask Ave., Westminster, CA 92683 t) 714-897-6510 natalia@kmccoc.org www.kmccoc.org Rev. Eugene Lee, Dir.;

YORBA LINDA

Pope John Paul II Polish Center - 3999 Rose Dr., Yorba Linda, CA 92886 t) 714-996-8161 polishcenter@sbcglobal.net www.polishcenter.org Rev. Zbigniew Fraszczak, S.V.D., Dir.;

CEMETERIES [CEM]

HUNTINGTON BEACH

Good Shepherd Cemetery and Mausoleum - 8301 Talbert Ave., Huntington Beach, CA 92646 t) 714-847-8546 hidalgor@rcbo.org occem.org/ Rodolfo Hidalgo, Manager;

LAKE FOREST

Ascension - 24754 Trabuco Rd., Lake Forest, CA 92630 t) 949-837-1331 ascension@rcbo.org Kevin M. Haynes, Manager;

ORANGE

Holy Cross Cemetery - 7845 Santiago Cyn, Orange, CA 92869 t) 714-532-6551 racebal@rcbo.org Rene Acebal, Mgr.;

Holy Sepulcher - 7845 Santiago Canyon Rd., Orange, CA 92869 t) 714-532-6551 holysepulcher@rcbo.org

COLLEGES & UNIVERSITIES [COL]

ORANGE

St. Joseph College, Orange - 480 S. Batavia St., Orange, CA 92868 t) 714-633-8121 Branch Campus of University of San Francisco; St. Joseph Library. Sr. Christine Hilliard, C.S.J., Librn.;

CONVENTS, MONASTERIES, AND RESIDENCES FOR WOMEN [CON]

ANAHEIM

Dominicans, Mission San Jose (St. Catherine Academy) - 215 N. Harbor Blvd., Anaheim, CA 92805-2596

t) 714-772-1363 laurie@msjdominicans.org www.stcatherinesacademy.com Sr. Laurence Diaz, O.P., Prioress; Srs.: 8

BUENA PARK

Sisters of Our Lady of Perpetual Help - 6751 Western Ave., Buena Park, CA 90621 t) 714-521-1345 cacblm1988@gmail.com www.solph.or.kr Sr. Baekyung Cheon, Supr.; Srs.: 4

CYPRESS

Union of the Sisters of the Presentation of the Blessed Virgin Mary - 5151 Evergreen Ave., Cypress, CA 90630 t) 714-527-4844 annettepbvm@gmail.com; srjoanvosullivan@aol.com Sr. Annette Figueiredo, Contact; Srs.: 6

FULLERTON

Institute of the Apostolic Oblates, Inc. (House of Professed Apostolic Oblates) - 2125 W. Walnut Ave., Fullerton, CA 92833 t) 714-449-0511 caprosanctity@prosanctity.org www.caprosanctity.org House of Formation for Professed Apostolic Oblates. Secular Institute of the Apostolic Oblates, Inc. Joan Patten, Moderator; Renee Jarecki, Admin.;

GARDEN GROVE

Eucharistic Missionaries of the Most Holy Trinity - 11892 E. Lampson Ave., Garden Grove, CA 92840 t) 714-530-5727 srteresa@sticypress.org Sr. Teresita Garcia, MESST, Supr.; Srs.: 3

Religious Sisters of Charity - St. Columban Convent, 12555 Westlake St., Garden Grove, CA 92840 t) 714-741-9492 Sr. Brid O'Shea, RSC, Contact; Srs.: 1

Sisters of St. Clare - 10411 Garden Grove Blvd., #27, Garden Grove, CA 92843-1076 c) 714-345-0809 sshrewsbury@sbdiocese.org Sr. Eymard Flood, O.S.C., Contact; Srs.: 1

GARDENA

Sisters of the Lovers of the Holy Cross - 14700 S. Van Ness Ave., Gardena, CA 90249-3700 c) 310-516-0271; 714-460-3236 srgracele@lhcla.org; srjosephineha@lhcla.org www.lhcla.org Sr. Grace Duc Duc Le Sr., LHC, Supr.; Sr. Dao Thu Hong Dao, LHC, Contact; Srs.: 76

HUNTINGTON BEACH

Sisters of the Presentation of the Blessed Virgin Mary - St. Bonaventure Convent, 16441 Bradbury Ln., Huntington Beach, CA 92647 t) 714-846-6212 presentation.hb@gmail.com www.pbvmunion.org Sr. Mary Dunlea, P.B.V.M., Contact; Srs.: 4

ORANGE

Sisters of St. Joseph of Carondelet - 353 Tustin Ave. #313, Orange, CA 92866 t) 818-437-3802 tlynchcsj@aol.com Sr. Teresa Lynch, C.S.J., Contact; Srs.: 1

St. Joseph - 507 N. Linwood Ave., Santa Ana, CA 92701 t) 714-454-6221

Sisters of St. Joseph of Orange - 440 S. Batavia St., Orange, CA 92868 t) 714-633-8121 x7704 sr.ellen.jordan@csjorange.org csjorange.org/ Sr. Ellen Jordan, Contact; Srs.: 87

Sisters of St. Joseph of Orange Motherhouse Community - 440 S. Batavia, Orange, CA 92868 t) 714-633-8121 www.csjorange.org Maria Elena Perales, Dir.; Srs.: 88

CSJ Education Network - t) (714) 744-3113 Bret Allen, Dir.;

CSJ Justice Center - 440 S. Batavia St., Orange, CA 92868 t) (714) 633-8121 x7716 mperales@csjorange.org Sisters of St. Joseph of Orange

Center for Spiritual Development - 434 S. Batavia St., Orange, CA 92868 t) 714-744-3175 x7430 jdeslisle@csjorange.org; chilliard@csjorange.org Sr. Jane DesLisle, CSJ, Dir.; Sr. Christine Hilliard, CSJ, Dir.;

Regina Residence Community - 460 S. Batavia St., Orange, CA 92868 t) 714-744-3109 Leondra Banuelos, Dir.;

Union of Sisters of the Presentation of the Blessed Virgin Mary - 343 E. Chestnut, Orange, CA 92867 t) 714-283-2496 clonea77@gmail.com; usrsdev52727@gmail.com pbvmunion.org Sr. Breda Christopher, P.B.V.M., Contact; Srs.: 3

SANTA ANA

Franciscan Missionary Sisters of the Immaculate Conception - 1718 W. 6th St., Santa Ana, CA 92703 t) 714-542-0381; 714-542-8352 stfrancishome@sbcglobal.net www.st-francis-home.org Sr. Elia Caro, OSF, Supr.; Srs.: 10

Poor Clare Missionary Sisters of the Blessed Sacrament - 1019 N. Newhope St., Santa Ana, CA 92703-1534 t) 714-554-8850 c) 714-925-6978 rocamc72@gmail.com www.misionerasclarisas.org Sr. Yenory Zuniga Loria, Supr.; Sr. Maricela de Jesus Valenzuela, Supr.; Srs.: 18

Sisters of the Company of Mary - St. Anne Convent, 1339 S. Broadway, Santa Ana, CA 92707 t) 714-558-1340 leticiasalazar@mac.com Sr. Elvira Rios, O.D.N., Secy.; Srs.: 4

Society Devoted to the Sacred Heart - 2927 S. Greenville St., Santa Ana, CA 92704 t) 714-557-4538 sacredheartsisters.com Sr. Susan Blaschke, Supr.; Sr. Rosemarie Rosemarie Karl, SDSH, Treas.; Srs.: 7

Sacred Heart Convent - 2911 S. Greenville St., Santa Ana, CA 92704 t) 714-751-6335 Sr. Martha Munoz, SDSH, Supr.;

SILVERADO

Rosarian Dominicans - St. Michael's Convent, 27977 Silverado Canyon Rd., Silverado, CA 92676 t) 657-314-9054 stmicdominican@yahoo.com Sr. Martha Celis, O.P., Supr.; Srs.: 8

TUSTIN

Sisters of the Company of Mary, Our Lady - 16791 E. Main St., Tustin, CA 92780-4034 t) 714-541-3125 elviraodn@yahoo.com; usregionsec@odnusa.org www.lestonnac.org Sr. Elvira Rios, O.D.N., Secy.; Srs.: 7

Lestonnac Residence: - 16791 E. Main St., Tustin, CA 92780 t) (657) 600-8565 srglondono@odnusa.org Sr. Gloria Londono, ODN, Admin.;

Lestonnac Retreat Center - 16791 E. Main St., Tustin, CA 92780 t) (657) 600-8565 lestonnacretreatcenter@odnusa.org www.lestonnacretreatcenters.com Sr. Charlotte Anne Turrietta, ODN, Dir.;

ENDOWMENTS / FOUNDATIONS / TRUSTS [EFT]

FULLERTON

St. Jude Memorial Foundation - 1440 N. Harbor Blvd., Ste. 200, Fullerton, CA 92835; Mailing: P.O. Box 4138, Fullerton, CA 92835 t) 714-992-3033 jim.watson@stjoe.org Dale Katsuyama, Contact;

GARDEN GROVE

***The Orange Catholic Foundation** - 13280 Chapman Ave., Ste. 430, Garden Grove, CA 92840 t) 714-282-3021 info@orangecatholicfoundation.org orangecatholicfoundation.org/ Kimberly Jetton, Pres.;

ORANGE

St. Joseph Health System Foundation - 3345 Michelson Dr., Ste 100, Orange, CA 92868 t) 714-347-7500 Gabriela Robles, Dir.;

Sisters of St. Joseph Healthcare Foundation - 440 S. Batavia St., Orange, CA 92868 t) 714-633-8121 x7109 bross@csjorange.org www.csjorange.org Sr. Marian Schubert, Rel. Ord. Ldr.;

SILVERADO

***St. Michael's Abbey Foundation** - 27977 Silverado Canyon Rd., Silverado, CA 92676 t) 657-314-9071 admin@stmichaelsabbey.com www.stmichaelsabbey.com Rt. Rev. Eugene J. Hayes, O.Praem., Abbot;

HOSPITALS / HEALTH SERVICES [HOS]

FULLERTON

St. Jude Medical Center - 101 E. Valencia Mesa Dr., Fullerton, CA 92835-3875 t) 714-871-3280 jim.watson@stjoe.org www.stjudemedicalcenter.org Laura Ramos, CEO; Bed Capacity: 320; Asstd. Annu.: 14,602; Staff: 2,273

LAGUNA BEACH

Mission Hospital Laguna Beach (MHLB) (St. Joseph Health System) - 31872 Coast Hwy., Laguna Beach, CA 92651 t) 949-381-4000 james.watson@stjoe.org Seth Teigen, CEO;

MISSION VIEJO

Mission Hospital Regional Medical Center (MHMV) - 27700 Medical Center Rd., Mission Viejo, CA 92691 t) 949-381-4000 jim.watson@stjoe.org www.mission4health.com Seth Teigen, CEO; Bed Capacity: 504; Asstd. Annu.: 16,398; Staff: 2,693

ORANGE

St. Joseph Hospital of Orange - 1100 W. Stewart Dr., Orange, CA 92868 t) 949-381-4000 jim.watson@stjoe.org sjo.org Jeremy Zoch, CEO; Bed Capacity: 463; Asstd. Annu.: 22,477; Staff: 3,114

MISCELLANEOUS [MIS]

ANAHEIM

Providence Medical Foundation (St. Joseph Heritage Healthcare) - 200 W. Center St. Promenade, Anaheim, CA 92805 t) 949-381-4000 jim.watson@stjoe.org Dr. David Kim, CEO;

FOUNTAIN VALLEY

Magnificat - Our Lady Queen of Peace - 9122 Blair River Cir., Fountain Valley, CA 92708 t) 714-345-6561 kmoses3737@gmail.com www.magnificat-ministry.net Karen Moses, Coord.; Dr. Elizabeth Kim, Asst. Coord.;

FULLERTON

African Missionaries - 839 Adlena Dr., Fullerton, CA 92833 t) 877-266-5289 support@africamissionaries.com www.africamissionaries.com Yolanda Epperson, Admin.;

GARDEN GROVE

Christ Catholic Cathedral Corporation - 13280 Chapman Ave., Garden Grove, CA 92840 t) 714-282-3076 bmilligan@rcbo.org Rev. Christopher H. Smith, CEO;

Christ Catholic Cathedral Facilities Corporation - 13280 Chapman Ave., Tower of Hope, 11th Floor, Garden Grove, CA 92840 t) 714-282-3076 bmilligan@rcbo.org Randy Sperry, Chair;

Magis Institute - 13280 Chapman Ave., 9th Fl., Garden Grove, CA 92840 t) 949-271-2727 spitzer@magiscenter.com magiscenter.com Rev. Robert J. Spitzer, S.J., Pres.;

IRVINE

St. Joseph Health Ministry - 3345 Michelson Dr, Ste 100, Irvine, CA 92612 t) 949-381-4000 jim.watson@stjoe.org Sr. Sharon Becker, C.S.J., Chair;

St. Joseph Health System - 3345 Michelson Dr., Ste. 100, Irvine, CA 92612 t) 949-381-4000 jim.watson@stjoe.org www.stjhs.org Dr. Rodney Hochman, CEO;

Our Lady of Peace Korean Catholic Center - 14010 Remington, Irvine, CA 92620-5703 t) 949-654-5239 office@olpkcc.org; frdaniel@olpkcc.org olpkcc.org Korean Catholic Center for daily Sacraments, Formation, and Community Rev. Daniel Seo, Dir.;

***Second Harvest Food Bank of Orange County, Inc.** - 8014 Marine Way, Irvine, CA 92618 t) 949-653-2900 jfoley@feedoc.org feedoc.org

ORANGE

American Federation Pueri Cantores - 1188 N. Tustin St., Orange, CA 92867 t) 714-633-7554 info@pcchoirs.org www.pcchoirs.org Paul French, Pres.;

SAN JUAN CAPISTRANO

Duc in Altum Schools Collaborative - 26351 Junipero Serra Rd., San Juan Capistrano, CA 92675 t) 949-493-9307 x1160 dia@diaschools.org diaschools.org Richard Meyer, Pres.;

SANTA ANA

***Council of Orange County - Society of St. Vincent de Paul** - 1505 E. 17th St., Ste. 109, Santa Ana, CA 92705 t) 714-542-0448 requestinfo@svdpoc.org www.svdpoc.org Brigid Noonan, Pres.;

MONASTERIES AND RESIDENCES FOR PRIESTS AND BROTHERS [MON]

ANAHEIM

Manresa Jesuit Residence - 401 W. Leonora St., Anaheim, CA 92805-2634 c) 714-425-2758 drobinson@jesuits.org Rev. John Francis Vu, S.J.,

Campus Min.; Rev. David C. Robinson, S.J., Supr.; Priests: 2

BUENA PARK

Servite Fathers and Brothers - Servite Priory, 5210 Somerset St., Buena Park, CA 90621; Mailing: 8562 Links Rd., Buena Park, CA 90621-1603 c) 714-853-0310 www.servite.org Servite Friars Rev. Sebastian Mulu, OSM, Prior; Priests: 4

Servite High School - 1952 W. La Palma Ave., Anaheim, CA 92801-3595 t) 714-774-7575 www.servitehs.org Stephen Walswick, Prin.;

FULLERTON

Servite Fathers and Brothers - St. Juliana Falconieri, 1316 N. Acacia, Fullerton, CA 92831 t) 714-879-1965 info@stjulianachurch.org www.stjulianachurch.org Rev. Michael M. Pontarelli, O.S.M., Contact; Priests: 1

MIDWAY CITY

Brothers of St. Patrick, St. Patrick's Novitiate - 7820 Bolsa Ave., Midway City, CA 92655 t) 714-897-8181 c) 714-642-2076 brjosephfsp@gmail.com; brophilip5@yahoo.com www.brothersofstpatrick.com Bro. Aquinas Cassin, F.S.P., Supr.; Bro. Joseph Anoop, F.S.P., Rel. Ord. Ldr.; Bro. Philip Shepler, F.S.P., Treas.; Bro. Thomas John Weldon, F.S.P., Mem.; Brs.: 4

SANTA ANA

Augustinian Recollects - Our Lady of Guadalupe, 1322 E. 3rd St., Santa Ana, CA 92701-5104 t) 714-836-4142 santaana.guadalupe@agustinosrecoletos.org agustinosrecoletos.org Rev. Anthony Zacarias Palos, OAR, Par. Vicar; Rev. Jose Felix Troncoso Martin, OAR, Prior; Rev. Alberto Fuentes, OAR, Par. Vicar; Priests: 3

SILVERADO

Norbertine Fathers of Orange, Inc. - St. Michael's Abbey, 27977 Silverado Canyon Rd., Silverado, CA 92676 t) 657-314-9071 admin@stmichaelsabbey.com www.stmichaelsabbey.com Rt. Rev. Eugene J. Hayes, O.Praem., Abbot; Rev. Chrysostom Anthony Baer, O.Praem, Prior; Rev. James G. Smith, O.Praem., Subprior; Rev. Joachim Aldaba, O.Praem., Priest; Rev. Hugh C. Barbour, O.Praem., Priest; Rev. Miguel Batres, O.Praem., Priest; Rev. Alan V. Benander, O.Praem., Priest; Rev. Martin Benzoni, O.Praem., Priest; Rev. Stephen M. Boyle, O.Praem., Priest; Rev. Godfrey E. Bushmaker, O.Praem., Priest; Rev. John Caronan, O.Praem., Priest; Rev. William Fitzgerald, O.Praem.; Rev. Vianney Ceja, Priest; Bro. Mark R Charlesworth, O.Praem., Brother; Rev. Ambrose Criste, O.Praem., Priest; Rev. Gregory M. Dick, O.Praem., Priest; Rev. William M. Fitzgerald, O.Praem., Priest; Rev. Peregrine Fletcher, O.Praem., Priest; Rev. Patrick D. Foutts, O.Praem., Priest; Rev. Hildebrand J. Garceau, O.Praem., Priest; Rev. Damien V. Giap, O.Praem., Priest; Rev. Francis M. Gloudeman, O.Praem., Priest; Rev. David Gonzalez, O.Praem., Priest; Rev. Charbel R. Grbavac, O.Praem., Priest; Rev. Louis L Hager, O.Praem., Priest; Rev. Brendan R. Hankins, O.Praem., Priest; Rev. John Henry Hanson, O.Praem., Priest; Rev. Basil Harnish, O.Praem., Priest; Rev. Ignatius B Harsha, O.Praem., Priest; Rev. Alphonsus B. Hermes, O.Praem., Priest; Rev. Robert S. Hodges, O.Praem., Priest; Rev. Joseph K. Horn, O.Praem., Priest; Rev. Jacob Hsieh, O.Praem., Priest; Rev. Bernard Johnson, O.Praem., Priest; Rev. Luke Laslavich, O.Praem., Priest; Peter Adrian Miller, O.Praem., Priest; Rev. Jerome M. Molokie, O.Praem., Priest; Rev. Thomas W. Nelson, O.Praem., Priest; Rev. Pascal B. Nguyen, O.Praem., Priest; Rev. Maximilian C. Okapal, O.Praem., Priest; Rev. Edmund Page, O.Praem., Priest; Rev. Michael U. Perea, O.Praem., Priest; Rev. Raymond Perez, O.Praem., Priest; Rev. Augustine R. Puchner, O.Praem., Priest; Rev. Justin S. Ramos, O.Praem., Priest; Rev. Anselm Rodriguez, O.Praem., Priest; Rev. Adrian Sanchez, O.Praem., Priest; Rev. Frederick Schmit, O.Praem., Priest; Rev. Theodore R. Smith, O.Praem., Priest; Rev. Benedict Solomon, O.Praem., Priest; Rev. Gabriel D. Stack, O.Praem., Priest; Rev. Victor S. Szczurek, O.Praem., Priest; Rev. Nicholas M. Tacito, O.Praem., Priest; Rev. Andrew P. Tran, O.Praem., Priest; Rev. Pio Vottola, Priest; Rev. Sebastian A. Walshe, O.Praem., Priest; Rev. Claude A. Williams, O.Praem., Priest; Rev. Charles W. Willingham, O.Praem., Priest; Rev. Norbert J. Wood, O.Praem., Priest; Brs.: 1; Priests: 57

PRESCHOOLS / CHILDCARE CENTERS [PRE]

SANTA ANA

Santa Clara Day Nursery and Kindergarten (Poor Clare Missionary Sisters (M.C.)) - 1021 N. Newhope St., Santa Ana, CA 92703 t) 714-554-8850; 714-554-8851 Sr. Hena Claudia Andrade, Prin.;

SILVERADO

St. Michael's Summer Camp - St. Michael's Abbey, 27977 Silverado Canyon Rd., Silverado, CA 92676 t) 657-314-9071 x271 admin@stmichellesabbey.com www.stmichaelsabbey.com Boys 7-12 yrs. Rev. Louis L Hager, O.Praem., Admin.; Rev. Joachim Aldaba, O.Praem., Contact; Stds.: 100

RETREAT HOUSES / RENEWAL CENTERS [RTR]

FULLERTON

Pro Sanctity Spirituality Center, Retreat House - 205 S. Pine Dr., Fullerton, CA 92833 t) 714-449-0511 caprosanctity@prosanctity.org caprosanctity.org Joan Patten, A.O., Dir.;

Pro Sanctity Movement - 205 S. Pine Dr., Fullerton, CA 92833 t) (714) 449-0511 www.caprosanctity.org Joan Patten, Dir.;

ORANGE

House of Prayer for Priests - 7734 E. Santiago Canyon Rd., Orange, CA 92869 t) 714-639-9740 domenico1410@hotmail.com www.rcbo.org/group/house-of-prayer/ Rev. Robert J. Spitzer, S.J., In Res.; Rev. Domenico Di Raimondo, Dir.;

Loyola Institute for Spirituality - 434 S. Batavia St., Orange, CA 92868 t) 714-997-9587 office@loyolainstitute.org www.loyolainstitute.org Lori Stanley, Exec. Dir.;

SANTA ANA

Heart of Jesus Retreat Center (Society Devoted to the Sacred Heart) - 2927 S. Greenville St., Santa Ana, CA 92704 t) 714-557-4538 office@joyfulapostolate.org joyfulapostolate.org Sr. Susan Blaschke, Supr.; Sr. Micaela Ramirez, SDSH, Dir.;

SEMINARIES [SEM]

SILVERADO

St. Michael's Norbertine Postulancy, Novitiate and Juniorate - 27977 Silverado Canyon Rd., Silverado, CA 92676 t) 657-314-9071 admin@stmichaelsabbey.com www.stmichaelsabbey.com Conducted by the Norbertine Fathers. Rev. Ambrose Criste, O.Praem.; Rev. Vianney Ceja, Admin.; Rev. Peregrine Fletcher, O.Praem., Admin.; Rev. Chrysostom Anthony Baer, O.Praem, Prof.; Rev. Maximilian C. Okapal, O.Praem., Prof.; Rev. Victor S. Szczurek, O.Praem., Prof.; Rev. Sebastian A. Walshe, O.Praem., Prof.; Rev. Norbert J. Wood, O.Praem., Prof.; Rt. Rev. Eugene J. Hayes, O.Praem., Abbot; Rev. John Henry Hanson, O.Praem., Dir.; Rev. Thomas W. Nelson, O.Praem., Dir.; Stds.: 45; Lay Tchrs.: 1

SPECIAL CARE FACILITIES [SPF]

SANTA ANA

St. Francis Home for the Aged (Franciscan Sisters of the Immaculate Conception, Inc.) - 1718 W. 6th St., Santa Ana, CA 92703 t) 714-542-0381 stfrancishome@sbcglobal.net www.st-francis-home.org Sr. Elia Caro, OSF, Admin.; Bed Capacity: 97; Asstd. Annu.: 32; Staff: 10

Diocese of Orlando

(Dioecesis Orlandensis)

MOST REVEREND JOHN G. NOONAN

Bishop of Orlando; ordained September 23, 1983; appointed Auxiliary Bishop of Miami June 21, 2005; ordained Titular Bishop of Bonusta and Auxiliary Bishop of the Archdiocese of Miami August 24, 2005; appointed Bishop of Orlando October 23, 2010; installed as Fifth Bishop of the Diocese of Orlando December 16, 2010. Chancery: 50 E. Robinson St., Orlando, FL 32801. T: 407-246-4800. Mailing Address: P.O. Box 1800, Orlando, FL 32802.

Chancery: 50 E. Robinson St., Orlando, FL 32801. Mailing Address: P.O. Box 1800, Orlando, FL 32802. T: 407246-4800; F: 407-246-4942.
www.orlandodiocese.org
tsimon@orlandodiocese.org

ESTABLISHED JUNE 18, 1968.

Square Miles 11,254.

Comprises the Counties of Brevard, Lake, Marion, Orange, Osceola, Polk, Seminole, Sumter and Volusia in the State of Florida.

For legal titles of parishes and diocesan institutions, consult the Chancery.

STATISTICAL OVERVIEW

Personnel

Bishop	1
Priests: Diocesan Active in Diocese	79
Priests: Diocesan Active Outside Diocese	6
Priests: Retired, Sick or Absent	54
Number of Diocesan Priests	139
Religious Priests in Diocese	38
Total Priests in your Diocese	177
Extern Priests in Diocese	23
Ordinations:	
Diocesan Priests	2
Transitional Deacons	3
Permanent Deacons	18
Permanent Deacons in Diocese	134
Total Brothers	12
Total Sisters	46

Parishes

Parishes	80
With Resident Pastor:	
Resident Diocesan Priests	64
Resident Religious Priests	16
Missions	11
Pastoral Centers	1

Professional Ministry Personnel:

Brothers	8
Sisters	10
Lay Ministers	218

Welfare

Health Care Centers	7
Total Assisted	1,241
Homes for the Aged	5
Total Assisted	598
Day Care Centers	9
Total Assisted	275
Special Centers for Social Services	17
Total Assisted	185,259
Residential Care of Disabled	1
Total Assisted	376

Educational

Diocesan Students in Other Seminaries	21
Total Seminarians	21
High Schools, Diocesan and Parish	5
Total Students	3,058
Elementary Schools, Diocesan and Parish	30
Total Students	8,771
Non-residential Schools for the Disabled	1
Total Students	65

Catechesis/Religious Education:

High School Students	3,027
Elementary Students	11,239
Total Students under Catholic Instruction	26,181
Teachers in Diocese:	
Priests	1
Brothers	1
Sisters	13
Lay Teachers	1,076

Vital Statistics

Receptions into the Church:	
Infant Baptism Totals	4,137
Minor Baptism Totals	360
Adult Baptism Totals	187
Received into Full Communion	373
First Communions	3,919
Confirmations	3,401
Marriages:	
Catholic	733
Interfaith	204
Total Marriages	937
Deaths	3,971
Total Catholic Population	390,668
Total Population	5,064,237

LEADERSHIP

Vicar General - t) 407-647-3392 Rev. Msgr. Richard Walsh, Vicar (frwalsh@stmargaretmary.org);
Vicar General and Chancellor for Canonical Affairs - t) 407-246-4846 Very Rev. John Giel (jgiel@orlandodiocese.org);
Chief Operating Officer/Chancellor - t) 407-246-4830 Theresa Simon (tsimon@orlandodiocese.org);
Vicar for Priestly Life and Ministry - Very Rev. Richard W. Trout;
Vicar for Clergy - Very Rev. Miguel A. Gonzalez;
Vicar for Religious - Very Rev. Benjamin A. Berinti, C.PP.S.;
Moderator for Religious Women - c) 864-420-1200 Sr. Catherine Noecker, O.S.F.;

ADVISORY BOARDS, COMMISSIONS, COMMITTEES, AND COUNCILS

Priests' Personnel Board - t) 407-246-4815
Presbyteral Council -
President - Most Rev. John Noonan;
Ex Officio Members - Very Rev. John Giel, Vicar; Rev. Msgr. Richard Walsh, Vicar Gen.; Very Rev. Miguel A. Gonzalez, Vicar for Priests & Vice Chair;
Representative by Age - Rev. Derek Saldanha; Rev. Juan Osorno; Very Rev. Ralph DuWell;
Representative - Secular Priests Not Incardinated - Rev. Msgr. Juanito Figura;
Representative - Religious Priests - Very Rev. Benjamin A. Berinti, C.PP.S.;
Representative - Retired Priests - Rev. Fred R. Ruse;
Diocesan Finance Council - Cesar Calvet, Chair;
Diocesan School Board - t) 407-246-4905 Very Rev. Timothy P. LaBo, Chair;
Health and Welfare Insurance Committee - t) 407-246-4830 Ryan Burrows, Chair;
Retirement Committee - t) 407-246-4830 Linda Shaughnessy, Chair;

CANONICAL SERVICES

Promoters of Justice - Sr. Lucy Vazquez, O.P.; Very Rev. John Giel, Chancellor for Canonical Affairs (jgiel@orlandodiocese.org);
Defenders of the Bond - Rev. Jose Bautista; Sr. Lucy Vazquez, O.P.;

CATHOLIC CHARITIES

Secretary for Human Dignity & Solidarity - t) 888-658-2828 Gary Tester, Pres. (gtester@cflcc.org);
Agape Mission Markets - Juan Vega, Contact;
Behavioral Health Services - Barbara Cage, Dir.;
Comprehensive Refugee Services - t) 407-277-1938 Monica Araujo, Contact;
Culture of Life - Leidy Rivas, Dir.;
Family Stability Program - t) 407-658-1818 x1023 Emma Pena, Dir.;
Human Trafficking Task Force - kborrero@cflcc.org Kate Borrero, Contact;
Immigration Legal Services - t) 407-658-0110 legalservices@cflcc.org Raul Pinzon, Contact;
Medical & Dental Clinics - eburley@cflcc.org Erin Burley, Dir.;
Pathways to Care & Step 2 - t) 407-388-0245 William Bernardo, Dir.;
Resurrection Community Housing Development - Jennifer Molinares, Contact;
Resurrection Property Management - wrojas@cflcc.org Wilmar Rojas, Dir.;
Senior Wellness Services - t) 863-687-2988 Barbara Cage, Dir.;

CLERGY AND RELIGIOUS SERVICES

Permanent Diaconate - t) 407-246-4878 dcamous@orlandodiocese.org Dcn. David Camous, Dir.;
Vocations - t) 407-768-3113 jswallows@orlandodiocese.org Rev. Josh Swallows, Dir.;
International Priests - t) 407-246-4815 Very Rev. Miguel A. Gonzalez, Rector;
Senior Priests - t) 407-246-4845

COMMUNICATIONS

Secretary for Communications & Senior Director - t) 407-246-4811 Jennifer Drow, Dir. (jdrow@orlandodiocese.org);
Florida Catholic Media - t) 407-246-4811 Jennifer Drow (jdrow@orlandodiocese.org);
Archivist - t) 407-246-4920 Renae Bennett (rbennett@orlandodiocese.org);

CONSULTATIVE BODIES

Censor of Books - t) 407-246-4814 Rev. Jeremiah L. Payne; Rev. Esau Garcia;

DEANERIES

Central Deanery North - t) (407) 869-9472 frivan@annunciationorlando.org Very Rev. Ivan Olmo, Dean;
Central Deanery South - t) (321) 939-1491 rtrout@celebrationcatholic.org Very Rev. Richard W. Trout, Dean;
Eastern Deanery - t) (386) 788-6144 frmatt@ladyofhope.org Very Rev. Matthew Mello, Dean;
Northern Deanery - t) (352),753-9602 rduwell@sttimothycc.com Very Rev. Ralph DuWell, Dean;
Southern Deanery - t) (321) 773-2783 scirce@hnj.org Very Rev. Scott M. Circe, Dean;
Western Deanery - t) (863) 213-5280 frtim@stjosephlakeland.org Very Rev. Timothy P. LaBo, Dean;

EDUCATION

Secretary for Education & Superintendent of Schools - t) 407-246-4904 Henry Fortier, Supt. (hfortier@orlandodiocese.org);
Youth Ministry - t) (407) 246-4904 Henry Fortier, Supt. (hfortier@orlandodiocese.org);
Children's Ministry - t) 407-246-4911 c) (407) 446-0529 jmolloy@orlandodiocese.org John Molloy, Dir.;
Mission Office, Sister Diocese of San Juan de la Maguana - t) 407-246-4890 Raquel Cespedes, Dir.;

EVANGELIZATION

Multi-Cultural Ministries -
African Ministry - t) 321-725-3066 Rev. Emmanuel Akalue;
Brazilian/Portuguese Ministry - t) 407-656-3113 Rev. Heitor Castoldi, C.S.;
Filipino Ministry - t) 321-452-5955 Rev. Francisco Aquino (Philippines);
Haitian Ministry - t) 407-246-4922 Sheila Henry, Admin. Asst.;
Hispanic Ministry - t) 407-344-9607 Rev. Jose Munoz;
Korean Ministry - t) 407-895-8858 Rev. Deog Su Han, Pst.;
Polish Ministry - t) 386-668-8270 Rev. Krzysztof Bugno, S.D.S., Pst.;
Vietnamese Ministry - t) 407-896-4210 Rev. Chau J. Nguyen;
Ministry to the Incarcerated - t) 407-246-4878 Dcn. Richard Dodd, Prison Ministry Coord. (jgassman@orlandodiocese.org);

FACILITIES

Secretary for Ecclesiastical Properties & Senior Director of Real Estate - t) 407-246-4869 Scott Fergerson, Dir. (sfergerson@orlandodiocese.org);
Queen of Angels Catholic Cemetery, Inc. - t) 407-246-4919 David Branson, Dir. Cemeteries (dbranson@orlandodiocese.org);
Catholic Cemeteries of Central Florida Holdings, Inc. - t) 407-246-4832 Roger Barnes, Comptroller (rbarnes@orlandodiocese.org);

FAITH FORMATION

Adult Ministry - t) 407-246-4912 tevans@orlandodiocese.org Tomas Evans, Dir.;

FINANCE

Secretary for Financial Services and CFO - t) 407-246-4831 Kevin Casey, CFO (kcasey@orlandodiocese.org);
Shared Accounting Services - t) 407-246-4848 mzirkle@orlandodiocese.org Michael Zirkle, Vice. Pres.;
Comptroller - t) 407-246-4832 Roger Barnes (rbarnes@orlandodiocese.org);
Information Technology - t) 407-246-4839 Jack Paige, Dir. (jpaige@orlandodiocese.org);
Risk Management - t) 407-246-4877 Tracy Dann, Mgr. (tdann@orlandodiocese.org);

HUMAN RESOURCES

Secretary for Human Resources & Senior Director - t) 407-246-4825 Regina-Marie Aldrin, Dir.;

ORGANIZATIONS

Diocesan Council of Catholic Women - Very Rev. Miguel A. Gonzalez, Spiritual Dir.;

PARISH SERVICES

Secretary for Leadership & Parish Life - t) 407-246-4897 Dcn. Joseph Gassman (jgassman@orlandodiocese.org);
Liturgical Music - t) 407-246-4862 abrakel@orlandodiocese.org Adam Brakel, Dir.;
Liturgy - t) 407-246-4861 bcroteau@orlandodiocese.org Bruce Croteau, Dir.;

SPIRITUAL LIFE

Diocesan Liaison of Ecumenism and Interreligious Dialogue - t) 407-246-4815 Very Rev. Anthony Aarons (franthony@mqus.org);
Tourism Ministry - t) 407-239-6600 Very Rev. Anthony Aarons, Rector (franthony@mqus.org);

STEWARDSHIP

The Catholic Foundation of Central Florida - t) 407-246-7194 Kimberlee Riley, Pres. (kriley@cfocf.org);

TRIBUNAL

Tribunal - Rev. Fernando Gil, Judicial Vicar;
Adjutant Judicial Vicar - t) (407) 246-4851 Rev. Joseph V. Bellerive, Adjutant Judicial Vicar;
Judges - Rev. Fernando Gil; Ricardo Gaiotti Silva, Canonical Assessor & Judge;
Manager of Tribunal Services - t) (407) 246-4851 Diana Anderson;
Regional Advocates - Carolina Breton, Polk County; Diana Jimenez, Seminole & Volusia Counties; Isabel Menjura, Osceola County;

MISCELLANEOUS / OTHER OFFICES

Safe Environment - t) 407-246-4822 Ida Valdez, Mgr.;
Victim Assistance Coordinator - t) 407-246-7179 vac@orlandodiocese.org
Propagation of the Faith - t) 407-246-4922 Sheila Henry;

PARISHES, MISSIONS, AND CLERGY

STATE OF FLORIDA

ALTAMONTE SPRINGS

Annunciation - 1020 Montgomery Rd., Altamonte Springs, FL 32714 t) 407-869-9472; 407-215-7621 (CRP) noreilly@annunciationorlando.org; ppronko@annunciationorlando.org www.annunciationorlando.org Very Rev. Ivan Olmo, Pst.; CRP Stds.: 486

Annunciation Catholic Academy - (Grades K-8) 593 Jamestown Blvd., Altamonte Springs, FL 32714 t) 407-774-2801 kahlep@annunciationacademy.org annunciationacademy.org Patricia Kahle, Prin.; Stds.: 509; Lay Tchrs.: 10

St. Mary Magdalen - 861 Maitland Ave., Altamonte Springs, FL 32701 t) 407-265-2303 (CRP); 407-831-1212 office@stmarymagdalen.org; gailr@stmarymagdalen.org www.stmarymagdalen.org Rev. Charles I. Mitchell, Pst.; Rev. Duberney Rodas Grajales, OP, Par. Vicar; Kristina Blair, DRE; CRP Stds.: 330

St. Mary Magdalen School - -8) 869 Maitland Ave., Altamonte Springs, FL 32701 t) 407-339-7301 stmarymagdalen@smmschool.org www.smmschool.org Lorianne Rotz, Prin.; Stds.: 474; Lay Tchrs.: 31

Early Learning Center - 710 Spring Lake Rd., Altamonte Springs, FL 32701 t) 407-831-3740 esteiner@smmschool.org Elisa Steiner, Dir.;

APOPKA

St. Francis of Assisi - 834 S. Orange Blossom Trail, Apopka, FL 32703-6560 t) 407-886-4602 www.stfrancisapopka.org Rev. Mathew Vettath Joseph, SDV, Par. Admin.; Rev. Robinson Gonzalez, SDV (Colombia), Par. Vicar; Dcn. Alvin Bedneau; Dcn. Juan Henriquez; Dcn. Ruthven Jackie; Dcn. Luis Alvira, DRE; Margaret Hettler, Bus. Mgr.; CRP Stds.: 265

BAREFOOT BAY

St. Luke - 5055 Micco Rd., Barefoot Bay, FL 32976 t) 772-664-9310 office@stlukebarefootbay.org www.stlukebarefootbay.org/ Rev. Tony Welle, Admin.; CRP Stds.: 6

BARTOW

St. Thomas Aquinas - 1305 E. Mann Rd., Bartow, FL 33830 t) 863-533-8578 freugene@stthomasbartow.org stthomasbartow.org Dcn. Mark M. King; Rev. Eugene Grytner, S.D.S., Pst.; CRP Stds.: 35

St. Elizabeth Ann Seton - 101 Edgewood Dr., Fort Meade, FL 33841 t) (863) 533-8578

BELLEVIEW

St. Theresa - 11528 S U.S. Hwy. 301, Belleview, FL 34420-4430 t) 352-245-2458 marcia@mystcc.org www.mystcc.org Rev. Thomas Connery, Pst.; CRP Stds.: 136

BUSHNELL

St. Lawrence - 320 E. Dade Ave., Bushnell, FL 33513 t) 352-793-7788; 352-446-3849 (CRP) church@stlawrencebushnell.org www.stlawrencebushnell.org Rev. Waldemar Maciag (Poland), Admin.; Ana Garcia, DRE; CRP Stds.: 30

CASSELBERRY

St. Augustine - 375 N. Sunset Dr., Casselberry, FL 32707 t) 407-695-3262 frtomas@saintaugustinecc.org; frontdesk@saintaugustinecc.org staugch.org/ Dcn. Pedro Laboy; Rev. Tomas Hurtado, Pst.; Jorge Medina, DRE; CRP Stds.: 210

CELEBRATION

Corpus Christi - 1050 Celebration Ave., Celebration, FL 34747 t) 321-939-1491 bfischetti@celebrationcatholic.org; annette@celebrationcatholic.org www.celebrationcatholic.org Very Rev. Richard W. Trout, Pst.; Annette Cayer, DRE; CRP Stds.: 396

CLERMONT

Blessed Sacrament - 720 12th St., Clermont, FL 34711 t) 352-394-3562 cstalnaker@mybscc.org www.mybscc.org Rev. Jose Augusto Cadavid, Par. Vicar; Rev. Roy V. Eco, Par. Vicar; Chris Stalnaker, DRE; Rev. Mark R. Wajda, Pst.; CRP Stds.: 528

Mission Outreach - Santo Toribio Romo - 1043 E. Myers Blvd., Mascotte, FL 34753; Mailing: 720 12th St., Clermont, FL 34711 t) (352) 394-3562 communications@mybscc.org

St. Faustina Catholic Church - 1714 U.S. Hwy. 27, Ste 23, Clermont, FL 34714 t) 352-515-9297 mmariniello@stfaustina.org; jseddio@stfaustina.org www.stfaustina.org Joe Seddio, Bus. Mgr.; Rev. Ramon Bolatete, Par. Admin.; CRP Stds.: 137

COCOA

Blessed Sacrament - 5135 N. U.S. Hwy. 1, Cocoa, FL 32927 t) 321-632-6333 secretary@blessedsacramentcocoa.org; dwegner@blessedsacramentcocoa.org www.blessedsacramentcocoa.org Dcn. William Shelden; Darlene Wegner, DRE; Rev. Marek Sarniewicz, S.D.S., Par. Admin.; CRP Stds.: 52

COCOA BEACH

Church of Our Saviour - 5301 N. Atlantic Ave., Cocoa Beach, FL 32931 t) 321-783-4554 oursaviourchurch@cfl.rr.com; mcastaneda@oursavioursparish.org www.oursavioursparish.org Rev. Percival P. DeVera, Pst.; Manuel Castaneda IV, DRE; CRP Stds.: 84

Church of Our Saviour School - (Grades PreK-8) t) 321-783-2330 awestner@oursaviourschool.org www.oursaviourschool.org Amy Westner, Prin.; Stds.: 208; Lay Tchrs.: 13

DAYTONA BEACH

Basilica of Saint Paul - 317 Mullally St., Daytona Beach, FL 32114 t) 386-252-5422 dsmith@basilicaofsaintpaul.com; info@basilicaofsaintpaul.com www.basilicaofsaintpaul.com Rev. Kenneth Gill, Par. Admin.; Rev. Alvaro Jimenez, Par. Vicar; Dawn Smith, DRE; CRP Stds.: 40

Basilica of St. Paul School - -8) t) 386-252-7915 arivera@stpaulpanthers.org www.stpaulpanthers.org Andrea Rivera-Bonilla, Prin.; Stds.: 197; Lay Tchrs.: 11

Our Lady of Lourdes - 201 University Blvd., Daytona Beach, FL 32118 t) 386-255-0433 office@ourladyoflourdesdaytona.com www.ourladyoflourdesdaytona.com Rev. Philip J. Egitto, Pst.; CRP Stds.: 27

Our Lady of Lourdes School - (Grades PreK-8) 1014 N. Halifax Ave., Daytona Beach, FL 32118 t) 386-252-0391 sdole@lourdesacademy.net lourdesacademydaytona.net Stephen Dole, Prin.; Stds.: 228; Lay Tchrs.: 15

DEBARY

St. Ann's - 26 Dogwood Trl., Debary, FL 32713; Mailing: P.O. Box 530218, Debary, FL 32753-0218 t) 386-668-8270 nthielen@stannsdebary.org; office@stannsdebary.org stannsdebary.org Rev. Andrzej Jurkiewicz, Admin.; Nelson Thielen, DRE; CRP Stds.: 107

DELAND

St. Peter Church - 359 New York Ave., DeLand, FL 32720 t) 386-822-6000; 386-822-6025 (CRP) jmansingh@stpeterdeland.org; ebyrne@stpeterdeland.org stpeterdeland.org/ Rev. Gilbert Medina, Pst.; Jenny Mansingh, DRE; Easter Byrne, Bus. Mgr.; CRP Stds.: 330

St. Peter's Church School - -8) 421 W. New York Ave., DeLand, FL 32720 t) 386-822-6010 gmedina@stpeterdeland.org www.stpeterdeland.org Charlotte Funston, Prin.; Stds.: 217; Lay Tchrs.: 2

San Jose Mission - 165 Emporia Rd., Pierson, FL 32180-2784; Mailing: 359 W. New York Ave., DeLand, FL 32720 t) (386) 822-6000 gmedina@stpeterdeland.org; ebyrne@stpeterdeland.org Rev. Ramon Alfredo Ortiz, Par. Vicar;

St. Hubert of the Forest - 55600 Veterans Dr., Astor, FL 32102 gmedina@stpeterdeland.org; ebyrne@stpeterdeland.org

DELTONA

St. Clare - 2961 Day Rd., Deltona, FL 32738 t) 386-789-9990 frhector@stclarefl.org; info@stclarefl.org stclarefl.org Rev. Hector Vazquez Saad, Pst.; CRP Stds.: 62

Our Lady of the Lakes - 1310 Maximillian St., Deltona, FL 32725 t) 386-574-2131 ollfaithform@ourladyofthelakes.org; olloffice@ourladyofthelakes.org www.ourladyofthelakes.org Rev. Christopher Hoffmann, Pst.; Rev. Frank Cerio, Par. Vicar; Brendan Dudley, DRE; CRP Stds.: 97

DUNNELLON

St. John the Baptist - 7525 S. US Hwy. 41, Dunnellon, FL 34432 t) 352-489-3166 maryalice@stjohncc.com www.stjohncc.com Rev. Jean Hugues Desir, Pst.; Dcn. Eric Makoid; Dcn. Santos N. Santiago; MaryAlice Hogan, CRE; CRP Stds.: 28

EUSTIS

St. Mary of the Lakes - 218 Ocklawaha Ave., Eustis, FL 32726-4840 t) 352-483-3500 faithformation@stmaryofthelakesparish.org; frontdesk@stmaryofthelakesparish.org www.stmaryofthelakesparish.org Rev. Carlos Bedoya, Pst.; CRP Stds.: 69

HAINES CITY

St. Ann - 1311 E. Robinson Dr., Haines City, FL 33845; Mailing: P.O. Box 1285, Haines City, FL 33844 t) 863-422-4370; 863-438-2700 (CRP) imuniz@stannhc.org www.stannhc.org (Formerly Transfiguration) Rev. Alfonso Cely, O.P., Pst.; CRP Stds.: 187

INDIALANTIC

Holy Name of Jesus - 3050 Hwy. A1A, Indialantic, FL 32903 t) 321-773-2783 x120 (CRP); 321-773-2783 hnjparish@hnj.org www.hnj.org Very Rev. Scott M. Circe, Pst.; Rev. Peter Cordeno, Par. Vicar; Rev. Matthew C. Newcomb, Par. Vicar; Rev. Msgr. David Page, Pastor Emer.; Dcn. Dan Bassile; Dcn. John Farrell; Dcn. Michael Nussear; Dcn. Edward Struttmann; Dcn. Vincent Trunzo; Debbie Weir Khan, DRE; CRP Stds.: 219

Holy Name of Jesus School - (Grades PreK-8) 3060 Hwy. A1A, Indialantic, FL 32903 t) 321-773-1630 hnj@hnj.org; kfalk@hnj.org www.hnj.org/school Kathleen Falk, Prin.; Stds.: 230; Lay Tchrs.: 13

KISSIMMEE

St. Catherine of Siena - 2750 E. Osceola Parkway, Kissimmee, FL 34743; Mailing: P. O. Box 450698, Kissimmee, FL 34745 t) 407-344-9607 jcruz@stcatherineofsienacc.org; jmunoz@stcatherineofsienacc.org www.stcatherineofsienacc.org Rev. Jose Munoz, Pst.; Rev. Nazaire Massillon (Haiti), Par. Vicar; CRP Stds.: 241

Holy Redeemer - 1603 N. Thacker Ave., Kissimmee, FL 34741 t) 407-847-2500 frluis@hredeemer.org www.hredeemer.org Rev. Luis Salazar, Pst.; Rev. Archie Filoteo Faustino, Par. Vicar; Rev. David Vargas, Par. Vicar; CRP Stds.: 505

Holy Redeemer School - (Grades PreK-8) 1800 W. Columbia Ave., Kissimmee, FL 34741 t) 407-870-9055 agutierrez@holyredeemerkissimmee.org www.holyredeemerkissimmee.org Anthony Gutierrez, Prin.; Stds.: 449; Lay Tchrs.: 30

St. Rose of Lima - 3880 Pleasant Hill Rd., Kissimmee, FL 34746; Mailing: 3860 Pleasant Hill Rd., Kissimmee, FL 34746 t) 407-932-5004 info@saintroseoflimacc.org; juan.contreras@saintroseoflimacc.org www.srlcc.org Rev. Emmanuel Akalue, Pst.; Dcn. Juan Contreras, DRE; CRP Stds.: 189

LADY LAKE

St. Timothy - 1351 Paige Pl., Lady Lake, FL 32159 t) 352-753-0989 bulletin@sttimothycc.com; rlaseter@sttimothycc.com www.sttimothycc.com Robert

Laseter, DRE; Very Rev. Ralph DuWell, Pst.; CRP Stds.: 627

LAKE WALES

Holy Spirit - 644 S. 9th St., Lake Wales, FL 33853 t) 863-676-1556 losorio@holyspiritlakewales.org Rev. Luis Osorio, Pst.; CRP Stds.: 140

LAKELAND

St. Anthony Catholic Church - 820 Marcum Rd., Lakeland, FL 33809-4306 t) 863-858-8047 alofaro@saintacc.com www.saintacc.com Very Rev. Timothy P. LaBo, Pst.; Rev. Mariano Catura, Par. Vicar; Andrew Nicholas LoFaro, Bus. Mgr.; CRP Stds.: 127

St. Anthony Catholic Church School - (Grades PreK-8) 924 Marcum Rd., Lakeland, FL 33809 t) 863-858-0671 pbecker@saintacs.com www.saintacs.com Patricia Becker, Prin.; Stds.: 191; Lay Tchrs.: 13

Church of the Resurrection - 333 Terrace Way, Lakeland, FL 33813-1109 t) 863-646-3556 alofaro@rcclakeland.org www.rcclakeland.org Very Rev. Timothy P. LaBo, Pst.; Rev. Joseph Tran, Par. Vicar; Andrew Nicholas LoFaro, Bus. Mgr.; CRP Stds.: 464

Resurrection Catholic School - (Grades PreK-8) t) 863-644-3931 office@rcslakeland.org; lschaal@rcslakeland.org www.rcslakeland.org Lisa Schaal, Prin.; Stds.: 515; Lay Tchrs.: 31

St. John Neumann - 501 E. Carter Rd., Lakeland, FL 33813 t) 863-647-3400 mailbox@sjncc.org; jsztybel@sjncc.org www.sjncc.org Rev. Jaroslaw Sztybel, Admin.; CRP Stds.: 258

St. Joseph's - 118 W. Lemon St., Lakeland, FL 33815 t) 863-213-5280 alofaro@stjosephlakeland.org stjosephlakeland.org Very Rev. Timothy P. LaBo, Pst.; Rev. Zackary Gray, Par. Vicar; Rev. Blake Britton, Par. Vicar; Andrew Nicholas LoFaro, Bus. Mgr.; CRP Stds.: 188

LEESBURG

Saint Paul Catholic Church - 1330 Sunshine Ave., Leesburg, FL 34748 t) 352-787-6354 info@ccstpaul.com www.ccstpaul.com Rev. Gianni Agostinelli, Par. Vicar; Rev. Matthew Hawkins, Pst.; Jeff Falanga, DRE; Dcn. Patrick Kenneth McAvoy, Bus. Mgr.; CRP Stds.: 177

Saint Paul Catholic School - (Grades PreK-8) 1322 Sunshine Ave., Leesburg, FL 34748 t) 352-787-4657 info@saintpaulschool.com saintpaulschool.com Monica Matthews, Prin.; Stds.: 238; Sr. Tchrs.: 1; Lay Tchrs.: 15

St. Paul's Thrift Shop - 1321 Sunshine Ave., Leesburg, FL 34748 t) (352) 787-6354

St. Paul's Gift Shop - t) (352) 787-6354

LONGWOOD

Church of the Nativity - 3255 N. Ronald Reagan Blvd., Longwood, FL 32750 t) 407-322-3961 info@nativity.org; jelder@nativity.org www.nativity.org Rev. David Scotchie, Pst.; Jo Ann Elder, DRE; CRP Stds.: 228

MELBOURNE

Ascension - 2950 N. Harbor City Blvd., Melbourne, FL 32935-6259 t) 321-254-1595 mrusso@ascensioncatholic.net; dre@ascensioncatholic.net www.ascensioncatholic.net Rev. John Bosco Maison, Pst.; Dcn. Sergio Colon; Dcn. Christopher Meehan; Dcn. Tom Stauffacher; Dcn. William Terneus Sr.; Dcn. Ralph Turingan; Dcn. Phil Warwick; Betsy Glasenapp, DRE; CRP Stds.: 278

Ascension School - (Grades PreK-8) c/o Ascension Parish, 3000 N. Harbor City Blvd., Melbourne, FL 32935 t) (321) 254-1595 cstokes@ascensioncatholicsch.org www.ascensioncatholicsch.org Claudia Stokes, Prin.; Stds.: 459; Lay Tchrs.: 33

Our Lady of Lourdes - 1710 S. Hickory St., Melbourne, FL 32901-4517; Mailing: 1626 Oak St., Melbourne, FL 32901-4517 t) 321-723-3636 pattytaylor@ollmlb.org www.ollmlb.org Rev. Thomas R. Walden, Admin.; Patty Taylor, DRE; CRP Stds.: 76

Our Lady of Lourdes School - (Grades PreK-8) 420 E. Fee Ave., Melbourne, FL 32901 t) 321-723-3631 school@ollmelbourne.org; office@ollmelbourne.org www.ollmelbourne.org Donna Witherspoon, Prin.; Stds.: 117; Lay Tchrs.: 15

MELBOURNE BEACH

Immaculate Conception - 3780 S. Hwy. A1A, Melbourne Beach, FL 32951 t) 321-725-0552 vhock@icparishmb.org; office@icparishmb.org www.icparishmb.org Very Rev. Benjamin A. Berinti, C.PP.S., Pst.; Rev. Raymond Kaele, Par. Vicar; Manfred Dreilich, Music Min.; Vickie Hock, DRE; CRP Stds.: 51

MERRITT ISLAND

Divine Mercy Catholic Community - 1940 N. Courtenay Pkwy., Merritt Island, FL 32953 t) 321-452-5955 maryfrances@divinemercychurch.org; knousec@divinemercychurch.org divinemercychurch.org Rev. Romil Aperocho, Par. Vicar; Rev. Francisco Aquino (Philippines), Pst.; Mary-Frances Coburn, DRE; Carol Knouse, Bus. Mgr.; CRP Stds.: 100

MIMS

Holy Spirit - 2309 Holder Rd., Mims, FL 32754-2103; Mailing: 2399 Holder Rd., Mims, FL 32754 t) 321-269-7785 (CRP); 321-269-2282 faithformation@holyspiritmims.com; info@holyspiritmims.com holyspiritmims.com Rev. Andrzej Wojtan, Admin.; Christopher McCormick, DRE; CRP Stds.: 144

MOUNT DORA

St. Patrick's - 6803 Old Hwy. 441 S., Mount Dora, FL 32757 t) 352-383-8556 jzeller@stpatrickmtdora.org; mbaugh@stpatrickmtdora.org www.stpatrickmtdora.org Rev. Jimson Varghese, S.D.V. (India), Pst.; Rev. Gianni Agostinelli, Assoc. Pst.; Rev. Hermogenes Sargado, SDV, Par. Vicar; CRP Stds.: 290

NEW SMYRNA BEACH

Our Lady Star of the Sea - 4000 S. Atlantic Ave., New Smyrna Beach, FL 32169 t) 386-427-4530 x11 (CRP); 386-427-4530 www.ourladystar.com Rev. J. Patrick Quinn, T.O.R., Pst.; CRP Stds.: 28

Sacred Heart - 998 Father Donlon Dr., New Smyrna Beach, FL 32168; Mailing: P.O. Box 729, New Smyrna Beach, FL 32170 t) 386-410-5957 (CRP); 386-428-6426 sacredheart@sacredheartnsb.com www.sacredheartnsb.com Rev. John Tizio, C.Ss.R., Pst.; Rev. Kevin MacDonald, C.Ss.R., Par. Vicar; Rev. Aldrin Nunes, C.Ss.R., Par. Vicar; Dcn. Lou Bartos; CRP Stds.: 30

Sacred Heart School - -8) 1003 Turnbull St., New Smyrna Beach, FL 32168 t) 386-428-4732 elabreche@sacredheartcatholic.com shseagles.org Elizabeth LaBreche, Prin.; Stds.: 243; Lay Tchrs.: 19

St. Gerard - 3171 S. Ridgewood Ave., Edgewater, FL 32141; Mailing: c/o Sacred Heart Catholic Church, P.O. Box 729, New Smyrna Beach, FL 32170

OCALA

Blessed Trinity - 5 S.E. 17th St., Ocala, FL 34471 t) 352-629-8092 mail@blessedtrinity.org blessedtrinity.org Rev. Msgr. Patrick J. Sheedy, Pst.; Rev. Bernard Kiratu, Par. Vicar; Rev. Zbigniew Stradomski, Par. Vicar; Dcn. Heriberto Berrios; Dcn. Stephen Floyd; CRP Stds.: 166

Blessed Trinity School - (Grades K-8) t) 352-622-5808 mlosito@btschool.org btschool.org Megan Losito, Prin.; Stds.: 581; Lay Tchrs.: 36

Christ the King - 14045 N. U.S. Hwy. 301, Citra, FL 32113; Mailing: P.O. Box 129, Citra, FL 32113 t) 352-595-5605 admin@ctk-fl.org

Guadalupe Catholic Mission - 11153 W. Hwy. 40, Ocala, FL 34482; Mailing: c/o Blessed Trinity Catholic Church, 5 S.E. 17th St., Ocala, FL 34471 t) (352) 629-8092 psj@blessedtrinity.org; misioncatequistasocala07@yahoo.com Sr. Magalis Baldovino, M.C.S., DRE;

Immaculate Heart of Mary - 10670 SE Maricamp Rd., Ocala, FL 34472; Mailing: P.O. Box 310, Candler, FL 32111 t) 352-687-4031; 352-653-0031 (CRP) office@ihmcatholicchurch.com; dre@ihmcatholicchurch.com ihmcatholicchurch.com Rev. Stephen Ogonwa, Admin.; Wendie Ricketts, DRE; CRP Stds.: 15

St. Jude Catholic Community - 443 Marion Oaks Dr., Ocala, FL 34473-3203 t) 352-347-0154 religioused@judeparish.org www.judeparish.org Rev. Raul Adrian Valdez, Admin.; Mary Lynn Martin, DRE; CRP Stds.: 25

Our Lady of the Springs - 4047 N.E. 21st St., Ocala, FL 34470 t) 352-236-2230 dhiggins@ourladyofthesprings.org www.ourladyofthesprings.org Rev. Bill Zamborsky, Pst.; Deborah Higgins, DRE; CRP Stds.: 16

St. Joseph of the Forest - 17301 E. Hwy. 40, Silver Springs, FL 34488 t) 352-625-4222

Queen of Peace - 6455 S.W. State Rd. 200, Ocala, FL 34476-5553 t) 352-854-2181 qopparishoffice@queenofpeaceocala.com www.ocalaqueenofpeace.com Rev. Patrick J. O'Doherty, Pst.; Rev. Paul Parambil, OCD, Par. Vicar; CRP Stds.: 28

ORLANDO

St. James Cathedral - 215 N. Orange Ave., Orlando, FL 32801 t) 407-422-2005 info@stjamesorlando.org www.stjamesorlando.org Very Rev. Miguel A. Gonzalez, Rector; CRP Stds.: 310

St. James Cathedral School - -8) 505 E. Ridgewood St., Orlando, FL 32803 t) 407-841-4432 stjcs@stjcs.com www.stjcs.com Jayme Hartmann, Prin.; Stds.: 453; Lay Tchrs.: 36

St. Ignatius Kim Korean Mission - 1518 E. Muriel St., Orlando, FL 32806 t) 407-895-8858 stjjkim@gmail.com orlando.sarang.net Rev. Deog Su Han, Pst.;

St. Andrew - 801 N. Hastings St., Orlando, FL 32808 t) 407-293-0730 mzayas@standrew-orlando.org www.standrew-orlando.org Rev. Anthony Leo Hodges, Pst.; Rev. Barthelemy Garcon, S.M.M., Par. Vicar; Dcn. Carlos Martinez; Martha Lushman-Zayas, DRE; Dcn. Armand Carpentier; CRP Stds.: 119

St. Andrew School - -8) 877 Hastings St., Orlando, FL 32808 t) 407-295-4230 admissions@standrewcatholicschool.org www.standrewcatholicschool.org Latrina Peters-Gibson, Prin.; Stds.: 309; Lay Tchrs.: 17

Basilica of the National Shrine of Mary Queen of the Universe - 8300 Vineland Ave., Orlando, FL 32821 t) 407-239-6600 franthony@mqus.org maryqueenoftheuniverse.org Very Rev. Anthony Aarons, Rector;

Blessed Trinity - 4545 Anderson Rd., Orlando, FL 32812 t) 407-277-1702 alan.cruz@btccorl.org btccorl.org Rev. Roland Nadeau, M.S., Pst.; Rev. William Slight, M.S., Par. Vicar; Louis A. Murgia, DRE; CRP Stds.: 167

St. Charles Borromeo - 4001 Edgewater Dr., Orlando, FL 32804 t) 407-293-9556 x121 (CRP); 407-293-9556 stcharleschurch@stcharlesorlando.com www.stcharlesorlando.org Rev. Robert Marquez, Par. Admin.; Dcn. Paul Volkerson; Dcn. Luis Alvira; CRP Stds.: 119

St. Charles Borromeo School - -8) 4005 Edgewater Dr., Orlando, FL 32804 t) 407-293-7691 jrodriguez@scbcs.net www.stcharlesschoolorlando.org Dr. Jamie Rodriguez, Prin.; Stds.: 315; Lay Tchrs.: 23

Preschool - 4005 Edgewater Dr., Orlando, FL 32804 t) 407-293-7691 Dr. Jamie Rodriguez, Prin.;

Good Shepherd - 5900 Oleander Dr., Orlando, FL 32807 t) 407-277-3939; 407-277-3939 x212 (CRP) nsantana@gs.church; lmediavilla@gs.church www.gs.church Rev. James Henault, M.S., Pst.; Rev. Frank Cooney, M.S., Par. Vicar; Rev. Sunny Poovathumkudy, MS, Par. Vicar; Laura Mediavilla, DRE; CRP Stds.: 234

Good Shepherd School - (Grades PreK-8) 5902 Oleander Dr., Orlando, FL 32807 t) 407-277-3973 gdelorbe@goodshepherd.org www.goodshepherd.org Gloria Del Orbe, Prin.; Stds.: 339; Lay Tchrs.: 30

Good Shepherd Early Childhood Educational Ctr. -

t) 407-277-3973 x105 gdelorbe@goodshepherd.org Gloria Del Orbe, Prin.;

Holy Cross - 12600 Marsfield Ave., Orlando, FL 32837 t) 407-438-0990 holycrossorlando.org Rev. Luis Barrera, Par. Vicar; Rev. Esau Garcia, Pst.; Rev. Edwin Cardona, Par. Vicar; CRP Stds.: 885

Holy Family - 5125 S. Apopka-Vineland Rd., Orlando, FL 32819 t) 407-876-6331 (CRP); 407-876-2211 hfoffice@holyfamilyorlando.org; ncarbone@holyfamilyorlando.org www.holyfamilyorlando.com Rev. Martin Nguyen, Pst.; Rev. Shenoy Thomas, MC, Par. Vicar; Rev. Tom Pringle, Par. Vicar; Dcn. Carl Lawrence Brockman; Dcn. Richard Chabot; Dcn. Richard Dodd; Dcn. Noel Oteyza; Nora Carbone, CRE; CRP Stds.: 566

Holy Family School - (Grades PreK-8) 5129 S. Apopka-Vineland Rd., Orlando, FL 32819 t) 407-876-9344 sisterdorothy@hfcschool.com www.hfcschool.com Sr. Dorothy Sayers, M.P.F., Prin.; Stds.: 652; Lay Tchrs.: 25

St. Isaac Jogues - 4301 S. Chickasaw Tr., Orlando, FL 32829 t) 407-249-0906 stisaac@st-isaac.org; mbaker@st-isaac.org st-isaac.org Rev. Jose Bautista, Pst.; Dennis Johnson, Parish Life Coord.; Mike Baker, DRE; Rev. Enrique Guerra, Par. Vicar; CRP Stds.: 636

St. John Vianney - 6200 S. Orange Blossom Tr., Orlando, FL 32809 t) 407-855-5391 x222 (CRP); 407-855-5391 riverag@sjvorlando.org; parishoffice@sjvorlando.org Rev. Francisco Ojeda, Par. Vicar; Rev. Carlos J. Caban Vazquez, SDB, Admin.; CRP Stds.: 643

St. John Vianney School - -8) t) 407-855-4660 marshallc@sjvs.org; sjvs@sjvs.org www.sjvs.org Cathy Marshall, Prin.; Stds.: 474; Lay Tchrs.: 23

St. Joseph - 1501 N. Alafaya Tr., Orlando, FL 32828 t) 407-275-0841 eheinsen@stjosephorlando.org; office@stjosephorlando.org www.stjosephorlando.org Rev. Benjamin Lehnertz, Admin.; Dennis Johnson, Parish Life Coord.; Edith Heinsen, DRE; CRP Stds.: 583

St. Maximilian Kolbe - 1501 N. Alafaya Tr., Orlando, FL 32828 t) 407-275-0841 djohnsonjr@stjosephorlando.org stjosephorlando.org Rev. Benjamin Lehnertz, Admin.;

St. Philip Phan Van Minh Catholic Church - 15 W. Par St., Orlando, FL 32804; Mailing: 297 W. Par St., Orlando, FL 32804 t) 407-896-4210 cjnguyen@philipminhparish.org; office@philipminhparish.org philipminhparish.org Dcn. Nuoc Van Dang; Rev. Chau J. Nguyen, Pst.; Rev. Michael Pham, CRM, Par. Vicar; Sr. Marie Nguyen, DRE; CRP Stds.: 285

ORMOND BEACH

St. Brendan - 1000 Ocean Shore Blvd., Ormond Beach, FL 32176 t) 386-441-1505 vorlando@stbrendanchurchormond.org; trinko@stbrendanchurchormond.org Rev. Thomas G. Barrett, Pst.; Valeta Orlando, DRE; Dcn. Fred D'Angelo; CRP Stds.: 10

St. Brendan School - -8) t) 386-441-1331 pgorrasi@stbrendanormond.org Philip Gorrasi, Prin.; Stds.: 209; Lay Tchrs.: 14

Prince of Peace - 600 S. Nova Rd., Ormond Beach, FL 32174 t) 386-672-5272 (CRP); 386-672-5272 youth@princeofpeaceormond.com; admin@princeofpeaceormond.com www.princeofpeaceormond.com Rev. Justin Vakko Kannamparabil, O.C.D., Pst.; Rev. Francis Joseph, OCD, Par. Vicar; Dcn. Carlos Bom Conselho; Dcn. Bruce Gesinski; CRP Stds.: 123

OVIEDO

Most Precious Blood Catholic Church - 113 Lockwood Blvd, Oviedo, FL 32765 t) 407-365-3231 info@oviedocatholic.org www.oviedocatholic.org Rev. Josh Swallows, Admin.; Rev. Julius Lopez, Par. Vicar; CRP Stds.: 446

PALM BAY

St. Joseph - 5330 Babcock St., N.E., Palm Bay, FL 32905 t) 321-727-1565 vargasa@st-joe.org Very Rev. Benjamin A. Berinti, C.PP.S., Pst.; Dcn. Michael Patrick Mintern; Dcn. Joseph Moran; Dcn. James D. Stokes; Analisa Alegria, DRE; CRP Stds.: 156

St. Joseph School - -8) 5320 Babcock St., N.E., Palm Bay, FL 32905 t) 321-723-8866 office@st-joe.org; henrye@st-joe.org Edward Henry, Prin.; Stds.: 215; Lay Tchrs.: 21

Our Lady of Grace - 300 Malabar Rd. S.E., Palm Bay, FL 32907-3005 t) 321-725-3066 olg@ourladyofgracechurch.com; twood@ourladyofgracechurch.com www.ourladyofgracechurch.com Rev. Vilaire Philius, Admin.; Theresa Wood, DRE; CRP Stds.: 141

PORT ORANGE

Epiphany - 201 Lafayette St., Port Orange, FL 32127 t) 386-767-6111 finance@ccepiphany.com epiphanypo.com Rev. Karl Bergin, Pst.; Jessica Smith, DRE; CRP Stds.: 158

Our Lady of Hope - 4675 S. Clyde Morris Blvd, Port Orange, FL 32129-4064; Mailing: PO Box 290216, Port Orange, FL 32129 t) 386-788-6144 admin@ladyofhope.org Very Rev. Matthew Mello, Pst.; Rev. Paul Dau, Par. Vicar; CRP Stds.: 292

ROCKLEDGE

St. Mary Catholic Church - 1136 Seminole Dr., Rockledge, FL 32955 t) 321-636-6834 sdilago@stmaryrockledge.org; admin@stmaryrockledge.org www.stmaryrockledge.org Rev. Juan Osorno, Admin.; Rev. Mark Librizzi, Par. Vicar; CRP Stds.: 52

St. Mary Catholic Church School - (Grades PreK-8) 1152 Seminole Dr., Rockledge, FL 32955 t) 321-636-4208 info@stmarys-school.org www.stmarys-school.org Stephanie Swartz, Prin.; Stds.: 221; Lay Tchrs.: 14

SANFORD

All Souls - 3280 W. 1st St., Sanford, FL 32771; Mailing: 301 W 8 St., Sanford, FL 32771 t) 407-322-3795 rdiaz@orlandodiocese.org; frjeremiah@asccsanford.org asccsanford.org Rev. Jeremiah L. Payne, Pst.; CRP Stds.: 167

All Souls School - -8) 810 S. Oak Ave., Sanford, FL 32771 t) 407-322-7090 office@allsoulscatholicschool.org allsoulscatholicschool.org Barbara Schirard, Prin.; Stds.: 204; Lay Tchrs.: 11

ST. CLOUD

Saint Frances Xavier Cabrini Catholic Church - Narcoossee Middle School, 2700 N. Narcoossee Rd., St. Cloud, FL 34771; Mailing: 11954 Narcoossee Rd., Ste. 2, PMB / #512, Orlando, FL 32832 t) 407-766-1134 frcharles@saintcabrinicatholic.org www.saintcabrinicatholic.org Rev. Charles Viviano, Pst.; CRP Stds.: 250

St. Thomas Aquinas Church - 900 Brown Chapel Rd., St. Cloud, FL 34769; Mailing: 700 Brown Chapel Rd., St. Cloud, FL 34769 t) 407-957-4495 sjefferson@stacatholic.org; frderek@stacatholic.org www.stacatholic.org Rev. Derek Saldanha, Pst.; Rev. Fidel Rodriguez, Par. Vicar; Shaheda Jefferson, Bus. Mgr.; Jorge Montes, RCIA Coord.; CRP Stds.: 430

St. Thomas Aquinas Church School - (Grades PreK-8) 800 Brown Chapel Rd., St. Cloud, FL 34769 t) 407-957-1772 npavgouzas@stacschool.com stacschool.com Nick Pavgouzas, Prin.; Margie Smith, Bus. Mgr.; Stds.: 262; Lay Tchrs.: 20

SUMMERFIELD

St. Mark the Evangelist - 7081 SE Hwy. 42, Summerfield, FL 34491 t) 352-347-9317 pastor@stmarkrcc.com; reception@stmarkrcc.com www.stmarkrcc.com Rev. Rafal Dominik Kandora, OSPPE, Pst.; Rev. Dominik Libiszewski, OSPPE, Par. Vicar; CRP Stds.: 525

TITUSVILLE

St. Teresa - 203 Ojibway Ave., Titusville, FL 32780 t) 321-349-5445 (CRP); 321-268-3441 faithformation@stteresa-titusville.org; marge@stteresach.org www.saintteresatitusville.org Dcn. Donald Boland; Rev. Krzysztof Bugno, S.D.S., Pst.; Ina Smith, Music Min.; Rev. Gabriel Kaminski, SDS (Poland), Pst. Assoc.; Gregory Clouser, DRE; CRP Stds.: 38

St. Teresa School - -8) 207 Ojibway Ave., Titusville, FL 32780 t) 321-267-1643 mmccrory@steresa-titusville.org www.stteresa-titusville.org Mary McCrory, Prin.; Stds.: 179; Lay Tchrs.: 11

VIERA

St. John the Evangelist - 5655 Stadium Pkwy., Viera, FL 32940 t) 321-637-9650 office@stjohnviera.org www.stjohnviera.org Rev. John Britto Antony, C.S.C., Pst.; Dawn Hurley, DRE; CRP Stds.: 351

WILDWOOD

San Pedro de Jesus Maldonado Mission - 210 Wonders St., Wildwood, FL 34785; Mailing: 1330 Sunshine Ave, Leesburg, FL 34748 t) 352-787-9208 giagox@gmail.com Rev. Gianni Agostinelli, Admin.; CRP Stds.: 90

St. Vincent de Paul - 5323 E. CR 462, Wildwood, FL 34785 t) 352-330-0220 stvincentchurch@sumtercatholic.org; faithformation@sumtercatholic.org www.sumtercatholic.org Rev. Peter Puntal, Pst.; Rev. John E. McCracken, Par. Vicar; Michelle Szczepanski, DRE; CRP Stds.: 64

WINTER GARDEN

Resurrection Catholic Church - 1211 Winter Garden Vineland Rd., Winter Garden, FL 34787-4338 t) 407-656-3113 parish@resurrectionwg.org; rcc@resurrectionwg.org www.resurrectionwg.org Rev. Heitor Castoldi, C.S., Pst.; Rev. Noe Jaimes, cs, Par. Vicar; Sr. Patricia Sipan, S.N.D., DRE; CRP Stds.: 795

WINTER HAVEN

St. Joseph's - 532 Ave. M N.W., Winter Haven, FL 33881 t) 863-294-3144 alofaro@stjosephwh.org www.stjosephwh.org Rev. Sebastian Nzabhayanga, Par. Vicar; Andrew Nicholas LoFaro, Bus. Mgr.; Very Rev. Timothy P. LaBo, Pst.; CRP Stds.: 199

St. Joseph's School - (Grades PreK-8) 535 Ave. M N.W., Winter Haven, FL 33881 t) 863-293-3311 thaas@stjosephwhschool.org www.stjosephwhschool.org Tammi Haas, Prin.; Stds.: 472; Lay Tchrs.: 28

St. Matthew - 1991 Overlook Dr., Winter Haven, FL 33884 t) 863-324-3040 info@saintmcc.com saintmcc.com Rev. Nicholas J. O'Brien, Pst.; CRP Stds.: 54

Our Lady of Guadalupe - 2150 Bomber Rd., Wahneta, FL 33880 t) 863-299-3854 thepastor@saintmcc.com Rev. Delvis Mederos, Par. Vicar;

WINTER PARK

St. Margaret Mary - 526 N. Park Ave., Winter Park, FL 32789 t) 407-647-3392 debbie@stmargaretmary.org; concetta@stmargaretmary.org www.stmargaretmary.org Rev. Msgr. Richard Walsh, Pst.; Rev. Adam Marchese, Par. Vicar; Rev. Shenoy Thomas, MC, Par. Vicar; Dcn. David Engasser; CRP Stds.: 390

St. Margaret Mary School - -8) 142 E. Swoope Ave., Winter Park, FL 32789 t) 407-644-7537 info@smmknight.org www.smmknight.org Kathleen Walsh, Prin.; Stds.: 471; Lay Tchrs.: 38

Saints Peter and Paul - 5300 Old Howell Branch Rd., Winter Park, FL 32792 t) 407-657-6114 david.lawton@stspp.net www.stspp.net Rev. Derk Schudde, Pst.; Rev. Msgr. Juanito Figura, Par. Vicar; CRP Stds.: 292

WINTER SPRINGS

St. Stephen - 575 Tuskawilla Rd., Winter Springs, FL 32708 t) 407-699-5683 gigis@st-stephen.com; jgiel@st-stephen.com st-stephen.com Dcn. James Ferruzzi; Very Rev. John Giel, Pst.; CRP Stds.: 653

SCHOOLS: PRESCHOOL THRU HIGH SCHOOL

SCHOOLS

STATE OF FLORIDA

ORLANDO

Morning Star Catholic School - (PAR) 930 Leigh Ave., Orlando, FL 32804-2299 t) 407-295-3077 abbeya@morningstarorlando.org; aceitunol@morningstarorlando.org www.morningstarorlando.org Special Needs Students ages 5-26 Dr. Alicia Abbey, Prin.; Thomas Doyle, Pres.; Stds.: 71; Lay Tchrs.: 8

HIGH SCHOOLS

STATE OF FLORIDA

DAYTONA BEACH

Father Lopez Catholic High School, Inc. - (DIO) 3918 LPGA Blvd., Daytona Beach, FL 32124 t) 386-253-5213 lsvajko@fatherlopez.org; mgallolethcoe@fatherlopez.org www.fatherlopez.org Leigh Svajko, Prin.; Stds.: 419; Lay Tchrs.: 43

LAKELAND

Santa Fe Catholic High School, Inc. - (DIO) 3110 Hwy. 92 E., Lakeland, FL 33801 t) 863-665-4188 mfranzino@santafecatholic.org www.santafecatholic.org Matthew Franzino, Prin.; Camille Jowanna, Prin.; Stds.: 386; Lay Tchrs.: 28

MELBOURNE

Central Catholic High School, Inc. - (DIO) 154 E. Florida Ave., Melbourne, FL 32901 t) 321-727-0793 reginan@melbournecc.org melbournecc.org Dave Parker, Vice Prin.; Nicholas Regina, Pres.; Stds.: 405; Pr. Tchrs.: 1; Lay Tchrs.: 35

OCALA

Trinity Catholic High School, Inc. - (DIO) 2600 S.W. 42nd St., Ocala, FL 34471 t) 352-622-9025 lpereira@tchs.us www.trinitycatholichs.org Tammie Vassou, Prin.; Lou Pereira, Pres.; Stds.: 535; Lay Tchrs.: 44

ORLANDO

Bishop Moore Catholic High School Inc. - (DIO) 3901 Edgewater Dr., Orlando, FL 32804 t) 407-293-7561 luters@bishopmoore.org www.bishopmoore.org Erika Wikstrom, Prin.; Thomas Doyle, Pres.; Stds.: 1,450,105; Sr. Tchrs.: 1; Lay Tchrs.: 105

INSTITUTIONS LOCATED IN DIOCESE

CAMPUS MINISTRY / NEWMAN CENTERS [CAM]

DAYTONA BEACH

Catholic Campus Ministry at Embry-Riddle Aeronautical University - 600 S. Clyde Morris Blvd., Daytona Beach, FL 32114-3900 t) (386) 767-6111 rdiaz@orlandodiocese.org Rev. Karl Bergin, Pst.;

DELAND

Catholic Campus Ministry at Stetson University - 359 W. New York Ave., Deland, FL 32720 t) 386-822-6000 www.stpeterdeland.org Rev. Gilbert Medina, Pst.;

LAKELAND

Florida Southern College Newman Center - c/o St. Joseph, 118 W. Lemon St., Campus Ministry/Newman Center, Lakeland, FL 33815 t) 863-213-5280 alofaro@stjosephlakeland.org www.stjosephlakeland.org Very Rev. Timothy P. LaBo, Pst.;

MELBOURNE

Catholic Campus Ministry at Florida Institute of Technology - Florida Institute of Technology, 150 W. University Blvd., Melbourne, FL 32901-6988 t) 321-674-8045 ljaime@fit.edu www.fit.edu/ccm Rev. Randall Meissen, LC, Campus Min.;

OVIEDO

Catholic Campus Ministry at the University of Central Florida - 3925 Lockwood Blvd., #1051, Oviedo, FL 32765 t) 407-392-0824 kzeiler@cmmknights.com www.ccmknights.com Rev. Josh Swallows, Chap.; Bro. Martin Buganski, Campus Min.;

WINTER PARK

Catholic Campus Ministry at Rollins College - c/o Msgr. Richard Walsh, 526 Park Ave. N., Winter Park, FL 32789 t) (407) 647-3392 rdiaz@orlandodiocese.org stmargaretmary.org Rev. Msgr. Richard Walsh, Campus Min.;

CATHOLIC CHARITIES [CCH]

ORLANDO

Catholic Charities of Central Florida, Inc. - 1819 N. Semoran Blvd., Orlando, FL 32807 t) 888-658-2828 cflcc.org Gary Tester, Pres.; Asstd. Annu.: 187,098; Staff: 148

CEMETERIES [CEM]

ORLANDO

Catholic Cemeteries of Central Florida Holdings, Inc. - 50 E. Robinson St., Orlando, FL 32801 t) 407-246-4832 Roger Barnes, Comptroller;

MISCELLANEOUS [MIS]

ORLANDO

Florida Catholic Media - 50 E. Robinson St., Orlando, FL 32801; Mailing: P.O. Box 4993, Orlando, FL 32802 t) 407-373-0075; 888-275-9953 aborowski@thefloridacatholic.org www.thefloridacatholic.org/ Ann B. Slade, Associate Publisher;

ST. CLOUD

Magnify of Central Florida - 401 Bishop Grady Ct., St. Cloud, FL 34769 t) 407-892-6078 kevin@magnifyfl.org www.magnifyfl.org Residential, Life Skills, Employment, and Transition services for youth and adults with disabilities. Kevin Johnson, Exec.; Asstd. Annu.: 376; Staff: 70

MONASTERIES AND RESIDENCES FOR PRIESTS AND BROTHERS [MON]

COCOA BEACH

Congregation of Holy Cross, United States Province - 325 Arthur Ave., Cocoa Beach, FL 32931-4005 t) 321-799-8383 Rev. R. Bradley Beaupre, C.S.C., Supr.; Rev. Anthony R. Grasso, C.S.C., Assistant Superior; Rev. George B Mulligan, CSC, In Res.; Rev. Joseph J. Long, C.S.C., In Res.; Rev. Laurence Olszewski, C.S.C., In Res.; Rev. James T. Preskenis, C.S.C., In Res.; Rev. Edmund Sylvia, C.S.C., In Res.; Rev. Robert A. Wiseman, C.S.C., In Res.; Priests: 7

DELAND

Augustinian Monks of the Primitive Observance - Mother of the Good Shepherd Monastery, 2075 Mercers Fernery Rd., Deland, FL 32720 t) 386-736-4321 monks@osaprim.org www.augustinianmonks.com Bro. Nicholas Drouin, OSA, Prim., Prior; Brs.: 3

NEW SMYRNA BEACH

St. Alphonsus Villa-Redemptorist Fathers and Brothers - 318 N. Riverside Dr., New Smyrna Beach, FL 32168 t) 386-428-6481 vpofrichmond@aol.com Luz Estelle Rodriguez, Bus. Mgr.; Brs.: 1; Priests: 9

Franciscan Friars, TOR - 4385 Saxon Dr., New Smyrna Beach, FL 32169 t) (352) 978-9874 rdiaz@orlandodiocese.org Rev. Blase Romano, T.O.R., Bus. Mgr.; Brs.: 1; Priests: 2

Redemptorist Fathers of the Vice Province of Baltimore - 313 Hillman St., New Smyrna Beach, FL 32168 t) 386-427-3094 vpofrichmond@aol.com Luz Estelle Rodriguez, Bus. Mgr.; Brs.: 1; Priests: 9

Villa Madonna Friary (Franciscan Friars TOR) - 4385 Saxon Dr., New Smyrna Beach, FL 32169 t) (352) 978-9874 rdiaz@orlandodiocese.org Rev. Blase Romano, T.O.R., Bus. Mgr.; Brs.: 1; Priests: 2

NURSING / REHABILITATION / CONVALESCENCE / ELDERLY CARE [NUR]

DAYTONA BEACH

Casa San Pablo - 401 N. Ridgewood Ave., Daytona Beach, FL 32114 t) 386-253-2828 casasanpablomgr@spm.net Barbara D. Mitchell, Admin.; Asstd. Annu.: 64; Staff: 7

MELBOURNE

Ascension Manor - 2960 Pineapple Ave., Melbourne, FL 32935 t) 321-757-9828 ascensionmgr@cflcc.org Josephine Stratford, Bus. Mgr.; Asstd. Annu.: 76; Staff: 3

OCALA

Trinity Villas, Inc. - 3728 N.E. 8th Pl., Ocala, FL 34470-1093 t) 352-694-5507 trinitymgr@cflcc.org Gary Tester, Pres.; Asstd. Annu.: 162; Staff: 8

ORLANDO

St. Joseph's Garden Courts, Inc. - 1515 N. Alafaya Trl., Orlando, FL 32828 t) 407-382-0808 sjgc-mgr@cflcc.org Gary Tester, Pres.; Asstd. Annu.: 80; Staff: 5

Monsignor Bishop Manor, Inc. - 815 Borders Cir., Ste. 144, Orlando, FL 32808 t) 407-293-3339 mbmmanager@cflcc.org Connie Casquete, Bus. Mgr.; Asstd. Annu.: 143; Staff: 5

ORMOND BEACH

Prince of Peace Housing, Inc. - 664 S. Nova Rd., Ormond Beach, FL 32174 t) 386-673-5080 princeofpeacemgr@caterretmgmt.com Asstd. Annu.: 69; Staff: 5

PORT ORANGE

Epiphany Manor - 4792 S. Ridgewood Ave., Port Orange, FL 32127 t) 386-767-2556 epiphanymanormgr@carteretmgmt.com Kave Thompson, Bus. Mgr.; Asstd. Annu.: 72; Staff: 5

ST. CLOUD

St. Anthony Garden Court - 444 Hamilton Park Cir., St. Cloud, FL 34769 t) 321-805-4733 stanthonygardenctmgr@spm.net Gary Tester, Pres.; Shaimaa Elawdan, Bus. Mgr.; Asstd. Annu.: 69; Staff: 2

WINTER HAVEN

Episcopal Catholic Apartments - 500 Ave. L, N.W., Winter Haven, FL 33881 t) 863-299-4481 episcopalcatholicmgr@spm.net Jessica Boerger, Admin.; Asstd. Annu.: 210; Staff: 7

RETREAT HOUSES / RENEWAL CENTERS [RTR]

WINTER PARK

San Pedro Spiritual Development Center - 95 Bishop Grady Ln., Winter Park, FL 32792 t) 407-671-6322 info@sanpedrocenter.org www.sanpedrocenter.org Randall Pinner, Exec. Dir.;

Diocese of Owensboro

(Dioecesis Owensburgensis)

MOST REVEREND WILLIAM F. MEDLEY

Bishop of Owensboro; ordained May 22, 1982; appointed Bishop of Owensboro December 15, 2009; ordained February 10, 2010. Mailing Address: 600 Locust St., Owensboro, KY 42301.

McRaith Catholic Center: 600 Locust St., Owensboro, KY 42301. T: 270-683-1545; F: 270-683-6883.
www.owensborodiocese.org
martha.hagan@pastoral.org

CREATED DECEMBER 9, 1937.

Square Miles 12,502.

Erected February 23, 1938.

Comprises the following thirty-two Counties in the western part of the State of Kentucky: Allen, Ballard, Breckinridge, Butler, Caldwell, Calloway, Carlisle, Christian, Crittenden, Daviess, Edmonson, Fulton, Graves, Grayson, Hancock, Henderson, Hickman, Hopkins, Livingston, Logan, Lyon, McCracken, McLean, Marshall, Muhlenberg, Ohio, Simpson, Todd, Trigg, Union, Warren and Webster.

For legal titles of parishes and diocesan institutions, consult the McRaith Catholic Center.

STATISTICAL OVERVIEW

Personnel

Bishop	1
Priests: Diocesan Active in Diocese	59
Priests: Diocesan Active Outside Diocese	1
Priests: Retired, Sick or Absent	13
Number of Diocesan Priests	73
Religious Priests in Diocese	5
Total Priests in your Diocese	78
Extern Priests in Diocese	5
Ordinations:	
Diocesan Priests	1
Permanent Deacons in Diocese	43
Total Sisters	109

Parishes

Parishes	78
With Resident Pastor:	
Resident Diocesan Priests	68
Resident Religious Priests	10
Professional Ministry Personnel:	
Sisters	15
Lay Ministers	88

Welfare

Catholic Hospitals	1
Total Assisted	43,256
Homes for the Aged	1
Total Assisted	175
Day Care Centers	1
Total Assisted	96
Specialized Homes	1
Total Assisted	20
Special Centers for Social Services	1
Total Assisted	1,200

Educational

Diocesan Students in Other Seminaries	5
Total Seminarians	5
Colleges and Universities	1
Total Students	1,024
High Schools, Diocesan and Parish	3
Total Students	430
Elementary Schools, Diocesan and Parish	13
Total Students	1,842
Catechesis/Religious Education:	
High School Students	145
Elementary Students	1,511
Total Students under Catholic Instruction	4,957
Teachers in Diocese:	
Priests	1
Sisters	8
Lay Teachers	338

Vital Statistics

Receptions into the Church:	
Infant Baptism Totals	654
Minor Baptism Totals	74
Adult Baptism Totals	65
Received into Full Communion	161
First Communions	749
Confirmations	645
Marriages:	
Catholic	156
Interfaith	41
Total Marriages	197
Deaths	559
Total Catholic Population	51,043
Total Population	886,477

LEADERSHIP

McRaith Catholic Center - t) 270-683-1545
Vicar General - t) 270-684-5369 Rev. J. Patrick Reynolds;
Vicar of Clergy - Rev. Jason McClure;
Chancellor - Thomas R. Lilly;
Vice Chancellor - Martha Hagan;
Administrative Assistant to the Bishop - Martha Hagan;
Archivist - Edward Wilson;
Diocesan Tribunal -
Adjutant Judicial Vicar (Vacant) -
Advocates -
Defenders of the Bond - Rev. J. Patrick Reynolds; Rev. William R. Thompson;
Director/Formal Case Instructor/Assessor - Louanne Payne;
Documentary Case Instructors/Notaries - Patti Bartley;
Judges - Rev. John R. Vaughan; Rev. J. Michael Clark; Emily Danchisin;
Judicial Vicar - Rev. Patrick Cooney, O.S.B., Vicar;
Peritus - Michael Flaherty; Donald L. Preuss;
Promoter of Justice - Rev. William R. Thompson;

ADVISORY BOARDS, COMMISSIONS, COMMITTEES, AND COUNCILS

Age Group Six Representative - Rev. Anthony J. Shonis;
Catholic Charities - t) 270-852-8343 Susan Montalvo-Gesser, Dir.; Rev. Ed Bradley, Ex Officio; Debbie Webb;
Catholic Campaign for Human Development - Susan Montalvo-Gesser, Dir.;
Catholic Relief Service - Susan Montalvo-Gesser, Dir.;
Co-Coordinator of Worship - Rev. Brandon Williams; Lauren Johnson;
Cursillo - t) 270-684-4745 Rev. Tom Buckman; Felicia Elliott, Dir.;
Diocesan Liturgical Committee - Rev. Brandon Williams; Lauren Johnson; Michael Bogdan;
Consultors - Rev. Emmanuel Udoh; Rev. Randy Howard; Rev. John M. Thomas;
Deans - Rev. Daniel C. Dillard; Rev. Larry McBride; Rev. Tony Jones;
Ongoing Formation of Priests - Rev. Joshua A. McCarty;
Pastoral Office for Education -
Assistant Superintendent of Schools - Joanne Mathieson;
Digital Media Specialist - Riley Greif, Dir.;
Director of Communications - Tina Kasey;
Director of Ecumenism - Rev. Ray Clark;
Director of Office for Faith Formation - Dcn. Jay VanHoosier;
Editor and Coordinator Diocesan Publications - Elizabeth Wong-Barnstead, Editor;
Gasper River Catholic Youth Camp and Retreat Center - Ben Warrell, Dir.;
Superintendent of Schools - David Kessler;
Youth & Young Adult Ministry - Charlie Hardesty, Dir.;
Pastoral Office for Finance - Raymond Purk, CFO; Kim Haire, Controller;
Pastoral Office for Social Concerns - Susan Montalvo-Gesser, Dir.;
African-American Office - Veronica Wilhite, Dir.;
Hispanic Office - Dcn. Chris Gutierrez, Dir.;
Office for Safe Environment for the Protection of Children and Young People - Janice Hendricks, Coord.;
Respect Life Office - Susan Montalvo-Gesser;
Social Concerns Committee - Dcn. Richard Murphy; Joe Abel; Ranni Dillard;
Pastoral Office for Stewardship - Thomas R. Lilly;
Diocesan Finance Council - Rev. J. Patrick Reynolds; Rev. Jerry Riney; Sr. Barbara Jean Head, O.S.U.;
Pastoral Office of Family Life - Danny May, Dir.;
Family Life Committee - Danny May; Amanda Reffitt; John McCarty;
Natural Family Planning - Michelle Roberts, Owensboro; Martha Winn, Bowling Green; Jenny Rush, Hopkinsville;
Society for the Propagation of the Faith - Rev. Ray Clark;
Priest Personnel Committee - Rev. J. Patrick Reynolds, Vicar; Rev. Emmanuel Udoh; Rev. Thomas J. Buckman;
Priests' Council - Rev. Daniel C. Dillard; Rev. Larry McBride; Rev. Tony Jones;
***Roman Catholic Diocese of Owensboro Charitable Trust Fund, Inc.** - Raymond Purk; Most Rev. William F. Medley; Thomas R. Lilly;
Vicar of Clergy - Rev. Jason McClure, Vicar;
Vocations Office - Rev. Daniel C. Dillard, Dir.;

EVANGELIZATION

Office of Evangelization & Discipleship - Jeff Andrini, Dir.;

ORGANIZATIONS

Birthright - t) 270-683-1103 Terri LaHugh, Dir.;
Daughters of Isabella - Rev. Msgr. Bernard Powers, Chap.; Ann Newby, State Regent; Sheila Thompson, Owensboro Circle #241 Regent;
Holy Childhood Association - Rev. Ray Clark;
Legion of Mary (Vacant) -
Mercy Health Partners - Lourdes, Inc. - t) 270-444-2444 Michael Yungmann, Pres.;
Pastoral Assistance Coordinator (English) - t) 270-852-8369 Louanne Payne (louanne.payne@pastoral.org);
Pastoral Assistance Coordinators (Spanish) - t) 270-880-8360 Susan Montalvo-Gesser; Miguel Quintanilla;
St. Vincent de Paul Society - t) 270-993-6972 Nancy Harris, Pres.;
Scouting Activities - Rev. Kenneth J. Mikulcik, Chap.;
Serra Club - Rev. Ray Clark, Chap.;
Owensboro Chapter - Ernie Taliaferro, Pres.;

PARISHES, MISSIONS, AND CLERGY

COMMONWEALTH OF KENTUCKY

BARDWELL

St. Charles - 6922 State Rte. 408, Bardwell, KY 42023 t) 270-642-2586 sghayden@wk.net Rev. Chrispin Oneko (Kenya), Pst.; CRP Stds.: 10

BEAVER DAM

Holy Redeemer - 107 13th St., Beaver Dam, KY 42320 t) 270-274-3414 holyredeemercc@gmail.com Rev. Julio Barrera, Pst.; Lisa Whitehouse, Bus. Mgr.; Sr. Adia Badillo - Lorenzo, Hispanic Ministry; Gail Critchelow, DRE; CRP Stds.: 92

BOWLING GREEN

Holy Spirit - 4754 Smallhouse Rd., Bowling Green, KY 42104-4141 t) 270-842-7777 frrandy@holyspiritcatholic.org; frstephen@holyspiritcatholic.org www.holyspiritcatholic.org Rev. Randy Howard, Pst.; Rev. Martin Ma Na Ling, Par. Vicar; Lori Lewis, Pst. Assoc.; CRP Stds.: 282

St. Joseph - 434 Church Ave., Bowling Green, KY 42101 t) 270-842-2525 ryan.harpole@pastoral.org www.stjosephbg.org Rev. Ryan Harpole, Pst.; Rev. Corey D. Bruns, Assoc. Pst.; CRP Stds.: 90

CADIZ

St. Stephen - 1698 Canton Rd., Cadiz, KY 42211 t) 270-522-3801 ststephencath387@bellsouth.net ststephencc.com Dcn. Randall Potempa; Rev. Gregory G. Trawick, Pst.; CRP Stds.: 10

CALHOUN

St. Sebastian - 180 State Rte. 136 W., Calhoun, KY 42327-9521 t) 270-273-3185 Rev. Jegin Puthenpurackal, H.G.N. (India), Pst.; CRP Stds.: 25

CALVERT CITY

St. Pius Tenth - 777 Fifth Ave., Calvert City, KY 42029; Mailing: P.O. Box 495, Calvert City, KY 42029 t) 270-395-4727 crecalvertcity@gmail.com; stpiusx@stpiusx.us stpiusx.us Rev. Brian Johnson, Pst.; Paula Schmidt, DRE; CRP Stds.: 45

CENTRAL CITY

St. Joseph - 109 S. 3rd St., Central City, KY 42330 t) 270-754-1164 c) (270) 399-5860 stjosephcc.org Rev. John Ighacho (Kenya), Pst.; Dcn. Donald Adams; CRP Stds.: 13

CLARKSON

St. Anthony - 1256 St. Anthony Rd., Clarkson, KY 42726 t) 270-242-4791 stanthony1256@windstream.net www.triparishcatholic.com Dcn. William Grant; Rev. Brandon Williams, Pst.;

St. Augustine - 30 St. Augustine Rd, Grayson Springs, KY 42726, Clarkson, KY 42726; Mailing: 1256 St. Anthony Rd, Clarkson, KY 42726 t) 270-242-4791 stanthony1256@windstream.net www.triparishcatholic.com Dcn. T.J. Anthony Dennison; Dcn. William Grant; Rev. Brandon Williams, Pst.;

St. Elizabeth of Hungary - 306 Clifty Ave., Clarkson, KY 42726; Mailing: P.O. Box 273, Clarkson, KY 42726 t) 270-242-4414 saintelizabethclarkson@windstream.net Rev. Steve Hohman, Pst.; CRP Stds.: 18

CLINTON

St. Jude - 308 Mayfield Rd., Clinton, KY 42031 t) 270-653-6869 jjhobbs@windstream.net Rev. Robert Drury, Pst.; Dcn. Hal M. Jones; Dcn. Brent Kimbler; CRP Stds.: 3

CLOVERPORT

St. Rose - 1285 Middle Patesville Rd., Cloverport, KY 42348 t) 270-788-6422 michael.abiero@pastoral.org; angelalasley3254@gmail.com Rev. Michael Charles Abiero, Pst.;

CURDSVILLE

St. Elizabeth - 6143 First St., Curdsville, KY 42334; Mailing: P.O. Box 9-A, Curdsville, KY 42334 c) 270-570-2299 selizabethcville@gmail.com Judy Schadler, Contact;

DAWSON SPRINGS

Resurrection - 530 Industrial Park Rd., Dawson Springs, KY 42408 t) 270-797-8665; 270-383-4743 Dcn. Michael Marsili; Rev. David Kennedy, Pst.;

EARLINGTON

Holy Cross - 112 S. Day St., Earlington, KY 42410 t) 270-383-4743 david.kennedy@pastoral.org Dcn. Michael Marsili; Rev. David Kennedy, Pst.;

Immaculate Conception - 112 S. Day St., Earlington, KY 42410 t) 270-383-4743 frdavidkennedy@aol.com Dcn. Michael Marsili; Rev. David Kennedy, Pst.;

EDDYVILLE

St. Mark Church - 302 Peachtree Ln., Eddyville, KY 42038 t) 270-388-2133 stmarkeddyville.weconnect.com Rev. Jojy Joseph HGN, HGN (India), Pst.; Dcn. Paul Bachi; CRP Stds.: 9

FANCY FARM

St. Denis - 2758 Hwy. 1748 W., Fancy Farm, KY 42039; Mailing: 6922 State Rte. 408, Bardwell, KY 42023 t) 270-642-2586 sghayden@wk.net Rev. Chrispin Oneko (Kenya), Pst.; CRP Stds.: 8

St. Jerome - 20 State Route 339N, Fancy Farm, KY 42039; Mailing: P.O. Box 38, Fancy Farm, KY 42039 t) 270-623-8181 stjerome@wk.net www.stjeromefancyfarm.com Rev. Darrell Venters, Pst.; CRP Stds.: 172

FORDSVILLE

St. John the Baptist - 67 Smith St., Fordsville, KY 42343; Mailing: P.O. Box 127, Fordsville, KY 42343 t) 270-276-3619 c) (270) 485-3359 (request records/

bulletin) roby042569@gmail.com; hagand4001@gmail.com owensborodiocese.org Mission of St. Mary's Whitesville, Ky Rev. Brian Roby, Pst.;

FRANKLIN

St. Mary - 403 N. Main St., Franklin, KY 42134; Mailing: PO Box 388, Franklin, KY 42135 t) 270-586-4515 tom.buckman@pastoral.org www.stmarysfranklin.cc Rev. Tom Buckman, Pst.; CRP Stds.: 50

FULTON

St. Edward - 504 Eddings St., Fulton, KY 42041 t) 270-472-2742 stedwardky@bellsouth.net Rev. Robert Drury, Pst.;

GRAND RIVERS

St. Anthony of Padua - 1518 J.H. O'Bryan Ave., Grand Rivers, KY 42045; Mailing: P.O. Box 447, Grand Rivers, KY 42045 t) 270-395-4727 stpiusx@stpiusx.us www.stanthonygrandrivers.org Rev. Brian Johnson, Pst.; CRP Stds.: 4

GUTHRIE

St. Francis of Assisi Catholic Church - 7600 Russellville Rd., Guthrie, KY 42234; Mailing: P.O. Box 297, Guthrie, KY 42234 t) 270-265-5263 stfrancisofassis@outlook.com Dcn. Heriberto Rodriguez, Parish Life Coord.; Rev. Albert Bremer, Sacr. Min.; Rev. Ken Mikulcik, Sacr. Min.;

HARDIN

St. Henry - 16097 U.S. Hwy. 68 E., Hardin, KY 42048 t) 270-474-8058 stchrch@bellsouth.net sainthenryparish.net Rev. Gregory G. Trawick, Pst.; Dcn. Randall Potempa; CRP Stds.: 5

HARDINSBURG

St. Anthony - 1654 S. Hwy. 79, Hardinsburg, KY 40143 t) 270-257-2132 sallyyountsac@att.net Dcn. Mike wIEDEMER; Gale Hinton, DRE; Rev. Shaiju Thomas, Pst.;

St. Mary-of-the-Woods - 1654 Hwy. 79 S., Hardinsburg, KY 40143 t) 270-257-2131 (CRP); 270-257-2132 galehinton@att.net; sallyyountsac@att.net Michael Wiedemer; Gale Hinton, DRE; Rev. Shaiju Thomas, Pst.;

St. Romuald - 394 N. Hwy. 259, Hardinsburg, KY 40143 t) 270-756-2356 stromuald@bbtel.com stromuald.org Dcn. Tony Anthony; Rev. Anthony Jones, Pst.; CRP Stds.: 43

HAWESVILLE

Immaculate Conception - 240 Court Sq., Hawesville, KY 42348; Mailing: P.O. Box 219, Hawesville, KY 42348 t) 270-927-8419 icscchurch2@gmail.com www.icscchurch.org Rev. Terry Devine, Pst.; Nicole Ballard, DRE; Neena Gaynor, Pst. Min./Coord.; CRP Stds.: 48

HENDERSON

Holy Name of Jesus - 511 Second St., Henderson, KY 42420 t) 270-826-2096 rwheeler@holynameparish.net; holyname@holynameparish.net www.holynameparish.net Rev. Stephen Van Lal Than Lalte, Par. Vicar; Rev. Larry McBride, Pst.; CRP Stds.: 60

Holy Name of Jesus School - (Grades PreK-8) 628 Second St., Henderson, KY 42420 t) 270-827-3425 jeadens@holynameschool.org www.holynameschool.org Judy Jenkins, Prin.; Julie Eadens, Pres.;

HICKMAN

Sacred Heart - 411 Moulton St., Hickman, KY 42050-1327 t) 270-236-2071 ltbjr@ken-tennwireless.com Rev. Robert Drury, Pst.; Butch Busby, Contact;

HOPKINSVILLE

SS. Peter and Paul - 902 E. Ninth St., Hopkinsville, KY 42240 t) 270-885-8522 stsppchurch.org Rev. Jude Okeoma, Assoc. Pst.; Dcn. Timothy D. Barnes; Dcn. Roberto Cruz; Dcn. William E. Sweet; Rev. Richard C. Meredith, Pst.; Dcn. Trinidad Soriano; Libby Downs, DRE; CRP Stds.: 78

SS. Peter and Paul School - (Grades PreK-8) t) 270-886-0172 stephanie.blankenberger@sppshopkinsville.org sppshopkinsville.org/ Stephanie Blankenberger, Prin.; Stds.: 115; Lay Tchrs.: 10

IRVINGTON

Holy Guardian Angels - 301 W. High St., Irvington, KY 40146; Mailing: P.O. Box 155, Irvington, KY 40146 t) (270) 547-2132 michael.abiero@pastoral.org; angelalasley3254@gmail.com Rev. Michael Charles Abiero, Pst.; Rebecca Hacker, DRE;

LACENTER

St. Mary - 624 Broadway, LaCenter, KY 42056; Mailing: P.O. Box 570, LaCenter, KY 42056 t) 270-665-5551 Rev. Emmanuel Udoh, Pst.; Theresa Wilkins, DRE;

LEITCHFIELD

St. Joseph - 204 N. Main St., Leitchfield, KY 42754 t) 270-259-3028 stjoseph1840@yahoo.com stjosephch.org Rev. Sinoj E. Pynadath, HGN, Pst.;

St. Paul - 1821 St. Paul Rd., Leitchfield, KY 42754 t) 270-242-7436 stpaulgrayson@windstream.net Rev. Steve Hohman, Pst.; CRP Stds.: 26

St. Paul School - (Grades PreSchool-8) 1812 St. Paul Rd., Leitchfield, KY 42754 t) 270-242-7483 stpaulschool@mediacombb.net Chris Reed, Prin.;

LEWISPORT

St. Columba - 815 Pell St., Lewisport, KY 42351; Mailing: P.O. Box 358, Lewisport, KY 42351 t) 270-295-3682; 270-927-8419 (CRP) icscchurch2@gmail.com www.icscchurch.org Rev. Terry Devine, Pst.; Nicole Ballard, DRE; Neena Gaynor, Pst. Min./Coord.; CRP Stds.: 8

LIVEMORE

St. Charles Borromeo - 506 Hill St., Livemore, KY 42352; Mailing: 180 Hwy. 136 W., Calhoun, KY 42327 t) 270-273-3185 Rev. Jegin Puthenpurackal, H.G.N. (India), Pst.;

MADISONVILLE

Christ the King - 1600 Kingsway Dr., Madisonville, KY 42431 t) 270-821-5494 office.ctk@madisonville.org ctkmadisonville.org Rev. Carl McCarthy, Pst.; CRP Stds.: 15

Christ the King School - (Grades PreK-8) 1500 Kingsway Dr., Madisonville, KY 42431 t) 270-821-8271 office@ctksmadinsolville.com Beth Herrmann, Prin.; Stds.: 92; Lay Tchrs.: 6

Preschool - t) 270-821-3954

MARION

St. William - 860 S. Main St., Marion, KY 42064 t) 270-965-2477 saintwilliam@att.net Rev. John Okoro (Nigeria), Pst.; CRP Stds.: 12

MAYFIELD

St. Joseph - 702 W. Broadway St., Mayfield, KY 42066 t) 270-247-2843 stjosephmayfield.com Rev. Eric D. Riley, Pst.; Dcn. Michael Clapp, Pst. Assoc.; Sr. Lina Maria Ramos, Pst. Assoc.; Christie Scarbrough, Bus. Mgr.; CRP Stds.: 160

MORGANFIELD

St. Ambrose - 5194 State Route 270 W, Morganfield, KY 42437; Mailing: P.O. Box 256, Sturgis, KY 42459 t) 270-333-2806 (CRP); 270-333-1832 stambrosercc@gmail.com Rev. John Okoro (Nigeria), Pst.;

St. Ann - 304 S Church St., Morganfield, KY 42437-1609 t) 270-389-2287; 270-389-2292 stann304@bellsouth.net Rev. Freddie Byrd, Pst.; CRP Stds.: 9

Sacred Heart - 674 State Rte. 141 N., Morganfield, KY 42437; Mailing: 201 E. Market St., Waverly, KY 42462 t) 270-389-4224 stpeter.sacredheart@gmail.com Rev. Dave Johnson, Pst.;

MORGANTOWN

Holy Trinity - 766 Logansport Rd., Morgantown, KY 42261; Mailing: P.O. Box 222, Morgantown, KY 42261 t) 270-274-3414 holytrinitycc@gmail.com Rev. Julio Barrera, Pst.; Lisa Whitehouse, Bus. Mgr.; Sr. Aida Badillo - Lorenzo, Hispanic Ministry;

MURRAY

St. Leo - 401 N 12th St., Murray, KY 42071 t) 270-753-3876 fr.josh@stleoky.org www.stleoky.org Rev. Joshua A. McCarty, Pst.; Dcn. Victor Fromm; Dcn. Joseph R. Ohnemus; CRP Stds.: 122

OAK GROVE

St. Michael the Archangel - 448 State Line Rd., Oak Grove, KY 42262 t) 270-640-9850 julian.ibemere@pastoral.org stmichaeloakgrove.com Dcn. Jack Cheasty; Dcn. Tom Torson; Rev. Julian Ibemere (Nigeria), Pst.;

OWENSBORO

St. Stephen Cathedral - 614 Locust St., Owensboro, KY 42301; Mailing: 610 Locust St., Owensboro, KY 42301-2130 t) 270-683-6525 ststephencathedral@pastoral.org ststephencathedral.org Rev. John M. Thomas, Rector; Rev. Shibu Cheriankunnel, Par. Vicar; Dcn. Richard Murphy; Crissy Stevenson, Pastoral Assistant; Andrew Nunez, Bus. Mgr.; James Wells, Director of Music Ministry; Alex Reid, Director of Stewardship and Ministries; Rick Rhodes, Director of Adult Ministries; Karina Romero, Director of Youth and Young Adult Ministries; Donna Murphy, Pst. Assoc.; Bob Stone, Building and Grounds Supervisor; Holly Pfeifer, Preschool Director; CRP Stds.: 44

Blessed Sacrament - 602 Sycamore St., Owensboro, KY 42301; Mailing: 610 Locust St, Owensboro, KY 42301-2130 t) 270-926-4741 blessedsac602@gmail.com www.blessedsacramentchapel.org Sr. Jeannette Fennewald, SSND, Pst. Assoc.;

St. Alphonsus - 7925 State Route 500, Owensboro, KY 42301 t) 270-229-4164 vivian.bowles@maplemount.org; st.alphonsus@att.net saintalphonsusparish.org Rev. Anthoni Ottagan, Pst.; Sr. Vivian Marie Bowles, O.S.U., DRE; CRP Stds.: 36

Blessed Mother - 601 E. 23rd St., Owensboro, KY 42303 t) 270-683-8444 bmcbusiness1@outlook.com blessedmotherchurch.com Rev. J. Michael Clark, Pst.; Rev. Jamie Dennis, Par. Vicar; Patty Woerter, Music Min.; Christina Banard, Youth Min.; Jennifer Hawes, Bus. Mgr.; CRP Stds.: 30

The Immaculate - 2516 Christie Pl., Owensboro, KY 42301 t) 270-683-0689 sbelcher@immaculateparish.org; mtate@immaculateparish.org immaculateparish.org Rev. John R. Vaughan, Pst.; Matthew Tate, DRE; CRP Stds.: 49

SS. Joseph and Paul - 609 E. 4th St., Owensboro, KY 42303 t) 270-683-5641 aprilsjpc@owens.twcbc.com www.stjpc.org Rev. Jean Rene Kalombo, Pst.; Rev. Daniel C. Dillard, Par. Vicar; Rev. Michael E. Williams, Par. Vicar; Dcn. John Cecil; Dcn. Chris Gutierrez; CRP Stds.: 65

St. Martin - 5856 Kentucky 81, Owensboro, KY 42301 t) 270-685-0339 stmartinrome@gmail.com Rev. Patrick M. Bittel, Pst.;

St. Mary Magdalene - 7232 Kentucky 56, Owensboro, KY 42301 t) 270-771-4436 office@stmarymagd.org; augusty.valomchalil@pastoral.org stmarymagd.org Rev. Augusty Valomchalil, MSSCC, Pst.; Jacob Hein, Music Min.; CRP Stds.: 18

Our Lady of Lourdes - 4029 Frederica St., Owensboro, KY 42301 t) 270-684-5369 lois@lourdescatholicchurch.com; chollis@lourdescatholicchurch.com Rev. J. Patrick Reynolds, Pst.; Robin Murphey, DRE;

Our Lady of Lourdes Day Care - 4005 Frederica St., Owensboro, KY 42301

St. Peter of Alcantara - 81 Church St., Owensboro, KY 42301 t) 270-764-1983 office@stpeterofalcantara.com stpeterofalcantara.com Rev. William R. Thompson, Pst.; CRP Stds.: 23

St. Pius Tenth Parish - 3418 Hwy. 144, Owensboro, KY 42303 t) 270-684-4745 spx@stpiustenthparish.org www.stpiustenthparish.org/ Rev. Babu Kulathumkal, H.G.N. (India), Pst.; Matt Knight, Youth Min.; Sara Lewis, DRE; Jeanie Lewis, Bus. Mgr.; CRP Stds.: 78

St. Pius Tenth Day Care - t) 270-684-7456

Precious Blood - 3306 Fenmore St., Owensboro, KY 42301 t) 270-684-6888 precious-blood.net Rev. Suneesh Mathew Kulathanapatikal, H.G.N. (India), Pst.; Dcn. Jay VanHoosier; Sr. Rosanne Spalding, O.S.U., DRE; CRP Stds.: 31

PADUCAH

St. Francis de Sales - 116 S. Sixth St., Paducah, KY 42001 t) 270-442-1923 office@parishsfds.com www.parishsfds.com Rev. Gary Clark, Pst.;

St. John the Evangelist - 6705 Old U.S. Hwy. 45 S, Paducah, KY 42003 t) 270-554-3810; 270-443-0295 (CRP) hwurth@comcast.net; paducahfaithformation@smss.org www.stjohnspaducah.com Rev. Bruce Fogle, Pst.; Ging Smith, Dir.;

Paducah Faith Formation - 377 Highland Blvd., Paducah, KY 42003

Rosary Chapel - 711 Ohio St., Paducah, KY 42003 t) 270-444-6383 office@rosarychapel.org rosarychapel.org/ Rev. Emmanuel Udoh, Pst.; CRP Stds.: 17

Chapel - ; Mailing: P.O. Box 1481, Paducah, KY 42003 rosary@bellsouth.net

St. Thomas More - 5645 Blandville Rd., Paducah, KY 42001-8722 t) 270-534-9000 jill@stmore.org stmore.org Rev. Brad Whistle, Pst.; Rev. Basilio Az Cuc, Par. Vicar; Dcn. Terry Larbes; Steve DuPerrieu, Admin.; CRP Stds.: 79

PHILPOT

St. Lawrence - 6119 St. Lawrence Rd., Philpot, KY 42366; Mailing: 9515 State Route 144, Saint William Catholic Church, Philpot, KY 42366 t) 270-281-4802 swslparishes.org Connie Lemmons, Bus. Mgr.; Rev. Shijo Vadakumkara, Pst.;

St. William - 9515 Hwy. 144, Philpot, KY 42366 t) 270-281-4802 swslparishes.org Kara Bekebrede, DRE; Rev. Shijo Vadakumkara, Pst.; Connie Lemmons, Bus. Mgr.; CRP Stds.: 71

Mary Carrico Catholic School - (Grades PreK-8) t) 270-281-5526 marthawarrenmccs144@yahoo.com

PRINCETON

St. Paul - 813 S. Jefferson, Princeton, KY 42445 t) 270-365-6786 stmarkeddyville.weconnect.com Rev. Jojy Joseph HGN, HGN (India), Pst.; CRP Stds.: 19

REED

St. Augustine - 16777 St. Augustine Church Rd., Reed, KY 42451 t) 270-764-1983 office@stpeterofalcantara.com www.staugustinereed.org Rev. William R. Thompson, Pst.; Sr. Alicia Coomes, O.S.U., Pst. Assoc.;

RUSSELLVILLE

Sacred Heart - 296 W 6th St, Russellville, KY 42276 t) 270-726-6963 email@sacredheartrussellville.org sacredheartrussellville.org Rev. Ken Mikulcik, Pst.; Rev. Albert Bremer, Par. Vicar; Dcn. Edwin Pacheco; Melanie Abney, DRE; CRP Stds.: 41

SCOTTSVILLE

Christ the King - 298 Bluegrass Dr., Scottsville, KY 42164; Mailing: P.O. Box 463, Scottsville, KY 42164 t) 270-237-4404 christtheking298@gmail.com ctkscottsville.org Rev. Thomas J Buckman, Pst.; Terri J Anderson, DRE; CRP Stds.: 10

SEBRE

St. Michael - 57 Watkins Sebree Rd, Sebre, KY 42455; Mailing: P.O. Box 705, Sebree, KY 42455 t) 270-835-2584 c) (270) 881-7737 (Pastor's cellphone) carmelo.jimenez@pastoral.org smsebree.org/ Rev. Jose Carmelo Jimenez (Mexico), Pst.; Rev. Lustein Blanco, Par. Vicar; Dcn. Baltazar Rafael; CRP Stds.: 63

STURGIS

St. Francis Borgia - 1306 N. Adams St., Sturgis, KY 42459; Mailing: P.O. Box 256, Sturgis, KY 42459 t) 270-333-2806 saintfrancisborgia@yahoo.com stfrancisborgiasturgis.org Rev. John C. Okoro, Pst.; CRP Stds.: 12

SUNFISH

St. John the Evangelist - 430 St. John Church Rd., Sunfish, KY 42210 t) 270-259-3028 stjoseph1840@yahoo.com stjohnch.org Rev. Sinoj E. Pynadath, HGN;

UNIONTOWN

St. Agnes - 504 Mulberry St., Uniontown, KY 42461 t) 270-822-4416 khumphrey32887@gmail.com; sonyagough2016@gmail.com www.stagnesuniontown.com Rev. Bruce McCarty, Pst.; Sonya Gough, DRE; CRP Stds.: 18

UTICA

St. Anthony - 261 St. Anthony Rd., Utica, KY 42376 t) 270-733-4341 sacc.utica@gmail.com Rev. Mark A. Buckner, Pst.; Dcn. Tim Nugent, DRE; Cecelia Millay, DRE; CRP Stds.: 15

WAVERLY

St. Peter - 201 E. Market St., Waverly, KY 42462 t) 270-389-4224 stpeter.sacredheart@gmail.com Rev. Dave Johnson, Pst.;

WAX

St. Benedict - 6874 Hwy 479, Wax, KY 42726; Mailing: c/o 1256 St. Anthony Rd., Clarkson, KY 42726 t) 270-242-4791 stanthony1256@windstream.net www.triparishcatholic.com Dcn. T.J. Anthony Dennison; Dcn. William Grant; Rev. Brandon Williams, Pst.; Karen Meredith, DRE;

St. Anthony Church -

WHITESVILLE

St. Mary of the Woods - 10534 Main Cross, Whitesville, KY 42378; Mailing: PO Box 1, Whitesville, KY 42378 t) 270-233-4196 debbie.aud@stmarywoods.com www.stmaryofthewoodswhitesville.com Emily Gipson, DRE; Rev. Brian Roby, Pst.; CRP Stds.: 69

St. Mary of the Woods School - (Grades PreSchool-8) 10521 Franklin St, Whitesville, KY 42378 t) 270-233-5253 emily.hernandez@stmarywoods.com stmarywoods.com Emily Hernandez, Prin.; Stds.: 293; Lay Tchrs.: 15

SCHOOLS: PRESCHOOL THRU HIGH SCHOOL

SCHOOLS

COMMONWEALTH OF KENTUCKY

BOWLING GREEN

St. Joseph Interparochial School - (PAR) (Grades PreK-8) 416 Church Ave., Bowling Green, KY 42101-1887 t) 270-842-1235 rschwartz@stjosephschoolbg.org stjosephschoolbg.org Rodney Schwartz, Prin.; Joella Scheidegger, Librn.; Stds.: 294; Lay Tchrs.: 23

HARDINSBURG

St. Romuald School - (PAR) (Grades PreK-8) 408 N. Hwy. 259, Hardinsburg, KY 40143 t) 270-756-5504 lori.carwile@stromualdschool.org; jennifer.oreilly@stromualdschool.org www.stromualdschool.org Jennifer O'Reilly, Prin.; Stds.: 231; Lay Tchrs.: 11

MORGANFIELD

John Paul II Catholic School - (PAR) (Grades PreK-8) 307 S. Church St., Morganfield, KY 42437 t) 270-389-1898 bhendrickson@johnpauliicatholicschool.org www.johnpauliicatholicschool.org Rev. Freddie Byrd, Vicar; Beth Hendrickson, Prin.; Renee French, Librn.; Stds.: 227; Lay Tchrs.: 15

OWENSBORO

Owensboro Catholic Elementary 4-6 Campus - (PAR) (Grades 4-6) 525 E. 23rd St., Owensboro, KY 42303 t) 270-683-6989 tracy.conkright@owensborocatholic.org Tracy Conkright, Prin.; Stds.: 289; Scholastics: 18; Lay Tchrs.: 15

Owensboro Catholic Elementary K-3 Campus - (PAR) (Grades K-3) 4017 Frederica St., Owensboro, KY 42301 t) 270-684-7583 jim.tinius@owensborocatholic.org www.owensborocatholic.org Jim Tinius, Prin.; Kristin Miller, Vice Prin.; Stds.: 370; Lay Tchrs.: 20

Owensboro Catholic Middle School - (PAR) (Grades 7-8) 2540 Christie Pl., Owensboro, KY 42301 t) 270-683-0480 olivia.schilke@owensborocatholic.org www.owensborocatholic.org Olivia Schilke, Prin.; Stds.: 185; Lay Tchrs.: 13

PADUCAH

St. Mary Elementary - (DIO) (Grades PreK-5) 377 Highland Blvd., Paducah, KY 42003 t) 270-442-1681 mary.smith@smss.org www.smss.org Monica Hayden, Dir.; Mary Smith, Prin.; Stds.: 244; Lay Tchrs.: 18

St. Mary Middle School - (DIO) (Grades 6-8) 1243 Elmdale Rd., Paducah, KY 42003 t) 270-442-1681 x226 doug.shelton@smss.org www.smss.org Douglas Shelton, Prin.; Monica Hayden, Dir.; Lisa Clark, Librn.; Stds.: 77; Lay Tchrs.: 6

HIGH SCHOOLS

COMMONWEALTH OF KENTUCKY

OWENSBORO

Owensboro Catholic High School - (PAR) 1524 W. Parrish Ave., Owensboro, KY 42301 t) 270-684-3215 gates.settle@owensborocatholic.org www.owensborocatholic.org Rev. Daniel Dillard, Chap.; Keith Osborne, Admin.; Tim Riley, Dean; Gates Settle, Prin.; Stds.: 425; Lay Tchrs.: 28

PADUCAH

St. Mary High School - (PAR) (Grades 9-12) 1243 Elmdale Rd., Paducah, KY 42003 t) 270-442-1681 x226 doug.shelton@smss.org www.smss.org Douglas Shelton, Prin.; Monica Hayden, Dir.; Lisa Clark, Librn.; Stds.: 79

WHITESVILLE

Trinity High School - (PAR) (Grades 9-12) 10510 Main Cross St., Whitesville, KY 42378 t) 270-233-5533 emily.hernandez@stmarywoods.com www.trinityhs.com Emily Hernandez, Prin.; Stds.: 82; Lay Tchrs.: 8

INSTITUTIONS LOCATED IN DIOCESE

CAMPUS MINISTRY / NEWMAN CENTERS [CAM]

BOWLING GREEN

St. Thomas Aquinas Catholic Campus Center at Western Kentucky University - 1403 College St., Bowling Green, KY 42102-4770; Mailing: P.O. Box 10170, Bowling Green, KY 42102-4770 t) 270-843-3638 jason.mcclure@pastoral.org www.wkucatholiccenter.com Rev. Jason Wayne McClure, Chap.;

MURRAY

Murray State University Newman House - 220 N. 13th St., Murray, KY 42071; Mailing: 401 N. 12th St., Murray, KY 42071 t) 270-767-6616 alex@stleoky.org www.stleoky.org/newman-house Alex Kaufmann, Campus Min.;

CEMETERIES [CEM]

OWENSBORO

Mater Dolorosa - 1860 W. 9th St., Owensboro, KY 42301; Mailing: 5404 Hwy. 54, Owensboro, KY 42303 t) 270-926-8097 cliff.russell@pastoral.org; joseph.hayden@pastoral.org Cliff Russell, Dir.;

St. Raphael Cemetery - 6025 Hayden Bridge Rd., Owensboro, KY 42301; Mailing: 600 Locust St., Owensboro, KY 42301-2130 t) 270-683-1545 martha.hagan@pastoral.org Tom Lilly, Chancellor;

Resurrection (Owensboro Catholic Cemeteries) - 5404 Hwy. 54, Owensboro, KY 42303 t) 270-926-8097 cliff.russell@pastoral.org; joseph.hayden@pastoral.org www.cemify.com/cem/resurrection Cliff Russell, Dir.;

PADUCAH

Mt. Carmel Cemetery, Inc. - 4149 Old Mayfield Rd., Paducah, KY 42003; Mailing: P.O. Box 7346, Paducah, KY 42002-7346 t) 270-534-5593 c) 270-331-1006 mt.carmelcemetery@outlook.com www.mtcarmelcemeterypaducah.org Rev. Gary Clark, Pst. Assoc.; Rev. Emmanuel Udoh, Pst. Assoc.; Rev. Brad Whistle, Pst. Assoc.;

COLLEGES & UNIVERSITIES [COL]

OWENSBORO

Brescia University - 717 Frederica St., Owensboro, KY 42301 t) 270-685-3131 stephanie.clary@brescia.edu www.brescia.edu Rev. Ray Clark, Prof.; Rev. J. Raymond Goetz, Prof.; Rev. Larry Hostetter, Pres.; Rev. Michael E. Williams, Chap.; Dcn. Tim Nugent, Prof.; Sr. Pam Mueller, O.S.U., Spiritual Adv./Care Srvcs.; Sr. Judith Riney, O.S.U., Librn.; Stds.: 1,024; Lay Tchrs.: 2,074,545; Sr. Tchrs.: 55,824

CONVENTS, MONASTERIES, AND RESIDENCES FOR WOMEN [CON]

MAPLE MOUNT

St. Joseph's Female Ursuline Academy, Inc. - 8001 Cummings Rd., Maple Mount, KY 42356 t) 270-229-4103 x201 leadershipcouncil@maplemount.org; sharon.sullivan@maplemount.org www.ursulinesmsj.org Motherhouse and Convent of the Ursuline Nuns of the Congregation of Paris. Sr. Sharon Sullivan, OSU, Supr.; Sr. Ann McGrew, OSU, Treas.; Srs.: 82

OWENSBORO

The Glenmary Center (Home Mission Sisters of America, Inc.) - 405 W Parrish Ave., Owensboro, KY 42301; Mailing: P.O. Box 22264, Owensboro, KY 42304-2264 t) 270-686-8401 srdarlene@glenmarysisters.org www.glenmarysisters.org Service to the Home Missions Sr. Darlene Presley, Pres.; Srs.: 6

Service to the Home Missions -

WHITESVILLE

Passionist Nuns/St. Joseph's Monastery - 8564 Crisp Rd., Whitesville, KY 42378-9782 t) 270-233-4571 nunsp@passionistnuns.org www.passionistnuns.org Sr. John Mary Read, C.P., Supr.; Srs.: 12

ENDOWMENTS / FOUNDATIONS / TRUSTS [EFT]

BOWLING GREEN

St. Joseph Cemetery Foundation, Inc. - 930 Saint Joseph Ln., Bowling Green, KY 42103; Mailing: P.O. Box 10334, Bowling Green, KY 42102 t) 270-842-2525 (St. Joseph Parish); 270-842-7777 (Holy Spirit Parish) monica@stjosephbg.org www.stjosephbg.org/cemetery Steve Dieball, Contact;

OWENSBORO

The Catholic Foundation of Western Kentucky - 600 Locust St., Owensboro, KY 42301 t) 270-683-1545 tom.lilly@pastoral.org www.owensborodiocese.org/ Tom Lilly, Chancellor;

Interparish Deposit Loan Fund Corp. - 600 Locust St., Owensboro, KY 42301-2130 t) 270-683-1545 ray.purk@pastoral.org www.owensborodiocese.org/ Raymond Purk, Contact;

***The Roman Catholic Diocese of Owensboro Kentucky Charitable Trust Fund, Inc.** - 600 Locust St., Owensboro, KY 42301 t) 270-683-1545 ray.purk@pastoral.org www.owensborodiocese.org/ Raymond Purk, Exec.;

PADUCAH

St. Mary School System Benefit Fund - 1243 Elmdale Rd., Paducah, KY 42003 t) 270-442-1681 x273 eleanor.spry@smss.org www.smss.org Eleanor Spry, Contact;

HOSPITALS / HEALTH SERVICES [HOS]

PADUCAH

***Dublin Manor, Inc.** - 665 McAuley Dr., Apt. 105, Paducah, KY 42003 t) 270-441-0026 ltalley@mercyhousing.org Apartments for the Elderly Molly Brochocki, Dir.;

Mercy Health KY Urgent Care LLC - 1530 Lone Oak Rd., Paducah, KY 42003

Mercy Health - Lourdes Hospital LLC - 1530 Lone Oak Rd., Paducah, KY 42003 t) 270-444-2444 www.mercy.com/paducah Michael Yungmann, CEO; Bed Capacity: 329; Asstd. Annu.: 43,940; Staff: 953

Mercy Regional Emergency Medical System - 3551 Coleman Rd., Paducah, KY 42001 t) 270-443-6529

***Mercy Manor, Inc.** - 665 McAuley Dr., Apt. 105, Paducah, KY 42003 t) 270-415-9166 ltalley@mercyhousing.org Apartments for Elderly. Molly Brochocki, Dir.;

MISCELLANEOUS [MIS]

BOWLING GREEN

Diocesan Shrine of Mary Mother of the Church and Model of all Christians - St. Joseph, 434 Church Ave., Bowling Green, KY 42101 t) 270-842-2525 ryan.harpole@pastoral.org Rev. Ryan Harpole, Rector;

OWENSBORO

St. Benedict Joseph's Homeless Shelter - 1001 W. 7th St., Owensboro, KY 42301 t) 270-541-1003; 270-315-4419 stbenedicts42301@roadrunner.com stbenedictsowenboro.org Harry Pedigo Jr., Dir.;

Carmelite Sisters of the Divine Heart of Jesus of Kentucky Corporation - 2501 Old Hartford Rd., Owensboro, KY 42303 t) 270-683-0227 carmelhomeinfo@yahoo.com www.carmelhomeky.com Sr. M. Francis Teresa Scully, D.C.J., Admin.; Sr. Maria Carmelita, D.C.J., Supr.;

***Catholic Men's Conference of Western KY** - 600 Locust St., Owensboro, KY 42301 t) 270-683-1545 ray.purk@pastoral.org kycatholic.com/ Raymond Purk, Dir.;

***Daniel Pitino Shelter, Inc.** - 501 Walnut St., Owensboro, KY 42301 t) 270-688-9000 contact@pitinoshelter.org www.pitinoshelter.org Emergency homeless shelter; soup kitchen; transitional houses; permanent supportive housing apt complex. Maryanne Mountain, Bus. Mgr.; Dr. Michele Johnston, Dir.;

St. Gerard Life Home - 600 Locust St., Owensboro, KY 42301 t) 270-852-8328; 270-541-1003; 270-315-6556 (House mom) stgerard@pastoral.org stbenedictsowensboro.org Birthmother housing and pregnancy outreach. Susan Montalvo Gesser, Dir.; Harry Pedigo Jr., Dir.;

Heralds of Good News of St. Paul, Inc. - 81 Church St., Owensboro, KY 42301 t) 270-764-1983 Rev. Sinoj E. Pynadath, HGN;

Owensboro Catholic Consolidated School System - 1524 W. Parrish Ave., Owensboro, KY 42301 t) 270-686-8896 keith.osborne@owensborocatholic.org www.owensborocatholic.org Rev. J. Patrick Reynolds, Vicar;

The Owensboro Catholic League, Inc. - 3152 Pleasant Valley Rd., Owensboro, KY 42303 c) 270-314-9606 kyklump@aol.com Michael Murphy, Pres.;

PADUCAH

St. Mary School System - 1243 Elmdale Rd., Paducah, KY 42003 t) 270-442-1681 x273 eleanor.spry@smss.org www.smss.org Douglas Shelton, Prin.; Mary Smith, Prin.; Eleanor Spry, Dir.;

MONASTERIES AND RESIDENCES FOR PRIESTS AND BROTHERS [MON]

AUBURN

Fathers of Mercy - 806 Shaker Museum Rd., Auburn, KY 42206 t) 270-542-4146 x4 business@fathersofmercy.com www.fathersofmercy.com Rev. Francis Fusare, CPM, In Res.; Rev. Peter Stryker, CPM, In Res.; Rev. John Broussard, CPM, Councilor; Rev. John Agapito, C.P.M., In Res.; Rev. William Casey, C.P.M., In Res.; Rev. James P. Costigan, C.P.M., In Res.; Rev. Wade Menezes, C.P.M., In Res.; Rev. Nathan Mudd, CPM, Secy.; Rev. Kenneth Geraci, C.P.M., Councilor; Rev. Louis Guardiola, C.P.M., In Res.; Rev. Louis Caporiccio, CPM, Chap.; Rev. Ricardo Pineda, C.P.M., Treas.; Rev. Allan Cravalho, In Res.; Rev. David Wilton, C.P.M., Supr.; Rev. Anthony M. Stephens, C.P.M., Vicar; Rev. Joel Rogers, C.P.M., Councilor; Brs.: 4; Priests: 29

NURSING / REHABILITATION / CONVALESCENCE / ELDERLY CARE [NUR]

OWENSBORO

Carmelite Sisters of the Divine Heart of Jesus - 2501 Old Hartford Rd., Owensboro, KY 42303 t) 270-683-0227 srmfrancisteresa@yahoo.com; sr.mariacarmelita@yahoo.com Rev. Ray Clark, Chap.; Sr. Francis Theresa, D.C.J., Dir.; Asstd. Annu.: 155; Staff: 128

PRESCHOOLS / CHILDCARE CENTERS [PRE]

OWENSBORO

Cathedral Preschool - 600 Locust St., Owensboro, KY 42301 t) 270-926-1652 pam.weafer@pastoral.org Holly Pfeiffer, Dir.; Stds.: 96; Lay Tchrs.: 13

RETREAT HOUSES / RENEWAL CENTERS [RTR]

BOWLING GREEN

Gasper River Catholic Youth Camp & Retreat Center - 2695 Jackson Bridge Rd., Bowling Green, KY 42101 t) 270-781-2466 ben.warrell@pastoral.org; gasperriver@hotmail.com www.gasperriverretreatcenter.org (A diocesan-owned entity) Ben Warrell, Dir.;

An asterisk (*) denotes an organization that has established tax-exempt status directly with the IRS and is not covered by the USCCB Group Ruling.

Diocese of Palm Beach

(Dioecesis Litoris Palmensis)

MOST REVEREND GERALD M. BARBARITO

Bishop of Palm Beach; ordained January 31, 1976; appointed Auxiliary Bishop of Brooklyn June 28, 1994; installed August 22, 1994; appointed Bishop of Ogdensburg October 26, 1999; appointed Bishop of Palm Beach July 1, 2003; installed August 28, 2003. Office: 9995 N. Military Tr., Palm Beach Gardens, FL 33410.

The Pastoral Center Office: 9995 N. Military Tr., Palm Beach Gardens, FL 33410. T: 561-775-9500; F: 561-775-9556.
Mailing Address: P.O. Box 109650, Palm Beach Gardens, FL 33410-9650.
diocesepb.org
info@diocesepb.org

ESTABLISHED OCTOBER 24, 1984.

Square Miles 5,115.

Comprises the Counties of Palm Beach, Martin, Indian River, Okeechobee and St. Lucie in the State of Florida.

Legal Corporate Title: The Diocese of Palm Beach.

For legal titles of parishes and diocesan institutions, consult the Chancery.

STATISTICAL OVERVIEW

Personnel
Bishop....1
Retired Bishops....1
Priests: Diocesan Active in Diocese....73
Priests: Diocesan Active Outside Diocese....2
Priests: Retired, Sick or Absent....30
Number of Diocesan Priests....105
Religious Priests in Diocese....38
Total Priests in your Diocese....143
Extern Priests in Diocese....61
Ordinations:
Diocesan Priests....2
Transitional Deacons....1
Permanent Deacons in Diocese....95
Total Brothers....5
Total Sisters....51

Parishes
Parishes....50
With Resident Pastor:
Resident Diocesan Priests....44
Resident Religious Priests....5
Missions....3
Pastoral Centers....1

Professional Ministry Personnel:
Brothers....2
Sisters....4
Lay Ministers....150

Welfare
Homes for the Aged....1
Total Assisted....394
Special Centers for Social Services....12
Total Assisted....10,500

Educational
Seminaries, Diocesan....1
Students from This Diocese....7
Students from Other Dioceses....105
Total Seminarians....7
High Schools, Diocesan and Parish....3
Total Students....1,501
Elementary Schools, Diocesan and Parish....14
Total Students....4,995
Elementary Schools, Private....2
Total Students....560
Catechesis/Religious Education:
High School Students....2,508
Elementary Students....6,435

Total Students under Catholic Instruction....16,006
Teachers in Diocese:
Priests....14
Scholastics....10
Brothers....2
Sisters....9
Lay Teachers....502

Vital Statistics
Receptions into the Church:
Infant Baptism Totals....2,613
Minor Baptism Totals....383
Adult Baptism Totals....157
Received into Full Communion....794
First Communions....2,534
Confirmations....2,133
Marriages:
Catholic....420
Interfaith....79
Total Marriages....499
Deaths....1,983
Total Catholic Population....246,982
Total Population....2,179,280

LEADERSHIP

The Pastoral Center - t) 561-775-9500
Vicar General - Very Rev. Charles E. Notabartolo;
Moderator of Curia - Very Rev. Charles E. Notabartolo;
Episcopal Secretary - Rev. Brian King;
Executive Secretary to the Bishop - Annette Russell;
Chancellor - Very Rev. Albert A. Dello Russo;
Administrative Assistant to the Vicar General and Chancellor - Merke Baroni;
Administrative Assistant to the Chancellor - Beatriz Urrea;
Coordinator of Archives and Records - Merke Baroni;
Matrimonial Tribunal - t) 561-775-9535 tribunal@diocesepb.org Rt. Rev. Archmandrite Glen J. Pothier, Judicial Vicar;
Judicial Vicar - Rt. Rev. Archmandrite Glen J. Pothier;
Judges - Rt. Rev. Archmandrite Glen J. Pothier; Very Rev. Albert A. Dello Russo; Rev. Alexander Padilla II;
Defender of the Bond - Rev. Francisco J. Osorio;
Assessors - Rev. Michael W. Edwards; Rev. Kevin C. Nelson;
Promoter of Justice - Rev. Francisco J. Osorio;
Notaries - Sandi Martinez; Deborah Duxbury; Alice Rivera;
Director of the Tribunal - Sandi Martinez;
Case Directors & Secretaries - Sandi Martinez, Dir.; Deborah Duxbury; Alice Rivera;
Advocates - Dcn. Martin Serraes; Rev. Kevin C. Nelson; Dcn. John Beaudoin;
Vicars Forane -
Cathedral Deanery - Very Rev. Thomas R. LaFreniere;
Central Deanery - Very Rev. Ducasse Francois;
Northern Deanery - Very Rev. Robert L. Pope Jr.;
Southern Deanery - Very Rev. Nestor Rodriguez;
College of Consultors - Very Rev. Charles E. Notabartolo, Vicar General;
Presbyteral Council - Rev. John F. Horan, O.Carm., Chair; Rev. J. Scott Adams, Secy.; Very Rev. Charles E. Notabartolo, Vicar General;
Religious Men and Women - t) 561-775-9586 Rev. Michael Driscoll, O. Carm., Episcopal Delegate for Men Religious; Sr. Jadwiga Drapala, C.a.Ch., Episcopal Delegate;
Vocations and Seminarians - t) 561-775-9552; 561-775-9555; 561-775-9586 Rev. Daniel Daza-Jaller, Dir.; Sr. Jadwiga Drapala, Coord., Women's Vocations; Viviana Morales, Admin. Asst.;
Episcopal Delegate for Retired Priests - t) 561-775-9500 Rev. Michael W. Edwards;
Finance Officer - t) 561-775-9500 Vito Gendusa, CFO;

OFFICES AND DIRECTORS

Building, Construction, Real Estate Office - t) 561-775-9514; 561-775-9523 Daniel Lewis, Supt., Bldgs., Construction & Properties; Michael Lockwood, Dir., Bldg. & Construction; Destiny Gibbons, Admin. Asst.;
Campus Ministry at Florida Atlantic University - t) 561-571-1436 Rev. Joseph M. Papes, Campus Min.;
Cemetery: Our Lady Queen of Peace - t) 561-793-0711 Daniel Lewis, Admin.;
Communications - t) 561-775-9529 jtrefelner@diocesepb.org Jennifer Trefelner, Dir. Communications & Devel.;
Development - t) 561-775-9520 jtrefelner@diocesepb.org Jennifer Trefelner, Dir. Communications & Devel.;
Employee Services - t) 561-775-9525; 561-775-9503 Ana Jarosz, Dir.; Gretchen Wood, Human Resources Asst.;
Finance - t) 561-775-9500; 561-775-9571 Vito Gendusa, CFO; Karen Lentz, Controller;
Haitian Ministry - t) 561-466-9617 Rev. Yves Geffrard, Episcopal Delegate;
Hispanic Ministry - t) 561-775-9544 Rev. Duvan Bermudez, Dir.; Armando Garcia, Admin. Asst.;
Information Technology - t) 561-775-9500 Carlos Mesa, Dir.; Michael Winningham, IT Systems Analyst/Devel.;
Insurance Services - t) 561-775-9574 Ana Jarosz, Dir.; Sandy Maulden, Benefits Asst.;
Internal Services - t) 561-630-2694 Marian Loynd, Dir.;
Liturgy - t) 561-630-2974 Rev. Brian King, Dir.; Beatriz Urrea, Coord.;
Marriage, Family Life, Faith Formation & Youth Ministry - t) 561-775-9524 Catherine Loh, Dir.;
Faith Formation - Liliana Soto-Cabrera, Coord.;
Family Life - Beth Zanotelli, Coord.;
Marriage Preparation - Dcn. Louie Romero, Coord.;
Youth and Young Adult Ministry - Andy Baker, Coord.;
Permanent Diaconate - t) 561-775-9540 Dcn. David Zanotelli, Episcopal Delegate; Dcn. Peter Del Valle, Formation Dir.;
Propagation of the Faith & Missionary Cooperative Plan - t) 561-775-9598 Very Rev. Albert A. Dello Russo, Dir.; Josie Pinera, Office Asst.;
Real Estate - t) 561-775-9538; 561-775-9587 Daniel Lewis, Supt., Bldgs., Construction & Properties; Pam Bloor, Admin. Asst.;
Safe Environments - t) 561-775-9507 Very Rev. Albert A. Dello Russo, Coord.;
Administrator of Background Screening - t) 561-775-9530 ckasey@diocesepb.org Kathy Casey;
Administrator of Education and Training Programs - t) 561-775-9593 llinnell@diocesepb.org Lisa Linnell;
Victim Assistance Coordinator - t) 561-775-9558 va@diocesepb.org Lisa Linnell;

CATHOLIC CHARITIES

CEO and Executive Director - t) 561-775-9573 Dr. Ellen T Wayne;
Catholic Charities Administrative Offices - t) 561-775-9560 Karen Rojas, Exec. Admin. Asst.;
Anti-Human Trafficking (Bakhita Empowerment) Program - Catholic Charities - t) 888-373-7888 (Hotline); 561-345-2025 aht@ccdpb.org Sandra Perez, Prog. Dir.;
Counseling Services - t) 844-848-6777 Ashli Jones, Dir.;
Boca Raton - St. Joan of Arc Catholic Church - t) 844-848-6777
Boynton Beach - St. Mark Church - t) 844-848-6777
Fort Pierce - St. Mark the Evangelist Church - t) 844-848-6777
Pahokee - St. Mary's Ctr. - t) 844-848-6777
Palm Beach - St. Edward Catholic Church - t) 844-848-6777
Riviera Beach - Catholic Charities St. Francis Center - t) 844-848-6777
Stuart - t) 844-848-6777
Elder Services -
Elder Affairs - t) 561-345-2010 Amy Fariello-Hansen, Prog. Admin.;
Finance Director - t) 561-775-9577 Peter Herrmann;
Fund Development and Marketing Director - t) 561-630-2695
Health Related Services -
Interfaith Health & Wellness/Wellness Ministry - t) 561-345-2006 wellness@ccdpb.org Bernadette Macy, Prog. Coord.;
Human Resources Manager - t) 561-775-9589 Judith Richardson;
Hunger, Homeless and Outreach - t) 561-924-5677; 561-345-2000 Rocio Lopez, Prog. Dir.;
Immigration Services -
St. Francis Center - t) 561-345-2003 Timothy Keohane, Attorney/Prog. Dir.;
St. Mary Center - t) 561-924-5677
Stuart Center - t) 772-463-0445
Marketing and Fundraising Manager - t) 561-775-9567
Operations Director - t) 561-360-3321 Krishna Rivera;
Parish Social Ministry/Catholic Relief Services - t) 561-360-3327 Donna Pearson, Dir.;
Pregnancy Services -
Birthline/Lifeline - t) 561-924-5677; 561-282-1467; 561-732-0570 Katherine Bowers, Dir.;
Prison Ministry - t) 561-360-3326 Dcn. Gregory Quinn, Dir.;
Program Development and Quality Director - t) 561-345-2005 Carol Rodriguez;
Refugee Services -
Bakhita Empowerment Program/Refugee, Resettlement - t) 561-345-2025 Sandra Perez, Prog. Admin.;
Respect Life Ministry - t) 561-360-3330 Deanna Herbst-Hoosac, Prog. Admin.;
Respite Program - t) 561-345-2006 Bernadette Macy, Prog. Coord.;
Transitional Housing -
Samaritan Center - t) 772-770-3039 Renee Bireley, Prog. Dev.;
Volunteer Services - t) 561-360-3329 Vicky Mongrut, Coord.;

EDUCATION

Education -
Schools Office - t) 561-775-9546 Gary Gelo, Supt.; John F. Clarke, Asst. Supt.; Katie Kervi, Prog. Coord.;
School of Christian Formation (English & Spanish) - t) 561-775-9544 Rev. Duvan Bermudez, Dir.; Armando Garcia, Admin. Asst.;

ORGANIZATIONS

Charismatic Movement -
English -
Spanish - t) 561-793-8544 Rev. Francisco J. Osorio, Spiritual Adv./Care Srvcs.; Rosa Garcia Ramirez, Diocesan Coord.; Fernando Ramirez, Diocesan Coord.;
Christ Child Society -
Boca Raton - t) 561-386-9450 Christine Wyns, Pres.;
North Palm Beach - t) 231-526-0291 Anne Kroha;
Stuart - Leslie Berch, Pres.;
Council of Catholic Women - Rev. Clemens Hammerschmitt, Spiritual Advisor (frclemh@bellsouth.net); Doreen Ann Recco, Pres. (pbdccw@gmail.com);
Cursillo Movement -
English - t) 561-747-9330 Ron Crescenzo, Dir.; Dcn. Joseph O'Connell, Spiritual Adv./Care Srvcs.;
Spanish - t) 561-964-4168 Sr. Margarita Gomez, R.M.I., Spiritual Adv./Care Srvcs.; Alicia M. Fernandez, Lay Dir.;
Damas Catolicas en Acion - t) 561-358-7286 Rev. Duvan Bermudez, Spiritual Moderator; Esther Garcia, Diocesan Coord.;
Knights of Columbus - t) 561-276-6892 Rev. Canon Thomas J. Skindeleski;
Legion of Mary, Palm Beach Curia - Rev. Danis Ridore, Spiritual Moderator; Dolores Crane, Pres.;

PARISHES, MISSIONS, AND CLERGY

STATE OF FLORIDA

BELLE GLADE

St. Philip Benizi - 710 S. Main St., Belle Glade, FL 33430-4202 t) 561-996-3870 Rev. Nobert Jean-Pierre (Haiti), Pst.; Rev. Pierre-Soul Estefont, Par. Vicar; Angelica Mendoza, DRE; CRP Stds.: 283

BOCA RATON

Ascension - 7250 N. Federal Hwy., Boca Raton, FL 33487 t) 561-997-5486 ascension@accboca.net; admin-asst@accboca.net Rev. Carl Hellwig, Pst.; Debbie Cramsie, DRE; CRP Stds.: 120
St. Joan of Arc - 370 S.W. 3rd St., Boca Raton, FL 33432 t) 561-392-0007; 561-952-2870 (CRP); 561-392-7974 (CRP) davidson_rosa@stjoan.org www.stjoan.org Very Rev. Nestor Rodriguez, Pst.; Rev. Junesh Vakapadath Xavier, Par. Vicar; Rev. Robinson Aza, Par. Vicar; Dcn. William Watzek; Rosa Davidson, DRE; CRP Stds.: 360

St. Joan of Arc School - (Grades PreK-8) 501 S.W. 3rd Ave., Boca Raton, FL 33432 t) (561) 392-7974 stjoan.org/school Lani D Hiponia, Prin.; Stds.: 437; Lay Tchrs.: 33

St. John the Evangelist - 10300 Yamato Rd., Boca Raton, FL 33498 t) 561-488-1373 religiousedstjohn@gmail.com www.saintjohn-bocaraton.com Rev. Dominic Toan Tran, Pst.; Margaret Ciccone, DRE; CRP Stds.: 150

St. Jude - 21689 Toledo Rd., Boca Raton, FL 33433 t) 561-392-8172; 561-314-1057 (CRP) info@stjudeboca.org; skessler@stjude.org stjudeboca.org Rev. John F. Horan, O.Carm., Pst.; Rev. Christopher Iannizzotto, Par. Vicar; Rev. Richard Champigny, O.Carm., In Res.; Rev. Michael Driscoll, In Res.; Susan Kessler, DRE; CRP Stds.: 265

St. Jude School - (Grades 1-8) t) 561-392-9160 mendezm@saintjudeschool.org Debbie Armstrong, Prin.; Stds.: 441; Lay Tchrs.: 30

Our Lady of Lourdes - 22094 Lyons Rd., Boca Raton, FL 33428 t) 561-483-2440 secretary@lourdesboca.org www.lourdeschurchboca.org Rev. Eduardo Medina, Pst.; Rev. Francis Reardon, Pastor Emer.; Dcn. Francis Fau, Pst. Assoc.; CRP Stds.: 210

BOYNTON BEACH

St. Mark - 643 St. Mark Pl., Boynton Beach, FL 33435; Mailing: 730 N.E. 6th Ave., Boyton Beach, FL 33435 t) 561-734-9330 www.stmarkboynton.com Rev. Robert Benko, OFM Conv., Pst.; Rev. Michael Sajda, Par. Vicar; Rev. Carl Zdancewicz, Par. Vicar; Rev. Richard T. Florek, O.F.M.Conv., In Res.; Rev. Germain Kopaczynski, O.F.M.Conv., In Res.; Rev. Joseph Dorniak, In Res.; Sr. Mary Joan Millecan, Pst. Min./Coord.; Mary A. Mares, DRE; CRP Stds.: 119

St. Mark Catholic Church - 643 St. Mark Place, Boynton Beach, FL 33435 Sr. Mary Joan Millecan, Pst. Assoc.;

St. Thomas More - 10935 S. Military Trl., Boynton Beach, FL 33436 t) 561-737-3095 operations@stmbb.org; academydirector@stmbb.org www.stmbb.org Rev. Julian P. Harris, Pst.; Rev. Alex J. Vargas, Par. Vicar; Anne Marie Fischer, DRE; CRP Stds.: 145

Thomas More Academy for Early Childhood Learning - 10935 S. Military Trail, Boynton Beach, FL 33436 t) 561-737-3770 schooloffice@stmbb.org Anne Marie Fischer, Dir.; Stds.: 85; Lay Tchrs.: 4

DELRAY BEACH

Emmanuel - 15700 S. Military Trl., Delray Beach, FL 33484 t) 561-496-2480 secretary@emmanuelcatholic.church; religiouseducation@emmanuelcatholic.church www.emmanuelcatholic.church Rev. Gaudioso Zamora, Pst.; Jean Krokus, DRE; CRP Stds.: 117

Our Lady of Perpetual Help Mission - 510 S.W. Eighth Ave., Delray Beach, FL 33444-2448 t) 561-276-4880 Rev. Roland Desormeaux, C.S., Pst.; CRP Stds.: 15

Our Lady Queen of Peace - 9600 W. Atlantic Ave., Delray Beach, FL 33446 t) 561-499-6234 x100 Rev. Moacir Balen, Pst.; Rev. Olmes Milani, C.S., Vicar; Sr. Mercedes Dominguez, R.M.I., DRE; CRP Stds.: 127

St. Vincent Ferrer - 840 George Bush Blvd., Delray Beach, FL 33483 t) 561-276-6892 office@stvincentferrer.com; faithformation@stvincentferrer.com www.stvincentferrer.com Rev. Dennis Gonzales, Pst.; Dcn. Robert Laquerre, Bus. Mgr.; Rev. Danis Ridore, In Res.; Dcn. Greg Osgood; CRP Stds.: 86

St. Vincent Ferrer School - (Grades PreK-8) 810 George Bush Blvd., Delray Beach, FL 33483 t) 561-278-3868 denise.oloughlin@stvfschool.org www.stvfschool.org Denise O'Loughlin, Prin.; Patrick Hansen, Vice Prin.; Stds.: 424; Sr. Tchrs.: 2; Lay Tchrs.: 32

FELLSMERE

Our Lady of Guadalupe Mission - 12896 County Rd. 512, Fellsmere, FL 32948; Mailing: P.O. Box 9, Fellsmere, FL 32948 t) 772-571-9875 office@olgmission.com; olgmission@bellsouth.net Rev. John Morrissey, Pst.; Rev. Sabas Ntimia Mallya, A.L.C.P. (Tanzania), Admin.; CRP Stds.: 133

FORT PIERCE

St. Anastasia - 407 S. 33rd St., Fort Pierce, FL 34947 t) 772-461-2233; 772-468-0806 (CRP); 772-216-7397 (CRP) annulments@stanastasiachurch.org; tlezama@att.net www.stanastasiachurch.org Rev. Richard E. George II, Pst.; Rev. Jacob Edwin, OCD, Par. Vicar; Rev. Jaime Dorado (Colombia), Admin.; Mitiz Macias, DRE; Teresa Velazquez Lezama, DRE; CRP Stds.: 274

St. Anastasia School - (Grades PreK-8) 401 S. 33 St., Fort Pierce, FL 34947 t) 772-461-2232 khoeffner@sta.school; krichmond@sta.school www.saintanastasiaschool.org Dr. Kevin Hoeffner, Prin.; Stds.: 579; Scholastics: 10; Lay Tchrs.: 39

St. Mark the Evangelist - 1924 Zephyr Ave., Fort Pierce, FL 34982 t) 772-461-8150 stmarks1924@gmail.com stmarkftpierce.org Rev. Robert Pope, Pst.; Rev. Antony Lopez, O.C.D., Par. Vicar; CRP Stds.: 55

Notre Dame Mission - 217 N. U.S. Hwy. #1, Fort Pierce, FL 34950 t) 772-466-9617 notredamecatholicmission@hotmail.com notredamecc.com Rev. Yves Geffrard, Pst.; Yvrose Sylvain, DRE; CRP Stds.: 23

HIGHLAND BEACH

St. Lucy - 3510 S. Ocean Blvd., Highland Beach, FL 33487 t) 561-278-1280 stlucys@bellsouth.net www.stlucycommunity.com Rev. Daniel B. Horgan, Pst.; Pat Ward, CFO; CRP Stds.: 40

HOBE SOUND

St. Christopher - 12001 S.E. Federal Hwy., Hobe Sound, FL 33455 t) 772-546-5150 office@stchrishs.com; mstevens@stchrishs.com www.stchrishs.com Rev. Aidan Hynes, Pst.; Dcn. James Parrilli; Susan Kirch, DRE; CRP Stds.: 102

INDIANTOWN

Holy Cross - 15939 S.W. 150th St., Indiantown, FL 34956; Mailing: P.O. Box 999, Indiantown, FL 34956 t) 772-597-2798 holycross351@gmail.com holycrossindiantown.org Rev. Francisco J. Osorio, Pst.; Juan Carlos Lasso, DRE; CRP Stds.: 55

JENSEN BEACH

St. Martin de Porres - 2555 N.E. Savannah Rd., Jensen Beach, FL 34957 t) 772-334-4214 info@stmartindp.com www.stmartindp.com Rev. J. Scott Adams, Pst.; Andrew Gekoskie, Music Min.; Greg Cannata, Parish Life Coord.; CRP Stds.: 61

JUPITER

St. Peter - 1701 Indian Creek Pky., Jupiter, FL 33458 t) 561-575-0837 rmiklos@stpeterjupiter.com www.stpeterjupiter.com Rev. Donald T. Finney, Pst.; Rev. Jean Wesner Boulin, Par. Vicar; Rev. Wesler Hilaire, Par. Vicar; Dcn. John Bartalini; Dcn. Donald Battison; Dcn. John Collins; Dcn. Stephen McMahon; Dcn. Stephen Scienzo; Dcn. Edwin Velasquez; CRP Stds.: 317

LAKE WORTH

St. Matthew - 6090 Hypoluxo Rd., Lake Worth, FL 33463-7312 t) 561-966-8878; 561-966-1538 (CRP) chammerschmitt@saintmatthewchurch.org; dorothy@saintmatthewchurch.org www.st-matthew-church.com Rev. Clemens Hammerschmitt, Pst.; Rev. Leonard Dim, Par. Vicar; Rev. Raciel Trevino, Par. Vicar; Debbie Whitlock, DRE; CRP Stds.: 145

Sacred Heart - 425 N. M St., Lake Worth, FL 33460 t) 561-582-4736 rectory@sacredheartfamily.com www.sacredheartchurchfamily.com Rev. Jean Wesner Boulin, Par. Admin.; Dcn. Gerard Palermo; CRP Stds.: 151

Sacred Heart School - (Grades PreK-8) 410 N. M St., Lake Worth, FL 33460 t) 561-582-2242 costelloej@sacredheartfamily.com www.sacredheartschoollakeworth.com Frank Sagarese, Prin.; Stds.: 202; Lay Tchrs.: 15

LANTANA

Holy Spirit - 1000 Lantana Rd., Lantana, FL 33462; Mailing: P.O. Box 3978, Lantana, FL 33462 t) 561-585-5970 office@holyspiritlantana.com; religioused@holyspiritlantana.com www.holyspiritlantana.com Rev. Elifete St. Fort, Pst.; Patrice Althouse, DRE; CRP Stds.: 85

NORTH PALM BEACH

St. Clare - 821 Prosperity Farms Rd., North Palm Beach, FL 33408 t) 561-622-7477; 561-420-2311 (CRP) sbernardin@stclarecatholicschool.org stclarechurch.net Rev. William D. O'Shea, Pst.; Rev. Mark Mlay, A.L.C.P. (Tanzania), Par. Vicar; Sara Bernardin, DRE; CRP Stds.: 86

St. Clare School - (Grades PreK-8) t) 561-622-7171 info@sccsfl.org stclareschool.com Rita Kissel, Prin.; Stds.: 402; Lay Tchrs.: 29

St. Paul of the Cross - 10970 Jack Nicklaus Dr., North Palm Beach, FL 33408 t) 561-626-1873 kate.devine@paulcross.org; patricia.quinn@paulcross.org paulcross.org Very Rev. Thomas R. LaFreniere, Pst.; Dcn. Frank Bandy; Rev. Daniel Daza-Jaller, In Res.; Kate Devine, DRE; CRP Stds.: 29

OKEECHOBEE

Sacred Heart - 901 SW 6th St., Okeechobee, FL 34974 t) 863-763-3727 Rev. Yves Francois, Pst.; Sandy Olson, DRE; CRP Stds.: 120

PAHOKEE

St. Mary - 1200 E. Main St., Pahokee, FL 33476 t) 561-924-7305; 561-342-8038 (CRP) stmarysofpahokee.com Rev. Juan Raul Cardenas, Pst.; Ivania Larios, DRE; CRP Stds.: 152

PALM BEACH

St. Edward - 144 N. County Rd., Palm Beach, FL 33480 t) 561-832-0400 stedwardchurch@aol.com Rt. Rev. Archmandrite Glen J. Pothier, Pst.; Elizabeth Bockmeyer, DRE; CRP Stds.: 42

PALM BEACH GARDENS

Cathedral of St. Ignatius Loyola - 9999 N. Military Tr., Palm Beach Gardens, FL 33410 t) 561-622-2565 office@cathedralpb.com www.cathedralpb.com Very Rev. Gavin J. Badway, Rector; Rev. Michael Cairnes, Par. Vicar; Dcn. John Beaudoin; CRP Stds.: 190

St. Patrick - 13591 Prosperity Farms Rd., Palm Beach Gardens, FL 33410 t) 561-626-8626 denise@stpatrickchurch.org; donna@stpatrickchurch.org www.stpatrickchurch.org Rev. Aidan Lacy, Pst.; Rev. John D'Mello, Par. Vicar; Rev. Brian Flanagan, Pastor Emer.; Dcn. Guy Hart; Dcn. Joe Pollock; Sr. Vivian Gonzalez, R.M.I., Parish Outreach; Megan Milstead, DRE; Donna Faber, Bus. Mgr.; CRP Stds.: 132

PALM CITY

Holy Redeemer - 1454 S. W. Mapp Rd., Palm City, FL 34990 t) 772-286-4590; 772-220-4517 (Offices) religed@holyredeemercc.org; ewesley@holyredeemercc.org www.holyredeemercc.org Rev. Martin Dunne III, Pst.; Margaret Castor, DRE; CRP Stds.: 233

PALM SPRINGS

St. Luke - 2892 S. Congress Ave., Palm Springs, FL 33461 t) 561-965-8980 robert.sullivan@stlukeparish.com stlukeparish.com Rev. Andrew Brierley, Pst.; Robert Sullivan, DRE; CRP Stds.: 600

St. Luke School - (Grades PreK-8) t) 561-965-8190 diann.bacchus@stlukeparish.com www.stlukepalmsprings.org/ Diann Bacchus, Prin.; Stds.: 294; Lay Tchrs.: 22

PORT ST. LUCIE

St. Bernadette - 350 N.W. California Blvd., Port St. Lucie, FL 34986 t) 772-336-9956 parish@stbernadetteslw.org; eric@stbernadetteslw.org www.stbernadetteslw.org Rev. Victor A. Ulto, Pst.; Dcn. Martin Ervin; Dcn. Mario Lopez; Eric Seibenick, DRE; CRP Stds.: 221

St. Elizabeth Ann Seton - 930 SW Tunis Ave, Port St. Lucie, FL 34953-3351 t) 772-336-0282; 772-336-0363 (CRP) donna@steasparish.org seascatholicparish.org Rev. Andre Dumarsais Pierre-Louis, Pst.; Donna Caiazzo, DRE; CRP Stds.: 165

Holy Family - 2330 S.E. Mariposa Ave., Port St. Lucie,

FL 34952-7403 t) 772-335-2385; 772-337-4313 (CRP) holyfamilypsloffice@yahoo.com holyfamilyccpsl.com Rev. Tri Tang Pham, Pst.; Rev. Thomas F. Cauley Jr., Pastor Emer.; Mary Acevedo, DRE; CRP Stds.: 129

Ryan Center for Young Children Ministry - 2330 S.W. Mariposa Ave., Port St. Lucie, FL 34952 t) (772) 335-2385 Ellen Bradley, Dir.; Stds.: 37; Lay Tchrs.: 3

St. Lucie - 280 SW Prima Vista, Port St. Lucie, FL 34983; Mailing: 425 SW Irving St., Port St. Lucie, FL 34983 t) 772-878-1215 drecco@stlucie.cc; emonteagudo@stlucie.cc www.stlucie.cc Rev. Mark Szanyi, O.F.M.Conv., Pst.; Rev. Paul Gabriel, O.F.M.Conv., Par. Vicar; Rev. Daniel Pal, O.F.M.Conv., Par. Vicar; Rev. Msgr. James M. Burke, Pastor Emer.; Rev. Peter C. Dolan, Pastor Emer.; Dcn. Gerry Bott; Dcn. Vincent Cookingham; Dcn. Charles Santo Immordino; Dcn. Dale Konas; Dcn. Carlos Melendez; Rev. Curt Kreml, O.F.M.Conv., In Res.; Andrea Draper, DRE; CRP Stds.: 160

RIVIERA BEACH

St. Francis of Assisi - 200 W. 20th St., Riviera Beach, FL 33404-6160 t) 561-842-2482 stfrancisofassisi@gmail.com stfrancisofassisi1948.org Rev. Peter Truong, Pst.; Elizabeth Thomas, Teacher;

ROYAL PALM BEACH

Our Lady Queen of the Apostles - 100 Crestwood Blvd. S., Royal Palm Beach, FL 33411 t) 561-798-5661 www.olqa.cc Rev. Zbigniew A. Rudnicki, Pst.; Rev. Laurent Assenga, A.L.C.P., Par. Vicar; Dcn. Robert Laquerre; Dcn. Rodney Brimlow; CRP Stds.: 257

SEBASTIAN

St. Sebastian - 13075 U.S. Hwy. 1, Sebastian, FL 32958 t) 772-589-5790; 772-589-4147 (CRP) rectory@stsebastian.com; sandy@stsebastian.com www.stsebastian.com Rev. John Morrissey, Pst.; Rev. Sabas Mallya, A.L.C.P., Par. Vicar; Debbie Bova, DRE; CRP Stds.: 117

STUART

St. Andrew - 2100 S.E. Cove Rd., Stuart, FL 34997-7600 t) 772-781-4415 www.saintandrewcatholic.org Rev. John A. Barrow, Pst.; Donna Hernandez, DRE; CRP Stds.: 80

St. Joseph - 1200 E. 10th St., Stuart, FL 34996 t) 772-287-2727 x102 melanied@sjcflorida.org sjcflorida.org Rev. Noel McGrath (Ireland), Pst.; Rev. Wisman Simeon, Par. Vicar; Rev. Paul Vincent, Par. Vicar; Rev. Alain Waterman, Par. Vicar; CRP Stds.: 281

St. Joseph School - (Grades PreK-8) t) 772-287-6975 lpreston@sjscf.org sjcschargers.com Heather Lamb, Admin.; Stds.: 323; Sr. Tchrs.: 2; Lay Tchrs.: 26

TEQUESTA

St. Jude - 204 N. U.S. Hwy. One, Tequesta, FL 33469; Mailing: P.O. Box 3726, Tequesta, FL 33469 t) 561-746-7974; 561-748-8805 (CRP) info@stjudechurch.net; deaconles@stjudechurch.net www.stjudecatholicchurch.net Rev. Kevin C. Nelson, Pst.; Rev. Frank D'Amato, Par. Vicar; Frank Faranda, DRE; Dcn. Lester Loh, DRE; Dcn. Augustine DiFiore; Dcn. Paul Gialanella; CRP Stds.: 168

VERO BEACH

St. Helen - 2085 Tallahassee Ave., Vero Beach, FL 32960 t) 772-567-5129; 772-562-5954 (CRP) church@sthelenvero.org; pfies@sthelenvero.org sthelenvero.org Rev. Matthew DeGance, Admin.; Rev. Armando Leon, Par. Vicar; Rev. Nicholas Paul Zrallack, Par. Vicar; Paige Fies, DRE; CRP Stds.: 278

St. Helen School - (Grades 1-8) 2025 20th Ave., Vero Beach, FL 32960 t) 772-567-5457 a.kathman@sthelenschoolvero.org; k.carter@sthelenschoolvero.org www.sthelenschoolvero.org Deborah Irish, Prin.; Stds.: 294; Lay Tchrs.: 23

Holy Cross - 500 Iris Ln., Vero Beach, FL 32963 t) 772-231-0671 cflynn@holycrossverobeach.org; lhumenik@holycrossverobeach.org www.holycrossverobeach.org Rev. Thomas E. Barrett, Pst.; Lori Humenik, DRE; CRP Stds.: 176

St. John of the Cross - 7550 26th St., Vero Beach, FL 32966; Mailing: 7590 26th St., Vero Beach, FL 32966 t) 772-563-0057 www.stjohnsvero.org Rev. Brian Campbell, Pst.; Dcn. Robert Borchert; Dcn. William Weiss; CRP Stds.: 50

WELLINGTON

St. Rita - 13645 Paddock Dr., Wellington, FL 33414 t) 561-793-8544; 561-795-4321 (CRP) dmcdermott@saintrita.com www.saintrita.com Rev. Mario Castañeda, Pst.; Rev. Marco De León, Par. Vicar; Donna McDermott, DRE; CRP Stds.: 839

St. Therese de Lisieux - 11800 Lake Worth Rd., Wellington, FL 33449 t) 561-784-0689 faithformation@sttherese-church.org; frontoffice@sttherese-church.org sttherese-church.org Rev. David C. Downey, Pst.; Dcn. Peter Del Valle; Dcn. Vincent Muller; Dcn. Alfred C. Payne; Dcn. Robert Rodriguez; Audra Afflitto, DRE; CRP Stds.: 150

WEST PALM BEACH

St. Ann - 310 N. Olive Ave., West Palm Beach, FL 33401 t) 561-832-3757 saintannchurch1@msn.com; religioused@stannchurch.net stannchurchwpb.org Rev. Quesnel Delvard, Pst.; Rev. Jean Vanes Nicolas, Priest Assisting; Rev. Brendan Cosmas, Priest in Residence; Marjory Mallebranche, DRE; CRP Stds.: 155

St. Ann School - (Grades 1-8) 324 N. Olive Ave., West Palm Beach, FL 33401 t) 561-832-3676 sasoffice@saswpb.org www.stannwpb.org Susan Demes, Prin.; Stds.: 291; Lay Tchrs.: 20

Our Lady Faith Haitian Center - 1020 Belvedere Rd., West Palm Beach, FL 33405 t) 561-223-2762

Holy Name of Jesus - 345 S. Military Tr., West Palm Beach, FL 33415 t) 561-683-3555; 561-683-3555 x111 (CRP) info@myhnj.org Rev. Antony Pulikal, Pst.; Rev. Ambrose Kadambukatt; Dcn. Jack Hamilton; Dcn. Mark Hoch; Dcn. Peter Mazzella; CRP Stds.: 335

St. John Fisher - 4001 N. Shore Dr., West Palm Beach, FL 33407 t) 561-842-1224 stjohnfisherwpb.com Rev. Benedict Redito, Pst.; Rev. Duvan Bermudez, In Res.; CRP Stds.: 101

St. Juliana - 4500 S. Dixie Hwy., West Palm Beach, FL 33405; Mailing: 4510 S. Dixie Hwy, West Palm Beach, FL 33405 t) 561-833-9745; 561-833-1278 (CRP) jmoyeno@stjulianawpb.com; officeadmin@stjulianawpb.com www.stjulianacatholicchurch.com Very Rev. Ducasse Francois, Pst.; Maximinio Matos, Priest Assisting; Jackie Moyeno, DRE; CRP Stds.: 225

St. Juliana School - (Grades PreK-8) 4355 S. Olive Ave, West Palm Beach, FL 33405 t) 561-655-1922 info@saintjuliana.org www.saintjuliana.org Eileen Lewis, Prin.; Stds.: 391; Lay Tchrs.: 28

Mary Immaculate - 500 Spencer Dr., West Palm Beach, FL 33409; Mailing: 390 S Sequoia Dr., West Palm Beach, FL 33409 t) 561-686-8128; 561-686-8128 x106 (CRP) miwpb@miwpb.org; rvanoordt@miwpb.com www.miwpb.com Rev. Tomasz Makowski, Pst.; Ruth Liliana Van Oordt, DRE; CRP Stds.: 34

SCHOOLS: PRESCHOOL THRU HIGH SCHOOL

SCHOOLS

STATE OF FLORIDA

INDIANTOWN

Hope Rural School - (PRV) (Grades PreK-5) 15929 S.W. 150th St., Indiantown, FL 34956 t) 772-597-2203 edunnop@hoperuralschool.org; mrohdeop@hoperuralschool.org www.hoperuralschool.org Sr. Martha Rohde, O.P., Prin.; Sr. Elizabeth Dunn, O.P., Dir.; Stds.: 135; Lay Tchrs.: 10

JUPITER

All Saints Catholic School - (PAR) (Grades PreK-8) 1759 Indian Creek Pkwy., Jupiter, FL 33458 t) 561-748-8994 ascs@allsaintsjupiter.org www.allsaintsjupiter.org Jill Broz, Prin.; Stds.: 465; Lay Tchrs.: 36

WEST PALM BEACH

***Rosarian Academy (Sisters of St. Dominic (Adrian, MI))** - (PRV) (Grades PreSchool-8) 807 N. Flagler Dr., West Palm Beach, FL 33401 t) 561-832-5131 info@rosarian.org www.rosarian.org Virginia Devine, Prin.; Linda Trethewey, Headmaster; Stds.: 425; Lay Tchrs.: 39

HIGH SCHOOLS

STATE OF FLORIDA

BOCA RATON

Saint John Paul II Academy - (DIO) (Grades 9-12) 4001 N. Military Tr., Boca Raton, FL 33431 t) 561-314-2100 finance@sjpii.net www.sjpii.net Bro. Daniel Aubin, F.S.C., Pres.; Edward Bernot, Prin.; Michael Scaramuzzo, Vice Prin.; Marion Demarest, Vice Prin.; Dr. Jennifer Mulhall, Campus Min.; AnnMarie Chiste, Bus. Mgr.; Stds.: 533; Lay Tchrs.: 33

FORT PIERCE

John Carroll High School, Inc. - (DIO) (Grades 9-12) 3402 Delaware Ave., Fort Pierce, FL 34947-6116 t) 772-464-5200 info@johncarrollhigh.com www.johncarrollhigh.com Corey Heroux, Prin.; Rev. Thomas E. Barrett, Pres.; Stds.: 373; Lay Tchrs.: 26

WEST PALM BEACH

Cardinal Newman High School, Inc. - (DIO) (Grades 9-12) 512 Spencer Dr., West Palm Beach, FL 33409-3616 t) 561-683-6266 brotherthomas@cardinalnewman.com www.cardinalnewman.com Bro. Thomas Zoppo, FSC, Pres.; Wesley Logsdon, Prin.; Stds.: 595; Bro. Tchrs.: 1; Sr. Tchrs.: 1; Lay Tchrs.: 45

INSTITUTIONS LOCATED IN DIOCESE

CATHOLIC CHARITIES [CCH]

RIVIERA BEACH

Catholic Charities of the Diocese of Palm Beach, Inc. - 100 W. 20th St., Riviera Beach, FL 33404 t) (561) 775-9560 catholiccharities@ccdpb.org Dr. Ellen T Wayne, CEO; Asstd. Annu.: 10,500; Staff: 78

CEMETERIES [CEM]

ROYAL PALM BEACH

Our Lady Queen of Peace Catholic Cemetery of the Diocese of Palm Beach, Inc. - 10941 Southern Blvd., Royal Palm Beach, FL 33411 t) 561-793-0711 info@ourqueen.org; dlewis@diocesepb.org www.ourqueen.org Daniel P. Lewis, Admin.;

CONVENTS, MONASTERIES, AND RESIDENCES FOR WOMEN [CON]

STUART

Congregation of the Sisters of the Most Holy Soul of Christ - 1042 E. 9th St., Stuart, FL 34996 t) 772-286-5720 sisterscach@yahoo.com; sschfl@hotmail.com sistersofthemostholysoulofchrist.com Sr. Anita Gabarczyk, C.A.C.h., Supr.;

ENDOWMENTS / FOUNDATIONS / TRUSTS [EFT]

BOYNTON BEACH

St. Vincent de Paul Regional Seminary Endowment Trust - 10701 S. Military Trl., Boynton Beach, FL 33436 t) 561-732-4424 ahernandez@svdp.edu Rev. Alfredo Hernandez, Rector;

PALM BEACH GARDENS

Helping Hands Scholarship Fund, Diocese of Palm Beach - 9995 N. Military Tr., Palm Beach Gardens, FL 33410; Mailing: P.O. Box 109650, Palm Beach Gardens, FL 33410-9650 t) 561-775-9547 ggelo@diocesepb.org Gary Gelo, Supt.;

RIVIERA BEACH

Catholic Charities Foundation of the Diocese of Palm Beach, Inc. - 100 W. 20th St., Riviera Beach, FL 33404 t) 561-775-9560 catholiccharities@ccdpb.org ccdpb.org Dr. Ellen T Wayne, CEO;

MISCELLANEOUS [MIS]

BOCA RATON

Christ Child Society of Boca Raton - 21809 Beachnut Dr., Boca Raton, FL 33433; Mailing: P.O. Box 811025, Boca Raton, FL 33481-1025 c) (561) 386-9450 agnesgreg@aol.com; chrissy6130@yahoo.com

***Cross Catholic Outreach** - 2700 N. Military Tr., Ste. 300, Boca Raton, FL 33427-3908; Mailing: P.O. Box 273908, Boca Raton, FL 33427-3908 t) 800-914-2420 x121 sburns@crosscatholic.org www.crosscatholic.org James J. Cavnar, Pres.; David Adams, Vice. Pres.; Wade Crow, Vice. Pres.; Michele Sagarino, Vice. Pres.; Brian Schutt, Vice. Pres.; Michael Veitenhans, Vice. Pres.;

DELRAY BEACH

Prelature of the Holy Cross and Opus Dei - 4409 Frances Dr., Delray Beach, FL 33445 t) 561-498-1249 Rev. Juan Velez, Chap.; Rev. William Shaughnessy, OP Dei, Chap.; Rev. Oscar Regojo, OP Dei, Chap.;

GREENACRES

Villa Madonna - 4809 Lake Worth Rd., Greenacres, FL 33463-3455 t) 561-963-1900 villamadonnamgr@spm.net

JENSEN BEACH

Villa Assumpta, Inc. - 2539 N.E. Mission Dr., 9-8, Jensen Beach, FL 34957 t) 561-334-0009 villaassumptamgr@spm.net Anthony Silas, Admin.;

JUNO BEACH

Christ Child Society of Palm Beach - 1016 Ocean Dr., Juno Beach, FL 33408; Mailing: P.O. Box 14441, North Palm Beach, FL 33408 t) (313) 882-2419 annekroha@msn.com Anne Kroha, Pres.;

PALM BEACH GARDENS

Diocese of Palm Beach, Inc. - 9995 N. Military Trl., Palm Beach Gardens, FL 33410-9650; Mailing: P.O. Box 109650, Palm Beach Gardens, FL 33410-9650 t) 561-775-9500 vgendusa@diocesepb.org Vito Gendusa, Chief Financial Officer;

Diocesan Property & Liability Insurance Committee -

Diocese of Palm Beach Burse Fund Trust -

Diocese of Palm Beach Endowment Trust -

Diocese of Palm Beach Health Plan Trust - Very Rev. Charles E. Notabartolo, Chair;

Diocese of Palm Beach Pension Plan Trust - Very Rev. Charles E. Notabartolo, Chair;

Diocese of Palm Beach Savings Fund Trust -

The Florida Catholic of Palm Beach, Inc. - Diocese of Palm Beach, Palm Beach Gardens, FL 33410-9650; Mailing: P.O. Box 109650, Palm Beach Gardens, FL 33410-9650 t) 561-775-9500 jtrefelner@diocesepb.org Jennifer Trefelner, Dir.;

Vose Properties, Inc. - 9995 N. Military Trail, Palm Beach Gardens, FL 33410; Mailing: P.O. Box 109650, Palm Beach, FL 33410 t) 561-775-9500 vgendusa@diocesepb.org Vito Gendusa, Chief Financial Officer;

PORT ST. LUCIE

***Adorer Missionary Sisters of the Poor** - 1381 S.E. Airoso Blvd., Port St. Lucie, FL 34983; Mailing: P.O. Box 19895, West Palm Beach, FL 33416 t) 561-810-1963 info@adorermissionaries.org adorermissionarysistersofthepoor.org Rev. Mark Mlay, A.L.C.P. (Tanzania), Dir.; Sr. Mary Jennifer Wandia, Dir.;

Diocesan Council of Catholic Women - 139 SE Lucero Dr., Port St. Lucie, FL 34983; Mailing: P.O. Box 109650, Palm Beach Gardens, FL 33410 c) 772-528-3991 ccwdoreen@gmail.com pbdccw.org Rev. Clemens Hammerschmitt, Spiritual Adv./Care Srvcs.; Doreen Ann Recco, Pres.;

Villa Seton, Inc. - 3300 S.W. Chartwell St., Port St. Lucie, FL 34953 t) 772-344-6969 villasetonmgr@spm.net Jocelyn Sanchez, Admin.;

RIVIERA BEACH

Villa Franciscan, Inc. - 2101 Ave. F, Riviera Beach, FL 33404 t) 561-840-0444 villafranciscanmgr@spm.net villafranciscan.catholicweb.com Fay Montgomery, Admin.;

STUART

Christ Child Society of Stuart - 6673 SE Pacific Dr., Stuart, FL 34997; Mailing: P.O. Box 2007, Stuart, FL 34995 t) (772) 781-0653 barbaralangella1@gmail.com Barbara Langella, Pres.;

***Mary's Home** - 1033 S.E. 14th St., Stuart, FL 34996 t) 772-223-5000 kim@maryshome.org Alean Timm, Dir.; Kim Gaudet, Oper. Mgr.;

VERO BEACH

***St. Sebastian Conference of St. Vincent de Paul Society, Inc.** - 5480 85th St., Vero Beach, FL 32967-5544 t) 772-589-3338 manager@svdp-sebastian.org www.svdp-sebastian.org Michael Davis, Pres.;

***St. Vincent de Paul Society of Indian River County, Incorporated** - 1745 14th Ave., Vero Beach, FL 32960 t) 772-567-6774 svdpvero@att.net Jan Pilon, Pres.;

WEST PALM BEACH

St. Ann Place Outreach Center, Inc. - 2107 N. Dixie Hwy., West Palm Beach, FL 33407 t) (561) 805-7708 jpescosolido@stannplace.net John Pescosolido, Exec. Dir.;

Magnificat Palm Beach Chapter, Inc. - 8439 Whispering Oak Way, West Palm Beach, FL 33411 t) (561) 685-3458 magnificatpalmbeach@gmail.com www.magnificat-ministry.net Rev. Mario Castaneda, Spiritual Adv./Care Srvcs.; Peggy Rowe-Linn, Pres.; Catherine Dorsey, Vice. Pres.; Deanna Bartalini, Secy.; Mary Anne Gioia, Treas.; Marie Murphy Wooldridge, Treas.;

Villa Regina - 2660 N. Haverhill Rd., West Palm Beach, FL 33417 t) 561-478-3900 villareginamgr@spm.net Monica Alvarez, Admin.;

MONASTERIES AND RESIDENCES FOR PRIESTS AND BROTHERS [MON]

ATLANTIS

Christ the King Monastery of St. Clare - 457 Glenbrook Dr., Atlantis, FL 33462-1007 t) (561) 498-3295 ctkmdelray@comcast.net (Solemn Vows, Papal Enclosure) Sr. Leanna Chrostowski, O.S.C., Abbess;

NORTH PALM BEACH

Our Lady of Florida Spiritual Center - 1300 U.S. Hwy. No. 1, North Palm Beach, FL 33408 t) 561-626-1300 www.ourladyofflorida.org Rev. Lucian Clark, C.P., Dir.; Rev. Francis Finnigan, C.P., Mem.; Bro. Luis Daniel Guivas Gerena, C.P., Mem.; Bro. Augustine Lowe, C.P., Mem.; Rev. Paul Ruttle, C.P., Mem.; Rev. Edward Wolanski, C.P., Mem.; Bro. Edward Hall, C.P., Retreat Team; Rev. Melvin Shorter, C.P., Local Leader; Brs.: 3; Priests: 5

VERO BEACH

Paulist Fathers Residence - 1225 20th Ave., Vero Beach, FL 32960 t) 772-532-4445 phuesing@paulist.org Rev. James M. Brucz, C.S.P., In Res.; Rev. Michael J. Martin, C.S.P., In Res.; Rev. Richard Sparks, In Res.; Rev. Marcos Zamora, C.S.P., In Res.; Rev. Paul Huesing, Supr.; Priests: 5

NURSING / REHABILITATION / CONVALESCENCE / ELDERLY CARE [NUR]

WEST PALM BEACH

Lourdes-Noreen McKeen Residence for Geriatric Care (The Carmelite System) - 315 Flagler Dr. S., West Palm Beach, FL 33401 t) 561-655-8544 www.lnmr.org The Carmelite System Sr. Diane Mack, O Carm, Admin.; Asstd. Annu.: 394; Staff: 166

PRESCHOOLS / CHILDCARE CENTERS [PRE]

WEST PALM BEACH

Holy Cross Catholic Preschool & Center - 930 Southern Blvd., West Palm Beach, FL 33405 t) 561-366-8026 director@holycrosscpc.org www.holcrosscpc.org Ana M. Fundora, Exec.; Stds.: 100; Lay Tchrs.: 2

SEMINARIES [SEM]

BOYNTON BEACH

St. Vincent de Paul Regional Seminary - 10701 S. Military Trl., Boynton Beach, FL 33436 t) 561-732-4424 sdeleon@svdp.edu www.svdp.edu Rev. Nicholas George Azar II, Prof.; Rev. Llane Briese, Prof.; Rev. Dominic James Buckley, Dir.; Rev. Gregg Caggianelli, Vice Rector; Rev. Timothy Cusick, Dean; Sr. Bernardone Rock, FSE, Music Min.; Rev. Alfredo Hernandez, Rector; Rev. John Horn, S.J., Prof.; Most Rev. Silvio Jose Baez, OCD, Prof.; Rev. Kevin McQuone, Spiritual Director; Rev. George Nursey, Dean; Rev. Steven Olds, Prof.; Rev. Alexander Tadeo Padilla II, Prof.; Rev. Thomas Pulickal, Prof.; Rev. Juan Carlos Rios, Dean; Art Quinn, Librn.; Stds.: 149; Lay Tchrs.: 7; Pr. Tchrs.: 14; Sr. Tchrs.: 4

Seminary Formation Council, LLC - 10701 S. Military Trl., Boynton Beach, FL 33436 t) (561) 732-4424 jhorn@svdp.edu

An asterisk (*) denotes an organization that has established tax-exempt status directly with the IRS and is not covered by the USCCB Group Ruling.

Diocese of Paterson

(Dioecesis Patersonensis)

MOST REVEREND KEVIN J. SWEENEY, D.D.

Bishop of Paterson; ordained June 28, 1997; appointed Eighth Bishop of Paterson April 15, 2020; ordained July 1, 2020.

Diocesan Center: 777 Valley Rd., Clifton, NJ 07013. T: 973-777-8818; F: 973-777-8976. www.patersondiocese.org

ESTABLISHED DECEMBER 9, 1937.

Square Miles 1,214.

Comprises the Counties of Passaic, Morris and Sussex in the State of New Jersey.

For legal titles of parishes and diocesan institutions, consult the Chancery Office.

STATISTICAL OVERVIEW

Personnel	
Bishop	1
Retired Bishops	1
Abbots	1
Retired Abbots	2
Priests: Diocesan Active in Diocese	149
Priests: Diocesan Active Outside Diocese	10
Priests: Retired, Sick or Absent	107
Number of Diocesan Priests	266
Religious Priests in Diocese	77
Total Priests in your Diocese	343
Extern Priests in Diocese	3
Ordinations:	
Diocesan Priests	7
Transitional Deacons	2
Permanent Deacons in Diocese	196
Total Brothers	26
Total Sisters	522
Parishes	
Parishes	107
With Resident Pastor:	
Resident Diocesan Priests	96
Resident Religious Priests	5
Without Resident Pastor:	
Administered by Priests	6
Pastoral Centers	6
Closed Parishes	1
Professional Ministry Personnel:	
Brothers	3
Sisters	14
Lay Ministers	119
Welfare	
Catholic Hospitals	1
Total Assisted	315,000
Homes for the Aged	8
Total Assisted	515
Day Care Centers	6
Total Assisted	900
Specialized Homes	1
Total Assisted	50
Special Centers for Social Services	8
Total Assisted	19,000
Residential Care of Disabled	12
Total Assisted	75
Educational	
Diocesan Students in Other Seminaries	11
Seminaries, Religious	1
Students, Religious	3
Total Seminarians	14
Colleges and Universities	2
Total Students	1,300
High Schools, Diocesan and Parish	3
Total Students	1,600
High Schools, Private	4
Total Students	1,208
Elementary Schools, Diocesan and Parish	15
Total Students	3,979
Elementary Schools, Private	4
Total Students	450
Catechesis/Religious Education:	
High School Students	3,914
Elementary Students	16,218
Total Students under Catholic Instruction	28,683
Teachers in Diocese:	
Priests	7
Brothers	2
Sisters	20
Lay Teachers	726
Vital Statistics	
Receptions into the Church:	
Infant Baptism Totals	4,316
Minor Baptism Totals	559
Adult Baptism Totals	152
Received into Full Communion	422
First Communions	3,558
Confirmations	3,633
Marriages:	
Catholic	725
Interfaith	103
Total Marriages	828
Deaths	2,965
Total Catholic Population	420,000
Total Population	1,174,641

LEADERSHIP

Vicar General and Moderator of the Curia - Rev. Msgr. T. Mark Condon;
Vicar General - Rev. Michael J. Parisi;
Coordinator for Special Projects - Thomas A. Barrett;
Chief Financial Officer - Patrick Brennan;
Episcopal Vicars -
Education - Rev. Stanley C. Barron;
Evangelization - Rev. Paul S. Manning;
Special Diocesan Initiatives - Rev. Msgr. Geno Sylva;
Deans - Rev. Peter S. Glabik, Clifton; Rev. Maciej Kranc, Eastern Morris; Rev. Marc A. Mancini, Mid-Passaic;
Chancellor/Delegate for Religious - Sr. Theresa Lee, F.M.A., Chancellor;
Vice Chancellor - Rev. Stephen Prisk;
Archivist - Rev. Msgr. Raymond J. Kupke;
Priest Secretary to the Bishop - Rev. Stephen Prisk;
Secretary to the Bishop - Gladys Pozza;
Secretary to the Vicar General and Chancellor - Bea Spina, Admin. Asst.;
Secretary to the Vice Chancellors - Kerry Timoney;
Diocesan Counsel - Kenneth F. Mullaney;
Censor Librorum - Rev. Kevin Corcoran; Rev. Lemmuel Camacho;
Diocesan Tribunal -
Judicial Vicar - Rev. Marc A. Mancini;
Adjutant Judicial Vicar - Rev. Msgr. Joseph T. Anginoli;
Advocates - Rev. Michael Rodak; Rev. Philip-Michael Tangorra; Rev. Mateusz Jasniewicz;
Auditors - Rev. John P. Hanley; Rev. Manuel Guevara; Dcn. Henry Hyle;
Defenders of the Bond - Rev. Msgr. T. Mark Condon; Rev. Msgr. George F. Hundt;
Canonical Advisor - Rev. Msgr. Joseph J. Goode;
Associate Judges - Rev. Marc A. Mancini; Rev. Msgr. John J. Carroll; Rev. Emmett J. Gavin, O.Carm.;
Administrative Assistants and Notaries - Shawn Vacca; Mary Beth Leonhard;
Consulting Psychologists and Experts - Rev. Richard Mucowski, O.F.M.; Joseph De Christofano; Mary De Christofano;
Minister to Priests - Rev. David McDonnell;
Delegate for Polish Seminarians and Clergy - Rev. Dariusz K. Kaminski;
Vocations Office - t) 973-777-2955 Rev. Edward Rama, Dir.; Rev. Dailon Lisabet;
Vocations Board - Rev. Msgr. T. Mark Condon; Rev. Sigmund Peplowski; Rev. T. Kevin Corcoran;
Consultative Bodies -
Presbyteral Council - Rev. Msgr. John E. Hart, Chair; Rev. David McDonnell, Vice Chm.; Rev. Brian P. Quinn;
College of Consultors - Rev. Msgr. John E. Hart, Chair; Rev. David McDonnell, Vice Chm.; Rev. Brian P. Quinn;
College of Deans - Rev. David McDonnell, Chair;
Finance Council - Herbert Thomas, Chair; Sr. Joan Daniel Healy, S.C.C.; Thomas A. Barrett;
Theological Commission - Rev. Msgr. John E. Hart; Rev. Msgr. T. Mark Condon; Sr. Kathleen Flanagan, S.C.;
Pastoral Council - Elizabeth Heldak, Chair;
Liturgical Commission - Rev. Msgr. T. Mark Condon, Chair;
Hispanic Commission - Alvaro Camargo, Pres.;
Black Catholic Ministries Commission - Ruth Lawson, Chair;

ADMINISTRATION

Affiliated Organizations -
Apostleship of Prayer - Rev. Msgr. Christopher C. DiLella, Dir.;
Diocesan Pilgrimage Office - t) 973-827-8030 Rev. Michael Rodak, Dir.;
Legion of Mary - t) 973-779-0427 Lucy Leone, Pres.;
Priests Eucharistic League - Rev. Msgr. Christopher C. DiLella, Dir.;
Communications Secretariat - t) 973-278-3202 Richard A. Sokerka, Exec.; Joseph Cece, Webmaster;
Diocesan Newspaper, "The Beacon" - t) 973-279-8845 Jay Agnish, Editor; Michael Wojcik, Editor;
School Division - t) 973-777-8818 Rev. Stanley C. Barron, Vicar for Educ.; Mary Baier, Supt.; Debbie Duane, Assoc. Supt.;
Secretariat for Catholic Charities - t) 973-777-8818 Rev. Msgr. Herbert K. Tillyer, Pres.; Scott Milliken, CEO; Christopher Brancato;
Catholic Family and Community Services - Robert Jacob, Dir. & CFO; Darrin Maloney, Dir.; Jason Hunter, Oper. Coord.;
Department for Persons with Disabilities - t) 973-406-1100 Joanna Miller, Exec. Dir.; Rocco Zappile, CFO; Patricia Barrett, Pastoral Care Coord.;
Barnet House - t) 973-409-2764 Ashley Hidalgo, Dir.;
Basile Apartment - t) 973-409-2767 Geoffrey Ondimu;
Calabrese House - t) 973-299-8360 Lori Evans, Dir.;
Columbus House - t) 973-697-1644 James Cerny, Dir.;
Finnegan House - t) 973-697-1246 Lynne Rockstroh, Dir.;
Fitzpatrick House - t) 973-248-1569 Tyler Artress, Dir.;
Giuliano House - Kelly O'Caiside, Dir.;
Greunert Center Special Needs - t) 973-663-9102 Diane Madsden, Dir.;
Gruenert Employment Center - t) 973-663-9102 Carolina Nelson, Dir.;
Keleher Apartments - t) 973-409-2761 Isabel Marte, Dir.;
Migrant Ministry - t) 908-647-0280 Luis Arias, Asst. Dir.;
Murray House - t) 973-470-5694 Tania Alessio, Dir.;
Straight and Narrow, Inc. - t) 973-345-6000 Sam Pirozzi, Exec.; Hayman Rambaran, Dir.; Ruth Jean-Marie, Dir.;
Support Coordination - Kristen Bulas, Dir.;
Wallace House - t) 973-276-3470 Kim Walter, Dir.;
Walsh House - t) 973-970-9616 Clara List, Dir.;
Wehrlen House - t) 973-208-1883 Cheryl Slate, Dir.;
Father English Multi-Purpose Community Center - t) 973-279-7100 Delia Rosario, Dir.;
Community and Emergency Support Services - Ariel Alonso, Dir.;
Early Intervention Service Coordination - Lisa O'Connor, Dir.;
Early Intervention Targeted Evaluation and Case Management - Danielle Cuskey, Dir.;
Early Learning Programs - Joseph Murray, Dir.;
El Mundo de Colores - t) 973-523-0919 Laura Zarife, Dir.;
Emergency Food and Clothing Programs - Carlos Roldan, Dir.;
Pastoral Ministry and Volunteers - Sr. Maureen Sullivan, Dir.;
Senior Day Program - Lynn Gaffney, Dir.;
Veterans Services - Melissa Schaber, Dir.;
Youth Risk Reduction - Delia Rosario, Dir.;
Friendship Corner II - t) 973-405-6711 Gloria Bodker, Dir.;
Hispanic Information Center - t) 973-779-7022 Delia Rosario, Dir.;
Hope House - t) 973-361-5555 Karina Calabuit, Dir.;
Meals on Wheels - Kathy Talmadge, Dir.;
Partnership for Social Services - t) 973-827-4702
Secretariat for Evangelization - t) 973-777-8818 Rev. Paul S. Manning, Exec.; Brian Honsberger, Dir.;
Catholic Scouting -
Boy Scouting - Rev. Christopher S. Barkhausen, Chap.;
Girl Scouting - Rev. Frank P. Agresti, Chap.;
Communities Coordinator - Kaitlin Ferrari;
Coordinator of Faith and Leadership Formation - Maria Moncaleano;
Office Manager - Jerilynn Ann Prokop;
Office of Director of Catechesis - Ivannia Vega-McTighe;
Office of Family Life - Eniola Honsberger, Dir.;
Office of Worship and Spirituality - Rev. Msgr. T. Mark Condon, Dir.;
Diocesan Director of Music - Preston Dibble;
Related Organizations -
Catholic Deaf Society -
Charismatic Renewal - t) 973-347-0032 Rev. Nicholas Bozza, Liaison;
English Cursillos - Mike Wilson, Dir.; Rev. Raymond Orama, Spiritual Advisor;
Spanish Cursillos - Luis Salerna, Dir.; William Torres; Rev. Brando Ibarra, Spiritual Advisor;
Respect Life - Mary Mazzarella, Consultant;
Young Adult Ministry - Daniel Ferrari, Coord.;
Secretariat for Pastoral Administration - t) 973-777-2955
Clergy Personnel Office - Rev. Msgr. John E. Hart, Dir.; Moira Clark, Admin. Asst.;
Personnel Board - Rev. Msgr. John E. Hart; Rev. Christopher S. Barkhausen; Rev. Msgr. T. Mark Condon;
Deacon Internship Program - Rev. Dariusz K. Kaminski; Rev. Hernan Arias;
Mission Office - t) 973-777-8818 x256 mburdeos@patersondiocese.org www.rcdop.org Rev. Stanley C. Barron, Dir.;
Office of the Permanent Diaconate - t) 973-443-9300 Dcn. Peter Cistaro, Dir.;
Victim Assistance Coordinator - t) 973-879-1489 Peggy Zanello;
Youth Protection - Eric Wilsusen, Dir.;

FINANCE

Diocesan Cemeteries Office - t) 973-279-2900 Rev. Peter VB. Wells, Dir.; John M. Cavanaugh, Asst. Dir.;

PARISHES, MISSIONS, AND CLERGY

STATE OF NEW JERSEY

ANDOVER

Good Shepherd - Rte. 517 (48 Tranquility Rd.), Andover, NJ 07821; Mailing: P.O. Box 464, Andover, NJ 07821 t) (973) 786-6631 (Main Office) office@goodshepherdrc.org www.goodshepherdrc.org/ Rev. Timothy Dowling, Pst.; Phyllis Haarmann, DRE; Dcn. Keith Harris; CRP Stds.: 178

BOONTON

SS. Cyril and Methodius - 215 Hill St., Boonton, NJ 07005; Mailing: 910 Birch St., Boonton, NJ 07005 t) 973-334-0139 stcyrilboonton@yahoo.com www.stscm.org Rev. Lukasz Iwanczuk, Pst.;

Our Lady of Mount Carmel - 910 Birch St., Boonton, NJ 07005 t) 973-334-1017 admin@olmcboonton.org www.olmc.church Rev. Daniel P. O'Mullane, Pst.; Rev. Wade Trainor, Par. Vicar; CRP Stds.: 491

Our Lady of Mount Carmel School - (Grades PreK-8) 205 Oak St., Boonton, NJ 07005 t) 973-334-2777 school@olmcboonton.org www.olmc.academy Classical Catholic School Peter Alvarez, Headmaster; Stds.: 304; Lay Tchrs.: 19

BRANCHVILLE

Our Lady Queen of Peace - 209 U.S. Hwy. 206, Branchville, NJ 07826 t) 973-948-3185 office@olqpbranchville.org www.olqpbranchville.org Rev. Philip-Michael Tangorra, Pst.; CRP Stds.: 81

BUDD LAKE

St. Jude - 17 Mt. Olive Rd., Budd Lake, NJ 07828 t) 973-691-1561 info@stjudeparish.org www.stjudeparish.org Rev. Jesus Antonio Gaviria, Pst.; Dcn. Anthony C. Siino; CRP Stds.: 310

BUTLER

St. Anthony - 65 Bartholdi Ave., Butler, NJ 07405 t) 973-838-0031 ascollante@saopp.org; bleck@saopp.org www.saopp.org Rev. Joseph Juracek, O.F.M., Pst.; Rev. Kevin Daly, O.F.M., Assoc. Pst.; Annette Miller, DRE;

Parish House - 71 Bartholdi Ave., Butler, NJ 07405 t) 973-838-8585

CEDAR KNOLLS

Notre Dame of Mt. Carmel - 75 Ridgedale Ave., Cedar Knolls, NJ 07927 t) 973-538-1358 parishsecretary@ndcarmel.com Dcn. Joseph Harris; Q. Furnald, Dir., Youth Ministry & Contemporary Music; Cristina Folan, Dir., Evangelization & Communication; Laura Balogh, Faith Formation Dir.; Jim Keefe, Music Dir.; Marc Luciani, Sacristan; Rev. Patrick G. O'Donovan, Pst.; Rev. Alex Nevitt, Par. Vicar; CRP Stds.: 300

CHATHAM

Corpus Christi - 234 Southern Blvd., Chatham, NJ 07928 t) 973-635-0070 frkevin@corpuschristi.org corpuschristi.org Rev. T. Kevin Corcoran, Pst.; Rev. Michal J. Szwarc, Par. Vicar; Rev. Msgr. James T. Mahoney, Pastor Emer.; CRP Stds.: 600

St. Patrick's - 85 Washington Ave., Chatham, NJ 07928; Mailing: 41 Oliver St., Chatham, NJ 07928 t) 973-635-0625 www.st-pats.org Rev. Robert J. Mitchell, Pst.; Rev. Artur Prazak, Par. Vicar; CRP Stds.: 513

St. Patrick's School - (Grades PreSchool-8) 45 Chatham St., Chatham, NJ 07928 t) 973-635-4623 www.st-pats-school.org/ Dr. Christine Ross, Prin.; Stds.: 250; Lay Tchrs.: 20

CHESTER

St. Lawrence the Martyr - 375 Main St., Chester, NJ 07930; Mailing: PO Box 730, Chester, NJ 07930 t) 908-879-5371; 908-879-6714 (CRP) fft@stlchester.org; parish@stlchester.org www.stlchester.org Rev. Angel Torres, Assoc. Pst.; Dcn. William DiVizio; Dcn. Gregory Szpunar; Shannon Rossi, DRE; Rev. Nicholas Bozza, Pst.; CRP Stds.: 315

CLIFTON

St. Andrew the Apostle - 400 Mt. Prospect Ave., Clifton, NJ 07012 t) 973-779-6873 x20 saintandrewsofficemanager@gmail.com www.standrewsclifton.org Rev. Jeider S. Barraza, Pst.; Rev. Msgr. Patrick J. Scott, In Res.;

Saint Brendan and Saint George - 154 E. First St., Clifton, NJ 07011 t) 973-772-6775 Rev. Jesus Peralta, Pst.; Rev. Milton Camargo, Par. Vicar;

Saint Brendan and Saint George School - t) 973-772-1149

St. Clare - 69 Allwood Rd., Clifton, NJ 07014 t) 973-777-7588 Rev. Peter S. Glabik, Pst.; Rev. Thomas J. Fitzgerald, Assoc. Pst.;

SS. Cyril and Methodius - 218 Ackerman Ave., Clifton, NJ 07011 t) 973-546-4390 Rev. Misael Jaramillo, Admin.; Rev. Gabriel Barrera, Par. Vicar; Dcn. Eugenio Morales;

St. John Kanty - 49 Speer Ave., Clifton, NJ 07013 t) 973-779-4102 sjkrcch@optonline.net Rev. Waclaw Sokolowski, O.F.M.Conv., Pst.; Rev. Boguslaw Czerniakowski, O.F.M.Conv., Assoc. Pst.; Rev. Edward Handy, O.F.M.Conv., In Res.;

St. Paul - 124 Union Ave., Clifton, NJ 07011 t) 973-340-1300 stpaulchurchnj@verizon.net Rev. Leonardo Jaramillo, Pst.; Dcn. Hector Casillas; Dcn. Joseph Puskas;

St. Philip the Apostle - 797 Valley Rd., Clifton, NJ 07013 t) 973-779-6200 dpannullo@atphilip.org; lvalenti@stphilip.org www.stphilip.org Rev. David Monteleone, Pst.; Rev. Nico Quintos, Par. Vicar; Rev. Msgr. P. Kevin Flanagan, In Res.; Dcn. Robert G. Ayers; Dcn. Nicholas Veliky; Denise Pannullo, DRE; CRP Stds.: 207

St. Philip Preparatory School - t) 973-779-4700 Barbara Zito, Prin.;

Sacred Heart - 145 Randolph Ave., Clifton, NJ 07011 t) 973-546-6012 sacredheartclifton.com Rev. Robert W. Wisnefski, Admin.; Rev. Krzystof Slimak, Par. Vicar; Rev. Andrew T. Perretta, In Res.; CRP Stds.: 15

DENVILLE

St. Mary's - 15 Myers Ave., Denville, NJ 07834 t) 973-627-8276 ccd@stmarys-denville.org Rev. Martin G. Glynn, Pst.; Rev. Stephen A. Delia, Par. Vicar; Dcn. Michael Allgaier; Dcn. John Flynn; Dcn. James Rizos; PJ Miller, DRE;

St. Mary's School - t) 973-627-2606

DOVER

St. Clement, Pope and Martyr - 154 Mt. Pleasant Ave., Dover, NJ 07801 t) 973-366-7547 (CRP); 973-366-7095 dreparish@stclement-rtwp.org; parishoffice@stclement-rtwp.org www.stclement-rtwp.org Rev. Giovanni Rodriguez, Admin.; Dcn. Henry Hyle; Susan Drew, DRE;

Sacred Heart Church and Our Lady Queen of the Most Holy Rosary - 4 Richards Ave., Dover, NJ 07801 t) 973-366-0060 phyle@sacredheart-dover.com; coordreled@sacredheart-dover.com www.sacredheart-dover.com Rev. Leonardo Lopez, Admin.; Rev. Carmen Buono, In Res.; Dcn. John R. Figueroa, DRE; CRP Stds.: 300

EAST HANOVER

St. Rose of Lima - 312 Ridgedale Ave., East Hanover, NJ 07936 t) 973-887-0357 (CRP); 973-887-5572 Rev. Maciej Kranc, Pst.; Dcn. Vincent Leo Jr.; CRP Stds.: 328

FLANDERS

St. Elizabeth Ann Seton - 61 Main St., Flanders, NJ 07836 t) 973-927-7077 (CRP); 973-927-1629 office@stelizabethschurch.org stelizabethschurch.org Rev. Stanley C. Barron, Pst.; Dcn. Richard J. Goglia; Corinne Kilkeary, Youth Min.; CRP Stds.: 254

FLORHAM PARK

Holy Family - 35 Orchard Rd., Florham Park, NJ 07932; Mailing: 1 Lloyd Ave., Florham Park, NJ 07932 t) 973-377-3101 (CRP); 973-377-1817 hfreducation@gmail.com; rectory@holyfamilyfp.org Rev. Thomas Rekiel, Pst.; Rev. Charles Lana, Pst. Assoc.; Rev. Frederick Walters, Pastor Emer.; Dcn. Peter Fiore; Virginia Akhoury, Pst. Assoc.; Anne Giedlinski, DRE; CRP Stds.: 278

Holy Family School - 17 Lloyd Ave., Florham Park, NJ 07932 t) 973-377-4181

FRANKLIN

Immaculate Conception - 75 Church St., Franklin, NJ 07416 t) 973-827-9501 (CRP); 973-827-9575 church@icrschool.com www.iccfranklin.org Rev. Boguslaw Kobus, Pst.;

GREEN POND

St. Simon the Apostle - 1010 Green Pond Rd., Green Pond, NJ 07435 t) 973-697-4699 www.stsimonapostle.org Rev. Richard Bay, Pst.; Connie Catania, DRE;

HARDYSTON

St. Jude the Apostle - 4 Beaver Run Rd., Hardyston, NJ 07419 t) 973-827-2280 (CRP); 973-827-8030 stjudehamburg@embarqmail.com www.stjudehardyston.org Rev. Michael Rodak, Pst.; CRP Stds.: 68

HASKELL

St. Francis of Assisi - 868 Ringwood Ave., Haskell, NJ 07420 t) 973-835-1946 stfrancis@optonline.net Rev. Gregorz Golba, Admin.; Dcn. Jose Rivera;

HAWTHORNE

St. Anthony's - 276 Diamond Bridge Ave., Hawthorne, NJ 07506 t) 973-427-7873 (CRP); 973-427-1478 religiouseducation.stanthony@gmail.com; stanthonyparishhawthorne@gmail.com Rev. Msgr. Raymond J. Kupke, Pst.; Rev. Francis H. Lennie, Par. Vicar; Dcn. Gerald Fadlalla; Dcn. Ronnie Gonzalez; Sr. Betty Ann Martinez, F.M.A., DRE; CRP Stds.: 300

St. Anthony's School - (Grades PreK-8) 270 Diamond Bridge Ave., Hawthorne, NJ 07506 t) 973-423-1818 stanthony@nac.net Sr. Mary Jackson, F.M.A., Prin.; Stds.: 220; Sr. Tchrs.: 2; Lay Tchrs.: 15

HEWITT

Our Lady Queen of Peace - 1911 Union Valley Rd., Hewitt, NJ 07421-3056 t) 973-728-8162; 973-728-8162 x308 (CRP) janet.scheil@olqpnj.org; olqpnj@gmail.com www.olqpnj.org Rev. Kamil Stachowiak, Pst.; Rev. Aleksander Bialas, Par. Vicar; Dcn. Charles Roche; Janet Scheil, DRE;

HIGHLAND LAKES

Our Lady of Fatima - 184 Breakneck Rd., Highland Lakes, NJ 07422; Mailing: P.O. Box 242, Highland Lakes, NJ 07422 t) 973-764-4457; 973-764-7277 (CRP) olfatima@warwick.net olfatimaparish.net Rev. Babu Thelappilly, Admin.; Dcn. William Aquino;

HOPATCONG

St. Jude's - 40 Maxim Dr., Hopatcong, NJ 07843 t) (973) 398-6377 office@stjudehopatcong.org www.stjudehopatcong.org Rev. Kamil Peter Wierzbicki, Pst.; Dcn. Thomas Friel; CRP Stds.: 85

KINNELON

Our Lady of the Magnificat - 2 Miller Rd., Kinnelon, NJ 07405 t) 973-838-6838 dre@olmchurch.org; secy@olmchurch.org www.olmchurch.org Rev. Steven Shadwell, Pst.; Rev. Msgr. John J. Carroll, Pastor Emer.; Mary Ramsden, DRE; CRP Stds.: 258

LAKE HOPATCONG

Our Lady Star of the Sea - 237 Espanong Rd., Lake Hopatcong, NJ 07849; Mailing: P.O. Box 337, Lake Hopatcong, NJ 07849 t) 973-663-0124 jhedrick@olsoslh.org Rev. P. Christopher Muldoon, Pst.; Dcn. Alberto R. Totino; Josephine Hedrick, DRE;

LINCOLN PARK

St. Joseph's - 216 Comly Rd., Lincoln Park, NJ 07035 t) 973-696-4411 stjoelp@optonline.net Rev. Artur P. Zaba, Pst.; Rev. Marcin Bradtke, Par. Vicar; Dcn. Stephen J. Marabeti; Dcn. Joseph Parlapiano;

LITTLE FALLS

Our Lady of the Holy Angels - 473 Main St., Little Falls, NJ 07424; Mailing: 465 Main St, Little Falls, NJ 07424 t) 973-256-5200 pfiliaci@gmail.com; contact@holyangelscommunity.org www.holyangelsrc.org Rev. Msgr. T. Mark Condon, Pst.; Dcn. Joseph Sisco; Beverly Cuccinelli, Admin.; Trish Filiaci, DRE; CRP Stds.: 274

LONG VALLEY

St. Luke - 265 W. Mill Rd., Long Valley, NJ 07853 t) (908) 876-3515 stlukeparishlv.com Rev. Owen B. Moran, Pst.; CRP Stds.: 401

St. Mark the Evangelist - 59 Spring Ln., Long Valley, NJ 07853 t) 908-850-0652 frmarcin@comcast.net www.stmarksnj.org/ Rev. Michal Rybinski, Par. Vicar; Rev. Marcin Michalowski, Pst.; CRP Stds.: 71

Our Lady of the Mountain - 2 E. Springtown Rd., Long Valley, NJ 07853 t) (908) 876-4395 ourladyofthemountain.org/ Rev. Michal Rybinski, Par. Vicar; Rev. Marcin Michalowski, Pst.; CRP Stds.: 323

MADISON

St. Vincent Martyr - 26 Green Village Rd., Madison, NJ 07940 t) (973) 377-4000 mainoffice@svmnj.org www.svmnj.org Rev. Msgr. George F. Hundt, Pst.; Rev. Krzysztof P. Liwarski, Par. Vicar; Rev. Yojaneider Garcia, Chap.; Dcn. Robert Morton; Jan Figenshu, Pst. Assoc.; CRP Stds.: 501

St. Vincent Martyr School -

MENDHAM

St. Joseph's - 8 W. Main St., Mendham, NJ 07945; Mailing: 6 New St., Mendham, NJ 07945 t) 973-543-5950 jcronin@stjoesmendham.org; dkuzma@stjoesmendham.org www.stjoesmendham.org Rev. Msgr. Joseph T. Anginoli, Pst.; Rev. Vic Karljohn Rouie Reyes Leviste (Phillipines), Par. Vicar; CRP Stds.: 313

MONTAGUE

St. James the Greater - 75 River Rd., Montague, NJ 07827 t) (973) 948-2296 stjamesthomas@aol.com Rev. Wayne F. Varga, Pst.; Dcn. Wayne Von Doehren; Mary Flexer, DRE; CRP Stds.: 6

MONTVILLE

St. Pius X - 24 Changebridge Rd., Montville, NJ 07045 t) 973-335-2894 office@st-pius-x.org www.st-pius-x.org

Rev. Mark Olenowski, Pst.; Rev. Joemin Parinas, Par. Vicar; CRP Stds.: 700

MORRIS PLAINS

St. Virgilius - 250 Speedwell Ave., Morris Plains, NJ 07950 t) 973-538-1418 svparishoffice@gmail.com stvirgilparish.org Rev. Michal A Falgowski, Pst.; Rev. Marcin Kania, Par. Vicar; Dcn. Rich Pinto; Dcn. Merle Sisler;

MORRISTOWN

Assumption of the Blessed Virgin Mary - 91 Maple Ave., Morristown, NJ 07960 t) 732-675-6389 (CRP); 973-539-2141 linda.macios@assumptionparish.org; assumption@assumptionparish.org Rev. Msgr. John E. Hart, Pst.; Rev. Lukasz Wnuk, Par. Vicar; Rev. Dennis J. Crowley, In Res.; Dcn. Brian D. Beyerl; Dcn. P. Michael Hanly; Dcn. Elliott Stein; Linda Macios, DRE;

Assumption of the Blessed Virgin Mary School - (Grades PreK-8) 63 MacCulloch Ave., Morristown, NJ 07960 t) 973-538-0590 pdechiaro@assumptionnj.org www.assumptionnj.org/ Sr. Merris Larkin, Prin.;

St. Margaret of Scotland - 6 Sussex Ave., Morristown, NJ 07960; Mailing: 12 Columba St., Morristown, NJ 07960 t) 973-538-0874 stmargaretchurchmorristown@gmail.com www.csmargaret.org Rev. Hernan Arias, Pst.; Rev. Duberney Villamizar, Admin.; Rev. Dailon Lisabet, Par. Vicar; Dcn. Tim Holden; Dcn. Ken Rado;

St. Thomas More - 4 Convent Rd., Morristown, NJ 07960; Mailing: P.O. Box 286, Convent Station, NJ 07961 t) 973-267-5585 info@stmnj.org Rev. Thomas H. Fallone, Pst.;

MOUNT ARLINGTON

Our Lady of the Lake - One Park Ave., Mount Arlington, NJ 07856 t) 973-770-0291 Rev. Paul Barboutz, Pst.; Rev. Hugh P. Murphy, Pastor Emer.;

MOUNTAIN LAKES

St. Catherine of Siena - 10 N. Pocono Rd., Mountain Lakes, NJ 07046 t) (973) 334-7131 parishoffice@stcatherine-ml.org www.stcatherine-ml.org Rev. Michael J. Parisi, Pst.; CRP Stds.: 206

NETCONG

St. Michael's - 4 Church St., Netcong, NJ 07857 t) (973) 347-0032 office.admin@stmichaelnetcong.org Rev. Michael Lee, Pst.; Dcn. Richard F. Bias; Dcn. John Meyer; Dcn. Russell Raffay;

NEW VERNON

Christ the King - 16 Blue Mill Rd., New Vernon, NJ 07976; Mailing: P.O. Box 368, New Vernon, NJ 07976 t) 973-539-4955 x10 frbriansullivan@me.com www.churchofchristtheking.org Rev. Brian Sullivan, Pst.; Rev. Armando Vizcara, Par. Vicar;

NEWTON

St. Joseph - 24 Halsted St., Newton, NJ 07860; Mailing: 22 Halsted St., Newton, NJ 07860-2003 t) 973-383-1985; 973-383-8413 (CRP) parishoffice@stjosephnewton.org Rev. ST Sutton, Pst.; Dcn. Gerald Hanifan; Dcn. Thomas Zayac;

OAK RIDGE

St. Thomas, the Apostle - 5635 Berkshire Valley Rd., Oak Ridge, NJ 07438 t) (973) 208-0090 terry@ststhomasjohn.org Rev. Brian Ditullio, Par. Vicar; Rev. Benjamin Williams, Pst.; CRP Stds.: 127

OGDENSBURG

St. Thomas of Aquin - 53 Kennedy Ave., Ogdensburg, NJ 07439 t) 973-827-3190 stthomasofaquin@embarqmail.com www.stthomasofaquin.org Rev. Przemyslaw Gawlik; Dcn. Dominic Zampella; CRP Stds.: 33

PARSIPPANY

St. Ann - 781 Smith Rd., Parsippany, NJ 07054 t) 973-884-1986 stann@saint-ann.net www.saint-ann.net Rev. Joseph J. Garbarino, Pst.; Dcn. Leonard Deo; Dcn. Alfred Frank; Louis Castano, Music Min.; Ginny Bissig, Pst. Assoc.; CRP Stds.: 85

St. Christopher - 1050 Littleton Rd., Parsippany, NJ 07054 t) 973-539-6208 Rev. Joseph G. Buffardi, Pst.; Rev. Luis Alberto Hernandez, Par. Vicar; Dcn. Richard A. Gaydo; Dcn. Alan Lucibello;

St. Peter the Apostle - 179 Baldwin Rd., Parsippany, NJ 07054 t) 973-334-2090 stpetertheapostle179@gmail.com saintpetertheapostle.org Rev. David Pickens, Pst.; Rev. Diego Monsalve, Par. Vicar; Rev. Sylwester Pierzak, Par. Vicar; Rev. Msgr. Herbert K. Tillyer, Pastor Emer.; Dcn. Luis Carlos Mendez; Dcn. Joseph Marsicovete; Dcn. Robert A. Lang; Dcn. Peter Cistaro; CRP Stds.: 327

PASSAIC

St. Anthony of Padua - 95 Myrtle Ave., Passaic, NJ 07055 t) 973-777-4793 Rev. Hernan Cely, Admin.; Rev. Jose M. Zuniga, Par. Vicar;

Assumption of the Blessed Virgin Mary - 63 Monroe St., Passaic, NJ 07055 t) 973-779-0427 stmaryrcchurch@gmail.com stmarypassaic.org/ Saint Mary's Parish has witnessed an eventful and fruitful century of progress. With hearts filled with gratitude to a good and generous God. Rev. Jorge I. Rodriguez, Pst.; CRP Stds.: 49

Holy Rosary - 6 Wall St., Passaic, NJ 07055 t) 973-473-1578 (Shrine of Saint John Paul II) Rev. A. Stefan Las, Pst.; Rev. Michal Dykalski, Assoc. Pst.; Rev. Slawomir Tomaszewski, Par. Vicar;

Holy Trinity - 226 Harrison St., Passaic, NJ 07055 t) 973-778-9763 Rev. Antonio Rodriguez, Pst.;

St. Joseph's - 7 Parker Ave., Passaic, NJ 07055 t) 973-473-2822 st-josephchurch@mail.com Rev. Dariusz K. Kaminski, Pst.;

Our Lady of Fatima and Saint Nicholas - 153 Washington Pl., Passaic, NJ 07055 t) 973-472-0815 Dcn. Ramon Lacardo; Dcn. Gilberto Martinez; Rev. Rolands Uribe, Admin.;

Our Lady of Mt. Carmel - 10 St. Francis Way, Passaic, NJ 07055 t) 973-473-0246 Rev. Andres Baquero, Pst.;

St. Stephen's - 223 Third St., Passaic, NJ 07055 t) 973-779-0332 ststephenspassaic@gmail.com ststephenspassaic.com Hungarian Heritage Library Rev. Laszlo Balogh, Pst.; CRP Stds.: 45

PATERSON

Cathedral of St. John the Baptist - 381 Grand St., Paterson, NJ 07505 t) 973-345-4070 info@rcdopcathedral.org patersoncathedral.org Rev. Msgr. Eugene R. Sylva, Rector; Rev. Cesar Jaramillo, Par. Vicar; Rev. Jorge Castano, Par. Vicar; Dcn. Luis Gil; Dcn. Guido Pedraza; Dcn. German Vargas; Ivannia Vega-McTighe, DRE; Dr. David Bower, Music Min.; Justin Carrasco, Youth Min.; CRP Stds.: 502

St. Agnes - 681 Main St., Paterson, NJ 07503 t) 973-279-0250 saintagnesrcchurch@gmail.com saintagnesrcchurch.com/ Rev. Enrique Corona, Pst.; Dcn. Gilberto Vazquez; CRP Stds.: 93

St. Anthony's - 138 Beech St., Paterson, NJ 07501 t) 973-742-9695 stanthonypaterson1@yahoo.com stanthonypaterson.com/ Rev. Eider Reyes, Pst.; Escari Tucker, DRE; CRP Stds.: 60

Blessed Sacrament - 224 E. 18th St., Paterson, NJ 07524 t) 973-523-5002; 973-523-5003 frrayorama@optonline.net; ftorrez@optonline.net Rev. Raymond Orama, Pst.; CRP Stds.: 26

St. Bonaventure - 174 Ramsey St., Paterson, NJ 07501 t) 973-279-1016 tgallo1130@yahoo.com; parishoffice@stbonspaterson.org www.stbonspaterson.org Rev. Daniel P. Grigassy, O.F.M., Pst.; Rev. Paul J Breslin, O.F.M., Assoc. Pst.; Rev. Robert J Norton, O.F.M., In Res.; Dcn. Joseph Balough; Dcn. Juan Borges; Teresa Gallo-Tomcho, DRE; CRP Stds.: 100

St. Gerard Majella - 501 W. Broadway, Paterson, NJ 07522 t) 973-595-8446 stgerardmajella@optonline.net Rev. Leo Antony, S.D.V., Admin.; Rev. James Butts, S.D.V., Assoc. Pst.; Rev. Benny Chittilappilly, S.D.V., Assoc. Pst.; Rev. Robert Vass, S.D.V., Assoc. Pst.;

St. Gerard Majella School - (Grades PreK-8) 10 Carrelton Dr., Paterson, NJ 07522 t) 973-595-5640 stgerardschool.org Sr. Jo-Ann Pompa, M.P.F, Prin.; Stds.: 130; Sr. Tchrs.: 1; Lay Tchrs.: 11

St. Joseph's - 399 Market St., Paterson, NJ 07501 t) 973-278-0030 rzadcaj@juno.com Rev. Janusz Rzadca, Pst.;

St. Mary's - 410 Union Ave., Paterson, NJ 07502 t) 973-790-8651 brandojb@aol.com (Auxilium Christianorum) Rev. Brando Ibarra, Pst.; Dcn. Juan Carlos Carnero;

St. Michael the Archangel - 70 Cianci St., Paterson, NJ 07501-1831 t) 973-523-8413 st_michael@yahoo.com Rev. Enrique Corona, Pst.;

Our Lady of Lourdes - 440 River St., Paterson, NJ 07524-1902 t) 973-742-2142 Rev. Raimundo Rivera, Admin.; Rev. Hector Melendez, Assoc. Pst.; Dcn. Raul Pamplona;

Our Lady of Pompei - 70 Murray Ave., Paterson, NJ 07501 t) 973-742-1969 ourladyofpompeii@aol.com www.ourladyofpompeichurch.com Rev. Frank P. Agresti, Pst.; CRP Stds.: 14

Our Lady of Victories - 100 Fair St., Paterson, NJ 07501 t) 973-279-0487; 973-279-0527 olvjude@gmail.com www.olvjude.org Rev. Raimundo Rivera, Pst.; Rev. Ruben Dario Castillo (Colombia), Vicar; Dcn. Maximo Paulino;

St. Stephen's - 86 Martin St., Paterson, NJ 07501 t) 973-742-2822 ststepheninpaterson@gmail.com Rev. Rafael Ciro, Pst.;

St. Therese - 80 13th Ave., Paterson, NJ 07504 t) 973-881-0400 sttheresechurch@optonline.net www.sttheresepaterson.com/ Rev. Yasid Salas, Pst.; Dcn. Luis Ramirez; CRP Stds.: 149

PEQUANNOCK

Holy Spirit - 318 Newark-Pompton Tpke., Pequannock, NJ 07440 t) 973-696-1234 www.holyspiritparishnj.org Rev. Stephen Prisk, Pst.; Dcn. Michael Scruggs; CRP Stds.: 109

Holy Spirit School - 330 Newark-Pompton Tpke., Pequannock, NJ 07440 t) 973-835-5680

Convent - t) 973-694-2111

Our Lady of Fatima Chapel (Tridentine) - 32 W. Franklin Ave., Pequannock, NJ 07440 Rev. Karl Marsolle, F.S.S.P., Pst.; Rev. Robert Boyd, Assoc. Pst.; Rev. Matthew McNeely, F.S.S.P., Admin.;

Kolbe Immaculata School - 18 First St., Pequannock, NJ 07440 t) 973-694-1034 Jayne Bayne, Prin.;

POMPTON LAKES

Our Lady of the Assumption - 17 Pompton Ave., Pompton Lakes, NJ 07442 t) 973-835-7750 (CRP); 973-835-0374 (Office) smc@stmarys-pompton.org www.stmarys-pompton.org/ Rev. John Alderson, Par. Vicar; Rev. John Coughlin, O.F.M., Par. Vicar; Rev. John Aherne, O.F.M., Admin.; Dcn. Thomas Kimak; CRP Stds.: 982

POMPTON PLAINS

Our Lady of Good Counsel - 155 W. Pkwy., Pompton Plains, NJ 07444 t) 973-839-3311 Rev. Darwin J. Lastra, Pst.; Rev. Peter J. Clarke; Dcn. Carmen Restaino;

PROSPECT PARK

St. Paul's - 286 Haledon Ave., Prospect Park, NJ 07508 t) 973-790-8135 Rev. Henry Pinto, Pst.;

RANDOLPH

St. Matthew the Apostle - 335 Dover-Chester Rd., Randolph, NJ 07869 t) 832-251-4129 moira.dziomba@stmatthewsrandolph.org Rev. Brian P. Quinn, Pst.; Dcn. Richard A. Brady; Dcn. Edward Keegan; Moira Dziomba, DRE;

Resurrection - 651 Millbrook Ave., Randolph, NJ 07869 t) 973-895-4224 info@resurrectionparishnj.org www.resurrectionparishnj.org Rev. John F. Tarantino, Pst.; Dcn. Richard Reck; Dcn. Richard Van Glahn; CRP Stds.: 431

RINGWOOD

St. Catherine of Bologna - 112 Erskine Rd., Ringwood, NJ 07456 t) 973-962-7032 www.stcatherineofbologna.org Rev. Pawel F. Szurek, Pst.; CRP Stds.: 146

ROCKAWAY

St. Cecilia's - 70 Church St., Rockaway, NJ 07866 t) 973-627-0313 stcecilia.faithformation@gmail.com; stcec@optonline.net st-cecilia.org Rev. Sigmund A. Peplowski, Pst.; Rev. Mateusz Darlak, Par. Vicar; James Clancy, DRE; CRP Stds.: 225

Convent - 100 Church St., Rockaway, NJ 07866

t) 973-627-6533
Sacred Heart - 63 E. Main St., Rockaway, NJ 07866 t) 973-627-0422 shrectory@gmail.com sacredheartrockaway.org Rev. Pawel Bala, Pst.; Rev. Stephen Sniscak, In Res.; CRP Stds.: 10

SANDYSTON
St. Thomas the Apostle - 210 Rte. 206 N., Sandyston, NJ 07826 t) 973-948-2296; 973-948-7004 (CRP) stjamesthomas@aol.com Rev. Wayne F. Varga, Pst.; Dcn. Wayne Von Doehren; Mary Flexer, DRE; CRP Stds.: 74

SPARTA
Saint Kateri Tekakwitha - 427 Stanhope Rd., Sparta, NJ 07871 t) (973) 729-1682 office@saintkateri.org www.saintkateri.org/ Rev. Vidal Gonzalez Jr., Pst.; CRP Stds.: 165
Our Lady of the Lake - 294 Sparta Ave., Sparta, NJ 07871 t) 973-729-6107 info@ourladyofthelake.org www.ourladyofthelake.org Rev. David McDonnell, Pst.; Rev. Kamil Kiszka, Par. Vicar; Dcn. Anthony Curcio Jr.; Dcn. James McGovern; CRP Stds.: 302

STIRLING
St. Vincent de Paul - 250 Bebout Ave., Stirling, NJ 07980 t) 908-647-0118; 908-647-0421 (CRP) parish@stvincentschurch.org stvincentschurch.org Rev. A. Richard Carton, Pst.; Dcn. Peter J. O'Neill; CRP Stds.: 343

STOCKHOLM
St. John Vianney - 2823 Rte. 23 S, Stockholm, NJ 07460; Mailing: 5635 Berkshire Valley Rd., Oak Ridge, NJ 07438 t) (973) 697-6550 terry@ststhomasjohn.org www.ststhomasjohn.org Rev. Benjamin Williams, Pst.; Rev. Brian Ditullio, Par. Vicar; Dcn. James Camarrano; Dcn. Kevin L. Combs; CRP Stds.: 43

SUCCASUNNA
St. Therese - 151 Main St., Succasunna, NJ 07876; Mailing: 7 Hunter St., Succasunna, NJ 07876 t) 973-584-9444 (CRP); 973-584-8271 sttheresoffice@optonline.net www.sttheresroxbury.org Rev. Richard Kilcomons, Pst.; Rev. Javier Bareno, Par. Vicar; Rev. Dulibber Gonzalez, Par. Vicar; Dcn. Jose Padron;
St. Therese School - 135 Main St., Succasunna, NJ 07876 t) 973-584-0812

SUSSEX
St. Monica - 33 Unionville Ave., Sussex, NJ 07461 t) 973-875-4521 stmonica@ptd.net www.stmonicasussex.org Rev. Jan Wodziak, Pst.; CRP Stds.: 26

SWARTSWOOD
Our Lady of Mt. Carmel - 203 Swartswood Rd., Swartswood, NJ 07877; Mailing: P.O. Box 124, Swartswood, NJ 07877 t) 973-383-3566; 973-579-2355 (CRP) Rev. Abuchi Nwosu, Admin.; Dcn. Anthony P. Barile Jr.;

TOTOWA
St. James of the Marches - 32 St. James Pl., Totowa, NJ 07512 t) 973-790-0288 stjameschurch@optonline.net www.stjamesofthemarches.com Rev. Marc A. Mancini, Pst.; Rev. Joseph Mactal, Par. Vicar;

VERNON
St. Francis de Sales - 614 County Rte. 517, Vernon, NJ 07462; Mailing: P.O. Box 785, McAfee, NJ 07428 t) 973-827-3248 office@stfrancisvernon.org www.stfrancisvernon.org Rev. Christopher S. Barkhausen, Pst.; Dcn. Dennis Gil; Petrina Garrity, CRE; Linda Allen-Poole, Youth Min.; CRP Stds.: 253

WAYNE
Annunciation - 45 Urban Club Rd., Wayne, NJ 07470 t) 973-694-5700 trish23@optonline.net www.abvm-wayne.org Rev. Ricardo Ortega, Pst.; CRP Stds.: 57
Holy Cross - Holy Cross Way & Van Duyne Ave., Wayne, NJ 07470; Mailing: 630 Valley Rd., Wayne, NJ 07470 t) 973-694-4585 vonbreton@aol.com Rev. Peter VB. Wells, Pst.; Rev. Duberney Villamizar, Par. Vicar;
Immaculate Heart of Mary - 580 Ratzer Rd., Wayne, NJ 07470 t) 973-694-4891 (CRP); 973-694-3400 ihmchurch@aol.com Rev. Mateusz Jasniewicz, Pst.; Rev. Daniel A. Kelly, Pastor Emer.;
Immaculate Heart of Mary School - (Grades PreK-8) t) 973-694-1225 ihm.wayne@gmail.com www.ihmwaynenj.org Marcello Monte, Prin.;
Our Lady of Consolation - 1799 Hamburg Tpke., Wayne, NJ 07470 t) 973-839-3444 Rev. Michael D. Lombardo, Pst.; Rev. Philip-Michael Tangorra, In Res.;
Our Lady of the Valley - 630 Valley Rd., Wayne, NJ 07470 t) 973-694-4585 secretary@olvwayne.org olvwayne.org Rev. Peter VB. Wells, Pst.; Dcn. Vincent Cocilovo; CRP Stds.: 450

WEST MILFORD
St. Joseph - 454 Germantown Rd., West Milford, NJ 07480 t) 973-208-0636 pastor@st.josreph-nj.org Rev. Jakub Grzybowski, Admin.; Dcn. Benjamin LoParo; Dcn. Harry White;

WHARTON
St. Bernard's - 446 Mt. Hope Rd., Wharton, NJ 07885-2814 t) 973-627-0066 stbernardsmth@verizon.net Rev. Alfred J. Lampron, Pst.;
St. Mary's - 371 S. Main St, Wharton, NJ 07885; Mailing: 425 W. Blackwell St, Dover, NJ 07801 t) 973-366-0184 info@stmarysdover.org www.stmarysdover.org Rev. Lemmuel Camacho, Pst.; Rev. Cerilo Javinez, Par. Vicar; Dcn. Thomas P. Beirne; Dcn. Stuart A. Hartnett; Andrea Henry, Bus. Mgr.; CRP Stds.: 142

WHIPPANY
Our Lady of Mercy - 9 Parsippany Rd., Whippany, NJ 07981 t) 973-887-0050 olmchwhip@aol.com ourladyofmercyparish.com/ Rev. Roberto Amador, Pst.; Rev. Alexis Coffi Gonzalez, In Res.; Dcn. Vincent LoBello; Rev. Manuel Cuellar, Par. Vicar; CRP Stds.: 170

SCHOOLS: PRESCHOOL THRU HIGH SCHOOL

SCHOOLS

STATE OF NEW JERSEY

PARSIPPANY
All Saints Academy - (DIO) (Grades PreK-8) 189 Baldwin Rd., Parsippany, NJ 07054 t) 973-334-4704 jberg@allsaintspar.org www.allsaintspar.org Judy Berg, Prin.;

ROCKAWAY
Divine Mercy Academy, Inc. - (DIO) (Grades PreK-8) 87 Halsey Ave., Rockaway, NJ 07866 t) 973-627-6003 principal@dmarockaway.org dmarockaway.org Rev. Sigmund A. Peplowski, Pst.; Ann Mitchell, Prin.; Janet Maulbeck, Bus. Mgr.; Stds.: 222; Lay Tchrs.: 12

SPARTA
Pope John XXIII Middle School, Inc. - 28 Andover Rd., Sparta, NJ 07871 t) (973) 729-6125 johnfernandes@popejohn.org Most Rev. Kevin J. Sweeney, Pres.; Rev. Msgr. T. Mark Condon, Vice. Pres.; Stds.: 260; Lay Tchrs.: 21

TOTOWA
Academy of Saint James of the Marches - (DIO) (Grades PreK-8) 400 Totowa Rd., Totowa, NJ 07512 t) 973-956-8824 principal@academyofstjames.org academyofstjames.org Serves St. James of the Marches, Totowa, students in Paterson, NJ and surrounding communities. Lelia D Pappas, Admin.; Blanca Hopper, Admin.; Stds.: 182; Sr. Tchrs.: 2; Lay Tchrs.: 18

HIGH SCHOOLS

STATE OF NEW JERSEY

CONVENT STATION
Academy of St. Elizabeth (Sisters of Charity) - (PRV) (Grades 9-12) 2 Convent Rd., Convent Station, NJ 07961; Mailing: PO Box 297, Convent Station, NJ 07961 t) 973-290-5200 lburek@aose.info academyofsaintelizabeth@aose.info Lynn Burek, Prin.; Stds.: 221; Lay Tchrs.: 26

DENVILLE
Morris Catholic High School - (DIO) 200 Morris Ave., Denville, NJ 07834 t) 973-627-6674 mchs@morriscatholic.org www.morriscatholic.org Rev. Peter J. Clarke, Pres.; Rev. Carmen Buono, Chap.; Robert Loia, Prin.;

MORRISTOWN
Delbarton School - (PRV) (Grades 7-12) 230 Mendham Rd., Morristown, NJ 07960 t) 973-538-3231 comments@delbarton.org www.delbarton.org Boys. Rev. Michael Tidd, O.S.B., Headmaster;
Villa Walsh Academy - (PRV) (Grades 7-12) 455 Western Ave., Morristown, NJ 07960 t) 973-538-3680 villawalsh@aol.com www.villawalsh.org College Preparatory for girls. Conducted by Religious Teachers Filippini

NORTH HALEDON
Mary Help of Christians Academy, Inc. (Missionary Society of the Salesian Sisters, Inc.) - (PRV) (Grades 9-12) 659-723 Belmont Ave., North Haledon, NJ 07508 t) 973-790-6200 headofschool@maryhelp.org www.maryhelp.org Sr. Colleen Clair, FMA, Admin.; Stds.: 148; Sr. Tchrs.: 3; Lay Tchrs.: 30

WAYNE
De Paul Catholic High School - (DIO) 1512 Alps Rd., Wayne, NJ 07470 t) 973-694-3702 petrocellir@dpchs.org; weirk@dpchs.org depaulcatholic.org Russell Petrocelli, Prin.;

INSTITUTIONS LOCATED IN DIOCESE

ASSOCIATIONS [ASN]

WAYNE
The Association of the Marian Apostolate of Mercy, Inc. - 701 Runnymede Dr., Wayne, NJ 07470 t) 973-956-5969 marianoutreach@gmail.com Rev. John Gordon; Sr. Maria Elizabeth Whilifer, Pres.; Judith A. Bonnesen, Treas.;

CAMPUS MINISTRY / NEWMAN CENTERS [CAM]

HALEDON
William Paterson University of New Jersey - 219 Pompton Rd., Haledon, NJ 07508 t) 973-720-3524; 973-595-6184 frhubert@jesuscampus.net www.jesuscampus.net Jesus Christ, Prince of Peace Chapel Catholic Campus Ministry Center. Rev. Paul Tomczyk, Dir.;

MADISON
Drew University Catholic Campus Ministry - 205 Madison Ave., Madison, NJ 07940; Mailing: P.O. Box 387, Convent Station, NJ 07961-0387 t) 973-408-3027 Brian Honsberger, Campus Min.;

MORRISTOWN
College of St. Elizabeth, Center for Theological and Spiritual Development - 2 Convent Rd., Morristown, NJ 07960 t) 973-290-4354 x4491 ibaratte@cse.edu www.cse.edu/center

CATHOLIC CHARITIES [CCH]

CLIFTON
Catholic Charities of the Roman Catholic Diocese of Paterson, Inc. - 777 Valley Rd., Clifton, NJ 07013 t) 973-737-2077 scott@ccpaterson.org Scott Milliken, Dir.;

COLLEGES & UNIVERSITIES [COL]

DENVILLE
Assumption College for Sisters - 200A Morris Ave.,

Denville, NJ 07834 t) 973-957-0188 president@acs350.org acs350.org Sr. Teresa Bruno, S.C., Dean; Sr. Joseph Spring, S.C.C., Pres.; Barbara Kelly-Vegona, Registrar; Patricia McGrady, Treas.; Stds.: 38

MORRISTOWN

Saint Elizabeth University - 2 Convent Rd., Morristown, NJ 07960-6989 t) 973-290-4000; 973-290-4498 mfescoe@steu.edu www.steu.edu Dr. Gary Crosby, Pres.; Michael Dennis Fescoe, Vice. Pres.; Katherine Buck, Vice Pres. Student Life;

CONVENTS, MONASTERIES, AND RESIDENCES FOR WOMEN [CON]

BOONTON

Society of the Sisters of the Church - 24 Deer Hill Ct., Boonton, NJ 07005 t) 973-299-8365 srbw@ssoc.org www.ssoc.org

CHESTER

Carmel of the Immaculate Heart of Mary - 80 Pleasant Hill Rd., Chester, NJ 07930-2135 t) 908-879-4990; 908-879-0887 hermcarm@gti.net Hermits of Our Lady of Mt. Carmel Mother Theresa Margaret Des Bois, O.Carm., Prioress;

DENVILLE

Missionary Sisters of the Immaculate Conception USA Unit - 19 Pocono Rd., Denville, NJ 07834; Mailing: 25 Orchard St. Ste. 104, Denville, NJ 07834 t) 973-279-3790 smicunit@gmail.com Sr. Kathryn Conti, S.M.I.C., Supr.;

Missionary Sisters of the Immaculate Conception USA Unit - 25 Orchard Rd., Ste. 104, Denville, NJ 07834 t) 973-279-3790 smicunit@gmail.com smic-missionarysisters.com Sr. Janice Jolin, SMIC, Supr.; Srs.: 16

FLORHAM PARK

Sister Joanna House of Formation - 88 Brooklake Rd., Florham Park, NJ 07932 t) 973-966-9762 vocationist@yahoo.com vocationist-sisters.org Sr. Perpetua Da Conceicao, S.D.V., Supr.;

GLADSTONE

Mt. St. John Convent - 22 St. John's Dr., Gladstone, NJ 07934; Mailing: P.O. Box 711, Gladstone, NJ 07934 t) 908-234-0640 baptistines@worldnet.att.net www.baptistines.home.att.net Sr. Angelita Vazzano, C.S.J.B., Admin.;

HALEDON

St. Joseph Provincial Center - 655 Belmont Ave., Haledon, NJ 07508 t) 973-790-7966 Provincialate of Daughters of Mary Help of Christians Sr. Helene Godin, FMA, Supr.; Srs.: 35

MENDHAM

Mallinckrodt Convent-Motherhouse and Novitiate of the Sisters of Christian Charity (Daughters of the Blessed Virgin Mary of the Immaculate Conception) - 350 Bernardsville Rd., Mendham, NJ 07945 t) 973-543-6528 secretary@scceast.org; bus.manager@scceast.org scceast.org Sr. Joann Marie Aumand, SCC, Prov.; Srs.: 145

MORRISTOWN

St. Lucy Provincialate of the Religious Teachers Filippini, Novitiate, Villa Walsh Academy (Pontifical Institute of the Religious Teachers Filippini) - 455 Western Ave., Morristown, NJ 07960-4912 t) 973-538-2886 srpatricia@filippiniusa.org www.filippiniusa.org Sr. Patricia Pompa, Prov.; Sr. Betty Jean Takacs, Supr.; Sr. Elaine Bebyn, M.P.F., Prin.; Srs.: 123

St. Joseph Infirmary Hall - 455 Western Ave., Morristown, NJ 07960-4912

Monastery Discalced Carmelite Nuns of the Most Blessed Virgin Mary of Mt. Carmel - 189 Madison Ave., Morristown, NJ 07960 t) 973-539-0773 Sr. Therese Katulski, O.C.D., Prioress;

Motherhouse of the Sisters of Charity of St. Elizabeth - 2 Convent Rd., Morristown, NJ 07960; Mailing: P.O. Box 476, Convent Station, NJ 07961-0476 t) 973-290-5000 escharity@aol.com www.scnj.org Sr. Maureen Shaughnessy, SC, Supr.; Srs.: 44

PARSIPPANY

St. Francis of Assisi Novitiate-Franciscan Sisters of St. Elizabeth - 499 Park Rd., Parsippany, NJ 07054 t) 973-539-3857 sr-cathylynn@yahoo.com www.franciscansisters.com

PATERSON

Daughters of Charity of the Most Precious Blood - 46 Preakness Ave., Paterson, NJ 07522 t) 973-956-1921 josephinefcpps@gmail.com; avemariadcpb@gmail.com Sr. Regi Karumakkel, D.C.P.B., Supr.; Srs.: 12

STIRLING

Holy Trinity Convent - 1026 Long Hill Rd., Stirling, NJ 07980 t) 908-647-6584 sistersjstirling@gmail.com Sr. Sophia Kozikowska, Supr.;

WOODLAND PARK

Missionary Sisters of the Immaculate Conception of the Mother of God - Generalate, 47 Garden Ave., Woodland Park, NJ 07424 t) (973) 279-1484 smicgeneralate@gmail.com www.missionarysistersofic.org Sr. Beatrice Yang, SMIC, Minister General; Srs.: 4

The Society of Sisters for the Church - 396 Rifle Camp Rd., Woodland Park, NJ 07424 t) 973-345-1816 (Res. Sister); (703) 799-8081 smbphd@aol.com www.ssc-usa.org Sr. Michael Bochnowski, SSC, Pres.; Srs.: 17

ENDOWMENTS / FOUNDATIONS / TRUSTS [EFT]

CLIFTON

Catholic Foundation of the Diocese of Paterson, Inc. - 777 Valley Rd., Clifton, NJ 07013 t) 973-777-8818 kmullaney@patersondiocese.org Rev. Msgr. T. Mark Condon, Pres.; Rev. T. Kevin Corcoran, Secy.; Rev. Hernan Arias, Vice Pres.;

Diocese of Paterson Catholic Cemetery Perpetual Care Trust - 777 Valley Rd., Clifton, NJ 07013 t) 973-777-8818 x240 lorettarybacki@gmail.com; theresalosewicz@popejohn.org Sr. Karen Kattwinkel, SSC, Contact;

Diocese of Paterson Catholic Education Trust - 777 Valley Rd., Clifton, NJ 07013 Most Rev. Kevin J. Sweeney, Pres.;

Diocese of Paterson Mission Fund, Inc. - 777 Valley Rd., Clifton, NJ 07013 Rev. Msgr. T. Mark Condon, Pres.; Rev. T. Kevin Corcoran, Secy.;

DENVILLE

Missionary Sisters of the Immaculate Conception 1996 Trust Fund - 25 Orchard St., Ste. 104, Denville, NJ 07834 t) 973-279-3790 smicunit@gmail.com

HOSPITALS / HEALTH SERVICES [HOS]

PATERSON

St. Joseph's University Medical Center - 703 Main St., Paterson, NJ 07503 t) 973-754-2000 www.stjosephshealth.org/ Rev. Francis Enrico Conde, Chap.; Rev. Wilder A. Londono; Rev. Jose Miguel Jimenez, Chap.; Bed Capacity: 651; Staff: 5,000

MISCELLANEOUS [MIS]

BLOOMFIELD

Riese Corporation - 264 Belleville Ave., Bloomfield, NJ 07003 t) 973-743-2300 Sponsoring Governor Paterson Towers, Maurice Brick Residence, Brestel Residence, William F. Hinchcliffe Pavilion, Ralph J. Diverio Residence. Rev. Msgr. Herbert K. Tillyer, Pres.;

CHESTER

Nazareth Village - 11 Meadow Ln., Chester, NJ 07930; Mailing: Box 635, Chester, NJ 07930 t) 908-879-6991 nazarethvillage@hotmail.com www.nazarethvillage.net Retirement residence for diocesan priests. Rev. Brian P. Quinn, Dir.; Rev. Nelson Betancur, In Res.; Rev. John Andrew Connell, In Res.; Rev. Edward M. Davey, In Res.; Rev. Joseph P. Davis, In Res.; Rev. Msgr. George A. Dudak, In Res.; Rev. George J. Gothie, In Res.; Rev. John J. Klein, In Res.; Rev. Msgr. Peter J. McHugh, In Res.; Rev. Joseph E. Murphy, In Res.; Rev. Brendan J. Murray, In Res.; Rev. Ronald Sordillo, In Res.; Rev. Msgr. Raymond M. Lopatesky, In Res.;

CLIFTON

Casa Guadalupe, Inc. - 737 Valley Rd., Clifton, NJ 07013 t) 973-737-1466; 201-951-2857 holly@casaguadalupe.net; avemaria53@gmail.com www.casaguadalupe.net House of Discernment for women contemplating religious life. Rev. Agustino Miguel Torres, C.F.R., Dir.; Holly Wright, Dir.;

Consortium of Catholic Schools of the Roman Catholic Diocese of Paterson, Inc., Catholic Academy of Passaic County - 777 Valley Rd., Clifton, NJ 07013 t) 973-777-8818 x276 patrickpeace@patersondiocese.org Most Rev. Arthur J. Serratelli, Pres.; Sr. Mary Edward Spohrer, S.C.C., Secy.; Patrick Peace, Dir.; Rev. Msgr. James T. Mahoney, Vice Pres.;

Saint Gerard Majella School, Inc. - 777 Valley Rd., Clifton, NJ 07013 t) 973-777-8818 x276

St. Joseph's Fund - 777 Valley Rd., Clifton, NJ 07013 t) 973-777-8818 shepherd@patersondiocese.org Most Rev. Arthur J. Serratelli, Pres.; Rev. Msgr. T. Mark Condon, Vice Pres.;

Paterson Diocese Central Investment & Lending Agency, Inc. - 777 Valley Rd., Clifton, NJ 07013 t) 973-777-8818 kmullaney@patersondiocese.org Most Rev. Kevin J. Sweeney, Pres.; Rev. Msgr. T. Mark Condon, Vice. Pres.; Sr. Theresa Lee, F.M.A., Secy.;

DENVILLE

Morris Catholic High School, Inc. - 200 Morris Ave., Denville, NJ 07834 Most Rev. Arthur J. Serratelli, Pres.; Rev. Msgr. James T. Mahoney, Vice Pres.;

HARDYSTON

Cor Jesu Mission Fund Inc - 40 Franek Rd., Hardyston, NJ 07419 t) 973-220-6995 frmastroeni@icloud.com Rev. Anthony J. Mastroeni, Pres.; Sr. Elias Margand, O.C.D., Vice. Pres.; Dr. Richard Mayer, Treas.;

MADISON

St. Paul Inside The Walls: The Catholic Center for Evangelization at Bayley-Ellard - 205 Madison Ave., Madison, NJ 07940 t) 973-377-1004 insidethewalls.org Rev. Paul S. Manning, Exec.; Rev. Yojaneider Garcia, Assoc. Dir.; Dcn. Guido Pedraza; Dcn. Eric Munoz, Campus Min.; Dcn. Peter Cistaro, Dir.;

MENDHAM

Sisters of Christian Charity United, Inc. - Mallinckrodt Convent, 350 Bernardsville Rd., Mendham, NJ 07945 t) 973-543-6528 smed@scceast.org Sr. Mary Edward Spohrer, S.C.C., Pres.; Sr. DeSales Tonero, S.C.C., Secy.;

MORRISTOWN

Seton Ministries, Inc. - Sisters of Charity of Saint Elizabeth, 2 Convent Rd., Morristown, NJ 07960; Mailing: P.O. Box 476, Convent Station, NJ 07961-0476 t) 973-290-5450; 973-290-5177; 973-290-5430 (John DiMucci) mshaughnessy@scnj.org; nneary@scnj.org www.scnj.org Sr. Maureen Shaughnessy, SC, Supr.; Sr. Noreen Neary, SC, Chair; John DiMucci, Dir.;

NEWTON

Sacred Heart Novitiate (Salesian Sisters) - 20 Swartswood Rd., Newton, NJ 07860 t) 973-383-2620 Sr. Karen Dunn, F.M.A., Supr.;

PASSAIC

St. Jude Media Ministries - 63 Monroe St., Passaic, NJ 07055 t) 908-879-1460 jcatoir@aol.com www.messengerofjoy.com

Passaic Neighborhood Center for Women - 217 Third St., Passaic, NJ 07055-5119 t) 973-470-0844 cecile@patersondiocese.org www.ncwpassaic.org (Jointly sponsored by the Diocese of Paterson & 15 congregations of religious women) Cecile Pagliarulo, Dir.; Sr. Elaine Maguire I, FSP, Assoc. Dir.;

PATERSON

St. Anthony's Guild - 174 Ramsey St., Paterson, NJ 07501; Mailing: 129 W. 31st St. - 2nd Fl., New York, NY 10001 t) 212-564-8799 frdavid@thefranciscans.org www.stanthonysguild.org Membership organization supports the work of The Franciscan Friars of Holy Name Province. Rev. David I. Convertino, O.F.M., Dir.;

Martin de Porres Village Corporation - 1 Green St., Paterson, NJ 07501 t) 973-881-8022 Sponsoring Martin

De Porres, Vill. Rev. Msgr. Herbert K. Tillyer, Pres.;
Sr. Merita Learning Center - 1 Green St., Paterson, NJ 07501 t) 973-881-7115 Sr. Christina Schoen, F.S.P., Dir.;
Saint Michael's Friary (Franciscan Friars of the Renewal) - 190 Butler St., Paterson, NJ 07524 t) 973-345-7082 stmichaelcfr@gmail.com franciscanfriars.com Bro. Shawn O'Conner, C.F.R., Supr.; Bro. Joachim Joseph Bellavance, C.F.R., Vicar; Rev. Herald Joseph Brock, C.F.R., Pst. Assoc.; Rev. Emmanuel Mary Mansford, C.F.R., Pst. Assoc.; Rev. Agustino Miguel Torres, C.F.R., Pst. Assoc.; Bro. Dominic Ruiz, CFR, Friar; Bro. Michael Francis Kearney, CFR, Friar;
Straight and Narrow, Inc. - 508 Straight St., Paterson, NJ 07503; Mailing: P.O. Box 2738, Paterson, NJ 07501 t) 973-345-6000 info@ccpaterson.org Angela Nikolovski, Exec. Dir.;

RINGWOOD
NCPC, Inc. - 112 Erskine Rd., Ringwood, NJ 07456 t) 973-962-7032 Most Rev. Arthur J. Serratelli, Pres.;

SPARTA
The Catholic Academy of Sussex County, Inc. - 28 Andover Rd., Sparta, NJ 07871 t) 973-729-6125 johnfernandes@popejohn.org The Academy operates Pope John XXIII H.S.; Rev. George Brown School; Pope John XXIII Middle School; Camp Auxilium Center. Rev. Walter Jenkins, C.S.C., Headmaster; Most Rev. Kevin J. Sweeney, Pres.; Rev. Msgr. T. Mark Condon, Vice. Pres.; Sr. Theresa Lee, F.M.A., Secy.;
Pope John XXIII Regional High School, Inc. - 28 Andover Rd., Sparta, NJ 07871 t) 973-729-6125 johnfernandes@popejohn.org Rev. Walter Jenkins, C.S.C., Headmaster; Most Rev. Kevin J. Sweeney, Pres.; Rev. Msgr. T. Mark Condon, Vice. Pres.; Sr. Theresa Lee, F.M.A., Secy.;

WAYNE
DePaul Catholic Diocesan High School, Inc. - 1512 Alps Rd., Wayne, NJ 07470 t) 973-694-3702 weirk@dpchs.org; bekkerk@dpchs.org Most Rev. Kevin J. Sweeney, Pres.; Rev. Msgr. T. Mark Condon, Vice. Pres.; Sr. Theresa Lee, F.M.A., Secy.;
Siena Village - 1000 Siena Village, Wayne, NJ 07470 t) 973-696-2811 aldors@aol.com Sr. Alice Matthew, O.P., Dir.;

MONASTERIES AND RESIDENCES FOR PRIESTS AND BROTHERS [MON]

BUTLER
St. Anthony Friary (Order of Friars Minor) - 63 Bartholdi Ave., Butler, NJ 07405 t) 973-838-4080; 646-473-0265 mharlan@hnp.org aka: St. Anthony Friary (Butler), Franciscan Friars-Holy Name Province, Inc. Bro. Paul J. Chelus, O.F.M.; Rev. Bernard R. Creighton, O.F.M., Vicar; Bro. Peter X. Ahlheim, O.F.M., In Res.; Rev. Richard Husted, O.F.M., In Res.; Rev. Michael Joyce, O.F.M., In Res.; Rev. Daniel J. Lanahan, O.F.M., In Res.; Rev. Claude T. Lenehan, O.F.M., In Res.; Rev. Bartholomew R. McMahon, O.F.M., In Res.; Rev. Gerald R. Mudd, O.F.M., In Res.; Rev. Emmet Murphy, OFM, In Res.; Rev. Paul Osborne, OFM, In Res.; Bro. Octavio A. Duran, O.F.M., Admin.; Rev. Francis K. Kim, O.F.M., Pst. Min./Coord.; Rev. Thomas R. Hartle, O.F.M., Spiritual Adv./Care Srvcs.; Bro. Kevin McGoff, OFM, Spiritual Adv./Care Srvcs.; Bro. Thomas J. Cole, O.F.M., Archivist; Rev. Kevin M. Cronin, O.F.M., Ministry of the Word; Rev. Brice Leavins, O.F.M., In Res.; Rev. Christopher C. Van Haight, O.F.M., Guardian; Brs.: 6; Priests: 17
Franciscan Ministry of the Word - t) 973-838-4093 www.franmow.org
Order of Friars Minor of the Province of the Most Holy Name (Franciscan Friars-Holy Name Province (NJ), Inc.) - 63 Bartholdi Ave., Butler, NJ 07405-1462; Mailing: 129 W 31st St. 2nd Fl, New York, NY 10001 t) 646-473-0265 mharlan@hnp.org Rev. Kevin J. Mullen, O.F.M., Prov.;

CLIFTON
Holy Face of Jesus Monastery (Sylvestrine Benedictine Monks) - 1697 State Hwy. 3, Clifton, NJ 07012; Mailing: P.O. Box 691, Clifton, NJ 07012 t) 973-778-1177 holyfaceosb@gmail.com Bro. Antony Maldonado, OSB, Supr.; Rev. Louis-Marie Navaratne, O.S.B., Supr.; Brs.: 1; Priests: 4

FLORHAM PARK
Father Justin Vocationary (Vocationist Fathers) - 90 Brooklake Rd., Florham Park, NJ 07932 t) 973-966-6262 info@vocationist.org www.vocationistfathers.org Rev. Shiju Chittattukara, SDV, Dir. & Supr.; Rev. Ignatius Okoroji, SDV, Vice Supr. & Retreat Master;

MORRISTOWN
St. Mary's Abbey - 230 Mendham Rd., Morristown, NJ 07960 t) 973-538-3235 osbmonks@delbarton.org www.saintmarysabbey.org Most Rev. Elias R. Lorenzo, O.S.B., Auxiliary Bishop, Archdiocese of Newark; Rt. Rev. Jonathan Licari, O.S.B., Admin.; Very Rev. Edward Seton Fittin, O.S.B., Prior; Rev. Jerome Borski, O.S.B., Archivist; Rev. Gabriel M. Coless, O.S.B., Mem.; Rev. Richard F. Cronin, O.S.B., Mem.; Rev. Simon P. Gallagher, O.S.B., Mem.; Rev. John E. Hesketh, O.S.B., Subprior; Rev. James O'Donnell, O.S.B., Mem.; Rev. Hilary O'Leary, O.S.B., Formation Dir.; Rev. Jude S. Salus, O.S.B., Mem.; Rev. Anthony G. Sargent, O.S.B., Mem.; Rev. Andrew T. Smith, O.S.B., Mem.; Rev. Demetrius M. Thomas, O.S.B., Mem.; Rev. Michael Tidd, O.S.B., Headmaster; Rev. Joseph Voltaggio, O.S.B., Mem.; Rev. Benedict M. Worry, O.S.B., Librn.; Bro. Paul J. Diveny, O.S.B., Treas.; Bro. Finnbar McEvoy, O.S.B., Mem.; Bro. William McMillan, O.S.B., Mem.; Bro. Kieran M. Shiek, O.S.B., Mem.; Brs.: 4; Priests: 16

NEWTON
St. Paul's Abbey (Order of St. Benedict, Congregation of St. Ottilien) - 289 U.S. Hwy. 206 S., Newton, NJ 07860-0007; Mailing: P.O. Box 7, Newton, NJ 07860-0007 t) 973-383-2470 osbnewton@catholic.or.kr (Formerly the Little Flower Monastery), Monastery established March 15, 1924; elevated to abbey June 9, 1947. Rt. Rev. Justin E. Dzikowicz, O.S.B., Abbot; Rt. Rev. Joel P. Macul, O.S.B., Abbot; Rev. Samuel Kim, O.S.B., Prior; Rev. Damian J. Milliken, O.S.B.;

OAK RIDGE
St. Stanislaus B. M. Friary (Capuchin Fathers) - 2 Manor Dr., Oak Ridge, NJ 07438 t) 973-697-7757 jkrzyskow@yahoo.com Dcn. Jerzy P. Krzyskow; Brs.: 1

RINGWOOD
Holy Name Friary, Inc. - 2 Morris Rd., Ringwood, NJ 07456; Mailing: 129 W 31st St., 2nd Fl., New York, NY 10001 t) 646-473-0265 mharlan@hnp.org Rev. Joseph Francis Cavoto, OFM, Pres.;

STIRLING
Shrine of St. Joseph - 1050 Long Hill Rd., Stirling, NJ 07980 t) 908-647-0208 religious@stshrine.org shrineofsaintjoseph.com Rev. Gustavo Amell, S.T.; Rev. Abram E. Dono, S.T.; Rev. Raul Ventura, S.T.; Rev.- Seraphim Molina, S.T., Dir.; Cary Lynn St. Pierre, Contact; Brs.: 1; Priests: 5
Trinity House at the Shrine of St. Joseph - 1292 Long Hill Rd., Stirling, NJ 07980; Mailing: 1050 Long Hill Rd., Stirling, NJ 07980 t) 908-647-0208 religious@stshrine.org stshrine.org Rev. Dennis Berry, S.T., Dir.;

WAYNE
Xaverian Missionary Fathers - Delegation House, 12 Helene Ct., Wayne, NJ 07470-2813 t) 973-942-2975 wayne@xaverianmissionaries.org; usasxprocure@hotmail.com www.xaverianmissionaries.org Rev. Dan Boschetto, S.X.; Rev. Luigi Brioni, S.X.; Rev. Ramon Cerratos, S.X.; Rev. Renato Filippini, S.X.; Rev. Edi Foschiatto, S.X.; Rev. Fernandes de Araujo Herondi, S.X.; Rev. Danilo Lago, S.X.; Rev. Mauro Loda, S.X.; Rev. Dario Maso, S.X.; Rev. Pablo Nieves, S.X.; Rev. Horacio Perez, S.X.; Rev. Franco Qualizza, S.X.; Rev. Martino Roia, S.X.; Rev. Frank Sottocornola, S.X.; Rev. Joe Vignato, S.X.; Rev. Michael Davitti, S.X., Rector; Rev. Frank B. Grappoli, S.X., Mem.; Rev. Mark Marangone, S.X., Supr.;

NURSING / REHABILITATION / CONVALESCENCE / ELDERLY CARE [NUR]

DENVILLE
St. Francis Health Resort, Inc. - 122-126 Diamond Spring Rd., Denville, NJ 07834 t) 973-627-5000 www.saintfrancisres.com Senior Living Community Sr. M. Johnice Thone, S.S.M., Exec.; Asstd. Annu.: 50; Staff: 20

PATERSON
St. Joseph Rest Home for Aged Women - 52 Preakness Ave., Paterson, NJ 07522; Mailing: 46 Preakness Ave., Paterson, NJ 07522 t) 973-956-1921 josephinefcpps@gmail.com; avemariadcpb@gmail.com Conducted by Daughters of Charity of the Most Precious Blood Sr. Regi Karumakkel, D.C.P.B., Supr.; Asstd. Annu.: 13; Staff: 6

TOTOWA
St. Joseph's Home for the Elderly - 140 Shepherd Ln., Totowa, NJ 07512 t) 973-942-0300 info@littlesistersofthepoor.org www.littlesistersofthepoor.org Conducted by Little Sisters of the Poor. Rev. Sean McDonnell, Chap.; Sr. Mary Thomas D'Mello, L.S.P., Pres.; Asstd. Annu.: 70; Staff: 90

PRESCHOOLS / CHILDCARE CENTERS [PRE]

FLORHAM PARK
Magic Kingdom Day Nursery (Vocationist Sisters) - 88 Brooklake Rd., Florham Park, NJ 07932 t) 973-966-9762 magickingdom2008@yahoo.com www.magickingdomnurseryschool.com Sr. Perpetua Da Conceicao, S.D.V., Prin.;

NEWTON
Camp Auxilium Center - 14 Old Swartswood Rd., Newton, NJ 07860 t) 973-383-2621 campauxiliumcenter@campauxilium.org; summercamp@campauxilium.org www.campauxilium.org Operated by Salesian Sisters. Sr. Fran Da Grossa, FMA, Admin.;

PARSIPPANY
St. Elizabeth Nursery and Montessori School, Inc. - 499 Park Rd., Parsippany, NJ 07054 t) 973-540-0721 elizabethsaint@yahoo.com www.stelizabethschool.com Sr. Cathy Lynn Cummings, F.S.S.E., Prin.;

RETREAT HOUSES / RENEWAL CENTERS [RTR]

BRANCHVILLE
Sanctuary of Mary-Our Lady of the Holy Spirit (Vocationist Fathers) - 252 Wantage Ave., Branchville, NJ 07826 t) 973-722-7142 frlouissdv@gmail.com vocationist.org Rev. Louis Caputo, SDV, Rector; Rev. Shiju Chittattukara, SDV, Dir.; Rev. Ignatiius Okoroji, SDV, Vice Superior;

CHESTER
Hermits of Bethlehem in the Heart of Jesus - 82 Pleasant Hill Rd., Chester, NJ 07930 t) 908-879-7059 hermitsofcarmel@gmail.com Rev. Robert Gajewski, Dir.;

FLORHAM PARK
Vocationist Fathers Retreat Center - 90 Brooklake Rd., Florham Park, NJ 07932 t) 973-966-6262 info@vocationist.org www.vocationist.org Rev. Shiju Chittattukara, SDV, Dir. & Supr.; Rev. Ignatius Okoroji, SDV, Vice Supr. & Retreat Master;

MENDHAM
Villa Pauline - 352 Bernardsville Rd., Mendham, NJ 07945 t) 973-543-9058 smpdemek@scceast.org Retreat House for Men & Women Sr. Marie Pauline Demek, Dir.;

MORRISTOWN
Loyola Jesuit Center - 161 James St., Morristown, NJ 07960 t) 973-539-0740 retreathouse@loyola.org www.loyola.org Loyola House of Retreats dba Loyola Jesuit Center Rev. Steven Pugliese, S.J.;

St. Mary's Abbey Retreat Center - 230 Mendham Rd., Morristown, NJ 07960 t) 973-538-5235 x2100 retreatcenter@delbarton.org saintmarysabbey.org/retreat-center Rev. Joseph Voltaggio, O.S.B., Dir.;

NEWTON

Sacred Heart Retreat Center (Missionary Society of the Salesian Sisters, Inc.) - 20 Old Swartswood Rd., Newton, NJ 07860 t) 973-383-2620 newtonshc@salesiansisters.org sacredheartspiritualitycenter.org Sr. Theresa Kelly, FMA, Dir.;

SPECIAL CARE FACILITIES [SPF]

POMPTON LAKES

Pathways Counseling Center, Inc. - 16 Pompton Ave., Pompton Lakes, NJ 07442 t) 973-835-6337 drhall@pathwayscounseling.org; info@pathwayscounseling.org www.pathwayscounseling.org Dr. Pamela Hall, Dir.;

An asterisk (*) denotes an organization that has established tax-exempt status directly with the IRS and is not covered by the USCCB Group Ruling.

Diocese of Pensacola-Tallahassee

(Dioecesis Pensacolensis-Tallaseiensis)

MOST REVEREND WILLIAM A. WACK, C.S.C.

Bishop of Pensacola-Tallahassee; ordained April 9, 1994; appointed Bishop of Pensacola-Tallahassee May 29, 2017; ordained August 22, 2017. Office: 11 North B St., Pensacola, FL 32502. T: 850-435-3500.

Monsignor James Amos Pastoral Center: 11 North B St., Pensacola, FL 32502. T: 850-435-3500; F: 850-436-6424. elld@ptdiocese.org

ESTABLISHED NOVEMBER 6, 1975.

Square Miles 14,044.

Comprises the following Counties: Bay, Calhoun, Escambia, Franklin, Gadsden, Gulf, Holmes, Jackson, Jefferson, Leon, Liberty, Madison, Okaloosa, Santa Rosa, Taylor, Wakulla, Walton and Washington Counties.

For legal titles of parishes and diocesan institutions, consult the Pastoral Center.

STATISTICAL OVERVIEW

Personnel
Bishop....1
Retired Bishops....1
Priests: Diocesan Active in Diocese....53
Priests: Diocesan Active Outside Diocese....5
Priests: Retired, Sick or Absent....13
Number of Diocesan Priests....71
Religious Priests in Diocese....14
Total Priests in your Diocese....85
Extern Priests in Diocese....31
Permanent Deacons in Diocese....64
Total Brothers....8
Total Sisters....15

Parishes
Parishes....49
With Resident Pastor:
Resident Diocesan Priests....47
Resident Religious Priests....7
Without Resident Pastor:
Administered by Priests....9
Missions....4
Pastoral Centers....1
New Parishes Created....2
Professional Ministry Personnel:
Brothers....5
Sisters....15
Lay Ministers....49

Welfare
Catholic Hospitals....3
Total Assisted....1,765,052
Homes for the Aged....2
Total Assisted....429
Day Care Centers....4
Total Assisted....349
Specialized Homes....4
Total Assisted....271
Special Centers for Social Services....6
Total Assisted....46,367
Other Institutions....2
Total Assisted....236

Educational
Students from This Diocese....8
Students from Other Dioceses....10
Total Seminarians....8
High Schools, Diocesan and Parish....2
Total Students....860
Elementary Schools, Diocesan and Parish....7
Total Students....2,241
Non-residential Schools for the Disabled....1
Total Students....22
Catechesis/Religious Education:
High School Students....981
Elementary Students....2,149
Total Students under Catholic Instruction....6,261
Teachers in Diocese:
Priests....3
Sisters....3
Lay Teachers....274

Vital Statistics
Receptions into the Church:
Infant Baptism Totals....714
Minor Baptism Totals....87
Adult Baptism Totals....104
Received into Full Communion....160
First Communions....708
Confirmations....731
Marriages:
Catholic....163
Interfaith....35
Total Marriages....198
Deaths....593
Total Catholic Population....71,445
Total Population....1,536,711

LEADERSHIP

Bishop's Office - t) (850) 435-3520 bishop@ptdiocese.org Most Rev. William Albert Wack, C.S.C.;

Monsignor James Amos Pastoral Center - t) 850-435-3500 elld@ptdiocese.org David Ell, COO;

Chancellor - t) 850-435-3500 chancellor@ptdiocese.org Rev. Msgr. Michael V. Reed, Chancellor;

Archivist - Rev. Msgr. Michael V. Reed;

Child and Youth Protection - Rev. Msgr. Michael V. Reed; Claudia Wolf, Diocesan Investigator;

Delegate for Religious - Sr. Margaret Kuntz, A.S.C.J.;

Independent Review Board - Rev. Douglas G. Halsema; Dcn. John Parnham; Dcn. Don Krehley;

Safe Environment - Jeanne Blake, Safe Environment Coord.;

Vicar for Priests - Rev. Dennis J. O'Brien;

Victim Assistance Coordinators - Louis Makarowski; Dr. Shannon Mullen; Dcn. Molina Santiago;

Chief Operating Officer - t) (850) 435-3502 David Ell, COO;

Chief Financial Officer - t) (850) 435-3509 largaespadae@ptdiocese.org Ed Largaespada, CFO;

Accounting - Nicholas Bray;

Cemetery, Office of - t) 850-432-0878

Internal Review - Bill Beck;

Risk and Insurance Manager - Thomas Martin Jr.;

Safety Manager - Marvin Patterson;

Office of Schools - t) 850-435-3540 juhasm@ptdiocese.org Michael Juhas, Supt.; Donna Bass, Asst. to Supt. Schools & Teacher Certification;

Catholic Youth Sports League - cysl@ptdiocese.org Tony Howard, Dir.;

Holy Childhood Association - Michael Juhas, Dir.;

Stewardship & Development, Office of - t) 850-435-1521 kennedyj@ptdiocese.org John Kennedy, Dir.;

Human Resources - t) (850) 435-3558 jonesr@ptdiocese.org Robin Jones, Dir.;

Real Estate/Construction - t) (850) 435-3542 bennettr@ptdiocese.org Robert Bennett;

Information Technology - t) (850) 435-3537 itsupport@ptdiocese.org Bryan Goodwin;

Communications Office - t) (850) 435-3528 communications@ptdiocese.org Sharmane Adams, Dir.;

Catholic Charities of Northwest Florida - t) 850-435-3516 kneem@cc.ptdiocese.org Matthew Knee, Pres.;

Fort Walton Beach (West-Central Deanery) - t) 850-244-2825 wisee@cc.ptdiocese.org Eva Wise, Asst. Exec. Dir.;

Panama City Office (East Central Deanery) - t) (850) 763-0475 wisee@cc.ptdiocese.org Eva Wise, Asst. Exec. Dir.;

Pensacola Office (West Deanery) - t) 850-436-8754 wisee@cc.ptdiocese.org Eva Wise, Asst. Exec. Dir.;

Tallahassee Office (East Deanery) - t) 850-222-2180 wisee@cc.ptdiocese.org Eva Wise, Asst. Exec. Dir.;

Vicars Forane - Very Rev. Michael Foley, Eastern Vicariate; Very Rev. Craig Smith, Western Vicariate; Very Rev. Ted Sosnowski, East Central Vicariate;

Vicar General - t) (850) 435-3510 huntl@clergy.ptdiocese.org Rev. Msgr. Luke Hunt;

Tribunal - t) 850-435-3549 fowlerj@ptdiocese.org

Judicial Vicar - fowlerj@ptdiocese.org Very Rev. T. Joseph Fowler;

Adjutant Judicial Vicar - olsons@ptdiocese.org Rev. Stephen Olson;

Ecclesiastical Notaries - Conseula Floyd; Kathy Methvin;

Judges - Very Rev. T. Joseph Fowler; Rev. Stephen Olson;

Promoter of Justice - Rev. Msgr. Michael V. Reed;

Defender of the Bond - Rev. Eugene D. Casserly;

College of Consultors - Rev. Msgr. Luke Hunt; Rev. Msgr. Michael V. Reed; Very Rev. John B. Cayer;

Finance, Diocesan Commission for - Most Rev. William Wack, C.S.C.; Rev. Msgr. Luke Hunt, Secy.; Rev. Msgr. Michael V. Reed;

Administrative Council -

Council of Priests -

Presider - Most Rev. William Albert Wack, C.S.C.;

Ex Officio Members - Rev. Msgr. Luke Hunt; Rev. Msgr. Michael V. Reed, Chancellor;

Elected by Deanery - Rev. Msgr. Stephen C. Bosso, Mem.; Rev. Philip Fortin, Mem.; Rev. Jack Campbell, West;

Members at Large - Rev. John Cayer, Mem.; Rev. Thomas Kennell, Mem.;

Members Appointed - Rev. Alvaro Pio Gonzalez (Colombia), Mem.; Rev. Richard Graham, Mem.; Rev. George Thekku, Mem.;

Council of Sisters - Sr. Margaret Kuntz, A.S.C.J., Pres.;

Priests' Pension Plan, Board - Most Rev. William Albert Wack, C.S.C., Chair; Rev. Msgr. Luke Hunt; Rev. Msgr. Michael V. Reed;

Priest Personnel Board - Rev. Msgr. Luke Hunt; Rev. Msgr. Michael V. Reed; Very Rev. Michael Foley;

Vicar for Permanent Deacons - t) (850) 435-3550 calliparej@ptdiocese.org Very Rev. Joseph P. Callipare, Dir.;

Office of the Permanent Diaconate and Permanent Deacon Formation - t) 850-435-3552 calliparej@ptdiocese.org Very Rev. Joseph P. Callipare, Vicar;

Permanent Deacon Deanery Representatives - Dcn. Raymond Aguado, Mem.; Dcn. Daniel Dailey, Mem.; Dcn. Andrew Grosmaire, Mem.;

Permanent Deacon Formation Board - Very Rev. Joseph P. Callipare, Chair; Rev. Christian Winkeljohn; Dcn. Raymond Aguado;

Permanent Deacon Formation Team - Very Rev. Joseph P. Callipare, Dir.; Rev. Christian Winkeljohn, Liturgical Formation; Dcn. Anthony DeCotis, Pastoral Formation;

Vocations & Seminarians, Office of - t) (850) 435-3552 frtim@cocathedral.com Stacey Ragland, Staff; Very Rev. Timothy Michael Holeda II, Dir.;

Seminarian Candidate Review Board - Rev. Douglas G. Halsema, Mem.; Very Rev. Timothy Michael Holeda II, Mem.; Rev. John J. Licari, Mem.;

OFFICES AND DIRECTORS

African American Catholics, Commission for - c) (850) 969-6590 gabriel.brown@ecua.fl.gov Gabriel M. Brown, Chair;

Apostleship of the Sea, Office of the - t) (850) 435-3550 calliparej@ptdiocese.org Very Rev. Joseph P. Callipare;

Campus Ministry - t) 850-222-9630 director@fsucatholic.org Bro. Parker Jordan, B.H., Dir.; Very Rev. Timothy Michael Holeda II, Campus Min.; Bro. Ray Morris, B.H.;

Florida State University - Bro. Parker Jordan, B.H., Dir.;

Tallahassee Community College - Bro. Parker Jordan, B.H., Dir.;

Campus Ministry at Florida A&M University - Rev. Paschal Chester, S.V.D., Dir.;

Catholic Campus Ministry at University of West Florida - Rev. Raymond G. Herard III, Dir.;

Charismatic Renewal, Diocesan Commission for - c) (850) 454-4445 ptdccr@gmail.com Rev. Nicholas Schumm, Chap.; Keith Whalen, Chair;

Cursillo Movement - c) (850) 496-5722 fraitest@clergy.ptdiocese.org Dcn. Thomas Fraites;

Diocesan Council of Catholic Women - c) (850) 624-6891 walkerj@cc.ptdiocese.org Joan Walker, Pres.; Rev. Richard Dawson, Spiritual Adv./Care Srvcs.; Very Rev. Michael Foley, Spiritual Adv./Care Srvcs.;

Hispanic Ministry, Office for - t) 850-939-3020 gonzalesp@clergy.ptdiocese.org Rev. Alvaro Pio Gonzalez (Colombia), Dir.;

Knights of Columbus - t) (850) 939-3020 kellyj@clergy.ptdiocese.org Rev. John F. Kelly, Chap.;

Legion of Mary - t) 850-432-9362 perezh@clergy.ptdiocese.org Rev. Canon Hector R.G. Perez, Dir.;

Office for Advocacy & Justice - t) 850-435-3532 Aida Bone, Dir. (bonea@ptdiocese.org); Dcn. Raymond Aguado (aguador@clergy.ptdiocese.org);

Office for Faith Formation - t) (850) 435-3523 kuntzm@ptdiocese.org Sr. Margaret Kuntz, A.S.C.J.;

Office for Marriage & Family Life - t) (850) 435-3553 filippinic@ptdiocese.org Chez Filippini;

Office for Youth Ministry - t) (850) 435-3513 kurnikl@ptdiocese.org Lisa Kurnik;

Orders & Ministries, Commission for - Rev. Msgr. Luke Hunt; Rev. Msgr. Michael V. Reed; Very Rev. Timothy Michael Holeda II;

Propagation of the Faith, Office of - Very Rev. T. Joseph Fowler;

PARISHES, MISSIONS, AND CLERGY

STATE OF FLORIDA

APALACHICOLA

St. Patrick - 27th 6th St., Apalachicola, FL 32320; Mailing: PO Box 550, Apalachicola, FL 32329 t) 850-653-9453; 850-653-2100 office@stpatrick.ptdiocese.org stpatricksmass.com Rev. Roger Latosynski, Pst.; CRP Stds.: 4

BLOUNTSTOWN

St. Francis of Assisi - 16498 S.W. Gaskin St., Blountstown, FL 32424 t) 850-674-4482; 850-320-7725 office@sfa.ptdiocese.org; pulingt@clergy.ptdiocese.org Rev. Tarsisius Puling, svd (indonesia), Pst.; Anna Najere, DRE; CRP Stds.: 29

BONIFAY

Blessed Trinity - 2331 Hwy. 177A, Bonifay, FL 32425 t) 850-547-3735 btbonifay@embarqmail.com www.blessedtrinity.ptdiocse.org Rev. Richard Dawson, Pst.;

CANTONMENT

St. Jude Thaddeus - 303 Rocky Ave., Cantonment, FL 32533 t) 850-968-6189 office@stjude.ptdiocese.org; c_r_davis2003@yahoo.com Rev. George Thekku, Pst.; Dcn. McBurnett J. Smith Jr.; Dcn. Bradley M. Seabrook; Rachel Bradley, DRE; CRP Stds.: 16

St. Elizabeth of Hungary - t) (850) 968-6189

CARRABELLE

Sacred Heart of Jesus - 2653 Hwy. 98 E., Carrabelle, FL 32323; Mailing: P O Box 729, Lanark Village, FL 32323 t) 850-697-3669 sacredheartofjesus.ptdiocese.org Rev. Dustin Feddon, Pst.; Dcn. David Harris;

CHIPLEY

St. Joseph the Worker - 1664 Main St., Chipley, FL 32428; Mailing: P O Box 266, Chipley, FL 32428 t) 850-638-7654 stjoe@chipley.ptdiocese.org stjoeworker.ptdiocese.org Rev. Philip Fortin, Pst.; CRP Stds.: 16

CRAWFORDVILLE

St. Elizabeth Ann Seton - 3609 Coastal Hwy., Crawfordville, FL 32327 t) 850-745-8359 (CRP) office@seas.ptdiocese.org www.catholicchurchwakulla.org Rev. Joseph Anthu Raj, Pst.; Amy Wiedeman, DRE; CRP Stds.: 15

CRESTVIEW

Our Lady of Victory - 550 Adams Dr., Crestview, FL 32536 t) 850-682-4622 www.olvnow.com Rev. Roy C. Marien, Pst.; Vivianna Lasher, DRE; Theresa Vannier, Bus. Mgr.; CRP Stds.: 127

DE FUNIAK SPRINGS

St. Margaret - 247 U.S. Hwy. 331 - N., De Funiak Springs, FL 32433; Mailing: PO Box 590, De Funiak Springs, FL 32435-0590 t) 850-892-9247 stmargaret@embarqmail.com www.stmargaret.ptdiocese.org Rev. Richard Dawson, Pst.; Kathy Russ, DRE;

DESTIN

Corpus Christi - 307 Beach Dr., Destin, FL 32541 t) 850-654-5422 corpusdomini@outlook.com ccdestin.com Rev. Viet Huynh, Pst.; Robert Pacheco, DRE; CRP Stds.: 60

FORT WALTON BEACH

St. Mary Church - 110 St. Mary Ave. SW, Fort Walton Beach, FL 32548-6645 t) 850-243-3742 office@saintmary.life www.saintmary.life Rev. Douglas G. Halsema, Pst.; Dcn. Michael Brown; Dcn. Daniel M. McAuliffe; Dcn. Michael Symons; Dcn. Wayne Walker; CRP Stds.: 110

St. Mary Church School - (Grades K-8) 110 Robinwood Dr., S.W., Fort Walton Beach, FL 32548 t) 850-243-8913 office@saintmaryschool.net www.saintmaryschool.net Amy Akins, Prin.; Stds.: 403; Lay Tchrs.: 31

FOUNTAIN

Our Lady Queen of Peace Mission - 18005 Lazy Ln., Fountain, FL 32404; Mailing: 5622 Julie Dr., Panama City, FL 32404 t) 850-769-5067 brownw@clergy.ptdiocese.org Rev. William P. Brown, Pst.;

GULF BREEZE

St. Ann - 100 Daniel Dr., Gulf Breeze, FL 32561; Mailing: PO Box 1057, Gulf Breeze, FL 32562 t) 850-932-2859 kathyb@stanngulfbreeze.org www.stanngulfbreeze.org Rev. Msgr. Luke Hunt, Pst.; Rev. John Cayer, Par. Vicar; Dcn. Raymond Aguado; Grace Hofius, DRE; CRP Stds.: 200

St. Ann Discovery School - t) 850-932-9330 Tammie Fulmer, Dir.; Stds.: 114; Lay Tchrs.: 29

Our Lady of the Assumption - 920 Via de Luna, Gulf Breeze, FL 32561 t) 850-934-0222

Saint Sylvester - 6464 Gulf Breeze Pkwy., Gulf Breeze, FL 32563 t) 850-939-3020 saintsylv@stsylv.org; bursonm@stsylv.org www.stsylv.org Rev. John F. Kelly, Pst.; Rev. Alvaro Pio Gonzalez (Colombia), Assoc. Pst.; Dcn. Charles Sukup; Sandy Nicholas, DRE; CRP Stds.: 258

MADISON

St. Vincent de Paul - 186 N.W. Sumter St., Madison, FL 32340-2048 t) 850-973-2428 saintvdp@gmail.com Stephanie Arriaza Allen, DRE; Rev. Dominic Dat Tran, Pst.; CRP Stds.: 9

MARIANNA

St. Anne - 3009 5th St., Marianna, FL 32446 t) 850-482-3734 stanne@stannemar.ptdiocese.org stannemar.ptdiocese.org/ Rev. Philip Fortin, Pst.; CRP Stds.: 38

MARY ESTHER

St. Peter - 100 Francis St., Mary Esther, FL 32569 t) 850-581-2556 office@saintpeter.me saintpeter.me Rev. Doug Martin, Pst.; Dcn. Anthony DeCotis; CRP Stds.: 47

MILTON

St. Rose of Lima - 6451 Park Ave., Milton, FL 32570 t) 850-623-3600 lewisk@srl.ptdiocese.org www.srolparish.org Rev. Msgr. Michael V. Reed, Pst.; Rev. Christian Plancher, Par. Vicar; Dcn. Phil Czajkowski; Dcn. Thomas Kennell; Dcn. Jeffrey Massey; CRP Stds.: 189

MIRAMAR BEACH

Church of the Resurrection - 259 Miramar Beach Dr., Miramar Beach, FL 32550 t) 850-837-0357 admin@resurrectionbythebeach.org www.resurrectionbythebeach.org Rev. Thomas J. Guido, Pst.; CRP Stds.: 28

MONTICELLO

St. Margaret - 1565 E. Washington Hwy., Monticello, FL 32344; Mailing: c/o 186 N.W. Sumter St., Madison, FL 32340 t) 850-973-2428 saintmarg@gmail.com Rev. Dominic Dat Tran, Pst.; Shanon Metty, DRE; CRP Stds.: 10

NICEVILLE

Christ Our Redeemer - 1028 White Point Rd., Niceville, FL 32578 t) 850-897-7797 www.corcatholic.org Rev. Robert Johnson, Pst.; Dcn. James Murray; Dcn. Miguel Nolla; Dcn. William E. Schaal; Krista Abel, Youth Min.; Sharon Mikus, DRE;

Holy Name of Jesus - 1200 Valparaiso Blvd., Niceville, FL 32578 t) 850-678-7813 (Parish & Rectory); 850-678-6790 (CRP); 850-678-7861 (Outreach); (850) 279-3106 (Thrift Shop) holyname@holynamechurch.org www.holynamechurch.org Very Rev. Stephen A. Voyt, Pst.; Dcn. James Cox; Dcn. Thomas Dwyer; Dcn. Thomas Elsesser; Dcn. Thomas Fraites; Dcn. John Shin; Dcn. Louis Marini; Dcn. Gary McBride, Admin.; CRP Stds.: 178

PANAMA CITY

St. Dominic - 3308 E. 15th St., Panama City, FL 32405-7414 t) 850-785-4574 www.saintdominicpc.com Rev. Michael J. Nixon, Pst.; Rev. Richard Graham, Par. Vicar; Dcn. Steven Snigg; Dcn. Michael Theobald; Rev. Joseph Pinchock, In Res.; CRP Stds.: 154

St. John the Evangelist - 1008 Fortune Ave., Panama City, FL 32401 t) 850-763-1821 saintjohnpc@saintjohnpc.org; heather.hanna@saintjohnpc.org www.saintjohnpc.org Rev. Thomas Kennell, Par. Admin.; Dcn. Earl C. Mirus; Dcn. Timothy M. Warner; CRP Stds.: 62

St John Catholic Academy - (Grades PreK-8) 1005 Fortune Ave., Panama City, FL 32401 t) 850-763-1775 office@sjseagles.org www.stjohncatholicacademy.org Sr. Grace Ford, Dir.; Stds.: 168; Lay Tchrs.: 17

Our Lady of the Rosary - 5622 Julie Dr., Panama City, FL 32404 t) (850) 740-1003 office@olr.ptdiocese.org; pcl@olr.ptdiocese.org www.rosary.ptdiocese.org Rev. Kurian Manikuttiyil, Pst.; Kevin Hall, DRE; CRP Stds.: 20

Our Lady Queen of Peace - 18005 Lazy Ln., Fountain, FL 32438; Mailing: 5622 Julie Dr., Panama City, FL 32404 t) 850-722-0466 deak0744@mchs.com Rev. William P. Brown, Pst.;

SS. Peter & Paul Parish - 1003 N East Ave., Panama City, FL 32401 t) 985-518-2641 antontin@hotmail.com Rev. Anthony Tin Nguyen, Pst.; CRP Stds.: 65

PANAMA CITY BEACH

St. Bernadette - 1214 Moylan Rd., Panama City Beach, FL 32407 t) 850-234-3266 stbernadette@knology.net www.stbernadette.com Very Rev. Ted Sosnowski, Pst.; Valerie Voorheis, DRE; CRP Stds.: 83

Child Development Center - t) 850-230-0009 www.stbcda.com Chelsea Current, Dir.;

St. Bernadette John Lee Outreach Center - 1329 Moylan Rd., Panama City Beach, FL 32407 t) 850-236-5252 Juli Rock, Contact;

PENSACOLA

Cathedral of the Sacred Heart - 1212 E. Moreno St., Pensacola, FL 32503 t) 850-438-3131 office@shc.ptdiocese.org shc.ptdiocese.org Very Rev. James Paul Valenzuela, Rector; Rev. Jacob Jaks, Assoc. Pst.; Dcn. Paul Graaff; CRP Stds.: 20

Sacred Heart Cathedral School - (Grades K-8) 1603 N. 12th Ave., Pensacola, FL 32503 t) 850-436-6440 esnow@shcs.ptdiocese.org Elizabeth Snow, Prin.; Stds.: 335; Lay Tchrs.: 29

St. Anne's - 5200 Saufley Field Rd., Pensacola, FL 32526-1626 t) 850-456-5966 office@stannebv.org www.saintannebellview.org Rev. Chuck R. Collins, Pst.; Louise Browne, DRE; CRP Stds.: 45

St. Anthony of Padua - 1804 N. Davis Hwy., Pensacola, FL 32503; Mailing: 1212 E. Moreno St., Pensacola, FL 32503 t) (850) 438-3131 valenzuelaj@clergy.ptdiocese.org www.ptdiocese.org Very Rev. James Paul Valenzuela, Pst.; Rev. Jacob Jaks, Assoc. Pst.;

Basilica of St. Michael the Archangel - 19 N. Palafox St, Pensacola, FL 32502; Mailing: P.O. Box 12423, Pensacola, FL 32591 t) 850-438-4985 office@stmichael.ptdiocese.org; rector@stmichael.ptdiocese.org stmichael.ptdiocese.org Very Rev. Joseph Fowler, Rector; Dcn. Stephen Wulf;

Holy Spirit - 10650 Gulf Beach Hwy., Pensacola, FL 32507 t) 850-492-0837 office@hs.ptdiocese.org www.holyspiritperdido.com Rev. Thomas S. Collins, Pst.; CRP Stds.: 92

Holy Spirit Child Development Academy - t) 850-492-4968 director@hscda.ptdiocese.org Infant to 4 yrs Allison Joann Gill, Dir.;

St. John the Evangelist - 303 S. Navy Blvd., Pensacola, FL 32507 t) 850-455-0356 finance@stjohn.ptdiocese.org; fella@stjohn.ptdiocese.org www.stjohnpensacola.com Rev. John J. Licari, Pst.; Rev. William Philip Ganci, Par. Vicar; Dcn. Donald Krehely; Alejandra Duda, DRE; CRP Stds.: 71

St. John the Evangelist School - (Grades PreK-8) 325 S. Navy Blvd., Pensacola, FL 32507 t) 850-456-5218 principal@sjsw.ptdiocese.org Dana Donahoo, Prin.; Stds.: 276; Sr. Tchrs.: 1; Lay Tchrs.: 40

St. Joseph - 140 W. Government St., Pensacola, FL 32502; Mailing: PO Box 13566, Pensacola, FL 32591 t) 850-436-6461 www.stjoepns.org Rev. Arulappan Jayaraj, HGN, Pst.; Dedra Thompson, DRE;

Little Flower - 6495 Lillian Hwy., Pensacola, FL 32506 t) 850-455-5641 office@ptlittleflower.org www.ptlittleflower.org Rev. Jack Campbell, Par. Admin.; Rev. Inbaraj Lourdusamy, H.G.N., Par. Vicar; Dcn. Reymond Castellano; Dcn. Thomas Gordon; CRP Stds.: 57

Little Flower School - (Grades PreK-8) 6495 Lilliam Hwy., Pensacola, FL 32506 t) 850-455-4851 avarias@pensacolafs.org; info@ptlittleflower.org ptlittleflower.org Stephen Sanchez, Prin.; Stds.: 234; Lay Tchrs.: 17

St. Mary - 401 Van Pelt Ln., Pensacola, FL 32505 t) 850-478-2797 secretary@stmarypensacola.org stmarypensacola.org Rev. Christian Winkeljohn, Pst.; Katinka Ritz, DRE; Dcn. Ken McClure; CRP Stds.: 35

Nativity of Our Lord - 9945 Hillview Dr., Pensacola, FL 32514-5702 t) 850-477-3221 admin@nativityofourlordcc.org; faith@nativityofourlordcc.org www.nativityofourlordcc.org Rev. Henry A Lech Jr., Pst.; Rev. Raymond G. Herard III, Par. Vicar; Dcn. John R Jacobs; CRP Stds.: 87

Our Lady Queen of Martyrs - 3295 S. Barrancas Ave., Pensacola, FL 32507 t) 850-607-7470 c) 585-520-7145 ourladyqueenofmartyrs@gmail.com nuvuongcacthanhtudaopensacola.com Rev. Leo Vu, CRM, Pst.; Vinh Huynh, DRE; CRP Stds.: 15

St. Paul - 3131 Hyde Park Rd., Pensacola, FL 32503; Mailing: 1700 Conway Dr., Pensacola, FL 32503 t) 850-434-2551; 850-434-2551 x102 (CRP) office@stpaulcatholic.net www.stpaulcatholic.net Very Rev. Craig Smith, Pst.; Rev. Stephen Olson, Par. Vicar; Dcn. William Whibbs; CRP Stds.: 59

St. Paul School - 3121 Hyde Park Rd., Pensacola, FL 32503 t) 850-436-6435 school@stpaulcatholic.net Blair Hodge, Prin.; Stds.: 352; Lay Tchrs.: 31

St. Stephen - 900 W. Garden St., Pensacola, FL 32502 t) 850-432-9362 fhrgp3@cox.net; ststephenrectory@cox.net www.latinmasspensacola.com (Diocesan Shrine of Our Lady of Fatima) Rev. Canon Hector R.G. Perez, Rector; CRP Stds.: 52

St. Thomas More - 3295 Barrancas Ave., Pensacola, FL 32507; Mailing: 510 Bayshore Dr., Pensacola, FL 32507 t) 850-456-2543 office@stm.ptdiocese.org www.stthomasmore.ptdiocese.org Rev. Nicholas Schumm, Pst.; Michele Kenaga, DRE; CRP Stds.: 21

PENSACOLA BEACH

Our Lady of the Assumption Mission - 100 Via De Luna Dr., Pensacola Beach, FL 32561; Mailing: PO Box 1057, Gulf Breeze, FL 32562 t) 850-934-0222 kathyb@stanngulfbreeze.org www.stanngulfbreeze.org See St. Ann, Gulf Breeze. Rev. Msgr. Luke Hunt, Pst.; Rev. John Cayer, Par. Vicar; CRP Stds.: 12

PERRY

Immaculate Conception - 2750 S. Byron Butler Pkwy., Perry, FL 32348 t) 850-584-3169 immaculateperry@gmail.com immaculateperry.org/ Rev. Matthew Busch, Pst.; Heather Smith, DRE; CRP Stds.: 26

PORT ST. JOE

St. Joseph - 2001 Monument Ave., Port St. Joe, FL 32456; Mailing: 304 20th St, Port Saint Joe, FL 32456 t) 850-227-1417 www.stjosephpsj.org Rev. Mathew Abraham Kochumoodapuvail, Pst.; CRP Stds.: 19

QUINCY

St. Thomas the Apostle - 27 N. Shadow St., Quincy, FL 32351; Mailing: P.O. Box 549, Quincy, FL 32351 t) 850-627-2350 www.stthomasquincy.com Rev. Vincent Alexius, Pst.; CRP Stds.: 148

SANTA ROSA BEACH

St. Rita - 40 Saint Rita Ln., Santa Rosa Beach, FL 32459; Mailing: 22 Saint Rita Ln., Santa Rosa Beach, FL 32459 t) 850-267-2558; 850-267-2558 x103 (CRP) office@saintritaparish.org; jenna@saintritaparish.org saintritaparish.org Stewart Danos, Admin.; Gabrielle Schrack, Music Min.; Laurie Elliott, Bus. Mgr.; Rev. Michael Hartley, Pst.; Dcn. Antonio Herrera; Nancy Wesson, Liturgy Dir.; Jenna Danos, CRE; CRP Stds.: 214

St. Rita Preschool - 14 Saint Rita Ln., Santa Rosa Beach, FL 32459 t) (850) 267-2558 x106 preschool@saintritaparish.org Amelia Cantu, Prin.; Stds.: 64; Lay Tchrs.: 15

SUNNY HILLS

St. Theresa - 2071 Sunny Hills Blvd., Sunny Hills, FL 32428 t) 850-332-3188 pastor@sttheresa.ptdiocese.org; moodyp@clergy.ptdiocese.org www.sttheresa.ptdiocese.org Rev. Paul Moody, Admin.;

TALLAHASSEE

Blessed Sacrament - 653 Miccosukee Rd., Tallahassee, FL 32308; Mailing: 624 Miccosukee Rd., Tallahassee, FL 32308 t) 850-222-1321 office@bsctlh.com; ymikeworth@bsctlh.com bsctlh.com Rev. Peter Zalewski, Pst.; Rev. Dustin Feddon, Par. Vicar; Rev. Sean Vincent Knox, Par. Vicar; Dcn. Patrick Dallet; Dcn. C. Louis Fete; Dcn. Michael Nixon; Rev. Bernard Jakubco, M.S.C., In Res.;

Trinity Catholic - (Grades PreK-8) 706 E. Brevard St., Tallahassee, FL 32308 t) 850-222-0444 bridgest@trinityknights.org trinityknights.org James Thomas Bridges, Prin.; Stds.: 473; Lay Tchrs.: 36

St. John Neumann Retreat Center - 685 Miccosukee Rd., Tallahassee, FL 32308 t) 850-224-2971 info@neumanncenter.org www.neumanncenteroftallahassee.com Kevin Keating, Dir.;

Co-Cathedral of St. Thomas More - 900 W. Tennessee St., Tallahassee, FL 32304 t) 850-222-9630 office@cocathedral.com www.cocathedral.com Very Rev. Timothy Michael Holeda II, Rector; Rev. Luke Farabaugh, Par. Vicar; Dcn. Andrew Grosmaire; CRP Stds.: 68

Good Shepherd - 4665 Thomasville Rd., Tallahassee, FL 32309-2512 t) 850-893-1837 goodshepherd@gsparishtlh.org; minnok@gsparishtlh.org goodshepherdparish.org Very Rev. Michael Foley, Pst.; Rev. Arockiaraj Kunipaku Selvaraj, HGN, Assoc. Pst.; Dcn. Tom Gillis; Dcn. Gerald Haynes; Dcn. Thomas McBrearty; Dcn. Edward Melvin III; Dcn. Mark Schneider; CRP Stds.: 488

St. Louis - 3640 Fred George Rd., Tallahassee, FL 32303 t) 850-262-8156 admin@stlouis.ptdiocese.org www.stlouiscatholicchurch.org Rev. Alberic Lazerna, Pst.; Dcn. Joseph Jacobs; CRP Stds.: 35

St. Augustine Yu Korean Mission - 708 Hazel Dr., Fort Walton Beach, FL 32547-2002 t) 850-570-0558

SCHOOLS: PRESCHOOL THRU HIGH SCHOOL

HIGH SCHOOLS

STATE OF FLORIDA

PENSACOLA

Mother Clelia Morning Star High School, LLC - 70 Hunter Ave., Pensacola, FL 32505 t) (850) 857-8364 office@mshspensacola.org www.mshspensacola.org Amanda Jansen Drews, Dir.; Stds.: 22; Lay Tchrs.: 2

Pensacola Catholic High School - (DIO) (Grades 9-12) 3043 W. Scott St., Pensacola, FL 32505 t) 850-436-6400 kmartin@pensacolachs.org www.pensacolachs.org Sr. Kierstin Martin, A.S.C.J., Prin.; Stds.: 666; Sr. Tchrs.: 1; Lay Tchrs.: 52

TALLAHASSEE

St. John Paul II Catholic High School - (DIO) (Grades 9-12) 5100 Terrebone Dr., Tallahassee, FL 32311-7848 t) 850-201-5744 csabo@jpiichs.org www.sjpiichs.org Rev. J. Thomas Dillon, Pst.; Joanna Copenhaver, Prin.; Stds.: 204; Pr. Tchrs.: 1; Lay Tchrs.: 22

INSTITUTIONS LOCATED IN DIOCESE

CONVENTS, MONASTERIES, AND RESIDENCES FOR WOMEN [CON]

SUNNY HILLS

Vestiarki Sisters of Jesus (Poland) - 3919 Vistula Dr., Sunny Hills, FL 32428 t) 850-773-3302 vestiarki@att.net Sr. Natalia Kwiateck, Supr.; Srs.: 6

ENDOWMENTS / FOUNDATIONS / TRUSTS [EFT]

PENSACOLA

The Catholic Foundation of Northwest Florida, Inc. - 11 N. B St., Pensacola, FL 32502 t) 850-435-3500 kennedyj@ptdiocese.org; hughesv@ptdiocese.org www.ptdiocese.org Ed Largaespada, Exec.; John Kennedy, Dir.;

Sacred Heart Foundation, Inc. - 2200 Airport Blvd. Fl. 2, Pensacola, FL 32504; Mailing: P.O. Box 2700, Pensacola, FL 32513-2700 t) 850-416-4660 loraine.brown@ascension.org; don.king@ascension.org givesacredheart.org Don King, CEO; Loraine Brown, Chief Mission Integration Officer;

HOSPITALS / HEALTH SERVICES [HOS]

PENSACOLA

The Mother Seton Guild of Sacred Heart Hospital, Inc. - 5151 N. 9th Ave., Pensacola, FL 32504 t) 850-416-7883 Harold Knowles, Pres.;

Sacred Heart Health System, Inc. - 5151 N. Ninth Ave., Pensacola, FL 32504 t) 850-416-7000 don.king@ascension.org; loraine.brown@ascension.org sacred-heart.org Sacred Heart Hospital of Pensacola; Sacred Heart Hospital on the Emerald Coast; Sacred Heart Hospital on the Gulf. Don King, CEO; Loraine Brown, Chief Mission Integration Officer; Bed Capacity: 636; Asstd. Annu.: 1,765,052; Staff: 5,236

Sacred Heart Health Ventures, Inc. - 5151 N. Ninth Ave., Pensacola, FL 32504 t) 850-416-6500 don.king@ascension.org; loraine.brown@ascension.org Don King, CEO; Loraine Brown, Chief Mission Integration Officer;

MISCELLANEOUS [MIS]

FREEPORT

Christ the King Chapel - 16250 US Hwy. 331 S., Freeport, FL 32439 t) 850-267-2558 Rev. Longin Buhake, Admin.; Maria Powell, Secy.; Registered Parishioner Households: 306; Estimated Number of Catholics: 509; Hours of Reconciliation: 1

PANAMA CITY

St. Dominic Media Production Center - 3308 E. 15th St., Panama City, FL 32405 t) 850-914-0072 contact@saintdominicmedia.com www.saintdominicmedia.com Rev. Michael J. Nixon, Pres.;

PENSACOLA

Fox Trace Housing, LLC - 11 N. B St., Pensacola, FL 32502 t) (850) 435-3500 Brianna Methvin, Contact;

Joseph House LLC - 11 N. B St., Pensacola, FL 32502 c) 850-933-0375 frdustin@josephhouseus.org josephhouseus.org Rev. Dustin Feddon, Exec.;

Trinity House, LLC - 11 N. B St., Pensacola, FL 32502 t) 850-435-3500 aguador@ptdiocese.org Transitional Housing Dcn. Raymond Aguado, Contact;

TALLAHASSEE

Florida Catholic Conference - 201 W. Park Ave., Tallahassee, FL 32301-7760 t) 850-205-6820 conference@flacathconf.org; info@flacathconf.org www.flaccb.org Michael Sheedy, Exec.;

***John Paul II Healing Center** - 2910 Kerry Forest Pkwy., #D4-344, Tallahassee, FL 32309 t) (850) 765-6272 Karen Steplitus, Contact;

Magnificat of Tallahassee, Inc. - 1232 Blockford Ct. W., Tallahassee, FL 32317 t) 850-321-8174 magnificattallahassee@gmail.com; terrylshine@gmail.com (Mary, Mother of Mercy and Hope Chapter) Terry Shine, Pres.;

Martyrs of La Florida Missions, Incorporated - 1230 Archangel Way, Tallahassee, FL 32317-9636; Mailing: P.O. Box 12062, Tallahassee, FL 32317-2062 t) 850-445-1326 c) 850-508-5547 secretary@martyrsoflafloridamissions.org www.martyrsoflafloridamissions.org Heather Jordan, Secy.; Michael Sheedy, Vice. Pres.;

MONASTERIES AND RESIDENCES FOR PRIESTS AND BROTHERS [MON]

TALLAHASSEE

Brotherhood of Hope - 2302 Mission Rd., Tallahassee, FL 32304 t) 850-580-3553 brother@brohope.net www.brotherhoodofhope.org Bro. Brandt Haglund, Campus Min.; Bro. Parker Jordan, Campus Min.; Bro. Ray Morris, B.H., Campus Min.; Bro. Rahl Bunsa, B.H., Supr.; Bro. Theodore Psemeneki, Rel. Ord. Ldr.; Brs.: 5

NURSING / REHABILITATION / CONVALESCENCE / ELDERLY CARE [NUR]

PENSACOLA

Haven of Our Lady of Peace, Inc. - 1900 Summit Blvd., Pensacola, FL 32503 t) 850-436-5900 don.king@ascension.org; loraine.brown@ascension.org Don King, CEO; Loraine Brown, Chief Mission Integration Officer; Asstd. Annu.: 320

TALLAHASSEE

Casa Calderon, Inc. - 800 W. Virginia St., Tallahassee, FL 32304 t) 850-222-4026 kristie.edwards@thecolumbiagroup.com; robert.wicker@thecolumbiagroup.com Rev. John Cayer, Pres.; Asstd. Annu.: 109; Staff: 6

SPECIAL CARE FACILITIES [SPF]

PACE

***Majella House Inc.** - 5568 Woodbine Rd., #121, Pace, FL 32571-8766 t) 850-816-0616 majellahouseinc@gmail.com majellahouse.org Maternity Home Ministry to pregnant, homeless mothers and their children. Mary Beth Cyr, Pres.; Asstd. Annu.: 35

PANAMA CITY

St. Barnabas House - 2943 E 11th St., Panama City, FL 32401; Mailing: c/o Catholic Charities, 3128 E. 11th St., Panama City, FL 32401 t) 850-417-7942; 850-252-8217 watsong@cc.ptdiocese.org Monika Weld, Adrienne; Bed Capacity: 14; Asstd. Annu.: 40; Staff: 2

An asterisk (*) denotes an organization that has established tax-exempt status directly with the IRS and is not covered by the USCCB Group Ruling.

Diocese of Peoria

(Dioecesis Peoriensis)

MOST REVEREND LOUIS TYLKA

Bishop of Peoria; ordained May 18, 1996; appointed Coadjutor Bishop of Peoria May 11, 2020; consecrated July 23, 2020; installed March 3, 2022. Office: 419 N.E. Madison Ave., Peoria, IL 61603.

Chancery: 419 N.E. Madison Ave., Peoria, IL 61603. T: 309-671-1550; F: 309-671-1576.

ESTABLISHED 1877.

Square Miles 16,933.

A cross-section of Illinois, bounded on the north by the Counties of Whiteside, Lee, De Kalb, Grundy and Iroquois, and on the east by Kendall, Grundy, Kankakee and Ford, and on the south by Adams, Brown, Cass, Menard, Sangamon, Macon, Moultrie, Douglas and Edgar; comprising the Counties of Bureau, Champaign, Dewitt, Fulton, Hancock, Henderson, Henry, Knox, La Salle, Livingston, Logan, Marshall, Mason, McDonough, McLean, Mercer, Peoria, Piatt, Putnam, Rock Island, Schuyler, Stark, Tazewell, Vermilion, Warren and Woodford.

For legal titles of parishes and diocesan institutions, consult the Chancery.

STATISTICAL OVERVIEW

Personnel
Bishop ... 1
Retired Bishops ... 1
Abbots ... 1
Retired Abbots ... 1
Priests: Diocesan Active in Diocese ... 126
Priests: Diocesan Active Outside Diocese ... 10
Priests: Retired, Sick or Absent ... 47
Number of Diocesan Priests ... 183
Religious Priests in Diocese ... 19
Total Priests in your Diocese ... 202
Extern Priests in Diocese ... 19
Ordinations:
Transitional Deacons ... 4
Permanent Deacons ... 20
Permanent Deacons in Diocese ... 167
Total Brothers ... 5
Total Sisters ... 141

Parishes
Parishes ... 156
With Resident Pastor:
Resident Diocesan Priests ... 77
Resident Religious Priests ... 3
Without Resident Pastor:
Administered by Priests ... 76
New Parishes Created ... 1
Closed Parishes ... 2
Professional Ministry Personnel:
Brothers ... 6
Sisters ... 22
Lay Ministers ... 76

Welfare
Catholic Hospitals ... 13
Total Assisted ... 2,660,118
Health Care Centers ... 3
Homes for the Aged ... 2
Total Assisted ... 144
Day Care Centers ... 5
Total Assisted ... 100
Special Centers for Social Services ... 5
Total Assisted ... 10,000

Educational
Diocesan Students in Other Seminaries ... 22
Seminaries, Religious ... 1
Total Seminarians ... 22
Colleges and Universities ... 1
Total Students ... 350
High Schools, Diocesan and Parish ... 6
Total Students ... 1,522
High Schools, Private ... 2
Total Students ... 320
Elementary Schools, Diocesan and Parish ... 37
Total Students ... 6,630
Catechesis / Religious Education:
High School Students ... 805
Elementary Students ... 6,300
Total Students under Catholic Instruction ... 15,949
Teachers in Diocese:
Priests ... 6
Sisters ... 16
Lay Teachers ... 734

Vital Statistics
Receptions into the Church:
Infant Baptism Totals ... 1,425
Minor Baptism Totals ... 160
Adult Baptism Totals ... 131
Received into Full Communion ... 299
First Communions ... 1,633
Confirmations ... 1,971
Marriages:
Catholic ... 272
Interfaith ... 126
Total Marriages ... 398
Deaths ... 1,899
Total Catholic Population ... 132,938
Total Population ... 1,434,776

LEADERSHIP

Bishop's Office - t) 309-671-1550 Cheryl Berkshier, Secy.; Mark Harcharik, Secy.;
Vicar General - t) 309-671-1550 Rev. Msgr. Philip D. Halfacre, Vicar;
Chancellor - Patricia Gibson, Chancellor (cberkshier@cdop.org); Patti Carmody;
Director of the Curia - Patricia Gibson, Dir. (cberkshier@cdop.org); Matt Faley, Assoc. Dir.;
Legal Department - Patricia Gibson (cberkshier@cdop.org);
Advocates - Linda Thomas; John Mackoway;
Notaries - Debra Anne Hill, Notary;

ADMINISTRATION

Office of Information Management - Amanda E. Connon, Dir.;

OFFICES AND DIRECTORS

Catholic Cemeteries -
Catholic Relief Services - t) 309-671-1550
Censor Librorum - Rev. Msgr. Philip D. Halfacre;
Cursillo Program - t) 309-676-5587 Dcn. Rick Miller, Dir.;
Divine Worship, Office of - t) 309-671-1550 Phillip Lee, Dir.; Ana Rodas, Assoc. Dir.; Jon Kroepel, Music Min.;
Diocesan Director of Music - t) 309-671-1550 Jon Kroepel;
Liturgy, Churches and Chapels - t) 309-671-1550 Phillip Lee, Ex Officio; Ana Rodas, Ex Officio; Jon Kroepel, Ex Officio;
Holy Childhood Association - t) 309-671-1550 Rev. Msgr. Philip D. Halfacre;
Newspaper--"The Catholic Post" - Jennifer Willems, Editor; Shannon Reznik, Graphic Designer;
Office of Victims Assistance - t) 309-677-7082 Dr. Sharon Weiss;
Permanent Diaconate, Office of - Rev. Msgr. Timothy Nolan, Vicar; Terri LaHood, Secy.;
Rural Life Conference - Msgr. Thomas Mack, Dir. (fatherkh@aol.com);
Vocations Office - t) 309-671-1550 Rev. Patrick Henehan, Formation; Rev. Chase Hilgenbrinck, Recruitment; Carla Oliver, Admin. Asst.;

ADVISORY BOARDS, COMMISSIONS, COMMITTEES, AND COUNCILS

Catholic Women, Council of - t) 309-762-2362 Rev. Msgr. Dale L. Wellman, Moderator;

CATHOLIC CHARITIES

Catholic Charities - t) 217-935-2241; 309-397-0822; 815-672-4567 Susie Meismer, Spiritual Adv./Care Srvcs.; Julie Enzenberger, C.V., Spiritual Adv./Care Srvcs.; John J Gibson, Spiritual Adv./Care Srvcs.;

CLERGY AND RELIGIOUS SERVICES

Clergymen's Aid, Inc. - t) 309-671-1550 Most Rev. Louis Tylka, Trustee & Ex Officio; Rev. Msgr. Philip D. Halfacre, Trustee & Ex Officio; Rev. Joel Phelps, Pres.;
Priests' Eucharistic League - t) 309-671-1550 Rev. Msgr. Philip D. Halfacre;
Priests' Purgatorial Society - t) 309-671-1550 Rev. Msgr. Philip D. Halfacre;

CONSULTATIVE BODIES

Diocesan Personnel Board - t) 309-671-1550 Most Rev. Louis Tylka; Rev. Msgr. Philip D. Halfacre; Rev. Msgr. Mark J. Merdian;
Finance Council (Canon 492) - Most Rev. Louis Tylka; Rev. Msgr. Philip D. Halfacre; Rev. Msgr. Paul E. Showalter;
Diocesan College of Consultors - Rev. Msgr. Philip D. Halfacre; Msgr. Thomas Mack (fatherkh@aol.com); Rev. Patrick Henehan;
Presbyteral Council - Most Rev. Louis Tylka; Rev. Msgr. Philip D. Halfacre; Rev. Patrick Henehan, Pres.;

DEANERIES

Vicariates and Vicars - Rev. Dustin P. Schultz, Bloomington-Lincoln; Rev. Joel Phelps, Champaign; Rev. Steven P. Loftus, Danville;

DEVELOPMENT

Diocesan Office of Development and Stewardship - t) 309-671-1550 Sr. M. Salezia Rudyova, F.S.J.B., Assoc. Dir.;

EDUCATION

Catholic Education Office - Kenneth (Jerry) Sanderson, Supt.; Roberta Gifford, Secy.; Linda Nolan, Secy.;

EVANGELIZATION

Diocesan Evangelization and Faith Formation - t) (309) 671-1550
Diocesan Hispanic Ministry Office - t) 309-671-1550 Rosa Romero Carrillo, Dir.; Elizabeth Ruiz, Secy.;
Respect Life & Human Dignity -

FINANCE

Diocesan Office of Finance - Mike Buckley, Diocesan Dir.; Russ Courter, Dir.; Jill Watson, Assoc. Dir.;

HUMAN RESOURCES

Diocesan Office of Human Resources - Karen Small, Dir.; Christy Dwyer, Assoc. Dir.;

ORGANIZATIONS

TEC - t) 309-676-4001 Rev. Kyle Lucas, Spiritual Adv./Care Srvcs.;

SOCIAL SERVICES

Christ Child Society of Central Illinois - t) 309-637-1713 christchildsociety@gmail.com
Christ Child Society of the Quad Cities - ccsqc@yahoo.com Shelly Huiskamp;
Propagation of the Faith - t) 309-671-1550 Rev. Msgr. Philip D. Halfacre;

TRIBUNAL

Diocesan Tribunal - t) 309-671-1550 Rev. Msgr. Jason A. Gray, Vicar;
Judicial Vicar - Rev. Msgr. Jason A. Gray, Vicar;
Defender of the Bond - Rev. Msgr. Eric S. Powell;
Promoter of Justice - Rev. Msgr. Eric S. Powell;
Judges - Rev. Msgr. Jason A. Gray, Vicar; Adela Maria Kim, Judge; Sr. Anna Flanigan, O.S.F., Judge;

MISCELLANEOUS / OTHER OFFICES

Office of Safe Environment - t) 309-671-1550 Kenneth (Jerry) Sanderson, Dir.;

PARISHES, MISSIONS, AND CLERGY

STATE OF ILLINOIS

ABINGDON

Sacred Heart - 504 N. Main St., Abingdon, IL 61410; Mailing: 254 E. Tompkins St., Galesburg, IL 61401 t) (309) 343-8256 adorecc7@gmail.com galesburgcatholic.com This location is commonly "linked" with the following in terms of pastorates: St. Patrick, Galesburg; Immaculate Heart of Mary, Galesburg; and Corpus Rev. Lee Brokaw, Pst.; Rev. Ghislain Inai, SMA (Ivory Coast), Par. Vicar; Dcn. Todd Church; Dcn. Michael P. Crummer; Dcn. Robert Rodriguez; Dcn. Robert Wood; CRP Stds.: 3

ALEDO

St. Catherine's Church - 106 N.E. Fourth, Aledo, IL 61231 t) 309-582-7500 lcstc@hotmail.com Worship site of St. Mary Magdalene Parish, Aledo. Rev. John Thieryoung, Pst.;
Linked Parish: St. Anthony, Matherville -
Linked Parish: St. John, Viola - 1101 21st. Ave., Viola, IL 61468; Mailing: 106 N.E. 4th St., Aledo, IL 61231 t) (309) 582-7500 (St. Mary Magdalene, Aledo) cpomc.org

Saint Mary Magdalene Roman Catholic Congregation of Aledo - 106 N.E. 4th St., Aledo, IL 61231 t) (309) 582-7500 cpomc.org Parish with two worship sites: St. Catherine Church, Aledo and St. Anthony Church, Matherville. Rev. John Thieryoung, Pst.; CRP Stds.: 38

ANNAWAN

Sacred Heart - 305 W. South Ave., Annawan, IL 61234; Mailing: PO Box 210, Atkinson, IL 61235 t) (309) 936-7900 office@stanthonysatkinson.org theheartandthelily.org This location is commonly "linked" with the following in terms of pastorates: St. Anthony, Atkinson. Rev. S. Stephen Engelbrecht, Pst.; Dcn. Marshall Plumley, Sacr. Min.; Dcn. Nicholas Simon, Sacr. Min.; CRP Stds.: 25
Linked Parish: St. Anthony - 204 W. Main St., Atkinson, IL 61235; Mailing: P.O. Box 210, Atkinson, IL 61235

ARLINGTON

St. Patrick's - 106 Church St., Arlington, IL 61312; Mailing: Box 159, Cherry, IL 61317 t) 815-894-2006 holytsp@gmail.com www.bureaucatholic.org This location is commonly "linked" with the following in terms of pastorates: Holy Trinity, Cherry and St. Thomas More, Dalzell. Rev. Binh K. Tran, Pst.;

ATKINSON

St. Anthony's - 204 W. Main St., Atkinson, IL 61235-0210; Mailing: P.O. Box 210, Atkinson, IL 61235-0210 t) (309) 936-7900 office@stanthonysatkinson.org theheartandthelily.org This location is commonly "linked" with the following in terms of pastorates: Sacred Heart, Annawan. Rev. S. Stephen Engelbrecht, Pst.; Dcn. Marshall Plumley, Sacr. Min.; Dcn. Nicholas Simon, Sacr. Min.; CRP Stds.: 8

BARTONVILLE

St. Anthony - 2525 S. Skyway Rd., Bartonville, IL 61607-1458 t) 309-697-0627 (CRP); 309-697-0645 kcampbell@stanthonybartonville.com; jdarling@stanthonybartonville.com www.stanthonybartonville.com Rev. Charles Klamut, Pst.; Dcn. Louis A. Tomlianovich; Karen Campbell, DRE; Mary Ann Fahey-Darling, Music Min.; John L Darling, Pst. Assoc.; CRP Stds.: 63

BEMENT

St. Michael - 332 S. Macon, Bement, IL 61813; Mailing: 1301 N. Market St., Monticello, IL 61856 t) (217) 762-2566 office@stphilomenaonline.org stphilomenaonline.org This location is commonly "linked" with the following parishes in terms of pastorates: St. Philomena, Monticello. Rev. Msgr. Michael C. Bliss, Pst.; Dcn. Gene Triplett; CRP Stds.: 2

BENSON

St. John - 209 Jefferson St, Benson, IL 61516; Mailing: PO Box 197, El Paso, IL 61738 t) (309) 527-4555 stmaryselpaso@gmail.com www.stmaryselpaso.org/ This location is commonly "linked" with the following parishes in terms of pastorates: St. Mary, El Paso. Rev. Robert Rayson, Pst.; CRP Stds.: 30

BLOOMINGTON

Holy Trinity - 711 N. Main St., Bloomington, IL 61701 t) (309) 829-2197 businessmgr@holytrinitybloomington.org; office@holytrinitybloomington.org hsp-ht.org/ This location is commonly "linked" with the following parishes in terms of pastorates: St. Patrick, Bloomington. Rev. Jeffrey D. Stirniman, Pst.; Rev. Peter Okola, AJ (Kenya), Par. Vicar; Dcn. Robert Hermes; Dcn. Joe Knapp; Dcn. Albert Lundy; Elaine Rinehimer, Bus. Mgr.; David Liptak, Coordinator of Evangelization & Discipleship; CRP Stds.: 36

St. Mary's - 527 W. Jackson St., Bloomington, IL 61701; Mailing: 601 W. Jackson St., Bloomington, IL 61701 t) 309-827-8526 stmarysparish@frontier.com; stmarybloomington.dre@gmail.com www.stmarysbloomington.org Rev. Gregory Nelson, Pst.; Dcn. Jose Montenegro; Regina Mann, DRE; CRP

Stds.: 120

St Mary's Catholic School - (Grades PreK-8) 603 W Jackson St, Bloomington, IL 61701 t) 309-828-5954 www.stmarysschool.net/ Jamie Hartrich, Prin.; Stds.: 150; Lay Tchrs.: 15

St. Patrick - 1209 W. Locust St., Bloomington, IL 61701; Mailing: 711 N. Main St., Bloomington, IL 61701-3039 t) (309) 829-1355 businessmgr@holytrinitybloomington.org; office@historicsaintpatrick.org hsp-ht.org/ This location is commonly "linked" with the following parishes in terms of pastorates: Holy Trinity, Bloomington. Rev. Jeffrey D. Stirniman, Pst.; Rev. Peter Okola, AJ (Kenya), Par. Vicar; Dcn. Robert Hermes; Dcn. Joe Knapp; Dcn. Albert Lundy; Elaine Rinehimer, Bus. Mgr.; David Liptak, Coordinator of Evangelization & Discipleship; CRP Stds.: 26

St. Patrick Church of Merna - 1000 N. Towanda Barnes Rd., Bloomington, IL 61705; Mailing: 1001 N. Towanda Barnes Rd., Bloomington, IL 61705 t) (309) 662-7361 office@stpatrickmerna.org stpatrickmerna.org This location is commonly "linked" with the following parishes in terms of pastorates: St. Mary, Downs. Rev. Dustin P. Schultz, Pst.; Rev. Matthew Deptula, Par. Vicar; Dcn. Gayle E. Cyrulik; Dcn. Daniel Froelich; Dcn. Troy Morris; Dcn. Michael Pool; CRP Stds.: 324

BRADFORD

St. John the Baptist - 218 First St., Bradford, IL 61421 t) (309) 695-4031 starkcatholic@gmail.com www.starkcountycatholic.com This location is commonly "linked" with the following parishes in terms of pastorates: St. Dominic, Wyoming. Rev. John Cyr, Pst.; CRP Stds.: 5

BRIMFIELD

St. Joseph's - 314 W. Clay St., Brimfield, IL 61517; Mailing: P.O. Box 199, Brimfield, IL 61517 t) (309) 446-3275 parishoffice@stjosephbrimfield.org www.stjosephbrimfield.org/ This location is commonly "linked" with the following parishes in terms of pastorates: St. James, Williamsfield. Rev. John M. Verrier, Pst.; Dcn. John Burton; CRP Stds.: 28

Linked Parish: St. James - 2240 E. Legion Rd., Williamsfield, IL 61489 t) (309) 446-3832 www.stjameswilliamsfield.org

BUSHNELL

St. Bernard - 376 W. Hail St., Bushnell, IL 61422 t) (309) 772-2333 st.bbushnell@gmail.com This location is commonly "linked" with the following parishes in terms of pastorates: St. Augustine, St. Augustine. Rev. Eugene A. Radosevich, Pst.;

CANTON

St. Mary's - 159 E. Chestnut St., Canton, IL 61520; Mailing: 139 E. Chestnut St., Canton, IL 61520 t) (309) 647-1473; (309) 647-1476 (CRP) st.marys1@hotmail.com (Merged with: St. Michael, St. David) Rev. Msgr. Timothy Nolan, Pst.; Dcn. Curtis Theyse;

Linked Parish: St. Michael Parish - 528 4th St., Saint David, IL 61563

CARTHAGE

Immaculate Conception - 125 N. Fayette St., Carthage, IL 62354; Mailing: PO Box 147, Nauvoo, IL 62354 t) (217) 453-2428 (Nauvoo Office); (217) 357-3087 www.hancockcountycatholic.org This location is commonly "linked" with: Sacred Heart, Dallas City; St. Mary, Hamilton; Sacred Heart, Warsaw; and Sts. Peter & Paul, Nauvoo. Rev. Anthony J. Trosley, Pst.; CRP Stds.: 33

CHAMPAIGN

Holy Cross - 405 W. Clark St., Champaign, IL 61820 t) (217) 352-8748 office@holycrosscatholic.org www.holycrosscatholic.org Rev. Joseph P. Donton, Pst.; Rev. Leopold Mushobozi, Par. Vicar; Dcn. Edward Mohrbacher; Dcn. Michael Smith; Elizabeth Kelley, DRE; CRP Stds.: 37

Holy Cross School - -8) 410 W. White St., Champaign, IL 61820 t) (217) 356-9521 meyersm@holycrosselem.org www.holycrosselem.org Greg Koerner, Prin.; Stds.: 222; Scholastics: 21; Lay Tchrs.: 14

St. John's Catholic Chapel - 604 E. Armory Ave., Champaign, IL 61820 t) 217-344-1266 info@sjcnc.org www.sjcnc.org Rev. Robert Lampitt, Chap.; Rev. Alexander Millar, Chap.; Rev. Matthew Hoelscher, Chap.;

St. Mary's - 612 E. Park St., Champaign, IL 61820 t) (217) 352-8364 stmary@stmary-cu.org stmarycu.org Rev. Anthony Co, Pst.; Rev. Edward U. Ohm, In Res.; Dcn. Faustino Lopez; CRP Stds.: 110

Saint Matthew Roman Catholic Congregation of Champaign - 1303 Lincolnshire Dr., Champaign, IL 61821 t) (217) 359-4224 (school); (217) 359-4114 (parish) www.stmatt.net This location is commonly "linked" with the following in terms of pastorates: St. Boniface, Seymour. Rev. Msgr. Stanley L. Deptula, Pst.; Rev. Andru O'Brien, Par. Vicar; Rev. Alou Pilizue, SMA (Togo), Par. Vicar; Dcn. David Schug; Dcn. William S. Scott; CRP Stds.: 142

St. Matthew School - (Grades PreK-8) 1307 Linconshire Dr., Champaign, IL 61821 mbiggs@stmatt.net stmatt.net Michelle Biggs, Prin.; Stds.: 400; Sr. Tchrs.: 2; Lay Tchrs.: 27

Sisters of St. Francis of the Martyr St. George - 1719 Robert Dr., Champaign, IL 61821

CHENOA

St. Joseph's - 225 W. Owsley St., Chenoa, IL 61726 t) (815) 945-2561; (815) 844-7683 chenoacatholic@gmail.com This location is commonly "linked" with: St. Mary, Lexington; St. Joseph, Flanagan; Sts. Peter and Paul, Chatsworth. Rev. David Sabel, Pst.; Rev. William Keebler, Par. Vicar; CRP Stds.: 10

Linked Parish: St. Mary - 201 Lee St., Lexington, IL 61753; Mailing: 225 W. Owsley St., Chenoa, IL 61726 stmaryspontiac@mchsi.com

CHERRY

Holy Trinity - 212 S. Main St., Cherry, IL 61317; Mailing: P.O. Box 159, Cherry, IL 61317 t) 815-894-2006 juliehtc@outlook.com; holytsp@gmail.com www.bureaucatholic.org (Linked Parishes: St. Patrick, Arlington & St. Thomas More, Dalzell) Rev. Binh K. Tran, Pst.; Julie Hollinger, DRE;

CHILLICOTHE

St. Edward - 1216 N. 6th St., Chillicothe, IL 61523; Mailing: 1221 N. 5th St., Attn: Parish Office, Chillicothe, IL 61523 t) 309-274-3809 info@sainted.org www.sainted.org Rev. Martin Mwongyera, Admin.; Dcn. John W. Merdian; Dcn. Bob Pomazal; Dcn. Gregory Serangeli; CRP Stds.: 15

St. Edward School - (Grades PreSchool-8) 1221 N. 5th St., Chillicothe, IL 61523 t) (309) 274-2994 dlawson@sainted.org; mdomico@sainted.org saintedschool.org Mike Domico, Prin.; Stds.: 111; Lay Tchrs.: 8

CLINTON

St. John the Baptist Catholic Church - 502 N. Monroe St., Clinton, IL 61727 t) (217) 935-3727 stjohnsclinton@yahoo.com www.clintonstjohns.org This location is commonly "linked" with the following parishes in terms of pastorates: Sacred Heart, Farmer City. Rev. James Owusu Yeboah, SMA (Ghana), Pst.; Dcn. Patrick J. Comfort; Dcn. Scott Whitehouse; Sue Neuschwanger, DRE; CRP Stds.: 26

Linked Parish: St. John - 102 N. State St., Bellflower, IL 61724; Mailing: 502 N. Monroe St., Clinton, IL 61727 www.clintonstjohns.org/ Secondary worship site for St. John the Baptist, Clinton.

COAL VALLEY

St. Maria Goretti - 220 E. 22nd Ave., Coal Valley, IL 61240; Mailing: P.O. Box 159, Coal Valley, IL 61240 t) (309) 799-3414 stmariagorettiparishcv@gmail.com smgcv.org This location is commonly "linked" with the following parishes in terms of pastorates: Our Lady of Peace, Orion. Rev. Anthony M. Ego, Pst.; Dcn. Thomas C. Gainey;

COLONA

St. Patrick's - 201 First St., Colona, IL 61241 t) (309) 792-3854 stpatcolona1954@gmail.com stpatrickcolona.com Rev. Peter Zorjan, Pst.; Dcn. Al Angelo, Sacr. Min.; Dcn. Aaron Hoste, Sacr. Min.; Rose Roe, DRE; CRP Stds.: 32

DALZELL

St. Thomas More - 302 Chestnut St., Dalzell, IL 61320 t) 815-663-6201 holytsp@gmail.com www.bureaucatholic.org (Linked Parishes: St. Patrick, Arlington & Holy Trinity, Cherry) Rev. Binh K. Tran, Pst.;

DANVILLE

Holy Family - 444 E. Main St., Danville, IL 61832 t) (217) 431-5100 office@holyfamilydanville.net holyfamilydanville.net Rev. Steven P. Loftus, Pst.; Rev. Ignatius Mulenda, Par. Vicar; CRP Stds.: 60

St. Paul's - 1303 N. Walnut St., Danville, IL 61832 t) 217-442-5313 jennifermartindill@stpauldanville.org; cindyharden@stpauldanville.org stpauldanville.org Rev. Thomas R. Szydlik, Admin.; Jennifer Martindill, DRE; CRP Stds.: 15

DELAVAN

St. Mary's - 505 E. 4th St., Delavan, IL 61734; Mailing: P.O. Box 769, Delavan, IL 61734 t) (309) 244-8516 stmarydelavan@gmail.com stmarydelavan.org This location is commonly "linked" with the following in terms of pastorates: St. Joseph, Hopedale. Rev. Michael Adrie, SMA, Par. Admin.; CRP Stds.: 36

Linked Parish: St. Joseph's - 132 Washington St., Hopedale, IL 61747

DEPUE

St. Mary's - 312 Park St., DePue, IL 61322; Mailing: PO Box 19, DePue, IL 61322 t) (815) 447-2552 frcreegan@netscape.net This location is commonly "linked" with the following parishes in terms of pastorates: St. Mary, Tiskilwa. Rev. Kevin G. Creegan, Pst.; CRP Stds.: 53

Linked Parish: St. Mary - 121 W. Main St., Tiskilwa, IL 61368; Mailing: PO Box 271, Tiskilwa, IL 61368

DOWNS

St. Mary's - 108 E. Washington St., Downs, IL 61736; Mailing: P.O. Box 66, Downs, IL 61736 t) (309) 662-7361 (Forwarded from Direct); (309) 378-4679 (Direct to Forwarded) office@stpatrickmerna.org stmarysdowns.org This location is commonly "linked" with the following parishes in terms of pastorates: St. Patrick of Merna, Bloomington. Rev. Dustin P. Schultz, Pst.; Rev. Matthew Deptula, Par. Vicar; Dcn. Gary D. Koerner; Dcn. John Louie; CRP Stds.: 51

DWIGHT

St. Patrick's - 100 W. Mazon Ave., Dwight, IL 60420; Mailing: 114 W. Mazon Ave., Dwight, IL 60420 t) (815) 584-3110 (CRP); (815) 584-3522 st.patricks.dwight.dre@gmail.com; stpatsdwight@att.net Rev. Chris G. Haake, Pst.; Danielle Elizabeth Schmidberger, DRE; CRP Stds.: 15

EARLVILLE

St. Theresa Parish - 221 W. Union St., Earlville, IL 60518; Mailing: 1010 Jefferson St., Mendota, IL 61342 t) 815-538-6151 st.theresa.earlville@gmail.com www.st-theresa-earlville.com/ (Linked Parishes: Holy Cross, Mendota; Sts. Peter & Paul, Peterstown) Rev. Peter A. Pilon, Pst.; Rev. Jeff Windy, Par. Vicar; Jean Dau, DRE; CRP Stds.: 11

EAST MOLINE

St. Anne - 555 18th Ave., East Moline, IL 61244 t) 309-755-5071 amy.rel.ed@gmail.com; office@saintanne-em.org www.saintanne-em.org Rev. James G. Pallardy, Par. Admin.; Amy Virnig, DRE; CRP Stds.: 30

Our Lady of Grace Catholic Academy - (Grades PreK-8) 603 18th Ave., East Moline, IL 61244 t) (309) 755-9771 office@olgca.org www.olgca.org Victoria McCollum, Prin.; Stds.: 106; Sr. Tchrs.: 1; Lay Tchrs.: 10

EAST PEORIA

St. Monica Church - 303 Campanile Dr., East Peoria, IL 61611 t) (309) 694-2061 x1; (309) 694-2061 x2; (309) 694-2061 x3 (CRP) stmonicadreep@gmail.com; epstmonica@gmail.com www.stmonicachurch.net/ This location is commonly "linked" with the following parishes in terms of pastorates: St. Patrick, Washington. Rev. Jonathan Steffen, Pst.; Rev. John Bazimenyera (Uganda), Par. Vicar; Laurie Harkness, DRE; Dcn. Stephen Racki III; CRP Stds.: 8

EL PASO

St. Mary's - 79 W. 3rd St., El Paso, IL 61738; Mailing: P.O. Box 197, El Paso, IL 61738 t) (309) 527-3958 (CRP); (309) 527-4555 stmaryselpaso@gmail.com www.stmaryselpaso.org/ Rev. Robert Rayson, Pst.; Kisha Craig, DRE; CRP Stds.: 55

ELKHART

St. Patrick - 213 S. Bogardus St., Elkhart, IL 62634; Mailing: 316 S. Logan St., Lincoln, IL 62656 t) 217-732-4019 jdondanville@logancountycatholic.org www.logancountycatholic.org (Linked Parishes: St. Mary, Atlanta, St. Thomas Aquinas, Mount Pulaski & Holy Family, Lincoln) Rev. Joseph Dondanville, Pst.; Rev. Narcis Katambe (Tanzania), Par. Vicar; Dcn. Wendell Justin Lowry III; CRP Stds.: 15

Linked Parish: St. Thomas Aquinas - 321 S. Lafayette St., Mount Pulaski, IL 62548 t) (217) 732-4019

ELMWOOD

St. Patrick's - 802 W. Main St., Elmwood, IL 61529 t) (309) 742-4921 stpatrickcc@gmail.com This location is commonly "linked" with the following parishes in terms of pastorates: St. Mary, Kickapoo. Rev. James Pankiewicz, Pst.; CRP Stds.: 35

EUREKA

St. Luke - 904 E. Reagan Dr., Eureka, IL 61530; Mailing: P.O. Box 226, Eureka, IL 61530 t) (309) 467-4855 www.stsjlj.com This location is commonly "linked" with the following parishes in terms of pastorates: St. Joseph, Roanoke. Rev. Ryan Mattingly, Pst.; CRP Stds.: 25

FAIRBURY

St. Andrew - 110 E. Ash St., Fairbury, IL 61739 t) (815) 692-2555 standrewparish@outlook.com www.fairburycatholic.org Rev. Scott Archer, Pst.; CRP Stds.: 45

FARMER CITY

Sacred Heart - 612 N. Plum St., Farmer City, IL 61842; Mailing: 502 N. Monroe St., Clinton, IL 61727 t) (309) 928-3855 x2 shchurch612@frontier.com www.sacredheartfc.org/ This location is commonly "linked" with the following parishes in terms of pastorates: St. John, Clinton. Rev. James Owusu Yeboah, SMA (Ghana), Pst.; Dcn. Scott Whitehouse; CRP Stds.: 18

FARMINGTON

St. Matthew's - 156 E. Vernon St., Farmington, IL 61531; Mailing: 139 E. Chestnut St., Canton, IL 61520 t) 309-647-1473 st.marys1@hotmail.com Linked to the Parish of St. Mary in Canton Rev. Msgr. Timothy Nolan, Pst.; Dcn. Gary Schultz;

GALESBURG

Corpus Christi - 273 S. Prairie St., Galesburg, IL 61401; Mailing: 254 E. Tompkins St., Galesburg, IL 61401 t) (309) 343-8256 adorecc7@gmail.com www.galesburgcatholic.com This location is commonly "linked" with: Sacred Heart, Abingdon; St. Patrick, Galesburg; and Immaculate Heart of Mary, Galesburg. Rev. Lee Brokaw, Pst.; Rev. Ghislain Inai, SMA (Ivory Coast), Par. Vicar; Dcn. Todd Church; Dcn. Michael P. Crummer; Dcn. Robert Rodriguez; Dcn. Robert Wood; CRP Stds.: 56

Costa Catholic Academy - (Grades PreSchool-8) 2726 Costa Dr., Galesburg, IL 61401 t) (309) 344-3151 www.costacatholicacademy.org Operates with Immaculate Heart, Corpus Christi, and St. Patrick, all in Galesburg. Julie Purl, Prin.; Stds.: 154; Lay Tchrs.: 12

Immaculate Heart of Mary - 2401 N. Broad St., Galesburg, IL 61401-1203; Mailing: 254 E. Tompkins St., Galesburg, IL 61401 t) (309) 344-3108 ihmgalesburg@gmail.com galesburgcatholic.com This location is commonly "linked" with: Sacred Heart, Abingdon; St. Patrick, Galesburg; and Corpus Christi, Galesburg. Rev. Ghislain Inai, SMA (Ivory Coast), Par. Vicar; Rev. Lee Brokaw, Pst.; Dcn. Todd Church; Dcn. Michael P. Crummer; Dcn. Robert Rodriguez; Dcn. Robert Wood; Laura Junk, DRE; CRP Stds.: 36

St. Patrick's - 858 S. Academy St., Galesburg, IL 61401; Mailing: 254 E. Tompkins St., Galesburg, IL 61401 t) (309) 343-9874 stpatrickschurch@outlook.com galesburgcatholic.com This location is commonly "linked" with the following parishes in terms of pastorates: Sacred Heart, Abingdon; Corpus Christi, Galesburg; Immaculate H Rev. Lee Brokaw, Pst.; Rev. Ghislain Inai, SMA (Ivory Coast), Par. Vicar; Dcn. Todd Church; Dcn. Michael P. Crummer; Dcn. Robert Rodriguez; Dcn. Robert Wood; CRP Stds.: 11

GALVA

St. John's - 212 N.E. 1st St., Galva, IL 61434; Mailing: P.O. Box 249, Woodhull, IL 61490 t) (309) 932-2409 stjohngalva2@gmail.com threestjohns.com This location is commonly "linked" with: St. John Paul II, Kewanee; St. John Vianney, Cambridge; and St. John, Woodhull. Rev. Johndamaseni Zilimu, Pst.; Rev. Christopher Magesa (Tanzania), Par. Vicar; Dcn. John V. Holevoet; CRP Stds.: 35

GENESEO

St. Malachy's - 595 E. Ogden Ave., Geneseo, IL 61254 t) (309) 944-5393 church@stmalgeneseo.org saintmalachy.org Rev. Daniel Gifford, Pst.; Dcn. Larry Honzel; Dcn. Tom Mattan; Dcn. Robert O'Rourke; Dcn. Mike Sigwalt, RCIA Coord.; Dcn. Bob Thoene; Dcn. Thomas Wachtel; Kimberly Souba, DRE; CRP Stds.: 214

St. Malachy's School - (Grades K-6) t) (309) 944-3230 tsmith@stmalgeneseo.org www.saintmalachy.org Tim Smith, Prin.; Stds.: 114; Lay Tchrs.: 7

GEORGETOWN

St. Isaac Jogues - 109 W. 7th St., Georgetown, IL 61254 t) (217) 662-8726 stisaacjogues054@gmail.com This location is commonly "linked" with the following in terms of pastorates: St. Mary, Westville. Rev. Timothy J. Sauppe, Pst.;

GERMANTOWN HILLS

St. Mary of Lourdes - 424 Lourdes Church Rd., Germantown Hills, IL 61548 t) (309) 383-4460 businessmanager@stmarylourdes.org; igrebner@stmarylourdes.org www.stmarylourdes.org Rev. Eric Bolek, Par. Admin.; Dcn. Dan Fandel; Dcn. Rich Flavin; Dcn. Robert Heiple; Ileen Grebner, DRE; CRP Stds.: 124

GRANVILLE

Sacred Heart of Jesus - 311 Hennepin St., Granville, IL 61326; Mailing: P.O. Box 217, Granville, IL 61326 t) (815) 339-2138 shgsph@gmail.com www.shgsph.org This location is commonly "linked" with the following in terms of pastorates: St. Patrick, Hennepin. Rev. Patrick DeMeulemeester, Pst.; CRP Stds.: 65

HAVANA

St. Patrick's - 545 S. Orange St., Havana, IL 62644 t) (309) 740-1495 office@3forthetrinity.org 3forthetrinity.org This location is commonly "linked" with the following in terms of pastorates: Immaculate Conception, Manito and St. Mary, Lewistown. Rev. David Whiteside, Pst.; Dcn. William Meyer; CRP Stds.: 7

Linked Parish: Immaculate Conception - 505 S. Adams St., Manito, IL 61546; Mailing: 545 S. Orange St., Havana, IL 62644 Dcn. Robert Sondag;

HENNEPIN

St. Patrick's - 920 E. Dore Dr., Hennepin, IL 61327; Mailing: 311 Hennepin St., P.O. Box 217, Granville, IL 61326 t) (815) 339-2138 shgsph@gmail.com www.shgsph.org This location is commonly "linked" with the following in terms of pastorates: Sacred Heart, Granville. Rev. Patrick DeMeulemeester, Pst.; CRP Stds.: 25

HENRY

St. John XXIII - 401 South St., Henry, IL 61537; Mailing: 415 N. High St., Lacon, IL 61540 t) (309) 246-5145 iccc@grics.net www.stjohnhenry.com This location is commonly "linked" with the following in terms of pastorates: Immaculate Conception, Lacon. Rev. John Bosco Mujuni, Pst.; Christy Beall, DRE; CRP Stds.: 40

HOOPESTON

St. Anthony Church - 423 S. Third St., Hoopeston, IL 60942; Mailing: 501 S. 3rd St., Hoopeston, IL 60942 t) 219-283-6249 (CRP); 217-283-6211 drestanthony@gmail.com; stanthony423@gmail.com Rev. Steven P. Loftus, Pst.; Rev. Ignatius Mulenda, Par. Vicar; CRP Stds.: 25

IVESDALE

St. Joseph's - 201 5th St., Ivesdale, IL 61851; Mailing: P.O. Box 175, Ivesdale, IL 61851 t) (217) 485-1129 officeofstp@gmail.com stjosephivesdale.com This location is commonly "linked" with the following in terms of pastorates: St. Patrick, Tolono. Rev. Patrick O'Neal, Pst.; Dcn. James Brewer, DRE; CRP Stds.: 30

KEWANEE

Saint John Paul II Parish - 406 W. Central Blvd., Kewanee, IL 61443-2010 t) (309) 852-4549 angie@saintjohnpaulii-kewanee.org; office@saintjohnpaulii-kewanee.org saintjohnpaulii-kewanee.org This location is commonly "linked" with the following in terms of pastorates: St. John Vianney, Cambridge; St. John the Evangelist, Galva; and St. Joh Rev. Johndamaseni Zilimu, Pst.; Rev. Christopher Magesa (Tanzania), Par. Vicar; Angela Ryan, DRE; Mary Ebert, RCIA Coord.; CRP Stds.: 30

Visitation Catholic School - (Grades PreSchool-8) 107 S. Lexington, Kewanee, IL 61443 t) (309) 856-7451 www.visitationcatholic.com Wayne Brau, Prin.; Stds.: 145; Lay Tchrs.: 10

KICKAPOO

St. Mary of Kickapoo - 9910 W. Knox St., Kickapoo, IL 61528 t) (309) 691-2030 stmarys@stmaryskickapoo.org www.stmaryskickapoo.org Rev. James Pankiewicz, Pst.; Dcn. Thomas L. Mueller; CRP Stds.: 70

St. Mary of Kickapoo School - 9910 W. Knox, Kickapoo, IL 61528 t) (309) 691-3015 stmaryskickapoo.org/school/ Bill Lamb, Prin.; Stds.: 67; Scholastics: 7; Lay Tchrs.: 7

LACON

Immaculate Conception - 412 N. Center St., Lacon, IL 61540; Mailing: 415 N. High St., Lacon, IL 61540 t) (309) 246-5145 iccc@grics.net www.icclacon.org This location is commonly "linked" with the following in terms of pastorates: St. John XXIII, Henry. Rev. John Bosco Mujuni, Pst.; Katie Bogner, DRE; CRP Stds.: 17

LASALLE

St. Hyacinth - 927 10th St., LaSalle, IL 61301; Mailing: 725 4th St., LaSalle, IL 61301 t) (815) 223-0641 office@lasallecatholic.org www.lasallecatholic.org This location is commonly "linked" with the following in terms of pastorates: St. Patrick, LaSalle and Shrine of the Holy Rosary, LaSalle. Rev. Thomas Otto, Pst.; Rev. Michael Pica, Par. Vicar; Dcn. Gabriel Guerrero; CRP Stds.: 125

Trinity Catholic Academy (St Patrick) - (Grades PreK-8) 650 Fourth St., LaSalle, IL 61301 t) (815) 223-8523 tcasaints@lasallecatholic.org www.lasallecatholic.org/tca.html Deb Myers, Prin.; Stds.: 146; Lay Tchrs.: 11

St. Patrick - 725 Fourth St., LaSalle, IL 61301 t) 815-223-0641 dmyers@lasallecatholic.org; office@lasallecatholic.org This location is commonly "linked" with the following in terms of pastorates: St. Hyacinth, LaSalle and Shrine of the Holy Rosary, LaSalle. Rev. Thomas Otto, Pst.; Deb Myers, DRE; Rev. Michael Pica, Par. Vicar; Dcn. Gabriel Guerrero;

Shrine of Queen of the Holy Rosary - 529 4th St., LaSalle, IL 61301; Mailing: 725 4th St., LaSalle, IL 61301 t) 815-223-0641 office@lasallecatholic.org wwwlasallecatholic.org (Linked Parishes: St. Hyacinth, LaSalle & St. Patrick, LaSalle) Rev. Thomas Otto, Rector; Rev. Michael Pica, Par. Vicar;

LEWISTOWN

St. Mary Parish - 705 N. Broadway St., Lewistown, IL 61542; Mailing: 545 S Orange St, Havana, IL 62644 t) 309-740-1495 office@3forthetrinity.org; stpatrickshavana@yahoo.com 3forthetrinity.org This location is commonly "linked" with the following in terms of pastorates: St. Patrick, Havana and Immaculate Conception, Manito. Rev. David Whiteside, Pst.;

LINCOLN

Holy Family - 316 S. Logan St., Lincoln, IL 62656 t) (217) 732-4019 office@logancountycatholic.org www.logancountycatholic.org This location is commonly "linked" with the following in terms of pastorates: St. Patrick, Elkhart; St. Thomas Aquinas, Mt. Pulaski; and St. Mary, Atl Rev. Joseph Dondanville, Pst.; Rev. Narcis Katambe (Tanzania), Par. Vicar; Dcn. Wendell Justin Lowry III; CRP Stds.: 52

Carroll Catholic School - (Grades PreSchool-8) 111 Fourth St., Lincoln, IL 62656 t) (217) 732-7518 dwelch@carrollcatholicschool.com www.carrollcatholic.com David Welch, Prin.; Stds.: 125; Lay Tchrs.: 9

Linked Parish: St. Mary's - 805 N.W. Pearl St., Atlanta, IL 61723; Mailing: 316 S. Logan St., Lincoln, IL 62656

LOSTANT

St. John the Baptist - 301 S. Sheridan St., Lostant, IL 61334; Mailing: 207 W. Third St. S., Wenona, IL 61377 t) (815) 853-4558 smary1876@mchsi.com www.4saints.org/ This location is commonly "linked" with the following in terms of pastorates: St. Patrick, Minonk; St. Ann, Toluca; and St. Mary, Wenona. Rev. Patrick Greenough, O.F.M.Conv., Pst.; Rev. Stephen McKinley, O.F.M.Conv., In Res.; Sandi Long, DRE; CRP Stds.: 2

MACOMB

St. Paul's - 309 W. Jackson St., Macomb, IL 61455 t) (309) 833-2496 churchoffice@stpaulmacomb.com stpaulmacomb.com/church/ Rev. Adam Stimpson, Pst.; Rev. Joseph Domfe, SMA (Ghana), Par. Vicar; Dcn. Tony Ensenberger; Dcn. Lawrence Adams, DRE; CRP Stds.: 36

St. Paul's School - (Grades PreK-6) 322 W. Washington St., Macomb, IL 61455 t) (309) 833-2470 office@stpaulmacomb.com www.stpaulmacomb.com/ Laura Cody, Prin.; Stds.: 153; Lay Tchrs.: 9

MAHOMET

Our Lady of the Lake - 501 W. State St., Mahomet, IL 61853; Mailing: P.O. Box 109, Mahomet, IL 61853 t) (217) 586-5153 office@ololcatholic.org ololcatholic.org Rev. Joseph T. Hogan, Pst.; Dcn. Michael Burge; Dcn. John Leonard; Dcn. Anthony Nickrent; Marie Burge, DRE; CRP Stds.: 158

MARSEILLES

St. Joseph's - 200 Broadway St., Marseilles, IL 61341 t) (815) 795-2240 parishgroup3@gmail.com www.stjosephmarseillesil.org This location is commonly "linked" with the following in terms of pastorates: St. Mary, Grand Ridge. Rev. Sixmund Nyabenda Henry (Tanzania), Par. Admin.; Dcn. Ron Wackerlin; Debbie Woodyer, DRE; CRP Stds.: 40

St. Mary - 2098 E. 22nd Rd., Grand Ridge, IL 61325; Mailing: 200 Broadway St., Marseilles, IL 61341 stmarygrandridgeil.org

MATHERVILLE

St. Anthony's Church - 1386 252nd St., Matherville, IL 61263; Mailing: c/o St. Catherine Church, 106 NE 4th St., Aledo, IL 61231 t) 309-582-7500 lcstc@hotmail.com (Linked Parishes: St. John, Viola & St. Catherine, Aledo) Rev. John Thieryoung, Pst.;

Linked Parish: St. John - 1102 21st Ave., Viola, IL 61486; Mailing: 106 NE 4th St., Aledo, IL 61231 t) (309) 582-7500 (St. Mary Magdalene, Aledo) cpomc.org

MENDOTA

Holy Cross - 1010 Jefferson St., Mendota, IL 61342 t) (815) 538-6151 briancorriganhcdre@gmail.com mendotacatholic.org This parish is commonly "linked" with the following parishes in terms of pastorates: Sts. Peter & Paul, Peterstown. Rev. Peter A. Pilon, Pst.; Rev. Jeff Windy, Par. Vicar; Dcn. Hector Diaz; Dcn. Raymond Fischer; Dcn. Jose Lopez; Brian Corrigan, DRE;

Holy Cross School - (Grades PreK-8) 1008 Jefferson St., Mendota, IL 61342 t) (815) 539-7003 Michael Struna, Prin.; Stds.: 174; Lay Tchrs.: 10

SS. Peter and Paul - 3864 E. 1st Rd, Mendota, IL 61342; Mailing: 1010 Jefferson St., Mendota, IL 61342 t) 815-538-6151 (Linked Parishes: Holy Cross, Mendota) Rev. Peter A. Pilon, Pst.;

METAMORA

St. Mary's - 415 W. Chatham St., Metamora, IL 61548 t) (309) 367-4407 deb.adams@saintmarysmetamora.org stmarysmetamora.com/ Rev. David M. Kipfer, Pst.; Dcn. Terry Stalsburg; CRP Stds.: 151

St. Mary's School - (Grades PreK-8) 400 W. Chatham St., Metamora, IL 61548 t) (309) 367-2528 harperj@stmfalcons.com stmfalcons.com Ron Kiesewetter, Prin.; Stds.: 105; Lay Tchrs.: 8

MILAN

St. Ambrose - 312 W. First St., Milan, IL 61264; Mailing: 320 1st St. W., Milan, IL 61264 t) (309) 787-4593 stambrosemilan@gmail.com www.stambrosemilan.org/ Rev. Joseph Baker, Pst.; CRP Stds.: 24

MINONK

St. Patrick's - 420 E. Sixth St., Minonk, IL 61760; Mailing: 207 W. Third St. S., Wenona, IL 61377 t) (815) 853-4558 smary1867@mchsi.com www.4saints.org/ This location is commonly "linked" with the following in terms of pastorates: St. John the Baptist, Lostant; St. Ann, Toluca; and St. Mary, Wenona. Rev. Patrick Greenough, O.F.M.Conv., Pst.; Rev. Stephen McKinley, O.F.M.Conv., In Res.; Sandi Long, DRE; CRP Stds.: 10

MOLINE

Christ the King - 3209 60th St., Moline, IL 61265 t) (309) 762-4634 x206 (CRP); (309) 762-4634 ctkenter@ctkmoline.com www.christthekingmoline.org Rev. Donald L. Levitt, Pst.; Dcn. Kevin Hernandez; Dcn. Mark Jackson; CRP Stds.: 134

St. Mary's - 412 10th St., Moline, IL 61265 t) (309) 764-1562; (309) 269-3754 (CRP) stmarysmolineil@hotmail.com; talenself@gmail.com This location is commonly "linked" with the following in terms of pastorates: St. Mary, Moline. Rev. Antonio Dittmer, Pst.; Dcn. Marco Martinez; Lisa Forgie, DRE; CRP Stds.: 95

Our Lady of Grace Catholic Academy - 602 17th Ave., East Moline, IL 61244 t) 309-755-9771 Victoria McCollum, Prin.; Stds.: 106; Sr. Tchrs.: 1; Lay Tchrs.: 10

St. Mary's - 412 10th St., Moline, IL 61265 t) (309) 764-1562 This location is commonly "linked" with the following in terms of pastorates: St. Mary, East Moline (closed). Rev. Antonio Dittmer, Pst.; Dcn. Russ W. Swim; Meaghan Terry, DRE;

Sacred Heart Roman Catholic Congregation of Moline Illinois - 1307 17th Ave., Moline, IL 61265; Mailing: 1608 13th St., Moline, IL 61265 t) (309) 762-2362 desutter@sacredheartmoline.org; shchurch@sacredheartmoline.org sacredheartmoline.org Rev. Mark DeSutter, Pst.; Rev. Matthew Cole, SMA, Par. Vicar; Dcn. Matt Martel; Dcn. Mike Maynard; Sr. Kathleen Mullin, Pst. Assoc.; Debbie Patronagio, DRE; CRP Stds.: 80

Lee Parish Center - 1608 13th St., Moline, IL 61265 Rev. Mark DeSutter, Pst.;

Seton Catholic School - (Grades PreK-8) 1320 16th Ave., Moline, IL 61265 t) (309) 757-5500

MONMOUTH

Immaculate Conception - 200 W. Broadway, Monmouth, IL 61462 t) (309) 734-7533 info@iccmonmouth.org www.iccmonmouth.org This location is commonly "linked" with the following in terms of pastorates: St. Patrick, Raritan and St. Theresa, Alexis. Msgr. Thomas Mack, Pastor Emer.; Rev. Timothy Hepner, Pst.; Dcn. William H. Clark; Dcn. Thomas Mann; Dcn. Joseph McCleary; Kristine Campbell, DRE; CRP Stds.: 85

Immaculate Conception School - (Grades PreK-8) 115 N. B St., Monmouth, IL 61462 t) (309) 734-6037 icstrojans@gmail.com www.immaculate-conception.net Randy Frakes, Prin.; Stds.: 182; Lay Tchrs.: 13

MONTICELLO

St. Philomena - 1301 N. Market St., Monticello, IL 61856 t) (217) 762-2566 office@stphilomenaonline.org stphilomenaonline.org This location is commonly "linked" with the following in terms of pastorates: St. Michael, Bement. Rev. Msgr. Michael C. Bliss, Pst.; Dcn. Gene Triplett; Kari Higgins, DRE; CRP Stds.: 92

MORTON

Blessed Sacrament - 1020 S. First Ave., Morton, IL 61550 t) (309) 266-9721 info@bscmorton.org bscmorton.org Rev. Msgr. Gerald T. Ward, Pst.; Dcn. Michael Harris; Dcn. Rick Miller; Dcn. David Steeples; Dcn. Kevin Zeeb; MaryBeth Steinkoenig, DRE; CRP Stds.: 162

Blessed Sacrament School - (Grades PreK-8) 1018 S First Ave, Morton, IL 61550 t) (309) 263-8442 blessedschool@bssmorton.org bssmorton.org Melissa Scholl, Prin.; Stds.: 213; Lay Tchrs.: 17

NAUVOO

SS. Peter and Paul - 190 N. Wells St., Nauvoo, IL 62354; Mailing: P.O. Box 147, Nauvoo, IL 62354 t) (217) 453-2428 business@hancockcountycatholic.org www.hancockcountycatholic.org This location is commonly "linked" with: Sacred Heart, Dallas City; St. Mary, Hamilton; Sacred Heart, Warsaw; and Immaculate Conception, Carthage. Rev. Anthony J. Trosley, Pst.; Dcn. Daniel Moffitt; CRP Stds.: 17

SS. Peter and Paul School - (Grades PreK-6) 1115 Young St., Nauvoo, IL 62354 t) (217) 453-2511 principal@stspeterpaul.org www.stspeterpaul.org/ Trevor Knipe, Admin.; Stds.: 57; Lay Tchrs.: 5

Linked Parish: Sacred Heart - 90 W. 5th St., Dallas City, IL 62330 hancockcountycatholic.org Dcn. Harold (Tony) Herdrich;

NORMAL

Epiphany - 1000 E. College Ave., Normal, IL 61761 t) (309) 452-2585 office@epiphanyparish.com www.epiphanyparish.com Rev. Msgr. Eric S. Powell, Pst.; Dcn. Mark Cleary; CRP Stds.: 137

Epiphany School - (Grades PreK-8) 1002 E. College Ave., Normal, IL 61761 t) (309) 452-3268 mary.brownfield@epiphanyschools.org epiphanyschools.org Jennifer Kamradt, Prin.; Stds.: 344; Lay Tchrs.: 22

ODELL

St. Paul's - 200 S. West St., Odell, IL 60460; Mailing: 114 W. Mazon Ave., Dwight, IL 60420 t) (815) 584-3522 stpatsdwight@att.net This location is commonly "linked" with the following in terms of pastorates: St. Patrick, Dwight. Rev. Chris G. Haake, Pst.; CRP Stds.: 63

St. Paul's School - (Grades PreK-8) 300 S. West St., Odell, IL 60460 t) (815) 998-2194 schooloffice@saintpaulodell.com www.stpaulodell.weebly.com Richard Morehouse, Prin.; Stds.: 65; Lay Tchrs.: 5

OGLESBY

Holy Family - 311 N. Woodland Ave., Oglesby, IL 61348 t) (815) 883-8233 office@hfoglesby.org hfoglesby.org Rev. Paul Carlson, Pst.; CRP Stds.: 27

Holy Family School - (Grades PreK-8) 336 Alice Ave., Oglesby, IL 61348 t) (815) 883-8916 holyfamilyschool@comcast.net Jyll Jasiek, Prin.; Stds.: 166; Lay Tchrs.: 10

OHIO

Immaculate Conception Church - 101 N. Main St., Ohio, IL 61349; Mailing: P.O. Box 370, Walnut, IL 61376 t) (815) 379-2602 This location is commonly "linked" with the following in terms of pastorates: St. John, Walnut. Rev. Thomas Shaw, Pst.;

ORION

Mary, Our Lady of Peace - 1410 10th St., Orion, IL 61273-0175; Mailing: P.O. Box 175, Orion, IL 61273-0175 t) (309) 581-2923 dremolop@gmail.com; maryourladyofpeace@gmail.com maryourladyofpeace.org This location is commonly "linked" with the following in terms of pastorates: St.

Maria Goretti, Coal Valley. Rev. Anthony M. Ego, Pst.; Tammy Mount, DRE; CRP Stds.: 75

OTTAWA

St. Columba - 122 W. Washington St., Ottawa, IL 61350 t) (815) 433-0700 ottawacatholiccommunity@gmail.com ottawacatholic.org This location is commonly "linked" with the following in terms of pastorates: St. Francis of Assisi, Ottawa and St. Patrick, Ottawa. Rev. Msgr. Mark J. Merdian, Pst.; Rev. Gary C. Caster, Par. Vicar; Rev. Nicolas Wilson, Par. Vicar; Dcn. Michael Driscoll; Dcn. Daniel Goetz; CRP Stds.: 102

St. Francis of Assisi - 820 Sanger St., Ottawa, IL 61350; Mailing: 122 W. Washington St., Ottawa, IL 61350 t) (815) 433-0700 ottawacatholiccommunity@gmail.com ottawacatholic.org This location is commonly "linked" with the following in terms of pastorates: St. Columba, Ottawa and St. Patrick, Ottawa. Rev. Msgr. Mark J. Merdian, Pst.; Rev. Gary C. Caster, Par. Vicar; Rev. Nicolas Wilson, Par. Vicar; Dcn. Michael Driscoll; Dcn. Daniel Goetz; CRP Stds.: 38

St. Patrick's - 726 W. Jefferson St., Ottawa, IL 61350; Mailing: 122 W. Washington St., Ottawa, IL 61350 t) (815) 433-0700 ottawacatholiccommunity@gmail.com ottawacatholic.org This location is commonly "linked" with the following in terms of pastorates: St. Columba, Ottawa and St. Francis of Assisi, Ottawa. Rev. Msgr. Mark J. Merdian, Pst.; Rev. Gary C. Caster, Par. Vicar; Rev. Nicolas Wilson, Par. Vicar; Dcn. Michael Driscoll; Dcn. Daniel Goetz; CRP Stds.: 70

PEKIN

St. Joseph Catholic Church - 303 S. 7th St., Pekin, IL 61554 t) (309) 347-6108 stjoseph@stjosephpekin.org www.stjosephpekin.org Rev. Michael J. Andrejek, Pst.; Dcn. Timothy Blanchard; Dcn. Mark Scamp; Dcn. Ernie Whited; Dcn. Mark Wilder; Cristen Mini, DRE; CRP Stds.: 56

St. Joseph Catholic School - (Grades PreK-8) 300 S. 6th St., Pekin, IL 61554 t) (309) 347-7194 www.stjosephschoolpekin.com Mary Jo Sarff, Prin.; Stds.: 117; Lay Tchrs.: 9

PENFIELD

St. Lawrence's - 302 Main St., Penfield, IL 61862; Mailing: P.O. Box 49, Penfield, IL 61862 t) (217) 595-5620 slcpenfield@gmail.com This location is commonly "linked" with the following in terms of pastorates: St. Charles Borromeo, Homer. Rev. Michael L. Menner, Pst.;

Linked Parish: St. Charles Borromeo - 110 S. East St., Homer, IL 61849 This location is commonly "linked" with the following in terms of pastorates: St. Lawrence, Penfield.

PEORIA

St. Mary's Cathedral - 607 N.E. Madison Ave., Peoria, IL 61603; Mailing: 504 Fulton St., Peoria, IL 61602 t) (309) 673-6317 b.stbernards@comcast.net catholicpeoria.com This location is commonly "linked" with the following in terms of pastorates: St. Bernard, Peoria; Sacred Heart, Peoria; and St. Joseph, Peoria. Most Rev. Louis Tylka, Pst.; Rev. William T. Miller, Rector; Rev. Luke A. Spannagel, Par. Vicar; Dcn. Raymond Toby Tyler; CRP Stds.: 146

St. Ann - 1010 S. Louisa St., Peoria, IL 61605 t) (309) 674-5072 parishoffice@saintannpeoria.com saintannpeoria.com Rev. Jeremy Freehill, Pst.; Dcn. Steve Cenek; CRP Stds.: 44

St. Bernard's - 509 E. Kansas Ave., Peoria, IL 61603; Mailing: 504 Fulton St., Peoria, IL 61602 t) (309) 673-6317 b.stbernards@comcast.net www.catholicpeoria.com This location is commonly "linked" with the following in terms of pastorates: Cathedral of St. Mary of the Immaculate Conception, Peoria; Sacred Heart Rev. William T. Miller, Pst.; Rev. Luke A. Spannagel, Par. Vicar;

Holy Family - 3720 N. Sterling Ave., Peoria, IL 61615 t) (309) 688-3427 x200 parish.office@peoriaholyfamily.com peoriaholyfamily.com Rev. Greg Jozefiak, Pst.; Rev. Bruno Byomuhangi, Par. Vicar; Dcn. Mark Bursott; Dcn. Joseph LaHood;

Holy Family School - (Grades PreK-8) 2329 W. Reservoir, Peoria, IL 61615 t) (309) 688-2931 office@peoriahfs.com school.peoriaholyfamily.com Anastacia Gianessi, Prin.; Stds.: 120; Lay Tchrs.: 11

St. Joseph - 103 Richard Pryor Pl., Peoria, IL 61605; Mailing: 504 Fulton St., Peoria, IL 61602 t) (309) 676-0726 b.stbernards@comcast.net catholicpeoria.com Mission Church of Sacred Heart, Peoria. Commonly "linked" with: St. Bernard, Peoria and Cathedral of St. Mary of the Immaculate Conception, Peoria. Rev. William T. Miller, Pst.; Rev. Luke A. Spannagel, Par. Vicar;

Southside Catholic Child Care Center - 1010 W. Johnson, Peoria, IL 61605

St. Jude - 10811 N. Knoxville Ave., Peoria, IL 61615 t) (309) 243-7811 x2200 stjude@stjudecatholic.com www.stjudechurchpeoria.org Rev. Patrick Henehan, Pst.; Rev. Daniel Patrick McShane, Par. Vicar; Dcn. Jeff Brady; Dcn. Roger Hunter; Rachael Morlock, DRE; CRP Stds.: 180

Dominican Sisters of Mary, Mother of the Eucharist - 10809 N. Knoxville Ave., Peoria, IL 61615 c.brennan@pndhs.org Sr. Catherine Thomas, O.P., Prioress;

St. Jude Catholic School - (Grades PreK-8) 10911 N. Knoxville Ave., Peoria, IL 61615 t) (309) 243-2493 office@stjudecatholic.com stjudecatholic.com Sr. Maria Christi Nelson, O.P., Prin.; Stds.: 280; Sr. Tchrs.: 3; Lay Tchrs.: 14

St. Mark's - 1113 W. Bradley Ave., Peoria, IL 61606-1722 t) (309) 497-2838 (CRP); (309) 673-1263 tmischler@saint-mark.net; stmark@saint-mark.net saint-mark.net Rev. Msgr. Brian Brownsey, Pst.; Dcn. Terry Dixon; Dcn. Thomas Dwyer; Theresa Mischler, DRE; CRP Stds.: 31

St. Mark's School - (Grades PreK-8) 711 N. Underhill, Peoria, IL 61606 t) (309) 676-7131 school.saint-mark.net Dr. Noreen Dillon, Prin.; Stds.: 160; Pr. Tchrs.: 1; Lay Tchrs.: 15

St. Philomena - 1000 W Albany Ave., Peoria, IL 61604-1419 t) (309) 682-8642 parish@stphils.com www.stphils.com Rev. David P. Richardson, Pst.; Rev. Luke A. Spannagel, In Res.; Dcn. Michael C. Schallmoser; Jenny Witt, DRE; CRP Stds.: 45

St. Philomena School - (Grades PreK-8) 3216 N. Emery Ave., Peoria, IL 61604 t) (309) 685-1208 school@stphils.com Jack Dippold, Prin.; Stds.: 501; Lay Tchrs.: 27

Sacred Heart - 504 Fulton St., Peoria, IL 61602 t) (309) 673-6317 b.stbernards@comcast.net catholicpeoria.com This location is commonly "linked" with the following in terms of pastorates: Cathedral of St. Mary of the Immaculate Conception, Peoria; St. Bernard, Rev. William T. Miller, Pst.; Rev. Luke A. Spannagel, Par. Vicar; Dcn. Brian Reynolds;

St. Vincent De Paul - 6001 N. University St., Peoria, IL 61614 t) (309) 691-3602 svdppeoria@hotmail.com svdppeoria.com Rev. Stephen A. Willard, Pst.; Rev. Derick T Mwesiga, Par. Vicar; Dcn. Robert W. Myers Sr.; Taylor Huber, DRE; CRP Stds.: 53

St. Vincent De Paul School - (Grades PreK-8) t) (309) 691-5012 svdpoffice@svdpvikings.com www.svdpvikings.com Sarah Hogan, Prin.; Stds.: 235; Lay Tchrs.: 17

PEORIA HEIGHTS

St. Thomas - 904 E. Lake Ave., Peoria Heights, IL 61616 t) (309) 688-3446 x1300 parishoffice@stthomas-church.net www.stthomaspeoria.org/ Rev. Msgr. Jason A. Gray, Pst.; Rev. Achilleus R Tegamaisho (Tanzania), Par. Vicar; Dcn. Edmund Mallow Jr.; Dcn. John R. Nelson; CRP Stds.: 30

St. Thomas the Apostle School - (Grades PreSchool-8) 4229 N. Monroe Ave., Peoria Heights, IL 61616 t) (309) 685-2533 office@stthomas-school.net school.stthomaspeoria.org Maureen Bentley, Prin.; Stds.: 282; Sr. Tchrs.: 1; Lay Tchrs.: 22

PERU

St. Joseph's - 829 Schuyler St., Peru, IL 61354; Mailing: 1925 5th St., Peru, IL 61354 t) (815) 223-0718 parishoffice@stjoeperu.org stjoeperu.org Rev. Gary W. Blake, Pst.; Rev. Jeffery A. Small, Par. Vicar; Dcn. Thomas L. Jagiella; Dcn. Daniel O'Connor; Kristi Bejster, DRE; CRP Stds.: 110

St. Mary - 1319 Sixth St., Peru, IL 61354; Mailing: 1109 Pulaski St., Peru, IL 61354 t) (815) 223-0315 stvalentineperu@gmail.com This location is commonly "linked" with the following in terms of pastorates: St. Valentine, Peru. Rev. Gary W. Blake, Pst.; Rev. Jeffery A. Small, Par. Vicar; CRP Stds.: 110

St. Valentine - 1109 Pulaski St., Peru, IL 61354 t) 815-223-0315 stvalentineperu@gmail.com This location is commonly "linked" with the following in terms of pastorates: St. Mary, Peru. Rev. Gary W. Blake, Pst.; Rev. Jeffery A. Small, Par. Vicar; CRP Stds.: 103

PESOTUM

St. Mary - 1247 CR 200N, Pesotum, IL 61863; Mailing: P.O. Box 266, Philo, IL 61864 t) (217) 369-8453 (CRP); (217) 684-5107 kthorson@stthomasphilo.org This location is commonly "linked" with the following in terms of pastorates: St. Thomas, Philo. Rev. Keith A. Walder, Pst.; Dcn. Donald P. Koeberlein, DRE;

PHILO

St. Thomas - 312 E. Madison St., Philo, IL 61864; Mailing: P.O. Box 266, Philo, IL 61864 t) (217) 684-5107 kthorson@stthomasphilo.org www.stthomasphilo.org This location is commonly "linked" with the following in terms of pastorates: St. Mary, Pesotum. Rev. Keith A. Walder, Pst.; Dcn. Donald P. Koeberlein, DRE; CRP Stds.: 88

St. Thomas School - (Grades PreSchool-8) 311 E. Madison St., Philo, IL 61864 t) (217) 684-2309 jholmes@stthomasphilo.org school.stthomasphilo.org Stds.: 172; Lay Tchrs.: 13

PONTIAC

St. Mary's - 119 E. Howard St., Pontiac, IL 61764; Mailing: P.O. Box 374, Pontiac, IL 61764 t) (815) 844-7683 zehr.patti@stmaryspontiac.org www.stmaryspontiac.org This location is commonly "linked" with the following in terms of pastorates: St. John, Cullom (closed). Rev. Adam Cesarek, Pst.; Rev. David Sabel, In Res.; Dcn. Ray White; CRP Stds.: 44

St. Mary's School - 414 N. Main St., Pontiac, IL 61764 t) 815-844-6585 jones.karen@stmaryspontiac.org Karen Jones, Prin.; Stds.: 142; Lay Tchrs.: 11

PRINCETON

St. Louis - 616 S. Gosse Blvd., Princeton, IL 61356 t) (815) 879-0181 stlparishoffice@gmail.com stlouisprinceton.org Rev. Msgr. James E. Kruse, Pst.; Dcn. John P. Murphy; CRP Stds.: 80

PRINCEVILLE

St. Mary of the Woods - 119 Saint Mary St., Princeville, IL 61559-9244 t) (309) 385-2578 smowmo@frontier.com; smowccd@yahoo.com www.smowcatholic.com Rev. Corey Krengiel, Pst.; Dcn. Frederick J. Kruse; CRP Stds.: 80

RANSOM

Church of St. Patrick - 110 S. Wallace St., Ransom, IL 60470; Mailing: 200 Broadway St., Marseilles, IL 61341 t) (815) 795-2240 parishgroup3@gmail.com www.ribourdecatholic.com/st-patrick-ransom This location is commonly "linked" with the following in terms of pastorates: St. Patrick, Seneca. Rev. Bowan M. Schmitt, Pst.; Brad Coughlin, DRE;

RANTOUL

St. Malachy R.C. Congregation - 311 E. Grove Ave, Rantoul, IL 61866; Mailing: 340 E. Belle Ave., Ste. 1, Rantoul, IL 61866 t) (217) 892-2044 donnaa@stmalachyschool.org sms217.org This location is commonly "linked" with the following in terms of pastorates: St. Elizabeth of Hungary, Thomasboro. Rev. Joel Phelps, Pst.; Dcn. Guadalupe I. Lopez; CRP Stds.: 34

St. Malachy School - (Grades PreK-8) 340 E. Belle Ave., Rantoul, IL 61866 t) (217) 892-2011 stmalachyschool.org Sandra Davis, Prin.; Stds.: 168; Lay Tchrs.: 12

RAPIDS CITY

St. John the Baptist - 1416 3rd Ave., Rapids City, IL 61278-0250; Mailing: P.O. Box 250, Rapids City, IL 61278-0250 t) (309) 496-2414 stjohnstmaryqc.org This location is commonly "linked" with the following in terms of pastorates: St. Mary, Hampton. Rev. Glenn Harris, Pst.; Dcn. Robert DePauw; Rose Roe, DRE; CRP Stds.: 39

Linked Parish: St. Mary - 708 State St., Hampton, IL 61256

ROANOKE

St. Joseph - 508 W. Randolph St., Roanoke, IL 61561; Mailing: P.O. Box 226, Eureka, IL 61530 t) (309) 467-4855 saintluke.eureka@gmail.com www.stsjlj.com This location is commonly "linked" with the following in terms of pastorates: St. Luke, Eureka. Rev. Ryan Mattingly, Pst.; CRP Stds.: 20

ROCK ISLAND

St. Mary - 2208 4th Ave., Rock Island, IL 61201; Mailing: 2810 5th Ave., Rock Island, IL 61201 t) (309) 788-3322 stmarysrockisland@gmail.com www.stmaryri.com This location is commonly "linked" with the following in terms of pastorates: Sacred Heart, Rock Island. Rev. Witold Adamczyk, O.F.M.Conv. (Poland), Pst.; CRP Stds.: 8

St. Pius X - 2502 29th Ave., Rock Island, IL 61201 t) (309) 793-7373 parishoffice@stpiusri.org www.stpiusri.org Rev. Piotr Sarnicki, O.F.M.Conv. (Poland), Pst.; Rev. Witold Adamczyk, O.F.M.Conv. (Poland), In Res.; Dcn. Joseph Dockery-Jackson; Dcn. Russ W. Swim; CRP Stds.: 88

Sacred Heart - 2810 5th Ave., Rock Island, IL 61201 t) 309-794-0660 shrec@sacredheartri.com www.sacredheartri.com This location is commonly "linked" with the following in terms of pastorates: St. Mary, Rock Island. Rev. Witold Adamczyk, O.F.M.Conv. (Poland), Pst.; CRP Stds.: 4

RUSHVILLE

St. Rose - 319 N. Franklin St., Rushville, IL 62681-0292; Mailing: 309 W. Jackson St., Macomb, IL 61455 t) (309) 833-2496 churchoffice@stpaulmacomb.com stroserushville.com/ This location is commonly "linked" with the following in terms of pastorates: St. Paul, Macomb. Rev. Adam Stimpson, Pst.; Rev. Joseph Domfe, SMA (Ghana), Par. Vicar; CRP Stds.: 9

SENECA

St. Patrick's - 176 W. Union St., Seneca, IL 61360; Mailing: 200 Broadway St., Marseilles, IL 61341 t) (815) 357-6239 parishgroup3@gmail.com www.stpatricksenecail.org/ This location is commonly "linked" with the following in terms of pastorates: St. Patrick, Ransom. Rev. Bowan M. Schmitt, Pst.; Jennifer Doloski, DRE; CRP Stds.: 86

SEYMOUR

St. Boniface - 416 County Rd. 1100 N., Seymour, IL 61875 t) (217) 863-2190 mmoconnor1120@gmail.com This location is commonly "linked" with the following in terms of pastorates: St. Matthew, Champaign. Rev. Msgr. Stanley L. Deptula, Pst.; Rev. Andru O'Brien, Par. Vicar; Rev. Alou Pilizue, SMA (Togo), Par. Vicar; CRP Stds.: 10

SHEFFIELD

St. Patrick's - 231 W. Atkinson St., Sheffield, IL 61361-0038; Mailing: P.O. Box 514, Sheffield, IL 61361-0038 t) (815) 454-8062 stpatssheffield@mediacombb.net stpatssheffield.org Rev. Mark O. Miller, Pst.; Mary Ann Cernovich, DRE; Amy Wright, DRE; CRP Stds.: 15

SILVIS

Our Lady of Guadalupe - 800-17th St., Silvis, IL 61282 t) (309) 792-3867 olgsilvissec@gmail.com www.olgsilvis.com This location is commonly "linked" with the following in terms of pastorates: St. Patrick, Colona. Rev. Peter Zorjan, Pst.; Rose Roe, DRE; CRP Stds.: 5

SPRING VALLEY

Parish of the Nativity of Our Lord Roman Catholic Congregation - 510 Richard A. Mautino Dr., Spring Valley, IL 61362-0150; Mailing: P.O. Box 150, Spring Valley, IL 61362 t) (815) 663-3731 www.nativitysv.org Rev. Scott Potthoff, Pst.; Dcn. Dennis J. Gillan; Dcn. Jack Kusek; CRP Stds.: 58

ST. AUGUSTINE

St. Augustine - 103 State Route 41, St. Augustine, IL 61474; Mailing: 376 W. Hail, Bushnell, IL 61422 t) (309) 772-2333 st.bbushnell@gmail.com (Linked Parish: St. Bernard, Bushnell) Rev. Eugene A. Radosevich, Pst.; CRP Stds.: 15

STREATOR

St. Michael the Archangel Parish - 513 S. Shabbona St., Streator, IL 61364 t) (815) 672-2474; (815) 672-5911 (CRP) parishoffice@stmichael-streator.org www.stmichael-streator.org This location is commonly "linked" with the following in terms of pastorates: Sts. Peter and Paul, Leonore. Rev. Msgr. Philip D. Halfacre, Pst.; Rev. Austin Lee Bosse, Par. Vicar; CRP Stds.: 148

St. Michael the Archangel School - (Grades PreK-8) 410 S. Park St., Streator, IL 61364 t) (815) 672-3847 info@stmichael-streator.org www.stmichael-streator.org/ Emily Blumenshine, Prin.; Stds.: 148; Lay Tchrs.: 14

TAYLOR RIDGE

St. Patrick Church - 9619 140th St. W., Taylor Ridge, IL 61284; Mailing: Box 249, Andalusia, IL 61232 t) (309) 798-2098 andalusiapat1@gmail.com saintpatrickandalusia.org/ Rev. Joseph Baker, Pst.; CRP Stds.: 25

THOMASBORO

St. Elizabeth of Hungary - 100 Church St., Thomasboro, IL 61878; Mailing: P.O. Box 307, Thomasboro, IL 61878 t) (217) 643-3395 This location is commonly "linked" with the following in terms of pastorates: St. Malachy, Rantoul. Rev. Joel Phelps, Pst.;

TISKILWA

St. Mary - 121 W. Main St., Tiskilwa, IL 61368; Mailing: P.O. Box 271, Tiskilwa, IL 61368 t) (815) 447-2552 frcreegan@netscape.net This location is commonly "linked" with the following in terms of pastorates: St. Mary, DePue. Rev. Kevin G. Creegan, Pst.;

TOLONO

St. Patrick - 212 E. Washington St., Tolono, IL 61880; Mailing: P.O. Box K, Tolono, IL 61880 t) (217) 485-1129 officeofstp@gmail.com stpatricktolono.com This location is commonly "linked" with the following in terms of pastorates: St. Joseph, Ivesdale. Rev. Patrick O'Neal; CRP Stds.: 11

TOLUCA

St. Ann Parish - 311 W. Santa Fe Ave., Toluca, IL 61369; Mailing: 207 W. 3rd St. S., Wenona, IL 61377 t) (815) 853-4558 smary1867@mchsi.com www.4saints.org/ This location is commonly "linked" with the following in terms of pastorates: St. John the Baptist, Lostant; St. Patrick, Minonk; and St. Mary, Wenona Rev. Patrick Greenough, O.F.M.Conv., Pst.; Rev. Stephen McKinley, O.F.M.Conv., In Res.; Sandi Long, DRE; CRP Stds.: 25

TONICA

SS. Peter and Paul's - Rt. 1, 957 N. 17th Rd., Tonica, IL 61370; Mailing: 513 S. Shabbona St., Streator, IL 61364 t) (815) 672-2474 parishoffice@stmichael-streator.org Rev. Msgr. Philip D. Halfacre, Pst.; Rev. Austin Lee Bosse, Par. Vicar; Dcn. Robb Caputo;

URBANA

St. Patrick - 708 W. Main St., Urbana, IL 61801 t) (217) 367-2665 secretary@stpaturbana.org stpaturbana.org Rev. Anthony Co, Pst.; Dcn. Clifford Maduzia; Jonathan McCoy, DRE; Jaclyn Grandone, Bus. Mgr.; CRP Stds.: 90

UTICA

St. Mary - 303 S. Division St., Utica, IL 61373; Mailing: P.O. Box 159, Utica, IL 61373 t) (815) 667-4677 office@stmaryutica.org stmarysutica.org Rev. Michael J. Driscoll, Pst.; Heather Leffers, DRE; CRP Stds.: 38

WALNUT

St. John the Evangelist - 204 N. Main St., Walnut, IL 61376-0370; Mailing: P.O. Box 370, Walnut, IL 61376 t) (815) 379-2602 This location is commonly "linked" with the following in terms of pastorates: Immaculate Conception, Ohio. Rev. Thomas Shaw, Pst.; CRP Stds.: 11

WAPELLA

St. Patrick Church - 320 S. Locust St., Wapella, IL 61777; Mailing: P.O. Box 116, Wapella, IL 61777 t) (217) 935-8510 stpatrickwapella@yahoo.com www.saintpatrickwapella.org Rev. Geoffrey Horton, Pst.; Dcn. Todd Weber; CRP Stds.: 48

WARSAW

Sacred Heart - 245 S. 9th St., Warsaw, IL 62379; Mailing: P.O. Box 93, Warsaw, IL 62379 t) (217) 256-3657; (217) 453-2428 (Nauvoo Office) warsaw@hancockcountycatholic.org www.hancockcountycatholic.org Commonly "linked" with: Immaculate Conception, Carthage; Sacred Heart, Dallas City; St. Mary, Hamilton; and Sts. Peter and Paul, Nauvoo. Rev. Anthony J. Trosley, Pst.; CRP Stds.: 18

WASHINGTON

St. Patrick's - 705 E. Jefferson, Washington, IL 61571 t) (309) 444-3524 prattl@stpatswashington.com; churchoffice@stpatswashington.com stpatswashington.com This location is commonly "linked" with the following in terms of pastorates: St. Monica, East Peoria. Rev. Jonathan Steffen, Pst.; Rev. John Bazimenyera (Uganda), Par. Vicar; Dcn. Paul Neakrase; Linda Pratt, DRE; CRP Stds.: 144

St. Patrick's School - (Grades PreK-8) 100 N. Harvey St., Washington, IL 61571 t) (309) 444-4345 schooloffice@stpatswashington.com www.stpatswashington.com Doreen Shipman, Prin.; Stds.: 144; Lay Tchrs.: 14

WEDRON

St. Joseph's - 2027 N. 3372nd Rd., Wedron, IL 61350; Mailing: 3609 E. 2351st Rd., Serena, IL 60549 t) (815) 792-2622 cberkshier@cdop.org Rev. John G. Waugh, Pst.;

WENONA

St. Mary's - 207 W. Third St. S., Wenona, IL 61377 t) (815) 853-4558 smary1867@mchsi.com www.4saints.org/ This location is commonly "linked" with the following in terms of pastorates: St. John the Baptist, Lostant; St. Patrick, Minonk; and St. Ann, Toluca. Rev. Patrick Greenough, O.F.M.Conv., Pst.; Rev. Stephen McKinley, O.F.M.Conv., In Res.; Sandi Long, DRE; CRP Stds.: 55

WESTVILLE

St. Mary's - 231 N. State St., Westville, IL 61883 t) (217) 267-3334 stmary1903@yahoo.com www.catholic-church.org/~westvillestmarys/ (Linked Parish: St. Isaac Jogues, Georgetown) Rev. Timothy J. Sauppe, Pst.; Laura DeAth, DRE; CRP Stds.: 14

WOODHULL

St. John's - 390 E. Highway Ave., Woodhull, IL 61490; Mailing: P.O. Box 249, Woodhull, IL 61490 t) (309) 334-2180 stjohnchurch@divcominc.net www.threestjohns.com/ This location is commonly "linked" with the following in terms of pastorates: St. John Paul II, Kewanee; St. John Vianney, Cambridge; and St. John the Rev. Johndamaseni Zilimu, Pst.; Rev. Christopher Magesa (Tanzania), Par. Vicar; Dcn. Joseph O'Tool; CRP Stds.: 41

Linked Parish: St. John Vianney - 313 S. West St., Cambridge, IL 61238; Mailing: P.O. Box 183, Cambridge, IL 61238 t) (309) 937-3304 stjohnvianney3@gmail.com www.threestjohns.com

WYOMING

St. Dominic's - 303 N. Galena Ave., Wyoming, IL 61491 t) (309) 695-4031 starkcatholic@gmail.com starkcountycatholic.com/ This location is commonly "linked" with the following in terms of pastorates: St. John the Baptist, Bradford. Rev. John Cyr, Pst.; CRP Stds.: 30

SCHOOLS: PRESCHOOL THRU HIGH SCHOOL

SCHOOLS

STATE OF ILLINOIS

BLOOMINGTON

Corpus Christi Catholic School of Bloomington Inc. - (DIO) (Grades PreK-8) 1909 E. Lincoln St., Bloomington, IL 61701 t) (309) 662-3712 awilson@corpuschristisaints.org www.corpuschristisaints.org Adrienne Wilson, Prin.; Stds.: 472; Lay Tchrs.: 33

EAST MOLINE

Our Lady of Grace Catholic Academy - (PAR) (Grades PreK-8) 603 18th Ave., East Moline, IL 61244 t) 309-755-9771 office@olgca.org www.olgca.org Stds.: 106; Sr. Tchrs.: 1; Lay Tchrs.: 10

LASALLE

Trinity Catholic Academy - (PAR) (Grades PreK-8) 650 Fourth St., LaSalle, IL 61301 t) (815) 223-8523 dmyers@lasallecatholic.org www.asd.com Deb Myers, Prin.; Stds.: 146; Lay Tchrs.: 11

MOLINE

Seton Catholic School - (PAR) (Grades PreK-8) 1320 16th & 17th Ave., Moline, IL 61265 t) (309) 757-5500; (309) 764-5418 office@setonschool.com www.setonschool.com Jane Barrett, Prin.; Stds.: 437; Lay Tchrs.: 21

ROCK ISLAND

Jordan Catholic School of Rock Island, Inc. - (DIO) (Grades PreK-8) 2901-24th St., Rock Island, IL 61201 t) (309) 793-7350 karmetta@jordanschool.com www.jordanschool.com Directs the Elementary School System for the Rock Island-Milan area, operating facilities at St. Pius X. Parishes in Rock Island. Kelly McLaughlin, Prin.; Stds.: 317; Sr. Tchrs.: 1; Lay Tchrs.: 23

Commission on Education for Jordan Catholic School - 2901 24th St., Rock Island, IL 61201 jordanschool.com

HIGH SCHOOLS

STATE OF ILLINOIS

BLOOMINGTON

Central Catholic High School - (DIO) (Grades 9-12) 1201 Airport Rd., Bloomington, IL 61704-2534 t) (309) 661-7000 sfoster@blmcchs.org; cmcgraw@blmcchs.org www.blmcchs.org Sean Foster, Pres.; Christopher McGraw, Prin.; Rev. Geoffrey Horton, Chap.; Stds.: 275; Lay Tchrs.: 23

CHAMPAIGN

High School of St. Thomas More - (DIO) (Grades 9-12) 3901 N. Mattis Ave., Champaign, IL 61822 t) (217) 352-7210 srmbridget@hs-stm.org www.hs-stm.org Rev. Andru O'Brien, Chap.; Sr. M. Bridget Martin, FSGM, Prin.; Stds.: 210; Pr. Tchrs.: 1; Sr. Tchrs.: 2; Lay Tchrs.: 20

DANVILLE

Schlarman Academy - (DIO) (Grades K-12) 2112 N. Vermilion St., Danville, IL 61832 t) (217) 442-3880 x201 brew@schlarman.com www.schlarmanacademy.com Rev. Thomas R. Szydlik, Chap.; Barb Rew, Prin.; Stds.: 431; Lay Tchrs.: 13

OTTAWA

Marquette Academy of Ottawa, Inc. - (DIO) (Grades PreSchool-12) 1000 Paul St., 1110 LaSalle St., Ottawa, IL 61350 t) (815) 433-0125 brick@marquetteacademy.net marquetteacademy.net Brooke Rick, Prin.; Rev. Austin Lee Bosse, Chap.; Stds.: 392; Pr. Tchrs.: 4; Lay Tchrs.: 30

PEORIA

Peoria Notre Dame High School - (DIO) (Grades 9-12) 5105 N. Sheridan Rd., Peoria, IL 61614 t) (309) 691-8741 g.mcinnis@pndhs.org pndhs.org Dr. Susie Cicciarelli, Prin.; Grant McInnis, COO; Tim Speck, Dean; Rev. Daniel Patrick McShane, Chap.; Rev. Luke A. Spannagel, Chap.; Stds.: 476; Sr. Tchrs.: 2; Lay Tchrs.: 35

Peoria Notre Dame Scholarship Trust - 5105 N. Sheridan Rd., Peoria, IL 61614

Peoria Notre Dame High School Foundation - 5105 N. Sheridan Rd., Peoria, IL 61614

PERU

St. Bede Academy (Benedictine Fathers and Brothers) - (PRV) (Grades 9-12) 24 W. U.S. Hwy. 6, Peru, IL 61354-2903 t) (815) 223-3140 mamershon@st-bede.com www.st-bede.com Rev. Ronald L. Margherio, O.S.B., Chap.; Eve Postula, Supt.; Michelle Mershon, Prin.; Rev. Dominic M. Garramone, O.S.B., Exec.; Theresa Bernabei, Dir.; Stds.: 280; Lay Tchrs.: 22

ROCK ISLAND

Alleman High School - (DIO) (Grades 9-12) 1103 40th St., Rock Island, IL 61201 t) (309) 786-7793 alleman@allemanhighschool.org www.allemanhighschool.org Rev. Daniel J. Mirabelli, C.S.V., Dir.; Stds.: 262; Sr. Tchrs.: 2; Lay Tchrs.: 19

INSTITUTIONS LOCATED IN DIOCESE

ASSOCIATIONS [ASN]

BLOOMINGTON

Bloomington-Normal Catholic Cemetery Association - 711 N. Main St., Bloomington, IL 61701 t) (309) 829-3019; (309) 807-0338 businessmgr@holytrinitybloomington.org Rev. Jeffrey D. Stirniman, Pst.; Elaine Rinehimer, Bus. Mgr.; Ellen Schroeder, Cemetery Coord.;

DANVILLE

Resurrection Catholic Cemetery Association of Danville, IL - 813 Wendt Ave., Danville, IL 61832; Mailing: 444 E. Main St., Danville, IL 61832 t) (217) 431-5114 cemetery@holyfamilydanville.net Mike O'Kane, Trustee;

FARMER CITY

St. Joseph Cemetery Association of Farmer City, IL - 612 N. Plum St., Farmer City, IL 61842; Mailing: 502 N. Monroe St., Clinton, IL 61727 t) (309) 928-3855 shchurch612@frontier.com Rev. James Owusu Yeboah, SMA (Ghana);

GALESBURG

St. Joseph's Cemetery Association of Galesburg, IL - 2315 Monmouth Blvd., Galesburg, IL 61401; Mailing: 273 S. Prairie St., Galesburg, IL 61401 t) (309) 342-8256; (309) 342-1913 kemlars@gmail.com; adorecc7@gmail.com Rev. William T. Miller, Admin.;

PEKIN

Catholic Cemetery Association of Pekin, IL - 5th St. & Hanna Dr., Pekin, IL 61554; Mailing: 303 S. 7th St., Pekin, IL 61554 t) (309) 347-6108 stjoseph@stjosephpekin.org; catholiccemeteries@stjosephpekin.org Rev. Michael J. Andrejek; Dcn. Mark Wilder, Dir.;

PEORIA

Catholic Cemetery Association of Peoria, IL - 7519 N. Allen, Peoria, IL 61614 t) (309) 691-5889 dvalentine@ccapeo.org www.ccapeo.org Operates St. Mary's Cemetery, St. Joseph's Cemetery and Resurrection Cemetery & Mausoleum in Peoria. Dr. Diane Valentine, Dir.;

ROCK ISLAND

Calvary Cemetery Association of Rock Island, IL - 2901-12th St., Rock Island, IL 61201 t) (309) 788-6197 info@calvarycemetaryri.com www.calvarycemetaryri.com Greg Vogele, Supt.;

CAMPUS MINISTRY / NEWMAN CENTERS [CAM]

CHAMPAIGN

Newman Foundation at the University of IL (St. John's Catholic Newman Center) - 604 E. Armory Ave., Champaign, IL 61820 t) (217) 344-1266 www.sjcnc.org Rev. Robert Lampitt, Chap.; Rev. Alexander Millar, Par. Vicar; Rev. Matthew Hoelscher, Par. Vicar;

EUREKA

Salve Regina Newman Foundation - 108 E. College Ave., Eureka, IL 61530; Mailing: P.O. Box 226, Eureka, IL 61530 t) (309) 467-4855 saintluke.eureka@gmail.com www.stsjlj.com/newman-center Rev. Ryan Mattingly, Dir.;

MACOMB

St. Francis of Assisi Newman Center - 1401 W. University Dr., Macomb, IL 61455 t) (309) 837-3989 wiucatholic@gmail.com www.wiucatholic.org Rev. Adam Stimpson, Chap.; Rev. Joseph Domfe, SMA (Ghana), Chap.; Beate Wilson, Dir.;

MONMOUTH

St. Augustine Newman Club - 502 N. 6th St., Monmouth, IL 61462; Mailing: 200 W. Broadway, Monmouth, IL 61462 t) (309) 734-7533 frhepner@immaculate-conception.net iccmonmouth.org/st-augustine-newman-center Rev. Timothy Hepner, Chap.;

NORMAL

St. John Paul II Catholic Newman Center, St. Robert Bellarmine Chapel - 501 S. Main St., Normal, IL 61761 t) (309) 452-5046 office@stjpnc.org www.isucatholic.org Rev. Kyle Lucas, Pst.;

PEORIA

Augustana College Catholic Campus Ministry - 419 NE Madison Ave., Peoria, IL 61603 t) (309) 671-1550 cberkshier@cdop.org Patricia Gibson, Chancellor;

Franciscan Spirituality and Resource Center - 2408 W. Heading Ave., Peoria, IL 61604 t) (309) 674-6168 srdiane2408@gmail.com westpeoriasisters.org Sr. Betty Jean Haverback, O.S.F., Contact; Sr. Diane VandeVoorde, O.S.F., Contact;

Monsignor Duncan College Campus Ministry, NFP - 419 N.E. Madison Ave., Peoria, IL 61603 t) (309) 671-1550 Mike Buckley, Contact;

Newman Foundation at Bradley University & Illinois Central College - 1116 W. College St., Peoria, IL 61606-1728 t) (309) 674-0208 stjosephnewman@gmail.com ncbu.org Rev. Msgr. Brian Brownsey, Chap.; Sara Petty, Campus Min.;

CATHOLIC CHARITIES [CCH]

PEORIA

Catholic Charities of the Diocese of Peoria - 419 N.E. Madison Ave., Peoria, IL 61603 t) 309-636-8000 www.ccdop.org Child Care, Food Pantry, Baby Pantry, Furniture Bank, Soup Kitchen, Senior Counseling Services, Senior Support Services, Family & Community Outreach. Suzie Meismer, Admin.; Asstd. Annu.: 10,000; Staff: 8

Catholic Charities Branch Offices - 419 N.E. Madison Ave., Peoria, IL 61603 t) (309) 671-1550 Susie Meismer, Spiritual Adv./Care Srvcs.;

Guardian Angel Outreach - 111 Spring St., Streator, IL 61364; Mailing: 513 S. Shabbona St., Streator, IL 61364 t) (815) 673-3966 Linda Volkman, Contact;

CONVENTS, MONASTERIES, AND RESIDENCES FOR WOMEN [CON]

EAST PEORIA

St. Francis Medical Center Convent - 1175 St. Francis Ln., East Peoria, IL 61611 t) (309) 655-2083; (309) 655-4840 robert.brandfass@osfhealthcare.org franciscansisterspeoria.org Sr. Agnes Joseph Williams, O.S.F., Dir.; Srs.: 5

***Motherhouse, The Sisters of the Third Order of St. Francis** - 1175 St. Francis Ln., East Peoria, IL 61611-1299 t) (309) 699-7215 robert.brandfass@osfhealthcare.org www.franciscansisterspeoria.org Sr. Judith Ann Duvall,

O.S.F., Supr.; Srs.: 20
Mt. Alverno Novitiate (Novitiate of The Sisters of the Third Order of St. Francis) - 1175 St. Francis Ln., East Peoria, IL 61611-1299 t) (309) 699-9313 robert.brandfass@osfhealthcare.org www.franciscansisterspeoria.org Sr. Rose Therese Mann, OSF, Admin.; Srs.: 2
LACON
St. Joseph Motherhouse and Novitiate - 507 N. Prairie St., Lacon, IL 61540 t) (309) 246-6783 dsfcongregation@gmail.com www.laconfranciscans.org Sr. Miroslava Loretta Gelatikova, DSF, Supr.; Sr. Loretta Matas, D.S.F., Supr.; Srs.: 10
PEORIA
Franciscan Apostolic Sisters - 600 N.E. Monroe St., Peoria, IL 61603; Mailing: 66 5th Ave., East Greenwich, RI 02818 t) (401) 336-3145 srloufas@yahoo.com Sr. Magdalena Obispo, FAS, Supr.; Srs.: 7
Missionaries of Charity Convent - 506 Hancock St., Peoria, IL 61603 t) (309) 495-9490 Sr. M. Zita MC, Supr.; Sr. M. Jonathan, MC, Regl. Supr.; Srs.: 4
PEORIA HEIGHTS
Franciscan Sisters of John the Baptist - 1209 E. Lake Ave., Peoria Heights, IL 61616 t) 309-688-3500 fsjbpeoria@yahoo.com www.sistersofjohnthebaptist.org Mother M. Vaclava Ballon, F.S.J.B., Supr.; Srs.: 7
PRINCEVILLE
Apostolic Sisters of St. John - 10809 W. Legion Hall Rd., Princeville, IL 61559 t) (309) 243-1488 sr.ap.princeville@stjean.com www.apostolicsistersofsaintjohn.com Sr. Marie de Ravinel, C.S.J., Prioress; Srs.: 3
Contemplative Sisters of St. John - 11227 W. Legion Hall Rd., St. Therese Convent, Princeville, IL 61559 t) 309-385-2550 c) (309) 215-2360 srs.princeville@gmail.com www.stjohncontemplativesisters.com Sr. Michelle Marie Evinger, Supr.; Srs.: 3
ROCK ISLAND
St. Mary Monastery (Benedictine Sisters) - 2200 88th Ave. W., Rock Island, IL 61201-7649 t) (309) 283-2100 benedictines@smmsisters.org www.smmsisters.org Sr. Susan Hutchens, O.S.B., Prioress; Srs.: 19
Benet House Retreat Center - 2200 88th Ave W., Rock Island, IL 61201 t) (309) 283-2108 retreats@smmsisters.org Sr. Roberta Bussan, O.S.B., Dir.;
WEST PEORIA
Emmaus House - 2327 W. Heading Ave., West Peoria, IL 61604 c) 309-573-6043 sranapia@piercedhearts.org www.piercedhearts.org
Immaculate Conception Convent - 2408 W. Heading Ave., West Peoria, IL 61604-5096 t) (309) 674-6168 kamourisse@gmail.com westpeoriasisters.org Motherhouse of the Sisters of St. Francis of the Immaculate Conception. Sr. Kathleen Ann Mourisse, Pres.; Srs.: 25

ENDOWMENTS / FOUNDATIONS / TRUSTS [EFT]

LACON
St. Francis of Assisi Fund, NFP - 507 N. Prairie St., Lacon, IL 61540-1152 t) (309) 246-6783 dsfcongregation@gmail.com www.laconfranciscans.org Sr. Loretta Matas, D.S.F., Pres.;
PEORIA
Archbishop Fulton J. Sheen Foundation - 419 N.E. Madison, Peoria, IL 61603 t) (309) 671-1550 info@celebratesheen.com www.archbishopsheencause.org Most Rev. Louis Tylka, Pres.; Rev. Msgr. Stanley L. Deptula, Exec.;
John Lancaster Spalding Scholarship Fund, NFP - 419 N.E. Madison Ave., Peoria, IL 61603 t) (309) 671-1550 mbuckley@cdop.org Mike Buckley, Contact;
St. Therese Seminarian Foundation, NFP - 419 N.E. Madison Ave., Peoria, IL 61603 t) (309) 671-1550 Mike Buckley, Contact;

HOSPITALS / HEALTH SERVICES [HOS]

BLOOMINGTON
OSF HealthCare St. Joseph Medical Center - 2200 E. Washington, Bloomington, IL 61701 t) (309) 662-3311 robert.brandfass@osfhealthcare.org osfhealthcare.org Sponsored and owned by the Sisters of the Third Order of St. Francis. Rev. Rogers Byambaasa, A.J., Chap.; Lynn Fulton, Pres.; Bed Capacity: 149; Asstd. Annu.: 265,894; Staff: 934
DANVILLE
OSF HealthCare Sacred Heart Medical Center (Presence Central and Suburban Hospitals Network d/b/a Presence United Samaritans Medical Center) - 812 N. Logan, Danville, IL 61832 t) (217) 443-5000 robert.brandfass@osfhealthcare.org www.osfhealthcare.org Rev. Deusdedit Byomuhangi, Chap.; Philip Jackson, Chap.; Andrew Martin, Chap.; Timothy Shaw, Chap.; Ron Ziemer, Chap.; Earl Hill, Pres.; Bed Capacity: 174; Asstd. Annu.: 82,524; Staff: 565
EAST PEORIA
OSF HealthCare Saint Francis Medical Center - 1175 St. Francis Ln., East Peoria, IL 61611 t) (309) 655-2000 robert.brandfass@osfhealthcare.org osfhealthcare.org Sponsored and owned by the Sisters of the Third Order of St. Francis. Rev. Dennis Spohrer, Chap.; Rev. Fredi Gomeztorres, Chap.; Rev. John Twinomujuni, Chap.; Robert G Anderson, Pres.; Bed Capacity: 629; Asstd. Annu.: 84,575; Staff: 5,987
GALESBURG
OSF HealthCare St. Mary Medical Center - 3333 N. Seminary St., Galesburg, IL 61401-1299 t) (309) 344-3161 robert.brandfass@osfhealthcare.org osfhealthcare.org Rev. Deus-Dedit B. Byabato, Chap.; Lisa DeKezel, Pres.; Dcn. David Steeples, Dir.; Bed Capacity: 81; Asstd. Annu.: 19,725; Staff: 581
The Galesburg St. Mary Medical Center Foundation - 3333 N. Seminary St., Galesburg, IL 61401-1299; Mailing: 530 N.E. Glen Oak Ave., Peoria, IL 61637 t) (877) 574-5678 Thomas Hammerton, Pres.;
KEWANEE
OSF HealthCare Saint Luke Medical Center - 1501 W. South St., Kewanee, IL 61443; Mailing: P.O. Box 747, Kewanee, IL 61443 t) (309) 852-7500 robert.brandfass@osfhealthcare.org osfhealthcare.org Rev. Johndamaseni Zilimu, Chap.; Jackie Kernan, Pres.; Bed Capacity: 25; Asstd. Annu.: 94,725; Staff: 224
MENDOTA
Mendota Community Hospital (OSF HealthCare Saint Paul Medical Center) - 1401 E. 12th St., Mendota, IL 61342 t) (815) 539-7461 www.osfhealthcare.org/saint-paul/ Dawn Trompeter, Pres.; Bed Capacity: 25; Asstd. Annu.: 95,525; Staff: 220
MONMOUTH
OSF HealthCare Holy Family Medical Center - 1000 W. Harlem Ave., Monmouth, IL 61462-1099 t) (309) 734-3141 robert.brandfass@osfhealthcare.org osfhealthcare.org Rev. Thomas Otto, Chap.; Jackie Kernan, Pres.; Bed Capacity: 25; Asstd. Annu.: 95,525; Staff: 224
OTTAWA
***OSF HealthCare Saint Elizabeth Medical Center** - 1100 E. Norris Dr., Ottawa, IL 61350 t) (815) 433-3100 robert.brandfass@osfhealthcare.org www.ottawaregional.org Owned by Ottawa Regional Hospital & Healthcare Center. Sponsored by The Sisters of the Third Order of St. Francis. Rev. Michael J. Driscoll, Dir.; Dawn Trompeter, Pres.; Bed Capacity: 97; Asstd. Annu.: 18,425; Staff: 742
PEORIA
OSF Healthcare System - 124 S.W. Adams St., Peoria, IL 61602 t) (309) 655-2850 robert.brandfass@osfhealthcare.org www.osfhealthcare.org Sponsored and owned by the Sisters of the Third Order of St. Francis. Robert Sehring, CEO; Bed Capacity: 2,098; Asstd. Annu.: 391,425; Staff: 23,475
***OSF Multi-Specialty Group** - 800 N.E. Glen Oak Ave., Peoria, IL 61603 t) (309) 655-2850 robert.brandfass@osfhealthcare.org Jeffry Tillery, Pres.; Asstd. Annu.: 825,450; Staff: 4,208
PONTIAC
OSF HealthCare Saint James-John W. Albrecht Medical Center - 2500 W. Reynolds, Pontiac, IL 61764 t) (815) 842-2828 robert.brandfass@osfhealthcare.org osfhealthcare.org Sponsored and owned by the Sisters of the Third Order of St. Francis. Bradley V. Solberg, Pres.; Dcn. George Wagner, Dir.; Bed Capacity: 42; Asstd. Annu.: 174,235; Staff: 335
PRINCETON
OSF HealthCare Saint Clare Medical Center - 530 Park Ave., E., Princeton, IL 61356 t) (815) 875-2811 osfhealthcare.org Jackie Kernan, Pres.; Bed Capacity: 25; Asstd. Annu.: 92,350; Staff: 212
SPRING VALLEY
St. Margaret's Health - 600 E. First St., Spring Valley, IL 61362 t) (815) 664-5311 administration@aboutsmh.org www.aboutsmh.org A ministry of SMP Health, sponsored by the Sisters of Mary of the Presentation Health Ministry, a Public Juridic Person. Timothy Muntz, Pres.; Dcn. John P. Murphy; Bed Capacity: 34; Asstd. Annu.: 304,390; Staff: 689
STREATOR
St. Mary's Hospital (Hospital Sisters Third Order of St. Francis) - 111 Spring St., Streator, IL 61364 t) (815) 673-2311 robert.brandfass@osfhealthcare.org www.osfhealthcare.org/streator Operated as an outpatient facility only. Ken Beutke, Pres.;
URBANA
OSF HealthCare Heart of Mary Medical Center (Presence Central and Suburban Hospitals Network) - 1400 W. Park St., Urbana, IL 61801 t) (217) 337-2000 robert.brandfass@osfhealthcare.org www.osfhealthcare.org Rev. Edward U. Ohm, Chap.; Erin Rogers, Pres.; Bed Capacity: 210; Asstd. Annu.: 115,350; Staff: 762

MISCELLANEOUS [MIS]

ALEDO
Family of Mary - 1331 230th St., Aledo, IL 61231 t) (309) 372-4654 c) (563) 940-1249 scott_triumph@yahoo.com Scott White, Pres.;
BLOOMINGTON
Central Catholic High School of Bloomington, Inc. - 1201 Airport Rd., Bloomington, IL 61704 t) (309) 661-7000 sfoster@blmcchs.org; cmcgraw@blmcchs.org blmcchs.org Rev. Geoffrey Horton, Chap.; Sean Foster, Pres.; Christopher McGraw, Prin.;
CHAMPAIGN
Presence Home Care - 1501 Interstate Dr., Champaign, IL 61822 t) (217) 355-4120 john.halstead1@ascension.org www.ascension.org Polly Davenport, COO; John Halstead, CMIO;
STM Boosters, Inc. - 3901 N. Mattis Ave., Champaign, IL 61822 t) (217) 352-7210 mvandervennet@hs-stm.org www.hs-stm.org Sr. M. Bridget Martin, FSGM, Admin.;
The High School of St. Thomas More of Champaign, Inc. - 3901 N. Mattis Ave., Champaign, IL 61822 t) (217) 352-7210 srmbridget@hs-stm.org www.hs-stm.org Sr. M. Bridget Martin, FSGM, Prin.; Rev. Andru O'Brien, Chap.;
weDignify - 604 E. Armory Ave., Champaign, IL 61820 t) (217) 255-6675 info@wedignify.org www.wedignify.org Anna Kinskey, Exec. Dir.;
DANVILLE
Schlarman Academy of Danville, Inc. - 2112 N. Vermilion, Danville, IL 61832 t) (217) 442-3880 x201 brew@schlarman.com www.schlarmanacademy.com Rev. Thomas R. Szydlik, Chap.; Barb Rew, Admin.;
LACON
Religious Sisters Aid, NFP - 507 N. Prairie St., Lacon, IL 61540-1152 t) (309) 246-6783 dsfcongregation@gmail.com laconfranciscans.org Sr. Loretta Matas, D.S.F., Pres.;
MOLINE
The Order of the Legion of Little Souls of the Merciful Heart of Jesus - 428 39th St., Moline, IL 61265 t) (309)

797-8491 teresahuyten@hotmail.com; thuyten@yahoo.com Rev. Michael L. Menner, Chap.; Teresa I. Huyten, Dir.;

Special Persons Encounter Christ (SPEC) Rock Island Vicariate - 1802 56th St. Ct., Moline, IL 61265

PEORIA

Diocesan Aid, NFP - 419 N.E. Madison Ave., Peoria, IL 61603 t) (309) 671-1550 Mike Buckley, Contact;

Family Resource Center - 415 N.E. Monroe Ave., Peoria, IL 61603 t) (309) 839-2287 Rev. William T. Miller;

Jordan Catholic School of Rock Island, Inc. - 419 N.E. Madison Ave., Peoria, IL 61603 t) (309) 671-1550 cberkshier@cdop.org Kelly McLaughlin, Prin.;

Notre Dame High School of Peoria, Inc. - 5105 N. Sheridan Rd., Peoria, IL 61614 t) (309) 691-8741 g.mcinnis@pndhs.org pndhs.org Dr. Susie Cicciarelli, Prin.; Grant McInnis, COO;

Seton Catholic School of Moline, Inc. - 419 N.E. Madison Ave., Peoria, IL 61603 t) (309) 671-1550 cberkshier@cdop.org Jane Barrett, Prin.;

St. Vincent De Paul Society - 419 N.E. Madison Ave., Peoria, IL 61603 t) 309-671-1550 jenzenberger@cdop.org Diocesan Council and Particular Council of Peoria.

ROCK ISLAND

Alleman High School of Rock Island, Inc. - 1103 40th St., Rock Island, IL 61201 t) (309) 786-7793 alleman@allemanhighschool.org www.allemanhighschool.org Michael Lootens, Prin.;

SPRING VALLEY

SMP Illinois Region Health System - 600 E. 1st St., Spring Valley, IL 61362 t) (815) 664-5311 smphealth.org/

URBANA

Opus Dei - Lincoln Green University Center, 715 W. Michigan Ave., Urbana, IL 61801 t) (217) 367-6650 gbcole123@gmail.com www.lincoln-green.org/ Prelature of the Holy Cross and Opus Dei

WEST PEORIA

Militia Immaculata, Inc. - 2106 W. Heading Av., West Peoria, IL 61604; Mailing: P.O. Box 5547, Peoria, IL 61601-5547 t) (331) 223-5564 minational@missionimmaculata.com militiaoftheimmaculata.com Encourages total consecration to Mary as a means of spiritual renewal for individuals and society. Ronald Rodrigues, Pres.; Antonella DiPiazza, FKMI, Natl. Office Manager;

MONASTERIES AND RESIDENCES FOR PRIESTS AND BROTHERS [MON]

PRINCEVILLE

Congregation of St. John - 11223 W. Legion Hall Rd., Princeville, IL 61559 t) (309) 385-1193 monastery.princeville@stjean.com www.brothersofsaintjohnprinceville.org Rev. Thomas J. Dunton, C.S.J. (United Kingdom), Supr.; Brs.: 4; Priests: 2

NURSING / REHABILITATION / CONVALESCENCE / ELDERLY CARE [NUR]

PEORIA

St. Augustine Manor - 1301 N.E. Glendale Ave., Peoria, IL 61603 t) (309) 674-7069 staugustinemanor@yahoo.com

PRESCHOOLS / CHILDCARE CENTERS [PRE]

WEST PEORIA

Jesu Children's Enrichment Centers - 2903 Heading Ave., West Peoria, IL 61604; Mailing: 1717 W. Candletree Dr., Suite C, Peoria, IL 61614 t) 309-636-7550 jesu@rng3.com Wendy Pettett, Bus. Mgr.;

RETREAT HOUSES / RENEWAL CENTERS [RTR]

MAGNOLIA

Sacre-Coeur Retreat Center, NFP - 8508 County Rd. 100 N., Magnolia, IL 61336; Mailing: 419 N.E. Madison Ave., Peoria, IL 61603 t) (309) 409-5519 scrcexedir@cdop.org www.scrcmagnolia.org/ Rosa Romero Carrillo, Dir.;

SEMINARIES [SEM]

PERU

St. Bede Abbey (Benedictine Society of St. Bede, Benedictine Fathers and Brothers) - 26 W. U.S. Hwy. 6, Peru, IL 61354 t) (815) 223-3140 mcalhoun@st-bede.com stbedeabbey.org Rt. Rev. Michael Calhoun, O.S.B., Abbot; Rev. Philip D. Davey, O.S.B., Mem.; Rev. Dominic M. Garramone, O.S.B., Prior; Rev. Harold L. Datzman, O.S.B.; Rev. Patrick A. Fennell, O.S.B.; Rev. Gregory Jarzombek, O.S.B.; Rev. Ronald L. Margherio, O.S.B.; Bro. David Freeman, O.S.B.; Bro. Nathaniel Grossman, O.S.B.; Bro. Luke E. McLachlan, O.S.B.; Stds.: 280; Lay Tchrs.: 28

SPECIAL CARE FACILITIES [SPF]

NORMAL

Homes of Hope, Inc. - 705 E. Lincoln St., Ste. 313, Normal, IL 61761 t) (309) 862-0607 homesofhope1@frontier.com Maureen McIntosh, Dir.;

An asterisk (*) denotes an organization that has established tax-exempt status directly with the IRS and is not covered by the USCCB Group Ruling.

The Personal Ordinariate of the Chair of Saint Peter

MOST REVEREND STEVEN J. LOPES

Ordinary of The Chair of Saint Peter; ordained June 23, 2001; appointed first Bishop of the Personal Ordinariate of the Chair of Saint Peter November 24, 2015; ordained Bishop February 2, 2016

Ordinariate Office: 7730 Westview Dr., Houston, TX 77055. T: 713-609-9292; F: 832-565-1175. Mailing Address: P.O. Box 55206, Houston, TX 77255.
secretary@ordinariate.net
www.ordinariate.net

ESTABLISHED JANUARY 1, 2012.

STATISTICAL OVERVIEW

Personnel
Bishop....1
Priests: Diocesan Active in Diocese....45
Priests: Diocesan Active Outside Diocese....10
Priests: Retired, Sick or Absent....24
Number of Diocesan Priests....79
Total Priests in your Diocese....79
Ordinations:
Transitional Deacons....3
Permanent Deacons....2
Permanent Deacons in Diocese....19

Parishes
Parishes....42
With Resident Pastor:
Resident Diocesan Priests....30
Without Resident Pastor:
Administered by Priests....8
Administered by Deacons....2
New Parishes Created....2

Educational
Diocesan Students in Other Seminaries....5
Total Seminarians....5
High Schools, Diocesan and Parish....2
Total Students....111
Elementary Schools, Diocesan and Parish....1
Total Students....200
Catechesis/Religious Education:
High School Students....1,195
Elementary Students....317
Total Students under Catholic Instruction....1,828
Teachers in Diocese:
Lay Teachers....35

Vital Statistics
Receptions into the Church:
Infant Baptism Totals....171
Minor Baptism Totals....31
Adult Baptism Totals....43
Received into Full Communion....93
First Communions....263
Confirmations....534
Marriages:
Catholic....62
Interfaith....4
Total Marriages....66
Deaths....53
Total Catholic Population....8,000

LEADERSHIP

Bishop - Most Rev. Steven J. Lopes;
Vicar General - t) 713-609-9292 x2219 Rev. Msgr. Timothy P. Perkins (vg@ordinariate.net);
Chancellor - t) 346-247-2201 secretary@ordinariate.net Lynn Schmidt, Chancellor;
Director of Vocations and Clergy Formation - t) 346-247-2205 vocations@ordinariate.net Rev. Richard D. Kramer;
Moderator of the Curia - t) 713-609-9292 x2219 vocations@ordinariate.net Rev. Richard D. Kramer;
Director of Finance - dcn.ag.stockstill@ordinariate.net Dcn. A.G. Stockstill (ag.stockstill@ordinariate.net);

ADMINISTRATION

Executive Administrative Assistant, Office of the Bishop - t) 346-247-2201 secretary@ordinariate.net Kelly Gilbert;

OFFICES AND DIRECTORS

Communications Coordinator - media@ordinariate.net Lynn Schmidt, Dir.;
Director of Safe Environment and Youth Protection - t) 346-249-2209 safeenvironment@ordinariate.net Lynn Schmidt;
Notary - Dcn. Mark Stockstill;
Director of Worship - t) 713-609-9292 x2219 Tim Caruthers;
Ordinariate Legal Counsel - Michael Casseb;

PARISHES, MISSIONS, AND CLERGY

COMMONWEALTH OF KENTUCKY

LOUISVILLE

Our Lady and Saint John Catholic Church - 639 S. Shelby St., Louisville, KY 40202 c) (502) 791-6444 info@ourladyandstjohn.org www.ourladyandstjohn.org/ Rev. Jonathan Erdman, Par. Admin.;

COMMONWEALTH OF MASSACHUSETTS

GROVELAND

Church of Saint Gregory the Great - 137 Seven Star Rd., Groveland, MA 01834 t) 617-860-2987 office@saintgregoryordinariate.org Kevin McDermott, Contact;

COMMONWEALTH OF PENNSYLVANIA

BRIDGEPORT

St. John the Baptist - 500 Ford St., Bridgeport, PA 19405; Mailing: 502 Ford St., Bridgeport, PA 19405 t) 215-247-1092 fr.bill.cantrell@ordinariate.net www.ordinariatephiladelphia.org (2010 as St. Michael's.) Rev. William Cantrell, Pst.; Rev. Matthew Hummel, Par. Vicar; Dcn. Roger Converse;

SCRANTON

St. Thomas More Catholic Church - 1625 N. Main Ave., Scranton, PA 18508; Mailing: 116 Theodore St., Scranton, PA 18508 t) 570-343-0634 contact@stmscranton.org www.stmscranton.org Rev. Eric Bergman, Pst.; Dcn. Joshua Davis; CRP Stds.: 72

STATE OF ARIZONA

PAYSON

The Catholic Church of Holy Nativity - 1414 N. Easy St., Payson, AZ 85541 t) (928) 478-6988 www.holynativitypayson.com Rev. Joseph Vieira, Pst.;

STATE OF CALIFORNIA

IRVINE

Saint John Henry Newman - 2532 Dupont Dr., Irvine, CA 92612; Mailing: 2646 Dupont Dr., PO Box 163, Irvine, CA 92612 t) (714) 900-3314 www.newmanonline.org Rev. Evan Simington, Par. Admin.; CRP Stds.: 12

STATE OF FLORIDA

JACKSONVILLE

St. James Catholic Church - 12447 Mandarin Rd., Jacksonville, FL 32223; Mailing: 3725 Lilly Rd., Jacksonville, FL 32207 t) (904) 999-1423 office@stjamescc.org stjamescc.org Rev. Philip Mayer, Par. Vicar; CRP Stds.: 16

ORLANDO

Incarnation Catholic Church - 1515 Edgewater Dr., Orlando, FL 32804 t) 407-843-2886 incarnationoffice1515@gmail.com www.ordinariate.org/ Rev. William P. Holiday, Pst.; Rev. Jason McCrimmon, Par. Vicar;

St. Vincent's Academy Preschool - t) 407-843-1997 www.stvincentsacademy.org Heather Russell, Dir.; Patricia Rollen, Asst. Dir.;

STATE OF GEORGIA

BISHOP

St. Aelred Catholic Community - 4951 Mason Hwy., Bishop, GA 30621; Mailing: P.O. Box 61, Bishop, GA 30621 t) 706-389-4009 www.staelred.org/ Rev. Gregory Tipton, Pst.; Daniela Wieczorek, Admin.; CRP Stds.: 45

STATE OF MARYLAND

BALTIMORE

Mount Calvary Church - 816 Eutaw St., Baltimore, MD 21201 t) 410-728-6140 www.mountcalvary.com Rev. Albert Scharbach, Pst.; Rev. Robert Kirk; CRP Stds.: 58

FORT WASHINGTON

Saint Luke - 2315 Brinkley Rd., Fort Washington, MD 20744 t) 202-999-9934 stlukesdcordinariate@gmail.com stlukesordinariate.com/ Rev. John Vidal, Pst.; Rev. Jason Catania, Par. Vicar; CRP Stds.: 14

SYKESVILLE

St. Timothy Catholic Community - 703 Sandosky Rd., Sykesville, MD 21784; Mailing: 6049 Kennard Ct., Eldersburg, MD 21784 t) (443) 328-5768 fr.armando.alejandro@ordinariate.net www.sttimsocsp.cc/ Rev. John Worgul, Par. Vicar; Rev. Armando Alejandro, Par. Admin.;

TOWSON

Christ the King Catholic Church - 1102 Hart Rd., Towson, MD 21286-1631 t) 410-321-0711 office@ctktowson.org www.ctktowson.org Rev. Edward Meeks, Pst.; Rev. Robert Kirk; Dcn. Melvin Reick; CRP Stds.: 100

STATE OF MISSOURI

KANSAS CITY

Our Lady of Hope Ordinariate Community - 1310 Westport Rd., Kansas City, MO 64111 t) 816-421-2112 www.ourladyofhopekc.com Rev. Ed Wills, Par. Vicar; Dcn. Scott McKellar;

REPUBLIC

Saint George Catholic Church - 1404 E. Hines St., Republic, MO 65738; Mailing: 645 S. Assisi Way, Republic, MO 65738-2190 t) 417-732-2018 www.saint-george-church.net/ Rev. Chori Seraiah, Pst.; CRP Stds.: 16

STATE OF NEBRASKA

OMAHA

St. Barnabas Church of the Personal Ordinariate of the Chair of St. Peter - 129 N. 40th St., Omaha, NE 68131; Mailing: 4124 Davenport St., Omaha, NE 68131 t) 402-558-4633 fr.stephen.hilgendorf@ordinariate.net www.saintbarnabas.net Rev. Stephen Hilgendorf, Pst.; Rev. Robert Scheiblhofer; Dcn. Patrick Simons; CRP Stds.: 35

STATE OF NEW YORK

HENRIETTA

St. Alban's Catholic Church - 2732 Culver Rd., Henrietta, NY 14422; Mailing: 445 King's Hwy. S., Rochester, NY 14617 t) 585-484-1827 stalbanscatholic.com Rev. Nathan Davis, Par. Admin.; CRP Stds.: 18

STATE OF NORTH CAROLINA

JACKSONVILLE

Our Lady of Good Counsel Community - 657 N. Marine Blvd., Jacksonville, NC 28546; Mailing: 816 Welton Cir., Jacksonville, NC 28546-2605 t) (910) 449-6841 Rev. William Waun, Admin.;

STATE OF SOUTH CAROLINA

CHARLESTON

Corpus Christi Catholic Community - 95 Hasell St., Charleston, SC 29401; Mailing: P. O. Box 430, Charleston, SC 29402 t) 843-722-7696 corpuschristicsp.org Rev. Patrick Allen, Par. Admin.; CRP Stds.: 21

STATE OF TEXAS

ARLINGTON

Church of St. Mary the Virgin - 1408 N. Davis Dr., Arlington, TX 76012 t) 817-460-2278 stmaryarl@sbcglobal.net stmarythevirgin.org/ Rev. Christopher Stainbrook, Pst.; Rev. Thomas Kennedy, Par. Vicar; CRP Stds.: 204

CLEBURNE

St. John Vianney Catholic Church - 2020 W. Kilpatrick, Cleburne, TX 76033; Mailing: 501 N. Nolan River Rd., Cleburne, TX 76033 t) (940) 867-3860 stjohnvianneycleburne.com/ Rev. Scott Wooten, Par. Admin.; CRP Stds.: 46

DENISON

St. Michael and All Angels Catholic Church - 101 E. Texas St., Denison, TX 75020 t) 903-821-7511 www.stmichaelsallangels.com/about-us Rev. Randall Fogle, Par. Vicar;

ESCONDIDO

St. Augustine of Canterbury - 200 W. Grand Ave., Escondido, TX 92025; Mailing: P.O. Box 2025, Carlsbad, TX 92018 t) 714-649-9800 pastor@staugustineofcanterbury.org www.staugustineofcanterbury.org Rev. Samuel Keyes, Par. Admin.; Dcn. Keith Way;

FORT WORTH

St. Thomas Becket Catholic Church - 3550 S.W. Loop 820, Fort Worth, TX 76133 t) (682) 216-6583 father@stbecketfw.org stbecketfw.org/ Rev. Kenneth M. Bolin, Par. Admin.;

HOUSTON

The Cathedral of Our Lady of Walsingham - 7809 Shadyvilla Ln., Houston, TX 77055-5011 t) 713-683-9407 office@olwcatholic.org www.olwcatholic.org Rev. Charles A. Hough IV, Rector; Rev. Patrick McCain, Par. Vicar; Dcn. Mark Stockstill; Dcn. Arthur G Stockstill; Dcn. Scott Woloson; CRP Stds.: 401

The American Shrine of Our Lady of Walsingham -

SAN ANTONIO

Our Lady of the Atonement Catholic Church - 15415 Red Robin Rd., San Antonio, TX 78255 t) (210) 695-2944 info@ourladyoftheatonement.org ourladyoftheatonement.org/ Rev. Mark W. Lewis, Pst.; Rev. Jon Jenkins, Par. Vicar; Dcn. Michael D'Agostino; Dcn. David Delaney; Dcn. Randy King; CRP Stds.: 262

Atonement Catholic Academy, Inc. - (Grades PreK-12) t) 210-695-2240 schoolinfo@atonementonline.com theatonementacademy.org/ Walter Spencer, Prin.; Lay Tchrs.: 37

Archdiocese of Philadelphia

(Archidioecesis Philadelphiensis)

MOST REVEREND NELSON J. PEREZ, D.D.

Archbishop of Philadelphia; ordained May 20, 1989; appointed Titular Bishop of Catrum and Auxiliary Bishop of Rockville Centre June 8, 2012; ordained July 25, 2012; appointed Bishop of Cleveland July 11, 2017; installed September 5, 2017; appointed Archbishop of Philadelphia January 23, 2020; installed February 18, 2020. Office: 222 N. 17th St., Philadelphia, PA 19103-1299.

The Chancery: 222 N. 17th St., Philadelphia, PA 19103-1299. T: 215-587-4538.
www.archphila.org
chancery@archphila.org

DIOCESE ESTABLISHED APRIL 8, 1808.

Square Miles 2,202.

Erected an Archdiocese February 12, 1875.

Comprises all the City and County of Philadelphia, and the Counties of Bucks, Chester, Delaware and Montgomery in the State of Pennsylvania.

Patrons of the Diocese: I. Immaculate Conception B.V.M., December 8; II. Saints Peter and Paul, Apostles, June 29. This Archdiocese was solemnly consecrated to the Sacred Heart of Jesus on the Feast of Saint Teresa of Avila, October 15, 1873. On May 23, 1952, the Archdiocese of Philadelphia was solemnly consecrated to the Immaculate Heart of Mary at the Shrine of Our Lady of Fatima, Portugal.

For legal titles of parishes and archdiocesan institutions, consult The Chancery.

Most Reverend Michael L. Fitzgerald, D.D.
Auxiliary Bishop of Philadelphia; ordained May 17, 1980; appointed Auxiliary Bishop of Philadelphia and Titular Bishop of Tamallula June 22, 2010; ordained August 6, 2010. Office: 222 N. 17th St., Rm. 530, Philadelphia, PA 19103-1299. T: 215-965-8280.

Most Reverend Timothy C. Senior, D.D.
Auxiliary Bishop of Philadelphia; ordained May 18, 1985; appointed Auxiliary Bishop of Philadelphia and Titular Bishop of Floriana June 8, 2009; ordained July 31, 2009; appointed Rector of Saint Charles Borromeo Seminary July 1, 2012. Res.: 22 N. 17th St., Philadelphia, PA 19103. T: 215-989-4357. bsenior@archphila.org.

Most Reverend John J. McIntyre, D.D.
Auxiliary Bishop of Philadelphia; ordained May 16, 1992; appointed Auxiliary Bishop of Philadelphia and Titular Bishop of Bononia June 8, 2010; ordained August 6, 2010. Office: 222 N. 17th St., Rm. 830, Philadelphia, PA 19103-1299. T: 215-965-8190.

Most Reverend Edward M. Deliman, D.D.
Auxiliary Bishop of Philadelphia; ordained May 19, 1973; appointed Auxiliary Bishop of Philadelphia and Titular Bishop of Sufes May 31, 2016; ordained August 18, 2016. Regina Caeli, 685 York Rd., Warminster, PA 18974. T: 215 458-8215.

STATISTICAL OVERVIEW

Personnel
Retired Cardinals....1
Archbishops....1
Retired Archbishops....1
Auxiliary Bishops....3
Retired Bishops....1
Abbots....1
Retired Abbots....2
Priests: Diocesan Active in Diocese....276
Priests: Diocesan Active Outside Diocese....13
Priests: Retired, Sick or Absent....120
Number of Diocesan Priests....409
Religious Priests in Diocese....245
Total Priests in your Diocese....654
Extern Priests in Diocese....56
Ordinations:
Diocesan Priests....6
Religious Priests....1
Transitional Deacons....7
Permanent Deacons....6
Permanent Deacons in Diocese....299
Total Brothers....77
Total Sisters....1,998

Parishes
Parishes....214
With Resident Pastor:
Resident Diocesan Priests....183
Resident Religious Priests....21
Without Resident Pastor:
Administered by Priests....10
Pastoral Centers....12
Professional Ministry Personnel:
Brothers....59
Sisters....1,180
Lay Ministers....214

Welfare
Catholic Hospitals....4
Total Assisted....330,148
Health Care Centers....1
Total Assisted....309
Homes for the Aged....8
Total Assisted....2,775
Residential Care of Children....2
Total Assisted....315
Day Care Centers....1
Total Assisted....89
Specialized Homes....7
Total Assisted....7,255
Special Centers for Social Services....8
Total Assisted....224,652
Residential Care of Disabled....3
Total Assisted....213

Educational
Seminaries, Diocesan....2
Students from This Diocese....66
Students from Other Dioceses....63
Seminaries, Religious....2
Students, Religious....3
Total Seminarians....69
Colleges and Universities....11
Total Students....32,456
High Schools, Diocesan and Parish....15
Total Students....10,121
High Schools, Private....15
Total Students....6,800
Elementary Schools, Diocesan and Parish....102
Total Students....32,586
Elementary Schools, Private....26
Total Students....6,761
Non-residential Schools for the Disabled....3
Total Students....139
Catechesis/Religious Education:
High School Students....459
Elementary Students....31,282
Total Students under Catholic Instruction....120,673
Teachers in Diocese:
Priests....26
Brothers....15
Sisters....104
Lay Teachers....4,543

Vital Statistics
Receptions into the Church:
Infant Baptism Totals....8,772
Minor Baptism Totals....529
Adult Baptism Totals....211
Received into Full Communion....190
First Communions....6,648
Confirmations....7,085
Marriages:
Catholic....1,949
Interfaith....709
Total Marriages....2,658
Deaths....9,250
Total Catholic Population....1,546,350
Total Population....4,195,425

LEADERSHIP

Vicars General - Most Rev. Timothy C. Senior; Most Rev. John J. McIntyre; Most Rev. Michael J. Fitzgerald;
Office of the Archbishop - t) 215-587-0506 Most Rev. Nelson J. Perez, Archbishop of Philadelphia;
Office of the Moderator of the Curia - Rev. Msgr. Daniel J. Kutys; Marc A. Fisher, CFO;
Information Line, Archdiocesan - t) 215-587-3600
The Chancery - t) 215-587-4538 Rev. Sean P. Bransfield, Chancellor; Rev. Richard K. McFadden, Vice Chancellor; Sean T. Doyle, Staff Canonist;
Catholic Historical Research Center of the Archdiocese of Philadelphia - t) 215-904-8149 x1001 www.chrc-phila.org Leslie O'Neill, Dir.;
Office for General Services - t) 215-895-3459 Robert Whomsley, Dir.;
Metropolitan Tribunal - t) 215-587-3750
Judicial Vicar - Rev. Msgr. Paul A. DiGirolamo; Rev. Eduardo G. Montero, Adjunct Judicial Vicar;
Archdiocesan Judges - Rev. Sean P. Bransfield; Rev. Joseph C. Dieckhaus; Rev. Msgr. James J. Graham;
Office for Child and Youth Protection - t) 215-587-3880 Leslie J. Davila, Dir.;
Office for Property Management - t) 215-587-3560 Phil Schneider, Dir.;
Office for Divine Worship - t) 215-587-3537 Rev. Gerald Dennis Gill, Dir. (fr.dgill@archphila.org);
Director of Liturgical Music - t) 215-587-3696
Office for General Counsel - t) 215-587-0511 Suzanne Hueston, Gen. Counsel;
Office for Insurance Services - t) 215-587-2494 Margaret Toland, Insurance & Risk Mgr.;
Office for Information Technology - t) (215) 854-7067 Mike Chorneiko, CIO; Dave Fiedler, Assoc. CIO;
Office for Consecrated Life - t) (215) 587-3795 Sr. Gabrielle Mary Braccio, R.S.M., Delegate for Consecrated Life;
Office for Parish Service and Support - t) 215-587-3995 Arjun Dias, Dir.;
Office of Investigations - t) 215-587-3763 John P. DeLaney, Dir.;
Collections - Office of the Moderator of the Curia - t) 215-587-4507

ADVISORY BOARDS, COMMISSIONS, COMMITTEES, AND COUNCILS

Board of Trustees of Lay Employees Retirement Plan - Rev. Msgr. Daniel J. Kutys; Rev. Msgr. Thomas A. Murray; Dcn. Franz N. Fruewald;
Diocesan Priests' Compensation and Benefits Committee - Rev. Michael F. Hennelly, Chair; Rev. Edward H. Bell; Rev. Andrew C. Brownholtz;
Building Committee -
Censores Librorum - Rev. Msgr. J. Brian Bransfield; Rev. Msgr. Joseph G. Prior; Rev. Robert A. Pesarchick;
College of Consultors - Most Rev. Nelson J. Perez, Archbishop; Most Rev. Michael J. Fitzgerald; Most Rev. John J. McIntyre;
Council of Priests - Most Rev. Timothy C. Senior; Most Rev. John J. McIntyre; Most Rev. Michael J. Fitzgerald;
Educational Fund - t) 215-587-3943
Parish Sites and Boundaries, Commission for -
Pastors Review Board - Rev. John F. Babowitch; Rev. Msgr. Federico A. Britto; Rev. Martin T. Cioppi;
Pennsylvania Catholic Conference - Most Rev. Nelson J. Perez; Rev. Msgr. Daniel J. Kutys; Kenneth A. Gavin;

CLERGY AND RELIGIOUS SERVICES

Office for Clergy - Rev. Michael F. Hennelly, Vicar for Clergy; Rev. Brian M. Kean, Asst. Vicar for Clergy;
Office for Retired and Infirm Priests - Rev. Edward J. Kennedy, Rector (Pro-Tem) Villa St. Joseph; Rev. Msgr. Daniel J. Sullivan, Vicar;
Permanent Diaconate Department - Dcn. Michael Pascarella Jr., Assoc. to Vicar for Clergy;
St. Charles Borromeo Seminary - t) 610-667-3394 Most Rev. Timothy C. Senior, Chancellor; Rev. Keith J. Chylinski, Rector; Rev. Patrick J. Brady, Vice Rector;
Vocation Office for Diocesan Priesthood - t) 610-667-5778 Rev. David M. Friel, Dir.;
Liaison for the Office for Catholic Cemeteries - t) 215-895-3459 Robert Whomsley;
Office for Ecclesiastical Exchange - t) 215-587-3996

COMMUNICATIONS

Secretariat for Communications - t) 215-587-3747
CatholicPhilly.com - t) 215-587-3509 Matthew Gambino, Dir.;
Office for Communications - Kenneth A. Gavin, Chief Communications Officer;

DEANERIES

Deanery 1 - Eastern Delaware County - Rev. Thomas P. Whittingham, Dean;
Deanery 2 - Western Delaware County - Rev. Msgr. Michael J. Matz, Dean;
Deanery 3 - Western Chester County - Rev. Joseph T. Shenosky, Dean;
Deanery 4 - Northern Chester County - Rev. Stephen F. Leva;
Deanery 5 - Western Montgomery County - Rev. Msgr. Charles L. Sangermano, Dean;
Deanery 6 - Main Line, Bridgeport and Roxborough - Rev. Msgr. Kevin C. Lawrence;
Deanery 7 - Eastern Montgomery County and Northwest Philadelphia - Rev. Msgr. Joseph P. Duncan;
Deanery 8 - South Philadelphia, Northern Liberties - Rev. Joseph J. Kelley;
Deanery 9 - West Philadelphia, Center City - Rev. Msgr. Federico A. Britto;
Deanery 10 - Central and Upper Bucks County - Rev. Msgr. John C. Marine;
Deanery 11 - Upper Northeast Philadelphia/Lower Bucks County - Rev. Msgr. Joseph G. Prior;
Deanery 12 - Lower Northeast Philadelphia - Rev. Thomas M. Higgins;
Deanery 13 - Hispanic Catholics - Rev. Francisco D'Amico;

EDUCATION

Office of Catholic Education - ocathsch@archphila.org
Assistant Superintendent for Curriculum Instruction and Assessment - t) 215-587-3744 Sr. Edward William Quinn, I.H.M.;
Assistant Superintendents for Elementary Schools - Bernadette Dougherty, Asst. Supt.; Micah Sumner, Asst. Supt.; Sr. Margaret Rose Adams, I.H.M., Asst. Supt.;
Assistant Superintendents for Secondary Schools - Patricia Rigby, Asst. Supt.; Nancy Kurtz, Interim Asst. Supt.;
Associate Director of Information Technology - Steven B. Pagano;
Chief Operating Officer - Jay De Fruscio;
Chief Marketing and Advancement Officer - Jennifer Tuberosa;
Director for Elementary Enrollment - t) 215-587-4543 Bonnie Del Ciotto;
Director of Enrollment Management for Secondary Schools - Owen D Logue;
Director of Government Programs - t) 215-587-3919 Eileen Schweyer;
Director of International Programs - t) 215-587-3789 Janet Dollard;
Director of Technology Pre-K to 12 - t) 215-587-3710 Aaron W. Heintz;
Director of Special Education - t) 215-587-3718 Danielle Heeney;
Educational Financial Services -
Assistant Chief Financial Officers - Maureen D. Fisher; Thomas J. Geisler;
Chief Financial Officer - t) (215) 587-3774 David J. Magee;
Executive Director of Athletics Secondary Schools - t) 215-587-0514 Stephen Haug;
Director of Human Resources for Secondary Schools - t) 215-587-3976 James Molnar;
Technology Project Manager - Elizabeth (Pitek) Torre;
Secretary for Elementary Schools - t) 215-587-3585 Andrew McLaughlin;
Senior Director of Enrollment Management - t) 215-587-3972 Steven Clement;
Senior Network Technicians - Albert Rossana; Andrew Ciccaglione; Thomas Baird;
Superintendent for Secondary Schools and Special Education - t) 215-587-3736 Brooke Cortese Tesche;
System Administrator - Jill Ladd;
Technology Integration Coaches, PreK-12 - Annabel Dotzman; Anthony Dunn;

EVANGELIZATION

Hispanic Catholic Institute - t) 215-667-2824 Blanca Herrera, Coord.;
Office for Black Catholics - t) 215-587-3541 Kim Walker, Dir.;
Office for Hispanic Catholics - t) 215-667-2823 Most Rev. Edward M. Deliman, Auxiliary Bishop of Philadelphia; Kathia Arango, Dir.;
Office for Life and Family - t) 215-587-5661 Steven Bozza, Dir.;
Respect Life, Natural Family Planning, Marriage and Family, Life Affirming Choices, Marriage Preparation Ministry - t) 215-587-0510 Dcn. Patrick J. Kennedy, Coord., Marriage Prep;
Office for Pastoral Care for Migrants and Refugees - t) 215-587-3540 Sr. Gertrude Borres, R.A., Dir.;
Apostleship of the Sea - Sr. Gertrude Borres, R.A., Coord.;
Brazilian Apostolate - t) 215-535-2962 Rev. David A. Waters, Pro Tem;
Chinese Apostolate - t) 215-992-0999 Rev. Thomas Betz;
Filipino Apostolate - t) 215-635-6210 Rev. Efren V. Esmilla, Chap.; Ferdie Aczon; Hermine Aczon;
Francophone African Community - t) 215-747-3250 Rev. Rene Againglo;
French Apostolate - t) 610-527-1016 Mathilde Ruyant-Lucq, Lay Coord.;
Ghanaian Community - t) 215-357-5905 Sr. Florence Enechukwu, M.S.H.R., Coord.;
Haitian Apostolate - t) 215-745-1389 Rev. Eugene R. Almonor, O.M.I., Chap.;
Indian Apostolate - Knanayan Community of St. John Neumann - t) 215-947-3500 Rev. Bins Jose Chethalil, Chap.;
Indian Apostolate, Latin Rite - t) 215-855-1311 Rev. Shaji Silva, Chap.;
Indian Apostolate - St. Thomas Syro-Malabar Catholic Church - t) 215-808-4052 Rev. Kuriakose Kumbakeel, Pst.;
Indian Apostolate, Syro Malankara Rite - t) 215-673-8127 Rev. Babu Madathiparambil;
Indonesian Apostolate - Rev. Markus Rudy Hermawar;
Korean Apostolate - t) 215-548-5535 Rev. Joseph Kim Soon-Jin, Pst.;
Nigerian Igbo Community - t) 214-747-3250 Rev. Celestine Chukwunonso Madubuko, Chap.;
Other African Communities - t) 610-525-3313 Sr. Florence Enechukwu, M.S.H.R.;
Pakistani Apostolate - t) 215-745-1389 Rev. Tariq Isaac;
Polish Apostolate - t) 215-535-6667 Rev. Jan Palkowski, Pst.;
Portuguese Apostolate - t) 215-518-9083 Rev. David Waters, Temporary Chap.;
Vietnamese Apostolate - t) 215-424-1300 Rev. Msgr. Joseph T. Trinh, Chap.;
Office for Persons With Disabilities and the Deaf Apostolate - Sr. Kathleen Schipani, I.H.M., Dir.;
Deaf Apostolate - www.deafcatholicphilly.org Rev. Msgr. Paul V. Dougherty, Chap.; Rev. Sean A. Loomis, Chap.; Dcn. William J. Griffin, Chap.;
Office for the New Evangelization - t) 215-587-5630

Meghan Cokeley, Dir.; Paola Herrera, Assoc. Dir.;
Pontifical Mission Societies - t) (215) 587-3944 Rev. Msgr. James D. Beisel, Dir.; Michele Meiers, Asst. Dir.; Alixandra Holden, Mission Educ. & Communications Mgr.;
Secretariat for Evangelization - t) 215-965-8190 Most Rev. John J. McIntyre, Auxiliary Bishop of Philadelphia;

FINANCE
Office for Financial Services -
Chief Financial Officer - t) 215-587-4510 Marc A. Fisher;
Controller - t) 215-587-3943 Beth D'Eramo;

HUMAN RESOURCES
Human Resources Office - t) 215-587-3910 Maureen Gallagher, Dir.;

SOCIAL SERVICES
Catholic Charities of the Archdiocese of Philadelphia - James Amato, Sec. Catholic Human Svcs.; Tim J. Duffy, Div. Controller;
Director of IT Operations Associate CIO - t) 267-663-0032 Mike Chorneiko, CIO; Dave Fiedler, Oper. Assoc.;
Director of the Community-Based Services Division & Director of Housing & Homeless Services - t) 215-587-3590 Amy Stoner;
Director of the Developmental Programs Division, Administrative Office - t) (484) 472-5066; (484) 472-5100 Nicole McFadden, Controller; Fran E. Swiacki Jr.;
Director of Youth Services - t) 215-854-7052 Dr. James Black;
Nutritional Development Services - t) 215-895-3470 Lizanne E. Hagedorn, Dir.;
Secretary for Catholic Human Services - t) 215-587-3908 James Amato, Secy.; Franz Fruehwald, CFO; Mike Chorneiko, CIO;
Catholic Housing & Community Services - t) 215-587-3633; 215-854-7091; (215) 854-7036; (267) 663-5430 Heather Hout, Dir.; Suzanne O'Grady-Laurito, Asst.Dir.; Karen Cosner, Controller;
Coordinator of the Catholic Campaign for Human Development - t) 215-854-7022 Franz Fruehwald;
Director of Catholic Relief Services - t) 215-895-3470 Anne H. Ayella;

PARISHES, MISSIONS, AND CLERGY

COMMONWEALTH OF PENNSYLVANIA

ABINGTON
Our Lady Help of Christians - 1500 Marian Rd., Abington, PA 19001 t) 215-887-3466 (CRP); 215-886-3456 secretary@olhc-parish.org www.olhc-parish.org Rev. Anthony W. Janton, Pst.; Dcn. John J. Nucero; Pamela A McAfee, Bus. Mgr.; Jennifer Bellantoni, DRE;

AMBLER
St. Anthony of Padua - 259 Forest Ave., Ambler, PA 19002-5903 t) 215-646-4742 mchenry@saintanthonyparish.org; pastor@saintanthonyparish.org www.saintanthonyparish.org Rev. Msgr. Stephen P. McHenry, Pst.; Rev. Michael J. Saban, Par. Vicar; Dcn. Edward M. Cuff; Dcn. Kevin Gentilcore;
St. Anthony Preschool and Childcare - 260 Forest Ave., First Fl., Ambler, PA 19002 t) 215-646-6150
St. Joseph - 16 S. Spring Garden St., Ambler, PA 19002-4797 t) 215-646-0494 stjosephambler@gmail.com Rev. Eugene M. Tully, Pst.; Dcn. Mark J. Kuhn; Rev. Charles J. McElroy, In Res.;

ARDMORE
St. Colman - 11 Simpson Rd., Ardmore, PA 19003 t) 610-642-0545 stcolmanchurch@gmail.com stcolmanardmore.com Rev. John J. Ames, Pst.; Dcn. John J. Rodgers; Cathy Dernoncourt, DRE;

ARDSLEY
Queen of Peace - 820 N. Hills Ave., Ardsley, PA 19038 t) 215-886-3014 (CRP); 215-887-1838 queenofpeaceparish@comcast.net qofpchurch.org Rev. Lawrence F. Crehan, Pst.; Dcn. Franz N. Fruehwald; Dcn. Raymond Jacobucci; Anne Florian, DRE; Joseph Costello, Bus. Mgr.;
Convent - 825 N. Hills Ave., Ardsley, PA 19038 t) 215-887-4785

ASTON
St. Joseph - 3255 Concord Rd., Aston, PA 19014 t) 610-494-4358 (CRP); 610-497-3340 cmaugeri@stjoseph.org; stjoseph256@comcast.net Rev. Msgr. J. Brian Bransfield, Pst.; Dcn. John M. Betzal; Rev. Msgr. Thomas P. Flanigan, In Res.; Catherine Maugeri, DRE;

AVONDALE
St. Gabriel of the Sorrowful Mother - 8910 Gap Newport Pike, Avondale, PA 19311; Mailing: P.O. Box 709, Avondale, PA 19311 t) 610-268-0296 stgabriel@kennett.net; stgsmdre@gmail.com www.stgabrielparish.org Rev. Anthony J. DiGuglielmo, Pst.; Linda Riofski, DRE;
St. Rocco - 9016 Gap Newport Pike, Avondale, PA 19311; Mailing: P.O. Box 1019, Avondale, PA 19311 t) 610-268-3365 mail@stroccochurch.org www.stroccochurch.org Rev. Msgr. Francis J. Depman, Pst.; Rev. Andres Arambula Garcia, Par. Vicar; CRP Stds.: 1,172
Sisters, Servants of the Lord and the Virgin of Matara - 420 Auburn Rd., Avondale, PA 19311 t) 610-268-0675
Santa Maria, Madre de Dios - 29 Gap Newport Pike, Avondale, PA 19311 t) 610-268-1515 mail@missionsantamaria.org www.missionsantamaria.org Outreach Center

BALA CYNWYD
St. Matthias - 128 Bryn Mawr Ave., Bala Cynwyd, PA 19004-3013 t) 610-664-0207 www.saintmatthias.org Rev. Brian M. Kean, Par. Admin.; Most Rev. Timothy C. Senior, In Res.; Dcn. Ernest W. Angiolillo; CRP Stds.: 97

BENSALEM
St. Charles Borromeo - 1731 Hulmeville Rd., Bensalem, PA 19020 t) 215-638-3625 st.charles@stcharlesbensalem.org www.stcharlesbensalem.org Rev. Philip M. Forlano, Pst.; Dcn. Kevin J. McDermott; Dcn. Louis Quaglia;
St. Charles Borromeo School - (Grades PreK-8) 1704 Bristol Pike, Bensalem, PA 19020 t) 215-639-3456 stcharlesbensalem.org
Convent - 1080 Kings Ave., Bensalem, PA 19020 t) 215-639-0113
St. Ephrem - 5400 Hulmeville Rd., Bensalem, PA 19020 t) 215-639-4895 (CRP); 215-245-1698 stephremrectory@yahoo.com Rev. Michael G. Speziale, Pst.; Rev. Stephen F. Katziner, Par. Vicar; Dcn. James P. DeBow; Rev. Timothy O'Sullivan, In Res.;
St. Ephrem School - 5340 Hulmeville Rd., Bensalem, PA 19020 t) 215-639-9488
Convent - 5300 Hulmeville Rd., Bensalem, PA 19020 t) 215-638-1024

BERWYN
St. Monica - 635 First Ave., Berwyn, PA 19312 t) 610-644-0110 parishoffice@saintmonicachurch.org www.saintmonicachurch.org Rev. Paul J. O'Donnell, Par. Admin.; Jason Carter, DRE; CRP Stds.: 137

BLUE BELL
St. Helena - 1489 DeKalb Pike, Blue Bell, PA 19422 t) 610-275-7711 (Rectory) parish@sainthelenachurch.org www.sainthelena-centersquare.net Rev. Msgr. Joseph J. Nicolo, Pst.; Rev. Brian T. Connolly, Par. Vicar; CRP Stds.: 275
St. Helena School - 1499 DeKalb Pike, Blue Bell, PA 19422 t) 610-279-3345 www.sainthelenaschool.org

BOOTHWYN
St. John Fisher - 4225 Chichester Ave., Boothwyn, PA 19061 t) 610-485-0441 contact@sjf71.org www.stjohnfisherchurch.org Rev. Robert B. McDermott, Pst.; Dcn. Daniel Bingnear; CRP Stds.: 91

BRISTOL
St. Mark - 1025 Radcliffe St., Bristol, PA 19007 t) 215-788-2319 office@saintmarkchurch.net Rev. Dennis M. Mooney, Pst.; Dcn. Richard S. Malamut; Mary Leonhauser, DRE;
St. Mark School - 1024 Radcliffe St., Bristol, PA 19007 t) 215-785-0973 Marie Sanson, Prin.;

BROOKHAVEN
Our Lady of Charity - 231 Upland Rd., Brookhaven, PA 19015 t) 484-924-9141 (CRP); 610-872-6192 olcharity@comcast.net www.olcbrookhaven.org Rev. James A. Lyons, Pst.;

BROOMALL
St. Pius X - 220 Lawrence Rd., Broomall, PA 19008 t) 610-353-6950 (CRP); 610-353-4880 stpiusxbusinessoffice@comcast.net www.saintpius.net Rev. Msgr. William C. Kaufman, Pst.; Rev. Msgr. John J. Jagodzinski, In Res.; Rev. August A Taglianetti, In Res.; CRP Stds.: 325
St. Pius X School - 204 Lawrence Rd., Broomall, PA 19008 t) 610-356-7222

BRYN MAWR
St. John Neumann - 380 Highland Ln., Bryn Mawr, PA 19010 t) 610-525-3100 mainoffice@sjnparish.org sjnparish.org Rev. Msgr. Michael J. Matz, Pst.; Dcn. Kevin Harrington; Rev. Robert J. Chapman, In Res.; Clare Frissora, Parish Life Coord.; Katie Bucaro, DRE; CRP Stds.: 129
Our Mother of Good Counsel - 31 Pennswood Rd., Bryn Mawr, PA 19010 t) 610-525-0147 kcarey@omgcparish.net; omgc@omgcparish.net www.omgcparish.org Rev. Joseph S. Mostardi, O.S.A., Pst.; Rev. John F. Deary, O.S.A., Par. Vicar; Rev. Joseph Loya, O.S.A., In Res.; Rev. J. Thomas Pohto, O.S.A., In Res.; Bro. Michael Riggs, OSA, In Res.; Bro. Nicholas Stone, OSA, In Res.; Karen Carey, DRE;

CHADDS FORD
St. Cornelius - 160 Ridge Rd., Chadds Ford, PA 19317 t) 610-459-2502 stcorn1@comcast.net; stcornprep@scornelius.org www.saintcornelius.org Rev. Msgr. David E. Diamond, Pst.; Dcn. Harry J. Morris; Dcn. John J. Todor; Julie Sullivan, DRE; CRP Stds.: 313
St. Cornelius School - (Grades PreK-PreK) 160 Ridge Rd, Chadds Ford, PA 19317 t) 610-459-8663 scornelius.org/ Stds.: 128; Lay Tchrs.: 16

CHALFONT
St. Jude - 321 W. Butler Ave., Chalfont, PA 18914-2329 t) 215-822-7553 (CRP); 215-822-0179 prep@stjudeschool.com; office@stjudechalfont.org www.stjudechalfont.org Rev. Anthony J. Costa, Pst.; Rev. Terence P. Weik, Par. Vicar; Dcn. Michael J. Cushing; Dcn. Timothy P. Lynch;
St. Jude School - 323 W. Butler Ave., Chalfont, PA 18914-2329 t) 215-822-9225 semrsm@stjudeschool.com www.stjudeschool.com Sr. Elizabeth Marley, R.S.M., Prin.;

CHELTENHAM
St. Joseph - 7631 Waters Rd., Cheltenham, PA 19012-1318; Mailing: 100 Old Soldiers Rd., Cheltenham, PA 19012 t) 215-635-5533 wsh-stjos2000@gmail.com stjoescheltenham.org Rev. William S. Harrison, Pst.; CRP Stds.: 10
Presentation of Blessed Virgin Mary - 100 Old Soldiers Rd., Cheltenham, PA 19012 t) 215-379-2054 (CRP); 215-379-1364 presentationbvm@gmail.com presentationbvm.org twinned with St. Joseph parish in Cheltenham Rev. William S. Harrison, Pst.; CRP Stds.: 17
Presentation of Blessed Virgin Mary School - 105 Old

Soldiers Rd., Cheltenham, PA 19012 t) 215-379-3798 www.presentationbvm.org/school

Convent - 107 Old Soldiers Rd., Cheltenham, PA 19012 t) 215-379-8343

CHESTER

St. Katharine Drexel - 1920 Providence Ave., Chester, PA 19013 t) 610-872-3731 info@stkatharinedrexelparish.org www.stkatharinedrexelparish.org Rev. Robert A. Ianelli, Pst.; Dcn. John J. Pileggi; Jose Martin, DRE; CRP Stds.: 50

Convent - 1902 Providence Ave., Chester, PA 19013 t) 610-876-4916

Saint Katharine Drexel Evangelization Center - 226 Norris St., Chester, PA 19013 t) 610-872-3140

CHESTER SPRINGS

Saint Elizabeth - 100 Saint Elizabeth Dr., Chester Springs, PA 19425 t) 610-646-6545 (CRP); 610-321-1200 religioused@stelizabethparish.org; steucc@stelizabethparish.org www.stelizabethparish.org Rev. Msgr. Thomas M. Mullin, Pst.; Rev. Dharshana Jayamanne (Sri Lanka), Par. Vicar; Dcn. Kevin T. Mead; Dcn. Barry R. Midwood;

St. Elizabeth School - (Grades PreK-8) 120 Saint Elizabeth Dr., Chester Springs, PA 19425; Mailing: P.O. Box 780, Uwchlan, PA 19480-0780 t) 610-646-6540 dgreco@stelizabethparish.org Diane Greco, Prin.; Stds.: 208; Lay Tchrs.: 17

CLIFTON HEIGHTS

Sacred Heart - 316 E. Broadway Ave., Clifton Heights, PA 19018 t) 610-623-0409 sacredheartchurch@rcn.com sacredheart-cliftonheights.net Rev. Msgr. George A. Majoros, Pst.; Rev. Paul Stenson, In Res.;

St. Hedwig Chapel - 4th & Hayes Sts., Chester, PA 19013

COATESVILLE

St. Joseph - 404 Charles St., Coatesville, PA 19320 t) 610-384-0360 sjrectoy@comcast.net www.stjosephcoatesville.org Rev. Eder Estrada, F.M., Pst.;

Our Lady of the Rosary - 80 S. 17th Ave., Coatesville, PA 19320 t) 610-384-1415 fatherb@olrcc.org Rev. Juan Francisco Mora Bello, F.M., Pst.;

COLLEGEVILLE

St. Eleanor - 647 Locust St., Collegeville, PA 19426 t) 610-489-1647; 610-489-4677 x2233 (CRP) church@steleanor.com; religioused@steleanor.com www.steleanor.com Rev. Msgr. Michael T. McCulken, Pst.; Rev. Henry Graebe, Par. Vicar; Dcn. John A. Hasson; Dcn. Edward T. Hinson; Rev. Msgr. Thomas A. Murray, In Res.; CRP Stds.: 550

Holy Cross Regional Catholic School - (Grades PreK-8) 701 Locust St., Collegeville, PA 19426 t) 610-489-9434 x2225 thealy@hcrc.school www.hcrc.school

COLLINGDALE

St. Joseph - 500 Woodlawn Ave., Collingdale, PA 19023 t) 610-586-1520 (CRP); 610-583-4530 stjoe.col@rcn.com stjoecollingdale.com Rev. Thomas M. Sodano, Pst.; Dcn. Patrick J. Kelly; Rev. John D. Gabin, In Res.; Mary Carney, DRE;

CONSHOHOCKEN

St. Mary Roman Catholic Church - 140 W. Hector St., Conshohocken, PA 19428 t) 610-717-3972 www.stmarylatinmass.com/ Latin Mass Rev. Carl Gismondi, F.S.S.P., Pst.; Rev. Caleb Kick, F.S.S.P., Par. Vicar;

St. Matthew - 219 Fayette St., Conshohocken, PA 19428 t) 610-828-0424 stmatthewdre@verizon.net; stmatthewrectory@verizon.net www.stmatthewparish.com Rev. Joseph P. Devlin, Pst.; Rev. James J. McKeaney, In Res.; Dcn. Joseph C. Carr; CRP Stds.: 168

St. Matthew Daycare and Early Childhood Center - 210 Harry St., Conshohocken, PA 19428 t) 610-828-5191

CROYDON

St. Thomas Aquinas - 601 Bristol Pike, Croydon, PA 19021-5496 t) 215-788-2989 sta712014@gmail.com www.staq.org Rev. David A. Fernandes, Pst.; Dcn. John J. Gallagher; CRP Stds.: 55

DARBY

Blessed Virgin Mary - 1101 Main St., Darby, PA 19023 t) 610-583-2128; 610-583-8536 bvmrectory2@rcn.com; bvmrectory@rcn.com www.bvm-darby.com/ Rev. Mariano DellaGiovanna, Par. Admin.; Rev. Msgr. David C Quitugua, Par. Vicar; Rev. Edward J. Kennedy, In Res.;

Blessed Virgin Mary School - 47 MacDade Blvd., Darby, PA 19023 t) 610-586-0638

DOWNINGTOWN

St. Joseph - 338 Manor Ave., Downingtown, PA 19335; Mailing: 332 Manor Ave., Downingtown, PA 19335 t) 610-269-8294 reception@stjosephrc.org; prep@stjosephrc.org stjosephrc.org Rev. Stephen F. Leva, Pst.; Rev. Andrew J. Auletta, Par. Vicar; Dcn. Michael P. Murtha; Dcn. Matthew D. Coyne; Dcn. Edward R. Schiappa; Rev. John E. Donia, In Res.; Rev. Samuel A. Verruni, In Res.; Kathryn Thomas, DRE; CRP Stds.: 568

St. Joseph School - 340 Manor Ave., Downingtown, PA 19335 t) 610-269-8999

Convent - 336 Manor Ave., Downingtown, PA 19335 t) 484-593-4352

DOYLESTOWN

Our Lady of Guadalupe - 5194 Cold Spring Creamery Rd., Doylestown, PA 18902 t) 267-247-5374 olguadbulletin@gmail.com; dre@olguadalupe.org www.olguadalupe.org Rev. Msgr. Joseph P. Gentili, Pst.; Dcn. Robert F. Brady; Karen Brody, DRE; David Serrano González, Director of Hispanic Ministry;

Our Lady of Mount Carmel - 235 E. State St., Doylestown, PA 18901 t) 215-345-7089 (CRP); 215-348-4190 www.ourladymtcarmel.org Rev. Matthew W. Guckin, Pst.; Dcn. William J. Barrow; Rev. David O'Brien, In Res.; Cindy Balceniuk, DRE;

Our Lady of Mount Carmel School - 225 E. Ashland St., Doylestown, PA 18901 t) 215-348-5907

Convent - 209 E. State St., Doylestown, PA 18901 t) 215-348-4663

DREXEL HILL

St. Andrew - 3500 School Ln., Drexel Hill, PA 19026 t) 610-259-1169 bus.mgr@standrewdh.org standrewdh.org Rev. Msgr. Albin J. Grous, Pst.; Dcn. Thomas N. Verna;

St. Andrew School - 529 Mason Ave., Drexel Hill, PA 19026 t) 610-259-5145 saintandrewschool.com Helen McLean, Prin.; Daniel Salvatore, Vice Prin.;

Convent - 535 Mason Ave., Drexel Hill, PA 19026 t) 610-259-6130

St. Bernadette - 1035 Turner Ave., Drexel Hill, PA 19026 t) 610-789-7676 x101 pastor@stbl.org www.stbl.org Rev. John P. Masson, Par. Admin.; Dcn. Thomas P. Fitzpatrick; Mary Kate Murphy, DRE;

St. Bernadette School - 1001 Turner Ave., Drexel Hill, PA 19026

St. Charles Borromeo - 3422 Dennison Ave., Drexel Hill, PA 19026 t) 610-623-3800 rectory@scbdh.org scbdh.org Rev. Msgr. George A. Majoros, Pst.; Dcn. John H. Farrell;

St. Dorothy - 4910 Township Line Rd., Drexel Hill, PA 19026 t) 610-853-1499 (CRP); 610-789-7788 Rev. Michael D. Murphy, Pst.; Rev. Msgr. Robert J. Carroll, Par. Vicar; Dcn. John P. Donnelly; Dcn. Joseph P. McGonigal; Rev. Msgr. Daniel J. Kutys, In Res.; Sue Phelan, DRE; CRP Stds.: 220

St. Dorothy School - (Grades K-8) 1225 Burmont Rd., Drexel Hill, PA 19026 t) 610-789-4100 www.stdots.org Karen Tomasetti, Prin.;

Convent - 1201 Burmont Rd., Drexel Hill, PA 19026 t) 610-789-4112

EAST NORRITON

St. Paul - 2007 New Hope St., East Norriton, PA 19401 t) 610-279-6725 stpaulparish.eastnorriton@gmail.com stpaulcatholicchurcheastnorriton.net/ Rev. Harry E. McCreedy, Pst.; Dcn. Matthew J. Hrobak; Rev. James N. Catagnus, In Res.; Sr. Rosellen Bracken, R.S.M., Spiritual Adv./Care Srvcs.; Meg Farrell, DRE; Mary Rose Edmonds, Bus. Mgr.;

St. Titus - 3006 Keenwood Rd., East Norriton, PA 19403 t) 610-306-3438 (CRP); 610-279-4990 sttitus@sttitus.org www.sttitus.org Rev. Msgr. Joseph J. Nicolo, Par. Admin.; Dcn. Claude B. Granese; Claire Boyle, DRE; Maureen Lewis, Bus. Mgr.;

EDDYSTONE

St. Rose of Lima - 1901 Chester Pike, Eddystone, PA 19022 t) 610-876-6170 stroselimaparish@gmail.com www.stroseoflimaparish.net Rev. Brian A. Izzo, Admin.;

ELKINS PARK

St. James - 8320 Brookside Rd., Elkins Park, PA 19027 t) 215-635-6210 stjameselkinspark@comcast.net Rev. Efren V. Esmilla, Pst.;

EXTON

SS. Philip and James - 107 N. Ship Rd., Exton, PA 19341 t) 610-363-1307 (CRP); 610-363-6536 bdoyle@sspjparish.net www.sspj.net Rev. Joseph C. Dieckhaus, Pst.; Sr. Mary Ann Spaetti, I.H.M., DRE; Sr. Eunice Marie Timony, I.H.M., DRE;

SS. Philip and James School - (Grades PreK-8) 721 E. Lincoln Hwy., Exton, PA 19341 t) 610-363-6530 steresa@sspj.net school.sspj.net

Convent - 105 N. Ship Rd., Exton, PA 19341 t) 610-363-2263

FAIRLESS HILLS

St. Frances Cabrini - 325 S. Oxford Valley Rd., Fairless Hills, PA 19030 t) 215-946-4040 jeanemadden@saintfrancescabrini.net; parish@saintfrancescabrini.net www.saintfrancescabrini.net Rev. Msgr. Michael P. McCormac, Pst.; Dcn. Paul Ablaza; Dcn. Mace M. Mazzoni; Jean Madden, DRE; CRP Stds.: 135

FEASTERVILLE

Assumption B.V.M. - 1900 Meadowbrook Rd., Feasterville, PA 19053 t) 215-357-1221 www.abvmfeasterville.org Rev. Michael J. Davis, Pst.; Dcn. Eric M. Umile; Rev. Bins Jose Chethalil, In Res.; Rev. John J. Kelly, In Res.; Patricia A. Criniti, DRE;

FLOURTOWN

St. Genevieve - 1225 Bethlehem Pike, Flourtown, PA 19031 t) 215-836-2828 rectory@stgensparish.com www.stgensparish.com Rev. Carl F. Janicki, Pst.; Dcn. Michael G. Conroy; Dcn. Kevin J. Potter; Rev. John T. Lyons, In Res.; CRP Stds.: 115

St. Genevieve School - 1237 Bethlehem Pike, Flourtown, PA 19031 t) 215-836-5644 www.stgens.com

GLADWYNE

St. John Baptist Vianney - 350 Conshohocken State Rd., Gladwyne, PA 19035; Mailing: 1110 Vaughan Ln., Gladwyne, PA 19035 t) 610-642-0938; 610-642-0938 x20 (CRP) info@sjvgladwyne.com; mmonroe@sjvgladwyne.com www.sjvgladwyne.com Rev. William G. Donovan, Pst.; Dcn. James Russo, Pst. Assoc.; Thomas Kincade, Bus. Mgr.; MaryAnne Monroe, DRE;

GLEN MILLS

St. Thomas the Apostle - 430 Valleybrook Rd., Glen Mills, PA 19342 t) 610-459-3477 (CRP); 610-459-2224 staparish@staglenmills.org Rev. Stephen E. Shott, O.S.F.S., Pst.; Rev. Joseph A. DiMauro, Par. Vicar; Dcn. Anthony J. Cincotta; Mary Sassani, DRE; Sr. Nicoletta Maria, R.S.M., Pastoral Ministry;

St. Thomas the Apostle School - t) 610-459-8134

GLENOLDEN

St. George - 22 E. Cooke Ave., Glenolden, PA 19036-1497 t) 610-237-1633 st.georgesec@rcn.com www.stgeorgeparish.org Rev. Leo P. Oswald, Pst.; CRP Stds.: 35

Convent - 11 E. Lamont Ave., Glenolden, PA 19036-1497 t) 484-318-5092

GLENSIDE

St. Luke the Evangelist - 2316 Fairhill Ave., Glenside, PA 19038 t) 215-572-0128 stlukerc@aol.com; secretary@stlukerc.org www.stlukeglenside.org Rev. Joseph D. Brandt, Pst.; Rev. John F. Wackerman, Par.

Vicar; Dcn. Thomas M. Croke; Dcn. John K. Hunter, Bus. Mgr.; CRP Stds.: 202

St. Luke Catholic School - (Grades PreK-8) 2336 Fairhill Ave., Glenside, PA 19038 t) (215) 884-0843 office@saintlukeschool.org www.saintlukeschool.org Stds.: 299; Lay Tchrs.: 26

HATBORO

St. John Bosco - 235 E. County Line Rd., Hatboro, PA 19040 t) 267-803-0774 (CRP); 215-672-7280 cflack@saintjohnbosco.org www.saintjohnbosco.org Rev. Gary J. Kramer, Pst.; Rev. Angelo J. Hernandez, Par. Vicar;

HATFIELD

St. Maria Goretti - 1601 Derstine Rd., Hatfield, PA 19440 t) 215-721-6559 (CRP); 215-721-0199 www.stmariagoretti.net Rev. John C. Nguyen, Pst.; Dcn. Phuong T. Nguyen;

HAVERTOWN

Annunciation B.V.M. - 401 Brookline Blvd., Havertown, PA 19083; Mailing: 410 Sagamore Rd., Havertown, PA 19083 t) 610-449-9858 (CRP); 610-449-1613 office@annunciationparish.com www.annunciationparish.com Rev. Sean A. Loomis, Par. Admin.; Dcn. Robert V. McElwee; Rev. Tadeusz Pacholczyk, In Res.;

Convent - 421 Brookline Blvd., Havertown, PA 19083 t) 610-449-4065

St. Denis - 2401 St. Denis Ln., Havertown, PA 19083 t) 610-446-0200 sduffy@stdenishavertown.org www.stdenis.org Rev. Kevin J. Gallagher, Pst.; Rev. James J. Cardosi, Par. Vicar; Rev. Msgr. Robert C. Vogan, In Res.; Sr. Rose Caritas, I.H.M., DRE;

Convent - t) 610-446-1263

Sacred Heart - 105 Wilson Ave., Havertown, PA 19083 t) 610-449-3000 shpmckee@comcast.net; sacredheartparish@sacredheartmanoa.org sacredheartmanoa.org Rev. John J. Nordeman, Pst.; Dcn. William V. Williams; Rev. Gerald D. Canavan, In Res.; Sr. Kathryn Benham, I.H.M., DRE;

Sacred Heart School - 109 N. Manoa Rd., Havertown, PA 19083 t) 610-446-9198

Convent - 108 Shelbourne Rd., Havertown, PA 19083 t) 610-446-3694

HILLTOWN

Our Lady of the Sacred Heart - 100 Broad St., Hilltown, PA 18927; Mailing: P.O. Box 31, Hilltown, PA 18927 t) 215-822-9020 (CRP); 215-822-9224 olsh@comcast.net olsh-hilltown.com Rev. Michael J. Pawelko, Pst.; Dcn. Vincent G. Ceneviva; Dcn. Gregg W. Hoyer; Dcn. Gary D. Schoenenberger; CRP Stds.: 249

HOLLAND

St. Bede the Venerable - 1071 Holland Rd., Holland, PA 18966 t) 215-357-2130 (CRP); 215-357-5720 email@st-bede.org www.st-bede.org Rev. Msgr. John C. Marine, Pst.; Rev. Ryan Nguyen, Par. Vicar; Carole Obrokta, DRE;

HORSHAM

St. Catherine of Siena - 321 Witmer Rd., Horsham, PA 19044 t) 215-674-8549 (CRP); 215-672-2881 religioused@stcatherineschurch.org; pastor@stcatherineschurch.org stcatherineschurch.org Rev. Joseph F. Rymdeika, Pst.; Dcn. Mario G Mirabelli; Regina Osborne, DRE; CRP Stds.: 328

HUNTINGDON VALLEY

St. Albert the Great - 212 Welsh Rd., Huntingdon Valley, PA 19006 t) 215-947-3641 (CRP); 215-947-3500 dre@satg1.org saintalthegreat.org Rev. Msgr. Joseph P. Duncan, Pst.; Rev. Quy K Pham, Par. Vicar; Dcn. Edward J. Morris; Rev. Alexander R. Gibbs, In Res.; Thomas Kuchler, Music Min.; Jonathan DeMent, Youth Min.; Dennis Mueller, DRE; Alice M Pesce, Bus. Mgr.; Christine Regan, Dir.; CRP Stds.: 212

St. Albert the Great School - t) 215-947-2332 Cynthia Koons, Prin.;

JAMISON

St. Cyril of Jerusalem - 1410 Almshouse Rd., Jamison, PA 18929 t) 215-343-3139 (CRP); 215-343-1288 deaconjoe@saint-cyril.com; ctomassoni01@gmail.com Rev. Msgr. Robert J. Powell, Pst.; Rev. Timothy J. Buckley, Par. Vicar; Dcn. Joseph T. Owen, DRE; CRP Stds.: 250

JENKINTOWN

Immaculate Conception - 604 West Ave., Jenkintown, PA 19046 t) 215-884-4022 icr604west@comcast.net Rev. Joseph E. Howarth, Pst.; Dcn. Alvin Clay; Rev. Alexander Masluk, In Res.; Rev. Charles J. Sullivan, In Res.; Marie McGuigan, DRE;

KENNETT SQUARE

St. Patrick - 205 Lafayette St., Kennett Square, PA 19348 t) 610-444-2214 (CRP); 610-444-4364 stpatrickkennett@gmail.com www.stpatrickkennettsquare.org Rev. Christopher B. Rogers, Pst.; Dcn. Alan T. Haley; Rev. Andres Arambula Garcia, In Res.; Marianne Kane, DRE;

KING OF PRUSSIA

Mother of Divine Providence - 333 Allendale Rd., King of Prussia, PA 19406-1640 t) 610-265-4178 mdpinfo@mdpparish.com mdpparish.com Rev. Martin T. Cioppi, Pst.; Dcn. Mark H. Dillon; Dcn. Gregory J. Maskarinec; Rev. Fidelis A. Olokunboro (Nigeria), In Res.; CRP Stds.: 180

LAFAYETTE HILL

St. Philip Neri - 437 Ridge Pike, Lafayette Hill, PA 19444 t) 610-834-1975 mcpastorius@comcast.net; spnprep@spnschool.org www.saintphilipnerichurch.com Rev. George J. Szparagowski, Par. Admin.; Rev. Richard K. McFadden, Par. Vicar; Dcn. Michael Cipressi; Dcn. Robert G. Flynn; Rev. William B. Dooner, In Res.; Sharon Otto, DRE; Michael C. Pastorius, Bus. Mgr.; Rev. Msgr. Charles P. Vance, Pastor Emer.;

St. Philip Neri School - (Grades PreK-8) 3015 Chestnut St., Lafayette Hill, PA 19444 t) 610-828-3082 venezialee@spnschool.org www.spnschool.org Elizabeth Veneziale, Prin.;

Convent - 3015 Chestnut St., Lafayette Hill, PA 19444 t) 610-828-2866 Sr. Lourdes Kennedy, Supr.;

LANSDALE

Corpus Christi - 900 Sumneytown Pike, Lansdale, PA 19446 t) 215-362-2292 (CRP); 215-855-1311 corpuschristibusmgr@gmail.com corpuschristilansdale.org Rev. John D. Schiele, Pst.; Rev. Dennis Z. Fedak, Par. Vicar; Rev. Shaji Silva, Par. Vicar; Dcn. B. Stephen Currie; Dcn. William W. Evans; Brian Jefferes, DRE; Sr. Mary Carroll McCaffrey, S.S.J., Parish Outreach; CRP Stds.: 308

Corpus Christi School - 920 Sumneytown Pike, Lansdale, PA 19446 t) 215-368-0582 ccsprin@corpuschr.org Maria Greenberg, Prin.; Stds.: 388; Lay Tchrs.: 27

St. Stanislaus - 51 Lansdale Ave., Lansdale, PA 19446 t) 215-855-9893 (CRP); 215-855-3133 ststansprep@yahoo.com; ststan@comcast.net www.ststanislaus.com Rev. Sean P. English, Pst.; Rev. Jonathan G. Rice, Par. Vicar; Dcn. Anthony J. Bellitto Jr.; Dcn. Charles G. Lewis; Dcn. Juan E. Valentin; Rev. Zachary W. Navit, In Res.; Leona Russell, DRE;

Mater Dei Catholic School - (Grades PreK-8) 493 E. Main St., Lansdale, PA 19446-2898 t) 215-368-0995 gsamanns@materdeicatholic.com materdeicatholic.com Diane E. McCaughan, Prin.;

LANSDOWNE

St. Philomena - 41 E. Baltimore Ave., Lansdowne, PA 19050 t) 610-622-2420 stphilomenaparish@rcn.com www.stphilspa.com Rev. Paul J. Castellani, Pst.; CRP Stds.: 45

LENNI

St. Francis de Sales - 35 New Rd., Lenni, PA 19052; Mailing: P.O. Box 97, Lenni, PA 19052 t) 610-459-0554 (CRP); 610-459-2203 parishoffice@sfdslenni.org sfdslenni.org Rev. Alan J. Okon Jr., Pst.; Dcn. Paul A. Quinn; Sr. Betty Kirk, O.S.F., Parish Services Director;

Convent - 28 New Rd., Aston, PA 19014 t) 610-459-2501

Fair Acres Geriatric Center - t) 610-891-5600

Granite Farms Est. - t) 610-358-3440

Riddle Village - t) 610-891-3777

The Residence at Glen Riddle - t) 610-358-9933

Riddle Hospital - t) 610-566-9400

Penn State Lima Campus - t) 610-892-1350

Williamson School - t) 610-566-1776

LEVITTOWN

St. Michael the Archangel - 66 Levittown Pkwy., Levittown, PA 19054 t) 215-945-1166 (CRP); 215-547-2518 (Prep) church@stmichaellvt.org; prep@stmichaellvt.org www.stmichaellvt.org Rev. Michael C. DiIorio, Pst.; Dcn. John Murray, DRE; CRP Stds.: 74

St. Michael the Archangel School - (Grades PreK-8) 130 Levittown Pkwy., Levittown, PA 19054 t) 215-943-0222 www.sma-pa.org Stds.: 230; Lay Tchrs.: 15

Our Lady of the Angels - 88 Levittown Pkwy., Levittown, PA 19054 t) 215-943-4810

Queen of the Universe - 2443 Trenton Rd., Levittown, PA 19056 t) 215-945-2704 (CRP); 215-945-8750 quparishprep@gmail.com; info@quparish.com Rev. John R. Weber, Pst.; Rev. Cesar Izaguirre, Par. Vicar; Dcn. John K. Murray;

Parish Center - 2505 Trenton Rd., Levittown, PA 19056 t) 215-945-0215

MALVERN

St. Patrick - 104 Channing Ave., Malvern, PA 19355; Mailing: 131 Channing Ave., Malvern, PA 19355 t) 610-296-8899 (PREP); 610-647-2345 (Main Phone) reception@stpatrickmalvern.org www.stpatrickmalvern.org Rev. Christopher Redcay, Pst.; Rev. Arul Amalraj Selvanayagam, O.Praem., Par. Vicar; Dcn. Louis Libbi; Dcn. Thomas Strohmetz; Rev. Mark J. Cavara, In Res.; Rev. Thomas J. Gardner, In Res.; CRP Stds.: 330

St. Patrick School - 115 Channing Ave., Malvern, PA 19355 t) 610-644-5797 podonnell@saintpatrickmalvern.org www.saintpatrickmalvern.org/ Stds.: 360; Lay Tchrs.: 31

MAPLE GLEN

St. Alphonsus - 33 Conwell Dr., Maple Glen, PA 19002 t) 215-643-7938 (CRP); 215-646-4600 mgordan@stalphonsusparish.org; rectory@stalphonsusparish.org stalphonsusparish.org/ Rev. Msgr. Brian P. Hennessy, Pst.; Dcn. John J. Mischler; Dcn. James Toth; Michele Gordon, DRE;

Our Lady of Mercy Regional Catholic School - (Grades K-8) 29 Conwell Dr., Maple Glen, PA 19002 t) 215-646-0150 John C. McGrath, Prin.;

MEDIA

St. Mary Magdalen - 2400 N. Providence Rd., Media, PA 19063 t) 610-566-8821 administrative@stmarymagdalen.net www.stmarymagdalen.net Rev. Msgr. Ralph J. Chieffo, Pst.; Dcn. Joseph P. Boyle Jr., DRE; Dcn. James A. DiFerdinand; Dcn. E. Peter Zurbach; Susan Edmundowicz, Bus. Mgr.; CRP Stds.: 176

St. Mary Magdalen School - 2430 N. Providence Rd., Media, PA 19063 t) 610-565-1822 office@stmarymagdalen.net stmarymagdalen.net Jennifer Roehrig, Prin.;

Nativity of the Blessed Virgin Mary - 30 E. Franklin St., Media, PA 19063 t) 610-566-0185 nativitybvm@comcast.net www.nativity-bvm.org Rev. Edward H. Bell, Pst.; Rev. Kevin T. Mulligan, Par. Vicar; Dcn. William G. Kussmaul; Rev. Stephen D. Thorne, In Res.;

MILMONT PARK

Our Lady of Peace - 501 Belmont Ave., Milmont Park, PA 19033-3308 t) 610-532-8081 olp-parish.com Rev. Joseph C. McCaffrey, Par. Admin.; Dcn. William A Koniers;

MORRISVILLE

Holy Trinity - 201 N. Pennsylvania Ave., Morrisville, PA 19067 t) 215-295-3079 (CRP); 215-295-3045 htcre@aol.com; holytrinityrcc@aol.com www.holytrinitymorrisville.org Rev. Msgr. John C. Eckert, Pst.; Dcn. Warren C. Leonard; Kathleen Gnida, DRE;

Holy Trinity School - (Grades PreK-8) Osborne Ave.

& Stockham Ave., Morrisville, PA 19067 t) 215-295-6900 teachlit25@aol.com Elaine McDowell, Prin.;

St. John the Evangelist - 752 Big Oak Rd., Morrisville, PA 19067 t) 215-295-9239 (CRP); 215-295-4102 sjeoffices@stjohnpa.org; prepdirector@stjohnpa.org www.stjohnpa.org Rev. William J. Monahan, Pst.; Rev. Richard E. Rudy, Par. Vicar;

MORTON

Our Lady of Perpetual Help - 2130 Franklin Ave., Morton, PA 19070 t) 610-543-5448 (CRP); 610-543-1046 olphprep@gmail.com; olphcc@comcast.net www.olphmorton.org Rev. James E. Goerner, Pst.; Michele Hundermark, DRE; CRP Stds.: 140

Our Lady of Angels Regional School - (Grades PreK-8) t) 610-543-8350

Convent - t) 610-543-0186

NARBERTH

St. Margaret - 208 N. Narberth Ave., Narberth, PA 19072 t) 610-664-3370 x16 (CRP); 610-664-3770 office@saintmarg.org www.saintmarg.org Rev. Msgr. Paul V. Dougherty, Pst.; CRP Stds.: 130

St. Margaret School - 227 N. Narberth Ave., Narberth, PA 19072 t) 610-664-2640 office@smsnarberth.org www.smsnarberth.org

NEW HOPE

St. Martin of Tours - 1 Riverstone Cir., New Hope, PA 18938 t) 215-862-5472 info@stmartinoftours.org www.stmartinoftours.org Rev. W. Frederick Kindon, Pst.; Dcn. Peter L. Niche;

NEWTOWN

St. Andrew - 81 Swamp Rd., Newtown, PA 18940 t) 215-968-6929 (CRP); 215-968-2262 info@stapn.org standrewnewtown.com Rev. Msgr. Michael C. Picard, Pst.; Rev. Kyle M. Adamczyk, Par. Vicar; Rev. Marc F. Capizzi, Par. Vicar; Rev. Alexander W. Pancoast, Par. Vicar; Dcn. Edward E. Duess; Dcn. Steven M. Javie; Dcn. John Scott McDonald; Dcn. John J. Pfeifer;

St. Andrew School - 51 Wrights Rd., Newtown, PA 18940 t) 215-968-2685

Preschool - 51 Wrights Rd., Newtown, PA 18940 t) 215-968-2685

NEWTOWN SQUARE

St. Anastasia - 3301 W. Chester Pike, Newtown Square, PA 19073 t) 610-356-5069 (CRP); 610-356-1613 thaggerty@saintannies.org; llawler@saintannies.org www.saintanastasia.net Rev. Michael A. Colagreco, Pst.; Rev. Brandon M. Artman, Par. Vicar; Dcn. Chris Hilden; Sr. Mary Barrar, Pst. Min./Coord.; Theresa Haggerty, DRE; Joe Lacava, Bus. Mgr.;

St. Anastasia School - 3309 W. Chester Pike, Newtown Square, PA 19073 t) 610-356-6225 www.saintannies.org Beth Dotle, Prin.; Marlene Louden, Librn.;

Convent - 3305 W. Chester Pike, Newtown Square, PA 19073 t) 484-422-8861

Holy Mary Korean Catholic Church - 100 Media Line Rd., Newtown Square, PA 19073 t) 610-325-2240 www.slachurch.com Rev. Chan Mi Kim; Rev. Michael Yoo;

NORRISTOWN

St. Francis of Assisi - 600 Hamilton St., Norristown, PA 19401 t) 610-272-0402 sfa600prep@gmail.com; sfarectory@yahoo.com www.stfrancisnorristown.com Rev. Richard J. Smith, Pst.; Dcn. David J. Matour; CRP Stds.: 80

St. Francis of Assisi School - 601-A Buttonwood Sts., Norristown, PA 19401 t) 610-272-0501 btigue@sfacatholic.org sfa.ocephila.org

Holy Saviour - 407 E. Main St., Norristown, PA 19401 t) 610-275-0958 msgrsangermano@holysaviour.com www.holysaviour.net Rev. Msgr. Charles L. Sangermano, Pst.; Rev. J. Thomas Heron, In Res.; CRP Stds.: 120

Our Lady of Mount Carmel - 460 Fairfield Rd., Plymouth Meeting, PA 19462 t) 610-277-7739

St. Patrick - 703 Green St., Norristown, PA 19401 t) 610-272-4500 (CRP); 610-272-1408 stpatnorris@comcast.net www.stpatrick-norristown.net Rev. Manuel J. Flores, Par. Admin.; Sr. Marie Horstmann, I.H.M., DRE; Christopher Lawrence, Bus. Mgr.;

Missionaries of Charity - 630 DeKalb St., Norristown, PA 19401 t) 610-277-5962

St. Teresa of Avila - 1260 S. Trooper Rd., Norristown, PA 19403-3659 t) 610-666-5820 starectory@verizon.net www.stteresaofavilaparish.com Rev. J. Jerome Wild, Pst.; CRP Stds.: 59

Visitation B.V.M. - 196 N. Trooper Rd., Norristown, PA 19403 t) 610-539-6211 (CRP); 610-539-5572 sister.diane@visitationbvmschool.org; bulletin@visitationbvm.org www.visitationbvm.org Rev. Robert M. Gross, Pst.; Rev. Francis J. Mulranen, Par. Vicar; Dcn. Vincent M. Drewicz; Dcn. Patrick J. Mandracchia; Sr. Diane Marie, C.S.F.N., DRE;

Visitation B.V.M. School - 190 N. Trooper Rd., Norristown, PA 19403 t) 610-539-6080

Convent - t) 610-539-5558

NORTH WALES

Mary, Mother of the Redeemer - 1325 Upper State Rd., North Wales, PA 19454 t) 215-412-2251 (CRP); 215-362-7400 mmr@mmredeemer.org mmredeemer.org Rev. Msgr. John T. Conway, Pst.; Rev. Mark Tobin, Par. Vicar; Dcn. Paul A. Logan; Dcn. John M. Travaline; Lou Tonelli, Bus. Mgr.; Dcn. Mario G. Mirabelli, Parish Svcs.; CRP Stds.: 263

Mary, Mother of the Redeemer School - 1321 Upper State Rd., North Wales, PA 19454 t) 215-412-7101 Denise Judge, Prin.;

St. Rose of Lima - 425 S. Main St., North Wales, PA 19454-3203 t) 215-699-4434 (CRP); 215-699-4617 stroselima@srol.org Rev. Msgr. James J. Graham, Pst.; Dcn. Robert P. Gohde; Dcn. Joseph V. Hosack Jr.;

Parish Center - 425 S. Pennsylvania Ave., North Wales, PA 19454-3498

NORWOOD

St. Gabriel - 233 Mohawk Ave., Norwood, PA 19074 t) 610-532-5057 (CRP); 610-586-1225 religiousedu@stgabrielnorwood.org; office@stgabrielnorwood.org Rev. John D. Hand, Pst.; Rev. Celestine Chukwunonso Madubuko, Par. Vicar; CRP Stds.: 145

ORELAND

Holy Martyrs - 120 Allison Rd., Oreland, PA 19075 t) 215-884-8575 holymartyrssecretary@gmail.com; holymartyrschurch@gmail.com www.holymartyrschurch.org Rev. Jason V. Kulczynski, Pst.; CRP Stds.: 24

OTTSVILLE

St. John the Baptist - 4050 Durham Rd., Ottsville, PA 18942 t) 610-847-5521 prep@stjohnsottsville.org www.stjohnsottsville.org Rev. Selvaraj Lucas, MSC, Pst.; Rev. Josemarie Legaspi, In Res.; Joan Black, DRE;

OXFORD

Church of the Sacred Heart - 203 Church Rd., Oxford, PA 19363-1822 t) 610-932-5040 info@sacredheart.us; dsingo@sacredheart.us sacredheartchurchoxford.org Rev. Joseph T. Shenosky, Pst.; Dcn. Justin J. Watkins; Alexis Witiak, DRE; Douglas Anthony Singo, Bus. Mgr.; CRP Stds.: 250

PAOLI

St. Norbert - 6 Greenlawn Rd., Attn: Parish Office, Paoli, PA 19301 t) 610-644-1655 x114 (CRP); 610-644-1655 parish.stnorbert.org Rev. Steven J. Albero, O. Praem., Pst.; Rev. James C. Rodia, O.Praem., Par. Vicar; Dcn. Henry C. Fila; Dcn. John P. Lozano; Dcn. Stephen J. Martino; CRP Stds.: 233

St. Norbert School - 6 Greenlawn Rds., Attn: School, Paoli, PA 19301 t) 610-644-1670 Stds.: 211; Sr. Tchrs.: 1; Lay Tchrs.: 18

PARKESBURG

Our Lady of Consolation - 603 W. Second Ave., Parkesburg, PA 19365 t) 610-857-1003 (CRP); 610-857-3510 www.olcchurch.org Rev. Sean F. O'Neill, Pst.;

St. Malachy - 76 St. Malachy Rd., Cochranville, PA 19330

PENNDEL

Our Lady of Grace - 225 Bellevue Ave., Penndel, PA 19047; Mailing: 338 Hulmeville Ave., Penndel, PA 19047 t) 215-757-5530 (CRP); 215-757-7700 parish@olg1.org; dre@olg1.org www.olgparishpenndel.org Rev. Msgr. Joseph G. Prior, Pst.; Rev. William B. Dooner, Pastor Emer.; Rev. George E. Pereia, In Res.; Rev. Raju Pilla, In Res.; Rev. Thomas A. Nasta, In Res.; Dcn. John P. Teson, Bus. Mgr.; Maddie Applebee, Pst. Assoc.; Christine Flack, DRE;

Our Lady of Grace School - 300 Hulmeville Ave., Penndel, PA 19047 t) 215-757-5287 www.olgschoolpenndel.org Eric Harper, Prin.;

Parish Service Center - 338 Hulmeville Ave., Penndel, PA 19047 t) 215-757-5052

PENNSBURG

St. Philip Neri - 1325 Klinerd Rd., Pennsburg, PA 18073 t) 215-679-7839 (CRP); 215-679-9275 ofcmgr@spnparish.org www.spnparish.org Rev. Anthony R. Hangholt, Pst.; Dcn. Michael J. Franks Sr.; Dcn. Matthew A. Horvath; CRP Stds.: 150

PHILADELPHIA

Cathedral Basilica of Saints Peter and Paul and the Shrine of Saint Katharine Drexel - 1723 Race St., Philadelphia, PA 19103 t) 215-561-1313 info@cathedralphila.org www.cathedralphila.org Rev. Gerald Dennis Gill, Rector; Rev. Matthew Biedrzycki, Par. Vicar; Rev. Msgr. John M. Savinski, In Res.; Dcn. Jesus M. Burgos; CRP Stds.: 64

St. Agatha-St. James - 3728 Chestnut St., Philadelphia, PA 19104; Mailing: 111 S. 38th St., 3rd Fl., Philadelphia, PA 19104 t) 267-787-5000 x101 office@saintsaj.org www.saintsaj.org Rev. Carlos F. Keen, Admin.; Bro. Michael Gokie, S.V.C., In Res.; Rev. Remigo Morales Bermudez Buse, S.V.C., In Res.; Bro. Leonardo Negrini, S.V.C., In Res.; Bro. Patrick Travers, ., In Res.;

St. Agnes-St. John Nepomucene - 319 Brown St., Philadelphia, PA 19123; Mailing: 1723 Race St., Philadelphia, PA 19103 t) 215-561-1313 info@cathedralphila.org Rev. Gerald Dennis Gill, Admin.;

St. Ambrose - 401 E. Roosevelt Blvd., Philadelphia, PA 19120 t) 215-439-3671 (CRP); 215-329-7900 stambroseparish@outlook.com Rev. Charles J. Ravert, Pst.; Rev. James N. Catagnus, Pastor Emer.;

St. Andrew - 1913 Wallace St., Philadelphia, PA 19130 t) 215-765-2322 salrcc@aol.com Rev. Gerald Dennis Gill, Admin.;

St. Casimir Church - 324 Wharton St., Philadelphia, PA 19147 t) 215-468-2052 (Worship Site)

St. Anne - 2328 E. Lehigh Ave., Philadelphia, PA 19125; Mailing: P.O. Box 3682, Philadelphia, PA 19125 t) 215-739-4590 frskip317@outlook.com Rev. Mardean E. Miller, Pst.;

Annunciation B.V.M. - 1511 S. 10th St., Philadelphia, PA 19147 t) 215-334-0159 annunciation19147@gmail.com www.annunciationbvmchurch.org Rev. Nicholas Martorano, O.S.A., Pst.; Rev. Juan Cardenas, O.S.A., Par. Vicar; Rev. Robert Terranova, Par. Vicar; Rev. Elizandro Contreras, O.S.A., Pst. Assoc.; CRP Stds.: 150

St. Anselm - 12670 Dunks Ferry Rd., Philadelphia, PA 19154 t) 215-637-3525 stanselmparish.com/ Rev. Anthony T. Rossi, Pst.; Rev. John J. Large, Par. Vicar; Dcn. Dennis P. Warner; Dcn. Gerald J. Whartenby; CRP Stds.: 100

St. Anselm School - (Grades PreK-8) 12650 Dunks Ferry Rd., Philadelphia, PA 19154 t) 215-632-1133 smee@stanselmschoolphila.com Seamus James Mee, Prin.; Stds.: 258; Lay Tchrs.: 20

St. Athanasius - 2050 E. Walnut Ln., Philadelphia, PA 19138 t) 215-548-2700 rectory@stathanasiuschurch.us www.stathanasiuschurch.us Rev. Joseph F. Okonski, Pst.; Dcn. James L. Mahoney; Rev. Anayo Nna, C.Ss.R. (Nigeria), In Res.; Marlyn Barnes, DRE; CRP Stds.: 15

St. Athanasius School - (Grades PreK-8) 7105 Limekiln Pike, Philadelphia, PA 19138 t) 215-424-5045 secretary@saschool.org www.saschool.org Andrea Tomaino, Prin.;

St. Augustine - 243 N. Lawrence St., Philadelphia, PA 19106-1195 t) 215-627-1838 staugustineparish09@gmail.com www.st-augustinechurch.com First foundation of Augustinian Order in U.S.A. Friar William F. Waters, O.S.A., Pst.; Friar James R. Keating, O.S.A., In Res.; Friar Paul F. Morrisey, O.S.A., In Res.; Friar James Paradis, O.S.A., In Res.; Jacob A. Marquart III, O.F.S., Parish Services Director;

St. Barbara - 5359 Lebanon Ave., Philadelphia, PA 19131 t) 215-473-1044 saintbarbara5359@gmail.com Rev. Msgr. Wilfred J. Pashley, Pst.;

Convent - 5336 Diamond St., Philadelphia, PA 19131 t) 215-477-3839

St. Barnabas - 6300 Buist Ave., Philadelphia, PA 19142-3098 t) 215-726-1119 stbarnabasrectory@comcast.net Rev. Miguel Angel Bravo, Par. Admin.;

St. Bartholomew - 5600 Jackson St., Philadelphia, PA 19124 t) 215-831-1224 stbartrectory@yahoo.com Rev. Michael S. Olivere, Par. Admin.; Dcn. Gerard J. McPhillips;

St. Bernard - 7341 Cottage St., Philadelphia, PA 19136 t) 215-333-0446 stbernardrectory@aol.com www.stbernardmayfair.org Rev. Joseph N. Accardi, Pst.;

St. Bridget - 3667 Midvale Ave., Philadelphia, PA 19129 t) 215-844-4126 pastor@stbridgeteastfalls.org Rev. Bernard J. Taglianetti, Pst.; Rev. Stephen P. DeLacy, In Res.; Rev. Michael F. Hennelly, In Res.;

Convent - 3665 Midvale Ave., Philadelphia, PA 19129

St. Cecilia - 535 Rhawn St., Philadelphia, PA 19111 t) 215-725-1240 (Parish Office); (215) 725-2821 (PREP) parish@stceciliafc.org www.stceciliafc.org Rev. Christopher M. Walsh, Pst.; Rev. Robert F. Lucas, Par. Vicar; Rev. Charles E. Bonner, Pastor Emer.; CRP Stds.: 101

St. Cecilia School - (Grades PreK-8) 525 Rhawn St., Philadelphia, PA 19111 t) 215-725-8588 Stds.: 539; Sr. Tchrs.: 1; Lay Tchrs.: 26

St. Charles Borromeo - 902 S. 20th St., Philadelphia, PA 19146 t) 215-735-6898 (CRP); 215-735-0600 stcharlesborromeo@gmail.com www.stcb-southphila.com Rev. Wellington M. Munoz, Par. Admin.;

Christ the King - 3252 Chesterfield Rd., Philadelphia, PA 19114 t) 215-632-1144 ctk@christthekingparish.net www.christthekingparish.net Rev. James A. Callahan, Pst.; CRP Stds.: 60

Christ the King School - (Grades PreK-8) 3205 Chesterfield Rd., Philadelphia, PA 19114 t) 215-632-1375; 215-637-3838 www.christthekingschool.net

St. Christopher - 13301 Proctor Rd., Philadelphia, PA 19116 t) 215-673-5177 info@stchrisparish.org www.stchrisparish.org Rev. Msgr. Joseph P. Garvin, Pst.; Rev. SangWoo Chi, Par. Vicar; Dcn. Eugene McNally; Dcn. James O'Neill; CRP Stds.: 94

St. Christopher School - 13305 Proctor Rd., Philadelphia, PA 19116 t) 215-673-5787 www.stchrisstrong.org

St. Cyprian - 525 Cobbs Creek Pkwy., Philadelphia, PA 19143 t) 215-747-3250 sntcyprian@verizon.net Rev. Msgr. Federico A. Britto, Pst.; Rev. Rene Againglo, Par. Vicar; Dcn. Anthony O. Willoughby; Rev. David A. Fisher, In Res.;

Divine Mercy Parish - 6667 Chester Ave., Philadelphia, PA 19142-1397 t) 215-727-8300 divinemercyparish@comcast.net Rev. Quan M. Trinh, Par. Admin.; Dcn. Diep T. Nguyen; Christina Pilling, DRE;

St. Barnabas Independence Mission School - 64th and Buist Ave., Philadelphia, PA 19142 t) 215-729-3603 Sr. Margaret McCullough, I.H.M., Prin.;

St. Dominic - 8504 Frankford Ave., Philadelphia, PA 19136 t) 215-624-5301 (CRP); 215-624-5502 stdominicphila@hotmail.com www.stdominicphilapa.e-paluch.com Rev. Edward T. Kearns, Pst.; Dcn. Mark A. Salvatore; Rev. Edward E. Brady, In Res.;

St. Dominic School - 8512 Frankford Ave., Philadelphia, PA 19136 t) 215-333-6703 Sr. Shaun Thomas, I.H.M., Prin.;

Epiphany of Our Lord - 1121 Jackson St., Philadelphia, PA 19148 t) 215-334-1035 Rev. James R. Casey, Pst.; Dcn. Olindo Mennilli; Marge Jarman, DRE;

Our Lady of Hope Regional Catholic School - 1248 Jackson St., Philadelphia, PA 19148 t) 215-467-5385 Patricia Cody, Prin.;

St. Francis de Sales - 4625 Springfield Ave., Philadelphia, PA 19143 t) 215-222-5819 www.saintfrancisdesales.net Rev. Eric Banecker, Pst.; Dcn. Samuel O. Ujor; Rev. Benjamin Nwanonenyi, In Res.; Rev. George L. Strausser, In Res.; CRP Stds.: 45

St. Francis de Sales School - 917 S. 47th St., Philadelphia, PA 19143 t) 215-387-1749 Sr. Mary McNulty, I.H.M., Prin.;

Convent - 912 S. 47th St., Philadelphia, PA 19143 t) 215-727-3929 ihm912@comcast.net; schristinelamb@desalesschool.net

St. Francis Xavier - 2319 Green St., Philadelphia, PA 19130 t) 215-765-4568 x3 sfx7840@msn.com www.sfxoratory.org/ Rev. Paul C. Convery, C.O., Pst.; Rev. Georges G. Thiers, C.O., In Res.; Dcn. Vincent J. Thompson; CRP Stds.: 15

Oratory - 2321 Green St., Philadelphia, PA 19130

St. Francis Xavier School - (Grades PreK-8) 641 N. 24th St., Philadelphia, PA 19130 t) 215-763-6564 apfranx032@aol.com sfxschool.com Dolores Butler, Prin.;

St. Gabriel - 2917 Dickinson St., Philadelphia, PA 19146 t) 215-463-4060 roseadamsihm@gmail.com; myangel1134@aol.com Rev. Francis P. Foley, Pst.; Sr. Rose Marie Adams, I.H.M., DRE;

Convent - 2916 Dickinson St., Philadelphia, PA 19104 t) 215-334-2620

St. Gabriel Independence Mission School - t) 215-468-7230 Sr. Noreen James Friel, I.H.M., Prin.;

St. Helena - 6161 N. Fifth St., Philadelphia, PA 19120-1422 t) 215-424-1300 sophiessj@aol.com; jtmtrinh@aol.com sainthelenaparish.net Rev. Msgr. Joseph T. Trinh, Pst.; Rev. Peter J. Welsh, Par. Vicar; Dcn. Victor M. Pomales; Dcn. Huan C. Tran; Rev. Albert Gardy Villarson, O.M.I., In Res.; Sr. Sophie Yondura, S.S.J., Pst. Assoc.; CRP Stds.: 50

St. Helena School - 6101 N. Fifth St., Philadelphia, PA 19120 t) 215-549-2947

Holy Angels - 7000 Old York Rd., Philadelphia, PA 19126 t) 215-927-1162 holyangels102@hotmail.com Rev. Joseph Soon-Jin Kim, Par. Admin.; Rev. Chan Mi Kim, Par. Vicar; Rev. Michael Jung-Kyuto Yoo, Par. Vicar; Martin Shin, DRE;

Holy Cross - 154 E. Mt. Airy Ave., Philadelphia, PA 19119 t) 215-438-2921 secretary@holycrossphl.org Rev. Rayford E. Emmons, Par. Vicar; Rev. William E. Grogan, Pst.; Dcn. Edward M. Purnell;

Holy Cross School - 144 E. Mt. Airy Ave., Philadelphia, PA 19119 t) 215-242-0414

Convent - 148 E. Mt. Airy Ave., Philadelphia, PA 19119 t) 215-247-0262

Holy Family - 234 Hermitage St., Philadelphia, PA 19127 t) 215-482-0450 prep@holyfamilychurch.org; contact@holyfamilychurch.org www.holyfamilychurch.org Rev. Msgr. Patrick E. Sweeney, Pst.; Dcn. James M. Browne; Janet Kempf, DRE;

Holy Innocents - 1337 E. Hunting Park Ave., Philadelphia, PA 19124 t) 215-743-2600 holyinnocents@comcast.net www.holyinnocentsrc.org Rev. Thomas M. Higgins, Pst.; Rev. Roneld Saint Louis, Par. Vicar; Rev. Vincent Tung The Pham, Par. Vicar; Dcn. Andres A. Carrillo;

Holy Name of Jesus - 701 E. Gaul St., Philadelphia, PA 19125-2896 t) 215-739-3960 holynamefishtown@gmail.com www.holynameofjesus-fishtown.org Rev. Alfred E. Bradley, C.Ss.R., Admin.;

St. Laurentius Catholic School - (Grades PreK-8) 1612 E. Berks St., Philadelphia, PA 19125 t) 215-423-8834 kbell@stlaurentius.org www.stlaurentius.org Kelly Griffith Bell, Prin.;

Holy Redeemer - 915 Vine St., Philadelphia, PA 19107 t) 215-922-0999 Mission Chapel of the Church of St. John the Evangelist. Rev. John Daya, O.F.M.Cap., Coordinator of Chinese Apostolate;

Holy Redeemer School - (Grades 1-8) contact@stjohnsphilly.org www.holyredeemer.cc

Parish House - 916 Wood St., Philadelphia, PA 19107 t) 215-592-7552

St. Ignatius of Loyola - 636 N. 43rd St., Philadelphia, PA 19104 t) 215-386-5065 staff.manager636@gmail.com Rev. Msgr. Federico A. Britto, Par. Admin.; Jennifer Simmons, DRE;

Our Mother of Sorrows-St. Ignatius School - 617 N. 43rd St., Philadelphia, PA 19104 t) 215-222-3626 info@omssiphila.org omssiphila.org Sr. Owen Patricia Bonner, S.S.J., Prin.;

Chaplaincy - 4401 Haverford Ave., Philadelphia, PA 19104 t) 215-349-8800

Immaculate Heart of Mary - 819 E. Cathedral Rd., Philadelphia, PA 19128 t) 215-483-4266 (CRP); 215-483-1000 ihmparish@comcast.net www.ihmphila.org Rev. Edward J. Casey, Pst.; Rev. Quan H. Tran, Par. Vicar; Dcn. Salvatore R. Bianco; Rev. Joseph W. Bongard, In Res.; Rev. Sean P. Bransfield, In Res.;

Immaculate Heart of Mary School - 815 E. Cathedral Rd., Philadelphia, PA 19128 t) 215-482-2029

St. Jerome - 8100 Colfax St., Philadelphia, PA 19136 t) 215-333-4461 parish@stjeromechurchphila.org www.stjeromechurchphila.org Rev. Michael J. Reilly, Pst.; Rev. Robert Ngageno, In Res.; Rev. Michael J. Ryan, In Res.; CRP Stds.: 49

St. Jerome School - (Grades PreK-8) 3031 Stamford St., Philadelphia, PA 19136 t) 215-624-0637 principalstjerome@gmail.com sjsphila.org Susan Gallagher, Prin.;

St. John Cantius - 4415 Almond St., Philadelphia, PA 19137 t) 215-535-6667 rectory@stjohncantiusparish.org www.stjohncantiusparish.org With a Polish Mission Rev. Mark S. Kunigonis, Pst.; Rev. Konstanty J. Pruszynski, Par. Vicar; CRP Stds.: 47

Saint John Paul II Parish - 2645 E. Allegheny Ave., Philadelphia, PA 19134 t) 215-739-2735; 215-739-3500 sarah@jpiiphila.org; nativityportrichmond@gmail.com Rev. James P. Olson, Pst.; Rev. Bindel-Mary Nnabuife, C.M., Assistant; Rev. Jan Palkowski, Senior Priest; Rev. James P. Gorman, In Res.; Dcn. Ralph J. Shirley; CRP Stds.: 49

St. John the Baptist - 146 Rector St., Philadelphia, PA 19127 t) 215-482-4600 sjbphila@stjohnmanayunk.org www.stjohnmanayunk.org Records held for St. Mary of the Assumption Church (German), St. Josaphat Church (Polish), St. Ladislaus Church (Polish). Rev. Msgr. Kevin C. Lawrence, Pst.; Rev. Msgr. Hugh Joseph Shields, In Res.;

St. John the Evangelist - 21 S. 13th St., Philadelphia, PA 19107 t) 215-563-4145 www.stjohnsphilly.org Rev. Thomas Betz, Pst.; Friar John McCloskey, O.F.M. Cap., Par. Vicar; Rev. Roger White, O.F.M.Cap., Par. Vicar; Rev. Joseph Lei Jin, In Res.; Rev. Benjamin R. Regotti, O.F.M.Cap., In Res.; Friar Akolla Etuge, O.F.M. Cap, Campus Min.; CRP Stds.: 58

Holy Redeemer Chinese Church - 915 Vine St., Philadelphia, PA 19107 t) 215-922-0999

St. Katherine of Siena - 9700 Frankford Ave., Philadelphia, PA 19114-2896 t) 215-637-1464 (CRP); 215-637-7548 prep@skschurch.com; skschurch@skschurch.com www.skschurch.com Rev. Joseph S. Zaleski, Par. Admin.; Rev. Kevin C Okafor, Par. Vicar; Dcn. James J. Duffy; Dcn. Robert H. Hall; Rev. Saji Mukkoot, In Res.; Carol Buchsbaum, Bus. Mgr.;

St. Katherine of Siena School - (Grades PreK-8) 9738 Frankford Ave., Philadelphia, PA 19114 t) 215-637-2181 www.sksgradeschool.com Regina A. Tanghe, Prin.;

St. Malachy - 1429 N. 11th St., Philadelphia, PA 19122 t) 215-763-1305 pastor@stmalachychurch.faith www.stmalachychurch.faith Rev. Thomas P. Kletzel, Pst.; CRP Stds.: 20

Saint Martha - 11301 Academy Rd., Philadelphia, PA 19154-3304 t) 215-632-3720 churchoffice@stmarthachurch.com stmarthachurch.com Rev. Jonathan J. Dalin, Pst.; Rev. Alexander Masluk, Pastor Emer.; Dcn. Stephen A. Guckin; Rev. Msgr. Kenneth P. McAteer, In Res.;

St. Martha School - 11321 Academy Rd., Philadelphia, PA 19154-3304 t) 215-632-0320

St. Martin De Porres - 2340 W. Lehigh Ave., Philadelphia, PA 19132 t) 215-228-8330 smdp2340@hotmail.com smdpphiladelphia.com Rev. Addisalem T. Mekonnen, Par. Admin.; Dcn. Melvin J. Burton;

St. Martin De Porres School - 23rd St. & Lehigh Ave., Philadelphia, PA 19132 t) 215-223-6872

St. Martin of Tours - 5450 Roosevelt Blvd, Philadelphia, PA 19124 t) 215-535-2962 x403 ccd@smtparish.org www.smtparish.org Rev. Efren V. Esmilla, Pst.; Rev. David A. Waters, Par. Vicar; Rev. Jose Luis Queimado, C.Ss.R., Brazilian Apostolate;

St. Martin of Tours Mission School - 5701 Loretto Ave., Philadelphia, PA 19124

Maternity B.V.M. - 9220 Old Bustleton Ave., Philadelphia, PA 19115-4616 t) 215-673-4010 (CRP); 215-673-8127 church@maternitybvm.net www.maternitybvmchurch.net Rev. Paul S. Quinter, Pst.; Rev. Dominic Ishaq, Par. Vicar; Dcn. Joseph W. Bernauer Jr.; Dcn. Charles R. Lindsay; Dcn. Raymond N. Scipioni; Sr. Mary Beth Geraghty, R.S.M., DRE; CRP Stds.: 42

Maternity B.V.M. School - 9322 Bustleton Ave., Philadelphia, PA 19115 t) 215-673-0235 Mary Zawisza, Prin.; Carol Sims, Librn.;

Convent - t) 215-673-8118

St. Matthew - 3000 Cottman Ave., Philadelphia, PA 19149 t) 215-333-3142 (CRP); 215-333-0585 st-matthews@comcast.net www.stmattsparish.com Rev. Patrick J. Welsh, Pst.; Rev. Kevin P. McCabe, Par. Vicar; Dcn. Robert C. Burns;

St. Matthew School - 3040 Cottman Ave., Philadelphia, PA 19149

Convent - t) 215-333-8214

St. Michael - 1445 N. Second St., Philadelphia, PA 19122 t) 215-739-2358 st.michaelrcchurch1831@aol.com icstmichael19122.wordpress.com Rev. Fernando Londono, Par. Admin.;

St. Monica - 2422 S. 17th St., Philadelphia, PA 19145 t) 215-334-1659 (CRP); 215-334-4170 josephkelley56@gmail.com www.saintmonicaparish.net Rev. Joseph J. Kelley, Pst.; Rev. Kenneth Cavara, Par. Vicar; Dcn. Leonard D. DeMasi; Dcn. James J. Stewart; Rev. John E. Calabro, In Res.; CRP Stds.: 96

Junior School - 1720 Ritner Ave., Philadelphia, PA 19145 t) 215-334-3777

Senior School - 2500 S. 16th St., Philadelphia, PA 19145 t) 215-467-5338

St. Nicholas of Tolentine - 910 Watkins St., Philadelphia, PA 19148 t) 215-463-1326 stnicks910@verizon.net www.stnicksphila.com Rev. Nicholas Martorano, O.S.A., Pst.; Rev. Robert Terranova, Par. Vicar; CRP Stds.: 65

St. Anthony of Padua Regional Catholic School - 913 Pierce St., Philadelphia, PA 19148 t) 215-468-0353

Old St. Joseph's - 321 Willings Aly., Philadelphia, PA 19106 t) 215-923-1733 office@oldstjoseph.org www.oldstjoseph.org Rev. Francis T Hannafey, S.J., Pst.; Rev. Paul D Holland, SJ, Par. Vicar; Bro. Robert L. Carson, S.J.; Christine Szczepanowski, DRE;

Old St. Mary's - 252 S. Fourth St., Philadelphia, PA 19106 t) 215-923-7930 Rev. Msgr. Paul A. DiGirolamo, Pst.;

Our Lady of Calvary - 11024 Knights Rd., Philadelphia, PA 19154 t) 215-637-1648 (CRP); 215-637-7515 office@ourladyofcalvary.org www.ourladyofcalvary.org Rev. John F. Babowitch, Pst.; Rev. William S. Kirk, Par. Vicar; Dcn. Michael J. Bell; Dcn. John P. Teson; Rev. Louis J. Monica Jr., In Res.;

Our Lady of Calvary School - (Grades PreK-8) 11023 Kipling Ln., Philadelphia, PA 19154 Sr. Mildred Chesnavage, C.S.F., Prin.;

Our Lady of Consolation - 7056 Tulip St., Philadelphia, PA 19135 t) 215-333-0442 olc_btate@comcast.net olctacony.com Rev. Joseph L. Farrell, Pst.;

Our Lady of Hope - 5200 N. Broad St., Philadelphia, PA 19141-1628 t) 215-329-8100 parishoffice@olhcatholic.org www.olhcatholic.org Rev. Andrew Labatorio, C.I.C.M., Par. Admin.; Rev. Daniel M. Tettedji, Par. Vicar; Dcn. Felipe Hernandez; Dcn. Homer A. Panganiban;

Our Lady of Lourdes - 6315 Lancaster Ave, Philadelphia, PA 19151 t) 215-473-1669 www.ourladylourdes.org Rev. Matthew H. Phelan, O.de.M, Pst.; Rev. Justin Freeman, O.de.M., Par. Vicar;

Our Lady of Mt. Carmel - 2319 S. Third St., Philadelphia, PA 19148 t) 215-334-7766 olmc-phila@verizon.net www.ourladymountcarmel.net Rev. Francis J. Cauterucci, Pst.; Rev. Chanlis Chacko, In Res.; CRP Stds.: 41

Convent - 251 Ritner St., Philadelphia, PA 19148 t) 215-334-6800

Our Mother of Consolation - 9 E. Chestnut Hill Ave., Philadelphia, PA 19118 t) 215-247-0430 ckonopelski@omcparish.com; jfisher@omcparish.com www.omcparish.com Rev. John J. Fisher, OSFS, Pst.; Dcn. Joseph L. Nines; Dcn. Christopher C. Roberts; Rev. Robert G. Mulligan, O.S.F.S., In Res.; Rev. Charles J. Norman, O.S.F.S., In Res.; Sr. Christine Konopelski, S.S.J., Pst. Assoc.;

Our Mother of Consolation School - (Grades PreK-8) 17 E. Chestnut Hill Ave., Philadelphia, PA 19118 t) 215-247-1060 tschmidt@omcparish.com school.omcparish.com Theresa Schmidt, Prin.;

Convent - 23 E. Chestnut Hill Ave., Philadelphia, PA 19118 t) 215-247-0552

St. Patrick - 242 S. 20th St., Philadelphia, PA 19103 t) 215-735-9900 office@stpatrickphilly.org www.stpatrickphilly.org Friar Hyacinth M Cordell, O.P., Pst.; Friar Pachomius Walker, O.P., Par. Vicar; Friar Dominic J Bump, O.P., In Res.; Bro. James Wallace, O.P., In Res.; Dr. Sean O'Connor, Music Min.; Loretta A. Colucci, Bus. Mgr.;

St. Mary Interparochial School - Fifth & Locust Sts., Philadelphia, PA 19106 t) 215-923-7522 schooloffice@saintmarys.us www.saintmarys.us

St. Paul - 808 S. Hutchinson St., Philadelphia, PA 19147 t) 215-923-0355 st.paul.philly@gmail.com stpaulparish.net Rev. Paul W. Galetto, O.S.A., Pst.; CRP Stds.: 45

St. Mary Magdalen de Pazzi Church - 712 Montrose St., Philadelphia, PA 19147 (Worship Site)

St. Peter the Apostle - 1019 N. Fifth St., Philadelphia, PA 19123 t) 215-627-2386 spaphilly.org/ Rev. Richard S. Bennett, C.Ss.R., Pst.; Rev. Gerard Chylko, C.Ss.R., Par. Vicar; Rev. Thomas Deely, C.Ss.R., Par. Vicar; Rev. Huan Le Thanh, C.Ss.R., Par. Vicar; Rev. Charles P. McDonald, C.Ss.R., In Res.; Rev. Huyen T. Nguyen, C.Ss.R., In Res.; CRP Stds.: 30

St. Peter the Apostle School - 1009 N. Fifth St., Philadelphia, PA 19123 t) 215-922-5958

Convent - 1005 N. 5th St., Philadelphia, PA 19123 t) 215-627-3954

St. John Neumann - t) 215-627-3080 Deborah Binder, Dir.;

St. Philip Neri - 218 Queen St., Philadelphia, PA 19147 t) 215-468-1922 stphilipneri@comcast.net queenvillagecatholic.com Rev. Edward P. Kuczynski, Pst.;

St. Raymond of Penafort - 1350 Vernon Rd., Philadelphia, PA 19150 t) 215-549-3760 pastor@saintraymond.net www.saintraymond.net Rev. Charles Zlock, Pst.; Dcn. William C. Bradley;

St. Raymond of Penafort School - (Grades PreK-8) 7940 Williams Ave., Philadelphia, PA 19150 t) 215-548-1919 pwright@straymondphila.org straymondphila.imsphila.org/

Resurrection of Our Lord - 2000 Shelmire Ave., Philadelphia, PA 19152 t) 215-742-1127 x120 (CRP); 215-745-3211 resurrectionchurch@resurrectphila.org www.resurrectphila.org Rev. James R. DeGrassa, Pst.; Dcn. Dennis J. Friel; Dcn. John J. Knesis; Rev. Thomas P. Gallagher, O.S.F.S., In Res.; Rev. Harold B. McKale, In Res.; Karen Fitzgerald, DRE; Dcn. Joao A. Ferreira, Portugese Apostolate;

Resurrection of Our Lord School - 2020 Shelmire Ave., Philadelphia, PA 19152 resurrectionschool@yahoo.com www.resurrectschool.org Joan Stulz, Prin.;

St. Richard - 3010 S. 18th St., Philadelphia, PA 19145 t) 215-468-4777 dre@strichardchurch.org; parish@strichardchurch.org www.strichardchurch.org Rev. Matthew D. Brody, Pst.; Rev. John J. McGoldrick (Ireland), In Res.; CRP Stds.: 76

Holy Spirit Church - 1857 Hartranft St., Philadelphia, PA 19145; Mailing: 3010 S. 18th St., Philadelphia, PA 19145 t) (215) 468-4777 (Worship Site)

St. Rita of Cascia - 1166 S. Broad St., Philadelphia, PA 19146 t) 215-546-8333 ritashrine@aol.com www.saintritashrine.org Spiritual records are kept at Annunciation B.V.M. Church, Philadelphia. Rev. Robert Joseph Guessetto, O.S.A., Chap.; Rev. Daniel McLaughlin, O.S.A., In Res.;

The National Shrine of St. Rita of Cascia -

Sacred Heart of Jesus - 1404 S. Third St., Philadelphia, PA 19147-6099 t) 215-465-4050 sacredheart310@comcast.net www.sacredheartchurchsp.com Rev. James C. Otto, Pst.; CRP Stds.: 90

Stella Maris - 2901 S. 10th St., Philadelphia, PA 19148 t) 215-465-2336 (CRP); 215-465-2337 stellamarisparish@comcast.net www.stellamarisphila.com Rev. John R. DiOrio, Pst.; Marie Milano, DRE; Dawn Lalli-Shaw, Bus. Mgr.; CRP Stds.: 51

Convent - 2929 S. 10th St., Philadelphia, PA 19148 t) 215-462-1111

St. Thomas Aquinas - 1719 Morris St., Philadelphia, PA 19145 t) 215-334-2312 staquinasparish@gmail.com Rev. Markus Rudy Hermawan, CM (Indonesia), In Res.; Rev. Dominic Tran Minh Duc, Pst.; Rev. Wilmer Chirino Gonzalez, Par. Vicar; Dcn. Cristobal Chavac; Joanne Gledhill, DRE; CRP Stds.: 150

Aquinas Center - 1700 Fernon St., Philadelphia, PA 19145 t) 267-928-4048 www.staquinas.com

St. Timothy - 3001 Levick St., Philadelphia, PA 19149 t) 215-338-9797 x123 (School); 215-624-6188 ckirschman@st-tims.org; rectory@st-tims.org www.st-tims.org Rev. Michael S. Olivere, Pst.; Rev. Andrew F. Lane, Par. Vicar; Rev. Charles J. Noone, In Res.;

Convent - 3033 Levick St., Philadelphia, PA 19149 t) 215-624-8333

St. Veronica - 533 W. Tioga St., Philadelphia, PA 19140 t) 267-836-9056 (CRP); 215-228-4878; 215-225-5677 stveronica@servidoras.org; stveronica.rcc@gmail.com www.saintveronicaparish.org Rev. Roberto Gurrola, I.V.E., Pst.; Rev. Jose Molina, I.V.E., Par. Vicar; Sr. Mother Incarnation, S.S.V.M., DRE; Sr. Assumption Binyahan, DRE; Dcn. Jose Luis Lozada, Pst. Min./Coord.;

St. Veronica School - 3521 N. 6th St., Philadelphia, PA 19140 t) 215-225-1575 Sr. Eileen Buchanan, I.H.M., Prin.;

Katharine Drexel Sisters, Servants of the Lord and the Virgin of Matara - t) 215-856-4541 c.katharinedrexel@servidoras.org Mother Mary Incarnation Creeden, SSVM, Supr.;

St. Hugh of Cluny - 145 W. Tioga St., Philadelphia, PA 19140; Mailing: St. Veronica, 533 W. Tioga St., Philadelphia, PA 19140 Worship site

St. Vincent de Paul - 109 E. Price St., Philadelphia, PA 19144 t) 215-438-2925 secretary@saint-vincent-church.org www.saint-vincent-church.org Rev. Sylvester

Peterka, C.M., Pst.; Rev. Joseph Ita-Sam, C.M., Par. Vicar; Rev. Bindel-Mary Nnabuife, C.M., Par. Vicar; Bro. Alfred Smith, C.M., In Res.; Valerie Lee-Jeter, Music Min.; Darin Williams, Music Min.; Maria Beatty, Youth Min.; Terrance Fulton, Youth Min.; Suzanne Garnett, DRE; JoAnn O'Connor, Bus. Mgr.;

St. Vincent De Paul Youth and Young Adult Center - 49 W. Logan St., Philadelphia, PA 19144 t) 215-842-3668 Sr. Sharon Horace, D.C., Dir.;

St. Vincent's Food Pantry - 100 E. Rittenhouse St., Philadelphia, PA 19144; Mailing: 109 E, Price St., Philadelphia, PA 19144 t) 215-438-1514 Elizabeth Bergen, Contact; Jean Flynn, Contact;

Visitation B.V.M. - 2625 B St., Philadelphia, PA 19125 t) 215-634-1133 nrivera@communitycenteratvis.org; visitationchurch@visitationbvm.com www.visitationbvm.net Rev. Francis Mulvaney, C.Ss.R., Pst.; Rev. Pierre Cao Vinh Phuc, Par. Vicar; Rev. Charles P. McDonald, C.Ss.R., Par. Vicar; Rev. Huyen T. Nguyen, C.Ss.R., In Res.; Norma Rivera, DRE; David Serrano, DRE;

Visitation B.V.M. School - (Grades PreK-8) 300 E. Lehigh Ave., Philadelphia, PA 19125 t) 215-634-7280 contact@vizobvm.org www.vizobvm.org Edward Coleman, Prin.;

Cardinal Bevilacqua Community Center - 2646 Kensington Ave., Philadelphia, PA 19125 t) 215-426-9422 Sr. Elizabeth Scanlon, R.S.M., Dir.;

St. William - 6200 Rising Sun Ave., Philadelphia, PA 19111 t) 215-745-1389 office@churchofstwilliam.com www.churchofstwilliam.org Rev. Alfonso J. Concha, Pst.; Rev. Tariq Isaac, Par. Vicar; Rev. Eugene Almonor, O.M.I., In Res.; Rev. Augusto M. Concha, In Res.; Dcn. Felipe Cruz; Dcn. William J. Moser; Evelin Santana, CRE; CRP Stds.: 101

Convent - 6226 Rising Sun Ave., Philadelphia, PA 19111

PHOENIXVILLE

St. Ann - 502 S. Main St., Phoenixville, PA 19460 t) 610-933-3732 stannphx@comcast.net www.churchofsaintann.org Rev. John J. Newns, Pst.; Dcn. Daniel T. Giblin; Dcn. Mark Szewczak; CRP Stds.: 183

St. Basil the Great - 2300 Kimberton Rd., Phoenixville, PA 19460 t) 610-935-1261 (CRP); 610-933-2110 dre@stbasil.org; church@stbasils.org www.stbasils.org Rev. Gary T. Pacitti, Pst.; Dcn. Mark D. Nowakowski; James King, DRE;

Sisters of St. Francis Residence - t) 610-933-2345

St. Mary of the Assumption - 212 Dayton St., Phoenixville, PA 19460 t) 610-933-2526 parishoffice@stmaryassumption.org www.stmaryassumption.org Rev. John S. Hutter, Pst.; Dcn. Jeffrey S. Hanna; CRP Stds.: 45

PLYMOUTH MEETING

Epiphany of Our Lord - 3050 Walton Rd., Plymouth Meeting, PA 19462-2361 t) 215-367-5853 (CRP); 610-828-8634 rep@eol.comcastbiz.net; eol@epiphanyofourlord.com Rev. Thomas D. O'Donald, Par. Admin.; Dcn. Michael Pascarella Jr.; Gail Toto, Youth Min.; Stephanie Quigley, DRE;

Holy Rosary Regional Catholic School - 3040 Walton Rd., Plymouth Meeting, PA 19462-2361 t) 610-825-0160 www.holyrosaryregional.com Lisa Hoban, Prin.;

POTTSTOWN

St. Aloysius - 214 N. Hanover St., Pottstown, PA 19464 t) 610-326-5877 x434 (CRP); 610-326-5877 saintaloysius.net Rev. Joseph L. Maloney, Pst.; Rev. Francesco M. D'Amico, Par. Vicar; Dcn. George S. Harmansky;

St. Aloysius School - (Grades PreK-8) 844 N. Keim St., Pottstown, PA 19464 t) 610-326-6167 kbruce@saintaloysius.net www.saintaloysius.net Kathleen Bruce, Prin.;

St. Thomas More - 2101 Pottstown Pike, Pottstown, PA 19465 t) 610-469-9302 (CRP); 610-469-9304 office.stthomasmoreparish@gmail.com stthomasmorepottstown.org/ Rev. Msgr. Thomas J. Dunleavy, Par. Admin.; Dcn. Timothy L. Murphy; CRP Stds.: 46

PRIMOS

St. Eugene - 200 S. Oak Ave., Primos, PA 19018 t) 610-626-2866 steugene55@rcn.com www.sainteugenechurch.net Rev. Joseph M. McDermott, Pst.; Dcn. James V. Walsh;

St. Eugene School - (Grades K-8) 110 S. Oak Ave., Primos, PA 19018 t) 610-622-2909 dthompson@sainteugeneschool.org sainteugeneschool.org Diana Thompson, Prin.;

QUAKERTOWN

St. Isidore - 2545 W. Pumping Station Rd., Quakertown, PA 18951; Mailing: 603 W. Broad St., Quakertown, PA 18951 t) 215-536-6498 (CRP); 215-536-4389 izprepoff@comcast.net; dre@stisidoreprep.com www.stisidores.org Rev. Kenneth C. Brabazon, Pst.; Dcn. David C. Mitchell; Dcn. Patrick J. O'Donnell; Jeffrey Daley, DRE; CRP Stds.: 254

St. Isidore School - (Grades PreK-8) 603 W. Broad St., Quakertown, PA 18951 t) 215-536-6052 izzybiz@comcast.net stisidoreschool.com Dr. Robin Conboy, Prin.; Stds.: 270; Lay Tchrs.: 15

RICHBORO

St. Vincent de Paul - 654 Hatboro Rd., Richboro, PA 18954-1039 t) 215-322-1932 (CRP); 215-357-5905 pastor@saintvincents.net; info@saintvincents.net www.saintvincents.net Rev. Stephen H. Paolino, Par. Admin.; Rev. Joseph J. McLaughlin, Pastor Emer.; Elaine M Potalivo, DRE; CRP Stds.: 220

Sisters of St. Joseph - 624 Hatboro Rd., Richboro, PA 18954-1039 t) 215-942-9152

RIDLEY PARK

St. Madeline - 400 Morton Ave., Ridley Park, PA 19078; Mailing: 110 Park St., Ridley Park, PA 19078 t) 610-532-6880 stmadeline@comcast.net stmadelineparish.com/ Rev. John B. Flanagan, Pst.; Dcn. Michael J. Alexander; CRP Stds.: 135

RIEGELSVILLE

St. Lawrence - 345 Elmwood Ln., Riegelsville, PA 18077 t) 610-749-2684 saintlawrence@verizon.net Rev. Walter J. Benn, Pst.;

ROSEMONT

St. Thomas of Villanova Parish - 1229 E. Lancaster Ave., Rosemont, PA 19010 t) 610-525-4801 x210 admin@stvparish.org www.stthomasofvillanova.org Rev. Joseph A. Genito, O.S.A.; Rev. Michael Hughes, O.S.A., Par. Vicar; Dcn. Donald P. DiCarlo Jr.; CRP Stds.: 300

ROYERSFORD

Sacred Heart - 838 Walnut St., Royersford, PA 19468; Mailing: P.O. Box 64, Royersford, PA 19468 t) 610-948-5915 www.sacredheartroyersford.org Rev. Tadeusz Gorka, Pst.; Dcn. David M. Kubczak;

RYDAL

St. Hilary of Poitiers - 820 Susquehanna Rd., Rydal, PA 19046 t) 215-884-3252 sthilaryrydal@gmail.com www.sthilarypoitiers.org Rev. Kevin P. Murray, Pst.; Rev. Jacob John, In Res.;

St. Hilary of Poitiers School - (Grades PreK-8) 920 Susquehanna Rd., Rydal, PA 19046 t) 215-887-4520 Eileen Fagan, Prin.; Diane Sawyer, Librn.;

SCHWENKSVILLE

St. Mary - 40 Spring Mount Rd., Schwenksville, PA 19473 t) 610-287-8156 solzinski@churchofsaintmary.org www.churchofsaintmary.org Rev. James M. Cox, Pst.; Dcn. Donald O. Nichols; CRP Stds.: 171

St. Mary School - t) 610-287-7757

Saint Teresa of Calcutta - 256 Swamp Pike, Schwenksville, PA 19473 t) 610-287-2525 frbrandt@stteresacalcutta.com www.stteresacalcutta.org Rev. Paul C. Brandt, Pst.; Dcn. Peter J. Dolan; Dcn. James V. Nash; Dcn. Thomas G. Phillips Jr.; Rev. Alessandro Giardini, In Res.; Rev. John J. Pidgeon, In Res.;

St. Teresa of Calcutta School - (Grades PreK-8) t) 610-287-2500 Anita M. Dixon, Prin.;

SECANE

Our Lady of Fatima - 1 Fatima Dr., Secane, PA 19018 t) 610-586-3633 x287 (CRP); 610-532-5800 secretary@olfsecane.org www.olfsecane.org Rev. Roland D. Slobogin, Pst.; Rev. Thomas P. Gillin, Par. Vicar; Rev. Michael J. Lonergan, In Res.;

Convent - 5 Fatima Dr., Secane, PA 19018 t) 610-532-1190

SELLERSVILLE

St. Agnes - 445 N. Main St., Sellersville, PA 18960 t) 215-257-2128 stagnesprep@gmail.com www.stagneschurch.org Rev. Jeffrey M. Stecz, Pst.; Dcn. R. Lyle Benner; Dcn. Raymond Thuel; Dcn. Harry Tucker; Rev. Shaju K. Kanjiramparayil, O.S.F.S., In Res.; CRP Stds.: 125

SOUTHAMPTON

Our Lady of Good Counsel - 611 Knowles Ave., Southampton, PA 18966-4198 t) 215-357-1300 x107 (CRP); 215-357-1300 tcoffice@olgc.org www.olgc.org Rev. Robert G. Suskey, Pst.; Rev. Msgr. Joseph A. Tracy, Par. Vicar; CRP Stds.: 272

Our Lady of Good Counsel School - Frank Mokriski, Prin.;

SPRING CITY

St. Joseph - 3640 Schuylkill Rd., Spring City, PA 19475 t) 610-850-4228 (CRP); 610-948-7760 stjosephprep@comcast.net; st.joes@comcast.net Rev. Charles R. O'Hara, Pst.; Rev. Donato P. Silveri, In Res.; Andrea Jackowski, DRE;

SPRINGFIELD

St. Francis of Assisi - 136 Saxer Ave., Springfield, PA 19064 t) 610-543-0848 (CRP); 610-543-0848 sfabulletin@hotmail.com www.sfaparish.org Rev. Matthew J. Tralies, Pst.; Dcn. William T. Baxter; Rev. Henry Mc Kee, In Res.; Rev. Joseph J. Meehan, In Res.;

St. Francis of Assisi School - 112 Saxer Ave., Springfield, PA 19064 t) 610-543-0546

Holy Cross - 651 E. Springfield Rd., Springfield, PA 19064-3336 t) 610-626-3321 contactus@holycrosscatholics.org holycrosscatholics.org Rev. Steven W. Kiernan, Pst.; Dcn. Thomas L. Taylor; Rev. Edward C. Kelly, In Res.;

Holy Cross School - (Grades PreK-8) 240 N. Bishop Ave., Springfield, PA 19064 t) 610-626-1709 www.hcscrusaders.com Dr. Mary Rose Worrilow, Prin.;

St. Kevin - 200 W. Sproul Rd., Springfield, PA 19064-2016 t) 610-544-8777 info@st.kevin.com Rev. John C. Moloney, Pst.; CRP Stds.: 246

STOWE

St. Gabriel of the Sorrowful Mother - 127 E. Howard St., Stowe, PA 19464-6707 t) 610-326-5127 contact@sgsm62.org Rev. Eugene C. Wilson, Pst.; Dcn. Rafael M. Then Jr.; Maria Boyer, DRE; CRP Stds.: 26

STRAFFORD

Our Lady of the Assumption - 35 Old Eagle School Rd., Strafford, PA 19087 t) 610-688-6590 (CRP); 610-688-1178 rmangelilli@olastrafford.org; rwesterfer@olastrafford.org olastrafford.org Rev. Gerald P. Carey, Pst.; Dcn. John P. Rose; Rev. Augustin Kassa, SMA, In Res.; CRP Stds.: 120

Preschool - 135 Fairfield Ln., Strafford, PA 19087 t) 610-688-5277

SWEDESBURG

Sacred Heart - 120 Jefferson St., Swedesburg, PA 19405 t) 610-275-1750 unitedinthesacredheart.com Rev. Peter J. DiMaria, Pst.;

Convent - 635 E. Fourth St., Swedesburg, PA 19405 t) 610-239-1785 Sisters Servants of the Most Sacred Heart Sr. Ryszarda Wittbrodt, Supr.;

UPPER DARBY

St. Laurence - 30 St. Laurence Rd., Upper Darby, PA 19082 t) 610-449-0600 x215 (CRP); 610-449-0600 www.saintlaurencedelco.org Rev. Thomas P. Whittingham, Pst.; Dcn. Samuel Ortiz; Dcn. Mark Wallace; Rev. Anthony Raymundo, In Res.; Rita Marian, I.H.M., DRE;

St. Laurence School - 8245 W. Chester Pike, Highland Park, PA 19082 t) 610-789-2670

Convent - t) 610-449-7042

H.O.P.E. Program -

WALLINGFORD

St. John Chrysostom - 617 S. Providence Rd., Wallingford, PA 19086 t) 610-874-3418 mpizzano@sjcparish.org; phoffice@sjcparish.org www.sjcparish.org Rev. Edward J. Hallinan, Pst.; Dcn. John R. Bowie; Rev. Donald P. McNamara, In Res.; Mary Pizzano, DRE;

Mother of Providence Regional Catholic School - 607 S. Providence Rd., Wallingford, PA 19086 t) 610-876-7110 www.mpregional.org

WARMINSTER

Nativity of Our Lord - 625 W. Street Rd., Warminster, PA 18974 t) 215-675-1925 www.noolp.org Rev. Joseph G. Watson, Pst.; Rev. Joseph J. Quindlen, In Res.; CRP Stds.: 202

Nativity of Our Lord School - (Grades PreK-8) 585 W. Street Rd., Warminster, PA 18974 t) 215-675-2820 kmcdonough@noolp.org school.noolp.org Roselee Maddaloni, Pres.; Kyle McDonough, Prin.; Nicole Ferruzzi, Vice Prin.; Stds.: 497; Lay Tchrs.: 30

Precious Friends of St. Gianna Childcare Center - 657 York Rd., Warminster, PA 18974

WARRINGTON

St. Joseph - 1795 Columbia Ave., Warrington, PA 18976 t) 215-672-9990 (CRP); 215-672-3020 sjc18976@verizon.net www.saintjosephchurch.us Rev. Joseph C. Bordonaro, Pst.; Cathy Cain, DRE;

St. Robert Bellarmine - 856 Euclid Ave., Warrington, PA 18976 t) 215-343-9433 (CRP); 215-343-0315 donnaheeneydre@gmail.com; strobertsecretary@verizon.net www.saintrobertwarrington.org Rev. Msgr. James D. Beisel, Pst.; Rev. Patrick J. Muka, Par. Vicar; Dcn. George E. Morris Jr.; Dcn. Thomas P. Quinn; Rev. James F. Endres, In Res.; Donna Heeney, DRE; CRP Stds.: 354

WAYNE

St. Isaac Jogues - 50 W. Walker Rd., Wayne, PA 19087 t) 610-687-2481 (CRP); 610-687-3366 sijccd@gmail.com; rectory@stisaac.org www.stisaac.org Rev. Stephen A. Moerman, Pst.; Dcn. Daniel E. Mazurek; Louis M. Valenti, DRE;

St. Katharine of Siena - 104 S. Aberdeen Ave., Wayne, PA 19087 t) 610-688-7890 (CRP); 610-688-4584 religioused@sksparish.org www.sksparish.org Rev. Msgr. Hans A.L. Brouwers, Pst.; Rev. Msgr. Francis W. Beach, Par. Vicar; Sr. Mary Elizabeth Karalis, S.S.J., DRE; Colleen Maguire, Coordinator of Parish Life Ministry;

St. Katharine of Siena School - (Grades K-8) 116 S. Aberdeen Ave., Wayne, PA 19087 t) 610-688-5451 Frank Tosti, Prin.;

Convent - 235 Windermere Ave., Wayne, PA 19087 t) 610-688-0655 srkathleen@sksparish.org

WEST BRANDYWINE

St. Peter - 2835 Manor Rd., West Brandywine, PA 19320 t) 610-380-9045 office@saintpeterchurch.net saintpeterchurch.net Rev. Michael J. Fitzpatrick, Pst.; Dcn. H.W. Todd Smith; Rev. Emmanuel K. Iheaka, In Res.; CRP Stds.: 1

Parish Religious Education Program - 2875 Manor Rd., West Brandywine, PA 19320 t) 610-384-3145 Patrice A. Peterson, DRE;

WEST CHESTER

St. Agnes - 233 W. Gay St., West Chester, PA 19380 t) 610-436-4640 (CRP); 610-692-2990 clytle@saintagnesparish.org saintagnesparish.org Rev. Louis P. Bellopede, Pst.; Rev. Daniel J. Arechabala, Par. Vicar; Rev. Wilfred E. Emeh, Par. Vicar; Dcn. Dwight E. Johnson; Dcn. Thomas E. Shurer; Rev. William J. Chiriaco, In Res.; CRP Stds.: 600

St. Agnes School - 211 W. Gay St., West Chester, PA 19380 t) 610-696-1260

Convent - 205 W. Gay St., West Chester, PA 19380 t) 610-692-9430

St. Maximilian Kolbe - 15 E. Pleasant Grove Rd., West Chester, PA 19382 t) 610-399-6936; 610-399-9642 (PREP Office) saintmax@comcast.net; smk-prep@stmax.org www.stmax.org Rev. Christopher J. Papa, Pst.; Rev. William T Lange, Par. Vicar; Rev. Russell Ortega, O.S.A., In Res.; Lauren Welsh, DRE; CRP Stds.: 406

St. Maximilian Kolbe School - (Grades PreK-8) 300 Daly Dr., West Chester, PA 19382 t) 610-399-8400 stmaxinfo@stmax.org www.school.stmax.org Monica Malseed, Prin.;

SS. Peter and Paul - 1325 Boot Rd., West Chester, PA 19380 t) (610) 692-2216 x238 mdelassandro@sspeterandpaulrc.org; pafox@sspeterandpaulrc.org www.sspeterandpaulrc.org Rev. Msgr. Angelo R. Citino, Pst.; Rev. David M Buffum, Par. Vicar; Dcn. Robert F. Pierce; Dcn. Patrick M. Stokely; Michele D'Alessandro, DRE; CRP Stds.: 225

SS. Peter and Paul School - (Grades PreK-8) 1327 Boot Rd., West Chester, PA 19380-5901 t) 610-696-1000 school@sspeterandpaulrc.org Margaret Egan, Prin.; Dorothy Conway, Librn.;

SS. Simon and Jude - 8 Cavanaugh Ct., West Chester, PA 19382 t) 610-692-3118 (CRP); 610-696-3624 rectory@simonandjude.org www.simonandjude.org/ Rev. Michael J. Gerlach, Pst.; Rev. Msgr. Thomas J. Dunleavy, Par. Vicar; Dcn. Gerald J. Cassidy; Dcn. James T. Owens; Dcn. Joseph A. Ruggiero; Rev. Philip J. Lowe, In Res.; Sr. Barbara Jude Gentry, I.H.M., DRE; Ronald B. Avellino, Bus. Mgr.; Sr. Mary Agnes Ryan, RCIA Coord.;

SS. Simon and Jude School - (Grades PreK-8) 6 Cavanaugh Ct., West Chester, PA 19382 t) 610-696-5249 ssjschool@simonandjude.org school.simonandjude.org Sr. Regina Elinich, I.H.M., Prin.;

Convent - 6 Cavanaugh Court, West Chester, PA 19382 t) 610-692-4394 Sr. Helene Thomas Connolly, IHM, Supr.;

WEST GROVE

Assumption B.V.M. - 300 State Rd., West Grove, PA 19390 t) 610-869-8575 (CRP); 610-869-2722 abvm@comcast.net www.assumptionbvmwestgrove.org Rev. Scott D. Brockson, Pst.; Dcn. Thomas Hannan; Dcn. Ronald L. Lewis; Mary Rose Edmonds, Parish Opers. Mgr.;

Assumption B.V.M. School - 290 State Rd., West Grove, PA 19390 t) 610-869-9576 assumptionwestgrove@comcast.net Danielle White, Prin.;

WILLOW GROVE

St. David - 316 N. Easton Rd., Willow Grove, PA 19090 t) 215-659-4059 (CRP); 215-657-0252 rectory@stdavidparish.org www.stdavidparish.org Rev. Matthew Windle, Pst.; Rev. Msgr. Paul M. Kennedy, In Res.; Dcn. Christopher J. Mars; CRP Stds.: 144

Queen of Angels Regional Catholic School - (Grades PreK-8) 401 N. Easton Rd., Willow Grove, PA 19090 t) 215-659-6393 qoaschool@qoaschool.org www.qoaschool.org Sr. Margaret Rose Adams, I.H.M., Prin.;

Convent - 400 N. Easton Rd., Willow Grove, PA 19090 t) 215-659-0445

WYNNEWOOD

Presentation B.V.M. - 204 Haverford Rd., Wynnewood, PA 19096 t) 610-642-8341 parishcenter@presbvm.org www.presbvm.org Rev. Eduardo G. Montero, Pst.; CRP Stds.: 72

YARDLEY

St. Ignatius of Antioch - 999 Reading Ave., Yardley, PA 19067 t) 215-493-5204 (CRP); 215-493-3377 contact@stignatius.church www.stignatiuschurch Rev. Andrew C. Brownholtz, Pst.; Dcn. Michael L. Cibenko; Rev. Charles J. Kennedy, In Res.;

St. Ignatius of Antioch School - 995 Reading Ave., Yardley, PA 19067 t) 215-493-3867 www.sischool.org

SCHOOLS: PRESCHOOL THRU HIGH SCHOOL

SCHOOLS

COMMONWEALTH OF PENNSYLVANIA

ABINGTON

Regina Coeli Academy - (PRV) (Grades PreK-8) 1525 Marian Rd., Abington, PA 19001 t) 215-277-1386 info@reginacoeliacademy.com www.reginacoeliacademy.com A private independent school. Tim Murnane, Chair; Stds.: 118; Lay Tchrs.: 12

ARDMORE

***Regina Academies** - (PRV) (Grades PreK-12) 40 E Montgomery Ave, Ardmore, PA 19003; Mailing: PO Box 465, Wynnewood, PA 19096 t) 610-726-1856 mbradford@reginaacademies.org www.reginaacademies.org Mark Bradford, Exec.; Stds.: 600; Pr. Tchrs.: 1; Lay Tchrs.: 57

***Regina Angelorum Academy** - 104 Argyle Rd., Ardmore, PA 19003 t) 610-649-1730 reginaangelorum@yahoo.com reginaangelorumacademy.org Ann Coffey, Prin.;

ARDSLEY

Good Shepherd Catholic Regional School - (PAR) 835 N. Hills Ave, Ardsley, PA 19038 t) 215-886-4782 spatriciahealey@gscregional.org www.gscregional.org Sr. Helen Thomas McCann, Prin.;

ASTON

Holy Family Regional Catholic School - 3265 Concord Rd., Aston, PA 19014 t) 610-494-0147 jdolores@holyfamilyaston.org www.holyfamilyaston.org Jennifer Dolores, Prin.;

BERWYN

***Regina Luminis Academy** - (Grades K-8) 601 First Ave., Berwyn, PA 19312 t) 610-269-3905 drattore@reginaluminis.org www.reginaluminisacademy.com Denise D'Attore, Headmaster; Mark Anthony, Pres.; Miranda McClain, Librn.;

BRYN MAWR

St. Aloysius Academy - (PRV) (Grades PreK-8) 401 S. Bryn Mawr Ave., Bryn Mawr, PA 19010 t) 610-525-1670 mainoffice@staloysiusacademy.org www.staloysiusacademy.org Sr. Stephen Anne Roderiguez, I.H.M., Prin.;

SS. Colman-John Neumann School - (PAR) (Grades PreK-8) 372 Highland Ln., Bryn Mawr, PA 19010 t) 610-525-3266 kelly.ciminera@scjnschool.org www.scjnschool.org Regional school for St. Colman Parish and St. John Neumann Parish. Kelly Ciminera, Prin.;

CHESTER

Drexel Neumann Academy - (PRV) (Grades PreK-8) 1901 Potter St., Chester, PA 19013-5497 t) 610-872-7358 mgannonosf@comcast.net Sr. Catherine McGowan, S.S.J., Prin.; Sr. Margaret Gannon, O.S.F., Pres.;

COLLEGEVILLE

Holy Cross Regional Catholic School - 701 Locust St., Collegeville, PA 19426 t) 610-489-9434 thealy@holycrossregionalschool.org holycrossregionalschool.org Theresa A. Healy, Prin.;

DREXEL HILL

Holy Child Academy - (PRV) (Grades PreK-8) 475 Shadeland Ave., Drexel Hill, PA 19026 t) 610-259-2712 mfoxtully@holychildacademy.com holychildacademy.com Judy Clay, Librn.; Margaret Fox-Tully, Head of School;

HAVERTOWN

Cardinal John Foley Regional Catholic School - 300 E. Eagle Rd., Havertown, PA 19083 t) 610-446-4608 principal@cardinalfoley.org Mary Ann DeAngelo, Prin.;

HOLLAND

St. Katharine Drexel Regional Catholic School - 1053 Holland Rd., Holland, PA 18966 t) 215-357-4720 mslauraclark@skdschool.org www.skdschool.org Laura

Clark, Prin.;

KING OF PRUSSIA

***Independence Mission Schools** - 640 Freedom Bus. Center Dr., Ste. 115, King of Prussia, PA 19406 t) 610-200-5100 info@independencemissionschools.org www.independencemissionschools.org See School Section for related schools. Richard Auletta, Pres.; Brian McElwee, Dir.;

DePaul Catholic School - 44 W. Logan St., Philadelphia, PA 19144 t) 215-842-1266 secretary@thedepaulcatholicschool.org depaulphila.org Katie Wardlow, Prin.;

***St. Martin de Porres School** - 2300 W. Lehigh Ave., Philadelphia, PA 19132 t) 215-223-6872 stmartindeporresphila.org Sr. Meaghan V. Patterson, S.S.J., Prin.;

St. Helena - Incarnation Regional Catholic School - 6101 N. 5th St., Philadelphia, PA 19120 t) 215-549-2947 www.sthelenaphila.org Nick Huck, Prin.;

St. Frances Cabrini Regional Catholic School - 405 N. 65th St., Philadelphia, PA 19151 t) 215-748-2994 stfrancescabriniphila.org William Cascarina, Prin.;

Holy Cross - 144 E. Mount Airy Ave., Philadelphia, PA 19119 t) 215-242-0414 holycrossoffice@holycrossphila.org holycrossphila.org Emily Diefendorf, Prin.;

Our Mother of Sorrows/St. Ignatius of Loyola - 617 N. 43rd St., Philadelphia, PA 19104 t) 215-222-3626 info@omssiphila.org ommsiphila.org Sr. Owen Patricia Bonner, S.S.J., Prin.;

St. Cyril of Alexandria - 716 Emerson Ave., East Lansdowne, PA 19050 t) 610-623-1113 bmontague@stcyrilphila.org stcyrilphila.independencemissionschools.org Theresa Power, Admin.; Sr. Barbara Montague, I.H.M., Prin.;

St. Gabriel - 2917 Dickinson St., Philadelphia, PA 19146 t) 215-468-7230 stgabrielphila.org Sr. Noreen James Friel, I.H.M., Prin.;

St. Malachy - 1012 W. Thompson St., Philadelphia, PA 19122 t) 215-232-0696 stmalachyphila.org Stephen Janczewski, Prin.;

St. Martin of Tours - 5701 Loretto Ave., Philadelphia, PA 19124 t) 215-744-0444 info@stmartinoftoursphila.org www.stmartinoftoursphila.org Sr. Ellen Giardino, I.H.M., Prin.;

St. Raymond of Penafort - 7940 Williams Ave., Philadelphia, PA 19150 t) 215-548-1919 straymondphila.org Patricia Wright, Prin.;

St. Rose of Lima - 1522 N. Wanamaker St., Philadelphia, PA 19131 t) 215-473-6030 stroseoflimaphila.org Sr. Rita James Murphy, I.H.M., Prin.;

St. Thomas Aquinas - 1631 S. 18th St., Philadelphia, PA 19145 t) 215-334-0878 info@stthomasphila.org stthomasphila.org Nicole Unegbu, Prin.;

St. Veronica - 3521 N. 6th St., Philadelphia, PA 19140 t) 215-225-1575 stveronicasphila.org Sr. Eileen Buchanan, I.H.M., Prin.;

St. Barnabas Catholic School - 6334 Buist Ave., Philadelphia, PA 19142 t) 215-729-3603 stbarnabasphila.org Sr. Catherine Clark, I.H.M., Prin.;

Mother Teresa Regional Catholic School - 405 Allendale Rd., King of Prussia, PA 19406 t) 610-265-2323 christine.pagan@mtcschool.org www.mtcschool.org Christine Pagan, Prin.; Miranda Miller, Librn.;

LANSDALE

Mater Dei Catholic School - 493 E. Main St., Lansdale, PA 19446 t) 215-368-0995 info@materdeicatholic.com www.materdeicatholic.com Diane E. McCaughan, Prin.;

LEVITTOWN

Holy Family Regional Catholic School - 2477 Trenton Rd., Levittown, PA 19056 t) 215-269-9600 www.hfrcs.org Linda Robinson, Prin.;

MALVERN

Villa Maria Academy - (PRV) (Grades PreK-8) 280 IHM Dr., Malvern, PA 19355 t) 610-644-4864 office@villamaria.org www.villamaria.org Sr. Susan Joseph, I.H.M., Prin.; Stds.: 270; Lay Tchrs.: 34

MAPLE GLEN

Our Lady of Mercy Regional Catholic School - 29 Conwell Dr., Maple Glen, PA 19002 t) 215-646-0150 jmcgrath@olmrcs.com www.olmrcs.com John C. McGrath, Prin.; Rosa Costanzo, Librn.;

MERION STATION

Waldron Mercy Academy - (PRV) (Grades PreSchool-8) 513 Montgomery Ave., Merion Station, PA 19066 t) 610-664-9847 wma@waldronmercy.org www.waldronmercy.org Private, co-educational elementary school with child care, preschool & Montessori programs. Ann Marie Braca, Prin.; Theresa Gannon, Vice Prin.; Stds.: 410; Lay Tchrs.: 49

MORTON

Our Lady of Angels Regional Catholic School - (PAR) (Grades PreK-8) 2130 Franklin Ave., Morton, PA 19070 t) 610-543-8350 slowe@olaschool2.com www.ourladyofangelsmorton.org Susan Beatrice Lowe, Prin.;

OTTSVILLE

***Regina Academy at St. John the Baptist** - (PRV) (Grades PreK-8) 4040 Durham Rd., Ottsville, PA 18942 t) 610-847-5523 emailtkoeber@rasjb.org www.rasjb.org Tami Koeber, Head of School;

PHILADELPHIA

St. Anthony of Padua Regional Catholic School - 913 Pierce St., Philadelphia, PA 19148-1619 t) 215-468-0353 srmcarsele@stanthonyofpaduarcs.org teacherweb.com Sr. Mary Esther Carsele, M.P.F., Prin.; Sr. Carmela Falcone, M.P.F., Prin.; Sr. Dolores Duffy, O.S.F., Librn.;

Blessed Trinity Regional Catholic School - 3033 Levick St., Philadelphia, PA 19149 t) 215-338-9797 lmilewski@btrc.org Linda Milewski, Prin.; James Zaccario, Dir.; Michael Skudar, Librn.;

St. George School - (PAR) (Grades PreK-8) 2700 E. Venango St., Philadelphia, PA 19134 t) 215-634-8803 www.stgeorgecatholic.com Joanne H. Walls, Prin.;

The Gesu School - (PRV) (Grades PreK-8) 1700 W. Thompson St., Philadelphia, PA 19121 t) 215-763-3660; 215-763-9077 (Devel.) www.gesuschool.org Rev. Raymond Donaldson, SJ, Chap.; Sr. Ellen Convey, I.H.M., Prin.; Alana Lee, Vice Prin.; Bryan Carter, Pres.; Sr. Mary E. Bur, I.H.M., Librn.;

Holy Innocents Area Catholic School - (PAR) 1312 E. Bristol St., Philadelphia, PA 19124 t) 215-743-5909 srm625@yahoo.com Sr. Regina Mullen, I.H.M., Prin.; Carol Hockensmith, Librn.;

***La Salle Academy** - (PRV) (Grades 3-8) 1434 N. 2nd St., Philadelphia, PA 19122 t) 215-739-5804 jmcgowan@lasalleacademy.net www.lasalleacademy.net Teresa Diamond, Prin.; Sr. Jeanne McGowan, S.S.J., Pres.;

St. Mary Interparochial School - (PAR) (Grades K-8) 5th & Locust Sts., Philadelphia, PA 19106 t) 215-923-7522 schooloffice@saintmarys.us; advancement@saintmarys.us www.saintmarys.us Jayda Pugliese, Prin.; Christina Haciski, Dir.; Millie Cammisa, Librn.;

Mother of Divine Grace School - (PAR) 2612 E. Monmouth St., Philadelphia, PA 19134 t) 215-426-7325 jelockhart@motherdivinegrace.com www.motherdivinegrace.com Lockhart Jane White, Prin.;

Nazareth Academy Grade School - (PRV) 4701 Grant Ave., Philadelphia, PA 19114 t) 215-637-7777 slinda@nazarethacademy.net www.nazarethacademy.net Sr. Linda Joseph, C.S.F.N., Prin.; Sr. M. Yvette Ortiz, C.S.F.N., Treas.; Stds.: 198; Lay Tchrs.: 14

Norwood-Fontbonne Academy - (PRV) (Grades PreK-8) 8891 Germantown Ave., Philadelphia, PA 19118-2718 t) 215-247-3811 x210 rkilleen@norfon.org; pingram@norfon.org www.norfon.org Dr. Ryan Killeen, Pres.; Allyn Monteiro, DRE; Stds.: 339; Lay Tchrs.: 33

Our Lady of Hope Regional Catholic School - 1248 Jackson St., Philadelphia, PA 19148 t) 215-467-5385 pab0223@comcast.net www.ourladyofhopephilly.com Patricia Cody, Prin.; Theresa T. Ford, Librn.;

Our Lady of Port Richmond Regional School - 3233 Thompson St., Philadelphia, PA 19134 t) 215-739-1920 srmary@ourladyofportrichmond.com ourladyorportrichmond.com Regional School for St. Adalbert, Nativity of the Blessed Virgin Mary and Our Lady Help of Christians. Sr. Mary Ripp, S.C.C., Prin.; Sr. Angela Abbruzzese, S.C.C., Librn.;

St. Pio Regional Catholic School - (Grades PreSchool-8) 1826 Pollock St., Philadelphia, PA 19145 t) 215-467-5430 eileensharpwilson@gmail.com www.stpiocatholic.org Francesca Russo, Prin.;

Resurrection Regional Catholic School - (PAR) (Grades PreK-8) 2020 Shelmire Ave., Philadelphia, PA 19152-4209 t) 215-742-1127 jbellantoni@resurrectschool.org www.resurrectschool.org Jack Bellantoni, Prin.;

PHOENIXVILLE

Holy Family School - (PAR) 221 Third Ave., Phoenixville, PA 19460 t) 610-933-7562 abraca@myholyfamily.org www.myholyfamilyschool.org Regional school for St. Ann Parish; St. Mary of the Assumption Parish; St. Joseph, Spring City; St. Basil the Great, Kimberton. Ann Marie Braca, Prin.; Susan Vickrey, Librn.;

PLYMOUTH MEETING

Holy Rosary Regional Catholic School - 3040 Walton Rd., Plymouth Meeting, PA 19462-2361 t) 610-825-0160 lhoban@holyrosaryregional.com; mailman@holyrosaryregional.com Mary Ann Gilman, Prin.;

RADNOR

Armenian Sisters Academy - (PAR) (Grades PreK-8) 440 Upper Gulph Rd., Radnor, PA 19087 t) 610-687-4100 sisteremma@asaphila.org; office@asaphila.org www.asaphila.org Sr. Emma Moussayan, Prin.; Lara Odabashian Croy, Librn.;

RIDLEY PARK

St. James Regional Catholic School - 500 Tome St., Ridley Park, PA 19078 t) 610-583-3662 principal@stjamesregional.com www.stjamesregional.com Regional school for St. Madeline Parish, St. Rose of Lima Parish, and St. Gabriel Parish. Loren Loomis, Prin.;

ROSEMONT

Holy Child School at Rosemont - (PRV) (Grades PreSchool-8) 1344 Montgomery Ave., Rosemont, PA 19010 t) 610-992-1000 info@holychildrosemont.org; mtrost@holychildrosemont.org www.holychildrosemont.org Thomas Lengel, Head of School; Megan Trost, Assistant to the Head of School; Stds.: 323; Lay Tchrs.: 34

SPRING HOUSE

Gwynedd-Mercy Academy Elementary School - (PRV) (Grades K-8) 816 Norristown Rd., Spring House, PA 19477; Mailing: P.O. Box 241, Spring House, PA 19477 t) 215-646-4916; 215-646-2406 (Bus. Office) aknapke@gmaelem.org www.gmaelem.org Sr. Anne W. Knapke, R.S.M., Prin.; Mary Johnson, Librn.;

WALLINGFORD

Mother of Providence Regional Catholic School - (PAR) (Grades PreK-8) 607 S. Providence Rd., Wallingford, PA 19086 t) 610-876-7110 sdempsey@mpregional.org www.mpregional.org Sara Dempsey, Prin.; Stds.: 266; Lay Tchrs.: 22

WARRINGTON

St. Joseph-St. Robert School - (PAR) 850 Euclid Ave., Warrington, PA 18976 t) 215-343-5100 stjstr.org Regional school for St. Joseph Parish and St. Robert Bellarmine Parish. Deborah R. Jaster, Prin.; Patricia Pfeil, Librn.;

WEST BRANDYWINE

Pope John Paul II Regional Catholic Elementary School - 2875 Manor Rd., West Brandywine, PA 19320

t) 610-384-5961 skerins@popejohnpaul2sch.org www.popejohnpaul2sch.org Sarah Kerins, Prin.;

WILLOW GROVE

Archbishop Wood High School - 314 Easton Rd, Willow Grove, PA 19090 t) 215-657-9311 principal@ourladyofconfidence.org www.ourladyofconfidence.org Intellectual Disability. Katie Bier, Prin.; Stds.: 49; Lay Tchrs.: 7

Main School and Office-St. David Site - jmoeller@ourladyofconfidence.org

Queen of Angels Regional Catholic School - (DIO) (Grades PreSchool-8) 401 N. Easton Rd., Willow Grove, PA 19090 t) 215-659-6393 qoaschool@qoaschool.org www.qoaschool.org Sr. Mary C Chapman Sr., IHM, Prin.; Stds.: 251; Lay Tchrs.: 15

WYNCOTE

Ancillae-Assumpta Academy - (PRV) (Grades PreSchool-8) 2025 Church Rd., Wyncote, PA 19095 t) 215-885-1636 alintner@ancillae.org; mgillespie@ancillae.org www.ancillae.org Private, co-educational school. Sr. Maureen Gillespie, A.C.J., Prin.; Sr. Kathleen Helbig, Treas.; Amelia Lintner, Dir.; Maureen Rilling, DRE; Stds.: 573; Sr. Tchrs.: 3; Lay Tchrs.: 60

HIGH SCHOOLS

COMMONWEALTH OF PENNSYLVANIA

BENSALEM

Holy Ghost Preparatory School - (PRV) (Grades 9-12) 2429 Bristol Pike, Bensalem, PA 19020 t) 215-639-2102 www.holyghostprep.org Rev. Daniel Sormani, C.S.Sp., Chap.; Kevin Burke, Prin.; Gregory J. Geruson, Pres.; Stds.: 423; Pr. Tchrs.: 1; Lay Tchrs.: 37

BERWYN

***Regina Luminis Academy** - (PRV) (Grades PreK-12) 601 First Ave., Berwyn, PA 19312; Mailing: 601First Ave Berwyn, PA 19355-3097 t) 610-269-3905 info@reginaluminis.org www.reginaluminisacademy.com/ Marybeth Brehany, Headmaster; Mark Anthony, Pres.; Stds.: 163; Lay Tchrs.: 16

BRYN MAWR

Sacred Heart Academy Bryn Mawr (Country Day School at Overbrook Foundation) - (PRV) (Grades K-12) 480 S. Bryn Mawr Ave., Bryn Mawr, PA 19010 t) 610-527-3915 ann.simpson@shabrynmawr.org; carla.macmullen@shabrynmawr.org www.shabrynmawr.org/ Sloane Davis, Bus. Mgr.; Eileen Day, Dir. of Upper School; Carla MacMullen, Head of School; Beth Porter, Dir. of Lower School; Kimberley Trinacria, Dir. of Middle School; Stds.: 193; Lay Tchrs.: 34

DEVON

Devon Preparatory School (Piarist Fathers) - (PRV) (Grades 6-12) 363 N. Valley Forge Rd., Devon, PA 19333 t) 610-688-7337 devoninfo@devonprep.com www.devonprep.com Rev. Francisco Aisa, Sch.P., Prin.; Rev. Geza Pazmany, Sch.P., In Res.; Rev. James J. Shea, Sch.P., Mem.; Rev. Andrew Mbinkar, Sch.P., Chap.; Stds.: 324; Pr. Tchrs.: 4; Lay Tchrs.: 58

DOWNINGTOWN

Bishop Shanahan High School - (DIO) (Grades 9-12) 220 Woodbine Rd., Downingtown, PA 19335 t) 610-518-1300 rplunkett@shanahan.org; jdonia@shanahan.org www.shanahan.org Rev. William Chiriaco, Campus Min.; Sr. Regina Plunkett, I.H.M., Pres.; Rev. John E. Donia, Prin.; Stds.: 968; Pr. Tchrs.: 2; Sr. Tchrs.: 6; Lay Tchrs.: 49

DREXEL HILL

Monsignor Bonner and Archbishop Prendergast Catholic High School - 403 N. Lansdowne Ave., Drexel Hill, PA 19026-1196 t) 610-259-0280 www.bonnerprendie.com Patricia Rooney, Prin.; Dr. John E Cooke, Pres.; Stds.: 831; Pr. Tchrs.: 1; Lay Tchrs.: 44

FAIRLESS HILLS

Conwell-Egan Catholic High School - (DIO) 611 Wistar Rd., Fairless Hills, PA 19030 t) 215-945-6200 info@conwell-egan.org conwell-egan.org Formerly Bishop Egan High School, Fairless Hills, and Bishop Conwell High School, Levittown. Tom Lynch, Pres.; Mathew Fischer, Prin.; Stds.: 515; Lay Tchrs.: 24

FLOURTOWN

Mt. St. Joseph Academy - (PRV) 120 W. Wissahickon Ave., Flourtown, PA 19031-1899 t) 215-233-3177 cdiorka@msjacad.org www.msjacad.org Elizabeth Blessing, Prin.; Sr. Charlene Diorka Sr., SSJ, Pres.; Stds.: 462; Lay Tchrs.: 47

GWYNEDD VALLEY

Gwynedd Mercy Academy High School - (PRV) 1345 Sumneytown Pike, Gwynedd Valley, PA 19437-0902; Mailing: P.O. Box 902, Gwynedd Valley, PA 19437-0902 t) 215-646-8815 dmarbach@gmahs.org www.gmahs.org Eileen O'Neill Carty, Prin.; Denise Corkery Marbach, Pres.; Stds.: 411; Lay Tchrs.: 65

HOLLAND

Villa Joseph Marie High School - (PRV) (Grades 9-12) 1180 Holland Rd., Holland, PA 18966 t) 215-357-8810 lcarr@vjmhs.org www.vjmhs.org Lauren Carr, Prin.; Jeanne Frawley, Pres.; Stds.: 332; Lay Tchrs.: 43

LANSDALE

Lansdale Catholic High School - (PAR) 700 Lansdale Ave., Lansdale, PA 19446-2995 t) 215-362-6160; 215-242-6160 (Philadelphia) jcasey@lansdalecatholic.com www.lansdalecatholic.com James W. Casey, Pres.; Rita McGovern, Prin.; Rev. David O'Brien, Minister; Stds.: 600

MALVERN

Malvern Preparatory School for Boys - (PRV) (Grades 6-12) 418 S. Warren Ave., Malvern, PA 19355-2707 t) 484-595-1100 cdrennen@malvernprep.org www.malvernprep.org Rev. Christopher J. Drennen, O.S.A., Director of Mission and Ministry; Rev. William C. Gabriel, O.S.A., Teacher; Rev. Donald F. Reilly, O.S.A., In Res.; Patrick Mcstravog, O.S.A., In Res.; Stds.: 640; Pr. Tchrs.: 3; Lay Tchrs.: 83

Villa Maria Academy High School - (PRV) 370 Central Ave., Malvern, PA 19355 t) 610-644-2551 srryan@vmahs.org www.vmahs.org Sr. Marie Claire Matsinger, I.H.M., Campus Min.; Sr. Regina Ryan, I.H.M., Prin.; Melissa Norman, Librn.; Stds.: 390; Sr. Tchrs.: 7; Lay Tchrs.: 57

MERION STATION

Merion Mercy Academy - (PRV) (Grades 9-12) 511 Montgomery Ave., Merion Station, PA 19066 t) 610-664-6655 mainoffice@merion-mercy.com www.merion-mercy.com/ Day School for Girls. Marianne Grace, Pres.; Stds.: 371; Lay Tchrs.: 31

ORELAND

Martin Saints Classical High School - (PRV) (Grades 9-12) 121 Allison Rd., Oreland, PA 19075 t) 267-495-4865 adickerson@martinsaintsclassical.org www.martinsaintsclassical.org Adam A. Dickerson, Headmaster; Dcn. Christopher C. Roberts, Pres.; Nicole Marshall, Director of Advancement; Stds.: 51; Lay Tchrs.: 7

PHILADELPHIA

Archbishop Ryan High School - (DIO) (Grades 9-12) 11201 Academy Rd., Philadelphia, PA 19154-3397 t) 215-637-1800 information@archbishopryan.com www.archbishopryan.org Joseph McFadden, Prin.; Joseph Sanginiti, Pres.; Stds.: 851

***Cristo Rey Philadelphia High School** - (PRV) (Grades 9-12) 1717 W. Allegheny Ave., Philadelphia, PA 19132 t) 215-219-3943 kreilly@crphs.org www.cristoreyphiladelphia.org Thomas Shoemaker, Pres.; Stds.: 541; Lay Tchrs.: 31

Father Judge High School for Boys (Oblates of St. Francis de Sales) - (DIO) (Grades 9-12) 3301 Solly Ave., Philadelphia, PA 19136-2396 t) 215-338-9494 mainoffice@fatherjudge.com www.fatherjudge.com/ James Irving Hozier Sr., Prin.; Brian P. King, Pres.; Stds.: 750; Scholastics: 60; Pr. Tchrs.: 1; Bro. Tchrs.: 1; Sr. Tchrs.: 1; Lay Tchrs.: 38

St. Hubert's Catholic High School for Girls - (DIO) 7320 Torresdale Ave., Philadelphia, PA 19136 t) 215-624-6840 contactus@huberts.org www.huberts.org Lizanne Pando, Pres.; Gerard Laskowski, Prin.; Stds.: 475; Lay Tchrs.: 27

SS. John Neumann and Maria Goretti Catholic High School - (DIO) (Grades 9-12) 1736 S. 10th St., Philadelphia, PA 19148-1694 t) 215-465-8437 www.neumanngorettihs.org (Formerly Southeast Catholic High School, Bishop Neumann High School, St. John Neumann High School for Boys, St. Maria Goretti High School for Girls) Rory Sweeney, Pres.; Rev. James E. Dalton, O.S.F.S., Campus Min.; Kim Eife, Prin.; Stds.: 571; Lay Tchrs.: 28

St. Joseph's Preparatory School - (PRV) (Grades 9-12) Office of the President,, 1733 W. Girard Ave., Philadelphia, PA 19130 t) (215) 978-1951 www.sjprep.org John Marinacci, Pres.; Andrew T. Cavacos, Prin.; Albert Greene, Dean; Sonia Nelson, Librn.; Stds.: 900; Pr. Tchrs.: 2; Bro. Tchrs.: 1; Lay Tchrs.: 100

Little Flower Catholic High School for Girls - (DIO) 1000 W. Lycoming St., Philadelphia, PA 19140 t) 215-455-6900 jmcnamara@lfch.org www.littleflowerhighschool.org Colette Weber, Prin.; Jeane McNamara, Pres.; Stds.: 428; Lay Tchrs.: 28

Mercy Career & Technical High School - (PAR) 2900 W. Hunting Park Ave., Philadelphia, PA 19129-1803 t) 215-226-1225 generalinfo@mercycte.org www.mercycte.org Catherine Glatts, Vice President for CTE; Sr. Rosemary Herron, R.S.M., Pres.; Christian Aument, Prin.; Stds.: 303; Sr. Tchrs.: 5; Lay Tchrs.: 30

Nazareth Academy High School - (PRV) 4001 Grant Ave., Philadelphia, PA 19114-2999 t) 215-637-7676 jmeredith@nazarethacademyhs.org www.nazarethacademyhs.org Denise LePera, Pres.; James Meredith, Prin.; Stds.: 345; Lay Tchrs.: 35

Roman Catholic High School for Boys - (DIO) 301 N. Broad St., Philadelphia, PA 19107 t) 215-627-1270; 215-627-1570 psticco@romancatholichs.com www.romancatholichs.com Patricia C. Sticco, Prin.; Rev. Joseph W. Bongard, Pres.; Sandra Kolander, Librn.;

West Catholic Preparatory High School - 4501 Chestnut St., Philadelphia, PA 19139 t) 215-386-2244 info@westcatholic.org www.westcatholic.org Andrew Brady, Pres.; Genevieve Torres, Prin.; Messiah Reames, Dean, Students; Kelly Foley, Campus Min.; Chris Diehl, Asst. Prin., Student Life; Michael J. Field Jr., Asst. Prin., Acad. Affairs; Stds.: 433; Scholastics: 22; Bro. Tchrs.: 2; Sr. Tchrs.: 2; Lay Tchrs.: 20

RADNOR

Archbishop John Carroll High School - (DIO) 211 Matson Ford Rd., Radnor, PA 19087 t) 610-688-7610 carroll@jcarroll.org www.jcarroll.org Rev. Mark J. Cavara, Campus Min.; Patricia Gioffre Scott, Pres.; William Gennaro, Prin.;

ROYERSFORD

Pope John Paul II High School - 181 Rittenhouse Rd., Royersford, PA 19468 t) 484-975-6500 www.pjphs.org Vince Cazzetta, Pres.; Kathleen Guyger, Prin.; Stds.: 720; Lay Tchrs.: 36

SPRINGFIELD

Cardinal O'Hara High School - (DIO) 1701 S. Sproul Rd., Springfield, PA 19064 t) 610-544-3800 info@cohs.com cohs.com Coed Michael Connor, Pres.; Rev. John P. Masson, School Minister; Eileen Vice, Prin.; Stds.: 830; Lay Tchrs.: 40

VILLANOVA

Academy of Notre Dame de Namur - (PRV) (Grades 6-12) 560 Sproul Rd., Villanova, PA 19085 t) 610-687-0650 lhotchkiss@ndapa.org www.ndapa.org Dr. Laura M. Hotchkiss, Headmaster; Stds.: 539; Lay Tchrs.: 56

WARMINSTER

Archbishop Wood Catholic High School - (DIO) 655 York Rd., Warminster, PA 18974 t) 215-672-5050 gzimmaro@archwood.org www.archwood.org Gary V. Zimmaro, Pres.; Cloe O'Grady, Prin.; Rev. Paul J. O'Donnell, School Minister; Stds.: 840; Lay Tchrs.: 41

WYNDMOOR

LaSalle College High School - (PRV) (Grades 9-12) 8605

Cheltenham Ave., Wyndmoor, PA 19038 t) 215-233-2911 admissions@lschs.org www.lschs.org James Fyke, Prin.; Bro. James Butler, F.S.C., Pres.; Kevin Dougherty, Vice President; Bro. Edward Koronkiewicz, Community Director; Daniel L McGowan, Vice President of Institutional Advancement; Mark Gibbons, CFO; Joseph Hartnett, Bd. Chair; Stds.: 1,090; Bro. Tchrs.: 6; Lay Tchrs.: 105

INSTITUTIONS LOCATED IN DIOCESE

ASSOCIATIONS [ASN]

ASTON

Association of Franciscan Colleges and Universities, Inc. - Neumann University, 1 Neumann Dr., Aston, PA 19014 t) 601-358-4539 haugd@neumann.edu Debi Haug, Dir.;

PHILADELPHIA

The Central Association of the Miraculous Medal - 475 E. Chelten Ave., Philadelphia, PA 19144-5785 t) 215-848-1010; 800-523-3674 tshea@cammonline.org www.miraculousmedal.org Rev. Timothy V. Lyons, C.M., Dir.;

CAMPUS MINISTRY / NEWMAN CENTERS [CAM]

PHILADELPHIA

Newman Apostolate for Archdiocese of Philadelphia - 222 N. 17th St., Philadelphia, PA 19103 t) (215) 587-3979 www.archdiocese-phl.org/offices/na.htm Rev. Stephen P. DeLacy, Dir.;

Arcadia University - St. Luke the Evangelist Church, 2316 Fairhill Ave, Glenside, PA 19038-4107 t) 215-572-0128 Rev. Joseph D. Brandt, Chap.;

Bucks County Community College - St. Andrew Church, 81 Swamp Rd., Newtown, PA 18940 t) 215-968-2262

Cheney University - t) 610-399-2353 Chaplaincy Vacant.

Community College of Philadelphia - 1700 Spring Garden St, Philadelphia, PA 19129 Chaplaincy Vacant.

Delaware County Community College - St. Anastasia, 3301 W. Chester Pk., Newtown Square, PA 19073 t) (610) 359-5206 x5341 Chaplaincy Vacant.

Delaware County Community College - Math Science Dept., Media, PA 19063 t) 610-359-5206

Delaware Valley College of Science and Agriculture - St. Jude Church, 321 W. Butler Ave., Chalfont, PA 18914-2329 t) 215-822-0179 Rev. Jeffrey M. Rott;

Drexel University - Newman Catholic Center, 3720 Chestnut St., Philadelphia, PA 19104-6189 mjg395@drexel.edu saintsaj.org/drexel Bro. Michael Gokie, S.V.C., Dir.;

Harcum College - Our Mother of Good Counsel, 31 Pennswood Rd., Bryn Mawr, PA 19010 t) (215) 525-4100 x6045

Lincoln University - Sacred Heart Church, 101 Church Rd., Oxford, PA 19363 t) 610-932-5040

Montgomery County Community College - St. Helena Church, 1489 DeKalb Pk., Blue Bell, PA 19422; Mailing: P.O. Box 5085, Center Square, PA 19422 t) (215) 275-7711 Rev. Msgr. Joseph J. Nicolo, Chap.;

Pennsylvania State University - Delaware County Campus - St. Francis de Sales Church, 33 New Rd., Lenni, PA 19062; Mailing: Box 97, Lenni, PA 19062 t) 610-459-2203

Pennsylvania State University - Abington - 1600 Woodland Rd., Abington, PA 19001 t) 215-881-7548 bep@psu.edu Rev. Msgr. Archdeacon Brian Polk, Chap.;

Pennsylvania State University - Great Valley Campus -

Philadelphia College of Pharmacy and Science - 3728 Chestnut St., Philadelphia, PA 19104 t) 215-898-7575

Philadelphia University - St. Bridget Church, 3667 Midvale Ave., Philadelphia, PA 19129-1712 t) 215-844-4126

Roxborough Memorial School of Nursing - St. John the Baptist, 146 Rector St., Philadelphia, PA 19107 t) 215-482-4600 Rev. Msgr. Kevin C. Lawrence, Chap.;

Temple University - Newman Center, 2129 N. Broad St., Philadelphia, PA 19122-1193 t) 215-232-3779 smahoney@temple.edu www.templenewmancenter.org Rev. Shaun L. Mahoney, Chap.;

Temple University, Ambler Campus - St. Alphonsus Church, 33 Conwell Dr., Maple Glen, PA 19002 t) 215-646-4600 www.libertynet.org/~tunewman

Tenet Hahnemann (Center City Campus) - Cathedral Basisilica SS Peter and Paul, 1723 Race St., Philadelphia, PA 19103 t) 215-561-1313 Chaplaincy Vacant.

Thomas Jefferson University - 111 S. 11th St, Philadelphia, PA 19107 Rev. Joseph Leggieri;

Tri-College Newman Cluster - Bryn Mawr, Haverford and Swarthmore Colleges - 3301 W. Chester Pike, Newtown Square, PA 19073 t) 610-328-8578 rev.johnames@gmail.com

University of Pennsylvania - Newman Hall, 3720 Chestnut St., Philadelphia, PA 19104-6189 t) 267-757-5000 ptravers@saintsaj.org www.newman.upenn.edu Bro. Patrick Travers, ., Other;

University of the Arts - Students Activity Center, 320 Broad St, Philadelphia, PA 19102 t) (215) 875-2236 Chaplaincy Vacant.

University of the Sciences in Philadelphia - St. Francis de Sales Church, 4625 Sprigfield Ave, Philadelphia, PA 19143 t) 215-596-8800 Rev. Louis C. Bier, Chap.;

Ursinus College - St. Eleanor Church, 647 Locust St., Collegeville, PA 19426-2541 t) 610-489-1647 Rev. Msgr. Michael T. McCulken, Chap.;

West Chester University - Newman Center, 409 Trinity Dr., West Chester, PA 19382-5362 t) 610-436-0891 www.wcunewman.org Rev. Thomas J. Gardner, Chap.; Daniel Pin, Dir.;

Widener University - St. Katharine Drexel Church, 1920 Providence Ave., Chester, PA 19013-5695 t) (610) 872-0545 fatherwhittingham@gmail.com Rev. Thomas P. Whittingham, Chap.;

CATHOLIC CHARITIES [CCH]

PHILADELPHIA

Catholic Social Services of the Archdiocese of Philadelphia - 222 N. 17th St., Philadelphia, PA 19103-1202 t) 267-331-2490 www.cssphiladelphia.org Amy Stoner, Dir.;

Adoption Services - t) 267-331-2443 www.adoption-phl.org Robert Montoro, Admin.;

Casa del Carmen Family Services - 4440 N. Reese St., Philadelphia, PA 19140 t) 267-331-2500 Christopher Gale, Admin.;

Catholic Community Services - 10125 Verree Rd., #200, Philadelphia, PA 19116 Teresa Thompson, Dir.;

Catholic Housing and Community Services - 222 N. 17th St., Philadelphia, PA 19103 t) 215-587-3663 hhuot@chs-adphila.org chcsphiladelphia.org/ Provides support svcs to older adults, including multi-service centers, in-home support, parish-based support progs; housing social svc coordination.

Developmental Programs Division Office - 20 E. Cleveland Ave., Norwood, PA 19074 t) 484-472-5066 fswiacki@chs-adphila.org www.dgdpcommunities.org Francis E. Swiacki Jr., Exec. Dir.;

Foster Care - t) 267-331-2488 Robert Montoro, Admin.;

Miscellaneous Corporations -

St. Joseph Catholic Home for Children - 222 N. 17th St., Philadelphia, PA 19103

St. Joseph House for Boys - 222 N. 17th St., Philadelphia, PA 19103

St. Vincent's Home, Tacony - 222 N. 17th St., Philadelphia, PA 19103

St. Vincent's Services - 222 N. 17th St., Philadelphia, PA 19103

Northeast Philadelphia Family Service Center - 7340 Jackson St., Philadelphia, PA 19136 t) 215-624-5920 Yvonne Branch, Admin.;

Philadelphia County Community-Based Services -

Southwest Philadelphia Family Service Center - 6214 Grays Ave., Philadelphia, PA 19142 t) 215-724-8550 Lola DeCarlo Coles, Admin.;

Specialized Services - 227 N. 18th St., Philadelphia, PA 19103 The offices are all located at the Holy Family Center unless otherwise noted.

Immigration and Refugee Services - t) 215-854-7019

Senior Adult Services - t) 215-854-7087 Karen Becker, Dir.;

Senior Centers and Clubs - 222 N. 17th St., Philadelphia, PA 19103 t) 215-854-7087 hhuot@chs-adphila.org

Suburban Counties -

Bucks County Family Service Centers - 100 Levittown Pkwy., Levittown, PA 19054 t) 215-945-2550 Teri Mitchell, Admin.;

Chester County Operating Base Cecilia - 605 E. Lincoln Hwy., Coatesville, PA 19320 t) 610-384-8387 Rick Pytlewski, Admin.;

Delaware County Family Service Center -

Montgomery County Family Service Center - 353 E. Johnson Hwy., Norristown, PA 19401 t) 610-279-7372 Susan Stier, Admin.;

CEMETERIES [CEM]

BENSALEM

Resurrection - 5201 Hulmeville Rd., Bensalem, PA 19020; Mailing: 222 N. 17th St., Philadelphia, PA 19103 t) 215-302-9379 rwhomsley@archphila.org

CHALFONT

St. John Neumann - 3797 County Line Rd., Chalfont, PA 18914; Mailing: 222 N. 17th St., Philadelphia, PA 19103 t) 215-302-9390 rwhomsley@archphila.org

COATESVILLE

All Souls - 3215 Manor Rd., Coatesville, PA 19320; Mailing: 222 N. 17th St., Philadelphia, PA 19103 t) 484-200-8320 rwhomsley@archphila.org

NEWTOWN

All Saints - 291 W. Durham Rd., Newtown, PA 18940; Mailing: 222 N. 17th St., Philadelphia, PA 19103 t) 215-302-9340 rwhomsley@archphila.org

PHILADELPHIA

Cathedral - 1032 N. 48th St., Philadelphia, PA 19131; Mailing: 222 N. 17th St., Philadelphia, PA 19103 t) 215-302-9341 rwhomsley@archphila.org

Holy Saviour - 222 N. 17th St., Philadelphia, PA 19103 rwhomsley@archphila.org

Holy Sepulchre - Cheltenham Ave. & Ivy Hill Rd., Philadelphia, PA 19150; Mailing: 222 N. 17th St., Philadelphia, PA 19103 t) 215-302-9356 rwhomsley@archphila.org

New Cathedral - Front & Luzerne St, Philadelphia, PA 19140; Mailing: 222 N. 17th St., Philadelphia, PA 19103 t) 215-302-9364 rwhomsley@archphila.org

SPRINGFIELD

SS. Peter and Paul - 1600 S. Sproul Rd., Springfield, PA 19064; Mailing: 222 N. 17th St., Philadelphia, PA 19103 t) 484-200-8321 rwhomsley@archphila.org

WEST CONSHOHOCKEN

Calvary - Gulph & Matsonford Rd., West Conshohocken, PA 19428; Mailing: 222 N. 17th St., Philadelphia, PA 19103 t) 610-232-7180

YEADON

Holy Cross - 626 Bailey Rd., Yeadon, PA 19050; Mailing: 222 N. 17th St., Philadelphia, PA 19103 t) 610-232-7182 rwhomsley@archphila.org

COLLEGES & UNIVERSITIES [COL]

ASTON

Neumann University - One Neumann Dr., Aston, PA 19014-1298 t) 610-558-5501 neumann@neumann.edu www.neumann.edu Sponsored by the Sisters of St. Francis of Philadelphia. Chris E. Domes, Pres.; Stds.: 2,155; Lay Tchrs.: 86; Pr. Tchrs.: 1; Sr. Tchrs.: 1

GWYNEDD VALLEY

Gwynedd Mercy University - 1325 Sumneytown Pike, Gwynedd Valley, PA 19437; Mailing: P.O. Box 901, Gwynedd Valley, PA 19437 t) 215-646-7300 mchale.b@gmercyu.edu; marketing@gmercyu.edu www.gmercyu.edu Deanne D'Emilio, Pres.;

IMMACULATA

Immaculata University (Conducted by Sisters, Servants of the Immaculate Heart of Mary) - 1145 King Rd., Immaculata, PA 19345 t) 610-647-4400 www.immaculata.edu Barbara Lettiere, Pres.; Amy Bosio, Vice Pres., Finance & Administration; Dr. Angela Tekely, Vice Pres., Academic Affairs; Sr. Antoine Lawlor, IHM, Vice Pres., Mission & Ministry; Patricia Canterino, Vice Pres., Student Devel. & UG Admissions; Susan Arnold, Vice Pres., Institutional Advancement; Steven Kendus, Vice Pres., Marketing & Communications; Dr. Jean Shingle, Dean, College of UG Studies; Dr. Mary Powell, Dean. College of Nursing & Health Professions; Dr. Marcia Parris, Dean, College of Graduate Studies; Cecelia Oswald, Dir., Institutional Research & Effectiveness; Dr. Jeffrey Rollison, Exec. Dir., Gabriele Library; Dina Stern, Dir., Financial Aid; Stds.: 2,501; Lay Tchrs.: 78; Sr. Tchrs.: 8

PHILADELPHIA

Chestnut Hill College - 9601 Germantown Ave., Philadelphia, PA 19118-2693 t) 215-248-7000 kmiller@chc.edu www.chc.edu William W. Latimer, Pres.; Stds.: 1,411; Lay Tchrs.: 69; Sr. Tchrs.: 4

Holy Family University - 9801 Frankford Ave., Philadelphia, PA 19114 t) 215-637-7700 ptownsend@holyfamily.edu www.holyfamily.edu/ Dr. Anne Prisco, Pres.; Sr. Rita Fanning, C.S.F.N., Vice. Pres.; Eric Nelson, Vice. Pres.; Michael McNulty-Bobholz, Vice. Pres.; Rev. Mark J. Hunt, Prof.; Shannon Brown, Librn.; Jill Snyder, Campus Min.; Stds.: 2,928; Lay Tchrs.: 72; Pr. Tchrs.: 1; Sr. Tchrs.: 1

***Saint Joseph's University** - 5600 City Ave., Philadelphia, PA 19131 t) 610-660-1000 president@sju.edu www.sju.edu Rev. Daniel R.J. Joyce, S.J., Vice. Pres.; Stds.: 7,863; Lay Tchrs.: 390; Pr. Tchrs.: 2

Jesuit Fathers - t) 610-660-1400 Rev. Mark C. Aita, S.J.; Rev. Anthony J. Berret, S.J.; Rev. John M. Braverman, S.J.; Rev. Thomas J. Brennan, S.J.; Rev. William J. Byron, S.J.; Rev. Peter A. Clark, S.J.; Rev. Joseph J. Feeney, S.J.; Rev. Vincent J. Genovesi, S.J.; Rev. Joseph J. Godfrey, S.J.; Rev. Daniel R.J. Joyce, S.J.; Rev. Brendan G. Lally, S.J.; Rev. Joseph L. Lombardi, S.J.; Rev. John Martin, S.J.; Rev. Nicholas J. Rashford, S.J.; Rev. Damien Ruff, S.J.; Rev. Patrick H. Samway, S.J.; Anne Krakow, Librn.;

LaSalle University - 1900 W. Olney Ave., Philadelphia, PA 19141 t) 215-951-1000 president@lasalle.edu www.lasalle.edu (Inc. under the auspices of the Brothers of the Christian Schools) Dr. Daniel J Allen, Pres.; Bro. Robert J. Kinzler, F.S.C., Asst. VP University Ministry, Service & Support; Stds.: 4,049; Bro. Tchrs.: 2; Lay Tchrs.: 198

RADNOR

Cabrini University (Missionary Sisters of the Sacred Heart of Jesus) - 610 King of Prussia Rd., Radnor, PA 19087-3698 t) 610-902-8100; 610-902-8200 www.cabrini.edu Helen G Drinan, Pres.; Rev. David Driesch, O.Praem., Chap.; Stds.: 1,616; Lay Tchrs.: 68; Pr. Tchrs.: 1

ROSEMONT

Rosemont College of the Holy Child Jesus - 1400 Montgomery Ave., Rosemont, PA 19010-1699 t) 610-527-0200 jim.cawley@rosemont.edu www.rosemont.edu Jim Cawley, Pres.; Stds.: 772; Lay Tchrs.: 26

VILLANOVA

Villanova University - 800 Lancaster Ave., Villanova, PA 19085 t) 610-519-7499 jleon.washington@villanova.edu www.villanova.edu Founded 1842 by the Augustinians, Province of St. Thomas of Villanova. Colleges of Liberal Arts and Sciences, Engineering, Nursing; The School of Law. Rev. Joseph D. Calderone, O.S.A., Campus Min.; Bro. Michael Duffy, O.S.A., Campus Min.; Rev. Peter M. Donohue, O.S.A., Pres.; Rev. Stephen J. Baker, O.S.A., Academic Advisor, College of Liberal Arts & Sciences; Rev. Francis J. Caponi, O.S.A., Assoc. Prof.; Rev. Martin Laird, O.S.A., Prof.; Rev. Francis Chambers, O.S.A., Assoc. Dir. Admission; Rev. David A. Cregan, O.S.A., Assoc. Prof., Theatre; Rev. Kevin M. DePrinzio, O.S.A., Vice Pres., Mission & Ministry; Rev. Allan Fitzgerald, O.S.A., Dir., The Augustinian Inst.; Millicent Gaskell, Librn. & Dir., Falvey Memorial Libr.; Rev. Kail C. Ellis, O.S.A., Dean Emeritus, College of Liberal Arts & Sciences; Rev. Joseph Loya, O.S.A., Assoc. Prof. Russian Area Studies Dir.; Rev. Lee J. Makowski, O.S.A., Asst. Teaching Prof.; Rev. Arthur P. Purcaro, O.S.A., Asst. Vice Pres., Church Mgmt. Prog.; Rev. Joseph Ryan, O.S.A., Assoc. Teaching Prof.; Rev. Bernard C. Scianna, O.S.A., Dir., Office of Fraternity & Sorority Life; Sr. Beth Hassel, P.B.V.M., Dir., Center for Faith & Learning; Rev. Richard Jacobs, O.S.A., Prof., Public Admin. & Pi Alpha Alpha Chapter Advisor;

CONVENTS, MONASTERIES, AND RESIDENCES FOR WOMEN [CON]

ARDMORE

Missionary Sisters of the Holy Rosary (M.S.H.R.) - 205 Cricket Ave., Ardmore, PA 19003 t) 610-896-1786 mcneillhelena@yahoo.com holyrosarymissionarysisters.org Sr. Anne Marino, Contact;

ASTON

Anna Bachmann House - 606 S. Convent Rd., Aston, PA 19014-1207 t) 610-558-3240 psmith@osfphila.org www.osfphila.org Sr. Patricia Smith, O.S.F., Contact; Srs.: 2

Convent of Our Lady of Angels - 609 S. Convent Rd., Aston, PA 19014 t) 610-459-4125 communications@osfphila.org www.osfphila.org Motherhouse of the Sisters of St. Francis of Philadelphia. Sr. Theresa Firenze, OSF, Congregational Minister; Srs.: 32

Sisters of St. Francis - 607 S. Convent Rd., Aston, PA 19014 t) 610-358-5417 cwright@osfphila.org www.osfphila.org Sr. Karen Pourby, OSF, Secy.; Srs.: 4

Sisters of St. Francis of Philadelphia - 6 Red Hill Rd., Aston, PA 19014 t) 610-459-1113

Sisters of St. Francis of Philadelphia - Portiuncula Convent, 610 Red Hill Rd., Aston, PA 19014 t) 610-558-5350 www.osfphila.org Sr. Karen Pourby, OSF, Secy.; Srs.: 3

Sisters of St. Francis of Philadelphia - Visitation Convent 609 S. Convent Rd., Aston, PA 19014 t) 610-558-7731 www.osfphila.org Sr. Karen Pourby, OSF, Secy.; Srs.: 3

Sisters of St. Francis of Philadelphia (Assumption Convent) - 609 S. Convent Rd., Aston, PA 19014 t) 610-558-7672 www.osfphila.org Sr. Karen Pourby, OSF, Secy.; Srs.: 5

BRYN MAWR

Missionary Sisters of the Holy Rosary - 741 Polo Rd., Bryn Mawr, PA 19010 t) 610-520-1974; 610-520-1976 enechufn@yahoo.com www.holyrosarymissionarysisters.com Sr. Florence Enechukwu, Contact; Srs.: 316

Society of the Holy Child Jesus - 700 Old Lancaster Rd., Bryn Mawr, PA 19010 t) 610-527-5076 www.shcj.org Sr. Carroll Juliano, Prov.; Srs.: 4

CHELTENHAM

Sisters of the Good Shepherd (Contemplative) - 7633 Waters Rd., Cheltenham, PA 19012 t) 215-782-8627 judeelleng@aol.com Sr. Martha Cardenas, Supr.;

CHESTER

Missionaries of Charity, Gift of Mary - 2714 W. 9th St., Chester, PA 19013 t) 610-494-7424

ELVERSON

Daughters of St. Mary of Providence (D.S.M.P.) - 227 Isabella Rd., Elverson, PA 19520 t) 610-942-4166 stmaryofprov@comcast.net stmaryofprov-pa.org Sr. Brenda McHugh, DSMP, Dir.;

ERDENHEIM

Sisters of St. Joseph of Philadelphia - Divine Shepherd Convent, 927 Bethlehem Pike, Erdenheim, PA 19038 t) 215-836-2082 kshelly@ssjphila.org Sr. Maureen G. Erdlen, SSJ, Pres.; Srs.: 3

Sisters of St. Joseph of Philadelphia, Nazareth House - 931 Bethlehem Pike, Erdenheim, PA 19038 t) 215-836-2613 kshelly@ssjphila.org Sr. Maureen G. Erdlen, SSJ, Pres.;

FLOURTOWN

Sisters of St. Joseph of Philadelphia, Mt. St. Joseph Academy - Convent, 120 W. Wissahickon Ave., Flourtown, PA 19031-1899 t) 215-233-4368 kshelly@ssjphila.org Sr. Maureen G. Erdlen, SSJ, Pres.;

FOX CHASE MANOR

Sisters of St. Basil the Great (O.S.B.M.) - 710 Fox Chase Rd., Fox Chase Manor, PA 19046-4198 t) 215-663-9153 province@stbasils.com www.stbasils.com Motherhouse Sr. Dorothy Ann Busowski, O.S.B.M., Prov.;

Basilian Spirituality Center - t) 215-780-1227

GWYNEDD VALLEY

Religious Sisters of Mercy - Transfiguration Convent - 1325 Sumneytown Pike, Gwynedd Valley, PA 19437-0901; Mailing: P.O. Box 901, Gwynedd Valley, PA 19437-0901 t) 215-641-5512 mcmahon.c@gmc.edu www.gmc.edu Sr. Catherine McMahon, Contact;

Religious Sisters of Mercy - St. Joseph Convent - 1349 Sumneytown Pike, Gwynedd Valley, PA 19437-0902; Mailing: P.O. Box 902, Gwynedd Valley, PA 19437-0902 t) 215-646-5259 pvetrano@mercymidatlantic.org Sr. Patricia Donlon, Contact;

HAVERFORD

Handmaids of the Sacred Heart of Jesus - 616 Coopertown Rd., Haverford, PA 19041 t) 610-642-5715 handmaidshaverford@gmail.com www.acjusa.org Srs.: 6

Handmaids of the Sacred Heart of Jesus Provincialate - 616 Coopertown Rd., Haverford, PA 19041 t) 610-642-5715 aciusaprovince@gmail.com www.acjusa.org Sr. Lyan Tri, Prov.; Srs.: 26

HUNTINGDON VALLEY

Sisters of the Redeemer - 521 Moredon Rd., Huntingdon Valley, PA 19006; Mailing: 1600 Huntingdon Pike, Meadowbrook, PA 19046 t) (215) 914-4101 emarvel@holyredeemer.com; etroy@holyredeemer.com redeemersisters.org Sr. Ellen Marvel, CSR, Prov.; Srs.: 2

Sisters of the Redeemer - St. Teresa of Avila Convent - 619 Moredon Rd., Huntingdon Valley, PA 19006; Mailing: 1600 Huntingdon Pike, Meadowbrook, PA 19046 t) (215) 947-0135 emarvel@holyredeemer.com; etroy@holyredeemer.com redeemersisters.org Sr. Ellen M. Marvel, C.S.R., Prov.; Srs.: 4

JENKINTOWN

Sisters of the Redeemer - St. Elizabeth Convent - 615 Fox Chase Rd., Jenkintown, PA 19046; Mailing: 1600 Huntingdon Pike, Meadowbrook, PA 19046 t) (215) 935-6583; (215) 914-4101 emarvel@holyredeemer.com; etroy@holyredeemer.com redeemersisters.org Sr. Ellen M. Marvel, C.S.R., Prov.; Srs.: 2

LANGHORNE

Monastery of St. Clare, Poor Clares (Cloistered Contemplative Nuns) - 1271 Langhorne-Newton Rd., Langhorne, PA 19047 t) 215-968-5775 stclare@poorclarepa.org www.poorclarepa.org Prayer and Altar Bread Ministry. Sr. Patricia Anne Coogan, Abbess;

San Damiano Convent (Sisters of St. Francis of Philadelphia) - 104 Alberts Way, Langhorne, PA 19047 t) 215-757-9494 congregationalrecords@osfphila.org www.osfphila.org Sr. Karen Pourby, OSF, Secy.; Srs.: 3

LANSDALE

Religious of the Assumption, North American Province,

Inc. - 506 Crestview Rd., Lansdale, PA 19446 t) 215-368-4427 (Main House); 215-362-6296 raworcester@hotmail.com Sr. Nuala Cotter, Prov.;

MALVERN

Sisters, Servants of the Immaculate Heart of Mary (I.H.M.) - Pacis Hall, 1 Pacis Dr., Malvern, PA 19355 t) 610-889-1668; 610-889-1667 (Camilla Hall) pacishall@gmail.com Sr. John Evelyn DiTrolio, I.H.M., Supr.;

Sisters, Servants of the Immaculate Heart of Mary (I.H.M.) - 100 Maxis Dr., Malvern, PA 19355 t) 610-386-2000 ch@camillahall.org Sr. Anne Veronica Burrows, I.H.M., Admin.;

Sisters, Servants of the Immaculate Heart of Mary (I.H.M.) - 4 Gillet Dr., Malvern, PA 19355 t) 610-647-4400 x3660 gillet@immaculata.edu www.ihmimmaculata.org Sr. Catherine Ward, Supr.;

Villa Maria Academy Convent (Sisters, Servants of the Immaculate Heart of Mary (I.H.M.)) - 370 Old Lincoln Hwy., Malvern, PA 19355 t) 610-647-4878 info@vmahs.org www.vmahs.org Sr. Mary E. Smith, I.H.M., Supr.; Srs.: 10

Villa Maria House of Studies (Villa Maria House of Studies, Motherhouse of the Sisters, Servants of the Immaculate Heart of Mary) - 1 Our Lady Cir., Malvern, PA 19355 t) 610-647-2160 s.donna.shallo@ihmimm.org Sr. M. Elaine deChantal Brooks, Supr.; Srs.: 580

MEADOWBROOK

Sisters of the Redeemer - Redeemer Community (Province Center) - 1600 Huntingdon Pike, Meadowbrook, PA 19046 t) (215) 914-4101 emarvel@holyredeemer.com; etroy@holyredeemer.com redeemersisters.org Sr. Ellen M. Marvel, C.S.R., Prov.; Sr. Anita Bolton, CSR, Prov. Asst.; Sr. Maryanne King, Prov. Asst.; Rev. Dennis J.W. O'Donnell, Dir.; Srs.: 5

MERION STATION

McAuley Convent - 517 Montgomery Ave., Merion Station, PA 19066 t) 610-667-2775 pvetrano@mercymidatlantic.org Infirmary for Religious Sisters of Mercy. Sr. Maryanne Werner, R.S.M., Dir.;

Sisters of Mercy of the Americas, Mid-Atlantic Community, Inc. - 515 Montgomery Ave., Merion Station, PA 19066 t) 610-664-6650 www.mercymidatlantic.org Sr. Patricia Vetrano, R.S.M., Pres.; Sr. Kathleen Keenan, R.S.M., Leadership Team; Sr. Patricia Lapczynski, R.S.M., Leadership Team; Sr. Patricia Smith, R.S.M., Leadership Team; Sr. Alicia Zapata, R.S.M., Leadership Team;

Sisters of Mercy of the Americas, Mid-Atlantic Community - 515 Montgomery Ave., Merion Station, PA 19066 t) 610-664-6650 www.mercymidatlantic.org Sr. Patricia Vetrano, R.S.M., Pres.; Sr. Mary Ann Clarahan, R.S.M., Contact;

NORRISTOWN

Missionaries of Charity - 630 DeKalb St., Norristown, PA 19401-3944 t) 610-277-5962 Services include Food Distribution and Emergency Night Shelter and Soup Kitchen.

PHILADELPHIA

St. Anna's Convent - 1815 S. Alder St., Philadelphia, PA 19148 t) 267-761-9573 annassaint09@gmail.com www.allsaintssisters.org A ministry of the All Saints Sisters of the Poor. Elaine Swan Sr., Bus. Mgr.;

Assumption Hall - Sisters of St. Joseph, 8900 Norwood Ave., Philadelphia, PA 19118-2711 t) 215-247-3665; 215-248-2564 kshelly@ssjphila.org Residence for Norwood-Fontbonne Academy Faculty. Sr. Maureen G. Erdlen, SSJ, Pres.; Srs.: 14

Assumption House - 1001 S. 47th St., Philadelphia, PA 19143 t) 215-386-5016 raphila1001@outlook.com

Blessed Trinity Mother Missionary Cenacle - 3501 Solly Ave., Philadelphia, PA 19136 t) 215-335-7550 gensec@msbt.org msbt.org Generalate, Formation, and residence for Missionary Servants of the Most Blessed Trinity. Mother Boniface Spirituality Center. Sr. Barbara McIntyre, MSBT, Supr.; Srs.: 82

Carmelite Monastery - 1400 Old York Rd., Philadelphia, PA 19126 t) 215-424-6143 Mother Pia of Jesus Crucified, Treas.;

Clare House - 2421 Jasper St., Philadelphia, PA 19125 t) 215-739-6441 Franciscan Sisters of Allegany and Sisters of St. Francis of Philadelphia. Sr. Mary Augustini, OSF, Admin.;

Congregation of the Sisters of St. Felix, St. Ignatius Convent - 4401 Haverford Ave., Philadelphia, PA 19104 t) 215-222-2296 sjudithmk@feliciansisters.org www.feliciansistersna.org

Emmaus Convent (Sisters of Mercy (R.S.M.)) - 5358 Cedar Ave., Philadelphia, PA 19143 t) 215-471-7260 rsmemmaus@aol.com Sr. Margaret O'Donnell, Contact;

St. Francis Convent - 1727 S. 11th St., Philadelphia, PA 19148 t) 215-463-7343 gpfrancia@verizon.net Sr. Francis Christi DeMarchi, O.S.F., Contact;

The Grey Nuns of the Sacred Heart, Inc. - 14500 Bustelton Ave., Philadelphia, PA 19116-1188 t) 215-968-4236 emcguigan@greynun.org www.greynun.org Sr. Denise Roche, Pres.; Srs.: 67

Immaculate Heart Convent - 7310 Torresdale Ave., Philadelphia, PA 19136 t) 215-332-8299 ihc@comcast.net Faculty Residence for Sisters, Servants of the Immaculate Heart of Mary, teaching at St. Hubert High School. Sr. M. Margaret Fleming, I.H.M., Supr.;

Immaculate Heart Convent - 4904 Chestnut St., Philadelphia, PA 19139 t) 215-474-8971 ihc@comcast.net Sr. Sarah Lamb, I.H.M., Supr.;

St. Joseph Convent - 7310 Torresdale Ave., Philadelphia, PA 19136 t) 215-332-8299 ssjtorr@netcarrier.com Faculty Residence for Sisters of St. Joseph, who teach at Connell-Egan Catholic High School, St. Hubert High School and St. Francis-St Vincent Homes. Sr. M. Margaret Fleming, I.H.M., Supr.;

Little Sisters of the Poor - Holy Family Home, 5300 Chester Ave., Philadelphia, PA 19143 t) 215-729-5153 www.littlesistersofthepoor.org Sr. Celine Therese Vadukkoot, Pres.; Srs.: 10

Little Workers of the Sacred Hearts - 160 Carpenter Ln., Philadelphia, PA 19119-2563 t) 215-843-2266 Sr. Leena Joseph, P.O.S.C., Supr.;

Mary Immaculate Convent - 1731 S. 11th St., Philadelphia, PA 19148 t) 215-336-2940; 215-468-9133 maryim1731@yahoo.com Sr. Margaret P. Reinking, I.H.M., Supr.;

Medical Mission Sisters, North American Sector - 8400 Pine Rd., Philadelphia, PA 19111 t) 215-742-6100 mmsorg@medicalmissionsisters.org www.medicalmissionsisters.org Sr. Sue Sopczynski, M.M.S., Pres.; Srs.: 59

Monastery of the Visitation Nuns - 5820 City Ave., Philadelphia, PA 19131-1295 t) 215-473-5888 viznunphil@aol.com visitationnuns.org Sr. Antoinette Marie Walker, V.H.M., Supr.; Srs.: 5

Mt. St. Joseph Convent - 9701 Germantown Ave., Philadelphia, PA 19118-2694 t) 215-248-7205 kshelly@ssjphila.org ssjphila.org Motherhouse of the Sisters of St. Joseph of Chestnut Hill, Philadelphia. Sr. Maureen G. Erdlen, SSJ, Pres.; Srs.: 48

Nazareth Convent - Religious Sisters of Mercy, 6369 Woodbine Ave., Philadelphia, PA 19151 t) 215-477-3022 pvetrano@mercymidatlantic.org Sr. Kathleen Lyons, R.S.M., Contact;

Peace Hermitage (Society of Catholic Medical Missionaries (Medical Mission Sisters)) - 8400 Pine Rd., Philadelphia, PA 19111 t) 312-659-3655; 215-742-6100 x149

School Sisters of Notre Dame - 3715 S. Hereford Ln., Philadelphia, PA 19114 t) 267-250-9310 sisterbernie@yahoo.com www.ssnd.org Sr. Bernadette Marie Ravenstahl, S.S.N.D., Contact;

Sister Servants of the Holy Spirit of Perpetual Adoration (S.Sp.S.A.P.) - Convent of Divine Love, 2212 Green St., Philadelphia, PA 19130 t) 215-567-0123 conventofdivinelove@verizon.net www.adorationsisters.org Sr. Mary Caritas, S.Sp.S.A.P., Supr.;

Sisters of Life - St. Malachy Convent & Apostolic Center, 1413 N. 11th St., Philadelphia, PA 19122 t) 267-831-3100 philly@sistersoflife.org sistersoflife.org Sr. Maeve Nativitas O'Doherty, S.V., Supr.; Sr. Gemma Grace Harris, S.V., Asst. to Local Supr.; Sr. Monica Pollard, S.V., Asst. for Mission; Srs.: 6

Sisters of St. Joseph - Neumann House, 58 E. Northwestern Ave., Philadelphia, PA 19118 t) 215-248-7282 kshelly@ssjphila.org www.ssjphila.org Sr. Maureen G. Erdlen, SSJ, Pres.; Srs.: 3

Sisters of St. Joseph of Philadelphia, Cecilian Convent - 6818 Cresheim Rd., Philadelphia, PA 19119; Mailing: 9701 Germantown Ave., Philadelphia, PA 19111 t) 215-438-7515 kshelly@ssjphila.org Sr. Maureen G. Erdlen, SSJ, Pres.; Srs.: 7

Sisters of St. Joseph of Philadelphia, Elizabeth House - 138 W. Carpenter Ln., Philadelphia, PA 19119-2563; Mailing: 9701 Germantown Ave., Philadelphia, PA 19118 t) 215-849-3362 kshelly@ssjphila.org Sr. Maureen G. Erdlen, SSJ, Pres.;

Sisters of St. Joseph of Philadelphia, Fournier Community - 9701 Germantown Ave., Philadelphia, PA 19118-2694 t) 215-248-7205 kshelly@ssjphila.org ssjphila.org Sr. Marie O'Brien, S.S.J., Contact; Srs.: 4

Sisters of the Holy Family of Nazareth - 2755 Holme Ave., Mount Nazareth, Philadelphia, PA 19152 t) 215-338-8992 nazarethcsfn.org/ Sr. Barbara Jean Wojnicki, C.S.F.N., Supr.; Sr. Kathleen Maciej, C.S.F.N., Prov.; Srs.: 38

Sisters of the Holy Family of Nazareth - 4800 Stevenson St, Delaney Hall, Philadelphia, PA 19114-2128 t) 267-341-3735 nazarethcsfn.org/ Sr. Brendan O'Brien, C.S.F.N., Supr.; Sr. Kathleen Maciej, C.S.F.N., Prov.; Srs.: 9

Sisters of the Holy Family of Nazareth - 2703 Holme Ave., Mary of Nazareth Convent, Philadelphia, PA 19152 t) 215-332-2300 x210 nazarethcsfn.org/ Sr. Michele Vincent Fisher, CSFN, Supr.; Sr. Kathleen Maciej, C.S.F.N., Prov.; Srs.: 11

RADNOR

Armenian Sisters of the Immaculate Conception - 440 Upper Gulph Rd., Radnor, PA 19087 t) 610-688-9360 sisteremma@asaphila.org www.asaphila.org Sr. Emma Moussayan, Supr.;

Missionary Sisters of the Sacred Heart of Jesus (Cabrini Sisters) - 610 King of Prussia Rd., Radnor, PA 19087-3698 t) 610-995-1210 baltas40@aol.com www.mothercabrini.org Sr. Christine Baltas, Contact;

ROSEMONT

American Province Archives, Society of the Holy Child Jesus - 1308 Wendover Rd., Rosemont, PA 19010 t) 610-525-8951 rmcdougall@shcj.org www.shcj.org/american/contact/contact-us/ Sr. Roseanne McDougall, S.H.C.J., Dir.;

Holy Child Center - 1341 Montgomery Ave., Rosemont, PA 19010 t) 610-525-9900 www.shcj.org Sr. Carroll Juliano, Prov.; Srs.: 25

Society of the Holy Child Jesus American Province, Inc. - 1341 Montgomery Ave., Rosemont, PA 19010-1628 t) 610-626-1400 americanprovince@shcj.org www.shcj.org Sr. Carroll Juliano, Prov.;

SPRINGFIELD

St. Anthony Convent - 1715 S. Sproul Rd., Springfield, PA 19064 t) 610-544-4066 Residence for Sisters of St. Francis of Philadelphia

Immaculate Heart of Mary Convent - 1725 S. Sproul Rd., Springfield, PA 19064 t) 610-544-0275 ihspringfield@hotmail.com Faculty Residence for Sisters, Servants of the Immaculate Heart of Mary. Sr. M. Rose Lawrence Harlan, I.H.M., Supr.;

St. Joseph Convent - 1725 S. Sproul Rd., Springfield, PA 19064 t) 610-544-0275 Sisters of St. Joseph Faculty House, Cardinal O'Hara High School.

Our Lady of Mercy Convent - 1735 S. Sproul Rd., Springfield, PA 19064 t) 610-544-0238 Faculty Residence for Sisters of Mercy who teach in Cardinal O'Hara and Mercy Vocational High Schools and who serve in other various ministries.

STRAFFORD

Our Lady of the Assumption Convent (Sisters, Servants of the Immaculate Heart of Mary) - 139 Fairfield Ln., Strafford, PA 19087 t) 610-688-7889

olaihm@yahoo.com Sr. Judith Ann Trumbore, I.H.M., Supr.;

TREVOSE

Sisters of the Blessed Sacrament - 4 Neshaminy Interplex Dr., Ste. 205, Trevose, PA 19053 t) 215-244-8174 schmidtsl@aol.com www.katharinedrexel.org Sr. Stephanie Henry, SBS, Pres.; Srs.: 63

WARMINSTER

Sisters of St. Joseph of Philadelphia - Nativity of Our Lord Convent, 605 W. Street Rd., Warminster, PA 18974 t) 215-672-0147 kshelly@ssjphila.org Residence of Sisters St. Joseph. Sr. Paula Napoli, S.S.J., Contact;

WYNCOTE

Handmaids of the Sacred Heart of Jesus - 2025 Church Rd., Wyncote, PA 19095 t) 215-576-6250 mgillespie@ancillae.org Sr. Margaret Scott, acj, Contact; Srs.: 8

WYNNEWOOD

Sisters of the Holy Child Jesus (S.H.C.J.) - Connell House, 105 Old Forest Rd., Wynnewood, PA 19096 t) 610-649-8462 www.shcj.org Sr. Carroll Juliano, Prov.; Srs.: 1

ENDOWMENTS / FOUNDATIONS / TRUSTS [EFT]

ASTON

Sisters of St. Francis Foundation - 609 S. Convent Rd., Aston, PA 19014 t) 610-558-7713 dkrist@osfphila.org www.osfphila.org Purpose: Raises funds to fulfill the needs of the Ministries and Retired Sisters of the Sisters of St. Francis of Philadelphia. Sr. Deborah Krist, O.S.F., Dir.;

Sisters of St. Francis of Philadelphia, Charitable Trust II - 609 S. Covent Rd., Aston, PA 19014 t) 610-558-7733 tfirenze@osfphila.org www.osfphila.org Sr. Theresa Firenze, OSF, Congregational Minister;

CHESTER

The Papal Foundation - 2501 Seaport Dr., Ste. SH300, Chester, PA 19013 t) 610-535-6340; 610-535-6341 jschnatz@thepapalfoundation.com www.thepapalfoundation.com Dave Savage, Exec. Dir.; James V. Coffey, Senior Vice President of Development;

HUNTINGDON VALLEY

Holy Redeemer Ministries - 667 Welsh Rd., Huntingdon Valley, PA 19006 t) 215-938-4650 cegan@holyredeemer.com www.holyredeemer.com Parent Corporation of Holy Redeemer Health System; Sponsor: Sisters of the Holy Redeemer, C.S.R. Catherine Egan, Vice. Pres.;

Marketing & Public Affairs Department - 521 Moredon Rd., Huntingdon Valley, PA 19006 t) 215-938-3226

MERION STATION

The Mercy Foundation - 515 Montgomery Ave., Merion Station, PA 19066-1297 t) 610-664-6650 Sr. Patricia Vetrano, R.S.M., Pres.;

PHILADELPHIA

Fournier Retirement Fund Corporation - Mount St. Joseph Convent, 9701 Germantown Ave., Philadelphia, PA 19118-2694 t) 215-248-7205 kshelly@ssjphila.org www.ssjphila.org Sr. Maureen G. Erdlen, SSJ, Pres.;

St. Raymond Nonnatus Foundation for Freedom, Family and Faith - 6398 Drexel Rd., Philadelphia, PA 19151 t) 215-870-9913 spirmod.srnf@gmail.com; director.srnf@gmail.com Founded to give redemptive charism of the Order of the B.V.M. of Mercy by providing support and accompaniment to Catholic families in crisis. Anne De Santis, Dir.;

ROSEMONT

The Support Fund Trust of the Society of The Holy Child Jesus-American Province - 1341 Montgomery Ave., Rosemont, PA 19010 t) 610-626-1400 shcj.org/american Sr. Carroll Juliano, Prov.;

YARDLEY

***Legacy of Life Foundation** - 25 S. Main St., #217, Yardley, PA 19067 t) 215-788-4051 marie@legacyoflifefoundation.org www.legacyoflifefoundation.org Angela McManimon, Dir.; Marie Joseph, Dir.;

HOSPITALS / HEALTH SERVICES [HOS]

DARBY

Mercy Catholic Medical Center (Mercy Fitzgerald Hospital) - 1500 Lansdowne Ave., Darby, PA 19023-1291 t) 610-237-4030 www.mercyhealth.org Opened July 1, 1933. Inc. May 1, 1969. A member of Mercy Health System and Trinity Health. Susan Croushore, Pres.; Kathryn Connelly-Conallen, Senior Vice Pres. & CEO, Mercy Acute Care Svcs.; Sr. Donna M. Watto, R.S.M., Vice Pres. Mission Integration;

HUNTINGDON VALLEY

HRH Management Corporation - 667 Welsh Rd., Huntingdon Valley, PA 19006 t) 215-938-4650 cegan@holyredeemer.com www.holyredeemer.com Affiliate of Holy Redeemer Health System. Sponsor: Sisters of the Holy Redeemer, C.S.R. Catherine Egan, Vice. Pres.;

LANGHORNE

St. Mary Medical Center - 1201 Langhorne-Newtown Rd., Langhorne, PA 19047 t) 215-710-2000 www.stmaryhealthcare.org Affiliate of Trinity Health. James Woodward, Pres.;

MEADOWBROOK

Holy Redeemer Hospital - 1648 Huntingdon Pike, Meadowbrook, PA 19046 t) 215-947-3000 cegan@holyredeemer.com www.holyredeemer.com Subsidiary of Holy Redeemer Health System, Acute care community hospital. Catherine Egan, Exec. Vice Pres. & Chief Admin. Officer;

PHILADELPHIA

Mercy Catholic Medical Center (Mercy Philadelphia Hospital) - 501 S. 54th St., Philadelphia, PA 19143 t) 215-748-9300 www.mercyhealth.org Opened July 2, 1918. Incorporated May 1, 1969. A member of Mercy Health System and Trinity Health. Kathryn Connelly-Conallen, Senior Vice Pres. & CEO, Mercy Acute Care Svcs.; Susan Croushore, Pres. & CEO; Sr. Suzanne Gallagher, R.S.M., Vice Pres., Mission Integration;

***Nazareth Hospital** - 2601 Holme Ave., Philadelphia, PA 19152 t) 215-335-6039 cathy.weaver@trinityhealth.org www.mercyhealth.org A member of Mercy Health System and Trinity Health. Susan Croushore, Pres.; Mary Ann Carter, Vice Pres. Mission Integration; Kathryn Connelly-Conallen, Senior Vice Pres. & CEO, Mercy Acute Care Svcs.;

MISCELLANEOUS [MIS]

BROOMALL

The National Catholic Bioethics Center - 600 Reed Rd., Ste. 102, Broomall, PA 19008 t) 215-877-2660 info@ncbcenter.org www.ncbcenter.org/ Tara Capizzi, COO; Joseph Meaney, Pres.; John F. Brehany, Executive Vice President; Rev. Tadeusz Pacholczyk, Dir. of Education;

***Pastoral and Matrimonial Renewal Center** - 28 N. Malen Rd., Broomall, PA 19008; Mailing: P.O. Box 2304, Southeastern, PA 19399 t) 484-366-6102 rfeher@pmrcusa.org livinginlove.org Katherine M. Feher, Vice Pres. & Sec.; Ronald D. Feher, Pres. & Treas.;

CHESTER

Sisters of St. Francis of Philadelphia, Anna's Place - 226 Norris St., Chester, PA 19013 t) 484-361-5900 annasplace.org Sponsored Outreach Center Sr. Elizabeth Pepe, OSF, Program Coordinator;

COATESVILLE

Franciscans of Mary - 404 Charles St., Coatesville, PA 19320 t) 610-384-0360 information@frmaria.org www.franciscansofmary.org Rev. Santiago Martin Rodriguez, F.M., Pres.;

COLLEGEVILLE

State Correctional Institution - 1200 Mokychic Rd., Collegeville, PA 19426 t) 610-409-7890 Rev. John J. Pidgeon, Pst.;

CONSHOHOCKEN

Mercy Health System of Southeastern PA - 1 W. Elm St., Ste. 100, Conshohocken, PA 19428 t) 610-567-6107 cweaver@mercyhealth.org www.mercyhealth.org Regional health ministry of Trinity Health. Sr. Mary Christine McCann, R.S.M., Chair; Susan Croushore, Pres.; Catherine Weaver, Vice Pres. Mission & Integration;

St. Agnes Continuing Care Center - t) 610-567-6120
***East Norriton Physician Services** - t) 610-567-6120
Mercy Catholic Medical Center (Mercy Philadelphia Hospital) - t) 215-748-9300
***Mercy Family Support** - t) 610-690-2500
Mercy Catholic Medical Center (Mercy Fitzgerald Hospital) - t) 610-237-4030
***Mercy Health Foundation** - t) 610-567-6120
***Mercy Health Plan** - t) 610-567-6120
***Mercy Home Health** - t) 610-690-2500
***Mercy Home Health Services** - t) 610-690-2500
***Mercy Management Services of Southeastern PA** - t) 610-567-6120
Mercy Suburban Hospital - t) 610-278-2002
***N.E. Physician Services, Inc.** - t) 610-567-6120
***Nazareth Health Care Foundation** - t) 215-335-6159
***Nazareth Hospital** - t) 215-335-6039
***Nazareth Physician Services** - t) 610-567-6120

DOWNINGTOWN

***Growing Catholics, Inc.** - 250 Truman Way, Downingtown, PA 19335 t) 215-219-8499 meigankelly@yahoo.com Meigan Kelly, Contact;

***Theology of the Body Institute** - 400 Boot Rd., Ste. B1, Downingtown, PA 19335 t) 215-302-8200 info@tobinstitute.org tobinstitute.org Purpose: To educate and train men and women to understand, live and promote the Theology of the Body. Christopher West, Pres.; Jennifer Settle, Dir.; Bill Howard, Media Dir.;

EAST NORRITON

***Gianna Center of Philadelphia** - Suburban Community Hospital, 2705 DeKalb Pike, Ste. 207, East Norriton, PA 19401 t) 215-857-9599 info@phgiannacenter.com www.phgiannacenter.org Health care that adheres to USCCB Ethical and Religious Directives for Catholic Health Care and is available to all women, regardless of income. Sophia Stuckey, Admin.; Max Mercado, Pres.; Delia Larrauri, Vice. Pres.; Barbara Rose, Secy.; Gina Meigs, Treas.;

Society of St. Vincent de Paul of Philadelphia - 3004 Keenwood Rd., East Norriton, PA 19403 t) 484-704-7153 careygroberts@comcast.net Catholic Lay Organization serving those in need with spiritual, moral, material and financial support regardless of race, creed, etc. Larry Huber, Pres.; Ronald Mandel, Vice Pres.;

HUNTINGDON VALLEY

Holy Redeemer Health System - 667 Welsh Rd., Huntingdon Valley, PA 19006 t) 215-938-4650 www.holyredeemer.com Parent organization which maintains, manages, and operates the health care system sponsored and established by the Sisters of the Holy Redeemer. Michael B. Laign, Pres.;

Holy Redeemer Home Health and Hospice Services - t) 800-678-8678
Holy Redeemer Hospital - t) 215-947-3000
Holy Redeemer Lafayette - t) 215-214-2800 Robin Frankwich, Group Vice Pres., Long Term Care & Residential Svcs.;
Holy Redeemer Multi-Care, Inc. -
Holy Redeemer St. Joseph Manor - t) 215-938-4000 Benjamin Pieczynski, Vice Pres. & Admin.;
Holy Redeemer Transitional Care Unit - t) 215-947-3000

KING OF PRUSSIA

***The Living Scripture Institute** - 743 Roy Rd., King of Prussia, PA 19406 t) 610-888-9049 ktdann@live.com www.livingscriptureinstitute.org Our mission is to educate & deliver an integrated psychological & spiritual process for the healing of men and women suffering distressing life events Katie Dannunzio, Vice Pres.;

Rachel's Vineyard Ministries (International Headquarters) - 808 N. Henderson Rd., King of Prussia, PA 19406 t) 610-354-0555 t.burke@rachelsvineyard.org www.rachelsvineyard.org Purpose: provide retreats offering emotional and spiritual healing after abortion; and continuing education for professionals, clergy and lay persons.

LEVITTOWN

Catholic Clinical Consultants - 100 Levittown Pkwy., Levittown, PA 19055 t) 855-518-2223 Provides outsourced management, clinical and behavioral health consulting and other out-patient behavioral health services. Dr. James Black; Racchel Meade, Admin.; Most Rev. John J. McIntyre, Pres.;

MALVERN

***Catholic Leadership Institute** - 301 Lindenwood Dr., Ste 310, Malvern, PA 19355 t) 610-363-1315 info@catholicleaders.org www.catholicleaders.org Pastoral leadership formation & consulting services. Most Rev. Robert D. Gruss, Moderator; Daniel Cellucci, CEO; Timothy C. Flanagan, Founder;

Peak Encounter Ministries, Inc. - ; Mailing: P.O. Box 1077, Malvern, PA 19355 t) 484-240-1834 hello@peakencounter.org; hello@peakencounter.com peakencounter.org Provides adventure & contemplative opportunities for young adults to encounter God in nature. Heather Makowicz, Pres.;

MEADOWBROOK

Redeemer Valley Farm, Inc. - 1600 Huntington Pike, Meadowbrook, PA 19046 t) (215) 914-4109 adura@holyredeemer.com redeemervalleygarden.com Sr. Anastase Dura, C.S.R., Contact;

MERION STATION

Sisters of Mercy of the Americas Mid-Atlantic Community, Inc. - 515 Montgomery Ave., Merion Station, PA 19066 t) 610-664-6650 rbonnard@mercymidatlantic.org www.mercymidatlantic.org Sr. Patricia Vetrano, R.S.M., Pres.;

NARBETH

Camp Camino, Inc. - 134 N. Narbeth Ave., Narbeth, PA 19072 t) (215) 410-8994 Michael P. Broadhurst, Contact;

NEWTOWN SQUARE

Global Health Ministry - 3805 W. Chester Pike, Ste. 100, Newtown Square, PA 19073-2304 t) 610-355-2003 mmcginley@trinity-health.org www.globalhealthvolunteers.net Sr. Mary Jo McGinley, R.S.M., Pres.;

ORELAND

***Pro-Life Union of Greater Philadelphia** - 88 Pennsylvania Ave., Oreland, PA 19075 t) 215-885-8150 mail@prolifeunion.org prolifeunion.org Affirms the sanctity of life through our work in alternatives, education, outreach & public affairs. Rev. Christopher M. Walsh, Chair;

PAOLI

AbbeyFest Ministries, Inc. - 220 S. Valley Rd. Paoli, Paoli, PA 19301; Mailing: P.O. Box 190, Berwyn, PA 19312 t) 215-569-5438 megan@theabbeyfest.com www.theabbeyfest.com Michael P. Broadhurst, Chair; Megan Schrieber, Pres.;

PHILADELPHIA

***American Academy of the Sacred Arts** - c/o Maria Merlino, 2807 S. 13th St., Philadelphia, PA 19148 t) 215-339-5041 maria.merlino@comcast.net Purpose is to glorify God in the cultural disciplines through the creation of original art, educational outreach and ecumenical dialogue. William Maffucci, Pres.; Maria Merlino, Trustee;

***American Catholic Historical Society** - 263 S. 4th St., Philadelphia, PA 19106 t) 215-925-5752 info@amchs.org www.amchs.org Promotes the documentation & interpretation of the history of the Catholic Church in the U.S. Michael H. Finnegan, Pres.;

***Augustinian Defenders of the Rights of the Poor** - 2130 S. 21st St., 2nd Fl., Philadelphia, PA 19145 t) 215-925-3566 info@rightsofthepoor.org www.rightsofthepoor.org ADROP is about collaborating with the poor and powerless in our society by matching identified needs across political, economic & religious spectra. Joseph Micucci, Exec.;

Catholic Charities Appeal of the Archdiocese of Philadelphia - 222 N. 17th St., Philadelphia, PA 19103 t) 215-587-4507 Rev. Msgr. Daniel J. Kutys, Contact;

Catholic Kolping Society - 9130 Academy Rd., Philadelphia, PA 19114 t) 267-255-2527 phillykolpingnews@gmail.com www.kolpingphilly.com Anna Nordin, Treas.; Frank Staub, Pres.;

Catholic League For Persons With Disabilities - 911 Loney St., Philadelphia, PA 19111 t) 215-725-9746 Barbara M. Walter, Secy.;

Catholics United for the Faith - 183 Hillcrest Ave., Philadelphia, PA 19118 t) 215-247-2585 annemwilson@yahoo.com www.saintjohnneumannchapter.org/ (St. John Neumann Philadelphia Area Chapter) Anne M. Wilson, Chair;

Change for Change - 9701 Germantown Ave., Philadelphia, PA 19118-2694 t) 215-248-7220 changeforglobalchange@earthlink.net Addresses the global problem of sustainability through education, donations and grants to not-for-profit organizations. Sr. Maureen G. Erdlen, SSJ, Pres.;

The Collegium Institute - 3814 Walnut St, Philadelphia, PA 19104; Mailing: PO Box 30730, Philadelphia, PA 19104-6197 t) 773-813-9011; 610-368-7288 dcheely@collegiuminstitute.org; ebrown@collegiuminstitute.org www.collegiuminstitute.org/ An independent scholarly foundation devoted to fostering the Catholic intellectual tradition, and the liberal tradition of humane studies. Matthew O'Brien, Treas.; Daniel Cheely, Pres.;

Concerts at the Cathedral - 1723 Race St., Philadelphia, PA 19103 t) 215-561-1313 bm01003@aop222.org Rev. Gerald Dennis Gill, Rector;

CORA Services, Inc., Philadelphia, Pennsylvania - 8540 Verree Rd., Philadelphia, PA 19111 t) 215-342-7660 info@coraservices.org www.coraservices.org Services provided for children and their families. AnnMarie Schultz, Pres.;

CSFN Mission & Ministry, Inc. - 2755 Holme Ave., Philadelphia, PA 19152 t) 215-335-4802 ltfelici@aol.com Sr. Loretta Theresa Felici, CSFN, CEO;

***Depaul, USA** - 5725 Sprague St., Philadelphia, PA 19138-1721 t) 215-438-1955 charles.levesque@depaulusa.org www.depaulusa.org Provide homeless and disadvantaged people the opportunity to fulfill their potential and move towards an independent and positive future. Brendan Sculley, Dir.; Charles Levesque, Contact;

Franciscan Volunteer Ministry, Inc. - Michael Duffy, 1802 E Hagert St., Philadelphia, PA 19125; Mailing: P.O. Box 29276, Philadelphia, PA 19125 t) 215-427-3070 fvmadir@gmail.com; fvmpd@aol.com www.franciscanvolunteerministry.org Purpose: To create and run a Franciscan lay volunteer program in the United States. Lizzy Heurich, Dir.; Katie Sullivan, Dir.;

Heritage of Faith - Vision of Hope - 222 N. 17th St., Philadelphia, PA 19103 t) 215-587-4549 dkutys@archphila.org Rev. Msgr. Daniel J. Kutys, Contact;

IHM Center for Literacy - 7341 Cottage St., Philadelphia, PA 19136 t) 215-338-3120 ihmcenter4literacy@yahoo.com www.ihmcenterforliteracy.com Full-time program with courses in English for Speakers of Other Languages (ESOL) Sr. Margaret Paul Longshore, I.H.M., Dir.;

2nd Sight - 929 S. Farragut St., Philadelphia, PA 19143-3695 t) 215-382-0292 ihmesldesales@verizon.net

***International Institute for Culture** - 6331 Lancaster Ave., Philadelphia, PA 19151 t) 215-877-9910 webmaster@iiculture.org www.iiculture.org Purpose: for the evangelization of culture through international conferences, language and cultural programs. John M. Haas, Pres.;

Saint Joseph Guild - Mount St. Joseph Convent, 9701 Germantown Ave., Philadelphia, PA 19118-2694 t) 215-248-7840 nschlein@ssjphila.org www.ssjphila.org Nicole Schlein, Dir.;

Katherine Kiernan Chateau, Inc. - c/o Catholic Social Services, 222 N. 17th St., Ste. 300, Philadelphia, PA 19103 t) 215-587-3903 chsweb@chs-adphila.org Catholic Social Services, Contact;

The Medaille Corporation - 9701 Germantown Ave., Philadelphia, PA 19118 t) 215-248-7205 kshelly@ssjphila.org Supports the charitable works of the Sisters of Saint Joseph of Chestnut Hill, Philadelphia Sr. Maureen G. Erdlen, SSJ, Pres.;

Medical Mission Sisters Supplemental Subsidy Fund, Inc. (Society of Catholic Medical Missionaries, Inc.) - 8400 Pine Rd., Philadelphia, PA 19111 t) 215-742-6100 aminazu@medicalmissionsisters.org www.medicalmissionsisters.org Sr. Sue Sopczynski, M.M.S., Pres.;

Missionary Cenacle Apostolate - 3501 Solly Ave, Philadelphia, PA 19136 t) 410-772-5799 Branch of the Missionary Cenacle Family. Lay people called to be missionaries in the Church in the providence of everyday life. Pat Regan, Treas.;

National Shrine of Saint Rita of Cascia - 1166 S. Broad St., Philadelphia, PA 19146 t) 215-546-8333; 215-546-8335 ritashrine@aol.com www.saintritashrine.org Center of Devotion to Saint Rita in the United States. Rev. Eugene DelConte, O.S.A., In Res.; Rev. Daniel McLaughlin, O.S.A., In Res.; Chesley Turner, Dir.;

Natural Family Planning Center of Washington, DC, Inc. - 8400 Pine Rd., Philadelphia, PA 19111-1345 t) 301-897-9323 hannaklaus@gmail.com www.teenstarprogram.org Teen STAR & Holistic Sexuality Programs. Sr. Hanna Klaus, M.M.S., Exec.;

***New Jerusalem Now** - 2011 W. Norris St., Philadelphia, PA 19121-2120 t) 215-763-8806 mehmms@verizon.net Residential program that seeks to integrate all dimensions of recovery from drugs in the members' daily lives. Serves North Philadelphia. Sr. Margaret McKenna, M.M.S., Dir.;

Perpetual Help Center - 1019 N. 5th St., Philadelphia, PA 19123; Mailing: P.O. Box 29308, Philadelphia, PA 19125 t) 410-990-1680 kwhaleye@redemptorists.net www.perpetualhelpcenter.org Rev. Raymond Collins, Rector;

Philadelphia Senatus of the Legion of Mary - 5109 N. Broad St., Philadelphia, PA 19141 t) 215-457-6343 info@philadelphiasenatus.org www.philadelphiasenatus.org Catholic Lay Assoc. Tony Gilliam, Pres.; Rev. Addisalem T. Mekonnen, Spiritual Dir.;

Redemptorist Office for Mission Advancement - 1019 N. 5th St., Philadelphia, PA 19123; Mailing: PO Box 29308, Philadelphia, PA 19125 t) 410-990-1680 kwhaley@redemptorists.net redemptorists.net Rev. Raymond Collins, Rector;

Sisters of Saint Joseph Welcome Center - 728 E. Allegheny Ave., Philadelphia, PA 19134-2428 t) 215-634-1696 kmcshane15@gmail.com www.ssjwelcomecenter.org Sr. Kathleen McShane, Dir.;

Society of Catholic Medical Missionaries Generalate, Inc. - 8400 Pine Rd., Philadelphia, PA 19111 t) 215-742-6100 generalate@medicalmissionsisters.org.uk www.medicalmissionsisters.org.uk Corporation collects funds for charitable and missionary work, for Medical Mission Sisters. Sr. Francine Poondikulam, Treas.;

The Saint Thomas More Society of Philadelphia - ; Mailing: P.O. Box 58060, Philadelphia, PA 19102 t) 215-564-8106 stmsphila@gmail.com www.saintthomasmoresociety.org Purpose: The Society is an association of Catholic lawyers organized to strengthen the religious and charitable commitment of its members. Suzanne Mintzer, Pres.;

Trinity Health Life Pennsylvania, Inc. (Mercy LIFE - West Philadelphia) - 4508 Chestnut St., Philadelphia, PA 19139 t) 267-787-8282 kelly.hopkins@trinity-health.org www.trinity-health.org Kelly Hopkins, Pres.;

***U.S. Catholic Sisters Against Human Trafficking (USCSAHT)** - 138 W. Carpenter Ln., Philadelphia, PA 19119 t) 215-779-6557 kcoll2016@gmail.com www.sistersagainsttrafficking.org U.S. Catholic Sisters Against Human Trafficking Sr. Kathleen Coll, Contact;

Vincentian Family Office - 500 E. Chelten Ave., Philadelphia, PA 19144-1203 t) 215-713-3984 vfo@famvin.org www.famvin.org The international VFO accompanies the Vincentian Family in its development and growth of our shared Vincentian Charism. Rev. Joseph V. Agostino, C.M., International Director;

ROSEMONT

Holy Child Network of Schools - 1341 Montgomery Ave., Rosemont, PA 19010 t) 610-626-1400 hcschools@shcj.org www.holychildschools.org Sr. Eileen McDevitt, S.H.C.J., Dir.;

SCHWENKSVILLE

***You Are Made New Ministry, Inc.** - 749 Martingale Rd., Schwenksville, PA 19473 t) 610-287-2989 de@youarenew.com www.youaremadenew.com Denise Yarrison, Founder & Exec. Dir.;

SPRINGFIELD

LIVE Vertical, Inc. - 521 Lehann Cir., Springfield, PA 19064 t) (610) 986-6660 livevertical.org Rob Longo, Chief Evangelization Officer;

WEST CHESTER

FIERCE Athlete, Inc. - 227 N. Walnut St., Apt. 2, West Chester, PA 19380; Mailing: PO Box 168, West Chester, PA 19381 t) 860-392-9225 sam@fierceathlete.org www.fierceathlete.org Promotes true and authentic identity and femininity within female athletics through the teachings of the Catholic Church. Samantha Kelley, Pres.;

The Franciscan Federation, Third Order Regular of the Sisters and Brothers of the United States - 1554 Paoli Pike, #307, West Chester, PA 19380 t) 929-207-3653 franfedoffice@franfed.org www.franfed.org Sr. Lilia Kagendo, LSOSF, Exec.; Sr. Carol Woods, S.F.M.A., Exec.;

WYNNEWOOD

***The Culture Project International** - ; Mailing: P.O. Box 86, Wynnewood, PA 19096 t) 800-315-8684 mail@restoreculture.com www.restoreculture.com An initiative of young people to restore culture through the experience of virtue. Cristina Barba, Pres.;

MONASTERIES AND RESIDENCES FOR PRIESTS AND BROTHERS [MON]

ARDMORE

Bellesini Friary - 111 Argyle Rd., Ardmore, PA 19003 c) (610) 955-6188 Rev. Allan Fitzgerald, O.S.A., Prior; Rev. Joseph L. Narog, O.S.A., Dir.; Rev. Kevin De Prinzio, O.S.A., In Res.; Priests: 3

BENSALEM

Congregation of the Holy Spirit - Spiritan Hall, 2401 Bristol Pike, Bensalem, PA 19020 t) 215-638-0845 jmcmloskey@holyghostprep.org www.spiritans.org Faculty Residence for Priests Teaching at Holy Ghost Preparatory School. Rev. Philip Agber, C.S.Sp.; Bro. Joseph T. Cannon; Rev. Christopher H. McDermott, C.S.Sp.; Rev. James P. McCloskey, C.S.Sp., Supr.;

Missionaries of the Blessed Sacrament (M.S.S.) - 2290 Galloway Rd., B7, Bensalem, PA 19020 t) 215-244-9211 apea@webtv.net www.perpetualadoration.org Rev. Victor P. Warkulwiz, M.S.S., Supr.;

BRYN MAWR

Augustinians Friars (O.S.A.) - Our Mother of Good Counsel Community, 31 Pennswood Rd., Bryn Mawr, PA 19010-3475 t) 610-525-0147 Rev. Joseph S. Mostardi, O.S.A., Pst.; Rev. John F. Deary, O.S.A., Prior; Rev. J. Thomas Pohto, O.S.A., Treas.; Rev. Joseph Loya, O.S.A., In Res.; Bro. Michael Riggs, OSA, In Res.; Bro. Nicholas Stone, OSA; Brs.: 2; Priests: 4

DEVON

Piarist Fathers (Order of the Pious Schools) - 363 N. Valley Forge Rd., Devon, PA 19333 t) 610-688-7337 c) 718-419-2264 jnelsonh55@yahoo.com Rev. Nelson Henao, Sch.P., Rector; Rev. Geza Pazmany, Sch.P., In Res.; Rev. Javier Renteria, Sch.P., Chap.; Rev. Francisco Aisa, Sch.P., Headmaster; Rev. James J. Shea, Sch.P., Mem.;

DOYLESTOWN

The Order of Saint Paul, First Hermit - The Pauline Fathers - 654 Ferry Rd., Doylestown, PA 18901; Mailing: P.O. Box 2049, Doylestown, PA 18901 t) 215-345-0607 reception@czestochowa.us www.czestochowa.us Rev. Tadeusz Lizinczyk, Prov.; Rev. Marcin Cwierz, OSPPE, Prior; Rev. Bogdan Olzacki, Subprior; Rev. Marcin Mikulski, Shrine Director; Rev. Joseph Olczak, OSPPE; Rev. Jan Michalak, O.S.P.P.E., OSPPE; Rev. Jan Kolmaga, O.S.P.P.E., OSPPE; Rev. Jerzy Maj, O.S.P.P.E., OSPPE; Rev. Bartlomiej Marciniak, O.S.P.P.E., OSPPE; Rev. Tadeusz Olzacki, OSPPE; Rev. Sebastian Hanks, OSPPE; Rev. Rafal Walczyk, O.S.P.P.E., OSPPE; Rev. Maciej Karpinski, OSPPE; Rev. Tymoteusz Tarnacki, O.S.P.P.E., OSPPE; Bro. Piotr Lisiecki, O.S.P.P.E., OSPPE; Bro. Tomasz Fabiszewsk, O.S.S.P.E., OSPPE; Bro. Kazimierz Kania, O.S.P.P.E., OSPPE; Brs.: 4; Priests: 24

LAVEROCK

Brothers of Charity (F.C.) - Triest Hall, 7720 Doe Ln., Laverock, PA 19038 t) 215-887-6361 jfitzfc@aol.com www.brothersofcharity.org Bro. John Fitzgerald, F.C., Supr.;

MALVERN

Augustinian Friars (O.S.A.) - 418 S. Warren Ave., Malvern, PA 19355-2707 t) 484-595-1194 provincial@augustinian.org www.augustinians.org Patrick Mcstravog, O.S.A., In Res.; Rev. William C. Gabriel, O.S.A., Teacher; Rev. Donald F. Reilly, O.S.A., Prior; Rev. Christopher J. Drennen, O.S.A., Treas.; Priests: 4

MERION STATION

Arrupe Jesuit Community - 41 Lapsey Ln., Merion Station, PA 19066 t) 412-888-7804 egeinzer@jesuits.org Rev. Eugene M. Geinzer, S.J., Pres.; Rev. Thomas J. Brennan, S.J.; Rev. George W. Bur, S.J.; Rev. Raymond Donaldson, SJ; Rev. Andreas Gosele; Rev. Daniel R.J. Joyce, S.J.; Rev. Frank Kaminski; Rev. Richard S. McCouch, S.J.; Rev. Douglas Ray, SJ; Rev. Daniel M. Ruff, S.J.; Rev. Stephen Surovick; Priests: 11

Jesuit Community at St. Joseph's University - 261 City Ave., Merion Station, PA 19066 t) 610-660-1400 rkeane@sju.edu Rev. Vincent de P. Alagia, S.J., In Res.; Rev. David G. Allen, S.J., In Res.; Rev. John Barron, S.J., Pst. Min./Coord.; Rev. Anthony J. Berret, S.J., In Res.; Rev. William J. Byron, S.J., In Res.; Rev. Peter A. Clark, S.J., Prof.; Rev. James J. Ditillo, S.J., Chap.; Rev. Joseph J. Feeney, S.J., In Res.; Rev. Vincent J. Genovesi, S.J., In Res.; Rev. Joseph J. Godfrey, S.J., In Res.; Rev. Frank Haig, S.J., In Res.; Rev. Robert E. Hamm, S.J., In Res.; Rev. Robert Lawrence Keane, S.J., Supr.; Rev. Thomas Kuller, S.J., Admin.; Rev. Joseph P. Lacey, S.J., In Res.; Rev. Brendan G. Lally, S.J., Pst. Min./Coord.; Rev. Gasper F. LoBiondo, S.J., In Res.; Rev. Joseph L. Lombardi, S.J., In Res.; Rev. Lucien Longtin, S.J., In Res.; Rev. James McAndrews, S.J., In Res.; Rev. Edward T. O'Donnell, S.J., Sacr. Min.; Rev. Nicholas J. Rashford, S.J., In Res.; Bro. Marco Rodriguez, S.J., Admin.; Rev. Patrick H. Samway, S.J., Pst. Min./Coord.; Rev. William Sneck, S.J., In Res.; Rev. Martin R. Tripole, S.J., In Res.; Rev. Kevin Wildes, S.J., In Res.; Rev. George B. Wilson, S.J., In Res.; Brs.: 1; Priests: 27

Loyola Center - 261 City Ave., Philadelphia, PA 19066-1835

PAOLI

Daylesford Abbey, Inc. - 220 S. Valley Rd., Paoli, PA 19301-1900 t) 610-647-2530 norbertines@daylesford.org www.daylesford.org Daylesford Abbey is a Roman Catholic monastery of Canons Regular of Premontre, located in Chester County, Pennsylvania Rt. Rev. Domenic A. Rossi, O. Praem., Abbot; Very Rev. John C. Zagarella, O. Praem., Prior; Rev. John Joseph Novielli, O. Praem., Dir.; Rev. Carl Braschoss, O. Praem.; Rev. Andrew D. Ciferni, O.Praem.; Rev. Steven J. Albero, O. Praem.; Rev. Maurice C. Avicolli, O.Praem.; Rev. Francis Danielski, O.Praem.; Rev. Paul J. DeAntoniis, O. Praem.; Rev. David Driesch, O.Praem.; Rt. Rev. Ronald J. Rossi, O. Praem., Abbot; Rt. Rev. Richard J. Antonucci, O. Praem., Abbot; Bro. Jeffrey Himes; Rev. Blaise R. Krautsack, O.Praem.; Rev. Joseph P. McLaughlin, O.Praem.; Rev. James C. Rodia, O.Praem.; Rev. Thomas J. Rossi, O.Praem.; Rev. Nicholas R. Terico, O.Praem.; Rev. Joseph A. Serano, O.Praem., Treas.; Brs.: 1; Priests: 20

PHILADELPHIA

Augustinian Community (O.S.A.) - 1511 S. 10th St., Philadelphia, PA 19147 t) 215-463-1326 stnicks910@verizon.net www.stnicksphila.com Rev. Nicholas Martorano, O.S.A., Pst.; Rev. Juan Cardenas, O.S.A., Par. Vicar; Rev. Robert Joseph Guessetto, O.S.A., Prior; Rev. Elizandro Contreras, O.S.A., In Res.; Rev. Paul W. Galetto, O.S.A., In Res.; Rev. Jeremy Hiers, OSA, In Res.; Rev. Daniel McLaughlin, O.S.A., In Res.; Rev. Robert Terranova, In Res.; Priests: 8

The Brothers of the Christian Schools/Jeremy House Postulancy - 6633 Ardleigh St., Philadelphia, PA 19119-3824 t) 215-843-1884 juliano@fscdena.org Bro. Brian Henderson, F.S.C., Dir.;

Congregation of the Mission - St. Vincent's Seminary, 500 E. Chelten Ave., Philadelphia, PA 19144-1203 t) 215-713-2400 idetres@vincentiansusaeast.org Central House of the Congregation of the Mission (Vincentian Community), Eastern Province. Rev. Stephen F. Cantwell, C.M., In Res.; Rev. James F. Dorr, C.M., In Res.; Rev. John Patrick Prager, C.M., In Res.; Rev. Stephen M. Grozio, C.M., Prov.; Rev. Thomas F. McKenna, C.M., Asst. Prov.; Rev. John Thomas Maher, CM, Supr.; Rev. Dennis H. Holtschneider, C.M.; Rev. John A. Kettelberger, C.M.; Rev. Joseph V. Agostino, C.M., In Res.; Rev. Stephen Charles Bicsko, C.M., In Res.; Rev. Michael Callaghan, C.M., In Res.; Rev. John B. Freund, C.M., In Res.; Rev. John William Gouldrick, C.M., In Res.; Rev. Joel Bernardo, C.M., In Res.; Rev. John E. Kane, C.M., In Res.; Rev. Daniel J. Kramer, C.M., In Res.; Rev. Charles F. Krieg, C.M., In Res.; Rev. Robert P. Maloney, C.M., In Res.; Rev. William J. O'Brien, C.M., In Res.; Vincent Joseph O'Malley, C.M., In Res.; Rev. Abel Osorio, C.M., In Res.; Rev. Alfred R. Pehrsson, C.M., In Res.; Rev. Flavio Pereira, C.M., In Res.; Rev. Carl L. Pieber, C.M., In Res.; Rev. Thomas A. Sendlein, C.M., In Res.; Rev. Michael J. Shea, C.M., In Res.; Rev. Stephen P. Trzecieski, C.M., In Res.; Rev. Martin F. McGeough, Chap.; Rev. Francis W. Sacks, C.M., Chap.; Rev. Elmer Bauer III, C.M., Treas.; Bro. Peter A. Campbell, C.M., Treas.; Rev. Timothy V. Lyons, C.M., Dir.; Brs.: 5; Priests: 87

Gesu School Jesuit Community and Outreach Center (S.J.) - 1700 W. Thompson St., Philadelphia, PA 19121 t) 215-763-3660 x108 neil@gesuschool.org

Monastery of Our Lady of Mercy (Fathers of Our Lady of Mercy, Inc. / Order of the B.V.M. of Mercy (Mercedarian Friars)) - 6398 Drexel Rd., Philadelphia, PA 19151-2596 t) 215-879-0594 vocations@orderofmercy.org www.orderofmercy.org Headquarters for the U.S. Vicariate of the Roman Province Rev. Matthew H Phelan, O. de. M, Supr.; Rev. Justin Freeman, O.de.M., Par. Vicar; Bro. Martin J Jarocinski, O. de M., In Res.; Bro. Dominic (Matthew) Whetzel, O.de.M., In Res.; Brs.: 2; Priests: 2

Order of Friars Minor of the Province of the Most Holy Name - Juniper Friary, 1802 E. Hagert St., Philadelphia, PA 19125 t) (215) 423-2859 Bro. Frederick C. Dilger, O.F.M., Supr.; Rev. Paul Lostritto, O.F.M., In Res.; Bro. James La Grutta, OFM, In Res.; Rev. Patrick K Sieber, OFM, In Res.; Rev. Michael Duffy, O.F.M., In Res.; Rev. Stephen Nathaniel DeWitt, OFM, Contact; Brs.: 2; Priests: 4

Padre Pio Friary, Province of St. Augustine - 1509 Church St., Philadelphia, PA 19124 t) 215-476-6511 Bro. Alexander Hostoffer, O.F.M. Cap., Dir.; Rev. Kevin Thompson, O.F.M. Cap, Dir.; Bro. Edgar Pereira, OFM Cap, Staff; Rev. Reynaldo Frias Santana, O.F.M. Cap., Asst.; Bro. Andrew McCarty, O.F.M. Cap., Asst. Dir.; Brs.: 3; Priests: 2

The Philadelphia Congregation of The Oratory of St. Philip Neri - 2321 Green St., Philadelphia, PA 19130-3196 t) 215-765-4568 Rev. Paul C. Convery, C.O., Vicar; A. Joseph Mosko, Seminarian; Rev. Georges G. Thiers, C.O., Provost; A Joshua Vargas, Novice;

RIDLEY PARK

Servants of Charity (SdC) - Divine Providence Village, 405 Tome St., Ridley Park, PA 19078 t) 484-472-5067 fr.dweber@chs-adphila.org Rev. Dennis M. Weber, S.D.C.;

ROSEMONT

Saxony Hall - 110 Montrose Ave., Rosemont, PA 19010-1509 t) 610-520-4510 provincial@augustinian.org Rev. Martin S. Laird, O.S.A.; Rev. Joseph Loya, O.S.A.; Rev. James J. McCartney, O.S.A.; Rev. John J. McKenzie, O.S.A.; Rev. Stephen J. Baker, O.S.A., Treas.; Rev. Robert P. Hagan, O.S.A., Prior;

VILLANOVA

St. Augustine Friary - 214 Ashwood Rd., Villanova, PA 19085 t) (610) 527-0325 secretary.treasurer@augustinian.org Rev. Robert P. Hagan, O.S.A., Prov.; Rev. Aldo Potencio, O.S.A, Secy.; Priests: 2

Fray de Leon Community - Burns Hall - West Campus, Villanova University, 800 E. Lancaster Ave., Villanova, PA 19085; Mailing: P.O. Box 340, Villanova, PA 19085 t) 610-519-5020; 610-527-3330 x279 Rev. Peter M. Donohue, O.S.A.; Bro. Michael Duffy, O.S.A.; Rev. Bernard C. Scianna, O.S.A.; Rev. David A. Cregan, O.S.A.; Brs.: 1; Priests: 3

St. John Stone Friary - 37 Aldwyn Ln., Villanova, PA 19085 t) 610-519-0634 Rev. Joseph D. Calderone, O.S.A.; Bro. Robert Thornton, O.S.A.; Rev. John E. Deegan, O.S.A., Treas.; Rev. Kail C. Ellis, O.S.A., Prior;

Provincial Offices of the Order of St. Augustine, Province of St. Thomas of Villanova - 214 Ashwood Rd., Villanova, PA 19085-0340; Mailing: P.O. Box 340, Villanova, PA 19085-0340 t) 610-527-3330 secretary.treasurer@augustinian.org www.augustinian.org Rev. Robert P. Hagan, O.S.A., Prov.; Rev. Aldo Potencio, O.S.A, Secy. & Treas.; Rev. John E. Deegan, O.S.A., Dir.; Rev. Joseph L. Narog, O.S.A., Dir.; Bro. Richard Ekmann, O.S.A., Archivist; Affiong Inyang, Dir.; Madonna Sutter, Dir.; Brs.: 9; Priests: 110

St. Thomas Monastery - 800 E. Lancaster Ave., Villanova, PA 19085 t) 610-519-7500 lynn.walsh@villanova.edu Rev. James Cassidy, O.S.A.; Rev. Michael F. DiGregorio, O.S.A.; Rev. Edward Dixey, O.S.A.; Rev. Edward Doherty, O.S.A.; Rev. Harry J. Erdlen, O.S.A.; Rev. James R. Flynn, O.S.A.; Rev. Robert P. Hagan, O.S.A.; Rev. Richard O'Leary, O.S.A.; Rev. Russell Ortega, O.S.A.; Rev. John P. Betoni, O.S.A.; Rev. Francis J. Caponi, O.S.A.; Rev. Thomas J. Casey, O.S.A.; Rev. Francis Chambers, O.S.A.; Rev. Thomas P. Dwyer, O.S.A.; Bro. Richard Ekmann, O.S.A.; Rev. John J. Ferrence, O.S.A.; Rev. Adrian Gilligan, O.S.A.; Rev. James D. McBurney, O.S.A.; Rev. Stephen J. Baker, O.S.A.; Rev. Francis J. Horn, O.S.A.; Bro. William C. Harkin, O.S.A.; Francis Barr; Rev. Martin Laird, O.S.A.; Rev. Lee J. Makowski, O.S.A.; Rev. James J. McCartney, O.S.A.; Rev. Gary N. McCloskey, O.S.A.; Rev. Joseph G. Ryan, O.S.A.; Rev. John J. Sheridan, O.S.A.; Rev. Martin L. Smith, O.S.A.; Rev. Michael P. Sullivan, O.S.A.; Rev. Dennis M. McGowan, O.S.A., Prior; Rev. Francis A. Farsaci, O.S.A., Subprior; Rev. Francis J. Doyle, O.S.A., Priest; Rev. Aquilino Gonzalez, OSA, Other; Rev. James MacDougall, OSA, Other; Rev. W. Howard McGraw, Other; Rev. John J. McKenzie, O.S.A., Priest; Rev. Richard Nahman, OSA, Other; John O'Rourke, Priest; Rev. James Wenzel, OSA, Other; Rev. Denis G. Wilde, O.S.A., Other; Joseph Wimmer, Priest; Brs.: 2; Priests: 42

St. Thomas of Villanova Friary - 109 Willowburn Rd., Villanova, PA 19085-1313 t) 610-527-0856 joseph.calderone@villanova.edu Rev. Russell Ortega, O.S.A.; Rev. Joseph D. Calderone, O.S.A., Treas.; Bro. Robert Thornton, O.S.A., Prior;

WYNDMOOR

Christian Brothers (F.S.C.) - LaSalle High School Community, 8605 Cheltenham Ave., Wyndmoor, PA 19038 t) 215-233-3030 www.lschs.org Bro. Edward Koronkiewicz, Community Director; Brs.: 8

Villa de Sales Oblate Residence - 8501 Flourtown Ave., Wyndmoor, PA 19038 t) 215-836-1472 ghoffman@oblates.org Rev. Joseph F. Chorpenning, O.S.F.S.; Rev. Edward T. Fitzpatrick, O.S.F.S.; Rev. Thomas P. Gallagher, O.S.F.S.; Rev. Charles J. Norman, O.S.F.S.; Rev. Robert Mancini, O.S.F.S., In Res.; Rev. Richard T. Reece, O.S.F.S.;

NURSING / REHABILITATION / CONVALESCENCE / ELDERLY CARE [NUR]

DARBY

Little Flower Manor - 1201 Springfield Rd., Darby, PA 19023 t) 610-534-6000 rport@littleflowermanor.org All Skilled Nursing Care. Staffed by Sisters of the Divine Redeemer. Rosemary Port, Admin.;

ELVERSON

St. Mary of Providence Center - 227 Isabella Rd., Elverson, PA 19520 t) 610-942-4166 stmaryofprov@comcast.net stmaryofprov-pa.org Residence for Senior Citizens. Center of Spirituality, Retreats Sr. Brenda McHugh, DSMP, Dir.;

FLOURTOWN

Bethlehem Retirement Village - 100 W. Wissahickon Ave., Flourtown, PA 19031 t) 215-233-0998 Staffed by the Sisters of St. Joseph. Sr. Judith Oliver, S.S.J., Dir.; Asstd. Annu.: 105; Staff: 4

Saint Joseph Villa - 110 W. Wissahickon Ave., Flourtown, PA 19031-1898 t) 215-836-4179 dunni@stjosephvilla.org www.stjosephvilla.org Irene Dunn, SSJ, Pres.; Asstd. Annu.: 475; Staff: 100

HUNTINGDON VALLEY

Redeemer Village - 1551 Huntingdon Pike, Huntingdon Valley, PA 19006; Mailing: Holy Redeemer Health System, c/o 521 Moredon Rd., Huntingdon Valley, PA 19006 t) 215-947-8168; 215-938-3226 www.holyredeemer.com Subsidiary of Holy Redeemer Health System. Low income housing for the elderly or handicapped, subsidized by HUD.

Redeemer Village II - Subsidiary of Holy Redeemer Health System, Inc. Low income housing for the elderly or handicapped, subsidized by HUD.

IMMACULATA

Camilla Hall Nursing Home - Camilla Dr., Immaculata, PA 19345-0100; Mailing: P.O. Box 100, Immaculata, PA 19345-0100 t) 610-386-2000 ch@camillahall.org Rev. John Burger, S.S.C., Chap.; Rev. Michael Callaghan, C.M., Chap.; Sr. Ann Raymond Welte, Supr.; Becky Rigsby, Interim Admin.;

PHILADELPHIA

Holy Family Home (Little Sisters of the Poor) - 5300 Chester Ave., Philadelphia, PA 19143-4993 t) 215-729-5153 phmothersuperior@littlesistersofthepoor.org Rev. James F. Sullivan, Chap.; Mother Celine Therese, Supr.; Pat Lo, Admin.;

St. Ignatius Nursing Home (Felician Services Inc.) - 4401 Haverford Ave., Philadelphia, PA 19104 t) 215-349-8800 smccrary@stinrc.org; eburleigh@stinrc.org www.stinrc.org Felician Services Inc. Ed Burleigh, Admin.; Susan McCrary, CEO; Asstd. Annu.: 250; Staff: 150

St. John Neumann Place - 2600 Moore St., Philadelphia, PA 19145 t) 215-463-1101 www.stjohnneumannplace.org Heather Huot, Contact;

St. Joseph Housing Corporation - 9701 Germantown Ave., Philadelphia, PA 19118-2694 t) 215-248-7205 kshelly@ssjphila.org www.ssjphila.org Staffed by the Sisters of St. Joseph. Sr. Maureen G. Erdlen, SSJ, Pres.; Asstd. Annu.: 108; Staff: 4

***Nativity BVM Place** - 3255 Belgrade St., Philadelphia, PA 19134 t) (215) 426-9422 info@chcsphiladelphia.org Heather Huot, Dir.;

The Servants of Relief for Incurable Cancer (Dominican Sisters of Hawthorne) - 1315 W. Hunting Park Ave., Philadelphia, PA 19140 t) 215-329-3222 superiorgeneral@hawthorne-dominicans.org www.sacredheartphila.org Attended by Oblates of St. Francis de Sales. Mother Marie Edward, Pres.; Staff: 5

PRESCHOOLS / CHILDCARE CENTERS [PRE]

BENSALEM

St. Francis - St. Joseph Homes for Children - 3400 Bristol Pike, Bensalem, PA 19020 t) 215-638-9310 cssphiladelphia@chs-adphila.org www.sfsj.org Provides residential treatment at 8 sites for male youth, ages 12 to 20; also Supervised Living for male youth 17 & older. James Logan, Admin.;

PHILADELPHIA

Casa del Carmen Day Care Center - 4400 N. 5th St., Philadelphia, PA 19140; Mailing: 4400 N. Reese St., Philadelphia, PA 19140 t) 215-457-4325 Shari Gold, Dir.;

St. Monica Early Learning Center - 1720 W. Ritner St., Philadelphia, PA 19145 t) 215-334-6001 rpeterson44@yahoo.com stmonicaparish.net Sr. Rosemary Peterson, I.H.M., Dir.;

ROSEMONT

St. Edmond's Home for Children - 320 S. Roberts Rd., Rosemont, PA 19010 t) 610-525-8800 cssmrserv.org Licensed I.C.F./M.R. Home for children ages birth to 21 with severe/profound intellectual and physical disabilities. Rev. Dennis M. Weber, S.D.C., Chap.; Denise Clofine, Admin.;

WYNNEWOOD

St. Katherine Day School - 930 Bowman Ave., Wynnewood, PA 19096 t) 610-667-3958 principal@stkds.org Children with Developmental Delay and/or Multiple Impairments. Stds.: 49

RETREAT HOUSES / RENEWAL CENTERS [RTR]

ASTON

Clare House to The Hermitages - 608 B. Legion Rd., Aston, PA 19014 t) 610-558-6152 fsc@osfphila.org www.fscaston.org Directed and Private Retreats. 5 Hermitages on property. Staffed by Sisters of St. Francis of Philadelphia. Name change to The Hermitages Sr. Angela Presenza, OSF, Program Director;

Franciscan Spiritual Center - 609 S. Convent Rd., Aston, PA 19014 t) 610-558-6152 fsc@osfphila.org www.fscaston.org Private, directed retreats. Spiritual, human development and holistic programs. Staffed by the Sisters of St. Francis Philadelphia. Sr. Angela Presenza, OSF, Program Director;

DOYLESTOWN

National Shrine of Our Lady of Czestochowa - 654 Ferry Rd., Doylestown, PA 18901; Mailing: P.O. Box 2049, Doylestown, PA 18901 t) 215-345-0600; 215-345-0601 info@czestochowa.us czestochowa.us Rev. Marcin Cwierz, OSPPE, Prior; Rev. Tadeusz Lizinczyk, Prov.; Rev. Rafal Walczyk, O.S.P.P.E., Dir.;

HAVERFORD

Saint Raphaela Center - 616 Coopertown Rd., Haverford, PA 19041 t) 610-642-5715 info@straphealacenter.org straphaelacenter.org Retreat House Sr. Michelle Cimaroli, acj, Dir.;

MALVERN

St. Joseph's-in-the-Hills - 315 S. Warren Ave., Malvern, PA 19355-0315; Mailing: P.O. Box 315, Malvern, PA 19355-0315 t) 610-644-0400 mail@malvernretreat.com malvernretreat.com (The Malvern Retreat House), Owned and Operated by Catholic Laity. Jacqueline J. Delaney, Chair; Mark J. Poletunow, Pres.; Rev. James T. McGuinn, Rector - ProTem;

PHILADELPHIA

***Cranaleith Spirituality Center** - 13475 Proctor Rd., Philadelphia, PA 19116 t) 215-934-6206 info@cranaleith.org; office@cranaleith.org cranaleith.org Education, Retreat, and Conference Center Deborah Kost, Exec.;

The Marianist Center for Lay Formation - 1341 N.

Delaware Ave., Ste. 402, Philadelphia, PA 19125-4300 t) 215-634-4116 marianistcenter@gmail.com www.marianist.com Committed to the Marianist mission to foster spiritual growth and formation of lay communities and social justice. Bro. Stephen Glodek, SM, Dir.;

Mother Boniface Center - 3501 Solly Ave., Philadelphia, PA 19136 t) 267-350-1830 mbscdirector@msbt.org www.msbt.org/mbsc A ministry of the Missionary Servants of the Most Blessed Trinity. programs; retreats, days of recollection, scripture study, meetings; workshops. Margarita Solis-Deal, Dir.;

SEMINARIES [SEM]

PAOLI

Daylesford Abbey (Norbertine Fathers, Inc.) - 220 S. Valley Rd., Paoli, PA 19301-1900 t) 610-647-2530 nobertines@daylesford.org www.daylesford.org Rt. Rev. Domenic A. Rossi, O. Praem., Abbot; Very Rev. John C. Zagarella, O. Praem., Prior; Rev. Joseph A. Serano, O.Praem., Treas.; Rt. Rev. Richard J. Antonucci, O. Praem., Abbot; Rt. Rev. Ronald J. Rossi, O. Praem., Abbot;

PHILADELPHIA

Brothers of the Christian Schools - Jeremy House, 6633 Ardleigh St., Philadelphia, PA 19119-3824 t) 215-843-1884 richfsc2003@gmail.com Bro. Richard Buccina, F.S.C., Dir.;

DePaul Novitiate - 5710 Magnolia St., Philadelphia, PA 19144 t) 215-843-1581 Novitiate for the Congregation of the Mission (Vincentians). Rev. Elmer Bauer III, C.M., In Res.;

St. Vincent's Seminary - 500 E. Chelten Ave., Philadelphia, PA 19144-1296 t) 215-713-2400 idetres@vincentiansusaeast.org www.cmeast.org Central House of the Eastern Province of the Congregation of the Mission, (Vincentians). Residence for retired priests & brothers. Rev. Elmer Bauer III, C.M., Treas.; Rev. John Thomas Maher, CM, Supr.; Rev. Stephen M. Grozio, C.M., Prov.; Rev. Timothy V. Lyons, C.M., Dir.; Allen Andrews, Executive Dir. Finance; Rev. Thomas F. McKenna, C.M., Asst. Provincial;

Vincentian Theologate-DeAndreis House - 124 Cotton St., Philadelphia, PA 19127 t) 267-437-2537 For Men studying at St. Charles Borromeo Seminary. Rev. Charles P. Strollo, C.M., In Res.; Rev. Gregory J. Semeniuk, C.M., Dir.;

WYNNEWOOD

Theological Seminary of St. Charles Borromeo - 100 E. Wynnewood Rd., Wynnewood, PA 19096 t) 610-667-3394 www.scs.edu Rev. Jason E. Buck, Dean; John M. Haas, John Cardinal Krol Chair in Moral Theology; Nathan J. Knutson, Lucille M. Francesco Chair Sacred Music; Rev. Augustus C. Puleo, Faculty; Todd Chiaravalloti, Registrar; Rev. Christopher R. Cooke, Dean; Rev. Dennis J. Carbonaro, Dir.; Rev. David M. Friel, Dir.; Rev. Keith J. Chylinski, Rector; Most Rev. Timothy C. Senior, Seminary Chancellor; Rev. Herbert J. Sperger, Dir.; Rev. Patrick J. Brady, Vice Rector; Rev. Msgr. Gerard C. Mesure, Dean; Rev. John P. Collins, Resident, Adjunct Faculty; Rev. Thomas F. Dailey, O.S.F.S., John Cardinal Foley Chair in Social Communications; Rev. Msgr. Gregory J. Fairbanks, Dean, Faculty; Rev. Frank A. Giuffre, Faculty, Dir. Spiritual Year; Rev. Msgr. John M. Savinski, Adjunct Spiritual Dir.; Rev. Msgr. Andrew J. Golias, Resident, Adjunct Faculty; Rev. Daniel E. Mackle, Faculty; Rev. Msgr. Michael K. Magee, Dean, Faculty; Mark McLaughlin, CFO/CEO; Rev. Robert A. Pesarchick, Vice Pres. Academic Affairs; Stds.: 130; Lay Tchrs.: 8; Pr. Tchrs.: 15; Sr. Tchrs.: 1

Spirituality Year - 51 E. Third Ave., Conshohocken, PA 19428

YEADON

Redemptoris Mater Archdiocesan Missionary Seminary - 821 W. Cobbs Creek Parkway, Yeadon, PA 19050 t) 610-713-5697 secretary@rmphiladelphia.org rmphiladelphia.org Rev. Mariano DellaGiovanna; Rev. Carlos A. Benitez, Rector;

SPECIAL CARE FACILITIES [SPF]

ASTON

Assisi House - 600 Red Hill Rd., Aston, PA 19014 t) 610-459-8990 kmccarron@osfphila.org www.osfphila.org Home for retired Sisters of St. Francis of Philadelphia. Sr. Kathleen McCarron, Admin.; Bed Capacity: 120; Asstd. Annu.: 104; Staff: 130

BENSALEM

St. Francis - St. Joseph - St. Vincent Homes For Children - 3400 Bristol Pike, Bensalem, PA 19020 t) 215-638-9310 jlogan@sfsj.org Operates the following programs for court adjudicated dependent females ages 12-21 who suffer from abuse and neglect. All facilities are staffed 24/7. James Logan, Admin.;

Guardian Angel Group Home - 157 W. Carpenter Ln., Philadelphia, PA 19111 t) 267-574-1100 Girls ages 12-21.

St. Joseph's Hall Group Home - 477 E. Locust Ave., Philadelphia, PA 19144 t) 215-849-1316 Girls ages 12-21.

CHESTER

The Bernardine Center (Bernardine Franciscans, Delaware County) - 2625 W. Ninth St., Chester, PA 19013 t) 610-497-3225 c) 484-794-7033 director@bernardinecenter.org www.bernardinecenter.org West Side Brunch, Emergency Food Cupboard, Advocacy, Anger Management Classes, Baby Cupboard. Sr. Sandra Lyons, O.S.F., Dir.; Asstd. Annu.: 11,052; Staff: 2

DARBY

Villa Saint Joseph - 1436 Lansdowne Ave., Darby, PA 19023-1298 t) 610-586-8535 h.mcconnell@chs-adphila.org Home for aged, infirm and convalescent priests of the Archdiocese of Philadelphia. CLaudia Populaire, Admin.;

DOWNINGTOWN

***Saint John Vianney Center** - 151 Woodbine Rd., Downingtown, PA 19335 t) 610-269-2600 info@sjvcenter.org www.sjvcenter.org Behavioral health and addictions treatment and resource center serving Catholic Clergy, Consecrated Men and Women Religious. David Shellenberger, Pres.;

NORWOOD

Communities of Don Guanella and Divine Providence - 20 E. Cleveland Ave., Norwood, PA 19074 t) 484-472-5066 fswiacki@chs-adphila.org dgdpcommunities.org Residential care & specialized training for adults with intellectual/developmental disabilities. Angela Babcock, Admin.; Fran Swiacki, Exec. Dir.; Rev. Dennis M. Weber, S.D.C., Dir., Ministry & Mission; Patricia Menszak, Admin. - Don Guanella; Bed Capacity: 320; Asstd. Annu.: 400; Staff: 896

Don Guanella Home at Bethel - 4317 Bethel Rd., Boothwyn, PA 19061 t) 610-494-4976 bjenkins@chs-dphila.org Barbara Jenkins, Dir.;

Don Guanella Home at Broadview - 1302 Broadview E., Downingtown, PA 19335 t) 610-873-1536 Barbara Jenkins, Dir.;

Don Guanella Home at Fairhill - 2 Fairhill Rd., Morton, PA 19070 t) 610-544-3987 bjenkins@chs-dphila.org Barbara Jenkins, Dir.;

Don Guanella Home at Fairview - 990 Fairview Rd., Swarthmore, PA 19081 t) 610-544-3987 bjenkins@chs-dphila.org Barbara Jenkins, Dir.;

Don Guanella Home at Frankford - 8538 Frankford Ave., Philadelphia, PA 19136 t) 215-331-3615 Barbara Jenkins, Dir.;

Don Guanella Home at Grant - 500-502 Grant Ave., Downingtown, PA 19335 t) 610-873-1917 bjenkins@chs-dphila.org Barbara Jenkins, Dir.;

Don Guanella Home at Meetinghouse - 1834 Meetinghouse Rd., Boothwyn, PA 19061 t) 610-859-7962 bjenkins@chs-dphila.org Barbara Jenkins, Dir.;

Don Guanella Home at Rolling Road - 813 W. Rolling Rd., Springfield, PA 19064 t) 610-543-2659 bjenkins@chs-dphila.org Barbara Jenkins, Dir.;

Don Guanella Home at Sickles - 1545 Sickles Dr., Aston, PA 19014 t) 484-840-0358 bjenkins@chs-dphila.org Barbara Jenkins, Dir.;

Don Guanella Home at Upland - 225 Upland Ave., Brookhaven, PA 19015 t) 610-872-1329 Barbara Jenkins, Dir.;

Don Guanella Home at Whiteland - 125 Whiteland Ave., Downingtown, PA 19335 t) 610-873-1726 Barbara Jenkins, Dir.;

Gula House - 1745 S. Sproul Rd., Springfield, PA 19064 t) 484-472-8074 Barbara Jenkins, Dir.;

Servants of Charity House - 1755 S. Sproul Rd., Springfield, PA 19064 t) 484-479-3936

Sisters Servants of the Immaculate Heart of Mary House - 1765 S. Sproul Rd., Springfield, PA 19064 t) 484-479-3806

PHILADELPHIA

Nativity BVM Senior Community Center - 3255 Belgrade St, Philadelphia, PA 19134; Mailing: 222 N. 17th St., Philadelphia, PA 19103 t) 215-423-2772 kbecker@chs-adphila.org Jennifer Scornaienchi, Contact;

Casa del Carmen - 4400 N. Reese St., Philadelphia, PA 19140 t) 267-331-2500 cssphiladelphia@chs-adphila.org Offers emergency crisis social services to the Spanish speaking community in Philadelphia and surrounding areas. Camille Crane, Admin.;

St. Edmond Senior Community Center - 2130 S. 21st St, Philadelphia, PA 19145; Mailing: 222 N. 17th St., Philadelphia, PA 19103 t) 215-790-9530 kbecker@chs-adphila.org Karen Becker, Dir.;

Drueding Center - 413 W. Master St., Philadelphia, PA 19122 t) 215-769-1830 acollins@holyredeemer.com www.druedingcenter.org Subsidiary of Holy Redeemer Health System, Provides transitional housing & support services for homeless women with children Anne Marie Collins, Exec.;

Marketing/Public Affairs Department - c/o 1602 Huntingdon Pike, Meadowbrook, PA 19046 t) 215-938-3226

St. Francis Inn - 2441 Kensington Ave., Philadelphia, PA 19125 t) 215-423-5845 info@stfrancisinn.org stfrancisinn.org Soup Kitchen & Social Service Center Rev. Stephen Nathaniel DeWitt, OFM, Contact; Bro. Frederick C. Dilger, O.F.M.; Rev. Michael A. Duffy, O.F.M.; Bro. James La Grutta, OFM; Asstd. Annu.: 59,504; Staff: 9

Holy Redeemer Home Health and Hospice Services - 12265 Townsend Rd., Ste. 400, Philadelphia, PA 19154 t) 215-671-9200 www.holyredeemer.com Holy Redeemer Support Svcs, Affiliate of Holy Redeemer Health System. Sponsor: Sisters of the Holy Redeemer, Medicare certified home health agency. Patricia O'Brien, Senior Vice Pres. & Chief Admin. Officer;

Marketing & Public Affairs Department - 521 Moredon Rd., Huntingdon Valley, PA 19006 t) 215-938-3226

St. John's Hospice - 1221 Race St., Philadelphia, PA 19107 t) 215-563-7763 hhuot@chs-adphila.org www.saintjohnshospice.org Staffed by Catholic Social Services Archdiocese of Philadelphia. Barry Martin, Dir.;

The Good Shepherd Program of St. John's Hospice - 1225 Race St., Philadelphia, PA 19107 t) 215-569-1101

St. Lucy Day School for Children with Visual Impairments and Archbishop Ryan Academy for the Deaf - 4251 L St., Philadelphia, PA 19124 t) 215-289-4220 llettiere@lucy-ryan.org stl.ocephila.org Sr. Lisa Ann Lettiere, I.H.M., Prin.;

St. Mary's Residence (Catholic Social Services) - 247 S. 5th St., Philadelphia, PA 19106 t) 215-922-4228 Kathleen Nelson, Dir.; Bed Capacity: 38; Asstd. Annu.: 41; Staff: 5

McAuley House - 1800 Morris St., Philadelphia, PA 19145 t) 215-271-5166 cssphiladelphia@chs-adphila.org

Mercy Hospice - 334 S. 13th St., Philadelphia, PA 19107 t) 215-545-5153 Provides residential case management & referral services to homeless women, women in recovery, who are single or are with their children. Renee Hudson-Small, Program Director;

Mount Nazareth (Sisters of the Holy Family of Nazareth) - 2755 Holme Ave., Philadelphia, PA 19152 t) (215) 543-0102 info@nazarethcsfn.org Home for retired and infirm sisters. Sr. Barbara Jean Wojnicki Sr., CSFN, Supr.; Bed Capacity: 60; Asstd. Annu.: 12; Staff: 16

Norris Square Senior Community Center - 2121 N. Howard St., Philadelphia, PA 19133; Mailing: 222 N. 17th St., Philadelphia, PA 19103 t) 215-423-7241

Star Harbor Senior Community Center - 4700 Springfield Ave., Philadelphia, PA 19143; Mailing: 222 N. 17th St., Philadelphia, PA 19103 t) 215-724-4414 Karen Becker, Contact;

Visitation Homes - 2638 Kensington Ave., Philadelphia, PA 19125 t) 215-425-2080 Residential service program for families making the transition from homelessness to permanent housing. Kate Baumgardner, Program Director;

Women of Hope Lombard - 1210 Lombard St., Philadelphia, PA 19147 t) 215-732-1341 Residential Facility for chronically mentally ill homeless women.

Women of Hope-Vine - 251 N. Lawrence St., Philadelphia, PA 19106 t) 215-592-9116 Residential facility for chronically mentally ill homeless women. Kathryn Girasole, Program Director;

PHOENIXVILLE

St. Mary's Franciscan Shelter - 209 Emmett St., Phoenixville, PA 19460 t) 610-933-3097 stmarysfs@verizon.net stmarysfs.org Sr. Bernadette Dougherty, S.S.J., Exec.;

WARMINSTER

Regina Coeli Residence for Priests - 685 York Rd., Warminster, PA 18974 t) 215-441-4642 Home for retired priests of the Archdiocese of Philadelphia. Rev. Msgr. J. Michael Flood, Admin.; Helen McConnell, Admin.;

An asterisk (*) denotes an organization that has established tax-exempt status directly with the IRS and is not covered by the USCCB Group Ruling.

Diocese of Phoenix

(Dioecesis Phoenicensis)

MOST REVEREND JOHN P. DOLAN

Bishop of Phoenix; ordained July 1, 1989; appointed Titular Bishop of Uchi Maius and Auxiliary Bishop of San Diego April 19, 2017; episcopal ordination June 8, 2017; appointed Bishop of Phoenix June 10, 2022; installed August 2, 2022. Office: 400 E. Monroe St., Phoenix, AZ 85004-2336.

Diocesan Pastoral Center: 400 E. Monroe St., Phoenix, AZ 85004-2336. T: 602-354-2000; F: 602-354-2427.
www.dphx.org
contact-us@dphx.org

ESTABLISHED DECEMBER 2, 1969.

Square Miles 43,967.

Comprises the Counties of Maricopa; Mohave; Yavapai & Coconino not to include the territorial boundaries of the Navajo Indian Reservation; Pinal–that portion of land known as the Gila River Indian Reservation in the State of Arizona.

Patroness of Diocese: Our Lady of Guadalupe.

For legal titles of parishes and diocesan institutions, consult the Chancery Office.

Most Reverend Eduardo A. Nevares
Auxiliary Bishop of Phoenix; ordained July 18, 1981; appointed Titular Bishop of Natchesium and Auxiliary Bishop of Phoenix May 11, 2010; episcopal ordination July 19, 2010. Office: 400 E. Monroe St., Phoenix, AZ 85004-2336.

STATISTICAL OVERVIEW

Personnel
Bishop....1
Auxiliary Bishops....1
Retired Bishops....1
Priests: Diocesan Active in Diocese....128
Priests: Diocesan Active Outside Diocese....1
Priests: Retired, Sick or Absent....38
Number of Diocesan Priests....167
Religious Priests in Diocese....103
Total Priests in your Diocese....270
Extern Priests in Diocese....82
Ordinations:
Diocesan Priests....4
Religious Priests....1
Transitional Deacons....2
Permanent Deacons....7
Permanent Deacons in Diocese....223
Total Brothers....7
Total Sisters....116

Parishes
Parishes....94
With Resident Pastor:
Resident Diocesan Priests....58
Resident Religious Priests....23
Without Resident Pastor:
Administered by Priests....13
Missions....24
Pastoral Centers....1

Professional Ministry Personnel:
Brothers....2
Sisters....46
Lay Ministers....131

Welfare
Catholic Hospitals....1
Total Assisted....98,515
Health Care Centers....5
Total Assisted....5,644
Homes for the Aged....24
Total Assisted....1,364
Day Care Centers....1
Total Assisted....405
Specialized Homes....7
Total Assisted....1,882
Special Centers for Social Services....38
Total Assisted....3,755,289
Residential Care of Disabled....2
Total Assisted....280
Other Institutions....2
Total Assisted....20,152

Educational
Seminaries, Diocesan....1
Students from This Diocese....16
Diocesan Students in Other Seminaries....27
Students, Religious....4
Total Seminarians....47
Colleges and Universities....4
Total Students....7,879

High Schools, Diocesan and Parish....6
Total Students....3,777
High Schools, Private....1
Total Students....1,314
Elementary Schools, Diocesan and Parish....29
Total Students....9,253
Catechesis/Religious Education:
High School Students....1,695
Elementary Students....14,312
Total Students under Catholic Instruction....38,277
Teachers in Diocese:
Priests....3
Sisters....22
Lay Teachers....1,114

Vital Statistics
Receptions into the Church:
Infant Baptism Totals....4,033
Minor Baptism Totals....881
Adult Baptism Totals....349
Received into Full Communion....1,818
First Communions....3,766
Confirmations....3,730
Marriages:
Catholic....1,175
Total Marriages....1,175
Deaths....3,673
Total Catholic Population....1,701,135
Total Population....5,101,585

LEADERSHIP

Vicars General - Most Rev. Eduardo A. Nevares; Rev. Fredrick J. Adamson;
Moderator of the Curia - t) (602) 354-2180 Rev. Fredrick J. Adamson;
Diocesan Office - t) (602) 354-2000; (602) 257-0030
Chancellor/Vice Moderator of the Curia - t) (602) 354-2470 Dr. Maria R. Chavira; Anna Alicia Novoa, Secy. (anovoa@dphx.org);
College of Consultors - Rev. Thomas Bennett; Rev. Jose Jesus Lopez Arias; Rev. Matthew Lowry;
Deans - Rev. James Aboyi, V.C., Dean - South East Central (fraboyi@holycrossmesa.org); Rev. John Bonavitacola, Dean - North West North; Rev. Francisco "Bing" Colasito, Dean - North West Central;
Presbyteral Council - Rev. John Muir, Chair; Rev. Robert Aliunzi, A.J., Vice Chmn.; Rev. Thaddeus M. McGuire, Secy.;
Diocesan Tribunal - t) (602) 354-2275 Rev. Christopher J. Fraser, Vicar; Nicole M. Delaney, Dir.;
Adjutant Judicial Vicar - Rev. Kevin C. Grimditch;
Advocates - Camille O'Melia; James O'Melia; Donna Wicker;
Defenders of the Bond - Rev. Peter P. Dobrowski; Robert Flummerfelt; Daniela Knepper;
Diocesan Judges - Rev. F. Nelson Libera, J.C.D.; Rev. Charles G. Kieffer; Rev. Awte Weldu, O. Cist;
Director - Nicole M. Delaney;
Judicial Vicar - Rev. Christopher J. Fraser;
Notaries - Leana Lowery; Vilma Hogreve; Heidi Stoll;
Promoter of Justice - Rev. F. Nelson Libera, J.C.D.;

OFFICES AND DIRECTORS

Archives - t) (602) 354-2475 Katherine Herrick, Archivist;
Arizona Catholic Conference - t) (602) 354-2390 Ronald Johnson, Exec.;
Buildings & Properties - t) (602) 354-2161 Brian Laspisa, Dir. (blaspisa@dphx.org);
Catholic Campaign for Human Development/Catholic Relief Services - t) (602) 354-2125 Sr. Mary Juanita Gonsalves, R.S.M., Contact;
Catholic Cemeteries & Funeral Homes - t) (602) 267-1329 dopccfh.org Joseph W. Lange, Pres.; Rev. Michael L. Diskin, Spiritual Adv./Care Srvcs.; Harry Antram, Dir., Mission & Care;
Administrative Offices - t) (602) 267-1329 www.dopccfh.org Joseph W. Lange;
All Souls Catholic Cemetery - t) (928) 220-2317 asccem.org Vincent J. Johnson Sr., Mgr.;
Calvary Catholic Cemetery - t) (928) 774-0072 cccem.org Vincent J. Johnson Sr., Mgr.;
St. Francis Catholic Cemetery - t) (602) 267-1329 qohccem.org Rich Craven, Mgr.;
Holy Cross Catholic Cemetery & Funeral Home - t) (623) 936-1710 hcccem.org Paty Rodriguez, Mgr.; Nathan Caviness, Gen. Mgr.;
Holy Redeemer Catholic Cemetery - t) (480) 513-3243 hrccem.org Dina Spear, Mgr.;
Queen of Heaven Catholic Cemetery & Funeral Home - t) (480) 892-3729 qohccem.org Chad Viliborghi, Mgr.; Nathan Caviness, Gen. Mgr.;
The Catholic Sun - t) (602) 354-2130 www.catholicsun.org Brett Meister, Dir. (bmeister@dphx.org);
Censor Librorum - Rev. Msgr. Peter Dai Bui; Rev. Kevin C. Grimditch;
Child and Youth Protection and Safe Environment Training - t) (602) 354-2396 Anne Vargas-Leveriza, Dir.; Eveling Ortega, Secy. (eortega@dphx.org);
Christ in Our Neighborhood - t) (602) 354-2025 Joyce Coronel, Mgr.;
Clergy, Vicar for - Rev. Msgr. Peter Dai Bui, Vicar; Brenda Santibanez, Secy. (bsantibanez@dphx.org);
Priestly Life and Ministry Committee - Rev. Msgr. Peter Dai Bui, Chair; Rev. Clement Attah; Rev. Sheunesu Bowora;
Priests' Personnel Board - Rev. Msgr. Peter Dai Bui, Chair; Rev. James Aboyi, V.C., Mem.; Rev. John Bonavitacola, Mem.;
Communications Office - t) (602) 354-2130 Brett Meister, Dir. (bmeister@dphx.org);
Diaconate Office - Dcn. James Trant, Dir.; Dcn. Douglas Bogart, Dir.;
Ecumenical and Interreligious Affairs - t) (602) 354-2471 Rev. David Loeffler, Dir. (frloeffler@dphx.org);
Education and Evangelization, Division - t) (602) 354-2334
Superintendent of Schools - t) (602) 354-2341 Domonic Salce;
Employee Benefits - t) (602) 354-2189
Finance Office - t) (602) 354-2186 Joseph Anderson, CFO; Maria Ventura, Controller (mventura@dphx.org);
Holy Childhood Association - t) (602) 354-2005 Sr. Mary Juanita Gonsalves, R.S.M.;
Human Resources - t) (602) 354-2201 Marian A. Enriquez, Dir.;
John Paul II Resource Center - t) (602) 354-2179 Michal Villanueva, Coord.;
Kino Catechetical Institute - t) (602) 354-2320 Steve Greene, Dir.;
Legal/General Counsel - t) (602) 354-2474 Dennis Naughton, Gen. Counsel;
Marriage and Respect Life, Office of - t) (602) 354-2355 Mike Phelan, Dir.;
Medical Ethics Board - Rev. Ignatius Mazanowski, F.H.S., Chair; Rev. Daniel Connealy, Assoc. Dir. (frconnealy@dphx.org);
Mental Health Ministry Program - t) (602) 354-2401 Maricela Campa, Mgr.;
Native American Ministry, Office of - t) (602) 354-2050 Rev. Antony Tinker, F.H.S., Dir.;
Natural Family Planning, Office of - t) (602) 354-2123 Armida Escarcega, Coord.;
Office of Consecrated Life - t) (602) 354-2472 Sr. Anthony Mary Diago, R.S.M., Dir.;
Office of Mission Advancement - Rev. Gregory J. Schlarb, Vicar;
Office of Multicultural Ministries - Most Rev. Eduardo A. Nevares, Dir.; Ignacio Rodriguez, Assoc. Dir.; Rev. Andrew McNair, Chap. (frmcnair@simonjude.org);
Parish Finance and Corporate Services - t) (602) 354-2491 Doug Pritchard, Dir.;
Priests' Assurance Association - t) (602) 354-2478 Rev. John Bonavitacola, Pres.; Rev. Daniel McBride, Treas.; Rev. Emile C. "Bud" Pelletier Jr., Secy.;
Prisons, Catholic Ministries to - t) (602) 354-2485 Kevin Starrs, Dir.; Dcn. Ricardo Gonzalez (donricardo@stjames-greater.com);
Propagation of the Faith - t) (602) 354-2005 Sr. Mary Juanita Gonsalves, R.S.M.;
Renewal Ministries, Catholic - t) (480) 201-6691 Most Rev. Eduardo A. Nevares, Spiritual Dir.; Marge Chavez, Coord.;
Schools, Catholic - Domonic Salce, Supt.; Mary Bartsch, Asst. Supt.;
Scouting, Catholic Committee on - t) (480) 279-6737 Rev. R. Christopher Axline, Liaison;
Vocations Office - Rev. Kurt Perera, Dir. (frperera@simonjude.org); Rev. Fernando Camou, Assoc. Dir.; Rev. Matthew Lowry, Assoc. Dir.;
Worship and Liturgy, Office of - t) (602) 354-2110; (602) 354-2113 Rev. John Muir, Dir.; Rev. Fernando Camou; Dcn. William A. Chavira;

PARISHES, MISSIONS, AND CLERGY

STATE OF ARIZONA

ANTHEM

St. Rose Philippine Duchesne Roman Catholic Parish - 2825 W. Rose Canyon Cir., Anthem, AZ 85086 t) (623) 465-9740 agonzales@stroseanthem.com www.stroseanthem.com Rev. Francisco "Bing" Colasito, Pst.; Rev. Samuel Aliba, Par. Vicar; Rev. James Starbuck; Dcn. Thomas Henrich; Dcn. John Mezydlo; CRP Stds.: 200
Mission of the Good Shepherd - 45033 N. 12th St., New River, AZ 85087; Mailing: 2825 W. Rose Canyon Cir., Anthem, AZ 85086 stroseanthem.com/index

ASHFORK

St. Anne Roman Catholic Mission, A Quasi-Parish - 47047 7th St., Ashfork, AZ 86320; Mailing: P.O. Box 525, Ash Fork, AZ 86320 t) 928-635-0177 Rev. Theilo Ramirez, Pst.;

AVONDALE

St. Thomas Aquinas Roman Catholic Parish - 13720 W. Thomas Rd., Avondale, AZ 85392 t) (623) 935-2151 staccavondale@gmail.com www.stacc.net Rev. John Muir, Pst.; Rev. Anwar Zomaya, Assoc. Pst.; Rev. Christopher Gossen, Par. Vicar; Rev. Rodney Lee A. Pruss; Rev. Estevan Wetzel; Dcn. Edgar Carnecer; Dcn. Kenneth Porter; Dcn. Jason Robinson; Dcn. Charles Shaw; Dcn. Kenneth Wedge;
St. Thomas Aquinas Roman Catholic Parish School - (Grades PreSchool-8) t) (623) 935-0945 stawebmaster@stacc.net Cynthia Scheller, Prin.;

BAPCHULE

St. Peter - 1500 N. St. Peter Rd., Bapchule, AZ 85121; Mailing: P.O. Box 2018, Sacaton, AZ 85147 t) (520) 562-3716 friarantony@diocesephoenix.org Dcn. Peter Fejes; Rev. Antony Tinker, F.H.S., Admin.;
St. Peter School - (Grades PreSchool-8) ; Mailing: P.O. Box 10840, Bapchule, AZ 85221 t) (520) 315-3835 spimcs.org Rev. Msgr. Ed Meulemans, Chap.; Sr. Martha Mary Carpenter, O.S.F., Prin.;
Holy Family - Arrow Weed Rd., Blackwater, AZ 25128 t) (520) 354-2050
Our Lady of Victory -
St. Anne -
St. Anthony - S. Church St., Sacaton, AZ 85147; Mailing: P.O. Box 783, Sacaton, AZ 85147 Dcn. Sidney Martin;
Consolata Missionary Sisters - 120 Church St., Sacaton, AZ 85147; Mailing: P.O. Box 10840, Bapchule, AZ 85151 t) (520) 419-7033
St. Francis of Assisi - AK Chin - 16657 N. Church St., Maricopa, AZ 85139 t) (520) 610-2937

BLACK CANYON CITY

St. Philip Benizi Roman Catholic Mission, A Quasi-Parish - 34621 Black Canyon Hwy., Black Canyon City, AZ 85324; Mailing: P.O. Box 138, Black Canyon City, AZ 85324 t) (623) 374-5392 lstokes20@cox.net Dcn. Leslie Stokes; Rev. Francisco "Bing" Colasito, Admin.; CRP Stds.: 6

BUCKEYE

Saint Henry Roman Catholic Parish - 24750 W. Lower Buckeye Rd., Buckeye, AZ 85326 t) (623) 386-0175 st_henry@dphx.org sthenrybuckeye.com Rev. William "Billy" J. Kosco, Pst.; Rev. Kevin Penkalski, Assoc. Pst.; Rev. Ryan Lee; Dcn. Mark Gribowski; Dcn. Victor Leon; Dcn. Dominick Bonaiuto;

BULLHEAD CITY

St. Margaret Mary Roman Catholic Parish - 1691 N. Oatman Rd., Bullhead City, AZ 86442 t) (928) 758-7117 st_margaret_mary@dphx.org www.stmargaretmarybhc.com Rev. Baldemar Garza; Rev. Daniel Vollmer; Dcn. John Del Quadro; Dcn. Anthony Picciano; Henry Castaneda, DRE;

CAMP VERDE

St. Frances Cabrini Roman Catholic Parish - S. 781 Cliff Pkwy., Camp Verde, AZ 86322 t) (928) 567-3543 st_frances_cabrini@dphx.org Rev. Alphonsus Bakyil, S.O.L.T., Pst.;

CAREFREE

Our Lady of Joy Roman Catholic Parish - 36811 N Pima Rd, Carefree, AZ 85377; Mailing: P.O. Box 1359, Carefree, AZ 85377 t) (480) 488-2229 oloj.org Rev. Jesus "Jess" G. Ty, Pst.; Rev. Clement Attah, Par. Vicar; Dcn. James Sejba; Dcn. Dennis Fleming; Dcn. Daniel Doheny; Dcn. Handel Metcalf; Carlos Gonzales, DRE;

Our Lady of Joy Roman Catholic Parish School - (Grades PreSchool-PreK) t) (480) 595-6409 Jessica Snook, Prin.;

CASHION

St. William Roman Catholic Parish - 11025 W. 3rd St., Cashion, AZ 85329; Mailing: P.O. Box 329, Cashion, AZ 85329 t) (623) 936-6115 dphx.org/parish/st-william-parish-cashion Rev. Andres Arango; Rev. Mario Garcia-Icedo, Par. Admin.; Dcn. James Cascio;

Our Lady of Guadalupe -

CAVE CREEK

St. Gabriel Roman Catholic Parish - 32648 N. Cave Creek Rd., Cave Creek, AZ 85331 t) (480) 595-0883 receptionist@stgacc.org stgacc.org Rev. David Kulandaisamy, Assoc. Pst.; Rev. John Slobig, Parochial Administrator Pro-Tem; Rev. Chad King; Dcn. James Walsh; Dcn. William Clower; Dcn. Robert Torigian;

Annunciation Catholic School - (Grades K-8) t) (480) 361-8234 www.acsphx.org Dr. Sharon Pristash, Prin.;

CHANDLER

St. Andrew the Apostle Roman Catholic Parish - 3450 W. Ray Rd., Chandler, AZ 85226 t) (480) 899-1990 church@standrewchandler.com Rev. Teilo Lwande, A.J., Par. Vicar; Rev. Edward Urassa, Par. Vicar; Rev. Nicholas Erias Koro, A.J.; Dcn. Ernest Garcia; Dcn. Mark Lishko; Dcn. Kenneth Kulinowski; Dcn. Donald Crawford; Dcn. Ramsey Echeverria; Dcn. Ramon Zamora;

St. Columba Kim Roman Catholic Mission - 1375 N. McClintock Dr., Chandler, AZ 85226 t) (480) 446-7121 A Quasi Parish Rev. Byung Choy;

St. Mary Roman Catholic Parish Chandler - 230 W. Galveston, Chandler, AZ 85225 t) (480) 963-3207; (480) 734-2187 (St Juan Diego Church) parish@smchandler.org; office@sjdchandler.org www.stmarychandler.org Rev. Daniel McBride; Rev. Daniel Cruz, Par. Vicar; Rev. Edgardo Iriarte, Par. Vicar; Rev. Msgr. Richard W. Moyer; Rev. Elario Zambakari, Par. Vicar; Rev. Joseph Ayima; Dcn. Antonio Alvarez; Dcn. Bruce Bennett; Dcn. Joseph Ryan; Dcn. Marvin Silva; Dcn. Oliver Babbits; Dcn. Douglas Davaz; Dcn. Manuel Olivas; Dcn. Paul Hursh; Dcn. Paul Muthart;

St. Mary-Basha Catholic Elementary - (Grades PreK-8) 200 W. Galveston, Chandler, AZ 85225 t) (480) 963-4951 tseybert@stmarybashacatholic.org www.stmarybashacatholic.org Tiffany Seybert, Prin.; Lisa Ballesteros, Librn.;

Juan Diego Roman Catholic Church - 3200 S. Cooper Rd., Chandler, AZ 85286; Mailing: 230 W Galveston, Chandler, AZ 85225

CHINO VALLEY

St. Catherine Laboure Roman Catholic Parish - 2062 N. Hwy. 89, Chino Valley, AZ 86323; Mailing: PO Box 152, Chino Valley, AZ 86323 t) (928) 636-4071 stcathlab@cableone.net stcatherinecv.org Dcn. Michael Holmes; Dcn. Michael Johnsen; Rev. H. Fred LeClaire, C.M.F., Pst.; Dcn. Daniel Gullotta; Dcn. George Vivet;

CONGRESS

Good Shepherd of the Desert Mission - 26750 S. Congress Way, Congress, AZ 85332; Mailing: P.O. Box 1134, Congress, AZ 85332 t) (928) 685-4712 c) (928) 231-7313 goodshepherdotd@gmail.com Quasi-Parish. Rev. Camilo De Villa, Pst.;

COTTONWOOD

Immaculate Conception Roman Catholic Parish - 700 N. Bill Gray Rd., Cottonwood, AZ 86326 t) 928-634-2933 parishassistant@ic-cc.org ic-cc.org Rev. Jose D. Cornelia, D.S.; Rev. Marvin Soto, Par. Vicar; Dcn. David Kaminsky; Dcn. Peter Murphy; Dcn. James Hoy; Sr. Bernadette De la Santa Faz, Dir. Faith Formation; CRP Stds.: 43

Immaculate Conception Catholic School - (Grades PreSchool-8) 750 N. Bill Gray Rd., Cottonwood, AZ 86326 t) (928) 649-0624 info@iccs-k8.org Jacqueline Kirkham, Prin.;

DOLAN SPRINGS

Our Lady of the Desert Mission, A Quasi-Parish - 15385 N. Pierce Ferry Rd., Dolan Springs, AZ 86441 t) (928) 767-3397 ourladyofthedesert@yahoo.com Rev. Julius Kayiwa; Rosemarie Poskarbiewicz, DRE;

EL MIRAGE

Santa Teresita Roman Catholic Parish - 14016 N. Verbena St., El Mirage, AZ 85335; Mailing: PO Box 67, El Mirage, AZ 85335 t) (623) 583-8183 santa_teresita@dphx.org www.stcaz.com Rev. Stephen Schack, Pst.;

FLAGSTAFF

Holy Trinity Newman Center, A Quasi-Parish - 520 W. Riordan Rd., Flagstaff, AZ 86001 t) (928) 779-2903 info@catholicjacks.org www.catholicjacks.org Rev. Matthew Lowry, Dir.; Rev. Jose Jesus Lopez Arias, Assoc. Dir.;

San Francisco de Asis Roman Catholic Parish - 1600 E. Rte. 66, Flagstaff, AZ 86001 t) (928) 779-1341 church@sfdaparish.org sfdaparish.org Rev. William Schmid, Pst.; Rev. Ian Wintering, Par. Vicar; Rev. Dan Vanyo; Rev. Peter P. Dobrowski; Dcn. James Bret; Dcn. Jeffrey Hartin; Dcn. Ronald Johnson; Dcn. Robert Olberding; Dcn. Dennis Revering; Dcn. Mark Veazie; Dcn. James Myers; Dcn. Gregory Blanchard;

San Francisco de Asis - (Grades PreSchool-8) 1600 E. Rte.66, Flagstaff, AZ 86001 t) (928) 779-1337 school@sfdaparish.org www.sfdaschool.org Bill Carroll, Prin.;

Nativity of B.V.M. - 16 W. Cherry Ave., Flagstaff, AZ 86001

Our Lady of Guadalupe - 224 S. Kendrick, Flagstaff, AZ 86001

FOUNTAIN HILLS

Ascension Roman Catholic Parish - 12615 Fountain Hills Blvd., Fountain Hills, AZ 85268 t) 480-837-1066 ascension@dphx.org www.ascensionfh.org Dcn. Phillip LoCascio; Dcn. Richard Smith; Rev. John T. McDonough, Pst.;

St. Dominic - 25603 N. Danny Ln., Ste. 2, Rio Verde, AZ 85263

GILA BEND

St. Michael Roman Catholic Parish - 314 Dobson St., Gila Bend, AZ 85337; Mailing: P.O. Box F, Gila Bend, AZ 85337 t) (928) 683-9997 stmichaelgb@gmail.com Rev. Manoj John, Sch.P., Admin.;

GILBERT

St. Anne Roman Catholic Parish - 440 E. Elliot Rd., Gilbert, AZ 85234 t) 480-507-4400 admin@stanneaz.org stanneaz.org Rev. Keith Edwin Kenney, Pst.; Rev. Joal Bernales, Par. Vicar; Rev. Timothy Dogo, Par. Vicar; Rev. Dennis Riccitelli; Dcn. Robert Carey; Dcn. Keith Boswell; Dcn. Ivan Rojas; Dcn. Robert Estes; Dcn. Joseph Spadafino; Dcn. Andrew Gilliland; Dcn. John Berger; Donna Kano, DRE; CRP Stds.: 693

Carmelite Missionaries of St. Therese of the Child Jesus - t) (480) 307-3319

St. Mary Magdalene Roman Catholic Parish - 2654 E. Williams Field Rd., Gilbert, AZ 85295 t) (480) 279-6737 pastor@smarymag.org Rev. R. Christopher Axline, Pst.; Rev. Sylvester Modebei (Nigeria), Par. Vicar; Rev. Arthur Nave; Rev. Edward Gilbert; Dcn. Craig Hintze; Dcn. Richard Nevins; Dcn. Lawrence St. Onge; Dcn. Sean Sylvester;

GLENDALE

St. Helen Roman Catholic Parish - 5510 W. Cholla St., Glendale, AZ 85304-3322 t) (623) 979-4202; (623) 500-3200 (Parish Mgr.); (623) 500-3206 (Admin.) bfavot@sthelenglendale.org; lvantuyl@sthelenglendale.org sthelenglendale.org Rev. John R. Ssegawa, A.J. (Uganda), Pst.; Rev. Scott Harris; Rev. Thomas Suss; Rev. James R. Blantz, C.S.C.; Rev. Mark Okeny; Dcn. Robert Campas; Dcn. Stanley Gwizdak; Dcn. Joseph Shinske; Dcn. John Mickel; Dcn. William Jenkins;

St. James Roman Catholic Parish - 19640 N. 35th Ave., Glendale, AZ 85308 t) (623) 581-0707 admin@stjames-greater.com stjames-greater.com/ Dcn. Frank Devine; Dcn. Ronald TenBarge; Rev. Benedict Onegiu, A.J., Pst.; Rev. Felix Kauta, A.J., Assoc. Pst.; Dcn. Marvin Hernandez; Rev. William Okot, A.J., In Res.;

St. Louis the King Roman Catholic Parish - 4331 W. Maryland Ave., Glendale, AZ 85301 t) (623) 930-1127 office@slkparish.com www.stlouistheking.org/ Rev. Joseph Bui, Pst.; Rev. Awte Weldu, O. Cist; Dcn. Joseph Stickney; Sr. Mary Ann Mahoney, I.H.M., DRE;

St. Louis the King Roman Catholic Parish School - (Grades PreK-8) t) (623) 939-4260 Joseph Zielinski, Prin.;

Our Lady of Perpetual Help Roman Catholic Parish - 5614 W. Orangewood Ave., Glendale, AZ 85301 t) 623-939-9758 olph_glendale@dphx.org Rev. Mario Cortes, Assoc. Pst.; Rev. Ernesto Reynoso, Pst.; Rev. Pratap Gatla; Dcn. Christopher Georges; Dcn. Anthony (Tony) Lopez; Dcn. Dennis Raczkowski; Dcn. Kevin Knapp;

Our Lady of Perpetual Help Roman Catholic Parish School - (Grades PreSchool-8) 7521 N. 57th Ave., Glendale, AZ 85301 t) (623) 931-7288 Jeannette Weivoda, Prin.;

Our Lady of Guadalupe - 6733 N. 55th Ave., Glendale, AZ 85301

St. Raphael Roman Catholic Parish - 5525 W. Acoma, Glendale, AZ 85306 t) (602) 938-4227 straphael@olvstr.net www.olvstr.net Rev. Edward J. Kaminski, C.S.C., Pst.; Dcn. Robert Manthie; Dcn. Eduardo Mirasol; Dcn. Richard Meidl; Amelia Sury, DRE;

St. Thomas More Roman Catholic Parish - 6180 W. Utopia Rd., Glendale, AZ 85308-7111 t) (623) 566-8222 st_thomas_more@stmglendale.org Rev. Franklin L. Bartel; Rev. John D. Ehrich, Admin.; Rev. James Turner; Dcn. Richard Kijewski; Maria Buhrman, DRE;

GOODYEAR

Saint John Vianney Roman Catholic Parish - 539 La Pasada Blvd., Goodyear, AZ 85338 t) (623) 932-3313 st_john_vianney_az@dphx.org www.sjvaz.net Rev. Paul Ybarra, CSC; Rev. David Halm, C.S.C.; Rev. Thomas F. Lemos, C.S.C.; Rev. David Smith; Dcn. William Booth; David Portugal, DRE;

Saint John Vianney Roman Catholic Parish School - (Grades PreSchool-8) t) (623) 932-2434 school.sjvaz.net Doug Weivoda, Prin.;

GRAND CANYON

El Cristo Rey Roman Catholic Parish - 44 Albright Ave., Grand Canyon, AZ 86023; Mailing: P.O. Box 505, Grand Canyon, AZ 86023 t) (928) 638-2390 elcristorey@msn.com Rev. Rafael Bercasio, Pst.;

GUADALUPE

Our Lady of Guadalupe Roman Catholic Parish - 5445 San Angelo St., Guadalupe, AZ 85283 t) 480-839-2860 olo_guad_guad@dphx.org Rev. Rafael Umaña, I.V.E.;

KINGMAN

St. Mary Roman Catholic Parish - 302 E. Spring St., Kingman, AZ 86401 t) (928) 753-3359 stmarychurch@yahoo.com Rev. Victor Yakubu; Dcn. Francis Staab;

LAKE HAVASU CITY

Our Lady of the Lake Roman Catholic Parish - 1975 Daytona Dr., Lake Havasu City, AZ 86403 t) 928-855-2685 ourlady@ourladylhc.org www.ourladyofthelakeromancatholic.org/ Dcn. John Navaretta; Dcn. Patrick Toilolo; Dcn. William Vivio; Dcn. Richard Rein; Dcn. Carl Swanson; Rev. Michael Accinni Reinhardt, Par. Vicar; Rev. Anthony O. Okolo, C.S.Sp., Par. Vicar;

Our Lady of the Lake Catholic School - (Grades PreK-6) t) (928) 855-0154 fmu@ourladylhc.org ourladyofthelakeromancatholic.org After School Care Fatima Mu, Prin.;

LAVEEN

St. John the Baptist - 5427 W. Pecos Rd., Laveen, AZ 85339; Mailing: P.O. Box 693, Laveen, AZ 85339 t) (520) 550-2034 stjohns@gilanet.net Rev. Antony Tinker,

F.H.S., Admin.; Rev. Anthony Costantino; Rev. Richard Fornwalt; Rev. Sean McConnell; Rev. Joseph Francis LePage, F.H.S., In Res.; Dcn. Ronald Poulin;

St. Catherine - 3986 S. Santa Cruz Rd., Laveen, AZ 85339 t) (602) 292-4466

St. Francis of Assisi - 3090 N. Longmore, Scottsdale, AZ 85256 t) (602) 292-4466 Pima-Maricopa Indian Community, Salt River.

San Lucy - 1120C St., Gila Bend, AZ 85337 t) (602) 354-2050

St. Paschal Baylon - 850 E. Oak, Mesa, AZ 85203 t) (602) 292-4466

Blessed Kateri Tekakwitha Spirituality Center/St. John's Convent -

MAYER

St. Joseph Roman Catholic Mission, A Quasi-Parish - 10901 S. Hwy. 69, Mayer, AZ 86333; Mailing: P.O. Box 171, Mayer, AZ 86333-0171 t) (928) 632-4018 frbakyil@diocesephoenix.org Rev. Alvin Cayetano, S.O.L.T.;

MESA

All Saints Roman Catholic Parish - 1534 N. Recker Rd., Mesa, AZ 85205 t) (480) 985-7655 pjohnson@asccm.org www.asccm.org Rev. Robert J. Caruso, Pst.; Rev. Michael O'Neil; Rev. Gordon Doffing; Rev. Joevensie Balang; Dcn. Gordon Aird; Dcn. Raymond DuBois; Dcn. Thomas Ferreira; Dcn. Bernard Filzen; Dcn. William Finnegan; Dcn. Gene Messer; Dcn. Stephen Schmidt; Dcn. Ronald Wilson;

St. Bridget Roman Catholic Parish - 2850 E. Lockwood St., Mesa, AZ 85213 t) (480) 924-9111 admin@stbridget.org Rev. W. Scott Brubaker, Pst.; Rev. Robert J. Voss;

Christ the King Roman Catholic Parish - 1551 E. Dana Ave., Mesa, AZ 85204 t) 480-964-1719 christ_the_king@ctk-catholic.org www.ctk-catholic.org Rev. Rolyn B. Francisco, Pst.; Rev. Jose Ballesteros, Par. Vicar; Rev. Lawrence O'Keefe; Dcn. Ronald Ruiz; Dcn. Thomas Bishop; Dcn. Robert Bonura; Dcn. Frank Galarza; Dcn. John Tift;

Christ the King Catholic School - (Grades PreK-8) t) (480) 844-4480 ctk@ctk-catholicschool.org www.ctk-catholicschool.org Shelley Conner, Prin.;

School Sisters of Notre Dame - 1534 E. Dana Ave., Mesa, AZ 85204 t) (602) 290-2273 Sr. Patricia Gehling, Admin.;

Holy Cross Roman Catholic Parish - 1244 S. Power Rd., Mesa, AZ 85206 t) 480-981-2021 bcosentino@holycrossmesa.org; lshirling@holycrossmesa.org www.holycrossmesa.org Rev. Lawrence Merta, Pst.; Rev. Jaya Rao Maddu, M.C.L., Par. Vicar; Rev. Joseph Karikunnel, C.S.T., In Res.; Dcn. Richard Conn; Dcn. James Gersitz; Dcn. Juan Carlos Gonzalez; Dcn. Joseph Scaccia; Dcn. Clarence Vetter; Cynthia M. Benzing, DRE;

Queen of Peace Roman Catholic Parish - 30 W. 1st St., Mesa, AZ 85201 t) 480-969-9166 info@qop.org qop.org Rev. Thomas Bennett, Pst.; Rev. Frankie Cicero, Par. Vicar; Rev. Gabriel Terrill, Par. Vicar; Dcn. Richard Areyzaga; Dcn. Santiago Rodriguez; Dcn. Jaime Whitford; Dcn. Joseph "Tom" Swisher; Dcn. Thomas J. Phelan III; Dcn. Jose Avila; CRP Stds.: 220

Queen of Peace Roman Catholic Parish School - (Grades PreK-8) 141 N. Macdonald St., Mesa, AZ 85201 t) (480) 969-0226 Renee Baeza, Prin.; Stds.: 214; Lay Tchrs.: 10

St. Timothy Roman Catholic Parish - 1730 W. Guadalupe, Mesa, AZ 85202 t) (480) 775-5200 dmesa@sttimothymesa.org www.sttimothymesa.org Dcn. Kevin Bassett; Dcn. James Beattie; Dcn. Abram Calderon; Rev. Augustine Acheme, VC, Par. Vicar; Rev. John Greb, Pst.; Rev. Chauncey Winkler;

St. Timothy Catholic School - (Grades K-8) 2520 S. Alma School Rd., Mesa, AZ 85210 t) (480) 775-2650 www.sttimothymesa.org/school Maureen Vick, Prin.;

St. Timothy Preschool - (Grades PreSchool- 2045 S. Pennington, Mesa, AZ 85202 t) (480) 775-5238 arice@sttimothymesa.org Debbi Mesa, Parish Mgr.;

NEW RIVER

Good Shepherd Mission, A Quasi-Parish - 45033 N. 12th St., New River, AZ 85087 t) (623) 465-9740 st.rose@dphx.org Dcn. Robert Head; Rev. Francisco "Bing" Colasito, Admin.;

PEORIA

St. Charles Borromeo Roman Catholic Parish - 8615 W. Peoria Ave., Peoria, AZ 85345-0819 t) (623) 979-3418 frontoffice@scbpeoria.org www.scbpeoria.org Rev. Msgr. George E. Highberger; Rev. James Kalliyathuparambil; Dcn. Catarino Portillo;

PHOENIX

SS. Simon and Jude Roman Catholic Cathedral - 6351 N. 27th Ave., Phoenix, AZ 85017 t) 602-242-1300 contactus@simonjude.org www.simonjude.org Dcn. Douglas Bogart; Dcn. Roy Drapeau; Dcn. Anthony Smith; Rev. Fernando Camou, Rector; Rev. Rafael Escarcega; Dcn. Juan Guzman; Most Rev. Thomas J. Olmsted, In Res.;

SS. Simon and Jude Roman Catholic Cathedral School - (Grades PreK-8) t) (602) 242-1299 www.simonjudeschool.org Sr. Raphael Quinn, IBVM, Prin.;

Sisters of Loreto (I.B.V.M.) - t) (602) 574-4091

St. Agnes Roman Catholic Parish - 1954 N. 24th St., Phoenix, AZ 85008 t) 602-244-0349 info@stagnesphx.org www.stagnesphx.org Rev. Bradley L. Peterson, O. Carm., Pst.; Rev. Jorge Monterosso, O. Carm., Par. Vicar; Rev. Harold Lafey; Dcn. Eduardo Lopez; Dcn. Jesse Sanchez; CRP Stds.: 238

St. Agnes Roman Catholic Parish School - (Grades PreSchool-8) 2311 E. Palm Ln., Phoenix, AZ 85006 t) (602) 244-1451 www.stagnesphx.org/school Kelly Aranowski, Prin.; Terry Kucera, Librn.;

St. Anthony Roman Catholic Parish - 909 S. 1st Ave., Phoenix, AZ 85003 t) 602-252-1771 stanthonyparishphoenix@gmail.com stanthonyphx.org Rev. Fabio Schilereff, I.V.E., Pst.; Rev. Josep Emmanuel Galvez Badillo, I.V.E., Par. Vicar; CRP Stds.: 49

St. Augustine Roman Catholic Parish - 3630 N. 71st Ave., Phoenix, AZ 85033 t) (623) 849-3131 phxsta.org Rev. Carlos Gomez-Rivera, Pst.; Rev. Octavio Delgado, Par. Vicar; Rev. Raul Herrero; Dcn. Ernesto Ramirez; Dcn. Jose Torres; Dcn. Martin Gallo; Martha Morales, DRE;

St. Benedict Roman Catholic Parish - 16223 S. 48th St., Phoenix, AZ 85048 t) (480) 961-1610 stbenedict@stbenedict.org stbenedict.org Dcn. Edwin Winkelbauer; Rev. James Aboyi, V.C., Pst.; Rev. Manasseh Iorchir, VC, Par. Vicar;

St. John Bosco Catholic School - (Grades PreSchool-8) 16035 S. 48th St., Phoenix, AZ 85048 t) (480) 219-4848 info@sjbosco.org www.sjbosco.org Jamie Bescak, Prin.;

St. Catherine of Siena Roman Catholic Parish - 6401 S. Central Ave., Phoenix, AZ 85042 t) (602) 276-5581 st_catherine@diocesephoenix.org Ordinary & Extraordinary Form Rev. Alonso Saenz, Pst.; Rev. Michael Gilbert; Dcn. Carlos Terrazas;

St. Catherine of Siena Roman Catholic Parish School - (Grades PreSchool-8) 6413 S. Central Ave., Phoenix, AZ 85040 t) (602) 276-2241 x251 www.stcatherineschool.org Ana Zarate, Prin.;

Corpus Christi Roman Catholic Parish - 3550 E. Knox, Phoenix, AZ 85044 t) (480) 893-8770 steve.mandarino@corpuschristiphx.org www.corpuschristiphx.org Rev. Reynaldo Clutario, Pst.; Rev. Johnson Vadakkumcherry; Rev. Zachary Shallow; Dcn. Christopher Kellogg; Dcn. Dennis Lambert; Dcn. Philip Simeone; Dcn. Philip Amantia; Denise Halloran, DRE;

St. Francis Xavier Roman Catholic Parish - 4715 N. Central Ave., Phoenix, AZ 85012-1796 t) (602) 279-9547 pastor@sfxphx.org; stfrancisxavier@sfxphx.org www.sfxphx.org Rev. Robert A Fambrini, S.J., Pst.; Rev. Kevin Dilworth, S.J.; Rev. George Teodoro, S.J., Par. Vicar; Rev. Daniel Sullivan; Rev. Thomas Carroll; Rev. Isidro Lepez; Dcn. Thomas Klein; Dcn. Jaime Garcia;

St. Francis Xavier Roman Catholic Parish School - (Grades PreSchool-8) t) (602) 266-5364 x4101 ryan.watson@sfxphx.org school.sfxphx.org Jesuit School Ryan Watson, Prin.;

St. Gregory Roman Catholic Parish - 3424 N 18th Ave, Phoenix, AZ 85015 t) 602-264-4488 parishemail@stgphx.org www.stgregoryphx.com Rev. Paul Sullivan, Pst.; CRP Stds.: 110

St. Gregory Roman Catholic Parish School - (Grades PreSchool-8) 3440 N 18th Ave, Phoenix, AZ 85015 t) (602) 266-9527 www.stgphx.org Rachel Gatson, Prin.; Stds.: 300; Lay Tchrs.: 30

Holy Family Roman Catholic Parish - 6802 S. 24th St., Phoenix, AZ 85042 t) (602) 268-2632 Rev. Oscar Gutierrez, Pst.; Rev. Martin Munoz, M.D.M., Assoc. Pst.;

Immaculate Heart of Mary Roman Catholic Parish - 909 E. Washington St., Phoenix, AZ 85034 t) 602-253-6129 ihmparishphoenix@gmail.com ihmphx.org Rev. Fabio Schilereff, I.V.E., Pst.; Rev. Josep Emmanuel Galvez Badillo, I.V.E.; Rev. Jose Sylvester; Rev. Msgr. Antonio Sotelo; Dcn. Jesus Morales; CRP Stds.: 89

St. Jerome Roman Catholic Parish - 10815 N. 35th Ave., Phoenix, AZ 85029 t) (602) 942-5555 frgary@saintjerome.org www.saintjerome.org Dcn. Schubert Wenzel; Rev. Gary R. Regula, Pst.; Rev. Job Kundoni, Par. Vicar; CRP Stds.: 300

St. Jerome Roman Catholic Parish School - (Grades PreSchool-8) t) (602) 942-5644 akolden@saintjerome.org www.saintjerome.org/school-home Rodney Wilhelm, Prin.;

St. Joan of Arc Roman Catholic Parish - 3801 E. Greenway Rd., Phoenix, AZ 85032-4698 t) (602) 867-9171 office@stjoanofarc.com Rev. Daniel Connealy, Pst.; Rev. Oliver Vietor, Par. Vicar; Rev. Larry Weidner; Dcn. Mark Salvato; Dcn. Andrew Lambros;

St. Joan of Arc Catholic School - (Grades PreSchool-k) t) (602) 867-9179 www.stjoanofarc.com Debbie Allen, Dir.;

St. Joseph Roman Catholic Parish - 11001 N. 40th St., Phoenix, AZ 85028 t) (602) 966-5120 finance@stjoephx.org Rev. Regidor Carreon, Pst.;

St. Josephine Bakhita Roman Catholic Mission Phoenix - 809 S. 7th Ave., Phoenix, AZ 85007 Rev. Marvin McNair;

St. Luke Roman Catholic Parish - 19644 N. 7th Ave., Phoenix, AZ 85027 t) (623) 582-0561 parishoffice@saintlukecatholic.org Rev. Pawel Stawarczyk, Pst.;

St. Mark Roman Catholic Parish - 400 N. 30th St., Phoenix, AZ 85008 t) (602) 267-0503 st_mark@dphx.org Rev. Fausto Penafiel, Par. Admin.;

St. Martin de Porres Roman Catholic Parish - 3851 W. Wier Ave., Phoenix, AZ 85041; Mailing: 6802 S. 24th St., Phoenix, AZ 85042 t) (602) 268-2632 men_sa_jero82@hotmail.com Rev. Martin Munoz, M.D.M., Assoc. Pst.;

St. Mary's Roman Catholic Basilica - 231 N. Third St., Phoenix, AZ 85004 t) (602) 354-2100 frontdesk@smbphx.org www.smbphx.org Rev. Michael Weldon, O.F.M., Rector; Rev. Micah Muhlen, O.F.M., Par. Vicar; Rev. Edward Sarrazin, O.F.M., Par. Vicar; Rev. Raad Mushe; Friar Scott William Slattum, O.F.M., RCIA Coord.; Dcn. Santino Bernasconi;

Mater Misericordiae Catholic Church - 1537 W. Monroe St., Phoenix, AZ 85007 t) (602) 253-6090 office@phoenixlatinmass.org www.phoenixlatinmass.org Rev. Michael Passo, F.S.S.P., Pst.; Rev. Joseph Portzer, FSSP, Par. Vicar; Rev. Federico Masutti; Rev. Michael Stinson; Rev. Martin Garcia;

St. Matthew Roman Catholic Parish - 320 N. 20th Dr., Phoenix, AZ 85009 t) (602) 258-1789 respericueta@stmatthewaz.org Rev. Eleazar Perez; Dcn. Anthony Beltran; Dcn. Angel Guzman;

St. Matthew Roman Catholic Parish School - (Grades PreK-8) t) (602) 254-0611 stmatthewaz.org Christine

Tax, Prin.;
Most Holy Trinity Roman Catholic Parish - 8620 N. Seventh St., Phoenix, AZ 85020 t) 602-944-3375 pgalaviz@mht.org www.mht.org Rev. Alphonsus Zaldy Abainza, SOLT, Pst.; Rev. Dennis Dugan, SOLT, Par. Vicar; Rev. Lauro Bejo, SOLT, Par. Vicar; Bro. Ryan Avery, In Res.; Rev. Dale Craig, S.O.L.T., In Res.; Dcn. Lowell O'Grady; Dcn. John Raphael Dalisay, D.S.; Nayeli Ramirez, DRE;
Most Holy Trinity Roman Catholic Parish School - (Grades PreSchool-8) 535 E. Alice Ave., Phoenix, AZ 85020 t) (602) 943-9058 www.mhtcatholicschool.org/ Margaret MacCleary, Prin.;
Sisters of the Society of Our Lady of the Most Holy Trinity - t) (815) 788-0575
Our Lady of Czestochowa Roman Catholic Parish - 2828 W. Country Gables Dr., Phoenix, AZ 85053 t) 602-212-1172 biuro@rcphx.org www.polskaparafiaphoenix.com Rev. Pawel Bandurski, SChr, Pst.; CRP Stds.: 180
Missionary Sisters of Christ the King for Polonia - 2828 W Country Gables Dr, Phoenix, AZ 85053 t) (602) 212-1172 mchr.pl Sr. Ewa Filipiuk, MChR, Supr.; Sr. Kinga Malgorzata Hoffmann, MChR, Secy.;
Our Lady of Fatima Mission - 1418 S. 17th Ave., Phoenix, AZ 85007 t) (602) 254-4944 olfphx@gmail.com Rev. Vinhson Nguyen, Admin.;
Our Lady of the Valley Roman Catholic Parish - 3220 W. Greenway Rd., Phoenix, AZ 85053 t) 602-993-1213 olv@olvstr.net www.olvstr.net Rev. Joachim Adeyemi (Nigeria); Dcn. Robert Manthie; Dcn. Robert Meidl; Dcn. Eduardo Mirasol; Dcn. William Vivio; Leah Johnson, DRE; Amelia Sury, DRE;
St. Paul Roman Catholic Parish - 330 W. Coral Gables Dr., Phoenix, AZ 85023 t) (602) 942-2608 admin@stpaulsphoenix.org; pklein@stpaulsphoenix.org www.stpaulsphoenix.org Rev. Dindo C. Cuario, Pst.; Rev. Ishaya S. Samaila, Par. Vicar; Rev. Michael D. Couhig, C.S.C.; Rev. Bitrus Maigamo; Dcn. Gary Chatel; Craig Cullity, Pst. Assoc.; Patrick Klein, DRE;
St. Philip the Deacon Mission, A Quasi-Parish - 615 N. 20th St., Phoenix, AZ 85006 t) (602) 253-1076 st_philip_the_deacon@dphx.org Rev. Gerardo R. Barmasse, C.S.C.;
Sacred Heart Roman Catholic Parish - 1421 S. 12th St., Phoenix, AZ 85034 t) (602) 258-2089 sacred_heart@dphx.org Dcn. Matias Valle; Dcn. Antonio Hernandez; Rev. Paul Sullivan, Pst.;
St. Theresa Roman Catholic Parish - 5045 E. Thomas Rd., Phoenix, AZ 85018-7912 t) (602) 840-0850 info@stphx.org www.stphx.org Rev. Andrzej Boroch; Rev. John Parks; Dcn. Colin Campbell; Dcn. Mark Kriese;
St. Theresa Catholic School - (Grades PreSchool-8) 5001 E. Thomas Rd., Phoenix, AZ 85018-7900 t) (602) 840-0010 info@stcs.us www.stcs.us Dr. Thomas D. Dertinger, Prin.;
St. Thomas the Apostle Roman Catholic Parish - 2312 E. Campbell Ave., Phoenix, AZ 85016-5597 t) (602) 954-9089 smadrid@staphx.org staphx.org Dcn. William A. Chavira; Rev. Steven A. Kunkel, Pst.; Rev. Robert Bolding, In Res.; Rev. Awte Weldu, O. Cist, In Res.; Rev. Joseph Kizhavana; Dcn. John Barelli; Dcn. Kevin Tulipana; Tom Parks, DRE; Eric J. Westby, DRE;
St. Thomas the Apostle Roman Catholic Parish School - (Grades PreSchool-8) 4510 N. 24th St., Phoenix, AZ 85016 t) (602) 954-9088 Mary Coffman, Prin.; Meg Bushard, Librn.;
Dominican Sisters of Mary, Mother of the Eucharist - 4550 N. 24th St., Phoenix, AZ 85016 t) 602-368-5238 Sr. Martin Therese, O.P., Supr.;
Vietnamese Martyrs Parish Roman Catholic Parish - 2915 W. Northern Ave., Phoenix, AZ 85051 t) (602) 395-0421 dmnguyenop@yahoo.com cttdvnphx.org/ Rev. J.B. Duc Minh Nguyen, O.P., Pst.; Rev. Anh Nguyen, Par. Vicar; CRP Stds.: 145
St. Vincent de Paul Roman Catholic Parish - 3140 N. 51st Ave., Phoenix, AZ 85031 t) (623) 247-6871 stvincent@svdpphx.org Rev. Guillermo Avila Martinez, Par. Vicar; Rev. Joseph Pee Thuruthel, Admin.; Rev. Jose Jesus Lopez Arias; Rev. Joemon Joy; Dcn. Lorenzo Salazar; Dcn. Jose Alvarado;
St. Vincent de Paul Roman Catholic Parish School - (Grades PreSchool-8) 3130 N. 51st Ave., Phoenix, AZ 85031 t) (623) 247-8595 www.svdpschool.org Sr. Julie Kubasak, D.C., Prin.;
Daughters of Charity of St. Vincent de Paul - 3130 N. 51st Ave., Phoenix, AZ 85031 Sr. Julie Kubasak, D.C., Supr.; Sr. Cabrini Thomas, D.C., Dir.;

PRESCOTT

Sacred Heart Roman Catholic Parish Prescott - 150 Fleury St., Prescott, AZ 86301 t) (928) 445-3141 parish@sacredheartprescott.com www.sacredheartprescott.com Dcn. Mark Weber; Rev. Irudayaraj John Britto, C.M.F., Pst.; Rev. Gaspar Masilamani, C.M.F., Assoc. Pst.; Rev. Ralph Berg, C.M.F., Pst. Assoc.; Rev. Gerald Caffrey, C.M.F., In Res.; Rev. Gary Norman; Rev. Vicente Montiel Romero; Dcn. Peter Balland; Dcn. Joseph Bueti; Dcn. Ernie Gonzales; Dcn. Charles Tony Humphrey; Dcn. Thomas Gregory;
Sacred Heart Roman Catholic Parish School - (Grades PreK-8) 131 N. Summit Ave., Prescott, AZ 86301 t) (928) 445-2621 www.sacredhearteducation.com Pamela Dickerson, Prin.;
Institute of the Blessed Virgin Mary - 229 N. Summit St., Prescott, AZ 86301

PRESCOTT VALLEY

St. Germaine Roman Catholic Parish - 7997 E. Dana Dr., Prescott Valley, AZ 86314 t) (928) 772-6350 stg-admin@cableone.net stgermaineinpv.com Rev. Manoj John, Sch.P.; Rev. Noble John Puthiydath; Dcn. Dale Avery; Dcn. Dennis Egan; Dcn. James Fogle; Dcn. Wayland Moncrief; Dcn. Robert Schaefer;

QUEEN CREEK

Our Lady of Guadalupe Roman Catholic Parish - 20615 E. Ocotillo Rd., Queen Creek, AZ 85142-0856 t) (480) 987-0315 johns@ologparish.org Rev. Craig W.M. Friedley, Pst.; Dcn. Narciso Macia; Dcn. David Barraza; Dcn. Alberto Juan; John N Simon, Admin.; CRP Stds.: 352

SCENIC

La Santisima Trinidad Mission, A Quasi-Parish - 3735 Scenic Blvd., Scenic, AZ 86432; Mailing: P.O. Box 1236, Mesquite, NV 89024 t) (602) 242-7191 alfredovaldez10@yahoo.com Rev. Alfredo Valdez Molina, Pst.;

SCOTTSDALE

St. Bernadette Roman Catholic Parish - 16245 N. 60th St., Scottsdale, AZ 85254 t) (480) 905-0221 stbenedict@stbenedict.org Rev. Donald J. Kline, Par. Admin. Pro-Tem; Rev. Douglas Spina; Dcn. Alfred Homiski; Dcn. Frank Nevarez; Dcn. Peter Auriemma;
Saint John XXIII Catholic School Community - (Grades PreK-8) 16235 N. 60th St., Scottsdale, AZ 85254 t) (480) 905-0939 popejohnxxiii@diocesephoenix.org saintjohnxxiii.org Preston Colao, Prin.; Susan Houck, Librn.;
St. Bernard of Clairvaux Roman Catholic Parish - 10755 N. 124th St., Scottsdale, AZ 85259 t) (480) 661-9843 church@stboc.org www.stbernardscottsdale.org Rev. Michael Straley, Pst.; Rev. Simon Osuchukwu, Assoc. Pst.; Dcn. Alan Hungate; Ryan Ayala, Dir.;
Blessed Sacrament Roman Catholic Parish - 11300 N. 64th St., Scottsdale, AZ 85254 t) 480-948-8370 parish@bscaz.org www.bscaz.org Rev. William Abba, Par. Vicar; Rev. Bryan Buenger; Rev. Msgr. George Schroeder; Dcn. Jeffrey Strom; Dcn. Robert Evans; Dcn. Fred Giesner; Dcn. Roger Mullaney; Dcn. William Schneider;
Blessed Sacrament Catholic School - (Grades PreSchool-k) t) (480) 998-9466 www.blsachurch.net/ preschool
St. Daniel the Prophet Roman Catholic Parish - 1030 N. Hayden Rd., Scottsdale, AZ 85257 t) (480) 945-8437 email@sdtp.net www.sdtp.net Rev. Thaddeus M. McGuire; Rev. Sheunesu Bowora, Par. Admin.;
St. Francis of Assisi Roman Catholic Parish - 3090 N. Longmore, Scottsdale, AZ 85256; Mailing: P.O. Box 768, Bagdad, AZ 86321 t) (928) 633-2389 Rev. Camilo De Villa, Admin.; Dcn. James Trant; Jennie Martinez, DRE;
St. Maria Goretti Roman Catholic Parish - 6261 N. Granite Reef Rd., Scottsdale, AZ 85250 t) (480) 948-8380 smgoretti@smgaz.org www.smgaz.org Rev. Tegin Avarez, Admin.; Dcn. Carmene Carbone; Dcn. Gary Scott;
Our Lady of Perpetual Help Roman Catholic Parish - 7655 E. Main St., Scottsdale, AZ 85251 t) 480-947-4331 parish@olphaz.org Rev. Gregory J. Schlarb, Pst.; Rev. William Fitzgerald; Rev. Msgr. Thomas F. Hever; Rev. Sunny Abraham;
Our Lady of Perpetual Help Catholic School - (Grades PreSchool-8) 3801 N. Miller Rd., Scottsdale, AZ 85251 t) (480) 874-3720 school@olphaz.org olphaz.org/school Donna Lauro, Prin.;
Sisters of Charity - 7634 E. Second St., Scottsdale, AZ 85251
Our Lady of the Angels Conventual Church - 5802 E. Lincoln Dr., Scottsdale, AZ 85253 t) (480) 948-7460 casa@thecasa.org; dcm@thecasa.org www.thecasa.org at the Franciscan Renewal Center. Dcn. Herve Lemire; Bro. Vincent Nguyen, O.F.M.; Rev. Peter Kirwin, O.F.M., Rector; Rev. William K. Bried, O.F.M., Assoc. Pst.; Rev. Page Polk, In Res.; Rev. Joseph Schwab, O.F.M., In Res.; Patty Tafolla, DRE;
St. Patrick Roman Catholic Parish - 10815 N. 84th St., Scottsdale, AZ 85260 t) (480) 998-3843 generalmail@stpatcc.org www.stpatcc.org Rev. Eric Tellez, Pst.; Rev. Patrick Robinson; Rev. Andre Dargis, In Res.; Dcn. Louis Cornille III; Dcn. Joseph Herrera; Dcn. James Hostutler;

SEDONA

St. John Vianney Roman Catholic Parish - 180 St. John Vianney Ln., Sedona, AZ 86336 t) (928) 282-7545 stjohnvianney@sjvsedona.org www.sjvsedona.org Rev. David J. Kelash, V.F., Pst.; Dcn. Ronald Martinez; Dcn. Dennis Sullivan; Dcn. Donald Henkiel; Rev. Ignatius Mazanowski, F.H.S., Admin.;

SELIGMAN

St. Francis Roman Catholic Parish - 22440 Schoeney, Seligman, AZ 86337; Mailing: P.O. Box 309, Seligman, AZ 86337 t) (928) 422-3354 Rev. Theilo Ramirez, Pst.;

SUN CITY

St. Clement of Rome Roman Catholic Parish - 15800 Del Webb Blvd., Sun City, AZ 85351 t) (623) 974-5867 dpo@stclementaz.org Rev. Emile C. "Bud" Pelletier Jr., Pst.; Rev. Shia Reh Marino, Assoc. Pst.; Dcn. Lee Beatrice; Dcn. Patrick Thielen; Dcn. Lee Kloft; Dcn. Irving Dennis;
St. Elizabeth Seton Roman Catholic Parish - 9728 W. Palmeras Dr., Sun City, AZ 85373 t) (623) 972-2129 office@sescc.org sescc.org Rev. Kilian McCaffrey, Pst.; Rev. William Fournier; Rev. Raymond Greco; Rev. William Green; Dcn. Jeffrey Arner; Mary Fogelson, DRE; Dcn. James Brown; Dcn. Martin Pogioli; Dcn. Salvatore Lema; Dcn. Craig Reaktenwalt; Dcn. Paul Csuy;
Church of St. Joachim & St. Anne Roman Catholic Parish - 11625 N. 111th Ave., Sun City, AZ 85351-3746 t) (623) 972-1179 admin@sjasuncity.org Dcn. Dennis Luft; Dcn. Stephen Weiss; Rev. Nicholas A. Floridi, Assoc. Pst.;

SUN CITY WEST

Our Lady of Lourdes Roman Catholic Parish - 19002 N. 128th Ave., Sun City West, AZ 85375 t) (623) 546-2767 ololscw.org Rev. John Bonavitacola, Pst.; Rev. Augustine Ogumere, C.S.Sp.; Rev. Richard Ryan; Dcn. Larry Grey; Dcn. James Carabajal;
Prince of Peace Roman Catholic Parish Sun City West - 14818 W. Deer Valley Dr., Sun City West, AZ 85375 t) (623) 214-5180 info@popscw.org popscw.org Rev. David M. Ostler, Pst.; Rev. Julian Reginato, In Res.; CRP Stds.: 100

SUN LAKES

St. Steven Roman Catholic Parish - 24827 S. Dobson

Rd., Sun Lakes, AZ 85248 t) (480) 895-9266 freric@ststevensaz.org www.saintstevensparish.org Rev. Leo Pierre Hissey; Rev. Eric Houseknecht, Assoc. Pst.; Rev. Fredrick Ogbonna; Rev. Wilfred Yinah, V.C.; Dcn. Richard Corwin; Dcn. David Runyan; Yadi De La Torre, DRE;

SURPRISE

St Clare of Assisi Roman Catholic Parish Surprise - 17111 W. Bell Rd., Surprise, AZ 85374 t) (623) 546-3444 church@stcpaz.org stcpaz.org Rev. Gregory Menegay, Par. Vicar; Rev. Jacob Thomas Vettathu, MS; Rev. Robert Tino; Rev. David Ashbeck; Rev. Hans P. Ruygt; Dcn. Donnan Lukaszewski; Dcn. Michael Pirylis; Dcn. Joseph Badame; Dcn. David Opsahl; Dcn. John Woiwode;

TEMPE

All Saints Roman Catholic Newman Center - 230 E. University Dr., Tempe, AZ 85281-3700 t) 480-967-7823 mkilker@asucatholic.org www.asucatholic.org Rev. Robert Clements, Pst.; Rev. Bruce Downs, Assoc. Pst.; Rev. Aaron Qureshi; Dcn. Wayne Rich;

Church of the Resurrection Roman Catholic Parish - 3201 S. Evergreen Rd., Tempe, AZ 85282 t) 480-838-0207 parishinfo@resurrectionaz.org; rcia@resurrectionaz.org www.resurrectionaz.org Rev. Thomas R. Kagumisa, Par. Vicar; Rev. Romeo Dionisio, Admin.; Dcn. William Malatin; Dcn. Sione Hola; Rob Kubasko, DRE; Dee Dee Tamminen, DRE; Sr. Anne Marie Smith, OSF, Bus. Mgr.; CRP Stds.: 83

Holy Spirit Roman Catholic Parish - 1800 E. Libra Dr., Tempe, AZ 85283 t) 480-838-7474 parish@holyspirit-tempe-az.org www.holyspirit-tempe-az.org Rev. Michael Ashibuogwu; Rev. John Clote; Dcn. Gary Johnson; Yvette Mayer, DRE; Bill Price, DRE;

St. Margaret Roman Catholic Parish - 2435 E. McArthur Dr., Tempe, AZ 85281 t) (480) 967-0379 stmargaretcatholic@gmail.com www.stmargarettempe.org Rev. Matthew Krempel, Admin.; Dcn. Antonio Acuna;

Our Lady of Mt. Carmel Roman Catholic Parish - 2121 S. Rural Rd., Tempe, AZ 85282 t) 480-967-8791 parish@olmctempe.com; frcharlie@olmctempe.com www.olmctempe.com Rev. Charles Goraieb, Pst.; Rev. Robert Aliunzi, A.J., Par. Vicar; Rev. Aaron Agorsor; Dcn. Thomas Glenn; Dcn. Christopher Gass; Dcn. David Knebelsberger; Sr. Po-Yee Yeung, DRE; CRP Stds.: 110

Our Lady of Mt. Carmel Roman Catholic Parish School - (Grades PreSchool-8) 2117 S. Rural Rd., Tempe, AZ 85282 t) 480-967-5567 info@olmcschool.info www.olmcschool.info/ Kelly Shewbridge, Prin.; Stds.: 400; Sr. Tchrs.: 1; Lay Tchrs.: 21

TOLLESON

Blessed Sacrament Roman Catholic Parish - 312 N. 93rd Ave., Tolleson, AZ 85353 t) (623) 936-7107 welcome@blessedaz.org Rev. Jose Garzon Pastrana; Rev. Pedro Velez Prensa, Assoc. Pst.; Dcn. Jose Garza; Dcn. Sergio Estupinan;

WICKENBURG

St. Anthony of Padua Roman Catholic Parish - 232 N. Tegner St., Wickenburg, AZ 85390 t) (928) 684-2096 stanthony@qwestoffice.net mystanthonyofpadua.com Rev. Jose R. Lobaton, O.F.M., Pst.; Rev. Vinhson Nguyen; Rosemary Peterson, DRE;

Our Lady of Guadalupe - 50627 Eagle Eye Rd., Aguila, AZ 85320; Mailing: P.O. Box 96, Aguila, AZ 85320

WILLIAMS

St. Joseph Roman Catholic Parish - 900 W. Grant, Williams, AZ 86046 t) (928) 635-2430 father.trsramirez@gmail.com ssjaf.weconnect.com/ Rev. Theilo Ramirez, Pst.; Dcn. Christopher Giannola;

SCHOOLS: PRESCHOOL THRU HIGH SCHOOL

HIGH SCHOOLS

STATE OF ARIZONA

AVONDALE

St. John Paul II Roman Catholic High School - (DIO) (Grades 9-12) 3120 N. 137th Ave., Avondale, AZ 85392 t) 623-233-2777 mgonzales@jp2catholic.org jp2catholic.org Rev. Estevan Wetzel, Chap.; Sr. Mary Jordan Hoover, O.P., Prin.; Stds.: 355; Sr. Tchrs.: 3; Lay Tchrs.: 25

CHANDLER

Seton Catholic Preparatory High School - (DIO) (Grades 9-12) 1150 N. Dobson Rd., Chandler, AZ 85224 t) 480-963-1900 vserna@setoncatholic.org www.setoncatholic.org Victor Serna, Prin.; Pamela K Hollerbach, Vice Prin.; Julie Grindey, Dean of Students; Stds.: 550; Pr. Tchrs.: 1; Lay Tchrs.: 45

PHOENIX

Bourgade Catholic High School - (DIO) 4602 N. 31st Ave., Phoenix, AZ 85017 t) 602-973-4000 jbravo@bourgadecatholic.org www.bourgadecatholic.org Rev. David Loeffler, Chap.; Miara Cash, Campus Min.; Javier Bravo, Prin.;

Brophy College Preparatory (Jesuit Fathers) - (PRV) (Grades 6-12) 4701 N. Central Ave., Phoenix, AZ 85012 t) 602-264-5291 awolf@brophyprep.org; bryan@brophyprep.org www.brophyprep.org Boys Day School. Rev. Juan Pablo Marrufo Del Toro, S.J., Chap.; Austin Pidgeon, Dean; Bob Ryan, Prin.; Adria Renke, Pres.; Rev. William H. Muller, S.J., Vice. Pres.; Stds.: 1,382; Scholastics: 1; Pr. Tchrs.: 3; Lay Tchrs.: 107

St. Mary's Roman Catholic High School - (DIO) (Grades 9-12) 2525 N. Third St., Phoenix, AZ 85004 t) 602-251-2500 tbartlett@smknights.org; jfaria@smknights.org www.smknights.org Rev. Robert Bolding, Pres.; Tanya Bartlett, Prin.; Stds.: 475; Pr. Tchrs.: 1; Sr. Tchrs.: 3; Lay Tchrs.: 33

Xavier College Preparatory Roman Catholic High School - (DIO) 4710 N. Fifth St., Phoenix, AZ 85012 t) (602) 277-3772 jnu@xcp.org www.xcp.org Rev. Nathaniel Glenn, Chap.; Sr. Joan Nuckols, B.V.M., Prin.; Sr. M. Joan Fitzgerald, B.V.M., Pres.; Remi Fitzgerald, Dir.;

SCOTTSDALE

Notre Dame Preparatory Roman Catholic High School - (DIO) 9701 E. Bell Rd., Scottsdale, AZ 85260 t) (480) 634-8200 info@ndpsaints.org Rev. Philip Evanstock, C.S.Sp.; Jill Platt, Prin.;

INSTITUTIONS LOCATED IN DIOCESE

CAMPUS MINISTRY / NEWMAN CENTERS [CAM]

FLAGSTAFF

Holy Trinity Newman Center, A Quasi-Parish - 520 W. Riordan Rd., Flagstaff, AZ 86001 t) (928) 779-2903 info@catholicjacks.org www.catholicjacks.org Rev. Matthew Lowry, Chap.; Rev. Anthony Dang;

PHOENIX

Holy Spirit Roman Catholic Newman Center Phoenix - 3057 W. Camelback Rd., Phoenix, AZ 85017 t) (602) 744-4232 info@catholiclopes.faith Rev. David Loeffler, Dir.;

TEMPE

All Saints Catholic Newman Center Tempe - 230 E. University Dr., Tempe, AZ 85281 t) 480-967-7823 mkilker@asucatholic.org www.asucatholic.org (Tempe) Rev. Robert Clements, Dir.; Rev. Bruce Downs, Par. Vicar;

CATHOLIC CHARITIES [CCH]

PHOENIX

***Catholic Charities Community Services** - 4747 N. 7th Ave., Phoenix, AZ 85013 t) (602) 285-1999 info@cc-az.org www.catholiccharitiesaz.org Anthony R Siebers, Chair; Paul S. Mulligan, CEO;

Catholic Charities Community Services, Flagstaff - 2101 N. 4th St., Flagstaff, AZ 86004 t) (928) 774-9125 www.catholiccharitiesaz.org/ Sandi Flores, Dir.;

Catholic Charities Community Services, Phoenix - 5151 N. 19th Ave, Phoenix, AZ 85015 t) (602) 997-6105 www.catholiccharitiesaz.org/ Carrie Mascaro, Exec.;

Catholic Charities Community Services, West Valley - 7400 W. Olive Ave., Ste. 10, Peoria, AZ 85345 t) (623) 486-9868 Yatin Dua, Dir.;

Catholic Charities Community Services, Yavapai - 434 W. Gurley St., Prescott, AZ 86301 t) (928) 778-2531 www.catholiccharitiesaz.org/ Catherine A Brummet-Peterson, Exec.;

Catholic Charities Parish & Community Engagement - Malissa Geer, Dir.;

Foundation for Senior Living - 1201 E. Thomas Rd., Phoenix, AZ 85014 t) (602) 285-1800 info@fsl.org www.fsl.org Affordable apartments and community-based health and social services Tamara Bohannon, CEO; Asstd. Annu.: 35,000; Staff: 360

Affordable Services for Seniors, Inc. - 1201 E. Thomas Rd., Phoenix, AZ 85014 shastings@fsl.org Tom Egan, Pres.;

St. Clair Senior Living - shastings@fsl.org

Foundation for Senior Adult Living, Inc. - Sweetwater Gardens (Apartments for the Handicapped), Phoenix; Kingman Heights Apartments, Kingman.

FSL Home Improvements - kmartin@fsl.org Katie Martin, Dir.;

FSL Management -

FSL Pathways - Assisted Group Living Program (11 Houses), Phoenix.

FSL Programs - ainiguez@fsl.org Adult Day Health Care Ctrs; In-Home Care Svcs; Home Safety & Repair Prog; Community Action Prog/Senior Ctrs; Adult Foster Care; Oasis; Pathways Prog.

FSL Real Estate Services - shastings@fsl.org

FSL Rural Development - jgreene@fsl.org Becket House Apts, Lake Havasu City; Vianney Villas Apts, Avondale; Padua Hills Apts, Wickenburg; St. Agnes Apts, Williams; Amy Neal Retirement Ctr.

COLLEGES & UNIVERSITIES [COL]

MESA

Benedictine University - Gillet Hall, 225 E. Main St., Mesa, AZ 85201 t) (602) 888-5500 mesa@ben.edu www.ben.edu/mesa (Branch Campus at Mesa, AZ) Rev. Alex Juguilon, O.S.C., Chap.; Robert Curtis, Campus Min.; Kevin Broeckling, CEO;

CONVENTS, MONASTERIES, AND RESIDENCES FOR WOMEN [CON]

MESA

Sisters of Notre Dame de Namur - 548 W. Third St., Sister Nancy Wellmeier, SNDdeN, Mesa, AZ 85201 t) (480) 964-3685 wellmier@aol.com

PHOENIX

Institute of the Blessed Virgin Mary - 2521 W. Maryland Ave., Phoenix, AZ 85017 t) 602-242-2544 srdympna@simonjude.org ibvm.us (Regional House) Sr. Judy Illig, IBVM, Prov.; Sr. Dympna Doran, Local Supr.;

Missionaries of Charity - 1414 S. 17th Ave., Phoenix, AZ 85007 t) (602) 258-5504

Our Lady of Guadalupe Monastery - 8502 W. Pinchot Ave., Phoenix, AZ 85037 t) (623) 848-9608 sisterlinda@olgmonastery.com www.olgmonastery.com Sisters of St. Benedict Sr. Linda Campbell, O.S.B., Prioress;

Sisters of Charity of the Blessed Virgin Mary - 311 E. Highland Ave., Phoenix, AZ 85012 t) (602) 501-8436 jnu@xcp.org (Xavier Convent)

Sisters of Notre Dame de Namur - 6635 S. 14th Way, Phoenix, AZ 85042-4459 t) (480) 964-3685

SCOTTSDALE

Carmelite Missionaries of St. Therese of the Child Jesus - 1030 N. Hayden Rd., Scottsdale, AZ 85257 t) (480) 633-3729

TONOPAH

The Poor Clares of Perpetual Adoration, Our Lady of Solitude Monastery - 9020 N. 381st Ave., Tonopah, AZ 85354; Mailing: PO Box 639, Tonopah, AZ 85354 t) 480-245-9614 desertnuns@msn.com www.desertnuns.com Mother Marie Andre Campbell, PCPA, Abbess; Srs.: 7

ENDOWMENTS / FOUNDATIONS / TRUSTS [EFT]

GOODYEAR

St. John Vianney School Development Fund - 539 La Pasada Blvd., Goodyear, AZ 85338 t) (623) 932-3313 eesquivel@sjvaz.net; business@sjvaz.net www.sjvaz.net Rev. Thomas J. Eckert, C.S.C., Pres.;

PHOENIX

Saint Mary's Scholarship & Benefit Fund - 2525 N. Third St., Phoenix, AZ 85004 t) (602) 251-2506 pmadigan@smknights.org www.smknights.org Kevin Muir, Prin.; Amy Lawrence, Dir. Devel. & Finance;

TEMPE

Catholic Community Foundation for the Diocese of Phoenix - 4500 S. Lakeshore Dr., Ste. 650, Tempe, AZ 85282 t) (480) 651-8800 info@ccfphx.org ccfphx.org Independent 501c(3) entity and Canonical institution that encourages charitable giving to provide sustainable support for those who serve community. Dcn. James Carabajal, CEO; Kyle Felix, COO;

HOSPITALS / HEALTH SERVICES [HOS]

GILBERT

Mercy Gilbert Medical Center - 3555 S. Val Vista Dr., Gilbert, AZ 85297 t) 480-728-8000 pam.koerner@commonspirit.org www.mercygilbert.org Sponsored by Catholic Health Care Federation Mark Slyter, Pres.; Bed Capacity: 219; Asstd. Annu.: 104,748; Staff: 1,480

MISCELLANEOUS [MIS]

CHANDLER

The Catholic Singles Ministry, Inc. - 4593 W. Ivanhoe St., Chandler, AZ 85226 t) (602) 443-7104 Karina Penaranda, Contact;

MESA

Americare Hospice & Pallative Care - 1212 N. Spencer, #2, Mesa, AZ 85203 t) (480) 726-7773

***Life Teen, Inc.** - 2222 S. Dobson Rd., Ste. 601, Mesa, AZ 85202; Mailing: 6105 Blue Stone Rd, Ste B, Atlanta, GA 30328 t) (800) 809-3902 info@lifeteen.com lifeteen.com Randy Raus, Pres.;

PHOENIX

Andre House of Arizona - 213 S. 11th Ave., Phoenix, AZ 85007-3132; Mailing: P.O. Box 2014, Phoenix, AZ 85001 t) (602) 255-0580 jminich@andrehouse.org; jdelaney@andrehouse.org andrehouse.org Hospitality House, U.S. Province of the Congregation of Holy Cross. John Delaney II, CEO; Jay Minich, CFO;

Caritas In Veritate International - USA - 3443 N. Central Ave., Ste. 1002, Phoenix, AZ 85012 t) 602-795-9810 henry@caritasinveritate.com Henry Cappello, President and CEO;

Catholic Education Arizona - 5353 N. 16th St., Ste. 330, Phoenix, AZ 85016 t) (602) 218-6542 dpreach@ceaz.org www.catholiceducationarizona.org Nancy Padberg, CEO; Deb Preach, Chief Devel. Officer/School Liaison;

Christ Child Society - 4633 N. 54th St., Phoenix, AZ 85018-1904 t) 602-840-5066 phxchristchildsociety@gmail.com www.christchildphx.org Nancy DiMascio, Pres.;

Cursillo Movement - 4633 N. 54th St., Phoenix, AZ 85018 t) (602) 840-5066 x42 info@phoenixcursillo.com www.phoenixcursillo.com Dcn. Marvin Hernandez; Dave Zeman, Dir.;

***Diocesan Council for the Society of St. Vincent De Paul** - 420 W. Watkins, Phoenix, AZ 85003; Mailing: PO Box 13600, Phoenix, AZ 85002 t) (602) 254-3338; (602) 266-4673 www.stvincentdepaul.net Stephen J. Zabilski, Exec. Dir.; Stephen Attwood, Bd. Pres.;

FSL Christopher Properties - 1201 E. Thomas Rd., Phoenix, AZ 85014 t) (602) 285-0505 x181 ainiguez@fsl.org Steve Hastings, Dir.;

St. Joseph the Worker - 1125 W. Jackson St., Phoenix, AZ 85007; Mailing: P.O. Box 13503, Phoenix, AZ 85002 t) (602) 417-9854 c) (602) 550-6331 info@sjwjobs.org; mlaront@sjwjobs.org www.sjwjobs.org Lauren Podgorski, Chair; Karl Johnson, Treas.; Brent Downs, Exec.;

Kino Catechetical Institute - 400 E. Monroe, Phoenix, AZ 85004 t) (602) 354-2300 kinoinstitute@dphx.org www.kinoinstitute.org Program for Catechetical Studies & Adult Leadership Formation. Steve Greene, Dir.; Luz Lobato, Spanish Progs. Admin./Office Mgr.; Stds.: 102; Lay Tchrs.: 1

***Tepeyac Leadership, Inc.** - 522 N. Central Ave., #613, Phoenix, AZ 85001 c) 602-451-1922 cpereyra@tepeyacleadership.org tliprogram.org/ Non-profit dedicated to civic leadership development for lay Catholic professionals. Cristofer Pereyra, CEO;

QUEEN CREEK

***EENU-USA, Inc. (E3 Africa)** - 18521 E. Queen Creek Rd., Ste. 105-273, Queen Creek, AZ 85142 t) (480) 243-8789 programs@e3africa.org; director@e3africa.org www.e3africa.org Michael Scaramella, Exec.; Rev. Robert Aliunzi, A.J., Mem.;

SCOTTSDALE

***Franciscan Friars of Arizona at the Franciscan Renewal Center** - 5802 E. Lincoln Dr., Scottsdale, AZ 85253 t) (480) 948-7460 casa@thecasa.org thecasa.org Charles Brown, Gen. Mgr.;

***NPH USA** - 8925 E. Pima Ctr. Pkwy., Ste. 145, Scottsdale, AZ 85258-4407 t) (480) 967-9449; (480) 967-9449 infosw@nphusa.org; chardy@nphusa.org www.nphusa.org Belinda Roda, Southwest Devel. Mgr.;

SEDONA

Chapel of the Holy Cross - 780 Chapel Rd., Sedona, AZ 86336 t) 928-282-7545 Rev. Ignatius Mazanowski, F.H.S., Pst.; Charles E. Reaume, Admin.;

SUN CITY

Magnificat Phoenix Chapter - 13611 N. 98th Ave. G, Sun City, AZ 85351 t) (623) 979-9780 aa-ok@cox.net; azmtbriwal@gmail.com aa-ok0.wixsite.com/magnificat-arizona

TEMPE

***City of the Lord** - 711 W. University Dr., Tempe, AZ 85281-3411 t) 480-968-5990 phoenixbranch@cityofthelord.org www.cityofthelord.org Jeff Looker, Senior Branch Coordinator;

MONASTERIES AND RESIDENCES FOR PRIESTS AND BROTHERS [MON]

PHOENIX

Carmelite Community - 1717 W. Flower, Phoenix, AZ 85015 t) 602-274-0442 Rev. Silvan Boyle, O.Carm.;

Conventual Priory of the Holy Cross (Crosier Fathers and Brothers Province, Inc.) - 717 E. Southern Ave., Phoenix, AZ 85040-3142; Mailing: P.O. Box 90428, Phoenix, AZ 85066-0428 t) 602-443-7100 crosier@crosier.org www.crosier.org Rev. Thomas A. Enneking, O.S.C., Prior; Rev. Michael Cotone, O.S.C., In Res.; Priests: 2

Crosier Community of Phoenix (Canons Regular of the Order of the Holy Cross) (Conventual Priory of the Holy Cross) - 717 E. Southern Ave., Phoenix, AZ 85040-3142; Mailing: P.O. Box 90428, Phoenix, AZ 85066-0428 t) 602-443-7100 phoenix@crosier.org www.crosier.org Rev. Thomas A. Enneking, O.S.C., Prior; Bro. Gabriel Guerrero, O.S.C., Mem.; Rev. Alex Juguilon, O.S.C., Mem.; Rev. Hubert Kavusa, O.S.C., Mem.; Bro. Gregory Madigan, O.S.C., Mem.; Rev. Jean-Marie Mukoka, OSC (Congo), Mem.; Rev. Robert J. Rossi, O.S.C., Mem.; Rev. Kosman Sianturi, OSC, Mem.; Rev. Jude Verley, O.S.C., Mem.; Rev. Virgil Petermeier, O.S.C., Mem.; Bro. Christopher Erran, OSC, Mem.; Rev. Daniel Hernandez, O.S.C., Mem.; Rev. Stephan Bauer, O.S.C., Mem.; Brs.: 3; Priests: 10

Crosier Village of Phoenix - 717 E. Southern Ave., Phoenix, AZ 85040-3142; Mailing: PO Box 90428, Phoenix, AZ 85066-0428 t) (602) 443-7100 village@crosier.org Rev. Thomas A. Enneking, O.S.C., Pres.; Priests: 1

Disciples of Hope - 9241 N. 36th Dr., Phoenix, AZ 85051 t) (602) 841-7824 frzantua@yahoo.com www.discipulispei.org Dcn. Agerico Dalisjay, D.S., In Res.;

Holy Cross Congregation/Casa Santa Cruz - 7126 N. Seventh Ave., Phoenix, AZ 85021 t) (602) 944-6000 Rev. John H. Pearson, C.S.C., Supr.; Rev. Duane Balcerski, C.S.C., Asst. Supr./Treas.; Rev. Gerardo R. Barmasse, C.S.C., In Res.; Rev. James R. Blantz, C.S.C., In Res.; Rev. Michael D. Couhig, C.S.C., In Res.; Rev. William W. Faiella, C.S.C., In Res.; Rev. James W. Thornton, C.S.C., In Res.;

Society of Jesus - Phoenix Jesuit Community, 120 E. Mariposa St., Phoenix, AZ 85012 t) (602) 872-7329 phxjescom@gmail.com Rev. George Wanser, S.J., Supr.; Rev. Robert A Fambrini, S.J., Pst.; Rev. Anthony P. Sauer, S.J., Par. Vicar; Rev. Kevin Dilworth, S.J., Chap.; Rev. Juan Pablo Marrufo del Torro, S.J., Teacher; Simon Peter Zachary, S.J., Teacher;

St. Therese Priory - 75 E. Mariposa St. Apt 1, Phoenix, AZ 85012-1631 t) (602) 604-2365 Rev. Kevin Lafey, O.Carm.; Rev. James Mueller, O.Carm.; Rev. Bradley L. Peterson, O. Carm., Prior; Bro. Eric Bell, Treas.; Rev. Ronald Oakham, Ohter;

NURSING / REHABILITATION / CONVALESCENCE / ELDERLY CARE [NUR]

PHOENIX

St. Agnes Apartments - 1201 E. Thomas Rd., Phoenix, AZ 85014 t) (928) 635-2913 info@fsl.org (Retirement)

Amy Neal Retirement Center - 1201 E. Thomas Rd., Phoenix, AZ 85014 t) (928) 757-7016 info@fsl.org HUD rent subsidized.

Becket House Apartments - 1201 E. Thomas Rd., Phoenix, AZ 85014 t) (928) 855-7178 info@fsl.org (Retirement)

Havasu Hills - 865 Cashmere Dr., Lake Havasu City, AZ 86404 t) (928) 855-4743

Kingman Heights Apartments - 1201 E. Thomas Rd., Phoenix, AZ 85014 t) (928) 753-2425 info@fsl.org (Retirement) - HUD rent subsidized.

Pineview Manor Apartments - 1201 E. Thomas Rd., Phoenix, AZ 85014 t) (928) 474-1317 info@fsl.org

Roeser Senior Village Apartments - 1201 E. Thomas Rd., Phoenix, AZ 85014 t) (602) 268-5100 info@fsl.org

Sweetwater Gardens Apartments - 1201 E. Thomas Rd., Phoenix, AZ 85014 t) (602) 867-4549 info@fsl.org (Handicapped)

Vianney Villas Apartments - 1201 E. Thomas Rd., Phoenix, AZ 85014 t) (623) 932-2036 info@fsl.org (Retirement)- HUD Rent Subsidized

WICKENBURG

Padua Hills Apartments - 460 S. West Rd., Wickenburg, AZ 85390 t) (928) 684-7034 ainiguez@fsl.org www.fsl.org (Retirement)- HUD Rent Subsidized Steve Hastings, Dir.;

RETREAT HOUSES / RENEWAL CENTERS [RTR]

BLACK CANYON CITY

Merciful Heart Hermitage: A House of Prayer for Priests - 19950 E. St. Joseph Rd., Black Canyon City, AZ 85324; Mailing: P.O. Box 159, Black Canyon City, AZ 85324 t) 623-374-9204 mercifulretreat@gmail.com Rev. Eugene Florea, Dir.;

PHOENIX

The Catholic Retreat for Young Singles, Inc. (Catholic Singles Community) - 4633 N 54th St, Phoenix, AZ 85018 t) 480-540-4760 csc@cscarizona.org www.cscarizona.org Josilyn Tan, Pres.;

Mount Claret Roman Catholic Retreat Center - 4633 N. 54th St., Phoenix, AZ 85018 t) (602) 840-5066 info@mtclaret.org Thomas McGuire, Dir.; Rev. James Trempe; Rev. Emile C. "Bud" Pelletier Jr., In Res.; Rev. Msgr. Gilbert J. Rutz, In Res.;

Our Lady of Guadalupe Retreat/Conference Center - 8502 W. Pinchot, Phoenix, AZ 85037 t) (623) 848-9608 sisterlydia@olgmonastery.com olgmonastery.com Sr. Linda Campbell, O.S.B., Contact;

SCOTTSDALE

Franciscan Renewal Center, Inc. (Casa de Paz Y Bien) - 5802 E. Lincoln Dr., Scottsdale, AZ 85253 t) (480) 948-7460 casa@thecasa.org www.thecasa.org Rev. Peter Kirwin, O.F.M., Rector; Rev. William K. Bried, O.F.M., In Res.; Rev. Joseph Schwab, O.F.M., Exec.;

Diocese of Pittsburgh

(Dioecesis Pittsburgensis)

MOST REVEREND DAVID A. ZUBIK

Bishop of Pittsburgh; ordained May 3, 1975; appointed Auxiliary Bishop of Pittsburgh and Titular Bishop of Jamestown February 18, 1997; consecrated April 6, 1997; appointed Bishop of Green Bay October 10, 2003; installed December 12, 2003; appointed Bishop of Pittsburgh July 18, 2007; installed September 28, 2007. Office: 2900 Noblestown Rd., Pittsburgh, PA 15205.

Pastoral Center: 2900 Noblestown Rd., Pittsburgh, PA 15205. T: 412-456-3000
communications@diopitt.org
www.diopitt.org

ESTABLISHED AUGUST 11, 1843.

Square Miles 3,754.

Comprises the Counties of Allegheny, Beaver, Lawrence, Washington, Greene, and Butler in the State of Pennsylvania.

Legal Title: The Diocese of Pittsburgh and each parish in the diocese are organized as separate Pennsylvania Charitable Trusts.

Most Reverend William John Waltersheid, V.G.
Auxiliary Bishop of Pittsburgh; ordained July 11, 1992; appointed Auxiliary Bishop of Pittsburgh and Titular Bishop of California February 25, 2011; consecrated April 25, 2011. Office: 2900 Noblestown Rd., Pittsburgh, PA 15205.

Most Reverend Mark A. Eckman
Auxiliary Bishop of Pittsburgh; ordained May 11, 1985; appointed Auxiliary Bishop of Pittsburgh and Titular Bishop of Sitifis November 5, 2021; consecrated January 11, 2022. Office: 2900 Noblestown Rd., Pittsburgh, PA 15205.

STATISTICAL OVERVIEW

Personnel

Bishop........1
Auxiliary Bishops........2
Retired Bishops........1
Priests: Diocesan Active in Diocese........169
Priests: Diocesan Active Outside Diocese........2
Priests: Retired, Sick or Absent........124
Number of Diocesan Priests........295
Religious Priests in Diocese........90
Total Priests in your Diocese........385
Extern Priests in Diocese........17
Ordinations:
Diocesan Priests........1
Religious Priests........1
Transitional Deacons........3
Permanent Deacons in Diocese........106
Total Brothers........22
Total Sisters........602

Parishes

Parishes........63
With Resident Pastor:
Resident Diocesan Priests........57
Resident Religious Priests........2
Without Resident Pastor:
Administered by Pastoral Teams, etc.........4
New Parishes Created........4
Closed Parishes........18

Professional Ministry Personnel:
Brothers........4
Sisters........39
Lay Ministers........214

Welfare

Catholic Hospitals........1
Homes for the Aged........8
Day Care Centers........4
Specialized Homes........3
Special Centers for Social Services........29
Residential Care of Disabled........1

Educational

Seminaries, Diocesan........1
Students from This Diocese........11
Diocesan Students in Other Seminaries........22
Total Seminarians........33
Colleges and Universities........3
Total Students........11,520
High Schools, Diocesan and Parish........7
Total Students........2,906
High Schools, Private........3
Total Students........696
Elementary Schools, Diocesan and Parish........42
Total Students........8,562
Elementary Schools, Private........4
Total Students........973
Non-residential Schools for the Disabled........2
Total Students........136
Catechesis/Religious Education:
High School Students........792
Elementary Students........17,217
Total Students under Catholic Instruction........42,835
Teachers in Diocese:
Brothers........5
Sisters........7
Lay Teachers........1,005

Vital Statistics

Receptions into the Church:
Infant Baptism Totals........3,194
Minor Baptism Totals........124
Adult Baptism Totals........116
Received into Full Communion........180
First Communions........3,148
Confirmations........3,001
Marriages:
Catholic........856
Interfaith........327
Total Marriages........1,183
Deaths........6,593
Total Catholic Population........618,731
Total Population........1,929,323

LEADERSHIP

Pastoral Center - t) 412-456-3000
Vicars General - Most Rev. Mark A. Eckman (meckman@diopitt.org); Most Rev. William J. Waltersheid; Very Rev. Lawrence A. DiNardo;
Vicar for Canonical Services - Very Rev. Thomas W. Kunz;
Vicar for Church Relations - Rev. Msgr. Ronald P. Lengwin;
Vicar for Clergy & Consecrated Life - Most Rev. Mark A. Eckman (meckman@diopitt.org);
Episcopal Vicar for Faith Initiatives - Most Rev. William J. Waltersheid;
Regional Vicars - Very Rev. Philip N. Farrell (pfarrell@diopitt.org); Very Rev. David G. Poecking;
North Vicariate - t) 412-456-5649 Very Rev. Philip N. Farrell;
South Vicariate - t) 412-456-5645 Very Rev. David G. Poecking;
Bishop's Office - Most Rev. David A. Zubik;
General Secretary - t) 412-456-3131 Very Rev. Lawrence A. DiNardo, Vicar;
Associate General Secretary - Very Rev. Thomas W. Kunz; Rev. Larry Adams (ladams@saintmauriceparish.org);
Chancellor - t) (412) 456-3166 Anna Bamonte Torrance, Chancellor;
Archives and Record Center - t) 412-456-3158 Dennis Wodzinski, Dir.;
Office of the Patrimony - t) 421-456-3158 Rev. Michael R. Ruffalo, Cur.;
Canonical Services - t) 412-456-3129 Very Rev. Thomas W. Kunz;
Administrative Procedures, Office for - t) 412-456-3126 Very Rev. Thomas W. Kunz;
Diocesan Review Board - t) 412-456-3129 Very Rev. Michael S. Sedor, Exec. Sec.;
Civil Law Services - Christopher G. Ponticello, Gen. Counsel; Kristin Boose Repin, Assoc. Gen. Counsel; Jarrod Turner, Legal Counsel;
Secretariat for Formation - Ellen M. Mady;
Health Care Liaison - t) 412-456-3131 Very Rev. Lawrence A. DiNardo;
Liturgy & Worship, Dept. for - t) 412-456-3041 Rev. James J. Chepponis, Diocesan Dir. Music; Erica Gamerro, Dir., Worship & Liturgical Ministry;
Mission Office - t) 412-456-3065 Dcn. Timothy F. Noca, Dir. (tnoca@protechtraining.com);
Stewardship, Office for - t) 412-456-3085 Dolores C. Nypaver, Dir.; Michael Freker, Dir.;

ADMINISTRATION

Auditors/Analysts, Office for the - t) 412-456-3029 James E. Stierheim;
Building Commission - t) 412-456-3034 Charles Goetz, Chair; James J. Zielinski, Exec. Sec.;
Business Services, Dept. for - t) 412-456-3137 Robert Costantino;
Central Accounting Services - t) 412-456-3030 Robert Costantino;
Chief Facilities Officer - t) 412-456-3093 Charles Goetz;
Chief Financial Officer - t) 412-456-3137 Robert Costantino;
Chief Operations Officer - t) (412) 456-3129 Dcn. Kevin L. Lander;
Facilities Management & Maintenance, Dept. for - Charles Goetz, Dir.; James J. Zielinski, Dir.; Joseph Kubiak, Plant Mgr.;
Financial Services, Office for - t) 412-456-3025 Robert Costantino; John Cushma, Controller; Wayne C. Boettcher, Dir.;
Human Resources, Office for - t) 412-456-3016 Dcn. Jeffrey A. Hirst, Dir.;
Insurance/Employee Benefits & Payroll, Office for - t) 412-456-3045 David S. Stewart, Dir.;
Office for Compliance - t) (412) 456-3093 Phyllis Haney, Dir.;
Operations and Information Technology - t) (412) 456-3129 Dcn. Kevin L. Lander, Dir.;
Parish Accounting Services - t) (412) 456-3030 Mary Ann Racki;
Payroll, Office for - t) 412-456-3006 John G. Cvetic, Dir.;
Secretariat for Protection of Children, Youth and Vulnerable Adults - t) 412-456-3093; 888-808-1235 (Toll Free Victim's Assistance Hotline) Phyllis Haney;
Victim Assistance Ministry - t) 412-456-3093 Laetitia Bridges, Dir.;

CLERGY AND RELIGIOUS SERVICES

Deacon Ongoing Formation - t) 412-456-3124 Dcn. Stephen J. Byers, Dir.;
Department for Post Ordination Formation - t) 412-456-3060 Most Rev. Mark A. Eckman (meckman@diopitt.org);
Institutional Ministries - Adam Blai, Dir.;
Office of the Delegate for Consecrated Life - t) 412-456-3067 Sr. Mindy Welding;
Permanent Diaconate - t) 412-456-3124 Dcn. Stephen J. Byers, Dir.;
Pre-Ordination Formation, Department for - t) 412-456-3048 Rev. Thomas A. Sparacino;
Priest Ongoing Formation, Department for - t) 412-456-3060 Most Rev. Mark A. Eckman (meckman@diopitt.org);
Priestly Vocations, Office for - t) 412-456-3123 Rev. Kenneth W. Marlovits, Dir.;
Retired Priests, Office for - t) 412-931-4624 Rev. Leroy A. DiPietro, Delegate;
St. Paul Seminary - Rev. Thomas A. Sparacino, Rector; Rev. Steven V. Neff, Spiritual Adv./Care Srvcs.; Sr. Cindy Ann Kibler, S.H.S., Apostolic Works Coord.;
Secretariat for Clergy and Consecrated Life - t) 412-456-3060 Most Rev. Mark A. Eckman (meckman@diopitt.org); Sr. Anna Marie Gaglia, C.S.J., Clergy Support Coord.;

COMMUNICATIONS

Communications, Office for - t) 412-456-3020 Jennifer Antkowiak, Exec. Dir.;
Media and Technology, Office for - t) 412-456-3116 Michael Anania, Video/Digital Media Production Editor;

CONSULTATIVE BODIES

Catholic Diocese of Pittsburgh Foundation Board - Dolores C. Nypaver, Secy.;
Clergy Personnel Board - Most Rev. David A. Zubik, Mem.; Most Rev. William J. Waltersheid; Most Rev. Mark A. Eckman (meckman@diopitt.org);
College of Consultors - Most Rev. David A. Zubik; Most Rev. William J. Waltersheid; Most Rev. Mark A. Eckman (meckman@diopitt.org);
Diocesan Finance Council - Most Rev. David A. Zubik; Most Rev. Mark A. Eckman (meckman@diopitt.org); Very Rev. Lawrence A. DiNardo;
Priest Council - Most Rev. David A. Zubik; Most Rev. William J. Waltersheid; Most Rev. Mark A. Eckman (meckman@diopitt.org);

EDUCATION

Catholic School Administrator - Finances - t) 412-456-3108 Roy Cartier, Dir.;
Department of Catholic Schools - Michelle Peduto, Supt.; Sharon Loughran Brown, Asst. Supt. (sharon@srcespgh.org); Roy Cartier, Asst. Supt.;
Director of Catholic Identity - t) 412-456-3090 Judene Indovina;
Director of Hispanic Apostolate - Jorge Vela;
Director of Youth and Young Adult Engagement - t) 412-456-3090 Jacob Williamson, Dir.;
Natural Family Planning Advisory Committee - t) (412) 456-3124 Dcn. Stephen J. Byers;
Secretariat for Catholic Schools - t) (412) 456-3090 Michelle Peduto (mapeduto@carlow.edu);

PARISH SERVICES

Secretariat for Parish Services - t) 413-456-3180 Linda Lee Ritzer;

TRIBUNAL

Tribunal Office - t) 412-456-3033
Adjutant Judicial Vicar - Very Rev. Michael S. Sedor;
Defender of the Bond - Rev. Louis L. DeNinno; Ellen M. Mady;
Judges - Very Rev. Michael S. Sedor; Rev. Dennis P. Yurochko; Very Rev. Val Michlik;
Judicial Vicar - Very Rev. Michael S. Sedor;
Matrimonial Concerns, Office for - Rev. Louis L. DeNinno; Rev. William E. Dorner;
Moderator of the Tribunal - Jay Conzemius;
Notary - Diane Kass;
Promoter of Justice - Very Rev. Thomas W. Kunz;

PARISHES, MISSIONS, AND CLERGY

COMMONWEALTH OF PENNSYLVANIA

ALIQUIPPA

Mary, Queen of Saints - 115 Trinity Dr., Aliquippa, PA 15001 t) 724-775-6363 sfcabrini@comcast.net www.maryqueenofsaints.org/ Rev. Canice McMullen, OSB, Pst.; Dcn. Joseph A Samchuck; Rev. Joachim J. Morgan, O.S.B., Par. Vicar; Dcn. Joseph N. Basko; Dcn. Robert J. Bittner; CRP Stds.: 450
Our Lady of Fatima School - (Grades PreK-8) 3005 Fatima Dr., Aliquippa, PA 15001 t) 724-375-7565 www.ourladyoffatima-hopewell.org Shirley Martin, Prin.; Stds.: 162; Scholastics: 14; Lay Tchrs.: 14

ALLISON PARK

Sts. Martha and Mary - 2554 Wildwood Rd., Allison Park, PA 15101 t) 412-486-6001 admin@stsmarthaandmaryparish.org www.stsmarthaandmaryparish.org/ Rev. Vincent F. Kolo, Par. Vicar; Rev. Christopher J. Mannerino, Par. Vicar; Dcn. Gary Molitor; Rev. Robert J. Vular, Pst.; Dcn. Clifford M. Homer Sr.; CRP Stds.: 777

AMBRIDGE

Good Samaritan - Merged Jul 2022 Merged with SS. John & Paul, Franklin Park & St. John the Baptist, Baden & Our Lady of Peace, Conway to form St. Luke the Evangelist Parish.

BADEN

St. John the Baptist - Merged Jul 2022 Merged with Good Samaritan, Ambridge & SS. John & Paul, Franklin Park & Our Lady of Peace, Conway to form St. Luke the Evangelist Parish.

BAIRDFORD

Our Lady of the Lakes (The Catholic Communities of St. Victor & Transfiguration Parishes) - 527 Bairdford Rd., Bairdford, PA 15006; Mailing: P.O. Box 149, Bairdford, PA 15006 t) 724-265-2070 admin@ollakes.org www.ollakes.org Rev. Vincent F. Kolo, Par. Vicar; Dcn. Rick Sumrok; Rev. James P. Holland, Pst.; CRP Stds.: 156

BEAVER

Our Lady of the Valley - 200 3rd St., Beaver, PA 15009 t) (724) 775-4111 info@olotv.org www.olotv.org/ Rev. Howard W. Campbell, Pst.; Rev. Paul Kuppe, O.F.M.Cap., Par. Vicar; CRP Stds.: 264
SS. Peter and Paul School - 370 E. End Ave., Beaver, PA 15009 t) 724-774-4450 school@ssppbeaver.org Cindy Baldrige, Prin.; Stds.: 157; Scholastics: 13; Lay Tchrs.: 13

BEAVER FALLS

St. Monica - 116 Thorndale Dr., Beaver Falls, PA 15010-1730 t) 724-846-7540 office@saintaugustineparish.com www.saintaugustineparish.com Rev. John F. Naugle, Par. Vicar; Dcn. Harry J. DeNome; Rev. Ladis Cizik, Chap.; Rev. Kim J. Schreck, Pst.; CRP Stds.: 115

BENTLEYVILLE

St. Katharine Drexel Parish - 126 Church St., Bentleyville, PA 15314 t) 724-209-1370 www.katharinedrexelpgh.org Rev. Thomas J. Lewandowski, Par. Vicar; Rev. Michael R. Peck, Par. Vicar; Rev. Michael A. Zavage, Par. Vicar; Dcn. Michael Gatto; Dcn. Jeffrey A. Hirst; Dcn. Barry A. Krofcheck; Dcn. Thomas W. Raymond; Rev. Donald Chortos, In Res.; Rev. Edward L. Yuhas, Pst.; CRP Stds.: 36

BETHEL PARK

Our Lady of Hope - 7003 Baptist Rd., Bethel Park, PA 15102 t) (412) 833-0661 www.olhpgh.org/ Dcn. James A. Kenny; Dcn. Thomas B. Mills; Dcn. Robert J. Stein; Dcn. Samuel Toney; Rev. Charles W. Speicher, In Res.; Rev. Richard J. Tusky, In Res.; Rev. John E. Hissrich, Chap.; Rev. Michael S. Suslowicz, Par. Vicar; Rev. John W. Skirtich, Pst.; CRP Stds.: 436

BRIDGEVILLE

Corpus Christi - 212 Station St., Bridgeville, PA 15017 t) 412-221-5213 parishoffice@corpuschristipgh.org www.corpuschristipgh.org/ Rev. Michael Faix, Par. Vicar; Rev. Dennis P. Yurochko, Pst.; Dcn. Lee Miles; Dcn. Leonard M. Thomas Jr.; Very Rev. Michael S. Sedor, In Res.; CRP Stds.: 626

BUTLER

All Saints - 125 Buttercup Rd., Butler, PA 16001; Mailing: 128 N. McKean St., Butler, PA 16001 t) (724) 287-1759 www.allsaintsbutler.org/ Rev. Kevin C. Fazio, Pst.; Rev. John J. Baver, Par. Vicar; Rev. Richard J. Thompson, Par. Vicar; Dcn. Mike Kaufman; Dcn. James Shope; Dcn. Mitchell M. Natali; CRP Stds.: 200

Holy Sepulcher - 1304 E. Cruikshank Rd., Butler, PA 16002 t) 724-586-7610 parish@holysepulcher.org www.holysepulcher.org Dcn. Doug Nelson; Rev. Dennis M. Buranosky, In Res.; Rev. Robert Guay, In Res.; Rev. Charles S. Bober, Pst.; Dcn. Ralph W. Bachner Jr.; Dcn. William H. Carver; CRP Stds.: 252

Holy Sepulcher School - (Grades PreK-8) 6515 Old Rte. 8, Butler, PA 16002 t) 724-586-5022 school@holysepulcher.org Jim Correll, Prin.; Stds.: 150; Scholastics: 13; Lay Tchrs.: 13

St. Mary of the Assumption - 821 Herman Rd., Butler, PA 16002 t) 724-352-2149 www.stsjjmcatholic.org/ Rev. Ward Stakem, O.F.M.Cap., Pst.; Rev. James Kurtz, O.F.M.Cap., Par. Vicar; Barbara Moran, DRE;

CABOT

St. Francis of Assisi - 315 Stoney Hollow Rd., Cabot, PA 16023 t) 724-352-2149 www.saintfrancisparish.net/ Rev. Matthew R. McClain, Pst.; Rev. Louis F. Pascazi, Par. Vicar; Dcn. Bruce Beaver; Rev. James Kurtz, O.F.M.Cap., Par. Vicar; Rev. Ward Stakem, O.F.M.Cap., Par. Vicar; CRP Stds.: 201

CANONSBURG

St. Oscar Romero - 317 W. Pike St., Canonsburg, PA 15317 t) 724-745-6560 pshultz@romeroparish.org romeroparish.org Dcn. Anton V. Mobley; Dcn. Brian M. Podobnik; Rev. Carmen A. D'Amico, Pst.; Rev. George T. DeVille, Par. Vicar; Rev. Thomas L. Gillespie, Par. Vicar; Dcn. Joseph Cerenzia; Rev. Thomas J. Galvin, Chap.; CRP Stds.: 561

CARNEGIE

St. Raphael the Archangel - 330 3rd Ave., Carnegie, PA 15106 t) (412) 857-5356 office@straphaelcgs.org www.straphaelcgs.org/ Dcn. Kevin L. Lander; Dcn. Paul Lim; Rev. Robin Evanish, In Res.; Rev. James P. McDonough, In Res.; Dcn. James S. Mackin; Rev. Aleksandr Schrenk, Par. Vicar; Rev. Robert J. Grecco, Pst.; Rev. Jerome Etenduk, In Res.; CRP Stds.: 168

Saints Simon & Jude Early Childhood Program - 1625 Greentree Rd., Pittsburgh, PA 15220 t) 412-563-1199 preschool@ssjpittsburgh.org Maureen Torcasi, Dir.;

CHICORA

St. Clare of Assisi - 864 Chicora Rd., Chicora, PA 16025 t) 724-445-3713 office@saintclareparish.com www.saintclareparish.com Rev. James Kurtz, O.F.M.Cap., Par. Vicar; Rev. Louis F. Pascazi, Par. Vicar; Rev. Ward Stakem, O.F.M.Cap., Par. Vicar; Rev. Matthew R. McClain, Pst.; CRP Stds.: 259

Preschool - 211 St. Wendelin Rd., Butler, PA 16002 t) 724-285-4986 www.stwendelinschool.com

St. Wendelin School - (Grades K-8) 211 Saint Wendelin Rd., Butler, PA 16002 t) 724-285-4986 stwend@zoominternet.net www.stwendelinschool.com Jolynn Clouse, Prin.; Stds.: 110; Scholastics: 10; Lay Tchrs.: 10

CONWAY

Our Lady of Peace - Merged Jul 2022 Merged with Good Samaritan, Ambridge & SS. John & Paul, Franklin Park & St. John the Baptist, Baden to form St. Luke the Evangelist Parish.

CRANBERRY TOWNSHIP

Divine Grace - 2535 Rochester Rd., Cranberry Township, PA 16066 t) (724) 776-2888 lbunni@divinegracepgh.org www.divinegracepgh.org Formerly Holy Redeemer. Rev. James A. Wehner, Pst.; Rev. John P. Gallagher, Par. Vicar; Rev. Mark L. Thomas, Par. Vicar; Rev. David J. Egan, Par. Vicar; Dcn. Jeffrey J. Ludwikowski; Dcn. Donald C. Pepe; Dcn. Joseph Ross;

Convent - 300 Crescent Ave., Ellwood City, PA 16117 t) 724-758-3741

St. Gregory School - (Grades PreSchool-8) 115 Pine St., Zelienople, PA 16063 t) (724) 452-9731 schooloffice@stgregzelie.org school.stgregzelie.org Erin Rice, Prin.;

St. Ferdinand - Merged Jul 2022 Merged with Holy Redeemer, Ellwood City and Saint Gregory, Zelienople to form Divine Grace Parish.

St. Kilian - 7076 Franklin Rd., Cranberry Township, PA 16066-5302 t) 724-625-1665 www.saintkilian.org Dcn. Doug Nelson; Rev. Charles S. Bober, Pst.; Dcn. Ralph W. Bachner Jr.; Dcn. William Carver; Rev. Dennis M. Buranosky, In Res.; Rev. Robert Guay, In Res.; CRP Stds.: 758

St. Kilian School - (Grades PreK-8) school@stkilian.org www.saintkilian.org/school Jessica Rock, Prin.; Stds.: 706; Scholastics: 36; Lay Tchrs.: 36

DONORA

St. Andrew the Apostle - 1 Park Manor Dr., Donora, PA 15033 t) (724) 379-4777 saintandrewmidmon.org/ Rev. Gerald S. Mikonis, In Res.; Dcn. Alexander J. Poroda II; Rev. Joseph Uzar, Par. Vicar; Rev. Kevin J. Dominik, Pst.; CRP Stds.: 179

ELIZABETH

St. Joachim and Anne - 101 McLay Dr., Elizabeth, PA 15037 t) 412-751-0663 www.joachimandannediopitt.org/ Rev. Miroslaus A. Wojcicki, Par. Vicar; Dcn. Dale J. DiSanto; Dcn. Jeffrey P. Formica; Dcn. Stephen C. Pikula; Dcn. John E. Ragan; Rev. Thomas A. Wagner, Pst.; CRP Stds.: 195

EMSWORTH

Sacred Heart - Merged Jul 2022 Merged with Assumption of the Blessed Virgin Mary, Bellevue & St. John Neumann, Franklin Park to form Regina Coeli Parish.

FENELTON

St. John the Evangelist - 668 Clearfield Rd., Fenelton, PA 16034 t) 724-287-7590; 724-287-0426 (CRP) stjohnchurch@zoominternet.net; stjohnccd@zoominternet.net stsjjmcatholic.org Rev. Ward Stakem, O.F.M.Cap., Pst.; Rev. James Kurtz, O.F.M.Cap., Par. Vicar; Laura Eakman, DRE;

GLENSHAW

Our Lady of Perpetual Help - 2510 Middle Rd., Glenshaw, PA 15116 t) 412-486-4100 rectory@olphpgh.org olphpgh.org Rev. Timothy F. Whalen, Pst.; Rev. John E. Forbidussi, Par. Vicar; Rev. Ernest J. Strzelinski, Par. Vicar; Dcn. Stephen Cafaro; Dcn. Francis J. Dadowski Jr.; Dcn. Richard D. Ernst; CRP Stds.: 261

HOMESTEAD

St. Thomas the Apostle - 363 W. 11th Ave. Ext., Homestead, PA 15120 t) (412) 461-1054 www.thomastheapostle.net/ Rev. E. Daniel Sweeney, Pst.; Dcn. Ronald D. Demblowski; Rev. Stan M. Gregorek, In Res.; Rev. Nicholas Mastrangelo, In Res.; Dcn. Daniel D'Antonio; CRP Stds.: 181

Sisters of the Holy Spirit - 635 St. Agnes Ln., West Mifflin, PA 15122 t) 412-466-3554 stagnes11@verizon.net

IMPERIAL

St. Isidore the Farmer - 103 Church Rd., Imperial, PA 15126 t) 724-695-7325 parish@stisidorethefarmer.org stisidorethefarmer.org Rev. Harry R. Bielewicz, Pst.; Rev. Zachary A. Galiyas, Par. Vicar; CRP Stds.: 366

JEFFERSON HILLS

Triumph of the Holy Cross - 139 Gill Hall Rd., Jefferson Hills, PA 15025 t) (412) 755-2046 parish@triumphoftheholycrosspgh.org www.triumphoftheholycrosspgh.org/ Rev. Paul J Zywan, Pst.; Rev. Patrick C. Barkey, Par. Vicar; Rev. William R. Terza, Par. Vicar; Rev. Joseph G. Luisi, Chap.; Dcn. Brian Kail; CRP Stds.: 519

MCKEES ROCKS

Archangel Gabriel - 5718 Steubenville Pike, McKees Rocks, PA 15136 t) 412-787-2140 info@archangelgabrielparish.org archangelgabrielparish.org Rev. Alan E. Morris, Admin.; Rev. Joseph Codori, Par. Vicar; Rev. Yohana Shija Masalu (Tanzania), In Res.; Rev. Constantine Mlelwa, OSA (Tanzania), In Res.; Rev. Regis J. Ryan, In Res.; Rev. Louis F. Vallone, In Res.; Dcn. Timothy Killmeyer; CRP Stds.: 268

MCMURRAY

St. John XXIII - 120 Abington Dr., McMurray, PA 15317 t) 724-941-9406 sallyt@john23.org www.john23.org/ Dcn. Kevin Lewis; Rev. Robert M. Miller, Pst.; Rev. Pierre M. Falkenhan, Par. Vicar; Dcn. Victor P. Satter; Rev. David Green, Chap.; CRP Stds.: 779

MIDLAND

St. Blaise - 772 Ohio Ave., Midland, PA 15059 t) 724-643-4050 office@saintaugustineparish.com www.saintaugustineparish.com Rev. Kim J. Schreck, Pst.; CRP Stds.: 39

MONROEVILLE

Christ the Divine Shepherd - 245 Azalea Dr., Monroeville, PA 15146 t) 412-373-0050 parishoffice@cdsmph.org www.christthedivineshepherd.org/ Rev. Michael P. Conway, Pst.; Rev. Jeremy J. Mohler, Par. Vicar; Dcn. Michael W. Kelly; Rev. Frederick Gruber, Chap.; Rev. Thomas R. Miller, Par. Vicar; CRP Stds.: 179

MOON TOWNSHIP

Most Sacred Heart of Jesus - One Parish Pl., Moon Township, PA 15108-2697 t) 412-264-2573 parish@mshj.org www.mshj.org Rev. Francis M. Kurimsky, Pst.; Rev. Mingwei Li, Par. Vicar; Rev. Robert L. Seeman, Par. Vicar; Rev. Drew P. Morgan, C.O., In Res.; Dcn. Robert A. Jancart; CRP Stds.: 444

NATRONA HEIGHTS

Guardian Angels - 1526 Union Ave., Natrona Heights, PA 15065 t) (724) 226-4900 office@guardianangelspgh.org www.guardianangelspgh.org/ Rev. Andrew Fischer, Par. Vicar; Dcn. Patrick G. Wood; Rev. John D. Brennan, In Res.; Rev. John B. Lendvai, Pst.; CRP Stds.: 216

St. Joseph High School - 800 Montana Ave., Natrona Heights, PA 15065 t) 724-224-5552 admissions@saintjosephhs.com Kimberly Minick, Prin.; Beverly K. Kaniecki, Pres.;

NEW CASTLE

Holy Spirit - 910 S. Mercer St., New Castle, PA 16101 t) 724-652-3422 jbook@hsplc.org holyspiritparishoflawrencecounty.org/ Rev. Benjamin Barr, Par. Vicar; Rev. Aaron J. Kriss, Par. Vicar; Rev. Joseph R. McCaffrey, Pst.; Dcn. John J. Carran; CRP Stds.: 644

PITTSBURGH

St. Paul Cathedral - 108 N. Dithridge St., Pittsburgh, PA 15213 t) 412-621-4951 info@saintpaulcathedral.org ghocatholics.org Rev. Steven M. Palsa, Chap.; Rev. Daniel L. Walsh, C.S.Sp., Par. Vicar; Dcn. Thomas J. Berna; Rev. Kris D. Stubna, Admin.; CRP Stds.: 36

Assumption of the Blessed Virgin Mary on the Beautiful

River - Merged Jul 2022 Merged with Sacred Heart, Emsworth & St. John Neumann, Franklin Park to form Regina Coeli Parish.

St. Benedict the Moor Parish - 91 Crawford St., Pittsburgh, PA 15219 t) 412-281-3141 office@sbtmparishpgh.com www.sbtmparishpgh.com/ Rev. Thomas J. Burke, Pst.; Rev. C. Matthew Hawkins, Par. Vicar; Rev. David H. Taylor, Par. Vicar;

Blessed Trinity - 3198 Schieck St., Pittsburgh, PA 15227 t) 412-884-7744 office@blessedtrinitypgh.net www.blessedtrinitypgh.org Rev. Stephen Kresak, Pst.; Rev. Robert J. Ahlin, Par. Vicar; Rev. Levi Hartle, Par. Vicar; Rev. Kenneth A. Sparks, Par. Vicar; Dcn. Michael J. Babcock; Dcn. James R. Grab; Dcn. Daniel E. Nizan; Dcn. Andrew J. White Sr.; Dcn. Timothy B. Zenchak; CRP Stds.: 320

St. Catherine Laboure - 320 McMurray Rd., Pittsburgh, PA 15241 t) 412-833-1010 stl@stlouisedemarillac.org www.sclpgh.org Rev. Daniel J. Maurer, Pst.; Rev. Jon Brzek, Par. Vicar; Dcn. Richard R. Cessar; Dcn. William F. Strathmann Jr.; CRP Stds.: 554

Christ Our Savior - 3854 Brighton Rd., Pittsburgh, PA 15212-1696 t) 412-761-1552 office@cospgh.org www.christoursaviorpgh.org Rev. Nicholas S. Vaskov, Pst.; Rev. Dam D. Nguyen, Par. Vicar; Dcn. Gery G. Pielin; Rev. Louis L. DeNinno, In Res.; Very Rev. Lawrence A. DiNardo, In Res.; CRP Stds.: 60

Christ the King - 342 Dorseyville Rd., Pittsburgh, PA 15215 t) 412-963-8885 christthekingpgh.org Rev. William P. Siple, Par. Vicar; Dcn. Robert F. Wertz Jr.; Rev. Dale E. DeNinno, Pst.; CRP Stds.: 331

Divine Mercy - 164 Washington Pl., Pittsburgh, PA 15219 t) 412-471-0257 office@divinemercypgh.org www.divinemercypgh.org Rev. Christopher D. Donley, Admin.;

Holy Family - 444 St. John St., Pittsburgh, PA 15239 t) 412-793-4511 office@holyfamilypgh.org www.holyfamilypgh.org/ Dcn. Eric Collier; Dcn. Timothy F. Noca; Dcn. Joseph R. Vannucci; Rev. Kevin G. Poecking, Pst.; Rev. George R. Dalton, Par. Vicar; Rev. David D. DeWitt, Par. Vicar; Dcn. Frank Bursic; CRP Stds.: 315

Immaculate Heart of Mary - 3058 Brereton St., Pittsburgh, PA 15219 t) 412-621-5170 recihm@verizon.net www.pghshrines.org/immaculate-heart-of-mary Rev. James R. Orr, Par. Vicar; Rev. Michael R. Ruffalo, Par. Vicar; Dcn. G. Gregory Jelinek; Rev. Nicholas S. Vaskov, Dir.;

St. John Neumann - Merged Jul 2022 Merged with Assumption of the Blessed Virgin Mary, Bellevue & Sacred Heart, Emsworth to form Regina Coeli Parish.

St. Joseph the Worker - 2001 Ardmore Blvd., Pittsburgh, PA 15221 t) (412) 271-0809 falmade@diopitt.org www.sjwpitt.org Rev. Cassian Edwards, Par. Vicar; Rev. Kenneth E. Kezmarsky, Par. Vicar; Dcn. Joseph M. Dougherty; Dcn. Jeff McLaughlin; Rev. Martin F. Barkin, Par. Vicar; Dcn. Keith G. Kondrich; Dcn. Herbert E. Riley Jr.; Rev. Frank D. Almade, Pst.; CRP Stds.: 78

St. Jude - 310 Shady Ave., Pittsburgh, PA 15206 t) 412-661-0187 infosh@saintjudepgh.org saintjudepgh.org Saint Jude Parish is the new parish from the merger of Sacred Heart Parish and Saint Raphael Parish. These 2 ceased to exit on January 4, 2021. Rev. Brendan H. Dawson, Pst.; Rev. Steven M. Palsa, Parish Chaplain; Rev. John P. Sweeney, Senior Parochial Vicar; Dcn. John A. Vaskov; Dcn. William O. Hahn; CRP Stds.: 45

St. Maria Goretti Parish - 4712 Liberty Ave., Pittsburgh, PA 15224 t) 412-682-2354 parish.secretary.smg@gmail.com www.olasmg.org Dcn. Blaine Carnprobst; Rev. Nicholas J. Argentieri, Chap.; Rev. Douglas A. Boyd, Chap.; Rev. Thomas Gramc, Admin.; Rev. Jonathan Ulrick, OFM Cap., Par. Vicar; Dcn. Richard T. Fitzpatrick; Rev. Pierre G. Sodini, In Res.; CRP Stds.: 24

St. Mary Magdalene - 509 S. Dallas Ave., Pittsburgh, PA 15208 t) 412-661-7222 parishoffice@stmarymagpgh.org www.saintmarymagdalenepgh.org/ Rev. C. Matthew Hawkins, Par. Vicar; Rev. Thomas J. Burke, Pst.; Rev. David H. Taylor, Par. Vicar; Rev. James Adeoye, In Res.; Rev. Augustine Temu, In Res.; CRP Stds.: 137

Mary, Queen of Peace - 81 S. 13th St., Pittsburgh, PA 15203 t) 412-381-0212 parish@maryqueenofpeacepgh.org www.@maryqueenofpeacepgh.org Dcn. Bob McMullen; Dcn. Frank J. Szemanski; Rev. Michael J. Stumpf, Pst.; CRP Stds.: 65

St. Matthew - 3616 Mt. Troy Rd., Pittsburgh, PA 15212 t) (412) 821-2351 parish@saintmatthewpgh.org saintmatthewpgh.org Rev. James K. Mazurek, Par. Vicar; Rev. Miroslaw Stelmaszczyk, Par. Vicar; Dcn. Stephen J. Byers; Dcn. Stephen J. Kisak; Rev. James R. Gretz, Pst.; Dcn. Charles H. Rhoads; CRP Stds.: 350

St. Michael the Archangel - 311 Washington Rd., Pittsburgh, PA 15216 t) (412) 561-3300 www.smapgh.org Rev. Brian J. Welding, Pst.; Rev. Anthony R. Sciarappa, Par. Vicar; Dcn. John Mayer; Dcn. Eric Schorr; Dcn. Frederick N. Eckhardt; CRP Stds.: 608

Most Holy Name of Jesus - 1700 Harpster St., Pittsburgh, PA 15212 t) 412-231-2994 mostholyname@hotmail.com www.pghshrines.org/about-holy-name Rev. Nicholas S. Vaskov, Moderator; Dcn. G. Gregory Jelinek; Rev. James R. Orr, Dir.; Rev. Michael R. Ruffalo, Dir.; CRP Stds.: 76

St. Anthony's Chapel - 1704 Harpster St., Pittsburgh, PA 15212 www.pghshrines.org/about-st-anthony-chapel

Most Precious Blood of Jesus - 3250 California Ave., Pittsburgh, PA 15212 t) 412-761-1508 office@mpboj.com www.mostpreciousbloodparish.org Rev. William Avis, Pst.; Rev. Canon Ross Bourgeois, Par. Vicar; CRP Stds.: 161

St. Nicholas - 24 Maryland Ave., Pittsburgh, PA 15209-2738 t) 412-821-8726 mostholyname@gmail.com www.pghshrines.org/st-nicholas Rev. James R. Orr, Par. Vicar; Rev. Michael R. Ruffalo, Par. Vicar; Dcn. G. Gregory Jelinek; Rev. Nicholas Vaskov, Admin.;

Our Lady of the Angels - 225 37th St., Pittsburgh, PA 15201 t) 412-682-0929 parish@oloa.org www.olasmg.org Dcn. Blaine Carnprobst; Rev. Nicholas J. Argentieri, Chap.; Rev. Douglas A. Boyd, Chap.; Rev. Pierre G. Sodini, Chap.; Rev. Thomas Gramc, Admin.; Rev. Jonathan Ulrick, OFM Cap., Par. Vicar; Dcn. Richard T. Fitzpatrick; Bro. David Cira, O.F.M.Cap., In Res.; Rev. Richard J. Zelik, O.F.M.Cap., In Res.; Rev. Marino Msigala, OFM Cap. (Tanzania), Chap.; CRP Stds.: 24

St. Patrick-St. Stanislaus Kostka - 57 21st St., Pittsburgh, PA 15222 t) 412-471-4767 saintsinthestrip@comcast.net www.pghshrines.org/st-stanislaus Rev. James R. Orr, Par. Vicar; Rev. Michael R. Ruffalo, Par. Vicar; Dcn. G. Gregory Jelinek; Rev. Nicholas S. Vaskov, Admin.; CRP Stds.: 8

St. Paul of the Cross - 400 Hoodridge Dr., Pittsburgh, PA 15234 t) 412-531-5964 stpaulofthecross.com Rev. Michael A. Caridi, Pst.; Rev. Richard A. Infante, Par. Vicar; Dcn. Philip D. Martorano; Dcn. Victor P. DeFazio; Dcn. Joseph J. Kosko Jr.; CRP Stds.: 171

St. Philip - 50 W. Crafton Ave., Pittsburgh, PA 15205; Mailing: Administrative Offices, 114 Berry St., Pittsburgh, PA 15205 t) 412-922-6300 parishoffice@saintphilipchurch.org www.saintphilipchurch.org Rev. James R. Torquato, Pst.; Rev. Larry Adams, In Res.; Rev. Joseph Charles Scheib, In Res.; CRP Stds.: 83

Ascension Worship Site - 114 Berry St., PIttsburgh, PA 15205 parishofficecrafton@gmail.com Rev. John B. Gizler III, Admin.;

Regina Coeli - 45 N. Sprague Ave., Pittsburgh, PA 15202 t) (412) 766-6660 reginacoeliparish.org/ Rev. Timothy X. Deely, Pst.; Rev. Jeffrey Craig, Par. Vicar; Rev. David C. Schmidt, Par. Vicar; Dcn. Richard J. Caruso; Dcn. William R. Palamara Jr.;

Resurrection - 126 Fort Couch Rd., Pittsburgh, PA 15241 t) 412-833-0031 parishoffice@resurrectionpgh.org resurrectionpgh.org Dcn. Joseph Kralik; Dcn. Russell White; Rev. James J. Chepponis, Par. Vicar; Dcn. William G. Batz; Dcn. Lawrence R. Sutton; Most Rev. Mark A. Eckman, In Res.; Rev. Michael R. Ackerman, Pst.; CRP Stds.: 480

Our Lady of Mount Carmel - 800 Avila Ct., Pittsburgh, PA 15237 t) (412) 367-9001 jrushofsky@mountcarmelpgh.org www.mountcarmelpgh.org Rev. Jack Demnyan, Par. Vicar; Rev. Robert J. Miller, Par. Vicar; Dcn. David R. Witter Sr.; Dcn. Clifford M. Homer Sr., Pst. Assoc.; Rev. John R. Rushofsky, Pst.; Rev. Michael J Maranowski, Chap.; Dcn. Gary L. Comer; Dcn. Robert E. Koslosky, DRE; CRP Stds.: 494

Convent - 900 Avila Ct., Pittsburgh, PA 15237 t) 412-367-9001 x544

St. Teresa of Kolkata - 1810 Belasco Ave., Pittsburgh, PA 15216 t) 412-531-2135 stk15216@gmail.com stteresakolkatapgh.org Rev. James M. Bachner, Pst.; Rev. Fernando Torres, L.C., Par. Vicar; Dcn. Mark S. Bibro; Dcn. Richard A. Longo; Dcn. Thomas O'Neill; Dcn. Scott Potter; CRP Stds.: 182

SEWICKLEY

Divine Redeemer - 200 Walnut St., Sewickley, PA 15143 t) 412-741-6650 office@divine-redeemer.com www.divine-redeemer.org Dcn. Jason Corsetti; Dcn. Stephen M. Deskevich; Dcn. Thomas A. Lopus; Rev. Joseph M. Mele, In Res.; Rev. Brian W. Noel, Pst.; Rev. David J. Jastrab, In Res.; CRP Stds.: 171

Saint Luke the Evangelist - 2586 Wexford Bayne Rd., Sewickley, PA 15143 t) (724) 935-2104 www.saintluke.net Formerly Saints John and Paul. Rev. John F. Donahue III, Pst.; Rev. John J. Batykefer, Par. Vicar; Rev. Michael J. Roche, Par. Vicar; Rev. Joseph A. Carr, Chap.; Dcn. Tom Boucek; Dcn. Anthony J. Giordano; Dcn. James R. Olson; CRP Stds.: 1,017

SLIPPERY ROCK

St. Faustina - 342 Normal Ave., Slippery Rock, PA 16057 t) 724-794-2880 www.stfaustinaparish.org/ Rev. Sean M. Francis, Par. Vicar; Dcn. Edwin P. Christmann; Rev. Adam M. Verona, Pst.; CRP Stds.: 166

WASHINGTON

St. Hilary - 320 Henderson Ave., Washington, PA 15301 t) 724-222-4087 sthilaryparish.org Rev. Michael John Lynam, Pst.; Rev. Michael R. Peck, Par. Vicar; Rev. Thomas J. Lewandowski, Campus Min.;

St. James - 119 W. Chestnut St., Washington, PA 15301 t) 724-225-1425 office@stjameswashpa.org stjameswashpa.org Rev. Edward L. Yuhas, Pst.; Rev. Michael A. Zavage, Par. Vicar; Dcn. Michael Gatto; Dcn. Thomas W. Raymond; Rev. Donald Chortos, In Res.; Rev. Thomas J. Lewandowski, Par. Vicar; Rev. Michael R. Peck, Par. Vicar; Dcn. Jeffrey A. Hirst; Rev. George F. Chortos, In Res.; Friar Andrew Siasa, ALCP/OSS, In Res.; Dcn. Barry A. Krofcheck; CRP Stds.: 189

WAYNESBURG

St. Matthias - 232 E. High St., Waynesburg, PA 15370 t) 724-627-7568 saintannchurch@comcast.net www.stmatthiasgreene.org Rev. James B. Farnan, Pst.; Rev. J. Francis Frazer, Par. Vicar; Dcn. Elbert A. Kuhns; Dcn. James M. Sheil; CRP Stds.: 151

WEXFORD

St. Aidan - 10090 Old Perry Hwy., Wexford, PA 15090 t) 724-935-4343 parish@saintaidanparish.org saintaidanparish.org Rev. John L. McKenna, Par. Vicar; Dcn. David McLaughlin; Dcn. Brett Schurter; Dcn. Albert E. Heiles Jr.; Rev. Daniel Waruszewski, Par. Vicar; Rev. William D. Wuenschel, Pst.; CRP Stds.: 361

WHITE OAK

Mary, Mother of God - 1640 Fawcett Ave., White Oak, PA 15131 t) 412-672-9641 secretary@marymotherofgod1.org www.marymotherofgod1.org Rev. Adam C. Potter, Par. Vicar; Rev. Terrence P. O'Connor, Pst.; Dcn. Reynold Wilmer; Rev. Joseph C. Beck, Chap.; CRP Stds.: 118

ZELIENOPLE

St. Gregory - Merged Jul 2022 Merged with Holy Redeemer, Ellwood/Koppel/Wampum and Saint

Ferdinand, Cranberry Township to form Divine Grace Parish.

SCHOOLS: PRESCHOOL THRU HIGH SCHOOL

SCHOOLS

COMMONWEALTH OF PENNSYLVANIA

ALLISON PARK

Providence Heights Alpha School (Sisters of Divine Providence) - (PRV) (Grades PreK-8) 9000 Babcock Blvd., Allison Park, PA 15101 t) 412-366-4455 mruefle@alphaschool.org www.alphaschool.org Margaret Ruefle, Prin.; Stds.: 132; Scholastics: 20; Lay Tchrs.: 15

BUTLER

Butler Catholic School - (PAR) (Grades PreK-8) 515 E. Locust St., Butler, PA 16001 t) 724-285-4276 bcsoffice@butlercatholic.org www.butlercatholic.org Serving All Saints Parish of Butler, Pennsylvania Sr. John Ann Mulhern, C.D.P., Prin.; Stds.: 236; Lay Tchrs.: 17

PITTSBURGH

St. Benedict The Moor School - 631 Watt St., Pittsburgh, PA 15219 t) (412) 682-3755 www.extramilefdn.org/st_benedict.php Rosanne Kwiatkowski, Prin.;

The Campus School of Carlow University (Sisters of Mercy) - (PRV) (Grades PreSchool-8) 3333 5th Ave., Pittsburgh, PA 15213 t) 412-578-6158 www.campusschool.carlow.edu Keely Baronak, Exec. Dir.;

North Hills Regional Catholic Elementary Schools, Inc. - (DIO) (Grades PreK-8) 800 Avila Ct., Pittsburgh, PA 15237 t) 412-837-1056 www.nhrces.org Michael C Killmeyer, Admin.; Stds.: 980

Christ the Divine Teacher Catholic Academy - (Grades PreK-8) 205 Brilliant Ave., Pittsburgh, PA 15215 t) 412-781-7927 office@cdtca.org (Aspinwall), (Regional). Part of North Hills Regional Catholic Elementary Schools, Inc Mark Grgurich, Prin.; Kathy Goreczny, Librn.;

Blessed Francis Seelos Academy - (Grades PreK-8) 201 Church Rd., Wexford, PA 15090

Blessed Francis Seelos Academy Early Childhood Center - (Grades PreK-8) 10090 Old Perry Hwy., Wexford, PA 15090

Blessed Trinity Academy - (Grades PreK-8) 2510 Middle Rd., Glenshaw, PA 15116 t) 412-486-7611

Holy Cross Academy - (Grades PreK-8) 307 Siebert Rd., Pittsburgh, PA 15237

Saint James School (Sewickley) - (Grades PreK-8) 201 Broad St., Sewickley, PA 15143 t) 412-741-5540 bswiger@stjamesschool.us Dr. Bradley Swiger, Prin.;

Northside Catholic Assumption Academy - (DIO) (Grades PreSchool-8) 3854 Brighton Rd., Pittsburgh, PA 15212 t) (412) 761-5043 www.extramilefdn.org/northside_academy.php Rosanne Kwiatkowski, Prin.;

Pittsburgh East Regional Catholic Elementary Schools - 201 Penn Center Blvd., Ste. 400, Pittsburgh, PA 15235 t) (412) 752-7214 Jonathan Cuniak, Supt.; Stds.: 1,366

Divine Mercy Academy - 245 Azalea Dr., Monroeville, PA 15146 t) (412) 372-7255 dmapgh.org/ Nikole Laubham, Prin.;

Mary of Nazareth Catholic School - 1640 Fawcett St., White Oak, PA 15131 t) (412) 672-2360 www.maryofnazarethschool.org/ Beau Quattrone, Prin.;

Saint Bede School - 6920 Edgerton Ave., Pittsburgh, PA 15208 t) (412) 661-9425 www.saintbedeschool.com/ Sr. Daniela Bronka, Prin.;

Holy Family Catholic School - 418 Unity Center Rd., Pittsburgh, PA 15239 t) (412) 793-4580 holyfamilycatholic.net/ Marie DiLonardo, Prin.;

Sacred Heart Elementary School - 325 Emerson St., Pittsburgh, PA 15206 t) (412) 441-1582 Erin Mascaro, Prin.;

Saint Therese of Lisieux School - 3 Saint Therese Ct., Munhall, PA 15120 t) (412) 462-8162 sttheresesschoolmunhall.org Lynda McFarland, Prin.;

Saint Irenaeus Pre-School - 637 Fourth St., Oakmont, PA 15139 t) (412) 793-4580 Jeanne Loebig, Dir.;

Sister Thea Bowman Catholic Academy - (DIO) (Grades PreK-8) 721 Rebecca Ave., Pittsburgh, PA 15221 t) 412-242-3515 office@stbca.net www.extramilefdn.org/sr_bowman.php David Barr, Prin.;

South Regional Catholic Elementary Schools - (DIO) (Grades PreSchool-8) 401 Washington Rd, Pittsburgh, PA 15216 t) (412) 569-8603 sharon@srcespgh.org srcespgh.org Sharon Loughran Brown, Supt.; Carlos Leyva, Bus. Mgr.; Stds.: 2,178; Lay Tchrs.: 70

Archangel Gabriel Catholic School - (Grades PreSchool-8) 5720 Steubenville Pike, McKees Rocks, PA 15136 t) (412) 787-2656 archangelgabrielpgh.org/ Dr. Bradley Swiger, Prin.;

Madonna Catholic Regional School - (Grades PreSchool-8) 731 Chess St., Monongahela, PA 15063 t) (724) 258-3199 www.madonnacatholic.com/ Kathryn Miller, Prin.;

Mother of Mercy Academy - (Grades PreSchool-8) 5200 Greenridge Dr., Pittsburgh, PA 15236 t) (412) 882-3353 www.motherofmercyacademy.org/ Donald Militzer, Prin.;

Saint Louise de Marillac Catholic School - (Grades PreSchool-8) 310 McMurray Rd., Upper Saint Clair, PA 15241 t) (412) 835-0600 stlouiseschoolpa.org/

Guardian Angel Academy - (Grades PreSchool-8) 915 Alice St., Pittsburgh, PA 15220 t) (412) 922-4765 www.guardianangelacademy.org/

Ave Maria Academy - (Grades PreSchool-8) 134 Fort Couch Rd., Pittsburgh, PA 15241 t) (412) 833-1412 avemariapgh.org Leslie Krueger, Prin.; Lynne Lynch, Prin.;

John F. Kennedy Catholic School - (Grades PreSchool-8) 111 W. Spruce St., Washington, PA 15301 t) (724) 225-1680 www.jfkcatholic.com/

HIGH SCHOOLS

COMMONWEALTH OF PENNSYLVANIA

CORAOPOLIS

Our Lady of the Sacred Heart High School - (PRV) (Grades 9-12) 1504 Woodcrest Ave., Coraopolis, PA 15108 t) 412-264-5140 info@olsh.org; cneubert@olsh.org www.olsh.org Tim Plocinik, Prin.; Bethany Cvitkovic, Librn.;

CRANBERRY TOWNSHIP

North Catholic High School - (DIO) 1617 Rte. 228, Cranberry Township, PA 16066 t) 412-321-4823 www.northcatholic.org/ Joseph Wilson, Pres.;

MCKEESPORT

Serra Catholic High School, Inc. - (DIO) 200 Hershey Dr., McKeesport, PA 15132 t) 412-751-2020 73781@diopitt.org www.serrahs.com Timothy Chirdon, Pres.;

NATRONA HEIGHTS

Saint Joseph High School, Inc. - 800 Montana Ave., Natrona Heights, PA 15065 t) 724-224-5552 bkaniecki@saintjosephhs.com; kminick@saintjosephhs.com www.saintjosephhs.com Kimberly Minnick, Prin.; Beverly K. Kaniecki, Pres.; Stds.: 130; Lay Tchrs.: 14

PITTSBURGH

Bishop Canevin High School, Inc. - (DIO) 2700 Morange Rd., Pittsburgh, PA 15205 t) 412-922-7400 mainoffice@bishopcanevin.org www.bishopcanevin.org Michael Joyce, Prin.;

Central Catholic High School, Inc. - (DIO) (Grades 9-12) 4720 Fifth Ave., Pittsburgh, PA 15213 t) 412-208-3400 (Main); 412-208-3421 www.centralcatholichs.com Bro. Michael Andrejko, FSC, Prin.; Stds.: 740; Bro. Tchrs.: 4; Lay Tchrs.: 59

***Nazareth Prep** - (PRV) (Grades 9-12) 8235 Ohio River Blvd., Pittsburgh, PA 15202 t) 412-307-0230 www.nazarethprep.org Nazareth Prep is an independent Catholic high school that provides an affordable, innovative education focused on college and career readiness. Sr. Linda Yankoski, CSFN, Pres.; Stds.: 137; Lay Tchrs.: 14

Oakland Catholic High School, Inc. - (DIO) 144 N. Craig St., Pittsburgh, PA 15213 t) 412-682-6633 webmaster@oaklandcath.org www.oaklandcatholic.org Marisa Greco, Prin.; Nicole Modarelli, Prin.; Sharyn Zalno, Prin.; Mary Claire Kasunic, Pres.;

Seton-LaSalle Catholic High School, Inc. - (DIO) (Grades 9-12) 1000 McNeilly Rd., Pittsburgh, PA 15226 t) 412-561-3583 martinl@slshs.org; osterhausl@slshs.org slshs.org Lauren Martin, Prin.; Lisa Osterhaus, Pres.;

INSTITUTIONS LOCATED IN DIOCESE

ASSOCIATIONS [ASN]

PITTSBURGH

The Catholic Cemeteries Association of the Diocese of Pittsburgh - 718 Hazelwood Ave., Pittsburgh, PA 15217-2807 t) 412-521-9133 cca@ccapgh.org www.ccapgh.org

All Saints Catholic Cemetery & Mausoleum (Braddock Catholic) - 1560 Brinton Rd., Pittsburgh, PA 15221-4899 t) 412-271-5950

Calvary Catholic Cemetery & Mausoleum -

Christ Our Redeemer Catholic Cemetery & Mausoleum (North Side Catholic) - 204 Cemetery Ln., Pittsburgh, PA 15237-2722 t) 412-931-2206 formerly North Side Catholic Cemetery and Mausoleum

Good Shepherd Catholic Cemetery & Mausoleum - 733 Patton St., Monroeville, PA 15146-4530 t) 412-824-0355

Holy Savior Catholic Cemetery - 4629 Bakerstown Rd., Gibsonia, PA 15044-8993 t) 724-625-3822

Holy Souls Catholic Cemetery - c/o Resurrection Cemetery, 100 Resurrection Rd., Moon Twp, PA 15108-7759 t) 724-695-2999 Michael Sinnott, Dir.;

Saint Joseph Catholic Cemetery & Mausoleum - 1443 Lincoln Hwy., North Versailles, PA 15137-2448 t) 412-823-9111

St. Mary Catholic Cemetery - c/o Calvary Cemetery, 718 Hazelwood Ave., Pittsburgh, PA 15217-2807 t) 412-421-9959

Mount Carmel Catholic Cemetery & Mausoleum - 7601 Mt. Carmel Rd., Verona, PA 15147-1518 t) 412-241-1260

Our Lady of Hope Catholic Cemetery & Mausoleum - 1898 Bakerstown Rd., Tarentum, PA 15084-3213 t) 724-224-2785

Queen of Heaven Catholic Cemetery & Mausoleum - 2900 Washington Rd., McMurray, PA 15317-3278 t) 724-941-7601

Resurrection Catholic Cemetery & Mausoleum - 100 Resurrection Rd., Moon Township, PA 15108-7759 t) 724-695-2999

Sacred Heart Catholic Cemetery and Mausoleum - 97 Sacred Heart Rd., Monongahela, PA 15063-9605 t) 724-258-2885

St. Stanislaus Catholic Cemetery & Mausoleum & St. Anthony Catholic Cemetery - 700 Soose Rd., Pittsburgh, PA 15209-1544 t) 412-821-4324 Michael Sinnott, Dir.;

Catholic Parish Cemeteries Association - 1000 Logue St., Pittsburgh, PA 15220 t) 412-680-0495 linn@cpca-pgh.org

Epiphany Association - 820 Crane Ave., Pittsburgh, PA 15216-3050 t) 412-341-7494 samuto.epiphanyassociation@gmail.com

www.epiphanyassociation.org/ Susan Muto, Dean;
***The Association of Ladies of Charity, Diocese of Pittsburgh** - 2900 Noblestown Rd., Pittsburgh, PA 15205

CAMPUS MINISTRY / NEWMAN CENTERS [CAM]

CRAFTON

Office for Campus Ministry - 2900 Noblestown Rd., Crafton, PA 15205 t) 412-456-3140 jwilliamson@diopitt.org Jacob Williamson, Director, Youth and Young Adult Ministry;

Art Institute of Pittsburgh - St. Mary of Mercy, Stanwix St., Pittsburgh, PA 15212-5296 t) 412-321-0711 Rev. Nicholas S. Vaskov;

California University (California) - 250 University Ave., California, PA 15419 t) 724-938-3204 Rev. Michael A. Zavage, Dir.;

Carlow University - 3333 5th Ave., Pittsburgh, PA 15213 t) 412-578-6069

Carnegie-Mellon University - Pittsburgh Oratory Catholic Newman Center, 4450 Bayard St., Pittsburgh, PA 15213 t) 412-681-3181 info@pittsburghoratory.org Rev. Peter Gruber, C.O., Dir.; Rev. Reed Frey, C.O., Campus Min.; Rev. Thomas Skamai, C.O., Campus Min.;

Chatham College - Pittsburgh Oratory Catholic Newman Center, 4450 Bayard St., Pittsburgh, PA 15213 t) 412-681-3181 info@pittsburghoratory.org Rev. Peter Gruber, Dir.; Rev. Stephen Lowery, C.O., Campus Min.; Rev. Reed Frey, C.O., Campus Min.; Rev. Thomas Skamai, C.O., Campus Min.;

Duquesne University - Campus Ministry, Pittsburgh, PA 15282 t) 412-396-6020 walshd@duq.edu Rev. Daniel L. Walsh, C.S.Sp.; Linda Donovan, Campus Min.; Debbie Kostosky, Campus Min.; Katherine Lecci, Campus Min.;

Geneva College - Campus Ministry, 289 Ridge Rd., New Brighton, PA 15066 t) 724-846-5978 Rev. Kim J. Schreck, Dir.;

La Roche College - 9000 Babcock Blvd., Pittsburgh, PA 15237 t) 412-536-1050

Pennsylvania State University, Beaver Campus - Office of Student Life, 6001 University Blvd., Moon Township, PA 15108 t) 724-773-3839 gslifkey@diopitt.org Gary M. Slifkey, Dir.;

Point Park College - St. Mary of Mercy Church, 202 Stanwix St., Pittsburgh, PA 15222 t) 412-261-0110 nvaskov@diopitt.org Rev. Nicholas S. Vaskov;

Robert Morris College, Moon Township Campus -

Slippery Rock University, Newman Center (Slippery Rock) - 342 Normal Ave., Slippery Rock, PA 16057 t) 724-794-8459 campusministry@rockcatholic.org Diane Magliocca, Campus Min.; Rev. Robert L. Seeman, Dir.;

University of Pittsburgh - Pittsburgh Oratory Catholic Newman Center, 4450 Bayard St., Pittsburgh, PA 15213 t) 412-681-3181 info@pittsburghoratory.org Rev. Peter Gruber, Dir.; Rev. Stephen Lowery, C.O., Campus Min.; Rev. Reed Frey, C.O., Campus Min.; Rev. Thomas Skamai, C.O., Campus Min.;

Washington and Jefferson College (Washington) - 213 Fourth St., California, PA 15419 t) 724-938-3204 mzavage@diopitt.org Rev. Michael A. Zavage;

Waynesburg College (Waynesburg) - 213 Fourth St., California, PA 15419 t) 724-938-3204 mzavage@diopitt.org Rev. Michael A. Zavage;

Westminster College - 314 W. Englewood Ave., New Castle, PA 16105 t) 724-652-9471 frmrp@stcamillusparish.org Rev. Michael R. Peck;

PITTSBURGH

Office for Institutional Ministries - 2900 Noblestown Rd., Pittsburgh, PA 15205 t) 412-456-3060 ablai@diopitt.org Adam Blai, Dir.;

COLLEGES & UNIVERSITIES [COL]

PITTSBURGH

Carlow University - 3333 Fifth Ave., Pittsburgh, PA 15213 t) 412-578-6059 admission@carlow.edu www.carlow.edu Dr. Kathy W Humphrey, Pres.; Dr. Matthew Gordley, Dean, College of Arts and Sciences; Rhonda Maneval, Dean, Professor, College of Health and Wellness;

Duquesne University of the Holy Spirit - 600 Forbes Ave., Pittsburgh, PA 15282 t) 412-396-6000 walshd@duq.edu www.duq.edu Rev. William Cleary; Rev. Brian Cronin, C.S.Sp.; Rev. Jean-Michael Gelmetti, C.S.Sp.; Rev. Jocelyn Gregoire, C.S.Sp.; Rev. Sean Kealy, C.S.Sp.; Rev. James P. McCloskey, C.S.Sp.; Rev. George J. Spangenberg, C.S.Sp.; Rev. Peter I. Osuji, Campus Min.; Rev. John A. Sawicki, C.S.Sp., Treas.; Rev. Naos McCool, C.S.Sp., Dean; Rev. Gregory Olikenyi, C.S.Sp., Prof.; Rev. Eugene Uzukwu, C.S.Sp., Prof.; Rev. Jeffrey T. Duaime, C.S.Sp., Supr.; Rev. John Fogarty, Supr.; Ken Gormley, Pres.; Rev. Sean M. Hogan, C.S.Sp., Pres.; Rev. William H. Christy, C.S.Sp., Dir.; Rev. James C. Okoye, Dir.; Rev. Daniel L. Walsh, C.S.Sp., Dir.; Rev. Raymond D. French, C.S.Sp., Vice Pres. Mission & Identity;

College of Liberal Arts - t) 412-396-6389 James Swindal, Dean;

School of Business Administration - t) 412-396-6238 Dean B. McFarlin, Dean;

School of Education - t) 412-396-6093 Cindy M. Walker, Dean;

School of Health Sciences - t) 412-396-6652 Philip Reeder, Dean; Paula Sammahone Turocy, Dean; Sara Baron, Librn.; Timothy R. Austin, Provost & Academic Vice Pres.;

School of Law - t) 412-396-6300 Maureen Lally-Green, Dean;

School of Music - t) 412-396-6080 Seth Beckman, Dean;

School of Nursing - t) 412-396-6550 Mary Ellen Smith Glasgow, Dean;

School of Pharmacy - t) 412-396-6380 J. Douglas Bricker, Dean;

La Roche University - 9000 Babcock Blvd., Pittsburgh, PA 15237-5898 t) 412-367-9300 admissions@laroche.edu www.laroche.edu Sr. Candace Introcaso, C.D.P., Pres.; Howard Ishiyama, Provost, Sr. VP Academic Affairs & Academic Dean; Stds.: 1,143; Lay Tchrs.: 57; Scholastics: 134

CONVENTS, MONASTERIES, AND RESIDENCES FOR WOMEN [CON]

ALLISON PARK

Congregation of the Sisters of Divine Providence of Allegheny County - 9000 Babcock Blvd., Allison Park, PA 15101-2793 t) 412-931-5241 mbisbey@cdpsisters.org www.cdpsisters.org Motherhouse of the Sisters of Divine Providence in the Diocese (Pittsburgh); Novitiate of the Sisters of Divine Providence (Allison Park, PA). Sr. Michele Bisbey, C.D.P., Prov.; Srs.: 148

BADEN

Ladies of Bethany - 1018 W. State St., Baden, PA 15001 t) 729-869-6083 mimovodi@msn.com Sr. Monique Dietz, L.B., Pres.; Sr. Sharon Iacobucci, Delegate for Relg.;

Sisters of St. Joseph - 1020 State St., Baden, PA 15005 t) 724-869-2151 kzaffuto@stjoseph-baden.org www.stjoseph-baden.org St. Joseph Convent Motherhouse Sr. Sharon Costello, Moderator; Rev. Frank Mitolo, Chap.; Srs.: 110

BAKERSTOWN

St. Benedict Monastery - Benedictine Sisters of Pontifical Jurisdiction, 3526 Bakerstown Rd., Bakerstown, PA 15007-9705 t) 724-502-2600 osbpgh@osbpgh.org; osbarc469@gmail.com www.osbpgh.org Motherhouse and Novitiate of the Benedictine Sisters in the Diocese. Sr. Karen R. Brink, O.S.B., Prioress; Srs.: 35

BEAVER FALLS

Felician Sisters of North America, Inc. Congregation of the Sisters of St. Felix of Cantalice, Our Lady of Hope Province - 871 Mercer Rd., Beaver Falls, PA 15010-6815 t) 724-384-5300 sjudithmk@feliciansisters.org www.feliciansistersna.org Sr. Judith Marie Kubicki, Pres.; Srs.: 413

BETHEL PARK

Sisters of Charity of Seton Hill Generalate - 7005 Baptist Rd., Bethel Park, PA 15102 t) 412-832-1242 jacherubin@scsh.org; cblazina@scsh.org sistersofcharityofsetonhillgeneralate.org/ Sr. Jane Ann Cherubin, S.C., Supr.; Srs.: 305

CORAOPOLIS

Our Lady of the Sacred Heart Convent - 1500 Woodcrest Ave., Coraopolis, PA 15108 t) 412-264-2890 sjudithmk@feliciansisters.org www.feliciansistersna.org Home of the Felician Sisters of Pennsylvania C.S.S.F. Sr. Judith Marie Kubicki, Prov.; Srs.: 35

ELIZABETH

Divine Redeemer Motherhouse - 999 Rock Run Rd., Elizabeth, PA 15037-2613 t) 412-751-8600 sdrarusa@gmail.com www.divine-redeemer-sisters.org Motherhouse and Novitiate of the Sisters of the Divine Redeemer. Rev. Edwin J. Wichman, Chap.; Sr. M. Alojziana Spisakova, S.D.R., Supr.; Srs.: 10

GIBSONIA

Disciples of the Lord Jesus Christ - 10745 Babcock Blvd., Gibsonia, PA 15044 t) 806-534-2312 x118

PITTSBURGH

Our Lady of Sorrows Monastery of the Passionist Nuns - 2715 Churchview Ave., Pittsburgh, PA 15227 t) 412-881-1155 passionistnuns@gmail.com www.passionistnunspgh.org Mother Joyce Foga, Supr.; Srs.: 8

School Sisters of St. Francis United States Province - 4900 Perry Hwy., Ste. 201, Pittsburgh, PA 15229 t) 412-761-2855 administrationusa@schoolsistersosf.org schoolsistersosf.org Sr. Marian Sgriccia, OSF, Prov.; Srs.: 55

Sisters of Charity of Nazareth - 8200 McKnight Rd., Pittsburgh, PA 15237 t) 412-364-3000 spalding@scnfamily.org (formerly VSCs) Rev. David Moczulski, O.F.M.;

Sisters of Mercy of the Americas - New York, Pennsylvania, Pacific West Community - 3333 Fifth Ave., Pittsburgh, PA 15213 t) 412-578-6225 Sr. Pat Flynn, RSM, Rel. Ord. Ldr.; Srs.: 229

Sisters of Our Lady of Charity of the Good Shepherd Central South US Province - 4100 Vinceton St., Pittsburgh, PA 15214; Mailing: P.O. Box 340, Pittsburgh, PA 15214 t) 412-931-2299 cs.provincial@gssweb.org Sr. Sheila Rooney, Supr.;

Sisters of St. Francis of the Providence of God - 5802 Curry Rd., Pittsburgh, PA 15236 t) 412-882-9911 info@osfprov.org; sjgardner@osfprov.org www.osfprov.org Sr. Janet Gardner, O.S.F., Contact; Rev. Frederick L. Cain, Chap.; Srs.: 15

Sisters of the Holy Family of Nazareth, Holy Family Province USA Inc. - 105 Nazareth Way, Pittsburgh, PA 15229 c) (412) 216-0073 jbcsfn@hotmail.com www.nazarethcsfn.org Sr. Jance Blados, Contact;

Sisters of the Holy Spirit (S.H.S.) - 5246 Clarwin Ave., Pittsburgh, PA 15229-2208 t) 412-931-1917 www.sistersoftheholyspirit.com (Ross Township) Sr. Diane Smith, SHS, Supr.; Srs.: 22

VILLA MARIA

Sisters of the Humility of Mary, Inc. - 288 Villa Dr., Villa Maria, PA 16155; Mailing: P.O. Box 914, Villa Maria, PA 16155 t) 724-964-8861 treardon@humilityofmary.org; tperry@humilityofmary.org www.humilityofmary.org Sr. Carol Anne Smith, H.M., Supr.; Sr. Joanne Gardner, H.M., Archivist; Srs.: 102

WARRENDALE

Sisters of St. Francis of the Neumann Communities, Western Pennsylvania Region - Waters of Wexford, 210 Fowler Rd., Warrendale, PA 15086 t) 412-508-3012 bschaad@sosf.org Rev. Gervase Degenhardt, O.F.M. Cap., Chap.;

ENDOWMENTS / FOUNDATIONS / TRUSTS [EFT]

ALLISON PARK

Sisters of Divine Providence Charitable Trust - 9000 Babcock Blvd., Allison Park, PA 15101-2793

t) 412-635-5414 mbisbey@cdpsisters.org www.cdpsisters.org Sr. Michele Bisbey, C.D.P., Prov.;

BADEN

The City of God Foundation - 1020 State St., Baden, PA 15005 t) (724) 869-6542 eninehouser@stjoseph-baden.org Erin Ninehouser, Coordinator;

BEAVER FALLS

Felician Sisters of North America Endowment Trust - 871 Mercer Rd., Beaver Falls, PA 15010-6815 t) 724-384-5300 sjudithmk@feliciansisters.org Sr. Judith Marie Kubicki, Trustee;

Felician Sisters of North America Real Estate Trust - 871 Mercer Rd., Beaver Falls, PA 15010 t) 724-384-5300 sjudithmk@feliciansisters.org Sr. Judith Marie Kubicki, Trustee;

Felician Sisters of North America Retirement and Continuing Care Trust - 871 Mercer Rd., Beaver Falls, PA 15010 t) 724-384-5300 sjudithmk@feliciansisters.org Sr. Judith Marie Kubicki, Trustee;

BETHEL PARK

Spiritan Support Trust - 6320 Brush Run Rd., Bethel Park, PA 15102 t) 412-831-0302 usprovince@spiritans.org www.spiritans.org Rev. Jeffrey T. Duaime, C.S.Sp., Prov.;

ELIZABETH

Sisters of Divine Redeemer Charitable Trust - 999 Rock Run Rd., Elizabeth, PA 15037-2613 t) 412-751-8600 info@divine-redeemer-sisters.org www.divine-redeemer-sisters.org

MCKEESPORT

Pauline Auberle Foundation - 1101 Hartman St., McKeesport, PA 15132-1500 t) 412-673-5800 johnly@auberle.org www.auberle.org John Patrick Lydon, CEO; Nichole Williams, Contact;

PITTSBURGH

Catholic Benefits Trust - 2900 Noblestown Rd., Pittsburgh, PA 15205 t) 412-456-3149 dstewart@catholicbenefitstrust.org David S. Stewart, CEO;

Catholic Diocese of Pittsburgh Foundation (Sharing In Faith (Tm) Our Catholic Legacy Foundation) - 2900 Noblestown Rd., Pittsburgh, PA 15205 t) 412-456-3085 stewardship@diopitt.org www.diopitt.org Dolores Nypaver, Dir.;

Chimbote Foundation - 2900 Noblestown Rd., Pittsburgh, PA 15205 t) 412-456-3085 www.diopitt.org Dcn. Timothy F. Noca, Dir.;

Institutional Common Fund Trust - 2900 Noblestown Rd., Pittsburgh, PA 15205 t) 412-456-3137 klander@diopitt.org Wayne C. Boettcher, Dir.;

Institutional Deposit and Loan Fund Trust - 2900 Noblestown Rd., Pittsburgh, PA 15205 t) 412-456-3137 klander@diopitt.org Wayne C. Boettcher, Dir.;

Nazareth Family Foundation - 201 Nazareth Way, Pittsburgh, PA 15229 t) 814-660-2559 mcollins.nff@gmail.com Sr. Theadora Krause, CSFN, Pres.;

North Catholic Endowment Fund - 2900 Noblestown Rd., Pittsburgh, PA 15205 www.diopitt.org

Parish Common Fund Trust - 2900 Noblestown Rd., Pittsburgh, PA 15205 t) 412-456-3025 wboettcher@diopitt.org Wayne C. Boettcher, Dir.;

Parish Deposit and Loan Fund Trust - 2900 Noblestown Rd., Pittsburgh, PA 15205 t) 412-456-3025 klander@diopitt.org Wayne C. Boettcher, Dir.;

Portiuncula Foundation of the Sisters of St. Francis of the Neumann Communities - 146 Hawthorne Rd., Pittsburgh, PA 15209 t) 412-821-2200 x430 portiuncula@sosf.org Natalie Kasievich, Dir.;

***Sister Thea Bowman Black Catholic Educational Foundation** - 8235 Ohio River Blvd., Pittsburgh, PA 15202-1454 t) (678) 699-7634 jbarker2@theabowmanfoundation.org Joseph Barker II, Contact;

Vincentian Collaborative System Charitable Foundation - 8250 Babcock Blvd., Pittsburgh, PA 15237 t) 412-548-4055 info@vcs.org vcs.org A ministry of Vincentian Collaborative System Alyssa DeLuca, Exec. Dir.;

VILLA MARIA

Sisters of the Humility of Mary Charitable Trust - 288 Villa Dr., Villa Maria, PA 16155; Mailing: P.O. Box 313, Villa Maria, PA 16155 t) 724-964-8861 treardon@humilityofmary.org; tperry@humilityofmary.org www.humilityofmary.org Sr. Carol Anne Smith, H.M., Trustee;

WEXFORD

***St. Anthony Charitable Foundation** - 2000 Corporate Dr., Ste. 580, Wexford, PA 15090 t) 724-940-9020 jgaughan@stanthonykids.org stanthonykids.org Jerome Gaughan, Dir.;

HOSPITALS / HEALTH SERVICES [HOS]

PITTSBURGH

UPMC Mercy - 1400 Locust St., Pittsburgh, PA 15219 t) 412-232-8111 eisemanp@upmc.edu www.upmcmercy.com Michael Grace, Pres.;

MISCELLANEOUS [MIS]

BADEN

Bethany Community - 1018 W. State St., Baden, PA 15001 t) 729-869-6083 mimovodi@msn.com Timothy Giltinan, Admin.;

BEAVER FALLS

Felician Sisters of North America Marian Corporation - 871 Mercer Rd., Beaver Falls, PA 15010-6815 t) 724-384-5300 sjudithmk@feliciansisters.org Sr. Judith Marie Kubicki, Pres.;

Felician Sisters of North America Real Estate Holding Corporation - 871 Mercer Rd., Beaver Falls, PA 15010-6815 t) 724-384-5300 sjudithmk@feliciansisters.org Sr. Judith Marie Kubicki, Pres.;

ELIZABETH

Divine Redeemer Health Care Ministries Corp. - 999 Rock Run Rd., Elizabeth, PA 15037-2613 t) 412-751-8600 sdrarusa@gmail.com www.divine-redeemer-sisters.org

GIBSONIA

***The Ark and the Dove, Inc.** - 10745 Babcock Blvd., Gibsonia, PA 15044 t) 724-444-8055 info@thearkandthedoveworldwide.org www.thearkandthedoveworldwide.org Rev. Joseph M. Mele, Spiritual Adv./Care Srvcs.;

MCKEESPORT

Auberle - 1101 Hartman St., McKeesport, PA 15132-1500 t) 412-673-5800 x1310 johnly@auberle.org www.auberle.org Helping build strong individuals, families and communities. John Patrick Lydon, CEO; Darla Poole, Exec.;

PITTSBURGH

The Capuchin Franciscan Volunteer Corps, Inc. (Province of St. Augustine of the Capuchin Order) - 220 37th St., Pittsburgh, PA 15201 t) 412-682-6011 capcorpseast@gmail.com www.capuchin.com Rev. Francis X. Yacobi, O.F.M.Cap., Province Liaison; Margaret McIntyre-Stacy, Dir.; R. Joseph Kusnir, CFO;

Catholic Charities Free Health Care Center - 212 Ninth St., Pittsburgh, PA 15222

Catholic Charities of the Diocese of Pittsburgh, Inc. - 212 Ninth St., Pittsburgh, PA 15222

The Catholic Institute of Pittsburgh, PA - 2900 Noblestown Rd., Pittsburgh, PA 15205 t) 412-456-3137

Catholic Sisters Leadership Council (Western PA) - 2900 Noblestown Rd., Pittsburgh, PA 15205 t) 412-477-2333 sjgardner@osfprov.org Sr. Janet Gardner, O.S.F., Chair; Sr. Maria Kruszewski, Chair; Sr. Constance M. Tomyl, C.S.S.F., Secy.;

Christ Child Society of Pittsburgh - ; Mailing: P.O. Box 11324, Pittsburgh, PA 15238-1324 t) 412-552-9211 Rev. Jeremy J. Mohler, Spiritual Adv./Care Srvcs.;

Cursillo Movement-Diocese of Pittsburgh - 1138 Windmill Ln., Pittsburgh, PA 15237 t) 412-837-9450 pghcursillo@gmail.com www.pghcursillo.org Dan Kubisiak, Dir.; Rev. Thomas J. Galvin, Spiritual Adv./Care Srvcs.;

Elizabeth Seton Center Inc. - 1900 Pioneer Ave., Pittsburgh, PA 15226 t) 412-561-8400 srbarb@setoncenter.com www.setoncenter.com Sr. Barbara Ann Boss, S.C., CEO;

Knights of Columbus Bishop of Pittsburgh Diocese Project - ; Mailing: P.O. Box 9691, Pittsburgh, PA 15226-0691 t) 724-422-7136 www.bishopsprojectkofc.org

National Institute for Newman Studies - 211 N. Dithridge St., Pittsburgh, PA 15213 t) 412-681-4375 admin@ninsdu.org www.newmanstudies.org Catharine Ryan, Pres.; Kenneth L. Parker, Exec.;

Nazareth Global Missions, Inc. - 201 Nazareth Way, Pittsburgh, PA 15229; Mailing: 310 N. River Rd., Des Plaines, IL 60016 t) (847) 298-6760 x150 treasurer@nazarethcsfn.org Sr. Kathleen Maciej, C.S.F.N., Prov.;

Our Campaign for the Church Alive!, Inc. - 2900 Noblestown Rd., Pittsburgh, PA 15205 t) 412-456-3085 stewardship@diopitt.org

Pension Plan for the Diocese of Pittsburgh - 2900 Noblestown Rd., Pittsburgh, PA 15205 t) 412-456-3137 benefits@diopitt.org (Lay Pension Plan)

Pittsburgh Catholic Publishing Associates, Inc. - 2900 Noblestown Rd., Pittsburgh, PA 15205 Jennifer Antkowiak, Exec. Dir.;

Pittsburgh Mercy Health System, Inc. - McAuley Hall, 3333 Fifth Ave., Pittsburgh, PA 15213 t) 412-578-6675 www.pittsburghmercy.org Sr. Susan Welsh, R.S.M., Pres.;

McAuley Ministries - t) 412-578-6223 mrcooprt@mcauleyministries.org www.mcauleyministries.org Michele Rone Cooper, Exec.;

Mercy Life Center Corporation - 1200 Reedsdale St., Pittsburgh, PA 15233 t) 412-323-8026

***Preambula Group** - One PPG Pl., Ste. 1700, Pittsburgh, PA 15222 t) 724-719-3679 preambula.org Dr. Michel Therrien, Pres. & CEO;

Prelature of the Holy Cross and Opus Dei - 5090 Warwick Terr., Pittsburgh, PA 15213 t) 412-683-8448 info@warwickhouse.org www.opusdei.org Rev. Joseph P. Landauer, Chap.; Rev. Martin J. Miller, Chap.;

Priests' Benefit Plan of the Diocese of Pittsburgh - 2900 Noblestown Rd., Pittsburgh, PA 15205 t) 412-456-3060 centralaccounting@diopitt.org Purpose: To provide certain retirement and health-related benefits to eligible priests. Rev. Charles S. Bober, Chair;

Procurator Assurance, Inc. - c/o 2900 Noblestown Rd., Pittsburgh, PA 15205 t) 412-456-3137 insurance@diopitt.org Robert Costantino, Dir.; David S. Stewart, Vice. Pres.;

Scholastic Opportunity Scholarship Program - 2900 Noblestown Rd., Pittsburgh, PA 15205 t) 412-456-3100 www.diopitt.org

Sisters Place, Inc. - 111 Brownsville Rd., Pittsburgh, PA 15210 t) 412-233-3903 info@sistersplace.org www.sistersplace.org Damian Gilliard, Pres.; Melissa Ferraro, CEO;

***Society of Saint Vincent de Paul** - Council of Pittsburgh, 1243 N. Franklin St., Pittsburgh, PA 15233 t) 412-321-1071 x206 council@svdppitt.org www.svdppitt.org Al Bannon, Pres.; Dcn. Keith G. Kondrich, Exec.;

The Catholic Historical Society of Western Pennsylvania - 2900 Noblestown Rd., Pittsburgh, PA 15205-4227 t) 412-921-4421 joyecho@aol.com www.catholichistorywpa.org Blanche McGuire, Pres.;

Saint Thomas More Society - 400 County Office Bldg., 542 Forces Ave., Pittsburgh, PA 15219 t) 412-350-2547 rita.murillo@alleghenycounty.us Sr. Rita C. Murillo, C.S.J., Pres.;

Totus Tuus - 4205 Bigelow Blvd., Pittsburgh, PA 15213 t) 603-630-2637; 412-996-7980 mimikag3@gmail.com; rmdonahue10@gmail.com Rhodora M. Donahue, Pres.; Marie Garesche, Treas.;

Vincentian Collaborative System - 8250 Babcock Blvd., Pittsburgh, PA 15237 t) 412-630-9980 vcsinfo@vcs.org www.vcs.org Dean Owrey, CEO;

Vincentian Collaborative System Rehabilitation Services -

111 Perrymont Rd., Pittsburgh, PA 15237 t) 412-630-9980 vcsinfo@vcs.org vcs.org Linda Parkinson, Admin.;

VALENCIA

Magnificat Pittsburgh - 201 Valley Dr., Valencia, PA 16059 c) 724-316-0158 mundy@zbzoom.net www.magnificatpittsburgh.org/ Joyce Mundy, Contact;

VILLA MARIA

Villa Maria Education & Spirituality Center - ; Mailing: P.O. Box 424, Villa Maria, PA 16155 t) 724-964-8886 jmkudlacz@humilityofmary.org www.vmesc.org Jane Marie Kudlacz, H.M., Pres.; Matt Abramowski, Dir.;

Villa Maria Residential Services - 380 Villa Dr., Villa Maria, PA 16155; Mailing: P.O. Box 230, Villa Maria, PA 16155 t) 724-964-8920 x3340 jbird@humilityofmary.org www.villaapartments.org The Villa Maria Apartments provide housing for low and moderate income adults age 55 and over. Sr. Jean Tobin Lardie, H.M., Rel. Ord. Ldr.;

WEXFORD

***St. Anthony Programs** - 2000 Corporate Dr., Ste. 580, Wexford, PA 15090 t) 724-940-9020 msieg@stanthonyschoolprograms.com

MONASTERIES AND RESIDENCES FOR PRIESTS AND BROTHERS [MON]

BEAVER

St. Fidelis Friary - 372 E. End Ave., Beaver, PA 15009 t) 724-282-1485 Rev. John Petrikovic, O.F.M. Cap., Archivist; Rev. John D. Harvey, O.F.M.Cap., Senior Parochial Vicar; Rev. Michael P. Greb, O.F.M.Cap., Dir., Pastoral Care, McGuire Memorial; Rev. Paul Kuppe, O.F.M.Cap., Sr. Parochial Vicar; Priests: 4

BETHEL PARK

Congregation of the Holy Spirit Province of the United States - 6230 Brush Run Rd., Bethel Park, PA 15102 t) 412-831-0302 usprovince@spiritans.org spiritans.org Rev. Donald J. McEachin, C.S.Sp., Prov.; Rev. William H. Christy, C.S.Sp., Prov. Asst.; Rev. John A. Sawicki, C.S.Sp., Treas.; Rev. Daniel Abba, C.S.Sp., Councilor; Anne Marie Hansen, Councilor; Rev. Benoit Mukamba, C.S.Sp., Councilor; Rev. Binh T. Quach, C.S.Sp., Councilor; Brs.: 1; Priests: 72

Holy Spirit Fathers and Brothers Provincialate - 6230 Brush Run Rd., Bethel Park, PA 15102 t) 412-831-0302 usprovince@spiritans.org www.spiritans.org Rev. Donald J. McEachin, C.S.Sp., Prov.; Bro. Michael Suazo, C.S.Sp., Dir.;

BUTLER

St. Mary's Friary - 821 Herman Rd., Butler, PA 16002 t) 724-282-1485 Province of St. Augustine Rev. Albert Alexandrunas, O.F.M.Cap., Ministry of Prayer; Rev. James Kurtz, O.F.M.Cap., Sr. Par. Vicar; Rev. Ward Stakem, O.F.M.Cap., Sr. Par. Vicar; Bro. Joseph Day, O.F.M.Cap., Fraternal Service; Bro. Walter Robb, O.F.M.Cap., Fraternal Service; Brs.: 2; Priests: 3

PITTSBURGH

St. Augustine Friary - 221 36th St., Pittsburgh, PA 15201 t) 412-682-6430 www.capuchin.com Rev. Robert Marva, O.F.M.Cap., Prov.; Bro. James Mungovan, O.F.M. Cap., Vicar Provincial; Guardian; Rev. William Henn, O.F.M. Cap., Prof.; Bro. Ross Henley, O.F.M. Cap., Dir., Evangelization; Bro. Matthew Hindelang, O.F.M. Cap., Asst. Dir., Evangelization; Rev. Dennis Klemash, O.F.M. Cap., CNA/Elder Care; Bro. Joseph Morton, OFM Cap., Treas.; Bro. Thomas Piolata, OFM Cap, Graduate Studies; Rev. John Pfannenstiel, O.F.M. Cap., Dir.; Bro. Robert Toomey, O.F.M. Cap., Fraternity Service; Rev. Joseph Tuscan, O.F.M. Cap., Preaching Ministry; Rev. Francis X. Yacobi, O.F.M.Cap., Exec. Secy.; Rev. John Bednarik, O.F.M. Cap., In Res.; Rev. Robert Craig, O.F.M. Cap., In Res.; Rev. Gervase Degenhardt, O.F.M. Cap., In Res.; Rev. Paul Dressler, OFM Cap., In Res.; Rev. Samuel Driscoll, O.F.M. Cap., In Res.; Rev. John Getsy, O.F.M.Cap., In Res.; Rev. Lester Knoll, O.F.M. Cap., In Res.; Rev. Leon Leitem, O.F.M. Cap., In Res.; Rev. Benjamin Madden, O.F.M. Cap., In Res.; Rev. Michael P. Masich, O.F.M. Cap., In Res.; Rev. Robert L. McCreary, O.F.M. Cap., In Res.; Bro. Charles McElroy, O.F.M. Cap., In Res.; Rev. Joseph Mindling, O.F.M.Cap., In Res.; Rev. Brian Newman, O.F.M. Cap., In Res.; Rev. Matthew Palkowski, O.F.M.Cap., In Res.; Rev. Cyril Repko, O.F.M. Cap., In Res.; Rev. Scott Seethaler, O.F.M. Cap., In Res.; Rev. Colman Studeny, OFM Cap., In Res.; Rev. Allan Wasiecko, O.F.M. Cap., In Res.; Rev. Jonathan Williams, O.F.M. Cap., In Res.; Brs.: 7; Priests: 26

The Capuchin Franciscan Friars Province of Saint Augustine - 220 37th St., Pittsburgh, PA 15201 t) 412-682-6011 joekusnir@capuchin.com Rev. Robert Marva, O.F.M. Cap., Prov.; Bro. James Mungovan, O.F.M. Cap., Vicar Prov.; Rev. Brian Stacy, OFM Cap, Councilor; Rev. Emilio Biosca, O.F.M.Cap., Councilor; Rev. Richard Owens, OFM, Cap, Councilor; Rev. Francis X. Yacobi, O.F.M.Cap., Exec. Sec.; Rev. Rafael Anguiano-Rodriguez, O.F.M.Cap., Vocations Dir.; Rev. John Petrikovic, O.F.M. Cap., Archivist; Rev. John Pfannenstiel, O.F.M. Cap., Dir.; R. Joseph Kusnir, CFO; Brs.: 22; Priests: 92

Congregation of the Oratory of St. Philip Neri - The Pittsburgh Oratory, 4450 Bayard St., Pittsburgh, PA 15213 t) 412-681-3181 info@pittsburghoratory.org www.thepittsburghoratory.org Very Rev. Michael J. Darcy, C.O., Provost; Rev. Joshua Kibler, C.O., Vice-Provost; Rev. Stephen Lowery, C.O., Campus Min.; Rev. Peter J. Gruber, C.O., Director of Campus Ministry; Rev. Reed Frey, C.O., Campus Min.; Rev. Thomas Skamai, C.O., Campus Min.; Dcn. John Leonard Dornan, Seminarian; Bro. Kurt Kessler, Seminarian; Brs.: 2; Priests: 6

Franciscan Friars, T.O.R. (Queen of Peace Friary) - 5324 Carnegie St., Pittsburgh, PA 15201 t) 412-449-1029 Rev. Bernard Tickerhoof, T.O.R., Vicar; Rev. Jude Ventiquattro, In Res.; Bro. Martin Zatsick, TOR, Supr.;

Holy Family Friary - 232 S. Home Ave., Pittsburgh, PA 15202-2899 t) 412-761-2550; 412-721-7092 dmoczulskiofm@gmail.com (Friars Minor), The Franciscans. Rev. John Joseph Gonchar, O.F.M.; Rev. David Moczulski, O.F.M.; Rev. Leonard Cornelius, O.F.M., Vicar;

St. John Vianney Manor - 2600 Morange Rd., Pittsburgh, PA 15205 t) 412-928-0825; 412-928-0908 pprzybyla@diopitt.org Retired priests' residence. Rev. Norbert J. Campbell, In Res.; Rev. David C. Dixon, In Res.; Rev. John M. Jordan, In Res.; Rev. Malcolm McDonald, In Res.; Rev. Robert J. Meyer, In Res.; Rev. Msgr. William M. Ogrodowski, In Res.; Rev. Philip J. Przybyla, In Res.; Rev. Miroslaw Stelmaszczyk, In Res.; Rev. Richard G. Terdine, In Res.; Rev. Raymond M. Utz, In Res.; Most Rev. William J. Winter, In Res.;

Our Lady of the Angels Friary - 225-37th St., Pittsburgh, PA 15201 t) 412-682-6888 joekusnir@capuchin.com Rev. Jonathan Ulrick, OFM Cap., Par. Vicar; Bro. David Cira, O.F.M.Cap., Chap.; Rev. Marino Msigala, OFM Cap. (Tanzania), Chap.; Rev. Richard J. Zelik, O.F.M.Cap., Chap.; Brs.: 1; Priests: 4

St. Paul of the Cross Monastery - 148 Monastery Ave., Pittsburgh, PA 15203-1498 t) 412-381-1188 (Monastery); 412-381-7676 (Retreat Center) stpaulsmonastery@cpprov.org stpaulofthecrossmonastery.com/ Monastery & Retreat Center. Rev. Justin Kerber, C.P., Rector; Rev. Curtis Kiddy, C.P., Mem.; Rev. John F. McMillan, C.P., Mem.; Rev. Richard A. Nalepa, C.P., Mem.; Rev. Joseph Sedley, C.P., Mem.; Rev. Donald Ware, C.P., Mem.; Rev. Gerald Laba, C.P., Dir.; Bro. Leo DiFiore, C.P., De Familia; Brs.: 1; Priests: 7

Society of The Divine Word - 207 Lytton, Pittsburgh, PA 15213 t) 412-683-4030 luhal@dwci.edu Bro. John DeBold, S.V.D.; Rev. Raymond Hober, S.V.D.; Bro. Gerard Raker, S.V.D., Supr.; Rev. Walter Ostrowski, S.V.D., Dir.;

NURSING / REHABILITATION / CONVALESCENCE / ELDERLY CARE [NUR]

BADEN

***Villa St. Joseph of Baden, Inc.** - 1020 State St., Baden, PA 15005 t) 724-869-6528 vsjincadmin@stjoseph-baden.org Sr. Diane Cauley, C.S.J., Admin.;

PITTSBURGH

Little Sisters of the Poor Home for the Aged - 1028 Benton Ave., Pittsburgh, PA 15212 t) 412-307-1100 mspittsburgh@littlesistersofthepoor.org www.littlesistersofthepoorpittsburgh.org Rev. William P. Feeney, Chap.; Sr. Mary Vincent Mannion, Supr.; Asstd. Annu.: 103; Staff: 115

Marian Manor Corp. - 2695 Winchester Dr., Pittsburgh, PA 15220 t) 412-440-4300 (Admin.); 412-440-4343 (Nursing) sromito@vcs.org www.vcs.org Ministry of Vincentian Collaborative System Samantha Romito, Admin.; Asstd. Annu.: 477; Staff: 135

PRESCHOOLS / CHILDCARE CENTERS [PRE]

CORAOPOLIS

***Girls Hope of Pittsburgh, Inc.** - 1005 Beaver Grade Rd., Ste. 103, Coraopolis, PA 15108 t) 412-329-7172 twiese@bhgh.org Provides a supportive home environment and education for girls who because of poverty, abuse, neglect or abandonment cannot remain in their own home. Tom Wiese, Exec.;

PITTSBURGH

Franciscan Child Day Care Center - 1401 Hamilton Rd., Pittsburgh, PA 15234-2399; Mailing: 5802 Curry Rd., Pittsburgh, PA 15236 t) 412-882-9911 www.osfprov.org/fcdcc.htm Sr. Janet Gardner, OSF, Pres.; Stds.: 45; Lay Tchrs.: 8

Holy Family Institute - 8235 Ohio River Blvd., Pittsburgh, PA 15202 t) 412-766-4030 www.hfi-pgh.org Holy Family Institute is committed to helping children, preserving families, and strengthening communities by providing a network of social services. Michael Sexauer, Pres.; Sr. Linda Yankoski, C.S.F.N., CEO;

Holy Family Foundation - 8235 Ohio River Blvd., Pittsburgh, PA 15202 t) (412) 766-4030 Promotes & supports the works & educational purposes of Holy Family Institute.

Mt. Alvernia Day Care & Learning Center - 146 Hawthorne Rd., Pittsburgh, PA 15209 t) 412-821-4302 mtalverniadaycare@sosf.org www.sosf.org Sr. Karen Krebs, Dir.;

Providence Connections, Inc. - Corporate Office, 3113 Brighton Rd., Pittsburgh, PA 15212-2456 t) 412-766-3860 lmacqueen@providenceconnections.org www.providenceconnections.org Lori MacQueen, Dir.; Stds.: 125; Lay Tchrs.: 5

Providence Family Support Center - 3113 Brighton Rd., Pittsburgh, PA 15212-2456 sellwood@providenceconnections.org Samantha Ellwood, Dir.;

Vincentian Child Development Center - 8150 McKnight Rd., Pittsburgh, PA 15237 t) 412-366-8588 jparagi@vcs.org vcs.org A Ministry of Vincentian Collaborative System Jill Paragi, Dir.; Stds.: 182; Lay Tchrs.: 29

RETREAT HOUSES / RENEWAL CENTERS [RTR]

ALLISON PARK

Kearns Spirituality Center - 9000 Babcock Blvd., Allison Park, PA 15101-2713 t) 412-366-1124 mbisbey@cdpsisters.org; ealmendarez@cdpsisters.org www.cdpsisters.org Sr. Elena Almendarez, Dir.;

BETHEL PARK

The Spiritan Center - 6230 Brush Run Rd., Bethel Park, PA 15102 t) 412-835-3510 thespiritancenter@gmail.com Rev. Ralph J. Poirier, C.S.Sp.; Rev. Joseph A. Seiter, C.S.Sp.; Bro. Michael Suazo, C.S.Sp.; Rev. Lazarus Langbiir, CSSp, In Res.; Rev. Christopher Promis, CSSp, In Res.; Rev. William Smith, CSSp., In Res.; Rev. George J. Spangenberg, C.S.Sp., In Res.; Rev. Edward Vilkauskas, CSSp, In Res.; Rev. Freddy Washington, CSSp, In Res.;

PITTSBURGH

Martina Spiritual Renewal Center, Inc. - 5244 Clarwin Ave., Pittsburgh, PA 15229-2208 t) 412-931-9766 martinaspiritual@verizon.net martinacenter.com Sr. Diane Smith, SHS, Pres.; Sr. Donna Smith, S.H.S., Admin.;

St. Paul of the Cross Retreat Center - 148 Monastery Ave., Pittsburgh, PA 15203 t) 412-381-7676; 412-381-7677 stpaulrcpa@cpprov.org stpaulsretreatcenter-pittsburgh.org Rev. Patrick Geinzer, C.P.; Rev. Michael Salvagna, C.P.; Rev. Donald Ware, C.P.; John Colaizzi, Admin.; Rev. Gerald Laba, C.P., Dir.;

SEMINARIES [SEM]

PITTSBURGH

Saint Paul Seminary - 2900 Noblestown Rd., Pittsburgh, PA 15205-4227 t) 412-456-3048 seminaryprog@diopitt.org www.diopitt.org Rev. Thomas A. Sparacino, Rector; Rev. Brian W. Noel, Dir.;

SPECIAL CARE FACILITIES [SPF]

NEW BRIGHTON

McGuire Memorial - 2119 Mercer Rd., New Brighton, PA 15066-3437 t) 724-843-3400 mcgm@mcguirememorial.org www.mcguirememorial.org

PITTSBURGH

DePaul School for Hearing and Speech - 6202 Alder St., Pittsburgh, PA 15206 t) 412-924-1012 mjmac@depaulinst.com www.speakmiracles.org Mary Jo Maynard, Prin.; Ruth Auld, Dir.;

Marian Hall Home, Inc. - 934 Forest Ave., Pittsburgh, PA 15202-1118 t) 412-761-1999 msgriccia@marianhall.org www.marianhall.org Sr. Marian Sgriccia, O.S.F., Admin.;

The Community at Holy Family Manor, Inc. - 301 Nazareth Way, Pittsburgh, PA 15229-5105 t) 412-931-6996 mrobb@chfmanor.org; mharrison@chfmanor.org chfmanor.org Programs: Mt. Nazareth Learning Center; Holy Family Manor Personal Care Home. Michael Robb, Exec. Dir.; Bed Capacity: 54; Asstd. Annu.: 1,340; Staff: 78

Vincentian de Marillac - 5300 Stanton Ave., Pittsburgh, PA 15206 t) 412-361-2833 hbutts@vcs.org vcs.org Catholic, skilled nursing home. A Ministry of Vincentian Collaborative System Hillary Butts, Admin.; Bed Capacity: 50; Asstd. Annu.: 126; Staff: 71

Vincentian Home - 111 Perrymont Rd., Pittsburgh, PA 15237 t) 412-366-5600 info@vcs.org www.vcs.org Catholic, Skilled Nursing Home A Ministry of Vincentian Collaborative System Jennifer Pruett, Admin.; Bed Capacity: 218; Asstd. Annu.: 906; Staff: 289

WEXFORD

***St. Anthony School Programs** - 2000 Corporate Dr., Ste. 580, Wexford, PA 15090 t) 724-940-9020 lgeorge@stanthonyschoolprograms.com Lisa George, Dir.;

An asterisk (*) denotes an organization that has established tax-exempt status directly with the IRS and is not covered by the USCCB Group Ruling.

Diocese of Portland (In Maine)

(Dioecesis Portlandensis)

MOST REVEREND ROBERT P. DEELEY

Bishop of Portland; ordained July 14, 1973; appointed Titular Bishop of Kearney and Auxiliary Bishop of Boston November 9, 2012; ordained Bishop January 4, 2013; appointed Bishop of Portland December 18, 2013; installed February 14, 2014. Office: 510 Ocean Ave., Portland, ME 04103-4936.

Chancery: 510 Ocean Ave., Portland, ME 04103-4936. T: 207-773-6471; F: 207-773-0182.

ESTABLISHED JULY 29, 1853.

Square Miles 35,385.

Comprises the State of Maine.

Corporate Title: Roman Catholic Bishop of Portland, a Corporation Sole. This Corporation is comprised of the Diocesan parishes, missions, churches, rectories, cemeteries, schools, departments and other Diocesan activities. Those listings do not connote separate civil status (legal, tax, or otherwise) for any such listed activities, departments, entities or personnel that are comprised within the Roman Catholic Bishop of Portland, a Corporation Sole.

The list below also includes organizations which are separate from the Roman Catholic Bishop of Portland, a Corporation Sole.

For the legal titles of other diocesan-related institutions that are not part of the Roman Catholic Diocese of Portland, please consult Chancery.

STATISTICAL OVERVIEW

Personnel

Bishop....1
Retired Bishops....1
Priests: Diocesan Active in Diocese....35
Priests: Retired, Sick or Absent....58
Number of Diocesan Priests....93
Religious Priests in Diocese....35
Total Priests in your Diocese....128
Extern Priests in Diocese....16
Permanent Deacons in Diocese....45
Total Brothers....7
Total Sisters....153

Parishes

Parishes....48
With Resident Pastor:
Resident Diocesan Priests....28
Resident Religious Priests....5
Without Resident Pastor:
Administered by Priests....15
Professional Ministry Personnel:
Sisters....4
Lay Ministers....29

Welfare

Catholic Hospitals....2
Total Assisted....581,910
Homes for the Aged....8
Total Assisted....1,378
Day Care Centers....2
Total Assisted....72
Specialized Homes....1
Total Assisted....279
Special Centers for Social Services....1
Total Assisted....53,441
Other Institutions....4
Total Assisted....497

Educational

Diocesan Students in Other Seminaries....9
Total Seminarians....9
Colleges and Universities....1
Total Students....1,542
High Schools, Diocesan and Parish....1
Total Students....126
High Schools, Private....1
Total Students....372
Elementary Schools, Diocesan and Parish....8
Total Students....1,603
Elementary Schools, Private....1
Total Students....182
Catechesis / Religious Education:
High School Students....230
Elementary Students....2,078
Total Students under Catholic Instruction....6,142
Teachers in Diocese:
Priests....1
Lay Teachers....153

Vital Statistics

Receptions into the Church:
Infant Baptism Totals....700
Minor Baptism Totals....95
Adult Baptism Totals....42
Received into Full Communion....62
First Communions....724
Confirmations....789
Marriages:
Catholic....163
Interfaith....56
Total Marriages....219
Deaths....5,210
Total Catholic Population....286,095
Total Population....1,362,357

LEADERSHIP

Vicars General - Rev. Msgr. Marc B. Caron (marc.caron@portlanddiocese.org); Rev. Msgr. Andrew Dubois (andrew.dubois@portlanddiocese.org);
Moderator of the Curia - Rev. Msgr. Marc B. Caron (marc.caron@portlanddiocese.org);
Chancellor - Sr. Rita-Mae Bissonnette, R.S.R. (ritamae.bissonnette@portlanddiocese.org);
Archives - Sr. Rita-Mae Bissonnette, R.S.R., Archivist; Barbara Miles, Asst.;
Vicar for Priests - Rev. Msgr. Paul F. Stefanko (paul.stefanko@portlanddiocese.org);
Vicars Forane - Rev. Louis J. Phillips, Vicar (Louis.phillips@portlanddiocese.org); Rev. Philip A. Tracy, Vicar; Rev. Jean-Paul Labrie, Vicar (jeanpaul.labrie@portlanddiocese.org);

OFFICES AND DIRECTORS

Diocesan Office of Lifelong Faith Formation - Lori Dahlhoff, Dir. (lori.dahlhoff@portlanddiocese.org);
Catholic Scouting - Scott Valcourt, Chair;
Children and Adult Ministry - Georgette Dionne, Coord.; Hannah Gonneville, Asst. Coord.;
Coordinator of Youth Ministry - Shawn Gregory;
Campaign for Human Development - Suzanne Lafreniere (suzanne.lafreniere@portlanddiocese.org);
Campus Ministry - t) 207-866-2155 www.umaine.edu/newman/ Rev. Kyle L. Doustou (kyle.doustou@portlanddiocese.org);
Catholic Foundation of Maine - www.catholicfoundationmaine.org/ Elizabeth Badger, Exec. (elizabeth.badger@portlanddiocese.org);
Catholic Schools Superintendent - schools@portlanddiocese.org mainecatholicschools.com/ Marianne Pelletier (marianne.pelletier@portlanddiocese.org);
Department of Canonical Services - Rev. John D. Dickinson, Judicial Vicar (jack.dickinson@portlanddiocese.org);
Due Process - Shannon Fossett, Dir.;
Tribunal - tribunal@portlanddiocese.org Rev. John D. Dickinson, Judicial Vicar; Rev. Claude R. Gendreau, Office Coord.;
Advocates - Shannon Fossett; Christopher Siuzdak; David Bearse;
Associate Judges - Rev. Msgr. Paul F. Stefanko; David Bearse, Assoc. Judge; Shannon Fossett, Assoc. Judge;
Defenders of the Bond - Rev. Mark P. Nolette; David Bearse; Shannon Fossett;
Guardian - Rev. Msgr. Marc B. Caron;
Notary - Rev. Claude R. Gendreau;
Officialis - Rev. John D. Dickinson;
Promoter of Justice - Christopher Siuzdak;
Department of Financial Services - Scott Graff, Diocesan Finance Officer (scott.graff@portlanddiocese.org);
Controller - Laurie J. Downey;
Information Technology - Jennifer Nelson, Dir.;
Parish Financial Services - John Bernier, Dir.;
Risk Management - John Cavallaro, Dir.;
Safe Environment - Robert McDermott, Dir.;
Development and Annual Appeal - Michael Sullivan, Dir. (mike.sullivan@portlanddiocese.org);
Diocesan Office of Communications - comments@portlanddiocese.org David W. Guthro, Dir. (dave.guthro@portlanddiocese.org);
Harvest Magazine - harvestmagazine@portlanddiocese.org Lois Czeniak, Editor;
Director of Chaplaincies - Dcn. Peter J. Bernier (peter.bernier@portlanddiocese.org);
Hispanic Ministry - Rev. Michael E. Sevigny, O.F.M.Cap., Dir.; Jose Perez Lopez, Pst. Min./Coord.; Rosario Starratt, Pst. Min./Coord.;
Hospital Chaplaincy - Dcn. Peter J. Bernier, Coord.;
Latin Mass - t) 207-212-3218 Rev. Robert A. Parent, Coord.;
Prison Ministry - Michael Smith, Assoc. Dir.; Dcn. Robert Curtis, Chap.;
Professional Responsibility - t) 207-321-7836 Michael Magalski, Dir. (michael.magalski@portlanddiocese.org);
Public Policy - Suzanne Lafreniere, Dir. (suzanne.lafreniere@portlanddiocese.org);
Seminarians - Rev. Gregory P. Dube, Dir. (greg.dube@portlanddiocese.org);
Support and Assistance Ministry - Sr. Rita-Mae Bissonnette, R.S.R., Dir. (ritamae.bissonnette@portlanddiocese.org); Carolyn Bloom, Independent Clinician (cbloomlcsw@gmail.com);
Vocations - Rev. Gregory P. Dube, Dir. (greg.dube@portlanddiocese.org);

CLERGY AND RELIGIOUS SERVICES

Continuing Education of Clergy - Dcn. Peter J. Bernier (peter.bernier@portlanddiocese.org);
Delegate for Religious - Sr. Rita-Mae Bissonnette, R.S.R. (ritamae.bissonnette@portlanddiocese.org);
Diaconate - Dcn. Peter J. Bernier, Dir. (peter.bernier@portlanddiocese.org);
Ministry to Priests - Dcn. Peter J. Bernier, Dir. (peter.bernier@portlanddiocese.org); Rev. Msgr. Paul F. Stefanko, Vicar for Priests (paul.stefanko@portlanddiocese.org);

CONSULTATIVE BODIES

Diocesan Consultors - Rev. Msgr. Marc B. Caron (marc.caron@portlanddiocese.org); Rev. Msgr. Andrew Dubois (andrew.dubois@portlanddiocese.org); Rev. Msgr. Paul F. Stefanko (paul.stefanko@portlanddiocese.org);
Presbyteral Council - Rev. Msgr. Rene T. Mathieu, Chair; Rev. Kyle L. Doustou, Vice Chair (kyle.doustou@portlanddiocese.org); Rev. Msgr. Marc B. Caron, Moderator of the Curia (marc.caron@portlanddiocese.org);
Diocesan Finance Council - Scott Graff, Diocesan Finance Officer (scott.graff@portlanddiocese.org); Rev. Msgr. Marc B. Caron, Moderator of the Curia (marc.caron@portlanddiocese.org); James Geary, Chair;
Personnel Board - Rev. Claude R. Gendreau, Chair (claude.gendreau@portlanddiocese.org); Rev. Gregory P. Dube, Vice Chair (greg.dube@portlanddiocese.org); Rev. Msgr. Marc B. Caron, Moderator of the Curia (marc.caron@portlanddiocese.org);
Diocesan Pastoral Council - Mary Colombo, Chair; Rose Ann Schultz, Mem. (schr426@gmail.com); Thomas Ancona;
Diocesan Priests' Benefit Plan - Rev. Msgr. Paul F. Stefanko, Chair (paul.stefanko@portlanddiocese.org); Most Rev. Robert P. Deeley, Pres.; Sr. Rita-Mae Bissonnette, R.S.R., Secy. (ritamae.bissonnette@portlanddiocese.org);
Diocesan Review Board - Michael McGovern, Chair; Rev. Msgr. Marc B. Caron (marc.caron@portlanddiocese.org); Edna Chace, Mem.;
Diocesan Board of Education - Marianne Pelletier, Secy. (marianne.pelletier@portlanddiocese.org); Donna Jacques; Michael Komich;

FACILITIES

DICON - Diocesan Construction - Alan Hinckley, Supt. (alan.hinckley@portlanddiocese.org);
Diocesan Bureau of Housing - Most Rev. Robert P. Deeley, Pres.; Scott Graff, Treas. (scott.graff@portlanddiocese.org);
Property Management - Denis Lafreniere, Dir. (denis.lafreniere@portlanddiocese.org);

HUMAN RESOURCES

Human Resources - Elizabeth Allen, Dir. (elizabeth.allen@portlanddiocese.org);
Benefits - Elizabeth Allen;

ORGANIZATIONS

General Counsel - t) 207-772-6565 Thomas R. Kelly;
Maine Diocesan Council of Catholic Women - Sandra Breton, Pres.;
Office for Missions - Sally Page, Dir. (sally.page@portlanddiocese.org);
Catholic Relief Services - Sally Page, Dir.;
Pontifical Association of Missionary Childhood - Sally Page, Dir.;
Pontifical Society for the Propagation of the Faith - Sally Page, Dir.;

PARISHES, MISSIONS, AND CLERGY

STATE OF MAINE

AUBURN

Immaculate Heart of Mary Parish - 24 Sacred Heart Pl., Auburn, ME 04210-4938 t) 207-782-8096; 207-782-8096 x1202 (CRP) ihmadmin@portlanddiocese.org ihm-auburn.org Rev. Robert D. Lariviere, Pst.; Gladys Garlarneau, Admin.; Manuel Salgado, Admin.; CRP Stds.: 5
Sacred Heart Church - 8 Sacred Heart Pl., Auburn, ME 04210
St. Philip's Church - 2365 Turner Rd., Auburn, ME 04210

AUGUSTA

St. Michael Parish - 24 Washington St., Augusta, ME 04330-4239 t) 207-623-8823 st.michael@portlanddiocese.org; diane.james@portlanddiocese.org stmichaelmaine.org Rev. Nathan D. March, Pst.; Rev. Nehru Stephen Savarayia, H.G.N. (India), Par. Vicar; Rev. Anthony F. Kuzia, CM, Vicar; Diane Charest James, Bus. Mgr.; Gina M Czerwinski, Parish Life Coord.; Sandra Parlato, DRE; CRP Stds.: 93
St. Augustine Church - 1 Kendall St., Augusta, ME 04330
St. Mary of the Assumption Church - 41 Western Ave., Augusta, ME 04330
St. Joseph Church - 1 Lincoln St., Gardiner, ME 04345
St. Denis Church - 298 Grand Army Rd., Whitefield, ME 04353
St. Michael Parish School - (Grades PreK-8) 56 Sewall St., Augusta, ME 04330-7327 t) 207-623-3491 kevin.cullen@portlanddiocese.org Kevin Cullen, Prin.; Stds.: 183; Lay Tchrs.: 12
St. Francis Xavier Church - 130 Rte. 133, Winthrop, ME 04364
Sacred Heart Church - 12 Summer St., Hallowell, ME 04347

BANGOR

Saint Paul the Apostle Parish - 217 York St., Bangor, ME 04401-5442; Mailing: 207 York St., Bangor, ME 04401-5442 t) 207-217-6740 catherine.taft@portlanddiocese.org; mary.brown@portlanddiocese.org www.stpaulbangor.me Rev. Msgr. Andrew Dubois, Pst.; Rev. Bruce Siket, Par. Vicar; Dcn. Luis Sanclemente, Parish Life Coord.; Dcn. Timothy R. Dougherty; Dcn. Michael E. Whalen; Rev. Apolinary Kavishe, A.J. (Tanzania), Chap.; Rev. Robert Tumwekwase, A.J. (Uganda), Chap.; CRP Stds.: 212
All Saints Catholic School - (Grades PreK-8) 768 Ohio St., Bangor, ME 04401; Mailing: P.O. Box 1749, Bangor, ME 04402-1749 t) 207-947-7063; 207-942-0955 matthew.houghton@portlanddiocese.org allsaintsmaine.org Matthew Houghton, Prin.; Stds.: 184; Lay Tchrs.: 13
St. Mary's Campus - (Grades PreK-3) 768 Ohio St., Bangor, ME 04401-3165 t) 207-947-7063 matthew.houghton@portlanddiocese.org A campus

of All Saints Catholic School Matthew Houghton, Prin.;

St. John Church - 207 York St., Bangor, ME 04401-5442 t) 207-217-6710

St. Mary Church - 768 Ohio St., Bangor, ME 04401-3106

St. Joseph Church - 531 N. Main St., Brewer, ME 04412-1219

St. Theresa Church - 425 S. Main St., Brewer, ME 04412-2327

St. Matthew Church - 70 Western Ave., Hampden, ME 04444-1427

St. Gabriel Church - 435 S. Main St., Winterport, ME 04496

BAR HARBOR

Parish of the Transfiguration - 56 Mount Desert St., Bar Harbor, ME 04609-1324 t) 207-288-3535 transfiguration@portlanddiocese.org www.hc-catholics.org Rev. Emile H. Dube, Pst.; Rev. Roland Berngeh (Cameroon), Par. Vicar; Rev. Anthanasius S. Wirsiy (Cameroon), Par. Vicar; CRP Stds.: 7

Holy Redeemer Church - t) (207) 288-3535

St. Ignatius Church - 8 Lookout Way, Northeast Harbor, ME 04679

Our Lady Star of the Sea Chapel - 98 Main St., Isleford, Little Cranberry Island, ME 04646 Summers only.

St. Peter's Church - 5 Ocean House Rd., Manset, ME 04656

BENEDICTA

St. Benedict's - 1063 Benedicta Rd., Benedicta, ME 04733-0000; Mailing: PO Box 27, Benedicta, ME 04733-0027 t) 207-365-4294 robert.meinders@portlanddiocese.org Rev. Dominic Savio, H.G.N. (India), Admin.; Anna Robinson, DRE; Gert Campbell, Bus. Mgr.; CRP Stds.: 10

BRIDGTON

St. Joseph - 225 S. High St., Bridgton, ME 04009-4104 t) 207-647-2334; 207-743-2606 (CRP) joanne.fortier@portlanddiocese.org www.cluster30.org Rev. Edward R. Clifford, Pst.; Joanne Fortier, DRE; Jodi Roma, Bus. Mgr.; CRP Stds.: 16

St. Elizabeth Ann Seton - 857 Main St., Fryeburg, ME 04037-1521

BRUNSWICK

All Saints Parish - 132 McKeen St., Brunswick, ME 04011-2980 t) 207-725-2624 allsaints@portlanddiocese.org; philip.tracy@portlanddiocese.org www.allsaintsmaine.com Rev. Philip A. Tracy, Pst.; Rev. Patrick Agbodi, SMA (Nigeria), Par. Vicar; Rev. Peter Shaba, S.M.A. (Nigeria), Par. Vicar; Dcn. Robert Curtis; Dcn. Thomas Blatz; Dcn. John Murphy; Dcn. Edwin Robinson; Charleen Foley, Bus. Mgr.; Gil Peterson, Music Min.; Deb Poulton, Youth Min.; Merissa Newton, Youth Min.; Martha Corkery, Parish Life Coord.; Amy Ford, DRE; Marcy Brenner, RCIA Coord.; CRP Stds.: 80

St. John's Catholic School - (Grades PreK-8) 37 Pleasant St., Brunswick, ME 04011-2279 t) 207-725-5507 Shelly Wheeler, Prin.; Stds.: 130; Lay Tchrs.: 14

St. Mary Church - 144 Lincoln St., Bath, ME 04530-2198

St. Charles Church - McKeen St., Brunswick, ME 04011

St. John the Baptist Church - 39 Pleasant St., Brunswick, ME 04011-2279 t) (207) 725-5507

Our Lady Queen of Peace Church - 82 Atlantic Ave., Boothbay Harbor, ME 04538-2129

St. Patrick Church - 380 Academy Hill Rd., Newcastle, ME 04553-3473

St. Ambrose Church - 27 Kimball St., Richmond, ME 04357-1106

St. Katharine Drexel Church - 419 Mountain Rd., Harpswell, ME 04079

BUCKSPORT

Stella Maris Parish - 64 Franklin St, Bucksport, ME 04416-0000; Mailing: PO Box S, Bucksport, ME 04416-1219 t) 207-702-9217 stellamaris@portlanddiocese.org; stellamaris@roadrunner.com Rev. Emile H. Dube, Pst.; Rev. Anthanasius S. Wirsiy (Cameroon), Par. Vicar; Wendy Johnson, DRE; CRP Stds.: 15

Our Lady of Hope Church - 137 Perkins St., Castine, ME 04421

St. Mary Star of the Sea - 8 Granite St., Stonington, ME 04681

St. Vincent de Paul - Franklin St, Bucksport, ME 04416

CALAIS

Saint Kateri Tekakwitha Parish - 31 Calais Ave., Calais, ME 04619-1637; Mailing: 31 Calais Avenue, Calais, ME 04619-0898 t) 207-454-0680 www.sktparish.org Rev. Brad Morin, Pst.; Sr. Carol A. LeTourneau, R.S.M., CRE; Mary White, CRE; Marc Podschlne II, DRE; Kathy Lawrence, Bus. Mgr.; CRP Stds.: 26

Immaculate Conception Church - ; Mailing: P.O. Box 898, Calais, ME 04619 www.sktparish.org

St. Ann Church - Peter Dana Point Rd., Indian Twp, ME 04668

St. James the Greater Church - 15 Hillside St., Baileyville, ME 04694

St. John the Evangelist Church - 39 Hersey Ln., Pembroke, ME 04666

St. Joseph Church - 51 Washington St., Eastport, ME 04631

CAMDEN

Saint Brendan the Navigator Parish - 7 Union St., Camden, ME 04843-2015 t) 207-236-4785 www.stbrendanparish.net Rev. Nathan D. March, Pst.; Rev. Divine Fossoh (Cameroon), Par. Vicar; Dcn. Robert Cleveland; Christine Fee, Parish Life Coord.; Karol Skoby, Bus. Mgr.; CRP Stds.: 62

St. Mary of the Isles - Pendleton Point Rd., Islesboro, ME 04848

St. Francis of Assisi Church - 81 Court St., Belfast, ME 04915-6134

Our Lady of Good Hope Church - Union St., Camden, ME 04843

St. Bernard Church - 150 Broadway, Rockland, ME 04841-2698

CARIBOU

Parish of the Precious Blood - 31 Thomas Ave., Caribou, ME 04736-1721; Mailing: PO Box 625, Caribou, ME 04736-0625 t) 207-498-2536 carl.gallagher@portlanddiocese.org; jeanine.morneault@portlanddiocese.org www.theppb.org Rev. David R. Raymond, Pst.; Rev. Simon Assogba, SMA (Benin), Par. Vicar; Rev. Anthony Korir, SMA (Kenya), Par. Vicar; Martha Frank, Bus. Mgr.; Janet Beckwith, Parish Life Coord.; CRP Stds.: 95

Our Lady of the Lakes - 2111 Portage Rd. US #11, Portage, ME 04768

St. Catherine - 24 McManus St., Washburn, ME 04786

St. Mark's Church - 113 Allen Farm Rd., Ashland, ME 04732

Holy Rosary Church - 34 Vaughn St., Caribou, ME 04736-1721

Sacred Heart Church - 1141 Van Buren Rd., Caribou, ME 04736

St. Joseph Church - 17 Main St., Mars Hill, ME 04758-0000

St. Denis Church - 147 Main St., Fort Fairfield, ME 04742-1223

St. Louis Church - 106 Main St., Limestone, ME 04750-1116

St. Therese Church - 239 Main St., Stockholm, ME 04783-0000

Nativity of the Blessed Virgin Mary Church - 333 Main St., Presque Isle, ME 04769-0813

DEXTER

Our Lady of the Snows Parish - 60 Free St., Dexter, ME 04930-1507; Mailing: P.O. Box 193, Dexter, ME 04930-0193 t) 207-924-7104 olofthesnows@portlanddiocese.org www.ourladyofthesnowsme.org Rev. Robert L. Lupo, Pst.; Dcn. David Denbow; CRP Stds.: 18

St. Anne Church - 64 Free St., Dexter, ME 04930

St. Thomas Aquinas Church - 43 High St., Dover Foxcroft, ME 04426

Sts. Francis & Paul the Apostle Church - 128 Riverside St., Milo, ME 04463

EAST MILLINOCKET

Christ the Divine Mercy Parish - 58 Cedar St., East Millinocket, ME 04430-1031; Mailing: P.O. Box 400, East Millinocket, ME 04430-0400 t) 207-746-3333 tina.mcleod@portlanddiocese.org; christthedivinemercy@portlanddiocese.org christthedivinemercyparish.org Rev. Dominic Savio, H.G.N. (India), Admin.; Gert Campbell, Bus. Mgr.; Tina McLeod, DRE; CRP Stds.: 14

St. Peter's Church - t) (207) 746-3333

St. Martin of Tours Church - 19 Colby St., Millinocket, ME 04462

ELLSWORTH

St. Joseph - 231 Main St., Ellsworth, ME 04605-1613 t) 207-667-2342 Rev. Emile H. Dube, Pst.; Rev. Anthanasius S. Wirsiy (Cameroon), Par. Vicar; CRP Stds.: 16

Our Lady of the Lake - Green Lake Rd., Dedham, ME 04429 (summers only)

St. Margaret - Grindstone Ave., Winter Harbor, ME 04693 (summers only)

FALMOUTH

Parish of the Holy Eucharist - 266 Foreside Rd., Falmouth, ME 04105-1405 t) 207-847-6890 pothe@portlanddiocese.org pothe.org/ Rev. Steven G. Cartwright, Pst.; Rev. Peter Kaseta, O.F.M.Cap., Par. Vicar; Rev. Paul Marquis, In Res.; CRP Stds.: 179

Holy Martyrs of North America Church - t) (207) 847-6890 pothe.org

Sacred Heart Church - 326 Main St., Yarmouth, ME 04096 t) (207) 847-6890

St. Gregory Church - 24 N. Raymond Rd, Gray, ME 04105-1405 t) (207) 847-6890

St. Jude Church - 134 Main St., Freeport, ME 04034 t) (207) 847-6890

FARMINGTON

St. Joseph's - 133 Middle St., Farmington, ME 04938-1598 t) 207-778-2778; 207-897-2173 (CRP) stjfarmington@portlanddiocese.org stroseandstjosephmaine.org Rev. Paul H. Dumais, Pst.; CRP Stds.: 25

FORT KENT

St. John Vianney Parish - 26 E. Main St., Fort Kent, ME 04743-1395 t) 207-834-5656 stjohnvianneyparish@portlanddiocese.org stjohnvianneyparish.net Rev. Jean-Paul Labrie, Pst.; Barbara Pelletier, DRE; Gale Rioux, Other; CRP Stds.: 214

St. Mary Church - 3443 Aroostock Rd., Eagle Lake, ME 04739

St. Louis Church - Main St., Fort Kent, ME 04743

St. Charles Church - 912 Main St., St. Francis, ME 04774

St. Joseph Church - 7 Church St., Wallagrass, ME 04781

GREENVILLE

Holy Family - 145 Pritham Ave., Greenville, ME 04441-0000; Mailing: P.O. Box 457, Greenville, ME 04441-0457 t) 207-695-2262 bette.diangelo@portlanddiocese.org Rev. Hyacinth Ndifon Fornkwa (Cameroon), Admin.; CRP Stds.: 7

St. Joseph's - Rockwood Rd., Rockwood, ME 04478 Rev. Aaron L. Damboise, Pst.;

HOULTON

St. Mary of the Visitation - 110 Military St., Houlton, ME 04730-2507; Mailing: 112 Military St., Houlton, ME 04730 t) 207-532-2871 maryagnespaul.org Rev. Kevin J. Martin, Pst.; Dcn. Albert Burleigh; Dcn. Ronald Ouellette; Clare Desrosiers, DRE; CRP Stds.: 57

ISLAND FALLS

St. Agnes - 76 Sewall St., Island Falls, ME 04747; Mailing: 112 Military St., Houlton, ME 04730-2507

t) 207-532-2871 maryagnespaul.org Rev. Kevin J. Martin, Pst.; Dcn. Albert Burleigh; Dcn. Ronald Ouellette; Clare Desrosiers, DRE; CRP Stds.: 2

St. Paul - 34 Katahdin St., Patten, ME 04765 Rev. Kent R. Ouellette, Pst.;

JACKMAN

St. Anthony - 370 Main St., Jackman, ME 04945; Mailing: P.O. Box 457, Greenville, ME 04441-0457 t) 207-668-2881 Rev. Hyacinth Fornkwa (Cameroon), Pst.; Lorraine Auclair, Bus. Mgr.; CRP Stds.: 6

JAY

St. Rose of Lima - One Church St., Jay, ME 04239-1801 t) 207-897-2173 strose@portlanddiocese.org stroseandstjosephmaine.org Rev. Paul H. Dumais, Pst.; CRP Stds.: 34

KITTERY

Parish of the Ascension of the Lord - 6 Whipple Rd., Kittery, ME 03904-1739 t) 207-439-0442 bill.green@portlanddiocese.org pal-me.org Rev. Scott M. Mower, Pst.; Veronica Richards, DRE; CRP Stds.: 35

St. Christopher-by-the-Sea Church - 4 Barrell Ln., York, ME 03909-1020

St. Raphael's Church - Whipple Rd., Kittery, ME 03904

Star of the Sea Church - 13 Church St., York Beach, ME 03910 (Seasonal)

Our Lady of the Angels Church - 160 Agamenticus Rd., South Berwick, ME 03908

LEWISTON

Prince of Peace Parish - 607 Sabattus St, Lewiston, ME 04240-5061; Mailing: PO Box 1540, Lewiston, ME 04241-1540 t) 207-777-1200 princeofpeaceme.com Rev. Daniel P. Greenleaf, Pst.; Rev. Patrick Finn, Par. Vicar; Rev. Raja Thaniyel, HGN (India), Par. Vicar; Rev. Arockiasmy Santhiyagu, H.G.N. (India), Chap.; Dcn. Irenee Richard, O.P.; Tyler Nadeau, DRE; Scott Vaillancourt, Music Min.; Joline Laliberte, Bus. Mgr.; CRP Stds.: 79

Catholic Center - 16 Ste. Croix St., Lewiston, ME 04241-1540; Mailing: P.O. Box 1540, Lewiston, ME 04241-1540 joline.laliberte@portlanddiocese.org

Basilica of Ss. Peter & Paul - 27 Bartlett St., Lewiston, ME 04240

Holy Cross Church - 1080 Lisbon St., Lewiston, ME 04240

Holy Family Church - 607 Sabattus St., Lewiston, ME 04240 t) (207) 777-1200

Holy Trinity Church - 67 Frost Hill Ave., Lisbon Falls, ME 04252-1126 www.princeofpeace.me

Our Lady of the Rosary Church - 131 High St., Sabattus, ME 04280-4250 www.princeofpeace.me

LIMERICK

St. Matthew - 19 Dora Ln., Limerick, ME 04048-3527 t) 207-793-2244 stmatthew@portlanddiocese.org www.stmatthewlimerick.org Rev. Wilfred P. Labbe, Pst.; Dcn. Paul Lissandrello; CRP Stds.: 46

LINCOLN

Our Lady of the Eucharist Parish - 164 Main St., Lincoln, ME 04457-1523; Mailing: P.O. Box 310, Lincoln, ME 04457-0310 t) 207-794-6333; 207-974-6333 (CRP) ourladyoftheeucharist@portlanddiocese.org www.ourladyoftheeucharist.org Rev. Anthony Kanagaraj Chinnaiyan, HGN (India), Admin.; Patricia Aldrich, DRE; Karen Carson, DRE; CRP Stds.: 39

St. Mary of Lourdes - Main St, Lincoln, ME 04457-1523 Rev. Richard C. Malo, Pst.;

St. Leo the Great - 16 River Rd., Howland, ME 04448 Rev. Richard C. Malo, Pst.;

St. Anne - 75-76 Danforth Rd., Danforth, ME 04424 Rev. Richard C. Malo, Pst.;

Sacred Heart - Lee-Winn Rd., Winn, ME 04495 Rev. Richard C. Malo, Pst.;

MACHIAS

Saint Peter the Fisherman Parish - 8 Free St., Machias, ME 04654-0248; Mailing: P.O. Box 248, Machias, ME 04654-0248 t) 207-255-3731 stpeterthefisherman@portlanddiocese.org; johnson.sacreties@portland.diocese.org www.stpeterthefisherman.me Rev. Johnson Sacreties Panneer Selvan, HGN (India), Admin.; Janet Ustruck, Bus. Mgr.; Jeannine Wright, DRE; CRP Stds.: 3

Holy Name of Jesus Church - t) (207) 255-3731

Sacred Heart Church - 14 Hamilton St., Lubec, ME 04652 t) (207) 255-3731

St. Michael Church - 51 Elm St., Cherryfield, ME 04622 t) (207) 255-3731

MADAWASKA

Notre Dame du Mont Carmel Parish - 309 St. Thomas St., Ste. 103, Madawaska, ME 04756-1278 t) 207-728-7531 (CRP); 207-728-7135 greg.cyr@portlanddiocese.org; judy.lavoie@portlanddiocese.org sjvcatholics.org Rev. Kent R. Ouellette, Pst.; Rev. Agustin Sebasthiyan, HGN (India); Gregory Cyr, Bus. Mgr.; Dcn. Donald R. Clavette; CRP Stds.: 82

St. Gerard-Mt. Carmel Church - 361 Main St., Grand Isle, ME 04746

St. Thomas Aquinas Church - 321 St. Thomas St., Madawaska, ME 04756

St. David Church - 774 Main St., Madawaska, ME 04756

MEXICO

Parish of the Holy Savior - 7 Brown St., Mexico, ME 04257 t) 207-364-4556 holysaviorparish@portlanddiocese.org www.parishoftheholysavior.com Rev. Aaron L. Damboise, Pst.; Cheryl Cox, Bus. Mgr.; CRP Stds.: 11

Our Lady of the Snows Church - 265 Walkers Mills Rd., Bethel, ME 04217

St. Athanasius & St. John Church - 126 Maine Ave., Rumford, ME 04276

NORWAY

Saint Teresa of Calcutta Parish - 32 Paris St., Norway, ME 04268-5633 t) 207-743-2606 joanne.fortier@portlanddiocese.org; jodi.roma@portlanddiocese.org www.cluster30.org Rev. Edward R. Clifford, Pst.; Joanne Fortier, DRE; Jodi Roma, Bus. Mgr.; CRP Stds.: 17

Our Lady of Ransom Church - 117 Elm St., Mechanic Falls, ME 04256

St. Catherine of Sienna Church - Paris St., Norway, ME 04268

St. Mary Church - 276 King St., Oxford, ME 04270

OLD TOWN

Parish of the Resurrection of the Lord - 429 Main St., Old Town, ME 04468-1718 t) 207-827-4000 resurrectionparish@portlanddiocese.org resurrectionofthelord.org/ Rev. Kyle L. Doustou, Pst.; Jessica Moore, DRE; Linda Lawrence, Bus. Mgr.; Robert Pascale, Dir.; CRP Stds.: 40

St. Ann Church - 84 Main St., Bradley, ME 04411 t) (207) 827-4000

St. Ann Church - 6 Down St., Indian Island, ME 04468; Mailing: 429 Main St., Old Town, ME 04468 t) (207) 827-4000

Holy Family Church - t) (207) 827-4000

Our Lady of Wisdom Newman Center Chapel - 83 College Ave., Orono, ME 04473; Mailing: 429 Main Street, Old Town, ME 04468 t) (207) 827-4000

OQUOSSOC

Our Lady of the Lakes - 43 Rangeley Ave., Oquossoc, ME 04964-0333; Mailing: P.O. Box 333, Oquossoc, ME 04964-0333 t) 207-864-3795 ollmaine.org Rev. Philip Clement, Admin.; CRP Stds.: 2

St. Luke - 19 Lake St., Rangeley, ME 04964 t) (207) 864-3795

St. John - 76 Main St., Stratton, ME 04964 t) (207) 864-3795

Richard H. Bell Memorial Chapel - Sugarloaf Ski Area, Sugarloaf, ME 04964

PEAKS ISLAND

St. Christopher's - 15 Central Ave., Peaks Island, ME 04108-1140; Mailing: 307 Congress St., Portland, ME 04101-3695 t) 207-773-7746 www.portlandcatholic.org Rev. Seamus P. Griesbach, Pst.; Rev. Selvaraj Kasi, HGN (India), Par. Vicar; Rev. Kevin Upham, Par. Vicar; Abrey Feliccia, Parish Life Coord.; Thomas Van Dzura, Bus. Mgr.;

Our Lady Star of the Sea - 8 Beach Ave., Long Island, ME 04050; Mailing: 307 Congress St, Portland, ME 04101 t) (207) 773-7746

PITTSFIELD

St. Agnes - 238 Detroit St., Pittsfield, ME 04967-3522; Mailing: P.O. Box 193, Dexter, ME 04930-0193 t) 207-924-7104 olofthesnows@portlanddiocese.org Rev. Robert L. Lupo, Pst.; Dcn. David Denbow; CRP Stds.: 8

PORTLAND

Cathedral of the Immaculate Conception - 307 Congress St., Portland, ME 04101-3695 t) 207-773-7746 www.portlandcatholic.org Rev. Seamus P. Griesbach, Rector; Abrey Feliccia, Parish Life Coord.; Thomas Van Dzura, Bus. Mgr.; Rev. Selvaraj Kasi, HGN (India), Par. Vicar; Rev. Kevin Upham, Par. Vicar; Dcn. Michael Augustino; CRP Stds.: 63

St. Louis - 279 Danforth St., Portland, ME 04102; Mailing: 307 Congress St., Portland, ME 04101-3695 t) 207-773-7746 portlandpeninsula@portlandcatholic.org www.portlandcatholic.org Rev. Seamus P. Griesbach, Pst.; Rev. Selvaraj Kasi, HGN (India), Par. Vicar; Rev. Kevin Upham, Par. Vicar; Rev. Amandus B. Sway, A.J. (Tanzania), In Res.; Abrey Feliccia, Parish Life Coord.; Thomas Van Dzura, Bus. Mgr.; CRP Stds.: 5

Our Lady of Hope Parish - 673 Stevens Ave., Portland, ME 04103-2640 t) 207-797-7026 linda.mccormack@portlanddiocese.org www.ladyofhopemaine.org Rev. Paul Sullivan, S.J., Pst.; Rev. Brian J. Conley, SJ, Par. Vicar; Jane Driscoll, Parish Life Coord.; Mary Cafazzo, Bus. Mgr.; Rev. John R. d'Anjou, S.J., Senior Priest; CRP Stds.: 32

St. Joseph Church - Stevens Ave., Portland, ME 04103 t) (207) 797-7026 (Worship Site)

St. Pius X Church - 492 Ocean Ave., Portland, ME 04103 t) (207) 797-7026

St. Brigid School - (Grades PreK-8) 695 Stevens Ave., Portland, ME 04103-2682 t) 207-797-7073 william.burke@portlanddiocese.org www.sbrigids.com William Burke, Prin.; Stds.: 370; Lay Tchrs.: 23

St. Peter's - 72 Federal St., Portland, ME 04101-3695; Mailing: 307 Congress St., Portland, ME 04101 t) 207-773-7746 www.portlandcatholic.org Rev. Seamus P. Griesbach, Pst.; Rev. Selvaraj Kasi, HGN (India), Par. Vicar; Rev. Kevin Upham, Par. Vicar; Abrey Feliccia, Parish Life Coord.; Thomas Van Dzura, Bus. Mgr.; CRP Stds.: 18

Sacred Heart/St. Dominic - 65 Mellen St., Portland, ME 04101-3695; Mailing: 307 Congress St., Portland, ME 04101-3695 t) 207-773-7746 www.portlandcatholic.org Rev. Seamus P. Griesbach, Pst.; Rev. Selvaraj Kasi, HGN (India), Par. Vicar; Rev. Kevin Upham, Par. Vicar; Dcn. Michael Augustino; Abrey Feliccia, Parish Life Coord.; Thomas Van Dzura, Bus. Mgr.; CRP Stds.: 29

SACO

Good Shepherd Parish - 271 Main St., Saco, ME 04072-1510 t) 207-282-3321 goodshepherd@portlanddiocese.org goodshepherdparish.us Rev. Timothy J. Nadeau, Pst.; Blaise Northrop, Director of Pastoral Life; David Gadbois, Bus. Mgr.; Rev. Anthony Lawir (Cameroon), Par. Vicar; Dcn. Kevin N. Jacques; Dcn. Robert M. Parenteau; Dcn. Richard Huot; Michelle Philbrick, Faith Formation Coordinator; CRP Stds.: 131

St. Brendan Church - 40 Lester B. Orcutt Blvd., Biddeford Pool, ME 04006; Mailing: 271 Main St., Saco, ME 04072 (Summers Only)

St. Joseph Church - 178 Elm St., Biddeford, ME 04005; Mailing: 271 Main St., Saco, ME 04072

Most Holy Trinity Church -

St. James School - (Grades PreK-8) 25 Graham St., Biddeford, ME 04005 t) 207-282-4084 nancy.naimey@portlanddiocese.org; helen.fournier@portlanddiocese.org www.sjsbiddeford.org Nancy Naimey, Prin.; Stds.:

163; Lay Tchrs.: 14

St. Margaret Church - 6 Saco Ave., Old Orchard Beach, ME 04064; Mailing: 271 Main St., Saco, ME 04072

St. Philip Church - 404 Goodwins Mills Rd., Lyman, ME 04002; Mailing: 271 Main St., Saco, ME 04072

SANFORD

Saint Therese of Lisieux Parish - 66 North Ave., Sanford, ME 04073-2997 t) 207-324-2420; 207-324-2420 x108 (CRP) shelly.carpenter@portlanddiocese.org; wilfred.labbe@portlanddiocese.org www.stthereseparishmaine.org Rev. Wilfred P. Labbe, Pst.; Shelly Carpenter, DRE; CRP Stds.: 56

Holy Family Church - t) (207) 324-2427

Notre Dame Church - 66 North Ave, Sanford, ME 04073 t) (207) 324-2420

St. Thomas Consolidated School - (Grades PreK-8) 69 North Ave., Sanford, ME 04073-2542 t) 207-324-5832 jessica.rice@portlanddiocese.org www.saintthomassanford.org Jessica Rice, Prin.; Stds.: 116; Lay Tchrs.: 9

SCARBOROUGH

St. John Paul II Parish - 150 Black Point Rd., Scarborough, ME 04074-9394; Mailing: PO Box 57, Scarborough, ME 04070 t) 207-883-0334 jp2me@portlanddiocese.org; michelle.valcourt@portlanddiocese.org jp2me.org Rev. John D. Dickinson, Pst.; Rev. Alexander Robert Boucher, Par. Vicar; Kris Benson, Parish Life Coord.; Dcn. Mark B Tuttle; Carrie Flanagan, Bus. Mgr.; Michelle Valcourt, DRE; Rev. Msgr. Marc B. Caron, In Res.; CRP Stds.: 130

Holy Cross School - (Grades PreK-8) 436 Broadway, South Portland, ME 04106-2996 t) 207-799-6661 william.ridge@portlanddiocese.org; timothy.stebbins@portlanddiocese.org www.holycrossmaine.org Timothy Stebbins, Prin.; Stds.: 118; Lay Tchrs.: 11

Holy Cross Church - 124 Cottage Rd., South Portland, ME 04106 t) (207) 883-0334

St. Bartholomew Church - 8 Two Lights Rd., Cape Elizabeth, ME 04107 t) (207) 883-0334 Rev. Claude R. Gendreau, In Res.;

St. Maximilian Kolbe Church - t) (207) 883-0334

SKOWHEGAN

Christ the King Parish - 273 Water St., Skowhegan, ME 04976; Mailing: PO Box 369, Skowhegan, ME 04976-0369 t) 207-474-2039 christthekingparish@portlanddiocese.org www.ctkparishonline.com Rev. James L. Nadeau, Pst.; Alicia Benson, DRE; CRP Stds.: 9

St. Peter Church - 26 Owens St., Bingham, ME 04920

St. Sebastian Church - 175 Main St., Madison, ME 04950

Notre Dame de Lourdes Church - Water St., Skowhegan, ME 04976

ST. AGATHA

Our Lady of the Valley - 379 Main St., St. Agatha, ME 04772; Mailing: 309 St. Thomas St., Ste. 103, Madawaska, ME 04756-1278 t) 207-543-7447; 207-728-7531 (Cluster II Office) judy.lavoie@portlanddiocese.org; greg.cyr@portlanddiocese.org sjvcatholics.org Rev. Kent R. Ouellette, Pst.; Rev. Agustin Sebasthiyan, HGN (India), Par. Vicar; CRP Stds.: 81

St. Luce Church - 437 U.S. Route 1, Frenchville, ME 04745

St. Agatha Church - ; Mailing: PO Box 10, St. Agatha, ME 04772

St. Joseph Church - 413 Shore Rd., Sinclair, ME 04779

St. Michael Church - 31 Chapel Rd., St. David, ME 04773

VAN BUREN

Saint Peter Chanel Parish - 174 Main St., Van Buren, ME 04785-1237 t) 207-868-2718 judy.lavoie@portlanddiocese.org; greg.cyr@portlanddiocese.org sjvcatholics.org Rev. Kent R. Ouellette, Pst.; Rev. Agustin Sebasthiyan, HGN (India); CRP Stds.: 24

St. Joseph Church - 1779 Hamlin Rd., Hamlin, ME 04785

St. Bruno-St. Remi Church - Main St., Van Buren, ME 04785

WELLS

Holy Spirit Parish - 236 Eldridge Rd., Wells, ME 04090-4050 t) 207-985-6252 (CRP); 207-646-5605 rosanne.smith@portlanddiocese.org; carolyn.houston@portlanddiocese.org holyspiritme.org Rev. Fred Morse, Pst.; Carolyn Houston, DRE; Rosanne Smith, DRE; Dcn. Darrell Blackwell; CRP Stds.: 79

St. Martha Church - 30 Portland Rd., Kennebunk, ME 04043-6631

St. Mary Church - Eldridge Rd., Wells, ME 04090

All Saints Church - 45 School St., Ogunquit, ME 03907 (Summers only)

WESTBROOK

St. Anthony of Padua Parish - 268 Brown St., Westbrook, ME 04092; Mailing: P.O. Box 69, Westbrook, ME 04098 t) 207-854-0490; 207-857-0490 (CRP); 207-839-4857 (CRP) stanthonysparish@portlanddiocese.org; mary.hopkins@portlanddiocese.org www.stanthonysparish.org Rev. Louis J. Phillips, Pst.; Dcn. Lawrence Guertin, Parish Life Coord.; Rev. Dominic Tumusiime, AJ (Uganda), Par. Vicar; Sr. Jackie Moreau, R.S.M., DRE; Rev. Reginald R. Brissette, In Res.; CRP Stds.: 88

Our Lady of Sebago - Rte. 114, East Sebago, ME 04085

St. Hyacinth Church - Brown St., Westbrook, ME 04092-0000

St. Anne Church - 299 Main St., Gorham, ME 04038

Our Lady of Perpetual Help - 919 Roosevelt Trl., Windham, ME 04062

WINSLOW

Corpus Christi Parish - 17 S. Garand St., Winslow, ME 04901 t) 207-872-2281 ccmoffice@gwi.net www.corpuschristimaine.org Rev. Daniel J. Baillargeon, Pst.; Deborah Hebert, Bus. Mgr.; Jennifer Kelly, DRE; Kimberly Suttie, Parish Life Coord.; CRP Stds.: 77

Notre Dame Church - 116 Silver St., Waterville, ME 04901

St. John Church - 26 Monument St., Winslow, ME 04901

St. Helena Church - Route 27, Belgrade Lakes, ME 04918 (Summers only)

SCHOOLS: PRESCHOOL THRU HIGH SCHOOL

SCHOOLS

STATE OF MAINE

AUBURN

Saint Dominic Academy - (DIO) (Grades PreK-12) 121 Gracelawn Rd., Auburn, ME 04210-0452 t) 207-782-6911; 207-783-9323 info@stdomsmaine.org www.stdomsmaine.org Alanna Stevenson, Prin.; John Patrick Yorkey, Prin.; Stds.: 465; Lay Tchrs.: 35

WATERVILLE

Mount Merici Academy - (PRV) (Grades PreSchool-8) 18 Mount Merici Ave., Waterville, ME 04901-4645 t) 207-873-3773 finance@mountmerici.org www.mountmerici.org Tina St.Pierre, Head of School; Stds.: 182; Lay Tchrs.: 27

HIGH SCHOOLS

STATE OF MAINE

PORTLAND

Cheverus High School - (PRV) 267 Ocean Ave., Portland, ME 04103-5707 t) 207-774-6238 moran@cheverus.org www.cheverus.org John Moran, Prin.; Rev. Robert Pecoraro, S.J., Pres.; Stds.: 372; Pr. Tchrs.: 1; Lay Tchrs.: 30

CAMPUS MINISTRY / NEWMAN CENTERS [CAM]

BIDDEFORD

University of New England - 11 Hills Beach Rd., Biddeford, ME 04005-9526; Mailing: Good Shepherd Parish - Campus Ministry, 271 Main St, Saco, ME 04072-1510 t) 207-282-3321 Rev. Timothy J. Nadeau, Pst.;

BRUNSWICK

Bowdoin College - 255 Maine St., Brunswick, ME 04011-0000; Mailing: All Saints Parish - Campus Ministry, 132 McKeen St, Brunswick, ME 04011-2980 t) 207-725-2624 anne.theriault@portlanddiocese.org Anne Theriault, Campus Min.;

CASTINE

Maine Maritime Academy - 1 Pleasant St., Castine, ME 04420-0000; Mailing: Stella Maris Parish - Campus Ministry, PO Box S, Bucksport, ME 04416-1219 t) 207-469-3322 Served by the priests and staff of Stella Maris Parish. Rev. Emile H. Dube, Pst.;

INSTITUTIONS LOCATED IN DIOCESE

FARMINGTON

University of Maine at Farmington - 224 Main St, Farmington, ME 04938-1953; Mailing: St Joseph Parish - Campus Ministry, 133 Middle St, Farmington, ME 04938-1598 t) 207-778-2778 stjfarmington@portlanddiocese.org Served by the priests and staff of St. Joseph Parish in Farmington, ME. Rev. Paul H. Dumais, Pst.;

FORT KENT

University of Maine at Fort Kent - 23 University Dr., Fort Kent, ME 04743-1248; Mailing: St. John Vianney Parish - Campus Ministry, 26 E. Main St., Fort Kent, ME 04743-1395 t) 207-834-5656 stjohnvianneyparish@portlanddiocese.org Rev. Jean-Paul Labrie, Pst.;

GORHAM

University of Southern Maine - 37 College Ave., Gorham, ME 04038-1032; Mailing: St Anthony of Padua Parish - Campus Ministry, PO Box 69, Westbrook, ME 04098-0069 t) 207-857-0490 louis.phillip@portlanddiocese.org Rev. Louis J. Phillips, Pst.;

Gorham Campus - t) 207-839-4857 Joy Segovia, Campus Min.;

LEWISTON

Bates College - 163 Wood St., Lewiston, ME 04240-7687; Mailing: Prince of Peace Parish - Campus Ministry, P.O. Box 1540, Lewiston, ME 04241-1540 t) 207-777-1200 gabriel.jacques@portlanddiocese.org www.bates.edu/chaplaincy Rev. Patrick Finn, Par. Vicar;

MACHIAS

University of Maine at Machias - 116 O'Brien Ave., Machias, ME 04654-1329; Mailing: St. Peter the Fisherman Parish - Campus Ministry, P.O. Box 248, Machias, ME 04654-0248 t) 207-255-3731 stpeterthefisherman@portlanddiocese.org Served by St. Peter the Fisherman Parish, Machias Rev. Johnson Sacreties Panneer Selvan, HGN (India), Admin.;

ORONO

University of Maine - University of Maine at Orono, 83 College Ave, Orono, ME 04473-4210; Mailing: Parish of the Resurrection of the Lord - Campus Ministry, 429 Main St, Old Town, ME 04468-1718 t) 207-827-4000 resurrectionparish@portlanddiocese.org www.umaine.edu/newman Rev. Kyle L. Doustou, Pst.; Audrey Aylmer, Campus Min.;

PRESQUE ISLE

University of Maine at Presque Isle - 181 Main St., Presque Isle, ME 04769-2844; Mailing: Parish of the Precious Blood - Campus Ministry, P.O. Box 625, Caribou, ME 04736-0625 t) 207-498-2536 pbb@portlanddiocese.org Rev. David R. Raymond, Pst.;

SOUTH PORTLAND

Southern Maine Community College - 2 Fort Rd, South Portland, ME 04106-1611; Mailing: St. John Paul II Parish - Campus Ministry, 150 Black Point Rd, Scarborough, ME 04074-9349 t) 207-883-0334 jack.dickinson@portlanddiocese.org Rev. John D. Dickinson, Pst.;

STANDISH

Saint Joseph's College - 278 Whites Bridge Rd., Standish, ME 04084-5263; Mailing: Campus Ministry Office, 278 Whites Bridge Rd., Standish, ME 04084-5263 t) 207-892-6766 lsullivan@sjcme.edu; kcody@sjcme.edu www.sjcme.edu Campus Ministry Office. Dr. James Dlugos, Pres.;

WATERVILLE

Colby College - 4000 Mayflower Hill Dr, Waterville, ME 04901-8840; Mailing: Lorimer Chapel, 4272 Mayflower Hill Dr, Waterville, ME 04901-8842 t) 207-859-4273 ccmoffice@corpuschristimaine.org Rev. Daniel J. Baillargeon, Pst.;

Thomas College - 180 W. River Rd., Waterville, ME 04901-5061; Mailing: Corpus Christi Parish - Campus Ministry, 17 S. Garand St., Waterville, ME 04901-7016 t) 207-872-2281 ccmoffice@corpuschristimaine.org Rev. Daniel J. Baillargeon, Pst.;

CATHOLIC CHARITIES [CCH]

PORTLAND

Catholic Charities Maine - 307 Congress St., Portland, ME 04101-3638; Mailing: PO Box 10660, Portland, ME 04104-6060 t) 207-781-8550 info@ccmaine.org www.ccmaine.org Rev. Msgr. Marc B. Caron, Chap.; Most Rev. Robert P. Deeley, Pres.; Stephen P. Letourneau, CEO; Michael Smith, Dir.; Asstd. Annu.: 53,441; Staff: 470

St. Elizabeth's Child Development Center - 87 High St., Portland, ME 04101-3811 t) 207-871-7444 Bill Hager, Dir.;

St. Michael's Center - 436 S. Main St., Brewer, ME 04412 t) 207-941-2855 (Functional Family Therapy and Case Management Services and Children Behavioral Health Home Services) Bob Colby, Dir.;

CEMETERIES [CEM]

BANGOR

Mount Pleasant Catholic Cemetery - 449 Ohio St., Bangor, ME 04401-3736; Mailing: 207 York St., Bangor, ME 04401-5442 t) 207-947-4322 joseph.gallant@portlanddiocese.org Joseph Gallant, Supt.;

BIDDEFORD

St. Joseph Cemetery and St. Mary Cemetery - 120 West St., Biddeford, ME 04005-0000 t) 207-282-0747 kenneth.greenleaf@portlanddiocese.org portlanddiocese.org/cemeteries Jessica Letendre, Dir.;

LEWISTON

St. Peter Cemetery - 217 Switzerland Rd, Lewiston, ME 04240 t) 207-782-8721 portlanddiocese.org/cemeteries Jessica Letendre, Dir.;

SOUTH PORTLAND

Calvary Cemetery - 1461 Broadway, South Portland, ME 04106-2601 t) (207) 773-5796 jessica.letendre@portlanddiocese.org; kenneth.greenleaf@portlanddiocese.org portlanddiocese.org/cemeteries Jessica Letendre, Dir.;

WATERVILLE

St. Francis Catholic Cemetery - 78 Grove St., Waterville, ME 04901-5825; Mailing: 17 S. Garand St, Winslow, ME 04901 t) 207-872-2770 stfrancem@portlanddiocese.org www.portlanddiocese.org/stfranciscemetery Deborah Hebert, Dir.;

COLLEGES & UNIVERSITIES [COL]

STANDISH

Saint Joseph's College - Attn: President's Office, 278 Whites Bridge Rd., Standish, ME 04084-5263 t) 207-893-7711 lsullivan@sjcme.edu; cfuller@sjcme.edu www.sjcme.edu Kathryn Cody, Admin.; Dr. James Dlugos, Pres.; Dr. Christopher Fuller, Vice. Pres.; Stds.: 1,542; Lay Tchrs.: 55; Sr. Tchrs.: 1

CONVENTS, MONASTERIES, AND RESIDENCES FOR WOMEN [CON]

ACTON

The Sisters of the Presentation of Mary of Maine, Inc. Presentation Villa - 246 Rte. 109, Acton, ME 04001; Mailing: Diocese of Portland, 510 Ocean Ave., Portland, ME 04103-4936 t) 978-688-1920 pmtreasurer209@gmail.com www.presentationofmary-usa.org Sr. Annette Laliberte, P.M., Treas.; Srs.: 2

BANGOR

St. Joseph Convent - 754 Ohio St., Bangor, ME 04401-3165 c) 207-944-1015 Sr. Barbara Theresa Martis, C.S.S.F., Supr.; Srs.: 2

Missionary Sisters of the Immaculate Conception of the Mother of God - 121 Fern St., Bangor, ME 04401-4039 t) 207-262-3532 bridie59@earthlink.net Sr. Miriam Devlin, S.M.I.C., Supr.; Srs.: 2

BIDDEFORD

St. Joseph Convent - 409 Pool St., Biddeford, ME 04005 t) 207-283-9051 anadeau409@maine.rr.com Sr. Annette Nadeau, S.C.I.M., Supr.; Srs.: 21

Marie Joseph Spiritual Center - 10 Evans Rd., Biddeford, ME 04005-9290 t) 207-284-5671 sisters@mariejosephspiritual.org www.mariejosephspiritual.org (Sisters of the Presentation of Mary) Sr. Ruth Ouellette, P.M., Supr.; Srs.: 13

Provincial Residence - 409 Pool St., Biddeford, ME 04005-9506 t) 207-283-9051 scimprov@outlook.com Servants of the Immaculate Heart of Mary. Sr. Theresa Gauvin, S.C.I.M., Prov.; Srs.: 1

LEWISTON

Holy Cross - 16 Saint Croix St., Apt. 2, Lewiston, ME 04240-5061 t) 207-782-0263 ccmondor@yahoo.com; pmtreasurer209@gmail.com Sr. Cecile Mondor, P.M., Supr.; Srs.: 2

OLD ORCHARD BEACH

Sisters of Our Lady of the Holy Rosary - 25 Portland Ave., Old Orchard Beach, ME 04064-2211 t) 207-934-0592; (207) 937-3214 jenroy43@yahoo.ca Sr. Jeannette Roy, R.S.R., Supr.; Srs.: 9

OTTISFIELD

Community of the Resurrection A Lataste Community, Inc. - 205 Poplar Ridge Rd., Ottisfield, ME 04270-0000; Mailing: P.O. Box 284, Casco, ME 04015-0284 t) 207-627-7184 comres123@gmail.com Sr. Renata Camenzind, Supr.; Srs.: 3

PORTLAND

Sisters of Mercy of the Americas - 84 Plymouth St., Portland, ME 04103-2005 t) 207-797-6957 kmsmith@sistersofmercy.org Sr. Mary M. Morey, R.S.M., Contact; Srs.: 1

Sisters of Mercy of the Americas, Northeast Area - 966 Riverside St., Portland, ME 04103-1046 t) 207-797-7861 kmsmith@sistersofmercy.org Sr. Kathleen Smith, R.S.M., Contact; Srs.: 49

SABATTUS

Dominican Sisters - 61 Lisbon Rd., Sabattus, ME 04280-4209 t) 207-375-6583 japro43@gmail.com Sr. Jacqueline Provencher, O.P., Prioress; Sr. Monique Belanger, O.P., Prov.; Srs.: 4

ST. AGATHA

Our Lady of Wisdom Community - Montfort Heights, 384 Main St., Apt. 221, St. Agatha, ME 04772-6169 t) 207-543-9395 Sr. Jacqueline Ayotte, D.W., Contact; Srs.: 2

ST. ALBANS

Sky-Arch Hermitage - 47 Bryant Rd., St. Albans, ME 04971-7327 t) 207-938-3013 Srs.: 1

WATERVILLE

Blessed Sacrament Convent - 101 Silver St., Waterville, ME 04901-5923 t) 207-872-7072 jjroneysss@gmail.com; srcathcaron101@gmail.com www.blesacrament.org Servants of the Blessed Sacrament. Sr. Catherine Marie Caron, S.S.S., Supr.; Srs.: 10

Ursuline Sisters - 1 St. Angela Way, Waterville, ME 04901-4640; Mailing: St Mary's Residence #211, 100 Campus Ave, Lewiston, ME 04240-6040 t) 207-786-9312 Srs.: 9

WINDSOR

Transfiguration Hermitage - 205 Windsor Neck Rd., Windsor, ME 04363-3202 t) 207-445-8031 x201 th.srelizabeth@gmail.com; srewagner@gmail.com www.transfigurationhermitage.org Sr. Elizabeth Wagner, Contact; Srs.: 3

WINSLOW

Sisters of St. Joseph of Lyon - Maine - 80 Garland Rd., Winslow, ME 04901-0600 t) 207-873-4512 office@csjmaine.org www.csjmaine.org Srs.: 14

WINTHROP

Little Franciscans of Mary - 130 Rte. 133, Winthrop, ME 04364 t) 207-395-5338 carol.martin@portlanddiocese.org Sr. Carol Martin, P.F.M., Contact; Srs.: 2

ENDOWMENTS / FOUNDATIONS / TRUSTS [EFT]

PORTLAND

***Catholic Foundation of Maine** - 510 Ocean Ave., Portland, ME 04103-4936; Mailing: PO Box 799, Portland, ME 04104-0799 t) 207-321-7820; 207-321-7871 elizabeth.badger@catholicfoundationmaine.org Elizabeth Badger, Exec.;

HOSPITALS / HEALTH SERVICES [HOS]

BANGOR

St. Joseph Hospital - 360 Broadway, Bangor, ME 04401; Mailing: PO Box 403, Bangor, ME 04402 t) 207-907-1000 mary.prybylo@sjhhealth.com; dberry1@covh.org www.stjoeshealing.com Sponsored by Covenant Health, Inc. Rev. Robert Tumwekwase, A.J. (Uganda), Chap.; Mary Prybylo, CEO; Bed Capacity: 112; Asstd. Annu.: 259,952; Staff: 834

***Alternative Health Services of St. Joseph, Inc.** - 360 Broadway, Bangor, ME 04401 maryprybylo@sjhhealth.com www.stjoehealing.org Home Health and Hospice Services.

***St. Joseph Ambulatory Care, Inc.** - 360 Broadway, Bangor, ME 04401 t) 207-907-1100 maryprybylo@sjhhealth.com www.stjoehealing.org Corporate entity for all employed physicians and their related office practices for St. Joseph Hospital.

***St. Joseph Healthcare Foundation** - 360 Broadway, Bangor, ME 04401 t) 207-907-1100 maryprybylo@sjhhealth.com www.stjoehealing.org Parent corporation of St. Joseph Hospital and affiliates.

MISCELLANEOUS [MIS]

LEWISTON

St. Mary's Health System - 93 Campus Ave., Lewiston, ME 04240; Mailing: PO Box 7291, Lewiston, ME 04243-7291 t) 207-777-8802; 207-777-8546 www.stmarysmaine.com Member of Covenant Health in Tewksbury, MA. Steven Jorgensen, Pres.; Elizabeth Keene, Vice. Pres.; Staff: 16

***St. Mary's d'Youville Pavilion** - 102 Campus Ave., Lewiston, ME 04240 t) 207-777-4200 www.stmarysdyouville.org Sponsored by St. Mary's Health System (a member of Covenant Health in Tewksbury, MA) Philip Hickey, Admin.; Rev. Arockiasmy Santhiyagu, H.G.N. (India), Priest; Charles Demm, Dir.; John Baugher, Chap.;

***St. Mary's Regional Medical Center** - 93 Campus

Ave., Lewiston, ME 04240; Mailing: P.O. Box 291, Lewiston, ME 04243-0291 t) (207) 777-8802 (Administration) Rev. Arockiasmy Santhiyagu, H.G.N. (India), Priest; Charles Demm, Dir.; John Baugher, Chap.; Bed Capacity: 170; Asstd. Annu.: 321,948; Staff: 1,258

St. Mary's Nutrition Center of Maine - t) 207-513-3847 Nutrition services. Kirsten Walter, Dir.;

St. Mary's Residences - 100 Campus Ave., Lewiston, ME 04240 t) (207) 777-8832 (Formerly: Maison Marcotte) Steven Jorgensen, Pres.; Larry Morin, Dir.;

PORTLAND

DBH Management II, Inc. - 510 Ocean Ave., Portland, ME 04103 t) 207-660-9229 mike@dbhmanagement.org Scott Graff, Treas.; Michael Pease, Dir.; Most Rev. Robert P. Deeley, Pres.;

DBH Management, Inc. - 510 Ocean Ave., Portland, ME 04103-4936 t) 207-660-9229 mike@dbhmanagement.org Sponsored by: Roman Catholic Diocese of Portland. Scott Graff, Treas.; Michael Pease, Dir.;

MONASTERIES AND RESIDENCES FOR PRIESTS AND BROTHERS [MON]

ALFRED

Brothers of Christian Instruction - 125 Shaker Hill Rd., Alfred, ME 04002; Mailing: P.O. Box 159, 125 Shaker Hill Rd., Alfred, ME 04002-0159 t) 207-324-1017 x3 djcaron43@yahoo.com Bro. Daniel Caron, F.I.C., Prov. Asst.; Brs.: 9; Priests: 1

KENNEBUNK

Society of Franciscan Fathers of Greene, Maine - 28 Beach Ave., Kennebunk, ME 04043-7628; Mailing: P.O. Box 980, Kennebunkport, ME 04046-0980 t) 207-967-2011 jonasbac@gmail.com www.framon.net Rev. Aurelijus Gricius, O.F.M., Supr.; Rev. John J. Bacevicius, O.F.M., Mem.; Rev. Andrew R. Bisson, O.F.M., Mem.; Rev. Raimundas Bukauskas, O.F.M., Vicar & Treas.; Priests: 4

PORTLAND

St. Ignatius Residence (The Jesuits of Maine) - 492 Ocean Ave., Portland, ME 04103-4936; Mailing: 292 Ociean Ave, Portland, ME 04103 t) 207-775-3032 bconleysj@gmail.com Jesuit Fathers (Northeast Prov.). Rev. Brian J. Conley, SJ, Supr.; Priests: 5

NURSING / REHABILITATION / CONVALESCENCE / ELDERLY CARE [NUR]

AUGUSTA

Roncalli Apartments, Inc. - 144 State St., Augusta, ME 04330; Mailing: 510 Ocean Ave., Portland, ME 04103-4936 t) 207-512-4248 mharris@dbhmanagement.org www.roncalliapartments.com Sponsor: Roman Catholic Diocese of Portland. Michael Pease, Dir.; Scott Graff, Treas.; Asstd. Annu.: 36; Staff: 3

BANGOR

St. Xavier's Home - 119 Somerset St., Bangor, ME 04401-5334; Mailing: 510 Ocean Ave., Portland, ME 04103-4936 t) 207-942-2108 mike@dbhmanagement.org Sponsor: Roman Catholic Diocese of Portland. Scott Graff, Treas.; Asstd. Annu.: 24; Staff: 3

BIDDEFORD

St. Andre Health Care & Facility - 407 Pool St., Biddeford, ME 04005-9716 t) 207-282-5171 salaimo@covh.org standre.org Sponsored by Covenant Health, Inc., Tewksbury, MA. Sandra Lucas, Pst. Min./Coord.; Stephen Alaimo, Pres.; Asstd. Annu.: 320; Staff: 125

PORTLAND

Deering Pavilion - 880 Forest Ave., Portland, ME 04103-4128 t) 207-797-8777 info@deeringpavilion.com www.deeringpavilion.com Diocesan Bureau of Housing Joanne Bean, Admin.; Scott Graff, Treas.; Asstd. Annu.: 239; Staff: 9

WATERVILLE

St. Francis Apartments, Inc. - 52 Elm St., Waterville, ME 04901-6015; Mailing: 510 Ocean Ave., Portland, ME 04103-4936 t) 207-660-9256 mharris@dbhmanagement.org Scott Graff, Treas.; Michael Pease, Dir.; Asstd. Annu.: 47; Staff: 3

Seton Village Inc. - 1 Carver St., Waterville, ME 04901-5739; Mailing: 510 Ocean Ave., Portland, ME 04103-4936 t) 207-873-0178 robin@dbhmanagement.org Most Rev. Robert P. Deeley, Pres.; Michael Pease, Dir.; Scott Graff, Treas.; Asstd. Annu.: 181; Staff: 6

RETREAT HOUSES / RENEWAL CENTERS [RTR]

BIDDEFORD

Marie Joseph Spiritual Center - 10 Evans Rd., Biddeford, ME 04005-9290 t) 207-284-5671 sisters@mariejosephspiritual.org www.mariejosephspiritual.org Congregation (Sisters) of the Presentation of Mary, Inc. Michelle VanDeven, Dir.;

FRENCHVILLE

Christian Life Center - 444 U.S. Rte. 1, Frenchville, ME 04745-0530; Mailing: 309 St. Thomas St. Ste 103, Madawaska, ME 04756-1278 t) 207-728-7531 judy.lavoie@portlanddiocese.org; antony.mariadoss@portlanddiocese.org clc4me.org Rev. Alex Anthony Maria Doss, H.G.N. (India), Dir.; Rev. Jean-Paul Labrie, Dean;

SPECIAL CARE FACILITIES [SPF]

BREWER

St. Andre Home, Inc. - Admin. Office, 436 S Main St., Brewer, ME 04412; Mailing: PO Box 2373, Bangor, ME 04402-2373 t) 207-282-3351 cnason@saintandrehome.org; cmeservey@saintandrehome.org www.saintandrehome.org Clinical and Case Management, Services for Human Sex Trafficking Victims, Community Outreach Services; Residences in Biddeford, Bangor Carey Nason, Dir.; Bed Capacity: 5; Asstd. Annu.: 109; Staff: 18

LEWISTON

***St. Martin de Porres Residence, Inc. (St. Catherine Of Siena Residence)** - 23 Bartlett St., Lewiston, ME 04240-6804; Mailing: P.O. Box 7227, Lewiston, ME 04243-7227 t) 207-786-4690; 207-241-7511 (Women's Residence) stmdeporres@outlook.com Andrew Phinney, Dir.; Bed Capacity: 18; Asstd. Annu.: 200; Staff: 10

SACO

Esther Residence - 27 Thornton Ave., Saco, ME 04072-2720 t) 207-283-0323 joanne_roy@aol.com www.estherresidence.org Transitional housing for women. Servants of the Immaculate Heart of Mary Sr. Joanne Roy, S.C.I.M., Dir.; Bed Capacity: 8; Asstd. Annu.: 10; Staff: 5

An asterisk (*) denotes an organization that has established tax-exempt status directly with the IRS and is not covered by the USCCB Group Ruling.

Archdiocese of Portland in Oregon

(Archidioecesis Portlandensis in Oregon)

MOST REVEREND ALEXANDER K. SAMPLE

Archbishop of Portland in Oregon; ordained June 1, 1990; appointed Bishop of Marquette December 13, 2005; installed January 25, 2006; appointed Archbishop of Portland in Oregon January 29, 2013; installed April 2, 2013.

Archdiocesan Pastoral Center: 2838 E. Burnside St., Portland, OR 97214-1895. T: 503-234-5334; F: 503-234-2545.
www.archdpdx.org
commdir@archdpdx.org

Square Miles 29,717.

Erected as a Vicariate-Apostolic December 1, 1843

Created Archdiocese of Oregon City, July 24, 1846; Name changed by Papal Decree to "Archdiocese of Portland in Oregon," September 26, 1928.

Comprises that part of the State of Oregon lying between the summit of the Cascades and the Pacific Ocean.

For legal titles of parishes and archdiocesan institutions, consult the Archdiocesan Pastoral Center.

MOST REVEREND PETER LESLIE SMITH
Auxiliary Bishop of Portland in Oregon; ordained June 9, 2001; appointed Titular Bishop of Tubunae in Mauretania and Auxiliary Bishop of Portland in Oregon March 4, 2014; ordained April 29, 2014.

STATISTICAL OVERVIEW

Personnel

Archbishops	1
Retired Archbishops	1
Auxiliary Bishops	1
Retired Bishops	1
Abbots	3
Retired Abbots	3
Priests: Diocesan Active in Diocese	98
Priests: Diocesan Active Outside Diocese	2
Priests: Retired, Sick or Absent	62
Number of Diocesan Priests	162
Religious Priests in Diocese	137
Total Priests in your Diocese	299
Extern Priests in Diocese	39
Ordinations:	
Diocesan Priests	1
Transitional Deacons	6
Permanent Deacons in Diocese	71
Total Brothers	56
Total Sisters	314

Parishes

Parishes	124
With Resident Pastor:	
Resident Diocesan Priests	88
Resident Religious Priests	19
Without Resident Pastor:	
Administered by Priests	17
Missions	23
Pastoral Centers	1
Professional Ministry Personnel:	
Sisters	33
Lay Ministers	170

Welfare

Catholic Hospitals	10
Total Assisted	1,671,207
Health Care Centers	10
Total Assisted	80,375
Homes for the Aged	9
Total Assisted	4,531
Residential Care of Children	1
Total Assisted	160
Day Care Centers	2
Total Assisted	1,247
Specialized Homes	4
Total Assisted	1,984
Special Centers for Social Services	20
Total Assisted	875,414

Educational

Diocesan Students in Other Seminaries	26
Seminaries, Religious	1
Total Seminarians	26
Colleges and Universities	1
Total Students	3,771
High Schools, Diocesan and Parish	3
Total Students	1,712
High Schools, Private	7
Total Students	3,648
Elementary Schools, Diocesan and Parish	39
Total Students	8,583
Elementary Schools, Private	4
Total Students	1,006
Catechesis/Religious Education:	
High School Students	3,159
Elementary Students	7,331
Total Students under Catholic Instruction	29,236
Teachers in Diocese:	
Priests	11
Brothers	4
Sisters	20
Lay Teachers	1,488

Vital Statistics

Receptions into the Church:	
Infant Baptism Totals	3,292
Minor Baptism Totals	311
Adult Baptism Totals	302
Received into Full Communion	340
First Communions	3,327
Confirmations	2,831
Marriages:	
Catholic	585
Interfaith	116
Total Marriages	701
Deaths	1,709
Total Catholic Population	400,822
Total Population	3,643,840

LEADERSHIP
Archdiocesan Pastoral Center - t) 503-234-5334

ADMINISTRATION
Delegate for Catholic Health Care - t) 503-233-8322 vschueler@archdpdx.org Sr. Veronica Schueler, F.S.E.;

OFFICES AND DIRECTORS
Administrative - t) 503-233-8379 jwillhite@archdpdx.org Jo Willhite, Chief Admin. Officer;
Archives - t) 503-233-8334 jschiwek@archdpdx.org Joseph Schiwek, Records Mgr.;
Area Vicars - Rev. Anthony Ahamefule, South Coast; Rev. David Brown, Metropolitan Eugene; Rev. Maxy D'Costa, South Portland Suburban;
Auxiliary Bishop, Vicar General and Moderator of the Curia - t) 503-233-8331 Most Rev. Peter L. Smith;
Building Commission - Most Rev. Peter L. Smith, (Ex Officio); Rev. Don Gutmann, Chair; Jo Willhite, (Ex Officio);
Catechesis & Faith Formation Institute Catholic Life & Leadership - t) 503-233-8315 rmoreno@archdpdx.org Rolando Moreno, Dir.;
Catholic Charities, Inc. - t) 503-231-4866 Natalie Wood, Dir.;
Catholic Youth Organization/Camp Howard - t) 503-231-9484 srkrista@cyohoward.org Sr. Krista von Borstel, S.S.M.O., Exec.;
Cemeteries - t) 503-292-6621 mstaff@ccpdxor.com Jo Willhite; Daniel Serres, Dir. (dserres@ccpdxor.com);
Chancellor - t) 503-233-8322 vschueler@archdpdx.org Sr. Veronica Schueler, F.S.E., Chancellor;
Child & Youth Protection - t) 503-233-8302 cshannon@archdpdx.org Cathy Shannon, Dir.; Mario Martinez, Asst. Child Protection Officer (mmartinez@archdpdx.org);
Clergy Personnel - t) 503-233-8326 clergy@archdpdx.org Rev. Todd Molinari, Vicar;
Clergy Personnel Board - Most Rev. Alexander K. Sample, Archbishop of Portland; Most Rev. Peter L. Smith, Auxiliary Bishop, Vicar General, Moderator of the Curia; Rev. Todd Molinari, Vicar;
College of Consultors - Most Rev. Peter L. Smith, Auxiliary Bishop, Vicar General, Moderator of the Curia; Rev. Msgr. Joseph Betschart, Pres./Rector; Rev. Msgr. Richard Huneger, Pst.;
Continuing Education for Clergy - t) 503-233-8368 Msgr. John Cihak, Dir.; Rev. John Douglas Marshall; Rev. Mark V. Bachmeier;
Department of Pastoral Ministries - t) 503-233-8335 kwelch@archdpdx.org Dcn. Kevin Welch, Dir.;
Departments -
Archdiocesan Administrative Department - t) 503-233-8379 jwillhite@archdpdx.org Jo Willhite, Chief Admin. Officer;
Department of Catholic Schools - t) 503-233-8300; 503-233-8348 dcs@archdpdx.org; vinahara@archdpdx.org Jeannie Ray-Timony, Supt.; Amy Jefferis, Asst. Supt.; Kim Shields, Asst. Supt.;
General Counsel - t) 503-233-8378 gkkiely@archdpdx.org G. Kevin Kiely, Gen. Counsel; Elise Ferguson, Legal Admin. & Risk Mgr.;
Office of the Chancellor and Public Affairs - t) 503-233-8322 vschueler@archdpdx.org Sr. Veronica Schueler, F.S.E., Chancellor;
Office of the Vicar for Clergy and Ministry Personnel - t) 503-233-8326 clergy@archdpdx.org Rev. Todd Molinari, Dir.;
Oregon Catholic Conference (OCC) - Board of Directors - t) 503-233-8386 tcooper@archdpdx.org Most Rev. Alexander K. Sample, Archbishop of the Archdiocese of Portland in Oregon, Pres.; Most Rev. Liam Cary, Bishop of Baker, Vice Pres.; Most Rev. Peter L. Smith, Auxiliary Bishop of the Archdiocese of Portland in Oregon, Sec./Treas.;
Development - t) 503-233-8312 stewardship@archdpdx.org Maharlika Bui, Devel. Assoc. (gifts@archdpdx.org); Christy Ulrich, Donor Svcs. Mgr. (cuhrich@archdpdx.org); Heather Brower, Grant Coord. (hbrower@archdpdx.org);
Diaconate Office - t) 503-233-8337 bdiehm@archdpdx.org Dcn. Brian Diehm, Dir.; Dcn. Geoff Schmitt, Assoc.;
Divine Worship - t) 503-233-8350 goconnor@archdpdx.org Msgr. Gerard O'Connor, Dir.;
Ecumenical and Interreligious Affairs - t) 503-233-8386 tcooper@archdpdx.org Todd Cooper, Dir.;
Episcopal Delegate for Religious - t) 503-233-8322 vschueler@archdpdx.org Sr. Veronica Schueler, F.S.E.;
Finance Officer - t) 503-233-8379 jwillhite@archdpdx.org Jo Willhite, Chief Admin. Officer;
Hispanic Ministries - t) 503-233-8399 ministeriohispano@archdpdx.org Rev. Michael I. Kueber, Dir.;
Historical Commission - Mary Beth Herkert, Pres.;
Human Resources - t) 503-233-8327 awilson@archdpdx.org Alana Wilson, Dir.;
Marriage & Family Life - t) 503-233-8304 Jason Kidd (jkidd@archdpdx.org);
Mission Office - t) 503-233-8322 vschueler@archdpdx.org Sr. Veronica Schueler, F.S.E.;
Oregon Catholic Conference - t) 503-233-8386 tcooper@archdpdx.org Most Rev. Alexander K. Sample, Pres.; Most Rev. Liam Cary, Vice. Pres.; Most Rev. Peter L. Smith, Secy.;
Oregon Catholic Press - t) 503-281-1191 Most Rev. Alexander K. Sample, Publisher-in-Chief; Wade Wisler, Publisher;
People with Disabilities -
Project Rachel - t) 800-249-8074
Propagation of the Faith, Pontifical Society for the - t) 503-233-8322 vschueler@archdpdx.org Sr. Veronica Schueler, F.S.E., Dir.;
Refugee Resettlement - t) 503-688-2688 mwesterbeck@ccoregon.org Matthew Westerbeck, Dir.;
St. Mary's Home for Boys - t) 503-649-5651 smiller@stmaryshomeforboys.org Francis Maher, Exec.;
School Office - t) 503-233-8300 dcs@archdpdx.org Jeannie Ray-Timony, Supt.; Amy Jefferis, Asst. Supt.; Kim Shields, Asst. Supt.;
Tribunal - t) 503-233-8381 tribunal@archdpdx.org Sr. Joanna Hoang, MTG, Notary (srjhoang@archdpdx.org); Kelly Littleton, Judge (klittleton@archdpdx.org); Stephen V Garbitelli, Dir.;
Vicar for Clergy and Ministry Personnel - t) 503-233-8368 clergy@archdpdx.org Rev. Todd Molinari;
Vocations - t) 503-233-8368 vocations@archdpdx.org Rev. Peter Julia, Dir.;
Youth and Young Adult Ministry - t) 503-233-8310 ym@archdpdx.org Alexis (Lexie) Torres, Young Adult Coord. (atorres@archdpdx.org); Jason Kidd, Youth Ministry Coord. (jkidd@archdpdx.org);

COMMUNICATIONS
Communications and IT - Marlin Circo, IT Dir.; Robin Moodie, Mktg. & Communications Mgr.;

PASTORAL SERVICES
Respect Life Coordinator - Sarah Livingstone, Coord.;

TRIBUNAL
Auditor - t) 503-233-8380 rweldon@archdpdx.org Rachel Weldon;
Defender of the Bond - Shannon Fossett;
Director of the Tribunal - t) 503-233-8314 sgarbitelli@archdpdx.org Stephen V Garbitelli;
Judges - Rev. Nazario Atukunda; Rev. Msgr. Patrick Brennan (pbrennan@archdpdx.org); Stephen V Garbitelli;
Judicial Vicar - Rev. Msgr. Patrick Brennan (pbrennan@archdpdx.org);
Adjutant Judicial Vicars - Most Rev. Peter L. Smith; Rev. John J. Boyle;
Notaries - t) 503-233-8381 tribunal@archdpdx.org Sr. Joanna Hoang, MTG, Ecclesiastical Notary (srjhoang@archdpdx.org); Susan Ouffoue, Ecclesiastical Notary; Rachel Weldon, Ecclesiastical Notary;

PARISHES, MISSIONS, AND CLERGY

STATE OF OREGON

ALBANY
Our Lady of Perpetual Help (St. Mary) - 815 Broadalbin St., S.W. (office), 822 Ellsworth St. SW (Church), Albany, OR 97321-2469 t) 541-926-1449 olphoffice@stmarysalbany.com www.stmarysalbany.com Rev. Mariano Escano, Pst.; Ace Tupasi, Pst. Assoc.; CRP Stds.: 234

ALOHA
St. Elizabeth Ann Seton - 3145 S.W. 192nd Ave., Aloha, OR 97003 t) 503-649-9044 fjmeeuwsen@seas-aloha.org; re@seas-aloha.org seas-aloha.org Rev. Jeffrey Meeuwsen, Pst.; Dcn. Jesus Espinoza, Pst. Assoc.; Sr. Stella Maris Namae, Director of Catechesis; Carmen Orozco, Bus. Mgr.; Pati Izquierdo, RE Administrative Assistant; CRP Stds.: 105

ASHLAND
Our Lady of the Mountain - 987 Hillview Dr., Ashland, OR 97520 t) 541-482-1146 (Front Office); (541) 708-8500 x100 (Admin. Assist.) sperry@mind.net; olmop@mind.net www.ourladymt.org Rev. Brent Crowe, Admin.; Dcn. Ricardo Cervantes, Pst. Assoc.; Christine Bates, CRE; Elizabeth Millenheft, Youth Min.; CRP Stds.: 60

ASTORIA
St. Mary, Star of the Sea - 1465 Grand Ave., Astoria, OR 97103 t) 503-325-3671 office@stmaryastoria.com www.stmaryastoria.com Rev. William Oruko, Pst.; CRP Stds.: 19
St. Francis de Sales - 867 5th Ave., Hammond, OR 97121 t) (503) 325-3671

AUMSVILLE
St. Mary - Shaw - 9168 Silver Falls Hwy., Aumsville, OR 97325-0338; Mailing: PO Box 338, Aumsville, OR 97325 t) 503-362-6159 bonipast@wvi.com; janna.adams@archdpdx.org www.stmaryshaw.com/ Rev. Paul Materu, A.L.C.P., Pst.; Rev. Richard Rossman, In Res.; Dcn. Steve Tabor; Janna Adams, Bus. Mgr.; Mary Reich, DRE;

BANDON
Holy Trinity Catholic Parish - 355 Oregon Ave., S.E., Bandon, OR 97411 t) 541-329-0697; 541-347-2309 holytrinitybandon@yahoo.com www.holytrinitybandon.org Rev. Anthony Ahamefule, Admin.; CRP Stds.: 12
St. John the Baptist - 15th and Hwy 101, Port Orford, OR 97465 t) 541-332-0139 gmdietel@icloud.com

BANKS
St. Francis of Assisi Catholic Church, Banks, Oregon - 39135 N.W. Harrington Rd., Banks, OR 97106 t) 503-324-2231 Rev. Michael Vuky, Pst.; CRP Stds.: 141
St. Francis of Assisi School - (Grades K-8) 39085 N.W. Harrington Rd., Banks, OR 97106 t) 503-324-2182 sfaoffice01@gmail.com Jannelle Mayo, Prin.; Stds.: 145; Lay Tchrs.: 6

BEAVERTON
St. Cecilia - 5105 S.W. Franklin Ave., Beaverton, OR 97005 t) 503-644-2619; 503-644-2619 x164 (CRP) Rev. Michael Walker, Pst.; Shelly Schultheis, Bus. Mgr.; CRP Stds.: 182
St. Cecilia School - (Grades PreSchool-8) 12250 S.W. 5th, Beaverton, OR 97005 www.stceciliaschool.us Wendy Casale, Librn.; Stds.: 344; Lay Tchrs.: 17
Holy Trinity - 13715 S.W. Walker Rd., Beaverton, OR 97005 t) 503-643-9528 cstorm@htsch.org; parish@h-t.org www.h-t.org Rev. William Holtzinger, Pst.; Dcn. Brett Edmonson, Bus. Mgr.; Chris Storm, DRE; CRP

Stds.: 253

Holy Trinity School - (Grades PreK-8) 13755 S.W. Walker Rd., Beaverton, OR 97005 t) 503-644-5748 holytrinity@pvt.k12.or.us htsch.org Chris Storm, DRE; Stds.: 281; Lay Tchrs.: 25

BROOKINGS

Star of the Sea Catholic Church - 820 Old County Rd., Brookings, OR 97415 t) 541-469-2313 starofthesea@frontier.com; pastor@sosstc.org staroftheseastcharles.org Rev. Justus Alaeto, Pst.; Dcn. Roger Hogan; Dcn. Leo H. Appel II; Sr. Mary Fidel Ike, Pst. Assoc.; CRP Stds.: 19

St. Charles Borromeo - 94323 Gauntlet, Gold Beach, OR 97444; Mailing: P.O. Box 529, Gold Beach, OR 97444 t) (541) 247-2453 pastor@sosspc.org

CANBY

St. Patrick - 498 N.W. 9th, Canby, OR 97013; Mailing: PO Box 730, Canby, OR 97013 t) 503-263-1287 (CRP); 503-266-9411; 503-263-1286 jpatershall@canby.com; stpatricks@canby.com stpatcanby.org Rev. Arturo Romero, Pst.; Jody Patershall, DRE; Frances Parker, CRE; Heriberto Aguilar, DRE (Spanish); CRP Stds.: 195

CENTRAL POINT

Shepherd of the Valley - 600 Beebe Rd., Central Point, OR 97502 t) 541-664-1050 shepherdcatholic.com Rev. Theodore Lange, Pst.; CRP Stds.: 197

COOS BAY

St. Monica - 357 S. 6th St., Coos Bay, OR 97420 t) 541-267-7421 teresa@saintmonicacoosbay.org www.saintmonicacoosbay.org Rev. Robert Wolf, Pst.; Pam Romanko, DRE; CRP Stds.: 38

COQUILLE

Holy Name - 50 S. Dean St., Coquille, OR 97423; Mailing: P.O. Box 368, Coquille, OR 97423 t) 541-396-3849 parishoffice@holynamecq.org Rev. Jorge Hernandez, O.F.M., Pst.;

Sts. Ann and Michael - 209 Second St., Myrtle Point, OR 97458 t) (541) 396-3849

CORNELIUS

St. Alexander - 170 N. 10th Ave., Cornelius, OR 97113; Mailing: P.O. Box 644, Cornelius, OR 97113 t) 503-359-0304 dschiferl.sac@comcast.net; reception.sac@comcast.net www.stalexandercornelius.org Rev. David E. Schiferl, Pst.; Sr. Juanita Villarrea, SSMO, Pst. Assoc.; Neela Kale, Pst. Assoc.; Lizbeth Chavez Villasenor, DRE; CRP Stds.: 289

CORVALLIS

St. Mary - 501 N.W. 25th St., Corvallis, OR 97330 t) 541-757-1988 cmyers@stmarycorvallis.org; klong@stmarycorvallis.org www.stmarycorvallis.org Rev. Lucas Laborde, S.S.J., Pst.; Dcn. Chris Anderson; Catherine Myers, Bus. Mgr.; Lauren Sanders, DRE; Kimberly Long, Admin.; CRP Stds.: 143

COTTAGE GROVE

Our Lady of Perpetual Help (St. Philip Benizi) - 1025 N. 19th St., Cottage Grove, OR 97424 t) 541-942-3420 office@olphcg.net olphcg.net Rev. John J. Boyle, Pst.; Loralyn Eckstine, DRE; Joan Elizabeth Goossens, Bus. Mgr.; CRP Stds.: 44

St. Philip Benizi - 552 Holbrook, Creswell, OR 97426 t) (541) 942-3420

DALLAS

St. Philip - 825 S.W. Mill St., Dallas, OR 97338 t) 503-623-2440 stphilipdallasor@gmail.com stphilipdallas.org Rev. Michael Johnston, Pst.; CRP Stds.: 22

ESTACADA

St. Aloysius - 192 N.W. 3rd Ave, Estacada, OR 97023; Mailing: 18090 S.E. Langensand Rd., Sandy, OR 97055 t) 503-630-2416; 503-668-4446 x101 (CRP) mjaparishescluster.org/contact-st-aloysius Rev. Gregg Bronsema, Pst.;

EUGENE

St. Jude - 4330 Willamette, Eugene, OR 97405 t) 541-344-1191 parishstjude@comcast.net www.stjudeeugene.org Rev. Paolo Dayto, Pst.; CRP Stds.: 20

St. Mark - 1760 Echo Hollow Rd., Eugene, OR 97402 t) 541-689-0725 sparkministrieseugene@gmail.com; saintmark1760@hotmail.com www.stpeterstmarkeugene.org Rev. Michael Jeeva Antony, Pst.; Dcn. Darrell Meter; Mariah Harris, DRE; Dinah Lehmann, Bus. Mgr.; CRP Stds.: 91

St. Mary - 1062 Charnelton St., Eugene, OR 97401 t) 541-342-1139 info@stmaryeugene.com www.stmaryeugene.com Rev. Stephen Kenyon, Par. Vicar; Rev. Ronald Nelson, Pst.; Rev. Arockiaraj (Raj) Michael Pandi (India), Par. Vicar; CRP Stds.: 15

St. Paul Catholic Church - 1201 Satre St., Eugene, OR 97401 t) 541-686-2345; 541-686-2345 x203 (CRP) stpaulcommunity@archdpdx.org; pvdmehden@archdpdx.org saintpaulparish.com Rev. David Brown, Pst.; Dcn. Greg Wilhelm; Pat Von der Mehden, Pst. Assoc.; Sarah Burch, Music Min.; Kristin White, DRE; Dawn Champoux, Bus. Mgr.; CRP Stds.: 106

St. Paul Catholic Church School - (Grades PreSchool-8) t) 541-344-1401 cpenwell@saintpaul-school.org saintpaul-school.org Christine Penwell, Prin.; Stds.: 287; Lay Tchrs.: 14

St. Peter - 1150 Maxwell Rd., Eugene, OR 97404; Mailing: P.O. Box 40518, Eugene, OR 97404 t) 541-688-1051 sparkministrieseugene@gmail.com; stpetereugene@gmail.com www.stpeterstmarkeugene.org Rev. Michael Jeeva Antony, Pst.; Dcn. David Sorensen; Mariah Harris, DRE; Dinah Lehmann, Bus. Mgr.; CRP Stds.: 23

St. Thomas More Catholic Church - 1850 Emerald St., Eugene, OR 97403 t) 541-343-7021 secretary@uonewman.org; pastor@uonewman.org www.uonewman.org (Catholic Campus Ministry) Rev. Pius Youn, OP, Pst.; Rev. Josh David Gatus, O.P., Assoc. Pst.; Corinne M. Lopez, DRE; Rev. Vincent Benoit, O.P., In Res.; Rev. Garry Cappleman, O.P., In Res.;

FLORENCE

St. Mary, Our Lady of the Dunes - 85060 U.S. Hwy. 101 S., Florence, OR 97439; Mailing: PO Box 2640, Florence, OR 97439 t) 541-997-2312 dgilday@archdpdx.org; rlacrosse@archdpdx.org Rev. Panneer Selvam, Pst.; Renee LaCosse, Office Asst./Liturgical Asst.; CRP Stds.: 24

FOREST GROVE

St. Anthony of Padua - 1660 Elm St., Forest Grove, OR 97116 t) 503-357-2989 office@safg.org www.safg.org Rev. Benjamin Tapia, Pst.; Diana Wuertz, Bus. Mgr.; CRP Stds.: 113

Visitation B.V.M. - 4285 N.W. Visitation Rd., Forest Grove, OR 97116 t) 503-357-6990; 503-575-5608 bookkeeper@vcsknights.org; churchsecretary@vcsknights.org www.verboort.org/ Rev. Michael Vuky, Pst.; CRP Stds.: 60

Visitation B.V.M. School - (Grades PreK-8) 4189 N.W. Visitation Rd., Forest Grove, OR 97116 secretarty@vcsknights.org www.vcsknights.org Carol Funk, Prin.; Stds.: 247; Lay Tchrs.: 17

GERVAIS

Sacred Heart-St. Louis - 605 7th St, Gervais, OR 97026; Mailing: PO Box 236, Gervais, OR 97026 t) 503-792-4231 secretary@shstl.org Rev. James Herrera, Pst.; CRP Stds.: 68

Sacred Heart School - (Grades PreK-8) 515 7th St., Gervais, OR 97026 t) 503-792-4541 principal@shstl.org www.shstl.org Mariana Hill, Prin.; Marion Zellner, Librn.; Stds.: 64; Lay Tchrs.: 6

GRAND RONDE

St. Michael - 48520 Hebo Rd., Grand Ronde, OR 97347; Mailing: 1145 N.E. 1st St., McMinnville, OR 97128-6064 t) 503-472-5232 churchoffice@stjamesmac.com stjamesmac.com Rev. Mike Walker, Pst.;

GRANTS PASS

St. Anne - 1131 N.E. 10th St., Grants Pass, OR 97526 t) 541-476-2240; 541-479-4848 (CRP) office@stannegp.com www.stannegp.com Rev. Robert Wolf, Pst.; Rev. Joseph Mujaeropiro, AJ, Par. Vicar; Dcn. Robert Chapin;

St. Anne School - (Grades PreK-5) 1131 NE 10th St., Grants Pass, OR 97526 t) 541-479-1582 stanneschool@stannegp.com www.stanneschoolgp.com Colleen Kotrba, Prin.; Stds.: 78; Lay Tchrs.: 5

Kelly Youth Center - 1131 NE 10th St., Grants Pass, OR 97526 t) 541-476-5802 youthministry@stannegp.com Brian Suda, Pst. Assoc.;

St. Patrick of the Forest - 407 W. River St., Cave Junction, OR 97523 t) 541-592-3658

Our Lady of the River Mission - 3625 N. River Rd., Gold Hill, OR 97525 t) 541-582-1373

GRESHAM

St. Anne - 1015 S.E. 182nd Ave., Gresham, OR 97233-5099 t) 503-665-4935 stannegresham@archdpdx.org www.stannechurchingresham.org Rev. Jose Luis Gonzalez, Pst.; Rev. Miguel Angel Figueroa Farias, Assoc. Pst.; CRP Stds.: 299

St. Henry - 346 N.W. First St., Gresham, OR 97030 t) 503-665-9129 sthenry_gresham@archdpdx.org; theitzman@archdpdx.org sthenrygresham.org Rev. Francesco DePuydt, Pst.; Rev. Niall O'Riordan, Par. Vicar; Dcn. Larry Loumena; Dcn. Lou DeSitter; Claire Clow, Bus. Mgr.; CRP Stds.: 281

HAPPY VALLEY

Our Lady of Lavang - 11731 S.E. Stevens Rd., Happy Valley, OR 97086 t) 503-249-5892 apham@archdpdx.org; info@gxlavangoregon.com www.lavang.us Rev. Ansgar Pham, S.D.D., Pst.; Rev. John Baptist Duong Khac Ngo, SDD, Par. Vicar; Rev. Thanh Dinh Vo, SDD, Par. Vicar; Dcn. Tien Nguyen; Sr. KimAnh Ngo, DRE; CRP Stds.: 864

St. Andrew Dung-Lac - 7390 S.W. Grabhorn Rd., Aloha, OR 97007 t) 503-519-5302 standrewdlmission@gmail.com

HILLSBORO

St. Matthew Catholic Church - 475 S.E. 3rd Ave., Hillsboro, OR 97123-4499 t) 503-648-1998 parishoffice@stmatthewhillsboro.org; bsmith@stmatthewhillsboro.org www.stmatthewhillsboro.org Rev. Juan Jose Gonzalez, MSpS, Pst.; Rev. Rito Guzman, M.Sp.S., Par. Vicar; Rev. Mario Rodriguez, M.Sp.S, Par. Vicar; Maggie Stopka, Liturgy Dir.; Maria Wanner, Faith Formation Coord.; Charlene Sippel, Youth Min.; Becky Smith, Bus. Mgr.; CRP Stds.: 315

St. Matthew School - (Grades PreK-8) 221 S.E. Walnut St., Hillsboro, OR 97123 t) 503-648-2512 kjost@smcshillsboro.org; kcardenas@smschillsboro.org www.stmatthewschoolhillsboro.org Kristin Jost, Prin.; Stds.: 100; Sr. Tchrs.: 1; Lay Tchrs.: 8

INDEPENDENCE

St. Patrick Church - 1275 E St., Independence, OR 97351 t) 503-838-1242 stpatrick97351@yahoo.com Rev. Francisco Bringuela, Pst.; Mireya Molina, Bus. Mgr.; CRP Stds.: 153

JUNCTION CITY

St. Helen - 1350 W. 6th Ave., Junction City, OR 97448 t) 541-998-8053 strosesthelen.org Rev. Edgar Eloy Rivera Torres, Pst.; CRP Stds.: 72

KEIZER

St. Edward - 5303 River Rd. N., Keizer, OR 97303 t) 503-393-5323 grace@sainteds.com; cyndie.harris@sainteds.com wwwsainteds.com Rev. Gary L. Zerr, Pst.; CRP Stds.: 325

LAKE OSWEGO

Our Lady of the Lake - 650 A Ave., 2nd Fl., Lake Oswego, OR 97034-2943 t) 503-636-7687 office@ollparish.com; laurap@ollparish.com www.ollparish.com Rev. John W. Kerns, Pst.; Rev. Suresh Amalraj, Par. Vicar; Dcn. Kevin Welch; Laura Patton, DRE; Georgeann Boras, Pastoral/Admin. Asst.; Boras Georgeann, Pastoral/Admin. Asst.; CRP Stds.: 122

Our Lady of the Lake Catholic School - (Grades K-8)

650 A Ave., Lake Oswego, OR 97034 t) 503-636-2121 office@ollstaff.org Corrine Buich, Prin.; Stds.: 278; Lay Tchrs.: 25

LEBANON

St. Edward - 100 S. Main St., Lebanon, OR 97355 t) 541-258-5333; 541-258-2224 (CRP) Dcn. Richard E. Triska; Rev. Peter O'Brien, Pst.; CRP Stds.: 115

LINCOLN CITY

St. Augustine - 1139 N.W. Hwy. 101, Lincoln City, OR 97367; Mailing: 1151 N.W. Inlet Ave., Lincoln City, OR 97367 t) 541-994-2216 staugustinechurch@lincolncitycoast.com www.staugustinelincolncity.com Rev. Joseph Sebasty, Pst.; Robin Reddish, Office Mgr.;

MCMINNVILLE

St. James - 1145 N.E. First St., McMinnville, OR 97128 t) 503-472-5232; 503-472-5232 x234 (CRP); 503-472-5232 x233 (CRP) churchoffice@stjamesmac.com; mdouglass@stjamesmac.com stjamesmac.com Rev. Amirtham Irudayaraj, Assoc. Pst.; Alejandrina Alvarez, DRE; Colleen Johnson, Bus. Mgr.; Ana Tinoco, Office Manager; Rev. Zani Pacanza, Pst.; Dcn. Raul Rodriguez, Hispanic Minister; Mike Douglass, Youth Min.; CRP Stds.: 320

St. James School - (Grades PreK-6) 206 N.E. Kirby St., McMinnville, OR 97128 t) 503-472-2661 schooloffice@stjamesmac.com www.stjamesmac.com Sally Briedwell, Librn.; Sandra Lonergan, Prin.; Stds.: 85; Lay Tchrs.: 10

MEDFORD

Sacred Heart of Jesus - 517 W. Tenth St., Medford, OR 97501 t) 541-779-4661 www.sacredheartmedford.org Rev. Kenneth Sampson, Pst.; Rev. Moises Kumulmac, Par. Vicar; Dcn. Ron Filardi; Dcn. Dennis Macey; Brenda Woodburn, Director of Administration; CRP Stds.: 131

Sacred Heart School - (Grades PreSchool-8) 431 S. Ivy, Medford, OR 97501 t) 541-772-4105 www.shcs.org Curt Shenk, Prin.; Terry Fry, Bus. Mgr.; Stds.: 135; Lay Tchrs.: 16

St. Joseph - 280 N 4th St, Jacksonville, OR 97530 t) (541) 779-4661

MILWAUKIE

Christ the King - 7414 S.E. Michael Dr., Milwaukie, OR 97222 t) 503-659-1475 office@ctk.cc www.ctk.cc Rev. Msgr. John Cihak, Pst.; Theresa Becker, CRE; David Ochoa, CRE; Alex McCune, Music Min.; CRP Stds.: 50

Christ the King School - (Grades PreK-8) 7414 SE Michael Dr., Milwaukie, OR 97222 t) 503-785-2411 office@ctk.pvt.k12.or.us; riehlj@ctk.pvt.k12.or.us www.ctkweb.org Sarah Taber, Prin.; Stds.: 235; Lay Tchrs.: 26

St. John the Baptist - 10955 SE 25th Ave, Milwaukie, OR 97222 t) 503-654-5449 parishoffice@sjbcatholicchurch.org sjbcatholicchurch.org Rev. John Douglas Marshall, Pst.; Rev. Nazario Atukunda, In Res.; CRP Stds.: 204

St. John the Baptist School - (Grades PreSchool-8) 10956 SE 25th Ave, Milwaukie, OR 97222 t) 503-654-0200 office@sjbcatholicschool.org www.sjbcatholicschool.org Robert Plowman, Prin.; Stds.: 262; Sr. Tchrs.: 1; Lay Tchrs.: 25

MOLALLA

St. James - 301 Frances St., Molalla, OR 97038 t) 503-829-2080 st_james@molalla.net; stjamesmolalla957@gmail.com www.stjamesmolalla.org Rev. Aniceto Guiriba, Pst.; Patricia Parks, Bus. Mgr.;

MONROE

St. Rose of Lima - 470 S. 5th St., Monroe, OR 97456; Mailing: 1350 W. 6th Ave., Junction city, OR 97448 t) 541-998-8053 strosesthelen.org Rev. Edgar Eloy Rivera Torres, Pst.; CRP Stds.: 6

MOUNT ANGEL

St. Mary - 575 E. College St., Mount Angel, OR 97362 t) 503-845-2296 parishcoordinator@stmarymtangel.org www.stmarymtangel.org Mark Dol, Pst. Min./Coord.; Rev. Ralph Recker, O.S.B., Pst.; Cynthia Unger, DRE; CRP Stds.: 201

Holy Rosary - 7442 Crooked Finger Rd. NE, Scotts Mills, OR 97375; Mailing: 575 E. College St., Mount Angel, OR 97362 office@stmarymtangel.org

MYRTLE CREEK

All Souls Catholic Church - 1242 N.E. Spruce St., Myrtle Creek, OR 97457; Mailing: P.O. Box 810, Myrtle Creek, OR 97457 t) 541-863-3271 allsoulsparish@gmail.com; kschray@gmail.com allsoulscatholic.com Rev. Karl Schray, Admin.; CRP Stds.: 29

Holy Family - 243 Marshall Ave., Glendale, OR 97442; Mailing: P.O. Box 136, Glendale, OR 97442 t) 541-227-8274

NEWBERG

St. Peter - 2315 N. Main, Newberg, OR 97132-6081 t) 503-538-4312 shellydidway@gmail.com; stpeter.office@frontier.com stpeternewbergor.org Rev. Martin Tavares-Hernandez, Pst.; Shelly Didway, DRE; Nancy Gooden, Bus. Mgr.; Dcn. Jose Montoya, Hispanic Coord.; CRP Stds.: 210

NEWPORT

Sacred Heart Parish - 927 N. Coast Hwy., Newport, OR 97365; Mailing: P.O. Box 843, Newport, OR 97365 t) 541-265-5101 office@sacredheartnewport.com Rev. Amalraj Rayappan (India), Pst.;

Our Lady of Guadalupe - 231 E. Logsden Rd., Siletz, OR 97380 t) 541-444-1164

NORTH BEND

Holy Redeemer - 2250 16th St., North Bend, OR 97459 t) 541-756-0633 religious.ed@holyredeemernb.org; businessoffice@holyredeemernb.org holyredeemernb.org Rev. Jorge Hernandez, O.F.M., Pst.; James DeLong, DRE; Susan Uehara, Bus. Mgr.; CRP Stds.: 34

NORTH PLAINS

St. Edward - 10990 N.W. 313th Ave., North Plains, OR 97133; Mailing: PO Box 507, North Plains, OR 97133 t) 503-647-2131 mail@stedwardnp.org; n.vandehey@stedwardnp.net www.stedwardnp.org Rev. Michael Vuky, Admin.; Nancy Vandehey, DRE; CRP Stds.: 23

OAKRIDGE

St. Michael Catholic Church - 76387 Crestview St. #422, Oakridge, OR 97463 t) 541-782-3262 ecoleman@archdpdx.org Rev. Ed Coleman, Pst.; CRP Stds.: 6

St. Henry - 38925 Dexter Rd., Dexter, OR 97431; Mailing: P.O. Box 65, Dexter, OR 97431 t) (541) 937-3033

OREGON CITY

St. John the Apostle - 410 Center St., Oregon City, OR 97045; Mailing: 417 Washington St., Oregon City, OR 97045 t) 503-742-8200 office@sja-catholicchurch.com www.sja-catholicchurch.com Rev. Maxy D'Costa, Pst.; CRP Stds.: 6

St. John the Apostle School - (Grades PreSchool-8) 516 5th St., Oregon City, OR 97045 t) 503-742-8230 office@sja-eagles.com sja_eagles.com Mary Haluska, Prin.; Stds.: 231; Lay Tchrs.: 18

St. Philip Benizi - 18211 S. Henrici Rd., Oregon City, OR 97045 t) 503-631-7124 (CRP); 503-631-2882 stphilipbenizi_redland@archpdx.org; mpattyn@archdpdx.org www.philipbenizi.com Rev. Paschal Ezurike, Admin.; Dcn. Jim Pittman; Mary Pattyn, Bus. Mgr.; CRP Stds.: 52

PORTLAND

Cathedral of the Immaculate Conception - 1716 N.W. Davis St., Portland, OR 97209 t) 503-228-4397 parishoffice@cathedral.org maryscathedral.com Rev. Msgr. Gerard O'Connor, Rector; Brigid Young, Pst. Assoc.; Sarah Schneider, Admin.; CRP Stds.: 39

Cathedral of the Immaculate Conception School - (Grades PreK-8) 110 N.W. 17th Ave., Portland, OR 97209 t) 503-275-9370 abiggs@cathedral-or.org www.cathedral-or.org Amy Biggs, Prin.; Stds.: 248; Lay Tchrs.: 20

St. Agatha - 1430 S.E. Nehalem St., Portland, OR 97202 t) 503-236-4747 www.stagathaportland.com Rev. Luan Q. Tran, Pst.;

St. Agatha School - (Grades PreK-8) 7960 S.E. 15th Ave., Portland, OR 97202 t) 503-234-5500 www.stagathaschoolpdx.us Stacey Dunn, Librn.; Stds.: 160; Lay Tchrs.: 13

All Saints - 3847 N.E. Glisan, Portland, OR 97232 t) 503-232-4305 frpaul@allsaintsportland.com; parish@allsaintsportland.com www.allsaintsportland.org Rev. Paul Jeyamani, Pst.; CRP Stds.: 61

All Saints School - (Grades PreK-8) 601 N.E. Cesar E. Chavez Blvd., Portland, OR 97232 t) 503-232-4772 sangeetas@allsaintsportland.com www.allsaintsportland.com Mary Wallulis, Librn.; Stds.: 451; Lay Tchrs.: 41

St. Andre Bessette Church - 601 W. Burnside St., Portland, OR 97209 t) 503-228-0746 pastor@saintandrechurchpdx.org; mission@saintandrechurchpdx.org saintandrebessettepdx.org (Downtown Chapel), Rev. Tom Gaughan, CSC, Pst.; Joan Allen, NA, Coordinator of Mission and Outreach; Laura Dieken, Part-time Parish Accountant;

St. Andrew - 806 N.E. Alberta St., Portland, OR 97211 t) 503-281-4429 asandoval@archdpdx.org; ouroffice@standrewchurch.com standrewchurch.com/ Rev. David E. Zegar, Pst.; CRP Stds.: 88

St. Anthony - 3720 S.E. 79th Ave., Portland, OR 97206 t) 503-771-6039 grymsza@archdpdx.org; pdonoghue@archdpdx.org stanthonypdx.com Glenn Rymsza, DRE; Rev. Patrick Donoghue, Pst.; CRP Stds.: 26

Ascension - 743 SE 76th Ave., Portland, OR 97215 t) 503-256-3897; 503-256-3897 x21 (CRP) sgrigar@ascensionpdx.org ascensionpdx.org Rev. David Leo Jaspers, Pst.; Sharon Grigar, Pst. Assoc.; CRP Stds.: 93

St. Birgitta - 11820 N.W. St. Helens Rd., Portland, OR 97231-2319 t) 503-286-3929 secretarystb@gmail.com; jclifton@archdpdx.org www.stbirgittapdx.com Rev. Joshua Clifton, Admin.; CRP Stds.: 12

Portland, Chapel of Our Lady of Sinj - 11820 NW Saint Helens Rd., Portland, OR 97231 t) (503) 286-3928

St. Charles - 5310 N.E. 42nd, Portland, OR 97218 t) 503-281-6461 stchas@stcharlespdx.org www.stcharlespdx.org/ Rev. Anthony Galati, Apostolic Admin.; Leif Kehrwald, Pst. Assoc.; CRP Stds.: 33

Church of St. Joseph the Worker - 2310 S.E. 148th Ave., Portland, OR 97233 t) 503-761-8710; 503-761-8710 x103 (CRP) www.stjosephtheworkerpdx.org Rev. Ted Prentice, Pst.; CRP Stds.: 71

Church of St. Michael the Archangel - 424 S.W. Mill St., Portland, OR 97201 t) 503-228-8629 www.stmichaelportland.org Rev. Ignacio Llorente, S.S.J., Pst.; Rev. Aaron Stettler, SSJ (Argentina), Assoc. Pst.; CRP Stds.: 2

St. Clare - 8535 S.W. 19th Ave., Portland, OR 97219 t) 503-244-1037; 503-244-1037 x104 (CRP) office@saintclarechurch.org; kim@saintclarechurch.org www.saintclarechurch.org Rev. Donald Gutmann, Pst.; Dcn. Bill McNamara; CRP Stds.: 48

St. Clare School - (Grades K-8) 1807 S.W. Freeman St., Portland, OR 97219 t) 503-244-7600 info@stclarepdx.org www.stclarepdx.org Christopher Harris, Prin.; Stds.: 226; Lay Tchrs.: 21

St. Elizabeth of Hungary - 4112 S.W. Sixth Ave. Dr., Portland, OR 97239 t) 503-222-2168 office@stelizabethportland.net www.stelizabethportland.net Rev. Charles A. Wood, Pst.;

St. Francis of Assisi - 330 SE 11th Ave, Portland, OR 97214 t) 503-232-5880 stfrancispdx.org Rev. George Kuforiji, Admin.; CRP Stds.: 3

Holy Cross Catholic Church - 5227 N. Bowdoin St., Portland, OR 97203 t) 503-289-2834 www.holycrosspdx.org/holy-cross-church/ Rev. Mark Bachmeier, Pst.; Mary Jane Weber, Parish Life Coord.; James Henderson, Youth Min.; Andrea Swanson, DRE; Deb Volker, Bus. Mgr.; Ana Carmina Perez-Flores, Hispanic Ministry; CRP Stds.: 107

Holy Cross Catholic Church School - (Grades PreK-8) 5202 N. Bowdoin St., Portland, OR 97203 t) 503-289-3010 dlarsen@archdpdx.org www.holycrosspdx.org/school Amanda Louie, Librn.; RJ Tagorda, Prin.; Stds.: 226; Lay Tchrs.: 16

Christ The Teacher, University of Portland - 5000 N. Willamette Blvd., Portland, OR 97203 t) (503) 943-8000 webmaster@up.edu Rev. Timothy Weed, Pst.;

Holy Family - 7525 S.E. Cesar E. Chavez Blvd., Portland, OR 97202; Mailing: 3732 S.E. Knapp St, Portland, OR 97202 t) 503-774-1428; 503-774-1428 x123 (CRP); 503-774-1428 x107 (CRP); 503-774-1428 x125 (CRP) churchlady@holyfamilyportland.com www.holyfamilyportland.org Rev. Rodel de Mesa, Pst.; Dcn. Timothy Dooley;

Holy Family Catholic School - (Grades PreSchool-8) 7425 Cesar E. Chavez Blvd., Portland, OR 97202 t) 503-774-8871 office@holyfamilyportland.org Joe Galati, Prin.; Stds.: 213; Lay Tchrs.: 19

Holy Redeemer - 25 N. Rosa Parks Way, Portland, OR 97217 t) 503-285-4539 holyredeemerchurch@comcast.net Rev. Pat Neary, Pst.; Rev. Michael Belinsky, CSC, Par. Vicar; Dcn. Robert Lukosh; Rev. Cameron Cortens; Dcn. John Rilatt; CRP Stds.: 75

Holy Redeemer School - (Grades PreSchool-8) 127 N. Rosa Parks Way, Portland, OR 97217 t) 503-283-5197 dmcpheeters@holyredeemerpdx.org www.holyredeemerpdx.org Deirdre McPheeters, Prin.; Stds.: 254; Sr. Tchrs.: 1; Lay Tchrs.: 22

Holy Rosary Parish Dominican - 375 N.E. Clackamas St., Portland, OR 97232 t) 503-235-3163 office@holyrosarypdx.org holyrosarypdx.org Rev. Peter Do, O.P., Pst.; Rev. Joseph Selinger, O.P., Par. Vicar; Rev. Paul Raftery, O.P., Par. Vicar; CRP Stds.: 102

St. Ignatius - 3400 S.E. 43rd Ave., Portland, OR 97206 t) 503-777-1491 office@sipdx.org www.sipdx.org Rev. Michael Moynahan, SJ, Pst.; Grace Byrd, DRE; CRP Stds.: 278

St. Ignatius School - (Grades PreK-8) 3330 S.E. 43rd St., Portland, OR 97206 t) 503-774-5533 school@sispdx.org www.sispdx.org Carol Pausz, Prin.; Stds.: 219; Lay Tchrs.: 11

Immaculate Heart of Mary - 2926 N. Williams Ave., Portland, OR 97227 t) 503-287-3724 immaculateheart_portland@archdpdx.org; ahardy@archdpdx.org immaculateheartchurch.archdpdx.org Rev. Paulinus Mangesho, A.L.C.P., Pst.; Dcn. Harold Burke-Sivers; CRP Stds.: 17

St. John Fisher - 4567 SW Nevada St., Portland, OR 97219 t) 503-244-4945 mtimoneydeville@johnfisher.org; kbirrell@johnfisher.org johnfisher.org Rev. Richard B. Thompson, Pst.; Kim Cox, Bus. Mgr.; CRP Stds.: 15

St. John Fisher School - (Grades K-8) 4581 SW Nevada St., Portland, OR 97219 t) 503-246-3234 mwasman@sjfschool.org sjfschool.org Merrit Holub, Prin.; Margaret Burd, Librn.; Stds.: 214; Sr. Tchrs.: 1; Lay Tchrs.: 14

St. Juan Diego Catholic Church - 5995 N.W. 178th Ave., Portland, OR 97229 t) 503-644-1617 c) (503) 880-3337 office@stjuandiego.org www.stjuandiego.org Rev. Hans Mueller, Pst.; Ana Garcia, Bus. Mgr.; Kristin Mombert, DRE; Dcn. Dennis Desmarais; Dcn. Diego Montiel; CRP Stds.: 147

Korean Martyrs Catholic Church - 10840 S.E. Powell Blvd., Portland, OR 97266 t) 503-762-6880 c) 971-270-6408 chrkor@yahoo.com www.kmccp.org Rev. Hyunjin Seo, Pst.; Paul Park, DRE; CRP Stds.: 38

St. Mary Magdalene - 3123 N.E. 24th Ave., Portland, OR 97212 t) 503-281-5777 fathermike@themadeleine.edu www.themadeleine.edu (The Madeleine) Rev. Michael Biewend, Pst.; Darlene Maurer, Pst. Assoc.; CRP Stds.: 34

St. Mary Magdalene School - (Grades K-8) 3240 N.E. 23rd Ave., Portland, OR 97212 t) 503-288-9197 cglasgow@themadeleine.edu Carol Glasgow, Prin.; Stds.: 265; Lay Tchrs.: 14

Our Lady of Sorrows - 5239 S.E. Woodstock Blvd., Portland, OR 97206-6822 t) 503-775-6731 frchrispine@oslpdx.org; ian@olspdx.org www.olspdx.org Rev. Chrispine Otieno, Pst.; CRP Stds.: 20

St. Patrick Catholic Church, Portland, Oregon - 1623 N.W. 19th Ave., Portland, OR 97209 t) 503-222-4086 office@stpatrickpdx.org; tfurlow@archdpdx.org stpatrickpdx.org/ Rev. Timothy Furlow, Pst.; CRP Stds.: 7

St. Peter - 8623 S.E. Woodstock Blvd., Portland, OR 97266 t) 503-777-3321 stpeterportland@archdpdx.org; mscott@archdpdx.org Rev. Raul O. Marquez, Pst.; Marcy Scott, DRE; Sr. Maria Kieu Tran, Youth Min.;

St. Philip Neri - 2408 S.E. 16th Ave., Portland, OR 97214 t) 503-231-4955 info@stphilipneripdx.org; debbieg@stphilipneripdx.org www.stphilipneripdx.org Debra Guthrie, Admin.; Rev. Andrew R. Thomas, Pst.; Lyndi Haugen, Pst. Assoc.;

St. Pius X - 1280 N.W. Saltzman Rd., Portland, OR 97229 t) 503-644-5264 frontdesk@stpius.org www.stpius.org Rev. Sean M. Weeks, Pst.; CRP Stds.: 300

St. Pius X School - (Grades PreK-8) 1260 N.W. Saltzman Rd., Portland, OR 97229 t) 503-644-3244 jsmith@stpius.org www.stpiuspanthers.org Joanne Smith, Prin.; Stds.: 527; Lay Tchrs.: 34

St. Rita - 10029 N.E. Prescott St., Portland, OR 97220 t) 503-252-3403 stritaparish@archdpdx.org stritapdx.org Rev. Tetzel Umingli, Pst.; Barbara Stanton, DRE; CRP Stds.: 28

St. Rose of Lima - 2727 N.E. 54th Ave., Portland, OR 97213 t) 503-281-5318 dcooper@strosepdx.org www.strosepdx.org Rev. Matthew (Matt) Libra, Pst.; CRP Stds.: 41

St. Rose School - (Grades PreK-8) 5309 N.E. Alameda St., Portland, OR 97213 t) 503-281-1912 jwimer@strosepdx.org Jessie Wimer, Prin.; Anne McCoy, Bus. Mgr.; Stds.: 253; Lay Tchrs.: 26

Sacred Heart - 3910 S.E. 11th Ave., Portland, OR 97202 t) 503-231-9636 sacredheart@sacredheartportland.org www.sacredheartportland.org Rev. Robert L. Barricks, Pst.; CRP Stds.: 7

Southeast Asian Vicariate - 5404 N.E. Alameda Dr., Our Lady of LaVang, Portland, OR 97213 t) 503-249-5892 apham@archdpdx.org www.gxlavangoregon.com Rev. Ansgar Pham, S.D.D., Pst.; CRP Stds.: 864

St. Stanislaus - 3916 N. Interstate Ave., Portland, OR 97227-1063 t) 503-281-7532 parish@ststanislausparish.com Rev. Piotr Dzikowski, S.Ch., Pst.; CRP Stds.: 11

St. Stephen - 1112 S.E. 41st Ave., Portland, OR 97214 t) 503-234-5019 saintstephenpdx@gmail.com www.saintstephenpdx.com/ Rev. Eric Andersen, Pst.; Joseph Salazar, Relg. Educ. Coord.; CRP Stds.: 63

St. Therese of the Child Jesus - 1260 N.E. 132nd Ave., Portland, OR 97230 t) 503-256-5850 stthereseor.org Rev. Jeffrey Eirvin, Pst.;

St. Therese of the Child Jesus School - (Grades PreSchool-8) t) 503-253-9400 www.sttheresеschool.org/ Stds.: 203; Lay Tchrs.: 12

St. Thomas More - 3525 S.W. Patton Rd., Portland, OR 97221 t) 503-222-2055 x112 (CRP); 503-222-2055 stmparish@stmpdx.org; mschuster@stmpdx.org Rev. Martin L. King, Pst.; Margaret Schuster, CRE; CRP Stds.: 16

St. Thomas More School - (Grades K-8) 3521 S.W. Patton Rd., Portland, OR 97221 t) 503-222-6105 stmschool@stmpdx.org www.stmpdxschool.org Katy Smith, Prin.; Stds.: 204; Lay Tchrs.: 26

RAINIER

Nativity B.V.M. - 204 E. C St., Rainier, OR 97048; Mailing: P.O. Box 340, Rainier, OR 97048 t) 503-556-5641 mgikenyi@archdpdx.org; nbvm.sjb.bulletin@gmail.com www.nativityofbvm.org/ Rev. Mark O. Gikenyi, Pst.; Dcn. Paul Cramer; Jewel Lee, DRE; CRP Stds.: 1

St. John the Baptist - 100 High St., Clatskanie, OR 97016; Mailing: PO Box 340, Rainier, OR 97048 t) (503) 556-5641

REEDSPORT

St. John the Apostle - 12 St. John's Way, Reedsport, OR 97467; Mailing: P.O. Box 205, Reedsport, OR 97467 t) 541-271-5621; 541-997-2312 pansel@ourladyofthedunes.org; nervin@archdpdx.org ourladyofthedunes.org Rev. Panneer Selvam, Pst.; Renee LaCosse, DRE; Patricia Horning, Bus. Mgr.;

ROCKAWAY

St. Mary by the Sea - 275 S. Pacific St, Rockaway, OR 97136; Mailing: PO Box 390, Rockaway Beach, OR 97136 t) 503-355-2661 stmarys1927@gmail.com www.stmarybythesea.com/ Rev. Macdonald Akuti, Par. Admin.; CRP Stds.: 15

ROSEBURG

St. Joseph - 800 W. Stanton St., Roseburg, OR 97471 t) 541-673-5157 jcampos@archdpdx.org; pschulze@qwestoffice.net sjfx-church.org Rev. Jose Campos-Garcia, Pst.; Lourdes Clyde, DRE; Chris Hart, Liturgy Dir.; Pauline Schulze, Bus. Mgr.; CRP Stds.: 45

SALEM

St. Joseph - 721 Chemeketa St., N.E., Salem, OR 97301 t) 503-581-1623; 503-581-1623 x102 (CRP) frontdesk@stjosephchurch.com www.stjosephchurch.com Rev. Christopher Siluvai Rayan (India), Par. Vicar; Rev. Msgr. Richard Huneger, Pst.; CRP Stds.: 428

St. Joseph School - (Grades PreSchool-8) 373 Winter St., N.E., Salem, OR 97301 t) 503-581-2147 schoolbusinessoffice@stjosephchurch.com; ddewar@stjosephchurch.com school.stjosephchurch.com/ Deb Dewar, Prin.; Naomi Arreguin, Bus. Mgr.; Stds.: 180; Lay Tchrs.: 8

Queen of Peace - 4227 Lone Oak Rd., SE, Salem, OR 97302 t) 503-364-7202 church@qpsalem.org; churchqpsalem@gmail.com qpsalem.org Rev. Timothy J. Mockaitis, Pst.; Eddie Caudel, DRE; Michelle Unger, DRE; Sarah Ferguson, DRE; CRP Stds.: 175

Queen of Peace School - (Grades PreSchool-5) 4227 Lone Oak Rd. SE, Salem, OR 97302 t) 503-362-3443 school@qpsalem.org qpschool.org Carl Mucken, Prin.; Stds.: 219; Lay Tchrs.: 20

St. Vincent de Paul - 1010 Columbia St., N.E., Salem, OR 97301 t) 503-363-4589 office@svdpchurchsalem.org www.svdpchurchsalem.org Rev. Manuel Becerra, Pst.; Jaqueline Najera, Pst. Assoc.; CRP Stds.: 319

St. Vincent de Paul School - (Grades PreK-6) 1015 Columbia St., N.E., Salem, OR 97301; Mailing: 1010 Columbia St NE, Salem, OR 97301 t) 503-363-8457 www.svdpschoolsalem.org Richard Hernandez, Prin.; Stds.: 93; Lay Tchrs.: 9

SANDY

St. Michael the Archangel - 18090 S.E. Langensand Rd., Sandy, OR 97055-9427 t) 503-668-4446 www.stmichaelsandy.org Rev. Gregg Bronsema, Admin.; Tammy Pagano, Pst. Assoc.;

St. John the Evangelist - 24905 E. Woodsey Way, Welches, OR 97067; Mailing: 18090 SE Langensand Rd., Sandy, OR 97055 t) (503) 668-4446 office@stmichaelsandy.org

SCAPPOOSE

St. Wenceslaus - 51555 S.W. Old Portland Rd., Scappoose, OR 97056 t) 503-543-2110 (CRP); 503-543-2110 x201 (Office Mgr.) office@stwenceslaus-scappoose.com; wanda@stwenceslaus-scappoose.com Rev. David Gutmann, Pst.; Wanda Van Ortwick, DRE; Janell Greisen, Youth Min.; CRP Stds.: 75

SCIO

St. Bernard - 38810 N.W. Cherry St., Scio, OR 97374; Mailing: P.O. Box 45, Scio, OR 97374 t) 503-394-2625; 503-394-2848 (CRP) pobrien@archdpdx.org www.facebook.com/stbernardscio Rev. Peter O'Brien, Pst.;

St. Thomas - 647 Third St., Jefferson, OR 97352; Mailing: P.O. Box 928, Jefferson, OR 97352 t) (541) 327-2343

Our Lady of Lourdes - 39043 Jordan Rd., Scio, OR 97374 t) 503-394-2437 olol@smt-net.com www.lourdesjordan.com Rev. Luan D. Nguyen, Pst.;

Jeanne Sanders Howe, Admin.; Bob Bjornstedt, DRE; CRP Stds.: 7

St. Patrick - 362 7th St., Lyons, OR 97358 t) 503-668-4446

SEASIDE

Our Lady of Victory - 120 Oceanway St., 1, Seaside, OR 97138; Mailing: PO Box 29, Seaside, OR 97138 t) 503-738-6616; 503-738-6161 (CRP) olvoffice@archdpdx.org www.ourladyofvictoryseaside.org Rev. Joseph Barita, A.L.C.P./O.S.S., Pst.; Joseph Salazar, DRE; CRP Stds.: 46

St. Peter the Fisherman - 79441 Hwy. 101 S., Arch Cape, OR 97102 t) (503) 738-6161 ourladyofvictoryseaside.org/

SHADY COVE

Our Lady of Fatima - 56 Williams Ln., Shady Cove, OR 97539; Mailing: PO Box 116, Shady Cove, OR 97539 t) 541-878-2479 fatimacatholic97539@yahoo.com Pamela Williams, Contact;

SHERIDAN

Good Shepherd - 127 N.E. Hill St., Sheridan, OR 97378; Mailing: 1145 N.E. 1st St., McMinnville, OR 97128-6064 t) 503-472-5232 churchoffice@stjamesmac.com; mwalker@archdpdx.org stjamesmac.com/goodshepherd Rev. Mike Walker, Pst.; Dcn. David J. Briedwell, Admin.; Marie Scett, DRE; CRP Stds.: 1

SHERWOOD

St. Francis - 15651 S.W. Oregon St., Sherwood, OR 97140 t) 503-625-6185; 503-625-6187 (CRP) murmini@sfsherwood.org; bbloudek@sfsherwood.org www.stfrancissherwood.org Rev. Amalanathan Irudayaraj, Pst.; Dcn. Bill Bloudek; CRP Stds.: 248

St. Francis School - (Grades K-8) 15643 S.W. Oregon St., Sherwood, OR 97140 t) 503-625-0497 dgonzalez@sfsherwood.org stfrancissherwoodschool.org Denise Gonzalez, Prin.; Stds.: 184; Lay Tchrs.: 19

SILVERTON

St. Paul - 1410 Pine St., Silverton, OR 97381 t) 503-873-2044 office@stpaulsilverton.com; hkleiman@stpaulsilverton.com www.stpaulsilverton.com Rev. Jossey Kuriakose (India), Admin.; CRP Stds.: 168

SPRINGFIELD

St. Alice - 1520 E St., Springfield, OR 97477-4161 t) 541-747-7041; 541-747-7041 (CRP) pries@archdpdx.org stalice.org Rev. Mark A. Bentz, Pst.; Danielle Plantz, Pst. Assoc.; Sarah J Zielinski, DRE; Peggy A. Ries, Bus. Mgr.; CRP Stds.: 186

ST. HELENS

St. Frederic Catholic Church - 175 S. 13th St., St. Helens, OR 97051 t) 503-397-0148 stfred@comcast.net stfredericchurch.org Rev. Nicolaus Marandu, A.L.C.P., Pst.; Diane Larson, CRE; Sally Caniparoli, Youth Min.; Rosa Gonzalez, Spanish Coord.; CRP Stds.: 50

ST. PAUL

St. Paul Catholic Church - 20217 Christie St., N.E., St. Paul, OR 97137; Mailing: PO Box 454, St. Paul, OR 97137 t) 503-633-4611 stpaulparish@stpaultel.com www.stpaulparishweb.org/ Rev. Scott Baier, Admin.; CRP Stds.: 18

St. Paul School - (Grades PreK-8) 20327 Christie St., N.E., St. Paul, OR 97137; Mailing: P.O. Box 188, St. Paul, OR 97137 t) 503-633-4622 office@saintpaulparochial.org www.saintpaulparochial.org Amanda Davidson, Prin.; Stds.: 117; Lay Tchrs.: 16

STAYTON

Immaculate Conception - 1035 N. Sixth Ave., Stayton, OR 97383; Mailing: 1077 N. 6th Ave., Stayton, OR 97383 t) 503-769-2656 Rev. Luan D. Nguyen, Pst.; Sacha Etzel, DRE; CRP Stds.: 90

St. Catherine of Siena - 716 S First Ave,, Mill City, OR 97360 t) (503) 769-2656

SUBLIMITY

St. Boniface - 375 S.E. Church St., Sublimity, OR 97385 t) 503-769-5664; 503-769-1029 (CRP) bonirel@wvi.com; bonipast@wvi.com www.saintboniface.net Kimberly Zuber, Administrative Assistant; Rev. Paul Materu, A.L.C.P., Pst.;

SUTHERLIN

St. Francis Xavier - 323 N. Comstock Ave., Sutherlin, OR 97479; Mailing: 800 W. Stanton, Roseburg, OR 97479 t) 541-673-5157 jcampos@archdpdx.org; pschulze@archdpdx.org sjfx-church.org/ Rev. Jose Manuel Campos-Garcia, Pst.; Chris Hart, Liturgy Dir.; Lourdes Clyde, Relg. Educ. Coord.; CRP Stds.: 9

SWEET HOME

St. Helen Catholic Church - 600 Sixth Ave., Sweet Home, OR 97386 t) 541-367-2530 sweethomecatholicchurch@gmail.com sweethomecatholicchurch.com/ Rev. Fred Jeffrey Anthony, Pst.; Dcn. Robert Malone; CRP Stds.: 25

Holy Trinity - 104 Blakely Ave., Brownsville, OR 97327; Mailing: P.O. Box 145, Brownsville, OR 97327 t) (541) 367-2530 holytrinitybrownsvilleor@mail.com

TIGARD

St. Anthony - 9905 S.W. McKenzie St., Tigard, OR 97223 t) 503-639-4179 x112; 503-639-4179 x124 (CRP) jhenderson@satigard.org; mmarston@satigard.org www.satigard.org Rev. John Henderson, Pst.; Rev. Peter Nhat Hoang, Assoc. Pst.; Dcn. Marco Espinoza; Dcn. Dave Hammes; CRP Stds.: 105

St. Anthony School - (Grades PreK-8) 12645 S.W. Pacific Hwy., Tigard, OR 97223 anichols@satigard.org satigard.org Andrew Nichols, Prin.; Stds.: 358; Lay Tchrs.: 35

TILLAMOOK

Sacred Heart - 2410 Fifth St., Tillamook, OR 97141 t) 503-842-6647; (503) 842-6648 www.tillamooksacredheart.org Rev. Jesus Angelo Te, Pst.;

St. Joseph - 34560 Parkway Dr, Cloverdale, OR 97112; Mailing: 2410 5th St., Tillamook, OR 97141 t) 503-922-1199 iamalanathan@gmail.com Rev. Angelo Te, Pst.;

TUALATIN

Resurrection Catholic Church - 21060 S.W. Stafford Rd., Tualatin, OR 97062 t) 503-638-1579 office@rcparish.org; mbashoury@rcparish.org www.rcparish.org Rev. William C. Moisant, Pst.; Maya Bashoury, Bus. Mgr.; CRP Stds.: 143

VENETA

St. Catherine of Siena - 25181 E. Broadway Ave., Veneta, OR 97487-0277; Mailing: P.O. Box 277, Veneta, OR 97487-0277 t) 541-935-3933 stcofsienaveneta@aol.com; rnelson@archdpdx.org www.stcveneta.com Rev. Ronald Nelson, Pst.; CRP Stds.: 37

VERNONIA

St. Mary of Immaculate Conception - 960 Missouri Ave., Vernonia, OR 97064; Mailing: PO Box 312, Vernonia, OR 97064 t) 503-429-8841 maryscatholicchurch@frontier.com Rev. Joshua Clifton, Admin.; CRP Stds.: 19

WALDPORT

St. Anthony - 685 N. Broadway, Waldport, OR 97394; Mailing: P.O. Box 770, Waldport, OR 97394 t) 541-563-3246 stanthonywaldport@gmail.com www.stanthonywaldport.org Phyllis O'Boyle, DRE; Rev. Joseph Hoang, Pst.;

WILSONVILLE

St. Cyril - 9205 S.W. Fifth St., Wilsonville, OR 97070 t) 503-682-2332 secretary@stcyrilparish.org www.stcyrilparish.org Rev. Brian V. Allbright, Pst.; Suzanne D'Souza, CRE; Julie Tiedtke, Bus. Mgr.; CRP Stds.: 48

WOODBURN

St. Luke - 417 Harrison St., Woodburn, OR 97071 t) 503-981-5011 stluke1899@gmail.com www.stlukewoodburn.net Rev. Moises Leal, Pst.; Omar Torres, Youth Min.; Sr. Angelica Lopez, DRE; CRP Stds.: 125

St. Luke School - (Grades PreK-8) 529 Harrison St., Woodburn, OR 97071 t) 503-981-7441 www.stlukeschoolwoodburn.org Becky Williams, Prin.; Stds.: 136; Scholastics: 2; Lay Tchrs.: 9

St. Agnes - 3052 D St., Hubbard, OR 97032 t) (503) 981-5011 (St. Luke Office) www.stlukewoodburn.weconnect.com

YAMHILL

St. John the Evangelist - 445 N. Maple St., Yamhill, OR 97148; Mailing: P.O. Box 580, Yamhill, OR 97148 t) 503-662-4291 st.johnyamhill@gmail.com; aalvarez@archdpdx.org stjohnyamhill.org Rev. Julio Cesar Torres Montejo, Admin.; CRP Stds.: 46

SCHOOLS: PRESCHOOL THRU HIGH SCHOOL

SCHOOLS

STATE OF OREGON

BEAVERTON

Sisters of St. Mary of Oregon Campus Schools Corporation - 4440 S.W. 148th Ave., Beaverton, OR 97078 t) 503-644-9181 jmatcovich@valleycatholic.org www.valleycatholic.org John Matcovich, Pres.; Stds.: 989; Lay Tchrs.: 90

Valley Catholic Middle & High Schools - 4275 S.W. 148th Ave., Beaverton, OR 97078 t) 503-644-3745 sbruins@valleycatholic.org (Coed) Sara Bruins, Prin.; Stds.: 649; Lay Tchrs.: 68

Valley Catholic Elementary School - 4420 S.W. St. Mary's Dr., Beaverton, OR 97078 t) 503-718-6500 mdoxtator@valleycatholic.org Melissa Doxtator, Prin.; Stds.: 340; Lay Tchrs.: 22

Valley Catholic Elementary School - (Grades K-5) 4420 S.W. St. Mary's Dr., Beaverton, OR 97078 t) 503-718-6500 mdoxtator@valleycatholic.org www.valleycatholic.org Sisters of St. Mary of Oregon Melissa Doxtator, Prin.; Stds.: 340; Lay Tchrs.: 22

EUGENE

O'Hara Area Elementary Catholic School - (PAR) (Grades PreSchool-8) 715 W. 18th, Eugene, OR 97402 t) 541-485-5291 tconway@oharaschool.org www.oharaschool.org Tammy Conway, Prin.; Leslie Yakama, Librn.; Leslie Jones, Religious Coordinator; Stds.: 543; Lay Tchrs.: 33

PORTLAND

***St. Andrew Nativity School** - (PRV) (Grades 6-8) 4925 N.E. 9th Ave., Portland, OR 97211-4513; Mailing: P.O. Box 11127, Portland, OR 97211-4513 t) 503-335-9600 info@nativityportland.org www.nativityportland.org No-tuition, middle school serving disadvantaged students Rosemarie El Youssef, Prin.; Carolyn Becic, Pres.; Stds.: 77; Pr. Tchrs.: 1; Lay Tchrs.: 8

Franciscan Montessori Earth School - (PRV) 14750 S.E. Clinton St., Portland, OR 97236 t) 503-760-8220 sisterthQresegutting@fmes.org www.fmes.org Sr. Therese Gutting, F.S.E., Headmaster; Stds.: 261; Sr. Tchrs.: 1; Lay Tchrs.: 23

HIGH SCHOOLS

STATE OF OREGON

EUGENE

Marist Catholic High School - (PAR) 1900 Kingsley Rd., Eugene, OR 97401 t) 541-686-2234 sgraf@marisths.org www.marisths.org (Coed) David Welch, Pres.; Stacey Baker, Vice Prin.; Stds.: 379; Lay Tchrs.: 34

MEDFORD

St. Mary's School - (PRV) (Grades 5-12) 816 Black Oak Dr., Medford, OR 97504 t) 541-773-7877 rbernard@smschool.us www.smschool.us Coed Ryan Bernard, Pres.; Jim Meyer, Prin.; Stds.: 531; Lay Tchrs.: 62

MILWAUKIE

La Salle Catholic College Preparatory - (PRV) (Grades 9-12) 11999 S.E. Fuller Rd., Milwaukie, OR 97222

t) 503-659-4155 jhuelskamp@lsprep.org www.lsprep.org John Huelskamp, Pres.; Alanna O'Brien, Prin.; Ann Poteet, Librn.; Stds.: 629; Lay Tchrs.: 42

PORTLAND

Central Catholic High School - (DIO) (Grades 9-12) 2401 SE Stark St., Portland, OR 97214 t) 503-235-3138 info@centralcatholichigh.org www.centralcatholichigh.org (Coed) Danyelle Ramsey, Prin.; Colin McGinty, Pres.; Rev. Timothy Murphy, Pres.; Stds.: 861; Pr. Tchrs.: 1; Sr. Tchrs.: 2; Lay Tchrs.: 53

De La Salle North Catholic High School (Coed) - (PRV) (Grades 9-12) 4300 NE Killingsworth St., Portland, OR 97218 t) 503-285-9385 x100 info@dlsnc.org www.delasallenorth.org James Broadous II, Vice Prin.; Deirdre Perkins, Vice Prin.; Ashleigh de Villiers, Pres.; Maria Cabrera, Prin.; Stds.: 239; Lay Tchrs.: 20

Jesuit High School (The Society of Jesus) - (PRV) (Grades 9-12) 9000 S.W. Beaverton-Hillsdale Hwy., Portland, OR 97225-2491 t) 503-292-2663 tarndorfer@jesuitportland.org; dgolik@jesuitportland.org www.jesuitportland.org (Coed) Rev. Craig Boly, S.J., Chap.; Khalid Maxie, Prin.; Donald Clarke, Campus Min.; Thomas D. Arndorfer, Pres.; Stds.: 1,275; Pr. Tchrs.: 1; Lay Tchrs.: 93

St. Mary's Academy - (PRV) (Grades 9-12) 1615 S.W. Fifth Ave., Portland, OR 97201 t) 503-228-8306; 971-256-9972 catherine.knight@smapdx.org www.smapdx.org (Girls) Emily Niedermeyer Becker, Pres.; Nicole Foran, Prin.; Stds.: 610; Lay Tchrs.: 51

SALEM

***Archbishop Francis Norbert Blanchet School** - (PRV) (Grades 6-12) 4373 Market St., N.E., Salem, OR 97301 t) 503-391-2639 info@blanchetcatholicschool.com www.blanchetcatholicschool.com Robin Smith, Prin.; Bob Weber, Pres.; Stds.: 368; Lay Tchrs.: 37

STAYTON

Regis St. Mary Catholic School - (DIO) 550 W. Regis St., Stayton, OR 97383 t) 503-769-2159 principal@regisstmary.org www.regisstmary.org (Coed) Candi Hedrick, Prin.; Stds.: 107; Lay Tchrs.: 14

Regis High School Foundation - 500 W. Regis St., Stayton, OR 97383 t) (503) 769-2159 rhsprincipal@regishighschool.net; office@regishighschool.net www.regishighschool.net John Meldrum, Pres.;

INSTITUTIONS LOCATED IN DIOCESE

ASSOCIATIONS [ASN]

PORTLAND

***The Gamelin-Oregon Association-Emilie House** - 5520 N.E. Glisan, Portland, OR 97213-3170 t) 503-236-9779 shannan.stickler@providence.org www.providencesupportivehousing.org Shannan Stickler, Dir.;

CAMPUS MINISTRY / NEWMAN CENTERS [CAM]

ASHLAND

Southern Oregon University (Ashland) - c/o Our Lady of the Mountain Church, 987 Hillview Dr., Ashland, OR 97520 t) 541-482-0825 sperry@mind.net www.newmansou.com Walsh Memorial Newman Center Rev. Mariano Escano, Chap.;

CORVALLIS

Newman Center at Oregon State University (Corvallis) - Newman Center, 2127 N.W. Monroe St., Corvallis, OR 97330 t) 541-752-6818 info@osunewman.org www.osunewman.org Rev. Maximo Stock, S.S.J., Dir.; Connor York, Dir.;

EUGENE

Lane Community College (St. Thomas More Catholic Church, Eugene, Newman Center) - 1850 Emerald St., Eugene, OR 97403 t) 541-343-7021 secretary@uonewman.org; corinnelopez@gmail.com uonewman.org Rev. Pius Youn, OP, Campus Min.; Rev. Josh David Gatus, O.P., Campus Min.;

University of Oregon (Eugene) - 1850 Emerald St., Eugene, OR 97403 t) 541-343-7021 secretary@uonewman.org; corinnelopez@gmail.com www.uonewman.org Rev. Emmanuel Taylor, Pst.; Rev. Garry Cappleman, O.P., Assoc. Pst.; Rev. Vincent Benoit, O.P., In Res.; Corinne M. Lopez, Dir.;

MCMINNVILLE

Linfield College (McMinnville) - 1145 N.E. First St., McMinnville, OR 97128 t) 503-472-5232 mdouglass@stjamesmac.com Michael Douglass, Campus Min.;

MONMOUTH

Western Oregon University (Monmouth) - 315 Knox St N, Monmouth, OR 97361 t) 503-838-1242; 503-606-0113 (Campus House) www.stpatrickindependence.org Rev. Francisco Bringuela, Pst.; Thomas Dooley, Campus Min.; Darin E Silbernagel, Bus. Mgr.;

PORTLAND

Lewis & Clark College - 0615 S.W. Palatine Hill Rd., Portland, OR 97219; Mailing: P.O. Box 171, Portland, OR 97219 t) 503-768-7085; 574-229-6513; 503-780-2886 dhaug@lclark.edu; amlechevallier@lclark.edu

PDX Newman Center - 926 S.W. Clifton St., Portland, OR 97201 t) 503-241-4281 campusminister@stmichaelportland.org www.pdxcatholic.org Sr. Teresa Harrell, Campus Min.;

University of Portland - Campus Ministry, 5000 N. Willamette Blvd., Portland, OR 97203 t) 503-943-7131 ministry@up.edu www.up.edu Beth Barsotti, Dir.; Maureen Briare, Dir.; Rev. Jim Gallagher, C.S.C., Dir.; Anthony Paz, Dir.; Rev. Timothy Weed, Liturgy Dir.;

SALEM

Willamette University (Salem) - 721 Chemeketa St., N.E., Salem, OR 97301 t) 503-581-1623 chrelibar3@gmail.com Rev. Msgr. Richard Hunegar, Pst.; Christina Barth, Youth Min.;

CATHOLIC CHARITIES [CCH]

GRANTS PASS

Society of St. Vincent de Paul Our Lady of the Valley Council - 132 S.E. H St., Grants Pass, OR 97526 t) 541-476-5137 c) 541-660-8249 maryf@svdpgpusa.org Mary Frances Morris, Treas.; Asstd. Annu.: 10,304; Staff: 5

PORTLAND

Catholic Charities Oregon - 2740 S.E. Powell Blvd., #5, Portland, OR 97202 t) 503-231-4866 info@catholiccharitiesoregon.org www.catholiccharitiesoregon.org Natalie Wood, Exec. Dir.; Asstd. Annu.: 15,871; Staff: 147

***Caritas Community Housing Corporation** - 2740 SE Powell Boulevard, Portland, OR 97202 t) (503) 231-4866 info@ccoregon.org Travis Phillips, Exec.; Michelle Rouse, Caritas Housing Prog. Mgr.;

Catholic Community Services of Lane County - 1025 G. St., Springfield, OR 97477 t) 541-345-3628 lperreault@ccslc.org; cpickering@ccslc.org www.ccslc.org Basic needs services. Lorri Perreault, Exec. Dir.;

Catholic Youth Organization/Camp Howard - 825 N.E. 20th, Ste. 120, Portland, OR 97232-2295 t) 503-231-9484 srkrista@cyocamphoward.org www.cyocamphoward.org Sr. Krista Von Borstel, S.S.M.O., Exec.;

***El Programa Hispano Catolico** - 333 S.E. 223rd Ave., Ste. 100, Gresham, OR 97030 t) 503-489-6811 equiroz@elprograma.org Edith Quiroz, Exec.;

Refugee Resettlement Services - 2740 SE Powell Blvd, Portland, OR 97202 t) (971) 222-1883 refugee@ccoregon.org Matthew Westerbeck, Bus. Mgr.;

CEMETERIES [CEM]

EUGENE

Mount Calvary Cemetery - 220 Crest Dr., Eugene, OR 97405; Mailing: 333 S.W. Skyline Blvd., Portland, OR 97221 t) 541-686-8722 dserres@ccpdxor.com Daniel Serres, Dir.; Trish Lockhart, Funeral Director and Counselor;

HAPPY VALLEY

Gethsemani Cemetery - 11666 S.E. Stevens Rd., Happy Valley, OR 97086 t) (503) 292-6621 dserres@ccpdx.or.com www.ccpdxor.com Daniel Serres, Dir.;

PORTLAND

Mount Calvary Cemetery - 333 S.W. Skyline Blvd., Portland, OR 97221 t) 503-292-6621 tcorbett@ccpdxor.com www.ccpdxor.com Most Rev. Peter L. Smith, Bd. Mem.; Most Rev. Alexander K. Sample, Mem.; Joanne K. Willhite, Treas.;

COLLEGES & UNIVERSITIES [COL]

PORTLAND

***University of Portland** - 5000 N. Willamette Blvd., Portland, OR 97203 t) 503-943-7101; 503-943-7147; 503-943-8000 admissions@up.edu; leadem@up.edu www.up.edu Endowed by the Congregation of Holy Cross. Dr. Robert D. Kelly, Pres.; Stds.: 3,771; Lay Tchrs.: 283; Pr. Tchrs.: 6

College of Arts and Sciences - 5000 N. Willamette Blvd., #216, Portland, OR 97203 t) 503-943-7221 stewarta@up.edu; cas@up.edu college.up.edu/ Laura McLary, Dean;

Graduate School - 5000 N. Willamette Blvd., Portland, OR 97203 t) 503-943-7107 gradschl@up.edu www.up.edu/graduate/ John Watzke, Dean;

Pamplin School of Business - 5000 N. Willamette Blvd., Portland, OR 97203 t) 503-943-7224 parkerc@up.edu; breiling@up.edu business.up.edu/index.html Gary Malecha, Interim Dean;

School of Education - 5000 N. Willamette Blvd., MSC 149, Portland, OR 97203 t) 503-943-7135 watzke@up.edu; weitzel@up.edu education.up.edu John Watzke, Dean;

School of Engineering - Shiley Hall, 5000 N. Willamette Blvd., Portland, OR 97203 t) 503-943-7292 engineering@up.edu engineering.up.edu Brian Fabien, Dean;

School of Nursing - Buckley Ctr. 301 5000 N. Willamette Blvd., Portland, OR 97203 t) 800-227-4568; 503-943-7211 nursing@up.edu; shillamc@up.edu Joane T. Moceri, Dean; Casey Shillam, Dean;

CONVENTS, MONASTERIES, AND RESIDENCES FOR WOMEN [CON]

ALOHA

Lovers of the Holy Cross of Thu Thiem - 6955 S.W. 201st, Aloha, OR 97078 t) 503-330-5411 mtgttbeaverton@gmail.com Sr. Mary Therese Nguyen, Contact; Srs.: 7

BEAVERTON

Convent, Franciscan Missionary Sisters of Our Lady of Sorrows - 3600 S.W. 170th Ave., Beaverton, OR 97003-4467 t) 503-649-7127 franmisisters39@gmail.com www.olpretreat.org Sr. Anne Marie Warren, O.S.F., Supr.; Srs.: 9

***Sisters of Mary of Kakamega, SMK** - 84 S.W. Horton Way, Beaverton, OR 97006 c) (509) 607-7784 Sr. Angelicah Njuguna, Supr.; Srs.: 3

Sisters of St. Mary of Oregon - 4440 S.W. 148th Ave., Beaverton, OR 97078 t) 503-644-9181 srmichaelfrancined@ssmo.org www.ssmo.org Motherhouse of the Sisters of St. Mary of Oregon Rev. Godfred Ocun, A.J., Chap.; Sr. Denise Klaas, S.S.M.O, Admin.; Sr. Michael Francine Duncan, S.S.M.O., Supr.; Srs.: 48

BRIDAL VEIL

Franciscan Sisters of the Eucharist Convent - 48100 E. Historic Columbia River Hwy., Bridal Veil, OR 97010-0023; Mailing: P.O. Box 23, Bridal Veil, OR

97010-0023 t) 503-695-2375 bridalveil@fsecommunity.org www.fsecommunity.org Sr. Mary Margaret Delaski, F.S.E., Supr.; Srs.: 10

EUGENE

Carmel of Maria Regina - 87609 Green Hill Rd., Eugene, OR 97402 t) 541-345-8649 carmeleugene@gmail.com carmelitesinoregon.org/ (Contemplative Order) Sr. Elizabeth Mary St. Onge, O.C.D., Prioress; Srs.: 6

LAKE OSWEGO

Convent of the Holy Names - 17410 Holy Names Dr., Lake Oswego, OR 97034 t) 503-675-7100 alindsay@snjmuson.org www.snjmusontario.org Provincial House of the Sisters of the Holy Names of Jesus & Mary, S.N.J.M. Srs.: 106

MEDFORD

Missionary Sisters of the Rosary of Fatima, Inc. - 622 Shadow Wood Dr., Medford, OR 97501 t) 541-646-6701 sistergml@hotmail.com Sr. Imelda Mercado, Contact; Srs.: 10

MOUNT ANGEL

Queen of Angels Monastery - 840 S. Main St., Mount Angel, OR 97362-9527 t) 503-845-6141 info@benedictine-srs.org www.benedictine-srs.org Monastery of the Benedictine Sisters of Mt. Angel., See separate listing for Benedictine Sisters Shalom Prayer Center (retreat center). Sr. Jane Hibbard, S.N.J.M., Admin.; Srs.: 19

PORTLAND

Convent of Sisters of Reparation of the Sacred Wounds of Jesus - 2120 S.E. 24th Ave., Portland, OR 97214-5504 t) 503-236-4207 repsrs@comcast.net www.reparationsisters.org Motherhouse Mother Mary of the Angels, S.R., Supr.; Srs.: 1

Holy Spirit Sisters - 2736 N.E. 54th Ave., Portland, OR 97213 t) 503-239-0328 hssportland@gmail.com Sr. Euphemia M. Mkenda, Contact; Srs.: 7

Rose Hall Reparation and Prayer Center - 2120 S.E. 24th Ave., Portland, OR 97214-5504 t) 503-236-4207 mmangels@comcast.net; repsrs@comcast.net www.reparationsisters.org Support for ministry and Donnes of Reparation Mother Mary of the Angels, S.R., Dir.; Srs.: 1

Sister Adorers of the Holy Cross Convent - 7408 S.E. Alder, Portland, OR 97215 t) 503-254-3284 mtgdlhn@yahoo.com; kimchibuimtg@gmail.com Sr. Mary Kim Chi Bui, M.T.G., Supr.; Srs.: 33

ENDOWMENTS / FOUNDATIONS / TRUSTS [EFT]

BANKS

Felix Rougier Religious Care Trust - 39085 N.W. Harrington Rd., Banks, OR 97106; Mailing: P.O. Box 130, Banks, OR 97106 t) 503-324-2492 jgmsps@me.com Rev. Jose Gerardo Alberto, M.Sp.S., Trustee; Rev. Gerardo Cisneros, Trustee; Rev. Alex Rubio, M.Sp.S., Trustee;

LAKE OSWEGO

Holy Names Sisters Foundation - 17590 Gleason Dr., Lake Oswego, OR 97034; Mailing: P.O. Box 398, Marylhurst, OR 97036 t) 503-675-7123 vcummings@snjmuson.org Vicki Cummings, Contact;

MILWAUKIE

La Salle Catholic College Preparatory Educational Foundation - 11999 S.E. Fuller Rd., Milwaukie, OR 97222 t) 503-353-1417 mwinningham@lsprep.org; ablue@lsprep.org www.lsprep.org Matthew Winningham, Treas.;

MOUNT ANGEL

Benedictine Foundation of Oregon - 840 S. Main St., Mount Angel, OR 97362 t) 503-845-2556 benedictinefoundation@gmail.com www.benedictine-srs.org Sr. Dorothy Jean Beyer, O.S.B, Dir.;

PORTLAND

Catholic Schools Endowment Foundation of Oregon - 2838 E. Burnside St., Portland, OR 97214 t) (503) 233-8318

Parish Funds Trust - 2838 E. Burnside St., Portland, OR 97214-1895 t) 503-234-5334 jwillhite@archdpdx.org Joanne K. Willhite, Admin.;

SALEM

Salem Catholic Schools Foundation - 1850 45th Ave., N.E., Salem, OR 97305 t) 503-371-9068 dana@salemcatholicschools.org www.salemcatholicschools.org Dana North, Contact;

ST. BENEDICT

The Abbey Foundation of Oregon - 1 Abbey Dr., St. Benedict, OR 97373-0497; Mailing: P.O. Box 497, St. Benedict, OR 97373-0497 t) 503-845-3030 info@mtangel.edu www.mountangelabbey.org Rev. Martin Grassel, O.S.B., Treas.;

HOSPITALS / HEALTH SERVICES [HOS]

COTTAGE GROVE

***Peace Health - Cottage Grove Community Medical Center** - 1515 Village Dr., Cottage Grove, OR 97424; Mailing: 1115 S.E. 164th Ave., Ste. 314, Vancouver, WA 98686 t) 360-729-1000; 541-767-5500 sbrewer@peacehealth.org www.peacehealth.org Liz Dunne, Pres.; Bed Capacity: 14; Asstd. Annu.: 46,266; Staff: 173

FLORENCE

Peace Health - Peace Harbor Medical Center - 400 Ninth St., Florence, OR 97439; Mailing: 1115 S.E. 164th Ave., Dept. 314, Vancouver, WA 98683 t) 360-729-1000 sbrewer@peacehealth.org www.peacehealth.org Liz Dunne, Pres.; Bed Capacity: 21; Asstd. Annu.: 17,409; Staff: 421

MEDFORD

Providence Health & Services-Oregon (Providence Medford Medical Center) - 1111 Crater Lake Ave., Medford, OR 97504-6225; Mailing: 4400 N.E. Halsey St., Bldg. 2, Ste. 595, Portland, OR 97213 t) 541-732-5000 lee.casey@providence.org Rev. Christopher Fabre, Contact; Rev. James Clifford, O.S.A., Chap.; Josue Delgado, Chap.; John Dungey, Chap.; Valerie Garrick, Chap.; Constance Wilkerson, Chap.; Lee Casey, Dir.; Bed Capacity: 134; Asstd. Annu.: 59,568; Staff: 1,600

***Providence Community Health Foundation, Medford** - 940 Royal Ave., Ste. 410, Medford, OR 97504 t) 541-732-6766 kelly.buechler@providence.org www.providence.org/medford/foundation Kelly Buechler, Exec.;

MILWAUKIE

Providence Health & Services-Oregon (*Providence Milwaukie Hospital) - 10150 S.E. 32nd Ave., Milwaukie, OR 97222; Mailing: 4400 N.E. Halsey St., Bldg. 2, Ste. 595, Portland, OR 97213 t) 503-513-8300 julie.dir-munoz@providence.org www.providence.org/milwaukie Victor Carrasco, CEO; Sherri Kulink, Exec.; Bed Capacity: 77; Asstd. Annu.: 128,651; Staff: 661

NEWBERG

Providence Health & Services-Oregon (Providence Newberg Medical Center) - 1001 Providence Dr., Newberg, OR 97132-1887; Mailing: 4400 N.E. Halsey St., Bldg. 2, Ste. 595, Portland, OR 97213 t) 503-537-1555 bonnie.mcculley@providence.org Rev. Christopher Fabre, Contact; Lori Bergen, Exec.; Bonnie McCulley, Dir.; Bed Capacity: 40; Asstd. Annu.: 52,851; Staff: 540

OREGON CITY

Providence Health & Services-Oregon (Providence Willamette Falls Medical Center) - 1500 Division St., Oregon City, OR 97045; Mailing: 4400 N.E. Halsey St., Portland, OR 97213 t) 503-656-1631 julie.dir-munoz@providence.org www.providence.org Mary Follen, Chap.; Thomas Struck, Chap.; Russ Reinhard, Exec.; Julia Smith, Music Thanatologist; Julie Dir-Munoz, Contact; Bed Capacity: 143; Asstd. Annu.: 51,880; Staff: 695

Providence Willamette Falls Medical Foundation - 1500 Division St., Oregon City, OR 97405; Mailing: 4400 N.E. Halsey St., Bldg. 2, Ste. 595, Portland, OR 97213 t) (503) 650-6809 andra.koller@providence.org Tiffany Gillespie, Chief Philanthropy Officer;

PORTLAND

Providence Health & Services-Oregon (Providence Portland Medical Center) - 4805 N.E. Glisan St., Portland, OR 97213; Mailing: 4400 N.E. Halsey St., Bldg. 2, Ste. 595, Portland, OR 97213 t) 503-215-1111 bruce.cwiekowski@providence.org; kelly.schmidt@providence.org oregon.providence.org Kelly Schmidt, Contact; Rev. Jon Andres, Chap.; Rev. Kevin T. Clarke, S.J., Chap.; Rev. Michael L. Harvey, O.F.M., Chap.; Rev. Augustine Manyama, A.J., Chap.; Rev. Dominic Mtenga, Chap.; Rev. Frederick Nkwasibwe, Chap.; Rev. Augustine Okwuzu, SMMM, Chap.; Krista Farnham, CEO; Bed Capacity: 483; Asstd. Annu.: 247,649; Staff: 3,592

Providence Health & Services-Oregon (Providence St. Vincent Medical Center) - 9205 S.W. Barnes Rd., Portland, OR 97225; Mailing: 4400 N.E. Halsey St., Bldg. 2, Ste. 595, Portland, OR 97213 t) 503-216-1234 sisterlynda.thompsonsnjm@providence.org; godfred.ocun@providence.org www.providence.org Rev. Christopher Fabre, Chap.; Rev. Francis Njau, A.J., Chap.; Rev. Cornelius Ssekitto, AJ, Chap.; Janice Burger, Exec.; Sr. Lynda Thompson, S.N.J.M., Dir.; Rev. Godfred Ocun, A.J., Contact; Bed Capacity: 539; Asstd. Annu.: 193,201; Staff: 3,595

ROSEBURG

Mercy Medical Center, Inc. - 2700 Stewart Pkwy., Roseburg, OR 97471 t) 541-673-0611 kellymorgan@chiwest.com; davidprice@chiwest.com www.chimercyhealth.com Kelly C. Morgan, Pres.; David Price, Dir., Mission Integration; Bed Capacity: 174; Asstd. Annu.: 403,060; Staff: 1,274

Mercy Foundation, Inc. - 1600 N.W. Garden Valley Blvd., Ste 110, Roseburg, OR 97471; Mailing: 2700 N.W. Stewart Pkwy., Roseburg, OR 97471 t) 541-677-4818 clestusosuji@chiwest.com Rev. Cletus Osuji, Chap.;

SEASIDE

Providence Health & Services-Oregon (Providence Seaside Hospital) - 725 S. Wahanna Rd., Seaside, OR 97138-7735; Mailing: 4400 N.E. Halsey St., Bldg. 2, Ste. 595, Portland, OR 97213 t) 503-717-7000 cherilyn.frei@providence.org www.providence.org/northcoast Don Lemmon, Exec.; Cherilyn Frei, Contact; Bed Capacity: 25; Asstd. Annu.: 18,955; Staff: 475

SPRINGFIELD

***Sacred Heart Medical Center (Sisters of St. Joseph of Peace)** - 3333 River Bend Dr., Springfield, OR 97477; Mailing: 1115 S.E. 164th Ave., Vancouver, WA 98683 t) 360-729-1000; 541-222-7300 sbrewer@peacehealth.org www.peacehealth.org Div. of PeaceHealth. Liz Dunne, Pres.; Bed Capacity: 455; Asstd. Annu.: 68,647; Staff: 4,500

MISCELLANEOUS [MIS]

BEAVERTON

Our Lady of Peace Institute in Catholic Teaching - 3600 S.W. 170th Ave., Beaverton, OR 97003-4467 t) 503-649-7127 sisters@olpretreat.org www.olpretreat.org Sr. Maria Benedicta Hemminger, OSF, Dir.;

Sisters of St. Mary of Oregon Ministries Corporation - 4440 S.W. 148th Ave., Beaverton, OR 97078 t) 503-644-9181 info@ssmoministries.org www.ssmoministries.org Sr. Adele Marie Altenhofen, S.S.M.O., Pres.;

EUGENE

St. Vincent de Paul Society of Lane County, Inc. - 2890 Chad Dr., Eugene, OR 97408; Mailing: P.O. Box 24608, Eugene, OR 97408 t) 541-687-5820 askme@svdp.us www.svdp.us Lane County District Council Charlie Burnham, Pres.; Terrence R. McDonald, Exec.;

LAKE OSWEGO

***Friends of Our Lady Queen of Africa** - 5308 Westfield Court, Lake Oswego, OR 97035; Mailing: P.O. Box 1061, Lake Oswego, OR 97034 t) 503-968-2211 bverheggen@comcast.net Dcn. Kevin Welch, Chair; Jean Verheggen, Secy.; Bill Verheggen, Treas.; Greg Heinrich, Dir.; Susan Welch, Dir.; Kathleen Wendland, Dir.;

Holy Names Heritage Center Inc. - 17425 Holy Names

Dr., Lake Oswego, OR 97034 t) 503-607-0595; 503-607-0597 scantor@snjmuson.org www.holynamesheritagecenter.org Sarah Cantor, Dir.;

***Mary's Woods at Marylhurst, Inc.** - 17400 Holy Names Dr., Lake Oswego, OR 97034 t) 503-675-2004 ssharma@marywoods.org www.maryswoods.org Jacki Gallo, Chair; Sr. Roswitha Frawley, S.N.J.M., Dir.; Kimberly Scott, Dir.; Lynn Szender, Dir.;

Sisters of the Holy Names of Jesus and Mary U.S.-Ontario Province Corporation - 17590 Gleason Dr., Lake Oswego, OR 97034; Mailing: P.O. Box 398, Marylhurst, OR 97036 t) 503-675-7123 www.snjmusontario.org Sr. Linda Patrick, SNJM, Vice. Pres.; Sr. Carol Higgins, S.N.J.M., Secy.; Sr. Maureen Delaney, S.N.J.M., Prov.; Sr. Mary Slater, S.N.J.M., Treas.; Sr. Diane Enos, S.N.J.M., Dir.; Sr. Marcia Frideger, S.N.J.M., Dir.;

MARYLHURST

Franciscan Spiritual Center (Sisters of St. Francis of Philadelphia) - 3159 Furman Dr., Marylhurst, OR 97036; Mailing: P.O. Box 144, Marylhurst, OR 97036 t) 503-794-8542 info@francisspctr.com francisspctr.com Christine Naylor, Dir.; Michelle Kroll, Admin.; Sr. Theresa Lamkin, OSF, Spiritual Direction;

MEDFORD

Society of St. Vincent de Paul - 2424 N. Pacific Hwy., Medford, OR 97501; Mailing: P.O. Box 1663, Medford, OR 97501 t) 541-772-3828 vincent@mind.net www.stvincentdepaulmedford.info Rogue Valley District Council Kathleen Begley, Pres.;

MILWAUKIE

***Jesuit Volunteer Corps Northwest (JVC Northwest, JV EnCorps)** - 2780 S.E. Harrison St., Suite 102, Milwaukie, OR 97222; Mailing: PO Box 22125, Portland, OR 97269 t) 503-335-8202 info@jvcnorthwest.org www.jvcnorthwest.org Martha McElligott, Executive Assistant; Greg Carpinello, Exec.; Anne Douglas, Dir.;

MOUNT ANGEL

***Fr. Bernard Youth Center, Inc.** - 980 S. Main St., Mount Angel, OR 97362-0790; Mailing: PO Box 790, Mt Angel, OR 97362 t) 503-845-4097 adminoffice@fbyc.info; mark@fbyc.info www.fbyc.info Lay Ministry Youth and Young Adult Retreat Center Sr. Jeanine Tiscot, RSM, Exec.;

St. Joseph Shelter - 925 S. Main, Mount Angel, OR 97362-9527 t) 503-845-6147 sjshelter@mtangel.net stjosephshelter.org Mike Norman, Dir.;

MYRTLE CREEK

Conference of St. Vincent de Paul of Myrtle Creek - 116 N. Main St., Myrtle Creek, OR 97457; Mailing: P.O. Box 1258, Myrtle Creek, OR 97457 t) 541-331-6029 tlday52@outlook.com Terri Lynn Day, Pres.; Tamara E. Whiteley, Treas.;

PORTLAND

Blanchet House of Hospitality - 310 N.W. Glisan St., Portland, OR 97209 t) 503-241-4340 info@blanchethouse.org www.blanchethouse.org Scott Kerman, Dir.;

Brotherhood of the People of Praise - 7709 N. Denver Ave., Portland, OR 97217 c) 612-720-3067 joelkibler@gmail.com Most Rev. Peter L. Smith, Contact;

Catholic Broadcasting Northwest, Inc., Mater Dei Radio, KBVM-FM 88.3, KMME-FM 94.9 & 100.5 - 6249 SW Canyon Court, Portland, OR 97228; Mailing: P.O. Box 5888, Portland, OR 97228-5888 t) 503-285-5200 info@materdeiradio.com www.materdeiradio.com Patrick Ryan, Dir.;

St. Joseph the Worker Corporate Work Study Program, Inc. - 7528 N Fenwick Ave., Portland, OR 97217 t) 503-285-9385 x125 cwspmembers@dlsnc.org www.delasallenorth.org Aiyana Ashley, Dir.;

***The Northwest Catholic Counseling Center** - 8383 N.E. Sandy, Ste. 205, Portland, OR 97220 t) 503-253-0964 info@nwcounseling.org www.nwcounseling.org/ Mental Health Counseling Erin Peters, CEO;

Oregon Catholic Conference - 2838 E. Burnside St., Portland, OR 97214 t) 503-233-8386 tcooper@archdpdx.org Most Rev. Alexander K. Sample, Pres.; Most Rev. Liam Cary, Vice Pres.; Most Rev. Peter L. Smith, Secy.;

Oregon Catholic Press - 5536 N.E. Hassalo St., Portland, OR 97213 t) 503-281-1191 wadew@ocp.org Wade Wisler, Publisher;

Providence Health & Services-Oregon (Providence Home & Community Services) - 6410 N.E. Halsey St., Ste. 100, Portland, OR 97213-4778; Mailing: 4400 N.E. Halsey St., Bldg. 2, Ste. 595, Portland, OR 97213 t) 503-215-4321 james.arp@providence.org James Arp, Exec.;

Providence Health & Services-Oregon (Providence Hospice) - 6410 NE Halsey St., Portland, OR 97213 t) 503-215-2273 jane.brandes@providence.org Hospice services.

Providence Health & Services-Oregon (Providence Home Health) - 6410 NE Halsey St., Portland, OR 97213 t) 503-215-4646 susan.murtha@providence.org Sophia Gonzalez, Contact;

Providence Health & Services-Oregon (Providence Home Medical Equipment) - 6410 NE Halsey St., Portland, OR 97213 t) (503) 215-4663 pat.reagan@providence.org Provides medical equipment & services. John Kleiderer, Chief Mission Officer;

Providence Health & Services-Oregon (Providence Specialty Pharmacy) - t) 503-215-4633 Providence Specialty Pharmacy Services offers a full line of pharmacy services at home, in our infusion suites or in long-term care facilities.

The Rosary Center - 1331 N.E. Third Ave., Portland, OR 97232; Mailing: P.O. Box 3617, Portland, OR 97208-3617 t) 503-236-8393 rosary@rosary-center.org rosarycenter.org (The Rosary Confraternity, Inc.), Western Dominican Province

***Society of St. Vincent de Paul Portland Council** - 8101 SE Cornwell St., Portland, OR 97206; Mailing: P.O. Box 42157, Portland, OR 97242-0157 t) 503-234-5287 brian.f@svdpportland.org svdppdx.org Brian Ferschweiler, Dir.;

ROSEBURG

Linus Oakes Village - 2665 Van Pelt Blvd., Roseburg, OR 97471 t) 541-677-4800 mkronner@chilivingcomm.org www.homeishere.org An operating unit of CHI Living Communities, which is a subsidiary of CommonSpirit Health Michelle Kronner, Exec. Dir.;

SALEM

***St. Vincent de Paul Society of Mid-Williamette Valley** - 3745 Portland Rd., N.E., Salem, OR 97303 t) 503-364-3210 shari@svdpsalem.org Edward Moore, District Manager;

MONASTERIES AND RESIDENCES FOR PRIESTS AND BROTHERS [MON]

AMITY

Brigittine Priory of Our Lady of Consolation - The Order of the Most Holy Savior - 23300 Walker Ln., Amity, OR 97101 t) 503-835-8080 monks@brigittine.org www.brigittine.org Bro. Bernard Ner Suguitan, O.Ss.S., Prior; Brs.: 4

CARLTON

The Cistercian (Trappist) Abbey of Our Lady of Guadalupe (Order of Cistercians of the Strict Observance) - 9200 N.E. Abbey Rd., Carlton, OR 97111-9504 t) 503-852-7174 community@trappistabbey.org www.trappistabbey.org Rt. Rev. Peter McCarthy, O.C.S.O., Abbot; Rev. M. Dominique-Savio Nelson, O.C.S.O., Prior; Rev. Richard Layton, O.C.S.O., Bus. Mgr.; Rev. Casey Bailey, Novice Master; Rev. Martin Cawley, O.C.S.O.; Rev. Timothy Clark, O.C.S.O.; Rev. Timothy Michell, O.C.S.O.; Rev. Peter Plakut, O.C.S.O.; Brs.: 12; Priests: 7

CORVALLIS

***Saint John Society** - 501 N.W. 25th St., Corvallis, OR 97330; Mailing: PO Box 1004, Corvallis, OR 97339 t) 541-760-3498 stjohnsociety@socsj.org www.socsj.org Rev. Lucas Laborde, S.S.J., Pst.; Rev. Ignacio Llorente, S.S.J., Pst.; Rev. Maximo Stock, S.S.J., Chap.; Priests: 4

HILLSBORO

Missionaries of the Holy Spirit, M.Sp.S. - 642 S.E. 20th Ct., Hillsboro, OR 97123 t) 503-648-1998 jgmsps@me.com Serving St. Matthew Catholic Church, in Hillsboro, OR. Rev. Mario Rodriguez, M.Sp.S, Assoc. Pst.; Bro. Oscar Rodriguez, M.Sp.S., Youth Min.; Rev. Rito Guzman, M.Sp.S., Assoc. Pst.; Rev. Juan Jose Gonzalez, M.Sp.S., Pst.; Brs.: 1; Priests: 3

MILWAUKIE

Missionaries of the Holy Spirit, M.Sp.S. - 2512 SE Monroe St., Milwaukie, OR 97222; Mailing: PO Box 22387, Milwaukie, OR 97269 t) 503-324-2492 jgmsps@me.com www.mspsusa.org Provincial House Rev. Jose Ugalde, M.Sp.S., Treas.; Rev. Alex Rubio, M.Sp.S., Vicar; Rev. Pedro Arteaga, M.Sp.S., Prov.; Priests: 3

MOUNT ANGEL

Discalced Carmelite Friars (O.C.D.) - 300 Humpert Ln., Mount Angel, OR 97362 t) 503-902-1120 pvecellio@gmail.com discalcedcarmelitefriars.com Rev. Raymond Bueno, O.C.D., In Res.; Bro. Juan Torres, In Res.; Rev. Peter Mary Vecellio, O.C.D, Rector; Bro. Joseph Mary, O.C.D.; Rev. John Melka, O.C.D., In Res.; Bro. James Lindsay, O.C.D., Spiritual Adv./Care Srvcs.; Brs.: 3; Priests: 1

Missionaries of the Holy Spirit, M.Sp.S. - 585 E. College St., Mount Angel, OR 97362; Mailing: P.O. Box 499, St. Benedict, OR 97373 t) 503-845-1181 Felix Rougier House of Studies. Rev. Juan Antonio Romero, MSpS, Rector; Bro. John Terron, MSpS, Mem.; Bro. Ricardo Velez, MSpS, Mem.; Bro. Daniel Zorrilla, MSpS, Mem.; Brs.: 4; Priests: 1

PORTLAND

Colombiere Jesuit Community - 3220 S.E. 43rd Ave., Portland, OR 97206-3104 t) (503) 595-1941 wameche@jesuits.org; ljcmanager@jesuits.org www.jesuitswest.org Rev. William Ameche, SJ, Supr.; Very Rev. Sean Carroll, S.J., Prov.; Rev. Robert J. Niehoff, S.J., Prov. Asst.; Rev. Christopher S. Weekly, S.J., Prov. Asst.; Rev. Michael Moynahan, SJ, Pst.; Rev. William Vogel, S.J., Assoc. Pst.; Rev. San H Mai, S.J., Pst. Assoc.; Rev. Craig Boly, S.J., Chap.; Rev. Kevin T. Clarke, S.J., Chap.; Rev. Jack Krouse, SJ, Teacher; Bro. Jeffrey R. Allen, S.J., Minister; Rev. Steven Dillard, S.J., Asst. Tertian Dir.; Rev. Michael F Weiler, S.J., Tertian Dir.; Rev. Michael C. Gilson, S.J., Socius; Rev. Gary N. Smith, S.J., In Res.; Rev. Jerry D. Graham, S.J., In Res.; Brs.: 1; Priests: 15

The Grotto, The National Sanctuary of Our Sorrowful Mother - 8840 N.E. Skidmore St., Portland, OR 97294-0008; Mailing: P.O. Box 20008, Portland, OR 97294-0008 t) 503-254-7371 office@thegrotto.org www.thegrotto.org Rev. Leonardus Hambur, O.S.M., Rector; Rev. Edgar Benedi-an, O.S.M., Spiritual Adv./Care Srvcs.; Rev. Ignatius M. Kissel, O.S.M., In Res.; Rev. John Topper, OSM, In Res.; Christopher Blanchard, Exec. Dir.; Priests: 3

Holy Rosary Priory - 375 N.E. Clackamas St., Portland, OR 97232-1103 t) 503-235-3163 peter@holyrosarypdx.org Rev. Peter Do, O.P., Prior; Rev. Paul Raftery, O.P., Subprior; Rev. Joseph Selinger, O.P., Mem.; Rev. Brian T.B. Mullady, O.P., Mem.; Rev. Paschal Donald Salisbury, O.P., Mem.; Priests: 6

Priests of Holy Cross in Oregon, Inc. - 5000 N. Willamette Blvd., Portland, OR 97203; Mailing: 5408 N. Strong St., Portland, OR 97203 t) 503-943-8024 ssimmonds@holycrossusa.org Bro. Jony Theotonius Gregory, C.S.C., In Res.; Bro. Ken Allen, C.S.C., In Res.; Rev. Robert Antonelli, C.S.C., In Res.; Rev. Richard Berg, C.S.C., In Res.; Rev. John Donato, C.S.C., In Res.; Rev. Thomas E. Gaughan, CSC, In Res.; Rev. Mark Ghyselinck, C.S.C., In Res.; Rev. Robert L. Loughery, C.S.C., In Res.; Rev. Patrick Hannon, C.S.C., In Res.; Rev. Peter Walsh, C.S.C., In Res.; Rev. Edwin Obermiller, C.S.C., In Res.; Rev. Dan Parrish, C.S.C., In Res.; Bro. Pablo J Quan, CSC, In Res.; Rev. James Rigert, C.S.C., In Res.; Rev. Richard Rutherford, C.S.C., In Res.; Rev. Jeffrey Schneibel, C.S.C., In Res.; Rev. Timothy Weed, In Res.; Rev.

Arthur F. Wheeler, C.S.C., In Res.; Brs.: 3; Priests: 15

Society of Jesus, Oregon Province - 3215 S.E. 45th Ave., Portland, OR 97206; Mailing: P.O. Box 86010, Portland, OR 97286-0010 t) 503-226-6977 uweprovince@jesuits.org www.jesuitswest.org Very Rev. Sean Carroll, S.J., Prov.; Rev. Michael C. Gilson, S.J., Socius; Rev. Edward S. Fassett, S.J., Treas.; Brs.: 2; Priests: 18

SAINT BENEDICT

Mt. Angel Abbey - 1 Abbey Dr., Saint Benedict, OR 97373 t) 503-845-3030 info@mtangel.edu www.mountangelabbey.org Rev. Teresio Caldwell, O.S.B.; Rt. Rev. Peter Eberle, O.S.B.; Rev. Martin Grassel, O.S.B.; Rev. Basil Lawrence, O.S.B.; Rev. Joseph Nguyen, O.S.B.; Rev. Ralph Recker, O.S.B.; Rev. Andrew Schwenke, O.S.B.; Rev. Edmund Smith, O.S.B.; Rev. Jacob Stronach, O.S.B.; Rev. Paul Thomas, O.S.B.; Rev. Philip Waibel, O.S.B.; Rev. Aelred Yockey, O.S.B.; Rt. Rev. Nathan Zodrow, O.S.B.; Rev. Timothy Kalange, O.S.B., Prof.; Rev. John Paul Le, O.S.B., Prof.; Rev. Ephrem Martinez, O.S.B., Prof.; Rt. Rev. Jeremy Driscoll, O.S.B., Abbot; Rev. Vincent Trujillo, O.S.B., Prior; Rev. William Hammelman, O.S.B., Subprior; Rt. Rev. Gregory Duerr, O.S.B., Priest; Rev. Pius X Harding, O.S.B., Guest Master; Rev. John Vianney Le, O.S.B., Priest; Rev. Vincent Liem Nguyen, O.S.B., Junior Master; Rev. Odo Recker, O.S.B., Vocation Director; Rev. Israel Sanchez, O.S.B., Student; Rev. Jack D. Shrum, Novice; Brs.: 25; Priests: 26

SAN DIEGO

Augustinian Community - 3180 University Ave., Suite 255, San Diego, CA 92104; Mailing: PO Box 5150, Central Point, OR 97502 t) 619-235-0247 jimcliffordosa@gmail.com; osa-west@calprovince.org Rev. James Clifford, O.S.A., Supr.; Priests: 1

NURSING / REHABILITATION / CONVALESCENCE / ELDERLY CARE [NUR]

BEAVERTON

Maryville Nursing Home - 14645 S.W. Farmington Rd., Beaverton, OR 97007 t) 503-643-8626 Kathleen Parry, Exec.; Cornelia Agum, Dir.; Asstd. Annu.: 140; Staff: 220

MOUNT ANGEL

Providence Health & Services-Oregon (Providence Benedictine Nursing Center) - 540 S. Main St., Mount Angel, OR 97362-9532 t) 503-845-6841 james.arp@providence.org www.providence.org/ benedictine Jennifer Gringerich, Chap.; Barbara Harrend, Chap.; David Horn, Chap.; Emily Dazey, Exec.; Asstd. Annu.: 406; Staff: 119

Providence Benedictine Home Health - 570 S Main St., Mt Angel, OR 97362 t) 503-845-9226 emily.dazey@providence.org Susan Murtha, Dir.;

Providence Benedictine Orchard House - 550 A S Main St, Mt Angel, OR 97362 t) 503-845-2544 emily.dazey@providence.org Personalized Living Center (ALF).

PORTLAND

***St. Anthony Village (activity of St. Anthony Village Enterprise)** - 3560 S.E. 79th Ave., Portland, OR 97206 t) 503-775-4414 mmaslowsky@villageenterprises.org; aadm@sageve.org www.villageenterprises.org Rev. Michael Maslowsky, Pres.; Asstd. Annu.: 132; Staff: 75

***Assumption Village (activity of St. Anthony Village Enterprise)** - 9121 N. Burr Ave., Portland, OR 97203 t) 503-283-5644 aadm@sageve.org www.villageenterprises.org Christina Burton, Admin.; Rev. Michael Maslowsky, Pres.; Asstd. Annu.: 80; Staff: 50

Providence Health & Services-Oregon (Providence ElderPlace) - 4400 NE Halsey St., Building 1, Portland, OR 97213; Mailing: 4400 N.E. Halsey St., Bldg. 2, Ste. 595, Portland, OR 97213 t) 503-215-6556 ellen.garcia@providence.org Providence Elder Place Ellen Garcia, Exec.; Asstd. Annu.: 2,037; Staff: 493

PRESCHOOLS / CHILDCARE CENTERS [PRE]

BEAVERTON

St. Mary's Home for Boys, Inc. - 16535 S.W. Tualatin Valley Hwy., Beaverton, OR 97003 t) 503-649-5651 www.stmaryshomeforboys.org Francis Maher, Exec.; Stds.: 65; Lay Tchrs.: 9

Sisters of St. Mary of Oregon Little Flower Development Center - 4450 S.W. St. Mary's Dr., Beaverton, OR 97078 t) 503-520-0214 Amber Ploussard, Prin.; Stds.: 149; Lay Tchrs.: 19

PORTLAND

Providence Health & Services-Oregon (*Providence Child Center) - 830 N.E. 47th Ave., Portland, OR 97213; Mailing: 4400 N.E. Halsey St., Bldg. 2, Ste. 595, Portland, OR 97213 t) 503-215-2400 joann.vance@providence.org Joann Vance, Exec.; Kelly Schmidt, Dir.; Stds.: 3,423

Providence Health & Services-Oregon (Center for Medically Fragile Children) - 830 NE 47th Ave., Portland, OR 97213 t) (503) 215-2837 jvance@providence.org Provides skilled nursing care for children.

Providence Health & Services-Oregon - 830 NE 47th Ave, Portland, OR 97213 t) 503-215-6832 Child development program.

Providence Health & Services-Oregon (Providence Neurodevelopmental Center for Children) - 830 NE 47th Ave., Portland, OR 97213 t) 503-215-2233 kelly.schmidt@providence.org Providence Neurodevelopmental Center for Children (PNCC) provides diagnostic & therapy services for children with complex developmental medical needs. John Kleiderer, Dir.;

RETREAT HOUSES / RENEWAL CENTERS [RTR]

BEAVERTON

Our Lady of Peace Retreat - 3600 S.W. 170th Ave., Beaverton, OR 97003-4467 t) 503-649-7127 sisters@olpretreat.org www.olpretreat.org Sr. Agnes Clare Navarra, OSF, Supr.;

CENTRAL POINT

St. Rita's Retreat Center - 10800 Blackwell Rd, Central Point, OR 97502; Mailing: P.O. Box 310, Gold Hill, OR 97525 t) 541-855-1333 paterretreat@gmail.com stritaretreat.org Rev. Stephen J. Fister, Dir.;

MCKENZIE BRIDGE

St. Benedict Lodge Dominican Retreat & Conference Center - 56630 N. Bank Rd., McKenzie Bridge, OR 97413-9614; Mailing: 55433 McKenzie Hwy., McKenzie Bridge, OR 97413 t) 541-822-3572 (Office & Res.) sblodge@opwest.org sblodge.opwest.org Rev. Kieran Healy, Dir.; Bro. Lupe Gonzalez, Asst.;

MOUNT ANGEL

Benedictine Sisters Shalom Prayer Center - 840 S. Main St., Mount Angel, OR 97362-9527 t) 503-845-2556 info@benedictine-srs.org www.benedictine-srs.org Sr. Dorothy Jean Beyer, O.S.B, Dir.;

ST. BENEDICT

Mount Angel Abbey Guest House & Retreat Center - 1 Abbey Dr., St. Benedict, OR 97373 t) 503-845-3025 retreat@mtangel.edu www.mountangelabbey.org Rev. Pius X Harding, O.S.B., Guest Master;

SEMINARIES [SEM]

MOUNT ANGEL

Felix Rougier House of Studies - 585 E. College St., Mount Angel, OR 97362; Mailing: P.O. Box 499, St. Benedict, OR 97373 t) 503-845-1181 mspsmahos@gmail.com; jgmsps@me.com Rev. Alex Rubio, M.Sp.S., Supr.; Rev. Pedro Arteaga, M.Sp.S., Teacher; Stds.: 6; Pr. Tchrs.: 2

SAINT BENEDICT

Mount Angel Seminary - 1 Abbey Dr., Saint Benedict, OR 97373 t) 503-845-3951 seminaryinfo@mtangel.edu www.mountangelabbey.org/seminary/ Rev. Peter Arteaga, M.Sp.S., Formation Dir.; Rev. E. Scott Borgman (France), Formation Dir.; Rev. Odo Recker, O.S.B., Formation Dir.; Rt. Rev. Jeremy Driscoll, O.S.B., Chancellor; Rev. Msgr. Joseph V. Betschart, Pres.-Rector; Rev. Stephen Clovis, Vice Pres. for Administration & Dir. Human Formation; Dr. Shawn Keough, Vice Pres., Academics & Academic Dean; Rev. Martin Grassel, O.S.B., Procurator; Rev. William Dillard, Dir. Spiritual Formation; Dr. Brian Morin, Librn.; Terence Merritt, Registrar; Rev. Teresio Caldwell, O.S.B., Dir. Student Services& Formation; Stds.: 122; Lay Tchrs.: 14; Pr. Tchrs.: 6

Diocese of Providence

(Dioecesis Providentiensis)

MOST REVEREND THOMAS J. TOBIN

Bishop of Providence; ordained July 21, 1973; appointed Titular Bishop of Novica and Auxiliary Bishop of Pittsburgh, November 3, 1992; consecrated December 27, 1992; appointed Fourth Bishop of Youngstown; installed February 2, 1996; appointed eighth Bishop of Providence March 31, 2005; installed May 31, 2005. Office: One Cathedral Square, Providence, RI 02903-3695.

Bishop's Office & Chancery Office: One Cathedral Square, Providence, RI 02903-3695. T: 401-278-4500
www.dioceseofprovidence.org

ESTABLISHED FEBRUARY 16, 1872.

Square Miles 1,085.

Corporate Title: Roman Catholic Bishop of Providence, a corporation sole

Comprises the State of Rhode Island.

MOST REVEREND RICHARD G. HENNING

Coadjutor Bishop of Providence; ordained May 30, 1992; appointed Titular Bishop of Tabla and Auxiliary Bishop of Rockville Centre June 8, 2018; consecrated July 24, 2018; appointed Coadjutor Bishop of Providence November 23, 2022; took canonical possession Jan 26, 2023. Office: One Cathedral Square, Providence, RI 02903-3695.

STATISTICAL OVERVIEW

Personnel

Bishop	2
Retired Bishops	3
Abbots	1
Retired Abbots	1
Priests: Diocesan Active in Diocese	108
Priests: Diocesan Active Outside Diocese	3
Priests: Retired, Sick or Absent	92
Number of Diocesan Priests	203
Religious Priests in Diocese	82
Total Priests in your Diocese	285
Extern Priests in Diocese	8
Ordinations:	
Diocesan Priests	1
Transitional Deacons	1
Permanent Deacons in Diocese	87
Total Brothers	49
Total Sisters	189

Parishes

Parishes	121
With Resident Pastor:	
Resident Diocesan Priests	91
Resident Religious Priests	8
Without Resident Pastor:	
Administered by Priests	22
Missions	11
Closed Parishes	3

Professional Ministry Personnel:	
Brothers	7
Sisters	23
Lay Ministers	100

Welfare

Homes for the Aged	4
Total Assisted	4,128
Special Centers for Social Services	8
Total Assisted	133,250

Educational

Seminaries, Diocesan	1
Students from This Diocese	5
Students from Other Dioceses	6
Diocesan Students in Other Seminaries	10
Total Seminarians	15
Colleges and Universities	2
Total Students	7,677
High Schools, Diocesan and Parish	4
Total Students	1,576
High Schools, Private	3
Total Students	2,245
Elementary Schools, Diocesan and Parish	25
Total Students	4,926
Elementary Schools, Private	3
Total Students	865

Catechesis/Religious Education:	
High School Students	1,953
Elementary Students	8,590
Total Students under Catholic Instruction	27,847
Teachers in Diocese:	
Priests	9
Brothers	7
Sisters	13
Lay Teachers	1,012

Vital Statistics

Receptions into the Church:	
Infant Baptism Totals	1,961
Minor Baptism Totals	176
Adult Baptism Totals	89
Received into Full Communion	124
First Communions	1,887
Confirmations	2,373
Marriages:	
Catholic	556
Interfaith	149
Total Marriages	705
Deaths	5,073
Total Catholic Population	600,835
Total Population	1,097,379

LEADERSHIP

Vicars General - Most Rev. Richard G. Henning; Rev. Msgr. Albert A. Kenney;
Episcopal Vicars and Secretaries -
Deans -
Deanery I -
Deanery II - Very Rev. Francis A. O'Loughlin;
Deanery III - Very Rev. Daniel J. Sweet;
Deanery IV - Very Rev. D. Andrew Messina;
Deanery V - Very Rev. Edward S. Cardente;
Deanery VI - Very Rev. William J. Ledoux;
Deanery VII - Very Rev. Bernard A. Healey;
Deanery VIII -
Secretary for Catholic Charities and Social Ministry - James Jahnz;
Secretary for Evangelization and Pastoral Planning - Michael Lavigne;
Vicar for Judicial Matters - Rev. Msgr. Ronald P. Simeone;
Vicar for Planning & Financial Services - Rev. Msgr. Raymond B. Bastia;
Bishop's Office - t) 401-278-4546 Rev. Hiep Nguyen, Admin. Asst. to Bishop; Rev. Nathan J. Ricci, Admin. Asst. to Bishop; Velia Lisi, Secy. (vlisi@dioceseofprovidence.org);
Moderator of the Curia - t) 401-278-4519 Rev. Msgr. Albert A. Kenney;
Chancellor - t) (401) 278-4663 Rev. Timothy D. Reilly;
Vice Chancellor - t) 401-278-4664 Rev. Nathan J. Ricci;
Diocesan Tribunal -
Advocate - Rev. Timothy D. Reilly;
Assessor and Auditor - Dcn. John P. Pryor;
Assessor and Counselor - Nancy Gould;
Defenders of the Bond - Rev. Albert P. Marcello III;
Judges - Rev. Anthony VanBerkum, OP; Rev. Msgr. Ronald P. Simeone; Rev. Msgr. Paul D. Theroux;
Judicial Vicar - t) 401-278-4666 Rev. Msgr. Ronald P. Simeone;
Notaries - Patricia Costa; Linda L. Nastari;
Notary & Secretary - Patricia Costa;
Promoter of Justice - Rev. Nathan J. Ricci;

OFFICES AND DIRECTORS

Diocesan Administration -
Archives - t) (401) 278-4522 Lisa A. Vespia;
Communications and Public Relations - t) (401) 278-4600 Michael Kieloch, Dir.; Victoria Hunt, Social Media Specialist; Laura H. Testa, Communications Mgr.;
Education and Compliance - t) (401) 941-0760 Kevin O'Brien;
Human Resources - t) (401) 278-4584 John Bittner, Dir.; Natalie Mack, Benefits Coord.;
RI Catholic Conference - Very Rev. Bernard A. Healey, Dir.;
RI Catholic Newspaper - t) (401) 272-1010 Rick Snizek, Editor; Rev. Nathan J. Ricci, Theological Advisor;
Society for the Propagation of the Faith - t) (401) 278-4520 Rev. Francesco Francese, Dir.;
Victim Assistance - t) 401-946-0728 Michael Hansen, Dir.;
Worship - t) 401-278-4587 Rev. Jeremy J. Rodrigues, Dir. (jrodrigues@dioceseofprovidence.org);

ADVISORY BOARDS, COMMISSIONS, COMMITTEES, AND COUNCILS

Council of Priests - t) 401-278-4567
Appointed Members - Rev. Francis P. Kayatta; Rev. Christopher J. Murphy; Rev. Msgr. Jacques L. Plante;
College of Consultors - Most Rev. Richard G. Henning; Rev. Msgr. Raymond B. Bastia; Rev. Msgr. Albert A. Kenney;
Elected Members - Very Rev. William J. Ledoux; Rev. Roger C. Gagne; Rev. Ryan J. Simas;
Ex Officio - Most Rev. Richard G. Henning; Rev. Msgr. Raymond B. Bastia; Rev. Msgr. Albert A. Kenney;
Officers - Most Rev. Thomas J. Tobin, Pres.; Rev. Msgr. Albert A. Kenney, Secy.; Very Rev. William J. Ledoux, Moderator;
Finance Council - Most Rev. Thomas J. Tobin, Pres.; Rev. Msgr. Raymond B. Bastia, Secy.; Rev. Msgr. Albert A. Kenney;
Chief Financial Officer - Michael F. Sabatino;

CLERGY AND RELIGIOUS SERVICES

Secretariat for Ministerial Services -
Clergy Benefit Fund -
Ecumenical Officer - t) 401-787-4093 Rev. John A. Kiley;
Permanent Diaconate - t) 401-278-4604 Dcn. Noel Edsall, Dir.;
Post-Ordination Formation - t) 401-331-1316 Rev. Carl B. Fisette;
Pre-Ordination Formation - t) 401-331-1316 Rev. Christopher M. Murphy, Coord.;
Priests' Personnel Committee - Rev. Christopher J. Murphy; Rev. Msgr. Paul D. Theroux; Very Rev. William J. Ledoux;
Religious - t) 401-278-4633 Sr. Elizabeth Castro, H.M.S.P., Dir.;
Council of Religious - Sr. Elizabeth Castro, H.M.S.P., Coord.; Rev. Perianayagasamy Anandarayar, SdC; Sr. Mary Antoinette Cappelli, F.M.H.;
Seminary of Our Lady of Providence - t) 401-331-1316 Rev. Christopher M. Murphy, Rector; Rev. James Mary Sullivan, O.P., Dir. Spiritual Formation; Michael Hansen, Human Formation;
Vocations - Rev. Brian J. Morris, Dir.;

EVANGELIZATION

Secretariat for Evangelization and Pastoral Planning - Michael Lavigne, Secy. (mlavigne@dioceseofprovidence.org);
Catholic Schools - t) 401-278 4550 cso@dioceseofprovidence.org www.catholicschools.org Dr. James Power, Supt.;
Catholic Youth Ministry - t) 401-278-4626
Catholic Scouting-Boy Scouts, Girl Scouts, Camp Fire - Rev. Stephen M. Battey, Chap.; Sr. Diane Russo, R.S.M., Pst. Assoc.;
Catholic Youth Organization of the Diocese of Providence -
Youth Summer Camp - t) 401-568-3580 www.motherofhopecamp.com Michelle Ficocelli, Dir.;
Office of Faith Formation - t) 401-278-4646 Edward Trendowski, Dir.; Michelle Donovan, Asst. Dir.;
Apostolate with People with Disabilities - t) (401) 278-4578 Irma I. Rodriguez;
Marriage Preparation and Enrichment - t) (401) 278-4576
SPRED (Special Religious Education) - t) 401-278-4578 Irma I. Rodriguez, Coord.;

FINANCE

Vicariate for Planning and Financial Services - t) (401) 278-4540 Rev. Msgr. Raymond B. Bastia, Vicar; Michael F. Sabatino, CFO;
Catholic Cemeteries - t) 401-944-8383 Anthony J. Carpinello, Dir.;
Diocesan Facilities Department - t) 401-278-4636 Gary Ferguson, Dir.;
Fiscal Office - t) 401-278-4616 Cheryl Brennan, Diocesan Controller;
Information Technology - t) 401-278-4611 Christopher Pagliarini, Dir.;
Insurance Commission - t) 401-278-4547 Rev. Msgr. Raymond B. Bastia, Chair;
Catholic Mutual Group - Joseph Walsh, Claims & Risk Mgr.;
Parish Financial Assistance - t) 401-278-4644 Catherine Messier, Dir.;
Stewardship and Development - t) 401-277-2121 Tim McCaig, Dir.;
Catholic Charity Appeal - Tim McCaig, Dir.;
Catholic Foundation of R.I. - Richard Popovic, Dir.;

SOCIAL SERVICES

Secretariat for Catholic Charities and Social Ministry - t) (401) 421-7833 x222 James Jahnz, Secy. (jjahnz@dioceseofprovidence.org);
Catholic Social Services of RI - t) 401-421-7833 x222 James Jahnz, Supvr.;
AIDS Ministry - James Jahnz;
Catholic Campaign for Human Development and Catholic Charities Advocacy Fund - jmonteiro@dioceseofprovidence.org James Jahnz;
Catholic Social Services of RI - Kent County Satellite - t) 401-823-6211 Rosanna Lenus;
Catholic Social Services of RI - Newport County Satellite - t) 401-619-4677
Catholic Social Services of RI - Northern RI Satellite - t) 401-762-2849 Rosanna Lenus;
Catholic Social Services of RI - South County and Newport Satellite - t) 401-783-3149 Melanie Monteiro;
Chaplains of Public Institutions - t) 401-462-5206 Rev. Lazarus Onuh (Nigeria), Chap.;
Elder Care Services - t) 401-421-7833 x212 Hector Munoz; Jan Vargas; Ann McCarthy;
Emmanuel House - t) 401-421-7888 James Jahnz;
Health Care Ministries - t) 401-861-5111 Rev. Albert A. Ranallo Jr., Coord.;
Immigration and Refugee Services - Nancy Gonzalez, Coord.;
Keep the Heat On - t) 401-421-7833 x207
Office for Multi-Cultural Ministry - t) 401-421-7833 x237 Rev. Nolasco Tamayo; Linda A'Vant-Deishinni, Coord.; Silvio Cuellar, Coord.;
Peace and Justice -
Life and Family Ministry - t) 401-278-4508; 401-421-7833 x218 Lisa Cooley, Coord.;
Adoption Searches - Peter Magnotta;
Evaluations for Maturity for Marriage - Peter Magnotta;
Project Rachel - t) 888-456-4673
Rachel's Vineyard's Retreats - Lisa Cooley, Liaison;
Respect Life Activities - Lisa Cooley, Coord.;
Project Hope/Projecto Esperanza - t) 401-728-0515 Melanie Monteiro, Intake Worker;
St. Martin de Porres Multi-Service Center - t) 401-274-6783 Linda A'Vant-Deishinni, Dir.;
Friendly Visitor Program - t) 401-274-6783 Linda A'Vant-Deishinni, Coord.;

PARISHES, MISSIONS, AND CLERGY

STATE OF RHODE ISLAND

ALBION

St. Ambrose Church, Albion, Rhode Island - 191 School St., Albion, RI 02802; Mailing: P.O. Box 67, Albion, RI 02802 t) 401-333-1568 stambrosechurch@cox.net stambrosechurchri.org Rev. Thomas J. Ferland, Pst.; CRP Stds.: 135

ASHAWAY

Church of Our Lady of Victory, Ashaway - 169 Main St., Ashaway, RI 02804 t) 401-377-8830 ggolv@yahoo.com; olvsvpri@gmail.com Dcn. Costa Adamopoulos; Rev. Chinnaiah Yerrnini, Pst.;

BARRINGTON

Holy Angel's Church Corporation - 341 Maple Ave., Barrington, RI 02806 t) 401-245-7743 hangels@fullchannel.net Rev. Timothy D. Reilly, Admin.;

Saint Luke's Church Corporation, Barrington - 108 Washington Rd., Barrington, RI 02806-1133 t) 401-246-1212 treilly@dioceseofprovidence.org Rev. Mark Gabriel Gadoury, Assoc. Pst.; Rev. Timothy D. Reilly, Pst.; CRP Stds.: 300

St. Luke School - (Grades PreK-8) 10 Waldron Ave., Barrington, RI 02806 t) 401-246-0990 www.stlukesri.org Nicole Varone, Prin.; Neil Kiely, Dir.; Stds.: 161; Lay Tchrs.: 25

BLOCK ISLAND

Saint Andrew's Church Corporation, Block Island - Spring St., Block Island, RI 02807; Mailing: Box 279, Block Island, RI 02807 t) 401-278-4500 Rev. Joseph Protano Jr., Pst.;

BRADFORD

Saint Vincent's Church Corporation, Bradford - 7 Church St., Bradford, RI 02808; Mailing: 4 Saint Clare Way, Westerly, RI 02891 t) 401-348-8765 x3 scc1svdp@gmail.com Rev. Peter J. D'Ambrosia, Admin.;

BRISTOL

Saint Elizabeth's Church of Bristol - 577 Wood St., Bristol, RI 02809-2395 t) 401-253-8366 office@saintelizabethchurch.net www.stelizabethri.com Rev. Vander Sebastiao Martins (Brazil), Pst.; CRP Stds.: 168

Saint Mary's Church, Bristol, Rhode Island - 330 Wood St., Bristol, RI 02809; Mailing: P.O. Box 120, Bristol, RI 02809 t) 401-253-3300; 401-253-2270 (CRP) frbjg@aol.com www.stmarybristolri.org Rev. Barry J. Gamache, Pst.; Dcn. Paul Bisbano; Dcn. Bernard G. Theroux;

Our Lady of Prudence -

Church of Our Lady of Mount Carmel, Bristol - 141 State St., Bristol, RI 02809 t) 401-253-9449 olmc141@gmail.com Rev. Henry P. Zinno Jr., Pst.;

Our Lady of Mount Carmel School - (Grades PreK-8) 127 State St., Bristol, RI 02809 t) 401-253-8455 jwalters@olmcri.org www.olmcri.org Jessica Walters, Prin.;

CAROLINA

Saint Mary's Church Corporation, Carolina, RI - 437 Carolina Back Rd., Carolina, RI 02812; Mailing: P.O. Box 475, Carolina, RI 02812 t) 401-364-7214 dolly@stmjparish.org stmjparish.org Rev. Paul E. Desmarais, Pst.; Dcn. Paul A. Theroux; Sally Lambert, DRE;

St. James - 2079 Matunuck School House Rd., Charlestown, RI 02813

CENTRAL FALLS

Holy Spirit Parish Central Falls - 1030 Dexter St., Central Falls, RI 02863-1717 t) 401-726-2600 the.holy.spirit.parish@gmail.com Unification of Holy Trinity Legal Titles: Church of the Holy Trinity, Central Falls; Notre Dame Church; Saint Matthew's Church of Central Falls Rev. Otoniel J. Gomez, Pst.;

St. Joseph's Church of Central Falls - 391 High St., Central Falls, RI 02863-3109 t) 401-278-4500 Rev. Dariusz J. Jonczyk, Pst.;

CHEPACHET

St. Eugene's Church Corporation, Chepachet - 1251 Putnam Pike, Chepachet, RI 02814; Mailing: P.O. Box A, Chepachet, RI 02814 t) 401-278-4500 Rev. Stephen J. Dandeneau, Pst.;

COVENTRY

SS. John and Paul Parish Corporation, Coventry - 341 S. Main St., Coventry, RI 02816 t) 401-821-4780 (CRP); 401-821-5764 father.woolley@verizon.net; ssjp341@stjp.necoxmail.com stsjohnpaulri.com/ Rev. Michael J. Woolley, Pst.; Rev. Doan Paul Nguyen, Assoc. Pst.; Rev. Dennis J. Kieton, In Res.; Dcn. Walter Foster; Patricia Jarvis, DRE; Ann Sartell, DRE; CRP Stds.: 320

Father John V. Doyle School - 343 S. Main St., Coventry, RI 02816 t) 401-821-3756 jaesmith@fjvd.org www.ri.net/rinet/fr_doyle Jae T. Smith, Prin.;

Church of Our Lady of Czenstochowa - 445 Washington St., Coventry, RI 02816 t) 401-821-7991 olczenstochowa@aol.com olcsvp.org/ Rev. Jacek Ploch, Pst.; CRP Stds.: 42

Church of Saint Vincent de Paul, Anthony, Rhode Island - 6 St. Vincent de Paul St., Coventry, RI 02816 t) 401-821-8719 stvincentcoventry@gmail.com olcsvp.org Rev. Jacek Ploch, Pst.; CRP Stds.: 30

CRANSTON

Holy Apostles Church, Cranston, Rhode Island - 800 Pippin Orchard Rd., Cranston, RI 02921 t) 401-946-5586 parishoffice@holyapostles.com www.holyapostles.com Very Rev. William J. Ledoux, Pst.; Rev. Msgr. Albert A. Kenney, In Res.; CRP Stds.: 540

Immaculate Conception Church Corporation, Cranston - 237 Garden Hills Dr., Cranston, RI 02920 t) 401-942-1854 iccrireligiousedu@gmail.com; iccrioffice@gmail.com www.iccatholicchurch.com Rev. Edward J. Wilson Jr., Pst.; Dcn. Scott Brown; Dcn. Noel Edsall; Dcn. Thomas R. Raspallo; Deanna Marinucci, DRE;

Saint Mark's Church Corporation of Cranston - 9 Garden Ct., Cranston, RI 02920-5701 t) 401-942-1616 welcome@stmarkri.org www.stmarkri.org Rev. Anthony W. Verdelotti, Pst.; Sr. Angelina Giramma, M.P.F., Pst. Min./Coord.; Claudia Jackvony, CRE; Peter Brissette, Liturgy Coord.; Ron Almeida, Music Min.; Matthew E. Gebhart, Bus. Mgr.; CRP Stds.: 91

Saint Mary's Church, Cranston - 1525 Cranston St., Cranston, RI 02920-5297 t) 401-944-1323 (CRP); 401-942-1492 (Rectory) nnasser@stmaryschoolri.org; office@stmarycranston.org www.saintmarycranston.org (Santa Maria della Civita) Rev. Michael A. Sisco, Pst.; Dcn. Steven Valliere; Dcn. Peter A. Ceprano; Dcn. Armand R. Ragosta; Nancy Nasser, DRE; CRP Stds.: 66

St. Mary School - (Grades PreK-8) 85 Chester Ave., Cranston, RI 02920-5297 t) 401-944-4107 llepore@stmaryschoolri.org www.stmaryschoolri.org Lisa Lepore, Prin.;

St. Matthew's Church Corporation - 15 Frances Ave., Cranston, RI 02910 t) 401-461-7172 stmatthewri@cox.net stmatthewri.org Rev. Ronald J. Bengford, Pst.; CRP Stds.: 30

Saint Paul's Church of Edgewood - One St. Paul Pl., Cranston, RI 02905 t) 401-941-5576 (CRP); 401-278-4500 Rev. Thomas J. Woodhouse, Admin.; Dcn. Paul Shea; Julie Bradley, DRE;

St. Paul School - (Grades PreK-8) 1789 Broad St., Cranston, RI 02905 t) 401-941-2030 johncorry@stpaulcranston.org www.saintpaulschoolcranston.com John F. Corry, Prin.;

CUMBERLAND

St. Aidan Church Corporation, Cumberland - 1460 Diamond Hill Rd., Cumberland, RI 02864; Mailing: PO Box 7058, Cumberland, RI 02864 t) 401-333-5897 c) (401) 533-0601 (Parish Cemeteries Office) office@aidan-patrick.org saintaidanparish.weconnect.com/ Rev. Msgr. Jacques L. Plante, Pst.; Moira McCarty, DRE; CRP Stds.: 87

Saint Joan's Church, Cumberland, Rhode Island - 3357 Mendon Rd., Cumberland, RI 02864-2195 t) 401-658-0734 stjoanschurch@gmail.com www.stjoanschurchri.org Rev. Norman W. Bourdon, Pst.; Francine M. Salinger, DRE; CRP Stds.: 130

Saint John Baptist Mary Vianney Church Corporation, Diamond Hill - 3655 Diamond Hill Rd., Cumberland, RI 02864; Mailing: 3587 Diamond Hill Rd., Cumberland, RI 02864 t) 401-333-6060; 401-333-2347 (CRP) sjvparishoffice@gmail.com; sjvreginab@gmail.com www.sjvparish.org Rev. Joseph A. Pescatello, Pst.; CRP Stds.: 380

St. Joseph's Church, Ashton, Rhode Island - 1303 Mendon Rd., Cumberland, RI 02864; Mailing: P.O. Box 7005, Cumberland, RI 02864 t) 401-333-4014 (CRP); 401-333-4013 historicstjosephchurch@gmail.com www.stjosephashtonri.org Rev. Charles H. Galligan, Pst.; Leslie Towle, DRE; CRP Stds.: 86

Church of Our Lady of Fatima, Valley Falls - 1 Fatima Dr., Cumberland, RI 02864 t) 401-724-3454 (CRP); 401-723-6719 olffaithformation@gmail.com; olf@olfchurch.org olfchurch.org Holy Day Mass; 9am - 6:30pm (bilingual) Special Devotions: Eucharistic Adoration, every Friday 2pm-8pm Adoration of the Blessed Sacrament -1 sat./mth Dcn. Amandio Bartolo; Rev. Fernando A. Cabral (Portugal), Pst.; Melissa DiFonzo, DRE; CRP Stds.: 96

EAST GREENWICH

Our Lady of Mercy, Greenwich, Rhode Island - 65 Third St., East Greenwich, RI 02818 t) 401-884-1061 (CRP); 401-884-4968 reled@olmparish.org; confirmation@olmparish.org olmparish.org Very Rev. Bernard A. Healey, Pst.; Rev. Daniel Mahoney, Assoc. Pst.; Douglas E. Green, DRE; CRP Stds.: 300

EAST PROVIDENCE

Saint Francis Xavier's Church - 81 N. Carpenter St., East Providence, RI 02914 t) 401-434-1878 sfxsecretary@yahoo.com saintfrancisxavierchurch.com Rev. Jorge V. Rocha, Pst.; Rev. Hiep Nguyen, Par. Vicar; CRP Stds.: 217

St. Martha's Church Corporation, East Providence - 2595 Pawtucket Ave., East Providence, RI 02914 t) 401-434-4060; 401-434-4070 secretary@stmarthaschurchepri.org stmarthaschurchepri.org Rev. Albert P. Marcello III, In Res.; Dcn. Dominic P. DiOrio; Mary-Beth Hoxie, DRE;

Church of Our Lady of Loreto, East Providence - 346 Waterman Ave., East Providence, RI 02914 t) 401-434-3535 Rev. Maria Julian Barnad, SdC., Pst.; Douglas E. Green, DRE;

Church of the Sacred Heart - 118 Taunton Ave., East Providence, RI 02914 t) 401-434-0326 x3; 401-434-0326 x4 (CRP) church@sacredheartepri.com; sduarte@sacredheartepri.com www.sacredheartepri.com Rev. Silvio De Nard, SdC, Pst.; Rev. Perianayagasamy Anandarayar, SdC, Assoc. Pst.; Sandy Maria Duarte, DRE; CRP Stds.: 30

Sacred Heart School - (Grades K-8) 56 Purchase St., East Providence, RI 02914 t) 401-434-1080 info@sacredheartepri.com Emily Cabo DaSilva, Prin.; Stds.: 130; Lay Tchrs.: 10

Nursery-Day Care - 101 Taunton Ave., East Providence, RI 02914 t) 401-434-2462 tjones@sacredheartepri.com Tracy Jones, Dir.;

EXETER

Saint Kateri Tekakwitha Catholic Community - 84 Exeter Rd., Exeter, RI 02822 t) 401-212-0855 gsabourin@dioceseofprovidence.org www.kateritekakwitha.org/katerichurch Rev. Msgr. Gerard O. Sabourin, Admin.; Dcn. John A. Corey;

FOSTER

St. Paul's Church Corporation, Foster - 116A Danielson Pike, Foster, RI 02825-1468 t) 401-647-3664 church@stpaulsfoster.org Rev. M.J. Bernard Dore, Pst.; Dcn. Fernando Botelho;

GREENVILLE

St. Philip's Church Greenville Rhode Island - 622 Putnam Pike, Greenville, RI 02828-1403 t) 401-949-0330 (CRP); 401-949-1500 reled@saintphilip.com; office@saintphilip.com www.saintphilip.com Rev. Michael J. McMahon, Pst.; Rev. Phillip J Dufour, Assoc. Pst.; Dcn. Joseph Day; Dennis Sousa, DRE; CRP Stds.: 285

St. Philip School - (Grades PreK-8) 618 Putnam Pike, Greenville, RI 02828 t) 401-949-1130 Cynthia Senenko, Prin.;

HARRISVILLE

St. Patrick's Church, Burrillville, Rhode Island - 45 Harrisville Main St., Harrisville, RI 02830 t) 401-568-5600 burrillvillecatholic@gmail.com www.stpatrickri.org Rev. Jose Parathanal, Admin.;

Church of Saint Teresa of the Child Jesus, Nasonville - 35 Dion Dr., Harrisville, RI 02830 t) 401-568-3057 (CRP); 401-568-8280 ourladyofgoodhelp@gmail.com Became a mission of Our Lady of Good Help Parish on July 1, 2019. Rev. Jose Parathanal; Dcn. Richard J. Lapierre;

HOPE VALLEY

Saint Joseph's Church, Hope Valley - 1105 Main St., Hope Valley, RI 02832; Mailing: P.O. Box 388, Hope Valley, RI 02832 t) 401-539-8312 (CRP); 401-539-8311 reledstjosephhv@aol.com; stjosephhv@verizon.net Rev. Chinnaiah Yerrnini, Pst.; Dcn. Ronald Preuhs; Shannon Reed, DRE;

JAMESTOWN

Saint Mark Church of Jamestown - 60 Narragansett Ave., Jamestown, RI 02835 t) 401-423-1421 secretary@stmarkjtn.org www.stmarkjtn.org Rev. Douglas Grant, Pst.;

JOHNSTON

Church of Our Lady of Grace - 4 Lafayette St., Johnston, RI 02919 t) 401-231-8959 (CRP); 401-231-2220 ourladyofgraceri@aol.com Rev. Peter J. Gower, Pst.; CRP Stds.: 145

St. Robert Bellarmine Church Corporation, Johnston - 1804 Atwood Ave., Johnston, RI 02919-3244 t) 401-232-5600 (CRP); 401-232-9321 srbp1804@aol.com strobertsparish.org Rev. Richard A. Narciso, Pst.; Dcn. Joseph Tumminelli; CRP Stds.: 68

Saint Rocco Church of Johnston - 927 Atwood Ave., Johnston, RI 02919 t) 401-944-6040 (CRP); 401-942-5203 churchofstrocco@gmail.com Rev. Angelo N. Carusi, Pst.; Dcn. Robert P. Troia; Sr. Mary Antoinette Cappelli, F.M.H., DRE; Robin Okolowitcz, DRE;

St. Rocco School - (Grades PreK-8) 931 Atwood Ave., Johnston, RI 02919 t) 401-944-2993 principal@stroccoschool.org www.stroccoschool.org Lorraine Moschella, Prin.;

KINGSTON

Christ the King Church Corporation, Kingston - 180 Old North Rd., Kingston, RI 02881 t) 401-789-0417 (CRP); 401-783-7459 info@ctkri.org www.ctkri.org Rev. Jared J. Costanza, Pst.; CRP Stds.: 438

LINCOLN

St. Jude's Church, Lincoln - 301 Front St., Lincoln, RI 02865 t) 401-725-8120 (CRP); 401-725-8140 stjudereled@gmail.com; officeatst.jude@verizon.net www.saintjuderi.com Rev. Brendan Murphy, O.P., Pst.; Dcn. L.J. (Bud) Remillard; Sr. Mary Higgins, R.S.M., DRE;

LITTLE COMPTON

St. Catherine's Church Corporation, Little Compton - 74 Simmons Rd., Little Compton, RI 02837-0208 t) 401-635-4420 becky@saintcatherinesiena.com www.saintcatherinesiena.com Rev. Stephan A. Silipigni, Pst.; Karen Lambert, DRE;

MANVILLE

Saint James Church of Manville, Rhode Island - 45 Division St., Manville, RI 02838; Mailing: P.O. Box 60, Manville, RI 02838 t) 401-766-1558 office.stjames@verizon.net www.saintjamesmanville.org Rev. Thomas J. Ferland, Pst.; CRP Stds.: 25

MAPLEVILLE

Our Lady of Good Help (Eglise de Notre Dame de Bonsecours) - 1063 Victory Hwy., Mapleville, RI 02839; Mailing: 35 Dion Dr., Harrisville, RI 02830 t) 401-568-8280 burrillvillecatholic@gmail.com www.burrillvillecatholic.org Our Lady of Good Help absorbed St. Theresa Parish, Harrisville, on July 1, 2019. Rev. Michael J. McMahon, Pst.; Dcn. Richard J. Lapierre;

MIDDLETOWN

Saint Lucy's Church Corp. - 909 W. Main Rd., Middletown, RI 02842-6351 t) 401-278-4500 stlucyoffice@gmail.com www.stlucy.org Dcn. John E. Croy; Rev. John C. Codega, Pst.; Rev. John W. O'Brien, Pastor Emer.; Colette Savaria, DRE; Jane Parillo, RCIA Coord.;

NARRAGANSETT

St. Mary, Star of the Sea Church Corporation, Point Judith - 864 Pt. Judith Rd., Narragansett, RI 02882 t) 401-789-7308 (CRP); 401-783-4449 stmarys@dioceseofprovidence.org Rev. Francis P. Kayatta, Pst.; Darie Lavallee, Pst. Assoc.; CRP Stds.: 90

St. Thomas More - 53 Rockland St., Narragansett, RI 02882 t) 401-789-7682 fathermtaillon@gmail.com stthomasmoreri.org Rev. Marcel L. Taillon, Pst.; MaryTheresa Conca, DRE;

St. Veronica Chapel - 1035 Boston Neck Rd., Narragansett, RI 02882

NEWPORT

Saint Augustin's Church of Newport - 2 Eastnor Rd., Newport, RI 02840; Mailing: 12 William St., P.O. Box 357, Newport, RI 02840 t) 401-278-4500 Rev. Kris M. von Maluski, Pst.; Sr. Josephine St. Leger, S.J.C., Pst. Assoc.; Deborah Circosta, DRE;

Church of Jesus-Saviour, Newport - One Vernon Ave., Newport, RI 02840 t) 401-847-1267; 401-846-4095 jsaviour@jesussaviour.necoxmail.com www.jsaviournewportri.org Very Rev. Francis A. O'Loughlin, Pst.; Lynn Banigan, DRE; Clotilde Rinfret, DRE; CRP Stds.: 28

Saint Joseph's Church of Newport, Rhode Island - 5 Mann Ave., Newport, RI 02840 t) 401-847-0065; 401-847-9248 (CRP) religioused@stjosephsnewport.org; office@stjosephsnewport.org www.stjosephsnewport.org Rev. Scott D. Pontes, Pst.;

St. Mary's, Newport, Rhode Island - 12 William St., Newport, RI 02840; Mailing: P.O. Box 547, Newport, RI 02840 t) 401-846-6057 (CRP); 401-278-4500 Rev. Mark A. Sauriol, Admin.;

NORTH KINGSTOWN

St. Francis de Sales Church Corporation, North Kingstown - 381 School St., North Kingstown, RI 02852 t) 401-885-3639 (CRP); 401-884-2105 (Office) www.saintfds.org Rev. David C. Procaccini, Pst.; Dcn. Ronald DePietro; Kristen Soucie, DRE; CRP Stds.: 139

NORTH PROVIDENCE

Saint Anthony's Church Corporation, North Providence - 1413 Mineral Spring Ave., North Providence, RI 02904; Mailing: 5 Gibbs St., North Providence, RI 02904 t) 401-353-3120 stanthonynp@cox.net saintanthonychurch.org Very Rev. Edward S. Cardente, Pst.; Maryann Pallotta, DRE; CRP Stds.: 173

Mary, Mother of Mankind Church Corporation, North Providence - 25 Fourth St., North Providence, RI 02911 t) 401-231-3544 (CRP); 401-231-3542 mmmchurch@hotmail.com Rev. TJ Varghese, Pst.; Dcn. Stephen M. Risi;

The Church of the Presentation of the Blessed Virgin Mary - 1081 Mineral Spring Ave., North Providence, RI 02904; Mailing: 5 Gibbs St., North Providence, RI 02904 t) 401-722-7140 pbvm1081@cox.net saintanthonychurch.org Canonically unified with St. Anthony Parish, North Providence, on December 31, 2022. Very Rev. Edward S. Cardente, Pst.; Maryann Pallotta, DRE; CRP Stds.: 6

NORTH SCITUATE

Saint Joseph's Church Corporation, North Scituate - 144 Danielson Pk., North Scituate, RI 02857; Mailing: P.O. Box 236, North Scituate, RI 02857 t) 401-647-2255; 401-647-2650 (CRP) dmc948@verizon.net Rev. Paul R. Grenon, Pst.; Dcn. Paul A. Ullucci; Rev. Eugene R. Lessard, In Res.; Laurence Hall, Youth Min.; Andrea Olson, Youth Min.; Lisa Woodhead, DRE;

PASCOAG

Saint Joseph's Roman Catholic Church of Pascoag - 183 Sayles Ave., Pascoag, RI 02859-0188; Mailing: P.O. Box 188, Pascoag, RI 02859-0188 t) 401-568-2411 stjosephpascoag@cox.net www.stjosephri.org Rev. Stephen J. Dandeneau, Admin.;

PAWTUCKET

Saint Anthony's Church Corporation, Pawtucket - 32 Lawn Ave., Pawtucket, RI 02860 t) 401-723-9138 stanthony32@pawtucket.necoxmail.com Rev. Joao Baptista Barros, Admin.;

Holy Family Parish, Pawtucket - 195 Walcott St., Pawtucket, RI 02860 t) 401-724-9190 holyfamily195@gmail.com www.holyfamilypawtucket.org Rev. Joseph F. Craddock, Pst.; CRP Stds.: 40

Immaculate Heart of Mary - 291 High St., Pawtucket, RI 02860; Mailing: 35 Clay St., Central Falls, RI 02863 t) 401-725-1126 immheartofmarypawtucket@gmail.com www.facebook.com/immheartmarypawtucket/ (An operation of Church of St. Maron in Providence) Rev. Joao Baptista Barros, C.S.Sp., Pst.;

Saint John Paul II Parish, Pawtucket, Rhode Island - 697 Central Ave., Pawtucket, RI 02861-2191 t) 401-722-1220; 401-722-1101 stjpii697@gmail.com www.saintjohnpaulri.com Rev. Stephen M. Battey, Pst.; Debra Zagorski, DRE;

St. Cecilia School, Pawtucket - (Grades PreK-8) 755 Central Ave., Pawtucket, RI 02861 t) 401-723-9463 mtetzner@scsri.org www.scsri.org Mary E. Tetzner, Prin.;

The Church of St. John the Baptist of Pawtucket Rhode Island - 69 Quincy Ave., Pawtucket, RI 02860 t) 401-722-9054 st.johnthebaptist@verizon.net Rev. Brian M. Sistare, Pst.; Dcn. Vicente Caban; Sr. Nereida Brian Olmedo, HMSP, DRE;

The Church of the Immaculate Conception of Pawtucket, Rhode Island - 103 Pine St., Pawtucket, RI 02860 t) 401-722-5425 stmarypawt@cox.net Rev. Brian M. Sistare, Admin.; Dcn. C. Patrick Sheehy;

Church of Saint Teresa of the Child Jesus, Pawtucket, Rhode Island - 358 Newport Ave., Pawtucket, RI 02861 t) 401-722-8650 (CRP); 401-278-4500 Rev. Joshua A. Barrow, Pst.; Dcn. N. David Bouley; Susan Levesque, DRE;

St. Teresa of the Child Jesus School - (Grades PreK-8) 140 Woodhaven Rd., Pawtucket, RI 02861 t) 401-726-1414 aamodie@stteresapawtucket.org www.stteresaschoolpawtucket.com Susan Mansfield, Prin.;

PORTSMOUTH

Saint Anthony's Church of Portsmouth - 2836 E. Main Rd., Portsmouth, RI 02871; Mailing: P.O. Box 570, Portsmouth, RI 02871 t) 401-683-3636 (CRP); 401-683-0089 stanthonych@msn.com; vze24s3u@verizon.net Rev. Daniel J. Gray, Pst.; Dcn. Paul St. Laurent;

St. Barnabas Church Corporation, Portsmouth - 1697 E. Main Rd., Portsmouth, RI 02871-2427 t) 401-683-3147 (CRP); 401-683-1343 mjblackburn.sb@gmail.com; sbchurch@stbarnabas.necoxmail.com stbarnabasportsmouth.weconnect.com Rev. David G. Thurber Jr., Pst.; Marcia Blackburn, DRE; Mary Lou Proulx, Bus. Mgr.; Dcn. John Silvia; CRP Stds.: 282

PROVIDENCE

Saint Adalbert's Church - 866 Atwells Ave., Providence, RI 02909-2596 t) 401-351-9306 www.stadalberts.us Rev. Marek S. Kupka, Pst.; Sr. Mary John Fryc, Pst. Min./Coord.; Sr. Janice M. Gaudette, C.S.S.F., DRE; CRP Stds.: 34

Convent - t) 401-831-3336

St. Agnes Church - 351 Branch Ave., Providence, RI 02904 t) 401-861-7265 stagnesprov@verizon.net; fsalmani@verizon.net Rev. Frank S. Salmani, Pst.;

Saint Ann's Catholic Church of Providence, Rhode Island - 2 Russo St., Providence, RI 02940-9207 t) 401-278-4500 Rev. Albert D. Ranallo Jr., Pst.; Rev. Antony Jeya Siluvai Rayan;

The Church of the Assumption, Providence, Rhode Island - 791 Potters Ave., Providence, RI 02907 t) 401-941-3768 (CRP); 401-941-1248 religiouseducation791@yahoo.com; assumptionsouthprovidence@yahoo.com Rev. Gildardo Suarez (Colombia), Pst.; Sr. Angela Daniels, C.P., Pst. Assoc.; Dcn. Rony Lopez; Luz Lopez, DRE;

Saint Anthony's Church Corporation, Rhode Island - 549 Plainfield St., Providence, RI 02909 t) 401-943-2300

Saint Augustine's Church, Providence, Rhode Island - 639 Mount Pleasant Ave., Providence, RI 02908; Mailing: 20 Old Rd., Providence, RI 02908 t) 401-831-3503 staugprov@verizon.net churchofsaintaugustineprov.com/ Rev. Robert H. Forcier, Pst.; Timothy McGinn, DRE; CRP Stds.: 80

St. Augustine School - (Grades PreK-8) 635 Mt. Pleasant Ave., Providence, RI 02908 t) 401-831-1213 principal@staugustinesri.com Janet Rufful, Prin.;

Saint Bartholomew's Church Corporation - 297 Laurel Hill Ave., Providence, RI 02909-3897 t) 401-278-4500 Rev. Vilmar Orsolin, Pst.; Rev. Joseph Pranzo, C.S., Assoc. Pst.;

The Church of the Blessed Sacrament in Providence, Rhode Island - 239 Regent Ave., Providence, RI 02908 t) 401-751-7575 blessacprov@gmail.com blessedsacramentpvd.org Rev. Charles R. Grondin, Pst.; Dcn. Luis Garcia; Rev. Vijan Kiran Anthony Raj, In Res.; CRP Stds.: 69

Blessed Sacrament School - (Grades PreK-8) 240 Regent Ave., Providence, RI 02908 t) 401-831-3993 cweber@blessedschoolpvd.org blessedschoolpvd.com Christopher Weber, Prin.; Stds.: 142; Lay Tchrs.: 17

Saint Charles Borromeo Roman Catholic Church, Providence, Rhode Island - 178 Dexter St., Providence, RI 02907 t) 401-421-6441 stcharlesprov@verizon.net Rev. Jaime A. Garcia, Pst.; Dcn. Jose Rico, Pst. Assoc.;

St. Edward (The Church of St. Joseph Geneva Rhode Island) - 997 Branch Ave., Providence, RI 02904; Mailing: 5 Gibbs St., North Providence, RI 02904 t) 401-331-4035 stanthonynp@cox.net Canonically unified with St. Anthony Parish, North Providence, on December 31, 2022. Very Rev. Edward S. Cardente, Pst.; CRP Stds.: 22

Corporation of the Church of the Holy Cross - 18 King Philip St., Providence, RI 02909; Mailing: 65 Fruit Hill Ave., Providence, RI 02909 t) 401-751-1144 (CRP); 401-272-7118 stthomaschurch@cox.net Mission of St. Thomas Parish, Providence. For inquiries for sacramental records, contact St. Thomas Parish, Providence. Rev. John P. Soares, Admin.; June Carnevale, DRE;

Corporation of the Church of the Holy Ghost, Rhode Island - 472 Atwells Ave., Providence, RI 02909 t) 401-421-3551 holyghostchurchri@gmail.com holy-ghost-church.org Rev. Francesco Francese, Pst.; CRP Stds.: 50

Church of the Holy Name of Jesus at Providence, Rhode Island - 99 Camp St., Providence, RI 02906-1799 t) 401-272-4515 theholyname@cox.net Rev. Lazarus Onuh (Nigeria), In Res.;

St. Joseph's Church Providence Rhode Island - 92 Hope St., Providence, RI 02906 t) 401-421-9137 stjoe1851@cox.net stjosephprovidence.org Rev. Edward A. Sousa Jr., Pst.; Rev. Stanley Azaro; Rev. Maurice L. Brindamour; Rev. Domingos M. da Cunha; Rev. Henry J. Bodah, In Res.; Virginia DiMasi, DRE;

Church of St. Maron in Providence - One Cathedral Square, Providence, RI 02903-3695 t) 401-278-4500 treilly@dioceseofprovidence.org Rev. Timothy D. Reilly, Pst.;

St. Mary's Church Providence Rhode Island - 538 Broadway, Providence, RI 02909-3329 t) 401-274-3434 secretary@stmaryonbroadway.org stmaryonbroadway.org Traditional Latin Parish Rev. Jonathan Romanoski, FSSP, Pst.; CRP Stds.: 24

St. Michael's Providence, Rhode Island - 239 Oxford St., Providence, RI 02905 t) 401-781-7210 Rev. James T. Ruggieri, Pst.; Rev. Joseph Brice, Assoc. Pst.; Dcn. Juan Andres Perez;

Church of Our Lady of Charity of Providence - One Cathedral Sq., Providence, RI 02903-3695 t) 401-278-4500 treilly@dioceseofprovidence.org Rev. Timothy D. Reilly, Pst.;

Church of Our Lady of Lourdes - 901 Atwells Ave., Providence, RI 02909 t) 401-272-8127 Rev. Marek S. Kupka, Pst.; Dcn. Anthony J. Wendoloski Jr.;

Church of Our Lady of the Rosary - 463 Benefit St., Providence, RI 02903 t) 401-273-1685 (CRP); 401-421-5621 olrccd463@aol.com; rosary463@aol.com www.rosary463.com Rev. Joseph A. Escobar, Pst.; Dcn. Victorino Andrade; Elisa Guerra Thibeault, DRE; CRP Stds.: 253

St. Patrick's Church, Providence, Rhode Island - 244 Smith St., Providence, RI 02908 t) 401-421-7070; 401-781-8403 (CRP) stpatrickprov@outlook.com www.saintpatrickchurch.net Rev. James T. Ruggieri, Pst.; Dcn. Eduardo Birbuet, Pst. Assoc.; Dcn. Charles Andrade; Dcn. Robert MacLure; Maria Batista, DRE;

St. Patrick Academy - (Grades 9-12) t) 401-421-9300 bdaigle@stpatrickacademyri.org www.stpatrickacademyri.org Bruce Daigle, Prin.; Jessica Hauk, Librn.;

SS. Peter and Paul's Church - 30 Fenner St., Providence, RI 02903 t) 401-331-2434 religious_education@providencecathedral.org; aiello@providencecathedral.org providencecathedral.org Rev. Msgr. Anthony Mancini, Rector; Rev. Robert W. Hayman, In Res.; Rev. Jeremy J. Rodrigues, In Res.; Sr. Elizabeth Castro, H.M.S.P., DRE; Rev. Msgr. Raymond B. Bastia, In Res.;

Cathedral Convent -

Saint Pius V Church, Providence, Rhode Island - 240 Eaton St.., Providence, RI 02908 t) 401-751-4871 esther@spvchurch.org spvchurch.org/ Rev. James Mary Sullivan, O.P., Pst.; Rev. Anthony VanBerkum, OP, Par. Vicar; CRP Stds.: 20

Saint Raymond's Church Corporation - 1240 N. Main St., Providence, RI 02904; Mailing: 2 Matilda St., Providence, RI 02904-1812 t) 401-351-4224 straymondschurch@gmail.com www.straymonds.com Rev. Edward L. Pieroni, Pst.; CRP Stds.: 26

Church of Saint Sebastian - 67 Cole Ave., Providence, RI 02906 t) 401-751-0196; 401-751-0196 x14 (CRP) pastor@stsebastianri.org; ssricgs@gmail.com stsebastianri.org Rev. Edward A. Sousa Jr., Admin.;

St. Thomas' Church of Manton Rhode Island - 65 Fruit Hill Ave., Providence, RI 02909-5598 t) 401-272-1443 (CRP); 401-278-4500; (401) 272-7118 (Parish Office) stthomaschurchri.org Rev. John P. Soares, Pst.; Dcn. Albert DePetrillo;

RIVERSIDE

St. Brendan - 60 Turner Ave., Riverside, RI 02915 t) 401-433-2600 stbrendan@cox.net stbren.com Lori Lavigne, DRE; Rev. Scott J. Carpentier, Pst.; CRP Stds.: 60

RUMFORD

Saint Margaret's Church Corporation, East Providence Rhode Island - 1098 Pawtucket Ave., Rumford, RI 02916 t) 401-438-3231 (CRP); 401-438-3230 cmoreira@cox.net; office-stmargaretchurch@cox.net Rev. Jeremy J. Rodrigues, Pst.; Charles Moreira, Pst. Assoc.;

St. Margaret School - (Grades PreK-8) 42 Bishop Ave., Rumford, RI 02916 t) 401-434-2338 lunes@stmargaretsch.org Lee Ann Nunes, Prin.;

SLATERSVILLE

St. John's Church Society, Rhode Island - 63 Church St., Slatersville, RI 02876; Mailing: PO Box 266, Slatersville, RI 02876 t) 401-762-0946 stjohn02876@yahoo.com; stjohnreled@yahoo.com stjohntheevangelist.weconnect.com/ Rev. Gerard J. Caron, Pst.; Celeste Baillargeon, DRE; CRP Stds.: 66

SMITHFIELD

St. Michael's Church, Georgiaville, Rhode Island - 80 Farnum Pike, Smithfield, RI 02917 t) 401-231-1340 (CRP); 401-231-5119 stmikesgeo@gmail.com www.stmichaelsmithfield.org Rev. Richard A. Valentine, Pst.;

TIVERTON

Saint Christopher's Church of Tiverton - 1554 Main Rd., Tiverton, RI 02878; Mailing: 265 Stafford Rd., Tiverton, RI 02878 t) 401-624-6644 lynne@sstandctiverton.org; cindy@sstandctiverton.org www.sstandctiverton.org Rev. Przemyslaw Lepak, Pst.; Dcn. Timothy Flanigan; Lynne Swass, DRE;

Church of the Holy Ghost, North Tiverton - 316 Judson St., Tiverton, RI 02878; Mailing: 311 Hooper St., Tiverton, RI 02878 t) 401-624-3664 (Religious Education); 401-624-8131 (Parish Office) frogers@holyghostcc.org; frfinelli@holyghostcc.org www.holyghostcc.org Rev. Jay A. Finelli, Pst.; CRP Stds.: 12

Saint Madeleine's Church Corporation of Tiverton - 35 Lake Rd., Tiverton, RI 02878 t) 401-278-4500 Rev. Stephan A. Silipigni, Pst.;

St. Theresa's Parish Corporation, Tiverton - 265 Stafford Rd., Tiverton, RI 02878 t) 401-624-8746 lynne@sstandctiverton.org; cindy@sstandctiverton.org www.sstandctiverton.org Rev. Przemyslaw Lepak, Pst.; Dcn. Timothy Flanigan; Lynne Swass, DRE;

WAKEFIELD

St. Francis of Assisi - 114 High St., Wakefield, RI 02879-3141 t) 401-783-4411; 401-792-8684 (CRP) cullen_stfrancis@verizon.net; castro_stfrancis@verizon.net stfranciswakefield.com Rev. Albert A. Ranallo Jr., Pst.; Barbette Cullen, DRE; CRP Stds.: 77

St. Romuald Chapel - 61 Atlantic Ave., Wakefield, RI 02879

WARREN

Saint Alexander's Church Corporation, Warren - 221 Main St., Warren, RI 02885 t) 401-247-1764 (CRP); 401-245-6369 parishoffice@saintalexanders.com www.saintalexanders.com Rev. Joseph R. Upton, Admin.;

Church of Saint Mary of the Bay - 645 Main St., Warren, RI 02885 t) 401-245-7000 stmary02885@gmail.com; smbfaithformation@gmail.com stmaryofthebay.org Dcn. John P. Pryor; Rev. Joseph R. Upton, Pst.; CRP Stds.: 100

Saint Thomas the Apostle Church Corporation of Warren - 500 Metacom Ave., Warren, RI 02885-2808 t) 401-245-4488 (CRP); 401-245-4469 stthomasap500@fullchannel.net Rev. John E. Abreu, Pst.; Anne Furtado, DRE; CRP Stds.: 30

WARWICK

St. Benedict's Church, Conimicut - 135 Beach Ave., Warwick, RI 02889 t) 401-737-9492 stbenedicts@verizon.net Canonically unified with St. Kevin Parish, Warwick, in November 2021. Rev. Robert L. Marciano, Admin.;

Saint Catherine's Roman Catholic Church of Warwick, Rhode Island - 3252 Post Rd., Warwick, RI 02886; Mailing: 111 Long St., Warwick, RI 02886 t) 401-739-0212 treilly@dioceseofprovidence.org In July 2021, canonically merged into SS. Rose and Clement Parish, Warwick. Very Rev. D. Andrew Messina, Pst.;

Saint Francis Church Corporation, Hillsgrove - 596 Jefferson Blvd., Warwick, RI 02886; Mailing: 111 Long St., Warwick, RI 02886 t) 401-739-0212 treilly@dioceseofprovidence.org stfranciswarwick.com In July 2021, canonically merged into SS. Rose and Clement Parish, Warwick. Very Rev. D. Andrew Messina, Pst.;

Convent - 249 Chestnut St., Warwick, RI 02888 Rev. Pierre J. Plante, Pst.;

St. Gregory the Great Church Corporation, Warwick - 360 Cowesett Rd., Warwick, RI 02886 t) 401-884-1666 office@stgregorychurchri.com; info@stgregorychurchri.com www.stgregorychurchri.com Rev. David F. Ricard, Admin.; Rev. Alfred V. Ricci, Pastor Emer.; Dcn. Dana Ackerson; Dcn. Paul F. Kirk; Angela Christianson, DRE; Juliette Demers, DRE;

St. Kevin's Church Corporation, Warwick - 333 Sandy Ln., Warwick, RI 02889 t) 401-739-6309 (CRP); 401-278-4500 Rev. Robert L. Marciano, Pst.; Dcn. John Fulton; Brian Callahan, DRE; Michael Curran, DRE; Christopher Tanguay, DRE;

St. Kevin School - (Grades PreK-8) 39 Cathedral Rd., Warwick, RI 02889 t) 401-737-7172 dirving@saintkevinschool.org www.saintkevinschool.org David Irving, Prin.;

St. Peter's Church, Warwick, Rhode Island - 350 Fair St., Warwick, RI 02888 t) 401-461-5691 (CRP); 401-467-4895 info@stpeterswarwick.com Rev. Roger C. Gagne, Pst.; Dcn. Robert M. Morisseau; Margaret Andreozzi, DRE; Elaine Morisseau, DRE;

St. Peter School - (Grades PreK-8) 120 Mayfair Rd., Warwick, RI 02888 t) 401-781-9242 stpeters5@cox.net Joan Sickinger, Prin.;

Saint Rita's Church Corporation, Oakland Beach - 722 Oakland Beach Ave., Warwick, RI 02889 t) 401-738-1800 saintrita02889@ahoo.com Rev. Dean P. Perri, Pst.; Cheryl Picard, DRE;

Sts. Rose & Clement - 111 Long St., Warwick, RI 02886 t) 401-739-0212 office@ssrcri.com www.ssrcri.com Very Rev. D. Andrew Messina, Pst.; CRP Stds.: 107

St. Rose of Lima - 200 Brentwood Ave., Warwick, RI 02886 t) 401-739-6937 kizzi@saintroseschool.com www.saintroseschool.com Kimberly Izzi, Prin.;

Saint Timothy's Church Corporation, Warwick - 1799 Warwick Ave., Warwick, RI 02889 t) 401-738-9079 (CRP); 401-739-9552 sttim1799@aol.com sainttimothy.weconnect.com Rev. Dean P. Perri, Pst.; CRP Stds.: 62

WEST WARWICK

Saint Anthony's Church Corporation, River Point - 10 Sunset Ave., West Warwick, RI 02893 t) 401-278-4500 chancellor@dioceseofprovidence.org Rev. Victor T. Silva, Pst.; Dcn. Carlos Botelho;

Church of Christ the King, West Warwick - 130 Legris Ave., West Warwick, RI 02893 t) 401-821-9228 ctkwwri@cox.net ctkwwri.org Rev. Victor T. Silva, Pst.; CRP Stds.: 30

SS. John and James Parish - 20 Washington St., West Warwick, RI 02893-4919 t) 401-821-7661 ssjohnandjames@cox.net SS. John and James Parish absorbed St. Mary Parish, West Warwick, on July 1, 2019. Rev. Nicholas T. Fleming, Pst.; Dcn. Scott Brown; Christine Daneault, DRE;

St. Joseph's Church, Natick RI - 854 Providence St., West Warwick, RI 02893-1140 t) 401-821-4072 stjoseph854@gmail.com www.stjosephww.org Rev. Gregory P. Stowe, Pst.; Dcn. Cyrille W.J. Cote; CRP Stds.: 85

St. Joseph School - (Grades PreK-8) 850 Wakefield St., West Warwick, RI 02893 t) 401-821-3450 eclark@sjsww.org www.sjsww.org Erin Clark, Prin.;

St. Mary's Church, Crompton Rhode Island - 70 Church St., West Warwick, RI 02893; Mailing: 20 Washington St., West Warwick, RI 02893 t) 401-828-8756 (CRP); 401-821-5555 stmaryschurch1@cox.net Rev. Nicholas T. Fleming, Admin.; Dcn. Scott Brown;

Church of Our Lady of Good Counsel, Warwick RI - 62 Pleasant St., West Warwick, RI 02893 t) 401-822-1869 (CRP); 401-821-6428 olgc60@verizon.net Rev. Paul R. Lemoi, Pst.; Susan Cinieri, DRE; CRP Stds.: 9

SS. Peter and Paul's Church, Phoenixville, Rhode Island - 48 Highland St., West Warwick, RI 02893-5699 t) 401-821-2198 sspeterandpaulchurch@verizon.net Rev. Robert J. Giardina, Pst.;

Church of the Sacred Heart, Natick RI - 820 Providence St., West Warwick, RI 02893 t) 401-821-4184 sacredheartww@cox.net Rev. Richard A. Bucci, Pst.;

WESTERLY

Saint Clare's Church Corporation, Misquamicut - 4 Saint Clare Way, Westerly, RI 02891 t) 401-348-8765 scc1svdp@gmail.com stclarewesterly.com Rev. Peter J. D'Ambrosia, Pst.; Dcn. Stephen R. Cote; Dcn. W. Carl LaFleur; Dcn. John D. McGregor;

Church of the Immaculate Conception of Westerly, Rhode Island - 111 High St., Westerly, RI 02891-0556 t) 401-596-0900 (CRP); 401-596-2130 icc@immcon.org immcon.org Rev. Giacomo D. Capoverdi Jr., Pst.; Catherine Kimmel, DRE;

St. Pius X Parish Corporation, Westerly - 44 Elm St., Westerly, RI 02891 t) 401-596-8530 (CRP); 401-596-2535 chrismagowan@cox.net; stpiusx@cox.net Rev. Michael J. Najim, Pst.; Dcn. Francis J. Valliere; Christine Magowan, DRE; Rev. Raymond N. Suriani, In Res.;

WICKFORD

St. Bernard's Roman Catholic Church of Wickford, Rhode Island - 275 Tower Hill Rd., Wickford, RI 02852 t) 401-295-0387 sbc.bus@verizon.net; sbc.pa@verizon.net www.stbernardnk.org Rev. David F. Gaffney, Pst.; Angelo Giacchi, Pst. Assoc.; Dawn Masterson, DRE; Christina Pichette, DRE; CRP Stds.: 171

WOONSOCKET

Saint Agatha's Church Corporation, Woonsocket - 34 Joffre Ave., Woonsocket, RI 02895 t) 401-278-4500 Rev. Michael A. Kelley, Pst.; Dcn. Eugene Garceau;

All Saints Parish - 323 Rathbun St., Woonsocket, RI 02895 t) 401-762-1100 An alliance of Our Lady of Victories, St. Aloysius, and St. Ann. Rev. Ryan J. Simas, Pst.;

Saint Anthony's Church, Woonsocket, RI - 128 Greene St., Woonsocket, RI 02895 t) 401-766-2640 saintanthonywoonsocket@verizon.com saintanthonywoonsocket.org Rev. Msgr. Ronald P. Simeone, Pst.;

St. Charles Borromeo's Church, Woonsocket, RI - 8 Daniels St., Woonsocket, RI 02895; Mailing: 323 Rathbun St., Woonsocket, RI 02895 t) 401-766-0176 rectory@stcharlesborromeo.com stcharlesborromeo.com Canonically unified with All Saints Parish, Woonsocket. Rev. Ryan J. Simas, Pst.;

Holy Trinity Parish Woonsocket - 1409 Park Ave., Woonsocket, RI 02895 t) 401-762-5117 holy.trinity1409@gmail.com www.holytrinityri.com Unification of Holy Family Church of the Holy Family; Our Lady, Queen of Martyrs Church Corp; Church of the Sacred Heart-Woonsocket Very Rev. Daniel J. Sweet, Pst.;

Saint Joseph's Church, Woonsocket - 1200 Mendon Rd., Woonsocket, RI 02895-3999 t) 401-766-0626 saintjoseph1929@gmail.com saintjosephwoonsocket.org Rev. Ryan J. Simas, Pst.; CRP Stds.: 50

Woonsocket Health Center -

Wyndemere Woods -

The Church of the Precious Blood Corporation, Woonsocket, RI - 94 Carrington Ave., Woonsocket, RI 02895; Mailing: 34 Joffre Ave., Woonsocket, RI 02895 t) 401-767-2950 preciousblood@cox.net Rev. Michael A. Kelley, Pst.;

Saint Stanislaus Kostka Church of Woonsocket - 174 Harris Ave., Woonsocket, RI 02895 t) 401-278-4500 Rev. Dariusz J. Jonczyk, Admin.;

SCHOOLS: PRESCHOOL THRU HIGH SCHOOL

SCHOOLS

STATE OF RHODE ISLAND

CRANSTON

Immaculate Conception Catholic Regional School - (PAR) (Grades PreK-8) 235 Garden Hills Dr., Cranston, RI 02920 t) 401-942-7245 aspaziante@iccatholicschool.org iccatholicschool.org Andrea Spaziante, Prin.; Kristine Mahone, Librn.; Stds.: 250

EAST GREENWICH

Our Lady of Mercy Regional School - (PAR) (Grades PreK-8) 55 Fourth Ave., East Greenwich, RI 02818 t) 401-884-1618 principal@olmschool.org www.olmschool.org Scott W. Fuller, Prin.; Camille Craybas, Librn.;

GREENVILLE

Overbrook Academy (Overbrook, Inc.) - (PRV) (Grades 6-9) 60 Austin Ave., Greenville, RI 02828 t) 401-349-3444 information@overbrookacademy.org www.overbrookacademy.com (Boarding School) Berenice Garcia, Dir.; Stds.: 81; Lay Tchrs.: 4

MIDDLETOWN

All Saints Academy - (DIO) (Grades PreSchool-8) 915 W. Main Rd., Middletown, RI 02842 t) 401-848-4300 office@allsaintsacademy.org; dgreen@allsaintsacademy.org allsaintsacademy.org Dianne M. Green, Prin.; Stds.: 151; Lay Tchrs.: 11

PAWTUCKET

Woodlawn Catholic Regional School - (PAR) (Grades PreK-8) 61 Hope St., Pawtucket, RI 02860 t) 401-723-3759 mrbennettwcrs@gmail.com www.woodlawncrs.com Mary-Regina Bennett, Prin.;

PORTSMOUTH

***St. Philomena School (Saint Philomena School of the Sacred Heart)** - (PRV) (Grades PreK-8) 324 Cory's Ln., Portsmouth, RI 02871 t) 401-683-0268 bcordeiro@saintphilomena.org; lgallant-stanzione@saintphilomena.org www.saintphilomena.org Dawn Pagano, Vice Prin.; Brian Cordeiro, Prin.; Stds.: 411; Lay Tchrs.: 34

PROVIDENCE

Bishop McVinney Regional School (Catholic Association for Regional Education) - (PAR) (Grades PreK-8) 155 Gordon Ave., Providence, RI 02905 t) 401-781-2370 lhebertbmv@gmail.com bmv-school.org Louis Hebert, Prin.; Stds.: 190; Lay Tchrs.: 12

San Miguel School - (PRV) (Grades 5-8) 525 Branch Ave., Providence, RI 02904 t) 401-467-9777 csoltys@sanmiguelprov.org; jwolf@sanmiguelprov.org www.sanmiguelprov.org Carol Soltys, Prin.; Stds.: 62; Lay Tchrs.: 7

St. Thomas Regional School - (PAR) (Grades PreK-8) 15 Edendale Ave., Providence, RI 02911 t) 401-351-0403 mdimuccio@saintthomasregional.com Mary DiMuccio, Prin.;

RIVERSIDE

St. Mary Academy-Bay View - (PRV) (Grades PreK-12) 3070 Pawtucket Ave., Riverside, RI 02915 t) 401-434-0113 x156 rperry@bayviewacademy.org; mrossi@bayviewacademy.org www.bayviewacademy.org Day Pupils. Corporate Member-Mercy Education System of the Americas (MESA) Dr. Marcela Rossi, Prin.; Sr. Marybeth Beretta, RSM, Pres.; Stds.: 393; Sr. Tchrs.: 3; Lay Tchrs.: 38

WAKEFIELD

Monsignor Matthew F. Clarke Regional School - (PRV) (Grades PreSchool-8) 5074 Tower Hill Rd., Wakefield, RI 02879 t) 401-789-0860 alisi@monsignorclarkeschool.org www.monsignorclarkeschool.org Monsignor Clarke School is the only Catholic elementary/middle school in southern Rhode Island Arthur Lisi, Prin.; Stds.: 365; Lay Tchrs.: 17

WARWICK

Chesterton Academy of Our Lady of Hope - (PRV) 487 Jefferson Blvd., Warwick, RI 02886; Mailing: P.O. Box 6973, Warwick, RI 02887 t) (401) 287-2280 www.chestertonri.org

WOONSOCKET

Greater Woonsocket Catholic Regional School System - 1210 Mendon Rd., Woonsocket, RI 02895 t) 401-762-1095 administrator@gwcrs.org www.gwcrs.org Jennifer DeOliveira, Admin.;

Monsignor Gadoury Catholic Regional School - 1371 Park Ave., Woonsocket, RI 02895 t) 401-767-5902 mgprincipal@cox.net Shawn A. Capron, Prin.;

Good Shepherd Catholic Regional School - t) 401-767-5906 goodshepherdprincipal@gwcrs.org Jennifer DeOliveira, Prin.;

HIGH SCHOOLS

STATE OF RHODE ISLAND

PAWTUCKET

St. Raphael Academy - (DIO) 123 Walcott St., Pawtucket, RI 02860 t) 401-723-8100 x113 drichard@saintrays.org www.saintrays.org Conducted by the Brothers of the Christian Schools. Rev. Ryan J. Simas, Chap.; Daniel J. Richard, Pres.; Michelle Carrara, Dir.;

PORTSMOUTH

Portsmouth Abbey School (Order of St. Benedict in Portsmouth, Rhode Island) - (PRV) 285 Cory's Ln., Portsmouth, RI 02871 t) 401-683-2000 mcd@portsmouthabbey.org; hmassist@portsmouthabbey.org www.portsmouthabbey.org Daniel McDonough, Headmaster;

PROVIDENCE

La Salle Academy (St. John Baptist de LaSalle Institute) - (PRV) (Grades 6-12) 612 Academy Ave., Providence, RI 02908 t) 401-351-7750 dkavanagh@lasalle-academy.org; pmeehan@lasalle-academy.org www.lasalle-academy.org Conducted by the Brothers of the Christian Schools. Rev. Thomas J. Woodhouse, Chap.; Donald Kavanagh, Prin.; Bro. Dennis Malloy, F.S.C., Pres.; Patrick Meehan, CFO; Thomas Glavin, Vice Pres., Institutional Advancement; Stds.: 1,500

RIVERSIDE

St. Mary Academy - Bay View - (PRV) 3070 Pawtucket Ave., Riverside, RI 02915 t) 401-434-0113 x156 mberetta@bayviewacademy.org www.bayviewacademy.org Corporate Member-Mercy Education System of the Americas (MESA) Colleen Gribbin, Prin.; Sr. Marybeth Beretta, Pres.; Laura Laurence, Librn.;

WAKEFIELD

The Prout School - (DIO) 4640 Tower Hill Rd., Wakefield, RI 02879 t) 401-789-9262 sdeluca@theproutschool.org www.theproutschool.org Rev. Carl B. Fisette, Chap.; David Estes, Prin.; Sharon DeLuca, Dir.;

WARWICK

Bishop Hendricken High School - (DIO) (Grades 8-12) 2615 Warwick Ave., Warwick, RI 02889 t) 401-739-3450 hawks@hendricken.com www.hendricken.com Mark DeCiccio, Prin.; Rev. Robert L. Marciano, Pres.;

WOONSOCKET

Mount Saint Charles Academy, Inc., Brothers of the Sacred Heart. - (PRV) (Grades 6-12) 800 Logee St., Woonsocket, RI 02895-5599 t) 401-769-0310 tenreiroa@mtstcharles.org mountsaintcharles.org Alan J Tenreiro, Pres.; Stds.: 576; Bro. Tchrs.: 2; Lay Tchrs.: 41

INSTITUTIONS LOCATED IN DIOCESE

CAMPUS MINISTRY / NEWMAN CENTERS [CAM]

BRISTOL

Roger Williams University - 1 Old Ferry Rd., Bristol, RI 02809 t) 401-254-3433 nsoukup@rwu.edu Donald Farrish, Pres.;

KINGSTON

University of Rhode Island Catholic Center - 90 Chapel Way, Kingston, RI 02881 t) 401-874-2324 chaplain@rhodycatholic.com www.rhodycatholic.com Rev. Carl B. Fisette, Chap.;

PROVIDENCE

Brown University (Brown-RISD Catholic Community) - 69 Brown St., Suite 410, Providence, RI 02912; Mailing: c/o Office of Chaplains & Religious Life, Box 1931, Providence, RI 02912 t) 401-863-2344 chaplain@brownrisdcatholic.org www.brownrisdcatholic.org Rev. Edmund McCullough, O.P., Chap.;

Johnson & Wales University - CBCSI Bldg., 8 Abbott Park Pl., Providence, RI 02903 t) 401-598-1830 pvd@admissions.jwu.edu The Newman Club Jessica Grady, Dir.;

Rhode Island College - Donovan Lower Level, 600 Mt. Pleasant Ave., Providence, RI 02908 t) 401-456-8346 ricinterfaithcenter@ric.edu www.ric.edu/interfaithcenter Interfaith Center Frank Sanchez, Pres.;

SMITHFIELD

Bryant University - 1150 Douglas Pk., Smithfield, RI 02917-1284; Mailing: Box 33, Smithfield, RI 02917-1284 t) 401-232-6045 rburgess2@bryant.edu Rev. Joseph Pescatello, Chap.;

CEMETERIES [CEM]

EAST PROVIDENCE

Gate of Heaven - 555 Wampanoag Trail, East Providence, RI 02915 t) 401-434-2579 cemetery@dioceseofprovidence.org Anthony Carpinello, Dir.;

PROVIDENCE

St. Ann's - 1 Cathedral Sq., Providence, RI 02908-3301 t) 401-278-4500 Anthony Carpinello, Dir.;

St. Columba - 1 Cathedral Sq., Providence, RI 02908-3301 t) 401-278-4500 Anthony Carpinello, Dir.;

St. Francis - 1 Cathedral Sq., Providence, RI 02908-3301 t) 401-278-4500 Anthony Carpinello, Dir.;

St. Joseph - 1 Cathedral Sq., Providence, RI 02908-3301 t) 401-278-4500 Anthony Carpinello, Dir.;

Maria Del Campo - 1 Cathedral Sq., Providence, RI 02903 t) 401-278-4500 treilly@dioceseofprovidence.org Anthony Carpinello, Dir.;

Mount St. Mary's - 1 Cathedral Sq., Providence, RI 02903 t) 401-278-4500 Anthony Carpinello, Dir.;

St. Patrick's - 1 Cathedral Sq., Providence, RI 02908-3301 t) 401-278-4500 Anthony Carpinello, Dir.;

Resurrection - 1 Cathedral Sq., Providence, RI 02903 t) 401-278-4500 Anthony Carpinello, Dir.;

COLLEGES & UNIVERSITIES [COL]

NEWPORT

Salve Regina University (Salve Regina University, Sisters of Mercy of the Americas) - 100 Ochre Point Ave., Newport, RI 02840-4192 t) 401-341-2137 humanresources@salve.edu www.salve.edu Dr. Theresa Ladrigan-Whelpley, Vice. Pres.; Sr. M. Therese Antone, R.S.M., Chancellor; Rev. Scott D. Pontes, Chap.; Amy Cady, Director of the Mercy Center for Spiritual Life; Stds.: 2,872; Lay Tchrs.: 134; Sr. Tchrs.: 1

PROVIDENCE

***Providence College** - One Cunningham Sq., Providence, RI 02918 t) 401-865-1000 pcadmiss@providence.edu www.providence.edu Conducted by the Dominican Friars. Rev. J. Stuart McPhail, O.P., Chap.; Rev. Peter Martyr Joseph Yungwirth, O.P., Chap.; Rev. Mark D. Nowel, O.P., Dean; Rev. R. Gabriel Pivarnik, O.P., Vice Pres. Mission & Ministry; Rev. Kenneth Sicard, O.P., Pres.;

CONVENTS, MONASTERIES, AND RESIDENCES FOR WOMEN [CON]

BARRINGTON

Monastery of Discalced Carmelites at Nayatt, Barrington, Rhode Island - 25 Watson Ave., Barrington, RI 02806-4009 t) 401-278-4663 sllbarr@juno.com home.att.net/~barringtoncarmel Sr. Susan L. Lumb, Prioress;

BRISTOL

Mt. St. Joseph Spiritual Life Center and Provincialate (Sisters of St. Dorothy) - 13 Monkeywrench Ln., Bristol, RI 02809-2916 t) 401-253-5434 nuninbristol@yahoo.com www.dioceseofprovidence.org Srs.: 4

CUMBERLAND

Sisters of Mercy of the Americas Northeast Community, Inc. - 15 Highland View Rd., Cumberland, RI 02864-1124 t) 401-333-6333 Sr. Judith Frikker, RSM, Pres.; Srs.: 366

Mercycrest Convent - 125 Wrentham Rd., Cumberland, RI 02864; Mailing: 15 Highland Rd., Cumberland, RI 02864 info@mercyne.org Sr. Maureen Mitchell, R.S.M., Pres.;

Mercymount Convent - 75 Wrentham Rd., Cumberland, RI 02864; Mailing: 15 Highland View Rd., Cumberland, RI 02864 info@mercyne.org sistersofmercy.org/northeast Sr. Maureen Mitchell, R.S.M., Pres.;

Sisters of Mercy of the Americas Northeast Community, Inc., Administrative Offices - 15 Highland View Rd., Cumberland, RI 02864-1124 t) (401) 333-6333

EAST GREENWICH

Franciscan Apostolic Sisters - 66 Fifth Ave., East Greenwich, RI 02818 t) 401-336-3145 c) 401-474-6513; 401-474-9065 srnemfas@yahoo.com; srloufas@yahoo.com www.geocities.com/franapsisters Sr. Nemesia Licayu, F.A.S., Supr.; Sr. Lourdes DeLeon, F.A.S., Treas.; Srs.: 6

Franciscan Apostolic Sisters Regional House - 622 Putnam Pike, Greenville, RI 02828; Mailing: 66 5th Ave., East Greenwich, RI 02818 c) (401) 474-6513

MIDDLETOWN

Cluny Provincial House (Sisters of St. Joseph of Cluny Province of USA and Canada) - 7 Restmere Ter., Middletown, RI 02842 t) 401-846-4757 (Prov.); 401-846-4826 (Office) clunyusa@hotmail.com clunyusandcanada.org Sr. Genevieve Marie Vigil, S.J.C., Prov.; Srs.: 2,400

St. Joseph of Cluny Convent - t) 401-847-3637

Provincial House - Sr. Luke Parker, S.J.C., Prov.;

NEWPORT

Javouhey House - 78 Carroll Ave., Newport, RI 02840 t) 401-849-5124 ellenliston@yahoo.com Srs.: 3

NORTH PROVIDENCE

Daughters of Mary Mother of Mercy - 2 Pope St., North Providence, RI 02904 t) 401-353-8654 ponyeje@yahoo.com Sr. Patricia Onyeje, D.M.M.M., Supr.; Srs.: 2

Franciscan Missionaries of Mary - 399 Fruit Hill Ave., North Providence, RI 02911 t) 401-353-5800 lapfmm@aol.com www.fmmusa.org Sr. Lois Ann Pereira, F.M.M., Supr.; Srs.: 30

De Chappotin Community - t) 401-353-9412

Holy Family Community -

Our Lady of the Lourdes Convent - 385 Fruit Hill Ave., North Providence, RI 02911 t) 401-353-6381

Trinity Community, Assisted Living Community - Sr. Maria C. Zunzarren, F.M.M., Supr.;

NORTH SMITHFIELD

Franciscan Missionaries of Mary - Ein Karim Community, 318 Mendon Rd., North Smithfield, RI 02896 t) 401-766-8242 karimfmm@aol.com Sr. Emilie Duchaney, F.M.M.; Srs.: 2

PROVIDENCE

St. Clare Convent, Cutting Memorial (The Saint Clare Home) - 1 Cathedral Sq., Providence, RI 02908-3301 t) 401-846-1025 Rev. Timothy D. Reilly, Contact; Srs.: 2

SMITHFIELD

Sisters of the Cross and Passion - 310 George Washington Hwy., Ste. 300, Smithfield, RI 02917; Mailing: P. O. Box 17372, Smithfield, RI 02917 t) (401) 349-4960 x3207 maryjaneh656@gmail.com www.passionistsisters.org Sr. Mary Jane Holden, Sr. Mary Jane Holden; Srs.: 25

WAKEFIELD

Congregation of the Sisters of Divine Providence Generalate - 12 Christopher St., Wakefield, RI 02879 t) 401-782-1785 officeforreligious@dioceseofprovidence.org Sr. Maria Fest, C.D.P., Supr.; Srs.: 4

Mother of Providence Convent -

WEST GREENWICH

***Missionary Sisters Servants of the Word HMSP, Northeast Province** - 28 Victory Hwy., West Greenwich, RI 02817 t) 401-397-5053 Sr. Elizabeth Castro, H.M.S.P., Supr.; Srs.: 7

ENDOWMENTS / FOUNDATIONS / TRUSTS [EFT]

NARRAGANSETT

Ocean Tides Christian Brothers Charitable Trust - 635 Ocean Rd., Narragansett, RI 02882 t) 401-789-1016 eiovino@oceantides.org; martino@oceantides.org Bro. James Martino, F.S.C., Pres.;

PASCOAG

Father Andre Coindre Charitable Trust - 685 Steere Farm Rd., Pascoag, RI 02859-4601 t) 401-568-3361 x3202 bileblancsc@gmail.com Bro. Ivy LeBlanc, S.C., Treas.;

PROVIDENCE
***The Interfaith Community Dire Emergency Fund** - One Cathedral Sq., Providence, RI 02903 t) 401-421-7833 x207 jjahnz@dioceseofprovidence.org

MISCELLANEOUS [MIS]

COVENTRY
Cursillo Movement - 461 Shady Valley Rd., Coventry, RI 02816; Mailing: One Cathedral Square, Providence, RI 02903 t) 401-392-1252 treilly@dioceseofprovidence.org
CUMBERLAND
Northeast FIDES, Inc. - 15 Highland View Rd., Cumberland, RI 02864-1124 t) 401-333-6333 Sr. Judith Frikker, RSM, Pres.;
GREENVILLE
LC Pastoral Services, Inc. - 60 Austin Ave., Greenville, RI 02828 t) 401-949-3444 fformolo@legionaries.org Rev. Frank Formolo, Secy.;
Magnificat - Our Lady of Divine Providence Chapter, Inc. - 5 Danecroft Ave., Greenville, RI 02828 t) 401-864-7731 lsg45mag@cox.net; dianebaron@cox.net Linda Gatta, Contact;
Mater Ecclesiae, Inc. - 60 Austin Ave., Greenville, RI 02828 t) 401-949-3444 sbaldwin@regnumchristi.net www.regnumchristi.org Sonia Baldwin, Secy.;
Overbrook, Incorporated - 60 Austin Ave., Greenville, RI 02828 t) 770-828-4950 Sonia Baldwin, Secy.;
Regnum Christi - 60 Austin Ave., Greenville, RI 02828 t) 401-349-3444 fformolo@legionaries.org www.regnumchristi.org Rev. Frank Formolo;
MAPLEVILLE
Society of St. Vincent de Paul of Providence - 525 Maureen Cir., Mapleville, RI 02839 t) 401-568-4709 jmar10@cox.net www.svdpri.org James Martufi, Pres.;
MIDDLETOWN
Charismatic Renewal - 909 W. Main Rd., Middletown, RI 02842-6351 t) 401-847-6153 stlucyoffice@gmail.com Rev. John W. O'Brien;
NORTH KINGSTOWN
***The Haitian Project, Inc.** - 650 Ten Rod Rd., North Kingstown, RI 02852; Mailing: P.O. Box 6891, Providence, RI 02940 t) 401-351-3624 operations@haitianproject.org www.haitianproject.org Marisa (Reese) Grondin, Pres.;
NORTH PROVIDENCE
Franciscan Missionaries of Mary - 399 Fruit Hill Ave., North Providence, RI 02911 t) 401-636-4470 mmottefmm@gmail.com www.fmmusa.org Sr. Mary Motte, R.S.M., Contact;
Mission Resource Center - t) 401-353-4470
NORTH SMITHFIELD
Hombre Nuevo (RI), Inc. - 275 Mechanic St., North Smithfield, RI 02896-7718 t) 770-828-4950 fformolo@legionaries.org Rev. Frank Formolo, Secy.;
Ocean Pastoral Center, Inc. - 275 Mechanic St., North Smithfield, RI 02896-7718 t) 770-828-4950 fformolo@legionaries.org Rev. Frank Formolo, Secy.;
PROVIDENCE
***Bishop McVinney Auditorium** - One Cathedral Sq., Providence, RI 02903 t) (401) 278-4500 Rev. Nathan J. Ricci;
Conference of Regional Treasurers - 1 Cathedral Square, Providence, RI 02903; Mailing: P.O. Box 17372, Smithfield, RI 02917 t) 401-349-4960 vgladu@bmtconsults.com Virginia Gladu, Contact;
***Mandamiento Nuevo Corporation** - One Cathedral Sq., Providence, RI 02903 t) 401-421-7833 x104 jbarry@dioceseofprovidence.org John J. Barry III, Secy.;
Miscellaneous Listings for the Diocese of Providence - One Cathedral Sq., Providence, RI 02903 t) 401-278-4663 treilly@dioceseofprovidence.org www.dioceseofprovidence.org See School Section for related schools. Rev. Timothy D. Reilly, Chancellor;
St. Benedict's Hearth Corporation, East Providence. -
Saint Casimir's Church of Warren -
Catholic Cemeteries -
Catholic Charity Fund -
Catholic Foundation of Rhode Island -
Catholic Information Center of Newport -
Catholic Inner City Apostolate, Inc. -
Catholic Investment Trust, Inc. -
Catholic Social Services of RI - t) 401-278-4500
Catholic Teachers' College of Providence -
Catholic Youth Organization of the Diocese of Providence -
Christ the Redeemer Academy -
The Church of the Immaculate Conception, North Providence -
Cluny School - 75 Brenton Rd., Newport, RI 02840
Corpus Christi Carmel -
De LaSalle Academy Corporation -
Deliverance Ministry -
DiMed Corp. -
Diocesan Administration Corporation - t) 401-278-4616
Diocesan Catholic Telecommunications Network of Rhode Island -
Diocesan Plant Fund -
Diocesan School Financial Services - t) 401-278-4500
Diocesan Service Corporation - t) 401-278-4616
St. Dominic Savio Boys' Center -
Saint Elizabeth Ann Seton Academy - 909 Lonsdale Ave., Central Falls, RI 02863
F.A.C.E. of Rhode Island (Financial Aid for Children's Education of Rhode Island) -
Father Barry CYO Center -
Father Holland Catholic Regional Elementary School - 180 Sayles Ave., Pascoag, RI 02859
Saint Francis House -
Grateful for God's Providence - c/o Office of Stewardship & Devel., One Cathedral Sq., Providence, RI 02903
Saint Hedwig's Church Corporation, Providence -
Holy Name Society -
Homes for Hope Foundation -
House of the Good Shepherd of Providence -
Inter-Parish Loan Fund, Inc. -
St. John's Church of Providence -
LaSalle Academy -
Little Sisters of the Assumption of Woonsocket -
Saint Margaret's Home -
Saint Maria Society -
Marian Association of Northern Rhode Island -
St. Martin de Porres Center - c/o Fiscal Office, One Cathedral Sq., Providence, RI 02903
St. Mary Academy of the Visitation -
The Mercy Home and School -
Mont St. Francois, of Woonsocket R.I. -
Mother of Hope Novitiate -
Nazareth Home -
New England Conference of Diocesan Directors of Religious Education -
Our Lady of Fatima High School - 360 Market St., Warren, RI 02885
Our Lady of Peace Retreat House -
Our Lady of Providence Preparatory Seminary -
Our Lady, Queen of the Clergy -
Parish Investment Group -
Pius X Salvage Bureau -
Project Hope/Projecto Esperanza, Inc. -
Saint Raphael's Industrial Home and School -
Retreat House of the Immaculate Heart of Mary -
The Rhode Island Catholic Orphan Asylum (St. Aloysius Home) -
Rhode Island Home for Working Boys -
Roman Catholic Bishop of Providence (A Corporation Sole) -
St. Casimir -
Saint William Church Corporation, Norwood -
Shepherds of Hope, Inc. - t) 401-278-4500
Society for the Propagation of the Faith, Diocese of Providence -
Stella Maris Home for Convalescents -
The Church of Saint Jean Baptiste of Warren, Rhode Island -
St. Vincent de Paul Home, Woonsocket -
Saint Vincent de Paul Infant Asylum -
Vision of Hope Fund, Inc. -
Prelature of the Holy Cross and Opus Dei - Mathewson House, 224 Bowen St., Providence, RI 02906 t) 401-272-7834 info@opusdei.org www.opusdei.org Rev. George Crafts;
WARWICK
***Poverello Corporation** - 222 Jefferson Blvd., Ste. 200, Warwick, RI 02888; Mailing: c/o Holy Name Provincial Office, 129 W 31st St., 2nd Fl., New York, NY 10001-3403 t) 646-473-0265 mharlan@hnp.org f.k.a.: Poverello Center; f.k.a: Weybosset Street Community Center Rev. Kevin Mullen, Pres.;
WEST WARWICK
Tides Family Services - 215 Washington St., West Warwick, RI 02893 t) 401-822-1360 mail@tidesfs.org www.tidesfs.org Bro. Michael Reis, F.S.C., CEO;
Learning Center - 242 Dexter St., Pawtucket, RI 02860 t) 401-724-8060
Learning Center - 790 Broad St., Providence, RI 02907 t) 401-467-8228
Learning Center - 222 Washington St., West Warwick, RI 02893 t) 401-823-0157
Outreach and Tracking Program - 242 Dexter St., Pawtucket, RI 02860 t) 401-724-8380
Preserving Families Network - 242 Dexter St., Pawtucket, RI 02860 t) 401-724-8201
Preserving Families Network - 55 Main St., Ste. 1, Woonsocket, RI 02895 t) 401-766-9320
Preserving Families Network - 790 Broad St., Providence, RI 02907 t) 401-467-8888
Preserving Families Network -
Woonsocket Outreach Project - 55 Main St., Ste. 1, Woonsocket, RI 02895 t) 401-766-9320
Youth Diversion Project -
Youth Diversion Project - 242 Dexter St., Pawtucket, RI 02860 t) 401-724-8380
Youth Transition Center - 790 Broad St., Providence, RI 02907 t) 401-467-8888
Youth Transition Center - 242 Dexter St., Pawtucket, RI 02860 t) 401-724-8100

MONASTERIES AND RESIDENCES FOR PRIESTS AND BROTHERS [MON]

BRISTOL
St. Columban's Retirement House (St. Columban's Foreign Mission Society) - 65 Ferry Rd., Bristol, RI 02809; Mailing: Box 65, Bristol, RI 02809 t) 401-253-6909 jburger@columban.org Rev. William Brunner, S.S.C.; Rev. John Buckley, S.S.C.; Rev. Salvatore S. Caputo, S.S.C.; Rev. Michael J. Donnelly, S.S.C.; Rev. James Dwyer, S.S.C.; Rev. Victor Gaboury, S.S.C.; Rev. Francis Grady, S.S.C.; Rev. John Marley, S.S.C.; Rev. Daniel McGinn, S.S.C.; Rev. Joseph McSweeney, S.S.C.; Rev. John Moran, S.S.C.; Rev. Paul O'Malley, S.S.C.; Rev. Francis D. O'Mara, S.S.C., In Res.; Rev. Vincent Youngkamp, S.S.C., In Res.; Rev. Robert O'Rourke, S.S.C.; Rev. Richard L. Pankratz, S.S.C.; Rev. Francis J. Royer, S.S.C.; Rev. Alban Sueper, S.S.C.; Rev. William F. Sullivan, S.S.C.; Rev. William F. Sweeney, S.S.C.; Rev. Thomas Vaughan, S.S.C.; Rev. John Q. Wanaurny, S.S.C.; Rev. Gerard P. Wilmsen, S.S.C.; Rev. John E. Burger, S.S.C., Vicar; Rev. Francis P. Carroll, S.S.C., Supr.; Rev. Charles Lintz, S.S.C., Supr.; Brs.: 23; Priests: 23
NARRAGANSETT
Christian Brothers' Center (Brothers of the Christian Schools, District of Eastern North America) - 635 Ocean Rd., Narragansett, RI 02882 t) 401-789-0244 x102 cheryl@dlcb.org www.dlcb.org Bro. Michael Shubnell, Dir.; Brs.: 12
PASCOAG
Brothers of the Sacred Heart Residence - 685 Steere Farm Rd., Pascoag, RI 02859-4601; Mailing: 4600 Elysian Fields Ave., New Orleans, LA 70122 t) 504-301-4758 unitedstatesprovince@gmail.com brothersofthesacredheart.org Bro. Matthew Scanlon, S.C., In Res.; Bro. Donald Tardif, S.C., In Res.; Bro. Guy Beaulieu, S.C., In Res.; Bro. Joseph Beaulieu, S.C., In Res.; Bro. Frederick Bouchard, S.C., In Res.; Bro.

Marcel Brisson, S.C., In Res.; Bro. Irenee Chabot, S.C., In Res.; Rev. Louis Couvillon, In Res.; Bro. Eldon Crifasi, S.C., In Res.; Bro. Kevin Finnegan, S.C., In Res.; Bro. Roger Fountain, S.C., In Res.; Bro. Robert T. Gagne, S.C., In Res.; Bro. Paul Gauvin, S.C., In Res.; Bro. Paul Hebert, S.C., In Res.; Bro. William Leimbach, S.C., In Res.; Bro. Roland Ouellette, S.C., In Res.; Bro. Clement Pelletier, S.C., In Res.; Bro. Roy Pinette, S.C., In Res.; Bro. Robert Provencher, S.C., In Res.; Bro. Benoit Roy, S.C., In Res.; Bro. John Spalding, S.C., In Res.; Bro. Robert Ziobro, S.C., In Res.; Rev. Jonathan DeFrange, OSB, Chap.; Bro. Carl Bouchereau, S.C., Dir.; Brs.: 23; Priests: 1

PORTSMOUTH

Abbey of St. Gregory the Great (Order of St. Benedict in Portsmouth, Rhode Island, Benedictines of the English Congregation) - 285 Cory's Ln., Portsmouth, RI 02871 t) 401-683-2000 abbot@portsmouthabbey.org portsmouthabbeymonastery.org/ Rt. Rev. Michael Brunner, O.S.B., Abbot; Bro. Basil Piette, OSB, Mem.; Bro. Joseph N. Byron, O.S.B., Prior; Rev. Geoffrey P. Chase, O.S.B., Mem.; Rev. Christopher Davis, O.S.B., Mem.; Rev. Gregory J. Havill, O.S.B., Mem.; Rt. Rev. Caedmon W. Holmes, O.S.B., Mem.; Bro. Benedict Maria, OSB, Mem.; Rev. Edward Mazuski, OSB, Mem.; Bro. Sixtus Roslevich, O.S.B., Mem.; Rev. Paschal P. Scotti, O.S.B., Mem.; Rt. Rev. Matthew Stark, O.S.B., Mem.; Brs.: 3; Priests: 9

Order of St. Benedict in Portsmouth, Rhode Island (Portsmouth Abbey School) - 285 Corys Ln., Portsmouth, RI 02871 t) 401-683-2000 abbot@portsmouthabbey.org; fathermichael@portsmouthabbey.org www.portsmouthabbey.org Bro. Joseph N. Byron, O.S.B., Contact; Brs.: 3; Priests: 8

PROVIDENCE

Brothers of Our Lady of Providence - 1055 N. Main St., Providence, RI 02904 t) 401-351-7230 whitmarsh@whitmarshcorp.org Bro. John McHale, O.L.P., Supr.; Brs.: 1

St. John Vianney Residence - 493 Mt. Pleasant Ave., Providence, RI 02908 t) 401-331-9870 fathercjm@gmail.com Residence for Senior Priests. Rev. Robert M. Beirne; Rev. Jose Q. dos Reis; Rev. Nicholas P. Smith; Rev. Roger A. Houle, In Res.; Rev. John D. Dreher, In Res.; Rev. Richard C. Maynard, In Res.; Rev. Farrell E. McLaughlin, In Res.;

St. Pius V Priory (Dominican Fathers) - 55 Elmhurst Ave., Providence, RI 02908 t) 401-751-4871 info@spvchurch.org spvchurch.org/ Rev. Patrick Mary Briscoe, O.P.; Rev. John P. Burchill, O.P.; Brs.: 2; Priests: 2

St. Thomas Aquinas Priory at Providence College - 1 Cunningham Sq., Providence, RI 02918 t) 401-865-2101 dmaioran@providence.edu Rev. John E. Allard, O.P.; Rev. J. Iriarte Andujar, O.P.; Rev. Nicanor P.G. Austriaco, O.P.; Rev. Vincent Bagan, O.P.; Rev. Albino F. Barrera, O.P.; Rev. Peter Batts, O.P.; Most Rev. Ernest B. Boland, O.P.; Rev. Justin Brophy, O.P.; Rev. Bonaventure Chapman, O.P.; Rev. Ronald Leo Checkai, O.P.; Rev. Paul M. Conner, O.P.; Rev. G. Adrian Dabash, O.P.; Rev. Raymond Daley, O.P.; Rev. Thomas Davenport, O.P.; Rev. Thomas J. Ertle, O.P.; Rev. William David Folsey, O.P.; Rev. Joseph J. Guido, O.P.; Rev. G. Nicholas Ingham, O.P.; Rev. Terence Keegan, O.P.; Rev. Humbert Kilanowski, O.P.; Rev. Bernard F. Langton, O.P.; Rev. Ambrose Little, O.P.; Rev. Richard A. McAlister, O.P.; Rev. J. Stuart McPhail, O.P.; Rev. Isaac Morales, O.P.; Rev. Damian Myett, O.P.; Rev. Robert D. Myett, O.P.; Rev. Mark D. Nowel, O.P.; Rev. Michael D. O'Connor, O.P.; Rev. David T. Orique, O.P.; Rev. John S. Peterson, O.P.; Rev. Alan Piper, O.P.; Rev. R. Gabriel Pivarnik, O.P.; Rev. Matthew D. Powell, O.P.; Rev. Philip Neri Reese, O.P.; Rev. Augustine Reisenauer, O.P.; Rev. Kevin D. Robb, O.P.; Rev. Paul E. Seaver, O.P.; Rev. Brian J. Shanley, O.P.; Rev. Kenneth Sicard, O.P.; Rev. Joseph Torchia, O.P.; Rev. Dominic M. Verner, O.P.; Rev. John C. Vidmar, O.P.; Rev. Walter Urban Voll, O.P.; Rev. Peter Martyr Joseph Yungwirth, O.P.; Rev. Thomas P. McCreesh, O.P., Prior; Rev. Edward T. Myers, O.P., Prior;

WOONSOCKET

Brothers of the Sacred Heart - 800 Logee St., Woonsocket, RI 02895 t) 504-301-4758 unitedstatesprovince@gmail.com Bro. Ronald Travers, S.C., In Res.; Bro. Francis Fontaine, S.C., In Res.; Bro. Marcel Leclerc, S.C., In Res.; Bro. Alan Aubin, S.C., Dir.; Brs.: 4

NURSING / REHABILITATION / CONVALESCENCE / ELDERLY CARE [NUR]

CUMBERLAND

Mount St. Rita Health Centre - 15 Sumner Brown Rd., Cumberland, RI 02864 t) 401-333-6352 mail@mountstrita.org www.mountstrita.org Licensed Nursing Home. Mount St. Rita Health Centre Inc., Sponsored by Covenant Health, Inc. William P. Fleming, Admin.;

NEWPORT

St. Clare Home - 309 Spring St., Newport, RI 02840 t) 401-849-3204 mbdaigneault@stclarenewport.org stclarenewport.org Nursing Facility. Rev. Raymond C. Theroux, Chap.; Rev. Thomas D. O'Neill, In Res.; Mary Beth Daigneault, Admin.;

NORTH KINGSTOWN

Scalabrini Villa Inc. - 860 N. Quidnessett Rd., North Kingstown, RI 02852 t) 401-884-1802 admin@scalabrinivilla.com www.scalabrinivilla.com Full Skilled Nursing Facility. Rev. Peter Polo, C.S., Chap.; Sr. Nemesia Licayu, F.A.S., Supr.;

NORTH PROVIDENCE

Our Lady, Queen of Peace, Assisted Living Community (Franciscan Missionaries of Mary) - 399 Fruit Hill Ave., North Providence, RI 02911 t) 401-353-5800 lapfmm@aol.com Stephanie Dyer, Admin.; Sr. Lois Ann Pereira, F.M.M., Supr.;

NORTH SMITHFIELD

Saint Antoine Residence - 10 Rhodes Ave., North Smithfield, RI 02896 t) 401-767-3500 jwoznicki@stantoine.net www.stantoine.net John Barry III, Contact;

The Villa at Saint Antoine (The Frassati Residence) - 400 Mendon Rd., North Smithfield, RI 02896-6999 t) 401-767-2574 tsummiel@stantoine.net; msmith@stantoine.net www.stantoine.net Tammy Summiel, Admin.;

The Frassati Residence (The Villa at Saint Antoine) -

PAWTUCKET

Jeanne Jugan Apartments - 310 Sayles Ave., Pawtucket, RI 02860 t) 401-723-4314 pwmothersuperior@littlesistersofthepoor.org www.littlesistersofthepoor.org Sr. Patricia Mary Metzger, l.s.p., Supr.; Asstd. Annu.: 30; Staff: 1

Jeanne Jugan Residence (Jeanne Jugan Residence of the Little Sisters of the Poor) - 964 Main St., Pawtucket, RI 02860 t) 401-723-4314 pwmothersuperior@littlesistersofthepoor.org www.littlesistersofthepoor.org Sr. Patricia Mary Metzger, l.s.p., Supr.; Asstd. Annu.: 54; Staff: 98

PRESCHOOLS / CHILDCARE CENTERS [PRE]

CHEPACHET

Mother of Hope Camp - 1589 Putnam Pike, Chepachet, RI 02814; Mailing: 1 Cathedral Sq., Providence, RI 02903 t) 401-278-4626; 401-568-3580 mlosardo@dioceseofprovidence.org www.motherofhopecamp.com Michelle Losardo, Dir.;

CRANSTON

Rejoice in Hope Youth Center - 804 Dyer Ave., Cranston, RI 02920 t) 401-942-6571 pkane@dioceseofprovidence.org catholicyouthri.com Pat Kane, Dir.;

CUMBERLAND

Mercymount Country Day School (Sisters of Mercy of the Americas) - 35 Wrentham Rd., Cumberland, RI 02864 t) 401-333-5919 principal@mercymount.org www.mercymount.org Sr. Rayleen Giannotti, R.S.M., Prin.; Stds.: 324; Lay Tchrs.: 32

NARRAGANSETT

Ocean Tides, Inc. - 635 Ocean Rd., Narragansett, RI 02882-1314 t) 401-789-1016 x222 bsullivan@oceantides.org www.oceantides.org Brian Sullivan, Pres.; Stds.: 73; Lay Tchrs.: 26

PROVIDENCE

Group Home for Adolescent Boys - 1055 N. Main St., Providence, RI 02904 t) 401-351-7230 whitmarsh@whitmarshhouse.org (Whitmarsh House) Bro. John McHale, O.L.P., Dir.; Stds.: 30; Lay Tchrs.: 30

St. Martin de Porres Multi-Purpose Center - 160 Cranston St., Providence, RI 02907 t) 401-274-6783 priceesther4@gmail.com John J. Barry III, Contact;

The McAuley Corporation (McAuley Ministries., Sisters of Mercy of the Americas Northeast Community) - 622 Elmwood Ave., Providence, RI 02907; Mailing: P.O. Box 73195, Providence, RI 02907 t) 401-941-9013 dwolfe@mcauleyri.org www.mcauleyri.org Donald P. Wolfe, Exec.;

McAuley Ministries - McAuley House - Meal site assisting 10,000 homeless annually. Mary Margaret Earl, Admin.;

McAuley Ministries - McAuley Village - 325 Niagara St., Providence, RI 02907 t) 401-467-3630 Michele L. Matott, Admin.;

McAuley Ministries - The Warde-robe - 1286 Broad St., Central Falls, RI 02863 t) 401-729-0405 Clothing and housewares for the working poor. Donna Benetti, Admin.;

WARWICK

OLP Center, Inc. - 836 Warwick Neck Ave., Warwick, RI 02889 t) 401-739-6850 info@aldrichmansion.com aldrichmansion.com Anthony Papa, Dir.;

WOONSOCKET

Fr. Marot CYO Center (CYO of Northern Rhode Island, Inc.) - 174 Harris Ave., Woonsocket, RI 02895; Mailing: P.O. Box 518, Woonsocket, RI 02895-0518 t) 401-762-3252 frmarotcyo@gmail.com catholicyouthri.com/fr-marot-cyo-center Leo Fontaine, Dir.;

RETREAT HOUSES / RENEWAL CENTERS [RTR]

CUMBERLAND

***Mercy Ecology, Inc.** - 75 Wrentham Rd., Cumberland, RI 02864; Mailing: 15 Highland View Rd., Cumberland, RI 02864 t) 301-787-7208 acurtis@sistersofmercy.org www.mercyecology.org Sr. Anne Curtis, RSM, Dir.;

NORTH PROVIDENCE

Bethany Renewal Center - 397 Fruit Hill Ave., North Providence, RI 02911 t) 401-353-5860 bethanyfmm@aol.com www.fmmusa.org Conducted by the Franciscan Missionaries of Mary.

SEMINARIES [SEM]

PROVIDENCE

Seminary of Our Lady of Providence - 485 Mt. Pleasant Ave., Providence, RI 02908 t) 401-331-1316 cdeangelis@dioceseofprovidence.org House of Formation for College Students and Pre-Theologians. Rev. Christopher J. Murphy, Rector; Dr. Michael Hansen, Dir., Human Formation/Staff Psychologist;

An asterisk (*) denotes an organization that has established tax-exempt status directly with the IRS and is not covered by the USCCB Group Ruling.

Diocese of Pueblo

(Dioecesis Pueblensis)

MOST REVEREND STEPHEN J. BERG

Bishop of Pueblo; ordained May 15, 1999; appointed Bishop of Pueblo January 15, 2014; ordained and installed February 27, 2014. Pastoral Center, 101 N. Greenwood St., Pueblo, CO 81003-3164.

Catholic Pastoral Center: 101 N. Greenwood St., Pueblo, CO 81003. T: 719-544-9861; F: 719-544-5202.
www.diopueblo.org
officeofbishop@dioceseofpueblo.org

Square Miles 48,155.

Diocesan Patron: St. Therese of the Child Jesus. Secondary Patroness: Our Lady of Guadalupe.

Erected a Diocese November 15, 1941.

Comprises the 29 Counties of Alamosa, Archuleta, Baca, Bent, Conejos, Costilla, Crowley, Custer, Delta, Dolores, Fremont, Gunnison, Hinsdale, Huerfano, Kiowa, La Plata, Las Animas, Mesa, Mineral, Montezuma, Montrose, Otero, Ouray, Prowers, Pueblo, Rio Grande, Saguache, San Juan and San Miguel in the southern and western part of the State of Colorado.

For legal titles of parishes and diocesan institutions, consult the Finance Office.

STATISTICAL OVERVIEW

Personnel
Bishop 1
Retired Bishops 1
Priests: Diocesan Active in Diocese 23
Priests: Diocesan Active Outside Diocese 2
Priests: Retired, Sick or Absent 13
Number of Diocesan Priests 38
Religious Priests in Diocese 23
Total Priests in your Diocese 61
Extern Priests in Diocese 10
Permanent Deacons in Diocese 41

Parishes
Parishes 52
With Resident Pastor:
Resident Diocesan Priests 21
Resident Religious Priests 5
Without Resident Pastor:
Administered by Priests 26
Missions 46

Pastoral Centers 1
Professional Ministry Personnel:
Sisters 14
Lay Ministers 40

Welfare
Catholic Hospitals 4
Total Assisted 590,963
Special Centers for Social Services 1
Total Assisted 149,237

Educational
Diocesan Students in Other Seminaries 4
Total Seminarians 4
Elementary Schools, Diocesan and Parish 3
Total Students 871
Elementary Schools, Private 1
Total Students 110
Catechesis/Religious Education:
High School Students 976
Elementary Students 1,872

Total Students under Catholic Instruction 3,833
Teachers in Diocese:
Lay Teachers 85

Vital Statistics
Receptions into the Church:
Infant Baptism Totals 579
Minor Baptism Totals 67
Adult Baptism Totals 54
Received into Full Communion 65
First Communions 568
Confirmations 733
Marriages:
Catholic 100
Interfaith 22
Total Marriages 122
Deaths 954
Total Catholic Population 48,789
Total Population 702,475

LEADERSHIP

Chancery - t) 719-544-9861 Most Rev. Stephen J. Berg;
Delegate - t) 719-544-9861
Vicar General - t) 719-544-9861 x1121 Very Rev. Derrek D. Scott;
Moderator of the Curia - t) 719-544-9861 x1171
Chancellor - t) 719-544-9861 x1112 Joe'l DeYoung;
Vicar for the New Evangelization - t) 719-544-9861 x1171
Vicar for Clergy - t) 719-544-9861 x1193 Very Rev. Stephen Olamolu, V.C., Vicar;
Director of Pastoral Services - t) 719-544-9861 x1117 Dcn. Daniel T. Leetch;
Diocesan Tribunal - Rev. Msgr. Mark Plewka;
Judge - Rev. Msgr. Mark Plewka;
Judicial Vicar - Rev. Msgr. Mark Plewka;
Secretarial to the Tribunal - Alice LeDoux, Secy.;
Ecclesiastical Notaries - Maryjane Chargin; Very Rev. Stephen Olamolu, V.C.;
College of Consultors - Very Rev. Carlos A. Alvarez, Mem.; Rev. Michael Chrisman, Mem.; Rev. Steven J. Murray, Mem.;
Deans - Very Rev. Carlos A. Alvarez, Dean - Alamosa Deanery; Very Rev. Henry James Wertin, Dean - Grand Junction Deanery; Very Rev. Timothy Okeahialam, Dean - La Junta Deanery;

OFFICES AND DIRECTORS

Communications -
Development Director -
Diocesan Liturgical Commission - Rev. Michael Chrisman, Contact;
Diocesan Pastoral Committee (Vacant) -
Director of Operations - t) 719-544-9861 x1112 Joe'l DeYoung;
Finance - Richard Eitel, Interim CFO (deitel@dioceseofpueblo.org);
Finance Advisory Council - t) 719-544-9861 x1141 Richard Eitel, Interim CFO;
Foundation - Steven S. Chargin;
Human Resources - t) 719-544-9861 x1110 Nancy Martinez;
Institutional Ministries - Dcn. Daniel T. Leetch;
Liaison to Superintendent of Catholic Schools - Dcn. Daniel T. Leetch;
Moderator of the Curia - t) 719-544-9861 x1171
Office of Missionary Discipleship - Seth Wright;
Presbyteral Council - Very Rev. Carlos A. Alvarez; Rev. Michael Chrisman; Rev. Msgr. James F. Koenigsfeld;
Respect Life Office - Diane Hochevar, Dir.;
Tribunal - Rev. Msgr. Mark Plewka;
Vicar for Clergy - t) 719-544-9861 x1193 Very Rev. Stephen Olamolu, V.C., Vicar;
Vocations - t) 719-544-9861 x1115 Rev. Carl Wertin (cwertin@ctkpueblo.org);
Worship - Rev. Michael Chrisman;

PARISHES, MISSIONS, AND CLERGY

STATE OF COLORADO

AGUILAR

St. Anthony of Padua - 125 S. Fir St., Aguilar, CO 81020; Mailing: P.O. Box 577, Aguilar, CO 81020-0577 t) 719-941-4124 Rev. Isaac Kariuki, Par. Admin.;

ALAMOSA

Sacred Heart - 715 E. 4th St., Alamosa, CO 81101; Mailing: P.O. Box 547, Alamosa, CO 81101-0547 t) 719-589-5829 (Center); 719-589-9788 admin@sacredheartalamosa.org; pastor@sacredheartalamosa.org www.sacredheartalamosa.org Very Rev. Carlos A. Alvarez, Pst.; CRP Stds.: 206

AVONDALE

Sacred Heart - 210 Hwy. 50 E., Avondale, CO 81022; Mailing: P.O. Box 279, Avondale, CO 81022-0279 t) 719-947-3092 shcparish@hotmail.com; jamartinez53@comcast.net Rev. Victor Raj, HGN (India), Par. Admin.; Dcn. Edward Riccillo; CRP Stds.: 20

CANON CITY

St. Michael - 10th St. & College Ave., Canon City, CO 81212; Mailing: 1016 Mystic Ave., Canon City, CO 81212 t) 719-275-7549 office@stmikescanoncity.org www.stmikescanoncity.org Rev. Jesse L. Perez, Pst.; Dcn. Richard A. Madison; CRP Stds.: 21

CAPULIN

St. Joseph - 19895 County Rd. 8, Capulin, CO 81124; Mailing: P.O. Box 40, Capulin, CO 81124-0040 t) 719-274-5304 saintjosephp@gmail.com Rev. Jay Gapayao, S.O.L.T., Par. Vicar; Rev. Arturo Anonuevo, S.O.L.T., Par. Admin.; CRP Stds.: 110
Our Lady of the Valley - 19617 S. Hwy. 285, La Jara, CO 81140 t) 719-274-5647
St. Therese of the Child Jesus - 115 Main St., Manassa, CO 81141 t) (719) 274-5304
St. Anthony - 18900 County Rd. 28, Los Sauces, CO 81151 t) (719) 274-5304
Our Lady of the Immaculate Conception - 211 Blanca St., Romeo, CO 81148 t) (719) 274-5304

CENTER

St. Francis Jerome - 781 Warden St., Center, CO 81125-9367; Mailing: P.O. Box 590, Monte Vista, CO 81144-0590 t) 719-852-2673 sjccommunity.org (San Juan Catholic Community) Rev. Damian de la Cruz Nunez, C.R., Par. Vicar; Dcn. Ray Torres; Dcn. Jerry LeBlanc, DRE; Rev. Albert Berkmans, HGN, Par. Admin.;

CONEJOS

Our Lady of Guadalupe - 6633 County Rd. 13, Conejos, CO 81129; Mailing: P.O. Box 305, Antonito, CO 81120-0305 t) 719-376-5985 ourladyofguadalupeparish@outlook.com www.ologp.com Rev. Sergio Robles-Cardenas, C.R. (Mexico), Par. Admin.; CRP Stds.: 40
St. Augustine - 803 Pine St., Antonito, CO 81120
Sagrada Familia - 17344 Co. Rd. G, Lobatos, CO 81120
San Juan Nepomuceno y San Cayetano - 684 Co. Rd. B, Ortiz, CO 81120
San Antonio de Padua - 13148 Co. Rd. C, San Antonio, CO 81120
San Pedro y San Rafael - 5308 Co. Rd. 10.75, San Rafael, CO 81120
San Isidro Labrador -
San Miguel Church -
El Santuario de Los Pobladores -

CORTEZ

St. Margaret Mary - 28 E. Montezuma, Cortez, CO 81321-3299; Mailing: 20 S. Market St., Cortez, CO 81321 t) 970-565-7308 smm@fone.net www.montelorescatholic.org Montelores Catholic Community Very Rev. Arokiya Soosaidhas Panneerselvam, HGN (India), Par. Admin.; CRP Stds.: 20
St. Jude - 423 N. Pine, Dove Creek, CO 81324 t) (970) 565-7308 montelorescatholic.org

CRESTED BUTTE

Queen of All Saints - 401 Sopri Ave., Crested Butte, CO 81224; Mailing: 400 W. Georgia Ave., Gunnison, CO 81230 t) 970-641-0808 stpeters@gunnisoncatholic.org www.crestedbuttecatholic.org St. Peter Parish, Gunnison. Rev. Andres Ayala-Santiago (Mexico), Pst.; Dcn. Joseph W. Fitzpatrick; Dcn. Vincent Rogalski; CRP Stds.: 14

DEL NORTE

Holy Name of Mary - 645 Pine St., Del Norte, CO 81132-2246; Mailing: P.O. Box 590, Monte Vista, CO 81144-0590 t) 719-852-2673 sjccommunity.org (San Juan Catholic Community) Rev. Damian de la Cruz Nunez, C.R., Par. Vicar; Dcn. Ray Torres; Dcn. Jerry LeBlanc, DRE; Rev. Albert Berkmans, HGN, Par. Admin.;
St. Francis of Assisi - 5615 W. CR 5 N., Monte Vista, CO 81144 t) (719) 852-2673
Holy Family - 0204 Church St., South Fork, CO 81154 t) (719) 852-2673
Immaculate Conception - 104 W. 3rd St., Creede, CO 81130 t) (719) 852-2673
San Jose - County Rd. 63, Agua Ramon, CO 81154 t) (719) 852-2673

DELTA

St. Michael - 628 Meeker St., Delta, CO 81416-1923 t) 970-874-3300 c) 970-275-0069 secretary@stmichaelsdelta.org www.stmichaelsdelta.org Rev. Albeiro Herrera-Ciro, Pst.; Dcn. Price Hatcher, Bus. Mgr.; CRP Stds.: 61
St. Philip Benizi - ; Mailing: P.O. Box 713, Cedaredge, CO 81413-0713 t) 970-856-6495

DURANGO

St. Columba - 1830 E. 2nd Ave., Durango, CO 81301-5019 t) 970-247-0044 parishoffice@stcolumbacatholic.org www.stcolumbacatholic.org Rev. Kevin F. Novack, Pst.; Dcn. Christopher Peterson; CRP Stds.: 10
Sacred Heart - 254 E. 5th Ave., Durango, CO 81301-5649 t) 970-247-3997 office.sacredheart.dgo@gmail.com sacredheartdgo.artyrox.com Rev. Heriberto Torres, C.R., Pst.; CRP Stds.: 23

FLORENCE

St. Benedict - 622 W. 2nd St., Florence, CO 81226-1015 t) 719-784-4879 stbenedicts_81226@yahoo.com; joyce_stb@yahoo.com stbenedictco.org Rev. Stephen Injoalu, Pst.; Joyce Archuletta, DRE; CRP Stds.: 30

FRUITA

Sacred Heart - 1210 17 1/2 Rd., Fruita, CO 81521-9717 t) 970-858-9605 gloriasacredheart@gmail.com sacredheartfruita.com Rev. Paul Ekeh, Pst.; Dcn. George Fortunato; Dcn. Alonso Kennedy; CRP Stds.: 125

GRAND JUNCTION

Immaculate Heart of Mary - 790 26 1/2 Rd., Grand Junction, CO 81506-8350; Mailing: 790 H Rd., Grand Junction, CO 81506 t) 970-242-6121 raluise@ihmgjt.org; jhirschfeld@ihmgjt.org www.ihmgjt.org Rev. Selvanathan Soosai, HGN (India), Par. Vicar; Rev. Chrysogonus Nwele, Pst.; Dcn. Luke Konantz; Dcn. Leo Truscott; Richard J Aluise, Bus. Mgr.; CRP Stds.: 70
St. Ann - 535 W. 1st St., Palisade, CO 81526-8786 t) 970-464-5024
St. Joseph - 230 N. 3rd St., Grand Junction, CO 81501-2439 t) 970-243-0209 belle@stjosephgj.org stjosephgj.org Very Rev. Henry James Wertin, Pst.; Rev. Nadin Williams Ospino, Par. Vicar; Dcn. Fred Bartels; Dcn. Douglas Van Houten; Dcn. Richard Vieira, DCN; Teresa Gill, DRE; CRP Stds.: 100

GUNNISON

St. Peter - 300 N. Wisconsin, Gunnison, CO 81230-3021; Mailing: 400 W. Georgia Ave., Gunnison, CO 81230 t) 970-641-0808 stpeters@gunnisoncatholic.org gunnisoncatholic.org Rev. Andres Ayala-Santiago (Mexico), Pst.; Dcn. Lloyd Hawes; Dcn. Vincent Rogalski; CRP Stds.: 80
St. Rose of Lima -

HOLLY

St. Frances of Rome - 131 S. Main St., Holly, CO 81047; Mailing: P.O. Box 130, 119 S 6th, Holly, CO 81047-0130 t) 719-537-6688 stfrances89@gmail.com Rev. Joseph Lawrence Arokiasamy, HGN, Par. Vicar; CRP Stds.: 45
St. Mary - 211 LaBelle, Bristol, CO 81047-0130

IGNACIO

St. Ignatius Parish - 15449 Hwy. 172, Ignacio, CO 81137; Mailing: P.O. Box 1350, Ignacio, CO 81137-1350 t) 970-563-4241 office@stignatiuschurchignacio.com www.stignatiuschurchignacio.com Rev. Cesar Arras, C.R., Par. Admin.; CRP Stds.: 30
St. Bartholemew - 1749 CR 526, Bayfield, CO 81122 t) (970) 563-4241
SS. Peter & Rose - 18851 CO State Hwy 151, Ignacio, CO 81137 stignatiuschurchignacio.com

LA JUNTA

Our Lady of Guadalupe / St. Patrick Parish - 202 Lincoln Ave., La Junta, CO 81050-1181 t) 719-384-4342 ljcp@bresnan.net www.olgsplajunta.org Rev. Joseph Matitu, SSS, Par. Vicar; CRP Stds.: 115

LAMAR

St. Francis De Sales-Our Lady of Guadalupe - 600 E. Parmenter St., Lamar, CO 81052-3523 t) 719-336-7759 catholicchurchlamar@gmail.com stfrancisolg.org Rev. Joseph Lawrence Arokiasamy, HGN, Par. Vicar; Dcn. Allan J. Medina; CRP Stds.: 162

LAS ANIMAS

St. Mary - 650 Elm Ave., Las Animas, CO 81054; Mailing: 714 Elm Ave., Las Animas, CO 81054-1738 t) 719-456-1104 stmaryla@yahoo.com Rev. Joseph Matitu, SSS, Par. Vicar; CRP Stds.: 23

MANCOS

St. Rita of Cascia - 203 S. Main St., Mancos, CO 81238; Mailing: 20 S. Market St., Cortez, CO 81321-3217 t) 970-565-7308 smm@fone.net montelorescatholic.org St. Rita of Cascia and Our Lady of Victory are part of the Montelores Catholic Community (St. Margaret Mary Church of Cortez, CO) Very Rev. Arokiya Soosaidhas Panneerselvam, HGN (India), Par. Admin.; CRP Stds.: 6

Our Lady of Victory Church - 101 N. 7th St., Dolores, CO 81323 t) (970) 565-7308

MONTE VISTA

St. Joseph - 425 Batterson, Monte Vista, CO 81144; Mailing: P.O. Box 590, Monte Vista, CO 81144-0590 t) 719-852-2673 sjccommunity.org (San Juan Catholic Community) Rev. Damian de la Cruz Nunez, C.R., Par. Vicar; Dcn. Ray Torres; Dcn. Jerry LeBlanc, DRE; Rev. Albert Berkmans, HGN, Par. Admin.; CRP Stds.: 75

Monte Vista Estates - 2277 East Dr., Monte Vista, CO 81144 t) 719-852-5138

Colorado State Veterans Center - 3749 Sherman Ave., Monte Vista, CO 81144 t) 719-852-5118

The Legacy Assisted Living Home - 100 Chico Camino, Monte Vista, CO 81144 t) 719-852-5179

MONTROSE

St. Mary - 1855 St. Mary Dr., Montrose, CO 81401-5011 t) 970-249-3319 bpatterson@stmarymontrose.org www.stmarymontrose.org Rev. Matthew Wertin, Pst.; Dcn. Mario Diaz; Dcn. Jose Pacheco; CRP Stds.: 205

Our Lady of Fatima - 211 Main St., Olathe, CO 81425; Mailing: 1855 St. Mary Dr., Montrose, CO 81401-5011

OURAY

St. Daniel the Prophet - 614 5th St., Ouray, CO 81427; Mailing: PO Box 565, Ouray, CO 81427-0565 t) 970-325-4373 sdouray@gmail.com Rev. Nathanael Foshage, O.S.B., Par. Admin.;

St. Patrick - 1005 Reece, Silverton, CO 81433; Mailing: P.O. Box 565, Ouray, CO 81427-0565 t) (970) 325-4373

PAGOSA SPRINGS

Immaculate Heart of Mary - 453 Lewis St., Pagosa Springs, CO 81147; Mailing: 353 S. Pagosa Blvd., Pagosa Springs, CO 81147-4300 t) 970-731-5744 parishsecretary@ihmjp2.org www.popejohnpauliichurch.org Dcn. Mark McVay; Rev. Samuel Auta, Pst.;

St. Francis -

St. John Baptist -

St. James -

Pope John Paul II (Immaculate Heart of Mary) - 353 S. Pagosa Blvd., Pagosa Springs, CO 81147-4300 t) 970-731-5744 parishsecretary@ihmjp2.org www.ihmjp2.org Rev. Samuel Auta, Pst.; Dcn. Mark McVay; CRP Stds.: 87

PAONIA

Sacred Heart - 235 N. Fork Ave., Paonia, CO 81428; Mailing: P.O. Box 988, Paonia, CO 81428-0988 t) 970-527-3214 sacredheart@tds.net www.facebook.com/sacredheartcatholicchurchpaonia/ Rev. Wojciech Pelczarski (Poland), Pst.; CRP Stds.: 29

St. Margaret Mary - 289 Bridge & Piñon, Paonia, CO 81428 t) 970-872-2117

PUEBLO

Cathedral of the Sacred Heart - 414 W. 11th St., Pueblo, CO 81003-2888 t) 719-544-5175 shcathedral@shcathedral.net shcathedral.net Most Rev. Stephen J. Berg, Pst.; Very Rev. Derrek D. Scott, Rector; Dcn. Ben Davis; Dcn. Daniel T. Leetch; Tess Padilla, Bus. Mgr.; Deborah L. Rendon, Liturgy Dir.; Amanda Davis, DRE; CRP Stds.: 108

St. Anne - 2701 E. 12th St., Pueblo, CO 81001-4708 t) 719-545-2644 stephen.olamolu70@gmail.com; mariannas@stannespueblo.com www.stannespueblo.com Dcn. Immanuel Santistevan; Theresa O'Brien, DRE; Very Rev. Stephen Olamolu, V.C., Sacr. Min.; CRP Stds.: 12

Christ the King - 1708 Horseshoe Dr., Pueblo, CO 81001 t) 719-542-9248 mmeissner@ctkpueblo.org; lescalera@ctkpueblo.org www.ctkpueblo.org Rev. Carl Wertin, Pst.; Rev. JeganMari Thangavel, HGN (India), Par. Vicar; Dcn. John Chavez; Dcn. Corey Compton; Laura Escalera, DRE; CRP Stds.: 71

St. Francis Xavier - 611 Logan Ave., Pueblo, CO 81004-3505 t) 719-564-1125 stfrancisxavierpueblo@yahoo.com www.sfxavierpueblo.org Rev. Peter Magadya Abogado, SSS, Par. Admin.; CRP Stds.: 13

Our Lady of Lourdes - 8800 Maryknoll, Beulah, CO 81023; Mailing: P.O. Box 86, Beulah, CO 81023-0086

Holy Family - 2827 Lakeview Ave., Pueblo, CO 81005-2495 t) 719-564-2696 holyfamilyparishpueblo@gmail.com holyfamilyparishpueblo.com Rev. Mark T. Bettinger, Pst.; Dcn. Robert Sanchez; CRP Stds.: 85

St. Aloysius - 8006 Hwy. 165 W., Rye, CO 81069; Mailing: P.O. Box 186, Rye, CO 81069-0186 t) 719-489-3543 homim73@yahoo.com Rev. Gregory Ezeanya, Sacr. Min.;

Holy Rosary - 2400 W. 22nd St., Pueblo, CO 81003; Mailing: C/O Our Lady of the Meadows, Pueblo, CO 81005 t) 719-561-3580 pastor@olm-parish.com Rev. Msgr. James E. King, Pst.; Dcn. Marco Vegas; CRP Stds.: 20

St. Joseph - 1145 S. Aspen Rd., Pueblo, CO 81006-9998 t) 719-544-1886 stjoesparishoffice@comcast.net; josefina_marrufo@yahoo.com stjosephparish-pueblo.com Dcn. Edward Riccillo; Rev. Steven J. Murray, Pst.; CRP Stds.: 171

St. Leander - 1402 E. 7th St., Pueblo, CO 81001-3510 t) 719-544-8411 stleanderparish@comcast.net Claudia Tafoya, DRE; Rev. Victor Raj, HGN (India), Par. Admin.; Dcn. Immanuel Santistevan; CRP Stds.: 16

St. Mary Help of Christians - 307 E. Mesa Ave., Pueblo, CO 81006; Mailing: 217 E. Mesa Ave., Pueblo, CO 81006-1014 t) 719-296-8778 stmaryhev@hotmail.com Belinda Castro, DRE; Rev. Mark del Rosario, SSS, Par. Admin.; CRP Stds.: 22

Our Lady of Mt. Carmel - 421 Clark St., Pueblo, CO 81003 t) 719-542-5952 ourladyofmtcarmel@live.com Rev. Donald P. Malin, Pst.; Dcn. Michael Sanchez; Sr. Andrea Vasquez, O.S.B, Pst. Assoc.; Teresa Cornejo, CRE; Marian Johnson, Youth Min.; CRP Stds.: 64

Our Lady of the Meadows - 23 Starling Dr., Pueblo, CO 81005-1878 t) 719-561-3580 olm@olm-parish.com www.olm@olmparish.com Rev. Msgr. James E. King, Pst.; Dcn. Marco Vegas; CRP Stds.: 21

St. Pius X - 3130 Morris Ave., Pueblo, CO 81008-1338 t) 719-542-4264 pmonte2@comcast.net Rev. Zaldy Norba, S.S.S. (Phillipines), Pst.; Dcn. Roy Stringfellow; CRP Stds.: 32

Shrine of St. Therese - 300 Goodnight Ave., Pueblo, CO 81004-1097 t) 719-542-1788 parish@sostpueblo.org www.sostpueblo.org Rev. Michael Chrisman, Pst.; Dcn. Carl Cook; CRP Stds.: 80

St. Therese - 1133 Ln. 36, Pueblo, CO 81006; Mailing: 1145 S. Aspen Rd., Pueblo, CO 81006-1655 t) (719) 948-2137; 719-544-1886 Rev. Steven J. Murray, Pst.;

PUEBLO WEST

St. Paul the Apostle - 1132 W. Oro Grande Dr., Pueblo West, CO 81007; Mailing: P.O. Box 7199, Pueblo West, CO 81007-0199 t) 719-647-1500 www.saintpaulapostlechurch.org/ Very Rev. Edmundo Valera, Pst.; Dcn. Patrick Byrne; Dcn. Philip Medina; CRP Stds.: 79

ROCKY FORD

St. Peter the Apostle - 1209 Swink Ave., Rocky Ford, CO 81067-1835 t) 719-254-3565 sprockyford@spetersrf.org; sppastor@spetersrf.org Dcn. Terry Marinelli; Rev. Joel Lasutaz, SSS, Par. Admin.; CRP Stds.: 39

St. Peter Chapel - 905 Main St., Ordway, CO 81063; Mailing: P.O. Box 218, Ordway, CO 81063-0218 t) 719-267-4645

Mary Queen of Heaven - 602 7th St, Fowler, CO 81039; Mailing: P.O. Box 384, Fowler, CO 81039-0384 t) 719-263-4455

SAN LUIS

Sangre de Cristo - 511 Church Pl., San Luis, CO 81152; Mailing: P.O. Box 326, San Luis, CO 81152-0326 t) 719-992-0122 admin@sdcparish.org Rev. John Farley, Par. Admin.; CRP Stds.: 24

St. James - t) (719) 992-0122

Holy Family - t) (719) 992-0122

Immaculate Conception - t) (719) 992-0122

San Acacio - t) (719) 992-0122

SS. Peter and Paul - t) (719) 992-0122 temporarily closed

St. Isidro - t) (719) 992-0122

St. Francis of Assisi - t) (719) 992-0122

Sacred Heart of Jesus - t) (719) 992-0122

SPRINGFIELD

Our Lady of the Annunciation - 140 Kansas St., Springfield, CO 81073-0174; Mailing: P.O. Box 174, Springfield, CO 81073-0174 t) (719) 529-9738 www.facebook.com/catholicchurchspringfield/ Rev. Joseph Lawrence Arokiasamy, HGN, Par. Vicar; CRP Stds.: 16

TELLURIDE

St. Patrick - 301 N Spruce, Telluride, CO 81435; Mailing: P.O. Box 398, Telluride, CO 81435-0398 t) 970-728-3387 spctelluride@gmail.com stpatrickstelluride.com Rev. Mariusz Wirkowski (Poland), Pst.; CRP Stds.: 21

Our Lady of Sorrows Nucla - 325 Fox St., Nucla, CO 81424; Mailing: P.O. Box 451, Nucla, CO 81424-0451 stpatrickstelluride@yahoo.com

TRINIDAD

Most Holy Trinity - 235 N. Convent St., Trinidad, CO 81082-2692 t) 719-846-3369 tacc@trinidadcatholic.org; john.pearce@trinidadcatholic.org www.trinidadcatholic.org Rev. Sebastian Vincent Savarimuthu, HGN (India), Par. Vicar; Very Rev. Timothy Okeahialam, Par. Admin.; CRP Stds.: 69

San Isidro -

St. Ignatius -

WALSENBURG

St. Mary - 121 E. 7th St., Walsenburg, CO 81089; Mailing: P.O. Box 86, 121 E. 7th St., Walsenburg, CO 81089-0086 t) 719-738-1204 stmarywal@gmail.com spanishpeakscatholic.com Sr. Carol Tlach, S.N.D., Pst. Assoc.; Rev. Isaac Kariuki, Par. Admin.; CRP Stds.: 30

Christ the King - 505 S. Main St., La Veta, CO 81055 t) (719) 890-0642

Sacred Heart - Colorado State Hwy. 69, Gardner, CO 81040 t) (719) 738-1204

WESTCLIFFE

Our Lady of the Assumption - 109 S. 5th St., Westcliffe, CO 81252-0359 t) 719-783-3507 ola.westcliffe@gmail.com www.olawestcliffe.org Rev. Stephen Injoalu, Pst.; CRP Stds.: 15

SCHOOLS: PRESCHOOL THRU HIGH SCHOOL

SCHOOLS

STATE OF COLORADO

DURANGO

St. Columba - (DIO) (Grades PreK-8) 1801 E. 3rd Ave., Durango, CO 81301-5072 t) 970-247-5527 office@stcolumbaschooldurango.org stcolumbaschooldurango.org Kevin C. Chick, Prin.; Stds.: 292; Lay Tchrs.: 19

GRAND JUNCTION

Holy Family Catholic School - (PAR) (Grades PreSchool-8) 786 26 1/2 Rd., Grand Junction, CO 81506 t) 970-242-6168 jake.aubert@hfcs-gj.org; coni.gipson@hfcs-gj.org holyfamily-gj.org Jake T. Aubert, Prin.; Stds.: 475; Lay Tchrs.: 34

PUEBLO

St. John Neumann Catholic Schools - (PRV) (Grades PreK-8) 2415 E. Orman Ave., Pueblo, CO 81004 t) 719-561-9419 admissions@sjncs.us www.sjncs.us Julie Naccarato, Admin.; Stds.: 110; Lay Tchrs.: 18

St. Therese Catholic School - (DIO) (Grades PreSchool-8) 320 Goodnight Ave., Pueblo, CO 81004 t) 719-561-1121 j.valdez@sttheresepueblo.org www.sttheresepueblo.org Dennis Vigil, Prin.; Stds.: 104; Lay Tchrs.: 14

INSTITUTIONS LOCATED IN DIOCESE

CEMETERIES [CEM]

AGUILAR

St. Anthony - (St. Anthony Parish)

CAPULIN

St. Joseph - (St. Joseph Parish)

CONEJOS

Conejos; Las Mesitas; Ortiz - (Our Lady of Guadalupe Parish)

FRUITA

Fruita Catholic - (Sacred Heart Parish)

MONTE VISTA

St. Francis of Assisi - Plaza de Los Valdeses, Monte Vista, CO 81144; Mailing: P.O. Box 590, 425 Batterson St., Monte Vista, CO 81144 t) 719-852-2673 (Holy Name of Mary Parish)

PAGOSA SPRINGS

St. John the Baptist; St. Andrew Avelino; St. Francis; and St. James - (Pope John Paul II & Immaculate Heart of Mary Parish)

RYE

Mount Olivet (The Rye Mount Olivet Cemetery) - (St. Aloysius Mission Parish)

SAN LUIS

San Luis; San Pedro; San Acacio; San Francisco; and Chama - (Sangre de Cristo Parish)

TRINIDAD

Trinidad Catholic - Legal Title: Trinidad Catholic Cemetery Assoc. (Cemetery Bd.)

WALSENBURG

St. Mary (St. Mary South Cemetery) -

WESTCLIFFE

Silver Cliff Assumption Catholic - (Our Lady of the Assumption Parish)

CONVENTS, MONASTERIES, AND RESIDENCES FOR WOMEN [CON]

PUEBLO

Capuchin Poor Clares O.S.C.Cap. - 806 E. B St., Pueblo, CO 81003 t) 719-295-2236 damaspobres@gmail.com Sr. Rosa de Guadalupe Perez, O.S.C.Cap., Vicar; Srs.: 6

Servants of the Blessed Sacrament - 311 E. Mesa Ave., Pueblo, CO 81006 t) 719-545-7729; 719-544-4506 ssspueblo@outlook.com www.blesacrament.org Sr. Gorgonia Parcero, SSS, Supr.; Sr. Resillia Llanto, SSS, Treas.; Srs.: 3

ENDOWMENTS / FOUNDATIONS / TRUSTS [EFT]

DURANGO

Mercy Health Foundation - 1010 Three Springs Blvd., Ste. 248, Durango, CO 81301 t) (303) 673-8970 patrickgaughan@centura.org www.mercydurango.org Affiliate of Catholic Health Initiatives Colorado Foundation. Angela Fuller, Contact;

GRAND JUNCTION

St. Mary's Hospital Foundation - 2635 N. 7th St., Grand Junction, CO 81502-1628; Mailing: P.O. Box 1628, Grand Junction, CO 81502-1628 t) 970-298-1954 richelle.barton@imail.org www.stmarygj.org/aboutfoundation Carmen Shipley, Dir.;

PUEBLO

***Catholic Diocese of Pueblo Foundation** - 101 N. Greenwood St., Pueblo, CO 81003 t) 719-544-9861 x1131 schargin@dioceseofpueblo.org www.catholicfoundationdop.org Steven S. Chargin, Dir.;

HOSPITALS / HEALTH SERVICES [HOS]

CENTENNIAL

Centura Health-St. Thomas More Hospital - 9100 E, Mineral Cir., Centennial, CO 80112 t) 719-285-2000 patrickgaughan@centura.org www.stmhospital.org An operating unit of Catholic Health Initiatives Colorado (an affiliate of CommonSpirit Health formerly known as Catholic Health Initiatives). Angie Simonson, Exec.; Bed Capacity: 25; Asstd. Annu.: 29,999; Staff: 304

DURANGO

Mercy Hospital - 1010 Three Springs Blvd., Durango, CO 81301; Mailing: 9100 E. Mineral Cir., Centennial, CO 80112 t) (303) 673-8970 patrickgaughan@centura.org www.mercydurango.org An operating unit of Catholic Health Initiatives Colorado (an affiliate of CommonSpirit Health formerly known as Catholic Health Initiatives). Brandon Mencini, Exec.; Bed Capacity: 82; Asstd. Annu.: 56,848; Staff: 1,128

GRAND JUNCTION

St. Mary Hospital and Medical Center - 2635 N. 7th St., Grand Junction, CO 81501; Mailing: P.O. Box 1628, Grand Junction, CO 81501 t) 970-298-2273 gina.reed@imail.org www.stmarygj.org Bryan Johnson, Pres.; Gina Reed, Contact; Bed Capacity: 346; Asstd. Annu.: 456,956; Staff: 2,485

PUEBLO

Centura Health-St. Mary-Corwin Medical Center - 1008 Minnequa Ave., Pueblo, CO 81004; Mailing: 9100 E. Mineral Cir., Centennial, CO 80112 t) 719-557-4000 michaelcafasso@centura.org; patrickgaughan@centura.org www.stmarycorwin.org An operating unit of Catholic Health Initiatives Colorado (an affiliate of CommonSpirit Health formerly known as Catholic Health Initiatives). Rev. Thomas Vadakemury, CMI (India), Chap.; Michael Cafasso, Admin.; Bed Capacity: 42; Asstd. Annu.: 47,160; Staff: 500

MISCELLANEOUS [MIS]

GRAND JUNCTION

Grand Valley Peace and Justice - 740 Gunnison Ave., Grand Junction, CO 81501 t) 970-985-4253; (970) 314-9616 (Second line) programcoordinator@gvpeacejustice.org gvpeacejustice.org Social Justice projects for the vulnerable in our community. Sherry Cole, Program Coordinator;

PAGOSA SPRINGS

Archuleta Housing Corporation - 703 San Juan St. Suite 205, Pagosa Springs, CO 81147-0355; Mailing: PO Box 355, Pagosa Springs, CO 81147 t) 970-398-1860 office.archhouse@gmail.com www.archuletahousing.com Rev. Samuel Auta, Pres.; Nicole Holt, Exec.;

PUEBLO

St. Charles Community - 18 Dartmouth, Pueblo, CO 81005 t) 719-566-1620 Ed Sajbel, Contact;

Deacon Candidate Formation Committee - 101 N. Greenwood St., Pueblo, CO 81003 t) 719-544-9861 x1117 dleetch@dioceseofpueblo.org www.diopueblo.org Dcn. Daniel T. Leetch, Dir.; Dcn. Michael Anderson;

Serra Club of Pueblo - 101 N. Greenwood St., Pueblo, CO 81003 c) (719) 240-6111 rose_guerrero51@yahoo.com Dcn. Jake Arellano; Rose Guerrero, Pres.;

SPECIAL CARE FACILITIES [SPF]

GRAND JUNCTION

Grand Valley Catholic Outreach, Inc. - 245 S. 1st St., Grand Junction, CO 81501 t) 970-241-3658 kabland@catholicoutreach.org; beverly@catholicoutreach.org www.catholicoutreach.org Provide emergency & permanent housing, food, clothing, hot showers, financial assistance with rent & utilities to the needy in our community. Sr. Karen Bland, O.S.B., Exec.; Bed Capacity: 68; Asstd. Annu.: 149,237; Staff: 15

An asterisk (*) denotes an organization that has established tax-exempt status directly with the IRS and is not covered by the USCCB Group Ruling.

Diocese of Raleigh

(Dioecesis Raleighiensis)

MOST REVEREND LUIS RAFAEL ZARAMA, J.C.L.

Bishop of Raleigh; ordained November 27, 1993; appointed Auxiliary Bishop of Atlanta and Titular Bishop of Bararus July 27, 2009; consecrated September 29, 2009; appointed Sixth Bishop of Raleigh July 5, 2017; installed August 29, 2017.

Catholic Center: 7200 Stonehenge Dr., Raleigh, NC 27613-1620. T: 984-900-3200; F: 984-900-3201. www.dioceseofraleigh.org

Square Miles 31,875.

Established as Vicariate-Apostolic of North Carolina by Pope Pius IX, March 3, 1868.

Established as Diocese of Raleigh by Pope Pius XI, December 12, 1924.

Comprises the following Counties in the State of North Carolina: Alamance, Beaufort, Bertie, Bladen, Brunswick, Camden, Carteret, Caswell, Chatham, Chowan, Columbus, Craven, Cumberland, Currituck, Dare, Duplin, Durham, Edgecombe, Franklin, Gates, Granville, Greene, Halifax, Harnett, Hertford, Hoke, Hyde, Johnston, Jones, Lee, Lenoir, Martin, Moore, Nash, New Hanover, Northampton, Onslow, Orange, Pamlico, Pasquotank, Pender, Perquimans, Person, Pitt, Robeson, Sampson, Scotland, Tyrrell, Vance, Wake, Warren, Washington, Wayne and Wilson.

For legal titles of parishes and diocesan institutions, consult the Chancery.

STATISTICAL OVERVIEW

Personnel

Bishop	1
Priests: Diocesan Active in Diocese	61
Priests: Diocesan Active Outside Diocese	5
Priests: Retired, Sick or Absent	31
Number of Diocesan Priests	97
Religious Priests in Diocese	55
Total Priests in your Diocese	152
Extern Priests in Diocese	17
Ordinations:	
Diocesan Priests	2
Transitional Deacons	1
Permanent Deacons in Diocese	94
Total Brothers	3
Total Sisters	19

Parishes

Parishes	81
With Resident Pastor:	
Resident Diocesan Priests	46
Resident Religious Priests	22
Without Resident Pastor:	
Administered by Priests	13
Missions	16
Pastoral Centers	5
Professional Ministry Personnel:	
Brothers	3
Sisters	10
Lay Ministers	101

Welfare

Special Centers for Social Services	11
Total Assisted	158,836

Educational

Diocesan Students in Other Seminaries	14
Total Seminarians	14
High Schools, Diocesan and Parish	1
Total Students	1,562
High Schools, Private	3
Total Students	610
Elementary Schools, Diocesan and Parish	27
Total Students	7,900
Catechesis / Religious Education:	
High School Students	3,934
Elementary Students	10,534
Total Students under Catholic Instruction	24,554
Teachers in Diocese:	
Priests	6
Sisters	1
Lay Teachers	860

Vital Statistics

Receptions into the Church:	
Infant Baptism Totals	3,900
Minor Baptism Totals	784
Adult Baptism Totals	171
Received into Full Communion	300
First Communions	3,363
Confirmations	3,047
Marriages:	
Catholic	661
Interfaith	238
Total Marriages	899
Deaths	1,607
Total Catholic Population	243,934
Total Population	5,095,747

LEADERSHIP

Office of the Bishop - t) 984-900-3103 Most Rev. Luis Rafael Zarama;
Vicar General - t) 984-900-3108 Very Rev. Michael J. Burbeck, Vicar;
Judicial Vicar - t) 984-900-3411 Very Rev. Javier Castrejon (Mexico), Vicar;
Chancellor - t) 984-900-3410 Luis O. Capacetti (luis.capacetti@raldioc.org);
Chancery - t) 984-900-3410 Luis O. Capacetti, Chancellor (luis.capacetti@raldioc.org);
Chief Financial Officer/Chief Administrative Officer - t) 984-900-3144 Dr. Russell C. Elmayan;
Deans - Very Rev. Paul Nicholas Cottrill, Albemarle; Very Rev. John E. McGee, O.S.F.S., Cape Fear; Very Rev. John J. Forbes III, Fayetteville;
Diocesan Attorney - t) 919-729-5202 Frank Tortora III;
Diocesan Consultors - Very Rev. Michael J. Burbeck; Very Rev. Javier Castrejon (Mexico); Rev. Msgr. Jeffrey A. Ingham;
Diocesan Tribunal - t) 984-900-3411 dioceseofraleigh.org/tribunal/tribunal
Adjutant Judicial Vicar (Vacant) -
Defenders of the Bond - Very Rev. Michael G. Schuetz; Luis O. Capacetti;
Diocesan Judges - Very Rev. Javier Castrejon (Mexico), Judicial Vicar; Rev. Thomas S. Duggan; Rev. Rafael A. Leon-Valencia;
Director of the Tribunal - t) (984) 900-3411 Vikki Newell;
Judicial Vicar - Very Rev. Javier Castrejon (Mexico), Vicar;
Notaries - Vikki Newell; Veronica Alvarado Trejo; Paula Zanker;
Promoter of Justice - Very Rev. Michael G. Schuetz;
Council of Priests - Very Rev. Michael J. Burbeck, Vicar General; Rev. Msgr. John Williams, Vicar for Priest; Very Rev. Javier Castrejon (Mexico), Judicial Vicar;
Council of Women Religious - Sr. Mary Ann Czaja, C.S.A.; Sr. Constance Gilder, S.S.J.; Sr. Carol Marozzi, S.S.J.;
Vicar for Priests - Rev. Msgr. John Williams;
Bishop's Delegate for Religious - t) 910-791-1003 x106 jmcgee@iccwilm.org Very Rev. John E. McGee, O.S.F.S.;

OFFICES AND DIRECTORS

African Ancestry Ministry and Evangelization Network - t) 984-900-3197 Rev. Msgr. Joseph K. Ntuwa (Uganda), Episcopal Delegate to African Ancestry Ministry & Native Americans Catholics (msgr.joseph.ntuwa@raldio.org); Rev. Marcos Leon-Angulo, Chap., African American Catholic Community (padreleon@peru.com); Rev. David L. Miller, Chap., Native American Catholic Community;
Archives - t) 984-900-3137 Rev. Msgr. Gerald L. Lewis; Diana Zwilling, Archivist;
Catholic Charities of the Diocese of Raleigh, Inc. - t) 984-900-3120 Lisa E. Perkins, Exec.;
Communications - t) 984-900-3166 John Dornan, Dir.;
Ecumenical Commission -
NC Catholics Magazine - t) 984-900-3169 Kate Turgeon Watson, Editor;
Web Administrator - t) 984-900-3196 Michelle King;
Director of Information Technology - t) 919-364-9141 Kevin Hemphill;
Director of Property, Construction and Risk Management - t) 919-728-7125 Michael Wengenroth;
Hispanic Ministry - t) 984-900-3182 Lettie Banda;
Human Resources - t) 984-900-3171 Gary Rosia, Dir.;
Miscellaneous Offices -
Apostleship of the Sea -
Censor Librorum (Vacant) -
Holy Childhood Pontifical Association (Vacant) -
Home Mission Society of the Diocese of Raleigh - t) 919-568-1065 Maureen O'Keefe Lindgren;
Pontifical Mission Societies in the United States - t) 910-762-5491 Very Rev. Thomas R. Davis;
Victim Assistance Coordinator - t) 919-790-8533 x2550 Ruth DeVito;
Office for Child & Youth Protection - t) 866-535-7233 John A. Pendergrass, Dir.;
Office for Vocations and Seminarian Formation - t) 984-900-3104 Very Rev. Jeffrey A. Bowker, Dir.;
Director of Seminarian Formation - t) 984-900-3106 Very Rev. Jeffrey A. Bowker;
Promoter of Vocations - t) 984-900-3105 Rev. James J. Magee III;
Office of Divine Worship - t) 984-900-3109 Rev. James Sabak, O.F.M.;
Office of Education: Superintendent of Schools - t) 984-900-3416 Lytia Reese, Supt.;
Office of Evangelization and Discipleship - t) 984-900-3178 Amy Daniels, Exec. Dir.;
Director of Faith Formation - t) 984-900-3187 Patrick Ginty;
Director of Marriage and Family Life - t) 984-900-3183 Gabriel Hernandez;
Office of Permanent Diaconate - t) 984-900-3126 Dcn. Felix Sáez Jr., Dir.;
Parish Stewardship - t) 984-900-3178 Amy Daniels;

PARISHES, MISSIONS, AND CLERGY

STATE OF NORTH CAROLINA

AHOSKIE

St. Charles Borromeo - 122 NC 561 W., Ahoskie, NC 27910; Mailing: P.O. Box 605, Ahoskie, NC 27910 t) 252-332-2939; 252-513-8566 saintcharlescatholic.org Rev. Robert L. Schmid Jr., Pst.; CRP Stds.: 23
St. Anne - 1715 Main St., Scotland Neck, NC 27874 t) (252) 332-2939

APEX

St. Andrew the Apostle - 3008 Old Raleigh Rd., Apex, NC 27502 t) 919-362-0414 www.saintandrew.org Rev. John G. Durbin, Pst.; Dcn. Richard Mickle; CRP Stds.: 643
St. Ha-Sang Paul Jung - 3031 Holland Rd., Apex, NC 27502 t) 919-414-9256 hellospjcc@gmail.com www.spjcc.org/xe/home Rev. Dongwook Lee (Korea), Pst.; CRP Stds.: 36
St. Mary Magdalene - 625 Magdala Pl., Apex, NC 27502 t) 919-657-4800 x7281 www.stmm.net Rev. Christopher Scott Koehn, Pst.; Rev. Msgr. Donald F. Staib, Pastor Emer.; Dcn. Dev Lobo; Dcn. Joseph Richard Stevens; Suzanne Will, CRE; CRP Stds.: 745
St. Mary Magdalene School - (Grades PreSchool-8) t) (919) 657-4800 John Mihalyo, Prin.; Stds.: 630; Lay Tchrs.: 77

BURGAW

St. Joseph Catholic Parish of Burgaw - 1303 Hwy. 117 S., Burgaw, NC 28425 t) 910-259-2601 stjosephcatholicnc.org Rev. Roger Malonda Nyimi (Democratic Republic of Congo), Admin.; CRP Stds.: 50

BUTNER

St. Bernadette - 804 W. D St., Butner, NC 27509; Mailing: 311 Eleventh St., Butner, NC 27509 t) 919-575-4537 st_bernadette3@frontier.com Rev. Marcos Leon-Angulo, Pst.; CRP Stds.: 28

BUXTON

Our Lady of the Seas - 48478 Hwy. 12, Buxton, NC 27920; Mailing: PO Box 399, Buxton, NC 27920 t) 252-995-6370 olsparish365@gmail.com www.ourladyoftheseas.org Rev. Alfred J. Smuda, O.S.F.S., Pst.; CRP Stds.: 30

CARY

St. Michael the Archangel Catholic Church - 804 High House Rd, Cary, NC 27513 t) 919-468-6100 office@stmichaelcary.org www.stmichaelcary.org Very Rev. Michael J. Burbeck, Pst.; Rev. John Michael De Guzman, Par. Vicar; Rev. Joseph Kalu Oji, C.S.Sp., Par. Vicar; Rev. Steven Costello, L.C., Director of Evangelization and Catechesis; Rev. Msgr. John A. Wall, Pastor Emer.; Dcn. Glenn Dudek; Dcn. Patrick Daniel Pelkey; Dcn. Brian John Phillips; Dcn. David A Wulff; CRP Stds.: 714
St. Michael the Archangel Catholic School - 810 High House Rd, Cary, NC 27513 t) 919-468-6150 x152 administration@stmcary.org www.stmcary.org/ Tara Navarro, Prin.; Stds.: 519; Lay Tchrs.: 33

CASTLE HAYNE

St. Stanislaus Catholic Parish of Castle Hayne - 4849 Castle Hayne Rd., Castle Hayne, NC 28429-4849 t) 910-675-2336 ststans4@ec.rr.com ststanislauscatholic.org Rev. Roger Malonda Nyimi (Democratic Republic of Congo), Admin.; CRP Stds.: 31

CHAPEL HILL

Newman Catholic Student Center, University of North Carolina - 218 Pittsboro St., Chapel Hill, NC 27516-2738 t) 919-929-3730 info@uncnewman.org uncnewman.org Rev. Timothy Kulbicki, O.F.M. Conv., Pst.; Rev. William J. Robinson, O.F.M.Conv., Par. Vicar; Dcn. Kevin Sullivan; CRP Stds.: 103
St. Thomas More - 940 Carmichael St., Chapel Hill, NC 27514-4203 t) 919-942-1040 parishofficestaff@stmchapelhill.org stmchapelhill.org Very Rev. Scott E. McCue, Pst.; Rev. Steven T. DiMassimo, Par. Vicar; Dcn. Luis Alfonso Royo Camacho; Dcn. Robert Edward Troy Jr.; Dcn. Stephen Yates; Mary Ellen McGuire, Pst. Assoc.; CRP Stds.: 640
St. Thomas More School - (Grades PreK-8) 920 Carmichael St., Chapel Hill, NC 27514 t) 919-929-1546 dfulford@stmcsnc.org www.stmcsnc.org Darrell Fulford, Prin.; Stds.: 393; Lay Tchrs.: 28

CLAYTON

St. Ann - 4057 U.S. 70 Bus. Hwy. W., Clayton, NC 27520 t) 919-934-2084 st.ann.frontdesk@gmail.com www.st-annschurch.org Rev. Peter A. Grace, C.P., Pst.; Rev. Thomas S. Duggan, Par. Vicar; Dcn. Albert Bandiera; Dcn. Michael Wundsam; CRP Stds.: 573

CLINTON

Immaculate Conception - 104 E. John St., Clinton, NC 28328 t) 910-592-1384 www.icclintonnc.org Very Rev. J. Joseph Dionne, C.Ss.R., Pst.; Rev. Mark B. Wise, C.Ss.R., Par. Vicar; CRP Stds.: 107
San Juan - 1710 Old U.S. Hwy. 701, Ingold, NC 28446 t) (910) 592-1384

DUNN

Sacred Heart Parish of Dunn - 106 S McKay Ave., Dunn, NC 28334; Mailing: PO Box 535, Dunn, NC 28335 t) 910-891-1972 janshdunn@gmail.com www.sacredheartdunn.org Rev. Joseph G. Mulroney, Pst.; CRP Stds.: 45

DURHAM

Holy Cross - 2438 S. Alston Ave., Durham, NC 27713 t) 919-957-2900 office@holycrossdurham.org Rev. Pius S. Wekesa (Kenya), Pst.; Dcn. Phil Rzewnicki; CRP Stds.: 46
Holy Infant Catholic Parish - 5000 Southpark Dr., Durham, NC 27713-9470 t) 919-544-7135; 919-973-0018 (CRP) holyinfantchurch.org Rev. Robert M. Rutledge, O.S.F.S., Pst.; Lynn Sale, Pst. Assoc.; CRP Stds.: 109
Immaculate Conception - 901A W. Chapel Hill St., Durham, NC 27701 t) 919-682-3449 info@icdurham.org www.icdurham.org Rev. Jacek Orzechowski, O.F.M., Pst.; Rev. Hugh Macsherry, O.F.M., Par. Vicar; Rev. Gonzalo de Jesús Torres-Acosta, O.F.M., Par. Vicar; Dcn. Gerardo Chavez; Dcn. Laurence DeCarolis; CRP Stds.: 800
Immaculata Catholic School - (Grades PreK-8) 721 Burch Ave., Durham, NC 27701 t) 919-682-5847 corcorand@icdurham.org Patrick Kurz, Prin.; Stds.: 530; Lay Tchrs.: 45
St. Matthew - 1001 Mason Rd., Durham, NC 27712 t) 919-479-1001 tlilley@stmatthewcc.org www.stmatthewcc.org Rev. Robert P. Staley, Pst.; Dcn.

Desider Vikor; CRP Stds.: 138

EDENTON

St. Ann - 207 N. Broad St., Edenton, NC 27932; Mailing: P.O. Box 422, Edenton, NC 27932 t) 252-482-2617 edentoncatholic.weebly.com Rev. Jairo A. Maldonado-Pacheco, Par. Admin.; Dcn. Frank T. Jones III; CRP Stds.: 54

All Souls - 917 Main St., Columbia, NC 27925 t) (252) 482-2617

ELIZABETH CITY

Holy Family - 1453 N. Road St., Elizabeth City, NC 27909 t) 252-338-2521 Very Rev. Paul Nicholas Cottrill, Pst.; Dcn. Ronald Soriano; CRP Stds.: 86

St. Katharine Drexel - 154 Maple Rd., Maple, NC 27956; Mailing: P.O. Box 64, Maple, NC 27956 t) 252-453-6035

FARMVILLE

St. Elizabeth of Hungary - 3455 S. Contentnea St., Farmville, NC 27828; Mailing: 3447 S. Contentnea St., Farmville, NC 27828-1686 t) 252-753-4367 stelizabethoffarmville.org Rev. Marco Antonio Gonzalez-Hernandez, Pst.;

FAYETTEVILLE

St. Andrew Kim - 1401 Valencia Dr., Fayetteville, NC 28303 t) 910-630-2316 Rev. Hakseng Choi (Korea), Pst.;

St. Ann - 357 N. Cool Spring St., Fayetteville, NC 28301 t) 910-483-3216 info@stanncatholicchurch.org www.stanncatholicchurch.org Rev. Michael Coveyou, Pst.; Dcn. Gary Stemple; CRP Stds.: 43

St. Ann Catholic School - (Grades PreK-8) 365 N. Cool Spring St., Fayetteville, NC 28301 t) 910-483-3902 principal@stanncatholicchurch.org www.stanncatholicschool.net N. Rene' Corders, Prin.; Stds.: 132; Lay Tchrs.: 14

St. Elizabeth Ann Seton - 1000 Andrews Rd., Fayetteville, NC 28311 t) 910-488-1797 cjohnson@seaschurch.net www.seaschurch.net Rev. Miguel Arturo Cabra, Pst.; Dcn. Steven James Canali; CRP Stds.: 100

St. Patrick - 2840 Village Dr., Fayetteville, NC 28304; Mailing: 2844 Village Dr., Fayetteville, NC 28304-3813 t) 910-323-2410 churchoffice@stpatnc.org stpatnc.org Rev. Gregory Lowchy, Pst.; Rev. Tyler Austin Sparrow, Par. Vicar; Dcn. Vincent Joseph Mescall; Dcn. Gerardo Mercado; Dcn. Joshua Klickman; CRP Stds.: 200

St. Patrick Catholic School - (Grades PreK-8) 1620 Marlborough Rd., Fayetteville, NC 28304 t) 910-323-1865 x123 schoolinfo@stpatschoolnc.org stpatschoolnc.org/ Christa Larkin, Prin.; Stds.: 208; Pr. Tchrs.: 2; Lay Tchrs.: 34

FUQUAY-VARINA

St. Bernadette - 1005 Wilbon Rd., Fuquay-Varina, NC 27526-9702 t) 919-552-8758 office@stbnc.net www.stbnc.net Rev. Carlos N. Arce, Pst.; Dcn. John Reichert; Dcn. Charles Edward Zlamal; Dcn. Wendell Lowry; CRP Stds.: 497

Social Outreach Office -

GARNER

Saint Mary, Mother of the Church Catholic Parish of Garner - 1008 Vandora Springs Rd., Garner, NC 27529-3546 t) 919-772-5524 business@smmocg.org www.stmarygarner.org Rev. David M. Chiantella, Pst.; Rev. Agustin Alonso Sigaran Donis (El Salvador), Par. Vicar; CRP Stds.: 371

GOLDSBORO

St. Mary - 1603 Edgerton St., Goldsboro, NC 27530-3141 t) 919-734-5033 office@saintmarygoldsboro.org www.saintmarygoldsboro.org Rev. Roch T. Drozdzik (Poland), Pst.; Dcn. Matthew Anthony Yurksaitis; CRP Stds.: 143

St. Mary Catholic School - (Grades PreK-8) 1601 Edgerton St., Goldsboro, NC 27530-3141 t) 919-735-1931 x33 lynnmagoon@smsgoldsboro.org smsgoldsboro.org Lynn Magoon, Prin.; Stds.: 238; Lay Tchrs.: 14

GRAHAM

Blessed Sacrament - 1620 Hanford Rd., Graham, NC 27235; Mailing: P.O. Box 619, Burlington, NC 27216 t) 336-226-8796 joe@blessedsacramentnc.org www.blessedsacramentnc.org Rev. Vincent P. Rubino, O.F.M.Conv., Pst.; Rev. Piotr Tymko, O.F.M. Conv., Assoc. Pst.; Rev. Timothy Lyons, O.F.M. Conv.; Rev. Peter C. Tremblay, O.F.M.Conv., In Res.; Dcn. Leo Tapler; CRP Stds.: 654

Blessed Sacrament Catholic School - (Grades PreK-8) 515 Hillcrest Ave., Burlington, NC 27215 t) 336-570-0019 office@bssknights.org www.bssknights.org Maria Gomez, Prin.; Stds.: 247; Lay Tchrs.: 17

GREENVILLE

St. Gabriel Catholic Parish of Greenville - 3250 Dickinson Ave., Greenville, NC 27834 t) 252-758-1504 secretarystgabriel@gmail.com www.stgabrielgreenville.org Rev. Romen A. Acero, Pst.; CRP Stds.: 129

St. Peter's - 2700 E. Fourth St., Greenville, NC 27858 t) 252-757-3259 parishoffice@spcsnc.org www.saintpetercatholicchurch.org Rev. James J. Magee III, Pst.; Dcn. Arthur Charles Schneider; Rev. Ian C. Van Heusen, In Res.; CRP Stds.: 254

St. Peter's School - (Grades PreK-8) 2606 E. 5th St., Greenville, NC 27858 t) 252-752-3529 dsommer@spcsnc.net www.stpeterscatholicschool.com Debra Sommer, Prin.; Stds.: 448; Pr. Tchrs.: 1; Lay Tchrs.: 32

HAMPSTEAD

All Saints Catholic Parish of Hampstead - 18737 U.S. Hwy. 17 N., Hampstead, NC 28443 t) 910-270-1477 business@asccnc.org; secretary@asccnc.org www.allsaintsccnc.org Rev. Msgr. Joseph K. Ntuwa (Uganda), Pst.; CRP Stds.: 186

All Saints Catholic Church - 420 N. Topsail Dr., Surf City, NC 28445; Mailing: 18737 U.S. Hwy. 17 N, Hampstead, NC 28443 t) (910) 270-1477 msgr.joseph.ntuwa@raldioc.org

HAVELOCK

Annunciation - 246 E. Main St., Havelock, NC 28532-0720 t) 252-447-2112 secretary@annunciationparish.org; fr.s.james.buchholz@raldioc.org annunciationparish.org Rev. Samuel James Buchholz, Pst.; Dcn. Walter Calabrese; Dcn. James Richard Strange; CRP Stds.: 75

Annunciation Catholic School - t) 252-447-3137 info@acsnc.net annunciationcatholicnc.org Dr. Matthew J. Jennings, Prin.; Stds.: 184; Lay Tchrs.: 10

HENDERSON

St. James - 3275 US 158 Bypass, Henderson, NC 27537-9666 t) 252-438-3124 stjamescatholichenderson.org Rev. Rafael A. Leon-Valencia, Pst.; Dcn. Felix Sáez Jr.; CRP Stds.: 75

St. Joseph the Worker - 842 US Hwy 158 West Business, Warrenton, NC 27589; Mailing: P.O. Box 934, Warrenton, NC 27589 t) 252-257-5605 info@st-joseph-church.com www.st-joseph-church.com/

HILLSBOROUGH

Holy Family - 216 Governor Burke Rd., Hillsborough, NC 27278 t) 919-732-1030 records@hfcch.org hfcch.org Rev. Ryan W. Elder, Pst.; Dcn. Bertrand Paul L'Homme; CRP Stds.: 119

HOPE MILLS

Good Shepherd Catholic Church - 5050 Oak St., Hope Mills, NC 28348 t) 910-425-1590 gdshprd81@gmail.com Rev. Arulanantham Yagappan, M.S.F.S., Pst.; Patricia Martin-Kamionka, DRE; CRP Stds.: 107

St. Isidore - 4733 Macedonia Church Rd., Fayetteville, NC 28312 t) 910-424-2698 Rev. John Vedanayagam, M.S.F.S., Admin.;

JACKSONVILLE

Infant of Prague, Church of the Holy Spirit - 210 Marine Blvd., Jacksonville, NC 28540; Mailing: 205 Chaney Ave., Jacksonville, NC 28540 t) 910-347-4196 psecretary.iop@gmail.com; iopbmanager@gmail.com iopnc.org Rev. John Victor Gournas, Pst.; Rev. Pedro Manuel Munoz Munoz, O.F.M.Cap., Par. Vicar; Dcn. James Anthony Marapoti; Sr. Barbara Marie Cady, S.U., DRE; CRP Stds.: 237

Infant of Prague, Church of the Holy Spirit School - (Grades PreK-8) 501 Bordeaux St, Jacksonville, NC 28540 t) 910-353-1300; 910-455-0838 iopprincipal@gmail.com www.iopschool.net Jennifer Feldhaus, Prin.; Stds.: 178; Lay Tchrs.: 19

KINSTON

Holy Spirit Catholic Church - 400 Academy Heights Rd., Kinston, NC 28504; Mailing: P.O. Box 1455, Kinston, NC 28504 t) 252-523-8898 www.hscatholicchurchkinston.com (Formerly Holy Trinity-Our Lady of the Atonement) Rev. Joseph J. Yaeger, Pst.; CRP Stds.: 131

KITTY HAWK

Holy Redeemer by the Sea - 301 W. Kitty Hawk Rd, Kitty Hawk, NC 27949; Mailing: P.O. Box 510, Kitty Hawk, NC 27949 t) 252-261-4700 hrbtskittyhawk@gmail.com obxcatholicparish.org Rev. William F. Walsh, O.S.F.S., Pst.; Rev. John A. Hanley, O.S.F.S., Assoc. Pst.; Dcn. James Phillip Cooper; Dcn. Mark Mueller; Dcn. Albert J Hallatt; CRP Stds.: 96

Holy Trinity by the Sea Catholic Mission - 7335 Virginia Dare Tr., Nags Head, NC 27959; Mailing: PO Box 510, Kitty Hawk, NC 27949 t) (252) 261-4700 obxcatholicparish.org/

LAURINBURG

St. Mary Catholic Parish of Laurinburg - 800 S. Main St., Laurinburg, NC 28352 t) 910-276-4468 parishoffice800@gmail.com www.saintmaryparishlaurinburg.org Rev. Cyriac John (India), Pst.; Dcn. Juan Alexander Vicent Martinez; CRP Stds.: 32

LOUISBURG

Our Lady of the Rosary - 2227 Hwy. 39 N., Louisburg, NC 27549; Mailing: PO Box 593, Louisburg, NC 27549 t) 919-340-0556 olrcatholic@gmail.com catholicolr.org Rev. Marlee Abao, C.I.C.M., Pst.; Dcn. Patrick Gerald McIlmoyle; CRP Stds.: 109

LUMBERTON

St. Francis De Sales Catholic Parish of Lumberton - 2000 E Elizabethtown Rd., Lumberton, NC 28358; Mailing: P.O. Box 2249, Lumberton, NC 28358 t) 910-739-4723 office@stfrancisdesalescatholic.org www.stfrancisdesalescatholic.org/ Rev. Zacharie Lukielo Tati (Congo), Admin.; Dcn. Patrick Snyder; CRP Stds.: 117

MOREHEAD CITY

St. Egbert - Arendal at 17th St., Morehead City, NC 28557; Mailing: 1706 Evans St., Morehead City, NC 28557 t) 252-726-3559 camedy@stegbert.org www.crystalcoastcatholic.org Rev. Ryszard W. Kolodziej, Pst.; Rev. Msgr. Francis R. Moeslein, Pastor Emer.; Joseph McKenzie, Pst. Assoc.; CRP Stds.: 119

Parish Hall - 1706 Evans St., Morehead City, NC 28557 t) (252) 726-3559

St. Egbert Catholic School - -5) 1705 Evans St., Morehead City, NC 28557 t) 252-726-3418 adminassistant@stegbert.org www.stegbert.org Nancy Guthrie, Admin.; Stds.: 124; Lay Tchrs.: 16

MOUNT OLIVE

Maria, Reina De Las Americas - 636 Whitfield Rd., Mount Olive, NC 28365; Mailing: P.O. Box 978, Beulaville, NC 28518 t) 910-298-4300 mreinacatholic@gmail.com mariareinacatholic.org (Mary, Queen of the Americas) Rev. Bernard Kayimbw Mbay, C.I.C.M., Admin.; Rev. Edward Tembo, C.I.C.M., Par. Vicar; Rev. Remy Konkolongo Kankolongo, C.I.C.M., Par. Vicar; Veronica Rivera, DRE; CRP Stds.: 131

St. Teresa del Nino Jesus - 206 Cavenaugh St., Beulaville, NC 28518 t) (910) 208-0058 fr.bernard.mbay@raldioc.org santateresacatholic.org

St. Mary of the Angels - 3262 US Hwy 117 N Bypass, Mount Olive, NC 28365; Mailing: P.O. Box 1145, Mount Olive, NC 28365 t) 919-658-4023 amy.breindel@raldioc.org saintmarymo.org Rev. Bernard Kayimbw Mbay, C.I.C.M., Pst.; CRP Stds.: 59

NEW BERN

St. Paul - 3005 Country Club Rd., New Bern, NC 28562 t) 252-638-1984 dconway@spccnb.org spccnb.org Rev.

Thomas S. Tully, Pst.; Dcn. Daniel Joseph Doban; Dcn. Frederick Melvin Fisher Jr.; Dcn. Jim Hackett; CRP Stds.: 89

St. Paul Catholic School - (Grades PreK-8) 3007 Country Club Rd., New Bern, NC 28562 t) 252-633-0100 info@stpaulcs.org stpaulcs.org Dcn. David William Kierski, Prin.; Stds.: 201; Lay Tchrs.: 18

St. Peter the Fisherman - 1149 White Farm Rd., Oriental, NC 28571 t) 252-249-3687

NEWTON GROVE

Our Lady of Guadalupe - 211 Irwin Dr., Newton Grove, NC 28366; Mailing: P.O. Box 100, Newton Grove, NC 28366 t) 910-594-0287 ologoffice@aol.com ourladyofguadalupenewtongrove.org Rev. Alvaro Riquelme, C.Ss.R., Pst.; Rev. Mark B. Wise, C.Ss.R., Par. Vicar; Dcn. Louise Vincent Parente; CRP Stds.: 112

ORIENTAL

Saint Peter the Fisherman - 1149 White Farm Rd., Oriental, NC 28571 t) 252-249-3687 stpeteronc@embarqmail.com stpeteronc.org Mission of St. Paul, New Bern. Rev. Thomas S. Tully, Pst.;

PINEHURST

Sacred Heart - 300 Dundee Rd., Pinehurst, NC 28374 t) 910-295-6550 shrcc@sacredheartpinehurst.org; jeanne.ryan@sacredheartpinehurst.org sacredheartpinehurst.org Very Rev. John J. Forbes III, Pst.; Very Rev. Javier Castrejon (Mexico), Par. Vicar; Dcn. Guy A. Berry Jr.; Dcn. Gregory Thomas Cross; CRP Stds.: 257

Early Childhood Center - t) 910-295-3514 Stephanie Hinds, Dir.;

Saint Juan Diego - 6963 NC 705 Hwy., Robbins, NC 27325; Mailing: 300 Dundee Rd., Pinehurst, NC 28374 c) (910) 690-9288 sanjuandiegorobbins@gmail.com www.sanjuandiegorobbins.org

PLYMOUTH

St. Joan of Arc - 506 E. Main St., Plymouth, NC 27962; Mailing: P.O. Box 822, Plymouth, NC 27962 t) (252) 226-0340 stjoanplymouth.org Rev. Richard Toboso, G.H.M., Pst.; Rev. Jose Carlos Miguel Lopez, G.H.M., Par. Vicar; CRP Stds.: 18

RAEFORD

St. Elizabeth of Hungary - 6199 Fayetteville Rd., Raeford, NC 28376-0665; Mailing: P.O. Box 665, Raeford, NC 28376 t) 910-875-8803 www.stelizabethofhungaryraeford-nc.org Rev. Edisson Urrego Restrepo, Admin.; Dcn. Juan Carlos Campos; CRP Stds.: 75

RALEIGH

Holy Name of Jesus Cathedral - 715 Nazareth St., Raleigh, NC 27606; Mailing: 219 W. Edenton St., Raleigh, NC 27603-1724 t) 919-832-6030 raleighcathedral.org Rev. Msgr. David D. Brockman, Rector; Rev. Juan Andres Arturo-Gonzalez, C.O. (Colombia), Par. Vicar; Rev. Erik Reyes Reyes, Par. Vicar; Dcn. Michael Boyd Alig; Stacie Miller, Dir.; CRP Stds.: 618

Cathedral School - (Grades PreK-8) 204 Hillsborough St., Raleigh, NC 27603 t) 919-832-4711 cathedralschool@cathedral-school.net www.cathedral-school.net Peggy Lane, Prin.; Stds.: 223; Lay Tchrs.: 17

Sacred Heart Church - 200 Hillsborough St, Raleigh, NC 27603

Catholic Student Center, North Carolina State University - 1720 Hillsborough St. LL One, Raleigh, NC 27605; Mailing: P.O.Box 10302, Raleigh, NC 27605 t) 708-846-1500 ccminterns@gmail.com Rev. John Curran, L.C., Campus Min.;

Doggett Center at Aquinas House - t) 919-833-9668

Saint Francis of Assisi Catholic Parish of Raleigh - 11401 Leesville Rd., Raleigh, NC 27613 t) 919-847-8205 rob.neppel@stfrancisraleigh.org; trish.adamkowski@stfrancisraleigh.org www.stfrancisraleigh.org Rev. Msgr. Michael G. Clay, Pst.; Rev. John Alex Gonzalez, Par. Vicar; Dcn. Stephen William Andrews; Rev. James Sabak, O.F.M., In Res.; CRP Stds.: 667

The Franciscan School - (Grades K-8) 10000 St. Francis Dr., Raleigh, NC 27613 t) 919-534-4837 dawn.smith@stfrancisraleigh.org www.franciscanschool.org Dawn Marie Smith, Prin.; Stds.: 676; Lay Tchrs.: 53

St. Francis Early Child Learning Center (ECLC) - t) (919) 847-8205 x240 www.preschoolatstfrancis.com Heidi Hobler, Prin.;

Saint Joseph Catholic Parish of Raleigh - 2811 Poole Rd., Raleigh, NC 27610 t) 919-231-6364 secretary@stjral.org www.saintjosephraleigh.org Rev. Peter C. Devereux, L.C., Pst.; Rev. Lourduraj Alapaty (India), In Res.; Dcn. Stephen Lewandowski; CRP Stds.: 189

St. Luke the Evangelist - 12333 Bayleaf Church Rd., Raleigh, NC 27614-9165 t) 919-848-1533 secretary@stlrnc.org stlukesraleigh.org Rev. Msgr. Jeffrey A. Ingham, Pst.; Dcn. Michael Sanchez; CRP Stds.: 108

Our Lady of La Vang Parish - 11701 Leesville Rd., Raleigh, NC 27613 t) 919-307-4023 martinbancrm@gmail.com; hdtc.ollv@gmail.com www.ducmelavangraleigh.org Rev. Martin M. Tran Van Ban, C.R.M., Pst.; Dcn. Anthony Hoang Nguyen; CRP Stds.: 159

Our Lady of Lourdes - 2718 Overbrook Dr., Raleigh, NC 27608 t) 919-861-4600 mhouse@ourladyoflourdescc.org ourladyoflourdescc.org Rev. Patrick A. Keane, Pst.; Dcn. Byron M. Champagne, DRE; Dcn. Myles J. Charlesworth; Dcn. D. Thomas Mack; CRP Stds.: 195

Our Lady of Lourdes School - 2710 Overbrook Dr., Raleigh, NC 27608 t) 919-861-4610 www.olls.org Christopher Sutton, Prin.; Stds.: 478; Lay Tchrs.: 19

St. Raphael the Archangel - 5801 Falls of Neuse Rd., Raleigh, NC 27609 t) 919-865-5700 www.saintraphael.org Rev. Thomas M Simisky, S.J., Pst.; Rev. Bruce Bavinger, S.J., Par. Vicar; Rev. Lawrence Searles, S.J., Par. Vicar; Dcn. Louis Philip Clark; Dcn. Thomas di Stefano; Dcn. Arthur G. Powers; Dcn. John Robert Wetsch; CRP Stds.: 500

St. Raphael - (Grades K-8) 5815 Fall of Neuse Rd., Raleigh, NC 27609 t) 919-865-5750 srcs@saintraphael.org saintraphaelschool.org Joseph Whitmore, Prin.; Stds.: 429; Lay Tchrs.: 35

St. Raphael Catholic Early Childhood Center - t) 919-865-5728 straphaelpreschool.org Molly DeAngelo, Dir.;

RED SPRINGS

St. Andrew - 301 Mercer Ave., Red Springs, NC 28377; Mailing: P.O. Box 649, Red Springs, NC 28377 t) 910-359-8022 standrewredsprings.org Rev. Francisco Javier Garcia-Gonzalez, Admin.;

Our Lady of Mount Carmel -

RIEGELWOOD

Christ the King - 100 Burns Rd., Riegelwood, NC 28456; Mailing: 1011 Eastwood Rd., Wilmington, NC 28403 t) 910-392-0720 staffassistant@stmarkcatholicchurch.com www.stmarkcatholicchurch.com Rev. Gregory D. Spencer, Pst.;

Christ the King - t) (910) 392-0720

ROANOKE RAPIDS

St. John the Baptist - 900 Hamilton St., Roanoke Rapids, NC 27870; Mailing: P.O. Box 116, Roanoke Rapids, NC 27870 t) 252-537-4667 c) 252-308-8771 stjohnbaptist@hotmail.com saintjohnthebaptistcc.wordpress.com Rev. Marlon A. Mendieta Rodas, Pst.; Dcn. Bernard Zdancewicz; CRP Stds.: 69

Immaculate Conception - King St., Halifax, NC 27839

ROCKY MOUNT

Our Lady of Perpetual Help - 331 Hammond St., Rocky Mount, NC 27804; Mailing: 328 Hammond St., Rocky Mount, NC 27804 t) 252-972-0452 church@olphrm.com www.olphrm.com Rev. Clyde Timberlake Meares, Admin.; Rev. Paul Parkerson, Par. Vicar; CRP Stds.: 57

Immaculate Conception - 721 Virginia Ave., Rocky Mount, NC 27804 t) (252) 972-0452

Our Lady of Perpetual Help Catholic School - 315 Hammond St., Rocky Mount, NC 27801 t) 252-972-1971 office@olphrm.com school.olphrm.com Julie Love, Prin.; Stds.: 126; Lay Tchrs.: 12

ROXBORO

Sts. Mary and Edward - 611 N. Main St., Roxboro, NC 27573-5040 t) 336-599-4122 stmaryandedward.org Rev. William H. Rodriguez, Pst.; CRP Stds.: 58

SANFORD

St. Stephen the First Martyr - 901 N. Franklin Dr., Sanford, NC 27330 t) 919-776-1532 secretary@ststephencc.org www.ststephensanford.org Rev. Baiju Augustine Avittappally, M.S., Pst.; Rev. Hector LaChapelle, M.S., In Res.; Dcn. Robert Lawrence Bridwell; Dcn. Gustavo Castro-Reynoso; Dcn. Emilio Mejia; Dcn. Mark Alan Westrick; CRP Stds.: 223

SHALLOTTE

St. Brendan the Navigator - 5101 Ocean Hwy. W., Shallotte, NC 28471; Mailing: P.O. Box 2984, Shallotte, NC 28459 t) 910-754-8544 brenavigator@atmc.net saintbrendan-shallotte.org Rev. Mark J. Betti, Pst.; Dcn. John Thomas Baffa; Dcn. Louis F Howe; Dcn. John James Mullins; Dcn. Thomas Kronyak; Dcn. Andrew Robert McGahran;

SILER CITY

St. Julia Catholic Parish of Siler City - 210 Harold Hart Rd., Siler City, NC 27344 t) 919-742-5584 office@stjsc.org www.saintjulianc.org Rev. Julio A. Martinez, O.F.M. Conv., Pst.; Rev. Luis Palacios-Rodriguez, O.F.M. Conv., Par. Vicar; CRP Stds.: 204

SOUTHERN PINES

St. Anthony of Padua - 160 E. Vermont Ave, Southern Pines, NC 28387; Mailing: 175 E. Connecticut Ave., Southern Pines, NC 28387 t) 910-692-6613 d.wake@stanthonyparish.net www.stanthonyparish.net Rev. John A. Kane, Pst.; Rev. Msgr. John Williams, In Res.; Dcn. Eric Rosario Ramos; Dcn. Joseph Pius Piyasiri Gabriel; Diana Wake, DRE; CRP Stds.: 133

SOUTHPORT

Sacred Heart - 5269 Dosher Cutoff, S.E., Southport, NC 28461 t) 910-457-6173 sacheart3@earthlink.net Rev. Thanh N. Nguyen, Pst.; Dcn. Rick Keith Autry; Dcn. Kenneth E. Moytlinski; Patricia Ciemnicki, Dir.; CRP Stds.: 41

SWANSBORO

St. Mildred - 653 Old Hammock Rd., Swansboro, NC 28584 t) 910-326-5589 stmildred@embarqmail.com www.stmildred.info Rev. David L. Miller, Admin.; Dcn. Gerald Fatica; CRP Stds.: 97

TARBORO

St. Catherine of Siena - 1004 St. David St., Tarboro, NC 27886 t) 252-563-4567 parish@scstar.org stcatherinetarboro.org Rev. Eric Imbao, C.I.C.M., Pst.; CRP Stds.: 50

WAKE FOREST

St. Catherine of Siena - 520 W. Holding Ave., Wake Forest, NC 27587 t) 919-570-0070 spender@scswf.org www.scswf.org/ Rev. Bill John Acosta-Escobar, Pst.; Rev. Matthew Nwafor, Par. Vicar; Dcn. Bradley Evans Watkins; CRP Stds.: 535

St. Catherine of Siena Catholic School - (Grades K-8) t) 919-556-7613 info@scswf.org www.school.scswf.org Catherine Schwarz, Prin.; Stds.: 250; Sr. Tchrs.: 1; Lay Tchrs.: 23

St. Catherine of Siena Preschool -

WALLACE

Transfiguration of Jesus - 506 E. Main St., Wallace, NC 28466; Mailing: P.O. Box 1601, Wallace, NC 28466 t) 910-665-1530 transfigurationofjesus.wallace@gmail.com www.transfigurationofjesusparish.org Rev. Randy V. Gonzales, C.I.C.M., Pst.; Dcn. Michael Dean Vandiver; CRP Stds.: 23

Santa Clara Catholic Mission - 352 N. Academy St., Magnolia, NC 28453 t) (910) 665-1530

WASHINGTON
Mother of Mercy - 112 W. 9th St., Washington, NC 27889 t) 252-495-8255 secretary@momlw.org motherofmercync.com Very Rev. Michael G. Schuetz, Pst.; Dcn. Tomasz Cechulski;
WENDELL
St. Eugene - 608 Lions Club Rd., Wendell, NC 27591; Mailing: P.O. Box 188, Wendell, NC 27591 t) 919-365-7114; 919-365-7114 x202 (DRE) steoffice@stewnc.org; stereled@stewnc.org www.catholicste.org Rev. Archie Tacay, C.I.C.M., Pst.; Dcn. John S. Class; Dcn. Anthony Favale; Alex Hernandez, DRE; CRP Stds.: 416
WHITEVILLE
Sacred Heart - 302 N. Lee St., Whiteville, NC 28472 t) 910-642-3895 p.sacredheart.whiteville@raldioc.org www.sacredheartwhiteville.org/ Rev. Joshua West, L.C., Admin.;
Our Lady of the Snows - 701 W. Broad St., Elizabethtown, NC 28337-1766 t) 910-862-4998 Joan Marion, Pst. Min./Coord.;
WILLIAMSTON
Holy Trinity - 830 E. Boulevard St. (Hwy. 17/13), Williamston, NC 27892; Mailing: P.O. Box 894, Williamston, NC 27892 t) (252) 226-0699 c) (252) 508-8268 (Sacramental Emergency) office@htccwnc.org www.williamstoncatholic.org Rev. Chester Artysiewicz, G.H.M, Par. Admin.; Rev. Vijaya Babu "Sleeva" Katta (India), Par. Vicar; CRP Stds.: 20
WILMINGTON
Basilica Shrine of Saint Mary - 220 S. 5th Ave, Wilmington, NC 28401; Mailing: 412 Ann St., Wilmington, NC 28401 t) 910-762-5491 secretary@thestmaryparish.org www.thestmaryparish.org Very Rev. Thomas R. Davis, Pst.; Rev. Alberto Ortega, Assoc. Pst.; Dcn. John Joseph Walsh; CRP Stds.: 150
St. Mary Catholic School - (Grades PreK-8) 217 S. 4th St., Wilmington, NC 28401 t) (910) 762-5491 x140 principal@thestmaryparish.org www.thestmaryschool.org Joyce Price, Prin.; Stds.: 146; Lay Tchrs.: 20
Immaculate Conception - 6650 Carolina Beach Rd., Wilmington, NC 28412 t) 910-791-1003 info@iccwilm.org www.iccwilm.org Very Rev. John E. McGee, O.S.F.S., Pst.; CRP Stds.: 79
St. Mark Catholic Parish of Wilmington - 1011 Eastwood Rd., Wilmington, NC 28403 t) (910) 398-6509 pastoral@stmarkcc.net stmarkcc.net Rev. Gregory D. Spencer, Pst.; Rev. Cesar Torres Martinez (Mexico), Par. Vicar; Dcn. Edwin Jeffress Jolly; Dcn. Rick Tucek; CRP Stds.: 875
Christ the King - 100 Burns Rd., Riegelwood, NC 28456-0155; Mailing: 1011 Eastwood Rd., Wilmington, NC 28403 t) (910) 392-0720 office@stmarkcc.net
St. Mark Catholic School - 1013 Eastwood Rd., Wilmington, NC 28403 t) 910-452-2800 secretary@smcsnc.org smcsnc.org Tripp Burton, Prin.; Stds.: 518; Pr. Tchrs.: 1; Lay Tchrs.: 40
WILSON
Church of St. Therese - 700 Nash St., N.E., Wilson, NC 27893-3047 t) 252-237-3019 st.therese.wilson@gmail.com sttheresewilson.com Very Rev. Jeffrey A. Bowker, Pst.; Dcn. Michel du Sablon; CRP Stds.: 187
WINDSOR
Holy Spirit Catholic Church - 403 Belmont St., Windsor, NC 27983; Mailing: P.O. Box 1394, Windsor, NC 27983 t) 252-794-5086 holyspiritwindsor@gmail.com holyspiritwindsor.org Rev. Chester Artysiewicz, G.H.M, Admin.; CRP Stds.: 4
WRIGHTSVILLE BEACH
St. Therese Catholic Parish of Wrightsville - 209 S. Lumina Ave., Wrightsville Beach, NC 28480 t) 910-256-2471 office@catholicwb.org www.catholicwb.org Rev. William J. Upah, Pst.; CRP Stds.: 48

SCHOOLS: PRESCHOOL THRU HIGH SCHOOL

SCHOOLS

STATE OF NORTH CAROLINA

RALEIGH
Diocese of Raleigh Virtual School, Inc. - 7200 Stonehenge Dr., Raleigh, NC 27613 t) 984-900-3416 dorvs@raldioc.org Lytia Reese, Pres.; Stds.: 4

HIGH SCHOOLS

STATE OF NORTH CAROLINA

DURHAM
***Cristo Rey Research Triangle High School** - (PRV) (Grades 9-12) 334 Blackwell St., Ste. G100, Durham, NC 27701 t) (984) 983-7010 james.mcpherson@cristoreyrt.org cristoreyrt.org James McPherson, CFO/Director of Business Operations; Stds.: 138; Lay Tchrs.: 24
GREENVILLE
St. John Paul II Catholic High School - (PRV) 2725 E. 14th St., Greenville, NC 27858; Mailing: 3250A Dickinson Ave., Greenville, NC 27834 t) 252-215-1224 dsommer@jp2highschool.com www.jp2highschool.com Katie Stanley, Prin.; Stds.: 204; Lay Tchrs.: 21
RALEIGH
Cardinal Gibbons High School - (DIO) 1401 Edwards Mill Rd., Raleigh, NC 27607 t) 919-834-1625 nbarkan@cghsnc.org www.cghsnc.org Jeff Bell, Prin.; Rev. Luke Rawicki, L.C., Chap.; Tripp Reade, Librn.; Stds.: 1,562; Pr. Tchrs.: 1; Lay Tchrs.: 163
***St. Thomas More Academy, Inc.** - (PRV) 3109 Spring Forest Rd., Raleigh, NC 27616 t) 919-878-7640 admissions@stmacademy.org www.stmacademy.org Dcn. Bradley Evans Watkins, Headmaster; Stds.: 245; Lay Tchrs.: 18

INSTITUTIONS LOCATED IN DIOCESE

CAMPUS MINISTRY / NEWMAN CENTERS [CAM]

CHAPEL HILL
Newman Catholic Student Center - 218 Pittsboro St., Chapel Hill, NC 27516 t) 919-929-3730 info@uncnewman.org www.uncnewman.org Rev. Timothy Kulbicki, O.F.M. Conv., Pst.;
DURHAM
Duke Catholic Center - 404 Chapel Dr., Page Bldg., Ste. 309, Durham, NC 27708; Mailing: Box 90976, Durham, NC 27708 t) 919-684-3354 catholic@duke.edu catholic.duke.edu Rev. Juan Jose Hernandez, L.C., Dir.;
ELON
Elon University - 100 Campus Dr, Elon, NC 27244; Mailing: Campus Box 2960, Elon, NC 27244-2010 t) 336-278-7355 ptremblay@elon.edu org.elon.edu/ccm Rev. Peter C. Tremblay, O.F.M.Conv., Chap.; Trung Huynh-Duc, Dir.;
GREENVILLE
Newman Catholic Student Center at East Carolina University - 953 E. 10th St., Greenville, NC 27858 t) 910-391-8609 chaplain@ecunewman.org; assistant@ecunewman.org www.ecunewman.org Rev. Ian C. Van Heusen, Chap.;
RALEIGH
Campbell University Catholic Campus Ministry - 7200 Stonehenge Dr., c/o Ian Van Heusen, Raleigh, NC 27613 t) (252) 757-1991 Rev. Ian C. Van Heusen, Chap.;
NC State University Catholic Campus Ministry - 1720 Hillborough St., Raleigh, NC 27605; Mailing: PO Box 10302, Raleigh, NC 27605 t) 203-530-6908 jcurran@legionaries.org www.catholicpack.org Rev. John Curran, L.C., Chap.;
WILMINGTON
Newman Catholic Student Center (Catholic Student Center UNC-W) - 4802 College Acres Dr., Wilmington, NC 28403; Mailing: UNC-W Station, P.O. Box 20044, Wilmington, NC 28403 t) 910-792-0507 mcnamarar@uncw.edu; uncw.ccm@gmail.com www.newman-uncw.org Rev. Gregory Anatuanya (Nigeria), Chap.; Sr. Rosemary G. McNamara, S.U., Dir.;

CATHOLIC CHARITIES [CCH]

RALEIGH
Catholic Charities of the Diocese of Raleigh, Inc. - 7200 Stonehenge Dr., Raleigh, NC 27613-1620 t) 984-900-3117 lisa.perkins@ccharitiesdor.org catholiccharitiesraleigh.org Lisa E. Perkins, CEO; Asstd. Annu.: 158,836; Staff: 56
Albemarle Office - 1453 N. Road St., Elizabeth City, NC 27909 t) 252-426-7717 lisa.higgins@ccharitiesdor.org Barkley Sample, Dir.;
Cape Fear Office - 20 N. 4th St. Ste. 300, Harrelson Center, Wilmington, NC 28401 t) 910-251-8130 emilie.hart@ccharitiesdor.org Emilie Hart, Dir.;
Fayetteville Office - 726 Ramsey St., Ste. 10 & 11, Fayetteville, NC 28301 t) 910-424-2020 Barkley Sample, Dir.;
New Bern Office - 502 Middle St., New Bern, NC 28560; Mailing: P.O. Box 826, New Bern, NC 28563 t) 252-638-2188 Barkley Sample, Dir.;
Newton Grove Office - 4057 US-70 BUS, Clayton, NC 27520 t) 919-821-9750 gabby.amos@ccharitiesdor.org Barkley Sample, Dir.;
Piedmont Office - 2020 Chapel Hill Rd., Ste. 30, Durham, NC 27707 t) 919-286-1964 Jeremy Ireland, Dir.;
Raleigh Office - 3000 Highwoods Blvd., Ste. 128, Raleigh, NC 27604 t) 919-790-8533 Barkley Sample, Dir.;
Tar River Office - 1746 Union St., Greenville, NC 27834 t) 252-355-5111 maria.bick@ccharitiesdor.org Barkley Sample, Dir.;

CONVENTS, MONASTERIES, AND RESIDENCES FOR WOMEN [CON]

CHAPEL HILL
Sisters, Servants of the Immaculate Heart of Mary - 222 Cosgrove Ave., Chapel Hill, NC 27514 t) 919-240-5612 cgellings@aol.com ihmsisters.org Srs.: 1
JACKSONVILLE
Sisters of St. Ursula - 518 East Ct., Jacksonville, NC 28546; Mailing: 205 Chaney Ave., Jacksonville, NC 28540 t) 910-389-1742 bmcady@aol.com Sr. Barbara Marie Cady, S.U., Contact; Srs.: 2
TARBORO
Congregation of St. Agnes - 4934 Howard Ave. Ext., Tarboro, NC 27886 t) 252-823-0540 tcoutreach@tarboronc.com csasisters.org Srs.: 1

ENDOWMENTS / FOUNDATIONS / TRUSTS [EFT]

RALEIGH
Catholic Community Deposit and Loan Fund, Inc. - 7200 Stonehedge Dr., Raleigh, NC 27613 t) 984-900-3140 Dr. Russell C. Elmayan, CFO/CAO; Susan Wrenn-Callahan, Controller;
The Foundation of the Roman Catholic Diocese of Raleigh, Inc. - 4700 Homewood Ct., Ste. 320, Raleigh, NC 27609 t) 919-568-1065 maureen@foundationdor.org;

alicia@foundationdor.org www.foundationdor.org Maureen O'Keeffe Lindgren, Exec.;

HOSPITALS / HEALTH SERVICES [HOS]

SOUTHERN PINES

St. Joseph of the Pines, Inc. - 100 Gossman Dr., Ste. B, Southern Pines, NC 28387 t) 910-246-3100 lportfleet@sjp.org www.sjp.org Lynnette RauvolaBouta, Chap.; Scott Brewton, Vice. Pres.; Katie Shumaker, Bus. Mgr.;

MISCELLANEOUS [MIS]

FAYETTEVILLE

LIFE St. Joseph of the Pines, Inc. - 4900 Raeford Rd., Fayetteville, NC 28304 t) 910-483-4911 joyce.alexander-hines@trinity-health.org lifestjosephofthepines.org/ Connie Goodson, Admin.;

RALEIGH

Catholic Housing Corporation - 7200 Stonehenge Dr., Raleigh, NC 27613-1620 t) 984-900-3140 russ.elmayan@raldioc.org Dr. Russell C. Elmayan, CFO/CAO; Frank L. Tortora III, Gen. Counsel;

The Clergy Retirement Plan of Diocese of Raleigh - 7200 Stonehenge Dr., Raleigh, NC 27613-1620 t) 919-821-9711 gary.rosia@raldioc.org www.dioceseofraleigh.org Gary Rosia, Dir.;

Vocations Office - 7200 Stonehenge Dr., Raleigh, NC 27613-1620 t) 984-900-3104 x30002 vocations@raldioc.org ncpriest.org Rev. James J. Magee III, Promoter of Vocations;

SOUTHERN PINES

St. Joseph of the Pines, Inc. - 100 Gossman Dr., Ste. B, Southern Pines, NC 28387 t) 910-246-1000; (910) 245-3100 (Exec. Asst.); 910-246-1036 (Chap.) lynnette.rauvolabouta@trinity-health.org; scott.brewton@trinity-health.org www.sjp.org Lynnette RauvolaBouta, Chap.; Scott Brewton, Vice. Pres.; Katie Shumaker, Bus. Mgr.;

MONASTERIES AND RESIDENCES FOR PRIESTS AND BROTHERS [MON]

ELON

Conventual Franciscans - 1236 Westbrook Ave., Elon, NC 27244 t) 336-446-6753 catholic@netpath.net www.blessedsacramentnc.org Rev. Vincent P. Rubino, O.F.M.Conv.; Priests: 3

PITTSBORO

Our Lady of Guadalupe Friary - 1283 Thompson St., Pittsboro, NC 27312; Mailing: P.O. Box 1638, Pittsboro, NC 27312 t) 919-545-5600 fr.julio.martinez@raldioc.org www.franciscanseast.org Rev. Julio A. Martinez, O.F.M. Conv., Supr.; Brs.: 2; Priests: 6

RALEIGH

Jesuit Community - 1017 Ivy Ln, Raleigh, NC 27609 t) 919-865-5700 www.saintraphael.org Rev. Bruce Bavinger, S.J., Supr.; Rev. Lawrence Searles, S.J.; Rev. Thomas M Simisky, S.J.; Priests: 3

NURSING / REHABILITATION / CONVALESCENCE / ELDERLY CARE [NUR]

SOUTHERN PINES

St. Joseph of the Pines Retirement Villa - 100 Gossman Dr., Ste. B, Southern Pines, NC 28387 t) 910-246-1000 katelyn.shumaker@trinity-health.org www.sjp.org Scott Brewton, Vice. Pres.;

PRESCHOOLS / CHILDCARE CENTERS [PRE]

APEX

Saint Andrew Early Childhood Center - 3008 Old Raleigh Rd., Apex, NC 27502 t) 919-387-8656 ecc@saintandrew.org www.saintandrew.org Nancy Wujek, Dir.; Stds.: 150; Lay Tchrs.: 29

CARY

St. Michael Early Childhood Center - 804 High House Rd., Cary, NC 27513 t) 919-468-6110 preschool@stmcary.org www.stmichaelpreschool.com Lisa Ciesla, Dir.; Stds.: 135; Lay Tchrs.: 12

RALEIGH

St. Raphael Preschool - 5801 Falls of the Neuse Rd., Raleigh, NC 27609 t) 919-865-5717 bjcady@saintraphael.org straphaelpreschool.org Sarah Macey, Dir.; Stds.: 141; Lay Tchrs.: 23

SPECIAL CARE FACILITIES [SPF]

RALEIGH

Catholic Parish Outreach - 2013 N. Raleigh Blvd., Raleigh, NC 27604 t) 919-873-0245 kelly.rappl@ccharitiesdor.org www.cporaleigh.org A program of Catholic Charities of the Diocese of Raleigh Barkley Sample, Dir.; Asstd. Annu.: 59,377; Staff: 5

An asterisk (*) denotes an organization that has established tax-exempt status directly with the IRS and is not covered by the USCCB Group Ruling.

Diocese of Rapid City

(Dioecesis Rapidopolitana)

MOST REVEREND PETER M. MUHICH

Bishop of Rapid City; ordained September 29, 1989; appointed Bishop of Rapid City May 12, 2020; installed July 9, 2020.

Chancery Office: 225 Main St., Ste. 100, Rapid City, SD 57701. T: 605-343-3541; F: 605-348-7985. chancery@diorc.org

Square Miles 43,000.

Formerly the Diocese of Lead.

Erected August 4, 1902; See transferred to Rapid City, August 1, 1930.

Comprises the Counties of Bennett, Butte, Corson, Custer, Dewey, Fall River, Gregory, Haakon, Harding, Jackson, Jones, Lawrence, Lyman, Meade, Mellette, Pennington, Perkins, Stanley, Oglala Lakota, Todd, Tripp and Ziebach in the State of South Dakota.

For legal titles of parishes and diocesan institutions, consult the Chancery Office.

STATISTICAL OVERVIEW

Personnel

Bishop	1
Priests: Diocesan Active in Diocese	26
Priests: Retired, Sick or Absent	8
Number of Diocesan Priests	34
Religious Priests in Diocese	12
Total Priests in your Diocese	46
Extern Priests in Diocese	3
Ordinations:	
Diocesan Priests	1
Permanent Deacons in Diocese	32
Total Brothers	3
Total Sisters	25

Parishes

Parishes	58
With Resident Pastor:	
Resident Diocesan Priests	21
Resident Religious Priests	5
Without Resident Pastor:	
Administered by Priests	32
Missions	22
Pastoral Centers	4
Professional Ministry Personnel:	
Brothers	3
Sisters	12
Lay Ministers	45

Welfare

Catholic Hospitals	1
Total Assisted	27,203
Specialized Homes	1
Total Assisted	423
Special Centers for Social Services	2
Total Assisted	5,551

Educational

Diocesan Students in Other Seminaries	11
Total Seminarians	11
High Schools, Diocesan and Parish	1
Total Students	190
High Schools, Private	1
Total Students	170
Elementary Schools, Diocesan and Parish	2
Total Students	555
Elementary Schools, Private	3
Total Students	328
Catechesis / Religious Education:	
High School Students	390
Elementary Students	1,868
Total Students under Catholic Instruction	3,512
Teachers in Diocese:	
Priests	2
Scholastics	2
Brothers	1
Sisters	5
Lay Teachers	132

Vital Statistics

Receptions into the Church:	
Infant Baptism Totals	299
Minor Baptism Totals	31
Adult Baptism Totals	18
Received into Full Communion	39
First Communions	328
Confirmations	361
Marriages:	
Catholic	52
Interfaith	24
Total Marriages	76
Deaths	557
Total Catholic Population	23,668
Total Population	230,087

LEADERSHIP

Chancery Office - t) 605-343-3541 chancery@diorc.org
Chancellor - Sr. Christine Hernandez, SCTJM;
Diocesan Tribunal -
Officialis - Rev. Timothy S. Hoag;
Diocesan Consultors - Rev. Bryan Sorensen, Buffalo; Rev. Daniel Juelfs, Piedmont; Rev. Kerry Prendiville, Rapid City;
Deaneries - Rev. Kerry Prendiville, Rapid City; Rev. Msgr. Michael Woster, Spearfish; Rev. Ronald S. Seminara, S.J., Pine Ridge;
Presbyteral Council - Rev. Kerry Prendiville, Rapid City; Rev. Msgr. Michael Woster, Spearfish; Rev. Ronald S. Seminara, S.J., Pine Ridge;
Vicar for Clergy - Rev. Kerry Prendiville, Vicar;

OFFICES AND DIRECTORS

Archives - Kathy Cordes, Archivist;
Campaign for Human Development - Germaine Little Bear, Contact;
Chief Financial Officer/Administrator of Temporal Affairs - Richard Soulek;
Development Program - Todd Tobin, Dir.;
Diocesan Finance Council - Dan Duffy; Timothy Frost; Rev. Adam Hofer;
Director of Communications - Jacques Daniel;
West River Catholic Newspaper - Laurie Hallstrom, Editor;
Office of Pastoral Ministries - Sr. Rachel Gosda, SCTJM, Dir.;
Diocesan Office of Faith Formation - Sr. Rachel Gosda, SCTJM, Dir.;
Diocesan Office of Ministry to Youth and Young Adults - Jacques Daniel, Dir.;
Native Ministry Office - Germaine Little Bear;
Office of Family Life - Amy Julian, Dir.;
Permanent Diaconate Program - Rev. Brian Patrick Christensen, Dir.; Dcn. Gregory Sass, Asst. Dir.;
Propagation of the Faith - Dcn. Greg Palmer, Contact;
Superintendent of Schools - Barbara Honeycutt;
Victim Assistance Coordinator - t) 605-209-3418 Barbara Scherr;
Vocation Program - Rev. Mark McCormick, Dir.;

PARISHES, MISSIONS, AND CLERGY

STATE OF SOUTH DAKOTA

BELLE FOURCHE

St. Paul - 855 Fifth Ave., Belle Fourche, SD 57717-1701 t) 605-723-3226 char@stpaulbf.com; tina@stpaulbf.com Rev. Msgr. Michael Woster, Pst.; Rev. Zane Pekron, Par. Vicar; Tina Barrie, DRE; Char Davis, Bus. Mgr.; CRP Stds.: 43

BISON

Blessed Sacrament - 202 Rogers St., Bison, SD 57620; Mailing: PO Box 382, Bison, SD 57620 t) 605-244-5547 Attended from St. Anthony in Buffalo. Rev. Bryan Sorensen, Pst.; Sara Stadler, DRE; CRP Stds.: 34

BONESTEEL

Immaculate Conception - 607 Mellette St, Bonesteel, SD 57317; Mailing: PO Box 376, Bonesteel, SD 57317-0376 t) 605-654-2204 (Office); 605-605-6542 (Parish Hall) imconsta@gwtc.net Served from St. Joseph, Gregory. Mary Ann Koenig, DRE; Rev. Jonathan Dillon, Pst.; CRP Stds.: 30

BUFFALO

St. Anthony - 404 4th St. W., Buffalo, SD 57720; Mailing: PO Box 85, Buffalo, SD 57720 t) 605-375-3438 (Rectory); 605-375-3439 (Parish Hall) Affiliated with Blessed Sacrament, Bison and St. Isidore in Ralph Rev. Bryan Sorensen, Pst.; Yolanda Martian, DRE; CRP Stds.: 44

St. Isidore, Ralph - General Delivery, Ralph, SD 57650 t) (605) 375-3438 (Buffalo - St. Anthony)

BURKE

Sacred Heart - 934 Lincoln Ave., Burke, SD 57523; Mailing: PO Box 354, Burke, SD 57523 t) 605-775-2532 Served from St. Joseph, Gregory. Rev. Jonathan Dillon, Pst.; Annie York, DRE; CRP Stds.: 41

COLOME

St. Isidore - 301 Carr St., Colome, SD 57528; Mailing: 302 W. 4th St., Winner, SD 57580 t) 605-842-3520; 605-842-3560 parishsec@gwtc.net catholictripp.org Served from Immaculate Conception, Winner. Rev. Zane Pekron, Pst.; CRP Stds.: 18

CUSTER

St. John the Baptist - 449 Harney St., Custer, SD 57730-0632; Mailing: PO Box 632, Custer, SD 57730 t) 605-673-4426 stjohns@gwtc.net www.custercatholic.org Attended from St. Anthony, Hot Springs. Rev. Collins Igwilo (Nigeria), Pst.; CRP Stds.: 55

DEADWOOD

St. Ambrose - 760 Main St., Deadwood, SD 57732; Mailing: 141 Siever St., Lead, SD 57754 t) 605-584-2002 www.stambrosedwd.com attended from St. Patrick's in Lead Rev. Leo Hausmann, Pst.; Valerie Minihan, DRE; CRP Stds.: 2

EAGLE BUTTE

All Saints - 109 E. Heritage Ave., Eagle Butte, SD 57625-0110; Mailing: PO Box 110, Eagle Butte, SD 57625 t) 605-964-3391 pastor@allsaintsparish.online www.allsaintsparish.online Cheyenne River Reservation Parishes Rev. John Paul Trask, Pst.; CRP Stds.: 36

Sacred Heart - 410 1st St., Dupree, SD 57623 t) 605-365-5273 Dupree, SD

St. Joseph, Ridgeview - 220 6th St. W., Ridgeview, SD 57652

St. Catherine, Promise - Promise Rd., Promise, SD 57601

St. Therese - Whitehorse Rd., White Horse, SD 57661

St. Joseph, Cherry Creek - Main Rd., Cherry Creek, SD 57553

Sacred Heart, Red Scaffold - BIA Hwy. 6, Red Scaffold, SD 57626

Immaculate Conception, Bridger - Unnamed Road, Bridger, SD 57748

Cheyenne River Reservation - 109 E. Heritage Ave., Eagle Butte, SD 57625; Mailing: PO Box 110, Eagle Butte, SD 57625-0100 t) 605-964-3391 pastor@allsaintsparish.online All Saints Parish, Eagle Butte and mission parishes. Rev. John Paul Trask, Pst.;

FAIRFAX

St. Anthony's - 2nd St., Fairfax, SD 57335-0186; Mailing: PO Box 186, Fairfax, SD 57335-0186 t) 605-654-2204; 605-835-9290 Served from St. Joseph's, Gregory. Rev. Jonathan Dillon, Pst.;

FAITH

St. Joseph - 405 S 5th Ave. W., Faith, SD 57626; Mailing: PO Box 307, Faith, SD 57626-0307 t) 605-967-2201 stjoseph@faithsd.com Mandy Brown, DRE; Rev. Janusz Korban, Pst.; Cathy Smith, DRE; CRP Stds.: 32

St. Anthony in Red Owl - Red Owl Rd, 9 miles north of Hwy 34, Red Owl, SD 57626 t) (605) 967-2201 (St. Joseph, Faith)

St. Joseph, Mud Butte - 16601 Old 212, Mud Butte, SD 57758

FORT PIERRE

St. John - 206 W. Main Ave., Fort Pierre, SD 57532 t) 605-223-2176 stjohnsfortpierre.org Rev. Ron Garry, Pst.; Josie Huck, DRE; CRP Stds.: 86

St. Anthony of Padua, Draper - 132 S. Elm Ave., Draper, SD 57531; Mailing: 206 W. Main Ave., Ft. Pierre, SD 57532-6604 t) 605-225-2176 Served by St. John, Ft. Pierre

GREGORY

St. Joseph - 414 Church Ave., Gregory, SD 57533 t) 605-835-9290 Rev. Jonathan Dillon, Pst.; Lisa King, DRE; Kimberly Veskrna, Bus. Mgr.; CRP Stds.: 54

HERMOSA

St. Michael's - 13480 Hwy. 40, Hermosa, SD 57744; Mailing: 520 Cathedral Dr., Rapid City, SD 57701-5499 t) 605-342-0507 bchristensen@diorc.org stmichaels-hermosa.com Attended by Cathedral of Our Lady of Perpetual Help, Rapid City. Rev. Brian Patrick Christensen, Pst.; Rev. Leonard Ssenyonjo (Uganda), Par. Vicar; Elizabeth Strain, Bus. Mgr.; Rev. Matthew Fallgren, Par. Vicar; CRP Stds.: 17

HILL CITY

St. Rose of Lima - 305 Pine Ave., Hill City, SD 57745; Mailing: PO Box 236, Hill City, SD 57745-0236 t) 605-574-2479 bulletin.k.hc@gmail.com www.centralblackhillscatholic.com Dcn. Robert Ackerman; Nancy Ronning, DRE; Rev. Mark E. Horn, Pst.; Robert Kinyon, Seminarian, Pastoral Year; CRP Stds.: 66

Our Lady of Mt. Carmel - 1014 Madill St., Keystone, SD 57751

HOT SPRINGS

St. Anthony of Padua - 538 University Ave., Hot Springs, SD 57747; Mailing: PO Box 969, Hot Springs, SD 57747-0969 t) 605-745-3393 (Office); 605-745-3278 (After Hours Emergency) sohillscatholic@gwtc.net stanthonyhotsprings.org Affiliated with St. John in Custer and St. James in Edgemont. Rev. Grant Gerlach, Pst.; Dcn. Thomas Adams; Dcn. James Hayes; Dcn. Craig Pearson; CRP Stds.: 29

St. James the Apostle - 310 3rd Ave., Edgemont, SD 57735; Mailing: PO Box 568, Edgemont, SD 57735 t) 605-662-7801 stjames@goldenwest.net Rev. Collins Igwilo (Nigeria), Pst.;

KADOKA

Our Lady of Victory - 600 Maple St., Kadoka, SD 57543; Mailing: PO Box 567, Martin, SD 57551 t) 605-837-2219 Served from Our Lady of the Sacred Heart, Martin. Rev. Tyler Dennis, Pst.;

KENEL

Assumption of the Blessed Virgin Mary - Kenel Rd., Kenel, SD 57642; Mailing: PO Box 539, McLaughlin, SD 57642-0539 t) 605-823-4401; 605-823-2484 (Convent) jhoerter@diorc.org Served from St. Bernard, McLaughlin. Rev. James Hoerter, Pst.; Sr. Jacqueline Schroeder, OSF, DRE; CRP Stds.: 1

KENNEBEC

St. Michael's - 300 Hotchkiss St., Kennebec, SD 57544; Mailing: PO Box 185, Lower Brule, SD 57548-0185 t) 605-473-5335 pastteam@gwtc.net Served from St. Mary, Lower Brule. Rev. Jean Claude Mbassi, SCJ, Pst.; CRP Stds.: 3

LEAD

St. Patrick's - 141 Siever St., Lead, SD 57754 t) 605-584-2002 affiliated with St. Ambrose in Deadwood Rev. Leo Hausmann, Pst.; Valerie Minihan, DRE; CRP Stds.: 20

LEMMON

St. Mary's - 410 2nd Ave W, Lemmon, SD 57638; Mailing: PO Box 210, Lemmon, SD 57638-0210 t) 605-374-3767 Affiliated with Sacred Heart in Morristown, St. Bonaventure in McIntosh, St. Michael in Watauga Rev. Adam Hofer, Pst.; Jenny Dirk, DRE; CRP Stds.: 53

LOWER BRULE

Lower Brule Reservation - 508 Gall St, Lower Brule, SD 57548; Mailing: PO Box 185, Lower Brule, SD 57548-0185 t) 605-473-5487 (Residence); 605-473-5335 (Office) pastateam@gwtc.net Lower Brule Reservation Ministry. Serves parishes in Lower Brule, Kennebec, Reliance. Rev. Jean Claude Mbassi, SCJ, Pst.;

St. Mary's - 508 Gall St., Lower Brule, SD 57548; Mailing: P.O. Box 185, Lower Brule, SD 57548 t) 605-473-5335 pastteam@gwtc.net Affiliated with St. Michael in Kennebec and St. Mary in Reliance Rev. Jean Claude Mbassi, SCJ, Pst.; Rev. Christianus Hendrick, S.C.J., Assoc. Pst.; Dcn. Steve McLaughlin;

MANDERSON

St. Agnes - 1892 BIA 33, Manderson, SD 57756; Mailing: PO Box 88, Manderson, SD 57756-0088 t) 605-867-2267 joycetibbitts@redcloudschool.org

Served by Holy Rosary Mission, Pine Ridge. Rev. Brad A. Held, S.J., Pst.; Rev. Edmund Yainao, SJ, Assoc. Pst.; Joyce Tibbitts, Parish Life Coord.;

MARTIN

Our Lady of the Sacred Heart - 802 1st Ave., Martin, SD 57551; Mailing: PO Box 567, Martin, SD 57551-0567 t) 605-685-6232 olshofmartin@gmail.com olshmartin.org Affiliated with Our Lady of Victory, Kadoka Rev. Tyler Dennis, Pst.; CRP Stds.: 17

MCINTOSH

St. Bonaventure's - 140 1st Ave. W., McIntosh, SD 57641; Mailing: PO Box 320, McIntosh, SD 57641-0320 t) 605-374-3767 stmarys@sdplains.com Served from St. Mary, Lemmon Rev. Adam Hofer, Pst.; Sue Bubbers, DRE; CRP Stds.: 12

MCLAUGHLIN

St. Bernard - 410 1st Ave. E., McLaughlin, SD 57642; Mailing: PO Box 539, McLaughlin, SD 57642 t) 605-823-4401 (Rectory); 605-823-2484 (Convent) jhoerter@diorc.org Rev. James Hoerter, Pst.; Sr. Jacqueline Schroeder, OSF, DRE; CRP Stds.: 13

St Aloysius, Bullhead - 401 Tatanka St, Bullhead, SD 57642

MIDLAND

St. William - 205 Elm St., Midland, SD 57553; Mailing: PO Box 309, Philip, SD 57567 t) 605-859-2664 (Sacred Heart Office); (605) 843-2544 (St. William Church) drc-philip@gwtc.net Served from Sacred Heart, Philip. Rev. Grant Gerlach, Pst.; CRP Stds.: 4

MISSION

St. Thomas the Apostle - 150 Jefferson St., Mission, SD 57555; Mailing: PO Box 151, Mission, SD 57555 t) 605-856-4618 Served from St. Francis Mission. Rev. Ronald S. Seminara, S.J., Pst.;

MORRISTOWN

Sacred Heart - 308 2nd Ave E., Morristown, SD 57645; Mailing: PO Box 210, Lemmon, SD 57638-0210 t) 605-374-3767 Served from St. Mary, Lemmon Rev. Adam Hofer, Pst.; CRP Stds.: 11

MURDO

St. Martin - 509 2nd St., Murdo, SD 57559; Mailing: PO Box 399, Presho, SD 57568 t) 605-895-2534 Served from Christ the King, Presho. Rev. John Heying, Pst.; CRP Stds.: 6

NEW UNDERWOOD

St. John the Evangelist - 106 S. A St., New Underwood, SD 57761-0305; Mailing: PO Box 305, New Underwood, SD 57761-0305 t) 605-342-1556 (St. Therese, Rapid City) sttherese@diorc.org Served from St. Therese, Rapid City. Rev. Kerry Prendiville, Pst.; CRP Stds.: 11

NEWELL

St. Mary Star of the Sea - 306 6th St., Newell, SD 57760; Mailing: PO Box 72, Newell, SD 57760-0072 t) 605-720-3579 stfrancis@rushmore.com Served from St. Francis of Assisi, Sturgis Rev. Timothy William Castor, Pst.; CRP Stds.: 20

PHILIP

Sacred Heart - 307 W. Elm, Philip, SD 57567; Mailing: PO Box 309, Philip, SD 57567 t) 605-859-2664 drc-philip@gwtc.net Affiliated with St. William, Midland and St. Mary, Milesville Rev. Grant Gerlach, Pst.; Dcn. Lloyd Frein; Faye Piroutek, Bus. Mgr.; CRP Stds.: 42

St. Mary, Milesville - 203rd St., Milesville, SD 57553

PIEDMONT

Our Lady of the Black Hills - 12365 Sturgis Rd., Piedmont, SD 57769-2007 t) 605-787-5168 olbh@olbh.org olbh.org Rev. Andrzej Wyrostek, Pst.; Dcn. John Osnes; Dcn. Gregory Sass; CRP Stds.: 133

PINE RIDGE

Sacred Heart - 30238 US Hwy. 18, Pine Ridge, SD 57770; Mailing: PO Box 359, Pine Ridge, SD 57770-0359 t) 605-867-5551 Attended from Holy Rosary Mission. Angie Stover, Bus. Mgr.; Carol LaDeaux, DRE; CRP Stds.: 3

PRESHO

Christ the King - 409 S. Fir Ave., Presho, SD 57568; Mailing: PO Box 399, Presho, SD 57568-0399 t) 605-895-2534 Affiliated with St. Martin, Murdo and Sacred Heart, White River Rev. John Heying, Pst.; CRP Stds.: 9

RAPID CITY

Cathedral of Our Lady of Perpetual Help - 520 Cathedral Dr., Rapid City, SD 57701-5499 t) 605-342-0507 cathedral@cathedralolph.org www.cathedralolph.org Affiliated with St Michael in Hermosa, Rapid City Newman Center Rev. Leonard Ssenyonjo (Uganda), Par. Vicar; Rev. Brian Patrick Christensen, Pst.; Rev. Matthew Fallgren, Assoc. Pst.; Dcn. Raul Daniel; Dcn. George Gladfelter; Dcn. James Scherr; Rev. Ed Vanorny, In Res.; Elizabeth Strain, Bus. Mgr.; Brett Eckert, Dir., Evangelization & Catechesis; CRP Stds.: 130

Rapid City Catholic Newman Center - 316 E. Kansas City St., Rapid City, SD 57701 t) 605-716-4130 frank@rcnewmancenter.com www.rcnewmancenter.com Rev. Mark McCormick, Chap.; Frank Birkholt, Dir.;

Blessed Sacrament - 4500 Jackson Blvd., Rapid City, SD 57702-4999 t) 605-342-3336 www.blessedsacramentchurch.org Rev. Timothy S. Hoag, Pst.; Rev. Tony Grossenburg, Par. Vicar; Dcn. Robert Hrabe; Dcn. Larry Kopriva; Dcn. Greg Palmer; Michael Weber, Liturgy Dir.; Ruth Zagala, Bus. Mgr.; Bridget Grapentine, Dir., Evangelization & Catechesis; CRP Stds.: 174

Immaculate Conception Church of Rapid City - 922 Fifth St., Rapid City, SD 57701; Mailing: P.O. Box 289, Rapid City, SD 57709-0289 t) 605-341-1578 office@fssp-rapidcity.org www.fssp-rapidcity.org Personal parish served by the Priestly Fraternity of St. Peter. Sacraments celebrated according to liturgical norms of 1962. Rev. Gregory Bartholomew, FSSP, Pst.; Jennifer Esposito, Bus. Mgr.; CRP Stds.: 60

St. Isaac Jogues - 211 Knollwood Dr., Rapid City, SD 57709-1304; Mailing: PO Box 1304, Rapid City, SD 57709-1304 t) 605-343-2165 Rev. Ed Witt, S.J., Pst.; Dcn. Luis Usera Sr.; CRP Stds.: 54

Mother Butler Center - 231 Knollwood Dr, Rapid City, SD 57701 Catechetical and Social Center for Indians.

St. Therese the Little Flower - 532 Adams St., Rapid City, SD 57701 t) 605-342-1556 staintheresechurch.org Formerly known as The Church of St. John the Evangelist. Rev. Kerry Prendiville, Pst.; Rev. Francis Nsubuga (Uganda), Assoc. Pst.; Dcn. Charles Rausch; Dcn. Don Moore; Bobby Myers, DRE; CRP Stds.: 66

RELIANCE

St. Mary's - 32984 SD Hwy. 47, Reliance, SD 57569; Mailing: PO Box 185, Lower Brule, SD 57548-0185 t) 605-473-5335 pastteam@gwtc.net Served from St. Mary's, Lower Brule. Rev. Jean Claude Mbassi, SCJ, Pst.; CRP Stds.: 8

ROSEBUD

St. Bridget - 130 Rosebud St., Rosebud, SD 57570; Mailing: PO Box 340, Rosebud, SD 57570-0340 t) 605-747-2361 sfmission.org Served by St. Francis Mission. Rev. James Lafontaine, S.J., Assoc. Pst.; CRP Stds.: 167

SPEARFISH

St. Joseph - 844 N 5th St., Spearfish, SD 57783-2005 t) 605-642-2306 michele@stjosephspearfish.com www.stjosephspearfish.com Affiliated with St. Paul, Belle Fourche Rev. Kevin Lee Achbach, Pst.; Rev. Joshua Lee, Par. Vicar; Dcn. Ray Klein; Andrew Graupmann, DRE; CRP Stds.: 95

ST. FRANCIS

St. Charles Borromeo - 350 Oak St., St. Francis, SD 57572; Mailing: Box 499, St. Francis, SD 57572 t) 605-747-2436 (CRP); 605-747-2361 sfmission.org Served from St. Francis Mission Rev. James Lafontaine, S.J., Assoc. Pst.; Jenny Black Bear, DRE;

St. Agnes - #1 W. Service Rd., Parmelee, SD 57566 t) (605) 747-2361 (St. Francis Mission) Served from St. Francis Mission Rev. James Lafontaine, S.J., Assoc. Pst.;

St. Francis Mission - 350 Oak St., St. Francis, SD 57572; Mailing: PO Box 499, St. Francis, SD 57572-0499 t) 605-747-2361 info@sfmission.net www.sfmission.org Serving the Rosebud Indian Reservation. Parishes in St. Francis, Rosebud, Parmelee, Mission. Sapa Un Catholic Academy. Rev. Ronald S. Seminara, S.J., Pst.; Rodney Bordeaux, Pres.; Harold Compton, COO; Rev. James Lafontaine, S.J., Dir.;

STURGIS

St. Francis of Assisi - 1049 Howard St., Sturgis, SD 57785-1999 t) 605-720-3579 (Office/Rectory) stfrancisccd@rushmore.com; stfrancis@rushmore.com saintfrancisscatholicchurch.weconnect.com Affiliated with St. Mary Star of the Sea, Newell Rev. Timothy William Castor, Pst.; Dcn. Tom Murphy, DRE; Kristi Palmer, Youth Min.; Ronda Snyder, Bus. Mgr.; CRP Stds.: 71

TIMBER LAKE

Holy Cross - 511 E. St., Timber Lake, SD 57656; Mailing: P.O. Box 70, Timber Lake, SD 57656-0070 t) 605-865-3653 holycrosschurch57656@gmail.com holycrosstimberlake.com Affiliated with Holy Rosary, Trail City and St. Mary, Isabel Rev. Brian Lane, Pst.; LuAnn Lindskov, DRE; Sarah Schweitzer, DRE; Lynn Hahne, RCIA Coord.; CRP Stds.: 72

St. Mary, Isabel - 220 E. Idaho, Isabel, SD 57633; Mailing: PO Box 70, Timber Lake, SD 57656-0070 Served by Holy Cross, Timber Lake

Queen of the Holy Rosary - 200 1st Ave W, Trail City, SD 57657; Mailing: PO Box 70, Timber Lake, SD 57656-0070

WALL

St. Patrick's - 701 Norris St., Wall, SD 57790-0405; Mailing: PO Box 405, Wall, SD 57790-0405 t) 605-279-2542 stpatrickwall@gwtc.net Affiliated with St. Margaret, Lakeside Rev. Tyler Dennis; CRP Stds.: 20

St. Margaret - 22100 Wicksville Rd, Owanka, SD 57767 Served from St. Patrick, Wall

WATAUGA

St. Michael - 1st Ave E, Watauga, SD 57660; Mailing: PO Box 210, Lemmon, SD 57638 t) 605-374-3767 Served from St. Mary, Lemmon. Rev. Adam Hofer, Pst.; CRP Stds.: 10

WHITE RIVER

Sacred Heart - 218 N. McKinley St., White River, SD 57579; Mailing: PO Box 185, White River, SD 57579 t) 605-895-2534 jheying@diorc.org served from Presho Rev. John Heying, Pst.; CRP Stds.: 2

WINNER

Immaculate Conception - 325 S. Van Buren St, Winner, SD 57580; Mailing: 302 W. 4th St., Winner, SD 57580 t) 605-842-3520 parishsec@gwtc.net catholictripp.org Affiliated with St. Isidore, Colome Rev. Zane Pekron, Pst.; CRP Stds.: 91

Our Lady of Good Counsel - Wood - Rural, Wood, SD 57585; Mailing: PO Box 151, Mission, SD 57555 t) (605) 842-3520 Served from Immaculate Conception, Winner

SCHOOLS: PRESCHOOL THRU HIGH SCHOOL

SCHOOLS

STATE OF SOUTH DAKOTA

PINE RIDGE

Holy Rosary/Red Cloud Indian School Inc. - 100 Mission Dr., Pine Ridge, SD 57770-2100 t) 605-867-5491; 605-867-2801 (Lourdes School) www.redcloudschool.org Ministry on the Pine Ridge Indian Reservation. Rev. Brad Held, S. J., Pst.; Moira Coomes, Supt.; Dr. Raymond A. Naldony, Pres.;

Tashina Rama, Vice. Pres.;

Red Cloud High School - 100 Mission Dr., Pine Ridge, SD 57770-2100 t) 605-867-1289 redcloudschool.org Jessica Heesacker, Prin.; Stds.: 170; Bro. Tchrs.: 1; Pr. Tchrs.: 1; Scholastics: 1; Lay Tchrs.: 20

Our Lady of Lourdes Elementary - 500 Lourdes Ln, Porcupine, SD 57772; Mailing: PO Box 7, Porcupine, SD 57772-0007 t) 605-967-2801 tlessert@redcloudschool.org Theresa Lessert, Prin.; Stds.: 96; Lay Tchrs.: 14

Red Cloud Elementary School - 100 Mission Dr., Pine Ridge, SD 57770-2100 t) 605-867-5889 annmarieamiotte@redcloudschool.org Ann-Marie Amiotte, Prin.; Stds.: 183; Sr. Tchrs.: 1; Lay Tchrs.: 8

The Heritage Center - t) 605-867-8267 marymaxon@redcloudschool.org www.redcloudschool.org/museum Museum Mary Maxon, Dir.;

RAPID CITY

Rapid City Catholic School System - (DIO) 424 Fairmont Blvd., Rapid City, SD 57701 t) (605) 343-3541 (Superintendant); 605-348-1477 x117 (Bus. Office) rccss.org Robert Aberle, Supt.; Rev. Mark McCormick, Chap.; Rev. Andrzej Wyrostek, Chap.; James Johnston, Prin.; Stds.: 190; Sr. Tchrs.: 1; Lay Tchrs.: 23

St. Elizabeth Elementary School - 2101 City Springs Rd., Ste. 100, Rapid City, SD 57702 t) 605-716-5213 clecy@rccss.org www.rccss.org Colleen Lecy, Prin.; Stds.: 309; Lay Tchrs.: 31

St. Thomas More Middle School - 424 Fairmont Blvd., Rapid City, SD 57701 t) (605) 348-1477 www.rccss.org Mary Helen Olsen, Prin.; Stds.: 161; Sr. Tchrs.: 1; Lay Tchrs.: 22

INSTITUTIONS LOCATED IN DIOCESE

ASSOCIATIONS [ASN]

RAPID CITY

Priest Retirement and Aid Association/Pension Plan Board - 225 Main St., Rapid City, SD 57701; Mailing: PO Box 678, Rapid City, SD 57709-0678 t) 605-343-3541 rsoulek@diorc.org Rev. Ron Garry, Pres.; Richard Soulek, Bus. Mgr.; Rev. Msgr. Michael Woster, Exec. Sec.;

CATHOLIC CHARITIES [CCH]

RAPID CITY

Western South Dakota Catholic Foundation, Inc. - 2101 City Springs Rd.. Ste. 300, Rapid City, SD 57702 t) 605-721-6843 chubbeling@wsdcf.org; pjquin@wsdcf.org wsdcf.org Paul Quin, Exec. Dir.; Asstd. Annu.: 21; Staff: 2

CONVENTS, MONASTERIES, AND RESIDENCES FOR WOMEN [CON]

PIEDMONT

***Immaculate Heart Hermitage, Inc.** - 21623 Domino Place, Piedmont, SD 57769; Mailing: PO Box 484, Piedmont, SD 57769 t) 605-519-9232 www.carmelartinspirations.com Sr. Mary Catherine Jacobs, OCarm, Hermit; Srs.: 1

RAPID CITY

***Benedictine Convent of St. Martin** - 1851 City Springs Rd., Rapid City, SD 57702-9613 t) 605-343-8011 www.blackhillsbenedictine.com Motherhouse of the Sisters of St. Benedict. Sr. Jennifer Kehrwald, OSB, Admin.; Srs.: 12

ENDOWMENTS / FOUNDATIONS / TRUSTS [EFT]

RAPID CITY

Catholic Parish Association Contingency Fund, Inc. - 225 Main St., Ste. 100, Rapid City, SD 57701; Mailing: PO Box 678, Rapid CIty, SD 57709-0678 t) 605-343-3541 rsoulek@diorc.org Kelly Kjerstad, Pres.;

HOSPITALS / HEALTH SERVICES [HOS]

GREGORY

Avera McKennan (Avera Gregory Hospital) - 400 Park Ave., Gregory, SD 57533-0400; Mailing: PO Box 408, Gregory, SD 57639-0408 t) 605-835-8394 anthony.timanus@avera.org www.avera.org Sponsored by Presentation of the B.V.M. of Aberdeen, SD & Benedictine Sisters of Sacred Heart Monastery, Yankton, SD. Anthony Timanus, CEO; Bed Capacity: 80; Asstd. Annu.: 27,203; Staff: 134

MISCELLANEOUS [MIS]

MCLAUGHLIN

Standing Rock Reservation - 410 1st Ave. E, McLaughlin, SD 57642; Mailing: PO Box 539, McLaughlin, SD 57642 t) 605-823-4401 (Rectory); 605-823-2484 (Convent) jhoerter@diorc.org Includes parishes of eastern Standing Rock Reservation, located in McLaughlin, Bullhead and Kenel. Rev. James Hoerter, Pst.; Sr. Jacqueline Schroeder, OSF, DRE;

RAPID CITY

Catholic Social Services - 529 Kansas City St., Ste. 100, Rapid City, SD 57701 t) 605-348-6086 css@cssrapidcity.com www.catholicsocialservicesrapidcity.com James Kinyon, Exec. Dir.; Lorinda Collings, CFO;

MONASTERIES AND RESIDENCES FOR PRIESTS AND BROTHERS [MON]

LOWER BRULE

SCJ Community House - 508 Gall St., Lower Brule, SD 57548; Mailing: PO Box 185, Lower Brule, SD 57548-0185 t) 605-473-5335; 605-473-5487 jcmbassi@diorc.org Rev. Jean Claude Mbassi, SCJ, Pst.; Rev. Christianus Hendrick, S.C.J.; Dcn. Steve McLaughlin; Priests: 2

MISSION

Kino Jesuit Community - 27560 US Hwy. 18, Mission, SD 57555; Mailing: PO Box 499, St. Francis, SD 57572-0499 t) 605-747-2361 jlafontainesj@jesuits.org Rev. Ronald S. Seminara, S.J., Pst.; Rev. James Lafontaine, S.J., Assoc. Pst.; Priests: 2

PIEDMONT

Casa Maria Residence for Retired Priests - 12541 Sturgis Rd., Piedmont, SD 57769; Mailing: PO Box 678, Rapid City, SD 57709-0678 t) 605-721-7910 Richard Soulek, C.F.O.; Rev. Daniel Juelfs, Bd. of Dir.; Priests: 4

PINE RIDGE

Holy Rosary Mission Jesuit Community - 100 Mission Dr., Pine Ridge, SD 57770-2100 t) 605-867-5491 www.redcloudschool.org DBA De Smet Jesuit Community Bro. Joseph Fleischman, S.J.; Bro. Michael Zimmerman, S.J.; Rev. Brad A. Held, S.J., Pst.; Rev. Ronald S. Seminara, S.J., Assoc. Pst.; Rev. Edmund Yainao, SJ, Assoc. Pst.; Rev. Joseph Daoust, SJ, Sacr. Min.; Rev. Peter J. Klink, S.J., Sacr. Min.; Dcn. William J. White; Rev. David Mastrangelo, SJ, Sacr. Min.; Brs.: 3; Priests: 6

Church of Christ the King - 490 Lourdes Ln, Porcupine, SD 57772; Mailing: PO Box 367, Porcupine, SD 57772-0367 t) 605-867-1614 joycetibbitts@redcloudschool.org Joyce Tibbitts, Pst. Min./Coord.;

Our Lady of Sorrows - 463 Main St, Kyle, SD 57770; Mailing: PO Box 567, Kyle, SD 57752-0567 t) 605-455-2888 (Office); 605-455-1521 (Parish House) Reservation Chapel. Rev. Brad Held, S. J., Pst.;

St. John of the Cross - Rural, Allen, SD 57714; Mailing: PO Box 567, Kyle, SD 57752-0567 t) 605-454-6261 Reservation Chapel in Allen, SD

Our Lady of the Sioux - 100 Church Hill Rd., Oglala, SD 57764; Mailing: PO Box 140, Oglala, SD 57764-0140 t) 605-867-1518; 605-867-5673 (Asst.) sioux@gwtc.net Sr. Barbara Ann Bogenschutz, O.P., Parish Life Coord.;

St. Bernard, Red Shirt Table - Rural, Red Shirt Table, SD 57738; Mailing: PO Box 140, Oglala, SD 57764-0140 Served from Holy Rosary Mission, Pine Ridge

Our Lady of Good Counsel, No Water (Drywood) - Rural, Oglala, SD 57764; Mailing: PO Box 140, Oglala, SD 57764-0140 Served by Holy Rosary Mission, Pine Ridge

Saint Ignatius Loyola - 434 Hwy. 44, Wanblee, SD 57577; Mailing: PO Box 567, Kyle, SD 57752 t) 605-455-2888 Rev. Brad Held, S. J., Pst.;

RETREAT HOUSES / RENEWAL CENTERS [RTR]

HOWES

The Diocese of Rapid City Mahpiya na Maka Okoigna - 20100 Center Rd., Howes, SD 57748-7703 t) 605-985-5906 ssc@diorc.org www.siouxspiritualcenter.org Sioux Spiritual Center Carole Brown, Dir.;

SPECIAL CARE FACILITIES [SPF]

EAGLE BUTTE

Sacred Heart Center - 121 Landmark St., Eagle Butte, SD 57625; Mailing: PO Box 2000, Eagle Butte, SD 57625-2000 t) 605-964-6062 (SHC Administration); (605) 964-6069 (SHC Child Services); (605) 964-7233 (SHC Family Violence) www.shconline.org Social Service Agency. Child Services, Family Violence Shelter. Travis Hedrick, Exec. Dir.; Kirk Beyer, Dir. Progs./Oper.; Bed Capacity: 26; Asstd. Annu.: 423; Staff: 30

An asterisk (*) denotes an organization that has established tax-exempt status directly with the IRS and is not covered by the USCCB Group Ruling.

Diocese of Reno

(Dioecesis Renensis)

MOST REVEREND DANIEL H. MUEGGENBORG, D.D., S.T.L.

Bishop of Reno, ordained July 14, 1989; appointed Bishop of Reno July 20, 2021; installed September 24, 2021.

Pastoral Center: 290 S. Arlington Ave., Reno, NV 89501-1713. T: 775-329-9274; F: 775-348-8619
jenyh@catholicreno.org
www.renodiocese.org

Square Miles 70,852.

Erected as the Diocese of Reno by His Holiness Pope Pius XI March 27, 1931. Canonical Erection of the Diocese August 19, 1931; Redesignated Diocese of Reno-Las Vegas by Pope Paul VI, October 13, 1976; Reformed Diocese of Reno by His Holiness Pope John Paul II March 21, 1995.

Comprises the Counties of Carson City, Churchill, Douglas, Elko, Eureka, Humboldt, Lander, Lyon, Mineral, Pershing, Storey, and Washoe.

Patrons of the Diocese: Our Lady of the Snows (August 5); The Holy Family (Sunday in the Octave of Christmas);
Established through an Apostolic brief dated August 24, 1933.

Legal Title: "The Roman Catholic Bishop of Reno and His Successors, a Corporation Sole".

For legal titles of parishes and diocesan institutions, consult the Pastoral Center.

STATISTICAL OVERVIEW

Personnel	
Bishop	1
Retired Bishops	2
Priests: Diocesan Active in Diocese	24
Priests: Retired, Sick or Absent	13
Number of Diocesan Priests	37
Religious Priests in Diocese	2
Total Priests in your Diocese	39
Extern Priests in Diocese	9
Ordinations:	
Permanent Deacons	10
Permanent Deacons in Diocese	35
Total Brothers	2
Total Sisters	8
Parishes	
Parishes	28
With Resident Pastor:	
Resident Diocesan Priests	22
Without Resident Pastor:	
Administered by Priests	6
Missions	6
Pastoral Centers	1
Professional Ministry Personnel:	
Brothers	2
Lay Ministers	112
Educational	
Diocesan Students in Other Seminaries	3
Total Seminarians	3
High Schools, Diocesan and Parish	1
Total Students	644
Elementary Schools, Diocesan and Parish	4
Total Students	1,133
Catechesis / Religious Education:	
High School Students	60
Elementary Students	120
Total Students under Catholic Instruction	1,960
Teachers in Diocese:	
Lay Teachers	112
Vital Statistics	
Receptions into the Church:	
Infant Baptism Totals	1,242
Minor Baptism Totals	134
Adult Baptism Totals	134
First Communions	1,040
Confirmations	743
Marriages:	
Catholic	160
Interfaith	45
Total Marriages	205
Deaths	451
Total Catholic Population	89,622
Total Population	764,596

LEADERSHIP

Bishop's Office - Most Rev. Randolph R. Calvo;
Bishop Emeritus - Most Rev. Phillip F. Straling;
Secretary - t) 775-326-9428 Jeny Hill;
Moderator of the Curia/Chancellor - Rev. Robert W. Chorey;
Secretary - t) 775-326-9410 Karen Smeath;
Vicar General - Rev. Charles Durante;
Tribunal -
Adjutant Judicial Vicar -
Advocates - Rev. Philip George; Bro. Matthew Cunningham, F.S.R.; Rev. Chuck Durante;
Defender of the Bond - Rev. Robert E. Hayes;
Judge - Rev. Joseph Abraham;
Judicial Vicar/Officialis - Rev. Joseph Abraham;
Promoter of Justice - Rev. Robert E. Hayes;
Secretary/Notary - t) 775-326-9411 Piedad Gonzalez;
Vicar for Clergy - Rev. Joseph Abraham;
Department of Education -
Diocesan School Board - Most Rev. Randolph R. Calvo; Karen L. Barreras; John Anxo, Past Pres.;
Superintendent of Catholic Schools - t) 775-326-9430 Karen L. Barreras;
Pastoral Ministry Offices -
Archives - Rev. Robert W. Chorey; Karen Smeath;
Office of Ethnic Ministries - t) 775-326-9423 Maripaz Ramos, Dir.;
Office of Faith Formation - t) 775-326-9439 Monique Jacobs, Dir.;
Conference Associate - t) 775-326-9440 Breanna Balmut, Secy.;
Office of Lay Ministry Formation - t) 775-326-9431 Lauri-Anne Reinhart, Dir.;
Office of Permanent Diaconate Formation, Family Life and Spirituality Director - t) 775-326-9786 Dcn. Joseph Bell;
Office of Safe Environment - t) 775-326-9430 Elda Juarez;
Office of Youth and Young Adult Ministry - t) 775-372-6456 Christina Davis, Dir.;
Secretaries - Suzanna Corral; Breanna Balmut; Pat Giannotti;
Curia - Most Rev. Randolph R. Calvo; Rev. Charles Durante, Vicar Gen.; Karen L. Barreras;

OFFICES AND DIRECTORS

Department of Stewardship and Development - t) 775-326-9432 Michael Quilici, Chief Devel. Officer; Carmen Godoy, Secy.; Carla Mischel, Secy.;
Detention Ministry - Dcn. Michael Johnson;
Lovelock Prison - t) 775-273-2189 Rev. Kuriakose Mambrakatt;
Reno Area - t) 775-322-2255 Dcn. Jose Castro;
Diocesan Board of Consultors - Most Rev. Randolph R. Calvo; Rev. Charles Durante; Rev. Mark Hanifan;
Diocesan Communications - Rev. Robert W. Chorey, Chancellor;
Finance Office -
Accountant and Bookkeeper - t) 775-326-9435 Rita San Paolo-Oueilhe;
Chief Financial Officer - t) 775-326-9420 Richard Todd;
Finance Council - Most Rev. Randolph R. Calvo; Rev. Charles Durante; Rev. Robert W. Chorey;
Human Resources - t) 775-326-9425 Mary Jean Snow;
Payroll and Employee Benefits Coordinator - t) 775-326-9422 Diane Lacebal;
Frontier of the Faith - t) 775-326-9433
Director - Rev. Robert W. Chorey;
High Desert Catholic Magazine - Lisa Laughlin, Editor (hdc@catholicreno.org);
Life, Peace & Justice Commission - Rev. Charles Durante; Midge Breeden; Jeff Hardcastle;
Liturgy Commission - Carol Sara; Maria Leman; Sandy McGowan, Liturgical Coord.;
Missionary Co-Op - Rev. Robert W. Chorey;
Ongoing Formation for Permanent Deacons - Rev. Joseph Abraham, Vicar;
Our Mother of Sorrows Cemetery - t) 775-323-0133 omos@catholicreno.org Christine Luna, Oper. Mgr.;
Presbyteral Council - Most Rev. Randolph R. Calvo; Rev. Charles Durante; Rev. Mark Hanifan;
Priest Personnel Board - Most Rev. Randolph R. Calvo; Rev. Charles Durante; Rev. Joseph Abraham;
Project Rachel - Karen Mowry, Dir.;
Property Management - Richard Todd;
Respect Life Commission - Rev. Mark Hanifan, Priest Moderator; Julianna Jervis; Wendy Avansino;
Seminary Board - Most Rev. Randolph R. Calvo; Rev. Charles Durante; Rev. Michael Mahone;
Victims' Advocate - Marilyn Janka; David Caloiaro;
Vocations Team - Rev. Michael Mahone; Rev. Robert W. Chorey; Sr. Maria Ahearn, O.C.D.;
Secretary - t) 775-326-9426 Pat Giannotti;

PARISHES, MISSIONS, AND CLERGY

STATE OF NEVADA

BATTLE MOUNTAIN

St. John Bosco - 392 S. Reese St., Battle Mountain, NV 89820; Mailing: 384 S. Reese St., Battle Mountain, NV 89820 t) 775-635-2576 stjboscosm@hotmail.com Rev. Tomy Mamparampil Joseph, Pst.; Dcn. Dennis Cahill; Yolanda Rodriguez, DRE;

CARLIN

Sacred Heart - 562 4th St., Carlin, NV 89822; Mailing: P.O. Box 235, Carlin, NV 89822 t) 775-754-6425; 775-754-6415 (CRP) carlincatholic@yahoo.com; thaub@frontiernet.net Rev. Biju Malancheruvil, Pst.; Laurie Haub, DRE;

CARSON CITY

Corpus Christi - 3597 N. Sunridge Dr., Carson City, NV 89705 t) 775-267-3200 generaloffice@cchurchcc.org; karens@cchurchcc.org www.cchurchcc.org Rev. James Setelik, Pst.; Karen Smeath, DRE;
St. Teresa of Avila Parish Corporation - 3000 N. Lompa Ln., Carson City, NV 89706 t) 775-882-1968; 775-882-2130 (CRP) stteresa@stteresaofavila.net; kanderson@stteresaofavila.net www.stteresaofavila.net Rev. Thomas P Babu, Pst.; Rev. Eduardo Gutierrez, Par. Vicar; Dcn. Gilbert Coleman; Dcn. Michael Johnson; Dcn. Craig LaGier; Dcn. Dennis Schreiner; Grace Kengle, Youth Min.; Kari Anderson, DRE;
St. Teresa of Avila School - (Grades K-8) 567 S. Richmond Ave., Carson City, NV 89703 t) 775-882-2079 pburger@stts.org www.stts.org Peggy Burger, Prin.; Teya Cantwell, Librn.;
St. Teresa Child Development Center - 561 Richmond Ave., Carson City, NV 89703 t) 775-283-0261 csupko@stts.org Cindi Supko, Dir.;
St. Teresa of Avila Columbarium & Memorial Gardens -

DAYTON

St. Ann - 3 Melanie Dr., Dayton, NV 89403; Mailing: P.O. Box 309, Dayton, NV 89403 t) 775-246-7578 admin@stannsdayton.org Rev. Thomas Nelson, Pst.; Marna Zachry, DRE;

ELKO

St. Joseph's - 1035 C St., Elko, NV 89801 t) 775-738-6432; 775-738-8770 (CRP) stjoech@frontier.com; sjcc@frontiernet.net stjoech.org Rev. Varghese Malancheruvil, Pst.; Rev. Joseph Walsh, Assoc. Pst.; Dcn. Franklin Martinez; Catherine Valdez, Youth Min.; Catherine Higginbotham, DRE;
Our Lady of Guadalupe - ; Mailing: P.O. Box 200, Jackpot, NV 89825

EUREKA

St. Brendan's - 70 N. O'Neill Ave., Eureka, NV 89316; Mailing: Po Box 305, Eureka, NV 89316 t) 775-318-0065 stbrendans1867@gmail.com Rev. Varghese Malancheruvil, Pst.;

FALLON

St. Patrick - 850 W. Fourth St., Fallon, NV 89406 t) 775-423-2846; 775-427-3916 (CRP) st.patricksfallon@yahoo.com stpatricksparish.org Rev. Antonio Quijano Jr., Pst.; Dcn. Kurt Carlson; Dcn. Ronald Cherry; Dcn. Wayne Crooks; Paul Loop, Youth Min.; Judy Northrup, DRE;

FERNLEY

St. Robert Bellarmine - 625 Desert Shadows Ln., Fernley, NV 89408 t) 775-575-4011 books@strobertbellarmine.org www.strobertbellarmine.org Rev. Joseph Infante, Pst.; Dcn. Ruben Cervantes; Linda Harrison, DRE;
St. Joseph the Worker -

GARDNERVILLE

St. Gall - 1343 Centerville Rd., Gardnerville, NV 89410 t) 775-782-2852; 775-782-3784 (CRP) dimelli@saintgall.org; mhanifan@saintgall.org www.saintgall.org Rev. Mark Hanifan, Pst.; Dcn. Emilio Gonzales; Dcn. Bill Henderson; DeAnna Imelli, DRE;

HAWTHORNE

Our Lady of Perpetual Help - 804 A St., Hawthorne, NV 89415; Mailing: P.O. Box 850, Hawthorne, NV 89415 t) 775-463-2882 Rev. Jesus Ballesteros, Pst.; Suzanne Welch, DRE;

INCLINE VILLAGE

St. Francis of Assisi - 701 Mount Rose Hwy., Incline Village, NV 89451 t) 775-831-0490 katiec@sftahoe.org; beckym@sftahoe.org www.sftahoe.org Rev. Jorge Herrera, Pst.; Sarah Morris, Youth Min.; Rebecca Massingill, DRE;

LOVELOCK

St. John the Baptist - 1045 Franklin Ave., Lovelock, NV 89419-0177; Mailing: P.O. Box 177, Lovelock, NV 89419-0177 t) 775-273-2189; 775-273-7903 (CRP); 775-422-3240 (CRP) stjohns_lovelock@yahoo.com; twmaita@hotmail.com www.stjohnthebaptist.today Rev. Kuriakose Mambrakatt, Pst.; Tera Maita, DRE; Beki Rosas, DRE;

RENO

St. Thomas Aquinas Cathedral - 310 W Second St., Reno, NV 89503-5398 t) 775-329-2571 office@stacathedral.com; grace@stacathedral.com www.stacathedral.com Rev. Charles Durante, Rector; Dcn. Joseph Bell; Grace Kengle, DRE; Dcn. Robert Dangel; CRP Stds.: 58
St. Albert the Great - 1250 Wyoming Ave., Reno, NV 89503; Mailing: 1259 St. Albert Dr., Reno, NV 89503 t) 775-747-0722 www.stalbertreno.org Rev. Honesto Agustin, Pst.; Rev. Patrick Klekas, Par. Vicar; Dcn. Charles Lanham; Dcn. Richard Ramm; David Willems, Youth Min.; Beth Lujan, DRE;
St. Albert the Great School - (Grades K-8) 1255 St. Albert Dr., Reno, NV 89503 t) 775-747-3392 lkane@stalbertreno.org Stephanie Hix, Prin.; Laurie Vasquez, Librn.;
St. Albert's Child Development Center - 1259 St. Albert Dr., Reno, NV 89503 Kristen Mareno, Dir.;
St. Michael's - 14075 Mt. Vida St., Reno, NV 89506 t) 775-972-7462; 775-737-9337 (CRP) stmreno@stmichaelreno.org; martha@stmichaelreno.org www.stmichaelreno.org Rev. Elberto Melendez, Pst.; Martha Ibarra, DRE;
Our Lady of the Snows - 1138 Wright St., Reno, NV 89509 t) 775-323-6894; 775-329-6147 (CRP) parishadministrator@olsparish.com; dre@olsparish.org www.olsparish.com Rev. Robert W Chorey, Pst.; Rev. Christopher Kanowitz, Par. Vicar; Dcn. Brian Callister; Dcn. David Norman; Lauri-Anne Reinhart, DRE;
Our Lady of the Snows School - (Grades K-8) 1125 Lander St., Reno, NV 89509 t) 775-322-2773 tfuetsch@ourladyofthesnowsschool.org www.snowsnv.org Tim Fuetsch, Prin.;
St. Rose of Lima - 100 Bishop Manogue Dr., Reno, NV 89511 t) 775-851-1874; 775-850-2535 (CRP); 775-850-2544 (CRP) srl@strosereno.com; dre@strosereno.com www.strosereno.com Rev. Joseph

Abraham, Pst.; Rev. Bobin Babu, Assoc. Pst.; Dcn. Auguste Lemaire; Linda Walsh, Youth Min.; Lydia Aberasturi, DRE; Brizeida Hernandez, Bus. Mgr.;

Holy Spirit - 1025 N. U.S. Hwy. 395, Washoe Valley, NV 89704

St. Therese of the Little Flower Catholic Church - 875 E. Plumb Ln., Reno, NV 89502 t) 775-322-2255; 775-322-2255 x114 (CRP) yocelin@littleflowerchurchreno.org; deacon@littleflowerchurchreno.org www.littleflowerchurchreno.org Rev. Jorge Herrera, Pst.; Rev. Paul McCollum, Pst.; Rev. Arlon Vergara, OSA, Assoc. Pst.; Rev. Justin Lazar, Par. Vicar; Dcn. Robert Ruggiero;

St. Therese Church of the Little Flower School - (Grades K-8) 1300 Casazza Dr., Reno, NV 89502 t) 775-323-2931 colts@littleflowerschoolnv.org www.littleflowerschoolnv.org Vicki Rossolo, Prin.;

SPARKS

Holy Cross Catholic Community - 5650 Vista Blvd., Sparks, NV 89436 t) 775-358-2544 www.holycrosssparks.com Rev. Jose Issac, Pst.; Dcn. Antonio Baptista; Rosa Martinez, DRE;

Immaculate Conception - 2900 N. McCarran Blvd., Sparks, NV 89431 t) 775-358-5977 office@icsparks.org www.icsparks.org Rev. Philip George, Pst.;

SUN VALLEY

St. Peter Canisius - 225 E. Fifth Ave., Sun Valley, NV 89433 t) 775-673-6800; 775-762-0738 (CRP) st.petercanisius@hotmail.com Rev. Edgar Villanueva, Pst.; Dcn. Russ Bergin; Imelda Lopez, DRE;

VIRGINIA CITY

St. Mary's in the Mountains - 111 S. E St., Virginia City, NV 89440; Mailing: P.O. Box 510, Virginia City, NV 89440 t) 775-847-9099 info@stmarysvc.org dioceseofreno.org/mary-mountains.aspx Rev. Charles Durante, Pst.; Rev. Thomas Nelson, Assoc. Pst.;

WELLS

St. Thomas Aquinas - 619 Sixth St., Wells, NV 89835-0369; Mailing: P.O. Box 369, Wells, NV 89835-0369 t) 775-752-3400 taaquinaschurch@hotmail.com Rev. Varghese Malancheruvil, Pst.; Ann Battenfield, DRE;

WINNEMUCCA

St. Paul - 350 Melarkey St., Winnemucca, NV 89445 t) 775-626-2928; 775-623-2928 (CRP) stpaulswimmsec@gmail.com; stpaulswmcaccd@gmail.com Rev. Jose Sobarzo Guerra, Pst.; Catherine Whitman, DRE;

St. Alphonsus - Main St, Paradise Valley, NV 89426

Sacred Heart - Olivarria St, McDermitt, NV 89421

YERINGTON

Holy Family - 103 N. West St., Yerington, NV 89447 t) 775-463-2882; 775-721-1829 (CRP) holyfamily104@yahoo.com; ccdcomdu@yahoo.com holyfamily104nv.com Rev. Jesus Ballesteros, Pst.; Cindy Hitchcock, DRE;

St. John the Baptist -

ZEPHYR COVE

Our Lady of Tahoe - One Elks Point Rd., Zephyr Cove, NV 89448; Mailing: PO Box 115, Zephyr Cove, NV 89448 t) 775-588-2080 www.ourladyoftahoe.org Rev. Larry Morrison, Pst.;

SCHOOLS: PRESCHOOL THRU HIGH SCHOOL

HIGH SCHOOLS

STATE OF NEVADA

RENO

Bishop Manogue Catholic High School, a Nevada non-profit corporation - (DIO) 110 Bishop Manogue Dr., Reno, NV 89511 t) 775-336-6000 karenb@catholicreno.org www.bishopmanogue.org Brianne Thoreson, Prin.; Frank Lazarek, Vice Prin.; Lauren McBride, Vice Prin.; Matthew Schambari, Pres.;

INSTITUTIONS LOCATED IN DIOCESE

CAMPUS MINISTRY / NEWMAN CENTERS [CAM]

RENO

Our Lady of Wisdom Catholic Parish Corporation - 1101 N. Virginia St., Reno, NV 89503 t) 775-322-4336 church@olwnreno.com www.olwnreno.com Most Rev. Daniel H. Mueggenborg, Admin.; Rev. Bobin Babu, Par. Vicar; Jordan Dicus, Campus Min.; Therese Gaikowski, Admin.; Lay Staff: 2; Infant Baptisms: 6; Received into Full Communion: 3; First Communions: 9; Confirmations: 8; Catholic Marriages: 1; Interfaith Marriages: 3; Registered Parishioner Households: 148; Estimated Number of Catholics: 250; Deaths: 2

University of Nevada, Newman Community - 1101 N. Virginia St., Reno, NV 89503 t) 775-322-4336 olwnewmancenter@gbis.com ladyofwisdomnewman.org Served by Our Lady of Wisdom. Rev. Nathan Mamo, Pst.;

CATHOLIC CHARITIES [CCH]

RENO

Catholic Charities of Northern Nevada - 500 E. 4th St., Reno, NV 89512; Mailing: P.O. Box 5099, Reno, NV 89513 t) 775-322-7073 mbaxter@ccsnn.org www.ccsnn.org Marie L Baxter, CEO; Barbara Klipfel, Exec.;

Immigration Assistance - 395 Gould St., Reno, NV 89502; Mailing: P.O. Box 5099, Reno, NV 89513 aallen@ccsnn.org ccsnn.org/pages/immigration-assistance Annie Allen, Dir.;

St. Vincent's Residence/Crossroads Program - 395 Gould St., Reno, NV 89502; Mailing: PO Box 5099, Reno, NV 89512 bklipfel@ccsnn.org ccsnn.org/pages/crossroads-housing-program

St. Vincent's Dining Room - 325 Valley Rd., Reno, NV 89512; Mailing: P.O. Box 5099, Reno, NV 89513-5099 t) 775-323-7073 x455 bklipfel@ccsnn.org ccsnn.org/pages/dining-room

St. Vincent's Food Pantry - ; Mailing: P.O. Box 5099, Reno, NV 89513 ccarrillo@ccsnn.org Carlos Carrillo, Dir.;

St. Vincent's Helping Hands - ; Mailing: P.O. Box 5099, Reno, NV 89513 bklipfel@ccsnn.org ccsnn.org/pages/resource-network

St. Vincent's Thrift Shop - ; Mailing: P.O. Box 5099, Reno, NV 89513 t) (775) 322-7073 x545 jfisher@ccsnn.org; lhernandez@ccsnn.org ccsnn.org/pages/thrift-stores Lee Hernandez, Exec.; John Fisher, Dir.;

CEMETERIES [CEM]

RENO

Our Mother of Sorrows Cemetery & Mausoleum - 2700 N. Virginia St., Reno, NV 89503; Mailing: P.O. Box 8505, Reno, NV 89507 t) 775-323-0133 omos@catholiccemetery.org www.catholiccemeteryreno.org Christine Luna, Mgr.;

CONVENTS, MONASTERIES, AND RESIDENCES FOR WOMEN [CON]

RENO

Sisters of Our Lady of Mount Carmel (OCD) - 1950 La Fond Dr., Reno, NV 89509-3099 t) 775-323-3236 renocarmel@carmelofreno.net www.carmelofreno.com Sr. Susan Weber, O.C.D., Prioress;

ENDOWMENTS / FOUNDATIONS / TRUSTS [EFT]

RENO

The Catholic Community Foundation of the Diocese of Reno - 290 S. Arlington, Ste. 200, Reno, NV 89501-1713 t) 775-326-9417 richardt@catholicreno.org Richard Todd, Exec.;

MISCELLANEOUS [MIS]

RENO

***Fertility Care Center of Reno, Inc.** - 1281 Terminal Way, #114, Reno, NV 89502 t) 775-827-5111 juliannajervis@att.net fertilitycarecenterofreno.org Teaches Creighton Model FertilityCare System Julianna Jervis, Pres.;

Nevada Catholic Conference - 290 S. Arlington Ave., Ste. 200, Reno, NV 89501-1713 nevadacatholicconference@gmail.com Mike Dyer, Contact;

MONASTERIES AND RESIDENCES FOR PRIESTS AND BROTHERS [MON]

RENO

Brothers of Our Lady of the Holy Rosary Monastery - 232 Sunnyside Dr., Reno, NV 89503-3510 t) 775-747-4441 bros-reno@charter.net Bro. Edward Zuber, F.S.R.; Bro. Matthew Cunningham, F.S.R., Supr.; Brs.: 2

PRESCHOOLS / CHILDCARE CENTERS [PRE]

RENO

Holy Child Early Learning Center - 440 Reno Ave., Reno, NV 89509 t) 775-329-2979 bklipfel@ccsnn.org; mbaxter@ccsnn.org ccsnn.org Barbara Klipfel, Exec.;

An asterisk (*) denotes an organization that has established tax-exempt status directly with the IRS and is not covered by the USCCB Group Ruling.

Diocese of Richmond

(Dioecesis Richmondiensis)

MOST REVEREND BARRY C. KNESTOUT

Bishop of Richmond; ordained June 24, 1989; appointed Auxiliary Bishop of Washington and Titular Bishop of Leavenworth November 18, 2008; Episcopal ordination December 29, 2008; appointed Bishop of Richmond December 5, 2017; installed January 12, 2018. Pastoral Center: 7800 Carousel Lane, Richmond, VA 23294.

Catholic Diocese of Richmond Pastoral Center: 7800 Carousel Lane, Richmond, VA 23294. T: 804-359-5661; F: 804-358-9159.
www.richmonddiocese.org
Bishop@richmonddiocese.org

ESTABLISHED IN 1820.

Square Miles 36,711.

Comprises the State of Virginia, with the exception of the Counties of Arlington, Clarke, Culpeper, Fairfax, Fauquier, Frederick, King George, Lancaster, Loudoun, Madison, Northumberland, Orange, Page, Prince William, Rappahannock, Richmond, Shenandoah, Spotsylvania, Stafford, Warren and Westmoreland.

For legal titles of parishes and diocesan institutions, consult the Chancery Office.

STATISTICAL OVERVIEW

Personnel

Bishop	1
Priests: Diocesan Active in Diocese	73
Priests: Diocesan Active Outside Diocese	3
Priests: Retired, Sick or Absent	57
Number of Diocesan Priests	133
Religious Priests in Diocese	18
Total Priests in your Diocese	151
Extern Priests in Diocese	50
Ordinations:	
Diocesan Priests	2
Transitional Deacons	3
Permanent Deacons in Diocese	183
Total Brothers	3
Total Sisters	107

Parishes

Parishes	138
With Resident Pastor:	
Resident Diocesan Priests	106
Resident Religious Priests	7
Without Resident Pastor:	
Administered by Priests	25
Missions	6
Pastoral Centers	1

Professional Ministry Personnel:	
Brothers	1
Sisters	33
Lay Ministers	253

Welfare

Catholic Hospitals	9
Total Assisted	391,283
Homes for the Aged	7
Total Assisted	1,709
Day Care Centers	1
Total Assisted	145
Special Centers for Social Services	1
Total Assisted	26,200

Educational

Diocesan Students in Other Seminaries	27
Total Seminarians	27
High Schools, Diocesan and Parish	4
Total Students	963
High Schools, Private	5
Total Students	888
Elementary Schools, Diocesan and Parish	21
Total Students	6,547
Elementary Schools, Private	3
Total Students	952
Catechesis/Religious Education:	
High School Students	2,978
Elementary Students	8,424
Total Students under Catholic Instruction	20,779
Teachers in Diocese:	
Priests	3
Brothers	1
Sisters	11
Lay Teachers	788

Vital Statistics

Receptions into the Church:	
Infant Baptism Totals	2,751
Minor Baptism Totals	70
Adult Baptism Totals	13
Received into Full Communion	195
First Communions	2,696
Confirmations	1,638
Marriages:	
Catholic	472
Interfaith	255
Total Marriages	727
Deaths	1,507
Total Catholic Population	226,674
Total Population	5,244,996

ADMINISTRATION

Vicar General and Moderator of the Curia - Very Rev. Michael G. Boehling;
Chancellor - t) 804-355-9155 chancellor@richmonddiocese.org Very Rev. Msgr. R. Francis Muench;
Vice Chancellor - t) 804-359-5661 x218 Edith McNeil Jeter;
Diocesan Tribunal - t) 804-355-9155 tribunal@richmonddiocese.org
Judicial Vicar - Very Rev. Msgr. R. Francis Muench;
Assistant to the Bishop - Anne C. Edwards;
Campus Ministry - t) (804) 622-5162 Andrew Waring, Dir.; Laura LaClair, Assoc. Dir.;
Catholic Community Foundation - Margaret Keightley, Exec.; Alex Previtera, Dir.; Joyce A. Schreiber, Dir.;
Center for Marriage, Family & Life - t) 804-622-5159 cmfl@richmonddiocese.org; marriageprep@richmonddiocese.org Andrew Waring, Dir.; Daniel Harms, Assoc. Dir. (dharms@richmonddiocese.org); Katie Reda, Prog. Mgr.;
Deacon Director - Dcn. John J. Kren, Dir.; Geraldine Mancuso, Registrar & Coord. Permanent Diaconate;
Defenders of the Bond - Christina Hip-Flores; Amy Jill Strickland; Elisa E. Ugarte;
Director of Archives and Museum - Edith McNeil Jeter, Archivist;
Ecclesiastical Notaries - Kathleen M. McIntosh; Elizabeth Murillo; Adriana Carlucci;
Ethnic and Special Liturgies - richmonddiocese.org
Facilities Management - Joshua Murphy, Dir.;
Judges - Rev. Michael M. Duffy; Very Rev. Brian W. Capuano; Rev. Kevin J. O'Brien;
Office for Black Catholics - t) (804) 359-5661 Rev. Tochi Iwuji, Dir.;
Office for the Hispanic Ministry - Daniel Vilar, Dir.;
Office of Asian Ministry - Daniel Villar, Dir.;
Office of Catholic Schools - t) (804) 359-5661 Kelly Lazzara, Supt.; Dr. Laura Clift, Asst. Supt.; Dr. Michael J. Riley, Asst. Supt.;
Office of Christian Formation - t) (804) 359-5661 cf@richmonddiocese.org Teresa Lee, Dir.; Tracy Brookmire, Assoc. Dir.; Megan Cottam, Assoc. Dir.;
Office of Communications - Deborah M. Cox, Dir.;
Office of Evangelization - Andrew Waring, Dir.; Carrie Poston, Prog. Mgr.;
Office of Finance - Sarah W. Rabin, Dir.; Aimee W. Chappell, Asst. Dir.; Michael J. McGee, CFO;
Diocesan Housing Corporation - Dr. William J. Spitzer, Exec. Dir.;
Office of Human Resources - Sarah Folger, Dir.; Carol Bensusan, Dir.; Nazia Shafi, Dir.;
Office of Information Technology - Eric Sund, Dir.; Ian Reyes, Systems Admin.; Lynn Mooney, Web Svcs. & Database Devel.;
Office of Printing - Joel Cliborne, Dir.;
Office of Real Estate - Shawn Lazar, Dir.;
Office of Risk Management - Regina Isaac, Dir.;
Office of Social Ministries - Tina Wandersee, Dir.;
Office of Worship - Very Rev. Brian W. Capuano;
Vicar for Clergy - Very Rev. Timothy M. Kuhneman; Rev. John C. Kazibwe, Asst. to Vicar for Clergy for African Priests; Very Rev. Salvador Anonuevo, Asst. to Vicar for Clergy for Filipino & Hispanic Priests;
Vicar for Ecumenism & Ecumenical Affairs -
Vicar for Vocations - Very Rev. Brian W. Capuano;
Youth & Young Adult - Katie Yankoski, Assoc. Dir.;

ADVISORY BOARDS, COMMISSIONS, COMMITTEES, AND COUNCILS

Building and Renovation Committee - t) 757-426-2180 Rev. Robert J. Cole, Chair;
Campus & Young Adult Ministry - t) (804) 622-5159 evangelization@richmonddiocese.org Andrew Waring, Dir.;
Catholic Daughters of America - Brenda R. West (brwest@cox.net);
Catholic Relief Services - t) 804-622-5180
Catholic Virginian (Diocesan Newspaper) - t) 804-359-5654 Lily Nguyen, Editor;
Cemeteries - t) 757-229-0851 Dcn. Edward Handel, Dir.;
Christian Formation Commission - Donna Keeley, Chair; Michelle Tomshack, Chair;
Commission for Ecumenical & Interreligious Affairs -
Council of Catholic Women - t) 804-741-2487 Louise Hartz;
Diocesan Pastoral Council - Kim Hulcher;
Diocesan School Board - Sam Samorian, Chair;
Finance Council - Michael J. McGee, CFO;
Haitian Ministry Commission - t) 804-622-5206
Knights of Columbus - statedeputy@vakofc.org Mark Janda;
Liturgical Commission - Stephen DeMauri;
Office for Ethnic Ministry - Daniel Villar, Dir.;
Presbyteral Council - Very Rev. Sean M. Prince;
Propagation of the Faith - Dcn. Robert (Bob) Young (bob.young@missioners.org);
Respect Life - Tina Wandersee, Dir.;
Victim Assistance Coordinator - t) 804-622-5175 Karen Loper;
Youth Ministry Council - Andrew Waring, Dir.;

CATHOLIC CHARITIES

Catholic Charities - t) 804-285-5900 Jay Brown, Exec. Dir.;
Commonwealth Catholic Charities -
Catholic Charities of Eastern Virginia, Inc. - t) 757-467-7707 Tracy Fick, CEO;

DEANERIES

Eastern Vicariate - Very Rev. Eric J. Ayers, (Episcopal Vicar);
Deanery 1 - Very Rev. Sean M. Prince, Dean;
Deanery 2 - Very Rev. Esteban DeLeon, Dean;
Deanery 3 - Rev. Anthony W. Morris, Dean;
Deanery 4 - Very Rev. W. Daniel Beeman, Dean;
Deanery 5 - Very Rev. Gerald S. Kaggwa, Dean;
Central Vicariate - Very Rev. Msgr. R. Francis Muench, (Episcopal Vicar);
Deanery 10 - Very Rev. Joseph Mary Lukyamuzi, Dean;
Deanery 6 - Very Rev. Anthony E. Marques, Dean;
Deanery 7 - Very Rev. Michael A. Renninger, Dean;
Deanery 8 - Very Rev. Shay Auerback, S.J., Dean;
Deanery 9 - Very Rev. Joseph F. Goldsmith, Dean;
Western Viciariate - Very Rev. Kevin L. Segerblom, (Episcopal Vicar);
Deanery 11 - Very Rev. Francis Xavier Musolooza, Dean;
Deanery 12 - Very Rev. Msgr. Patrick D. Golden, Dean;
Deanery 13 - Very Rev. John Asare, Dean;
Deanery 14 - Very Rev. Christopher Martin Hess, Dean;
Deanery 15 - Very Rev. Salvador Anonuevo, Dean;

TRIBUNAL

Adjutant Judicial Vicar - t) (804) 355-9155 tribunal@richmonddiocese.org

PARISHES, MISSIONS, AND CLERGY

COMMONWEALTH OF VIRGINIA

ABINGDON

Christ the King - 820 E. Main St., Abingdon, VA 24210; Mailing: P.O. Box 1201, Abingdon, VA 24212-1201 t) 276-628-2941 office@ctk-abingdon.org christthekingsaintjohn.org Very Rev. Rolo B. Castillo, Pst.; CRP Stds.: 38

AMELIA

Good Samaritan - 13441 Patrick Henry Hwy., Amelia, VA 23002; Mailing: 8901 Winterpock Rd., Chesterfield, VA 23832 t) 804-639-6712 stgabrielmail@saintgabriel.org Rev. Felix Rex Amofa, Pst.; Dcn. Armando DeLeon, Pst. Min./Coord.;

AMHERST

St. Francis of Assisi - 332 S. Main St., Amherst, VA 24521; Mailing: P.O. Box 663, Amherst, VA 24521 t) 434-946-2053 parish@stfrancisamherst.comcastbiz.net stfrancisamherst.org Rev. Rogelio L. Abadano, Pst.;

APPOMATTOX

Our Lady of Peace - 2938 Oakleigh Ave., Appomattox, VA 24522-0668; Mailing: P.O. Box 668, Appomattox, VA 24522-0668 t) 434-352-0104 jimg301@juno.com Dcn. Lou Burgess; Rev. James E. Gallagher Jr., Pst.;

ASHLAND

St. Ann - 105 S. Snead St., Ashland, VA 23005-1811 t) 804-798-5039 office@stannscc.org www.stannsashland.org Rev. James Edward Gordon, Pst.; Dcn. Lawrence Mikkelson; Dcn. Eugene P. Kamper; Wanda Clarke, Admin.; Matthew Brady, Music Min.; Lise Mikkelson, Pst. Assoc.;

BEDFORD

Holy Name of Mary - 1307 Oakwood St., Bedford, VA 24523-1613 t) 540-586-8988 rporterfield.hnm@gmail.com; rbailey.hnm@gmail.com holynameofmary.net Rev. Nixon Negparanon, Pst.; Dcn. Mark DeLaHunt; Rebecca Porterfield, Bus. Mgr.; CRP Stds.: 104

BIG STONE GAP

Sacred Heart - 1821 Holton Ave. E., Big Stone Gap, VA 24219-2611 c) 757-404-2296 (Pastor); 660-254-1676 (Asst.) ebaffourasamoah@richmonddiocese.org; fbrownsberger@proton.me www.holytrinitycluster.org Rev. Eric Baffour Asamoah, Pst.; CRP Stds.: 5

BLACKSBURG

St. Mary - 1205 Old Mill Rd., Blacksburg, VA 24060-3618 t) 540-552-1091 officestaff@stmarysblacksburg.org; businessmanager@stmarysblacksburg.org www.stmarysblacksburg.org Very Rev. John Asare, Pst.; Dcn. Mike Ellerbrock; Dcn. Richard Lee Furman; CRP Stds.: 142
Newman Community - 203 Otey St., Blacksburg, VA 24060 t) 540-951-0032

BLACKSTONE

Immaculate Heart of Mary - 903 S. Main St., Blackstone, VA 23824-0266; Mailing: P.O. Box 266, Blackstone, VA 23824-0266 Rev. Magnus Tochi Iwuji, Pst.; Rev. Patrick Baffour-Akoto, Par. Vicar; Dcn. Emmett R. McLane III, Pst. Assoc.; Dcn. Peter J. Menting;

BRISTOL

St. Anne - 316 Euclid Ave., Bristol, VA 24201-4014 t) 276-669-8200 stannes@stannes-bristol.org www.stannes-bristol.org Very Rev. Christopher Martin Hess, Pst.; CRP Stds.: 49
St. Anne School - (Grades PreK-8) 580 Oakview Ave., Bristol, VA 24201 t) 276-669-0048 schooloffice@stanneschoolbristol.org Billie Schneider, Prin.; Angie Bush, Librn.;

BUCKNER

Immaculate Conception - 1107 Fredericks Hall Rd., Buckner, VA 23024; Mailing: P.O. Box 128, Bumpass, VA 23024 t) 540-894-4266 office@louisacatholics.org www.louisacatholics.org Mission of St. Jude, Mineral. Rev. Michael M. Duffy, Pst.; Dcn. Alfonso Benet; Dcn. Thomas Fursman; Jess Johnson, DRE; CRP Stds.: 8

CAPE CHARLES

St. Charles Borromeo - 545 Randolph Ave., Cape Charles, VA 23310-3305 t) 757-331-1724 (Rectory); 757-331-2040 (Office) saintcharles545@gmail.com www.stcharlesbcc.org Rev. J. Michael Breslin, Pst.;

CHARLOTTESVILLE

Catholic Church of the Holy Comforter - 208 E. Jefferson St., Charlottesville, VA 22902-5105 t) 434-295-7185; 434-295-6559 (CRP); 434-293-8989 (Outreach) office@holycomforterparish.org www.holycomforterparish.org Church of the Paraclete Very Rev. Joseph Mary Lukyamuzi, Pst.; Dcn. Henry Vinklarek; Mary Frances Lilly, Bus. Mgr.; Daniel Kirkland, Liturgy Dir.; Melinda Wells, DRE; Bridget Davis, Pst. Min./Coord.; CRP Stds.: 49

Incarnation Catholic Church - 1465 Incarnation Dr., Charlottesville, VA 22901-1716 t) 434-973-4381 office@incarnationparish.org Rev. Msgr. Timothy E. Keeney, Pst.; Rev. Daniel Molochko, Par. Vicar; Missy Bishop, DRE; Patrick Drury, Youth Min.; Jean DePiro, Music Min.; CRP Stds.: 204

Our Lady of the Rosary - 1186 Crozet Ave., Crozet, VA 22932; Mailing: P.O. Box 74, Crozet, VA 22932 t) (434) 812-2936

St. Thomas Aquinas - 401 Alderman Rd., Charlottesville, VA 22903 t) 434-293-8081 admin@stauva.org; frwalter@stauva.org www.stauva.org/ Rev. Walter C. Wagner, Pst.; Rev. David Mott, Pst. Assoc.; Jillian Miller, Parish Life Coord.; Rev. Joseph-Anthony Kress, Campus Min.; Reed Golomb, Youth Min.; Caroline Golomb, CRE; Friar Matthew Erickson, O.P., Pst. Assoc.; Anthony Di Tolve, RCIA Coord.; Karl Meier, Music Min.; Marta C Brannon, Liturgy Dir.; Marianne Jablonski, Parish Life Coord.; Rev. Mario Aquinas Calabrese, O.P., Prior; Lori W Donlon, Bus. Mgr.; CRP Stds.: 438

CHESAPEAKE

St. Benedict - 521 McCosh Dr., Chesapeake, VA 23320-6111 t) 757-543-0561 frdamian521@hrcoxmail.com stbenedictschapel.org Rev. Neal Nichols, Pst.; Rev. Anthony Forte, Assoc. Pst.; Rev. Daniel Kluge, Assoc. Pst.; Kerry Sottung, Bus. Mgr.; CRP Stds.: 150

Church of St. Therese of Lisieux - 4137 Portsmouth Blvd., Chesapeake, VA 23321-2127 t) 757-488-2553 info@sttheresechesva.org www.sttheresechesva.org Rev. Kevin J. O'Brien, Pst.; Dcn. Frederick Clarence Allen III; CRP Stds.: 416

St. Mary - 536 Homestead Rd., Chesapeake, VA 23321; Mailing: 3501 Cedar Ln., Portsmouth, VA 23703 t) (757) 484-7335 Rev. Anthony William Morris, Pst.; Rev. Peter Calixtus Barfi; Rev. Daniel N. Klem;

Prince of Peace - 621 Cedar Rd., Chesapeake, VA 23322 t) 757-547-0356 pop.office@popparish.org www.popparish.org Rev. John Bosco Walugembe, Pst.; Dcn. Adrian A. Marchi;

St. Stephen, Martyr - 1544 S. Battlefield Blvd., Chesapeake, VA 23322-2041 t) 757-421-7416 ssm@ssmrcc.org ssmrcc.org Very Rev. Charles Ssebalamu, Pst.; Dcn. Kevin F. Trail; Dcn. Adrian A. Marchi;

CHESTERFIELD

St. Gabriel - 8901 Winterpock Rd., Chesterfield, VA 23832 lisa.gorton@saintgabriel.org Rev. Felix Rex Amofa, Pst.; Dcn. Roy Smith; Lisa Gorton, DRE;

CHINCOTEAGUE ISLAND

St. Andrew the Apostle - 6319 Mumford St., Chincoteague Island, VA 23336 t) 757-336-5432 saintandrewcatholicchurch@gmail.com standrewci.com Rev. Gerard Leoval C. Guadalupe, Pst.; CRP Stds.: 8

CHRISTIANSBURG

Holy Spirit Catholic Church - 355 Independence Blvd., Christiansburg, VA 24073 Rev. Patricio Alcantara, Pst.;

St. Jude - 1740 Tyler Rd., Christiansburg, VA 24073-6154 t) 540-639-5341 stjuderadfordva@gmail.com stjuderadfordva.org Dcn. Michael J. Ellerbrock; Susan Ellerbrock, DRE; Rev. Cassidy Stinson, Admin.; CRP Stds.: 39

CLARKSVILLE

St. Catherine of Siena - 805 Virginia Ave., Clarksville, VA 23927; Mailing: P.O. Box 1537, Clarksville, VA 23927 t) 434-374-8408 saintcatherines@usa.net Rev. Raner Ombao Lucila, Pst.; Rev. Johnny Mintah Mensah, Par. Vicar; Dcn. Paul Minner; Dcn. John E. Sadowski; Dcn. Peter Coleman; CRP Stds.: 6

CLIFTON FORGE

St. Joseph - 620 Jefferson Ave., Clifton Forge, VA 24422-1715 t) 540-863-5371 stjoseph@ntelos.net Rev. Augustine Lukenge, Pst.; Rev. Daniel L. Kelly, In Res.;

CLINTWOOD

St. Joseph - 478 Clintwood Main St., Clintwood, VA 24228-1250; Mailing: P.O. Box 1250, Clintwood, VA 24228 t) 276-926-5451 stanthony3@verizon.net; cinray@outlook.com www.holytrinitycluster.org Rev. Eric Baffour Asamoah, Pst.; CRP Stds.: 3

COLUMBIA

St. Joseph's/Shrine of St. Katharine Drexel - 28 Cameron St., Columbia, VA 23038-0808; Mailing: 4309 Thomas Jefferson Pkwy., Palmyra, VA 22963 t) 434-589-5201 receptionist@saintspeterpaul.org saintjosephcolumbia.org Rev. David Martin Ssentamu, Pst.; CRP Stds.: 47

COVINGTON

Sacred Heart - 255 W Main St, Covington, VA 24426-1542; Mailing: 214 W Locus St, Covington, VA 24426-1537 t) (540) 962-6541 office@sacredheartcovington.org sacredheartcovington.org Rev. Augustine Lukenge, Pst.; CRP Stds.: 25

DANVILLE

Sacred Heart - 538 Central Blvd., Danville, VA 24541 t) 434-792-9456 information@sheartchurch.org www.sheartchurch.org Rev. Anthony O. Senyah, Pst.;

Sacred Heart School - 540 Central Blvd., Danville, VA 24541 t) 434-793-2656 kskania@sheartschool.com www.sheartschool.com Kira S. Kania, Prin.;

EBONY

St. Peter the Apostle - 31 Ebony Rd., Ebony, VA 23845 t) 434-636-6277 office@stpeterebony.org www.stpeterebony.org Rev. Joker R. Bayta, Pst.; CRP Stds.: 2

ELKTON

Holy Infant - 101 W. Marshall Ave., Elkton, VA 22827; Mailing: 101 W. Marshall Ave, PO BOX 301, Elkton, VA 22827 t) 540-298-1341 holy_infant@verizon.net www.holyinfant-elkton.org Rev. Michael Mugomba, Pst.; Dcn. Paul Kudrav;

EMPORIA

St. Richard - 117 Laurel St., Emporia, VA 23847; Mailing: PO Box 627, Emporia, VA 23847 t) 434-636-6277 office@strichardscatholicchurch.org www.strichardscatholicchurch.org Rev. Joker R. Bayta, Pst.; CRP Stds.: 63

FARMVILLE

St. Theresa - 709 Buffalo St., Farmville, VA 23901-1109 t) 434-315-0311 sttheresa@embarqmail.com; sttheresa2@embarqmail.com Rev. Magnus Tochi Iwuji, Pst.; Dcn. Emmett R. McLane III; Dcn. Peter J. Menting; Karel Bailey, DRE;

Longwood University -

Hampden-Sydney College -

FINCASTLE

Church of the Transfiguration - 7624 Roanoke Rd., Fincastle, VA 24090 t) 540-473-2646 www.churchofthetransfiguration.com CRP Stds.: 20

St. John the Evangelist - 99 Second St., New Castle, VA 24127

FORT MONROE

St. Mary Star of the Sea - 7 Frank Ln., Fort Monroe, VA 23651-1010 t) 757-722-9855; 757-722-3138 kprimo@peninsulacluster.org www.smsschurch.com Very Rev. Romeo D. Jazmin, Pst.; Rev. Thomas Bagley Lawrence III, Par. Vicar; Dcn. Michael Swisher; Kimberly A. Primo, Admin.; CRP Stds.: 15

St. Mary Star of the Sea - 14 N. Willard Ave., Hampton, VA 23663 t) 757-723-6358 Sr. Mary John, O.P., Prin.;

FRANKLIN

St. Jude - 1014 Clay St., Franklin, VA 23851-1309 t) 757-569-9600 st_jude1@stjudefranklin.org Rev. Emmanuel Tobi Mensah, Pst.; CRP Stds.: 20

Infant of Prague - Rte. 460, Wakefield, VA 23888

GATE CITY

St. Bernard - 139 Linda St., Gate City, VA 24251 t) 276-386-9665 frkevin@stannes-bristol.org Very Rev. Christopher Martin Hess, Pst.; Rev. Timothy A. Drake, In Res.;

St. Patrick -

GLEN ALLEN

St. Michael - 4491 Springfield Rd., Glen Allen, VA 23060 t) 804-527-1037; 804-527-1037 x13 (CRP) admin@saint-mikes.org; pmundy@saint-mikes.org www.saint-mikes.org Rev. Daniel O. Brady, Pst.; Rev. James M. Arsenault, Assoc. Pst.; Rev. Renier Supranes, Par. Vicar; Dcn. David S. Nemetz, Pst. Assoc.; Dcn. Andrew M. Ferguson, Bus. Mgr.; Dcn. Robert H. Griffin;

GLOUCESTER

St. Therese, the Little Flower - 6262 Main St., Gloucester, VA 23061 t) (804) 693-5939 b.manager@stthersglo.org stthersglo.org Rev. Gregory R. Kandt, Pst.; Dcn. Jose Miguel Melendez; CRP Stds.: 25

HAMPTON

Immaculate Conception - 2150 Cunningham Dr., Hampton, VA 23666-0382 t) 757-826-0393 churchoffice@icchampton.org www.icchampton.org Rev. John Grace, Pst.; CRP Stds.: 62

St. Joseph - 512 Buckroe Ave., Hampton, VA 23664 t) 757-851-8800 ktallent@peninsulacluster.org www.stjosephcatholic.org/ Very Rev. Romeo D. Jazmin, Pst.; Rev. Thomas Bagley Lawrence III, Par. Vicar; Dcn. Guillermo Gonzalez; Dcn. David Reaves; CRP Stds.: 44

St. Rose of Lima and the Korean Martyrs - 2114 Bay Ave., Hampton, VA 23661 t) 757-245-5513 stroseerols@gmail.com; roselimakm@gmail.com www.strosekmcp.org Rev. Simon Hyo Sung Ahn, Pst.; CRP Stds.: 18

HARRISONBURG

Blessed Sacrament - 154 N. Main St., Harrisonburg, VA 22802 t) 540-434-4341 office@bsccva.com www.bsccva.org Rev. Silvio Kaberia, Pst.; Rev. Armando Herrera-DosReis, Par. Vicar; Rev. Ritche Malacas Sarabia, Par. Vicar; CRP Stds.: 354

HIGHLAND SPRINGS

St. John the Evangelist - 813 W. Nine Mile Rd., Highland Springs, VA 23075 t) 804-737-8028 office@stjohnscatholicchurch.org www.stjohnscatholicchurch.org Rev. Joseph Maxwell Appiagyei, Pst.; Rev. Nicholas E. Redmond, Par. Vicar; Paulita Matheny, DRE;

HOPEWELL

St. James Church - 510 W. Poythress St., Hopewell, VA 23860-2508 t) 804-458-9223 office@stjameshopewell.comcastbiz.net Very Rev. Joseph F. Goldsmith, Pst.; Rev. Julio Ciraco Barrameda Buena, Assoc. Pst.;

HOT SPRINGS

The Shrine of the Sacred Heart - 1499 Shady Ln., Hot Springs, VA 24445-0047 t) 540-839-2603 shrine@tds.net Rev. Augustine Lukenge, Pst.;

HURT

St. Victoria - ; Mailing: P.O. Box 640, Hurt, VA 24563-0640 t) 434-324-4824 stviccach@fairpoint.net Rev. James E. Gallagher Jr., Pst.; Dcn. Christopher Barrett; Kassaundra Carey, DRE;

JONESVILLE

Church of the Holy Spirit - 384 Eagle Ridge Dr., Jonesville, VA 24263; Mailing: P.O. Box 923, Jonesville, VA 24263 t) 276-346-0269 stanthonys3@verizon.net; linda.alsup@lee.k12.va.us www.holytrinitycluster.org Rev. Eric Baffour Asamoah, Pst.;

LEBANON

Good Shepherd - 890 W. Main St., Lebanon, VA 24266-0730; Mailing: P.O. Box 730, Lebanon, VA 24266-0730 t) (276) 889-1690 office@spiritofthemountain.org spiritofthemountain.org/ Rev. Zaverio Banasula (Uganda), Pst.; CRP Stds.: 4

Saint Mary - 109 Beech Ave., N.E., Coeburn, VA 24230; Mailing: P.O. Box 1724, Coeburn, VA 24230

LEXINGTON

St. Patrick - 221 W. Nelson St., Lexington, VA 24450; Mailing: P.O. Box 725, Lexington, VA 24450 t) 540-463-3533 office@stpatrickslexington.com stpatrickslexington.com Rev. Stefan Migac (Slovakia),

Pst.; Dcn. Paul Gorski; Kathleen Nowacki-Correia, DRE; CRP Stds.: 64

Virginia Military Institute -

Washington and Lee Univesity -

Southern Virginia University -

LOVINGSTON

St. Mary Catholic Church - 9900 Thomas Nelson Hwy., Lovingston, VA 22949-0735 t) 434-263-8509; 434-263-6923 (CRP) stmarystfrancischurch@verizon.net www.stmarycatholicchurch.org Rev. Rogelio L. Abadano, Pst.; Dcn. Richard J. Nees;

LYNCHBURG

Holy Cross - 710 Clay St., Lynchburg, VA 24504-2530 t) (434) 846-5245 gflores@holycrosslynchburg.org; sanonuevo@richmonddiocese.org holycrosslynchburg.org Very Rev. Salvador Anonuevo, Pst.; Rev. James E. Gallagher Jr., In Res.; Dcn. Christopher Murphy; Dcn. Charles Louis Mugnolo; CRP Stds.: 91

St. Thomas More - 3015 Roundelay Rd., Lynchburg, VA 24502-2036 t) 434-237-5911 info@stmva.org www.stmva.org Rev. Msgr. Michael D. McCarron, Pst.; CRP Stds.: 50

MARION

St. John the Evangelist Church - 124 Park Blvd., Marion, VA 24354 t) 276-783-7282; 276-781-0209 (Office) www.christthekingsaintjohn.org Very Rev. Rolo B. Castillo, Pst.;

MARTINSVILLE

St. Joseph - 2481 Spruce St., Martinsville, VA 24112 t) 276-638-4779; 276-638-1192 office@stjoe24112.comcastbiz.net www.stjoechurch.net Rev. Carlos H. Lerma, Pst.; CRP Stds.: 160

MATHEWS

Church of Francis de Sales - 176 Lover's Ln., Mathews, VA 23109-0158 Very Rev. Gerald S. Kaggwa, Pst.;

MECHANICSVILLE

Church of the Redeemer - 8275 Meadowbridge Rd., Mechanicsville, VA 23116 t) 804-746-4911 jcowles@churchredeemer.org; rwatson-fields@churchredeemer.org www.churchredeemer.org Rev. James Cowles, Pst.; Dcn. Christopher Stephen Colville; Dcn. Ronald A. Reger; Dcn. William J. Blatnik; Kate S. Chittum, DRE; Diane Atkins, Spiritual Adv./Care Srvcs.; Renee S. Reisenweaver, Youth Min.; Erin S. Woods, Music Min.; CRP Stds.: 45

MEHERRIN

Sacred Heart - 2597 Bruceville Rd., Meherrin, VA 23954 Rev. Magnus Tochi Iwuji, Pst.; Dcn. Emmett R. McLane III, Pst. Assoc.; Dcn. Peter J. Menting;

MINERAL

St. Jude - 1937 Davis Hwy., Mineral, VA 23117-0040; Mailing: P.O. Box 40, Mineral, VA 23117 t) 540-894-4266; 540-223-1563 (CRP) office@louisacatholics.org; dre@louisacatholics.org www.louisacatholics.org Rev. Michael M. Duffy, Pst.; Dcn. Alfonso Benet; Dcn. Thomas Fursman; Jess Johnson, DRE; CRP Stds.: 82

Immaculate Conception - 1107 Fredericks Hall Rd., Bumpass, VA 23024-0128; Mailing: P.O. Box 128, Bumpass, VA 23024-0128

MONETA

Resurrection - 15353 Moneta Rd., Moneta, VA 24121-9804 t) 540-297-5530 info@resurrectioncatholic.org www.resurrectioncatholic.org Rev. Nixon Negparanon, Pst.; Joe Day, Admin.; Dcn. Barry Dwayne Welch, Pst. Assoc.; CRP Stds.: 37

NEW CASTLE

St. John the Evangelist Parish - 99 Second St., New Castle, VA 24127 t) 540-864-8686 stjohnnewcastle@tds.net

NEWPORT NEWS

St. Jerome - 116 Denbigh Blvd., Newport News, VA 23608-3333 t) 757-877-5021; 757-877-3771 (CRP) stjerome@stjeromennva.org; margie@stjeromennva.org www.stjeromennva.org Rev. George Prado, Pst.; Dcn. Peter Eric Palm;

Our Lady of Mount Carmel - 100 Harpersville Rd., Newport News, VA 23601-2324 t) 757-595-0385 frdbeeman@olmc.org www.olmc.org Very Rev. W. Daniel Beeman, Pst.; Rev. Oswaldo Anleu-Sandoval (Guatemala), Par. Vicar; Rev. Peter Tran, Priest in residence; Dcn. Edwin Anleu Sandoval; Dcn. Antonio Siochi; CRP Stds.: 231

Our Lady of Mount Carmel School - 52 Harpersville Rd., Newport News, VA 23601-2324 t) 757-596-2754 principal@olmc-school.com www.olmc-school.com

St. Vincent de Paul - 230 33rd St., Newport News, VA 23607-0258; Mailing: P.O. Box 258, Newport News, VA 23607 t) 757-245-4234 stvdpcc@verizon.net Very Rev. Romeo D. Jazmin, Pst.; Rev. Thomas Bagley Lawrence III, Par. Vicar;

NORFOLK

Basilica of St. Mary of the Immaculate Conception - 1000 Holt St., Norfolk, VA 23504-4201 t) 757-622-4487 www.basilicaofsaintmary.org Rev. James P. Curran, Rector; Dcn. Calvin J. Bailey; CRP Stds.: 75

Blessed Sacrament - 6400 Newport Ave., Norfolk, VA 23505-4557 t) 757-423-8305 office@blessed-sacrament.com; cmccrary@blessed-sacrament.com www.blessed-sacrament.com Rev. Eric James Ayers, Pst.; Claire McCrary, DRE;

Christ the King - 1803 Columbia Ave., Norfolk, VA 23509-1200 t) 757-622-1120 (CRP); 757-622-1120 office@christthekingnorfolk.org www.christthekingnorfolk.org Rev. Joseph Wamala, Pst.; CRP Stds.: 72

Christ the King School - 3401 Tidewater Dr., Norfolk, VA 23509 t) 757-625-4951 info@ctkparish.org www.ctkparish.org Francine Gagne, Prin.;

Holy Trinity - 154 W. Government Ave., Norfolk, VA 23503-2905 t) 757-480-3433 parish.office@trinitynorfolk.org www.trinitynorfolk.org Rev. James M. Glass, O.S.B., Pst.;

Our Lady of Lavang - 1806 Ashland Ave., Norfolk, VA 23509-1236 t) 757-232-1424; 757-531-7214 parish@ourladyoflavang.org Rev. Joseph Phien Nguyen, Pst.; Joseph Trinh Tu, DRE;

Our Lady of Vietnam Chapel - 1806 Ashland Ave., Norfolk, VA 23509 t) 757-531-7214; 757-232-1424 parish@ourladyoflavang.org Rev. Joseph Phien Nguyen, Pst.; Rev. John Baptist Khoi Nguyen, DRE;

Chapel - 1307 LaSalle Ave., Hampton, VA 23669

St. Pius X - 7800 Halprin Dr., Norfolk, VA 23518-4408 t) 757-583-0291 parish@spxnorfolk.org www.spxnorfolk.org Very Rev. Sean M. Prince, Pst.; Dcn. Hoang Le; CRP Stds.: 49

St. Pius X School - t) 757-588-6171 school@piusxparish.org Sr. Linda Taber, I.H.M., Pres.;

Sacred Heart - 520 Graydon Ave., Norfolk, VA 23507-1711 t) (757) 625-6763 Rev. Paul Muyimbwa, Pst.; CRP Stds.: 49

NORTH CHESTERFIELD

St. Augustine - 4400 Beulah Rd., North Chesterfield, VA 23237-1850 t) 804-275-7962 aroberts@staugustinerva.org; staug4400@gmail.com www.staugustinerva.org Rev. Wayne L. Ball, Pst.; Dcn. Armando J. de Leon; Angymarie Corrigan, Youth Min.; Amanda Roberts, DRE; Dcn. Eric Christopher Broughton; Dcn. Christopher Corrigan;

Church of the Epiphany - 11000 Smoketree Dr., North Chesterfield, VA 23236-3144 t) 804-794-0222 epiphany@epiphanychurch.org www.epiphanychurch.org Rev. John C. Kazibwe, Pst.; Dcn. Stephen Haut; Dcn. Victor Valle;

St. Edward the Confessor - 2700 Dolfield Dr., North Chesterfield, VA 23235 t) 804-272-2948 stedward@stedwardch.org www.stedchurch.com Rev. Donald H. Lemay, Pst.; Rev. Deacon James D. Greer; Rev. Deacon Kevin Hogan; Rev. Deacon Gregg Whisler; Rev. Deacon Robert D. Ewan; CRP Stds.: 546

Regional School St. Edward-Epiphany - 10701 Huguenot Rd., Richmond, VA 23235 t) 804-272-2881 Emily Elliott, Prin.;

St. Joseph - 828 Buford Rd., North Chesterfield, VA 23235 t) 804-320-4932 office@stjosephrichmond.org www.stjosephrichmond.org Rev. Karl Marsolle, Pst.; Rev. David Franco, Par. Vicar; Rev. J. Peter Byrne, F.S.S.P., Par. Vicar; CRP Stds.: 100

NORTON

St. Anthony - 1009 Virginia Ave., N.W., Norton, VA 24273-1897 t) 276-679-2336 businessmanager@holytrinitycluster.org; ebaffourasamoah@richmonddiocese.org www.holytrinitycluster.org Rev. Eric Baffour Asamoah, Pst.; CRP Stds.: 10

University of Virginia at Wise -

ONLEY

St. Peter the Apostle Catholic Church - 25236 Coastal Blvd., Onley, VA 23418-0860; Mailing: P.O. Box 860, Onley, VA 23418-0860 t) (757) 787-4592 stpeteronley@gmail.com Rev. Michael Montalban Imperial, Pst.;

PALMYRA

Ss. Peter & Paul - 4309 Thomas Jefferson Pkwy., Palmyra, VA 22963-9506 t) 434-589-5201 office@saintspeterpaul.org www.saintspeterpaulpalmyra.org Rev. David Martin Ssentamu, Pst.; CRP Stds.: 40

PEARISBURG

Holy Family - 516 Mason Court Dr., Pearisburg, VA 24134-1832 t) 540-921-3547 holyfamilyva589@gmail.com holyfamilypearisburg.org Rev. Patricio Alcantara, Pst.;

PETERSBURG

St. John - 7215 Squirrel Level Rd., Petersburg, VA 23805-7035 t) 804-861-0123 info@stjohndinwiddie.org www.stjohndinwiddie.org Very Rev. Joseph F. Goldsmith, Pst.; Rev. Julio Ciraco Barrameda Buena, Assoc. Pst.; Rev. Ernest Livasia Bulinda, Assoc. Pst.; Dcn. Matthew C. MacLaughlin;

St. Joseph - 151 W. Washington St., Petersburg, VA 23803-1306; Mailing: P.O. Box 2006, Petersburg, VA 23804-1306 t) 804-733-3115 x15 (CRP); 804-733-3115 st_joseph_church@sjcpetersburg.com www.sjcpetersburg.com Rev. Gino P. Rossi; Dcn. Robert (Bob) Young; Dcn. Charles (Herb) Funk; Dcn. Donatus Theukwumere Amaram; CRP Stds.: 76

St. Joseph School - 123 Franklin St., Petersburg, VA 23803 t) 804-732-3931 Joseph Whitmore, Prin.;

PORTSMOUTH

Church of the Holy Angels - 34 Afton Pkwy., Portsmouth, VA 23702; Mailing: 3501 Cedar Ln., Portsmouth, VA 23703 t) 757-484-7335 holyangels@clusterparishes.com; christianformation@clusterparishes.com www.clusterparishes.com Rev. Anthony W. Morris, Pst.; Rev. Peter Calixtus Barfi, Par. Vicar; Rev. Daniel N. Klem, Assoc. Pst.;

Church of the Resurrection - 3501 Cedar Ln., Portsmouth, VA 23703 t) 757-484-7335 resurrection@clusterparishes.com www.clusterparishes.com Rev. Anthony W. Morris, Pst.; Rev. Peter Calixtus Barfi, Par. Vicar; Rev. Daniel N. Klem; Lourdes Gonzalez, CRE; Theresa Carpenter, RCIA Coord.; Roberto Pagtalunan, Youth Min.;

St. Paul - 522 High St., Portsmouth, VA 23704-3516; Mailing: 3501 Cedar Ln., Portsmouth, VA 23703-3803 t) (757) 484-7335 Rev. Anthony W. Morris, Pst.; Rev. Peter Calixtus Barfi; Rev. Daniel N. Klem;

POWHATAN

St. John Neumann - 2480 Batterson Rd., Powhatan, VA 23139-7513 t) 804-598-3754 sjn_general@yahoo.com www.sjnpowhatan.org Rev. Walter G. Lewis, Pst.; Dcn. James O. Tubbs, Pst. Assoc.; Gary Fitzgerald, Music Min.; Jean Kennedy, DRE; Jaime Quinn, Liturgy Dir.; Lee Mecca, Bus. Mgr.; CRP Stds.: 86

QUINTON

St. Elizabeth Ann Seton - 2631 Pocahontas Tr., Quinton, VA 23141-0245; Mailing: P.O. Box 648, Quinton, VA 23141-0648 t) 804-932-3388 (CRP); 804-932-4125 seas.dthomson@verizon.net; seascatholic@verizon.net www.seascatholicchurch.org Rev. J. Scott Duarte, Pst.;

CRP Stds.: 40

RICHMOND

Cathedral of the Sacred Heart - 823 Cathedral Pl., Richmond, VA 23220 t) 804-359-5651 info@richmondcathedral.org www.richmondcathedral.org Very Rev. Anthony E. Marques, Rector; Dcn. Christopher M. Malone; Dcn. Mark C. Matte; CRP Stds.: 68

Saint Benedict - 300 N. Sheppard St., Richmond, VA 23221 t) 804-254-8810 ioleary@saintbenedictparish.org www.saintbenedictparish.org Rev. John David Ramsey, Pst.; Dcn. Edward Owen Jr.; CRP Stds.: 52

Saint Benedict School - (Grades PreK-8) 3100 Grove Ave., Richmond, VA 23221 t) 804-254-8850 scress@saintbenedictschool.org www.saintbenedictschool.org Sean M. Cruess, Prin.;

St. Bridget - 6006 Three Chopt Rd., Richmond, VA 23226-2730 t) 804-282-9511 parishmail@saintbridgetchurch.org Rev. Kenneth J. Shuping, Pst.; Rev. James P. O'Reilly, Par. Vicar; Dcn. Robert B. Giovenco; Dcn. Charles Giovanetti; Rev. John Christian, Par. Vicar; Dcn. Victor Petillo; Very Rev. Msgr. R. Francis Muench, In Res.;

Saint Bridget Catholic School - 6011 York Rd., Richmond, VA 23226 t) 804-288-1994 information@saintbridget.org www.saintbridget.org George Sadler, Prin.;

Church of the Vietnamese Martyrs - 12486 Patterson Ave., Richmond, VA 23238 t) 804-784-5450 cvmrectory@gmail.com Rev. Paul Tuan Nguyen, O.P., Pst.; Rev. John Baptist Khoi Nguyen, Assoc. Pst.;

St. Elizabeth - 2712 2nd Ave., Richmond, VA 23222-3935; Mailing: 1301 Victor St., Richmond, VA 23222-3935 t) 804-329-4599 office@stelizcc.org stelizcc.org/ Rev. James M. Arsenault, Admin.; Dcn. Christopher Barrett; CRP Stds.: 100

All Saints - 3418 Noble Ave., Richmond, VA 23222 t) 804-329-7524 Kenneth Soistman, Prin.;

Holy Rosary - 3300 R St., Richmond, VA 23223-0416 t) 804-222-1105 office@hrccrichmond.org Rev. John J. Wagner III, Pst.; Dcn. Melvin D. Dowdy; Dcn. Francis Nelson Jr.; CRP Stds.: 45

St. Kim Taegon - 3100 Logandale Ave, Richmond, VA 23224 t) 804-232-0993 stkimchurch@gmail.com Rev. Myoungsang Lee, Pst.;

St. Mary - 9505 Gayton Rd., Richmond, VA 23229-5319 t) 804-740-4044 parish@stmarysrichmond.org www.stmarysrichmond.org Very Rev. Michael A. Renninger, Pst.; Dcn. Joseph Thomas Morlino; Dcn. Peter J. McCourt; Dcn. Kirk Collins; Dcn. Frank Ronald Baskind; Heather Heishman, Liturgy Dir.; Joe Lenich, Music Min.; Christopher Jenkins, Youth Min.; Laura Stapleton, Youth Min.; Gregg Kamper, Bus. Mgr.;

St. Mary School - 9501 Gayton Rd., Richmond, VA 23229 t) 804-740-1048 info@saintmary.org Brandon Hess, Prin.;

Our Lady of Lourdes - 8200 Woodman Rd., Richmond, VA 23228-3237 t) 804-262-7315 updates@ollrichva.org Rev. Jonathan Goertz, Pst.; Rev. Santos Rafael Ramirez Chicas (El Salvador), Par. Vicar; Dcn. Steven Cottam; Dcn. James Van Wyk;

Our Lady of Lourdes School - (Grades PreK-8) 8250 Woodman Rd., Richmond, VA 23228 t) 804-262-1770 admissions@lourdesrva.org; frontoffice@lourdesrva.org www.lourdesrva.org Dr. Carey Jacobsen, Prin.;

St. Patrick - 213 N. 25th St., Richmond, VA 23223-7115 t) 804-737-8028 office@saintpatrickchurchhill.org www.saintpatrickchurchhill.org Rev. Joseph Maxwell Appiagyei, Pst.; Rev. Nicholas E. Redmond, Par. Vicar; Paulita Matheny, DRE;

St. Paul - 909 Rennie Ave., Richmond, VA 23227 t) 804-329-0473 churchoffice@saintpaulscc.com saintpaulscc.org Rev. James J. Begley Jr., Pst.; Dcn. John Tucker III; Jan Dowdell, Music Min.; CRP Stds.: 10

All Saints - 3418 Noble Ave., Richmond, VA 23222 t) 804-329-7524 wcoleman@allsaintsric.org Michael Kelleher III, Prin.;

St. Peter - 800 E. Grace St., Richmond, VA 23219-0933; Mailing: P.O. Box 933, Richmond, VA 23219-0933 t) (804) 643-4315 stpeterchurch2@aol.com Rev. Joseph Maxwell Appiagyei, Pst.; Rev. Nicholas E. Redmond, Par. Vicar;

Sacred Heart - 1400 Perry St., Richmond, VA 23224-2057 t) 804-232-8964 sacredheartrva.org/ Rev. Shay W. Auerbach, S.J., Pst.;

ROANOKE

St. Andrew - 631 N. Jefferson St., Roanoke, VA 24016-1401 t) 540-344-9814 jmcintyre@standrewsva.org www.standrewsva.org Very Rev. Kevin L. Segerblom, Pst.; Rev. Christopher Masla, Par. Vicar; CRP Stds.: 151

St. Gerard - 809 Orange Ave., N.W., Roanoke, VA 24016-1117 t) 540-343-7744 maria@stgerardroanokeva.org; isaura@stgerardroanokeva.org stgerardroanokeva.org Rev. Daniel A. Cogut, Pst.; Rev. Julio Herman Reyes (El Salvador), Par. Vicar;

Our Lady of Nazareth - 2505 Electric Rd., S.W., Roanoke, VA 24018-3599 t) 540-774-0066; 540-774-0773 (CRP) secretary@oln-parish.com; cf@oln-parish.org www.oln-parish.com Very Rev. Msgr. Patrick D. Golden, Pst.; CRP Stds.: 173

ROCKY MOUNT

St. Francis of Assisi - 15 Glennwood Dr., Rocky Mount, VA 24151-2111 t) 540-483-9591 churchsecretary556@gmail.com; crefoa@gmail.com www.francis-of-assisi.org Rev. Carlos H. Lerma, Pst.;

RUCKERSVILLE

Shepherd of the Hills - 6562 Amicus Rd., Ruckersville, VA 22968; Mailing: P.O. Box 83, Quinque, VA 22965-0083 t) 434-985-3929 holy_infant@verizon.net shepherdofthehillscatholicparish.org/ Rev. Michael Mugomba, Pst.; Jane Lilly, DRE;

RUTHER GLEN

St. Mary of the Annunciation - 10306 Ladysmith Rd., Ruther Glen, VA 22546; Mailing: P.O. Box 396, Ladysmith, VA 22501 t) 804-448-9064 office@saintmarycc.org www.saintmarycc.org Rev. Alexander Muddu, Pst.; Dcn. David J. Geary; Dcn. Francis Leaming Jr.;

SALEM

Our Lady of Perpetual Help - 314 Turner Rd., Salem, VA 24153-2399 t) 540-387-0491 office@olphsalem.org www.olphsalem.org Rev. Daniel A. Cogut, Pst.; Rev. Julio Herman Reyes (El Salvador), Par. Vicar; Dcn. John Eric Beach; Dcn. Eric M. Surat; Barbara Hairfield, DRE;

SCOTTSVILLE

St. George - 7240 Scottsville Rd., Scottsville, VA 24590-0009; Mailing: P.O. Box 9, Scottsville, VA 24590-0009 t) 434-286-3724 stgeorge604@juno.com Rev. Walter C. Wagner, Pst.; Rev. David Mott, Par. Vicar; Dcn. Michael Stinson; Anglea Scolfora, DRE;

SMITHFIELD

Church of the Good Shepherd - 300 Smithfield Blvd., Smithfield, VA 23430 t) 757-365-0579 formation@cgsparish.org; admin@cgsparish.org www.cgsparish.org Rev. Pio Antonio Yllana, Pst.; Mary Langhill, DRE;

SOUTH BOSTON

St. Paschal Baylon - 800 John Randolph Blvd., South Boston, VA 24592-2943 t) 434-572-2285 stpaschalchurch@embarqmail.com Rev. Raner Lucila, Pst.; Rev. Johnny Mintah Mensah, Par. Vicar; Dcn. Richard Bolgiano; Dcn. Paul Buckman; CRP Stds.: 22

SOUTH CHESTERFIELD

St. Ann - 17111 Route 1, South Chesterfield, VA 23834-5396 t) 804-526-2548 saintann@stanncc.com www.stanncc.com Rev. Ernest Livasia Bulinda, Pst.;

SOUTH HILL

Good Shepherd - 1664 N. Mecklenburg Ave., South Hill, VA 23970-0621; Mailing: P.O. Box 621, South Hill, VA 23970-0621 t) 434-447-3622 goodsh23970@embarqmail.com Rev. Raner Lucila, Pst.; Rev. Johnny Mintah Mensah, Par. Vicar; CRP Stds.: 32

SOUTH PRINCE GEORGE

Church of the Sacred Heart - 9300 Community Ln., South Prince George, VA 23805 t) 804-732-6385 sacredheart@catholiccluster.com www.catholiccluster.com Rev. Julio Ciraco Barrameda Buena, Par. Vicar; Very Rev. Joseph F. Goldsmith, Pst.; Penny E. Merhout, Bus. Mgr.; Dcn. Edward G. Hanzlik; Dcn. Robert Straub; Dcn. Esaud Feliciano; CRP Stds.: 135

ST. PAUL

St. Therese - 16661 Wise St., St. Paul, VA 24283-0056; Mailing: P.O. Box 56, St. Paul, VA 24283-0056 t) 276-889-1690 office@spiritofthemountain.org spiritofthemountain.org/ Rev. Zaverio Banasula (Uganda), Pst.;

STAUNTON

St. Francis of Assisi - 118 N. New St., Staunton, VA 24401-3636 t) 540-886-9121 office@stfrancisparish.org www.stfrancisparish.org Rev. Joseph Wamala, Pst.; Dcn. James Kledzik;

SUFFOLK

St. Mary of the Presentation - 202 S. Broad St., Suffolk, VA 23434-5715 t) 757-539-5732 office@stmarysuffolk.org www.stmarysuffolk.org Rev. Rogelio A. S. Largoza, Pst.;

TAPPAHANNOCK

St. Timothy - 413 St. Timothy Ln., Tappahannock, VA 22560-0129 t) 804-443-2760 (Office); 804-443-2570 (Rectory) www.sttimothysparish.org Rev. Gerald F. Musuubire, Pst.; CRP Stds.: 48

TAZEWELL

Holy Family Parish - 312 Tazewell Ave., Tazewell, VA 24651 t) 276-988-4626 parishoffice@holyfamilyswva.org www.holyfamilyva.com Rev. Eric Anokye, Pst.; CRP Stds.: 5

TOPPING

Church of the Visitation - 8462 General Puller Hwy, Topping, VA 23169; Mailing: PO Box 38, Topping, VA 23169 t) 804-758-5160 churchofthevisitation@va.metrocast.net www.church-of-the-visitation.org Very Rev. Gerald S. Kaggwa, Pst.;

VIRGINIA BEACH

Catholic Church of St. Mark - 1505 Kempsville Rd., Virginia Beach, VA 23464-7210 t) 757-479-1010 (Office); 757-479-9897 (Rel Form.) secretary@stmark-parish.org; franthony@stmark-parish.org www.stmark-parish.org Rev. Anthony Mpungu, Pst.; Dcn. Michael Johnson, Pst. Assoc.; Dcn. John J. Kren; Sharon Katzman, DRE; CRP Stds.: 210

Church of the Ascension - 4853 Princess Anne Rd., Virginia Beach, VA 23462-4446 t) 757-495-1886 x410 info@ascensionvb.org Rev. Daniel J. Malingumu, Pst.; Dcn. James Ahearn; Dcn. Gary R. Harmeyer; Dcn. Thomas E. McFeely; Diane Nestor, Music Min.; Travis Hayes, Youth Min.; Janet Jones, DRE; Lisa Liedl, Bus. Mgr.; CRP Stds.: 508

Church of the Holy Apostles - 1593 Lynnhaven Pkwy., Virginia Beach, VA 23453-2008 (Anglican-Roman Catholic Congregation of Hampton Roads) Rev. Msgr. Raphael A. Owusu Peprah, Chap.; Dcn. Gary R. Harmeyer, Pst. Assoc.;

St. Gregory the Great - 5345 Virginia Beach Blvd., Virginia Beach, VA 23462 t) 757-497-8330 stgregoryg@aol.com; toni@stgregorysva.org stgregoryvabeach.org Rev. Dominic Leo, OSB, Par. Admin.; Rev. Cristiano Aparecido Brito, O.S.B., Par. Vicar; Rev. Mark Wenzinger, OSB, Par. Vicar; Dcn. Kevin Gorman; Dcn. Darrell G. Wentworth; Carol Noona, Music Min.; Laura Sage, Pst. Assoc.; David Lamb, Treas.; Rev. Lee R. Yoakam, O.S.B., In Res.; Dcn. Robert Beardsworth; CRP Stds.: 360

St. Gregory the Great School - 5343 Virginia Beach Blvd., Virginia Beach, VA 23462-1896 t) 757-497-1811 office@sggsvb.org Gina Coss, Prin.;

St. Gregory the Great Daycare Center - 5361 Virginia Beach Blvd., Virginia Beach, VA 23462 t) 757-497-6013 Kathy Walker, Dir.;

Holy Family - 1279 N. Great Neck Rd., Virginia Beach, VA 23454-2117 t) 757-481-5702 secretary@holyfamilyvb.org holyfamilyvb.org Rev. Rene R. Castillo, Pst.; Dcn. Robert May;

Holy Spirit - 1396 Lynnhaven Pkwy., Virginia Beach, VA 23453-2710 t) 757-468-3600 office@holyspiritvb.org www.holyspiritvb.org/ Rev. Matthew Allen Kiehl, Pst.; Dcn. Vernon Krajeski; Dcn. Stephen Kuczma; Dcn. Robert Smithberger;

St. John the Apostle Church - 1968 Sandbridge Rd., Virginia Beach, VA 23456 t) 757-426-2180 www.sjavb.org Rev. Robert J. Cole, Pst.; Dcn. Chris James Finocchio Jr.; Dcn. Joseph F. Grillo; Dcn. Gary "Mac" McClelland; Dcn. Glenn Bailey; Veronica Litwinowicz, Youth Min.; John Domingo, DRE; CRP Stds.: 284

St. John the Apostle Church School - 1968B Sandbridge Rd., Virginia Beach, VA 23456 t) 757-821-1100 Miriam Cotton, Prin.;

St. Luke - 2304 Salem Rd., Virginia Beach, VA 23456-1215 t) 757-427-5776 stlukecc@aol.com www.stlukevabeach.org Rev. Msgr. Raphael A. Owusu Peprah, Admin.; Dcn. Lawrence P. Illy; Dcn. Anacleto Magsombol;

St. Matthew - 3314 Sandra Ln., Virginia Beach, VA 23464-1736 t) 757-420-6310 office@saintmatts.net www.saintmatts.net Rev. Peter Naah, Pst.; Dcn. Cris Romero; Dcn. Daniel Sorady; CRP Stds.: 75

St. Matthew School - 3316 Sandra Ln., Virginia Beach, VA 23464 t) 757-420-2455 office@smsvb.net www.smsvb.net Louis Goldberg, Prin.;

St. Nicholas - 712 Little Neck Rd., Virginia Beach, VA 23452 awhitehouse@stnicholasvb.com Rev. Venancio R. Balarote Jr., Pst.; Lora Di Nardo, Pst. Assoc.; Angela Whitehouse, DRE;

Star of the Sea - 1404 Pacific Ave., Virginia Beach, VA 23451-3439 Very Rev. Esteban DeLeon, Pst.;

Star of the Sea School - -8) 309 15th St., Virginia Beach, VA 23451 t) 757-428-8400 carey.averill@sosschool.org; information@sosschool.org www.sosschool.org Carey Averill, Prin.;

WAYNESBORO

St. John the Evangelist - 301 Sheppard Court, Waynesboro, VA 22980 jdunford@stjohnevan.com www.stjohnevan.com Very Rev. Francis Xavier Musolooza, Pst.;

WEST POINT

Our Lady of the Blessed Sacrament - 3570 King William Ave., West Point, VA 23181; Mailing: 207 W. Euclid Blvd., West Point, VA 23181-9378 t) 804-843-3125 olbs@olbs-catholic.org; adminassistant@olbs-catholic.org www.olbs-catholic.org Rev. Oscar Paraiso, Pst.; Erin Hayden, DRE; Bob Ryalls, Bus. Mgr.;

WILLIAMSBURG

St. Bede - 3686 Ironbound Rd., Williamsburg, VA 23188-5207 t) 757-229-3631 stboffice@bedeva.org www.bedeva.org Rev. Anthony Ferguson, Par. Vicar; Dcn. Gregory Ballentine; Dcn. James Findley; Dcn. Francis Roettinger; Dcn. Bill Westerman; CRP Stds.: 594

St. Olaf, Patron of Norway - 104 Norge Ln., Williamsburg, VA 23188-7229 t) 757-564-3819 office@stolaf.cc www.stolaf.cc Rev. Thomas E. Mattingly, Pst.; Dcn. Donald Fox; Dcn. Edward Handel; Dcn. Robert R. Thompson; Dcn. Neil Zachary; CRP Stds.: 117

WOODLAWN

St. Joseph's - 78 St. Josephs Ln., Woodlawn, VA 24381 t) 276-236-7814 office@stjosephswoodlawn.org stjosephswoodlawn.org Rev. Herman Katongole, Pst.;

Church of the Risen Lord - 59 Mountainview Loop, Stuart, VA 24171

Church of All Saints - 598 Needmore Rd., N.E., Floyd, VA 24091

WYTHEVILLE

St. Mary the Mother of God - 370 E. Main St., Wytheville, VA 24382; Mailing: PO Box 7, Wytheville, VA 24382 t) 276-228-3104 officemanager@stmaryswytheville.org www.stmaryswytheville.org Rev. Francis Boateng, Pst.; CRP Stds.: 8

Saint Edward - N. Washington Ave. & 7th St., Pulaski, VA 24301; Mailing: P.O. Box 1670, Pulaski, VA 24301 t) (540) 980-6511 stedwardpulaski.org Rev. Francis K. Boateng, Pst.;

YORKTOWN

St. Joan of Arc - 315 Harris Grove Ln., Yorktown, VA 23692-4014 t) 757-898-7190 (CRP); 757-898-5570 cmacababbad@stjoanofarcva.org Rev. Michael Joly, Pst.; Dcn. Mark Mueller; Dcn. James L. Satterwhite;

Saint Kateri Tekakwitha - 3800 Big Bethel Rd., Yorktown, VA 23693-3814 t) 757-766-3800 dgausmann@stkateri.cc; lyankoski@stkateri.cc www.stkateri.cc Rev. Robert M. Spencer, Pst.; Lori Yankoski, Music Min.; Debra Gausmann, DRE; CRP Stds.: 163

SCHOOLS: PRESCHOOL THRU HIGH SCHOOL

SCHOOLS

COMMONWEALTH OF VIRGINIA

BLACKSBURG

***St. John Neumann Academy** - (PRV) (Grades PreK-8) 3600 Yellow Sulphur Rd., Blacksburg, VA 24060 t) 540-552-7562 julia.wharton@sjnacademy.org Julia Wharton, Dir.; Stds.: 181; Lay Tchrs.: 18

BRISTOL

St. Anne Catholic School - (PAR) (Grades PreK-8) 300 Euclid Ave., Bristol, VA 24201 t) 276-669-0048 schooloffice@stanneschoolbristol.org Andrew Snyder, Prin.; Stds.: 146; Lay Tchrs.: 16

CHARLOTTESVILLE

Charlottesville Catholic School - (DIO) (Grades PreK-8) 1205 Pen Park Rd., Charlottesville, VA 22901 t) 434-964-0400 info.ccs@cvillecatholic.org Vada Fallica, Prin.; Stds.: 353; Lay Tchrs.: 28

DANVILLE

Sacred Heart Elementary School - (DIO) (Grades PreK-8) 540 Central Blvd., Danville, VA 24541 t) 434-793-2656 mweatherford@sheartschool.com Matthew Weatherford, Prin.; Stds.: 133; Lay Tchrs.: 15

HAMPTON

St Marys Star of the Sea Catholic School - (DIO) (Grades PreK-8) 14 N. Willard Ave., Hampton, VA 23663 t) 757-723-6358 admin@saintmarystarofthesea.com; finance@saintmarystarofthesea.com Dcn. Michael Derrick Brown, Bus. Mgr.; Sr. Mary Cecilia Goodrum, O.P., Prin.; Stds.: 179; Sr. Tchrs.: 4; Lay Tchrs.: 11

NEWPORT NEWS

Our Lady of Mt Carmel - (DIO) (Grades PreK-8) 52 Harpersville Rd., Newport News, VA 23601 t) 757-596-2754 www.olmc-school.com Sr. Anna Joseph, O.P., Prin.; Stds.: 360; Sr. Tchrs.: 3; Lay Tchrs.: 23

NORFOLK

***Barry Robinson Schools of Norfolk** - (PRV) 443 Kempsville Rd., Norfolk, VA 23502; Mailing: P.O. Box 1180, Norfolk, VA 23501 t) (757) 440-5500 Robert E. McCartney, CEO;

Christ the King Catholic School - (DIO) (Grades PreK-8) 3401 Tidewater Dr., Norfolk, VA 23509 t) 757-625-4951 kcallahan@ctkparish.org Kim Callahan, Prin.; Stds.: 216; Lay Tchrs.: 12

St. Patrick Catholic School - (PRV) (Grades PreK-8) 1000 Bolling Ave., Norfolk, VA 23508 t) 757-440-5500 office@mystpcs.org www.stpcs.org Lauren Mazzari, Head of School; Jamye Brown, Assistant Head of School; Stds.: 399; Lay Tchrs.: 34

St. Pius X School - (DIO) (Grades PreK-8) 7800 Halprin Dr., Norfolk, VA 23518 t) 757-588-6171 school@spxschoolnorfolk.org www.spxschoolnorfolk.org Mark Zafra, Prin.; Stds.: 185; Sr. Tchrs.: 1; Lay Tchrs.: 16

PETERSBURG

St. Joseph School - (PAR) (Grades PreK-8) 123 Franklin St., Petersburg, VA 23803 t) 804-732-3931 school@saintjosephschool.com; sowens@saintjosephschool.com Sarah Owens, Prin.; Teresa Fisher, Librn.; Stds.: 164; Lay Tchrs.: 17

PORTSMOUTH

Portsmouth Catholic Regional - (DIO) (Grades PreK-8) 2301 Oregon Ave., Portsmouth, VA 23701 t) 757-488-6744 priscillataylor@portsmouthcatholic.net; donnahenry@portsmouthcatholic.net Donna Henry, Prin.; Stds.: 165; Lay Tchrs.: 13

POWHATAN

Blessed Sacrament Huguenot High School - (DIO) (Grades PreK-12) 2501 Academy Rd., Powhatan, VA 23139 t) 804-598-4211 mperry@bshknights.org Meredith Perry, Prin.; Stds.: 393; Lay Tchrs.: 42

RICHMOND

All Saints Catholic School - (DIO) (Grades PreK-8) 3418 Noble Ave., Richmond, VA 23222 t) 804-329-7524 smeadows@allsaintsric.org Scott Meadows, Prin.; Stds.: 204; Lay Tchrs.: 16

St. Benedict School - (DIO) (Grades PreK-8) 3100 Grove Ave., Richmond, VA 23221 t) 804-254-8850 development@saintbenedictschool.org Sean M. Cruess, Prin.; Leda Ansbro, Librn.; Stds.: 237; Lay Tchrs.: 13

St. Bridget School - (DIO) (Grades PreK-8) 6011 York Rd., Richmond, VA 23226 t) 804-288-1994 aallen@saintbridget.org Allie Strollo, Prin.; Stds.: 525; Lay Tchrs.: 41

St. Edward-Epiphany Catholic School - (DIO) (Grades PreK-8) 10701 W. Huguenot Rd., Richmond, VA 23235 t) 804-272-2881 office@seeschool.com www.seeschool.com Tracy Hamner, Prin.; Justin Andrew, Asst. Prin.; Mindy Gerloff, Bus. Mgr.; Stds.: 546; Lay Tchrs.: 32

St. Mary's Catholic School - (DIO) (Grades PreK-8) 9501 Gayton Rd., Richmond, VA 23229; Mailing: 9505 Gayton Rd., Richmond, VA 23229 t) 804-740-1048 info@saintmary.org www.saintmary.org Brandon Hess, Prin.; Mary Jordan, Vice Prin.; Stds.: 424; Lay Tchrs.: 33

Our Lady of Lourdes School - (PAR) (Grades PreK-8) 8250 Woodman Rd., Richmond, VA 23228 t) 804-262-1770 carey_jacobsen@lourdesrva.org Dr. Carey Jacobsen, Prin.; Stds.: 356; Scholastics: 1; Pr. Tchrs.: 1; Lay Tchrs.: 24

VIRGINIA BEACH

St. Gregory the Great School - (DIO) (Grades PreK-8) 5343 Virginia Beach Blvd., Virginia Beach, VA 23462 t) 757-497-1811 office@sggsvb.org Joe Branco, Prin.; Stds.: 591; Lay Tchrs.: 40

St. John the Apostle Catholic School - (DIO) (Grades PreK-8) 1968-B Sandbridge Rd., Virginia Beach, VA 23456 t) 757-821-1100 sja@sjavb.org www.sjavb.org Miriam Cotton, Prin.; Jennifer Davey, Vice Prin.; Tracey Dooley, Bus. Mgr.; Stds.: 468; Lay Tchrs.: 29

St. Matthew School - (DIO) (Grades PreK-8) 3316 Sandra Ln., Virginia Beach, VA 23464 t) 757-420-2455 office@smsvb.net www.smsvb.net Louis Goldberg, Prin.; Stds.: 492; Lay Tchrs.: 31

Star of the Sea School - (DIO) (Grades PreK-8) 309 15th St., Virginia Beach, VA 23451 t) 757-428-8400 information@sosschool.org Carey Averill, Prin.; Stds.: 25; Lay Tchrs.: 20

HIGH SCHOOLS

COMMONWEALTH OF VIRGINIA

NEWPORT NEWS

Peninsula Catholic High School - (DIO) (Grades 8-12) 600 Harpersville Rd., Newport News, VA 23601 t) 757-596-7247 www.peninsulacatholic.com Stds.: 269; Lay Tchrs.: 28

RICHMOND

Benedictine College Preparatory (Benedictine Schools of Richmond) - (PRV) (Grades 9-12) 12829 River Rd.,

Richmond, VA 23238 t) 804-708-9500 bcpinfo@benedictinecollegeprep.org; finance@benedictineschools.org www.benedictinecollegeprep.org A Catholic Military High School operated by the Benedictine Monks. Drew Mugford, Prin.; Stds.: 284; Pr. Tchrs.: 1; Sr. Tchrs.: 1; Lay Tchrs.: 46

***Cristo Rey Richmond High School** - (PRV) (Grades 9-12) 313 N. Belmont Ave, Richmond, VA 23221; Mailing: 304 N Sheppard St, Richmond, VA 23221 t) 804-447-4704 info@cristoreyrichmond.org Dcn. Peter J. McCourt, Pres.; Corey Taylor, Prin.; Dr. Lynn Waidelich, Vice Prin.; Taylor Wilkerson, Campus Min.; Stds.: 221; Scholastics: 1; Lay Tchrs.: 19

Saint Gertrude High School (Benedictine Schools of Richmond) - (PRV) (Grades 9-12) 12829 River Rd., Richmond, VA 23238 t) 804-708-9500 sghs@saintgertrude.org; finance@benedictineschools.org www.saintgertrude.org Drew Mugford, Prin.; Amy Pickral, Headmaster; Stds.: 214; Pr. Tchrs.: 1; Sr. Tchrs.: 1; Lay Tchrs.: 46

ROANOKE

Roanoke Catholic School - (DIO) (Grades PreK-12) 621 N. Jefferson St., Roanoke, VA 24016-1401 t) 540-982-3532 ppatterson@roanokecatholic.com www.roanokecatholic.com Christopher Michael, Dean; Patrick Patterson, Prin.; Stds.: 397; Lay Tchrs.: 33

VIRGINIA BEACH

Catholic High School - (DIO) (Grades 9-12) 4552 Princess Anne Rd., Virginia Beach, VA 23462 t) 757-467-2881 boonp@chsvb.org www.chsvb.org Peggy Boon, Prin.; Stds.: 479; Lay Tchrs.: 39

WILLIAMSBURG

Walsingham Academy - (PRV) (Grades PreK-12) 1100 Jamestown Rd., Williamsburg, VA 23185 t) 757-229-6026 mjo@walsingham.org www.walsingham.org Private Day School for Boys and Girls. Angie Baker, Dir.; Mary Johnston, Dir.; Sr. Mary Jeanne Oesterle, R.S.M., Pres.; Stds.: 517; Sr. Tchrs.: 1; Lay Tchrs.: 60

INSTITUTIONS LOCATED IN DIOCESE

CAMPUS MINISTRY / NEWMAN CENTERS [CAM]

ASHLAND

Catholic Campus Ministry, Randolph Macon College - 105 S. Snead St., Ashland, VA 23005 t) (804) 798-5039 office@stannscc.org Erin McGuire_Metrey, Campus Min.;

BLACKSBURG

Virginia Tech, Newman Community - 203 Otey St., Blacksburg, VA 24060 t) 540-951-0032 chitzelberger@gmail.com Chris Hitzelberger, Campus Min.;

CHARLOTTESVILLE

Catholic Campus Ministry, University of Virginia - 401 Alderman Rd., Charlottesville, VA 22903 t) (434) 293-8081 Rev. Joseph-Anthony Kress, Chap.;

FARMVILLE

Catholic Campus Ministry, Hampden-Sydney & Longwood Univ. - 114 Midtown Ave., Farmville, VA 23901 t) (434) 394-0586 farmvilleccm@gmail.com Rev. Tochi Iwuji, Chap.; Dan Holland, Campus Min.;

HARRISONBURG

Catholic Campus Ministry, James Madison University - 1052 S. Main St., Harrisonburg, VA 22801 t) (540) 434-7360 afarinholt@jmuccm.com Austin Farinholt, Campus Min.;

LEXINGTON

Catholic Campus Ministry, Washington & Lee Univ. & VMI (Lexington Catholic Campus Ministry) - 221 W Nelson St, Lexington, VA 24450; Mailing: P.O. Box 725, Lexington, VA 24450 t) 540-463-3533 director@catholex.com www.catholex.com Rev. Stefan Migac (Slovakia), Chap.; Andrew DeCelle, Campus Min.;

LYNCHBURG

Lynchburg Catholic Campus Ministry - 500 Brevard St., Lynchburg, VA 24501 t) (434) 544-8698 serratore_kr@lynchburg.edu Kayla Rose Serratore, Campus Min.;

NEWPORT NEWS

Catholic Campus Ministry, Christopher Newport University - 100 Harpersville Rd., Newport News, VA 23601 t) (757) 595-0385 x123 ccm@cnu.edu Cate Harmeyer, Campus Min.;

NORFOLK

Catholic Campus Ministry, Norfolk State University - 1000 Holt St., Norfolk, VA 23504 t) (804) 622-5162 llaclair@richmonddiocese.org Laura LaClair, Campus Min.;

Catholic Campus Ministry, Old Dominion University - 1306 W. 49th St., Norfolk, VA 23508 t) 757-440-9065 info@catholicmonarchs.org Marissa O'Neil, Campus Min.;

NORTON

Catholic Campus Ministry, University of Virginia at Wise - 1009 Virginia Ave., N.W., Norton, VA 24273 t) (804) 622-5162 llaclair@richmonddiocese.org Rev. Zaverio Banasula (Uganda), Chap.; Laura LaClair, Admin.;

RADFORD

Catholic Campus Ministry, Radford University - 1024A Clement St., Radford, VA 24141 c) (540) 505-0312 catholic@radford.edu ruccm.com Rev. Cassidy Stinson, Chap.; Tony Laux, Campus Min.;

RICHMOND

Catholic Campus Ministry, Virginia Commonwealth University - 20 N Laurel, Richmond, VA 23220 t) (804) 622-5162 llaclair@richmonddiocese.org Very Rev. Anthony E. Marques; Laura LaClair, Admin.;

SALEM

Catholic Campus Ministry, Roanoke College - 221 College Ln., Salem, VA 24153 t) (540) 387-0491 madeleineglawson@gmail.com Madeleine Wertz, Campus Min.; Rev. Daniel A. Cogut, Chap.;

WILLIAMSBURG

Catholic Campus Ministry, College of William & Mary - 10 Harrison Ave., Williamsburg, VA 23185 t) (757) 220-1415 info@wmccm.org Rev. Kyle O'Connor, Chap.; John Hopke, Campus Min.;

CATHOLIC CHARITIES [CCH]

RICHMOND

Commonwealth Catholic Charities - 1601 Rolling Hills Dr., Richmond, VA 23229-5011 t) 804-285-5900 agency@cccofva.org www.cccofva.org Jay Brown, CEO;

St. Francis House - 820 Campbell Ave., S.W., Roanoke, VA 24016-3536 t) 540-342-7561 x319

Satellite Office - 918 Harris St., Ste. 1G, Charlottesville, VA 22903 t) 434-974-6880

Satellite Office - 541 Luck Ave. S.W., Ste. 118, Roanoke, VA 24016-5055 t) 540-342-0411

Satellite Office - 507 Park Ave., S.W., Norton, VA 24273 t) 276-679-1195

Satellite Office - 836 Camnpbell Ave., S.W., Roanoke, VA 24016-3536 t) 540-342-7561

Satellite Office - 12284 Warwick Blvd., Ste. 1-A, Newport News, VA 23606-3855 t) 757-247-3600

Satellite Office - 827 Commerce St., Petersburg, VA 23803 t) 804-733-6207

Satellite Office - 511 W. Grace St., Richmond, VA 23220-4911 t) 804-648-4177

VIRGINIA BEACH

Catholic Charities of Eastern Virginia, Inc. - 5361-A Virginia Beach Blvd., Virginia Beach, VA 23462 t) 757-456-2366 hr@cceva.org www.cceva.org Tracy Fick, CEO; Asstd. Annu.: 10,200; Staff: 53

Branch Office - 4855 Princess Anne Rd., Virginia Beach, VA 23462 t) 757-467-7707

Branch Office - 1301 Colonial Ave., Norfolk, VA 23517 t) 757-533-5217

Branch Office - 3804 Poplar Hill Rd., Ste. A, Chesapeake, VA 23321 t) 757-484-0703

Branch Office - 12829 Jefferson Ave., Ste. 101, Newport News, VA 23608 t) 757-875-0060

CEMETERIES [CEM]

LYNCHBURG

Holy Cross - 710 Clay St., Lynchburg, VA 24504 t) 434-846-5245 aflagg@holycrosslynchburg.org

NORFOLK

St. Mary's Catholic Cemetery - 3000 Church St., Norfolk, VA 23504 t) 757-627-2874

PORTSMOUTH

All Saints Catholic Cemetery (formerly St. Paul's Cemetery) - 2701 Elm St., Portsmouth, VA 23704; Mailing: P.O. Box 155, Portsmouth, VA 23705 t) 757-483-6201 cgettys@richmonddiocese.org Christina Gettys, Family Service Advisor;

RICHMOND

Holy Cross Cemetery - 1628 Matthews St., Richmond, VA 23222 t) 804-321-5936 John West, Bus. Mgr.;

Mount Calvary - 1400 S. Randolph St., Richmond, VA 23220 t) 804-355-5271 jim.glass@mcalvary.com Jim Glass, Bus. Mgr.;

ROANOKE

St. Andrew's Diocesan Cemetery - 3601 Salem Tpke., N.W., Roanoke, VA 24017 t) 540-595-7173 standrewscemetery@gmail.com

SOUTH PRINCE GEORGE

Sacred Heart Cemetery Corporation - 9300 Community Ln., South Prince George, VA 23805 t) 804-732-6385 dhanzlik87@gmail.com Very Rev. Joseph F. Goldsmith, Pres.; David Hanzlik, Dir.; Michael Hanzlik, Dir.; Lewis Hanzlik, Dir.; Elaine Ward, Dir.;

CONVENTS, MONASTERIES, AND RESIDENCES FOR WOMEN [CON]

BARHAMSVILLE

Bethlehem Monastery of the Poor Clare Nuns - 5500 Holly Fork Rd., Barhamsville, VA 23011 t) 757-566-1684 mtstfrancis@gmail.com www.poor-clares.org Observing the Primitive Rule of St. Clare, Constitutions of the Poor Clare Federation of Mary Immaculate (strictly cloistered, solemn vows). Mother Mary Joyce Valappattukaran, P.C.C.; Srs.: 21

CROZET

Our Lady of the Angels Monastery - 3365 Monastery Dr., Crozet, VA 22932 t) 434-823-1452 sisters@olamonastery.org www.olamonastery.org Sr. Kathy Ullrich, O.C.S.O., Prioress; Srs.: 11

HAMPTON

Dominican Sisters of Saint Cecilia, Nashville, O.P. - 14 N. Willard Ave., Hampton, VA 23663 t) (757) 723-6358 Srs.: 8

Lovers of the Holy Cross, L.H.O. - 318 Whealton Rd., Hampton, VA 23666 t) (832) 331-6321 Srs.: 3

NEWPORT NEWS

Bernardine Sisters of the Third Order of St. Francis - 6A Ridgewood Pkwy., Newport News, VA 23602-4484 t) 757-886-6391 www.bfranciscan.org Srs.: 4

Handmaids of Our Lady of Mount Carmel, H.L.M.C. - 12 Cedarwood Way, Apt. B, Newport News, VA 23608 t) (443) 226-2790 Sr. Imelda Manuhwa, H.L.M.C., Supr.; Srs.: 3

NORFOLK

Sisters Servants of the Immaculate Heart of Mary - 7813 Halprin Dr., Norfolk, VA 23518 t) 757-769-7009; 757-588-6171 piusihmva@aol.com www.ihmimmaculata.org Srs.: 6

St. Pius X Convent - Sr. Linda Taber, I.H.M., Supr.;

PORTSMOUTH

Sisters of Bon Secours - 412 West Rd., Portsmouth, VA 23707 t) 757-397-3869 rita_thomas@bshsi.com Sr. Rita Thomas, Pres.; Srs.: 1

POWHATAN

Sisters of Blessed Sacrament, S.B.S. - 2260 Scottville

Rd., Powhatan, VA 23139 t) (804) 349-8868 Srs.: 4

QUINTON

Little Sisters of St. Francis, L.S.O.S.F., St. Francis Convent - 11300 Continental Rd., Quinton, VA 23141 t) (757) 564-7371 Sr. Agnes Narocho, L.S.O.S.F., Supr.; Srs.: 7

RICHMOND

Comboni Missionary Sisters, Delegation House - 1307 Lakeside Ave., Richmond, VA 23228-4710 t) 804-262-8827 www.combonimissionarysistersusa.org Sr. Eugenia Adriana Del Pilar Tovar Villacis, Supr.; Sr. Delia Margarita Contreras del Toro, Treas.; Srs.: 7

Congregation of Bon Secours, C.B.S. - 5912 Monument Ave., Richmond, VA 23226 t) (201) 983-2440 Srs.: 1

Daughters of Mary Immaculate, D.M.I. - 12500 Patterson Ave., Richmond, VA 23238 t) (804) 784-5427 Sr. Cecilia Tien Ngo, D.M.I., Supr.; Srs.: 6

Sisters for Christian Community, S.F.C.C. - 5110 Sulky Dr., Richmond, VA 23228 t) (804) 334-4985 Srs.: 5

ROCKVILLE

Monastery of the Visitation Monte Maria - 12221 Bienvenue Rd., Rockville, VA 23146-1620 t) 804-749-4885 info@visitmontemaria.com www.visitmontemaria.com Sr. Mary Paula Zemienieuski, V.H.M., Supr.; Srs.: 8

SAINT CHARLES

Congregation de Notre-Dame of Montreal, C.N.D. - ; Mailing: P.O. Box E, Saint Charles, VA 24282 t) (276) 546-1213 Srs.: 1

VIRGINIA BEACH

Franciscan Sisters of St. Joseph - 6112 Level Green Ct., Virginia Beach, VA 23464-4511 t) 757-420-1431 mbogaever@yahoo.com Srs.: 4

Sisters Servants of I.H.M. - St. Gregory the Great, 5349 Virginia Beach Blvd., Virginia Beach, VA 23462 t) 757-497-7517 smaryihm@stgregory.pvt.k12.va.us; stgregsihms@aol.com Sr. Dolores Sabisky, I.H.M., Supr.; Srs.: 6

WILLIAMSBURG

Sisters of Mercy - 1100 Jamestown Rd., Williamsburg, VA 23187-8702; Mailing: P.O. Box 8702, Williamsburg, VA 23187-8702 t) 757-220-8735 www.walsingham.org Srs.: 3

ENDOWMENTS / FOUNDATIONS / TRUSTS [EFT]

RICHMOND

The Catholic Community Foundation of the Diocese of Richmond - 7800 Carousel Ln., Richmond, VA 23294 t) 804-359-5661 mkeightley@richmonddiocese.org www.richmondcatholicfoundation.org Keightley Keightley, Exec.;

St. Francis Home of Richmond Foundation, Ltd. - 65 W. Clopton St., Richmond, VA 23225 t) 804-231-1043 bslough@saintfrancisrva.org Provides grants to subsidize cost of care for aged, infirm and disabled residents of limited means. Bruce M. Slough, Exec. Dir.;

VIRGINIA BEACH

Catholic Charities of Eastern Virginia Foundation - 5361-A Virginia Beach Blvd., Virginia Beach, VA 23462 t) 757-456-2366 hr@cceva.org www.cceva.org Tracy Fick, CEO;

YORKTOWN

***Philippians2Foundation** - 108 Quartermarsh Dr., Yorktown, VA 23692 t) (757) 876-1021 philippians2foundation@gmail.com Dcn. David Reaves, Pres.;

HOSPITALS / HEALTH SERVICES [HOS]

MIDLOTHIAN

Bon Secours - St. Francis Medical Center, LLC - 13700 St. Francis Blvd., Ste. 100, Midlothian, VA 23114 t) 804-594-7400 Joseph Wilkins, Pres.; Bed Capacity: 145; Asstd. Annu.: 57,399; Staff: 994

NEWPORT NEWS

Mary Immaculate Hospital LLC - 2 Bernardine Dr., Newport News, VA 23602-4499 t) 757-886-6000 www.bonsecourshamptonroads.com Darlene Stephenson, CEO; Sr. Bernard Marie Magill, O.S.F., Dir.; Bed Capacity: 238; Asstd. Annu.: 34,757; Staff: 706

Bernardine Franciscan Sisters Foundation, Inc. - t) 757-886-6025 david_niski@bshsi.org Sr. David Ann Niski, Dir.;

PORTSMOUTH

Bon Secours Hampton Roads Health System, LLC - 3636 High St., Portsmouth, VA 23707-3236 t) 757-398-2122 Patricia Davis-Hagens, Pres.;

Maryview Hospital LLC - 3636 High St., Portsmouth, VA 23707 t) 757-398-2200 www.bonsecourshamptonroads.com Paul Gaden, CEO; Bed Capacity: 358; Asstd. Annu.: 78,716; Staff: 1,399

Maryview Behavioral Medicine Center - 3636 High St., Portsmouth, VA 23707 t) (757) 398-2367 www.bonsecourshamptonroads.com Lucy Kooiman, Admin.;

RICHMOND

Bon Secours Richmond Health System - 5875 Bremo Rd., Ste 710, Richmond, VA 23226 t) 804-281-8330 www.bonsecours.com Michael Lutes, Pres.;

Bon Secours - Memorial Regional Medical Center LLC - 8260 Atlee Rd., Mechanicsville, VA 23116 t) 804-764-6000 Leigh Sewell, Pres.; Bed Capacity: 246; Asstd. Annu.: 65,575; Staff: 1,449

Bon Secours Mercy Health Emporia LLC - 727 N. Main St., Emporia, VA 23847 t) (434) 348-4400 dba South Virginia Regional Medical Center Kathe Ware, Admin.; Bed Capacity: 80; Asstd. Annu.: 14,424; Staff: 146

Bon Secours Mercy Health Franklin LLC - 100 Fairview Dr., Franklin, VA 23851 t) (757) 569-6100 Kimberly Marks, Pres.; Bed Capacity: 204; Asstd. Annu.: 14,618; Staff: 339

Bon Secours Mercy Health Petersburg LLC - 200 Medical Park Blvd., Petersburg, VA 23805 t) (804) 765-5000 dba Southside Regional Medical Center Donald Emery, Pres.; Bed Capacity: 307; Asstd. Annu.: 72,405; Staff: 1,091

Bon Secours - Richmond Community Hospital LLC - 1500 N. 28th St., Richmond, VA 23233 t) 804-225-1701 Bryan Lee, Pres.; Bed Capacity: 101; Asstd. Annu.: 34,933; Staff: 396

Bon Secours - St. Mary's Hospital of Richmond LLC - 8580 Magellan Pkwy., Richmond, VA 23227 t) (804) 225-1700 Bryan Lee, Pres.; Bed Capacity: 421; Asstd. Annu.: 99,311; Staff: 2,202

SUFFOLK

Maryview Hospital LLC - 7007 Harbour View Blvd., Suffolk, VA 23435 t) (757) 398-2200 Kate Brinn, Pres.; Bed Capacity: 358; Asstd. Annu.: 78,716; Staff: 1,399

MISCELLANEOUS [MIS]

CHARLOTTESVILLE

Saint Anselm Institute for Catholic Thought - 1540 Jefferson Park Ave., Charlottesville, VA 22903; Mailing: P.O. Box 6432, Charlottesville, VA 22906-6432 t) 434-243-1044 info@stanselminstitute.org www.stanselminstitute.org

CHESTER

***The Catholic Evangelical Missionary People of Color Grant, Inc.** - 3408 Castlebury Dr., Chester, VA 23831 t) (840) 314-1681 mario@cempoc.org Dr. Mario Dance, Dir.;

RICHMOND

***Commonwealth Catholic Charities Housing Corporation** - 1601 Rolling Hills Dr., Richmond, VA 23229-5011

Sacred Heart Center, Inc. - 1400 Perry St., Richmond, VA 23224 t) 804-230-4399 tanya-gonzalez@shcrichmond.org; elaine_hinckle@shcrichmond.org Adult Education, Social Services, Latino Outreach Rev. Shay W. Auerbach, S.J., Pres.; Tanya Gonzalez, Dir.;

Shroud of Turin Center - 12829 River Rd., Richmond, VA 23238 t) 804-977-4820 bryan1106@comcast.net; shroud_center@comcast.net Provides educational services and conducts historical research into the Shroud of Turin. Bryan Walsh, Dir.;

VIRGINIA BEACH

***Missioners of Christ** - 5880 Oak Terrace Dr., Virginia Beach, VA 23464 t) (757) 424-8774 info@missioners.org www.missionersofchrist.org/

San Lorenzo Spiritual Center - 4556 Indian River Rd, Virginia Beach, VA 23456; Mailing: P.O. Box 64458, Virginia Beach, VA 23467-4458 t) 757-471-8949 Rev. Msgr. Raphael A. Owusu Peprah, Pst.;

MONASTERIES AND RESIDENCES FOR PRIESTS AND BROTHERS [MON]

RICHMOND

Mary Mother of the Church Abbey - 12829 River Rd., Richmond, VA 23238-7206 t) 804-784-3508 abbeyinfo@richmondmonks.org www.richmondmonks.org Benedictine Monks. Rev. Gregory Gresko, O.S.B.; Rev. Adrian W. Harmening, O.S.B.; Bro. Vincent McDermott, O.S.B.; Bro. Robert Nguyen, O.S.B.; Bro. Ambrose Okema, O.S.B.; Bro. David Owen, O.S.B.; Bro. Jeffery Williams, O.S.B.; Rt. Rev. Placid Solari, O.S.B., Admin.; Rev. John Mary Lugemwa, O.S.B., Prior;

NURSING / REHABILITATION / CONVALESCENCE / ELDERLY CARE [NUR]

CHARLOTTESVILLE

Our Lady of Peace - 751 Hillsdale Dr., Charlottesville, VA 22901 t) 434-973-1155 sara.warden@our-lady-of-peace.com www.our-lady-of-peace.com Sara Warden, Admin.; Asstd. Annu.: 214; Staff: 108

RICHMOND

St. Francis - Manchester - 65 W. Clopton St., Richmond, VA 23225 t) 804-231-1043 bslough@saintfrancishome.com Bruce M. Slough, Exec.; Asstd. Annu.: 102; Staff: 48

St. Mary's Woods - 1257 Marywood Ln., Richmond, VA 23229 t) 804-741-8624 jotanya.belton@stmaryswoods.com stmaryswoods.com Jotanya Belton, Dir.; Asstd. Annu.: 120; Staff: 98

Our Lady of Hope Health Center, Inc. - 13700 N. Gayton Rd., Richmond, VA 23233 t) 804-360-1960 plong@ourladyofhope.com www.ourladyofhope.com Julia Fretwell, Admin.; Asstd. Annu.: 265; Staff: 142

ROANOKE

Our Lady of the Valley Retirement Community - 650 N. Jefferson St., Roanoke, VA 24016 t) 540-345-5111 myengst@ourladyofthevalley.com www.ourladyofthevalley.com Mary Lynn Yengst, Admin.; Asstd. Annu.: 256; Staff: 152

SUFFOLK

Mary Immaculate Nursing Center LLC - 7007 Harbour View Blvd., Suffolk, VA 23435 t) (757) 886-6500 sdschitter1@mercy.com Michael Lutes, Pres.;

VIRGINIA BEACH

Marian Manor - 5345 Marian Ln., Virginia Beach, VA 23462 t) 757-456-5018 karen@marian-manor.com Karen Land, Admin.; Asstd. Annu.: 123; Staff: 93

Our Lady of Perpetual Help Health Center, Inc. - 4560 Princess Anne Rd., Virginia Beach, VA 23462-7905 t) 757-495-4211 tanderson@ourladyperpetualhelp.com www.ourladyperpetualhelp.com Theresa Anderson, Admin.; Asstd. Annu.: 203; Staff: 161

PRESCHOOLS / CHILDCARE CENTERS [PRE]

VIRGINIA BEACH

Holy Family Day School - 1279 N. Great Neck Rd., Virginia Beach, VA 23454-2117 t) 757-481-1180 dayschoolprincipal@holyfamilyvb.org www.holyfamilyvb.org Cynthia Girard, Dir.; Stds.: 51; Lay Tchrs.: 5

RETREAT HOUSES / RENEWAL CENTERS [RTR]

ABINGDON

Jubilee House Retreat Center - 822 E. Main St., Abingdon, VA 24210-4415 t) 276-619-0919 info@jubileeretreat.org www.jubileeretreat.org Robert

Vaughan, Dir.;

ROANOKE

Madonna House - 828 Campbell Ave., S.W., Roanoke, VA 24016 t) 540-343-8464 mhrke79@gmail.com www.madonnahouse.org Marie McLaughlin, Dir.;

An asterisk (*) denotes an organization that has established tax-exempt status directly with the IRS and is not covered by the USCCB Group Ruling.

Diocese of Rochester

(Dioecesis Roffensis)

MOST REVEREND SALVATORE R. MATANO, D.D., S.T.L., J.C.D.

Bishop of Rochester; ordained December 17, 1971; appointed Coadjutor Bishop of Burlington March 3, 2005; ordained April 19, 2005; succeeded November 9, 2005; appointed Bishop of Rochester November 6, 2013; installed as Ninth Bishop of Rochester January 3, 2014. Office: 1150 Buffalo Rd., Rochester, NY 14624.

Pastoral Center: 1150 Buffalo Rd., Rochester, NY 14624-1890. T: 585-328-3210; T: 800-388-7177; F: 585-328-3149.

ESTABLISHED MARCH 3, 1868.

Square Miles 7,107.

Comprises the Counties of Cayuga, Chemung, Livingston, Monroe, Ontario, Schuyler, Seneca, Steuben, Tioga, Tompkins, Wayne and Yates in the State of New York.

Legal Title of Diocese: The Diocese of Rochester.

For legal titles of parishes and diocesan institutions, consult the Pastoral Center.

STATISTICAL OVERVIEW

Personnel

Bishop	1
Abbots	1
Retired Abbots	1
Priests: Diocesan Active in Diocese	84
Priests: Diocesan Active Outside Diocese	2
Priests: Retired, Sick or Absent	52
Number of Diocesan Priests	138
Religious Priests in Diocese	27
Total Priests in your Diocese	165
Extern Priests in Diocese	16
Ordinations:	
Diocesan Priests	1
Permanent Deacons	3
Permanent Deacons in Diocese	131
Total Brothers	29
Total Sisters	415

Parishes

Parishes	86
With Resident Pastor:	
Resident Diocesan Priests	68
Resident Religious Priests	1
Without Resident Pastor:	
Administered by Priests	15
Administered by Deacons	1
Administered by Religious Women	1
Administered by Lay People	1
Missions	2
Professional Ministry Personnel:	
Brothers	2
Sisters	6
Lay Ministers	106

Welfare

Health Care Centers	2
Total Assisted	1,500
Homes for the Aged	4
Total Assisted	1,500
Day Care Centers	1
Total Assisted	44
Specialized Homes	7
Total Assisted	650
Special Centers for Social Services	72
Total Assisted	260,000
Residential Care of Disabled	10
Total Assisted	75

Educational

Diocesan Students in Other Seminaries	4
Total Seminarians	4
Colleges and Universities	1
Total Students	115
High Schools, Private	6
Total Students	2,844
Elementary Schools, Diocesan and Parish	16
Total Students	2,331
Elementary Schools, Private	2
Total Students	173
Catechesis / Religious Education:	
High School Students	1,073
Elementary Students	5,023
Total Students under Catholic Instruction	11,563
Teachers in Diocese:	
Priests	1
Sisters	6
Lay Teachers	474

Vital Statistics

Receptions into the Church:	
Infant Baptism Totals	1,355
Minor Baptism Totals	459
Adult Baptism Totals	56
Received into Full Communion	257
First Communions	1,298
Confirmations	1,167
Marriages:	
Catholic	293
Interfaith	80
Total Marriages	373
Deaths	2,527
Total Catholic Population	315,239
Total Population	1,501,137

LEADERSHIP

Pastoral Center - t) 585-328-3210; 800-388-7177 (Toll Free within Diocese); 585-328-3228 www.dor.org
Vicar General - t) 585-328-3228 x1230 Very Rev. Paul J. Tomasso, Vicar General, Moderator of the Curia;
Moderator of the Curia - t) 585-328-3228 x1230 Very Rev. Paul J. Tomasso, Vicar General, Moderator of the Curia;
Chancellor and Director of the Department of Legal Services - t) 585-328-3228 x1213 Rev. Daniel J. Condon;
Judicial Vicar - t) 585-328-3228 x1465 Very Rev. Peter B. Mottola, J.C.L., Judicial Vicar;

ADMINISTRATION

Priest Secretary to Bishop Matano - t) 585-328-3228 x1245 Rev. Daniel E. White;
Executive Assistant to the Bishop, Moderator of the Curia, Vicar General - t) 585-328-3228 x1224 Kathleen McMahon;
Legal Assistant to the Chancellor - t) 585-328-3228 x1225 Janice Boyea;
Diocesan Archives - t) 585-328-3228 x1204 Sr. Connie Derby, R.S.M., Dir. (archives@dor.org);
Child & Youth Protection -
- **Victim Assistance** - t) 585-328-3228 x1555 victimassistance@dor.org Deborah Housel, Coord.;
- **Safe Environment Education & Compliance** - t) 585-328-3228 x1252 Tammy Sylvester, Diocesan Dir.;

CATHOLIC CHARITIES

Catholic Charities of the Diocese of Rochester - t) 585-328-3228 x1323 Karen Dehais, Dir.; Anthony Adams, Chair; Sabrina McLeod, Vice Pres., Financial Oper.;

CLERGY AND RELIGIOUS SERVICES

Diocesan Director of Priest Personnel - t) 585-328-3228 x1230 Very Rev. Paul J. Tomasso;
Deacon Personnel & Formation - t) 585-328-3228 x1237 Dcn. Edward Giblin, Dir.;
Office of Seminarians - t) (585) 328-3228 x1230 Very Rev. Paul J. Tomasso;
Office of Vocations - t) (585) 663-5432 Very Rev. William G. Coffas, Pst.; Very Rev. Peter D. VanLieshout, Pst.; Rev. Daniel L. White, Par. Vicar;
Vicar for Religious - t) 585-328-3228 x1213 Rev. Daniel J. Condon, J.C.L., Chancellor;

COMMUNICATIONS

Director of Communications - t) 585-328-3228 x1237 Dcn. Edward Giblin, Dir.; Katey Bourne, Technical Coord.;

CONSULTATIVE BODIES

Bishop's Stewardship Council - Patrick Burke, Chair;
College of Consultors - t) (585) 328-3228 x1213 Rev. Daniel J. Condon, Contact;
Priests' Council - Very Rev. William G. Coffas, Chair; Rev. Timothy E. Horan, Vice Chmn.; Rev. Daniel E. White, Secy.;
Review Board - Dr. Jack McIntyre, Chair;

DEANERIES

Central Deanery - Very Rev. Edison Tayag;
East Deanery - Very Rev. Frank E. Lioi;
Monroe Central Deanery - Very Rev. William G. Coffas;
Monroe East Deanery - Very Rev. James A. Schwartz;
Monroe West Deanery - Very Rev. Lee P. Chase;
South Deanery - Very Rev. Jeffrey R. Galens;
West Deanery - Very Rev. James P. Jaeger;

EVANGELIZATION

Department of Evangelization and Catechesis - t) 585-328-3228 x1244 Leslie Barkin, Dir.;
- **Project Coordinator/Youth and Young Adult Ministry** - t) (585) 328-3228 x1375 Mark Capellazzi;
- **Coordinator of Sacramental Catechesis and Family Life** - t) (585) 328-3228 x1243 Donald Smith;

Propagation of the Faith - t) (585) 671-2110 Rev. Paul Gitau, Dir.;

FAITH FORMATION

Department of Catholic Schools - t) 585-328-3228 x1246 James Tauzel, Supt.; Sr. Francella Quinn, Admin. Asst.;
Department of Human Resources for Catholic Schools - t) 585-328-3228 x1252 Tammy Sylvester, Dir.;
Coordinator of Assessment & Professional Growth - t) 585-328-3228 x1253 Patty Selig;
Coordinator of Sports - t) 585-328-3228 x1242 Brooke England;

FINANCE

Chief Financial Officer - t) 585-328-3228 x1450 Lisa M. Passero;
Director of Finance - t) 585-328-3228 x1263 Mary Ziarniak, Dir.;
Controller - t) 585-328-3228 x1376 Scott Mosman;
Buildings and Properties - t) 585-328-3228 x1207 Sean Moran, Mgr.;
Information Technology - t) 585-328-3228 x1272 David Kilpatrick, Dir. & Chief Information Officer; Mark Darling, Dir. IT Oper.;
Risk Management/Parish Regional Cemetaries - t) 585-328-3228 x1215 Dan Poherence, Dir.;

HUMAN RESOURCES

Human Resources - t) 585-328-3228 x1252 Tammy Sylvester, Dir.;
- **HRIS and Payroll Manager** - t) (585) 328-3228 x1203 Renate Parks;

PASTORAL SERVICES

Pastoral Service - t) 585-328-3228 x1337
- **Director** - t) 585-328-3228 x1328 Bernard Grizard, Diocesan Dir.;
- **Associate Director and Office of Life Issues** - t) 585-328-3228 x1218 Dr. Shannon Kilbridge;
- **Office of Migrant Ministry** - t) 585-328-3228 x1354 Rev. Jesus Flores, Coord.;
- **Project Managers** - t) (585) 328-3228 x1318 Carmen Rollinson; Elizabeth Johnston;
- **Urban Hispanic Ministry** - t) (585) 328-3228 x1340; (315) 331-6753 Jorge Salgado, N.W. Monroe County; Luci Romero-Ponce, Wayne County-Regl. Coord.;

STEWARDSHIP

Office of Stewardship and Communications - t) 585-328-3228 x1326 Colleen Brade, Dir., Stewardship/ CMA;

TRIBUNAL

Tribunal Office - t) 585-328-3228 x1223 Very Rev. Peter B. Mottola, J.C.L., Judicial Vicar;
Chancellor of the Tribunal - t) 585-328-3228 x1223 Janice Boyea, Legal Asst. & Chancellor of the Tribunal;
Judges - Rev. T. Pius Pathmarajah; Rev. Louis A. Sirianni, Adjutant Judicial Vicar; Rev. William F. Laird, Adjutant Judicial Vicar;
Defenders of the Bond - Mary Ellen Goverts; Rev. Donald J. Curtiss;
Tribunal Staff - t) 585-328-3228 x1223 Dcn. Jose Rivera, Judicial Asst.; Dcn. James Steiger, Judicial Asst., Ecclesiastical Notary; Rev. Richard Brickler, Assesor;

MISCELLANEOUS / OTHER OFFICES

Rochester Catholic Press Association, Inc. - Catholic Courier - El Mensajero Catolico - t) 585-529-9530; 800-600-3628 Karen Franz, Gen. Mgr. & Editor;

PARISHES, MISSIONS, AND CLERGY

STATE OF NEW YORK

ADDISON

Saints Isidore and Maria Torribia - 51 Maple St., Addison, NY 14801 t) 607-359-2115 ssimt@dor.org www.simtparish.org/ Rev. Patrick L. Connor, Pst.; Dcn. Douglas Farwell; Dcn. Dave LaFortune;

AUBURN

St. Alphonsus - 90 Melrose Rd., Auburn, NY 13021-9212 t) 315-252-9576 aholyfam@dor.org www.holyfamilyauburn.org Rev. Stephen Karani, Pst.; Rev. Michael R. Brown, Par. Vicar; Dcn. Gregg Lawson;
Holy Family - 85 North St., Auburn, NY 13021 t) 315-252-9576 aholyfam@dor.org auburnholyfamily.org Rev. Stephen Karani, Pst.; Rev. Michael R. Brown, Par. Vicar;
St. Mary - 15 Clark St., Auburn, NY 13021 t) (315) 252-9545 stmarys@dor.org www.stmaryauburn.org Very Rev. Frank E. Lioi, Pst.; Dcn. Dennis Donahue; Rev. Joseph Maurici III, Par. Vicar;
- **St. Joseph's School** - t) 315-253-8357 Also serving the parishes of Auburn. Michael Carney, Prin.;

Saints Mary and Martha Roman Catholic Parish Cayuga County, NY - 299 Clark St., Auburn, NY 13021 t) 315-252-7593 maryandmartha@dor.org www.marymarthaauburn.com Very Rev. Frank E. Lioi, Pst.; Rev. Joseph Maurici III, Par. Vicar; Dcn. Dennis Donahue;
Our Lady of the Snow - 15 Clark St., Auburn, NY 13021 t) 315-252-9545 wstjosep@dor.org ourladyofthesnow.org Very Rev. Frank E. Lioi, Pst.; Rev. Joseph Maurici III, Par. Vicar; Dcn. Dennis Donahue;
Sacred Heart - 90 Melrose Rd., Auburn, NY 13021 t) (315) 252-7271 asacredh@dor.org www.auburnholyfamily.org Rev. Stephen Karani, Pst.; Rev. Michael R. Brown, Par. Vicar;
- **St. Ann** - 4890 Twelve Corners Rd., Owasco, NY 13021 t) 315-252-7271

AURORA

Good Shepherd Catholic Community - 303 Main St., Aurora, NY 13026; Mailing: P.O. Box 296, Aurora, NY 13026-0296 t) 315-364-7197 gscc@dor.org www.thegoodshepard.cc Rev. William A. Moorby, Pst.;

AVON

St. Agnes - 96 Prospect St., Avon, NY 14414 t) 585-226-2100 astagnes@dor.org saintagnespaulrose.org Rev. Michael G. Fowler, Pst.; Dcn. Peter Dohr; Dcn. William Goodman;
- **St. Agnes School** - (Grades PreK-6) 60 Park Place, Avon, NY 14414 t) (585) 226-8500 avon-st.agnesschool@dor.org Elizabeth Dowd, Prin.;

BATH

St. John Vianney Roman Catholic Parish, Steuben County, NY - 32 E. Morris St., Bath, NY 14810 t) 607-776-3327 sjv@dor.org sjvbath.org Very Rev. James P. Jaeger, Pst.; Dcn. Robert Colomaio; Dcn. Thomas Jack;

BROCKPORT

Nativity of the Blessed Virgin Mary - 152 Main St., Brockport, NY 14420-1972 t) 585-637-4500 cnativit@dor.org www.nativitybrockport.org Rev. Joseph P. McCaffrey, Pst.; Dcn. Vincenzo Franco; Dcn. Paul Virgilio;

CALEDONIA

The Parish of Saint Martin de Porres, Livingston County, NY - 198 North Rd., Caledonia, NY 14423 t) 585-538-2126 sstmaryo@dor.org www.stmartinrochester.org Rev. John H. Hayes, Pst.; Dcn. Matthew Dudek;

CANANDAIGUA

St. Benedict Roman Catholic Parish Ontario County, NY - 95 N. Main St., Canandaigua, NY 14424 t) 585-394-1220 fr.michael.costik@dor.org www.stbenedictonline.org Rev. Michael Costik, Pst.; Rev. Mathew J Walter, Par. Vicar; Teresa Dunn, Pst. Assoc.;

CLIFTON SPRINGS

St. Peter's Roman Catholic Parish, Ontario County - 12 Hibbard Ave., Clifton Springs, NY 14432 t) 315-462-2961 stpeters@dor.org www.stpeterparish.us

Rev. Anthony Amato, Par. Admin.;

CLYDE

Catholic Community of the Blessed Trinity - 43 W. DeZeng St., Clyde, NY 14433 t) (315) 902-4130 ccblessedtrinity@dor.org Rev. Felicjan Sierotowicz, Par. Admin.; Rev. Michael Merritt, Par. Vicar;

St. Joseph the Worker Roman Catholic Parish, Wayne County - 43 Dezeng St., Clyde, NY 14433 t) 315-902-4130 fr.felicjan.sierotowicz@dor.org www.saintjoetheworker.org Rev. Felicjan Sierotowicz, Par. Admin.; Rev. Michael Merritt, Par. Vicar; Dcn. Gregory Kiley;

St. Patrick - Grand Ave., Savannah, NY 13146 t) 315-365-3244

CORNING

All Saints - 158 State St., Corning, NY 14830 t) 607-936-4689 allsaintsparish@dor.org www.allsaintsparish.org Rev. Johna Orenge Omboga, Temporary Parochial Administrator;

EAST ROCHESTER

St. Jerome - 207 S. Garfield St., East Rochester, NY 14445 t) 585-586-3231 estjerom@dor.org www.stjeromerochester.org Rev. William B. Leone, Pst.; Rev. William Endres, In Res.; Sr. Clare Brown, S.S.J., Pst. Assoc.;

ELMIRA

The Parish of the Most Holy Name of Jesus, Chemung County, NY - 1010 Davis St., Elmira, NY 14901 t) 607-733-3484 www.elmiracatholic.org Rev. Scott Kubinski, Pst.; Rev. Richard T. Farrell, Par. Vicar; Dcn. Joseph Erway, Pst. Assoc.; Dcn. Alberto Pacete; Dcn. Paul Sartori; Dcn. George Welch;

FAIRPORT

Church of the Assumption - 20 East Ave., Fairport, NY 14450 t) 585-388-0040 assumptionfpt@dor.org www.cota.church Rev. William McGrath, Pst.; Sr. Barbara Baker, Pst. Min./Coord.; Dcn. David Snyder; Julie Gutierrez, Pst. Assoc.; Dcn. Ronald J. Tocci, In Res.; Dcn. Philip Yawman, In Res.;

Church of the Resurrection - 63 Mason Rd., Fairport, NY 14450 t) 585-223-5500 fchurcho@dor.org www.resurrectionfairport.org Rev. William McGrath, Pst.; Sr. Barbara Baker, Pst. Min./Coord.; Julie Gutierrez, Pst. Assoc.;

Church of St. John of Rochester of Perinton, New York - 8 Wickford Way, Fairport, NY 14450 t) 585-248-5993 x13 fstjohno@dor.org www.stjohnfairport.org Rev. Peter C. Clifford, Pst.; Dcn. James Pegoni; Robert Layer, Pst. Assoc.; Rev. Jeff Chichester, In Res.; Rev. Alexander H. Bradshaw, In Res.;

FREEVILLE

Holy Cross - 375 S. George Rd., Freeville, NY 13068 t) (607) 533-0145 www.netcatholic.org Rev. Jorge I. Ramirez, Pst.; Mary Ann Kozak, Pst. Assoc.;

GENESEO

St. Luke the Evangelist Roman Catholic Church Society of Livingston County - 13 North St., Geneseo, NY 14454 t) 585-243-1100 stlukelivingstoncounty.org Rev. Hoan Q. Dinh, Par. Vicar; Rev. Sylvester Bioh (Ghana), Par. Vicar; Michael Sauter, Temporary Pastoral Administrator; Dcn. Paul Clement; Dcn. George Spezzano; Leslie Nieves, Pst. Min./Coord.;

GENEVA

Our Lady of Peace Roman Catholic Church of Geneva, NY - 130 Exchange St., Geneva, NY 14456 t) 315-789-0930 gourladyofpeace@dor.org www.ourladyofpeacegeneva.org Rev. Thomas P. Mull, Pst.; Rev. Carlos Sanchez, Par. Vicar; Dcn. Robert Cyrana;

St. Francis DeSales/St. Stephen School - (Grades K-8) 17 Elmwood Ave., Geneva, NY 14456 t) 315-789-1828 sfssdcs@dor.org Suzanne Poherence, Prin.;

GROTON

St. Anthony - 312 Locke Rd., Groton, NY 13073 t) (607) 533-0145 gstantho@dor.org netcatholic.org Rev. Jorge I. Ramirez, Par. Admin.; Mary Ann Kozak, Pst. Assoc.;

HAMLIN

St. Elizabeth Ann Seton - 3747 Brick Schoolhouse Rd., Hamlin, NY 14464; Mailing: PO Box 149, Hamlin, NY 14464 t) 585-964-8627 seas@dor.org www.myseas.org Rev. John F. Gagnier, Par. Admin.; Dcn. Christopher Fisher Jr.;

HILTON

St. Leo - 110 Old Hojack Ln., Hilton, NY 14468; Mailing: P.O. Box 725, Hilton, NY 14468 t) 585-392-2710 x2 hstleoch@dor.org www.stleochurch.org Rev. Joseph R. Catanise, Pst.; Rev. Robert P. Ring, In Res.; Dcn. Jose Rivera; Dcn. James Steiger; Dcn. Jeffrey P. Serbicki;

HONEOYE

St. Mary, Our Lady of the Hills - 8961 Main St., Honeoye, NY 14471; Mailing: P.O. Box 725, Honeoye, NY 14471 t) 585-229-5007 hstmaryo@dor.org www.stmaryandmatthew.com Rev. William F. Laird, Pst.; Dcn. John Hoffman;

HONEOYE FALLS

St. Paul of the Cross - 31 Monroe St., Honeoye Falls, NY 14472 t) 585-226-2100 astagnes@dor.org www.stagnespaulrose.org Rev. Michael G. Fowler, Pst.; Dcn. Peter Dohr; Dcn. William Goodman;

HORNELL

Our Lady of the Valley - 27 Erie Ave., Hornell, NY 14843 t) 607-324-5811 ourladyofthevalley@dor.org www.olv14843.org Rev. Stanley Kacprzak, Pst.; Dcn. Mark Clark; Dcn. Robert W. McCormick; Deborah Brinkhus, Pst. Assoc.;

HORSEHEADS

St. Mary Our Mother - 816 W. Broad St., Horseheads, NY 14845 t) 607-739-3817 smomc@dor.org www.stmaryourmother.com Rev. Christopher E. Linsler, Pst.;

INTERLAKEN

The Parish of Mary, Mother of Mercy, Seneca County, NY - 3660 Orchard St., Interlaken, NY 14847; Mailing: PO Box 403, Interlaken, NY 14847 t) 607-294-0064 immmercy@dor.org www.marymotherofmercy.com Rev. Bernard Maloney, O.F.M.Cap., Pst.;

ITHACA

St. Catherine of Siena - 309 Siena Dr., Ithaca, NY 14850 t) 607-257-2493 istcathe@dor.org www.stcathofsiena.org Rev. Joseph W. Marcoux, Pst.; Karen Webb, Pastoral Care Associate;

Immaculate Conception - 113 N. Geneva St., Ithaca, NY 14850 t) 607-273-6121 iimmacul@dor.org www.immconch.org Rev. Augustine Chumo, Pst.; Dcn. Daniel R. Hurley; Dcn. George Kozak;

LANSING

All Saints - 347 Ridge Rd., Lansing, NY 14882 t) (607) 533-0145 www.netcatholic.org Rev. Jorge I. Ramirez, Par. Admin.; Andra Benson, Pst. Assoc.;

LIMA

St. Rose - 1985 Lake Ave., Lima, NY 14485; Mailing: 96 Prospect St., Avon, NY 14414 t) 585-226-2100 astagnes@dor.org www.saintagnespaulrose.org Rev. Michael G. Fowler, Pst.; Dcn. Peter Dohr; Dcn. William Goodman;

LIVONIA

St. Matthew Catholic Church Society - 6591 Richmond Mills Road, Livonia, NY 14487; Mailing: P.O. Box 77, Livonia, NY 14487 t) (585) 346-3815 lstmatthew@dor.org www.stsmaryandmatthew.com Rev. William F. Laird, Pst.; Dcn. John Hoffman;

MACEDON

The Parish of St. Katharine Drexel - 52 Main St., Macedon, NY 14502 t) 315-538-8242 drexelparish@dor.org www.catholicparisheswwc.org Rev. Symon Peter Ntaiyia, Pst.; Rev. Daniel L. White, Par. Vicar;

MENDON

St. Catherine of Siena - 26 Mendon-Ionia Rd., Mendon, NY 14506 t) 585-624-4990 mstcathe@dro.org www.saintcath.org Rev. Robert Scott Bourcy, Pst.; Dcn. James Carra; Dcn. Kevin Cargas; Sr. Ruth Maier, Pst. Assoc.;

Convent - 15 Mendon-Ionia Rd., Mendon, NY 14506 t) 716-624-1538

NEWARK

St. Michael - 401 Main St., Newark, NY 14513 t) 315-331-6753 www.stmichaelsnewark.org Rev. Felicjan Sierotowicz, Par. Admin.; Rev. Michael Merritt, Par. Vicar; Julie Sherman, Pst. Assoc.;

NORTH CHILI

St. Christopher - 3350 Union St., North Chili, NY 14514; Mailing: P.O. Box 399, North Chili, NY 14514 t) 585-594-1400 nstchris@dor.org www.stchristophersnchili.org Rev. Eloo Malachy Nwosu, Par. Admin.;

ONTARIO

St. Maximilian Kolbe - 5823 Walworth Rd., Ontario, NY 14519; Mailing: P.O. Box 499, Ontario, NY 14519 t) 315-524-2611 ostmarys@dor.org www.catholicparisheswwc.org Rev. Symon Peter Ntaiyia, Pst.; Rev. Daniel L. White, Par. Vicar; Dcn. Edward Kohlmeier;

OWEGO

Blessed Trinity - 309 Front St., Owego, NY 13827 t) 607-687-1068; 607-625-3192 (Rectory) blessedtrinity@dor.org www.blessed-trinity-parish.org Very Rev. Jeffrey R. Galens, Pst.; Rev. Steven Lewis, Par. Vicar;

St. Patrick - 309 Front St., Owego, NY 13827 t) 607-687-1068 blessedtrinity@dor.org www.blessed-trinity-parish.org Very Rev. Jeffrey R. Galens, Pst.; Rev. Steven Lewis, Par. Vicar;

PENFIELD

St. Joseph - 43 Gebhardt Rd., Penfield, NY 14526 t) 585-586-8089 info@sjcpenfield.com info@sjcpenfield.com Very Rev. James A. Schwartz, Pst.; Rev. Sriram Sadhanala, H.G.N., Par. Vicar; Rev. Robert G. Kreckel, In Res.; Dcn. Duncan Harris, Pst. Assoc.; Dcn. Duncan DeBell, Pst. Assoc.; Cathy Kamp, Pst. Assoc.;

St. Joseph School - (Grades PreK-6) 39 Gebhardt Rd., Penfield, NY 14526-1398 t) 585-586-6968 sjpendcs@dor.org Amy Johnson, Prin.;

PENN YAN

Our Lady of the Lakes Catholic Community - 210 Keuka St., Penn Yan, NY 14527 t) 315-536-7459 pstmicha@dor.org www.ourladyofthelakescc.org Rev. Leo J. Reinhardt, Pst.; Dcn. Timothy Hebding; Dcn. Roger Loucks;

PITTSFORD

Church of the Transfiguration - 50 W. Bloomfield Rd., Pittsford, NY 14534 t) 585-248-2427 transfiguration@dor.org www.transfigurationpittsford.org Rev. Robert Scott Bourcy, Pst.; Dcn. Eric Bessette; Margie Benza, Pst. Assoc.;

St. Louis - 64 S. Main St., Pittsford, NY 14534 t) 585-586-5675 pstlouis@dor.org www.stlouischurch.org Rev. Mitchell Zygadlo, Pst.; Rev. Simon Atta Denchira (Ghana), Par. Vicar; Dcn. Patrick DiLaura;

Saint's Place - 46 S. Main St., Pittsford, NY 14534 t) 585-385-6860 saintlady@stlouischurch.org www.saintsplace.org Isabel Miller, Dir.;

St. Louis School - (Grades PreK-5) 11 Rand Pl., Pittsford, NY 14534-2084 t) 585-586-5200 sisdcs@dor.org Eileen Schenk, Prin.;

ROCHESTER

Sacred Heart Cathedral - 296 Flower City Pk., Rochester, NY 14615 t) 525-254-3221 cathedralcommunity@dor.org www.sacredheartrochester.org Most Rev. Salvatore R. Matano, In Res.; Very Rev. Peter D. VanLieshout, Rector; Rev. Daniel E. White, In Res.; Dcn. Lynn W. Kershner; Dcn. Michael Kristan; Sr. Joan Hilbert, Pst. Min./Coord.;

The Cathedral Community - t) 585-254-3221 (Holy Rosary, Most Precious Blood, Sacred Heart Cathedral)

St. Anne - 1600 Mt. Hope Ave., Rochester, NY 14620-4598 t) 585-271-3260 rstannec@dor.org www.ourladyoflourdesassistance@dor.org Rev. Gary L. Tyman, Pst.; Rev. James F. Lawlor, Assisting Priest;

Rev. Dennis Bonsignore, In Res.; Dcn. William Rabjohn, Pst. Assoc.; Steve Witkowicz, Pst. Min./Coord.;

Blessed Sacrament - 534 Oxford St., Rochester, NY 14607; Mailing: 259 Rutgers St., Rochester, NY 14607 t) 585-271-7240 rblessed@dor.org southeastrochestercatholics.org Rev. John Loncle, Pst.; Rev. Edward L. Palumbos, In Res.; Rev. David Tedesche, In Res.; Dcn. Ed Knauf; Dcn. David Palma;

Convent - 247 Rutgers St., Rochester, NY 14607 t) 585-271-7736

St. Boniface - 330 Gregory St., Rochester, NY 14620; Mailing: 259 Rutgers St., Rochester, NY 14607 t) 585-271-7240 rstbonif@dor.org www.southeastrochestercatholics.org Rev. John Loncle, Pst.; Rev. Edward L. Palumbos, In Res.; Rev. David Tedesche, In Res.; Dcn. Ed Knauf; Dcn. David Palma;

St. Charles Borromeo - 3003 Dewey Ave., Rochester, NY 14616 t) 585-663-3230 gstcharl@dor.org www.stcharlesgreece@dor.org Rev. John A. Firpo, Pst.; Rev. T. Pius Pathmarajah, Assoc. Pst.; Dcn. Daniel Callan;

Emmanuel Church of the Deaf of the Diocese of Rochester - 34 Monica St., Rochester, NY 14619 t) 585-235-3340 fr.ray.fleming@dor.org www.stmonicaofrochester.org Rev. Raymond H. Fleming, Pst.; Dcn. Patrick A. Graybill;

Roman Catholic Parish of St. Frances Xavier Cabrini - 80 Prince St., Rochester, NY 14605 t) 585-325-4041 stfrancesxavier@dor.org www.cabriniroc.org Rev. Daniel Sierra-Ruiz, Pst.; Rev. Robert Thomas Werth, Par. Vicar; Dcn. Jorge Malave; Dcn. Agenol Rodriguez; Dcn. Salvador Otero; Dcn. Carlos Vargas;

St. George - 150 Varinna Dr., Rochester, NY 14618 t) 585-319-5689 fr.gary.tyman@dor.org Rev. Gary L. Tyman, Pst.;

Holy Apostles - 530 Lyell Ave., Rochester, NY 14606; Mailing: 7 Austin St., Rochester, NY 14606 t) 585-254-7170 aholyapo@dor.org www.holyapostleschurchfamily.org Rev. Anthony P. Mugavero, Pst.; Dcn. Nemesio Vellon Martinez;

Holy Cross - 4492 Lake Ave., Rochester, NY 14612-4597 t) 585-663-2244 rholycross@dor.org www.holycrossrochester.org Very Rev. William G. Coffas, Pst.; Rev. Joseph Martuscello, Par. Vicar; Rev. Robert J. Schrader, Sr. Priest; Dcn. Joseph Placious;

Holy Cross School - (Grades PreK-6) 4488 Lake Ave., Rochester, NY 14612 t) 585-663-6533 hcdcs@dor.org T.J. Verzillo, Prin.; James Tauzel, Supt.;

Immaculate Conception/St. Bridget - 445 Frederick Douglass St., Rochester, NY 14608; Mailing: 34 Monica St., Rochester, NY 14619 t) (585) 235-3340 rimmacul@dor.org www.immaculateconceptionrochester.org Rev. Raymond H. Fleming, Pst.; Dcn. Richard Rall;

St. John the Evangelist - 2400 Ridge Rd., W., Rochester, NY 14626 t) 585-225-8980 gstjohnt@dor.org www.stjohngreece.org Rev. Peter Enyan-Boadu (Ghana), Pst.; Dcn. Elmer Smith; Tod Simone, Pst. Min./Coord.;

Kateri Tekakwitha Roman Catholic Parish - 445 Kings Hwy. S., Rochester, NY 14617 t) 585-544-8880 ikateri@dor.org www.kateriirondequoit.org Rev. Lance Gonyo, Pst.; Dcn. Lon Smith, Pst. Assoc.; Rev. Nathan Davis, Par. Vicar;

Saint Kateri School - (Grades PreK-6) t) 585-467-8730 sksdcs@dor.org Terri Morgan, Prin.;

St. Lawrence - 1000 N. Greece Rd., Rochester, NY 14626 t) 585-723-1350; 585-225-7320 (CRP) rstlawre@dor.org www.stlawrencegreeceny.org Very Rev. Lee P. Chase, Pst.; Dcn. David Squilla, Pst. Assoc.; Dcn. Emmanuel Asis;

St. Lawrence School - (Grades PreK-5) t) 585-225-3870 slawrdcs@dor.org Frank Arvizzigno, Prin.;

Marianne Cope Roman Catholic Parish, Monroe County NY - 2061 E. Henrietta Rd., Rochester, NY 14623 t) 585-334-3518 x1101 smcrcc@dor.org Rev. Michael Mayer, Par. Vicar; Sr. Sheila Stevenson, R.S.M., Par. Admin.; Dcn. Robert Lyons; Dcn. Michael Zuber; Christine Wenzel, Pst. Min./Coord.;

St. Mark - 54 Kuhn Rd., Rochester, NY 14612 t) 585-225-3710; (585) 227-6824 rstmarkc@dor.org www.stmarksgreece.com Rev. Louis A. Sirianni, Par. Vicar; Dcn. Frank Pettrone, Par. Admin.; Dcn. Gerard de la Fuente;

St. Mary - 15 St. Mary's Pl., Rochester, NY 14607; Mailing: 259 Rutgers St., Rochester, NY 14607 t) 585-271-7240 rstmaryc@dor.org www.southeastrochestercatholics.org Rev. John Loncle, Pst.; Rev. Edward L. Palumbos, In Res.; Rev. David Tedesche, In Res.; Dcn. David Palma; Dcn. Ed Knauf;

St. Monica - 831 Genesee St., Rochester, NY 14611; Mailing: 34 Monica St., Rochester, NY 14619 t) 585-235-3340 www.stmonicaofrochester.org Rev. Raymond H. Fleming, Pst.; Dcn. Matthew Dudek; Dcn. Brian J. McNulty;

Our Lady of Lourdes - 150 Varinna Dr., Rochester, NY 14618 t) 585-473-9656 bourlady@dor.org www.bourlady.org Rev. Gary L. Tyman, Pst.; Rev. James F. Lawlor, Assisting Priest; Dcn. William Rabjohn, Pst. Assoc.; Steve Witkowicz, Pst. Min./Coord.;

Seton Catholic School - (Grades PreK-6) 165 Rhinecliff Dr., Rochester, NY 14618-1525 t) 585-473-6604 csoffice@rochester.rr.com Mary Kate Koecheler, Prin.;

Our Lady of Victory-St. Joseph - 210 Pleasant St., Rochester, NY 14604 t) 585-454-2244 ourladyvictory@dor.org olvsj.org Rev. Ronald A. Antinarelli, KCHS, Pst.;

Our Lady Queen of Peace - 601 Edgewood Ave., Rochester, NY 14618-4329 t) 585-244-3010 rourlady@dor.org www.olqpstm.org Rev. Joseph A. Hart, Pst.; Dcn. Arthur Cuestas; Margaret Ostromecki, Pst. Assoc.; CRP Stds.: 201

Our Mother of Sorrows - 5000 Mt. Read Blvd., Rochester, NY 14612 t) 585-663-5432 x10 mos@dor.org www.mothersofsorrows.net Very Rev. William G. Coffas, Pst.; Rev. Joseph Martuscello, Par. Vicar; Rev. Robert J. Schrader, Senior Priest; Dcn. Thomas Jewell;

The Parish of the Holy Family, Monroe County, NY - 4100 Lyell Ave., Rochester, NY 14606 t) 585-247-4322 theparishoftheholyfamily@rochester.rr.com www.theparishoftheholyfamily.org Rev. Steven W. Lape, Pst.; Rev. Martin Truong, C.R.M., Par. Vicar; Dcn. Patrick M. Shanley; Dcn. Binh-Yen Nguyen;

Peace of Christ Roman Catholic Parish of Rochester, NY - 25 Empire Blvd., Rochester, NY 14609 t) 585-288-5000 rpeace@dor.org www.peaceofchristparish.org Very Rev. Peter B. Mottola, Pst.; Rev. Timothy Brown, Par. Vicar; Dcn. Robert Corsaro; Dcn. Marcelo DeRisio;

St. Ambrose Academy - (Grades PreK-5) 31 Empire Blvd., Rochester, NY 14609-4335 t) (585) 288-0580 saadcs@dor.org Christine Deutsch, Prin.;

St. Pius Tenth - 3010 Chili Ave., Rochester, NY 14624 t) 585-247-2566 cstpiusx@dor.org www.saintpiustenth.org Rev. Paul Bonacci, Par. Admin.; Dcn. James Briars, Pst. Assoc.; Dcn. Johan Engstrom, DRE;

St. Pius X School - (Grades PreK-5) 3000 Chili Ave., Rochester, NY 14624-4598 t) 585-247-5650 spxdcs@dor.org Maria Cahill, Prin.; Stds.: 130; Lay Tchrs.: 9

St. Stanislaus - 1124 Hudson Ave., Rochester, NY 14621; Mailing: 34 Saint Stanislaus St., Rochester, NY 14621 t) 585-467-3068 rststani@dor.org www.saintstanislausrochester.org Rev. Roman Caly, M.M. (Poland), Pst.; Dcn. Bruno Petrauskas; Dcn. Donald Eggleston;

St. Theodore - 168 Spencerport Rd., Rochester, NY 14606 t) 585-429-6811 gsttheo@dor.org www.sttheodoreschurch.com Rev. Kevin E. McKenna, Pst.; Dcn. Dennis Lohouse;

St. Thomas More - 2617 East Ave., Rochester, NY 14610 t) 585-381-4200 stm@dor.org www.olqpstm.com Rev. Joseph A. Hart, Pst.; Rev. Daniel J. Condon, Sacr. Min.; Dcn. Arthur Cuestas; Margaret Ostromecki, Pst. Assoc.; CRP Stds.: 201

SPENCERPORT

St. John the Evangelist - 55 Martha St., Spencerport, NY 14559 t) 585-352-5481 sstjohnc@dor.org www.stjohnchurchspencerport.org Rev. Justin D. Miller, Par. Admin.; Dcn. Alex DeLucenay;

VICTOR

St. Patrick - 115 Maple Ave., Victor, NY 14564 t) 585-924-7111 vstpatrick@dor.org www.stpatrickvictor.org Very Rev. Edison Tayag, Pst.; Dcn. John Payne;

WATERLOO

St. Francis & St. Clare Roman Catholic Parish, Seneca County, NY - 35 Center St., Waterloo, NY 13165 t) 315-539-2944 sfscparish@dor.org sfscrcc.org Rev. James Fennessy, Pst.;

WATKINS GLEN

St. Benedict - c/o St. Mary's of the Lake, Watkins Glen, NY 14891; Mailing: P.O. Box 289, Watkins Glen, NY 14891 t) 607-535-2786 wstmaryo@dor.org www.stmarystben.org Rev. Jeffrey Tunnicliff, Pst.; Dcn. Daniel Pavlina; Dcn. Rick Roy; Dcn. Thomas Ruda; Rosemary Nabogis, Pst. Min./Coord.;

St. Mary of the Lake - 905 N. Decatur St., Watkins Glen, NY 14891; Mailing: P.O. Box 289, Watkins Glen, NY 14891 t) 607-535-2786 wstmaryo@dor.org www.stmarystben.org Rev. Jeffrey Tunnicliff, Pst.; Dcn. Daniel Pavlina; Dcn. George Roy; Dcn. Thomas Ruda; Rosemary Nabogis, Pst. Min./Coord.;

Parish Center - 10th St., Watkins Glen, NY 14891

WAYLAND

Holy Family Catholic Community - 206 Fremont St., Wayland, NY 14572-1298 t) 585-728-2228 hfcc@dor.org www.hfccwny.org Rev. John Gathenya, Pst.;

WEBSTER

Holy Spirit - 1355 Hatch Rd., Webster, NY 14580 t) 585-671-5520 pholyspi@dor.org www.holyspirit-saintjoseph.org Very Rev. James A. Schwartz, Pst.; Dcn. Raymond Garbach, Pst. Assoc.; Dcn. Roger DeBell; Rev. Sriram Sadhanala, H.G.N., Par. Vicar;

Holy Trinity - 1460 Ridge Rd., Webster, NY 14580 t) 585-264-1616 wholytri@dor.org www.holytrinityweb.com Rev. Timothy E. Horan, Pst.; Rev. John M. Mulligan, In Res.;

St. Paul - 783 Hard Rd., Webster, NY 14580 t) 585-671-2100 wstpaulc@dor.org www.stpaulrcc.org Rev. Paul Gitau, Pst.; Dcn. Mark Robbins;

St. Rita - 1008 Maple Dr., Webster, NY 14580 t) 585-671-1100 wstritap@dor.org www.saintritawebster.org Rev. Timothy L. Niven, Pst.; Dcn. James J. Fien; Dcn. Richard Rall; Julie Cohn, Pst. Min./Coord.;

St. Rita School, Webster - (Grades PreK-6) t) 585-671-3132 sritadcs@dor.org Nancy Ferrarone, Prin.;

SCHOOLS: PRESCHOOL THRU HIGH SCHOOL

SCHOOLS

STATE OF NEW YORK

AVON

St. Agnes School - (PAR) (Grades PreK-6) 60 Park Pl., Avon, NY 14414-1053 t) 585-226-8500 sagnesdcs@dor.org stagnesavon.org Elizabeth Dowd, Prin.;

CANANDAIGUA

St. Mary School (Canandaigua) - (PAR) (Grades

PreK-8) 16 E. Gibson St., Canandaigua, NY 14424-1310 t) 585-394-4300 smcdcs@dor.org www.stmaryscanandaigua.org Lisa Milano, Prin.;

ELMIRA

Holy Family Elementary - (PAR) (Grades PreK-6) 421 Fulton St., Elmira, NY 14904-1709 t) 607-732-3588 paula.k.smith@dor.org www.schools.dor.org/holyfamilypri Paula Smith, Prin.;

GENEVA

St. Francis de Sales - St. Stephen School - (PAR) (Grades PreK-8) 17 Elmwood Ave., Geneva, NY 14456-2299 t) 315-789-1828 sfssdcs@dor.org www.stfrancisststephen.org Suzanne Poherence, Prin.;

HORSEHEADS

St. Mary Our Mother (Horseheads) - (PAR) (Grades PreK-6) 811 Westlake St., Horseheads, NY 14845-2099 t) 607-739-9157 smoms@dor.org Heather Bill, Prin.;

PENN YAN

St. Michael (Penn Yan) - (PAR) (Grades PreSchool-5) 214 Keuka St., Penn Yan, NY 14527-1143 t) 315-536-6112 smpydcs@dor.org stmichaelschoolpy.com Debra Marvin, Prin.;

ROCHESTER

Diocese of Rochester Department of Catholic Schools - (DIO) 1150 Buffalo Rd., Rochester, NY 14624 t) 585-328-3210 schools@dor.org www.dor.org James Tauzel, Supt.; Stds.: 5,392; Sr. Tchrs.: 6; Lay Tchrs.: 474

Nativity Preparatory Academy of Rochester - 15 Whalin St., Rochester, NY 14620 t) 585-271-1630 info@nativityrochester.org www.nativityrochester.org James Smith, Pres.; Jennifer Kremer, Prin.;

Nazareth Elementary School - (PAR) (Grades PreSchool-6) 311 Flower City Park, Rochester, NY 14615-3614 t) 585-458-3786 mmancuso@nazarethschools.org nazarethschools.org Sr. Margaret Mancuso, S.S.J., Prin.;

HIGH SCHOOLS

STATE OF NEW YORK

ELMIRA

Notre Dame High School - (PRV) 1400 Maple Ave., Elmira, NY 14904 t) 607-734-2267 kellyn@notredamehighschool.com www.notredamehighschool.com Patricia Mack, Head of School; Sr. Mary Walter Hickey, R.S.M., Pres.; Stds.: 232

ROCHESTER

The Aquinas Institute - (PRV) 1127 Dewey Ave., Rochester, NY 14613-9989 t) 585-254-2020 www.aquinasinstitute.com Theodore Mancini, Prin.; Raymond Shea, Interim Principal; Stds.: 733

Bishop Kearney High School - (PRV) 125 Kings Hwy. S., Rochester, NY 14617-5596 t) 585-342-4000 jsimoni@bkhs.org www.bkhs.org (Coed), Sponsored by the Congregation of Christian Brothers in association with the School Sisters of Notre Dame, Wilton Province. Mary Martell, Prin.; Steve Salluzzo, Pres.; Stds.: 409

McQuaid Jesuit High School - (PRV) 1800 S. Clinton Ave., Rochester, NY 14618 t) 585-473-1130 ababer@mcquaid.org www.mcquaid.org Northeast Province of the Society of Jesus (The Jesuits) Rev. Philip G. Judge, S.J., Pres.; Adam R. Baber, Prin.; Stds.: 745

Our Lady of Mercy School for Young Women - (PRV) (Grades 6-12) 1437 Blossom Rd., Rochester, NY 14610 t) 585-288-7120 info@mercyhs.com www.mercyhs.com Pamela Fennell Baker, Pres.; Dr. Sherylanne Diodato, Interim Principal; Stds.: 657

INSTITUTIONS LOCATED IN DIOCESE

CAMPUS MINISTRY / NEWMAN CENTERS [CAM]

ROCHESTER

Campus Ministry - Pastoral Center, 1150 Buffalo Rd., Rochester, NY 14624 t) 585-328-3210 x1218 shannon.kilbridge@dor.org Shannon Kilbridge, Dir.;

The Catholic Community of Ithaca College - 1001 Muller Chapel, Ithaca College, 953 Danby Rd., Ithaca, NY 14850 t) (607) 274-3011 fr.daniel.mcmullin@dor.org www.ithaca.edu/catholic Rev. Daniel McMullin;

Catholic Newman Community at the University of Rochester - Interfaith Chapel, 1045 Joseph C. Wilson Blvd, Rochester, NY 14627 t) 585-275-8515 bcool@admin.rochester.edu www.urnewman.org Rev. Brian Cool, Dir.;

The Cornell Catholic Community, Inc. (Ithaca) - Cornell University, Ithaca, NY 14853 t) 607-255-4228 fr.daniel.mcmullin@dor.org www.cornellcatholic.org Rev. Daniel McMullin, Dir.;

Eastman School of Music Catholic Students Organization - Interfaith Chapel, 320 Wilson Blvd., Rochester, NY 14627 t) 585-275-8515 bcool@admin.rochester.edu www.urnewman.org Rev. Brian Cool, Dir.;

Elmira College - 1010 Davis St., Elmira, NY 14901; Mailing: One Park Pl., Elmira, NY 14901 t) (607) 734-6255 fr.scott.kubinski@dor.org Rev. Scott M. Kubinski, Contact;

Hobart and William Smith College - c/o Our Lady of Peace, 130 Exchange St., Geneva, NY 14456 t) 315-789-0930 x106 fr.thomas.mull@dor.org Roman Catholic Community. Rev. Thomas P. Mull;

St. John Fisher College - 3690 East Ave., Rochester, NY 14618 t) 585-385-8368 kmannara@sjfc.edu www.sjfc.edu/student-life/campus-ministry/ Rev. Kevin Mannara, C.S.B., Dir.;

Keuka College c/o Our Lady of the Lakes - 210 Keuka St., Penn Yan, NY 14527 t) 315-536-7459 fr.leo.reinhardt@dor.org Rev. Leo J. Reinhardt;

Monroe Community College c/o Our Lady of Lourdes / St. Anne - 1600 Mount Hope Ave., Rochester, NY 14620 t) 585-271-3260 fr.gary.tyman@dor.org Rev. Gary L. Tyman;

Nazareth College of Rochester - 4245 East Ave., Rochester, NY 14618 t) 585-389-2303 jfazio1@naz.edu Jamie Fazio, Campus Min.;

New York Chiropractic College - c/o St. Francis & St. Clare, 25 Center St., Waterloo, NY 13165 t) (315) 651-4349 fr.james.fennessy@dor.org Rev. James Fennessy;

Newman (Catholic Campus) Parish, RIT/NTID - Interfaith Center, 40 Lomb Memorial Dr., Rochester, NY 14623 t) 585-475-5172 bcool@admin.rochester.edu www.ritnewman.com Rev. Brian Cool, Dir.;

Roberts Wesleyan College c/o St. Christopher Church - 3350 Union St., North Chili, NY 14514 t) 585-595-1400 Rev. Eloo Malachy Nwosu;

State University College at Brockport, the Newman Oratory of Brockport - 101 Kenyon St., Brockport, NY 14420 t) 585-637-4500 fr.joe.mccaffrey@dor.org Rev. Joseph P. McCaffrey, Chap.;

State University College at Geneseo (Geneseo), Newman Catholic Community at the Interfaith Center - 11 Franklin St., Geneseo, NY 14454 t) 585-243-1460 mike.sauter@dor.org Michael Sauter, Dir.;

Wells College, c/o Good Shepherd Catholic Community - 299 Main St, Aurora, NY 13026 t) 315-364-7197 fr.william.moorby@dor.org Rev. William A. Moorby, Chap.;

CATHOLIC CHARITIES [CCH]

ELMIRA

Catholic Charities of Chemung/Schuyler - 215 E. Church St., Elmira, NY 14901 t) 607-734-9784 nancy.koons@dor.org www.cs-cc.org Asstd. Annu.: 7,201; Staff: 77

Food Bank of the Southern Tier - 388 Upper Oakwood Ave., Elmira, NY 14903 t) 607-796-6061 natasha.thompson@foodbankst.org www.foodbankst.org Joseph Thomas, Chair Bd.; Natasha Thompson, Pres. & CEO; Asstd. Annu.: 1,311,901; Staff: 46

GENEVA

Catholic Charities of the Finger Lakes - 94 Exchange St., Geneva, NY 14456 t) 315-789-2686 ccfl@dor.org catholiccharitiesfl.org (Serving Wayne, Yates, Ontario, Seneca, and Cayuga Counties) Frank Capozzi Jr., Exec. Dir.; Dr. Richard Kasulke, Chair Bd.; Asstd. Annu.: 27,000; Staff: 39

Early Intervention - Inga Rojas, Contact;

General Counseling/College Bound - Janalee Weaver, Staff Member;

Justice & Peace/Parish Social Ministry -

LaCasa/Community Outreach - Sandy Thomas, Staff Member;

PINS & DAS -

Wolcott Clothing Center - Jill Lee, Staff Member;

ITHACA

Catholic Charities of Tompkins/Tioga - 324 W. Buffalo St., Ithaca, NY 14850 t) 607-272-5062 x13 renee.spear@dor.org www.catholiccharitiestt.org Renee Spear, Exec. Dir.; Sue Hyatt, Chair; Michaela Cortright, Deputy Director; Asstd. Annu.: 12,436; Staff: 35

Development -

Family Empowerment Services -

Immigrant Support Services - Sue Chaffee, Dir.;

Justice and Peace, Tompkins -

Justice and Peace, Tioga - Kathy Dubel, Dir.;

Samaritan Center -

MT. MORRIS

Catholic Charities of Steuben / Livingston County - 34 E State St, Mt. Morris, NY 14510 t) 607-776-8085; (585) 658-4466 x13 (Admin Office) tabitha.brewster@dor.org ccsteubenlivingston.org/ Dr. Tabitha Brewster, Exec. Dir.; Asstd. Annu.: 30,916; Staff: 131

ROCHESTER

Catholic Charities Family & Community Services - 87 N. Clinton Ave., Rochester, NY 14604 t) 585-546-7220 ccfcs@cfcrochester.org Lori VanAuken, President & CEO; Luke Mazzochetti, Chair Bd.; Tracy Boff, COO; Asstd. Annu.: 20,000; Staff: 908

Compliance - 79 N. Clinton Ave., Rochester, NY 14604 t) (585) 546-7220 tdavis@cfcrochester.org Rebecca Ziobrowski, Regional Compliance Officer;

Emergency Shelter/ Residential Services - llewis@cfcrochester.org

Fund Development - spartner@cfcrochester.org Sally Partner, Vice President;

Mental Health - kmurrell@cfcrochester.org

Refugee, Aging & Family Services - Jennifer Berenson, Dir., Children Youth & Family Svcs.; Lisa Hoyt, Dir., Refugee & Immigration Svcs.; Jennifer McDermott, Dir., Aging & Adult Svcs.;

Social Policy - mebenhoe@cfcrochester.org

Strategic Growth & Advocacy - spartner@cfcrochester.org Sally Partner, Vice Pres.;

Substance Use Disorder Service - kmurrell@cfcrochester.org

Catholic Charities of the Diocese of Rochester - 1150 Buffalo Rd., Rochester, NY 14624 t) 585-328-3210 x1302 karen.dehais@dor.org www.dor.org/charities/index.htm Karen Dehais, Dir.; Anthony Adams, Chair; Sabrina McLeod, VP of Financial Operations; Barbara Poling, Human Resources Dir.; Robert G Trusiak, Centralized Compliance Dir.; Staff: 12

Catholic Charities Finance Office - 94 Exchange St., Geneva, NY 14456-2235 t) 315-789-1377 kirstin.goodman@dor.org

Regional Diocesan Administration - 215 E. Church St., Elmira, NY 14901 t) 607-734-9748 jack.balinsky@dor.org Lois Mazzarese, Finance Dir.; Donna L. Rieker, Employee Rels. Specialist;

CEMETERIES [CEM]

AUBURN

St. Joseph's - 6020 Lake Ave., Auburn, NY 13021

CORNING
St. Mary -
ELMIRA
SS. Peter and Paul's - 623 Franklin St., Elmira, NY 14904
GENEVA
St. Mary's and St. Patrick's -
ROCHESTER
Holy Sepulchre Cemetery - 2461 Lake Ave., Rochester, NY 14612 t) 585-458-4110 cathy@holysepulchre.org www.holysepulchre.org Cathy H Vail, Exec. Dir.;

COLLEGES & UNIVERSITIES [COL]

ROCHESTER
St. Bernard's School of Theology & Ministry - 120 French Rd., Rochester, NY 14618 t) 585-271-3657 registrar@stbernards.edu www.stbernards.edu Dr. Stephen J. Loughlin, Pres.; Dr. Matthew Kuhner, Dean; Matthew D. Brown, Dir.; Stds.: 115; Lay Tchrs.: 5; Sr. Tchrs.: 2

CONVENTS, MONASTERIES, AND RESIDENCES FOR WOMEN [CON]

PITTSFORD
Monastery of Our Lady and St. Joseph Carmelite Monastery - 1931 W. Jefferson Rd., Pittsford, NY 14534-1041 t) 585-427-7094 carmelitesofrochester.org Discalced Carmelite Nuns. Mother Paul Augustine of the Sacred Passion, Prioress; Srs.: 15
ROCHESTER
Sisters of Mercy of the Americas - New York, Pennsylvania, Pacific West Community - 1437 Blossom Rd., Rochester, NY 14610 t) (585) 485-5442 www.sistersofmercy.org Sr. Patricia McDermott, Pres.; Srs.: 229
Sisters St. Joseph of Rochester - 150 French Rd., Rochester, NY 14618-3822 t) 585-641-8100 cong@ssjrochester.org www.ssjrochester.org Sisters of St. Joseph of Rochester, Inc. Very Rev. Paul J. Tomasso, Chap.; Sr. Eileen Daly, SSJ, Pres.; Srs.: 153

ENDOWMENTS / FOUNDATIONS / TRUSTS [EFT]

ROCHESTER
Sisters of Saint Joseph of Rochester Charitable Trust - 150 French Rd., Rochester, NY 14618 t) 585-641-8166 apender@ssjrochester.org Alicia Pender, Contact;
Sisters of Saint Joseph of Rochester Ministry Foundation, Inc. - 150 French Rd., Rochester, NY 14618-3822 t) 585-641-8124 bsutter@ssjrochester.org www.ssjrochester.org Stephen LaSalle II, Chair;
St. Theodore's Apartment Housing Development Fund Co., Inc. (Dunn Tower II Apts.) - 200 Dunn Tower Dr., Rochester, NY 14606 t) 585-429-6840 dt2@dunntower.com www.dunntower.com
WATERLOO
Patrician Fund Trust - 25 Center St., Waterloo, NY 13165 t) 315-651-4349 sstpatri@dor.org www.senecafallsonline.com/stpats/ Rev. James Fennessy, Contact;

MISCELLANEOUS [MIS]

CALEDONIA
Magnificat - Rochester - Louise Carson, 656 Middle Rd, Caledonia, NY 14423; Mailing: Magnificat Rochester, P.O. Box 24787, Rochester, NY 14624 t) (585) 233-8647 magnificatrochester@frontier.com magnificatrochester.org/ Ministry to Catholic Women Louise Carson, Contact;
CORNING
Anawim Community Center - 122 E. First St., Corning, NY 14830 t) 607-936-4965 shirleyfernandes@anawim.com www.anawim.com Rev. Daniel Healy, Dir.;
OWEGO
Owego -Tioga County Rural Ministry - 143 North Ave., Owego, NY 13827 t) 607-687-3021 info@tcrm.org tcrm.org This ministry serves as a food pantry and an emergency outreach to the poor and elderly of the county. Sr. Mary O'Brien, C.S.J., Exec.;
PENFIELD
Rochester Comitium - 71 Thorntree Cir., Penfield, NY 14526 t) (585) 266-0672 legionofmaryrochesterny.org Janice Caretta, Pres.; Rev. William B. Leone, Spiritual Adv./Care Srvcs.;
ROCHESTER
Apostleship of Prayer - Diocesan Pastoral Center, 1150 Buffalo Rd., Rochester, NY 14624 t) 585-328-3210 Rev. Thomas P. Mull;
Archivist (Diocese of Rochester Archives) - 1150 Buffalo Rd., Rochester, NY 14624 t) 585-328-3210 x1204 department.archive@dor.org Sr. Connie Derby, R.S.M., Dir.;
Catholic Committee on Scouting - 1150 Buffalo Rd., Rochester, NY 14624 t) 585-328-3210 communications@dor.org www.dor.org Rev. William McGrath, Chap.; Mark Capellazzi, Diocesan Liaison;
Churchville Housing Development Fund Corporation - 1150 Buffalo Rd., Rochester, NY 14624 t) (585) 529-9562 Mark Greisberger, Pres.;
Communis Fund of the Diocese of Rochester, Inc. - 1150 Buffalo Rd., Rochester, NY 14624 t) 585-328-3228 x1269 Mary Ziarniak, Contact;
The Diocese of Rochester Priests' Retirement Plan - 1150 Buffalo Rd., Rochester, NY 14624 t) (585) 328-3228 Janice Boyea, Contact;
DOR Holding, Inc. - 1150 Buffalo Rd., Rochester, NY 14624 t) 585-328-3228 x1269 Lisa M. Passero, Contact;
Dunn Tower Apartments, Inc. - 100 Dunn Tower Dr., Rochester, NY 14606 t) (585) 429-5520 dt1@dunntower.com www.dunntower.com Housing for Seniors; Under 62 with Physical or Mobility; Disabled Vets
Family Rosary For Peace, Inc. - 51 Hazelhurst Dr., Apt. C, Rochester, NY 14606 t) 585-436-8179 Very Rev. Paul J. Tomasso, Dir.;
Finger Lakes Guild - 120 French Rd., Rochester, NY 14618; Mailing: P.O. Box 25223, Rochester, NY 14625 fingerlakescma.org Dr. Angela Kristan, Pres.;
St. Joseph's House of Hospitality - 402 South Ave., Rochester, NY 14620; Mailing: P.O. Box 31049, Rochester, NY 14603 t) 585-232-3262; 585-232-3262 saintjoeshouse.org Services provide soup kitchen, personal assistance to the needy, emergency men's housing and social justice advocacy. Jasmin Reggler, Coordinator;
St. Joseph's Neighborhood Center, Inc. - 417 South Ave., Rochester, NY 14620 t) 585-325-5260 Bryan Hetherington, Pres.;
Marriage Encounter Apostolate - t) (585) 703-5259 www.wwme.org (Worldwide)
Mercy Community Services, Inc. - 142 Webster Ave., Rochester, NY 14609 t) 585-288-2634 info@mercycommunityservices.org www.mercycommunityservices.org Supportive Housing for Single Mothers and their Children and primary healthcare for the uninsured. Nikisha Johnson, Pres.;
Missionary Childhood Association - 1150 Buffalo Rd., Rochester, NY 14624 t) 585-436-9200 jconlon@dor.org www.dor.org/missions
Notre Dame Learning Center, Inc. - 71 Pkwy., Rochester, NY 14608; Mailing: P.O. Box 77175, Rochester, NY 14617 t) 585-254-5110 ndlc@frontiernet.net www.ndlcenter.org Ministry for children and adults by providing educational opportunities in literacy, reading & math. Sr. Evelyn Breslin, SSND, Exec. Dir.; Judith Ekberg, Chair; Sr. Mary Lennon, Treas.;
Providence Housing Development Corporation - 1150 Buffalo Rd., Rochester, NY 14624 t) (585) 529-9562 www.providencehousing.org Mission Statement: To strengthen families & communities by creating & providing access to quality affordable housing. Mark Greisberger, Dir.; Rev. Joseph A. Hart, Pres.; Daniel Sturgis, CFO;
- **Clark Park Apartments Housing Development Fund Company, Inc.** - 1150 Buffalo Rd., Rochester, NY 14624
- **Providence Atwood Park Housing Development Fund Company, Inc.** - 1150 Buffalo Rd., Rochester, NY 14624
- **Providence Brown Street Housing Development Fund Corporation** - 1150 Buffalo Rd., Rochester, NY 14624
- **Providence Canalside Housing Corporation** - 1150 Buffalo Rd., Rochester, NY 14624
- **Providence Clemens Housing Corporation** - 1150 Buffalo Rd., Rochester, NY 14624
- **Providence Lyons Housing Development Fund Company, Inc.** - 1150 Buffalo Rd., Rochester, NY 14624 Mark Greisberger, Pres.;
- **Providence Northstar Housing Development Fund Company, Inc.** - 1150 Buffalo Rd., Rochester, NY 14624
- **Providence Mt. Morris Housing Corporation** - 1150 Buffalo Rd., Rochester, NY 14624 Mark Greisberger, Pres.;
- **Providence Rivendell Court Apartments, Inc.** - 1150 Buffalo Rd., Rochester, NY 14624
- **Providence St. Andrew's Housing Development Fund Company, Inc.** - 1150 Buffalo Rd., Rochester, NY 14624
- **Providence Union Park Housing Development Fund Company, Inc.** - 1150 Buffalo Rd., Rochester, NY 14624
- **Providence Yates Housing Development Fund Company, Inc.** - 1150 Buffalo Rd., Rochester, NY 14624 Mark Greisberger, Pres.;
- **Son House Housing Development Fund Company, Inc.** - 1150 Buffalo Rd., Rochester, NY 14624
- **Union Meadows Housing Development Fund Company, Inc.** - 1150 Buffalo Rd., Rochester, NY 14624
- **West Town Village Housing Development Fund Company, Inc.** - 1150 Buffalo Rd., Rochester, NY 14624

Providence Powell Housing Development Fund Corporation - 1150 Buffalo Rd., Rochester, NY 14624 t) (585) 529-9562 daniel.sturgis@dor.org Mark Greisberger, Pres.;
Providence Wayne Charities Corporation - 1150 Buffalo Rd., Rochester, NY 14624 t) (585) 328-3210 Mark Greisberger, Pres.;
Rochester Catholic Worker Bethany House - 1111 Joseph Ave., Rochester, NY 14621 t) 585-454-4197 rbethan1@rochester.rr.com bethanyhouserocny.org Donna Ecker, Contact;
The Diocese of Rochester Lay Employees' Retirement Accumulation Plan - 1150 Buffalo Rd., Rochester, NY 14624 t) (585) 328-3210 Tammy Sylvester, Contact;
WEBSTER
Catholic Charismatic Renewal - 929 Gravel Rd., Webster, NY 14580 t) 585-671-5275 bomba_14580@yahoo.com Dcn. Robert Meyer;

MONASTERIES AND RESIDENCES FOR PRIESTS AND BROTHERS [MON]

INTERLAKEN
St. Fidelis Friary - 7790 County Rd. 153, Interlaken, NY 14847 t) 607-532-4423 Province of St. Mary (Order of Friars Minor Capuchin) NY -NE Rev. Bernard Maloney, O.F.M.Cap.; Rev. Richard Crawley, O.F.M. Cap., Chap.; Bro. Antonine Lizama, O.F.M.Cap.;
PIFFARD
Abbey of the Genesee, Inc. - 3258 River Rd., Piffard, NY 14533 t) 585-243-0660 www.geneseeabbey.org Rt. Rev. Gerard D'Souza, O.C.S.O., Abbot; Rev. Jerome J. Machar, O.C.S.O., Treas.; Bro. James Almeter, O.C.S.O., Mem.; Bro. David Baumbach, O.C.S.O., Mem.; Bro. Gregory Chan, O.C.S.O., Mem.; Rt. Rev. John Denburger, O.C.S.O., Mem.; Bro. Benedict Drgan, O.C.S.O., Mem.; Bro. Alberic Gardner, O.C.S.O., Mem.; Bro. Augustine Jackson, O.C.S.O., Mem.; Bro. Lawrence Jenny, O.C.S.O., Mem.; Bro. Brian Kerns, O.C.S.O., Mem.; Rev. Stephen Muller, O.C.S.O., Mem.; Bro. Louis Petruska, ocso, Mem.; Bro. Paul Richards, O.C.S.O., Mem.; Rev. Justin R. Sheehan, O.C.S.O., Mem.; Rev. Isaac Slater, O.C.S.O., Mem.; Bro. Walter Thomann, O.C.S.O., Mem.; Rev. John Hamill,

O.C.S.O., Mem.; Bro. Christian Walsh, O.C.S.O., Mem.; Bro. Anthony Weber, O.C.S.O., Mem.; Rev. Aelred W. Wentz, O.C.S.O., Mem.; Bro. David Wilson, O.C.S.O., Mem.; Brs.: 14; Priests: 9

PINE CITY

Mount Saviour Monastery (The Benedictine Foundation of NYS) - 231 Monastery Rd., Pine City, NY 14871-9787 t) 607-734-1688 info@msaviour.org www.msaviour.org Bro. John Thompson, O.S.B, Prior; Bro. Luke Zimnicky, O.S.B., Subprior; Bro. Pierre Pratte, O.S.B., Bus. Mgr.; Bro. Antonio Bravo Lara, O.S.B., Mem.; Bro. Gabriel Duffee, O.S.B., Mem.; Bro. Bruno Lane, O.S.B., Mem.; Bro. Michael O'Connor, O.S.B., Mem.; Brs.: 12

ROCHESTER

Basilian Fathers - 445 Kings Hwy. S., Rochester, NY 14617 t) 585-266-1288 Rev. George T. Smith, C.S.B., Mem.; Rev. Kevin Mannara, C.S.B., Mem.; Rev. Thomas P. Dugan, C.S.B., Mem.; Priests: 3

Basilian Residence - 3497 East Ave., Rochester, NY 14618 t) 585-586-4600 Rev. Thomas P. Dugan, C.S.B.;

Missionaries of the Precious Blood - 1261 Highland Ave., Rochester, NY 14620-1873 t) 585-244-2692 johncolacino7@gmail.com Rev. John A. Colacino, C.PP.S.; Priests: 1

Whitefriars Priory - 625 Colebrook Dr., Rochester, NY 14617 t) 585-266-2560 dmjdemaio@gmail.com Rev. Joseph DeMaio, O.Carm.; Rev. Matthew Temple, O.Carm.; Rev. Jack Healy, O.Carm., Prior;

NURSING / REHABILITATION / CONVALESCENCE / ELDERLY CARE [NUR]

ROCHESTER

St. Ann's Home for the Aged - 1500 Portland Ave., Rochester, NY 14621 t) 585-697-6000 info@stannscommunity.com www.stannscommunity.com Michael E. McRae, Pres.; Sr. Mary Louise Mitchell, S.S.J., Dir.;

St. Ann's Nursing Home Co., Inc. - 1450 Portland Ave., Rochester, NY 14621 t) 585-697-6000 info@stannscommunity.com www.stannscommunity.com (The Heritage) Michael E. McRae, President & CEO; Sr. Mary Louise Mitchell, S.S.J., Director of Pastoral Care;

Chapel Oaks - 1550 Portland Ave., Rochester, NY 14621 t) (585) 697-6600 www.stannscommunity.org Dcn. Daniel M. Kinsky, Chap.;

PRESCHOOLS / CHILDCARE CENTERS [PRE]

LIVONIA

Camp Stella Maris - 4395 E. Lake Rd., Livonia, NY 14487 t) 585-346-2243 info@campstellamaris.org campstellamaris.org Purpose: Residential camp (ages 7-15) and day camp (ages 5-12) under Catholic auspices, for boys & girls of all faiths. John Quinlivan, CEO; Stds.: 4,000; Lay Tchrs.: 100

RETREAT HOUSES / RENEWAL CENTERS [RTR]

CANANDAIGUA

Notre Dame Retreat House - 5151 Foster Rd., Canandaigua, NY 14424; Mailing: Box 342, Canandaigua, NY 14424 t) 585-394-5700 ndretreat.org Rev. Joseph F. Jones, C.Ss.R., Rector; Rev. Thomas Travers, C.Ss.R., Retreat Dir.; Bro. George Armoogam;

LODI

***Branches Christian Rest and Renewal Centers, Inc.** - 8251 Lower Lake Rd., Lodi, NY 14860; Mailing: 182 Schwartz Rd., Lancaster, NY 14086 t) 716-901-4313 branches1515@live.com branchescenter.org Donna Wieand, Admin.;

ROCHESTER

Mercy Spirituality Center - 65 Highland Ave., Rochester, NY 14620 t) 585-473-6893 info@mercyspiritualitycenter.org; bryan@mercyspiritualitycenter.org www.mercyspiritualitycenter.org Sponsored by Sisters of Mercy, New York, Pennsylvania Community. Brigid Ryan, Admin.;

An asterisk (*) denotes an organization that has established tax-exempt status directly with the IRS and is not covered by the USCCB Group Ruling.

Diocese of Rockford

(Dioecesis Rockfordiensis)

MOST REVEREND DAVID J. MALLOY

Bishop of Rockford; ordained July 1, 1983; appointed Bishop of Rockford March 20, 2012. Office: 555 Colman Center Dr., Rockford, IL 61125.

Diocesan Chancery: 555 Colman Center Dr., P.O. Box 7044, Rockford, IL 61125. T: 815-399-4300; F: 815-399-5266.
www.rockforddiocese.org
info@rockforddiocese.org

ESTABLISHED SEPTEMBER 23, 1908.

Square Miles 6,457.

Comprises Jo Daviess, Stephenson, Winnebago, Boone, McHenry, Carroll, Ogle, DeKalb, Kane, Whiteside and Lee Counties in the State of Illinois.

For legal titles of parishes and diocesan institutions, consult the Chancery Office.

STATISTICAL OVERVIEW

Personnel

Bishop 1
Abbots 1
Retired Abbots 1
Priests: Diocesan Active in Diocese 107
Priests: Diocesan Active Outside Diocese 5
Priests: Retired, Sick or Absent 57
Number of Diocesan Priests 169
Religious Priests in Diocese 9
Total Priests in your Diocese 178
Extern Priests in Diocese 16
Ordinations:
Diocesan Priests 1
Transitional Deacons 1
Permanent Deacons 17
Permanent Deacons in Diocese 142
Total Brothers 9
Total Sisters 84

Parishes

Parishes 105
With Resident Pastor:
Resident Diocesan Priests 66
Resident Religious Priests 6
Without Resident Pastor:
Administered by Priests 33
Missions 2

Professional Ministry Personnel:
Brothers 9
Sisters 39
Lay Ministers 91

Welfare

Catholic Hospitals 3
Total Assisted 431,833
Health Care Centers 2
Total Assisted 271
Homes for the Aged 3
Total Assisted 695
Day Care Centers 1
Total Assisted 81
Special Centers for Social Services 7
Total Assisted 29,139

Educational

Diocesan Students in Other Seminaries 10
Total Seminarians 10
Colleges and Universities 1
Total Students 202
High Schools, Diocesan and Parish 6
Total Students 1,863
High Schools, Private 2
Total Students 709
Elementary Schools, Diocesan and Parish 29
Total Students 6,199

Catechesis/Religious Education:
High School Students 1,767
Elementary Students 11,362
Total Students under Catholic Instruction 22,112
Teachers in Diocese:
Priests 5
Brothers 2
Sisters 6
Lay Teachers 649

Vital Statistics

Receptions into the Church:
Infant Baptism Totals 3,972
Minor Baptism Totals 340
Adult Baptism Totals 106
Received into Full Communion 174
First Communions 4,332
Confirmations 4,104
Marriages:
Catholic 587
Interfaith 128
Total Marriages 715
Deaths 2,177
Total Catholic Population 411,932
Total Population 1,493,761

LEADERSHIP

Chancery Office - t) 815-399-4300 officeofthebishop@rockforddiocese.org

Administrative Assistant to the Bishop - Coco Acosta-Zeman;

Secretary to the Bishop - Dcn. Thomas McKenna;

Diocesan Master of Ceremonies - t) 630-232-0124 Rev. Jonathan P. Bakkelund;

Vicar General and Moderator of the Curia - t) 815-399-4300 Rev. Msgr. Glenn L. Nelson (GNelson@RockfordDiocese.org);

Chancellor and General Counsel - t) 815-399-4300 Ellen B. Lynch, Chancellor (ELynch@RockfordDiocese.org);

Vice Chancellor - t) 815-399-4300 Very Rev. Matthew M. Bergschneider, Vice Chancellor (MBergschneider@RockfordDiocese.org);

Diocesan Consultors - Rev. Msgr. Glenn L. Nelson (GNelson@RockfordDiocese.org); Very Rev. F. William Etheredge (WEtheredge@RockfordDiocese.org); Rev. Patrick S. Gillmeyer, O.S.B. (PGillmeyer@RockfordDiocese.org);

Deans -

Aurora Deanery - Very Rev. Stephen St. Jules, Dean;

DeKalb Deanery - Very Rev. F. William Etheredge, Dean;

Elgin Deanery - Very Rev. Msgr. Daniel J. Deutsch, Dean;

Freeport Deanery - Very Rev. Peter Snieg, Dean;

McHenry Deanery - Very Rev. Robert W. Jones, Dean;

Rockford Deanery - Very Rev. Phillip A. Kaim, Dean;

Sterling Deanery - Very Rev. James R. Keenan, Dean;

Presbyteral Council - Rev. Matthew J. McMorrow, Chair (MMcmorrow@RockfordDiocese.org); Rev. John Kladar, Secy. (JKladar@RockfordDiocese.org); Very Rev. Phillip A. Kaim, Treas. (PKaim@RockfordDiocese.org);

ADMINISTRATION

Finance and Administration - t) 815-399-4300 Jodi Rippon, Dir. (JRippon@RockfordDiocese.org); Lori Graber, Asst. Dir. (LGraber@RockfordDiocese.org);

Accounting and Data Processing Office - t) 815-399-4300 Dan O'Malley, Dir. (DOmalley@RockfordDiocese.org); Lori Glenn, Bus. Mgr. (LGlenn@RockfordDiocese.org);

Information Technology - Robert White, Dir. (RWhite@RockfordDiocese.org); Joe Schneider, Computer Specialist (JSchneider@RockfordDiocese.org);

Diocesan Administration Offices and Property Management - t) 815-399-4300 Brian Heinkel, Bldg. Mgr. (BHeinkel@RockfordDiocese.org);

Human Resources - t) (815) 399-4300 Ellen B. Lynch, Dir. (ELynch@RockfordDiocese.org);

Safe Environment Office - Sara Danielson, Coord.;

Victim Assistance Coordinator - t) 815-293-7540 Richard D. Parsons (RParsons@RockfordDiocese.org);

OFFICES AND DIRECTORS

Catholic Charismatic Renewal Services - t) 815-654-8420 www.rockforddiocese.org/charismaticrenewal Rev. Christopher J. Kuhn, Spiritual Dir. (CKuhn@RockfordDiocese.org); Rev. Andres Salinas, Asst. Spiritual Dir., Hispanic Comm. (ASalinas@RockfordDiocese.org); Ronald Bergman, Diocesan Liaison;

Catholic Office of the Deaf - t) 815-399-4300 (Voice); 815-217-2234 (VP) deafapostolate@rockforddiocese.org www.rockforddiocese.org/deafapostolate Rev. Msgr. Glenn L. Nelson, Dir. (GNelson@RockfordDiocese.org);

Catholic Cemeteries - t) 815-965-1450 Ken Giambalvo, Dir. (kmg@rockcem.org); Jodi Rippon, Admin. (JRippon@RockfordDiocese.org);

Censores Librorum - Rev. Ryan B. Browning (RBrowning@RockfordDiocese.org); Rev. Jared Twenty (JTwenty@RockfordDiocese.org);

Charitable Giving Office - t) 815-399-4300 Claudia Broman, Dir. (CBroman@RockfordDiocese.org);

Council of Catholic Women, Diocesan - Rev. Msgr. Thomas L. Dzielak, Spiritual Advisor (TDzielak@RockfordDiocese.org); Josie Whaley, Pres. (jsw1205@gmail.com);

Courage - www.couragerc.org Very Rev. Phillip A. Kaim, Chap. (PKaim@RockfordDiocese.org);

Cursillo Movement - Rev. Godwin Nsikan-Ubom Asuquo, Spiritual Dir. (English) (GAsuquo@RockfordDiocese.org); Rev. Ruben Herrera, Spiritual Dir. (Spanish) (RHerrera@RockfordDiocese.org); Tiffany Guthrie, Lay Dir. (English) (rkdcursillo@gmail.com);

Divine Worship and Liturgical Commission Office - t) 630-232-0124 Rev. Jonathan P. Bakkelund, Dir. (JBakkelund@RockfordDiocese.org);

Ecumenical and Interreligious Affairs - t) 815-399-4300 Very Rev. Stephen St. Jules (SStjules@RockfordDiocese.org);

EnCourage - www.truthandlove.com Rev. Ryan B. Browning, Chap. (RBrowning@RockfordDiocese.org);

Ethicist for Health Care Issues, Diocesan - t) (847) 888-1682 Rev. Ryan B. Browning, Dir. (RBrowning@RockfordDiocese.org);

Filipino Catholic Ministry - Rev. Ariel A. Valencia, Dir. (AValencia@RockfordDiocese.org);

Hispanic Ministry Offices - Rev. Msgr. Arquimedes Vallejo, Episcopal Vicar (AVallejo@RockfordDiocese.org); Rev. Diego F. Ospina, Freeport Deanery Coord. (DOspina@RockfordDiocese.org); Sr. Maria Ventura Chavez, Aurora Deanery Coord.;

Office of Life and Family Evangelization - t) 815-399-4300 Therese Stahl, Dir. (TStahl@RockfordDiocese.org); Rev. Jeremy A. Trowbridge, Spiritual Dir. (JTrowbridge@RockfordDiocese.org);

Propagation of the Faith - t) 815-399-4300 Rev. Msgr. Glenn L. Nelson, Dir. (GNelson@RockfordDiocese.org);

Research and Planning - t) 815-399-4300 Kevin Fuss, Dir. (KFuss@RockfordDiocese.org);

Scouts - t) (815) 633-6311 Rev. Aaron Downing, Chap. (ADowning@RockfordDiocese.org);

Vietnamese Catholic Ministry - t) 815-312-9661 antonvlong7@msn.com Rev. Anthony Vu Khac Long, Dir. (ALong@RockfordDiocese.org);

CATHOLIC CHARITIES

Catholic Social Services and Catholic Charities - t) 815-399-4300 Cathy Weightman-Moore, Dir. (CWeightman-Moore@RockfordDiocese.org); Charlene Croyle, Fiscal Mgr. (CCroyle@RockfordDiocese.org);

Catholic Relief Services - Cathy Weightman-Moore, Dir.; Dcn. Thomas McKenna, Consultant;

Rural Life Conference - Dcn. Thomas McKenna, Dir.;

Catholic Campaign for Human Development - t) 815-399-4300 Cathy Weightman-Moore, Dir. (CWeightman-Moore@RockfordDiocese.org); Dcn. Thomas McKenna, Consultant (TMckenna@rockforddiocese.org);

Immigration Services - t) 815-399-1709 Iosdel Trujillo, Dir. (ITrujillo@RockfordDiocese.org);

Refugee Resettlement Services - t) (815) 399-1709 Janet Biljeskovic, Prog. Dir. (JBiljeskovic@RockfordDiocese.org);

St. Elizabeth Community Center - t) (815) 965-6993 Tracy Dixon, Prog. Dir. (TDixon@RockfordDiocese.org);

CLERGY AND RELIGIOUS SERVICES

Vicar for Clergy and Religious - t) 815-399-4300 vicarforclergy@rockforddiocese.org Rev. Msgr. Stephen J. Knox (SKnox@RockfordDiocese.org);

Bishop's Secretary for Retired Priests - Rev. Msgr. Stephen J. Knox;

Clergy Relief Society, Priests' Retirement Committee - Very Rev. Msgr. Daniel J. Deutsch, Treas.;

Ministry to Priests Program - Rev. Msgr. Stephen J. Knox, Clergy Sabbaticals & Diocesan Priests' Retreats;

Priest and Religious Personnel - t) 815-399-4300 Rev. Msgr. Stephen J. Knox, Vicar;

Office of Permanent Diaconate - Rev. Brian D. Grady, Dir. (BGrady@RockfordDiocese.org);

Vocation Office - t) 815-399-4300 Rev. Jack Reichardt, Dir. (JReichardt@RockfordDiocese.org); Rev. Robert Gonnella, Asst. Dir. (RGonnella@RockfordDiocese.org); Rev. Sean Grismer, Asst. Dir. (SGrismer@RockfordDiocese.org);

COMMUNICATIONS

Communications and Publications - t) 815-399-4300 Penny Wiegert, Dir. (PWiegert@RockfordDiocese.org); Margarita Mendoza, Translator/Asst. Dir. (MMendoza@RockfordDiocese.org);

The Observer - observer@rockforddiocese.org www.observer.rockforddiocese.org Penny Wiegert, Editor;

El Observador - observer@rockforddiocese.org Margarita Mendoza, Editor;

EDUCATION

Department of Educational Services - Vito DeFrisco, Dir. (VDefrisco@RockfordDiocese.org);

Catholic Education Office - t) (815) 399-4300 www.ceorockford.org Vito DeFrisco, Dir./Supt. of Schools; Renee Payne, Asst. Supt.;

Religious Education and Adult Formation - t) 815-399-4300 John Jelinek, Dir.;

Newman-Campus Ministry - t) 815-787-7770 Rev. Robert Gonnella, Dir.;

TRIBUNAL

Diocesan Tribunal - t) 815-399-4300

Judicial Vicar - Very Rev. Matthew M. Bergschneider;

Adjunct Judicial Vicars - Rev. Joseph F. Jaskierny;

Promoter of Justice - Rev. Msgr. Arquimedes Vallejo;

Defender of the Bond - Rev. Msgr. Arquimedes Vallejo;

Advocates - Rev. Joseph F. Jaskierny (JJaskierny@RockfordDiocese.org); Rev. Jhonatan Sarmiento (JSarmiento@RockfordDiocese.org); Dcn. James Easton;

Expert - Kerry Burd, Certified Psychologist;

Ecclesiastical Notaries - t) 815-399-4300 Denise George (DGeorge@RockfordDiocese.org); Donna Hayes (DHayes@RockfordDiocese.org);

PARISHES, MISSIONS, AND CLERGY

STATE OF ILLINOIS

ALBANY

St. Patrick - 1201 N. Bluff St., Albany, IL 61230; Mailing: 703 12th Ave., Fulton, IL 61252 t) 815-589-3542 www.icspchurches.org Rev. Matthew J. Camaioni, Par. Vicar; Rev. Slawomir Zimodro, Par. Admin.; CRP Stds.: 3

ALGONQUIN

St. Margaret Mary - 111 S. Hubbard St., Algonquin, IL 60102 t) 847-658-9339 (CRP); 847-658-7881 (CRP); 847-658-7625; 847-658-5313 stmargaretmary-algonquin@rockforddiocese.org; bohearn@stmmschool.org www.saintmargaretmary.org Rev. Zbigniew Zajchowski, O.F.M.Conv. (Poland), Pst.; Rev. Daniel P. Zdebik, O.F.M.Conv. (Poland), Par. Vicar; Rev. Tomasz Ryba, O.F.M. Conv. (Poland), Par. Vicar; Debbie Witthoft, Bus. Mgr.; Dcn. Howard

Fischer; Dcn. Michael LeRoy; Dcn. James McDonough; Dcn. Donald Miller; Dcn. Christopher Nocchi; Dcn. Timothy Pignatari; Teresa Chiappone, Youth Min.; Ellie Nelson, DRE; CRP Stds.: 724

St. Margaret Mary School - (Grades PreK-8) 119 S. Hubbard St., Algonquin, IL 60102 stmargaretmaryschool-algonquin@rockforddiocese.org; bohearn@rockforddiocese.org Brenna O'Hearn, Prin.; Stds.: 197; Lay Tchrs.: 15

AMBOY

St. Patrick - 32 N. Jones Ave., Amboy, IL 61310 t) 815-857-2315 saintpatrickamboy@gmail.com www.stpatrickamboy.org Rev. John Gow, Admin.; Dcn. Kevin Prunty; CRP Stds.: 55

St. Patrick - 1336 Maytown Rd., Amboy, IL 61310; Mailing: P. O. Box 80, Sublette, IL 61367 t) 815-849-5412 stpatrick-maytown@rockforddiocese.org olphmarystpatrick.com Rev. Randy J. Fronek, Pst.;

APPLE RIVER

St. Joseph - 105 W. Webster St., Apple River, IL 61001; Mailing: c/o St. Ann Church, P.O. Box 665, Warren, IL 61087 t) 815-745-2312 stjoseph-appleriver@rockforddiocese.org Rev. Andrew T. Skrobutt, Pst.; Monica McGivney, Bus. Mgr.; Connie Hill, DRE;

AURORA

Annunciation of the Blessed Virgin Mary - 1820 Church Rd., Aurora, IL 60505 t) 630-851-1436 annunciationbvm-aurora@rockforddiocese.org annunciationchurchbvm.org Rev. Patrick S. Gillmeyer, O.S.B., Pst.; Dcn. Kenneth Gay; Dcn. Michael Giblin; Dcn. Domenic Petitti; Mark Fletcher, DRE; Mary Glosson, Bus. Mgr.; CRP Stds.: 110

Annunciation of the Blessed Virgin Mary School - (Grades K-8) 1840 Church Rd., Aurora, IL 60505 t) 630-851-4300 annunciationschool-aurora@rockforddiocese.org annunciationbvm.org Mavis DeMar, Prin.; Stds.: 280; Lay Tchrs.: 10

Holy Angels - 120 S. Lancaster Ave., Aurora, IL 60506; Mailing: 180 S. Russell Ave., Aurora, IL 60506 t) 630-897-1194; 630-897-1194 x156 (CRP) holyangels-aurora@rockforddiocese.org; releducation@holy-angels.org www.holy-angels.org Rev. Michael G. Lavan, Pst.; Rev. Dean M. Smith, Par. Vicar; Dcn. Jim Hall; Dcn. Tom Hawksworth; Dcn. Tim White; Rose Gatze, DRE; Mimi Steinwart, DRE; CRP Stds.: 62

Holy Angels School - (Grades PreK-8) 720 Kensington Pl., Aurora, IL 60506 t) 630-897-3613 holyangelsschool-aurora@rockforddiocese.org www.holyangelsschool.net Tonya Forbes, Prin.; Stds.: 395; Lay Tchrs.: 24

St. Joseph - 722 High St., Aurora, IL 60505 t) 630-844-3780; 630-844-3782 x243 (CRP) stjoseph-aurora@rockforddiocese.org www.saintjosephaurora.org Rev. Matthew J. McMorrow, Pst.; Rev. Msgr. Robert J. Willhite, In Res.; Dcn. Bruce Watermann; CRP Stds.: 43

Pope St. John Paul II Catholic Academy-North Campus - (Grades PreK-8) 706 High St., Aurora, IL 60506-2232 t) 630-844-3781 mchristoffel@rockforddiocese.org www.jp2aurora.org/ Dr. Marisa Christoffel, Head of School; David Bielat, Vice Prin.; Stds.: 150; Lay Tchrs.: 10

St. Mary - 432 E. Downer Place, Aurora, IL 60505-3475; Mailing: 432 E. Downer Pl., Aurora, IL 60505-3475 t) 630-892-0480 stmary-aurora@rockforddiocese.org www.stmaryaurora.org Rev. Antoni Kretowicz, Pst.; Dcn. Jose Falcon; Anabel Rivas, DRE; CRP Stds.: 82

St. Nicholas - 308 High St., Aurora, IL 60505 t) 630-898-8707 stnicholas-aurora@rockforddiocese.org stnicholasparish.net/ Rev. Josue Lara, Pst.; Rev. Alexander Suarez Saenz (Colombia), Par. Vicar; CRP Stds.: 730

Our Lady of Good Counsel - 620 S. Fifth St., Aurora, IL 60505; Mailing: 615 Talma St., Aurora, IL 60505 t) 630-851-1100 olgc-aurora@rockforddiocese.org ourladyofgoodcounsel.net Rev. Timothy P. Mulcahey, Pst.; Dcn. Ray Weaver; Rev. Jerome L. Leake, In Res.; Jaliza Camacho, DRE; CRP Stds.: 231

Pope St. John Paul II Catholic Academy - South Campus - (Grades K-8) 601 Talma St., Aurora, IL 60505 t) 630-851-4400 abrummel@jp2aurora.org www.jp2aurora.org Dr. Marisa Christoffel, Head of School; David Bielat, Vice Prin.; Stds.: 63; Lay Tchrs.: 4

St. Peter - 925 Sard Ave., Aurora, IL 60506; Mailing: 915 Sard Ave., Aurora, IL 60506 t) 630-896-6816 www.stpeteraurorail.org Rev. Ruben Herrera, Pst.; Mark Fletcher, DRE; CRP Stds.: 89

St. Rita of Cascia - 750 Old Indian Trail Rd., Aurora, IL 60506 t) 630-892-9507 (CRP); 630-892-5918 strita-aurora@rockforddiocese.org www.saintritaofcascia.org Rev. Oscar Cortes, Pst.; Rev. Rafael Alexander Parafina (Phillipines), Par. Vicar; Dcn. Ignacio Felix; Dcn. Richard Martin; Dcn. Luis Patino; Rae Eigenhauser, DRE; CRP Stds.: 269

St. Rita of Cascia School - (Grades PreK-8) 770 Old Indian Trail Rd., Aurora, IL 60506 t) 630-892-0200 stritaofcasciaschool-aurora@rockforddiocese.org Heather Baer, Prin.; Stds.: 200; Lay Tchrs.: 10

Sacred Heart - 125 N. State St., Aurora, IL 60505 t) 630-898-4165 sacredheart-aurora@rockforddiocese.org Rev. Juan Arciniegas, Admin.; CRP Stds.: 277

St. Therese of Jesus - 271 N. Farnsworth Ave., Aurora, IL 60505 t) 630-898-5422 www.stojcc.org Rev. Darwin A. Flores (Venezula), Par. Admin.; Dcn. Julio Rosado; CRP Stds.: 108

BATAVIA

Holy Cross - 2300 Main St., Batavia, IL 60510-7625 t) 630-879-4750 holycross-batavia@rockforddiocese.org; staff@holycross-batavia.org www.holycross-batavia.org Rev. Jared Twenty, Pst.; Rev. John Kladar, Par. Vicar; Dcn. Gregory Norris; Dcn. Kenneth Ramsey; Dcn. Raymond J. Martin; Dcn. Dean Schroeder; Karen A. McQuillan, DRE; John Callahan, Bus. Mgr.; CRP Stds.: 392

Holy Cross School - (Grades PreK-8) t) 630-593-5290 holycrossschool-batavia@rockforddiocese.org www.holycrosscatholicschool.org Michael Puttin, Prin.; Stds.: 401; Lay Tchrs.: 19

BELVIDERE

St. James - 402 Church St., Belvidere, IL 61008 t) 815-547-6397; (815) 547-7633 (CRP) stjames-belvidere@rockforddiocese.org; b.graybiel@stjamesbelvidere.org www.stjamesbelvidere.org Rev. Brian A. Geary, Pst.; Dcn. Steven M. Johnson; Dcn. James D. Olson; Rev. William R. Schuessler, In Res.; Barbara Graybiel, DRE; CRP Stds.: 445

BYRON

St. Mary - 226 E. 2nd St., Byron, IL 61010; Mailing: P.O. Box 1070, Byron, IL 61010 t) 815-234-7431 stmary-byron@rockforddiocese.org; npell@rockforddiocese.org www.saintmaryinbyron.org Rev. Richard A. Rosinski, Pst.; Dcn. Thomas Petit; Stephanie Schermerhorn, CRE; CRP Stds.: 121

CARPENTERSVILLE

St. Monica - 90 N. Kennedy Dr., Carpentersville, IL 60110-1695 t) 847-428-7562 (CRP); 847-428-2646 stmonica-carpentersville@rockforddiocese.org stmonicaparish.com Rev. William E. Vallejo, Par. Admin.; Rev. Luis M. Guanipa (Venezuela), Par. Vicar; Velveth Garcia, DRE; CRP Stds.: 553

CARY

SS. Peter & Paul - 410 N. First St., Cary, IL 60013 t) 847-516-2636; 847-639-0414 (CRP) sspeterandpaul-cary@rockforddiocese.org www.peterpaulchurchcary.org Rev. Jeremy A. Trowbridge, Pst.; Rev. Domingo Jaramillo (Venezuela), Par. Vicar; Rev. Timothy J. Seigel, Par. Vicar; Dcn. Michael Boyce; Dcn. Mark Ennis; Dcn. Howard Ganschow II; Dcn. Juan Manuel Luna; Dcn. Michael O'Connor; Dcn. Donald Siciliano; Dcn. Robert Buerer; CRP Stds.: 250

SS. Peter & Paul School - (Grades PreK-8) 416 N. First St., Cary, IL 60013 t) 847-639-3041 sspeterandpaulschool-cary@rockforddiocese.org; nsatterlee@rockforddiocese.org Nick Satterlee, Prin.; Stds.: 238; Lay Tchrs.: 11

CRYSTAL LAKE

St. Elizabeth Ann Seton - 1023 McHenry Ave., Crystal Lake, IL 60014 t) 815-459-3033 www.elizabethannseton.org Dcn. Michael Bednarz; Rachael Jorgensen, Youth Min.; Rev. Keith D. Romke, Pst.; Rev. Moises A. Apostol, Par. Vicar; Dcn. Kenneth Giacone; Dcn. Richard Marcantonio; Karen Stinson, DRE; Sue Schulz, Bus. Mgr.; CRP Stds.: 157

St. Thomas the Apostle - 451 W. Terra Cotta Ave., Crystal Lake, IL 60014; Mailing: 272 King St., Crystal Lake, IL 60014 t) 815-455-5400; 815-455-9787 (CRP) www.stthomascl.church Very Rev. Robert W. Jones, Pst.; Rev. Charles P. Fitzpatrick, Par. Vicar; Rev. Andrew Hernandez (Phillipines), Par. Vicar; Rev. William Tunarosa, Par. Vicar; Dcn. Allen Bondi; Dcn. Neal Carpenter; Dcn. Jose Luis Aguilar; CRP Stds.: 427

St. Thomas the Apostle School - (Grades PreK-8) 265 King St., Crystal Lake, IL 60014 t) 815-459-0496 ghouston@rockforddiocese.org www.stthomascl.org Gina Houston, Prin.; Stds.: 216; Lay Tchrs.: 9

DEKALB

Christ the Teacher, University Parish of Northern Illinois University - 512 Normal Rd., DeKalb, IL 60115 t) 815-787-7770 www.newmanniu.org/ Rev. Robert Gonnella, Par. Vicar; Dcn. James Dombek; CRP Stds.: 44

St. Mary - 329 Pine St., DeKalb, IL 60115; Mailing: 302 Fisk Ave., DeKalb, IL 60115 t) 815-758-5432 x100; 815-758-5432 x102 (CRP) mail@stmarydekalb.org www.stmarydekalb.org Rev. Dean E. Russell, Pst.; Rev. Anthony Vu Khac Long, In Res.; Annalisa McMaster, DRE; CRP Stds.: 85

St. Mary School - (Grades PreK-8) 210 Gurler Rd., DeKalb, IL 60115 t) 815-756-7905 stmaryschool-dekalb@rockforddiocese.org; adavis@rockforddiocese.org www.stmaryschooldekalb.org/ Ashley Davis, Prin.; Stds.: 205; Lay Tchrs.: 12

DIXON

St. Anne - 1104 N. Brinton Ave., Dixon, IL 61021 t) 815-288-3131 stanne-dixon@rockforddiocese.org www.stanneparishdixon.org Rev. Timothy J. Draper, Pst.; Alexandra Binkley, CRE; CRP Stds.: 37

St. Anne School - (Grades PreK-5) 1112 N. Brinton Ave., Dixon, IL 61021 t) 815-288-5619 stanneschool-dixon@rockforddiocese.org www.stanneschooldixon.org Talarie Bilharz, Prin.; Stds.: 89; Lay Tchrs.: 7

St. Patrick - 612 Highland Ave., Dixon, IL 61021 t) 815-284-7719 stpatrick-dixon@rockforddiocese.org www.stpatrickdixon.org Rev. John R. Evans, Pst.; Rhonda Jahn, Bus. Mgr.; Dcn. Terrence Wagner; Sarah Campbell, CRE; CRP Stds.: 32

St. Mary Elementary & Junior High - (Grades PreK-8) 704 S. Peoria Ave., Dixon, IL 61021 t) 815-284-6986 stmaryschool-dixon@rockforddiocese.org; jspohn@rockforddiocese.org www.stmarysdixon.org Jean Spohn, Prin.; Stds.: 192; Lay Tchrs.: 10

DURAND

St. Mary - 606 W. Main St., Durand, IL 61024 t) 815-248-2490 stmary-durand@rockforddiocese.org www.stmarystpatrick.org Very Rev. Matthew M. Bergschneider, Pst.; Dcn. Steven Pulkrabek; Terry Cravens, CRE; CRP Stds.: 57

St. Patrick - 5333 N. Irish Grove Rd., Davis, IL 61019 t) (815) 248-2490 stmarystpatrick.org

EAST DUBUQUE

St. Mary - 170 Montgomery Ave., East Dubuque, IL 61025 t) 815-747-3221 stmary-eastdubuque@rockforddiocese.org stmaryedbq.org Rev. Dennis Vargas (Phillipines), Par. Admin.; Dcn. Anthony Keppler; Dcn. Douglas Kremer; Dcn. James Schilling; Kimberly J. Weber, Bus. Mgr.; CRP Stds.: 42

ELBURN

St. Gall - 43W885 Hughes Rd., Elburn, IL 60119 t) 630-365-6030 stgall-elburn@rockforddiocese.org stgall.com Rev. Max J. Striedl, Pst.; Dcn. Greg Farrell; Dcn. James Schiltz; CRP Stds.: 110

ELGIN

St. Joseph - 272 Division St., Elgin, IL 60120; Mailing: 33 N. Geneva St., Elgin, IL 60120 t) 847-931-2800; 847-931-2808 (CRP) stjoseph-elgin@rockforddiocese.org www.stjosephelgin.org Rev. Msgr. Arquimedes Vallejo, Pst.; Dcn. Francisco Fausto; CRP Stds.: 243

St. Edward Preparatory Academy - (Grades PreK-8) 274 Division St., Elgin, IL 60120 t) 847-931-2804 stedwardprepacademy-elgin@rockforddiocese.org; kmiller@rockforddiocese.org stedprep.org St. Joseph School, Elgin and St. Laurence School, Elgin merged. Dr. Kathleen Miller, Prin.; Stds.: 115; Lay Tchrs.: 8

St. Laurence - 225 Jewett St., Elgin, IL 60123 t) 847-468-6900 office@stlaurenceelgin.org stlaurenceelgin.org Rev. Andrew T. Mulcahey, Pst.; Rev. Robert J. Camacho, In Res.; Kathleen Sue Jones, Bus. Mgr.; CRP Stds.: 49

St. Mary - 400 Fulton St., Elgin, IL 60120; Mailing: 397 Fulton St., Elgin, IL 60120 t) 847-888-2828; 847-888-2819; 847-888-2718 stmary-elgin@rockforddiocese.org www.stmaryelgin.org Rev. Christopher J. Kuhn, Pst.; Rev. Lisandro Cristancho (Colombia), Par. Vicar; Dcn. David Mattoon; Dcn. Loc Nguyen; CRP Stds.: 250

St. Mary School - (Grades PreK-8) 103 S. Gifford St., Elgin, IL 60120 t) 847-695-6609 stmaryschool-elgin@rockforddiocese.org; cnorman@rockforddiocese.org Carol Norman, Prin.; Stds.: 118; Lay Tchrs.: 10

St. Thomas More - 215 Thomas More Dr., Elgin, IL 60123 t) 847-888-4887 (CRP); 847-888-1682 mtack@rockforddiocese.org; stthomasmore-elgin@rockforddiocese.org www.stthomasmorechurch.org Rev. Edilberto H. Jarapa (Phillipines), Par. Vicar; Dcn. David Deitz; Dcn. Jack Roder; Michelle Tack, DRE; Rev. Ryan B. Browning, Pst.; CRP Stds.: 350

St. Thomas More School - (Grades PreK-8) 1625 W. Highland Ave., Elgin, IL 60123 t) 847-742-3959 stthomasmoreschool-elgin@rockforddiocese.org www.stmcentral.org Sonja Keane, Prin.; Stds.: 184; Lay Tchrs.: 12

ELIZABETH

St. Mary - 112 E. Washington St., P.O> 246, Elizabeth, IL 61028; Mailing: P.O. Box 246, Elizabeth, IL 61028 t) 815-858-3422 stmary-elizabeth@rockforddiocese.org www.stmaryelizabethil.org Rev. Joachim B. Tyrtania, Pst.; CRP Stds.: 16

ERIE

St. Ambrose - 820 Fifth Ave., Erie, IL 61250; Mailing: P.O. Box 746, Erie, IL 61250 t) 815-537-2077 stambrose-erie@rockforddiocese.org Rev. David J. Reese, Admin.; Brigitte Young, CRE; CRP Stds.: 22

FREEPORT

St. Joseph - 229 W. Washington Pl., Freeport, IL 61032 t) 815-232-8271 stjoseph-freeport@rockforddiocese.org stjosephstmary.com Rev. Timothy J. Barr, Pst.; Dcn. Paul Ranney; CRP Stds.: 30

St. Mary - 704 S. State Ave., Freeport, IL 61032; Mailing: 229 W. Washington Place, Freeport, IL 61032 t) 815-232-8271 stmary-freeport@rockforddiocese.org stjosephstmary.com Rev. Timothy J. Barr, Pst.; Rev. Diego F. Ospina, In Res.; Dcn. Paul Ranney;

St. Thomas Aquinas - 1400 Kiwanis Dr., Freeport, IL 61032 t) 815-232-3225 stthomasfreeport.org Rev. Peter Snieg, Pst.; Dcn. Kim Hemesath; Dcn. Stephen Pospischil; Ellen McGinnis, CRE; Sylvia Jazo, CRE; CRP Stds.: 54

FULTON

Immaculate Conception - 703 12th Ave., Fulton, IL 61252 t) 815-589-3542 immaculateconception-fulton@rockforddiocese.org www.icspchurches.org/ Rev. Matthew J. Camaioni, Par. Vicar; Rev. Slawomir Zimodro, Par. Admin.; CRP Stds.: 16

GALENA

St. Mary - 406 Franklin St., Galena, IL 61036; Mailing: 227 S. Bench St., Galena, IL 61036 t) 815-777-2053 stmary-galena@rockforddiocese.org www.catholicgalena.com Rev. Howard C. Barch, Pst.; Rev. Joel N. Lopez, Par. Vicar; Dcn. Joseph Achino, DRE; CRP Stds.: 46

St. Michael - 227 S. Bench St., Galena, IL 61036 t) 815-777-2053 stmichael-galena@rockforddiocese.org www.catholicgalena.com Rev. Howard C. Barch, Pst.; Rev. Joel N. Lopez, Par. Vicar; Dcn. Joseph Achino, DRE; CRP Stds.: 48

GENEVA

St. Peter - 1891 Kaneville Rd., Geneva, IL 60134 t) 630-232-0124 re.director@stpetergeneva.org; stpeter-geneva@rockforddiocese.org www.stpeterchurch.com Rev. Jonathan P. Bakkelund, Pst.; Rev. John McFadden, Par. Vicar; Dcn. Gregory D'Anna; Nicole Billapando, DRE; CRP Stds.: 500

St. Peter School - (Grades PreK-8) 1881 Kaneville Rd., Geneva, IL 60134 t) 630-232-0476 stpeterschool-geneva@rockforddiocese.org; bward@rockforddiocese.org www.stpeterrockets.org Samantha Anderson, Prin.; Stds.: 293; Lay Tchrs.: 15

GENOA

St. Catherine of Genoa - 340 S. Stott St., Genoa, IL 60135 t) 815-784-2355 religioused@stcatherinegenoa.org; stcatherine-genoa@rockforddiocese.org stcatherinegenoa.org Rev. Zdzislaw F. Wawryszuk, Pst.; Dcn. Brian Mullens; Dcn. William A. Stankevitz; Carol Romano, CRE; CRP Stds.: 80

GILBERTS

St. Mary's of Gilberts - 10 Matteson Rd., Gilberts, IL 60136; Mailing: 845 W. Main St., Rockford, IL 60118 t) 847-426-2217 stmary-gilberts@rockforddiocese.org Parish under the direction of St Catherine of Siena in Dundee Rev. John P. McNamara, Pst.; Dcn. Steven Fox; Dcn. Hank Schmalen; Dcn. William Whitehead Jr.;

HAMPSHIRE

St. Charles Borromeo - 297 E. Jefferson Ave., Hampshire, IL 60140-7646 t) 847-683-2391; 847-683-1536 (CRP) stcharlesborromeo-hampshire@rockforddiocese.org; jolson@rockforddiocese.org www.scbparish.org Rev. Sylvester A. Nnaso, Pst.; Dcn. John Nelson; Dcn. Jerome Ryndak; Dcn. James Ward; Janice Olson, DRE; CRP Stds.: 135

St. Charles Borromeo School - (Grades PreK-8) 288 E. Jefferson Ave., Hampshire, IL 60140 t) 847-683-3450 scbschool@scbk8.org www.scbk8.org Mary Beth Jordan, Prin.; Stds.: 90; Lay Tchrs.: 10

HANOVER

St. John the Evangelist - 103 Savanna Rd., Hanover, IL 61041; Mailing: 105 Savanna Rd, Hanover, IL 61041 t) 815-591-2258 stjohntheevangelist-hanover@rockforddiocese.org Rev. Joachim B. Tyrtania, Pst.; Laura Kuzniar, CRE;

HARMON

St. Flannen - 213 S. Second St., Harmon, IL 61042; Mailing: 32 N. Jones Ave., Amboy, IL 61310 t) 815-857-2670 stflannen-harmon@rockforddiocese.org stpatrickamboy.org Rev. John Gow, Par. Admin.; Susan McCoy, CRE;

HARTLAND

St. Patrick - 15012 St. Patrick Rd., Hartland, IL 60098 t) 815-338-7883 Rev. Juan Ayala, Par. Vicar; Rev. Burt H. Absalon, Pst.; Dcn. Joseph Kayser; CRP Stds.: 20

HARVARD

St. Joseph - 206 E. Front St., Harvard, IL 60033; Mailing: 101 Church St., Harvard, IL 60033 t) 815-943-1644 (CRP); 815-943-6406 stjoseph-harvard@rockforddiocese.org stjosephharvard.org Rev. Steven P. Clarke, Pst.; Rev. Andres Salinas, Par. Vicar; Dcn. David Dollman; Dcn. Michael Keane; Dcn. Anthony Koss; CRP Stds.: 245

HUNTLEY

St. Mary - 10307 Dundee Rd., Huntley, IL 60142 t) 847-669-3137 stmary-huntley@rockforddiocese.org www.stmaryhuntley.org Rev. Christopher P. Di Tomo, Pst.; Rev. Jerome P. Koutnik, Par. Vicar; Rev. Dario Z Endiape (Phillipines), Par. Vicar; Dcn. George Coltman; Dcn. James Conrey; Dcn. Frank Englert; Dcn. Chris Lincoln; Dcn. David Marcheschi; Roberta Christian, DRE; CRP Stds.: 754

JOHNSBURG

St. John the Baptist - 2302 W. Church St., Johnsburg, IL 60051 t) 815-385-1477 stjohnthebaptist-johnsburg@rockforddiocese.org www.stjohnsjohnsburg.org Rev. Jacek Junak, CR (Poland), Pst.; Dcn. Jerry Giessinger; Dcn. David Gillespie; Stephanie Eldridge, DRE; CRP Stds.: 127

St. John the Baptist School - (Grades PreK-8) 2304 W. Church St., Johnsburg, IL 60051 t) 815-385-3959 cgillaspie@rockforddiocese.org stjohnschool.com Cathy Gillaspie, Prin.; Stds.: 74; Lay Tchrs.: 8

LEE

St. James - 221 W. Kirke Gate, Lee, IL 60530; Mailing: P.O. Box 100, Lee, IL 60530 t) 815-824-2053; 815-824-2004 (CRP) stjames-lee@rockforddiocese.org www.saintjamesinlee.org Rev. Bonaventure Okoro, Pst.; Dcn. George Schramm, CRE; Jean Marie Henning, Bus. Mgr.; CRP Stds.: 15

LENA

St. Joseph - 410 W. Lena St., Lena, IL 61048 t) 815-369-2810 stjoseph-lena@rockforddiocese.org Rev. Andrew T. Skrobutt, Pst.; CRP Stds.: 36

LOVES PARK

St. Bridget - 600 Clifford Ave., Loves Park, IL 61111 t) 815-633-6311 stbridget-lovespark@rockforddiocese.org stbridgetlovespark.org Rev. Jack Reichardt, Par. Vicar; Teresa McMahon, Youth Min.; Rev. Msgr. Stephen J. Knox, Pst.; Rev. Aaron Downing, Par. Vicar; Dcn. Philip Abel; Dcn. John Gibson; Dcn. William Riseley; Jake Washington, Youth Min.; Mary Henson, Family Faith Formation Coord.; CRP Stds.: 162

St. Bridget School - (Grades PreK-8) 604 Clifford Ave., Loves Park, IL 61111 t) 815-633-8255 stbridgetschool-lovespark@rockforddiocese.org www.stbridgetlovespark.org Mary Toldo, Prin.; Stds.: 398; Lay Tchrs.: 22

MAPLE PARK

St. Mary - 123 S. County Line Rd., Maple Park, IL 60151-0070; Mailing: P.O. Box 70, Maple Park, IL 60151-0070 t) 815-827-3205 www.stmarymaplepark.org Rev. William R. Antillon, Pst.; Dcn. Gregory Urban; Rev. Msgr. Thomas L. Dzielak, In Res.; CRP Stds.: 14

Novak Center - 211 S. County Line Rd., Maple Park, IL 60151-0070

MARENGO

Sacred Heart - 323 N. Taylor St., Marengo, IL 60152 t) 815-568-7878; 815-568-6230 (CRP) sacredheart-marengo@rockforddiocese.org; dsakowski@rockforddiocese.org www.sacredheartmarengo.org Rev. Matthew M. DeBlock, Pst.; Dcn. Robert Anchor; Debbie Sakowski, DRE; CRP Stds.: 150

MCHENRY

Church of Holy Apostles - 5211 W. Bull Valley Rd., McHenry, IL 60050 t) 815-385-5673; 815-388-0155 (CRP) holyapostles-mchenry@rockforddiocese.org www.thechurchofholyapostles.org Rev. Paul C. White, Pst.; Rev. Jhakson Garcia, Par. Vicar; Dcn. Curtis Fiedler; Dcn. Daniel Krey; Dcn. Daniel Torres Paredes; Dcn. Solis Victor; Argelia Gayton, Dir. Family Faith Formation; CRP Stds.: 150

St. Mary - 1401 N. Richmond Rd., McHenry, IL 60050; Mailing: 1407 N. Richmond Rd., McHenry, IL 60050 t) 815-385-0024 tmiller@rockforddiocese.org; stmary-mchenry@rockforddiocese.org www.stmarymchenryil.org Rev. David M. Austin, Pst.; Dcn. Michael Boyce; Tammy Miller, DRE; Celeste Mann, Liturgy Dir.; Barbara Russell, Bus. Mgr.; CRP Stds.: 32

Montini-Middle Grades - (Grades 4-8) 1405 N. Richmond Rd., McHenry, IL 60050 t) 815-385-1022 montinimiddleschool-mchenry@rockforddiocese.org; jsemchen@rockforddiocese.org Julie Stark, Prin.; James Smecken, Vice Prin.; Stds.: 107; Lay Tchrs.: 7

St. Patrick Church - 3500 W. Washington St., McHenry, IL 60050 t) 815-385-0025; 815-385-2959 (CRP) stpatrick-mchenry@rockforddiocese.org; reoffice@stpatrickmchenry.org www.stpatrickmchenry.org Rev. Godwin Nsikan-Ubom Asuquo, Pst.; Dcn. Craig Robinson; Lisa Johnson, CRE; CRP Stds.: 76

Montini Catholic School - (Grades PreK-3) c/o St. Patrick Church, 3504 W. Washington St., McHenry, IL 60050 t) 815-385-5380 montinischool-mchenry@rockforddiocese.org; jstark@rockforddiocese.org www.montinischool.org Julie Stark, Prin.; Stds.: 138; Lay Tchrs.: 4

MENOMINEE

Nativity of the Blessed Virgin Mary - 15406 W. Creek Valley Rd., Menominee, IL 61025 t) 815-747-3670 nativitybvm-menominee@rockforddiocese.org www.stmaryedbq.org Rev. Dennis Vargas (Phillipines), Par. Admin.; Dcn. Tony Keppler; Dcn. Douglas Kremer; Dcn. James Schilling; Kimberly J. Weber, Bus. Mgr.; Kathy Williams, CRE; CRP Stds.: 5

MORRISON

St. Mary - 13320 Garden Plain Rd., Morrison, IL 61270 t) 815-772-4890 www.stmarymorrison.org Rev. Slawomir Zimodro, Pst.; CRP Stds.: 11

MOUNT CARROLL

SS. John and Catherine - 314 S. Main St., Mount Carroll, IL 61053; Mailing: P. O. Box 193, Mount Carroll, IL 61053 t) 815-244-1835 c) 563-777-0397 Savanna. Rev. Thomas J. Doyle, Pst.;

NORTH AURORA

Blessed Sacrament Catholic Church - 801 Oak St., North Aurora, IL 60542-1063 t) 630-897-1029 re@blessedsacrament-na.org; blessedsacrament-northaurora@rockforddiocese.org blessedsacrament-na.org Rev. Max Lasrado, Pst.; Dcn. Ken McLaughlin; Melissa Heinen, CRE; CRP Stds.: 87

OREGON

St. Mary - 301 N. 4th St., Oregon, IL 61061; Mailing: 881 Mongan Dr., Oregon, IL 61061 t) 815-732-7383 stmary-oregon@rockforddiocese.org www.stmaryop.org Rev. Joseph P. Naill, Pst.; Dcn. Ron Abramowicz; Dcn. John Ley; CRP Stds.: 11

PECATONICA

St. Mary's Church of Pecatonica - 126 W. Fifth St., Pecatonica, IL 61063-0656; Mailing: P.O. Box 656, Pecatonica, IL 61063 t) 815-239-1271 c) 815-708-2308 www.stmarypecatonica.org Rev. Dennis M. Morrissy, Pst.; Dcn. Warren LaMont; CRP Stds.: 50

POLO

St. Mary Church - 211 N. Franklin Ave., Polo, IL 61064 t) 815-946-2535 stmary-polo@rockforddiocese.org www.stmaryop.org Rev. Joseph P. Naill, Pst.; Dcn. Ron Abramowicz; Dcn. John Ley; CRP Stds.: 4

PROPHETSTOWN

St. Catherine - 308 E. Third St., Prophetstown, IL 61277 t) 815-537-2077 Rev. David J. Reese, Par. Admin.;

RICHMOND

St. Joseph - 10519 Main St., Richmond, IL 60071 t) 815-678-4720 (CRP); 815-678-7421 stjoseph-richmond@rockforddiocese.org stjosephrichmondil.weconnect.com Rev. Msgr. Martin G. Heinz, Pst.; Dcn. Albert Dietz; Dcn. Norman Kocol; Dcn. Dennis Holian; Lisa Sachs, CRE; CRP Stds.: 20

ROCHELLE

St. Patrick - 244 Kelley Dr., Rochelle, IL 61068; Mailing: P.O. Box 329, Rochelle, IL 61068 t) 815-562-2370; 815-561-0079 (CRP) stpatrick-rochelle@rockforddiocese.org www.stpatricksrochelle.com Rev. Jesus Dominguez, Pst.; Dcn. Fermin Garcia; Dcn. George Schramm, DRE; CRP Stds.: 143

ROCK FALLS

St. Andrew - 708 10th Ave., Rock Falls, IL 61071 t) 815-625-4508 (Office) jthurwanger@rockforddiocese.org www.standrewrockfalls.org/ Rev. Richard M. Russo, Pst.; Sr. Marcianne Bzdon, S.S.N.D., CRE; CRP Stds.: 36

St. Andrew School - (Grades PreK-8) 701 11th Ave., Rock Falls, IL 61071 t) 815-625-1456 standewschool-rockfalls@rockforddiocese.org; kblakeslee@rockforddiocese.org standrewrockfalls.org Kathryn Blakeslee, Prin.; Stds.: 103; Lay Tchrs.: 10

ROCKFORD

St. Peter Cathedral - 1243 N. Church St., Rockford, IL 61103 t) 815-965-2765 office@cathedralofstpeter.org www.cathedralofstpeter.org Very Rev. Kenneth J. Anderson, Rector; Rev. Joseph F. Jaskierny, In Res.; Dcn. James Easton; Dcn. Robert Mitchison; CRP Stds.: 41

St. Anthony of Padua - 1010 Ferguson St., Rockford, IL 61102 t) 815-965-2761 stanthony-rockford@rockforddiocese.org stanthonyrockford.org Rev. Carl E. Beekman, Pst.; Dcn. Peter J. Addotta; CRP Stds.: 65

St. Bernadette - 2400 Bell Ave., Rockford, IL 61103 t) 815-968-0904 stbernadette-rockford@rockforddiocese.org; office@stbernadetterockford.com stbernadetterockford.com Rev. Kenneth J. Stachyra, Pst.; Rev. Ricardo F. Hernandez, Par. Vicar; Dcn. Gregg Cox; Dcn. Richard Gerdeman; Dcn. Ronald Meadors; Kevin Rilott, DRE; Melissa Clark, Bus. Mgr.; CRP Stds.: 28

St. Edward - 3004 11th St., Rockford, IL 61109 t) 815-229-0282; 815-229-8914 (CRP) stedward-rockford@rockforddiocese.org www.stedwardrockford.org Rev. Johnson Lopez, Pst.; Nancy Perez-Renteria, DRE; CRP Stds.: 303

Holy Family - 4401 Highcrest Rd., Rockford, IL 61107 t) 815-398-4280 holyfamily-rockford@rockforddiocese.org; bbeckett@holyfamilyrockford.org www.holyfamilyrockford.org Very Rev. Phillip A. Kaim, Pst.; Rev. Akan S. Simon, Par. Vicar; Dcn. Jason Stewart; Barbara Beckett, DRE; CRP Stds.: 97

Holy Family School - (Grades PreK-8) 4407 Highcrest Rd., Rockford, IL 61107 t) 815-398-5331 holyfamilyschool-rockford@rockforddiocese.org; cgendron@rockforddiocese.org Corine Gendron, Prin.; Stds.: 370; Lay Tchrs.: 22

St. James - 428 N. Second St., Rockford, IL 61107 t) 815-962-1214 www.stjamesrockford.com Rev. Jhonatan Sarmiento, Par. Admin.; Dcn. William Dean; Kim Carlson, Bus. Mgr.; Kathy Wilson, CRE; CRP Stds.: 45

St. Mary Oratory - 126 S. Winnebago St., Rockford, IL 61102; Mailing: 517 Elm St., Rockford, IL 61102 t) 815-965-5971 stmary-rockford@rockforddiocese.org www.institute-christ-king.org/rockford/ Rev. Canon John O'Connor, Rector;

St. Patrick - 2505 School St., Rockford, IL 61101 t) 815-965-9539 stpatrickrockford.org Rev. Ariel A. Valencia, Par. Admin.; Dcn. Luis DeLeon; CRP Stds.: 117

SS. Peter and Paul - 617 Lincoln Ave., Rockford, IL 61102 t) 815-962-7171 sspeterandpaul-rockford@rockforddiocese.org Hispanic National Parish Rev. Adalberto Sanchez, Admin.; Anabel Arreguin, DRE; Gerald Pratt, Music Min.; Petrinella Sowell, Bus. Mgr.; CRP Stds.: 120

St. Rita - 6254 Valley Knoll Dr., Rockford, IL 61109-1898 t) 815-398-0853 strita-rockford@rockforddiocese.org; parishoffice@stritarockford.org www.stritarockford.org Rev. Brian D. Grady, Pst.; Rev. James C. Canova, Par. Vicar; Dcn. Robert Collins; Dcn. Kevin Hunter; Dcn. John Huntley; Dcn. Paul Sanderson; CRP Stds.: 28

St. Rita School - (Grades PreK-8) 6284 Valley Knoll Dr., Rockford, IL 61109-1898 t) 815-398-3466 schooloffice@saintritaschool.org stritarockford.org Patrick Flanagan, Prin.; Stds.: 226; Lay Tchrs.: 10

St. Stanislaus Kostka - 201 Buckbee, Rockford, IL 61104 t) 815-965-3913; 815-965-3915 (CRP) ststanislaus-rockford@rockforddiocese.org; church@st-stanislaus.org www.st-stanislaus.org Rev. Mieczyslaw Wit, O.F.M.Conv., Pst.; Mary Strand, Music Min.; Margaret Borowski, Bus. Mgr.;

ROSCOE

Church of the Holy Spirit - 5637 Broad St., Roscoe, IL 61073; Mailing: P.O. Box 478, Roscoe, IL 61073 t) 815-623-6930 holyspirit-roscoe@rockforddiocese.org Rev. Romeo Pavino (Phillipines), Pst.; Kate Elliot, DRE; CRP Stds.: 7

SANDWICH

St. Paul the Apostle - 340 W. Arnold Rd., Sandwich, IL 60548 t) 815-786-2004 (CRP); 815-786-9266 stpaul-sandwich@rockforddiocese.org saintpaulscc.net Rev. Bernard J. Sehr, Pst.; CRP Stds.: 62

SAVANNA

St. John the Baptist - 318 Chicago Ave., Savanna, IL 61074 t) 815-273-3961 c) 563-777-0397 stjohnthebaptist-savanna@rockforddiocese.org stjohnsavanna.org Rev. Thomas Doyle, Pst.; Mimi Rucobo, DRE; CRP Stds.: 27

SCALES MOUND

Holy Trinity - 302 Franklin St., Scales Mound, IL 61075; Mailing: 227 S. Bench St., Galena, IL 61036 t) 815-777-2053 www.catholicgalena.com Rev. Howard C. Barch, Pst.; Rev. Joel N. Lopez, Par. Vicar; Dcn. Joseph Achino, DRE; CRP Stds.: 8

SHANNON

St. Wendelin - 18 S. Linn St., Shannon, IL 61078; Mailing: P.O. Box 23, Shannon, IL 61078 t) 815-864-2548 www.saintwen.org Rev. Michael J. Bolger, Pst.; CRP Stds.: 21

SOMONAUK

St. John the Baptist - 320 S. Depot St., Somonauk, IL 60552-0276; Mailing: P. O. Box 276, Somonauk, IL 60552 t) 815-498-2010 stjohnthebaptist-somonauk@rockforddiocese.org; info@stjbsom.org www.stjbsom.org Rev. Kevin M. Butler, Pst.; Judy Kreczmer, CRE; CRP Stds.: 59

SOUTH BELOIT

St. Peter - 620 Blackhawk Blvd., South Beloit, IL 61080; Mailing: 325 Oak Grove Ave., South Beloit, IL 61080 t) 815-525-3400 st-peter-church.com Rev. Romeo Pavino (Phillipines), Admin.; Rev. Jorge H. Loaiza, Par. Vicar; Dcn. Ignacio Badillo; Clara Fragozo, DRE; CRP Stds.: 135

SPRING GROVE

St. Peter - 2118 Main St Rd, Spring Grove, IL 60081; Mailing: P.O. Box 129, Spring Grove, IL 60081 t) 815-675-2288 stpetercatholicchurch.org Rev. Msgr. Joseph F. Jarmoluk, Pst.; Dcn. Mark Raz; Aimee Thomas, CRE; CRP Stds.: 73

ST. CHARLES

St. John Neumann - 2900 E. Main St., St. Charles, IL 60174 t) 630-377-2797 stjohnneumann-stcharles@rockforddiocese.org; kloar@sjnstcharles.org www.sjnstcharles.org Rev. David A. Peck, Pst.; Rev. Leonard Jacobs, Par. Vicar; Dcn. Shawn Glanville; Dcn. Paul Iwanski; Dcn. Ray Mills; Dcn. Michael Monteleone; Dcn. Ronald Williams; Dcn. David Womac; Kristi Loar, CRE; Mark Restaino, Youth Min.; CRP Stds.: 355

St. Patrick - 6N491 Crane Rd., St. Charles, IL 60175; Mailing: 6N487 Crane Rd., St. Charles, IL 60175 t) 630-338-8000 stpatrick-stcharles@rockforddiocese.org www.stpatrickparish.org Dcn. Steve Jolly; Very Rev. Msgr. Daniel J. Deutsch, Pst.; Rev. Lisandro Cristancho (Colombia), Par. Vicar; Rev. Nathan Pacer, Par. Vicar; Rev. Arnold Relles (Phillipines), Par. Vicar; Dcn. Michael Alber; Dcn. James Mellin; Dcn. Michael Smith; Dcn. David Stowell; CRP Stds.: 811

St. Patrick School - (Grades K-8) 787 Crane Rd., St. Charles, IL 60175 t) 630-338-8100 stpatrickschool-stcharles@rockforddiocese.org Lisa Brown, Prin.; Stds.: 417; Lay Tchrs.: 22

St. Patrick Preschool - (Grades PreK-PreK) 118 N. Fifth St., St. Charles, IL 60174 t) 630-338-8200 vday@stpatrickparish.org (Extended Day Care) Veronica Day, Dir.; Stds.: 160

STERLING

St. Mary - 509 Avenue B, Sterling, IL 61081; Mailing: 600 Avenue B, Sterling, IL 61081 t) 815-625-0640 stmary-sterling@rockforddiocese.org www.stmarysterlingil.org Very Rev. James R. Keenan, Pst.; Rev. Carlos A. Monsalve, Par. Vicar; Jane Olson, Pst. Assoc.; CRP Stds.: 93

St. Mary School - (Grades PreK-8) 6 W. Sixth St., Sterling, IL 61081 t) 815-625-2253 stmaryschool-sterling@rockforddiocese.org; mselmi@rockforddiocese.org www.smsterling.webs.com Melanie Selmi, Prin.; Stds.: 201; Lay Tchrs.: 8

Sacred Heart - 2224 Avenue J, Sterling, IL 61081 t) 815-625-1134 sacredheart-sterling@rockforddiocese.org; sheartreligioused@gmail.com www.sacredheartparish.net Rev. Bruce J. Ludeke, Pst.; Melinda Hutchison, CRE; CRP Stds.: 17

STOCKTON

Holy Cross - 223 E Front Ave., Stockton, IL 61085 t) 815-947-2545 holycross.weconnect.com Rev. Michael E. Morrissey, Par. Admin.; CRP Stds.: 61

SUBLETTE

Our Lady of Perpetual Help - 201 S. Locust St., Sublette, IL 61367; Mailing: P.O. Box 80, Sublette, IL 61367 t) 815-849-5412 olph.mary@gmail.com olphmarystpatrick.com Rev. Randy J. Fronek, Pst.; CRP Stds.: 29

SUGAR GROVE

St. Katharine Drexel Parish - 8S055 Dugan Rd., Sugar Grove, IL 60554; Mailing: P.O.Box 1189, Sugar Grove, IL 60554 t) 630-466-0303; 630-466-0303 x109 (CRP) stkatharinedrexel-sugargrove@rockforddiocese.org www.stkatharinedrexel.org Very Rev. Stephen St. Jules, Pst.; Rev. Steven Sabo, Par. Vicar; Dcn. Mark Chaplin; Dcn. Michael Lane; Dcn. Michael Winger; Sheryl Colwell, DRE; CRP Stds.: 263

SYCAMORE

St. Mary - 244 Waterman St., Sycamore, IL 60178; Mailing: 322 Waterman St., Sycamore, IL 60178 t) 815-895-3275; 815-895-3726 x1 (CRP) stmary-sycamore@rockforddiocese.org www.stmarysycamore.com Very Rev. F. William Etheredge; Dcn. Jim Newhouse; CRP Stds.: 236

St. Mary School - (Grades PreK-8) 222 Waterman St., Sycamore, IL 60178 t) 815-895-5215 stmaryschool-sycamore@rockforddiocese.org; pstrang@rockforddiocese.org www.stmarysycamore.com/school Pat Strang, Prin.; Stds.: 131; Pr. Tchrs.: 1; Sr. Tchrs.: 1; Lay Tchrs.: 11

TAMPICO

St. Mary - 105 N. Benton St., Tampico, IL 61283; Mailing: P.O. Box 159, Tampico, IL 61283 t) 815-438-5425 stmary-tampico@rockforddiocese.org; heartofmary@thewisp.net stmarytampico.com Rev. Richard M. Russo, Pst.; Dcn. William Lemmer;

VIRGIL

SS. Peter and Paul - 5 N 939 Meredith Rd., Virgil, IL 60151 t) 630-365-6618; 815-827-3205 x3 (CRP) tdzielak@rockforddiocese.org; sspeterandpaul-virgil@rockforddiocese.org ssppvirgil.org Rev. William R. Antillon, Pst.; Rev. Msgr. Thomas L. Dzielak, In Res.; CRP Stds.: 26

WALTON

St. Mary - 912 Walton Rd., Walton, IL 61021; Mailing: 32 N. Jones Ave., Amboy, IL 61310 t) 815-857-2670 www.stpatrickamboy.org Rev. John Gow, Admin.;

WARREN

St. Ann - 608 E. Railroad St., Warren, IL 61087; Mailing: P.O. Box 665, Warren, IL 61087 t) 815-745-2312 stann-warren@rockforddiocese.org; parishes.wa@gmail.com Rev. Andrew T. Skrobutt, Pst.; Monica McGivney, Bus. Mgr.; Connie Hill, DRE; CRP Stds.: 31

WEST BROOKLYN

St. Mary - 2520 Johnson St., West Brooklyn, IL 61378; Mailing: P. O. Box 80, Sublette, IL 61367 t) 815-849-5412 stmary-westbrooklyn@rockforddiocese.org olphmarystpatrick.com Rev. Randy J. Fronek, Pst.;

WEST DUNDEE

St. Catherine of Siena - 845 W. Main St., West Dundee, IL 60118 t) 847-426-2217 stcatherine-dundee@rockforddiocese.org stcatherinechurch.com Rev. John P. McNamara, Pst.; Rev. Reynante P. Talento (Phillipines), Par. Vicar; Dcn. Steven Fox; Dcn. Hank Schmalen; Dcn. William Whitehead Jr.; CRP Stds.: 96

St. Catherine of Siena School - (Grades PreK-8) t) 847-426-4808 ccanon@rockforddiocese.org; stcatherineschool-dundee@rockforddiocese.org www.stcatherinechurch.com Colleen Cannon, Prin.; Stds.: 210; Lay Tchrs.: 10

St. Mary - 10 Matteson Rd., Gilberts, IL 60136; Mailing: 845 W. Main St., W. Dundee, IL 60118 t) (847) 426-2217

WONDER LAKE

Christ the King - 5006 E. Wonder Lake Rd., Wonder Lake, IL 60097 t) 815-653-2561 christtheking-wonderlake@rockforddiocese.org christthekingchurch.org Rev. Ma Carlos Datu Saligumba, S.O.L.T. (Phillipines), Pst.; Megan Kathleen Pontarelli, Bus. Mgr.; Dcn. David Auld; Rodita Conroy, CRE; CRP Stds.: 27

WOODSTOCK

St. Mary - 312 Lincoln Ave., Woodstock, IL 60098 t) 815-338-3413 (CRP); 815-338-3377 stmary-woodstock@rockforddiocese.org; parish@stmary-woodstock.org www.stmary-woodstock.org Rev. Burt H. Absalon, Pst.; Rev. Juan Ayala, Par. Vicar; Dcn. Policarpo Jimenez; Dcn. William Johnston; Dcn. Hans Rokus; Dcn. Thomas Murray; CRP Stds.: 347

St. Mary School - (Grades PreK-8) 320 Lincoln Ave., Woodstock, IL 60098 t) 815-338-3598 school@stmary-woodstock.org stmary-woodstock.org/school Hillary Russell, Prin.; Stds.: 173; Lay Tchrs.: 10

Resurrection - 2918 S. Country Club Rd., Woodstock, IL 60098 t) 815-338-7330; 815-338-7330 x5 (CRP) resurrection-woodstock@rockforddiocese.org www.resurrectionwoodstock.church Rev. Stephen Glab, C.R., Pst.; CRP Stds.: 12

SCHOOLS: PRESCHOOL THRU HIGH SCHOOL

SCHOOLS

STATE OF ILLINOIS

ROCKFORD

All Saints Catholic Academy - (PAR) (Grades PreK-8) 409 N. First St., Rockford, IL 61107 t) 815-962-8515 allsaintsacademy-rockford@rockforddiocese.org; jkeesee@allsaintsrockford.org www.allsaintsrockford.org Jeremy Keesee, Prin.; Stds.: 163; Lay Tchrs.: 11

HIGH SCHOOLS

STATE OF ILLINOIS

AURORA

Aurora Central Catholic High School - (DIO) (Grades 9-12) 1255 N. Edgelawn Dr., Aurora, IL 60506 t) 630-907-0095 pmayer@rockforddiocese.org www.auroracentral.com ACCHS is a Catholic Coeducational High School. Paul Mayer, Prin.; Rev. Sean Grismer, Vice Principal & Spiritual Director; Stacey Boomershine, Vice Prin.; Leah Bohr, Vice Prin.; Stds.: 448; Pr. Tchrs.: 1; Sr. Tchrs.: 1; Lay Tchrs.: 33

Marmion Academy - (PRV) 1000 Butterfield Rd., Aurora, IL 60502 t) 630-897-6936 atinerella@marmion.org; marmionhighschool-aurora@rockforddiocese.org www.marmion.org Day School for Boys. Rt. Rev. John Brahill, O.S.B., Pres.; Rev. Michael Burrows, O.S.B., Chap.; Anthony Tinerella, Prin.; Stds.: 464; Lay Tchrs.: 35

Rosary High School - (PAR) (Grades 9-12) 901 N. Edgelawn Ave., Aurora, IL 60506 t) 630-896-0831 rosaryhighschool-aurora@rockforddiocese.org; amcmahon@rosaryhs.com www.rosaryhs.com Amy T McMahon, Headmaster; Kayley Johnson, Vice Prin.; Michael Johnson, Vice Prin.; Stds.: 240; Lay Tchrs.: 47

ELGIN

St. Edward Central Catholic High School - (DIO) (Grades 9-12) 335 Locust St., Elgin, IL 60123 t) 847-741-7535 stedwardhighschool@rockforddiocese.org; mainoffice@stedhs.org www.stedhs.org Brian Tekampe, Supt.; Annemarie Duffelmeier, Vice Prin.; Rev. Robert Blood, Vice Principal & Spiritual Director; Stds.: 225; Pr. Tchrs.: 1; Lay Tchrs.: 24

FREEPORT

Aquin Central Catholic High School - (DIO) (Grades 7-12) 1419 S. Galena Ave., Freeport, IL 61032 t) 815-235-3154 aquinhighschool-freeport@rockforddiocese.org; info@aquinschools.org www.aquinschools.org Elizabeth Heitkamp, Supt.; Rev. Michael J. Bolger, Vice Prin.; Stds.: 91; Pr. Tchrs.: 1; Bro. Tchrs.: 1; Lay Tchrs.: 13

Aquin Catholic Elementary School - (Grades 7-12) 1419 S. Galena Ave., Freeport, IL 61032 aquinelementaryschool-freeport@rockforddiocese.org; eheitkamp@rockforddiocese.org Aquin Catholic Elementary School became a part of Aquin Catholic High School in 2007. It previously operated as St. Joseph Elementary School. Elizabeth Heitkamp, Supt.; Stds.: 86; Lay Tchrs.: 13

ROCKFORD

Boylan Central Catholic High School - (DIO) (Grades 9-12) 4000 St. Francis Dr., Rockford, IL 61103 t) 815-877-0531 aott@rockforddiocese.org; boylan@boylan.org www.boylan.org Amy Ott, Pres.; Christopher Rozanski, Prin.; Rev. David Finn, Vice Principal & Spiritual Director; Christopher Lindstedt, Dean; Penny Yurkew, Vice Prin.; Stds.: 615; Pr. Tchrs.: 1; Sr. Tchrs.: 1; Lay Tchrs.: 52

STERLING

Newman Central Catholic High School - (DIO) 1101 W. 23rd St., Sterling, IL 61081-9002 t) 815-625-0500 newmanhighschool-sterling@rockforddiocese.org www.newmancchs.org Jennifer Oetting, Supt.; Rev. Bruce J. Ludeke, Vice Principal & Spiritual Director; Stds.: 179; Lay Tchrs.: 12

WOODSTOCK

Marian Central Catholic High School - (DIO) 1001 McHenry Ave., Woodstock, IL 60098 t) 815-338-4220 marianhighschool-woodstock@rockforddiocese.org; dnovy@rockforddiocese.org www.marian.com Michael J. Shukis, Supt.; Rev. Charles Warren, Vice Principal & Spiritual Director; Stds.: 320; Lay Tchrs.: 22

INSTITUTIONS LOCATED IN DIOCESE

CAMPUS MINISTRY / NEWMAN CENTERS [CAM]

DEKALB

Newman Foundation for Catholic Students of Northern

Illinois University - 512 Normal Rd., DeKalb, IL 60115 t) 815-787-7770 officemanager@newmanniu.org www.newmanniu.org Rev. Robert Gonnella, Par. Vicar; Denise Sanders, Campus Min.;

CEMETERIES [CEM]

AURORA

Mount Olivet - 278 Ashland Ave., Aurora, IL 60505 t) 630-897-9250 kgiambalvo@rockforddiocese.org Ken Giambalvo, Dir.;

ELGIN

Mount Hope - 1001 Villa St., Elgin, IL 60120 t) 847-468-6910 kgiambalvo@rockforddiocese.org Ken Giambalvo, Dir.;

GENEVA

Geneva-St. Charles Resurrection - 37W210 Fabyan Pkwy., Geneva, IL 60134 t) 331-248-0289 kgiambalvo@rockforddiocese.org Ken Giambalvo, Dir.;

ROCKFORD

Calvary-St. Mary's/St. James - 917 Auburn St., Rockford, IL 61103; Mailing: 8616 W. State St., Winnebago, IL 61088 t) 815-965-1450 kgiambalvo@rockforddiocese.org Ken Giambalvo, Dir.;

WINNEBAGO

Calvary - 8616 W. State St., Winnebago, IL 61088 t) 815-965-1450 kgiambalvo@rockforddiocese.org Ken Giambalvo, Dir.;

COLLEGES & UNIVERSITIES [COL]

ROCKFORD

Saint Anthony College of Nursing - 3301 N. Mulford Rd., Health Sciences Ctr., Rockford, IL 61114 t) (815) 282-7900 shannonlizer@sacn.edu www.sacn.edu Rev. Ryan B. Browning, Trustee; Staff: 70; Stds.: 202; Lay Tchrs.: 30

CONVENTS, MONASTERIES, AND RESIDENCES FOR WOMEN [CON]

FREEPORT

Congregation of the Sisters of the Immaculate Heart of Mary, Mother of Christ-Nigeria - Immaculate Heart Sisters Regional House, 1209A S. Walnut Ave., Freeport, IL 61032 t) 815-297-8287 guadaluperegion@gmail.com www.ihmsistersng.org Sr. Marilyn Umunnakwe, IHM, Supr.; Srs.: 8

ROCKFORD

The Poor Clares of Rockford - Corpus Christi Monastery, 2111 S. Main St., Rockford, IL 61102-3591 t) 815-963-7343 vicarforclergy@rockforddiocese.org www.poorclares.org/rockford/ Poor Clare Colettines. Mother Mary Dominica Stein, P.C.C., Mother Abbess; Srs.: 25

ENDOWMENTS / FOUNDATIONS / TRUSTS [EFT]

AURORA

Aurora Catholic Education Foundation - 1141 Trask St., Aurora, IL 60505; Mailing: P.O. Box 234, Aurora, IL 60507 t) 630-898-2998 Alan H Schuler, Treas.;

ELGIN

St. Edward Central Catholic High School Education Foundation - 335 Locust St., Elgin, IL 60123 t) 847-741-7535 stedwardhighschool@rockforddiocese.org www.stedhs.org Barbara Villont, Chair;

FREEPORT

Education Through the 90's Foundation - 1419 S. Galena Ave., Freeport, IL 61032 t) 815-235-3154 rosemarie.brubaker@aquinschools.org www.aquinschools.org Provides financial support for the Aquin Catholic School System. Rosemarie Brubaker, Admin.;

Freeport Catholic Education Foundation - 1419 S. Galena Ave., Freeport, IL 61032 t) 815-235-3154 rosemarie.brubaker@aquinschools.org www.aquinschools.org Provides financial support for the Aquin Catholic School System. Rosemarie Brubaker, Admin.;

ROCKFORD

Boylan Educational Foundation, Inc. - 4000 St. Francis Dr., Rockford, IL 61103 t) 815-877-0531 aott@rockforddiocese.org www.boylan.org Jeffrey Marrs, Admin.; Amy Ott, Pres.;

The Catholic Foundation for the People of the Diocese of Rockford - 555 Colman Center Dr., Rockford, IL 61125-7044; Mailing: P.O. Box 7044, Rockford, IL 61125-7044 t) 815-399-4300 domalley@rockforddiocese.org www.foundationrockford.org Dan O'Malley, Exec.;

HOSPITALS / HEALTH SERVICES [HOS]

AURORA

Presence Mercy Medical Center (Presence Central and Suburban Hospitals Network) - 1325 N. Highland Ave., Aurora, IL 60506; Mailing: 200 S. Wacker Dr., Fl. 12, Legal, Chicago, IL 60606 t) 630-859-2222 john.halstead1@ascension.org www.ascension.org Sponsored by Ascension Health Ministries (Ascension Sponsor), a public juridic person. DBA Ascension Mercy. Polly Davenport, COO; John Halstead, Chief Mission Integration Officer; Bed Capacity: 267; Asstd. Annu.: 41,007; Staff: 581

Center for Diabetic Wellness - 1325 N. Highland Ave., Aurora, IL 60506 t) 630-897-4000

Health Institute - 1975 Melissa Ln., Aurora, IL 60505 t) 630-907-1129

ELGIN

Presence Saint Joseph Hospital-Elgin (Presence Central and Suburban Hospitals Network) - 77 N. Airlite St., Elgin, IL 60123; Mailing: 200 S. Wacker Dr., Fl. 12, Legal, Chicago, IL 60606 t) 847-695-3200 john.halstead1@ascension.org www.ascension.org Sponsored by Ascension Health Ministries (Ascension Sponsor), a public juridic person. DBA Ascension Saint Joseph - Elgin. Polly Davenport, COO; John Halstead, Chief Mission Integration Officer; Bed Capacity: 184; Asstd. Annu.: 30,076; Staff: 502

ROCKFORD

Saint Anthony Medical Center (OSF Saint Anthony Medical Center) - 5666 E. State St., Rockford, IL 61108 t) 815-226-2000 robert.brandfass@osfhealthcare.org www.osfhealthcare.org Paula Carynski, Pres.; Rev. Steven J. Lange, Chap.; Rev. Pierre G. Polycarpe, Chap.; Bed Capacity: 254; Asstd. Annu.: 360,750; Staff: 2,040

MISCELLANEOUS [MIS]

AURORA

***Dominican Literacy Center, Aurora** - 260 Vermont Ave., Aurora, IL 60505-3100 t) 630-898-4636 domlitctr@sbcglobal.net www.dominicanliteracycenter.org Sr. Kathleen Ryan, O.P., Dir.;

The J. Chevalier Charitable Trust - c/o Missionaries of the Sacred Heart, 305 S. Lake St., Aurora, IL 60507; Mailing: P.O. Box 280, Aurora, IL 60507 t) 800-892-6126; 630-892-2371 kyle.r.langerman@morganstanley.com; rwkpng03@mscparish.com www.misacor-usa.org Rev. Richard Kennedy, MSC, Contact;

Public Action to Deliver Shelter, Inc. (PADS) - 659 S. River St., Aurora, IL 60506 t) 630-897-2165 info@hesedhouse.org www.hesedhouse.org Ecumenical advocacy, overnight and transitional shelters, daytime drop-in center for homeless persons, and comprehensive resource center. Ryan J. Dowd, Exec.;

JOHNSBURG

Magnificat, A Ministry to Catholic Women - 1205 Quincy Ave, Johnsburg, IL 60051; Mailing: 13726 Victor Ave, Hudson, FL 34667 t) 815-236-6027 rooney@sbcglobal.net Gina Rooney, Contact;

ROCKFORD

Catholic Office of the Deaf - 555 Colman Center Dr., Rockford, IL 61125; Mailing: P.O. Box 7044, Rockford, IL 61125 t) 815-399-4300 (Voice); 815-217-2234 (V.P.) deafapostolate@rockforddiocese.org www.rockforddiocese.org/deafapostolate/ Rev. Msgr. Glenn L. Nelson, Dir.;

St. Elizabeth Catholic Community Center - 1536 S. Main St., Rockford, IL 61102; Mailing: PO Box 7044, Rockford, IL 61125 t) 815-969-6526; 815-399-4300 catholiccharities@rockforddiocese.org catholiccharities.rockforddiocese.org Charlene Croyle, Fiscal Mgr.;

ST. CHARLES

Cultivation Ministries - 818 Gray St., St. Charles, IL 60174; Mailing: P.O. Box 662, St. Charles, IL 60174 t) 630-513-8222 frank@cultivationministries.com www.cultivationministries.com To cultivate team-based, intergenerational & disciple-making Catholic youth ministries by training, resourcing and supporting adult & student leaders. Frank Mercadante, Exec.;

Queen of Americas Guild - 311 Kautz Rd., St. Charles, IL 60174 t) 630-584-1822 staff@queenoftheamericasguild.org www.queenoftheamericasguild.org Christopher Smoczynski, Pres.; Stephen Banaszak, Vice Pres.; His Eminence Raymond Burke, Dir.; Matthew Smoczynski, Dir.; Most Rev. Juan Miguel Betancourt, Episcopal Moderator;

STERLING

St. Vincent DePaul Society - 7 W. 6th St., Sterling, IL 61081 t) 815-625-0311 svdsaukvalley@gmail.com www.stmarysterling.com Ed Mulvaney, Pres.;

St. Mary's Conference - 600 Ave. B, Sterling, IL 61081 t) 815-625-0640 Very Rev. James R. Keenan, Pst.;

STOCKTON

Christ in the Wilderness - 7500 S. Randecker Rd., Stockton, IL 61085-8922 t) 815-947-2476 citw@citwretreat.com www.citwretreat.com Sr. Julia Marie Bathon, O.S.F., Exec.;

SYCAMORE

***5 Stones Group, NFP (Cedar House)** - 1915 Aster Rd., Sycamore, IL 60178 t) 630-647-5464 accounting@weare5stones.com weare5stones.com Michael Pacer, Pres.;

MONASTERIES AND RESIDENCES FOR PRIESTS AND BROTHERS [MON]

AURORA

Marmion Abbey - 850 Butterfield Rd., Aurora, IL 60502 t) 630-897-7215 jbrahill@marmion.org www.marmion.org Rt. Rev. John Brahill, O.S.B., Abbot; Rev. Patrick S. Gillmeyer, O.S.B., Pst.; Rev. Paul Weberg, O.S.B., Prior; Rev. Thomas Bailey, O.S.B.; Rev. Michael Burrows, O.S.B.; Rev. Rene Otzoy Colaj, O.S.B.; Rev. Orlando Perez Gomez, O.S.B.; Rev. Theodore Haggerty, O.S.B.; Rev. Armando Menchu, O.S.B.; Rev. Antony Minardi, O.S.B.; Rev. Juan Francisco Peren Mux, O.S.B.; Rev. Frederick Peterson, O.S.B.; Rev. Cristobal Coche Quic, O.S.B.; Bro. Mariano Di Cristofano, O.S.B.; Bro. Francis Matthew Knott, OSB; Rev. Leo M. Ryska, O.S.B.; Rev. Charles Reichenbacher, O.S.B.; Rev. Joel Rippinger, O.S.B.; Rev. Nathanael Roberts, O.S.B.; Rev. Kenneth Theisen, O.S.B.; Bro. Andre Charron, O.S.B., Subprior; Rt. Rev. Vincent Bataille, O.S.B., Abbot Emeritus; Brs.: 3; Priests: 18

Missionaries of the Sacred Heart Community - 2000 W. Galena Blvd, Suite 205, Aurora, IL 60507; Mailing: P.O. Box 280, Aurora, IL 60507 t) 630-892-2371 rwkpng03@mscparish.com www.misacor-usa.org Rev. Richard Kennedy, MSC, Prov.; Priests: 1

MCHENRY

Villa Desiderata Retreat House - 3015 N. Bayview Ln., McHenry, IL 60051-9641 t) 815-385-2264 villaretreats@att.net www.villadesiderata.com Bro. Patrick T. Drohan, C.S.V.; Brs.: 1

NURSING / REHABILITATION / CONVALESCENCE / ELDERLY CARE [NUR]

AURORA

Ascension Living Fox Knoll Village (Presence Life Connections) - 421 N. Lake St., Aurora, IL 60506 t) 314-292-9308 ahscm-mission@ascension.org www.ascensionliving.org/ Ryan Endsley, COO; Asstd. Annu.: 102; Staff: 35

FREEPORT

Presence Saint Joseph Adult Day Center (Presence Life Connections) - 659 E. Jefferson St., Freeport, IL 61032 t) 314-292-9308 ahscm-mission@ascension.org www.ascensionliving.org/ Ryan Endsley, COO;

Ascension Living Saint Joseph Village (Presence Life Connections.) - 659 E. Jefferson St., Freeport, IL 61032 t) 314-292-9308 ahscm-mission@ascension.org www.ascensionliving.org/ Daniel Stricker, Pres.; Asstd. Annu.: 271; Staff: 118

ROCKFORD

Ascension Living Saint Anne Place (Presence Life Connections) - 4405 Highcrest Rd., Rockford, IL 61107 t) 314-292-9308 ahscm-mission@ascension.org www.ascensionliving.org/ Ryan Endsley, COO; Asstd. Annu.: 322; Staff: 86

RETREAT HOUSES / RENEWAL CENTERS [RTR]

BATAVIA

Holy Heart of Mary Novitiate - 717 N. Batavia Ave., Batavia, IL 60510 t) 630-879-1296 evelynbv@sbcglobal.net www.sscm-usa.org Servants of the Holy Heart of Mary. Sr. Evelyn Varboncoeur, S.S.C.M., Supr.;

Nazareth Spirituality Center - 717 N. Batavia Ave., Batavia, IL 60510 t) 630-879-1296 lindai220@sbcglobal.net; ckarnitsky@sscm-usa.org www.sscm-usa.org Linda Isleib, Dir.;

DEKALB

Newman Center of Northern Illinois University Educational Program and Development Fund, Inc. - 512 Normal Rd., DeKalb, IL 60115 t) 815-787-7770 bwelsh@rockforddiocese.org www.newmanniu.org Rev. Robert Gonnella;

ROCKFORD

Bishop Lane Retreat Center - 7708 E. McGregor Rd., Rockford, IL 61102 t) 815-965-5011 bishoplane@rockforddiocese.org www.bishoplane.org Kristen Sapoznik, Dir.;

SPECIAL CARE FACILITIES [SPF]

FREEPORT

Ascension Living Saint Joseph Village (Presence Life Connections) - 659 E. Jefferson St., Freeport, IL 61032 t) (314) 292-9308 www.ascensionliving.org/ Ryan Endsley, COO; Bed Capacity: 124; Asstd. Annu.: 271; Staff: 118

SAVANNA

MercyOne Clinton Home Care and Hospice - 9317A IL Route 84, Savanna, IL 61074; Mailing: 638 S Bluff Blvd, Clinton, IA 52732 t) 815-273-2628 timothy.shinbori@trinity-health.org; lisa.mason-hagen@mercyhealth.com www.mercyone.org Timothy T. Shinbori, Exec.; Asstd. Annu.: 200; Staff: 39

An asterisk (*) denotes an organization that has established tax-exempt status directly with the IRS and is not covered by the USCCB Group Ruling.

Diocese of Rockville Centre

(Dioecesis Petropolitana In Insula Longa)

MOST REVEREND JOHN O. BARRES, S.T.D., J.C.L., D.D.

Bishop of Rockville Centre; ordained October 21, 1989; appointed Bishop of Allentown May 27, 2009; installed July 30, 2009; appointed Bishop of Rockville Centre December 9, 2016; installed January 31, 2017. Pastoral Center, P.O. Box 9023, Rockville Center, NY 11571-9023.

Diocesan Offices: P.O. Box 9023, Rockville Centre, NY 11571-9023. T: 516-678-5800; F: 516-678-3138.
drvc.org

ESTABLISHED APRIL 6, 1957.

Square Miles 1,198.

The Roman Catholic Diocese of Rockville Centre, New York.

Comprises the Counties of Nassau and Suffolk (excepting Fishers Island) in the State of New York.

For legal titles of parishes and diocesan institutions, consult the Chancery Office.

MOST REVEREND ANDRZEJ J. ZGLEJSZEWSKI
Auxiliary Bishop of Rockville Centre; ordained May 26, 1990; appointed Titular Bishop of Nicives and Auxiliary Bishop of Rockville Centre February 11, 2014; ordained March 25, 2014. Mailing Address: 42 Dover Pl., Williston Park, NY 11596.

MOST REVEREND ROBERT J. COYLE
Auxiliary Bishop of Rockville Centre; ordained May 25, 1991; appointed Titular Bishop of Zabi and Auxiliary Bishop of the Archdiocese for the Military Services February 11, 2013; ordained April 25, 2013; appointed Auxiliary Bishop of Rockville Centre February 20, 2018. Mailing Address: 39 North Carl Ave., Babylon, NY 11702.

MOST REVEREND LUIS M. ROMERO
Auxiliary Bishop of Rockville Centre; ordained September 11, 1981; appointed Titular Bishop of Egara and Auxiliary Bishop of Rockville Centre March 3, 2020; installed June 29, 2020. Mailing Address: 104 Greenwich St., Hempstead, NY 11550.

STATISTICAL OVERVIEW

Personnel
Bishop....1
Auxiliary Bishops....3
Retired Bishops....2
Priests: Diocesan Active in Diocese....175
Priests: Diocesan Active Outside Diocese....5
Priests: Retired, Sick or Absent....120
Number of Diocesan Priests....300
Religious Priests in Diocese....29
Total Priests in your Diocese....329
Extern Priests in Diocese....140
Ordinations:
Diocesan Priests....3
Transitional Deacons....1
Permanent Deacons in Diocese....259
Total Brothers....52
Total Sisters....637

Parishes
Parishes....132
With Resident Pastor:
Resident Diocesan Priests....121
Resident Religious Priests....11
Professional Ministry Personnel:
Brothers....22
Sisters....29
Lay Ministers....271

Welfare
Catholic Hospitals....6
Total Assisted....328,535
Health Care Centers....2
Total Assisted....16,050
Homes for the Aged....3
Total Assisted....1,634
Specialized Homes....7
Total Assisted....1,432
Special Centers for Social Services....38
Total Assisted....33,058
Residential Care of Disabled....57
Total Assisted....289
Other Institutions....16
Total Assisted....1,552

Educational
Diocesan Students in Other Seminaries....15
Total Seminarians....15
Colleges and Universities....1
Total Students....3,401
High Schools, Diocesan and Parish....4
Total Students....2,218
High Schools, Private....5
Total Students....7,639
Elementary Schools, Diocesan and Parish....31
Total Students....10,085
Elementary Schools, Private....5
Total Students....691
Catechesis/Religious Education:
High School Students....1,191
Elementary Students....50,748
Total Students under Catholic Instruction....75,988
Teachers in Diocese:
Priests....13
Brothers....25
Sisters....12
Lay Teachers....1,689

Vital Statistics
Receptions into the Church:
Infant Baptism Totals....8,568
Minor Baptism Totals....554
Adult Baptism Totals....652
Received into Full Communion....159
First Communions....9,904
Confirmations....10,152
Marriages:
Catholic....2,382
Interfaith....363
Total Marriages....2,745
Deaths....9,272
Total Catholic Population....1,241,763
Total Population....2,917,000

LEADERSHIP

Diocesan Bishop - Most Rev. John O. Barres;
Diocesan Bishop Emeritus - Most Rev. William Francis Murphy;
Auxiliary Bishops - Most Rev. John C. Dunne; Rev. Msgr. Richard G. Henning; Most Rev. Andrzej J. Zglejszewski (zandrzej@drvc.org);
Secretary to the Bishop - Rev. John J. McCartney (chancellor@drvc.org);
Vicar General and Moderator of the Curia - t) 516-678-5800 x622 Rev. Eric R. Fasano (efasano@drvc.org);
Episcopal Vicars - Most Rev. Robert J. Coyle (rcoyle@drvc.org); Most Rev. Andrzej J. Zglejszewski (zandrzej@drvc.org); Rev. Msgr. Richard G. Henning;
Hispanic Ministry and Evangelization - t) 516-489-3675 Most Rev. Luis M. Romero;
Chancery Office -
Co Chancellors - Sr. Maryanne Fitzgerald, S.C.; Rev. John J. McCartney;
Secretary to the Bishop - Rev. John J. McCartney;
Cabinet -
Catholic Ministries Appeal - Barbara Kilarjian;
Co-Chancellors - Rev. John J. McCartney; Sr. Maryanne Fitzgerald, S.C.;
Department of Education - t) 516-280-2479 Denise Smith, Supt.;
Secretary for Communications - Sean P. Dolan;
Secretary for Evangelization and Catechesis - Rev. Lachlan Cameron;
Secretary for Ministerial Personnel - t) 516-678-5800 x585 Rev. Msgr. William E. Koenig;
Secretary for Operations and General Counsel - Thomas Renker;
Secretary for Social Services - t) 516-733-7013 Laura A. Cassell;
Secretary to the Bishop - Rev. John J. McCartney;
Censors of Books - Rev. Msgr. John A. Alesandro; Rev. Charles Caccavale; Rev. Msgr. Joseph De Grocco;
Diocesan Tribunal - t) 516-678-5800
Judicial Vicar - Rev. Msgr. Robert O. Morrissey (rmorrissey@drvc.org);
Adjutant Judicial Vicars - Rev. Thomas V. Arnao; Rev. Lee R. Descoteaux;
Diocesan Judge - Dcn. Thomas B. Rich;
Senior Staff Attorney - Silvana Barkaus;
Defender of the Bond - Rev. Irinel Racos; Rev. Msgr. Richard C. Bauhoff;
Promoter of Justice - Rev. Irinel Racos;
Notaries - Carol Gatz; Carol McCarthy; Lucille Vetrano;
Medical Experts - Thomas P. Demaria; Sr. Thomas More Fahey, R.G.S.;
Coordinator of Post-Annulment Counseling Program - t) 631-495-7901 Linda Sherlock-Reich;
Procurator & Advocates - Rev. Michael J. Bartholomew; Dcn. Richard Becker; Rev. Stephen J. Brigandi;
Presbyteral Council - Most Rev. John O. Barres, Ex Officio; Most Rev. Andrzej J. Zglejszewski, Ex Officio (zandrzej@drvc.org); Rev. Msgr. Richard G. Henning, Ex Officio;
College of Consultors - Most Rev. John O. Barres; Most Rev. Andrzej J. Zglejszewski (zandrzej@drvc.org); Rev. Msgr. Richard G. Henning;
Deans - Rev. Joseph H. Fitzgerald; Rev. Gerard A. Gordon; Rev. Robert A. Holz;

OFFICES AND DIRECTORS

Archives - t) 631-423-0483 archives@drvc.org Krista H. Ammirati;
Campus Ministry - Rev. Lachlan Cameron, Dir. (lcameron@drvc.org);
Catholic Cemeteries of Long Island - t) 516-434-2439; 631-234-8297; 631-732-3460; 516-334-7990 info@cclongisland.org www.cclongisland.org Richard C. Bie, Pres.;
Catholic Charities - t) 516-733-7013 Laura A. Cassell, CEO;
The Catholic Faith Network - t) 516-538-8700 info@cfntv.org Rev. Msgr. James C. Vlaun, Pres.;
Catholic Ministries Appeal - t) 516-678-5800 x296 cmanews@drvc.org www.drvc.org/cma/ Barbara Kilarjian (bkilarjian@drvc.org);
Catholic Scouting - t) 516-678-5800 x245
Chaplains (Uniformed) -
Chaplain of the Emerald Society - Rev. Sean J. Gann;
Chaplain of the Nassau County Firemen's Association - Rev. Kevin M. Smith, Our Lady of the Snow, Blue Point; Rev. Msgr. Steven Camp, Chap.; Rev. Christopher M. Costigan, Chap.;
Chaplains of the Nassau County Police Department - Rev. Joseph D'Angelo; Rev. Gerard Gordon;
Chief Financial Officer - Thomas Doodian (tdoodian@drvc.org);
Chief Operations Officer and General Counsel - Thomas Renker (trenker@drvc.org);
Clergy Personnel - t) 515-678-5800 x585 Rev. Msgr. William E. Koenig (wkoenig@drvc.org);
Deacons - t) 516-678-5800 x632 Dcn. Lawrence Faulkenberry, Dir. (lfaulkenberry@drvc.org);
Department of Education - Denise Smith, Supt. (dsmith@drvc.org); Biagio M. Arpino, Supt. (barpino@drvc.org); Marian Mingo, Asst. Supt. (mmingo@drvc.org);
Diaconate Formation - t) 631-423-0483 Dcn. Arthur A. Candido (acandido@drvc.org);
Facilities and Risk Management - William G. Chapin, Dir. (wgchapin@drvc.org);
Fe Fuerza Vida Newspaper - t) 516-678-5800 x221 Martha Moscosco, Editor;
Health Care Apostolate - t) 516-705-3701 Alan D. Guerci, Pres.; Salvatore Sodano, Chair; James Spencer, Vice. Pres.;
Healthcare Apostolate - t) 516-705-3700 Alan D. Guerci, Pres.;
Hispanic Apostolate of the South Fork - t) 631-287-9647
Human Resources - Patricia Kerner, Dir.; Arthur A. Candido;
Information Technology - Edward Costello, Dir.; Jack Weber, Dir. (helpdesk@drvc.org);
The Long Island Catholic Magazine - Sean P. Dolan, Assoc. Publisher & Editor (sdolan@drvc.org);
Ministry to Senior Priests - t) 631-608-2622 Rev. Msgr. Thomas C. Costa;
Office of Evangelization and Catechesis - Rev. Lachlan Cameron, Dir. (lcameron@drvc.org);
Office of Hispanic Ministry - Karol Garcia, Coord. (kgarcia@drvc.org);
Office of Liturgy and Worship - worship@drvc.org
Office of Multicultural Diversity - Darcel Whitten-Wilamowski, Coord. (dwhitten@drvc.org);
Office of Public Information - Sean P. Dolan, Dir. (sdolan@drvc.org);
Parish Cemeteries - t) 631-234-8297; 516-334-7990; 631-732-3460
Parish Stewardship - t) 516-678-5800 x297 stewardship@drvc.org www.stewardshipli.org
Pastoral Center - t) 516-678-5800
Pontificial Mission Societies and Diocesan Mission to the Dominican Republic - Sarah McAteer, Dir. (propfaithmission@drvc.org);
Priestly Life and Ministry - Rev. Msgr. Richard G. Henning, Central Vicariate;
Priests' Personnel Assignment Board - Most Rev. John O. Barres; Most Rev. Andrzej J. Zglejszewski (zandrzej@drvc.org); Rev. Msgr. Richard G. Henning;
Priests' Personnel Policy Board - Rev. Msgr. William E. Koenig (wkoenig@drvc.org); Rev. Antony Asir; Rev. Msgr. James P. Swiader;
Priests' Retirement Board - Rev. Msgr. William E. Koenig, Ex Officio (wkoenig@drvc.org); Rev. Msgr. Thomas C. Costa; Rev. Msgr. Richard M. Figliozzi;
SDR Board Executive Committee Members - Rev. Msgr. William E. Koenig; Rev. Robert Holz; Rev. Msgr. Thomas C. Costa;
Prison Ministry and Criminal Justice Affairs - t) 516-678-5800 x578 Dcn. Lawrence Faulkenberry, Dir. (lfaulkenberry@drvc.org);
Nassau County Correctional Center - t) 516-572-3622 Dcn. Jose B. Valdez; Dcn. Manuel J. Ramos;
Suffolk County Correctional Facility - t) 631-852-2294 Sr. Michelle Bremer, C.S.F.N., Chap.; Dcn. Roger P. Mott;
Suffolk County Minimum Security Facility - t) 631-852-7296 Sr. Michelle Bremer, C.S.F.N., Chap.; Dcn. Roger Mott;
Religious - Sr. Patricia Moran, C.I.J. (pmoran@drvc.org);
Religious & Priest Retirement Fund - t) 516-678-5800 x257 Barbara Kilarjian (bkilarjian@drvc.org);
Respect Life - t) 516-678-5800 x381
Victim Assistance Coordinator - Mary McMahon;
Vocations - vocations@drvc.org www.drvc.org/vocations Rev. Sean T. Magaldi, Dir.;
Worship - t) 516-678-5800 x504 worship@drvc.org
Youth Ministry Director - Nolan Reynolds (nreynolds@drvc.org);

ORGANIZATIONS

Catholic Lawyer's Guild - Rev. Eric R. Fasano, Chap. (efasano@drvc.org); Rev. Irinel Racos, Chap. (iracos@drvc.org);
Catholic Youth Organization of Nassau and Suffolk - t) 516-433-1145 Paul Echausse, Exec.; Rev. Joseph V. Davanzo, Priest Moderator;
Society of St. Vincent de Paul - t) 516-822-3132 Thomas J. Abbate, Exec.;

PARISHES, MISSIONS, AND CLERGY

STATE OF NEW YORK

AMITYVILLE

St. Martin of Tours - 37 Union Ave., Amityville, NY 11701 t) 631-691-1617 stmartinreo@gmail.com Rev. Gerard Gordon, Pst.; Dcn. Michael Aprile; Dcn. Richard Ferri; Dcn. Larry McPartland; Jennifer Kennedy, DRE;
St. Martin of Tours School - 30 Union Ave., Amityville, NY 11701 t) 631-264-7166 mmartinez5606@smtschool.org smtschool.org Dr. Jennifer Economos, Prin.;

BABYLON

St. Joseph - 39 N. Carll Ave., Babylon, NY 11702-2701 t) 631-587-4717 Rev. Jason Grisafi, Pst.; Rev. Ethel Anarado (Nigeria), Assoc. Pst.; Rev. David Atanasio, Chap.; Rev. Francis A. Samuel, O.C.I.; Dcn. Barry P. Croce; Dcn. Michael J. Leyden; Dcn. John F. Sullivan; Claire Moule, DRE;
Mission - (Summer)

BALDWIN

St. Christopher's Parish - 11 Gale Ave., Baldwin, NY 11510-3202 t) 516-223-0723 (Rectory); 516-223-5813 (CRP) info@stchrisbaldwin.org; stchrisreligion@gmail.com www.stchris.com Rev. Johnny Mendonca, Admin.; Dcn. Anthony Banno; Dcn. Ralph J. Muscente; Rev. Cornelius Dery (Ghana), In Res.; Rev. Emmanuel Mensa, In Res.;

BAY SHORE

St. Patrick's - 9 N. Clinton Ave., Bay Shore, NY 11706 t) 631-665-4914 (CRP); 631-665-4911 spparish@optonline.net www.stpatrickbayshore.org Rev. Sean J. Gann, Pst.; Rev. Cyril Obi Bayim, Assoc. Pst.; Rev. Roger Velasquez, Assoc. Pst.; Rev. Msgr. John C. Nosser, Pastor Emer.; Dcn. Frank Keach; Dcn. Joseph Peralta, RCIA Coord.; Dcn. Gregory Nardone, Bus. Mgr.;
St. Patrick's School - t) 631-665-0569 www.spsbayshore.org Roseann Petruccio, Prin.;

BAYVILLE

St. Gertrude's - 28 School St., Bayville, NY 11709 t) 516-628-2432 Rev. David Regan, Pst.; Rev. Edward M. Seagriff, Assoc. Pst.; Dcn. Theodore Kolakowski;

Pre School - t) 516-628-3710

BELLMORE

St. Barnabas the Apostle - 2320 Bedford Ave., Bellmore, NY 11710 t) 516-785-0130 stbarnabasocf@yahoo.com Rev. Jeff Yildirmaz, Pst.; Rev. Shaju Devassy, Assoc. Pst.; Rev. Michael Ngoka, Assoc. Pst.; Dcn. Richard Iandoli; Dcn. Bernard Sherlock;

BELLPORT

Mary Immaculate - 16 Browns Ln., Bellport, NY 11713 t) 631-286-3504 (CRP); 631-286-0154 leslie@miparish.net www.miparish.net Rev. Msgr. William A. Hanson, Pst.; Rev. Charles Osita Okonkwo, Chap.;

BETHPAGE

St. Martin of Tours - 220 Central Ave., Bethpage, NY 11714; Mailing: 40 Seaman Ave., Bethpage, NY 11714 t) 516-931-0818 gamit1946@hotmail.com www.smtbethpage.org Rev. Christopher M. Costigan, Pst.; Rev. Sylvester Ileka, Assoc. Pst.; Rev. Vincent Schifano, Assoc. Pst.; Dcn. Thomas Hennessy; Dcn. Ronald Lacsa; Dcn. Christopher P Quinn; Laura Leigh Agnese, DRE; Patricia Ryan, DRE;

BLUE POINT

Our Lady of the Snow - 175 Blue Point Ave., Blue Point, NY 11715 t) 631-363-6385 ourladyofthesnowbp@gmail.com ourladyodthesnowbluepoint Rev. Kevin M. Smith, Pst.; Rev. Joseph C Gaspar, Assoc. Pst.; Dcn. Robert Gronenthal; Dcn. Edward Karan; Loren Christie, DRE;

BOHEMIA

St. John Nepomucene - 1140 Locust Ave., Bohemia, NY 11716 t) 631-567-1765 Rev. Joseph M. Schlafer, Pst.; Rev. Lawrence A. Chadwick, Assoc. Pst.; Dcn. James Bohuslaw; Dcn. Roger Mott; Dcn. George Reich; Rev. Msgr. John Gilmartin, In Res.; Rev. Richard R. Viladesau, In Res.; Kathy Russell-Sica, DRE;

BRENTWOOD

St. Anne's - 88 Second Ave., Brentwood, NY 11717 t) 631-231-7344 (CRP); 631-273-8113 stannesbrentwood@gmail.com Rev. Stanislaw Wadowski (Poland), Pst.; Rev. Victor Evangelista, Assoc. Pst.; Rev. Charlince Vendredy, Assoc. Pst.; Dcn. Jay Alvarado; Dcn. Andres Colpa; Dcn. John E. Walters; Sue Lindsay, Music Min.; Janet Lambert, Parish Life Coord.; Marge Baum, Pst. Assoc.; Anthony (Tony) Bellizzi, Youth Min.; Bertha Keenan, DRE;

St. Luke - 266 Wicks Rd., Brentwood, NY 11717 t) 631-273-1110 info@sanlukes.org Rev. Cristobal Martin, M. Id, Pst.; Rev. Camillo Lugo (Colombia), Assoc. Pst.; Dcn. Jose Arevalo; Dcn. Richard A. Luken; Dcn. Orlando Mancilla; Bro. Carlos Lindao, M. Id, Youth Min.; Sr. Elaine Schenk, M.Id., DRE; Debby Cristaldo, Bus. Mgr.;

BRIDGEHAMPTON

Queen of the Most Holy Rosary - 2350 Montauk Hwy., Bridgehampton, NY 11932; Mailing: P.O. Box 3035, Bridgehampton, NY 11932 t) 631-537-0156 qmhrnybh@aol.com www.qmhr.org Rev. Peter Devaraj, S.A.C., Pst.; Robert Diederiks, Pst. Assoc.; Sr. Maryann McCarthy, C.S.J., DRE;

BROOKVILLE

St. Paul the Apostle - 2534 Cedar Swamp Rd., Rte. 107, Brookville, NY 11545 t) 516-938-4530 Rev. Msgr. James F. Pereda, Pst.; Dcn. Raymond P. D'Alessio; Bro. Joseph Bellizzi, S.M., DRE; Louise Shannon, DRE;

CARLE PLACE

Church of Our Lady of Hope - 534 Broadway, Carle Place, NY 11514-1712 t) 516-334-4781 (CRP); 516-334-6288 secretary@olhope.org olhope.org Rev. Kevin J. Dillon, Pst.; Dcn. Patrick J. Dunphy; Dcn. Thomas B. Rich; James Millen, Music Min.; CRP Stds.: 350

St. Brigid/ Our Lady of Hope Regional School - 101 Maple Ave., Westbury, NY 11590 t) 516-333-0580 Paul P. Clagnaz, Prin.;

CEDARHURST

St. Joachim - 614 Central Ave., Cedarhurst, NY 11516 Rev. Thomas Moriarty Jr., Admin.; Dcn. Frank J. Bono; Dcn. Charles R. Goldburg;

CENTER MORICHES

St. John the Evangelist - 25 Ocean Ave., Center Moriches, NY 11934 t) 631-878-4141 (CRP); 631-878-0009 rectory@sjecm.org Rev. John Sureau, Pst.; Rev. Felix Akpabio, Assoc. Pst.; Rev. Michael Plona, Assoc. Pst.; Dcn. John C. Pettorino;

CENTEREACH

Assumption of the Blessed Virgin Mary - 20 Chestnut St., Centereach, NY 11720 t) 631-588-6408 (CRP); 631-585-8760 lrobustelli@abvmcentereach.com; rectory@abvmcentereach.com Rev. Joseph Alenchery (India), Pst.; Dcn. Michael Montelione; Lisette Robustelli, DRE;

CENTERPORT

Our Lady Queen of Martyrs - 53 Prospect Rd., Centerport, NY 11721 neuler@olqmparish.org Rev. Stephen J. Pietrowski, Pst.; Bro. Etienne Jaeckel, Pst. Assoc.; Dcn. John Rieger; Ninette Euler, DRE;

CENTRAL ISLIP

St. John of God - 84 Carleton Ave., Central Islip, NY 11722 t) 631-234-4040 (CRP); 631-234-6535 sjogre@verizon.net; sjogno1@aol.com www.stjohnofgodparish.org Rev. Daniel Rivera, M.Sp.S., Pst.; Rev. Jorge Bastidas, Assoc. Pst.; Dcn. Jose B. Valdez; Guillermo Felix, Music Min.; Margaret Martin, DRE; Carmen Roncal, Pst. Assoc.; Maria Cristina Saenz, Pst. Assoc.; Giovanni Mayo, Pst. Assoc.; Yanira Copland Barahona, Pst. Assoc.; Sr. Valerie Scholl, C.S.J., Pst. Assoc.; CRP Stds.: 440

Parish Outreach - t) 631-234-1884 Ana Sullivan, Dir.;

Sisters of St. Joseph - 330 St. John St., Central Islip, NY 11722

COMMACK

Christ the King - 2 Indian Head Rd., Commack, NY 11725 t) 631-864-1623 cff@ctkrcc.org Rev. Robert W. Ketcham, Pst.; Rev. Robert C. Scheckenback, Assoc. Pst.; Dcn. Louis Anetrella; Dcn. Joseph Marfoglio;

COPIAGUE

Our Lady of the Assumption - 1 Molloy St., Copiague, NY 11726 t) 631-842-3545 (CRP); 631-842-5211; 631-626-4174 assumptioncopia@optonline.net www.olacopiague.org Rev. Dariusz Koszyk, Pst.; Rev. Jose Gustavo Perez Alzate, Assoc. Pst.; Dcn. Philip A. Mills Jr.; Biagio M. Arpino, DRE;

CORAM

St. Frances Cabrini - 134 Middle Country Rd., Coram, NY 11727 t) 631-698-3149 (CRP); 631-732-8445 coramcab@aol.com sfccoram.org Rev. Gilbert D. Lap, Pst.; Dcn. Peter Acquaro; Dcn. Monte Naylor Jr.; Dcn. Carmen L. Pagnotta;

CUTCHOGUE

Our Lady of Ostrabrama - 3000 Depot Ln., Cutchogue, NY 11935; Mailing: Box 997, Cutchogue, NY 11935 Rev. Msgr. Joseph W. Staudt, Admin.;

North Fork Regional Catholic School, Cutchogue - t) 631-734-5166

Sacred Heart - 27905 Main Rd., Cutchogue, NY 11935-0926; Mailing: P.O. Box 926, Cutchogue, NY 11935-0926 t) 631-734-2568 Rev. Msgr. Joseph W. Staudt, Pst.; Dcn. Jeffrey Sykes; Suzanne Sykes, DRE;

Our Lady of Good Counsel - Main Rd., Mattituck, NY 11952

DAVIS PARK

Most Precious Blood - 10 Spindrift Walk, Fire Island, Davis Park, NY 11772 t) 631-928-2377 (Summer Mission) Rev. Francis Pizzarelli, S.M.M., Pst.;

DEER PARK

SS. Cyril and Methodius - 125 Half Hollow Rd., Deer Park, NY 11729-4288 t) 631-667-4044 amora.laucella@gmail.com; parishoffice@sscmdp.org www.sscmdp.org Rev. Francisco Gius Garcia (Philippines), Pst.; Rev. Moise Aime (Haiti), Assoc. Pst.; Rev. Patrick Grace, Assoc. Pst.; Dcn. John F. Fitzpatrick; Dcn. William Sperl; Dcn. James A. Murano, Music Min.; Amora Laucella, DRE; Dcn. Philip A. Mills Jr., Bus. Mgr.; Rev. Francis D. Sang (Vietnam), In Res.;

SS. Cyril and Methodius School -

DIX HILLS

St. Matthew - 35 N. Service Rd., Dix Hills, NY 11746 t) 631-864-3321 Rev. Robert S. Hewes, Pst.; Rev. Joseph Shemgwan Habila, Assoc. Pst.; Rev. Benet Uwasomba, Assoc. Pst.; Dcn. Carmine DeStefano; Dcn. James M. McQuade; Dcn. Luis Roberto Polanco; Mary Donaldson, DRE; Dolores Tiernan, Bus. Mgr.;

EAST HAMPTON

Most Holy Trinity - 57 Buell Ln., East Hampton, NY 11937; Mailing: 79 Buell Ln., East Hampton, NY 11937 t) (631) 324-0134 x732 mht-eh.org Rev. Ryan Creamer, Pst.; Dcn. Lawrence Faulkenberry; CRP Stds.: 201

St. Peter the Apostle - 286 Main St., Amagansett, NY 11930

EAST ISLIP

Church of St. Mary - 20 Harrison Ave., East Islip, NY 11730 t) 631-581-4266 rectory@stmaryei.org stmaryei.org Rev. Anthony Iaconis, Pst.; Rev. John Crozier, Par. Vicar; Rev. Charles Gnanapragasam, Par. Vicar; Rev. Alfred Amankwah (Ghana), Par. Vicar; CRP Stds.: 865

Church of St. Mary School - 16 Harrison Ave., East Islip, NY 11730 t) (631) 581-3423 saintmaryschoolei.org Laura McMahon, Prin.; Stds.: 398; Lay Tchrs.: 28

EAST MEADOW

St. Raphael - 600 Newbridge Rd., East Meadow, NY 11554 t) 516-785-0236 vincenzarectory@optonline.net www.strapahaelparish.org Rev. Robert A. Holz, Pst.; Rev. Sung Ho Kim, Assoc. Pst.; Dcn. Victor R. Costa; Dcn. Angelo D'Aversa; Dcn. Dennis Schlosser; Ellen Fox, DRE; Diane Lawlor, Bus. Mgr.;

EAST NORTHPORT

St. Anthony of Padua - 20 Cheshire Pl., East Northport, NY 11731-2591 t) 631-261-1306 (CRP); 631-261-1077 pastor@saintanthonyofpadua.org Rev. Msgr. Joseph A. Mirro, Pst.; Rev. Valentine Ofomata, Assoc. Pst.; Rev. Kulandairajan Savarimuthu, Assoc. Pst.; Rev. Bruce J. Powers, In Res.; Dcn. Robert Braun; Patricia Seibert, DRE;

EAST PATCHOGUE

St. Joseph the Worker - 510 Narragansett Ave., East Patchogue, NY 11772 t) 631-286-2550 Rev. Martin Curtin, O.F.M.Cap., Pst.; Rev. Donald Philip Wesnofske, Assoc. Pst.; Rev. William Hector Tarraza, In Res.; Rev. Henry Vas, O.F.M.Cap., Chap.; Judy Hansen, DRE;

EAST ROCKAWAY

St. Raymond's - 263 Atlantic Ave., East Rockaway, NY 11518 t) 516-593-9075 econtaldisrre@optonline.net Rev. Charles Romano, Pst.; Rev. Vincent Hassan Bulus, Assoc. Pst.; Rev. Theodore Iloh, Assoc. Pst.; Dcn. Robert C. Campbell; Dcn. Thomas W. Connolly; Dcn. Thomas Malone; Dcn. Guy Donza, Pst. Assoc.; Evelyn Contaldi, DRE;

St. Raymond's School - t) 516-593-9010 Sr. Ruthanne Gypalo, I.H.M., Prin.;

ELMONT

St. Boniface - 631 Elmont Rd., Elmont, NY 11003 t) 516-354-0715 rectory@stbonelmont.com www.saintbonifaceelmont.com Rev. Eden Jean Baptiste, Assoc. Pst.; Rev. John Victor, O.M.I., Assoc. Pst.; Rev. Joseph Baidoo, Pst.; Dcn. Dominique Silien; Nancy Cosgrove, DRE;

St. Vincent de Paul - 1500 de Paul St., Elmont, NY 11003; Mailing: c/o St. Catherine of Sienna RC Church, 33 New Hyde Park Rd., Franklin Square, NY 11010 t) 516-352-2127 parishoffice@stcatherineofsienna.org stcatherineofsienna.org Rev. Msgr. Richard M. Figliozzi, Admin.;

FARMINGDALE

St. Kilian - 485 Conklin St., Farmingdale, NY 11735 t) 516-694-0633 Rev. Msgr. Mark P. Rowan, Pst.; Rev. George Oppong Afriyie, Assoc. Pst.; Rev. Jose Luis Tenas, Assoc. Pst.; Dcn. Frank D. Barone; Dcn. Lucio

Cotone; Dcn. Francis P. Marino; Dcn. George Owen; Dcn. William Weiss Jr.; Dcn. Mark Wetzel; Most Rev. John C. Dunne, In Res.; Rev. Augustine Fernando (India), In Res.; Kathleen Singleton, DRE; Claire Stiglic, DRE; Edward Fronckwicz, Bus. Mgr.; Paul C. Phinney, Dir.;

Parish Social Ministry/Outreach - 140 Elizabeth St., Farmingdale, NY 11735 t) 516-756-9656 Nina Petersen, Dir.;

FARMINGVILLE

Church of the Resurrection - 50 Granny Rd., Farmingville, NY 11738 t) 631-696-0270 x25 religioused@resurrectionrcchurch.org Rev. Gonzalo Oajaca-Lopez, Pst.; Dcn. Vincent Barreca Jr.; Dcn. Juan Diaz; Dcn. James DiGiovanna; Laurie Thorp, DRE;

FLORAL PARK

St. Hedwig's - One Depan Ave., Floral Park, NY 11001 t) 631-875-8413 contact@sthedwigfloralpark.org Rev. Piotr Rozek, Admin.; Rev. Msgr. Edward Wawerski, In Res.; Krzysztof Gospodarzec, DRE;

Our Lady of Victory - 2 Floral Pkwy., Floral Park, NY 11001-3198 t) 516-352-0510 (CRP); 516-354-0482 tfusco@olvfpny.org www.olvfpny.org Rev. Thomas M. Fusco, Pst.; Rev. Rafal Borowiejski, Assoc. Pst.; Rev. John V. O'Farrell, Pastor Emer.; Dcn. Lawrence P. Mulligan; Christine Fuchs, DRE;

Our Lady of Victory School - 2 Bellmore St., Floral Park, NY 11001 t) 516-352-4466; 516-354-2150 paugello5628@olvfp.org olvfp.org Margaret M. Augello, Prin.;

FRANKLIN SQUARE

St. Catherine of Sienna - 33 New Hyde Park Rd., Franklin Square, NY 11010 t) 516-352-0146 ffministry@stcatherineofsienna.org; parishoffice@stcatherineofsienna.org stcatherineofsienna.org Rev. Douglas R. Arcoleo, Pst.; Rev. Anthony Bonsu, Assoc. Pst.; Dcn. Joseph Benincasa; Dcn. Frank Gonzalez; Deneen Vukelic, DRE; CRP Stds.: 678

FREEPORT

Our Holy Redeemer - 37 S. Ocean Ave., Freeport, NY 11520 t) 516-546-1057 (CRP); 516-378-0665 ohrreled@optimum.net; ohr2003@optimum.net www.ohrfreeport.com/ Joanne Stuhlinger, CRE; Ana Sullivan, Outreach & Thrift Shop Coordinator; Rev. Christopher Nowak, Pst.; Rev. Carlos Urrego Arenas, Assoc. Pst.; Dcn. Bruce A. Burnham; Braulio Cacao, Pst. Assoc.; Kathleen Weston, Bus. Mgr.; CRP Stds.: 332

GARDEN CITY

St. Anne - 35 Dartmouth St., Garden City, NY 11530 t) 516-488-1032 (Faith Formation Office); 516-352-5904 (Office) parishoffice@stannesgc.org www.stannesgc.org Rev. Msgr. Thomas J. Harold, Pst.; Rev. Cody W. Bobick, Assoc. Pst.; Rev. Nicholas Frimpong, Assoc. Pst.; Dcn. Michael Boldizar; Dcn. Robert McCarthy; CRP Stds.: 900

St. Anne School - 25 Dartmouth St., Garden City, NY 11530 t) 516-352-1205 Gene Fennell, Prin.;

St. Joseph's - 130 Fifth St., Garden City, NY 11530 t) (516) 747-3535 www.stjosephchurchgc.org Rev. Msgr. James P. Swiader, Pst.; Rev. Prasanna Costa Warnakulasuriya, Assoc. Pst.; Rev. Hilary Nwajagu, Assoc. Pst.; Dcn. Jack McKenna, Dir.; Lisa Spohr, DRE; Joseph Cangialosi, Dir.; CRP Stds.: 1,100

St. Joseph's School - 450 Franklin Ave., Garden City, NY 11530 t) 516-747-2730 Regina A. Cioffi, Prin.; Brian Colomban, Prin.; Anna Maria Sirianni, Dir.;

GLEN COVE

St. Patrick's - 235 Glen St., Glen Cove, NY 11542 t) 516-671-7223 Rev. Gabriel Rach, Pst.; Rev. Leonard Mozie, Assoc. Pst.; Rev. Dom Elias Carr, Can.Reg., In Res.; Dcn. Frank Borchardt; Dcn. Juan Guilfu; Frances Howlett, Music Min.; Bernadette Heym, DRE;

For Hispanic Ministry - t) 516-759-6039

St. Rocco - 18 Third St., Glen Cove, NY 11542 Rev. Dom Daniel Stephen Nash, Can.Reg., Pst.;

GLEN HEAD

St. Hyacinth - 319 Cedar Swamp Rd., Glen Head, NY 11545 t) 516-676-0361 x123 Rev. Marian Bicz, In Res.; Rev. Bartlomiej Koba, Admin.; Eileen Meserole, DRE;

GREAT NECK

St. Aloysius - 592 Middle Neck Rd., Great Neck, NY 11023 t) 516-482-5660 Rev. Rene O. Tapel (Philippines), Pst.;

GREENLAWN

St. Francis of Assisi - 29 Clay Pitts Rd., Greenlawn, NY 11740; Mailing: 29 Northgate Dr., Greenlawn, NY 11740 t) 631-754-6436 (CRP); 631-757-7435 stfrancisgreenlawn@gmail.com www.stfrancisgreenlawn.org Rev. Peter Kaczmarek, Pst.; Rev. Francois Eale, Chap.; Dcn. James Byrne; Dcn. Jean Cantave; Dcn. Allan Longo;

GREENPORT

St. Agnes - 523 Front St., Greenport, NY 11944 t) 631-477-1422 (CRP); 631-477-0048 rectory@optonline.net www.saintagnesgreenport.org Rev. Richard P. Hoerning, Pst.;

HAMPTON BAYS

St. Rosalie's - 31 E. Montauk Hwy., Hampton Bays, NY 11946 t) 631-728-9248 (CRP); 631-728-9461 parish@saintrosalie.com www.saintrosalie.com Rev. Steve Maddaloni, Pst.; Rev. Henry Leuthardt, Assoc. Pst.; Dcn. Christopher Ervin, Pst. Assoc.; Dcn. James E. Leopard, DRE; CRP Stds.: 265

Mission - Montauk Hwy. & Walnut Ave., East Quogue, NY 11946

HAUPPAUGE

St. Thomas More - 115 Kings Hwy., Hauppauge, NY 11788-4221 t) 631-234-5551; 631-234-0397 (CRP) stmreled@yahoo.com; rectory@stmli.org www.stmli.org Rev. Antony Asir, Pst.; Dcn. Matt Surico; Dcn. Edward R. Vigneaux; Dcn. Robert Weisz; Mary Ellen Carroll, DRE;

HEMPSTEAD

St. John Chrysostom Malankara Mission - 115 Greenwich St., Hempstead, NY 11550 t) 516-775-1779 Rev. Joseph Nedumankuzhiyil (India), Admin.;

St. Ladislaus - 18 Richardson Pl., Hempstead, NY 11550 Rev. Mariusz Gorazd, Admin.;

Our Lady of Loretto - 104 Greenwich St., Hempstead, NY 11550 t) 516-483-3643 Rev. Luis M. Romero, M.Id, Pst.; Rev. Felipe R. Vazquez, Assoc. Pst.; Dcn. Juan Perez; Cecilia Bradley, DRE;

HEWLETT

St. Joseph's - 1346 Broadway, Hewlett, NY 11557 t) 516-569-6080 Rev. Thomas Moriarty Jr., Pst.; Rev. James F. Drew, Assoc. Pst.; Rev. Nobert D'Souza, Chap.; Dcn. Thomas Costello; Dcn. Daniel Otton; Julianne Markey, DRE;

HICKSVILLE

Holy Family - 5 Fordham Ave., Hicksville, NY 11801; Mailing: 17 Fordham Ave., Hicksville, NY 11801 t) 516-938-3846 response@holyfamilyparishny.org www.holyfamilyparishny.org Rev. Christopher Sullivan, Pst.; Rev. Fortunatus Mugisha, Assoc. Pst.; Rev. Francis Sam Sarpong, In Res.; Dcn. David J. White; Dcn. John H. McGonigle; Dcn. Jose A. Contreras, Pst. Min./Coord.; Colleen Mosley, DRE; Katya Syrochkina, Music Min.; Steven Benner, Youth Min.; CRP Stds.: 375

Holy Family School - (Grades PreSchool-8) 25 Fordham Ave., Hicksville, NY 11801 ccalabro@hfsli.org hfsli.org Adrianna Aceste, Prin.; Stds.: 244; Lay Tchrs.: 17

Outreach - 15 Fordham Ave., Hicksville, NY 11801 t) (516) 938-3846 x331 outreach@holyfamilyparishny.org

St. Ignatius Loyola - 129 Broadway, Hicksville, NY 11801 t) 516-931-0056; 516-935-6873 (CRP) stignatius1859@aol.com www.stignatiushicksville.org Rev. Shibi Pappan, OIC, Pst.; Rev. Francis A. Samuel, O.C.I., Res. Assoc.; Dcn. Jose A. Contreras; Dcn. Mario Gomez; Dcn. George A. Mais Jr.; Nivia Soto, Religious Education Coordinator; Joseph Samodulski, Dcn. Jose Contreras; CRP Stds.: 223

Our Lady of Mercy - 500 S. Oyster Bay Rd., Hicksville, NY 11801 t) 516-681-1228 religioused@olmrcc.com Rev. John J. McCartney, Pst.; Rev. Nasir Gulfam, Assoc. Pst.; Kevin Kwasnik, Youth Min.;

Our Lady of Mercy School - 520 S. Oysterbay Rd., Hicksville, NY 11801 t) 516-433-7040 jharrigan@olmshicks.org Jane Harrigan, Prin.;

HOLBROOK

Good Shepherd - 1370 Grundy Ave., Holbrook, NY 11741 t) 631-981-3889 (CRP); 631-588-7689 gsspiritualformation@gmail.com; goodshepherdstaf@aol.com www.goodshepherdrcchurch.org Most Rev. Robert J Coyle, Pst.; Rev. Gerald Cestare, Assoc. Pst.; Rev. Gennaro J. DiSpigno, Assoc. Pst.; Rev. Rudy Pesongco, Assoc. Pst.; Rev. Msgr. Gerard A. Ringenback, Pastor Emer.; Rev. Msgr. Thomas L. Spadaro, Pastor Emer.; Dcn. John Newhall; Dcn. Thomas O'Connor; Christine Fitzgerald, Youth Min.; Sr. Ellen Zak, C.S.F.N., DRE; Annmarie Camporeale, Bus. Mgr.;

HUNTINGTON

St. Patrick's - 400 Main St., Huntington, NY 11743-3208 t) 631-385-3311; 631-385-3311 x350 (CRP); 631-385-3311 x351 (CRP) rectory@stpathunt.org; reducation@stpathunt.org stpathuntington.org Rev. Msgr. Steven Camp, Pst.; Rev. Michael Bissex, Assoc. Pst.; Rev. Noel Sixon, Assoc. Pst.; Rev. Daniel Neyoh, Chap.; Dcn. Dale Bonocore; Dcn. William Casey; Dcn. Gerard Rorke; Dcn. Michael Whitcomb; Linda Oristano, DRE;

St. Patrick's School - (Grades PreK-8) 360 Main St., Huntington, NY 11743-3298 t) 631-385-3322 stpathunt.org Sr. Maureen McDade, Prin.;

HUNTINGTON STATION

St. Hugh of Lincoln - 21 E. Ninth St., Huntington Station, NY 11746 t) 631-271-6081 Rev. Robert J. Smith, Pst.; Rev. Nelson Adan Marquez Salvador, Assoc. Pst.; Rev. Khoa T. Le, Chap.; Dcn. Richard Bilella; Dcn. Edward W. Billia; Dcn. Luis Giraldo; Dcn. Vito B. Taranto; Helen Schramm, DRE;

Parish Center - 1450 New York Ave., Huntington Station, NY 11746

INWOOD

Our Lady of Good Counsel - 68 Wanser Ave., Inwood, NY 11096 t) 516-239-0662 Rev. Thomas Moriarty Jr., Pst.; Rev. Lee Descoteaux, In Res.; Maureen O'Louglin, DRE;

ISLAND PARK

Sacred Heart - 282 Long Beach Rd., Island Park, NY 11558 t) 516-431-7877 (CRP); 516-432-0655 ship282@verizon.net www.sacredheartislandpark.com Rev. Msgr. John J. Tutone, Pst.; Carmel Caracciolo, DRE;

ISLIP TERRACE

St. Peter the Apostle - 70 Rockaway St., Islip Terrace, NY 11752; Mailing: PO Box 9, Islip Terrace, NY 11752-0009 t) 631-277-9448 stpeters11752@gmail.com stpeterit.org Rev. Anthony Iaconis, Pst.; Dcn. Everett Lackenbauer; CRP Stds.: 143

KINGS PARK

St. Joseph's - 59 Church St., Kings Park, NY 11754 t) 631-269-4383 (CRP); 631-269-6635 info@stjoekp.com www.stjosephskp.org Rev. Peter Dugandzic, Pst.; Rev. Patrick Osei-Poku, Assoc. Pst.; Rev. Thomas W. Tassone, Assoc. Pst.; Rev. Francis P. Vattakudiyil, Assoc. Pst.; Dcn. John E. Trodden;

LAKE RONKONKOMA

St. Elizabeth Ann Seton - 800 Portion Rd., Lake Ronkonkoma, NY 11779 t) 631-737-4388; 631-737-8915 (CRP) steas@optonline.net; mhahnstliz@optonline.net steas.org Rev. Allan Sikorski, Pst.; Michele Hahn, DRE;

LEVITTOWN

St. Bernard - 3100 Hempstead Tpke., Levittown, NY 11756 reled@stbernardchurch.org Rev. Msgr. Ralph Sommer, Pst.; Rev. Joseph E. Nohs, Assoc. Pst.; Rev. Onyekachi Innocent Duru, Chap.; Dcn. John Blakeney; Dcn. James W. Flannery; Susan Martin, DRE;

LINDENHURST

Our Lady of Perpetual Help - 210 S. Wellwood Ave., Lindenhurst, NY 11757-4989 t) 631-226-7725

akleinlaut@oloph.org; ccarrano@oloph.org www.olphlindenhurst.com Rev. Msgr. Joseph DeGrocco, Pst.; Rev. Fidelis Ezeani (Nigeria), Assoc. Pst.; Rev. Emmanuel Okonkwo, Assoc. Pst.; Rev. Frank Zero, Assoc. Pst.; Dcn. Robert A. Becker; Dcn. William Crosby; Dcn. Douglas Smith; Christopher Reilly, Music Min.; April Kleinlaut, DRE; Jill Marie Delano, Bus. Mgr.; CRP Stds.: 600

LONG BEACH

St. Ignatius Martyr - 721 W. Broadway, Long Beach, NY 11561 t) 516-432-6788 Rev. Msgr. Donald M. Beckmann, Pst.; Rev. Ryszard Ficek, Assoc. Pst.; Dcn. Philip Newton; Sr. Diane Morgan, O.P., Pst. Assoc.; Gail Milne, DRE;

St. Mary of the Isle - 315 E. Walnut St., Long Beach, NY 11561 t) 516-432-1320 Rev. Brian P. Barr, Pst.; Rev. Anthony Osuagwu (Nigeria), Assoc. Pst.; Andrew Santos, DRE; Vicki Ayala-Solis, Bus. Mgr.;

LYNBROOK

Our Lady of Peace - 25 Fowler Ave., Lynbrook, NY 11563 t) 516-593-5150 srgracem@olplynbrook.com Rev. Richard T. Stelter, Pst.; Rev. Mathew Abraham, Chap.; Rev. Anthony Okolo, Chap.; Dcn. Thomas J. Evrard; Dcn. Kevin McCormack;

Our Lady of Peace School - 21 Flower Ave., Lynbrook, NY 11563 t) 516-593-4884 olpschool@optonline.net

MALVERNE

Our Lady of Lourdes - 65 Wright Ave., Malverne, NY 11565 t) 516-599-7222 (CRP); 516-599-1269 ollreld@gmail.com; rectoryoffice@ollchurchmalverne.org www.ollchurchmalverne.org Rev. Michael F. Duffy, Pst.; Rev. Richard R. Donovan, In Res.; Rev. Onuegbu C. Patrick, Chap.; Rev. Eugene Chi Jioke Umeyor, Chap.; Dcn. Richard H. Portuese; Mary Lasar, DRE;

Our Lady of Lourdes School - 76 Park Blvd., Malverne, NY 11565 t) 516-599-7328 Mary Carmel Murphy, Prin.;

MANHASSET

St. Mary's - 1300 Northern Blvd., Manhasset, NY 11030 t) 516-627-4028 (CRP); 516-627-0385 information@stmary.ws stmary.ws/ Rev. Robert A. Romeo, Pst.; Rev. Jude Dioka, Assoc. Pst.; Rev. Jiha Lim, Assoc. Pst.;

St. Mary's Elementary School - 1340 Northern Blvd., Manhasset, NY 11030 t) 516-627-0184 www.stmary11030.org (Elementary) Sarah de Venoge, Prin.;

St. Mary's High School - 51 Clapham Ave., Manhasset, NY 11030 t) 516-627-2711 www.stmary.ws/highschool (Coed)

MANORVILLE

Sts. Peter & Paul - 781 Wading River Rd., Manorville, NY 11949-1012 t) 631-208-1978 pastor@saintspeterandpaul.org; secretary@saintspeterandpaul.org www.saintspeterandpaul.org Rev. Matthew Considine, SMM, Pst.; Dcn. Vincent Sweeney; CRP Stds.: 99

MASSAPEQUA

The Roman Catholic Church of Saint Rose of Lima - 2 Bayview Ave., Massapequa, NY 11758-7299 t) 516-541-1712 (CRP); 516-798-4992; 516-541-1546 (School) religioused@srolchurch.org; michelez@srolchurch.org www.srolchurch.org Rev. Gerard J. Gentleman, Pst.; Rev. Allan Arneaud, Assoc. Pst.; Rev. Anthony Saliba, Assoc. Pst.; Dcn. Sean Cotter; Dcn. Thomas Elliott; Dcn. Michael Gambardella; Dcn. Francis B. McGuinness; CRP Stds.: 2,003

St. Rose of Lima School - (Grades PreK-8) 4704 Merrick Rd., Massapequa, NY 11758 kgallina@stroseschool.net www.stroseschool.net Brian Jensen, Prin.;

MASSAPEQUA PARK

Our Lady of Lourdes - 855 Carmans Rd., Massapequa Park, NY 11762 t) 516-541-3270; 516-799-5179 (CRP) www.ollmp.org Rev. Msgr. James P. Lisante, Pst.; Rev. Kevin Thompson, Assoc. Pst.; Dcn. Ferdinando Ferrara; Dcn. Frank Gariboldi; Dcn. Domenick Valdaro; Donna Kesselman, DRE; John Brosnan, Bus. Mgr.;

MASTIC BEACH

St. Jude - 89 Overlook Dr., Mastic Beach, NY 11951 t) 631-281-2835 (CRP); 631-281-5743 x12 faithformation@stjudemb.org; rectory@stjudemb.org www.stjudemb.org Rev. John David Ryan, Pst.; Dcn. John Gagliardi; Eileen C. Will, DRE; CRP Stds.: 383

MEDFORD

St. Sylvester - 68 Ohio Ave., Medford, NY 11763 t) 631-475-4506 parishoffice@stsylvesterli.org; fmcmahon@stsylvesterli.org www.stsylvesterli.org Rev. Dennis Suglia, Pst.; Dcn. Joseph Mystkowski; Dcn. George J. Riegger; Frances McMahon, DRE; Lori Zito, Dir.; CRP Stds.: 520

MELVILLE

St. Elizabeth of Hungary - 175 Wolf Hill Rd., Melville, NY 11747 t) 631-271-4455 center@stelizabeth.org www.stelizabeth.org Rev. Irinel Racos, Pst.; Dcn. John Failla; Francis Serpico, Youth Min.; Elizabeth Teixerira, Youth Min.; John Fruner, DRE; Lois Szypot, DRE; Harry Perepeluk, Bus. Mgr.; Jeanne Victor, Mem.; Virgil Barkauskas, Dir.; Maryann Giannettino, Dir.;

MERRICK

Cure of Ars Roman Catholic Church - 2323 Merrick Ave., Merrick, NY 11566 t) 516-623-1400 x101 (CRP); 516-623-1400 secretary@cureofarschurch.org www.cureofarschurch.org Rev. Msgr. Francis J. Caldwell, Pst.; Rev. Henry Leuthardt, Assoc. Pst.; Dcn. Ronald Federici; Rev. Zachary Callahan, In Res.; Carol Ng, Music Min.; Patricia A. Ryan, Music Min.; Vladimir Tiagunov, Music Min.; Nicolas Baylis, Youth Min.; Steven McClernon, Youth Min.; Lee Hlavacek, DRE; Ellen Zafonte, DRE; William Geasor, Bus. Mgr.; Lisa Hudson, Parish Social Ministry/Stewardship;

MINEOLA

Corpus Christi - 155 Garfield Ave., Mineola, NY 11501 t) 516-746-1223 rectory@corpuschristi-mineola.net www.corpuschristi-mineola.net Rev. Malcolm J. Burns, Pst.; Rev. Ngozichukwu Chimezie, Assoc. Pst.; Dcn. Brian J. Mannix; Most Rev. Andrzej J. Zglejszewski, In Res.; Susan Anaischik, DRE;

MONTAUK

St. Therese of Lisieux - 67 S. Essex St., Montauk, NY 11954; Mailing: P.O. Box 5027, Montauk, NY 11954 t) 631-668-2460 (CRP); 631-668-2200 sttheresedesk@optimum.net Rev. Thomas P. Murray, Pst.; Louise Carman, DRE; Christopher Murray, Bus. Mgr.;

Day Care/Nursery School - t) 631-668-5353 (2 & 3 years old)

NESCONSET

Church of the Holy Cross - 95 Old Nichols Rd., Nesconset, NY 11767 t) 631-265-2200 x12 hcreled@optonline.net Rev. Michael F. Holzmann, Pst.; Judith Pickel, Pst. Assoc.; Ellen Fox, DRE; Dcn. Ralph Rivera, Pst. Min./Coord.;

NEW HYDE PARK

Holy Spirit - 16 S. 6th St, New Hyde Park, NY 11040 t) 516-354-2363 Rev. Frank M. Grieco, Pst.; Dcn. Douglas Ferreiro;

Notre Dame - 45 Mayfair Rd., New Hyde Park, NY 11040 t) 516-437-5604 (CRP); 516-352-7203 notredameparish@optonline.net www.notredamenhp.com Rev. Joseph Scolaro, Pst.; Rev. Joseph Mappilamattel, Assoc. Pst.; Dcn. Frank Kurre; Dcn. Thomas Lemme; Rev. John Denniston, In Res.; Sr. Mary Jane Coleman, R.S.M., DRE;

Notre Dame School - 25 Mayfair Rd., New Hyde Park, NY 11040 t) 516-354-5618 Caryn Durkin Flores, Prin.;

NORTH MERRICK

Sacred Heart - 720 Merrick Ave., North Merrick, NY 11566 t) 516-379-1356; 516-868-9406 (CRP) frontdesk@sacredheartnm.org www.sacredheartnm.org Rev. Stephen J. Brigandi, Pst.; Rev. Peter Sarpong, Assoc. Pst.; Rev. Kevin Thompson, Assoc. Pst.; Maryann Specht, DRE;

NORTHPORT

St. Philip Neri - 344 Main St., Northport, NY 11768 t) 631-261-2485 x108 Rev. Msgr. Peter C. Dooley, Pst.; Dcn. Richard Becker; Patricia Merenda, DRE; Linda Oristano, DRE;

OCEAN BEACH

Our Lady of the Magnificat - 36 Bungalow Walk, Ocean Beach, NY 11770; Mailing: P.O. Box 445, Ocean Beach, NY 11770 t) 631-860-8962; 631-423-0483 x114 oceanbeachmagnificat@yahoo.com; rhenning@icseminary.edu Rev. Edward M. Sheridan, Admin.;

OCEANSIDE

St. Anthony - 110 Anchor Ave., Oceanside, NY 11572 t) (516) 764-0048 reception@sacli.org www.sacli.org Rev. Vincent L. Biagi, S.J., Assoc. Pst.; Rev. Kirk R. Reynolds, S.J., Assoc. Pst.; Kathy Logan, DRE; Rev. James Donovan, S.J., Pst.; Rev. Bret Stockdale, S.J., Assoc. Pst.; Dcn. Philip E. Savarese; Daniel Gibbons, Music Min.; Dcn. John O'Connor, Bus. Mgr.; CRP Stds.: 850

OYSTER BAY

St. Dominic's - 93 Anstice St., Oyster Bay, NY 11771 coneil@stdoms.org; cmangiarotti@stdoms.org Rev. Msgr. Thomas M. Coogan, Pst.; Rev. Vincent J. Ritchie, S.J., Assoc. Pst.; Rev. Msgr. Robert J. Batule, In Res.; Carolyn Mangiarotti, DRE; Cathy O'Neil, DRE;

Elementary School - 35 School St., Oyster Bay, NY 11771 t) 516-922-4233 esorge7485@stdomsob.org Ronald Martorelli, Prin.;

High School - 110 Anstice St., Oyster Bay, NY 11771 t) 516-922-4888 mchirichella@stdoms.org

PATCHOGUE

St. Francis de Sales - 7 Amity St., Patchogue, NY 11772 t) 631-289-4339 sanfraninpatch@hotmail.com Rev. Steven J. Hannafin, Pst.; Rev. Patrick J. Whitney, In Res.; Dcn. Francisco Diaz-Granados; Dcn. Martin McIndoe; Dcn. Robert Mongillo; Elaine Heschl, DRE;

Our Lady of Mt. Carmel - 495 New North Ocean Ave., Patchogue, NY 11772 t) 631-289-7327 (CRP); 631-475-4739 x101 hreid@drvc.org www.olmcpatchogue.org Rev. Henry W. Reid, Pst.; Dcn. Anthony Graviano; Dcn. Robert Lyon;

PLAINVIEW

St. Pius X - 1 St. Pius X Ct., Plainview, NY 11803 t) 516-822-8348 (CRP); 516-938-3956 www.stpiusxrc.com Rev. Valentine D. Rebello (India), Pst.; Rev. Chux Okochi; Dcn. John F. Burkart; Teresa Arrigo, Music Min.; Anne Bantleon, Pst. Assoc.; Salvatore Spano, Pst. Assoc.; Gail Gomula, DRE; Steve Rhoads, Youth Min.;

POINT LOOKOUT

Our Lady of the Miraculous Medal - 75 Parkside Dr., Point Lookout, NY 11569; Mailing: P.O. Box 20, Point Lookout, NY 11569 t) 516-432-8074 (CRP); 516-431-2772 relegioused@olmmc.com; rectory@olmmc.com www.olmmc.com Rev. Brian P. Barr, Pst.; Rev. Anthony Osuagwu (Nigeria), Assoc. Pst.; Rev. Msgr. James M. McNamara, In Res.; Georgette Levesque, DRE;

PORT JEFFERSON

Infant Jesus - 110 Myrtle Ave., Port Jefferson, NY 11777 t) 631-473-0165; 631-928-0447; 631-331-6045 rectory@infantjesus.org; religiouseducation@infantjesus.org www.infantjesus.org Rev. Patrick M. Riegger, Pst.; Rev. Francis Lasrado, Assoc. Pst.; Rev. Rolando Ticllasuca (Peru), Assoc. Pst.; Rev. Matthew Udobi, Chap.; Dcn. Michael Byrne; Dcn. Kenneth Clifford; Dcn. Robert A. Kruse; Dcn. William J. Powers; Dcn. Carlito Roman; Dcn. Richard E. Waldmann; Rev. Henry Vas, O.F.M.Cap., In Res.; Corrine Addiss, DRE;

PORT JEFFERSON STATION

St. Gerard Majella - 300 Terryville Rd., Port Jefferson Station, NY 11776 t) 631-928-2550 Rev. Gregory Rannazzisi, Pst.; Rev. Samuel Pius Aseleku, Chap.; Dcn. Vincent Beckles; Dcn. John Panzica; John Aleksak, DRE;

PORT WASHINGTON

Our Lady of Fatima - 6 Cottonwood Rd., Port Washington, NY 11050 t) 516-944-8322 Dcn. Arthur A. Candido, Admin.; Sr. Kathy Somerville, O.P., Pst. Assoc.; Sr. Gerri O'Neil, O.P., DRE; Barbara Minerva, Bus. Mgr.;

St. Peter of Alcantara - 1327 Port Washington Blvd., Port Washington, NY 11050 t) 516-883-5584 (CRP); 516-883-6675 pastor@stpeterofalcantara.org; susan@stpeterofalcantara.org stpeterofalcantara.org Rev. Msgr. Robert J. Clerkin, Pst.; Rev. Nestor Watin, Assoc. Pst.; Rev. Khoa T. Le, Par. Vicar; Dcn. Joseph Bianco, Pst. Assoc.; Dcn. John Hogan, Supt.; Mary Christine Thomsen, DRE;

IHM Spirituality Center - 1317 Port Washington Blvd., Port Washington, NY 11050 t) 516-883-2782 marynuzz@aol.com Mary F. Nuzzolese, Dir.;

RIVERHEAD

St. Isidore - 622 Pulaski St., Riverhead, NY 11901 t) 631-727-2114 sisidore@optonline.net saintisidoreriverhead.org Rev. Mikolaj Socha, O.S.P.P.E., Pst. Assoc.; Dcn. Michael A. Bonocore; Friar Krzysztof Drybka (Poland), Pst.; CRP Stds.: 143

St. John the Evangelist - 546 St. John's Pl., Riverhead, NY 11901 t) 631-727-6774 (CRP); 631-727-2030 x10 stjohnrelformation@gmail.com; stjohnriverhead@aol.com www.saintjohnriverhead.org Rev. Lawrence Duncklee, Pst.; Dcn. William Austin; Dcn. Peter F. Schultz; Dcn. Dan Waloski; CRP Stds.: 509

ROCKVILLE CENTRE

St. Agnes Cathedral - 29 Quealy Pl., Rockville Centre, NY 11570 t) 516-678-2306 (CRP); 516-766-0205 jlong@stagnescathedral.org; parishoffice@stagnescathedral.org www.stagnescathedral.org Most Rev. John O. Barres, Pst.; Rev. Msgr. William E. Koenig, Rector; Rev. Alessandro da Luz, Assoc. Pst.; Rev. Vian Ntegerej'Imana, Assoc. Pst.; Rev. German Villabon, O.S.A., Assoc. Pst.; Dcn. Thomas McDaid; Rev. John D. McCarthy, In Res.; Rev. Msgr. Robert O. Morrissey, In Res.; Most Rev. William Francis Murphy, In Res.; Rev. Msgr. James C. Vlaun, In Res.; Joseph R. Long, DRE;

St. Agnes Cathedral School - (Grades K-8) 70 Clinton Ave., Rockville Centre, NY 11570 t) 516-678-5550 cstjohn5546@stagnes-school.org stagnes-school.org Cecilia St. John, Prin.;

Campus Parish of Long Island - ; Mailing: P.O. Box 9023, Rockville Centre, NY 11571 t) 516-678-5800 Rev. Eric R. Fasano, Pst.; Ellen Zafonte, DRE;

ROCKY POINT

St. Anthony of Padua - 614 Rte. 25A, Rocky Point, NY 11778 t) 631-821-0872 (CRP); 631-744-2609 stasrp@optonline.net Rev. Lennard Sabio (Philippines), Pst.; Sr. Mary Schoberg, I.H.M., Pst. Assoc.; Sr. Phylis O'Dowd, O.P., DRE;

RONKONKOMA

St. Joseph - 45 Church St., Ronkonkoma, NY 11779-3300 t) 631-588-8456; 631-981-1805 (CRP) info@stjoronk.org stjosephronkonkoma.org Rev. Michael J. Rieder, Pst.; Rev. Vitus Mbamalu, Assoc. Pst.; Dcn. William Dobbins; Dcn. Michael Devenney; Dcn. Matthew Yellico; Dcn. Edward Grieb, Bus. Mgr.; Maryanne Trezza, DRE;

ROOSEVELT

Queen of the Most Holy Rosary - 196 W. Centennial Ave., Roosevelt, NY 11575 t) 516-623-1391 cherylwhite@optonline.net Rev. Joseph Baidoo, Pst.; Rev. Cesar Bejarano, Assoc. Pst.; Dcn. Thomas Jackson; Dcn. Clinton Lewis; Elena A. Powers, Music Min.; Cheryl White, DRE;

ROSLYN

St. Mary's - 110 Bryant Ave., Roslyn, NY 11576 t) 516-621-6798 Rev. Msgr. Timothy Valentine, Pst.; Nora Toal, DRE;

SAG HARBOR

St. Andrew's - 122 Division St., Sag Harbor, NY 11963-3154 t) 631-725-0123 frsgalfri@aol.com Rev. Peter Devaraj, S.A.C., Pst.; Rev. Manuel Zuzarte, Assoc. Pst.;

SALTAIRE

Our Lady Star of the Sea, Mission Chapel - 210 Pilot Walk, Saltaire, NY 11706 (Summer Mission) Rev. Richard R. Viladesau, Admin.;

SAYVILLE

St. Lawrence the Martyr - 27 Handsome Ave., Sayville, NY 11782 t) 631-589-0042 mdavidson@stlawrencesayville.org; office@stlawrencesayville.org www.stlawrencesayville.org Rev. Brian Ingram, Pst.; Rev. Thomas J. Pers, Assoc. Pst.; Dcn. Patrick LaBella; Joseph Mankowski, Music Min.; Jeanmarie Smith, Pst. Assoc.; Lorraine Magyar, Pst. Min./Coord.; Maria Davidson, DRE; Christopher Koch, Bus. Mgr.;

SEA CLIFF

St. Boniface Martyr - 145 Glen Ave., Sea Cliff, NY 11579 t) 516-671-0418 (CRP); 516-676-0676 stbonccd@gmail.com; stbonchurch@gmail.com Rev. Kevin J. Dillon, Pst.; Rev. Azubuike Anthony Clifford Igwegbe, Chap.; Dcn. Tom Fox; Chris Mandato, Youth Min.; Karen Croce, DRE; Eileen Krieb, Bus. Mgr.; Jeff Schneider, Dir.;

SEAFORD

St. James - 80 Hicksville Rd., Seaford, NY 11783 t) 516-796-2979 mmirkow@stjamesrcchurch.org; gdrost@stjamesrcchurch.org Rev. John Derasmo, Pst.; Rev. Innocent Mbaegbu, Assoc. Pst.; Rev. Francis Sam Sarpong, Assoc. Pst.; Dcn. Richard Brunner; Dcn. Chris Daniello; Alfred Allongo, Music Min.; Gina Drost, DRE; Marianne Mirkow, DRE;

Maria Regina - 3945 Jerusalem Ave., Seaford, NY 11783 t) 516-541-0921 (CRP); 516-798-2415 rderose@mariaregina.com www.mariaregina.com Rev. Frank M. Nelson, Pst.; Rev. Ignatius Okwuonu, Assoc. Pst.; Rev. Anthony Sebamalai, Assoc. Pst.; Dcn. Paul Neuhedel; Dcn. Joseph Oliva; Dcn. Gerald F. Whitfield; Rev. Msgr. Peter J Pflomm, Admin.; Alice Moran, DRE; Tina Rine, DRE;

Maria Regina School - t) 516-541-1229 Matthew Edward Scannapieco, Prin.;

St. William the Abbot - 2000 Jackson Ave., Seaford, NY 11783 t) 516-783-2528 (CRP); 516-785-1266 faithformation@stwilliam.org; information@stwilliam.org www.stwilliam.org Rev. Joseph H. Fitzgerald, Pst.; Dcn. Anthony M. Cedrone; Dcn. John Lynch; Dcn. Michael C. Metzdorff; Dcn. Joseph Tumbarello; CRP Stds.: 872

St. William the Abbot School - 2001 Jackson Ave., Seaford, NY 11783 t) 516-785-6784 ebricker5651@stwilliamtheabbot.net www.stwilliamtheabbot.net Elizabeth Bricker, Prin.;

SELDEN

St. Margaret of Scotland - 81 College Rd., Selden, NY 11784 t) 631-732-3131; 631-732-3131 x131 (CRP) jburtoff@saintmargaret.com; ff@saintmargaret.com www.saintmargaret.com Rev. James L. Wood, Pst.; Rev. Paul F. Butler, Assoc. Pst.; Dcn. Edward Hayes; Jackie Mirenda, CRE;

SETAUKET

St. James - 429 Rte. 25-A, Setauket, NY 11733 t) 631-941-4141 parish@stjamessetauket.org Rev. James P. Mannion Jr., Pst.; Rev. Robert Scheckenback, Assoc. Pst.; Rev. Mike Ezeatu, In Res.; Rev. John J. Fitzgerald, In Res.; Richard Foley, Liturgy Dir.; Miriam Salerno, Liturgy Dir.; Louise DiCarlo, DRE; Cristinia O'Keefe, RCIA Coord.; Kathy Vaeth, Dir.;

SHELTER ISLAND HEIGHTS

Our Lady of the Isle - 7 Prospect Ave., Shelter Island Heights, NY 11965; Mailing: P.O. Box 3027, Shelter Island Heights, NY 11965 t) 631-749-0001 ourladyoftheisle@gmail.com www.ourladyoftheisle.org Rev. Peter DeSanctis, Pst.; Ginny Gibbs, DRE; Sr. Kathryn Schlueter, C.S.J., DRE; Amber Brach-Williams, Bus. Mgr.; Patrick Clifford, Trustee; Frank Vecchio, Trustee; CRP Stds.: 40

SHOREHAM

St. Mark - 105 Randall Rd., Shoreham, NY 11786 t) 631-744-2800 pastor@sjbwr.org Rev. Msgr. Francis J. Schneider, Pst.; Rev. James Calledo, Assoc. Pst.; Rev. Thomas Tuite, Assoc. Pst.; Dcn. Igino Aceto; Lynn Fein, DRE;

SMITHTOWN

St. Patrick - 280 E. Main St., Smithtown, NY 11787 t) 631-265-2271; 631-724-7454 (CRP) rectory@stpatricksmithtown.org; stpatrickssmithtown@gmail.com www.stpatricksmithtown.org Rev. Msgr. Ellsworth R. Walden, Pst.; Rev. Michael Lombardi, Assoc. Pst.; Rev. Abraham Thannickal, OIC, Assoc. Pst.; Rev. Charles Okoye (Nigeria), Chap.; Dcn. Matthew Faughnan; Dcn. Jerry Reda; Rev. Frederick Hill, In Res.; Elaina Kedjierski, DRE; Margaret Soviero, DRE; Cynthia Marsh, Youth Admin.; Dianne Williams, Outreach Dir.; CRP Stds.: 834

St. Patrick School - 284 E. Main St., Smithtown, NY 11787 t) 631-724-0285 www.spssmith.org Barbara Pellerito, Prin.;

SOUND BEACH

St. Louis de Montfort - 75 New York Ave., Sound Beach, NY 11789-2506 t) 631-744-8566; 631-744-9515 (CRP) rdolson@sldmrc.org; elizabethteixeira717@gmail.com www.stlouisdm.org Rev. Msgr. Christopher J. Heller, Pst.; Dcn. Joseph T. Bartolotto; Dcn. Robert Mullane; Dcn. Gary F. Swane; Rev. Msgr. Donald Hanson, In Res.; Elizabeth Teixeira, Youth Min.; Michelle Mascolo, DRE;

SOUTHAMPTON

Basilica Church of Sacred Hearts of Jesus and Mary - 168 Hill St., Southampton, NY 11968 t) 631-283-0508 (CRP); 631-283-0097 parishoffice@shjmbasilica.org; mvetrano@drvc.org Rev. Michael A. Vetrano, Pst.; CRP Stds.: 147

Our Lady of Poland - 35 Maple St., Southampton, NY 11968 t) 631-283-0667 olpchurch@optonline.net www.olpchurch.org Dcn. James Ashe; Rev. Janusz Lipski, Pst.;

SOUTHOLD

St. Patrick's - 52125 Main Rd., Southold, NY 11971-1401; Mailing: P.O. Box 1117, Southold, NY 11971-1401 t) 631-765-2338 Rev. John J. Barrett, Pst.;

ST. JAMES

SS. Philip and James - 1 Carow Pl., St. James, NY 11780 t) 631-584-5454 info@sspj.org; religioused@sspj.org www.sspj.org Rev. Thomas J. Haggerty, Pst.; Rev. Joseph Lobo, Assoc. Pst.; Dcn. Ronald Blasius; Dcn. John Keenan; Barbara Luna, Admin.; CRP Stds.: 534

SS. Philip and James School - (Grades PreK-8) 359 Clinton Ave., St. James, NY 11780 t) 631-584-7896 danderson@sspjschool.net www.sspjschool.net Diane Anderson, Prin.;

SYOSSET

St. Edward Confessor - 205 Jackson Ave., Syosset, NY 11791-4218 t) 516-921-8030 x150; 516-921-8543 (CRP) mmaffeo@st-edwards.org; rpetti@st-edwards.org www.st-edwards.org Rev. Michael T. Maffeo, Pst.; Rev. Hyacinth Jemigbola (Nigeria), Assoc. Pst.; Rev. Celestine Nwosu, Assoc. Pst.; Rosemary Pettei, DRE; Dcn. Barry Croce, Pst. Min./Coord.; Dcn. James Murphy, Pst. Min./Coord.; CRP Stds.: 820

St. Edward Confessor School - 2 Teibrook Ave., Syosset, NY 11791 t) 516-921-7767 Vincent Albrecht, Prin.;

UNIONDALE

St. Martha - 546 Greengrove Ave., Uniondale, NY 11553 t) 516-481-2550 x311 (CRP); 516-481-2550 info@saintmartha.org www.saintmartha.org Rev. Rony Fabien, Pst.; Dcn. Hernst Bellevue, DRE; Marlene Jean-Baptiste, Dir.; Barbara Powell, Dir.;

VALLEY STREAM

Blessed Sacrament - 201 N. Central Ave., Valley Stream, NY 11580 Rev. Lawrence Onyegu, Admin.; Rev. Rejimon K. Benedict, Assoc. Pst.; Rev. Sathyan Naduviledath, O.I.C., In Res.; Randell Hochenberger, DRE;

Holy Name of Mary - 55 E. Jamaica Ave., Valley Stream, NY 11580 t) 516-825-1810 (CRP); 516-825-1450 holynamemary@aol.com Rev. David Regan, Pst.; Rev. Edmund Ani, Assoc. Pst.; Rev. Jose Luis Tenas, Assoc. Pst.; Dcn. James O'Hara; Dcn. Clyde Ruggieri; Dcn. Scott Baker, Bus. Mgr.; Sr. Margie Kelly, C.S.J., Parish Outreach Dir.; Cecilia Garzona, DRE; CRP Stds.: 499

Holy Name of Mary School - (Grades PreK-8) 90 S. Grove St., Valley Stream, NY 11580 t) 516-825-4009 Pamela Sanders, Prin.;

WADING RIVER

St. John Baptist - 1488 N. Country Rd., Wading River, NY 11792 t) 631-929-4339 office@sjbwr.org Rev. Msgr. Francis J. Schneider, Pst.; Dcn. Frederick Finter; Dcn. Vincent Pozzolano;

WANTAGH

St. Frances de Chantal - 1309 Wantagh Ave., Wantagh, NY 11793 t) 516-785-2333 x205 Rev. Seth N. Awo Doku, Pst.; Rev. Stanislaw Choragwicki, Assoc. Pst.; Rev. Aloysius Pakianather (Sri Lanka), Assoc. Pst.; Dcn. Thomas Anderson; Dcn. Anthony M. Cedrone; Dcn. Robert O'Donovan; Dcn. Joseph Torres; Lucy Creed, DRE; Donna Mugno, DRE;

WEST BABYLON

Our Lady of Grace - 666 Albin Ave., West Babylon, NY 11704 t) 631-661-9354 (CRP); 631-587-5185 faithformation@ourladyofgrace.net; parish@ourladyofgrace.net Rev. Joseph V. Davanzo, Pst.; Rev. Martin Adu Gyamfi, Assoc. Pst.; Rev. Gabriel Miah, Assoc. Pst.; Dcn. Brian Miller; Dcn. Irwin Saffran; Margaret Harnisch, DRE;

WEST HEMPSTEAD

St. Thomas, the Apostle - 24 Westminster Rd., West Hempstead, NY 11552 t) 516-538-7460 (CRP); 516-489-8585 stthomasap@optonline.net stthomasapostle.org Rev. Msgr. Francis J. Maniscalco, Pst.; Rev. Msgr. Michael Barimah-Apau, Assoc. Pst.; Rev. Anthony Cardone, Assoc. Pst.; Rev. Damian Umeokeke, Chap.; Dcn. Edward Cunningham; Dcn. John E. Ford; Dcn. Jacques Philippeaux; Rev. Msgr. John A. Alesandro, In Res.; Mary Ann Pellegrino, DRE;

St. Thomas, the Apostle School - 12 Westminster Rd., West Hempstead, NY 11552 t) 516-481-9310 Valerie Serpe, Prin.;

Chapel - 875 Hempstead Ave., West Hempstead, NY 11552

WEST ISLIP

Our Lady of Lourdes - 455 Hunter Ave., West Islip, NY 11795 t) 631-661-3224 parishoffice@ollchurch.org www.ollchurch.org Rev. Msgr. Brian J. McNamara, Pst.; Rev. Charles Mangano, Assoc. Pst.; Dcn. Thomas Lucie; Dcn. Richard P. Maher; Dcn. Jack Meehan; Dcn. John Teufel; Dcn. Nilo DeLeon; Sr. Nancy Campkin, DRE; Sr. Diane Liona, DRE; CRP Stds.: 1,043

WESTBURY

Church of Saint Brigid, Inc. - 85 Post Ave., Westbury, NY 11590 t) 516-334-0021 parish1@saintbrigid.net www.saintbrigid.net Rev. Anthony M. Stanganelli, Pst.; Rev. Romulo Cesar Gomez, Assoc. Pst.; Rev. Kulandairajan Savarimuthu, Assoc. Pst.; Dcn. Frank Pesce; Dcn. Darrell Buono, Vicar for Outreach Svcs.; Socorro Moreno, DRE; Robert Cammarata, Pastoral Assoc., Admin.; Sr. Ann Horn, O.P., Pastoral Assoc., Faith Formation;

St. Brigid/ Our Lady of Hope Regional School - 101 Maple Ave., Westbury, NY 11590 t) 516-333-0580 Paul P. Clagnaz, Prin.;

WESTHAMPTON BEACH

Immaculate Conception - 580 Main St., Westhampton Beach, NY 11978; Mailing: P.O. Box 1227, Westhampton Beach, NY 11978 t) 631-288-1423 parishoffice@iccwhb.org www.iccwhb.org Rev. Michael J. Bartholomew, Pst.; Dcn. Joseph Byrne; Dcn. Mark Herrmann; Rev. Richard P. Hoerning, In Res.; Kim DeVito, DRE; CRP Stds.: 366

WILLISTON PARK

St. Aidan's Church - 505 Willis Ave., Williston Park, NY 11596 t) 516-746-6585 x9404 Rev. Adrian McHugh (Ireland), Pst.; Rev. Kenneth Grooms, Assoc. Pst.; Rev. Solomon Obiechina Odinukwe, Assoc. Pst.; Rev. Edward M. Sheridan, In Res.; Dcn. Rudy Martin; Dcn. Salvatore Villani; Elaine Smith, DRE;

St. Aidan's Church School - (Grades N-3) 525 Willis Ave., Williston Park, NY 11596 Julie O'Connell, Prin.; Patti Serrano, Librn.;

WOODBURY

Holy Name of Jesus - 690 Woodbury Rd., Woodbury, NY 11797-2504 t) 516-921-2334 www.hnjchurch.net Rev. Msgr. Richard C. Bauhoff, Pst.; Rev. John Melapuram, Assoc. Pst.;

WYANDANCH

Our Lady of the Miraculous Medal - 1434 Straight Path, Wyandanch, NY 11798 t) 631-643-3364 Rev. William F. Brisotti, Pst.; Dcn. Alfredo Mora; Dcn. Irwin Saffran;

Gerald Ryan Outreach Center, Inc. - t) 631-643-7591 Naycha Florival, Youth Min.; Noelle Campbell, Dir.;

SCHOOLS: PRESCHOOL THRU HIGH SCHOOL

SCHOOLS

STATE OF NEW YORK

BELLMORE

St. Elizabeth Ann Seton Regional School - (PAR) (Grades N-8) 2341 Washington Ave., Bellmore, NY 11710 t) 516-785-5709 lgraziose@steas.com Supported by the following parishes: St. Barnabas, Bellmore; St. Raphael, East Meadow; Cure of Ars, Merrick; St. Frances de Chantal, Wantagh. Leeann Graziose, Prin.; Stds.: 301; Lay Tchrs.: 20

CENTER MORICHES

Our Lady, Queen of Apostles Regional School - (PAR) 2 St. Johns Pl., Center Moriches, NY 11934 t) 631-878-1033 derlanger@olqany.org Supported by: St. John Evangelist, Center Moriches; St. Jude, Mastic Beach; Immaculate Conception, Westhampton Beach; Ss. Peter & Paul, Manorville. Rev. John Sureau, Prin.;

CENTRAL ISLIP

Our Lady of Providence Regional School - (PAR) 82 Carleton Ave., Central Islip, NY 11722 t) 631-234-6324 lfitzpatrick@olprov.org www.olprov.org Supported by the following parishes: St. Anne, Brentwood; St. Luke, Brentwood; St. John of God, Central Islip; St. Peter the Apostle, Islip Terrace. Sharon Swift Imperati, Prin.;

COMMACK

Holy Family Regional School - (PAR) Indian Head Rd., Commack, NY 11725; Mailing: P.O. Box 729, Commack, NY 11725 t) 631-543-0202 hfrs@aol.com Supported by the following parishes: Christ the King, Commack; St. Matthew, Dix Hills; St. Thomas More, Hauppauge; St. Joseph, Kings Park. Brian Caltabiano, Prin.; Wendy Sokol, Librn.;

CUTCHOGUE

Our Lady of Mercy Regional School - (PAR) 27685 Main Rd., Cutchogue, NY 11935; Mailing: P.O. Box 970, Cutchogue, NY 11935 t) 631-734-5166 olm@olmregional.org www.olmregional.org Supported by the following parishes: Sacred Heart, Cutchogue; Our Lady of Ostrabrama, Cutchogue; St. Agnes, Greenport; St. Patrick, Southold; St. John Jane Harrigan, Prin.;

EAST NORTHPORT

Trinity Regional School - (PAR) 1025 Fifth Ave., East Northport, NY 11731 t) 631-261-5130 tregion@optonline.net Supported by the following parishes: Our Lady Queen of Martyrs, Centerport; St. Anthony of Padua, East Northport; St. Francis of Assisi, Greenlawn; St Patricia A. Ayers, Prin.;

FREEPORT

The De La Salle School - (PRV) (Grades 5-8) 87 Pine St., Freeport, NY 11520-3615 t) 516-379-8660 learn@delassalleschool.org www.delasalleschool.org Jeanmarie Becker, Prin.; William L. Gault, Exec.; Jeanne Mulry, Dir.;

GLEN COVE

All Saints Regional Catholic School - (PAR) (Grades N-8) 12 Pearsall Ave., Glen Cove, NY 11542-3052 t) 516-676-0762 www.asrcatholic.com Supported by the following parishes: St. Boniface, Sea Cliff; St. Hyacinth, Glen Head; St. Mary, Roslyn; St. Patrick, Glen Cove; St. Rocco, Glen Cove. Joanne Fitzgerald, Dean; Rev. Dom Elias Carr, Can.Reg., Headmaster;

LONG BEACH

Long Beach Catholic Regional School - (PAR) (Grades PreK-8) 735 W. Broadway, Long Beach, NY 11561 t) 516-432-8900 kkahn@lbcrs.org lbcrs.org Supported by the following parishes: St. Ignatius, Long Beach; St. Mary of the Isle, Long Beach, and Our Lady of the Miraculous Medal, Point Lookout. Marianne Carberry, Prin.; Kerry Kahn, Prin.; Patricia Esposito, Librn.;

MANHASSET

Our Lady of Grace Montessori School and Center - (Grades N-3) 29 Shelter Rock Rd., Manhasset, NY 11030 t) 516-365-9832 (School); 516-627-9255 (Center) Sr. Ann Barbara DeSiano, I.H.M., Admin.; Sr. Kelly Quinn, I.H.M., Prin.;

OLD WESTBURY

Holy Child Academy - (PRV) (Grades PreSchool-8) 25 Store Hill Rd., Old Westbury, NY 11568 t) 516-626-9300 cbowen@holychildacademy.org www.holychildacademy.org Palma Gartland, Campus Min.; Art Viscusi, Prin.; Marie O'Donoghue, Dir.;

PATCHOGUE

Holy Angels Regional School - (PAR) (Grades PreK-8) 1 Division St., Patchogue, NY 11772 t) 631-475-0422 mconnell@holyangelsregional.org www.holyangelsregional.org Supported by the following parishes: Mary Immaculate, Bellport; St. Frances Cabrini, Coram; St. Joseph the Worker, E. Patchogue; St. Sylvester, Medfor Michael Connell, Prin.; Karen Weibke, Bus. Mgr.; Katie Mitchell, Librn.;

PORT JEFFERSON

Our Lady of Wisdom Regional Catholic School - (PAR) 114-116 Myrtle Ave., Port Jefferson, NY 11777 t) 631-473-1211 jpiropato@ourladyofwisdomschool.com www.ourladyofwisdomschool.com Supported by the following parishes: Infant Jesus, Port Jefferson; St. Louis de Montfort, Sound Beach; St. James, Setauket; St. Gerard Majella. John W. Piropato, Prin.;

RIVERHEAD

Saint John Paul II Regional School - 515 Marcy Ave., Riverhead, NY 11901

SOUTHAMPTON

Our Lady of the Hamptons Regional School - (PAR) (Grades PreK-8) 160 N. Main St., Southampton, NY 11968 t) 631-283-9140 sks@olh.org www.olh.org Sr. Kathryn Schlueter, C.S.J., Prin.; Melissa Meyer, Librn.;

UNIONDALE

St. Martin de Porres Marianist School - (PRV) (Grades PreK-8) 530 Hempstead Blvd., Uniondale, NY 11553 t) 516-481-3303 storres@stmartinmarianist.org www.stmartinmarianist.org ShawnLisa Torres, Prin.; Bro. James W. Conway, S.M., Dir.;

HIGH SCHOOLS

STATE OF NEW YORK

HEMPSTEAD

Sacred Heart Academy - (PRV) (Grades 9-12) 47 Cathedral Ave., Hempstead, NY 11550 t) 516-483-7383 adeacetis@sacredheartacademyhempstead.org www.sacredheartacademyhempstead.org College preparatory-girls Sr. Jean Amore, Prin.; Kristin Lynch Graham, Pres.; Regina Foge, Librn.;

HICKSVILLE

Holy Trinity Diocesan High School - 98 Cherry Ln., Hicksville, NY 11801 t) 516-433-2900 hths98@holytrinityhs.echalk.com www.holytrinityhs.org Rev. Daniel Opoku-Mensah, Assoc. Pst.; Rev. Gerard J. Gentleman, Chap.; Kathleen Moran, Prin.;

MINEOLA
Chaminade High School (Boys) - (PRV) 340 Jackson Ave., Mineola, NY 11501 t) 516-742-5555 www.chaminade-hs.org Directed by the Society of Mary (Marianists) Rev. Peter Heiskell, SM, Chap.; Bro. Joseph D. Bellizzi, S.M., Prin.; John Callinan, Prin.; Gregory Kay, Prin.; Graham Otton, Prin.; Robert Paul, Prin.; Daniel Petruccio, Prin.; Bro. Thomas J. Cleary, S.M., Pres.;
SOUTH HUNTINGTON
St. Anthony's High School - (PRV) 275 Wolf Hill Rd., South Huntington, NY 11747-1394 t) 631-271-2020 officeoftheprincipal@stanthonyshs.org www.stanthonyshs.org College Prep. Directed by the Franciscan Brothers of Brooklyn. Bro. David Migliorino, Prin.;
SYOSSET
Our Lady of Mercy Academy - (PRV) 815 Convent Rd., Syosset, NY 11791-3895 t) 516-921-1047 mmyhan@olma.org www.olma.org College prep for young women. Sisters of Mercy/Mid-Atlantic Community. Sandra Betters, Prin.; Margaret Myhan, Pres.; Sheila Wilson, Librn.;
UNIONDALE
Kellenberg Memorial High School - (PRV) (Grades 6-12) 1400 Glenn Curtiss Blvd., Uniondale, NY 11553 t) 516-292-0200 brokenneth@kellenberg.org www.kellenberg.org Directed by the Society of Mary Bro. Kenneth M. Hoagland, S.M., Prin.; Rev. Thomas A. Cardone, S.M., Chap.; Rev. Daniel Griffin, Chap.; Angela Cameron, Assistant Principal for Academics; James J. O'Brien, Assistant Principal for Admissions; Kenneth Conrade, COO; John Fechtmann, Athletic Director; Maria Korzekwinski, Assistant Principal for Bro. Joseph Fox Latin School; Stds.: 2,667; Pr. Tchrs.: 3; Bro. Tchrs.: 6; Lay Tchrs.: 143
WEST ISLIP
St. John the Baptist Diocesan High School - (DIO) 1170 Montauk Hwy., West Islip, NY 11795 t) 631-587-8000 www.stjohnthebaptistdhs.net Rev. David Atanasio, Chap.; Biagio M. Arpino, Prin.; Cheryl Westerfeld, Librn.;

INSTITUTIONS LOCATED IN DIOCESE

CATHOLIC CHARITIES [CCH]

HICKSVILLE
Catholic Charities of Long Island - 90 Cherry Ln., Hicksville, NY 11801-6299 t) 516-733-7000 info@catholiccharities.cc www.catholiccharities.cc Laura A. Cassell, CEO; Paul F. Engelhart, COO; Richard Balcom, CFO;

Catholic Charities Health Systems Corp. of the Diocese of Rockville Centre, Inc. -

Catholic Charities Support Corp. - t) 516-733-7032

Central Intake & Referral Developers - t) 516-733-7045 Paula Malloy, Dir. Parish Social Ministry;

Chemical Dependency Services - 155 Indian Head Rd., Commack, NY 11725 t) 631-543-6200 Jennifer Perciavalle, Dir., Chemical Dependence Prog.;

Talbot House - Crisis Center - 30-C Carlough Rd., Bohemia, NY 11716 t) 631-589-4144

Development and Communications - Jennifer Regan Haight, Dir.;

Finance - t) 516-733-7015 Erin Shirvell, Dir.;

Housing Services - t) 516-733-7076 Jay Korth, Dir., Housing & Legal Affairs;

Human Resources - Kristy D'Errico, Dir.;

Immigrant Services - 143 Schleigel Blvd., Amityville, NY 11701 t) 631-789-5210 Carmen Maquilon, Dir.;

Meals on Wheels - Nassau and Suffolk - t) 516-733-5805 Kim Parbst, Dir. Sr. Svcs.;

Mental Health Outpatient Services - 333 N. Main St., Freeport, NY 11520 t) 631-665-6707 (Bay Shore Clinic); 516-654-1919 (Medford Clinic) Howard G. Duff, Dir.;

Mental Health Programs - 333 N. Main St., Freeport, NY 11520 t) 516-634-0012 x126 Howard G. Duff, Dir.;

Mental Health Residential Services - 333 N. Main St., Freeport, NY 11520 t) 516-634-0012 Howard G. Duff, Dir.;

Nutrition Outreach Education Program (NOEP) - 143 Schleigel Blvd., Amityville, NY 11701 t) 631-789-9546; 516-634-0014 x138 (Freeport) Amy Agiato, Dir. Nutrition & Maternity Svcs.;

Parish Social Ministry - t) 516-733-7061 Paula Malloy, Dir.;

Regina Maternity Services Corporation - t) 516-223-7888 Amy Agiato, Dir., Nutrition & Maternity Svcs.;

Regina Maternity Services/Mentoring - t) 516-223-7888 Amy Agiato, Director of Nutrition and Maternity Services;

Residential Services - Developmental Disabilities - 147 Schleigel Blvd., Amityville, NY 11701 t) 631-665-3434; 631-532-2150 Lori Savin, Dir., Disabilities Svcs.;

Senior Community Service Centers & Congregate Meal Sites - t) 516-733-5805 Kim Parbst, Dir. Sr. Svcs.;

Senior Services Case Management - 333 N. Main St., Freeport, NY 11520 t) 516-771-3410 Paulette Jones, Prog. Coord., Sr. Case Mgmt.;

VIP Club - t) 516-733-5805 Kim Parbst, Dir. Sr. Svcs.;

Women Infant and Children Program (WIC) - 333 N. Main St., Freeport, NY 11520 t) 516-377-0157 Amy Agiato, Dir., Nutrition & Maternity Svcs.;

CEMETERIES [CEM]

CENTRAL ISLIP
Catholic Cemeteries of Long Island - 115 Wheeler Rd., Central Islip, NY 11722 t) 631-234-8297 info@cclongisland.org www.cclongisland.org Richard C Bie, Pres./CEO; Dcn. Albert Pickford, Assoc. Dir. Oper.; John F. Kennedy, CFO; Ann Andersen, Assoc. Dir., Admin & Customer Sales & Svc.;
CORAM
Holy Sepulchre Cemetery - 3442 Rte. 112, Coram, NY 11727 t) 631-732-3460 info@cclongisland.org www.cclongisland.org Richard C Bie, Pres./CEO; Dcn. Albert Pickford, Assoc. Dir. Oper.; Ann Andersen, Assoc. Dir., Admin. & Customer Sales & Svc.; John F. Kennedy, CFO;
WESTBURY
Cemetery of the Holy Rood - 111 Old Country Rd., Westbury, NY 11590-0182; Mailing: PO Box 182, Westbury, NY 11590-0182 t) 516-334-7990 info@cclongisland.org www.cclongisland.org Richard C Bie, Pres./CEO; Dcn. Albert Pickford, Assoc. Dir. Oper.; Ann Andersen, Assoc. Dir. of Admin & Customer Sales & Svc.; John F. Kennedy, CFO;

COLLEGES & UNIVERSITIES [COL]

ROCKVILLE CENTRE
Molloy University - 1000 Hempstead Ave., Rockville Centre, NY 11571-5002; Mailing: P.O. Box 5002, Rockville Centre, NY 11571-5002 t) 516-323-3200; 516-323-4710 cmuscente@molloy.edu; dfornieri@molloy.edu www.molloy.edu Dr. James Lentini, Pres.; Dr. Michelle Piskulich, Provost & Vice Pres., Academic Affairs; Stds.: 4,769; Lay Tchrs.: 182; Sr. Tchrs.: 1

CONVENTS, MONASTERIES, AND RESIDENCES FOR WOMEN [CON]

AMITYVILLE
Queen of the Rosary, Motherhouse - 555 Albany Ave., Amityville, NY 11701-1197 t) 631-842-6000 sistersop@amityop.org www.amityvilleop.org Sisters of the Order of St. Dominic, Amityville Dominican Sisters, Inc., Sisters of St. Dominic. Peggy McVetty, Prioress;
BAY SHORE
New Jerusalem - 106 N. Penataquit Ave., Bay Shore, NY 11706-6939 t) 631-968-8859
BLUE POINT
St. Ursula Center - 186 Middle Rd., Blue Point, NY 11715 t) 631-363-2422 shoran@tildonkursuline.org www.tildonkursuline.org Ursuline Sisters, Congregation of Tildonk. Sandy Horan, Admin.;
BRENTWOOD
Saint Joseph Convent - Motherhouse, 1725 Brentwood Rd., Brentwood, NY 11717 t) 631-273-4531 rooney@csjbrentwood.org www.brentwoodcsj.org Sisters of Saint Joseph Generalate. Sr. Helen M. Kearney, C.S.J., Pres.; Sr. Helen Rooney, C.S.J., Secy.; Sr. Eileen M. Kelly, C.S.J., Treas.; Virginia Dowd, Archivist;

Saint Joseph Novitiate - 1725 Brentwood Rd., Brentwood, NY 11717 t) 631-273-1187 www.brentwoodcsj.org Sr. Mary Walsh, C.S.J., Dir.;

Maria Regina Residence, Inc. - 1725 Brentwood Rd., Bldg. 1, Brentwood, NY 11717-5589 t) 631-299-3000 ebartoldus@mariareginaresidence.org www.mariareginaresidence.org Sisters of St. Joseph
HAMPTON BAYS
St. Joseph's Villa Retreat and Renewal Center - 81 Lynn Ave., Hampton Bays, NY 11946 t) 631-728-6074 stjosephvilla@optonline.net www.csjbrentwoodny.org
HUNTINGTON
Missionary Sisters of St. Benedict - 350 Cuba Hill Rd., Huntington, NY 11743 t) 631-368-9528 mssb350@yahoo.com Sr. Lyudmyla Varhatyuk, O.S.B., Supr.; Srs.: 23
ISLIP
Daughters of Wisdom (Administration) - 385 Ocean Ave., Islip, NY 11751 t) 631-277-2660 eeckhardt@daughtersofwisdom.org www.daughtersofwisdom.org Sr. Catherine Sheehan, D.W., Prov.;
OCEANSIDE
St. Anthony's Parish House - 111 Anchor Ave., Oceanside, NY 11572 t) 516-536-3308 oceansideop@verizon.net Sr. Margaret Sammon, O.P., Contact;
POINT LOOKOUT
St. Clare Convent-Franciscan Sisters of Allegany - 104 Ocean Blvd., Point Lookout, NY 11569; Mailing: P.O. Box 823, Point Lookout, NY 11569 t) 516-665-3389; 347-963-4552 smcm1082@aol.com Sr. Catherine Moran, O.S.F., Contact;

St. Elizabeth Convent-Franciscan Sisters of Allegany - 29 Ocean Blvd., Point Lookout, NY 11569 t) 718-665-3063; 347-963-4552 congsecretary@fsallegany.org Sr. Catherine Moran, O.S.F., Contact;
ROCKVILLE CENTRE
Congregation of the Infant Jesus (Nursing Sisters of the Sick Poor) - 984 N. Village Ave., Rockville Centre, NY 11570 t) 516-823-3808 marylou.kelly@nursingsisterscij.org www.cijnssp.org Congregation of the Infant Jesus (Nursing Sisters of the Sick Poor). Sr. Helen M. Kearney, C.S.J., Trustee; Mary Louise Kelly, CIJ, Vice. Pres.; Srs.: 20
ROOSEVELT
Oblate Sisters of the Most Holy Redeemer - 290 Babylon Tpke., Roosevelt, NY 11575-0329; Mailing: P.O. Box 329, Roosevelt, NY 11575 t) 516-223-1013 ossr290@earthlink.net Mother of Good Counsel Home is a group home for pregnant and parenting teenage mothers and their infants. Sr. Matilde Murillo, O.SS.R., Dir.;
SOUND BEACH
Our Lady of Perpetual Help Convent - 49 Convent Dr., Sound Beach, NY 11789 t) 631-744-2477 convsb@optimum.net

ENDOWMENTS / FOUNDATIONS / TRUSTS [EFT]

BAY SHORE

Missionaries of the Company of Mary General House Charitable Trust - 26 S. Saxon Ave., Bay Shore, NY 11706 t) 631-627-1836 jpbsmm@gmail.com Rev. James Paul Brady, S.M.M., Trustee;

BRENTWOOD

Sisters of Saint Joseph Lay Employee Pension Plan Charitable Trust - 1725 Brentwood Rd., Brentwood, NY 11717 t) 631-273-1187 www.brentwoodcsj.org

ISLIP

Wisdom Charitable Trust - 385 Ocean Ave., Islip, NY 11751 t) 631-277-2660 bswiss@daughtersofwisdom.org

NESCONSET

***Cleary Foundation for the Deaf, Inc.** - 301 Smithtown Blvd., Nesconset, NY 11767-2007 t) 631-588-0530

ROCKVILLE CENTER

Diocese of Rockville Centre Health Care and Other Assistance Plan for Retired and Disabled Diocesan Priests Trust - c/o The RC Diocese of Rockville Centre, 50 N. Park Ave., Rockville Center, NY 11571

ROCKVILLE CENTRE

Diocese of Rockville Centre Health & Welfare Benefits Program Trust - Office of General Counsel, 50 N. Park Ave., Rockville Centre, NY 11571

***Tomorrow's Hope Foundation, Inc.** - ; Mailing: P.O. Box 9023, Rockville Centre, NY 11571 t) 516-678-5800 Joseph Young, Treas.;

SYOSSET

***Emmaus House Foundation, Inc. (Harvest Houses)** - 235 Cold Spring Rd., Syosset, NY 11791 t) 516-496-9796 jabharvest@yahoo.com www.harvesthouse.org Sr. Jeanne A. Brendel, O.P., Exec.;

HOSPITALS / HEALTH SERVICES [HOS]

BETHPAGE

***WSNCHS North Inc. (St. Joseph Hospital)** - 4295 Hempstead Tpke., Bethpage, NY 11714 t) 516-579-6000 www.chsli.org Christopher Nelson, Pres.; Patrick M. O'Shaughnessy, CEO; Bed Capacity: 203; Asstd. Annu.: 62,115; Staff: 682

MISCELLANEOUS [MIS]

AMITYVILLE

Dominican Sisters Of Amityville-Finance Dept. - 555 Albany Ave., Amityville, NY 11701 t) 631-842-6000 prioress@amityop.org www.amityvilleop.org Sr. Mary Patricia Neylon, O.P., Pres.; Sr. Patricia Hanvey, O.P., Vice Pres.; Sr. Patricia Koehler, O.P., Secy.;

***Dominican Youth Movement USA** - 555 Albany Ave., Amityville, NY 11701 t) 631-842-6000 x308 info@dymusa.org www.dymusa.org Creates programs for youth and young adults to connect more closely to the Dominican charism of preaching. Sr. Katherine R Frazier, OP, Exec. Dir.; Sr. Virginia Mary Fleming, Director Emeritas;

Queen of the Rosary Motherhouse - 555 Albany Ave., Amityville, NY 11701 t) 631-842-6000 x212 www.amityvilleop.org

BAY SHORE

Pronto of Long Island, Inc. - 128 Pine Aire Dr., Bay Shore, NY 11706 t) 631-231-8290 kbennett@prontolongisland.org www.prontoli.org

BETHPAGE

***Partnership for Global Justice** - 4108 Hicksville Rd., Bethpage, NY 11714 t) 212-682-6481 partnershipforglobaljustice@gmail.com www.partnershipforglobaljustice.com Sr. JoAnn Mark, A.S.C., Exec.;

***Society of St. Vincent de Paul-Central Council** - 249 Broadway, Bethpage, NY 11714 t) 516-822-3132 tabbate@svdpli.org svdpli.org Rev. Msgr. Gerard A. Ringenback, Spiritual Adv./Care Srvcs.; Gustave Gelardi, Pres.; Thomas J. Abbate, CEO;

BRENTWOOD

Congregation of the Sisters of St. Joseph - 1725 Brentwood Rd., Brentwood, NY 11717-5587 t) 631-273-1187 www.brentwoodcsj.org Sr. Eileen M. Kelly, C.S.J., Treas.;

The CSJ Learning Connection for Adult Education, Inc. - 1725 Brentwood Rd., Brentwood, NY 11717; Mailing: 1725 Brentwood Rd., Bldg. 2, Brentwood, NY 11717 t) 631-951-4783 csjtlc@optonline.net; murrayd523@gmail.com Denise Murray, Dir.;

CENTERPORT

Mt. Alvernia, Inc. - 105 Prospect Rd., Centerport, NY 11721; Mailing: PO Box 301, Centerport, NY 11721 t) 631-261-5730 alverniacenterportny@gmail.com; natalie@campalvernia.org campalvernia.org Directed by the Franciscan Brothers. Bro. Geoffrey Clement, Dir.; Bro. Lawrence Makofske, O.S.F., Dir.; Benjamin Esposito, Dir.;

Camp Alvernia - 105 Prospect Rd., Cente, NY 11721; Mailing: PO Box 301, Centerport, NY 11721 t) (631) 261-5730 www.campalvernia.org Directed by the Franciscan Brothers.

Mt. Alvernia Center for Retreats - 105 Prospect Rd., Centerport, NY 11721; Mailing: PO Box 301, Centerport, NY 11721 t) (631) 261-5730 www.campalvernia.org/retreats Directed by the Franciscan Brothers.

EASTPORT

Magnificat - Suffolk County NY Chapter - 200 Bach Ct., Eastport, NY 11941 t) 631-325-1923 c) 631-875-8850 corndang@optonline.net Rev. Roy Tvrdik, S.M.M., Spiritual Adv./Care Srvcs.;

GREENPORT

North Fork Parish Outreach, Inc. - 69465 Main Rd., Greenport, NY 11944; Mailing: P.O. Box 584, Greenport, NY 11944

HAMPTON BAYS

Centro Corazon de Maria, Inc. - 31 Montauk Hwy. E., Hampton Bays, NY 11946 t) 631-728-5558

Dominican Sisters Family Health Service - 103-6 W. Montauk Hwy., Hampton Bays, NY 11946 t) 631-728-0181 pjablow@dsfhs.org www.dsfhs.org Patricia Jablow, Admin.;

DSFHS Special Programs - ; Mailing: P.O. Box 1028, Hampton Bays, NY 11946 t) 631-728-0937

HICKSVILLE

***Department of Education, Diocese of Rockville Centre** - 128 Cherry Ln., Hicksville, NY 11801 kwalsh@drvc.org drvcschools.org Biagio M. Arpino, Supt.; Anthony Biscione, Supt.; Marian Hernandez, Supt.; Kathleen Razzetti, Supt.; Kathleen Walsh, Supt.;

HUNTINGTON

Sacred Heart Institute - 440 W. Neck Rd., Huntington, NY 11743 t) 631-423-0483 x185 rsullivan@cor-jesu.org www.cor-jesu.org Rosemary C. Sullivan, Exec.; Rev. Lachlan Cameron, Dir.;

NEW HYDE PARK

Sisters of the Imitation of Christ United States Mission, Inc. - 1653 Highland Ave., New Hyde Park, NY 11040 t) 516-358-4597

RIVERHEAD

Sisters of the Holy Family of Nazareth, Holy Family Province - 3560 Sound Ave., Riverhead, NY 11901 t) 631-727-5122 mron3560@yahoo.com Sr. Mary Ronald Wlodarczyk, C.S.F.N., Admin.;

ROCKVILLE CENTRE

Catholic Health System of Long Island, Inc. - 992 N. Village Ave., Rockville Centre, NY 11570 t) 516-705-3700 www.chsli.org Salvatore Sodano, Chair; Patrick M. O'Shaughnessy, Pres. & CEO;

Catholic Healthcare Network of Long Island - 992 N. Village Ave., Rockville Centre, NY 11570 t) 516-705-3700 www.chsli.org Patrick M. O'Shaughnessy, Pres. & CEO;

St. Catherine of Siena Medical Center - 50 Rte. 25A, Smithtown, NY 11787 t) 631-862-3000 James O'Connor, Pres.; Patrick M. O'Shaughnessy, CEO; Bed Capacity: 296; Asstd. Annu.: 88,333; Staff: 1,188

The St. Catherine of Siena Medical Center Foundation - 48 Rte. 25A, Medical Office Bldg., Ste. 205, Smithtown, NY 11787 t) 631-862-3000 James O'Connor, Pres.;

St. Catherine of Siena Nursing and Rehabilitation Care Center - 52 Rte. 25A, Smithtown, NY 11787 t) 631-862-3900 John Chowske, Admin.;

St. Charles Corporation - 200 Belle Terre Rd., Port Jefferson, NY 11777 t) 631-474-6600 James O'Connor, Pres.;

St. Charles Hospital and Rehabilitation Center - 200 Belle Terre Rd., Port Jefferson, NY 11777 t) 631-474-6600 Patrick M. O'Shaughnessy, CEO; James O'Connor, Pres.; Bed Capacity: 243; Asstd. Annu.: 221,448; Staff: 1,227

The St. Charles Hospital Foundation - 200 Belle Terre Rd., Port Jefferson, NY 11777 t) 631-474-6000 James O'Connor, Pres.;

CHS Services, Inc. - 992 N. Village Ave., Rockville Centre, NY 11570 t) (516) 705-3700 Patrick M. O'Shaughnessy, Pres. & CEO;

St. Francis Hospital - 100 Port Washington Blvd., Roslyn, NY 11576 t) 516-562-6000 Charles L. Lucore, Pres.; Patrick M. O'Shaughnessy, CEO; Bed Capacity: 364; Asstd. Annu.: 244,973; Staff: 3,317

***The St. Francis Hospital Foundation, Inc.** - 100 Port Washington Blvd., Roslyn, NY 11576 t) 516-562-6000 Patrick M. O'Shaughnessy, Pres.;

St. Francis - Mercy Corporation - 100 Port Washington Blvd., Roslyn, NY 11576 t) 516-562-6000 Patrick M. O'Shaughnessy, Pres.;

The St. Francis Research and Educational Corporation - 100 Port Washington Blvd., Roslyn, NY 11576 t) 516-562-6000 Charles L. Lucore, Pres.;

The Good Samaritan Hospital Foundation - 1000 Montauk Hwy., West Islip, NY 11795 t) 631-376-4001 Ruth Hennessey, Pres.;

Good Samaritan Hospital Medical Center - 1000 Montauk Hwy., West Islip, NY 11795 t) 631-376-3000 Ruth Hennessey, Pres.; Patrick M. O'Shaughnessy, CEO; Bed Capacity: 437; Asstd. Annu.: 304,397; Staff: 3,215

***Good Samaritan Hospital Self Insurance Against Malpractice Trust** - 1000 Montauk Hwy., West Islip, NY 11795 t) 631-376-3000 Ruth Hennessey, Pres.;

Good Samaritan Nursing Home - 101 Elm St., Sayville, NY 11782 t) 631-244-2400 Joseph Costa, Admin.;

Good Shepherd Hospice - 110 Bi-County Blvd., Farmingdale, NY 11735 t) 631-465-6300 Kim Kranz, Pres.;

Good Shepherd Hospice Foundation, Inc. - 110 Bi-County Blvd., Farmingdale, NY 11735 t) 631-465-6300 Kim Kranz, Pres.;

Mercy Medical Center - 1000 N. Village Ave., Rockville Centre, NY 11570 t) 516-705-2525 Joseph Manopella, Pres.; Patrick M. O'Shaughnessy, CEO; Bed Capacity: 375; Asstd. Annu.: 140,646; Staff: 1,522

The Mercy Medical Center Foundation - 1000 N. Village Ave., Rockville Centre, NY 11570 t) 516-705-2525 Joseph Manopella, Pres.;

Nursing Sisters Home Care, Inc. (Catholic Home Care) - 110 Bi-County Blvd., Farmingdale, NY 11735 t) 631-828-7400 Kim Kranz, Pres.;

The Our Lady of Consolation Foundation - 111 Beach Dr., West Islip, NY 11795 t) 631-587-1600 James Ryan, Pres.;

Our Lady of Consolation Nursing and Rehabilitation Care Center - 111 Beach Dr., West Islip, NY 11795 t) 631-587-1600 James Ryan, Admin.;

Personalized Recovery Oriented Services for People with Psychiatric Disabilities - 127 W. Main St., Riverhead, NY 11901 t) 631-862-3000 James O'Connor, Pres.;

The Samaritan Corporation - 1000 Montauk Hwy., West Islip, NY 11795 Ruth Hennessey, Pres.;

Siena Retirement Community Realty, LLC - 50 Rte. 25A, Smithtown, NY 11787 t) 631-862-3100 James O'Connor, Pres.;

Suffolk Hearing & Speech Center, Inc. - 369 E. Main St., East Islip, NY 11730 t) 631-376-4001 A diagnostics and treatment center.

***Wisdom Gardens Housing Development Fund Company, Inc.** - 200 Belle Terre Rd., Port Jefferson, NY 11777 t) (631) 474-6600 James O'Connor, Pres.;

***Ecclesia Assurance Company** - 50 N. Park Ave.,

Rockville Centre, NY 11571; Mailing: P.O. Box 9023, Rockville Centre, NY 11571 t) 516-678-5800 wgchapin@drvc.org William Chapin, Vice. Pres.;

Magnificat Rockville Centre - 219 Hempstead Ave., Rockville Centre, NY 11570

Mission Assistance Corporation - ; Mailing: P.O. Box 9023, Rockville Centre, NY 11571 t) 516-678-5800

Unitas Investment Fund Inc. - ; Mailing: P.O. Box 9023, Rockville Centre, NY 11571-9023 t) 516-678-5800 Thomas Doodian, Pres.;

SOUTH HUNTINGTON

St. Anthony's High School, South Huntington - 275 Wolf Hill Rd., South Huntington, NY 11747 t) 631-271-2020 officeoftheprincipal@stanthonyshs.org stanthonyshs.org Bro. Gary Cregan, O.S.F., Prin.;

St. Anthony's Threshold of Hope Inc. - 275 Wolf Hill Rd., South Huntington, NY 11747

Seraphic Properties, Inc. - 275 Wolf Hill Rd., South Huntington, NY 11747 t) 631-271-2020 officeoftheprincipal@stanthonyshs.org Bro. Gary Cregan, O.S.F., Admin.;

UNIONDALE

Catholic Faith Network - 1200 Glenn Curtiss Blvd., Uniondale, NY 11553 t) 516-538-8704 dmfeiler@cfntv.org www.cfntv.ort Rev. Msgr. James C. Vlaun, Pres.;

WESTBURY

Sisters, Lovers of the Holy Cross, Inc. - 43 Crown Ln, Westbury, NY 11590 t) 516-333-9464 sr.theresanguyen@yahoo.com

St. Theresa Convent - srteresanguyen@yahoo.com Sr. Theresa Nguyen, L.H.C., Pres.;

WYANDANCH

The Opening Word Program, Inc. - 1434 Straight Path, Wyandanch, NY 11798 t) 631-643-0541 opword@optonline.net Directed by the Sisters of St. Dominic. Sr. Mary Patricia Neylon, O.P., Chair; Sr. Margaret A. Krajci, O.P., Treas.; Sr. Lenore Toscano, O.P., Exec.;

MONASTERIES AND RESIDENCES FOR PRIESTS AND BROTHERS [MON]

BAY SHORE

Montfort Missionaries - 26 S. Saxon Ave., Bay Shore, NY 11706 t) (631) 666-7500 montfort.provincialusa@gmail.com montfortusa.org Montfort Spiritual Center and Headquarters of "Montfort Publications" The Missionaries of the Company of Mary; Montfort Spiritual Association Rev. Zakarias Beong, SMM, Preacher; Rev. James Paul Brady, S.M.M., Trustee; Rev. Bernard Brault, Mem.; Rev. John Breslin, S.M.M., Mem.; Rev. Matthew Considine, SMM, Prov. Asst.; Rev. Timoteus Daman, SMM, Preacher; Rev. Gerald J. Fitzsimmons, S.M.M., Preacher; Rev. Harry Flores, SMM, Preacher; Rev. Alonso Lazo, S.M.M., Preacher; Rev. James Manning, S.M.M., Mem.; Rev. John McCann, S.M.M., Mem.; Rev. Francis Pizzarelli, S.M.M., Councillor; Rev. Thomas Poth, S.M.M., Prov.; Rev. Philip Pramod, SMM, Preacher; Rev. Richard Schebera, S.M.M., Preacher; Rev. Roy Tvrdik, S.M.M., Preacher; Brs.: 16; Priests: 16

Montfort Missionaries - Spiritual Center - t) 718-489-5885

GLEN COVE

St. Josaphat's Monastery, Novitiate and Retreat House - East Beach Dr., Glen Cove, NY 11542 t) 516-671-0545 stjosaphatnvtt@gmail.com Basilian Fathers. Rev. Eugene (Andriy) Khdmyn, O.S.B.M., Vicar; Rev. Theodosius (Roman) Ilnicki, O.S.B.M., Secy.;

MANORVILLE

Shrine of Our Lady of the Island - 258 Eastport Manor Rd., Manorville, NY 11949 t) 631-325-0661 shrineoffice@optonline.net ourladyoftheisland.org Rev. Peter D'Abele, S.M.M.; Rev. Hugh Gillespie, S.M.M., Dir.; Brs.: 2; Priests: 2

MINEOLA

Provincial Residence and Novitiate - 240 Emory Rd., Mineola, NY 11501 t) 516-742-5555 tdriscoll@chaminade-hs.org Society of Mary (Marianists). Bro. Timothy S. Driscoll, S.M., Prov.; Rev. Thomas A. Cardone, S.M., Asst. Prov. & Asst. Rel. Life; Rev. Garrett J. Long, S.M.; Bro. Thomas J. Cleary, S.M.; Bro. James W. Conway, S.M.;

RONKONKOMA

St Pius X Residence for Retired Priests LLC - 310 Cenacle Rd., Ronkonkoma, NY 11779 t) 631-608-2622 tcosta@drvc.org Residence for retired and infirm diocesan priests. Rev. Msgr. Thomas C. Costa, Vicar; Rev. Joseph V. Arevalo, In Res.; Rev. Andrew P. Blake, In Res.; Rev. Msgr. Kenneth Boccafola, In Res.; Rev. Brian J. Brinker, In Res.; Rev. Msgr. Joseph K. Curley, In Res.; Rev. Claude J. D'Souza, In Res.; Rev. Msgr. Francis X. Gaeta, In Res.; Rev. Msgr. William J. Gill, In Res.; Rev. Msgr. John Heinlein, In Res.; Rev. Gregory Heinlein, In Res.; Rev. Peter T. Liu, In Res.; Rev. Robert Lubrano, In Res.; Rev. John R. Moore, In Res.; Rev. Thomas P. Murray, In Res.; Rev. Joseph E. Nohs, In Res.; Rev. Msgr. Dennis Reagan, In Res.; Rev. R. Michael Reid, In Res.; Rev. Msgr. T. Peter Ryan, In Res.; Rev. Edward M. Seagriff, In Res.; Rev. James L. Wood, In Res.; Dcn. Jay Valdes, Pst. Assoc.; Priests: 21

NURSING / REHABILITATION / CONVALESCENCE / ELDERLY CARE [NUR]

AMITYVILLE

Dominican Village, Inc. - 565 Albany Ave., Amityville, NY 11701 t) 631-842-6091 info@dominicanvillage.org Kenneth Ruthinoski, Pres.; Sr. Maureen Muir, Vice Pres. Opers.;

HUNTINGTON

Missionary Sisters of St. Benedict Home for the Aged, Inc. - 350 Cuba Hill Rd., Huntington, NY 11743 t) 631-368-9528 sjgh350@yahoo.com; s.justyna@mssbny.org www.mssbny.org Missionary Sisters of St. Benedict. Sr. Agnieszka Owsiejko, O.S.B., Admin.; Asstd. Annu.: 35; Staff: 26

PRESCHOOLS / CHILDCARE CENTERS [PRE]

BAY SHORE

Montfort Missionaries Charitable Trust - 26 S. Saxon Ave., Bay Shore, NY 11706 c) 718-551-8651 Rev. Matthew Considine, SMM, Trustee;

RETREAT HOUSES / RENEWAL CENTERS [RTR]

CENTERPORT

St. Francis Center, Inc. - 105 Prospect Rd., Centerport, NY 11721; Mailing: P.O. Box 301, Centerport, NY 11721 t) 631-261-5730 alverniacenterportny@gmail.com www.alvernia.org Directed by Franciscan Bros. of Brooklyn.

PATCHOGUE

St. Joseph's Prayer Center - 312 Maple Ave., Patchogue, NY 11772 t) 631-730-6210 stjoepc@optonline.net Louise Kramer, Dir.; Rev. James J. Wheeler, S.J., Dir.;

SAG HARBOR

Cormaria Retreat Center, Inc. - 77 Bay St., Sag Harbor, NY 11963; Mailing: P.O. Box 1993, Sag Harbor, NY 11963 t) 631-725-4206 cormaria@aol.com www.cormaria.org Directed by the Religious of the Sacred Heart of Mary. Sr. Ann Thaddeus Marino, R.S.H.M., Dir.;

SEMINARIES [SEM]

HUNTINGTON

Diocesan Seminary of the Immaculate Conception - 440 W. Neck Rd., Huntington, NY 11743 t) 631-423-0483 info@icseminary.edu Rev. Msgr. Richard G. Henning, Rector; Rev. Walter F. Kedjierski, Rector; Most Rev. William Murphy, Chair; Elyse B. Hayes, Dir.; Dcn. Dennis J. Schlosser, Dir.;

SPECIAL CARE FACILITIES [SPF]

NESCONSET

Cleary Deaf Child Center, Inc. - 301 Smithtown Blvd., Nesconset, NY 11767 t) 631-588-0530 jsimms@clearyschool.org www.clearyschool.org Day School (Infants thru 21 years). Directed by Catholic Charities. Jaqueline Simms, Dir.;

ROOSEVELT

Friends of Mother of Good Counsel Home, Inc. - 290 Babylon Tpke., Roosevelt, NY 11575 t) 516-223-1013 ossr290@earthlink.net Sr. Matilde Murillo, O.SS.R., Dir.;

SYOSSET

MercyFirst - 525 Convent Rd., Syosset, NY 11791-3864 t) 516-921-0808 rskolaski@mercyfirst.org www.mercyfirst.org Foster Care, Residential, Family Support, Immigrant Services, Integrated Health Care. Under the sponsorship of the Sisters of Mercy. Renee Skolaski, Pres. & CEO; Bed Capacity: 409; Asstd. Annu.: 3,000; Staff: 436

WADING RIVER

***Little Flower Children & Family Services of New York** - 2450 N. Wading River Rd., Wading River, NY 11792-1402 t) 631-929-6200 info@lfchild.org www.littleflowerny.org Foster Care; Adoption Services; Developmentally Disabled Adults; RTC; Health Care Management; Medicaid Service Provider; Therapeutic FBH Homes Corinne Hammons, CEO; Sr. Ellen Zak, CSFN, Local Supr.; Nilda Diaz, CFO;

WYANDANCH

Gerald J. Ryan Outreach Center, Inc. - 1434 Straight Path, Wyandanch, NY 11798 t) 631-643-7591 ryanouthreach@optonline.net

An asterisk (*) denotes an organization that has established tax-exempt status directly with the IRS and is not covered by the USCCB Group Ruling.

Diocese of Sacramento

(Dioecesis Sacramentensis)

MOST REVEREND JAIME SOTO, D.D., M.S.W.

Bishop of Sacramento; ordained June 12, 1982; appointed Auxiliary Bishop of Orange and named Titular Bishop of Segia March 23, 2000; installed May 31, 2000; appointed Coadjutor Bishop of Sacramento October 11, 2007; installed November 19, 2007; Succeeded to the See November 30, 2008. Diocesan Pastoral Center: Office of the Bishop, 2110 Broadway, Sacramento, CA 95818-2541. T: 916-733-0200; F: 916-733-0215.

Diocesan Pastoral Center: 2110 Broadway, Sacramento, CA 95818-2541. T: 916-733-0100; F: 916-733-0195.

www.scd.org

Square Miles 42,597.

Erected by His Holiness, Leo XIII, May 28, 1886.

Comprises the Counties of Amador, Butte, Colusa, El Dorado, Glenn, Lassen, Modoc, Nevada, Placer, Plumas, Sacramento, Shasta, Sierra, Siskiyou, Solano, Sutter, Tehama, Trinity, Yolo and Yuba in the State of California.

Co-Patrons of Diocese: St. Patrick; Our Lady of Guadalupe.

Legal Title: "Roman Catholic Bishop of Sacramento, A Corporation Sole."

For legal titles of parishes and diocesan institutions, consult the Diocesan Pastoral Center.

STATISTICAL OVERVIEW

Personnel

Bishop	1
Retired Bishops	1
Abbots	1
Priests: Diocesan Active in Diocese	89
Priests: Diocesan Active Outside Diocese	6
Priests: Retired, Sick or Absent	65
Number of Diocesan Priests	160
Religious Priests in Diocese	64
Total Priests in your Diocese	224
Extern Priests in Diocese	33
Ordinations:	
Diocesan Priests	1
Transitional Deacons	1
Permanent Deacons	20
Permanent Deacons in Diocese	195
Total Brothers	18
Total Sisters	111

Parishes

Parishes	102
With Resident Pastor:	
Resident Diocesan Priests	92
Resident Religious Priests	10
Without Resident Pastor:	
Administered by Deacons	1
Administered by Lay People	1
Missions	36
Pastoral Centers	1
Professional Ministry Personnel:	
Brothers	1
Sisters	11
Lay Ministers	119

Welfare

Catholic Hospitals	6
Total Assisted	773,820
Homes for the Aged	1
Total Assisted	200
Specialized Homes	14
Total Assisted	343
Special Centers for Social Services	16
Total Assisted	350,700

Educational

Diocesan Students in Other Seminaries	11
Seminaries, Religious	2
Students, Religious	2
Total Seminarians	13
High Schools, Diocesan and Parish	2
Total Students	1,190
High Schools, Private	3
Total Students	2,425
Elementary Schools, Diocesan and Parish	35
Total Students	8,624
Catechesis/Religious Education:	
High School Students	3,683
Elementary Students	13,721
Total Students under Catholic Instruction	29,656
Teachers in Diocese:	
Priests	3
Brothers	1
Sisters	11
Lay Teachers	773

Vital Statistics

Receptions into the Church:	
Infant Baptism Totals	5,665
Minor Baptism Totals	561
Adult Baptism Totals	256
Received into Full Communion	362
First Communions	4,344
Confirmations	4,318
Marriages:	
Catholic	718
Interfaith	242
Total Marriages	960
Deaths	2,718
Total Catholic Population	1,056,698
Total Population	3,786,209

LEADERSHIP

Vicar General - t) 916-733-0200 Very Rev. Christopher R. Frazer;
Moderator of the Curia - t) 916-733-0200 Very Rev. Christopher R. Frazer;
Chancellor - t) 916-733-0200 Uli Schmitt;
Vice-Chancellor and Director of Administration - t) (916) 733-0200 Chantal LeFevre;
Judicial Vicar - Very Rev. Mark R. Richards;
Episcopal Vicar for Clergy - t) 916-733-0200 Very Rev. Christopher R. Frazer;
Delegate for Religious - t) 916-733-0246 Sr. Lisa Marie Doty, FdCC;
Clergy Care Manager - t) 916-733-0200 Louella Garcia;
Director of Finance - t) 916-733-0277 Thomas J. McNamara, CFO;
College of Consultors - Very Rev. Christopher R. Frazer; Rev. Joel S. Genabia; Rev. Rene Jauregui;
Vicars Forane - Rev. Francisco Velazquez, (American River) (secretary@stphilomene.com); Rev. Eric Flores, (City); Rev. Renier C. Siva, (Gold Country) (fr.renier@stjoseph-vacaville.org);

OFFICES AND DIRECTORS

AIDS, Ministry to - t) 916-733-0253 Miriam Sammartino;
Archives - t) 916-733-0299 Philip Deleon, Archivist;
Associate Director of Deacon Formation - t) 916-733-0211 Dcn. Gregory McAvoy-Jensen;
Bereavement Ministry - t) 916-733-0133 Moises Roberto DeLeon, Assoc. Dir., Family & Respect Life Ministries;
Bishop's Radio Hour - t) 916-733-0168 Bob Dunning;
Black Catholic Ministry - t) 916-733-0122 Rev. Bart Landry, C.S.P.;
Building Committee - Thomas J. McNamara;
Catholic Committee on Scouting - t) 530-389-2780 Jennifer Campbell (scouting@scd.org); Very Rev. Christopher R. Frazer, Chap.; Jon Kantola, Chair;
The Catholic Foundation of the Diocese of Sacramento - t) 916-733-0274 Tony Riehl, Exec. Dir. (triehl@scd.org);
Catholic Herald Magazine - t) 916-733-0175 Julie Sly, Editor; Cathy Joyce, Advertising Mgr.;
Communications - t) 916-733-0154 Bryan Visitacion, Dir. (bvisitacion@scd.org);
Coordinator of Pastoral Hispana - t) 916-733-0123 Teresa Donan; Alex Barraza;
Deacon Council - Dcn. David Lehman; Dcn. Antonio Ramirez; Dcn. Charles Werner;
Department of Catholic Charities & Social Concerns - t) 916-733-0253 Miriam Sammartino, Dir.;
Diocesan Pastoral Council - Chantal LeFevre, Vice Chancellor;
Diocesan Tribunal - t) 916-733-0225
Auditors - Dcn. Roman Diaz; Cheryl M. Tholcke;
Defenders of the Bond - Rev. Michael J. Estaris; Christina Hip-Flores;
Judges - Rev. Brian C. Atienza; Rev. Joseph Huyen Van Nguyen; Very Rev. Mark R. Richards;
Moderator of the Tribunal Chancery - Cheryl M. Tholcke;
Notaries - Cheryl M. Tholcke; Monica Campos;
Promoter of Justice - Rev. Brian C. Atienza;
Diocese of Sacramento Priests' Pension Trust - Most Rev. Jaime Soto, Plan Sponsor; Rosa Miramontes;
Divorced and Separated Ministry - t) 916-733-0133 Moises Roberto DeLeon, Assoc. Dir.;
Eastern Catholic Churches - t) 916-733-0200 Very Rev. Christopher R. Frazer;
Ecclesia Dei Community (Latin Mass) - t) 916-455-5114 Rev. Joshua C. Curtis, F.S.S.P.;
Ecumenical & Interreligious Affairs - t) 916-733-0200 Very Rev. Christopher R. Frazer;
Finance Council - Very Rev. Christopher R. Frazer; Thomas J. McNamara; Bernard Bowler;
Finance Office - t) 916-733-0277 Thomas J. McNamara, Dir.;
Intercultural Committee on Access, Integration, and Mission - Dcn. Casey Walker, Chair (deaconcasey@stbasilvallejo.org);
Lay Personnel - t) 916-733-0240 Anna Schiele, Dir.; Rosa Miramontes, Benefits Mgr.;
Office of Clergy Coordination & Formation - Uli Schmitt, Dir.;
Office of Family and Faith Formation - Dcn. Kevin Staszkow, Dir.; Moises Roberto DeLeon, Assoc. Dir., Family & Respect Life Ministries; Lauralyn Solano, Asst. Dir., Lay Formation;
Office of Youth and Young Adult Ministries - Dcn. Kevin Staszkow, Dir.; Alex Barraza, Regl. Coord. Youth & Young Adult Ministry, Pastoral Juvenil; Antony Ta, Regl. Coord., Youth & Young Adult Ministry;
Pastoral Care Coordinator - t) 916-733-0142 Chantal LeFevre;
Presbyteral Council - Chantal LeFevre, Vice Chancellor; Very Rev. Christopher R. Frazer, Vicar; Most Rev. Jaime Soto;
Priests' Personnel Board, Diocesan - Most Rev. Jaime Soto; Very Rev. Christopher R. Frazer; Uli Schmitt;
Propagation of the Faith - t) 916-733-0253 Miriam Sammartino, Dir.;
Properties Committee - Thomas J. McNamara;
Radio Santisimo Sacramento - Lorena Albarran (lorenaa@radiosantisimosacramento.com);
Safe Environment Coordinator - t) 916-733-0227 Katita Schloemann;
Schools - t) 916-733-0110 Katie Perata, Dir. (kperata@scd.org);
Vocations - t) 916-733-0258 Rev. Guillermo Hernandez; Sr. Maria Campos, R.S.M.;
Worship, Office of - t) 916-733-0211 Dcn. Gregory McAvoy-Jensen;

ORGANIZATIONS

Lay Organizations -
Catholic Alumni Club - sactocac@yahoo.com Cynthia Speed;
Catholic Daughters of the Americas -
Court Our Lady of the Visitation #1890 - t) 916-202-1893 Teresa Reaves;
Court Our Lady of Wisdom #2392 - t) 916-316-5625 Diane McDonald, Regent;
Court Sacramento #172 - t) 916-682-5953 Rev. Joyle T. Martinez, Chap.; Michelle Eck, Regent;
Court St. Felicitas #1939 - t) 916-834-9157 Tonie Sledge, Regent; Rev. Msgr. James T. Murphy, Chap.;
Catholic Ladies Relief Society - t) 530-273-4290 Maria Dilts, Pres.;
Charismatic Renewal - t) 707-426-1401 Carlos Orino, Assoc. Diocesan Liaison;
Cursillo Movement -
Filipino Cursillo in Christianity Movement - t) 707-567-5556 Margie Weiner, Lay Dir.; Dcn. Renato Peregrino, Spiritual Adv./Care Srvcs.;
Movimiento de Cursillos de Cristiandad - t) 530-852-2205 Mauricia Aceves, Lay Dir.; Rev. Antonio B. Racela III, Spiritual Dir.;
Sacramento English Cursillo Community - Verne Bowers, Lay Dir.;
Daughters of Isabella - t) 209-200-1897 Linda Dulaney, Regent;
Diocesan Council of Catholic Women - judiemartinezart@gmail.com Judie Martinez, Pres.; Rev. John Cantwell, Moderator; Rev. Hernando Gomez-Amaya (Colombia), Moderator;
Italian Catholic Federation - t) 916-949-8894 Tim Anatonopolos, Pres.;
Knights of Columbus - Northern California Chapter - t) 530-683-9246 Hector C. Poblete, Pres.;
Knights of Peter Claver and Ladies Auxiliary - t) 916-689-0215 Barbara Montgomery, Grand Lady Court #175; Howard Penn, Deputy Grand Knight Council #175;
Legion of Mary - t) 916-832-0654 Sonia Posadas, Pres.;
Marriage Encounter - t) 916-489-3464 applications@sacramentowwme.org www.sacramentowwme.org Terry Doane; Janet Doane; Hector Villegas;
St. Thomas More Society - stms.sacramento@gmail.com Plauche F. Villere Jr., Pres.;
Scouting, Diocesan Catholic Committee on - Dcn. Kevin Staszkow; Jennifer Campbell; Very Rev. Christopher R. Frazer, Chap.;
Search - t) 916-420-3059 Simon Garcia, Pres.;
Secular Franciscan Order -
Little Portion Fraternity - t) 530-272-1416 Kathleen Molaro, SFO Regl. Min.;
St. Francis of Assisi Ministry - Dcn. Genaro Gonzalez, Min.;
Secular Order of Discalced Carmelites - Suzane Porter, Pres., Sacramento Rgn.; Mary Newell, Pres., Auburn Rgn.;
Society of St. Vincent de Paul - t) 707-480-8234 Joe Alves, Pres.;
Talleres de Oracion & Vida - t) 916-847-5671 www.tpvpil.org Paula Caceres, N.W. Nat'l. Coord.;
Young Ladies Institute - t) 916-638-7905 Marilyn Walter;

PARISHES, MISSIONS, AND CLERGY

STATE OF CALIFORNIA

ALTURAS

Pastor of Sacred Heart Parish, Alturas, a corporation sole - 507 E. Fourth St., Alturas, CA 96101-3406 t) 530-233-2119 shpalturas@gmail.com sacredheart-alturas.org Rev. Ashok Stephen, O.M.I., Par. Admin.; Kristin Daly, DRE; CRP Stds.: 21
St. James - Bonner St. & Garfield St., Cedarville, CA 96104 t) (830) 233-2119

ANDERSON

Pastor of Sacred Heart Parish, Anderson, a corporation sole - 3141 St. Stephen's Dr., Anderson, CA 96007 t) 530-365-8573 sacredheartanderson@outlook.com sacredheartparish.com Rev. Raj R. Derivera, Pst.; Dcn. Jesus Madrigal; Dcn. Rich Valles; Renae Magana, CRE; CRP Stds.: 99
St. Anne - 3415 Main St., Cottonwood, CA 96022; Mailing: 3141 St. Stephens Dr., Anderson, CA 96022 t) (530) 365-8573

AUBURN

Pastor of St. Joseph Parish, Auburn, a corporation sole - 1162 Lincoln Way, Auburn, CA 95603 t) 530-320-8810 (CRP); 530-885-2956 office@sjauburncatholic.com Rev. Carlo Paul G. Tejano, Pst.; Dcn. Joseph "Mark" Ruiz; CRP Stds.: 231
St. Joseph School - 11610 Atwood Rd., Auburn, CA 95603 t) 530-885-4490 info@saintjosephauburn.org Kristen Mendonsa, DRE; Stds.: 231; Lay Tchrs.: 12
Pastor of St. Teresa of Avila Parish, Auburn, a corporation sole - 11600 Atwood Rd., Auburn, CA 95603 t) 530-889-2254 info@stteresaauburn.com stteresaauburn.com Rev. Arbel S. Cabasagan, Pst.; Dcn. John Sheehan; Dcn. Adam Crawford; Jean Sawyer, Music Min.; Rosalind K Laferriere, DRE; CRP Stds.: 46

BENICIA

St. Dominic - 475 E I St., Benicia, CA 94510-0756 t) 707-747-7220; 707-747-7240 (CRP) tstone@stdombenicia.org; ekissinger@stdombenicia.org www.stdombenicia.org Rev. Carl Schlichte, O.P., Pst.; Rev. David Farrugia, O.P., In Res.; Rev. Vincent Serpa, O.P., In Res.; Dcn. Errol Kissinger, DRE; Rev. Gregory Liu, O.P., Par. Vicar; Dcn. Michael Scafani; Dcn. Shawn Carter; CRP Stds.: 198
St. Dominic School - (Grades PreK-8) 935 E. 5th St.,

Benicia, CA 94510-3427 t) 707-745-1266 admissions@sdbenicia.org sdbenicia.org Penelope Ogden, Prin.; Stds.: 305; Lay Tchrs.: 29

BURNEY

Pastor of St. Francis of Assisi Parish, Burney, a corporation sole - 37464 Juniper Ave., P.O. Drawer 160, Burney, CA 96013 t) (530) 330-5077 pastor@stfrancisburney.org www.stfrancisburney.org Rev. Fernando Meza, Par. Admin.; CRP Stds.: 65

St. Stephen's - 201 State Hwy. 299 E., Bieber, CA 96009 stfrancisburney.org

Our Lady of the Valley - 43434 Hwy. 299E, Fall River Mills, CA 96028 stfrancisburney.org

CARMICHAEL

Pastor of St. John the Evangelist Parish, Carmichael, a corporation sole - 5751 Locust Ave., Carmichael, CA 95608 t) 916-483-4628 (CRP); 916-483-8454 office@sjecarmichael.org www.sjecarmichael.org Rev. Bernardin Mugabo, Pst.; Rev. Bit-Shing Abraham Chiu, Par. Vicar; Rev. Thomas A. Bland, Pastor Emer.; Rev. Alban Uba (Nigeria), In Res.; Dcn. Jack Wilson; Dcn. Keith Johnson; Joanne Gifford, DRE; CRP Stds.: 41

St. John the Evangelist School - 5701 Locust Ave., Carmichael, CA 95608 t) 916-481-8845 principal@stjohnev.com www.stjohnev.com Christine Horton, Prin.; Stds.: 249; Scholastics: 2; Lay Tchrs.: 14

Pastor of Our Lady of the Assumption Parish, Carmichael, a corporation sole - 5057 Cottage Way, Carmichael, CA 95608 t) 916-488-4626 (CRP); 916-481-5115 faithformation@olaparish.net; parish@olaparish.net www.olaparish.net Tracy Urban, DRE; Rev. Eduino T. Silveira, Pst.; Rev. Michael F. Kiernan, Pastor Emer.; Rev. Brendan McKeefry, Pastor Emer.; Dcn. Paul Friedrich; Dcn. Michael Tateishi; CRP Stds.: 85

Our Lady of the Assumption School - 2141 Walnut Ave., Carmichael, CA 95608 t) 916-489-8958 albers@olaparish.net; ministrycoordinator@olaparish.net school.olaparish.net Robert Love, Prin.; Stds.: 341; Lay Tchrs.: 19

CHICO

Pastor of St. John the Baptist Parish, Chico, a corporation sole - 416 Chestnut St, Chico, CA 95928; Mailing: 435 Chestnut St, Chico, CA 95928 t) 530-343-8741 office@sjbchico.org www.sjbchico.org Rev. Francisco J. Hernandez-Gomez, Pst.; Rev. Dean J. Marshall, Par. Vicar; Dcn. F. Paul Sajben; Dcn. William Bruening; Dcn. Jesus Padilla Campos; Dcn. Leigh Langerwerf; Sandra O'Horan, Bus. Mgr.; CRP Stds.: 317

Notre Dame Elementary School - (Grades K-8) 435 Hazel St, Chico, CA 95928 t) 530-342-2502 office@ndschico.org www.ndschico.org Marci Johnson, Prin.; Kari Bertagna, Registrar; Stds.: 207; Lay Tchrs.: 10

St. James - 2416 Faber St., Durham, CA 95938; Mailing: 435 Chestnut St., Chico, CA 95928

Pastor of Our Divine Savior Parish, Chico, a corporation sole - 566 E. Lassen Ave., Chico, CA 95973 t) 530-343-4248 ourdivines@yahoo.com ourdivinesavior.org Rev. Martin J. Ramat, Pst.; Jennifer Forward, DRE; Dcn. David Kraatz; CRP Stds.: 95

CITRUS HEIGHTS

Pastor of Holy Family Parish, Citrus Heights, a corporation sole - 7817 Old Auburn Rd., Citrus Heights, CA 95610 t) 916-726-7217 (CRP); 916-723-2494 office@holyfamilycitrusheights.org www.holyfamilycitrusheights.org/ Rev. Enrique Alvarez, Pst.; Sr. Susana Wong Garcia, CRE; Dcn. Mark Holt; Dcn. Mark Hronicek; Dcn. Donald Galli; CRP Stds.: 86

CLARKSBURG

Pastor of St. Joseph Parish, Clarksburg, a corporation sole - 32890 S. River Rd., Clarksburg, CA 95612 t) 916-665-1132 office@stjosephsclarksburg.org www.stjosephsclarksburg.org Rev. Santiago E. Raudes, Pst.; Rev. Daniel Madigan, Pastor Emer.; CRP Stds.: 45

COLFAX

Pastor of St. Dominic Parish, Colfax, a corporation sole - 58 E. Oak St., Colfax, CA 95713; Mailing: PO Box 752, Colfax, CA 95713 t) 530-346-2286; 530-346-2314 (CRP) st.dominicpastor@gmail.com; st.dominicsecretary@gmail.com Rev. Salvador Bringas, Pst.; CRP Stds.: 5

COLUSA

Pastor of Our Lady of Lourdes Parish, Colusa, a corporation sole - 345 Oak St, Colusa, CA 95932; Mailing: 745 Ware Ave., Colusa, CA 95932 t) 530-458-4170 x1005 (CRP); 530-458-4170 dianneluoma@frontier.com; ollcolusa@yahoo.com www.ourladyoflourdescolusa.com Rev. Jacobo A. Caceres, Pst.; Dcn. Julian Delgado; Dcn. Ruben Fuentes; Laura Cervantes, DRE; CRP Stds.: 126

Our Lady of Lourdes School - (Grades PreK-8) 741 Ware Ave., Colusa, CA 95932 t) 530-458-8208 theollschool.com Stds.: 52; Lay Tchrs.: 4

St. Joseph - 1st St. & Center St., Princeton, CA 95970 t) (916) 458-4170 Rev. Jacob A. Caceres, Pst.;

Our Lady of Sorrows - Hwy. 45 between Grimes & Colusa, Grimes, CA 95950 t) (916) 458-4170 Rev. Jacob A. Caceres, Pst.;

CORNING

Pastor of Immaculate Conception Parish, Corning, a corporation sole - 814 Solano St., Corning, CA 96021; Mailing: 818 Solano St., Corning, CA 96021 t) 530-824-5879; 530-824-4989 (CRP); 530-209-8062 (CRP) iccorning@att.net Rev. Orlando R. Gomez, Pst.; Rocio Guillen, DRE; CRP Stds.: 210

St. Stanislaus - 4th St. & D St., Tehama, CA 96090 t) (530) 824-5879

DAVIS

Pastor of St. James Parish, Davis, a corporation sole - 1275 B St., Davis, CA 95616 t) 530-756-3636; 530-756-3636 (CRP) jmislang@stjamesdavis.net; mberry@stjamesdavis.net stjamesdavis.org Rev. Antonio B. Racela III, Pst.; Rev. Rene Jauregui, Par. Vicar; Dcn. Sam Colenzo; Dcn. Joseph O'Donnell; Josephine Mislang, DRE; CRP Stds.: 165

St. James School - 1215 B St., Davis, CA 95616 t) 530-756-3946 hchurch@sjsdavis.com www.sjsdavis.com Heather Church, Prin.; Stds.: 290; Bro. Tchrs.: 1; Sr. Tchrs.: 1; Lay Tchrs.: 15

Newman Center - 514 C St., Davis, CA 95616 t) 530-753-7393

DIXON

Pastor of St. Peter Parish, Dixon, a corporation sole - 105 S. 2nd St., Dixon, CA 95620 t) 707-678-9424 stpeterschurchdixon@gmail.com stpeterschurchdixon.com Rev. Hector Montoya, Pst.; Rev. Pius Amah, In Res.; Dcn. Daniel Blanton; Dcn. John Fio; CRP Stds.: 299

DOWNIEVILLE

Pastor of Immaculate Conception Parish, Downieville, a corporation sole - 207 Sunnyside Dr., Downieville, CA 95936; Mailing: PO Box 302, Downieville, CA 95936 t) 530-289-3102; 530-289-3644 (Parish Council Chair) c) 530-277-8954 icp110@att.net; foekej@gmail.com Rev. Jossy G. Vattothu, C.M.I., Vicar; Rev. Alexander A. Estrella, Pst.;

St. Thomas - 108 Butte Alley, Sierra City, CA 96125 t) (530) 289-3102

EL DORADO HILLS

Pastor of Holy Trinity Parish, El Dorado Hills, a corporation sole - 3111 Tierra de Dios Dr., El Dorado Hills, CA 95762-8008 t) 530-677-3234 holytrinity@holytrinityparish.org www.holytrinityparish.org Rev. Marcel Emeh, S.D.S., Par. Vicar; Rev. Lawrence J. Beck, Pst.; Dcn. James Hopp; Dcn. Dan Haverty; Rob Sabino, Music Min.; Cynthia Mulcaire, DRE; Jeremy Youngers, Bus. Mgr.; CRP Stds.: 203

Holy Trinity School - 3115 Tierra de Dios Dr., El Dorado Hills, CA 95762-8008 t) 530-677-3591 hts@holytrinityparish.org www.holytrinityparish.org/school Christopher Nelson, Prin.; Stds.: 148; Lay Tchrs.: 13

ELK GROVE

Pastor of Good Shepherd Parish, Elk Grove, a corporation sole - 9539 Racquet Ct., Elk Grove, CA 95758 t) 916-684-5722; 916-683-2963 x30 (CRP) goodshepherdchurch@gscceg.org; cffadmin@gscceg.org gscceg.org Dcn. Rommel Declines; Dcn. Alejandro Llenos; Rev. Michael D. Vaughan, Pst.; Rev. Julius Kaburu, Par. Vicar; Rev. Leon Juchniewicz, Pastor Emer.; CRP Stds.: 491

St. Elizabeth Ann Seton Elementary School - (Grades PreSchool-8) 9539 Racquet Court, Elk Grove, CA 95758 t) 916-684-7903 mswain@stelizabetheg.org Marci Greene, Prin.; Stds.: 392; Lay Tchrs.: 17

Pastor of St. Joseph Parish, Elk Grove, a corporation sole - 9961 Elk Grove-Florin Rd., Elk Grove, CA 95624 t) 916-685-3681; 916-685-3681 x120 (CRP) sjp.dre@stjoseph-elkgrove.net; aurora.aguirre@stjoseph-elkgrove.net stjoseph-elkgrove.net Dcn. Jose Gerardo Martin; Dcn. Gregory McAvoy-Jensen; Dcn. Jovy Perez; Rev. Apolonio C Catada, Par. Vicar; Rev. Julito R. Orpilla, Pst.; CRP Stds.: 310

Mission - 14673 Cantova Way, Rancho Murieta, CA 95683 t) (916) 685-3681 Mission Church of Saint Vincent De Paul

Pastor of St. Maria Goretti Parish, Elk Grove, a corporation sole - 8700 Bradshaw Rd., Elk Grove, CA 95624 t) 916-647-4538 x204; 916-647-4538 (CRP) admin@smgcc.net; business@smgcc.net www.smgcc.net Dcn. Gary Brys; Rev. Sylvester Kwiatkowski, Pst.; Sr. Maria Rosabel Sare, RVM, DRE; CRP Stds.: 140

FAIR OAKS

Pastor of St. Mel Parish, Fair Oaks, a corporation sole - 4745 Pennsylvania Ave., Fair Oaks, CA 95628; Mailing: P.O. Box 1180, Fair Oaks, CA 95628 t) 916-967-1229 office@stmelchurch.org; st.melcff@gmail.com www.stmelchurch.org Rev. Desmond T. O'Reilly, Pst.; Dcn. David Lehman; Dcn. Jack Roland; CRP Stds.: 60

St. Mel School - (Grades PreK-8) t) 916-967-2814 jnagel@stmelschool.org www.stmelschool.org Janet Nagel, Prin.; Stds.: 289; Lay Tchrs.: 24

FAIRFIELD

Pastor of Holy Spirit Parish, Fairfield, a corporation sole - 1050 N. Texas St., Fairfield, CA 94533; Mailing: 1070 N. Texas St., Fairfield, CA 94533 t) 707-425-3138 tlagrazon@holyspiritfairfield.org; vpaul@holyspiritfairfield.org www.holyspiritfairfield.org Rev. Jose Antonio Campos, Par. Vicar; Dcn. Rodolfo Que; Rev. Joel S. Genabia, Pst.; Rev. Michael D. Downey, Pastor Emer.; Rev. Regimon Chandy, In Res.; Dcn. Jack Davault; CRP Stds.: 735

Holy Spirit School - (Grades K-8) 1070 N. Texas St., Fairfield, CA 94533 t) 707-422-5016 mregello@hsschool.org; jthompson@hsschool.org www.hsschool.org Julie Thompson, Prin.; Stds.: 279; Lay Tchrs.: 13

Pastor of Our Lady of Mount Carmel Parish, Fairfield, a Corporation Sole - 2700 Dover Ave., Fairfield, CA 94533 t) (707) 422-7767 olmc.gem@gmail.com; olmc.val@gmail.com olmcfairfield.org (Carmelite Fathers) Rev. Patrick Arthur Gavin, O.Carm, Pst.; Rev. Joseph O. Cilia, O. Carm., Par. Vicar; Dcn. Raymond Elias; Rev. Mario Lopez, O.Carm, In Res.; CRP Stds.: 214

FOLSOM

Pastor of St. John the Baptist Parish, Folsom, a corporation sole - 307 Montrose Dr., Folsom, CA 95630 t) 916-985-2065; 916-985-7338 (CRP) info@folsomcatholic.org; slanger@folsomcatholic.org folsomcatholic.org Dcn. William Goeke; Rev. Renier C. Siva, Pst.; Rev. Cleetus P. Karakkat, Par. Vicar; Rev. F. Ignatius Haran, Pastor Emer.; Shannon Langer, DRE; CRP Stds.: 358

St. John's-Notre Dame - 309 Montrose Dr., Folsom, CA 95630 t) 916-985-4129 michelle.zalles@sjnds.org Kieth Martin, Prin.; Stds.: 366; Lay Tchrs.: 38

FORT JONES

Pastor of Sacred Heart Parish, Fort Jones, a corporation

sole - 11630 Main St., Fort Jones, CA 96032-0126; Mailing: 314 Fourth St., Yreka, CA 96097 t) 530-842-4874 stjoseph310@nctv.com Dcn. Charles Werner; Rev. Ronald V. Torres, Par. Admin.; CRP Stds.: 25

St. Mary's - 387 Center St., Etna, CA 96027 Rev. Ronald Torres, Par. Admin.;

All Saints - 1321 Indian Creek Rd., Happy Camp, CA 96093 t) (530) 842-4874 Rev. Ronald Torres, Par. Admin.;

St. Joseph - Main St., Sawyers Bar, CA 96027 Rev. Ronald Torres, Par. Admin.;

GALT

Pastor of St. Christopher Parish, Galt, a corporation sole - 950 S. Lincoln Way, Galt, CA 95632; Mailing: P.O. Box 276, Galt, CA 95632 t) 209-745-1389; 209-745-1389 x304 (CRP) mariapolanco@saint-christophers.com www.st-christopherchurch.com Rev. Miguel J. Silva, Pst.; Araceli Garcia, DRE; CRP Stds.: 342

GRANITE BAY

Pastor of St. Joseph Marello Parish, Granite Bay, a corporation sole - 7200 Auburn Folsom Rd., Granite Bay, CA 95746 t) 916-786-5001 sjmarelloparish@yahoo.com; discoverysjm@gmail.com www.stjosephmarello.org Rev. Philip V. Massetti, O.S.J., Pst.; Dcn. Jeffery McClure; CRP Stds.: 120

GRASS VALLEY

Pastor of St. Patrick Parish, Grass Valley, a corporation sole - 235 Chapel St., Grass Valley, CA 95945 t) 530-273-2347 admin@stpatrickgrassvalley.org; faithformation@stpatrickgrassvalley.org www.stpatrickgrassvalley.org Rev. Alexander A. Estrella, Pst.; Rev. Jossy G. Vattothu, C.M.I., Par. Vicar; Dcn. Richard Soria, DRE; CRP Stds.: 45

Mt. St. Mary's Academy - (Grades PreK-8) 400 S. Church St., Grass Valley, CA 95945 t) 530-273-4694 info@mtstmarys.org www.mtstmarys.org Edee Wood, Prin.; Stds.: 223; Lay Tchrs.: 11

GRIDLEY

Pastor of Sacred Heart Parish, Gridley, a corporation sole - 1560 Hazel St., Gridley, CA 95948; Mailing: P.O. Box 205, Gridley, CA 95948 t) 530-846-2140 joannhamman@sbcglobal.net; sacredheartgridley@gmail.com Rev. Roland B. Ramirez, Pst.; Joann Hamman, DRE; Dcn. Adam Bowers, RCIA Coord.; CRP Stds.: 210

Our Lady of Guadalupe - 9660 Broadway, Live Oak, CA 95953 t) (503) 084-6214

ISLETON

Pastor of St. Therese Parish, Isleton, a corporation sole - 100 4th St., Isleton, CA 95641; Mailing: 14012 Walnut Ave, Walnut Grove, CA 95690 t) 916-776-1330 info@churchofsaintanthony.org www.churchofsaintanthony.org Rev. Juan Carlos Villavicencio, P.E.S., Par. Vicar; Rev. Paolo Dorrego, P.E.S., Pst.; CRP Stds.: 45

JACKSON

Pastor of St. Katharine Drexel Parish, Martell, a corporation sole - 11361 Prospect Dr., Jackson, CA 95642 t) 209-223-2970 office@amadorcatholic.com www.amadorcatholic.com Rev. Colin C. Wen, Pst.; Rev. Thomas Relihan, Pastor Emer.; Dcn. Ray Moreno; CRP Stds.: 136

Our Lady of the Pines - 26750 Tiger Creek Rd., Pioneer, CA 95666

Immaculate Conception - 125 Amelia St., Sutter Creek, CA 95685

Sacred Heart of Jesus - 20 Relihan Dr., Ione, CA 95640

St. Patrick - 115 Church St., Jackson, CA 95642

KNIGHTS LANDING

Pastor of St. Paul Parish, Knights Landing, a corporation sole - 222 Sycamore Way, Knights Landing, CA 95645; Mailing: P.O. Box 176, Knights Landing, CA 95645 t) 530-735-6478 Rev. Jonathan B. Molina, Par. Admin.; Dcn. Hermenegildo Varela; CRP Stds.: 45

Catechetical Center - 6th St. & Locust St., Knights Landing, CA 95645 t) (530) 204-9097

St. Agnes - 9865 Main St., Zamora, CA 95645 t) (530) 735-6478

LAKE ALMANOR

Pastor of Our Lady of the Snows Parish, Lake Almanor, a corporation sole - 220 Clifford Dr., Lake Almanor, CA 96137; Mailing: P.O. Box 1970, Chester, CA 96020 t) 530-259-3932 tmylfrd@yahoo.com Rev. Joshua Sia, Pst.; Debbie Rives, DRE; CRP Stds.: 2

LINCOLN

Pastor of St. Joseph Parish, Lincoln, a corporation sole - 280 Oak Tree Ln., Lincoln, CA 95648 t) 916-645-2102; 916-645-2684 (CRP) stjosephlincoln@gmail.com; stjoelincolndre@gmail.com www.stjosephlincoln.com Rev. Fredhelito E. Gucor, Pst.; Rev. Jose Antonio Campos, Par. Vicar; Dcn. Paul DeVito; Dcn. Patrick Mahan; Dcn. Roberto Ruiz; Dcn. Juvencio Vela; CRP Stds.: 356

St. Boniface - 1028 Marcum Rd., Nicolaus, CA 95659 t) (916) 645-2102

St. Daniel - 214 Main St., Wheatland, CA 95692 t) (916) 645-2102

Our Lady of Guadalupe - 3rd St. & K St., Lincoln, CA 95648 t) (916) 645-2102

MARYSVILLE

Pastor of St. Joseph Parish, Marysville, a corporation sole - 702 C St., Marysville, CA 95901; Mailing: 223 8th St., Marysville, CA 95901 t) 530-742-6461 stjosephmarysville@gmail.com stjoseph-marysville.org Rev. Michal Olszewski, Pst.; Dale Walker, Bus. Mgr.; Dcn. Rafael Moreno; CRP Stds.: 473

Sacred Heart Church - ; Mailing: P.O. Box 208, Dobbins, CA 95953

MCCLOUD

Pastor of St. Joseph Parish, McCloud, a corporation sole - 213 Colombero Dr., McCloud, CA 96057; Mailing: 507 Pine St., Mt. Shasta, CA 96067 t) 530-926-4477 mtshastastanthony@gmail.com Rev. Lester T. Menor, Pst.; CRP Stds.: 7

MOUNT SHASTA

Pastor of St. John the Evangelist Parish, Dunsmuir, a corporation sole - 507 Pine St., Mount Shasta, CA 96067; Mailing: 1051 N. Davis Ave., Weed, CA 96094 t) 530-926-4477; 530-235-4705 (CRP) Dcn. Time Louie; Rev. Mario Valmorida, Admin.; Eileen Congi, DRE; Jan Garrigus, RCIA Coord.; CRP Stds.: 1

MT. SHASTA

Pastor of St. Anthony Parish, Mount Shasta, a corporation sole - 507 Pine St., Mt. Shasta, CA 96067 t) 530-926-4477 mtshastastanthony@gmail.com Rev. Lester T. Menor, Pst.; CRP Stds.: 11

NEVADA CITY

Pastor of St. Canice Parish, Nevada City, a corporation sole - 317 Washington St., Nevada City, CA 95959 t) 530-265-2049 secretary@stcanice.org stcanice.com Rev. Jossy G. Vattothu, C.M.I., Par. Vicar; Rev. Alexander A. Estrella, Pst.; CRP Stds.: 4

NORTH HIGHLANDS

Pastor of St. Lawrence Parish, North Highlands, a corporation sole - 4325 Don Julio Blvd., North Highlands, CA 95660 t) 916-332-4777 stl.businessmgr@gmail.com; esj.stlawrence18@gmail.com stlawrencenh.org Rev. Alvaro Perez, P.E.S., Pst.; Rev. Adam Tokashiki, P.E.S., Par. Vicar; Dcn. Kevin Staszkow; Elvia Jimenez, CRE; Josue Barraza, Youth Min.; Hector A. Callejas, Bus. Mgr.; CRP Stds.: 256

ORANGEVALE

Divine Savior - 9079 Greenback Ln., Orangevale, CA 95662-4703 t) 916-989-7400 kathleen@divinesavior.com; katie@divinesavior.com www.divinesavior.com Rev. Octavio Trejo Flores, SDS (Mexico); Rev. Patric Nikolas, SDS; CRP Stds.: 160

ORLAND

Pastor of St. Dominic Parish, Orland, A corporation sole - 822 A St., Orland, CA 95963; Mailing: 830 A St., Orland, CA 95963 t) 530-865-4550 stdominicorland@gmail.com www.facebook.com/saintdominicorland Rev. Mauricio Hurtado, Pst.; Dcn. Benito Rico; Dcn. Alberto Vargas; Dcn. Paul Randall; CRP Stds.: 463

St. Mary - 400 Los Robles Ave., Hamilton City, CA 95951 t) (530) 865-1550

OROVILLE

Pastor of St. Thomas the Apostle Parish, Oroville, a corporation sole - 1330 Bird St., Oroville, CA 95965 t) 530-533-0262 orocatholic@att.net www.orovillecatholic.org Rev. German Plaza Ramos, Par. Admin.; Dcn. Tom O'Connell; Dcn. Jesus Venegas; Zerimar Ramirez, DRE; CRP Stds.: 25

St. Thomas the Apostle School - 1380 Bird St., Oroville, CA 95965 t) 530-534-6969 kheinert@stschool.net www.stschool.net Kasia Heinert, Prin.; Stds.: 115; Lay Tchrs.: 7

St. Anthony of Padula - 10184 La Porte Rd., Challenge, CA 95925 t) (530) 533-0262

PARADISE

Pastor of St. Thomas More Parish, Paradise, a corporation sole - 767 Elliott Rd., Paradise, CA 95969 t) 530-877-4501 office@stmparadise.org www.stmparadise.net Rev. Martin J. Ramat, Pst.; Dcn. Michael Mangan; Sandra Rodriguez, CRE; CRP Stds.: 20

PLACERVILLE

Pastor of St. Patrick Parish, Placerville, a corporation sole - 3109 Sacramento St., Placerville, CA 95667 t) 530-622-7692 (CRP); 530-622-0373 faithformation@stpatpv.org; parishoffice@stpatpv.org stpatpv.org Dcn. Brian Smith; Rev. Hernando Gomez-Amaya (Colombia), Pst.; Rev. John Cantwell, Pastor Emer.; Kathleen Hill-Kasnic, DRE; Lupita Gonzalez, Bus. Mgr.; CRP Stds.: 254

St. James - 2831 Harkness St., Georgetown, CA 95634 t) 530-333-9432

St. Patrick Ladies Society - 3109 Sacramento, Street, CA 95667 t) (530) 622-0373

St. Patrick Aid Ministry (S.P.A.M.) - 3109 Sacramento Street, Placerville, CA 95667 t) (530) 622-0373

St. James Society - 2831 Harkness St., Georgetown, CA 95634 t) 530-333-2946 bearstate@hughes.net

PORTOLA

Pastor of Holy Family Parish, Portola, a corporation sole - 108 Taylor Ave., Portola, CA 96122 t) 530-832-5006 hfport@sbcglobal.net Rev. Innocent Subiza, Par. Admin.; Jessica Renteria, DRE; CRP Stds.: 40

Holy Rosary - 614 4th St., Loyalton, CA 96118 t) (530) 832-5006

QUINCY

Pastor of St. John Parish, Quincy, a corporation sole - 170 Lawrence St., Quincy, CA 95971; Mailing: P.O. Box 510, Quincy, CA 95971 t) 530-283-0890 saintjohnquincy@gmail.com Rev. Matthew J. Blank; Dcn. John Breaux; CRP Stds.: 19

RANCHO CORDOVA

Pastor of St. John Vianney Parish, Rancho Cordova, a Corporation Sole - 10497 Coloma Rd., Rancho Cordova, CA 95670 t) 916-362-1385 (Office); 916-369-8669 (CRP) parish.office@sjvparish.com; faithformation@sjvparish.com www.sjvparish.com Rev. Giovanni B. Gamas, Pst.; Rev. Martin J. Moroney, Pastor Emer.; Rev. Alfredo L. Tamayo, In Res.; Dcn. Daniel Rangel; Dcn. Walter Little; Veronica Zeller, CRE; CRP Stds.: 261

St. John Vianney School - (Grades K-8) 10499 Coloma Rd., Rancho Cordova, CA 95670 t) 916-363-4610 principal@sjvschool.org Amy Hale, Prin.; Stds.: 180; Lay Tchrs.: 9

RED BLUFF

Pastor of Sacred Heart Parish, Red Bluff, a corporation sole - 515 Main St., Red Bluff, CA 96080; Mailing: 2355 Monroe Ave., Red Bluff, CA 96080 t) 530-527-1351 admin@sacredheartredbluff.org; sacredheartredbluff@outlook.com www.sacredheartredbluff.org Dcn. Ignacio Montes; Rev. Charles P. Kelly, Pst.; Elsa Spaulding, Bus. Mgr.; CRP Stds.: 196

Sacred Heart School - 2255 Monroe Ave., Red Bluff, CA 96080 t) 530-527-6727 rcherveny@shsredbluff.org sacredheartredbluffschool.org Paul Weber, Prin.; Stds.: 135; Sr. Tchrs.: 3; Lay Tchrs.: 6

REDDING

Pastor of St. Joseph Parish, Redding, a corporation sole - 2040 Walnut Ave., Redding, CA 96001 t) 530-243-3463 stjoeparish@sbcglobal.net www.stjosephredding.org Rev. Eric D. Lofgren, Pst.; Rev. Ryan P. Mahar, Par. Vicar; Rev. Msgr. Russell G. Terra, Pastor Emer.; Dcn. Michael Mangas; Gayle Hermann, DRE; CRP Stds.: 17

St. Joseph School - 2460 Gold St., Redding, CA 96001 t) 530-243-2302 contact@sjsr.org Bill Koppes, Prin.; Stds.: 168; Lay Tchrs.: 13

St. Michael - 3440 Shasta Dam Blvd., Shasta Lake City, CA 96019 t) (530) 243-3463

Pastor of Our Lady of Mercy Parish, Redding, a corporation sole - 2600 Shasta View Dr., Redding, CA 96002 t) 530-222-3424 jessica@olmredding.net www.olmredding.net Rev. Cirilo Cervantes, M.C., Par. Admin.; Dcn. Ray Arnold; Dcn. Jose Ceja; Dcn. Raymond Hemenway; CRP Stds.: 142

Mary Queen of Peace - 30725 Shingletown Ridge Rd., Shingletown, CA 96088 t) (530) 222-3424

RIO VISTA

Pastor of St. Joseph Parish, Rio Vista, a corporation sole - 130 S. 4th St., Rio Vista, CA 94571 t) 707-374-2155; 707-374-2607 (CRP) stjosephoffice@comcast.net; stjosephcatechism@comcast.net www.stjosephriovista.org Rev. Mervin P. Concepcion, Pst.; Vega Elsa, DRE; CRP Stds.: 40

ROCKLIN

Pastor of SS. Peter and Paul Parish, Rocklin, a corporation sole - 4450 Granite Dr., Rocklin, CA 95677 t) 916-624-5827 sarah.peterson@rocklincatholic.org www.rocklincatholic.org Rev. Michael J. Dillon, Pastor Emer.; Dcn. David Haproff; Dcn. Bob Leathers; Sarah Peterson, Bus. Mgr.; Rev. Bony Arackal, Par. Admin.; Jennifer Gordon, CRE; Darcy Wharton, CRE; Michelle Pfister, RCIA Coord.; Nancy Von Thaden, Youth Min.; CRP Stds.: 499

ROSEVILLE

St. Clare - 1950 Junction Blvd., Roseville, CA 95747 t) 916-772-4717 paulas@stclareroseville.org; agness@stclareroseville.org stclareroseville.org Dcn. Larry Bertrand; Dcn. Kenneth Crawford; Rev. George T. Snyder Jr., Pst.; Rev. Santhosh Srayil Kurian, Par. Vicar; Dcn. Marinko Kraljevich; Dcn. Carl Kube; Andres Gonzales, Youth Min.; Patty Murphy, Coord. of Liturgy; Paula Staszkow, Parish Dir.; CRP Stds.: 552

Pastor of St. Rose of Lima Parish, Roseville, a corporation sole - 615 Vine Ave, Roseville, CA 95678 t) 916-783-5211; 916-783-5211 x7010 (CRP) office@strosechurch.org; dgentile@strosechurch.org strosechurch.org Dcn. Paul Herman; Rev. Sagar Kumar Gade, Par. Vicar; Rev. J. Michael B. Baricuatro, Pst.; Rev. Michael J. Cormack, Pastor Emer.; Dcn. Michael Turner; Dcn. Mark Van Hook; Dona Gentile, DRE; CRP Stds.: 524

St. Rose of Lima School - 633 Vine Ave., Roseville, CA 95678 t) 916-782-1161; 916-483-5211 ccanalas@strose.org; olgentile@strosechurch.org Suzanne Smolley, Prin.; Stds.: 252; Lay Tchrs.: 12

SACRAMENTO

Pastor of Cathedral of the Blessed Sacrament Parish, Sacramento, a corporation sole - 1017 Eleventh St., Sacramento, CA 95814 t) 916-444-3071 blessed@cathedralsacramento.org Catechetical Center Cathedral Parish Hall conducted by parish CCD and Daughters of Charity of Canossa. Most Rev. Jaime Soto; Rev. Michael O'Reilly, Rector; Dcn. Omar Bardales; Dcn. John Gisla; Dcn. Edgar Hilbert; Rex Rallanka, Music Min.; Sr. Lisa Marie Doty, DRE; CRP Stds.: 161

Pastor of St. Anne Parish, Sacramento, a corporation sole - 7724 24th St., Sacramento, CA 95832 t) 916-422-8380; 916-287-6103 (CRP) Rev. Lawrence M. Kithinji, Par. Admin.; Vera Teresa, DRE; CRP Stds.: 127

Pastor of St. Anthony Parish, Sacramento, a corporation sole - 660 Florin Rd., Sacramento, CA 95831 t) 916-392-6362 (CFF); 916-428-5678 christine@stasac.org; office@stasac.org www.stasac.org Rev. Mieczyslaw Mitch Maleszyk, Admin.; Dcn. David Cabrera; Dcn. Richard Koppes; Christine Soriano, DRE; CRP Stds.: 165

Pastor of St. Charles Borromeo Parish, Sacramento, a corporation sole - 7584 Center Pkwy., Sacramento, CA 95823 t) 916-421-7174 (CRP); 916-421-1063 (CRP); 916-421-5177 scbchurch@sbcglobal.net www.scbchurchsac.org Rev. Manuel A. Rodriguez, Par. Vicar; Rev. Oscar Gomez-Medina, Pst.; Sr. Josie Tanudtanud, DRE; Sr. Sara Janette Marquez Gomez, S.C.J.C., DRE; CRP Stds.: 733

St. Charles Borromeo School - 7580 Center Pkwy., Sacramento, CA 95823 t) 916-421-6189 scboffice@scbsac.net Antoinette Perez, Prin.; Stds.: 185; Lay Tchrs.: 9

Pastor of Divine Mercy Parish, Sacramento, a corporation sole - 2231 Club Center Dr., Sacramento, CA 95835 t) 916-256-3134 parish@divinemercynatomas.com; divinemercy.parish@sbcglobal.net www.divinemercynatomas.com Dcn. James Ogbonna; Rev. Eric Flores, Pst.; Luz Manrique, DRE; CRP Stds.: 285

Pastor of St. Elizabeth Parish, Sacramento, a corporation sole - 1817 12th St., Sacramento, CA 95811 t) 916-442-2333 stelizportugal@gmail.com www.stelizabethsac.org Rev. Michael O'Reilly, Par. Admin.; John Pires, DRE; CRP Stds.: 10

Pastor of St. Francis of Assisi Parish, Sacramento, a corporation sole - 1066 26th St., Sacramento, CA 95816 t) 916-443-8084 info@stfrancisparish.com; dff@stfrancisparish.com www.stfrancisparish.com Rev. Rey B. Bersabal, Pst.; JD Warrick, Admin.; John Iosefa, Music Min.; CRP Stds.: 55

St. Francis of Assisi School - 2500 K St., Sacramento, CA 95816 t) 916-442-5494 mainoffice@stfranciselem.org www.stfranciselem.org Ivan Hrga, Prin.; Stds.: 320; Lay Tchrs.: 17

Pastor of Holy Spirit Parish, Sacramento, a corporation sole - 3159 Land Park Dr., Sacramento, CA 95818 t) 916-443-5442 office@hs-sacramento.org www.hs-sacramento.org Dcn. Eric Hintz; Dcn. Daniel Patterson; Vince Nims, Youth Min.; Louise Maestretti, Bus. Mgr.; Rev. Loreto Bong B. Rojas, Pst.; CRP Stds.: 306

Holy Spirit School - (Grades 4-8) 3920 W. Land Park Dr., Sacramento, CA 95822 t) 916-448-5663 maltieri@hs-ps.com; rdomingo@hs-ps.com Rafael Domingo, Prin.; Stds.: 301; Lay Tchrs.: 16

Pastor of St. Ignatius Loyola Parish, Sacramento, a corporation sole - 3235 Arden Way, Sacramento, CA 95825-2014 t) 916-482-9666 x200 lchacon@stignatiussac.org www.stignatiussac.org Rev. Thomas M. Lucas, S.J., Pst.; Dcn. Jackson Gualco; Rev. Thomas H. O'Neill, S.J., Par. Vicar; Rev. Arthur J. Wehr, S.J., Par. Vicar; Rev. Matthew Yim, S.J., Par. Vicar; Dcn. Anthony Pescetti; Fatima Avila-Ohlsen, DRE; CRP Stds.: 89

St. Ignatius Loyola School - (Grades PreK-8) 3245 Arden Way, Sacramento, CA 95825 t) 916-488-3907 x103 pkochis@stignatiussacschool.org Patricia Kochis, Prin.; Katrena Paine, Vice Prin.; Stds.: 400; Lay Tchrs.: 16

Pastor of Immaculate Conception Parish, Sacramento, a corporation sole - 3263 1st Ave., Sacramento, CA 95817 t) 916-452-6866 religioused@immaculateconceptionsacramento.org; info@immaculateconceptionsacramento.org www.immaculateconceptionsacramento.org Rev. Luis F. Urrego (Colombia), Pst.; Dcn. Gerald Pauly; Josefina Gonzalez, DRE; Dcn. Genaro Gonzalez; CRP Stds.: 172

Pastor of St. Jeong-Hae Elizabeth Parish, Sacramento, a corporation sole - 9354 Kiefer Blvd., Sacramento, CA 95826 c) (916) 580-8519 (Deacon: Sang Dominic Kim) besttechno1@yahoo.com www.sackcc.net Dcn. Sang Dominic Kim; CRP Stds.: 19

Pastor of St. Joseph Parish, Sacramento, a corporation sole - 1717 El Monte Ave., Sacramento, CA 95815; Mailing: 1715 El Monte Ave, Sacramento, CA 95815 t) 916-925-3584 latu_cffsjc@yahoo.com; stjoseph1924@gmail.com saintjosephsacramento.org Dcn. Rafael Lopez; Rev. Rodolfo D. Llamas, Par. Admin.; Dcn. Antonio Ponce; Sr. Soledad Castillo, H.R.F., DRE; Dcn. Atonio Latu, DRE; CRP Stds.: 298

Pastor of St. Mary Parish, Sacramento, a corporation sole - 1333 58th St., Sacramento, CA 95819 t) 916-452-0296 x20 (CRP); 916-452-0296 cff@stmarysacto.org; rcia@stmarysacto.org www.stmarysacto.org Rev. Kavungal Davy, C.M.I., Pst.; Dcn. George Kriske; Cindy Blecha, DRE; Michelle Mills, RCIA Coord.; CRP Stds.: 40

St. Mary School - (Grades PreK-8) 1351 58th St., Sacramento, CA 95819 t) 916-452-1100 mdarosa@saintmaryschool.com www.saintmaryschool.com Preschool Mary DaRosa, Prin.; Stds.: 340; Lay Tchrs.: 12

Pastor of Our Lady of Guadalupe Parish, Sacramento, a corporation sole - 711 T St, Sacramento, CA 95811; Mailing: 1909 7th St, Sacramento, CA 95811 t) 916-442-3211; 916-446-3500 (CRP) office@shrinegpe.org; catechesis@shrinegpe.org www.guadalupe-sacramento.org Rev. Juan Francisco Bracamontes, Par. Admin.; Rev. Antonio Plasencia, Par. Vicar; Dcn. Alfredo Anguino; Sr. Vicenta Lemus, CRE; CRP Stds.: 350

Pastor of Our Lady of Lourdes Parish, Sacramento, a corporation sole - 1951 North Ave., Sacramento, CA 95838 t) 916-925-5313 ourladyoflourdes@comcast.net Rev. Dariusz Malczuk, Par. Admin.; Dcn. Jose Mejia; Sr. Blanca Dominguez, FdCC, DRE; CRP Stds.: 105

Daughters of Charity of Canossa - 1949 North Ave., Sacramento, CA 95838 t) 916-925-4001 Sr. Lisa Marie Doty, FdCC, Supr.;

Pastor of St. Paul Parish, Sacramento, a corporation sole - 8720 Florin Rd., Sacramento, CA 95828; Mailing: P.O. Box 292280, Sacramento, CA 95829 t) 916-381-5200; 916-381-5200 x2003 (CRP) saintpaulcatholic@comcast.net; saintpauldre@comcast.net www.stpaul-florin.org Rev. Joyle T. Martinez, Pst.; Sr. Elizabeth Siguenza, DRE; Dcn. Antonio Ramirez; CRP Stds.: 359

Pastor of St. Peter and All Hallows Parish, Sacramento, a corporation sole - 5501 14th Ave., Sacramento, CA 95820; Mailing: 5500 13th Ave., Sacramento, CA 95820 t) 916-456-7206 icorral@sp-ah.org sp-ah.org Rev. Jovito D. Rata, Pst.; Dcn. Jia Yah; Rev. Julian Medina, In Res.; Dcn. Tou Moua; Dcn. Manuel Ocon; Lupita Perez, DRE; CRP Stds.: 325

All Hallows - t) (916) 456-7206 (Worship Site)

Pastor of St. Philomene Parish, Sacramento, a corporation sole - 2428 Bell St., Sacramento, CA 95825 t) 916-481-6757 ffdirector@stphilomene.com www.stphilomene.com Rev. Gerald J. Ryle, Pastor Emer.; Dcn. Charles Cheever; Miluska Beltran, DRE; CRP Stds.: 215

St. Philomene School - (Grades K-8) 2320 El Camino Ave., Sacramento, CA 95821 t) 916-489-1506 office@stphilomene.org www.stphilomene.org Kerri Bray-Smith, Prin.; Stds.: 165; Sr. Tchrs.: 1; Scholastics: 13; Lay Tchrs.: 10

Pastor of Presentation of the Blessed Virgin Mary Parish, Sacramento, a corporation sole - 4123 Robertson Ave., Sacramento, CA 95821-0208 t) 916-482-8883 (CRP); 916-481-7441 office@presentationparish.org www.presentationparish.org Rev. Stanley T. Poltorak, Pst.; Dcn. Lawrence Klimecki; Sidney Curry, DRE; CRP Stds.: 60

Presentation of the Blessed Virgin Mary School - 3100 Norris Ave., Sacramento, CA 95821 t) 916-482-0351 wpavelchik@presentationschool.net; cdonahue@presentationschool.net www.presentationschool.net Carrie Donohue, Prin.; Stds.: 291; Sr. Tchrs.: 4; Lay Tchrs.: 3

Dominican Sisters of Mary, Mother of the Eucharist - 3110 Norris Ave., Sacramento, CA 95821 t) 916-482-0351

Pastor of St. Robert Parish, Sacramento, A Corporation

sole - 2243 Irvin Way, Sacramento, CA 95822 t) 916-451-1475; 916-451-1475 (CRP) churchst.robert@comcast.net; deacon_preciliano@yahoo.com www.saintrobertsac.org Rev. Michael D. Ritter, Pst.; Hilda Ramirez, DRE; CRP Stds.: 67

St. Robert School - 2251 Irvin Way, Sacramento, CA 95822 t) 916-452-2111 office@strobertschool.org www.strobertschool.org Samara Palko, Prin.; Stds.: 231; Lay Tchrs.: 14

Pastor of St. Rose Parish, Sacramento, a corporation sole - 5961 Franklin Blvd., Sacramento, CA 95824; Mailing: P.O. Box 246070, Sacramento, CA 95824 t) 510-287-1241 (CRP); 916-421-1777 (CRP); 916-421-1414 mary.maucieri.sr@gmail.com; pastorstrose@gmail.com www.stroseinsacramento.com Sr. Armida Ortega, DRE; Rev. Jose J. Beltran, Pst.; Dcn. Gilberto Coss; Mary Maucieri, Bus. Mgr.; CRP Stds.: 380

St. Patrick Academy - 5945 Franklin Blvd., Sacramento, CA 95824 t) 916-421-4963 info@saintpatricksacademy.net Julie Nguyen, Prin.; Stds.: 195; Sr. Tchrs.: 1; Lay Tchrs.: 10

Pastor of Sacred Heart Parish, Sacramento, a corporation sole - 1040 39th St., Sacramento, CA 95816 t) 916-452-4136 x2 c) 916-452-4830 (RCIA); 916-947-2683 (CRP) shchurchoffice@gmail.com; ritaspillane@gmail.com sacredheart.church Very Rev. Mark R. Richards, Pst.; Tila Madrigal, CRE; Rev. Simon Lodge (United Kingdom), Par. Vicar; Dcn. Sergio Diaz; Paul Sunderman, Youth Min.; Rita Spillane, RCIA Coord.; CRP Stds.: 42

Sacred Heart - (Grades PreK-8) 856 39th St., Sacramento, CA 95816 t) 916-456-1576 tsparks@sacredheartschool.net www.sacredheartschool.net Theresa Sparks, Prin.; Stds.: 285; Lay Tchrs.: 12

Pastor of St. Stephen the First Martyr Parish, Sacramento, a corporation sole - 5461 44th St., Sacramento, CA 95820 t) 916-455-5114 stephenproto@yahoo.com www.sacfssp.com Rev. Stephen Braun, FSSP, Vicar; Rev. Joshua C. Curtis, F.S.S.P., Pst.; Rev. Alan McWhirter, FSSP, Vicar; CRP Stds.: 185

Vietnamese Martyrs Parish - 8181 Florin Rd., Sacramento, CA 95828-9714 t) 916-383-4276; 916-812-2945 (CRP) cttdsacto@gmail.com cttd.org Rev. Vu Cao, CRM, Pst.; Rev. Ba Do, CRM; Dcn. Phong Nguyen, DRE; Dcn. Henry Hoang Tran; Dcn. An Binh Nguyen; Dcn. Ted Trong Nguyen; CRP Stds.: 477

SOUTH LAKE TAHOE

Pastor of St. Theresa Parish, South Lake Tahoe, a Corporation Sole - 1041 Lyons Ave., South Lake Tahoe, CA 96150 t) 530-544-4788 (CRP); 530-544-3533 x100 sttheresa@tahoecatholic.com www.tahoecatholic.com/ Rev. Joseph Sebastian, C.M.I., Par. Admin.; Danette Winslow, DRE; CRP Stds.: 162

SUSANVILLE

Pastor of Sacred Heart Parish, Susanville, a corporation sole - 120 N. Union St., Susanville, CA 96130; Mailing: P.O. Box 430, Susanville, CA 96130 t) 530-257-3230 secretaryshpsusanville@gmail.com www.sacredheartsusanville.org Rev. Arnold P. Parungao, Pst.; CRP Stds.: 51

Msgr. Moran Hall - 140 N. Weatherlow St., Susanville, CA 96130-3935 t) (530) 257-3230

TAHOE CITY

Pastor of Corpus Christi Parish, Tahoe City, a corporation sole - 905 W. Lake Blvd., Tahoe City, CA 96145; Mailing: P.O. Box 1878, Tahoe City, CA 96145 t) 530-583-4409 secretary@corpuschristi-tahoe.org www.corpuschristi-tahoe.org Rev. R. Francis Stevenson, Pst.; Teresa Mills, DRE; CRP Stds.: 28

Queen of the Snows - 1550 Squaw Valley Rd., Olympic Valley, CA 96146 t) (530) 583-4409

Marie Sluchak Community Park - Pine & Wilson Sts., Tahoma, CA 96142 t) (530) 583-4409 (July & August only)

TRUCKEE

Pastor of Assumption of the Blessed Virgin Mary Parish, Truckee, a corporation sole - 10930 Alder Dr., Truckee, CA 96161 t) 530-587-3595 info@assumptiontruckee.com; dreassumtiontruckee@outlook.com assumptiontruckee.com Rev. Vincent R. Juan, Pst.; Carol Fowler, DRE; CRP Stds.: 105

Our Lady of the Lake - 8263 Steelhead Ave., Kings Beach, CA 96143; Mailing: 10930 Alder Dr., Truckee, CA 96161 www.assumptiontruckee.com

TULELAKE

Pastor of Holy Cross Parish, Tulelake, a corporation sole - 765 First St., Tulelake, CA 96134; Mailing: P.O. Box 266, Tulelake, CA 96134 t) 530-640-2613 (CRP); 530-667-2727 cmarquez.cm10@gmail.com; holycrossandolgc@gmail.com Rev. Edgardo Garcia-Velazquez, Par. Admin.; Eneida Hernandez, DRE; CRP Stds.: 96

Our Lady of Good Counsel - W. 3rd St., Dorris, CA 96023 t) (530) 667-2727

VACAVILLE

Pastor of St. Joseph Parish, Vacaville, a corporation sole - 1791 Marshall Rd., Vacaville, CA 95687 t) 707-447-2354 office@stjoseph-vacaville.org; armida@stjoseph-vacaville.org www.stjv.org Dcn. Scott Sexton; Rev. Joshy Mathew, Pst.; Rev. Pepin Dandou, Par. Vicar; CRP Stds.: 83

Notre Dame - (Grades PreK-8) 1781 Marshall Rd., Vacaville, CA 95687 t) 707-447-1460 office@notredamevacaville.org notredamevacaville.org/ Tom Jensen, Prin.; Stds.: 308; Lay Tchrs.: 13

Pastor of St. Mary Parish, Vacaville, a Corporation Sole - 350 Stinson Ave., Vacaville, CA 95688 t) 707-448-2390; (707) 509-3352 (Faith Formation); (707) 446-4231 (Youth Minister/NFP) office@stmarysvacaville.com; faithformation@stmarysvacaville.com stmarysvacaville.com Rev. Brian J. Soliven, Pst.; Rev. Reji Joseph, Vicar; Rev. Michael McFadden, Pastor Emer.; Dcn. Robert Vandergraaf; Andreya Arevalo, Youth Min.; Martha Batres-Martin, DRE; CRP Stds.: 278

VALLEJO

Pastor of St. Basil Parish, Vallejo, a corporation sole - 1200 Tuolumne St., Vallejo, CA 94590; Mailing: 1225 Tuolumne St., Vallejo, CA 94590 t) 707-644-8309 (CRP); 707-644-5251 stbasilvallejore@gmail.com; fatheramby@gmail.com Dcn. Casey Walker; Rev. Ambrose O. Ugwuegbu (Nigeria), Par. Admin.; Julie Kissinger, DRE; CRP Stds.: 136

St. Basil School - 1230 Nebraska St., Vallejo, CA 94590 t) 707-642-7629 kwidenmann@stbasilschool.org Julia Boen, Prin.; Stds.: 294; Lay Tchrs.: 12

Pastor of St. Catherine of Siena Parish, Vallejo, a corporation sole - 3450 Tennessee St., Vallejo, CA 94591 t) 707-553-1355 stcatherine@stcsv.org stcatherinevallejo.org Rev. Jose Estaniel, MSP, Par. Vicar; Lucille Natividad, DRE; Dcn. Pedro Lobo; Dcn. Alejandro Madero; Dcn. Juan Moreno; Dcn. Renato Peregrino; Rev. Glenn Giovanni Jaron, M.S.P. (Philippines), Pst.; Dcn. Dennis Purificacion; CRP Stds.: 221

St. Catherine of Siena School - (Grades PreK-8) 3460 Tennessee St., Vallejo, CA 94591 t) 707-643-6691 Hydie Hess, Prin.; Stds.: 243; Lay Tchrs.: 12

Pastor of St. Vincent Ferrer Parish of Vallejo, a Corporation Sole - 420 Florida St., Vallejo, CA 94590; Mailing: 816 Santa Clara St., Vallejo, CA 94590 t) 707-643-0188 (CRP); 707-644-8396; 707-644-8795 stvincentferrercff@gmail.com; office@stvincentferrer.org www.stvincentferrer.org Dcn. Rafael Rey; Rev. Steven J. W. Wood, Par. Vicar; Dcn. John Bockman; Rev. Vicente C. Teneza, Pst.; Sr. Fe Bigwas, R.V.M., DRE; CRP Stds.: 329

St. Vincent Ferrer School - 411 Kentucky St., Vallejo, CA 94590 t) 707-642-4311 jessica.dare@svfsvallejo.org svfsvallejo.org Jessica Dare, Prin.; Stds.: 250; Lay Tchrs.: 24

WALNUT GROVE

Pastor of St. Anthony Parish, Walnut Grove, a corporation sole - 14012 Walnut Ave., Walnut Grove, CA 95690 t) 916-776-1330 info@churchofsaintanthony.org; frpaolo@churchofsaintanthony.org www.churchofsaintanthony.org Rev. Juan Carlos Villavicencio, P.E.S., Par. Vicar; Cathy Baranek, DRE; Rev. Paolo Dorrego, P.E.S., Pst.; CRP Stds.: 90

WEAVERVILLE

Pastor of St. Patrick Parish, Weaverville, a corporation sole - 102 Church St., Weaverville, CA 96093; Mailing: P.O. Box 1219, Weaverville, CA 96093-1219 t) 530-623-4383 saintpatricks96093@gmail.com www.stpatrickparishweaverville.org Cathy Black, DRE; CRP Stds.: 17

Holy Trinity -

St. Gilbert -

Trinity Center -

WEED

Pastor of Holy Family Parish, Weed, a corporation sole - 1051 N. Davis Ave., Weed, CA 96094 t) 530-261-1013 (CRP); 530-938-4334 tapia75@sbcglobal.net holyfamilycatholicchurchweed.org Rev. Mario Valmorida, Par. Admin.; Dcn. Time Louie; Chela Tapia, DRE; CRP Stds.: 20

WEST SACRAMENTO

Pastor of Holy Cross Parish, West Sacramento, a corporation sole - 1321 Anna St., West Sacramento, CA 95605 t) 916-371-1211 holycrossws@gmail.com Rev. Jhay B. Galeon, Pst.; Maria del Refugio Martinez, CRE; CRP Stds.: 275

Pastor of Our Lady of Grace Parish, West Sacramento, a corporation sole - 911 Park Blvd., West Sacramento, CA 95691 t) 916-371-4814; 916-371-9416 (School) office@westsacolg.org; olgoffice@wavecable.com www.westsacolg.org Dcn. David Campbell; Rev. Mathew Rappu, Pst.; Steve Ramirez-Palmer, Youth Min.; Dena Serrano, DRE; Byron Paige, RCIA Coord.; Jeremy Arcinas, Youth Min.; Ana Ramirez-Palmer, Youth Min.; CRP Stds.: 391

Our Lady of Grace School - (Grades PreK-8) 1990 Linden Rd., West Sacramento, CA 95691 administration@olgwestsac.com olgwestsac.com Sharon Dandorf, Prin.; Stds.: 341; Lay Tchrs.: 19

WILLIAMS

Pastor of Sacred Heart Parish, Maxwell, a corporation sole - 627 8th St., Williams, CA 95987; Mailing: Po Box 1327, Williams, CA 95987 t) 530-473-2432 sacredheart627@gmail.com; sacredheartmaxwellcre@gmail.com www.sacredheart-maxwell.org Rev. Victor Gutierrez, Pst.; Rev. John J. Myles, Pastor Emer.; Laura Rivera, Office Manager; Isabel Santana, Catechesis Coordinator; CRP Stds.: 512

Holy Cross - 412 Laurel St., Arbuckle, CA 95912 t) (530) 473-2432 sacredheart-maxwell.org/

Church of the Annunciation - 617 8th St., Williams, CA 95987 t) 580-473-2432

WILLOWS

Pastor of St. Monica Parish, Willows, a corporation sole - 1129 W. Wood St., Willows, CA 95988 t) 530-934-3314 x201 parishoffice@stmonicawillows.com www.stmonicawillows.com/ Maribel Palomino, DRE; Rev. Michael J. Estaris, Pst.; CRP Stds.: 214

St. Mary of the Mountain Church - 2nd St. & Geary St., Stonyford, CA 95979; Mailing: 1129 W. Wood St., Willows, CA 95988 t) (530) 934-3314 x301

WINTERS

St. Anthony Parish, Winters, a corporation sole - 511 Main St., Winters, CA 95694 t) 530-795-2230 admin@sa-sm.org; allenos@sa-sm.org www.sa-sm.org Rev. Perlito G. De la Cruz, Pst.; Dcn. Alejandro Llenos; Dcn. Jorge Villalobos; CRP Stds.: 273

St. Martin - 25633 Grafton Rd., Esparto, CA 95627 t) 530-787-3750

WOODLAND

Pastor of Holy Rosary Parish, Woodland, a corporation

sole - 575 California St, Woodland, CA 95695; Mailing: 503 California St., Woodland, CA 95695 t) 530-662-2805 x120; 530-662-5394 (CRP); 530-662-2894 (CRP) jmendoza@holyrosary.com; bcontreras@holyrosary.com holyrosary.com Rev. Jonathan B. Molina, Pst.; Rev. J. Guadalupe Vazquez Gonzalez, Vicar; Dcn. Gonzalo Chavez; Dcn. Jose Luis Collazo; Dcn. Peter Ta; CRP Stds.: 472

Holy Rosary School - (Grades PreK-8) 505 California St., Woodland, CA 95695 t) 530-662-3494 office@hrsaints.com www.hrsaints.com Carlos Overstreet, Prin.; Stds.: 120; Lay Tchrs.: 6

YREKA

Pastor of St. Joseph Parish, Yreka, a corporation sole - 314 Fourth St., Yreka, CA 96097 t) 530-842-4874 stjoseph310@nctv.com Rev. Ronald V. Torres, Admin.; CRP Stds.: 17

Catechetical Center - 310 Fourth St., Yreka, CA 96097 t) (530) 842-4874 Rev. Ronald Torres, Par. Admin.;

Immaculate Conception - 1508 Hawkinsville Humbug Rd., Hawkinsville, CA 96097; Mailing: 314 4th St., Yreka, CA 96097 Rev. Ronald Torres, Par. Admin.;

YUBA CITY

Pastor of St. Isidore Parish, Yuba City, a corporation sole - 222 Clark Ave., Yuba City, CA 95991 t) 530-673-1573 pastor@stisidore-yubacity.org; mknox@stisidore-yubacity.org stisidore-yubacity.org Rev. Avram E. Brown, Pst.; Rev. Erik Pereira, Par. Vicar; Dcn. Brad Bell; Dcn. Ruben Rojo; Dcn. John Thoo; Michelle Knox, DRE; CRP Stds.: 312

St. Isidore School - (Grades PreK-8) 200 Clark Ave., Yuba City, CA 95991 t) 530-673-2217 tblankenship@stisidoreschool.org; sburky@stisidoreschool.org stisidoreschool.org Susan Burky, Prin.; Stds.: 133; Lay Tchrs.: 8

SCHOOLS: PRESCHOOL THRU HIGH SCHOOL

HIGH SCHOOLS

STATE OF CALIFORNIA

CARMICHAEL

Jesuit High School - (PRV) (Grades 9-12) 1200 Jacob Ln., Carmichael, CA 95608-6024 t) 916-482-6060 president@jesuithighschool.org www.jesuithighschool.org (Boys) Rev. Edwin Harris, S.J., Chap.; Rev. Aaron Engebretson, S.J., Sacr. Min.; Michael Wood, Prin.; Rev. Thomas H. O'Neill, S.J., Supr.; Stds.: 962; Scholastics: 1; Pr. Tchrs.: 2; Lay Tchrs.: 65

SACRAMENTO

Christian Brothers High School of Sacramento, Inc. - (PRV) (Grades 9-12) 4315 Martin Luther King, Jr. Blvd., Sacramento, CA 95820 t) 916-733-3600; 916-733-3674 (Asst. to Prin.) jelorduy@cbhs-sacramento.org; cugarte@cbhs-sacramento.org www.cbhs-sacramento.org Dr. Crystal LeRoy, Pres.; Julian Elorduy, Interim Principal; Stds.: 1,149; Sr. Tchrs.: 1; Lay Tchrs.: 82

Cristo Rey High School - (PRV) 8475 Jackson Rd., Sacramento, CA 95826 t) 916-733-2660 cdickens@crhss.org; kcoulouras@crhss.org www.crhss.org Kate Coulouras, Prin.; David Perry, Pres.; Stds.: 314; Lay Tchrs.: 18

St. Francis Catholic High School - (DIO) (Grades 9-12) 5900 Elvas Ave., Sacramento, CA 95819 t) 916-452-3461 sfhsinfo@stfrancishs.org www.stfrancishs.org Girls. Rev. George Thadathil, C.M.I., Chap.; Elias Mendoza, Prin.; Dr. Fadia Desmond, Pres.; Stds.: 859; Lay Tchrs.: 51

VALLEJO

St. Patrick-St. Vincent High School - (DIO) (Grades 9-12) 1500 Benicia Rd., Vallejo, CA 94591 t) 707-644-4425 interimprincipalpresidentteam@spsv.org www.spsv.org Lydia Davis Mcleod, Pres.; Nora Rodgers, Prin.; Tamra Smith, Prin.; Stds.: 331; Pr. Tchrs.: 1; Lay Tchrs.: 23

INSTITUTIONS LOCATED IN DIOCESE

CAMPUS MINISTRY / NEWMAN CENTERS [CAM]

CHICO

Newman Catholic Center - Chico - 346 Cherry St., Chico, CA 95928 t) 530-342-5180 kstaszkow@scd.org www.chiconewman.org Monica Zuchelli, Dir.; Zack Seibert, Prog. Coord.;

DAVIS

Newman Catholic Center - Davis - 514 C St., Davis, CA 95616 t) 530-753-7393 director@davisnewman.org; vnims@scd.org www.davisnewman.org Clare Brady, Campus Min.; Weston Ruiz, Dir.;

SACRAMENTO

Newman Catholic Center - Sacramento - 5900 Newman Ct., Sacramento, CA 95819-2610 t) 916-454-4188 campusministry@sacnewman.org; wruiz@scd.org www.sacnewman.org Andrea Florez, Dir.;

CATHOLIC CHARITIES [CCH]

ROSEVILLE

Society of St. Vincent DePaul - 503 Giuseppe Ct. #8, Roseville, CA 95678 t) 916-781-3303 (Office); 916-472-6629 (Store) Emergency Services, Clothing Vouchers, Food Assistance, Baby Supplies, Hygiene, Dining Room, Mail Service. Stanko Thomas, Exec.; Asstd. Annu.: 55,898; Staff: 7

SACRAMENTO

Catholic Charities of California, Inc. - 1107 9th St. Ste. 707, Sacramento, CA 95814 t) 916-706-1539 smlahey@catholiccharitiesca.org; info@catholiccharitiesca.org www.catholiccharitiesca.org Ken Sawa, Pres.; Shannon M. Lahey, Exec.; Asstd. Annu.: 453,337; Staff: 17

Catholic Charities of Sacramento, Inc. - 2110 Broadway, Sacramento, CA 95818 t) 916-733-0254 msammartino@scd.org www.scd.org Laura Rios, Admin.; Miriam Sammartino, Dir.; Asstd. Annu.: 350,700; Staff: 2

Catholic Charities of Solano, Inc. - 125 Corporate Pl., Ste. A, Vallejo, CA 94590 t) 707-644-8909 miriam@ccyoso.org www.ccyoso.org Jim Lago, Chair;

Mother Teresa Maternity Home, Inc. - 3122 Sacramento St., Placerville, CA 95667 t) 530-295-8006 mtmh.edc@gmail.com motherteresamaternityhome.com/ Elizabeth Frey-Thomas, Chair;

Northern Valley Catholic Social Service - 2400 Washington Ave., Redding, CA 96001 t) 530-241-0552 cwyatt@nvcss.org www.nvcss.org Dan Ghidinelli, Chair; Cathy Wyatt, Dir.;

Sacramento Food Bank and Family Services - 3333 Third Ave., Sacramento, CA 95817 t) 916-456-1980 byoung@sacramentofoodbank.org www.sacramentofoodbank.org Karen Woodruff, Chair; Blake Young, CEO;

VALLEJO

Society of St. Vincent de Paul (St. Basil Conference) - 1220 Tuolumne St., Vallejo, CA 94590; Mailing: 1225 Tuolumne St., Vallejo, CA 94590 t) 707-644-0376 stbasilsvdpconf@gmail.com Rene Perryman, Pres.; Charmaine Ferrez, Mem.; Asstd. Annu.: 19,000

CEMETERIES [CEM]

CITRUS HEIGHTS

Calvary Cemetery & Funeral Center - 7101 Verner Ave., Citrus Heights, CA 95621; Mailing: 2110 Broadway, Sacramento, CA 95818 t) 916-726-1232 jdelcore@scd.org; smiller@scd.org www.cfcssacramento.org Jerry Del Core, CEO; Scott Miller, COO;

COLUSA

Holy Cross Cemetery - 1741 Westscott, Colusa, CA 95932; Mailing: 2110 Broadway, Sacramento, CA 95818 t) 916-726-1232 jdelcore@scd.org; smiller@scd.org www.cfcssacramento.org Jerry Del Core, CEO; Scott Miller, COO;

FAIRFIELD

St. Alphonsus Cemetery - 1801 Union Ave., Fairfield, CA 94533; Mailing: 2110 Broadway, Sacramento, CA 95818 t) 707-644-5209 jdelcore@scd.org; smiller@scd.org www.cfcssacramento.org Jerry Del Core, CEO; Scott Miller, COO;

GRASS VALLEY

St. Patrick's Cemetery - 18044 Rough & Ready Hwy., Grass Valley, CA 95945 t) 916-726-1232 jdelcore@scd.org; smiller@scd.org www.cfcssacramento.org Jerry Del Core, CEO; Scott Miller, COO;

RANCHO MURIETA

St. Vincent de Paul Cemetery - 15237 Jackson Rd., Rancho Murieta, CA 95683; Mailing: 2110 Broadway, Sacramento, CA 95818 t) 916-452-4831 jdelcore@scd.org; smiller@scd.org www.cfcssacramento.org Jerry Del Core, CEO; Scott Miller, COO;

RIO VISTA

St. Joseph Cemetery - 1 Cemetery Dr., Hwy. 12, Rio Vista, CA 94571; Mailing: 2110 Broadway, Sacramento, CA 95818 t) 916-452-4831 jdelcore@scd.org; smiller@scd.org www.cfcssacramento.org Jerry Del Core, CEO; Scott Miller, COO;

SACRAMENTO

St. Joseph Cemetery - 2615 21st St., Sacramento, CA 95818; Mailing: 2110 Broadway, Sacramento, CA 95818 t) 916-452-4831 jdelcore@scd.org; smiller@scd.org www.cfcssacramento.org Jerry Del Core, CEO; Scott Miller, COO;

St. Mary Cemetery & Funeral Center - 6509 Fruitridge Rd., Sacramento, CA 95820-5981; Mailing: 2110 Broadway, Sacramento, CA 95818 t) 916-452-4831 jdelcore@scd.org; smiller@scd.org www.cfcssacramento.org Jerry DelCore, CEO; Scott Miller, COO;

VALLEJO

All Souls Cemetery & Funeral Center - 550 Glen Cove Rd., Vallejo, CA 94591; Mailing: 2110 Broadway, Sacramento, CA 95818 t) 707-644-5209 jdelcore@scd.org; smiller@scd.org www.cfcssacramento.org Jerry Del Core, CEO; Scott Miller, COO;

St. Vincent Cemetery - 1255 Benicia Rd., Vallejo, CA 94591; Mailing: 2110 Broadway, Sacramento, CA 95818 t) 707-644-5209 jdelcore@scd.org; smiller@scd.org www.cfcssacramento.org Jerry Del Core, CEO; Scott Miller, COO;

WOODLAND

St. Joseph Cemetery - 860 West St., Woodland, CA 95695; Mailing: 2110 Broadway, Sacramento, CA 95818 t) 530-662-8645 jdelcore@scd.org; smiller@scd.org www.cfcssacramento.org Jerry Del Core, CEO; Scott Miller, COO;

CONVENTS, MONASTERIES, AND RESIDENCES FOR WOMEN [CON]

AUBURN

Sisters of Mercy of the Americas West Midwest Community, Inc. - 535 Sacramento St., Auburn, CA 95603 t) 530-887-2000 www.sistersofmercy.org Sr. Susan Sanders, R.S.M., Vice. Pres.; Srs.: 417

ELK GROVE

Religious of the Virgin Mary - 10816 Richert Ln., Elk Grove, CA 95624 t) 916-682-1203 c) 650-837-1034 rvmusacanadadistrict2016@gmail.com; rosabelrvm@gmail.com Sr. Maria Rosabel Sare, RVM, Supr.; Srs.: 5

GEORGETOWN

Discalced Carmelite Nuns (Carmel of the Holy Family and Saint Therese) - 6981 Teresian Way, Georgetown, CA 95634; Mailing: P.O. Box 4210, Georgetown, CA 95634 t) 530-333-1617 georgetown2004@juno.com www.carmelitemonastery.org Sr. Mary Beck-Meyer, Prioress; Srs.: 13

SACRAMENTO

Canossian Daughters of Charity - Our Lady of Lourdes Convent, 1949 North Ave., Sacramento, CA 95838 t) 916-925-4001 canossian.sisters@outlook.com www.canossiansisters.org Sr. Blanca Dominguez, FdCC; Sr. Lisa Marie Doty, FdCC, Supr.; Srs.: 2

Missionaries of Charity, Inc. - 3971 39th Ave., Sacramento, CA 95824 t) 916-454-3591 Srs.: 4

Sister Servants of the Blessed Sacrament, Inc. - 5929 61st St., Sacramento, CA 95824; Mailing: 3173 Winnetka Dr., Bonita, CA 91902 t) 619-267-0720 c) 619-484-2665 secretary@usasjs.org usasjs.org SJS Active Convent Sr. Lilia Mercedes Barba, SJS, Prov.; Sr. Esmeralda Razo, SJS, Treas.; Srs.: 3

Sisters Catechists of Jesus Crucified - 5712 Muskingham Way, Sacramento, CA 95823 t) 916-395-1875 suwoga@yahoo.com.mx Srs.: 4

Sisters of the Holy Rosary of Fatima - 1708 U St., Sacramento, CA 95818 t) 916-442-8646; 916-212-0412 vicentalemus@sbcglobal.net Sr. Vicenta Lemus, Contact; Srs.: 2

ENDOWMENTS / FOUNDATIONS / TRUSTS [EFT]

RANCHO CORDOVA

Mercy Foundation - 3400 Data Dr., Rancho Cordova, CA 95670 t) 916-851-2700 mercyfoundationsac@dignityhealth.org www.supportmercyfoundation.org Kevin Duggan, Pres.;

SACRAMENTO

The Catholic Foundation of the Diocese of Sacramento, Inc. - 2110 Broadway, Sacramento, CA 95818 t) 916-733-0266 foundation@scd.org www.scd.org/ catholic-foundation Tony Riehl, Exec.;

The Parochial Fund, Inc. - 2110 Broadway, Sacramento, CA 95818; Mailing: P.O. Box 189666, Sacramento, CA 95818 t) 916-733-0277 tmcnamara@scd.org Thomas J. McNamara, CFO;

The Preserving Our Past, Building Our Future Foundation of Northern California, Inc. - 2110 Broadway, Sacramento, CA 95818 t) 916-733-0266 foundation@scd.org Tony Riehl, Exec.;

HOSPITALS / HEALTH SERVICES [HOS]

CARMICHAEL

Mercy San Juan Medical Center - 6501 Coyle Ave., Carmichael, CA 95608 t) 916-537-5000 sheila.browne@commonspirit.org www.mercysanjuan.org Sponsored by Catholic Health Care Federation Michael Korpiel, Pres.; Bed Capacity: 384; Asstd. Annu.: 132,445; Staff: 2,672

FOLSOM

Mercy Hospital of Folsom - 1650 Creekside Dr., Folsom, CA 95630 t) 916-983-7400 pam.koerner@commonspirit.org www.mercyfolsom.org Sponsored by Catholic Health Care Federation Michael Korpiel, CEO; Bed Capacity: 106; Asstd. Annu.: 65,844; Staff: 843

MOUNT SHASTA

Mercy Medical Center Mt. Shasta - 914 Pine St., Mount Shasta, CA 96067 t) 530-926-6111 brenda.okeeffe@dignityhealth.org www.mercy.org Sponsored by Catholic Health Care Federation Rodger Page, Pres.; Sr. Brenda O'Keeffe, VP Mission Integration, Spiritual Care & Palliative Care Svcs.; Bed Capacity: 33; Asstd. Annu.: 77,972; Staff: 290

RED BLUFF

St. Elizabeth Community Hospital - 2550 Sr. Mary Columba Dr., Red Bluff, CA 96080-4397 t) 530-529-8000 brenda.okeeffe@dignityhealth.org www.mercy.org Sponsored by Catholic Health Care Federation Rodger Page, Pres.; Sr. Brenda O'Keeffe, VP Mission Integration, Spiritual Care & Palliative Care Svcs.; Bed Capacity: 76; Asstd. Annu.: 196,685; Staff: 588

REDDING

Mercy Medical Center Redding - 2175 Rosaline Ave., Redding, CA 96001; Mailing: P. O. Box 496009, Redding, CA 96049-6009 t) 530-225-6000 brenda.okeeffe@dignityhealth.org www.mercy.org Sponsored by Catholic Health Care Federation Todd Smith, Pres.; Sr. Brenda O'Keeffe, VP Mission Integration, Spiritual Care & Palliative Care Svcs.; Bed Capacity: 266; Asstd. Annu.: 166,972; Staff: 1,850

SACRAMENTO

Mercy General Hospital - 4001 J St., Sacramento, CA 95819 t) 916-453-4545 pam.koerner@commonspirit.org www.mercygeneral.org Sponsored by Catholic Health Care Federation Brian Evans, CEO; Bed Capacity: 283; Asstd. Annu.: 133,902; Staff: 2,288

MISCELLANEOUS [MIS]

COLFAX

Trinity Pines Catholic Center - 28000 Rollins Lake Rd., Colfax, CA 95713 t) 530-389-8722; (916) 733-0135 (Director Direct Line) jcampbell@scd.org www.trinitypinescatholic.org Jennifer Campbell, Dir.;

LOOMIS

Dominican Sisters of Mary, Mother of the Eucharist - Loomis - 5820 Rocklin Rd., Loomis, CA 95650 t) 734-994-7437 secretary@sistersofmary.org Sr. John Dominic Rasmussen, Treas.;

ORANGEVALE

Camp ReCreation - 9272 Madison Ave, Orangevale, CA 95662 t) 916-988-6835 camprecreation@outlook.com Carrie Judd, Dir.; Alex Nelson, Chair;

OREGON HOUSE

Grand Council, Catholic Ladies Relief Society of the Diocese of Sacramento - c/o Alice Victorino, 8126 Hemlock Ln., Oregon House, CA 95962 t) 530-692-2818 grandmavict@yahoo.com Yvonne Moore, Pres.; Alice Victorino, Pres.;

PLACERVILLE

Upper Room Dining Hall, Inc. - 1868 Broadway, Placerville, CA 95667; Mailing: P.O. Box 484, Placerville, CA 95667 t) 530-621-7730 director@upperroomdininghall.org; chair@upperroomdininghall.org upperroomdininghall.org Jennifer Mouzis, Chair;

RANCHO CORDOVA

Holy Trinity Community North America (HTCNA) - 4216 Silver Water Way, Rancho Cordova, CA 95742 t) 916-213-9281 Erick Yo, Pres.;

Rancho Cordova Food Locker - 10497 Coloma Rd., Rancho Cordova, CA 95670; Mailing: 2110 Broadway, Sacramento, CA 95818 t) (916) 837-5431 carrie@ranchocordovafoodlocker.org Carrie Johnson, Exec. Dir.; Asstd. Annu.: 19,220; Staff: 4

SACRAMENTO

California Catholic Conference, Inc. - 1119 K St., 2nd Floor, Sacramento, CA 95814 t) 916-313-4000 kdomingo@cacatholic.org www.cacatholic.org Kathleen Buckley Domingo, Exec. Dir.;

California Conference of Catholic Bishops - 1119 K St., 2nd Floor, Sacramento, CA 95814 t) 916-313-4000 leginfo@cacatholic.org www.cacatholic.org Kathleen Buckley Domingo, Exec. Dir.;

Catholic Committee on Scouting - 2110 Broadway, Sacramento, CA 95818 t) 916-733-0123 jcampbell@scd.org www.scd.org Jennifer Campbell, Staff to Committee;

Catholic Funeral and Cemetery Services of the Diocese of Sacramento, Inc. - 2110 Broadway, Sacramento, CA 95818 t) 916-733-0252 jdelcore@scd.org www.cfcssacramento.org/ Jerry Del Core, CEO;

Catholic Schools of Solano, Inc. - 2110 Broadway, Sacramento, CA 95818 t) 916-733-0110 csd@scd.org Katie Perata, Exec. Dir.;

Catholic Schools of the Northern Sacramento Valley, Inc. - 2110 Broadway, Sacramento, CA 95818 t) 916-733-0110 csd@scd.org Katie Perata, Exec. Dir.;

One Campaign of the Diocese of Sacramento, Inc. - 2110 Broadway, Sacramento, CA 95818 t) 916-733-0266 foundation@scd.org Tony Riehl, Exec.;

Radio Santisimo Sacramento, Inc. - 1909 7th St., Sacramento, CA 95811 t) 916-442-7389; 916-999-1240 lorenaa@radiosantisimosacramento.com; kcvv1240am@radiosantisimosacramento.com www.radiosantisimosacramento.com Lorena Albarran, Dir.;

Sacramento Catholic Forum - ; Mailing: P.O. Box 254848, Sacramento, CA 95865-4848 t) 916-572-3171 ncardin@relevantradio.com www.saccatholicforum.org Nicole Cardin, Contact;

Society of St. Vincent de Paul, Sacramento District Council - 2275 Watt Ave., Sacramento, CA 95816; Mailing: P.O. Box 162487, Sacramento, CA 95816 t) 916-972-1212 c) 707-480-8234 jalves@svdp-sacramento.org; dobrien@svdp-sacramento.org svdp-sacramento.org Joe Alves, Pres.; Denise O'Brien, Exec. Dir.;

***Stanford Settlement** - 450 W. El Camino Ave., Sacramento, CA 95833-2299 t) 916-927-1303 sisterjeanne@stanfordsettlement.org www.stanfordsettlement.org Sr. Jeanne Felion, S.S.S., Dir.;

VACAVILLE

Pro Ecclesia Sancta of California - 3945 Joslin Ln., Vacaville, CA 95688 t) 707-685-0370 fralvaro@pes-usa.org Rev. Alvaro Daniel Perez Silva, PES, Supr.; Rev. Humberto Palomino, P.E.S., Prov.;

MONASTERIES AND RESIDENCES FOR PRIESTS AND BROTHERS [MON]

CARMICHAEL

Sacramento Jesuit Community - 1200 Jacob Ln., Carmichael, CA 95608 t) 916-482-6060 toneill@jesuits.org The Jesuit Provinces of California and Oregon merged in 2017. The title is now "Jesuits West" with Provincial Offices in Portland, OR. Rev. John McGarry, S.J., Pres.; Rev. Thomas M. Lucas, S.J., Pst.; Rev. Arthur J. Wehr, S.J., Assoc. Pst.; Bro. Daniel C. Corona, S.J., In Res.; Rev. Edwin Harris, S.J., Chap.; Rev. Aaron Engebretson, S.J., Sacr. Min.; Rev. Matthew Yim, S.J., Assoc. Pst.; Rev. Christopher A. Calderon, S.J., Dean; Rev. Thomas H. O'Neill, S.J., Supr.; Brs.: 1; Priests: 8

CITRUS HEIGHTS

Christ the King Passionist Retreat Center, Inc. (The Passionists (Chicago, IL)) - 6520 Van Maren Ln., Citrus Heights, CA 95621 t) 916-725-4720 christtheking@passionist.org christthekingretreatcenter.org A community residence for the Passionist priests and brothers who conduct missions and retreats. Rev. Joseph Moons, C.P., Prov.; Rev. James G. Strommer, C.P., Supr.; Rev. John Conley, C.P., Ministry Team; Rev. John Hilgert, C.P.; Bro. Carl Hund, C.P.; Rev. Phillip Donlan, CP, Ministry Team; Brs.: 1; Priests: 5

VALLEJO

Missionary Society of the Philippines - 3450 Tennessee St., Vallejo, CA 94591 secgen@msp.org.ph www.msp.org.ph/contact.do Rev. Jose Estaniel, MSP, Par. Vicar; Rev. Glenn Giovanni Jaron, M.S.P. (Philippines), Admin.; Priests: 5

VINA

Abbey of New Clairvaux, Trappist (Cistercian Abbey, Cistercians of the Strict Observance) - 26240 7th St., Vina, CA 96092; Mailing: P.O. Box 80, Vina, CA 96092 t) 530-839-2161 monks@newclairvaux.org; mikeprym@newclairvaux.org www.newclairvaux.org Rt. Rev. Paul Mark Schwan, O.C.S.O., Abbot; Bro. Christopher Cheney, OCSO, Prior; Bro. Peter Damian,

O.C.S.O., Secy.; Brs.: 11; Priests: 10

WALNUT GROVE

Our Lady of Sacramento Monastery - 14080 Leary Rd., Walnut Grove, CA 95690; Mailing: P.O. Box 99, Walnut Grove, CA 95690 t) 916-776-1356 c) 916-477-0595 osm.ocist@gmail.com Rt. Rev. Dominic Hung Tran, OCist., Abbot; Rev. Leo Tien Nguyen, OCist, Prior; Rev. Nicolas Thanh Quang Le, OCist., Subprior; Dcn. Bosco Nhat Nguyen, OCist.; Rev. Thanh Dac Nguyen; Rev. Ephrem Duc Van Trinh, OCist.; Rev. Francis Nam Vu, OCist.; Bro. Anthony Hao Ngo, Mem.; Bro. Anphonse Thach Nguyen, OCist., Mem.; Bro. John of God Ngoc Nguyen, OCist., Mem.; Brs.: 4; Priests: 6

NURSING / REHABILITATION / CONVALESCENCE / ELDERLY CARE [NUR]

SACRAMENTO

Mercy McMahon Terrace - 3865 J St., Sacramento, CA 95816 t) 916-733-6510 mary.erickson@dignityhealth.org www.mercymcmahonterrace.org Mary Erickson, CEO; Asstd. Annu.: 200; Staff: 115

PRESCHOOLS / CHILDCARE CENTERS [PRE]

SACRAMENTO

St. Patrick's Fund for Children, Inc. - 2110 Broadway, Sacramento, CA 95818 t) 916-733-0200 Dcn. Gerald Pauly, Admin.;

RETREAT HOUSES / RENEWAL CENTERS [RTR]

APPLEGATE

Jesuit Retreat Center of the Sierra - 1001 Boole Rd., Applegate, CA 95703 t) 530-878-2776 applegatejrc@uccr.org www.uccr.org/applegate

AUBURN

Sisters of Mercy of the Americas West Midwest Community, Inc., Mercy Center Auburn - 535 Sacramento St., Auburn, CA 95603-5699 t) 530-887-2019 info@mercycenter.org www.mercycenter.org Sr. Susan Sanders, R.S.M., Vice. Pres.;

CAMPTONVILLE

Pendola Center - 1788 Mill Rd., Camptonville, CA 95922; Mailing: 2110 Broadway, Sacramento, CA 95818 t) (530) 288-3263 (Summer Camp); 916-733-0135 (Dir.); 916-733-0123 (Booking / Registration) jcampbell@scd.org www.pendola.org Summer camp for boys and girls 6-18. Jennifer Campbell, Dir.;

SEMINARIES [SEM]

LOOMIS

Mount St. Joseph Novitiate and Seminary (Novitiate of Oblates of St. Joseph) - 6530 Wells Ave., Loomis, CA 95650; Mailing: P.O. Box 547, Loomis, CA 95650 t) 916-652-6336 fphil@osjoseph.org www.osjusa.org Rev. Philip V. Massetti, O.S.J., In Res.; Rev. Stephen Spencer, Dir.;

VINA

Abbey of New Clairvaux, Trappist Seminary - 26240 7th St., Vina, CA 96092; Mailing: P.O. Box 80, Vina, CA 96092 t) 530-839-2161 pmschwan@newclairvaux.org www.newclairvaux.org Rev. Paul Jerome Konkler, O.C.S.O., In Res.; Rev. Placid Morris, O.C.S.O., In Res.; Rev. Thomas X. Davis, O.C.S.O., Dean; Rt. Rev. Paul Mark Schwan, O.C.S.O., Abbot; Stds.: 2

An asterisk (*) denotes an organization that has established tax-exempt status directly with the IRS and is not covered by the USCCB Group Ruling.

Diocese of Saginaw

(Dioecesis Saginavensis)

MOST REVEREND ROBERT D. GRUSS

Bishop of Saginaw; ordained July 2, 1994; ordained as Bishop of Rapid City Diocese July 28, 2011; appointed by Pope Francis Bishop of Saginaw Diocese May 24, 2019; installed July 26, 2019. Chancery: 5800 Weiss St., Saginaw, MI 48603-2762. T: 989-799-7910; F: 989-797-6670; www.saginaw.org.

Chancery: 5800 Weiss St., Saginaw, MI 48603-2762. T: 989-799-7910; F: 989-797-6670.
www.saginaw.org

ESTABLISHED FEBRUARY 26, 1938.

Square Miles 6,955.

Comprises the following Counties in the State of Michigan: Arenac, Bay, Clare, Gladwin, Gratiot, Huron, Isabella, Midland, Saginaw, Sanilac and Tuscola.

For legal titles of parishes and diocesan institutions, consult the Chancery Office.

STATISTICAL OVERVIEW

Personnel	
Bishop	1
Priests: Diocesan Active in Diocese	34
Priests: Diocesan Active Outside Diocese	2
Priests: Retired, Sick or Absent	36
Number of Diocesan Priests	72
Religious Priests in Diocese	5
Total Priests in your Diocese	77
Extern Priests in Diocese	7
Ordinations:	
Transitional Deacons	1
Permanent Deacons in Diocese	17
Total Sisters	57
Parishes	
Parishes	56
With Resident Pastor:	
Resident Diocesan Priests	34
Resident Religious Priests	4
Without Resident Pastor:	
Administered by Priests	8
Administered by Deacons	4
Administered by Religious Women	3
Administered by Lay People	3
Professional Ministry Personnel:	
Sisters	7
Lay Ministers	35
Welfare	
Catholic Hospitals	1
Total Assisted	484,429
Health Care Centers	1
Total Assisted	1,006
Homes for the Aged	1
Total Assisted	239
Day Care Centers	4
Total Assisted	187
Specialized Homes	2
Total Assisted	176
Special Centers for Social Services	4
Total Assisted	7,570
Other Institutions	2
Total Assisted	330
Educational	
Diocesan Students in Other Seminaries	5
Total Seminarians	5
High Schools, Diocesan and Parish	3
Total Students	378
Elementary Schools, Diocesan and Parish	10
Total Students	1,749
Catechesis / Religious Education:	
High School Students	393
Elementary Students	2,411
Total Students under Catholic Instruction	4,936
Teachers in Diocese:	
Sisters	1
Lay Teachers	162
Vital Statistics	
Receptions into the Church:	
Infant Baptism Totals	384
Minor Baptism Totals	130
Adult Baptism Totals	42
Received into Full Communion	114
First Communions	539
Confirmations	109
Marriages:	
Catholic	105
Interfaith	45
Total Marriages	150
Deaths	1,258
Total Catholic Population	86,333
Total Population	680,214

LEADERSHIP

Vicar General - brutkowski@diosag.org Rev. William J. Rutkowski;
Vicar for Priests - t) 989-797-6649 jcabrera@diosag.org Rev. Jose Cabrera;
Episcopal Vicars -
Territorial Vicars - Rev. Andrew D. Booms, Vicar; Rev. Steven M. Gavit, Vicar; Rev. Nathan E. Harburg, Vicar;
Delegate for Religious - t) 989-799-7910
Chancery - t) 989-799-7910 saginaw.org/
Chancellor & Delegate for Safe Environment - t) 989-797-6620 mobrien@diosag.org Sr. Mary Judith O'Brien, R.S.M.;
Multicultural Ministries Director - t) 989-797-6604 Dcn. Librado Gayton;

OFFICES AND DIRECTORS

Christ's Mission Appeal - t) 989-797-6626 Geri Rudolf, Dir.;
Clergy Personnel Board - Rev. Peter J. Gaspeny, Pres.;
Coordinator of Marriage and Family Life Ministry - t) 989-797-6655 bbauer@diosag.org Beth Bauer;
Diocesan College of Consultors - Rev. Robert H. Byrne; Rev. Peter J. Gaspeny; Rev. Thomas J. McNamara, Mem.;
Diocesan Council of Catholic Women - Rita Faith Maher, Pres.;
Diocesan Presbyteral Council - t) 989-781-2457 sgavit@diosag.org Rev. Steven M. Gavit, Chair;
Director of Human Resources - t) 989-797-6687 chuiskens@diosag.org Connie Huiskens Wojda;
Ecumenism Ministry - t) 989-797-6662 dosborn@dioceseofsaginaw.org Daniel Osborn;
Education/Formation - clynn@diosag.org Kellie Deming, Dir. Parish Life & Evangelization; Margaret McEvoy, Coord. Faith & Catechist Formation; Don Buchalski;
All Saints School - t) 989-894-8777 lisa.rhodus@ascbaycity.org ascbaycity.org Lisa Rhodus, Prin.; Sr. Maria Jose Perez, RSM, Vice Prin.;
Catholic Schools - t) 989-797-6651 saginaw.org/our-catholic-schools Cormac J. Lynn, Supt.;
Nouvel Catholic Schools - nouvelcatholic.org/contact
Financial and Business Operations -
Accounting Assistant - t) 989-797-6629 Tammy Charbonneau, Admin.;
Catholic Cemeteries - t) 989-797-6627 saginaw.org/cemeteries Alice Lefevre;
Chief Financial Officer - t) 989-797-6688 dbierlein@diosag.org Debra Bierlein, CFO;
Comptroller - t) 989-797-6642 mseeger@diosag.org Melissa Seeger, Dir.;
Diocesan Building Commission - t) 989-797-7657 jsills@dioceseofsaginaw.org Jane Sills;
Diocesan Finance Council - John Hunt, Chair;
Diocesan Investment Committee - Tom Braley, Chair;
Ministry to Charismatic Renewal - t) 989-684-4640 Judy Troxell, Dir.;
Mission Office - t) 989-797-6633
Office of Communication - t) 989-797-6630 ecarlson@diosag.org Erin Looby Carlson; Tim Spear; Christopher Pham;
Office of Liturgy - t) 989-797-6664 Rev. James W. Bessert, Dir.; Pam Bourscheidt, Assoc. Liturgical Music;
Organizations and Services -
Diocese of Saginaw Priests' Retirement Association - Rev. Peter J. Gaspeny;
Director of Development - t) 989-797-6656 Geri Rudolf, Dir.;
Holy Childhood Association - t) 989-797-6633 Kellie Deming, Contact;
Office of Stewardship and Planned Giving - grudolf@diosag.org Geri Rudolf, Dir.;
Tribunal - t) 989-797-6623
Auditors - t) 989-797-6667 Rev. Edwin G. Dwyer; Sr. Jean T. Baumann, O.S.F.;
Defenders of the Bond - Rev. Thomas E. Sutton;
Judges - Sr. Mary Judith O'Brien, R.S.M.; Rev. Richard M. Filary;
Judicial Vicar - t) 989-797-6622 rfilary@diosag.org Rev. Richard M. Filary;
Notary - Kimberly Voelker;
Promoter of Justice - Rev. Edwin G. Dwyer;
Victim Assistance Coordinator - t) 989-797-6682 victim.assistance@dioceseofsaginaw.org Nancy Felch, Contact;

EVANGELIZATION

Office of Diocesan Outreach - t) 989-797-6652 Lori Becker;

PARISHES, MISSIONS, AND CLERGY

STATE OF MICHIGAN

ALMA

Nativity of the Lord Parish of Alma and St. Louis - 510 Prospect Ave., Alma, MI 48801-1633 t) 989-463-5370 secretary@nativityparish.net; rwarner@diosag.org Rev. Paul Werley, Par. Vicar; Dcn. Richard A. Warner, Dir.; CRP Stds.: 29
St. Mary Church - t) (989) 463-5370
Mt. St. Joseph Church - 605 S. Franklin St., Saint Louis, MI 48880 t) (989) 463-5370
St. Mary School - 220 W. Downie St., Alma, MI 48801 t) 989-463-4579 lseeley@nativityparish.net Lisa Seeley, Prin.; Stds.: 131; Lay Tchrs.: 7

AU GRES

Saint Mark Parish of Au Gres - 415 S. Court St., Au Gres, MI 48703 t) 989-876-7925 jgere@stmark.diosag.org wwwstmarkparishofaugres.org Rev. Gerald E. Balwinski, Sacramental Min.; Rev. Thomas M. Kowalczyk, Sacramental Min.; Ann Brownell, DRE; Colleen McCormick Snyder, Dir.; CRP Stds.: 14

AUBURN

Saint Gabriel Parish of Auburn - 84 W. Midland Rd., Auburn, MI 48611 t) 989-662-6861 jworonoff@stgabriel.diosag.org www.auburnac.org Rev. Thomas E. Sutton, Pst.; CRP Stds.: 141
St. Joseph Church - jworonoff@stgabriel.diosag.org
Area School - (Grades PreSchool-5) 114 W. Midland Rd., Auburn, MI 48611 t) 989-662-6431 cswitalski@auburnac.org auburnacschool.org Clark Switalski, Prin.; Stds.: 122; Lay Tchrs.: 7
Auburn Area Catholic, Early Childhood Center - (Grades PreSchool-5) 114 W. Midland Rd., Auburn, MI 48611 t) 989-662-6431 jworonoff@stgabriel.diosag.org Clark Switalski, Prin.; Stds.: 43; Lay Tchrs.: 4
St. Anthony Church - 1492 W. Midland Rd., Auburn, MI 48611 t) 989-662-0064

BAD AXE

Saint Hubert Parish of Bad Axe - 311 Whitelam St., Bad Axe, MI 48413 t) 989-269-7729 mosantoski@sthubert.diosag.org sthubertbadaxe.org Rev. Thomas J. Fleming, Pst.; CRP Stds.: 69
Sacred Heart Church - t) 989-269-4010 Melinda Osantoski, Bus. Mgr.;
St. Joseph Church - 3455 Rapson Rd., Rapson, MI 48413

BANNISTER

Saint Cyril Parish of Bannister - 517 E Main, Bannister, MI 48807; Mailing: PO Box 96, Bannister, MI 48807 t) 989-862-5270; 989-862-4534 (CRP) braj@diosag.org Rev. Baltha Raj, Par. Admin.; CRP Stds.: 27

BAY CITY

All Saints Parish of Bay City - 710 Columbus Ave., Bay City, MI 48708 t) 989-893-4693 allsaintsparishbaycity@gmail.com www.allsaintsparishbaycity.org/ Rev. Jose Maria Cabrera, Pst.; Rev. Stephen Fillion, In Res.; CRP Stds.: 35
St. Boniface Church - 500 N. Lincoln St., Bay City, MI 48708 jcabrera@diosag.org
St. James Church - dknox@asp.diosag.org
All Saints - (Grades PreK-5) t) 989-892-4371 Lisa Rhodus, Prin.;
Convent - 200 S. Farragut St., Bay City, MI 48708 rfilary@diosag.org Rev. Richard M. Filary, Pst.;
Saint Catherine of Siena Parish of Bay City - 2956 E. N. Union Rd., Bay City, MI 48706 t) 989-684-1203 dknox@asp.diosag.org www.scsparish.com Rev. James W. Bessert, Sacr. Min.; Sr. Christine Gretka, C.S.J., Dir.; CRP Stds.: 51
St. Vincent de Paul Church - t) (989) 828-5720 sstonebrook@svdp.diosag.org Dcn. Todd S. Lovas, Parish Life Coord.;
Corpus Christi Parish of Bay City - 1008 S. Wenona St., Bay City, MI 48706 t) 989-893-4073 parish2014@corpus-christi-parish.com Hank Messing, Parish Life Coord.; Rev. Kevin Kerbawy, In Res.; CRP Stds.: 20
Our Lady of Czestochowa Parish of Bay City - 1503 Kosciuszko Ave., Bay City, MI 48708 t) 989-893-6421 rfilary@diosag.org www.baycityolc.com Rev. Richard M. Filary, Pst.; Dcn. Stanley Kuczynski; CRP Stds.: 32
St. Hyacinth Church - 1515 Cass Ave., Bay City, MI 48708 t) (989) 893-6421
St. Stanislaus Kostka Church - t) (989) 893-6421
Our Lady of Peace Parish of Bay City - 607 E. S. Union St., Bay City, MI 48706 t) 989-892-6031 kkochany@diosag.org Rev. John S. Sarge, Sacr. Min.; Dcn. Kenneth Kochany, Admin.;
St. Mary of the Assumption Church - kkocheny@diosag.org

BIRCH RUN

Saints Francis and Clare Parish of Birch Run - 12157 Church St., Birch Run, MI 48415 t) 989-624-9098 dmcgrandy@sfa.diosag.org Rev. David Jenuwine, Admin.; CRP Stds.: 96
Sacred Heart Church - t) (989) 624-9098 dmcgrandy@sfds.diosag.org

CARO

Saint Christopher Parish of Caro and Mayville - 910 W. Frank St., Caro, MI 48723 t) 989-672-2104; 989-673-2276 www.cmstchristopher.org Rev. Christopher M. Coman, Pst.; CRP Stds.: 68
Sacred Heart Church - 905 W Frank St., Caro, MI 48723 t) (989) 672-2104
St. Joseph Church - 315 W. Ohmer Rd., Mayville, MI 48744 t) (989) 672-2104

CARROLLTON

Saint John Paul II Parish of Carrollton - 3431 Jefferson, Carrollton, MI 48724 t) 989-755-0828 brutkowski@diosag.org stjohnpauliicc.org/ Rev. William J. Rutkowski, Pst.;
St. Josaphat Church - 469 Shattuck Rd., Saginaw, MI 48604 nserrato@sjpii.diosag.org

CASEVILLE

Our Lady of Perpetual Help Parish of Caseville - 6253 Main St., Caseville, MI 48725-1238; Mailing: P.O. Box 1238, Caseville, MI 48725-1238 t) 989-856-4933 //www.ourladyofperpetualhelpparish.com Rev. George Amos, Pst.; CRP Stds.: 14
St. Roch Church -
St. Francis Borgia Church - 25 Moeller St., Pigeon, MI 48755
St. Felix of Valois Church - 3505 Limerick Rd., Pinnebog, MI 48725 Rev. George Amos, Par. Admin.;

CASS CITY

Our Lady Consolata Parish of Cass City - 4292 S. Seeger St., Cass City, MI 48726; Mailing: 4618 South St PO Box 139, Gagetown, MI 48735-0139 t) 989-665-1027 dgillespie@diosag.org Has records of former St. Jude Church, Fairgrove. Dcn. David Gillespie, Admin.; CRP Stds.: 16
St. Pancratius Church - parishoffice@stpancc.com

Dcn. David Gillespie, Admin.;
St. Agatha Church - 4618 South St., Gagetown, MI 48735; Mailing: Box 139, Gagetown, MI 48735 ourladyconsolata@stpancc.com Dcn. David Gillespie, Admin.;
Holy Family Church - 8370 Unionville Rd., Sebewaing, MI 48759 t) (989) 665-1027 www.olconsolata.org Dcn. David Gillespie, Parish Life Coord.;

CHESANING

Saint Peter Parish of Chesaning - 404 S. Wood St., Chesaning, MI 48616; Mailing: P.O. Box 454, Chesaning, MI 48616 t) 989-845-1794 braj@diosag.org www.stpeterchesaning.org Rev. Baltha Raj, Par. Admin.; CRP Stds.: 45
Our Lady of Perpetual Help Church - t) (989) 845-1794 stpeterchesaning.org

CLARE

Our Lady of Hope Parish of Clare - 106 E. Wheaton Ave., Clare, MI 48617 t) 989-386-9862 parish@olhclare.org olhclare.org Rev. Msgr. Francis B. Koper, Pst.; CRP Stds.: 16
St. Cecilia Church - fkoper@diosag.org
St. Henry Church - 4079 E. Vernon Rd., Rosebush, MI 48878 mvenglar@olhclare.diosag.org

ESSEXVILLE

Saint Jude Thaddeus Parish of Essexville - 614 Pine St., Essexville, MI 48732 t) 989-894-2701 x111; 989-894-2701 (CRP) bbehmlander@sjt.diosag.org www.stjudethaddeus.org Rev. Dale A. Orlik, Pst.; Dcn. Timothy S. Hartwig; CRP Stds.: 117
St. John the Evangelist Church - t) (989) 894-2701

FRANKENMUTH

Blessed Trinity Parish of Frankenmuth - 958 E. Tuscola St., Frankenmuth, MI 48734 t) 989-652-3259 www.btmuth.org Rev. Patrick M. Jankowiak, Pst.; CRP Stds.: 119

FREELAND

Saint Agnes Parish of Freeland - 300 Johnson St., Freeland, MI 48623 t) 989-695-5652 dhemgesberg@stagnes.diosag.org www.stagnesfreeland.com Rev. Christian F. Tabares, Pst.; CRP Stds.: 121

GLADWIN

Sacred Heart Parish of Gladwin - 330 N. Silverleaf St., Gladwin, MI 48624 t) 989-426-7154 jwitkowski@shgladwin.diosag.org gladwinharrisoncatholic.com Rev. Joseph Marcel Portelli, Pst.; CRP Stds.: 9

HARBOR BEACH

Holy Name of Mary Parish of Harbor Beach - 413 S. 1st St., Harbor Beach, MI 48441 t) 989-479-3393 www.holynameofmaryparish.org Rev. Kevin Wojciechowski, Par. Admin.; CRP Stds.: 89
Our Lady of Lake Huron Church - 405 S. First St., Harbor Beach, MI 48441
St. Anthony of Padua Church - 8239 Helena Rd., Harbor Beach, MI 48441 t) (989) 479-3393
Our Lady of Lake Huron School - (Grades PreK-8) t) 989-479-3427 ageiger@ollhschool.org Stds.: 106; Lay Tchrs.: 8

HARRISON

Saint Athanasius Parish of Harrison - 310 S. Broad St., Harrison, MI 48625 t) 989-539-6232 jwitkowski@shgladwin.diosag.org www.gladwinharrisoncatholic.com Rev. Joseph Marcel Portelli, Pst.; CRP Stds.: 11

HEMLOCK

Saint John XXIII Parish of Hemlock and Merrill - 151 St. Mary's Dr., Hemlock, MI 48626 t) 989-642-5606; 989-642-5240 (CRP) ikruth@stjohn23.diosag.org Rev. Michael Steltenkamp, SJ, Admin.; CRP Stds.: 20
St. Mary Church -
Sacred Heart Church - 419 S. Midland St., Merrill, MI 48637
St. Patrick Church - 4708 S. Meridian Rd., Merrill, MI 48637

ITHACA

Saint Paul the Apostle Parish of Ithaca - 121 N. Union St., Ithaca, MI 48847 t) 989-875-2852 emills@stpaul.diosag.org Rev. Edwin G. Dwyer, Admin.; CRP Stds.: 31
St. Martin De Porres Church - 4010 W. Cleveland Rd., Perrinton, MI 48871

LEXINGTON

Ave Maria Parish of Lexington - 5366 Main St., Lexington, MI 48450; Mailing: PO Box 399, Lexington, MI 48450 t) 810-359-5400 avemariaparish@gmail.com www.avemariaparishmi.org Rev. Donald J. Eppenbrock, Sacr. Min.; Sr. Maria Inviolata Honma, S.M.D.G., Pst. Min./Coord.; CRP Stds.: 34
St. Denis Church - hjohnson@avemaria.diosag.org
St. Mary, Our Lady of Sorrows Church - 7066 Main St., Port Sanilac, MI 48469 hjohnson@avemaria.diosag.org

LINWOOD

Prince of Peace Parish of Linwood - 315 W. Center St., Linwood, MI 48634 t) 989-697-4443 banderson@pop.diosag.org www.princeofpeaceparish.net Rev. Nicholas F. Coffaro, Pst.; Dcn. Michael Arnold; CRP Stds.: 38
St. Valentine Church - 999 S. 9 Mile Rd., Kawkawlin, MI 48631 t) (989) 697-4443 office@princeofpeaceparish.net
Sacred Heart Church - 1000 E. Beaver Rd., Kawkawlin, MI 48631 princeofpeaceparish.net
St. Anne Church - t) (989) 697-4443 office@princeofpeace.net Rev. Nicholas F. Coffaro, Pst.;

MIDLAND

Assumption of the Blessed Virgin Mary Parish of Midland - 3516 E. Monroe Rd., Midland, MI 48642 t) 989-631-4447 assumption@assumptionmidland.org www.assumptionmary.org John Graveline, Parish Life Coord.; CRP Stds.: 62
Blessed Sacrament Parish of Midland - 3109 Swede Ave., Midland, MI 48642 t) 989-835-6777 www.blessed-midland.org Rev. Robert J. Howe, Pst.; CRP Stds.: 188
Saint Brigid of Kildare Parish of Midland - 207 Ashman St., Midland, MI 48640 t) 989-835-7121 jhovey@stbrigid.diosag.org stbrigid-midland.org Rev. Andrew D. Booms, Pst.; Dcn. Daniel J. Corbat; Dcn. Aloysius J. Oliver; Dcn. Francis W. Hudson; CRP Stds.: 76
St. Brigid School - (Grades K-8) 130 W. Larkin St., Midland, MI 48640-6579; Mailing: 207 Ashman St., Midland, MI 48640 t) 989-835-9481 school@stbrigid-midland.org Laura Wilkowski, Prin.; Stds.: 140; Lay Tchrs.: 13

MOUNT PLEASANT

Saint Joseph the Worker Parish of Beal City - 2163 N. Winn Rd., Mount Pleasant, MI 48858 t) 989-644-2041 lmonahan@sjw.diosag.org Rev. Thomas R. Held, Pst.; CRP Stds.: 9
St. Joseph the Worker School - (Grades PreK-6) 2091 N. Winn Rd., Mount Pleasant, MI 48858 t) 989-644-3970 dlorenz@bcstjoe.net Dennis Lorenz, Prin.; Stds.: 87; Lay Tchrs.: 8
Saint Mary University Parish of Mt. Pleasant - 1405 S. Washington St., Mount Pleasant, MI 48858 t) 989-773-3931 jhovey@stbrigid.diosag.org Rev. Andrew D. Booms, Pst.; Rev. Marc Hopps, Par. Vicar;
Sacred Heart Parish of Mt. Pleasant - 302 S. Kinney Ave., Mount Pleasant, MI 48858 t) 989-772-1385 www.sha.net Rev. Loren M. Kalinowski, Pst.; Dcn. James Damitio; CRP Stds.: 119
Sacred Heart Academy - (Grades PreK-12) 316 E. Michigan Ave., Mount Pleasant, MI 48858 t) 989-772-1457 myonker@sha.net Mary Kay Yonker, Prin.; Stds.: 458; Lay Tchrs.: 31

NEW LOTHROP

Saint Michael Parish of Maple Grove - 17994 Lincoln Rd., New Lothrop, MI 48460 t) 989-845-7010; 989-845-7011 dbitterman@smmg.diosag.org stmichaelmaplegrove.org Rev. John F. Cotter, Pst.; CRP Stds.: 121

PINCONNING

Holy Trinity Parish of Pinconning - 225 S. Jennings St., Pinconning, MI 48650 t) 989-879-2141 www.holytrinitypinconning.org/ Maintains records of St. Agnes Church. Rev. Matthew Federico, Pst.; CRP Stds.: 13
St. Michael School - (Grades PreK-8) 310 E. 2nd St., Pinconning, MI 48650 t) 989-879-3063 stmichaelschoolpinconning@gmail.com holytrinitypinconning.org Ashley Kanuszewski, Prin.; Stds.: 119; Lay Tchrs.: 7
St. Mary Church -
St. Michael Church - dlp3364@hotmail.com

PORT AUSTIN

Annunciation of the Lord Parish of Port Austin - 8661 Independence St., Port Austin, MI 48467-0355; Mailing: PO Box 355, Port Austin, MI 48467 t) 989-738-7521 annunciationparish@centurytel.net www.annunciationofthelordparish.weebly.com Rev. Craig Carolan, Pst.; CRP Stds.: 21
St. Michael Church - jpionk@aotl.diosag.org
St. Edward Church - 5083 Park St., Kinde, MI 48445 jpionk@aotl.diosag.org
St. Mary Church - 1709 Moeller Rd., Kinde, MI 48445 t) 989-738-5886 jpionk@aotl.diosag.org

REESE

Saint Elizabeth of Hungary Parish of Reese - 12835 E. Washington Rd., Reese, MI 48757; Mailing: P.O. Box 392, Reese, MI 48757-0392 t) 989-868-4081 reickholt@stelizabeth.diosag.org stelizabethreese.org Rev. Andrew S. LaFramboise; CRP Stds.: 20
St. Elizabeth Area Catholic School - (Grades PreK-8) t) 989-868-4108 alaframboise@diosag.org Gabbie Marguery-Costoya, Prin.; Stds.: 34; Lay Tchrs.: 5

RUTH

Holy Apostles Parish of Ruth - 7121 E. Atwater Rd., Ruth, MI 48470-8507; Mailing: P.O. Box 55, Ruth, MI 48470-0055 t) 989-864-3649 Rev. Robert J. Kelm, Pst.; CRP Stds.: 50
Sts. Peter and Paul Church - ; Mailing: 7135 E Atwater Rd, P O Box 55, Ruth, MI 48470-0055 t) (989) 864-8600
St. John Chrysostom - 7938 Third St, Forestville, MI 48434; Mailing: 7135 E Atwater Rd, P O Box 55, Ruth, MI 48470-0055 t) (989) 864-3649
Saint Isidore Parish of Parisville - 4190 Parisville Rd, Ruth, MI 48470 t) 989-864-3523 lrutkowski@ha-sti.diosag.org Rev. Robert J. Kelm, Pst.; CRP Stds.: 28
St. Mary Church - stisidoreparish@yahoo.com
St. Patrick Church - 1801 Palms Rd., Palms, MI 48465-9604 stisidoreparish@yahoo.com

SAGINAW

Cathedral of Mary of the Assumption Parish of Saginaw - 615 Hoyt Ave., Saginaw, MI 48607 t) 989-752-8119 officeadmin@cathedralsaginaw.org Most Rev. Robert D. Gruss, Pst.; Rev. Prentice Tipton Jr., Rector; CRP Stds.: 30
St. Mary Cathedral Parish Inter-Parish Endowment Fund - 705 Hoyt Ave., Saginaw, MI 48607 mvogelpohl@cathedral.diosag.org
Our Lady of the Assumption Convent - 705 Hoyt Ave., Saginaw, MI 48607 t) 989-752-2515 Religious Sisters of Mercy Sr. Mary Judith O'Brien, RSM, Contact;
Christ the Good Shepherd Parish of Saginaw - 2445 N. Charles St., Saginaw, MI 48602 t) 989-793-0618 ctgssaginaw@sbcglobal.net Rev. William J. Rutkowski, Pst.; CRP Stds.: 23
St. Helen Church - t) (989) 793-0618 ageiling@ctgs.diosag.org
Saint Dominic Parish of Saginaw - 2711 Mackinaw St., Saginaw, MI 48602 t) 989-799-2334 mvogelpohl@stdominic.diosag.org www.stdominicsaginaw.org Rev. Steven M. Gavit, Pst.; CRP Stds.: 59
St. Stephen Church -
Ss. Peter and Paul Church - 4735 Washington Ave., Saginaw, MI 48638 t) 989-793-3611
Saint Francis de Sales Parish of Bridgeport - 3945 Williamson Rd., Saginaw, MI 48601 t) 989-777-2091 dmcgrandy@sfds.diosag.org www.stfrancisdesales-saginaw.org Rev. John Mancini, O.S.F.S., Pst.;

St. Christopher Church - dmcgrandy@ssfc.diosag.org
Saint Francis of Assisi Parish of Saginaw - 3680 S. Washington Rd., Saginaw, MI 48601 t) 989-752-1971 dmcgrandy@sfds.diosag.org Rev. Alberto E. Vargas, Pst.; CRP Stds.: 36
St. Anthony of Padua - avargas@diosag.org Parish holds records of former St. George Church.
St. Casimir Church - 2122 S. Jefferson Ave., Saginaw, MI 48601 dmcgrandy@ssfc.diosag.org
Holy Family Parish of Saginaw - 1525 S. Washington Ave., Saginaw, MI 48601 t) 989-755-8020 ptipton@diosag.org holyfamilysaginaw.org/ Rev. Prentice Tipton Jr., Pst.;
Holy Spirit Parish of Saginaw - 1035 N. River Rd., Saginaw, MI 48609 t) 989-781-2457 www.saginawhsp.org Rev. Peter J. Gaspeny, Pst.; Kathleen Myles, Pst. Min./Coord.; CRP Stds.: 88
Saint John Vianney Parish of Saginaw - 6400 McCarty Rd., Saginaw, MI 48603 t) 989-790-5086 www.sjvsaginaw.org Sr. Janet Pewoski, C.S.J., Admin.; Rev. Robert S. Gohm, Sacr. Min.; Rev. Richard Jozwiak, Sacr. Min.; CRP Stds.: 13
Saint Joseph Parish of Saginaw - 936 N. Sixth Ave., Saginaw, MI 48601 t) 989-755-7561 dsasiela@stjoseph.diosag.org www.stjosephsaginaw.org Rev. Francis Voris, O.F.M.Cap., Pst.; Dcn. Librado Gayton; CRP Stds.: 37
Saint Thomas Aquinas Parish of Saginaw - 5376 State Rd., Saginaw, MI 48603 t) 989-799-2460 pmessing@sta.diosag.org www.stasaginaw.org Rev. Richard A. Bokinskie, Pst.; Sr. Ann deGuise OSF, Pst. Assoc.; CRP Stds.: 15
Nouvel Catholic Elementary Bernardine Sisters of Third Order of St. Francis - (Grades PreSchool-8) 2136 Berberovich, Saginaw, MI 48603 t) 989-792-2361 jsprague@nouvelcatholic.org www.nouvelcatholic.org (Farmington, MI) Amanda Kaul, Prin.; Stds.: 412; Lay Tchrs.: 39

SANDUSKY

Holy Family Parish of Sandusky - 59 N. Moore St., Sandusky, MI 48471 t) 810-648-2968 www.holyfamilyparishsanilaccounty.com Rev. Stephen Blaxton, Pst.; CRP Stds.: 47
St. Joseph Church -
St. Elizabeth Church - 6785 Marlette St., Marlette, MI 48453
St. John the Evangelist Church - 5335 Sandusky Rd., Peck, MI 48466

SANFORD

Our Lady of Grace Parish of Sanford - 2500 N. West River Rd., Sanford, MI 48657 t) 989-687-5657 dfox@diosag.org; cbeeck@olgrace.diosag.org www.ourladyofgracemi.org Rev. Daniel Fox, O.F.M.Cap., Pst.; CRP Stds.: 81
St. Agnes Church - 2500 N. W. River Rd., Sanford, MI 48657
St. Anne Church - 5738 M-30, Edenville, MI 48620

SHEPHERD

Saint Vincent de Paul Parish of Shepherd - 168 Wright, Shepherd, MI 48883 t) 989-828-5720 sstonebrook@svdp.diosag.org stvincentdp.com Dcn. Todd S. Lovas; Rev. Frederick J. Kawka, Sacr. Min.; CRP Stds.: 32
St. Patrick Church - 7631 N. County Line, Irishtown, MI 48883; Mailing: 168 E Wright Ave, Shepherd, MI 48883 t) (989) 828-5720 tlovas@diosag.org

ST. CHARLES

Mary of the Immaculate Conception Parish of St. Charles - 708 Sanderson St., St. Charles, MI 48655; Mailing: PO Box 39, St. Charles, MI 48655 t) 989-865-9460 dbitterman@mic.diosag.org maryimmaculateconception.org Rev. John F. Cotter, Pst.; CRP Stds.: 17
Immaculate Conception Church - t) (989) 865-9460 maryimmaculateconception.org/
St. Mary Church - 5661 Fergus Rd., Saint Charles, MI 48655-9694 dbitterman@smmg.diosag.org

STANDISH

Resurrection of the Lord Parish of Standish - 423 W. Cedar St., Standish, MI 48658; Mailing: P.O. Box 306, Standish, MI 48658 t) 989-846-9565 mfitzgerald@rotl.diosag.org arenaccatholic.com Rev. Ronald F. Wagner, Fr., Pst.; CRP Stds.: 25
St. Joseph Church - 7842 Newberry St., Alger, MI 48610 Rev. Ronald F. Wagner, Pst.;

UBLY

Good Shepherd Parish of Ubly - 4470 N. Washington St., Ubly, MI 48475 t) 989-658-8824 goodshepherd48475@yahoo.com Rev. Nathan E. Harburg, Pst.; CRP Stds.: 72
St. John the Evangelist Church - t) (989) 658-8824 luhl@goodshepherd.diosag.org
St. Columbkille Church - 3031 McAlpin Rd., Sheridan Corners, MI 48475 nharburg@diosag.org
St. Ignatius Church - 1826 Cumber Rd., Freiburg, MI 48410 luhl@goodshepherd.diosag.org
St. Joseph Church - 4960 Ubly Rd., Argyle, MI 48410 luhl@goodshepherd.diosag.org

VASSAR

Saint Frances Xavier Cabrini Parish of Vassar - 334 Division St., Vassar, MI 48768 t) 989-823-2911 stfrancescabrinivassar.org/ Records of St. Bernard, Millington are kept at the parish office. Rev. Andrew S. LaFramboise, Pst.;

SCHOOLS: PRESCHOOL THRU HIGH SCHOOL

SCHOOLS

STATE OF MICHIGAN

AUBURN

Auburn Area Catholic Schools - (PAR) (Grades PreK-5) 88 W. Midland Rd., Auburn, MI 48611 t) 989-662-6431 cswitalski@auburnac.org www.auburnacschool.org Clark Switalski, Prin.; Stds.: 120; Scholastics: 1; Lay Tchrs.: 7

BAY CITY

All Saints Central School - (PAR) (Grades PreK-12) 217 S. Monroe St., Bay City, MI 48708 t) 989-892-2533 lisa.rhodus@ascbaycity.org www.ascbaycity.org Lisa Rhodus, Prin.; Sr. Maria Jose Perez, RSM, Vice Prin.; Laura Tacey, Librn.; Stds.: 255; Lay Tchrs.: 19

SAGINAW

Nouvel Catholic Central School - (PAR) 2555 Wieneke Rd., Saginaw, MI 48603 t) 989-791-4330 ddecuf@nouvelcatholic.org nouvelcatholic Daniel Decuf, Prin.; Stds.: 593; Lay Tchrs.: 39
Nouvel Catholic Central Educational Foundation Endowment Fund - 2555 Wieneke Rd., Saginaw, MI 48603 t) (989) 797-6651 clynn@diosag.org Cormac J. Lynn, Supt.;

INSTITUTIONS LOCATED IN DIOCESE

CEMETERIES [CEM]

BAY CITY

St. Patrick's, Calvary & St. Stanislaus - 2000 Columbus Ave., 2977 Old Kawkawlin Rd., Kawkawlin, Bay City, MI 48708 t) 989-797-6672 alefevre@diosag.org saginaw.org/cemeteries Alice LeFevre, Dir.;

LINWOOD

St. Anne - 1673 E. Linwood Rd., Linwood, MI 48634; Mailing: c/o Diocese of Saginaw Catholic Cemteries, 5800 Weiss St., Saginaw, MI 48603 t) 989-797-6672 alefevre@diosag.org saginaw.org/catholic-cemeteries Alice LeFevre, Dir.;

MIDLAND

Calvary - 2743 E. Bombay Rd., Midland, MI 48642 t) 989-689-3739 alefevre@dioceseofsaginaw.org saginaw.org/cemeteries Alice LeFevre, Dir.;
Old Calvary Cemetery - 3140 Eastman Ave., Midland, MI 48642 t) 989-797-6672 alefevre@diosag.org Alice Lefevre, Dir.;

SAGINAW

St. Andrew's, Mt. Olivet & Calvary - 381 St. Andrews Rd, 3440 S. Washington,, Saginaw, MI 48638 t) 989-797-6672 alefevre@dioceseofsaginaw.org Alice LeFevre, Dir.;

CONVENTS, MONASTERIES, AND RESIDENCES FOR WOMEN [CON]

ALMA

Motherhouse and Novitiate of the Religious Sisters of Mercy - 1965 Michigan Ave., Alma, MI 48801 t) 989-463-6035 religious.sisters.of.mercy@gmail.com www.rsmofalma.org Mother Mary McGreevy, R.S.M., Supr.; Sr. Mary Judith O'Brien, RSM, Vicar; Srs.: 24

PORT SANILAC

Sisters of Our Mother of Divine Grace - 7066 W. Main St., Port Sanilac, MI 48469 t) 810-622-9904 x3 smphilomena@gmail.com sistersmdg.org Sr. Mary Philomena Fuire, SMDG, Supr.; Srs.: 6

SAGINAW

Franciscan Poor Clare Nuns, O.S.C. - 4875 Shattuck Rd., Saginaw, MI 48603-2962 t) 989-797-0593 srsclare@protonmail.com www.srsclare.com Srs.: 2
Motherhouse and Novitiate of the Mission Sisters of the Holy Spirit - 915 N. River Rd., Saginaw, MI 48609 t) 989-781-0934 marylou.owczarzak@gmail.com Sr. Mary Lou Owczarzak, M.S.Sp., Pres.; Srs.: 3

ENDOWMENTS / FOUNDATIONS / TRUSTS [EFT]

ALMA

Saint Thomas Aquinas Trust - 1635 Michigan Ave., Alma, MI 48801 t) (989) 463-6035 x1 sisterbrigidmary@gmail.com Sr. Brigid Mary Meeks, RSM, Contact;

SAGINAW

***Catholic Community Foundation of Mid-Michigan** - 5800 Weiss St., Saginaw, MI 48603; Mailing: P.O. Box 6883, Saginaw, MI 48608-6883 t) 989-797-6627; 989-797-6684 ccfmm@dioceseofsaginaw.org ccfmm.com Michael Wolohan, Pres.; Kristin Smith, Exec. Dir.;
Holy Spirit Sisters Charitable Trust - 1030 N. River Rd., Saginaw, MI 48609 t) 989-781-0934 marylou.owczarzak@gmail.com Sr. Mary Lou Owczarzak, M.S.Sp., Pres.;
***St. Robert Bellarmine Trust** - 5800 Weiss St., Saginaw, MI 48603 t) 989-797-6620; 989-797-6614 dbierlein@diosag.org Debra Bierlein, Admin.;
Saginaw Inter-Parish Deposit & Loan Trust - 5800 Weiss St., Saginaw, MI 48607 t) 989-797-6688 dbierlein@diosag.org Debra Bierlein, Bus. Mgr.;

HOSPITALS / HEALTH SERVICES [HOS]

SAGINAW

Ascension St. Mary's Hospital - 800 S. Washington Ave., Saginaw, MI 48601-2524 t) 989-907-8000 paula.caruso@ascension.org St. Mary's of Michigan, St. Mary's Medical Center of Saginaw, Inc., St. Mary's Hospital of Saginaw, Inc., The Sisters of Charity of St. Mary's Hospita Christopher McClead, Contact; Bed Capacity: 232; Asstd. Annu.: 484,429; Staff: 1,503
Field Neurosciences Institute - 800 S. Washington Ave., Saginaw, MI 48061 t) (989) 907-8000 healthcare.ascension.org Dr. Stephanie Duggan, Pres.;

MISCELLANEOUS [MIS]

ALMA

Saint Joseph Corporation - 1965 Michigan Ave., Alma,

MI 48801 t) 989-463-6035 olgrecords@gmail.com Mother Mary McGreevy, R.S.M., Pres.;

***Sacred Heart Mercy Health Care Center** - 2025 W. Cheesman Rd., Alma, MI 48801 t) 989-463-3451 business@sacredheartmercy.com www.sacredheartmercy.org Sr. Mary Christa Nutt, Dir.;

BAY CITY

***Society of St. Vincent de Paul, Bay County Council** - 523 Michigan Ave., Bay City, MI 48708 t) 989-893-5772 memorand@aol.com Member Conferences: Bay City, Our Lady of Peace, St. Catherine of Siena, Our Lady of Czestochowa, All Saints, Corpus Christi; Essexville-St. Jude Mark Morand, Pres.;

SAGINAW

Catholic Family Service of the Diocese of Saginaw - 710 N. Michigan Ave., Saginaw, MI 48602-4372 t) 989-753-8446 skoterba@catholicfamsvc.org www.cfssite.org Sr. Mary Rebecca Koterba, R.S.M., Exec.;

Counseling Center -

Adoption Center - 915 Columbus Ave., Bay City, MI 48708-6690 t) 989-892-2504 skoterba@catholicfamsvc.org catholicfamilyservice.net/about/ Part of Catholic Family Service.

Counseling Center - 710 N. Michigan, Saginaw, MI 48602 t) 989-753-8336

***Little Books of the Diocese of Saginaw, Inc.** - 5802 Weiss St., Saginaw, MI 48608-6009; Mailing: P.O. Box 6009, Saginaw, MI 48608-6009 t) 989-797-6653 littlebooks.org/ Stacey Trapani, Exec. Dir.;

***Partnership Center** - 723 Emerson St., Saginaw, MI 48607 t) 989-907-5610 saginawpartnershipcenter.org Jeff Raymaker, Dir.;

NURSING / REHABILITATION / CONVALESCENCE / ELDERLY CARE [NUR]

SAGINAW

St. Francis Home of Saginaw - 915 N. River Rd., Saginaw, MI 48609 t) 989-781-3150 tiffanyp@stfrhome.org stfrhome.org Rev. Thai Hung Nguyen, Chap.; Tiffany Patrick, Admin.; Asstd. Annu.: 239; Staff: 128

An asterisk (*) denotes an organization that has established tax-exempt status directly with the IRS and is not covered by the USCCB Group Ruling.

Diocese of St. Augustine

(Dioecesis Sancti Augustini)

MOST REVEREND ERIK THOMAS POHLMEIER

Bishop of St. Augustine; ordained July 25, 1998; appointed Bishop of St. Augustine May 15, 2022; consecrated July 22, 2022.
Office: 11625 Old St. Augustine Rd., Jacksonville, FL 32258.

Catholic Center: 11625 Old St. Augustine Rd., Jacksonville, FL 32258. T: 904-262-3200
www.dosafl.com

Square Miles 11,032.

Florida, east of the Apalachicola River, was erected by Pope Pius IX into a Vicariate-Apostolic in the year 1857, and in 1870 into the Diocese of St. Augustine.

Comprises all of the northeastern Counties of the State of Florida including Alachua, Baker, Bradford, Clay, Columbia, Dixie, Duval, Flagler, Gilchrist, Hamilton, Lafayette, Levy, Nassau, Putnam, St. Johns, Suwannee and Union Counties.

For legal titles of parishes and diocesan institutions, consult the Catholic Center.

STATISTICAL OVERVIEW

Personnel

Bishop	1
Retired Bishops	2
Priests: Diocesan Active in Diocese	60
Priests: Diocesan Active Outside Diocese	5
Priests: Retired, Sick or Absent	52
Number of Diocesan Priests	117
Religious Priests in Diocese	24
Total Priests in your Diocese	141
Extern Priests in Diocese	32
Permanent Deacons in Diocese	60
Total Brothers	1
Total Sisters	96

Parishes

Parishes	54
With Resident Pastor:	
Resident Diocesan Priests	47
Resident Religious Priests	7
Missions	14
Pastoral Centers	2
Professional Ministry Personnel:	
Brothers	1
Sisters	44
Lay Ministers	60

Welfare

Health Care Centers	5
Total Assisted	1,184,115
Homes for the Aged	2
Total Assisted	506
Day Care Centers	8
Total Assisted	799
Special Centers for Social Services	5
Total Assisted	233,988
Residential Care of Disabled	1
Total Assisted	30
Other Institutions	6
Total Assisted	657

Educational

Diocesan Students in Other Seminaries	21
Total Seminarians	21
High Schools, Diocesan and Parish	5
Total Students	2,312
Elementary Schools, Diocesan and Parish	24
Total Students	8,330
Non-residential Schools for the Disabled	1
Total Students	146
Catechesis / Religious Education:	
High School Students	619
Elementary Students	5,965
Total Students under Catholic Instruction	17,393
Teachers in Diocese:	
Priests	1
Sisters	5
Lay Teachers	792

Vital Statistics

Receptions into the Church:	
Infant Baptism Totals	1,649
Minor Baptism Totals	140
Adult Baptism Totals	137
Received into Full Communion	643
First Communions	1,617
Confirmations	1,744
Marriages:	
Catholic	339
Interfaith	113
Total Marriages	452
Deaths	1,321
Total Catholic Population	176,400
Total Population	2,425,334

LEADERSHIP

Vicar General - t) 904-285-2698 Rev. Msgr. Keith R. Brennan, Vicar (krb@olsspvb.org);
Chancellor - t) 904-262-3200 x129 Dcn. Michael Elison (chancellor@dosafl.com);
Episcopal Vicar for Development and Finance - t) 904-262-3200 x134 Rev. Msgr. Michael Houle, Vicar (mhoule@dosafl.com);
Chief Financial Officer - t) 904-262-3200 x133 Stephen R. Bell (sbell@dosafl.com);
Judicial Vicar - t) 904-800-2393 x204 Rev. Peter Akin-Otiko (pakin-otiko@dosafl.com);
College of Consultors - Rev. Msgr. Keith R. Brennan, Chair (krb@olsspvb.org);
Deans -
Gainesville Deanery - t) 352-332-6279 Rev. Alberto Esposito, Dean;
North Jacksonville Deanery - t) 904-388-8698 Rev. Jose J. Kulathinal, C.M.I., Dean;
South Jacksonville Deanery - t) 904-398-1963 Rev. Jason Trull, Dean;
St. Augustine Deanery - t) 904-471-5364 Rev. Timothy M. Lindenfelser, Dean;
St. Johns River Deanery - t) 904-284-3811 Rev. Michael Pendergraft, Dean;

OFFICES AND DIRECTORS

Bishop, Office of the - t) 904-262-3200 x136 bishopsoffice@dosafl.com Jerry Wilamowski, Exec. Asst.;
Chancellor, Office of the - t) 904-262-3200 x190 www.dosafl.com/chancellor/ Mary Kay Nedrich, Admin. (mknedrich@dosafl.com);
Archives & Records Management - t) 904-262-3200 x120 archives@dosafl.com archives.dosafl.com/ Katy Lockard, Exec. Dir. (klockard@dosafl.com); Dcn. David A. Williams, Dir. (history@dosafl.com);
Catholic Cemeteries - t) 904-824-6680 cemeteries.dosafl.com/ Keith Rezendez, Dir. (krezendes@dosafl.com);
Bunnell, St. Mary Cemetery -
High Springs, St. Madeleine Memorial Garden & Cemetery - t) 386-454-2358
Jacksonville, Gate of Heaven Cemetery, - t) 904-619-6293 Kristin Jewell, Family Needs Consultant;
St. Augustine, San Lorenzo Cemetery - dtruhowsky@dosafl.com Deborah Truhowsky, Cemetery Admin.;
Christian Formation Office - t) 904-262-3200 x118 formation.dosafl.com/ Erin McGeever, Dir. (emcgeever@dosafl.com);
Deaf and Blind Ministry - t) 904-824-6625 Erin McGeever, Dir.; Susan Boehm-Donlon, CRE;
Ministry Formation Program - formation.dosafl.com/ministryformation/
Communications - t) 904-262-1705 communications.dosafl.com/ Kathleen Bagg, Dir. (kbagg@dosafl.com);
St. Augustine Catholic - communications.dosafl.com
Human Resources - t) 904-262-3200 x122 hr.dosafl.com/ Greg C. Reed, Dir. (gcreed@dosafl.com);
Benefits Insurance Committee - Greg C. Reed, Chair;
Liturgy Office - t) 904-824-2806 liturgy.dosafl.com/ Rev. Thomas S. Willis, Dir.;
Diocesan Liturgical Commission - t) 352-376-5405 x118 Letty Valentin, Chair;
Real Estate Planning & Property Development - t) 904-262-3200 Lester Del Rosario, Dir. (ldelrosario@dosafl.com);
Building Committee - Lester Del Rosario, Chair;
Real Estate Committee - Lester Del Rosario, Chair;
Safe Environment Office - t) 904-262-3200 x104 safe.dosafl.com/ Donna Wilhelm, Dir. (dwilhelm@dosafl.com);
Virtus/Protecting God's Children -
Superintendent, Office of the - t) 904-262-0668 www.dosaeducation.org/home Dcn. Scott J. Conway, Supt. (superintendent@dosafl.com); Rhonda Rose, Asst. Supt. (rrose@dosafl.com); Audra Smith, Secy. (asmith@dosafl.com);
Diocesan Council for Catholic Schools -
Tribunal, Diocesan - t) 904-262-3200; 904-800-2393 tribunal.dosafl.com/ Jeriann Salak, Asst./Notary (jsalak@dosafl.com);
Victim Assistance Coordinator - t) 904-208-6979 safe.dosafl.com/reporting-abuse/ Tina Nugent, Coord. (tnugent@dosafl.com);
Vocations Office - t) 904-262-3200 x101 vocations@dosafl.com vocations.dosafl.com/ Rev. Steven Zehler, Dir.;

ADVISORY BOARDS, COMMISSIONS, COMMITTEES, AND COUNCILS

Finance Council - John Alexander, Chair;
Diocesan Pastoral Council - Erin McGeever, Secy. (emcgeever@dosafl.com);
Presbyteral Council - Rev. Timothy M. Lindenfelser, Chair (tlindenfelser66@gmail.com);
Review Board - Mark Borello, Chair;

CLERGY AND RELIGIOUS SERVICES

Vicar for Priests - t) 904-284-3811 Rev. Michael Pendergraft (pastor@sacredhearcatholicchurch.org);
Vicar for Senior Priests - t) 904-348-3983 Rev. William A. Kelly;
Senior Priest Care - t) 904-703-7910 Lauren Austin, Coord., Assistance for Senior Priests (laustin@dosafl.com);
Continuing Education for Clergy - t) 904-359-0331 Dcn. Robert DeLuca, Chair (delucab@comcast.net);
Spirituality Committee - t) 386-752-4470 Rev. Robert Hoffman, Chair (rhoffman@epiphanycatholiclc.com);
Vicar for Permanent Deacons - t) 904-287-0519 Rev. John H. Tetlow, Vicar (frjohnstaug@gmail.com);
Permanent Diaconate, Office of the - t) 904-287-0519 Dcn. David Yazdiya, Dir., Deacon Personnel (davidyazdiya@gmail.com); Rev. Slawomir Bielasiewicz, Dir., Spiritual Formation (frslawek@stmaryccfl.net);
Deacon Council - t) 904-571-9606 Dcn. Larry Hart, Secy. (dcnlarryhart@gmail.com);
Delegate for Religious - t) 904-764-3241 c) 904-477-0549 Sr. Victora Will, S.N.D., Dir. (will19v46@gmail.com);
Commission for Religious - t) 604-772-8337 Sr. Andrea Zbiegien, S.F.C.C., Chair (smaz_@bellsouth.net);

EVANGELIZATION

Campus Ministry -
Gainesville (University of Florida - St. Augustine Church & Catholic Student Center) - t) 352-372-3533 info@catholicgators.org catholicgators.org/student-ministries Rev. David Ruchinski, Dir.; Ashley Hemmingway, Senior Campus Min.;
Jacksonville (University of N. FL; Jacksonville U; FL State College, Jax; St. Johns River State College - UNF Catholic Student Center) - t) 904-687-8883 staugustineccm@gmail.com Rev. Blair Gaynes, Dir.; Sr. Brittany Samuelson, SCTJM, Campus Min.;
St. Augustine (Flagler College - Cathedral Basilica of St. Augustine) - t) 904-824-2806 staugustineccm@gmail.com Rev. Blair Gaynes, Dir.;
Charismatic Renewal - t) 352-244-9899 Dr. Mary Shaw, Contact (peaceofjesus@gmail.com);
Council of Catholic Women, Diocesan - t) 904-534-9940 Rev. Msgr. James R. Boddie Jr., Spiritual Adv./Care Srvcs. (jrb@ctkcatholic.com); Susan Prichett, Pres. (susanjop@comcast.net);
Cursillo - t) 904-252-6761 Rev. Amarnath Nagothu, M.S.F.S., Spiritual Adv./Care Srvcs.; Sandra David, Contact (s_l_david@hotmail.com);
Ecumenism and Interfaith - t) 904-262-3200 x129 Dcn. Michael Elison, Chancellor (chancellor@dosafl.com); Rev. Alberto Esposito (fral@qopparish.org); Chau Thien Phan;
Family Life Office - t) 904-262-3200 x156 family.dosafl.com/ Michael Day, Dir. (mday@dosafl.com);
Catholic Therapist Network - family.dosafl.com/therapists/
Divorced, Separated and Widowed Ministry -
Engaged Encounter - t) 904-580-4599 cee.st.augustinefl@gmail.com Camille & Denver Anderson, Coord.; Jose & Julie Delgadillo, Coord.;
Integral Ecology Committee - lclemen@ju.edu Dr. Lee Ann Clements, Chair;
It's Just Fun Catholic Singles Network - t) 904-551-2619 itsjustfun.org/ Rev. Anthony P. Palazzolo, Chap.;
Natural Family Planning -
Retrouvaille/Rediscovery - t) 904-718-6109 jacksonville@retrouvaille.org Shan & Jen Vendt, Coord.;
Hispanic Charismatic Renewal - t) 904-861-4449 Cesar Lopez, Contact (alopezhernandez65@gmail.com);
Legion of Mary - t) 904-654-3386 Rev. Edward W. Murphy, Chap. (frmurphy@ccstaug.com); Ginger Grant, Contact (gingergrant13@yahoo.com);
Marywood Retreat & Conference Center - t) 904-287-2525 info@marywoodcenter.org marywoodcenter.org/ Matthew Achorn, Exec. Dir. (machorn@marywoodcenter.org);
Camp St. John -
Multicultural Ministry - t) 904-353-3243; 904-854-0669 www.dosafl.com Alba M. Orozco, Dir. (amorozco@ccbjax.org);
Black Catholic Commission - t) 904-724-0080; 904-768-9934 Rev. Msgr. James R. Boddie Jr., Moderator; Ernie Favors, Chair;
Brazilian/Portuguese Outreach - t) 508-498-1734; 904-683-1410 Andreia Salles, Coord.; Ana Silva, Coord.;
Burmese Outreach - t) 904-354-4846 x268 burmese.chaplaincy@gmail.com Sarah Maley, Contact;
Filipino Catholic Commission - t) 904-737-6863 c) 904-629-2693 Susana Suarez, Pres.; Rev. Rafael Lavilla Jr., Spiritual Adv./Care Srvcs.;
Haitian Outreach - t) 904-208-1458 Rev. Calonge Lemaine, Coord.; Jonel Laguerre, Contact;
Hispanic Commission -
Pontifical Mission Societies - t) 904-824-0431 x323 www.dosafl.com/ministries/missions-office/ Dcn. Bryan Ott, Dir. (bryan.ott@sjaweb.org);
Holy Childhood Association - t) 904-461-5762
Society for the Propagation of the Faith - t) 904-461-5762
Prison Ministry - t) 904-293-3807 prisonministry.dosafl.com/ John Chick, Dir. (jchick@dosafl.com);
Stella Maris Seafarers Ministry - t) 904-613-3489 www.dosafl.com Dcn. Milton Vega, Dir. (mvega@dosafl.com);
Youth and Young Adult Ministry - t) 904-262-3200 x189 Robin Shipley, Dir. (rshipley@dosafl.com); Norma Garcia, Coord., Multicultural Ministry (ngarcia@dosafl.com);
Catholic Committee on Scouting - youth.dosafl.com/committee-on-scouting/ Reggie Dubay, Chair; Rev. Joseph Kuhlman, Chap.; Dcn. Dale Tatum, Chap.;

FINANCE

Catholic Foundation of Diocese of St. Augustine - t) 904-262-3200 catholicfoundation@dosafl.com cf.dosafl.com/ Patricia DiSandro, Exec. Dir. (pdisandro@dosafl.com); Cliff Evans, Planned Giving Officer (cevans@dosafl.com); Kim Howard, Planned Giving Coord. (khoward@dosafl.com);
Development & Stewardship Office - t) 904-262-3200 x171 stewardship.dosafl.com/ Charlie Sloan, Dir. (csloan@dosafl.com); Dcn. Edward Prisby, Assoc. Dir. (eprisby@stpaulsjaxbeach.org);
Fiscal Office - t) 904-262-3200 x132 fiscal.dosafl.com/ Matthew Reilly, Controller (mreilly@dosafl.com);
Risk Management - Deborah Tauro, Mgr.;
Shared Services - Michelle Brabson, Mgr.;

ORGANIZATIONS

Florida Catholic Conference - t) 850-222-3803 contact@flacathconf.org flacathconf.org/ Michael B. Sheedy, Exec. (msheedy@flcathconf.org);

SOCIAL SERVICES

Catholic Campaign for Human Development - Rev. Jhon Guarnizo, Coord. (btccjax10472@gmail.com);

Catholic Charities Bureau, Inc. - t) 904-899-5500 info@ccbdosa.org ccbdosa.org/ Anita Hassell, Exec. Dir. (ahassell@ccbdosa.org);

Gainesville Regional Office - t) 352-372-0294 www.catholiccharitiesgainesville.com/ John C. Barli, Dir.;

Jacksonville Regional Office - t) 904-354-4846 www.ccbjax.org/ Lori Weber, Dir.;

Camp I Am Special - t) 904-230-7447 campiamspecial@ccbjax.org

Immigration and Legalization - t) 904-354-5904 www.ccbjax.org/immigration-legal-services Iraida Martinez, Dir.;

Refugee Resettlement - t) 904-354-4846 www.ccbjax.org/refugee-resettlement Hellai Noorai, Dir.;

Lake City Regional Office - t) 386-754-9180 catholiccharitieslakecity.org/ Suzanne M. Edwards, Dir.;

St. Augustine Regional Office - t) 904-829-6300 www.ccbstaug.org/ Ricardo Rosado-Rodriguez, Dir.;

Catholic Relief Services - t) 904-899-5500 www.crs.org/ Anita Hassell, Dir. (ahassell@ccbdosa.org);

Courage/Encourage Ministry - t) 904-797-4842 Rev. Edward W. Murphy, Dir. (frmurphy@ccstaug.com);

Human Life & Dignity - t) 904-262-3200 x159 life.dosafl.com/ May Oliver, Dir. (moliver@dosafl.com);

PARISHES, MISSIONS, AND CLERGY

STATE OF FLORIDA

BUNNELL

St. Mary (Mother of God, St. Mary Parish) - 89 St. Mary's Pl., Bunnell, FL 32110-1537; Mailing: 230 S. Old Dixie Hwy., Bunnell, FL 32110-1537 t) 386-437-5098 secretary@stmaryccfl.net www.stmaryccfl.net Rev. Rafal Mazurowski (Poland), Pst.; CRP Stds.: 3

CALLAHAN

Our Lady of Consolation - 541668 U.S. Hwy. One, Callahan, FL 32011; Mailing: P. O. Box 692, Callahan, FL 32011 t) 904-879-3662 olccatholicchurch@comcast.net Rev. Dung Quang Bui, Pst.; Joseph Smith, DRE; Traci Nickens, Bus. Mgr.; CRP Stds.: 35

CHIEFLAND

St. John the Evangelist - 4050 N.W. US Hwy. 27 Alt., Chiefland, FL 32626; Mailing: PO Box 863, Chiefland, FL 32644 t) 352-493-9723 stjhc@bellsouth.net stjhc.org Rev. Cesar Torres-Pinzon, Pst.; Rev. Wilson Colmenares, Par. Vicar; CRP Stds.: 66

Holy Cross - 18278 S.W. Hwy. 19, Cross City, FL 32628 t) (352) 493-9723 www.stjhc.org/holy-cross-mission-church

Cristo El Buen Pastor - 239 N. U.S. Hwy. 129, Bell, FL 32619; Mailing: P.O. Box 863, Chiefland, FL 32644 www.stjhc.org/christ-the-good-shepherd

St. Andrew Mission - 390 2nd St., Cedar Key, FL 32625; Mailing: P.O. Box 863, Chiefland, FL 32644 www.stjhc.org/st-andrews-mission-church

CRESCENT CITY

St. John the Baptist - 2725 S Hwy 17, Crescent City, FL 32112; Mailing: P O Box 908, Crescent City, FL 32112 t) 386-698-2055 church@sjbch.com www.sjbch.com/ Rev. William Villa, Admin.; Sr. Matilde Ahu Rivera, DJBP, Pst. Assoc.; Sr. Catalina Perez-Hernandez, DJBP, Pst. Assoc.; CRP Stds.: 119

ELKTON

St. Ambrose - 6070 Church Rd., Elkton, FL 32033 t) 904-692-1366 choffice1@saintambrose-church.org www.saintambrose-church.org Rev. Steven Zehler, Pst.; Dcn. Dan Rindge; Christine Humphries, DRE; CRP Stds.: 32

FERNANDINA BEACH

St. Michael's - 201 N. 4th St., Fernandina Beach, FL 32034 t) 904-261-3472 www.stmichaelscatholic.com Rev. Jose Kallukalam (India), Pst.; Sr. Nayva Josephine Thekkumthala, Pst. Assoc.; Sr. Rose Paul Madassery, SABS, Admin.; Walt Edwards, Bus. Mgr.; CRP Stds.: 76

St. Michael's Academy - (Grades PreK-8) 228 N. 4th St., Fernandina Beach, FL 32034 t) 904-321-2102 smacad@smacad.org smacad.org/ Dcn. Scott J. Conway, Supt.; Susan Dorner, Prin.; Stds.: 232; Lay Tchrs.: 13

FLAGLER BEACH

Santa Maria Del Mar - 915 N. Central Ave., Flagler Beach, FL 32136 t) 386-439-2791 www.smdmcc.org Rev. Manny Lopez, Pst.; Dcn. Manuel Almeida; Dcn. John Harvey; Dcn. Bob Krol; CRP Stds.: 154

FLEMING ISLAND

Sacred Heart - 7190 Hwy. 17 S., Fleming Island, FL 32003 t) 904-284-3811; 904-284-9983 (CRP) www.sacredheartcatholicchurch.org Rev. Michael Pendergraft, Pst.; Rev. Sebastian Garcia (Spain), Par. Vicar; Sandra Curtis, DRE; Kristin Michler-Belleza, DRE; CRP Stds.: 338

Sacred Heart Mission - 207 Palmetto Ave., Green Cove Springs, FL 32043; Mailing: 7190 Hwy. 17 S., Fleming Island, FL 32003 sacredheartcatholicchurch.org

GAINESVILLE

St. Augustine Church and Catholic Student Center - 1738 W. University Ave., Gainesville, FL 32603 t) 352-372-3533 info@catholicgators.org www.catholicgators.org Rev. David Ruchinski, Pst.; Rev. Marialal Joseph, CMI, Par. Vicar; Rev. Raguiel Rodriguez, Par. Vicar;

Holy Faith - 747 NW 43rd St., Gainesville, FL 32607 t) 352-376-5405 holyfaithoffice@holyfaithchurch.org www.holyfaithcatholicchurch.org Rev. Jose J. Kulathinal, C.M.I., Pst.; Rev. Mazen Michael Elias, Par. Vicar; Dcn. Michael J. Demers; CRP Stds.: 155

St. Patrick Church - 500 N.E. 16th Ave., Gainesville, FL 32601 t) 352-372-4641 x100 stpatsjoy@saintpatricksparish.org; frlawrence@saintpatricksparish.org www.saintpatricksparishgnv.org Rev. Lawrence Peck, Admin.; CRP Stds.: 29

Queen of Peace Catholic Community - 10900 S.W. 24th Ave., Gainesville, FL 32607 t) 352-332-6279 office@qopparish.org qopparish.org Rev. Alberto Esposito, Pst.; Rev. Joseph Emmanuel Simon Dos Santos, Par. Vicar; Rev. Figi Philip George, CMI (India), Par. Vicar; Dcn. Jorge Morales; CRP Stds.: 407

Queen of Peace Academy - (Grades PreK-8) 10900 SW 24th Ave., Gainesville, FL 32607 t) 352-332-8808 office@qopacademy.org www.qopacademy.org Dcn. Scott J. Conway, Supt.; Therese Majewski, Prin.; Stds.: 466; Lay Tchrs.: 36

HIGH SPRINGS

St. Madeleine Sophie Parish and Santa Fe Shrine of Our Lady of La Leche - 17155 N.W. U.S. Hwy. 441, High Springs, FL 32643 t) 386-454-2358 stmadeleinecc@windstream.net www.stmadeleinecatholicchurch.com Rev. Mark Dzien, Pst.; Dcn. Henry Zmuda; CRP Stds.: 38

San Juan - 304 S.E. Plant Ave., Branford, FL 32008 t) 386-935-2632 sanjuanmissionfl@gmail.com sanjuanmission.org

INTERLACHEN

St. John the Evangelist - 106 Manitoba St., USPS Address: 1200 State Rd. 20, Interlachen, FL 32148; Mailing: PO Box 207, Interlachen, FL 32148 t) 386-684-2528 sjcc1200@aol.com Rev. Pablo Fuentes, Pst.;

JACKSONVILLE

Assumption - 2403 Atlantic Blvd., Jacksonville, FL 32207 t) 904-398-1963 assumption@assumptioncatholicchurch.org www.assumptioncatholicchurch.org Rev. Jason Trull, Pst.; Rev. Eric Stelzer, Par. Vicar; Rev. Matthew King, Par. Vicar; Dcn. Chuck Patterson; Dcn. Dale Tatum; CRP Stds.: 174

Assumption School - (Grades K-8) 2431 Atlantic Blvd., Jacksonville, FL 32207 t) 904-398-1774 mjimenez@assumptionjax.org assumptionjax.org Maryann Jimenez, Prin.; Stds.: 560; Lay Tchrs.: 40

Basilica of the Immaculate Conception - 121 E. Duval St., Jacksonville, FL 32202 t) 904-359-0331 office@icjax.org icjax.org Rev. Blair Gaynes, Pst.; Rev. Carlos Mario Lopera, In Res.; Dcn. Robert DeLuca;

Blessed Trinity - 10472 Beach Blvd., Jacksonville, FL 32246 t) 904-641-1414; 904-646-4320 (CRP) btccjax10472@gmail.com; dre@btccjax.org btccjax.org Rev. Jhon Guarnizo, Pst.; Rev. Wilson Colmenares, Par. Vicar; Rev. Steven Stillmunks, In Res.; Dcn. Brian Hughes; Dcn. Ramon Molano; CRP Stds.: 271

Blessed Trinity School - (Grades PreK-8) 10472 Beach Blvd, Jacksonville, FL 32246 t) 904-641-6458 principal@blessedtrinitycatholicschool.org blessedtrinitycatholicschool.org/ Marie Davis, Prin.; Stds.: 243; Lay Tchrs.: 14

Christ the King - 742 Arlington Rd. N., Jacksonville, FL 32211 t) 904-724-0080 rectory@ctkcatholic.com ctkcatholic.com Rev. Msgr. James R. Boddie Jr., Pst.; Rev. Julio Bedoya, ICC, Assoc. Pst.; Rev. Bernie Tan Dang, C.R.M., Assoc. Pst.; Dcn. George Barletta, Liturgy Dir.; Sandy Hill, DRE; CRP Stds.: 31

Christ the King School - (Grades K-8) 6822 Larkin Rd., Jacksonville, FL 32211 t) 904-724-2954 ctk@ctkschooljax.com ctkschooljax.com/ Dcn. Scott J. Conway, Supt.; Stephanie Engelhardt, Prin.; Stds.: 356; Lay Tchrs.: 23

Church of the Crucifixion - 3183 W. Edgewood Ave., Jacksonville, FL 32209-2209 t) 904-765-5284 crucifixion@comcast.net www.crucifixionjax.org Rev. Bernardine Eikhuemelo, Pst.;

St. Francis Choe Korean Catholic Mission - 8051 Rampart Rd., Jacksonville, FL 32244 t) 904-573-1833 stfccm@gmail.com www.stfccm.org Rev. Jinmo Kim, Pst.; CRP Stds.: 5

Holy Family - 9800 Baymeadows Rd., Jacksonville, FL 32256 t) 904-641-5838 plombardo@holyfamilyjax.com; mpetrotta@holyfamilyjax.com www.holyfamilyjax.com Rev. David Keegan, Pst.; Rev. Mason Wiggins, Par. Vicar; Patricia Lombardo, Admin.; Marleda Upton, Music Min.; Josie Kuhlman, Youth Min.; Chris Mueller, Youth Min.; Maria Petrotta, DRE; CRP Stds.: 77

Holy Family School - (Grades PreSchool-8) 9800-3 Baymeadows Rd., Jacksonville, FL 32256 t) 904-645-9875 mmoloney@hfcatholicschool.com hfcatholicschool.com/ Dcn. Scott J. Conway, Supt.; Matt Moloney, Prin.; Stds.: 419; Lay Tchrs.: 28

Holy Rosary - 4731 Norwood Ave., Jacksonville, FL 32206 t) 904-764-3241 holyrosaryjax@comcast.net holyrosaryjax.org Rev. Bernardine Eikhuemelo, Assoc. Pst.; Sr. Victora Will, S.N.D., Pst. Assoc.; CRP Stds.: 6

Holy Spirit - 11665 Fort Caroline Rd., Jacksonville, FL 32225 t) 904-641-7244 info@holyspiritchurchjax.org holyspiritchurchjax.org Rev. Amarnath Nagothu, M.S.F.S., Pst.; Dcn. Patrick J. Goin; Dcn. Edward Prisby; Dcn. Ray Stiles; CRP Stds.: 82

Holy Spirit School - (Grades PreK-8) t) 904-642-9165 dr.luciano@hscatholicschool.com www.hscatholicschool.com Dcn. Scott J. Conway; John Luciano, Prin.; Stds.: 219; Lay Tchrs.: 15

St. John the Baptist - 2400 Mayport Rd., Jacksonville, FL 32233; Mailing: P.O. Drawer 330005, Jacksonville,

FL 32233 t) 904-246-6014 stjohnthebaptistab@gmail.com www.saintjohnsatlanticbeach.org Rev. Rafael Lavilla Jr., Pst.; Rev. Ronald A. Camarda; Samantha Matthews, DRE; CRP Stds.: 105

St. Joseph - 11757 Old St. Augustine Rd., Jacksonville, FL 32258; Mailing: 11730 Old St. Augustine Rd., Jacksonville, FL 32258 t) 904-268-5422; 904-880-6404 (CRP) stjosephsoffice@gmail.com stjosephsjax.org Rev. Sebastian K. George, C.M.I., Pst.; Rev. Briggs Hurley, Par. Vicar; Dcn. Kevin Boudreaux; Dcn. Bob Gardner; Dcn. Lowell Hecht; Dcn. Robert Repke; Lourdes Flemming, DRE; CRP Stds.: 433

St. Joseph School - (Grades PreK-8) 11600 Old St. Augustine Rd., Jacksonville, FL 32258 t) 904-268-6688 schoolbilling@stjosephcs.org www.stjosephcs.org Dcn. Scott J. Conway, Supt.; Robin Fecitt, Prin.; Stds.: 542; Lay Tchrs.: 31

Mary, Queen of Heaven - 9401 Staples Mill Dr., Jacksonville, FL 32244 t) 904-777-3168 mqoh@comcast.net www.maryqueenofheaven.org Rev. Philip Timlin, Pst.; Dcn. Paul Testa; Dcn. David A. Williams; CRP Stds.: 52

St. Matthew - 1773 Blanding Blvd., Jacksonville, FL 32210 t) 904-388-8698 stmatthews@stmatthewsjax.com stmatthewsjax.weconnect.com Rev. Pradeep Baby Aetharyil, CMI, Pst.; Dcn. George Good; Dcn. David Yazdiya; Melissa Merritt, DRE; CRP Stds.: 72

St. Matthew School - (Grades PreSchool-8) 1773-0010 Blanding Blvd., Jacksonville, FL 32210 t) 904-387-4401 kneill@stmatthewscs.com www.stmatthewscs.com/ Dcn. Scott J. Conway, Supt.; Kathy Tuerk, Prin.; Stds.: 271; Lay Tchrs.: 15

Most Holy Redeemer - 8523 Normandy Blvd., Jacksonville, FL 32221-6701 t) 904-786-1192 mhrjax@mhrjax.org mhrjax.org Rev. Adam Izbicki, Pst.; Dcn. John Baker; Dcn. Mark Sciullo; Dcn. Milton Vega; Michael Fierro, DRE; CRP Stds.: 84

St. Patrick - 601 Airport Center Dr. E., Jacksonville, FL 32218 t) 904-768-2593 fatherliguori@hotmail.com stpatrickjacksonville.org Rev. Christopher Liguori, Pst.; Rev. Joseph Kuhlman, Par. Vicar; Dcn. David Belanger; CRP Stds.: 41

St. Patrick School - (Grades PreSchool-8) t) 904-768-6323 www.stpatrickjacksonville.org/school/ Dcn. Scott J. Conway, Supt.; Christopher Meyer, Prin.; Stds.: 297; Pr. Tchrs.: 1; Lay Tchrs.: 16

St. Paul's - 2609 Park St., Jacksonville, FL 32204 t) 904-387-2554 parishoffice@spsjax.org stpauls-jax.org/ Rev. George Vaniyapurackal, Pst.; Rev. Leonard Chuwa, A.J., Par. Vicar; Dcn. James Scott; CRP Stds.: 15

St. Paul's School - (Grades PreSchool-8) t) 904-387-2841 spsjax.org/ Dcn. Scott J. Conway, Supt.; Repper Kim, Prin.; Stds.: 193; Lay Tchrs.: 15

St. Pius V - 2110 Blue Ave., Jacksonville, FL 32209 t) 904-354-1501 spvbm@outlook.com www.stpiusjax.org Rev. Bernardine Eikhuemelo, Pst.; CRP Stds.: 54

Prince of Peace - 6320 Bennett Rd., Jacksonville, FL 32216 t) 904-733-6860; 904-733-6011 (CRP) popofficemanager@yahoo.com princeofpeacecatholicchurch.net/ Rev. Callistus O. C. Onwere (Nigeria), Pst.; Rev. Calonge Lemaine, Vicar; Rev. Lam Nguyen, Chap.; Dcn. Michael Federico; CRP Stds.: 24

Resurrection - 3383 University Blvd. N., Jacksonville, FL 32277-2483 t) 904-744-0833 secretary@respar.net www.respar.net Rev. Bartlomiej Gadaj, Pst.; CRP Stds.: 5

Resurrection School - (Grades PreK-8) 5710 Jack Rd., Jacksonville, FL 32277 t) 904-744-1266 principal@resurrectioncatholic.com www.resurrectionschooljax.com Dcn. Scott J. Conway, Supt.; Timothy Connor, Prin.; Stds.: 208; Lay Tchrs.: 14

Sacred Heart - 5752 Blanding Blvd., Jacksonville, FL 32244 t) 904-771-2152; 904-771-5800 x23 (CRP) shcatholicchurch@gmail.com www.sacredheartjax.com Rev. James Kaniparampil, C.M.I., Pst.; Rev. Alexander Carandang, O.S.J., Par. Vicar; Dcn. Jeffrey P. Burgess Sr.; Dcn. Scott J. Conway; Santa Cochran, DRE; CRP Stds.: 99

Sacred Heart School - (Grades PreK-8) 5752 Blanding Blvd, Jacksonville, FL 32244 t) (904) 771-5800 school@sacredheartjax.com sacredheartcatholicjax.org Dr. Arsenio Yumul, Prin.; Stds.: 414; Lay Tchrs.: 23

San Jose - 3619 Toledo Rd., Jacksonville, FL 32217 t) 904-733-1630 reception@sjcatholic.org www.sjcatholic.org Rev. Remek Blaszkowski, Pst.; Rev. Rodolfo Godinez, Assoc. Pst.; Dcn. Christopher Supple; Dcn. Jose de Jesus Garcia; Dcn. Peter Watry; Diane Foley, DRE; CRP Stds.: 164

San Jose School - (Grades PreSchool-8) t) 904-733-2313 swain@sanjoseschool.com sanjosecatholicschool.com/ Dcn. Scott J. Conway, Supt.; Jennifer Swain, Prin.; Stds.: 396; Lay Tchrs.: 22

JACKSONVILLE BEACH

St. Paul's - 523 Pablo Ave., Jacksonville Beach, FL 32250; Mailing: 224 N 5th St., Jacksonville Beach, FL 32250 t) 904-249-2600 office@stpaulsjaxbeach.org www.stpaulsjaxbeach.org Rev. Msgr. Michael Houle, Pst.; Rev. Valanarasu Irudayanathan, Par. Vicar; Rev. Joseph Jacob, CMI, Par. Vicar; Dcn. Lawrence Magner; CRP Stds.: 418

St. Paul's School - (Grades PreSchool-8) 428 2nd Ave. N., Jacksonville Beach, FL 32250 t) 904-249-5934 stpaulscatholicschool.com/ Dcn. Scott J. Conway, Supt.; Krissy Thompson, Prin.; Stds.: 652; Lay Tchrs.: 32

St. Peter's Mission - 960 S. Girvin Rd., Jacksonville, FL 32225 t) (904) 249-2600

KEYSTONE HEIGHTS

St. William - 210 S.W. Peach St., Keystone Heights, FL 32656 t) 352-473-4136 officemanager@stwilliamkeystone.com; dre@stwilliamkeystone.com stwilliamchurch.wixsite.com/stwilliam Rev. Mason Edward Wiggins, Pst.; CRP Stds.: 27

St. Philip Neri Mission - 7919 SE Hwy. 301, Hawthorne, FL 32640; Mailing: PO Box 232, Hawthorne, FL 32640 t) 352-481-3353 stphilipneri@hotmail.com Rev. Mason Edward Wiggins, Pst.;

LAKE CITY

Epiphany - 1905 SW Epiphany Ct, Lake City, FL 32025 t) 386-752-4470; 386-269-1646 (CRP) office@epiphanycatholiclc.com; dre@epiphanycatholiclc.com www.epiphanycatholiclc.com Rev. Robert Hoffman, Pst.; Dcn. Miguel Ortiz; Sherri Ortega, Bus. Mgr.; Susi Pittman, DRE; CRP Stds.: 24

Epiphany School - (Grades K-8) Epiphany Catholic School, 1937 S.W. Epiphany Ct., Lake City, FL 32025 t) 386-752-2320 epiphanyeagles@ecslc.org www.ecslc.org/ Dcn. Scott J. Conway, Supt.; Rita Klenk, Prin.; Stds.: 112; Lay Tchrs.: 10

LIVE OAK

St. Francis Xavier - 928 E. Howard St., Live Oak, FL 32064 t) 386-364-1108 stfxoff@comcast.net www.stfrancisliveoak.org Rev. Anthony Basso, Pst.; Dcn. John Okragleski; Dcn. Thomas Richards; CRP Stds.: 83

St. Therese of the Child Jesus - 5430 N.W. Hwy. 41, Jasper, FL 32052; Mailing: 928 Howard St. E., Live Oak, FL 32064 stfxpff@comcast.net

Our Lady of Guadalupe - 137 E. Main St., Mayo, FL 32066; Mailing: 928 Howard St. E., Live Oak, FL 32064 t) (386) 294-2126

MACCLENNY

St. Mary, Mother of Mercy - 1143 W. Macclenny Ave., Macclenny, FL 32063; Mailing: 894 Jacqueline Circle, Macclenny, FL 32063 t) 904-259-2959 stmarychurchmacclenny@gmail.com www.stmarymacclenny.com Rev. Martin Raj, OSB, Pst.; Julie Johnson, DRE; CRP Stds.: 39

MIDDLEBURG

St. Luke - 1606 Blanding Blvd., Middleburg, FL 32068 t) 904-282-0439 office@stlukesparish.org www.stlukesparish.org Rev. Andy Blaszkowski, Pst.; Rev. Jaisemon Xaviour, Par. Vicar; Dcn. Stephen Arnold; CRP Stds.: 155

ORANGE PARK

St. Catherine of Siena - 1649 Kingsley Ave., Orange Park, FL 32073 t) 904-264-0577 parish@stcatherineop.com www.stcatherineop.com Rev. Andrzej Mitera, Pst.; Rev. Maurice Milton Culver, Par. Vicar; Dcn. Bernard Graleski; Dcn. Larry Hart; Dcn. Ralph Martinez; Vincent Reilly, DRE; CRP Stds.: 163

PALATKA

St. Monica - 114 S. 4th St., Palatka, FL 32177 t) 386-325-9777 saintmonicacatholic@gmail.com www.stmonicacatholicchurch.com Rev. Anthony Bonela, M.S.F.S. (India), Pst.; CRP Stds.: 67

PALM COAST

St. Elizabeth Ann Seton - 4600 Belle Terre Pkwy., Palm Coast, FL 32164 t) 386-445-2246 info@seaspcfl.org www.seaspcfl.org Rev. Jose Panthaplamthottiyil, C.M.I., Pst.; Rev. Robert Trujillo, Par. Vicar; Dcn. Perlito (Tom) Alayu; Dcn. Bob Devereaux; Dcn. Jose Homem; Dcn. Michael McKenna; Dcn. Edward Wolff; Katherine Allio, DRE; CRP Stds.: 310

St. Elizabeth Ann Seton Catholic School - (Grades PreK-8) 4600 Belle Terre Pkwy., Ste. B, Palm Coast, FL 32164 t) 386-445-2411 bkavanagh@seaspc.org seaspc.org/ Dcn. Scott J. Conway, Supt.; Barbara Kavanagh, Prin.; Stds.: 195; Lay Tchrs.: 14

St. Stephen Chapel - 2400 E. Hwy. 100, Bunnell, FL 32110; Mailing: 4600 Belle Terre Pky., Palm Coast, FL 32164

PONTE VEDRA

St. John Paul II Catholic Church - 127 Stone Mason Way, Bldg. 200, Ponte Vedra, FL 32081 t) 904-330-0153 office@nocateecatholic.com nocateecatholic.com/ Rev. Richard Pagano, Pst.; Dcn. Tony Colichio; Dominic Salamida, DRE; CRP Stds.: 606

PONTE VEDRA BEACH

Our Lady Star of the Sea - 545 Hwy. A1A N., Ponte Vedra Beach, FL 32082 t) 904-285-2698 office@olsspvb.org; dre@olsspvb.org www.olsspvb.org Rev. Msgr. Keith R. Brennan, Pst.; Rev. Christopher Knight, Par. Vicar; Rev. Eric Stelzer, Par. Vicar; Sr. Lucille Clynes, D.W, Pst. Assoc.; Dcn. Anthony Marini; CRP Stds.: 274

Preschool - 545 A1A North, Ponte Vedra Beach, FL 32082 t) 904-567-1970 Chris Saliba, Dir.;

Palmer Catholic Academy - (Grades PreK-8) 4889 Palm Valley Rd., Ponte Vedra Beach, FL 32082 t) 904-543-8515 www.pcapvb.org Linda Earp, Prin.; Stds.: 438; Lay Tchrs.: 33

ST. AUGUSTINE

Cathedral - Basilica of St. Augustine - 38 Cathedral Pl., St. Augustine, FL 32084; Mailing: 35 Treasury St., St. Augustine, FL 32086 t) 904-824-2806 cathparish@gmail.com; cathedralcfp@gmail.com thefirstparish.org Rev. John H. Tetlow, Pst.; Rev. Mackenzie Hill, Par. Vicar; Rev. Matthew Ibok, Par. Vicar; Dcn. Doug Nullet; Dcn. Charles Kanaszka; CRP Stds.: 101

Cathedral Parish School - (Grades K-8) 259 St. George St., St. Augustine, FL 32084 t) 904-824-2861 bott@cpsschool.org www.thecathedralparishschool.org Dcn. Scott J. Conway, Supt.; Dcn. Bryan Ott, Prin.; Stds.: 345; Lay Tchrs.: 19

St. Benedict the Moor - 86 Martin Luther King St., St. Augustine, FL 32084

St. Anastasia - 5205 A1A S., St. Augustine, FL 32080-8006 t) 904-471-5364; 904-471-5364 x112 (CRP) office@saccfl.org; dre@saccfl.org www.saccfl.org Rev. Timothy M. Lindenfelser, Pst.; Rev. Jared Salvatore De Leo, Par. Vicar; Dcn. Stephen Kassebaum; Dcn. Bryan Ott; Denise Pressley, DRE; CRP Stds.: 112

Corpus Christi - 6175 Datil Pepper Rd., St. Augustine, FL 32086 t) 904-797-4842 ccoffice@ccstaug.com

www.corpuschristicatholicchurch.org Rev. Matthew Ibok, Pst.; Dcn. David Allen; Rev. Alan Bower, In Res.;
Our Lady of Good Counsel - 5950 State Rd. 16, St. Augustine, FL 32092-0626 t) 904-824-8688 olgc.susie@gmail.com www.olgc-church.org Rev. Guy Noonan, Pst.; Rev. Livinus "Martin" Ibeh, Chap.; Dcn. Lawrence Geinosky; CRP Stds.: 112
San Sebastian - 1112 State Rd. 16, St. Augustine, FL 32084 t) 904-824-6625 tyra@sansebastiancatholicchurch.com www.sansebastiancatholicchurch.com Rev. John D. Gillespie, Pst.; Rev. Heriberto Vergara, Assoc. Pst.; Rev. William Mooney, In Res.; Rev. Thomas P. Walsh, In Res.; Dcn. Santiago Rosado; Dcn. James Swanson; CRP Stds.: 201

ST. JOHN

San Juan Del Rio - 1718 State Rd. 13, St. John, FL 32259 t) 904-287-0519; 904-287-2801 (CRP) k.vinski@sjdrparish.org www.sjdrparish.org/ Rev. Peter Akin-Otiko, Pst.; Rev. Nicholas Bennett, Par. Vicar; Rev. Dilip Pally, M.S.F.S., Par. Vicar; Dcn. Peter Can Dang; Dcn. Michael Edison; Dcn. Stan Boschert, DRE; CRP Stds.: 579
San Juan Del Rio School - (Grades PreSchool-8) 1714 State Rd. 13, Jacksonville, FL 32259 t) 904-287-8081 saints@sjdrschool.org www.sjdrsaints.org Dcn. Scott J. Conway, Supt.; Michael Masi, Prin.; Stds.: 436; Sr. Tchrs.: 1; Lay Tchrs.: 24
St. Mark the Evangelist Catholic Church - t) (904) 287-2801 frtomstaug@gmail.com Rev. Thomas S. Willis, Admin.;

STARKE

St. Edward - 441 N. Temple Ave., Starke, FL 32091-3207 t) 904-964-6155 stedward441@gmail.com Rev. Jan A. Ligeza, Admin.; CRP Stds.: 5

WILLISTON

Holy Family - 17353 N.E. Hwy. 27 Alt, Williston, FL 32696 t) 352-528-2893 office@holyfamilywilliston.org www.holyfamilywilliston.org Rev. Anthony Edward Hamaty, Pst.; CRP Stds.: 24
St. Anthony the Abbot - 6090 S.E. 193rd Pl., Inglis, FL 34449; Mailing: P.O. Box 1070, Inglis, FL 34449 t) (352) 528-2893

YULEE

St. Francis of Assisi Catholic Church - 86000 St. Francis Way, Yulee, FL 32097 t) 904-849-1256 secretary@stfrancisyulee.org www.stfrancisyulee.com Rev. Slawomir Bielasiewicz, Pst.; Dcn. Brian Campbell; Dcn. Thomas Healy; Dcn. Ralph LaMachia; CRP Stds.: 71

SCHOOLS: PRESCHOOL THRU HIGH SCHOOL

SCHOOLS

STATE OF FLORIDA

GAINESVILLE

St. Patrick School - (DIO) (Grades PreSchool-8) 550 N.E. 16th Ave., Gainesville, FL 32601 t) 352-376-9878 fmackritis@spsgnv.org spsgnv.org/ Interparish school composed of students from St. Patrick, Holy Faith & St. Augustine, Gainesville. Rev. Lawrence Peck, Pst.; Dcn. Scott J. Conway, Supt.; Frank Mackritis, Prin.; Stds.: 422; Lay Tchrs.: 30

JACKSONVILLE

Guardian Catholic Schools, Inc. - (DIO) (Grades PreSchool-8) 4920 Brentwood Ave., Jacksonville, FL 32206 t) 904-765-1920 drumschlag@guardiancatholic.com www.guardiancatholicschools.org Dcn. Scott J. Conway, Supt.; Sr. Dianne Rumschlag, Headmaster; Stds.: 378; Sr. Tchrs.: 2; Lay Tchrs.: 33
Morning Star School - (DIO) (Grades K-12) 725 Mickler Rd., Jacksonville, FL 32211 t) 904-721-2144 principal@morningstar-jax.org www.morningstar-jax.org A school for exceptional children. Dcn. Scott J. Conway, Supt.; Elaine Shott, Prin.; Stds.: 146; Sr. Tchrs.: 1; Lay Tchrs.: 19

MIDDLEBURG

Annunciation School - (PAR) (Grades PreK-8) 1610 Blanding Blvd., Middleburg, FL 32068 t) 904-282-0504 principal@annunciationcatholic.org www.annunciationcatholic.org Interparish school composed of students from Sacred Heart, Green Cove Springs; St. Catherine's, Orange Park; and St. Luke, Middleburg. Rev. Andy Blaszkowski, Pst.; Rev. Andrzej Mitera, Pst.; Rev. Michael Pendergraft, Pst.; Dcn. Scott J. Conway, Supt.; Stephen Eiswert, Prin.; Stds.: 381; Lay Tchrs.: 25

HIGH SCHOOLS

STATE OF FLORIDA

GAINESVILLE

St. Francis Catholic High School, Inc. (St. Francis Catholic Academy) - (DIO) (Grades 9-12) 4100 N.W. 115 Ter., Gainesville, FL 32606 t) 352-376-6545 info@sfcawolves.org www.sfcawolves.org Dcn. Scott J. Conway, Supt.; Jason Acosta, Prin.; Stds.: 249; Sr. Tchrs.: 1; Lay Tchrs.: 26

JACKSONVILLE

Bishop John Snyder High School, Inc. - (DIO) (Grades 9-12) 5001 Samaritan Way, Jacksonville, FL 32221 t) 904-771-1029 davidyazdiya@bishopsnyder.org www.bishopsnyder.org Dcn. Scott J. Conway, Supt.; Dcn. David Yazdiya, Prin.; Stds.: 444; Lay Tchrs.: 33
Bishop Kenny High School, Inc. - (DIO) (Grades 9-12) 1055 Kingman Ave., Jacksonville, FL 32207 t) 904-398-7545 torlando@bishopkenny.org www.bishopkenny.org Dcn. Scott J. Conway, Supt.; Todd Orlando, Prin.; Stds.: 1,353; Lay Tchrs.: 90

ST. AUGUSTINE

St. Joseph's Academy, Inc. - (DIO) (Grades 9-12) 155 State Rd. 207, St. Augustine, FL 32084 t) 904-824-0431 todd.declemente@sjaweb.org www.sjaweb.org Dcn. Scott J. Conway, Supt.; Todd DeClemente, Prin.; Stds.: 266; Lay Tchrs.: 21

INSTITUTIONS LOCATED IN DIOCESE

ASSOCIATIONS [ASN]

JACKSONVILLE

***Association of St. Lawrence Comunita Cenacolo America Inc.** - 9485 Regency Square Blvd., Ste. 110, Jacksonville, FL 32225 t) 904-353-5353 cenacolo@bellsouth.net www.hopereborn.org Our Lady of Hope Community, Mary Immaculate Community, St. Maria Goretti Community, Our Lady of Joyful Hope Community, St. Vincent de Paul Farm Albino Aragno, Exec.;

CAMPUS MINISTRY / NEWMAN CENTERS [CAM]

JACKSONVILLE

U.N.F. Catholic Student Center - 11277 Alumni Way, Jacksonville, FL 32246 t) 904-516-8140 c) 904-687-8883 bsamuelson@dosafl.com; staugustineccm@gmail.com www.icjax.org/ccm-jax.html Sr. Mary Rachel Hart, Campus Min.; Sr. Brittany Samuelson, SCTJM, Campus Min.;

ST. AUGUSTINE

Flagler College Catholic Fellowship - c/o Cathedral Basilica of St. Augustine, 35 Treasury St., St. Augustine, FL 32084 c) 904-947-7775 staugustineccm@gmail.com Rev. Blair Gaynes, Dir.;

CATHOLIC CHARITIES [CCH]

JACKSONVILLE

Catholic Charities Bureau, Inc. - 3100 University Blvd. S., Ste. 120, Jacksonville, FL 32216 t) 904-899-5500 ahassell@ccbdosa.org www.ccbdosa.org Anita Hassell, CEO; Asstd. Annu.: 116,994; Staff: 100
Catholic Charities Bureau, Gainesville - 1701 N.E. 9th St., Gainesville, FL 32609 t) 352-372-0294 www.catholiccharitiesgainesville.org (Emergency services, pregnancy counseling, adoptions, adult finance education, and weekend hunger backpack program.) Denise Fanning, Dir.;
Catholic Charities Bureau, Jacksonville - 40 E. Adams St., Jacksonville, FL 32202 t) 904-354-4846 x228 lweber@ccbjax.org www.ccbjax.org Emergency financial assistance for housing/utilities, food pantry, immigration legal assistance, workforce development and refugee resettlement. Lori Weber, Dir.;
Catholic Charities Bureau, Lake City - 553 N.W. Railroad St., Lake City, FL 32055 t) 386-754-9180 www.catholiccharitieslakecity.org Suzanne M. Edwards, Dir.;
Catholic Charities Bureau, St. Augustine - 525 State Rd. 16, Ste. 112, St. Augustine, FL 32084; Mailing: P.O. Box 543, St. Augustine, FL 32085 t) 904-829-6300 info@ccbstaug.org ccbstaug.org Tara Provini, Dir.;
Jacksonville, Family Housing Management Co. - 3100 University Blvd., S., Ste. 235, Jacksonville, FL 32216 t) 904-632-1255 aballard@ccbjax.org seniorlife.dosafl.com/housing/ Richard Brock, Pres.; Asstd. Annu.: 326; Staff: 4
Jacksonville, Office of Housing Development - 3100 University Blvd., S., Ste. 235, Jacksonville, FL 32216 t) (904) 632-1255 Alma C. Ballard, Exec. Dir.;
Barry Apartments - 1000 Husson Ave., Palatka, FL 32177 t) 386-328-5137 office@barryapts.org www.barryapts.org Parent Co., Palatka Retirement Villas, Inc. Theresa Brauman, Pres.; Terri Jackson, Property Mgr.;
Hurley Apartments - 3333-35 University Blvd. N., Jacksonville, FL 32277 t) 904-744-6022 fpgimenez@hurleyapts.org www.hurleyapts.org Parent Co., Catholic Charities Housing Association of Jacksonville, Inc. Fred Madeja, Pres.; Alma C. Ballard, Exec. Dir.;
San Jose I Apartments - 3630 Galicia Rd., Jacksonville, FL 32217 t) 904-739-0555 jnash@sanjoseapts.org www.sanjoseapts.org (Parent Company: Housing Association of the Diocese of St. Augustine.) Laurie Corrigan, Pres.; Jacqueta Nash, Property Mgr.;
San Jose II Apartments - 3622 Galicia Rd., Jacksonville, FL 32217 t) 904-739-0555 jnash@sanjoseapts.org Parent Company: San Jose Catholic Housing Assoc., Inc. Anne Sulzbacher, Pres.; Alma C. Ballard, Exec. Dir.; Jacqueta Nash, Property Mgr.;

CONVENTS, MONASTERIES, AND RESIDENCES FOR WOMEN [CON]

JACKSONVILLE

Carmelites of Mary Immaculate Florida, Inc. - 1736 Hamilton St., CMI Spirituality Center, Jacksonville, FL 32210

ST. AUGUSTINE

Motherhouse of the Sisters of St. Joseph of St. Augustine, Florida - 241 St. George St., St. Augustine, FL 32085; Mailing: P.O. Box 3506, St. Augustine, FL 32085 t) 904-824-1752 info@ssjfl.org ssjfl.org Sr. Kathleen Carr, Supr.; Sr. Ann Elizabeth Kuhn, SSJ, Rel. Ord. Ldr.; Srs.: 36
St. Joseph Neighborhood Center - 241 St. George St., St. Augustine, FL 32085 t) 904-829-3735 www.ssjfl.org
St. Joseph Renewal Center - 234 St. George St., St. Augustine, FL 32084; Mailing: P.O. Box 3506, St. Augustine, FL 32084 t) 904-829-3735 www.ssjfl.org

The Sisters of St. Joseph Continuing Community Support Trust Fund. - 241 St. George St., St. Augustine, FL 32085 t) (904) 824-1752 www.ssjfl.org

St. Joseph Ministries - 241 St. George St., St. Augustine, FL 32085; Mailing: P.O. Box 3506, St. Augustine, FL 32085 t) 904-829-3735 www.ssjfl.org

HOSPITALS / HEALTH SERVICES [HOS]

JACKSONVILLE

St. Vincent's Medical Center, Inc. (Ascension Health Ministries) - 1 Shircliff Way, Jacksonville, FL 32204; Mailing: P.O. Box 2982, Jacksonville, FL 32204 t) 904-308-7300 don.king@ascension.org; loraine.brown@ascension.org www.jaxhealth.com Member St. Vincent's Health System, Inc. Don King, CEO; Loraine Brown, Chief Mission Integration Officer; Bed Capacity: 512; Asstd. Annu.: 242,109; Staff: 2,151

St. Luke's - St. Vincent's HealthCare, Inc. (Ascension Health Ministries) - 4201 Belfort Rd., Jacksonville, FL 32216 t) 904-296-3700 St. Vincent's Medical Center Southside. Member: St. Vincent's Health System, Inc. Bed Capacity: 224; Asstd. Annu.: 135,165; Staff: 946

St. Vincent's Ambulatory Care, Inc. - 1 Shircliff Way, Jacksonville, FL 32204 t) 904-308-1290 Asstd. Annu.: 714,181; Staff: 1,091

St. Vincent's Foundation, Inc. - 1 Shircliff Way, Jacksonville, FL 32204 t) 904-308-7306

St. Vincent's Health System, Inc. - 1 Shircliff Way, Jacksonville, FL 32204 Staff: 261

St. Vincent's Medical Center-Clay County, Inc. - 1670 St. Vincent's Way, Middleburg, FL 32068; Mailing: 1 Shircliff Way, Jacksonville, FL 32204 t) 904-602-1000 Bed Capacity: 134; Asstd. Annu.: 92,660; Staff: 655

MISCELLANEOUS [MIS]

JACKSONVILLE

DSA Land, Inc. - 11625 Old St. Augustine Rd., Jacksonville, FL 32258 t) 904-262-3200 x190 mnedrich@dosafl.com Dcn. Michael Elison, Chancellor;

ST. AUGUSTINE

St. Augustine House of Prayer & Evangelization Center - 30 Ocean Ave., St. Augustine, FL 32084 t) (904) 559-5556 porsini62@gmail.com Pat Orsini, Contact;

Religious Education for Catholic Deaf and Blind - 1112-1120 State Rd. 16, St. Augustine, FL 32084 t) 904-824-6625 susan@sansebastiancatholicchurch.com Erin McGeever, Dir.; Susan Boehm-Donlon, CRE;

Sisters of St. Joseph's Architectural Stained Glass - 241 St. George St., St. Augustine, FL 32084; Mailing: PO Box 3506, St. Augustine, FL 32085 t) 904-829-3735 info@ssjfl.org www.ssjstainedglass.com Sr. Diane Couture, S.S.J., Dir.;

MONASTERIES AND RESIDENCES FOR PRIESTS AND BROTHERS [MON]

BUNNELL

***Discalced Carmelite Fathers of Florida** - 141 Carmelite Dr., Bunnell, FL 32110 t) 386-437-2910; 386-437-2080 Bro. Patrick Gemmato, O.C.D.; Rev. Artur Chojda, O.C.D., Supr.; Brs.: 1; Priests: 1

NURSING / REHABILITATION / CONVALESCENCE / ELDERLY CARE [NUR]

JACKSONVILLE

St. Catherine Labouré Manor, Inc. (Ascension Living St. Catherine Laboure Place) - 1750 Stockton St., Jacksonville, FL 32204 t) 314-292-9308 ahscm-mission@ascension.org www.ascensionliving.org/ Ryan Endsley, COO; Asstd. Annu.: 500; Staff: 120

ST. JOHNS

Casa San Pedro - 365 Marywood Dr., St. Johns, FL 32259 t) 904-230-2562 csanpedr@bellsouth.net www.marywoodcenter.org Matt Achorn, Dir.; Asstd. Annu.: 6; Staff: 1

PRESCHOOLS / CHILDCARE CENTERS [PRE]

GAINESVILLE

St. Anne Early Learning Center - 4300 Newberry Rd., Gainesville, FL 32607 t) 352-448-9395 director@stanneelc.org www.stanneelc.org Dcn. Scott J. Conway, Supt.; Maria Ramos, Dir.; Stds.: 45; Lay Tchrs.: 11

JACKSONVILLE

Assumption Early Learning Center - 2433 Atlantic Blvd., Jacksonville, FL 32207 t) 904-518-4880 ddodds@assumptionjax.org assumptionjax.org/preschool Rev. Jason Trull, Pst.; Dcn. Scott J. Conway, Supt.; Theresa Little, Dir.; Stds.: 123; Lay Tchrs.: 11

Christ the King Early Learning Center - 720 Arlington Rd., Jacksonville, FL 32211 t) 904-724-7239 director@ctkearlylearning.com www.ctkearlylearning.com Dcn. Scott J. Conway, Supt.; Rachel Hawkins, Dir.; Stds.: 124; Lay Tchrs.: 9

MIDDLEBURG

St. Luke Early Learning Center - 1608 Blanding Blvd., Middleburg, FL 32068 t) 904-406-9510 director@stlukechildcare.org stlukesparish.org/child-care-center Rev. Andy Blaszkowski, Pst.; Amy Roberts, Dir.; Stds.: 100; Lay Tchrs.: 20

PONTE VEDRA

St. John Paul II Early Learning Center - 127 Stonemason Way, Ponte Vedra, FL 32081 t) 904-800-2445 director@stjp2elc.net www.stjp2elc.net Dcn. Scott J. Conway, Supt.; Caroline Vickery, Dir.; Stds.: 143; Lay Tchrs.: 6

ST. AUGUSTINE

Cathedral Parish Early Education Center - 10 Sebastian Ave., St. Augustine, FL 32084 t) 904-829-2933 valleycpeec@aol.com thefirstparish.org Dcn. Scott J. Conway; Jill Valley, Dir.; Stds.: 64; Lay Tchrs.: 7

ST. JOHNS

St. Therese Early Learning Center - 2468 County Rd. 210 W., St. Johns, FL 32259 t) 904-429-7637 director@stthereseelc.org www.stthereseelc.org Dcn. Scott J. Conway, Supt.; Mary Maier, Dir.; Stds.: 114; Lay Tchrs.: 9

YULEE

St. Clare Early Learning Center - 307 Franciscan Way, Yulee, FL 32097 t) 904-849-9192 director@stclareelc.org www.stclareelc.org Dcn. Scott J. Conway, Supt.; Tammy Thornton, Dir.; Stds.: 118; Lay Tchrs.: 9

RETREAT HOUSES / RENEWAL CENTERS [RTR]

ST. JOHNS

Marywood Center for Spirituality and Ministry - 235 Marywood Dr., St. Johns, FL 32259 t) 904-287-2525 info@marywoodcenter.org www.marywoodcenter.org Matthew Achorn, Dir.;

SHRINES [SHR]

ST. AUGUSTINE

Mission Nombre de Dios and Shrine of Our Lady of La Leche - 27 Ocean Ave., St. Augustine, FL 32084 t) 904-824-2809 info@missionandshrine.org missionandshrine.org/ Rev. Erlin Garcia, I.C.C., Rector; Rev. Julio Bedoya, ICC, In Res.; Rev. Carlos Martinez, ICC, In Res.; Brs.: 3

Mission Nombre de Dios Museum - 27 Ocean Ave., St. Augustine, FL 32084 Jon Carres, Exec. Dir.;

Shrine Church of Our Lady of La Leche - 27 Ocean Ave., St. Augustine, FL 32084

SPECIAL CARE FACILITIES [SPF]

JACKSONVILLE

L'Arche Jacksonville, Inc. - 700 Arlington Rd. N., Jacksonville, FL 32211 t) 904-721-5992 hello@larchejacksonville.org larchejacksonville.org A residential community for adults with intellectual disabilities and those who choose to share life with them (assistants). Amy Finn-Schultz, Exec.; Paul Poirrier, Dir. Devel.; Bed Capacity: 17; Asstd. Annu.: 30; Staff: 20

An asterisk (*) denotes an organization that has established tax-exempt status directly with the IRS and is not covered by the USCCB Group Ruling.

Diocese of St. Cloud

(Dioecesis S. Clodoaldi)

MOST REVEREND PATRICK M. NEARY, C.S.C.

Bishop of St. Cloud; ordained April 6, 1991; appointed Bishop of the Diocese of Saint Cloud December 15, 2022; ordained and installed February 14, 2023 as the 10th bishop of the Diocese of St. Cloud in Central Minnesota; Office: 214 Third Ave. So. PO Box1248, St. Cloud, MN 56302-1248 Tel: 320-251-2340.

Chancery: 214 Third Ave. S., P.O. Box 1248, St. Cloud, MN 56302-1248. T: 320-251-2340; F: 320-251-0470.
www.stcdio.org

Square Miles 12,251.

Corporate Title: "The Diocese of St. Cloud."

Erected as the Vicariate of Northern Minnesota, February 12, 1875.

Created as the Diocese of St. Cloud, September 22, 1889.

Comprises the Counties of Stearns, Sherburne, Benton, Morrison, Mille Lacs, Kanabec, Isanti, Pope, Stevens, Traverse, Grant, Douglas, Wilkin, Otter Tail, Todd and Wadena in the State of Minnesota.

For legal titles of parishes and diocesan institutions, consult the Chancery Office.

STATISTICAL OVERVIEW

Personnel

Bishop	1
Retired Bishops	1
Abbots	1
Priests: Diocesan Active in Diocese	57
Priests: Retired, Sick or Absent	31
Number of Diocesan Priests	88
Religious Priests in Diocese	56
Total Priests in your Diocese	144
Ordinations:	
Religious Priests	2
Transitional Deacons	1
Permanent Deacons	5
Permanent Deacons in Diocese	57
Total Brothers	55
Total Sisters	297
Parishes	
Parishes	131
With Resident Pastor:	
Resident Diocesan Priests	44
Resident Religious Priests	3
Without Resident Pastor:	
Administered by Priests	84
Professional Ministry Personnel:	
Brothers	49
Sisters	238
Welfare	
Catholic Hospitals	3
Total Assisted	450,304
Homes for the Aged	8
Total Assisted	1,116
Special Centers for Social Services	3
Total Assisted	56,927
Residential Care of Disabled	8
Total Assisted	73
Other Institutions	9
Total Assisted	1,232
Educational	
Diocesan Students in Other Seminaries	11
Seminaries, Religious	1
Students, Religious	3
Total Seminarians	14
Colleges and Universities	2
Total Students	3,327
High Schools, Diocesan and Parish	1
Total Students	619
High Schools, Private	1
Total Students	236
Elementary Schools, Diocesan and Parish	27
Total Students	3,889
Catechesis / Religious Education:	
High School Students	4,188
Elementary Students	8,167
Total Students under Catholic Instruction	20,440
Teachers in Diocese:	
Lay Teachers	469
Vital Statistics	
Receptions into the Church:	
Infant Baptism Totals	1,240
Adult Baptism Totals	13
Received into Full Communion	94
First Communions	1,352
Confirmations	1,145
Marriages:	
Catholic	242
Interfaith	95
Total Marriages	337
Deaths	1,507
Total Catholic Population	116,680
Total Population	579,222

LEADERSHIP

Chancery - t) 320-251-2340 Rev. Robert E. Rolfes, Vicar Gen.; Jane Marrin, Chancellor (jmarrin@gw.stcdio.org);
Vicar General - t) 320-251-2340 Rev. Robert E. Rolfes;
Chancellor - Jane Marrin (jmarrin@gw.stcdio.org);
Diocesan Tribunal - t) 320-251-6557 Karrie Mollner, Secy.;
Judicial Vicar - Rev. Virgil A. Helmin;
Adjutant Judicial Vicars - Rev. Matthew Crane;
Promoter Justitiae - Rev. Robert C. Harren;
Defensor Vinculi - Rev. Gregory Lieser; Rev. Thomas Olson; Rt. Rev. Jonathan Licari, O.S.B.;
Judges - Rev. Matthew Crane; Rev. Marvin Enneking; Rev. Virgil Helmin;
Notaries - Rev. Virgil A. Helmin; Karrie Mollner;
Advocates - Rev. Marvin Enneking; Rev. Mark Innocenti; Rev. Joseph Korf;
Marriage Counseling - t) 320-650-1660 Dcn. Stephen Pareja, Catholic Charities Exec. Dir.;
Diocesan Consultors - Rev. Robert Harren; Rev. Joseph Herzing;
Deans - Rev. Marvin Enneking, West Central; Rev. Michael Kellogg, Eastern; Rev. Joseph Korf, Southwestern;
Diocesan Corporate Board - Most Rev. Donald J. Kettler; Jane Marrin, Secy. (jmarrin@gw.stcdio.org); Rev. Glenn A. Krystosek;
Diocesan Finance Council - Most Rev. Donald J. Kettler; Joseph Spaniol, Finance Officer;
Conciliation/Arbitration Process - Most Rev. Donald J. Kettler; Jane Marrin, Dir. (jmarrin@gw.stcdio.org); Thomas Janson, Advisor;
Liturgical Commission - Sr. Jeanne Wiest, O.P. (jeanne.wiest@gw.stcdio.org); Rev. Kevin Anderson; Rev. Glen Lewandowski, O.S.C.;
Presbyteral Council - Most Rev. Donald J. Kettler; Rev. Robert E. Rolfes, Vicar Gen.; Rev. Thomas Olson;
Pastoral Council - Most Rev. Donald J. Kettler; Kristi Anderson, Diocesan Liaison;

OFFICES AND DIRECTORS

Archives (Vacant) -
Assistance Coordinator - t) 320-248-1563 Roxanne Storms;
Boy Scouts - Rev. Benjamin Kociemba, Chap.;
Campus Ministry - Rev. Joseph Herzing;
Catholic Campaign for Human Development - t) 320-229-6020 Kateri Mancini;
Catholic Charities - t) 320-650-1550 Dcn. Stephen Pareja, Exec.;
Catholic Foundation of the Diocese of St. Cloud - t) 320-258-0390 David Eickhoff, Exec.;
Catholic Relief Services - t) 320-251-1100 Rev. William Vos, Dir.;
Catholic Women, Council of - t) 320-281-3775 Rev. Laurn Virnig, Spiritual Advisor;
Cemeteries Assumption-Calvary - t) 320-251-5511 Rev. Robert E. Rolfes, Contact;
Censores Librorum - Rev. Robert C. Harren; Sr. Renee Domeier, O.S.B.;
Clerical Aid Association - Most Rev. Donald J. Kettler; Jane Marrin (jmarrin@gw.stcdio.org);
Communications Office - t) 320-251-3022 Joseph Towalski, Dir.;
Continuing Formation of Priests - t) 320-251-8335 Rev. Joseph Herzing;
Development Office - t) 320-258-0390 Joseph Towalski, Dir.;
Diocesan Commission on Ecumenical and Interreligious Affairs - Sr. Helen Rolfson, O.S.F., Chair;
Diocesan Education Council - David Fremo, Dir.; Kristi Bivens; Kent Schmitz;
Diocesan Planning Council - Most Rev. Donald J. Kettler; Jane Marrin, Chancellor (jmarrin@gw.stcdio.org); Brenda Kresky, Dir.;
Diocesan Priests Pension Plan Trustees - Most Rev. Donald J. Kettler; Rev. Kevin Anderson;
Health Ministry - Rev. Thomas Knoblach, Consultant for Healthcare Ethics;
Holy Childhood Association - Elizabeth Brown, Dir.;
Koinonia Program of Central Minnesota - Rev. David Maciej;
Legion of Decency -
Legion of Mary -
Magazine "The Central Minnesota Catholic" - t) 320-251-3022 Joseph Towalski, Editor;
Multicultural Ministry - t) 320-529-4614 Mayuli Bales, Dir.;
Office of Catholic Education Ministries - t) 320-251-0111 David Fremo, Dir.; Kristi Bivens, Assoc. Dir., Lay Leadership Formation; Kent Schmitz, Consultant for Youth Ministry & Rel. Educ.;
Office of Diaconate - t) 320-251-2340 Dcn. Richard Scheierl; Dcn. David Hernandez, Assoc.; Rev. Ralph G. Zimmerman, Vicar;
Office of Marriage and Family - t) 320-252-4721 Patrick Flynn, Dir.;
Pastoral Planning - t) 320-251-2340 Brenda Kresky, Dir.;
Personnel Committee - Most Rev. Donald J. Kettler; Rev. Timothy Baltes, Chair;
Propagation of the Faith - t) 320-251-2061 Elizabeth Brown, Dir.;
Rural Life Program - t) 320-229-6020 Kateri Mancini;
TEC (Central Minnesota TEC) (Together Encountering Christ) - t) 320-532-4455 Mike Lentz, Coord. (mike.lentz@cmtec.org);
Vicar for Retired Priests -
Vocations - t) 320-251-5001 Rev. Douglas Liebsch, Dir.;
Worship, Office of - t) 320-255-9068 Sr. Jeanne Wiest, O.P. (jeanne.wiest@gw.stcdio.org);

PARISHES, MISSIONS, AND CLERGY

STATE OF MINNESOTA

ALBANY

St. Anthony Catholic Church - 24326 Trobec St., Albany, MN 56307 t) 320-845-2416 stanthony@hohcatholic.org www.hohcatholic.org/stanthony Rev. Edward Vebelun, O.S.B., Pst.; Rev. Julius Beckermann, OSB, Par. Vicar; Rev. Gregory Miller, O.S.B., Sacr. Min.; CRP Stds.: 78

Seven Dolors - 151 2nd St. S., Albany, MN 56307; Mailing: PO Box 277, Albany, MN 56307 t) 320-845-2705; 320-845-5405 (CRP) sevendolors@hohcatholic.org www.hohcatholic.org/sevendolors Rev. Edward Vebelun, O.S.B., Pst.; Rev. Gregory Miller, O.S.B., Sacr. Min.; Antionette (Toni) Hudock, DRE; CRP Stds.: 280

Holy Family School - (Grades PreK-6) c/o Seven Dolors Parish, Albany, MN 56307; Mailing: P.O. Box 674, Albany, MN 56307 t) 320-845-2011 hfamily@albanytel.com Maria Heymans-Becker, Prin.; Donna Huckenpoehler, Librn.;

ALEXANDRIA

The Church of St. Mary - 420 Irving St., Alexandria, MN 56308 t) 320-763-5781 (Main Parish) stmary@stmaryalexandria.org; stmreled@stmaryalexandria.org www.stmaryalexandria.org Rev. Matthew Kuhn, Pst.; CRP Stds.: 371

St. Mary's School - (Grades K-6) c/o St. Mary's Parish, 420 Irving St., Alexandria, MN 56308 t) 320-763-5861 Troy Sladek, Prin.; Aaron Korynta, Librn.;

AVON

St. Benedict's - 212 1st St. SW, Avon, MN 56310; Mailing: P.O. Box 98, Avon, MN 56310 t) 320-250-5618 stbenedicts7121@benedictavon.org Rev. Edward Vebelun, O.S.B., Pst.; Rev. Julius Beckermann, OSB, Par. Vicar; Rev. Gregory Miller, O.S.B., Sacr. Min.; Timothy Stanoch, DRE; CRP Stds.: 306

St. Columbkille's - 12357 County Rd. 4, Avon, MN 56310; Mailing: P.O. Box 308, Holdingford, MN 56340 t) 320-228-0105; 320-249-9939 (CRP) secretary@tworiverscatholic.com; stwendelfaith@gmail.com tworiverscatholic.com Rev. Gregory John Mastey, Pst.; Jen Revermann, DRE; Kyle VanOverbeke, Youth Min.; Janice Wuebkers, Bus. Mgr.; CRP Stds.: 55

Immaculate Conception - 37186 County Rd. 9, Avon, MN 56310; Mailing: P.O. Box 308, Holdingford, MN 56340 t) 320-228-0105 secretary@tworiverscatholic.com tworiverscatholic.com Rev. Gregory Mastey, Pst.; Katrina Kolles, DRE; Janice Wuebkers, Bus. Mgr.; CRP Stds.: 54

BATTLE LAKE

Our Lady of the Lake - 407 Lake Ave. N., Battle Lake, MN 56515; Mailing: PO Box 671, Battle Lake, MN 56515-0671 t) 218-864-5619 church@ollsj.org disciplesofthemissionacc.org Rev. LeRoy Schik, Pst.; Dcn. Craig Stich; CRP Stds.: 56

BELGRADE

St. Francis De Sales - 541 Martin Ave., Belgrade, MN 56312; Mailing: PO Box 69, Belgrade, MN 56312 t) 320-254-8218 francisdesales@mediacombb.net www.bbecatholicchurches.com/ Rev. Gregory Paffel, Pst.; Rev. Canon Richard Aubol, Par. Vicar; Rev. Jeremy Theis, Par. Vicar; Dcn. Thomas McFadden; CRP Stds.: 57

BERTHA

St. Joseph - 201 Cherry St., N.W., Bertha, MN 56437; Mailing: 514 1st St. SE, Wadena, MN 56482 t) 218-631-1593 deaconrandy@maryacc.org Rev. Aaron J. Kuhn, Pst.; Rev. Gabriel Walz, Par. Vicar; CRP Stds.: 35

BIG LAKE

The Church of Mary of the Visitation of Becker/Big Lake - 440 Lake St. N., Big Lake, MN 55309; Mailing: P.O. Box 100, Big Lake, MN 55309 t) 763-447-3339 parish@maryofthevisitation.org www.maryofthevisitation.org Rev. Michael Kellogg, Pst.; Barb Olson, DRE; CRP Stds.: 424

The Church of Mary of the Visitation - 12100 Sherburne Ave., Becker, MN 55308 (Worship Site)

BLUFFTON

St. John the Baptist - 310 Main St., Bluffton, MN 56518; Mailing: 514 1st. St. SE, Wadena, MN 56482 t) 218-631-1593 deaconrandy@marysacc.org Rev. Aaron J. Kuhn, Pst.; Rev. Gabriel Walz, Par. Vicar; CRP Stds.: 99

BOWLUS

St. Edward's - 8550 MN-238, Bowlus, MN 56314; Mailing: PO Box 249, Upsala, MN 56384 t) 320-573-2132 238catholic@sytekcom.com www.238catholic.org/ Rev. David Grundman, Pst.; CRP Stds.: 29

St. Stanislaus Kostka - 248 Main St., Bowlus, MN 56314; Mailing: P.O. Box 258, Royalton, MN 56373 t) 320-584-5484 htrinityhcross@gmail.com Rev. Gregory Sauer, Pst.; Cindy Fussy, DRE; CRP Stds.: 79

BRAHAM

St. Peter & Paul - 1050 Southview Ave., Braham, MN 55006; Mailing: PO Box 483, Braham, MN 55006 t) 320-396-3105 officemanager@stspeter-paulchurch.com; financialbookkeeper@stspeter-paulchurch.com www.stspeter-paulchurch.com Rev. Donald Wagner, Pst.; CRP Stds.: 48

BRANDON

Church of St. Ann - 402 Nelson St., Brandon, MN 56315; Mailing: P.O. Box 256, Brandon, MN 56315 t) 320-524-2462 (CRP); 320-643-5173 stanns@gctel.com Rev. Peter VanderWeyst, Pst.; Dcn. Joseph Wood; Sheri Streasick, DRE; CRP Stds.: 43

Seven Dolors - 16921 County Rd. 7, N.W., Brandon, MN 56315 t) 320-876-2240 sevendolors@gctel.net www.catholicchurches-bmup.org Rev. Peter VanderWeyst, Pst.; Dcn. Joseph Wood; CRP Stds.: 78

BRECKENRIDGE

St. Mary of the Presentation - 221 Fourth St. N., Breckenridge, MN 56520-1496 t) 218-643-5173 ngrotluschen@stmarysbreck.com www.redrivervalleyacc.com/ Rev. Leo Moenkedick, Pst.; CRP Stds.: 60

St. Mary of the Presentation School - (Grades PreK-8) t) 218-643-5443 tomhaire@stmarysschoolbreck.com Tom Haire, Prin.;

BROWERVILLE

Christ the King - 720 Main St. N., Browerville, MN 56438; Mailing: PO Box 83, Browerville, MN 56438 t) 320-594-2291 Rev. Mitchell Bechtold, Pst.; Sarah Becker, Dean; Beverly Geraets, DRE; Roxanne Determan, Bus. Mgr.; CRP Stds.: 85

Christ the King School - (Grades PreK-6) 750 Main St. N., Browerville, MN 56438; Mailing: P.O. Box 186, Browerville, MN 56438 t) 320-594-6114 citenctks@embarqmail.com Cindy Iten, Prin.;

BROWNS VALLEY

St. Anthony's - 122 2nd St. S., Browns Valley, MN 56219; Mailing: PO Box 359, Browns Valley, MN 56219 t) 320-695-2621 wheatoncatholiccommunity@hotmail.com; st.anthony359@yahoo.com CRP Stds.: 5

BUTLER

Holy Cross - 54216 County Hwy. 148, Butler, MN 56567 t) 218-385-2201 fayeadell@yahoo.com; pastor@st-henrys.org www.parishfaith.com/holy-cross---butler Rev. George Michael, V.C. (India), Pst.; Rev. Thomas Skaja, Par. Vicar; Dcn. Randall Altstadt; Dcn. Richard Quistorff; Glenda Hofland, DRE; Mary Peeters, DRE; CRP Stds.: 35

CAMBRIDGE

Christ the King - 305 Fern St. N., Cambridge, MN 55008-1094 t) 763-689-1221 crkgcbmn@aol.com www.ctkcambridgemn.com Rev. Donald Wagner, Pst.; CRP Stds.: 55

CARLOS

St. Nicholas - 9473 CO. Rd. 3 NE, Carlos, MN 56319; Mailing: P.O. Box F, Osakis, MN 56360 t) 320-852-7041 st.nick@arvig.net Rev. Matthew Kuhn, Pst.; Tonya Beulke, DRE; CRP Stds.: 54

CHOKIO

St. Mary's - 401 4th St. W, Chokio, MN 56221; Mailing: P.O. Box 187, Chokio, MN 56221 t) 320-324-2680 stmarych@fedtel.net Rev. John Paul Knopik, Pst.; CRP Stds.: 38

CLARISSA

St. Joseph - 105 John St. S., Clarissa, MN 56440; Mailing: P.O. Box 5, Clarissa, MN 56440 t) 218-756-3614 (CRP); 218-756-2205 stjoschu@eaglevalleytel.com Rev. Mitchell Bechtold, Pst.; Bev Desotell, DRE; Eileen Uhlenkamp, DRE; CRP Stds.: 41

CLEAR LAKE

St. Marcus - 8701 Main Ave., Clear Lake, MN 55319-0237; Mailing: P.O. Box 237, Clear Lake, MN 55319-0237 t) 320-743-2481 stmarcussec@frontiernet.net www.churchofstmarcus.org/ Rev. Joseph Backowski, Admin.; CRP Stds.: 47

COLD SPRING

Church of Saint Boniface - 501 Main St., Cold Spring, MN 56320 t) 320-685-8222 x103 parish@stboniface.com www.rspcatholic.com Rev. Matthew Luft, O.S.B, Pst.; Rev. Cletus Connors, OSB, Par. Vicar; Dcn. Lawrence Sell; Sandee Kremers, Pst. Assoc.; Ashley Barker, Youth Min.; CRP Stds.: 429

Church of Saint Boniface School - (Grades PreSchool-6) t) 320-685-3541 ssharonwaldoch@stboniface.com Sr. Sharon Waldoch, S.S.N.D., Prin.; Shelly Giswold, Librn.;

St. James - 25042 County Rd. 2, Cold Spring, MN 56320 t) 320-685-3479 saintjames@rspcatholic.com Rev. Matthew Luft, O.S.B, Pst.; Rev. Cletus Connors, OSB, Par. Vicar; Dcn. Lawrence Sell; Sandee Kremers, Pst. Assoc.; CRP Stds.: 32

DENT

Church of the Sacred Heart - 36963 State Hwy. 108, Dent, MN 56528 t) 218-758-2700 sacredheart@arvig.net sacredheartstlawrencecatholicchurches.com Rev. George Michael, V.C. (India), Pst.; Rev. Thomas Skaja, Par. Vicar; Diane Sazama, DRE; Joe Sazama, DRE; Dcn. Mark Stenger; CRP Stds.: 47

EDEN VALLEY

The Church of the Assumption - 464 State St. N., Eden Valley, MN 55329; Mailing: PO Box 9, Eden Valley, MN 55329 t) 320-453-2788 assumptionev@meltel.net www.churchoftheassumptionedenvalley.org Rev. Aaron Nett, Pst.; CRP Stds.: 124

ELBOW LAKE

St. Olaf - 518 Division E St., Elbow Lake, MN 56531 t) 218-685-5372 stolaf@runestine.net www.stolafelbowlake.org Rev. Jeremy Ploof, Pst.; CRP Stds.: 76

ELIZABETH

St. Elizabeth - 706 Pleasant Ave., Elizabeth, MN 56533 t) 218-739-1140 (CRP); 218-731-5304 contact@olvchurch.org www.ffolvchurch.org Rev. Alan Wielinski, Pst.; Rev. Patrick Hoeft, Par. Vicar; Dcn. Peter Bellavance; Dcn. Joseph Hilber; Dcn. Charles Kampa; Dcn. Dean Pawlowski; Jan Dumas, DRE; CRP Stds.: 10

ELK RIVER

The Church of St. Andrew - 566 Fourth St., Elk River, MN 55330 t) 763-441-1483 minnocenti@saint-andrew.net www.saint-andrew.net Rev. Mark Innocenti, Pst.; Melissa Anderson, Admin.; CRP Stds.: 414

The Church of St. Andrew School - (Grades PreK-5) 428 Irving Ave., Elk River, MN 55330 t) 763-441-2216 adettmann@saint-andrew.net www.saint-andrew.net/school Ann Dettmann, Prin.; Aaron Johnson, Librn.; Stds.: 170; Lay Tchrs.: 8

FERGUS FALLS

Our Lady of Victory - 207 N. Vine St., Fergus Falls, MN 56537 t) 218-736-6837 (CRP); 218-736-2429 olv@prtel.com Rev. Alan Wielinski, Pst.; Dcn. Charles Kampa; Dcn. Dean Pawlowski; Jennifer Dummer, DRE; Mayme Hofland, DRE; CRP Stds.: 318

Our Lady of Victory School - (Grades PreSchool-6) 426 W. Cavour Ave., Fergus Falls, MN 56537 t) 208-736-6661 contact@ffolv.org Tonya Zierden, Prin.;

FLENSBURG

Sacred Heart - 15 Pine St., Flensburg, MN 56328; Mailing: 9406 Church Cir., Little Falls, MN 56345 t) 320-632-6930 ststans@littlefalls.net Rev. Jimmy Joseph, V.C., Pst.; CRP Stds.: 64

FOLEY

Church of St. John - 621 Dewey St., Foley, MN 56329; Mailing: P.O. Box 337, Foley, MN 56329 t) 320-968-7913 hyperdulia@arvig.net Rev. Michael Wolfbauer, Pst.; Sheila Matteson, DRE; CRP Stds.: 199

St. John's Area School - (Grades PreSchool-6) 215 7th Ave., Foley, MN 56329; Mailing: P.O. Box 368, Foley, MN 56329 t) 320-968-7972 principal@saintjohnsschool.net www.saintjohnsschool.net Christine Friederichs, Prin.;

St. Elizabeth of Hungary - 16426 125th Ave., N.E., Foley, MN 56329; Mailing: P.O. Box 86, Gilman, MN 56333 t) 320-387-2255; 320-387-3332 (CRP) sesjppchurch@jetup.net Rev. Matthew Langager, Pst.; CRP Stds.: 71

St. Joseph's - 33009 Nature Rd., Foley, MN 56329; Mailing: P.O. Box 86, Gilman, MN 56333 t) 320-355-2454 sesjppchurches@jetup.net Rev. Matthew Langager, Pst.; CRP Stds.: 17

St. Lawrence's - 10915 Duelm Rd., N.E., Foley, MN 56329 t) 320-968-7502; 320-968-6595 (CRP) st_lawrence@victorcc.net Rev. Joseph Backowski, Admin.; Betty Pundsack, DRE;

FORESTON

St. Louis Bertrand - 187 First St. S., Foreston, MN 56330; Mailing: P.O. Box 128, Foreston, MN 56330 t) 320-294-5460 stlouis@ecenet.com Rev. Derek Wiechmann, Pst.; Dcn. Kenneth Rosha; CRP Stds.: 38

FREEPORT

St. Francis of Assisi - 44055 State Hwy. 238, Freeport, MN 56331; Mailing: PO Box 249, Upsala, MN 56384 t) 320-573-2132 238catholic@sytekcom.com www.238catholic.org/ Rev. David Grundman, Pst.; John Young, DRE; CRP Stds.: 56

St. Rose of Lima - 28905 Co Rd 17, Freeport, MN 56331; Mailing: PO Box 155, Freeport, MN 56331 t) 320-836-2143 sacredheartfreeport.org Rev. Daniel Walz, Pst.; Amy Hoeschen, Admin.; Chrystal Sand, DRE; CRP Stds.: 35

Sacred Heart - 106 3rd Ave., N.E., Freeport, MN 56331; Mailing: P.O. Box 155, Freeport, MN 56331-0155 t) 320-836-2143 sacredheartfreeport.org Rev. Daniel Walz, Pst.; Amy Hoeschen, Admin.; Chrystal Sand, DRE; CRP Stds.: 73

Sacred Heart School - (Grades PreK-6) 303 2nd St. N.E., Freeport, MN 56331; Mailing: P.O. Box 39, Freeport, MN 56331 t) 320-836-2591 admin@shsfreeport.org shsfreeport.org Kristie Harren, Prin.;

GILMAN

SS. Peter and Paul - 10495 Golden Spike Road, Gilman, MN 56333; Mailing: P.O. Box 86, Gilman, MN 56333 t) 320-387-2255; 320-387-3332 (CRP) sesjppchurches@jetup.net Rev. Matthew Langager, Pst.; CRP Stds.: 71

GLENWOOD

St. Bartholomew's - 105 N. Franklin St., Glenwood, MN 56334 t) 320-634-3813 sheartchurch@gmail.com www.sacredheartglenwood.com Rev. Joseph Vanderberg, Pst.; Sue Heidelberger, DRE; Paula Johnson, DRE; CRP Stds.: 20

Sacred Heart - 122 N.W. 1st St., Glenwood, MN 56334 t) 320-634-4828 (CRP); 320-634-3813 sheartchurch@gmail.com www.sacredheartglenwood.com Rev. Joseph Vanderberg, Pst.; Sue Heidelberger, DRE; Paula Johnson, DRE; CRP Stds.: 226

GREENWALD

St. Andrew's - 211 2nd Ave. N., Greenwald, MN 56335; Mailing: Box 136, Greenwald, MN 56335 t) 320-987-3205 stjohn1@meltel.net; bookkeeper@stmarysofmelrose.com www.oneinfaith.org Rev. Marvin Enneking, Pst.; Rev. Arockiya Newton, Par. Vicar; Ruth Klaphake, DRE; CRP Stds.: 31

St. Andrew's School - (Grades K-2) c/o St. Andrew's Parish, Greenwald, MN 56335 t) 320-987-3133 sjsamarym@gmail.com

GREY EAGLE

St. Joseph's - 118 Minnesota St., Grey Eagle, MN 56336; Mailing: P.O. Box 366, Grey Eagle, MN 56336 t) 320-285-2545 stjoseph@meltel.net Rev. Ronald Dockendorf, Pst.; CRP Stds.: 105

HENNING

Church of St. Edward of Henning - 201 Douglas Ave., Henning, MN 56551 t) 218-583-2490 stedward@arvig.net Rev. LeRoy Schik, Pst.; Lyn Andrews, DRE; CRP Stds.: 24

HERMAN

St. Charles - 61 Berlin Ave. S., Herman, MN 56248 t) 320-677-2433 stcharlesch@frontier.com Rev. Jeremy Ploof, Pst.; Katy Blume, DRE; CRP Stds.: 24

HILLMAN

Church of St. Rita of Hillman - 16691 371st Ave., Hillman, MN 56338 t) 320-277-3807 strita@brainerd.net Rev. Jerome Schik, O.S.C., Pst.; CRP Stds.: 85

HOLDINGFORD

Church of All Saints - 311 River St., Holdingford, MN 56340; Mailing: P.O. Box 308, Holdingford, MN 56340 t) 320-228-0105; 320-292-1575 (CRP) secretary@tworiverscatholic.com tworiverscatholic.com Rev. Gregory Mastey, Pst.; Katrina Kolles, DRE; Kyle VanOverbeke, Youth Min.; Janice Wuebkers, Bus. Mgr.; CRP Stds.: 117

Our Lady of Mt. Carmel - 42942 125th Ave.,

Holdingford, MN 56340 t) 320-746-2449; 320-309-3280 (CRP) parishes@greatrivercatholic.org; opolefaith@gmail.com greatrivercatholic.org Rev. Gregory Sauer, Pst.; Dcn. Jeffrey Fromm; Melyssa Sakry, DRE; CRP Stds.: 1,550

ISANTI

St. Elizabeth Ann Seton - 207 Whiskey Rd., N.W., Isanti, MN 55040 t) 763-444-4035 annseton76@gmail.com stelizabeth-isanti.org Rev. Donald Wagner, Pst.; CRP Stds.: 25

KENSINGTON

Our Lady of the Runestone - 11 Runestone Dr., S.W., Kensington, MN 56343 t) 320-965-2596 olroffice@runestone.net Rev. Jeremy Ploof, Pst.; CRP Stds.: 17

KENT

St. Thomas - 115 Harris St., Kent, MN 56553; Mailing: PO Box 23, Kent, MN 56553 t) 218-557-8312 sharonl@702com.net www.kentbreckcatholics.org Rev. Leo Moenkedick, Pst.; CRP Stds.: 31

KIMBALL

Church of Saint Anne - 441 Hazel Ave. E., Kimball, MN 55353; Mailing: P.O. Box 99, Kimball, MN 55353 t) 320-398-2211 sannekim@meltel.net Rev. James Statz, Pst.; CRP Stds.: 72

Holy Cross - 10651 County Rd. 8, Kimball, MN 55353 t) 320-252-1799 shellyg@smhoc.org Rev. Eric Lundgren, Par. Admin.; CRP Stds.: 3

LAKE HENRY

St. Margaret's - 23189 State Hwy. 4, Lake Henry, MN 56362; Mailing: 505 Burr St., Paynesville, MN 56362 t) 320-243-4413 frglenn@saintalm.org saintalm.org Rev. Glenn A. Krystosek, Pst.; Hannah Voss, DRE; CRP Stds.: 17

LASTRUP

St. John Nepomuk - 28520 Church St., Lastrup, MN 56344; Mailing: P.O. Box 38, Lastrup, MN 56344 t) 320-468-2111 office@stjohnslastrup.org; stjohnslastrup@gmail.com stjohnslastrup.org Rev. Jose Chettoor, Pst.; CRP Stds.: 54

LITTLE FALLS

Holy Family - 18777 Riverwood Dr., Little Falls, MN 56345 t) 320-632-5720 holyfamilybp@gmail.com littlefallscatholic.org Rev. Benjamin Kociemba, Pst.; Rev. Patrick Hoeft, Par. Vicar; CRP Stds.: 98

St. Mary - 305 Fourth St., S.E., Little Falls, MN 56345 t) 320-632-5640 office@stmaryslf.org littlefallscatholic.org Rev. Patrick Hoeft, Par. Vicar; Rev. Benjamin Kociemba, Pst.; CRP Stds.: 246

Our Lady of Lourdes - 208 W. Broadway, Little Falls, MN 56345 t) 320-616-9689 (CRP); 320-632-8243 ololoffice@yahoo.com Rev. Patrick Hoeft; Katie Jacobson, DRE; Rev. Benjamin Kociemba, Pst.; Dcn. Craig Korver; Dcn. Jeffrey Winkelman; CRP Stds.: 341

St. Stanislaus - 9406 Church Cir., Little Falls, MN 56345-9803 t) 320-632-6930 ststans@littlefalls.net Rev. Jimmy Joseph, V.C., Pst.; CRP Stds.: 49

LONG PRAIRIE

St. Mary of Mt. Carmel - 409 Central Ave., Long Prairie, MN 56347 t) 320-357-0815 stmarysrectory@stmaryslp.org; ahinson@stmaryslp.org www.stmarymtcarmellongprairie.4lpi.com Rev. Omar Guanchez; Dcn. James Schulzetenberg; CRP Stds.: 130

St. Mary of Mt. Carmel School - (Grades PreK-6) t) 320-357-0813 bgugglberger@stmaryslp.org Brenda Gugglberger, Prin.;

LOWRY

St. John Nepomuk Catholic Church (Lake Reno) - 25890 110th St., Lowry, MN 56349-4580 t) 320-283-5273 snepomuk@runestone.net Rev. Joseph Vanderberg, Pst.; CRP Stds.: 21

MELROSE

St. John's - 20 Hwy 4 - Meire Grove, Melrose, MN 56352; Mailing: PO Box 136, Greenwald, MN 56335 t) 320-256-4207 bookkeeper@stmarysofmelrose.com; stjohn1@meltel.net www.oneinfaith.org Rev. Marvin Enneking, Pst.; Rev. Arockiya Newton, Par. Vicar; CRP Stds.: 280

St. John's - St. Andrew's Catholic School - (Grades 3-6) 121 2nd Ave. N., Greenwald, MN 56335; Mailing: P.O. Box 120, Greenwald, MN 56335 t) 320-987-3491; 320-987-3133 stjohnstandrew@gmail.com sjsaschool.org Mary Miller, Prin.;

St. Mary's - 755 Kraft Dr., S.E., Melrose, MN 56352-1427 t) 320-256-4207; 320-256-3108 (Pastor) stmarys@stmarysofmelrose.com Rev. Marvin Enneking, Pst.; Rev. Arockiya Newton, Par. Vicar; Dcn. Ernest Kociemba;

St. Mary's School - (Grades PreSchool-6) 320 5th S.E., Melrose, MN 56352 t) 320-256-4257 sms@meltel.net Robert Doyle, Prin.; Autumn Nelson, Librn.;

St. Michael's - 102 St. Michael Ave. N. - Spring Hill, Melrose, MN 56352; Mailing: PO Box 136, Greenwald, MN 56335 t) 320-256-4207 bookkeeper@stmarysofmelrose.com; stjohn1@meltel.net Rev. Marvin Enneking, Pst.; Rev. Arockiya Newton, Par. Vicar; CRP Stds.: 38

MENAHGA

The Church of the Assumption of Our Lady of Menahga - 113 Aspen Ave., N.W., Menahga, MN 56464; Mailing: 514 1st St., S.E., Wadena, MN 56482 t) 218-631-1593 deaconrandy@marysacc.org Rev. Aaron J. Kuhn, Pst.; Rev. Gabriel Walz, Par. Vicar; CRP Stds.: 15

MILACA

The Church of St. Mary of Milaca - 645 3rd Ave., S.E., Milaca, MN 56353; Mailing: 625 3rd Ave., S.E., Milaca, MN 56353 t) 320-983-3255 stmary.milaca@frontiernet.net www.fourpillarsinfaith.org Rev. Derek Wiechmann, Pst.; Dcn. Kenneth Rosha; CRP Stds.: 70

MORA

St. Kathryn's - 201 Forest Ave. E., Mora, MN 55051 t) 320-679-1593 moraoffice@stmarysmora.org Rev. Derek Wiechmann, Pst.; CRP Stds.: 26

St. Mary's - 201 Forest Ave. E., Mora, MN 55051 t) 320-679-1593 ritac@stmarysmora.org Rev. Derek Wiechmann, Pst.; Sue Grabowski, DRE; CRP Stds.: 81

MORRIS

Assumption of the Blessed Virgin Mary - 207 E. Third St., Morris, MN 56267; Mailing: PO BOX 287, Morris, MN 56267 t) 320-589-3003 assump@info-link.net Rev. Todd Schneider, Pst.; Nicole Berlinger, DRE; CRP Stds.: 178

Assumption of the Blessed Virgin Mary School - (Grades K-6) 411 Colorado Ave., Morris, MN 56267 t) 320-589-1704 principal@stmarysmorris.com Joseph Ferriero, Prin.;

MOTLEY

St. Michael - 1333 85th Ave., S.W., Motley, MN 56466; Mailing: 514 1st St., S.E., Wadena, MN 56482 t) 218-631-1593 deaconrandy@marysacc.org Rev. Aaron J. Kuhn, Pst.; Rev. Gabriel Walz, Par. Vicar; Dcn. Robert Shaffer; Dcn. John Wolak; CRP Stds.: 60

NEW MUNICH

Immaculate Conception - 650 Main St., New Munich, MN 56356; Mailing: PO Box 155, Freeport, MN 56331 t) 320-836-2143 sacredheartfreeport.org Rev. Daniel Walz, Pst.; Amy Hoeschen, Admin.; Chrystal Sand, DRE; CRP Stds.: 32

NORTH PRAIRIE

Holy Cross - 14891 Gable Rd., North Prairie, MN 56314; Mailing: P.O. Box 258, Royalton, MN 56373 t) 320-584-5484 htrinityhcross@gmail.com www.holycrossnorthprairie.org Rev. Gregory Sauer, Pst.; CRP Stds.: 26

ONAMIA

The Church of the Holy Cross of Onamia - 102 Crosier Dr. N., Onamia, MN 56359; Mailing: P.O. Box 500, Onamia, MN 56359 t) 320-532-3122 hconamia@gmail.com Rev. Jerome Schik, O.S.C., Pst.; CRP Stds.: 9

St. Therese - 43600 Hwy. 169, Onamia, MN 56359; Mailing: P.O. Box 26, Onamia, MN 56359 t) 320-532-3601 hconamiaparishoffice@yahoo.com Rev. Jerome Schik, O.S.C., Pst.; CRP Stds.: 6

OSAKIS

Immaculate Conception - 306 W. Oak St., Osakis, MN 56360; Mailing: P.O. Box F, Osakis, MN 56360 t) 320-859-2390 iccosakis@arvig.net Rev. Matthew Kuhn, Pst.; Greta Petrich, DRE; Jennifer Wolbeck, DRE; CRP Stds.: 84

St. Agnes - (Grades PreSchool-6) 307 4th Ave. W., Osakis, MN 56360; Mailing: PO Box 0, Osakis, MN 56360 t) 320-859-2130 mrspat@stagnesosakis.com Pat Pospisil, Prin.; Rosalie Kreemer, Librn.;

PARKERS PRAIRIE

Church of St. William - 209 W. Soo St., Parkers Prairie, MN 56361; Mailing: P.O. Box 339, Parkers Prairie, MN 56361 t) 218-338-2761 stwm@midwestinfo.net Rev. Peter VanderWeyst, Pst.; Dcn. Joseph Wood; CRP Stds.: 72

Sacred Heart - 60 Central Ave. N., Parkers Prairie, MN 56361 t) 218-267-2661 gloriajb@midwestinfo.net www.catholicchurches-bmup.org Rev. Peter VanderWeyst, Pst.; Dcn. Joseph Wood; CRP Stds.: 38

PAYNESVILLE

St. Louis - 505 Burr St., Paynesville, MN 56362 t) 320-243-4413 frglenn@saintalm.org saintalm.org Rev. Glenn A. Krystosek, Pst.; Hannah Voss, DRE; CRP Stds.: 219

PELICAN RAPIDS

St. Leonard's - 36 1st Ave. N.E., Pelican Rapids, MN 56572; Mailing: P.O. Box 378, Pelican Rapids, MN 56572 t) 218-863-4240 stleonard@loretel.net Rev. Alan Wielinski, Pst.; Dcn. Peter Bellavance; Ann Bergquist, DRE; Rev. Patrick Hoeft, Par. Vicar; CRP Stds.: 62

PERHAM

Church of Saint Henry, Perham - 234 2nd Ave. S.W., Perham, MN 56573 t) 218-346-7030 (CRP); 218-346-4240 admin@st-henrys.org; pastor@st-henrys.org parishfaith.com Rev. George Michael, V.C. (India), Pst.; Rev. Thomas Skaja, Par. Vicar; Dcn. Randy Alstadt; Dcn. Richard Quistorff; CRP Stds.: 339

St. Henry Area School - (Grades K-6) 253 2nd St. S.W., Perham, MN 56573 t) 218-346-6190 sthenryschool@arvig.net Jason Smith, Prin.; Lisa Silbernagel, Librn.;

St. Lawrence - 46404 County Hwy. 14, Perham, MN 56573 t) 218-346-7729 stlawrence@arvig.net sacredheartstlawrencecatholicchurches.com Rev. George Michael, V.C. (India), Pst.; Rev. Thomas Skaja, Par. Vicar; Dcn. Randall Altstadt; Dcn. Richard Quistorff; Dcn. Mark Stenger; Sandra E. Carrlson, DRE; Lisa Werner, Parish Life Coord.; Jeannie Guck, Bus. Mgr.; CRP Stds.: 41

PIERZ

Holy Cross - 29482 243rd St., Harding, Pierz, MN 56364 t) 320-468-2111 hardingchurch.org Rev. Jose Chettoor, Pst.; CRP Stds.: 54

St. Joseph's - 68 Main St., Pierz, MN 56364; Mailing: P.O. Box 428, Pierz, MN 56364 t) 320-468-6033 stjoes@midco.net stjosephsstmichaelschurchpierz.org Dcn. Craig Korver; Rev. Kenneth Popp, Pst.; CRP Stds.: 216

St. Michael's - 9251 Hwy. 25, Pierz, MN 56364; Mailing: PO Box 428, Pierz, MN 56364 t) 320-468-6033 stjoes@midco.net stjosephsstmichaelschurchpierz.org Dcn. Craig Korver; Rev. Kenneth Popp, Pst.; CRP Stds.: 84

PRINCETON

The Church of Christ Our Light - 804 7th Ave. S., Princeton, MN 55371 t) 763-389-2115 teresac@christourlightmn.org www.christourlightmn.org Rev. Kevin Anderson, Pst.; Dcn. Mark Barder; Teresa Davila, Admin.; Molly Weyrens, Pst. Assoc.; Maureen Putnam, Liturgy Dir.; Wendy Rappe, DRE; CRP Stds.: 215

RANDALL

St. James - 403 E. Minnesota Ave., Randall, MN 56475; Mailing: Box 225, Randall, MN 56475 t) 320-632-6930 ststans@littlefalls.net Rev. Jimmy Joseph, V.C.; CRP Stds.: 64

RICE

Immaculate Conception - 130 First Ave., N.E., Rice, MN

56367; Mailing: P.O. Box 189, Rice, MN 56367 t) 320-393-2826 (CRP); 320-393-2725 iccrice@jetup.net Jean Skroch, DRE; Rev. Gregory Sauer, Pst.; CRP Stds.: 160

RICHMOND

SS. Peter and Paul - 110 Central Ave. N., Richmond, MN 56368; Mailing: P.O. Box 69, Richmond, MN 56368 t) 320-597-2575 parish@ssppr.com www.ssppr.com Rev. Matthew Luft, O.S.B, Pst.; Rev. Cletus Connors, OSB, Par. Vicar; Dcn. Lawrence Sell; Sandee Kremers, Pst. Assoc.; Teri Krowka-Ansberry, DRE; CRP Stds.: 165

SS. Peter and Paul School - (Grades K-5) 111 Central Ave. N., Richmond, MN 56368 t) 320-597-2565 jwalz@ssppr.com Heather Pfannenstein, Prin.;

ROCKVILLE

Mary of the Immaculate Conception - 113 Broadway, Rockville, MN 56369; Mailing: P.O. Box 7, Rockville, MN 56369 t) 320-251-7801 micchurch@mywdo.com; micrparish@gmail.com Rev. Eric Lundgren, Par. Vicar; CRP Stds.: 70

ROSCOE

St. Agnes - 100 Lillie Ave., Roscoe, MN 56371; Mailing: 505 Burr St., Paynesville, MN 56362 t) 320-243-4413 frglenn@saintalm.org saintalm.org Rev. Glenn A. Krystosek, Pst.; CRP Stds.: 16

ROYALTON

Holy Trinity - 216 Second St. N., Royalton, MN 56373; Mailing: P.O. Box 258, Royalton, MN 56373 t) 320-584-5484 htrinityhcross@gmail.com www.holytrinityroyalton.org Rev. Gregory Sauer, Pst.; CRP Stds.: 270

SARTELL

St. Francis Xavier - 219 - 2nd St. N., Sartell, MN 56377; Mailing: P.O. Box 150, Sartell, MN 56377 t) 320-252-8761 (CRP); 320-252-1363 svaske@stfrancissartell.org; sfxyouthmin@stfrancissartell.org www.stfrancissartell.org/ Rev. Ronald Weyrens, Pst.; Dcn. Stephen Pareja; Melissa Fox, Youth Min.; Shelby Vaske, DRE; CRP Stds.: 1,144

St. Francis Xavier School - (Grades PreK-6) t) 320-252-9940 schooloffice@sfx61.org www.stfrancissartellschool.org/

SAUK CENTRE

St. Donatus - 304 Sinclair Lewis Ave., Sauk Centre, MN 56378 t) 320-346-2431 (CRP); 320-352-2196 stpaulschurch@mainstreetcom.com Rev. Mark Botzet, Par. Vicar; Rev. Gregory Paffel, Pst.; Rev. Jeremy Theis, Par. Vicar; Annette Fischer, DRE; CRP Stds.: 30

Our Lady of the Angels - 207 S. 7th St., Sauk Centre, MN 56378-1505; Mailing: 304 Sinclair Lewis Ave., Sauk Centre, MN 56378 t) 320-352-3502; 320-352-5580 (CRP) angels@mainstreetcom.com www.parishesontheprairie.org Rev. Mark Botzet, Par. Vicar; Rev. Gregory Paffel, Pst.; Rev. Jeremy Theis, Par. Vicar; Adam Saltmarsh, Bus. Mgr.; Dcn. Thomas McFadden; CRP Stds.: 125

St. Paul's - 304 Sinclair Lewis Ave., Sauk Centre, MN 56378 t) 320-352-5580 (CRP); 320-352-2196 stpaulschurch@mainstreetcom.com Rev. Mark Botzet, Par. Vicar; Rev. Gregory Paffel, Pst.; Rev. Jeremy Theis, Par. Vicar; Dcn. Thomas McFadden; CRP Stds.: 280

SS. Peter and Paul - 304 Sinclair Lewis Ave., Sauk Centre, MN 56378 t) 320-254-8218 (CRP); 320-352-2196 stpaulschurch@mainstreetcom.com Rev. Mark Botzet, Par. Vicar; Rev. Gregory Paffel, Pst.; Rev. Jeremy Theis, Par. Vicar; Jo Braegelman, DRE; Dcn. Thomas McFadden; Adam Saltmarsh, Bus. Mgr.; CRP Stds.: 66

SAUK RAPIDS

Annunciation - 9965 Mayhew Lake Rd., N.E., Sauk Rapids, MN 56379 t) 320-259-4941 (CRP); 320-252-1729 annunciation@cloudnet.com Rev. Thomas Knoblach, Pst.; Shirley Scapanski, DRE; CRP Stds.: 104

Church of Sacred Heart - 2875 - 10th Ave. N.E., Sauk Rapids, MN 56379 t) 320-251-8115 parish@sacredheartsaukrapids.org Dcn. Joseph Kresky; Rev. Thomas Knoblach, Pst.; Jen Haman, DRE; CRP Stds.: 337

St. Patrick - 7286 Duelm Rd., N.E., Sauk Rapids, MN 56379 t) 320-252-2069 stpatsmn@earthlink.net Rev. Michael Wolfbauer, Pst.; Toni Hammond, DRE; CRP Stds.: 37

SEBEKA

St. Hubert - 22008 County Rd. 23, Sebeka, MN 56477; Mailing: 514 1st St. SE, Wadena, MN 56482 t) 218-631-1593 deaconrandy@marysacc.org Dcn. Randy Alstadt, Bus. Mgr.; Rev. Aaron J. Kuhn, Pst.; Rev. Gabriel Walz, Par. Vicar; CRP Stds.: 50

ST. AUGUSTA

St. Mary Help of Christians - 24588 County Rd. 7, St. Augusta, MN 56301 t) 320-252-1799 shellyg@smhoc.org www.smhoc.org Rev. Erik Lundgren, Par. Admin.; CRP Stds.: 94

St. Mary Help of Christians School - (Grades K-6) t) 320-251-3937 kkirks@smhoc.org Kelly Kirks, Prin.;

ST. CLOUD

St. Mary's Cathedral of St. Cloud - 25 Eighth Ave. S., St. Cloud, MN 56301-4279 t) 320-251-1840 office@stmarystcloud.org stmarystcloud.org Rev. Scott Pogatchnik, Rector; Rev. Brady Keller, Par. Vicar; Dcn. Michael Benda; Dcn. John Wocken; CRP Stds.: 54

St. Anthony of Padua - 2405 1st St N, St. Cloud, MN 56303 t) 320-251-5966 saps@spiritandsaints.org; ff2@spiritandsaints.org www.stanthonys.net Rev. Joseph Herzing, Pst.; Gail Drinkwine, Music Min.; Lorne Thompson, Pst. Min./Coord.; Lucia Shyiak, DRE; Peggy Arseneau, Bus. Mgr.; CRP Stds.: 25

St. Augustine - 442 Second St., S.E., St. Cloud, MN 56304 t) 320-251-8335 info@staugs.com staugs.com Rev. Scott Pogatchnik, Pst.; Rev. Brady Keller, Assoc. Pst.; Dcn. Richard Scheierl; Dcn. John Wocken; Nikki Silbernick, DRE; CRP Stds.: 24

Christ Church - 396 First Ave. S., St. Cloud, MN 56301 t) 320-251-3260 newmancenter@scsucatholic.org (Newman Center) Rev. Joseph Herzing, Pst.; CRP Stds.: 106

Holy Spirit - 2405 Walden Way, St. Cloud, MN 56301 t) 320-251-3764 hspirit@spiritandsaints.org www.holyspiritstcloud.net/ Rev. Joseph Herzing, Pst.; Dcn. Vernon Schmitz; Gail Drinkwine, Music Min.; Lucia Shyiak, DRE; Peggy Arseneau, Bus. Mgr.; CRP Stds.: 196

St. John Cantius - 1515 Third St. N., St. Cloud, MN 56303 t) 320-251-4455 stjohncantius@charter.net www.stjohncantius.org Rev. Brady Keller, Pst. Assoc.; Dcn. Frank Ringsmuth; CRP Stds.: 13

St. Michael - 1036 County Rd. 4, St. Cloud, MN 56303 t) 320-251-6923 churchofstmichael@churchofstmichael.net Rev. Timothy Gapinski, Pst.; Dcn. Jim Trout; Dcn. Todd Warren; CRP Stds.: 80

St. Paul - 1125 11th Ave. N., St. Cloud, MN 56303 t) 320-251-4831 x201 tjancik@taocatholic.org www.taocatholic.org/ Dcn. Chris Goenner; Rev. LeRoy Scheierl, Pst.; CRP Stds.: 81

St. Peter - 930 31st Ave. N., St. Cloud, MN 56303; Mailing: 1125 11th Ave. N., St. Cloud, MN 56303 t) 320-251-4831 x201 lscheierl@taocatholic.org; tjancik@taocatholic.org www.taocatholic.org/ Rev. LeRoy Scheierl, Pst.; Dcn. Chris Goenner; CRP Stds.: 19

St. Wendelin's - 22714 State Hwy. 15, St. Cloud, MN 56301 t) 320-252-1799 shellyg@smhoc.org Rev. Eric Lundgren, Par. Admin.; CRP Stds.: 44

St. Wendelin's School - (Grades PreK-6) t) 320-251-9175 stwend@citescape.com Lynn Rasmussen, Prin.;

ST. JOSEPH

St. John the Baptist - 14241 Fruit Farm Rd., St. Joseph, MN 56374 t) 320-363-2569 jortloff@csbsju.edu Rev. Bradley Jenniges, O.S.B., Pst.; Julie Warner, DRE; CRP Stds.: 54

Church of Saint Joseph of Saint Joseph - 12 W. Minnesota St., St. Joseph, MN 56374 t) 320-363-7505 parish@churchstjoseph.org Rev. Bradley Jenniges, O.S.B., Pst.; CRP Stds.: 145

ST. MARTIN

St. Martin - 119 Maine St., St. Martin, MN 56376; Mailing: Box 290, St. Martin, MN 56376 t) 320-548-3550 parishofstmartin@arvig.com Rev. Edward Vebelun, O.S.B., Pst.; Rhonda Dingmann, Pst. Assoc.; Rev. Gregory Miller, O.S.B., Sacr. Min.; CRP Stds.: 124

ST. STEPHEN

St. Stephen's - 103 Central Ave. S., St. Stephen, MN 56375 t) 320-251-1520 (Office); 320-251-5066 (Religious Education) ststephenchurchoffice@gmail.com; ststephenfaith@gmail.com greatrivercatholic.wixsite.com/churchofststephen Rev. Ronald Weyrens, Pst.; Danna Gasperlin, DRE; CRP Stds.: 100

STAPLES

Sacred Heart - 310 Fourth St., N.E., Staples, MN 56479; Mailing: 514 1st. St. SE, Wadens, MN 56482 t) 218-631-1593 deaconrandy@marysacc.org Rev. Aaron J. Kuhn, Pst.; Rev. Gabriel Walz, Assoc. Pst.; Dcn. Robert Shaffer; Dcn. John Wolak; CRP Stds.: 90

Sacred Heart Area School - (Grades PreSchool-6) 324 - 4th St. N.E., Staples, MN 56479 t) 218-894-2077 sacredheartareaschool@staplesnet.com Charles Durham, Supt.;

SWANVILLE

St. John the Baptist - 22 1st. St. W., Swanville, MN 56382; Mailing: P.O. Box 68, Swanville, MN 56382 t) 320-547-2920 stjohns@gctel.net Rev. Ronald Dockendorf, Pst.; CRP Stds.: 97

TINTAH

St. Gall - 110 Minnesota Ave., Tintah, MN 56583 t) 218-369-2188 stgall@runestone.net Rev. Leo Moenkedick, Pst.; CRP Stds.: 9

UNDERWOOD

Church of Saint James at Maine - 32009 County Hwy. 74, Underwood, MN 56586 t) 218-864-5619 church@ollsj.org Rev. LeRoy Schik, Pst.; CRP Stds.: 30

UPSALA

St. Mary - 308 S. Main St., Upsala, MN 56384; Mailing: PO Box 249, Upsala, MN 56384 t) 320-573-2132 238catholic@sytekcom.com www.238catholic.org/ Rev. David Grundman, Pst.; CRP Stds.: 93

VERNDALE

St. Frederick - 20 Brown St. N., Verndale, MN 56481; Mailing: 514 1st. St. SE, Wadena, MN 56482 t) 218-631-1593 deaconrandy@marysacc.org Rev. Aaron J. Kuhn, Pst.; Rev. Gabriel Walz, Par. Vicar; CRP Stds.: 34

WADENA

St. Ann's - 514 First St., S.E., Wadena, MN 56482 t) 218-631-1593 deaconrandy@marysacc.org www.marysacc.org Dcn. Randy Alstadt, Contact; Rev. Aaron J. Kuhn, Pst.; Rev. Gabriel Walz, Par. Vicar; CRP Stds.: 100

WAHKON

Sacred Heart - 225 E. Second St., Wahkon, MN 56386; Mailing: P.O. Box 68, Wahkon, MN 56386 t) 320-495-3324 sacredheart56386@yahoo.com Rev. Jerome Schik, O.S.C., Pst.; CRP Stds.: 60

WAITE PARK

St. Joseph's - 106 7th Ave. N., Waite Park, MN 56387 t) 320-251-5231 churchofstjosephwp@sjcwaitepark.com Rev. Timothy Gapinski, Pst.; Dcn. Lucio Hernandez; CRP Stds.: 88

WATKINS

St. Nicholas - 15862 County Rd. 165, Watkins, MN 55389 t) 320-764-7345 stnicholas@meltel.net www.churchofsaintnicholas.com Rev. James Statz, Pst.; CRP Stds.: 25

WEST UNION

St. Alexius - 11 Oak St., West Union, MN 56378 t) 320-352-2563 stralexius@wisper-wireless.com Rev. Gregory Paffel, Pst.; Rev. Canon Richard Aubol, Par. Vicar; Rev. Jeremy Theis, Par. Vicar; Adam Saltmarsh, Bus. Mgr.; CRP Stds.: 65

WHEATON
Ave Maria - 201 Ninth St. S., Wheaton, MN 56296 t) 320-563-4421 laurie.karsky@gmail.com Rev. John Paul Knopik, Pst.; CRP Stds.: 42

SCHOOLS: PRESCHOOL THRU HIGH SCHOOL

SCHOOLS

STATE OF MINNESOTA

FOLEY
St. John's Area School - (PAR) (Grades PreK-6) 215 7th Ave. S., Foley, MN 56329; Mailing: P.O. Box 368, Foley, MN 56329 t) 320-968-7972 office@saintjohnsschool.net; principal@saintjohnsschool.net www.saintjohnsschool.net Christine Frederichs, Prin.; Stds.: 89; Lay Tchrs.: 8

LITTLE FALLS
Mary of Lourdes School (Elementary Campus) - 307 Fourth St., S.E., Little Falls, MN 56345 t) 320-632-5408 mhbecker@molschool.org www.molschool.org Jodi Vanderheiden, Prin.; Stds.: 132; Lay Tchrs.: 12

Mary of Lourdes School (Middle School Campus) - 205 N.W. Third St., Little Falls, MN 56345 t) 320-632-6742 jvanderheiden@molschool.org

PIERZ
Holy Trinity Catholic School - (PAR) (Grades PreK-6) 80 Edward St. S., Pierz, MN 56364; Mailing: P.O. Box 427, Pierz, MN 56364 t) 320-468-6446 mlitke@holytrinitypierz.org; office@holytrinitypierz.org holytrinitypierz.org Also MDE licensed child care program Michelle Litke, Admin.; Stds.: 169; Lay Tchrs.: 13

SAUK CENTRE
Holy Family School - (PAR) (Grades K-6) 231 Sinclair Lewis Ave., Sauk Centre, MN 56378 t) 320-352-6535 lpeterson@holyfamilysc.org; carlamoritz@holyfamilysc.org www.holyfamilysc.org Lynn Peterson, Prin.; Stds.: 254; Lay Tchrs.: 16

ST. CLOUD
All Saints Academy (St. Peter, Paul and Michael School) - (Grades PreK-6) 1215 11th Ave. N., St. Cloud, MN 56303 t) 320-251-5295 marissa.bristow@allsaintsmn.org; karl.terhaar@allsaintsmn.org www.allsaintsmn.org Karl Terhaar, Prin.; Stds.: 231; Lay Tchrs.: 18

St. Elizabeth Ann Seton School - 1615 Eleventh Ave. S., St. Cloud, MN 56301 t) 320-251-1988 kvangsness@seasmn.org Kelly Vangsness, Prin.; Alyssa Sauerer, Librn.; Stds.: 110; Lay Tchrs.: 11

St. Katharine Drexel School - (PAR) (Grades PreK-5) 428 2nd St., S.E., St. Cloud, MN 56304 t) 320-251-2376 mhbecker@ourcatholicschool.org www.ourcatholicschool.org St. Augustine's/St. Mary's Cathedral School and Sacred Heart School Maria Heymans-Becker, Prin.; Stds.: 185; Scholastics: 1; Lay Tchrs.: 16

HIGH SCHOOLS

STATE OF MINNESOTA

COLLEGEVILLE
Saint John's Preparatory School - (PRV) (Grades 6-12) 2280 Water Tower Rd., Collegeville, MN 56321; Mailing: PO Box 4000, Collegeville, MN 56321 t) 320-363-3315 admissions@sjprep.net www.sjprep.net College Preparatory. Dr. Christine Glomski, Prin.; Jon McGee, Headmaster; Stds.: 236

ST. CLOUD
The Cathedral High School - (DIO) (Grades 7-12) 312 7th Ave. N., St. Cloud, MN 56303 t) 320-251-3421 kcrispo@cathedralcrusaders.org Rev. Douglas Liebsch, Chap.; Stds.: 619; Pr. Tchrs.: 1; Lay Tchrs.: 48

Cathedral High School Education Foundation - pfoley@cathedralcrusaders.org Paula Foley, Prin.;

CAMPUS MINISTRY / NEWMAN CENTERS [CAM]

MORRIS
Newman Catholic Student Center - 306 E. Fourth St., Morris, MN 56267 t) 320-589-1947 newman@hometownsolutions.net www.mrs.umn.edu/~catholic Scott Crumb, Dir.;

ST. CLOUD
Newman Center, Inc. - 396 First Ave. S., St. Cloud, MN 56301 t) 320-251-3260 newmancenter@scsucatholic.org scsucatholic.org Rev. Joseph Herzing, Admin.;

CATHOLIC CHARITIES [CCH]

ST. CLOUD
Domus Transitional Housing - 17 S. 19 1/2 Ave., St. Cloud, MN 56301; Mailing: 911 18th St. N., St. Cloud, MN 56303 t) 320-650-1568 ccstcloud.org Dcn. Stephen Pareja, Exec.; Asstd. Annu.: 30; Staff: 2

COLLEGES & UNIVERSITIES [COL]

COLLEGEVILLE
Saint John's University - 2850 Abbey Plz., Collegeville, MN 56321; Mailing: Box 2222, Collegeville, MN 56321 t) 320-363-2077 jrscegura@csbsju.edu www.csbsju.edu (Men), SJU has a partnership with College of Saint Benedict, a liberal arts college for women. Brian Bruess, Pres.; Jennifer Meyer, CFO; Stds.: 1,645; Bro. Tchrs.: 4; Lay Tchrs.: 151; Pr. Tchrs.: 3; Scholastics: 378

ST. JOSEPH
College of Saint Benedict - 37 College Ave. S., St. Joseph, MN 56374 t) 320-363-5011 csbcampusministry@csbsju.edu www.csbsju.edu Sisters of the Order of Saint Benedict, (Women), CSB has a partnership with Saint John's University, a liberal arts college for men. Laurie Harmen, Pres.; Sr. Sharon Nohner, Dir.; Joanna Padden, Campus Min.; Stds.: 1,682

CONVENTS, MONASTERIES, AND RESIDENCES FOR WOMEN [CON]

LITTLE FALLS
St. Francis Convent - 116 Eighth Ave., S.E., Little Falls, MN 56345 t) 320-632-2981 info@fslf.org www.fslf.org Motherhouse of Franciscan Sisters of Little Falls, MN. Sr. Carol Schmit, O.S.F., Pres.; Srs.: 86

Franciscan Life Center - 116 Eighth Ave., S.E., Little Falls, MN 56345 t) (320) 632-2981

INSTITUTIONS LOCATED IN DIOCESE

SAUK RAPIDS
St. Clare's Monastery - 421 4th St. S., Sauk Rapids, MN 56379 t) 320-251-3556 Major Papal Cloister. Franciscan Poor Clare Nuns. Srs.: 14

ST. JOSEPH
St. Benedict's Monastery - 104 Chapel Ln., St. Joseph, MN 56374 t) 320-363-7100 cquinlivan@csbsju.edu www.sbm.osb.org Motherhouse and Formation House for Sisters of the Order of Saint Benedict. Sr. Susan Rudolph, O.S.B., Prioress; Srs.: 159

ENDOWMENTS / FOUNDATIONS / TRUSTS [EFT]

COLLEGEVILLE
Holy Cross Trust - 2900 Abbey Plz., Collegeville, MN 56321; Mailing: P.O. Box 2400, Collegeville, MN 56321 t) 320-363-2547 bjenniges@csbsju.edu Rev. Bradley Jenniges, O.S.B., Trustee;

ONAMIA
Crosier Continuing Care and Support Trust - 104 Crosier Dr. N., Onamia, MN 56359; Mailing: P.O. Box 500, Onamia, MN 56359-0500 t) 320-532-3103 kholl@crosier.org Rev. Kermit Holl, O.S.C.;

Crosier International Trust for Religious Life and Service - 104 Crosier Dr., Onamia, MN 56359; Mailing: PO Box 500, Onamia, MN 56359-0500 t) 320-532-3103 internationaltrust@crosier.org Rev. David Donnay, O.S.C.;

HOSPITALS / HEALTH SERVICES [HOS]

BRECKENRIDGE
St. Francis Medical Center - 2400 St. Francis Dr., Breckenridge, MN 56520 t) (218) 643-3000 missionintegrationmidwest@commonspirit.org www.sfcare.org David Nelson, Pres.; Andrew J. Santos III, Sr. Vice. Pres., Mission Integration; Luke Preussler, Dir.; Bed Capacity: 25; Asstd. Annu.: 21,000; Staff: 180

LITTLE FALLS
St. Gabriel's Hospital - 815 S.E. Second St., Little Falls, MN 56345 t) (320) 631-5600 missionintegrationmidwest@commonspirit.org www.chistgabriels.com/ Steve Smith, Pres.; Andrew J. Santos III, SVP, Mission Integration; Luke Preussler, Dir.; Bed Capacity: 25; Asstd. Annu.: 120,000; Staff: 400

ST. CLOUD
St. Cloud Hospital - 1406 Sixth Ave. N., St. Cloud, MN 56303 t) 320-251-2700 administrator@centracare.com www.stcloudhospital.com Rev. Mark Stang, Chap.; Bret Reuter, Dir.; Dr. Joy Plamann, Pres.; Bed Capacity: 489; Asstd. Annu.: 309,304; Staff: 6,108

MISCELLANEOUS [MIS]

BRECKENRIDGE
Appletree Court - 601 Oak St., Breckenridge, MN 56520 t) 218-643-0407 sfcare.org David Nelson, CEO;

BROWNS VALLEY
***Browns Valley Health Center** - 114 Jefferson St. S., Browns Valley, MN 56219 t) 320-695-2165 cward@bvhc.sfhs.org Claudia Ward, Admin.;

COLLEGEVILLE
Dialogue Interreligieux Monastique (Monastic Interreligious Dialogue) (DIMMID) - 2900 Abbey Plz., Collegeville, MN 56321-2015 t) 320-363-3921 wskudlarek@csbsju.edu dimmid.org Rev. William Skudlarek, O.S.B., Contact;

MELROSE
Rose Mill Apartments, LLC - 407 E. 5th St. N., Melrose, MN 56352; Mailing: 911 18th St. N., St. Cloud, MN 56303 t) 320-650-1568 ccstcloud.org Dcn. Stephen Pareja, Exec.;

MORRIS
St. Francis Health Services of Morris, Inc. - 801 Nevada Ave., Morris, MN 56267 t) 320-589-2004 craw@sfhs.org; jmichaelson@sfhs.org www.sfhs.org Carol Raw, CEO;

West Wind Village - 1001 Scotts Ave., Morris, MN 56267 t) 320-589-1133 www.pcs.sfhs.org

RICHMOND
Maple Apartments of Richmond, Inc. - 488 1st St., N.E., Richmond, MN 56368; Mailing: 911 18th St. N., St. Cloud, MN 56303 t) 320-650-1568 ccstcloud.org Dcn. Stephen Pareja, Exec.;

SAUK CENTRE
Sauk Centre Apts. - 217 Railroad Ave. Ct., Sauk Centre, MN 56378; Mailing: 911 18th St. N., St. Cloud, MN 56303 t) 320-650-1568 ccstcloud.org Dcn. Stephen Pareja, Exec.;

ST. CLOUD
Affordable Community Housing, Inc. - 911 18th St. N., St. Cloud, MN 56303 t) 320-650-1530 Dcn. Stephen Pareja, Exec.;

Central Minnesota Residents Encountering Christ - 6667 County Rd. 91, S.E., St. Cloud, MN 56304 t) 320-251-0098 ccarolt@yahoo.com

ST. JOSEPH
St. Joseph Apartment, Inc. - 410 W. Minnesota St., St. Joseph, MN 56374; Mailing: 911 18th St. N., St. Cloud,

MN 56303 t) 320-650-1568 ccstcloud.org Dcn. Stephen Pareja, Exec.;
Monastic Interreligious Dialogue - St. Benedict's Monastery, 104 Chapel Ln., St. Joseph, MN 56374 t) 320-363-7070 hmercier@csbsju.edu www.monasticdialog.org Sr. Helene Mercier, O.S.B., Contact;

MONASTERIES AND RESIDENCES FOR PRIESTS AND BROTHERS [MON]

COLLEGEVILLE

St. John's Abbey, of the Order of St. Benedict - 2900 Abbey Plz., Collegeville, MN 56321-2015; Mailing: P.O. Box 2015, Collegeville, MN 56321-2015 t) 320-363-2011 sjainfo@csbsju.edu saintjohnsabbey.org and St. John's University, School of Theology, Seminary, Preparatory School and Novitiate. Rt. Rev. John Klassen, O.S.B., Abbot; Rev. Eric Hollas, O.S.B., Prior; Bro. Simon-Hoa Phan, Subprior; Rev. Lewis Grobe, O.S.B.; Rev. Columba Stewart, O.S.B., Dir.; Rev. Nickolas Kleespie, O.S.B., Chap.; Rev. Efrain Rosado, OSB, Sacramental Min.; Rev. Thomas Andert, O.S.B.; Rev. Timothy Backous, O.S.B.; Rev. Stephen Beauclair, O.S.B.; Rev. Nickolas Becker, O.S.B.; Rev. Michael Bik, O.S.B.; Rev. Roger Botz, O.S.B.; Rev. Cletus Connors, O.S.B.; Rev. Alberic Culhane, O.S.B.; Rev. Ian Dommer, O.S.B.; Rev. John Patrick Earls, O.S.B.; Rev. Geoffrey Fecht, O.S.B.; Rev. Joseph Feders, O.S.B.; Rev. Jonathan Fischer, O.S.B.; Rev. Isaiah Frederick; Rev. Thomas Gillespie, O.S.B.; Rev. Anthony Gorman, O.S.B.; Rev. Michael Leonard Hahn, O.S.B.; Rev. Nathanael Hauser, O.S.B.; Rev. Bradley Jenniges, O.S.B.; Rev. Roger Kasprick, O.S.B.; Rev. Roger Klassen, O.S.B.; Rev. Robert Koopmann, O.S.B.; Rev. Michael Kwatera, O.S.B.; Bro. David Paul Lange, O.S.B.; Rev. Dale Launderville, O.S.B.; Rt. Rev. Jonathan Licari, O.S.B.; Rev. Matthew Luft, O.S.B; Rev. Luke Mancuso, O.S.B.; Rev. John Meoska, O.S.B.; Rev. Gregory Miller, O.S.B.; Rev. Dunstan Moorse, O.S.B.; Rev. Douglas Mullin, O.S.B.; Rev. Michael Naughton, O.S.B.; Rev. Michael Patella, O.S.B.; Rev. Roman Paur, O.S.B.; Rev. Michael Peterson, O.S.B.; Rev. Anthony Ruff, O.S.B.; Rev. Dominic Ruiz, O.S.B.; Rev. Francisco Schulte, O.S.B.; Rev. William Skudlarek, O.S.B.; Rev. Don Talafous, O.S.B.; Rev. Donald Tauscher, O.S.B.; Rev. Gordon Tavis, O.S.B.; Rev. Mel Taylor, O.S.B,; Rev. Wilfred Theisen, O.S.B.; Rev. Jerome Tupa, O.S.B.; Rev. Thomas Wahl, O.S.B.; Rev. Daniel Ward, O.S.B.; Rev. Blane Wasnie, O.S.B.; Rev. Cyprian Weaver, O.S.B.; Brs.: 38; Priests: 63

ONAMIA

Crosier Priory - 104 Crosier Dr. N., Onamia, MN 56359; Mailing: P.O. Box 500, Onamia, MN 56359 t) 320-532-3103 onamia@crosier.org www.crosier.org The National Shrine of St. Odilia is sponsored and maintained by the Crosier Fathers of Onamia Rev. Kermit Holl, O.S.C., Prior; Bro. Jeffrey Mario Breer, O.S.C., Mem.; Bro. Paulinus Daeli, O.S.C., Mem.; Bro. Ralph Dahl, O.S.C., Mem.; Bro. Christopher Erran, OSC, Mem.; Rev. Dale Ettel, Mem.; Rev. John J. Fleischhacker, O.S.C., Mem.; Rev. John Hawkins, O.S.C., Mem.; Rev. Steven Henrich, OSC, Mem.; Bro. Eric Kalimbiriro Kadalikashereza, OSC; Rev. Zawadi Jean-Marie Kambale Sambya, osc, Mem.; Rev. Kasereka Moise Kisonia, OSC, Mem.; Bro. Salama Vivalya Kasereka, OSC; Bro. Marcos Antonio Rodrigues Leles, osc, Mem.; Rev. Glen Lewandowski, O.S.C., Mem.; Bro. James L Lewandowski, OSC, Mem.; Rev. Ernest Martello, O.S.C., Mem.; Rev. James Moeglein, O.S.C., Mem.; Rev. Eugene D. Plaisted, O.S.C., Mem.; Rev. Gregory Poser, O.S.C., Mem.; Rev. James H. Remmerswaal, O.S.C., Mem.; Bro. James Scher, OSC, Mem.; Rev. Jerome Schik, O.S.C., Mem.; Bro. Leo Schoenberg, O.S.C., Mem.; Rev. Raymond Steffes, O.S.C., Mem.; Rev. John Vincent, O.S.C., Mem.; Brs.: 10; Priests: 16

NURSING / REHABILITATION / CONVALESCENCE / ELDERLY CARE [NUR]

ALBANY

Mother of Mercy Senior Living - 230 Church Ave., Albany, MN 56307; Mailing: Box 676, Albany, MN 56307 t) 320-845-2195 dmcdevitt@momcampus.org www.motherofmercymn.org Paul Gaebe, CEO; Asstd. Annu.: 205; Staff: 23

BRECKENRIDGE

St. Francis Home - 2400 St. Francis Dr., Breckenridge, MN 56520 t) (218) 643-3000 missionintegrationmidwest@commonspirit.org www.sfcare.org Andrew J. Santos III, SVP, Mission Integration; David Nelson, CEO; Rev. Leo Moenkedick, Chap.; Asstd. Annu.: 61; Staff: 70

COLD SPRING

Assumption Home - 715 First St. N., Cold Spring, MN 56320 t) 320-685-3693 lindseys@assumptionhome.com assumptionhome.org Lindsey Sand, Admin.; Asstd. Annu.: 87; Staff: 21
Assumption Home, Inc. - 715 First St. N., Cold Spring, MN 56320 t) 320-685-3693 lindseys@assumptionhome.com www.assumptionhome.org Made up of Assumption Home and Assumption Court, a nursing home and a housing with services apartment complex. Lindsey Sand, Admin.; Rev. Matthew Luft, O.S.B, CEO; Asstd. Annu.: 349; Staff: 180
John Paul Apartments - 200 Eighth Ave. N., Cold Spring, MN 56320 t) 320-685-4429 lindseys@assumptionhome.com Rev. Thomas Andert, O.S.B., Chap.; Lindsey Sand, Admin.; Asstd. Annu.: 89; Staff: 43

LITTLE FALLS

Alverna Apartments - 300 Eighth Ave., S.E., Little Falls, MN 56345 t) 320-631-5030 (An Affiliate of Catholic Health Initiatives)

MORRIS

West Wind Village - 1001 Scotts Ave., Morris, MN 56267 t) 320-589-1133 msyltie@sfhs.org Paula Viker, Admin.; Asstd. Annu.: 115; Staff: 23

PARKERS PRAIRIE

St. William's Living Center - 212 W S00 St, Parkers Prairie, MN 56361; Mailing: P.O. Box 30, Parkers Prairie, MN 56361 t) 218-338-4671 administrator@stwilliamslivingcenter.com Paul Baer, Admin.; Asstd. Annu.: 110; Staff: 11

ST. CLOUD

St. Benedict's Senior Community - 1810 Minnesota Blvd., S.E., St. Cloud, MN 56304 t) 320-252-0010 kratzkes@centracare.com Corporate Division of the St. Cloud Hospital. Operated under the auspices of the local Catholic Church of St. Cloud. Sr. Janelle Sietsema, O.S.B., Chap.; Rev. Stephen Beauclair, O.S.B., Chap.; Rebecca Calderone, Dir.; Susan Kratzke, Vice. Pres.;
Benedict Court - 1980 15th Ave., S.E., St. Cloud, MN 56304 Robin Theis, Admin.; Linda Kappel, Vice Pres.;
Benedict Homes (4) - Residential Homes for residents with memory loss diseases. All Benedict Homes are managed by St. Benedict's Senior Community. Linda Doerr, Dir.;
Benedict Village - 2000 15th Ave., S.E., St. Cloud, MN 56304 t) 320-252-4380 Managed by St. Benedict's Senior Community. A Division of the St. Cloud Hospital. Operated under the auspices of the local Catholic Church Robin Theis, Admin.; Linda Kappel, Vice Pres.;
Benet Place North - 1420 Minnesota Blvd., S.E., St. Cloud, MN 56304 t) 320-252-2557 Subsidized apartments with supportive services for older adults only. Managed by St. Benedict's Senior Community. Linda Doerr, Dir.;
Benet Place South - 1975 15th Ave., S.E., St. Cloud, MN 56304 t) 320-529-8700 Linda Doerr, Dir.;

RETREAT HOUSES / RENEWAL CENTERS [RTR]

ISANTI

Pacem in Terris Center for Spirituality - 26399 MN 47, N.W., Isanti, MN 55040; Mailing: P.O. Box 418, St. Francis, MN 55070 t) 763-444-6408 staff@paceminterris.org; tim.drake@paceminterris.org www.paceminterris.org Timothy Drake, Dir.;

SEMINARIES [SEM]

COLLEGEVILLE

St. John's School of Theology and Seminary - 2850 Abbey Plaza, Collegeville, MN 56321; Mailing: P.O. Box 7288, Collegeville, MN 56321 t) 320-363-2100 sot@csbsju.edu www.csbsju.edu/sot Rev. Michael Patella, O.S.B., Rector; Rev. Dale Launderville, O.S.B., Dean; David Wuolu, Librn.; Stds.: 108; Lay Tchrs.: 10; Pr. Tchrs.: 3

SHRINES [SHR]

ONAMIA

National Shrine of St. Odilia - 104 Crosier Dr. N., Onamia, MN 56359-0500; Mailing: P.O. Box 500, Onamia, MN 56359-0500 t) 320-532-3103 info@crosier.org www.crosier.org Sponsored and maintained by Crosier Fathers of Onamia. Rev. Zawadi Jean-Marie Kambale Sambya, OSC, Dir.;

SPECIAL CARE FACILITIES [SPF]

COLD SPRING

St. Anne's Home - 103 10th Ave. N., Cold Spring, MN 56320; Mailing: 911 18th St. N., St. Cloud, MN 56303 t) 320-650-1568 ccstcloud.org Contact Catholic Charities, Supervised Living Situation for Persons with Developmental Disabilities. Dcn. Stephen Pareja, Exec.; Bed Capacity: 4; Asstd. Annu.: 4; Staff: 4
Bethany Home - 13 8th Ave. S., Cold Spring, MN 56320; Mailing: 911 18th St. N., St. Cloud, MN 56303 t) 320-650-1568 ccstcloud.org Dcn. Stephen Pareja, Exec.; Bed Capacity: 4; Asstd. Annu.: 4; Staff: 4
St. Luke's Home - 411 8th Ave. N., Cold Spring, MN 56320; Mailing: 911 18th St. N., St. Cloud, MN 56303 t) 320-650-1568 ccstcloud.org Contact Catholic Charities, Adults with mild to moderate developmental disabilities. Dcn. Stephen Pareja, Exec.; Bed Capacity: 4; Asstd. Annu.: 4; Staff: 4
Mother Teresa Home - 101 Tenth Ave., Cold Spring, MN 56320; Mailing: 911 18th St. N., St. Cloud, MN 56303 t) 320-650-1568 ccstcloud.org Supervised Living Situation for Persons with Developmental Disabilities. Dcn. Stephen Pareja, Exec.; Bed Capacity: 4; Asstd. Annu.: 4; Staff: 4

PAYNESVILLE

Adult Foster Care for Handicapped Individuals - 1790 W. Mill St., Paynesville, MN 56362; Mailing: 911 18th St. N., St. Cloud, MN 56303 t) 320-650-1568 ccstcloud.org Dcn. Stephen Pareja, Exec.; Bed Capacity: 4; Asstd. Annu.: 13; Staff: 5

ST. CLOUD

St. Elizabeth Home - 306 15th Ave. N., St. Cloud, MN 56303; Mailing: 911 18th St. N., St. Cloud, MN 56303 t) 320-650-1568 ccstcloud.org Board and Lodging Home for Functionally Impaired Adults. Dcn. Stephen Pareja, Exec.; Bed Capacity: 18; Asstd. Annu.: 43; Staff: 2
St. Francis Home - 1727 Roosevelt Rd., St. Cloud, MN 56301; Mailing: 911 18th St. N., St. Cloud, MN 56303 t) 320-650-1568 ccstcloud.org Supervised Living Situation for Persons with Developmental Disabilities. Dcn. Stephen Pareja, Exec.; Bed Capacity: 4; Asstd. Annu.: 4; Staff: 4
LaPaz Community Inc. - 530 S. 16th St., St. Cloud, MN 56301; Mailing: 911 18th St. N., St. Cloud, MN 56303 t) 320-650-1568 ccstcloud.org Dcn. Stephen Pareja, Exec.; Bed Capacity: 36; Asstd. Annu.: 65; Staff: 1

Archdiocese of St. Louis

(Archidioecesis S. Ludovici)

MOST REVEREND MITCHELL T. ROZANSKI

Archbishop of St. Louis; ordained November 24, 1984; appointed Titular Bishop of Walla Walla and Auxiliary Bishop of Baltimore July 3, 2004; consecrated August 24, 2004; appointed Bishop of Springfield in Massachusetts June 19, 2014; installed August 12, 2014; appointed Archbishop of St. Louis June 10, 2020; installed August 25, 2020. Office: 20 Archbishop May Dr., St. Louis, MO 63119-5738.

Office: 20 Archbishop May Dr., St. Louis, MO 63119-5738. T: 314-792-7005
www.archstl.org
communications@archstl.org

Square Miles 5,968.

Diocese July 18, 1826; Archdiocese July 20, 1847.

Comprises that portion of the State of Missouri bounded on the north by the northern line of the County of Lincoln; on the west by the western lines of the Counties of Lincoln, Warren, Franklin and Washington; on the south by the southern lines of the Counties of Washington, St. Francois and Perry; on the east by the Mississippi River.

Heavenly Patrons–Saint Louis, King, Saint Vincent de Paul and Saint Rose Philippine Duchesne.

For legal titles of parishes and archdiocesan institutions, consult the Catholic Center.

MOST REVEREND MARK S. RIVITUSO

Auxiliary Bishop of St. Louis; ordained January 16, 1988; appointed Titular Bishop of Turuzi and Auxiliary Bishop of St. Louis March 7, 2017; installed May 2, 2017. Office: 20 Archbishop May Dr., St. Louis, MO 63119-5738.

STATISTICAL OVERVIEW

Personnel
Archbishops.......1
Retired Archbishops.......1
Auxiliary Bishops.......1
Retired Bishops.......1
Abbots.......1
Priests: Diocesan Active in Diocese.......204
Priests: Diocesan Active Outside Diocese.......15
Priests: Retired, Sick or Absent.......77
Number of Diocesan Priests.......296
Religious Priests in Diocese.......247
Total Priests in your Diocese.......543
Extern Priests in Diocese.......12
Ordinations:
Diocesan Priests.......2
Religious Priests.......4
Transitional Deacons.......4
Permanent Deacons.......18
Permanent Deacons in Diocese.......290
Total Brothers.......79
Total Sisters.......921

Parishes
Parishes.......178
With Resident Pastor:
Resident Diocesan Priests.......142
Resident Religious Priests.......15
Without Resident Pastor:
Administered by Priests.......15
Administered by Deacons.......4
Administered by Religious Women.......1
Administered by Lay People.......1
Missions.......6
Pastoral Centers.......2

Welfare
Catholic Hospitals.......12
Total Assisted.......2,126,000
Homes for the Aged.......11
Total Assisted.......3,606
Residential Care of Children.......3
Total Assisted.......1,584
Day Care Centers.......5
Total Assisted.......4,246
Specialized Homes.......17
Total Assisted.......35,560
Special Centers for Social Services.......16
Total Assisted.......56,467

Educational
Seminaries, Diocesan.......2
Students from This Diocese.......36
Students from Other Dioceses.......81
Diocesan Students in Other Seminaries.......2
Seminaries, Religious.......1
Students, Religious.......25
Total Seminarians.......63
Colleges and Universities.......2
Total Students.......14,490
High Schools, Diocesan and Parish.......10
Total Students.......3,350
High Schools, Private.......17
Total Students.......6,904
Elementary Schools, Diocesan and Parish.......89
Total Students.......23,151
Elementary Schools, Private.......11
Total Students.......1,765
Non-residential Schools for the Disabled.......1
Total Students.......18
Catechesis / Religious Education:
High School Students.......78
Elementary Students.......11,291
Total Students under Catholic Instruction.......61,110
Teachers in Diocese:
Priests.......22
Brothers.......3
Sisters.......18
Lay Teachers.......2,929

Vital Statistics
Receptions into the Church:
Infant Baptism Totals.......4,132
Minor Baptism Totals.......286
Adult Baptism Totals.......189
Received into Full Communion.......244
First Communions.......4,428
Confirmations.......4,305
Marriages:
Catholic.......978
Interfaith.......336
Total Marriages.......1,314
Deaths.......3,794
Total Catholic Population.......483,911
Total Population.......2,259,000

LEADERSHIP

Vicars General - Most Rev. Mark S. Rivituso; Rev. Msgr. Dennis R. Stehly; Rev. Michael P. Boehm;
Moderator of the Curia - Rev. Msgr. Dennis R. Stehly;
Chancellor - t) 314-792-7836 Nancy J. Werner;
Chancellor for Canonical Affairs - t) 314-792-7408 Rev. Msgr. Jerome D. Billing;
Vice Chancellor for Special Projects - t) 314-792-7812 Jennifer Stanard;
Metropolitan Tribunal - t) 314-792-7400
Judicial Vicar - Very Rev. Philip J. Bene;
Adjutant Judicial Vicar - Very Rev. Aaron P. Nord;
Judges - Mateusz Makowski; Marla Vaneza Pruneda; Rev. Dean P. Perri;
Defenders of the Bond - Rev. Nicholas J. Muenks; Sr. Robin Nordyke;
Promoter of Justice - Rev. Michael P. Joyce, C.M.;
Notaries - Rena Hill; Eric Gabrielson;
Tribunal of Second Instance for the Province of St. Louis - t) 314-792-7166
Judicial Vicar - Very Rev. John A. Brockland;
Collegiate Judges - Rev. Msgr. John B. Shamleffer; Rev. Msgr. James J. Ramacciotti;
Defender of the Bond - Dcn. J. Gerard Quinn;
Promoter of Justice - Very Rev. Nicholas E. Kastenholz;
Collegiate Judges ad causam - Most Rev. Mark S. Rivituso; Rev. Dennis M. Doyle;
Ecclesiastical Notary - Patricia A. Lanasa;
Archdiocesan Consultors - Most Rev. Mark S. Rivituso; Rev. Msgr. Dennis R. Stehly; Rev. Michael P. Boehm;
Deaneries/Deans -
North City Deanery - Very Rev. Scott Jones, Dean;
South City Deanery - Very Rev. Paul J. Niemann, Dean;
North County Deanery - Very Rev. Msgr. Mark C. Ullrich, Dean;
West County Deanery - Very Rev. Thomas M. Molini, Dean;
South County Deanery - Very Rev. Charles W. Barthel, Dean;
Mid-County Deanery - Very Rev. Michael E. Turek, Dean;
Festus Deanery - Very Rev. Richard V. Coerver, Dean;
St. Charles Deanery - Very Rev. Nicholas E. Kastenholz, Dean;
Ste. Genevieve Deanery - Very Rev. William C. Thess, Dean;
Washington Deanery - Very Rev. Joseph S. Post, Dean;
Archdiocesan Council of Priests - Rev. Paul Hoesing; Most Rev. Mark S. Rivituso; Rev. Msgr. Dennis R. Stehly;
Vicar for Priests - t) 314-792-7550 Rev. Kenneth A. Brown;
Archbishop's Liaison to Senior Priests - t) 314-963-0706 Rev. Philip G. Krahman;
Chief Financial Officer - t) 314-792-7278 Cory M. Nardoni;
Vicar for Strategic Planning - t) 314-792-7005 Rev. Christopher M. Martin;

OFFICES AND DIRECTORS

Annual Catholic Appeal - t) 314-792-7680 Brian Niebrugge, Exec. Dir.;
Archdiocesan Archives - t) 314-792-7020 Eric B. Fair, Dir.;
Archdiocesan Newspaper "St. Louis Review" - t) 314-792-7500 Teak Phillips, Editor;
Archdiocesan Office of Worship - t) 314-792-7231 Rev. Nicholas W. Smith, Dir.;
Building and Real Estate - t) 314-792-7087 Tom Du Bois, Dir.;
Cardinal Rigali Center - t) 314-792-7000 James Arnet, Bldg. Mgmt.;
Catholic Cemeteries of St. Louis - t) 314-792-7737 Rev. Msgr. Dennis M. Delaney, Dir.;
Catholic Charities - t) 314-367-5500 Dr. Jared H. Bryson, Pres.;
Catholic Relief Services - t) 314-792-7812 Jennifer Stanard;
Catholic Youth Apostolate - t) 314-792-7600 Deepan Rajaratnam, Dir.;
Central Purchasing - t) 314-792-7068 Mary Marx, Dir.;
Continuing Education & Formation of Priests - t) 314-792-7550 Rev. Peter J. Fonseca;
Evangelization and Discipleship - t) 314-792-7083 Brian Miller, Prog. Mgr.;
Evangelization and Parish Ministry Support - t) 314-792-7083 Dcn. Christopher M. Ast, Exec.;
Finance Office - t) 314-792-7281 Marilisa Heiderscheid, Controller;
Human Dignity and Intercultural Affairs - t) 314-792-7177 F. Javier Orozco, Exec. Dir.;
Human Resources - t) 314-792-7540 Kevin J. Loos, Chief Human Resource Officer;
Internal Audit - t) 314-792-7241 Whit Madere, Dir.;
Mission Office - t) 314-792-7655 Kim Specht, Dir.;
Latin America Apostolate, Archdiocese of St. Louis -
Missionary Childhood Association -
Pan Y Amor -
The Society for the Propagation of the Faith, Archdiocese of St. Louis -
Office of Catholic Education and Formation - t) 314-792-7300 www.archstl.org/education Todd R. Sweda, Dir.; Dr. Maureen DePriest, Dir.; Michael J. Duffy, Dir.;
Office of Child and Youth Protection - t) 314-792-7704 Sandra Price, Exec. Dir.;
Office of Communications and Planning - t) 314-792-7500 Brecht Mulvihill, Exec. Dir., Communications; John Schwob, Dir., Pastoral Planning; Lisa Shea, Dir., Community & Media Engagement;
Office of Consecrated Life - t) 314-792-7250 Sr. Marysia Weber, R.S.M., Dir.;
Office of General Counsel - t) 314-792-7075 Thomas M. Buckley, Gen. Counsel;
Office of Information Technology - t) 314-792-7570 Paul Giljum, Dir.;
Office of Marriage and Family Life - t) 314-792-7171 Paul Duker, Marriage Ministry Coord.;
Office of Racial Harmony - t) 314-792-7596 Joyce Jones, Dir.;
Office of the Permanent Diaconate - t) 314-792-7431 Dcn. Christopher M. Ast, Dir.; Dcn. Dale J. Follen, Assoc. Dir. Formation; Dcn. Bill Johnson, Assoc. Dir. Ministry & Life Permanent Diaconate;
Office of Vocations - t) 314-792-6460 Rev. Brian S. Fallon, Dir.;
Office of Youth Ministry - Amy Eschelbach, Dir.;
Parish Accounting Services - t) 314-792-7716 Jeff Martin, Dir.;
Peace & Justice Commission - t) 314-792-7062 Marie Kenyon, Dir.;
Priests' Mutual Benefit Society - t) 314-792-7034 Gigi Henson, Mgr.;
Priests' Purgatorial Society - t) 314-792-7408 Rev. Msgr. Jerome D. Billing, Pres.;
Priests' Wellness Program - t) 314-792-7648 Arje Crawford, Physical Wellness Coord.; Patrick Dotson, Emotional Wellness Coord.;
Project Rachel - t) 314-792-7555
Regina Cleri - t) 314-968-2240 Michael Miller, Admin.;
Respect Life Apostolate - t) 314-792-7555 Cynthia Kush Haehnel, Dir.;
Risk Management - t) 314-792-7203 Brandon S. Rothkopf, Dir.;
Safe Environment Program Office - t) 314-792-7271 Sandra Price, Dir.;
St. Louis Roman Catholic Theological Seminary - t) 314-792-6100 Rev. Paul Hoesing, Rector;
Cardinal Glennon College - Rev. Paul Hoesing, Pres.;
Kenrick School of Theology - Rev. Paul Hoesing, Pres.;
Stewardship & the Annual Catholic Appeal - t) 314-792-7680 Brian Niebrugge, Exec. Dir.;
Victim Assistance Coordinator - Ann Wier;

PARISHES, MISSIONS, AND CLERGY

STATE OF MISSOURI

APPLE CREEK

St. Joseph Catholic Church, Apple Creek - 138 St. Joseph Ln., Apple Creek, MO 63775 t) 573-788-2330 stjoeapc@gmail.com Rev. Patrick J. Christopher, Pst.; Ashly Richardet, DRE; CRP Stds.: 15

ARNOLD

St. David Catholic Church - 2334 Tenbrook Rd., Arnold, MO 63010 t) 636-287-1551 (CRP); 636-296-5485 garycathy@sbcglobal.net; stdavid@swbell.net www.stdavidarnold.org Rev. Charles F. Ferrara, Pst.; Dcn. Thomas G. Politte; Dcn. Scott D. Schardan; Cathy Whitlock, DRE;

Immaculate Conception Catholic Church, Arnold - 2300 Church Rd., Arnold, MO 63010 t) 636-321-0002 x1 parishsecretary@icarnold.com www.icarnold.com Dcn. Robert Eichelberger; Rev. Msgr. Jeffrey N. Knight, Pst.; Dcn. Steven M. Schisler; Dcn. Donald J. Walker; Christine Anderson, DRE; CRP Stds.: 261

AUGUSTA

Immaculate Conception Catholic Church, Augusta - 5912 S. Hwy. 94, Augusta, MO 63332 Rev. Eugene G. Robertson, Pst.;

BALLWIN

Holy Infant Catholic Church - 627 Dennison Dr., Ballwin, MO 63021-4870 t) 636-227-0802 x3 (CRP); 636-227-7440; 636-227-0802 x2 (School) psroffice@holyinfantballwin.org; rectoryoffice@holyinfantballwin.org www.holyinfantballwin.org Rev. Edward J. Stanger, Pst.; Rev. Msgr. Michael E. Dieckmann, Assoc. Pst.; Rev. Christopher D. Smith, Assoc. Pst.; Patricia Foley, DRE; CRP Stds.: 326

Holy Infant Catholic Church School - (Grades PreK-8) 248 New Ballwin Rd., Ballwin, MO 63021 www.holyinfantschool.org Rebecca R. McQuaide, Prin.; Carolanne Ryle, Librn.;

BIEHLE

St. Maurus Catholic Church - 10198 Hwy. B, Biehle, MO 63775 t) 573-788-2330 stjoeapc@gmail.com Rev. Patrick J. Christopher, Pst.; Ashly Richardet, DRE; CRP Stds.: 22

BLOOMSDALE

St. Agnes Catholic Church - 40 St. Agnes Dr., Bloomsdale, MO 63627; Mailing: P.O. Box 124, Bloomsdale, MO 63627 t) 573-483-2555 x1 office@stagnesandstlawrence.org; parish307@archstl.org www.stagnesandstlawrence.org Rev. Michael J. Benz, Pst.; Dcn. James Basler;

St. Agnes Catholic Church School - (Grades PreK-8) 30 St. Agnes Dr., Bloomsdale, MO 63627 t) 573-483-2506 principal@stagneselementary.org Debra Klahs, Prin.;

St. Lawrence Catholic Church - 8055 State Rt. Y, Bloomsdale, MO 63627; Mailing: P.O. Box 124, Bloomsdale, MO 63627 t) 573-483-2555 x1 office@stagnesandstlawrence.org; parish337@archstl.org Rev. Michael J. Benz, Pst.;

BONNE TERRE

St. Joseph Catholic Church, Bonne Terre - 15 St. Joseph St., Bonne Terre, MO 63628 t) 573-358-2112 bernieburle@yahoo.com saintjosephchurch.org Rev. James A. Holbrook, Pst.; CRP Stds.: 8

St. Anne - 5425 Brickey Rd., French Village, MO 63036

BRENTWOOD

St. Mary Magdalen Catholic Church, Brentwood - 2618 Brentwood Blvd., Brentwood, MO 63144 t) 314-961-0149 (CRP); 314-961-8400 info@stmmchurch.com Dcn. Daniel D. Fitzgerald; Rev. Msgr. Timothy P. Cronin, Pst.; Dcn. William A. Preiss;

St. Mary Magdalen Catholic School - 8750 Magdalen Ave., Brentwood, MO 63144 office@stmmschool.com stmmlab.com Kathy Wiseman, Prin.;

CADET

St. Joachim Catholic Church, Old Mines - 10120 Crest Rd., Cadet, MO 63630 t) 573-438-6181 stjoachimparish@hotmail.com stjoachim.org/ Rev. Anthony A. Dattilo, Pst.;

St. Joachim School - t) 573-438-3973 stjoachimschool_63630@yahoo.com stjoachimschool.com Carmen Litton, Prin.;

St. Joseph Catholic Church, Tiff - 10120 Crest Rd., Cadet, MO 63630 t) 573-438-6181 stjoachimparish@hotmail.com Rev. Anthony A. Dattilo, Pst.;

CATAWISSA

St. James Catholic Church, Catawissa - 1107 Summit Dr., Catawissa, MO 63015; Mailing: 1587 Hwy AM, Villa Ridge, MO 63089 t) 636-451-4685 stm.stj.vr@gmail.com www.stmarys-moselle.com Rev. Mark S. Bozada, Pst.;

St. Patrick - Hwy. NN & Rock Church Rd., Armagh, MO 63015 t) 636-257-2227

CHESTERFIELD

Ascension Catholic Church, Chesterfield - 230 Santa Maria Dr., Chesterfield, MO 63005 t) 636-532-3304 parishoffice@asc.church asc.church Very Rev. Thomas M. Molini, Pst.; Rev. Kent M. Pollman, Assoc. Pst.; Rev. Stephen Schumacher, Assoc. Pst.; Dcn. C. Frank Chauvin; Dcn. Robert Keeney; Dcn. John Marino; Rev. Richard J. Bockskopf, In Res.; Robin Seiler, DRE; CRP Stds.: 397

Preschool - Ascension Early Childhood Center, 238 Santa Maria Dr, Chesterfield, MO 63005 t) 636-532-3375 littleschool@acsls.org ascensionchesterfield.org/ls-home Erica Argue, Dir.;

Ascension Catholic Church, Chesterfield School - (Grades K-8) Ascension Catholic School, 238 Santa Maria Dr, Chesterfield, MO 63005 t) 636-532-1151 principal207@archstl.org www.ascensioncatholicschool.org Joseph Kilmade, Prin.; Stds.: 412; Lay Tchrs.: 29

Incarnate Word Catholic Church - 13416 Olive Blvd., Chesterfield, MO 63017 t) 314-576-5366 x26 (CRP); 314-576-5366 lflanagan@incarnate-word.org; generalmailbox@incarnate-word.org www.incarnate-word.org Rev. Kevin Schroeder, Pst.; Rev. David J. Hogan, Assoc. Pst.; Rev. James M. Sullivan, Senior Assoc.; Dcn. Donald J. Funke Jr.; Dcn. Ronald Lee Reuther; Laura Flanagan, DRE; Andrea Brockmann, Registrar;

Incarnate Word Catholic Church School - (Grades K-8) C. Michael Welling, Prin.;

CLAYTON

St. Joseph Catholic Church, Clayton - 106 N. Meramec Ave., Clayton, MO 63105 t) 314-726-1221 parishoffice@stjosephclayton.org stjosephclayton.org/ Very Rev. Philip J. Bene, Pst.; Rev. Michael L. Donald, Assoc. Pst.; Dcn. Delfin S. Leonardo; Dcn. John J. Stoverink;

CRESTWOOD

St. Elizabeth of Hungary Catholic Church - 1420 S. Sappington Rd., Crestwood, MO 63126 t) 314-963-8868 Dcn. Robert Snyder;

Convent - 1406 S. Sappington Rd., Crestwood, MO 63126 t) 314-961-2630

CREVE COEUR

St. Monica Catholic Church - 12136 Olive Blvd., Creve Coeur, MO 63141-6629 t) 314-205-9276 jcombs@stmonicastl.org Rev. Joseph A. Weber, Pst.; Rev. Michael L. Donald; Dcn. James P. Martin; Dcn. Carl J. Sommer; James Combs, DRE;

St. Monica Catholic School - (Grades PreK-8) 12132 Olive Blvd., Creve Coeur, MO 63141-6698 t) 314-434-2173 Genevieve Callier, Prin.;

CRYSTAL CITY

Sacred Heart Catholic Church, Crystal City - 555 Bailey Rd., Crystal City, MO 63019-1798 t) 636-937-4662 sh324cc@sbcglobal.net Rev. Saji Matthew Cheruparambil, O.S.B.Silv., Pst.; Dcn. Gerard G. Stoverink;

DARDENNE PRAIRIE

Immaculate Conception Catholic Church, Dardenne - 7701 Town Square Ave., Dardenne Prairie, MO 63368 t) 636-561-1974 (PSR); 636-561-6611 (Church) psr@icdparish.org; parishoffice@icdparish.org icdparish.org Rev. Msgr. Ted L. Wojcicki, Pst.; Rev. David J. Hogan, Assoc. Pst.; Rev. Michael Lampe, Assoc. Pst.; Dcn. Paul Bast; Dcn. Brett C. LePage; Dcn. Dan Schmitt; Dcn. Lonnie G. Weishaar; Barb Morgan, DRE; CRP Stds.: 758

Immaculate Conception Catholic School - (Grades PreK-8) 2089 Hanley Rd, Dardenne Prairie, MO 63368 t) 636-561-4450 michelle.knapp@icdschool.org www.icdschool.org Michelle Knapp, Prin.; Stds.: 826; Lay Tchrs.: 38

DE SOTO

St. Rose of Lima Catholic Church, DeSoto - 504 S. Third St., De Soto, MO 63020 t) 636-337-2212 limaatstrose@sbcglobal.net Rev. Alexander R. Anderson, Pst.; Dcn. Edward J. Boyer;

St. Rose of Lima Catholic School - (Grades PreSchool-8) www.stroseparish.info

ELLISVILLE

St. Clare of Assisi Catholic Church - 15642 Clayton Rd., Ellisville, MO 63011 t) 636-394-4368 (CRP); 636-394-7307 stclare@saintclareofassisi.org www.saintclareofassisi.org Rev. Christopher M. Martin, Pst.; Rev. Andrew A Auer, Assoc. Pst.;

St. Clare of Assisi Catholic Church School - (Grades PreK-8) 15668 Clayton Rd., Ellisville, MO 63011 t) 636-227-8654 Marie Sinnett, Prin.; Susan Gier, Librn.;

ELSBERRY

Sacred Heart Catholic Church, Elsberry - 714 Lincoln St., Elsberry, MO 63343 t) 573-898-2202 parish@sacredheartelsberry.org www.sacredheartelsberry.org Rev. Charles P. Tichacek, Pst.; Rachele Presley, DRE; CRP Stds.: 33

EUREKA

Most Sacred Heart Catholic Church, Eureka - 350 E. Fourth St., Eureka, MO 63025 t) 636-938-9507 (CRP); 636-938-5048 parishsecretary@sacredhearteureka.org; bizmgr@sacredhearteureka.org www.sacredhearteureka.org Rev. Joseph G. Kempf, Pst.; Rev. Leo J. Spezia, Assoc. Pst.; Dcn. Thomas L. Eultgen; Dcn. Leo S. Fehner; Dcn. Alan W. Whitson; CRP Stds.: 245

Most Sacred Heart School - (Grades K-8) t) 636-938-4602 Monica Wilson, Prin.;

FARMINGTON

St. Joseph Catholic Church, Farmington - 10 N. Long St., Farmington, MO 63640 t) 573-756-4250 secretary@stjosephfarmington.com www.stjosephfarmington.com Very Rev. William C. Thess, Pst.; Dcn. Mark A. Byington; CRP Stds.: 42

St. Joseph Catholic Church, Farmington School - (Grades K-8) 501 Ste. Genevieve Ave., Farmington, MO 63640 t) 573-756-6312

FENTON

St. Paul Catholic Church, Fenton - 15 Forest Knoll, Fenton, MO 63026-3105 t) 636-343-1234 x132 (Bus. Mgr.); 636-343-4333 x132 (CRP) bizmgr@stpaulfenton.org; parish213@archstl.org www.stpaulfenton.org Dcn. James Bohnert; Rev. Msgr. Kevin G. Callahan, Pst.; Rev. Scott L. Scheiderer, Assoc. Pst.; Dcn. Paul Crafts; Dcn. Anthony Shipp; CRP Stds.: 148

St. Paul Catholic Church, Fenton School - (Grades PreK-8) 465 New Smizer Mill Rd., Fenton, MO 63026 www.stpaulcatholicschoolfenton.org

FERGUSON

Blessed Teresa of Calcutta Catholic Church - 120 N. Elizabeth Ave., Ferguson, MO 63135 t) 314-524-0500 parishoffice@btcparish.org btcparish.org Rev. Thomas J. Haley, Pst.; Dcn. Allen F. Love; Debbie Davisson, DRE;

Blessed Teresa of Calcutta Catholic Church School - 150 N. Elizabeth, Ferguson, MO 63135 t) 314-522-3888 Addie Govero, Prin.;

FESTUS

Our Lady Catholic Church - 1550 St. Mary Ln., Festus, MO 63028-1543 t) 636-937-5008 (CRP); 636-937-5513 gklump@olparish.org olparish.org Rev. Gregory S. Klump, Pst.; Dcn. Timothy L. Dunn;

Our Lady Catholic School - (Grades K-8) 1599 St. Mary Ln., Festus, MO 63028-1557 tkempfer@olparish.org

FLORISSANT

St. Angela Merici Catholic Church - 3860 N. Hwy. 67, Florissant, MO 63034 t) 314-838-6565 brindley@stangelam.org www.saintangelamerici.org Rev. Msgr. Matthew M. Mitas, Pst.; Dcn. Joseph C. Kroutil;

St. Angela Merici Catholic Church School - (Grades K-8) t) 314-831-8012

St. Ferdinand Catholic Church - 1765 Charbonier Rd., Florissant, MO 63031 t) 314-837-3165 stferdinandchurch@stferdinandstl.org; stferd@juno.com www.stferdinandstl.org Rev. Michael G. Murphy, Pst.; Rev. Nicholas J. Muenks, Assoc. Pst.;

St. Norbert Catholic Church - 16455 New Halls Ferry Rd., Florissant, MO 63031 deaconbill@saintnorbert.com www.saintnorbert.com Rev. James M. Mitulski, Pst.; Dcn. William H. Twellman, Pst. Assoc.; Dcn. David A. Felber;

St. Norbert Catholic Church School - (Grades K-8) 16475 New Halls Ferry Rd., Florissant, MO 63031 t) 314-839-0948 school@saintnorbert.com Joanne Hoormann, Prin.;

St. Rose Philippine Duchesne Catholic Church - 1210 Paddock Dr., Florissant, MO 63033 t) 314-837-3410 secretary@strpdparish.org www.strpdparish.org Dcn. Dennis J. Barbero; Dcn. William P. Johnson; Rev. John C. Nickolai, Pst.;

St. Sabina Catholic Church - 1625 Swallow Ln., Florissant, MO 63031; Mailing: 1365 Harkee, Florissant, MO 63031 t) 314-837-0146 (CRP); 314-837-1365 jhofmann@stsabina.com Rev. Joseph W. Banden, Pst.; Dcn. John G. Hofmann; Dcn. Gerard M. Lauterwasser; Dcn. Harold A. Strauss;

Sacred Heart Catholic Church, Florissant - 751 N. Jefferson St., Florissant, MO 63031 t) 314-837-3757 x222 (CRP); 314-837-3757 x224 mmallien@sh-flo.org www.sacredheartflorissant.org Very Rev. Msgr. Mark C. Ullrich, Pst.; Rev. Anthony J. Gerber, Assoc. Pst.; Dcn. J. John Heithaus; CRP Stds.: 10

Sacred Heart Catholic Church, Florissant School - (Grades K-8) 501 St. Louis St., Florissant, MO 63031 t) 314-831-3372 Christopher Masterson, Prin.;

HAWK POINT

St. Mary Catholic Church, Hawk Point - 458 Main St., Hawk Point, MO 63349; Mailing: P.O. Box 205, Hawk Point, MO 63349 t) 636-338-4331 marysrectory@centurytel.net Rev. John A. Keenoy, Pst.; CRP Stds.: 53

HAZELWOOD

St. Martin de Porres Catholic Church - 615 Dunn Rd., Hazelwood, MO 63042-1799 t) 314-895-1100 mdpparishmo@gmail.com www.stmartindeporresstl.com Rev. Lijo Stephen Kallarackal, O.S.B.Silv., Admin.; Dcn. David Pacino; Marilyn Saunders, DRE;

HIGH RIDGE

St. Anthony Catholic Church, High Ridge - 3009 High Ridge Blvd., High Ridge, MO 63049 t) 636-677-4868 mrskathyjoslin@yahoo.com; rusalynesahr@att.net Rev. John Reiker, Pst.; Dcn. James R. G'Sell; Dcn. Richard L. Stevens; Kathy Joslin, DRE;

HILLSBORO

Church of the Good Shepherd Catholic Church, Hillsboro - 703 Third St., Hillsboro, MO 63050-4342 Rev. Raymond Buehler, Pst.; Dcn. Paul A. Martin; Dcn.

Daniel A. Raidt;

Church of the Good Shepherd Catholic Church, Hillsboro School - (Grades PreK-8) 701 Third St., Hillsboro, MO 63050 t) 636-797-2300 Mariann Jones, Prin.;

HOUSE SPRINGS

Our Lady, Queen of Peace Catholic Church - 4696 Notre Dame Ln., House Springs, MO 63051 Rev. Dennis C. Schmidt, Pst.; Rev. James T. Beighlie, C.M., Assoc. Pst.; Dcn. Thomas Gerling; Dcn. Paul Turek;

Our Lady, Queen of Peace Catholic Church School - (Grades K-8) 4675 Notre Dame Ln., House Springs, MO 63051 t) 636-671-0247 John Boyd, Prin.; Tiffany Leicht, Librn.;

IMPERIAL

St. John, The Beloved Disciple Catholic Church - 4614 Blue Springs Dr., Imperial, MO 63052 t) 636-296-8061 office@stjohnimperial.org Very Rev. Richard V. Coerver, Pst.;

St. Joseph Catholic Church, Imperial - 6020 Old Antonia Rd., Imperial, MO 63052-0968 t) 636-464-9027 (CRP); 636-464-1013 kowensby@sjiparish.org Very Rev. Daniel G. Shaughnessy, Pst.; Rev. Peter Faimega, Assoc. Pst.; Rev. Jonathan R. Ruzicka, Assoc. Pst.; Dcn. John Robert Wolffer; Dcn. Brian T. Selsor;

St. Joseph Catholic Church, Imperial School - (Grades K-8) 6024 Old Antonia Rd., Imperial, MO 63052 Sr. Carol Sansone, A.S.C.J., Prin.;

KIRKWOOD

St. Gerard Majella Catholic Church - 1969 Dougherty Ferry Rd., Kirkwood, MO 63122 t) 314-965-3985 office@sgmparish.org www.sgmparish.org Dcn. Mark Markowski; Rev. Christopher M. Rubie; Rev. Michael J. Grosch, Pst.; Dcn. Paul J. Arthur; Dcn. Donald Denham; Dcn. Timothy Dolan; CRP Stds.: 138

St. Gerard Majella School - (Grades K-8) 2005 Dougherty Ferry Rd., Kirkwood, MO 63122 t) 314-822-8844 principal@sgmschool.org Chrisell Guthrie, Prin.;

St. Peter Catholic Church, Kirkwood - 243 W. Argonne Dr., Kirkwood, MO 63122 t) 314-821-0460 x4212 (CRP Susan Lueker); 314-966-8600 (Parish Rectory Office); (314) 821-0460 x4121 (Principal, John Freitag) info@stpeterkirkwood.org www.stpeterkirkwood.org/ Rev. Matthew L. O'Toole, Pst.; Rev. Charles J. Archer, Assoc. Pst.; Dcn. John W. Komotos; Kevin Jebron Stillman, Dir.; CRP Stds.: 330

St. Peter Catholic Church, Kirkwood School - (Grades PreK-8) 215 N. Clay St., Kirkwood, MO 63122 stpschool.com/

LADUE

Church of the Annunziata Catholic Church - 9305 Clayton Rd., Ladue, MO 63124 t) 314-993-4422 dodie@annunziata.org htto://www.annunziata.org Rev. Msgr. John J. Leykam, Pst.; Dcn. Thomas J. Gottlieb;

LEMAY

St. Bernadette Catholic Church - 68 Sherman Rd., Lemay, MO 63125 t) 314-892-6882 stbrect@mindspring.com www.churchofsaintbernadette.org Rev. Robert J. Reiker, Pst.; Dcn. Michael Buckley;

St. Martin of Tours Catholic Church - 610 W. Ripa Ave., Lemay, MO 63125 t) 314-544-5664 Rev. Noah A. Waldman, Pst.; Dcn. Edward Fronick; Dcn. Phillip Warren;

LUEBBERING

St. Francis of Assisi Catholic Church - 1000 Luebbering Rd., Luebbering, MO 63061-3100 t) 636-629-1717 parish338@archstl.org Rev. Robert D. Knight, Pst.; Alison Byerley, DRE; CRP Stds.: 15

MANCHESTER

Christ, Prince of Peace Catholic Church - 415 Weidman Rd., Manchester, MO 63011 t) 636-391-1307 cdunlap@cpopschool.com www.christprinceofpeace.com Rev. Christopher J. Dunlap, Pst.; Dcn. Patrick J. Belding; Dcn. Gregory Bialis; Rev. Dennis J. Doyle, In Res.; Andrea Bonsanti, DRE; CRP Stds.: 105

Christ, Prince of Peace Catholic Church School - (Grades PreK-8) 417 Weidman Rd., Manchester, MO 63011 t) 636-394-6840 cfichter@cpopschool.com www.cpopschool.com Cynthia Fichter, Prin.; Stds.: 226; Lay Tchrs.: 20

St. Joseph Catholic Church, Manchester - 567 St. Joseph Ln., Manchester, MO 63021 t) 636-391-1404 (CRP); 636-227-5247 mfoster@stjoemanchester.org; info@stjoemanchester.org www.stjoemanchester.org Rev. Thomas M. Pastorius, Pst.; Rev. Ricardo Escobar, Assoc. Pst.; Rev. James A. Holbrook, Assoc. Pst.; Dcn. Jimmy D. Broyles; Dcn. Daniel R. Donnelly; Dcn. George Miller; Dcn. John M Burke; Michelle Foster, DRE;

MAPLEWOOD

Immaculate Conception Catholic Church, Maplewood - 2934 Marshall Ave., Maplewood, MO 63143 t) (314) 645-3329 icmaplewood@gmail.com www.icmaplewood.org Rev. Peter M. Blake, Sacramental Min.; Dcn. John P. Flanigan Jr., Parish Life Coord.;

MARTHASVILLE

St. Ignatius Loyola Catholic Church - 19127 Mill Rd., Marthasville, MO 63357-1439 t) 636-932-4445 info@saintig.com Rev. Steven P. Robeson, Pst.; Dcn. Paul J. Hecktor;

St. Ignatius Loyola Catholic School - (Grades K-8) 19129 Mill Rd., Marthasville, MO 63357 t) 636-932-4444 www.saintig.com Arlesa Leopold, Prin.;

St. Vincent Catholic Church, Dutzow - 13497 S. State Hwy. 94, Marthasville, MO 63357 t) 636-433-2678 svchurch@centurytel.net sv-ic.org Rev. Dennis M. Doyle, Pst.;

St. Vincent Catholic Church, Dutzow School - 13495 S. State Hwy. 94, Marthasville, MO 63357 t) 636-433-2466

MARYLAND HEIGHTS

Holy Spirit Catholic Church - 3130 Parkwood Ln., Maryland Heights, MO 63043 t) 314-739-0230 parish@holyspiritstl.org www.holyspiritstl.org Rev. Robert T. Evans, Pst.; Dcn. James DeNatale; Dcn. Scott Kaufman; Rev. Gerald A. Meier, In Res.; CRP Stds.: 85

Holy Spirit Catholic Church School - (Grades K-8) t) 314-739-1934

St. John Bosco Catholic Church - 12934 Marine Ave., Maryland Heights, MO 63146 t) 314-878-6492 (CRP); 314-434-1312 x4 cindy.meirink@stjohnboscostl.com; sjb@stjohnboscostl.com sjjohnboscostl.com Rev. Joseph A. Weber, Pst.; Dcn. Paul D. Craska; Dcn. John O'Hara; Cindy Meirink, Pst. Min./Coord.; Cindy Meirink, DRE;

NEW HAVEN

Assumption Catholic Church, New Haven - 603 Miller St., New Haven, MO 63068 Rev. John C. Deken, Pst.; Dcn. H. Wayne Groner;

Holy Family Catholic Church, Port Hudson - 124 Holy Family Church Rd., New Haven, MO 63068 t) 573-459-6594 (CRP); 573-459-6441 parish352@archstl.org Rev. James J. Foster, Pst.;

St. Gerald - 404 E. Fitzgerald, Gerald, MO 63037

St. Paul Catholic Church, Berger - 603 Miller St., New Haven, MO 63068 Dcn. H. Wayne Groner; Rev. John C. Deken, Pst.;

NEW MELLE

Immaculate Heart of Mary Catholic Church, New Melle - 8 W. Hwy. D, New Melle, MO 63365-0100; Mailing: PO Box 100, New Melle, MO 63365 t) 636-398-5270 secretary@ihm-newmelle.org www.ihm-newmelle.org Rev. Thomas C. Miller, Pst.; Dcn. Christopher M. Ast; Dcn. Anthony Falbo; Dcn. Carl J. Sommer; Shawn Mueller, DRE; Bryan Beams, Liturgy Dir.; Laura Orf, Bus. Mgr.; CRP Stds.: 104

NORMANDY

St. Ann Catholic Church, Normandy - 7530 Natural Bridge Rd., Normandy, MO 63121 t) 314-385-5090 secretary@sacs-stl.org; pastor@sacs-stl.org stannchurch-stl.org Rev. Nicklaus E. Winker, Pst.;

St. Ann Catholic Church, Normandy School - (Grades K-8) 7532 Natural Bridge, Normandy, MO 63121 t) 314-381-0113 principal@sacs-stl.org Jacob Reft, Prin.;

OAKVILLE

Queen of All Saints Catholic Church - 6603 Christopher Dr., Oakville, MO 63129-4919 t) 314-380-4011 (CRP); 314-846-8207 queenparish@qasstl.org queenparish@qasstl.org Rev. Msgr. Patrick K. Hambrough, Pst.; Rev. Joseph Detwiler, Assoc. Pst.; Dcn. Richard Schellhase; Dcn. Joseph Wingbermuehle; CRP Stds.: 178

Queen of All Saints Catholic Church School - (Grades K-8) 6611 Christopher Dr., St. Louis, MO 63129 t) 314-846-0506 Shannon Sanchez, Prin.;

O'FALLON

Assumption Catholic Church, O'Fallon - 403 N. Main St., O'Fallon, MO 63366 t) 636-240-1020 (CRP); 636-240-3721 www.assumptionbvm.org Very Rev. Nicholas E. Kastenholz, Pst.; Rev. Msgr. William W. McCumber, Assoc. Pst.; Rev. Patrick Russell, Assoc. Pst.; Dcn. Richard Tadlock; Dcn. Fred N. Volansky;

Assumption Catholic Church, O'Fallon School - (Grades PreK-8) 203 W. Third St., O'Fallon, MO 63366 t) 636-240-4474 Patricia Hensley, Prin.;

St. Barnabas Catholic Church - 1400 N. Main St., O'Fallon, MO 63366 t) 636-240-4556 parish@stbarnabasofallon.org; parish380@archstl.org www.stbarnabasofallon.org Traditional Latin Mass Parish. Rev. Linus Dolce, O.S.B., Par. Admin.;

OLD MONROE

Immaculate Conception Catholic Church, Old Monroe - 110 Maryknoll Rd., Old Monroe, MO 63369 t) 636-661-5002 parish@icomparish.org Rev. Richard J. Rath, Pst.; Dcn. Neal R. Westhoff;

Immaculate Conception Catholic School - (Grades PreK-8) 120 Maryknoll Rd., Old Monroe, MO 63369 t) 636-661-5156; 636-665-5463 jpalmer@icomparish.org icomparish.org/school Janice Palmer, Prin.;

OVERLAND

All Souls Catholic Church - 9550 Tennyson Ave., Overland, MO 63114 t) 314-427-0442 mminner311@gmail.com; smmshelton89@gmail.com allsoulsparishoverland.org Rev. Anthony B. Ochoa, Pst.; Dcn. Samuel Lee; CRP Stds.: 100

St. Jude Catholic Church - 2218 N. Warson Rd., Overland, MO 63114 Rev. James C. Gray, Pst.;

Our Lady of the Presentation Catholic Church - 8860 Tudor Ave., Overland, MO 63114 t) 314-427-0486 x201 olpresentation@hotmail.com olpchurch.weconnect.com Rev. Mark A. Dolan, Pst.;

PACIFIC

St. Bridget of Kidare Catholic Church - 111 W. Union St., Pacific, MO 63069 t) 636-271-3993 x201 parishoffice@sbkschool.org www.sbkparish.org/ Rev. Andrew V. Burkemper, Pst.; James Bornholdt; Dcn. Dean Mandis; Dcn. Michael E. Suden;

St. Bridget of Kidare Catholic Church School - t) 636-257-4533 Anne Hanneken, Prin.;

PARK HILLS

Immaculate Conception Catholic Church, Park Hills - 1020 W. Main St., Park Hills, MO 63601; Mailing: P O Box 66, Park Hills, MO 63601-0066 t) 573-431-2427 icsja@icsja.net; icsjapastor@icsja.net www.icsja.org Dcn. Michael D. Burch, DRE;

St. John - Maple St. & Walnut St., Bismarck, MO 63624 icsja.org

PERRYVILLE

Christ the Savior Catholic Church - 55 Shady Ln., Perryville, MO 63775; Mailing: 1010 Rosati Ct., Perryville, MO 63775 t) 573-547-4300 svdepaul@svdepaul.org Rev. Joseph C. Geders, C.M., Pst.; Rev. Ben Melaku, Assoc. Pst.;

Our Lady of Victory Catholic Church - 172 PCR 920, Perryville, MO 63775; Mailing: 1010 Rosati Ct., Perryville, MO 63775 t) 573-547-4300 svdepaul@svdepaul.org www.svdepaul.org Rev. Joseph C. Geders, C.M., Pst.; Rev. Ben Melaku, Pst. Assoc.;

St. Rose of Lima Catholic Church, Silver Lake - 10138 Hwy. T, Perryville, MO 63775; Mailing: 1010 Rosati Ct.,

Perryville, MO 63775 t) 573-547-4300 svdepaul@svdepaul.org Rev. Joseph C. Geders, C.M., Pst.; Rev. Ben Melaku, Pst. Assoc.;

St. Vincent De Paul Catholic Church, Perryville - 1000 Rosati Ct., Perryville, MO 63775; Mailing: 1010 Rosati Ct., Perryville, MO 63775 t) 573-547-4300 x3 svdepaul@svdepaul.org www.svdepaul.org Rev. Joseph C. Geders, C.M., Pst.; Rev. Ben Melaku, Pst. Assoc.; CRP Stds.: 253

Parish Center - 1010 Rosati Ct., Perryville, MO 63775

St. Vincent De Paul Catholic Church, Perryville School - (Grades K-6) 1007 W. St. Joseph St., Perryville, MO 63775 Ben Johnson, Prin.;

St. Vincent De Paul Catholic Church, Perryville High School - 210 S. Water St., Perryville, MO 63775 Patricia Hensley, Prin.;

St. Joseph -

St. James -

PORTAGE DES SIOUX

St. Francis of Assisi Catholic Church, Portage des Sioux - 1355 Farnham St., Portage Des Sioux, MO 63373; Mailing: P.O. Box 129, Portage Des Sioux, MO 63373

Immaculate Conception - 14060 Hwy. 94 N., West Alton, MO 63386 t) 636-899-0906

POTOSI

St. James Catholic Church, Potosi - 201 N. Missouri Ave., Potosi, MO 63664 Rev. Rodger P. Fleming, Pst.;

RICHMOND HEIGHTS

Immacolata Catholic Church - 8900 Clayton Rd., Richmond Heights, MO 63117 t) 314-991-5700 x303 (CRP); 314-991-5700 x311 (Parish) choffmeyer@immacolata.org www.immacolata.org Rev. Msgr. Vernon E. Gardin, Pst.; Rev. Conor M. Sullivan, In Res.; CRP Stds.: 70

Immacolata Catholic Church School - (Grades PreK-8) 8910 Clayton Rd., Richmond Heights, MO 63117 t) (314) 991-5700 x302 jstutsman@immacolata.org Jennifer Stutsman, Prin.;

Little Flower Catholic Church - 1264 Arch Ter., Richmond Heights, MO 63117 littleflower@little-flower-parish.org www.little-flower-parish.org Rev. Lawrence A. Herzog, Pst.;

Little Flower Catholic Church School - (Grades PreK-8) 1275 Boland Pl., Richmond Heights, MO 63117 t) 314-781-4995 Robert Baird, Prin.;

Oratory of Saint Gregory and Saint Augustine - 7230 Dale Ave., Richmond Heights, MO 63117 t) 314-644-2144 office@oratorysga.org stlouislatinmass.com Rev. Msgr. C. Eugene Morris, Rector; Donna Mueller, Bus. Mgr.; Jake Fowler, DRE; CRP Stds.: 107

RICHWOODS

St. Stephen Catholic Church - 11514 Hwy. A, Richwoods, MO 63071-0233; Mailing: PO Box 233, Richwoods, MO 63071 t) 573-678-2207 parish354@archstl.org www.ststephenrichwoodsmo.com Rev. Robert D. Knight, Pst.;

SAINT LOUIS

St. Andrew Kim Catholic Church - 13996 Olive Blvd., Saint Louis, MO 63017

SHREWSBURY

St. Michael Catholic Church - 7622 Sutherland Ave., Shrewsbury, MO 63119 t) 314-647-5611 Rev. Michael J. Grosch, Pst.;

SILEX

St. Alphonsus Catholic Church, Millwood - 29 St. Alphonsus Rd., Silex, MO 63377 Rev. Charles P. Tichacek, Admin.;

St. Alphonsus School - t) 573-384-5305

ST. CHARLES

St. Charles Borromeo Catholic Church - 601 N. 4th St., St. Charles, MO 63301 t) 636-946-2916 (CRP); 636-946-1893 office@borromeoparish.com; sister@borromeoparish.com www.borromeoparish.com Rev. William F. Dotson, Pst.; Rev. John Paul Hopping, Assoc. Pst.; Rev. Edward J. Godefroid, Assoc. Pst.; Dcn. Donald L. McElroy; Dcn. Jorge A. Perez;

St. Charles Borromeo Catholic Church School - (Grades PreK-8) 431 Decatur St., St. Charles, MO 63301 t) 636-946-2713 office@borromeoschool.com www.borromeoschool.org

St. Cletus - 2705 Zumbehl Rd., St. Charles, MO 63301 t) 636-255-1717 Rev. James J. Benz, Pst.; Rev. Mark Whitman, Assoc. Pst.; Dcn. Mark McCarthy; Dcn. Frank Olmsted;

St. Cletus School - 2721 Zumbehl Rd., St. Charles, MO 63301 t) 636-946-7756

St. Elizabeth Ann Seton Catholic Church - 2 Seton Ct., St. Charles, MO 63303 t) 636-946-6717 x504 info@setonscene.org setonscene.org/ Rev. Robert W. Burkemper, Pst.; Rev. Frank A. D'Amico, Assoc. Pst.; Dcn. David W. Ewing; Dcn. Robert J. Mayo II; Linda Rathz, DRE; CRP Stds.: 209

Seton Regional Catholic School - 1 Seton Ct., St. Charles, MO 63303 t) 636-946-6716

Sts. Joachim and Ann Catholic Church, St. Charles - 4112 McClay Rd., St. Charles, MO 63304 t) 636-441-7503; 636-926-0021 (CRP); 636-441-4835 frbrockland@stsja.org; psr@stsja.org www.stsja.org Rev. John A. Brockland, Pst.; Rev. James L. Gahan, Assoc. Pst.; Dcn. Vince Baker; Dcn. A. John Lipin; Dcn. William L Scarry; Dcn. Timothy Schultz; Dcn. Phillip Uro; Rose Wieschhaus, DRE; CRP Stds.: 409

Sts. Joachim and Ann Catholic School - (Grades PreK-8) 4110 McClay Rd., St. Charles, MO 63304-7915 Sue Schutz, Prin.; Stds.: 181; Lay Tchrs.: 15

St. Joseph Catholic Church, Cottleville - 1355 Motherhead Rd., St. Charles, MO 63304 t) 636-441-0055 x300 (CRP); 636-441-0055 parish@stjoecot.org; mdoerr@stjoecot.org stjoecot.org Rev. Msgr. James P. Callahan, Pst.; Rev. Alexander M. Nord, Assoc. Pst.; Rev. Dane Westhoff, Assoc. Pst.; Dcn. Thomas A. Burke III; Dcn. Michael Piva; Mary Doerr, DRE;

St. Joseph Catholic School - (Grades PreK-8) 1351 Motherhead Rd., St. Charles, MO 63304 info@stjoecot.org www.stjoecot.org/school Sr. Kateri Rose Masters, Prin.; Brad Benne, Vice Prin.;

Convent - 1353 Motherhead Rd., St. Charles, MO 63304 t) 636-244-2257

St. Peter Catholic Church, St. Charles - 221 First Capitol Dr., St. Charles, MO 63301 t) 636-946-6641 stpeterparish@stpstc.org Rev. John M. Seper, Pst.; Dcn. Lawrence R. Boldt; Dcn. Timothy H. Dallas; Dcn. Fred M. Haehnel;

St. Robert Bellarmine Catholic Church - 1424 First Capitol Dr. S., St. Charles, MO 63303 t) 636-946-6799 x11; 636-946-6799 x12 deaconphil@strbellarmine.com; lschueddig@strbellarmine.com www.strbellarmine.com Rev. Mark Whitman, Assoc. Pst.; Dcn. Philip King, Parish Life Coord.; Dcn. Joseph C. Meiergerd; Dcn. Manolo Rivera; Rev. Msgr. Raymond A. Hampe, In Res.;

Seton Regional Catholic School -

ST. CLAIR

St. Clare Catholic Church, St. Clair - 165 E. Springfield St., St. Clair, MO 63077 t) 636-629-0315 parish358@archstl.org Rev. Eric J. Kunz, Pst.; Dcn. Harvey Dubbs; Dcn. Trevor J Wild;

ST. LOUIS

Cathedral Basilica of Saint Louis Catholic Church - 4431 Lindell Blvd., St. Louis, MO 63108 t) 314-373-8200; 314-373-8202 parish@cathedralstl.org; laurav@cathedralstl.org www.cathedralstl.org Rev. Msgr. Henry J. Breier, Rector; Rev. Joseph Xiu Hui Jiang, Assoc. Pst.; Rev. Msgr. Gregory R. Mikesch, Assoc. Pst.; Rev. Zachary D. Povis, Par. Vicar; Dcn. John A. Curtin; Dcn. John J. Stoverink; Dcn. H. Matthew Witte;

St. Agatha Catholic Church - 3239 S. Ninth St., St. Louis, MO 63118 t) 314-772-1603 parishoffice@polishchurchstlouis.org www.polishchurchstlouis.org Stanislaw Poszwa, Admin.;

St. Alphonsus Liguori Catholic Church - 1118 N. Grand Blvd., St. Louis, MO 63106 t) 314-533-0304 stalphonsusrock.org Rev. Stephen Joseph Benden, C.Ss.R., Pst.; Rev. Rodney Olive, C.Ss.R., Assoc. Pst.; Bro. Stephen Fruge, C.Ss.R., Pastoral Staff; Rev. Thomas Donaldson, C.Ss.R., In Res.; Rev. Peter Schavitz, C.Ss.R., In Res.;

St. Ambrose Catholic Church - 5130 Wilson Ave., St. Louis, MO 63110 t) 314-771-1228 jfragale@stambroseonthehill.com Rev. Msgr. Vincent R. Bommarito, Pst.; Dcn. Joseph A. Fragale;

St. Ambrose Catholic Church School - (Grades K-8) 5110 Wilson Ave., St. Louis, MO 63110 t) 314-772-1437 stambroseonthehill.com Barbara Zipoli, Prin.;

St. Andrew Catholic Church - 309 Hoffmeister Ave., St. Louis, MO 63125-1609 t) 314-631-5135 (CRP); 314-631-0691 saintandrew@sbcglobal.net Rev. Philip D. Krill, Pst.; Mary Boedeker, DRE;

St. Anselm Catholic Church - 530 S. Mason Rd., St. Louis, MO 63141-8522 t) 314-878-2120 parishoffice@stanselmstl.org www.stanselmstl.org Rev. Aidan McDermott, O.S.B., Pst.; Rev. Francis Hein, O.S.B., Assoc. Pst.; Greg Siemer, DRE;

St. Anthony of Padua Catholic Church - 3140 Meramec St., St. Louis, MO 63118 t) 314-353-7470 www.stanthonyofpaduastl.com Rev. James Lause, O.F.M., Pst.; Rev. Andrew Lewandowski, O.F.M., Assoc. Pst.;

Assumption Catholic Church, Mattese - 4725 Mattis Rd., St. Louis, MO 63128 t) 314-487-7970 parish227@archstl.org www.assumptionstl.org Rev. Thomas G. Keller, Pst.; Rev. Raymond Buehler, Assoc. Pst.; Dcn. Charles T. Ryder; Dcn. David Schaefer; Dcn. Michael Thompson; Dcn. James Sigillito, Bus. Mgr.; Valerie Stringer, DRE; CRP Stds.: 92

Assumption Catholic Church, Mattese School - (Grades PreSchool-8) 4709 Mattis Rd, St. Louis, MO 63128 t) 314-487-6520 sykoraj@assumptionstl.org Jenn Sykora, Prin.; Stds.: 227; Lay Tchrs.: 13

St. Augustine Catholic Church - 1371 Hamilton Ave., St. Louis, MO 63112 t) 314-385-1934 st.augustine.cc@sbcglobal.net st-augustine-stl.org Rev. Msgr. Robert J. Gettinger, Rev. Msgr.; Rev. Christopher Adinuba, In Res.; Dcn. Edward R. Grotpeter;

Basilica of St. Louis, King of France Catholic Church - 209 Walnut St., St. Louis, MO 63102 t) 314-231-3250 oldcathedral@att.net www.oldcathedralstl.org/ Rev. Nicholas W. Smith, Pst.; Rev. Charles K. Samson, In Res.;

St. Catherine Laboure Catholic Church - 9740 Sappington Rd., St. Louis, MO 63128 t) 314-843-3245 x223 (CRP); 314-843-3245 informatioon@sclparish.org; jcormack@sclparish.org www.sclparish.org Rev. James B. Cormack, C.M., Pst.; Rev. Charles E. Prost, C.M., Assoc. Pst.; Dcn. Timothy J. Woods; Peggy Brinkmann, DRE;

St. Catherine Laboure Catholic Church School - (Grades K-8) 9750 Sappington Rd., St. Louis, MO 63128 t) 314-843-2819 Laurie Jost, Prin.;

St. Cecilia Catholic Church - 5418 Louisiana Ave., St. Louis, MO 63111 t) 314-351-1318 parish140@archstl.org www.stceciliaparishstl.org Rev. James R. Michler, In Res.; Rev. Timothy J. Noelker, Pst.; CRP Stds.: 85

St. Clement of Rome Catholic Church - 1510 Bopp Rd., St. Louis, MO 63131 t) 314-965-0709 saintclementoffice@yahoo.com www.stclementcatholicchurch.org Rev. Msgr. Michael T. Butler, Pst.; Rev. Msgr. Timothy P. Cronin, Assoc. Pst.; Dcn. Richard Vehige; Jesse Egbert, DRE; Barb Yoffie, DRE;

St. Clement of Rome Catholic Church School - (Grades PreK-8) 1508 Bopp Rd., St. Louis, MO 63131 t) 314-822-1903 www.stclementschool.com Sue Cunningham, Prin.;

St. Cronan Catholic Church - 1202 S. Boyle Ave., St. Louis, MO 63110 t) 314-256-9350 (CRP); 314-289-9384 parish143@archstl.org stcronan.org/ Rev. Msgr. A. John Schuler, Pst.; Mary Ward, Admin.; Diane Gozdzialski, Pst. Assoc.;

Cure' of Ars Catholic Church - 670 S. Laclede Station Rd., St. Louis, MO 63119-4910 t) 314-962-5883 cureofarsparishoffice@gmail.com cureofarsparish.org Rev. James J. Byrnes, Pst.; Dcn. Patrick G. Monahan;

St. Elizabeth, Mother of John the Baptist Catholic Church - 4330 Shreve Ave., St. Louis, MO 63115 Rev. Stephen P. Giljum, Pst.; Rev. J. Edward Vogler, In Res.;

Epiphany of Our Lord Catholic Church - 6596 Smiley Ave., St. Louis, MO 63139 t) 314-781-1199 parish104@archstl.org www.epiphanystl.org Rev. Michael Rennier, Pst.; CRP Stds.: 65

St. Francis of Assisi Catholic Church, Oakville - 4556 Telegraph Rd., St. Louis, MO 63129 t) 314-487-5736 x125 (CRP); 314-487-5736 parishoffice@sfastl.org Rev. Anthony R. Yates, Pst.; Rev. George Staley, Assoc. Pst.; Dcn. John DuFaux;

St. Francis of Assisi Catholic School - (Grades K-8) 4550 Telegraph Rd., St. Louis, MO 63129 D. Gregory Sturgill, Prin.;

St. Francis Xavier Catholic Church - 3628 Lindell Blvd., St. Louis, MO 63108 t) 314-977-7300; 314-977-7302 (CRP) church@slu.edu sfxstl.org (College) Rev. Daniel P. White, S.J., Pst.; Rev. Tom Cwik, S.J., Assoc. Pst.; Katie Jansen-Larson, Admin.;

St. Gabriel the Archangel Catholic Church - 6303 Nottingham Ave., St. Louis, MO 63109 t) 314-353-6303 parish149@archstl.org Rev. Msgr. John B. Shamleffer, Pst.; Rev. Mark R Madden, Assoc. Pst.; Rev. Msgr. Joseph M. Simon, In Res.; Dcn. David J. Willis;

St. Gabriel the Archangel Catholic School - 4711 Tamm Ave., St. Louis, MO 63109 t) 314-353-1229

St. George Catholic Church - 4980 Heege Rd., St. Louis, MO 63123 t) 314-353-7629 Rev. Christopher F. Holtmann, Pst.;

Holy Name of Jesus Catholic Church - 10235 Ashbrook Dr., St. Louis, MO 63137 t) 314-868-2310 parishoffice10235@sbcglobal.net www.holynamestlouis.org Rev. Michael L. Henning, Pst.; Rev. Raymond Iwuji, In Res.; Dcn. Matthew E. Duban; Dcn. George H. Watson;

Christ Light of the Nations - 1650 Redman Rd., St. Louis, MO 63138 t) 314-741-0400 st_mary@christlightofthenations.com www.christlightofthenations.com Sr. Mary Lawrence, S.S.N.D., Prin.; Sr. Nancy Becker, S.S.N.D., DRE;

Immaculate Heart of Mary Catholic Church, St. Louis - 4092 Blow St., St. Louis, MO 63116 t) 314-481-7543 adonohue@ihm-stl.org Rev. Kristian C. Teater, Pst.; Dcn. James W. Murphey Jr.;

St. James the Greater Catholic Church - 6401 Wade Ave., St. Louis, MO 63139 t) 314-645-0167 contactchurch@stjamesthegreater.org www.stjamesthegreater.org Rev. Richard J. Quirk, Pst.; Dcn. Michael A. Nicolai;

St. Joan of Arc Catholic Church - 5800 Oleatha Ave., St. Louis, MO 63139 t) 314-832-2838 Rev. Msgr. Vincent Bommarito, Pst.; Dcn. Daniel H. Henroid; Dcn. John McManemin;

South City Catholic Academy - 5821 Pernod, St. Louis, MO 63139

St. John Nepomuk Catholic Church - 1625 S. 11th St., St. Louis, MO 63104 t) 314-231-0141 josephiovanna@archstl.org Dcn. Joseph Iovanna, Dir.;

St. John Paul II Catholic Church - 4980 Heege Rd., St. Louis, MO 63123; Mailing: 6120 Pebble Hill Dr., St. Louis, MO 63123 t) 314-353-7629 Rev. Christopher F. Holtmann, Pst.;

Holy Cross Academy - (Grades PreK-8) 7748 Mackenzie Rd., Affton, MO 63123 t) 314-832-4161 Dr. Gregory A. Densberger, Prin.;

St. John the Apostle and Evangelist Catholic Church - 15 Plaza Sq., St. Louis, MO 63103 t) 314-421-3467 parish154@archstl.org www.stjohnapostleandevangelist.org Rev. Msgr. Dennis M. Delaney, Pst.;

St. John the Baptist Catholic Church, St. Louis - 4200 Delor St., St. Louis, MO 63116 t) 314-353-1255; 314-773-3070 (CRP) sjb4200@sjbstl.org; rectory@sjbstl.org www.sjbstl.org Rev. Mitchell S. Doyen, Pst.; Dcn. Dana Engelhardt; Dcn. George H. Watson, DRE; CRP Stds.: 72

St. Joseph Croatian Catholic Church - 2112 S. 12th St., St. Louis, MO 63104 t) 314-771-0958 Rev. Stjepan Pandzic, O.F.M., Pst.;

St. Luke the Evangelist Catholic Church - 7230 Dale Ave., St. Louis, MO 63117 t) 314-644-2144 office@stlukestl.org stlukestl.org Rev. Peter M. Blake, Pst.; Dcn. David Osmack;

St. Margaret Mary Alacoque Catholic Church - 4900 Ringer Rd., St. Louis, MO 63129 t) 314-487-2522 x201 sbrandt@smmaparish.org www.smmaparish.org Rev. Msgr. Norbert A. Ernst, Pst.; Rev. Samuel M Inameti, Assoc. Pst.; Rev. Msgr. William J. Leach, In Res.; Dcn. Andrew Daus; Dcn. Robert Orr;

St. Margaret Mary Alacoque Catholic Church School - (Grades PreSchool-8) 4900 Ringer Road, St. Louis, MO 63129 t) 314-487-1666 Stds.: 450; Lay Tchrs.: 28

St. Margaret of Scotland Catholic Church - 3854 Flad Ave., St. Louis, MO 63110 t) 314-776-0363 parishoffice@stmargaretstl.org www.stmargaretstl.org Rev. John Rogers Vien, Pst.; CRP Stds.: 17

St. Margaret of Scotland Catholic Church School - (Grades PreK-8) 3964 Castleman, St. Louis, MO 63110 t) 314-776-7837 smos-school.org

St. Mark Catholic Church, Affton - 4200 Ripa Ave., St. Louis, MO 63125 t) 314-743-8600 secretary@stmarkstl.com www.stmarkstl.com Rev. Brian E. Hecktor, Par. Admin.;

St. Mark Catholic School - (Grades PreK-8) 4220 Ripa Ave., St. Louis, MO 63125 t) 314-743-8640 malthage@stmarkstl.com; principal@stmarkstl.com

Sts. Mary and Joseph Catholic Church - 6304 Minnesota Ave., St. Louis, MO 63111 Rev. Ronald J. Hopmeir, Chap.;

St. Mary Magdalen Catholic Church, St. Louis - 4924 Bancroft Ave., St. Louis, MO 63109 t) 314-773-3070 (CRP); 314-352-2111 smmadmin@sbcglobal.net www.magdalen.org Dcn. William G. Weiss; Rev. Brian S. Fallon, Pst.;

South City Deanery Parish School of Religion - 4170 Delor, St. Louis, MO 63116

St. Mary of Victories Catholic Church and St. Stephen of Hungary Chapel - 744 S. 3rd St., St. Louis, MO 63102 t) 314-231-8101 charlessamson@archstl.org www.smov.info Rev. Charles K. Samson, Chap.;

Mary, Mother of the Church Catholic Church - 5901 Kerth Rd., St. Louis, MO 63128 t) 314-894-1373 parish228@archstl.org; agaravaglia@marymother.org www.marymother.org Very Rev. Charles W. Barthel, Pst.; Dcn. Randy C. Howe; Dcn. Richard Coffman; Dcn. Robert S. Smerek; CRP Stds.: 100

St. Matthew, Apostle Catholic Church - 2715 N. Sarah St., St. Louis, MO 63113 t) 314-531-6443 stmatthews@sbcglobal.net stmatthewtheapostle.org Rev. Timothy McMahon, SJ, Pst. Assoc.; Cheryl Archibald, Parish Life Coord.; Cheryl Archibald, Parish Life Coord.;

St. Matthias Catholic Church - 796 Buckley Rd., St. Louis, MO 63125 t) 314-892-5109 Rev. Dennis R. Port, Pst.; Dcn. Charles R. Bacher;

Most Holy Trinity Catholic Church - 3519 N. Fourteenth St., St. Louis, MO 63107-3796 Rev. Aidan McDermott, O.S.B., Sacramental Min.; Sr. Janice Munier, S.S.N.D., Parish Life Coord.;

St. Nicholas Catholic Church - 701 N. 18th St., St. Louis, MO 63103 Rev. Arthur J. Cavitt, Pst.; Rev. McDonald Nah, In Res.;

Oratory of St. Francis de Sales - 2653 Ohio Ave., St. Louis, MO 63118 t) 314-771-3100 sfds@institute-christ-king.org www.institute-christ-king.org Extraordinary Form of the Roman Rite Administered by the Institute of Christ the King Sovereign Priest. Rev. Canon Pierre Dumain, ICRSP, Vicar; Rev. Canon Benjamin L Coggeshall, ICRSP, Rector; CRP Stds.: 130

Our Lady of Guadalupe Catholic Church - 1115 S. Florissant Rd., St. Louis, MO 63121 t) 314-522-9264 Rev. Eric F. Olsen, Pst.; Sr. Cathy Doherty, S.S.N.D., Pst. Assoc.;

Our Lady of Guadalupe Catholic Church School - (Grades PreK-8) t) 314-524-1948 Peggy O'Brien, Prin.;

Our Lady of Providence Catholic Church - 8866 Pardee Rd., St. Louis, MO 63123 Rev. Richard J. Schilli, Pst.; Dcn. David Amelotti;

Our Lady of Sorrows Catholic Church - 5020 Rhodes Ave., St. Louis, MO 63109 t) 314-351-1600 parishoffice@olsorrows.org olsorrows.org Rev. Sebastian Mundackal, O.S.B., Pst.; Rev. Andrew J. Sigmund, In Res.; Dcn. Daniel Skillman; CRP Stds.: 25

Our Lady of the Holy Cross Catholic Church - 8115 Church Rd., St. Louis, MO 63147; Mailing: 1018 Baden Ave., Saint Louis, MO 63147 t) 314-381-0323; 314-381-0326 parish116@archstl.org www.olhcstl.org Rev. Vincent R. Nyman, Pst.;

Our Lady of the Pillar Catholic Church - 401 S. Lindbergh Blvd., St. Louis, MO 63131 t) 314-993-2280; 314-993-2280 x208 (CRP) ftustanowsky@olpillar.com; parishsecretary@olpillar.com www.olpillar.com Rev. Thomas French, S.M., Pst.; Rev. George James Cerniglia, SM, Assoc. Pst.; Dcn. Frederick S. Tustanowsky; CRP Stds.: 106

Our Lady of the Pillar Catholic School - (Grades PreK-8) 403 S. Lindbergh Blvd., St. Louis, MO 63131 t) 314-993-3353 hfanning@olpillar.com

Sts. Peter and Paul Catholic Church - 1919 S. 7th St, St. Louis, MO 63104-4029 t) 314-231-9923 office@stspeterandpaulstl.org stspeterandpaulstl.org Rev. Bruce H. Forman, Pst.; Dcn. Thomas Gorski;

St. Pius V Catholic Church - 3310 S. Grand Blvd., St. Louis, MO 63118 t) 314-772-1525 piusvrectory@sbcglobal.net stpiusv.org Very Rev. Paul J. Niemann, Pst.;

St. Raphael the Archangel Catholic Church - 6047 Bishops Pl., St. Louis, MO 63109 Rev. Robert J. Reiker, Pst.; Dcn. Ronald A. Holmes, Pst. Assoc.; Dcn. Gerald Geiser;

St. Raphael the Archangel Catholic Church School - (Grades K-8) 6000 Jamieson, St. Louis, MO 63109 t) 314-352-9474 Kim Vangel, Prin.;

Resurrection of Our Lord Catholic Church - 3900 Meramec St., St. Louis, MO 63116 t) 314-832-7023 thuynguyenmtg@gmail.com Rev. Khien Mai (John) Luu, S.V.D., Pst.; Rev. Chinh Quang Tran, SVD, Assoc. Pst.; Bro. Larry Camilleri, S.V.D., In Res.;

St. Richard Catholic Church - 11223 Schuetz Rd., St. Louis, MO 63146 t) 314-432-6224 vtonsor@strichardstl.org www.strichardstl.org Rev. Philip D. Krill, Pst.; Dcn. John A. Bischof;

St. Rita Catholic Church - 8240 Washington St., St. Louis, MO 63114 t) 314-428-4845 parish249@archstl.org www.stritacatholicchurch.org Very Rev. Michael E. Turek, Pst.; Dcn. David I. Harpring, Parish Life Coord.;

St. Roch Catholic Church - 6052 Waterman Blvd., St. Louis, MO 63112 t) 314-721-6340 linda@strochparish.org Rev. Msgr. Salvatore E. Polizzi, Pst.;

St. Roch Catholic School - (Grades PreK-8) 6040 Waterman Blvd., St. Louis, MO 63112 t) 314-721-2595 markg@strochschool.org Mark Gilligan, Prin.;

Seven Holy Founders Catholic Church - 6741 Rock Hill Rd., St. Louis, MO 63123; Mailing: 6820 Aliceton Ave., St. Louis, MO 63123 t) 314-638-3938 www.foundersaffton.org/ Rev. Msgr. John J. Brennell, Pst.; Dcn. Thomas A. Schiller; Dcn. Charles Lombardo;

Shrine of St. Joseph - 1220 N. 11th St., St. Louis, MO 63106-4614 t) 314-231-9407 kdfinazzo@yahoo.com; allen4651@yahoo.com www.shrineofstjoseph.org Rev. Dale P. Wunderlich, Rector;

St. Simon the Apostle Catholic Church - 11011 Mueller Rd., St. Louis, MO 63123 Rev. Bradley E. Modde, Pst.; Rev. Thomas J. Santen, Assoc. Pst.; Dcn. David Camden, Assoc. Pst.; Dcn. Paul F. Stackle;

Preschool - 11015 Mueller Rd., St. Louis, MO 63123 t) 314-842-3848 x3 simonsays@stsimonchurch.org www.simonsaysecc.com

St. Simon the Apostle Catholic Church School - (Grades K-8) 11019 Mueller Rd., St. Louis, MO 63123 t) 314-842-3848 x2 principal@stsimonschool.org

St. Stephen Protomartyr Catholic Church - 3949 Wilmington Ave., St. Louis, MO 63116 t) 314-481-1133 info@saintstephenstl.org saintstephenstl.org Rev. Ronald J. Hopmeir, Pst.;

St. Stephen Protomartyr Catholic Church School - (Grades K-8) 3923 Wilmington Ave., St. Louis, MO 63116 t) 314-752-4700 Michel Wendell, Prin.;

Sts. Teresa and Bridget Catholic Church - 3636 N. Market, St. Louis, MO 63113 t) 314-371-1190 pastor@ststb.org; drt@cicbservice.com www.ststb.org Rev. Timothy R. Cook, Pst.; Dcn. Charles M. Allen;

St. Vincent De Paul Catholic Church, St. Louis - 1408 S. Tenth St., St. Louis, MO 63104 t) 314-231-9328 (CRP); 314-420-8450 lmertz@stvstl.org; efmurphy@stvstl.org Rev. Edward F. Murphy, C.M., Pst.; Linda Mertz, DRE; Rev. James T. Beighlie, C.M., Confrere in Service;

St. Wenceslaus Catholic Church - 3014 Oregon Ave., St. Louis, MO 63118 t) 314-776-0883 stwencebulletin@sbcglobal.net Rev. Philip Sosa, M.S.F., Pst.;

ST. MARY

Immaculate Conception Catholic Church, St. Mary - 481 Pine St., St. Mary, MO 63673; Mailing: P.O. Box 27, St. Mary, MO 63673 Rev. Richard C. Kasznel, Pst.;

Sacred Heart Catholic Church, Ozoro - 17742 State Rte. N., St. Mary, MO 63673 Rev. James W. Schaefer, Pst.;

Convent - 17740 State Rte. N, St. Mary, MO 63673 t) 573-543-2997

ST. PAUL

St. Paul Catholic Church, St. Paul - 1223 Church Rd., St. Paul, MO 63366 t) 314-574-4483 (CRP); 636-978-1900 bmarishchen@st-paulchurch.org; parishcenter@st-paulchurch.org www.st-paulchurch.org Rev. Gerald J. Blessing, Pst.; Dcn. Robert J. Marischen; CRP Stds.: 58

St. Paul Catholic Church, St. Paul School - (Grades PreK-8) 1235 Church Rd., St. Paul, MO 63366 principal@stpaulknights.org Kelly Kaimann, Prin.;

ST. PETERS

All Saints Catholic Church, St. Peters - 7 McMenamy Rd., St. Peters, MO 63376 t) 636-397-6995 (CRP); 636-397-1440 x221 asparish@allsaints-stpeters.org Rev. Donald R. Wester, Pst.; Rev. Robert J. Suit, Assoc. Pst.; Rev. Joseph E. Wormek, Assoc. Pst.; Dcn. Gary Meyerkord; Dcn. Jorge A. Perez; Marya Pohlmeier, DRE;

All Saints Catholic School - (Grades K-8) 5 McMenamy Rd., Saint Peters, MO 63376; Mailing: 7 McMenamy Rd., Saint Peters, MO 63376 t) 636-397-1477 Rae Ann Kielty, Prin.;

STE. GENEVIEVE

St. Catherine of Alexandria - 23496 State Rte. WW, Ste. Genevieve, MO 63670; Mailing: 10 N. Long St., Farmington, MO 63640 t) 573-756-4250 secretary@stjosephfarmington.com Very Rev. William C. Thess, Pst. Min./Coord.;

St. Joseph Catholic Church, Zell - 11824 Zell Rd., Ste. Genevieve, MO 63670 Rev. Msgr. Jeffrey N. Knight, Pst.;

St. Joseph School - t) 573-883-5097

Our Lady, Help of Christians Catholic Church - 13370 Hwy. 32, Ste. Genevieve, MO 63670-9402 t) 573-883-3796 helpofchristians@hughes.net Rev. Francis F. Koeninger, Pst.;

Sts. Philip and James Catholic Church - 18411 River Aux Vases Church Rd., Ste. Genevieve, MO 63670 Rev. Gregory S. Klump, Pst.;

Ste. Genevieve Catholic Church, Ste. Genevieve - 49 DuBourg Pl., Ste. Genevieve, MO 63670; Mailing: 20 N. 4th St., Ste. Genevieve, MO 63670 t) 573-883-2731 happylaney@hotmail.com; nemethe@stegenevieveparish.com Rev. Edward G. Nemeth, Pst.; Rev. Mitchell Baer, Assoc. Pst.; Dcn. John F. Meere; Dcn. James M. Robert; CRP Stds.: 70

Ste. Genevieve Catholic Church, Ste. Genevieve School - 40 N. Fourth St., Ste. Genevieve, MO 63670 t) 573-883-2403 overmanna@valleschools.org Amanda Overmann, Prin.;

Valle High School - 40 N. 4th St., Ste. Genevieve, MO 63670 t) 573-883-7496 millerg@valleschools.org Elaine Mooney, Prin.;

SULLIVAN

St. Anthony Catholic Church, Sullivan - 201 W. Springfield Ave., Sullivan, MO 63080 t) 573-468-6101 sachurch@fidmail.com Rev. Paul E. Telken, Pst.; Dcn. Kevin R. Miller; CRP Stds.: 29

St. Anthony Catholic School - (Grades K-8) 119 W. Springfield Ave., Sullivan, MO 63080 t) 573-468-4423 principal365@archstl.org Mary Wooley, Prin.; Stds.: 39; Lay Tchrs.: 5

Church of the Holy Martyrs of Japan Catholic Church - 8244 Hwy. AE, Sullivan, MO 63080-3229 t) 573-627-3378 parish333@archstl.org Rev. Timothy J. Henderson, Admin.;

SUNSET HILLS

St. Justin Martyr Catholic Church - 11910 Eddie & Park Rd., Sunset Hills, MO 63126 t) 314-843-8482; 314-635-2499 (CRP) meiners@stjustinmartyr.org; business@stjustinmartyr.org www.stjustinmartyr.org Rev. William Kempf, Pst.; Dcn. Mark J. Jaeger; Rev. John J. Johnson, In Res.; Marge Meiners, Pst. Min./Coord.; Marie L Tate, Bus. Mgr.;

St. Justin Martyr Catholic Church School - (Grades PreK-8) 11914 Eddie & Park Rd., Sunset Hills, MO 63126 t) 314-843-6447 secretary@stjustinmartyr.org Amy Schroff, Prin.;

TROY

Sacred Heart Catholic Church, Troy - 100 Thompson Dr., Troy, MO 63379 t) 636-528-8219 x115 (CRP); 636-528-8219 x103 shsparish@sacredhearttroy.org; mjlydon55@gmail.com www.sacredhearttroy.org Rev. Michael J. Lydon, Pst.; Dcn. James P. Davies; CRP Stds.: 120

Sacred Heart Catholic Church, Troy School - 110 Thompson Dr., Troy, MO 63379 t) 636-528-6684 Ann Hoffman, Prin.;

UNION

Immaculate Conception Catholic Church, Union - 100 N. Washington Ave., Union, MO 63084; Mailing: 111 N Washington Ave, Union, MO 63084 t) 636-583-5144 x3 icunionoffice@gmail.com www.immaculatecunion.org/ Very Rev. Joseph S. Post, Pst.; Dcn. Keith Henderson; Dcn. Gerald H. Becker; CRP Stds.: 43

Immaculate Conception Catholic Church, Union School - (Grades PreK-8) 6 W. State St., Union, MO 63084 t) 636-583-2641 hello@icschoolunion.org icschoolunion.com/ Michele Jensen, Prin.; Stds.: 191; Lay Tchrs.: 16

St. Joseph Catholic Church, Neier - 2401 Neier Rd., Union, MO 63084 t) 636-583-2806 parishoffice@stjosephneier.com www.stjosephneier.com/ Rev. Thomas Wissler, Pst.; CRP Stds.: 52

UNIVERSITY CITY

All Saints Catholic Church, University City - 6403 Clemens Ave., University City, MO 63130 Rev. Michael J. Witt, Pst.; Dcn. Stephen L. Murray;

Christ the King Catholic Church - 7316 Balson Ave., University City, MO 63130 t) 314-721-8737 rectory@ctkstl.com www.ctkstl.com Very Rev. Michael E. Turek, Pst.; Dcn. David P. Dille;

Christ the King Catholic School - (Grades PreK-8) 7324 Balson Ave., University City, MO 63130 t) 314-725-5855 Caroline McCarthy, Prin.;

Our Lady of Lourdes Catholic Church, University City - 7148 Forsyth Blvd., University City, MO 63105 t) 314-726-6200 rectory@ucitylourdes.org Rev. Msgr. Richard E. Hanneke, Pst.;

Our Lady of Lourdes Catholic School - (Grades K-8) 7144 Forsyth Blvd, University City, MO 63105 t) 314-726-3352 jeanne.gearon@ucitylourdes.org

VALLEY PARK

Sacred Heart Catholic Church, Valley Park - 8 Fernridge, Valley Park, MO 63088 Rev. Thomas J. Haley, Pst.; Rev. Patrick J. Christopher, Assoc. Pst.; Very Rev. Scott Jones, Assoc. Pst.; Rev. Ryan W. Truss, Assoc. Pst.; Dcn. Gary Peterson; Dcn. Charles R. Snyder;

Sacred Heart Catholic School - (Grades PreK-8) 12 Ann Ave., Valley Park, MO 63088 t) 636-225-3824

VILLA RIDGE

St. John the Baptist Catholic Church, Gildehaus - 5567 Gildehaus Rd., Villa Ridge, MO 63089 t) 636-583-2392 Dcn. Randall G. Smith;

St. John the Baptist Catholic School - (Grades PreSchool-8) 5579 Gildehaus Rd., Villa Ridge, MO 63089 Gary Menke, Prin.;

St. Mary of Perpetual Help Catholic Church, Moselle - 1587 Hwy. AM, Villa Ridge, MO 63089 t) 636-451-4685 stm.stj.vr@gmail.com www.stmarys-moselle.com Rev. Mark S. Bozada, Pst.;

WARRENTON

Holy Rosary Catholic Church - 724 E. Booneslick Rd., Warrenton, MO 63383 t) 636-456-3698 brownd@holyrosarywm.com holyrosarywm.com Rev. Thomas A. Vordtriede, Pst.; Dcn. Ray Burle; Dcn. Mark L. Schmierbach; CRP Stds.: 46

Holy Rosary Catholic School - (Grades PreK-8) 716 Booneslick Rd., Warrenton, MO 63383 racinel@holyrosarywm.com www.school.holyrosarywm.com Lori Racine, Prin.; Stds.: 172; Lay Tchrs.: 10

WARSON WOODS

Ste. Genevieve Du Bois Catholic Church, Warson Woods - 1575 N. Woodlawn Ave., Warson Woods, MO 63122 Rev. Daniel E. Mosley, Pst.; Dcn. H. Matthew Witte;

Ste. Genevieve Du Bois School - (Grades PreK-8) t) 314-821-4245 Anthony Van Gessel, Prin.;

WASHINGTON

St. Ann Catholic Church, Clover Bottom - 7851 Hwy. YY, Washington, MO 63090-4050 t) 636-239-3222 Rev. Philip D. Krill, Pst.; Dcn. Stephen J. Young;

St. Francis Borgia Catholic Church - 310 W. Main St., Washington, MO 63090; Mailing: 115 Cedar St., Washington, MO 63090 t) 636-239-6701; 636-239-2530 (CRP) parish@borgiaparish.org; kgulledge@borgiaparish.org www.borgiaparish.org Rev. Michael Patrick Boehm, Pst.; Rev. Anthony Ritter, Assoc. Pst.; Dcn. Dennis Meinert; Dcn. David Tobben; Dcn. Tim Reis; Dcn. Leon Noelker; Kyra Gulledge, DRE; CRP Stds.: 57

St. Francis Borgia Catholic School - 225 Cedar St., Washington, MO 63090 t) 636-239-2590

St. Gertrude Catholic Church - 6535 Hwy. YY, Washington, MO 63090 t) 636-239-2347 Rev. Philip D. Krill, Pst.; Rev. Bernard J. Wilkins, In Res.; Dcn. Charles Gildehaus; Rosie Heidmann, DRE;

St. Gertrude Catholic Church School - (Grades K-8) 6520 Hwy. YY, Washington, MO 63090 stgertrude@primary.net Steve Young, Prin.;

Our Lady of Lourdes Catholic Church, Washington - 1014 Madison Ave., Washington, MO 63090-4806 t) 636-239-3520 rectory@ollwashmo.org www.olllwashmo.org Rev. James D. Theby, Pst.; Rev. Donald Morris, Assoc. Pst.; Dcn. Donald A. Elbert; Katelyn Boland, DRE; CRP Stds.: 73

Our Lady of Lourdes Catholic School - 950 Madison Ave., Washington, MO 63090 t) 636-239-5292

WEBSTER GROVES

Annunciation Catholic Church - 12 W. Glendale Rd., Webster Groves, MO 63119 t) 314-962-5955 psr@goannunciation.com; parishsecretary@goannunciation.com www.goannunciation.com Rev. Michael J. Esswein, Pst.; CRP Stds.: 116

Holy Redeemer Catholic Church - 17 Joy Ave., Webster Groves, MO 63119 t) 314-962-0038 parishoffice@holyr.org holyr.org/ Rev. Kevin V. Schmittgens, Pst.; Rev. Eugene W. Schaeffer III, Pst. Assoc.; Dcn. Stephen L. Murray; Dcn. Patrick G. Waldschmidt; CRP Stds.: 128

Holy Redeemer Catholic School - (Grades PreK-8)

t) 314-962-8989 principal@holyr.org www.holyr.org Wayne Schiefelbein, Prin.;

Mary, Queen of Peace Catholic Church - 676 W. Lockwood Ave., Webster Groves, MO 63119 t) 314-962-2311 (Office); 314-961-2891 x223 (CRP) mqpparishoffice@mqpwg.org www.mqpwg.org Rev. Craig T. Holway, Pst.; Rev. Timothy R. Cook, Assoc. Pst.; Dcn. Thomas O. Mulvihill; Dcn. Joseph M. Wientge; CRP Stds.: 150

Mary, Queen of Peace Catholic School - (Grades PreK-8) 680 W. Lockwood Ave., Webster Groves, MO 63119 jsmith@mqpwg.org www.mqpwg.org/school Julie Smith, Prin.;

WENTZVILLE

St. Gianna Catholic Church - 450 E Hwy N, Wentzville, MO 63385 t) 636-327-3639 rschulte@stgiannaparish.org www.stgiannaparish.org Rev. Timothy P. Elliott, Pst.; CRP Stds.: 45

St. Joseph Catholic Church, Josephville - 1390 Josephville Rd., Wentzville, MO 63385 t) 636-332-6676 trish.seaman@stjojo.net www.stjojo.net Rev. Robert J. Samson, Pst.; Dcn. David L. Billing; Nancy Burian, DRE; CRP Stds.: 30

St. Joseph Catholic Church, Josephville School - (Grades PreK-8) 1410 Josephville Rd., Wentzville, MO 63385 t) 636-332-5672 Jill Nance, Prin.;

St. Patrick Catholic Church - 405 S. Church St., Wentzville, MO 63385 t) 636-332-9225 stpatrickparish@stpatsch.org www.stpatrickwentzville.org/ Very Rev. Brian R. Fischer, Pst.; Rev. Gerson Parra, Assoc. Pst.; Rev. David P. Skillman, Assoc. Pst.; Dcn. Kirk Lackas; Dcn. Patrick Rankin; CRP Stds.: 328

St. Patrick Catholic School - (Grades PreSchool-8) 701 Church St., Wentzville, MO 63385 t) 636-332-9913 principal@stpatsch.org www.stpatrickwentzville.org Denise Brickler, Prin.;

St. Theodore Catholic Church - 5051 Hwy. P, Wentzville, MO 63385-2118; Mailing: 5085 Hwy P, Wentzville, MO 63385-2118 t) 636-332-9269 x283 (CRP); 636-332-9269 x226; 636-332-9269 x225 psr@sainttheodore.org; bulletin@sainttheodore.org www.sainttheodore.org/ Rev. Peter J. Fonseca, Admin.; Dcn. Dan Ford;

St. Theodore Catholic Church School - 5059 Hwy. P, Wentzville, MO 63385 sttheodore.school@centurytel.net

WILDWOOD

St. Alban Roe Catholic Church - 2001 Shepard Rd., Wildwood, MO 63038 t) 636-458-2977; (636) 458-2460 (CRP) tsmith@stalbanroe.org; rstoltz@stalbanroe.org www.stalbanroe.org Rev. Richard L. Stoltz, Pst.; Rev. Fredrick Devaraj, C.Ss.R., Assoc. Pst.; Dcn. Keith G. Mallon; Dcn. Tim Michaelree; Sr. Christian Price, A.S.C.J., DRE; CRP Stds.: 434

St. Alban Roe Catholic Church School - 2005 Shepard Rd., Wildwood, MO 63038 t) 636-458-6084 Tara Smith, Prin.;

SCHOOLS: PRESCHOOL THRU HIGH SCHOOL

SCHOOLS

STATE OF MISSOURI

ARNOLD

Holy Child School - (PAR) 2316 Church Rd., Arnold, MO 63010

Immaculate Conception - 2300 Church Rd., Arnold, MO 63010; Mailing: 2316 Church Rd., Arnold, MO 63010 t) 636-321-0002 delmore@holychildarnold.org icarnold.com

St. David - 2334 Tenbrook Rd., Arnold, MO 63010

CREVE COEUR

Chaminade College Preparatory - (PRV) (Grades 6-12) 425 S. Lindbergh Blvd., Creve Coeur, MO 63131 t) 314-993-4400 admissions@chaminade-stl.org www.chaminade-stl.org Resident and Day Students (Boys). Society of Mary. Todd Guidry, Pres.; Philip Rone, Prin.; Jack Twellman, Prin.; Stds.: 871; Bro. Tchrs.: 1; Lay Tchrs.: 86

FESTUS

Our Lady - (PAR) (Grades K-8) 1599 St. Mary Ln., Festus, MO 63028 t) 636-937-5008 ourladyschool@sbcglobal.net www.ourladycatholicschool.org

FLORISSANT

All Saints Academy - (Grades PreK-8) 1735 Charbonier Rd., Florissant, MO 63031 t) 314-921-2201 www.archstl.org/education Addie Govero, Dir.;

All Saints Academy - St. Ferdinand Campus - (Grades PreK-8) principal216@archstl.org www.stferdinandstl.org Annamarie Davis, Prin.;

All Saints Academy - St. Norbert Campus - (Grades PreK-8) 16475 New Halls Ferry Rd., Florissant, MO 63031 t) 314-839-0948 principal296@archstl.org www.saintnorbert.com/school.html Joanne Hoormann, Prin.;

All Saints Academy - St. Rose Philippine Duchesne Campus - (Grades PreK-8) 3500 St. Catherine, Florissant, MO 63033 t) 314-921-3023 principal504@archstl.org www.strpdparish.org/school Barbara Zipoli, Prin.;

O'FALLON

Assumption - (PAR) 203 W. Third St., O'Fallon, MO 63366 t) 636-240-4474 Genevieve Callier, Prin.;

ST. CHARLES

Academy of the Sacred Heart - (PRV) (Grades PreK-8) 619 N. 2nd St., St. Charles, MO 63301 t) 636-946-6127 bfasl@ash1818.org www.ash1818.org (Coed) Timothy Horner, Pres.; Marcia Renken, Prin.; Stds.: 195; Lay Tchrs.: 17

***John Paul II Preparatory School Incorporated** - 1418 S. First Capitol Dr., St. Charles, MO 63303 Lynette Schmitz, Prin.;

St. Elizabeth/St. Robert School - (PAR) (Grades K-8) 1 Seton Ct., St. Charles, MO 63303 t) 636-946-6716 Joanna Collins, Prin.;

ST. LOUIS

Archdiocesan Elementary Schools of the Archdiocese of St. Louis - 20 Archbishop May Dr., St. Louis, MO 63119 t) 314-792-7300 www.archstl.org/education Dr. Maureen DePriest, Supt.; Kristi Mantych, Dir.;

St. Cecilia School and Academy - 906 Eichelberger ST., St. Louis, MO 63119 t) 314-353-2455 principal140@archstl.org stc-stl.org/ Emily Roth, Prin.;

St. Louis Catholic Academy - 4720 Carter Ave., St. Louis, MO 63115 t) 314-389-0401 principal444@archstl.org www.slca-stl.org/ Sandra Morton, Prin.;

***St. Austin School** - (PRV) (Grades PreK-8) 1809 Des Peres Rd., St. Louis, MO 63131; Mailing: P.O. Box 6906, Chesterfield, MO 63006-6906 t) 314-580-2802 info@saintaustinschool.org www.saintaustinschool.org Classical Catholic school serving boys and girls. James H Spellmeyer, Bus. Mgr.; Stds.: 160; Lay Tchrs.: 10

Christ, Light of the Nations - (PAR) 1650 Redman Ave., St. Louis, MO 63138

St. Frances Cabrini Academy - (PAR) (Grades K-8) 3022 Oregon Ave., St. Louis, MO 63118 t) 314-776-0883 Peter Schroeder, Prin.;

St. Francis of Assisi - (PAR) (Grades PreK-8) 4550 Telegraph Rd., St. Louis, MO 63129 t) 314-487-5736 schooloffice@sfastl.org Elizabeth Bartolotta, Prin.;

Holy Cross Academy - St. Louis - (PAR) (Grades PreK-8) 8874 Pardee Rd., St. Louis, MO 63123 t) 314-475-3436 holycross@hca-stl.org www.holycross-stl.org Rev. Michael Esswein, Pst.; Stds.: 576; Lay Tchrs.: 47

Holy Cross Academy at the Annunciation Campus - (Grades PreK-8) 16 W. Glendale Rd., Webster Groves, MO 63119 t) 314-961-7712

Holy Cross Academy at Our Lady of Providence Campus - (Grades PreK-8)

Holy Cross Academy at St. Michael the Archangel Campus - (Grades PreK-8) 7630 Sutherland Ave., Shrewsbury, MO 63119 t) 314-647-7159

Holy Cross Academy at St. John Paul II Campus - (Grades PreK-8) 7748 Mackenzie Rd., St. Louis, MO 63123 t) 314-832-4161

St. Justin Martyr - (PAR) (Grades PreSchool-8) 11914 Eddie & Park Rd., St. Louis, MO 63126 t) 314-843-6447 schroff@stjustinmartyr.org; secretary@stjustinmartyr.org stjustinmartyr.org Amy Schroff, Prin.; Teresa McIntyre, Dir.;

Loyola Academy of St. Louis - (PRV) (Grades 6-8) 3851 Washington Blvd., St. Louis, MO 63108 t) 314-531-9091 eclark@loyolaacademy.org www.loyolaacademy.org Ashley Chapman, Prin.; H. Eric Clark, Pres.;

Marian Middle School - (PRV) 4130 Wyoming, St. Louis, MO 63116 t) 314-771-7674 sheger@mms-stl.org www.mms-stl.org S. Sarah Heger, Prin.;

South City Catholic Academy - (PAR) (Grades PreK-8) 5821 Pernod, St. Louis, MO 63139 t) 314-752-4171 principal402@archstl.org www.stlsouthcitycatholicacademy.org/ Laura Hirschman, Prin.;

Villa Duchesne and Oak Hill School - (PRV) (Grades PreSchool-12) 801 S. Spoede Rd., St. Louis, MO 63131-2699 t) 314-432-2021 admissions@vdoh.org; news@vdoh.org www.vdoh.org

TOWN AND COUNTRY

Visitation Academy - (PRV) (Grades PreK-8) 3020 N. Ballas Rd., Town and Country, MO 63131 t) 314-625-9100 swilliams@visitationacademy.org www.visitationacademy.org David Colon, Head of School; Dr. Marlise Albert, Lower School Prin.; Angie Jung, Middle School Prin.; Stds.: 587; Sr. Tchrs.: 3; Lay Tchrs.: 71

UNION

Immaculate Conception - (PAR) 6 W. State St., Union, MO 63084 t) 636-583-2641 Dennis Lottmann, Prin.;

UNIVERSITY CITY

Christ the King - (PAR) 7324 Balson Ave., University City, MO 63130 t) 314-725-5855 Susan E. Hooker, Prin.;

WASHINGTON

St. Francis Borgia - (PAR) (Grades PreK-8) 225 Cedar St., Washington, MO 63090 t) 636-239-2590 lpahl@borgiagradeschool.org Linda Pahl, Prin.;

HIGH SCHOOLS

STATE OF MISSOURI

CREVE COEUR

Chaminade College Preparatory School Inc. - (PRV) (Grades 9-12) 425 S. Lindbergh Blvd., Creve Coeur, MO 63131-2799 t) 314-993-4400 admissions@chaminade-stl.org www.chaminade-stl.org Resident and Day Students. Society of Mary. Todd Guidry, Pres.; Philip Rone, Prin.; Stds.: 562; Bro. Tchrs.: 1; Lay Tchrs.: 60

De Smet Jesuit High School - (PRV) 233 N. New Ballas Rd., Creve Coeur, MO 63141 t) 314-567-3500 www.desmet.org Trevor Bonat, Prin.; Rev. Walter T. Sidney, S.J., Pres.; Lynn G. Maitz, Librn.;

St. Louis Priory School - (PRV) (Grades 7-12) 500 S. Mason Rd., Creve Coeur, MO 63141-8500 t) 314-434-3690 frcuthbert@priory.org www.priory.org Rev. Cassian Koenemann, O.S.B.; Rev. Augustine Wetta, O.S.B.; Rev. Cuthbert Elliott, O.S.B., Headmaster; Rev. J. Gregory Mohrman, O.S.B., Abbot; Rev. Dominic Lenk, O.S.B., Theology Department Chair; Stds.: 298; Pr. Tchrs.: 5; Lay Tchrs.: 40

FESTUS

St. Pius X High School - (DIO) 1030 St. Pius Dr., Festus, MO 63028 t) 636-931-7487; 636-931-7488 advancement@stpius.com stpius.com College preparatory school fully accredited by AdvancED and the state of Missouri. Karen DeCosty, Prin.; Jim Lehn, Pres.;

FRONTENAC

Villa Duchesne and Oak Hill School - (PRV) 801 S. Spoede Rd., Frontenac, MO 63131 t) 314-432-2021 vdoh@vdoh.org www.vdoh.org Religious of the Sacred Heart. Sr. Donna Collins, R.S.C.J., Prin.; Katie Komos, Prin.;

KIRKWOOD

St. John Vianney High School - (PRV) 1311 S. Kirkwood Rd., Kirkwood, MO 63122 t) 314-965-4853 imulligan@vianney.com www.vianney.com Conducted for Boys by the Society of Mary (Marianists). Richard Davis, Pres.;

Ursuline Academy - (PRV) (Grades 9-12) 341 S. Sappington Rd., Kirkwood, MO 63122 t) 314-984-2800 pslater@ursulinestl.org www.ursulinestl.org Ursuline Sisters of the Roman Union. Mark Michalski, Prin.; Peggy Ann Slater, Pres.; Stds.: 325; Lay Tchrs.: 65

O'FALLON

St. Dominic High School - (DIO) (Grades 9-12) 31 St. Dominic Dr., O'Fallon, MO 63366 t) 636-240-8303 sgarrett@stdominichs.org www.stdominichs.org Jim Welby, Pres.;

ST. CHARLES

Duchesne High School - (DIO) 2550 Elm St., St. Charles, MO 63301-1494 t) 636-946-6767 snoonan@duchesne-hs.org www.duchesne-hs.org A Co-Educational College Prep High School Conducted by Archdiocesan Priests and Catholic Lay Staff. David Halfmann, Campus Min.; Frederick Long, Prin.; Susan Noonan, Pres.;

ST. LOUIS

Bishop DuBourg High School - (DIO) (Grades 9-12) 5850 Eichelberger St., St. Louis, MO 63109 t) 314-832-3030 dschnable@bishopdubourg.org; jprovaznik@bishopdubourg.org www.bishopdubourg.org Dr. Monica Freese, Prin.; Mark Bayens, Pres.;

Cardinal Ritter College Prep - (DIO) (Grades 9-12) 701 N. Spring, St. Louis, MO 63108 t) 314-446-5500 cedwards@cardinalritterprep.org info.csd.org/ritter.htm Coed. Dr. Craige Edwards, Prin.; Tamiko Armstead, Pres.;

Christian Brothers College High School (C.B.C.) - (PRV) 1850 De La Salle Dr., St. Louis, MO 63141 t) 314-985-6100 admin@cbchs.org www.cbchs.org Tim Seymour, Prin.; Michael Jordan, Pres.;

Cor Jesu Academy - (PRV) 10230 Gravois Rd., St. Louis, MO 63123 t) 314-842-1546 principal@corjesu.org www.corjesu.org Kathleen Pottinger, Dean of Student Life; Sr. Mary Grace Walsh, ASCJ, Pres.; Katie Mulhall, Librn.; Meghan Bohac, Dean of Academics; Stds.: 575; Sr. Tchrs.: 2; Lay Tchrs.: 56

Incarnate Word Academy - (PRV) 2788 Normandy Dr., St. Louis, MO 63121 t) 314-725-5850 sgerken@iwacademy.org www.iwacademy.org Sisters of Charity of Incarnate Word of San Antonio. Sharon Gerken, Pres.;

St. Joseph's Academy - (PRV) (Grades 9-12) 2307 S. Lindbergh Blvd., St. Louis, MO 63131 t) 314-394-4300 jsudekum@sja1840.org www.sja1840.org Jennifer Sudekum, Prin.; Marcia Niedringhaus, Pres.; Jennifer Millikan, Librn.;

St. Louis University High School, George H. Backer Memorial - (PRV) 4970 Oakland Ave., St. Louis, MO 63110 t) 314-531-0330 www.sluh.org Rev. Ian R. Gibbons, S.J., Prin.; Stds.: 985; Scholastics: 2; Pr. Tchrs.: 4; Lay Tchrs.: 90

Notre Dame High School - (PRV) 320 E. Ripa Ave., St. Louis, MO 63125 t) 314-544-1015 mbohac@ndhs.net www.ndhs.net Meghan Bohac, Pres.; Monika Pagano, Dir.;

TOWN AND COUNTRY

Visitation Academy - (PRV) (Grades 9-12) 3020 N. Ballas Rd., Town and Country, MO 63131 t) 314-625-9100 swilliams@visitationacademy.org www.visitationacademy.org David Colon, Head of School; Terence Murray, Upper School Prin.; Stds.: 587; Sr. Tchrs.: 3; Lay Tchrs.: 71

WASHINGTON

St. Francis Borgia Regional High School - (DIO) (Grades 9-12) 1000 Borgia Dr., Washington, MO 63090 t) 636-239-7871 matt.schutte@borgia.com; kara.miller@borgia.com www.borgia.com Pam Tholen, Prin.; Matt Schutte, Pres.; Stds.: 435; Lay Tchrs.: 28

WEBSTER GROVES

Nerinx Hall - (PRV) 530 E. Lockwood, Webster Groves, MO 63119 t) 314-968-1505 broche@nerinxhs.org www.nerinxhs.org Jane W. Kosash, Prin.; John E. Gabriel, Pres.; Alison Rollins, Librn.;

INSTITUTIONS LOCATED IN DIOCESE

ASSOCIATIONS [ASN]

PERRYVILLE

Association of the Miraculous Medal - 1811 W. Saint Joseph St., Perryville, MO 63775 t) 573-547-8343 ammfather@amm.org www.amm.org Don Fulford, CEO; Rev. Kevin P. McCracken, C.M., Dir.;

ST. LOUIS

Association of Saint Teresa Corporation - 9150 Clayton Rd., St. Louis, MO 63124 t) 314-993-4394 c) 314-229-4990 saintagatha@thecarmel.ca carmelite-nuns.org/about.html Sr. Marie Celeste Moloney, OCD, Pres.; Sr. Gisele Lucienne Bolduc, OCD, Secy.; Sr. Zelie Marie (Cheryl) Mataragas, OCD, Treas.;

The Catholic Health Association of the United States - 4455 Woodson Rd., St. Louis, MO 63134-3797 t) 314-427-2500 www.chausa.org

Catholic High School Association - 20 Archbishop May Dr., St. Louis, MO 63119 t) 314-792-7300 jphelps@archstl.org www.archstl.org/education/ Dr. Todd Sweda, Supt. Secondary Educ.;

St. Francis de Sales Association - 9328 Pine Ave., St. Louis, MO 63144; Mailing: 1772 Highland Pkwy., St. Paul, MN 55116 t) 651-592-6645 webteam@sfdsassociation.org www.sfdsassociation.org A call to the laity to live their individual vocation in the spirit of Jesus, using the writings of St. Francis de Sales. Ann Doody Wiedl, Laity;

The St. Louis Visitation Association of Christian Faithful - 3020 N. Ballas Rd., St. Louis, MO 63131 t) 314-625-9247 tcallahan@visitationmonastery.org; schwartz1924@sbcglobal.net stlvisitationacf.com/ Ann Hein, Moderator; Mary ann Schwartz, Bus. Mgr.;

CAMPUS MINISTRY / NEWMAN CENTERS [CAM]

ST. LOUIS

Catholic Student Center at Washington University - 6352 Forsyth Blvd., St. Louis, MO 63105-2269 t) 314-935-9191 braun@washucsc.org www.washucsc.org a Newman Center Rev. Gary G. Braun;

University of Missouri, St. Louis, Catholic Newman Center - 8200 Natural Bridge Rd., St. Louis, MO 63121 t) 314-385-3455 cnc@cncumsl.org; frnick@cncumsl.org www.cncumsl.org Rev. Nicklaus E. Winker, Dir.;

CATHOLIC CHARITIES [CCH]

ST. LOUIS

St. Francis Community Services - 4445 Lindell Blvd., St. Louis, MO 63108-2497 t) 314-932-3300 jheithaus@ccstl.org www.sfcsstl.org Provides legal aid for immigrants, veterans, victims of violence and others; bilingual immigrant services, including youth programs & case management. Dcn. J. John Heithaus, Exec. Dir.;

Catholic Legal Assistance Ministry - 100 N. Tucker Blvd., Ste. 726, St. Louis, MO 63101 t) 314-977-3993 amy.diemer@slu.edu sfcsstl.org/locations/clam/ A St. Francis Community Services program providing legal advocacy & representation in civil & immigration matters for low-income clients. Amy Diemer, Dir.;

St. Francis Community Services Southside Center (Vietnamese and Hispanic Programs) - 4222 Delor, St. Louis, MO 63116 t) 314-773-6100 cruizmartinez@ccstl.org sfcsstl.org/locations/southside/ Meets the immediate & systemic needs of immigrants Carlos Ruiz Martinez, Dir.;

Pathways to Progress - 10235 Ashbrook Dr., St. Louis, MO 63137 t) 314-269-5055 pathways@ccstl.org sfcsstl.org/services/case-management/ Wrap-around, long-term case management for impoverished families. Dcn. J. John Heithaus, Exec. Dir.;

CEMETERIES [CEM]

ELLISVILLE

Holy Cross Cemetery - 16200 Manchester Rd., Ellisville, MO 63011 t) 314-792-7738

FENTON

Saint Vincent Cemetery - 1488 Romaine Creek Rd., Fenton, MO 63026 t) 314-792-7737

FLORISSANT

Sacred Heart Cemetery - Graham Rd., Florissant, MO 63033 t) 314-792-7738

HAZELWOOD

Saint Ferdinand Cemetery - Graham Rd., Hazelwood, MO 63042 t) 314-792-7738

Saint Mary Cemetery - 5200 Fee Fee Rd., Hazelwood, MO 63042 t) 314-792-7738

KIRKWOOD

Saint Peter Cemetery - Geyer at W. Monroe Ave., Kirkwood, MO 63122 t) 314-792-7738

LAKE SAINT LOUIS

Cemetery of Our Lady - Lake St. Louis Blvd. & Orf Rd., Lake Saint Louis, MO 63366 t) 314-792-7738

LEMAY

Mount Olive Cemetery - 3906 Mt. Olive Rd., Lemay, MO 63125 t) 314-792-7737

ST. CHARLES

Saint Charles Borromeo Cemetery - Randolph St., St. Charles, MO 63301 t) 314-792-7738

Ste. Philippine Cemetery - 4057 Towers Rd., St. Charles, MO 63304 t) 314-792-7738

ST. LOUIS

Calvary Cemetery - 5239 W. Florissant Ave., St. Louis, MO 63115 t) 314-792-7738 Rev. Msgr. Dennis M. Delaney, Dir.;

Resurrection Cemetery - 6901 Mackenzie Rd., St. Louis, MO 63123 t) 314-792-7737

Saints Peter and Paul Cemetery - 7030 Gravois Ave., St. Louis, MO 63116 t) 314-792-7737

WASHINGTON

Ascension Cemetery - 5563 Country Club Rd., Washington, MO 63090 t) 314-792-7737

COLLEGES & UNIVERSITIES [COL]

ST. LOUIS

Fontbonne University - 6800 Wydown Blvd., St. Louis, MO 63105 t) 314-862-3456 smccaslin@fontbonne.edu www.fontbonne.edu J. Michael Pressimone, Pres.; Sharon McCaslin, Librn.;

Saint Louis University - One N. Grand Blvd., DuBourg Hall, Rm. 100, St. Louis, MO 63103; Mailing: 3634 Lindell Blvd., Verhaegen Hall, Rm. 315, St. Louis, MO 63108 t) 800-758-3678; 314-977-2223 admission@slu.edu www.slu.edu Rev. John A. Apel, S.J.; Rev. Michael D. Barber, S.J.; Rev. Richard Buhler, S.J.; Rev. James J. Burshek, S.J.; Rev. Christopher S. Collins, S.J.; Rev. David J. Corrigan, S.J.; Rev. Kevin L. Cullen, S.J.; Rev. Anthony C. Daly, S.J.; Rev. J. Daniel Daly, S.J.; Rev. Terrence E. Dempsey, S.J.; Rev. Donald Highberger, S.J.; Rev. Michael K. May, S.J.; Rev. David V. Meconi, S.J.; Rev. Robert E. Murphy, S.J.; Rev. Ronald R. O'Dwyer, S.J.; Rev. James M. O'Leary, S.J.; Bro. William R. Rehg, S.J.; Rev. Albert C. Rotola, S.J.; Rev. Steven A. Schoenig, S.J.; Rev. James A. Sebesta, S.J.; Rev. Daniel P. White, S.J.; Fred P. Pestello, Pres.;

Albert Gnaegi Center for Health Care Ethics - t) 314-977-1060 Jeffrey P. Bishop, Dir.;

Arts and Sciences, College of - t) 314-977-2710 Rev.

Theodore Vitali, C. P.; Christopher Duncan, Dean;
Center for Advanced Dental Education - t) 314-977-8363 John F. Hatton, Exec.;
Center for Outcomes Research - t) 314-977-9300 Thomas Burroughs, Exec.;
Center for Sustainability - t) 314-977-3608 Jason Knouft, Dean;
College for Public Health & Social Justice - t) 314-977-8100
College of Philosophy and Letters - t) 314-977-3827
Doisy College of Health Sciences - t) 314-977-8501 Mardell A. Wilson, Dean;
John Cook School of Business - t) 314-977-3800 Mark M. Higgins, Dean;
Madrid Spain Campus - t) 314-977-3445 Paul A. Vita, Dir.;
Parks College of Engineering, Aviation and Technology - t) 314-977-8283 Michelle B. Sabick, Dean;
Pius XII Memorial Library - t) 314-977-3095 David Cassens, Dean;
School for Professional Studies - t) 800-734-6736; 314-977-2330 Jennifer Giancola, Dean;
School of Education - t) 314-977-3292 Ann Rule, Dean;
School of Law - 100 N. Tucker Ave., Scott Hall, St. Louis, MO 63101 t) 314-977-2800 Michael A. Wolff, Dean;
School of Medicine - t) 314-977-9870 Philip O. Alderson, Dean;
School of Nursing - t) 314-977-8900 Teri A. Murray, Dean;

CONVENTS, MONASTERIES, AND RESIDENCES FOR WOMEN [CON]

BRIDGETON

Franciscan Sisters of Mary Administration - 3221 McKelvey Rd., Suite 107, Bridgeton, MO 63044 t) 314-768-1824 jbell@fsmonline.org; bjfranklin@collaborativegovernance.org www.fsmonline.org Judith Bell, Pres.; Srs.: 37

CHESTERFIELD

Missionary Sisters of St. Peter Claver - 667 Woods Mill Rd. S., Chesterfield, MO 63006-6067; Mailing: P.O. Box 6067, Chesterfield, MO 63006-6067 t) 314-469-4932 c) (636) 579-7401 www.missionarieclaveriane.org/ Sr. Line Fakatou, Supr.; Srs.: 4

ELLISVILLE

Passionist Nuns Monastery - 15700 Clayton Rd., Ellisville, MO 63011-2300 t) 636-527-6867 passionistnunsofstlouis.org Cloistered Contemplatives. Sr. Mary Veronica, C.P., Supr.; Srs.: 4

FRONTENAC

Monastery of the Visitation, St. Louis - 2039 N. Geyer Rd., Frontenac, MO 63131; Mailing: 3020 N Ballas Rd, St. Louis, MO 63131 t) 314-625-9247 tcallahan@visitationmonastery.org Residence of Visitation Nuns Living at the Monastery of the Visitation. Sr. Karen Mohan, Supr.; Srs.: 3

Offices of Visitation Nuns at the Monastery of the Visitation - 3020 N. Ballas Rd., Town and Country, MO 63131

Residence of Visitation Nuns -

Religious of the Sacred Heart Convent - Villa Duchesne, #1 Jaccard Ln., Frontenac, MO 63131 t) 314-872-8597 nghio@rscj.org

HIGH RIDGE

Society of Our Mother of Peace, Daughters of Our Mother of Peace - Mary the Font Solitude, 6150 Antire Rd., High Ridge, MO 63049-2135 c) 636-677-3235 smpsistersvoc@gmail.com www.marythefont.org Sr. Mary Margaret Torgerson, SMP, Supr.; Srs.: 6

KIRKWOOD

Carmelite Sisters of the Divine Heart of Jesus Provincial House and Novitiate - 10341 Manchester Rd., Kirkwood, MO 63122 t) 314-965-7616 vocations@carmelitedcj.org carmelitedcj.org Sr. Benedicta Huerta, Prov.;
Central Province of the Ursuline Nuns of the Roman Union - 353 S. Sappington Rd., Kirkwood, MO 63122 t) 314-821-6884 ursulines@osucentral.org www.osucentral.org Sr. Elisa Ryan, OSU, Prov.; Srs.: 65

Ursuline Sisters - 9308 Sutton Ave., St. Louis, MO 63144 t) (314) 488-7478 madooling@ursulinestl.org Sr. Mary Ann Dooling, O.S.U., Supr.;

Ursuline Sisters - 801 Fairdale Ave., Rock Hill, MO 63119 t) (314) 625-7584 osuritab@gmail.com Sr. Rita A. Bregenhorn, O.S.U., Supr.;

Ursuline Sisters - 105 N. Holmes Ave., St. Louis, MO 63122 t) 314-698-2506

Ursuline Sisters - 921 H Carriage Circle Ln., Kirkwood, MO 63122 t) 314-394-0931 adele@osucentral.org

LIGUORI

Monastery of St. Alphonsus - 200 Liguori Dr., Liguori, MO 63057-9999 t) 636-464-1093 rednun@redemptoristinenuns.org; prayerrequest@redemptoristinenuns.org www.redemptoristinenuns.org Order of the Most Holy Redeemer (Redemptoristine Nuns). Sr. Ann Marie Gool, O.Ss.R., Prioress; Srs.: 5

NORMANDY

Convent of the Immaculate Heart - 7626 Natural Bridge Rd., Normandy, MO 63121 t) 314-383-0300 srmpbrgs@aol.com www.goodshepherdsisters.org A residence for aged & infirm. Good Shepherd Sisters of the Mid-North America Prov.

O'FALLON

St. Mary's Institute of O'Fallon - 204 N. Main St., O'Fallon, MO 63366-2299 t) 636-240-6010 jbader@cppsadmin-ofallon.org www.cpps-ofallon.org Chapel of St. Joseph. Precious Blood Center Sr. Janice Bader, C.PP.S., Supr.; Srs.: 75

ST. CHARLES

Religious of the Sacred Heart - 301 Decatur St., St. Charles, MO 63301-2089 t) 636-946-7276 mmmunch@rscj.org Sr. Margaret Munch, RSCJ, Contact; Srs.: 1

ST. LOUIS

Adorers of the Blood of Christ, United States Region - 4233 Sulphur Ave., St. Louis, MO 63109 t) 314-351-6294 adminassistant@adorers.org www.adorers.org Sr. Vicki Bergkamp, ASC, Rel. Ord. Ldr.; Srs.: 166
Carmel of St. Joseph - 9150 Clayton Rd., St. Louis, MO 63124-1898 t) 314-993-4394 prioress@stlouiscarmel.org www.stlouiscarmel.com Chapel of the Precious Blood. Discalced Carmelites. Rev. Mother Marya Williams, O.C.D., Prioress; Srs.: 18
Carmelite Religious of Trivandrum - 5200 Glennon Dr., St. Louis, MO 63119 t) 314-792-6216 sr.ruby57@gmail.com www.kenrick.edu/ Sr. Rufina Devassy Kappithanparambil, CCR, Supr.;
Clelian House Convent - 5324 Wilson Ave., St. Louis, MO 63110 c) 203-993-0036 alegan@ascjus.org Sr. Alice Marie Legan, ASCJ, Supr.; Srs.: 4
Congregation of Mary, Queen - 3815 Westminster Pl., St. Louis, MO 63108 t) 314-371-1294 vocation@trinhvuong.org www.trinhvuong.org Sr. Pauline Nguyen, C.M.R., Supr.;
Congregational Office of the Sisters of St. Joseph of Carondelet - 10777 Sunset Office Dr., Ste. 10, St. Louis, MO 63127 t) 314-394-1985 congctroffice@csjcarondelet.org www.csjcarondelet.org Sr. Sean Peters, CSJ, Rel. Ord. Ldr.; Sr. Sally Harper, CSJ, Rel. Ord. Ldr.; Sr. Patricia Johnson, C.S.J., Rel. Ord. Ldr.; Sr. Mary McGlone, CSJ, Rel. Ord. Ldr.; Srs.: 6
Contemplative Sisters of the Good Shepherd - 7660 Natural Bridge Rd., St. Louis, MO 63121 t) (314) 397-9436 tponder@gspmna.org Antonia Ponder, COO; Srs.: 8
Cor Jesu Academy Convent - 10230 Gravois Rd., St. Louis, MO 63123 t) 314-843-8272 Sr. Mary Grace Walsh, ASCJ, Supr.; Srs.: 6
Daughters of Charity of St. Vincent de Paul, Province of St. Louise - 4328 Westminster, St. Louis, MO 63108-2624; Mailing: 4330 Olive St., St. Louis, MO 63108-2622 t) 314-533-3004 tom.beck@doc.org www.daughtersofcharity.org Provincial House for Daughters of Charity of St. Vincent de Paul, Province of St. Louise. Sr. Catherine Mary Norris, D.C., Prov.; Srs.: 348

Provincial Offices - 4330 Olive St., St. Louis, MO 63108-2622 t) 314-533-4770

Daughters of St. Paul Convent - 9804 Watson Rd., St. Louis, MO 63126 t) 314-965-6935 stlouis@pauline.org www.pauline.org Srs.: 10
Eucharistic Missionaries of St. Theresa - 12934 Marine Ave., St. Louis, MO 63146 t) 314-434-1312
Franciscan Sisters of Our Lady of Perpetual Help - 335 S. Kirkwood Rd., St. Louis, MO 63122 t) 314-965-3700 srrenita@fsolph.org www.fsolph.org Motherhouse and Novitiate of Franciscan Sisters of Our Lady of Perpetual Help. Sr. Renita Brummer, O.S.F., Rel. Ord. Ldr.; Srs.: 66
St. Joseph's Provincial House - 6400 Minnesota Ave., St. Louis, MO 63111-2899 t) 314-481-8800 mjohnson@csjsl.org www.csjsl.org Prov. House of the Sisters of St. Joseph of Carondelet. Dcn. Joseph Wingbermuehle, Admin.; Sr. Margaret Mary Schulz, Prov.; Sr. Amy Hereford, Prov. Asst.; Sr. Frances Elaine Maher, Prov. Asst.; Sr. Mary F. Johnson, C.S.J., Treas.;
Loretto Center - c/o Loretto St. Louis Staff Office, 530 E. Lockwood, St. Louis, MO 63119 t) 314-962-8112 dday@lorettocommunity.org; skassing@lorettocommunity.org www.lorettocommunity.org Sr. Donna Day, Admin.; Sr. Sharon Kassing, SL, Exec.;
Missionaries of Charity - 3629 Cottage Ave., St. Louis, MO 63113-3539 t) 314-533-2777 Also in: Peoria; Chicago; Detroit; Memphis; Dallas; Little Rock; Baton Rouge; Lafayette LA; Lexington; Atlanta; Charlotte; Gary; Indianapolis; Houston Sr. M. Davis MC, Supr.; Sr. M. Jonathan, MC, Regl. Supr.; Srs.: 7
Monastery of St. Clare of the Immaculate Conception - 200 Marycrest Dr., St. Louis, MO 63129-4813 t) 314-846-2618 Poor Clare Nuns.
Mount Grace Convent and Chapel of Perpetual Adoration - 1438 E. Warne Ave., St. Louis, MO 63107; Mailing: P.O. Box 16459, St. Louis, MO 63125 t) 314-381-2654 sistersuperior@outlook.com www.mountgraceconvent.org Sister Servants of the Holy Spirit of Perpetual Adoration (Generalate, Bad Driburg, Germany). Attended by Divine Word Fathers. Sr. Louise Mary Alindayu, SSpSAP, Supr.;

Convent -

Convent -

Religious Sisters of Mercy - 5047 Washington Pl., St. Louis, MO 63108 t) 314-932-7326 smrnerbun@archstl.org Sr. Mary Rachel Nerbun, RSM, Supr.; Srs.: 5
Sacred Heart Villa Convent - 2108 Macklind Ave., St. Louis, MO 63110 t) 314-771-2224 Sr. Alice Marie Legan, ASCJ, Supr.; Srs.: 4
Salesian Missionaries of Mary Immaculate - 798 Buckley Rd., St. Louis, MO 63125 t) 314-416-1778 smmi.us@gmail.com www.smmisisters.org/ Sr. Jolly Joseph, Supr.; Srs.: 3
School Sisters of Notre Dame, Central Pacific Province - Sancta Maria in Ripa, 320 E. Ripa Ave., St. Louis, MO 63125-2897 t) 314-544-0455 mhummert@ssndcp.org www.ssnd.org Sr. Debra Marie Sciano, SSND, Supr.; Srs.: 737

Liturgical Fabric Arts - 320 E. Ripa Ave., St. Louis, MO 63125 t) 314-633-7030 josephinessnd@yahoo.com www.liturgicalfabricarts.com

Resource Development - 320 E. Ripa Ave., St. Louis, MO 63125 t) 314-631-3530 missionadv@ssndcp.org www.ssndcp.org

School Sisters of Notre Dame Central Pacific Province, Inc. - 320 E. Ripa Ave., St. Louis, MO 63125 t) 314-544-0455 mhummert@ssndcp.org; mrehlinger@ssndcp.org www.ssnd.org Sr. Debra Marie Sciano, SSND, Supr.; Srs.: 737
School Sisters of Notre Dame Worldwide, Inc. - 320 E.

Ripa Ave., St. Louis, MO 63125 t) 314-633-7006; (262) 787-1013 (Finance Office) mhummert@ssndcp.org; ckiekhofer@ssndcp.org gerhardinger.org Sr. Debra Marie Sciano, SSND, Pres.; Mary Therese Hummert, Contact; Srs.: 1,969

Sisters of Good Shepherd Province of Mid North America - 7654 Natural Bridge Rd., St. Louis, MO 63121 c) (314) 397-9436 mmunday@gspmna.org; tponder@gspmna.org goodshepherdsisters.org Sr. Madeleine Munday, R.G.S., Prov.; Srs.: 82

Sisters of St. Francis of the Martyr St. George - 6825 Natural Bridge Rd., St. Louis, MO 63121 t) 314-383-4765 smchristine@mogch.org mogch.org Sr. M. Christine Crowder, F.S.G.M., Supr.;

Mother of Good Counsel Home - smbeata@mogch.org

Sisters of the Good Shepherd - 7654 Natural Bridge Rd., St. Louis, MO 63121 c) (314) 397-9436 (Antonia M. Ponder COO) tponder@gspmna.org www.goodshepherdsisters.org Antonia Ponder, COO; Srs.: 7

Society of the Sacred Heart, United States-Canada Province, Provincial House - 4120 Forest Park Ave., St. Louis, MO 63108 t) 314-652-1500 lterneus@rscj.org; provincialoffice@rscj.org www.rscj.org Sr. Suzanne Marie Cooke, RSCJ, Prov.; Srs.: 207

ST. LOUIS COUNTY

Religious of the Sacred Heart - 541 S. Mason Rd., St. Louis County, MO 63141-8550 t) 314-878-6705 khughes@rscj.org www.rscj.org

ENDOWMENTS / FOUNDATIONS / TRUSTS [EFT]

BRIDGETON

Mary and Joseph Trust - 3221 McKelvey Rd. Ste 107, Bridgeton, MO 63044 t) 314-768-1817 joshaughnessy@fsmonline.org John O'Shaughnessy, Treas.;

CHESTERFIELD

Mercy Health Foundation - 14528 S. Outer Forty, Ste. 100, Chesterfield, MO 63017 t) 314-579-6100 marynell.ploch@mercy.net Jacquelynn K. Richmond, Deputy Gen. Counsel;

CRYSTAL CITY

Mercy Health Foundation Jefferson - 1400 Hwy. 61 S., Crystal City, MO 63019; Mailing: P.O. Box 350, Crystal City, MO 63019 t) 314-628-3608 marynell.ploch@mercy.net Jacquelynn K. Richmond, Deputy Gen. Counsel;

DITTMER

Our Lady of Victory Charitable Foundation - 6476 Eime Rd., Dittmer, MO 63023 t) 636-274-5226 Marian Wolaver, Dir.;

FLORISSANT

Child Center Foundation - 2705 Mullanphy Ln., Florissant, MO 63031 t) 314-837-1702 info@mgstl.org www.marygrovechildren.org A residential and day treatment facility serving severely emotionally disturbed children and their families. Joseph Bestgen, CEO;

KIRKWOOD

Ursuline Provincialate Foundation, Central Province of the United States - 353 S. Sappington Rd., Kirkwood, MO 63122 t) 314-821-6884 ellette@osucentral.org Sr. Elisa Ryan, OSU, Prov.;

MARYLAND HEIGHTS

Society of St. Vincent de Paul National Foundation - 66 Progress Pkwy., Maryland Heights, MO 63043-3706 t) 314-576-3993 x200 dbarringer@svdpusa.org www.ssvpusa.org Sherry Brown, Admin.;

O'FALLON

Charitable Trust, Sisters of the Most Precious Blood of O'Fallon, MO - 204 N. Main St., O'Fallon, MO 63366-2299 t) 636-240-6010 ajungermann@cppsadmin-ofallon.org www.cpps-ofallon.org Support of retired Sisters. Sr. Susan Borgel, Treas.; Suann Fields, CFO;

St. Dominic Endowment Fund - St. Dominic High School, 31 St. Dominic Dr., O'Fallon, MO 63366 t) 314-240-8303 sgarrett@stdominichs.org www.stdominichs.org Jim Welby, Pres.;

PACIFIC

Franciscan Missionary Brothers Foundation - 265 St. Joseph Hill Rd., Pacific, MO 63069 t) 636-938-5361 shrine1olc@aol.com Bro. John Spila, O.S.F., Dir.;

Providence Trust - Our Lady of the Angels Monastery, 265 St. Joseph Hill Rd., Pacific, MO 63069 t) 636-938-5361 shrine1olc@aol.com theblackmadonnashrine.org Purpose: To support the religious and charitable purposes of the Franciscan Missionary Brothers of the Sacred Heart. Bro. John A. Spila, O.S.F., Dir.;

PERRYVILLE

St. Vincent de Paul Educational Foundation - 1010 A Rosati Ct., Perryville, MO 63775 t) 573-547-4591 svdepaul@svdepaul.org www.svdepaul.org Develops, Promotes and Sustains Catholic Education in Perry County. Rev. Milton F. Ryan, C.M.;

ST. CHARLES

Academy of the Sacred Heart of St. Charles, Missouri Endowment Trust Fund - 619 N. 2nd St., St. Charles, MO 63301 t) 636-946-6127 thorner@ash1818.org www.ash1818.org Timothy Horner, Pres.;

Duchesne High School Endowment Fund Inc. - 2550 Elm St., St. Charles, MO 63301 t) 636-946-6767 cnolan@duchesne-hs.org www.duchesne-hs.org Receives Bequests and Gifts from Various Donors for the Express Purpose of Aiding and Benefitting Duchesne High School, St. Charles, and by Investment Charles L. Nolan Jr., Pres.;

ST. LOUIS

Anna Foundation - 6400 Minnesota Ave., St. Louis, MO 63111 t) 314-481-8800 x321 mjohnson@csjsl.org Sr. Mary Frances Johnson, C.S.J., Treas.;

Cardinal Glennon Children's Foundation - 3800 Park Ave., St. Louis, MO 63110 t) 314-577-5605 www.glennon.org Member of SSM Health. Sandy Koller, Chief Philanthropy Officer;

Catholic Charities Foundation - 4445 Lindell Blvd., St. Louis, MO 63108 t) 314-367-5500 info@ccstl.org www.ccstl.org Dr. Jared H. Bryson, Pres.;

Language Access Multicultural People (LAMP) - 8050 Watson, Ste. 340, St. Louis, MO 63119 t) 314-842-0062 Jelena Mujanovic, Dir.;

Chaminade Foundation - 4425 W. Pine Blvd., St. Louis, MO 63108 t) 314-533-1207 jmarkel@sm-usa.org Bro. Joseph Markel, SM, Dir.;

Congregation of the Mission International Fund - 3701 Forest Park Ave., St. Louis, MO 63018 t) 314-344-1184 provinceoffice@vincentian.org Rev. Kevin P. McCracken, C.M., Treas.; Barbara Thibodeau, CFO;

Incarnate Word Foundation, Missouri - 5257 Shaw Ave., Ste. 309, St. Louis, MO 63110 t) 314-773-5100 lisa.durham@iwfdn.org; bridget.flood@iwfdn.org incarnatewordstl.org/ Bridget M. Flood, Exec.;

Lazarist Trust Fund - 3701 Forest Park Ave., St. Louis, MO 63108 t) 314-344-1184 provinceoffice@vincentian.org Rev. Kevin P. McCracken, C.M., Treas.;

Maria Droste Foundation - 7654 Natural Bridge Rd., St. Louis, MO 63121 t) 314-381-3400 tponder@gspmna.org Sr. Dolores Kalina, RSG, Treas.;

Marillac Mission Fund - 4600 Edmundson Rd., St. Louis, MO 63134 t) 314-733-8000 www.ascension.org F/K/A Daughters of Charity Foundation Craig Cordola, COO; Thomas VanOsdol, Executive Vice President & Chief Mission Integration Officer;

Missionaries of the Holy Family Retirement Trust Fund - 3014 Oregon Ave., St. Louis, MO 63118 t) 314-577-6300 msf@msf-america.org www.msf-america.org Rev. Philip Sosa, M.S.F., Supr.;

Pelletier Trust, a Charitable Trust of the Sisters of the Good Shepherd - 7654 Natural Bridge Rd., St. Louis, MO 63121 c) (314) 397-9436 (Antonia M. Ponder COO) tponder@gspmna.org Sr. Madeleine Munday, R.G.S., Prov.;

SSM Health Foundation - 10101 Woodfield Ln., St. Louis, MO 63132

Sisters of the Good Shepherd Province of Mid-North America Foundation - 7654 Natural Bridge Rd., St. Louis, MO 63121 c) (314) 397-9436 (Antonia M. Ponder COO) tponder@gspmna.org goodshepherdsisters.org Sr. Madeleine Munday, R.G.S., Prov.;

SSM Health Foundation - St. Louis - 12312 Olive Blvd., Ste. 100, St. Louis, MO 63141 t) 314-523-8044 www.ssmhealth.com/foundation Member of SSM Health. Paul Ross, Exec.;

Ursuline Sisters Trust Fund - 353 S. Sappington Rd., St. Louis, MO 63122 t) 314-821-6884 ellette@osucentral.org www.osucentral.org Ellette Gibson, Contact;

US Central and Southern Province, Society of Jesus Aged/Infirm Fund - 4511 W. Pine Blvd., St. Louis, MO 63108 t) 314-361-7765 ucstreasurer@jesuits.org Rev. J. Daniel Daly, S.J., Treas.;

US Central and Southern Province, Society of Jesus Formation Fund - 4511 W. Pine Blvd., St. Louis, MO 63108 t) 314-361-7765 ucstreasurer@jesuits.org Rev. J. Daniel Daly, S.J., Treas.;

Visitation Real Property Foundation - 3020 N. Ballas Rd., St. Louis, MO 63131 t) 314-625-9247 srvh@visitationmonastery.org Sr. Veronica Haronik, VHM, Pres.;

TROY

Mercy Health Foundation Lincoln - 1000 E. Cherry St., Troy, MO 63379; Mailing: 14528 S. Outer 40 Rd., Ste. 100, Chesterfield, MO 63017 t) 314-628-3608 marynell.ploch@mercy.net Jacquelynn K. Richmond, Deputy Gen. Counsel;

HOSPITALS / HEALTH SERVICES [HOS]

BRIDGETON

SSM Health De Paul Hospital - St. Louis - 12303 De Paul Dr., Bridgeton, MO 63044 t) 314-344-6000 www.ssmdepaul.com Member of SSM Health Care. Tina Garrison, Pres.; Rev. David Boyle, Chap.; Rev. Kevin Cook, Chap.; Rev. Daniel DeVilder, Chap.; Rev. Glenn Reitz, Chap.; Glen Greenwood, Chap.; Lee Howard Gunther, Chap.; Bed Capacity: 523; Asstd. Annu.: 223,409; Staff: 2,032

SSM Health De Paul Hospital - St. Louis - 12303 De Paul Dr., Bridgeton, MO 63044 t) (314) 344-6000 Bed Capacity: 523; Asstd. Annu.: 223,409; Staff: 2,032

St. Vincent Division - 12303 De Paul Dr., Bridgeton, MO 63044 t) 314-344-7955 Pre-Adolescent, Adolescent, Adult & Gero Psychiatric Care and Outpatient Chemical Dependency. Michelle Schafer, Admin.;

CREVE COEUR

Mercy Hospital St. Louis - 615 S. New Ballas Rd., Creve Coeur, MO 63141; Mailing: 14528 S. Outer 40 Rd., Ste. 100, Chesterfield, MO 63017 t) 314-251-6000 marynell.ploch@mercy.net www.mercy.net (See Branch Unit under Mercy Hospital East Community). Conducted by the Sisters of Mercy of the Americas South Central Community, Inc. Jacquelynn K. Richmond, Deputy Gen. Counsel;

FENTON

SSM St. Clare Health Center - 1015 Bowles Ave., Fenton, MO 63026 t) 636-496-2000 www.ssmhealth.com Member of SSM Health Care. Kyle Grate, Pres.; Bed Capacity: 180; Asstd. Annu.: 134,690; Staff: 1,040

LAKE SAINT LOUIS

SSM St. Joseph Hospital West (SSM Health St. Joseph Hospital - Lake Saint Louis) - 100 Medical Plz., Lake Saint Louis, MO 63367 t) 314-625-5200 www.ssmstjoseph.com Member of SSM Health Care. Deborah Graves, Pres.; Bed Capacity: 215; Asstd. Annu.: 156,156; Staff: 1,043

ST. CHARLES

SSM Health St. Joseph Hospital - St. Charles - 300 First Capitol Dr., St. Charles, MO 63301 t) 314-947-5000 www.ssmstjoseph.com Rev. Charles Dey, Chap.; Gail Holstein, Chap.; Bed Capacity: 333; Asstd. Annu.: 183,242; Staff: 1,197

ST. LOUIS

Mercy Hospital South - 10010 Kennerly Rd., St. Louis, MO 63128 t) 314-525-1000 marybeth.bulte@mercy.net

www.mercy.net fka St. Anthony's Medical Center Rev. William Cardy, O.F.M., Chap.;
SSM Health - Cardinal Glennon Children's Hospital - 1465 S. Grand Blvd., St. Louis, MO 63104 t) 314-577-5613 www.cardinalglennon.com Member of SSM Health Care. Steven Burghart, Pres.; Bed Capacity: 195; Asstd. Annu.: 248,872; Staff: 2,081
SSM Health St. Mary's Hospital - 6420 Clayton Rd., St. Louis, MO 63117 t) 314-768-8000 www.stmarys-stlouis.com Member of SSM Health Care Travis Capers, Pres.; Bed Capacity: 495; Asstd. Annu.: 219,417; Staff: 2,516
TROY
Mercy Hospital Lincoln - 1000 E. Cherry St., Troy, MO 63379 t) 314-628-3608 marynell.ploch@mercy.net Jacquelynn K. Richmond, Deputy Gen. Counsel;
WASHINGTON
Mercy Hospital Washington - 901 E. 5th St., Washington, MO 63090 t) 636-239-8000 marynell.ploch@mercy.net (See Listing Under Creve Coeur, MO). Eric Eoloff, Pres.;
WENTZVILLE
SSM St. Joseph Health Center-Wentzville - 500 Medical Dr., Wentzville, MO 63385 t) 636-327-1000 www.ssmstjoseph.com Deborah Graves, Pres.; Bed Capacity: 77; Asstd. Annu.: 14,132; Staff: 261

MISCELLANEOUS [MIS]

BRIDGETON
Collaborative Governance - 3221 McKelvey Rd., Suite 107, Bridgeton, MO 63044 t) 314-768-1824 ahewitt@collaborativegovernance.org; bjfranklin@collaborativegovernance.org Providing canonical governance and civil administration for religious communities. Sr. Barbara Jean Franklin, Chair; Sr. Janice Bader, CPPS, Pres.; Sr. Judith Bell, Pres.; Allison Hewitt, Exec.;
Room at the Inn - 3415 Bridgeland Dr., Bridgeton, MO 63044 t) 314-209-9198 dweber@roomstl.org www.roomstl.org Sr. Michele Bisbey, C.D.P., Prov.;
The Sarah Community - 3221 McKelvey Rd., Ste. 107, Bridgeton, MO 63044 t) 314-768-1817 thesarahcommunity.com Purpose: provides a continuing care retirement community for members of religious congregations and laity. Douglas Trost, Dir.;
Sisters of Divine Providence - 3415 Bridgeland Dr., Bridgeton, MO 63044 t) 314-971-4576 apairn@cdpsisters.org www.cdpsisters.org Sr. Michele Bisbey, C.D.P., Prov.; Sr. Ann Pairn, Contact;
CADET
Rural Parish Workers of Christ the King - 15540 Cannon Mines Rd., Cadet, MO 63630 t) 636-586-5171 ruralparishworkers@gmail.com rpwck.org A Secular Institute of the Archdiocese of St. Louis. Natalie Villmer, Dir.;
CHESTERFIELD
McAuley Portfolio Management Company - 14528 S. Outer Forty, Ste. 100, Attn: Mercy Corporate Paralegal - Legal Dept, Chesterfield, MO 63017 t) 314-579-6100 marynell.ploch@mercy.net
Mercy Health - 14528 S. Outer Forty, Ste. 100, Chesterfield, MO 63017 t) 314-579-6100 marynell.ploch@mercy.net www.mercy.net
MHM Support Services - 14528 S. Outer Forty, Ste. 100, Chesterfield, MO 63017 t) 314-579-6100 marynell.ploch@mercy.net
CRESTWOOD
St. Louis Catholic Charismatic Renewal - 1406 S. Sappington, Crestwood, MO 63126; Mailing: 20 Archbishop May Dr., Shrewsbury, MO 63119 t) 314-792-7734 janeguenther@archstl.org www.archstl.org/renewal Most Rev. Robert Hermann; Rev. Msgr. Edmund Griesedieck, Chap.; Jane Guenther, Dir.; Anne Hruz, Healing and Deliverance Coordinator;
Abiding Bible Companion - t) 314-725-6527
Healing & Deliverance Ministry -
Two Alike -
DARDENNE PRAIRIE
Saint William Apartments, Inc. - 1979 Hanley Rd., Dardenne Prairie, MO 63368; Mailing: 7601 Watson Rd., St. Louis, MO 63119 t) 636-695-4200
St. William Apartments II, Inc. - 1983 Hanley Rd., Dardenne Prairie, MO 63368; Mailing: 7601 Watson Rd., St. Louis, MO 63119 t) 636-695-4205
DITTMER
Servants of the Paraclete Missouri Generalate Corporation - 6476 Eime Rd., Dittmer, MO 63023 t) 636-274-5226 prafff@gmail.com www.servantsoftheparaclete.org Rev. Raffaele Talmelli, sP, Vicar;
FLORISSANT
Friends of Old St. Ferdinand, Inc. - 1 Rue St. Francois, Florissant, MO 63031
KIRKWOOD
Prelature of the Holy Cross and Opus Dei - Wespine Study Center, 100 E. Essex Ave., Kirkwood, MO 63122 t) 314-821-1608 info@wespine.org www.opusdei.org Rev. Gregory Coyne; Rev. Michael E. Giesler;
LIGUORI
Redemptorist Fathers - One Liguori Dr., Liguori, MO 63057 t) 636-464-2500 bmiller@liguori.org www.liguori.org Liguori Publications Rev. Byron J. Miller, C.Ss.R., Pres.; Rev. Joseph M. Curalli, C.Ss.R., Staff;
MARYLAND HEIGHTS
Society of St. Vincent de Paul National Stores - 66 Progress Pkwy., Maryland Heights, MO 63043 t) 314-576-3993 x200 usacouncil@svdpusa.org www.svdpusa-thriftstore.org David Barringer, CEO;
***Society of St. Vincent de Paul, National Council of the United States** - 66 Progress Pkwy., Maryland Heights, MO 63043-3706 t) 314-576-3993 usacouncil@svdpusa.org www.ssvpusa.org Rev. Donald J. Hying; Ralph Middlecamp, Pres.; David Barringer, CEO;
SHREWSBURY
The St. Louis Archdiocesan Fund - 20 Archbishop May Dr., Shrewsbury, MO 63119-5738 t) 314-792-7129 lawandabarnes@archstl.org LaWanda Barnes, Finance Manager;
ST. CHARLES
Sts. Joachim and Ann Care Service - 4116 McClay Rd., St. Charles, MO 63304 t) 636-441-1302 jlipin@jacares.org jacares.org Dcn. Jack Lipin, Exec.;
ST. LOUIS
Alexian Brothers Services, Inc. - 4600 Edmundson Rd., St. Louis, MO 63134 t) 314-292-9308 ahscm-mission@ascension.org www.ascensionliving.org/ Ryan Endsley, COO;
Almost Home - 3200 St. Vincent Ave., St. Louis, MO 63104-1336 t) 314-771-4663 rwise@almosthomestl.org www.almosthomestl.org Transitional living program for teenage mothers and their children who are homeless. Reona Wise, Exec.;
American Academy of FertilityCare Professionals - 11700 Studt Ave., Ste. C, St. Louis, MO 63141 t) 402-489-3733 president@aafcp.net aafcp.net Diane Daly, Office of Natural Family Planning Archdiocese of St. Louis;
Annual Catholic Appeal - 20 Archbishop May Dr., St. Louis, MO 63119 t) 314-792-7681 niebruggeb@archstl.org www.archstl.org/aca Brian Niebrugge, Dir.;
Archdiocesan Stewardship Education Committee - 20 Archbishop May Dr., St. Louis, MO 63119 t) 314-792-7215 www.archstl.org/stewardship Rev. John Paul Hopping; Rev. Msgr. Gregory R. Mikesch; Rev. John Rogers Vien; David Baranowski, Dir.;
The Archdiocese of St. Louis Real Estate Corporation - 20 Archbishop May Dr., St. Louis, MO 63119 t) 314-792-7004 Tom DuBois, Dir.;
ASC Health - 4233 Sulphur Ave., St. Louis, MO 63109 t) 314-351-6294 schumerf@adorers.org Sr. Mary Louise Degenhart, Chair;
ASC Investment Group Inc. - 4233 Sulphur Ave., St. Louis, MO 63109 t) 314-351-6294 bergkampv@adorers.org Sr. Vicki Bergkamp, ASC, Pres.; Sr. Michelle Woodruff, Treas.;
Ascension Ministry and Mission Fund - 4600 Edmundson Rd., St. Louis, MO 63134 t) 314-733-8000 christine.mccoy2@ascension.org www.ascension.org Christine K. McCoy, Exec.; Thomas VanOsdol, Executive Vice President & Chief Mission Integration Officer;
Aware, Inc. - St. Anthony's Medical Center, 10016 Kennerly Rd., St. Louis, MO 63128 t) 314-525-1622 Karen Molner, Pres.;
Catechetical/Adult Formation/Paul VI Institute of Catechetical and Pastoral Studies - 20 Archbishop May Dr., St. Louis, MO 63119 t) 314-792-7060 casinger@archstl.org; samanthagrone@archstl.org www.archstl.org Samantha Grone, Diocesan D.R.E.;
Catholic Home Study - Lazarist Residence, 13245 Tesson Ferry Rd., St. Louis, MO 63128 c) 773-896-6410 catholichomestudy@gmail.com www.catholichomestudy.org Offers free correspondence courses on the Catholic Faith. Rev. Ronald Hoye, C.M., Dir.;
Catholic Kolping Society of America - 5410 Oakvilla Manor Dr., St. Louis, MO 63129 t) 314-894-2136
Central Bureau of the C.C.V.A. - 3835 Westminster Pl., St. Louis, MO 63108-3472 t) 314-371-1653 centbur@sbcglobal.net www.socialjusticereview.org Rev. Edward Krause, C.S.C., Dir.;
St. Charles Lwanga Center - 4746 Carter Ave., Ste. 100, St. Louis, MO 63115-2238 t) 314-367-7929 info@lwangacenter.org www.archstl.org/lwangacenter/ A spiritual formation Center for leadership in the African American Catholic Community, in the Archdiocese of St. Louis. Rev. Arthur J. Cavitt, Dir.;
CSJ Ministries - 6400 Minnesota Ave., St. Louis, MO 63111 t) 314-481-8800 mjohnson@csjsl.org Sr. Mary Frances Johnson, C.S.J., Treas.;
Congregation Sisters of St. Joseph Education Association - 2767 Ashrock Dr., St. Louis, MO 63129
Daughters of Charity Ministries, Inc. - 4330 Olive St., St. Louis, MO 63108-2622 t) 314-533-4770 tom.beck@doc.org www.daughtersofcharity.org Sr. Catherine Mary Norris, D.C., Prov.;
Daughters of Charity National Health System, Inc. - 4600 Edmundson Rd., St. Louis, MO 63134 t) 314-733-8000 www.ascension.org John Tersigni, Chief Mission Integration Officer; Craig Cordola, Executive Vice President & Chief Operating Officer;
Daughters of Charity, Inc. - 4330 Olive St., St. Louis, MO 63108-2622 t) 314-533-4770 tom.beck@doc.org www.daughtersofcharity.org Sr. Catherine Mary Norris, D.C., Prov.;
Dominican Studentate - 3407 Lafayette Ave., St. Louis, MO 63104 t) 708-638-6163 thefriar@thefriar.org Rev. James V. Marchionda, O.P., Prov.;
Equestrian Order of the Holy Sepulchre of Jerusalem - 2870 S. Lindbergh Blvd., St. Louis, MO 63131 t) 314-984-5077 nardance@aol.com
The Franciscan Connection - 5201 Virginia, St. Louis, MO 63111; Mailing: P.O. Box 18637, St. Louis, MO 63118 t) 314-773-8485 franciscanconnection@thefriars.org www.franciscanconnection.org Community Outreach Friar Frank Coens, OFM, Dir.; Friar Paul Gallagher, OFM, Dir.; Friar Robert Charles Sieg, OFM, Dir.;
Franklin County Catholic Church Real Estate Corporation - 20 Archbishop May Dr., St. Louis, MO 63119 t) 314-792-7004 tomdubois@archstl.org Tom DuBois, Dir.;
Friends of St. Francis de Sales Oratory, Inc. - 2653 Ohio Ave., St. Louis, MO 63118 t) 314-771-3100 sfds@institute-christ-king.org www.traditionfortomorrow.com Rev. Canon Pierre Dumain, ICRSP, Rector; Rev. Canon Benjamin L Coggeshall, ICRSP, Vicar;
Good Shepherd Mission Development Corporation - 7654 Natural Bridge Rd., St. Louis, MO 63121 c) (314) 397-9436 (Antonia M. Ponder) dkalina@gspmna.org Sr. Dolores Kalina, RSG, Treas.;
Good Shepherd Programs of St. Louis - 7654 Natural

Bridge Rd., St. Louis, MO 63121 c) (314) 397-9436 (Antonia M. Ponder) tponder@gspmna.org Sr. Madeleine Munday, R.G.S., Prov.;

Hispanic Ministry of the Archdiocese of St. Louis - 20 Archbishop May Dr., St. Louis, MO 63119 t) 314-792-7645

Institute for Theological Encounter with Science & Technology (ITEST) - 20 Archbishop May Dr., St. Louis, MO 63119 t) 314-792-7220 itest@archstl.org faithscience.org/ Dr. Sebastian Mahfood, OP, Dir.;

Jefferson County Catholic Church Real Estate Corporation - 20 Archbishop May Dr., St. Louis, MO 63119 t) 314-792-7004 tomdubois@archstl.org Tom DuBois, Dir.;

Saint Joseph Educational Ministries Corporation - 6400 Minnesota Ave., St. Louis, MO 63111

Ladies of Charity of St. Catherine Laboure - 12160 Leelaine Dr., St. Louis, MO 63126 Affiliate with Ladies of Charity of the United States & the Assoc. of Intl. Charities of St. Vincent de Paul. Susan Tumminia, Pres.;

Ladies of Charity Service Center - 7500 Natural Bridge Rd., St. Louis, MO 63121 t) 314-383-4207 Ladies of Charity Service Center, Thrift Store & Food Pantry. Phyllis A. Makowski, Pres.;

Lincoln County Catholic Church Real Estate Corporation - 20 Archbishop May Dr., St. Louis, MO 63119 t) 314-792-7004 tomdubois@archstl.org Tom DuBois, Dir.;

St. Louis Area Women Religious Collaborative Ministries - 4330 Olive St., St. Louis, MO 63108; Mailing: 4200 Delor, St. Louis, MO 63116 t) 314-633-7095 info@englishtutoringproject.org Includes English Tutoring Project for Immigrant/Refugee Children and Intercommunity Environmental Council. Erin Prest, Treas.;

St. Louis County Catholic Church Real Estate Corporation - 20 Archbishop May Dr., St. Louis, MO 63119 t) 314-792-7004 tomdubois@archstl.org Tom DuBois, Dir.;

Lovers of the Holy Cross of St. Louis - 4211 Hydraulic Ave., St. Louis, MO 63116 t) 314-832-7321

Mercy Investment Services, Inc. - 2039 N. Geyer Rd., St. Louis, MO 63131 t) 314-909-4609 www.mercyinvestments.org Bryan Pini, Pres.;

National Christian Life Community of the United States of America (CLC) - 4511 W. Pine Blvd., St. Louis, MO 63108-2109 t) 202-425-2572 exco@clc-usa.com www.clc-usa.com A public, intl. assoc. of the Faithful of Pontifical Right which builds small faith-communities for mission & service to the church. E. Christina Kim, Pres.;

Oblates of Wisdom Study Center - 744 S. 3rd St., St. Louis, MO 63102; Mailing: PO Box 13230, St. Louis, MO 63157 t) 314-475-8524 materdei82@hotmail.com www.rtforum.org/os/index.html Rev. Brian W. Harrison, O.S., Dir.;

Our Lady's Inn - 8790 Manchester Rd., Ste. 202, St. Louis, MO 63144 t) 314-736-1544 pforrest@ourladysinn.org www.ourladysinn.org Residential Shelter and Aftercare Program for homeless pregnant women and their children. Peggy Forrest, CEO;

St. Charles Inn - 3607 Hwy. D, Defiance, MO 63341 t) 636-398-5375

St. Patrick Center - 800 N. Tucker, St. Louis, MO 63101 t) 314-802-0700 adagostino@stpatrickcenter.org www.stpatrickcenter.org Transforms lives through sustainable housing, employment & healthcare programs for those who are homeless or at risk. Anthony D'Agostino, CEO;

St. Patrick Partnership Center - 800 N. Tucker, St. Louis, MO 63101 t) 314-802-0700 www.stpatrickcenter.org Anthony D'Agostino, CEO;

Pauline Books and Media - 9804 Watson Rd., St. Louis, MO 63126 t) 314-965-3512; 314-965-5273 stlouis@pauline.org www.pauline.org Daughters of St. Paul.

Perpetual Help Retirement Corporation - 335 S. Kirkwood Rd., St. Louis, MO 63122 t) 314-965-3700 srmaryanne@fsolph.org www.fsolph.org To support the religious and charitable purposes of the Franciscan Sisters of Our Lady of Perpetual Help. Sr. Renita Brummer, O.S.F., Vice Pres.;

Perry County Catholic Church Real Estate Corporation - 20 Archbishop May Dr., St. Louis, MO 63119 t) 314-792-7004 tomdubois@archstl.org Tom DuBois, Dir.;

***Restoration Matters** - 357 Leffingwell Ave., St. Louis, MO 63122; Mailing: P.O. Box 220844, St. Louis, MO 63122 t) (314) 822-7641 info@restorationmatters.org restorationmatters.org

Rosati Center - 4220 N. Grand Ave., St. Louis, MO 63107 t) (314) 534-6624 A transitional housing facility providing shelter and individual case management. Managed by St. Patrick Center. Anthony D'Agostino, CEO;

Rural Parish Clinic of the Archdiocese of St. Louis - 20 Archbishop May Dr., St. Louis, MO 63119 t) 314-792-7717 (Office Mgr.); 314-792-7607 (Pres.) www.archstl.org/rpc Sr. Mary Rachel Nerbun, RSM, Pres.;

San Luis Apartments, Inc. - 20 Archbishop May Dr., St. Louis, MO 63119 t) 314-792-7408 billing@archstl.org Rev. Msgr. Jerome D. Billing, Chancellor;

Society Devoted to the Sacred Heart - 9600 Tennyson Ave., St. Louis, MO 63114 t) 314-429-0526 shsuperior@outlook.com www.sacredheartsisters.com

***Society of St. Vincent de Paul, Council of St. Louis** - 100 N. Jefferson Ave., St. Louis, MO 63103 t) 877-238-3228; 314-881-6000 info@svdpstl.org www.svdpstl.org

St. Charles Thrift Store - 1063 Regency Pkwy., St. Charles, MO 63303 t) 314-881-6047

Christy Thrift Store - 4928 Christy, St. Louis, MO 63116 t) 314-881-6043

Dellwood Thrift Store - 10052 W. Florissant Ave., St. Louis, MO 63136

Lemay Ferry Thrift Store - 3924 Lemay Ferry Rd., St. Louis, MO 63125 t) 314-881-6046

West County Thrift Store - 14660 Manchester Rd., Ballwin, MO 63011 t) 314-811-6034

SSM Health Businesses - 10101 Woodfield Ln., St. Louis, MO 63132 t) 314-994-7800 Member of SSM Health. Laura Kaiser, Pres.;

SSM Health Care Corporation - 10101 Woodfield Ln., St. Louis, MO 63132 t) 314-994-7800 Member of SSM Health. Laura Kaiser, Pres.;

SSM Health Care Portfolio Management Company - 10101 Woodfield Ln., St. Louis, MO 63132 t) 314-994-7800 Member of SSM Health. Laura Kaiser, Pres.;

SSM Health Care St. Louis - 12312 Olive Blvd., Ste. 600, St. Louis, MO 63141 t) 314-989-2000 www.ssmhealth.com Member of SSM Health Care. Jeremy Fotheringham, Pres.;

SSM Regional Health Services - 10101 Woodfield Ln., St. Louis, MO 63132 t) 314-994-7800 Member of SSM Health. Laura Kaiser, Pres.;

SSM-SLUH, Inc. - 1201 S. Grand Blvd, St. Louis, MO 63104 t) 314-577-8000 www.ssmhealth.com Steven Scott, Pres.;

St. Charles County Catholic Church Real Estate Corporation - 20 Archbishop May Dr., St. Louis, MO 63119 t) 314-792-7004 tomdubois@archstl.org Tom DuBois, Dir.;

St. Francois County Catholic Church Real Estate Corporation - 20 Archbishop May Dr., St. Louis, MO 63119 t) 314-792-7004 tomdubois@archstl.org Tom DuBois, Dir.;

St. Louis City Catholic Church Real Estate Corporation - 20 Archbishop May Dr., St. Louis, MO 63119 t) 314-792-7084 Randy Rathert, Director, Building and Real Estate;

Ste. Genevieve County Catholic Church Real Estate Corporation - 20 Archbishop May Dr., St. Louis, MO 63119 t) 314-792-7004 tomdubois@archstl.org Tom DuBois, Dir.;

US Central & Southern Province, Society of Jesus - 4511 W. Pine Blvd., St. Louis, MO 63108-2191 t) 314-361-7765 ucsadvancement@jesuits.org www.jesuitscentralsouthern.org Paula Parrish, Dir.;

VIMS - 3701 Forest Park Ave., St. Louis, MO 63108 c) 312-208-1595 mpranaitis@depaul.edu Rev. Mark S. Pranaitis, C.M., Exec. Dir.;

Vincentian Marian Youth, U.S.A. - 3701 Forest Park Ave., St. Louis, MO 63108; Mailing: National Office, P.O. Box 202, Perryville, MO 63775 t) 573-768-7011; 314-344-1184 provinceoffice@vincentian.org www.vmy.us Rev. David G. Nations, C.M., Natl. Advisor;

Vincentian Solidarity Office - 3701 Forest Park Ave., St. Louis, MO 63108 t) 215-713-3998 vsol@cmphlsvs.org Rev. Joel Bernardo, C.M., Exec. Dir.;

Warren County Catholic Church Real Estate Corporation - 20 Archbishop May Dr., St. Louis, MO 63119 t) 314-792-7004 tomdubois@archstl.org Tom DuBois, Dir.;

Washington County Catholic Church Real Estate Corporation - 20 Archbishop May Dr., St. Louis, MO 63119 t) 314-792-7004 tomdubois@archstl.org Tom DuBois, Dir.;

***Women for Faith and Family** - 6415 Sutherland, St. Louis, MO 63109 www.wf-f.org Susan J. Benofy, Treas.;

Young Catholic Musicians - 1919 S. 7th St., St. Louis, MO 63104 t) 314-962-9260 revycm@charter.net Mary Smith, Contact;

STE. GENEVIEVE

Vincentian Marian Youth Southeast Missouri - 751 Center Dr., Ste. Genevieve, MO 63670 t) 573-883-7200 c) (573) 608-0827 (Executive Director) info@vmysemo.org; mgiasi@vmysemo.org www.vmysemo.org Catholic Youth Ministry Organization serving the greater Southeast Missouri area. Curt Buerck, Pres.; Michael J Giasi, Exec.;

MONASTERIES AND RESIDENCES FOR PRIESTS AND BROTHERS [MON]

DARDENNE PRAIRIE

Franciscan Brothers of the Holy Cross St. Charles Friary - 12 Dardenne Woods Ct., Dardenne Prairie, MO 63368 t) 636-561-0589 bdavids61@gmail.com www.franciscanbrothers.net Bro. David Sarnecki, F.F.S.C., Supr.; Bro. Raphael Kreikemeier, F.F.S.C.;

DITTMER

Franciscan Friars Province of the Sacred Heart - 7992 St. Francis Ln., Eime Rd., Dittmer, MO 63023-0278; Mailing: P.O. Box 278, Dittmer, MO 63023-0278 t) 636-285-7362 (Friary); 636-274-0554 (Il Ritiro) Rev. Bertin Miller, O.F.M., Dir.; Rev. Pio Jackson, O.F.M., Chap.; Rev. Luis Runde, O.F.M.;

Servants of the Paraclete - St. Michael's Community, 6476 Eime Rd,, Dittmer, MO 63023 t) 636-274-5226 camillusrene@gmail.com www.servantsoftheparaclete.org Rev. Rene Godito, sP, Supr.; Brs.: 2; Priests: 4

EUREKA

Franciscan Brothers House of Studies - 450 Summerville Blvd., Eureka, MO 63025; Mailing: P.O. Box 129, Eureka, MO 63025 t) 636-938-5539 shrine1olc@aol.com House of Studies of Franciscan Missionary Brothers of the Sacred Heart of Jesus. Bro. John A. Spila, O.S.F., Dir.; Brs.: 1

HIGH RIDGE

Society of Our Mother of Peace - Sons of Our Mother of Peace, Mary the Font Solitude, 6150 Antire Rd., High Ridge, MO 63049-2135 c) 636-677-3235 smpvocations@gmail.com marythefont.org Rev. Placid Guste, S.M.P., Supr.; Rev. John Richard Hansen, SMP, Prov.; Brs.: 1; Priests: 2

LIGUORI

Alphonsian Foundation - One Liguori Dr., Liguori, MO 63057-9998 t) 636-223-1455 foundation@alfonsiana.org www.alphonsianfoundation.org Purpose: to provide public relations and financial support for the Alphonsian Academy of Moral Theology in Rome. Rev. Alfonso V. Amarante, C.Ss.R., Pres.; Priests: 1

St. Clement Health Care Center - 300 Liguori Dr., Liguori, MO 63057 t) 636-464-3666 Rev. Gan Nguyen, C.Ss.R., Local Superior; Bro. Gerard Patin, C.Ss.R., Dir.; Bro. Terrence Burke, C.Ss.R., Staff; Rev. Nghia Cao, C.Ss.R., Missionary; Rev. Richard Mevissen, C.Ss.R., In Res.; Rev. Vincent Minh Cao, C.Ss.R., Staff; Rev. Bernard Carlin, C.Ss.R., In Res.; Rev. Albert J. Castellino, C.Ss.R., In Res.; Rev. John Cody, C.Ss.R., In Res.; Rev. Joseph M. Curalli, C.Ss.R., Liguori Publications; Dcn. Richard W. Fischer, C.Ss.R., Staff; Rev. John Gouger, C.Ss.R., In Res.; Rev. Robert Halter, C.Ss.R., Missionary; Rev. Victor Karls, C.Ss.R., Missionary; Bro. Daniel Korn, C.Ss.R., In Res.; Rev. Frank Kriski, C.Ss.R., In Res.; Rev. Gerard B. LaPorte, C.Ss.R., In Res.; Rev. Gregory Mayers, C.Ss.R., In Res.; Rev. Byron J. Miller, C.Ss.R., Liguori Publications; Rev. Joseph Morin, C.Ss.R., In Res.; Rev. Rudy Papes, C.Ss.R., In Res.; Bro. Andrew Patin, C.Ss.R., Staff; Rev. David Polek, C.Ss.R., In Res.; Rev. Richard M. Potts, C.Ss.R., Missionary; Rev. Michael P. Quinn, C.Ss.R., Staff; Rev. Richard Quinn, C.Ss.R., In Res.; Bro. Robert T. Ruffing, C.Ss.R., In Res.; Rev. Denis Ryan, C.Ss.R., In Res.; Rev. Richard Schiblin, C.Ss.R., In Res.; Rev. Carl Schindler, C.Ss.R., In Res.; Bro. Paul Yasenak, C.Ss.R., Staff; Brs.: 7; Priests: 26

Liguori Mission House/Redemptorists - 300 Liguori Dr., Liguori, MO 63057 t) 636-464-6999 Rev. Gregory May, C.Ss.R., Ass't. Secretary;

Order of the Most Holy Redeemer, Monastery of the Most Holy Redeemer, Thailand - 200 Liguori Dr., Liguori, MO 63057 t) 636-464-1093 rednuns@gmail.com Sr. Joan E. Calver, O.SS.R., Prioress;

PACIFIC

Franciscan Missionary Brothers of the Sacred Heart of Jesus - 265 St. Joseph Hill Rd., Pacific, MO 63069 t) 636-938-5361 shrine1olc@aol.com theblackmadonnashrine.org Generalate of Franciscan Missionary Brothers of the Sacred Heart of Jesus. Bro. John Spila, O.S.F., Dir.; Brs.: 3

Black Madonna Shrine - 100 St. Joseph Hill Rd., Pacific, MO 63069 t) (636) 938-5361 Bro. John A. Spila, O.S.F., Dir.;

PERRYVILLE

Congregation of the Mission - 1701 W. St. Joseph St., Perryville, MO 63775-1599 t) 573-547-6533 josendorf@vincentian.org vincentian.org U.S. Motherhouse of the Congregation of the Mission (Vincentian Fathers, Brothers, Western Prov.). Rev. Lawrence F. Asma, C.M., In Res.; Rev. James T. Beighlie, C.M., In Res.; Rev. Robert J. Brockland, C.M., In Res.; Rev. Philip J. Coury, C.M., In Res.; Rev. Thomas Croak, C.M., In Res.; Rev. John F. Gagnepain, C.M., In Res.; Rev. Edward Gallagher, C.M., In Res.; Rev. Joseph C. Geders, C.M., Pst.; Bro. Harvey Goertz, C.M., In Res.; Bro. David P. Goodman, C.M., In Res.; Rev. William Hartenbach, In Res.; Rev. Jerome Herff, C.M., In Res.; Bro. Richard A. Hermann, C.M., In Res.; Dcn. Arnold Hernandez, C.M., In Res.; Rev. Thomas R. Hinni, C.M., In Res.; Rev. John J Jung, C.M., Par. Vicar; Rev. Richard L. Lause, C.M., In Res.; Rev. Ben Melaku, Par. Vicar; Rev. Patrick Mullin, In Res.; Rev. Binh Nguyen, C.M., In Res.; Bro. Timothy Opferman, C.M., Treas.; Rev. James R Osendorf, C.M., Supr.; Rev. Ronald W. Ramson, C.M., In Res.; Rev. William Rhinehart, C.M., In Res.; Rev. Charles F. Shelby, C.M., In Res.; Rev. John V. Shine, C.M., In Res.; Rev. James G Ward, In Res.; Rev. Robert Wood, C.M., In Res.; Bro. Richard Zoellner, C.M., In Res.; Brs.: 5; Priests: 26

ROCKY MOUNT

Contemplative Heart of Mary Hermitage - 20542 Echo Valley Rd., Rocky Mount, MO 65072 t) 573-557-2119 robertaten_2001@yahoo.com Rev. Robert L. Aten;

ST. LOUIS

The Abbey of St. Mary and St. Louis - 500 S. Mason Rd., St. Louis, MO 63141-8522 t) 314-434-3690 frdominic@priory.org www.stlouisabbey.org Benedictines of the English Congregation. Rt. Rev. Gregory Mohrman, O.S.B., Abbot; Rev. Cuthbert Elliott, O.S.B., Headmaster; Rev. Cassian Koenemann, O.S.B., Prior; Rev. Linus Dolce, O.S.B.; Rev. Finbarr Dowling, O.S.B.; Rev. Gerard Garrigan, O.S.B.; Rev. Francis Hein, O.S.B.; Rev. John McCusker, O.S.B.; Rev. Andrew Senay, O.S.B.; Rev. Augustine Wetta, O.S.B.; Rev. Benedict Allin, O.S.B., Other; Rev. Ambrose Bennett, O.S.B., Other; Rev. Thomas Frerking, O.S.B., Abbot Emeritus; Rev. Laurence Kriegshauser, O.S.B., Other; Rev. Dominic Lenk, O.S.B., Other; Rev. Aidan McDermott, O.S.B., Other; Rev. Athanasius Soto, O.S.B., Other; Rev. Ralph Wright, O.S.B., Other; Brs.: 2; Priests: 18

Bellarmine House of Studies - 3737 Westminster Pl., St. Louis, MO 63108-3407 t) 314-652-8862 bellarminehouse@gmail.com Jesuit Residence for Students in the College of Philosophy and Letters of St. Louis University. Rev. Steven A. Schoenig, S.J., Rector; Rev. John J. Vowells, S.J., Treas.; Rev. Matthew Baugh, S.J., Prof.; Rev. Thomas J Flowers, S.J., In Res.; Priests: 4

Congregation of the Mission Vincentian Fathers Lazarist Residence - 13245 Tesson Ferry Rd., St. Louis, MO 63128-3888 t) 314-843-0108 dthiess@vincentian.org Rev. Daniel R. Thiess, C.M., Supr.; Rev. Charles E. Prost, C.M., Par. Vicar; Rev. Patrick J. McDevitt, Rel. Ord. Ldr.; Rev. Kevin P. McCracken, C.M., Treas.; Rev. James B. Cormack, C.M., Sabbatical; Rev. Thomas E. Esselman, C.M., Asst. Prov.; Rev. Richard Gielow, C.M., Dir., Vincentian Parish Mission Ctr.; Rev. Miles J. Heinen, C.M., Asst. Gen. - Curia, Rome; Rev. Mark S. Pranaitis, C.M., Intl. Devel. Office - Gen. Curia; Rev. Bernard Quinn, C.M., Dir., Daughters of Charity West; Rev. Paul Sisul, C.M., Communication Specialist; Rev. Robert Gielow, C.M., Parish Missioner; Rev. Anthony Dosen, CM, Par. Admin.; Rev. Michael P. Joyce, C.M., Due Process Administrator; Rev. Toshio Sato, CM, Vocation Director; Rev. Clayton Kilburn, C.M., In Service; Rev. Ronald Hoye, C.M., Director Catholic Home Study Service; Rev. Daniel P. Kearns, C.M., In Service; Rev. Michael Mulhearn, C.M., In Res.; Bro. F. Joseph Hess, C.M., In Res.; Bro. David Berning, C.M.; Bro. Kenneth Lund, CM, Assoc. Dir. Prog. & Presentation;

Congregation of the Mission Western Province (Vincentians) - 3701 Forest Park Ave., St. Louis, MO 63108 t) 314-344-1184 provinceoffice@vincentian.org www.vincentian.org Rev. Patrick J McDevitt, CM, Rel. Ord. Ldr.; Rev. Kevin P. McCracken, C.M., Treas.;

Congregation of the Resurrection - 4252 W. Pine Blvd., St. Louis, MO 63108 t) 314-652-8814 gary9756@yahoo.com www.resurrectionseminary.com

St. Dominic Priory - 3407 Lafayette Ave., St. Louis, MO 63104 t) 708-638-6163 www.opcentral.org Rev. DePorres Durham, O.P., Prior; Rev. Jay M. Harrington, OP, Subprior; Rev. Patrick H. Baikauskas, O.P., In Res.; Rev. Vincent Davila, O.P., In Res.; Rev. Albert G. Glade, O.P., In Res.; Rev. Arthur Kirwin, O.P., In Res.; Rev. Scott O'Brien, OP, In Res.; Rev. Michael A. Mascari, O.P., In Res.; Rev. Edward Ruane, O.P., Assigned but living elsewhere; Rev. Kevin Stephens, O.P., In Res.; Rev. Mark Wedig, O.P., In Res.; Brs.: 18; Priests: 10

Dominican Community of St. Louis - 97 Waterman Pl., St. Louis, MO 63112-1820 t) (314) 314-8750 byrne@ai.edu St. Louis Bertrand House - Province of St. Albert the Great. Rev. Charles E. Bouchard, O.P., In Res.; Rev. Thomas Saucier, O.P., In Res.; Rev. Gerald Stookey, O.P., In Res.; Rev. Harry M. Byrne, OP, Supr.; Rev. Gregory J. Heille, OP, Bus. Mgr.; Priests: 5

Franciscan Friary of St. Anthony of Padua - 3140 Meramec St., St. Louis, MO 63118-4339 t) 314-353-7470 provsec@thefriars.org www.thefriars.org Franciscan Friars of the State of Missouri Rev. Jesus Aguirre-Garza, O.F.M.; Bro. Patrick Darnell, O.F.M.; Rev. Joseph Tan Doan Nguyen, O.F.M.; Bro. Robert Gross, O.F.M.; Bro. Jeffery Haller, O.F.M.; Bro. Patrick Hanrahan, O.F.M.; Bro. James Lammers, O.F.M.; Rev. Edmund Mundwiller, O.F.M.; Bro. Charles Reid, O.F.M.; Rev. Eulogio Roselada, O.F.M.; Rev. James Lause, O.F.M., Pst.; Rev. Ralph Parthie, O.F.M., Friar Life / Sec. of Formation; Rev. Andrew Lewandowski, O.F.M., Par. Vicar; Rev. David Rodriguez, In Res.; Rev. Glenn Phillips, O.F.M., Chap.; Rev. Thomas Nairn, O.F.M., Prov.; Rev. Michael Hill, O.F.M., Treas.; Bro. Joseph Rogenski, O.F.M., Dir.; Bro. Joseph Manning, Fraternal Service; Rev. John Abts, O.F.M., Health Care Dir.; Rev. Robert Joseph Barko, OFM, Sec. of Province; Brs.: 9; Priests: 17

Saint Jean de Brebeuf Jesuit Community - 4948 Wise Ave., St. Louis, MO 63110 c) (310) 743-3343 mcaruso@jesuits.org Rev. Michael P. Caruso, S.J., Supr.; Rev. Ralph D. Houlihan, S.J.; Rev. Matthew C. Stewart, S.J.; Rev. Ian R. Gibbons, S.J., Prin.; Rev. James J. Burshek, S.J., Teacher; Priests: 5

Jesuit Community Corporation at Saint Louis University - Jesuit Hall - 3751 Laclede Ave., St. Louis, MO 63108 c) (720) 425-0407 tmcmahon@jesuits.org Rev. Timothy McMahon, S.J., Supr.; Bro. Brent S. Gordon, S.J.; Rev. Sam Conedera, Prof.; Rev. Carlos Esparza, Prof.; Rev. Jacob Kapita, S.J.; Rev. Matthew Ma, S.J.; Rev. Michael K. May, S.J., Prof.; Rev. Bryan Y. Norton, S.J.; Rev. Ronald R. O'Dwyer, S.J., Prof.; Rev. David C. Paternostro, S.J.; Rev. John Peck, S.J.; Bro. William R. Rehg, S.J.; Rev. Michael Rozier, S.J.; Rev. Afonso Seixas-Nunes, S.J.; Rev. David Suwalsky, S.J.; Brs.: 2; Priests: 13

Leo Brown Jesuit Community - 3550 Russell Blvd., St. Louis, MO 63104 t) 314-771-5884 jarmstrong@jesuits.org Rev. Francis William Huete, S.J., Supr.; Rev. Ronald J. Boudreaux, S.J., In Res.; Rev. Michael D. Dooley, S.J., In Res.; Rev. John F. Armstrong, S.J., In Res.; Priests: 4

Marianist Province of the United States (Society of Mary) - 4425 W. Pine Blvd., St. Louis, MO 63108 t) 314-533-1207 ovasquez@sm-usa.org www.marianist.com Rev. George Cerniglia, SM, Assoc. Pst.; Rev. Quentin Hakenwerth, S.M., Mexico; Rev. Jose Ramirez, S.M.; Bro. William Campbell, S.M., In Res.; Rev. Michael R. Reaume, S.M., Ireland; Rev. James Schimelpfening, S.M.; Rev. Charles Stander, SM, Councilor; Rev. Oscar Vasquez, S.M., Prov.; Rev. Timothy Kenney, S.M., Asst. for Relg. Life; Bro. James Contadino, S.M., Ireland; Bro. James Eppy; Bro. David Herbold, S.M., Japan; Bro. Joseph Markel, S.M., Asst. for Temporalities; Bro. Gerard McAuley, S.M., Ireland; Bro. Robert Metzger, S.M.; Bro. Jesse O'Neill, SM, Asst. for Education; Bro. Bernard Ploeger, SM, Asst. Provincial; Bro. Fred Rech, S.M., Ireland; Bro. Robert Resing, S.M.; Bro. Richard Schrader, SM; Bro. Kenneth Straubinger, S.M.; Bro. Edward Violett, S.M.; Brs.: 137; Priests: 56

Chaminade Community - 401 S. Lindbergh Blvd., Creve Coeur, MO 63131 t) 314-993-1254 Rev. George James Cerniglia, SM, Assoc. Pst.;

Maryland Avenue Marianist Community - 4528 Maryland Ave., St. Louis, MO 63108 t) 314-367-0390 Rev. Sean Richard Downing, SM, Campus Min.; Bro. Bernard J. Ploeger, SM, Mem.;

Salve Marianist Community - 4108 W. Pine Blvd., St. Louis, MO 63108

St. Matthew Jesuit Community - 2715 N. Sarah St., St. Louis, MO 63113-2940 t) 314-531-6443 stmatthews@sbcglobal.net www.stmatthewtheapostle.org Rev. Jeffrey D. Harrison, S.J., Mem.; Priests: 1

Missionaries of LaSalette, Province of Mary, Mother of the Americas - 4650 S. Broadway, St. Louis, MO 63111-1398 t) 314-353-5000 lasalette.stl@gmail.com www.lasalette.org Missionaries of La Salette Corp. of Missouri Rev. Clifford Hasler, MS, Supr.; Rev. Dennis J. Meyer, M.S., Treas.; Rev. Jerry Lebanowski, MS; Rev. Thomas Vellappallil, M.S.; Bro. Luke D. Bauer; Bro. Adam Mateja, M.S.; Bro. Anthony J Sepanik, MS; Brs.: 3; Priests: 4

North American La Salette Mission Center - 4650 S. Broadway, St. Louis, MO 63111-1398 t) 314-352-0064 lsmc2@charter.net www.lasalette.org

and www.lsmc.org

Redemptorist Fathers - 1118 N. Grand Blvd., St. Louis, MO 63106 t) 314-533-0304 www.stalphonsusrock.org Rev. Stephen Joseph Benden, C.Ss.R., Pst.; Rev. Thomas Donaldson, C.Ss.R., Local Superior; Bro. Stephen Fruge, C.Ss.R., Pastoral Staff; Rev. Rodney Olive, C.Ss.R., Assoc. Pst.; Rev. Peter Schavitz, C.Ss.R., In Res.; Brs.: 1; Priests: 4

Sacred Heart Jesuit Community - 3900 Westminster Pl., St. Louis, MO 63108-3902 t) 314-531-5400 Rev. J. Daniel Daly, S.J., Supr.; Rev. Michael D. Barber, S.J., Mem.; Rev. Thomas P. Greene, S.J., Mem.; Rev. Michael G. Harter, S.J., Mem.; Rev. Jeffrey P. Putthoff, S.J., Mem.; Rev. Daniel P. White, S.J., Mem.; Priests: 6

USA Central & Southern Province, Society of Jesus - 4511 W. Pine Blvd., St. Louis, MO 63108-2191 t) 314-361-7765 ucsprov@jesuits.org www.jesuitscentralsouthern.org Rev. Thomas P. Greene, S.J., Prov.; Rev. John F. Armstrong, S.J., Prov. Asst.; Rev. Brian J. Christopher, S.J., Prov. Asst.; Rev. Michael D. Dooley, S.J., Prov. Asst.; Rev. Francis William Huete, S.J., Prov. Asst.; Rev. J. Daniel Daly, S.J., Treas.; Rev. Ronald J. Boudreaux, S.J., Prov. Asst.; Rev. Hung T. Pham, S.J., Prov. Asst.; Brs.: 16; Priests: 261

White House Retreat Jesuit Community - 7410 Christopher Dr., St. Louis, MO 63129-5701 t) 314-846-2575 whretreat@whretreat.org www.whretreat.org Rev. Ralph G. Huse, S.J., Supr.; Priests: 5

Office - 7400 Christopher Dr., St. Louis, MO 63129-5701 t) 314-416-6400; 800-643-1003 reservations@whretreat.org Rev. Anthony J. Wieck, S.J., Spiritual Adv./Care Srvcs.; Rev. Edward Arroyo, S.J., Assoc. Dir.; Rev. James A. Blumeyer, S.J., Assoc. Dir.;

NURSING / REHABILITATION / CONVALESCENCE / ELDERLY CARE [NUR]

EUREKA

St. Andrew's at Francis Place - 300 Forby Rd., Eureka, MO 63025 t) 636-938-5151 Sponsored by the Ursuline Sisters and managed by St. Andrew's Management Services, Inc. Sr. Rita A. Bregenhorn, O.S.U., Chair; Mary Alice Ryan, CEO;

KIRKWOOD

St. Agnes Home for the Elderly - 10341 Manchester Rd., Kirkwood, MO 63122 t) 314-965-7616 www.stagneshome.com Carmelite Sisters of the Divine Heart of Jesus of Missouri Rev. Conor M. Sullivan, Chap.; Ruth Dotson, Admin.;

ST. LOUIS

Alexian Brothers Lansdowne Village (Ascension Living Lansdowne Place) - 4624 Lansdowne, St. Louis, MO 63116 t) 314-292-9308 ahscm-mission@ascension.org ascensionliving.org Ryan Endsley, COO;

Ascension Living Sherbrooke Village (Alexian Brothers Sherbrooke Village) - 4005 Ripa Ave., St. Louis, MO 63125 t) 314-292-9308 ahscm-mission@ascension.org www.ascensionliving.org/ Ryan Endsley, COO; Asstd. Annu.: 542; Staff: 97

Alexian Court Apartments (Alexian Brothers Services, Inc.) - 2636 Chippewa St., St. Louis, MO 63118 t) 314-771-5604 0931@nationalchurchresidences.org www.alexianbrothers.net Sponsored by Alexian Brothers Senior Ministries. Managed by National Church Residence.

Cardinal Carberry Senior Living Center - 7601 Watson Rd., St. Louis, MO 63119 t) 314-961-8000 swesley@crssstl.org www.cardinalritterseniorservices.org Karen Ledbetter, CEO;

Mary, Queen and Mother Center - 7601 Watson Rd., St. Louis, MO 63119 t) 314-961-8000 mbarth@ccstl.org www.ccstl.org/crss Skilled Nursing Facility. A part of Cardinal Carberry Living Center Shari Kruep, Admin.;

Mother of Good Counsel Home - 6825 Natural Bridge Rd., St. Louis, MO 63121 t) 314-383-4765 smanselma@mogch.org mogch.org Skilled Nursing Facility for Men and Women. Conducted by Sisters of St. Francis of the Martyr St. George. Sr. M. Anselma Belongea, F.S.G.M., Admin.;

Mother of Perpetual Help Residence - 7609 Watson Rd., St. Louis, MO 63119 t) 314-918-2260 www.cardinalritterseniorservices.org A part of Cardinal Ritter Senior Services Kimberly Brown, Admin.; Sr. Suzanne Wesley, C.S.J., CEO;

Nazareth Living Center - 2 Nazareth Ln., St. Louis, MO 63129 t) 314-487-3950 julie.collins@benedictineliving.org www.nazarethlivingcenter.com Skilled Nursing Care Facility, Assisted & Independent Living. Sisters of St. Joseph of Carondelet & Benedictine Health System (Ministry Partner) Rev. Andrew O'Connor, Chap.; Julie E. Collins, Exec. Dir.; Asstd. Annu.: 725; Staff: 234

Our Lady of Life Apartments, Inc. - 7655 Watson Rd., St. Louis, MO 63119 t) 314-968-9447 www.cardinalritterseniorservices.org A part of Cardinal Ritter Senior Services.

Regina Cleri Residence - 10 Archbishop May Dr., St. Louis, MO 63119 t) 314-968-2240 reginacleri@earthlink.net A Residence for Retired Diocesan Priests of the Archdiocese of St. Louis. Conducted by the Archdiocese of St. Louis. Nancy Bryant, Admin.;

SSND Central Pacific Retirement, Inc. - 320 E. Ripa Ave., St. Louis, MO 63125 t) 314-544-0455 finance-sl@ssndcp.org; finance-ndeg@ssndcp.org Sr. Anna Marie Reha, Dir.;

WARRENTON

St. Clare of Assisi Senior Village, Inc. - 409 Warrenton Village Dr., Warrenton, MO 63383 t) 636-695-4205

PRESCHOOLS / CHILDCARE CENTERS [PRE]

BRIDGETON

Boys Hope Girls Hope - 12120 Bridgeton Square Dr., Bridgeton, MO 63044 t) 314-298-1250 hope@bhgh.org www.boyshopegirlshope.org A College Preparatory Residential Child Care Agency Serving Abandoned, Abused and Neglected Children. Paul A. Minorini, Pres.;

KIRKWOOD

Carmelite Child Development Center - 1111 N. Woodlawn Ave., Kirkwood, MO 63122 t) 314-822-0058 vocations@carmelitedcj.org www.carmelitedcj.org Operated by the Carmelite Sisters of the Divine Heart of Jesus. Provides child development, child care and services. Kris Wollaeger, Dir.;

ST. LOUIS

Birthright - 2525 S. Brentwood Blvd., Ste. 102, St. Louis, MO 63144 t) 314-962-5300 info@birthrightstl.org www.birthrightstl.org Ruth A. Bradberry, Dir.;

Branch Office - 6680 Chippewa, St. Louis, MO 63109 t) 314-962-3653

Branch Office - 3435-C Bridgeland, Bridgeton, MO 63044 t) 314-298-0945

Branch Office - 205 N. 5th St., St. Charles, MO 63301 t) 636-724-1200

Branch Office - 625 N. Euclid, St. Louis, MO 63108 t) 636-946-4900

Branch Office - 800 N. Tucker Blvd., St. Louis, MO 63101 t) 636-916-4300

Peace for Kids - 4415 Maryland, St. Louis, MO 63108 t) 314-531-0511 x104 sspruell@ccstl.org A child development center providing high quality child development education and care to children 6 weeks to 6 years. Sharon Spruell, CEO;

Sacred Heart Villa - 2108 Macklind Ave., St. Louis, MO 63110 t) 314-771-2224 kdoder@sacredheartvilla.org sacredheartvilla.org Full-time care from 6:30 a.m. to 6:00 p.m. for children ages 2-6 years old. Sr. Alice Marie Legan, ASCJ, Maintenance/Finance Supervisor; Kristine Doder, Dir.; Stds.: 120; Lay Tchrs.: 15

RETREAT HOUSES / RENEWAL CENTERS [RTR]

DITTMER

Il Ritiro-The Little Retreat (Il Ritiro Franciscan Retreat Center) - 7935 St. Francis Ln., Dittmer, MO 63023; Mailing: PO Box 38, Dittmer, MO 63023 t) 636-274-0554 il.ritiro@gmail.com www.ilritiro.org Operated by the Franciscan Friars Rev. Pio Jackson, O.F.M.; Rev. Bertin Miller, O.F.M.; Sr. Ann Pierre Wilken, OSF, Dir.;

Vianney Renewal Center - 6476 Eime Rd., Dittmer, MO 63023; Mailing: P.O. Box 130, Dittmer, MO 63023 t) 636-274-5226 Operated by the Servants of the Paraclete. Rev. David Fitzgerald, s.P.; Rob Furey, Dir.;

EUREKA

Marianist Retreat & Conference Center - 4000 Hwy. 109, Eureka, MO 63025-0718; Mailing: P. O. Box 718, Eureka, MO 63025-0718 t) 636-938-5390 hospitality@marianistretreat.com www.mretreat.org Nathan Martin, Exec. Dir.; Jen Duncan, Dir. Hospitality; Paul Masek, Dir. Prog.;

FLORISSANT

Pallottine Renewal Center, Inc. - 15270 Old Halls Ferry Rd., Florissant, MO 63034-1611 t) 314-837-7100 director@pallottinerenewal.org www.pallottinerenewal.org Pallottine Missionary Sisters, Queen of Apostles Province. Marilyn S. Webb, Dir.;

HIGH RIDGE

Society of Our Mother of Peace at Mary the Font Solitude - 6150 Antire Rd., High Ridge, MO 63049-2135 c) 636-677-3235 smpretreat@gmail.com www.marythefont.org Sr. Therese Marie Labicane, SMP, Contact;

PEVELY

Vision of Peace Ministries - 1000 Abbey Ln., Pevely, MO 63070 t) 636-475-3697 reservations@vophermitages.org vophermitages.org Vision of Peace Hermitages Rev. Msgr. Edmund O. Griesedieck, Spiritual Adv./Care Srvcs.; Dcn. Brian T. Selsor, Pres.; Rev. Msgr. Gregory R. Mikesch, Treas.;

ST. LOUIS

Mercy Center - 2039 N. Geyer Rd., St. Louis, MO 63131-3332 t) 314-966-4313 dhartman@sistersofmercy.org Institute of the Sisters of Mercy of the Americas Sr. Donella Hartman, R.S.M., Admin.;

***Mercy Conference and Retreat Center** - 2039 N. Geyer Rd., St. Louis, MO 63131 t) 314-966-4686 dstringfield@mercycenterstl.org www.mercycenterstl.org Dawn Stringfield, Dir.;

White House Retreat - 7400 Christopher Dr., St. Louis, MO 63129; Mailing: 7410 Christopher Dr, St. Louis, MO 63129 t) 314-416-6400; 800-643-1003 whretreat@whretreat.org www.whretreat.org Rev. Ralph G. Huse, S.J., Supr.;

Retreat House - Bro. John C. Fava, S.J.; Rev. Eugene C. Renard, S.J.; Rev. Richard E. Hadel, S.J., Dir.; Rev. Leonard E. Kraus, S.J., Dir.; William F. Schmidt, Dir.;

WILDWOOD

La Salle Institute - Retreat and Conference Center - 2101 Rue De La Salle, Wildwood, MO 63038-2299 t) 636-938-5374 mcook@lasalleretreat.org www.lasalleretreat.org Retreat center open for workshops, overnight retreats, conferences and youth programs Michelle Cook, Pres.;

Christian Brothers (De La Salle) - t) 636-938-6142

SEMINARIES [SEM]

ST. LOUIS

Aquinas Institute of Theology - 23 S. Spring Ave., St. Louis, MO 63108 t) 314-256-8800 info@ai.edu www.ai.edu Rev. Mark Wedig, OP, Pres./Prof., Liturgical & Sacramental Theology; Rev. Michael Mascari, OP, Academic Dean/Vice Pres.; Rev. Jay M. Harrington, OP, Prof., New Testament; Rev. Kevin Stephens, OP, Asst. Prof., Old Testament; Rev. Gregory J. Heille, OP, Prof., Preaching & Evangelization/Dir. of the Doctor of Ministry in Preaching Prog.; Rev. Harry M. Byrne, OP, Prof. Emeritus & Librarian; Sr. Juliet

Mousseau, RSCJ, Prof., Church History; Sr. Sara Fairbanks, OP, Assoc. Prof., Preaching & Evangelization; Sr. Carla Mae Streeter, OP, Prof. Emerita; Rev. Patrick H. Baikauskas, O.P., V.P., Institutional Advancement; Stds.: 106; Lay Tchrs.: 5; Pr. Tchrs.: 5; Sr. Tchrs.: 1

Kenrick-Glennon Seminary - 5200 Glennon Dr., St. Louis, MO 63119 t) 314-792-6100 marshafeingold@kenrick.edu www.kenrick.edu (St. Louis Roman Catholic Theological Seminary) Marsha Feingold, Archivist;

Cardinal Glennon College - Rev. Christopher M. Martin, Rector; Randall Colton, Prof.; John Finley, Prof.; Mary Ann Aubin, Librn.;

Kenrick School of Theology - Rev. Msgr. Edmund O. Griesedieck; Rev. Msgr. James J. Ramacciotti; Rev. Michael J. Witt; Rev. James Mason, Rector; Rev. Msgr. Gregory R. Mikesch, Rector; Rev. Jason J. Schumer, Rector; Most Rev. Robert Hermann, Spiritual Adv./Care Srvcs.; Very Rev. Scott Jones, Spiritual Adv./Care Srvcs.; Rev. Paul Hoesing, Dean; Rev. Fadi Auro, Prof.; Rev. Donald E. Henke, Prof.; Rev. Charles K. Samson, Prof.; Rev. Kristian C. Teater, Prof.; Rev. Edward Ahn, A.V.I., Dir.; Rev. Donald Anstoetter, Dir.; Rev. Mark Kramer, S.J., Dir.; Very Rev. Thomas M. Molini, Dir.; Rev. Mirco Sosio, A.V.I., Dir.; Mary Ann Aubin, Librn.;

SPECIAL CARE FACILITIES [SPF]

CREVE COEUR

SSM Rehab - 10101 Woodfield Ln., Creve Coeur, MO 63132 t) 314-768-5300 www.ssmrehab.com Member of SSM Health Care, For rehabilitation of pediatrics, adolescents and adults. Robert Pritts, CEO; Bed Capacity: 80

FLORISSANT

Child Center - Marygrove - 2705 Mullanphy Ln., Florissant, MO 63031 t) 314-830-6201 info@mgstl.org www.marygrovechildren.org Provides therapeutic residential treatment (ages 6-21), incl. therapeutic foster care, school, transitional living & independent living programs Michael P. Meehan, CEO; Bed Capacity: 225; Asstd. Annu.: 452; Staff: 183

NORMANDY

St. Vincent Home for Children (The German St. Vincent Orphan Association) - 7401 Florissant Rd., Normandy, MO 63121 t) 314-261-6011 info@saintvincenthome.org www.saintvincenthome.org Chapel of the Sacred Heart. A'eesha Bell, Dir.; Courtney Graves, Dir.; Deborah Jackson, Dir.;

ST. LOUIS

Ascension Health - 4600 Edmundson Rd., St. Louis, MO 63134 t) 314-733-8000 thomas.vanosdol@ascension.org www.ascension.org Sponsored by Ascension Health Ministries, a public juridic person. Thomas VanOsdol, Executive Vice President & Chief Mission Integration Officer; Craig Cordola, Executive Vice President & Chief Operating Officer;

Ascension Health Alliance - 4600 Edmundson Rd., St. Louis, MO 63134 t) 314-733-8000 thomas.vanosdol@ascension.org www.ascension.org Joseph R. Impicciche, Pres.; Staff: 4,657

Ascension Health Global Mission - 4600 Edmundson Rd., St. Louis, MO 63134 t) 314-733-8000 shuber@ascension.org www.ascension.org Susan Huber, Pres.; Thomas VanOsdol, Executive Vice President & Chief Mission Integration Officer;

Ascension Health-IS, Inc. (Ascension Technologies) - 4600 Edmundson Rd., St. Louis, MO 63134 t) 314-733-8000 www.ascension.org Gagan Singh, CIO; Chad Raith, Chief Mission Integration Officer; Staff: 2,075

Ascension Health Senior Care - 4600 Edmundson Rd., St. Louis, MO 63134 t) 314-733-8000 www.ascensionliving.org Parent to senior care facilities across the US. Ryan Endsley, COO; Kenneth (Bob) Smoot, Chief Mission Integration Officer;

Boys Hope Girls Hope of St. Louis, Inc. - 755 S. New Ballas Rd., Ste. 120, St. Louis, MO 63141 t) 314-692-7477 hopestlouis@bhgh.org www.boyshopegirlshopestl.org Residential care for adolescents with familydisruptions who are capable of college prep school work. Brian Hipp, Exec.;

Cardinal Ritter Senior Services - 7601 Watson Rd., St. Louis, MO 63119 t) 314-961-8000 cbaechle@crsstl.org www.cardinalrittterseniorservices.org Catholic Charities ministry providing compassionate care through a continuum of residential, healthcare, and supportive social services. Chris Baechle, CEO;

St. Agnes Apartments, Inc. - 2840 Wisconsin, St. Louis, MO 63118 t) 314-664-1255

Cardinal Carberry Senior Living Center - Cardinal Ritter General Partner Corporation - Cardinal Ritter Institute Residential Services Corporation - Provides housing management, housing & assisted living facilities for the elderly. Chris Baechle, CEO;

Cardinal Ritter Senior Services - Adult Day Program - 7663 Watson Rd., St. Louis, MO 63119 t) 314-962-7501

St. Clare of Assisi Senior Village, Inc. - 409 Warrenton Village Dr., Warrenton, MO 63383 t) 636-695-4200

St. Elizabeth Hall - 325 N. Newstead, St. Louis, MO 63108; Mailing: 7601 Watson Rd., St. Louis, MO 63119 t) 314-652-9525

Holy Angels Apartments I, Inc. - 3455 DePaul Ln., Bridgeton, MO 63044; Mailing: 7601 Watson Rd., St. Louis, MO 63119 t) 314-298-9505 Christopher Baechle, CEO;

Holy Angels Apartments II, Inc. - 3499 DePaul Ln., Bridgeton, MO 63044 t) 314-291-1345

Holy Infant Apartments, Inc. - 7663 Watson Rd., St. Louis, MO 63119 t) 314-962-7878

St. John Neumann Apartments, Inc. - 8424 Lucas & Hunt Rd., St. Louis, MO 63136 t) 314-385-0707

St. Joseph Apartments, Inc. - 7677 Watson Rd., St. Louis, MO 63119 t) 314-962-0969

Mary, Queen and Mother Center - 7601 Watson Rd., St. Louis, MO 63119 Tasanya Johnson, Admin.;

Mother of Perpetual Help Residence, Inc. - 7609 Watson Rd., St. Louis, MO 63119 t) 314-918-2260 Karen Ledbetter, Admin.;

Our Lady of Life Apartments, Inc. - 7655 Watson Rd., St. Louis, MO 63119; Mailing: 7601 Watson Rd., St. Louis, MO 63119 t) 314-968-9447

Pope John Paul II Apartments, Inc. - 6325 Waterways Dr., St. Louis, MO 63033 t) 314-653-0400 x294

St. William Apartments II, Inc. - 1983 Hanley Rd., Dardenne Prairie, MO 63368; Mailing: 7601 Watson Rd., St. Louis, MO 63119 t) 636-695-4205

St. William Apartments I, Inc. - 1979 Hanley Rd., Dardenne Prairie, MO 63368; Mailing: 7601 Watson Rd., St. Louis, MO 63119 t) 636-695-4200

Cathedral Tower - 325 N. Newstead Ave., St. Louis, MO 63108 t) 314-367-5500 x121 www.ccstl.org Building that houses agencies of Catholic Charities: Queen of Peace Center and St. Elizabeth Hall.

Department of Special Education - 20 Archbishop May Dr., St. Louis, MO 63119 t) 314-792-7300 www.archstl.org/education Grades PreK-8. Dr. Maureen DePriest, Supt.; Geraldine Book, Prin.;

St. Elizabeth's Adult Day Care Center, Inc. - 3683 Cook St., St. Louis, MO 63113 t) 314-772-5107 marsh@seadcc.org; hshannon@seadcc.org www.seadcc.org Conducted by the Sisters of the Most Precious Blood to Provide Day Care for the Elderly and Handicapped. Regina Marsh, Exec. Dir.; Asstd. Annu.: 200; Staff: 40

St. Elizabeth Adult Day Care Center - St. Charles - 1424 First Capitol Dr., S., St. Charles, MO 63303 t) 636-724-2110

St. Elizabeth Adult Day Care Center - Ste. Genevieve - 765 Market St., Sainte Genevieve, MO 63670 t) 573-883-7603

St. Elizabeth Adult Day Care Center - Florissant - 1831 N. New Florissant Rd., Florissant, MO 63033 t) 314-838-5005 www.seadcc.org/

St. Elizabeth Arnold Adult Day Care Center - 308 Plaza Way, Arnold, MO 63010 t) 636-282-0345

Father Dempsey's Hotel, Inc. - 3427 Washington Ave., St. Louis, MO 63103 t) 314-535-7221 maboussie@archstl.org Martie Aboussie, Exec.;

Father Jim's Home - 3427 Washington Ave., St. Louis, MO 63103 t) 314-535-7221 maboussie@archstl.org Martie Aboussie, Exec.;

Good Shepherd Children and Family Services - 1340 Partridge Ave., St. Louis, MO 63130 t) 314-854-5700 goodshepinfo@gsstl.org www.goodshepherdstl.org Providing foster care; adoption; expectant parent counseling, advocacy, & shelter; & transitional living services for teen mothers Kathy Fowler, Dir.;

Guardian Angel Settlement Association - 1127 N. Vandeventer Ave., St. Louis, MO 63113 t) 314-231-3188 info@gasastl.org www.gasastl.org Child Care Services and Social Services. Daughters of Charity of St. Vincent de Paul. Jessica Brandon, CEO;

Guardian Angel Settlement Association - Child Care Center

Guardian Angel Settlement Association - 3300 S. Jefferson Ave., St. Louis, MO 63118 t) 314-773-9027

St. Joseph Institute for the Deaf - 1314 Strassner Ave., St. Louis, MO 63144 t) 314-918-1369; 317-471-8560 jchapman@sjid.org www.sjid.org Listening and spoken language solutions for children with hearing loss. Cheryl Broekelmann, Dir.;

Saint Louis Counseling, Inc. - 9200 Watson Rd., G-101, St. Louis, MO 63126 t) 314-544-3800 tduff@ccstl.org www.saintlouiscounseling.org Provides professional counseling services to children, adolescents, adults, and the elderly. Thomas Duff, Dir.;

Saint Louis Counseling - Florissant Office - 1385 Harkee Rd., Florissant, MO 63031 t) 314-831-1533

Saint Louis Counseling - O'Fallon Office - 311 S. Main St., Ste. 100, O'Fallon, MO 63366 t) 636-281-1990

Saint Louis Counseling School Partnership Program -

Saint Louis Counseling - Troy Office - 140 Professional Pkwy., Troy, MO 63379 t) 636-528-5911

Saint Louis Counseling - Union Office - 500 Clark Ave., Union, MO 63084 t) 636-583-1800 saintlouiscounseling.org

St. Martha's Hall - ; Mailing: P.O. Box 4950, St. Louis, MO 63108 t) 314-533-1313 stmarthashall@att.net www.saintmarthas.org Provides a shelter care program for abused women and their children. Our mission is to help break the cycle of violence in their lives. Dcn. Brian T. Selsor, Chap.;

St. Mary's Special Services for Exceptional Children (St. Mary's Special School for Exceptional Children) - 20 Archbishop May Dr., St. Louis, MO 63119 t) 314-792-7300 www.archstl.org/education Early Intervention services for children PreK-2. Dr. Maureen DePriest, Admin.;

St. Philippine Home - 1015 Goodfellow Blvd., St. Louis, MO 63112 t) 314-454-1012 lpennington@ccstl.org Transitional housing for St. Louis homeless women with addiction & their children, accredited by COA. Lara B. Pennington, Exec.;

Queen of Peace Center - 325 N. Newstead Ave., St. Louis, MO 63108 t) 314-531-0511 sspruell@ccstl.org www.qopcstl.org Behavioral healthcare for women with substance abuse & their families. Sharon Spruell, CEO;

Rosati Center - 4220-24 N. Grand Ave., St. Louis, MO 63107 t) 314-534-6624 Anthony D'Agostino, CEO;

Rosati Group Home, Inc. - 4218 N. Grand Blvd., St. Louis, MO 63107 t) 314-534-6624 nboland@stpatrickcenter.org stpatrickcenter.org Group Home for homeless mentally ill adults. Managed by St. Patrick Center. Greg Vogelweid, Admin.;

Archdiocese of St. Paul and Minneapolis

(Archidioecesis Paulopolitana et Minneapolitana)

MOST REVEREND BERNARD A. HEBDA

Archbishop of Saint Paul and Minneapolis; ordained July 1, 1989; appointed Bishop of Gaylord October 7, 2009; Episcopal Ordination December 1, 2009; appointed Coadjutor Archbishop of Newark September 24, 2013; appointed Apostolic Administrator of St. Paul and Minneapolis June 15, 2015; appointed Archbishop of St. Paul and Minneapolis March 24, 2016; installed May 13, 2016. Office: 777 Forest St., St. Paul, MN 55106-3857. T: 651-291-4400; F: 651-291-4545; archbishop@archspm.org.

Archdiocesan Catholic Center: 777 Forest St., St. Paul, MN 55106-3857. T: 651-291-4400; F: 651-290-1629.
www.archspm.org
catholiccenter@archspm.org

Square Miles 6,187.

Diocese Established, July 19, 1850. Archdiocese Established, May 4, 1888.

Comprises the following twelve Counties of the State of Minnesota: Ramsey, Hennepin, Anoka, Carver, Chisago, Dakota, Goodhue, Le Sueur, Rice, Scott, Washington and Wright.

Corporate Title: The Archdiocese of Saint Paul and Minneapolis.

For legal titles of parishes and archdiocesan institutions, consult the Catholic Center.

Most Reverend Joseph A. Williams
Auxiliary Bishop of Saint Paul and Minneapolis; ordained May 25, 2002; appointed Auxiliary Bishop of Saint Paul and Minneapolis and Titular Bishop of Idassa December 10, 2021; episcopal ordination January 25, 2022. Office: 777 Forest St., St. Paul, MN 55106-3857. T: 651-291-4400. Email: bishopwilliams@archspm.org.

Most Reverend Michael J. Izen
Auxiliary Bishop of Saint Paul and Minneapolis; ordained May 28, 2005; appointed Auxiliary Bishop of Saint Paul and Minneapolis and Titular Bishop of Newport January 5, 2023; episcopal ordination April 11, 2023. Office: 777 Forest St., St. Paul, MN 55106-3857. T: 651-291-4400. Email: bishopizen@archspm.org.

STATISTICAL OVERVIEW

Personnel
Archbishops.....1
Retired Archbishops.....1
Auxiliary Bishops.....2
Retired Bishops.....1
Priests: Diocesan Active in Diocese.....203
Priests: Diocesan Active Outside Diocese.....5
Priests: Diocesan in Foreign Missions.....1
Priests: Retired, Sick or Absent.....155
Number of Diocesan Priests.....364
Religious Priests in Diocese.....68
Total Priests in your Diocese.....432
Extern Priests in Diocese.....40
Ordinations:
Diocesan Priests.....5
Transitional Deacons.....4
Permanent Deacons in Diocese.....197
Total Brothers.....34
Total Sisters.....438

Parishes
Parishes.....185
With Resident Pastor:
Resident Diocesan Priests.....148
Resident Religious Priests.....16
Without Resident Pastor:
Administered by Priests.....21
Missions.....2
Closed Parishes.....1
Professional Ministry Personnel:
Brothers.....11
Sisters.....31
Lay Ministers.....332

Welfare
Catholic Hospitals.....2
Total Assisted.....218,647
Health Care Centers.....2
Total Assisted.....15,000
Homes for the Aged.....14
Total Assisted.....31,313
Day Care Centers.....2
Total Assisted.....76
Specialized Homes.....3
Special Centers for Social Services.....20
Total Assisted.....23,000

Educational
Seminaries, Diocesan.....2
Students from This Diocese.....50
Students from Other Dioceses.....127
Diocesan Students in Other Seminaries.....5
Seminaries, Religious.....1
Students, Religious.....12
Total Seminarians.....67
Colleges and Universities.....4
Total Students.....15,954
High Schools, Diocesan and Parish.....2
Total Students.....961
High Schools, Private.....14
Total Students.....7,150
Elementary Schools, Diocesan and Parish.....73
Total Students.....21,692
Elementary Schools, Private.....4
Total Students.....1,206
Catechesis / Religious Education:
High School Students.....4,894
Elementary Students.....17,754
Total Students under Catholic Instruction.....69,678
Teachers in Diocese:
Priests.....27
Brothers.....5
Sisters.....14
Lay Teachers.....2,222

Vital Statistics
Receptions into the Church:
Infant Baptism Totals.....5,279
Minor Baptism Totals.....372
Adult Baptism Totals.....188
Received into Full Communion.....456
First Communions.....5,290
Confirmations.....5,112
Marriages:
Catholic.....876
Interfaith.....297
Total Marriages.....1,173
Deaths.....4,254
Total Catholic Population.....720,000
Total Population.....3,532,316

LEADERSHIP

Archdiocesan Catholic Center - t) 651-291-4400 www.archspm.org/

Office of the Archbishop - archbishop@archspm.org Most Rev. Bernard Hebda, Archbishop; Patrice Zangs, Exec. Asst. to Archbishop;

Office of the Auxiliary Bishop - bishopwilliams@archspm.org Most Rev. Joseph A. Williams; Maureen Portilla, Exec. Asst.;

Vicars General - vicargeneral@archspm.org Very Rev. Charles V. Lachowitzer; Very Rev. Michael Tix (tixm@archspm.org);

Presbyteral Council -

Executive Director - Rev. Ralph W. Talbot Jr.;

Deanery 1 - Rev. Thomas J. McKenzie, Dean;

Deanery 2 - Rev. Joseph Barron, PES, Dean;

Deanery 3 - Rev. Mark D. Moriarty, Dean;

Deanery 4 - Rev. Toulee (Peter) Ly, Dean;

Deanery 5 - Rev. Mark J. Joppa, Dean;

Deanery 6 - Rev. Randal J. Kasel, Dean;

Deanery 7 - Rev. Eugene J. Theisen, Dean;

Deanery 8 - Rev. Benjamin Little, Dean;

Deanery 9 - Rev. Allen R. Kuss, Dean;

Deanery 10 - Rev. Stanley P. Mader, Dean;

Deanery 11 - Rev. Nathaniel Meyers, Dean;

Deanery 12 - Rev. Paul J. Shovelain, Dean;

Deanery 13 - Very Rev. John M. Bauer, Dean;

Deanery 14 - Rev. Jude McPeak, OP, Dean;

Deanery 15 - Rev. James C. Liekhus, Dean;

Deanery 16 - Rev. Mark D. Pavlak, Dean;

Deanery 17 - Very Rev. Michael C. Johnson, Dean;

Deanery 18 - Rev. Robert H. Hart, Dean; Rev. Timothy E. Dolan, Dean;

Appointees - Rev. Hoang Dinh Nguyen, Appointee; Rev. Antony Skaria, C.F.I.C., Appointee; Rev. John J. Mitchell, Appointee;

Ex Officio - Most Rev. Bernard Hebda; Most Rev. Joseph A. Williams; Very Rev. Charles V. Lachowitzer;

Members of the Corporation - Most Rev. Bernard Hebda, Archbishop; Very Rev. Charles V. Lachowitzer, Vicar Gen.; Susan Mulheron, Chancellor (mulherons@archspm.org);

Operations - Bill Lentsch, COO (lentschb@archspm.org); Maureen Bartz, Exec. Asst. (bartzm@archspm.org);

Concierge - t) (651) 251-7777 missionsupport@archspm.org www.archspm.org/mission-support/ Theresa Kleinfehn;

OFFICES AND DIRECTORS

Archives and Records Management - records@archspm.org Allison Spies, Archives Prog. Mgr. (spiesa@archspm.org); Sehri Strom, Information Governance Prog. Mgr. (stroms@archspm.org); DeAnn Kautzmann, Records Specialist (kautzmannd@archspm.org);

Chancellor for Civil Affairs - Joseph Kueppers, Chancellor (kueppersj@archspm.org); Grace Miniatt, Paralegal (miniattg@archspm.org);

IT/Computer Services - helpdesk@archspm.org

Ministerial Standards and Safe Environment - t) 651-290-1618 Timothy O'Malley, Dir. (omalleyt@archspm.org); Paul Iovino, Deputy Dir. (iovinop@archspm.org);

Office of Conciliation - Molly Hess, Dir. (hessm@archspm.org);

Office of Indian Ministry - Shawn Phillips, Dir. (phillipss@archspm.org);

Office of Worship - Rev. Thomas Margevicius, Dir. (margeviciust@archspm.org); Cassandra Schwetz, Admin. Asst. (schwetzc@archspm.org);

Oficina del Ministerio Latino - Estela Villagran Manancero, Dir. (mananceroe@archspm.org);

Vicar for Latino Ministry - bishopwilliams@archspm.org Most Rev. Joseph A. Williams;

Vocations Office - stpaulpriest@10000vocations.org www.10000vocations.org/ Rev. David Blume, Dir.;

ADVISORY BOARDS, COMMISSIONS, COMMITTEES, AND COUNCILS

Archdiocesan Council of Catholic Women - accw@archspm.org www.accwarchspm.org Mary Kay Nickelson, Pres.; Rev. Daniel C. Haugan, Spiritual Advisor; Christine Allie, Admin. Asst. (alliec@archspm.org);

CANONICAL SERVICES

Chancellor for Canonical Affairs - chancellor@archspm.org Susan Mulheron, Chancellor (mulherons@archspm.org); Kaitlyn Powell, Canonical Affairs Specialist (powellk@archspm.org);

Vice Chancellors - Sean McDonough (mcdonoughs@archspm.org); Matthew Kuettel (kuettelm@archspm.org);

CLERGY AND RELIGIOUS SERVICES

Delegate for Consecrated Life - Sr. Carolyn Puccio, C.S.J. (puccioc@archspm.org);

Diaconate - Dcn. Lawrence W. Lawinger, Dir. (lawingerl@archspm.org);

Institute for Diaconate Formation - Dcn. Joseph T. Michalak Jr., Dir. (michalakj@archspm.org);

Institute for Ongoing Clergy Formation - Dcn. Daniel A. Gannon, Dir. (gann9131@stthomas.edu);

Office of Clergy Services - Rev. Michael Van Sloun, Dir. (mvansloun@st-barts.org);

Retirement Fund for Religious - Sr. Lynore Girmscheid, SSND, Coord. (girmscheidl@archspm.org);

COMMUNICATIONS

Communications - communications@archspm.org Tom Halden, Dir. (haldent@archspm.org);

The Catholic Spirit - www.thecatholicspirit.com Joseph Ruff, Editor-in-Chief (ruffj@archspm.org);

CONSULTATIVE BODIES

Archdiocesan Finance Council and Board of Directors - Peter Scherer, Chair; Paul Chestovich, Past Chair; Christopher Dietzen, Mem.;

College of Consultors - Rev. Patrick J. Hipwell, Secy.; Rev. Thomas W. Dufner; Rev. Douglas A. Ebert;

Commission on Bio-Medical Ethics - Rev. John P. Floeder, Chair (jpfloeder@stthomas.edu);

Ecumenical and Interreligious Affairs - Rev. Erich Rutten;

DEVELOPMENT

Mission Advancement - Jean Houghton, Dir. (houghtonj@archspm.org);

EDUCATION

Office for the Mission of Catholic Education - omce@archspm.org Jason Slattery, Dir.;

Department of Educational Quality and Excellence - Emily Dahdah, Dir.;

Department of Parish Catechesis - Eric Pederson, Dir.;

EVANGELIZATION

Archbishop Harry J. Flynn Catechetical Institute - www.cistudent.com Kelly Wahlquist, Dir. (kmwahlquist@stthomas.edu);

Synod Evangelization - Dcn. Joseph T. Michalak Jr., Dir. (michalakj@archspm.org); Rev. Joseph J. Bambenek, Asst. Dir. (bambenekj@archspm.org);

FACILITIES

Security, Safety, and Facilities - facilities@archspm.org Randy Gray, Mgr.;

FAMILY LIFE

Office of Marriage, Family, & Life - mfl@archspm.org

FINANCE

Administration and Financial Services - Thomas Mertens, CFO (mertenst@archspm.org);

Office of Financial Standards and Parish Accounting - Mary Jo Jungwirth, Dir.;

HUMAN RESOURCES

Human Resources and Benefits - Mary Ellen Moe, Dir. (moem@archspm.org);

PARISH SERVICES

Office of Parish Services - Dcn. Steven H. Maier, Dir. (maiers@archspm.org);

TRIBUNAL

Metropolitan Tribunal - t) 651-291-4466 tribunal@archspm.org www.archspm.org/tribunal-annulments/

Judicial Vicar - Very Rev. Michael C. Johnson;

Adjutant Judicial Vicar - Rev. James P. McConville;

Judges/Auditors/Advocates - Richard Aleman; Dcn. Nathan E. Allen; John Balk;

Defender of the Bond - Rev. Matthew J. Northenscold;

PARISHES, MISSIONS, AND CLERGY

STATE OF MINNESOTA

ALBERTVILLE

St. Albert - 11400 57th St., N.E., Albertville, MN 55301; Mailing: PO Box 127, Albertville, MN 55301 t) 763-497-2474 contactus@churchofstalbert.org www.churchofstalbert.org Rev. Joseph Arthur Zabinski, Par. Admin.; Dcn. Paul Ravnikar; CRP Stds.: 69

ANNANDALE

The Church of St. Ignatius of Annandale, Minnesota - 35 Birch St. E., Annandale, MN 55302; Mailing: PO Box 126, Annandale, MN 55302 t) 320-274-8828 parishoffice@stignatiusmn.com www.stignatiusmn.com Rev. John D. Meyer, Pst.; Rev. Kevin P. Magner, Par. Vicar; CRP Stds.: 152

ANOKA

Church of St. Stephen - 525 Jackson St., Anoka, MN 55303 t) 763-421-2471 info@ststephenchurch.org www.ststephenchurch.org Rev. Vinh-Thinh Nguyen Tran, Par. Vicar; Dcn. Philip Allen Grisez, Permanent Deacon; Rev. Jon Bennet Tran, Pst.; Dcn. Peter Bednarczyk; Dcn. Charles Waugh; CRP Stds.: 212

Church of St. Stephen School - (Grades PreK-8) 506 Jackson St, Anoka, MN 55303 t) 763-421-3236 schoolweb@ststephenchurch.org ststephenschool.org Theresa Gunderson, Prin.; Stds.: 385; Lay Tchrs.: 22

BAYPORT

St. Charles - 409 3rd St. N., Bayport, MN 55003 t) 651-439-4511 office@stcb.comcastbiz.net www.stcharlesbayport.com Most Rev. Michael J. Izen, Par. Admin.; Rev. Andrew B. Stueve, Par. Vicar;

BELLE PLAINE

Our Lady of the Prairie - 200 E. Church St., Belle Plaine, MN 56011 t) 952-873-6564 parish@ourladyoftheprairie.com www.ourladyoftheprairie.com Rev. Michael C. Kaluza, Pst.; Dcn. Michael James Daly; CRP Stds.: 71

Our Lady of the Prairie School - (Grades PreK-6) t) (952) 873-6564 school@ourladyoftheprairie.com school.ourladyoftheprairie.com Katie Cates, Prin.; Stds.: 43

BLAINE

St. Timothy's - 707 89th Ave., N.E., Blaine, MN 55434 t) 763-784-1329 info@churchofsttimothy.com www.churchofsttimothy.com Rev. Joseph Whalen, Pst.; Dcn. Joseph J. Frederick; CRP Stds.: 214

BLOOMINGTON

St. Bonaventure - 901 90th St. E., Bloomington, MN 55420 t) 952-854-4733 office@saintbonaventure.org;

faithformation@saintbonaventure.org www.saintbonaventure.org Rev. Mathai Chacko Chitteth, CFIC, Pst.; Dcn. Michael Redfearn; CRP Stds.: 89

St. Edward - 9401 Nesbitt Ave. S., Bloomington, MN 55437 t) 952-835-7101 receptionist@stedwardschurch.org www.stedwardschurch.org Rev. Richard A. Banker, Pst.; CRP Stds.: 104

Nativity of the Blessed Virgin Mary - 9900 Lyndale Ave. S., Bloomington, MN 55420 t) 952-881-8671 parishoffice@nativitybloomington.org www.nativitybloomington.org Rev. Nathan LaLiberte, Pst.; Dcn. James Reinhardt; Dcn. John Shearer; CRP Stds.: 62

Nativity of the Blessed Virgin Mary School - (Grades PreK-8) 9901 Bloomington Fwy. E., Bloomington, MN 55420 t) 952-881-8160 nativity@nativitybloomington.org school.nativitybloomington.org Ryan Pajak, Prin.; Stds.: 377; Lay Tchrs.: 19

BROOKLYN CENTER

St. Alphonsus - 7025 Halifax Ave. N., Brooklyn Center, MN 55429 t) 763-561-5100 parishoffice@mystals.org www.stalsmn.org Rev. John Schmidt, C.Ss.R., Pst.; Rev. Quy Duong, C.Ss.R., Par. Vicar; Rev. William Peterson, C.Ss.R., In Res.; Rev. John Son Tran, C.Ss.R., In Res.; Rev. Gregory Wiest, C.Ss.R., In Res.; Dcn. Michael Wurdock; CRP Stds.: 349

St. Alphonsus School - (Grades PreK-8) 7031 Halifax Ave. N., Brooklyn Center, MN 55429 t) 763-561-5101 schooloffice@mystals.org www.stalsmnschool.org Kari Staples, Prin.; Stds.: 142; Lay Tchrs.: 13

BROOKLYN PARK

St. Gerard Majella - 9600 Regent Ave. N., Brooklyn Park, MN 55443 t) 763-424-8770 www.st-gerard.org Very Rev. Charles Vincent Lachowitzer, Pst.; CRP Stds.: 82

St. Vincent de Paul - 9100 93rd Ave. N., Brooklyn Park, MN 55445 t) 763-425-2210 churchinfo@saintvdp.org www.saintvdp.org Rev. Dennis Zehren, Pst.; Rev. Michael Patrick Selenski, Par. Vicar; Dcn. Lawrence W. Lawinger; CRP Stds.: 399

St. Vincent de Paul School - (Grades PreK-8) 9050 93rd Ave. N., Brooklyn Park, MN 55445 t) 763-425-3970 schoolinfo@saintvdp.org school.saintvdp.org Maggie Dawson, Prin.; Stds.: 542; Lay Tchrs.: 24

BUFFALO

St. Francis Xavier - 223 19th St., N.W., Buffalo, MN 55313 t) 763-684-0075 www.stfxb.org Rev. Nathaniel Meyers, Pst.; Dcn. Paul Buck; CRP Stds.: 188

St. Francis Xavier School - (Grades PreK-8) 219 19th St., N.W., Buffalo, MN 55313 t) (763) 684-0075 school.stfxb.org Alisa Louwagie, Prin.; Stds.: 259; Lay Tchrs.: 11

BURNSVILLE

Church of the Risen Savior - 1501 County Rd. 42 E., Burnsville, MN 55306 t) 952-431-5222 info@risensavior.org www.risensavior.org Rev. Mario Castagnola, PES, Par. Vicar; Rev. Matthew Malek, Sacr. Min.; Rev. Timothy C. Rudolphi, Par. Admin.; CRP Stds.: 300

Mary, Mother of the Church - 3333 Cliff Rd. E., Burnsville, MN 55337 t) 952-890-0045 www.mmotc.org Rev. James M. Perkl, Pst.; Rev. Timothy C. Rudolphi, Par. Vicar; Dcn. James Pufahl; Dcn. Jeremiah Saladin; CRP Stds.: 156

CANNON FALLS

St. Pius V - 410 Colvill St. W., Cannon Falls, MN 55009 t) 507-263-2578 spvparish@gmail.com www.stpiusvcf.org Rev. Terry P. Beeson, Pst.; CRP Stds.: 97

CARVER

St. Nicholas - 412 4th St W, Carver, MN 55315; Mailing: c/o Guardian Angels, 215 W 2nd St, Chaska, MN 55318 t) 952-448-2345 www.stnicholascarver.org Rev. Tony VanderLoop, Pst.; CRP Stds.: 9

CENTERVILLE

St. Genevieve - 7087 Goiffon Rd, Centerville, MN 55038 t) 651-429-7937 info@stgens.org www.stgens.org Rev. Gregory L. Esty, Pst.; CRP Stds.: 89

St. Genevieve - 6995 Centerville Rd., Centerville, MN 55038 Parish Community Center

CHANHASSEN

St. Hubert - 8201 Main St, Chanhassen, MN 55317 t) 952-934-9106 webmaster@sthubert.org www.sthubert.org Rev. Rolf R. Tollefson, Pst.; Rev. Aric Aamodt, Par. Vicar; Dcn. Patrick Hirl; CRP Stds.: 587

St. Hubert School - (Grades PreK-8) t) 952-934-6003 school.sthubert.org Dr. David Sorkin, Prin.; Stds.: 729; Lay Tchrs.: 31

CHASKA

Guardian Angels - 215 W 2nd St, Chaska, MN 55318 t) 952-227-4000 info@gachaska.org www.gachaska.org Rev. Tony VanderLoop, Pst.; Dcn. John Cleveland; CRP Stds.: 141

CLEARWATER

St. Luke - 17545 Huber Ave., N.W., Clearwater, MN 55320 t) 320-558-2124 admin@churchofstlukes.com www.churchofstlukes.com Rev. Dennis J. Backer, Pst.; CRP Stds.: 83

CLEVELAND

Church of the Nativity - 200 W Main, Cleveland, MN 56017; Mailing: c/o Immaculate Conception of Marysburg, 27528 Patrick St., Madison Lake, MN 56063 t) 507-243-3166 office@maryschurches.com www.maryschurches.com Rev. Thomas Margevicius, Pst.; Rev. Michael Barsness, Par. Vicar; CRP Stds.: 95

COLOGNE

St. Bernard - 212 Church St E, Cologne, MN 55322 t) 952-466-2031 busadmin@st-bernard-cologne.org www.st-bernard-cologne.org Rev. Abraham George Kochupurackal, C.M.I., Pst.;

COLUMBIA HEIGHTS

Immaculate Conception - 4030 Jackson St NE, Columbia Heights, MN 55421 t) 763-788-9062 info@immac-church.org www.iccsonline.org Rev. James E. Peterson, Pst.; CRP Stds.: 90

Immaculate Conception School - (Grades PreK-8) t) 763-788-9065 school.iccsonline.org Jane Bona, Prin.; Stds.: 194; Lay Tchrs.: 14

COON RAPIDS

Church of the Epiphany - 1900 111th Ave NW, Coon Rapids, MN 55433 t) 763-755-1020 church@epiphanymn.org www.epiphanymn.org Dcn. Eric Gunderson; Rev. Thomas W. Dufner, Pst.; Rev. Paul Baker, Par. Vicar; Dcn. Kim Jensen; CRP Stds.: 286

Church of the Epiphany School - (Grades PreK-8) 11001 Hanson Blvd NW, Coon Rapids, MN 55433 t) 763-754-1750 schoolinfo@epiphanymn.org www.epiphanyschoolmn.org Ann Coone, Prin.; Stds.: 344; Lay Tchrs.: 22

CORCORAN

St. Thomas the Apostle - 20000 County Rd 10, Corcoran, MN 55340 t) 763-420-2385 hello@saintsppta.org www.churchofstthomas.org/ Rev. Glen T. Jenson, Pst.; Rev. Nels H. Gjengdahl, Sacr. Min.; CRP Stds.: 81

COTTAGE GROVE

Church of St. Rita - 8694 80th St S, Cottage Grove, MN 55016 t) 651-459-4596 stritas@saintritas.org www.saintritas.org Rev. Mark J. Joppa, Pst.; Dcn. John Nicklay; CRP Stds.: 208

CRYSTAL

St. Raphael - 7301 Bass Lake Rd., Crystal, MN 55428 t) 763-537-8401; 763-537-8401 x211 (CRP) info@straphaelcrystal.org www.straphaelcrystal.org Rev. Nicholas Hagen, Par. Admin.; CRP Stds.: 132

St. Raphael School - (Grades PreK-8) t) 763-504-9450 school@saintraphaelcrystal.org srsmn.org/ Jason Finne, Assoc. Prin.; Stds.: 152; Lay Tchrs.: 13

DAYTON

St. John the Baptist - 18380 Columbus St, Dayton, MN 55327; Mailing: PO Box 201, Dayton, MN 55327 t) 763-428-2828 sjbchurch@yahoo.com www.sjbdayton.org Rev. Timothy J. Yanta, Pst.; CRP Stds.: 52

DEEPHAVEN

St. Therese - 18323 Minnetonka Blvd., Deephaven, MN 55391 t) 952-473-4422 parish@st-therese.org www.st-therese.org Rev. Leonard Andrie, Pst.; Dcn. John Francis Allgaier; CRP Stds.: 240

St. Therese School - (Grades PreK-8) 18325 Minnetonka Blvd, Deephaven, MN 55391 t) 952-473-4355 school@st-therese.org www.st-therese.org/school Adam Groebner, Prin.; Stds.: 323; Lay Tchrs.: 24

DELANO

The Church of Saint Maximilian Kolbe - 401 River St N, Delano, MN 55328; Mailing: PO Box 470, Delano, MN 55328 t) 763-972-2077 office@stmaxkolbechurch.org www.stmaxkolbechurch.org Rev. Kyle Patrick Kowalczyk, Pst.; Dcn. Bruce LeDell Bowen; Dcn. Joseph Kittok; CRP Stds.: 44

Saint Maximilian Kolbe School - (Grades PreK-6) 235 S 2nd St, Delano, MN 55328 t) 763-972-2528 office@stmaxkolbeschool.org stmaxkolbeschool.org/ Mary Ziebell, Prin.; Stds.: 152; Lay Tchrs.: 8

St. Mary of Czestochowa - 1867 95th St., S.E., Delano, MN 55328 t) 952-955-1139 info@stmarydelano.org stmarydelano.org/ Rev. Paul Basil Kubista, Pst.; CRP Stds.: 63

EAGAN

St. John Neumann - 4030 Pilot Knob Rd, Eagan, MN 55122 t) 651-454-2079 sjn.org Rev. Anthony O'Neill, Pst.; Rev. Josh Jacob Salonek, Par. Vicar; Dcn. Martin Meyer; CRP Stds.: 422

St. Thomas Becket - 4455 S Robert Trl, Eagan, MN 55123 t) 651-683-9808 reception@stbeagan.org www.stbeagan.org Rev. Timothy Wozniak, Pst.; Dcn. Mickey Friesen; CRP Stds.: 166

EDEN PRAIRIE

Pax Christi - 12100 Pioneer Trl., Eden Prairie, MN 55347 t) 952-941-3150 pax@paxchristi.com www.paxchristi.com Rev. William A. Murtaugh, Pst.; Dcn. Charles A. Bobertz; Dcn. Alphonse Schroeder; Dcn. Victor Susai; CRP Stds.: 368

EDINA

Our Lady of Grace - 5071 Eden Ave, Edina, MN 55436 t) 952-929-3317 www.olgparish.org Rev. John Joseph Utecht, Par. Vicar; Rev. Kevin Finnegan, Pst.; CRP Stds.: 830

Our Lady of Grace School - (Grades K-8) 5051 Eden Ave., Edina, MN 55436 t) 952-929-5463 info@olg.org www.olgschool.net Mike McGinty, Head of School; Stds.: 815; Lay Tchrs.: 45

St. Patrick - 6820 Saint Patrick's Ln., Edina, MN 55439 t) 952-941-3164 office@stpatrick-edina.org www.stpatrick-edina.org Rev. Allen R. Kuss, Pst.; Dcn. Robert Schnell; CRP Stds.: 67

ELKO NEW MARKET

Saint Nickolaus - 51 Church St, Elko New Market, MN 55054 t) 952-461-2403 www.stnec.net Rev. Michael L. Rudolph, Pst.; CRP Stds.: 184

ELYSIAN

St. Andrew - 305 Park Ave NE, Elysian, MN 56028; Mailing: PO Box 261, Elysian, MN 56028 t) 507-362-4311 holyt7@frontiernet.net Rev. John Powers, Pst.;

EXCELSIOR

St. John the Baptist - 680 Mill St, Excelsior, MN 55331 t) 952-474-8868 stjohns@stjohns-excelsior.org www.stjohns-excelsior.org Rev. Alex Bernard Carlson, Pst.; Dcn. Michael Patrick Nevin, Permanent Deacon; CRP Stds.: 70

St. John the Baptist Catholic Montessori School - (Grades PreK-8) 638 Mill St, Excelsior, MN 55331 t) 952-474-5812 school@stjohns-excelsior.org www.stjohns-excelsior.org/school Angela Wroblewski, Prin.; Stds.: 119; Lay Tchrs.: 5

FARIBAULT

Divine Mercy Catholic Church - 139 Mercy Dr., Faribault, MN 55021; Mailing: 15 3rd Ave., S.W., Faribault, MN 55021 t) 507-334-7706; 507-334-2266 x16

(CRP) pparrish@divinemercy.cc www.divinemercy.cc Rev. Cory J. Rohlfing, Pst.; Rev. Clayton A. Forner, Par. Vicar; CRP Stds.: 213

Divine Mercy Catholic School - (Grades PreK-6) 15 3rd Ave SW, Faribault, MN 55021 t) (507) 334-7706 info@dmcs.cc www.dmcs.cc Gina Ashley, Prin.; Stds.: 267; Lay Tchrs.: 29

St. Patrick, Shieldsville - 7525 Dodd Rd, Faribault, MN 55021 t) 507-334-6002 spshieldsville@gmail.com www.spshieldsville.org Rev. Thomas M. Niehaus, Pst.;

FARMINGTON

Church of St. Michael - 22120 Denmark Ave, Farmington, MN 55024 t) 651-463-3360 info@stmichael-farmington.org www.stmichael-farmington.org Rev. Nicholas Froehle, Pst.; Dcn. James William Bauhs; Dcn. Russell Shupe; CRP Stds.: 271

FOREST LAKE

St. Peter - 1250 S. Shore Dr., Forest Lake, MN 55025 t) 651-982-2200 www.stpeterfl.org Rev. Daniel J. Bodin, Pst.; Rev. Paul James Hedman, Par. Vicar; Dcn. Matt Joseph Damiani; Dcn. Gary Houle; CRP Stds.: 155

St. Peter School - (Grades PreK-8) t) (651) 982-2216 www.school.stpeterfl.org James Morehead, Prin.; Stds.: 335; Bro. Tchrs.: 2; Lay Tchrs.: 16

FRIDLEY

St. William - 6120 5th St NE, Fridley, MN 55432 t) 763-571-5600 chofstwilliams.com Rev. David T. Ostrowski, Pst.; CRP Stds.: 31

GOLDEN VALLEY

Good Shepherd - 145 Jersey Ave. S., Golden Valley, MN 55426 t) 763-544-0416 info@goodshepherdgv.org www.goodshepherdgv.org Rev. Luke C. Marquard, Pst.; CRP Stds.: 91

Good Shepherd School - (Grades PreK-6) t) 763-545-4285 schoolinfo@gsgvschool.org www.gsgvschool.org Stevi Evans, Prin.; Stds.: 327; Lay Tchrs.: 19

St. Margaret Mary - 2323 Zenith Ave N, Golden Valley, MN 55422 t) 763-588-9466 myparish@smm-gv.org www.smm-gv.org Rev. Thomas Rayar, Pst.; CRP Stds.: 31

GOODHUE

The Church of the Holy Trinity - 211 N 4th St, Goodhue, MN 55027; Mailing: P.O. Box 275, Goodhue, MN 55027 t) 651-923-4472 holytrinitygoodhue@gmail.com www.holytrinitygoodhue.org Receiving parish for St. Mary's, Bellechester and St. Columbkill, Goodhue. Rev. Thomas E. McCabe, Par. Admin.; CRP Stds.: 115

St. Mary's Church - 221 Chester Ave., Bellechester, MN 55027 t) 651-923-4305

St. Columbkill Church - 36483 Co. 47 Blvd., Goodhue, MN 55027 t) 651-258-4307

Holy Trinity Church - 211 4th St., N., Goodhue, MN 55027

HAM LAKE

Church of Saint Paul - 1740 Bunker Lake Blvd NE, Ham Lake, MN 55304 t) 763-757-1148 (CRP); 763-757-6910 cosp@churchofsaintpaul.com www.churchofsaintpaul.com Rev. James T. Livingston, Pst.; Dcn. Bill Charles Schroeder; Dcn. Timothy Zinda; CRP Stds.: 479

HAMEL

St. Anne - 200 Hamel Rd., Hamel, MN 55340; Mailing: PO Box 256, Hamel, MN 55340 t) 763-478-6644 office@saintannehamel.org www.saintannehamel.org Rev. Corey T. Belden, Par. Admin.; CRP Stds.: 56

HAMPTON

St. Mary - 8433 239th St. E., Hampton, MN 55031; Mailing: 23315 Northfield Blvd., Hampton, MN 55031 t) 651-437-9030 parishoffice@stmathias.com stmarysnewtrier.com Very Rev. Michael Tix, Par. Admin.; Dcn. Steven H. Maier;

St. Mathias - 23315 Northfield Blvd., Hampton, MN 55031 t) 651-437-9030 parishoffice@stmathias.com www.stmathias.com Very Rev. Michael Tix, Par. Admin.; Dcn. Steven H. Maier;

HASTINGS

St. Elizabeth Ann Seton - 2035 15th St W, Hastings, MN 55033 t) 651-437-4254 info@seasparish.org www.seasparish.org Rev. David R. Hennen, Pst.; Dcn. Rodney LaVerne Walker; CRP Stds.: 73

St. Elizabeth Ann Seton School - (Grades PreK-8) 600 Tyler St, Hastings, MN 55033 t) 651-437-3098 www.seas-school.org Tim Sullivan, Prin.; Stds.: 211; Lay Tchrs.: 13

St. Joseph - 23955 Nicolai Ave, Hastings, MN 55033 t) 651-437-3526 www.stjosephmiesville.com Rev. Terry P. Beeson, Pst.; Rev. Michael Anthony (Cassian) DiRocco, Sacr. Min.; CRP Stds.: 37

HOPKINS

The Parish of Saint Gabriel the Archangel of Hopkins, Minnesota - 6 Interlachen Rd, Hopkins, MN 55343 t) 952-935-5536 officereceptionist@stgabrielhopkins.org www.stgabrielhopkins.org Rev. Paul Haverstock, Pst.; Dcn. Darrel Thomas Branch; CRP Stds.: 124

St. Gabriel the Archangel, St. Joseph Campus - 1300 Mainstreet, Hopkins, MN 55343

St. Gabriel the Archangel, St. John Campus -

INVER GROVE HEIGHTS

Church of St. Patrick - 3535 72nd St E, Inver Grove Heights, MN 55076 t) 651-455-6624 churchofstpatrick.com Rev. Brian Fier, Pst.; CRP Stds.: 116

JORDAN

St. John the Baptist - 313 2nd St E, Jordan, MN 55352 t) 952-492-2640 office@sjbjordan.org www.sjbjordan.org Rev. Neil Edward Bakker, Pst.; CRP Stds.: 111

St. John the Baptist School - (Grades PreK-6) 215 Broadway St N, Jordan, MN 55352 t) 952-492-2030 www.sjsjordan.org Mitch Dorr, Prin.; Stds.: 174; Lay Tchrs.: 9

St. Patrick of Cedar Lake Township - 24425 Old Hwy 13 Blvd, Jordan, MN 55352 t) 952-492-5723 (CRP); 952-492-6276 stpatrickstcatherine@gmail.com www.stpandc.mn.org Rev. Michael J. Miller, Pst.; CRP Stds.: 91

St. Catherine of Spring Lake Township - 4500 220th St. E., Prior Lake, MN 55372; Mailing: 24425 Old Hwy 13 Blvd, Jordan, MN 55352 t) 952-447-2180

KENYON

St. Michael - 108 Bullis St., Kenyon, MN 55946 t) 507-789-6120 stmichaels@kmwb.net; faithformation@kmwb.net stmichaelskenyon.wordpress.com Rev. Cory J. Rohlfing, Pst.; Dcn. Newell McGee; CRP Stds.: 26

LAKE ST. CROIX BEACH

St. Francis of Assisi - 16770 13th St. S., Lake St. Croix Beach, MN 55043 t) 651-436-7817 office@stfrancislscbmn.org www.stfrancislscbmn.org Rev. Mark J. Underdahl, Pst.; CRP Stds.: 50

LAKEVILLE

All Saints - 19795 Holyoke Ave., Lakeville, MN 55044 t) 952-469-4481 info@allsaintschurch.com www.allsaintschurch.com Rev. Thomas W. Wilson, Pst.; Rev. Michael Fredrik Reinhardt, Par. Vicar; Dcn. James Marschall; Dcn. Alan Nicklaus; CRP Stds.: 500

All Saints School - (Grades PreK-8) 19795 Holyoke Ave, Lakeville, MN 55044 t) 952-469-3332 school@allsaintschurch.com school.allsaintschurch.com Dr. Elizabeth de Leon, Prin.; Stds.: 484; Lay Tchrs.: 22

LE CENTER

St. Mary - 165 Waterville Ave. N., Le Center, MN 56057 t) 507-357-6633 www.stmarysthenry.org Rev. Thomas Margevicius, Pst.; Rev. Michael Barsness, Par. Vicar; Dcn. Adelmo de Jesus Gracia Suarez, Permanent Deacon; CRP Stds.: 171

LE SUEUR

St. Anne - 217 N. 3rd St., Le Sueur, MN 56058; Mailing: 503 N. 4th St., Le Sueur, MN 56058 t) 507-665-3811 stanneschurchoffice@gmail.com www.stanneschurchlesueur.org Rev. Christopher L. Shofner, Pst.; CRP Stds.: 94

St. Anne School - (Grades PreK-5) 511 4th St. N., Le Sueur, MN 56058 t) 507-665-2489 info@stanneslesueur.org www.stanneslesueur.org Anne Lewis, Prin.; Stds.: 138; Lay Tchrs.: 14

Church of St. Henry - 38807 261st Ave., Le Sueur, MN 56058; Mailing: 165 N. Waterville Ave., Le Center, MN 56057 t) 507-357-6633 www.stmarysthenry.org Rev. Thomas Margevicius, Pst.; Rev. Michael Barsness, Par. Vicar;

LINDSTROM

St. Bridget of Sweden - 13060 Lake Blvd., Lindstrom, MN 55045; Mailing: PO Box 754, Lindstrom, MN 55045 t) 651-257-2474 www.stbridgetofsweden.org Rev. David W. Kohner, Pst.; CRP Stds.: 148

LINO LAKES

St. Joseph of the Lakes - 171 Elm St., Lino Lakes, MN 55014 t) 651-784-3015 office@saintjosephsparish.org www.mystjoes.me Church of St. Joseph of Rice Lake Rev. Michael F. Anderson, Pst.; CRP Stds.: 292

LITTLE CANADA

Church of Saint John the Evangelist of Little Canada - 380 Little Canada Rd. E., Little Canada, MN 55117 t) 651-484-2708 sjolc.org/ Rev. Thomas J. Balluff, Pst.; CRP Stds.: 25

Saint John School of Little Canada - (Grades PreK-8) 2621 McMenemy Rd., Little Canada, MN 55117 t) 651-484-3038 saintjohnschool@sjolc.org school.sjolc.org/ Dan Hurley, Prin.; Stds.: 263; Lay Tchrs.: 21

LONG LAKE

St. George - 133 N. Brown Rd., Long Lake, MN 55356 t) 952-473-1247 info@stgeorgelonglake.org www.stgeorgelonglake.org Rev. Mark Shane Stoppel-Wasinger, Pst.; Rev. Timothy L. Norris, Sacr. Min.; Dcn. Bruce LeDell Bowen; CRP Stds.: 42

LONSDALE

Immaculate Conception - 116 Alabama St., S.E., Lonsdale, MN 55046; Mailing: 202 Alabama St., S.E., Lonsdale, MN 55046 t) 507-744-2829 office@icchurch.cc www.icchurch.cc Rev. Nicholas William VanDenBroeke, Pst.;

LORETTO

SS. Peter and Paul - 150 Railway St. E., Loretto, MN 55357; Mailing: PO Box 96, Loretto, MN 55357 t) 763-479-0535 www.saintsppta.org Rev. Glen T. Jenson, Pst.; Rev. Nels H. Gjengdahl, Sacr. Min.; CRP Stds.: 86

MADISON LAKE

Immaculate Conception of Marysburg - 27528 Patrick St., Madison Lake, MN 56063 t) 507-243-3166 office@maryschurches.com www.maryschurches.com Rev. Thomas Margevicius, Pst.; Rev. Michael Barsness, Par. Vicar;

MAHTOMEDI

St. Jude of the Lake - 700 Mahtomedi Ave., Mahtomedi, MN 55115 t) 651-426-3245 info@stjudeofthelake.org www.stjudeofthelake.org Rev. Chad VanHoose, Pst.; CRP Stds.: 126

St. Jude of the Lake School - (Grades PreK-6) 600 Mahtomedi Ave., Mahtomedi, MN 55115 t) 651-426-2562 schoolinfo@stjudeofthelake.org www.stjudeofthelakeschool.org Carrie Hackman, Prin.; Stds.: 281; Lay Tchrs.: 16

MAPLE GROVE

St. Joseph the Worker - 7180 Hemlock Ln N, Maple Grove, MN 55369 t) 763-425-6505 www.sjtw.net Rev. Michael Sullivan, Pst.; Rev. Ronald Kreul, OP, Par. Vicar; Dcn. Kevin O'Connor; Dcn. John Wallin; CRP Stds.: 578

MAPLE LAKE

St. Timothy - 8 Oak Ave N, Maple Lake, MN 55358 t) 320-963-3726 parishoffice@churchofsttimothy.org www.churchofsttimothy.org Rev. John D. Meyer, Pst.; Rev. Kevin P. Magner, Par. Vicar; CRP Stds.: 157

St. Timothy School - (Grades PreK-8) 215 Division St E, Maple Lake, MN 55358; Mailing: 8 Oak Ave N, Maple Lake, MN 55358 t) 320-963-3417 schooloffice@stimml.org school.churchofsttimothy.org Julie Shelby, Prin.; Stds.: 168; Lay Tchrs.: 10

MAPLEWOOD

St. Jerome - 380 Roselawn Ave E, Maplewood, MN 55117 t) 651-771-1209 secretary@stjerome-church.org www.stjerome-church.org Rev. Victor Valencia, Pst.; CRP Stds.: 169

St. Jerome School - (Grades PreK-8) 384 Roselawn Ave E, Maplewood, MN 55117 t) 651-771-8494 secretary@stjeromeschool.org stjeromeschool.org Rev. Seraphim Wirth, F.B.P., Chap.; Anne Gattman, Prin.; Stds.: 191; Sr. Tchrs.: 1; Lay Tchrs.: 13

Presentation of the Blessed Virgin Mary - 1725 Kennard St., Maplewood, MN 55109 t) 651-777-8116 mail@presentationofmary.org www.presentationofmary.org Rev. Toulee (Peter) Ly, Pst.; Dcn. Michael Powers; CRP Stds.: 7

Presentation of the Blessed Virgin Mary School - (Grades PreK-8) 1695 Kennard St, Maplewood, MN 55109 t) 651-777-5877 lprazak@presentationofmary.org presentationofmaryschool.org Sue Lovegreen, Prin.; Stds.: 150; Lay Tchrs.: 9

MENDOTA

St. Peter - 1405 Sibley Memorial Hwy., Mendota, MN 55150; Mailing: P.O. Box 50679, Mendota, MN 55150 t) 651-452-4550 church@stpetersmendota.org www.stpetersmendota.org Rev. Steven B. Hoffman, Pst.; Dcn. Tim Hennessey; CRP Stds.: 141

MINNEAPOLIS

The Basilica of St. Mary Co-Cathedral - 1600 Hennepin Ave., Minneapolis, MN 55403; Mailing: 88 N. 17th St., Minneapolis, MN 55403 t) 612-333-1381 www.mary.org Very Rev. Daniel F. Griffith, Pst.; CRP Stds.: 160

St. Albert the Great - 2836 33rd Ave S, Minneapolis, MN 55406 t) 612-724-3643 info@saintalbertthegreat.org www.saintalbertthegreat.org Rev. Jude McPeak, OP, Pst.; CRP Stds.: 26

All Saints - 435 4th St NE, Minneapolis, MN 55413 t) 612-379-4996 allsaints@fsspminneapolis.org www.fsspminneapolis.org Rev. Christopher Pelster, FSSP, Pst.; Rev. Daniel Mould, FSSP, Par. Vicar;

Church of St. Anne - St. Joseph Hien - 2306 26th Ave N, Minneapolis, MN 55411; Mailing: 2627 Queen Ave N, Minneapolis, MN 55411 t) 612-529-0503 sasjhparish@gmail.com www.gxannagiusehien.net Rev. Louis Ha Pham, CRM, Pst.; Rev. Ignatius Trieu Hoang, CRM, Par. Vicar; CRP Stds.: 382

Annunciation - 509 54th St W, Minneapolis, MN 55419 t) 612-824-0787; 612-824-9993 x251 (CRP) info@annunciationmsp.org www.annunciationmsp.org Rev. William Deziel, Pst.; Dcn. Sean Curtan; CRP Stds.: 361

Annunciation School - (Grades PreK-8) 525 54th St W, Minneapolis, MN 55419 t) 612-823-4394 www.annunciationmsp.org/school Kari Zobel, Prin.; Stds.: 403; Lay Tchrs.: 22

Ascension - 1723 Bryant Ave. N., Minneapolis, MN 55411 t) 612-529-9684 webmail@ascensionmpls.org www.ascensionmpls.org Rev. Dale J. Korogi, Pst.; CRP Stds.: 121

Ascension School - (Grades K-8) 1726 Dupont Ave N, Minneapolis, MN 55411 t) 612-521-3609 info@ascensionschoolmn.org www.ascensionschoolmn.org Benito Matias, Prin.; Stds.: 308; Lay Tchrs.: 23

St. Boniface - 633 2nd St NE, Minneapolis, MN 55413; Mailing: 629 2nd St NE, Minneapolis, MN 55413 t) 612-379-2761 boniface1858@usfamily.net www.stbonifacempls.org Rev. Biju Mathew, Par. Admin.; CRP Stds.: 16

St. Bridget - 3811 Emerson Ave. N., Minneapolis, MN 55412 t) 612-529-7779 stbridgetnorthside.com/ Rev. Marcel Okwara, C.Ss.R., Par. Admin.; Rev. Paul Jarvis, Par. Vicar; Dcn. Richard Heineman;

Christ the King - 5029 Zenith Ave S, Minneapolis, MN 55410 t) 612-920-5030 parishoffice@ctkmpls.org www.ctkmpls.org Rev. Thomas M. Kommers, Par. Admin.; Dcn. James F. DeShane; CRP Stds.: 17

The Church of Saint Stephen-Holy Rosary - 2211 Clinton Ave S, Minneapolis, MN 55404 t) 612-767-2430 info@ststephenscatholic.org www.sts-hr.org Rev. James J. Stiles, Pst.; Rev. Timothy L. Norris, Par. Vicar; Dcn. Jose Luis Rodriguez Alvarado; Rev. Evan Steven Koop, Sacr. Min.; CRP Stds.: 342

SS. Cyril and Methodius - 1315 2nd St., N.E., Minneapolis, MN 55413-1905 t) 612-379-9736 cyril1891@aol.com Rev. Fernando Ortega, Par. Vicar; Rev. Kevin T. Kenney, Par. Admin.; CRP Stds.: 163

St. Frances Cabrini - 1500 Franklin Ave., S.E., Minneapolis, MN 55414 t) 612-339-3023 office@cabrinimn.org www.cabrinimn.org Rev. Michael J. Krenik, Pst.; CRP Stds.: 27

Church of Gichitwaa Kateri - 3045 Park Ave, Minneapolis, MN 55407 t) 612-824-7606 www.katerimpls.org (Native American Quasi-Parish) Rev. James R. DeBruycker, Pst.; Rev. Stanley V. Sledz, Sacr. Min.; CRP Stds.: 3

St. Helena - 3204 E 43rd St, Minneapolis, MN 55406 t) 612-729-7344; 612-729-7321 (CRP) church@sainthelena.us www.sainthelena.us Rev. Marcus F. Milless, Par. Admin.; CRP Stds.: 27

St. Helena School - (Grades PreK-8) 3200 44th St E, Minneapolis, MN 55406 t) 612-729-9301 school@sainthelenaschool.us sainthelenaschool.us Karla Gergen, Prin.; Stds.: 129; Sr. Tchrs.: 1; Lay Tchrs.: 9

Holy Cross - 1621 University Ave., N.E., Minneapolis, MN 55413 t) 612-930-0860 info@ourholycross.org www.ourholycross.org Rev. Justus Musinguzi (Rwanda), Par. Vicar; Rev. Spencer J. Howe, Pst.; Rev. Cyprian Czop, O.M.I., Par. Vicar; Dcn. Eric James Evander;

St. Hedwig - 129 29th Ave., N.E., St. Anthony, MN 55418

St. Clement - 911 24th Ave., N.E., Minneapolis, MN 55418

Holy Name - 3637 11th Ave S, Minneapolis, MN 55407 t) 612-724-5465 www.churchoftheholyname.org Rev. Leo J. Schneider, Pst.; CRP Stds.: 26

Church of the Incarnation - 3817 Pleasant Ave, Minneapolis, MN 55409 t) 612-822-2101 contact@inc-scj.org www.inc-scj.org/ Rev. Kevin M. McDonough, Pst.; Dcn. Carl Valdez; CRP Stds.: 299

St. Joan of Arc - 4537 3rd Ave S, Minneapolis, MN 55419 t) 612-823-8205 www.saintjoanofarc.org Rev. James R. DeBruycker, Pst.; Rev. James Cassidy, Par. Vicar;

St. Lawrence - 1203 5th St SE, Minneapolis, MN 55414 t) 612-331-7941 info@umncatholic.org www.umncatholic.org Rev. Jake Anderson, Pst.;

St. Leonard of Port Maurice - 3949 Clinton Ave S, Minneapolis, MN 55409 t) 612-825-5811 stleonardmn.org Rev. Leo J. Schneider, Pst.;

St. Olaf - 215 S 8th St, Minneapolis, MN 55402 t) 612-332-7471 www.saintolaf.org Rev. Kevin T. Kenney, Pst.; Rev. Mark H. Wehmann, Par. Vicar;

Our Lady of Lourdes - 1 Lourdes Pl., Minneapolis, MN 55414 t) 612-379-2259 www.lourdesmpls.org Very Rev. John M. Bauer, Pst.; CRP Stds.: 4

Our Lady of Mount Carmel - 701 Fillmore St NE, Minneapolis, MN 55413 t) 612-623-4019 olmc@olmcmpls.org www.olmcmpls.org Provide ASL and deaf ministries Rev. Michael J. Krenik, Par. Admin.; Dcn. Michael Powers; CRP Stds.: 5

Our Lady of Peace - 5426 12th Ave S, Minneapolis, MN 55417 t) 612-824-3455 parishadmin@olpmn.org www.olpmn.org Rev. Joah Ellis, Pst.; Dcn. John Howard Bauch; CRP Stds.: 35

Our Lady of Peace School - (Grades PreK-8) 5435 11th Ave S, Minneapolis, MN 55417 t) 612-823-8253 schooladmin@olpmn.org school.olpmn.org Paul Berry, Prin.; Stds.: 212; Lay Tchrs.: 17

Our Lady of Victory - 5155 Emerson Ave N, Minneapolis, MN 55430 t) 612-529-7788 olvmplsoffice@gmail.com Rev. Terrence M. Hayes, Pst.;

St. Thomas the Apostle - 2914 W 44th St, Minneapolis, MN 55410 t) 612-922-0041 info@stthomasmpls.org www.stthomasmpls.org Rev. Michael A. Reding, Pst.; CRP Stds.: 30

MINNETONKA

Immaculate Heart of Mary - 13505 Excelsior Blvd., Minnetonka, MN 55345 t) 952-935-1432 www.ihm-cc.org/ Rev. John James Bauer, Pst.; CRP Stds.: 64

MONTGOMERY

Most Holy Redeemer - 206 Vine Ave W, Montgomery, MN 56069 t) 507-364-7981 hredeemer@frontiernet.net www.hredeemerparish.org Receiving parish for St. Canice, Kilkenny. Rev. Thomas M. Niehaus, Pst.; Dcn. R. Daniel Wesley; CRP Stds.: 75

Most Holy Redeemer School - (Grades PreK-8) 205 Vine Ave W, Montgomery, MN 56069 t) 507-364-7383 info@mosthrs.org mosthrs.org Kari Marsh, Prin.; Stds.: 79; Lay Tchrs.: 7

St. Canice - 183 W. Maple St., Kilkenny, MN 56052

MONTICELLO

St. Henry - 1001 E. 7th St., Monticello, MN 55362 t) 763-295-2402 info@sthenrycatholic.com www.sthenrycatholic.info Rev. Patrick Thomas Barnes, Pst.; Dcn. Michael Scott Engel, Permanent Deacon; CRP Stds.: 317

MOUND

Our Lady of the Lake - 2385 Commerce Blvd, Mound, MN 55364 t) 952-472-1284 www.ourladyofthelake.com Rev. Peter M. Richards, Pst.; Dcn. Delvin L. Wilkinson; CRP Stds.: 91

Our Lady of the Lake School - (Grades PreK-8) 2411 Commerce Blvd, Mound, MN 55364 t) 952-472-8228 admissions@schoololl.com school.ourladyofthelake.com Becky Kennedy, Prin.; Stds.: 178; Lay Tchrs.: 10

NEW BRIGHTON

St. John the Baptist - 835 2nd Ave NW, New Brighton, MN 55112 t) 651-633-8333 sjb@stjohnnyb.org www.stjohnnb.com Rev. Paul J. Shovelain, Pst.; Rev. Joseph Hoan Nguyen, Par. Vicar; Dcn. John Belian; Dcn. Rodney Palmer; Dcn. Gary Schneider; CRP Stds.: 164

St. John the Baptist School - (Grades PreK-8) 845 2nd Ave NW, New Brighton, MN 55112 t) 651-633-1522 www.stjohnnyb.org Ann Laird, Prin.; Stds.: 432; Lay Tchrs.: 22

NEW HOPE

St. Joseph - 8701 36th Ave N, New Hope, MN 55427 t) 763-544-3352 communications@stjosephparish.com www.stjosephparish.com Rev. Terrence Rassmussen, Pst.; Dcn. Robert Bramwell;

Saint Joseph - 13015 Roackford Rd., Plymouth, MN 55441

NEW PRAGUE

St. Wenceslaus - 215 Main St E, New Prague, MN 56071 t) 952-758-3225 info@npcatholic.org www.npcatholic.org Rev. Eugene J. Theisen, Pst.; Rev. Michael C. Skluzacek, Sacr. Min.; CRP Stds.: 217

St. Wenceslaus School - (Grades PreK-8) 227 Main St E, New Prague, MN 56071 t) 952-758-3133 swsaints.org Kimberly Doyle, Prin.; Stds.: 255; Lay Tchrs.: 19

St. John Campus - 20087 Hub Dr., New Prague, MN 56071 t) (952) 758-3225

St. Scholastica Campus - 31525 181st Ave., New Prague, MN 56071 t) (952) 758-3225

NORTH BRANCH

St. Gregory the Great - 38725 Forest Blvd, North Branch, MN 55056; Mailing: PO Box 609, North Branch, MN 55056 t) 651-674-4056 info@stgregorynb.org www.stgregorynb.org Rev. Matthew Shireman, Par. Admin.; Dcn. Kevin Michael Downie; CRP Stds.: 70

NORTH ST. PAUL

St. Peter - 2600 Margaret St N, North St. Paul, MN 55109 t) 651-777-8304 church@stpetersnsp.org www.churchofstpeternsp.org Rev. Jose Maria Cortes, F.S.C.B., Pst.; Rev. Pietro Rossotti, F.S.C.B., Par. Vicar; Rev. Ettore Ferrario, F.S.C.B., Par. Vicar; Dcn. Robert Anthony Bisciglia; Dcn. Eric Cooley; CRP Stds.: 168

St. Peter School - (Grades PreK-8) 2620 Margaret St N, North St. Paul, MN 55109 t) 651-777-3091 frontdesk@stpetersnsp.org www.stpetersnsp.org Dennis Rankin, Prin.; Stds.: 236; Lay Tchrs.: 11

NORTHFIELD

Annunciation - 4996 Hazelwood Ave, Northfield, MN 55057 t) 952-652-2625 secretary-ac@nuveramail.net www.thechurchoftheannunciation.org Rev. Louis Sebastian Floeder, Par. Admin.; Rev. Gregory E. Abbott, Pst.; CRP Stds.: 33

St. Dominic - 104 Linden St. N., Northfield, MN 55057; Mailing: 216 Spring St. N., Northfield, MN 55057 t) 507-645-8816 secretary@churchofstdominic.org www.churchofstdominic.org Rev. Louis Sebastian Floeder, Par. Admin.; CRP Stds.: 166

St. Dominic School - (Grades PreK-8) 216 Spring St N, Northfield, MN 55057 t) 507-645-8136 office@schoolofstdominic.org schoolofstdominic.org Jackie Chatelaine, Interim Principal; Stds.: 108; Lay Tchrs.: 13

NORWOOD

Ascension Catholic Church - 323 Reform St., N., Norwood, MN 55368 t) 952-467-3351 busadmin@ascensionnya.org www.ascensionnya.org Rev. Abraham George Kochupurackal, C.M.I., Pst.; CRP Stds.: 103

OAK GROVE

St. Patrick - 19921 Nightingale St NW, Oak Grove, MN 55011 t) 763-753-2011 stpats@st-patricks.org www.st-patricks.org Rev. Allan Paul Eilen, Pst.; Dcn. Kris Ringwall; CRP Stds.: 272

OAKDALE

Guardian Angels - 8260 4th St N, Oakdale, MN 55128 t) 651-738-2223 info@guardian-angels.org www.guardian-angels.org Dcn. Michael William Braun; Rev. Joseph Connelly, Par. Admin.; CRP Stds.: 177

Transfiguration - 6133 15th St N, Oakdale, MN 55128 t) 651-738-2646 www.transfigurationmn.org Rev. John Paul Erickson, Pst.; Rev. Brian T. Lynch, Par. Vicar; Dcn. Daniel Brewer; CRP Stds.: 41

Transfiguration School - (Grades PreK-8) 6135 15th St N, Oakdale, MN 55128 t) 651-501-2220 tiger@transfigurationmn.org transfigurationmn.org Sue Berthiaume, Prin.; Stds.: 145; Lay Tchrs.: 9

PINE ISLAND

St. Michael - 451 5th St SW, Pine Island, MN 55963 t) 507-356-4280 stmichaeloffice@bevcomm.net stpaulstmichael.com Rev. Randal J. Kasel, Pst.; CRP Stds.: 105

PLYMOUTH

St. Mary of the Lake - 105 Forestview Ln. N., Plymouth, MN 55441 t) 763-545-1443 info@smlplymouth.org www.smlplymouth.org Rev. Andrew Herbert Zipp, Par. Admin.; CRP Stds.: 107

PRIOR LAKE

Church of St. Michael of Prior Lake - 16400 Duluth Ave., S.E., Prior Lake, MN 55372; Mailing: 16311 Duluth Ave., S.E., Prior Lake, MN 55372 t) 952-447-2491 info@stmichael-pl.org www.stmichael-pl.org Rev. Thomas J. Walker, Pst.; Dcn. Terry Beer; CRP Stds.: 500

St. Michael Catholic School - (Grades PreK-8) 16280 Duluth Ave SE, Prior Lake, MN 55372 t) 952-447-2124 info@saintmpl.org saintmpl.org Carlos Connell-Torres, Prin.; Stds.: 358; Lay Tchrs.: 23

RAMSEY

St. Katharine Drexel - 7101 143rd Ave NW, Suite G, Ramsey, MN 55303 t) 763-323-4424 info@stkdcc.org www.stkdcc.org (Quasi-Parish) Rev. Paul A. Jaroszeski, Pst.; Dcn. Randall Joseph Bauer; CRP Stds.: 55

RED WING

Church of St. Joseph - 435 W 7th St, Red Wing, MN 55066; Mailing: 426 W 8th St, Red Wing, MN 55066 t) 651-388-1133 parish@stjosephredwing.org www.stjosephredwing.org Rev. Brandon M. Theisen, Pst.; Dcn. Patrick Evans; CRP Stds.: 96

RICHFIELD

The Church of the Assumption/La Iglesia de La Asuncion - 305 E 77th St, Richfield, MN 55423 t) 612-866-5019 www.assumptionrichfield.org Rev. James C. Liekhus, Pst.; Rev. David Shaw, Par. Vicar; Dcn. Peter Loving; CRP Stds.: 262

St. Peter - 6730 Nicollet Ave, Richfield, MN 55423 t) 612-866-5089 www.stpetersrichfield.org Rev. James C. Liekhus, Pst.; Rev. David Shaw, Par. Vicar; Dcn. Mark Johanns;

St. Richard - 7540 Penn Ave. S., Richfield, MN 55423 t) 612-869-2426 www.strichards.com Rev. James C. Liekhus, Pst.; Rev. David Shaw, Par. Vicar; CRP Stds.: 14

ROBBINSDALE

Sacred Heart - 4087 W. Broadway Ave., Robbinsdale, MN 55422 t) 763-537-4561 contact@shrmn.org www.shrmn.org Rev. Bryan J. B. Pedersen, Pst.; Dcn. James Ramsey; CRP Stds.: 48

Sacred Heart Catholic School - (Grades PreK-8) 4050 Hubbard Ave. N., Robbinsdale, MN 55422 t) 763-537-1329 info@shcsr.org sacredheartschoolrobbinsdale.org/ Karen Bursey, Prin.; Stds.: 161; Lay Tchrs.: 11

ROGERS

The Catholic Church of Mary Queen of Peace - 21304 Church Ave., Rogers, MN 55374 t) 763-428-2585 parishoffice@mqpcatholic.org www.mqpcatholic.org Rev. Mark L. Pavlik, Pst.; CRP Stds.: 174

St. Martin Church -

St. Walburga Church - 12020 Fletcher Ln., Rogers, MN 55374

Mary, Queen of Peace School - (Grades PreK-5) 21201 Church Ave., Rogers, MN 55374 t) 763-428-2355 school.mqpcatholic.org Kate Hamill, Prin.; Stds.: 128; Lay Tchrs.: 5

ROSEMOUNT

St. Agatha - 3700 160th St. E., Rosemount, MN 55068 t) 651-437-7498 saintagatha.org/ Rev. Richard J. Mahoney, Par. Admin.;

St. Joseph - 13900 Biscayne Ave. W., Rosemount, MN 55068 t) 651-423-4402 info@stjosephcommunity.org www.stjosephcommunity.org Rev. Paul A. Kammen, Pst.; Dcn. Gordon Bird; Dcn. Stephen Boatwright; CRP Stds.: 307

St. Joseph School - (Grades PreK-8) t) 651-423-1658 school@stjosephcommunity.org school.stjosephcommunity.org Kelly Roche, Prin.; Stds.: 315; Lay Tchrs.: 14

ROSEVILLE

Corpus Christi - 2131 Fairview Ave. N., Roseville, MN 55113 t) 651-639-8888 office@churchofcorpuschristi.org www.churchofcorpuschristi.org Rev. Michael John Goodavish, Pst.; Dcn. Glenn Skuta; CRP Stds.: 26

Saint Rose of Lima - 2048 Hamline Ave. N., Roseville, MN 55113 t) 651-645-9389 info@saintroseoflima.net www.saintroseoflima.net Rev. Marc V. Paveglio, Pst.; Dcn. Glenn Skuta; CRP Stds.: 38

Saint Rose of Lima School - (Grades PreK-8) 2072 Hamline Ave. N., Roseville, MN 55113 t) 651-646-3832 mysaintrose.net Sean Slaikeu, Prin.; Stds.: 181; Lay Tchrs.: 13

RUSH CITY

Sacred Heart - 425 Frandsen Ave. S., Rush City, MN 55069; Mailing: 415 W. 5th St., PO Box 45, Rush City, MN 55069 t) 320-358-4370 shc415@hotmail.com www.sacredheartrcmn.org Rev. Matthew Shireman, Par. Admin.; Dcn. Kevin Michael Downie;

SAVAGE

St. John the Baptist - 4625 125th St. W., Savage, MN 55378 t) 952-890-9465 frontdesk@stjohns-savage.org www.stjohns-savage.org Rev. Benjamin Little, Pst.; Dcn. Robert Scott Durham; Dcn. Gerald Little; CRP Stds.: 133

St. John the Baptist School - (Grades PreK-8) 12508 Lynn Ave. S., Savage, MN 55378 t) 952-890-6604 admissions@stjohns-savage.org stjohns-savage.org/school Greg Wesely, Prin.; Stds.: 362; Lay Tchrs.: 19

SHAFER

The Church of Saint Francis Xavier - 25267 Redwing Ave., Shafer, MN 55074; Mailing: PO Box 234, Taylors Falls, MN 55084 t) 651-465-7345 stjosephstfrancis@outlook.com www.stjosephtaylorsfalls.org Rev. John M. Drees, Pst.;

SHAKOPEE

Sts. Joachim and Anne - 2700 17th Ave. E., Shakopee, MN 55379 t) 952-445-1319 parish@ssjacs.org www.ssjacs.org Receiving parish for St. Mark, Shakopee, St. Mary of the Purification, Shakopee & St. Mary, Shakopee. Rev. Michael C. Becker, Pst.; Rev. Matthew Quail, Par. Vicar; CRP Stds.: 156

Shakopee Area Catholic School - (Grades PreK-8) t) 952-445-3387 www.sacsschools.org Nikki Giel, Prin.; Stds.: 597; Lay Tchrs.: 16

Church of St. Mark - 350 Atwood St. S., Shakopee, MN 55379

Church of St. Mary of the Purification - 15850 Marystown Rd., Shakopee, MN 55379

Church of St. Mary - 535 Lewis St. S., Shakopee, MN 55379

SHOREVIEW

St. Odilia - 3495 Victoria St N, Shoreview, MN 55126 t) 651-484-6681 info@stodilia.org www.stodilia.org Rev. Erich Rutten, Pst.; Rev. Brian Zuelke, OP, Par. Vicar; Rev. Scott M. Carl, Sacr. Min.; Dcn. Ramon Garcia Degollado, Permanent Deacon; Dcn. James Saumweber; CRP Stds.: 192

St. Odilia School - (Grades PreK-8) t) 651-484-3364 schooloffice@stodilia.org www.stodiliaschool.org Sandy Kane, Prin.; Stds.: 709; Lay Tchrs.: 35

SOUTH ST. PAUL

Holy Trinity - 749 6th Ave. S, South St. Paul, MN 55075 t) 651-455-1302 office@holytrinityssp.org www.holytrinityssp.org Rev. John P. Echert, Pst.; Rev. Robert J. Altier, Par. Vicar; Dcn. Ronald Michael Smisek; CRP Stds.: 88

Holy Trinity School - (Grades PreK-8) 745 6th Ave S, South St. Paul, MN 55075 t) 651-455-8557 secretary@holytrinitys.org www.holytrinityssp.org Anita Davis, Interim Principal; Stds.: 117; Lay Tchrs.: 10

St. John Vianney - 789 17th Ave N, South St. Paul, MN 55075 t) 651-451-1863 info@sjvssp.org www.sjvssp.org Rev. Antony Skaria, C.F.I.C., Pst.; CRP Stds.: 14

ST. ANTHONY

St. Charles Borromeo - 2739 Stinson Blvd, St. Anthony, MN 55418 t) 612-781-6529 stchbinfo@stchb.org www.stchb.org Rev. Troy D. Przybilla, Pst.; Dcn. Stephen Najarian; CRP Stds.: 2

St. Charles Borromeo School - (Grades PreK-8) 2727 Stinson Blvd NE, Minneapolis, MN 55418 t) 612-781-2643 stchbschool@gmail.com www.stchbschool.org Danny Kieffer, Prin.; Stds.: 335; Lay Tchrs.: 19

ST. BONIFACIUS

St. Boniface - 4025 Main St, St. Bonifacius, MN 55375; Mailing: PO Box 68, St. Bonifacius, MN 55375 t) 952-446-1054 office@saintboni.org www.saintboni.org Rev. Peter Hughes, Pst.; CRP Stds.: 48

ST. LOUIS PARK

Holy Family - 5900 Lake St W, St. Louis Park, MN 55416 t) 952-929-0113 staff@hfcmn.org www.hfcmn.org Rev. Joseph R. Johnson, Pst.; Rev. Timothy David Sandquist, Par. Vicar; CRP Stds.: 64

Holy Family Academy - (Grades PreK-8) 5925 Lake St W, St. Louis Park, MN 55416 t) 952-925-9193 info@hfamn.org www.hfamn.org Theresa Krueger, Headmaster; Stds.: 207; Sr. Tchrs.: 2; Lay Tchrs.: 13

ST. MICHAEL

St. Michael - 11300 Frankfort Pkwy., N.E., St. Michael, MN 55376 t) 763-497-2745 www.stmcatholicchurch.org Rev. Brian J. Park, Pst.; Rev. Connor Thomas Z McGinnis, Par. Vicar; Dcn. Steven Dupay; Dcn. Paul Ravnikar; CRP Stds.: 256

St. Michael Catholic School - (Grades PreK-8) 14 Main St N, Saint Michael, MN 55376 t) 763-497-3887 www.stmcatholicschool.org Heidi Gallus, Prin.; Stds.: 486; Lay Tchrs.: 26

ST. PAUL

Cathedral of Saint Paul - 239 Selby Ave, St. Paul, MN 55102 t) 651-228-1766 info@cathedralsaintpaul.org www.cathedralsaintpaul.org Rev. Matthew J. Northenscold, Sacr. Min.; Rev. John L. Ubel, Rector; Dcn. Ronald Schmitz; Dcn. Phillip Stewart; Dcn. Naokao Yang; CRP Stds.: 31

Church of St. Vincent - 651 Virginia St., St. Paul, MN 55103 (Worship Site)

St. Adalbert - 265 Charles Ave, St. Paul, MN 55103 t) 651-228-9002 stadalbert@comcast.net stadalbertchurch.org/ Rev. Minh Vu, Pst.; CRP Stds.: 86

St. Agnes - 535 Thomas Ave, St. Paul, MN 55103 t) 651-925-8800 office@churchofsaintagnes.org www.churchofsaintagnes.org Rev. Mark D. Moriarty, Pst.; Rev. James P. McConville, Sacr. Min.; Rev. John A. Gallas, Sacr. Min.; Dcn. Nathan E. Allen; CRP Stds.: 40

St. Agnes School - (Grades PreK-12) 530 Lafond Ave., St. Paul, MN 55103 t) 651-925-8700 info@saintagnesschool.org www.saintagnesschool.org Kevin Ferdinandt, Headmaster; Stds.: 805; Sr. Tchrs.: 4; Lay Tchrs.: 42

St. Andrew Kim - 1435 Midway Pkwy., St. Paul, MN 55108 t) 651-644-1605 standrewkimmn@gmail.com www.facebook.com/sakp.mn/ Rev. Dominicus Kim (Korea), Par. Admin.; CRP Stds.: 21

Assumption - 51 7th St W, St. Paul, MN 55102 t) 651-224-7536 info@assumptionsp.org www.assumptionsp.org Rev. Paul C. Treacy, Pst.; Dcn. James Saumweber; CRP Stds.: 75

Blessed Sacrament - 2119 Stillwater Ave, St. Paul, MN 55119-3508 t) 651-738-0677 www.blessedsacramentsp.org Rev. Jimmy Mathew Puttananickal, C.F.I.C., Pst.; CRP Stds.: 65

St. Casimir - 934 E. Geranium Ave E, St. Paul, MN 55106 t) 651-774-0365 office@stcasimirchurch.org www.stcasimirchurch.org Rev. Dwight Hoeberechts, OMI, Pst.; Rev. Cyprian Czop, O.M.I., Par. Vicar; CRP Stds.: 83

St. Cecilia - 2357 Bayless Pl, St. Paul, MN 55114 t) 651-644-4502 info@stceciliaspm.org www.stceciliaspm.org Rev. John Michael Hofstede, Pst.; CRP Stds.: 57

Church of St. Bernard - 187 Geranium Ave. W., St. Paul, MN 55117; Mailing: 1160 Woodbridge St., St. Paul, MN 55117 t) 651-488-6733 www.stbernardstpaul.org Rev. Arokiadoss Raji, Pst.; Rev. Saw Joseph, Par. Vicar; CRP Stds.: 113

Church of Lumen Christi - 2055 Bohland Ave, St. Paul, MN 55116 t) 651-698-5581 volunteer@lumenchristicc.org www.lumenchristicc.org Rev. Daniel C. Haugan, Pst.; Dcn. Michael A. Lane; CRP Stds.: 33

Highland Catholic School - (Grades PreK-8) 2017 Bohland Ave., St. Paul, MN 55116 t) 651-690-2477 info@highlandcatholic.org www.highlandcatholic.org Jane Schmidt, Prin.; Stds.: 477; Lay Tchrs.: 25

St. Columba - 1327 Lafond Ave., St. Paul, MN 55104 t) 651-645-9179 www.stcolumba.org Rev. Hoang Dinh Nguyen, Pst.; Dcn. Thomas Stiles; CRP Stds.: 126

St. Francis De Sales - 650 Palace Ave, St. Paul, MN 55102 t) 651-228-1169 sfsjadmin@sf-sj.org www.sf-sj.org Rev. James Francis Adams, Pst.; CRP Stds.: 46

Holy Childhood - 1435 Midway Pkwy., St. Paul, MN 55108 t) 651-644-7495 contact@holychildhoodparish.org www.holychildhoodparish.org Rev. Philippe Vigneron (France), Priest in-solidum; Rev. Andrew R. Brinkman, Priest in-solidum;

Holy Spirit - 515 Albert St S, St. Paul, MN 55116 t) 651-698-3353 www.holy-spirit.org Rev. Nathan Robert Hastings, Par. Admin.; CRP Stds.: 7

Holy Spirit School - (Grades PreK-8) t) (651) 698-3353 www.holyspiritschoolstp.org/ Dr. Jennifer Krieger, Prin.; Stds.: 262; Lay Tchrs.: 18

St. Louis King of France - 506 Cedar St, St. Paul, MN 55101 t) 651-224-3379 stlouiskingoffrance.org Rev. Joseph Hurtuk, S.M., Pst.;

St. Mark - 1976 Dayton Ave, St. Paul, MN 55104; Mailing: 2001 Dayton Ave, St. Paul, MN 55104 t) 651-645-5717 parishcenter@onestrongfamily.org www.onestrongfamily.org Rev. Humberto Palomino, P.E.S., Pst.; Rev. Joseph Barron, PES, Par. Vicar; Rev. David Hottinger, PES, Par. Vicar; CRP Stds.: 70

St. Mark School - 1983 Dayton Ave., St. Paul, MN 55104 t) (651) 644-5030 preschool@onestrongfamily.org www.onestrongfamily.org/preschool Gayane Manukyan, Preschool Dir.;

St. Mary - 267 8th St E., St. Paul, MN 55101; Mailing: 267 8th St E. #100, St. Paul, MN 55101 t) 651-222-2619 office@stmarystpaul.org stmarystpaul.org Rev. Byron S. Hagan, Priest in-solidum; Rev. Bryce Evans, Priest in-solidum; CRP Stds.: 10

Maternity of the Blessed Virgin - 1414 Dale St. N., St. Paul, MN 55117 t) 651-489-8825 info@maternityofmarychurch.org www.maternityofmarychurch.org Rev. Philippe Vigneron (France), Priest in-solidum; Dcn. Dennis Chlebeck; Rev. Andrew R. Brinkman, Priest in-solidum; CRP Stds.: 64

Maternity of Mary/St. Andrew School - (Grades PreK-8) 592 Arlington Ave W, St. Paul, MN 55117 t) 651-489-1459 principal@mmsaschool.org www.mmsaschool.org Mike Langer, Prin.; Stds.: 147; Lay Tchrs.: 11

St. Matthew - 510 Hall Ave., St. Paul, MN 55107; Mailing: 490 Hall Ave., St. Paul, MN 55107 t) 651-224-9793 www.st-matts.org Rev. Antony Skaria, C.F.I.C., Par. Admin.; Rev. Stephen J. Adrian, Sacr. Min.; CRP Stds.: 33

The Nativity of Our Lord - 1938 Stanford Ave, St. Paul, MN 55105; Mailing: 1900 Wellesley Ave, St. Paul, MN 55105 t) 651-696-5401 info@nativitystpaul.org www.nativitystpaul.org Rev. Patrick J. Hipwell, Pst.; Rev. William D. Duffert, Par. Vicar; Dcn. Donald Tienter; CRP Stds.: 44

The Nativity of Our Lord School - (Grades PreK-8) 1900 Stanford Ave, St. Paul, MN 55105 t) 651-699-1311 school@nativitystpaul.org school.nativity-mn.org Kate Wollan, Prin.; Stds.: 708; Lay Tchrs.: 42

Our Lady of Guadalupe - 401 Concord St, St. Paul, MN 55107 t) 651-228-0506 www.olgcatholic.org Rev. James Andrew Bernard, Priest in-solidum; Most Rev. Joseph A. Williams, Priest in-solidum; Dcn. Luis Rubi; CRP Stds.: 41

St. Pascal Baylon - 1757 Conway St., St. Paul, MN 55106 t) 651-774-1585 www.stpascals.org Receiving parish for St. John of St. Paul. Rev. John J. Mitchell, Pst.; Dcn. Richard Moore; CRP Stds.: 42

St. Patrick - 1095 DeSoto St., St. Paul, MN 55130 t) 651-774-8675 stpats15@yahoo.com www.stpatrickmn.weconnect.com Rev. Dwight Hoeberechts, OMI, Pst.; Rev. Cyprian Czop, O.M.I., Par. Vicar;

The Church of St. Peter Claver of Saint Paul, Minnesota - 369 Oxford St. N., St. Paul, MN 55104; Mailing: 375 Oxford St. N., St. Paul, MN 55104 t) 651-646-1797 www.spcchurch.org/ Rev. Joseph Leo Gifford, Par. Admin.; CRP Stds.: 44

St. Peter Claver School - (Grades K-8) 1060 Central Ave W, St. Paul, MN 55104 t) 651-621-2273 schooloffice@stpclaverschool.org www.stpclaverschool.org Terese Shimshock, Prin.; Stds.: 92; Lay Tchrs.: 7

Sacred Heart - 840 6th St E., St. Paul, MN 55106 t) 651-776-2741 sacredheart1909@gmail.com sacredheartstpaul.org Rev. Edison Galarza, O.C.C.S.S., Pst.;

St. Stanislaus - 398 Superior St., St. Paul, MN 55102 t) 651-292-1913 (CRP); 651-292-0303 ststans.org Rev. Daniel C. Haugan, Par. Admin.; CRP Stds.: 23

St. Thomas More - 1079 Summit Ave., St. Paul, MN 55105 t) 651-227-7669 parish@morecommunity.org www.morecommunity.org Rev. Richard J. Fichtinger, S.J.,, Pst.; Rev. Peter J Etzel, S.J., Par. Vicar;

St. Thomas More Catholic School - (Grades PreK-8) 1065 Summit Ave, St. Paul, MN 55105 t) 651-224-4836 school.morecommunity.org Patrick Lofton, Prin.; Stds.: 309; Lay Tchrs.: 18

ST. PAUL PARK

St. Thomas Aquinas - 920 Holley Ave, St. Paul Park, MN 55071 t) 651-459-2131 www.st-thomas-aquinas.com Rev. J. Anthony Andrade, Pst.; Dcn. Joseph George Utecht; CRP Stds.: 53

STILLWATER

St. Mary - 423 5th St S, Stillwater, MN 55082 t) 651-439-1270 info@costm.org www.stmarystillwater.org Most Rev. Michael J. Izen, Pst.; Rev. Austin Leonard Barnes, Par. Vicar;

Church of St. Michael - 611 3rd St S, Stillwater, MN 55082 t) 651-439-4400 info@costm.org www.stmichaelandstmarystillwater.org Most Rev. Michael J. Izen, Pst.; Rev. Austin Leonard Barnes, Par. Vicar; CRP Stds.: 234

TAYLORS FALLS

St. Joseph's - 490 Bench St., Taylors Falls, MN 55084; Mailing: PO Box 234, Taylors Falls, MN 55084 t) 651-465-7345 stjosephstfrancis@outlook.com www.stjosephtaylorsfalls.org Rev. John M. Drees, Pst.; CRP Stds.: 126

VERMILLION

St. John the Baptist - 106 Main St. W., Vermillion, MN 55085; Mailing: 23315 Northfield Blvd., Hampton, MN 55031 t) 651-437-9030; 651-438-8680 (CRP) parishoffice@stmathias.com www.stjohns-vermillion.com Very Rev. Michael Tix, Par. Admin.; Dcn. Steven H. Maier; CRP Stds.: 109

St. John the Baptist School - (Grades PreK-4) 111 Main St W, Vermillion, MN 55085; Mailing: PO Box 50, Vermillion, MN 55085 t) 651-437-2644 office@sjb-school.org sjb-school.org Paul Dieltz, Prin.; Stds.: 148; Sr. Tchrs.: 2; Lay Tchrs.: 6

VESELI

Most Holy Trinity - 4939 Washington St., Veseli, MN 55046 t) 507-744-2823 mhtveseli@gmail.com www.mhtveseli.com Rev. John G. Lapensky, Pst.;

VICTORIA

St. Victoria - 8228 Victoria Dr, Victoria, MN 55386 t) 952-443-2661 receptionist@stvictoria.org www.stvictoria.net Rev. Robert L. White, Pst.; Dcn. Ray Ortman; CRP Stds.: 276

WACONIA

St. Joseph Catholic Community - 41 1st St E, Waconia, MN 55387 t) 952-442-2384 churchoffice@stjosephwaconia.org www.stjosephwaconia.org Rev. Stanley P. Mader, Pst.; Dcn. Gregory Miller; CRP Stds.: 236

St. Joseph Catholic School - (Grades PreK-8) t) 952-442-4500 schooloffice@stjosephwaconia.org school.stjosephwaconia.org Bruce Richards, Prin.; Stds.: 215; Lay Tchrs.: 12

WATERTOWN

Immaculate Conception - 109 Angel Ave. N.W., Watertown, MN 55388; Mailing: P.O. Box 548, Watertown, MN 55388 t) 952-955-1458 iccwatertown@gmail.com www.iccwatertown.org Rev. Peter Hughes, Pst.; CRP Stds.: 89

WATERVILLE

Holy Trinity - 506 Common St., Waterville, MN 56096 t) 507-362-4311 holyt7@frontiernet.net Rev. John Powers, Pst.; CRP Stds.: 28

WAVERLY

St. Mary - 607 Maple St, Waverly, MN 55390; Mailing: PO Box 278, Waverly, MN 55390 t) (763) 726-7300 stmarys-waverly.net Rev. Kenneth L. O'Hotto, Pst.; CRP Stds.: 144

WAYZATA

St. Bartholomew - 630 Wayzata Blvd E, Wayzata, MN 55391 t) 952-473-6601 stbarts@st-barts.org www.st-barts.org Rev. John A. Klockeman, Pst.; Dcn. Richard P. Witucki; CRP Stds.: 115

St. Bartholomew School - (Grades PreK-6) t) 952-473-6189 stbartsschool@st-barts.org stbartsbulldogs.com/ Jennifer Haller, Prin.; Stds.: 186; Lay Tchrs.: 13

Holy Name of Jesus - 155 County Rd. 24, Wayzata, MN 55391 t) 763-473-7901 email@hnoj.org www.hnoj.org Rev. Stephen D. Ulrick, Pst.; Rev. Timothy Wratkowski, Par. Vicar; Dcn. Dennis Hanson; CRP Stds.: 561

Holy Name of Jesus School - (Grades PreK-6) t) 763-473-3675 hnojschool@hnoj.org www.hnoj.org/school Martha Laurent, Prin.; Stds.: 421; Lay Tchrs.: 21

WEST ST. PAUL

St. Joseph - 1154 Seminole Ave., West St. Paul, MN 55118 t) 651-457-2781; 651-457-8841 (CRP) www.churchofstjoseph.org Rev. Michael Creagan, Pst.; Rev. Bruno Nwachukwu, Par. Vicar; Dcn. Thomas P. Michaud Jr.; Dcn. Gregg A. Sroder; CRP Stds.: 198

St. Joseph School - (Grades PreK-8) 1138 Seminole Ave, West St. Paul, MN 55118 t) 651-457-8550 office@stjosephwsp.org www.stjosephwsp.org Ginger Vance, Prin.; Stds.: 422; Lay Tchrs.: 30

WHITE BEAR LAKE

St. Mary of the Lake - 4690 Bald Eagle Ave, White Bear Lake, MN 55110 t) 651-429-7771 contactus@stmarys-wbl.org www.stmarys-wbl.org Rev. Ralph W. Talbot Jr., Pst.; CRP Stds.: 228

St. Pius X - 3878 Highland Ave, White Bear Lake, MN 55110 t) 651-429-5337 questions@churchofstpiusx.org www.churchofstpiusx.org Rev. Thomas J. McKenzie, Pst.; Dcn. Timothy Harrer; CRP Stds.: 35

WOODBURY

Saint Ambrose of Woodbury - 4125 Woodbury Dr, Woodbury, MN 55129 t) 651-768-3030 parishinfo@saintambroseofwoodbury.org www.saintambroseofwoodbury.org Rev. Peter Williams, Pst.; Rev. Benjamin Wittnebel, Par. Vicar; Dcn. John Edward Vomastek; CRP Stds.: 697

Saint Ambrose of Woodbury School - (Grades PreK-8) t) 651-768-3000 info@saintambroseschool.org saintambroseschool.org Betsy Osterhaus-Hand, Prin.; Stds.: 775; Lay Tchrs.: 36

ZUMBROTA

St. Paul - 749 Main St S, Zumbrota, MN 55992 t) 507-732-5324 stpauls@hcinet.net www.stpaulstmichael.com Rev. Randal J. Kasel, Pst.; CRP Stds.: 3

SCHOOLS: PRESCHOOL THRU HIGH SCHOOL

SCHOOLS

STATE OF MINNESOTA

BLAINE

***The Way of the Shepherd** - (PRV) (Grades PreK-8) 13200 Central Ave., N.E., Blaine, MN 55434 t) 763-862-9110 info@wayoftheshepherd.org www.wayoftheshepherd.org Catholic Montessori School Rev. Allan Paul Eilen, Chap.; JoAnn Schulzetenberg, Head of School; Stds.: 84; Lay Tchrs.: 10

EAGAN

Faithful Shepherd Catholic School - (Grades PreK-8) 3355 Columbia Dr., Eagan, MN 55121 t) 651-406-4747 schooloffice@fscsmn.org www.fscsmn.org Serving the parishes of St. Peter, St. John Neumann and St. Thomas Becket. Catherine Butel, Prin.; Rev. Anthony O'Neill, Canonical Admin.; Mike Randall, Business Dir.; Stds.: 503; Lay Tchrs.: 32

MAPLE GROVE

***Ave Maria Academy** - (PRV) (Grades PreK-8) 7000 Jewel Ln N, Maple Grove, MN 55311 t) 763-494-5387 info@avemariaacademy.org www.avemariaacademy.org/ Rev. Corey T. Belden, Chap.; Justin Shay, Prin.; Stds.: 232; Lay Tchrs.: 16

MINNEAPOLIS

Carondelet Catholic School - (Grades PreK-8) 3210 51st St. W., Minneapolis, MN 55410 t) 612-927-8673 www.carondeletcatholicschool.com Rev. Michael A. Reding, Canonical Admin.; Paula Leider, Prin.; Stds.: 412; Lay Tchrs.: 34

St. John Paul II Catholic Preparatory School - (Grades PreK-8) 1630 4th St., N.E., Minneapolis, MN 55413 t) 612-789-8851 secretary@johnpaulschoolmn.org johnpaulschoolmn.org/ Serving the parishes of St. Cyril, Holy Cross, All Saints, Our Lady of Lourdes, St. Boniface, Our Lady of Mt. Carmel and St. Lawrence. Tricia Menzhuber, Prin.; Rev. Kevin Finnegan, Canonical Admin.; Stds.: 192; Lay Tchrs.: 13

Risen Christ Catholic School - (Grades K-8) 1120 E. 37th St., Minneapolis, MN 55407 t) 612-822-5329 info@risenchristschool.org risenchristschool.org Founded by the parishes of Holy Name, Holy Rosary, Incarnation, St. Albert the Great and St. Stephen. Rev. Joseph P. Gillespie, O.P., Canonical Admin.; Michael Rogers, Pres.; Stds.: 302; Lay Tchrs.: 21

MINNETONKA

Notre Dame Academy - (Grades PreK-8) 13505 Excelsior Blvd., Minnetonka, MN 55345 t) 952-358-3500 info@nda-mn.org www.nda-mn.org Dr. Bonita Jungels, Prin.; Rev. John James Bauer, Canonical Admin.; Stds.: 242; Lay Tchrs.: 18

RICHFIELD

Blessed Trinity Catholic School of Richfield, Minnesota - (Grades PreK-8) 6720 Nicollet Ave. S., Richfield, MN 55423 t) 612-869-5200 school@btcsmn.org www.btcsmn.org Serving the parishes of Assumption, St. Peter's and St. Richard's. Patrick O'Keefe, Prin.; Rev. James C. Liekhus, Canonical Admin.; Stds.: 201; Lay Tchrs.: 13

ST. PAUL

St Pascal Regional Catholic School - (Grades PreK-8) 1757 Conway St., St. Paul, MN 55106 t) 651-776-0092 principal@stpascals.org stpascalschool.org/ An Ascension Catholic Academy School Rev. John J. Mitchell, Canonical Administrator; Inna Collier Paske, Prin.; Stds.: 126; Lay Tchrs.: 11

STILLWATER

St. Croix Catholic School - (Grades PreK-8) 621 3rd St. S., Stillwater, MN 55082 t) 651-439-5581 www.stcroixcatholic.org Serving the parishes of St. Charles, Bayport; St. Mary, Stillwater; St. Michael, Stillwater. Most Rev. Michael J. Izen, Canonical Admin.; Sr. Maria Ivana Begovic, O.P., Prin.; Stds.: 351; Sr. Tchrs.: 4; Lay Tchrs.: 14

WEBSTER

Holy Cross Catholic School - (Grades PreK-8) 6100 37th St. W., Webster, MN 55088 t) 952-652-6100 info@holycrossschool.net www.holycrossschool.net Serving the parishes of Lonsdale, New Market & Veseli. Rev. Nicholas William VanDenBroeke, Canonical Admin.; Jim Grogan, Prin.; Stds.: 163; Lay Tchrs.: 12

WEST ST. PAUL

Community of Saints Regional Catholic School - (Grades PreK-8) 335 Hurley Ave. E., West St. Paul, MN 55118 t) 651-457-2510 info@communityofsaints.org www.communityofsaints.org Serving the parishes of Saint Matthew, St. Paul; Saint John Vianney, South St. Paul, and Our Lady of Guadalupe, St. Paul. Bridget Kramer, Prin.; Rev. Steve Adrian, Canonical Admin.; Stds.: 257; Lay Tchrs.: 12

WHITE BEAR LAKE

Frassati Catholic Academy - (Grades PreK-8) 4690 Bald Eagle Ave., White Bear Lake, MN 55110 t) 651-429-7771 www.frassati-wbl.org Rev. Thomas J. McKenzie, Chap.; Rev. Ralph W. Talbot Jr., Moderator; Patrick Gallivan, Prin.; Stds.: 305; Lay Tchrs.: 23

HIGH SCHOOLS

STATE OF MINNESOTA

FARIBAULT

Bethlehem Academy - (PRV) (Grades 6-12) 105 3rd Ave., S.W., Faribault, MN 55021 t) 507-334-3948 cardinals@bacards.org www.bacards.org Melinda Reeder, Pres.; Rev. John Powers, Chap.; Stds.: 246; Pr. Tchrs.: 1; Lay Tchrs.: 19

FRIDLEY

Totino-Grace High School - (PRV) (Grades 9-12) 1350 Gardena Ave NE, Fridley, MN 55432 t) 763-571-9116 website@totinograce.org www.totinograce.org Rev. Andrew Herbert Zipp, Chap.; Cheri Broadhead, Prin.; Dr. Craig Junker, Pres.; Stds.: 691; Lay Tchrs.: 61

HOPKINS

***Chesterton Academy** - (PRV) (Grades 9-12) 1320 Mainstreet, Hopkins, MN 55343 t) 952-378-1779 info@chestertonacademy.org www.chestertonacademy.org Christopher Olley, Headmaster; Rev. Tim Sandquist, Chap.; Stds.: 149; Lay Tchrs.: 12

MAPLEWOOD

Hill-Murray School - (PRV) (Grades 6-12) 2625 Larpenteur Ave E, Maplewood, MN 55109 t) 651-777-1376 www.hill-murray.org Dr. Susan Skinner, Vice President for Mission; Kelly Harrington, Prin.; Melissa Dan, Pres.; Rev. Paolo Di Gennaro, FSCB (Italy), Chap.; Stds.: 969; Pr. Tchrs.: 1; Lay Tchrs.: 77

MENDOTA HEIGHTS

Convent of the Visitation School - (PRV) (Grades PreK-12) 2455 Visitation Dr, Mendota Heights, MN 55120 t) 651-683-1700 info@vischool.org www.visitation.net Rev. Stefano Colombo, FSCB, Chap.; Rene Gavic, Head of School; Stds.: 570; Lay Tchrs.: 69

Saint Thomas Academy - (DIO) (Grades 6-12) 949 Mendota Heights Rd, Mendota Heights, MN 55120 t) 651-454-4570 www.cadets.com Rev. Mark D. Pavlak, Chap.; Kelby Woodard, Headmaster; Stds.: 626; Lay Tchrs.: 64

MINNEAPOLIS

Cristo Rey Jesuit High School - (PRV) (Grades 9-12) 2924 4th Ave. S., Minneapolis, MN 55408 t) 612-545-9700 www.cristoreytc.org Erin Healy, Prin.; Thomas A Bambrick, S.J., Dir., Jesuit Mission & Identity; Stds.: 435; Lay Tchrs.: 25

DeLaSalle High School - (PRV) (Grades 9-12) 1 DeLaSalle Dr., Minneapolis, MN 55401 t) 612-676-7600 principal@delasalle.com www.delasalle.com Rev. Kevin T. Kenney, Chap.; Brian Edel, Prin.; Patrick Felicetta, Interim President; Stds.: 697; Bro. Tchrs.: 1; Lay Tchrs.: 35

MONTICELLO

***Holy Spirit Academy** - (PRV) (Grades 9-12) 1001 7th St. E., Ste. 1, Monticello, MN 55362 t) 763-220-2402 office@holyspiritacademy.org holyspiritacademy.org/ Andrew Lang, Headmaster; Stds.: 55; Lay Tchrs.: 5

RICHFIELD

Academy of Holy Angels - (PRV) (Grades 9-12) 6600 Nicollet Ave S, Richfield, MN 55423 t) 612-798-2600 www.academyofholyangels.org Very Rev. Michael Tix, Chap.; Heidi Foley, Prin.; Stds.: 628; Lay Tchrs.: 43

ST. LOUIS PARK

Benilde-St. Margaret's School - (PRV) (Grades 7-12) 2501 Hwy 100 S, St. Louis Park, MN 55416 t) 952-927-4176 info@bsmschool.org www.bsmschool.org Meghan DesLauriers, Interim President; Rev. Timothy Wozniak, Chap.; Stephanie Nitchals, Prin.; Stds.: 1,154; Lay Tchrs.: 97

ST. PAUL

Cretin-Derham Hall - (PRV) (Grades 9-12) 550 Albert St S, St. Paul, MN 55116 t) 651-690-2443 www.cretin-derhamhall.org Rev. Patrick A. Kennedy, Chap.; Mona Passman, Prin.; Frank Miley, Pres.; Stds.: 900; Bro. Tchrs.: 1

VICTORIA

Holy Family Catholic High School - (PRV) (Grades 9-12) 8101 Kochia Ln, Victoria, MN 55386 t) 952-443-4659 communications@hfchs.org www.hfchs.org Rev. Nels H. Gjengdahl, Chap.; John Dols, Prin.; Michael Brennan, Pres.; Stds.: 554; Lay Tchrs.: 38

INSTITUTIONS LOCATED IN DIOCESE

CAMPUS MINISTRY / NEWMAN CENTERS [CAM]

MENDOTA HEIGHTS

Saint Paul's Outreach, Inc. - 2520 Lexington Ave. S., Mendota Heights, MN 55120 t) 651-451-6114 info@spo.org www.spo.org Most Rev. Bernard Hebda, Chair; David E Fischer, Pres.;

MINNEAPOLIS

Newman Center at St. Lawrence - 1203 5th St. SE, Minneapolis, MN 55414 t) 612-331-7941 info@umncatholic.org www.umncatholic.org Rev. Jake Anderson, Pst.;

CATHOLIC CHARITIES [CCH]

MINNEAPOLIS

Catholic Charities of Saint Paul & Minneapolis - 1007 E 14th St., Minneapolis, MN 55404 t) 612-204-8500 www.cctwincities.org Michael Goar, CEO; Asstd. Annu.: 23,000; Staff: 568

CEMETERIES [CEM]

ALBERTVILLE

St. Albert Cemetery - 11400 57th St., N.E., Albertville, MN 55301; Mailing: PO Box 127, Albertville, MN 55301 t) 763-497-2474 stalbertmn@gmail.com www.churchofstalbert.org Rev. Peter M. Richards, Contact;

ANNANDALE

St. Ignatius Cemetery - ; Mailing: P.O. Box 126, Annandale, MN 55302 t) 320-274-8828 bonnie@stignatiusmn.com Rev. John D. Meyer, Contact;

ANOKA

Calvary Cemetery/Church of St. Stephen - 525 Jackson St., Anoka, MN 55303 t) 763-421-2471 info@ststephenchurch.org Rev. Jon Bennet Tran, Pst.;

BAYPORT

St. Michael Cemetery - 409 Third St. N, Bayport, MN 55003 t) 651-439-4511 office@stcb.comcastbiz.net www.stcharlesbayport.com Rev. Mark J. Joppa, Pst.;

BELLE PLAINE

Sacred Heart Cemetery - 200 E. Church St., Belle Plaine, MN 56011 t) 952-873-6564 parish@ourladyoftheprairie.com Rev. Brian T. Lynch, Contact;

Saint Peter and Paul Cemetery - 200 E. Church St., Belle Plaine, MN 56011 t) 952-873-6564 parish@ourladyoftheprairie.com Rev. Brian T. Lynch, Contact;

BROOKLYN PARK

St. Vincent de Paul Cemetery - 9100 93rd Ave N, Brooklyn Park, MN 55445 t) 763-425-2210 churchinfo@saintvdp.org Rev. Dennis Zehren, Contact;

BUFFALO

St. Mark's Cemetery - 223 19th St. N.W., Buffalo, MN 55313 t) 763-684-0075 nate.meyers@stfxb.org Rev. Nathaniel Meyers, Contact;

Saint Francis Xavier Cemetery - 223 19th St. N.W., Buffalo, MN 55313 t) 763-684-0075 nate.meyers@stfxb.org Rev. Nathaniel Meyers, Contact;

CANNON FALLS

St. Pius V Cemetery - 410 Colvill St. W., Cannon Falls, MN 55009 t) 507-263-2578 spvparish@gmail.com Rev. Terry P. Beeson, Contact;

CARVER

St. Nicholas Cemetery - 412 4th St. W, Carver, MN 55315; Mailing: P.O. Box 133, Carver, MN 55315 t) 952-448-2345 stnicholas@embarqmail.com Rev. William Deziel, Contact;

CENTERVILLE

St. Genevieve Cemetery - 7087 Goiffon St., Centerville, MN 55038 t) 651-429-7937 info@stgens.org St. John the Baptist Cemetery in Hugo now under the care of the Church of St. Genevieve. Rev. Gregory L. Esty, Contact;

CHANHASSEN

St. Hubert Cemetery - 8201 Main St., Chanhassen, MN 55317 t) 952-934-9106 webmaster@sthubert.org Rev. Rolf R. Tollefson, Contact;

CHASKA

Guardian Angels Cemetery - 215 W. 2nd St., Chaska, MN 55318 t) 952-227-4000 info@gachaska.org Rev. William Deziel, Contact;

CLEARWATER

St. Luke Cemetery - 17545 Huber Ave., N.W., Clearwater, MN 55320 t) 320-558-2124 admin@churchofstlukes.com Rev. Dennis J. Backer, Contact;

COLOGNE

St. Bernard Cemetery - 212 Church St. E., Cologne, MN 55322 t) 952-466-2031 busadmin@st-bernard-cologne.org Rev. Abraham George Kochupurackal, C.M.I., Contact;

COON RAPIDS

Epiphany Cemetery - 1900 111th Ave. N.W., Coon Rapids, MN 55433 t) 763-862-4300 jmackey@epiphanymn.org www.epiphanymn.org Rev. Thomas W. Dufner, Contact;

CORCORAN

St. Jean de Chantel Cemetery - 20000 County Rd. 10, Corcoran, MN 55340 t) 763-420-2385 frjenson@saintsppta.org Rev. Glen T. Jenson, Contact;

Old St. Thomas Cemetery - 21420 93rd Ave. N., Corcoran, MN 55340; Mailing: 20000 County Rd. 10, Corcoran, MN 55340 t) 763-479-0535 bsullivan@saintsppta.org Rev. Glen T. Jenson, Contact;

St. Patrick's Cemetery - 20000 County Rd. 10, Corcoran, MN 55340 t) 763-420-2385 frjenson@saintsppta.org Rev. Glen T. Jenson, Contact;

St. Thomas the Apostle Cemetery - 20000 County Rd. 10, Corcoran, MN 55340 t) 763-420-2385 frjenson@saintsppta.org Rev. Glen T. Jenson, Contact;

DAYTON

St. John the Baptist Cemetery - 18380 Columbus St., Dayton, MN 55327; Mailing: P.O. Box 201, Dayton, MN 55327 t) 763-428-2828 sjbchurch@yahoo.com Rev. Timothy J. Yanta, Contact;

Old St. John the Baptist Cemetery - 18380 Columbus St., Dayton, MN 55327; Mailing: P.O. Box 201, Dayton, MN 55327 t) 763-428-2828 sjbchurch@yahoo.com Rev. Timothy J. Yanta, Contact;

DELANO

Calvary Cemetery - 204 S. River St., Delano, MN 55328 t) 763-972-2077 fr.nathan@delanocatholic.com Rev. Kyle Patrick Kowalczyk, Contact;

St. Joseph Cemetery - 204 S. River St., Delano, MN 55328 t) 763-972-2077 fr.nathan@delanocatholic.com Rev. Kyle Patrick Kowalczyk, Contact;

St. Mary of Czestochowa Cemetery - 1867 95th St. SE, Delano, MN 55328 t) 952-955-1139 stbonifacepastor@gmail.com Rev. Peter Hughes, Contact;

St. Peter Cemetery - ; Mailing: P.O. Box 470, Delano, MN 55328 t) 763-972-2077 cemetery@delanocatholic.com Rev. Kyle Patrick Kowalczyk, Contact;

ELKO NEW MARKET

St. Nicholas Cemetery - 51 Church St., Elko New Market, MN 55054 t) 952-461-2403 jberry@stncc.net Rev. Patrick Thomas Barnes, Contact;

EXCELSIOR

Resurrection Cemetery - 680 Mill St., Excelsior, MN 55331 t) 952-474-8868 stjohns@stjohns-excelsior.org www.stjohns-excelsior.org Rev. Alex Bernard Carlson, Contact;

FARIBAULT

Calvary Cemetery - 4 Second Ave SW, Faribault, MN 55021 t) 507-334-2266 bwagner@divinemercy.cc Rev. Cory J. Rohlfing, Contact;

St. Lawrence Cemetery - 4 Second Ave SW, Faribault, MN 55021 t) 507-334-2266 bwagner@divinemercy.cc Rev. Cory J. Rohlfing, Contact;

St. Patrick Cemetery - 7525 Dodd Rd., Faribault, MN 55021 t) 507-334-6002 spshieldsville@qwestoffice.net www.spshieldsville.org Rev. Thomas M. Niehaus, Contact;

FARMINGTON

St. Michael Cemetery - 22120 Denmark Ave, Farmington, MN 55024 t) 651-463-3360 info@stmichael-farmington.org www.stmichael-farmington.org Rev. Benjamin Little, Contact;

FOREST LAKE

Calvary Cemetery - 1250 S. Shore Dr., Forest Lake, MN 55025 t) 651-982-2200 pastor@stpeterfl.org Rev. Daniel J. Bodin, Contact;

GOODHUE

St. Mary Cemetery - 308 4th St. N, Goodhue, MN 55027 t) 651-923-4472 holytrinitygoodhue@gmail.org Rev. Randal J. Kasel, Contact;

HAMEL

St. Anne Cemetery - 200 Hamel Rd., Hamel, MN 55340; Mailing: P.O. Box 256, Hamel, MN 55340 t) 763-478-6644 office@saintannehamel.org Rev. Corey T. Belden, Contact;

HAMPTON

St. John the Baptist Cemetery - 23315 Northfield Blvd., Hampton, MN 55031 t) 651-437-9030 parishoffice@stmathias.com Rev. Cole T. Kracke, Contact;

St. Mary Cemetery - 8433 239th St. E., Hampton, MN 55031 t) 651-437-5546 info@stmarysnewtrier.com www.stmarysnewtrier.com Rev. Cole T. Kracke, Contact;

St. Mathias Cemetery - 23315 Northfield Blvd., Hampton, MN 55031 t) 651-437-9030 parishoffice@stmathias.com Rev. Cole T. Kracke, Contact;

HASTINGS

St. Elizabeth Ann Seton Cemetery - 2035 15th St. W, Hastings, MN 55033 t) 651-437-4254 info@seasparish.org www.seasparish.org Rev. David R. Hennen, Contact;

St. Joseph Cemetery - 23955 Nicolai Ave. E., Hastings, MN 55033 t) 651-437-3526 stjosephm@embarqmail.com www.stjosephmiesville.com Rev. Terry P. Beeson, Contact;

HOPKINS

St. Margaret's Cemetery - 6 Interlachen Rd, Hopkins, MN 55343 t) 952-935-5536 receptionistchurch@stgabrielhopkins.org Rev. James C. Liekhus, Contact;

INVER GROVE HEIGHTS

St. Patrick Cemetery - 3535 72nd St E, Inver Grove Heights, MN 55076 t) 651-455-6624 bfier@churchofstpatrick.com Rev. Brian Fier, Contact;

JORDAN

St. John the Baptist Cemetery - 313 2nd St. E, Jordan, MN 55352 t) 952-492-2640 office@sjbjordan.org Rev. Neil Edward Bakker, Contact;

Saint Catherine Cemetery - 24425 Old Hwy 13, Jordan, MN 55352 t) 952-492-6276 admin@stpandc.mn.org Rev. Michael J. Miller, Contact;

Saint Patrick Cemetery - 24425 Old Hwy. 13 Blvd., Jordan, MN 55352 t) 952-492-6276 admin@stpandc.mn.org Rev. Michael J. Miller, Contact;

KENYON

St. Edwards of Richland - 108 Bullis St., Kenyon, MN 55946 t) 507-789-6120 stmichaels@kmwb.net Rev. Cory J. Rohlfing, Contact;

LAKEVILLE

All Saints Cemetery - 19795 Holyoke Ave., Lakeville, MN 55044 t) 952-469-4481 info@allsaintschurch.com Rev. Thomas W. Wilson, Contact;

LE CENTER

Calvary Cemetery - 165 Waterville Ave. N., Le Center, MN 56057 t) 507-357-6633 gloriagw@frontier.com Rev. James J. Stiles, Contact;

St. Mary's Calvary Cemetery - 165 N. Waterville Ave., Le Center, MN 56057 t) 507-357-6633 gloriagw@frontier.com Rev. James J. Stiles, Contact;

LE SUEUR

St. Anne Cemetery - 217 N. 3rd St., Le Sueur, MN 56058 t) 507-665-3811 stanneschurchoffice@gmail.com Rev. Christopher L. Shofner, Contact;

Calvary Cemetery - 217 N. 3rd St., Le Sueur, MN 56058 t) 507-665-3811 stanneschurchoffice@gmail.com Rev. Christopher L. Shofner, Contact;

St. Thomas Cemetery - 217 N. 3rd St., Le Sueur, MN 56058 t) 507-665-3811 stanneschurchoffice@gmail.com www.stanneslesueur.org Rev. Christopher L. Shofner, Contact;

LINO LAKES

St. Joseph Cemetery - 171 Elm St., Lino Lakes, MN 55014 t) 651-784-3015 office@saintjosephsparish.org www.mystjoes.org Rev. Michael F. Anderson, Contact;

LITTLE CANADA

Saint John's Church of Little Canada Cemetery - 380 Little Canada Rd., Little Canada, MN 55117 t) 651-484-2708 pastor@stjohnsoflc.org Rev. Thomas J. Balluff, Contact;

LONG LAKE

St. George Cemetery - 133 N. Brown Rd., Long Lake, MN 55356 t) 952-473-1247 stgeorge@msn.com Rev. Mark R. Juettner, Contact;

LONSDALE

Calvary Cemetery - 202 Alabama St. SE, Lonsdale, MN 55046 t) 507-744-2829 icparish@lonstel.com Rev. Nicholas William VanDenBroeke, Contact;

LORETTO

Sts. Peter and Paul Cemetery - 145 Railway St. E., Loretto, MN 55357; Mailing: P.O. Box 96, Loretto, MN 55357 t) 763-479-0535 frjenson@saintsppta.org Rev. Glen T. Jenson, Contact;

MADISON LAKE

Marysburg Cemetery - 27528 Patrick St., Madison Lake, MN 56063 t) 507-243-3166 office@maryschurches.com www.maryschurches.com Rev. James J. Stiles, Contact;

MAPLE LAKE

St. Timothy Cemetery - 8 Oak Ave. N., Maple Lake, MN 55358 t) 320-963-3726 parishoffice@churchofsttimothy.org Rev. John D. Meyer, Contact;

MENDOTA

St. Peter Cemetery - 1405 Hwy. 13, Mendota, MN 55150; Mailing: P.O. Box 50679, Mendota, MN 55150 t) 651-452-4550 church@stpetersmendota.org www.stpetersmendota.org Rev. Steven B. Hoffman, Contact;

MENDOTA HEIGHTS

The Catholic Cemeteries - 2105 Lexington Ave., S., Mendota Heights, MN 55120 t) 651-228-9991 info@catholic-cemeteries.org www.catholic-cemeteries.org Joan Gecik, Exec. Dir.;

Resurrection - 2101 Lexington Ave. S., Mendota Heights, MN 55120 t) 651-454-0263 www.catholic-cemeteries.org/resurrection Joan Gecik, Exec. Dir.;

MINNEAPOLIS

St. Anthony & St. Mary - 2730 Central Ave., N.E., Minneapolis, MN 55418; Mailing: 8151 42nd Ave. N., New Hope, MN 55427 t) 763-537-4184 www.catholic-cemeteries.org/stanthonys Joan Gecik, Exec. Dir.;

St. Joan of Arc Memorial Garden - 4537 3rd Ave. S., Minneapolis, MN 55419 t) 612-823-8205 dheaney@stjoan.com www.saintjoanofarc.org Rev. James R. DeBruycker, Contact;

MONTGOMERY

Calvary Cemetery - 206 Vine Ave. W., Montgomery, MN 56069 t) 507-364-7981 hredeemer@frontiernet.net Rev. Thomas M. Niehaus, Contact;

St. Canice Cemetery - 206 Vine Ave W, Montgomery, MN 56069 t) 507-364-7981 hredeemer@frontiernet.net Now under the care of Most Holy Redeemer, Montgomery. Rev. Thomas M. Niehaus, Contact;

St. John's Cemetery - 206 Vine Ave. W., Montgomery, MN 56069 t) 507-364-7981 hredeemer@frontiernet.net Rev. Thomas M. Niehaus, Contact;

MONTICELLO

Church of Saint Henry Cemetery - 1001 E. 7th St., Monticello, MN 55362 t) 763-295-2402 info@sthenrycatholic.com Rev. Tony VanderLoop, Contact;

MOUND

Our Lady of the Lake Cemetery - 2385 Commerce Blvd., Mound, MN 55364 t) 952-472-1284 reurich@ourladyofthelake.com Rev. Anthony O'Neill, Contact;

NEW BRIGHTON

St. John the Baptist Cemetery - 835 2nd Ave. N.W., New Brighton, MN 55112 t) 651-633-8333 stjohnsnb@pclink.com Rev. Paul J. Shovelain, Contact;

NEW HOPE

Assumption & Gethsemane - 8151 42nd Ave. N., New Hope, MN 55427 t) 763-537-4184 www.catholic-cemeteries.org/gethsemane Joan Gecik, Exec. Dir.;

St. Joseph Cemetery - 8701 36th Ave N, New Hope, MN 55427 t) 763-544-3352 lkotecki@stjosephparish.com Rev. Terrence Rassmussen, Pst.;

NEW PRAGUE

St. Benedict Cemetery - 215 Main St. E., New Prague, MN 56071 t) 952-758-3225 info@npcatholic.org Rev. Eugene J. Theisen, Contact;

St. John the Evangelist Cemetery - 215 Main St. E., New Prague, MN 56071 t) 952-758-3225 info@npcatholic.org Rev. Eugene J. Theisen, Contact;

St. Joseph Cemetery - 215 Main St. E., New Prague, MN 56071 t) 952-758-3225 info@npcatholic.org Rev. Eugene J. Theisen, Contact;

St. Scholastica Cemetery - 215 Main St. E., New Prague, MN 56071 t) 952-758-3225 info@npcatholic.org Rev. Eugene J. Theisen, Contact;

St. Wenceslaus Cemetery - 215 E. Main St., New Prague, MN 56071 t) 952-758-3225 info@npcatholic.org Rev. Eugene J. Theisen, Contact;

NORTH BRANCH

St. Joseph Cemetery - 38725 Forest Blvd. N., North Branch, MN 55056; Mailing: P.O. Box 609, North Branch, MN 55056 t) 651-674-4056 info@stgregorynb.org Rev. Mark Shane Stoppel-Wasinger, Contact;

NORTH ST. PAUL

St. Mary's Cemetery - 2600 Margaret St. N., North St. Paul, MN 55109 t) 651-777-8304 info@churchofstpeternsp.org Rev. Ettore Ferrario, F.S.C.B., Contact;

NORTHFIELD

Annunciation of Hazelwood Cemetery - 4996 Hazelwood Ave., Northfield, MN 55057 t) 952-652-2625 secretary-ac@integra.com Rev. Robert H. Hart, Contact;

Calvary Cemetery - 216 Spring St. N., Northfield, MN 55057 t) 507-645-8816 secretary@churchofstdominic.org Rev. Robert H. Hart, Contact;

NORWOOD

Ascension Cemetery - 323 Reform St. N., Norwood, MN 55368 t) 952-467-3351 busadmin@ascensionnya.org Rev. Abraham George Kochupurackal, C.M.I., Contact;

St. Patrick's Cemetery - 323 Reform St. N., Norwood, MN 55368 t) 952-467-3351 busadmin@ascensionnya.org Rev. Abraham George Kochupurackal, C.M.I., Contact;

OAK GROVE

St. Patrick of Cedar Creek Cemetery - 19921 Nightingale St. N.W., Oak Grove, MN 55011 t) 763-753-2011 stpats@st-patricks.org Rev. Allan Paul Eilen, Contact;

OAKDALE

Guardian Angels Cemetery - 8260 4th St. N., Oakdale, MN 55128 t) 651-738-2223 info@guardian-angels.org guardian-anagels.org Rev. Rodger Bauman, Contact;

PINE ISLAND

St. Michael Cemetery - 451 5th St. SW, Pine Island, MN 55963 t) 507-356-4280 stmichaeloffice@bevcomm.net Rev. Randal J. Kasel, Contact;

PRIOR LAKE

St. Michael Cemetery - 16311 Duluth Ave., S.E., Prior Lake, MN 55372 t) 952-447-2491 info@stmichael-pl.org www.stmichael-pl.org Rev. Thomas J. Walker, Contact;

RED WING

Calvary Cemetery - 426 W. 8th St., Red Wing, MN 55066 t) 651-388-1133 parish@stjosephredwing.org Rev. Thomas M. Kommers, Contact;

RICHFIELD

Assumption Cemetery - 305 E. 77th St., Richfield, MN 55423 t) 612-866-5019 maria@assumptionrichfield.org Rev. Michael Kueber, Pst.;

ROGERS

St. Martin Cemetery - 21304 Church Ave., Rogers, MN 55374 t) 763-428-2585 parishoffice@mqpcatholic.org mqpcatholic.org Rev. Michael C. Kaluza, Contact;

St. Walburga Cemetery - 21304 Church Ave., Rogers, MN 55374 t) 763-428-2585 parishoffice@mqpcatholic.org mqpcatholic.org Rev. Michael C. Kaluza, Contact;

ROSEMOUNT

St. Agatha Cemetery - 3700 160th St. E., Rosemount, MN 55068 t) 651-699-0660 Rev. Richard J. Mahoney, Pst.;

St. Joseph Cemetery - 13900 Biscayne Ave. W., Rosemount, MN 55068 t) 651-423-4402 Rev. Paul A. Kammen, Contact;

RUSH CITY

Calvary Cemetery - 425 Field Ave., Rush City, MN 55069; Mailing: P.O. Box 45, Rush City, MN 55069 t) 320-358-4370 sacredheart@q.com Rev. Mark Shane Stoppel-Wasinger, Contact;

SAVAGE

St. John the Baptist Catholic Cemetery - 4625 W. 125th St., Savage, MN 55378 t) 952-890-9465 pastor@stjohns-savage.org Rev. Donald E. DeGrood, Contact;

SHAKOPEE

St. Mary of the Purification Cemetery - 2700 17th Ave E, Shakopee, MN 55379 t) 952-445-1319 frlundgren@ssjacs.org Rev. Erik Carl Martin Lundgren, Contact;

ST. BONIFACIUS

St. Boniface Cemetery - 4025 Main St., St. Bonifacius, MN 55375; Mailing: P.O. Box 68, St. Bonifacius, MN 55375 t) 952-446-1054 stbonifaceoffice@mchsi.com Rev. Peter Hughes, Contact;

ST. MICHAEL

St. Michael Cemetery - 11300 Frankfort Pkwy., N.E., St. Michael, MN 55376 t) 763-442-6831 djtcctbj@gmail.com www.stmcatholicchurch.org Rev. Peter M. Richards, Contact;

ST. PAUL

Calvary - 753 Front Ave., St. Paul, MN 55103 t) 651-488-8866 www.catholic-cemeteries.org/calvary Joan Gecik, Exec. Dir.;

ST. PAUL PARK

St. Thomas Aquinas Cemetery - 920 Holley Ave., St. Paul Park, MN 55071 t) 651-459-2131 Rev. J. Anthony Andrade, Contact;

TAYLORS FALLS

St. Francis Xavier Cemetery - 540 River St., Taylors Falls, MN 55084; Mailing: PO Box 234, Taylors Falls, MN 55084 t) 651-465-7345 stjosephstfrancis@outlook.com www.stjosephtaylorsfalls.org Rev. John M. Drees, Contact;

VESELI

St. John's Cemetery - 4939 Washington N. St., Veseli, MN 55046 t) 507-744-2823 mhtveseli@gmail.com Rev. John G. Lapensky, Contact;

Most Holy Trinity Cemetery - 4939 Washington N., Veseli, MN 55046 t) 507-744-2823 mhtveseli@gmail.com Rev. John G. Lapensky, Contact;

VICTORIA

St. Victoria Cemetery - 8228 Victoria Dr., Victoria, MN 55386 t) 952-443-2661 mcatino@stvictoria.org Rev. Robert L. White, Contact;

WACONIA

St. Joseph Cemetery - 41 E. 1st St., Waconia, MN 55387 t) 952-442-2384 churchoffice@stjosephwaconia.org Rev. Stanley P. Mader, Contact;

WATERTOWN

Immaculate Conception Cemetery - 109 Angel Ave., N.W., Watertown, MN 55388; Mailing: P.O. Box 548, Watertown, MN 55388 t) 952-955-1458 iccw@frontiernet.net www.iccwatertown.org Rev. James William Devorak, Contact;

WATERVILLE

Calvary Cemetery - 506 Common St., Waterville, MN 56096 t) 507-362-4311 holyt7@frontiernet.net Rev. Michael W. Ince, Contact;

WAVERLY

St. Mary Cemetery - ; Mailing: P.O. Box 278, Waverly, MN 55390 t) 763-658-4319 Rev. Kenneth L. O'Hotto, Contact;

WAYZATA

Holy Name of Jesus Cemetery - 155 County Rd. 24, Wayzata, MN 55391 t) 763-473-7901 email@hnoj.org www.hnoj.org Rev. Stephen D. Ulrick, Contact;

WHITE BEAR LAKE

St. Mary of the Lake Cemetery - 4690 Bald Eagle Ave., White Bear Lake, MN 55110 t) 651-429-7771 contactus@stmarys-wbl.org Rev. Ralph W. Talbot Jr., Contact;

ZUMBROTA

St. Paul Cemetery - 749 Main St., Zumbrota, MN 55992 t) 507-732-5324 stpauls@hcinet.net Rev. Randal J. Kasel, Contact;

COLLEGES & UNIVERSITIES [COL]

ST. PAUL

St. Catherine University - 2004 Randolph Ave., St. Paul, MN 55105 t) 651-690-6525 president@stkate.edu www.stkate.edu College of St. Catherine ReBecca Koenig Roloff, Pres.; Anita Thomas, Executive VP & Provost; Stds.: 3,589; Lay Tchrs.: 273

***University of St. Thomas** - 2115 Summit Ave., St. Paul, MN 55105 t) 651-962-5000 maht3181@stthomas.edu; crou5420@stthomas.edu www.stthomas.edu Robert K. Vischer, Interim President; Rev. Christopher Collins, Vice Pres., Mission; Rev. Joseph Taphorn, Rector, Vice Pres., School of Divinity; Rev. Dennis J. Dease, Pres. Emeritus; Mark Vangsgard, CFO & Vice Pres., Business Affairs; Stds.: 9,061

***University of St. Thomas - Minneapolis Campus** - 1000 La Salle Ave, Minneapolis, MN 55403

CONVENTS, MONASTERIES, AND RESIDENCES FOR WOMEN [CON]

DEEPHAVEN

Franciscan Clarist Congregation, F.C.C. - Vimala Province, Convent of St. Therese House, 17931 Minnetonka Blvd., Deephaven, MN 55391-3322 t) 952-473-4771 c) (952) 607-0616; 651-703-2365 srsancta@st-therese.org; srnavyamem@yahoo.com Congregation Sr. Sancta Ezhanikattu, FCC, Contact; Srs.: 12

LAKE ELMO

Carmel of Our Lady of Divine Providence - 8251 Mount Carmel Rd., Lake Elmo, MN 55042-9547 t) 651-777-3882 Discalced Carmelite Nuns of St. Paul Rev. John M. Burns, O.Carm., Chap.; Mother Marie-Ange of the Eucharistic Heart, Prioress; Srs.: 16

MENDOTA HEIGHTS

Monastery of the Visitation - 2455 Visitation Dr., Mendota Heights, MN 55120 t) 651-683-1700 x743 maryfranreis@aol.com Sr. Mary Frances Reis, Supr.;

MINNEAPOLIS

Missionaries of Charity - 1500 E 24th St., Minneapolis, MN 55404 t) 612-721-8614 Convent with maternity home Sr. Angeles M.C., Supr.; Sr. M. Jonathan, M.C., Regl. Supr.; Srs.: 4

Visitation Monastery of Minneapolis - 1615 Fremont Ave. N., Minneapolis, MN 55411-3234 t) 612-521-6113 vmonastery@aol.com; kpmvhm@aol.com www.visitationmonasteryminneapolis.org Sr. Karen Mohan, Supr.; Srs.: 6

ST. PAUL

Franciscan Sisters of St. Paul - 225 Frank St., St. Paul, MN 55106; Mailing: 1884 Randolph Ave, St. Paul, MN 55105 t) 651-690-7037 jreetz@csjstpaul.org Sr. Mary Lucy Scheffler, O.S.F., Supr.; Srs.: 4

St. Mary's Mission House - 265 Century Ave., St. Paul, MN 55125 t) 651-738-9704 saintpaulcom265@gmail.com; sspcweb@usfamily.net www.clavermissionarysisters.org Missionary Sisters of St. Peter Claver. Sr. Anna Dinh Sr., Supr.; Srs.: 8

St. Paul's Monastery - 2675 Benet Rd., St. Paul, MN 55109-4808 t) 651-777-8181 cnehotte@stpaulsmonastery.org www.stpaulsmonastery.org Benedictine Sisters of Pontifical Jurisdiction. Sr. Catherine Nehotte, Prioress; Sr. Soler Linda, Sub Prioress; Srs.: 20

Sisters of St. Joseph of Carondelet - 1884 Randolph Ave., St. Paul, MN 55105-1700 t) 651-690-7000 www.csjstpaul.org Ministry in the fields of Education; Health; Social Services; Spirituality. Srs.: 112

ENDOWMENTS / FOUNDATIONS / TRUSTS [EFT]

ANOKA

Church of St. Stephen of Anoka Building Fund Trust - 525 Jackson St., Church of St. Stephen of Anoka, Anoka, MN 55303 t) (763) 421-2471 Rev. Jon Bennet Tran, Trustee;

HASTINGS

Regina Foundation - 1175 Nininger Rd., Hastings, MN 55033 t) 651-404-1104; 651-404-1451 annette.walker@allina.com www.allinahealth.org Doug Laumeyer, Chair; John Moes, Vice. Pres.;

MAPLEWOOD

The Hill-Murray Foundation - 2625 Larpenteur Ave. E., Maplewood, MN 55109 t) 651-777-1376 mdan@hill-murray.org Melissa Dan, Pres.;

MINNEAPOLIS

***Catholic Eldercare Community Foundation, Inc.** - 817 Main St NE, Minneapolis, MN 55413 t) 612-379-1370 info@catholiceldercare.org www.catholiceldercare.org Greg Baumberger, Pres.;

The Islander Foundation - 1 De La Salle Dr., Minneapolis, MN 55401; Mailing: 25 Grove St, Minneapolis, MN 55401 t) 612-676-7603 melanie.pascu@delasalle.com www.islanderfoundation.org/ James Benson, Prin.;

ST. ANTHONY

St. Charles Borromeo Endowment Fund Trust - 2420 St. Anthony Blvd., St. Anthony, MN 55418; Mailing: 2739 Stinson Blvd., St. Anthony, MN 55418 t) 612-781-6529 businessadmin@stchb.org Rev. Troy D. Przybilla, Pst.;

ST. PAUL

***Aim Higher Foundation** - 2610 University Ave. W. Ste. 525, St. Paul, MN 55114 t) 612-819-6711 info@aimhigherfoundation.org; raustin@aimhigherfoundation.org aimhigherfoundation.org Richard Raymond Austin, Exec.;

Archdiocese of Saint Paul and Minneapolis Participants' Restated and Amended Irrevocable Trust - 777 Forest St., St. Paul, MN 55106 t) 651-291-4405 Joseph Kueppers, Chancellor for Civil Affairs;

Catholic Services Appeal Foundation of the Saint Paul and Minneapolis Area - 777 Forest St., St. Paul, MN 55106; Mailing: PO Box 6488, St. Paul, MN 55106 t) 612-294-6622 information@csafspm.org csafspm.org/ Tizoc Rosales, Pres.; Yen Fasano, Bd. Chair;

Leo C. Byrne Residence Trust - 60 Mississippi River Blvd. S., St. Paul, MN 55105 t) (651) 291-4400 Bill Lentsch, Trustee;

Nativity of Our Lord Endowment Fund - 1900 Wellesley Ave, St. Paul, MN 55105 t) 651-696-5401 info@nativitystpaul.org www.nativitystpaul.org Laura Barr, Admin.;

Sisters of St. Joseph of Carondelet Ministries Foundation, St. Paul Province - 1884 Randolph Ave., St. Paul, MN 55105 t) 651-690-7026 rscorpio@csjministriesfoundation.org www.csjministriesfoundation.org Ralph Scorpio, Exec. Dir.;

HOSPITALS / HEALTH SERVICES [HOS]

HASTINGS

United Hospital, Hastings Regina Campus - 1175 Nininger Rd., Hastings, MN 55033 t) 651-404-1000 pamela.kochendorfer@allina.com www.allinahealth.org/regina-hospital/ A part of Allina Health Helen Strike, Pres.; Rev. Paul Causton, Chap.; Bed Capacity: 57; Asstd. Annu.: 58,500; Staff: 372

SHAKOPEE

St. Francis Regional Medical Center - 1455 St. Francis Ave., Shakopee, MN 55379-3380 t) 952-428-3000 askstfrancis@allina.com www.stfrancis-shakopee.com Sponsored by Sisters of St. Benedict, Duluth, MN. Amy Jerdee, Pres.; Abbie Engelstad, Spiritual Adv./Care Srvcs.; Bed Capacity: 93; Asstd. Annu.: 160,147; Staff: 879

ST. PAUL

St. Mary's Health Clinics - 1884 Randolph Ave., St. Paul, MN 55105-1700 t) 651-287-7777 info@stmarysclinics.org www.stmaryshealthclinics.org Primary care free clinics for adults, uninsured and living within 200% of Federal Poverty Limits Sue Gehlsen, Exec. Dir.; Asstd. Annu.: 15,000; Staff: 27

MISCELLANEOUS [MIS]

EAGAN

***The Laboure Society, Inc.** - 1365 Corporate Center Curve, Ste. 104, Eagan, MN 55121 t) 651-452-1160 info@labouresociety.org www.rescuevocations.org Laboure exists to help our future priests, sisters, & brothers resolve their student loan debt & Religious Institutions & Dioceses pay for formation. John Flanagan, Exec.;

HASTINGS

Regina Healthcare, Inc. - 1175 Nininger Rd., Hastings, MN 55033 t) 651-404-1451 pamela.kochendorfer@allina.com Lynn Moratzka, Chair; Very Rev. Michael Tix, Vice. Pres.; James Noreen, Treas.;

INVER GROVE HEIGHTS

Catholic Finance Corporation - 5826 Blackshire Path, Ste. A, Inver Grove Heights, MN 55076-1799 t) 651-389-1070; 877-232-2250 info@catholicfinance.org www.catholicfinance.org Judy M. Logan, Exec. Dir.; Amanda Braith, Admin.;

MAPLE GROVE

Twin Cities Cursillo - 16511 Lake Ridge Dr., Maple Grove, MN 55311 t) 763-420-3669 mstgerm@embarqmail.com www.tc-cursillo.org/ Monica Louise St. Germain, Treas.;

MINNEAPOLIS

Catholic Eldercare, Inc. - 817 Main St., N.E., Minneapolis, MN 55413 t) 612-379-1370 info@catholiceldercare.org www.catholiceldercare.org Greg Baumberger, Pres.;

Catholic Eldercare By Day - t) 612-362-2405

MainStreet Lodge Assisted Living - 909 Main St., N.E., Minneapolis, MN 55413 t) 612-362-2450

Rivervillage East Assisted Living - 2919 Randolph St. N.E., Minneapolis, MN 55418 t) 612-605-2500

Skilled Nursing Facility -

Catholic Single Adults Club of the Twin Cities - ; Mailing: P.O. Box 581321, Minneapolis, MN 55458-1321 t) 651-368-5003 Greg Jacobs, Chair; Carl Bergstrom, Chair;

Cristo Rey Corporate Work Study Program - Twin Cities - 2924 - 4th Ave. S., Minneapolis, MN 55408 t) 612-545-9700 jasonmorrison@cristoreytc.org Jason Morrison, Pres.;

Francophone African Chaplaincy - 629 2nd St., N.E., Minneapolis, MN 55413; Mailing: 777 Forest St., St. Paul, MN 55106 t) 612-331-3143 aumoneriefrancophone@gmail.com sites.google.com/site/aumoneriefrancophone/ French-speaking Community of St. Boniface Rev. Biju Pattasseril, CFIC,

Par. Admin.;

Labor Mariae Sisters - 428 5th St. NE, Minneapolis, MN 55413 t) 612-353-6343 filiaelaborismariae@gmail.com Mother Maria Regina van den Berg, L.M., Mother General;

Queen Anne Communities - 2627 Queen Ave. N, Minneapolis, MN 55411 t) 612-529-0503 sasjhparish@gmail.com Rev. Louis Pham Ha, C.R.M., Pst.;

Sagrado Corazon de Jesus - 3817 Pleasant Ave., Minneapolis, MN 55409 t) 612-874-7169 www.sagradompls.org/ Dcn. William Heiman, Treas.; Rev. Kevin M. McDonough, Pres.; Bradley Capouch, Vice Pres.; Dcn. Carl Valdez, Secy.;

Youth and Family Center Inc. - 4405 E. Lake St., Minneapolis, MN 55406 t) 612-722-9612 youthandfamilycenter@gmail.com Counseling Center Sr. Martha Merriman, C.S.J., Dir.; Stds.: 5; Lay Tchrs.: 1

SPRING LAKE PARK

Rachel's Vineyard Twin Cities - 1066 County Hwy. 10 N.E., #401, Spring Lake Park, MN 55432 t) 763-250-9313 rachels@rvineyardmn.org rvineyardmn.org/ Retreats for Healing after Abortions Nancy Blom, Exec. Dir.;

ST. PAUL

Abria Pregnancy Resources - 2200 University Ave. W, Ste. 160, St. Paul, MN 55114 t) 651-695-0111 supporters@abria.org abria.org/ Angela M Franey, CEO;

Center for Mission - 777 Forest St, St. Paul, MN 55106 t) 651-222-6556 friesenm@archspm.org www.centerformission.org The Society for the Propagation of the Faith, Incorporated Dcn. Mickey Friesen, Dir.;

The Companions of Christ - 2137 Marshall Ave., St. Paul, MN 55104; Mailing: Companions of Christ, P.O. Box 16239, St. Paul, MN 55116 t) 651-642-5933 frpeter@saintambroseofwoodbury.org www.companionsofchrist.org Rev. Peter Williams, Moderator;

Franciscan Brothers of Peace - Queen of Peace Friary, 1289 Lafond Ave., St. Paul, MN 55104-2035 t) 651-646-8586 franciscan@brothersofpeace.org www.brothersofpeace.org Bro. John Mary Kaspari, F.B.P., Vicar; Rev. Seraphim Wirth, F.B.P., Community Servant; Bro. Didacus Gottsacker, F.B.P., Mem.; Bro. Dominic Michael Hart, F.B.P., Mem.; Bro. Joseph Katzmarek, F.B.P., Mem.; Bro. Pio King, F.B.P., Mem.; Bro. Paschal Listi, F.B.P., Mem.; Bro. Antonio Pagba, F.B.P., Mem.; Bro. Conrad Richardson, F.B.P., Mem.; Bro. James Voeller, F.B.P., Mem.;

Minnesota Conference of Catholic Bishops - 525 Park St., Ste. 450, St. Paul, MN 55103 t) 651-227-8777 info@mncatholic.org www.mncatholic.org Promotes the general welfare of the people of MN. All Catholic Bishops of Minnesota constitute Ex Officio the Board of Directors. Jason A. Adkins, Exec. Dir.;

WEST ST. PAUL

Community of Christ the Redeemer - 110 Crusader Ave. W., West St. Paul, MN 55118 t) 651-451-6123 info@ccredeemer.org www.ccredeemer.org Edward Gross, Exec. Dir.;

NET Ministries, Inc. - 110 Crusader Ave. W., West St. Paul, MN 55118-4427 t) 651-450-6833 ministry@netusa.org www.netusa.org Youth Ministry Evangelization Mark Berchem, Pres.;

Twin Cities TEC of the Archdiocese of St. Paul-Minneapolis, Minnesota, Inc. - 337 Hurley Ave. E., West St. Paul, MN 55118 t) 651-281-0085 retreats@twincitiestec.org www.twincitiestec.org Jeffrey Campeau, Contact;

MONASTERIES AND RESIDENCES FOR PRIESTS AND BROTHERS [MON]

BLOOMINGTON

Congregation of the Sons of the Immaculate Conception - 901 E 90th St., Bloomington, MN 55420 t) (952) 297-8415 Rev. Edwin Ngah, C.F.I.C., In Res.; Rev. Jimmy Mathew Puttananickal, C.F.I.C., In Res.; Rev. Antony Skaria, C.F.I.C., In Res.; Rev. Mathai Chacko Chitteth, CFIC, Pst.; Friar Sojan Thomas, CFIC, In Res.; Priests: 5

BROOKLYN CENTER

Redemptorist Fathers of Hennepin County - 7025 Halifax Ave. N., Brooklyn Center, MN 55429-1394 t) 763-561-5100 jschmidtcssr@gmail.com www.redemptoristsdenver.org Rev. John Schmidt, C.Ss.R., Local Supr. & Pastor; Rev. Quy Duong, C.Ss.R., Assoc. Pst.; Rev. Marcel Okwara, C.Ss.R., Assoc. Pst.; Rev. John Son Tran, C.Ss.R., In Res.; Rev. William Peterson, C.Ss.R., In Res.; Rev. Gregory Wiest, C.Ss.R., In Res.; Priests: 6

LAKE ELMO

Carmelite Hermitage of the Blessed Virgin Mary - 8249 Mount Carmel Rd., Lake Elmo, MN 55042-9545 t) 651-779-7351 carmelbvm@gmail.com www.carmelitehermitage.org Carmel of the Blessed Virgin Mary. Rev. Elijah Schwab, O.Carm., Admin.; Rev. John M. Burns, O.Carm., Prior; Rev. Patrick Peter Peach, O.Carm., Librn.; Brs.: 6; Priests: 4

MINNEAPOLIS

St. Albert the Great Priory - 2833 32nd Ave. S., Minneapolis, MN 55406 t) 612-724-3644 michaelauds@gmail.com Order of Preachers (Dominicans). Province of St. Albert the Great. Rev. Michael Monshau, OP, Prior; Rev. Cassian Kenneth Sama, O.P., Chap., Univ of Minnesota Med. Ctr.; Rev. Timothy Combs, O.P., Assoc. Chap. St. Thomas University; Rev. Brian Zuelke, OP, Assoc. Chap., St. Thomas University; Rev. Joseph P. Gillespie, O.P., Vicar; Rev. Jude McPeak, OP, Pst.; Rev. Gilbert Jerome Thesing, OP, In Res.; Priests: 7

Markoe House Jesuit Community - 2900 11th Ave. S.,, #1015-1019, Minneapolis, MN 55407 t) 414-698-6949 wsazama@morecommunity.org Rev. Warren Sazama, S.J., Pst.; Rev. David Haschka, S.J., In Res.; Rev. Stephen Pitts, SJ, In Res.; Rev. Peter J Etzel, S.J., Pst. Min./Coord.; Aaron B Malnick, S.J., Pst. Min./Coord.; Rev. Matthew L. Linn, S.J., Spiritual Adv./Care Srvcs.; Thomas A Bambrick, S.J., Dir.; Christopher S Collins, S.J., Dir.; Priests: 8

PRIOR LAKE

St. Joseph Cupertino Friary - 16385 St. Francis Ln., Prior Lake, MN 55372 t) 952-447-2182 director@franciscanretreats.net www.franciscanretreats.net Bro. Bob Roddy, O.F.M.Conv., Vicar; Friar James Kent, OFM Conv, Sacr. Min.; Rev. Steven J. McMichael, O.F.M.Conv., Sacr. Min.; Rev. James Van Dorn, O.F.M.Conv., Supr.;

NURSING / REHABILITATION / CONVALESCENCE / ELDERLY CARE [NUR]

DEEPHAVEN

St. Therese of Deephaven Senior Living (Deephaven Woods Senior Livin)g - 18025 Minnetonka Blvd., Deephaven, MN 55391 t) 952-288-2187 leah.bird@fairview.org; susan.krantz@fairview.org www.deephavenwoods.com Rev. Leonard Andrie, Contact; Asstd. Annu.: 78; Staff: 70

HASTINGS

Regina Senior Living - 1175 Nininger Rd., Hastings, MN 55033 t) 651-480-4333 briana.sturm@benedictineliving.org www.benedictineliving.org/hastings-mn/ Regina Care Center & Regina Assisted Living; Benedictine Living Community | Regina Briana Sturm, Exec. Dir.; Asstd. Annu.: 458; Staff: 103

MINNEAPOLIS

Benedictine Care Centers - 6499 University Ave., N.E., Ste. 300, Minneapolis, MN 55432 t) (763) 347-2200 Jerry Carley, Pres.;

Benedictine Living Community New Brighton - 1101 Black Oak Dr., New Brighton, MN 55112 t) (651) 633-1686 Reid A. Hewitt, Exec. Dir.;

Benedictine Living Community Red Wing - 135-213 Pioneer Rd., Red Wing, MN 55066 t) (651) 388-1234 Eileen LaFavor, Exec. Dir.;

Benedictine Living Community - Minneapolis - 618 E. 17th St, Minneapolis, MN 55404 t) 612-879-2800 peter.momanyi@benedictineliving.org www.benedictineliving.org/minneapolis-mn/ Peter Momanyi, Exec. Dir.; Asstd. Annu.: 350; Staff: 136

OSSEO

Benedictine Senior Living at Steeple Pointe (Benedictine Living Community | Osseo) - 625 Central Ave., Osseo, MN 55369 t) 763-425-4440 reid.hewitt@benedictineliving.org www.benedictineliving.org/osseo-mn/ Reid A. Hewitt, Exec. Dir.; Asstd. Annu.: 100; Staff: 34

RED WING

Benedictine Living Community - Red Wing - 135-213 Pioneer Rd., Red Wing, MN 55006 t) 651-388-1234 eileen.lafavor@benedictineliving.org www.benedictineliving.org/red-wing-mn/ Eileen LaFavor, Exec. Dir.; Asstd. Annu.: 527; Staff: 153

SHAKOPEE

St. Gertrude's Health and Rehabilitation Center (Benedictine Living Community | Shakopee) - 1850 Sarazin St., Shakopee, MN 55379 t) 952-233-4400 lowell.berggren@benedictineliving.org www.benedictineliving.org/shakopee-mn/ Lowell Berggren, Exec. Dir.; Asstd. Annu.: 29,800; Staff: 251

St. Gertrude's Health Center (Benedictine-The Gardens) - 1850 Sarazin St., Shakopee, MN 55379 t) (952) 233-4400 Tia Bowe, Admin.;

ST. PAUL

Holy Family Residence - 330 Exchange St. S., St. Paul, MN 55102 t) 651-227-0336 www.littlesistersofthepoorstpaul.org/ The Little Sisters of the Poor of St. Paul Sr. Mary William, Secy.; Sr. Theresa Theresa Robertson, Pres.; Sr. Cecilia Wong, Vice. Pres.;

***Our Lady of Peace** - 2076 St. Anthony Ave., St. Paul, MN 55104 t) 651-789-5031 jefft@ourladyofpeacemn.org www.ourladyofpeacemn.org Hospice Care Facility Jeffrey Thorne, President/CEO; Asstd. Annu.: 564; Staff: 155

PRESCHOOLS / CHILDCARE CENTERS [PRE]

MAPLEWOOD

Maple Tree Monastery Childcare Center - 2625 Benet Rd., Maplewood, MN 55109 t) 651-770-0766 mapletreeccc@gmail.com mapletreechildcare.com Jennie Schlauch, Prin.; Sr. Catherine Nehotte, Pres.; Stds.: 76; Lay Tchrs.: 17

MCGREGOR

Catholic Youth Camps, Inc. - 19590 520th Ln., McGregor, MN 55760; Mailing: 2233 Hamline Ave., Ste. B1, Roseville, MN 55113 t) 651-636-1645 office@cycamp.org www.cycamp.org Augusta McMonigal, Exec. Dir.;

RETREAT HOUSES / RENEWAL CENTERS [RTR]

BUFFALO

Christ the King Retreat Center - 621 First Ave. S., Buffalo, MN 55313 t) 763-682-1394 christtheking@kingshouse.com www.kingshouse.com Rev. Lon Konold, O.M.I., Supr.; Rev. Richard Sudlik, Dir.; Rev. Hank Lemoncelli, OMI, Preaching Team; Bro. Daniel Bozek, O.M.I., Preaching Team;

LAKE ELMO

Jesuit Retreat House - 8243 Demontreville Tr. N., Lake Elmo, MN 55042-9545 t) 651-777-1311 demontreville@aol.com Rev. Patrick M. McCorkell, S.J., Assoc. Dir.; Rev. Thomas Lawler, SJ, Dir.;

MARINE ON SAINT CROIX

Christian Brothers Retreat Center (Dunrovin Retreat Center) - 15525 Saint Croix Trl N, Marine on Saint Croix, MN 55047 t) 651-433-2486 dunrovin@dunrovin.org www.dunrovin.org Jerome Meeds, Pres.;

PRIOR LAKE

Franciscan Retreats and Spirituality Center - 16385 Saint Francis Ln., Prior Lake, MN 55372 t) 952-447-2182 director@franciscanretreats.net www.franciscanretreats.net Rev. Steven J. McMichael, O.F.M.Conv., In Res.; Friar James Kent, OFM Conv, Mem.; Rev. James Van Dorn, O.F.M.Conv., Mem.; Bro. Bob Roddy, O.F.M.Conv., Dir.;

ST. PAUL

Benedictine Center - St. Paul's Monastery - 2675 Benet Rd., St. Paul, MN 55109 t) 651-777-7251 info@benedictinecenter.org www.benedictinecenter.org Mary Elizabeth Ilg, Co-Dir., Office Mgr.;

Maryhill - 1800 Graham Ave., #309, St. Paul, MN 55116 t) 651-696-2970 societydhmmn@gmail.com www.dhmna.org Society of the Daughters of the Heart of Mary Marilyn Smith, Contact;

SEMINARIES [SEM]

ST. PAUL

Jesuit Novitiate of St. Alberto Hurtado - 1035 Summit Ave., St. Paul, MN 55105-3034 t) 651-224-5593 uminovitiate@jesuits.org Rev. Richard J. Fichtinger, S.J.,, Supr.; Rev. William M. O'Brien, S.J., Dir.; Bro. Ralph Cordero, Minister-Socius; Rev. Lawrence Ober, S.J., Socius; Stds.: 12; Bro. Tchrs.: 1; Pr. Tchrs.: 3; Scholastics: 12

St. John Vianney Seminary - 2110 Selby Ave., St. Paul, MN 55104; Mailing: 2115 Summit Ave., #5024, St. Paul, MN 55105 t) 651-358-3368 sjv@vianney.net www.sjvseminary.org Rev. Jonathan J. Kelly, Rector; Rev. Msgr. Aloysius R. Callaghan, Formation Advisor, Pontifical Irish College; Rev. Matthew Alexander, Formator, Spiritual Dir.; Rev. Colin Daniel Jones, Formator, Spiritual Dir.; Rev. Joseph H. Kuharski, Formator, Spiritual Dir.; Rev. Jeffrey Thomas Norfolk, Formator, Spiritual Dir.; Rev. Paul Gitter, Spiritual Dir.; Michael Roesch, Dir., Bus. & Opers.; Stds.: 92

The Saint Paul Seminary - 2260 Summit Ave., St. Paul, MN 55105 t) 651-962-5050 semssp.org/sps/ Rev. Joseph Taphorn, Rector and Vice President; Rev. Scott M. Carl, Vice Rector, Formation Director and Faculty; Rev. Evan Steven Koop, Dean of Men, Formation Director and Instructor of Dogmatic Theology; Dr. Christopher Thompson, Academic Dean and Professor of Moral Theology; Stds.: 83; Lay Tchrs.: 6; Pr. Tchrs.: 8

An asterisk (*) denotes an organization that has established tax-exempt status directly with the IRS and is not covered by the USCCB Group Ruling.

Diocese of St. Petersburg

(Dioecesis Sancti Petri in Florida)

MOST REVEREND GREGORY L. PARKES, J.C.L.

Fifth Bishop of St. Petersburg; ordained June 26, 1999; appointed Bishop of Pensacola-Tallahassee March 20, 2012; ordained and installed June 5, 2012; appointed Fifth Bishop of St. Petersburg November 28, 2016; installed January 4, 2017. Office: P.O. Box 40200, St. Petersburg, FL 33743-0200.

Pastoral Center: P.O. Box 40200, St. Petersburg, FL 33743-0200. T: 727-344-1611; F: 727-345-2143.
www.dosp.org
communicate@dosp.org

ESTABLISHED JUNE 17, 1968.

Square Miles 3,177.

Comprises the Counties of Citrus, Hernando, Hillsborough, Pasco and Pinellas in the State of Florida.

For legal titles of parishes and diocesan institutions, consult the Pastoral Center.

STATISTICAL OVERVIEW

Personnel
Bishop ... 1
Retired Bishops ... 1
Abbots ... 1
Priests: Diocesan Active in Diocese ... 95
Priests: Diocesan Active Outside Diocese ... 5
Priests: Retired, Sick or Absent ... 41
Number of Diocesan Priests ... 141
Religious Priests in Diocese ... 91
Total Priests in your Diocese ... 232
Extern Priests in Diocese ... 78
Ordinations:
Diocesan Priests ... 2
Transitional Deacons ... 1
Permanent Deacons in Diocese ... 119
Total Brothers ... 25
Total Sisters ... 122

Parishes
Parishes ... 75
With Resident Pastor:
Resident Diocesan Priests ... 62
Resident Religious Priests ... 12
Without Resident Pastor:
Administered by Priests ... 1
Missions ... 4
Professional Ministry Personnel:
Brothers ... 3
Sisters ... 85

Welfare
Catholic Hospitals ... 7
Total Assisted ... 495,000
Health Care Centers ... 7
Homes for the Aged ... 15
Total Assisted ... 1,250
Day Care Centers ... 10
Total Assisted ... 826
Specialized Homes ... 4
Special Centers for Social Services ... 66
Total Assisted ... 16,200
Residential Care of Disabled ... 1

Educational
Diocesan Students in Other Seminaries ... 14
Total Seminarians ... 14
Colleges and Universities ... 2
Total Students ... 18,100
High Schools, Diocesan and Parish ... 4
Total Students ... 2,081
High Schools, Private ... 3
Total Students ... 1,546
Elementary Schools, Diocesan and Parish ... 25
Total Students ... 7,316
Elementary Schools, Private ... 2
Total Students ... 813
Non-residential Schools for the Disabled ... 2
Total Students ... 165

Catechesis / Religious Education:
High School Students ... 1,725
Elementary Students ... 10,677
Total Students under Catholic Instruction ... 42,437
Teachers in Diocese:
Priests ... 3
Brothers ... 4
Sisters ... 14
Lay Teachers ... 1,062

Vital Statistics
Receptions into the Church:
Infant Baptism Totals ... 2,551
Minor Baptism Totals ... 114
Adult Baptism Totals ... 331
Received into Full Communion ... 272
First Communions ... 2,959
Confirmations ... 2,641
Marriages:
Catholic ... 469
Interfaith ... 165
Total Marriages ... 634
Deaths ... 3,307
Total Catholic Population ... 273,858
Total Population ... 3,409,597

LEADERSHIP

Office of the Bishop - Most Rev. Gregory L. Parkes; Kelly Bui, Exec. Secy.;
Vicar General - t) (727) 344-1611 www.dosp.org Rev. Msgr. Robert F. Morris;
Moderator of the Curia - Rev. Msgr. Robert F. Morris;
Chancellor for Canonical Affairs - t) 727-341-6832 Dcn. Rick Wells, Chancellor for Canonical Affairs; Maria T. Gonzalez, Exec. Sec.; Lisa Mobley, Archivist;
Propagation of the Faith - mcp@dosp.org www.dosp.org Dcn. Rick Wells, Coord.;
Victim Assistance Coordinator - t) 866-407-4505 John Lambert (jl@dosp.org);
Chancellor for Administration - Dr. Lois Locey, Chancellor for Admin. & COO; Madelyn Morales, Exec. Asst. (mmorales@dosp.org);
Director of Ministry to Priests - Maria T. Gonzalez, Exec. Secy.;
The Tribunal - t) 727-341-6858 tribunal@dosp.org
Judicial Vicar - Very Rev. Joseph L. Waters;
Coordinator of Tribunal Services - David Ridenour;
Tribunal Staff -
Judges - Very Rev. Joseph L. Waters; Rev. Msgr. Robert C. Gibbons; Rev. Francis Mutesaasira Lubowa;
Promoters of Justice - Rev. Msgr. Ronald B. Aubin; Dcn. Rick Wells;
Defenders of the Bond - Rev. Msgr. Ronald B. Aubin; Rev. William J. Swengros;
Auditor - Rev. Alexander T. Padilla II;
Notaries - Mary Sue Oliver; Kim Pacana;
Estates & Trusts - David Ridenour, Dir.; Kim Pacana, Admin. Asst.;
Censor Librorum - t) 727-344-1611 Very Rev. Joseph L. Waters;
College of Consultors - Rev. Msgr. Robert F. Morris; Rev. Msgr. Robert C. Gibbons; Rev. Msgr. Ronald B. Aubin;
Vocations Office - t) 727-345-3452 spvocation@dosp.org Rev. Steven (Chuck) Dornquast, Dir.;
Permanent Diaconate Office - Dcn. James Grevenites, Dir. Deacon Personnel; Rev. John B. Lipscomb, Dir. Diaconal Formation; Anna Maslanka, Secy. (amaslanka@dosp.org);
Prison Ministry - t) 727-344-1611 prisonmn@dosp.org Dcn. Joseph Zucchero, Liaison - Pinellas County; Dcn. David G. Lesieur, Liaison - Hillsborough County; Denise Starkey, Liaison - Pasco County;
Vicar for Religious - t) (727) 344-1611 www.dosp.org Sr. Marlene Weidenborner, O.S.F., Dir.;

ADMINISTRATION

Accounting and Finance - t) 727-344-1611 John Dey, CFO; Aaron Daniels, Controller (adaniels@dosp.org); Will Milano, Payroll Mgr. / Senior Acct. (wmilano@dosp.org);
Calvary Catholic Cemetery and Miserere Guild - t) 727-572-4355 info@calvarycemetery.net www.calvarycemetery.net Terry Young, Dir.; Rev. Hugh Chikawe, Chap.;
Campaign Processing Office - t) 727-341-6841 Maria Ghizzoni, Processing Specialist (mghizzoni@dosp.org); Kathleen King, Lead Processing Specialist; Marie Burkett, Processing Specialist;
The Catholic Foundation - Meegan Wright, Exec.; Michelle Mesiano, Prog. Coord.;
Department of Administration - t) 727-344-1611 Dr. Lois Locey, Chancellor for Admin. & COO; Madelyn Morales, Exec. Asst. (mmorales@dosp.org);
Diocesan Finance Council - Thomas Moriarty, Chair; Laura E. Prather; Rev. Curtis V. Carro;
Human Resources - Claudia Shoro, Exec. Dir.; Giselle Gillis, Human Resources Mgr. (ggillis@dosp.org); Patty Rudis, Human Resources Generalist (prudis@dosp.org);
Information Technology & Security - Andrew Ong, Dir.; Ray Miller, Enterprise Information Systems;
Insurance and Risk Management - Valerie Burns, Coord.; Dr. Lois Locey, Parish & School Ins. Emergency Contact;
Internal Services Administration - Angie Peterson, Mgr.;
Office of Construction Management - Hung Pham, Exec.; Joe Bonczek, Acct. Assoc.;
Office of Stewardship and Development - Meegan Wright, Exec.; Margaret Becker, Systems Admin.; Michelle Mesiano, Admin. Asst.;
Real Estate and Planning - Hung Pham, Contact;

OFFICES AND DIRECTORS

Communications Office - t) 727-344-1611 Teresa L. Peterson, Exec. Dir.; Keishla Espinal, Communications Coord. (kespinal@dosp.org); Katie Camario, Digital Communications Mgr.;
Life, Justice and Advocacy Ministry - Dr. Armando Chavarria, Contact (achavarria@dosp.org);
Pastoral Center - t) 727-344-1611 Dr. Lois Locey, Chancellor for Admin. & COO;

FAITH FORMATION

Catholic Schools and Centers - t) 727-347-5539 ocsc@dosp.org www.dosp.org/schools/ Chris Pastura, Supt.; Ann Davis, Assoc. Supt.; Mark Majeski, Assoc. Supt.;
Charismatic Renewal -
English -
Spanish Speaking Spiritual Moderator - t) 813-512-1729 Winston Guevara, Pres.;
Cursillo, English - Tom Doyle, Dir. (tom@ststephencatholic.org);
Cursillo, Spanish - Rev. Rafael E. Martos, Spiritual Adv./Care Srvcs.; Fernando Guerrero, Dir.;
Ecumenical and Inter-Religious Affairs - t) 727-344-1611 Rev. Robert J. Schneider, Dir.; Dcn. James Grevenites, Asst. Dir.;
Evangelization & Missionary Discipleship - t) 727-344-1611 Armando Chavarria, Exec. Dir.; Melissa Mulson, Regl. Assoc. Dir.; Diane Kledzik, Dir. Marriage & Family Life;
Intercultural Ministry - Carlos Flores, Dir.;
Our Lady of Good Counsel Camp - t) 352-726-2198 Rev. James B. Johnson, Dir. (frjohnson@goodcounselcamp.org);
Scouting Office, Boys - Rev. Elixavier Castro, Chap.; Dcn. Edward Anctil, Asst. Chap.; Kellye Williams, Chair;
Scouting Office, Girls - t) 813-870-0860 Rev. Elixavier Castro, Chap.; Gretchen Tarrou, Chair; Theresa Adams, Diocesan Vice Chair;
Sea, Apostleship of the - Dcn. Kevin Dwyer, Chap.;
Tampa Port Ministry-Seafarers Center - t) 813-234-8693 Dcn. Kevin Dwyer, Chap.;
Worship, Office of - t) 727-344-1611 Rev. Victor Amorose, Dir.;

ORGANIZATIONS

Catholic Charities, Diocese of St. Petersburg, Inc. - t) 727-893-1314 Rev. Msgr. Robert F. Morris, Pres.; Margaret Rogers, Exec. Dir.;
Central Services - t) 727-893-1314 www.ccdosp.org Rev. Msgr. Robert F. Morris, Pres.; Margaret Rogers, Exec.;
Catholic Daughters of the Americas - t) 212-877-3041 Michele Bowman, State Regent (michelebowman227@gmail.com); Rev. Edward Lamp, Chap. (fred@stmarktampa.org);
Diocesan Council of Catholic Women - t) 727-797-2375 Rev. Theodore Costello, Diocesan Moderator; Melissa Garrett, Pres.;
Family of St. Jerome, "Familiae Sancti Hieronymi" - Jan G. Halisky, Praeses Generalis;
Knights of Columbus - t) 352-726-1670 Rev. Timothy P. Cummings, Chap.;
Knights of Peter Claver - t) 813-681-3010 Thoreau Nellum;
Knights of Peter Claver Ladies Auxiliary - t) 813-625-0612 www.kofpc.org Giselle Johnson (gjoh912@aol.com);
Marian Servants of Divine Providence - t) (727) 797-7412 Alicia Goodwin, Dir. (alicia.goodwin@divineprovidence.org);
Our Lady's Tridentine Mass Society - ourladystridentinemasssociety@gmail.com Jan G. Halisky, Representative;
Pension Plan for Employees of the Entities of the Diocese of St. Petersburg -
Pension Plan Administrator - Gabriel, Roeder, Smith & Co. - t) 954-527-1616
Society of St. Vincent de Paul -
***Central Council of St. Petersburg Diocese** - t) 813-831-5100 Very Rev. John F. McEvoy, Spiritual Adv./Care Srvcs.; Marvin Ropert, Exec.; Nancy Jones, Pres.;
***East Hillsborough District Council** - t) 813-956-7754 Tom Dambly, Pres.;
***Hernando Citrus St. Vincent de Paul Society District Council** - t) 352-688-8396 James Yeske, Pres.;
***Pasco District Council** - t) 727-372-8908 Janice Lattuca, Pres.;
***South Pinellas District Council** - John Gerdes, Pres.; Patrick Sullivan, Pres.; Michael J. Raposa, CEO;
***Upper Pinellas District Council** - t) 727-559-2315 Bob Sorrell, Pres.;
***West Hillsborough District Council** - t) 813-251-8678 Nancy Jones, Pres.;

PASTORAL SERVICES

Diocesan Legal Counsel - t) 727-820-3963 jdivito@trenam.com Joseph A. DiVito;
Diocesan Review Board - t) 727-415-7377 Irene Sullivan, Chair;
Personnel Board - Rev. Msgr. Robert F. Morris; Very Rev. Joseph L. Waters; Rev. James B. Johnson (frjohnson@goodcounselcamp.org);
Presbyteral Council - Rev. Msgr. Robert C. Gibbons, Chair;
Appointed Members - Rev. Craig Morley; Very Rev. Arthur J. Proulx;
Elected Parochial Vicars - Rev. Timothy Williford; Rev. Mark (Drew) Woodke; Rev. John B. Lipscomb;
Elected Pastors - Rev. Victor Amorose; Rev. Curtis V. Carro; Rev. Msgr. Robert C. Gibbons;
Elected Retired Incardinated Member - Rev. Msgr. Ronald B. Aubin;
Ex Officio Members - Rev. Anthony Coppola, North Central Deanery; Rev. Sojan Punakkattu, Northern Deanery; Rev. Msgr. Robert F. Morris, Vicar General;
Officers - Most Rev. Gregory L. Parkes, Pres.; Rev. Msgr. Robert F. Morris, Vice. Pres.; Rev. Msgr. Robert C. Gibbons, Chair;
Priestly Growth and Enrichment Commission - Rev. Gary Dowsey, Chair; Rev. Felipe Gonzalez; Rev. Curtis V. Carro;

MISCELLANEOUS / OTHER OFFICES

Catholic Formation, Inc. - t) 727-344-1611 Rev. Msgr. Robert F. Morris;
Catholic Foundation, Inc. - t) 727-344-1611 mmesiano@catholicfoundation.org catholicfoundation.org/ Meegan Wright, Exec. Dir.; Michelle Mesiano, Prog. Coord.;
Diocesan Radio - WBVM 90.5 FM - t) 813-289-8040 contact@myspiritfm.com John Morris, Station Mgr.;
Emmaus Foundation, Inc. - t) 727-344-1611
WBVM 90.5 FM, Inc. - t) 813-289-8040 www.myspiritfm.com/ John Morris, Station Mgr.;

PARISHES, MISSIONS, AND CLERGY

STATE OF FLORIDA

BEVERLY HILLS

Our Lady of Grace - 6 Roosevelt Blvd., Beverly Hills, FL 34465 t) 352-746-2144 faithformation@ourladyofgracefl.org; parishoffice@ourladyofgracefl.org www.ourladyofgracefl.org Rev. Erwin Belgica, Pst.; Mary Grace Arnold, DRE;

BRANDON

Church of the Nativity - 705 E. Brandon Blvd., Brandon, FL 33511 t) 813-681-4608 nativitycatholicchurch.org Rev. Michael R. Smith, Pst.; Rev. Donald Amodeo, Par. Vicar; Rev. Anthony Astrab, Par. Vicar; Rev. Belisario Riveros, Par. Vicar; Dcn. Elix Castro; Dcn. Robert Harris; Dcn. Mark Taylor; Dcn. Carlos Zayas; Michael Ottman, DRE; CRP Stds.: 839

Church of the Nativity School - (Grades PreK-8) t) 813-689-3395 ncsprincipal@nativitycatholicschool.org www.nativitycatholicschool.org Maureen Ringley, Prin.; Bill Amrhein, Vice Prin.; Jennifer Seebaran, Vice Prin.;

BROOKSVILLE

St. Anthony the Abbot - 20428 Cortez Blvd., Brooksville, FL 34601-5601 t) 352-796-2096 diane@theabbot.org www.theabbot.org Rev. Paul Pecchie, Pst.; CRP Stds.: 56

CITRUS SPRINGS

St. Elizabeth Ann Seton - 1401 W. Country Club Blvd., Citrus Springs, FL 34434; Mailing: 1460 W. St. Elizabeth Pl., Citrus Springs, FL 34434 t) 352-489-4889 steas@tampabay.rr.com www.stelizabethcs.org Rev. Sojan Punakkattu, Pst.; CRP Stds.: 13

CLEARWATER

All Saints - 2801 Curlew Rd., Clearwater, FL 33761 t) 727-789-1025 allsaintsclearwater@gmail.com www.allsaintsclearwater.org Rev. Alan Weber, Pst.; Dcn. Scott Huang; Dcn. James Paterson; CRP Stds.: 39

St. Brendan - 245 Dory Passage, Clearwater, FL 33767 t) 727-443-5485 sheilao@stbrendancatholic.org stbrendancatholic.org Rev. Timothy H. Sherwood, Pst.; Rev. Msgr. Michael F. Devine, Pastor Emer.;

St. Catherine of Siena - 1955 S. Belcher Rd., Clearwater, FL 33764 t) 727-531-7721; 727-531-7721 (CRP) westrich@scosparish.org; contact@scosparish.org www.scosparish.org Rev. Msgr. Robert Morris, Pst.; Rev. Connor Penn, Par. Vicar; Dcn. Francisco Martinez-Pacini; Dcn. Rick Wells; Dcn. Joseph Zucchero; Sr. Kathleen Beatty, S.S.J., Pst. Assoc.; Sr. Rosamunda Massawe, C.D.N.K., Pst. Assoc.; Mandy Westrich, DRE; Dcn. Frank Averill;

St. Cecelia - 820 Jasmine Way, Clearwater, FL 33756 t) 727-447-3494; 727-449-2839; 727-447-3494 x121 (CRP) dre@stceceliachurch.org www.stceceliachurch.org Rev. Jesus Martinez, Par. Vicar; Rev. Robert J. Schneider, Pst.; Rev. Theobald Weria, A.L.C.P., Par. Vicar; Rev. Msgr. Aiden Foynes, Pastor Emer.; Dcn. Wilfredo Huertas; Beth Barringer, DRE;

Light of Christ - 2176 Marilyn St., Clearwater, FL 33765 t) 727-441-4545 info@locchurch.org; jesus@locchurch.org www.locchurch.org Rev. Bill D. Wilson Jr., Pst.;

St. Michael the Archangel - 2281 State Rd. 580, Clearwater, FL 33763 t) 727-797-2375 smaclw@verizon.net; kwhite1948@aol.com www.stmichaelfl.org Rev. Thomas J. Anastasia, Pst.; Rev. Ted Costello, Par. Vicar; Sr. Therese Carolan, Pst. Assoc.; Dcn. Paul Koppie, Pst. Assoc.; Katie White, DRE; CRP Stds.: 163

CRYSTAL RIVER

St. Benedict - 455 S. Suncoast Blvd., Crystal River, FL 34429 t) 352-795-4478; 352-795-4479 stbens@tampabay.rr.com stbenedictcrystalriver.org Rev. Ryszard Stradomski, Pst.; Dcn. Fred Oberst;

Daystar Life Center of Citrus County - 6751 W. Gulf to Lake Hwy., Crystal River, FL 34429 t) 352-795-8668 Anthony Kopka, Exec. Dir.;

DADE CITY

St. Rita - 14404 14th St., Dade City, FL 33523 t) 352-567-2894 saintritafl@gmail.com www.stritaparish.org Rev. Carlos J. Rojas, Pst.; Dcn. Irvin Lau;

Sacred Heart - 32145 Saint Joe Rd., Dade City, FL 33525 t) 352-588-3641 dre@sacredheartdadecity.org; office@sacredheartdadecity.org www.sacredheartdadecity.org Very Rev. Krzysztof Gazdowicz, Pst.; Claire Obordo, Lay Pastoral Assistant; Gina Savko, DRE; Mary Andrysiak, RCIA Coord.; CRP Stds.: 48

Sacred Heart Child Care Center - 32245 Saint Joe Rd., Dade City, FL 33525 t) 352-588-4060 director@sacredheartecc.com; business@sacredheartecc.com www.sacredheartecc.com Lucinda O'Quinn, Dir.;

DUNEDIN

Our Lady of Lourdes - 750 San Salvador Dr., Dunedin, FL 34698 t) 813-733-0872 (CRP); 727-733-3606 frjohn@ourladydunedin.org www.ourladydunedin.org Rev. John G. Tapp, Pst.; Rev. Zachary Brasseur, Par. Vicar; Tom Labanauskas, Music Min.; CRP Stds.: 152

Our Lady of Lourdes School - (Grades PreK-8) 730 San Salvador Dr., Dunedin, FL 34698 t) 727-733-3776 frontdesk@myoll.com www.myoll.com Robert Yevich, Prin.; Stds.: 193; Lay Tchrs.: 17

GULFPORT

Most Holy Name of Jesus - 5800 15th Ave. S., Gulfport, FL 33707 t) 727-347-9989 www.mostholyname.org/ Rev. Brian C. Fabiszewski, Pst.;

HOLIDAY

St. Vincent De Paul - 4843 Mile Stretch Dr., Holiday, FL 34690 t) 727-938-1001 (CRP); 727-938-1974 svdpfaithformation@yahoo.com; frbillsss@svdpfl.com www.svdpfl.com Rev. William Fickel, S.S.S., Pst.; Rev. Dominic Long, S.S.S., Par. Vicar;

HOMOSASSA

St. Thomas the Apostle - 7040 S. Suncoast Blvd., Homosassa, FL 34446 t) 352-628-7000 info@mystthomas.org www.mystthomas.org Rev. Jose Glenn Diaz, Pst.; Dcn. Mark Manko; Karen Robben, Bus. Mgr.; Robin Furciato, CRE; Michelle Painter, Music Min.; Joseph McEvoy, Pst. Assoc.; CRP Stds.: 18

HUDSON

St. Michael the Archangel - 8014 State Rd. #52, Hudson, FL 34667 t) 727-868-5276 balvarez@saintmichaelchurch.org; office@saintmichaelchurch.org saintmichaelchurch.org/ Very Rev. James Ruhlin, Pst.; Rev. Pastor Mafikiri, Assoc. Pst.; Barbara Alvarez, DRE;

INVERNESS

Our Lady of Fatima - 550 S. U.S. Hwy. 41, Inverness, FL 34450 t) 352-726-1670 annettefatima550@yahoo.com www.ourladyoffatimainv.org Rev. Michael Suszynski, Pst.; Rev. Claudius Mpuya Mganga, Par. Vicar; Dcn. Joseph Medeiros; Annette Tremante, DRE; CRP Stds.: 65

LAND O' LAKES

Our Lady of the Rosary - 2348 Collier Pkwy., Land O' Lakes, FL 34639; Mailing: P.O. Box 1229, Land O' Lakes, FL 34639 t) 813-949-4565; 813-949-2699 (CRP) office@ladyrosary.org www.ladyrosary.org Rev. Justin Paskert, Pst.; Rev. Felipe Gonzalez, Par. Vicar; Dcn. Kenneth Anderson; Dcn. Frank DeSanto; Dcn. William T. Ditewig; Dcn. Jose Solorzano; Rev. Msgr. Ronald B. Aubin, Pastor Emer.;

LARGO

St. Jerome - 10895 Hamlin Blvd., Largo, FL 33774 t) 727-595-3100 (CRP); 727-595-4610 www.stjeromeonline.org/ Rev. Thomas Morgan, Pst.; Rev. Robert Cadrecha, Par. Vicar; Rev. Msgr. Brendan Muldoon, Pastor Emer.; Dcn. Frederick Kunder; Sr. Lucia Brady, O.S.C., Pst. Assoc.; Thomas Kurt, Music Min.; Patrick Glim, DRE;

Early Childhood Center - t) 727-596-9491 Phyllis Steele, Dir.;

St. Matthew - 9111 90th Ave., Largo, FL 33777 t) 727-393-1288 faithformation@stmat.org; mandy.rose@stmat.org stmat.org Rev. Jonathan Emery, Pst.; Dcn. Anthony Quattrocki; CRP Stds.: 47

St. Patrick - 2121 16th Ave., S.W., Largo, FL 33770 t) 727-584-2318 officemgr@stpaticklargo.org stpatricklargo.org/ Rev. Charles Leke, Pst.; Rev. Martin Okoro, In Res.; Sr. Kathleen Luger, DRE;

St. Patrick School - (Grades PreK-8) 1501 Trotter Rd., Largo, FL 33770 t) 727-581-4865 kgalley@stpatrickcatholic.org www.stpatrickcatholic.org A Ministry of the Catholic School System - Diocese of St. Petersburg, Inc. Keith Galley, Prin.; Stds.: 171; Lay Tchrs.: 16

LECANTO

St. Scholastica - 4301 W. Homosassa Tr., 4301 W Homosassa Trl, Lecanto, FL 34461 t) 352-746-9422 mychurch@stscholastica.org; kbrasseur@stscholastica.org www.stscholastica.org Rev. William M. Santhouse, Par. Vicar; Rev. James B. Johnson, Pst.; Dcn. Nick Novak; Kathy Brasseur, DRE; CRP Stds.: 45

LUTZ

St. Timothy - 17512 Lakeshore Rd., Lutz, FL 33558-4802 t) 813-968-1077; 813-961-1716 (CRP) www.sainttims.org Rev. John Blum, Pst.; Rev. Mark (Drew) Woodke, Par. Vicar; Dcn. Mike Ryba, Pst. Assoc.; Dcn. Jerry L. Crall; Dcn. Marc Garofani; Dcn. Peter J. Burns; Dcn. Edward LaRose; Dcn. Glenn Smith; Justin Lantz, Youth Min.; Peggy Cloutier, Dir.;

MASARYKTOWN

St. Mary, Our Lady of Sorrows - 18810 U.S. Hwy. 41, Masaryktown, FL 34604 t) 352-796-2792 info@saintmaryols.com www.saintmaryols.com Rev. Thomas L. Madden, Pst.;

NEW PORT RICHEY

Our Lady Queen of Peace - 5340 High St., New Port Richey, FL 34652 t) 727-842-9396 (CRP); 727-849-7521 faithformation@ladyqueenofpeace.org; office@ladyqueenofpeace.org www.ladyqueenofpeace.org/ Rev. Sebastian Earthedath, M.S.T., Pst.; Rev. Saji James, M.S.T., Par. Vicar; Rev. Joseph Kalarickal, M.S.T., Par. Vicar; Dcn. Eusebio Torres; Sally McMullen, DRE;

St. Thomas Aquinas - 8320 Old C.R. #54, New Port Richey, FL 34653-6415 t) 727-372-8600 bulletin@stanpr.org; cheralyn@stanpr.org www.stanpr.org Rev. Eric Peters, Pst.; Rev. George Varkey, M.S.T., Assoc. Pst.; CRP Stds.: 350

St. Thomas Early Childhood Development Center - t) 727-376-2330 staecc@aol.com Alicia Mumma, Dir.;

PALM HARBOR

St. Luke the Evangelist - 2757 Alderman Rd., Palm Harbor, FL 34684 t) 727-787-2845 (CRP); 727-786-3648 officemgr@stlukealderman.org; areyes@stlukealderman.org www.stlukealderman.org Rev. Paul Kochu, Pst.; Dcn. Joe Reid; Rev. Pedro Camilo Simoes, S.A.C., Par. Vicar;

St. Luke Early Childhood Center - t) 727-787-2914 stlecc@gte.net Kathleen Mitchell, Dir.;

PINELLAS PARK

Sacred Heart - 7809 46th Way, Pinellas Park, FL 33781 t) 727-541-4447 shcc7809@gmail.com; sacredfaithformation@gmail.com sacredheartpinellaspark.com Rev. Bradley Reed, Par. Vicar; Dcn. John Ustick; Rev. Kevin Yarnell, Pst.; Dcn. Chris Jensen; CRP Stds.: 57

PLANT CITY

St. Clement - 1104 N. Alexander St., Plant City, FL 33563 t) 813-752-8251 cathy@stclementpc.org; info@stclementpc.org stclementpc.org/ Rev. Pedro Zapata, Pst.; Rev. Rafael Martos, Par. Vicar; Dcn. Neil

Legner; Cathy Rosales, DRE;

PORT RICHEY

St. James the Apostle - 8400 Monarch Dr., Port Richey, FL 34668 t) 727-869-3130 office@stjamesportrichey.org; faith.formation@stjamesportrichey.org www.stjamesportrichey.org/ Rev. Dominic Corona, Pst.;

RIDGE MANOR

St. Anne - 4142 Treiman Blvd., Hwy. 301, Ridge Manor, FL 33523 t) 352-583-2550 stanne@embarqmail.com Rev. John S. Hays, Pst.;

RIVERVIEW

Resurrection - 6819 Krycul Ave., Riverview, FL 33578 t) 813-677-2175 resurrectioncatholic@yahoo.com www.resurrectioncatholicriverview.com/ Rev. Daniel R. Kayajan, Pst.; Rev. Eugeniusz Gancarz, Pastor Emer.; Dcn. Pedro Leon; Dcn. Guillermo Caceres; Tina Ver Pault, DRE;

St. Stephen - 10118 St. Stephen Cir., Riverview, FL 33569 t) 813-689-4900; 813-671-4434 (CRP) frdermot@ststephencatholic.org; rosie@ststephencatholic.org www.ststephencatholic.org Rev. Anthony J. Ustick, Par. Vicar; Dcn. Geoff D'Angelo; Rev. Dermot Dunne, Pst.; Dcn. Edward Dodenhoff; Dcn. Mike Sweeney; Rosie Bridges, DRE; Rev. Israel A. Hernandez, Par. Vicar;

St. Stephen Catholic School - (Grades PreK-8) 10424 St. Stephen Cir., Riverview, FL 33569 t) 813-741-9203 lumoh@sscsfl.org www.sscsfl.org Mary Gurley, Vice Prin.; Linda Umoh, Prin.; Stds.: 274; Lay Tchrs.: 20

RUSKIN

St. Anne - 106 11th Ave., N.E., Ruskin, FL 33570-3625 t) 813-645-1714 office@saintanneruskin.org; storres-torrijos@saintanneruskin.org www.saintanneruskin.org Rev. Vijaya Polamarasetty, Par. Vicar; Very Rev. John F. McEvoy, Pst.; Dcn. Patrick Frye; Dcn. Vernon Schmitz; Carissa Hoffmann, DRE; Tina Gaitens, Bus. Mgr.; Linda Parkansky, Min. & Liturgy Coord.; Dcn. Robert Brunton;

SAFETY HARBOR

Espiritu Santo - 2405 Philippe Pkwy., Safety Harbor, FL 34695 t) 727-726-8477; 727-812-4656 (CRP) www.espiritusanto.cc/ Rev. Richard F Rosin, Par. Vicar; Rev. Leonard G. Piotrowski, Pst.; Dcn. Vincent Alterio, Pst. Assoc.; Dcn. John Alvarez, Pst. Assoc.; Dcn. Dominic P. Friscia, Pst. Assoc.; Dcn. Greg Nash, Pst. Assoc.; Dcn. Andrew Williams, Pst. Assoc.; Sue Sferra, DRE;

Espiritu Santo School - (Grades PreK-8) 2405A Philippe Pkwy., Safety Harbor, FL 34695-2047 t) 727-812-4650 schooloffice@escschool.org www.escschool.org Veronica Slain, Prin.;

SAN ANTONIO

St. Anthony of Padua - 32852 Rhode Island Ave., San Antonio, FL 33576; Mailing: P.O. Box 875, San Antonio, FL 33576 t) 352-588-3081 business@saopccfl.org; adminassistant@saopccfl.org saopccfl.org Rev. Oscar Unakalamba, Par. Vicar; Rev. Garry Welsh, Pst.; Rev. Henry J. Riffle, Pastor Emer.;

SEFFNER

St. Francis of Assisi - 4450 C.R. 579, Seffner, FL 33584; Mailing: P.O. Box 1218, Seffner, FL 33583 t) 813-681-9115 sfaseffner@tampabay.rr.com stfrancisc.com/ Rev. Alfred Kimaryo, I.C., Par. Vicar; Rev. Edison Bernavas, I.C., Pst.; Dcn. Richard Beaudry; Judy Erlendssaon, DRE;

SEMINOLE

Blessed Sacrament - 11565 66th Ave. N., Seminole, FL 33772 t) 727-391-4661 faithformationbscseminole@gmail.com blessedsacramentonline.org/ Rev. G. Richard Pilger, I.C., Pst.; Rev. Henry K. Sebastian, Par. Vicar; Rev. James Gordon, I.C., Pastor Emer.; Fred Eschenfelder, DRE;

Blessed Sacrament School - (Grades PreK-8) 11501 66th Ave. N., Seminole, FL 33772 t) 727-391-4060 bclark@bscschool.com www.bscschool.com Florida Catholic Conference Accrediation Rebecca Clark, Prin.;

St. Justin Martyr - 10851 Ridge Rd., Seminole, FL 33778 t) 727-397-3312 pwaloga@stjustinmartyr.net www.stjustinmartyr.net Rev. Gerald Hendry, Pst.; CRP Stds.: 45

SPRING HILL

St. Frances Xavier Cabrini - 5030 Mariner Blvd., Spring Hill, FL 34609 t) 352-683-9666; 352-686-9954 (CRP) info@stfrances.org; scollinsworth@stfrances.org www.stfrances.org Rev. Jose Tejada, Par. Vicar; Rev. David DeJulio, Pst.; Dcn. Robert Anderson; Dcn. Dennis Dolan; Dcn. Gregorio Lugo; Dcn. Edward Smith; Sherri Collinsworth, DRE;

Saint Joan of Arc - 13485 Spring Hill Dr., Spring Hill, FL 34609 t) 352-688-0663 sjoa-office@tampabay.rr.com www.stjoanofarcfl.com/ Dcn. Tom Casey; Rev. Patrick M. Rebel, Pst.; Dcn. Jose Cruz; Dcn. James Riveiro; Nancy Lovelock, Youth Min.; Mary Jo Waggoner, DRE; CRP Stds.: 63

St. Theresa - 1107 Commercial Way, Spring Hill, FL 34606 t) 352-683-2849 joanie@saint-theresa.org www.saint-theresa.org Rev. Bruce King, I.C., Pst.; Rev. Paul Stiene, I.C., Par. Vicar; Dcn. Victor Gonzalez; Dcn. James McMahon; Rev. James McAteer, I.C., In Res.; Mary Chapman, DRE; CRP Stds.: 75

ST. PETE BEACH

St. John Vianney - 445 82nd Ave., St. Pete Beach, FL 33706 t) 727-360-1147 info@sjvcc.org; faithformation@sjvcc.org www.stjohnsparish.org Rev. Victor Amorose, Pst.; Rev. Joshua Bertrand, Par. Vicar; Dcn. Richard Santello; Rev. Anthony Nyong, CM, In Res.; Very Rev. Joseph L. Waters, In Res.; CRP Stds.: 14

St. John Vianney School - (Grades PreK-8) 500 84th Ave., St. Pete Beach, FL 33706 t) 727-360-1113 rromano@sjvcc.org www.sjvcs.org Robert Hernandez, Prin.; Stds.: 259; Lay Tchrs.: 14

ST. PETERSBURG

Cathedral of St. Jude the Apostle - 5815 5th Ave. N., St. Petersburg, FL 33710 t) 727-347-9702 office@cathedralofstjude.org www.stjudesp.org Rev. Msgr. Michael Carruthers, Par. Vicar; Very Rev. Arthur J. Proulx, Rector; Dcn. John Carter, Bereavement Ministry; Dcn. John Fox, Facilities;

Cathedral of St. Jude the Apostle School - (Grades PreSchool-8) ; Mailing: 600 58th St. N., St. Petersburg, FL 33710 t) 727-347-8622 jgaudette@cathedralschoolofstjude.org; vslain@cathedralschoolofstjude.org stjudecathedralschool.org Jesse Gaudette, Prin.;

Blessed Trinity - 1600 54th Ave. S., St. Petersburg, FL 33712 t) 727-867-3663 amc@btsp.org btsp.org Rev. Wayne C. Genereux, Pst.; Dcn. William Lovelace, DRE; Alice Coston, Bus. Mgr.;

Holy Cross - 7851 54th Ave. N., St. Petersburg, FL 33709 t) 727-546-3315 www.holycrossrcc.com Very Rev. Emery Longanga, Pst.; CRP Stds.: 112

Holy Family - 200 78th Ave., N.E., St. Petersburg, FL 33702-4416 t) 727-526-5783 receptionist8@gmail.com www.holyfamilystpete.com/ Rev. Francis Mutesaasira Lubowa, Pst.; Rev. Robert G. Romaine, Par. Vicar; Dcn. Ted Fahrendorf; Linda Johnston, DRE;

Holy Family School - (Grades K-8) 250 78th Ave. N.E., St. Petersburg, FL 33702-4416 t) 727-526-8194 jdesrosiers@holyfamilycatholicschool.com; principal@holyfamilycatholicschool.com www.holyfamilycatholicschool.com Abigail Rudderham, Prin.;

Holy Family Early Childhood Center - t) 727-525-8489 nmeyers@holyfamilycatholicschool.com Judi Bruckner, Dir.;

Holy Martyrs of Vietnam Parish - 4000 43rd St. N., St. Petersburg, FL 33714 t) 727-397-7906; 727-397-9706 (CRP) cttdvnfl@gmail.com; officetdvn@gmail.com cttdvnfl.org/ Rev. Nguyen Vu Viet, Pst.; Sr. Maria Nguyen T. Xuan Huong, SJP, DRE;

St. Joseph - 2624 Union St. S., St. Petersburg, FL 33712 t) 727-822-2153 stjoseph@stjosephstpete.org stjosephstpete.org/ David VanWanzeele, DRE;

St. Mary Our Lady of Grace - 515 Fourth St. S., St. Petersburg, FL 33701 t) 727-896-2191 info@stmaryolg.org www.stmaryolg.org/ Rev. Damian Amantia, T.O.R., Pst.; Rev. Laurence Uhlman, T.O.R., Par. Vicar; Dcn. Michael Menchen;

***Daystar Life Center, Inc.** - 1055 28th St. S, St. Petersburg, FL 33712 t) 727-825-0442 daystarlife.com Jane Walker, Dir.;

St. Paul - 1800 12th St. N., St. Petersburg, FL 33704 t) 727-822-3481 parishoffice@stpaulstpete.com stpaulstpete.com/ Rev. Msgr. Robert C. Gibbons, Pst.; Rev. Joshua Hare, Par. Vicar;

The Mercy of God Polish Mission - 1358 20th Ave. N., St. Petersburg, FL 33704 polskamisjastpete@gmail.com

St. Paul School - (Grades PreK-8) 1900 12th St. N., St. Petersburg, FL 33704 t) 727-823-6144 office@stpaul1930.org www.stpaul1930.org Brendan Butcher, Prin.; Sr. Joan Carberry, O.S.F., Vice Prin.; Stds.: 316; Sr. Tchrs.: 1; Lay Tchrs.: 19

St. Raphael - 1376 Snell Isle Blvd., N.E., St. Petersburg, FL 33704 t) 727-821-7989 straphaels@st-raphaels.com www.st-raphaels.com Rev. Jonathan Stephanz, In Res.; Rev. Curtis V. Carro, Pst.; Rev. Louis Turcotte, Par. Vicar; Michael Specht, Youth Min.; Lynn Edmonds, DRE; Dcn. James Grevenites; Paul Wright, Bus. Mgr.;

St. Raphael School - (Grades PreK-8) 1376 Snell Isle Blvd., St. Petersburg, FL 33704 t) 727-821-9663 x2111 srsoffice@st-raphaels.com www.straphaelschool.net Mary Reynolds, Prin.; Stds.: 184; Lay Tchrs.: 18

SUN CITY CENTER

Prince of Peace - 702 Valley Forge Blvd., Sun City Center, FL 33573-5353 t) 813-634-2328 maureen@popcc.org; accounting@popcc.org www.popcc.org Rev. Timothy P. Cummings, Pst.; Rev. Augustine Mailadiyil, Assoc. Pst.; Karen Fernandez-Valentine, Pst. Min./Coord.; Maureen Vilcheck, Bus. Mgr.; CRP Stds.: 10

Our Lady of Guadalupe Mission - 16650 U.S. 301 S., Wimauma, FL 33598 t) 813-633-2384 missionguadalupe@gmail.com Rev. Gilberto Quintero, Admin.;

TAMPA

Blessed Sacrament - 7001 12th Ave. S., Tampa, FL 33619-4601 t) 813-626-2984 office@blessedsacramentcatholic.org www.blessedsacramentcatholic.org/ Rev. Kazimierz Domek, Pst.;

Christ the King - 821 S. Dale Mabry Hwy., Tampa, FL 33609 t) 813-876-5841 www.ctk-tampa.org/ Very Rev. Leonard Plazewski, Pst.; Rev. Andrew Burns, Par. Vicar; Dcn. Paul Haber; Dcn. Ronald Fly; Katie Holland, Dir.; CRP Stds.: 520

Christ the King School - (Grades PreK-8) 3809 Morrison Ave., Tampa, FL 33629 t) 813-876-8770 ntanis@cks-school.org www.cks-school.org Nick Tanis, Prin.;

Epiphany of Our Lord - 2510 E. Hanna Ave., Tampa, FL 33610; Mailing: P.O. Box 11246, Tampa, FL 33680 t) 813-238-1751 (CRP); 813-234-8693 epiphany_tampa2@yahoo.com www.epiphanytampa.com/ Rev. Edwin Palka, Pst.; Rev. Ignatius Tuoc, Pastor Emer.; CRP Stds.: 10

Immaculate Conception Haitian Catholic Mission - Rev. Pierre A Dorvil, S.M.M.;

Incarnation Catholic Church - 8220 W. Hillsborough Ave., Tampa, FL 33615; Mailing: 5124 Gateway Dr., Tampa, FL 33615 t) 813-885-7861; 813-884-3624 (CRP) secretary@icctampa.org; dff@icctampa.org www.icctampa.org Rev. Michael Cormier, Pst.; Rev. Michael Owen, Par. Vicar; Dcn. James Minary; Dcn. Ramon Rodriguez; Dcn. Matthew Shirina;

Incarnation School - (Grades PreK-8) 5111 Webb Rd., Tampa, FL 33615 t) 813-884-4502 icsmmood@icstampa.org icstampa.org Elaine Zambito, Admin.; Marrie McLaughlin, Prin.;

St. Joseph - 3012 W. Cherry St., Tampa, FL 33607

t) 813-877-5729 stjosephtpa@gmail.com; levantatesjc@gmail.com www.stjosephchurchtampa.org Rev. Nelson Restrepo, Pst.; Dcn. Jorge Suarez; Julia Valdes, DRE;

St. Joseph Vietnamese Parish - 5601 Hanley Rd., Tampa, FL 33634 t) 813-397-2019 c) 813-403-6519 Rev. Chien X. Dinh, S.V.D., Pst.;

St. Lawrence - 5225 N. Himes Ave., Tampa, FL 33614-6623 t) 813-875-4040 info@stlawrence.org www.stlawrence.org Rev. Msgr. Michael G. Muhr, Pst.; Rev. Elixavier Castro, Par. Vicar; Dcn. Gregory Lambert; CRP Stds.: 180

St. Lawrence School - (Grades PreK-8) 5223 N. Himes Ave., Tampa, FL 33614 t) 813-879-5090 pfreund@stlawrence.org www.stlawrencecatholicschool.org/ Patricia Freund, Prin.; Stds.: 496; Lay Tchrs.: 36

St. Mark the Evangelist - 9724 Cross Creek Blvd., Tampa, FL 33647 t) 813-907-7746 jdepiero@stmarktampa.org www.stmarktampa.org/ Rev. Richard Jankowski, Pst.; Dcn. Moises Guitierrez; Dcn. Jose Moronta; Dcn. Scott Paine; Dcn. Hector Rios; CRP Stds.: 768

St. Mary - 15520 North Blvd., Tampa, FL 33613 t) 813-961-1061 info@stmarytampa.org www.stmarytampa.org Rev. Kyle Smith, Pst.; Rev. Dayan Machado, Par. Vicar; Dcn. John Iadanza; Dcn. David G. Lesieur; Dcn. Mike Miller; Joan Rini, CRE; CRP Stds.: 51

Santa Maria - 14004 N. 15th St., Tampa, FL 33613-3554 t) 813-263-6979 jgimenez@stmarytampa.org

Mary Help of Christians - 6400 E. Chelsea St., Tampa, FL 33610 t) 813-626-7588 parish@mhctampa.org www.mhcptampa.org Rev. Steve Dumais, Pst.; Rev. Lee John Bosco, Par. Vicar; Dcn. Edmond Anctil;

Most Holy Redeemer - 10110 Central Ave. N., Tampa, FL 33612-7402 t) 813-933-2859 office@mhrtampa.org www.mhrtampa.org/ Rev. Anthony Coppola, Pst.; Dcn. Kevin Dwyer; Dcn. Joseph Krzanowski; Dcn. Ted Martin; Rev. Francisco Hernandez, Par. Vicar;

Our Lady of Perpetual Help - 1711 11th Ave., Tampa, FL 33605-3803 t) 813-248-5701 office@olphtampa.org olphtampa.org/ Rev. Hector Cruz, S.M., Pst.; Rev. Raymond Coolong, S.M., In Res.; Paul Morrissey, S.M., In Res.; Rev. Kenneth Ridgeway, S.M., In Res.; CRP Stds.: 30

St. Patrick - 4518 S. Manhattan Ave., Tampa, FL 33611 t) 813-839-5337 info2@stpatricktampa.org www.stpatricktampa.org/ Rev. Salvator Stefula, T.O.R., Pst.; Rev. Alberto Bueno, T.O.R., Par. Vicar; CRP Stds.: 67

St. Paul - 12708 N. Dale Mabry Hwy., Tampa, FL 33618-2802 t) 813-961-3023 ccayon@stpaulchurch.com; info@stpaulchurch.com www.stpaulchurch.com Rev. Craig Morley, Pst.; Rev. Tamil Selvam, Vicar; Rev. Timothy Williford, Vicar; Rev. Peter Okojie, Par. Vicar; Dcn. Carlos Celaya; Dcn. Raymond Dever; Dcn. Frank Henriquez; Carmen Cayon, DRE; Brian Smith, Bus. Mgr.; CRP Stds.: 667

St. Peter Claver - 1203 N. Nebraska Ave., Tampa, FL 33602-3044 t) 813-223-7098 stpeterclaver@gmail.com; info@spclavertampa.org spclavertampa.wix.com/ spcchurch Rev. Agustinus Seran, S.V.D., Pst.; Dcn. Ben Hooks;

St. Peter Claver School - (Grades PreK-8) 1401 Governor St., Tampa, FL 33602-3044 t) 813-224-0865 principal@spccs.org stpeterclavercatholicschool.org A member of the Catholic School System - Diocese of St. Petersburg, Inc. LaTonya White, Prin.; Stds.: 84; Lay Tchrs.: 13

Sacred Heart - 509 N. Florida Ave., Tampa, FL 33602; Mailing: P.O. Box 1524, Tampa, FL 33601 t) 813-229-1595 jwilliams@sacredheartfla.org; bferreris@sacredheartfla.org www.sacredheartfla.org Rev. Stephen E. Kluge, O.F.M., Par. Vicar; Rev. Michael P. Jones, OFM, Pst.; Rev. Zachary Elliott, O.F.M., Par. Vicar; Dcn. Henry Fulmer, OFM; Barbara Ferreris, DRE; Larry Cabrera, Bus. Mgr.; Sean Fitzsimmons-Brown, Dir. Liturgical Ministries & Music;

TARPON SPRINGS

St. Ignatius of Antioch - 715 E Orange St, Tarpon Springs, FL 34689; Mailing: PO Box 1306, Tarpon Springs, FL 34688-1306 t) 727-937-4050 kcreamer@ignatius.net; fmorin@ignatius.net www.st.ignatius.net/ Rev. Daniel Bot (Nigeria), Par. Vicar; Rev. William J. Swengros, Pst.; Rev. Joseph Paek, O.S.B., Par. Vicar; Dcn. Samuel Moschetto; Fran Morin, DRE;

St. Ignatius Early Childhood Center - 725 E Orange St, Tarpon Springs, FL 34689 t) 727-937-5427 www.stignatiusecc.org/ Angela Butler, Dir.;

TEMPLE TERRACE

Corpus Christi - 9715 N. 56th St., Temple Terrace, FL 33617 t) 813-988-1593 mychurch@spiritualhome.org www.spiritualhome.org Rev. Joel Kovanis, Pst.; Rev. Jonathan Loverita, Par. Vicar; Dcn. Pablo Riano; CRP Stds.: 266

Corpus Christi School - (Grades PreK-8) t) 813-988-1722 kkearney@cccstt.org cccstt.org Kelly Kearney, Prin.;

TRINITY

St. Peter the Apostle Catholic Church in Trinity, Inc. - 12747 Interlaken Rd., Trinity, FL 34655 t) 727-264-8968 office@sptatrinity.org; finance@sptatrinity.org www.sptatrinity.org Rev. Gary Dowsey, Pst.; CRP Stds.: 200

ZEPHYRHILLS

St. Joseph Catholic Church - 5345 16th St., Zephyrhills, FL 33542; Mailing: 5316 11th St., Zephyrhills, FL 33542 t) 813-782-2813 info@stjosephzephyrhills.org; admin@stjosephzephyrhills.org www.stjosephzephyrhills.org Rev. Allan Tupa, Pst.; Rev. Msgr. Cesar Petilla, Par. Vicar; Dcn. David Cardona; Beverly Burgess, Bus. Mgr.;

SCHOOLS: PRESCHOOL THRU HIGH SCHOOL

SCHOOLS

STATE OF FLORIDA

CLEARWATER

St. Cecelia Interparochial School - (PAR) (Grades PreK-8) 1350 Court St., Clearwater, FL 33756 t) 727-461-1200 scsoffice@st-cecelia.org; apeterson@st-cecelia.org www.st-cecelia.org Serving Light of Christ, St. Brendan, St. Catherine of Siena and St. Cecelia. Valerie Wostbrock, Prin.; Stds.: 444; Lay Tchrs.: 32

The Cenacle of Our Lady of Divine Providence - (PAR) 702 S. Bayview Ave., Clearwater, FL 33759; Mailing: 711 S. Bayview Ave., Clearwater, FL 33759 t) 727-724-9505 cenacleschool@divineprovidence.org www.divineprovidence.org School of Spiritual Direction; Public Association of the Faithful. Mary Sue Mooney, Dir.; Stds.: 150

Guardian Angels Catholic School - (PAR) (Grades PreK-8) 2270 Evans Rd., Clearwater, FL 33763 t) 727-799-6724 mstalzer@gacsfl.com www.gacsfl.com Serving All Saints, St. Ignatius, St. Luke and St. Michael the Archangel. Mary Stalzer, Prin.; Stds.: 163; Lay Tchrs.: 17

LECANTO

Saint John Paul II Catholic School - (DIO) (Grades PreK-8) 4341 W. Homosassa Tr., Lecanto, FL 34461 t) 352-746-2020 office@sjp2.us www.sjp2.us A Ministry of the Catholic School System - Diocese of St. Petersburg, Inc. Lee C Sayago, Prin.; Stds.: 223; Lay Tchrs.: 13

LUTZ

Mother Teresa of Calcutta Catholic School - (DIO) (Grades K-8) 17524 Lakeshore Rd., Lutz, FL 33558 t) 813-933-4750 office@mtctampa.org www.mtctampa.org A Ministry of the Catholic School System - Diocese of St. Petersburg, Inc. Teresa Caraker, Prin.; Jackie St. Charles, Asst. Prin.; Stds.: 436; Lay Tchrs.: 25

PINELLAS PARK

Morning Star Catholic School - Pinellas Park, Inc. - (DIO) (Grades K-12) 4661 80th Ave. N., Pinellas Park, FL 33781 t) 727-544-6036 info@morningstarschool.org www.morningstarschool.org Susan Conza, Prin.; Stds.: 98; Lay Tchrs.: 13

Sacred Heart Catholic School - (DIO) (Grades PreK-8) 7951 46th Way N., Pinellas Park, FL 33781 t) 727-544-1106 ryevich@shsaints.org www.sacredheartpinellaspark.org/ A Ministry of the Catholic School System - Diocese of St. Petersburg, Inc. Nicole Wilson, Prin.; Maggie Coy, Vice Prin.; Stds.: 201

PORT RICHEY

Bishop Larkin Catholic School - (DIO) (Grades PreK-8) 8408 Monarch Dr., Port Richey, FL 34668 t) 727-862-6981 office@bishoplarkin.org www.bishoplarkin.org/ A Ministry of the Catholic School System - Diocese of St. Petersburg, Inc. Stacy Cervone, Prin.; Stds.: 231; Sr. Tchrs.: 2; Lay Tchrs.: 13

SAN ANTONIO

St. Anthony Catholic School - (DIO) (Grades K-8) 12155 Joe Herrmann Dr., San Antonio, FL 33576; Mailing: P.O. Box 847, San Antonio, FL 33576-0847 t) 352-588-3041 shannonhall@stanthonyschoolfl.org; sistersherly@stanthonyschoolfl.org www.stanthonyschoolfl.org A Ministry of the Catholic School System - Diocese of St. Petersburg, Inc. Shannon Hall, Prin.; Sr. Sherly Vazhappilly, Vice Prin.; Stds.: 266; Sr. Tchrs.: 1; Lay Tchrs.: 16

SPRING HILL

Notre Dame Catholic School - (DIO) (Grades PreK-8) 1095 Commercial Way, Spring Hill, FL 34606 t) 352-683-0755 notredame@ndcsfl.org www.ndcsfl.org A Ministry of the Catholic School System - Diocese of St. Petersburg, Inc. Florence Buono, Prin.; Stds.: 238

TAMPA

Academy of the Holy Names of Florida, Inc. - (PRV) (Grades PreK-12) 3319 Bayshore Blvd., Tampa, FL 33629 t) 813-839-5371 snitchals@holynamestpa.org www.holynamestpa.org Bridgid Fishman, Prin.; Stephanie Nitchals, Prin.; Arthur Raimo, Pres.; Stds.: 968; Sr. Tchrs.: 1; Lay Tchrs.: 109

St. Joseph Catholic School - (DIO) (Grades PreK-8) 2200 N. Gomez Ave., Tampa, FL 33607 t) 813-879-7720 bbudd@sjstampa.org www.stjosephtampa.org A Ministry of the Catholic School System - Diocese of St. Petersburg, Inc. Brenda Budd, Prin.; Stds.: 294; Lay Tchrs.: 18

Morning Star Catholic School - Tampa, Inc. - (DIO) (Grades 1-8) 210 E. Linebaugh Ave., Tampa, FL 33612 t) 813-935-0232 eodom@morningstartampa.org www.morningstartampa.org School for Special Needs Youth Eileen Odom, Prin.; Stds.: 69; Lay Tchrs.: 9

Villa Madonna School - (PRV) (Grades PreK-8) 315 W. Columbus Dr., Tampa, FL 33602 t) 813-229-1322 www.villamadonnaschool.com Salesian Sisters of Tampa, Inc. Sr. Louise Ann Fantauzza, FMA, Admin.; Stds.: 313; Sr. Tchrs.: 5; Lay Tchrs.: 23

HIGH SCHOOLS

STATE OF FLORIDA

CLEARWATER

Clearwater Central Catholic High School, Inc. - (DIO) 2750 Haines Bayshore Rd., Clearwater, FL 33760 t) 727-531-1449 jdeputy@ccchs.org www.ccchs.org John Venturella, Pres.; James Deputy, Prin.; Enrique Garza, Asst. Prin.; Leanne Knoop, Dean; Lauren Spatola, Dean; Stds.: 565; Lay Tchrs.: 36

SPRING HILL

Bishop McLaughlin Catholic High School, Inc. - (DIO) 13651 Hays Rd., Spring Hill, FL 34610 t) 727-857-2600

beth.sylvester@bmchs.com www.bmchs.com Jenalisa Zummo, Prin.; Johnnathan Combs, Vice Prin.; Stds.: 344; Lay Tchrs.: 29

ST. PETERSBURG

St. Petersburg Catholic High School, Inc. - (DIO) 6333 9th Ave. N., St. Petersburg, FL 33710 t) 727-344-4065 info@spchs.org www.spchs.org Rev. Ralph F. D'Elia, Chap.; Ross Bubolz, Prin.; Jill Hudson, Asst. Prin.; Stds.: 444

TAMPA

Academy of the Holy Names of Florida, Inc. - (PRV) (Grades PreK-12) 3319 Bayshore Blvd., Tampa, FL 33629 t) 813-839-5371 araimo@holynamestpa.org www.holynamestpa.org Stephanie Nitchals, Prin.; Arthur Raimo, Pres.; Stds.: 486; Lay Tchrs.: 51

Cristo Rey Tampa Salesian High School - 6400 E. Chelsea St., Tampa, FL 33610 t) 813-621-8300 smorreale@cristoreytampa.org www.cristoreytampa.org College preparatory education for youth from economically-challenged families. Matthew J. Torano, Prin.; John Davidson, Vice Prin.; Scott Morreale, Pres.; Rev. Eddie Chincha, SDB, Youth Min.; Rev. Franco Pinto, S.D.B., Dir.; Rev. Joseph Hannon, S.D.B., Teacher/Counselor; Stds.: 212; Pr. Tchrs.: 1; Lay Tchrs.: 15

Jesuit High School of Tampa, Inc. - (PRV) (Grades 9-12) 4701 N. Himes Ave., Tampa, FL 33614; Mailing: 4701 N Himes Ave, Tampa, FL 33614 t) 813-877-5344 info@jesuittampa.org www.jesuittampa.org fka, St. Louis Catholic, Benevolent and Educational Association, Inc., Jesuit High School Foundation, Inc. Rev. Angel Rivera-Fals, S.J., Rector; Rev. Richard C. Hermes, S.J., Pres.; Michael Scicchitano, Prin.; Stds.: 859; Scholastics: 2; Pr. Tchrs.: 2; Lay Tchrs.: 74

Tampa Catholic High School, Inc. - (DIO) (Grades 9-12) 4630 N. Rome Ave., Tampa, FL 33603 t) 813-870-0860 enrollment@tampacatholic.org; principal@tampacatholic.org www.tampacatholic.org Robert Lees, Prin.; Stds.: 720; Bro. Tchrs.: 3; Lay Tchrs.: 51

CAMPUS MINISTRY / NEWMAN CENTERS [CAM]

ST. PETERSBURG

Eckerd College - Catholic Campus Ministry - c/o Diocese of St. Petersburg, 6363 9th Ave. N., St. Petersburg, FL 33710 t) (727) 341-6832 Dcn. Rick Wells, Contact;

TAMPA

Mary Help of Christians Camp - 6400 Chelsea St., Tampa, FL 33610 t) 813-626-6191 www.mhctampa.org Rev. Franco Pinto, S.D.B., Dir.;

University of Tampa - Catholic Student Organization - 401 W. Kennedy Blvd., Tampa, FL 33606; Mailing: Box 10-F, Tampa, FL 33606 t) 803-988-3727 www.newmanconnection.com Carly Bosse, Campus Min.;

TEMPLE TERRACE

Catholic Student Center, University of South Florida - 13005 N. 50th St., Temple Terrace, FL 33617-1022 t) 813-988-3727 director@catholicusf.org; office@catholicusf.org www.catholicusf.org Rev. Kyle Bell, Dir.;

CATHOLIC CHARITIES [CCH]

NEW PORT RICHEY

Catholic Charities - Palm Island, Inc. - 6423 Illinois Ave., New Port Richey, FL 34653 t) 727-697-3994 Asstd. Annu.: 21; Staff: 1

SEMINOLE

Catholic Charities - Pinellas Village, Inc. - 8384 Bayou Boardwalk, Seminole, FL 33777 t) 727-399-2500 Judy Vargas, Dir.;

ST. PETERSBURG

Catholic Charities Community Dev. Corp. - 1213 16th St. N., St. Petersburg, FL 33705 t) 727-893-1313; 727-893-1314 catholic.charities@ccdosp.org www.ccdosp.org Rev. Msgr. Robert F. Morris, Pres.; Margaret Rogers, Exec.;

Catholic Charities Housing, Inc. - 6363 Ninth Ave. N., St. Petersburg, FL 33710 t) 727-893-1314; 727-893-1314 catholic.charities@ccdosp.org www.ccdosp.org Rev. Msgr. Robert F. Morris, Pres.; Margaret Rogers, Exec.;

Catholic Charities - Arbor Villas, Inc. -

Catholic Charities - Alicia Arms, Inc. -

Catholic Charities - The Palms at University, Inc. -

Catholic Charities, Diocese of St. Petersburg, Inc. - 6363 Ninth Ave. N., St. Petersburg, FL 33710 t) 727-893-1313; 727-893-1314 catholic.charities@ccdosp.org www.ccdosp.org Rev. Msgr. Robert F. Morris, Pres.; Margaret Rogers, CEO;

Catholic Charities Community Development Corp. - 1213 16th St. N., St. Petersburg, FL 33705

Jeff Forbes Center - Administrative Offices - Services Provided - 1213 16th St. N., St. Petersburg, FL 33705 Our services include adoption, post-abortion counseling, pregnancy and parenting support services, free and charitable clinics, respite care program.

CCDOSP Developer, Inc. - 6363 Ninth Ave. N., St. Petersburg, FL 33710

St. Francis of Assisi Housing, Inc. - 6363 Ninth Ave. N., St. Petersburg, FL 33710

INSTITUTIONS LOCATED IN DIOCESE

CEMETERIES [CEM]

CLEARWATER

Miserere Guild, Inc. (Calvary Catholic Cemetery) - 5233 118th Ave. N., Clearwater, FL 33760 t) 727-572-4355 info@calvarycemetery.net www.calvarycemetery.net/ Rev. Hugh Chikawe, Chap.; Terry Young, Dir.;

COLLEGES & UNIVERSITIES [COL]

ST. LEO

Saint Leo University, Inc. - 33701 State Rd. 52, St. Leo, FL 33574; Mailing: MC2004 P.O. Box 6665, St. Leo, FL 33574-6665 t) 352-588-8200; 352-588-8894 eileen.dunbar@saintleo.edu www.saintleo.edu Saint Leo University Educational Fund, Inc. An Independent and Catholic Coeducational Liberal Arts University Dr. Edward Dadez, Pres.;

CONVENTS, MONASTERIES, AND RESIDENCES FOR WOMEN [CON]

MADEIRA BEACH

Surfside Condos - Franciscan Sisters of Allegany, NY - 15462 Gulf Blvd., #1003, Madeira Beach, FL 33708 t) 727-898-9501 joanc1230@tampabay.rr.com; kristen.luther@fsallegany.org Franciscan Sisters of Allegany Sr. Joan Carberry, O.S.F., Contact; Srs.: 10

ST. LEO

Holy Name Monastery - 12138 Wichers Rd, St. Leo, FL 33574; Mailing: PO Box 2450, 12138 Wichers Rd, St. Leo, FL 33574-2450 t) 352-588-8320 holyname@saintleo.edu www.benedictinesistersoffl.org Motherhouse and Novitiate of the Benedictine Sisters of Florida. Sr. Roberta Bailey, O.S.B., Prioress; Srs.: 14

ST. PETERSBURG

St. Anthony of Padua Convent - 1332 7th Ave. N., St. Petersburg, FL 33705-1409 t) 727-498-8709; 727-954-3981 pshirley@fsallegany.org; marymcnally2@aol.com Franciscan Sisters of Allegany (Allegany, NY). Sr. Mary McNally, O.S.F., Admin., VP; Srs.: 4

TAMPA

St. Clare Convent - 2924 W. Curtis St., Tampa, FL 33614-7102 t) 813-870-4272 sistercathycahill@gmail.com Franciscan Sisters of Allegany, Inc. Sr. Catherine Cahill, O.S.F., Secy.; Srs.: 5

St. Elizabeth Convent - 3000 N. Perry Ave., Tampa, FL 33603-5345 t) 813-229-1978 tuckeryellen@gmail.com Franciscan Sisters of Allegany, Inc. Sr. Mary Ellen Tucker, O.S.F., Admin.; Srs.: 4

Sisters' House - 3006 Perry Ave., Tampa, FL 33603-5345 t) 813-335-9392 thesistershouse3006@gmail.com thesistershouse.org Franciscan Sisters of Allegany, Inc. Sr. Catherine Cahill, O.S.F., Contact; Srs.: 2

Villa Madonna Convent - 315 W. Columbus Dr., Tampa, FL 33602 t) 813-229-1322 tampa@salesiansisters.org www.villamadonnaschool.com Villa Madonna School, Salesian Youth Center, Salesian Sisters of Tampa, Inc. Sr. Louise Ann Fantauzza, FMA, Supr.; Srs.: 5

ENDOWMENTS / FOUNDATIONS / TRUSTS [EFT]

PALM HARBOR

Allegany Franciscan Ministries, Inc. - 33920 U.S. Hwy. 19 N., Ste. 269, Palm Harbor, FL 34684 t) 727-507-9668 ecoogan@afmfl.org www.afmfl.org Eileen Coogan, CEO;

SEMINOLE

Village of Mary Children's Foundation, Inc. - 12990 Forest Dr., Seminole, FL 33775 t) 727-393-3186 John Lessl, Contact;

ST. PETERSBURG

Catholic Education Foundation, Inc. - 6363 9th Ave., N., St. Petersburg, FL 33710

TAMPA

***Marian World Foundation, Inc.** - 8706 Maple Lake Pl., Tampa, FL 33635 t) (813) 495-1373 Armando Remo Jr., Chair;

HOSPITALS / HEALTH SERVICES [HOS]

ST. PETERSBURG

St. Anthony's Hospital, Inc. - 1200 7th Ave. N., St. Petersburg, FL 33705 t) 727-825-1103 marfln@juno.com www.stanthonys.com St. Anthony's Ancillary Services, Inc., St. Anthony's Professional Buildings and Services, Inc., St. Anthony's Health Care Foundation, Inc., Francisca Rev. Jackson Cleetus, Chap.; Mardie Chapman, Chap.; Al Hall, Chap.; Reid Isenhart, Chap.; Robert Sherman, Dir.; Rev. Anthony Nyong, CM, Chap.;

TAMPA

St. Joseph's Hospital, Inc. - 3001 W. Martin Luther King Blvd., Tampa, FL 33607 t) 727-519-1277; 813-870-4000 colleen.walters@baycare.org www.sjbhealth.org St. Joseph's Ancillary Services, Inc., St. Joseph's Community Care, Inc., St. Joseph's Enterprises, Inc., St. Joseph's Health Care Center, Inc., St J Rev. Alex Agbata (Nigeria), Chap.; Anthony Britten-Campbell, Chap.; Rev. Gregory Brown, Chap.; Rev. Joshua Dyachim, Chap.; Rev. Kenneth Gerth, M.C.C.J., Chap.; Rev. George Gyasi, Chap.; Tina Imperato, Chap.; Sheryl Nicholson, Chap.; Kelvin Price, Chap.; Angel Sullivan, Chap.; Kenya Williams, Chap.; Mary Margaret Bowers-Atkinson, Dir. Spiritual Care - System; Rev. Aloysius Ezenwata, M.S.P., Dir., Mission - Region; Jim Palmer, Rgl. Mgr., Spiritual Care; Colleen Walters, VP Mission & Ethics;

MISCELLANEOUS [MIS]

BELLEAIR

Mantle of Mary, Inc. - 845 Indian Rocks Rd., Belleair, FL 33756 t) 727-446-0939 mpublishing2@gmail.com www.mantlepublishing.com Carol Marquardt, Pres.;

BRANDON

Partners with La Victoria, Inc. - 705 E. Brandon Blvd., Brandon, FL 33511-5443 t) 813-681-4608 pastor@nativitycatholicchurch.org www.pwlv.org Rev. Michael R. Smith, Pst.;

***Sun Coast Catholic Ministries, Inc.** - 2716 Broadway Center Blvd., Brandon, FL 33510 c) 727-403-8060 suncoastcatholicministries.com/ Dimitre Bobev, Dir.;

CLEARWATER

Community of the Marian Servants of Divine Providence - 711 S. Bayview Ave., Clearwater, FL 33759 t) 727-797-7412 info@divineprovidence.org www.divineprovidence.org Public Association of the

Faithful. Alicia Goodwin, Dir.;

Our Lady of Divine Providence House of Prayer - 711 S. Bayview Ave., Clearwater, FL 33759 t) (727) 797-7412 (Main Number)

Water 4 Mercy, Inc. - 3026 Oakmont Dr., Clearwater, FL 33761 c) 727-439-4222 nermine@water4mercy.org water4mercy.org 501(c)3 organization whose mission is eradicating thirst, hunger & poverty in Africa Rev. Gregg Tottle, Dir.; John Venturella, Dir.;

FLORAL CITY

Our Lady of Good Counsel Camp - 8888 E. Gobbler Dr., Floral City, FL 34436; Mailing: 4301 W. Homosassa Tr., Lecanto, FL 34461 t) 352-726-2198; 352-270-8831 frjohnson@goodcounselcamp.org; swatkins@goodcounselcamp.org goodcounselcamp.org Stephen Watkins, Dir.;

PALM HARBOR

***Living His Life Abundantly International, Inc.** - 36181 E. Lake Rd., Ste. 320, Palm Harbor, FL 34685 t) 813-854-1518; 800-558-5452 info@womenofgrace.com www.womenofgrace.com Johnnette Benkovic Williams, Pres.;

RIVERVIEW

Good News Ministries of Tampa Bay, Inc. - 7403 Restful Water Way, Riverview, FL 33569; Mailing: 11705 Boyette Rd., Box 277, Riverview, FL 33569 t) 863-510-7986 dir-admin@gnm.org gnm.org Ralph Modica, Chair; Terry Modica, CEO;

ST. PETERSBURG

Catholic Formation, Inc. - 6363 9th Ave., N., St. Petersburg, FL 33710

Catholic School System - Diocese of St. Petersburg, Inc. - ; Mailing: P.O. Box 40200, St. Petersburg, FL 33743-0200 t) 727-344-1611 Dcn. Rick Wells, Chancellor;

***Digital Disciple Corporation** - ; Mailing: P.O. Box 40200, St. Petersburg, FL 33743 t) 714-633-8121 x7119 ballen@csjorange.org Sisters of St. Joseph of Orange Bret Allen, Dir.;

Diocese of St. Petersburg, Inc. - 6363 9th Ave. N., St. Petersburg, FL 33710; Mailing: P.O. Box 40200, St. Petersburg, FL 33743-0200 t) 727-341-6832 Dcn. Rick Wells, Chancellor;

Magnificat Inc., Lower Pinellas Deanery Chapter of the Diocese of St. Petersburg, Florida - 3228 13th St. N., St. Petersburg, FL 33704 t) 727-542-0418 magnificatofstpetersburg@gmail.com Kathy Bolich, Dir.;

Partners with Haiti, Inc. - 1800 12th St. N., St. Petersburg, FL 33704 t) 727-822-3481; 727-525-2364 www.partnerswithhaiti.com/ Ministry of St. Paul's Church, St. Petersburg, Fl. Rev. Msgr. Robert C. Gibbons, Pst.; James Stitt, Pres.;

Pastoral Center - 6363 9th Ave. N., St. Petersburg, FL 33710 t) 727-344-1611 www.dosp.org For detailed information on the following listings contact the Chancery Office. Dcn. Rick Wells, Chancellor;

Allegany Community Out Reach Grant Fund, Inc. -

Allegany Franciscan Ministries, Inc. -

Catholic Charities Community Development, Corp. -

Catholic Charities Foundation of Tampa Bay, Inc. -

Catholic Media Ministry, Inc. -

Christopher Assurance, Inc. -

The Congregation of the Sisters of St. Clare (Florida), Inc. - 625 Court St., 2nd Fl., Clearwater, FL 33756

Employee Benefit Trust -

Franciscan Center of Tampa, FL, Inc. - 3010 Perry Ave., Tampa, FL 33603 t) 813-229-2695 info@franciscancentertampa.org www.franciscancentertampa.org

The Greater Tampa Catholic Lawyers Guild, Inc. - ; Mailing: P.O. Box 1816, Tampa, FL 33601

Regis Manor, Inc. -

Savings and Loan Trust -

TAMPA

DOSP USF Housing, Inc. - 13005 N. 50th St., Tampa, FL 33617; Mailing: P.O. Box 40200, St. Petersburg, FL 33743-0200 t) 813-988-3727 director@catholicusf.org Rev. Kyle Bell, Contact;

***Renew Haiti, Inc.** - 821 Dale Mabry Hwy., Tampa, FL 33609 t) 813-876-5841 haiti@ctk-tampa.org; kholland@ctk-tampa.org www.ctk-tampa.org Very Rev. Leonard Plazewski;

Schoenstatt Tampa Bay, Inc. - 3805 Woodroffe Ct., Tampa, FL 33618 c) 813-997-5755 schoenstatttampabay@gmail.com www.schoenstatttampabay.org Rev. Carlos Jose Rojas, Spiritual Adv./Care Srvcs.;

Tampa Magnificat - 2617 W. Prospect Rd., Tampa, FL 33629 t) 813-390-6611 tampamagnificat@gmail.com tampamagnificat.org

WBVM, 90.5 FM, Inc. - 717 S. Dale Mabry Hwy., Tampa, FL 33609 t) (813) 289-8040 www.myspiritfm.com/ John Morris, Station Manager;

TRINITY

Elisheba House, Inc. - 1936 Marshberry Ct., Trinity, FL 34655 c) 813-335-2163 office@elishebahouse.com www.elishebahouse.com Ivonne J Hernandez, Pres.; Laura Worhacz, Secy.; Ricardo Hernandez, Treas.;

VALRICO

***Knanya Catholic Congress of Central Florida, Inc.** - 2620 Washington Rd., Valrico, FL 33594 t) 813-681-6189 jillikal@aol.com Sunil Chacko, Pres.;

MONASTERIES AND RESIDENCES FOR PRIESTS AND BROTHERS [MON]

PINELLAS PARK

Priests of the Sacred Heart - 6701 82nd Ave. N., Pinellas Park, FL 33781 t) 727-541-2661 Rev. Vincent Suparman, S.C.J., Supr.; Rev. Steve Pujdak, S.C.J., Treas.; Rev. Paul Grizzelle-Reid, S.C.J.; Rev. Ralph Intranuovo, S.C.J.; Rev. Patrick Lloyd, S.C.J.; Rev. Gregory Speck, S.C.J.; Bro. Michael Fette, S.C.J.; Bro. Gabriel Kersting, S.C.J.; Brs.: 2; Priests: 6

SAINT LEO

St. Leo Abbey - 33601 State Rd. 52, Saint Leo, FL 33574; Mailing: P.O. Box 2350, St. Leo, FL 33574 t) 352-588-8624 www.saintleoabbey.org Rt. Rev. Isaac Camacho, O.S.B., Abbot; Rev. Lucius Amarillas, O.S.B., Prior; Rev. Felix Augustin, O.S.B.; Rev. Joseph Paek, O.S.B.; Rev. Clement Rees, O.S.B.; Rev. David Steinwachs, O.S.B., Mem.; Bro. Apollo Rodriguez, OSB, Mem.; Brs.: 1; Priests: 6

ST. PETERSBURG

St. Anthony Friary (St. Petersburg) Franciscan Friars-Holy Name Province, Inc. - 357 2nd St. N., St. Petersburg, FL 33701 t) 727-822-7917; 646-473-0265 mharlan@hnp.org Franciscan Residence and Retirement Community Rev. John Paul Hogan, O.F.M., Vicar; Rev. John Anglin, O.F.M., In Res.; Rev. Rene Barczak, In Res.; Rev. William Bried, O.F.M., In Res.; Rev. Eric Carpine, O.F.M., In Res.; Rev. Anthony Carrozzo, O.F.M., In Res.; Rev. Mario Di Lella, O.F.M., In Res.; Rev. Gerald M. Dolan, O.F.M., In Res.; Rev. Joseph Hertel, O.F.M., In Res.; Rev. Thomas P. Jones, O.F.M., In Res.; Rev. Kevin Mackin, O.F.M., In Res.; Rev. John J. Marino, O.F.M., In Res.; Rev. Jerome Massimino, O.F.M., In Res.; Rev. William Edward McConville, OFM, In Res.; Rev. John McDowell, O.F.M., In Res.; Rev. Thomas K. Murphy, O.F.M., In Res.; Rev. James Nero, In Res.; Rev. Ronald Stark, OFM, In Res.; Rev. Adam Szufel, O.F.M., In Res.; Rev. Kevin Tortorelli, In Res.; Rev. Vincent Laviano, O.F.M., Guardian; Bro. Thomas Donovan, OFM, In Res.; Bro. Karl Koenig, In Res.; Bro. William Mann, O.F.M., In Res.; Bro. Glen William Humphrey, O.F.M., In Res.; Bro. Michael Madden, O.F.M., In Res.; Dcn. Alan Thomas, O.F.M., In Res.; Brs.: 3; Priests: 22

Missionaries of Africa - 5757 7th Ave. N., St. Petersburg, FL 33710-7112 t) 727-343-1001 jeangorilla@aol.com www.missionariesofafrica.org USA Sector Rev. Jean Claude Robitaille, M.Afr., Supr.; Rev. Thomas W. Reilly, M.Afr.; Rev. Joseph Elmo Hebert, M.Afr.; Rev. George Markwell, M.Afr.; Rev. William J Curran, MAfr, In Res.; Rev. Benjamin Markwell, O.F.M. Cap., In Res.; Priests: 6

St. Peter Nolasco Residence - 5650 7th Ave. N., St. Petersburg, FL 33710-7112 t) 727-345-4766 www.orderofmercy.org Fathers of Our Lady of Mercy, Inc. Mercedarian Friars USA Rev. Oscar Kozyra, O.de.M.; Rev. Michael E. Perry, O.de.M.; Rev. Anthony Fortunato, Supr.; Priests: 3

TAMPA

Salesians of Don Bosco - 6400 E. Chelsea St., Tampa, FL 33610 t) 813-626-6191 www.mhctampa.org Rev. Franco Pinto, S.D.B., Dir.;

NURSING / REHABILITATION / CONVALESCENCE / ELDERLY CARE [NUR]

CLEARWATER

La Clinica Guadalupana, Inc. - 1020 Lakeview Rd., Clearwater, FL 33756 t) 727-461-7730 lifeknight@mindspring.com Jay E. Carpenter, Pres.;

St. Michael's Housing, Inc. (Casa Miguel) - 2285 State Rd., #580, Clearwater, FL 33763 t) 727-797-8551 jlungaro@ccdosp.org Independent Living. JoAnn Lungaro, Admin.;

HUDSON

Bethlehem Housing, Inc. - 8010 State Rd. 52, Hudson, FL 34667 t) 727-819-2861 bethlehem.house@verizon.net Asstd. Annu.: 60; Staff: 3

PLANT CITY

St. Clement Housing, Inc. - 1102 N. Alexander St., Plant City, FL 33563 t) 813-754-1237 Judy Archambault, Contact;

ST. PETERSBURG

Blessed Trinity Housing, Inc. (Trinity House) - 5701 16th St. S., St. Petersburg, FL 33705 t) 727-865-7590 trinityhousemgr@spm.net

Bon Secours St. Petersburg Home Care Services , LLC - 10901 Roosevelt Blvd., Ste. 200, St. Petersburg, FL 33716 t) 727-577-7990 sdschitter1@mercy.com bonsecours.com/st-petersburg (Serves Pinellas & Pasco Counties) Karen Reich, CEO;

Holy Cross Housing (Casa Santa Cruz) - 7825 54th Ave. N., St. Petersburg, FL 33709 t) 727-541-2631 Staff: 5

Transfiguration Housing, Inc. - 4021 45th St. N., St. Petersburg, FL 33714 t) 727-914-8912

TAMPA

Blessed Sacrament Housing, Inc. - 6801 12th Ave. S., Tampa, FL 33619 t) 813-620-0221 jagosto@ccdosp.org Asstd. Annu.: 68; Staff: 2

Christ the King Housing II, Inc. (Kings Arms) - 4125 N. Lincoln Ave., Tampa, FL 33607 t) 813-873-0234 k.arms@verizon.net

Christ the King Housing, Inc. (Kings Manor) - 2946 W. Columbus Dr., Tampa, FL 33607 t) 813-875-0139 browen@ccdosp.org Betsy Rowen, Admin.;

Epiphany Housing of Tampa, Inc. (Epiphany Arms) - 2508 E. Hanna Ave., Tampa, FL 33610 t) 813-232-2693 epiphanyarms@carteretmgmt.com Carlos Gonzalez, Contact;

St. Lawrence Housing, Inc. - 4815 N. MacDill Ave., Tampa, FL 33614-6898 t) 813-877-5800; (813) 870-3399 lyvargas@ccdosp.org www.stlawrence.org/san-lorenzo-terrace.html Liz Vargas, Dir.; Asstd. Annu.: 80; Staff: 5

St. Lawrence Housing II, Inc. - 4820 N Gomez Ave, Tampa, FL 33614 t) (813) 877-7174 www.stlawrence.org/san-lorenzo-terrace.html Rev. Msgr. Michael G. Muhr, Pres.; Asstd. Annu.: 68; Staff: 5

St. Patrick's Housing Corporation (Patrician Arms) - 4516 S. Manhattan Ave., Tampa, FL 33611 t) 813-835-8227 blendstrom@ccdosp.org Rev. Salvator Stefula, T.O.R., Dir.;

St. Patrick's Housing Corporation II (Patrician Arms II) - 4514 S. Manhattan Ave., Tampa, FL 33611 t) 813-443-5761 Rev. Salvator Stefula, T.O.R., Dir.;

PRESCHOOLS / CHILDCARE CENTERS [PRE]

DADE CITY

Sacred Heart Early Childhood Center - 32245 Saint Joe Rd., Dade City, FL 33525 t) 352-588-4060 sheccleo@embarqmail.com sacredheartecc.com/ Infant-PreK, Extended Care. Lucinda O'Quinn, Admin.; Stds.: 92; Lay Tchrs.: 10

LAND O' LAKES

Our Lady of the Rosary Early Childhood Center - Mary's House - ECC - 2348 Collier Pkwy., Land O' Lakes, FL 34639; Mailing: P.O. Box 1229, Land O' Lakes, FL 34639 t) 813-948-5999 maryshouse@ladyrosary.org www.ladyrosary.org/earlychildhoodcenter Corrine Ertl, Admin.; Rev. Justin Paskert, Pst.; Stds.: 99

LARGO

St. Jerome Early Childhood Center - 10895 Hamlin Blvd., Largo, FL 33774 t) 727-596-9491 preschool@stjeromeecc.org www.stjeromeearlychildhoodcenter.org/ Rev. Thomas Morgan, Pst.; Phyllis Steele, Dir.; Stds.: 44; Lay Tchrs.: 8

LUTZ

St. Timothy Catholic Early Childhood Learning Center - 17512 Lakeshore Rd., Lutz, FL 33558 t) 813-960-4857 mary.mcguire@sainttims.org www.sainttims.org Rev. John Blum, Pst.; Mary McGuire, Dir.; Stds.: 53

NEW PORT RICHEY

St. Thomas Aquinas Early Childhood Center - 8320 Old CR 54, New Port Richey, FL 34653 t) 727-376-2330 staecc@aol.com staecc.stanpr.org Rev. Eric Peters, Pst.; Alicia Mumma, Dir.; Stds.: 102; Lay Tchrs.: 16

PALM HARBOR

St. Luke Early Childhood Center - 2757 Alderman Rd., Palm Harbor, FL 34684 t) 727-787-2914 stlecc@gmail.com www.stlukeecc.com/ Ages 2-4, Extended Care. Lisa Hopen, Dir.; Rev. Paul Kochu; Stds.: 62; Lay Tchrs.: 11

ST. PETERSBURG

St Paul Children's Center - 1800 12th St. N., St. Petersburg, FL 33704 t) 727-822-3481 stpaulschildrenscenter.com 2 months through 2 yrs. Susan Hoch, Dir.; Stds.: 45

TAMPA

St. Paul Catholic Preschool - 12708 N. Dale Mabry Hwy., Tampa, FL 33618-2802 t) 813-264-3383 preschool@stpaulchurch.com www.stpaulchurch.com/ preschool/welcome Rev. Craig Morley, Pst.; Mindy Geer, Dir.; Stds.: 87; Lay Tchrs.: 12

TARPON SPRINGS

St. Ignatius Early Childhood Center - 725 E. Orange St., Tarpon Springs, FL 34689-1306 t) 727-937-5427 www.stignatiusecc.org/ Angela Butler, Dir.; Rev. William J. Swengros, Pst.; Stds.: 9; Lay Tchrs.: 12

RETREAT HOUSES / RENEWAL CENTERS [RTR]

CLEARWATER

Retreat Ministry of the Marian Servants of Divine Providence - 520 S. Bayview Ave., Clearwater, FL 33759; Mailing: 711 S. Bayview Ave., Clearwater, FL 33759 t) 727-799-4003 retreats@divineprovidence.org www.divineprovidence.org Public Association of the Faithful. Michele Sobota, Dir.;

LUTZ

Bethany Center, Inc. - 18150 Bethany Center Dr., Lutz, FL 33558 t) 813-960-6300 www.bethanycenterfl.org Danielle DeBrino, Dir.; Rev. John B. Lipscomb, Spiritual Adv./Care Srvcs.;

ST. LEO

Saint Leo Abbey Retreat Center - 33601 State Rd. 52, St. Leo, FL 33574; Mailing: P.O. Box 2350, St. Leo, FL 33574 t) 352-588-8631 saintleoretreat@saintleo.edu www.saintleoabbey.org Rt. Rev. Isaac Camacho, O.S.B., Abbot; Bro. Apollo Rodriguez, OSB, Secy.;

TAMPA

Franciscan Center, Retreat House - 3010 N. Perry Ave., Tampa, FL 33603-5345 t) 813-229-2695 info@franciscancentertampa.org www.franciscancentertampa.org Franciscan Sisters of Allegany, Inc. Brian A. Lemoi, Exec. Dir.; Karen Davies-Chaieb, Admin.;

Mary Help of Christians Center - 6400 E. Chelsea St., Tampa, FL 33610 t) 813-626-6191 center@mhctampa.org www.mhctampa.org Rev. Steve Dumais, Pst.; Rev. Lee John Bosco, Par. Vicar; Rev. Franco Pinto, S.D.B., Dir.; Rev. Eduardo Chincha, SDB, Youth Min.; Rev. Luis Aineto, SDB; Bro. Michael Brinkman, S.D.B.; Rev. Richard Crager, SDB; Rev. Bruce Craig, S.D.B.; Rev. Thomas Gwozdz, SDB; Rev. Joseph Hannon, S.D.B.; Rev. Dennis Hartigan, SDB; Rev. James Horan, SDB; Bro. David Iovacchini, S.D.B.; Bro. Georges Marquis, S.D.B.; Rev. Thomas McGahee, SDB; Rev. Raul Acosta Zunini, S.D.B.;

SPECIAL CARE FACILITIES [SPF]

LARGO

Bethlehem Centre, Inc. - 10895 Hamlin Blvd., Largo, FL 33774 t) 727-596-9394 bethlehem.centre@gmail.com bethlehem.centre@gmail.com Senior Center offering programs in Fitness, Exercise, Social, Educational, Music, Art, and Religious Nature. Joanne Biamonte, Dir.; Asstd. Annu.: 275; Staff: 1

An asterisk (*) denotes an organization that has established tax-exempt status directly with the IRS and is not covered by the USCCB Group Ruling.

Diocese of Salina

(Dioecesis Salinensis)

MOST REVEREND GERALD L. VINCKE

Bishop of Salina; ordained June 12, 1999; appointed Bishop of Salina June 13, 2018; installed August 22, 2018. Office: 103 N. Ninth, P.O. Box 980, Salina, KS 67402-0980.

Chancery Office: 103 N. Ninth, P.O. Box 980, Salina, KS 67402-0980. T: 785-827-8746; F: 785-827-6133.

chancery@salinadiocese.org

www.salinadiocese.org

Square Miles 26,685.

Formerly Diocese of Concordia.

Established August 2, 1887.

See transferred to Salina December 23, 1944.

(New boundaries established by Apostolic Letters dated July 1, 1897).

Bounded on the west by Colorado, on the north by Nebraska, on the east by the east lines of Washington, Riley, Geary and Dickinson Counties, and on the south by the south lines of Dickinson, Saline, Ellsworth, Russell, Ellis, Trego, Gove, Logan and Wallace Counties in the State of Kansas.

For legal titles of parishes and diocesan institutions, consult the Chancery Office.

STATISTICAL OVERVIEW

Personnel
Bishop....1
Priests: Diocesan Active in Diocese....37
Priests: Retired, Sick or Absent....12
Number of Diocesan Priests....49
Religious Priests in Diocese....19
Total Priests in your Diocese....68
Extern Priests in Diocese....7
Permanent Deacons in Diocese....22
Total Brothers....1
Total Sisters....57

Parishes
Parishes....85
With Resident Pastor:
Resident Diocesan Priests....31
Resident Religious Priests....10
Without Resident Pastor:
Administered by Priests....39
Administered by Deacons....3
Administered by Lay People....2
Pastoral Centers....1
Professional Ministry Personnel:
Sisters....4
Lay Ministers....3

Welfare
Catholic Hospitals....1
Total Assisted....31,896
Homes for the Aged....2
Total Assisted....148
Special Centers for Social Services....3
Total Assisted....6,959

Educational
Diocesan Students in Other Seminaries....8
Total Seminarians....8
High Schools, Diocesan and Parish....5
Total Students....379
Elementary Schools, Diocesan and Parish....11
Total Students....1,641
Catechesis / Religious Education:
High School Students....1,231
Elementary Students....2,843
Total Students under Catholic Instruction....6,102
Teachers in Diocese:
Lay Teachers....168

Vital Statistics
Receptions into the Church:
Infant Baptism Totals....534
Minor Baptism Totals....39
Adult Baptism Totals....22
Received into Full Communion....72
First Communions....690
Confirmations....696
Marriages:
Catholic....119
Interfaith....67
Total Marriages....186
Deaths....654
Total Catholic Population....38,916
Total Population....325,345

ADMINISTRATION

Vicar General - t) 785-827-8746 fred.gatschet@salinadiocese.org Very Rev. Fred Gatschet;

Vicar for Clergy - t) 785-827-8746 frrich@sacredheartcolby.com Rev. Richard Daise;

Chancellor - t) 785-827-8746 x18 chancellor@salinadiocese.org Corey Lyon;

Executive Assistant to the Bishop - t) 785-827-8746 x34 officeofthebishop@salinadiocese.org Brenda Streit;

ADVISORY BOARDS, COMMISSIONS, COMMITTEES, AND COUNCILS

Art and Architecture Commission - Rev. Keith Weber, Chair (keith.weber@salinadiocese.org); Rev. Frank Coady (frank.coady@salinadiocese.org); Jennifer Hood (finance@salinadiocese.org);

Diocesan Rural Life Commission - Francis Goeckel, Chair; Rev. Richard Daise, Moderator; David Edell, Co-Chair Elect;

CATHOLIC CHARITIES

Catholic Charities of Northern Kansas - t) 785-825-0208 ccnks.org/ Megan Robl, Exec. Dir. (mrobl@ccnks.org); Eric Frank, Dir., Devel. (efrank@ccnks.org); Christine Robl, Dir., Fin. (crobl@ccnks.org);

Hays Office - t) 785-625-2644 ccnks.org/hays Traci Pfannenstiel, Community Engagement & Outreach Coord.; Kimberly Feldt, Emergency Assistance & Office Coord.; Megan Pfannenstiel, Pregnancy & Adoption Specialist / Therapist;

Manhattan Office - t) 785-323-0644 ccnks.org/manhattan Estefania De La Torre, Emergency Assistance & Office Coord.; Jessica Sampson, Dir. Family Support Srvcs.; Renee Schur, Community Engagement & Outreach Coord.;

Salina Office - t) 785-825-0208 ccnks.org/salina Micki Buschart, Immigration Attorney of Counsel; Claudette Humphrey, Dir. Stabilization & Outreach Srvcs.; Yessenia Baquera, Dir. Immigration Legal Svcs.;

CLERGY AND RELIGIOUS SERVICES

Permanent Diaconate - Dcn. Steven H. Frueh, Dir. (deaconsteve@stmsalina.org);

COMMUNICATIONS

Communications - t) 785-827-8746 communications.office@salinadiocese.org Matea Gregg, Coord. (matea.gregg@salinadiocese.org); Katherine Hamel, Creative Editor (theregister@salinadiocese.org);

Diocesan Publications - Jennifer Hood, Bus. Mgr.; Brenda Streit, Advertising/Circulation; Katherine Hamel, Creative Editor;

CONSULTATIVE BODIES

College of Consultors - Rev. Msgr. James E. Hake, Senior Priest by Ordination; Rev. Frank Coady, Mem. (frank.coady@salinadiocese.org); Rev. Richard Daise, Mem.;

Diocesan Finance Council - Ron Gfeller, Mem.; Norman Kelly, Mem.; Mitzi Richards, Mem.;

Priests' Council - Rev. Frank Coady, Pres. (frank.coady@salinadiocese.org); Rev. Joseph Kieffer, Treas.; Rev. Andy Hammeke, Dean (andy.hammeke@salinadiocese.org);

EDUCATION

Catholic Schools - t) 785-827-8746 x30 Geoff Andrews, Supt. (geoff.andrews@salinadiocese.org); Susan Goodman, Educ. Coord. (susan.goodman@salinadiocese.org);

FACILITIES

Information Technology & Facilities Management - t) 785-827-8746 x11 Jeff Easter, Dir.;

FAITH FORMATION

Adult Faith Formation - Rev. Frank Coady (frank.coady@salinadiocese.org);

Youth Ministry and Religious Education - t) 785-827-8746 x49 Bill Meagher, Dir.; Susan Goodman, Educ. Coord. (susan.goodman@salinadiocese.org);

FAMILY LIFE

Family Life - t) 785-827-8746 x49 familylife@salinadiocese.org Bill Meagher, Dir.;

Natural Family Planning - Lindy Meyer, Consultant;

FertilityCare Services - fertilitycare@salinadiocese.org salinafertilitycare.org/ Lindy Meyer, Lead Practitioner;

Respect Life - respectlife@salinadiocese.org Rick Binder, Dir. (rick.binder@salinadiocese.org);

FINANCE

Finance and Accounting - t) 785-827-8746 Ernie Armstrong, CFO (ernie.armstrong@salinadiocese.org); Tyler Greenman, Asst. CFO (tyler.greenman@salinadiocese.org); Jennifer Hood, Controller (finance@salinadiocese.org);

HUMAN RESOURCES

Human Resources - t) 785-827-8746 x28 Kim Hoelting, Dir.;

ORGANIZATIONS

Catholic Foundation for Diocese of Salina - t) 785-827-8746 Katie Platten, CEO (katie.platten@salinadiocese.org); Heather Hartman, Dir. Devel. (heather.hartman@salinadiocese.org); Ernie Armstrong, CFO (ernie.armstrong@salinadiocese.org);

Salina Diocesan Clergy Health and Retirement Association, Inc. - Ernie Armstrong, Ex-Officio Member (ernie.armstrong@salinadiocese.org); Jennifer Hood, Ex-Officio Member (finance@salinadiocese.org); Rev. Norbert Dlabal;

SPIRITUAL LIFE

Liturgy - t) 785-827-8746 x31 liturgy@salinadiocese.org Rev. Frank Coady, Dir. (frank.coady@salinadiocese.org);

TRIBUNAL

Annulment Services - t) 785-827-8746 x22 tribunal@salinadiocese.org Rev. Peter O'Donnell, Judicial Vicar; Rev. Msgr. James E. Hake, Defender of the Bond; Sr. Carolyn Juenemann, C.S.J., Notary (carolyn.juenemann@salinadiocese.org);

Prenuptial Paperwork Services - t) 785-827-8746 x18 corey.lyon@salinadiocese.org Corey Lyon, Chancellor;

MISCELLANEOUS / OTHER OFFICES

Hispanic Ministry - carlos.ruiz-santos@salinadiocese.org Rev. Carlos Ruiz Santos, Dir. (frcarlos@ruraltel.net);

Priestly Vocations - t) 785-827-8746 x27 vocations@salinadiocese.org Rev. Andy Hammeke, Co-Vocation Dir. (andy.hammeke@salinadiocese.org); Rev. Joshua Werth, Co-Vocation Dir.;

Propagation of the Faith - t) 785-827-8746 x34 propfaith@salinadiocese.org Brenda Streit, Missions Coord.;

Safe Environment - t) 785-827-8746 x24 Wendy Backes, Prog. Coord. (wendy.backes@salinadiocese.org);

To Report Abuse - t) 866-752-8855 reportabuse@salinadiocese.org www.reportandprotect.com/

PARISHES, MISSIONS, AND CLERGY

STATE OF KANSAS

ABILENE

St. Andrew Parish, Abilene, Inc. - 311 S. Buckeye Ave., Abilene, KS 67410 t) 785-263-1570 officead@sacabilene.com www.sacabilene.com Rev. Peter O'Donnell, Pst.; CRP Stds.: 64

St. Andrew Parish School - (Grades PreK-5) 301 S. Buckeye Ave., Abilene, KS 67410 t) 785-263-2453 standrews@sasabilene.com standrewsabilene.com Christina Whitehair, Prin.; Stds.: 125; Lay Tchrs.: 8

ANGELUS

St. Paul Parish, Angelus, Inc. - 12001 S. Rd. 130 W., Angelus, KS 67748; Mailing: c/o St. Joseph, 625 Freeman Ave., Oakley, KS 67748 t) 785-671-3828 parish@sjoakley.org sjoakley.org/ Clustered with St. Joseph, Oakley. Rev. Luke Thielen, Pst.; CRP Stds.: 8

ANTONINO

Our Lady Help of Christians Parish, Antonino, Inc. - 695 210th Ave., Antonino, KS 67601; Mailing: c/o St. Fidelis Friary, 900 Cathedral Ave., Victoria, KS 67671 t) 785-735-9456 (Friary, Victoria) curtis.carlson@capuchins.org Clustered with St. Anthony Parish, Schoenchen Rev. Curtis Carlson, O.F.M.Cap., Pst.; CRP Stds.: 8

ATWOOD

Sacred Heart Parish, Atwood, Inc. - 508 N. Railroad Ave., Atwood, KS 67730 t) 785-626-3335 church508@yahoo.com Rev. Henry Saw Lone, Pst.; Dcn. Mark Vrbas; CRP Stds.: 66

AURORA

St. Peter Parish, Aurora, Inc. - 112 Kansas Ave., Aurora, KS 67417-0009; Mailing: PO Box 9, Aurora, KS 67417-0009 t) 785-243-1099 stpeteraururoraks@gmail.com Clustered with Our Lady of Perpetual Help Parish, Concordia. Rev. David Metz, Pst.;

BEARDSLEY

St. John Nepomucene Parish, Beardsley, Inc. - Co Rd Y & Rd 12, Beardsley, KS 67730; Mailing: c/o St. Francis of Assisi Parish, PO Box 1170, St. Francis, KS 67756-1170 t) 785-332-2680 sfsec625@gmail.com Clustered with St. Francis of Assisi Parish, St. Francis. Rev. Joseph Asirvatham, H.G.N. (India), Parish Admin.; Jennifer Sabatka, CRE; CRP Stds.: 21

BELLEVILLE

St. Edward Parish, Belleville, Inc. - 1827 Q St., Belleville, KS 66935; Mailing: PO Box 99, Belleville, KS 66935-0099 t) 785-527-5559 stedward6810@nckcn.com Rev. Henry Baxa, Priest Supervisor; CRP Stds.: 69

BELOIT

St. John the Baptist Parish, Beloit, Inc. - 622 E. Main, Beloit, KS 67420 t) 785-738-2851 sjparish@nckcn.com www.stjohnsbeloit.org Rev. Jarett Konrade, Pst.; Rev. Andrew Rockers, Par. Vicar; CRP Stds.: 79

St. John the Baptist Parish School - (Grades PreK-6) 712 E. Main, Beloit, KS 67420-3318 t) 785-738-3941 mkee@gostj.com www.gostj.com/ Marcy Kee, Prin.; Joe Holdren, Vice Prin.; Stds.: 104; Lay Tchrs.: 10

St. John the Baptist Parish High School - (Grades 7-12) 209 Cherry St., Beloit, KS 67420-3305 t) 785-738-2942 mkee@gostj.com www.gostj.com/ Marcy Kee, Prin.; Joe Holdren, Vice Prin.; Stds.: 94; Lay Tchrs.: 11

BIRD CITY

St. Joseph Parish, Bird City, Inc. - 203 N. Bird Ave., Bird City, KS 67731; Mailing: c/o St. Francis of Assisi, P.O. Box 1170, St. Francis, KS 67756-1170 t) 785-332-2680 sfsec625@gmail.com Clustered with St. Francis of Assisi, St. Francis. Rev. Joseph Asirvatham, H.G.N. (India), Parish Admin.; CRP Stds.: 31

BROOKVILLE

St. Joseph Parish, Brookville, Inc. - 110 W. 3rd, Brookville, KS 67425; Mailing: 118 N. 9th, Salina, KS 67401 t) 785-823-7221 Clustered with Sacred Heart Cathedral Parish, Salina. Very Rev. Fred Gatschet, Pst.; Rev. Joseph Stanly Basil, H.G.N. (India), Par. Vicar;

CATHARINE

St. Catherine Parish, Catharine, Inc. - 1681 St. Joseph St., Catharine, KS 67627; Mailing: PO Box 18, Catharine, KS 67627-0018 t) 785-650-1746 stonehill@ruraltel.net www.volgagerman.net/catharine-church Clustered with St. Anthony Parish, Schoenchen, and Our Lady Help of Christians Parish, Antonino.

Rev. Earl Befort, O.F.M.Cap., Pst.; Glenda Schuetz, Parish Life Coord.;

CAWKER CITY

Saints Peter and Paul Parish, Cawker City, Inc. - 612 12th St, Cawker City, KS 67430; Mailing: PO Box 232, Cawker City, KS 67430-0232 t) 785-545-8613 sspeterpaul@nckcn.com Clustered with St. John the Baptist Parish, Beloit. Rev. Jarett Konrade, Pst.; Rev. Andrew Rockers, Par. Vicar; Lisa LaRocque, Parish Mgr.; CRP Stds.: 12

CHAPMAN

St. Michael Parish, Chapman, Inc. - 210 E. 6th St., Chapman, KS 67431-0217; Mailing: P O Box 217, Chapman, KS 67431-0217 t) 785-922-6509 smichael-chapman@sbcglobal.net smchapmanparish.org Clustered with St. Andrew Parish, Abilene. Rev. Peter O'Donnell, Pst.; Marita Campbell, Parish Life Coord.; CRP Stds.: 57

CLAY CENTER

Saints Peter and Paul Parish, Clay Center, Inc. - 730 Court St., Clay Center, KS 67432 t) 785-632-5011 finance@sspeterandpaulcc.org www.sspeterpaul.weconnect.com/ Rev. Kerry Ninemire, Pst.; Dcn. Michael Robinson; Dcn. Walter Slingsby; CRP Stds.: 138

CLIFTON

St. Mary Parish, Clifton, Inc. - 213 Clifton St., Clifton, KS 66937; Mailing: c/o St. John the Baptist Parish, 204 N. High, Clyde, KS 66938 t) 785-446-3474 stjohn@nckcn.com Clustered with St. John the Baptist Parish, Clyde. Rev. Steven Heina, Pst.; CRP Stds.: 32

CLYDE

St. John the Baptist Parish, Clyde, Inc. - 204 N. High, Clyde, KS 66938 t) 785-446-3793 (CRP); 785-446-3474 stjohn@nckcn.com Rev. Steven Heina, Pst.; CRP Stds.: 85

COLBY

Sacred Heart Parish, Colby, Inc. - 585 N. French Ave., Colby, KS 67701 t) 785-462-2179 parish@sacredheartcolby.com www.sacredheartcolby.com Rev. Brian Lager, Pst.; Dcn. Thomas Schrick; CRP Stds.: 102

Sacred Heart Parish School - (Grades PreK-5) 1150 W. 6th St., Colby, KS 67701 t) 785-460-2813 school@sacredheartcolby.com sacredheartcolby.com Mandy Meagher, Prin.; Stds.: 109; Lay Tchrs.: 11

COLLYER

St. Michael Parish, Collyer, Inc. - 711 Ainslie Ave, Collyer, KS 67631; Mailing: c/o Christ the King Parish, 412 N 9th St., WaKeeney, KS 67672 t) 785-743-2330 (Parish Office, WaKeeney) c) 785-483-9360 ctkstm@ruraltel.net Clustered with Christ the King Parish, WaKeeney. Rev. Charles Steier, Pst.; CRP Stds.: 15

CONCORDIA

Our Lady of Perpetual Help Parish, Concordia, Inc. - 307 E. Fifth, Concordia, KS 66901; Mailing: P.O. Box 608, Concordia, KS 66901-0608 t) 785-243-1099 olph@olphconcordia.org www.olphconcordia.org Rev. David Metz, Pst.; CRP Stds.: 161

CUBA

St. Isidore Parish, Cuba, Inc. - 603 Linden, Cuba, KS 66935; Mailing: c/o St. Edward Parish, P.O. Box 99, Belleville, KS 66935-0099 t) 785-527-5559 stedward6810@nckcn.com Clustered with St. Edward Parish, Belleville. Dcn. Steve Heiman, Dir.; Rev. Henry Baxa, Priest Supervisor;

DAMAR

St. Joseph Parish, Damar, Inc. - 107 Oak St., Damar, KS 67632; Mailing: P.O. Box 68, Damar, KS 67632 t) 785-839-4343 sjdamar@ruraltel.net Clustered with Immaculate Heart of Mary Parish, Hill City. Rev. Ernest Amoako-Opare (Ghana), Pst.; CRP Stds.: 26

DORRANCE

St. Joseph Parish, Dorrance, Inc. - 1011 Lincoln Ave, Dorrance, KS 67634; Mailing: c/o St. Wenceslaus Parish, P.O. Box 528, Wilson, KS 67490 t) 785-658-3361 swchurch@wtciweb.com Clustered with St. Wenceslaus Parish, Wilson. Rev. Lourthuantony Kulandaijesu, H.G.N. (India), Par. Admin.;

DOWNS

St. Mary Parish, Downs, Inc. - 1312 Prentiss St., Downs, KS 67437; Mailing: P.O. Box 221, Downs, KS 67437-0221 c) (785) 545-8867 jkneihous@ruraltel.net Clustered with St. Boniface Parish, Tipton. Rev. Daryl Olmstead, Pst.; CRP Stds.: 38

ELLIS

St. Mary Parish, Ellis, Inc. - 703 Monroe, Ellis, KS 67637-2231 t) 785-726-4522 stmary@gbta.net stmarysofellis.org/ Rev. Dana Clark, Pst.; CRP Stds.: 51

St. Mary Parish School - (Grades PreK-6) 605 Monroe St., Ellis, KS 67637 t) 785-726-3185 stmarysofellis.org/school Patti Park, Prin.; Stds.: 72; Lay Tchrs.: 9

ELLSWORTH

St. Bernard Parish, Ellsworth, Inc. - 911 Kansas St., Ellsworth, KS 67439 t) 785-472-3136 stbernardsparishoffice@gmail.com www.stbsti.com Rev. Joshua Werth, Pst.; CRP Stds.: 74

ELMO

St. Columba Parish, Elmo, Inc. - 890 Main Elmo St, Elmo, KS 67451; Mailing: c/o St. John the Evangelist Parish, 712 N. Broadway, Herington, KS 67449 t) 785-258-2013 highway4catholics.org Clustered with St. John the Evangelist Parish, Herington. Rev. George Chalbhagam, C.M.I. (India), Pst.; Dcn. Richard J. Kramer; CRP Stds.: 1

ESBON

Sacred Heart Parish, Esbon, Inc. - 1100-1198 KS 112, Esbon, KS 66941; Mailing: 422 N Commercial, PO Box 13, Esbon, KS 66941-0013 t) 785-378-3939 (Parish Office, Mankato) sttheresa422@gmail.com www.facebook.com/sacredheartesbon Clustered with St. Theresa Parish, Mankato. Rev. Jarett Konrade, Priest in solidum (Moderator); Rev. Andrew Rockers, Priest in solidum; CRP Stds.: 10

GLASCO

St. Mary Parish, Glasco, Inc. - 301 E 1st St., Glasco, KS 67445; Mailing: PO Box 554, Glasco, KS 67445-0554 t) 785-392-2079 iccmkansas@gmail.com Clustered with Immaculate Conception of the Blessed Virgin Mary Parish, Minneapolis. Rev. Mark Wesely, Pst.;

GOODLAND

Our Lady of Perpetual Help Parish, Goodland, Inc. - 307 W. 13th St, Goodland, KS 67735 t) 785-890-7205 olph@nwkansascatholics.com www.nwkansascatholics.com Rev. Carlos Ruiz Santos; CRP Stds.: 95

GORHAM

St. Mary Help of Christians Parish, Gorham, Inc. - 135 3rd St., Gorham, KS 67640; Mailing: PO Box 135, Gorham, KS 67640-0135 t) 785-637-5241 st_marys@gorhamtel.com Clustered with St. Mary Queen of Angels Parish, Russell. Rev. Michael Elanjimattathil, C.M.I. (India), Pst.;

GRAINFIELD

St. Agnes Parish, Grainfield, Inc. - 266 Cedar St., Grainfield, KS 67737; Mailing: P.O. Box 156, Grainfield, KS 67737-0156 t) 785-673-4255 c) 785-673-3176 stagneschurch256@gmail.com www.govecountycatholicparishes.org Clustered with Sacred Heart Parish, Park Rev. James Maruthukunnel Thomas, C.M.I., Pst.; CRP Stds.: 23

GREENLEAF

Sacred Heart Parish, Greenleaf, Inc. - 143 Main St., Greenleaf, KS 66943; Mailing: PO Box 62, Greenleaf, KS 66943 t) 785-325-3147 www.washcountycc.net Clustered with St. John the Baptist Parish, Hanover Rev. Joseph Kieffer, Pst.;

GRINNELL

Immaculate Conception of the Blessed Virgin Mary Parish, Grinnell, Inc. - 308 Monroe St, Grinnell, KS 67738; Mailing: PO Box 69, Grinnell, KS 67738 t) 785-824-3221 imcgrinn@st-tel.net www.govecountycatholicparishes.org Clustered with Sacred Heart Parish, Park. Rev. James Maruthukunnel Thomas, C.M.I., Pst.; CRP Stds.: 6

GYPSUM

St. Patrick Parish - 819 Spring St., Gypsum, KS 67448; Mailing: c/o Immaculate Conception of the Blessed Virgin Mary, PO Box 337, Solomon, KS 67480 t) 785-655-2221 daylenetracy@gmail.com www.immaculateconceptionsolomon.org/ Daylene Tracy, Parish Life Coord.; Rev. John Wolesky, Priest Supv.;

HANOVER

St. John the Baptist Parish - 114 S. Church St., Hanover, KS 66945; Mailing: PO Box 395, Hanover, KS 66945 t) 785-337-2289 www.washcountycc.net Rev. Joseph Kieffer, Pst.; CRP Stds.: 44

St. John the Baptist Parish School - (Grades 1-8) 100 S. Church St., Hanover, KS 66945 t) 785-337-2368 www.stjohnshanover.com/ Amanda Cook, Prin.; Stds.: 101; Lay Tchrs.: 7

HAYS

Immaculate Heart of Mary Parish, Hays, Inc. - 1805 Vine St, Hays, KS 67601 t) 785-625-7339 skisner@ihm-church.com; frparker@ihm-church.com www.ihm-church.com Rev. Nicholas Parker, Pst.; Rev. David Michael, H.G.N. (India), Par. Vicar; Dcn. David Kisner; CRP Stds.: 167

Holy Family Elementary Grade School - (Grades PreK-6) 1800 Milner, Hays, KS 67601-3796 t) 785-625-3131 rwentling@hfehays.org www.hfehays.org Rachel Wentling, Prin.; Stds.: 279; Lay Tchrs.: 22

St. Joseph Parish, Hays, Inc. - 210 W. 13th St., Hays, KS 67601 t) 785-625-7356 stjoseph@stjoehays.com www.stj-church.com Rev. Richard Daise, Pst.; Rev. Michael Raj Kothalamuthu, H.G.N. (India), Par. Vicar; CRP Stds.: 92

St. Nicholas of Myra Parish, Hays, Inc. - 2901 E. 13th, Hays, KS 67601 t) 785-628-1446 rfweigel@eaglecom.net stn-church.com Rev. Damian Richards, Pst.; Dcn. Steve Urban; CRP Stds.: 151

HERINGTON

St. John the Evangelist Parish, Herington, Inc. - 712 N. Broadway, Herington, KS 67449 t) 785-258-2013 highway4catholics.org Rev. George Chalbhagam, C.M.I. (India), Pst.; Dcn. Richard J. Kramer; CRP Stds.: 19

HERNDON

Assumption of Mary Parish, Herndon, Inc. - 541 Palermo Ave., Herndon, KS 67739; Mailing: c/o Sacred Heart Parish, 508 N. Railroad Ave., Atwood, KS 67730 t) 785-626-3335 church508@yahoo.com Clustered with Sacred Heart Parish, Atwood. Rev. Henry Saw Lone, Pst.; Loretta A. Studer, Bus. Mgr. & CRE;

HILL CITY

Immaculate Heart of Mary Parish, Hill City, Inc. - 110 N. 10th Ave., Hill City, KS 67642 t) 785-421-2535 ihmchurchhc@gmail.com Rev. Ernest Amoako-Opare (Ghana), Pst.; CRP Stds.: 67

HOLYROOD

St. Mary Parish, Holyrood, Inc. - 202 S. Frank St., Holyrood, KS 67450; Mailing: c/o St. Wenceslaus Parish, PO Box 528, Wilson, KS 67490-0528 t) 785-658-3361 Clustered with St. Wenceslaus Parish, Wilson. Rev. Lourthuantony Kulandaijesu, H.G.N. (India), Par. Admin.;

HOPE

St. Phillip Parish, Hope, Inc. - 114 Main St., Hope, KS 67451; Mailing: c/o St. John the Evangelist Parish, 712 N. Broadway, Herington, KS 67449 t) 785-258-2013 highway4catholics.org Clustered with St. John the Evangelist Parish, Herington. Rev. George Chalbhagam, C.M.I. (India), Pst.; Dcn. Richard J. Kramer;

HOXIE

St. Frances Cabrini Parish, Hoxie, Inc. - 924 17th St, Hoxie, KS 67740; Mailing: PO Box 38, Hoxie, KS 67740 t) 785-675-3300 hoxieseguinparishes.org Rev. Vincent Thu Laing, Pst.; CRP Stds.: 105

JUNCTION CITY

St. Francis Xavier Parish, Junction City, Inc. - 218 N. Washington, Junction City, KS 66441 t) 785-238-2998 office@saintxparish.org www.saintxparish.org Rev.

Gnanasekar Kulandai, H.G.N., Pst.; CRP Stds.: 101

St. Francis Xavier Parish School - (Grades PreK-12) 200 N. Washington St., Junction City, KS 66441 t) 785-238-2841 office@saintxrams.org www.saintxrams.org Shawn Augustine, Prin.; Stds.: 148; Lay Tchrs.: 14

KANOPOLIS

St. Ignatius Loyola Parish, Kanopolis, Inc. - 127 N. Missouri St., Kanopolis, KS 67454 t) 785-472-3136 www.stbsti.com/ Clustered with St. Bernard Parish, Ellsworth. Rev. Joshua Werth, Pst.; CRP Stds.: 9

LEOVILLE

Immaculate Conception of the Blessed Virgin Mary Parish, Leoville, Inc. - 92 1500th Rd, Leoville, KS 67757; Mailing: c/o Sacred Heart Parish, 210 E. Washington St., Oberlin, KS 67749 t) 785-475-3103 (Parish Office, Oberlin) catholic@ruraltel.net Clustered with Sacred Heart Parish, Oberlin. Rev. Mathew Chacko, C.M.I., Pst.; CRP Stds.: 17

LINCOLN

St. Patrick Parish, Lincoln, Inc. - 206 N. Fifth, Lincoln, KS 67455; Mailing: PO Box 327, Lincoln, KS 67455-0327 t) 785-524-4823 stpat327@gmail.com Clustered with Immaculate Conception of the Blessed Virgin Mary Parish, Minneapolis. Rev. Mark Wesely, Pst.; CRP Stds.: 27

LOGAN

St. John the Evangelist Parish, Logan, Inc. - 203 E. Main, Logan, KS 67646; Mailing: PO Box 128, Logan, KS 67646-0128 t) 785-689-4299 stjohnchurch27@gmail.com Clustered with SS Philip & James Parish, Phillipsburg. Rev. John Schmeidler, Pst.; CRP Stds.: 20

MANHATTAN

St. Isidore Catholic Student Center Parish, Manhattan, Inc. - 711 Denison Ave., Manhattan, KS 66502 t) 785-539-7496 stisidores@stisidores.com www.stisidores.com/ Rev. Gale Hammerschmidt, Pst./Chap.; Rev. Matthew Davied, Par. Vicar/Asst. Chap.;

Seven Dolors of the Blessed Virgin Mary Parish - 731 Pierre St., Manhattan, KS 66502 t) 785-565-5000 office@sevendolors.com www.sevendolors.com Rev. Ryan McCandless, Pst.; Rev. Michael Leiker, Par. Vicar; Dcn. Edward Souza; Rev. Randall D. Weber, In Res.; CRP Stds.: 215

Manhattan Catholic Schools - (Grades PreK-8) 306 S. Juliette Ave., Manhattan, KS 66502-6297 t) 785-565-5050 www.manhattancatholicschools.org Michael Hubka, Prin.; Julie Jueneman, Vice Prin.; Stds.: 274; Lay Tchrs.: 21

St. Thomas More Parish, Manhattan, Inc. - 2900 Kimball Ave., Manhattan, KS 66502 t) 785-776-5151 stm@stmmanhattan.com stmmanhattan.com Rev. Frank Coady, Pst.; Dcn. Wayne Talbot, Pst. Assoc.; Dcn. Lawrence Erpelding; Dcn. Buzz Harris; CRP Stds.: 323

MANKATO

St. Theresa Parish, Mankato, Inc. - 422 N. Commercial, Mankato, KS 66956; Mailing: PO Box 265, Mankato, KS 66956-0265 t) 785-378-3939 stheresa422@gmail.com Rev. Jarett Konrade, Priest in solidum (Moderator); Rev. Andrew Rockers, Priest in solidum; CRP Stds.: 12

MILTONVALE

St. Anthony Parish, Miltonvale, Inc. - 612 W. 4th St., Miltonvale, KS 67466; Mailing: c/o SS Peter & Paul Parish, 730 Court St, Clay Center, KS 67432 t) 785-632-5011 (Parish Office, Clay Cntr) sspp@eaglecom.net Clustered with SS. Peter and Paul Parish, Clay Center Rev. Kerry Ninemire, Pst.; Dcn. Michael Robinson;

MINNEAPOLIS

Immaculate Conception of the Blessed Virgin Mary Parish, Minneapolis, Inc. - 216 Cherry St., Minneapolis, KS 67467; Mailing: PO Box 167, Minneapolis, KS 67467-0167 t) 785-392-2079 iccmkansas@gmail.com Rev. Mark Wesely, Pst.; CRP Stds.: 40

MUNDEN

St. George Parish, Munden, Inc. - 105 W. Myrza St., Munden, KS 66959; Mailing: c/o St. Edward Parish, P.O. Box 99, Belleville, KS 66935 t) 785-527-5559 stedward6810@nckcn.com Clustered with St. Edward Parish, Belleville. Dcn. Steve Heiman, Dir.; Rev. Henry Baxa, Priest Supervisor;

MUNJOR

St. Francis of Assisi Parish, Munjor, Inc. - 883 Moscow St., Munjor, KS 67601 t) 785-625-5314 office@stfrancis-church.com www.stfrancis-church.com Clustered with St. Nicholas of Myra Parish, Hays. Rev. Damian Richards, Pst.; Lilly Binder, Pst. Assoc.; CRP Stds.: 21

NEW ALMELO

St. Joseph Parish, New Almelo, Inc. - 28035 St. John St., New Almelo, KS 67645-9742 t) 785-567-4875 stjosephcc@ruraltel.net Clustered with St. Francis of Assisi Parish, Norton. Rev. Matthew John Cowan, Pst.; CRP Stds.: 13

NORTON

St. Francis of Assisi Parish, Norton, Inc. - 108 S. Wabash Ave., Norton, KS 67654; Mailing: P.O. Box 148, Norton, KS 67654-0148 t) 785-877-2234 stfranci@ruraltel.net www.stfrancisassisi.org/ Rev. Matthew John Cowan, Pst.; CRP Stds.: 84

OAKLEY

St. Joseph Parish, Oakley, Inc. - St. Joseph Parish Annex, 625 Freeman Ave, Oakley, KS 67748 t) 785-671-3828 parish@sjoakley.org sjoakley.org Rev. Luke Thielen, Pst.; Dcn. Dennis Engel; Dcn. Michael Brungardt; CRP Stds.: 40

St. Joseph Parish School - (Grades PreK-5) 725 Freeman Ave., Oakley, KS 67748 t) 785-671-4451 sjoakley.org/school Michelle Selzer, Prin.; Stds.: 64; Lay Tchrs.: 8

OBERLIN

Sacred Heart Parish, Oberlin, Inc. - 210 E Washington, Oberlin, KS 67749 t) 785-475-3103 catholic@ruraltel.net Rev. Mathew Chacko, C.M.I., Pst.;

OGDEN

St. Patrick Parish, Ogden, Inc. - 303 16th St, Ogden, KS 66517; Mailing: c/o Seven Dolors of the Blessed Virgin Mary Parish, 731 Pierre St., Manhattan, KS 66502 t) 785-565-5000 office@sevendolors.com Clustered with Seven Dolors of the Blessed Virgin Mary Parish, Manhattan. Rev. Ryan McCandless, Pst.;

OSBORNE

St. Aloysius Gonzaga Parish, Osborne, Inc. - 203 N. Elm, Osborne, KS 67473; Mailing: P.O. Box 267, Osborne, KS 67473-0267 t) 785-346-5582 stal@ruraltel.net Clustered with St. Boniface Parish, Tipton Rev. Daryl Olmstead, Pst.; CRP Stds.: 44

PARK

Sacred Heart Parish, Park, Inc. - 202 S. Cottonwood, Park, KS 67751; Mailing: PO Box 78, Park, KS 67751-0078 t) 785-673-4684 shcpark@ruraltel.net www.govecountycatholicparishes.org Rev. James Maruthukunnel Thomas, C.M.I., Pst.; CRP Stds.: 65

PHILLIPSBURG

Saints Philip and James Parish, Phillipsburg, Inc. - 690 S. 7th, Phillipsburg, KS 67661 t) 785-543-5367 sspjchurch@sbcglobal.net www.phillipsburgcatholic.org Rev. John Schmeidler, Pst.; CRP Stds.: 42

PLAINVILLE

Sacred Heart Parish, Plainville, Inc. - 206 N. Washington, Plainville, KS 67663; Mailing: PO Box 100, Plainville, KS 67663-0100 t) 785-434-4658 shcparish@shcplainville.org www.shcplainville.org Rev. Leo Blasi, Pst.; CRP Stds.: 40

Sacred Heart Parish School - (Grades PreK-6) 300 N. Washington, Plainville, KS 67663; Mailing: P.O. Box 408, Plainville, KS 67663 t) 785-434-2157 shcplainville.org Scott Brown, Prin.; Stds.: 60; Lay Tchrs.: 8

RUSSELL

St. Mary, Queen of Angels Parish, Russell, Inc. - 415 S. Windsor St., Russell, KS 67665 t) 785-483-2871 smqoa@ruraltel.net www.stmaryrussell.com Rev. Michael Elanjimattathil, C.M.I. (India), Pst.; CRP Stds.: 98

SALINA

Sacred Heart Cathedral Parish, Salina, Inc. - 118 N. Ninth St., Salina, KS 67401 t) 785-823-7221 officemanager@shcathedral.com www.shcathedral.com Very Rev. Fred Gatschet, Pst.; Rev. Joseph Stanly Basil, H.G.N. (India), Par. Vicar; Dcn. Jorge Rivera; CRP Stds.: 191

St. Elizabeth Ann Seton Parish, Salina, Inc. - 1000 Burr Oak Ln., Salina, KS 67401 t) 785-825-5282 office@stesalina.org www.stesalina.org Rev. Keith Weber, Pst.; CRP Stds.: 141

St. Mary, Queen of the Universe Parish, Salina, Inc. - 230 E. Cloud St., Salina, KS 67401 t) 785-827-5575 caitlyn@stmsalina.org stmsalina.org Rev. Kevin Weber, Pst.; Rev. Brian McCaffrey, Par. Vicar; Dcn. Steven H. Frueh; CRP Stds.: 135

St. Mary Queen of the Universe Parish School - (Grades PreK-6) 304 E. Cloud St., Salina, KS 67401 t) 785-827-4200 www.stmarysalina.org/ Tym Bonilla, Prin.; Corey Ritter, Vice Prin.; Stds.: 348; Lay Tchrs.: 27

SCHOENCHEN

St. Anthony Parish, Schoenchen, Inc. - 204 Church St., Schoenchen, KS 67667; Mailing: c/o St. Fidelis Friary, 900 Cathedral Ave., Victoria, KS 67671 t) 785-735-9456 (Friary, Victoria) curtis.carlson@capuchins.org Clustered with Our Lady Help of Christians Parish, Antonino Rev. Curtis Carlson, O.F.M.Cap., Pst.; CRP Stds.: 10

SEGUIN

St. Martin Parish, Seguin, Inc. - 540 14th St., Seguin, KS 67740; Mailing: c/o St. Francis of Cabrini Parish, P.O. Box 38, Hoxie, KS 67740-0038 t) 785-675-3300 www.hoxieseguinparishes.org/ Clustered with St. Francis Cabrini Parish, Hoxie, KS. Rev. Vincent Thu Laing, Pst.;

SELDEN

Sacred Heart Parish, Selden, Inc. - 201 S Missouri Ave, Selden, KS 67757; Mailing: c/o Sacred Heart Parish, 210 E. Washington St, Oberlin, KS 67749 t) 785-475-3103 (Parish Office, Oberlin) catholic@ruraltel.net Clustered with Sacred Heart Parish, Oberlin Rev. Mathew Chacko, C.M.I., Pst.; CRP Stds.: 19

SHARON SPRINGS

Holy Ghost Parish, Sharon Springs, Inc. - 403 N. Main St., Sharon Springs, KS 67758; Mailing: PO Box 190, Sharon Springs, KS 67758-0190 t) (785) 890-7205 (Parish Office, Goodland) c) (785) 821-1315 roxym.bussen@gmail.com; olph@nwkansascatholics.com www.nwkansascatholics.com/ Clustered with Our Lady of Perpetual Help Parish, Goodland. Rev. Carlos Ruiz Santos, Pst.; CRP Stds.: 42

SMITH CENTER

St. Mary Parish, Smith Center, Inc. - 403 W. Hwy 36, Smith Center, KS 66967; Mailing: PO Box 263, Smith Center, KS 66967-0263 t) (785) 543-5367 (Phillipsburg Office) Clustered with SS Phillip and James, Phillipsburg. Rev. John Schmeidler; CRP Stds.: 29

SOLOMON

Immaculate Conception of the Blessed Virgin Mary Parish, Solomon, Inc. - 3599 N. Field Rd., Solomon, KS 67480; Mailing: P.O. Box 337, Solomon, KS 67480-0337 t) 785-655-2221 daylenetracy@gmail.com www.immaculateconceptionsolomon.org Rev. John Wolesky, Priest Supvr.; Daylene Tracy, Parish Life Coord.; CRP Stds.: 24

ST. FRANCIS

St. Francis of Assisi Parish, St. Francis, Inc. - 625 S. River St., St. Francis, KS 67756; Mailing: PO Box 1170, St. Francis, KS 67756-1170 t) 785-332-2680 sfsec625@gmail.com Rev. Joseph Asirvatham, H.G.N. (India), Parish Admin.; CRP Stds.: 12

STOCKTON

St. Thomas Parish, Stockton, Inc. - 722 Main St., Stockton, KS 67669; Mailing: c/o Sacred Heart Parish, 206 N Washington, Plainville, KS 67663 t) 785-434-4658 shcparish@shcplainville.org shcplainville.org/ Clustered with Sacred Heart Parish,

Plainville. Rev. Leo Blasi, Pst.; CRP Stds.: 29
TIPTON
St. Boniface Parish, Tipton, Inc. - 308 Gambrinus, Tipton, KS 67485; Mailing: PO Box 87, Tipton, KS 67485-0087 t) 785-373-4455 boniface@wtciweb.com Rev. Daryl Olmstead, Pst.; CRP Stds.: 62
St. Boniface Parish High School - (Grades 7-12) 301 State St, Tipton, KS 67485; Mailing: P.O. Box 146, Tipton, KS 67485 t) 785-373-5835 Gery Hake, Prin.; Stds.: 15; Lay Tchrs.: 5
VICTORIA
The Basilica of St. Fidelis - 900 Cathedral Ave, Victoria, KS 67671; Mailing: 601 10th St, Victoria, KS 67671 t) 785-735-2777 www.stfidelischurch.com Rev. James E. Moster, O.F.M.Cap., Pst.; CRP Stds.: 150
St. Boniface Parish, Vincent, Inc. - Vincent Ave., Victoria, KS 67671; Mailing: 601 10th St., Victoria, KS 67671 t) 785-735-2777 (Parish Office, Victoria) fidelis@ruraltel.net www.stbonifacevincent.com Clustered with the Basilica of St. Fidelis, Victoria. Rev. James E. Moster, O.F.M.Cap., Pst.; CRP Stds.: 16
WAKEENEY
Christ the King Parish, WaKeeney, Inc. - 412 N. Ninth St., WaKeeney, KS 67672 t) 785-743-2330 c) 786-483-9360 ctkstm@ruraltel.net Clustered with St. Michael Parish, Collyer Rev. Charles Steier, Pst.; CRP Stds.: 66
WALKER
St. Ann Parish, Walker, Inc. - 1275 Walker Ave., Walker, KS 67674; Mailing: c/o The Basilica of St. Fidelis, 601 10th St., Victoria, KS 67671 t) 785-735-2777 (Victoria Office) fidelis@ruraltel.net www.stfidelischurch.com Clustered with the Basilica, Victoria Rev. James E. Moster, O.F.M.Cap., Pst.;
WASHINGTON
St. Augustine Parish, Washington, Inc. - 410 B St., Washington, KS 66968 t) 785-325-3147 staugustinesecretary@gmail.com www.washcountycc.net Clustered with St. John the Baptist, Hanover Rev. Joseph Kieffer, Pst.; CRP Stds.: 75
WILSON
St. Wenceslaus Parish, Wilson, Inc. - 2811 Ave. D., Wilson, KS 67490; Mailing: P.O. Box 528, Wilson, KS 67490-0528 t) 785-658-3361 Rev. Lourthuantony Kulandaijesu, H.G.N. (India), Par. Admin.; CRP Stds.: 38

SCHOOLS: PRESCHOOL THRU HIGH SCHOOL

HIGH SCHOOLS

STATE OF KANSAS
HAYS
Thomas More Prep-Marian High Inc. - (DIO) (Grades 7-12) 1701 Hall, Hays, KS 67601 t) 785-625-6577 meitnerc@tmpmarian.org www.tmp-m.org Chad Meitner, Prin.; Tom Meagher, Vice Prin.; Melissa Schoepf, Vice Prin. Jr High; Rev. Andy Hammeke, Chap.; Rev. Damian Richards, Moderator; Stds.: 264; Lay Tchrs.: 29
Endowment Foundation of Thomas More Prep-Marian, Inc. - 1701 Hall St., Hays, KS 67601 t) (785) 625-6577 ruderm@tmpmarian.org Mason Ruder, Advancement Director;
SALINA
Sacred Heart Junior-Senior High School - (DIO) (Grades 7-12) 234 E. Cloud, Salina, KS 67401 t) 785-827-4422 www.sacredheartknights.org John Krajicek, Prin.; John Hamilton, Vice Prin.; Rev. Kevin Weber, Chap.; Rev. Brian McCaffrey, Chap.; Stds.: 183; Lay Tchrs.: 17

INSTITUTIONS LOCATED IN DIOCESE

ASSOCIATIONS [ASN]

SALINA
Salina Diocesan Clergy Health and Retirement Association, Inc. - 103 N. 9th St., Salina, KS 67401-2503; Mailing: P.O. Box 980, Salina, KS 67402-0980 t) 785-827-8746 x12 ernie.armstrong@salinadiocese.org Ernie Armstrong, CEO;

CAMPUS MINISTRY / NEWMAN CENTERS [CAM]

HAYS
Comeau Catholic Campus Center, Hays, Inc. - 506 W. Sixth, Hays, KS 67601 t) 785-625-7396 sandy.losey@catholictigers.org www.catholictigers.org/ Rev. Andy Hammeke, Chap.;
MANHATTAN
St. Isidore Catholic Student Center Parish, Manhattan, Inc. - 711 Denison Ave., Manhattan, KS 66502 t) 785-539-7496 stisidores@stisidores.com www.stisidores.com Rev. Gale Hammerschmidt, Pst./Chap.; Rev. Matthew Davied, Par. Vicar/Asst. Chap.;

CONVENTS, MONASTERIES, AND RESIDENCES FOR WOMEN [CON]

CONCORDIA
Sisters of St. Joseph of Concordia - 215 Court St., Concordia, KS 66901; Mailing: P.O. Box 279, Concordia, KS 66901 t) 785-243-2149 csjcenter@csjkansas.org www.csjkansas.org Rev. Msgr. Barry E. Brinkman, Chap.; Sr. Jean Rosemarynoski, C.S.J., Pres.; Srs.: 78

ENDOWMENTS / FOUNDATIONS / TRUSTS [EFT]

SALINA
Marymount Memorial Educational Trust Fund - 103 N. 9th St., Salina, KS 67401-2503; Mailing: P.O. Box 980, Salina, KS 67402-0980 t) 785-827-8746 x12 keith.weber@salinadiocese.org Ernie Armstrong, CEO;
Sacred Heart Junior-Senior Endowment Fund, Inc. - 234 E. Cloud, Salina, KS 67401-6436 t) 785-825-4011 rthompson@sacredheartknights.org www.sacredheartknights.org John Krajicek, Prin.;
Catholic Foundation for Diocese of Salina - 103 N. Ninth St., Salina, KS 67401-2503; Mailing: P.O. Box 1696, Salina, KS 67402-1696 t) 785-827-8746 katie.platten@salinadiocese.org www.salinadiocese.org Katie Platten, CEO; Ernie Armstrong, CFO; Heather Hartman, Dir., Devel;

HOSPITALS / HEALTH SERVICES [HOS]

MANHATTAN
***Ascension Via Christi Hospital Manhattan, Inc.** - 1823 College Ave., Manhattan, KS 66502 t) (316) 858-4721 tracey.biles@ascension.org www.viachristi.org Kevin Strecker, CEO; Tracey Biles, Contact; Bed Capacity: 94; Asstd. Annu.: 31,896; Staff: 379

MISCELLANEOUS [MIS]

CONCORDIA
Nazareth Convent & Academy Corporation - 215 Court St., Concordia, KS 66901; Mailing: P.O. Box 279, Concordia, KS 66901 t) 785-243-2149 csjcenter@csjkansas.org www.csjkansas.org Rev. Msgr. Barry E. Brinkman, Chap.; Sr. Jean Rosemarynoski, C.S.J., Pres.;
Neighborhood Initiatives, Inc. - 215 Court St., Concordia, KS 66901; Mailing: P.O. Box 279, Concordia, KS 66901 t) 785-243-2149 csjcenter@csjkansas.org Sr. Jean Rosemarynoski, C.S.J., Pres.;
SALINA
St. Joseph Annex, Inc. - 401 W. Iron, Salina, KS 67401; Mailing: P.O. Box 980, Salina, KS 67402-0980 t) 785-827-8746 x12 Ernie Armstrong, CEO;
The Register of the Roman Catholic Diocese of Salina, Inc. - 103 N. Ninth St., Salina, KS 67401-2503; Mailing: P.O. Box 980, Salina, KS 67402-0980 t) 785-827-8746 theregister@salinadiocese.org Katherine Hamel, Editor;
Roman Catholic Diocese of Salina Deposit and Loan Inc. - 103 N. Ninth St., Salina, KS 67401-2503; Mailing: P.O. Box 980, Salina, KS 67402-0980 t) 785-827-8746 x12 ernie.armstrong@salinadiocese.org Ernie Armstrong, CEO;
Salina Catholic Diocese Seminary Burses, Inc. - 103 N. Ninth St., Salina, KS 67401-2503; Mailing: P.O. Box 980, Salina, KS 67402-0980 t) 785-827-8746 Ernie Armstrong, CEO;
Vocatio of Salina - 103 N. 9th St., Salina, KS 67401-2503; Mailing: P.O. Box 980, Salina, KS 67402-0980 t) 785-827-8746 vocations@salinadiocese.org Rev. Andy Hammeke, Co-Vocation Dir.; Rev. Joshua Werth, Co-Vocation Dir.;

MONASTERIES AND RESIDENCES FOR PRIESTS AND BROTHERS [MON]

VICTORIA
St. Fidelis Friary - 900 Cathedral Ave., Victoria, KS 67671 t) 785-735-9456 Rev. Earl Befort, O.F.M.Cap., Pst.; Rev. Harvey Dinkel, O.F.M.Cap., Chap.; Rev. James E. Moster, O.F.M.Cap., Pst.; Rev. Curtis Carlson, O.F.M.Cap., Supr.; Friar Donald Debes, O.F.M.Cap.; Bro. Joseph McGlynn, O.F.M.Cap.; Rev. Earl Meyer, O.F.M.Cap.; Rev. Felix Petrovsky, O.F.M.Cap.; Rev. Gilmary Tallman, O.F.M.Cap.; Brs.: 1; Priests: 8

NURSING / REHABILITATION / CONVALESCENCE / ELDERLY CARE [NUR]

HAYS
Via Christi Village Hays, Inc. (Ascension Living Via Christi Village Hays) - 2225 Canterbury, Hays, KS 67601 t) 314-292-9308 ahscm-mission@ascension.org www.ascensionliving.org/ Ryan Endsley, COO; Asstd. Annu.: 184; Staff: 90
MANHATTAN
Via Christi Village Manhattan, Inc. (Ascension Living Via Christi Village Manhattan) - 2800 Willow Grove Rd., Manhattan, KS 66502 t) 314-292-9308 ahscm-mission@ascension.org www.ascensionliving.org/ Ryan Endsley, COO; Asstd. Annu.: 299; Staff: 132

RETREAT HOUSES / RENEWAL CENTERS [RTR]

CONCORDIA
Manna House of Prayer - 323 E. Fifth St., Concordia, KS 66901; Mailing: P.O. Box 675, Concordia, KS 66901 t) 785-243-4428 retreatcenter@mannahouse.org www.mannahouse.org Sr. Betty Suther, C.S.J., Admin.;
VICTORIA
Capuchin Center for Spiritual Life - 900 Cathedral Ave., Victoria, KS 67671 t) 785-735-9393 ccsl@ruraltel.net Rev. Harvey Dinkel, O.F.M.Cap., Dir.;

An asterisk (*) denotes an organization that has established tax-exempt status directly with the IRS and is not covered by the USCCB Group Ruling.

Diocese of Salt Lake City

(Dioecesis Civitatis Lacus Salsi)

MOST REVEREND OSCAR AZARCON SOLIS

Bishop of Salt Lake City; ordained April 28, 1979; appointed Titular Bishop of Urci and Auxiliary Bishop of Los Angeles December 11, 2003; ordained February 10, 2004; appointed Bishop of Salt Lake City January 10, 2017; installed March 7, 2017. Office: 27 C St., Salt Lake City, UT 84103-2397.

Diocesan Offices and Organizations: 27 C St., Salt Lake City, UT 84103-2397. T: 801-328-8641; F: 801-328-9680.
www.dioslc.org

ESTABLISHED AS A VICARIATE-APOSTOLIC ON NOV. 23, 1886.

Square Miles 84,990.

Erected a Diocese on January 27, 1891.

Originally comprised all Utah and the Counties of Eureka, Lander, Lincoln, White Pine, Nye, Elko and Clark in the State of Nevada. By Apostolic Constitution dated March 27, 1931, the Nevada section was separated from the Salt Lake Diocese and incorporated in the Reno Diocese. The name was changed to Diocese of Salt Lake City on March 31, 1951.

Comprises the State of Utah.

Patroness of the Diocese of Salt Lake City: St. Mary Magdalene.

Second Patroness: Our Lady of Guadalupe.

For legal titles of parishes and diocesan institutions, consult the Chancery Office.

STATISTICAL OVERVIEW

Personnel

Bishop	1
Priests: Diocesan Active in Diocese	29
Priests: Diocesan Active Outside Diocese	2
Priests: Retired, Sick or Absent	20
Number of Diocesan Priests	51
Religious Priests in Diocese	7
Total Priests in your Diocese	58
Extern Priests in Diocese	20
Ordinations:	
Diocesan Priests	1
Transitional Deacons	2
Permanent Deacons in Diocese	82
Total Sisters	24

Parishes

Parishes	48
With Resident Pastor:	
Resident Diocesan Priests	39
Resident Religious Priests	4
Without Resident Pastor:	
Administered by Priests	3
Administered by Deacons	2
Missions	20
Professional Ministry Personnel:	
Sisters	3
Lay Ministers	42

Welfare

Day Care Centers	16
Total Assisted	786
Special Centers for Social Services	3
Total Assisted	387,739
Other Institutions	1
Total Assisted	60,453

Educational

Diocesan Students in Other Seminaries	8
Total Seminarians	8
High Schools, Diocesan and Parish	3
Total Students	1,392
Elementary Schools, Diocesan and Parish	13
Total Students	3,455
Catechesis/Religious Education:	
High School Students	2,643
Elementary Students	11,419
Total Students under Catholic Instruction	18,917
Teachers in Diocese:	
Sisters	2
Lay Teachers	194

Vital Statistics

Receptions into the Church:	
Infant Baptism Totals	2,331
Minor Baptism Totals	193
Adult Baptism Totals	184
Received into Full Communion	149
First Communions	2,190
Confirmations	1,920
Marriages:	
Catholic	300
Interfaith	44
Total Marriages	344
Deaths	654
Total Catholic Population	340,476
Total Population	3,404,760

LEADERSHIP

Diocesan Pastoral Center - t) 801-328-8641

Office of the Bishop - t) (801) 328-8641 x304 Marylin Acosta, Exec. Asst.;

Vicar General and Moderator of the Curia - Rev. Msgr. Colin F. Bircumshaw;

Vicar for Clergy and Assistant Moderator of the Curia - Very Rev. Kenneth L. Vialpando;

Chancellor - deacon.reade@dioslc.org; toni.glenn@dioslc.org Dcn. George W. Reade, Chancellor; Toni Glenn, Asst. to Chancellor;

Vice Chancellor - Very Rev. Langes J. Silva;

Assistant to the Bishop - Rev. Msgr. J. Terrence Fitzgerald;

OFFICES AND DIRECTORS

Board For Ongoing Formation of Priests - t) (801) 328-8941 x102 Rev. Msgr. Colin F. Bircumshaw; Very Rev. Kenneth L. Vialpando; Rev. Joseph D. Delka;

Catholic Community Services - t) 801-977-9119 Bradford R. Drake, Exec. Dir.; Rev. John S. Evans, Pres.;

Catholic Foundation of Utah - t) 801-272-1025 (Howie Lemcke); (801) 456-9306 (Nevah Stevenson) Howard Lemcke, Pres. (howiel@howardlemcke.com); Nevah L. Stevenson, Exec. Dir. (nevah.stevenson@dioslc.org);

Catholic Relief Services -

Catholic Schools Offices - t) 801-456-9315 (Mark Longe); 801-456-9330 (Nikki Ward) Mark Longe, Supt. (mark.longe@dioslc.org); Nikki Ward, Asst. Supt. (nikki.ward@dioslc.org);

Cemetery--Mount Calvary - t) 801-355-2476 John Curtice, Dir.; Linda Quintana, Secy.;

Chancery - Dcn. George W. Reade, Chancellor; Toni Glenn, Asst.;

Records and Archives - t) 801-456-9346 michael.courtney@dioslc.org Michael Courtney, Dir.;

College of Consultors - Rev. Msgr. Colin F. Bircumshaw; Rev. Msgr. J. Terrence Fitzgerald; Very Rev. Kenneth L. Vialpando;

Correctional Institution Ministry - t) 801-782-5393 (Chap., Utah State Prison); 435-896-5539 (Chap., Central Utah Correctional Facility, Gunnison); 801-913-5703 (Coord., Jail Min., Salt Lake Valley) Rev. Jose Fidel Barrera-Cruz, Chap., Central Utah Correctional Facility, Gunnison; Rev. Stephen M. Tilley, Chap., Utah State Prison; Dcn. Joaquin Mixco, Coord., Jail Ministry for Salt Lake Valley;

Deans - Very Rev. Dominic Briese, O.P., Dean - Wasatch Deanery; Rev. David J. Bittmenn, Dean - Southwestern Deanery; Very Rev. Christopher P. Gray, Dean - Salt Lake City Deanery;

Diaconate - t) 801-456-9362 (Dcn. Dodge); (801) 456-9397 (Dcn. Dillon) Dcn. Scott Dodge, Dir.; Dcn. Dale R. Dillon; Dcn. Bernardo Villar;

Diocesan Office for Persons with Disabilities - t) 801-456-9333 (Dolores Lopez); 801-456-9359 (Nell Cline) Dolores Lopez, Dir.; Nell Cline, Asst.;

Diocesan Pastoral Council - Most Rev. Oscar A. Solis, Bishop of Salt Lake City; Rev. Msgr. Colin F. Bircumshaw, Vicar General & Moderator of the Curia; Rev. Adrian Komar;

Diocesan Stewardship and Development - t) 801-456-9328 shannon.lee@dioslc.org Shannon Lee, Dir.;

Ecumenical Commission - Rev. Msgr. Joseph M. Mayo; Very Rev. Langes J. Silva; Very Rev. Martin L. Diaz;

Engaged Encounter - t) 801-214-8220 Veola Burchett, Coord.; Ken Burchett, Coord.;

Faith Formation - t) 801-456-9326 susan.northway@dioslc.org Susan Northway, Dir.;

Family Life-Natural Family Planning - t) 801-456-9324 crystal.painter@dioslc.org Crystal Painter, Dir.;

Finance Council - Rev. Msgr. Colin F. Bircumshaw, Vicar General; Dcn. George W. Reade, Chancellor; Candice Greenwald, CFO;

Finance Office - t) 801-456-9309 (Candice Greenwald); 801-456-9352 (Sarah Niemann) candice.greenwald@dioslc.org; sarah.niemann@dioslc.org Candice Greenwald, CFO; Sarah Niemann, Senior Accountant;

Government Liaison -

Hispanic Ministry - t) 801-456-9361 (Maria Cruz Gray); 801-456-9332 (Jacqueline Rivera) mariacruz.gray@dioslc.org; jacqueline.rivera@dioslc.org Maria-Cruz Gray, Dir.; Jacqueline Rivera, Secy.;

Holy Childhood Association - Dcn. George W. Reade, Dir.;

Liaison for Hispanic Priests - t) 801-255-8902 Rev. Javier G. Virgen, Liaison for Hispanic Priests;

Life, Peace and Justice Commission -

Liturgical Commission - t) (801) 544-4269 (Rev. Vidal); (801) 456-9363 (Ruth Dillon) Rev. Gustavo Vidal, Chair; Ruth Dillon, Staff Liaison;

Native American Ministry - Dolores Lopez;

Newspaper - t) 801-456-9340 (Marie Mischel); 801-456-9341 (Linda Petersen); 801-456-9356 (Arthur Heredia) Marie Mischel, Editor; Arthur Heredia, Business Mgr.; Linda Petersen, Assoc. Editor;

Office of Worship - t) 801-456-9363 (Ruth Dillon); 801-456-9357 (Corina Pace) ruth.dillon@dioslc.org; corina.pace@dioslc.org Ruth Dillon, Dir.; Corina Pace, Secy.;

Presbyteral Council - t) 801-942-5285 fr.john.evans@gmail.com Rev. John S. Evans, Pres.; Rev. Adrian Komar, Vice. Pres.; Rev. Joseph D. Delka, Secy.;

Priests' Mutual Benefit Society (Retirement) - Most Rev. Oscar A. Solis, Chair; Rev. John S. Evans, Dir.; Rev. Msgr. Joseph M. Mayo, Bd. Dir.;

Priests' Personnel Board - Most Rev. Oscar A. Solis, Pres.; Rev. Msgr. Colin F. Bircumshaw; Rev. Msgr. J. Terrence Fitzgerald;

Real Estate Office - Dcn. George W. Reade, Chancellor; Toni Glenn, Asst.;

Sisters' Council - Sr. Genevra Rolf, C.S.C., Episcopal Liaison for Women Rel.; Sr. Catherine Kamphaus, C.S.C., Pres.; Sr. Mary Ann Pajakowski, C.S.C., Secy.;

Skaggs Tuition Assistance Program for Catholic Schools - t) 801-456-9347 sr.genevra@dioslc.org Sr. Genevra Rolf, C.S.C.;

Society for the Propagation of the Faith - Dcn. George W. Reade, Dir.; Toni Glenn, Asst.;

Tribunal -

Judicial Vicar - t) 801-456-9312 fr.silva@dioslc.org Very Rev. Langes J. Silva, Judicial Vicar;

Secretary and Notary - t) 801-456-9316 terri.gioffre@dioslc.org Terri Gioffre, Secy.;

Promoter of Justice - Rev. Msgr. J. Terrence Fitzgerald;

Defenders of the Bond - Rev. Msgr. Joseph M. Mayo; Rev. Robert Herbst, O.F.M. Conv.;

Judges - Very Rev. Langes J. Silva, Diocesan Judicial Vicar & Vice Chancellor; Ashley Voeller; Patricia Ruiz;

Court-Appointed Experts - Mary Iverson;

Assessor - Patricia Ruiz;

Victim Assistance Coordinator and Safe Environment - t) (801) 456-9324 crystal.painter@dioslc.org Crystal Painter, Dir.;

Vocation Office - t) 801-253-6031 (Rev. Delka); (801) 487-1000 (Rev. Sternhagen); (801) 456-9398 (Dcn. Espinoza) Rev. Joseph D. Delka, Dir.; Rev. Dominic Sternhagen, Assoc. Dir.; Dcn. Sunday S. Espinoza, Office Mgr.;

Youth and Young Adult Ministry -

PARISHES, MISSIONS, AND CLERGY

STATE OF UTAH

AMERICAN FORK

Saint Peter LLC 242 - 634 N. 600 E., American Fork, UT 84003; Mailing: 622 N. 600 East, American Fork, UT 84003 t) 801-756-2747 (CRP); 801-756-7771 stpeters6@yahoo.com Rev. Ariel F Durian, C.S., Admin.; CRP Stds.: 118

Eagle Mountain -

BOUNTIFUL

Saint Olaf LLC 239 - 276 E. 1700 S., Bountiful, UT 84010 t) 801-295-3621 jennifer@stolafut.org www.stolafut.org Rev. Andrzej Skrzypiec, Pst.; Dcn. Scott Dodge; CRP Stds.: 50

Saint Olaf LLC 239 School - (Grades K-8) 1793 S. Orchard Dr., Bountiful, UT 84010 t) 801-295-5341 saintolaf@saintolaf.net stolafs.org Kathy Dorich, Librn.;

BRIGHAM CITY

Saint Henry LLC 225 - 380 S. 200 E., Brigham City, UT 84302 t) 435-723-2941 sthenrys@comcast.org Rev. Francisco Pires, Pst.; Dcn. Andy Hunnel; Dcn. Karl E. Meyersick; CRP Stds.: 93

Santa Ana - 760 W. 600 N., Tremonton, UT 84337; Mailing: 380 S 200 E, Brigham City, UT 84302 t) 435-257-0701 sthenrys@comcast.net

CEDAR CITY

Christ the King LLC 203 - 690 S. Cove Dr., Cedar City, UT 84720 t) 435-586-8298 ctkdre@gmail.com; ctk@skyviewmail.com christthekingutah.org Rev. Adrian Komar, Pst.; Dcn. Denny Davies; Dcn. Carlos Mendez; Miriam Nowak, DRE; CRP Stds.: 136

St. Gertrude -

St. Sylvester -

St. Dominic -

CENTRAL VALLEY

Saint Elizabeth LLC 220 - 815 N. SR 118, Central Valley, UT 84754 t) 435-896-5539 mcgod.is.love@gmail.com Rev. Manuel de Jesus Ceron Valdez, Pst.; CRP Stds.: 13

St. Anthony of the Desert - North on Sandcreek Rd., Torrey, UT 84775 c) 435-851-2268

St. Jude - 160 E. Center St., Ephraim, UT 84627

San Juan Diego Mission - 25 W. Center St., Gunnison, UT 84634

COPPERTON

Immaculate Conception LLC 206 - 8892 W. State Hwy., Copperton, UT 84006; Mailing: P.O Box 151, Copperton, UT 84006 t) 801-569-2706 icpcopperton@gmail.com immaculateconceptionparish.net Greg Schindler, Admin.; Christy Kelley, DRE; Heidi Madill, Bus. Mgr.; CRP Stds.: 9

COTTONWOOD HEIGHTS

Saint Thomas More Catholic Church LLC 248 - 3015 E Creek Rd, Cottonwood Heights, UT 84093-6575 t) 801-942-5285 parish@stmutah.org stmutah.org Rev. John S. Evans, Pst.; Dcn. John Keyser; Dcn. Mark E. Solak; CRP Stds.: 77

DRAPER

Saint John the Baptist LLC 252 - 300 E. 11800 S., Draper, UT 84020 t) 801-984-7101 office@sjb-parish.org; fatihformation@sjb-parish.org www.sjb-parish.org Rev. Stephen Tilley, Pst.; Rev. Msgr. Terence M. Moore, Pastor Emer.; Dcn. Jeremy Castellano; Nancy K. Lefort, DRE; CRP Stds.: 796

EUREKA

Saint Patrick LLC 257 - 121 Church St, Eureka, UT 84628; Mailing: P.O. Box 387, Payson, UT 84651 Rev. Jose Gregorio Rausseo Gomez, Pst.;

HELPER

Saint Anthony of Padua Catholic Church LLC 216 - 5 S. Main, Helper, UT 84526-1533 t) 435-472-5661 (Rectory); 435-472-8367 (CRP) akileo@ubtanet.com Rev. Albert Noepachio Kileo, A.L.C.P. (Tanzania), Pst.; Pam Felice, DRE;

HYDE PARK

Saint Thomas Aquinas LLC 247 - 725 S. 250 E., Hyde

Park, UT 84318 t) 435-752-1478 stthomas2006@gmail.com stthomaslogan.org Rev. Rogelio Felix-Rosas (Mexico), Admin.; Rev. Robin Pena Cruz (Philippines), Par. Vicar; Dcn. James P. Miller; CRP Stds.: 353

Utah State University (Saint Jerome Newman Center) - 795 N. 800 E., Logan, UT 84321 t) 435-753-7670 usunewmanleadership@gmail.com Rev. Joshua Maria Santos, Chap.;

KANAB

Saint Christopher LLC 219 - 39 W. 200 South, Kanab, UT 84741 t) 435-644-3414 stchristopherscathchurch@xpressweb.com kanabcatholicchurch.org/ Rev. David J. Bittmenn, Pst.; Rev. Richard T. Sherman, Sacr. Min.;

KEARNS

Saint Francis Xavier LLC 222 - 4501 W. 5215 S., Kearns, UT 84118 t) 801-968-2123 x121 sainfrancisxavier@sfxkearns.org sfxkearns.org Rev. Eugenio Yarce, Pst.; CRP Stds.: 638

Our Lady of Perpetual Help LLC 261 - 4360 W. 5415 S., Kearns, UT 84118 t) 801-968-8981 oloph2018@gmail.com vietnamcatholicslc.org (Vietnamese Parish) Rev. Tai Nguyen, Pst.; CRP Stds.: 120

LAYTON

Saint Rose of Lima LLC 245 - 210 S. Chapel St., Layton, UT 84041; Mailing: P.O. Box 557, Layton, UT 84041 t) 801-544-4269; 801-544-5425 (CRP) church@stroseut.org; kevin.cummings@stroseut.org www.stroseoflimacatholic.net Rev. Gustavo Vidal, Pst.; Dcn. Bernardo Villar; Kevin Cummings, DRE; CRP Stds.: 238

MAGNA

Our Lady of Lourdes LLC 209 - 2840 S. 9000 W., Magna, UT 84044; Mailing: P.O. Box 38, 2840 S. 9000 W., Magna, UT 84044 t) 801-508-1595 ololmagna@gmail.com Catholic Church Rev. Kelechi Alozie (Nigeria), Pst.; Dcn. Carlos Cortez; CRP Stds.: 150

MIDVALE

Saint Therese of the Child Jesus LLC 246 - 7832 S. Allen St., Midvale, UT 84047 t) 801-255-3721 stthereses.parish@gmail.com www.stcj.org Rev. Jose Alberto Barrera, Pst.; Dcn. Rubel J. Salaz; Dcn. Stanley L. Stott;

MILFORD

Saint Bridget LLC 217 - 210 S. 1st W., Milford, UT 84751; Mailing: P.O. Box 785, Milford, UT 84751 t) 435-864-3710 Rev. Marco T. Lopez, Pst.;

St. John Bosco - 96 S. Center, Delta, UT 84624; Mailing: P.O. Box 924, Delta, UT 84624

Holy Family - 445 S. 200 E., Fillmore, UT 84631; Mailing: P.O. Box 292, Fillmore, UT 84631 t) 801-835-6449

MOAB

Saint Pius X LLC 244 - 122 W. 400 N., Moab, UT 84532; Mailing: P.O. Box 636, Moab, UT 84532 c) 385-214-4592 piusx@frontiernet.net Rev. Rowland Nwokocha (Nigeria), Pst.; CRP Stds.: 8

Sacred Heart - Hwy. 46/Main, LaSal, UT 84530 c) (435) 259-5211

MONTICELLO

Saint Joseph LLC 229 - 385 S. Main, Monticello, UT 84535; Mailing: P.O. Box 518, Monticello, UT 84535 t) (385) 259-5211 piusx@frontiernet.net Rev. Rowland Nwokocha (Nigeria), Pst.; CRP Stds.: 2

Station -

MURRAY

Saint Jude LLC - 4893 Wasatch St., Murray, UT 84107 t) 801-268-2820 father.joubran@hotmail.com Rev. Joubran Boumerhi, Pst.; Waddell Goins, DRE;

OGDEN

Holy Family LLC 205 - 1100 E. 5550 S., Ogden, UT 84403 t) 801-479-1112 hfcre@hfutah.org; hfcc@hfutah.org holyfamilycatholicchurch.org Rev. Joseph M Minuth, O.P., Pst.; Dcn. Douglas B. Smith; Carl Leuschner, DRE; CRP Stds.: 61

Saint James the Just LLC 226 - 495 N. Harrison Blvd., Ogden, UT 84404 t) 801-782-5393 stjames_dre@comcast.net; stjames_secretary@comcast.net www.stjamescatholic.com Rev. David Trujillo, Pst.; Eileen Hollywood, DRE; CRP Stds.: 127

Saint Joseph LLC 230 - 514 24th St., Ogden, UT 84401; Mailing: 2350 Adams Ave., Ogden, UT 84401 t) 801-399-5627 mariagandara55@msn.com; frjoshuas.stambrose@gmail.com www.stjosephogden.org/home Rev. Joshua Maria Santos, Admin.; Rev. Charles T. Cummins, Assoc. Pst.; Rev. Oscar Manuel Hernandez-Hernandez (El Salvador), Par. Vicar; Dcn. Honorio Moreno; Dcn. Howard Schuyler; CRP Stds.: 391

St. Florence - 6481 E. Hwy. 39, Huntsville, UT 84317; Mailing: 2350 Adams Ave, Ogden, UT 84401 frmike@utahweb.com stflorence.wordpress.com/ Dcn. Terrance Waiss;

OREM

St. Francis of Assisi LLC 221 - 65 E. 500 N., Orem, UT 84057-4030 t) 801-221-0750; 801-221-0750 x16 (CRP) parish@oremstfrancis.org www.oremstfrancis.org Rev. Eleazar Silva, Pst.; Rev. Anil Kumar Kakumanu (India), Assoc. Pst.; Dcn. Julio Palomino; Dcn. Vincente Vasquez; CRP Stds.: 876

PARK CITY

Saint Mary of the Assumption LLC 238 - 1505 W. White Pine Canyon Rd., Park City, UT 84060 t) 435-649-9676 sfoley@stmarysparkcity.com www.stmarysparkcity.com Very Rev. Christopher P. Gray, Pst.; Rev. Noel Ancheta, Par. Vicar; Dcn. Robert H. Hardy; Dcn. Tom Tosti; Sandy Foley, Admin.; CRP Stds.: 656

St. Lawrence - 1st West Center, Heber City, UT 84032 t) 435-654-4035 Rachel LeMelle, Admin.;

PAYSON

San Andres LLC 212 - 315 E. 100 N., Payson, UT 84651; Mailing: P.O. Box 387, Payson, UT 84651 t) 801-465-4782 utsanandres.org Rev. Jose Gregorio Rausseo Gomez, Pst.;

San Isidro - www.utsanandres.org

PRICE

Good Shepherd LLC 204 - 185 N. Carbon Ave., c/o Notre Dame de Lourdes, Price, UT 84501 t) 435-637-1846 notredame@emerytelcom.net notredameprice.com Rev. Arokia Dass David, Pst.; Catherine Kane, DRE;

St. Michael - 140 N. Long St., Green River, UT 84525; Mailing: 185 N Carbon Ave, Price, UT 84501

Notre Dame de Lourdes LLC 207 - 210 N. Carbon Ave., Price, UT 84501; Mailing: 185 N. Carbon Ave., Price, UT 84501-2402 t) 435-637-1846 c) 435-630-0815 notredame@emerytelcom.net www.notredameprice.com Rev. Arokia Dass David, Pst.; Catherine Kane, DRE; CRP Stds.: 111

San Rafael - 1716 S. Hwy. 10, Huntington, UT 84528; Mailing: c/o Notre Dame de Lourdes 185 N Carbon Ave, Price, UT 84501 notredameprice.com Rev. Rafael A. Murillo, Pst.;

RIVERTON

Saint Andrew Catholic Church LLC 233 - 11835 S. 3600 W., Riverton, UT 84065 t) 801-253-6030; 801-253-6031 (CRP) secretary@standrewut.com; fr.delkaslc@gmail.com www.standrewut.com Rev. Joseph D. Delka, Pst.; Mariana Rodriguez, DRE; Dcn. Michael E. Bulson; Dcn. Duane Padilla; CRP Stds.: 133

ROOSEVELT

Saint Helen LLC 224 - 433 E. 200 North, Roosevelt, UT 84066; Mailing: P.O. Box 415, Roosevelt, UT 84066 t) 435-722-2975 sainthelencatholic@gmail.com Rev. Edward Leondhas (India), Admin.; CRP Stds.: 27

Saint Kateri Tekakwitha Catholic Mission - 915 S. 7500 E., Fort Duchesne, UT 84026; Mailing: Saint Helen's Catholic Church, P.O. Box 415, Roosevelt, UT 84066 Rev. Kakumanu Anil Kumar, Admin.;

SALT LAKE CITY

Cathedral of the Madeleine LLC 202 - 331 E. S. Temple St., Salt Lake City, UT 84111 t) 801-328-8941 x101 (CRP); 801-328-8941 dallred@utcotm.org; mdiaz@utcotm.org utcotm.org Very Rev. Martin L. Diaz, Pst.; Rev. Alfredo Valdez, Par. Vicar; Dcn. John Kranz; Dcn. Guillermo Mendez; Dcn. Drew Petersen; CRP Stds.: 110

Madeleine Choir School - (Grades PreK-8) 205 E. 1st Ave., Salt Lake City, UT 84103 t) 801-323-9850 gglenn@utmcs.org www.utmcs.org Gregory A. Glenn, Admin.;

Good Samaritan Program - Patricia Wesson, Dir.;

Saint Ambrose LLC 214 - 1975 S. 2300 East, Salt Lake City, UT 84108; Mailing: 2315 E Redondo Ave, Salt Lake City, UT 84108 t) 801-485-9324 (CRP); 801-485-5610 (Office) paroff@xmission.com www.stambrosecatholicchurch.org Rev. Erik J. Richtsteig, Pst.; Dcn. John Bash; Dcn. Steve Neveraski; CRP Stds.: 77

J. E. Cosgriff Memorial School - (Grades PreK-8) 2335 Redondo Ave., Salt Lake City, UT 84108 t) 801-486-3197 bhunt@cosgriff.org www.cosgriff.org Lisa Romero, Prin.; Heather Kirby, Librn.; Stds.: 370; Scholastics: 7; Lay Tchrs.: 29

Saint Ann LLC 215 - 450 E. 2100 S., Salt Lake City, UT 84115-2872; Mailing: 2119 S. 400 E., Salt Lake City, UT 84115-2872 t) 801-487-1000 pastor@ksaschool.org; parishsecretary@ksaschool.org www.saintannsaltlakecity.com/ Rev. Dominic Sternhagen, Pst.; CRP Stds.: 207

Saint Ann LLC 215 School - (Grades PreK-8) 430 E. 2100 S., Salt Lake City, UT 84105 t) 801-486-0741 snakaba@ksaschool.org; drichardson@ksaschool.org www.ksaschool.org

Saint Catherine of Siena Catholic Newman Center LLC 218 - 170 S. University St., Salt Lake City, UT 84102 t) 801-359-6066 office@stcatherineslc.org stcatherineslc.org Rev. Gabriel T. Mosher, O.P., Pst.; Rev. Cody Jorgensen, O.P., Campus Min.; Rev. Jacek Buda, OP, In Res.;

Our Lady of Guadalupe LLC 208 - 715 W. 300 N., Salt Lake City, UT 84116; Mailing: 257 N. 700 W., Salt Lake City, UT 84116 t) 801-364-2019 ologsecretary@gmail.com Rev. Jorge Roldan, Pst.; Dcn. Moises Ruiz, Sacr. Min.; CRP Stds.: 325

Our Lady of Lourdes LLC 211 - 670 S. 1100 East, Salt Lake City, UT 84102; Mailing: 1085 E. 700 South, Salt Lake City, UT 84102 t) 801-322-3330 sketcham@lourdesschool.org Rev. Anil Kumar Kakumanu (India), Pst.; CRP Stds.: 7

Our Lady of Lourdes LLC 211 School - (Grades K-8) 1065 E. 700 S. St., Salt Lake City, UT 84102 t) 801-364-5624 tbergquist@lourdesschool.org; gpoteracki@lourdesschool.org lourdesschool.org Christine Bergquist, Prin.;

Saint Patrick LLC 241 - 1058 W. 400 S., Salt Lake City, UT 84104-1261 t) 801-596-7233 stpatoffice@comcast.net stpatrickslc.org Rev. Anastasius Iwuoha (Nigeria), Pst.; Dcn. Sefo A. Manu; CRP Stds.: 59

Sacred Heart LLC 210 - 174 E. 900 South, Salt Lake City, UT 84111; Mailing: 946 S. 200 East, Salt Lake City, UT 84111 t) 801-363-8632 sacredheart210@gmail.com sacredheartslc.business.site/ Rev. Roberto Montoro (Mexico), Pst.; Dcn. German A. Toro; Dcn. Manuel Ceron Velez; Ana Mazariegos, DRE; CRP Stds.: 208

Saint Vincent de Paul LLC 250 - 1375 E. Spring Ln., Salt Lake City, UT 84117 t) 801-272-9216; 801-527-2037 (CRP) parishoffice@stvincents-school.org; utahcatholic@gmail.com saintvincent.us.com Rev. Samuel Dinsdale, Pst.; Rev. Msgr. M. Francis Mannion, Pastor Emer.; Dcn. Jeffrey James Allen; CRP Stds.: 51

Saint Vincent de Paul LLC 250 School - (Grades PreK-8) 1385 E. Spring Ln., Salt Lake City, UT 84117 t) 801-277-6702 ggreen@stvincents-school.org Gary Green, Prin.;

SANDY

Blessed Sacrament LLC 201 - 9757 S. 1700 E., Sandy, UT 84092 t) 801-571-5517 blessedsacramentsandy@gmail.com blessedsacramentsandy.org Rev. Rodelio Santos Ignacio (Philippines), Admin.; Dcn. Greg Werking; Dcn. Marcel

Soklaski; Donna Anderson, Pst. Assoc.; Michelle Beasley, DRE; CRP Stds.: 123

Blessed Sacrament LLC 201 School - (Grades PreSchool-8) 1745 E. 9800 S., Sandy, UT 84092 t) 801-572-5311 bpenn@blessedsacschool.org www.blessedsacschool.org Bryan Penn, Prin.; Stds.: 149; Lay Tchrs.: 8

Our Lady of the Snows -

ST. GEORGE

St. George LLC 223 - 259 W. 200 N., St. George, UT 84770; Mailing: P.O. Box 188, St. George, UT 84771 t) 435-673-2604 office@sgcatholics.com www.saintgeorgecatholics.com Rev. David J. Bittmenn, Pst.; Rev. Tristan P. A. Dillon, Par. Vicar; Dcn. Rigoberto Aquirre; Dcn. Douglas C. Biediger; Dcn. Jesse Robles; Dcn. Rogaciano Tellez; CRP Stds.: 403

Zion National Park -

Saint Paul Catholic Center - 171 S. Main, Hurricane, UT 84737

San Pablo -

TAYLORSVILLE

Saint Martin de Porres LLC 236 - 4914 S. 2200 West, Taylorsville, UT 84129; Mailing: 4976 Valois Cir., Taylorsville, UT 84129 t) 801-968-2369 fatherbriese@gmail.com www.stmartincatholicchurch.com Very Rev. Dominic Briese, O.P., Admin.; Guadalupe Vasquez Gonzalez, DRE; Dcn. Joaquin Mixco; CRP Stds.: 152

TOOELE

St. Marguerite LLC 235 - 15 S. 7th St., Tooele, UT 84074 t) 435-882-3860 stmarguerite1910@gmail.com Rev. Rafael A. Murillo, Admin.; CRP Stds.: 121

St. Marguerite LLC 235 School - (Grades PreK-8) t) 435-882-0081 stmargschool.org Trisha Kirkbride, Prin.;

VERNAL

Saint James the Greater LLC 227 - 138 N. 100 West St., Vernal, UT 84078 t) 435-789-3034 (CRP); 435-789-3016 stjamesvernal@gmail.com Rev. Showri Rayalu Kalva, Pst.; CRP Stds.: 34

WENDOVER

San Felipe LLC 251 - 606 E. Aria Blvd., Wendover, UT 84083; Mailing: P.O. Box 1270, Wendover, UT 84083 t) 435-406-9610; 435-665-2339 (CRP) info@sanfelipecatholicchurch.com Dcn. Daniel Carillo-Saldana, Admin.; CRP Stds.: 64

WEST HAVEN

Saint Mary LLC 237 - 4050 S. 3900 W., West Haven, UT 84401 t) 801-621-7961; 801-391-8655 (CRP) erika@stmarysutah.org; safeenvir@stmarysutha.org www.stmarysutah.org Rev. Oscar Martin Picos, Pst.; Joe Rodrigues, DRE; Dcn. Jack Clark; Dcn. Thom Rodgers; CRP Stds.: 225

WEST JORDAN

Saint Joseph the Worker LLC 232 - 7405 S Redwood Rd., West Jordan, UT 84084 t) 801-251-1236 (CRP); 801-255-8902 office@sjtwchurch.org www.sjtwchurch.org Rev. Javier G. Virgen, Pst.; Dcn. Sunday S. Espinoza; Dcn. Armando Solorzano; Edgar Sosa, Admin.; Melissa Castellano, DRE; CRP Stds.: 157

WEST VALLEY CITY

Saints Peter and Paul LLC 243 - 3560 W 3650 S, West Valley City, UT 84119 t) 801-966-5111; 801-966-5111 x202 (CRP) stpeterpaul@live.com Rev. Sebastien Sasa Nganomo Babisayone, Admin.; Dcn. George J. Sluga; CRP Stds.: 380

SCHOOLS: PRESCHOOL THRU HIGH SCHOOL

SCHOOLS

STATE OF UTAH

KEARNS

St. Francis Xavier Regional School - (PAR) (Grades PreK-8) 4501 W. 5215 S., Kearns, UT 84118 t) 801-966-1571 mrozsahegyi@stfxcs.org; lzamora@stfxcs.org stfrancisxavierschool.org Heather Brown, Prin.; Stds.: 212; Lay Tchrs.: 12

OGDEN

St. Joseph Catholic Elementary School - (PAR) (Grades PreSchool-8) 2980 Quincy Ave., Ogden, UT 84403 t) 801-393-6051 nessary@stjosephutah.com www.stjosephutah.com/es Nancy Essary, Prin.; Stds.: 376; Lay Tchrs.: 19

HIGH SCHOOLS

STATE OF UTAH

DRAPER

Juan Diego Catholic High School, Skaggs Catholic Center, LLC - (DIO) (Grades 9-12) 300 E. 11800 S., Draper, UT 84020 t) 801-984-7650 drgaleycolosimo@skaggscatholiccenter.org www.jdchs.org Gabriel Colosimo, Prin.; Stds.: 682; Lay Tchrs.: 48

OGDEN

St. Joseph Catholic High School - (DIO) (Grades 9-12) 1790 Lake St., Ogden, UT 84401 t) 801-394-1515 clayjones@stjosephutah.com www.stjosephutah.org Clay Jones, Prin.; Stds.: 173; Lay Tchrs.: 28

SALT LAKE CITY

Judge Memorial Catholic High School - (DIO) 650 S. 1100 E., Salt Lake City, UT 84102 t) 801-517-2188 plambert@judgememorial.com; rjames@judgememorial.com www.judgememorial.com Day School. (Coed) Patrick Lambert, Prin.; Stds.: 537; Scholastics: 8; Lay Tchrs.: 50

INSTITUTIONS LOCATED IN DIOCESE

CAMPUS MINISTRY / NEWMAN CENTERS [CAM]

EPHRAIM

St. Jude Catholic Center - 160 E Center St, Ephraim, UT 84627 t) 435-283-6242 stecatholicparish@gmail.com Dcn. Fernando Montano;

OGDEN

Weber State University, Newman Center - 3738 Custer Ave., Ogden, UT 84403 t) 801-399-9531 judyfranquelin@aol.com Rev. Charles T. Cummins, Dir.;

SALT LAKE CITY

University of Utah, Newman Center - 170 S. University St., Salt Lake City, UT 84102 t) 801-359-6066 office@stcatherineslc.org www.stcatherineslc.org (St. Catherine of Siena Catholic Newman Center) Rev. Cody Jorgensen, O.P., Campus Min.;

CATHOLIC CHARITIES [CCH]

SALT LAKE CITY

Catholic Community Services of Utah - 224 N. 2200 West, Salt Lake City, UT 84116 t) 801-977-9119 cmecklenburg@ccsutah.org; mbosgieter@ccsutah.org www.ccsutah.org Bradford R. Drake, CEO; Asstd. Annu.: 19,929; Staff: 145

Basic Needs Ogden Joyce Hansen Hall Food Bank, St. Martha's Baby Layette Project, Bridging the Gap - 2504 F. Ave., Ogden, UT 84401 t) 801-394-5944 www.ccsnorthernutah.org

Homeless Services - St. Vincent de Paul Dining Hall, Bishop K. Weigand Homeless Resource Center - 437 W. 200 S., Salt Lake City, UT 84104 t) 801-363-7710 rchappell@ccsutah.org Dcn. George W. Reade, Chancellor;

Refugee Resettlement, Immigration Services, Refugee Fostercare - abatar@ccsutah.org Dcn. George W. Reade, Chancellor;

Holy Cross Ministries - 860 E. 4500 S., Ste. 204, Salt Lake City, UT 84107 t) 801-261-3440 egardner@hcmutah.org www.holycrossministries.org Social Service Agency Emmie Gardner, CEO; Asstd. Annu.: 3,311; Staff: 32

CEMETERIES [CEM]

SALT LAKE CITY

Mount Calvary Catholic - 275 U St., Salt Lake City, UT 84103 t) 801-355-2476 john.curtice@dioslc.org John Curtice, Dir.;

CONVENTS, MONASTERIES, AND RESIDENCES FOR WOMEN [CON]

DRAPER

Congregation of the Sisters of the Holy Cross, Vivian Skaggs Armstrong Convent - 554 E. 11800 S., Draper, UT 84020 t) 801-501-8349 celinedounies@sjbelementary.org; patrice6250@gmail.com Marianne Farina, Supr.; Srs.: 1

PARK CITY

Congregation of the Sisters of the Holy Cross - 3221 Homestead Rd., Park City, UT 84098 t) 435-655-7980 mpajakowski@hcmutah.org Sisters of the Holy Cross, Inc. Marianne Farina, Supr.; Srs.: 4

SALT LAKE CITY

***Carmel of the Immaculate Heart of Mary Monastery** - 5714 Holladay Blvd., Salt Lake City, UT 84121 t) 801-277-6075 carmelsl@xmission.com www.carmelslc.org Mother Therese Bui, OCD, Prioress; Srs.: 12

Our Lady of Lourdes Convent - 675 S. 1100 E., Salt Lake City, UT 84102 t) 801-583-1204 sbrennan@cscsisters.org Marianne Farina, Supr.; Srs.: 2

ENDOWMENTS / FOUNDATIONS / TRUSTS

[EFT]

SALT LAKE CITY

Catholic Foundation of Utah - 27 C St., Salt Lake City, UT 84103 t) 801-456-9306; 801-328-8641 x306 nevah.stevenson@dioslc.org www.dioslc.org/foundation Rev. John E. Norman, Pres.; Nevah L. Stevenson, Exec.;

MISCELLANEOUS [MIS]

DRAPER

Skaggs Catholic Center LLC - 300 E. 11800 S., Draper, UT 84020 t) 801-984-7100; 801-984-7654 jocendagorta@skaggscatholiccenter.org www.skaggscatholiccenter.org Erin Carrabba, Prin.; Gabriel Colosimo, Prin.; Patrick Reeder, Prin.; Jo Cendagorta, Dir.;

OGDEN

Give Me A Chance, Inc. - 2913 Grant Ave., Ogden, UT 84401-3614 t) 801-627-2235 srarthurg@yahoo.com www.givemeachanceutah.org

SALT LAKE CITY

Catholic Diocese of Salt Lake City Capital Development Corporation - 27 C St., Salt Lake City, UT 84103 t) 801-328-8641 toni.glenn@dioslc.org Dcn. George W. Reade, Chancellor;

Catholic Diocese of Salt Lake City Real Estate Corporation - 27 C St., Salt Lake City, UT 84103 t) 801-328-8641 toni.glenn@dioslc.org Dcn. George W. Reade, Chancellor;

Ministries of the Catholic Diocese of Salt Lake City LLC - 27 C St., Salt Lake City, UT 84103 t) 801-328-8641 toni.glenn@dioslc.org Dcn. George W. Reade, Chancellor;

An asterisk (*) denotes an organization that has established tax-exempt status directly with the IRS and is not covered by the USCCB Group Ruling.

Diocese of San Angelo

(Dioecesis Angeliana)

MOST REVEREND MICHAEL J. SIS

Bishop of San Angelo; ordained July 19, 1986; appointed Bishop of San Angelo December 12, 2013; consecrated and installed January 27, 2014. Mailing Address: P.O. Box 1829, San Angelo, TX 76902.

The Chancery: P.O. Box 1829, San Angelo, TX 76902. T: 325-651-7500; F: 325-651-6688. www.sanangelodiocese.org

ESTABLISHED OCTOBER 16, 1961.

Square Miles 37,433.

Comprises 29 Counties in the State of Texas as follows: Andrews, Brown, Callahan, Coke, Coleman, Concho, Crane, Crockett, Ector, Glasscock, Howard, Irion, Kimble, McCulloch, Martin, Menard, Midland, Mitchell, Nolan, Pecos, Reagan, Runnells, Schleicher, Sterling, Sutton, Taylor, Terrell, Tom Green and Upton.

For legal title of parishes and diocesan institutions, consult the Chancery Office.

STATISTICAL OVERVIEW

Personnel
Bishop....1
Retired Bishops....1
Priests: Diocesan Active in Diocese....36
Priests: Diocesan Active Outside Diocese....3
Priests: Retired, Sick or Absent....11
Number of Diocesan Priests....50
Religious Priests in Diocese....8
Total Priests in your Diocese....58
Extern Priests in Diocese....12
Ordinations:
Permanent Deacons....16
Permanent Deacons in Diocese....82
Total Brothers....3
Total Sisters....12

Parishes
Parishes....45
With Resident Pastor:
Resident Diocesan Priests....35
Resident Religious Priests....2
Without Resident Pastor:
Administered by Priests....8
Missions....22
Closed Parishes....1
Professional Ministry Personnel:
Sisters....12
Lay Ministers....40

Welfare
Day Care Centers....1
Total Assisted....30
Special Centers for Social Services....11
Total Assisted....63,382

Educational
Diocesan Students in Other Seminaries....11
Total Seminarians....11
High Schools, Private....1
Total Students....70
Elementary Schools, Diocesan and Parish....3
Total Students....724
Catechesis/Religious Education:
High School Students....2,174
Elementary Students....5,650
Total Students under Catholic Instruction....8,629
Teachers in Diocese:
Sisters....3
Lay Teachers....69

Vital Statistics
Receptions into the Church:
Infant Baptism Totals....1,195
Minor Baptism Totals....213
Adult Baptism Totals....72
Received into Full Communion....126
First Communions....1,333
Confirmations....1,046
Marriages:
Catholic....218
Interfaith....32
Total Marriages....250
Deaths....1,064
Total Catholic Population....118,792
Total Population....803,169

LEADERSHIP
Vicar General - t) 325-651-7500 x118 Very Rev. Santiago D. Udayar (sudayar@sanangelodiocese.org);
Chancellor - t) 915-651-7500 x132 Michael Wyse (mwyse@sanangelodiocese.org);
Diocesan Finance Officer - t) 325-651-7500 x146 Dcn. Marc Mata, CFO;
Judicial Vicar - t) 325-651-7500 x131 Very Rev. Tom Barley (tbarley@sanangelodiocese.org);

OFFICES AND DIRECTORS
Campaign for Human Development - t) (325) 651-7500 Michael Wyse (mwyse@sanangelodiocese.org);
Communications Office - t) 325-651-7500 x123 bbodiford@sanangelodiocese.org Brian Bodiford, Dir.;
Continuing Education of the Clergy - t) 325-651-7500 Rev. Msgr. Larry J. Droll (ldroll@sanangelodiocese.org);
Evangelization and Catechesis - t) (325) 651-7500 Alison Pope, Dir. (apope@sanangelodiocese.org);
Human Resources - t) 325-651-7500 x146 Dcn. Marc Mata, Dir.;
Immigration Services - t) (325) 212-6192 psantana@sanangelodiocese.org Patricia Stokes Santana, (Abilene, San Angelo, Midland);
Office for Religious - t) 210-827-8722 mfiller@sanangelodiocese.org Sr. Marjorie Filler, C.D.P., Dir.;
Newspaper - t) 325-651-7500 x123 bbodiford@sanangelodiocese.org Brian Bodiford, Editor;
Permanent Deacon Director - t) 325-651-7500 x127 Dcn. Federico Medina Jr. (fmedina@sanangelodiocese.org);
Permanent Deacon Formation - t) 325-651-7500 x127 Dcn. Federico Medina Jr. (fmedina@sanangelodiocese.org);
Prison Ministry - mmedina@sanangelodiocese.org Dcn. Michael Medina;
Pro-Life - jmoutdoorsmen@aol.com Jerry Michael Peters, Dir.;
Propagation of the Faith - t) (325) 651-7500 x135 Michael Wyse, Dir. (mwyse@sanangelodiocese.org);
Rural Life - t) 432-270-0569 fschwartz@sanangelodiocese.org Dcn. Floyd Schwartz, Dir.;
Schools - t) 432-684-4563 jwilmes@sanangelodiocese.org Joan Wilmes, Supt.;
Stewardship and Development - t) 325-651-7500 x145 koniha@sanangelodiocese.org Kelly Oniha;
Vicar for Priests - t) 325-651-7500 Rev. Msgr. Larry J. Droll (ldroll@sanangelodiocese.org);
Victim Assistance Coordinator - t) 325-651-7500 lhines@sanangelodiocese.org Lori Hines;
Vocation Office - t) 325-651-7500 x122 Rev. Ryan Rojo, Dir. (rrojo@sanangelodiocese.org);

ADVISORY BOARDS, COMMISSIONS, COMMITTEES, AND COUNCILS
Deans - Very Rev. Joseph Choutapalli, Dean (jchoutapalli@yahoo.com); Rev. Msgr. Frederick Nawarskas, Abilene Deanery (fnawarskas@sanangelodiocese.org); Very Rev. Rodney White, Midland-Odessa Deanery (rwhite@sanangelodiocese.org);
Diocesan Liturgical Commission - t) (325) 651-7500 lhines@sanangelodiocese.org Linda Dye, Mem.; Rev. Josh Gray, Mem. (jgray@sanangelodiocese.org); Lori Hines, Chair;
Diocesan Consultors - Rev. Patrick Akpanobong, Mem. (pakpanobong@sanangelodiocese.org); Rev. Felix Archibong, Mem. (farchibong@sanangelodiocese.org); Rev. Albert Ezeanya (Nigeria), Mem. (aezeanya@sanangelodiocese.org);
Priests' Personnel Board - Rev. Patrick Akpanobong, Mem. (pakpanobong@sanangelodiocese.org); Rev. Joseph Barbieri, Mem. (jbarbieri@sanangelodiocese.org); Very Rev. Joseph Choutapalli, Mem. (jchoutapalli@yahoo.com);
Presbyteral Council - Rev. Joseph Barbieri, Mem. (jbarbieri@sanangelodiocese.org); Very Rev. Tom Barley, Chair (tbarley@sanangelodiocese.org); Rev. Angel Alfredo Castro, MSP, Mem. (acastro@sanangelodiocese.org);
Priests' Pension Plan - Rev. Patrick Akpanobong, Mem. (pakpanobong@sanangelodiocese.org); Rev. Felix Archibong, Mem. (farchibong@sanangelodiocese.org); Very Rev. Tom Barley, Chair (tbarley@sanangelodiocese.org);

CANONICAL SERVICES
Case Manager/Ecclesiastical Notary - t) 325-651-7500 x137 mpayton@sanangelodiocese.org Mary Ellen Payton;
Defensores Vinculi - t) 325-651-7500 Thomas C. Burke (tburke@sanangelodiocese.org); Rev. Msgr. Larry J. Droll (ldroll@sanangelodiocese.org);
Promoter of Justice for Priest Cases - t) 325-651-7500 Rev. Joseph Barbieri (jbarbieri@sanangelodiocese.org);
Promoter of Justice for Marriage Cases - t) 325-651-7500 x124 Thomas C. Burke (tburke@sanangelodiocese.org);
Advocate for Respondents - t) 325-651-7500 x127 Dcn. Federico Medina Jr. (fmedina@sanangelodiocese.org);
Judges - t) (325) 651-7500 Rev. Joseph Barbieri (jbarbieri@sanangelodiocese.org); Very Rev. Tom Barley, Vicar (tbarley@sanangelodiocese.org); Very Rev. Santiago D. Udayar (sudayar@sanangelodiocese.org);

ORGANIZATIONS
Catholic Relief Services - t) (325) 212-8580 Rev. Freddy Perez, Contact;
Cursillos de Cristiandad - Francisco Estrada, Contact; Teresa Rico Miller, Contact;

PARISHES, MISSIONS, AND CLERGY

STATE OF TEXAS

ABILENE
St. Francis of Assisi - 826 Cottonwood St., Abilene, TX 79601 t) 325-672-6695 abilene.stfrancis@sanangelodiocese.org Rev. Innocent Eziefule, Pst.; Dcn. Marc P. Main; Dcn. Eduardo Castillo; Mary Newman, CRE; CRP Stds.: 71
Holy Family - 5410 Buffalo Gap Rd., Abilene, TX 79606; Mailing: P.O. Box 5970, Abilene, TX 79606 t) 325-692-1820 mail@holyfamilyabilene.org; abilene.holyfamily@sanangelodiocese.org www.holyfamilyabilene.org Very Rev. Adam Droll, Par. Admin.; Rev. Msgr. Frederick Nawarskas, Par. Vicar; Dcn. Daniel Vaughan; Dcn. Gary Rhodes; Dcn. Alonzo Landin; Dr. Bob Moore, DRE; Angela Garcia, Youth Min.; CRP Stds.: 298
Sacred Heart - 837 Jeanette St., Abilene, TX 79602-2410 t) 325-677-7951 abilene.sacredheart@sanangelodiocese.org www.sacredheartabilene.org/ Rev. Albert Ezeanya (Nigeria), Pst.; Dcn. Dwain Hennessey; Dcn. Ronald Stegenga; Maria Valdez, CRE; Stephen Valdez, CRE; Lydia Gonzales, Youth Min.; CRP Stds.: 57
 Sts. Joachim and Ann - N. 1st St. & Cherry St., Clyde, TX 79510; Mailing: 837 Jeanette St., Abilene, TX 79602 t) (325) 677-7951 clyde@sanangelodiocese.org Rev. Albert Ezeanya, Pst.;
 Sacred Heart Perpetual Adoration Chapel - 1541 S. 8th St., Abilene, TX 79602 t) 325-611-7951
St. Vincent Pallotti - 2525 Westview Dr., Abilene, TX 79603-2138 t) 325-672-1794 abilene.stvincent@sanangelodiocese.org Rev. Emilio Sosa, Pst.; Dcn. Victor Ramirez; Rosita Priest, CRE; Teresa A. Villarreal, Youth Min.; CRP Stds.: 160
 Our Mother of Mercy - 1300 S. Locust, Abilene, TX 79603-2138; Mailing: PO Box 206, Abilene, TX 79536-0206 t) 325-794-1632 merkel@sanangelodiocese.org Lorena Flores, CRE;

ANDREWS
Our Lady of Lourdes - 201 N.E. Ave. K, Andrews, TX 79714 t) 432-523-4215; 432-523-4968 andrews@sanangelodiocese.org; ollandrews@valornet.com Rev. Joseph Ogbonna (South Africa), Pst.; Mary Alice Morris, CRE; Larissa Sanchez, Youth Min.; CRP Stds.: 269

BALLINGER
St. Mary Star of the Sea - 605 N. 5th St., Ballinger, TX 76821 t) 325-365-2687 ballinger@sanangelodiocese.org Rev. Timothy Hayter, Par. Admin.; Dcn. Claudio Sanchez; Michelle Aguilera, CRE; Phoebe Ann Branham, CRE; Elke Hughes, Youth Min.; CRP Stds.: 47
 St. James - 302 N. Washington, Bronte, TX 76933; Mailing: St. Mary , Star of the Sea Parish Parish, 605 N. 5th St., Ballinger, TX 76821 t) (325) 365-2687
 Our Lady of Guadalupe - 601 W. 10th, Robert Lee, TX 76945; Mailing: St. Mary, Star of the Sea Parish, 605 N. 5th St., Ballinger, TX 76821 t) (325) 365-2687

BIG LAKE
St. Margaret of Cortona - 107 E. 1st. St., Big Lake, TX 76932 t) 325-884-3221 biglake@sanangelodiocese.org Rev. Balachandra Nagipogu (India), Pst.; Julia Flores, RCIA Coord.; Rosemary Pena, Contact; Sarah Rodriguez, CRE; CRP Stds.: 93
 St. Thomas - 110 Hwy. 67, Rankin, TX 79778; Mailing: St. Margaret of Cortona Parish, 107 E. 1st St., Big Lake, TX 76932 t) (325) 884-3221 rankin@sanangelodiocese.org
 St. Francis - 201 W. 5th St., Iraan, TX 79744; Mailing: St. Margaret of Cortona Parish, 107 E. 1st St., Big Lake, TX 76932 t) (325) 884-3221 iraan@sanangelodiocese.org

BIG SPRING
Holy Trinity Parish - 1009 Hearn St., Big Spring, TX 79720; Mailing: PO Box 951, Big Spring, TX 79721 t) 432-714-4930 bigspring@sanangelodiocese.org Rev. Serafin P. Avenido Jr. (Philippines), Pst.; Dcn. Bobby Porras; Dcn. Jose Villagrana; Dianna Valdez, CRE; CRP Stds.: 180

BRADY
St. Patrick's - 406 S. Bridge, Brady, TX 76825; Mailing: P.O Box 1188, Brady, TX 76825 t) 325-597-2324 brady@sanangelodiocese.org www.stpatricksbrady.org Rev. Terence V. Brenon, Pst.; Dcn. Robert Selvera; Felix Gomez Jr., Youth Min.; Cindy Willmann, CRE; CRP Stds.: 30
 St. Francis Xavier - 107 S. Savage Ave., Melvin, TX 76858; Mailing: St. Patrick Parish, PO Box 1188, Brady, TX 76825 t) (325) 597-2324 melvin@sanangelodiocese.org

BROWNWOOD
St. Mary's - 1103 Main St., Brownwood, TX 76801; Mailing: 1101 Booker St., Brownwood, TX 76801 t) 325-646-7455; 325-646-9630 (CRP) brownwood@sanangelodiocese.org www.sm1familybwd.org Rev. Francis Onyekozuru, Par. Admin.; Dcn. John Specht; Stephanie Masterson, CRE; Beatrice Fanning, Youth Min.; Brent Fanning, Youth Min.; CRP Stds.: 146

CARLSBAD
St. Therese - 11774 Beaumont St., Carlsbad, TX 76934-0416; Mailing: P.O. Box 416, Carlsbad, TX 76934-0416 t) 325-465-8062 carlsbad@sanangelodiocese.org; sthcarlstx@frontier.com Rev. Josh Gray, Pst.; Dcn. Jesse Martinez; Dcn. Johnny Rodriguez; Linda Dye, CRE; Cindy Bentfield, Youth Min.; CRP Stds.: 18

COLEMAN
Sacred Heart - 303 E. College, Coleman, TX 76834 t) 325-625-5773 coleman@sanangelodiocese.org www.sacredheartchurchcoleman.org Rev. Laurent Mvondo (Cameroon), Pst.; Margie Mitchell, CRE; Angel Barrios, Youth Min.; Caitlin Barrios, Youth Min.; CRP Stds.: 28

COLORADO CITY

St. Ann's - 2005 Walnut St., Colorado City, TX 79512 t) 325-728-3252 Rev. Michael Udegbunam, Pst.; Janie Davila, DRE; Brian Potter, Youth Min.; Michelle Potter, Youth Min.; CRP Stds.: 42

St. Joseph - 403 S. Hinson, Loraine, TX 79532; Mailing: St. Ann, Parish, 2005 Walnut St., Colorado City, TX 79512 t) (325) 728-3252 loraine@sanangelodiocese.org

CRANE

Good Shepherd - 810 S. Virginia, Crane, TX 79731; Mailing: P. O. Box 1294, Crane, TX 79731 t) 432-558-2718 crane@sanangelodiocese.org Rev. Kumar Jujjuvarapu (India), Pst.; Dcn. Julio Carrasco; Dcn. Apolonio Gutierrez; Dcn. Felix Segura; Teresa Figueroa, CRE; CRP Stds.: 164

St. Isidore - 4614 S. Frank, Coyanosa, TX 79752; Mailing: Sacred Heart Parish, PO Box 1320, McCamey, TX 79752 t) 432-652-8216 coyanosa@sanangelodiocese.org Rev. Kumar Jujjuvarapu, Pst.;

Our Lady of Lourdes - 103 Merrill Ave, Imperial, TX 79743 t) (432) 558-2718 imperial@sanangelodiocese.org Rev. Kumar Jujjuvarapu, Pst.;

EDEN

St. Charles Borromeo Catholic Church - 302 Moss St., Eden, TX 76837; Mailing: P.O Box 575, Eden, TX 76837 t) 325-869-8311 eden@sanangelodiocese.org; bgovindu@sanangelodiocese.org Rev. Bala Anthony Govindu, Pst.; CRP Stds.: 15

Our Lady of Guadalupe - 12196 County Rd. 6009, Millersview, TX 76862 t) (325) 869-8311

St. Phillip Benizi Mission - 11937 Co. Rd. 5511, Eola, TX 76937; Mailing: P.O. Box 711, Eola, TX 76937 t) (325) 869-8311

ELDORADO

Our Lady of Guadalupe - 824 N. Divide St., Eldorado, TX 76936 t) 325-853-2663 eldorado@sanangelodiocese.org Rev. Anthony Franco, Admin.; Dcn. Victor Belman; Dcn. Michael Kahlig; CRP Stds.: 79

Immaculate Conception - 12264 W. Torres, Knickerbocker, TX 76939; Mailing: PO Box 96, Knickerbocker, TX 76939 t) 325-944-2820 knickerbocker@sanangelodiocese.org

St. Peter's - 324 N. Commerce, Mertzon, TX 76941; Mailing: P.O. Box 471, Mertzon, TX 76941 t) 325-835-2000 mertzon@sanangelodiocese.org Dcn. Michael Kahlig, Contact;

FORT STOCKTON

Our Lady of Guadalupe - 403 S. Main, Fort Stockton, TX 79735 t) 432-336-5027 fortstockton@sanangelodiocese.org www.ologpfs.weebly.com Rev. Francis Njoku, Pst.; Dcn. Daniel Holguin Jr.; Dcn. Reuben Reyes; Dcn. Luis Villarreal; Victoria Maldonado, Youth Min.; Consuelo Villarreal, CRE; CRP Stds.: 254

GARDEN CITY

St. Lawrence - 2400 FM 2401, Garden City, TX 79739 t) 432-397-2300 stlawrence@sanangelodiocese.org stlawrencecatholicchurch.com Rev. Prem S. Thumma, Pst.; Dcn. Joel Gutierrez; Dcn. Floyd Schwartz; Rachel Eggemeyer, CRE; Tammy Halfmann, CRE; CRP Stds.: 167

St. Thomas - 13100 N FM 2401, Midkiff, TX 79755; Mailing: St. Lawrence Parish, 2400 FM 2401,, Garden City, TX 79739 t) (432) 397-2300 midkiff@sanangelodiocese.org Irma Alvarado, CRE;

St. Paschal Baylona - 803 5th St. (Corner of 5th St. & Concho), Sterling City, TX 76951-0271; Mailing: PO Box 271, Sterling City, TX 76951 t) (432) 397-2300 sterlingcity@sanangelodiocese.org Victoria Aguilar, CRE; Juana Estrada, CRE;

JUNCTION

St. Theresa of the Child Jesus - 114 S. 7th St., Junction, TX 76849; Mailing: P.O. Box 486, Junction, TX 76849 t) 325-446-3393 junction@sanangelodiocese.org Rev. Mark Woodruff, Pst.; Dcn. Stanley Sienkiewich; Reginald Stapper, CRE; CRP Stds.: 35

MCCAMEY

Sacred Heart - 710 Burleson, McCamey, TX 79752; Mailing: PO Box 1320, McCamey, TX 79752 t) 432-652-8216 mccamey@sanangelodiocese.org Rev. Kumar Jujjuvarapu (India), Pst.; Dcn. Julio Carrasco; Dcn. Felix Segura; Becky Carrillo, CRE; CRP Stds.: 26

MENARD

Sacred Heart - 609 Ellis St, Hwy 83, Menard, TX 76859; Mailing: PO Box 788, Menard, TX 76859 t) 325-396-4906 menard@sanangelodiocese.org Rev. Mark Woodruff, Pst.; Jessica Wright, CRE; CRP Stds.: 32

MIDLAND

St. Ann's - 1906 W. Texas Ave., Midland, TX 79701-6564 t) 432-682-6303 parish@stannsparish.us; midland.stann@sanangelodiocese.org www.stannsparish.us Rev. Msgr. Larry J. Droll, Pst.; Rev. Yesu Mulakaleti, Assoc. Pst.; Dcn. Thomas Collier, Pastoral Assoc./Business Mgr.; Dcn. Jesus Napoles; Dcn. Mike Hernandez; Brandon Jaquish, Youth Min.; Mary Allison, DRE; Kristin Atkinson, Coord. Relg. Educ.; Leonor Spencer, CRE for Spanish Ministry; Faustino Rodriguez, Social Ministry Coord.; CRP Stds.: 689

St. Ann's School - (Grades PreK-8) 2000 W. Texas Ave., Midland, TX 79701 t) 432-684-4563 stannschool@sanangelodiocese.org www.stanns.us Joan Wilmes, Prin.; Stephanie Montes, Vice Prin.; Tracy Owen, Vice. Pres.; Stds.: 405; Sr. Tchrs.: 1; Lay Tchrs.: 32

Our Lady of Guadalupe - 1401 E. Garden Ln., Midland, TX 79701 t) 432-682-2581 midland.olg@sanangelodiocese.org www.olgmidland.org Rev. David Herrera, Pst.; Dcn. Sergio Cedillo; Dcn. Billy Garcia; Dcn. Ricardo Torres; Dcn. Ignacio Villa; Janie Garivay, CRE; CRP Stds.: 481

San Miguel Arcangel Church (Our Lady of San Juan) - 1100 Camp St., Midland, TX 79701 t) 432-570-0349 (CRP); 432-570-0952 midland.sanmiguel@sanangelodiocese.org; greenwood@sanangelodiocese.org www.sanmiguelchurch.com Rev. Patrick Akpanobong, Pst.; Dcn. Michael LaMonica; Dcn. Victor Lopez; Dcn. Alex Perez; Dcn. Sador Sotelo; Dcn. Alexander Chick; Elsa Lujan, CRE; Alex Chick, Youth Min.; CRP Stds.: 290

St. Rita of Cascia Mission - 8006 FM 307, Midland, TX 79706; Mailing: c/o San Miguel Arcangel, 2200 Camp St., Midland, TX 79701 t) (432) 570-0952

St. Stephen's - 4601 Neely Ave., Midland, TX 79707 t) 432-520-7394 midland.ststephen@sanangelodiocese.org; rwhite@sanangelodiocese.org www.ssccmidland.com Very Rev. Rodney White, Pst.; Rev. Kevin Lenius, Par. Vicar; Dcn. Leonard Hendon Jr.; Dcn. Luis Mata Sr.; Dcn. Fidel Saldivar; Gretchen Lara, CRE; Noe Carrasco, Youth Min.; CRP Stds.: 382

MILES

St. Thomas - 404 W. 7th St., Miles, TX 76861; Mailing: PO Box 306, Miles, TX 76861 t) 325-468-3171 miles@sanangelodiocese.org; st.thomas_miles@wcc.net Rev. Ariel R. Lagunilla, Pst.; Dcn. Frankie D. Aguirre; Dcn. Alan Pelzel; Dcn. David Workman; Very Rev. Tom Barley, In Res.; Sarah Kalina, CRE; Leslie Glass, CRE; CRP Stds.: 48

ODESSA

St. Anthony - 1321 W. Monahans St., Odessa, TX 79763; Mailing: 907 S. Dixie Blvd, Odessa, TX 79761 t) 432-337-2213; 432-334-6478 (CRP) evillegas@sanangelodiocese.org; odessa.stanthony@sanangelodiocese.org Rev. Frank Chavez, Pst.; Rev. Carlos Felipe Rodriguez, Par. Vicar; Dcn. Flavio Franco; Dcn. Alex Sosa; Rev. Msgr. Robert Bush, Par. Vicar; Dcn. Alfonso Moreno; Dcn. Scott Randolph; Sr. Elizabeth P. Villegas, O.N.D., DRE;

St. Elizabeth Ann Seton - 7601 N. Grandview, Odessa, TX 79765 t) 432-367-4657 ccd@setonparishodessa.org; office@setonparishodessa.org www.setonparishodessa.org Rev. Giuseppe Barbieri, Pst.; Dcn. Gary Brooks; Dcn. Alfred Camarillo Sr.; Dcn. Jose Gallegos; Dcn. Salvador Primera; Marilyn Kay Hemann, DRE; Brian Richards, Youth Min.; Blas T Campos Sr., Bus. Mgr.; CRP Stds.: 509

Holy Redeemer - 2633 Conover, Odessa, TX 79763 t) 432-580-3839; 432-580-4295; 432-337-2084 (CRP) hrccredeemer15@gmail.com www.holyredeemertx.org Rev. Angel Alfredo Castro, MSP, Pst.; Rev. Ismael Velazco Ornelas, MSP, Vicar; Dcn. Andrew Davis; Dcn. Edward Gonzalez; Dcn. Orlando Mendoza; Sr. Estela Tovar, CDP, DRE; CRP Stds.: 553

Our Lady of San Juan Mission - 905 Edgeport Dr., Odessa, TX 79765; Mailing: Holy Redeemer Parish, 2633 Conover Ave., Odessa, TX 79763 t) 432-362-2017 odessa.olsj@sanangelodiocese.org Adriana Orozco, Contact;

St. Joseph - 907 S. Dixie Blvd., Odessa, TX 79761 t) 432-337-2213; 432-334-6478 (CRP) evillegas@sanangelodiocese.org; odessa.stjoseph@sanangelodiocese.org www.stjosephanthonychurches.org/ Rev. Frank Chavez, Pst.; Rev. Carlos Felipe Rodriguez, Par. Vicar; Rev. Msgr. Robert Bush, Par. Vicar; Dcn. Alex Sosa; Dcn. Flabio Franco; Dcn. Alfonso Moreno; Dcn. Scott Randolph; Sr. Elizabeth P. Villegas, O.N.D., DRE; Gloria Medina, CRE; Mary Rivas, CRE; Yolanda Ruiz, CRE; CRP Stds.: 643

St. Mary's Church - 612 E. 18th St., Odessa, TX 79761 t) 432-332-5334 odessa.stmary@sanangelodiocese.org Pablo Davila, Youth Min.; Rev. Bernard Getigan, Pst.; Dcn. Hector Mendez; Dcn. Jesse Ortiz; Dcn. Bobby Wright; Sr. Maria Theresa Arzagon, OND, DRE; CRP Stds.: 226

St. Mary's Central Catholic School - (Grades PreK-8) 1703 N. Adams, Odessa, TX 79761 t) 432-337-6052 stmaryschool@sanangelodiocese.org smccsodessa.org Patricia Salcido, Prin.; Stds.: 213; Sr. Tchrs.: 1; Lay Tchrs.: 19

OZONA

Our Lady of Perpetual Help - 1715 Martinez St., Ozona, TX 76943; Mailing: PO Box 1069, Ozona, TX 76943 t) 325-392-3353 Rev. Hilary A. Ihedioha (Nigeria), Pst.; Janell Tambunga, CRE; Adrian Tijerina, Youth Min.; Lilia Tijerina, Youth Min.; Victor Hernandez, Youth Min.; Patricia Hernandez, Youth Min.;

Good Shepherd - 1040 Main (Hwy 290), Sheffield, TX 79781 sheffield@sanangelodiocese.org

ROWENA

St. Boniface - 1118 County Rd. 234, Rowena, TX 76875 t) 325-442-2893 olfen@sanangelodiocese.org Rev. Ariel R. Lagunilla, Pst.; Dcn. Frankie D. Aguirre; Dcn. Alan Pelzel; Dcn. David Workman;

St. Joseph's - 506 Edwards St., Rowena, TX 76875; Mailing: PO Box 96, Rowena, TX 76875 t) 325-442-3521 rowena@sanangelodiocese.org www.churchesofrom.org Rev. Ariel R. Lagunilla, Pst.; Dcn. Frankie D. Aguirre; Dcn. Alan Pelzel; Dcn. David Workman; Chris Martin, Youth Min.; Melissa Martin, Youth Min.; Jamie Glass, CRE; Jamie Strube, CRE; CRP Stds.: 138

SAN ANGELO

Cathedral of the Sacred Heart - 20 E. Beauregard Ave., San Angelo, TX 76903-5929 t) 325-658-6567 sanangelo.cathedral@sanangelodiocese.org sanangelocathedral.org Very Rev. Lorenzo Hatch, Rector; Dcn. Federico Medina Jr.; Patricia Gonzales, CRE; Cameron Wilson, Youth Min.; Dcn. Steven Zimmerman, RCIA Coord.; John Webber, Music Min.; Johnny Garza, Bus. Mgr.; Linda Melone, Development Director; CRP Stds.: 107

Sacred Heart Cathedral-Parish Educational Endowment Fund, Inc. - t) 915-658-6567

Holy Angels - 2309 A&M., San Angelo, TX 76904; Mailing: 2202 Rutgers, San Angelo, TX 76904 t) 325-942-8192 (CRP); 325-944-8967 lhines@sanangelodiocese.org; parish@holyangelssanangelo.org www.holyangelssanangelo.org Very Rev. Santiago D.

Udayar, Pst.; Dcn. Walter Hammons II; Lori Hines, DRE; Dcn. Leslie Maiman; CRP Stds.: 123

Angelo Catholic School - (Grades PreK-8) 2315 A & M Ave., San Angelo, TX 76904 t) 325-949-1747 angelocatholicschool@sanangelodiocese.org www.angelocatholicschool.org/ Elizabeth Mata, Prin.; Stds.: 106; Lay Tchrs.: 11

St. Joseph - 301 W. 17th, San Angelo, TX 76903 t) 325-653-5006 sanangelo.stjoseph@sanangelodiocese.org; noreen@stjosephsanangelo.org www.stjosephsanangelo.org Rev. Juan Lopez Cortes, MSP, Pst.; Rev. Lazaro Hernandez, MSP, Par. Vicar; Dcn. Abel Fernandez; Dcn. Antero Gonzalez; Dcn. John Rangel; Vickie Rivero, DRE; Noreen Rodriguez, Bus. Mgr.; CRP Stds.: 282

St. Margaret - 2619 Era St., San Angelo, TX 76905 t) 325-651-4633 sanangelo.stmargaret@sanangelodiocese.org; stmargaret-sa@hotmail.com stmargaretsa.org Rev. Josh Gray, Admin.; CRP Stds.: 50

St. Mary's - 11 W. Ave. N., San Angelo, TX 76903 t) 325-655-6278 sanangelo.stmary@sanangelodiocese.org Rev. Joey Faylona, Pst.; Dcn. Michael Lopez; Dcn. Marc Mata; Dcn. Claudio Sanchez; Silvia Alvarez, DRE; CRP Stds.: 250

SANDERSON

St. James Church - 209 E. Hackberry, Sanderson, TX 79848; Mailing: P.O. Box 520, Sanderson, TX 79848 t) 432-336-5027 Rev. Francis Njoku, Pst.; Thelma Calzada, Contact;

SONORA

St. Ann's - 311 W. Plum, Sonora, TX 76950; Mailing: PO Box 1397, Sonora, TX 76950 t) 325-387-2278 sonora@sanangelodiocese.org Rev. Felix Archibong, Pst.; Nancy Jimenez, CRE; Ben Taylor, Youth Min.; Lizzy Taylor, Youth Min.; Delia Samaniego, CRE; Nelda Tobias, CRE; CRP Stds.: 118

STANTON

St. Joseph's - 405 N. Convent St., Stanton, TX 79782-0846; Mailing: PO Box 846, Stanton, TX 79782-0846 t) 432-756-3743 stanton@sanangelodiocese.org Rev. Michael Michael Rodriguez, Pst.; Dcn. Clemente Villa Jr.; CRP Stds.: 107

St. Isidore - 3324 Co Rd 3400, Lenorah, TX 79749; Mailing: St. Joseph Parish, PO Box 846, Stanton, TX 79782 t) (432) 756-3743

SWEETWATER

Holy Spirit Parish - 511 W. Alabama, Sweetwater, TX 79556 t) 325-235-3318 sweetwater@sanangelodiocese.org Rev. Nilo Nalugon, Pst.; Dcn. W. W. Butler; Dcn. David Mendez; Sr. Luisita Iglesias, O.N.D., DRE; CRP Stds.: 191

WALL

St. Ambrose - 8602 Loop 570, Wall, TX 76957; Mailing: P.O. Box 228, Wall, TX 76957 t) 325-651-7551 wall@sanangelodiocese.org www.saint-ambrose.org Very Rev. Joseph Choutapalli, Pst.; Dcn. Allan Lange; Dcn. Daniel Shannahan; Lucy Thomas, DRE; Brittney Schniers, CRE; Felisha Wilkins, CRE; Amanda Williams, Youth Min.; CRP Stds.: 201

Holy Family - 18370 Bledsoe Rd., Mereta, TX 76940; Mailing: St. Ambrose Parish, PO Box 228, Wall, TX 76957 t) 325-468-3101 mereta@sanangelodiocese.org Dcn. Dan Shannahan; Sylvia Chappa, CRE;

WINTERS

Our Lady of Mt. Carmel - 119 W. College St., Winters, TX 79567 t) 325-939-0968 winters@sanangelodiocese.org Rev. Laurent Mvondo (Cameroon), Pst.; Rene Woffenden, Youth Min.; Brandi Jacob, DRE; CRP Stds.: 27

SCHOOLS: PRESCHOOL THRU HIGH SCHOOL

SCHOOLS

STATE OF TEXAS

MIDLAND

Holy Cross Catholic High School - (PRV) (Grades 9-12) 4014 N County Rd 1160, Midland, TX 79705; Mailing: P.O. Box 14221, Odessa, TX 79768 t) 432-235-1094 cgonzalez@holycrosschs.org www.holycrosschs.org Carolyn Gonzalez, Admin.; Stds.: 70; Lay Tchrs.: 7

INSTITUTIONS LOCATED IN DIOCESE

CAMPUS MINISTRY / NEWMAN CENTERS [CAM]

SAN ANGELO

Catholic Newman Center - 2451 Dena Dr., San Angelo, TX 76904 t) 325-949-8033 info@catholicram.org www.catholicram.org Rev. Freddy Perez, Dir.;

CATHOLIC CHARITIES [CCH]

ODESSA

Catholic Charities Community Services Odessa, Inc. - 2500 Andrews Hwy., Odessa, TX 79761 t) 432-332-1387 executivedirector@ccodessa.org www.ccodessa.com Sara Campos Aguilar, Dir.; Asstd. Annu.: 700; Staff: 1

CONVENTS, MONASTERIES, AND RESIDENCES FOR WOMEN [CON]

CHRISTOVAL

Carmelite Nuns of the Ancient Observance, San Angelo, TX - 6202 County Rd. 339, Christoval, TX 76935-3023 t) 325-853-1722 desertcarmel@carmelnet.org carmelnet.org/christoval/christoval.htm Sr. Mary Grace Erl, O.Carm., Contact; Srs.: 5

ENDOWMENTS / FOUNDATIONS / TRUSTS [EFT]

SAN ANGELO

The Catholic Charitable Foundation for the Roman Catholic Diocese of San Angelo - 804 Ford St., San Angelo, TX 76905; Mailing: P.O. Box 1824, San Angelo, TX 76902 t) 325-651-7500 mmata@sanangelodiocese.org Dcn. Marc Mata, CFO;

MISCELLANEOUS [MIS]

ABILENE

St. Vincent De Paul Society - 1241 Walnut St., Abilene, TX 79601 t) 325-677-6871 svdpabilenestore@gmail.com Dcn. Marc P. Main;

St. Vincent De Paul Thrift Store -

BIG SPRING

St. Vincent De Paul Society - 1009 Hearn St., Big Spring, TX 79720 t) 432-270-5191 bigspring@sanangelodiocese.org Food Distribution. Erlinda Rios, Contact;

MIDLAND

St. Vincent De Paul Society - 1906 W. Texas Ave., Midland, TX 79701 t) 432-684-3887 midland.stann@sanangelodiocese.org Kevin Harrington, Dir.;

SAN ANGELO

Magnificat-San Angelo Chapter, Inc. - 3937 Inglewood Dr., San Angelo, TX 76904 t) 325-650-0172 roxyadame1965@gmail.com Roxy Adame, Contact;

STANTON

St. Vincent De Paul Society - 405 N. Convent St., Stanton, TX 79782; Mailing: P.O. Box 846, Stanton, TX 79782 t) 432-756-3743 stanton@sanangelodiocese.org Rev. Michael Michael Rodriguez, Pst.;

MONASTERIES AND RESIDENCES FOR PRIESTS AND BROTHERS [MON]

CHRISTOVAL

Hermits of the Blessed Virgin Mary of Mount Carmel - 7637 Allen Rd., Christoval, TX 76935-0337; Mailing: PO Box 337, Christoval, TX 76935 t) 325-896-2249 stellamaris@carmelitehermits.org www.carmelitehermits.org Mount Carmel Hermitage Rev. Martin Hubbs, O.Carm., Prior; Rev. Fabian Maria Rosette, O.Carm., Mem.; Brs.: 3; Priests: 2

RETREAT HOUSES / RENEWAL CENTERS [RTR]

SAN ANGELO

Christ the King Retreat Center - 802 Ford, San Angelo, TX 76905 t) 325-651-5352 ckrc@sanangelodiocese.org Thomas C. Burke, Dir.;

Archdiocese of San Antonio

(Archidioecesis Sancti Antonii)

MOST REVEREND GUSTAVO GARCIA-SILLER, M.SP.S.

Archbishop of San Antonio; ordained June 22, 1984; appointed Auxiliary Bishop of Chicago and Titular See of Esco January 24, 2003; consecrated March 19, 2003; appointed Archbishop of San Antonio October 14, 2010; installed November 23, 2010; Pallium conferred June 20, 2011. Pastoral Center, 2718 W. Woodlawn Ave., San Antonio, TX 78228-5124. T: 210-734-2620; T: 210-734-1664; F: 210-734-0708.

Archdiocesan Pastoral Center/Chancery: 2718 W. Woodlawn Ave., San Antonio, TX 78228. T: 210-734-2620; F: 210-734-0231.

www.archsa.org

ESTABLISHED AUGUST 28, 1874.

Square Miles 23,180.

Created an Archbishopric, August 3, 1926.

The San Antonio Archdiocese comprises Atascosa, Bandera, Bexar, Comal, Edwards, Frio, Gillespie, Gonzales, Guadalupe, Karnes, Kendall, Kerr, Kinney, McMullen (that part of McMullen County north of the Nueces River), Medina, Real, Uvalde, Val Verde and Wilson.

For legal titles of parishes and archdiocesan institutions, consult the Pastoral Center.

Most Reverend Michael J. Boulette
Auxiliary Bishop of San Antonio; ordained March 19, 1976; appointed Titular Bishop of Hieron and Auxiliary Bishop of San Antonio January 23, 2017; consecrated March 20, 2017. Pastoral Center, 2718 W. Woodlawn Ave., San Antonio, TX 78228-0410.

Most Reverend Gary W. Janak
Auxiliary Bishop of San Antonio; ordained May 14, 1988; appointed Titular Bishop of Dionysiana and Auxiliary Bishop of San Antonio February 15, 2021; consecrated April 20, 2021. Pastoral Center: 2718 W. Woodlawn Ave., San Antonio, TX 78228.

STATISTICAL OVERVIEW

Personnel

Archbishops	1
Auxiliary Bishops	2
Priests: Diocesan Active in Diocese	83
Priests: Diocesan Active Outside Diocese	3
Priests: Retired, Sick or Absent	71
Number of Diocesan Priests	157
Religious Priests in Diocese	165
Total Priests in your Diocese	322
Extern Priests in Diocese	57
Ordinations:	
Diocesan Priests	1
Religious Priests	1
Transitional Deacons	2
Permanent Deacons	16
Permanent Deacons in Diocese	334
Total Brothers	46
Total Sisters	472

Parishes

Parishes	135
With Resident Pastor:	
Resident Diocesan Priests	82
Resident Religious Priests	38
Without Resident Pastor:	
Administered by Priests	16
Administered by Deacons	1
Missions	36
Professional Ministry Personnel:	
Brothers	33
Sisters	71
Lay Ministers	301

Welfare

Catholic Hospitals	6
Total Assisted	946,668
Health Care Centers	10
Total Assisted	5,087
Homes for the Aged	5
Total Assisted	94
Day Care Centers	5
Total Assisted	127
Specialized Homes	3
Total Assisted	249
Special Centers for Social Services	6
Total Assisted	160,027
Other Institutions	1
Total Assisted	40,000

Educational

Seminaries, Diocesan	1
Students from This Diocese	16
Students from Other Dioceses	21
Seminaries, Religious	3
Students, Religious	2
Total Seminarians	18
Colleges and Universities	5
Total Students	16,788
High Schools, Diocesan and Parish	2
Total Students	939
High Schools, Private	6
Total Students	1,517
Elementary Schools, Diocesan and Parish	25
Total Students	5,568
Elementary Schools, Private	5
Total Students	708
Catechesis/Religious Education:	
High School Students	7,298
Elementary Students	15,474
Total Students under Catholic Instruction	48,310
Teachers in Diocese:	
Priests	8
Brothers	3
Sisters	15
Lay Teachers	902

Vital Statistics

Receptions into the Church:	
Infant Baptism Totals	4,642
Minor Baptism Totals	682
Adult Baptism Totals	281
Received into Full Communion	567
First Communions	4,543
Confirmations	4,219
Marriages:	
Catholic	1,098
Interfaith	149
Total Marriages	1,247
Deaths	5,082
Total Catholic Population	1,148,253
Total Population	2,798,718

LEADERSHIP

Office of the Archbishop - Pablo Garcia, Personal Asst. to Archbishop (pablo.garcia@archsa.org); Linda Ramirez, Exec. Asst. to Archbishop (linda.ramirez@archsa.org); Yenisse Roman Ramirez, Exec. Asst. to Archbishop & Archives for the Office of Archbishop (yenisse.ramirez@archsa.org);
Office of the Chancellor - Most Rev. Gary Janak, Chancellor (gary.janak@archsa.org); Lori B. Peery, Vice Chancellor (lori.peery@archsa.org); Yessica Marval, Admin. Asst. (yessica.marval@archsa.org);
Vicars General - Most Rev. Michael L. Boulette, Vicar; Most Rev. Gary Janak, Vicar (gary.janak@archsa.org); Sally A. Carrion, Contact (sally.carrion@archsa.org);
Assistant to the Moderator of the Curia - t) 210-734-1674 Rev. Martin J. Leopold (mleopold@archsa.org);
Archives & Records Management Office - t) 210-734-1959 archive@archsa.org Elvira Sanchez Kisser, Dir. (elvira.kisser@archsa.org); Brent Stauffer, Records Mgr./Asst. Archivist (brent.stauffer@archsa.org); Claudia Sanchez, Archives Digitization Asst. (Claudia.Sanchez@archsa.org);
Archdiocesan Office of Stewardship and Development - t) (210) 734-1907 developmentoffice@archsa.org Jennifer Rodriguez, Dir. (jennifer.rodriguez@archsa.org);
Episcopal Delegate for Ecumenism, Interreligious and Community Affairs - t) 210-734-1670 Lori B. Peery (lori.peery@archsa.org);
Office for Annual Appeal, Grants & Parish/School Outreach - Edgar Barroso (edgar.barroso@archsa.org);
Hope for the Future - Beverly Duke, Grant Mgr. (beverly.duke@archsa.org); Maria Lloyd, Grants Coord. (maria.lloyd@archsa.org); Michael Bossaller, Mktg. Communications Coord. & Devel. Outreach Liaison (michael.bossaller@archsa.org);
Database Office - Norma Ferdin, Donor Svcs. Lead (norma.ferdin@archsa.org); Natalie Cura, Donor Svcs. Asst. (natalie.cura@archsa.org); Margaret Parales, Donor Svcs. Asst. (margaret.perales@archsa.org);
Assumption Seminary - t) 210-734-5137 assumptionseminary@archsa.org www.assumptionseminary.org Rev. James Myers, P.S.S., Rector (jmeyers@ost.edu); Rev. Renato Lopez, P.S.S., Vice-Rector (renato.lopez@archsa.org);
Vocation Office - t) 210-735-0553 vocations@archsa.org www.archsa.org/vocations Sr. Ana Cecilia Montalvo, F.Sp.S., Assoc. Dir.; Ana Bojorquez, Apostolic Admin.; Sharon Menezes, Admin. Asst.;
Catholic Community Foundation - t) 210-732-2157 Alison Cochrane, CEO & Pres. (alison.cochrane@ccftx.org); Dcn. John Paul Benage, Vice. Pres. (jpbenage@gmail.com);
Archdiocesan Tribunal - t) 210-734-1661 tribunal@archsa.org Andrea Mullins, Admin. Asst. (andrea.mullins@archsa.org);
Director - t) 210-734-1696 Laura G. Ruiz;
Judicial Vicar - Rev. Krikor Gregory Chahin;
Judges - Rev. Jose Ramon Perez-Martinez; Rev. Gilberto Vallejo (gilbert.vallejo@archsa.org); Sr. Janice Grochowsky, C.S.J.;
Promoter of Justice - Lori B. Peery (lori.peery@archsa.org);
Defenders of the Bond - Rev. Michael Ravenkamp, S.J.; Ashley Subler; Rev. Martin J. Leopold (mleopold@archsa.org);
Peritus - Denise M. Marantes (denise.marantes@archsa.org);
Advocate - Very Rev. Matthew De Leon (matthew.deleon@stpccs.org); Dcn. Jeffrey Gardner (rectory@stlouischurchcastroville.org); Dcn. Pete Nanez;
Auditors/Case Coordinators - Bosco D. Miller; Dcn. Jeffrey Gardner (rectory@stlouischurchcastroville.org); Blanca Gonzalez, Case Coord. (blanca.gonzalez@archsa.org);
Notary/Intake and Tribunal Archives Coordinator - Sr. Gemma Abonge (GemmaAbonge@stbrigidcc.org); Blanca Gonzalez (blanca.gonzalez@archsa.org); Denise M. Marantes (denise.marantes@archsa.org);

ADMINISTRATION

Administrative Services Department - t) 210-734-1605 Ruben A. Hinojosa, Dir. (ruben.hinojosa@archsa.org);
Archdiocesan Chief Financial Officer - Ruben Hinojosa;
Archdiocesan Cemeteries Office - t) 210-432-8134 Ismael Galvan, Exec. Dir. (ismael.galvan@archsa.org);
Archdiocesan Controller - t) 210-734-1677 Delia Thomas (delia.thomas@archsa.org);
Archdiocesan Finance Council - Lou Barbour; Sarah Gonzales; Jack Ligon;
Archdiocesan Presbyteral Council - Most Rev. Gustavo Garcia-Siller, M.Sp.S.; Most Rev. Michael J. Boulette; Most Rev. Gary Janak (gary.janak@archsa.org);
Building Committee - Jim Rodriguez; Steve Persyn; Logan Underdown;
Caritas Legal Service - t) 210-433-3256 Maria Garcia, Dir. (mgarcia@ccaosa.org);
Catholic Charities, Archdiocese of San Antonio, Inc. - t) 210-222-1294 J. Antonio Fernandez, Pres.; Gladys Gonzalez, COO (ggonzalez@setonhomesa.org); Lisette DeLeon, CFO;
Catholic Counseling and Consultation Center - t) 210-377-1133 Rey Acosta, Dir.;
Catholic Television of San Antonio (CTSA), Channel 15 - Yesenia Ramirez, Agency Dir. (yesenia.ramirez@archsa.org); Eric Allen, Broadcast Engineer (eric.allen@archsa.org); Daryl Swanson, Producer/Multimedia Journalist (daryl.swanson@archsa.org);
Clergy Ongoing Formation - t) 210-734-1626 Most Rev. Gary Janak, Episcopal Vicar for Vocations & Priest Formation (gary.janak@archsa.org);
College of Consultors - Most Rev. Gustavo Garcia-Siller, M.Sp.S.; Most Rev. Michael J. Boulette; Rev. Kevin P. Fausz, C.M.;
Deans - Rev. Kevin P. Fausz, C.M., Central; Rev. Frederic Mizengo, C.I.C.M., Northwest; Rev. Patrick O'Brien, Northeast (patrick.o'brien@archsa.org);
Department for Pastoral Ministries - Joan Martinez, Dept. Head (joan.martinez@archsa.org); Jazmin Villamil, Admin. Supvr. (jazmin.villamil@archsa.org);
Campus Ministry - t) 830-486-5509 Veronica Ybarra Oubre, Dir.;
Criminal Justice Ministry - t) 210-734-1980 Dcn. Adrian Cepeda, Dir.;
Deaf Ministry - t) 210-734-1636 Angela Mauer, Dir.;
Hospital Ministry - t) 210-415-5552 Lauren Stadelman, Dir.;
Mission Awareness - t) 210-734-1651 Nicky Mata;
Office for Events and Parish Life - t) 210-734-1632 Charles Ramirez, Dir.;
Office for Liturgy and Pastoral Care - t) 210-734-1643 Dolores Martinez, Dir.; Grace Rodriguez, Mgr.;
Office of Pro-Life Activities - t) 210-734-1655 Aaron A. Castillo, Dir.;
Pastoral Secretariats - Gloria F. Zapiain, Dir.; Aaron A. Castillo, Dir.; Maria Dolores Martinez, Dir. Worship;
Department of Clergy and Consecrated Life - Rev. James P. Fischler, C.I.C.M., Dir.; Martha Ross, Admin. Asst.;
Department of Communications - Jordan McMorrough, Dir. (jmcmorrough@archsa.org); Alejandro Orbezo, Assoc. Communications Dir. for Hispanic Media; Janet Mefrige, Communication Asst. (janet.mefrige@archsa.org);
Human Resources - Laura Melghem (laura.melghem@archsa.org);
Information Technology - Omar Gutierrez, Dir. (omar.gutierrez@archsa.org); Alfonso Rebolloso, IT Mgr. (alfonso.rebolloso@archsa.org); Jacob Montanez, Network/System Admin.;
Lay Benefits Plan Committee - Ruben Hinojosa; Laura Melghem (laura.melghem@archsa.org); Delia Thomas (delia.thomas@archsa.org);
Lay Pension Office - t) 210-734-1633 Lydia Washington (lydia.washington@archsa.org);
Mail Room - t) 210-734-1631 Ricoh;
Office for Religious - t) 210-734-1639 Sr. Elizabeth Ann Vasquez, S.S.C.J., Dir.;
Office of Catholic Schools -
Associate Counselor - t) 210-734-1659 Nicole Cleveland, Dir.;
Associate Superintendent of Academics - Amy Hudson;
Associate Superintendent of Business Operations - Chana Finch;
Business Manager - t) 210-734-1963 Ruth Dionne;
CYO Athletics - t) 210-734-1627 Jason Alvarez, Dir.;
Director of Academic Excellence - t) 210-734-1601 Ashley Altizer;
Director of Counseling and Student Services - Veronica Ball;
Director of Enrollment & Advancement - Claudia Gonzalez;
Director of Student Life & Enrichment - Monica Hildebrand, Responsive Svcs. Counselor;
Senior Business Manager - Elsa Astorga;
Superintendent - Marti West, Supt.; Amy Hudson, Assoc. Supt., Academics; Chana Finch, Assoc. Supt., Business Oper.;
Office of Diaconate and Formation - t) 210-734-2620 Dcn. Michael Pawelek, Dir.;
Office of Risk Management - Logan Underdown, Dir. (logan.underdown@archsa.org);
Office of Victim Assistance and Safe Environment - Steve Martinez, Dir. (smartinez@archsa.org); Norma Alvarado, Secy. (ovase@archsa.org); Storie Arredondo, Assoc. Dir.;
Parish and School Accounting - t) 210-734-1983 Laura Torres, Sr. Accountant (laura.torres@archsa.org);
Priests Personnel Board - Most Rev. Gustavo Garcia-Siller, M.Sp.S.; Most Rev. Michael J. Boulette; Most Rev. Gary Janak (gary.janak@archsa.org);
Print Service Center - t) 210-734-2620 x1501 Ricoh;
Refugee Services - t) 210-222-1294 Paula Torisk, Senior Dir.;
St. Peter and Joseph's Home -
Seton Home -
Today's Catholic Newspaper - t) 210-734-1634 Jordan B. McMorrough, Editor (jmcmorrough@archsa.org); Joann Hopkins, Advertising & Editorial Asst. (joann.hopkins@archsa.org); Veronica Markland, Digital & Social Media (veronica.markland@archsa.org);
Vicar for Retired Priests - Rev. Anthony O. Cummins (frtony.cummins@gmail.com);

OFFICES AND DIRECTORS

Censores Librorum (Vacant) -
Strategic Planning & Priorities - Juan Carlos Rodriguez, Dir. (juancarlos.rodriguez@archsa.org);

PARISHES, MISSIONS, AND CLERGY

STATE OF TEXAS

ATASCOSA

Our Lady Queen of Heaven - 11150 Macdona Lacoste Rd., Atascosa, TX 78002 t) 210-622-3282 tello_65@yahoo.com.mx; larcon1952@aol.com Rev. Oscar Tello-Curiel, Pst.; CRP Stds.: 109

BANDERA

St. Stanislaus - 311 7th St., Bandera, TX 78003; Mailing: P O Box 757, Bandera, TX 78003 t) 830-460-4712 ststanis@sbcglobal.net www.ststanislausbandera.com Rev. Msgr. Franciszek Kurzaj, Pst.; CRP Stds.: 146
St. Victor's Chapel - 10514 Park Rd. 37, Lakehills, TX 78063

BOERNE

Korean Martyrs Catholic Church - 7655 Curres Creek,

Boerne, TX 78015 t) 210-698-3877 kmccsa.sec@gmail.com www.kmccsa.org Rev. Chongman John the Baptist Lee, Pst.; CRP Stds.: 13

St. Peter the Apostle - 202 W. Kronkosky St., Boerne, TX 78006 t) 830-816-2233; 830-816-5657 (CRP) jeanna@stpetersboerne.com Marilyn Belcher, Finance Mgr.; Rev. Norman Ermis, Pst.; Dcn. Brad Wakely, Parish Operations Dir.; Dcn. Del Eulberg; Dcn. Marty Lee; Dcn. Paul M. Rayburg; Dcn. Michael Matteson; Lacey Sorrell, Dir. of Ministries & RCIA; Angela Spino, Dir. of Catechesis of the Good Shepherd; Laura Balderama Contreras, Dir. of EFF; CRP Stds.: 359

BRACKETTVILLE

St. Mary Magdalen - 301 S. Ann St., Brackettville, TX 78832; Mailing: P. O. Box 95, Brackettville, TX 78832 t) 830-563-2487 Rev. James Nebolisa Ikeatuegwu, Pst.; Dcn. James Bader; Dcn. Richard Lawrence; CRP Stds.: 60

St. Blaise -

CANYON LAKE

St. Thomas the Apostle - 180 St. Thomas Dr., Canyon Lake, TX 78133 t) 830-964-3497 church@stacltx.org stthomasatcanyonlake.org Dcn. Clifford Hall; Dcn. Robert J. Leibrecht; A'Laura Vrana, DRE; CRP Stds.: 85

CASTROVILLE

St. Louis - 610 Madrid, Castroville, TX 78009 t) 830-423-6156 (CRP); 830-931-2826 ddrtex1629@gmail.com; rectory@stlouischurchcastroville.org Rev. James Fischler, C.I.C.M., Pst.; Rev. Chinnappan Arockiasamy, MSFS, Par. Vicar; Dcn. Louis P. Bernal; Dcn. Richard P. Hoedebecke; Dcn. Jeffrey Gardner; Deborah Ruiz, DRE; CRP Stds.: 272

St. Louis School - (Grades PreK-5) 607 Madrid St., Castroville, TX 78009 t) 830-931-3544 jimmy.gouard@stlouiscs.org www.saintlouiscs.org Dr. Jimmy Gouard, Prin.; Stds.: 216; Lay Tchrs.: 16

St. Francis of Assisi (Medina Lake Chapel) -

CHARLOTTE

St. Rose of Lima - 333 Madero Ave., Charlotte, TX 78011; Mailing: P. O. Box 69, Charlotte, TX 78011 t) 830-277-1242 st.roselima1@gmail.com Rev. Jozef Glabinski, Pst.; Rosa Juarez, DRE; CRP Stds.: 76

St. Joseph - 703 Congress St., Tilden, TX 78072; Mailing: P.O. Box 297, Tilden, TX 78072 Rev. Jozef Michal Glabinski, Pst.;

COMFORT

Sacred Heart - 114 N. Hwy. 87, Comfort, TX 78013-0599; Mailing: P.O. Box 599, Comfort, TX 78013 t) 830-995-3708 sacredheart@hctc.net www.sacredheartcomfort.org Rev. Rudy Carrola, Pst.; Dcn. David Burkart; Dcn. Pedro Fernandez; CRP Stds.: 95

CONVERSE

St. Monica - 501 North St, Converse, TX 78109 t) 210-658-3816 parish@saintmonicaconverse.net www.saintmonicaconverse.net Rev. Prathap Reddy Thumma, Pst.; Rev. Alejandro Ortega, Par. Vicar; Janice Van Slambrouck, DRE; CRP Stds.: 517

St. Monica Catholic School - (Grades PreK-8) 515 North St., Converse, TX 78109 t) 210-658-6701 kgeyer@saintmonica.net; office@saintmonica.net www.saintmonica.net Abigail Salazar, Prin.; Stds.: 141; Lay Tchrs.: 13

DEL RIO

St. Joseph - 510 Wernett St., Del Rio, TX 78841-1429; Mailing: PO Box 1429, Del Rio, TX 78841-1429 t) 830-775-4753 dalilah@stjosephdelrio.com www.stjosephdelrio.com Rev. Jaime Paniagua, Pst.; Rev. Naveen Thumma, Vicar; Dcn. Marco Escobar; Dcn. Emiliano Pina; CRP Stds.: 247

Our Lady of Guadalupe - 509 W. Garza St., Del Rio, TX 78840; Mailing: 510 Wernett St., Del Rio, TX 78840 t) 830-775-3713 fatherpaniagua@gmail.com; dalilah@stjosephdelrio.com Rev. Jaime Paniagua, Pst.; Rev. Naveen Thumma, Par. Vicar; Dcn. Adrian Falcon; Dcn. Juan Padilla; CRP Stds.: 160

San Juan Diego Chapel - 523 Jeffery Dr., V V Park Estates, Del Rio, TX 78840

Sacred Heart - 307 E. Losoya St., Del Rio, TX 78840; Mailing: P. O. Box 1503, Del Rio, TX 78841 t) 830-775-2143 sacredheartcatholic@stx.rr.com Rev. Jose Manuel Otaolaurruchi, Pst.; Dcn. Edgardo Amaro; Dcn. Robert Sanchez; CRP Stds.: 187

Sacred Heart School - (Grades PreK-8) 209 E. Greenwood, Del Rio, TX 78840 t) 830-775-3274 schooloffice@shsdelrio.org www.shsdelrio.org Araceli Rubio, Prin.;

Mary, Queen of the Universe -

DEVINE

St. Joseph - 108 S. Washington Dr., Devine, TX 78016 t) 830-663-2244 stjosephdevinetx@sbcglobal.net www.stjosephsdevine.org Rev. Antonio X. Hernandez, Pst.; CRP Stds.: 144

St. Augustine - 100 Second St., Moore, TX 78057 t) (830) 663-2244

Our Lady of Mt. Carmel - 14024 FM 472, Bigfoot, TX 78005 t) (830) 663-2244

D'HANIS

Holy Cross - 375 CR 5214, D'Hanis, TX 78850; Mailing: P.O. Box 426, 310 FM 2200 S, D'Hanis, TX 78850 t) 830-363-7269 holycross-dhanis.org Rev. John Cyriac, MSFS, Pst.; CRP Stds.: 98

Immaculate Heart of Mary Mission - 213 CR 743, Yancey, TX 78886

DILLEY

St. Joseph's - 114 E. Frio St., Dilley, TX 78017; Mailing: P.O. Box N, Dilley, TX 78017 t) 830-965-2080 jesus.anguiano@archsa.org; gauna.secretarystj@yahoo.com Rev. Jesus Anguiano, Pst.; Alyssa Hall, DRE; CRP Stds.: 45

St. Mary -

ELMENDORF

St. Anthony – Saspamco - 16505 Kilowatt Rd., Elmendorf, TX 78112; Mailing: P.O Box 248, Elmendorf, TX 78112 t) 210-635-8539 (Office) stanthonysofc@gmail.com; stanthonys635@gmail.com www.stanthonyelmendorf.com Dan Chavarria, CRE; Rev. Anthony Male (India), Pst.; Dcn. Zafirin Moczygemba; Dcn. Michael Vrzalik; CRP Stds.: 121

Our Lady of Perpetual Help - t) (210) 625-3534 olphnb1@att.net Rev. Andrew Kafara (Poland), Pst.;

FALLS CITY

Holy Trinity - 211 W. Meyer, Falls City, TX 78113; Mailing: Box 158, Falls City, TX 78113 t) 830-254-3539 holytrinityfc@sbcglobal.net Rev. Andrzej Waszczenko, S.D.S. (Poland), Pst.; CRP Stds.: 134

Nativity of the Blessed Virgin Mary - 300 FM 3191 Cestohowa, Falls City, TX 78113 t) 830-745-2633 Rev. Wieslaw Iwaniec, Pst.; Kim Moy, DRE; CRP Stds.: 49

FLORESVILLE

Sacred Heart - 1009 Trail St., Floresville, TX 78114 t) 830-393-6117; 830-216-7706 church@churchsh.org www.churchsh.org Rev. Kris Bytomski, Pst.; Dcn. Juan A. Bosquez; Dcn. Guadalupe Casanova; Dcn. Doroteo Chavarria; Dcn. Ralph E. Guerra; CRP Stds.: 115

Sacred Heart School - (Grades PreK-5) 1007 Trail St., Floresville, TX 78114 t) 830-393-2117 hilary.reile@shsfloresville.org www.shsfloresville.org Stds.: 103

FREDERICKSBURG

St. Mary's - 307 W. Main St., Fredericksburg, TX 78624-9523 t) 830-997-9523 info@stmarysmail.com www.stmarysfbg.com Rev. John Nolan, Pst.; Rev. Cajetan Amaechi Anyanwu, CMF, Par. Vicar; Dcn. Marty Robertson; Dcn. Patrick Klein; Dcn. Francisco De La Torre; CRP Stds.: 363

St. Mary's School - (Grades K-8) t) 830-997-3914 lreeh@stmarysmail.com school.stmarysfbg.com

Our Lady of Guadalupe -

GONZALES

St. James - 417 N. College St., Gonzales, TX 78629 t) 830-672-2945 catholic@stx.rr.com ccgaw.org Rev. Jason Martini, Pst.; Dcn. Alfonso Moreno; Dcn. Terrence Brennan; Dcn. John Klapuch; CRP Stds.: 340

Sacred Heart - 426 St. John, Gonzales, TX 78629 Rev. Paul A. Raaz;

St. Patrick - U.S. Hwy. 90 A, Waelder, TX 78959

HARPER

St. Anthony - 163 N. Third St., Harper, TX 78631-0318; Mailing: P. O. Box 309, Harper, TX 78631 t) 830-864-4026 stanthony1@windstream.net stanthonyharper.org Rev. Rudy T. Carrola Jr., Pst.; Dcn. Curtis Klein; CRP Stds.: 33

HELOTES

Our Lady of Guadalupe - 13715 Riggs Rd., Helotes, TX 78023 t) 210-695-8791 olgmail@olghelotes.org www.olghelotes.org Rev. Scott Janysek, Pst.; Rev. Jesuraja Alangram, Vicar; Dcn. Leonard T. Cortinaz; Dcn. Frank Gallinaro; Dcn. Daniel D. Quaderer; Dcn. William Thornberry; Dcn. Ernest G. Zepeda; Sonia Lopez-Morales, Coord. of Religious Education Elementary; Angela Quintanilla, Coordinator of Religious Education Youth to Young Adults; Ana Alvarado, Asst. CRE; CRP Stds.: 556

HOBSON

St. Boniface - 358 CR 220, Hobson, TX 78117 t) 830-780-3559 boniface@hughes.net Rev. Andrzej Waszczenko, S.D.S. (Poland), Pst.;

HONDO

St. John the Evangelist - 2102 Ave. J, Hondo, TX 78861 t) 830-741-2236; 830-741-2284 (CRP) vpimentel@stjohnevangelist.org; sfernandez@stjohnevangelist.org www.stjohnshondo.com Rev. Arackathara Mathai Babychan, M.S.F.S., Pst.; Rev. John Cyriac, MSFS, Par. Vicar; Sylvia Fernandez, DRE; CRP Stds.: 213

JOURDANTON

St. Matthew's - 1608 Campbell Ave., Jourdanton, TX 78026 t) 830-769-3687 www.stmatthew-jourdanton.org/ Rev. Tu T. Nguyen; CRP Stds.: 113

St. Ignatius - 101 W. Ave. F, Christine, TX 78012; Mailing: P.O. Box 670, Jourdanton, TX 78026 Rev. Kazimierz Oleksy, S.D.S. (Poland), Pst.;

KARNES CITY

St. Cornelius - 605 E. Calvert St., Karnes City, TX 78118 t) 830-780-3947 stcornelius3947@sbcglobal.net Rev. Stanislaw P. Marciniak, Pst.; Laura Gamez, DRE; CRP Stds.: 76

St. Elizabeth - 13270 FM 99, Campbellton, TX 78008; Mailing: 605 E. Calvert St., Karnes City, TX 78118

KENEDY

Our Lady Queen of Peace - 605 Karnes St., Kenedy, TX 78119; Mailing: P.O. Box 89, Kenedy, TX 78119 t) 830-583-2417 kenedyolqop@yahoo.com Rev. Robert J. Ploch (Poland), Pst.; Dcn. Guadalupe Cantu; Martha Gonzales, DRE; CRP Stds.: 90

KERRVILLE

Notre Dame - 909 Main St., Kerrville, TX 78028 t) 830-896-4233 (CRP); 830-257-5961 frdavid@notredamechurch.cc www.notredamechurch.cc Dcn. Raul M Gutierrez; Dcn. Alfredo Jimmy Bill Jr.; Rev. Rafal Duda, Admin.; Dcn. Francisco Hernandez; Dcn. Sonny Kaufhold; Dcn. Roberto Zapata; CRP Stds.: 516

Notre Dame School - (Grades PreK-8) 907 Main St., Kerrville, TX 78028 t) 830-257-6707 tiffany.rangel@notredameschool.cc www.notredameschool.cc Ellen Kenalty, Prin.; Stds.: 148; Lay Tchrs.: 12

LA VERNIA

St. Ann - 14151 U.S. Hwy. 87 W., La Vernia, TX 78121 t) 830-779-3131 office@stannlv.org www.stannlv.org Rev. Johnson Le, Pst.; Dcn. Jesse Mata; Dcn. Israel Bocanegra; Dcn. Enrique Labrada III; Dcn. Wesley Rist; Jessica Lubianski, DRE; CRP Stds.: 300

LACOSTE

Our Lady of Grace - 15825 Bexar St., LaCoste, TX 78039; Mailing: P.O. Box 39, La Coste, TX 78039 t) 830-985-3355 (CRP); 830-985-3357 olgrace@earthlink.net www.olglacostetexas.org Rev. Leoyd Sanggaria, CICM, Admin.; Dcn. Joseph C. Boland; Alfonso Torres, DRE; CRP Stds.: 158

St. John Vianney - 12703 Cinco de Mayo, San Antonio, TX 78252; Mailing: PO Box 39, LaCoste, TX 78039 Dcn. Joe Boland;

LYTLE

St. Andrew - 14831 Main St., Lytle, TX 78052; Mailing: P.O. Box 326, Lytle, TX 78052 t) 830-709-4287 andrew.bosco@aol.com; varghese.antony@archasa.org Rev. Varghese Antony, Pst.; Dcn. Jerome Whitley; CRP Stds.: 168

St. John Bosco - 5th & Kearney St., Natalia, TX 78059 Rev. Varghese Antony, Pst.;

Immaculate Conception - 800 Diaz St., Coal Mine, TX 78052 t) (830) 709-4287

NEW BRAUNFELS

Holy Family - 245 S. Hidalgo, New Braunfels, TX 78130 t) 830-609-5320 (CRP); 830-609-6098 holyfamily@satx.rr.com hfnb.org Rev. Ralainirina Francois Rakotovoavy, M.S.F., Pst.; Dcn. Pedro Flores; CRP Stds.: 250

Our Lady of Perpetual Help - 138 W. Austin St., New Braunfels, TX 78130 t) 830-629-4506 (CRP); 830-625-3534 olphnbl@att.net Rev. Galson Angelot Andriamamitahina, MSF, Admin.; CRP Stds.: 65

St. John - 210 House St., New Braunfels, TX 78130 t) (830) 625-3534

SS. Peter and Paul - 386 N. Castell St., New Braunfels, TX 78130 t) 830-625-4531 x201 (CRP); 830-625-4531 kimberlymcfadden@sppnb.org; church@sppnb.org sppnb.org Rev. Steven A. Gamez, Pst.; Rev. Albert Tomkeka, Par. Vicar; Dcn. Ben Wehman; Marianna Underwood, Music Min.; Kimberly McFadden, DRE; Mary Kay Williams, Bus. Mgr.; Dcn. Rusty W. Brandt; Dcn. Fred Fey; Dcn. Robert Gorman; Dcn. William Schroeder; CRP Stds.: 1,040

SS. Peter and Paul School - (Grades PreK-8) 315 N. Seguin Ste. 300, New Braunfels, TX 78130 t) 830-625-1077 jlightsey@sppnb.org Jeff Lightsey, Prin.; Rebecca Matschek, Librn.; Stds.: 411; Scholastics: 4; Lay Tchrs.: 30

St. Joseph - FM 482 Northeast of Bunker St., Schertz, TX 78132 steven.gamez@archsa.org

NIXON

St. Joseph's - 207 S. Washington Ave., Nixon, TX 78140-2920 t) 830-582-1127 stjosephnixontx@yahoo.com Rev. Kuriakose P. Ouseph (India), Pst.; Dcn. John Moreno; CRP Stds.: 113

PANNA MARIA

Immaculate Conception of the Blessed Virgin Mary - 13879 N. FM 81, Panna Maria, TX 78144; Mailing: P.O.Box 9, Panna Maria, TX 78144 t) 830-780-2748 pan1854@yahoo.com pannamariachurch.com Rev. Wieslaw Iwaniec, Pst.; CRP Stds.: 35

St. Helena -

PEARSALL

Immaculate Heart of Mary - 422 W. Brazos, Pearsall, TX 78061; Mailing: P.O. Box AK, Pearsall, TX 78061 t) 830-334-4046 ihmcatholicptx@gmail.com ihmptx.org Rev. Jesus Camacho, Pst.; Dcn. Marcus Salazar; Dcn. Roberto Villarreal; Rebecca Ramirez, Dir.; Melissa Alcala, Parish Bookkeeper; CRP Stds.: 146

PLEASANTON

St. Andrew - 626 Market St., Pleasanton, TX 78064-2747 t) 830-569-3356 info@standrewpleasanton.org; debbie@standrewpleasanton.org standrewpleasonton.org Dcn. Bennie Garcia Jr.; Dcn. Joey Moczygemba; Dcn. Kurt G. Warnken; Deborah Shows, DRE; Rev. Ian Robbins, Pst.; CRP Stds.: 168

Sacred Heart - 365 St. Francis Ave., Campbellton, TX 78008; Mailing: St Andrew Church, 626 Market St., Pleasanton, TX 78064 t) (830) 569-3356 (St. Andrew office #)

St. Luke-Loire - 3930 FM 536, Pleasanton, TX 78064 t) 830-393-6021 frmikeajewole@yahoo.co.uk Rev. Michael Ajewole, M.S.P., Pst.; Danelle Pascarella, DRE; CRP Stds.: 35

Our Lady of Guadalupe - 170 Hackberry St., Leming, TX 78050; Mailing: 3930 FM 536, Pleasanton, TX 78064

POTEET

St. Philip Benizi - 274 Ave. H, Poteet, TX 78065; Mailing: P.O. Box 348, Poteet, TX 78065 t) 830-742-3796 alelocicm1@aol.com; stphilipbenizicatholicchurch@gmail.com Rev. Albert Lelo Luemba, C.I.C.M., Pst.; Alma Herrera, DRE; CRP Stds.: 260

POTH

Blessed Sacrament - 488 W. Westmeyer St., Poth, TX 78147; Mailing: P.O. Box 339, Poth, TX 78147 t) 830-484-3303 (DRE); 830-484-3302 bless@gvec.net blessedsacramentpoth.org Rev. Damian Jaje, S.D.S., Pst.; Dcn. Alan Crosby; Dcn. Jesse Nunez; Rebecca Raabe, DRE; CRP Stds.: 258

ROCKSPRINGS

Sacred Heart of Mary - 401 N US Hwy 377, Rocksprings, TX 78880; Mailing: P.O. Box 887, Rocksprings, TX 78880 t) 830-682-2165 sacredheartmary@swtexas.net Rev. Kishore Bathula, Pst.; Dcn. Gary Overbay; Dee Dworaczyk, Bookkeeper;

St. Mary Magdalen - 311 E. Third St., Camp Wood, TX 78833 t) 830-683-2165; 830-234-3366 Dcn. Samuel Bernal;

St. Raymond of Pennafort - 2nd St. and Mountain St., Leakey, TX 78873 t) 830-683-2165; 830-279-5860 kishore.bathula@archsa.org Dcn. Ruben Navarro;

RUNGE

St. Anthony's - 809 N Helena, Runge, TX 78151; Mailing: P.O. Box 188, Runge, TX 78151 t) 830-239-4146 contreras.irene@yahoo.com; stanthonyscc@yahoo.com Dcn. Guadalupe Cantu; Rev. Anthony Male (India), Pst.; CRP Stds.: 33

SABINAL

St. Patrick Catholic Church - 501 N. Orange St., Sabinal, TX 78881-0117; Mailing: P.O. Box 117, Sabinal, TX 78881-0117 t) 830-988-2255 parish@stpccs.org; father@stpccs.org www.facebook.com/stpatricksabinal Very Rev. Matthew De Leon, Pst.; Martina Flores, DRE; CRP Stds.: 44

St. Joseph - 105 W Houston St, Knippa, TX 78870 t) (830) 988-2255

St. Mary - 32141 FM 187, Vanderpool, TX 78885 t) 830-966-6268

SAN ANTONIO

Cathedral of San Fernando - 115 W. Main Plaza, San Antonio, TX 78205-2718; Mailing: 231 W. Commerce, San Antonio, TX 78205 t) 210-227-1297 info@sfcathedral.org www.sfcathedral.org Carlos Berardo Velazquez, Rector; Rev. Ruben Garcia, Par. Vicar; Dcn. Ramon Figueroa; Dcn. Roger Macias; Dcn. Joseph Marroquin; CRP Stds.: 72

San Francesco di Paola (Italian) - 205 Piazza Italia, San Antonio, TX 78207 t) 210-227-0548

St. Agnes - 804 Ruiz St. (Church address), San Antonio, TX 78207; Mailing: 829 Ruiz St., San Antonio,, TX 78207 t) 210-227-8258 glasmary@hotmail.com; ninfa.delgado@stagneschurchsa.org www.stagneschurchsa.org Rev. Lauro Regulo Gonzalez, M.N.M., Pst.; Sr. Maria Teresa Gonzalez, DRE; CRP Stds.: 250

St. Alphonsus - 1202 S. Zarzamora St., San Antonio, TX 78207; Mailing: 2004 Chihuahua St., San Antonio, TX 78207 t) 210-433-9365 st.alphonsus@sbcglobal.net Friar Andrew Martinez, Pst.; Dcn. Trinidad Gutierrez; CRP Stds.: 20

St. Ann - 210 Saint Ann, San Antonio, TX 78201 t) 210-734-6687 www.stannsa.org Very Rev. Ricardo Ramirez, Pst.; CRP Stds.: 128

St. Anthony Mary Claret - 6150 Roft Rd., San Antonio, TX 78253 t) 210-688-9033 saclaret@saclaret.com www.samcsa.com Rev. Jan Piotr Klak, Pst.; Rev. Arul Francis Arputham; Dcn. Thomas John Elms; Dcn. Eugene A. Festa; Dcn. Jerome P. Kozar; Dcn. Antonio Valdez; Dcn. Jose 'Joe' Berma; Luis Astorga, Admin.; Jennifer Rupert, DRE; CRP Stds.: 975

St. Anthony of Padua - 102 Lorenz Rd., San Antonio, TX 78209 t) 210-824-1743 secretary@stanthonydepadua.org www.stanthonydepadua.org Rev. Kevin Shanahan, M.S.C., Pst.; Dcn. Joe Borrego; Jose Castillo, Music Min.; Marcia Amy, Pst. Assoc.; Sonya Sanchez, DRE; CRP Stds.: 229

St. Anthony Parish - 14523 Roadrunner Way, San Antonio, TX 78249-1515 t) 210-699-9594 brian.garcia@archsa.org Rev. Brian Garcia, Chap.; Marina Olivares, Campus Min.; Leann Richardson, Campus Min.;

Basilica of the National Shrine of the Little Flower, Our Lady of Mt. Carmel and St. Therese Parish - 1715 N. Zarzamora, San Antonio, TX 78201; Mailing: 824 Kentucky Ave, San Antonio, TX 78201 t) 210-735-9126 x110 (CRP); 210-735-9126 x100 dre@littleflowerbasilica.org; scantu@littleflowerbasilica.org www.littleflowerbasilica.org Friar Gregory Ross, OCD, Pst.; Friar Jorge Cabrera, OCD, Par. Vicar; Friar Sam Anthony Morello, OCD, In Res.; Friar Emmanuel Javert Nnadozie, O.C.D., In Res.; Friar Raul Reyes, OCD, In Res.; Yolanda Vargas, DRE; Friar Luis Joaquin Castaneda, OCD, Prov.; Laura Cole, Bus. Mgr.; Dcn. Antonio G. Rodriguez; CRP Stds.: 81

Basilica of the National Shrine of the Little Flower, Our Lady of Mt. Carmel and St. Therese Parish School - (Grades PreK-8) 905 Kentucky Ave., San Antonio, TX 78201 t) 210-732-9207 jcastro@littleflowerschool.net www.littleflowercatholicschool.org Jackie Castro, Prin.; Stds.: 66; Sr. Tchrs.: 1; Lay Tchrs.: 5

St. Benedict - 4535 Lord Rd., San Antonio, TX 78220 t) 210-648-4632 (CRP); 210-648-0123 lord4535@att.net; st_benedict_church@sbcglobal.net stbenedictchurchsa.org Rev. Juan Carlos Bello-Carrillo, T.O.R., Pst.; Dcn. Todd Boyer; Dcn. Trinidad E. Gutierrez, Parish Coordinator; CRP Stds.: 63

Blessed Sacrament - 600 Oblate Dr., San Antonio, TX 78216 t) (210) 824-7231 resparza@blessedsacrament.church www.blessedsacrament.church Dcn. Paul Anthony Cardenas; Rev. Chris Munoz, Pst.; Dcn. Frank Martinez; Dcn. Alan Schultz; Dcn. Thomas Tucker; CRP Stds.: 161

Blessed Sacrament School - (Grades PreK-8) t) (210) 824-3381 michael.fierro@blessedschool.com www.blessedschool.com Michael Fierro, Prin.; Stds.: 170; Sr. Tchrs.: 2; Lay Tchrs.: 22

St. Bonaventure - 1918 Palo Alto Rd., San Antonio, TX 78211 t) 210-922-1882 (CRP); 210-922-1685 stbonaventure@att.net www.stbonaventuresa.org Rev. Jean-Oscar Nlandu, Pst.; Dcn. Martin Alfaro; Dcn. Luis L. Arredondo; Juan Serros, DRE; CRP Stds.: 197

St. Brigid - 6907 Kitchener St., San Antonio, TX 78240 t) 210-696-0896 parishoffice@stbrigidcc.org www.stbrigidcc.org Rev. Gilberto Vallejo, Pst.; Dcn. Donald V. Bradley Jr.; Dcn. Ruben Davila; CRP Stds.: 295

St. Cecilia - 125 W. Whittier St., San Antonio, TX 78210-2897 t) 210-533-7109 pastor@stceciliasa.org www.stceciliasa.org Very Rev. Edvin Rodriguez, Pst.; CRP Stds.: 75

Purisima Concepcion - 807 Mission Rd., San Antonio, TX 78210 t) (210) 533-7109 x212 c) (210) 533-8955 businessoffice@missionconcepcion.org Dcn. Raymond F. Jimenez, Pst. Assoc.; Rev. Marcos Ramos, Chap.;

Christ the King - 2610 Perez St., San Antonio, TX 78207; Mailing: 2623 Perez St, San Antonio, TX 78207 t) 210-433-3640 (CRP); 210-433-6301 ctksare@gmail.com; christ.church26@sbcglobal.net www.ctksatx.com Rev. Martin Garcia-Avila, Pst.; Juan Arriola, DRE; CRP Stds.: 129

St. Clare - 7701 Somerset Rd., San Antonio, TX 78211 t) 210-924-5252 x303 (CRP); 210-924-5252; 210-621-3689 stclchurch@att.net; pastor@stclaresatx.net www.stclaresatx.net Rev. Richard Samour, Pst.; Dcn. Alfred Gaona; Dcn. Gilbert M. Maldonado; Maria Gonzales, DRE; CRP Stds.: 44

Divine Providence - 5667 Old Pearsall Rd., San Antonio, TX 78242-2335 t) 210-623-3970 dpcatholic@gmail.com dpusa.org Rev. Ryan Carnecer, C.I.C.M., Pst.; Dcn. Rudy Mendez; Quena Chavez, DRE; Rosa Balderas, Registrar; Elvira Stephenson, Bus. Mgr.; CRP Stds.: 122

St. Dominic - 5919 Ingram Rd., San Antonio, TX 78228 t) 210-435-6211 welcome@stdominicsa.org www.stdominicsa.org Rev. Mike Horan, Pst.; Rev. Agustin Estrada, Par. Vicar; Dcn. Wayne Archer; Dcn. Ray Gonzalez; Dcn. Scott Imburgia; CRP Stds.: 434

El Carmen Catholic Church - 18555 Leal Rd. (Losoya), San Antonio, TX 78221 t) 210-626-2333 olomtcarmel@gmail.com www.facebook.com/elcarmenlosoya Our Lady of Mt. Carmel-Losoya, Nuestra Señora del Carmen, El Carmen Catholic Church Rev. Dennis Venegas, Admin.; Maria Celia Aldrich, DRE; CRP Stds.: 132

St. Elizabeth Ann Seton - 8500 Cross Mountain Tr., San Antonio, TX 78255 t) 210-698-1941 ed@seaschurch.com seaschurch.com Rev. Msgr. Conor McGrath, Pst.; Rev. Roberto Rosales, Vicar; Dcn. Lee Jan; Valerie Trevino, DRE;

St. Francis of Assisi - 4201 De Zavala Rd., San Antonio, TX 78249-2000 t) 210-492-4600 assistant@sfasat.org sfasat.org Rev. Tony Vilano, Pst.; Rev. Tomichan Moonnanappillil, Assoc. Pst.; Dcn. Michael A. Portele; Dcn. Johnny Flores; Dcn. James H. Hewson; Dcn. Timothy E. Tucker; Dcn. Pete Nañez; Dcn. Manuel R. Limones; Sr. Rose Kruppa, C.D.P., Pst. Assoc.; Monica Harness, Youth Min.; Larry Perry, DRE; Miriam Flores, Dir.; CRP Stds.: 367

St. Gabriel - 747 S.W. 39th St., San Antonio, TX 78237 t) 210-433-3689 stgabrielchurch1958@gmail.com Rev. Joaquin J. Rojas, M.N.M. (Mexico), Pst.; Rev. Fernando Quezada Covarrubias, MNM, Vicar; Consuelo Alfaro, Dir.; CRP Stds.: 52

St. Gerard Majella - 1523 Iowa St., San Antonio, TX 78203 t) 210-533-0161 parishoffice@saintgerardchurch.org; pastor@saintgerardchurch.org saintgerardchurch.org Rev. Donald Willard, C.Ss.R., Pst.; Rev. Robert H. Lindsey, C.Ss.R., Assoc. Pst.; Bro. Charles Fucik, C.Ss.R., Bookkeeper; CRP Stds.: 50

St. Gregory's - 700 Dewhurst Rd., San Antonio, TX 78213 t) 210-342-5271 frmiguel@stgregorys.net; saintgregsa@stgregorys.net www.stgregorys.net Dcn. Carlos Cerna; Dcn. Joe Lopez; Rev. Miguel Moreno, Pst.; Dcn. Fred Campos Jr.; Paul Canales, Admin.; Gloria Silva, DRE; Ezekiel O'Campo, Pst. Assoc.; CRP Stds.: 108

St. Gregory's School - (Grades PreK-8) 700 Dewhurst RD, San Antonio, TX 78213 t) 210-342-0281 x311; 210-342-0281 x368 ana.cortez@stgregorys.net www.stgregorysa.org Ana Cortez, Prin.; Stds.: 160; Lay Tchrs.: 19

St. Helena - 14714 Edgemont, San Antonio, TX 78247 t) 210-653-3316 estherc@sthelena.org www.sthelena.org Rev. Marcin Pawel Czyz, SDS, Pst.; Dcn. Gabe Becerra; Dcn. Paul Anthony Cardenas; Dcn. Paul Gustowski; Dcn. John Murphy; CRP Stds.: 274

St. Henry - 1619 S. Flores St., San Antonio, TX 78204 t) 210-225-6877 sthenrys@sbcglobal.net www.sthenrysatx.org Rev. Robert E. Hogan, B.B.D., Pst.; Dcn. Myron Benavidez; Dcn. Joseph L. De Leon; Bro. Ruben Garza, Pst. Assoc.; Sr. Sheeja Kannanthara, DRE; CRP Stds.: 101

Holy Family - 152 Florencia, San Antonio, TX 78228-5899 t) 210-433-8216 secretary@holyfamilysa.com; bookkeeper@holyfamilysa.com holyfamilysa.com Rev. Humphrey Milimo, OMI, Admin.; Dcn. Lorenzo Valdez; Sr. Maria Romero, DRE; CRP Stds.: 110

Holy Name - 3814 Nash Blvd., San Antonio, TX 78223 t) 210-333-5020 ibickel@holynameusa.org; holynameadmin@holynameusa.org www.holynameusa.org Rev. Juan Carlos Bello-Carrillo, T.O.R., Pst.; Dcn. Reynaldo Hinojosa Sr.; Dcn. Daniel Kearns; Dcn. Roberto R. Ruiz; Dcn. Rudy Sanchez; Jun Sorio, Music Min.; Irma Bickel, DRE; CRP Stds.: 150

Holy Name School - (Grades PreK-8) 3814 Nash Blvd, San Antonio, TX 78223 t) 210-333-7356 jtiller@hncstx.org www.hncstx.org Susie Garza, Prin.; Stds.: 149; Lay Tchrs.: 12

Holy Redeemer - 1819 Nevada, San Antonio, TX 78203 t) 210-532-5358 kevin.fausz@archsa.org www.catholicearth.com/hr-sa Rev. Kevin P. Fausz, C.M., Pst.; CRP Stds.: 35

Holy Rosary - 159 Camino Santa Maria, San Antonio, TX 78228 t) 210-433-3241 hrosaryparish@swbell.net www.holyrosarysa.org Rev. Neville O'Donohue, Pst.; Dcn. Francisco Sandoval; Dcn. Albert Sanchez; Rev. Brandon Paluch, S.M., In Res.; CRP Stds.: 92

Holy Spirit - 8134 Blanco Rd., San Antonio, TX 78216; Mailing: P.O. Box 460729, San Antonio, TX 78246 t) 210-341-1395 frmark@holyspiritsa.org; socialmedia@holyspiritsa.org www.holyspiritsa.org Rev. Mark Dreves, Pst.; Dcn. Omar Garcia; Dcn. Ricardo Rivas; Dcn. Jose A. Santos; Dcn. Warren A. Wilkins; Dcn. Evan Wittig; CRP Stds.: 431

Holy Spirit School - (Grades PreK-8) 770 W. Ramsey Rd., San Antonio, TX 78216 t) 210-349-1169 info@hscssa.org www.hscssa.org Lourdes Garcia, Prin.; Emily Garza, Vice Prin.; Stds.: 415; Lay Tchrs.: 34

Holy Trinity - 20523 Huebner Rd., San Antonio, TX 78258-3915 t) 210-497-4145 (CRP); 210-497-4200 x307 www.holytrinitysat.org Rev. Rodolfo Caballero, Pst.; Rev. Edward Gonzales, Assoc. Pst.; Dcn. Michael Cleary; Dcn. John B. Eichelberger; Dcn. Joe Franklin; Dcn. David R. Seguin; Dcn. Ricardo Serdan; Dcn. Brad Wakely; CRP Stds.: 1,208

Immaculate Conception - 314 Merida St., San Antonio, TX 78207 t) 210-225-2986 secy_icc@yahoo.com; andrew.martinez@archsa.org www.facebook.com/immaculate-conception-church Friar Andrew Martinez, Pst.; CRP Stds.: 40

Immaculate Heart of Mary - 617 S. Santa Rosa Blvd., San Antonio, TX 78204 t) 210-226-8268 admin@ihmsatx.org ihmsatx.org Rev. Benjamin Romero, C.M.F., Pst.; Dcn. Salvador Rodriguez; Jesse Garcia, Bus. Mgr.; Lisa Martinez, Admin. Asst.; Rev. Mark Clarke, C.M.F., In Res.; Mary Salas, DRE; CRP Stds.: 120

St. James the Apostle - 907 W. Theo Ave., San Antonio, TX 78225 t) 210-922-2136 sonny.aryanto@archsa.org www.stjamestheapostlesa.org Dcn. Chris Von Allmen; Dcn. Ernest Moran; Rev. Roger Brigente Montecalvo, CICM, In Res.; MaryAnn Gaytan, DRE; Rev. Sonny Aryanto, C.I.C.M., Pst.; Elizabeth Tucker, Bus. Mgr.; CRP Stds.: 245

St. James the Apostle School - (Grades PreK-8) t) 210-924-1201 sr.debbie.walker@stjamesschoolsa.org www.stjamesschoolsa.org Sr. Debbie Walker, Prin.; Stds.: 225

St. Jerome - 7955 Real Rd., San Antonio, TX 78263-3003 t) 210-648-2694 st.jerome@stjeromesatx.org www.stjeromesatx.org Rev. Krzysztof Pawlowski, Admin.; CRP Stds.: 208

St. Joan of Arc - 2829 Ackermann Rd., San Antonio, TX 78219-2100 t) 210-661-5277 Rev. Heliodoro Lucatero, Pst.; Dcn. Victor Cepero; Dcn. Wilfredo (Todd) Dapilmoto; Dcn. Robert Galan Jr.; Dcn. Valentin Cepero; CRP Stds.: 104

St. John Berchmans - 1147 Cupples Rd., San Antonio, TX 78226 t) 210-434-3247 rosydre@yahoo.com; accounting@stjohnberchmans.com Rev. Fidele O. Dikete, Pst.; Dcn. Jesus Rodriguez; Dcn. Jose L. Ocampo; Rosalinda Rodriguez, DRE; CRP Stds.: 70

St. John Berchmans School - (Grades PreK-8) t) 210-433-0411 sjb.info@sjbsa.com www.sjbschool-sa.com Nora Garcia, Prin.; Ariana Hopcus, Librn.;

St. John Neumann - 6680 Crestway Dr., San Antonio, TX 78239 t) 210-654-1643 info@sjnsa.org; pa@sjnsa.org www.sjnsa.org Rev. Alex Pereida, Pst.; Blanca Loza Rocha, DRE; Dcn. Stephen Kerr, Sacr. Min.; Dcn. Larry Lindsey, Sacr. Min.; CRP Stds.: 153

St. John the Evangelist - 4603 St. John's Way, San Antonio, TX 78212 t) 210-738-2201 st-john@sbcglobal.net www.stjohntheevangelist-sa.org Very Rev. Jean Baptiste Magbia Zabusu, Admin.; Dcn. Thomas Villalon; Yolanda Gutierrez, DRE; CRP Stds.: 90

Saint Jose Luis Sanchez Del Rio Catholic Parish - 21140 Gathering Oak, San Antonio, TX 78260 t) 210-497-0323 lenin.naffate@archsa.org; pedroram@stjoselito.faith www.stjoselito.faith/ Rev. Lenin Naffate (Mexico), Pst.; Dcn. Ron Sandoval; CRP Stds.: 56

St. Joseph - 623 E. Commerce St., San Antonio, TX 78205 t) 210-227-0126 x210 sjcdowntown@gmail.com Rev. Norman Pelletier, Pst.; Rev. Joseph Thai Tran, Vicar; Dcn. Vincent Scheel; Beatrice Bailey, DRE; CRP Stds.: 21

St. Joseph Spouse of the Virgin Mary - 535 New Laredo Hwy., San Antonio, TX 78211-1900 t) 210-924-4383 stjosephss.frontoffice@gmail.com www.stjosephss.org Friar Francisco Ramirez, OFM, Cap, Pst.; Dcn. Guadalupe De Luna; Dcn. Genaro Herrera; Dcn. Mauro Gonzalez; CRP Stds.: 109

St. Jude - 130 S. San Augustine Ave., San Antonio, TX 78237 t) (210) 432-8044; (210) 432-1582 (CRP) stjude.religioused@yahoo.com Rev. Alberto Marin, Pst.; Rev. Gustavo Montanez, Par. Vicar; Dcn. Felipe Barajas; Dcn. Bartolo Ramos; Lisa Martinez, DRE;

St Lawrence the Martyr Catholic Church - 236 E. Petaluma Blvd, Bldg #4, San Antonio, TX 78221 t) 210-924-6470 (CRP); 210-924-4401 www.stlawrencesa.org Rev. Arnold Ibarra, Pst.; Dcn. Adam Garza; Dcn. Nestor Huizar Jr.; Mary Zavala, DRE; Alicia J Ortiz, Bus. Mgr.; CRP Stds.: 227

St. Leo - 4401 S. Flores, San Antonio, TX 78214 t) 210-533-9108 terrisanch@yahoo.com; stleoschurch@yahoo.com wwwstleoschurch.net Rev. Frank Macias, Pst.; Dcn. Robert M. Caldwell Jr.; Dcn. Gerald Gonzalez; Dcn. Robert Paiz Ibarra; Dcn. J. Mark Luther; Dcn. Thomas Torres; Teresa Sanchez, DRE; CRP Stds.: 420

St. Leonard's - 8510 S. Zarzamora, San Antonio, TX 78224-2099 t) 210-924-6000 parishoffice@stleonardsa.org www.stleonardsa.org Rev. Servando Guerrero, Pst.; Dcn. Charles Gamez; CRP Stds.: 197

St. Luke - 4603 Manitou Dr., San Antonio, TX 78228-1889 t) 210-433-2777 office@stlukecatholic.org www.saintlukeparish.com Rev. Joel Quezada, M.Sp.S., Pst.; Rev. Jorge Haro, M.Sp.S, Par. Vicar; Dcn. Jack Don Nichols; Dcn. Ruben Caudillo; Dcn. Richard Gonzalez; Dcn. Jorge Pena; Dcn. Robert Torres; CRP Stds.: 246

St. Luke School - (Grades PreK-8) t) 210-434-2011 debbie.rodriguez@stlukecatholic.org www.stlukecatholic.org Nadine Buhrman, Prin.; Stds.: 455; Lay Tchrs.: 32

St. Margaret Mary - 1314 Fair Ave., San Antonio, TX 78223 t) 210-532-6309 info@stmmcc.org www.stmmcc.org Rev. Jimmy David Drennan, Pst.; Dcn. Candelario Garcia; Dcn. Francisco Lafuente; Dcn. Gerardo Mechler; Dcn. Gabriel J. Rosas; Luis Garcia, Youth Min.; Linda Rubio, DRE; Dcn. Jose Almanza; CRP Stds.: 205

St. Catherine - 2202 Hicks St., San Antonio, TX 78223; Mailing: 1314 Fair Ave., San Antonio, TX 78223 Rev. Jimmy Drennan, Pst.;

St. Mark the Evangelist - 1602 Thousand Oaks Dr., San Antonio, TX 78232-2398 t) 210-494-1606 dhamlin@stmarkevangelist.com stmarkevangelist.com Rev. Msgr. Kevin E. Ryan, Pst.; Dcn. Larry Brisiel; Dcn. Gilbert S. Hernandez; Dcn. Hipolito Huerta; Dcn. Ramon C. Rodriguez; Dcn. Jorge Cabello; Dorothea G. Hamlin, Admin.; Robert Martinez, Liturgy Dir.; Paul Vance, DRE; Megan Beyers, Youth Min.; Josh Frilling, Music Dir.; Anne Kemper, RCIA Dir.; Mary Anne Votion, Dir. Devel.; CRP Stds.: 499

St. Martin de Porres - 1730 Dahlgreen Ave., San Antonio, TX 78237 t) 210-432-5203 sporres1730@gmail.com Rev. Joaquin J. Rojas, M.N.M. (Mexico), Pst.; Rev. Fernando Quezada Covarrubias, Par. Vicar; Dcn. Benito Resendiz; CRP Stds.: 102

St. Mary - 202 N. St. Mary's St., San Antonio, TX 78205 t) 210-226-8381 stmarysa78205@gmail.com stmaryschurchsa.org Rev. John J. Gordon, O.M.I., Pst.; Rev. Edward Hauf, O.M.I., Assoc. Pst.; CRP Stds.: 6

St. Mary Magdalen - 1710 Clower St., San Antonio, TX 78201 t) 210-735-5284 (CRP); 210-735-5269 smm@stmarymagdalensa.org Rev. William H. Combs, Pst.; Dcn. Arturo Lozano; Dcn. David Zamora; Rev. Robert E. Hogan, B.B.D., In Res.; Rev. George T. Montague, S.M., In Res.; Francis Portillo, DRE; CRP Stds.: 315

St. Mary Magdalen School - (Grades PreK-8) 1700 Clower St., San Antonio, TX 78201 t) 210-735-1381 william.daily@stmmsa.org www.stmmsa.org William Daily, Prin.; Roberta Gujardo, Librn.; Stds.: 452; Sr. Tchrs.: 2; Lay Tchrs.: 37

Mary, Mother of the Church Catholic Parish - 311 Seascape Dr., San Antonio, TX 78251 t) 210-395-5137 office@mary-our-mother.org www.mary-our-mother.org Rev. Martin J. Leopold, Pst.; CRP Stds.: 170

St. Matthew Catholic Church - 10703 Wurzbach Rd., San Antonio, TX 78230 t) 210-478-5010 (CRP); 210-478-5000 srtherese@stmatts.org; kay@stmatts.org www.stmatts.org Rev. Eric Ritter, Pst.; Rev. Paul Melgarejo, Par. Vicar; Dcn. Tom Fox; Dcn. Alonzo Guzman; Dcn. John Ochiagha; Dcn. Roberto Rios; Dcn. Scott Sowell; Dcn. Oscar Vela Jr.; Sr. Therese Gleitz, DRE; CRP Stds.: 406

St. Matthew's School - (Grades PreK-8) t) 210-478-5099 office@smcssa.org Geneva Salinas, Prin.;

St. Michael - 418 Indiana, San Antonio, TX 78210 t) 210-532-3707 stmichaelrcc78210@yahoo.com www.stmichaelsa.com Rev. Kevin P. Fausz, C.M., Pst.; Dcn. Jesus Almanza; Margarita Sanchez, DRE; CRP Stds.: 27

Our Lady of Good Counsel - 1204 Castroville Rd., San Antonio, TX 78237 t) 210-432-6430 (CRP); 210-432-0873 olgcsa@yahoo.com Rev. Joaquin J. Rojas Fernandez, Pst.; Rev. Fernando Quezada Covarrubias, Vicar; Marisol Rodriguez, Bus. Mgr.;

Our Lady of Grace - 223 E. Summit Ave., San Antonio, TX 78212 t) 210-734-7285 www.olgsa.org Rev. Jorge Campos-Covarrubias, Pst.; Rev. Binoj Jose Elukkunnel, H.G.N., Par. Vicar; CRP Stds.: 261

Our Lady of Guadalupe - 1321 El Paso St., San Antonio, TX 78207 t) 210-226-4064 olginfo@olgsanantonio.org www.facebook.com/our-lady-of-guadalupe-shrine Friar Andrew Martinez, Pst.; Dcn. Ruben Felan; Dcn. Joe Avila; CRP Stds.: 25

Our Lady of Perpetual Help - 618 S. Grimes St., San Antonio, TX 78203 t) 210-532-7031 dre.olphsa@gmail.com; secretary.olphsa@gmail.com Rev. Kevin P. Fausz, C.M., Pst.; Dcn. Jesus Almanza; CRP Stds.: 50

Our Lady of Sorrows - 3107 N. St. Mary's St., San Antonio, TX 78212 t) 210-732-6295 office@olssa.org www.olssa.org Rev. Jose Ramon Perez-Martinez, Pst.; Rev. Binoj Jose Elukkunnel, H.G.N., Par. Vicar; Rev. Marian Piekarczyk, S.D.S., Spiritual Adv./Care Srvcs.; CRP Stds.: 14

Our Lady of the Angels - 1214 Stonewall St., San Antonio, TX 78211 t) 210-924-6591 ourlady1214@gmail.com; srpatriciaoladre@gmail.com www.olasa.org Friar Donald Rank OFM CAP, OFM Cap, Pst.; Dcn. Alejandro Diaz, OFM, Cap; Dcn. Albert Ramirez; Sr. Maria Patricia Gonzalez, HCG, DRE; CRP Stds.: 133

St. Patrick - 1114 Willow St., San Antonio, TX 78208 t) 210-226-5223 stpatrickwillow@hotmail.com www.saintpatricks.net Rev. Johanes Teguh Raharjo, C.I.C.M., Pst.; CRP Stds.: 92

St. Paul - 350 Sutton Dr., San Antonio, TX 78228; Mailing: 1201 Donaldson Ave., San Antonio, TX 78228 t) 210-733-7152 aarismendez@saintpaulsa.org; mgonzales@saintpaulsa.org www.saintpaulsa.org Rev. Prasanna Kumar Mese, Pst.; Dcn. Agustin Arismendez; Dcn. Adrian Cepeda; Dcn. Carl Weekly; Jennifer Smyrl, Pst. Assoc.; Virginia Valenzuela, Pst. Assoc.; Michelle Weekley, Pst. Assoc.; Rosie Arismendez, DRE; CRP Stds.: 110

St. Paul School - (Grades PreK-8) 307 John Adams, San Antonio, TX 78228 t) 210-732-2741 mary.crow@stpaulroyals.org Mary I. Crow, Prin.; Stds.: 121; Sr. Tchrs.: 1; Lay Tchrs.: 7

Community Center - 1201Donaldson Ave., San Antonio, TX 78228 t) 210-736-0055 mdavila@saintpaulsa.org Mary Davila, Bus. Mgr.;

Learning Center - 1201 Donaldson Ave., San Antonio, TX 78228 t) 210-738-8715 (Daycare) Josie Gonzalez, Dir.;

St. Peter Prince of the Apostles - 111 Barilla Pl., San Antonio, TX 78209 t) 210-822-3367; 210-822-3367 x306 (CRP) church@stpeterprince.org; re@stpeterprince.org www.stpeterprinceoftheapostles.org Rev. Jorge Campos-Covarrubias, Pst.; Rev. Binoj Jose Elukkunel, Par. Vicar; Dcn. John Paul Benage; Dcn. Robert Kusenberger; Dcn. Richard De Hoyos, DRE; Juan Caralos Hinojosa, Bus. Mgr.; CRP Stds.: 112

St. Peter Prince of the Apostles School - (Grades PreK-8) 112 Marcia Pl., San Antonio, TX 78209 t) 210-824-3171 becky.pawelek@stpeterprince.org www.stpeterprince.org Gabriel Duarte, Prin.; Stds.: 100; Lay Tchrs.: 21

St. Philip of Jesus - 142 E. Lambert St., San Antonio, TX 78204; Mailing: 150 E. Lambert St., San Antonio, TX 78204 t) 210-226-5024 parishinfo@stphilipofjesus.org www.stphilipofjesus.org Rev. Sean Stilson, Admin.; Dcn. Gilbert C. De La Portilla; Dcn. Jose Sanchez; Dcn. Hector Sandoval; CRP Stds.: 106

St. Pius X - 3907 Harry Wurzbach Rd, San Antonio, TX 78209; Mailing: 3303 Urban Cresrt Dr, San Antonio, TX 78209 t) 210-824-0139 stpiusx@stpiusxsa.org www.spxsa.church Rev. Patrick O'Brien, Pst.; Rev. Praveen Lakkisetti, Par. Vicar; Dcn. Kevin Kevin LaFrance, Pst. Assoc.; Dcn. Patrick Cunningham; CRP Stds.: 84

St. Pius X School - (Grades PreSchool-8) 7734 Robin Rest Dr., San Antonio, TX 78209 t) 210-824-6431 spxschool@stpiusxsa.org school.stpiusxsa.org/ Dr. Genese Bell, Prin.; Stds.: 215; Lay Tchrs.: 16

Prince of Peace - 7893 N. Grissom Rd., San Antonio, TX 78251 t) 210-681-5063 (CRP); 210-681-8330 communications@princeofpeacecatholic.org www.princeofpeacecatholic.org/ Rev. Jomon Joseph, MSFS, Pst.; Dcn. Robert G. Correa; Dcn. Richard Juarez; Dcn. Timothy McCarthy; Dcn. Dennis Lopez; Dcn. Agripino Sanabria; Barbara Forde, DRE; CRP Stds.: 403

Resurrection of the Lord - 7990 W. Military Dr., San Antonio, TX 78227 t) 210-675-1470 rojipeter@yahoo.com; lvega@resurrectionsatx.org www.resurrectionsatx.org Rev. Roji Peter, H.G.N., Pst.; Dcn. Jose Angel Martinez; Dcn. George Salazar Sr.; Rosemary Martinez, DRE; CRP Stds.: 206

St. Rose of Lima - 9883 Marbach Rd., San Antonio, TX 78245 t) 210-675-1920 info@stroseoflima.church stroseoflima.church Rev. Victor Valdez, Pst.; Rev. Wanjiru Ndung'u, Vicar; Sr. Abigail Toledo, DRE; CRP Stds.: 884

Sacred Heart - 2114 W. Houston St., San Antonio, TX 78207-3496 t) 210-227-9763 (CRP); 210-227-5059 x203 frfredshsa@gmail.com; sacredheartsa@hotmail.com Rev. Frederic Mizengo, C.I.C.M., Pst.; Dcn. Julio Garcia III; Rev. Roy Quiogue, C.I.C.M., In Res.; Martha Garcia, DRE; CRP Stds.: 123

San Francisco de la Espada - 10040 Espada Rd., San Antonio, TX 78214 t) 210-627-2064 espadacabrini@gmail.com missionsanfranciscodelaespada.org/ Friar Macario Torres Torres, OFM, Pst.; Dcn. Alberto R. Rodriguez; Sonia Valero, DRE;

St. Frances Cabrini - 1606 San Casimiro, San Antonio, TX 78214 Dcn. Albert Rodriguez, Dir.;

San Jose y San Miguel - 701 E. Pyron Ave., San Antonio, TX 78214 t) 210-922-0543 sanjoseinsatx@yahoo.com www.missionsanjosechurh.org Rev. Claudio Rogelio Martinez, O.F.M., Pst.; Dcn. Frank J. Chip Perry; Dcn. George Wunderlich; CRP Stds.: 38

San Juan Capistrano - 9101 Graf Rd., San Antonio, TX 78214-0308; Mailing: P.O. Box 14308, San Antonio, TX 78214 t) 210-532-2806 msjcapistranotx@gmail.com Rev. Rogelio Martinez Ruteaga, OFM, Admin.; Dcn. Carlos Marquez Jr.;

San Juan De Los Lagos Shrine - 3231 El Paso St., San Antonio, TX 78207-4607 t) 210-433-9722 sanjuanshrinesa@gmail.com sanjuanshrinesa.org Rev. Steven Montez, OMI, Pst.; Dcn. Juan Carlos Carreno; Dcn. Albert Salinas; CRP Stds.: 64

Senyor Santo Nino de Cebu - 5655 Rigsby Ave., San Antonio, TX 78222 t) 210-648-1705 stonino@usa.com stonino.org Rev. Martin Parayno, O.S.B. (Philippines), Pst.; CRP Stds.: 100

Shrine of St. Padre Pio of Pietrelcina - 3843 Bulverde Pkwy., San Antonio, TX 78259; Mailing: 20770 US Hwy. 281N, Ste. 108, PMB 611, San Antonio, TX 78258 t) 210-497-6101 stpadrepio@sbcglobal.net www.shrineofpadrepio.com Rev. Msgr. Patrick J. Ragsdale, VU, Pst.; Dcn. Richard Armendariz; Dcn. Clinton A. Couch; Dcn. Kenneth Gottardy; Dcn. John Patrick McGarrity; Dcn. Richard F. Neville Jr.; CRP Stds.: 227

Shrine of St. Padre Pio -

St. Thomas More - 4411 Moana Dr., San Antonio, TX 78218 t) 210-655-5070 stmparish@live.com www.thomasmoresatx.org Rev. Michael English, Assoc. Pst.; Dcn. Rolando Ruben Guerra; Dcn. Timothy M. Tate Sr.; CRP Stds.: 120

St. Thomas More School - (Grades PreK-8) 4427 Moana Dr., San Antonio, TX 78218 t) 210-655-2882 kgutierrez@stmcs62.org www.st-thomas-more-school.org Kimberly A. Gutierrez, Prin.; Stds.: 57; Sr. Tchrs.: 1; Lay Tchrs.: 6

St. Timothy's - 1515 Saltillo St., San Antonio, TX 78207 t) 210-434-2391 sttimothycatholic@yahoo.com www.sttimothysa.org/ Rev. Juan Carlos Tejada, Pst.; Sr. Midory Wu, DRE; Dcn. Antonio Caballero; Dcn. Hector Ledesma; CRP Stds.: 24

Vietnamese Martyrs Catholic Center - 14603 Santa Gertrudis St., San Antonio, TX 78217 t) 832-752-9520 uqluong7363@gmail.com www.vietsa.org Rev. Luong Uong, C.Ss.R., Pst.; CRP Stds.: 98

St. Vincent de Paul - 4222 S.W. Loop 410, San Antonio, TX 78227-4495 t) 210-674-4291 (CRP); 210-674-1200 mysvdpparish.re@gmail.com; mysvdpparish@gmail.com www.mysvdpparish.org Rev. Hugo O. Maese, MSpS, Pst.; Dcn. Apolonio Eduardo Garcia; Dcn. Francisco Suniga Jr.; Josie Dobroski, CRE; Mark Tebbs, Bus. Mgr.; CRP Stds.: 200

SCHERTZ

Church of the Good Shepherd - 1065 E. Live Oak Rd., Schertz, TX 78154; Mailing: PO Box 929, Schertz, TX 78154 t) 210-658-4350 adminasst@gsschertz.org www.gsschertz.org Rev. Octavio Muguerza, Pst.; Dcn. Harvey Balcer; Dcn. Elmer Fernandez; Dcn. Arsenio Reyes Jr.; Dcn. James L. Lindsey, Bus. Mgr.; CRP Stds.: 272

Immaculate Conception - 213 N. Barnett St., Marion, TX 78124 t) 830-914-2411 Rev. Octavio A. Muguerza, Pst.;

SEGUIN

St. James - 510 S. Camp St., Seguin, TX 78155 t) 830-379-1796 info@saintjamescc.org www.saintjamescc.org Rev. Stanislaw Fiuk (Poland), Pst.; Joey Gutierrez, Youth Min.; Deborah Boswell, DRE; CRP Stds.: 86

St. James School - (Grades PreK-8) 507 S. Camp St., Seguin, TX 78155 t) 830-379-2878 jvelez@sjcstx.org; jlopez@sjcstx.org www.sjcstx.org Johanna Lopez, Prin.; Shelly Marek, Librn.;

Our Lady of Guadalupe - 409 W. Krezdorn, Seguin, TX 78155-4429 t) 830-379-2818 (CRP); 830-379-4338 dtonary1@satx.rr.com; olgseg@satx.rr.com www.seguinolg.com Rev. David Tonary, M.S.F. (Canada), Pst.; Rev. Robert DeLong, MSF, Assoc. Pst.; Bro. Rolland Kapsner, M.S.F.; Dcn. Nick L. Carrillo; Gloria Reyna, DRE; CRP Stds.: 279

St. Joseph - 5093 Redwood Rd., Redwood, TX 78666

SELMA

Our Lady of Perpetual Help - 16075 N. Evans Rd., Selma, TX 78154-3824 t) 210-651-6913 info@olph.org www.olph.org Rev. Jeff Pehl, Pst.; Rev. Frank Garcia, Par. Vicar; Dcn. Bill Hartman; Dcn. Louis Heimer; Dcn. Kenneth Mamot; Dcn. Jesse Mata; Dcn. Barry Scheel; Annabelle Hernandez, Admin.; Gina Martin, Youth Min.; Jaclyn Ruli, DRE; CRP Stds.: 500

Our Lady of Perpetual Help School - (Grades K-8) t) 210-651-6811 x124 wohln@olphselma.org Amanda Miller, Prin.; Stds.: 323; Lay Tchrs.: 30

Child Development Center - 1607 N. Evans Rd, Selma, TX 78154 t) 210-651-6819 dunnes@olphselma.org Stephanie Dunne, Dir.;

SMILEY

St. Philip Benizi - 101 Morey, Smiley, TX 78159; Mailing: 207 S. Washington Ave., Nixon, TX 78140 t) 830-582-1127 stjosephnixontx@yahoo.com Religious Program is held in Nixon. Rev. Kuriakose P. Ouseph (India), Pst.; Dcn. John J. Moreno; CRP Stds.: 18

SOMERSET

St. Mary's - 19711 N. Dixon Rd., Somerset, TX 78069; Mailing: Box 295, Somerset, TX 78069 t) 830-701-3123 stmarys.somerset.tx@gmail.com Rev. James M. Kotara, Admin.; Sylvia Cruz, DRE;

SPRING BRANCH

St. Joseph - Honey Creek - 25781 Hwy. 46 W., Spring Branch, TX 78070-3613 t) 830-980-2268 suet@stjhc.church; info@stjhc.church www.stjoseph-honeycreek.org Rev. Eduardo Martinez, Pst.; Dcn. Glendower Bliss III; Dcn. Jesus Mireles; Dcn. Michael Pawelek; Dcn. Ignacio Romo; Sue Torres, DRE; CRP Stds.: 498

ST. HEDWIG

Annunciation of the Blessed Virgin Mary - 14011 FM 1346, St. Hedwig, TX 78152; Mailing: P.O. Box 100, St. Hedwig, TX 78152 t) 210-667-1232 drekaybulzacchelli@gmail.com; annunciationbvm@hotmail.com www.sthcc.org Rev. Boleslaw Zadora, S.D.S. (Poland), Pst.; Dcn. Richard T. Coronado; Dcn. Michael Drumm; CRP Stds.: 136

STOCKDALE

St. Ann's - 8161 FM 541-E, Kosciusko, Stockdale, TX 78160-6554 t) 830-745-2541 stannskos@gmail.com www.stannskos.com Rev. Pius Ezeigbo, Pst.; CRP Stds.: 50

St. Mary - 1201 W. St. Mary's St., Stockdale, TX 78160; Mailing: PO Box 535, Stockdale, TX 78160-0535 t) 830-996-3415 stmarys@gvec.net stmarysstockdale.org/ Rev. Praveen Lakkisetti, Admin.; Dcn. Benjamin Gimenez Jr.; CRP Stds.: 100

STONEWALL

St. Francis Xavier - 400 Saint Francis St., Stonewall, TX 78671-3717; Mailing: P. O. Box 209, Stonewall, TX 78671 t) 830-644-2368 stfrancisx@beecreek.net www.stfrancisxavierstonewall.org Rev. John Nolan, Pst.; Trudy Steele, DRE; CRP Stds.: 30

UVALDE

Sacred Heart - 408 Fort Clark Rd., Uvalde, TX 78801 t) 830-278-3448; 830-278-4846 secretary_shc@att.net; cecilia.martz_shc@att.net Rev. Eduardo D. Morales, Pst.; Dcn. Kenneth Dirksen; Dcn. Federico Flores; Dcn. Hector V. Garcia; Dcn. Daniel A. Ibarra; Cecilia Martinez, DRE; CRP Stds.: 415

Sacred Heart School - (Grades PreK-6) 401 W. Leona St., Uvalde, TX 78801; Mailing: 408 Fort Clark Rd., Uvalde, TX 78801 t) 830-278-2661 jolan@sacredheartuvalde.org Joseph Olan, Prin.; Stds.: 103; Lay Tchrs.: 9

VON ORMY

St. Peter the Fisherman - 17534 N. State Hwy. 16, Von Ormy, TX 78073 t) 830-276-4985 peter.fisherman.cc@gmail.com Rev. James M. Kotara, Pst.; CRP Stds.: 68

Sacred Heart - 13466 I-35 S., Von Ormy, TX 78073-0722; Mailing: P.O. Box 722, Von Ormy, TX 78073 t) 210-622-3457 sacredheart78073@outlook.com Rev. Oscar Tello-Curiel, Pst.; Dcn. Carlos Rodriguez; CRP Stds.: 63

SCHOOLS: PRESCHOOL THRU HIGH SCHOOL

SCHOOLS

STATE OF TEXAS

PLEASANTON

Our Lady of Grace Catholic School - (PRV) (Grades PreK-5) 626 Market St., Pleasanton, TX 78064 t) 830-569-8073 www.olgcstx.org Rev. Ian Robbins, Spiritual Adv./Care Srvcs.; Stds.: 87; Lay Tchrs.: 9

SAN ANTONIO

St. Anthony School - (PRV) (Grades PreK-8) 205 W. Huisache Ave., San Antonio, TX 78212 t) 210-732-8801 pramirez@stanthonysa.org www.stanthonysa.org Rev. Jorge Campos-Covarrubias, Chap.; Patricia Ramirez, Prin.; Natalie Lopez, Librn.; Stds.: 270; Lay Tchrs.: 30

St. John Bosco School (Institute of the Daughters of Mary Help of Christians (Salesian Sisters of St. John Bosco)) - (PRV) (Grades PreSchool-8) 5630 W. Commerce St., San Antonio, TX 78237 c) (210) 573-5112 rleblanc@stjohnbosco-satx.org; apalacios@stjohnbosco-satx.org www.stjohnbosco-satx.org Day School Roxanne LeBlanc, Prin.; Sr. Ngan Do, CEO; Sr. Ana Laura Palacios, FMA, CFO; Stds.: 220; Sr. Tchrs.: 1; Lay Tchrs.: 9

St. John Bosco Child Development Center - 5630 W. Commerce, San Antonio, TX 78237 t) 210-432-1686 lflores@stjohnbosco-satx.org Leticia Flores, Dir.;

Mount Sacred Heart Catholic School - (DIO) (Grades PreSchool-8) 619 Mount Sacred Heart Rd., San Antonio, TX 78216 t) 210-342-6711 www.mountsacredheart.org/ Joey Martinez, Prin.; Dorothy Hoel, Bus. Mgr.; Stds.: 157; Lay Tchrs.: 16

Providence Catholic School - (PRV) (Grades 6-12) 1215 N. St. Mary's St., San Antonio, TX 78215-1737 t) 210-224-6651 agarcia@providencecatholicschool.net www.providencecatholicschool.net College Preparatory School for girls. Alicia Garcia, Prin.; Daniele Delgado, Vice Prin.; Stds.: 231; Sr. Tchrs.: 1; Lay Tchrs.: 22

HIGH SCHOOLS

STATE OF TEXAS

KERRVILLE

Our Lady of the Hills College Prep - (PRV) (Grades 9-12) 235 Peterson Farm Rd., Kerrville, TX 78028 t) 830-895-0501 olh@olhcollegeprep.org; development@olhcollegeprep.org www.olhcollegeprep.org Bridget Collins, Prin.; Stds.: 50; Lay Tchrs.: 8

NEW BRAUNFELS

St. John Paul II Catholic High School - (DIO) (Grades 9-12) 6720 FM 482, New Braunfels, TX 78132 t) 830-643-0802 ailiff@johnpaul2chs.org www.johnpaul2chs.org Andrew Iliff, Prin.; Sandee Phelan, Librn.; Stds.: 205; Lay Tchrs.: 19

SAN ANTONIO

St. Anthony Catholic High School - (PRV) (Grades 9-12) 3200 McCullough Ave., San Antonio, TX 78212-3099 t) 210-832-5600 kvidaurr@uiwtx.edu www.sachs.org Kristina Vidaurri, Prin.; Stds.: 267; Lay Tchrs.: 28

Antonian College Preparatory High School - (DIO) (Grades 9-12) 6425 West Ave., San Antonio, TX 78213 t) 210-344-9265 www.antonian.org (Coed) John Mein, Vice Prin.; Stds.: 735; Lay Tchrs.: 44

Central Catholic High School - (PRV) (Grades 9-12) 1403 N. St. Mary's St., San Antonio, TX 78215-1785 t) 210-225-6794 jason.longoria@cchs-satx.org; lhernandez@cchs-satx.org www.cchs-satx.org all-boys high school Jason Francisco Longoria, Pres.; Dr. Lee Hernandez, Prin.; Stds.: 514; Pr. Tchrs.: 1; Lay Tchrs.: 43

Healy Murphy Center, Inc. - (PRV) (Grades PreK-12) 618 Live Oak St., San Antonio, TX 78202 t) 210-223-2944 dwatson@healymurphy.org www.healymurphy.org High school, GED, and child development center for youth in crisis. Douglas J. Watson, Exec.; Stds.: 300; Sr. Tchrs.: 2; Lay Tchrs.: 47

Holy Cross School of San Antonio - (PRV) (Grades 6-12) 426 N. San Felipe, San Antonio, TX 78228 t) 210-433-9395 stanley.culotta@holycross-sa.org; rene.escobedo@holycross-sa.org www.holycross-sa.org Brothers of Holy Cross. Richard Vasquez, Admin.; Rene Escobedo, Prin.; Stds.: 295; Scholastics: 295; Bro. Tchrs.: 2; Lay Tchrs.: 18

Incarnate Word High School - (PRV) 727 E. Hildebrand Ave., San Antonio, TX 78212-2598 t) 210-829-3102 nstrilka@iwhs.org www.incarnatewordhs.org Rosi Cortez, Prin.; Ariana Uribe, Dir.; Sylvia Herrera-Haman, Bus. Mgr.; Stds.: 359; Pr. Tchrs.: 1; Sr. Tchrs.: 3; Lay Tchrs.: 32

INSTITUTIONS LOCATED IN DIOCESE

CATHOLIC CHARITIES [CCH]

SAN ANTONIO

Ascension DePaul Services - 7607 Somerset Rd., San Antonio, TX 78211 t) 210-334-2300 patrick.butler@dcssa.org; john.tersigni@ascension.org www.adssa.org John Tersigni, Chief Mission Integration Officer; Patrick Butler, CEO; Asstd. Annu.: 4,085; Staff: 75

DePaul Children's Center - 3050 Golden Ave., San Antonio, TX 78211; Mailing: 7607 Somerset Rd., San Antonio, TX 78211 t) (210) 334-2311 Children's Development, Ascension DePaul Service, corporate member

DePaul Family Center - 7607 Somerset Rd., San Antonio, TX 78211 t) (210) 334-2300

DePaul Wesley Children's Center - 1418 Fitch St., San Antonio, TX 78211; Mailing: 7607 Somerset Rd., San Antonio, TX 78211 t) (210) 334-2390 Child Development Center; Ascension DePaul Services, corporate member

El Carmen Wellness Center - 18555-1 Leal Rd., San Antonio, TX 78221; Mailing: 7607 Somerset Rd., San Antonio, TX 78211 t) (210) 334-2360

La Mision Family Health Care - 19780 U.S. Hwy. 281 S., San Antonio, TX 78221; Mailing: 7607 Somerset Rd., San Antonio, TX 78211 t) (210) 626-0600

Catholic Charities, Archdiocese of San Antonio Inc. - 202 W. French Pl., San Antonio, TX 78212 t) 210-222-1294 afernandez@ccaosa.org www.ccaosa.org Family & Children Services, Senior Services, Family Self-Sufficiency, Caritas Legal Services, Refugee Resettlement Services, and Housing Services J. Antonio Fernandez, Pres./CEO; Asstd. Annu.: 160,027; Staff: 227

Caritas Legal Services - 110 Bandera Rd., San Antonio, TX 78228 t) 210-433-3256 mgarcia@ccaosa.org Maria Garcia, Senior Dir.;

Grace Counseling - 2911 S. New Braunfels Ave., San Antonio, TX 78210 t) 210-377-1133 racosta@stpjhome.org ccaosa.org Karen Diliberti, Dir.; Stuart Young, Lead Therapist;

Guadalupe Community Center - 1801 W. Cesar Chavez Blvd., San Antonio, TX 78207 t) 210-226-6178 dramirez@ccaosa.org Denise Ramirez, Senior Dir.;

Guadalupe Home - t) 210-476-0707 sseaney@ccaosa.org Shirley Seaney, Dir.;

Refugee Services - pwalker@ccaosa.org Paula Torisk, Senior Dir.;

San Antonio Birth Doulas - 4522 Fredericksburg Rd #A-47, Balcones Heights, TX 78201 t) 210-222-0988

morgan.thurmond@sabdoulas.org J. Antonio Fernandez, Exec. Dir.; Morgan Thurmond, Prog. Dir.;

CEMETERIES [CEM]

SAN ANTONIO

Catholic Cemeteries of the Archdiocese of San Antonio - 746 Castroville Rd., San Antonio, TX 78237 t) 210-438-8134 ismael.galvan@archsa.org Ismael Galvan, Dir.; Richard Corpus, Bus. Mgr.; Teresa Gariepy, Bus. Mgr.;

Holy Cross - 17501 Nacogdoches, San Antonio, TX 78266 t) 210-651-6011 teresa.gariepy@archsa.org Teresa Gariepy, Bus. Mgr.;

San Fernando No. 1 - 1100 S. Colorado St., San Antonio, TX 78207; Mailing: 746 Castroville Rd., San Antonio, TX 78237 t) 210-432-2303 richard.corpus@archsa.org Richard Corpus, Bus. Mgr.;

San Fernando No. 2 - 746 Castroville Rd., San Antonio, TX 78237 t) 210-432-2303 richard.corpus@archsa.org Richard Corpus, Bus. Mgr.;

San Fernando No. 3 (Roselawn) - 1735 Cupples Rd., San Antonio, TX 78226; Mailing: 746 Castroville Rd., San Antonio, TX 78237 t) 210-432-2364 ismael.galvan@archsa.org Ismael Galvan, Dir.;

COLLEGES & UNIVERSITIES [COL]

SAN ANTONIO

St. Mary's University of San Antonio, Texas - 1 Camino Santa Maria, Office of the President, San Antonio, TX 78228-8572; Mailing: Box 72, San Antonio, TX 78228-8572 t) 210-436-3722 tmengler@stmarytx.edu www.stmarytx.edu (Coed) Conducted by the Society of Mary. Rev. W. Franz Schorp, S.M.; Grace Walle, F.M.I., Chap.; Rosalind Alderman, Admin.; William Buhrman, Admin.; Robert Coleman, Admin.; Aaron Hanna, Admin.; Sheri King, Admin.; Rev. William Meyer, S.M., Admin.; Dianne Pipes, Admin.; Lori Swete, Admin.; Rev. John Thompson, S.M., Admin.; Carolyn Tubbs, Admin.; Jessica Uhlig, Admin.; Stephanie Ward, Admin.; Curtis White, Admin.; Tim Bessler, Dean; Rowena Ortiz-Walters, Dean; Leona Pallansch, Dean; Paricia Roberts, Dean; Rev. Conrad J. Kaczkowski, S.M., Prof.; Thomas Mengler, Pres.; Stds.: 3,432; Bro. Tchrs.: 2; Lay Tchrs.: 210; Pr. Tchrs.: 4; Sr. Tchrs.: 1; Scholastics: 12

The Mexican American Catholic College - 3115 W. Ashby Pl., San Antonio, TX 78228-5104 t) 210-732-2156 macc@maccsa.org www.maccsa.org Rev. Edward Owens, OSST, Prof.; Most Rev. Michael J. Boulette, Chair; Rev. Juan Molina, Pres.; Juanita Garcia, Librn.; Dr. John Chitakure, Academic Dean; Clemencia Barrera, HR Dir.; Stds.: 119; Lay Tchrs.: 15; Pr. Tchrs.: 2; Sr. Tchrs.: 2

Oblate School of Theology - 285 Oblate Dr., San Antonio, TX 78216-6693 t) 210-341-1366 info@ost.edu www.ost.edu (Coed) (Graduate Theology) Conducted by the Missionary Oblates of Mary Immaculate. Rev. Daniel Renaud, OMI, Director of Minister to Ministry Program; Rev. Wayne A. Cavalier, O.P., Dir., DMin Prog.; Rev. Ken Hannon, O.M.I., Dean; Rev. Roger H. Keeler (Canada), Co-Dir. MDiv Prog.; Rev. Joseph LaBelle, O.M.I., Prof.; Rev. John J. Markey, O.P., Dir., PhD Prog.; Rev. Msgr. Jeremiah McCarthy, Prof.; Rev. Antonio Ponce, O.M.I., Vice Pres., Mission; Rev. Ronald Rolheiser, O.M.I., Pres. Emeritus; Rev. Frank Santucci, OMI, Prof.; Rev. Bryan Silva, O.M.I., Prof.; Rev. Robert E. Wright, O.M.I., Co-Dir., MDiv Prog.; Rev. Thomas Klosterkamp, OMI (Germany), Prof.; Stds.: 187; Lay Tchrs.: 10; Pr. Tchrs.: 10; Sr. Tchrs.: 3

***Our Lady of the Lake University** - 411 S.W. 24th, San Antonio, TX 78207-4689 t) 210-434-6711 iperez@ollusa.edu www.ollusa.edu Sponsored by Congregation of Divine Providence. Diane E. Melby, Pres.; Gloria Urrabazo, Vice. Pres.; Stds.: 2,550; Lay Tchrs.: 121

University of the Incarnate Word - 4301 Broadway, CPO 139, San Antonio, TX 78209 t) 210-829-6000 maher@uiwtx.edu www.uiw.edu Thomas Evans, Pres.; Darrell Haydon, Vice. Pres.; Sr. Walter Maher, Vice. Pres.; Stds.: 10,500; Lay Tchrs.: 300; Sr. Tchrs.: 2

CONVENTS, MONASTERIES, AND RESIDENCES FOR WOMEN [CON]

BOERNE

St. Scholastica Monastery - 216 W. Highland, Boerne, TX 78006 t) 830-249-2645; 830-816-8504 reyesosb@gvtc.com; devcbs@yahoo.com www.boernebenedictines.org Benedictine Sisters, Monastery, and Novitiate. Sr. Bernadine Reyes, O.S.B., Prioress; Srs.: 13

SAN ANTONIO

Blessed Sacrament Convent - 227 Keller St., San Antonio, TX 78204 t) 210-223-5013 smarilupemieryteran@gmail.com Mercedarian Sisters of the Blessed Sacrament Sr. Gloria de Maria Medina Avila, Supr.; Srs.: 4

Blessed Sacrament and Incarnate Word Convent - 1135 Mission Rd., San Antonio, TX 78210 t) 210-534-8005 okorenek@bsasa.org; iwsteph@yahoo.com www.bsasa.org Blessed Sacrament Academy Sr. Stephanie Marie Martinez, I.W.B.S., Supr.; Srs.: 6

Congregation of the Sisters of Saint Brigid - 5118 Loma Linda Dr., San Antonio, TX 78201 t) 210-733-0701; 210-738-1472 sbc@brigidines.us www.brigidine.org.au Congregation of the Sisters of Saint Brigid Sr. Teresa Carter, C.S.B., Co-Leader; Sr. Mary Teresa Cullen, C.S.B., Co-Leader; Sr. Margaret Doyle, Co-Leader; Srs.: 8

Brigid's Place - A day retreat center. Sr. Mary T. Cullen, Dir.;

Congregation of Divine Providence Generalate - 515 S.W. 24th St., San Antonio, TX 78207 t) 210-434-1866 generalate@cdptexas.org www.cdptexas.org Sr. Pearl Ceasar, Supr.; Sr. Mary Bordelon, C.D.P., Rel. Ord. Ldr.; Sr. Anita Brenek, Rel. Ord. Ldr.; Sr. Lourdes Leal, C.D.P., Rel. Ord. Ldr.; Sr. Charlotte Kitowski, Archivist; Sr. Patricia Regan, Treas.; Srs.: 87

Cordi-Marian Missionary Sisters Convent - 2902 Morales St., San Antonio, TX 78207 t) 210-433-5064 mcalicia@aol.com Sr. Gemma Abonge, Supr.; Srs.: 2

Cordi-Marian Missionary Sisters - 11624 Culebra Rd., #501, San Antonio, TX 78253 t) 210-798-8220 mcm.materesa37@yahoo.com; mcmeliaj@aol.com www.cordi-marian.org Convent, Delegation Office, Retirement and Retreat Center, Senior Apartments, Resurrection Cemetery Rev. Alberto Trevino, Chap.; Sr. M. Teresa Cruz, MC-M, Prov.; Sr. M. Socorro Lozoya, MC-M, Treas.; Srs.: 20

Resurrection Cemetery - 11624 Culebra Rd., Bldg. 7, San Antonio, TX 78253 t) (210) 798-8220 x28 resurrection@cordi-marian.org www.cordi-marian.org/resurrectioncemetery Rev. Raymond Gaitan I, OAR, Spiritual Adv./Care Srvcs.; Richard Ruiz, Gen. Mgr.;

Daughters of Charity Residence - 7603 Somerset Rd., San Antonio, TX 78211; Mailing: 3026 Golden Ave., San Antonio, TX 78211 c) (314) 825-2971 roseann.aguilar@doc.org daughtersofcharity.org Daughters of Charity of St. Vincent de Paul, Province of St. Louis Sr. Rose Ann Aguilar, Supr.; Rt. Rev. Jean Thomas Dwyer, Mem.; Srs.: 4

Dominican Community of San Juan Macias (San Juan Macias Community) - 822 Chevy Chase Dr., San Antonio, TX 78209 t) 210-792-4813 sjmpriory@gmail.com; waycav@aol.com Rev. Wayne A. Cavalier, O.P., Supr; Dir., Congar Institute for Ministry Devel.; Prof. & DMin Prog. Dir., Oblate School of Theology; Rev. John J. Markey, O.P., Prof. & PhD Prog. Dir., Oblate School of Theology; Rev. Marcos Ramos, Coord., Spiritual Formation, Assumption Seminary; Prof., Oblate School of Theology; Priests: 3

Eucharistic Franciscan Missionary Sisters (Misioneras Eucaristicas Franciscanas) - 558 Cumberland, San Antonio, TX 78204 t) 210-224-7993 lupevilla720@hotmail.com Sr. Maria Guadalupe Villasenor, M.E.F., Supr.; Srs.: 2

Hermanas Catequistas Guadalupanas Convent - 4110 S. Flores St., San Antonio, TX 78214 c) 210-532-9344; 210-288-9388 guadalupanasregionaldelegation@yahoo.com; marthadejesusruiz@yahoo.com Sr. Maria Martha Ruiz, H.C.G., Supr.; Srs.: 6

Hermanas Josefinas (Josephine Sisters) - 511 Shadwell Dr., San Antonio, TX 78228-4244 t) 210-732-1973 c) 210-973-6165; 210-848-0105 glasmary@hotmail.com Sr. MariaTeresa Gonzalez, Supr.; Srs.: 6

Casa San Jose - 402 John Adams Dr., San Antonio, TX 78228 (Retired Sisters) Sr. Guadalupe Mondragon, Supr.;

Communidad de la Cesarita - 511 Shadwell Dr., San Antonio, TX 78228 t) 210-973-6165 c) (210) 848-0105

Incarnate Word Generalate - 4503 Broadway, San Antonio, TX 78209-6297 t) 210-828-2224 carolyn.psencik@amormeus.org www.amormeus.org General Administration of the Congregation of Sisters of Charity of the Incarnate Word. Sr. Yolanda Tarango, C.C.V.I., Supr.; Srs.: 216

Institute of the Daughters of Mary Help of Christians (Salesian Sisters of St. John Bosco.) - Province of Mary Immaculate, 6019 Buena Vista St., San Antonio, TX 78237-1700 t) 210-432-0089; 210-432-0090 suosec@salesiansisterswest.org www.salesiansisterswest.org Sr. Rosann Ruiz, F.M.A., Prov.; Srs.: 82

St. James Convent - 402 Nunes, San Antonio, TX 78225 t) 210-533-9659 james@salesiansisterswest.org Daughters of Mary Help of Christians (Salesian Sisters of St. John Bosco). Sr. Deborah Walker, FMA, Supr.; Srs.: 3

St. John Bosco Convent - 5630 W. Commerce St., San Antonio, TX 78237-1313 t) 210-432-8008 sjb@salesiansisterswest.org Daughters of Mary Help of Christians. Sr. Ngan Do, Supr.; Srs.: 10

Marian Community of Reconciliation (Fraternas) - 2715 Marlborough Dr., San Antonio, TX 78230 c) 210-849-1777; (210) 992-0091 ppollack@fraternas.org; salvarez@fraternas.org Sr. Rossana Milagros Goni, MCR, Supr.; Srs.: 6

Marianist Sisters Residence - 235 W. Ligustrum Dr., San Antonio, TX 78228 t) 210-433-5501 provincialfmiusa@gmail.com www.marianistsisters.org Centralhouse of the Congregation of the Daughters of Mary Immaculate. Marianist Sisters, (Community Dayton, OH). Annunciation House, Kettering, OH. Sr. Gretchen Trautman, F.M.I., Prov.; Sr. Lavon Kampf, F.M.I., Dir.; Srs.: 13

Missionary Catechists of Divine Providence - 2318 Castroville Rd., San Antonio, TX 78237 t) 210-432-0113 mainoffice@mcdp.org mcdp.org Central House and Admin. Offices Sr. Guadalupe Ramirez, Supr.; Sr. Esther M. Guerrero, Treas.; Srs.: 24

Missionary Servants of St. Anthony - 100 Peter Baque Rd., San Antonio, TX 78209-1805 t) 210-824-4553 pbmssa29@sanantonio.twcbc.com Missionary Servants of St. Anthony, Motherhouse and Novitiate of the Missionary Servants of St. Anthony; St. Anthony Retreat Center; St. Anthony Learn Sr. Mary Ann Domagalski, M.S.S.A., Supr.; Srs.: 2

Missionary Sisters of Our Lady of Perpetual Help (M.P.S.) - 2822 Wade St., San Antonio, TX 78210 t) 210-532-3546 rosymps2003@hotmail.com Sr. Ma Mercedes Martinez I, MPS, Admin.; Sr. Magdalena Noguez, M.P.S., Admin.; Sr. Alejandrina Castillo Perez, Local Supr.; Srs.: 6

Monastery of the Discalced Carmelite Nuns - 6301 Culebra Rd., San Antonio, TX 78238-4909 t) 210-680-1834 carmelsat@yahoo.com www.carmelsanantonio.org Mother Therese Leonard, O.C.D., Prioress; Srs.: 13

Motherhouse of the Sisters of the Holy Spirit and Mary Immaculate. - 300 Yucca St., San Antonio, TX 78203-2318 t) 210-533-5149 holyspirit@shsp.org www.shsp.org Sr. Geraldine Klein, S.H.Sp., Supr.; Srs.: 51

Our Lady of the Lake Convent Center - 603 S.W. 24th

St., San Antonio, TX 78207 t) 210-434-1866 flange@cdptexas.org Home for retired Sisters of Divine Providence. Sisters of Divine Providence. Sr. Cathy Parent, CDP, Pst. Min./Coord.; Sr. Frances Lorene Lange, C.D.P., Pastoral Min. / Coord.; Sr. Madeline Zimmerer, C.D.P., Pastoral Min. / Coord.; Srs.: 87

Presentation Province Center - 2715 Zurich, San Antonio, TX 78230 t) 210-979-8879 sectypbvmus@gmail.com www.pbvmunion.org Congregation: Union of Sisters of the Presentation of the Blessed Virgin Mary Sr. Katherine Fennell Sr., PBVM, Prov.; Srs.: 1

Residence of the Community of the Union of the Sisters of the Presentation of the B.V.M. - 2926 Dusseldorf, San Antonio, TX 78230-4570 t) 210-342-2503 pbvmsat@mail.com www.pbvmunion.org Sr. Therese Gleitz, Supr.; Srs.: 7

Presentation Sisters - 415 Arbor Pl., San Antonio, TX 78207 t) 210-223-4916 pbvmsisters@yahoo.com www.pbvmunion.org Congregation: Union of Sisters of the Presentation of the Blessed Virgin Mary Philippa Wall Sr., PBVM, Supr.; Srs.: 3

Provincial Offices of the Sisters of the Sacred Heart of Jesus of St. Jacut - 11931 Radium St., San Antonio, TX 78216-2714 t) 210-344-7203 mmargiefay@aol.com Sr. Marjorie Vincik, S.S.C.J., Rel. Ord. Ldr.; Srs.: 25

Beth Rachamim Community - 1203 Viewridge, San Antonio, TX 78213; Mailing: 11931 Radium, San Antonio, TX 78216 t) 210-308-0257

Casa Ste. Emile - 302 Harriet Dr., San Antonio, TX 78216 t) 210-822-9844

Holy Spirit Convent - 1922 W. Houston, San Antonio, TX 78207 t) (210) 277-2708

St. Joseph Community - 1014 Spent Wing, San Antonio, TX 78213 t) 210-239-5432

Santa Maria Community - 10803 Silhouette, San Antonio, TX, TX 78216; Mailing: 11931 Radium, San Antonio, TX 78216 t) 210-340-1872

Religious of Mary Immaculate Convent - 719 Augusta St., San Antonio, TX 78215 t) 210-226-0025; 210-223-8163 villamarmi@yahoo.com www.villamariaresidence.org Sr. Maria de Jesus Lozano, Supr.; Sr. Andrea Navarro Ayala, Vocations; Srs.: 5

School Sisters of Notre Dame Convent - Antonina Community - 2372 W. Southcross, San Antonio, TX 78211-1898 t) 210-923-2364 c) (210) 834-2649 mstos@ssndcp.org Sr. Marcelle Stos, SSND, Mem.; Srs.: 3

School Sisters of Notre Dame Convent - Holy Spirit Community - 11635 Lida Rose Dr., San Antonio, TX 78216 c) 214-766-0342 adlwalker@ssndcp.org Sr. Addie Lorraine Walker, S.S.N.D., Contact; Srs.: 2

School Sisters of Notre Dame Convent - Incarnation House - 9527 Sinsonte St., San Antonio, TX 78230 t) 210-454-3682 sbmssnd@yahoo.com www.ssnd.org Srs.: 2

Seraphic Sisters of Our Lady of Sorrows Convent - 621 W. Woodlawn Ave., San Antonio, TX 78212 t) 210-734-3364 hkomperda@hotmail.com Sr. Natalia Sura, S.O.L.S., Supr.; Srs.: 5

The Sisters of Perpetual Adoration Convent - 2403 W. Travis St., San Antonio, TX 78207 t) 210-228-0092; 210-226-3934 sistersapg@gmail.com; perpetualdaycare@att.net Sr. Ma. Estela Garcia-Rodriguez, APG, Supr.; Sr. Carolina Juarez Sanchez, Dir.; Srs.: 6

St. Teresa's Convent - 206 Beechwood, San Antonio, TX 78216 t) 210-532-7303 clarice.suchy@gmail.com www.teresiansisters.org Sr. Clarice Suchy, S.T.J., Supr.; Srs.: 4

Ursuline Residence - 515 S.W. 24th St., San Antonio, TX 78207 t) 210-454-2382 sresh_2000@yahoo.com Sr. Julie Hickey, OSU, Supr.; Srs.: 4

UVALDE

Society of St. Teresa of Jesus - 466 Encino St., Uvalde, TX 78801 t) 830-278-6724 clarice.suchy@gmail.com www.teresiansisters.org (Teresian Sisters) Sr. Clarice Suchy, S.T.J., Supr.; Srs.: 3

ENDOWMENTS / FOUNDATIONS / TRUSTS [EFT]

BOERNE

Benedictine Sisters Charitable Trust One - 216 W. Highland Dr., Boerne, TX 78006 t) 830-816-8504 snmika2010@gmail.com; sahrosb@gvtc.com Sr. Sylvia Ahr, OSB, Trustee; Sr. Susan Mika, O.S.B., Trustee;

Benedictine Sisters Charitable Trust Two - 216 W. Highland, Boerne, TX 78006 t) 830-816-8504 sahrosb@gvtc.com; snmika2010@gmail.com Sr. Sylvia Ahr, O.S.B., Trustee; Sr. Susan Mika, OSB, Trustee;

SAN ANTONIO

The Catholic Community Foundation for the Roman Catholic Church of the Archdiocese of San Antonio - 111 Barilla Pl., Ste. 101, San Antonio, TX 78209 t) 210-732-2157; 210-732-2153 john.benage@ccftx.org; alison.cochrane@ccftx.org www.ccftx.org Alison Cochrane, CEO & Pres.;

Catholic Fraternity Fund, LLC - info@ccftx.org www.catholicfund.us (An affiliated entity of the Catholic Community Fund)

Friends of Santa Rosa Foundation - 333 N. San Saba, 5th Fl., San Antonio, TX 78207; Mailing: PO Box 1661, San Antonio, TX 78296-1661 t) 210-321-8004; 210-704-3349 michele.obrien@christushealth.org www.friendsfoundation.org Dr. Ian Thompson Jr., Pres.; Terry Kyle, CEO; Allison Salinas, Dir.;

Holy Spirit Sisters' Trust - 300 Yucca St., San Antonio, TX 78203-2318 t) 210-533-5149 holyspirit@shsp.org Sisters of the Holy Spirit. Sr. Geraldine Klein, S.H.Sp., Pres.;

***La Promesa Foundation (Guadalupe Radio Network)** - 3522 Paesanos Pkwy., #104, San Antonio, TX 78231 t) 210-579-9844 c) 210-218-1734 lenoswald@grnonline.com www.grnonline.com Leonard Oswald, Pres.;

National Foundation for Mexican-American Vocations - 2718 W. Woodlawn, San Antonio, TX 78228 t) 210-734-2620 ruben.hinojosa@archsa.org www.archsa.org/vocations A nonprofit organization to financially help Mexican American Seminarians. Most Rev. Gary Janak, Chancellor;

Providence Trust - 515 S.W. 24th St., San Antonio, TX 78207 t) 210-434-1866 ramonabezner@gmail.com Congregation of Divine Providence, Inc. Charitable Trust.

San Antonio Catholic Worker House of Hospitality - 626 Nolan St., San Antonio, TX 78202 t) 210-224-7736 info@sa-catholicworker.org www.sa-catholicworker.org Chris Plauche, Dir.;

***Santa Rosa Children's Hospital Foundation (Children's Hospital of Santa Rosa)** - 333 N. San Saba, 5th Fl., San Antonio, TX 78207; Mailing: PO Box 1661, San Antonio, TX 78296-1661 t) 210-704-2800; 210-704-3349 michele.obrien@christushealth.org Dr. Ian Thompson Jr., Pres.; Terry Kyle, CEO;

Virgen de Guadalupe Foundation - 222 W. Cevallos, San Antonio, TX 78204; Mailing: P.O. Box 1728, Helotes, TX 78023 t) 830-388-3009 c) (210) 385-8348 vgradio@aol.com; gloria.coronado@vgmedia.org www.vgr1380.com Adrian Coronado, Pres.; Gloria Alicia Ricardez, Exec. Dir.;

HOSPITALS / HEALTH SERVICES [HOS]

NEW BRAUNFELS

Christus Santa Rosa Hospital - New Braunfels - 600 N. Union Ave., New Braunfels, TX 78130; Mailing: 100 N.E. Loop 410, Ste. 800, San Antonio, TX 78216 t) 830-606-9111; 210-704-2739 sarah.hill@christushealth.org www.christussantarosa.org Owned and operated by Christus, Santa Rosa Health Care Corp. Genifer Rucker, Pres.; Dr. Sarah Hill, Vice. Pres.; Bed Capacity: 81; Asstd. Annu.: 61,142; Staff: 558

SAN ANTONIO

Christus Santa Rosa Health Care Corporation - 100 N.E. Loop 410, Ste. 800, San Antonio, TX 78216 t) 210-321-8004; 210-704-2739 sarah.hill@christushealth.org www.christussantarosa.org Health related activities Stephanie Parker, Pres.; Dr. Sarah Hill, Vice. Pres.; Margaret Jones, Dir.; Sr. Michele O'Brien, Dir.; Bed Capacity: 643; Asstd. Annu.: 557,169; Staff: 4,338

Christus Santa Rosa Hospital, Alamo Heights - 403 Treeline Park Dr., San Antonio, TX 78209; Mailing: 100 N.E. Loop 410, Ste. 800, San Antonio, TX 72816 t) 210-294-8001; 210-704-2739 sarah.hill@christushealth.org Sherry Fraser, Pres.; Dr. Sarah Hill, Vice. Pres.; Bed Capacity: 24; Asstd. Annu.: 7,648; Staff: 169

Christus Santa Rosa Hospital, Westover Hills - 11212 Hwy. 151, San Antonio, TX 78251; Mailing: 100 N.E. Loop 410, Ste. 800, San Antonio, TX 78216 t) 210-321-8004; 210-704-2739 sarah.hill@christushealth.org www.christussantarosa.org Owned & operated by Christus Santa Rosa Health Care Corp. Pat Burns, Pres.; Dr. Sarah Hill, Vice. Pres.; Bed Capacity: 164; Asstd. Annu.: 63,764; Staff: 964

Christus Santa Rosa Hospital - Medical Center - 2827 Babcock Rd., San Antonio, TX 78229; Mailing: 100 N.E. Loop 410, Ste. 800, San Antonio, TX 78216 t) 210-704-2739; 210-705-6300 sarah.hill@christushealth.org www.christussantarosa.org Luanne Ansaldo, Pres.; Dr. Sarah Hill, Vice. Pres.; Bed Capacity: 127; Asstd. Annu.: 59,876; Staff: 556

The Children's Hospital of San Antonio - Christus Health - 333 N. Santa Rosa St., San Antonio, TX 78207; Mailing: 100 N.E. Loop 410, Ste. 800, San Antonio, TX 78216 t) 210-704-2011; 210-704-2739 sarah.hill@christushealth.org www.christussantarosa.org Owned and operated by Christus, Santa Rosa Health Care Corp. Cris Daskevich, CEO; Dr. Sarah Hill, Vice. Pres.; Bed Capacity: 144; Asstd. Annu.: 197,069; Staff: 1,268

MISCELLANEOUS [MIS]

BULVERDE

***The Alexander House Apostolate** - 30457 Leroy Scheel Rd., Bulverde, TX 78163; Mailing: P.O. Box 592107, San Antonio, TX 78259 t) 210-858-6195 info@thealexanderhouse.org www.thealexanderhouse.org Gregory Alexander, CEO; Julie Alexander, Dir.;

CASTLE HILLS

San Antonio Community Law Center - 201 Gladiola Ln., Castle Hills, TX 78213 t) 210-823-9333 sacommunitylawcenter@netzero.net Provides legal assistance to the working poor, children, and underserved. Bro. William Dooling, C.S.C., Dir.;

INGRAM

St. Peter Upon the Water, A Center For Spiritual Direction and Formation - 234 Indian Creek Rd., Ingram, TX 78025; Mailing: P. O. Box 509, Ingram, TX 78025 t) 830-367-5959 michael.boulette@archsa.org stpeteruponthewater.org Most Rev. Michael J. Boulette, Dir.;

SAN ANTONIO

***ACTS Missions** - 7711 Madonna Dr., San Antonio, TX 78216 t) 210-342-1077 dalaniz@actsmissions.org www.actsmissions.org Deborah Ann Alaniz, Exec. Dir.; Sylvia Ortiz, Accounting Mgr.;

Archdiocesan Union of Holy Name Societies - 115 Springwood, San Antonio, TX 78216 c) 210-882-8775 jlsanc50@gmail.com Jose Sanchez, Pres.;

The Archdiocese of San Antonio Capital Campaign Inc. - 2718 W. Woodlawn Ave., San Antonio, TX 78228 t) 210-734-1641 deborah.montez@archsa.org www.ontheway-andale.org Most Rev. Gustavo Garcia-Siller, M.Sp.S., Pres.; Rev. Martin J. Leopold, Vice Pres.;

Asociacion de Hermanas Latinas Misioneras en America, Inc. - 3115 W. Ashby Pl., San Antonio, TX 78228 t) 210-731-3133 hermanas.latinas.america@gmail.com www.ahlma.org Sr. Teresa Maya, C.C.V.I., Chair; Sr. Elizabeth Ann Guerrero, MCDP, Dir.;

Asociacion Nacional de Sacerdotes Hispanos, EEUU (Inc.) - Assumption Seminary, 2600 W. Woodlawn Ave., San Antonio, TX 78228 t) 806-549-8631 c) 210-984-6023 ansh@ansh.org; jmolina1@fordham.edu www.ansh.org Rev. Jiobani Batista, Exec.; Rev. Juan Molina, Pres.;
Brothers of the Beloved Disciple - 1701 Alametos, San Antonio, TX 78201 c) 210-667-6752 fr.hogan@cccrsa.net www.brothersofthebeloveddisciple.com A private association of the faithful. Rev. Robert E. Hogan, B.B.D., Supr.; Rev. John Bentley; Rev. William H. Combs; Rev. Sean Stilson; Rev. Lawrence Jerome Sergott, BBD; Bro. Ruben Garza;
Catholic Physicians Guild of San Antonio - 202 W. French Pl., San Antonio, TX 78212 t) 210-338-0308 info@cathmedsa.org www.cathmedsa.org Clark Kardys, Pres.;
Christus Santa Rosa Family Health Center - 11130 Christus Hills, San Antonio, TX 78251; Mailing: 100 N.E. Loop 410, Ste. 800, San Antonio, TX 78216 t) 210-321-8004; 210-704-2739 sarah.hill@christushealth.org www.christussantarosa.org Dr. Sarah Hill, Vice. Pres.; Jose R. Hinojosa, Dir.;
Cordi-Marian Education Center - 2902 Morales St., San Antonio, TX 78207 t) 210-433-5064 mcmalicia@aol.com Sr. Gemma Abonge, Supr.;
CYO Athletics - 2718 W. Woodlawn Ave, San Antonio, TX 78228 t) 210-734-2620 cyo@archsa.org www.archsa.org/cyo Jason Alvarez, Dir.;
Daughters of Mary Help Development Office (Department of Mission Advancement) - 6019 Buena Vista St., San Antonio, TX 78237-1700 t) 210-431-4999 directordma@salesiansisterswest.org salesiansisterswest.org Promotes the apostolic works of both the Daughters of Mary Help of Christians (Salesian Sisters) and VIDES-USA . Sr. Bernadette Mota, FMA, Dir.;
Federation of Catholic Parent Teacher Clubs of the Archdiocese of San Antonio - 2718 W. Woodlawn, San Antonio, TX 78228 t) 210-734-2620 x1231 dade.sustaita@sbcglobal.net www.archsa.org Annie Sustaita, Pres.; Melinda Fresquez, Treas.;
Headwaters at Incarnate Word, Inc. - 4503 Broadway, San Antonio, TX 78209 t) 210-828-2224 x280 pamela.ball@headwaters-iw.org www.headwaters-iw.org Pamela Ball, Dir.; Sr. Cynthia Ann Stacy, Dir.; Srs.: 1
House of Mercy Gift Shop, Inc. - 1201 Donaldson Ave., San Antonio, TX 78228 t) 210-736-0055 x101 mdavila@saintpaulsa.org Mary Davila, Bus. Mgr.;
Madonna Center, Inc. - 1906 Castroville Rd., San Antonio, TX 78237 t) 210-432-2374 info@madonnacentersa.org madonnacentersa.org Family Strengthening Services, Casework, Early Head Start, Pre School and After School Care, Seniors Socialization and Wellness Programs. Roger Caballero, Exec.;
Mary Help Network (ADMA) - 6019 Buena Vista St., San Antonio, TX 78237 c) 210-316-3747 adma@salesiansisterswest.org salesiansisterswest.org Sr. Mary Gloria Mar, FMA, Dir.;
MCSP, Inc. (Youth Sports, Inc.) - 714 E. Theo Ave., San Antonio, TX 78210 t) 210-477-8900 info@mcsportspark.org Erik Markus, Dir.;
Merced Housing Texas - 120 W. Mistletoe Ave., San Antonio, TX 78212; Mailing: P.O. Box 12870, San Antonio, TX 78212 t) 210-281-0234 merced@mercedhousingtexas.org www.mercedhousingtexas.org Founded by a consortium of religious orders to provide quality, affordable, service enriched housing for the economically poor, to strengthen families Kristin L. Davila, Pres.;
Missionary Oblates of Mary Immaculate - USA (MAMI-USA) - 323 Oblate Dr., San Antonio, TX 78216-6629 t) 210-736-1685 x141 contact@oblatemissions.org www.oblatemissions.org Rev. David Paul Uribe, OMI, Exec.;
St. Monica's Guild - 7711 Robin Rest Dr., San Antonio, TX 78209 t) 210-657-1326; 210-657-1326 A social, civic, and charitable group. Celeste Barron, Contact;
Old Spanish Missions (Las Misiones) - 2718 Woodlawn Ave., San Antonio, TX 78228; Mailing: P.O. Box 7804, San Antonio, TX 78207 t) 210-357-5601 oldspanishmissions@archsa.org www.lasmisiones.org Rebecca Simmons, Dir.; Karla Vasquez, Bus. Mgr.;
Purisima Concepcion - 807 Mission Rd., San Antonio, TX 78210 t) 210-533-8955 rebecca.simmons@archsa.org Rebecca Simmons, Dir.;
San Francisco de la Espada - 10040 Espada Rd., San Antonio, TX 78214 t) 210-627-2064 rebecca.simmons@archsa.org Rebecca Simmons, Dir.;
San Jose - 701 E. Pyron Rd., San Antonio, TX 78214 t) 210-922-0543 rebecca.simmons@archsa.org Rebecca Simmons, Dir.;
San Juan Capistrano - 9101 Graf Rd., San Antonio, TX 78214 t) 210-532-2806 rebecca.simmons@archsa.org Rebecca Simmons, Dir.;
St. Peter & St. Joseph Children's Home - 919 Mission Rd., San Antonio, TX 78210 t) 210-533-1203 ggonzalez@stpjhome.org www.stpjhome.org Gladys Gonzalez, Exec. Dir.;
Pilgrim Center of Hope - Evangelization Ministry - 7680 Joe Newton, San Antonio, TX 78251 t) 210-521-3377 ministry@pilgrimcenterofhope.org www.pilgrimcenterofhope.org Mary Jane Fox, Dir.; Dcn. Tom Fox, Dir.;
Presentation Ministry Center - 2003 Ruiz St., San Antonio, TX 78207 t) 210-663-6055 c) 210-279-4114 pbvmcenter@yahoo.com; cynthiajasso@hotmail.com Cynthia Jasso, Dir.;
Religious of Mary Immaculate - Villa Maria, 719 Augusta St., San Antonio, TX 78215 t) 210-226-0025; 210-223-8163 c) 202-250-1986 villamarmi@yahoo.com www.villamariaresidence.org (Pontifical), Apostolic Work: Counseling & guidance of young women of good moral conduct of any race or religion. Sr. Maria de Jesus Lozano Palomino, RMI, Supr.;
San Antonio Inter-Community Finance Office (SAIFO) - 11931 Radium St., San Antonio, TX 78216 t) 210-341-8884 kmoylan@mysaifo.com Kimberly Moylan, Dir.;
Servants of Jesus and Mary, S.A. - 7635 Dueling Oak, San Antonio, TX 78254 t) 210-823-6601 milabellera@hotmail.com www.servantsofjesusandmary.ning.com Gloria Urbina, Contact;
Socially Responsible Investment Coalition - 285 Oblate Dr., San Antonio, TX 78216 t) 210-344-6778 afalkenberg@sric-south.org sric-south.org/ Anna Falkenberg, Dir.;
VIDES Volunteers International Development Education and Solidarity - 6019 Buena Vista St., San Antonio, TX 78237-1700 c) 323-603-9792 director@vides.us www.vides.us Sr. Sydney Moss, FMA, Dir. VIDES+USA;

MONASTERIES AND RESIDENCES FOR PRIESTS AND BROTHERS [MON]

FALLS CITY

Salvatorian Fathers Community of Texas - 211 W. Meyer St., Falls City, TX 78113; Mailing: P.O. Box 158, Falls City, TX 78113 t) 830-254-3539 dariusz.ziebowicz@mailsds.org Rev. Dariusz Ziebowicz, S.D.S. (Poland), Supr.; Rev. Marcin Pawel Czyz, SDS, Admin.; Rev. Damian Jaje, S.D.S., Treas.; Rev. Josef Musiol, S.D.S. (Poland), Mem.; Rev. Marian Piekarczyk, S.D.S., Mem.; Rev. Andrzej Waszczenko, S.D.S. (Poland), Mem.; Rev. Boleslaw Zadora, S.D.S. (Poland), Mem.; Rev. Tacusz Tadak, Mem.; Priests: 8

SAN ANTONIO

Casa Maria Marianist Community - St. Mary's University, One Camino Santa Maria, San Antonio, TX 78228-8518; Mailing: Box 18, San Antonio, TX 78228-8518 t) 210-436-3066 a.brian.zamp@gmail.com Rev. James Tobin, S.M., Chap.; Bro. Brian Zampier, S.M., Dir.; Bro. Michael O'Grady, S.M., Area Vocation Dir.; Bro. Michael Sullivan, S.M., Prof.; Bro. Kaehler Lester; Brs.: 4; Priests: 1
Congregation of Holy Cross - Brother Charles Andersen Residence, 320 Brahan Blvd, San Antonio, TX 78215-1020 t) 210-843-9070 bmwcsc@yahoo.com Community residence. Bro. Michael Winslow, C.S.C., Dir.; Bro. Roger Croteau, Mem.; Bro. Patrick Tumwine, Mem.; Brs.: 4
De Mazenod House - 7707 Madonna Dr., San Antonio, TX 78216 t) 210-349-8572 klosterkamp@oblaten.de (Faculty Residence) US Province of the Missionary Oblates of Mary Immaculate. Rev. Warren Brown, O.M.I., In Res.; Rev. Ken Hannon, O.M.I., In Res.; Rev. Thomas Klosterkamp, OMI (Germany), In Res.; Rev. Joseph LaBelle, O.M.I., In Res.; Rev. Bryan Silva, O.M.I., In Res.; Priests: 5
Discalced Carmelite Fathers of San Antonio - 906 Kentucky Ave., San Antonio, TX 78201-6097 t) 210-735-9127; 210-735-9126 x100 (Office) scantu@littleflowerbasilica.org; pastor@littleflowerbasilica.org www.littleflowerbasilica.org Friar Gregory Ross, OCD, Pst.; Friar Luis Joaquin Castaneda, OCD, In Res.; Friar Sam Anthony Morello, OCD, In Res.; Friar Emmanuel Javert Nnadozie, O.C.D., In Res.; Friar Raul Reyes, OCD, In Res.; Friar Jorge Cabrera, OCD, Supr.; Brs.: 1; Priests: 6
Holy Cross of San Antonio - 426 N. San Felipe St., San Antonio, TX 78228 t) 210-434-3801 stanley.culotta@holycross-sa.org Bro. Stanley Culotta, C.S.C., Pres. Emeritus;
Holy Rosary Marianist Community - 159 Camino Santa Maria, San Antonio, TX 78228-4997 c) 314-282-5412 mmotz@marianist.us Rev. Neville O'Donohue, Pst.; Bro. Roger Bau, In Res.; Rev. Brandon Paluch, S.M., In Res.; Bro. Mark Motz, Dir.; Brs.: 2; Priests: 2
Holy Trinity Fathers - 401 Squires Row, San Antonio, TX 78213 t) 210-781-4945 thdymowski@gmail.com trinitarians.org Rev. J. Edward Owens, O.SS.T.; Bro. Patrick G. Wildgen, O.SS.T.; Brs.: 1; Priests: 1
Ligustrum Marianist Community - 253 W. Ligustrum Dr., San Antonio, TX 78228-4020 t) 210-433-9114 Rev. John Thompson, S.M., Mem.; Bro. Thomas Suda, S.M., Mem.; Rev. William J. Meyer, S.M., Dir.; Rev. Richard Villa, S.M., Mem.; Brs.: 1; Priests: 3
Marianist Residence - 520 Fordham Ave., San Antonio, TX 78228-4800 t) 210-436-3745 giancarlo1600@gmail.com Bro. Fred Halwe; Bro. Steven Grazulis, In Res.; Rev. Alvin McMenamy, In Res.; Bro. Donald Nussbaum, In Res.; Bro. Frederick Silbereis, In Res.; Rev. Timothy Dwyer, S.M.; Rev. Conrad J. Kaczkowski, S.M., Prof.; Rev. W. Franz Schorp, S.M.; Bro. Giancarlo Bonutti, Dir.; Rev. Gerald Haby, In Res.; Bro. Sylvester Burkemper, In Res.; Bro. Chester Burnog, In Res.; Bro. Lawrence Corbin, In Res.; Bro. Richard Dix, In Res.; Bro. Jerome Bommer, In Res.; Bro. James Jaeckle, In Res.; Bro. Del Jorn, In Res.; Bro. Al Kuntemeier, In Res.; Bro. John Laudenbach, In Res.; Bro. Edward Loch, In Res.; Bro. Louis Mason, In Res.; Bro. Paul Metzger, In Res.; Bro. Lawrence Scrivani, In Res.; Bro. Leo Slay, In Res.; Bro. Fred Stovall, In Res.; Bro. Dan Stupka, In Res.; Bro. Irwin Wachtel, In Res.; Brs.: 21; Priests: 4
Marianist Vocation Ministry - 159 Camino Santa Maria, San Antonio, TX 78228-4901 t) 314-250-4505 vocations@marianist.us marianist.com/vocations Vocation Office Bro. Mark Motz, Natl. Vocation Dir.; Brs.: 1
Missionaries of the Sacred Heart - 123 W. Laurel St., San Antonio, TX 78212-4667 t) 210-226-5514 laurelmsc@sbcglobal.net Sectional Headquarters of the Irish Province for Southern States. Rev. Kevin Shanahan, M.S.C., Pst.; Rev. Patrick Stenson, Pst.; Rev. James A. Harnan, M.S.C.; Rev. Michael O'Brien, M.S.C.; Priests: 4
Missionary Oblates of Mary Immaculate of Texas, Southern Province (San Antonio USP Support Office) -

327 Oblate Dr., San Antonio, TX 78216-6602 t) 210-349-1475 www.omiusa.org Rev. Louis Studer, O.M.I., Prov.; Rev. Mark Dean, O.M.I., Dir.; Rev. Arthur Flores, O.M.I., Dir.; Rev. James Chambers, O.M.I., Treas.; Rev. William Antone, OMI, Attached; Chula Vista, CA; Rev. Lucio Castillo, OMI, Attached; Chula Vista, CA; Rev. Jesse Esqueda, OMI, Attached; Chula Vista, CA; Rev. Eleazar Manuel-Lopez, OMI, Attached; Chula Vista, CA; Rev. Marek Stroba, OMI, Attached; Chula Vista, CA; Bro. Peter Vasquez, OMI, Attached; Chula Vista, CA; Priests: 5

Missionary Oblates of Mary Immaculate of Texas - 302 Oblate Dr., San Antonio, TX 78216 c) 210-275-7018 (Rev. Rolheiser); 202-286-2870 (Rev. Morell); 210-383-4094 (Rev. Renaud) rrolheiser@ost.edu; drenaud@omiusa.org Pierre Keralum Residence Rev. Daniel Renaud, OMI, In Res.; Rev. Ronald Rolheiser, O.M.I., In Res.;

Oblate Vocation Office - 327 Oblate Dr., San Antonio, TX 78216-6602 t) (210) 349-1475 vocations@omiusa.org Rev. Victor Manuel Patricio-Silva, OMI, Dir.;

North American Redemptorist Theology Residence - 1523 Iowa St., San Antonio, TX 78203 t) 210-533-0161 Rev. Jose Chavez, C.Ss.R., Formation Dir.; Rev. Peter Hill, C.Ss.R., Formation Dir.; Brs.: 7; Priests: 2

Oblate Benson Residence - 334 W. Kings Hwy., San Antonio, TX 78212 t) 210-370-3923 rhall@omiusa.org Missionary Oblates of Mary Immaculate Rev. Richard Hall, O.M.I., Dir.; Rev. John G. Castro, O.M.I., In Res.; Rev. Arthur Flores, O.M.I., In Res.; Rev. Thomas Ovalle, OMI, In Res.; Rev. David Paul Uribe, OMI, In Res.; Priests: 5

The Redemptorists/San Antonio - 1617 Iowa St., San Antonio, TX 78203 t) 210-817-4747 Rev. Alton Carr, C.Ss.R., In Res.; Bro. Charles Fucik, C.Ss.R., Pastoral Staff; Rev. Robert H. Lindsey, C.Ss.R., Assoc. Pst.; Rev. Thomas T. Pham, C.Ss.R., Local Supr. & Vocation Dir.; Rev. Luong Uong, C.Ss.R., Pastor, Vietnamese Martyrs; Rev. Donald Willard, C.Ss.R., Pastor, St. Gerard; Brs.: 1; Priests: 5

San Damiano Friary - 1104 Kentucky Ave., San Antonio, TX 78201 t) 210-734-4962 sandamianobooks@gmail.com Conventual Franciscan Friars. Friar Gary Johnson, OFM Conv., Guardian & Dir. Formation; Friar Andrew Martinez, Formation Dir.; Friar Philip Ley, O.F.M.Conv.; Friar Christian Emmanuel Abrica Benitez, OFM Conv., In Res.; Friar Cristian Ublado Castro Martinez, OFM Conv., In Res.; Rev. Richard Kaley, OFM Conv., In Res.; Bro. Tim Unser, O.F.M.Conv., Librn.; Brs.: 1; Priests: 6

Woodlawn Marianist Community - 3303 W. Woodlawn Ave., San Antonio, TX 78228 c) 210-867-6544 bro_tim@hotmail.com Rev. Patrick McDaid, Chap.; Bro. Timothy Pieprzyca, S.M., Dir.; Bro. James Burkholder, SM; Bro. Earl Leistikow, SM; Bro. Richard Thompson, SM; Bro. David Quigley, In Res.; Bro. Dan Klco, In Res.; Brs.: 6; Priests: 1

NURSING / REHABILITATION / CONVALESCENCE / ELDERLY CARE [NUR]

KENEDY

John Paul II Nursing Home - 209 S. 3rd St., Kenedy, TX 78119 t) 830-583-9841 johnpaul2nh@yahoo.com; sragnesbochenek@gmail.com Sr. Agnes Bochenek, S.O.L.S., Admin.; Asstd. Annu.: 60; Staff: 54

SAN ANTONIO

Casa De Padres - 8520 Cross Mountain Tr. #100, San Antonio, TX 78255 t) 210-698-0175 casadepadres@gmail.com Independent Living for Retired Priests of the San Antonio Archdiocese Rev. Msgr. Lambert S. Bily, In Res.; Rev. Emmet Carolan, In Res.; Rev. Paul Cleary, In Res.; Rev. Anthony Cummins, In Res.; Rev. Msgr. James V Janish, In Res.; Rev. Msgr. Patrick L. Marron, In Res.; Rev. Carl R. Maurer, In Res.; Rev. Msgr. Enda McKenna, In Res.; Rev. Jose Antonio Villanueva, In Res.; Rev. Msgr. Emil J. Wesselsky, In Res.; Tara Castro, Dir.; Asstd. Annu.: 11; Staff: 3

St. Francis Nursing Home and Independent Living - 630 W. Woodlawn, San Antonio, TX 78212 t) 210-736-3177 st.francis@sbcglobal.net; hkomperda@hotmail.com stfrancisnursinghome.org Home for the Aged and Convalescents. Seraphic Sisters of Our Lady of Sorrows. Sr. Samuela Komperda, Admin.; Sr. Agnes Bochenek, S.O.L.S., Pres.; Asstd. Annu.: 100; Staff: 96

Incarnate Word Retirement Community (The Village at Incarnate Word) - 4707 Broadway, San Antonio, TX 78209 t) 210-829-7561 paul.harrison@thevillageiw.org www.thevillageiw.org Retirement community that serves both religious and lay persons. Rev. Jim Rutkowski, Chap.; Paul Harrison, CEO; Asstd. Annu.: 483; Staff: 258

Incarnate Word Retirement Community Inc. - U.S. Province, 4707 Broadway, San Antonio, TX 78209-6215 t) 210-829-7561 paul.harrison@thevillageiw.org www.thevillageiw.org Paul Harrison, CEO; Alma Cosme, Dir.; Janette Eisenmenger, COO; Alma Cosme, VP Mktg./Business Devel.; Niki Simpson, VP Devel.; Srs.: 47

Marianist Residence: Skilled Nursing - 520 Fordham Ln., San Antonio, TX 78228-4800 t) 210-436-3771 giancarlo1600@gmail.com Home for Infirm Marianist Brothers and Priests. Rev. J. Donald Cahill, In Res.; Bro. Alva Gillis, In Res.; Bro. Francis Heyer, In Res.; Bro. Daniel Stupka, In Res.; Rev. Donald Wallace, In Res.; Bro. Giancarlo Bonutti, Dir.; Rev. Christian Janson, In Res.; Rev. Gerald Chinchar, In Res.; Rev. Anthony Jansen, In Res.; Rev. George Montague, S.M., In Res.; Bro. DuWayne Brisendine, In Res.; Bro. Michael Galvin, In Res.; Bro. Gerard Sullivan, In Res.; Asstd. Annu.: 12; Staff: 38

McCullough Hall Nursing Center, Inc. - 603 S.W. 24th St., San Antonio, TX 78207-4696 t) 210-435-7711 mbordelon@cdptexas.org Sr. Mary Bordelon, C.D.P., Contact; Asstd. Annu.: 40; Staff: 46

McCullough Hall Nursing Center, Inc. - 603 S.W. 24th St., San Antonio, TX 78207-4696 t) 210-435-7711 mbordelon@cdptexas.org Sr. Mary Bordelon, C.D.P., Contact; Asstd. Annu.: 40; Staff: 46

Oblate Madonna Residence - 5722 Blanco Rd., San Antonio, TX 78216 t) 210-341-2350 cbanks@omiusa.org Home for retired Priests and Brothers. Missionary Oblates of Mary Immaculate. Rev. Charles Banks, O.M.I., Supr.; Rev. Joseph Benedict Aluthwatte, In Res.; Rev. Donald Bernard, In Res.; Rev. Daniel Crahen, O.M.I., In Res.; Most Rev. Michael D. Pfeifer, O.M.I.; Bro. Peter Vasquez, OMI, In Res.; Rev. Eugene Canas, OMI, In Res.; Rev. Ramiro Cortez, In Res.; Rev. William Davis, O.M.I., In Res.; Rev. James Foelker, OMI, In Res.; Rev. Jose Maria Gago, In Res.; Rev. James Gibbons, OMI (Brazil), In Res.; Rev. Ricardo V. Guerra, O.M.I., In Res.; Rev. Patrick Guidon, OMI, In Res.; Rev. Robert Hickel, OMI, In Res.; Rev. Tom Horan, OMI, In Res.; Rev. Amador Lopez, In Res.; Rev. James P. Miller, In Res.; Rev. Godfrey Mwansa, In Res.; Rev. Paul Nourie, In Res.; Rev. Isidore Garcia, O.M.I., In Res.; Rev. Philion Richard, OMI, In Res.; Rev. Thomas Rush, In Res.; Rev. Luis Valbuena, In Res.; Rev. Edward Vrazel, In Res.; Rev. Robert Wright, O.M.I., In Res.; Rev. Manuel Villarreal, In Res.; Rev. William E. Zapalac, O.M.I., In Res.; Bro. Valmond LeClerc, O.M.I., In Res.; Asstd. Annu.: 31; Staff: 37

Missionary Servants of St. Anthony (Padua Place) - 80 Peter Baque Rd., San Antonio, TX 78209-1805 t) 210-826-7721 pp8061@sanantonio.twcbc.com Home for infirm and retired Priests, Brothers and Deacons. Sr. Mary Ann Domagalski, M.S.S.A., Admin.; Mary Quintero, Dir.; Rev. James Beegan, M.S.F., In Res.; Rev. Francisco D. Garcia II, In Res.; Rev. William McNamara, In Res.; Rev. Michael O'Brien, M.S.C., In Res.; Rev. Raymond Schuster, In Res.; Rev. Simon Brzozowski, In Res.; Rev. James Conway, In Res.; Rev. Msgr. Albert H. Hubertus, In Res.; Rev. Michael Lenihan, In Res.; Rev. Martin F McGuill, In Res.; Rev. Msgr. Thomas Palmer, In Res.; Dcn. Gilbert Weissler, In Res.; Asstd. Annu.: 13; Staff: 23

PRESCHOOLS / CHILDCARE CENTERS [PRE]

SAN ANTONIO

Immaculate Conception Kindergarten and Nursery - 2407 W. Travis St., San Antonio, TX 78207 t) 210-226-3934 perpetualdaycare@att.net; sistersapg@gmail.com Sr. Carolina Juarez Sanchez, Dir.; Stds.: 44; Lay Tchrs.: 8

RETREAT HOUSES / RENEWAL CENTERS [RTR]

BOERNE

Omega Retreat Center - 316 W. Highland Dr., Ste. 100, Boerne, TX 78006 t) 830-816-8470 (San Antonio); 830-249-3894 (Boerne) omegaretreatcenter@gmail.com omega.boernebenedictines.org Benedictine Sisters (Congregation of Benedictine Sisters) Melynda Weilbacher, Manager;

CASTROVILLE

Moye Retreat Center - 600 London St., Castroville, TX 78009 t) 830-931-2233 moyecenter@cdptexas.org Center for Retreats, Renewal, and Conferences. Under the direction of the Sisters of Divine Providence. Donna Bippert, Dir.; Sr. Mary Bordelon, C.D.P., Contact;

MOUNTAIN HOME

TECABOCA: A Marianist Center for Spiritual Renewal - 5045 Junction Hwy. 27, Mountain Home, TX 78058 t) 830-866-3425 director@tecaboca.com www.tecaboca.com Operated by Marianist Province of the U.S. Kay Tally-Foos, Exec.;

SAN ANTONIO

Oblate Renewal Center - 5700 Blanco Rd., San Antonio, TX 78216-6615 t) 210-349-4173; (210) 349-4173 orc@ost.edu www.ost.edu/oblate_renewal_center.htm Missionary Oblates of Mary Immaculate Sr. Deborah Fuchs, Spiritual Adviser / Care Svcs.; K.T. Cockrell, Director of Hospitality Services;

SEMINARIES [SEM]

SAN ANTONIO

The Seminary of the Assumption of the Blessed Virgin Mary-St. John of San Antonio, TX (Assumption-St. John's Seminary) - 2600 W. Woodlawn Ave., San Antonio, TX 78228-5196 t) 210-734-5137 assumptionseminary@archsa.org; oralia.lichtenberger@archsa.org www.assumptionseminary.org Rev. James Myers, P.S.S., Rector; Rev. Renato Lopez, P.S.S., Vice Rector of Formation; Sr. Dianne Heinrich, C.D.P., Coordinator of Intellectual Formation; Martin Martinez, Chair of Admissions/Assistant Coordinator for Pastoral Formation; Robert Gomez, Director of Operations; Rev. Martin Joseph Burnham, Formation Faculty; Rev. Jerome Magat, PSS, Dean of Men; Rev. Marcos Ramos, Formation Faculty; Stds.: 44; Lay Tchrs.: 1; Pr. Tchrs.: 5; Sr. Tchrs.: 1

Blessed Mario Borzaga Formation Community - 222 Oblate Dr., San Antonio, TX 78216 t) 210-248-9087 aponce@omiusa.org omiusa.org Scholasticate-(Theology). Missionary Oblates of Mary Immaculate, United States Province. Rev. Arun William Rozario, OMI (Bangladesh), Pst.; Rev. Antonio Ponce, O.M.I., Supr.; Rev. Ronald Framboise, O.M.I., Dir.; Rev. Abraham Chimese, OMI, Pst.; Rev. Francis Santucci, O.M.I., Pst.; Rev. Godfrey Mwansa, In Res.; Rev. Victor Manuel Patricio-Silva, OMI, In Res.; Stds.: 11; Pr. Tchrs.: 5; Scholastics: 11

Office of Diaconate Ministry and Formation - 2718 W. Woodlawn, San Antonio, TX 78228-5124 t) 210-734-1658 mike.pawelek@archsa.org; claudia.garza@archsa.org Dcn. Michael Pawelek, Dir.; Stds.: 83

San Damiano Friary, Initial House of Formation - 1104 Kentucky Ave., San Antonio, TX 78201 t) 210-734-4962 sandamianobooks@gmail.com Conventual Franciscan Friars. Friar Gary Johnson, OFM Conv., Guardian & Dir. Formation; Friar Andrew Martinez, Formation Dir.; Friar Phillip Ley, O.F.M.Conv.; Friar Timothy Unser, O.F.M.Conv.; Friar Christian Emmanuel Abrica

Benitez, OFM Conv., In Res.; Friar Cristian Ubaldo Castro Martinez, OFM Conv., In Res.; Rev. Richard Kaley, OFM Conv., In Res.; Stds.: 13; Pr. Tchrs.: 2; Scholastics: 13

SHRINES [SHR]

SAN ANTONIO

Basilica of the National Shrine of the Little Flower - 1715 N. Zarzamora, San Antonio, TX 78201; Mailing: 824 Kentucky Ave., San Antonio, TX 78201 t) 210-735-9126 sdehoyos@littleflowerbasilica.org; scantu@littleflowerbasilica.org www.littleflowerbasilica.org Friar Gregory Ross, OCD, Rector; Susana Cantu, Exec.; Laura Cole, Bus. Mgr.;

Oblate Lourdes Grotto Shrine of the Southwest, Tepeyac de San Antonio - 5712 Blanco Rd., San Antonio, TX 78216 t) 210-342-9864 rhall@omiusa.org www.oblatemissions.org Missionary Oblates of Mary Immaculate Rev. David Paul Uribe, OMI, Chap.; Rev. Richard Hall, O.M.I., Dir.;

Our Lady of Czestochowa - C/O Seraphic Sisters of Our Lady of Sorrows, 138 Beethoven St., San Antonio, TX 78210 t) 210-337-8193 serzeznik@gmail.com www.seraphicsisters.org Seraphic Sisters of Our Lady of Sorrows. Inga M Michnowicz, Supr.;

SPECIAL CARE FACILITIES [SPF]

SAN ANTONIO

Christus Continuing Care (Christus Homecare) - 100 N.E. Loop 410, Ste. 800, San Antonio, TX 78216 t) 210-785-5200 sarah.hill@christushealth.org www.christushomecare.org Dr. Sarah Hill, Vice. Pres.; Bed Capacity: 16; Asstd. Annu.: 3,500; Staff: 46

Project Rachel of San Antonio - 202 W. French Pl., San Antonio, TX 78212 t) 210-342-4673 rachel@anewchoice.org www.ccaosa.org Post-abortive healing ministry Stephanie Sahin, Dir.; Asstd. Annu.: 50; Staff: 1

Seton Home - 1115 Mission Rd., San Antonio, TX 78210 t) 210-533-3504 info@setonhomesa.org www.setonhomesa.org Gladys Gonzalez, Exec. Dir.; Bed Capacity: 99; Asstd. Annu.: 149; Staff: 85

Visitation House Ministries, Inc. - 830 W. Mulberry Ave, San Antonio, TX 78212; Mailing: P.O. Box 12074, San Antonio, TX 78212 t) 210-735-6910 cynthia.bossard@amormeus.org www.visitationhouseministries.org Supportive Housing and Education Program for homeless women and their children and an Outreach Program for other women from the community. Andrea Hofstetter, Dir.; Bed Capacity: 18; Asstd. Annu.: 50; Staff: 6

An asterisk (*) denotes an organization that has established tax-exempt status directly with the IRS and is not covered by the USCCB Group Ruling.

Diocese of San Bernardino

MOST REVEREND ALBERTO ROJAS

Bishop of San Bernardino; ordained May 24, 1997; appointed Auxiliary Bishop of Chicago and Titular Bishop of Marazanae June 13, 2011; Episcopal ordination August 10, 2011; appointed Coadjutor Bishop of San Bernardino December 2, 2019; Succeeded to the See December 28, 2020. Office: 1201 E. Highland Ave., San Bernardino, CA 92404-4641.

Diocesan Pastoral Center: 1201 E. Highland Ave., San Bernardino, CA 92404-4641. T: 909-475-5300; F: 909-475-5109.
www.sbdiocese.org
sbdiocese@sbdiocese.org

ESTABLISHED NOVEMBER 6, 1978.

Square Miles 27,293.

Comprises the Counties of San Bernardino and Riverside.

Legal Title: The Roman Catholic Bishop of San Bernardino, a Corporation Sole (Churches, Rectories, Halls, Catechetical Centers, etc.).

STATISTICAL OVERVIEW

Personnel
Bishop....1
Retired Bishops....2
Priests: Diocesan Active in Diocese....61
Priests: Diocesan Active Outside Diocese....1
Priests: Retired, Sick or Absent....34
Number of Diocesan Priests....96
Religious Priests in Diocese....120
Total Priests in your Diocese....216
Extern Priests in Diocese....62
Ordinations:
Diocesan Priests....4
Permanent Deacons....9
Permanent Deacons in Diocese....148
Total Brothers....8
Total Sisters....76

Parishes
Parishes....92
With Resident Pastor:
Resident Diocesan Priests....27
Resident Religious Priests....39
Without Resident Pastor:
Administered by Priests....26
Missions....7
Pastoral Centers....1
Professional Ministry Personnel:
Brothers....2
Sisters....13
Lay Ministers....121

Welfare
Catholic Hospitals....2
Total Assisted....280,001
Specialized Homes....1
Total Assisted....43,860
Special Centers for Social Services....8
Total Assisted....24,219

Educational
Seminaries, Diocesan....1
Students from This Diocese....6
Diocesan Students in Other Seminaries....12
Total Seminarians....18
High Schools, Diocesan and Parish....3
Total Students....1,517
Elementary Schools, Diocesan and Parish....26
Total Students....4,778
Elementary Schools, Private....1
Total Students....656
Catechesis/Religious Education:
High School Students....7,152
Elementary Students....12,980
Total Students under Catholic Instruction....27,101
Teachers in Diocese:
Priests....17
Sisters....6
Lay Teachers....482

Vital Statistics
Receptions into the Church:
Infant Baptism Totals....7,049
Minor Baptism Totals....591
Adult Baptism Totals....304
Received into Full Communion....1,624
First Communions....6,057
Confirmations....4,833
Marriages:
Catholic....1,374
Interfaith....148
Total Marriages....1,522
Deaths....5,645
Total Catholic Population....1,371,361
Total Population....4,653,105

LEADERSHIP

Diocesan Pastoral Center - t) 909-475-5300
Office of the Bishop - t) 909-475-5113 bishopsoffice@sbdiocese.org
Office of Episcopal Vicars - t) 909-475-5117 episcopalvicar@sbdiocese.org Very Rev. Rafael A. Partida; Very Rev. Romeo N. Seleccion, M.S.;
Office of Priest Personnel - t) 909-475-5120 Rev. Erik L. Esparza, Dir.;
Office of the Chancellor - t) 909-475-5100 chancellor@sbdiocese.org Sr. Leticia Salazar, O.D.N., Chancellor;
Office of the Vicar General - t) 909-475-5180 Rev. Msgr. Gerard M. Lopez, Vicar;

OFFICES AND DIRECTORS

Accounting Services - t) 909-475-5480 accounting@sbdiocese.org Jorge Montenegro, Dir. (jmontenegro@sbdiocese.org);
Archives - t) 909-475-5397 archives@sbdiocese.org Arlene Gutierrez, Archivist;
Canonical Services (Marriage Tribunal) - t) 909-475-5320 canonicalservices@sbdiocese.org Very Rev. David Andel, Dir. & Judicial Vicar (dandel@sbdiocese.org);
Catechetical Ministry - t) 909-475-5452 catechetical@sbdiocese.org Rosa Maria Gouveia, Dir. (rgouveia@sbdiocese.org);
Catholic Cemeteries - t) (909) 825-9246
Catholic Schools - t) 909-475-5437 catholicschools@sbdiocese.org Samuel Torres, Supt.;
Chief Financial Officer - t) (909) 475-5150 Jorge Montenegro, CFO;
Child and Youth Protection - t) 909-475-5125 Elder Samaniego, Dir. (esamaniego@sbdiocese.org);
Consecrated Life - t) 909-475-5345 consecratedlife@sbdiocese.org Sr. Mary Frances Coleman, R.S.M., Vicar (mfcoleman@sbdiocese.org);
Construction and Real Estate - t) 909-475-5310 ocre@sbdiocese.org David Meier, Dir. (dmeier@sbdiocese.org);
Diaconate Formation - t) (909) 475-5160 Dcn. Luis Sanchez, Dir.;
Ecclesial Services - t) 909-475-5160 ecclesialservices@sbdiocese.org Dcn. Luis Sanchez, Dir.;
Emergency Operations Collaborative (EOC) - t) (909) 475-5441 Ann Marie Gallant, Dir.;
Ethnic Affairs - t) 909-475-5140 rpartida@sbdiocese.org Rev. Rafael A. Partida, Dir.;
Facilities Management - t) (909) 475-5300 vturner@sbdiocese.org
Human Resources - t) 909-475-5170 humanresources@sbdiocese.org Virginia Turner, Dir. (vturner@sbdiocese.org);
Information Technology Services - t) (909) 475-5400 issupport@sbdiocese.org sbdiocese.wix.com/communications Edward Jabo, Dir. (ejabo@sbdiocese.org);
Marriage and Family Life Ministry - t) 909-475-5390 mflm@sbdiocese.org www.sbmarriageinitiative.org/ Mario Orlando Martinez, Dir.;
Media - t) 909-475-5400 sbdiocese.wixsite.com/communications John H. Andrews, Dir./ Vice Chancellor;
Ministry Formation Institute - t) 909-475-5370 mfi@sbdiocese.org Dr. Amanda Alexander, Dir.;
Ministry of Life, Dignity, and Justice - t) 909-475-5350 lifedignityandjust.wixsite.com/mldj Sr. Chilee Okoko, D.M.M.M., Dir.;
Ministry with Young Catholics - t) 909-475-5165 myo@sbdiocese.org; youngcatholics@sbdiocese.org sbyoungcatholics.org/ Edgardo Juarez, Dir. (ejuarez@sbdiocese.org);
Campus Ministry - t) (909) 475-5361
Mission - t) 909-475-5130 mission@sbdiocese.org
Mission Advancement - t) 909-475-5460 missionadvancement@sbdiocese.org
Parish Assistance - t) 909-475-5490 parishassistance@sbdiocese.org Jorge Montenegro, Dir. (jmontenegro@sbdiocese.org);
Pastoral Planning - t) 909-475-5146 pastoralplanning2@sbdiocese.org www.pastoralplanningministry.com Aaron G. Colin, Dir. (acolin@sbdiocese.org);
Payroll Services - t) 909-475-5188 payroll@sbdiocese.org Trang Pham, Dir. (tpham@sbdiocese.org);
Seminarians - t) 909-783-0260 Very Rev. Jorge A. Garcia, Rector;
Vicar for Retired Priests - t) 909-475-5345 mfcoleman@sbdiocese.org Sr. Mary Frances Coleman, R.S.M., Dir.;
Vocations - t) 909-783-1305 vocations@sbdiocese.org www.dsbvocations.org Rev. Hau Q. Vu, Dir. (hvu@sbdiocese.org);
Worship Office - t) 909-475-5335 worship@sbdiocese.org

ADVISORY BOARDS, COMMISSIONS, COMMITTEES, AND COUNCILS

Bishop's Advisory Commissions -
Commission for Ministry for Families with Gay and Lesbian Catholics - t) 909-475-5140 Very Rev. David Andel;
Diocesan Liturgical Commission - Clare Colella, Chair;
Bishop's Advisory Committees -
Diocesan Building Committee - Very Rev. Rafael A. Partida, Chair;
Diocesan Review Committee - t) 909-475-5120 Gerardo J. Lopez, Chair;
College of Consultors - Rev. Msgr. Gerard M. Lopez;
Consecrated Life Council - Sr. Mary Frances Coleman, R.S.M. (mfcoleman@sbdiocese.org);
Diocesan Curia - Rev. Msgr. Gerard M. Lopez;
Ecumenical Council - Rev. Gregory Elder, Chair;
Finance Council - t) 909-475-5150 Bruce Satzger, Chair; Jorge Montenegro, CFO;
Budget Committee - Bruce Satzger, Chair;
Catholic Foundation Trustees - Michael Vanderpool, Chair;
Financial Review Committee - Bruce Satzger, Chair;
Investment Committee - Michael Vanderpool, Chair;
Legal Counsel - t) 909-889-3691 Wilfrid C. Lemann;
Ministerial Personnel and Placement Board - Rev. Erik L. Esparza;
Presbyteral Council - Rev. Tyler Tripp, Chair;
Vicars Forane - t) (909) 475-5117 Rev. Msgr. Gerard M. Lopez;

PARISHES, MISSIONS, AND CLERGY

STATE OF CALIFORNIA

ADELANTO

Christ the Good Shepherd - 17900 Jonathan St., Adelanto, CA 92301; Mailing: P.O. Box 577, Adelanto, CA 92301 t) 760-246-7083 christthegoodshepherd@sbdiocese.org www.cgshepherd-adelanto.org Rev. Canice Nwizu, Admin.; Dcn. Gustavo Morales; Dcn. Santos Aguilera; CRP Stds.: 32

ALTA LOMA

St. Peter & St. Paul - 9135 Banyan St., Alta Loma, CA 91737-2338 t) 909-987-9312 stpeterstpaul.altaloma@sbdiocese.org www.stpeterstpaul.com Rev. Henry M. Sseriiso, I.M.C., Pst.; Rev. Andres Rivera, Par. Vicar; Dcn. Luis Chanco; Dcn. Neriel Rabe; Aileen Gamalinda, CRE; CRP Stds.: 349

St. Peter and St. Paul Catholic School - t) (909) 987-7908 www.stpeterstpaulschool.com Kelly Burt, Prin.; Stds.: 123; Lay Tchrs.: 13

ANZA

Sacred Heart - 56250 Hwy 371, Anza, CA 92539; Mailing: P.O. Box 390118, Anza, CA 92539-0118 t) (951) 763-5636 sacredheart.anza@sbdiocese.org sites.google.com/site/371sacredheartanza Rev. Kien Kieu, Admin.; CRP Stds.: 31

APPLE VALLEY

Our Lady of the Desert - 18386 Corwin Rd., Apple Valley, CA 92307-2328 t) 760-242-4427 andrea.m@oldccav.org oldccav.org Rev. Delwyn Haroldson, C.R., Pst.; Rev. James M. Gibson, C.R., Par. Vicar; Rev. Henry A. Ruszel, C.R., In Res.; Dcn. Marcial Ampuero; Sylvia Fath, DRE; CRP Stds.: 199

BARSTOW

St. Joseph - 505 E. Mountain View St., Barstow, CA 92311-2924 t) 760-256-6818; 760-733-4308 (CRP) parishoffice@stjoserpbarstow.com; stjoseph.barstow@sbdiocese.org www.stjosephbarstow.com Rev. Remigius Owuamanam, SMMM, Pst.; Rev. Gabriel Ezeh, S.M.M.M., Par. Vicar; Rev. Michael Okafor, S.M.M.M., Par. Vicar; Dcn. Lucio Espinoza; Dcn. Joseph Moorman; Dcn. Ricardo Uribe; Cecilia Sepulveda, DRE; CRP Stds.: 146

Our Lady of the Desert - 57457 State Hwy. 127, Baker, CA 92309; Mailing: 505 E. Mountain View St., Barstow, CA 92311 t) (760) 733-4308 oldesert.barstow@sbdiocese.org www.stjosephbarstow.com/

St. Madeline Sophie Barat - 83395 Trona Rd., Trona, CA 93562; Mailing: 505 E. Mountain View St., Barstow, CA 92311 t) 760-372-4717

St. Philip Neri (Lenwood) - 25333 Third St., Barstow, CA 92311; Mailing: 505 E. Mountain View St., Barstow, CA 92311 t) 760-253-5412 stphilipneribarstow@sbdiocese.org spnlenwood.org Rev. Remigius Owuamanam, SMMM, Pst.; Rev. Gabriel Ezeh, S.M.M.M., Par. Vicar; Rev. Michael Okafor, S.M.M.M., Par. Vicar; CRP Stds.: 53

BEAUMONT

Saint Kateri Tekakwitha Catholic Community, Inc. - 1234 Palm Ave., Beaumont, CA 92223 t) 951-845-2849; 951-849-2434 (CRP) stkateritekakwitha@sbdiocese.org www.stkateritekakwitha.org Very Rev. Dennis L. Legaspi, Pst.; Rev. Stephen C. Porter, Par. Vicar; Rev. Miguel R. Ceja, Par. Vicar; Dcn. Mark Hodnick; Dcn. Armando Luevano Jr.; Dcn. Vicente Gonzalez; CRP Stds.: 65

St. Mary Chapel - Morongo Indian Reservation (11231 Mission Rd.), Banning, CA 92220; Mailing: 157 W. Nicolet St., Banning, CA 92220 Rev. Earl Joseph Henley, M.S.C., Pst.;

BIG BEAR LAKE

St. Joseph - 42242 N. Shore Dr., Big Bear Lake, CA 92314; Mailing: P.O. Box 1709, Big Bear Lake, CA 92315 t) 909-866-3030 stjoseph.bigbear@sbdiocese.org saintjosephbb.wordpress.com Rev. Paul Smith, C.R., Pst.; Dcn. James Webber; CRP Stds.: 97

BLOOMINGTON

St. Charles Borromeo - 11342 Spruce St., Bloomington, CA 92316 t) 909-877-0792 stcharlesborromeo@sbdiocese.org stcharlesborromeoca.com Rev. Fernando Bonilla Sanchez, M.S.P., Admin.; Rev. Luis A. de la Cruz Quen, MSP, Par. Vicar; Rev. Oscar M. Muñoz-Martinez, MSP, Par. Vicar; Dcn. Juan Rodriguez; Dcn. Jesus Figueroa Jr.; CRP Stds.: 305

BLYTHE

St. Joan of Arc - 875 E. Chanslor Way, Blythe, CA 92225 t) 760-922-3261 stjoanofarc.blythe@sbdiocese.org stjoanofarcblythe.com Rev. Anthony Ibegbunam, Admin.; CRP Stds.: 64

CATHEDRAL CITY

St. Louis - 68633 C St., Cathedral City, CA 92234 t) 760-459-1261 (CRP); 760-328-2398 stlouiscathedralcity@sbdiocese.org www.stlouischurchcathedralcity.org Rev. Luis Guido,

Pst.; Rev. Athanasius O. Ezealla, Par. Vicar; CRP Stds.: 272

CHINO

St. Margaret Mary - 12686 Central Ave., Chino, CA 91710-3508 t) 909-591-7400 stmargaretmary@sbdiocese.org www.smmchino.org Rev. Restituto O. Galang, MSP, Pst.; Rev. Abil Raj Pannerselvam, H.G.N., Par. Vicar; Dcn. Bernardo Esparza; Dcn. John Anthony Cruz; CRP Stds.: 375

St. Margaret Mary School - (Grades PreK-8) 12664 Central Ave., Chino, CA 91710 t) 909-591-8419 smms.ocs@sbdiocese.org www.smms-chino.org Participating Parishes: St. Margaret Mary, Chino; St. Paul the Apostle, Chino Hills; St. Denis, Diamond Bar; St. Elizabeth Ann Seton, Ontario; etc, Waylynn Senn, Prin.; Stds.: 351; Lay Tchrs.: 21

Our Lady of Guadalupe - 5048 D St., Chino, CA 91710 t) 909-591-9402 ourladyofguadalupechino@gmail.com ourladyofguadalupechino.com Rev. Edmund Gomez, Pst.; Rev. Jose Luis Rivas, Par. Vicar; Dcn. Jorge Briones; Dcn. Anthony Brenes-Rios; CRP Stds.: 14

CHINO HILLS

St. Paul the Apostle - 14085 Peyton Dr., Chino Hills, CA 91709-1610 t) 909-465-5503 stpaultheapostlechin@sbdiocese.org www.sptacc.org Rev. Joseph Christian Pilotin, M.S., Admin.; Rev. Michael J. Fredericks, Par. Vicar; Rev. Mahka "Philip" Aung, Par. Vicar; Dcn. John Duffy; Dcn. Tony Moralez; Dcn. Gary Quinn; Jeanie Kiefer, DRE; CRP Stds.: 817

St. Paul the Apostle Preschool - (Grades PreK-PreK) 3683 Chino Ave, Chino, CA 91710 t) (909) 325-8950 cstutzman@sptacc.org Participating Parishes: St. Paul the Apostle, Chino Hills; St. Margaret Mary, Chino; Saint Oscar Romero Catholic Community Inc., Eastvale. Christina Stutzman, Prin.; Lay Tchrs.: 3

COACHELLA

Our Lady of Soledad - 52525 Oasis Palm Ave., 52980 Cesar Chavez St, Coachella, CA 92236 t) 760-398-5577 olsoledad.coachella@sbdiocese.org ourladyofsoledad.org Rev. Francisco Gomez, ST, Pst.; Rev. Ramon Flores Duarte, S.T., Par. Vicar; Dcn. Fernando Heredia; Dcn. Juan Manuel Lombera; Dcn. Marty Sullivan; Dcn. Sergio Vasquez; CRP Stds.: 29

COLTON

Immaculate Conception - 1106 N. La Cadena Dr., Colton, CA 92324 t) 909-825-5110 immaculateconception.colton@sbdiocese.org www.immaculateconception.coltoncatholic.com Rev. Dionicio Maximo Tzul Lacan, Pst.; Rev. Nelson Angel Bonilla, F.M.M., Par. Vicar; Dcn. Ernesto Vital; Salvador Madrigal, DRE; CRP Stds.: 254

San Salvador - 169 W. L St., Colton, CA 92324-3446 t) 909-825-3481 sansalvador.colton@sbdiocese.org sansalvador.coltoncatholic.com Rev. Moises Henriquez de Paz, Pst.; Dcn. Mark Martinez; Teresa Rosales, DRE; CRP Stds.: 108

CORONA

Corpus Christi - 3760 N. McKinley St., Corona, CA 92879-1956 t) 951-272-9043 corpuschristicorona.com Rev. Fidel V. Rivero, Admin.; Rev. Alexander A Espino, Par. Vicar; Maria Veronica Sell, CRE; CRP Stds.: 607

St. Edward - 417 W. Grand Blvd., Corona, CA 92882; Mailing: 610 W. Fifth St., Corona, CA 92882 t) 951-549-6000 x203 (CRP); 951-549-6000 stedward.corona@sbdiocese.org www.stedwardcorona.com Rev. Hector Magallon, Pst.; Rev. Andres T. Lino-Salinas, CORC, Par. Vicar; CRP Stds.: 350

St. Edward School - (Grades PreK-8) 500 S. Merrill St., Corona, CA 92882 t) 951-737-2530 stedwards@sbdiocese.org www.stedward1947.com Participating Parishes: St. Edward, Corona; St. Matthew, Corona; St. Mel, Norco; St. Mary Magdalene, Corona; St. Oscar Romero, Eastvale; etc. Nathan Arnold, Prin.; Heidi Morgan, Librn.; Stds.: 240; Pr. Tchrs.: 2; Lay Tchrs.: 24

St. Mary Magdalene - 8540 Weirick Rd., Corona, CA 92883-4995 t) 951-277-1801 secretary@smmcorona.org smmcorona.net Rev. Ba "Phillip" S. Lam, C.R.M., Pst.; Rev. Gregory Vi Tran, C.R.M., Par. Vicar; Dcn. Armando Hernandez; CRP Stds.: 153

St. Matthew - 2140 W. Ontario, Corona, CA 92882 t) 951-737-1621 stmatthew.corona@sbdiocese.org www.stmatthewcorona.org Rev. Jospeh A. Sebastian, S.V.D., Pst.; Rev. Jose Rodriguez Goopio, S.V.D., Par. Vicar; Raquel Aguilera, DRE; CRP Stds.: 257

CRESTLINE

St. Frances Xavier Cabrini - 23079 Crest Forest Dr., Crestline, CA 92325-3817 t) 909-338-2303 office@stfrancecabriniparish.org; stfrancesxaviercabri@sbdiocese.org Rev. Neil D. Fuller, S.V.D., Admin.; CRP Stds.: 26

DESERT HOT SPRINGS

St. Elizabeth of Hungary - 66-700 Pierson Blvd., Desert Hot Springs, CA 92240-3740 t) 760-251-9268 (CRP); 760-329-8794 stelizabethofhungary.dhs@sbdiocese.org www.stelizabethdhs.org Rev. Khan D. Ngo, Pst.; Dcn. Victor Gonzalez; Dcn. Jose Rene Quiroz; CRP Stds.: 130

EASTVALE

Saint Oscar Romero Catholic Community, Inc. - 6905 Harrison Ave., Eastvale, CA 92880; Mailing: 14395 Chandler St., Eastvale, CA 92880 t) 951-893-1522 info@stoscarromero.com www.stoscarromero.com Rev. Tomas Guillen, Admin.; Dcn. Michael Shaffer;

FONTANA

St. George - 17895 San Bernardino Ave., Fontana, CA 92335-6155 t) 909-877-3935 x103 (CRP); 909-877-1531 stgeorge.fontana@sbdiocese.org sbdiocese.wixsite.com/stgeorgefontana Rev. Deebar Yonas, S.V.D., Pst.; Dcn. Alfredo Vargas; Dcn. Enrique Serrano; Maria Ramirez, CRE; CRP Stds.: 208

Saint John XXIII Catholic Community, Inc. - 7650 Tamarind Ave., Fontana, CA 92336 t) 909-822-4732 stjohnxxiii@sbdiocese.org www.stjohnxxiii.net Rev. Cletus Imo, Admin.; Rev. Yovanny A. Acosta, Par. Vicar; Rev. Suresh Manickam, H.G.N., Par. Vicar; Dcn. Jose Domingo Bonilla; Dcn. Juan Carlos Viveros; CRP Stds.: 430

Resurrection Academy - (Grades PreK-8) 17434 Miller Ave., Fontana, CA 92336-2223 t) 909-822-4431 resurrection.ocs@sbdiocese.org www.resurrectionacademy.net Jackie Swinehart, Prin.; Stds.: 152; Lay Tchrs.: 11

Rialto Worship Center - 222 E. Easton St., Rialto, CA 92376 t) 909-421-7030

St. Joseph - 17080 Arrow Blvd., Fontana, CA 92335-3807 t) 909-822-0566 stjoseph.fontana@sbdiocese.org www.stjosephfontana.com Rev. Juan M. Escobedo, M.S.P., Admin.; Rev. Alfredo Olmos-Marcelo, M.S.P, Par. Vicar; Andrea Guzman, CRE; CRP Stds.: 104

St. Mary - 16550 Jurupa Ave., Fontana, CA 92337-7452 t) 909-822-5670 stmaryfontana@sbdiocese.org stmary.weconnect.com Rev. Albert R. Utzig, S.S.C., Pst.; Rev. Jude Lourdhuraj Durairaj, H.G.N., Par. Vicar; Dcn. Abel Zamora; Dcn. Robert Gonzalez; Rev. Arturo Aguilar, SSC, In Res.; CRP Stds.: 168

GRAND TERRACE

Christ the Redeemer - 12745 Oriole Ave., Grand Terrace, CA 92313-6133 t) 909-783-3811 ctrcgt@sbdiocese.org www.ctrgt.org Rev. Anthony C. Waturuocha, Admin.; Dcn. Carlos Flores Guardado; CRP Stds.: 35

HEMET

Holy Spirit - 26340 Soboba St., Hemet, CA 92544; Mailing: P.O. Box 5268, 26340 Soboba St. Hemet, CA 92544, Soboba, CA 92544 t) 951-927-8544 holyspirithemet@sbdiocese.org www.holyspirithemet.com Rev. Michael Onwuemelie, C.S.Sp., Pst.; Josephine Chagolla, CRE; CRP Stds.: 78

Our Lady of the Valley - 780 S. State St., Hemet, CA 92543-7163 t) 951-929-6131 olv.hemet@sbdiocese.org www.olvhemet.org Rev. Cornelius T. McQuillan, C.S.Sp., Pst.; Rev. Paul A. Ahiaba, C.S.Sp, Par. Vicar; Dcn. Raymond B. Moon; CRP Stds.: 375

HESPERIA

Holy Family Parish - 9974 I Ave., Hesperia, CA 92345-5482 t) 760-244-9180 holyfamily.hesperia@sbdiocese.org www.holyfamilyhd.org Rev. Reginald Ibe, Admin.; Rev. Jose A. Orozco, Par. Vicar; Yolanda Serrato, DRE; CRP Stds.: 497

HIGHLAND

St. Adelaide - 27457 E. Baseline St., Highland, CA 92346-3206 t) 909-862-8669 stadelaide.highland@sbdiocese.org www.stadelaidehighland.com Rev. Anthony Bui, Pst.; Rev. Javier Gonzalez-Cabrera, Par. Vicar; Dcn. Humberto Rocha; Dcn. Johanness Lauran; CRP Stds.: 50

St. John Bosco - 28991 Merris St., East Highland, CA 92346 t) 909-425-0931 stjohnbosco.highland@sbdiocese.org stadelaidehighland.com/

St. Adelaide School - (Grades PreK-8) 27487 E. Base Line Rd., Highland, CA 92346 t) 909-862-5851 stadelaide.ocs@sbdiocese.org www.stadelaideacademy.org Barbara Gustafson, Prin.; Stds.: 169; Sr. Tchrs.: 1; Lay Tchrs.: 12

IDYLLWILD

Queen of Angels - 54525 N. Circle Dr., Idyllwild, CA 92549-1106; Mailing: P.O. Box 1106, Idyllwild, CA 92549 t) 951-659-2708 queenofangels.idyllwild@sbdiocese.org Rev. Charles M. Miller, Pst.;

INDIO

Our Lady of Perpetual Help - 82500 Bliss Ave, Indio, CA 92201; Mailing: 82470-B Bliss Ave., Indio, CA 92201 t) 760-347-3507 olph.indio@sbdiocese.org www.olphindio.org Rev. Alex Gamino, Pst.; Dcn. Jeronimo "Jerry" Lugo; Dcn. Mark Padilla; Dcn. Luis Ramirez; Dcn. Alfredo Razo; Dcn. Brijido Rodriguez; CRP Stds.: 261

Our Lady of Perpetual Help School - (Grades PreK-8) 82-470 Bliss Ave., Indio, CA 92201 t) 760-347-3786 olphindio.ocs@sbdiocese.org www.olphschoolindio.com Alisa Covarrubias, Prin.; Stds.: 185; Pr. Tchrs.: 1; Lay Tchrs.: 13

JURUPA VALLEY

Sacred Heart - 9935 Mission Blvd., Jurupa Valley, CA 92509 t) 951-685-5058 sacredheart.riv@sbdiocese.org www.sacredheartjurupavalley.org Rev. Miguel Torres-Madrigal, Pst.; Rev. Jose Garcia Oviedo, Par. Vicar; Dcn. Jose Serrano; CRP Stds.: 88

LA QUINTA

St. Francis of Assisi - 47225 Washington St., La Quinta, CA 92253 t) 760-564-1255 x208 (CRP); 760-564-1255 stfrancisofassisi.laquinta@sbdiocese.org www.stfrancislq.com Rev. James McLaughlin, Pst.; Rev. Dominic Vu, Par. Vicar; Dcn. Jaime Rosas; Dcn. John Scanlon; Myrna Phelps, DRE; CRP Stds.: 201

LAKE ARROWHEAD

Our Lady of the Lake - 27627 Rim of the World Dr., Lake Arrowhead, CA 92352; Mailing: P.O. Box 1929, Lake Arrowhead, CA 92352-1929 t) 909-337-2333 g.horan@sbdiocese.org; ollakelakearrowhead@sbdiocese.org olllakearrowhead.org Rev. Michal Osuch, C.R., Pst.; Dcn. Michael Juback; Genese Horan, CRE; CRP Stds.: 122

LOMA LINDA

St. Joseph the Worker - 10816 Mt. View Ave., Loma Linda, CA 92354 t) 909-796-2605 stjosephtheworker.lomalinda@sbdiocese.org stjosephlomalinda.org Rev. Noel Cruz, M.S., Pst.; Dcn. Victor A. Barrion; Angela E. Flores, CRE; CRP Stds.: 71

LUCERNE VALLEY

St. Paul - 8973 Mesa, Lucerne Valley, CA 92356; Mailing: 18386 Corwin Rd., Apple Valley, CA 92307 t) 760-242-4427 Rev. Delwyn Haroldson, C.R., Pst.; Rev. James M. Gibson, C.R., Par. Vicar; Sylvia Fath, DRE; CRP Stds.: 21

MECCA

Sanctuary of Our Lady of Guadalupe - 65-100 Dale Kiler Rd., Mecca, CA 92254; Mailing: P.O. Box 218, Mecca,

CA 92254 t) 760-396-2717 x112 (CRP); 760-396-2717 olgshrinemecca@sbdiocese.org Rev. Rocendo Herrera, S.T., Pst.; Rev. Eder Tufay Quiñones Menjura, S.T., Par. Vicar; Dcn. Luis Ayala; Dcn. J. Trinidad Porras; Dcn. Francisco Sanchez; CRP Stds.: 276

MONTCLAIR

Our Lady of Lourdes - 10191 Central Ave., Montclair, CA 91763-3801 t) 909-626-7278 olllourdes.montclair@sbdiocese.org www.ollmontclair.org Rev. Clarence Gesbert Saldua, M.S., Admin.; Rev. Wilfredo Iminga, M.S., Par. Vicar; Dcn. Roberto Villatoro; CRP Stds.: 222

Our Lady of Lourdes School - (Grades PreK-8) 5303 Orchard St., Montclair, CA 91763; Mailing: 2252 N. Albright Ave., Montclair, CA 91763 t) 909-621-4418 ourladyoflourdes.ocs@sbdiocese.org www.ollschool.com Waylynn Senn, Prin.; Stds.: 119; Lay Tchrs.: 12

MORENO VALLEY

St. Christopher - 25075 Cottonwood Ave., Moreno Valley, CA 92553-0397 t) 951-924-1968 x114 (CRP); 951-924-1968 parishoffice@saintchristophermv.org; stchristopher.morenovalley@sbdiocese.org www.stchristophermv.org Very Rev. Romeo N. Seleccion, M.S., Pst.; Rev. Juan M. Sandoval-Ochoa, Par. Vicar; Rev. Christopher Navarro, M.S., Par. Vicar; Dcn. Leonardo Bautista; Dcn. Roberto Jara; CRP Stds.: 1,206

St. Christopher Preschool - (Grades PreK-PreK) t) 951-571-8347 preschool@saintchristophermv.org www.saintchristophermv.org/preschool Participating Parishes: St. Christopher, Moreno Valley; St. Patrick, Moreno Valley. Eleanor Manucal, Dir.; Lay Tchrs.: 2

St. Patrick - 10915 Pigeon Pass Rd., Moreno Valley, CA 92557 t) 951-485-6673 x113 (CRP); 951-485-6673 stpatrick@sbdiocese.org www.stpatrickmv.org Rev. Octavio Cortez, Admin.; Rev. Hector Vasquez, Par. Vicar; Dcn. Ernest Lara; Dcn. Hugo Ernesto Ocampo; Diana Palma, CRE; CRP Stds.: 418

MURRIETA

St. Martha - 37200 Whitewood Rd., Murrieta, CA 92563-5040 t) 951-698-8180 stmartha.murrieta@sbdiocese.org www.stmarthamurr.com Rev. Carlos Martinez, Admin.; Rev. Ian F. Hollick, Par. Vicar; Rev. Alphonsus Ngwaogu, Par. Vicar; Dcn. Christopher Ciraulo; Dcn. Porfirio Diaz; Dcn. Wilfredo Vita; CRP Stds.: 1,237

NEEDLES

St. Ann - 218 D St., Needles, CA 92363; Mailing: P.O. Box 190, Needles, CA 92363-0190 t) 760-326-2721 stannneedles@sbdiocese.org saintannromancatholicchurch.com Rev. Henry Licznerski, C.R., Pst.; CRP Stds.: 43

NORCO

St. Mel - 4140 Corona Ave., Norco, CA 92860; Mailing: PO Box 700, Norco, CA 92860 t) 951-737-7144 stmel.norco@sbdiocese.org stmelnorco.org Rev. Gerardo Mendoza, Pst.; Rev. Joseph T. Ellison, Par. Vicar; Dcn. Daniel Ezekwe; Emily Guilherme, DRE; CRP Stds.: 304

ONTARIO

St. Elizabeth Ann Seton - 2713 S. Grove Ave., Ontario, CA 91761-6931 t) 909-947-2956 x27 (CRP); 909-947-2956 stelizabethannseton.ontario@sbdiocese.org www.seascc-ont.org Rev. Julian Chikezie Okoroanyanwu, Par. Vicar; Rev. Cristobal Subosa, Pst.; Rev. Jorge Tellez, Par. Vicar; Dcn. Octavio Echeverria; CRP Stds.: 202

St. George - 505 N. Palm Ave., Ontario, CA 91762 t) 909-983-2637 stgeorge.ontario@sbdiocese.org Rev. Trung Mai, S.V.D., Pst.; Rev. Hien Pham, S.V.D., Par. Vicar; Dcn. Javier Muñoz; Dcn. Juan Ramirez; Gina Solomon, CRE; CRP Stds.: 114

St. George School - (Grades K-8) 322 West D St., Ontario, CA 91762 t) 909-984-9123 stgeorge.ocs@sbdiocese.org Participating Parishes: St. Joseph, Upland; Our Lady of Guadalupe, Ontario; Sacred Heart, Rancho Cucamonga; St. Peter & St. Paul, Alta Loma; etc. Andrew Ramirez, Prin.; Stds.: 315; Pr. Tchrs.: 2; Lay Tchrs.: 13

Our Lady of Guadalupe - 710 S. Sultana Ave., Ontario, CA 91761-2554 t) 909-986-6154; 909-983-2904 (CRP) olg.ontario@sbdiocese.org Rev. Roberto Cristobal Flores, S.V.D., Pst.; Rev. Briccio Tamoro, S.V.D., Par. Vicar; CRP Stds.: 252

San Secondo d'Asti - 250 N. Turner Ave., Ontario, CA 91761; Mailing: P.O. Box 1056, Guasti, CA 91743 t) 909-390-0011 ssdachurch.org Rev. Stanley I. Onwuegbule, Admin.; Alma Zendejas, DRE; CRP Stds.: 124

PALM DESERT

Christ of the Desert - 73441 Fred Waring Dr., Palm Desert, CA 92260-2286 t) (760) 346-0089 christofthedesert@sacredheartpalmdesert.com www.sacredheartpalmdesert.com (Newman Center) Rev. Gregory Elder, Pst.;

Sacred Heart - 43775 N Deep Canyon Rd., Palm Desert, CA 92260-3164 t) 760-346-6502 sacredheart.pd@sbdiocese.org sacredheartpalmdesert.com Rev. Gregory Elder, Pst.; Rev. Alwyn B. Anfone, Par. Vicar; Rev. Tyler Tripp, Par. Vicar; Dcn. Jesus Mercado; Dcn. Ricardo Garcia; CRP Stds.: 476

Sacred Heart School - (Grades PreK-8) 43-775 Deep Canyon Rd., Palm Desert, CA 92260 t) 760-346-3513 sacredheartpd.ocs@sbdiocese.org Participating Parishes: Our Lady of Perpetual Help, Indio; OL of Solitude, Palm Springs; Sacred Heart, PD, St. Elizabeth of Hungary Alan Bruzzio, Prin.; Christine Crevoiserat, Librn.; Stds.: 545; Sr. Tchrs.: 2; Lay Tchrs.: 30

PALM SPRINGS

Our Lady of Guadalupe - 204 S. Calle El Segundo, Palm Springs, CA 92262 t) 760-325-5809 olg.palmsprings@sbdiocese.org www.olgps.org Rev. David K. Foxen, M.S.C., Pst.; Rev. Jos R. Peter, MSC, Par. Vicar; Dcn. John Skora;

Our Lady of Solitude - 151 W. Alejo Rd., Palm Springs, CA 92262-5666 t) 760-325-3816 olsolitude.ps@sbdiocese.org www.olsps.org Rev. David K. Foxen, M.S.C., Pst.; Rev. Jos R. Peter, MSC, Par. Vicar; CRP Stds.: 175

St. Theresa - 2800 E. Ramon Rd., Palm Springs, CA 92264-7996 t) 760-323-2669 parishoffice@sbdiocese.org; sttheresaps@sbdiocese.org www.sttheresaps.com Rev. John P. Kavcak, M.S.C., Pst.; Yolanda Lopez, CRE; CRP Stds.: 127

St. Theresa School - (Grades PreK-8) 455 S. Compadre Rd., Palm Springs, CA 92262-7996 t) 760-327-4919 www.stsps.org Participating Parishes: Our Lady of Guadalupe Parish, Palm Springs; Our Lady of Solitude Parish, Palm Springs; St. Elizabeth of Hungary Vanessa Montes de Oca, Prin.; Stds.: 169; Lay Tchrs.: 13

PERRIS

St. James - 22190 Dunlap Dr., Perris, CA 92571; Mailing: 269 W. Third St., Perris, CA 92571 t) 951-657-2380 stjames.perris@sbdiocese.org www.stjamesthelessperris.com Rev. Eliseo Napiere, M.S.P., Pst.; Rev. Teodorico E. Tacaisan Jr., M.S.P., Par. Vicar; Dcn. Brooke Wagner; Dcn. Juan Navarro; Dcn. Jose Gomez; Teresita de Jesus Salas, CRE; CRP Stds.: 9

St. James School - (Grades K-8) 250 W. Third St., Perris, CA 92570-2005 t) 951-657-5226 stjames.ocs@sbdiocese.org www.stjamescs.com Participating Parishes: St. James, Perris; St. Vincent Ferrer, Menifee; St. Frances of Rome, Wildomar; St. Patrick, Moreno Valley; St. Christopher Thomas Strickland, Prin.; Stds.: 110; Lay Tchrs.: 7

PHELAN

Saint Junipero Serra - 8820 Sheep Creek Rd., Phelan, CA 92371-2570 t) 760-868-4342 x42 (CRP); 760-868-4342 stjuniperoserraphelan@sbdiocese.org www.stserraphelan.org Rev. Joachim Lechukwu (Nigeria), Admin.; Dcn. Bernardo Agustin; Dcn. Isaias Palma; Claudia Torres, DRE; CRP Stds.: 134

RANCHO CUCAMONGA

Our Lady of Mount Carmel - 10079 Eighth St., Rancho Cucamonga, CA 91730 t) 909-987-2717 x21 (CRP); 909-987-2717 olmtcarmel.rc@sbdiocese.org olmtcarmel.org/ Rev. Sagayaraj Emmanuel, M.S.C., Pst.; Dcn. Jeronimo Lechuga; Esthela Garcia, CRE; CRP Stds.: 58

Sacred Heart - 12704 Foothill Blvd., Rancho Cucamonga, CA 91739-9795 t) 909-899-1049 x141 (CRP); 909-899-1049 sacredheart.rc@sbdiocese.org www.sacredheartrc.org Rev. Benedict C. Nwachukwu-Udaku, Pst.; Rev. Robert Chikerizi Ihuoma, Par. Vicar; Dcn. Edward Clark; Dcn. Antonio Hernandez; Dcn. David Arias; CRP Stds.: 228

Sacred Heart School - (Grades K-8) 12676 Foothill Blvd., Rancho Cucamonga, CA 91739 sacredheartrc.ocs@sbdiocese.org www.shpsrancho.com Participating Parishes: Sacred Heart, Rancho Cucamonga; St. Joseph, Upland; St. Paul the Apostle, Chino Hills; St. George, Ontario; St. Mary Magdalene Enrique Landin, Prin.; Dr. Danielle Lascano Espinoza, Prin.; Stds.: 315; Pr. Tchrs.: 3; Lay Tchrs.: 16

REDLANDS

The Holy Name of Jesus Catholic Community, Inc. - 115 W. Olive Ave., Redlands, CA 92373-5245 t) 909-793-2469 thnoj@sbdiocese.org www.theholynameofjesus.org Rev. Erik L. Esparza, Pst.; Rev. Eulices Godinez, Par. Vicar; Dcn. Eric Vilchis; Dcn. Ayed Khader; Dcn. Fidel Canovas; CRP Stds.: 157

Sacred Heart Academy - (Grades PreK-8) 215 S. Eureka St., Redlands, CA 92373 t) 909-792-3958 sacredheartred.ocs@sbdiocese.org sacredheartredlands.com Angela C. Williams, Prin.; Stds.: 222; Lay Tchrs.: 18

Columbia Worship Site - 1205 Columbia St., Redlands, CA 92373-5245 theholynameofjesus.redlands@sbdiocese.org Rev. Yovanny A. Acosta, Par. Vicar;

RIALTO

St. Catherine of Siena - 339 N. Sycamore Ave., Rialto, CA 92376-5943 t) 909-875-1360 x122 (CRP); 909-875-1360 stcatherineofsiena.rialto@sbdiocese.org www.stcatherineofsienaparish.org Rev. Duy John Tran, S.V.D., Pst.; Rev. Richard D. Casillas, S.V.D., Par. Vicar; Dcn. Jose de Jesus Lopez; CRP Stds.: 268

St. Catherine of Siena School - (Grades PreK-8) 335 N. Sycamore Ave., Rialto, CA 92376 t) 909-875-7821 stcrialto@sbdiocese.org www.stcatherinerialto.com Beverly Winn, Prin.; Stds.: 173; Pr. Tchrs.: 2; Lay Tchrs.: 10

RIVERSIDE

St. Andrew Kim Korean Community - 4750 Challen Ave., Riverside, CA 92503 t) (951) 533-0580 standrewkim.norco@sbdiocese.org stkdgkcc.org Rev. Daeseon (Paul) Kim, M.S.C., Pst.; CRP Stds.: 20

St. Andrew Newman Center - 105 W. Big Springs Rd., Riverside, CA 92507-4737 t) 909-682-8751 newman.riv@sbdiocese.org sanccatholic.org Rev. Cyriacus Ogu, Admin.; Rev. Charles "Gino" Galley III, Par. Vicar; CRP Stds.: 63

St. Anthony - 3074 Madison St., Riverside, CA 92504-4478 t) 951-352-8393 stanthony.riv@sbdiocese.org Rev. Clemente Perez-Tellez, O de M, Pst.; Rev. Nicolas Batta, Par. Vicar; CRP Stds.: 122

St. Catherine of Alexandria - 3680 Arlington Ave., Riverside, CA 92506; Mailing: 7005 Brockton Ave., Riverside, CA 92506 t) 951-781-9855 x25 (CRP); 951-781-9855 stcatherineofalexandria.riv@sbdiocese.org www.stcofa.org Rev. Ephraim P. Arciga, M.S.C., Pst.; Rev. Luis A. Segura, Par. Vicar; Dcn. John De Gano; CRP Stds.: 404

St. Catherine of Alexandria School - (Grades K-8) 7025 Brockton Ave., Riverside, CA 92506 t) 951-684-1091 postmaster@stcofa.org www.stcofa1.org Participating Parishes: Our Lady of

Perpetual Help, Riverside; St. Francis de Sales, Riverside; St. Thomas the Apostle, Riverside; St. Anthony, Rivers Theresea Heron, Prin.; Stds.: 318; Lay Tchrs.: 16

St. Francis de Sales - 4268 Lime St., Riverside, CA 92501-3868 t) 951-686-4004 stfrancisdesales.riv@sbdiocese.org www.stfrancisdesales-riverside.com Rev. Louis Abdoo, I.M.C., Pst.; Rev. Kim Moonjung, I.M.C., Par. Vicar; Dcn. Joseph Marino; Julia Lee-Lewis, DRE; CRP Stds.: 61

St. Francis de Sales School - (Grades K-8) 4205 Mulberry St., Riverside, CA 92501 t) 951-683-5083 stfrancisriv@sbdiocese.org www.sfdslions.com Participating Parishes: St. Frances de Sales, Riverside; St. Charles Borromeo, Bloomington; St. Margaret Mary, Chino; etc. Kathryn A. Piguet, Prin.; Stds.: 131; Pr. Tchrs.: 2; Lay Tchrs.: 10

St. John the Evangelist - 3980 Opal St., Riverside, CA 92509-7297 t) 951-684-6864 stjohntheevangelist.riv@sbdiocese.org www.sanjuanevangelist.org/ Rev. Fernando Bonilla Sanchez, M.S.P., Pst.; Rev. Luis A. de la Cruz Quen, MSP, Par. Vicar; Rev. Marcos J. Medina-Leon, M.S.P., Par. Vicar; CRP Stds.: 520

Our Lady of Guadalupe - 2518 Hall Ave., Riverside, CA 92509; Mailing: 3980 Opal St., Riverside, CA 92509 olgbelltown.riv@sbdiocese.org www.sanjuanevangelist.org

Our Lady of Guadalupe Shrine - 2858 Ninth St., Riverside, CA 92507-4957 t) 951-683-1123 (CRP); 951-684-0279 Rev. Daniel Prado-Reyes, O de M, Pst.; Rev. Nicolas Battas Tierrablanca, Par. Vicar; Dcn. Enrique Vazquez; CRP Stds.: 167

Our Lady of Perpetual Help - 5250 Central Ave., Riverside, CA 92504-1825 t) 909-689-9821 x23 (CRP); 951-689-8921 olph.riv@sbdiocese.org www.olphriverside.org Rev. Benjamin E. Alforque, MSC, Admin.; Rev. Antonio Guzman, Par. Vicar; Rev. Johnny Dang, Par. Vicar; Dcn. Nam Bui; Dcn. Bernardo Hernandez; CRP Stds.: 368

Our Lady of Perpetual Help School - (Grades PreK-8) 6686 Streeter Ave., Riverside, CA 92504-1825 t) 951-689-2125 olphriverside.ocs@sbdiocese.org olphriverside.com Participating parishes: OLPH, Riverside; St. Francis de Sales, Riverside; St. Thomas the Apostle, Riverside; St. Catherine of Alexandria, Riverside Ann R. Meier, Prin.; Stds.: 218; Lay Tchrs.: 11

Queen of Angels - 4824 Jones Ave., Riverside, CA 92505-1499 t) 951-689-3674 queenofangelsriv@sbdiocese.org www.queenofangelsriverside.com Rev. Beni Leu, S.V.D., Pst.; Rev. Alexander Sila, S.V.D., Par. Vicar; CRP Stds.: 252

St. Thomas the Apostle - 3774 Jackson St., Riverside, CA 92503-4359 t) 951-689-1131 stthomastheapostle.riv@sbdiocese.org www.stthomasriverside.com Rev. Theodore P. Drennan, Admin.; Rev. Celestine Afugwobi, Par. Vicar; Dcn. Raúl Michel; Marisol Aceves Cordova, CRE; Dana Robles, CRE; CRP Stds.: 176

St. Thomas School - (Grades K-8) 9136 Magnolia Ave., Riverside, CA 92503-3870 t) 951-689-1981 stthoma@sbdiocese.org; jmorrow@sbdiocese.org www.stasriverside.com Participating Parishes: St. Thomas the Apostle - Riverside; O.L.P.H. - Riverside; St. Catherine - Riverside. Jeanette T. Morrow, Prin.; Stds.: 127; Pr. Tchrs.: 2; Lay Tchrs.: 17

RUNNING SPRINGS

St. Anne in the Mountains - 30480 Fredalba Rd., Running Springs, CA 92382; Mailing: P.O. Box 2400, Running Springs, CA 92382-2400 t) 909-867-2832 stanne.runningsprings@sbdiocese.org mountaincatholic.org Rev. Michal Osuch, C.R., Pst.;

SAN BERNARDINO

Our Lady of the Rosary Cathedral - 2525 N. Arrowhead Ave., San Bernardino, CA 92405 t) 909-883-8991 olrosary.sb@sbdiocese.org sbdiocese.wixsite.com/cathedral Rev. Duong Nguyen, Pst.; Rev. Fransiskus Santoso, S.V.D., Par. Vicar; Monica Havins, DRE; CRP Stds.: 27

Holy Rosary Academy - (Grades PreK-8) 2620 N. Arrowhead Ave., San Bernardino, CA 92405 t) 909-886-1088 holyrosary.ocs@sbdiocese.org www.holyrosaryacademyandpreschool.org Participating Parishes: Our Lady of the Rosary Cathedral, San Bernardino; St. Adelaide, Highland; St. Anthony, San Bernardio; etc. Cheryll Austin, Prin.; Margie Jasso, Librn.; Stds.: 179; Pr. Tchrs.: 2; Lay Tchrs.: 13

St. Anthony - 1640 Western Ave., San Bernardino, CA 92411-1300 t) 909-887-3810 Rev. Vihn "Daniel" Nguyen, SVD, Admin.; Dcn. Michael Bellinder; Dcn. Mario Gutierrez; CRP Stds.: 287

St. Bernardine Church - 531 N. F St., San Bernardino, CA 92410-3109 t) 909-884-0104 stbernardine.sb@sbdiocese.org sites.google.com/view/stbernardinechurch Rev. Leonard D. DePasquale, I.M.C., Admin.; Dcn. Edwin Estrella; CRP Stds.: 128

Our Lady of Guadalupe - 1430 W. Fifth St., San Bernardino, CA 92411 t) 909-888-0044 olgsb@sbdiocese.org www.olgsb.com Rev. Pedro E. Amezcua, C.O.R.C., Pst.; Rev. Jose Reyes-Cedillo, C.O.R.C, Par. Vicar; Rev. Francisco J. Varela Delgadillo, Par. Vicar; Clara Saenz, CRE; CRP Stds.: 109

Our Lady of Hope Catholic Community, Inc. - 6885 Del Rosa Ave., San Bernardino, CA 92404 t) 909-884-6375; 909-885-7472 (CRP) olofhopeparish@sbdiocese.org ourladyofhopesb.org Rev. Manuel Cardoza, Pst.; Rev. Ken T. Vu, Par. Vicar; Dcn. Alfonso Martinez; CRP Stds.: 320

Del Rosa Avenue Worship Site -

Valencia Avenue Worship Site - 1000 Valencia Ave., San Bernardino, CA 92410; Mailing: 6885 del Rosa Ave., San Bernardino, CA 92404 t) 909-885-6375

Our Lady of the Assumption - 796 W. 48th St., San Bernardino, CA 92407-3594 t) 909-882-2931 olassumption.sb@sbdiocese.org www.olasanbernardino.org Rev. Rogelio Gonzalez, Pst.; Dcn. Nelson Glass; Dcn. Jose Herrera; CRP Stds.: 124

Our Lady of the Assumption School - (Grades PreK-8) 796 W 48th St, San Bernardino, CA 92407 t) 909-881-2416 olassumption@sbdiocese.org www.olabruins.com Participating Parishes: Our Lady of the Assumption, San Bernardino; Our Lady of the Rosary Cathedral, San Bernardino; St. Catherine of Siena, Rialto. Patricia L Godsy, Prin.; Stds.: 173; Lay Tchrs.: 10

SAN JACINTO

St. Anthony - 630 S. Santa Fe Ave., San Jacinto, CA 92583-4012 t) 951-654-7911 (CRP); 951-654-7911 x105 stanthony.sjc@sbdiocese.org saintanthonysj.org Rev. Mark Bertelli, Pst.; Rev. Francis A. Grant, Par. Vicar; Dcn. Fernando Vera; CRP Stds.: 329

St. Hyacinth Academy - (Grades PreK-8) 275 S. Victoria Ave., San Jacinto, CA 92583 t) 951-654-2013 sthyacinths@sbdiocese.org; sha.ocs@sbdiocese.org www.shaeagles.org Participating Parishes: St. Anthony, San Jacinto; Our Lady of the Valley, Hemet; Holy Spirit, Hemet; St. Christopher, Moreno Valley. Grace Lacsamana, Prin.; Stds.: 100; Lay Tchrs.: 8

St. Joseph Mission - 23600 Soboba Rd., San Jacinto, CA 92583 t) 951-485-6673 (CRP); 951-654-2086 stjoseph.sanjacinto@sbdiocese.org Rev. Earl Henley, M.S.C., Pst.; Dcn. Andrew Orosco; CRP Stds.: 17

Our Lady of the Snows Chapel - Cahuilla Indian Reservation, Anza, CA 92539; Mailing: P.O. Box 1027, San Jacinto, CA 92581 t) 951-763-5636 Rev. Earl Joseph Henley, M.S.C., Pst.;

St. Rose of Lima Chapel - Santa Rosa Indian Reservation, Anza, CA 92539; Mailing: P.O. Box 1027, San Jacinto, CA 92581 t) 909-659-2708 Rev. Earl Joseph Henley, M.S.C., Pst.; Sr. Maria Genara Sarigumba, M.S.M, CRE;

St. Michael Chapel - Pechanga Indian Reservation, Temecula, CA 92592; Mailing: P.O. Box 1027, San Jacinto, CA 92581 t) 951-676-4403 Rev. Earl Joseph Henley, M.S.C., Pst.;

Sacred Hearts of Mary and Jesus Chapel - Torres-Martinez Indian Reservation, Thermal, CA 92274; Mailing: P.O. Box 1027, San Jacinto, CA 92581 t) 760-398-5577 Rev. Earl Joseph Henley, M.S.C., Pst.;

St. Jude Mission School - (Grades K-6) ; Mailing: P.O. Box 399, San Jacinto, CA 92581 t) 951-213-1276 saintjudesoboba@aol.com Participating Parishes: St. Joseph Mission, Soboba; Our Lad of the Valley, Hemet. Donna Ferri, Admin.; Stds.: 10; Lay Tchrs.: 2

SUN CITY

St. Vincent Ferrer - 27931 Murrieta Rd., Sun City, CA 92586-2320 t) 951-679-4531 stvincentferrer@sbdiocese.org www.mystvincentferrer.org Rev. Frederick A. Costales, M.S., Pst.; Dcn. Donald Hitzeman; Rev. Msgr. Philip A. Behan, In Res.; Rev. Arturo Chavez, In Res.; Rev. Raymond Kirk, In Res.; CRP Stds.: 575

TEMECULA

St. Catherine of Alexandria - 41875 C St., Temecula, CA 92592-3029 t) 951-676-4403 stcatherineofalexandria.temecula@sbdiocese.org stcatherineofalexandria.net Rev. Anthony C. Dao, Pst.; Rev. Juan C. Lopez, Par. Vicar; Rev. Emmanuel C. Azudiugwu, Par. Vicar; Dcn. Eduardo Baltodano; Dcn. John Gabriele; Dcn. Francisco Meza; CRP Stds.: 485

TWENTYNINE PALMS

Blessed Sacrament - 6785 Sage Ave., Twentynine Palms, CA 92277 t) 760-367-3343 blessedsacrament.29palms@sbdiocese.org www.blessedsacramentchurch29palms.com Rev. Eliseus Uju, Admin.; Elaine Ashfield, CRE; CRP Stds.: 60

UPLAND

St. Anthony - 2110 N. San Antonio Ave., Upland, CA 91784; Mailing: P.O. Box 608, Upland, CA 91785 t) 909-985-2803 stanthonyupland@sbdiocese.org; stanthony.upland@sbdiocese.org stanthonyupland.org Rev. Gerald Vidad, Pst.; Rev. Kenneth I. Okoroudo, Par. Vicar; Dcn. Guadalupe Ramirez; Dcn. Roberto Hernandez; CRP Stds.: 344

St. Joseph - 877 N. Campus Ave., Upland, CA 91786-3930 t) 909-981-8110 x29 (CRP); 909-981-8110 stjoseph.upland@sbdiocese.org www.stjosephupland.org Rev. Timothy Truong Do, Pst.; Rev. Alex Rodarte, Par. Vicar; Dcn. Mark Lopez; Dcn. Greg Moore; Dcn. Luc Morisset; CRP Stds.: 206

St. Joseph School - (Grades K-8) 905 N. Campus Ave., Upland, CA 91786 t) 909-920-5185 stjosephupland.ocs@sbdiocese.org Participating Parishes: St. Joseph, Upland; St. Anthony, Upland; St. Peter and St. Paul, Alta Loma; Sacred Heart, Rancho Cucamonga; etc. Sandra Alamo-Ng, Prin.; Stds.: 334; Lay Tchrs.: 11

VICTORVILLE

Holy Innocents - 13230 El Evado Rd., Victorville, CA 92392; Mailing: P.O. Box 2980, Victorville, CA 92393 t) 760-955-3010 holyinnocents.victorville@sbdiocese.org www.holyinnocentsvictorville.org Rev. Peter Phan, Admin.; Rev. Ismael Valenzuela Salazar, Par. Vicar; CRP Stds.: 323

St. Joan of Arc - 15512 Sixth St., Victorville, CA 92395-3200 t) 760-245-7674; 760-245-4904 (CRP) stjoanofarc.victorville@sbdiocese.org stjoanhd.org Rev. Hyacinth Ibeh, Pst.; Dcn. Gabriel Rico; CRP Stds.: 272

WILDOMAR

St. Frances of Rome - 21591 Lemon St., Wildomar, CA 92595-8410 t) 951-674-6881 x224 (CRP); 951-674-6881 stfrancesofrome@sbdiocese.org www.sfrome.com Rev. James F. Gayta Oropel, Pst.; Dcn. Rigoberto Ruano; Leticia Pablin, CRE; CRP Stds.: 416

WINCHESTER

St. Mother Teresa of Calcutta Catholic Community, Inc. - 34750 Whisper Heights Pkwy., Winchester, CA 92596; Mailing: 31579 Wintners Pointe Ct., Wichester, CA 92596 t) 951-325-7707 contactus@smtoc.org www.btocchurch.org Rev. Msgr. Thomas J. Burdick, Pst.; Rev. Toan Pham, Par. Vicar; Dcn. Jose Ibarra;

CRP Stds.: 264

WRIGHTWOOD

Our Lady of the Snows - 975 Lark Rd., Wrightwood, CA 92397; Mailing: 8820 Sheep Creek Rd., Phelan, CA 92371 t) 760-868-4342 olsnows.phelan@sbdiocese.org stserraphelan.org Rev. Joachim Lechukwu (Nigeria), Admin.; Claudia Torres, DRE;

YUCAIPA

St. Frances Xavier Cabrini - 12687 California St., Yucaipa, CA 92399-4405 t) 909-797-2533 parish@sfxc.org www.stfrancesxcabrinichurch.org Rev. Santos L. Ortega, Pst.; Dcn. Peter S. Bond; Dcn. Francisco Herrera; Dcn. Daniel D. Hudec; Virginia Velazquez, CRE; CRP Stds.: 198

YUCCA VALLEY

St. Mary of the Valley - 7495 Church St., Yucca Valley, CA 92284-3247 t) 760-365-2287 stmaryofthevalley.yuccavalley@sbdiocese.org www.stmaryofthevalley.com Rev. Mark E. Kotlarczyk, Pst.; CRP Stds.: 62

SCHOOLS: PRESCHOOL THRU HIGH SCHOOL

SCHOOLS

STATE OF CALIFORNIA

TEMECULA

Saint Jeanne de Lestonnac School - (PRV) (Grades PreK-12) 32650 Avenida Lestonnac, Temecula, CA 92592 t) 951-587-2505 stjeannedelestonnac.ocs@sbdiocese.org www.sjdls.com Participating Parishes: St. Martha, Murrieta; St. Catherine of Alexandria, Temecula; St. Mother Teresa of Calcutta, Winchester Kristen Mora, Prin.; Annette Zaleski, Prin.; Stds.: 656; Lay Tchrs.: 51

HIGH SCHOOLS

STATE OF CALIFORNIA

PALM DESERT

***Xavier College Preparatory** - (PRV) (Grades 9-12) 34-200 Cook St., Palm Desert, CA 92211 t) 760-601-3900 xavierprep@sbdiocese.org www.xavierprep.org Chris Alling, Prin.; Stds.: 576; Lay Tchrs.: 61

RIVERSIDE

Notre Dame High School - (DIO) 7085 Brockton Ave., Riverside, CA 92506 t) 951-275-5896 notredamehs@sbdiocese.org notredameriverside.org Participating Parishes: St. Catherine of Alexandria, Riverside; St. Thomas the Apostle, Riverside; Our Lady of Perpetual Help, Riverside; etc. RaeAnna Ashton, Prin.; Stds.: 338; Pr. Tchrs.: 1; Lay Tchrs.: 31

SAN BERNARDINO

Aquinas High School - (DIO) 2772 Sterling Ave., San Bernardino, CA 92404 t) 909-886-4659 aquinashs@aquinas.net www.aquinashs.net Participating Parishes: Our Lady of the Rosary Cathedral, San Bernardino; Our Lady of the Assumption, San Bernardino; St. Adelaide, Highland; etc. Dr. Amanda Egan, Prin.; Stds.: 603; Lay Tchrs.: 36

INSTITUTIONS LOCATED IN DIOCESE

CAMPUS MINISTRY / NEWMAN CENTERS [CAM]

RIVERSIDE

St. Andrew Newman Center - 105 W. Big Springs Rd., Riverside, CA 92507 t) 951-682-8751 newman.riv@sbdiocese.org www.sanccatholic.org Serving Riverside City-College and University of California at Riverside. Rev. Cyriacus Ogu, Admin.; Rev. Charles "Gino" Galley III;

SAN BERNARDINO

Catholic Newman Club at California State University, San Bernardino - 1201 E. Highland Ave., San Bernardino, CA 92404 t) 909-804-2048; (909) 475-5361 alasalle@sbdiocese.org Archie LaSalle, Campus Min.;

Catholic Newman Club at University of Redlands - 1201 E. Highland Ave., San Bernardino, CA 92404 t) (909) 475-5361 alasalle@sbdiocese.org Rita Rogers, Campus Min.;

CATHOLIC CHARITIES [CCH]

SAN BERNARDINO

Catholic Charities San Bernardino & Riverside Counties - 1450 N. D St., San Bernardino, CA 92405 t) 909-388-1239 info@ccsbriv.org ccsbriv.org Jesse R. Gonzalez, COO; Ken F. Sawa, CEO/Exec. Vice Pres.; Asstd. Annu.: 24,219; Staff: 52

CEMETERIES [CEM]

COLTON

Our Lady Queen of Peace Catholic Cemetery - 3510 Washington St., Colton, CA 92324; Mailing: 1201 E. Highland Ave., San Bernardino, CA 92404-4641 t) (909) 475-5136 olqp@sbdiocese.org sbcatholiccemeteries.org Alfred G. Martini, Dir.; Rev. Msgr. Gerard M. Lopez, Pst. Dir.;

CONVENTS, MONASTERIES, AND RESIDENCES FOR WOMEN [CON]

BIG BEAR LAKE

Society Devoted to the Sacred Heart, S.D.S.H. - 896 Cienega Rd., Big Bear Lake, CA 92315; Mailing: P.O. Box 1795, Big Bear Lake, CA 92315 t) 909-866-5696 sdshbigbear@gmail.com sacredheartsisters.com Sr. Gabrielle Vogl, Supr.; Srs.: 4

SAN BERNARDINO

Congregation of the Sisters of Charity of the Incarnate Word, Houston, Texas (CCVI) - 519 E. 21st St., San Bernardino, CA 92404 t) (713) 928-6053 sistersofcharity.org/ Srs.: 2

TEMECULA

Sisters of the Company of Mary Our Lady - 32650 Avenida Lestonnac, Temecula, CA 92592 t) (714) 235-4519 ernestineodn@gmail.com Sr. Ernestine Velarde, O.D.N., Pres.; Srs.: 4

Vina de Lestonnac Retirement Center-Convent - 39300 De Portola Rd., Temecula, CA 92592 Sr. Doris Valdez, O.D.N., Supr.;

ENDOWMENTS / FOUNDATIONS / TRUSTS [EFT]

SAN BERNARDINO

Catholic Education Foundation of the Diocese of San Bernardino - 1201 E. Highland Ave., San Bernardino, CA 92404 t) 909-475-5300 jmontenegro@sbdiocese.org Jorge Montenegro, Exec.;

The Catholic Foundation - 1201 E. Highland Ave., San Bernardino, CA 92404-4641 t) 909-475-5150 jmontenegro@sbdiocese.org Jorge Montenegro, CFO;

Diocesan Development Fund, Inc. - 1201 E. Highland Ave., San Bernardino, CA 92404-4641 t) 909-475-5150 jmontenegro@sbdiocese.org Annual Appeal Jorge Montenegro, CFO;

SAN JACINTO

Kateri Tekakwitha Fund - ; Mailing: P.O. Box 302, San Jacinto, CA 92581 t) 951-654-7899 katerisoboba@gmail.com Barbara Fritzsche, Contact;

HOSPITALS / HEALTH SERVICES [HOS]

APPLE VALLEY

St. Joseph Health, St. Mary - 18300 Hwy. 18, Apple Valley, CA 92307 t) 760-242-2311 judy.wagner@stjoe.org www.stmaryapplevalley.com Judy Wagner, Vice President Mission Services; Bed Capacity: 213; Asstd. Annu.: 140,219; Staff: 1,632

SAN BERNARDINO

St. Bernardine Medical Center - 2101 N. Waterman Ave., San Bernardino, CA 92404 t) 909-883-8711 kathleen.mcdonnell@commonspirit.org www.stbernardinemedicalcenter.org Sponsored by Catholic Health Care Federation Douglas Kleam, Pres.; Bed Capacity: 342; Asstd. Annu.: 139,782; Staff: 1,893

St. Bernardine Medical Center Foundation - 2101 N. Waterman Ave., San Bernardino, CA 92404 t) 909-881-4516 pam.koerner@commonspirit.org www.supportstbernardine.org Dan Murphy, Vice Pres. & Exec. Dir.;

MISCELLANEOUS [MIS]

CORONA

Confraternity of Operarios Del Reino De Cristo, C.O.R.C. - 605 W. 5th St., Corona, CA 92882 t) 951-549-6000 Rev. Pedro E. Amezcua Nuñez, C.O.R.C., Pst.; Rev. Andres T. Lino-Salinas, CORC, Par. Vicar; Rev. Jose Reyes Cedillo, C.O.R.C., Par. Vicar; Rev. Hector Magallon, Admin.; Priests: 4

RIVERSIDE

Misioneros Laicos del Verbo Divino - 4093 Tyler St., Riverside, CA 92503 t) 951-359-8900 mfloresmlvd@gmail.com Mariana Flores, Admin.;

SAN BERNARDINO

***Caritas Telecommunications Corporation** - 1201 E. Highland Ave., San Bernardino, CA 92404 t) 909-475-5415 jandrews@sbdiocese.org www.sbdiocese.org John H. Andrews, Dir.;

Diocese of San Bernardino Cemetery Corp., Inc. - 1201 E. Highland Ave., San Bernardino, CA 92404-4641 t) 909-475-5150 cemeteries@sbdiocese.org Rev. Msgr. Gerard M. Lopez, Pst. Dir.; Jorge Montenegro, CFO;

Diocese of San Bernardino Education & Welfare Corporation - 1201 E. Highland Ave., San Bernardino, CA 92404-4641 t) 909-475-5150 jmontenegro@sbdiocese.org Jorge Montenegro, CFO;

Diocese of San Bernardino Land Development Corporation - 1201 E. Highland Ave., San Bernardino, CA 92404-4641 t) 909-475-5150 jmontenegro@sbdiocese.org Jorge Montenegro, CFO;

Saint Junipero Serra House of Formation, Inc. - 1201 E. Highland Ave., San Bernardino, CA 92404-4641 t) 909-475-5150 jmontenegro@sbdiocese.org Jorge Montenegro, CFO;

***Mary's Mercy Center, Inc.** - 641 Roberds Ave., San Bernardino, CA 92411; Mailing: P.O. Box 7563, San Bernardino, CA 92411 t) 909-889-2558 mmcinc@msn.com marysmercycenter.org Rev. Michael Barry, SS.CC., Pres.;

Ministerio Biblico Verbo Divino (MBVD) - 555 N. E St., San Bernardino, CA 92401; Mailing: P.O. Box 1610, San Bernardino, CA 92402 t) 909-383-9030 mbvdsb@gmail.com www.verbodivino.org Rev. Danh Pham, SVD, Pres.;

***Wordnet, Inc.** - 532 N. D St., San Bernardino, CA 92401-1304 t) 909-383-4333 manage@wordnet.tv www.wordnet.tv Rev. Soney Sebastian, S.V.D., Executive Producer; Rev. Biju Mandapathil Thomas, S.V.D., Pres.; Anna Hamilton, Managing Director; Dolores Ongkingco, Finance Manager; Rev. Akhil Thomas, Assoc. Dir.; Sr. Jeanne Harris, O.P., Communications Specialist; Cecilia Negrete, Administrative Assistant; James Hagmann, Video Editor;

MONASTERIES AND RESIDENCES FOR PRIESTS AND BROTHERS [MON]

CORONA

Shrine of Presentation - 1775 S. Main St., Corona, CA 92882 t) 951-737-4125 www.medangcon.net Shrine of Presentation (Den Thanh Me Dang Con). Rev. Felix Luan, CMC, Pres.; Rev. Gregory Vi Tran, C.R.M., Vice President; Priests: 2

HEMET

Congregation of the Holy Spirit - Casa Laval Retirement

Community, 309 E. Whitter Ave., Hemet, CA 92546; Mailing: P.O. Box 3509, Hemet, CA 92546-3509 t) 951-312-2603 jgaglione@aol.com Rev. Michael Onwuemelie, C.S.Sp., Pst.; Rev. Joseph B. Gaglione, C.S.Sp., Supr.; Priests: 2

Congregation of the Sacred Hearts of Jesus and Mary, SS.CC. - Western U.S. Province, Hemet, 32481 Sage Rd., Hemet, CA 92544 t) 951-767-9303 frrich@hnmparish.org Rev. Richard Danyluk, SS.CC., Regl. Supr.; Rev. Patrick J. Crowley, SS.CC., Retreat Ministry; Rev. Martin O'Loghlen, SS.CC., Provincial Econome; Rev. Michael Barry, SS.CC., Pst. Min./Coord.; Rev. Jeremiah Holland, SS.CC., Asst. Novice Master; Rev. Patrick Travers, SS.CC., Pst. Min.; Priests: 6

LUCERNE VALLEY

The Cistercian Congregation of the Holy Family, St. Joseph Monastery - 21010 Lucerne Valley Cutoff, Lucerne Valley, CA 92356-0960; Mailing: P.O. Box 960, Lucerne Valley, CA 92356-0960 t) 760-666-0203 www.saintjosephmonateryca.org Rev. M. Anthony Hanh Si Pham, O.Cist., Supr.; Rev. M. Timothy Qui Van Than, O.Cist., Subprior; Rev. M. Justin Cong Huu Ho, O.Cist., Mem.; Rev. M. Robert Canh X Lai, O. Cist., Mem.; Rev. M. Antony Sang H Nguyen, O. Cist., Mem.; Bro. M. Francis of Assisi Phu Quoc Nguyen, O.Cist., Mem.; Bro. Bonaventure Dong Van Pham, O.Cist., Mem.; Bro. M. Peter Khanh Minh Ngoc Pham, O.Cist., Mem.; Rev. M. Peter-Binh Quynh Dang Pham, O.Cist., Mem.; Rev. Stephan Hoa Van Nguyen, O.Cist., Mem.; Brs.: 3; Priests: 7

MORENO VALLEY

The Pacific Region Missionaries of Our Lady of La Salette, MS - 25075 Cottonwood Ave., Moreno Valley, CA 92553 t) 951-924-1968 Rev. Joseph Christian Pilotin, M.S., Admin.; Rev. Christopher Navarro, M.S., Par. Vicar; Rev. Clarence Gesbert Saldua, M.S., Admin.; Rev. Wilfredo Iminga, M.S., Par. Vicar; Rev. Noel Cruz, M.S., Pst.; Rev. Philip Naw Aung, M.S., Par. Vicar; Rev. Frederick A. Costales, M.S., Pst.; Very Rev. Romeo N. Seleccion, M.S., Episcopal Vicar/ Pastor; Priests: 8

NEEDLES

Congregation of the Resurrection, CR - 218 D St., Needles, CA 92363 t) (760) 326-2721 hlicznerski@sbdiocese.org www.resurrectionists.com Rev. Henry Licznerski, C.R., Pst.; Rev. Delwyn Haroldson, C.R., Pst.; Rev. James M. Gibson, C.R., Par. Vicar; Rev. Henry A. Ruszel, C.R., Retired; Priests: 6

Congregation of the Resurrection - 27627 Rim of the World Dr., Lake Arrowhead, CA 92352; Mailing: P.O. Box 1929, Lake Arrowhead, CA 92352 t) 909-337-2333 Rev. Michal Osuch, C.R., Pst.;

Congregation of the Resurrection - 42242 North Shore Dr., Big Bear City, CA 92314; Mailing: P.O. Box 1709, Big Bear Lake, CA 92315 t) 909-866-3030 Rev. Paul Smith, C.R.;

REDLANDS

Discalced Carmelites, OCD - 926 E. Highland Ave., Redlands, CA 92374; Mailing: P.O. Box 8700, Redlands, CA 92374 t) 909-793-0424 frprovincialadam@gmail.com www.discalcedcarmelitefriars.com Rev. Adam Gregory Gonzales, O.C.D., Prov.; Priests: 1

NURSING / REHABILITATION / CONVALESCENCE / ELDERLY CARE [NUR]

SAN BERNARDINO

St. Bernardine Plaza Corporation - 550 W. Fifth St., San Bernardino, CA 92401-4641; Mailing: 1201 E. Highland Ave., San Bernardino, CA 92404-4641 t) 909-888-0153 stbern2@la.twcbc.com Individual housing to elderly and handicapped. Jorge Montenegro, CFO; Asstd. Annu.: 150; Staff: 5

RETREAT HOUSES / RENEWAL CENTERS [RTR]

BIG BEAR LAKE

Sacred Heart Retreat Camp - 896 Cienega Rd., Big Bear Lake, CA 92315; Mailing: P.O. Box 1795, Big Bear Lake, CA 92315 t) 909-866-5696 office@sacredheartretreatcamp.com www.sacredheartretreatcamp.com Sr. Gabrielle Vogl, SDSH, Supr.; Sr. Hannah Barnett, Dir.;

REDLANDS

El Carmelo Retreat House - 926 E. Highland Ave., Redlands, CA 92374; Mailing: P.O. Box 8067, Redlands, CA 92376 t) 909-792-1047 elcarmelorh@gmail.com www.elcarmelo.org Rev. Adam Gregory Gonzales, O.C.D., Prov.; Rev. Gerald Werner, OCD, Local Supr.; Rev. Roberto Barcelos, OCD, In Res.; Bro. John Mark Charlesworth, O.C.D., In Res.; Rev. Jose Luis Ferroni, In Res.;

RIVERSIDE

Divine Word Province/ Retreat Center - 11316 Cypress Ave., Riverside, CA 92505 t) 951-687-7600 (Province) svdusw@gmail.com www.svdusw.org/ Rev. Hieu Trong Nguyen, S.V.D., Director of Retreat Center; Rev. Vinh T. Trinh, S.V.D., Assistant Director of Retreat Center; Rev. Alan Jenkins, S.V.D., Rector; Rev. Paul Schmidt, SVD, Vice Rector; Rev. Long Van Nguyen, SVD, Admonitor; Rev. Joh P. Kirby, SVD, Prov. Supr.;

RUNNING SPRINGS

St. Anne in the Mountains Catholic Church and Retreat Center - 30480 Fredalba Rd, Running Springs, CA 92382; Mailing: P.O. Box 2400, Running Springs, CA 92382 t) 909-867-2832 stanneinthemountains@aol.com www.mountaincatholic.org Terri MacDonald, Contact;

TEMECULA

Congregation of Kkottongnae Brothers and Sisters of Jesus - 37885 Woodchuck Rd., Temecula, CA 92592 t) 951-302-3400 ustmc@kkot.or.kr www.tmclkkot.org Sr. Thomas Jangmi Yu, C.K.S.J., In Res.; Sr. Philip Hyangbae Lee, C.K.S.J., Dir.; Sr. James Hyojln Kim, C.K.S.J., Retreat Manager/Facilitator;

Vina de Lestonnac Retreat Center - 39300 De Portola Rd., Temecula, CA 92592; Mailing: 16791 E. Main St., Tustin, CA 92780 t) 951-302-5571 vinadelestonnac@odnusa.org Olivia Cornejo, Dir.; Tina Volz, Retreat Coord.;

SEMINARIES [SEM]

GRAND TERRACE

Saint Junipero Serra House of Formation - 12725 Oriole Ave., Grand Terrace, CA 92313 t) 909-783-0260 jgarcia@sbdiocese.org Very Rev. Jorge A. Garcia, Rector; Rev. Msgr. Anthony Eze, Dir. Spiritual Formation; Rev. Emmanuel Ukaegbu-Onuoha, Dir. Academics; Emma Mejico, Formator; Stds.: 19; Lay Tchrs.: 1; Pr. Tchrs.: 3

Diocese of San Diego

(Dioecesis Sancti Didaci)

HIS EMINENCE ROBERT CARDINAL MCELROY

Bishop of San Diego; ordained April 12, 1980; appointed Titular Bishop of Gemellae in Byzacena and Auxiliary Bishop of San Francisco July 6, 2010; ordained September 7, 2010; appointed Bishop of San Diego March 3, 2015; ordained April 15, 2015; installed April 15, 2015; elevated to Cardinal August 27, 2022. Office: 3888 Paducah Dr., San Diego, CA 92117.

Mailing Address: P.O. Box 85728, San Diego, CA 92186-5728.
Pastoral Center: 3888 Paducah Dr., San Diego, CA 92117. T: 858-490-8200; F: 858-490-8272.
rvaldivia@sdcatholic.org
www.sdcatholic.org

ESTABLISHED JULY 11, 1936.

Square Miles 8,852.

Comprises the Counties of Imperial and San Diego in the State of California.

Legal Titles: The Roman Catholic Bishop of San Diego, a Corporation Sole–Diocese of San Diego.

For legal titles of parishes and diocesan institutions, consult the Diocesan Office.

Most Reverend Ramon Bejarano
Auxiliary Bishop of San Diego; ordained August 15, 1998; appointed Titular Bishop of Carpi and Auxiliary Bishop of San Diego February 27, 2020; installed July 14, 2020. Pastoral Center: 3888 Paducah Dr., San Diego, CA 92117.

STATISTICAL OVERVIEW

Personnel	
Cardinals	1
Auxiliary Bishops	1
Priests: Diocesan Active in Diocese	100
Priests: Diocesan Active Outside Diocese	2
Priests: Diocesan in Foreign Missions	1
Priests: Retired, Sick or Absent	47
Number of Diocesan Priests	150
Religious Priests in Diocese	93
Total Priests in your Diocese	243
Extern Priests in Diocese	39
Ordinations:	
Diocesan Priests	2
Transitional Deacons	4
Permanent Deacons	9
Permanent Deacons in Diocese	128
Total Brothers	26
Total Sisters	163
Parishes	
Parishes	96
With Resident Pastor:	
Resident Diocesan Priests	74
Resident Religious Priests	16
Without Resident Pastor:	
Administered by Priests	4
Administered by Lay People	2
Missions	13
New Parishes Created	1
Closed Parishes	2
Professional Ministry Personnel:	
Sisters	17
Lay Ministers	213
Welfare	
Catholic Hospitals	2
Total Assisted	230,735
Homes for the Aged	1
Total Assisted	1,051
Day Care Centers	1
Total Assisted	600
Specialized Homes	2
Total Assisted	60
Special Centers for Social Services	6
Total Assisted	123,971
Residential Care of Disabled	1
Total Assisted	90
Educational	
Seminaries, Diocesan	1
Students from This Diocese	12
Diocesan Students in Other Seminaries	1
Seminaries, Religious	3
Students, Religious	7
Total Seminarians	20
Colleges and Universities	3
Total Students	9,191
High Schools, Diocesan and Parish	3
Total Students	3,067
High Schools, Private	4
Total Students	1,625
Elementary Schools, Diocesan and Parish	38
Total Students	9,258
Elementary Schools, Private	4
Total Students	563
Catechesis/Religious Education:	
High School Students	6,704
Elementary Students	13,134
Total Students under Catholic Instruction	43,562
Teachers in Diocese:	
Sisters	7
Lay Teachers	684
Vital Statistics	
Receptions into the Church:	
Infant Baptism Totals	5,660
Minor Baptism Totals	480
Adult Baptism Totals	335
Received into Full Communion	494
First Communions	4,878
Confirmations	3,953
Marriages:	
Catholic	1,203
Interfaith	203
Total Marriages	1,406
Deaths	3,544
Total Catholic Population	1,386,368
Total Population	3,465,920

LEADERSHIP

Pastoral Center - t) 858-490-8200
Vicars General - t) (858) 490-8200 Most Rev. Ramon Bejarano; Very Rev. Michael Pham;
Chancellor - t) 858-490-8232 Maria Olivia (Barioly) Galvan;
Vicar for Clergy and Moderator of the Curia - t) (858) 490-8200 Most Rev. Ramon Bejarano, Vicar for Clergy Pro-Tem;
Vice Moderator of the Curia - t) 858-490-8310 Rodrigo Valdivia;
Judicial Vicar - t) (858) 490-8200 Very Rev. Msgr. Steven F. Callahan;
Adjutant Judicial Vicar - t) (858) 490-8200 Rev. Edward McNulty;

OFFICES AND DIRECTORS

Archivist - t) 858-490-8208
Censor Librorum - t) (858) 490-8200 Bernadeane Carr;
Child and Youth Protection - t) (858) 490-8301 Rodrigo Valdivia;
Civil Affairs - t) 858-490-8277 William Nolan, Dir.;
Communications and Public Affairs - t) (858) 490-8200 Aida Bustos, Dir.; Kevin Eckery, Dir.;
Diocesan Institute - t) 858-490-8210 Gerardo Rojas, Dir.;
Ecumenical and Interreligious Affairs - t) 858-487-4314 Very Rev. Msgr. Dennis Mikulanis, Vicar;
Ethnic and Intercultural Communities - t) 858-490-8306 Very Rev. Michael Pham, Dir.;
Evangelization & Catechetical Ministry - t) 858-490-8232 Maria Olivia (Barioly) Galvan, Dir.; Joseph Horejs, Assoc. Dir.; Leticia Trent, Assoc. Dir.;
Family Life & Spirituality - t) 858-490-8299 John Prust, Dir.; Ricardo Marquez, Assoc. Dir.; Janelle Peregoy, Assoc. Dir. Separated & Div. Ministry;
Finance - t) (858) 490-8200 Shirley Pajanor, CFO; Ann Duong, Controller;
Human Resources - t) 858-490-8380 Ann Radosevich, Dir.; Judith Gonzalez, Assoc. Dir.;
Information Technology - t) 858-490-8329 Matthew Dolan, Dir.;
Life, Peace and Justice - t) (858) 490-8324 Dr. Robert Ehnow, Dir.; Maria Lourdes Valencia, Assoc. Dir. Culture of Life; Christina Slentz, Assoc. Dir. Creation Care;
Liturgy and Spirituality - t) 858-490-8290 Noreen McInnes, Dir.;
Missions - t) 858-490-8250 Rev. Soney Sebastian, S.V.D., Dir.; Sr. Eva Rodriguez, S.J.S., Dir., Missionary Childhood Association; Sr. Doreen Lai, Assoc. Dir.;
Permanent Diaconate - t) 858-490-8239 Rev. Eduardo Samaniego, S.J., Dir.; Jose Ernesto Gonzalez, Assoc. Dir.;
Priestly Formation -- St. Francis Center - t) 619-291-7446 Very Rev. Matthew D. Spahr, Rector/ Dir.; Rev. Eric Tamayo, Vice Rector; Rev. Michael Sinor, Dir. Spiritual Formation;
Priestly Vocations - t) 619-291-7446 Rev. Eric Tamayo, Dir.;
Schools - t) (858) 490-8241 Leticia Oseguera, Dir.; Julie Cantillon, Assoc. Dir.; Matthew Cordes, Assoc. Dir.;
Stewardship - t) 858-490-8294 Manny Aguilar, Dir.;
Women Religious - t) 858-490-8289 Sr. Kathleen Warren, O.S.F., Dir.;
Youth and Young Adult Ministry - t) 858-490-8260 Maricruz Flores, Dir.; Brilema Perez, Assoc. Dir.;

ADVISORY BOARDS, COMMISSIONS, COMMITTEES, AND COUNCILS

Cemetery Advisory Board - t) 619-264-3127 Very Rev. Msgr. Dennis Mikulanis, Dir.;
College of Consultors - Most Rev. Ramon Bejarano; Very Rev. Efrain Bautista; Very Rev. Devdas Masillamony;
Diocesan Pastoral Council - Athena Besa, Chair; Debra Ipsen, Secy.;
Diocesan Review Board - John Hargrove, Pres.;
Finance Council - Very Rev. Michael Pham; Rev. Peter Escalante; Rev. Reynaldo Manahan;
Personnel Board for Priests - Very Rev. Msgr. Dennis Mikulanis; Very Rev. Michael Pham; Very Rev. Matthew D. Spahr;
Presbyteral Council - Very Rev. Efrain Bautista, Chair; Very Rev. Edmundo Zarate-Suarez, Vice Chair; Rev. Msgr. Edward Brockhaus;
Vicars Forane - Very Rev. Efrain Bautista, South Bay; Very Rev. Luke Jauregui, Escondido; Very Rev. Devdas Masillamony, El Cajon;

TRIBUNAL

Defenders of the Bond - Rev. Msgr. Mark A. Campbell; Rev. Msgr. Daniel J. Dillabough; Rev. Agustin Opalalic;
Diocesan Judges - Anna Amato; Chorbishop Philip Najim; Rodrigo Valdivia;
Notaries - Kelly Anastay; Erika Mayoral; Leticia Mendoza;
Promoter of Justice - Rev. David N. Croisetiere;
Tribunal Auditor - Barbara Kearns;

MISCELLANEOUS / OTHER OFFICES

Apostleship of the Sea - t) (619) 726-4982 Rev. James Boyd, Chap.; Narciso Guzman, Dir. Pro-Tem;
Cursillo -
  English - cjscursillosd@gmail.com Cyndi Sapter, Lay Dir.;
  Filipino - t) (619) 829-1277 Novy Balan, Lay Dir.;
  Vietnamese - t) 619-602-2857 Rachelle P. Nguyen, Lay Dir.;
Hispanic Charismatic Renewal Center (Carismatica Hispana) - t) (619) 213-5570 Eliseo Raggio, Coord. Gen.;
Missionary Childhood Association - t) 858-490-8250 Sr. Eva Rodriguez, S.J.S., Dir.;
Propagation of the Faith - t) 858-490-8250 Rev. Soney Sebastian, S.V.D., Dir.;
Victim Assistance Coordinator - t) 858-490-8353 Mary Acosta;

PARISHES, MISSIONS, AND CLERGY

STATE OF CALIFORNIA

ALPINE

Pastor of Queen of Angels Catholic Parish, Alpine, a corporation sole - 2569 W Victoria Dr., Alpine, CA 91901-3662 t) 619-445-2145 parish@queenofangels.org www.queenofangels.org Rev. David Exner, Pst.; CRP Stds.: 40

BONITA

Pastor of Corpus Christi Catholic Parish, Bonita, a corporation sole - 450 Corral Canyon Rd., Bonita, CA 91902-4072 t) 619-482-3953 (CRP); 619-482-3954 www.corpuschristicatholic.org Very Rev. Efrain Bautista, Pst.; Rev. Dan Holgren, Par. Vicar; Dcn. Wil Hollowell; Dcn. Raul Millan; Dcn. Alan Pangilinan; Dcn. Jose Oscar Paredes; Michael Wickham, DRE; CRP Stds.: 816
  Preschool - 480 Corral Canyon Rd., Bonita, CA 91902 t) 619-482-3956 preschool@corpuschristicatholic.org Araceli Ongyan, Dir.;

BORREGO SPRINGS

Pastor of Saint Richard Catholic Parish, Borrego Springs, a corporation sole - 611 Church Ln., Borrego Springs, CA 92004-1128; Mailing: PO Box 1128, Borrego Springs, CA 92004 t) 760-767-5701 pastor@strichardborrego.com Rev. Fernando Maldonado, Pst.; CRP Stds.: 122
  Christ the King Catholic Mission - 3811 Del Mar Dr., Salton Sea Beach, CA 92274

BRAWLEY

Pastor of Saint Margaret Mary Catholic Parish, Brawley, a corporation sole - 620 S. Cesar Chavez St., Brawley, CA 92227 t) 760-550-9830 brawleycatholic@gmail.com www.brawleycatholic.org Rev. Bernardo Lara, Pst.; Dcn. Marcos Lopez; Rev. Claro Ortiz, Assoc. Pst.; CRP Stds.: 139

Pastor of Sacred Heart Catholic Parish, Brawley, a corporation sole - 402 S. Imperial Ave., Brawley, CA 92227 t) 760-679-3505 brawleycatholic@gmail.com www.brawleycatholic.org Rev. Bernardo Lara, Pst.; Rev. Claro Ortiz, Assoc. Pst.; Dcn. Alberto Moya; CRP Stds.: 72
  Sacred Heart Catholic Parish Brawley School - (Grades PreSchool-8) 428 S. Imperial Ave., Brawley, CA 92227 t) 760-344-2662 office@sacredheartschoolbrawley.org www.sacredheartschoolbrawley.org Annalisa Burgos, Prin.; Stds.: 70; Lay Tchrs.: 4
  Preschool - 428 S. Imperial Ave., Brawley, CA 92227 t) 760-344-2662 office@sacredheartschoolbrawley.org www.sacredheartschoolbrawley.org Susie Wood, Dir.;

CALEXICO

Pastor of Our Lady of Guadalupe Catholic Parish, Calexico, a corporation sole - 124 E. Fifth St., Calexico, CA 92231 t) 760-357-2532 (CRP); 760-357-1822 ourladyofguadalupeparish-calexico.org Rev. Jose A. Sosa, Sch.P., Pst.; Rev. Manuel Sanahuja, Sch.P., Assoc. Pst.; Dcn. Refugio Gonzalez; CRP Stds.: 168
  Our Lady of Guadalupe Academy - (Grades PreSchool-8) 535 Rockwood Ave., Calexico, CA 92231 t) 760-357-1986 mmeza@olgacademy.com Sr. Maria Elvia Gonzalez, S.J.S., Prin.; Silvia Chavarin, Librn.;
  Preschool - Jazel Sanchez, Dir.;

CALIPATRIA

Pastor of Saint Patrick Catholic Parish, Calipatria, a corporation sole - 133 E. Church St., Calipatria, CA 92233; Mailing: P.O. Box 238, Calipatria, CA 92233 t) 760-502-6350 (CRP); 760-502-6348 stpatrickcalipatria@gmail.com; stpatrickoffice@gmail.com www.stpatricks-catholic-church-of-calipatria Very Rev. Antonio Morales, Pst.; CRP Stds.: 44
  Immaculate Heart of Mary - 19 Sixth St., Niland, CA 92257 t) 760-359-3730 a_sadorra@yahoo.com Augustine Sadorra, Contact;

CAMPO

Pastor of Saint Adelaide of Burgundy Catholic Parish, Campo, a corporation sole - 1347 Dewey Pl., Campo, CA 91906; Mailing: P.O. Box 369, Campo, CA 91906 t) 619-478-1017 adelaidemagdalene@gmail.com stadelaidestmarymagdalene.com Rev. Fr Dave Leon, Admin.; CRP Stds.: 23
  St. Mary Magdalene - 44686 Calexico Ave, Jacumba, CA 91934 t) (619) 478-1017 Rev. Dave Leon, Pst.; Dcn. Jose Luis Del Rio;

CARLSBAD

Pastor of Saint Elizabeth Seton Catholic Parish, Carlsbad, a corporation sole - 6628 Santa Isabel St., Carlsbad, CA 92009-5148 t) 760-438-3393 reled-ses@gmail.com; parsec.ses@gmail.com www.seschurch.org Rev. Michael Robinson, Pst.; Patty Mann, DRE; CRP Stds.: 350

Pastor of Saint Patrick Catholic Parish , Carlsbad, a corporation sole - 3821 Adams St., Carlsbad, CA 92008-0249 t) 760-729-8442 (CRP); 760-729-2866 lacuna@stpatrickcarlsbad.com www.stpatrickcarlsbad.com Rev. Ronald Bagley, CJM, Pst.; Dcn. Miguel Enriquez; Dcn. Michael Frazee; Dcn. Richard Pomphrey; CRP Stds.: 364
  Saint Patrick Catholic Parish Carlsbad School - (Grades K-8) 3820 Pio Pico Dr., Carlsbad, CA 92008 t) 760-729-1333 dnelson@stpaddys.org www.stpaddys.org Denise Nelson, Prin.; Brian Sestito, Prin.;

CHULA VISTA

Pastor of Mater Dei Catholic Parish, Chula Vista, a corporation sole - 1571 Magdalena Ave., Chula Vista,

CA 91913; Mailing: P.O. Box 212047, Chula Vista, CA 91921 t) 619-656-3735; 619-656-3740 (CRP) parish@materdeicv.org; rep@materdeicv.org www.materdeicv.org Dcn. Jovel Javier Rodriguez; Rev. Jovencio D. Ricafort, Pst.; Maria C. Galace, Dir.; CRP Stds.: 405

Pastor of Most Precious Blood Catholic Parish, Chula Vista, a corporation sole - 1245 4th Ave., Chula Vista, CA 91911-3012 t) 619-422-2159 (CRP); 619-422-2100 mpbchurch@gmail.com; mpbwcc@hotmail.com www.preciousbloodchurch.com Most Precious Blood Residence Rev. Paul Dass Selvaraj, OMI, Admin.; Dcn. Ruben Pelina; CRP Stds.: 245

Pastor of Our Lady of Guadalupe Catholic Parish, Chula Vista, a corporation sole - 345 Anita St., Chula Vista, CA 91911-4198 t) 619-422-1887 (CRP); 619-422-3977 pastor.olgcv@gmail.com www.ourladyofguadalupecv.org Rev. Hily Buyco Gonzales, c.s., Pst.; Rev. Liem Nguyen, c.s., Assoc. Pst.; Dcn. Guillermo Valdivia; CRP Stds.: 175

Pastor of Saint Pius X Catholic Parish, Chula Vista, a corporation sole - 1120 Cuyamaca Ave., Chula Vista, CA 91911-3506 t) 619-420-9193 parishcenter@saintpiusx.org saintpiusx.org Rev. Andres Ernesto Torres, Assoc. Pst.; Rev. Jay T. Bananal, Pst.; CRP Stds.: 207

Saint Pius X Catholic Parish Chula Vista School - (Grades PreK-8) 37 E. Emerson St., Chula Vista, CA 91911 t) 619-422-2015 info@spxcv.com Marisa Amann, Prin.;

Preschool - 37 E. Emerson St., Chula Vista, CA 91911-3506 t) 619-422-2015 info@spxcv.com spxcv.com Florence Burgos, Dir.;

Pastor of Saint Rose of Lima Catholic Parish, Chula Vista, a corporation sole - 293 H St., Chula Vista, CA 91910-4703 t) 619-426-6717 (CRP); 619-427-0230 parish@strosecv.com www.strosecv.com Rev. Roldan Nunez, Assoc. Pst.; Rev. Miguel Campos, Pst.; CRP Stds.: 102

Saint Rose of Lima Catholic Parish School - (Grades PreK-8) 278 Alvarado St., Unit 2, Chula Vista, CA 91910 t) 619-422-1121 school@strosecv.com Jeff Saavedra, Prin.;

Preschool - 278 Alvarado St., Unit 2, Chula Vista, CA 91910 t) 619-422-1121 Glenda Martinez, Dir.;

CORONADO

Pastor of Sacred Heart Catholic Parish, Coronado, a corporation sole - 655 C Ave., Coronado, CA 92118-2229 t) 619-435-3167 sacredheart@sacredheartcor.org www.sacredheartcor.org Rev. Michael F. Murphy, Pst.; Dcn. Frederico Drachenberg; Dcn. Robert E. Griffin Jr.; Dcn. Kevin Murray; Dcn. John Roberts; Most Rev. Neal Buckon, In Res.; Rev. Msgr. Donal C. Sheahan, In Res.; CRP Stds.: 216

Sacred Heart Catholic Parish Coronado School - (Grades PreK-8) 706 C Ave., Coronado, CA 92118 t) 619-437-4431 school@sacredheartcoronado.org www.sacredheartcoronado.org Peter Harris, Prin.; Stds.: 278; Lay Tchrs.: 13

DESCANSO

Pastor of Our Lady of Light Catholic Parish, Descanso, a corporation sole - 9136 Riverside Dr., Descanso, CA 91916 t) 619-445-3620 gloria@ourladyoflight.church; office@ourladyoflight.church ourladyoflight.church Rev. Enrique Fuentes, Pst.; CRP Stds.: 10

EL CAJON

Pastor of The Church of Saint Luke Catholic Parish, El Cajon, a corporation sole - 1980 Hillsdale Rd., El Cajon, CA 92019 t) 619-442-1697 x103 parishoffice@thechurchofstluke.org; pldir@thechurchofstluke.org thechurchofstluke.org Jane Alfano, Dir.; Rev. Donald Coleman, In Res.; Dcn. Jerry Stenovec; CRP Stds.: 250

Pastor of Holy Trinity Catholic Parish, El Cajon, a corporation sole - 405 Ballard St., El Cajon, CA 92019-2123 t) 619-444-9425 manager@holytrinityelcajon.org www.holytrinityelcajon.org Rev. Reynaldo Manahan, Pst.; Dcn. Timothy Treadwell; CRP Stds.: 138

Holy Trinity Catholic Parish School - (Grades PreK-8) 509 Ballard St., El Cajon, CA 92019-2125 t) 619-444-7529 principal@holytrinityhawks.com www.holytrinityschoolelcajon.com Francine Moss, Prin.;

Preschool - t) 619-444-1052 Debbie Edelbrock, Dir.;

Pastor of Saint Kieran Catholic Parish, El Cajon, a corporation sole - 1510 Greenfield Dr., El Cajon, CA 92021-3511 t) 619-588-6881 secretary@stkierans.sdcoxmail.com www.stkieran.com Rev. Ben Davison, Pst.; CRP Stds.: 27

Saint Kieran Catholic Parish School - (Grades PreSchool-8) 1347 Camillo Way, El Cajon, CA 92021 t) 619-588-6398 pprovo@saintkierancatholicschool.org Patricia Provo, Prin.;

Preschool - Erin Marshall, Dir.;

Pastor of Saint Louise de Marillac Catholic Parish, El Cajon, a corporation sole - 2005 Crest Dr., El Cajon, CA 92021-4309 t) 619-749-7908 frscotty@aol.com; stlouisecrest@cox.net www.stlouisecrest.com Rev. Scott A. Burnia, Pst.; CRP Stds.: 7

Pastor of Our Lady of Grace Catholic Parish in El Cajon, CA, a corporation sole - 2766 Navajo Rd., El Cajon, CA 92020-2183 t) 619-469-0133 mpospichal@olg-church.org www.olg-church.org Rev. Lauro Minimo, Pst.; Dcn. John Sawaya; Lissa Hutcheson, DRE; Patricia Kane, Bus. Mgr.; CRP Stds.: 121

Our Lady of Grace Catholic Parish School - (Grades K-8) t) 619-466-0055 emares@olg.org www.olg.org Erin Mares, Prin.; Stds.: 288; Lay Tchrs.: 13

EL CENTRO

Pastor of Our Lady of Guadalupe Catholic Parish, El Centro, a corporation sole - Merged Jul 2022 Merged with St. Mary, El Centro to form Our Lady of the Valley Catholic Parish, El Centro.

Pastor of Our Lady of the Valley Catholic Parish in El Centro, a corporation sole - 795 S. La Brucherie Rd., El Centro, CA 92243 t) (760) 791-8742 (CRP); 760-353-7280 (CRP); 760-352-4211 churchlady@elcentrocatholic.org Rev. Ron Mark Edney, Pst.; Rev. Edward Horning, Assoc. Pst.; Dcn. Domingo Enriquez; Dcn. Sergio Hernandez; Rev. David Sereno, In Res.; CRP Stds.: 364

Saint Mary Catholic Parish El Centro School - (Grades PreSchool-8) 700 S. Waterman Ave., El Centro, CA 92243 t) 760-352-7285 receptionist@elcentrostmarys.org; adminassistant@elcentrostmarys.org Dr. Allan J. White, O.P., Prin.; Sylvia Marroquin, Bus. Mgr.;

Saint Mary Preschool, El Centro - 700 S. Waterman Ave., El Centro, CA 92243 t) (760) 352-7285 Jennifer Ramirez, Dir.;

Sacred Heart - 40 E. Main, Heber, CA 92249

ENCINITAS

Pastor of Saint John the Evangelist Catholic Parish, Encinitas, a corporation sole - 1001 Encinitas Blvd., Encinitas, CA 92024-2828 t) 760-753-6254 admin@saintjohnencinitas.org; bookkeeper@saintjohnencinitas.org www.saintjohnencinitas.org/ Rev. James Bahash, Pst.; Rev. Robert Kibaki, A.J., Assoc. Pst.; CRP Stds.: 295

Saint John the Evangelist School - (Grades PreK-8) 1003 Encinitas Blvd., Encinitas, CA 92024 t) 760-944-8227 mecruz@saintjohnschool.com www.saintjohnschool.com Dan Schuh, Prin.;

ESCONDIDO

Pastor of Church of the Resurrection Catholic Parish, Escondido, a corporation sole - 1445 Conway Dr., Escondido, CA 92027 t) 760-747-2322 x201 (CRP); 760-747-2322 info@resurrectionchurch.org www.resurrectionchurch.org Rev. Eduardo Bernardino, Pst.; Rev. Abel Barajas, Assoc. Pst.; CRP Stds.: 391

Pastor of Saint Mary Catholic Parish, Escondido, a corporation sole - 1170 S. Broadway, Escondido, CA 92025-5815 t) 760-745-1611; 760-745-1611 x236 (CRP) esaucedo@stmaryp.org; reception@stmaryp.org www.stmaryp.org Rev. Scott Herrera, Pst.; Rev. Manuel Gutierrez del Toro, Assoc. Pst.; CRP Stds.: 816

St. Mary School - (Grades K-8) 130 E. 13th Ave., Escondido, CA 92025 t) 760-743-3431 office@stmesc.org; principal@stmesc.org www.stmesc.org Amanda Johnston, Prin.;

Preschool - 130 E. 13th Ave., Escondido, CA 92025; Mailing: 1170 S. Broadway, Escondido, CA 92025 aharriff@stmaryesc.org www.stmaryp.org/st-mary-preschool Amanda Harriff, Dir.;

Pastor of Saint Timothy Catholic Parish, Escondido, a corporation sole - 2960 Canyon Rd., Escondido, CA 92025 t) 760-489-1200 frontdesk@sttimothychurch.com www.sttimothychurch.com Rev. Cavana Wallace, Pst.; CRP Stds.: 84

FALLBROOK

Pastor of Saint Peter the Apostle Catholic Parish, Fallbrook, a corporation sole - 450 S. Stage Coach Ln., Fallbrook, CA 92028 t) 760-689-6200 x6204 office@stpeter-fallbrook.org www.stpeter-fallbrook.org Dcn. Ted Rotunda; Rev. Arturo Uribe, C.Ss.R., Pst.; Dcn. Daniel Rosas; CRP Stds.: 466

St. Peter the Apostle Catholic School - (Grades PreSchool-8) t) 760-689-6250 www.spacschool.com

Preschool - Gisela Gutierrez, Dir.;

HOLTVILLE

Pastor of Saint Joseph Catholic Parish, Holtville, a corporation sole - 560 Maple Ave., Holtville, CA 92250 t) 760-356-2147 stjosephholtville@gmail.com www.stjosephholtville.com Rev. Jose Alfredo Moreno, Pst.; CRP Stds.: 120

IMPERIAL

Pastor of Saint Anthony of Padua Catholic Parish, Imperial, a corporation sole - 211 W. Sixth St., Imperial, CA 92251 t) 760-355-1304 (CRP); 760-355-1347 stanparish@sbcglobal.net Rev. Danilo Valdepenas, Pst.; Maria Fugett, DRE; CRP Stds.: 141

JAMUL

Pastor of Saint Pius X Catholic Parish, Jamul, a corporation sole - 14107 Lyons Valley Rd., Jamul, CA 91935-0369; Mailing: P.O. Box 369, Jamul, CA 91935-0369 t) 619-669-0085 parishoffice@stpiusxjamul.com www.stpiusxjamul.com/ Rev. Higinio Garcia, Pst.; CRP Stds.: 43

JULIAN

Pastor of Saint Elizabeth of Hungary Catholic Parish, Julian, a corporation sole - 2814 B St., Julian, CA 92036-0366; Mailing: P.O. Box 366, Julian, CA 92036-0366 t) 760-765-0613 secretarystelizabethjulian@gmail.com www.stelizabethjulian.org Rev. Timothy Deutsch, Pst.; CRP Stds.: 25

LA JOLLA

Pastor of All Hallows Catholic Parish, La Jolla, a corporation sole - 6602 La Jolla Scenic Dr. S., La Jolla, CA 92037-5799 t) 858-459-2975 allhallowsparish@gmail.com www.allhallows.com Rev. Joseph Masar, Pst.; Catherine Adams, DRE; CRP Stds.: 54

All Hallows Catholic Parish School - (Grades PreK-8) 2390 Nautilus, La Jolla, CA 92037 t) 858-459-6074 mainoffice@allhallows.com www.allhallowsacademy.com

Pastor of Mary, Star of the Sea Catholic Parish, La Jolla, a corporation sole - 7669 Girard Ave., La Jolla, CA 92037-4480 t) 858-454-2631 marystarofthesea@marystarlajolla.org www.marystarlajolla.org Rev. Patrick J. Mulcahy, Pst.; CRP Stds.: 66

Stella Maris Academy - (Grades K-8) 7654 Herschel Ave., La Jolla, CA 92037 t) 858-454-2461 info@stellamarisacademy.org www.stellamarisacademy.org Patricia Lowell, Prin.;

LA MESA

Pastor of Saint Martin of Tours Catholic Parish, La Mesa, a corporation sole - 7710 El Cajon Blvd., La Mesa, CA 91942-6932 t) 619-466-3241 (CRP); 619-465-5334 info@saintmartinoftours.cc; dorac@saintmartinoftours.cc www.stmartinoftoursparish.org Rev. Elmer Mandac, Pst.; Dcn. Allen Rosker; CRP Stds.: 183

Saint Martin of Tours Catholic Parish School - (Grades PreSchool-8) 7708 El Cajon Blvd., La Mesa, CA 91942-6932 info51@stmartinacademy.org www.stmartinacademy.org Jennifer Miller, Prin.;

Preschool - 7714 El Cajon Blvd., La Mesa, CA 91942 t) 619-698-8462 athompson@stmartinacademy.org stmartinacademy.org/preschool Anne Thompson, Dir.;

LAKESIDE

Pastor of Saint Kateri Tekakwitha National Indian Parish - 1054 Barona Rd., Lakeside, CA 92040-1502 t) 619-443-3412 c) (951) 237-9687 (Pst.); (619) 249-3143 (Bookkeeper) bktparish@aol.com www.bktparish.com Rev. Herman Manuel, S.V.D., Pst.; CRP Stds.: 9

Assumption of BVM -

Nativity of BVM -

Immaculate Conception of BVM -

Pastor of Our Lady of Perpetual Help Catholic Parish Lakeside in Lakeside California, A Corporation Sole - 13208 Lakeshore Dr., Lakeside, CA 92040 t) 619-443-1412; 619-443-1672 karen.woollard@olphchurch.org; nora.codina@olphchurch.org olphchurch.org Rev. Minh Q. Do, Assoc. Pst.; Rev. Derek Twilliger, Pst.; Dcn. Dennis O'Neil; Dcn. Patrick Root; Dcn. Mark Silva; Dcn. Daniel Ramos; CRP Stds.: 115

LEMON GROVE

Pastor of Saint John of the Cross Catholic Parish, Lemon Grove, a corporation sole - 8086 Broadway, Lemon Grove, CA 91945-2598 t) 619-461-2681 (CRP); 619-466-3209 www.sjcparishlg.org Rev. Jose Luis Muro, Pst.; Rev. Michael O'Connor, Assoc. Pst.; CRP Stds.: 370

Saint John of the Cross Catholic Parish School - (Grades PreK-8) 8175 Lemon Grove Way, Lemon Grove, CA 91945 t) 619-466-8624 www.stjohncross.org Gregory Krumm, Prin.;

Mercedarian Sisters of the Blessed Sacrament - 8171 Lemon Grove Way, Lemon Grove, CA 91945 t) (216) 533-8607 Sr. Rosario Vega, H.M.S.S., Supr.;

Preschool - t) 619-466-8624 x103 Idania Walters, Dir.;

NATIONAL CITY

Pastor of Saint Anthony of Padua Catholic Parish, National City, a corporation sole - 410 W. 18th St., National City, CA 91950 t) 619-477-4520 office@stanthonyofpaduanc.com www.stanthonyofpaduanc.com/ Very Rev. Edmundo Zarate-Suarez; Dcn. Braulio Gutierrez; CRP Stds.: 179

Pastor of Saint Mary Catholic Parish, National City, a corporation sole - 426 E. Seventh St., National City, CA 91950-2322 t) 619-474-1501 liturgy@stmarynationalcity.org; 19neman51@gmail.com stmarynationalcity.org Rev. Nemesio Sungcad, Pst.; Rev. Rogelio Pingol, Pst. Assoc.; CRP Stds.: 89

OCEANSIDE

Pastor of Saint Margaret Catholic Parish, Oceanside, a corporation sole - 4300 Oceanside Blvd., Oceanside, CA 92056-2999 t) 760-941-5560 ccd@oceanside4christ.com; churchoffice@oceanside4christ.com www.oceanside4christ.com Rev. William A. Kernan, Pst.; CRP Stds.: 138

Pastor of Saint Mary, Star of the Sea Catholic Parish, Oceanside, a corporation sole - 609 Pier View Way, Oceanside, CA 92054-2861 t) 760-722-1688 tonyh@stmarystars.org www.stmarystars.org Rev. Reynald Evangelista, Pst.; CRP Stds.: 600

Saint Mary, Star of the Sea Catholic Parish School - (Grades K-8) 515 Wisconsin Ave., Oceanside, CA 92054 t) 760-722-7259 info@stmarystars.com stmarystars.com Angela Willburn, Prin.;

Preschool - 515 Wisconsin Ave., Oceanside, CA 92054 t) 760-722-7475 stmarystars.com Angela Willburn, Prin.;

Pastor of Mission San Luis Rey Catholic Parish, Oceanside, a corporation sole - 4070 Mission Ave., Oceanside, CA 92057-6497 t) 760-757-3250 www.sanluisreyparish.org Rev. Oscar Mendez, OFM, Pst.; Rev. Samuel Nasada, OFM, Assoc. Pst.; CRP Stds.: 324

Mission San Luis Rey De Francia -

Pastor of Saint Thomas More Catholic Parish, Oceanside, a corporation sole - 1450 S. Melrose Dr., Oceanside, CA 92056 t) 760-758-4100 x100 parishoffice@stmoside.org www.stmoside.org Rev. Brent Kruger, Pst.; Dcn. Timothy Anthony Keane; Dcn. John Fredette; CRP Stds.: 213

PALA

Pastor of Mission San Antonio de Pala Catholic Parish, Pala, a corporation sole - 3015 Pala Mission Rd., Pala, CA 92059-0070; Mailing: P.O. Box 70, Pala, CA 92059 t) 760-742-3317 x112 (CRP); 760-742-3317 parishoffice@missionsanantoniodepala.org; fathergerardo@missionsanantoniodepala.org www.missionsanantonio.org Rev. Gerardo Fernandez, Pst.; Dcn. Carlos Monsalvo; CRP Stds.: 82

Rincon Indian Reservation, St. Bartholomew -

La Jolla Indian Reservation, Our Lady of Refuge -

Pauma Indian Reservation, St. James -

POWAY

Pastor of Saint Gabriel Catholic Parish, Poway, a corporation sole - 13734 Twin Peaks Rd., Poway, CA 92064 t) 858-748-5348 office@saintgabrielschurch.com www.saintgabrielschurch.com Rev. Michel Froidurot, Pst.; Rev. Patrick J. Murphy, Assoc. Pst.; Dcn. Ricardo Elizondo; CRP Stds.: 385

Pastor of Saint Michael Catholic Parish, Poway, a corporation sole - 15546 Pomerado Rd., Poway, CA 92064-2404 t) 858-487-4755 (CRP); 858-485-1392 stmikes@smpoway.org; reoffice@smpoway.org www.smpoway.org Rev. Melchisedech Monreal, Pst.; Rev. Victor T. Maristela, Assoc. Pst.; Dcn. William Adsit; Dcn. John Charron; Dcn. Terry Hannify; Rev. Dominic Obour, In Res.; CRP Stds.: 368

St. Michael's School - (Grades PreK-8) 15542 Pomerado Rd., Poway, CA 92064 t) 858-485-1303 info@smspoway.org Kathleen Mock, Prin.; Stds.: 549; Lay Tchrs.: 44

Preschool - 15542 Pomerado Rd, Poway, CA 92064 t) 858-485-1303 Lori Romero, Dir.;

RAMONA

Pastor of Immaculate Heart of Mary Catholic Parish, Ramona, a corporation sole - 537 E St., Ramona, CA 92065 t) 760-789-0583 www.ihmramona.org Rev. Ignatius Dibeashi, Pst.; Dcn. Andres Escobedo; Dcn. William Turner; CRP Stds.: 110

RANCHO SANTA FE

Pastor of Church of the Nativity Catholic Parish, Rancho Santa Fe, a corporation sole - 6309 El Apajo Rd., Rancho Santa Fe, CA 92067; Mailing: PO Box 8770, Rancho Santa Fe, CA 92067-8770 t) 858-756-9562 (CRP); 858-756-1911 nativitycatholic.org Rev. Agustin Opalalic, Pst.; CRP Stds.: 376

Church of the Nativity Catholic Parish School - (Grades PreSchool-8) 6309 El Apajo, Rancho Santa Fe, CA 92067-8770; Mailing: P. O. Box 9180, #9180, Rancho Santa Fe, CA 92067-8770 t) 858-756-6763 mzures@nativitymail.org www.thenativityschool.org Paul Parker, Prin.;

SAN DIEGO

Pastor of Saint Joseph Cathedral Catholic Parish, San Diego, a corporation sole - 1535 Third Ave., San Diego, CA 92101-3192 t) 619-239-0229 blanca@sdcathedral.org Rev. Peter Navarra, Pst.; Dcn. Joseph Moore; Dcn. David Warren; CRP Stds.: 57

Pastor of Saint Agnes Catholic Parish, San Diego, a corporation sole - 1140 Evergreen St., San Diego, CA 92106 t) 619-223-9748 (CRP); 619-223-2200 www.saint-agnes.org/ Rev. Romeo Velos, C.S., Pst.; CRP Stds.: 35

Pastor of Saint Anne Catholic Parish, San Diego, a corporation sole - 2337 Irving Ave., San Diego, CA 92113 t) 619-239-8253 stannefsspsandiego@gmail.com stannesd.com Rev. John Lyons, FSSP, Pst.; Rev. Earl Eggleston, Assoc. Pst.; Rev. Aaron Liebert, FSSP, Assoc. Pst.; CRP Stds.: 70

Pastor of Ascension Catholic Parish, San Diego, a corporation sole - 11292 Clairemont Mesa Blvd., San Diego, CA 92124 t) 858-279-2735 office@ascension-sd.org www.sdascension.org Rev. Edwin Tutor, Pst.; Dcn. Adam Curtis; Dcn. Jim Scull; CRP Stds.: 168

Pastor of Blessed Sacrament Catholic Parish, San Diego, a corporation sole - 4540 El Cerrito Dr., San Diego, CA 92115 t) 619-582-5722 x124 (CRP); 619-582-5722 (Office) info@blessedsacrament-sandiego.org www.blessedsacrament-sandiego.org Rev. Yos Sodanango, SVD (Indonesia), Pst.; CRP Stds.: 34

Pastor of Saint Brigid Catholic Parish, San Diego, a corporation sole - 4735 Cass St., San Diego, CA 92109-2698 t) 858-483-3032 (CRP); 858-483-3030 gayle@saintbrigidparish.org; info@saintbrigidparish.org www.saintbrigidparish.org Very Rev. Msgr. Steven F. Callahan, Pst.; Rev. Sebastian Bukenya, Assoc. Pst.; Dcn. Michael Daniels; Dcn. Chris Hulburt; Dcn. Patrick McCay; Gayle Heyman, DRE; CRP Stds.: 88

Pastor of Saint Catherine Laboure Catholic Parish, San Diego, a corporation sole - 4124 Mt. Abraham Ave., San Diego, CA 92111 t) 858-278-0587 (CRP); 858-277-3738 (CRP); 858-277-3133 kkeith@stcatherinelaboure.net; youth@stcatherinelaboure.net www.stcatherinelaboure.net Rev. Brian Hayes, Pst.; Marivel Castillo, Youth Min.; Jorge Verduzco, Youth Min.; Kathy Keith, CRE; CRP Stds.: 126

Pastor of Saint Charles Borromeo Catholic Parish, San Diego, a corporation sole - 2802 Cadiz St., San Diego, CA 92110-4870 t) 619-225-8157 bookkeeper@saintcharlespl.com www.saintcharlespl.com Rev. John Amsberry, Pst.; Dcn. Lane Litke; CRP Stds.: 125

Saint Charles Borromeo Catholic Parish School - (Grades K-8) 2808 Cadiz St., San Diego, CA 92110 t) 619-223-8271 office@saintcharlesacademy.com Debra Cota, Prin.;

Pastor of Saint Charles Catholic Parish, San Diego, a corporation sole - 990 Saturn Blvd., San Diego, CA 92154 t) 619-575-2240 (CRP); 619-423-0242 saintcharles.org Rev. Emilio A. Magana, Pst.; Rev. Burt Boudoin, Assoc. Pst.; CRP Stds.: 170

Saint Charles Catholic Parish School - (Grades K-8) 929 18th St., San Diego, CA 92154 t) 619-423-3701 principal@saintcharlesschool.com saintcharlesschool.com Sylvia Benning, Prin.;

Pastor of Christ the King Catholic Parish, San Diego, a corporation sole - 29 N. 32nd St., San Diego, CA 92102 t) 619-231-8906 ctksandiego@gmail.com www.ctksandiego.org Rev. Tommie Jennings, Pst.; CRP Stds.: 89

Pastor of Saint Columba Catholic Parish, San Diego, a corporation sole - 3327 Glencolum Dr., San Diego, CA 92123 t) 858-277-3863 stcolumbarectory@gmail.com www.stcolumbasandiego.com Rev. Rolando Gabutera, Pst.; Dcn. H. William Vasquez Jr.; CRP Stds.: 25

Saint Columba Catholic Parish School - (Grades PreK-8) 3365 Glencolum Dr., San Diego, CA 92123 t) 858-279-1882 lglenwinkel@yahoo.com; principal@stcolumbaschool.org stcolumbaschool.org

Preschool - 3365 Glencolum Dr., San Diego, CA 92123 t) 858-279-0161 Clarissa Carver, Dir.;

Pastor of Saint Didacus Catholic Parish, San Diego, a corporation sole - 4772 Felton St., San Diego, CA 92116 t) 619-284-3472 mainoffice@stdidacuschurch.org www.stdidacuschurch.org Rev. Reynaldo Roque, Pst.; Dcn. Dino Serafino; Dcn. Marco Huizar; Elena Platas, DRE; CRP Stds.: 114

Saint Didacus Catholic Parish School - (Grades PreSchool-8) 4630 34th St., San Diego, CA 92116 t) 619-284-8730 principal@stdidacusparishschool.org www.stdidacusparishschool.org Stds.: 161; Lay Tchrs.: 10

Preschool - 4630 34th St, San Diego, CA 92116 t) 619-284-8730 stdidacusparishschool.org

Pastor of Good Shepherd Catholic Parish, San Diego, a corporation sole - 8200 Gold Coast Dr., San Diego, CA 92126-3699 t) 858-271-0207; 858-693-1522 goodshepherd@goodshepherdparish.net www.goodshepherdparish.net Dcn. Manuel Rivas, DRE; Very Rev. Michael Pham, Pst.; Rev. Manuel Del

Rio, Assoc. Pst.; CRP Stds.: 606

Good Shepherd Catholic Parish School - (Grades PreSchool-8) 8160 Gold Coast Dr., San Diego, CA 92126 gsoffice@goodshepherdcatholic.net www.gscs-online.org Ladonna Lambert, Prin.; Miranda Espejo, Librn.;

Pastor of Saint Gregory the Great Catholic Parish, San Diego, a corporation sole - 11451 Blue Cypress Dr., San Diego, CA 92131 t) 858-653-3540 reception@stgg.org www.stgg.org Rev. Nicholas P. Clavin, Pst.; Dcn. Ronald H. Diem; Dcn. Dominic Guzzardo; Dcn. Doug Pingel; CRP Stds.: 330

St. Gregory the Great Catholic School - (Grades PreSchool-8) 15315 Stonebridge Pkwy., San Diego, CA 92131 t) 858-397-1290 office@stggcs.org www.stggcs.org Maeve O'Connell, Prin.;

Pastor of Holy Family Catholic Parish, San Diego, a corporation sole - 1957 Coolidge St., San Diego, CA 92111-7098 t) 858-277-0404 x101 church@oneholyfamily.org oneholyfamily.org Rev. Peter Vu Lam, Pst.; CRP Stds.: 258

Pastor of Holy Spirit Catholic Parish, San Diego, a corporation sole - 2725-55th St., San Diego, CA 92105-5094 t) 619-262-2435 linda@holyspiritsd.org www.holyspiritsd.org Rev. Dickens Remy, Pst.; Rev. Phien Van Pham, Assoc. Pst.; Elodia Castillo, DRE; CRP Stds.: 562

Pastor of The Immaculata Catholic Parish, San Diego, a corporation sole - 5998 Alcala Park, USD Campus, San Diego, CA 92110-2492 t) 619-574-5700; 619-574-5702 (CRP) theimmaculata@sandiego.edu www.theimmaculata.org Very Rev. Matthew D. Spahr, Pst.; CRP Stds.: 130

Pastor of Immaculate Conception Catholic Parish, San Diego, a corporation sole - 2540 San Diego Ave., San Diego, CA 92110-2840 t) 619-295-4141 parish@icc-sandiego.org www.immaculate-conception-sandiego.org Rev. Garrett Galvin, O.F.M., Admin.; Friar Michael Blastic, OFM, In Res.; Friar Joseph Chinnici, OFM, In Res.; Friar Vincent Mesi, O.F.M., Sacr. Min.;

Pastor of Saint John the Evangelist Catholic Parish, San Diego, a corporation sole - 1638 Polk Ave., San Diego, CA 92103 t) 619-291-1660 office@sjesandiego.org www.sjesandiego.org Rev. Charles A. Moat, Admin.; Rev. Anthony Yang, SVD, Pst. Assoc.; Dcn. Robert Booth; CRP Stds.: 10

Pastor of Saint Jude Shrine of the West Catholic Parish, San Diego, a corporation sole - 3785 Boston Ave., San Diego, CA 92113-3210; Mailing: 1129 S. 38th St., San Diego, CA 92113-3210 t) 619-264-2195; 619-264-4795 (CRP) info@stjudesd.com www.stjudesd.com Very Rev. Edmundo Zarate-Suarez, Pst.; Rev. Gerardo Gomez-Zapien, Assoc. Pst.; Rev. Alfredo Heyrosa, Assoc. Pst.; CRP Stds.: 258

Pastor of Saint Mary Magdalene Catholic Parish in San Diego, California, a Corporation Sole - 1945 Illion St., San Diego, CA 92110 t) 619-276-1248 (CRP); 619-276-1041 religioused@stmarymagonline.org; fredward@stmarymagonline.org www.stmarymagonline.org Kia Scott, Youth Min.; Barlow Gerry, DRE; Rev. Edward McNulty, Pst.; CRP Stds.: 127

The School of the Madeleine - (Grades PreK-8) 1875 Illion St., San Diego, CA 92110 t) 619-276-6545 info@schoolofthemadeleine.com www.schoolofthemadeleine.com Jean Coleman, Prin.;

Pastor of Saint Maximilian Kolbe Mission, a corporation sole - 1735 Grand Ave., San Diego, CA 92109 t) 858-272-7655; 619-668-0485 (CRP) pastor@polishmission.org Rev. Czeslaw Rybacki, S.Ch., Pst.;

Pastor of Saint Michael Catholic Parish, San Diego, a corporation sole - 2643 Homedale St., San Diego, CA 92139 t) 619-470-1977 msalamat@stmichaelsandiego.org www.stmichaelsandiego.org Rev. Manuel Ediza, Pst.; Rev. Msgr. Francisco Cinco III, Assoc. Pst.; Dcn. Gustavo Magana; Dcn. Carl Shelton; CRP Stds.: 225

Preschool - 2637 Homedale St., San Diego, CA 92139 t) 619-472-5437 vdayag@stmichaelsandiego.org www.smapreschool.org/ Veronica Dayag, Dir.;

Pastor of Mission San Diego de Alcala Catholic Parish, San Diego, a corporation sole - 10818 San Diego Mission Rd., San Diego, CA 92108-2429 t) (619) 624-0900 (Religious Education); (619) 281-8449 (Visitor Ctr); (619) 283-7319 (Parish Office) ngonsalves@missionsandiego.org www.missionsandiego.org (California's First Mission) Rev. Raymond Philip Napuli, Assoc. Pst.; Rev. William A. Springer, Assoc. Pst.; Rev. Peter M. McGuine, Pst.; CRP Stds.: 145

Pastor of Our Lady of Angels Catholic Parish, San Diego, a corporation sole - 656 24th St., San Diego, CA 92102-2911 t) 619-239-1231; 619-239-1526 (CRP) Rev. Ricardo Juarez, CJM, Pst.; Sr. Gloria Galvan, Pst. Min./Coord.; CRP Stds.: 274

Pastor of Our Lady of Guadalupe Catholic Parish, San Diego, a corporation sole - 1770 Kearney Ave., San Diego, CA 92113-1128 t) 619-233-3838 vtoscano@olgsd.org; ssantarosasj@olgsd.org olgsd.org Rev. Scott Santarosa, SJ, Pst.; Rev. Neal J. Wilkinson, S.J., Assoc. Pst.; Rev. Brad Mills, SJ, Assoc. Pst.; Rev. Mike Lee, SJ, Assoc. Pst.; Rev. Hung T. Nguyen, S.J., Assoc. Pst.; CRP Stds.: 106

Our Lady's School - (Grades K-8) 650 24th St., San Diego, CA 92102 t) 619-233-8888 principal@olssd.org olssd.org Stds.: 195; Lay Tchrs.: 10

Pastor of Our Lady of Mt. Carmel Catholic Parish, San Diego, a corporation sole - 13541 Stoney Creek Rd., San Diego, CA 92129 t) 858-484-1070 ourlady@olmc-sandiego.org olmcsandiego.org Rev. Anthony Saroki, Pst.; Rev. Ignatius Kipchirchir, Assoc. Pst.; Dcn. Juan Faus; Dcn. Manny Porciuncula; Dcn. Frank Reilly; CRP Stds.: 435

Pastor of Our Lady of Refuge Catholic Parish, San Diego, a corporation sole - 4226 Jewell St., San Diego, CA 92109 t) 858-274-2959 (CRP); 858-274-9670 marissa@ourladyofrefuge.net www.ourladyofrefugesandiego.net Rev. David N. Croisetiere, Pst.; Dcn. Salvador Huitron; CRP Stds.: 28

Pastor of Our Lady of the Rosary Catholic Parish, San Diego, a corporation sole - 1668 State St., San Diego, CA 92101; Mailing: 1629 Columbia St., San Diego, CA 92101 t) 619-234-4820 parish@olrsd.org olrsd.org Rev. Joseph Tabigue, C.R.S.P., Pst.; Rev. Louis M. Solcia, C.R.S.P., Assoc. Pst.; Rev. Albino Vecina, C.R.S.P., Assoc. Pst.; CRP Stds.: 67

Pastor of Our Lady of the Sacred Heart Catholic Parish, San Diego, a corporation sole - 4177 Marlborough Ave., San Diego, CA 92105-1412 t) 619-280-0515 ourladyofsacred@olshsandiego.com Rev. Dominic Asare, SVD, Pst.; CRP Stds.: 317

Preschool - t) 619-284-0124 Enid Dixon, Dir.;

Pastor of Our Mother of Confidence Catholic Parish, San Diego, a corporation sole - 3131 Governor Dr., San Diego, CA 92122 t) 858-453-3554 (CRP); 858-453-0222 frontdesk@omcsandiego.org www.omcsandiego.org JoEllyn Mascarenhas, CRE; Melanie Eckler, Bus. Mgr.; Rev. Steven Larion, Pst.; Dcn. Scott Wall; Dcn. Greg Settelmayer; CRP Stds.: 129

Pastor of Saint Patrick Catholic Parish, San Diego, a corporation sole - 3585 30th St., San Diego, CA 92104-4142 t) 619-295-2157 parishsecretary@stpatsd.org www.stpatrickschurchsd.weconnect.com Rev. Carlos Alberto Flores, O.S.A., Pst.; Rev. William Thomas Porter Davis, OSA, Assoc. Pst.; Rev. Sarfraz Alam, O.S.A., In Res.; CRP Stds.: 120

Saint Patrick Catholic Parish San Diego School - (Grades PreSchool-8) 3014 Capps St., San Diego, CA 92104-4222 t) 619-297-1314 secretary@stpatrick.sdcoxmail.com www.stpatrickssd.com Hernan Valdivia, Prin.;

St. Augustine High School Chapel - 3266 Nutmeg St., San Diego, CA 92104-5151 Rev. Gary Sanders, O.S.A., Prov.;

Pastor of Saint Rita Catholic Parish, San Diego, a corporation sole - 5124 Churchward St., San Diego, CA 92114-3797 t) 619-264-4399 (CRP); 619-264-3165 aurelia@stritaschurchsd.org; connie@stritaschurchsd.org stritasd.weconnect.com Sr. Ma. de Lourdes Barbosa, DRE; Rev. Silverio Espenilla, Pst.; CRP Stds.: 100

Saint Rita Catholic Parish School - (Grades PreK-8) 5165 Imperial Ave., San Diego, CA 92114 t) 619-264-0109 principal@stritassd.org www.stritassd.org Gina Olsen, Prin.; Ruberta Castro, Librn.;

Preschool - t) 619-264-8831 Vicky Torres, Dir.;

Pastor of Sacred Heart Catholic Parish, San Diego, a corporation sole - 4776 Saratoga Ave, San Diego, CA 92107-9990 t) 619-224-2746; 619-224-2746 x102 (CRP) parishoffice@sacredheartob.org; religioused@sacredheartob.org www.sacredheartob.org Rev. Thomas Kiely, Pst.; Rev. Keith Shuley, C.C., In Res.; Stephen Williams, DRE; Rev. Emmanuel Ochigbo, Residence; Dcn. Mark Wieczorek; CRP Stds.: 37

Sacred Heart Academy Preschool - 4895 Saratoga Ave., San Diego, CA 92107 t) 619-222-7252 shaobpreschool2@gmail.com www.sacredheartpreschool.org Rebecca Godina, Dir.;

Pastor of San Rafael Catholic Parish, San Diego, a corporation sole - 17252 Bernardo Center Dr., San Diego, CA 92128 t) 858-487-4314 office@sanrafaelparish.org; religioused@sanrafaelparish.org www.sanrafaelparish.org Very Rev. Msgr. Dennis Mikulanis, Pst.; Rev. Niranjan Kanmury, Assoc. Pst.; CRP Stds.: 293

Pastor of Saint Therese Catholic Parish, San Diego, a corporation sole - 6400 Saint Therese Way, San Diego, CA 92120-3018 t) 619-582-3716 rulrich@sttheresepariSh.org www.sttheresepariSh.org Very Rev. Devdas Masillamony, Pst.; CRP Stds.: 148

St. Therese Academy - (Grades PreSchool-8) 6440 Saint Therese Way, San Diego, CA 92120 t) 619-583-6270 msperrazzo@sta-sd.org Mark Sperrazzo, Prin.; Stds.: 306; Sr. Tchrs.: 1; Lay Tchrs.: 10

Preschool - 6440 Saint Therese Way, San Diego, CA 92120 t) 619-583-1493 msperrazzo@sta-sd.org Melba Jemienez, Dir.;

Pastor of Saint Therese of Carmel Catholic Parish, San Diego, a corporation sole - 4355 Del Mar Trails Rd., San Diego, CA 92130 t) 858-481-3232 parishoffice@stocsd.org www.sttheresecarmel.org Rev. Chris Tozzi, Pst.; Dcn. John Fanelle; Dcn. Philip Hardjadinata; CRP Stds.: 475

Pastor of Saint Vincent de Paul Catholic Parish, San Diego, a corporation sole - 4080 Hawk St., San Diego, CA 92103-1899; Mailing: 4077 Ibis St., San Diego, CA 92103 t) 619-299-3880 vincentcatholic.org Rev. Alexander De Paulis, Pst.;

Saint Vincent de Paul Catholic Parish School - (Grades K-8) 4061 Ibis St., San Diego, CA 92103-1899 t) 619-296-2222 sstutz@svscatholic.org; mterzoli@svscatholic.org svscatholic.org Steve Stutz, Prin.;

Preschool - 4077 Ibis St., San Diego, CA 92103 t) 619-296-2261 joette@vincentcatholic.org Joette M Correia, Dir.;

SAN MARCOS

Pastor of Saint Mark Catholic Parish in San Marcos A Corporation Sole - 1147 Discovery St., San Marcos, CA 92078-1313 t) 760-744-1130 (CRP); 760-744-1540 kgray@stmarksrcc.org www.stmarkscatholicchurch.org Very Rev. Bruce J. Orsborn, Pst.; Rev. Miguel Romero, Pst. Assoc.; Rev. William Zondler, Pst. Assoc.; CRP Stds.: 787

Deer Springs Mission - 2557 Sarver Ln., San Marcos, CA 92069

SAN YSIDRO

Pastor of Our Lady of Mt. Carmel Catholic Parish, San Ysidro, a corporation sole - 2020 Alaquinas Dr., San

Ysidro, CA 92173-2107 t) 619-428-1415 olmcsy@gmail.com www.ourladyofmountcarmel-sy.org Dcn. David Gonzalez; Rev. Armando P. Escurel, Pst.; Dcn. Raul Gonzalez; Dcn. Jose Luis Medina; Dcn. Timothy Schulz; CRP Stds.: 198

Our Lady of Mt. Carmel Catholic Parish San Ysidro School - (Grades 1-8) 4141 Beyer Blvd., San Ysidro, CA 92173-2133 t) 619-428-2091 frontoffice@olmc.school Sr. Eva Lujano, S.J.S., Prin.; Ma. Eugenia Villareal, Librn.;

SANTA YSABEL

Pastor of Santa Ysabel Indian Mission Catholic Parish, Santa Ysabel, a corporation sole - 23013 Hwy. 79, Santa Ysabel, CA 92070-0129; Mailing: P.O. Box 129, Santa Ysabel, CA 92070-0129 t) 760-765-0810 missionsantaysabel1818@yahoo.com Rev. Timothy Deutsch, Pst.; Dcn. Fred Thornton;

SANTEE

Pastor of Guardian Angels Catholic Parish, Santee, a corporation sole - 9310 Dalehurst Rd., Santee, CA 92071-1010 t) 619-448-1213 office@guardianangelssantee.org; faithformation@guardianangelssantee.org www.guardianangelssantee.org Rev. Andre Ramos, Pst.; Tammy Mansir, DRE; CRP Stds.: 175

Preschool - t) 619-596-3281 preschool@ga.sdcoxmail.com Joyce Keup, Dir.;

SOLANA BEACH

Pastor of Saint James Catholic Parish, Solana Beach, a corporation sole - 625 S. Nardo Ave., Solana Beach, CA 92075-2398 t) 858-755-2545 info@stjames-stleo.com; psmith@stjames-stleo.com www.stjamesandleo.org Rev. Ricardo Antonio Chinchilla, CJM, Pst.; Rev. George Perez, CJM, Assoc. Pst.; Jannet Diaz, DRE; Pamela Smith, DRE; Dcn. Peter Hodsdon, Bus. Mgr.; CRP Stds.: 256

St. James Academy - (Grades PreSchool-8) 623 S. Nardo Ave., Solana Beach, CA 92075 t) 858-755-1777 principal@saintjamesacademy.com saintjamesacademy.com Christine Lang, Prin.;

St. Leo - 936 Genevieve St., Solana Beach, CA 92075 t) (858) 755-2545 x200

Preschool - Laura Kuhn, Dir.;

SPRING VALLEY

Pastor of Santa Sophia Catholic Parish, Spring Valley, a corporation sole - 9800 San Juan St., Spring Valley, CA 91977 t) 619-463-6629 bpadlo@santasophia.org; parish@santasophia.org www.santasophia.org Rev. Corey Tufford, Pst.; Bernadette Padlo, Dir.; CRP Stds.: 120

Santa Sophia Catholic Parish School - (Grades PreSchool-8) 9806 San Juan St., Spring Valley, CA 91977 t) 619-463-0488 santasophiaacademyoffice@gmail.com santasophiaacademy.org/ Karen Laaperi, Prin.;

Preschool - Victoria Simanek, Dir.;

VALLEY CENTER

Pastor of Saint Stephen Catholic Parish, Valley Center, a corporation sole - 31020 Cole Grade Rd., Valley Center, CA 92082-1015; Mailing: P.O. Box 1015, Valley Center, CA 92082 t) 760-749-3352 (CRP); 760-749-3324 www.ststephenvc.com Very Rev. Luke Jauregui, Pst.; Dcn. John Tobin; CRP Stds.: 314

VISTA

Pastor of Saint Francis of Assisi Catholic Parish, Vista, a corporation sole - 525 W. Vista Way, Vista, CA 92083-5974 t) 760-945-8000 stfrancismain@stfrancis-vista.org www.stfrancis-vista.org Rev. Ruben Arceo, S.J., Pst.; Dcn. Ronald Arnold; Dcn. Jose Luis Maldonado; Dcn. Juan Santillan; CRP Stds.: 784

Saint Francis of Assisi Catholic Parish School - (Grades PreSchool-8) t) 760-630-7960 info@sfs-vista.org Elizabeth Joseph, Prin.;

Preschool - t) 760-630-7964 Jennifer Paino, Dir.;

WESTMORLAND

Pastor of Saint Joseph Catholic Parish, Westmorland, a corporation sole - 300 N. Center St., Westmorland, CA 92281; Mailing: 402 S. Imperial Ave., Brawley, CA 92227 t) 760-679-3505 brawleycatholic@gmail.com www.brawleycatholic.org Rev. Bernardo Lara, Pst.; Rev. Claro Ortiz, Assoc. Pst.;

WINTERHAVEN

Pastor of Saint Thomas Indian Mission Catholic Parish, Winterhaven, a corporation sole - 350 Picacho Rd., Winterhaven, CA 92283-1176; Mailing: PO Box 1176, Winterhaven, CA 92283-1176 t) 760-572-0283 captinfreon@aol.com www.stthomasindianmission.org Steven Taylor, Parish Life Coord.;

SCHOOLS: PRESCHOOL THRU HIGH SCHOOL

SCHOOLS

STATE OF CALIFORNIA

CHULA VISTA

Mater Dei Juan Diego Academy - (PRV) (Grades PreK-7) 1615 Mater Dei Dr., Chula Vista, CA 91913 t) 619-423-2121 info@mdjda.org www.mdjda.org Cristina Torres, Admin.; Faina Salter, Prin.; Stds.: 472; Lay Tchrs.: 19

Mater Dei Juan Diego Adult Center - (PRV) 1615 Mater Dei Dr., Chula Vista, CA 91913 t) 619-423-2121 nbartels@mdchs.net Nancy Bartels, Dir.; Stds.: 400

SAN DIEGO

St. Katharine Drexel Academy - (DIO) (Grades K-8) 4551 56th St., San Diego, CA 92115 t) 619-582-3862 mainoffice@skda-sd.org www.skda-sd.org Kelly Bonde, Prin.; Stds.: 132; Lay Tchrs.: 9

Nativity Prep Academy - (PRV) (Grades 6-8) 4463 College Ave, San Diego, CA 92115; Mailing: 6126 Adelaide Ave, San Diego, CA 92115 t) 619-544-9455 info@nativityprep.org www.nativityprep.org Jodi Drake, Prin.; Gilbert P Brady, Pres.; Diana Junge, Bus. Mgr.; Xochitl Alvarez, Dir.; Stds.: 63; Lay Tchrs.: 8

Nazareth School - (PRV) (Grades PreSchool-8) 10728 San Diego Mission Rd., San Diego, CA 92108 t) 619-641-7987 principal@nazarethschool.org www.nazarethschool.org Rene Coons, Prin.; Georgina Barragan, Dir.; Stds.: 293; Lay Tchrs.: 20

Notre Dame Academy - (PRV) (Grades PreSchool-8) 4345 Del Mar Trails Rd., San Diego, CA 92130 t) 858-509-2300 ndaadministration@ndasd.org www.ndasd.org Sr. Marie Pascale Clisson, U.C.S.C., Prin.; Ursula Segura, Dir.; Stds.: 270; Lay Tchrs.: 30

SAN MARCOS

St. Joseph Academy (Sierra Madre Academy) - (PRV) (Grades PreK-12) 500 Las Flores Dr., San Marcos, CA 92078 t) 760-305-8505 office@saintjosephacademy.org www.saintjosephacademy.org (Co-Ed) Luke Heintschel, Headmaster;

HIGH SCHOOLS

STATE OF CALIFORNIA

CALEXICO

Vincent Memorial Catholic High School - (DIO) 525 W. Sheridan, Calexico, CA 92231 t) 760-357-3461 vmoffice@vmchs.com vmchs.com (Coed). Conducted by Sisters Servants of the Blessed Sacrament. Sr. Guadalupe Hernandez, S.J.S., Prin.; Stds.: 307; Lay Tchrs.: 16

CHULA VISTA

Mater Dei Catholic High School - (DIO) 1615 Mater Dei Dr., Chula Vista, CA 91913 t) 619-423-2121 mdietz@materdeicatholic.org www.materdeicatholic.org (Coed) Aaron Gonzalez, Prin.; Rev. Joaquin O. Martinez, S.J., Pres.; Stds.: 1,144; Lay Tchrs.: 63

SAN DIEGO

Academy of Our Lady of Peace - (PRV) (Grades 9-12) 4860 Oregon St., San Diego, CA 92116 t) 619-297-2266 llek@aolp.org www.aolp.org (Girls) Lauren Lek, Head of School; Brandy Sato, Asst. Head of School; Jessica Occhialini, CFO; Stds.: 745; Lay Tchrs.: 52

St. Augustine High School - (PAR) 3266 Nutmeg St., San Diego, CA 92104-5199 t) 619-282-2184 jhorne@sahs.org www.sahs.org (Boys), Conducted by The Augustinians. Rev. Maxime Villeneuve, O.S.A., Chap.; Nicole Quirk, Campus Min.; James Horne, Prin.; Edwin Hearn, Pres.; Jason Alcoser, Librn.; Bro. Bobby Baiocco, Dir. Christian Svcs.; Kevin DeRieux, Exec. Dir. Finance & Facilities; Stds.: 725; Pr. Tchrs.: 1; Bro. Tchrs.: 1; Lay Tchrs.: 58

Cathedral Catholic High School - (DIO) 5555 Del Mar Heights Rd., San Diego, CA 92130 t) 858-523-4000 bwallace@cathedralcatholic.org www.cathedralcatholic.org Marlena Conroy, Prin.; Dr. Kevin Calkins, Pres.; Stds.: 1,616; Scholastics: 97; Lay Tchrs.: 97

***Cristo Rey San Diego High School, Inc.** - (PRV) (Grades 9-12) 1228 S. 38th St., San Diego, CA 92113; Mailing: 3525 Del Mar Heights Rd., #882, San Diego, CA 92130 t) 619-432-1899 cristoreysandiego.org Michael Derrick, Prin.; Robert Nascenzi, Pres.; Stds.: 155; Lay Tchrs.: 16

SAN MARCOS

Saint Joseph Academy - (PRV) 500 Las Flores Dr., San Marcos, CA 92078 t) 760-305-8505 office@saintjosephacademy.org www.saintjosephacademy.org (Co-Ed) Anthony Biese, Headmaster;

INSTITUTIONS LOCATED IN DIOCESE

CAMPUS MINISTRY / NEWMAN CENTERS [CAM]

SAN DIEGO

Newman Center - SDSU - 5855 Hardy Ave., San Diego, CA 92115 t) 858-490-8203 privera@sdcatholic.org www.sdsucatholic.org Rev. Pedro Rivera, Dir.;

University of California at San Diego (Campus Ministry) - 4321 Eastgate Mall, San Diego, CA 92121-2102 t) 858-452-1957 cathcom@ucsd.edu www.catholicucsd.org Berenice Cervantes, Pst. Assoc., Spirituality & Campus Ministry; Rev. Christopher T Nguyen, S.J., Dir.; Chinh Nguyen, S.J., Pst. Assoc.; David W. Vacchi, Pst. Assoc., Administration & Campus Ministry;

CATHOLIC CHARITIES [CCH]

SAN DIEGO

Catholic Charities - 3888 Paducah Dr., San Diego, CA 92117; Mailing: P.O. Box 121831, San Diego, CA 92112-1831 t) 619-323-2841 vpajanor@ccdsd.org www.ccdsd.org Homeless, Immigrant, Refugee, Senior and Food Distribution Services Appaswamy Vino Pajanor, CEO; Asstd. Annu.: 123,971; Staff: 211

Catholic Charities Day Center - 250 W. Orange Ave., El Centro, CA 92243 t) (619) 323-2841

Emergency Services (Main Office) - t) (619) 323-2841

House of Hope - El Centro-Imperial County - t) (619) 323-2841

Immigrant Services - San Diego - t) (619) 323-2841

La Posada Farm Worker and Homeless Men's Housing, Carlsbad - t) (619) 323-2841

Our Lady of Guadalupe Shelter - Calexico-Imperial County - t) (619) 323-2841

Pregnancy and Adoption - t) (619) 323-2841

Rachel Women's Center - 759 Eighth Ave., San Diego, CA 92101 t) (619) 323-2841

Refugee Services - 4575-A Mission Gorge Pl., San Diego, CA 92120 t) (619) 323-2841

***S.V.D.P. Management Inc. (Father Joe's Villages)** - 3350 E St., San Diego, CA 92102 t) 619-446-2100; 619-466-3537 yourfriends@neighbor.org my.neighbor.org Owns and manages the property for St. Vincent de Paul Village, Inc. Dcn. Jim F. Vargas, O.F.S., Pres.;

***St. Vincent de Paul Village (Father Joe's Villages)** - 1501 Imperial Ave., San Diego, CA 92101; Mailing: 3350 E St., San Diego, CA 92102-3332 t) 619-466-3537 donations@neighbor.org my.neighbor.org Programs and services to prevent & end homelessness Dcn. Jim F. Vargas, O.F.S., Pres.;

Addiction Treatment & Education Center - t) 619-233-8500 info@neighbor.org individual and group addiction treatment for people who are homeless

Affordable Housing - Corporate Office, 3350 E St., San Diego, CA 92102 t) 619-446-2100 info@neighbor.org 365 affordable studio, 1-, 2- and 3-bedroom units in 5 buildings.

Chaplaincy Services -

Day Center for Homeless Adults -

Franklin Antonio Public Lunch Line -

Housing Programs -

Village Health Center -

CEMETERIES [CEM]

OCEANSIDE

Old Mission San Luis Rey Cemetery - 4050 Mission Ave., Oceanside, CA 92057 t) 760-757-3651 x133; 760-231-8445 danielle@sanluisrey.org www.sanluisrey.org/cemetery Gwyn Grimes, Exec.; Danielle Napoli, Dir.;

PALA

Pala Indian Missions - 3015 Pala Mission Rd., Pala, CA 92059; Mailing: P.O. Box 70, Pala, CA 92059 t) 760-742-3317 info@missionsanantonio.org 6 separate Indian burial grounds. Rev. Gerardo Fernandez, Pst.;

SAN DIEGO

Holy Cross Cemetery and Mausoleum - 4470 Hilltop Dr., San Diego, CA 92102 t) 619-264-3127 mario@holycrosssd.com www.holycrossd.com Very Rev. Msgr. Dennis Mikulanis, Dir.;

COLLEGES & UNIVERSITIES [COL]

ESCONDIDO

***John Paul the Great Catholic University** - 220 W. Grand Ave., Escondido, CA 92025 t) 858-653-6740 dbadillo@jpcatholic.edu www.jpcatholic.edu Derry (Jeremiah) Connolly, Pres.; Stds.: 305; Lay Tchrs.: 8

SAN DIEGO

Franciscan School of Theology - 5998 Alcala Park, San Diego, CA 92110 t) 619-574-5800 ggalvin@fst.edu www.fst.edu Rev. Garrett Galvin, O.F.M., Pres.; Sr. Kathleen Flood, OFS, Vice Pres., Student Affairs & Spiritual Formation; Sr. Juliet Mousseau, RSCJ, Vice Pres., Academic Affairs; Andrea DeLucia, Dir. Devel.; Kimberly Renna, CFO & Vice Pres. Business Oper.; Dan Stone, Asst. Vice Pres., Enrollment Mgmt.; Stds.: 71; Lay Tchrs.: 2; Pr. Tchrs.: 2

University of San Diego - 5998 Alcala Park, San Diego, CA 92110-2492 t) 619-260-4600 universityministry@sandiego.edu www.sandiego.edu/ministry Rev. Robert Capone, Chap.; Rev. Michael White, C.S.Sp., Chap.; Sr. Maria De la Paz, O.F.M., Campus Min.; James T. Harris, Pres.; Rev. Msgr. Daniel J. Dillabough, Senior Priest; Stds.: 8,815

Center for Christian Spirituality - t) 619-260-4784 www.sandiego.edu/ccs

Center for the Study of Latino/Latina Catholicism - t) 619-260-4525 www.sandiego.edu/cas/latino-cath Orlando Espin, Dir.;

Frances G. Harpst Center for Catholic Thought and Culture - Jeffrey Burns, Dir.;

Msgr. John Portman Chair of Roman Catholic Systematic Theology - t) 619-260-7844 www.sandiego.edu/theo/about/portman

Pastoral Care and Counseling Program - t) 619-260-4784

CONVENTS, MONASTERIES, AND RESIDENCES FOR WOMEN [CON]

BONITA

Sister Servants of the Blessed Sacrament, Inc - 3173 Winnetka Dr., Bonita, CA 91902 t) 619-267-0720; 619-856-4419 provincial@usasjs.org usasjs.org Province of the Immaculate Conception Sr. Adriana Rebeca Zuro, SJS, Prov.; Srs.: 40

SJS Bonita Formation Convent, Our Lady of Peace Convent - 3211 Winnetka Dr., Bonita, CA 91902 t) 619-245-8727 province@usasjs.org SJS US Formation House

SJS Bonita Retirement Convent, Blessed Sacrament Convent - 3417 Kennelworth Ln., Bonita, CA 91902 t) 619-245-8727 SJS Retirement Convent

SJS Calexico Convent, Our Lady of Guadalupe Convent - 536 Rockwood Ave., Calexico, CA 92231 t) 760-357-1046 Sr. Maria Elvia Gonzalez, S.J.S., Supr.;

SJS San Ysidro Convent, Our Lady of Mount Carmel Convent - 333 W. Park Ave., San Ysidro, CA 92173 t) 619-207-0333 Sr. Aurora Lopez-Ornelas, Supr.;

CHULA VISTA

Franciscan Missionaries of Our Lady of Peace - 575 E St., #20, Chula Vista, CA 91910; Mailing: P.O. Box 432453, San Ysidro, CA 92143-2453 t) 619-691-9008 mareaport@hotmail.com Sr. Gabriela Chavez, Supr.; Srs.: 1

Religious of the Incarnate Word - 153 Rainier Ct., Chula Vista, CA 91911 t) 619-869-7337 incarword.ca@gmail.com Srs.: 7

FALLBROOK

Hermanas del Corazon de Jesus Sacramentado - 133 Alvarado Ct., Fallbrook, CA 92028 t) 760-645-3372 hcjsfbrk@aol.com; 3holycruz@hotmail.com Sr. Ruth Irene Becerra Leyva, H.C.J.S., Supr.; Srs.: 2

LEMON GROVE

Mercedarian Sisters of the Blessed Sacrament - 8171 Lemon Grove Way, Lemon Grove, CA 91945 t) 619-460-4271 sistermusict@yahoo.com; m_rosariovega@yahoo.com www.mercedariansisters.org Sr. Teresa Gomez, HMSS, Supr.; Sr. Rosario Vega, H.M.S.S., Prov.; Srs.: 4

SAN DIEGO

Carmelite Monastery of San Diego, California - 5158 Hawley Blvd., San Diego, CA 92116-1934 t) 619-280-5425 smgcarmel@outlook.com www.carmelsandiego.com (Discalced), Cloistered Contemplative Nuns Sr. Joanna Baker, OCD, Prioress; Srs.: 14

Community of the Holy Spirit - 1263 Robinson Ave., #25, San Diego, CA 92103 c) 619-957-7176 lutz93@cox.net Sr. Mary Jo Anderson, CHS, Contact; Srs.: 9

Congregation of the Sisters of Mercy, U.S. Region - 10726 Caminito Cascara, San Diego, CA 92108 t) (619) 417-0293 www.sistersofmercy.ie Sr. Alyce Waters, Reg. Leader; Srs.: 4

Congregation of the Sisters of Nazareth - 6333 Rancho Mission Rd., San Diego, CA 92108 t) 619-563-0480 srrose.hoye@sistersofnazareth.com sistersofnazareth.com Sr. Rose Hoye, Supr.; Srs.: 5

Daughters of Divine Charity - 6430 St. Therese Way, San Diego, CA 92120 t) 619-287-1320 Srs.: 2

Dominican Sisters of Adrian - 17565 Caminito Canasto, San Diego, CA 92127 t) 619-255-4238 kclausen2@cox.net Sr. Joan Kowalski, OP, Contact; Srs.: 1

Missionaries of Charity - 3877 Boston Ave., San Diego, CA 92113-3218 t) 619-263-9566 kwarren@sdcatholic.org Srs.: 15

Religious of Jesus and Mary - 1510 Third Ave., San Diego, CA 92101 t) 619-234-0556 jstolba@rjmusa.org Sr. Rosemary Nicholson, R.J.M., Supr.; Srs.: 3

School Sisters of Notre Dame - 1997 Magdalene Way, San Diego, CA 92110 t) 619-276-5830 jweisma1@san.rr.com Srs.: 5

Sisters of Providence, St. Mary-of-the-Woods - 6665 Canyon Rim Row, #216, San Diego, CA 92111 t) 562-325-1256 doreenlai@yahoo.com.sg Sr. Dawn Tomaszewski, Supr.; Sr. Doreen Lai, Dir.; Srs.: 3

Sisters of Social Service - 3525 Third Ave., San Diego, CA 92103-4908 t) 619-295-1896 sisterssocialservice@gmail.com Sr. Michelle Walsh, S.S.S., Supr.; Srs.: 3

Sisters of St. Joseph of Orange - 440 S. Batavia St., San Diego, CA 92868 t) 714-633-8121 www.csjorange.org Sr. Ellen Jordan, Contact; Srs.: 1

Sisters of St. Francis (Philadelphia) - 6333 Rancho Mission Rd., San Diego, CA 92108 t) 619-563-0480 sistermary.kiely@gmail.com Srs.: 2

Sisters of St. Joseph of Carondelet - 1033 Hayes Ave., San Diego, CA 92103 t) 619-295-2887 doan@aolp.org Sr. Patricia Nelson, CSJ, Dir.; Srs.: 8

Society of the Holy Child Jesus - 6243 Caminito Telmo, San Diego, CA 92111 t) 858-277-0309 americanprovince@shcj.org Sr. Carroll Juliano, Prov.; Srs.: 1

VISTA

Sisters of St. Clare (O.S.C.) - 1171 Via Santa Paulo, Vista, CA 92081 t) 760-295-0611 c) 760-445-4143 madfitz@icloud.com; mfitzgerald@stfrancis-vista.org Sr. Madeline Fitzgeral, O.S.C., Contact; Srs.: 87

ENDOWMENTS / FOUNDATIONS / TRUSTS [EFT]

EL CAJON

Kraemer Endowment Foundation, Inc. - 2119 E. Madison Ave., El Cajon, CA 92019-1111 t) 858-735-0317 john.seiber@ubs.com John Seiber, Chair;

LA JOLLA

Mercy Hospital Foundation, San Diego - ; Mailing: P.O. Box 2669, La Jolla, CA 92038 t) 800-326-3776 braunwarth.mary@scrippshealth.org www.scrippsfoundation.org Mary Braunwarth, Dir.;

LEMON GROVE

St. John's Plaza (Calexico Plaza Development Corp., A California Nonprofit Corporation) - 8150 Broadway, Lemon Grove, CA 91945 t) 619-466-5354 stjohnsplaza@sjp.sdcoxmail.com

SAN DIEGO

The St. Augustine Foundation - 3180 University Ave., Suite 255, San Diego, CA 92104-2089 t) 619-564-8715 www.californiaaugustinians.org Support needs of the Order, individuals and communities throughout the world to promote peace, justice, community, and care and empowerment of people David Canedo, Exec. Dir.; Rev. John Keller, Pres.; Rev. Max Villeneuve, O.S.A., CFO;

The Bellesini Foundation - 3180 University Ave., Ste. 255, San Diego, CA 92104-2089 t) 619-235-0247 osa-west@calprovince.org www.californiaaugustinians.org Funding for the education of brothers in the Province of St. Augustine. Rev. Gary Sanders, O.S.A., CEO; Rev. Max Villeneuve, O.S.A., CFO;

Cathedral Plaza Development Corp., A California Nonprofit Corporation - 1551 Third Ave., San Diego, CA 92101 t) 619-234-0093 cathedral@cathedralplaza.sd.coxmail.com

***Catholic Community Foundation of San Diego** - 4747 Morena Blvd., Ste. 300, San Diego, CA 92117 t) 858-397-9700 mrubio@ccfsd.org www.ccfsd.org Provides a one-stop resource for Catholic philanthropy in the Catholic communities in San Diego and Imperial counties. Manny Rubio, CEO; Ryan Douglas, Dir. Finance and Operations;

Guadalupe Plaza (Guadalupe Housing Partner, LP) - 4142 42nd St., San Diego, CA 92105 t) 619-584-2414 Andrea Hernandez, Contact;

Mater Dei Catholic High School Foundation, Inc. - 3888 Paducah Dr., San Diego, CA 92186; Mailing: P.O. Box 85728, San Diego, CA 92186 t) 858-490-8310 rvaldivia@sdcatholic.com Rodrigo Valdivia, Contact;

The Tagaste Foundation - 3180 University Ave., Ste. 255, San Diego, CA 92104-2089 t) 619-235-0247 osa-west@calprovince.org Funding for the support, care and maintenance of Aged or Infirm brothers of the Province of St. Augustine. Rev. Gary Sanders, O.S.A., CEO; Rev. Max Villeneuve, O.S.A., CFO;

HOSPITALS / HEALTH SERVICES [HOS]

SAN DIEGO

Scripps Mercy Hospital - 4077 Fifth Ave., San Diego, CA 92103 t) 619-686-3418 ybarra.miriam@scrippshealth.org www.scrippshealth.org Tom Gammiere, Exec.; Mark Zangrando, Dir.; Bed Capacity: 655; Asstd. Annu.: 230,735; Staff: 4,311

Scripps Mercy Chula Vista - 435 H St., Chula Vista, CA 91910 t) 619-691-7000 Rev. Emmanuel Ochigbo, Chap.; Mark Weber, Chap.;

MISCELLANEOUS [MIS]

ALPINE

***Queen of Angels Catholic Parish in Alpine, CA Real Property Support Corporation** - 2569 Victoria Dr., Alpine, CA 91901-3662 t) 619-445-2145 Rev. David Exner, Pst.;

BORREGO SPRINGS

***Saint Richard Catholic Parish in Borrego Springs, CA Real Property Support Corporation** - 611 Church Ln (Diamond Bar Rd.), Borrego Springs, CA 92004-1128; Mailing: PO Box 1128, Borrego springs, CA 92004 t) 760-767-5701 pastor@strichardborrego.com Rev. Fernando Maldonado, Pst.;

BRAWLEY

***Sacred Heart Catholic Parish Brawley in Brawley, CA Real Property Support Corporation** - 402 S. Imperial Ave., Brawley, CA 92227 t) 760-344-3171 Rev. Bernardo Lara;

***Saint Margaret Mary Catholic Parish in Brawley, CA Real Property Support Corporation** - 620 S. Cesar Chavez St., Brawley, CA 92227

CALEXICO

***Our Lady of Guadalupe Catholic Parish Calexico in Calexico, CA Real Property Support Corporation** - 124 E. Fifth St., Calexico, CA 92231-2632 t) 760-357-1822 Rev. Jose A. Sosa, Sch.P., Pst.;

CALIPATRIA

***Saint Patrick Catholic Parish Calipatria in Calipatria, CA Real Property Support Corporation** - 133 E. Church St., Calipatria, CA 92233-0238; Mailing: P.O. Box 238, Calipatria, CA 92233-0238

CAMPO

***Saint Adelaide of Burgundy Catholic Parish in Campo, CA Real Property Support Corporation** - 1347 Dewey Pl., Campo, CA 91906 t) 619-478-1017 stadelaidestmarymagdalene.com Rev. Dave Leon, Pst.;

CARLSBAD

***Saint Elizabeth Seton Catholic Parish in Carlsbad, CA Real Property Support Corporation** - 6628 Santa Isabel St., Carlsbad, CA 92009-5148 t) 760-438-3393 Rev. Michael Robinson, Pst.;

CHULA VISTA

***Mater Dei Catholic Parish in Chula Vista, CA Real Property Support Corporation** - 1571 Magdalena Ave., Chula Vista, CA 91921-2047; Mailing: P.O. Box 212047, Chula Vista, CA 91921-2047 t) 619-656-3735 Rev. Jovencio D. Ricafort, Pst.;

***Most Precious Blood Catholic Parish in Chula Vista, CA Real Property Support Corporation** - 1245 Fourth Ave., Chula Vista, CA 91911-3012 t) 619-422-2100 mpbchurch@gmail.com preciousbloodchurch.com Rev. Marek Stroba (Poland), Assoc. Pst.; Rev. Paul Dass Selvaraj, OMI, Pst.;

***Our Lady of Guadalupe Catholic Parish Chula Vista in Chula Vista, CA Real Property Support Corporation** - 345 Anita St., Chula Vista, CA 91911-4198 t) 619-422-3977 office@ourladyofguadalupecv.org www.ourladyofguadalupecv.org Rev. Hily Buyco Gonzales, c.s., Pst.; Rev. Liem Nguyen, c.s., Assoc. Pst.;

***Saint Rose of Lima Catholic Parish in Chula Vista, CA Real Property Support Corporation** - 293 H St., Chula Vista, CA 91910-4703 t) 619-427-0230 parish@strosecv.com

CORONADO

***Sacred Heart Catholic Parish Coronado in Coronado, CA Real Property Support Corporation** - 655 C Ave., Coronado, CA 92118-2229 t) 619-435-3167 Rev. Michael F. Murphy, Pst.;

DESCANSO

***Our Lady of Light Catholic Parish in Descanso, CA Real Property Support Corporation** - 9136 Riverside Dr., Descanso, CA 91916 t) 619-445-3620 Rev. Enrique Fuentes, Pst.;

EL CAJON

***Catholic Answers, Inc.** - 2020 Gillespie Way, El Cajon, CA 92020 t) 619-387-7200 x323; (619) 599-0205 (Jennifer Phelps) jennifer@catholic.com www.catholic.com Christopher Check, Pres.;

***The Church of Saint Luke Catholic Parish in El Cajon, CA Real Property Support Corporation** - 1980 Hillsdale Rd., El Cajon, CA 92019-3846 t) 619-442-1697 busmgr@thechurchofstluke.org www.thechurchofstluke.org/ Rev. Ronald Cochran;

***Our Lady of Grace Catholic Parish in El Cajon, CA Real Property Support Corporation** - 2766 Navajo Rd., El Cajon, CA 92020-2183 t) 619-469-0133 Rev. Lauro Minimo, Pst.;

***Saint Kieran Catholic Parish in El Cajon, CA Real Property Support Corporation** - 1510 Greenfield Dr., El Cajon, CA 92021-3511

***Saint Louise de Marillac Catholic Parish in El Cajon, CA Real Property Support Corporation** - 2005 Crest Dr., El Cajon, CA 92021-4309

EL CENTRO

***Our Lady of the Valley Catholic Parish in El Centro, CA Real Property Support Corporation** - 795 S. La Brucherie Rd., El Centro, CA 92243

ENCINITAS

***Saint John the Evangelist Catholic Parish Encinitas in Encinitas, CA Real Property Support Corporation** - 1001 Encinitas Blvd., Encinitas, CA 92024-2828 t) 760-753-6254 Rev. James Bahash, Pst.;

ESCONDIDO

***Benedictus** - 8975-7 Lawrence Welk Dr., Escondido, CA 92026 t) 760-500-8565 kostickj@juno.com www.benedictussd.wordpress.com Dcn. James Kostick, Contact;

***Church of the Resurrection Catholic Parish in Escondido, CA Real Property Support Corporation** - 1445 Conway Dr., Escondido, CA 92027-1345 t) 760-747-2322 Rev. Eduardo Bernardino, Pst.;

San Diego North County Magnificat - Our Lady of Guadalupe Chapter - 1361 Wicker Pl., Escondido, CA 92027 t) 858-354-1791 cjrippee@cox.net Cynthia Rippee, Contact;

***Saint Timothy Catholic Parish in Escondido, CA Real Property Support Corporation** - 2960 Canyon Rd., Escondido, CA 92025-7402

FALLBROOK

***Saint Peter the Apostle Catholic Parish in Fallbrook, CA Real Property Support Corporation** - 450 S. Stage Coach Ln., Fallbrook, CA 92028-2457

IMPERIAL

***Saint Anthony of Padua Catholic Parish Imperial in Imperial, CA Real Property Support Corporation** - 211 W. Sixth St., Imperial, CA 92251-1519 t) 760-355-1347 Rev. Danilo Valdepenas, Pst.;

LA JOLLA

***All Hallows Catholic Parish in La Jolla, CA Real Property Support Corporation** - 6602 La Jolla Scenic Dr. S., La Jolla, CA 92037-5799 t) 858-459-2975 Rev. Joseph Masur, Pst.;

***Friends of the Poor** - 8460 Whale Watch Way, La Jolla, CA 92037 t) 858-454-4174 Jean Colarusso, Pres.;

***Mary, Star of the Sea Catholic Parish in La Jolla, CA Real Property Support Corporation** - 7669 Girard Ave., La Jolla, CA 92037-4480 t) 858-454-2631 Rev. Patrick J. Mulcahy, Pst.;

LA MESA

***Saint Martin of Tours Catholic Parish in La Mesa, CA Real Property Support Corporation** - 7710 El Cajon Blvd., La Mesa, CA 91942-6932

LEMON GROVE

***Saint John of the Cross Catholic Parish in Lemon Grove, CA Real Property Support Corporation** - 8086 Broadway Ave., Lemon Grove, CA 91945-2598 Rev. Jose Luis Muro, Pst.;

NATIONAL CITY

***Saint Anthony of Padua Catholic Parish National City in National City, CA Real Property Support Corporation** - 410 W. 18th St., National City, CA 91950 t) 619-477-4520

***Saint Mary Catholic Parish National City in National City, CA Real Property Support Corporation** - 426 E. Seventh St., National City, CA 91950-2322 t) 619-474-1501 Rev. Nemesio Sungcad, Pst.;

OCEANSIDE

***The Emiliani Project** - 884 Arvita Ct., Oceanside, CA 92057 t) 760-805-3042 missions@emilianiproject.org emilianiproject.org Jordan Reece, Contact;

***Mission San Luis Rey Catholic Parish in Oceanside, CA Real Property Support Corporation** - 4070 Mission Ave., Oceanside, CA 92057-6497 t) 760-757-3250 Rev. Oscar Mendez, OFM, Pst.;

***Saint Thomas More Catholic Parish in Oceanside, CA Real Property Support Corporation** - 1450 S. Melrose Dr., Oceanside, CA 92056 t) (760) 758-4100 x100 (Parish Office) parishoffice@stmoside.org Rev. Brent Kruger, Pst.;

PALA

***Mission San Antonio de Pala Catholic Parish in Pala, CA Real Property Support Corporation** - Pala Mission Rd., Pala, CA 92059-0070; Mailing: P.O. Box 70, Pala, CA 92059-0070 t) 760-742-3317 Rev. Gerardo Fernandez, Pst.;

POWAY

***Saint Gabriel Catholic Parish in Poway, CA Real Property Support Corporation** - 13734 Twin Peaks Rd., Poway, CA 92064 Rev. Michel Froidurot, Pst.;

The Genesis Initiative - ; Mailing: P.O. Box 612, Poway, CA 92074 t) 858-748-3348 info@genesisinitiative.org Martha Lyles, Contact; Dick Lyles, Contact;

***Saint Michael Catholic Parish Poway in Poway, CA Real Property Support Corporation** - 15546 Pomerado Rd., Poway, CA 92064-2404

RANCHO SANTA FE

***Church of the Nativity Catholic Parish in Rancho Santa Fe, CA Real Property Support Corporation** - 6309 El Apajo Rd., Rancho Santa Fe, CA 92067-8770; Mailing: P.O. Box 8770, Rancho Santa Fe, CA 92067-8770 t) 858-756-1911 Rev. Agustin Opalalic, Pst.;

SAN DIEGO

Academy of American Franciscan History - 5998 Alcala Park, San Diego, CA 92122 t) 510-548-1755 acadafh@fst.edu www.aafh.org Jeffrey Burns, Dir.;

***Ascension Catholic Parish in San Diego, CA Real Property Support Corporation** - 11292 Clairemont Mesa Blvd., San Diego, CA 92124-1524 t) 858-279-2735 Rev. Edwin Tutor, Pst.;

***Blessed Sacrament Catholic Parish in San Diego, CA Real Property Support Corporation** - 4540 El Cerrito Dr., San Diego, CA 92115-3701 t) 619-582-5722 Rev. Yos Sodanango, SVD (Indonesia), Pst.;

***Catholic Action for Faith and Family** - ; Mailing: P.O. Box 910308, San Diego, CA 92191 t) 858-461-0777 tmckenna@catholicaction.org Thomas McKenna, Contact;

Catholic Cemeteries of San Diego and Imperial Counties - 4470 Hilltop Dr., San Diego, CA 92102 t) 619-264-3127 Very Rev. Msgr. Dennis Mikulanis, Dir.;

Catholic Secondary Education - Diocese of San Diego, Incorporated - 3888 Paducah Dr., San Diego, CA 92186; Mailing: P.O. Box 85728, San Diego, CA 92186 t) 858-490-8301 rvaldivia@sdcatholic.org Rodrigo Valdivia, Vice Moderator of the Curia;

***Children of the Immaculate Heart** - 2337 Irving Ave, San Diego, CA 92170; Mailing: P.O. Box 13954, San Diego, CA 92170 t) 619-431-5537 c) 831-277-7066 officemanager.cih@gmail.com; childrenoftheimmaculateheart@gmail.com www.childrenoftheimmaculateheart.org Grace Williams,

CEO;

***Christ the King Catholic Parish in San Diego, CA Real Property Support Corporation** - 29 N. 32nd St., San Diego, CA 92102-4301 t) 619-231-8906 ctksandiego@gmail.com www.ctksandiego.org Rev. Tommie Jennings, Pst.; Dcn. Carlos Morales;

Cristo Rey San Diego Corporate Work Study Program, Inc. - 1228 S. 38th St., San Diego, CA 92113; Mailing: 3525 Del Mar Heights Rd., #882, San Diego, CA 92130 t) 619-432-1899 Robert Nascenzi, Pres.;

Diocese of San Diego Education & Welfare Corporation - 3888 Paducah Dr., San Diego, CA 92117; Mailing: PO Box 85728, San Diego, CA 92186-5728 t) 858-490-8200 www.sdcatholic.org William Nolan, Admin.;

***Good Shepherd Catholic Parish in San Diego, CA Real Property Support Corporation** - 8200 Gold Coast Dr., San Diego, CA 92126-3699 t) 858-271-0207 Very Rev. Michael Pham, Pst.;

***Holy Spirit Catholic Parish in San Diego, CA Real Property Support Corporation** - 2725-55th St., San Diego, CA 92105-5094 t) 619-262-2435 Rev. Dickens Remy, Pst.;

***The Immaculata Catholic Parish in San Diego, CA Real Property Support Corporation** - 5998 Alcala Park, USD Campus, San Diego, CA 92110-2492 t) (858) 490-8200 Very Rev. Matthew D. Spahr;

***Immaculate Conception Catholic Parish in San Diego, CA Real Property Support Corporation** - 2540 San Diego Ave., San Diego, CA 92110-2840 t) 619-295-4141 Rev. Garrett Galvin, O.F.M., Admin.;

Mater Dei Catholic High School of San Diego Inc. - 3888 Paducah Dr., San Diego, CA 92117; Mailing: P.O. Box 85728, San Diego, CA 92186-5728 t) 858-490-8310 rvaldivia@sdcatholic.org Rodrigo Valdivia, Contact;

***Mission San Diego De Alcala Catholic Parish in San Diego, CA Real Property Support Corporation** - 10818 San Diego Mission Rd., San Diego, CA 92108-2429 t) 619-237-7319 pmcguine@missionsandiego.org Rev. Peter M. McGuine, Pst.;

***Modern Catholic Pilgrim** - 4227 Arguello St., San Diego, CA 92103; Mailing: 3548 47th Ave. S., Minneapolis, MN 55406 t) 858-210-5367 will@moderncatholicpilgrim.com www.moderncatholicpilgrim.com Will Peterson, Pres.;

The Mother Teresa of Calcutta Center - 3835 National Ave., San Diego, CA 92113 t) 619-915-5107; 619-623-5813 mtc@motherteresa.org www.motherteresa.org Rev. Brian Kolodiejchuk, Dir.;

Nazareth School of San Diego, Inc. - 10728 San Diego Mission Rd., San Diego, CA 92108 t) 619-641-7987 office@nazarethschool.org Colleen Mauricio, Prin.;

***Our Lady of Guadalupe Catholic Parish San Diego in San Diego, CA Real Property Support Corporation** - 1770 Kearny Ave., San Diego, CA 92113-1128 t) 619-233-3838 Rev. Scott Santarosa, SJ, Pst.;

***Our Lady of the Rosary Catholic Parish in San Diego, CA Real Property Support Corporation** - 1629 Columbia St., San Diego, CA 92101-2501 t) 619-234-4820 Rev. Joseph Tabigue, C.R.S.P., Pst.;

***Our Lady of the Sacred Heart Catholic Parish in San Diego, CA Real Property Support Corporation** - 4177 Marlborough Ave., San Diego, CA 92105-1412 t) 619-280-0515 Rev. Dominic Asare, SVD, Pst.;

***Our Mother of Confidence Catholic Parish in San Diego, CA Real Property Support Corporation** - 3131 Governor Dr., San Diego, CA 92122-2229 t) 858-453-0222 Rev. Steven Larion, Pst.;

The Roman Catholic Services Corporation for Parishes and Schools of San Diego and Imperial Counties - 3888 Paducah Dr., San Diego, CA 92117; Mailing: P.O. Box 81868, San Diego, CA 92138-1868 t) 858-490-8311 mmacie@sdcatholicservices.org www.sdcatholicservices.org/ Michael Macie, Exec. Dir.; Jeffrey Nelson, Dir. Real Estate; Daniel Rancourt, Dir. Construction Services;

***Sacred Heart Catholic Parish San Diego in San Diego, CA Real Property Support Corporation** - 4776 Saratoga Ave., San Diego, CA 92107-2250 t) 619-224-2746 Rev. Thomas Kiely, Pst.;

***Saint Agnes Catholic Parish in San Diego, CA Real Property Support Corporation** - 1140 Evergreen St., San Diego, CA 92106-2533 t) 619-223-2200 Rev. Romeo Velos, C.S., Pst.;

***Saint Anne Catholic Parish in San Diego, CA Real Property Support Corporation** - 2337 Irving Ave., San Diego, CA 92113-2334 t) 619-239-8253 Rev. John Lyons, FSSP, Pst.;

***Saint Brigid Catholic Parish in San Diego, CA Real Property Support Corporation** - 4735 Cass St., San Diego, CA 92109-2698 t) 858-483-3030 Very Rev. Msgr. Steven F. Callahan, Pst.;

***Saint Catherine Laboure Catholic Parish in San Diego, CA Real Property Support Corporation** - 4124 Mt. Abraham Ave., San Diego, CA 92111-3211 t) 858-277-3133 Rev. Brian Hayes, Pst.;

***Saint Charles Borromeo Catholic Parish in San Diego, CA Real Property Support Corporation** - 2802 Cadiz St., San Diego, CA 92110-4870 t) 619-225-8157 Rev. John Amsberry, Pst.;

***Saint Charles Catholic Parish in San Diego, CA Real Property Support Corporation** - 990 Saturn Blvd., San Diego, CA 92154-2001 t) 619-423-0242 Rev. Emilio A. Magana, Pst.;

***Saint Columba Catholic Parish in San Diego, CA Real Property Support Corporation** - 3327 Glencolum Dr., San Diego, CA 92123-2369 t) 858-277-3863 Rev. Rolando Gabutera, Pst.;

***Saint Didacus Catholic Parish in San Diego, CA Real Property Support Corporation** - 4772 Felton St., San Diego, CA 92116-1824 t) 619-284-3472 www.stdidacuschurch.org Rev. Reynaldo Roque, Pst.;

***Saint John the Evangelist Catholic Parish San Diego in San Diego, CA Real Property Support Corporation** - 1638 Polk Ave., San Diego, CA 92103-2622 t) 619-291-1660 pastorcharles@sjesandiego.org www.sjesandiego.org Rev. Charles Moat Jr., SVD, Pst.;

***Saint Jude Shrine of the West Catholic Parish in San Diego, CA Real Property Support Corporation** - 1129 S. 38th St., San Diego, CA 92113-3210

***Saint Mary Magdalene Catholic Parish in San Diego, CA Real Property Support Corporation** - 1945 Illion St., San Diego, CA 92110

***Saint Michael Catholic Parish San Diego in San Diego, CA Real Property Support Corporation** - 2643 Homedale St., San Diego, CA 92139-2299 t) (619) 470-1977 stmichaelsandiego.org Rev. Manuel Ediza, Pst.; Rev. Msgr. Francisco Cinco III, Assoc. Pst.; Dcn. Gustavo Magana; Dcn. Carl Shelton;

***Saint Patrick Catholic Parish San Diego in San Diego, CA Real Property Support Corporation** - 3585 30th St., San Diego, CA 92104-4142 t) 858-490-8311 jnelson@sdcatholic.org Rev. Carlos Alberto Flores, O.S.A., Pst.;

***Saint Rita Catholic Parish in San Diego, CA Real Property Support Corporation** - 5124 Churchward St., San Diego, CA 92114-3797

***Saint Therese Catholic Parish in San Diego, CA Real Property Support Corporation** - 6400 Saint Therese Way, San Diego, CA 92120-3018

***Saint Therese of Carmel Catholic Parish in San Diego, CA Real Property Support Corporation** - 4355 Del Mar Trails Rd., San Diego, CA 92130

***Saint Vincent de Paul Catholic Parish in San Diego, CA Real Property Support Corporation** - 4077 Ibis St., San Diego, CA 92103-1899 t) 619-299-3880 office@vincentcatholic.org vincentcatholic.org Rev. Alexander De Paulis, Pst.;

***The San Diego Catholic Account for Parishes and Schools, Incorporated** - 3888 Paducah Dr., San Diego, CA 92117 t) 858-490-8200 Rev. Mark Edney, Pres.;

***San Rafael Catholic Parish in San Diego, CA Real Property Support Corporation** - 17252 Bernardo Center Dr., San Diego, CA 92128-2075

The Sisters of Nazareth of San Diego Real Estate Holdings, Inc. - 6333 Rancho Mission Rd., San Diego, CA 92108 t) 619-708-2775 srvera.chan@sistersofnazareth.us Sr. Vera Chan, Secy.;

Victoire Management Support, Inc. - 6333 Rancho Mission Rd., San Diego, CA 92108 t) 619-563-0480 Sr. Rose Hoye, Admin.;

SAN YSIDRO

***Our Lady of Mount Carmel Catholic Parish San Ysidro in San Ysidro, CA Real Property Support Corporation** - 2020 Alaquinas Dr., San Ysidro, CA 92173-2107 t) 619-428-1415 Rev. Armando P. Escurel, Pst.;

SOLANA BEACH

***Saint James Catholic Parish in Solana Beach, CA Real Property Support Corporation** - 625 S. Nardo Ave., Solana Beach, CA 92075-2398 Rev. Ricardo Antonio Chinchilla, CJM, Pst.;

SPRING VALLEY

***Santa Sophia Catholic Parish in Spring Valley, CA Real Property Support Corporation** - 9800 San Juan St., Spring Valley, CA 91977

VALLEY CENTER

***Saint Stephen Catholic Parish in Valley Center, CA Real Property Support Corporation** - 31020 Cole Grade Rd., Valley Center, CA 92082-1015; Mailing: P.O. Box 1015, Valley Center, CA 92082-1015

VISTA

***Saint Francis of Assisi Catholic Parish in Vista, CA Real Property Support Corporation** - 525 W. Vista Way, Vista, CA 92083-5974 Rev. Ruben Arceo, S.J., Pst.;

WESTMORLAND

***Saint Joseph Catholic Parish Westmorland in Westmoreland, CA Real Property Support Corporation** - 300 N. Center St., Westmorland, CA 92281-0627

MONASTERIES AND RESIDENCES FOR PRIESTS AND BROTHERS [MON]

OCEANSIDE

Old Mission San Luis Rey - 4050 Mission Ave., Oceanside, CA 92057-6402 t) 760-757-3651 gwyn@sanluisrey.org www.sanluisrey.org Franciscan Friars. Rev. Oscar Mendez, OFM, Pst.; Rev. Samuel Nasada, OFM, Assoc. Pst.; Gwyn Grimes, Exec.; Kathryn De Anda, Dir.; Danielle Napoli, Dir.; Rev. Anthony Garibaldi, O.F.M., Contact; Brs.: 17; Priests: 11

Prince of Peace Abbey - 650 Benet Hill Rd., Oceanside, CA 92058-1253 t) 760-967-4200 princeabby@aol.com; dearmonks@gmail.com princeofpeaceabbey.blogspot.com/ Benedictine Monks. Rt. Rev. Sharbel Ewen, O.S.B., Abbot; Bro. Raphael Meyer, O.S.B., Prior; Bro. Peter Aslin, O.S.B., Mem.; Bro. Joseph Black, O.S.B., Mem.; Bro. Simeon Chung, O.S.B., Mem.; Rev. Bede Clark, O.S.B., Mem.; Bro. Anselm Clark, O.S.B., Mem.; Rev. Damien Evangelista, O.S.B., Mem.; Rev. Paul Farrelly, O.S.B., Mem.; Bro. Noel Greenawalt, O.S.B., Mem.; Bro. Peter Khoa Le, O.S.B., Mem.; Bro. Agustin Lopez Gonzalez, O.S.B., Mem.; Bro. Benedict Menezes, O.S.B., Mem.; Rev. Stephanos Pedrano, O.S.B., Mem.; Rev. Michel Pham, O.S.B., Mem.; Bro. Philip Poutous, O.S.B., Mem.; Bro. Mario Quizon, O.S.B., Mem.; Bro. Daniel Sokol, O.S.B., Mem.; Bro. Meinrad Taylor, O.S.B., Mem.; Bro. Emmanuel Tran, O.S.B., Mem.; Bro. Gabriel Williams, Mem.; Rev. Charles Wright, O.S.B., Mem.; Brs.: 15; Priests: 6

SAN DIEGO

Augustinian Community - 3266 Nutmeg St., San Diego, CA 92104-5151; Mailing: 3180 University Ave., Suite 255, San Diego, CA 92104-2089 t) (619) 235-0247 osa-west@calprovince.org calaugustinians.org Rev. Sarfraz Alam, O.S.A., Mem.; Rev. Raymond Elam, O.S.A., Mem.; Rev. Carlos Alberto Flores, O.S.A., In Res.; Rev. Robert W. Gavotto, O.S.A., Mem.; Rev. Adnan Ghani, O.S.A., Treas.; Rev. John Grace, O.S.A., In Res.; Rev. Michael McFadden, O.S.A., Mem.; Bro. Mauricio Morales, O.S.A., Mem.; Bro. Arturo Renteria, O.S.A., Mem.; Rev. James Retzner, O.S.A., Prior; Rev. Gary Sanders, O.S.A., Prov.; Rev. Dominic Smith, O.S.A., Mem.; Rev. Maxime Villeneuve, O.S.A., Mem.; Brs.: 3; Priests: 29

VISTA

The Eudists - Congregation of Jesus and Mary - 1616 1/2 York Dr., Vista, CA 92084-7612; Mailing: P.O. Box

3619, Vista, CA 92085-3619 t) 209-783-8337 wfrowlandcjm@eudistsusa.org; accounting@eudistsusa.org www.eudistsusa.org Rev. Gerard Lecomte, CJM, Treas.; Priests: 8

NURSING / REHABILITATION / CONVALESCENCE / ELDERLY CARE [NUR]

SAN DIEGO

Nazareth House of San Diego, Inc. - 6333 Rancho Mission Rd., San Diego, CA 92108 t) 619-563-0480 marie@nazarethhouse.sd.org www.nazarethhouse.sd.org Retired Priests Residential and Assisted Living Sr. Marie McCormack, C.S.N., Admin.;

RETREAT HOUSES / RENEWAL CENTERS [RTR]

DESCANSO

Camp Oliver - 8761 Riverside Dr., Descanso, CA 91916; Mailing: P.O. Box 206, Descanso, CA 91916 t) 619-445-5945 info@campoliver.org www.campoliver.org Sisters of Social Service. Trista Brant, Dir.;

JULIAN

Whispering Winds Catholic Conference Center - 17606 Harrison Park Rd., Julian, CA 92036; Mailing: 4636 Mission Gorge Pl., #203, San Diego, CA 92120 t) 619-464-1479 office@whisperingwinds.org www.whisperingwinds.org Martin Rosales, Exec.;

OCEANSIDE

Old Mission San Luis Rey Retreat - 4050 Mission Ave., Oceanside, CA 92057-6402 t) 760-757-3659 x108 retreats@sanluisrey.org www.sanluisrey.org Kathryn De Anda, Dir.;

SAN DIEGO

Spiritual Ministry Center - 4822 Del Mar Ave., San Diego, CA 92107-3407 t) 619-224-9444 spiritmin@rscj.org www.spiritmin.org Bunny Flick, Contact;

SEMINARIES [SEM]

SAN DIEGO

The Roman Catholic Seminary of San Diego - 1667 Santa Paula Dr., San Diego, CA 92111 t) 619-291-7446 www.sdcatholic.org St. Francis De Sales House of Formation is a residence for both college and graduate level seminarians in the Program of Priestly Formation. Very Rev. Matthew D. Spahr, Rector; Rev. Eric Tamayo, Vice Rector; Rev. Michael Sinor, Dir. Spiritual Formation; Laura Martin-Spencer, Pst. Min./Coord.; Stds.: 12

SPECIAL CARE FACILITIES [SPF]

EL CAJON

St. Madeleine Sophie's Center - 2119 E. Madison Ave., El Cajon, CA 92019-1111 t) 619-442-5129 demerson@stmsc.org www.stmsc.org Debra Turner-Emerson, CEO; Asstd. Annu.: 600; Staff: 135

SPRING VALLEY

Noah Homes - 12526 Campo Rd., Spring Valley, CA 91978 t) 619-660-6200 m.nocon@noahhomes.org www.noahhomes.org Molly Nocon, Exec.; Bed Capacity: 90; Asstd. Annu.: 90; Staff: 130

An asterisk (*) denotes an organization that has established tax-exempt status directly with the IRS and is not covered by the USCCB Group Ruling.

Archdiocese of San Francisco

(Archidioecesis Sancti Francisci)

MOST REVEREND SALVATORE J. CORDILEONE, J.C.D.

Archbishop of San Francisco; ordained July 9, 1982; appointed Auxiliary Bishop of San Diego and Titular Bishop of Natchesium July 5, 2002; ordained August 21, 2002; appointed Bishop of Oakland March 23, 2009; installed May 5, 2009; appointed Archbishop of San Francisco July 27, 2012; installed October 4, 2012. Office: One Peter Yorke Way, San Francisco, CA 94109-6602.

The Chancery Office: One Peter Yorke Way, San Francisco, CA 94109-6602.

www.sfarch.org
info@sfarch.org

ESTABLISHED JULY 29, 1853.

Square Miles 1,016.

Code Address: Roman, San Francisco.

Comprises the Counties of San Francisco, San Mateo and Marin in the State of California.

Patrons of the Archdiocese of San Francisco: St. Francis of Assisi, October 4; St. Patrick, March 17.

Legal Title: The Roman Catholic Archbishop of San Francisco, a Corporation Sole.

For legal titles of parishes and archdiocesan institutions, consult the Chancery Office.

STATISTICAL OVERVIEW

Personnel

Archbishops	1
Retired Bishops	2
Abbots	1
Priests: Diocesan Active in Diocese	116
Priests: Diocesan Active Outside Diocese	3
Priests: Retired, Sick or Absent	66
Number of Diocesan Priests	185
Religious Priests in Diocese	149
Total Priests in your Diocese	334
Ordinations:	
Diocesan Priests	2
Religious Priests	3
Transitional Deacons	3
Permanent Deacons	9
Permanent Deacons in Diocese	114
Total Brothers	17
Total Sisters	456

Parishes

Parishes	92
With Resident Pastor:	
Resident Diocesan Priests	72
Resident Religious Priests	16
Without Resident Pastor:	
Administered by Priests	8
Professional Ministry Personnel:	
Brothers	10
Lay Ministers	141

Welfare

Catholic Hospitals	3
Total Assisted	1,800
Homes for the Aged	12
Residential Care of Children	5
Total Assisted	30
Day Care Centers	31
Total Assisted	1,500
Residential Care of Disabled	1

Educational

Seminaries, Diocesan	1
Students from This Diocese	13
Students from Other Dioceses	37
Diocesan Students in Other Seminaries	6
Total Seminarians	19
Colleges and Universities	2
Total Students	12,500
High Schools, Diocesan and Parish	4
Total Students	3,849
High Schools, Private	7
Total Students	4,100
Elementary Schools, Diocesan and Parish	47
Total Students	11,995
Elementary Schools, Private	7
Total Students	1,929
Catechesis/Religious Education:	
High School Students	1,647
Elementary Students	9,798
Total Students under Catholic Instruction	45,837
Teachers in Diocese:	
Priests	3
Brothers	3
Sisters	38
Lay Teachers	1,997

Vital Statistics

Receptions into the Church:	
Infant Baptism Totals	2,166
Minor Baptism Totals	233
Adult Baptism Totals	189
Received into Full Communion	176
First Communions	2,138
Confirmations	2,389
Marriages:	
Catholic	379
Interfaith	112
Total Marriages	491
Deaths	1,637
Total Catholic Population	472,000
Total Population	1,737,000

LEADERSHIP

Chancery and Pastoral Center - t) 415-614-5500

Office of the Archbishop -

Administrative Assistant - t) 415-614-5604 Chari Penson;

Archbishop - Most Rev. Salvatore J. Cordileone;

Executive Assistant to the Archbishop - t) 415-614-5609 Karen McLaughlin;

Censor Librorum - Rev. John S. Kselman, P.S.S.;

Chancellor - Rev. Msgr. C. Michael Padazinski (padazinskim@sfarch.org);

Deans - Rev. Thomas M. Hamilton, Sunset Deanery; Rev. Michael J. Hurley, O.P., Cathedral Deanery; Rev. Moises Agudo, Mission Deanery (agudom@sfarch.org);

Episcopal Vicar for Filipinos - t) 415-614-5590 Rev. Eugene D. Tungol (tungole@sfarch.org);

Episcopal Vicar for Spanish Speaking - t) 415-614-5591 Rev. Moises Agudo (agudom@sfarch.org);

Moderator of the Curia - Rev. Patrick J. Summerhays;

Executive Assistant - t) 415-614-5589 Diana Powell;

Office for Consecrated Life - t) 415-614-5535 Sr. Rosina Conrotto, P.B.V.M., Dir. (conrottor@sfarch.org);

Office of Diaconate Formation - t) 415-614-5615 Dcn. Fred Totah, Dir. (totahf@sfarch.org);

Office of the Permanent Diaconate - t) 415-614-5531 Dcn. Michael J. Ghiorso, Dir. (ghiorsom@sfarch.org);

Office of Vocations - Rev. Cameron M. Faller (cameron@sfarch.org); Chari Penson, Admin. Asst. (pensonc@sfarch.org);

Vicar for Administration - t) 415-614-5589 Rev. Patrick J. Summerhays, Vicar; Diana Powell, Exec. Asst. (powelld@sfarch.org);

Vicar for Clergy - Rev. Andrew P. Spyrow, Vicar (spyrow.andrew@sfarch.org);

Manager, Office of the Auxiliary Bishops, Office of the Vicar for Clergy - t) 415-614-5611 Sharon Lee; Merle Talens;

Vicar General - t) 415-614-5611 Rev. Stephen H. Howell, Vicar (howell.stephen@sfarch.org); Sharon Lee, Contact (lees@sfarch.org);

OFFICES AND DIRECTORS

Archdiocesan Archives - t) 650-328-6502 Chris Doan, Archivist;

Archdiocesan Legal Office - t) 415-614-5623 Paula F. Carney, Gen. Counsel (carneyp@sfarch.org); Larry R. Jannuzzi, Sr. Gen. Counsel (jannuzzil@sfarch.org); Philip Lam;

Catholic Cemeteries - t) 650-756-2060 Monica Williams (mjwilliams@holycrosscemeteries.com);

Department of Catholic Schools - t) 415-614-5660 dcsreception@sfarch.org www.sfdcs.org Pamela A. Lyons, Supt.; Susana Lapeyrade-Drummond, Asst. Supt.; Jonathan Schild, Asst. Supt.;

The Roman Catholic Welfare Corporation of San Francisco -

Department of Pastoral Ministry - Dcn. Fred Totah (totahf@sfarch.org);

Ministry of Consolation - t) 415-614-5547 Ed Hopfner;

Office of Ethnic Ministries -

African American Ministry - Dcn. Fred Totah, Dir.;

Arab-American Catholic Ministry - t) 415-452-9634 Rev. Richard Van De Water;

Brazilian Ministry - t) 415-452-9634; 415-454-8141 Rev. Messius Albuquerque;

Burmese Ministry - t) 415-333-3627 Rev. Francis Than Htun;

Charismatic Renewal - Rev. Raymond Reyes;

Chinese Ministry - t) 415-614-5575 Rev. Peter L. Zhai, S.V.D.;

Courage/Encourage - Rev. Anselm Ramelow, O.P.;

Cursillo Movement - Rev. Martin J. Mager, O.S.B.;

Deaf Ministry - Rev. Ghislain C. Bazikila;

Filipino Ministry - Rev. Eugene D. Tungol;

Haitian Ministry - Pierre Labossiere;

Hispanic Ministry - t) 415-824-1700 Rev. Moises Agudo;

Igbo Nigerian Ministry - t) 650-726-4674 Rev. Charles Onubogu;

Indonesian Ministry - t) 415-487-8560 Rev. Stephanus Hendrianto, S.J.;

Irish Ministry - t) 415-282-0141 Rev. Brendan McBride (Ireland), Coord.;

Italian Ministry -

Korean Catholic Ministry - t) 415-333-1194 Rev. Jeong Gon Kim;

Native American Ministry - t) 415-621-8203 Andy Galvan;

Polish, Croatian, Slovenian Mission - t) 415-252-5799 Rev. Tadeusz Rusnak, S.Ch.;

Samoan Ministry - t) 866-964-7584 Maya Suisala;

Tongan Ministry - t) 650-342-2470 Rev. Saimone Moala; Rev. Kapiolani Kakala;

Vietnamese Catholic Ministry - t) 415-387-5545 Rev. Te Van Nguyen;

Young Men's Institute - Rev. Agnel De Heredia;

Office of Faith Formation - Sr. Celeste Arbuckle, S.S.S., Dir.; Janet Fortuna, Coord. Special Needs; Anelita Reyes, Assoc. Dir. Faith Formation;

Office of Marriage and Family Life - t) 415-614-5547 Ed Hopfner, Dir.;

Office of Worship - t) 415-614-5586 Laura Bertone, Dir.;

Office of Youth & Young Adult Ministry - t) 415-614-5595 Dcn. Chris Mariano, Dir.;

Director of Stewardship - Florian Romero (romerof@sfarch.org);

Development Associate - Jenny Dahl;

Metropolitan Tribunal and Office of Canonical Affairs -

Adjutant Judicial Vicar -

Vice Chancellor and Tribunal Office Manager - Robert W. Graffio;

Defenders of the Bond - Rev. Thuan V. Hoang; Diane L. Barr; Robert W. Graffio;

Judges - Rev. Msgr. C. Michael Padazinski; Krystyna Amborski; Rev. Roy Remo;

Judicial Vicar - Rev. Msgr. Romulo A. Vergara;

Notary and Secretary to the Tribunal - Reina A. Parada;

Promoter of Justice - Rev. Thuan V. Hoang;

San Francisco Metropolitan Tribunal - t) 415-614-5690

Tribunal Auditors - Reina Parada;

Missionary Childhood Association - A Pontifical Mission Society - t) 415-614-5670 Genevieve Elizondo, Dir.;

Office for the Propagation of the Faith - A Pontifical Mission Society - t) 415-614-5673 Genevieve Elizondo, Dir.;

Office of Child and Youth Protection - Dcn. Fred Totah (totahf@sfarch.org);

Safe Environment Coordinator - t) 415-614-5576 Twyla Powers;

Victim Assistance Coordinator - t) 415-614-5506 Rocio Rodriguez;

Office of Development - t) 415-614-5580 development@sfarch.org Rod Linhares, Dir. (linharesr@sfarch.org);

Office of Ecumenism and Interreligious Affairs (Vacant) -

Office of Human Life & Dignity - t) 415-614-5570 lifeanddignity@sfarch.org www.sfarch.org/hld Valerie Schmalz;

Catholic Campaign for Human Development (CCHD) -

Gabriel Project (Pregnancy Counseling) - t) 800-910-2848

Project Rachel (Post Abortion Counseling) - t) 415-614-5567

Respect Life Program - t) 415-614-5533

Restorative Justice Program - t) 415-614-5572 Julio Escobar, Coord.;

Social Action and Digital Media - t) 415-614-5616 Melissa Vlach;

Social Action Coordinator - t) 415-614-5569 Martin Ford;

Office of Human Resources - Vicky Salgado, Dir. (salgadov@sfarch.org); Josie Berdal, Human Resources Mgr. (berdalj@sfarch.org); Christine Escobar, Human Resources Mgr. (escobarc@sfarch.org);

ADVISORY BOARDS, COMMISSIONS, COMMITTEES, AND COUNCILS

Archbishop's Cabinet - Most Rev. Salvatore J. Cordileone, Archbishop of San Francisco; Rev. Stephen H. Howell, Vicar (howell.stephen@sfarch.org); Rev. Patrick J. Summerhays, Moderator of the Curia & Vicar for Admin.;

College of Consultors - Most Rev. Salvatore J. Cordileone; Rev. Stephen H. Howell (howell.stephen@sfarch.org); Rev. Moises Agudo (agudom@sfarch.org);

Presbyteral Council - Rev. Kevin Kennedy, Chair;

COMMUNICATIONS

Department of Communications - t) 415-614-5638 Rev. Patrick J. Summerhays;

Archdiocesan Publication: "Catholic San Francisco" - t) 415-614-5647 Most Rev. Salvatore J. Cordileone, Editor;

FACILITIES

Administrative Services - t) 415-614-5532 Jose Leon, Facilities Mgr. for Pastoral Ctr.;

FINANCE

Director of Finance/Chief Financial Officer - t) 415-614-5511 Joseph Passarello (passarelloj@sfarch.org);

Executive Assistant and Payroll Coordinator - t) 415-614-5510 Siena Perez;

PARISHES, MISSIONS, AND CLERGY

STATE OF CALIFORNIA

BELMONT

Immaculate Heart of Mary - 1040 Alameda de las Pulgas, Belmont, CA 94002 t) 650-593-6157 office@ihmbelmont.org; rlang@ihmbelmont.org ihmbelmont.org Rev. Mark G. Mazza, Pst.; Rev. Gabriel Wankar, Par. Vicar; Dcn. Steven Hackett; Dcn. Henry Jacquemet; Dcn. Leon Kortenkamp; Robyn Lang, DRE; CRP Stds.: 65

Immaculate Heart of Mary School - 1000 Alameda de las Pulgas, Belmont, CA 94002 t) 650-593-4265 ihmoffice@ihmschoolbelmont.org www.ihmschoolbelmont.org Andrea Harville, Prin.; Stds.: 262; Lay Tchrs.: 25

St. Mark - 325 Marine View Ave., Belmont, CA 94002 t) 650-591-7072 (CRP); 650-591-5937 st_markschurch@yahoo.com; sm.faithform@yahoo.com www.saintmarks.us Rev. Angel N. Quitalig, Pst.; Dcn. Richard Dizon; Dcn. Gerard F. Quinn, In Res.; Edmund Ibarra, DRE;

BURLINGAME

St. Catherine of Siena - 1310 Bayswater Ave., Burlingame, CA 94010 t) 650-344-6884 stcsiena@yahoo.com stcsiena.org Rev. John A. Ryan, Pst.; Rev. Nicholas Case, Par. Vicar; Rev. Toan X. Nguyen, Par. Vicar;

St. Catherine of Siena School - (Grades K-8) 1300 Bayswater Ave., Burlingame, CA 94010 t) 650-344-7176 office@stcatherineofsiena.net www.stcos.com Patricia Bandel, Prin.; Stds.: 290; Sr. Tchrs.: 2; Lay Tchrs.: 11

Our Lady of Angels - 1721 Hillside Dr., Burlingame, CA 94010 t) 650-347-3671 (CRP); 650-347-7768 parishoffice@olaparish.org; schoolofreligion@olaparish.org ola.community Rev. Michael Mahoney, O.F.M.Cap., Pst.; Rev. James

Stump, O.F.M.Cap., Assoc. Pst.; Rev. Peter Ronald Eugenio, Assoc. Pst.; Rev. Gerald Barron, O.F.M., Cap, In Res.; Dcn. Chris Mariano; Rev. Brian McKenna, O.F.M.Cap., In Res.; Rev. Eugene M. Ludwig, O.F.M.Cap., In Res.; Johna Maychrowitz, DRE; Margaux Ty, Youth Min.; CRP Stds.: 183

Our Lady of Angels School - 1328 Cabrillo Ave., Burlingame, CA 94010 t) 650-343-9200 www.ola.community Amy Costa, Prin.; Stds.: 306; Lay Tchrs.: 15

Preschool - 1341 Cortez Ave., Burlingame, CA 94010 t) 650-343-3115 olapreschool@yahoo.com Lysette Cukar, Dir.;

COLMA

Holy Angels - 107 San Pedro Rd., Colma, CA 94014 t) (650) 488-0240 x100 holyangelsccd@hotmail.com; ning2allen@yahoo.com hacolma.org Rev. Edgardo Rodriguez, Assoc. Pst.; Rev. Alex L. Legaspi, Pst.; Rev. Antonio G. Petilla; Dcn. Joseph Ramos; CRP Stds.: 168

Holy Angels School - (Grades PreSchool-8) 20 Reiner St., Colma, CA 94014 t) 650-755-0220 srolive@holyangelscolma.org; holyangelscolma@holyangelscolma.org www.holyangelscolma.org Sr. Ma. Oliva Fuentes, O.P., Prin.; Stds.: 132; Sr. Tchrs.: 3; Lay Tchrs.: 12

DALY CITY

St. Andrew - 1571 Southgate Ave., Daly City, CA 94015 t) 650-991-2937 (CRP); 650-756-3222 noels@standrew-dalycity.org; standrew1968@att.net Dcn. Emilo V Lucero; Michele Bussey, DRE;

Our Lady of Mercy - One Elmwood Dr., Daly City, CA 94015 t) 650-992-5769 (CRP); 650-755-2727 olmcatholicchurch@gmail.com olmcath.org Rev. Domingo Orimaco, Pst.; Rev. Gabriel Wankar, Assoc. Pst.; Rev. Rey V. Culaba, C.S.S.R., In Res.; Dcn. Marcos M. Cobillas; Dcn. Michael J. Ghiorso; Sr. Concepcion CAmbaya, RVM, DRE;

Our Lady of Mercy School - 7 Elmwood Dr., Daly City, CA 94015 t) 650-756-3395 office@olmbulldogs.com www.olmbulldogs.com Jeffrey Burgos, Prin.; Stds.: 262; Lay Tchrs.: 41

Religious of the Virgin Mary, Our Lady of Mercy - 15 Elmwood Dr., Daly City, CA 94015 Sr. Maria Ruth Linaac, Contact;

Our Lady of Perpetual Help - 60 Wellington Ave., Daly City, CA 94014 t) 650-755-4010 (CRP); 650-755-9786 padre_ba@yahoo.com; olphrectory@gmail.com www.olphparishdc.org Rev. Augusto E. Villote, Pst.; Rev. Manuel D. Igrobay, Par. Vicar; Maria Aquino, Youth Min.; Maria Camua-Madayag, DRE;

Our Lady of Perpetual Help School - 80 Wellington Ave., Daly City, CA 94014 t) 650-755-4438 info@olphdc.org www.olphdc.org Katie Franco, Prin.; Stds.: 150; Lay Tchrs.: 14

EAST PALO ALTO

St. Francis of Assisi - 1425 Bay Rd., East Palo Alto, CA 94303 t) 650-325-6236 (CRP); 650-322-2152 Rev. Lawrence C. Goode, Pst.; Rev. Msgr. John R. Coleman, In Res.; Rev. Gabriel Flores, In Res.; Dcn. Louis Dixon;

FAIRFAX

St. Rita - 100 Marinda Dr., Fairfax, CA 94930 t) 415-456-4815 saintritafairfax@att.net www.saintritachurch.org Rev. Kenneth M. Weare, Pst.; CRP Stds.: 25

FOSTER CITY

St. Luke - 1111 Beach Park Blvd., Foster City, CA 94404 t) 650-574-9191 (CRP); 650-345-6660 info@saintlukefc.org saintlukefc.org/ Dcn. David Arms, NA; Rev. Alner U. Nambatac (Philippines), Admin.; Rev. Manuel D. Igrobay, Par. Vicar; Sr. Maria Ruth Linaac, DRE; Dcn. Mar Tano; CRP Stds.: 102

GREENBRAE

St. Sebastian - 373 Bon Air Rd., Greenbrae, CA 94904 t) 415-461-0704 www.sebastian94904.com Rev. William H. Thornton, Pst.; Rev. Jerry Murphy, Assoc. Pst.; Dcn. David Previtali; CRP Stds.: 33

HALF MOON BAY

Our Lady of the Pillar - 400 Church St., Half Moon Bay, CA 94019 t) 650-726-5587 (CRP); 650-726-4650 office@ourladyofthepillar.org ourladyofthepillar.org Rev. Jose M. Corral, Pst.; Rev. Maurice C Igboerika, Par. Vicar; Rev. Charles Onubogu, In Res.; Celina Rivera, RCIA Coord.; Terry Ruppel, RCIA Coord.;

St. Anthony - 696 North St., Pescadero, CA 94060 t) 650-726-4674

Our Lady of Refuge - 146 Sears Ranch Rd., La Honda, CA 94020 t) 650-747-9555

LAGUNITAS

St. Cecilia - 450 W. Cintura Ave., Lagunitas, CA 94938; Mailing: P.O. Box 289, Lagunitas, CA 94938 t) 415-488-9799 stcecilia.lagunitas@yahoo.com www.stcecilia-lagunitas.org Rev. Ngoan V. Phan, Pst.; Carol Bennetts, DRE; Margaret Farley, DRE;

St. Mary - 4100 Nicasio Valley Rd., Nicasio, CA 94946; Mailing: PO Box 289, Lagunitas, CA 94938 stmary.nicasio@yahoo.com; stmary.nicasio@gmail.com www.stmary-nicasio.org

LARKSPUR

St. Patrick - 401 Magnolia, Larkspur, CA 94939; Mailing: 114 King St., Larkspur, CA 94939 t) 415-924-0600 x15 (CRP); 415-924-0600 parish@stpatricksmarin.org; l_gramlich@stpatricksmarin.org www.stpatricksparish.com Rev. Msgr. C. Michael Padazinski, Pst.; Helena Miller-Fleig, DRE;

St. Patrick School - (Grades K-8) 120 King St., Larkspur, CA 94939 t) 415-924-0501 office@stpatricksmarin.org stpatricksmarin.org Angela Hadsell, Prin.; Stds.: 262; Lay Tchrs.: 25

MENLO PARK

St. Anthony - 3500 Middlefield Rd., Menlo Park, CA 94025 t) 650-365-6071 (CRP); 650-366-4692 stanthonycatholicparish@live.com Rev. Fabio E. Medina, Pst.; Rev. Jose Eduardo Mendoza, Assoc. Pst.; Asusena Aguilar, DRE;

San Jose Obrero - 400 Heller St., Redwood City, CA 94063 saintanthonycatholicparish@live.com

Clothing Distribution Center - t) 650-364-2556 Free clothing for men & women.

Church of the Nativity - 210 Oak Grove Ave., Menlo Park, CA 94025 t) 650-323-7914 www.nativitymenlo.org Rev. Msgr. Steven D. Otellini, Pst.; Rev. Christian Anyanwu, Par. Vicar; Dcn. Robert Andrews; Dcn. Dominick Peloso; Monica Hickam, DRE; CRP Stds.: 70

Nativity Catholic School - (Grades PreK-8) 1250 Laurel St., Menlo Park, CA 94025 t) 650-325-7304 info@nativityschool.com www.nativityschool.com Jessica Adrian, Prin.; Stds.: 235; Lay Tchrs.: 15

St. Denis - 2250 Avy Ave., Menlo Park, CA 94025 t) 650-854-5976 x102 c) 415-686-9951 wpodell@aol.com www.stdenisparish.org Rev. W. Paul O'Dell, Pst.; Lucy Soltau, DRE;

Our Lady of the Wayside - 930 Portola Rd., Portola Valley, CA 94028 Rev. Msgr. Jose A. Rodriguez, In Res.;

St. Raymond - 1100 Santa Cruz Ave., Menlo Park, CA 94025 t) 650-323-1755 office@straymondmp.org www.straymondmp.org Rev. Jerome Cudden, O.P., Pst.; Rev. John Winkowitsch, O.P., Par. Vicar; Dcn. Tom Kelly; Rev. Dominic DeLay, O.P., In Res.; Rev. Xavier M. Lavagetto, O.P., In Res.; Rev. Corwin Low, O.P., In Res.; Rev. Reginald Martin, O.P., In Res.; Rev. Patrick O'Neil, O.P., In Res.; Bro. Anthony Maria Akerman, In Res.;

St. Raymond School - (Grades PreK-8) 1211 Arbor Rd., Menlo Park, CA 94025 t) 650-322-2312 www.straymond.org Valerie Mattei, Prin.; Stds.: 259; Sr. Tchrs.: 1; Lay Tchrs.: 25

MILL VALLEY

Our Lady of Mt. Carmel - 3 Oakdale Ave., Mill Valley, CA 94941 t) 415-388-4190; 415-388-1008 (CRP) officeolmc@gmail.com; ffolmcmv@gmail.com www.mountcarmelmv.org Rev. Patrick T. Michaels, Pst.; Emmanuel Orjuela, Liturgy Dir.; Iris Flores, DRE;

MILLBRAE

St. Dunstan - 1133 Broadway, Millbrae, CA 94030 t) 650-697-7451 (CRP); 650-697-4730 glynn.joseph@sfarch.org; stdunstanccd@att.net saintdunstanchurch.org Rev. Thomas Basquel, C.S.Sp, Assoc. Pst.; Rev. Diarmuid C. Casey, C.S.Sp., In Res.; Rev. Alwyn Furtado, C.S.Sp., In Res.; Dcn. Richard Cepriano; Rev. Joseph Glynn, C.S.Sp., Pst.; Sherre Leone, DRE;

St. Dunstan School - (Grades PreK-8) 1150 Magnolia Ave., Millbrae, CA 94030 t) 650-697-8119 lsandoval@st-dunstan.org st-dunstan.org Dr. Laura Sandoval, Prin.; Stds.: 221; Lay Tchrs.: 12

NOVATO

St. Anthony of Padua - 1000 Cambridge St., Novato, CA 94947 t) 415-883-2177 felix_lim@yahoo.com www.stanthonynovato.org Rev. Felix Lim, Pst.; Dcn. Joseph Brumbaugh;

Our Lady of Loretto - 1806 Novato Blvd., Novato, CA 94947 t) 415-897-6714 (CRP); 415-897-2171 church@ollnovato.org; amy@ollnovato.org www.ollnovato.org Rev. Tony S. Vallecillo, Pst.; Annie Troy, Youth Min.; Amy Bjorklund Reeder, DRE;

Our Lady of Loretto School - (Grades PreK-8) 1811 Virginia Ave., Novato, CA 94945 t) 415-892-8621 school.ollnovato.org Stds.: 182; Lay Tchrs.: 13

OLEMA

Sacred Heart - 10189 State Rte. 1, Olema, CA 94950; Mailing: P.O. Box 70, Olema, CA 94950 t) 415-663-1139 arauz.erick@sfarch.org; sacredheart@horizoncable.com Rev. Erick E. Arauz, Pst.; Lourdes Romo, DRE;

St. Mary Magdalene - 16 Horseshoe Hill, Bolinas, CA 94924 Rev. Jose Shaji, Pst.;

PACIFICA

Good Shepherd - 901 Oceana Blvd., Pacifica, CA 94044 t) 650-355-2593 good.shepherd.pac@sbcglobal.net www.gschurchca.org Rev. Suan Charito, Pst.; Dcn. Joseph LeBlanc;

Good Shepherd School - (Grades PreK-8) 909 Oceana Blvd., Pacifica, CA 94044 t) 650-359-4544 gss.office@goodshepherdschool.us; g.torres@goodshepherdschool.us goodshepherdschool.us Gustavo Torres, Prin.; Stds.: 165; Lay Tchrs.: 10

St. Peter - 700 Oddstad Blvd., Pacifica, CA 94044 t) 650-359-5000 (CRP); 650-359-6313 strhilda@gmail.com; stpeterpacifica@comcast.net stpeterpacifica.org Rev. Jerome P. Foley, Pst.; Sr. Hilda Sandoval, M.F.P., DRE; CRP Stds.: 124

PORTOLA VALLEY

Our Lady of the Wayside - 930 Portola Rd., Portola Valley, CA 94028 See St. Denis, Menlo Park. Rev. Paul O'Dell, Pst.;

REDWOOD CITY

St. Matthias - 1685 Cordilleras Rd., Redwood City, CA 94062 t) 650-366-9544 info@stmatthiasparish.org www.stmatthiasparish.org Rev. David A. Ghiorso, Pst.; Rev. Samuel Musiimenta, Par. Vicar; Dcn. Richard P. Foley; Dcn. David Rolandelli; CRP Stds.: 35

St. Matthias Preschool - 533 Canyon Rd., Redwood City, CA 94062 t) 650-367-1320 Rosemary Juarez, Dir.;

Our Lady of Mount Carmel - 300 Fulton St., Redwood City, CA 94062 t) 650-368-8237 (CRP); 650-366-3803 parish@mountcarmel.org; mhernandez@mountcarmel.org Rev. Msgr. Romulo A. Vergara, Pst.; Rev. Ian Quito, Assoc. Pst.; Dcn. Thomas J. Boyle; Dcn. Raymond L. Smith; Magdalena Hernandez, DRE;

Our Lady of Mount Carmel School - 301 Grand St., Redwood City, CA 94062 t) 650-366-6127 schoolinfo@mountcarmel.org school.mountcarmel.org Jennifer Bruzzone, Prin.; Stds.: 261; Lay Tchrs.: 11

St. Pius - 1100 Woodside Rd., Redwood City, CA 94061 t) 650-361-1411 www.pius.org Rev. Antonio de Guzman Jr., Par. Vicar; Rev. Thomas V. Martin, Pst.;

St. Pius School - t) 650-368-8327 principal@stpiusschool.org stpiusschool.org James Brandt, Prin.; Stds.: 209; Lay Tchrs.: 12

ROSS

St. Anselm - 97 Shady Ln., Ross, CA 94957; Mailing: P.O. Box 1061, Ross, CA 94957-1061 t) 415-453-2342 info@saintanselm.org www.saintanselm.org Rev. William E. Brown, Pst.; Dcn. Edward Cunningham; Dcn. Robert Yee Meave; Dcn. Bernard O'Halloran; Daniel Joseph Veto, DRE; CRP Stds.: 56

St. Anselm School - (Grades K-8) 40 Belle Ave., San Anselmo, CA 94960 t) 415-454-8667 stanselmschool.com Kim Orendorff, Prin.; Stds.: 269; Lay Tchrs.: 15

SAN BRUNO

St. Bruno - 555 San Bruno Ave. W., San Bruno, CA 94066 t) 650-588-2121 x114 (CRP); 650-588-2121 religioused@saintbrunos.org Rev. Michael Brillantes, Pst.; Kacey Carey, DRE;

St. Robert - 1380 Crystal Springs Rd., San Bruno, CA 94066 t) 650-588-0477 (CRP); 650-589-2800 reception@saintroberts.org; saintrobertsccd@gmail.com Rev. Arnold Zamora, Pst.; Dcn. John Meyer; Leslie Fong, DRE;

St. Robert School - 345 Oak Ave., San Bruno, CA 94066 t) 650-583-5065 saintrobert-school.org Patrick Sullivan, Prin.; Stds.: 303; Lay Tchrs.: 14

SAN CARLOS

St. Charles - 880 Tamarack Ave., San Carlos, CA 94070 t) 650-591-7349 parishoffice@stcharlesparish.org www.stcharlesparish.org Rev. David A. Ghiorso, Pst.; Rev. Samuel Musiimenta, Par. Vicar; Dcn. Ernie von Emster; Alison Spong, DRE;

St. Charles School - (Grades K-8) 850 Tamarack Ave., San Carlos, CA 94070 t) 650-593-1629 marmando@stcharlesschoolsc.org stcharlesschoolsc.org Megan Armando, Prin.; Stds.: 269; Lay Tchrs.: 29

SAN FRANCISCO

Cathedral of St. Mary (Assumption) - 1111 Gough St., San Francisco, CA 94109 t) 415-567-2020; 415-567-2020 (CRP) info@smcsf.org www.smcsf.org Rev. Kevin Kennedy, Pst.; Rev. Jerald Geronimo, Par. Vicar; Dcn. R. Christoph Sandoval; Rev. Patrick J. Summerhays, In Res.; CRP Stds.: 82

St. Agnes - 1025 Masonic Ave., San Francisco, CA 94117 t) 415-487-8560 admin@saintagnessf.com; maureen@saintagnessf.org www.saintagnessf.org Rev. George T. Williams, S.J., Pst.; Rev. O. Alejandro Baez, S.J., Assoc. Pst.; Sr. Julia Prinz, VDMF, DRE; Sr. Teresa Malave, VDMF, CRE; Frank Uranich, Liturgy Dir.; Maureen Beckman, Bus. Mgr.;

St. Anne - 850 Judah St., San Francisco, CA 94122 t) 415-665-1600 x38 (CRE); 415-665-1600 x22 info@stanne-sf.org; tessievelicaria@stanne-sf.org www.stanne-sf.org Rev. Peter L. Zhai, S.V.D., In Res.; Rev. Daniel Nascimento, Pst.; Rachel Gee, CRE; CRP Stds.: 35

St. Anne School - (Grades PreK-8) 1320 14th Ave., San Francisco, CA 94122 t) 415-664-7977 white@stanne.com www.stanne.com Thomas C. White, Prin.; Stds.: 290; Lay Tchrs.: 27

St. Anthony of Padua - 3215 Cesar Chavez St., San Francisco, CA 94110 t) 415-647-2704 www.missionparishes.com Rev. Moises R. Agudo, Pst.;

Immaculate Conception Chapel - 3255 Folsom St., San Francisco, CA 94110 Rev. Moises Agudo, Pst.;

St. Anthony-Immaculate Conception School - (Grades K-8) 299 Precita Ave., San Francisco, CA 94110 t) 415-648-2008 Barbara Moodie, Prin.; Stds.: 239; Lay Tchrs.: 9

St. Benedict Parish at St. Francis Xavier Church - 1801 Octavia, San Francisco, CA 94109 t) 415-567-9855; 415-255-5837 (Video -Pastor); 415-255-5768 (Video - Office) www.sfdeafcatholics.org (Founded 1962 for Deaf and Hard of Hearing). Rev. Paul Zirimenya, Pst.;

St. Boniface - 133 Golden Gate Ave., San Francisco, CA 94102 t) 415-863-7515 www.saintbonifacesf.org Rev. Thomas B. West, OFM, Pst.; Bro. Raul Diaz, OFM, In Res.; Rev. David Gaa, OFM, In Res.; Rev. John Luat Nguyen, O.F.M., In Res.; Bro. Martin Sanabria, OFM, In Res.; Bro. Dick Tandy, O.F.M., In Res.; Rev. Hoang T. Trinh, O.F.M., In Res.; Bro. Brian Trawick, OFM, Admin.;

Saint Brendan the Navigator Church - 29 Rockaway Ave., San Francisco, CA 94127 t) 415-681-4225 saintbrendanchurchsf@gmail.com www.stbrendanparish.org Rev. Michael F. Quinn, Pst.; Rev. Celestine Tyowua, Assoc. Pst.; Rev. Raymond Tyochemba, In Res.; Rev. Paul F. Warren, In Res.;

St. Brendan School - (Grades K-8) 940 Laguna Honda Blvd., San Francisco, CA 94127-1239 t) 415-731-2665 sbs@stbrendansf.com www.stbrendansf.com Stds.: 286; Lay Tchrs.: 16

St. Cecilia - 2555 17th Ave., San Francisco, CA 94116 t) 415-664-8481 www.stcecilia.com Rev. Rene R. Ramoso, Pst.; Rev. Sebastine Tor Orya Bula, V.C., Assoc. Pst.; Dcn. J. Rory Desmond; Rev. Paul Arnoult, In Res.; Rev. Lodovico Joseph Landi, In Res.;

St. Cecilia School - (Grades PreK-8) 660 Vicente St., San Francisco, CA 94116 t) 415-731-8400 office@stceciliaschool.org www.stceciliaschool.org Laura M Held, Prin.; Stds.: 514; Lay Tchrs.: 26

St. Charles Borromeo - 713 S. Van Ness Ave., San Francisco, CA 94110 t) 415-824-1700 www.stcharleschurchsf.com Rev. Moises Agudo, Admin.; Dcn. Juan Michel;

Church of the Epiphany - 827 Vienna St., San Francisco, CA 94112 t) 415-333-7630 x15 (CRP); 415-333-7630 tungol.eugene@sfarch.org; jpedroza@epiphanysf.com www.epiphanysf.com Rev. Eugene D. Tungol, Pst.; Rev. Michael P. Rocha, Par. Vicar; Dcn. Ven Garcia; Rev. Rolando A. Caverte, In Res.; Oliver Meneses, DRE;

School of the Epiphany - (Grades PreK-8) 600 Italy Ave., San Francisco, CA 94112 t) 415-337-4030 info@sfepiphany.org www.sfepiphany.org Brian Joost, Prin.; Stds.: 162; Lay Tchrs.: 15

Corpus Christi - 62 Santa Rosa Ave., San Francisco, CA 94112 t) 415-585-2991 thodukulam.thomas@sfarch.org; corpuschristisfo@gmail.com Rev. Thomas Anthony Thodukulan, S.D.B., Pst.; Rev. Edward Liptak, S.D.B., Assoc. Pst.; Rev. Jesse Montes, Assoc. Pst.; Rev. Aloysius J. Pestun, S.D.B., In Res.; Dcn. Mynor Montepeque; Dcn. Alvaro Ortega; Sr. Elizabeth Villanueva, F.M.A., DRE;

St. Dominic's Catholic Church - 2390 Bush St., San Francisco, CA 94115 t) 415-567-7824; 415-567-7824 x111 (CRP) info@stdominics.org; kathy@stdominics.org www.stdominics.org Rev. Michael J. Hurley, O.P., Pst.; Rev. Vincent Kelber, OP, Assoc. Pst.; Rev. Christopher Wetzel, O.P., Assoc. Pst.; Dcn. Charles McNeil; Dcn. Dino Ornido; Dcn. Dan Rosen; Dcn. Jimmy Salcido; CRP Stds.: 150

St. Elizabeth - 449 Holyoke St., San Francisco, CA 94134 t) 415-468-0820 Laurrie Digneo, CRE; Rev. Charles Puthota, Pst.; CRP Stds.: 24

St. Emydius - 286 Ashton Ave., San Francisco, CA 94112 t) 415-587-7066; 415-587-0407 stemydius@stemydius.church www.stemydiussf.org Rev. William J. Brady, Pst.; Rev. David M. Pettingill, In Res.;

St. Finn Barr - 415 Edna St., San Francisco, CA 94112 t) 415-333-3627 juliet@stfinnbarr.org; secretary@sfbsf.org sfbsf.org Rev. Raymond D. Tyohemba, VC, Admin.; Rev. William H. McCain, Pst.; Juliet Samonte, DRE; CRP Stds.: 7

St. Finn Barr School - (Grades K-8) 419 Hearst Ave., San Francisco, CA 94112 t) 415-333-1800 m.mortonson@stfinnbarr.org www.stfinnbarr.org Megan Kimble, Prin.; Stds.: 236; Lay Tchrs.: 25

St. Francis of Assisi, National Shrine - 610 Vallejo St., San Francisco, CA 94133 t) 415-986-4557 frjohn@shrinesf.org Rev. John DeLaRiva, O.F.M.Cap., Rector;

St. Gabriel - 2559 40th Ave., San Francisco, CA 94116 t) 415-731-6161 secretary@sgparish.org; youthminister@sgparish.org Rev. Thomas M. Hamilton, Pst.; Dcn. John Hurst; Rev. Ernesto M. Jandonero, In Res.; Rev. Andrew P. Spyrow, In Res.; Rev. Zacharias (Freddie) Thomas, In Res.; Rev. Paul Zirimenya, In Res.; Nancy Becerra, DRE;

St. Gabriel School - 2550 41st Ave., San Francisco, CA 94116 t) 415-566-0314 office@stgabrielsf.com www.stgabrielsf.com Gina Beal, Prin.; Stds.: 452; Lay Tchrs.: 25

Holy Family Chinese Mission (St. Mary's Chinese Catholic Center) - 660 California St., San Francisco, CA 94108

Holy Name of Jesus - 1555 39th Ave., San Francisco, CA 94122 t) 415-664-8590 hnparishsecretary@gmail.com holynamesf.org Rev. Allan Roy Remo; Sr. Cristina Ovejera, DRE; CRP Stds.: 8

Holy Name School - (Grades PreSchool-8) 1560 40th Ave., San Francisco, CA 94122 t) 415-731-4077 www.holynamesf.com Michael Miller, Prin.; Stds.: 366; Lay Tchrs.: 13

St. Ignatius - 650 Parker Ave., San Francisco, CA 94118 t) 415-422-2188 gbonfiglio@usfca.edu; info@stignatiussf.org stignatiussf.org Rev. Gregory R. Bonfiglio, S.J., Pst.; Rev. Paul D. Devot, S.J., Assoc. Pst.; Rev. John D. Whitney, S.J., Assoc. Pst.; Dcn. Eddy Gutierrez; Lisa Freese, DRE; Maggie Warner, Dir. Liturgy & Music; CRP Stds.: 94

St. James - 1086 Guerrero St., San Francisco, CA 94110 t) 415-824-4233 (CRP); 415-824-4232 Rev. Mario P. Farana, Pst.; Rev. Shouraiah Pudota, Pst.; Rev. Ulysses L. D'Aquila, In Res.; Rev. Raymond Tyohemba, In Res.;

St. James School - 321 Fair Oaks St., San Francisco, CA 94110 t) 415-647-8972 www.saintjamessf.org Alex Endo, Prin.; Stds.: 136; Lay Tchrs.: 12

Dominican Sisters of Mission San Jose - 1212 Guerrero St., San Francisco, CA 94110 t) 415-824-2052 ica@icaacademy.org Lisa Graham, Prin.;

St. John of God - 1290 Fifth Ave., San Francisco, CA 94122 t) 415-566-5610 stjohnofgod-sf@sbcglobal.net; torreano82@gmail.com www.sjog.net Rev. Narcis L. Kabipi, Admin.; Beverlie Leano-Torres, DRE;

St. John the Evangelist - 19 St. Mary's Ave., San Francisco, CA 94112-1098 t) 415-334-4646 saintjohnevangelist@yahoo.com; fragnel55@gmail.com www.saintjohnevangelist.org Rev. Agnel De Heredia, Pst.; Rodrigo Castillo, DRE; CRP Stds.: 65

St. John School - 925 Chenery St., San Francisco, CA 94131 t) 415-584-8383 principalsj@stjohnseagles.com www.stjohnseagles.com Alexandra Iwaszewicz, Prin.; Stds.: 147; Lay Tchrs.: 10

St. Kevin - 704 Cortland Ave., San Francisco, CA 94110 t) 415-648-5751 stkevin100@gmail.com www.stkevinsf.org Rev. Miguel A Ruiz, SVD, Pst.;

St. Michael Korean Catholic Church - 32 Broad St., San Francisco, CA 94112 t) 415-333-1194 stmichaelinfo@gmail.com Rev. Youngsaeng Goo (Korea), Pst.; Evonne Kim, Admin.; Jihyeon Rim, Youth Min.; CRP Stds.: 40

Mission Dolores Basilica - 3321 16th St., San Francisco, CA 94114 t) 415-621-8203 parish@missiondolores.org; nicaroses31@gmail.com (Mission San Francisco de Asis), Rev. Francis M.P. Garbo (Philippines), Pst.; Dcn. Vicente Cervantes; Dcn. Mario Zuniga; Jerome Lenk, Liturgy Dir.; Maria Rosales-Uribe, DRE;

St. Monica - St. Thomas the Apostle Parish - 470 24th Ave., San Francisco, CA 94121 t) 415-751-5275; 415-387-5545 monicarectory@sbcglobal.net smstaparishsf.org Rev. Andrew P. Spyrow, Admin.; Rev. Michael P. Rocha, Par. Vicar; Dcn. Kyrill Bruce E. Pagacz; Dcn. Peter Solan; Rev. Paulinus Iwuji, In Res.; Rev. Te Van Nguyen, In Res.; Sr. Noreen O'Connor, C.S.J., DRE; CRP Stds.: 12

St. Monica School - 5950 Geary Blvd., San Francisco, CA 94121 t) 415-751-9564 office@stmonicasf.org stmonicasf.org Vincent Sweeters, Prin.; Stds.: 190; Lay Tchrs.: 12

St. Thomas the Apostle Church - 3835 Balboa St., San Francisco, CA 94121 stthomasapostlechurchsf@gmail.com (Worship Site)

St. Thomas the Apostle School - 3801 Balboa St., San Francisco, CA 94121 t) 415-221-2711 info@sfsta.org Stds.: 100; Lay Tchrs.: 20

Most Holy Redeemer - 100 Diamond St., San Francisco, CA 94114-2414 t) 415-863-6259; 415-863-6259 (CRP) mhr-admin@mhr.org www.mhr.org Rev. Matthew B. Link, C.PP.S., Pst.; Michael Poma, Bus. Mgr.;

Nativity - 245 Linden St., San Francisco, CA 94102 t) 415-252-5799; 415-252-5799 (CRP) Rev. Eugemoisz Bolda, SChr, Pst.; Rev. Tadeusz Rusnak, S. Ch., Pst.;

Notre Dame des Victoires - 566 Bush St., San Francisco, CA 94108 t) 415-397-0113 ndvsf.org Rev. Juan Gonzalez, S.M., Pst.; Rev. Joseph McLaughlin, S.M., Par. Vicar; Christopher Hewitt, Music Min.; Miriam Kane, Music Min.; Lupe Gil Kaatz, RCIA Coord.; Daniel Kaatz, RCIA Coord.;

Notre Dame des Victoires School - (Grades K-8) 659 Pine St., San Francisco, CA 94108 t) 415-421-0069 office@ndvsf.org Stds.: 270; Lay Tchrs.: 26

Old St. Mary's Cathedral & Chinese Mission - 660 California St., San Francisco, CA 94108 t) 415-288-3800 frjohn@oldsaintmarys.org; frjoe@oldsaintmarys.org www.oldsaintmarys.org Rev. John B Ardis, CSP, Pst.; Rev. Joseph Scott, C.S.P., Assoc. Pst.; Rev. Thomas A. Tavella, C.S.P., Assoc. Pst.; Rev. Richard Chilson, C.S.P., In Res.; Rev. Michael Evernden, C.S.P., In Res.; Rev. Thomas F. Foley, C.S.P., In Res.; Rev. John E. Hurley, C.S.P., In Res.; Rev. Bartholomew K. Landry, C.S.P., In Res.; Rev. Terrance Ryan, C.S.P., In Res.; Dcn. Simon Tsui, Pst. Assoc.;

St. Mary School & Chinese Catholic Center - (Grades PreK-PreK) 836 Kearny St., San Francisco, CA 94108 t) 415-929-4690 www.stmaryschoolsf.org

Chinese Language School - 838 Kearny St., San Francisco, CA 94108 t) 415-929-4694

Holy Family Association - t) 415-929-4696 info@oldsaintmarys.org

Holy Family Chinese Mission - info@oldsaintmarys.org

Our Lady of Fatima Byzantine Catholic Church - 5920 Geary Blvd., San Francisco, CA 94121 t) 415-752-2052 www.byzantinecatholic.org Rev. Kevin Kennedy, Pst.; Dcn. Kyrill Bruce E. Pagacz;

Our Lady of Lourdes - 1715 Oakdale Ave., San Francisco, CA 94124 t) 415-285-3377 Rev. Chinonso Okoroichi, Par. Vicar; Rev. Andrew Ibegbulem, OSA, Admin.; Sr. Eva Camberos, M.F.P., DRE; Patricia Mann, DRE;

All Hallows Chapel - 1440 Newhall St., San Francisco, CA 94124 ollsanfran@aol.com Rev. Daniel E. Carter, Pst.;

St. Patrick - 756 Mission St., San Francisco, CA 94103 t) 415-421-3730 information@stpatricksf.org www.stpatricksf.org Rev. Roberto A. Andrey, Pst.; Rev. Raphael L. Laizer, In Res.; Dcn. Ferdinand Mariano; Nenette Murata, DRE;

St. Paul - 221 Valley St., San Francisco, CA 94131 t) 415-648-7538 stpaulssf@gmail.com; lmiller@sfpaulsf.org www.stpaulsf.org/ Rev. Mario P. Farana, Pst.; Rev. James Liebner, Pst. Assoc.; Dorothy Vigna, DRE;

St. Paul Littlest Angel Pre-School - 221 Valley St., Ste. X, San Francisco, CA 94131 t) 415-824-5437 littlestangelpreschool@gmail.com Tina Baluyut, Prin.;

St. Paul School - 1690 Church St., San Francisco, CA 94131 t) 415-648-2055 info@stpaulsf.net Jacqueline Curran, Prin.; Stds.: 162; Lay Tchrs.: 10

Novitiate of the Missionaries of Charity - 312 29th St., San Francisco, CA 94131 t) 415-647-1889 Sr. Rosina Conrotto, PBVM, Contact;

St. Paul of the Shipwreck - 1122 Jamestown Ave., San Francisco, CA 94124 t) 415-468-3434 spswoffice@aol.com; office@stpauloftheshipwreck.org www.stpauloftheshipwreck.org Rev. Andrew Ibegbulem, OSA, Admin.; Rev. Chinonso Okoroichi, Par. Vicar; Dcn. Larry Chatmon; Dcn. Sergio Gomez; Sr. Estela Martinez Padilla, M.F.P., Pst. Assoc.; Patricia Mann, DRE;

St. Peter - 1200 Florida St., San Francisco, CA 94110 t) 415-282-1652 www.stpetersf.com Rev. Moises Agudo, Pst.; Rev. Msgr. Jose A. Rodriguez;

St. Peter School - (Grades K-8) 1266 Florida St., San Francisco, CA 94110 t) 415-647-8662 info@sanpedro.org www.stpeterssf.org Sandra Jimenez, Prin.; Stds.: 183; Lay Tchrs.: 12

SS. Peter and Paul - 666 Filbert St, San Francisco, CA 94133 t) 415-421-0809 www.salesiansspp.org Rev. Tho Bui, S.D.B., Pst.; Rev. Albert Mengon, S.D.B., Par. Vicar; Ernest Martinez, In Res.; Rev. Armand Oliveri, S.D.B., In Res.; Bro. Quang Nguyen, In Res.; Dcn. Edward Te, DRE; CRP Stds.: 170

Saints Peter and Paul School - (Grades PreK-8) 660 Filbert St., San Francisco, CA 94133 t) 415-421-5219 lharris@sspeterpaulsf.org sspeterpaulsf.org Lisa Harris, Prin.; Stds.: 158; Lay Tchrs.: 18

St. Philip the Apostle - 725 Diamond St., San Francisco, CA 94114 t) 415-282-0141 info@saintphilipparish.org www.saintphilipparish.org Rev. James Liebner, Par. Vicar; Rev. Brendan McBride (Ireland), In Res.;

St. Philip the Apostle School - (Grades PreK-8) 665 Elizabeth St., San Francisco, CA 94114 t) 415-824-8467 info@saintphilipschool.org www.saintphilipschool.org Mary McKeever, Prin.; Stds.: 223; Lay Tchrs.: 25

Star of the Sea - 4420 Geary Blvd., San Francisco, CA 94118 t) 415-751-0450 x22 (CRP); 415-751-0450 admin@starparish.com; fr.illo@starparish.com starparish.com Rev. Joseph Illo, Pst.; Rev. Michael J. Konopik, Par. Vicar; Rev. Mark V. Taheny, Par. Vicar; Rev. Mathias Wambua, In Res.; Clarisse Siu, Dir.;

Star of the Sea Preschool - 360 9th Ave., San Francisco, CA 94118 info@starparish.com

Stella Maris Academy - -8) 360 9th Ave, San Francisco, CA 94118 t) 415-745-2474 info@stellamarissf.org www.stellamarissf.org/ Gavin T Colvert, Prin.; Stds.: 53; Lay Tchrs.: 10

St. Stephen - 601 Eucalyptus Dr., San Francisco, CA 94132; Mailing: 451 Eucalyptus Dr., San Francisco, CA 94132-1526 t) 415-681-2444 x1; 415-681-2444 x4 (CRP) info@saintstephensf.org; faithformation@saintstephensf.org www.saintstephensf.org Rev. Michael Liliedahl, Pst.; Dcn. Manuel Abad; Rev. Cameron M. Faller, In Res.; Rev. Michael J. Healy, In Res.; Mary Molly Mullaney, DRE; Carol Cagalingan, Parish Mgr.;

St. Stephen School - 401 Eucalyptus Dr., San Francisco, CA 94132 t) 415-664-8331 office@sfststephenschool.org ststephenschoolsf.org Sharon McCarthy Allen, Prin.; Stds.: 293; Lay Tchrs.: 11

St. Teresa - 1490 19th St., San Francisco, CA 94107; Mailing: 390 Missouri St., San Francisco, CA 94107-2820 t) 415-285-5272 info@stteresasf.org www.stteresasf.org/ Rev. Michael A. Greenwell, O.Carm., Pst.; Rev. Michael E. Kwiecien, O.Carm., Assoc. Pst.; Dcn. Martin Schurr; Anna Rose Schelstrate, DRE; CRP Stds.: 20

St. Thomas More - 1300 Junipero Serra Blvd., San Francisco, CA 94132 t) 415-452-9634 vandewaterrick@yahoo.com; stmchurch2002@aol.com Rev. Richard Van De Water, Admin.; Dcn. Khaled Abu-Alshaer; Dcn. Arthur Sanchez; Dcn. Beda Abdon Nepomuceno;

St. Vincent de Paul - 2320 Green St., San Francisco, CA 94123 t) 415-922-1010 kmartin@svdpsf.com svdpsf.org Rev. Michael J. Healy, Admin.; Rev. Stephen Idoko, Par. Vicar; Rev. Michael Strange, P.S.S., In Res.;

St. Vincent de Paul School - (Grades K-8) 2350 Green St., San Francisco, CA 94123 t) 415-346-5505 administration@svdpsf.com svdpsf.com Marguerite Pini, Prin.; Stds.: 205; Lay Tchrs.: 15

Visitacion, Church of the - 655 Sunnydale Ave., San Francisco, CA 94134 t) 415-494-5517 c) 415-342-7289 info@visitacionchurch.org; vcalalo13@gmail.com www.visitacionchurch.org Rev. Thuan V. Hoang, Pst.; Rev. Victorio R. Balagapo, In Res.; Rev. Cameron M. Faller, In Res.;

Our Lady of the Visitacion - (Grades K-8) 785 Sunnydale Ave., San Francisco, CA 94134 t) 415-239-7840 ldeguzman@olvsf.org; pkeeley@olvsf.org www.olvsf.org Lara de Guzman, Prin.; Stds.: 237; Lay Tchrs.: 12

Our Lady of Guadalupe - 285 Alvarado St., Brisbane, CA 94005; Mailing: 655 Sunnydale Ave., San Francisco, CA 94134 t) 415-467-9727 www.visitacionchurch.org/olg-mission

SAN MATEO

St. Bartholomew - 600 Columbia Dr., San Mateo, CA 94402 t) 650-347-0701 stbarts@barts.org Rev. Arsenio G. Cirera, Pst.; Rev. Jose Shaji, Assoc. Pst.; Joseph Tolentino, Youth Min.; Rachel Smit, DRE;

St. Gregory - 2715 Hacienda St., San Mateo, CA 94403 t) 650-345-8506; 650-574-8716 (CRP) info@stgregs-sanmateo.org; re@stgregs-sanmateo.org saintgregorychurch.org Rev. V. Mark P. Reburiano, Pst.; Rev. Oliver U. Ortese, Par. Vicar; Dcn. Salvatore Campagna Jr.; Remee Vargas, DRE;

St. Gregory School - (Grades K-8) 2701 Hacienda St., San Mateo, CA 94403 t) 650-573-0111 office@stgregs-sanmateo.org stgregs-sanmateo.org Johanna McCormack, Prin.; Stds.: 293; Lay Tchrs.: 14

St. Matthew - One Notre Dame Ave., San Mateo, CA 94402 t) 650-344-7622 parish@stmatthewcath.org www.stmatthew-parish.org Rev. Jorge Eduardo Arias Salazar, Par. Vicar; Rev. Rufino J.O. Gepiga, Par. Vicar; Rev. Msgr. John J. Talesfore, Pst.; Rev. Benjamin Rosado, Par. Vicar; Most Rev. William J. Justice, In Res.; Teresita Contreras, Pst. Assoc.; CRP Stds.: 3

St. Matthew School - (Grades K-8) 910 S. El Camino Real, San Mateo, CA 94402 t) 650-343-1373 office@stmatthewcath.org www.stmatthewcath.org Marc Nava, Prin.; Stds.: 614; Lay Tchrs.: 26

St. Timothy - 1515 Dolan Ave., San Mateo, CA 94401 t) 650-579-0901 (CRP); 650-342-2468 information@sttims.us www.sttims.us Rev. Alner U. Nambatac (Philippines), Pst.; Rev. Manuel D. Igrobay, Par. Vicar; Rev. Kapiolani Kakala, In Res.; Dcn. Faiva Po'oi; Dcn. Fred Totah; CRP Stds.: 86

St. Timothy School - t) 650-342-6567 www.sttimothyschool.org Stds.: 174; Lay Tchrs.: 11

SAN RAFAEL

St. Isabella - 1 Trinity Way, San Rafael, CA 94903; Mailing: P.O. Box 6166, San Rafael, CA 94903 t) 415-479-1560 therese@stisabellasparish.org; office@stisabellasparish.org www.stisabellasparish.org Rev. Cyril J. O'Sullivan, Pst.; Rev. Ephrem R. Tillya, Par. Vicar; Dcn. Graham Cumming; Rev. Cornelius J. Healy, In Res.;

St. Isabella School - (Grades K-8) t) 415-479-3727 rpheatt@stisabellaschool.org www.stisabellaschool.org Rob Pheatt, Prin.; Stds.: 233; Lay Tchrs.: 12

St. Raphael - 1104 Fifth Ave., San Rafael, CA 94901 t) 415-459-7331 (CRP); 415-454-8141 kaguilar@saintraphael.com; mgarza@saintraphael.com www.saintraphael.com Rev. Luello N. Palacpac (Philippines), Pst.; Rev. Kyle J. Faller, Assoc. Pst.; Rev. Santos Rodriguez, Assoc. Pst.; Dcn. David Bernstein; Dcn. Jose Hernandez; Dcn. Eugene B. Smith; Miguel Garza, DRE; Catherine Wright, RCIA Coord.;

St. Raphael School - (Grades PreSchool-8) 1100 Fifth Ave., San Rafael, CA 94901 t) 415-454-4455 office@straphaelschool.com www.straphaelschool.com Lydia Collins, Prin.; Stds.: 179; Lay Tchrs.: 19

St. Sylvester - 1115 Point San Pedro Rd., San Rafael, CA 94901

SAUSALITO

St. Mary Star of the Sea - 180 Harrison Ave., Sausalito, CA 94965 t) 415-332-1765 reled@starofthesea.us; frmike@starofthesea.us Rev. Michael F. Quinn, Pst.; Rev. Andrew W. Ginter, Admin.;

SOUTH SAN FRANCISCO

All Souls - 315 Walnut Ave., South San Francisco, CA 94080 t) 650-873-5356 (CRP); 650-871-8944 pastor@allsoulsparishssf.org; secretary@allsoulsparishssf.org www.allsoulsparishssf.org Rev. Kazimierz Abrahamczyk, SVD, Pst.; Rev. Jerome Bai, SVD,

Assoc. Pst.; Lourdes Yniguez, DRE;

All Souls School - (Grades PreSchool-8) 479 Miller Ave., South San Francisco, CA 94080 t) 650-583-3562 info@ssfallsoulsschool.org; principal@ssfallsoulsschool.org www.ssfallsoulsschool.org Vincent Riener, Prin.; Stds.: 250; Lay Tchrs.: 13

All Souls Preschool - (Grades PreK-PreK) 479 Miller Ave, South San Francisco, CA 94080 t) 650-871-1751 Carla Malouf Jisrawi, Dir.; Stds.: 20; Lay Tchrs.: 3

St. Augustine - 3700 Callan Blvd., South San Francisco, CA 94080 t) 650-873-2282 staugustinessf@gmail.com staugustinessf.org Rev. Raymund M. Reyes, Pst.; Rev. Eduardo Dura, Assoc. Pst.; Rev. Martin S. Njoalu, Assoc. Pst.; Dcn. Virgil Capetti; Dcn. Nestor Fernandez II; CRP Stds.: 306

Mater Dolorosa - 307 Willow Ave., South San Francisco, CA 94080 t) 650-583-4131 cff@mdssf.org; frances@mdssf.org Rev. Rolando S. De la Rosa, Pst.; Dcn. Alex Aragon; Rev. Vito J. Perrone, In Res.; Frances Lidwell, Admin.; Felisa Cepeda, DRE;

St. Veronica - 434 Alida Way, South San Francisco, CA 94080 t) 650-588-1455 x103 (CRP); 650-588-1455 kguglielmoni@stveronicassf.com; churchoffice@stveronicassf.com www.stveronicassf.com Rev. Patrick J. Driscoll, Pst.; Rev. Cameron Pollette, Par. Vicar; Dcn. Roger Beaudry; Karen Guglielmoni, DRE; CRP Stds.: 168

St. Veronica School - t) 650-589-3909 office@saintveronicassf.org www.saintveronicassf.org Mary Boland, Prin.; Stds.: 252; Lay Tchrs.: 12

TIBURON

St. Hilary - 761 Hilary Dr., Tiburon, CA 94920-1421 t) 415-435-1122 dianar@sthilary.org www.sthilary.org Rev. Roger G. Gustafson, Pst.; Lisa Veto, DRE;

St. Hilary School - 765 Hilary Dr., Tiburon, CA 94920 t) 415-435-2224 office@sainthilaryschool.org www.sainthilaryschool.org Marie Bordeleau, Prin.; Stds.: 280; Lay Tchrs.: 23

TOMALES

Church of the Assumption - 26825 Shoreline Hwy., Tomales, CA 94971-0082; Mailing: PO Box 82, Tomales, CA 94971-0082 t) 707-878-0028; 707-878-2208 (CRP) lopez.juan@sfarch.org; lopezjuanmanuel585@gmail.com Rev. Juan Manuel Lopez, Pst.;

St. Helen - t) 650-720-1429

SCHOOLS: PRESCHOOL THRU HIGH SCHOOL

SCHOOLS

STATE OF CALIFORNIA

ATHERTON

Sacred Heart Schools, Atherton - (PRV) (Grades PreSchool-12) 150 Valparaiso, Atherton, CA 94027 t) (650) 322-9931 www.shschools.org (Sacred Heart Schools, P-8) Francesa Brake, Prin.; Richard Dioli, Dir.; Stds.: 552; Sr. Tchrs.: 2; Lay Tchrs.: 93

BELMONT

Notre Dame Elementary School - (PRV) 1200 Notre Dame Ave., Belmont, CA 94002 t) 650-591-2209 kjeremiassen@nde.org nde.org Kathleen Jeremiassen, Prin.; Stds.: 167; Lay Tchrs.: 12

SAN FRANCISCO

St. Brigid Elementary School - (DIO) (Grades K-8) 2250 Franklin St., San Francisco, CA 94109 t) 415-673-4523 office@saintbrigidsf.org www.saintbrigidsf.org Sr. Angeles Marin, R.C.M., Prin.; Stds.: 116; Lay Tchrs.: 11

DeMarillac Academy of San Francisco - (PRV) (Grades 4-8) 175 Golden Gate Ave., San Francisco, CA 94102 t) 415-552-5220 theresa_houghton@demarillac.org www.demarillac.org Co-sponsored by Daughters of Charity and De La Salle Christian Brothers. Jojo de Guzman, Prin.; Theresa Flynn Houghton, Pres.; Stds.: 104; Lay Tchrs.: 12

Mission Dolores Academy - (PRV) (Grades K-8) 3371 16th St., San Francisco, CA 94114 t) 415-346-9500 development@mdasf.org Rev. Charles R. Gagan, S.J.; Meredith Essalat, Prin.; Stds.: 194; Lay Tchrs.: 25

Schools of the Sacred Heart, Convent of the Sacred Heart Elementary School - (PRV) (Grades K-8) 2222 Broadway St., San Francisco, CA 94115 t) 415-563-2900 heart@sacredsf.org www.sacredsf.org (Girls) Dr. Ann Marie Krejcarek, Pres.; Amanda Walker, Librn.;

Schools of the Sacred Heart, Stuart Hall For Boys - (PRV) (Grades K-8) 2222 Broadway St., San Francisco, CA 94115 t) 415-563-2900 heart@sacredsf.org www.sacredsf.org (Boys) Kevin Brenner, Admin.; Alexa Johnson, Headmaster; Dr. Ann Marie Krejcarek, Pres.; Stds.: 361; Lay Tchrs.: 18

St. Thomas More School - (DIO) (Grades PreSchool-8) 50 Thomas More Way, San Francisco, CA 94132 t) 415-337-0100 office@stmsf.org www.stmsf.org Preschool and TK David Greenbaum, Prin.; Stds.: 236; Lay Tchrs.: 14

HIGH SCHOOLS

STATE OF CALIFORNIA

ATHERTON

Sacred Heart Schools, Atherton - (PRV) (Grades PreK-12) 150 Valparaiso, Atherton, CA 94027 t) 650-322-1866 www.shschools.org Religious of the Sacred Heart. Richard Dioli, Dir.; Stds.: 633; Lay Tchrs.: 152

BELMONT

Notre Dame High School (Girls) - (PRV) 1540 Ralston Ave., Belmont, CA 94002 t) 650-595-1913 lkern@ndhsb.org www.ndhsb.org Dr. Linda Kern, Prin.; Stds.: 419; Lay Tchrs.: 41

BURLINGAME

Mercy High School (Girls) - (PRV) (Grades 9-12) 2750 Adeline Dr., Burlingame, CA 94010-5597 t) 650-343-3631 www.mercyhsb.com Natalie Ciriglian Brosnan, Head of School; Stds.: 373; Lay Tchrs.: 35

KENTFIELD

Marin Catholic High School - (DIO) (Grades 9-12) 675 Sir Francis Drake Blvd., Kentfield, CA 94904 t) 415-464-3800 tnavone@marincatholic.org www.marincatholic.org Chris Valdez, Prin.; Tim Navone, Pres.; Stds.: 780; Scholastics: 70; Pr. Tchrs.: 1; Sr. Tchrs.: 4; Lay Tchrs.: 65

PORTOLA VALLEY

Woodside Priory School - (PRV) (Grades 6-12) 302 Portola Rd., Portola Valley, CA 94028 t) 650-851-8221 www.prioryca.org (Coed, Boarding). Benedictine Fathers of the Priory, Inc. Caitha Ambler, Prin.; Ana Cortez-Hernandez, Prin.; Patrick Ruff, Prin.; Stds.: 395; Lay Tchrs.: 53

SAN FRANCISCO

Archbishop Riordan High School (Co-ed) - (PAR) 175 Frida Kahlo Way, San Francisco, CA 94112 t) 415-586-8200 riordan@riordanhs.org www.riordanhs.org Tim Reardon, Prin.; Stds.: 1,057; Lay Tchrs.: 95

ICA Cristo Rey - (PRV) 3625 24th St., San Francisco, CA 94110 t) 415-824-2052 ica@icacademy.org www.icacristorey.org Parent organization is Dominican Sisters of Mission San Jose Dr. George V Fornero, Prin.; Sr. Diane Aruda, O.P., Pres.; Stds.: 290; Sr. Tchrs.: 2; Lay Tchrs.: 35

St. Ignatius College Preparatory (Coed) - (PRV) (Grades 9-12) 2001 37th Ave., San Francisco, CA 94116-1165 t) 415-731-7500 info@siprep.org www.siprep.org Rev. John Mitchell, S.J., Supr.; Rev. Edward A. Reese, S.J., Pres.; Michelle Levine, Prin.; Stds.: 1,510; Lay Tchrs.: 125

Mercy High School (Girls) - (PRV) 3250 19th Ave., San Francisco, CA 94132 t) 415-334-0525 mercysf@mercyhs.org www.mercyhs.org Sr. Carolyn Krohn, RSM, Headmaster;

Sacred Heart Cathedral Preparatory (Coed) - (PAR) 1055 Ellis St., San Francisco, CA 94109 t) 415-775-6626 rgallagher@shcp.edu shcp.edu Sponsored by Daughters of Charity and Christian Brothers. Gary Cannon, Prin.; Dr. Melinda Skrade, Pres.; Stds.: 1,349; Bro. Tchrs.: 1; Sr. Tchrs.: 1; Lay Tchrs.: 90

Schools of the Sacred Heart, Convent of the Sacred Heart High School (Girls) - (PRV) 2222 Broadway, San Francisco, CA 94115 t) 415-563-2900 heart@sacredsf.org www.sacredsf.org Dr. Ann Marie Krejcarek, Pres.; Rachel Simpson, Chief Academic Officer; Stds.: 377; Lay Tchrs.: 25

Schools of the Sacred Heart, Stuart Hall High School - (PRV) 1715 Octavia St., San Francisco, CA 94109 t) 415-345-5811 katie.zepeda@sacredsf.org www.sacredsf.org (Boys) Dr. Ann Marie Krejcarek, Pres.; Stds.: 220; Lay Tchrs.: 21

SAN MATEO

Junipero Serra High School (Boys) - (PAR) (Grades 9-12) 451 W. 20th Ave., San Mateo, CA 94403-1385 t) 650-345-8207 padres@serrahs.com www.serrahs.com Rev. Nicholas Case, Chap.; Charlie McGrath, Prin.; Dr. Barry Thornton, Pres.; Stds.: 854; Lay Tchrs.: 56

CAMPUS MINISTRY / NEWMAN CENTERS [CAM]

SAN FRANCISCO

Catholic Student Association of UCSF - 1290 Fifth Ave., San Francisco, CA 94122-2649 t) 415-566-5610 stjohnofgod-sf@sbcglobal.net www.sjog.net Rev. Narcis L. Kabipi, Admin.;

Newman Center, San Francisco State University - St. Thomas More Church, 1300 Junipero Serra Blvd., San Francisco, CA 94132-2913 t) 415-452-9634 stmchurch2002@aol.com www.stmchurch.com Rev. Marvin Paul Felipe, S.D.B. (Philippines), Chap.;

CATHOLIC CHARITIES [CCH]

INSTITUTIONS LOCATED IN DIOCESE

SAN FRANCISCO

Catholic Charities CYO of the Archdiocese of San Francisco - 990 Eddy St., San Francisco, CA 94109 t) 415-972-1200 moreinfo@catholiccharitiessf.org; dcartahena@catholiccharitiessf.org www.catholiccharitiessf.org Ellen Hammerle, CEO; Kathleen Grogan, Treas.; Most Rev. Salvatore J. Cordileone, J.C.D., Bd. Chair; Joe Boerio, Bd. Pres.; Theodore Borromeo, Bd. Sec.; Asstd. Annu.: 72,000; Staff: 417

Catholic Charities Adult Day Services San Francisco - 50 Broad St., San Francisco, CA 94112 t) 415-452-3500 pclement@catholiccharitiessf.org Patty Clement-Cihak, Dir.;

Catholic Charities Assisted Housing & Health Program - 810 Ave. D, San Francisco, CA 94130 t) 415-972-1344 ebrown@catholiccharitiessf.org Erick Brown, Dir.;

Catholic Charities Center for Immigration Legal and Support Services - 36 37th Ave., San Mateo, CA 94403 t) 650-295-2160 dotero@catholiccharitiessf.org Marirose Piciucco, Dir.;

Catholic Charities Center for Immigration and Legal Support Services - 2187 Mission St., San Francisco, CA 94110 mpiciucco@catholiccharitiessf.org Marirose Piciucco, Gen. Counsel, Center for Immigration;

Catholic Charities CYO Athletics - 255 Jules Ave., San Francisco, CA 94112 t) 415-988-7652 mlandry@catholiccharitiessf.org Sarah Burton, Dir.;

Catholic Charities CYO Camp & Retreat Center - 2136 Bohemian Hwy., Occidental, CA 95465

t) 707-874-0200 rgarcia@catholiccharitiessf.org Ricardo Garcia, Dir.;

Catholic Charities CYO Transportation - 699 Serramonte Blvd., Ste. 210, Daly City, CA 94015 t) 650-757-2110 mrea@catholiccharitiessf.org Bill Avalos, Dir.;

Catholic Charities Derek Silva Community - 20 Franklin St., San Francisco, CA 94102 t) 415-553-8700 kfauteux@catholiccharitiessf.org Kevin Fauteux, Dir.;

Catholic Charities Edith Witt Senior Community - 66 9th St., San Francisco, CA 94103 t) 415-503-0816 glippert@catholiccharitiessf.org Geofrey Lippert, Dir.;

Catholic Charities Homelessness Prevention Program - 2871 Mission St., San Francisco, CA 94110 t) 415-972-1310 jcartagena@catholiccharitiessf.org

Catholic Charities Maureen & Craig Sullivan Youth Services - 801 Jessie St., San Francisco, CA 94103 t) 415-863-1171 x100 enave@catholiccharitiessf.org Erica Nave, Dir.;

Catholic Charities OMI Senior Center - 65 Beverly St., San Francisco, CA 94132 t) 415-334-5550 lrodriguez@catholiccharitiessf.org Liz Rodriguez, Dir.;

Catholic Charities Peter Claver Community - 1340 Golden Gate Ave., San Francisco, CA 94115 t) 415-749-3800 tsagun@catholiccharitiessf.org

Catholic Charities Rita da Cascia Community - 1652 Eddy St., #8, San Francisco, CA 94115 t) 415-202-0941 sgodt@catholiccharitiessf.org Stephanie J. Godt, Dir.;

Catholic Charities San Francisco Boys' Home - t) 415-221-3443 sdouglas@catholiccharitiessf.org

Catholic Charities St. Joseph's Family Center - 899 Guerrero St., San Francisco, CA 94110 t) 415-550-4478 jlandaverde@catholiccharitiessf.org

Catholic Charities St. Vincent's School for Boys - t) 415-507-2000 Sarah Burton, Dir.;

Catholic Charities 10th & Mission Family Housing - 1390 Mission St., San Francisco, CA 94103 t) 415-863-1141 glippert@catholiccharitiessf.org Geofrey Lippert, Contact;

Catholic Charities Treasure Island Child Development Center - 850 Ave. D, Bldg. 502, San Francisco, CA 94130 t) 415-801-4745 Kathie Autumn, Dir.;

Catholic Charities Treasure Island Supportive Housing - 810 Ave. D, San Francisco, CA 94107 t) 415-743-0018 ebrown@catholiccharitiessf.org Erick Brown, Dir.;

Charities Carl Gellert & Celia Berta Gellert Foundation Adult Day Services of San Mateo - 787 Walnut St., San Carlos, CA 94070 t) 650-592-9325 csantoni@catholiccharitiessf.org

CEMETERIES [CEM]

COLMA

Holy Cross - ; Mailing: P.O. Box 1577, Colma, CA 94014 t) 650-323-6375 moreinfo@holycrosscemeteries.com Monica Williams, Dir.;

Holy Cross Cemetery and Mausoleum - ; Mailing: P.O. Box 1577, Colma, CA 94014 t) 650-756-2060 moreinfo@holycrosscemeteries.com Monica Williams, Dir.;

SAN RAFAEL

Mount Olivet - 270 Ranchitos Rd., San Rafael, CA 94903 t) 415-479-9020 moreinfo@holycrosscemeteries.com Monica Williams, Dir.;

COLLEGES & UNIVERSITIES [COL]

BELMONT

Notre Dame de Namur University - 1500 Ralston Ave., Belmont, CA 94002 t) 650-508-3500 www.ndnu.edu Sisters of Notre Dame de Namur. Dr. Beth Martin, Pres.; Stds.: 350; Lay Tchrs.: 100

SAN FRANCISCO

***University of San Francisco** - 2130 Fulton St., San Francisco, CA 94117-1080 t) 415-422-5555 www.usfca.edu Established 1855; Chartered by State, 1859. Jesuit Fathers. Rev. Paul J. Fitzgerald, S.J., Pres.; Stds.: 9,688; Lay Tchrs.: 505; Pr. Tchrs.: 3

CONVENTS, MONASTERIES, AND RESIDENCES FOR WOMEN [CON]

ATHERTON

Religious of the Sacred Heart-Oakwood - 140 Valparaiso Ave., Atherton, CA 94027-4403 t) 650-323-8343 rshmwap@earthlink.net Retirement Center for elderly Religious of the Sacred Heart. Sr. Clare Pratt, R.S.C.J., Dir.;

BURLINGAME

Sisters of Mercy of the Americas West Midwest Community, Inc. - 2300 Adeline Dr., Burlingame, CA 94010-5599 t) 650-340-7474 www.sistersofmercy.org Sr. Susan Sanders, R.S.M., Vice. Pres.; Srs.: 417

DALY CITY

Daughters of Charity of St. Vincent de Paul - 2000 Sullivan Ave., Daly City, CA 94015-2202 t) 650-991-6715 docsmc@sbcglobal.net www.daughtersofcharity.com/ Sr. Arthur Gordon, D.C., Supr.;

Quinhon Missionary Sisters of the Holy Cross - 298 Southgate Ave., Daly City, CA 94015 t) 650-755-7231 sistersmtgqndc@yahoo.org; josephinedao3@yahoo.com

Religious of the Virgin Mary - 15 Elmwood Dr., Daly City, CA 94015 t) 650-992-5769

MENLO PARK

Corpus Christi Monastery - 215 Oak Grove Ave., Menlo Park, CA 94025-3272 t) 650-322-1801 dominicannun@opnunsmenlo.org www.opnunsmenlo.org Nuns of the Order of Preachers. Sr. Maria Christine, O.P., Prioress;

Daughters of St. Paul - 3248 Middlefield Rd., Menlo Park, CA 94025; Mailing: 3250 Middlefield Rd, Menlo Park, CA 94025 t) 650-549-8480 fspredwood@gmail.com www.pauline.org Sr. Marlyn Monge, FSP, Supr.; Srs.: 4

ORANGE

Sisters of St. Joseph of Orange - 440 S. Batavia St., Orange, CA 92868 t) 714-633-8121 sr.ellen.jordan@csjorange.org Sr. Ellen Jordan, C.S.J., Secy.;

PACIFICA

Missionaries of Charity - 164 Milagra Dr., Pacifica, CA 94044 t) 650-355-3091 (India) Sr. Rosina Conrotto, PBVM, Contact;

Novitiate - 312 29th St., San Francisco, CA 94131 t) 415-647-1889

Queen of Peace - 55 Sadowa St., San Francisco, CA 94112 t) 415-586-3449

REDWOOD CITY

Sisters of Saint Francis - Mount Alverno - 1330 Brewster Ave., Redwood City, CA 94062-1312; Mailing: P.O. Box 1028, Redwood City, CA 94064 t) 650-369-1725 mariaelenam@franciscanway.org; provincialcouncil-sfp@franciscanway.org Sr. Maria Elena Martinez, Prov.; Srs.: 43

Sisters of St. Francis-Mt. Alverno Marian Residence Corporation - 1330 Brewster Ave., Redwood City, CA 94062; Mailing: P.O. Box 1028, Redwood City, CA 94064 t) 650-369-1725 claireblohm@franciscanway.org; mariaelenam@franciscanway.org Maria Elena Martinez Sr., Prov.; Claire Blohm, CFO; Srs.: 43

Trinity Community - 1506 Roosevelt Ave., Redwood City, CA 94061 t) 650-339-1240 srdorothym@aol.com Sisters of St. Francis.

SAN FRANCISCO

Carmelite Monastery of Cristo Rey, Discalced Carmelite Nuns - 721 Parker Ave., San Francisco, CA 94118-4227 t) 415-387-2640 prioress@cmcrnuns.org carmelofcristorey.org/ Sr. Elizabeth Ramirez, Treas.;

Discalced Carmelite Nuns of Berkeley, Inc. - 721 Parker Ave., San Francisco, CA 94118-4227 t) 415-387-2640 prioress@cmcrnuns.org Sr. Elizabeth Ramirez, O.C.D., Secy.;

Franciscan Missionaries of Our Lady of Peace - 46 Harrington St., San Francisco, CA 94112 t) 415-587-3729 camberos.eva1990@yahoo.com Sr. Eva Camberos, M.F.P., Supr.;

Our Lady of Guadalupe Convent -

Mercy Place (Sisters of Mercy-Burlingame) - 826 30th Ave., San Francisco, CA 94121-3522 t) 415-876-4303 Suzetter Deitchler, Contact;

Monastery of Perpetual Adoration, Nuns of Perpetual Adoration - 771 Ashbury St., San Francisco, CA 94117-4013 t) 415-566-2743 mpador@aol.com Sr. Rosalba Vargas, A.P., Supr.;

Sisters of Social Service of Los Angeles - 1850 Ulloa St., San Francisco, CA 94116 t) 415-681-9219 cel_arbuckle@yahoo.com www.socialservicesisters.org Sr. Celeste Arbuckle, SSS, Contact;

Sisters of St. Joseph of Orange - 478 12th Ave., San Francisco, CA 94118 t) 415-387-2493 jmrmmcsj@sbcglobal.net; csjsf@earthlink.net Sr. Ellen Jordan, C.S.J., Contact;

Sisters of the Good Shepherd - 1310 Bacon St., San Francisco, CA 94134 t) 415-586-2822 sistersofthegoodshepherd.com Sr. Anne Kelley, Rel. Ord. Ldr.; Antonia Ponder, COO; Sr. Marguerite Bartling, RGS, Contact;

Sisters of the Presentation San Francisco - 281 Masonic Ave., San Francisco, CA 94118-4416 t) 415-422-5001 syu@pbvmsf.org www.presentationsisterssf.org Sr. Rosina Conrotto, PBVM, Pres.; Srs.: 50

Verbum Dei Missionary Fraternity - 3365-3373 19th St., San Francisco, CA 94110 t) 415-282-3005 areacouncil@verbumdeiusa.org www.verbumdeiusa.org (Institute of Consecrated Life, Rome, Italy), Prayer and ministry of the Word, working with youth, young adults & adults. Sr. Rosalia Meza, Prov.; Srs.: 19

SAN RAFAEL

Carmelite Monastery of the Mother of God, Discalced Carmelite Nuns - 530 Blackstone Dr., San Rafael, CA 94903 t) 415-479-6872 sram@motherofgodcarmel.org Sr. Anna Marie Vanni, O.C.D., Prioress;

Dominican Sisters of San Rafael Generalate & Convent - 1520 Grand Ave., San Rafael, CA 94901-2236 t) 415-453-8303 carla.kovack@sanrafaelop.org www.sanrafaelop.org Sr. Carla Kovack, O.P., Prioress; Srs.: 58

St. Dominic Convent - 2517 Pine St., San Francisco, CA 94115-2609 t) 415-567-8282

Dominican Convent - 1540 Grand Ave., San Rafael, CA 94901-2236 t) (415) 453-8303

Jane d'Aza Convent - 60 Locust Ave., San Rafael, CA 94901-2237 t) 415-453-4784

St. Margaret Convent - 40 Locust Ave., San Rafael, CA 94901-2237 t) 415-458-2952

Our Lady of Lourdes Convent - 77 Locust Ave., San Rafael, CA 94901-2237 t) 415-457-3171

St. Rose Convent - 2515 Pine St., San Francisco, CA 94115-2609 t) 415-441-2685

ENDOWMENTS / FOUNDATIONS / TRUSTS [EFT]

REDWOOD CITY

Sisters of St. Francis Charitable Trust - 1330 Brewster Ave., Redwood City, CA 94062 t) 650-369-1725 provincialcouncil-sfp@franciscanway.org franciscanway.org/st-francis-province/ Sr. Patricia Rayburn, OSF, Contact;

SAN FRANCISCO

St. Anthony Foundation - 150 Golden Gate Ave., San Francisco, CA 94102 t) 415-241-2600 info@stanthonysf.org www.stanthonysf.org We provide essential services, health care, and gateways to stability for families and individuals experiencing homelessness and extreme poverty. Nils Behnke, CEO; Tere Brown, Dir.; Jeff Pace, Dir.; Suzie Sheedy, Dir.;

The Christopher Missions Foundation - 100 Portola Dr., #7, San Francisco, CA 94131 t) 415-306-3788 c) 415-515-9400 nanettelmiller13@gmail.com Nanette Lee Miller, Admin.;

Father Raphael Piperni Charitable Trust - 1100 Franklin St., San Francisco, CA 94109 t) 415-441-7144

suoeconomer@salesiansf.org (The FRPC (R) Trust) Rev. Tho Bui, S.D.B., Admin.;
The Megan Furth Memorial Fund - 3371 16th St., San Francisco, CA 94114 t) 415-346-9500 paulr@mdasf.org Rev. Charles Gagan, S.J., Pres.;
Philip Rinaldi Charitable Trust - 1100 Franklin St., San Francisco, CA 94109 t) 415-441-7144 suoeconomer@salesiansf.org For the care of needy youth and for the formation needs of Salesians of St. John Bosco. Rev. Tho Bui, S.D.B., Admin.;
Sisters of the Presentation Community Support Trust Fund - 2340 Turk Blvd., San Francisco, CA 94118-4340 t) 415-422-5001; 415-722-9577 pchiesa@pbvmsf.org Trust used for the religious and charitable needs of the Sisters of the Presentation of the Blessed Virgin Mary.

SAN RAFAEL

Sisters of the Third Order of St. Dominic, Congregation of the Most Holy Name, Support Charitable Trust Fund - 1520 Grand Ave., San Rafael, CA 94901-2236 t) 415-453-8303 carla.kovack@sanrafaelop.org www.sanrafaelop.org Trust used for the religious and charitable needs of the Sisters of the Third Order of St. Dominic, Congregation of the Most Holy Name. Sr. Carla Kovack, O.P., Chair;

HOSPITALS / HEALTH SERVICES [HOS]

SAN FRANCISCO

St. Mary's Medical Center - 450 Stanyan St., San Francisco, CA 94117 t) 415-668-1000 pam.koerner@commonspirit.org www.stmarysmedicalcenter.org Sponsored by Catholic Health Care Federation Marvin O'Quinn, Pres.; Bed Capacity: 275; Asstd. Annu.: 99,648; Staff: 1,076;
St. Mary's Medical Center Foundation - 450 Stanyan St., San Francisco, CA 94117 t) 415-750-5790 margine.sako@dignityhealth.org www.supportstmaryssf.org Margine Sako, Dir.;

MISCELLANEOUS [MIS]

BERKELEY

St. Conrad Center for Ministry and Studies - 1534 Arch St., Berkeley, CA 94708; Mailing: 1345 Cortez Ave., Burlingame, CA 94010 t) 650-344-8321 finance@olacapuchins.org Rev. Joseph S. Dederick, O.F.M.Cap., CEO;

BURLINGAME

Music at Kohl Mansion, Inc. - 2750 Adeline Dr., Burlingame, CA 94010 t) 650-762-1130 director@musicatkohl.org www.musicatkohl.org Patricia Kristof Moy, Dir.;

DALY CITY

Vincentian Service Corps West - 2000 Sullivan Ave., Daly City, CA 94015-2202; Mailing: 26000 Altamont Rd., Los Altos Hills, CA 94022 t) (650) 949-8868 jday@doc1633.org www.vscwest.org Sr. Christina Maggi, CEO;

EAST PALO ALTO

Legion of Mary - 1425 Bay Rd., East Palo Alto, CA 94303 t) 650-322-2152 Rev. Lawrence C. Goode, Dir.;

MENLO PARK

The Benedict XVI Institute for Sacred Music and Divine Worship - 320 Middlefield Rd., Menlo Park, CA 94025 t) 415-614-5517 wongr@sfarch.org Maggie Gallagher, Dir.;
Daughters of Carmel (Congregation of Putri Karmel) - 320 Middlefield Rd., Menlo Park, CA 94025 t) 650-329-8518 daughtersofcarmel@gmail.com www.daughtersofcarmel.org Sr. Mary Jacinta PKarm, Pres.;
Pauline Books & Media - 3250 Middlefield Rd., Menlo Park, CA 94025 t) 650-562-7060 norcal@paulinemedia.com www.pauline.org Daughters of St. Paul. Sr. Bernardine Sattler, Mgr.;

PORTOLA VALLEY

St. Stephen Hungarian Catholic Mission - 302 Portola Rd., Portola Valley, CA 94028 t) 650-851-6109 x109 donate@hungariancatholicmission.com Rev. Maurus B. Nemeth, O.S.B., Pst.;

REDWOOD CITY

Caritas Business Services - 203 Redwood Shores Pkwy., Ste. 800, Redwood City, CA 94065 t) 650-551-6631 wahidchoudhury@dochs.org www.dochs.org
The Catholic Worker Community - 545 Cassia St., Redwood City, CA 94063 t) 650-366-4415 lawrencepurcell@sbcglobal.net A foster home for teenagers. Lawrence P. Purcell, Dir.;
***St. Francis Center of Redwood City** - 151 Buckingham Ave., Redwood City, CA 94063 t) 650-365-7829 schristina@aol.com www.stfrancisrwc.org Sr. Christina Heltsley, O.P., Exec.;

SAN FRANCISCO

Alliance of Mission District Catholic Schools (AMDCS) - 1 Peter York Way, San Francisco, CA 94109 t) 415-614-5546 torresg@sfarch.org www.sfarchdiocese.org Gustavo Torres, Admin.;
***American Auxiliary of Paris Foreign Missions** - 425 California St., 25th Floor, San Francisco, CA 94104 t) 415-908-1081 llanctot@lanlawoffice.com Rev. Vincent Senechal, Pres.;
Archdiocesan Council of Catholic Women - One Peter Yorke Way, San Francisco, CA 94109-6602 t) 415-614-5500 dcmibach@aol.com A. Cathleen Mibach, Pres.;
The Archdiocese of San Francisco Parish and School Juridic Persons Real Property Support Corporation - 1301 Post St., Ste. 102, San Francisco, CA 94109 t) 415-292-0802 christianj@adsfrpsc.org John Christian, Exec.;
The Archdiocese of San Francisco Parish, School and Cemetery Juridic Persons Capital Assets Support Corporation - 1301 Post St., Ste. 103, San Francisco, CA 94109-6667 t) 415-292-3600 kennedya@adsfcasc.org Richard P. Hannon, Dir.;
***Bella Health and Wellness, Inc.** - 2000 Van Ness Ave. Suite 304, San Francisco, CA 94109; Mailing: PO Box 641801, San Francisco, CA 94164 t) (415) 775-1500 sally@bellahw.org www.bellahw.org Catholic healthcare clinic. Dolores Meehan, Exec. Dir.;
St. Benedict Parish for Deaf and Hearing Impaired at St. Francis Xavier Church - 1801 Octavia, San Francisco, CA 94109 t) 415-567-9855; 415-567-0438 (TDD); 415-255-5868 (Video Phone) stbenz1801@gmail.com; info@sfdeafcatholics.org www.sfdeafcatholics.org Rev. Paul Zirimenya, Pst.;
Breaking Bread with Hope - 990 Eddy St., San Francisco, CA 94109 t) 415-972-1200 pclement@catholiccharitiessf.org
Catholic Charismatic Renewal (CCR) - One Peter Yorke Way, San Francisco, CA 94109 t) 415-614-5500 sfspirit.com Rev. Jose M. Corral; Rev. Angel N. Quitalig; Rev. Raymund M. Reyes; Dcn. Ernie von Emster;
Catholic Kolping Society - 440 Taraval St., San Francisco, CA 94116 t) 415-381-3989 lbrinkmann@mac.com Lisa Brinkmann, Pres.; Catherine Vennemeyer, Treas.;
Catholic Scouting - One Peter Yorke Way, San Francisco, CA 94109 t) 415-614-5594 georgea@sfarch.org; marianoc@sfarch.org www.sfarch.org/youthministry Dcn. Chris Mariano, Diocesan Coord., Youth & Young Adult Ministries;
Congregation of the Holy Family of Blessed Mariam Thresia, India - 3112 Turk Blvd., San Francisco, CA 94118 t) 415-666-3237 chfsfo@yahoo.com www.blessedmariamthresia.org
Equestrian Order of the Holy Sepulchre of Jerusalem - Northwestern Lieutenancy - 8 Lenox Way, San Francisco, CA 94127 t) 415-682-4228 eohsfaller@gmail.com eohsjnwusa.org/
ICA San Francisco Work Study, Inc. - 3625 24th St., San Francisco, CA 94110 t) 415-824-2052 tszarnicki@icacademy.org Tim Szarnicki, CEO;
***Mercy Housing California** - 1256 Market St., San Francisco, CA 94102; Mailing: 1600 Broadway, Ste. 2000, Denver, CO 80202 t) 415-355-7100 www.mercyhousing.org Housing development for low-income families, elderly, and singles. Doug Shoemaker, Pres.;
M.H.R. AIDS Support Group - 100 Diamond St., San Francisco, CA 94114-2414 t) 415-863-6259 x10 mhr@mhr-asg.com www.mhr-asg.com Pete Toms, Contact;
St. Paul High School Alumnae Assoc. - 221 Valley St., San Francisco, CA 94131 t) 415-648-7538 sphsalumnae@yahoo.com Not-for-profit charitable outreach. Marilyn Highlander-Pool, Pres.;
Prelature of the Holy Cross and Opus Dei - 765 14th Ave., San Francisco, CA 94118 t) 415-386-0431 info@opusdei.org www.opusdei.org Rev. Msgr. James A. Kelly, Chap.;
Menlough Study Center - 1160 Santa Cruz Ave., Menlo Park, CA 94025 t) 650-327-1675 office@menlough.org
The Ricci Institute for Chinese-Western Cultural History - University of San Francisco, 2130 Fulton St., LM280, San Francisco, CA 94117-1080 t) 415-422-6401 ricci@usfca.edu www.usfca.edu/ricci Rev. Antoni J. Ucerler, S.J., Dir.; Xiaoxin Wu, Dir.;
St. Rose Corporation - 2501 Pine St., San Francisco, CA 94115 t) 415-440-9568 bob.warwick@sanrafaelop.org Sr. Cathy Murray, O.P., Chair;
San Buenaventura Center for Ministry and Studies - 750 Anza St., San Francisco, CA 94118; Mailing: 1345 Cortez Ave., Burlingame, CA 94010 t) 650-344-8321 finance@olacapuchins.org Rev. Joseph S. Dederick, O.F.M.Cap., CEO;
San Francisco Particular Council of the Society of St. Vincent de Paul - 1175 Howard St., San Francisco, CA 94103 t) 415-977-1270 info@svdp-sf.org www.svdp-sf.org Martha Arbouex, Chair; Shari Wooldridge, Exec.;
Shrine of St. Jude Thaddeus - 2390 Bush St., San Francisco, CA 94115 t) 415-931-5919 info@stjude-shrine.org www.stjude-shrine.org Rev. Emmerich W. Vogt, O.P., Dir.;

SAN MATEO

***The Society of St. Vincent de Paul, Particular Council of San Mateo County, Inc.** - 50 N. B St., San Mateo, CA 94401-3917 t) 650-373-0622 info@svdpsm.org www.svdpsm.org James D. Lonergan, Dir.;
SVdP's Catherine Center - 50 N. B St., San Mateo, CA 94401 t) 650-838-9800 Safe, supportive housing program for women previously incarcerated.
SVdP's North County Homeless Help Center - 344 Grand Ave., South San Francisco, CA 94080 t) 650-589-9039
SVdP's Peninsula Family Resource Center (PFRC) - t) 650-343-4403
SVdP's Restorative Justice Ministry - t) 650-796-0767
SVdP's San Mateo Homeless Help Center - t) 650-343-9251
SVdP's South County Homeless Help Center - 2600 Middlefield Rd., Redwood City, CA 94063 t) 650-343-4403
SVdP's Youth-Service Learning Opportunities - t) 650-589-9039
Thrift Store - 40 North B St., San Mateo, CA 94401 t) 650-294-8912
Thrift Store - 344 Grand Ave., South San Francisco, CA 94080 t) 650-589-8445
Vehicle Donation Program - t) 800-322-8284 www.svdpsm.org/give/donate-a-vehicle

SAN RAFAEL

***Center Interfaith Housing** - 164 N. San Pedro Rd., San Rafael, CA 94903 t) 415-492-9340
Mission Holding Corporation - 1520 Grand Ave., San Rafael, CA 94901-2236 t) 415-453-8303 carla.kovack@sanrafaelop.org www.sanrafaelop.org Sr. Carla Kovack, O.P., Pres.;
The Sisters of Nazareth of San Rafael Real Estate Holdings, Inc. - 245 Nova Albion Way, San Rafael, CA 94903 t) 415-479-8282 Sr. Rose Hoye CSN, Supr.;
***St. Vincent de Paul Society Marin County District Council** - 820 B St., San Rafael, CA 94915; Mailing: P.O. Box 150527, San Rafael, CA 94915 t) 415-454-3303 svdpmarin@vinnies.org vinnies.org Christine Paquette,

Exec.;

Affordable Housing - 822 B St., San Rafael, CA 94901 cpaquette@vinnies.org

Emergency Help Desk - 822 B. St., San Rafael, CA 94901 t) 415-454-0366 cpaquette@vinnies.org

Free Dining Room - cpaquette@vinnies.org

Rotating Emergency Shelter Team (Rest Program) - 822 B St., San Rafael, CA 94901

Vehicle Donations - t) 800-322-8284 cpaquestte@vinnies.org

SOUTH SAN FRANCISCO

The Contemplatives of Saint Joseph - 377 Willow Ave., South San Francisco, CA 94080-1446 t) 267-500-4155 cosj@att.net www.cosjmonastery.com Rev. Joseph Homick; Rev. Vito J. Perrone, Supr.;

TRACY

Seeds of Life - Verbum Dei - 31448 Hwy. 33, Tracy, CA 95304; Mailing: 3365 19th St., San Francisco, CA 94110 t) 209-637-3404 seedsoflife@verbumdeiusa.org seeds.verbumdeiusa.org Spirituality Center Sr. Ellen Hess, V.D.M.F., Contact;

MONASTERIES AND RESIDENCES FOR PRIESTS AND BROTHERS [MON]

BURLINGAME

Capuchin Provincial House - 1345 Cortez Ave., Burlingame, CA 94010 t) 650-344-8321 finance@olacapuchins.org www.capuchinswest.org Rev. Richard Lopes, O.F.M.Cap., Chap.; Rev. Joseph S. Dederick, O.F.M.Cap., Prov.; Rev. Miguel Angel Ortiz, O.F.M.Cap., Secy.; Brs.: 40; Priests: 28

Capuchin Franciscan Foundation for Retired Friars - 1345 Cortez Ave., Burlingame, CA 94010 t) (650) 344-8321 x5 Michael Smith, Chair;

Capuchin Franciscan General Needs Foundation - 1345 Cortez Ave., Burlingame, CA 94010 t) (650) 344-8321 x5 Walter Bankovich, Chair;

Capuchin Franciscan Mission Foundation - 1345 Cortez Ave., Burlingame, CA 94010 t) (650) 344-8321 x5 Walter Bankovich, Chair;

Capuchin Franciscan Seminarians Foundation - t) (650) 344-8321 x5 Michael Smith, Chair;

PORTOLA VALLEY

Woodside Priory - 302 Portola Rd., Founders Hall, Portola Valley, CA 94028-7897 t) 650-851-8221; 650-851-6133 mmager@prioryca.org www.prioryca.org Benedictine Fathers of the Priory, Inc. Rev. Maurus B. Nemeth, O.S.B.; Rt. Rev. Matthew Kenneth Leavy, O.S.B., Campus Min.; Patrick Ruff, Prin.; Rev. Martin J. Mager, O.S.B., Supr.; Priests: 3

SAN FRANCISCO

St. Dominic Priory - 2390 Bush St., San Francisco, CA 94115-3124 t) 415-567-7824 stdominics.org Rev. Justin Charles Gable, O.P.; Rev. Bruno Gibson, OP; Rev. Michael J. Hurley, O.P., Pst.; Rev. Vincent Kelber, O.P., Prior; Bro. Gregory R. Lira, O.P.; Rev. James J. Moore, O.P.; Rev. Anselm Ramelow, O.P.; Rev. Anthony R. Rosevear, O.P.; Rev. Emmerich W. Vogt, O.P.; Rev. Martin Walsh, O.P.; Rev. Christopher Wetzel, O.P., Assoc. Pst.; Brs.: 1; Priests: 9

Jesuit Community at St. Ignatius College Preparatory - 2001 37th Ave., San Francisco, CA 94116-1165 t) 415-731-7500 jmitchell@siprep.org www.siprep.org Rev. John Mitchell, S.J., Supr.; Bro. Douglas E. Draper, S.J., Admin.; Rev. Ronald C. Clemo, S.J., Sacr. Min.; Rev. Edward Reese, S.J., Pres.; Rev. Charles R. Gagan, S.J., Exec.; Rev. Michael Agliardo, Dir.; Rev. Joseph D. Fessio, S.J., Editor; Rev. A. Francis Stiegeler, S.J., Faculty Member; Bro. Hermenegildo V. Potestades, S.J., Registered Nurse; Brs.: 2; Priests: 7

Loyola House Jesuit Community - 2600 Turk Blvd., San Francisco, CA 94118-4347 t) 415-422-4200 jesuits@usfca.edu www.usfca.edu/jesuit (Corporate Title: Jesuit Community at University of San Francisco) Rev. John D. Whitney, S.J., Assoc. Pst.; Rev. Gregory R. Bonfiglio, S.J., Pst.; Rev. George T. Williams, S.J., Pst.; Rev. O. Alejandro Baez, S.J., Assoc. Pst.; Rev. Paul D. Devot, S.J., Assoc. Pst.; Rev. Robert J McTeigue, Assoc. Pst.; Rev. Patrick J Lee, S.J., Rector; Rev. Germain Clerveau, S.J.; Rev. Timothy Godfrey, S.J.; Rev. Olivier Kayitare, S.J.; Rev. Gerdenio S. Manuel, S.J.; Rev. Edwin Martinez-Callejas, S.J.; Rev. Sanil Mayilkunnel, S.J. (India); Fala Valery Ngong Ekem, S.J.; Rev. Brent H Otto, S.J.; Rev. Patric R Razafimahafaly, S.J.; Rev. Abdon Rwandekwe, S.J. (Rwanda); Rev. Barwende Sane, S.J.; Rev. Manuel Chavira, S.J., Chap.; Bro. James Siwicki, S.J., Admin.; Rev. Donal Godfrey, S.J., Pst. Min./Coord.; Rev. Matthew J. Motyka, S.J., Prof.; Rev. Joseph H. Nguyen, S.J., Prof.; Rev. Dennis C. Recio, S.J., Prof.; Rev. Paul J. Fitzgerald, S.J., Pres.; Brs.: 1; Priests: 24

Marist Center of the West - 625 Pine St., San Francisco, CA 94108-3210 t) 415-398-3543 randyh@maristsociety.org Society of Mary, U.S. Province (Marist). The Marist Society of California Rev. Rene Iturbe, S.M., Supr.; Rev. Phillip d'Auby, S.M., Senior Religious; Bro. Joseph Grima, S.M., Senior Religious; Rev. Bruce J. Lery, S.M., In Res.; Rev. Alfred Puccinelli, S.M., Senior Religious; Rev. Etienne Siffert, S.M., Senior Religious; Scott Kuang, House Administrator; Brs.: 1; Priests: 5

Salesian Provincial Residence - 1100 Franklin St., San Francisco, CA 94109 t) 415-441-7144 suoeconomer@salesiansf.org Rev. Mel Trinidad, S.D.B., Prov.; Rev. Tho Bui, S.D.B., Treas.; Bro. Lawrence King, S.D.B., In Res.; Rev. Thomas Prendiville, S.D.B., In Res.; Rev. Richard Presenti, S.D.B., In Res.; Rev. Jerry Wertz, S.D.B., In Res.; Rev. Nicholas Reina, S.B.D., In Res.;

San Buenaventura Friary - 750 Anza St., San Francisco, CA 94118 t) 415-387-7005 arwilson@juno.com Residence of Capuchin Provincial House, Burlingame, CA. Rev. Alan Wilson, O.F.M.Cap, Guardian;

Verbum Dei Missionary Fraternity - 3365-3373 19th St., San Francisco, CA 94110 t) 415-282-3005 sanfrancisco@verbumdeiusa.org www.verbumdeiusa.org Convent for sisters. Sr. Rosalia Meza, Prov.;

NURSING / REHABILITATION / CONVALESCENCE / ELDERLY CARE [NUR]

SAN FRANCISCO

Alexis Apartments of St. Patrick's Parish - 390 Clementina St., San Francisco, CA 94103-4138 t) 415-495-3690 alexis@jsco.net Yorbee Hui, Property Mgr.; Asstd. Annu.: 200; Staff: 8

Alexis Apartments - 756 Mission St., San Francisco, CA 94103 t) 415-421-3730 William Wong, Property Mgr.;

Home for the Aged of the Little Sisters of the Poor - St. Anne's Home for the Aged/ Little Sisters of the Poor, 300 Lake St., San Francisco, CA 94118 t) 415-751-6510 clsanfran@littlesistersofthepoor.org; mssanfran@littlesistersofthepoor.org www.littlesistersofthepoorsanfrancisco.org Sr. Marguerite McCarthy, LSP, Supr.; Asstd. Annu.: 85; Staff: 83

Madonna Residence - 350 Golden Gate Ave., San Francisco, CA 94102 t) 415-361-5113 mercyhousing.org Nonprofit residence for women of low income. Ismael Guerrero, President & CEO; Asstd. Annu.: 70; Staff: 7

SAN RAFAEL

Nazareth House of San Rafael, Inc. - 245 Nova Albion Way, San Rafael, CA 94903 t) 415-479-8282 alice@nazarethhousesr.com www.nazarethsr.org Sr. Rose Hoye CSN, Supr.; Barbara Anne Crowley, CEO;

PRESCHOOLS / CHILDCARE CENTERS [PRE]

SAN FRANCISCO

Holy Family Day Homes of San Francisco - 299 Dolores St., San Francisco, CA 94103 t) 415-861-5361 admin@holyfamilydayhome.org www.holyfamilydayhome.org Heather Monado, Exec.; Stds.: 100; Lay Tchrs.: 44

RETREAT HOUSES / RENEWAL CENTERS [RTR]

BURLINGAME

Sisters of Mercy of the Americas West Midwest Community, Inc. Mercy Retreat and Conference Center of Burlingame - 2300 Adeline Dr., Burlingame, CA 94010 t) 650-340-7474 sistersofmercy@mercywmw.org mercy-center.org Sr. Susan Sanders, R.S.M., Vice. Pres.;

MENLO PARK

Vallombrosa Center, Conference and Retreat Center of the Archdiocese of San Francisco - 250 Oak Grove Ave., Menlo Park, CA 94025 t) 650-325-5614 www.vallombrosa.org Rev. Patrick O'Neil, O.P., Dir.;

SAN RAFAEL

Santa Sabina Center - 25 Magnolia, San Rafael, CA 94901 t) 415-457-7727 info@santasabinacenter.org www.santasabinacenter.org Dominican Sisters Retreat and Conference Center. Sr. Margaret Diener, O.P., Dir.;

SEMINARIES [SEM]

MENLO PARK

St. Patrick's Seminary and University (The Roman Catholic Seminary of San Francisco) - 320 Middlefield Rd., Menlo Park, CA 94025 t) 650-325-5621 info@stpsu.edu www.stpsu.edu Major Seminary of the Archdiocese of San Francisco Rev. Gary Thomas, Dir.; Most Rev. Salvatore J. Cordileone, J.C.D., Chancellor; Rev. Mark D. Doherty, Rector; Rev. Blaise R. Berg, Prof.; Rev. Armando J. Gutierrez, Prof.; Rev. Goran Jovicic, Prof.; Rev. Dennis D. McManus, Prof.; Rev. Khoa Nguyen, O.F.M., Prof.; Rev. Marc Valadao, Prof.; Rev. Samuel F. Weber, O.S.B., Prof.; Rev. Vito J. Perrone, Dir.; Matthew Horwitz, Librn.; Rev. Kevin P. Joyce, Spiritual Director; Rev. David Robinson, S.J., Spiritual Director; Rev. Anthony J. Stoeppel, Vice Rector; Stds.: 73; Lay Tchrs.: 10; Pr. Tchrs.: 12

St. Joseph's-St. Patrick's College Alumni Association - St. Patrick's Seminary, 320 Middlefield Rd., Menlo Park, CA 94025 t) 650-289-3336 www.saintjosephscollege.org Thomas Dillon, Pres.;

SAN FRANCISCO

Capuchin Franciscan Order San Buenaventura Friary - 750 Anza St., San Francisco, CA 94118 t) 415-387-7005 arwilson@juno.com Rev. Robert A. Barbato, O.F.M.Cap., Rector; Rev. Christopher Kearney, O.F.M.Cap., Archivist; Rev. John DeLaRiva, O.F.M.Cap., In Res.; Rev. Quoc Nguyen, O.F.M.Cap., Supr.; Rev. Harold Snider, O.F.M.Cap., In Res.;

SPECIAL CARE FACILITIES [SPF]

SAN FRANCISCO

The Good Shepherd Gracenter - 1310 Bacon St., San Francisco, CA 94134 t) 415-337-1938 inquiry@gsgracenter.org www.gsgracecenter.org Residential. Sr. Marguerite Bartling, RGS, CEO; Bed Capacity: 13; Asstd. Annu.: 300; Staff: 11

Mount St. Joseph-St. Elizabeth (Epiphany Center) - 100 Masonic Ave., San Francisco, CA 94118 t) 415-567-8370 sisterbettymarie@theepiphanycenter.org www.theepiphanycenter.org Comprehensive residential drug treatment providing programs to address the traumatic stressors experienced by low-income women(with/without children). Sr. Betty Marie Dunkel, D.C., Exec. Dir.; Bed Capacity: 34; Asstd. Annu.: 200; Staff: 50

Epiphany Center - 100 Masonic Ave., San Francisco, CA 94118 t) 415-537-8370 theepiphanycenter.org Comprehensive residential drug treatment providing programs to address the traumatic stressors experienced by low-income women(with/without children).

Diocese of San Jose in California

(Dioecesis Sancti Josephi in California)

MOST REVEREND OSCAR CANTU, S.T.D.

Bishop of San Jose; ordained May 21, 1994; appointed Auxiliary Bishop of San Antonio and Titular Bishop of Dardano June 2, 2008; appointed Bishop of Las Cruces February 28, 2013; appointed Coadjutor Bishop of San Jose July 11, 2018; Succeeded to See May 1, 2019.

Diocese of San Jose: 1150 N. First St., Ste. 100, San Jose, CA 95112. T: 408-983-0100; F: 408-983-0295.
www.dsj.org
chancellor@dsj.org

ESTABLISHED JANUARY 27, 1981.

Square Miles 1,300.

The Diocese of San Jose comprises the County of Santa Clara in the State of California.

Patrons of the Diocese of San Jose: St. Joseph, Husband of Mary, March 19; St. Clare of Assisi, August 11.

Legal Title: The Roman Catholic Bishop of San Jose, a Corporation Sole.

For legal titles of parishes and diocesan institutions, consult the Chancery Office.

STATISTICAL OVERVIEW

Personnel

Bishop	1
Retired Bishops	1
Priests: Diocesan Active in Diocese	88
Priests: Diocesan Active Outside Diocese	2
Priests: Retired, Sick or Absent	60
Number of Diocesan Priests	150
Religious Priests in Diocese	168
Total Priests in your Diocese	318
Extern Priests in Diocese	25
Ordinations:	
Diocesan Priests	2
Permanent Deacons	1
Permanent Deacons in Diocese	38
Total Brothers	21
Total Sisters	236

Parishes

Parishes	49
With Resident Pastor:	
Resident Diocesan Priests	44
Resident Religious Priests	5
Missions	3
Pastoral Centers	2

Professional Ministry Personnel:

Brothers	5
Sisters	31
Lay Ministers	94

Welfare

Homes for the Aged	1
Total Assisted	150
Special Centers for Social Services	1
Total Assisted	109,294

Educational

Diocesan Students in Other Seminaries	6
Total Seminarians	6
Colleges and Universities	1
Total Students	8,918
High Schools, Diocesan and Parish	1
Total Students	1,761
High Schools, Private	6
Total Students	5,159
Elementary Schools, Diocesan and Parish	26
Total Students	6,914
Elementary Schools, Private	2
Total Students	311

Catechesis/Religious Education:

High School Students	2,805
Elementary Students	6,923
Total Students under Catholic Instruction	32,797
Teachers in Diocese:	
Priests	6
Sisters	5
Lay Teachers	1,201

Vital Statistics

Receptions into the Church:	
Infant Baptism Totals	3,801
Minor Baptism Totals	219
Adult Baptism Totals	184
Received into Full Communion	239
First Communions	2,715
Confirmations	2,320
Marriages:	
Catholic	214
Interfaith	145
Total Marriages	359
Deaths	1,791
Total Catholic Population	689,000
Total Population	1,885,508

LEADERSHIP

Diocese of San Jose - t) 408-983-0100
Vicar General - t) 408-983-0267 Very Rev. Hao Dinh;
Chief Operating Officer - t) 408-983-0210 Rosio Gonzalez;
Communications Director - t) 408-983-0228 Cynthia Shaw;
Vicar for Clergy - t) 408-983-0154 Rev. Joseph Benedict;
Judicial Vicar - t) 408-983-0215 Rev. Noel Sanvicente, Vicar;
Delegate to Religious - t) 408-983-0123 Sr. Ellen Hess, V.D.M.F.;
Bishop's Cabinet - Most Rev. Oscar Cantu; Very Rev. Hao Dinh; Rev. Joseph Benedict;
College of Consultors - Rev. Msgr. Francis V. Cilia; Very Rev. Hao Dinh; Rev. Hector Basanez;
Council of Priests - Most Rev. Oscar Cantu, Pres.; Rev. Joseph Kim, Chair; Rev. Hugo Marcel Rojas, Vice Chair;
Council of Religious - Sr. Ellen Hess, V.D.M.F., Chair; Sr. Maria de la Revelacion Castaneda, S.S.V.M.; Sr. Ana Maria Chavolla;
Deans - Rev. Walter Suarez, Deanery 2; Rev. Msgr. Francis V. Cilia, Deanery 3; Rev. Brian Dinkel, I.V.E., Deanery 4;
Stewardship & Development Director - t) 408-983-0250 Carlos Proano, Dir.;
Chancellor - t) 408-983-0267 Very Rev. Hao Dinh;

OFFICES AND DIRECTORS

Catholic Charities - Gregory R. Kepferle, CEO;
Chancellor - t) 408-983-0267 Very Rev. Hao Dinh, Chancellor;
- **Diocesan Archives and Records Management** - t) 408-983-0267 Erin Louthen, Archivist;

Chief Operating Officer - t) 408-983-0210 Rosio Gonzalez;
- **Human Resources Office** - t) 408-983-0149 Victoria Nuguid, Dir.;
- **Stewardship & Development Director** - t) 408-983-0250 Carlos Proano, Dir.;
- **Communications Director** - t) 408-983-0228 Cynthia Shaw;
- **Office for the Protection of Children and Vulnerable Adults** - t) 408-983-0113 Anthony Gonzalez, Dir.; Griselda Cervantez;

Department for Evangelization - t) 408-983-0182 Rev. Gerardo Menchaca, Vicar;
- **Director for Faith Formation** - t) 408-983-0111 Irma Alarcon de Rangel, Dir.; Sr. Catherine Phuong Dang, L.H.C.;
- **Director for Youth and Young Adults** - t) 408-983-0199
- **Director of Life, Justice & Peace** - t) (408) 983-0134 Rev. Angelbert Chikere;
- **Director of Liturgy** - t) 408-983-0136 Rev. Jeff Fernandez;
- **Family Life and Spirituality** - t) (408) 983-0127
- **Human Concerns Commission** - t) 408-983-0267 Very Rev. Hao Dinh, Liaison;
- **Liturgical Commission** - t) 408-983-0136 Rev. Jeff Fernandez, Liaison; Rev. Christopher Bennett;
- **Institute for Leadership in Ministry** - t) 408-983-0111 Irma Alarcon de Rangel, Dir.;
- **Respect Life Program** - t) (408) 983-0134
- **Restorative Justice** - t) 408-983-0131 Michael Shirley, Assoc. Dir.;
- **Youth and Young Adult Ministry** - t) 408-983-0199 Rev. Truyen Nguyen, Chap.;

Department of Catholic Schools - Jennifer Beltramo, Supt.; Cynthia Olivarra, Dir.;
Diocesan Tribunal - t) (408) 983-0243 Rev. Noel Sanvicente;
- **Administrative Assistant** - Perla Amarotellez;
- **Case Instructor and Notary** - t) 408-983-0224 Zaira Martinez-Robles;
- **Defender of the Bond** - Rev. Robert E. Hayes;
- **Judges** - t) 408-983-0219 Rev. Noel Sanvicente;

Ecumenical and Interreligious Affairs - Rev. Jose Rubio, Dir.;
Finance Office - t) 408-983-0230 Dcn. Eric Simontis, CFO; Kurt Hogan, Dir., Facilities, Insurance & Risk Mgmt.; Julio Bermudez, Compliance Officer;
- **Building Committee** - Kurt Hogan, Chair; Very Rev. Hao Dinh; Rev. Christopher Bennett;
- **Risk Management** - t) 408-983-0237
- **Finance Council** - Kevin Bedolla; Steve Duffy; Nancy Erba;
- **Information Technology** - t) 408-983-0244 Jason Crain;

Department of Cemeteries - t) 650-428-3730 Heather Gloster, Dir.;
Roman Catholic Seminary Corporation - Most Rev. Oscar Cantu, Pres.; Very Rev. Hao Dinh, Vice. Pres.; Dcn. Eric Simontis;
Roman Catholic Welfare Corporation - Most Rev. Oscar Cantu, Pres.; Very Rev. Hao Dinh, Vice. Pres.; Jennifer Beltramo;
The Valley Catholic (Diocesan Magazine) - t) (408) 983-0228 Cynthia Shaw, Editor;
Vicar for Clergy - t) 408-983-0154 Rev. Joseph Benedict;
- **Deacon Formation** - t) 408-983-0256 Dcn. Richard Noack, Dir.; Dcn. Carl Bugarin, Dir.;
- **Diocesan Clergy Personnel Board** - Most Rev. Oscar Cantu, Ex Officio; Rev. Joseph Benedict, Ex Officio; Very Rev. Hao Dinh, Ex Officio;
- **Director of Deacon Life** - Dcn. Carl Bugarin, Dir.;
- **Ongoing Formation of Clergy** - Rev. Mark Arnzen, Chair; Rev. Joseph Benedict, Ex Officio; Dcn. Carl Bugarin, Ex Officio;
- **Permanent Diaconate Admissions and Evaluations Board** - Dcn. Richard Noack, Ex Officio; Rev. Joseph Benedict, Ex Officio; Irma Alarcon de Rangel, Ex Officio;
- **Priests' Retirement Board** - Rev. Msgr. J. Patrick Browne, Chair; Rev. Joseph Benedict, Ex Officio; Dcn. Eric Simontis, Ex Officio;
- **Vocation Office** - t) 408-983-0255 Rev. Andrew C. Nguyen, Dir.; Sr. Rosario Munoz, D.V.M.G., Assoc. Dir.;
  - **Vocation Assessment Team** - Most Rev. Oscar Cantu, Ex Officio; Rev. Andrew C. Nguyen, Ex Officio; Rev. Joseph Benedict, Ex Officio;

Vicar General - t) 408-983-0267 Very Rev. Hao Dinh;
- **Missions Office** - t) (408) 983-0267 Very Rev. Hao Dinh, Dir.;
- **Propagation of the Faith-Holy Childhood Association-Catholic Relief Service** - t) (408) 983-0267 Very Rev. Hao Dinh, Dir.;
- **Lay Retirement Board** - Joseph Guerra, Chair; Very Rev. Hao Dinh, Ex Officio; Dcn. Eric Simontis, Ex Officio;

PARISHES, MISSIONS, AND CLERGY

STATE OF CALIFORNIA

ALVISO

Our Lady, Star of the Sea - 1385 Michigan Ave., Alviso, CA 95002; Mailing: P.O. Box 426, Alviso, CA 95002-0426 t) 408-263-2121 starofthesea@dsj.org www.olsalviso.org Rev. Hector Villela-Huerta (Mexico), Pst.; Oscar Maldonado, DRE; CRP Stds.: 95

CAMPBELL

St. Lucy - 2350 Winchester Blvd, Campbell, CA 95008 t) 408-378-2464 stlucyparishoffice@dsj.org www.stlucy-campbell.org Rev. Rick Rodoni, Pst.; Rev. Andrey Garcia, Par. Vicar; CRP Stds.: 122
- **St. Lucy School** - (Grades PreK-8) 76 Kennedy Ave., Campbell, CA 95008 t) 408-871-8023 principal@stlucyschool.org Susan Grover, Prin.; Stds.: 265; Lay Tchrs.: 12

CUPERTINO

St. Joseph of Cupertino - 10110 N. De Anza Blvd., Cupertino, CA 95014 t) 408-252-7653 catmin@stjosephcupertino.org; info@stjosephcupertino.org www.stjosephcupertino.org Rev. Michael Syjueco, Pst.; Rev. Anthony Tuong Nguyen, Par. Vicar; Rev. Mendie Nguyen, Par. Vicar; Dcn. Ronald Hansen; Daniel Gutierrez, DRE; CRP Stds.: 86
- **St. Joseph of Cupertino School** - (Grades PreK-8) 10120 N. DeAnza Blvd., Cupertino, CA 95014 t) 408-252-6441 michael.lee@dsj.org www.sjcschool.org Jennifer Packard, Prin.; Stds.: 134; Pr. Tchrs.: 1; Lay Tchrs.: 16

GILROY

St. Mary - 11 First St., Gilroy, CA 95020 t) 408-847-5151 x102 deborah.pelliccione@dsj.org smpgilroy.org Rev. Michael D. Hendrickson, Pst.; Rev. Francisco Miramontes, Par. Vicar; Rev. Jose Rubio, In Res.; CRP Stds.: 826
- **St. Mary School** - (Grades K-8) 7900 Church St., Gilroy, CA 95020-4499 t) 408-842-2827 kelly.kramer@dsj.org; marcee.ervin@dsj.org stmarygilroy.org Marcee Ervin, Prin.; Stds.: 191; Lay Tchrs.: 10

LOS ALTOS

St. Nicholas and St. William Catholic Parish - 473 Lincoln Ave., Los Altos, CA 94022 t) 650-559-2080 x2202; 650-948-2158 x2202 finance257@dsj.org www.stnicholasandstwilliam.org Rev. John Poncini, Pst.; Rev. Robain Lamba, Par. Vicar; Rev. Michael Gazzingan (Philippines), Par. Vicar; Lidia Fiandeiro, Bus. Mgr.; Catherine Campbell, DRE; Quynh Pham, Youth Min.; Gary Soals, Music Min.; CRP Stds.: 154
- **St. Nicholas School** - (Grades PreK-8) 12816 S. El Monte Ave., Los Altos Hills, CA 94022 t) 650-941-4056 jpopolizio@stnicholaslah.com www.stnicholaslah.com/ Jan Popolizio, Prin.; Stacy French, Vice Prin.; Stds.: 265; Lay Tchrs.: 14

St. Simon - 1860 Grant Rd., Los Altos, CA 94024 t) 650-967-8311 x10; 650-967-8311 (CRP) mhnguyen@stsimon.org; rectory@stsimon.org www.stsimon.org Rev. Brendan McGuire, Pst.; Rev. Christopher Bologo, Par. Vicar; Rev. Thuc Si Ho, Par. Vicar; Sr. Mary-Han Nguyen, DRE; Joan Mibach, Bus. Mgr.; CRP Stds.: 196
- **St. Simon School** - (Grades PreK-8) 1840 Grant Rd., Los Altos, CA 94024 t) 650-968-9952 akoslovsky@stsimon.org Ann Koslovsky, Prin.; Stds.: 529; Lay Tchrs.: 37

LOS GATOS

St. Mary of the Immaculate Conception - 219 Bean Ave., Los Gatos, CA 95030 t) 408-354-3726 gkimm@stmaryslg.org; parish.office@stmaryslg.org www.stmaryslg.org/ Rev. Gregory C. Kimm, Pst.; Rev. Gabriel Lee, Par. Vicar; CRP Stds.: 96
- **St. Mary of the Immaculate Conception School** - (Grades K-8) 30 Lyndon Ave., Los Gatos, CA 95030 t) 408-354-3944 mhernandez@stmaryslg.org www.smslg.org Monica Hernandez, Prin.; Sheila Chavez, Librn.; Stds.: 182; Lay Tchrs.: 15

MILPITAS

St. Elizabeth - 750 Sequoia Dr., Milpitas, CA 95035 t) 408-262-8100 elizabethchurch@comcast.net www.stelizabethmilpitas.org Rev. Andres C. Ligot, Pst.; Rev. Duong Nguyen, Par. Vicar; Maria Belen Flores, DRE; CRP Stds.: 434

St. John the Baptist - 279 S. Main St., Milpitas, CA 95035 t) 408-262-2546 cbrazil@sjbs.org; mollat@sjbparish.org www.sjbparish.org Rev. Edgar Elamparo I, Par. Vicar; Rev. Msgr. Wilfredo S. Manrique, Pst.; Cory Mollat, DRE; CRP Stds.: 59
- **St. John the Baptist School** - (Grades PreSchool-8) 360 S. Abel St., Milpitas, CA 95035 t) 408-262-8110 info@sjbs.org www.sjbs.org Christopher Brazil, Prin.; Stds.: 211; Sr. Tchrs.: 2; Lay Tchrs.: 9

MORGAN HILL

St. Catherine of Alexandria - 17400 Peak Ave., Morgan Hill, CA 95037 t) 408-779-3959 office@stca.org www.stca.org Rev. Severo Kuupuo (Ghana), Par. Vicar; Rev. Sergio Ovando, Pst.; Rev. Msgr. Francisco Rios, Par. Vicar; Dcn. Juan Aquino; Dcn. Erik Haeckel; Rose Pucan-Meagor, DRE; CRP Stds.: 478

St. Catherine of Alexandria School - (Grades K-8) 17500 Peak Ave., Morgan Hill, CA 95037 t) 408-779-9950 fabienne.esparza@dsj.org www.stcatherinemh.org Anne Nowell, Prin.; Linda Knox, Vice Prin.; Stds.: 342; Lay Tchrs.: 10

MOUNTAIN VIEW

St. Athanasius - 160 N. Rengstorff Ave., Mountain View, CA 94043 t) 650-961-8600 x100; 650-961-8600 x101 (CRP) athanasius@comcast.net; michelle.agreda@dsj.org www.stathanasiusparish.com Rev. Daniel C. Urcia, Par. Vicar; Dcn. Reynaldo Reyes; Rev. Walter Suarez, Pst.; Betty Dominguez Cruz, Bus. Mgr.; CRP Stds.: 103

St. Joseph - 582 Hope St, Mountain View, CA 94041; Mailing: P.O. Box 27, Mountain View, CA 94042 t) 650-967-3831 x121; 650-967-3831 (CRP) diane.wollantsbayona@dsj.org www.sjpmv.org Rev. Eduardo Obero, Par. Vicar; Rev. Engelberto Gammad, Pst.; Rev. Noel Sanvicente, In Res.; CRP Stds.: 93

St. Joseph School, A Drexel School - (Grades K-8) 1120 Miramonte Ave., Mountain View, CA 94040 t) 650-967-1839 christine.usis@dsj.org www.sjmv.org Christine Usis, Prin.; Stds.: 142; Lay Tchrs.: 9

PALO ALTO

St. Thomas Aquinas - 3290 Middlefield Rd., Palo Alto, CA 94306 t) 650-494-2496 estanislao.mikalonis@dsj.org www.paloaltocatholic.org Rev. Estanislao Mikalonis, Pst.; Rev. Rolando Santoianni, Par. Vicar; Dcn. Daniel Hernandez; Ana Arellano Bell, DRE; CRP Stds.: 70

St. Elizabeth Seton Catholic Community School - (Grades PreK-8) 1095 Channing Ave., Palo Alto, CA 94301 t) 650-326-9004 info@setonpaloalto.org www.setonpaloalto.org Sponsored by the Daughters of Charity. Elizabeth Watters, Prin.; Celia Rodriguez, Librn.; Stds.: 179; Lay Tchrs.: 14

SAN JOSE

Cathedral Basilica of St. Joseph - 80 S. Market St., San Jose, CA 95113 t) 408-283-8100 cbsjoffice@gmail.com www.stjosephcathedral.org/ (Mexican National Church) Rev. Ernesto Orci, Pst.; Rev. Prosper Molengi, Par. Vicar; Rev. Joseph Quoc-Tuan Nguyen, Par. Vicar; Nidia Fuentes, DRE; CRP Stds.: 182

St. Anthony - 20101 McKean Rd., San Jose, CA 95120 t) 408-997-4800 churchstanthony@dsj.org churchstanthony.com Rev. Tadeusz Terembula, Pst.; CRP Stds.: 33

St. Brother Albert Chmielowski Polish Catholic Pastoral Mission - 10250 Clayton Rd., San Jose, CA 95127-4336 t) 408-251-8490 office@saintalbert.us www.saintalbert.us Rev. Jan Fiedurek, S.Chr., Pst.; CRP Stds.: 32

Christ the King (Parroquia Cristo Rey) - 5284 Monterey Rd, San Jose, CA 95111 t) 408-362-9958 www.ctksj.org Rev. Hector Basanez, Pst.; Rev. Phuc Trong Tran, Par. Vicar; Sandra Maldonado, DRE; CRP Stds.: 235

St. Christopher - 1576 Curtner Ave., San Jose, CA 95125; Mailing: Msgr. Allen Center, 2278 Booksin Ave., San Jose, CA 95125 t) 408-269-2226; 408-264-8764 (CRP) loretta.pfaff@stchrissj.org www.saintchris.com Rev. Christopher Bennett, Pst.; Rev. Paolo Gobbo, Par. Vicar; Rev. Khoa Vu, Par. Vicar; Dcn. Richard Noack; Edward Dantes, DRE; CRP Stds.: 167

St. Christopher School - (Grades K-8) 2278 Booksin Ave., San Jose, CA 95125 t) 408-723-7223 info@stchris.us www.stchris.us Andrew Armann, Prin.; Stds.: 492; Lay Tchrs.: 27

Church of the Transfiguration - 4325 Jarvis Ave., San Jose, CA 95118 c) (669) 274-6530 transfiguration@dsj.org www.sanjosetransfig.com Judy Bateman, Admin.; Rev. Tito Jesus Cartagenas Jr., Pst.; CRP Stds.: 10

Five Wounds Portuguese National Church - 1375 E. Santa Clara St., San Jose, CA 95116 t) 408-292-2123 info@fivewoundschurch.org www.fivewoundschurch.org Rev. Antonio Silveira, Pst.; CRP Stds.: 45

St. Frances Cabrini - 15333 Woodard Rd., San Jose, CA 95124 t) 408-879-1120 x13; 408-879-1120 x14 (CRP) james.okafor@dsj.org; merry.kaelani@dsj.org sfcabrini.org Rev. James Okafor (Nigeria), Pst.; Rev. Vincent Tinh Thanh Dang, Par. Vicar; Merry Kaelani, CRE; CRP Stds.: 24

St. Frances Cabrini School - (Grades PreK-8) 15325 Woodard Rd., San Jose, CA 95124 t) 408-377-6545 info@sfcschool.org www.sfcschool.org Ronda Byrne-Clark, Prin.; Stds.: 425; Lay Tchrs.: 25

St. Francis of Assisi - 5111 San Felipe Rd., San Jose, CA 95135 t) 408-223-1562; 408-223-1770 x316 (CRP) matthew.stanley@dsj.org www.sfoasj.com Rev. Matthew D. Stanley, Pst.; Rev. Athanasius Kikoba (Uganda), Par. Vicar; Rev. Lieu Vu, Par. Vicar; Dcn. Silvanus Offorjebe; Dcn. Joseph Cabrido; Dcn. Andrzej Sobczyk; Lisa Nakamura, DRE; CRP Stds.: 177

Holy Cross - 580 E. Jackson St., San Jose, CA 95112 t) 408-294-2440 holycross.sanjose@gmail.com; charlesmuscat52@gmail.com www.holycrosssj.org Rev. Leonardo Rocha, Pst.; Rev. Thanh Khan Vu, C.S., Par. Vicar; Bro. Charles Muscat, C.S., DRE; CRP Stds.: 180

Holy Family (Roman Catholic Bishop of San Jose, a Corporation Sole) - 4848 Pearl Ave., San Jose, CA 95136 t) 408-265-4040 holyfamilysanjose.org Rev. Andrew V. Nguyen, Pst.; Rev. Tony Terwase Famave, Par. Vicar; Dcn. Raymond Gans; CRP Stds.: 95

Holy Family School - (Grades PreK-8) 4850 Pearl Ave., San Jose, CA 95136 t) 408-978-1355 office@hfsj.org www.holyfamilyschoolsj.com Vida Covington, Prin.; Terri Lanoie, Librn.; Stds.: 280; Lay Tchrs.: 13

Holy Korean Martyrs - 1523 McLaughlin Ave., San Jose, CA 95122 t) 408-734-9721; 669-231-4137 hkmccsj@gmail.com www.sjkoreancatholic.org Rev. Taehoon Ko, Pst.; Rev. Jaehoon Jung, Par. Vicar; Sr. Yeon Rye Park, DRE; CRP Stds.: 335

Holy Spirit - 1200 Redmond Ave., San Jose, CA 95120 t) 408-997-5101; 408-997-5112 (CRP) merry.reardon@dsj.org www.holyspiritchurch.org Rev. John The Hoang, Par. Vicar; Mary Sparacino, Bus. Mgr.; Rev. Ritche S. Bueza, Pst.; Merry Reardon, DRE; CRP Stds.: 242

Holy Spirit School, A Drexel School - (Grades PreSchool-8) 1198 Redmond Ave., San Jose, CA 95120 t) 408-268-0794 hssschooloffice@dsj.org; sally.douthit@dsj.org www.holyspirit-school.org Sally Douthit, Prin.; Claudia Jones, Admin.; Stds.: 500; Lay Tchrs.: 26

St. John Vianney - 4600 Hyland Ave., San Jose, CA 95127 t) 408-258-7832 x22 (Admin.); 408-258-7832 (CRP) luis.estrada@dsj.org sjvnews.net Rev. Manuel Rafael Barrios, Par. Vicar; Rev. Joseph Kim, Pst.; Luis Estrada, Admin.; Dcn. Raul Mendoza; Joselyn Martinez, DRE; CRP Stds.: 276

St. John Vianney School - (Grades PreK-8) 4601 Hyland Ave., San Jose, CA 95127 t) 408-258-7677 school@sjvsj.org www.sjvsj.org Karen Suty, Prin.; Stds.: 392; Lay Tchrs.: 19

St. Julie Billiart - 6410 Cottle Rd., San Jose, CA 95123; Mailing: 366 St. Julie Dr., San Jose, CA 95119 t) 408-629-3030; 408-629-3030 x102 (CRP) office@stjulies-dsj.org; info@stjulies-dsj.org www.stjulies-dsj.org Rev. Angelo David, Pst.; Rev. Pedro Perez-Sencion, Par. Vicar; Yolanda Toulet, DRE; Shantha Smith, Bus. Mgr.; CRP Stds.: 188

St. Leo the Great - 88 Race St., San Jose, CA 95126 t) 408-293-3503 office@stleochurchsj.org www.stleochurchsj.org Rev. Steve Kim, Pst.; Nidia Fuentes, DRE; CRP Stds.: 211

St. Leo the Great School - (Grades PreK-8) 1051 W. San Fernando St., San Jose, CA 95126 t) 408-293-4846 cathy.torrisi@stleosj.org Matt Komar, Prin.; Stds.: 210; Lay Tchrs.: 13

St. Maria Goretti - 2980 Senter Rd., San Jose, CA 95111 t) 408-363-2300 smgparish@smgsj.org; elena.musselman@dsj.org www.smgsj.org Rev. Pedro Tejeda, Par. Vicar; Rev. Justin Le, Pst.; Rev. Dat Luong, Par. Vicar; Rev. Eric Piczon, Par. Vicar; Dcn. Anthony Pham; Sr. Cecilia Phan, Pst. Assoc.; Araceli Zarate, DRE; CRP Stds.: 568

St. Martin of Tours - 200 O'Connor Dr., San Jose, CA 95128 t) 408-294-8953 maria.moore@pacbell.net stmartin.org Rev. Saju Joseph, Pst.; Rev. Generoso Geronimo (Philippines), Par. Vicar; Therese Lehane, Pst. Min./Coord.; Lori Krouse, Treas.; Lerma Simpson, DRE; Maria Moore, Bus. Mgr.; CRP Stds.: 69

St. Martin of Tours School - (Grades PreK-8) 300 O'Connor Dr., San Jose, CA 95128 t) 408-287-3630 deborah.gisirodriguez@dsj.org www.stmartinsj.org Deborah Gisi-Rodriguez, Prin.; Stds.: 325; Lay Tchrs.: 18

St. Mary of the Assumption - 901 Lincoln Ave., San Jose, CA 95126 t) 408-279-0279 drago.gveric@dsj.org www.facebook.com/croatiancatholicchurch/ (Croatian Mission) Rev. Drago Gveric, O.F.M., Pst.;

Croatian Franciscan Fathers Corporation - Franciscan Fathers - t) (408) 279-0279

Most Holy Trinity - 2040 Nassau Dr., San Jose, CA 95122 t) 408-729-0101 duc.vu@dsj.org www.mht-church.org Rev. Martin O. Silva, SJ, Par. Vicar; Rev. Duc Vu, S.J., Pst.; Rev. Andrew Garcia, S.J., Par. Vicar; Rev. Francis Nguyen, S.J., Par. Vicar; Dcn. Raul Mendoza; Dcn. Dung Quoc Tran; Portifio Nevarez, DRE; Mario Lucas, Bus. Mgr.; CRP Stds.: 479

Most Holy Trinity School, A Drexel School - (Grades PreK-8) 1940 Cunningham Ave., San Jose, CA 95122 t) 408-729-3431 elizabeth.trela@dsj.org Elizabeth Trela, Prin.; Becki Diaz, Contact; Stds.: 200; Lay Tchrs.: 10

Our Lady of Guadalupe - 2020 E. San Antonio St., San Jose, CA 95116 t) 408-258-7057; 408-257-7057 (CRP) olgparishsj@gmail.com Rev. Gerardo Menchaca, Pst.; Dcn. Armando Brambila; Mother Maria Gisela N Enriquez Sr., DRE; CRP Stds.: 374

Our Lady of La Vang Parish - 389 E. Santa Clara St., San Jose, CA 95112; Mailing: 25 N. 14th St., Ste. 540, San Jose, CA 95112 t) 408-291-6280; 408-294-8120 www.ducmelavangparish.org Dcn. Dinh Chu; Rev. Peter Loi Huynh, Pst.; Rev. John Tran Nguyen, Par. Vicar; Rev. Joseph Page, Par. Vicar; Rev. Hung Vu, Par. Vicar; Dcn. Tho Le; Kim Oanh Le, Admin.; CRP Stds.: 729

Vietnamese Ministry - 2849 S. White Rd., San Jose, CA 95148 josephnguyen.vanthu@dsj.org Rev. Joseph N. Vanthu, Dir.;

St. Patrick School, A Drexel School - (Grades K-8) 51 N. 9th St., San Jose, CA 95112 t) 408-283-5858 olga.islas@dsj.org; martha.angeles@dsj.org www.stpatrickschool.org Sponsored by the Daughters of Charity. Olga Islas, Prin.; Sr. Christena Papavera, Librn.; Stds.: 195; Sr. Tchrs.: 1; Lay Tchrs.: 8

Our Lady of Refuge - 2165 Lucretia Ave., San Jose, CA 95122 t) 408-715-2278 luis.lopezmiranda@dsj.org; theresalando@yahoo.com ourladyofrefugesj.org Rev. Hugo Marcel Rojas, Pst.; Rev. Anthony Tan Nguyen, Par. Vicar; Sr. Theresa Lan Do, LHC, DRE; Luis Lopez Miranda, Bus. Mgr.; CRP Stds.: 376

Queen of Apostles - 4911 Moorpark Ave., San Jose, CA 95129 t) 408-253-7560 www.qofa.org Rev. Jeff Fernandez, Pst.; Kristie Manning, DRE; Rev. Celso Singson, Par. Vicar; CRP Stds.: 49

Queen of Apostles School - (Grades PreK-8) 4950 Mitty Way, San Jose, CA 95129 t) 408-252-3659 guel@qofa-school.org www.qofa-school.org Stephanie Hoover, Prin.; Deborah Wagner, Librn.; Stds.: 235; Lay Tchrs.: 12

Sacred Heart of Jesus - 325 Willow St., San Jose, CA 95110 t) 408-816-7822 diyi.iquinas@dsj.org; sacredheartofjesus@dsj.org www.sacredheartjesuschurch.org Rev. Jonathan Cuarto, Vicar; Rev. Luis Vargas, Pst.; Rev. Truyen Nguyen, In Res.; CRP Stds.: 299

Santa Teresa - 794 Calero Ave., San Jose, CA 95123

t) 408-629-7777 x101; 408-629-7777 x108 (CRP) lynda@santateresachurch.com; george.aranha@dsj.org santateresachurch.com Rev. George Aranha, Pst.; Lynda DeManti, Pst. Assoc.; CRP Stds.: 57

St. Thomas of Canterbury - 1522 McCoy Ave., San Jose, CA 95130 t) 408-378-1595 andrew.c.nguyen@dsj.org; victoria.schwoob@dsj.org www.stthomassj.org Rev. Andrew C. Nguyen, Pst.; CRP Stds.: 91

St. Victor - 3150 Sierra Rd., San Jose, CA 95132; Mailing: 3108 Sierra Rd., San Jose, CA 95132 t) 408-251-7055 admin@stvictorchurch.org; janine.pascual@dsj.org www.stvictorchurch.org/ Rev. Mark Gazzingan, Pst.; Rev. Allen Navarro, Par. Vicar; Rev. John Offor (Nigeria), Par. Vicar; Sr. Sara King, Pst. Assoc.; Dcn. Carl Bugarin; Janine Pascual, DRE; CRP Stds.: 245

St. Victor School - (Grades PreK-8) t) 408-251-1740 victoria.hinkle@dsj.org Maria Victoria Hinkle, Admin.; Victoria Hinkle, Prin.; Rosanne Huey, Bus. Mgr.; Joan Passalaqua, Librn.; Stds.: 207; Sr. Tchrs.: 1; Lay Tchrs.: 10

SANTA CLARA

St. Clare - 725 Washington St., Santa Clara, CA 95050-4935 t) 408-248-7786 stclareparish@dsj.org; francis.cilia@dsj.org www.stclareparish.org Rev. Msgr. Francis V. Cilia, Pst.; Rev. Victor Trinidad, Par. Vicar; Rev. Carlos Alberto Olivera, In Res.; Rev. Martin Chukwunenye Ezeador, In Res.; Christopher Wemp, Music Min.; Sandra Quintanilla, DRE; Ryan Bao, Youth Min.; Diane Madruga, RCIA Coord.; Lucy Santos, Pst. Min./Coord.; CRP Stds.: 129

St. Clare School - (Grades PreK-8) 750 Washington St., Santa Clara, CA 95050-4935 t) 408-246-6797 office@stclareschool.org www.stclare.school Cecile Mantecon, Prin.; Stds.: 227; Lay Tchrs.: 12

St. Justin - 2655 Homestead Rd., Santa Clara, CA 95051 t) 408-248-1094; 408-296-1193; 408-296-1193 x104 (CRP) www.st-justin.org Rev. Christopher Bransfield, Pst.; Rev. Gerald Nwafor (Nigeria), Par. Vicar; CRP Stds.: 93

St. Justin School - (Grades PreK-8) t) (408) 248-1094 schooloffice@stjustinschool.org www.stjustinschool.org Maira Gutierrez, Prin.; Stds.: 300; Lay Tchrs.: 25

St. Lawrence, the Martyr - 1971 Saint Lawrence Dr., Santa Clara, CA 95051 t) 408-296-3000 edepaz@saintlawrence.org; parish@saintlawrence.org www.saintlawrence.org Rev. Anthony Uytingco, Par. Vicar; Rev. Mark Arnzen, Pst.; Dcn. Gregorio Ortiz; Eleanor De Paz, DRE; Rev. Angelbert Chikere, In Res.; CRP Stds.: 96

Saint Lawrence Elementary & Middle School - (Grades PreK-8) 1977 St. Lawrence Dr., Santa Clara, CA 95051 t) 408-296-2260 gayle.wholley@dsj.org www.slems.org Christine Frea, Prin.; Stds.: 92; Lay Tchrs.: 8

Our Lady of Peace - 2800 Mission College Blvd., Santa Clara, CA 95054 t) 408-988-4585; 408-988-7648 (CRP) adult.edu@olop-shrine.org; catechismoffice@olop-shrine.org www.olop-shrine.org Rev. Brian Dinkel, I.V.E., Pst.; Rev. Jonathan Yu Dumlao, I.V.E., Par. Vicar; Rev. Miguel Lombardi, IVE, Par. Vicar; Mother Maria Revelacion, S.S.V.M., DRE; Sr. Mary of Joseph, S.S.V.M., DRE; CRP Stds.: 575

San Jose Chinese Catholic Mission - 725 Washington St., Santa Clara, CA 95050-4966 t) 408-758-8917 carlosalberto.olivera@dsj.org sjccm.com/ (Cantonese Catholic Community) Rev. Carlos Alberto Olivera, Pst.; CRP Stds.: 50

SARATOGA

Church of the Ascension - 12033 Miller Ave., Saratoga, CA 95070 t) 408-725-3939 hao.dinh@dsj.org www.ascensionsaratoga.org Very Rev. Hao Dinh, Pst.; Rev. Reynaldo Sarmiento, Par. Vicar; Loy Oppus-Moe, Pst. Min./Coord.; CRP Stds.: 35

Sacred Heart - 13716 Saratoga Ave., Saratoga, CA 95070 t) 408-867-3634 x501 c.orasin@sacredheartsaratoga.org; j.benedict@sacredheartsaratoga.org www.sacredheartsaratoga.org Rev. Joseph Benedict, Pst.; Rev. Biju Varghese (India), Par. Vicar; Dcn. Donald Sifferman; CRP Stds.: 27

Sacred Heart School - (Grades K-8) 13718 Saratoga Ave., Saratoga, CA 95070 t) 408-867-9241 office@sacredheartsaratoga.org school.sacredheartsaratoga.org Tom Pulchny, Prin.; Stds.: 228; Lay Tchrs.: 12

Pre-School - 13718 Saratoga Ave, Saratoga, CA 95070 t) 408-867-9241 office@sacredheartsaratoga.org school.sacredheartsaratoga.org Tom Pulchny, Prin.;

STANFORD

Catholic Community at Stanford - Old Union, 3rd Fl., Stanford University, Stanford, CA 94309; Mailing: P.O. Box 20301, Stanford, CA 94309 t) 650-725-0080 admin@stanfordcatholic.org; xavierop@stanford.edu web.stanfordcatholic.org Rev. Xavier Lavagetto, O.P., Pst.; Rev. Dominic DeLay, OP, Par. Vicar; Rev. Robert Glynn, SJ, Par. Vicar; Dcn. John Kerrigan; Sr. Gloria Marie Jones, OP, Pst. Assoc.; Sr. Regena Ross, OP, Pst. Assoc.; Teresa Pleins, DRE; CRP Stds.: 60

SUNNYVALE

Church of the Resurrection - 1399 Hollenbeck Ave, Sunnyvale, CA 94087; Mailing: 725 Cascade Dr., Sunnyvale, CA 94087 t) 408-245-5554 maryclare@resparish.org; jeanne.matsuda@dsj.org www.resurrection-church.org Rev. John Doanh Phong Nguyen, S.J., Pst.; Rev. Arthur Yabes, S.V.D., Par. Vicar; Dcn. Michael Haas; Rev. Andrzej Salapata (Poland), In Res.; Jeanne Matsuda, DRE; CRP Stds.: 87

Church of the Resurrection Elementary School, A Drexel School - (Grades PreSchool-8) 1395 Hollenbeck Ave., Sunnyvale, CA 94087 t) 408-245-4571 marie.reid@rescatholicschool.org; school@rescatholicschool.org rescatholicschool.org/ Jacqueline T. Wright, Prin.; Stds.: 164; Lay Tchrs.: 20

St. Cyprian - 195 Leota Ave, Sunnyvale, CA 94086; Mailing: 1133 W. Washington Ave, Sunnyvale, CA 94086 t) 408-739-8506 info@saintcyprian.org www.saintcyprian.org Rev. Vincent Pineda, Pst.; Alde Vera, DRE; CRP Stds.: 71

St. Martin - 590 Central Ave., Sunnyvale, CA 94086; Mailing: 593 Central Ave., Sunnyvale, CA 94086 t) 408-736-3725 nancy.cordova@dsj.org; mkang@smsdsj.org www.smsdsj.org Rev. Roberto Gomez, Pst.; Rev. Peter-Luc Phan, Par. Vicar; Nancy Cordova, Director of Faith Formation; CRP Stds.: 133

SCHOOLS: PRESCHOOL THRU HIGH SCHOOL

SCHOOLS

STATE OF CALIFORNIA

CAMPBELL

Canyon Heights Academy, Inc. - (PRV) (Grades PreSchool-8) 775 Waldo Rd., Campbell, CA 95008 t) 408-370-6727 kholman@chamail.net www.canyonheightsacademy.com Kevin Holman, Exec. Dir.; Dr. Analiza Filion, Prin.; Rev. Matthew Schmitz, LC, Chap.; Stds.: 225; Lay Tchrs.: 20

SAN JOSE

Sacred Heart Nativity School - (PRV) (Grades 6-8) 310 Edwards Ave., San Jose, CA 95110 t) 408-993-1293 rsolorio@shnativity.org www.shnativity.org Michael Serrania, Prin.; Dcn. Ruben Solorio, Pres.; Stds.: 86; Lay Tchrs.: 6

HIGH SCHOOLS

STATE OF CALIFORNIA

CAMPBELL

Saint John XXIII College Prep - 2350 Winchester Blvd., Campbell, CA 95008-4098 t) 408-378-2464 steve.kim@dsj.org Rev. Steve Kim, Contact;

MOUNTAIN VIEW

Saint Francis High School - (PRV) (Grades 9-12) 1885 Miramonte Ave., Mountain View, CA 94040 t) 650-968-1213 dianewilson@sfhs.com www.sfhs.com Brothers of Holy Cross. Jason D Curtis, Pres.; Katie Teekell, Prin.; Rev. Anthony J. Mancuso, Chap.; Simon Raines, Admin.; Sr. Jodi Cecilia Min, O.P, Dir.; Stds.: 1,783; Lay Tchrs.: 104

SAN JOSE

Archbishop Mitty High School - (DIO) (Grades 9-12) 5000 Mitty Ave., San Jose, CA 95129 t) 408-252-6610 www.mitty.com Latantya Hilton, Pres.; Kate Caputo, Prin.; Stds.: 1,761; Pr. Tchrs.: 1; Lay Tchrs.: 120

Bellarmine College Preparatory - (PRV) (Grades 9-12) 960 W. Hedding St., San Jose, CA 95126 t) 408-294-9224 tdelcarlo@bcp.org www.bcp.org Society of Jesus Sonya Arriola, Prin.; Rev. Mario J. Prietto, S.J., Supr.; Rev. Gerald T. Wade, S.J., Chancellor; Rev. Richard E. Cobb, S.J.; Rev. Michael Moodie, S.J.; Most Rev. Carlos A. Sevilla, S.J.; Rev. Robert J. Shinney, S.J.; Chris Meyercord, Pres.; Tana Perotin, Librn.; Stds.: 1,640; Pr. Tchrs.: 2; Lay Tchrs.: 112

***Cristo Rey San Jose Jesuit High School** - (PRV) (Grades 9-12) 1389 E. Santa Clara St., San Jose, CA 95116 t) 408-293-0425 peter.pabst@cristoreysj.org www.cristoreysanjose.org Society of Jesus Andria Bengtson, Prin.; Rev. Peter G. Pabst, S.J., Chancellor; Silvia Mahan, Pres.; Stds.: 434; Pr. Tchrs.: 2; Lay Tchrs.: 30

Notre Dame High School - (PRV) 596 S. Second St., San Jose, CA 95112 t) 408-294-1113 mbriley@ndsj.org www.ndsj.org Sisters of Notre Dame de Namur. Mary Beth Riley, Prin.; Amy Huang, Dir.; Stds.: 675; Sr. Tchrs.: 1; Lay Tchrs.: 55

Presentation High School - (PRV) 2281 Plummer Ave., San Jose, CA 95125 t) 408-264-1664 kgeorgiez@presentationhs.org www.presentationhs.org Sisters of the Presentation. Rev. Rick Rodoni, Chap.; Katherine Georgiev, Prin.; Stds.: 627; Lay Tchrs.: 37

INSTITUTIONS LOCATED IN DIOCESE

ASSOCIATIONS [ASN]

LOS GATOS

Jesuit Seminary Association - 300 College Ave, Los Gatos, CA 95030; Mailing: P.O. Box 519, Los Gatos, CA 95031-0519 t) 408-884-1600 uweprovince@jesuits.org www.jesuitswest.org Rev. Edward S. Fassett, S.J., Treas.;

CAMPUS MINISTRY / NEWMAN CENTERS [CAM]

SAN JOSE

SJSU Catholic Newman Center - 300 S. 10th St., San Jose, CA 95112; Mailing: 80 S. Market St., San Jose, CA 95113 t) 408-283-8100 x2219 ernesto.orci@dsj.org www.facebook.com/sjsunewmancenter/ Rev. Ernesto Orci, Dir.;

CATHOLIC CHARITIES [CCH]

SAN JOSE

Advocacy & Community Engagement - 2625 Zanker Rd., San Jose, CA 95134 t) 408-468-0100 info@catholiccharitiesscc.org Rev. Jon Pedigo, S.T.L., Dir.;

Handicapables - mneu@catholiccharitiesscc.org

Parish Partnerships - t) 408-468-1011

Step Up Silicon Valley -

Volunteers -

Behavioral Health Services - 2625 Zanker Rd., San Jose, CA 95134 t) 408-468-0100 info@catholiccharitiesscc.org www.catholiccharitiesscc.org Ofelia Picanco, Dir.; Sabry Ramirez, Dir.;

Older Adult Wellness Center -

Restorative Justice Center -

Youth & Family Wellness Center -

Catholic Charities of Santa Clara County - 2625 Zanker Rd., San Jose, CA 95134 t) 408-468-0100 info@catholiccharitiesscc.org www.catholiccharitiesscc.org Lisa Christian, COO; Jenny Ho, CFO; Gregory R. Kepferle, CEO; Rev. Jon Pedigo, S.T.L., Dir.; Asstd. Annu.: 109,294; Staff: 685

Children, Youth & Family Development - 2625 Zanker Rd., San Jose, CA 95134-0275 t) 408-468-0100 info@catholiccharitiesscc.org www.catholiccharitiesscc.org Sara Reyes, Senior Div. Dir.;

Adult Day Care Services -

Bridges of Hope -

CORAL (Communities Organizing Resources to Advance Learning) -

Family Resource Centers -

Franklin McKinley's Children's Initiative -

Long Term Care Ombudsman - t) 408-944-0567

Probation Gang Resistance & Intervention Program -

Senior Community Services -

Washington United Youth Center - t) 408-938-6731

Youth Empowerment for Success - t) 408-283-6150

Economic Development Services - 2625 Zanker Rd., San Jose, CA 95134-2107 t) 408-468-0100 info@catholiccharitiesscc.org www.catholiccharitiesscc.org Eila Latif, Dir.;

Car Donation -

Disaster Recovery Services -

Employment Services -

Home Care Aide Certification & Placement Services -

Immigration Legal Services -

Refugee & Immigration Integration -

Responsible Landlord English Initiative - t) 408-283-6150

Emergency Program & Housing Services - 2625 Zanker Rd., San Jose, CA 95134-0275 t) 408-468-0100 info@catholiccharitiesscc.org Lindsey Caldwell, Dir.;

Housing Sharing -

Supportive Housing Services -

Refugee Services - 2625 Zanker Rd., San Jose, CA 95134 t) 408-468-0100 info@catholiccharitiesscc.org Candace Chen, Div. Dir.;

Refugee Foster Care -

Refugee Resettlement -

CEMETERIES [CEM]

LOS ALTOS

Gate of Heaven - 22555 Cristo Rey Dr., Los Altos, CA 94024 t) 650-428-3730 cemeteryinfo@ccdsj.org www.ccdsj.org Heather Gloster, Dir.;

SAN JOSE

Calvary Catholic Cemetery - 2650 Madden Ave., San Jose, CA 95116; Mailing: 22555 Cristo Rey Dr., Los Altos, CA 94024 t) 408-258-2940 cemeteryinfo@dsj.org www.ccdsj.org (Santa Clara Co.) Heather Gloster, Dir.;

COLLEGES & UNIVERSITIES [COL]

SANTA CLARA

Santa Clara University - 500 El Camino Real, Santa Clara, CA 95053-0001 t) 408-554-4000; 408-554-4160 www.scu.edu Dr. Julie Sullivan, Pres.; Molly A. McDonald, Chief of Staff; John Ottoboni, Gen. Counsel; Alison Benders, Vice Pres. Mission & Min.; Eva Blanco Masias, Vice Pres. Enrollment Mngmnt.; T. Sha Duncan Smith, Vice Pres. Diversity, Equity & Inclusion; Lawrence Lokman, Vice Pres. Univ. Mktg. & Comm.; James Lyons, Vice Pres. Univ. Rels.; Ed Grier, Dean, Leavey School of Business; Michael Kaufman, Dean, School of Law; Rev. Joseph G. Mueller, S.J., Dean, Jesuit School of Theology; Daniel Press, Dean, College of Arts and Sciences; Elaine Scott, Dean, School of Engineering; Sabrina Zirkel, Dean, School of Education & Counseling Psychology; Don Heider, Exec. Dir., Markkula Ctr. for Applied Ethics; Brigit Helms, Exec. Dir., Miller Ctr. for Social Entrepreneurship; Kate Morris, Co-Provost; Dr. Ed Ryan, Co-Provost; Jeanne Rosenberger, Vice Provost Student Life; Renee Baumgartner, Athletics Dir.; Rev. John R. Treacy, S.J., Univ. Rels. Chap.; Stds.: 8,918; Lay Tchrs.: 571; Pr. Tchrs.: 12; Sr. Tchrs.: 1

Jesuit Community at Santa Clara University, Inc. - 801 Franklin St., Santa Clara, CA 95050; Mailing: 500 El Camino Real, Santa Clara, CA 95053-1600 t) 408-554-4124 www.scu.edu/scujesuits/ Rev. Luis F. Calero, S.J., Rector; Rev. Samuel P. Bellino, S.J., Mem.; Rev. James R. Blaettler, S.J., Mem.; Bro. Thomas C. Bracco, S.J., Mem.; Rev. Julian Climaco, S.J., Mem.; Rev. Edward S. Fassett, S.J., Mem.; Rev. Maria Joseph Israel, S.J., Mem.; Rev. Arthur F. Liebscher, S.J., Mem.; Rev. Paul P. Mariani, S.J., Mem.; Rev. John P. Mossi, S.J., Mem.; Rev. Peter G. Pabst, S.J., Mem.; Rev. Dennis R. Parnell, S.J., Mem.; Rev. Roy Ragas, S.J., Mem.; Rev. Gerald Robinson, S.J., Mem.; Rev. Robert W. Scholla, S.J., Mem.; Rev. Anthony E. Sholander, S.J., Mem.; Rev. Dennis C. Smolarski, S.J., Mem.; Rev. Paul A. Soukup, S.J., Mem.; Rev. Salvatore A. Tassone, S.J., Mem.; Rev. Dat T. Tran, S.J., Mem.; An Nguyen Vu, S.J., Mem.;

Jesuit School of Theology of Santa Clara University - 1735 Le Roy Ave., Berkeley, CA 94709 t) 510-549-5013 Society of Jesus Jasmine Allen, Admin.;

CONVENTS, MONASTERIES, AND RESIDENCES FOR WOMEN [CON]

CAMPBELL

Sisters of the Holy Names of Jesus and Mary US-Ontario Province. - 65 W Rincon Ave., Campbell, CA 95008; Mailing: P.O. Box 907, Los Gatos, CA 95031-0907 t) 408-250-2221 nclemmons@snjmuson.org www.snjmusontario.org Sr. Maureen Delaney, S.N.J.M., Prov.; Sr. Diane Enos, SNJM, Dir.; Sr. Marcia Frideger, SNJM, Dir.; Sr. Carol Higgins, SNJM, Dir.; Sr. Linda Patrick, SNJM, Dir.; Sr. Mary Slater, SNJM, Dir.; Srs.: 108

CUPERTINO

Blessed Virgin Missionaries of Carmel (B.V.M.C.) - 10130 N. De Anza Blvd., Cupertino, CA 95014 t) 408-257-1022 srkristine2010@gmail.com Sr. Kristine Japitana, Local Contact; Srs.: 4

LOS ALTOS HILLS

Daughters of Charity of St. Vincent de Paul, Seton Provincialate - 26000 Altamont Rd., Los Altos Hills, CA 94022 t) 650-941-4490 srcmaggi@doc1633.org www.daughtersofcharity.com Sr. Christina Maggi, DC, Prov.; Srs.: 48

Immaculate Heart Monastery of the Poor Clares - 28210 Natoma Rd., Los Altos Hills, CA 94022-3220 t) 650-948-2947 poorclareslosaltos.org Poor Clares of Los Altos Srs.: 23

MILPITAS

The Congregation of the Augustinian Recollect Sisters in California - 307 Moretti Ln., Milpitas, CA 95035 t) 408-262-3536; 408-416-7501 marcegono@sjbs.org www.augustinianrecollect.org.ph Sr. Myrna Arcegono, Supr.; Srs.: 4

SAN JOSE

Community of the Holy Spirit - 1275 Naglee Ave., San Jose, CA 95126 t) 408-275-1710 Sr. Jolene M. Schmitz, C.H.S., Contact; Srs.: 1

Daughters of Charity of St. Vincent de Paul - 350 O'Connor Dr., San Jose, CA 95128 t) 408-862-9377 srmrandall@doc1633.org Sr. Christina Maggi, D.C., Prov.; Srs.: 4

Eucharistic Missionaries of the Most Holy Trinity - 815 S. Daniel Way, San Jose, CA 95128 t) 408-243-3157 giselamesst@hotmail.com Mother Maria Gisela N Enriquez Sr., Contact; Srs.: 3

La Salle Sisters - 3867 Silver Creek Rd., San Jose, CA 95121-1969; Mailing: 248 Kirk Ave, San Jose, CA 95127 t) 408-238-9351 anhloanls@gmail.com; atdo@alumni.scu.edu thelasallesisters.org Religious Sisters Sr. Anhloan Therese Do, LS.S., Supr.; Sr. Theresa Thu Ha Nguyen, L.S.S., Treas.; Srs.: 13

***La Salle Community Center** - 248 Kirk Ave., San Jose, CA 95127-2220 t) 408-684-4701; 408-708-4139 bichvanlss@yahoo.com www.thelasallesisters.org Language School; Preschool Sr. Bich Van Nguyen, LS.S., Dir.; Sr. Anhloan Do, LS.S., Chair;

Quinhon Missionary Sisters of the Holy Cross - 368 Neilson Ct., San Jose, CA 95111 t) 408-362-9719; 408-368-0692 catherinepdang@yahoo.com www.mtgqn.org Sr. Catherine Phuong Dang, L.H.C., Supr.; Srs.: 11

Sisters of Mercy of Americas (Burlingame) - 1600 Petersen Ave., #40, San Jose, CA 95129 t) 408-500-5441 eloros@global.net Sr. Laura Reicks, Pres.; Srs.: 2

SANTA CLARA

Carmelite Monastery of the Infant Jesus, Discalced Carmelite Nuns - 1000 Lincoln St., Santa Clara, CA 95050 t) 408-296-8412 santaclaracarmel@sbcglobal.net www.members.aol.com/santaclaracarmel Sr. Irene of Jesus and Mary, O.C.D., Prioress; Srs.: 6

Institute of the Servants of the Lord and the Virgin of Matara - 2800 Mission College Blvd., Santa Clara, CA 95054 t) 669-208-3450 c.ourladyofpeace@servidoras.org www.ssvmusa.org Mother Maria de la Revelacioń Castaneda, SSVM, Contact; Srs.: 9

SARATOGA

Dominican Sisters of St. Catherine of Siena - 14735 Aloha Ave., Saratoga, CA 95070 c) (847) 867-5988 sasnyderop@aol.com Changed the entity type to Convent / Monastery Sr. Susan Snyder, O.P., Contact; Srs.: 3

SUNNYVALE

Sisters of Charity of the Blessed Virgin Mary - 1220 Tasman Dr., #571, Sunnyvale, CA 94089 t) 408-220-5150 www.bvmcong.org Sr. Marilyn Katherine Wilson, Contact; Srs.: 3

ENDOWMENTS / FOUNDATIONS / TRUSTS [EFT]

LOS GATOS

USA West Province, Society of Jesus Irrevocable Aged-Infirm Fund Charitable Trust - 300 College Ave, Los Gatos, CA 95030; Mailing: P.O. Box 519, Los Gatos, CA 95031-0519 t) 408-884-1600 uwetreasurer@jesuits.org Rev. Sean Carroll, S.J., Prov.;

USA West Province, Society of Jesus Irrevocable Apostolic Fund Charitable Trust - 300 College Ave, Los Gatos, CA 95030; Mailing: P.O. Box 519, Los Gatos, CA 95031-0519 t) 408-884-1600 uwetreasurer@jesuits.org Rev. Sean Carroll, S.J., Prov.;

USA West Province, Society of Jesus Irrevocable Formation Fund Charitable Trust - 300 College Ave, Los Gatos, CA 95030; Mailing: P.O. Box 519, Los Gatos, CA 95031-0519 t) 408-884-1600 uwetreasurer@jesuits.org Rev. Sean Carroll, S.J., Prov.;

USA West Province, Society of Jesus Irrevocable Foundations Fund Charitable Trust - 300 College Ave, Los Gatos, CA 95030; Mailing: P.O. Box 519, Los Gatos, CA 95031-0519 t) 408-884-1600 uwetreasurer@jesuits.org Rev. Sean Carroll, S.J., Prov.;

MOUNTAIN VIEW

Villa Siena Foundation - 1855 Miramonte Ave., Mountain View, CA 94040 t) 650-961-6484 foundation@villa-siena.org villa-siena.org Corine Bernard, Exec.;

SAN JOSE

The Catholic Community Foundation - 777 N. First St., Ste. 490, San Jose, CA 95112 t) 408-995-5219 info@catholiccf.org www.catholiccf.org Mary Quilici Aumack, Exec.;

San Jose Cathedral Foundation - 80 S. Market St., San Jose, CA 95113 t) 408-283-8100 anna.moran@dsj.org www.stjosephcathedral.org (A nonprofit, charitable, public-benefit California corporation.) Rev. Ernesto Orci, Chair;

SANTA CLARA
IVE West Coast Trust - 2800 Mission College Blvd., Santa Clara, CA 95054 t) 408-988-4585 brian.dinkel@dsj.org Rev. Brian Dinkel, I.V.E.;
SARATOGA
Our Lady of Fatima Villa Foundation - 14434 Oak St., Saratoga, CA 95070 t) (408) 647-2760 bmahoney@olfvfoundation.org fatimavilla.org Rev. Scott Wallenfelsz, SDS, Chair;

MISCELLANEOUS [MIS]

CUPERTINO
St. Joseph Cupertino Retirement Residence - 10130 N. De Anza Blvd., Cupertino, CA 95014 t) 408-257-1022 michael.mitchell@dsj.org Rev. Msgr. Michael J. Mitchell, Dir.;
EAST PALO ALTO
Rosalie Rendu Inc. - 2345 Pulgas Ave., East Palo Alto, CA 94303-1320; Mailing: 26000 Altamont Rd., Los Altos Hills, CA 94022 t) 650-473-9522; 650-949-8868 jday@doc1633.org Sr. Christina Maggi, D.C., CEO;
LOS ALTOS
Jesuit Institute for Family Life - 300 Manresa Way, Los Altos, CA 94022 t) 650-948-4854 rfabing@jesuit.org www.elretiro.org Rev. Robert J. Fabing, S.J., Dir.;
LOS ALTOS HILLS
Daughters of Charity Ministry Services Corporation - 26000 Altamont Rd., Los Altos Hills, CA 94022-4317 t) 650-949-8868 jday@doc1633.org Sr. Christina Maggi, D.C., CEO;
Ministry Services of the Daughters of Charity of St. Vincent de Paul - 26000 Altamont Rd., Los Altos Hills, CA 94022 t) 650-949-8868 jday@doc1633.org Sr. Christina Maggi, D.C., CEO;
Vincentian Marian Youth - 26000 Altamont Rd., Los Altos Hills, CA 94022 t) 650-941-4490 jday@doc1633.org Sr. Christina Maggi, D.C., CEO;
LOS GATOS
California Jesuit Missionaries - 300 College Ave, Los Gatos, CA 95030; Mailing: P.O. Box 519, Los Gatos, CA 95031-0519 t) 408-884-1612 uweprovince@jesuits.org www.jesuitswest.org Rev. Theodore Gabrielli, S.J., Dir.;
MENLO PARK
Roman Catholic Communications Corporation of the Bay Area (Catholic Telemedia Network) - 324 Middlefield Rd., Menlo Park, CA 94025 t) 650-326-7850 ronald@ctnba.org Most Rev. Michael C. Barber, S.J., Chair; Most Rev. Oscar Cantu, Chair; Ronald J. Loiacono, Exec.;
SACRAMENTO
Holy Trinity Community North America - Silicon Valley Region - 4216 Silver Water Way, Sacramento, CA 95742; Mailing: 5010 Birkdale Way, San Jose, CA 95138 t) 408-833-5044 erick.yo@gmail.com htcna.org/ Paulus Usong, Exec.;
SAN JOSE
Alexian Brothers of San Jose, Inc. - c/o 1150 N. First St., Ste. 100, San Jose, CA 95112; Mailing: c/o CT Corporation, 818 W. Seventh St., Ste. 930, Los Angeles, CA 90017 t) 224-273-2331 john.halstead1@ascension.org www.ascension.org Polly Davenport, COO; John Halstead, Chief Mission Integration Officer;
Caritas Housing Corporation - 1400 Parkmoor Ave., Ste. 190, San Jose, CA 95126 t) 408-550-8300 info@charitieshousing.org www.charitieshousing.org Mark Mikl, Exec. Dir.;
Catholic Professional and Business Club - ; Mailing: P.O. Box 6346, San Jose, CA 95150 t) 408-491-9229 sjcathpros@gmail.com sjcatholicprofessionals.com Rev. Christopher Bennett, Chap.; Christopher Miller, Pres.; Susan B. Skorey, Pres.;
Charities Housing Development Corporation of Santa Clara County - 1400 Parkmoor Ave., Ste. 190, San Jose, CA 95126 t) 408-550-8300 info@charitieshousing.org www.charitieshousing.org Mark Mikl, Exec. Dir.;
Hope Charities Housing Corporation - 1400 Parkmoor Ave., Ste. 190, San Jose, CA 95126 t) 408-550-8300 info@charitieshousing.org www.charitieshousing.org Mark Mikl, Exec. Dir.;
St. Joseph Financial Services - 1150 N. First St., Ste. 100, San Jose, CA 95112 t) 219-779-7505 Jonathan Boulos, CEO;
Roman Catholic Seminary Corporation of San Jose - 1150 N. First St., Ste. 100, San Jose, CA 95112 t) 408-983-0168 eric.simontis@dsj.org Very Rev. Hao Dinh, Vice. Pres.;
The Roman Catholic Welfare Corporation of San Jose - 1150 N. First St., Ste. 100, San Jose, CA 95112 t) 408-983-0267 hao.dinh@dsj.org Very Rev. Hao Dinh, Contact;
San Jose English Cursillo - 2278 Booksin Ave, San Jose, CA 95125; Mailing: P.O. Box 6648, San Jose, CA 95150-6648 c) 408-316-3951 lcargnoni@sbcglobal.net www.sanjosecursillo.org Lawrence J Cargnoni, Dir.;
Serra International Region 11, District 31 - 1282 Shasta Ave., San Jose, CA 95126; Mailing: 3191 Buckingham Ave., Clovis, CA 93619 t) 408-293-8004 bgnewnan@gmail.com Bruce Newnan, Pres.;
Stoney Pine Charities Housing Corporation - 1400 Parkmoor Ave., Ste. 190, San Jose, CA 95126 t) 408-550-8300 info@charitieshousing.org www.charitieshousing.org
Sunset Charities Housing Corporation - 1400 Parkmoor Ave., Ste. 190, San Jose, CA 95126 t) 408-550-8300 info@charitieshousing.org www.charitieshousing.org
Vietnamese Catholic Center - 2849 S. White Rd., San Jose, CA 95148 t) 408-983-0157 josephnguyen.vanthu@dsj.org www.dsj.org Rev. Joseph N. Vanthu, Dir.;
SANTA CLARA
Jesuit Volunteer Corps. - 500 El Camino Real, Santa Clara, CA 95050 t) 408-241-4200 lstrubeck@jesuitvolunteers.org www.jesuitvolunteers.org Laura Strubek, Admin.;
Saint Joseph Academy - 2800 Mission College Blvd., Santa Clara, CA 95054; Mailing: 355 Dixon Rd, Milpitas, CA 95035 t) 650-716-7704 st.josephacademy@servidoras.org (homeschool cooperative) Mother Maria Revelacion, S.S.V.M., Dir.; Stds.: 51
SARATOGA
Christ Child Society of San Jose - 19825 Oakhaven Dr., Saratoga, CA 95070 t) 408-446-5522 2parkersmp@sbcglobal.net Pamela Parker, Pres.;
STANFORD
Saint Francis Xavier Lay Missionary Society - ; Mailing: P.O. Box 20211, Stanford, CA 94309-0211 t) 650-260-3799 info@laymissionary.org www.laymissionary.org Independently Tax-Exempt Tricia Bolle, Pres.;

MONASTERIES AND RESIDENCES FOR PRIESTS AND BROTHERS [MON]

CUPERTINO
The Marianist Center - 22683 Alcalde Rd., Cupertino, CA 95014 t) 408-207-4800 somervillej1@gmail.com Marianist Center Bro. William Bolts, S.M.; Rev. James Allen DeLong, S.M.; Bro. Frank Gomes; Bro. Howard Hughes, S.M.; Rev. Robert Hughes, S.M.; Rev. John Klobuka; Bro. James Leahy, S.M.; Bro. Stanley Murakami, S.M.; Rev. John Putka, S.M.; Bro. John Schlund; Bro. John Somerville, Dir.; Rev. Patrick Tonry; Bro. Thomas Spring, SM; Bro. James Vorndran; Bro. Vincent Wayer, S.M.; Brs.: 10; Priests: 5
The Alcalde House - 22683 Alcalde Rd., Cupertino, CA 95014 t) 408-207-4808 Bro. Jack Somerville, Dir.;
The Bordeaux House - 22655 Alcalde Rd., Cupertino, CA 95014 t) (408) 207-4800 Bro. Jack Somerville, Dir.;
LOS ALTOS
Maryknoll - 23000 Cristo Rey Dr., Los Altos, CA 94024 t) 650-386-4342 losaltos@maryknoll.org www.maryknollsociety.org Maryknoll Residence for Priests and Brothers. Rev. William J. Grimm, M.M., Dir.; Rev. William M. Boteler, M.M., In Res.; Rev. Michael Gould, M.M., In Res.; Rev. Joseph Hermes, M.M., In Res.; Rev. Robert E. Hoffmann, M.M., In Res.; Rev. James R. Jackson, M.M., In Res.; Rev. Robert A. Jalbert, M.M., In Res.; Rev. Stephen Judd, M.M., In Res.; Rev. Roberto Rodriguez, M.M., In Res.; Rev. David J. Schwinghamer, M.M., In Res.; Rev. John Soltis, M.M., In Res.; Priests: 12
LOS GATOS
Sacred Heart Jesuit Center - 300 College Ave., Los Gatos, CA 95030-7009; Mailing: P.O. Box 128, Los Gatos, CA 95031-0128 t) 408-884-1700 gwanser@jesuits.org USA West Province of the Society of Jesus Rev. George Wanser, S.J., Supr.; Rev. Richard Case, S.J., Supr.; Rev. E. Joseph O'Keefe, S.J., Admin.; Rev. Thomas G. Allender, S.J., In Res.; Rev. Joseph T. Angilella, S.J., In Res.; Rev. Roy Antunez, S.J., In Res.; Rev. Kevin Ballard, S.J., In Res.; Rev. Kenneth Baker, In Res.; Bro. Michael Bennett, In Res.; Rev. E. Louis Bishop, S.J., In Res.; Rev. Michael Braden, S.J., In Res.; Rev. Cornelius M. Buckley, S.J., In Res.; Rev. Thomas J/ Bunnell, S.J., In Res.; Rev. Peter Burns, S.J., In Res.; Rev. Frank Case, S.J., In Res.; Rev. Peter Minh Quang Chu, S.J., In Res.; Rev. Richard E. Cobb, S.J., In Res.; Rev. John A. Coleman, S.J., In Res.; Rev. Patrick Connolly, S.J., In Res.; Rev. Thomas Connolly, S.J., In Res.; Bro. Justin A. DeChance, S.J., In Res.; Rev. Robert G. Dolan, S.J., In Res.; Rev. George J. Dumais, S.J., In Res.; Bro. William C. Farrington, S.J., In Res.; Rev. L. Paul Fitterer, S.J., In Res.; Rev. Thomas Gallagher, In Res.; Rev. Reynold J. Gatto, S.J., In Res.; Rev. Laurence L. Gooley, S.J., In Res.; Rev. Thomas Griffin-Smolenski, S.J., In Res.; Rev. Albert Grosskopf, In Res.; Bro. Charles J. Jackson, S.J., In Res.; Bro. John E. Keck, S.J., In Res.; Rev. James H. Keene, S.J., In Res.; Rev. David F. Klein, S.J., In Res.; Bro. Thomas Koller, S.J., In Res.; Rev. James R Laudwein, S.J., In Res.; Bro. Arthur W. Lee, S.J., In Res.; Rev. David J. Leigh, S.J., In Res.; Rev. Jerold W. Lindner, S.J., In Res.; Bro. Frederick Mercy, In Res.; Rev. J. Gordon Moreland, S.J., In Res.; Rev. Alfred E. Naucke, S.J., In Res.; Rev. Patrick B. O'Leary, S.J., In Res.; Rev. Charles R. Olsen, S.J., In Res.; Bro. Charles J. Onorato, S.J., In Res.; Rev. Louis A. Peinado, S.J., In Res.; Rev. Richard Perry, S.J., In Res.; Bro. Daniel J. Peterson, S.J., In Res.; Rev. Charles T. Phipps, S.J., In Res.; Rev. Thomas G. Piquado, S.J., In Res.; Rev. L. Michael Pope, S.J., In Res.; Rev. J. Daniel Powers, S.J., In Res.; Rev. John Privett, S.J., In Res.; Rev. Patrick Reuse, S.J., In Res.; Rev. William J. Rewak, S.J., In Res.; Rev. John Ridgway, S.J., In Res.; Rev. Anastacio S. Rivera, S.J., In Res.; Bro. Theodore C. Rohrer, S.J., In Res.; Rev. James Schaukowitch, S.J., In Res.; Rev. Michael G. Scully, S.J., In Res.; Most Rev. Carlos A. Sevilla, S.J., In Res.; Rev. Donald B. Sharp, S.J., In Res.; Rev. Robert J. Shinney, S.J., In Res.; Rev. Thomas E. Splain, S.J., In Res.; Rev. Roy W. Thaden, S.J., In Res.; Rev. Peter J. Togni, S.J., In Res.; Rev. James Torrens, In Res.; Rev. Bernard Tyrrell, In Res.; Rev. Gary Uhlenkott, S.J., In Res.; Rev. Anthony P. Via, S.J., In Res.; Rev. Kevin Waters, In Res.; Brs.: 10; Priests: 60
USA West Province, Society of Jesus - 300 College Ave., Los Gatos, CA 95030-7009; Mailing: P.O. Box 519, Los Gatos, CA 95031-0519 t) 503-226-6977 uweprovince@jesuits.org www.jesuitswest.org Society of Jesus, Oregon Province, Portland, OR; The Pioneer Educational Society, Spokane, WA; Montana Catholic M Rev. Sean Carroll, S.J., Prov.; Rev. Michael Gilson, Socius; Rev. Edward S. Fassett, S.J., Treas.; Rev. Alan Figueroa Deck, S.J., Prov. Asst. for Spiritual Min.; Rev. Theodore Gabrielli, S.J., Asst. for Intl. Min.; Rev. Radmar Jao, S.J., Prov. Asst. for Vocations; Rev. Robert Niehoff, Prov. Asst. for Higher Education; Rev. Ignatius Ohno, Delegate for Senior Jesuits; Rev. Anthony E. Sholander, S.J., Delegate for Formation; Rev. Robert R Ballecer, S.J., Serving outside the US; Rev. Roberto C Duran, S.J., Serving outside the US; Rev. Christopher Weekly, S.J., Prov. Asst. for Pastoral Min.; Rev. Fred J. Green, S.J., Serving outside the US; Rev. Stephanus Hendrianto, S.J., Serving outside the US; Rev. Mark A. Hoelsken, S.J., Serving outside the

US; Rev. Scott M. Lewis, S.J., Serving outside the US; Rev. Alex A. Llanera, S.J., Serving outside the US; Rev. Bartholomew J. Murphy, S.J., Serving outside the US; Rev. Wafik H. Nasry, S.J., Serving outside the US; Rev. William R. O'Neill, S.J., Serving outside the US; Rev. Mark A. Ravizza, S.J., Serving outside the US; Rev. Richard J. Schneck, S.J., Serving outside the US; Rev. Thomas P Sherman, S.J., Serving outside the US; Rev. Peter K. Siu, S.J., Serving outside the US; Rev. Thomas H. Smolich, S.J., Serving outside the US; Brs.: 23; Priests: 348

SAN JOSE

Carmelite Monastery, Novitiate - 12455 Clayton Rd., San Jose, CA 95127; Mailing: P.O. Box 3420, San Jose, CA 95156-3420 t) 408-251-1361 www.sanjosecarmelites.com Rev. Thomas Reeves, OCD, Prior; Rev. Matthias Lambrecht, OCD, Mem.; Bro. Roger Larre, OCDS, Mem.; Rev. Charles Nawodylo, OCD, Mem.; Bro. Dustin Vu, OCD, Mem.; Rev. James Geoghegan, O.C.D., Mem.; Rev. Paul Koenig, OCD, Mem.; Rev. Patrick Sugrue, O.C.D., Mem.; Brs.: 2; Priests: 6

SANTA CLARA

Casa San Inigo, Jesuit Residence - 1075 Benton St., Santa Clara, CA 95050-4801 t) (408) 884-1700 ppabst@jesuits.org Rev. Peter G. Pabst, S.J.; Priests: 1

The Institute of the Incarnate Word (IVE) - 2800 Mission College Blvd., Santa Clara, CA 95054 t) 408-988-4585 brian.dinkel@dsj.org Rev. Miguel Lombardi, IVE, Par. Vicar; Rev. Brian Dinkel, I.V.E., Pst.; Rev. Jonathan Yu Dumlao, I.V.E., Par. Vicar; Priests: 3

Jesuit Community - 500 El Camino Real, Santa Clara, CA 95053 t) 408-554-4124 jblaettler@jesuits.org Rev. James R. Blaettler, S.J.; Brs.: 1; Priests: 22

NURSING / REHABILITATION / CONVALESCENCE / ELDERLY CARE [NUR]

MOUNTAIN VIEW

Villa Siena - 1855 Miramonte Ave., Mountain View, CA 94040 t) 650-961-6484 cbernard@villa-siena.org www.villa-siena.org Residential Care and Skilled Nursing Facility. Daughters of Charity of St. Vincent de Paul. Corine Bernard, Exec.; Asstd. Annu.: 150; Staff: 105

SAN JOSE

Giovanni Center, Inc. - 85 S. Fifth St., San Jose, CA 95112 t) 408-288-7436 jeannedarc@jsco.net A California nonprofit charitable, public-benefit, housing project for low-income elderly. Asstd. Annu.: 24; Staff: 10

Jeanne d'Arc Manor - 85 S. Fifth St., San Jose, CA 95112 t) 408-288-7421 jeannedarc@jsco.net Housing project for low-income elderly and disabled. Sponsored by the Roman Catholic Bishop of San Jose, A Corporation Sole. Asstd. Annu.: 86; Staff: 10

PRESCHOOLS / CHILDCARE CENTERS [PRE]

SAN JOSE

Vietnamese Youth and Culture Association - 1103 Maxey Ct., San Jose, CA 95132 t) 408-926-4665 c) 408-644-4812 frerephong@gmail.com www.lasan.org Brothers of the Christian Schools (San Francisco-New Orleans Prov.). Bro. Fortunat Phong, F.S.C., Dir.; Bro. Valery An, FSC, Other; Bro. Simon Thai Hoang, FSC, Mem.; Stds.: 100

RETREAT HOUSES / RENEWAL CENTERS [RTR]

LOS ALTOS

Jesuit Retreat Center of Los Altos - 300 Manresa Way, Los Altos, CA 94022 t) 650-917-4080 www.jrclosaltos.org Rev. Kevin Leidich, S.J., Supr.; Rev. John Auther, S.J., Pst. Min./Coord.; Rev. Robert J. Fabing, S.J., Dir.; Rev. Chi V. Ngo, S.J., Dir.; Rev. Robert Glynn, SJ, In Res.;

SHRINES [SHR]

SANTA CLARA

Shrine of Our Lady of Peace - 2800 Mission College Blvd., Santa Clara, CA 95054 t) 408-988-4585 info@olop-shrine.org www.olop-shrine.org/ Rev. Brian Dinkel, I.V.E., Dir.;

Our Lady of Peace Gift Shop - 2800 Mission College Blvd., Santa Clara, CA 95054 t) 408-980-9825 brian.dinkel@dsj.org Deborah Pecoraro, Contact;

An asterisk (*) denotes an organization that has established tax-exempt status directly with the IRS and is not covered by the USCCB Group Ruling.

Archdiocese of Santa Fe

(Archidioecesis Sanctae Fidei)

MOST REVEREND JOHN C. WESTER

Archbishop of Santa Fe; ordained May 15, 1976; appointed Auxiliary Bishop of San Francisco and Titular Bishop of Lamiggiga June 30, 1998; ordained September 18, 1998; appointed Bishop of Salt Lake City January 8, 2007; installed March 14, 2007; appointed Archbishop of Santa Fe April 27, 2015; installed June 4, 2015. Catholic Center: 4000 St. Josephs Pl., N.W., Albuquerque, NM 87120.

Archdiocese of Santa Fe Catholic Center: 4000 St. Josephs Pl., N.W., Albuquerque, NM 87120. T: 505-831-8100.

ESTABLISHED IN 1850.

Square Miles 61,142.

Created an Archbishopric in 1875.

Solemnly consecrated to the Immaculate Heart of Mary on October 7, 1945.

Comprises the Counties of Colfax, Curry, DeBaca, Guadalupe, Harding, Los Alamos, Mora, Quay, Roosevelt, San Miguel, Santa Fe, Socorro, Taos, Torrance and Union with a part of Bernalillo, Sandoval, Rio Arriba and Valencia Counties.

Patron of the Archdiocese: St. Francis of Assisi.

For legal titles of parishes and archdiocesan institutions, consult the Chancery Office.

STATISTICAL OVERVIEW

Personnel
Archbishops....1
Retired Archbishops....1
Abbots....3
Priests: Diocesan Active in Diocese....90
Priests: Diocesan Active Outside Diocese....3
Priests: Retired, Sick or Absent....47
Number of Diocesan Priests....140
Religious Priests in Diocese....55
Total Priests in your Diocese....195
Extern Priests in Diocese....29
Ordinations:
Diocesan Priests....4
Transitional Deacons....1
Permanent Deacons in Diocese....200
Total Brothers....46
Total Sisters....70

Parishes
Parishes....93
With Resident Pastor:
Resident Diocesan Priests....83
Resident Religious Priests....9
Without Resident Pastor:
Administered by Deacons....1
Missions....223
Pastoral Centers....4

Professional Ministry Personnel:
Brothers....49
Sisters....57
Lay Ministers....114

Welfare
Catholic Hospitals....1
Total Assisted....566,428
Health Care Centers....1
Total Assisted....1,000
Day Care Centers....1
Total Assisted....98
Specialized Homes....1
Total Assisted....116
Special Centers for Social Services....6
Total Assisted....395,754
Residential Care of Disabled....1
Total Assisted....16

Educational
Diocesan Students in Other Seminaries....12
Students, Religious....2
Total Seminarians....14
Colleges and Universities....1
Total Students....260
High Schools, Diocesan and Parish....1
Total Students....489
High Schools, Private....1
Total Students....436
Elementary Schools, Diocesan and Parish....13
Total Students....2,313
Catechesis / Religious Education:
High School Students....3,435
Elementary Students....6,729
Total Students under Catholic Instruction....13,676
Teachers in Diocese:
Brothers....1
Sisters....2
Lay Teachers....269

Vital Statistics
Receptions into the Church:
Infant Baptism Totals....2,190
Minor Baptism Totals....265
Adult Baptism Totals....135
Received into Full Communion....230
First Communions....2,390
Confirmations....2,026
Marriages:
Catholic....521
Interfaith....52
Total Marriages....573
Deaths....3,494
Total Catholic Population....327,368
Total Population....1,312,167

LEADERSHIP

Vicar General - t) 505-831-8158 Very Rev. Glennon F. Jones, Vicar General/Vicar for Clergy;
Episcopal Vicar - t) 505-839-7952 lluna@archdiosf.org Rev. Msgr. Lambert J. Luna;
Episcopal Vicar for Doctrine and Life - t) 505-865-7497 mdemkovich@archdiosf.org Very Rev. Michael T. Demkovich, O.P.;
Secretary to the Archbishop - t) 505-831-8120 mamascarenas@archdiosf.org Melanie Mascarenas;
Chancellor - t) (505) 831-8241 sschultz@archdiosf.org Very Rev. Stephen C. Schultz, Chancellor; Monica Justice, Secy. (mjustice@archdiosf.org);
Archivist and Artistic Patrimony - t) 505-983-3811 blucero@archdiosf.org Bernadette Lucero, Archival/ Curatorial Dir.;
Attorney for the Archdiocese - t) 505-938-7770 jflores@stelzner.com Juan L. Flores;
Communications-Media - t) 505-831-8180 lradigan@archdiosf.org Leslie M. Radigan, Dir.;
Ecumenical Commission and Interreligious Affairs (Vacant) -
General Services - t) 505-831-8181 dquezada@archdiosf.org David Quezada, Dir.;
Parish Bulletin Service, "The Catholic Communicator" - t) 505-856-0333 jcpress@comcast.net Jenny Chilson;
Human Resources - t) 505-831-8130 csalcido@archdiosf.org Cathy Salcido, Dir.;

OFFICES AND DIRECTORS

Appeal Court - t) 505-831-8356 ocoelho@archdiosf.org Very Rev. Oscar W. Coelho, Judicial Vicar;
College of Consultors - t) 505-831-8158 stetrick@archdiosf.org Most Rev. John C. Wester, Archbishop; Rev. Msgr. Lambert J. Luna, Episcopal Vicar; Very Rev. John Cannon;
Council of Men and Women Religious (Vacant) -
Mission Office (Vacant) -
Office of Religious - t) 505-831-8158 Very Rev. Glennon F. Jones, Vicar for Religious;
Pastoral Planning - t) 505-831-8221 mmontez@archdiosf.org Michelle Montez, Exec. Dir. (planning@archdiosf.org);
Permanent Diaconate Program - t) 505-831-8245 kdavis@archdiosf.org Dcn. Keith Davis, Dir.;
Pilgrimage for Vocations (Vacant) - Rev. Michael Niemczak, Spiritual Adv./Care Srvcs.;
Presbyteral Council of the Archdiocese of Santa Fe - t) 505-831-8120 mamascarenas@archdiosf.org Most Rev. John C. Wester, President (Ex-Officio); Rev. Msgr. Lambert J. Luna, Episcopal Vicar (Ex-Officio Member); Very Rev. Stephen C. Schultz, Chancellor;
Propagation of the Faith (Vacant) -
Tribunal - t) 505-831-8356 ocoelho@archdiosf.org Very Rev. Oscar W. Coelho, Judicial Vicar;
Adjutant Judicial Vicars - t) (505) 831-8341 lmartinez@archdiosf.org Rev. Jerome A. Plotkowski; Rev. Steve Rosera; Very Rev. Oscar W. Coelho;
Associate Judges - t) (505) 831-8341 Rev. Msgr. Jerome Martinez y Alire; Dcn. George Sandoval; Very Rev. Ronald Walters, O.F.M.;
Defenders of the Bond - t) (505) 831-8341 Rev. Ronald J. Bowers; Very Rev. Oscar W. Coelho; Rev. Jerome A. Plotkowski;
Delegate for Matrimonial Dispensations - t) (505) 831-8341 Very Rev. Oscar W. Coelho, Judicial Vicar; Rev. Jerome A. Plotkowski, Adjutant Judicial Vicar;
Judicial Vicar - t) (505) 831-8341 Very Rev. Oscar W. Coelho;
Notary - t) 505-831-8344; 505-831-8341 Lorena Mendoza, Notary I; Louellen N. Martinez, Notary II;
Promoter of Justice - t) (505) 831-8341 Rev. Ronald J. Bowers;
Vicars Forane (Deans) - t) 505-831-8158 stetrick@archdiosf.org Very Rev. Rick Zerwas, Dean; Very Rev. John Cannon, Dean; Very Rev. Julio Gonzalez, S.F., Dean;
Vocations - t) 505-831-8143 mniemczak@archdiosf.org; tpham@archdiosf.org Rev. Michael Niemczak, Dir.; Rev. Tai Pham, Assoc. Dir. (frtai@johnxxiiicc.org);

FINANCE

Chief Financial Officer - t) 505-831-8132 tsalgado@asfcca.org Tony Salgado;
Finance Council - t) 505-831-8132 tsalgado@asfcca.org Most Rev. John C. Wester, Archbishop; Tony Salgado, CFO; William F. Raskob III, Chair;
Parish Property Support Services - t) 505-831-8397 tmacken@archdiosf.org Thomas P. Macken, Exec. Dir.;

PASTORAL SERVICES

African American Ministry - t) 505-831-8167; 505-836-3627 Brenda Dabney, Pt. Coord.; Anne Avellone, Archdiocesan Liasion;
Archdiocesan Network for Catholic Legislative Advocacy - t) 505-831-8167 aavellone@archdiosf.org Anne Avellone, Dir.;
Catholic Campaign for Human Development - t) 505-831-8167 aavellone@archdiosf.org Anne Avellone, Dir.;
Catholic Charities - t) 505-724-4670 Dolores Nunez, CEO;
Catholic Committee on Scouting - t) 505-890-6574 littledads@comcast.net Matthew Unsworth, Chair; Dcn. David Little, Spiritual Adv./Care Srvcs.;
Catholic Schools Office - t) 505-831-8172 Donna Illerbrun, Supt.;
Cursillo Movement - t) 505-471-7688 acarrillo@archdiosf.org Dcn. Andres Carrillo, Spiritual Adv./Care Srvcs.;
Evangelization - t) 505-831-8221 mmontez@archdiosf.org Michelle Montez, Exec. Dir. (planning@archdiosf.org);
Executive Director - t) 505-831-8221 mmontez@archdiosf.org Michelle Montez (planning@archdiosf.org);
Formation for Christian Service - t) 505-831-8221 mmontez@archdiosf.org Michelle Montez, Exec. Dir. (planning@archdiosf.org);
Hospital Ministry (Vacant) - t) 505-831-8158
Liturgical Commission - t) 505-831-8128 dthillet@archdiosf.org Most Rev. John C. Wester, Ex Officio; Barbara Guenther, Chair;
Marriage and Family Life Office - t) 505-831-8117 yduran@archdiosf.org Yvette Duran, Family Life Coord.;
Ministry to Spanish Speaking - t) 505-831-8152 rgonzalez@archdiosf.org Rocio Gonzalez, Dir.;
Native American Ministry - t) 505-831-8104 szuni@archdiosf.org Shirley Zuni, Dir.;
Office of Worship - t) (505) 831-8158 Very Rev. Glennon F. Jones, Vicar;
Ongoing Priestly Formation -
People Living With Disabilities - t) 505-831-8229 rvigil@archdiosf.org Dcn. Robert Vigil, Dir.; Karen Mitchell, Coord. Disabilities; Charles Griego, Deaf Coord.;
Prison & Detention Ministry - t) 505-831-8174 rvigil@archdiosf.org Dcn. Robert Vigil, Dir.; Herman Delgado, Thresholds Coord.; Josephine War, Detention Ministry Coord.;
RCIA - t) (505) 831-8158 Very Rev. Glennon F. Jones, Vicar;
Religious Education - t) 505-831-8127 Sr. Mary Edna Pearl Esquibel, C.S.S.F., Dir.;
St. Vincent de Paul Council - t) (505) 346-1500 Eva Pereira, Pres.;
Schools of Lay Ministry Formation - t) 505-831-8221 mmontez@archdiosf.org Michelle Montez, Exec. Dir. (planning@archdiosf.org);
Albuquerque Deanery A,B,C & SW, "Emmaus Journey" - t) (505) 263-8097 luceroc7056@gmail.com Cory Lucero, Contact;
Northwest Deanery - Camino de Fe - t) (505) 831-8221 Nila Ortega-Montoya, Contact; Mary Anne Vigil, Contact;
Santa Fe Deanery - Jornada de Fe - t) (505) 831-8221 Anne Kaul, Contact; Brian Stafford, Contact;
Social Justice - t) 505-831-8167 aavellone@archdiosf.org Anne Avellone, Dir.;
Spanish School of Ministry - t) 505-831-8152 rgonzalez@archdiosf.org Rocio Gonzalez, Dir.; Beatriz Quezada, Coord. Albuquerque Area; Angie Kollasch, Coord. Santa Fe Area;
Victim Assistance Coordinator - t) 505-831-8144 aklimka@archdiosf.org Annette M. Klimka;
Youth and Young Adult Ministry - t) 505-831-8145 Sr. Mary Edna Pearl Esquibel, C.S.S.F., Dir.;

PARISHES, MISSIONS, AND CLERGY

STATE OF NEW MEXICO

ABIQUIU

St. Thomas Apostle - 1 Church Plz., Abiquiu, NM 87510; Mailing: P.O. Box 117, Abiquiu, NM 87510 t) 505-685-4462 stthomasapostle@windstream.net; paulinec16@yahoo.com Rev. Valentine Phu Ngoc Au, Pst.; CRP Stds.: 36
San Miguel Archangel - t) (505) 685-4462
San Antonio - t) (505) 685-4462
San Pedro - t) (505) 685-4462
San Juan Bautista - t) (505) 685-4462
Santa Teresa - t) (505) 685-4462
Nuestra Senora de Guadalupe - t) (505) 685-4462 (parent parish phone)

ALBUQUERQUE

St. Anne-Albuquerque - 1400 Arenal Rd., S.W., Albuquerque, NM 87105 t) 505-877-3121 st.anne.abq@gmail.com Rev. Irby C. Nichols, Pst.; Dcn. Juan Barajas; Dcn. Victoriano Ceballos-Moreno; Brenda Romero, DRE; CRP Stds.: 48
St. Charles Borromeo - 1818 Coal Pl., S.E., Albuquerque, NM 87106 t) 505-242-3462 office@stcbabq.org stcharleschurchabq.org/ Rev. Vincent Dominguez, Pst.; Reina Goode, DRE; Dcn. Louis Hernandez; Dcn. Paul Dung Van Nguyen; Dcn. John Rasinski; CRP Stds.: 18
St. Charles Borromeo School - (Grades PreK-8) 1801 Hazeldine Ave., S.E., Albuquerque, NM 87106 t) (505) 243-5788 phorton@stcharlesabq.org Paul Horton, Prin.; Stds.: 105; Lay Tchrs.: 10
Church of the Ascension - 2150 Raymac Rd., S.W., Albuquerque, NM 87105 t) 505-877-8144 (CRP); 505-877-8550 Rev. Edmund Savilla, Pst.; Dcn. Leon Jones; Angelica Padilla, DRE; Kendra Sanchez, DRE; CRP Stds.: 55
St. Edwin - 2105 Barcelona, S.W., Albuquerque, NM 87105 t) 505-877-2967 office@stedwinabq.com; religioused@stedwinabq.com Dcn. Jose Ayala; Dcn. Paul LeFebre; Rev. Peter Muller, O.Praem., Pst.; CRP Stds.: 31
St. Francis Xavier-Albuquerque - 820 Broadway, S.E., Albuquerque, NM 87102 t) 505-243-5201 francisxavierabq@gmail.com Rev. Bijoy Francis, Pst.; Dcn. Larry Carmony; Rosemary Martinez, DRE; CRP Stds.: 65
Holy Family-Albuquerque - 562 Atrisco Dr., S.W., Albuquerque, NM 87195; Mailing: P.O. Box 12127, Albuquerque, NM 87195 t) 505-842-5448 (DRE); 505-842-5426 (Parish office) holyfamilychurch505@gmail.com; holyfamilychurch505@yahoo.com Rev. Patrick Schafer, O.F.M., Pst.; Rev. Andres D Gallegos, OFM, Par. Vicar; Dcn. Constantino Avalos-Sanchez; Dcn. Eddie Blea; Karen Mitchell, DRE; CRP Stds.: 208
Holy Ghost - 833 Arizona St. SE, Albuquerque, NM 87108 t) 505-265-5957; 505-265-5958 hgministeriosesp@gmail.com holyghost.weconnect.com

Rev. Hyginus Chuks Anuta, Pst.; Marlene Torres, DRE; CRP Stds.: 159

Holy Ghost School - (Grades PreK-8) 6201 Ross SE, Albuquerque, NM 87108 t) 505-256-1563 dwine@hgcsabq.com www.holyghostcatholicschool.com Douglas Wine, Prin.; Stds.: 162; Lay Tchrs.: 15

Immaculate Conception-Albuquerque - 619 Copper Ave., N.W., Albuquerque, NM 87102 t) 505-247-4271 srosera@iccabq.org iccabq.org Rev. Steve Rosera, Par. Admin.; Rev. Robert Bustamante, Par. Vicar; Dcn. George Sandoval; Dcn. Donald Roseborough; Sr. Teresa Aparicio, OLVM, CRE; Debbie Garcia, CRE; CRP Stds.: 70

St. Mary Catholic School - (Grades PreK-8) 224 Seventh St., N.W., Albuquerque, NM 87102 t) 505-242-6271 support@stmarys.me www.stmarys.me Rebecca Sanchez-Maestas, Prin.; Stds.: 248; Lay Tchrs.: 21

Saint John XXIII Catholic Community - 4831 Tramway Ridge Dr., N.E., Albuquerque, NM 87111 t) 505-293-0088 claram@johnxxiiicc.org www.johnxxiiicc.org Rev. Tai Pham, Pst.; Dcn. Jerry Pierce; Angela Holt, DRE; Clara Maestas, Bus. Mgr.; CRP Stds.: 104

St. Joseph on the Rio Grande - 5901 St. Joseph's Dr., N.W., Albuquerque, NM 87120 t) 505-244-2154 (CRP); 505-839-7952 office@sjrgparish.org Rev. Msgr. Lambert J. Luna, Pst.; Rev. William McNichols, Sacramental Min.; CRP Stds.: 174

St. Jude Thaddeus - 5712 Paradise Blvd., N.W., Albuquerque, NM 87114 t) 505-898-0826 (Church); 505-897-4006 stjude@stjudenm.org www.stjudenm.org Rev. Tien-Tri Nguyen, Pst.; Dcn. Faustin Archuleta; Dcn. Salvador Mercado; Yvette Serna, DRE; CRP Stds.: 800

Nativity of the Blessed Virgin Mary - 9502 Fourth St., N.W., Albuquerque, NM 87114 t) 505-898-5253 dking@n-bvm.org www.n-bvm.org Rev. Chike Emmanuel Uba (Nigeria), Pst.; Francesca Twiss, DRE; Dolores King, Bus. Mgr.; Dcn. Michael Illerbrun; Dcn. Leonard Martinez; Dcn. Juan Ortiz; Dcn. Ralph Vigil; CRP Stds.: 239

Our Lady of Mount Carmel - 7807 Edith, Albuquerque, NM 87114 t) (505) 898-5253 nbvm_abq02@archdiosf.org

Our Lady of Fatima - 4020 Lomas Blvd., N.E., Albuquerque, NM 87110 t) 505-265-5868 olofatima_abq9@archdiosf.org www.fatimachurchabq.org Very Rev. Stephen C. Schultz, Pst.; Rev. Edward Okpu (Nigeria), Par. Vicar; Rev. John B. Trambley II, In Res.; Dcn. Timoteo Lujan; CRP Stds.: 5

Our Lady of Fatima School - (Grades PreK-8) t) 505-255-6391 mmader@fatimaschoolabq.com www.fatimaschoolabq.com Melinda Mader, Prin.; Stds.: 66; Lay Tchrs.: 9

Our Lady of Guadalupe-Albuquerque - 1860 Griegos, Rd N.W., Albuquerque, NM 87107 t) 505-345-4596 olog9108@gmail.com; olog9109@gmail.com www.guadalupeabq.com Rev. Christopher James Hallada, Pst.; Dcn. Juan Cabrera; Dcn. George W. Valverde; CRP Stds.: 90

Our Lady of Lavang - 1015 Chelwood Park, N.E., Albuquerque, NM 87112 t) 505-275-3079 htran@archdiosf.org lavangabq.org Dcn. Tien Bui; Rev. Hoi Tran, Pst.; CRP Stds.: 60

Our Lady of Most Holy Rosary - 5415 Fortuna Rd., N.W., Albuquerque, NM 87105 t) 505-836-5011 hrparish@holyrosaryabq.org; hrreligioused@holyrosaryabq.org www.holyrosaryabq.org Rachael Baca, DRE; Rev. Andrew J. Pavlak, Pst.; Dcn. Frank Perez; Dcn. Joseph Silva; Erick Martinez, Liturgy Dir.; Dcn. James Owens, O.Praem., Pst. Assoc.; Norma Vivian, Pst. Assoc.; Dcn. Keith Davis, RCIA Coord.; CRP Stds.: 255

Our Lady of the Annunciation - 2532 Vermont, N.E., Albuquerque, NM 87110 t) 505-298-7553 hwillets@annunciationparishabq.org annunciationparishabq.org Dcn. Victor Bachechi; Dcn. Lawrence Anthony Rivera; Dcn. Patrick Sena; Rev. Msgr. Bennett J. Voorhies, Pst.; Rev. Thomas Kayammakal (India), Par. Vicar; Leslie Monette, DRE; CRP Stds.: 165

Our Lady of the Annunciation School - (Grades PreK-8) 2610 Utah N.E., Albuquerque, NM 87110 t) 505-299-6783 www.acsabq.org Cindy Shields, Prin.; Leticia Gomez, Vice Prin.; Stds.: 421; Lay Tchrs.: 40

Our Lady of the Assumption-Albuquerque - 811 Guaymas Pl., N.E., Albuquerque, NM 87108-2398 t) 505-256-9818 ola.parish@olacs.org www.olacs.org Bilingual Rev. Edward C. Domme, Pst.; Rev. Michael Cimino, Par. Vicar; Dcn. James P. Delgado; Dcn. John Granato; Dcn. Maurice Graff; CRP Stds.: 76

Our Lady of the Assumption-Albuquerque School - (Grades PreK-8) t) 505-256-3167 achavez@olacs.org olacs.org/school Anissa Chavez, Prin.; Stds.: 122; Lay Tchrs.: 16

Prince of Peace Catholic Community - 12500 Carmel Ave., N.E., Albuquerque, NM 87122 t) 505-856-7657 popabq@icloud.com; office@popabq.org www.popabq.org Dcn. Leandro Centenera; Dcn. Steven Fraker; Rev. Michael J. Shea, Pst.; Joe P Sena, Bus. Mgr.; CRP Stds.: 100

Queen of Heaven - 5311 Phoenix Ave. N.E., Albuquerque, NM 87110 t) 505-881-1772 qhoffice@qofhabq.com; qhreligioused@qofhabq.com www.qofhabq.com Rev. John B. Trambley II, In Res.; Rev. Simeon F. Wimmershoff, Pst.; Dcn. Ruben Barela; Dcn. Larry Cleveland, Liturgy Dir.; Dcn. Pilar Garcia, Youth Min.; Dcn. Stephen Sais, RCIA Coord.; CRP Stds.: 129

Risen Savior Catholic Community - 7701 Wyoming, N.E., Albuquerque, NM 87109 t) 505-821-1571 hope@risensaviorcc.org www.risensaviorcc.org Dcn. Timothy Parker; Rev. Charles Ugochukwu (Nigeria), Pst.; Dcn. Mark Bussemeier; Dcn. Manuel Garcia; Kevin Newman, Liturgist; CRP Stds.: 132

Sacred Heart-Albuquerque - 412 Stover Ave., S.W., Albuquerque, NM 87102 t) 505-242-0561 sacredheartalbnm@gmail.com www.sacredheartabq.com/ Sheryl Angell, DRE; Dcn. Marcus Montano; Rev. Benjamin O. Onwumelui (Nigeria), Pst.; Dcn. Robert Vigil; CRP Stds.: 52

San Felipe de Neri - 2005 N. Plaza, N.W., Albuquerque, NM 87104; Mailing: PO Box 7007, Albuquerque, NM 87194 t) 505-243-4628 www.sanfelipedeneri.org Rev. Michael Chiagorom (Nigeria), Admin.; Dcn. Maurice Menke; Walter Lujan, DRE; Juliana Jaramillo, RCIA Coord.; CRP Stds.: 50

San Felipe de Neri School - (Grades PreK-8) 2000 Lomas Blvd., N.W., Albuquerque, NM 87104 t) 505-242-2411 apowledge@sanfelipedenerischool.org sanfelipedenerischool.org/ Cheryl Robertson, Prin.; Stds.: 150; Lay Tchrs.: 12

San Jose de los Duranes - 2110 Los Luceros Rd., N.W., Albuquerque, NM 87104 t) (505) 243-4628 mchiagorom@sanfelipedeneri.org

San Ignacio - 1300 Walter St., N.E., Albuquerque, NM 87102 t) 505-243-4287 sanignacio_abq23@archdiosf.org Rev. Joel O. Bugas, Pst.; CRP Stds.: 24

San Jose-Albuquerque - 2401 Broadway Blvd., S.E., Albuquerque, NM 87102-5009 t) 505-242-3658 sanjoseparish@msn.com sjoseparish.org Dcn. Ruben Zamudio; Dcn. Edgar Torres; Rev. Eulalio Arteaga y Pinon, FdCC (Mexico), Admin.; CRP Stds.: 448

Sangre de Cristo - 8901 Candelaria, N.E., Albuquerque, NM 87112 t) (505) 292-6477 sangredecristocatholicchurch@gmail.com parishesonline.com Rev. Celestine Ojike (Nigeria), Pst.; Dcn. William Ennis; CRP Stds.: 15

Santuario San Martin de Porres - 8321 Camino San Martin, S.W., Albuquerque, NM 87121 t) 505-836-4676 sanmoffice@gmail.com santuariosanmartin.org Very Rev. Oscar W. Coelho, Pst.; Dcn. Oscar Marquez; Dcn. Cresencio Salinas; Dcn. Ricardo Chavez; Lourdes Morachiz, DRE; Alvin Santos, DRE; CRP Stds.: 488

Shrine of St. Bernadette - 11401 Indian School Rd. NE, Albuquerque, NM 87112; Mailing: 11509 Indian School Rd. NE, Albuquerque, NM 87112 t) 505-298-7557; (505) 247-6829 (CRP) bsais@ssbnm.org www.shrineofst.bernadette.com Brenda Sais, DRE; Dcn. William Barry; Dcn. Terry Palmer; Dcn. Joe Santana; Dcn. Charles E. Schwenn; Very Rev. Rick Zerwas, Pst.; CRP Stds.: 46

Shrine of the Little Flower St. Therese of the Infant Jesus Parish - 300 Mildred, N.W., Albuquerque, NM 87107 t) 505-344-8050 stthereseabq@gmail.com; sttheresechurch@yahoo.com www.littleflowerabq.org (Shrine Dedicated 1955) Dcn. Thomas Baca; Dcn. Michael Wesley; Rosa Aragon, DRE; Dcn. Larry Carmony, Admin.; CRP Stds.: 120

St. Therese Catholic School - (Grades PreK-8) 311 Shropshire N.W., Albuquerque, NM 87107 t) 505-344-4479 m.giglio@stschool.org www.sttheresesschoolabq.org Mary Giglio, Prin.; Stds.: 172; Lay Tchrs.: 11

St. Thomas Aquinas University Parish - 1815 Las Lomas Rd., N.E., Albuquerque, NM 87106-3803 t) 505-247-1094 lobocatholic.org@gmail.com (Serving the University of New Mexico) Rev. Michael DePalma, Pst.; CRP Stds.: 35

ANTON CHICO

San Jose-Anton Chico - 1081 Iglesia Rd., Anton Chico, NM 87711; Mailing: P.O. Box 99, Anton Chico, NM 87711 t) 575-427-1164 sanjoseac@plateautel.net Rev. Timothy J. Meurer, Pst.; CRP Stds.: 21

Our Lady of Guadalupe, Tecolotito - t) (575) 427-1164

Sacred Heart-San Isidro, Dilia - t) (575) 427-1164

Sangre de Cristo, Plaza de Arriba - t) (575) 427-1164

Santo Nino de Atocha, Dahlia - t) (575) 427-1164

ARROYO SECO

La Santisima Trinidad - 498 Hwy. 150, Arroyo Seco, NM 87514; Mailing: PO Box 189, Arroyo Seco, NM 87514 t) 505-776-2273 (CRP); 575-776-2273 nmmountaincatholic@gmail.com Rev. Angelo Marquez, Pst.; Dcn. Romolo Arellano; Dcn. Larry Torres; Viola Espinoza, DRE; CRP Stds.: 36

Nuestra Senora de Dolores - Upper Plaza, Arroyo Hondo, NM 87513 t) (505) 776-2273 (Parent parish phone)

San Antonio de Padua - Valdez Plaza, Valdez, NM 87580 t) (575) 776-2273 (Parent parish phone)

Santo Nino de Atocha - Santo Nino Rd., Las Colonias, NM 87529 t) (575) 776-2273 (Parent parish phone)

San Cristobal - t) (575) 776-2272 (Parent parish phone)

BELEN

Our Lady of Belen - 101-A N. 10th St., Belen, NM 87002 t) 505-864-8043; 505-864-7869 (CRP) lobchurch@ourladyofbelen.org; olbffcdre@ourladyofbelen.org www.ourladyofbelen.org Rev. Albert Mutebi Ssekabembe (Uganda), Par. Vicar; Rev. Clement Niggel, Pst.; Dcn. Jerry Baca; Dcn. Michael Montoya; Dcn. Manuel Trujillo; Elizabeth Crespin, DRE; CRP Stds.: 194

St. Mary's School - (Grades PreK-8) 101-B 10th St., Belen, NM 87002 t) 505-864-0484 smsschool@stmarysbelen.com www.stmarysbelen.com Melanie Chavez, Prin.; Stds.: 167; Lay Tchrs.: 12

Nuestra Senora de Guadalupe, Los Chavez - t) (505) 864-8043

St. Francis Xavier, Jarales - t) (505) 864-8043

San Isidro, Pueblitos - t) (505) 864-8043

Cristo Rey, Bosque - t) (505) 864-8043

BERNALILLO

Our Lady of Sorrows-Bernalillo - 301 S. Camino del Pueblo, Bernalillo, NM 87004; Mailing: P.O. Box 607, Bernalillo, NM 87004 t) 505-867-5252 parishadmin@olosbern.com www.olosbernalillo.com Very Rev. Clarence Maes, Pst.; Rev. June N. Ramos, Par. Vicar; Dcn. Eric Buenaventa; Dcn. Gonzalo Calderon; Dcn. Jose de Jesus Cervantes; CRP Stds.: 168

San Antonio, Placitas - 43 San Antonio, Placitas, NM

87043 t) (505) 867-5252

San Jose, Algodones - 1416 Hwy. 313, Algodones, NM 87001 t) (505) 867-5252

St. Anthony, Sandia Pueblo - 300 Parrot Blvd., Sandia Indian Pueblo, NM 87004 t) (505) 867-5252

CERRILLOS

St. Joseph-Cerrillos - 7th First St., Cerrillos, NM 87010; Mailing: PO Box 98, Cerrillos, NM 87010 st-josephs@live.com Rev. William Sanchez, Admin.;

San Francisco de Asis - t) (505) 604-7335 wsanchez@archdiosf.org

Nuestra Senora de los Remedios - State Rd. 41, Galisteo, NM 87540 t) (505) 604-7335 st-joseph@live.com

CHAMA

St. Patrick-Chama - 352 Pine St., Hwy. 29, Chama, NM 87520; Mailing: P.O. Box 36, Chama, NM 87520-0036 t) 575-756-2926 dre@nuestrasenoradelvalle.org; st.patrickparish@nuestrasenoradelvalle.org Rev. Ted Butler, Pst.; Dcn. Joseph Valdez; CRP Stds.: 10

Santo Nino de Atocha - Hwy. 84 & State Rd. 310, Cebolla, NM 87518 t) (575) 756-2926

San Juan Nepomuceno - County Rd. 295, Canjilon, NM 87515 t) (575) 756-2926

CHIMAYO

Holy Family-Chimayo - 1440 Private Dr. NM-76 #10, Chimayo, NM 87522; Mailing: P.O. Box 235, Chimayo, NM 87522 t) 505-351-4360; 505-351-4477 juliogonzalezhsf@gmail.com www.prayatalltimes.com Dcn. Jose O. Lopez; Very Rev. Julio Gonzalez, S.F., Pst.; Rev. Sebastian Lee, SF, Par. Vicar; CRP Stds.: 28

Santo Domingo - t) (505) 351-4360 (parent parish phone)

San Antonio - t) (505) 351-4360 (parent parish phone) Very Rev. Julio Gonzales, S.F., Pst.;

Santo Tomas - t) (505) 351-4360

San Jose - t) (505) 351-4360 (parent parish phone) Very Rev. Julio Gonzales, S.F., Pst.;

San Miguel - t) (505) 351-4360 Very Rev. Julio Gonzales, S.F., Pst.;

San Ysidro & Sagrado Corazon - t) (505) 351-4360

Santo Rosario - t) (505) 351-4360

CIMARRON

Immaculate Conception Church-Cimarron - 440 W. 18th St., Cimarron, NM 87714-9705; Mailing: P.O. Box 75, Cimarron, NM 87714 t) 575-376-2553 iccparishoffice@yahoo.com Rev. Benoit Trieu Van Vu, Pst.;

St. Mel - 200 Willow Creek, Eagle Nest, NM 87718 t) (575) 376-2553 (Parent parish phone) Rev. Benoit Trieu Van Vu, Pst.;

San Antonio - t) (575) 376-2553 (Parent parish Phone) Rev. Benoit Trieu Van Vu, Pst.;

Holy Angels - 34 Westridge Rd., Angel Fire, NM 87710 t) (575) 376-2553 (Mother parish phone) Rev. Benoit Trieu Van Vu, Pst.;

CLAYTON

St. Francis Xavier-Clayton - 115 N. First St., Clayton, NM 88415 t) 575-374-8894 sfxclayton@gmail.com www.sfxclayton.com Rev. Joseph Baltz, Pst.; Rose Ramirez, DRE; CRP Stds.: 22

Our Lady of Guadalupe - t) (575) 374-8894

St. Joseph - t) (575) 374-8894

CLOVIS

Our Lady of Guadalupe-Clovis - 108 N. Davis St., Clovis, NM 88101 t) 575-763-4445 olgclovis@yahoo.com www.ologsj.org Very Rev. Eli Valadez, Pst.; Angelina Garcia, DRE; CRP Stds.: 242

San Jose - t) (575) 763-4445 (Parent parish phone)

Sacred Heart-Clovis - 921 Merriwether St., Clovis, NM 88101 t) 575-763-6947 office@sacredheartclovis.com www.sacredheartclovis.com Rev. Michael Niemczak, Pst.; Rev. Franklin Iwuagwu, Par. Vicar; Dcn. Juan A. Rodriguez; Dcn. Michael A. Rowley; CRP Stds.: 270

St. Catherine - 309 Brownhorn St, Melrose, NM 88124 t) (575) 763-6947

CORRALES

San Ysidro - 5015 Corrales Rd., Corrales, NM 87048; Mailing: P.O. Box 182, Corrales, NM 87048 t) 505-898-1779 215jkelley@gmail.com Rev. James McGowan, Pst.; Dcn. Steve Rangel; Tina Barbian, DRE; CRP Stds.: 25

DIXON

St. Anthony-Dixon - Private Dr. 1114 SR 75, Dixon, NM 87527-0039; Mailing: PO Box 39, Dixon, NM 87527 t) 505-579-4389 standixon@valornet.com dixonpenascocc.org/ Rev. John Kimani, Pst.; Esther Romero, DRE; CRP Stds.: 6

Nuestra Senora de Guadalupe - t) (505) 579-4389 (Parent parish phone)

Nuestra Senora de los Dolores - t) (505) 579-4389 (Parent parish phone)

San Jose - t) (505) 579-4389 (Parent parish phone)

EL RITO

San Juan Nepomuceno - 1191 Main St., El Rito, NM 87530; Mailing: P.O. Box 7, El Rito, NM 87530 t) 575-581-4714 sjn_elrito40@archdiosf.org Rev. Joseph Van Tao Nguyen, Pst.; CRP Stds.: 34

Immaculate Conception, Tres Piedras - t) (575) 581-4637

Nuestra Divina Pastora, La Petaca - t) (575) 581-4712

Our Lady Guadalupe, La Madera - t) (575) 581-4714

Our Lady of Mount Carmel, Canon de Vallecitos - t) (575) 581-4714

Our Lady of Sorrows, Vallecitos - t) (575) 581-4714

San Luis Gonzaga, Las Tablas - t) (575) 581-4714

St. Anthony, Servilleta - t) (575) 581-4714

St. Anthony, Placitas - t) (575) 581-4714

St. Mary, Ojo Caliente - t) (575) 581-4714 Rev. Joseph Van Tao Nguyen, Pst.;

ESPANOLA

Sacred Heart-Espanola - 908 Calle Rosario, Espanola, NM 87532; Mailing: P.O. Box 69, Espanola, NM 87532 t) 505-753-4225 Dcn. Alex Valdez; Rev. Dominic Bernard Pierson, Pst.; Dcn. Christopher Gilbert; CRP Stds.: 47

Our Lady of Guadalupe, Guachupangue - t) (505) 753-4225 (Parent parish phone)

San Antonio, El Guache - t) (505) 753-4225 (Parent parish phone)

San Francisco, El Duende - t) (505) 753-4225 (Parent parish phone)

San Jose, Hernandez - t) (505) 753-4225 (Parent parish phone)

FORT SUMNER

St. Anthony of Padua-Fort Sumner - 443 W. Richard Ave., Fort Sumner, NM 88119; Mailing: PO Box 370, Fort Sumner, NM 88119 t) 575-355-2320 lbassler68@hotmail.com Rev. Christopher Denzell Bernabe, Pst.; CRP Stds.: 35

ISLETA PUEBLO

St. Augustine - TR 35, #71, Isleta Pueblo, NM 87022; Mailing: PO Box 849, Isleta Pueblo, NM 87022 t) 505-869-3398 staugustine_isleta21@archdiosf.org Rev. Milton Thomas, O.Praem., Pst.; CRP Stds.: 67

JEMEZ PUEBLO

San Diego Mission - 475 Mission Rd., Jemez Pueblo, NM 87024; Mailing: P.O Box 79, Jemez Pueblo, NM 87024-0079 t) 575-834-7300 Rev. Jason Pettigrew, Pst.; CRP Stds.: 30

Our Lady of Guadalupe - t) (575) 834-7300 (Parent Parish Phone)

Santo Toribio - t) (575) 834-7300 (Parent parish phone)

San Ysidro - t) (575) 834-7300 (parent parish phone)

Santa Ana - t) (575) 834-7300 (Parent parish phone)

Our Lady of the Assumption Zia Pueblo - t) (575) 834-7300 (Parent parish phone)

JEMEZ SPRINGS

Our Lady of the Assumption-Jemez Springs - 17530 State Rd. 4, Jemez Springs, NM 87025; Mailing: P.O. Box 10, Jemez Springs, NM 87025 c) (505) 231-2452 vicargeneral@archdiosf.org Very Rev. Glennon F. Jones, Vicar;

LA JOYA

Our Lady of Sorrows-La Joya - 19 Calle de la Iglesia, La Joya, NM 87028; Mailing: P.O. Box 534, Veguita, NM 87028 t) 505-864-4461; 505-864-4170 (Rectory) parishoffice@olslajoyanm.org www.olslajoyanm.org Rev. Tobechukwu P. Oluoha, OSA (Nigeria), Pst.; CRP Stds.: 34

San Antonio, Abeytas - t) (505) 864-4461

San Jose, Contreras - t) (505) 864-4461

San Isidro, Las Nutrias - t) (505) 864-4461

San Juan, Veguita - t) (505) 864-4461

San Antonio, Sabinal - t) (505) 864-4461

LAS VEGAS

Immaculate Conception-Las Vegas - 811 Sixth St., Las Vegas, NM 87701 t) 505-454-0685 (CRP); 505-425-7791 icchurch2000@yahoo.com; iccchurch2000@yahoo.com www.icparishlvnm.org Rev. Dennis M. Garcia, Pst.; Dcn. John Pete Campos; Darlene Chavez, DRE; Dcn. Ernest Chavez; Dcn. Christopher Torres; CRP Stds.: 220

Our Lady of Refuge, Los Vigiles - t) (505) 425-7791 (Parent parish phone)

San Antonio, Upper Town - t) (505) 425-7791 (Parent parish phone)

Our Lady of Sorrows Church-Las Vegas - 403 Valencia St., Las Vegas, NM 87701 t) 505-434-0017 (CRP); 505-454-1469 olos-bm@outlook.com Rev. Agustin Henderson, Par. Vicar; Very Rev. Rob Yaksich, Pst.; Dcn. Reyes L. Sanchez; Donna Lopez, DRE; CRP Stds.: 88

Christ the King, El Llanito - t) (505) 454-1469 (Parent parish phone) Very Rev. Rob Yaksich, Pst.;

Santo Nino, Gallinas - t) (505) 454-1469 (Parent parish phone) Very Rev. Rob Yaksich, Pst.;

Santo Nino, Lower Rociada - t) (505) 454-1469 (Parent parish phone) Very Rev. Rob Yaksich, Pst.;

San Isidro, Trujillo - t) (505) 454-1469 (Parent parish address) Very Rev. Rob Yaksich, Pst.;

Nuestra Senora de Guadalupe, Sapello - t) (505) 454-1469 (Parent parish phone) Very Rev. Rob Yaksich, Pst.;

Holy Family, Variadero - t) (505) 454-1469 (Parent parish phone) Very Rev. Rob Yaksich, Pst.;

San Jose, Upper Rociada - t) (505) 454-1469 (Parent parish phone) Very Rev. Rob Yaksich, Pst.;

San Antonio, Los Montoyas - t) (505) 454-1469 (Parent parish phone) Very Rev. Rob Yaksich, Pst.;

San Antonio, El Porvenir - t) (505) 454-1469 (Parent parish phone) Very Rev. Rob Yaksich, Pst.;

Our Lady of Sorrows, Tecolote - t) (505) 454-1469 (Parent parish phone) Very Rev. Rob Yaksich, Pst.;

San Geronimo, San Geronimo - t) (505) 454-1469 (Parent parish phone) Very Rev. Rob Yaksich, Pst.;

San Rafael, Trementina - t) (505) 454-1469 (Parent parish phone) Very Rev. Rob Yaksich, Pst.;

Santo Nino, La Manga - t) (505) 454-1469 (Parent parish address) Very Rev. Rob Yaksich, Pst.;

San Augustine, San Augustine - t) (505) 454-1469 (Parent parish phone) Very Rev. Rob Yaksich, Pst.;

LOS ALAMOS

Immaculate Heart of Mary - 3700 Canyon Rd., Los Alamos, NM 87544 t) 505-662-6193; 505-662-7773 (CRP); 505-661-8303 ihm@ihmcc.org; re@ihmcc.org ihmcc.org Rev. John C. Daniel, Pst.; Dcn. James O'Hara; Dcn. John Sutton; Dcn. Ray Alcouffe; Greg Smithhisler, Liturgy Dir.; Nate Stephens, Youth Min.; Caren Stephens, DRE; Nan Holmes, Bus. Mgr.; CRP Stds.: 603

St. Joseph - 196 Meadow, White Rock, NM 87547; Mailing: 3700 Canyon Rd, Los Alamos, NM 87544 Mission church--located in White Rock, NM

LOS LUNAS

San Clemente - 244 Luna N.E., Los Lunas, NM 87031; Mailing: PO Box 147, Los Lunas, NM 87031-0147 t) 505-865-9370 (CRP); 505-865-7385 www.sanclementeparish.org Very Rev. James Marshall, Pst.; Rev. Francisco Alanis, Par. Vicar; Dcn. Hector Avitia; Dcn. Paul Baca; Dcn. Robert Burkhard; Dcn. Jim Snell; CRP Stds.: 423

San Antonio - 1531 Los Lentes NE, Los Lunas, NM 87031 t) (505) 865-7385 sanclemente@qwestoffice.net

San Juan Diego - ; Mailing: P.O. Box 3320, Los Lunas, NM 87031 t) 505-866-0443

sanjuandiego@qwestoffice.net

LOS OJOS

San Jose-Los Ojos - State Rd. 514 #101, Los Ojos, NM 87551; Mailing: PO Box 6, Los Ojos, NM 87551 t) (575) 588-7473 (CRP); 505-699-3897 sanjosechurch@nuestrasenoradelvalle.org Rev. Ted Butler, Pst.; CRP Stds.: 10

San Joaquin, Ensenada - t) 575-588-7473

St. Michael, La Puente - t) 575-588-7473

San Antonio, Plaza Blanca - t) 575-588-7473

MORA

St. Gertrude the Great - #12 County Rd. A-033, Mora, NM 87732; Mailing: PO Box 599, Mora, NM 87732 t) 575-387-2336 stgertrudes.frdale@gmail.com Rev. James Mulligan, SOLT, In Res.; Rev. Dale Craig, SOLT, Admin.; Rev. Paul Grala, SOLT, Par. Vicar; Dcn. Cristobal Eloy Roybal; CRP Stds.: 63

San Jose, Le Doux - t) (575) 387-2336 stgertrudes.aa@gmail.com

Nuestra Senora del Carmel - t) (575) 387-2336 (parent parish phone) stgertrudes.aa@gmail.com

Santa Rita - t) (575) 387-2336 stgertrudes.aa@gmail.com

San Isidro - t) (575) 387-2336 stgertrudes.aa@gmail.com

El Santo Nino de Atocha, Buena Vista - t) (575) 387-2336 (parent parish phone) stgertrudes.aa@gmail.com

San Acacio - t) (575) 387-2336 (Parent parish phone) stgertrudes.aa@gmail.com

Sacred Heart of Jesus - t) (575) 387-2336 (parent parish phone) stgertrudes.aa@gmail.com

San Antonio de Padua, Chacon - t) (575) 387-2336 stgertrudes.aa@gmail.com

Immaculate Heart of Mary - t) (575) 387-2336 (Parent parish phone) stgertrudes.aa@gmail.com

San Antonio de Padua, Cleveland - t) 575-387-2236 stgertrudes.aa@gmail.com

Nuestra Senora de Guadalupe - t) (575) 387-2336 (Parent parish phone) stgertrudes.aa@gmail.com

El Santo Nino de Atocha, Monte Aplanado - t) 575-387-2236 stgertrudes.aa@gmail.com

Santa Teresita del Nino Jesus - t) (575) 387-2336 stgertrudes.aa@gmail.com

San Rafael - t) (575) 387-2336 stgertrudes.aa@gmail.com

San Jose, Canoncito - t) (575) 387-2336 stgertrudes.aa@gmail.com

San Santiago - t) (575) 387-2336 stgertrudes.aa@gmail.com

MORIARTY

Estancia Valley Catholic Parish - 1400 3rd St. S., Moriarty, NM 87035; Mailing: P.O. Box 129, Moriarty, NM 87035 t) 505-832-6655 parishoffice@evcpnm.org; formation@evcpnm.org www.evcpnm.org Rev. Adrian Sisneros, Par. Vicar; Dcn. Lincoln Richey; Tamara Magoffe, DRE; Rev. Robert Lancaster, Pst.; CRP Stds.: 97

Sts. Peter & Paul - 101 S. Ninth St., Estancia, NM 87016; Mailing: PO Box 129, Moriarty, NM 87035 t) (505) 832-6655 (parent parish phone)

San Antonio - 8566 Hwy. 55 W., Tajique, NM 87016; Mailing: PO Box 129, Moriarty, NM 87035 t) (505) 832-6655 (Parent parish phone)

St. Elizabeth Ann Seton - 85 Hwy. 344, Edgewood, NM 87015; Mailing: PO Box 129, Moriarty, NM 87035 t) (505) 832-6655 (parent parish phone)

MOUNTAINAIR

St. Alice - 301 S. Roosevelt St., Mountainair, NM 87036; Mailing: P.O. Box 206, Mountainair, NM 87036 t) 505-847-2291 office@stalicenm.com Rev. Jordan Sanchez, Pst.; Yvonne Garcia, DRE; CRP Stds.: 43

San Lorenzo - t) (505) 847-2291 (Parent parish phone)

St. Vincent de Paul - t) (505) 847-2291 (Parent parish phone)

Nuestra Senora de Dolores - t) (505) 847-2291 (Parent parish phone)

St. Anthony - t) (505) 847-2291 (Parent parish phone)

Our Lady of Sorrows - t) (505) 847-2291 (Parent parish phone)

OHKAY OWINGEH

San Juan Bautista - 185 Popaye Ave., Ohkay Owingeh, NM 87566; Mailing: P.O. Box 1075, Ohkay Owingeh, NM 87566-1075 t) 505-852-4179 info@sanjuanandtewa.com sanjuanandtewa.com Rev. Benny Sebastian, CST (India), Par. Vicar; Rev. Nathan Lopez, Pst.; Dcn. John Bird; Dcn. Gregory Aguilar; CRP Stds.: 90

San Antonio - t) (505) 852-4179

San Pablo - t) (505) 852-4179

San Rafael - t) (505) 852-4179

San Miguel - t) (505) 852-4179

San Francisco - t) (505) 852-4179

Sagrada Familia - t) (505) 852-4179

San Diego - t) (505) 852-4179

San Idelfonso - t) (505) 852-4179

Santa Clara - t) (505) 852-4179

St. Anne - t) (505) 852-4179

PECOS

St. Anthony of Padua-Pecos - #10 St. Anthony's Loop, Pecos, NM 87552; Mailing: HC 74 Box 23, Pecos, NM 87552 t) 505-757-6305 (CRP); 505-757-6345 saint.anthonys.pecos@gmail.com Rev. Christopher Nnonyelu (Nigeria), Admin.; Dcn. Richard Roybal; CRP Stds.: 62

Nuestra Senora de La Luz - t) (505) 757-6345

Santo Nino - t) (505) 757-6345

Nuestra Senora de Guadalupe, Glorieta - t) (505) 757-6345

Sagrada Familia - t) (505) 757-6345

Nuestra Senora de Guadalupe, El Macho - t) (505) 757-6345

PENA BLANCA

Nuestra Senora De Guadalupe - Pena Blanca - 816 Hwy. 22, Pena Blanca, NM 87041; Mailing: P.O. Box 1270, Pena Blanca, NM 87041 t) 505-465-2226 olog_penablanca57@archdiosf.org Rev. Anthony Obinna Ezeaputa, Pst.; Dcn. Jose Segura; Dcn. Dan Kennedy; CRP Stds.: 200

St. Bonaventure - t) (505) 465-2226 Indian Pueblo

San Felipe - t) (505) 465-2226 Indian Pueblo

Santo Domingo - t) (505) 465-2226 Indian Pueblo

Santa Barbara - t) (505) 465-2226

San Miguel - t) (505) 465-2226

PENASCO

San Antonio de Padua - 14079 N. Hwy. 75, Penasco, NM 87553-0460; Mailing: PO Box 460, Penasco, NM 87553 t) 575-587-2111 josefarodriguezsadp@gmail.com www.dixonpenascocc.org Rev. John Kimani, Pst.; CRP Stds.: 31

Santa Cruz Mission - t) (575) 587-2111 (Parent parish phone)

Sagrado Corazon Mission - t) (505) 587-2111 (Parent parish phone)

Nuestra Senora de los Dolores Mission - t) (504) 587-2111 (Parent parish phone)

San Lorenzo Mission - t) (575) 587-2111 (Parent parish phone)

San Juan Nepomuceno Mission - t) (575) 587-2111 (Parent parish phone)

Nuestra Senora de la Asuncion Mission - t) (575) 587-2111 (Parent parish phone)

Santa Barbara Mission - t) (575) 587-2111 (Parent parish phone)

PERALTA

Our Lady of Guadalupe-Peralta - 3674 Hwy. 47, Peralta, NM 87042; Mailing: P.O. Box 10, Peralta, NM 87042 t) 505-869-6993 (CRP); 505-869-2189 ologoffice@yahoo.com; ologccd@yahoo.com Rev. Emmanuel Izuka (Nigeria), Pst.; Dcn. Edward Espinosa; Annette Chavez, DRE; Gilbert Duncan, DRE; CRP Stds.: 99

Sangre de Cristo - t) (505) 869-2189

PORTALES

St. Helen - 1600 S. Ave. O, Portales, NM 88130 t) 575-356-4241 Rev. Francisco Carbajal, Pst.; Dcn. Roberto Herrera; CRP Stds.: 38

QUESTA

St. Anthony-Questa - 10 Church Plz., Questa, NM 87556; Mailing: PO Box 200, Questa, NM 87556 t) 575-586-0649 (CRP); 575-586-0470 stanthony_questa61@archdiosf.org Rev. Andrew Ifele (Nigeria), Pst.; Dcn. Leroy Lucero; Danette Rael, DRE; Dcn. Marcus J. Rael; CRP Stds.: 80

St. Edwin - t) (575) 586-0470 (parish)

Sagrado Corazon - t) (505) 586-0470 (parent parish phone)

Santo Nino - t) (575) 586-0470 (Parent parish phone)

Nuestra Senora de Guadalupe - t) (575) 586-0470 (Parent parish phone)

RANCHOS DE TAOS

San Francisco de Asis - #60 St. Francis Plz., Ranchos De Taos, NM 87557; Mailing: P.O. Box 72, Ranchos de Taos, NM 87557-0072 t) 575-758-2754 sanfranciscoranchos@gmail.com sfranchos.org Rev. Michael Garcia, Pst.; CRP Stds.: 64

Nuestra Senora de San Juan de Los Lagos, Talpa - t) (575) 758-2754 (Parent parish phone)

Nuestra Senora del Carmen, Llano Quemado - t) (575) 758-2754 (parent parish phone)

San Ysidro, Los Cordovas - t) (575) 758-2754 (parent parish phone)

RATON

St. Patrick - St. Joseph - 105 Buena Vista St., Raton, NM 87740 t) 575-445-9763 stspatjoe@bacavalley.com stpatrickstjoseph.weconnect.com Rev. William Woytavich, Pst.; Dcn. Thomas Alderette; Vickie Castellini-Blaisure, DRE; Brad Long, RCIA Coord.; CRP Stds.: 29

RIBERA

San Miguel Del Vado - 7 Sagebrush Way, Ribera, NM 87560; Mailing: PO Box 507, Ribera, NM 87560 t) 575-421-2780 sanmiguel@plateautel.net Rev. Moses Nwankwo, Pst.; Lana Gallegos, DRE; CRP Stds.: 5

San Jose Mission - t) (575) 421-2780

San Juan Nepomuceno Mission - t) (575) 421-2780; (575) 421-2780

Santa Rita Mission - t) (575) 421-2780

Our Lady of the Rosary Misson - t) (575) 421-2780

Nuestra Senora de Guadalupe Mission - t) (575) 421-2780

San Isidro Labrador Mission - t) (575) 421-2780

San Antonio de Padua - t) (575) 421-2780

RIO RANCHO

Church of the Incarnation - 2309 Monterrey Rd., N.E., Rio Rancho, NM 87144 t) 505-771-8331 claire@incarnation.church incarnation.church Rev. Leo W. Ortiz, Pst.; Dcn. George Meyerson, Pst. Assoc.; Dcn. Norbert Archibeque; Dcn. Louis Bernal; Dcn. Mark Buie; Dcn. Jerome Paszkiewicz; CRP Stds.: 229

St. John Vianney Church - 1001 Meteor Ave., N.E., Rio Rancho, NM 87144 t) 505-892-4449 info@sjvnm.org www.sjvnm.org Dcn. Matthew Lamoreux; Rev. Scott Mansfield, Pst.; Victoria Romero, DRE; CRP Stds.: 149

St. Thomas Aquinas - 1502 Sara Rd. S.E., Rio Rancho, NM 87124 t) 505-892-1497 (CRP); 505-892-1511 (Front Desk) cre@stanm.org; amy.montoya@stanm.org stanm.org Rev. Msgr. Douglas A. Raun, Pst.; Rev. Scott McKee, Par. Vicar; Dcn. Roger Ayers; Dcn. Thomas M. Tynan; Dcn. Tomas Perez; Dcn. Edward Leyba; Sr. Roseanne Fernandez, DRE; Dcn. David Little, DRE; Dcn. Frank Smith, Director of Marriage, Family, and Social Action; CRP Stds.: 343

St. Thomas Aquinas School - (Grades PreK-8) 1100 Hood Rd., S.E., Rio Rancho, NM 87124 t) 505-892-3221 principal@stasnm.net; registrar@stasnm.net www.stasnm.org Sr. Anne Louise Abascal, M.P.F., Prin.; Abi Walden, Vice Prin.; Stds.: 344; Sr. Tchrs.: 1; Lay Tchrs.: 24

ROY

Holy Family-St. Joseph - 515 St. George Ln., Roy, NM 87743; Mailing: P.O. Box 37, Roy, NM 87743 t) 575-485-9633 holyfamilyroy@yahoo.com Rev. Christopher A. Martinez, Pst.; CRP Stds.: 15

Immaculate Conception, Gallegos - t) (575) 485-9633 (Parent parish phone)

Nuestra Senora de Guadalupe, Sabinoso - t) (575) 485-9633 (Parent parish phone)

Sacred Heart, Bueyeros - t) (575) 485-9633 (Parent parish phone)

SANTA CRUZ

Holy Cross - 1332 Holy Cross St., Santa Cruz, NM 87567-1228; Mailing: P.O. Box 1228, Santa Cruz, NM 87567 t) 505-216-5001 (CRP); 505-753-3345 holycrossadm@yahoo.com www.hcccsantacruz.org Rev. Luis Gabriel Gomez Lopez, SF, Par. Vicar; Dcn. Ernest Salazar; Rev. Javier Gutierrez, S.F., Pst.; Janice D. Valdez, DRE; Debbie Valdez, Bus. Mgr.; CRP Stds.: 186

Holy Cross School - (Grades PreK-8) 1330 Holy Cross St., Santa Cruz, NM 87567-1260; Mailing: P.O. Box 1260, Santa Cruz, NM 87567-1260 t) 505-753-4644 hccsoffice@myhccs.org Angela Trujillo, Admin.; Victoria Garcia, Prin.; Stds.: 74; Lay Tchrs.: 5

La Sangre de Cristo - t) (505) 753-3344 (parent parish phone)

Nacimiento de Santo Nino Jesus - t) (505) 753-3345 (parent parish phone)

San Isidro - t) (505) 753-3345 (parent parish phone)

San Pedro - t) (505) 753-3345 (parent parish phone)

Santo Nino de Atocha - t) (505) 753-3345 (parent parish phone)

SANTA FE

The Cathedral Basilica of St. Francis of Assisi - 131 Cathedral Pl., Santa Fe, NM 87501-2127; Mailing: P.O. Box 2127, Santa Fe, NM 87504 t) 505-982-5619 pastor@cbsfa.org; receptionist@cbsfa.org Dcn. Martin Gallegos Jr.; Rev. Joseph A. Vigil, Assoc. Pst.; Dcn. William Kollasch; Dcn. Juan Martinez; Dcn. Joseph Garcia; Very Rev. John Cannon, Pst.; CRP Stds.: 94

St. Anne Catholic Church - 511 Alicia St., Santa Fe, NM 87501 t) 505-983-4430 cmtz1611@aol.com Rev. Larry R. Brito, Pst.; Catherine Keinjan, DRE; Dcn. Enrique M. Montoya; Rev. Donatus Onyeke, C.S.S.P. (Nigeria), In Res.; CRP Stds.: 160

Cristo Rey Parish - 1107 Cristo Rey St., Santa Fe, NM 87505; Mailing: 1147 Cristo Rey St., Santa Fe, NM 87505 t) 505-983-8528 office@cristoreyparish.org www.cristroreyparish.org Very Rev. John Cannon, Pst.;

Our Lady of Guadalupe - 1147 Cristo Rey St., Santa Fe, NM 87501 t) (505) 983-8528 (parent parish phone)

St. John the Baptist-Santa Fe - 1301 Osage Ave., Santa Fe, NM 87505 t) 505-983-5034 administration@sjtbcc.com www.sjtbcc.net Dcn. Jack Conrad; Rev. James Sanchez, Pst.; Dcn. Andres Carrillo; CRP Stds.: 29

Nuestra Senora de Guadalupe del Valle de Pojoaque - 9 Grazing Elk Dr., Santa Fe, NM 87506-7140 t) 505-455-2267 (CRP); 505-455-2472 ologp59@gmail.com Rev. Msgr. Jerome Martinez y Alire, Pastor Emer.; Dcn. John Archuleta; Dcn. Pedro Garcia; Rev. Franklin D. Pretto-Ferro, Admin.; Dcn. Greg Romero; Dcn. Reuben Roybal; CRP Stds.: 83

Sagrado Corazon de Jesus - t) (505) 455-2472 (Parent parish phone)

San Antonio de Padua - t) (505) 455-2472 (Parent parish phone)

San Francisco de Asis - t) (505) 455-2472 (Parent parish phone)

San Isidro - 3552 Agua Fria St., Santa Fe, NM 87507 t) 505-471-0710 sanisidro4@gmail.com sanisidroparish.org Rev. Jose Geronimo Herrera, Pst.; Dcn. Theodore Branch; Sr. Juanita Gonzalez, DRE; Dcn. Michael Salazar; Dcn. Anthony Trujillo; CRP Stds.: 344

San Jose, La Cienega - t) (505) 471-0710 (Parent parish phone)

Santa Maria de la Paz Catholic Community - 11 College Ave., Santa Fe, NM 87508-9225 t) 505-473-4200 smdlp@smdlp.org Rev. Darrell Segura Jr., Par. Vicar; Dcn. John Cordova; Dcn. Eloy Gallegos; Dcn. Dennis Snyder; Sr. Magdalena Casas, D.L.J.C., Dir.; Sr. Gabriel Mary Gaughan, DLJC, DRE; Tommy Baca, Youth Min.; Bernadette C. Bach, RCIA Coord.; Tommy Martinez, Bus. Mgr.; Brenda Weimer, Liturgy Dir.; CRP Stds.: 164

Shrine of Our Lady of Guadalupe-Santa Fe - 417 Agua Fria St., Santa Fe, NM 87501 t) 505-988-3336 (CRP); 505-983-8868 olog_sf73@archdiosf.org santuariodeguadalupesantafe.com/ Rev. Daniel Dupre, Pst.; Dcn. Jose Luis Burrola, Pst. Assoc.; Dcn. Thomas Stith, Pst. Assoc.; Dcn. Gilbert Valdez, Pst. Assoc.; CRP Stds.: 130

San Ysidro - t) (505) 983-8868 (Parent parish phone)

Our Lady of Sorrows - t) (505) 983-8868

SANTA ROSA

St. Rose of Lima - 439 S. Third St., Santa Rosa, NM 88435 t) 505-472-3992 (CRP); 575-472-3724 luciaf11@hotmail.com Dcn. Mark Marvin Marquez; Rev. Christopher Denzell Bernabe, Pst.; CRP Stds.: 140

San Ignacio - t) (575) 472-3724

San Isidro - t) (575) 472-3724

Santo Nino - t) 505-575-4723 srol_santarosa77@archdiosf.org

San Jose - t) (575) 472-3724 srol_santarosa77@archdiosf.org

Holy Family - t) (575) 472-3724 (Parent parish phone) srol_santarosa77@archdiosf.org

Our Lady of Sorrows - t) (575) 472-3724 srol_santarosa77@archdiosf.org

Our Lady of Refuge - t) (575) 472-3724

SOCORRO

San Miguel - 403 El Camino Real, N.W., Socorro, NM 87801 t) 575-835-2891 smiguel@sdc.org Rev. John Anasiudu (Nigeria), Pst.; Dcn. Nicholas Keller; Dcn. Miguel Ybarra; Romero Christina, DRE; CRP Stds.: 120

La Sagrada Familia - t) (575) 835-2891

San Lorenzo - t) (575) 835-2891

San Jose - t) (575) 835-2891

San Antonio, San Antonio - t) (575) 835-2891

San Antonio, Alamillo - t) (575) 835-2891

St. Mary Magdalene - t) (575) 835-2891

Santa Rita - t) (575) 835-2891

SPRINGER

St. Joseph - 605 5th St., Springer, NM 87747; Mailing: PO Box 516, Springer, NM 87747 t) 575-483-2775; 575-483-0035 stjosephicc@hotmail.com Rev. Benoit Trieu Van Vu, Pst.; Dcn. Edward Olona; Marcella Jensen, DRE; CRP Stds.: 9

Our Lady of Mt Carmel Mission - t) (575) 483-2775 (Parent parish phone) Rev. Benoit Trieu Van Vu, Pst.;

San Isidro Mission - t) (575) 483-2775 (parent parish phone) Rev. Benoit Trieu Van Vu, Pst.;

TAOS

Nuestra Senora De Guadalupe-Taos - 205 Don Fernando St., Taos, NM 87571 t) 575-776-4764 (CRP); 575-758-9208 olgtaos@yahoo.com www.ologtaos.com Rev. Felice Peter Mgendwa (Tanzania), Admin.; Dcn. Jerry Quintana; CRP Stds.: 69

Nuestra Senora De Dolores - t) (575) 758-9208

San Antonio, La Loma - t) (575) 758-9208

San Geronimo, Taos Pueblo - t) (575) 758-9208

Santa Teresita de Jesus, El Prado - t) (575) 758-9208

Imaculada Concepcion, Ranchitos - t) (575) 758-9208

TIERRA AMARILLA

Santo Nino-Tierra Amarilla - Rio Arriba CR 15, Bldg 23, Tierra Amarilla, NM 87575; Mailing: PO Box 160, Tierra Amarilla, NM 87575 t) 575-588-7473 santonino@nuestrasenoradelvalle.org Rev. Ted Butler, Pst.; Dcn. Joseph Valdez;

TIJERAS

Holy Child - 19 Camino del Santo Nino, Tijeras, NM 87059; Mailing: PO Box 130, Tijeras, NM 87059 t) 505-281-2297 parish@holychildnm.com holychildparishnm.org Rev. Mark E. Granito, Pst.; Dcn. Randall Rodriguez; Dcn. Maurice Rodriguez; CRP Stds.: 101

Holy Child - t) (505) 281-2297

San Juan de Nepumoceno - t) (505) 281-2297

San Isidro, Escobosa - t) (505) 281-2297 (parent parish phone)

San Antonio - t) (505) 281-2297 (parent parish phone)

San Isidro, Sedillo - t) (505) 281-2297 (parent parish phone)

San Lorenzo - t) (505) 281-2297 (parent parish phone) Rev. Mark E. Granito, Pst.;

Holy Child Catholic School - (Grades PreK-8) t) 505-281-3077 jmartinez@holychildnm.com www.holychildcatholicschool.org Stds.: 66; Lay Tchrs.: 8

Senor de Mapimi - t) (505) 281-2297 (parent parish phone)

TOME

Immaculate Conception-Tome - 7 Church Loop, Tome, NM 87060-0100; Mailing: PO Box 100, Tome, NM 87060 t) 505-865-4220 (CRP); 505-865-7497 secy@immaculateconceptiontome.com www.immaculateconceptiontome.org Very Rev. Michael T. Demkovich, O.P., Pst.; Monica Padilla, Liturgy Dir.; Nichole Villela, DRE; CRP Stds.: 161

Immaculate Conception Casa Colorado - State Hwy. 304 S., Belen, NM 87002 t) (505) 865-7497 (Parent parish phone)

TUCUMCARI

St. Anne-Tucumcari - 306 W. High St., Tucumcari, NM 88401 t) 575-461-2515 stannestucumcari@gmail.com Rev. Johnpaul O Afuecheta, Pst.; Dcn. Raphael (Ray) P. Aragon; Nancy Arias, DRE; CRP Stds.: 45

St. Anthony - t) (575) 461-2515

Sacred Heart - t) (575) 461-2515

Our Lady of Guadalupe - t) (575) 461-2515

St. Joan of Arc - t) (575) 461-2515

VAUGHN

St. Mary - 376 W. 8th St., Vaughn, NM 88353; Mailing: PO Box 276, Vaughn, NM 88353 t) 575-584-2954 stmarys@plateautel.net Rev. Timothy J. Meurer, Pst.; CRP Stds.: 1

Our Lady of Guadalupe Mission Church, Encino - t) (575) 584-2954

San Jose Mission Church, Pinos Wells - t) (575) 584-2954

St. Helen Mission Church, Pastura - t) (505) 584-2954

St. John the Baptist Mission Church, Duran - t) (575) 584-2954

VILLANUEVA

Our Lady of Guadalupe-Villanueva - 4 Our Lady of Guadalupe, Villanueva, NM 87583; Mailing: P.O. Box 39, Villanueva, NM 87583 t) 575-421-2548 nsdeguadalupe@plateautel.net Rev. Moses Nwankwo, Pst.; Lana Gallegos, DRE; CRP Stds.: 52

Nuestra Senora de Los Desamparados - t) (575) 421-2548 (Parent parish phone)

Nuestro Senor Esquipula - t) (575) 421-2548 (Parent parish phone)

San Antonio - t) (575) 421-2548 (Parent parish phone)

San Francisco - t) (575) 421-2548 (Parent parish phone)

San Isidro & Santa Teresita - t) (575) 421-2548 (Parent parish phone)

WAGON MOUND

Santa Clara - 805 Calhoun Ave., Wagon Mound, NM 87752; Mailing: P.O. Box 186, Wagon Mound, NM 87752 t) 575-666-2478 cmartinez@archdiosf.org Rev. Christopher A. Martinez, Pst.; Dcn. Charlie Duran; CRP Stds.: 2

Nuestra Senora de Guadalupe, Ocate - 501 Nolan St., Wagon Mound, NM 87752 t) (575) 666-2478

Nuestro Senor de Esquipula, Los Le Febres - 501 Nolan St., Wagon Mound, NM 87752 t) (575) 666-2478

Sagrado Corazon, Watrous - 501 Nolan St., Wagon Mound, NM 87752 t) (575) 666-2478

San Juan Bautista, Los Hueros - 501 Nolan St., Wagon Mound, NM 87752 t) (575) 666-2478

SCHOOLS: PRESCHOOL THRU HIGH SCHOOL

SCHOOLS

STATE OF NEW MEXICO

SANTA FE

Santo Nino Regional Catholic School - (PAR) (Grades PreK-6) 23 College Ave., Santa Fe, NM 87508 t) 505-424-1766 snrcs@santoninoregional.org www.santoninoregional.org Robin Chavez, Prin.; Stds.: 178; Lay Tchrs.: 7

HIGH SCHOOLS

STATE OF NEW MEXICO

ALBUQUERQUE

St. Pius X High School, Inc. - (DIO) 5301 St. Joseph Dr., N.W., Albuquerque, NM 87120 t) 505-831-8400 www.saintpiusx.com Michael A Deely, Prin.; Rev. John B. Trambley II, Pres.; Noreen Copeland, Pres.; Stds.: 498; Sr. Tchrs.: 1; Lay Tchrs.: 51

SANTA FE

St. Michael's High School - (PRV) (Grades 7-12) 100 Siringo Rd., Santa Fe, NM 87505 t) 505-983-7353 akingsbury@smhs.me www.stmichaelsff.org (Coed Day School) Arlana Kingsbury, Prin.; Stds.: 436; Bro. Tchrs.: 1; Lay Tchrs.: 24

INSTITUTIONS LOCATED IN DIOCESE

ASSOCIATIONS [ASN]

ALBUQUERQUE

Catholic Cemetery Association - 1900 Edith Blvd. S.W., Albuquerque, NM 87120 t) 505-248-1532 dmartinez@asfcca.org Diocesan Cemeteries, Rosario (Santa Fe), Mt. Calvary (Albuquerque) and Gate of Heaven (Albuquerque). Donna Martinez, Dir.;

CAMPUS MINISTRY / NEWMAN CENTERS [CAM]

ALBUQUERQUE

St. Thomas Aquinas University Parish - 1815 Las Lomas Rd., N.E., Albuquerque, NM 87106 t) 505-247-1094 mdepalma@archdiosf.org www.lobocatholic.org Rev. Michael DePalma, Pst.;

LAS VEGAS

Highlands University Newman Center - 811 6th Street, Las Vegas, NM 87701 t) 505-425-7791 icchurch2000@yahoo.com Attended by Immaculate Conception Parish, Las Vegas. Rev. Dennis M. Garcia, Campus Min.;

PORTALES

University Catholic Center - St. Thomas More Chapel - 1614 W. 17th St., Portales, NM 88130 t) 575-356-4241 emmabritton.sthelens@gmail.com Rev. Francisco Carbajal, Chap.;

SOCORRO

St. Patrick Newman Center - 801 School of Mines Rd., Socorro, NM 87801 t) 575-835-8650 agalleoo@nmt.edu Dcn. Nicholas Keller, Dir.;

CONVENTS, MONASTERIES, AND RESIDENCES FOR WOMEN [CON]

ALBUQUERQUE

Cristo Rey Provincial House - 5625 Isleta Blvd., S.W., Albuquerque, NM 87105 t) 505-873-2854 serafiniannamaria@yahoo.com.mx www.canossiansisters.org Canossian Daughters of Charity. Sr. Anna Maria Serafini, FdCC, Prov.; Srs.: 25

RIO RANCHO

Felician Sisters of the Southwest United States of America - 4106 Pico Norte, NE, Rio Rancho, NM 87124 t) 505-892-8862 sjudithmk@feliciansisters.org www.feliciansistersna.org Sr. Judith Marie Kubicki, Prov.; Srs.: 17

ENDOWMENTS / FOUNDATIONS / TRUSTS [EFT]

ALBUQUERQUE

Annual Catholic Appeal Foundation of the Archdiocese of Santa Fe - 4000 St. Joseph Pl., N.W., Albuquerque, NM 87120 t) 505-831-8155 jsanchez@asfcca.org www.acaarchdiosf.org Julie Anne Sanchez, Dir.;

Anselm Weber Fund - 1204 Stinson St., S.W., Albuquerque, NM 87195-0315; Mailing: P.O. Box 12315, Albuquerque, NM 87195-0315 t) 505-877-6394 treasolg@comcast.net Rev. Gregory Friedman, O.F.M., Treas.;

Archbishop's School Fund - 4000 St. Joseph Pl., N.W., Albuquerque, NM 87120 t) 505-831-8172 dillerbrun@archdiosf.org Donna Illerbrun, Supt.;

Archdiocese of Santa Fe Real Estate Trust - 4000 St. Joseph Pl., N.W., Albuquerque, NM 87120 t) 505-831-8397 tmacken@archdiosf.org Thomas P. Macken, Chancellor;

The Catholic Foundation of the Archdiocese of Santa Fe - 4333 Pan American Fwy., N.E., Ste. D, Albuquerque, NM 87107 t) 505-872-2901 ed@thecatholicfoundation.org www.thecatholicfoundation.org Edward Larranaga, Pres.;

St. Pius X High School Foundation, Inc. - 5301 St. Joseph Dr., N.W., Albuquerque, NM 87120 t) 505-831-8423 mdeeley@spxabq.org www.saintpiusx.com Nonprofit corporation for the financial support of St. Pius X High School. Michael A Deely, Prin.;

Roger Huser Fund - 1204 Stinson St., S.W., Albuquerque, NM 87121-3440; Mailing: P.O. Box 12315, Albuquerque, NM 87195-0315 t) 505-877-6394 treasolg@comcast.net Rev. Gregory Friedman, O.F.M., Treas.;

JEMEZ SPRINGS

EDSA Charitable Trust - 18161 Hwy. 4, Jemez Springs, NM 87025; Mailing: P.O. Box 489, Jemez Springs, NM 87025 t) 575-829-4138 prafff@gmail.com

Fitzgerald Charitable Trust - 18161 Hwy. 4, Jemez Springs, NM 87025 t) 575-829-3586 prafff@gmail.com www.theservants.org

SANTA FE

St. Michael's High School Foundation - 100 Siringo Rd., Santa Fe, NM 87505; Mailing: P.O. Box 22563, Santa Fe, NM 87502 t) 505-988-2264 mayers@smhs.me stmikesfoundation.org/ Tom Coughlan, Pres.;

HOSPITALS / HEALTH SERVICES [HOS]

SANTA FE

***CHRISTUS St. Vincent Regional Medical Center** - 455 St. Michael's Dr., Santa Fe, NM 87505 t) 505-983-3361 contactus@stvin.org www.christushealth.org Regional health care system including hospital, outpatient sites and primary care, pediatric and specialty clinics Lillian Montoya, CEO; Bed Capacity: 200; Asstd. Annu.: 566,428; Staff: 2,281

MISCELLANEOUS [MIS]

ALBUQUERQUE

Archdiocesan Priests Retirement Fund, Inc. - 5024 4th St., N.W., Albuquerque, NM 87107 t) 505-503-8637 jen@jcantrellcpa.com Rev. George Robert Yaksich, Pres.;

Archdiocese of Santa Fe D&L Fund - 4000 St. Joseph Pl., N.W., Albuquerque, NM 87120 t) 505-831-8132 tsalgado@asfcca.org Tony Salgado, Exec.;

Archdiocese of Santa Fe Real Estate Corporation - 4000 St. Joseph Pl., N.W., Albuquerque, NM 87120 t) 505-831-8397 tmacken@archdiosf.org

***St. Bernadette Institute of Sacred Art** - 302 Chama St. NE, Albuquerque, NM 87108-2023; Mailing: PO Box 8249, Albuquerque, NM 87198-8249 t) 505-717-5157 stbernadetteinst@gmail.com; danieltpaulos@gmail.com www.stbernadetteinstitute.com Sponsors and supports Catholic art and artists. Dan Paulos, Dir.;

The Brothers of the Good Shepherd - 901 Brother Mathias Pl., N.W., Albuquerque, NM 87102-7103; Mailing: P.O. Box 389, Albuquerque, NM 87102-7103 t) 505-243-4238 judy@sjog-na.org www.sjog-na.org Bro. David Lynch, OH, Pres.; Bro. Richard MacPhee, Treas.;

Caritas Deus Inc. - 412 Iron St., S.W., Albuquerque, NM 87103; Mailing: P.O. Box 749, Albuquerque, NM 87103 t) 505-243-2527 judy@sjog-na.org Property management nonprofit corporation. Bro. David Lynch, OH, Pres.; Bro. Richard MacPhee, Treas.;

Catholic Charismatic Center - 1412 Fifth St., N.W., Albuquerque, NM 87102 t) 505-247-0397 abqcatholiccharismaticcenter@gmail.com www.asqccc.org Sr. Anna Sophia Garcia Ferralde, DLJC, Dir.;

Charity Unlimited - 901 Brother Mathias Pl., N.W., Albuquerque, NM 87103; Mailing: P.O. Box 389, Albuquerque, NM 87103 t) 505-243-4238 judy@sjog-na.org Property management nonprofit corporation. Bro. David Lynch, OH, Pres.; Bro. Richard MacPhee, Treas.;

Dominican Ecclesial Institute (D.E.I.) - 4060 St. Josephs Pl., N.W., Ste. 210, Albuquerque, NM 87125 t) 505-831-8212 c) 505-504-2766 director@deiabq.org www.deiabq.org Dr. Mary McLeod, CEO;

Fraternidad Piadosa de Nuestro Padre Jesus Nazareno - 4000 St. Joseph Pl., N.W., Albuquerque, NM 87120 t) (505) 617-6299 ernestarmijo@gmail.com Ernest Armijo, Elder;

St. Joseph Fertility Care Center - 5311 Phoenix Ave NE, Albuquerque, NM 87110 t) 505-263-3509 angel@stjosephfertilitycare.org www.stjosephfertilitycare.org Angelique N. Garcia, Pres.;

SPX Real Estate Corp. - 5301 St. Joseph Pl., N.W., Albuquerque, NM 87120 t) (505) 235-6715 Jerry D. Sais, Pres.;

***Trinity House Catholic Worker** - 1925 Five Points Rd., S.W., Albuquerque, NM 87105 t) 505-842-5697 trinityhousecw@gmail.com trinityhousecw.org Ed Singletary, Dir.;

RIO RANCHO

St. Felix Pantry, Inc. - 4020 Barbara Loop SE, Rio Rancho, NM 87124-1023 t) 505-891-8075 info@stfelixpantry.org www.stfelixpantry.org Food Pantry and Referral Services Sr. Mary Angela Parkins, C.S.S.F., Pres.;

SANTA FE

Religious Communities Impact Fund, Inc. - 1010 Marquez Pl., Ste. D3, Santa Fe, NM 87505 t) 505-372-7561 sgeisler@rcif.org www.rcif.org Sarah Geisler, Dir.;

MONASTERIES AND RESIDENCES FOR PRIESTS AND BROTHERS [MON]

ABIQUIU

Monastery of Christ in the Desert - 1305 Forest Service Rd. 151, Abiquiu, NM 87510; Mailing: P.O. Box 270, Abiquiu, NM 87510 t) 575-613-4233 webmonk@christdesert.org www.christdesert.org Rt. Rev. Christian Leisy, O.S.B., Abbot; Rev. Thomas Benedict Baxter, O.S.B., Mem.; Rev. Bernard Cranor, O.S.B., Mem.; Rt. Rev. Philip Lawrence, O.S.B., Mem.; Rev. Andrew Dzung An Nguyen, O.S.B., Mem.; Rev. Bonaventure Nguyen, O.S.B., Mem.; Rev. Mayeal Thu Van Tran, O.S.B., Mem.; Rev. Jeffrey Steele, OSB, Mem.; Brs.: 13; Priests: 10

ALBUQUERQUE

Community of the Franciscans of the Renewal San Juan Diego Friary - 404 San Mateo Blvd., N.E., Albuquerque, NM 87108 t) 505-990-3001 cfrgensec@franciscanfriars.com www.cfrnewmexico.com San Juan Diego Friary Rev. Roch Greiner, CFR, Supr.; Rev. Juan Diego Sutherland, C.F.R., Vicar; Rev. Leo Fisher, C.F.R., Pst. Assoc.; Bro. Gerard Kanapes, C.F.R., Mem.; Friar Teresiano Madrigal, Friar; Brs.: 2; Priests: 3

Santa Maria de la Vid Abbey - 5825 Coors Blvd., S.W., Albuquerque, NM 87121-6700 t) 505-873-4399 norbertines@norbertinecommunity.org www.norbertinecommunity.org Sponsor of the Norbertine Spirituality Center. Canons Regular of Premontre (Norbertine Community). Rt. Rev. Joel P. Garner, O.Praem., Abbot; Rev. Robert E. Campbell, O.Praem., Prior; Rev. Stephen A. Gaetner, O.Praem.; Rev. Eugene Gries, O.Praem., Other; Rev. Peter Muller, O.Praem.; Dcn. James Owens, O.Praem., Treas.; Rev. Thomas Pulikal, O.Praem. (India); Rev. Milton Thomas, O.Praem.; Brs.: 3; Priests: 7

The Province of Our Lady of Guadalupe of the Order of Friars Minor, Inc. - 1204 Stinson, S.W., Albuquerque, NM 87121-3440 t) 505-831-9199 ofmprovsec@aol.com; provincial@swfranciscans.org www.swfranciscans.org Rev. Nicholas Baxter, O.F.M.; Rev. Gregory Friedman, O.F.M., Secy.; Rev. Paul Juniet, O.F.M.; Rev. Sean Murnan, O.F.M.; Rev. Richard Rohr, O.F.M.; Rev. Erasmo Romero, O.F.M., Vocation Dir., Councillor; Very Rev. Ronald Walters, O.F.M., Prov.; Bro. Gordon Boykin, O.F.M., Spiritual Asst.; Bro. Michael Burns, O.F.M., Guardian; Bro. Bernard Keele, OFM; Bro. Richardo Garcia, O.F.M.; Bro. Gerald Grantner, O.F.M.; Rev. Patrick Schafer, O.F.M., Councillor; Bro. Bruce Michalek, O.F.M., Dir.; Bro. Duane Torisky, OFM, Secretarial Staff; Bro. George Ward, O.F.M.; Brs.: 18; Priests: 26

Villa Mathias, Inc. - 901 Bro. Mathias Pl., N.W., Albuquerque, NM 87103; Mailing: P.O. Box 389, Albuquerque, NM 87103 t) 505-243-4238 judy@sjogna.org Bro. David Lynch, OH, Pres.; Bro. Richard MacPhee, Treas.; Brs.: 5; Priests: 2

JEMEZ SPRINGS

Our Lady of Lourdes - 18161 Hwy 4, Jemez Springs, NM 87025; Mailing: P.O. Box 489, Jemez Springs, NM 87025 t) (575) 829-3004 servantsoftheparaclete.org Temporarily Closed Bro. John Paul Pelletier, sP, Contact;

PECOS

Our Lady of Guadalupe Abbey - 16 Guadalupe Ln., Pecos, NM 87552-1080; Mailing: P.O. Box 1080, Pecos, NM 87552-1080 t) 505-757-6415 guestmaster@pecosmonastery.org www.pecosmonastery.org (Olivetan Benedictine Monks) Bro. Gary Miller, OSB oliv.; Bro. Timothy Mundie, OSB oliv; Rt. Rev. Aidan Gore, O.S.B. Oliv.; Rev. Symeon Galazka, OSB oliv., Other; Bro. Bruno Boyko, O.S.B. Oliv.; Bro. Francis Dawson, O.S.B. Oliv.; Bro. Joseph Janeczko, O.S.B. Oliv.; Bro. Jaboc Kozel, O.S.B. Oliv.; Bro. James M. Marron, O.S.B. Oliv.; Bro. Christopher Thurman, OSB oliv., Other; Rev. Andrew Miles, O.S.B., In Res.; Brs.: 8; Priests: 3

SANTA FE

Discalced Carmelite Monastery - 49 Mount Carmel Rd., Santa Fe, NM 87505-0352 t) 505-983-7232 vocation@carmelofsantafe.org www.carmelofsantafe.org Mother Marie Bernadette Bennett, OCD, Prioress;

RETREAT HOUSES / RENEWAL CENTERS [RTR]

ALBUQUERQUE

Norbertine Spirituality Center - 5825 Coors Blvd., S.W., Albuquerque, NM 87121-6700 t) 505-873-4399 retreats@norbertinecommunity.org www.norbertinecommunity.org Patti Dailey, Dir.;

PECOS

Our Lady of Guadalupe Olivetan Benedictine Abbey - 16 Guadalupe Ln., Pecos, NM 87552; Mailing: P.O. Box 1080, Pecos, NM 87552 t) 505-757-6415 guestmaster@pecosmonastery.org www.pecosmonastery.org Rt. Rev. Aidan Gore, O.S.B. Oliv., Abbot;

SHRINES [SHR]

ALBUQUERQUE

Shrine of St. Bernadette - 11401 Indian School Rd., N.E., Albuquerque, NM 87112; Mailing: 11509 Indian School Rd NE, Albquerque, NM 87112 t) (505) 247-6829 lgerrish@ssbnm.org www.shrineofstbernadette.com Dcn. William Barry; Dcn. Terry Palmer; Dcn. Joe Santana; Dcn. Charles E. Schwenn; Brenda Sais, DRE; Very Rev. Rick Zerwas, Pst.;

Shrine of the Little Flower/St. Therese of the Infant Jesus - 300 Mildred, N.W., Albuquerque, NM 87107 t) 505-344-8050 sttheresealb@gmail.com Dcn. Larry Carmony, Admin.;

CHIMAYO

Santuario de Chimayo - 15 Santuario Dr., Chimayo, NM 87522 t) 505-351-4360 holyfamilychimayo@hotmail.com www.holychimayo.us Attended by Holy Family, Chimayo Very Rev. Julio Gonzales, S.F., Pst.;

ISLETA PUEBLO

Shrine of Saint Kateri Tekakwitha (St. Augustine Parish) - Tribal Rd. 35 #71, Isleta Pueblo, NM 87022; Mailing: PO Box 849, Isleta Pueblo, NM 87022 t) 505-869-3398 mthomas@archdiosf.org Attended by St. Augustine. Rev. Milton Thomas, O.Praem., Admin.;

SANTA FE

Shrine of Our Lady of Guadalupe - 417 Agua Fria St., Santa Fe, NM 87501 t) 505-983-8868 olog_sf73@archdiosf.org Rev. Daniel Dupre, Pst.;

SPECIAL CARE FACILITIES [SPF]

ALBUQUERQUE

Casa Angelica - 5629 Isleta Blvd., S.W., Albuquerque, NM 87105 t) 505-877-5763 jdouglas@casaangelica.org www.casaangelica.org Home for developmentally disabled children and young adults. Jim Douglas, Admin.; Bed Capacity: 16; Asstd. Annu.: 16; Staff: 56

Good Shepherd Center, Inc. - 218 Iron St., S.W., Albuquerque, NM 87103; Mailing: P.O. Box 749, Albuquerque, NM 87103 t) 505-243-2527 gsc@gscnm.org; bronich@gscnm.org www.gscnm.org Agency for Homeless. Bro. Nicholas Foran, OH, Exec.; Bed Capacity: 60; Asstd. Annu.: 97,150; Staff: 11

SANTA FE

Villa Therese Catholic Clinic - 1779 Hopewell St., Santa Fe, NM 87505 t) 505-983-8561 execdirector@vtccsf.org www.vtccsf.org Free clinic for basic medical, dental, and vision care as well as basic assistance to those who are uninsured and/or underinsured. Victoria Otero, Dir.; Asstd. Annu.: 1,000; Staff: 6

Diocese of Santa Rosa in California

(Dioecesis Sanctae Rosae in California)

MOST REVEREND ROBERT FRANCIS VASA

Bishop of Santa Rosa in California; ordained May 22, 1976; appointed Bishop of Baker November 19, 1999; consecrated and installed January 26, 2000; appointed Coadjutor Bishop of Santa Rosa in California January 24, 2011; installed March 6, 2011; succeeded June 30, 2011.

Chancery Office: 985 Airway Ct., Santa Rosa, CA 95403. T: 707-566-3300; F: 707-542-9702. Mailing Address: P.O. Box 1297, Santa Rosa, CA 95402-1297. www.srdiocese.org

ESTABLISHED FEBRUARY 21, 1962.

Square Miles 11,711.

Comprises six Counties in the State of California-viz.,Del Norte, Humboldt, Lake, Mendocino, Napa and Sonoma.

Legal Titles: "The Roman Catholic Bishop of Santa Rosa, a Corporation Sole" and "The Roman Catholic Welfare Corporation of Santa Rosa."

For legal titles of parishes and diocesan institutions, consult the Chancery Office.

STATISTICAL OVERVIEW

Personnel

Bishop	1
Retired Bishops	1
Priests: Diocesan Active in Diocese	36
Priests: Diocesan Active Outside Diocese	2
Priests: Retired, Sick or Absent	25
Number of Diocesan Priests	63
Religious Priests in Diocese	14
Total Priests in your Diocese	77
Extern Priests in Diocese	11
Ordinations:	
Diocesan Priests	1
Permanent Deacons in Diocese	47
Total Brothers	27
Total Sisters	46

Parishes

Parishes	40
With Resident Pastor:	
Resident Diocesan Priests	35
Resident Religious Priests	5
Missions	22
Pastoral Centers	2
Professional Ministry Personnel:	
Brothers	8
Sisters	14

Welfare

Catholic Hospitals	4
Total Assisted	492,505
Health Care Centers	1
Total Assisted	203,129
Residential Care of Children	1
Total Assisted	21
Special Centers for Social Services	1
Total Assisted	19,384

Educational

Diocesan Students in Other Seminaries	5
Total Seminarians	5
High Schools, Diocesan and Parish	2
Total Students	757
High Schools, Private	3
Total Students	779
Elementary Schools, Diocesan and Parish	8
Total Students	1,607
Elementary Schools, Private	2
Total Students	249
Catechesis/Religious Education:	
High School Students	1,002
Elementary Students	3,768
Total Students under Catholic Instruction	8,167
Teachers in Diocese:	
Priests	2
Scholastics	1
Brothers	2
Sisters	6
Lay Teachers	238

Vital Statistics

Receptions into the Church:	
Infant Baptism Totals	2,063
Minor Baptism Totals	108
Adult Baptism Totals	85
Received into Full Communion	104
First Communions	2,100
Confirmations	1,508
Marriages:	
Catholic	356
Interfaith	57
Total Marriages	413
Deaths	843
Total Catholic Population	191,049
Total Population	955,245

LEADERSHIP

Chancery Office - t) 707-566-3300
Vicar General - t) 707-566-3334 Very Rev. Samuel Moses Brown (mbrown@srdiocese.org);
Deans - Rev. Bernard D'Sa, Humboldt/Del Norte Dean; Rev. Abel Mena, Napa Dean; Rev. Michaelraj Philominsamy, Sonoma North Dean;
Chancellor - Very Rev. Samuel Moses Brown (mbrown@srdiocese.org);
Moderator of the Curia - Very Rev. Samuel Moses Brown (mbrown@srdiocese.org);
Director of Clergy Personnel - Very Rev. Samuel Moses Brown (mbrown@srdiocese.org);
Vicar for Priests - t) 707-566-3334 Very Rev. Samuel Moses Brown (mbrown@srdiocese.org);
Vicar for Retired Priests - Rev. Msgr. Daniel P. Whelton (dwhelton@srdiocese.org);
Diocesan Finance Officer - t) 707-566-3329 Dcn. Joe Oberting, CFO (joe_oberting@yahoo.com);
Secretary to the Bishop - t) 707-566-3325 Lynne Peter (lpeter@srdiocese.org);
Diocesan Tribunal - t) 707-566-3370 tribunal@srdiocese.org
Judicial Vicar - Rev. Fergal McGuinness, Vicar (fmcguinness@srdiocese.org);
Adjutant Judicial Vicar - Rev. Abel Mena;
Promoter of Justice - Very Rev. Samuel Moses Brown (mbrown@srdiocese.org);
Defender of the Bond - Rev. David Galeana;
Diocesan Judges - Rev. Abel Mena; Rev. Msgr. James P. Gaffey; Rev. Msgr. John J. Brenkle;
Advocates - Rev. William P. Donahue; Dcn. Joseph Olsen Jr.;
Tribunal Auditor - t) 707-566-3370 Sr. Philomena Marie, M.S.S.R.;
Notaries - Very Rev. Samuel Moses Brown (mbrown@srdiocese.org); Sr. Caritas Marie, M.S.S.R.; Lynne Peter (lpeter@srdiocese.org);
Presbyteral Council - Rev. Eliseo Avendano (danielroa21@aol.com); Rev. Bernard D'Sa; Rev. Abel Mena;
College of Consultors - Very Rev. Samuel Moses Brown, Vicar Gen. (mbrown@srdiocese.org); Rev. Alvin Villaruel; Rev. Michaelraj Philominsamy;
Parish Priest Consultors - Rev. Alvin M. Villaruel; Rev. Michaelraj Philominsamy; Rev. Abel Mena;
Clergy Personnel Board - Very Rev. Samuel Moses Brown (mbrown@srdiocese.org); Rev. Frank Epperson; Rev. William P. Donahue;
Diocesan Finance Council - Most Rev. Robert F. Vasa; Very Rev. Samuel Moses Brown (mbrown@srdiocese.org); Dcn. Joe Oberting (joe_oberting@yahoo.com);
Diocesan Building Committee - Dcn. Joe Oberting (joe_oberting@yahoo.com); Kelly Righetti; Ed Ronchelli;
Diocesan Review Board - George Berg; Daniel Hanlon; Richard Ortiz;
Priests Pension Board - Rev. William P. Donahue; Rev. Gerard Gormley; Rev. Fergal McGuinness (fmcguinness@srdiocese.org);
Communications & Evangelization Committee - Most Rev. Robert F. Vasa; Dcn. Dennis Purificacion; Rev. Raul Lemus;
Diocesan Commission on Catechesis - Adrian Peterson; Most Rev. Robert F. Vasa; Very Rev. Samuel Moses Brown (mbrown@srdiocese.org);

OFFICES AND DIRECTORS

Advancement - t) 707-566-3396 Russ Ferreira;
Attorney for the Diocese - t) 707-544-5858 Daniel J. Galvin III;
Catholic Charities, Central Administrative Office - t) 707-528-8712 Jennielynn Holmes, CEO (jholmes@srcharities.org);
Catholic Community Foundation - t) 707-566-3344 Most Rev. Robert F. Vasa, Pres.; Very Rev. Samuel Moses Brown, Vice. Pres. (mbrown@srdiocese.org); Dcn. Joe Oberting, Financial Vice Pres. (joe_oberting@yahoo.com);
Catholic Restorative Justice Ministries - t) 707-544-9080 Dcn. John Storm, Dir.;
Cemeteries - t) 707-546-6290 Angela Scheihing, Dir.;
Communications - t) 707-566-3302 Christopher Lyford, Dir.;
Continuing Clergy Formation - Very Rev. Samuel Moses Brown (mbrown@srdiocese.org);
Custodian of Records - t) 707-566-3334 Very Rev. Samuel Moses Brown (mbrown@srdiocese.org);
Director of Seminarians - t) 707-566-3300 Rev. Frank Epperson;
Director of the Office for the Protection of Children and Youth - t) 707-566-3308 Fatima Jimenez;
Ecumenical and Interreligious Affairs - t) 707-566-3300
Family Life - t) 707-566-3305 Dcn. Dave Gould, Dir.; Carlin Gould, Dir.; Dcn. Sergio Velazquez (svelazquez60@gmail.com);
Hispanic Ministry - t) 707-544-3300
  Catholic Cursillo Movement & Movimento Cursillisto of the Diocese of Santa Rosa - Dcn. Sergio Orozco; Denise Hewitt;
  Movimiento Carismatico -
  Movimiento Familiar Cristiano - t) 707-254-9878 Rev. Mario Valencia; Alejandro Gonzalez; Ana Gonzalez;
  Stewardship, Appeals & CCF - t) 707-566-3344 Sr. Caritas Marie, M.S.S.R., Dir.;
Newspaper - t) 707-566-3302 Christopher Lyford, Dir.;
Permanent Diaconate - Dcn. Russ Bowden; Dcn. Sergio Velazquez (svelazquez60@gmail.com);
Propagation of the Faith - t) 707-539-5377 joberting@srdiocese.org Dcn. Joe Oberting, Dir. (joe_oberting@yahoo.com);
Religious Education - t) 707-566-3313 Dcn. Dennis Purificacion, Diocesan D.R.E.;
Santa Rosa Diocesan Council of Catholic Women - santarosadccw@gmail.com Char Mayclin, Pres.;
Schools - t) 707-566-3393 Adrian Peterson;
Scouts - t) 707-566-3343 Stephen Morris; Rev. Jeffrey Keyes, Chap.;
Vocations - t) 707-495-6750 pastor@sjccotati.org Rev. Raul Lemus;
Youth and Young Adult Ministry - t) 707-566-3343 c) 310-849-2342 dsryouth@srdiocese.org Stephen Morris, Dir.;

PARISHES, MISSIONS, AND CLERGY

STATE OF CALIFORNIA

AMERICAN CANYON

Pastor of Holy Family Catholic Church of American Canyon, A Corporation Sole - 200 Antonina Ave., American Canyon, CA 94503 t) 707-645-9331 pastor@holyfamily-amcan.church www.holyfamily-amcan.church Rev. Frederick K.A. Kutubebi, Pst.; Dcn. Victor Leach; Marina Maldonado, DRE; CRP Stds.: 170

ARCATA

Pastor of St. Mary Catholic Church of Arcata, A Corporation Sole - 1690 Janes Rd., Arcata, CA 95521 t) 707-822-7696 office@stmarysarcata.org stmarysarcata.org Rev. Francis Gayam, Pst.; Rev. Fabian Nwokorie, Par. Vicar; Dcn. John Gai; Dcn. Jon Pedicino; CRP Stds.: 47
  St. Joseph - 340 Greenwood Ave., Blue Lake, CA 95525; Mailing: 1690 Janes Rd., c/o St. Mary's Parish, Arcata, CA 95521 t) (707) 822-7696 stmarysarcata.com
  Pastor of St. Kateri Tekakwitha Catholic Mission of Hoopa, A Corporation Sole - Kateri Ln., Hoopa, CA 95546; Mailing: c/o St. Mary's Parish, 1690 Janes Rd, Arcata, CA 95521 t) (707) 822-7696 www.stmarysarcata.org

CALISTOGA

Pastor of Our Lady of Perpetual Help Catholic Church of Calistoga, A Corporation Sole - 901 Washington St., Calistoga, CA 94515 t) 707-942-6894 olphincalistoga@gmail.com olphcalistoga.org Rev. Andres Querijero, Pst.; CRP Stds.: 79

CLEARLAKE

Pastor of Our Lady Queen of Peace Catholic Church of Clearlake, A Corporation Sole - 14435 Uhl Ave., Clearlake, CA 95422; Mailing: P.O. Box 460, Clearlake, CA 95422 t) 707-994-6618 qopccclearlake@gmail.com Rev. Marlon Atendido, SVD, Par. Admin.; Margarita Lopez, DRE; CRP Stds.: 41
  Queen of the Rosary - 3972 Country Club Dr., Lucerne, CA 95458; Mailing: PO Box 460, Clearlake, CA 95422

CLOVERDALE

Pastor of St. Peter Catholic Church of Cloverdale, A Corporation Sole - 491 S. Franklin St., Cloverdale, CA 95425 t) 707-894-2535 sp-olmc@outlook.com stpeterscloverdale.org Rev. David Galeana, Pst.; Dcn. Harry Martin; CRP Stds.: 115
  Our Lady of Mt. Carmel - 26300 Asti Rd., Cloverdale, CA 95425; Mailing: 491 S. Franklin St., Clverdale, CA 95425

COTATI

Pastor of St. Joseph Catholic Church of Cotati, A Corporation Sole - 150 St. Joseph Way, Cotati, CA 94931-4117 t) 707-795-4807; 707-795-4951 (CRP) secretary@sjccotati.org; pastor@sjccotati.org wwww.sjccotati.org Rev. Raul Lemus, Pst.; Rev. John Plass, Par. Vicar; Dcn. Juventino Vera; Norma Suarez, CRE; CRP Stds.: 133

CRESCENT CITY

Pastor of St. Joseph Catholic Church of Crescent City, A Corporation Sole - 319 E St., Crescent City, CA 95531 t) 707-465-1762 sjccc707@yahoo.com www.sjccc.net Rev. Gregory Villaescusa, Pst.; Dcn. Juan Gamez; Dcn. Aadam Trask; CRP Stds.: 51
  St. Robert and Ann - Mild Rd., Klamath, CA 95548; Mailing: 319 E St., Crescent City, CA 95531 t) (707) 465-1762

EUREKA

Pastor of St. Bernard Catholic Church of Eureka, A Corporation Sole - 615 H St., Eureka, CA 95501 t) 707-442-6466 office@saintbernards.org www.saintbernards.org Rev. Bernard D'Sa, Pst.; Rev. Sudhakar Mannam, MOP (India), Par. Vicar; Dcn. Dance Farrell; Dcn. Frank Weber; CRP Stds.: 14
  St. Joseph - 201 Henderson St., Eureka, CA 95501
Pastor of Sacred Heart Catholic Church of Eureka, A Corporation Sole - 2085 Myrtle Ave., Eureka, CA 95501 t) 707-443-8429 sacredheartoffice@suddenlinkmail.com Rev. Bernard D'Sa, Pst.; Dcn. Dance Farrell; CRP Stds.: 68

FERNDALE

Pastor of Assumption of Our Lady Catholic Church of Ferndale, A Corporation Sole - 546 Berding St., Ferndale, CA 95536; Mailing: P.O. Box 1097, Ferndale, CA 95536 t) 707-786-9551 assump@suddenlink.net Rev. Mario Laguros (Philippines), Par. Admin.; CRP Stds.: 80
  St. Patrick - 29131 Mattole Rd., Petrolia, CA 95536 t) (707) 726-0338

FORT BRAGG

Pastor of Our Lady of Good Counsel Catholic Church, A Corporation Sole - 255 S. Harold St., Fort Bragg, CA 95437 t) 707-964-0229 olgcinfb@gmail.com olgcinfb.org Rev. Andrew Pacheco, Pst.; CRP Stds.: 54
  San José Sánchez del Río School - (Grades K-8) Kathleen Kasperson, Dir.; Stds.: 25; Scholastics: 1; Lay Tchrs.: 1

FORTUNA

Pastor of St. Joseph Catholic Church of Fortuna, a Corporation Sole - 820 14th St., Fortuna, CA 95540; Mailing: PO Box 430, Fortuna, CA 95540

t) 707-725-1148 stjosephchurch@suddenlink.net stjoeparish.org Rev. Edilberto Ramon, Admin.; Dcn. Rafael Meraz; Dcn. Francisco Nunez; Dcn. Thomas Silva; CRP Stds.: 44

St. Patrick - 690 Pershing St., Loleta, CA 95551 Rev. Edildberto Ramon, Par. Admin.;

GARBERVILLE

Pastor of Our Lady of the Redwoods Catholic Church of Garberville, A Corporation Sole - 515 Maple Ln., Garberville, CA 95542; Mailing: P.O. Box 115, Garberville, CA 95542 t) 707-923-7864 ourladyoftheredwoods@gmail.com Rev. Mario Laguros (Philippines), Pst.;

GUERNEVILLE

Pastor of St. Elizabeth Catholic Church of Guerneville, A Corporation Sole - 14095 Woodland Dr., Guerneville, CA 95446-9553 t) 707-869-2107 churchelizabeth@comcast.net Rev. Luis M. Penaloza, Pst.;

Pastor of St. Catherine of Siena Catholic Mission of Monte Rio, A Corporation Sole - Chapel Dr., Monte Rio, CA 95462 t) (707) 869-2107

Pastor of St. Colman Catholic Mission of Cazadero, A Corporation Sole - Cazadero Hwy., Cazadero, CA 95421

HEALDSBURG

Pastor of St. John the Baptist Catholic Church of Healdsburg, A Corporation Sole - 208 Matheson St., Healdsburg, CA 95448 t) 707-433-5536; 707-433-5536 x128 (CRP) vicenta.vega@sjshbg.org; kellyann.azevedo@sjshbg.org www.stjohnshealdsburg.org Rev. Sean Rogers, Pst.; Rev. Raphael Karekatt, MSFS (India), Par. Vicar; Dcn. Malcolm Barrack; Vicenta V Vega, Spanish Ministry Director; CRP Stds.: 110

St. John the Baptist Catholic School - (Grades PreSchool-8) 217 Fitch St., Healdsburg, CA 95448 t) 707-433-2758 joe.filice@sjshbg.org sjshbg.org Joseph F. Filice, Prin.; Stds.: 284; Lay Tchrs.: 10

HOOPA

Pastor of St. Kateri Tekakwitha Catholic Mission of Hoopa, A Corporation Sole - Pine Creek Rd. & St. Kateri Ln., Hoopa, CA 95546; Mailing: 1690 Janes Rd., Arcata, CA 95521 t) 707-822-7696 office@stmarysarcata.org stmarysarcata.org Rev. Francis Gayam, Pst.; Rev. Fabian Nwokorie, Par. Vicar; Dcn. Ken Bond;

LAKEPORT

Pastor of St. Mary Immaculate Catholic Church of Lakeport, a Corporation Sole - 801 N. Main St., Lakeport, CA 95453-4303 t) 707-263-4401 dre@stmaryslakeport.com www.stmary'slakeport.com Rev. Eliseo Avendano, Pst.; Guadalupe M. Silva, DRE; CRP Stds.: 115

St. Peter - 4085 Main St., Kelseyville, CA 95451 secretary@stmaryslakeport.com

MCKINLEYVILLE

Pastor of Christ the King Catholic Church of McKinleyville, A Corporation Sole - 1951 McKinleyville Ave., McKinleyville, CA 95519; Mailing: P.O. Box 2367, McKinleyville, CA 95519 t) 707-839-2911 ctkparish@att.net Rev. Francis Gayam, Pst.; Rev. Fabian Nwokorie, Par. Vicar;

Holy Trinity - Hector St., Trinidad, CA 95570

MENDOCINO

Pastor of St. Anthony Catholic Church of Mendocino, a Corporation Sole - 10700 Lansing St., Mendocino, CA 95460; Mailing: P.O. Box 665, Mendocino, CA 95460-0665 t) 707-937-2406 (Office); 707-937-5808 (Pastor) saofc@stanthonysofmendocino.com stanthonysofmendocino.com/ Rev. Robert Torczynski, Par. Admin.;

Pastor of Blessed Sacrament Catholic Mission of Elk, A Corporation Sole - ; Mailing: P.O. Box 28, Elk, CA 95432-0028 t) 707-877-3275 dcong1061@gmail.com

MIDDLETOWN

Pastor of St. Joseph Catholic Church of Middletown, A Corporation Sole - ; Mailing: P.O. Box 1350, Middletown, CA 95461 t) (707) 987-3676 stjoseph11@att.net www.stjoseph-middletown.com Rev. Lawrence Mendoza, Par. Admin.; CRP Stds.: 35

Our Lady of the Lake - Hwy. 175, Loch Lomond, CA 95461 t) 707-987-3676

Our Lady of the Pines - Forest Lake Dr., Cobb, CA 95461 t) 707-987-3676

NAPA

Pastor of St. Apollinaris Catholic Church of Napa, A Corporation Sole - 3700 Lassen St., Napa, CA 94558 t) 707-257-2555; 707-255-7200 (CRP) www.stapollinarisparish.org Rev. Fergal McGuinness, Pst.; Rev. Thomas Kyallo (Kenya), Par. Vicar; Dcn. John Dermody; Dcn. Peter Mathews; Christine Walsh, DRE; CRP Stds.: 156

St. Apollinaris School - (Grades PreK-8) t) 707-224-6525 obrazil@stasnapa.com www.stapollinaris.com Olivia Brazil, Prin.; Stds.: 340; Lay Tchrs.: 13

Pastor of St. John the Baptist Catholic Church of Napa, A Corporation Sole - 960 Caymus St., Napa, CA 94559 t) 707-226-9379 x15 manager@saintjohnscatholic.org www.stjb1858.com Rev. Ismael Mora, Pst.; Rev. Raju Kolanti, MSFS, Par. Vicar; Dcn. Joe Oberting; Dcn. Jaime Tafolla; Dcn. Joel Tapia; Dcn. Sergio Velazquez; Alejandra Gloria, DRE; Javier Gloria, DRE; Wayne Beasley, RCIA Coord.; Maria Guadalupe Gallegos, Bus. Mgr.; CRP Stds.: 448

Pastor of St. Thomas Aquinas Catholic Church of Napa, A Corporation Sole - 2725 Elm St., Napa, CA 94558-6029 t) 707-255-2949 stthomas_napa@att.net www.stthomasaquinasnapa.com Rev. Abel Mena, Pst.; Rev. Gary Sumpter, In Res.; CRP Stds.: 87

OCCIDENTAL

Pastor of St. Philip Catholic Church of Occidental, a Corporation Sole - 3730 Bohemian Hwy., Occidental, CA 95465; Mailing: PO Box 339, Occidental, CA 95465 t) 707-874-3812 philip.teresa@yahoo.com stphilipstteresa.org Rev. Balaswamy Govindu, Pst.; CRP Stds.: 11

St. Teresa - 17120 Bodega Hwy., Bodega, CA 94922 t) (707) 874-3812

PETALUMA

Pastor of St. James Catholic Church of Petaluma, A Corporation Sole - 125 Sonoma Mt. Pkwy., Petaluma, CA 94954 t) 707-762-4256 office@stjamespetaluma.org www.stjamespetaluma.org Rev. Gerard Gormley, Pst.; Rev. Lawrence Mutiso (Kenya), Par. Vicar; Dcn. Patrick Barnes; Dcn. Randy Kokke; Dcn. Tom Nangle; CRP Stds.: 176

Pastor of St. Vincent de Paul Catholic Church of Petaluma, A Corporation Sole - 35 Liberty St., Petaluma, CA 94952 t) 707-762-4278 x12 wpdonah@gmail.com svdppetaluma.org Rev. Williams Donahue, Pst.; Rev. Thomas Joseph Stuart, Par. Vicar; Abraham Solar, DRE; Dcn. James Carr; Rev. Msgr. Daniel P. Whelton, In Res.; CRP Stds.: 181

St. Vincent de Paul School - (Grades K-8) 246 Howard St., Petaluma, CA 94952 t) 707-762-6426 info@svelem.org www.svelem.org Shannon Jordan, Prin.; Stds.: 202; Lay Tchrs.: 10

St. Vincent de Paul High School - (Grades 9-12) 849 Keokuk, Petaluma, CA 94952 t) 707-763-1032 pdaly@svhs-pet.org www.svhs-pet.org Patrick W. Daly, Prin.; Rev. William P. Donahue, Pres.; Stds.: 190; Lay Tchrs.: 28

POINT ARENA

Pastor of St. Aloysius Catholic Church of Point Arena, A Corporation Sole - 70 School St., Point Arena, CA 95468; Mailing: P.O. Box 66, Point Arena, CA 95468 t) (707) 882-1734 frobada07@srdiocese.org Rev. Taiye Anthony Obada, Admin.; Dcn. Sergio Orozco; CRP Stds.: 32

Mary, Star of the Sea - 39141 Church St., Gualala, CA 95445; Mailing: PO Box 66, Point Arena, CA 95468 t) 707-882-1734 staloysiusparish70@gmail.com

ROHNERT PARK

Pastor of St. Elizabeth Catholic Church of Rohnert Park, A Corporation Sole - 4595 Snyder Ln., Rohnert Park, CA 94928 t) 707-585-3708 stelizseton@sbcglobal.net www.stelizabethrp.com. Rev. Thomas K. Diaz, Pst.; CRP Stds.: 63

SANTA ROSA

Pastor of St. Eugene Cathedral of Santa Rosa, A Corporation Sole - 2323 Montgomery Dr., Santa Rosa, CA 95405 t) (707) 542-6985 bookkeeper@steugenes.com www.steugenes.com Rev. Frank Epperson, Pst.; Rev. Sundar Bala Putchakayala, MSFS, Par. Vicar; Rev. Gabriel Sanchez, Par. Vicar; Dcn. Michael Heinzelman; Dcn. Gary Moore; Dcn. Russ Bowden; Rev. Jeffrey Keyes, In Res.; Rev. Alan Acevedo; CRP Stds.: 126

Cathedral of St. Eugene School - (Grades PreK-8) 300 Farmers Ln., Santa Rosa, CA 95405 t) 707-545-7252 office@steugenesch.org www.steugenesch.org Stds.: 68; Sr. Tchrs.: 3; Lay Tchrs.: 6

Pastor of Holy Spirit Catholic Church of Santa Rosa, A Corporation Sole - 1244 St. Francis Rd., Santa Rosa, CA 95409 t) 707-539-4495 holy-spirit@sbcglobal.net www.holyspirit-sr.org Rev. Ron Serban, Pst.; CRP Stds.: 87

Pastor of Resurrection Catholic Church of Santa Rosa, A Corporation Sole - 303 Stony Point Rd., Santa Rosa, CA 95401 t) 707-544-7272 resurrection@sonic.net www.resurrectionfamilies.org Rev. Aaron Earl DePeyster, Par. Admin.; Rev. Jose Gonzalez, Par. Vicar; Dan Kransover, DRE; Gayle Ballinger, Youth Min.; CRP Stds.: 343

Pastor of St. Rose of Lima Catholic Church of Santa Rosa, A Corporation Sole - 398 10th St., Santa Rosa, CA 95401 t) 707-542-6448 strosechurchsr@gmail.com stroseonline.com Rev. Michaelraj Philominsamy, Pst.; Rev. Innasi Rapheal, H.G.N. (India), Par. Vicar; Very Rev. Samuel Moses Brown, In Res.; CRP Stds.: 648

St. Rose of Lima School - (Grades PreSchool-8) 4300 Old Redwood Hwy., Santa Rosa, CA 95403 t) 707-545-0379 stroseschool@sonic.net www.strosecatholicschool.org Kathleen Aymar, Prin.; Stds.: 325; Lay Tchrs.: 15

Pastor of Star of the Valley Catholic Church of Santa Rosa, A Corporation Sole - 495 White Oak Dr., Santa Rosa, CA 95409 t) 707-539-6262 sov@sonic.net www.staroftheyalley.org Rev. Msgr. James E. Pulskamp, Pst.;

SEBASTOPOL

Pastor of St. Sebastian Catholic Church of Sebastopol, A Corporation Sole - 7983 Covert Ln., Sebastopol, CA 95472 t) 707-823-2208 rosyv.stsebastian@outlook.com www.stseb.org Rev. Mario Valencia, Par. Admin.; Rev. Angelito Peries, In Res.; CRP Stds.: 175

SONOMA

Pastor of St. Francis Solano Catholic Church of Sonoma, A Corporation Sole - 469 Third St. W., Sonoma, CA 95476 t) 707-996-6759 sfrancis_solano@sbcglobal.net Rev. Alvin Villaruel, Pst.; Rev. Rowell Gumalay, MOP (phillipines), Par. Vicar; Dcn. Dave Gould; Sarah Wilson, DRE; CRP Stds.: 197

St. Francis Solano School - (Grades K-8) 342 W. Napa St., Sonoma, CA 95476 t) 707-996-4994 stf.schooloffice@saintfrancissolano.org Debbie Picard, Prin.; Stds.: 193; Lay Tchrs.: 16

Pastor of St. Leo the Great Catholic Church of Boyes Hot Springs, A Corporation Sole - 601 W. Agua Caliente Rd., Sonoma, CA 95476; Mailing: P.O. Box 666, Boyes Hot Springs, CA 95416 t) 707-996-8422 office@stleosonoma.org stleosonoma.org Rev. Jojo Puthussery, M.F. (India), Par. Admin.; Nancy Gibson, Youth Min.; Rosa Chavez, CRE; CRP Stds.: 64

ST. HELENA

Pastor of St. Helena Catholic Church of St. Helena, A Corporation Sole - 1340 Tainter St., St. Helena, CA 94574; Mailing: 1255 Oak Ave., St. Helena, CA 94574 t) 707-963-1228 info@sthelenacatholic.com www.sthelenacatholic.com/ Rev. Manuel Chavez, Pst.; CRP Stds.: 146

UKIAH

Pastor of St. Mary of the Angels Catholic Church of Ukiah, a Corporation Sole - 900 S. Oak St., Ukiah, CA 95482 t) 707-462-1431 stmaryschurchukiah.com Rev.

Rayapu Thirumalareddy (India), Par. Admin.; Dcn. Daniel Vilotti; CRP Stds.: 415

St. Mary of the Angels School - (Grades K-8) 991 S. Dora St., Ukiah, CA 95482 t) 707-462-3888 principalteam@smsukiah.org www.stmarysukiah.org Jim Caruso, Prin.; Andrea Keffeler, Prin.; Sam Kircher, Prin.; Stds.: 170; Lay Tchrs.: 8

St. Francis Mission - Center St., Hopland, CA 95482; Mailing: 900 Oak St, Ukiah, CA 95449 t) (707) 462-1431 stmukiahservice@gmail.com

Pastor of St. Elizabeth Seton Catholic Mission, A Corporation Sole - School Rd, Philo, CA 95466 t) (707) 462-1431

WILLITS

Pastor of St. Anthony of Padua Catholic Church of Willits, a Corporation Sole - 61 W. San Francisco Ave., Willits, CA 95490 t) 707-459-2252 saintanthonywillits@gmail.com www.stanthonywillits.org Rev. Arogyriah Bandanadam, MF, Par. Admin.; CRP Stds.: 55

Our Lady, Queen of Peace - Foothill Blvd., Covelo, CA 95426 stanthonywillits.org

WINDSOR

Pastor of Our Lady of Guadalupe Catholic Church of Windsor, A Corporation Sole - 8400 Old Redwood Hwy., Windsor, CA 95492 t) 707-837-8962; 707-837-7620 x202 (CRP) officeolg@gmail.com olgwindsor.org Rev. Carlos Ortega, Pst.; Dcn. Todd Graveson; CRP Stds.: 231

YOUNTVILLE

Pastor of St. Joan of Arc Catholic Church of Yountville, A Corporation Sole - 6404 Washington St., Yountville, CA 94599; Mailing: Box 2009, Yountville, CA 94599 t) 707-944-2461 stjoanofarc01@aol.com www.stjoanofarcparish.com Rev. Daniel Enrique Roa, Pst.; Dcn. Bruce Miroglio; Lilia Manzo, DRE; CRP Stds.: 80

Holy Family - t) (707) 944-2461 stjoanofarcparish.com Rev. Daniel Roa;

SCHOOLS: PRESCHOOL THRU HIGH SCHOOL

SCHOOLS

STATE OF CALIFORNIA

EUREKA

***St. Bernard's Catholic School (St. Bernard's Academy)** - (PRV) (Grades 6-12) 222 Dollison St., Eureka, CA 95501 t) 707-443-2735 info@saintbernards.us saintbernards.us Paul Shanahan, Pres.; Dcn. Dance Farrell, DRE; Stds.: 253; Bro. Tchrs.: 1; Lay Tchrs.: 22

NAPA

Kolbe-Trinity - (PRV) (Grades K-12) 2055 Redwood Rd., Napa, CA 94558 t) 707-258-9030 office@kolbetrinity.org; jbertolini@kolbetrinity.org www.kolbetrinity.org Civil incorporation: Trinity Education Center, Inc. John Bertolini, Headmaster; Rev. Gary Sumpter, Chap.; Stds.: 160; Lay Tchrs.: 8

HIGH SCHOOLS

STATE OF CALIFORNIA

NAPA

Justin-Siena High School - (PRV) (Grades 9-12) 4026 Maher St., Napa, CA 94558 t) 707-255-0950 jvanhofwegen@justin-siena.org justin-siena.org Matthew Powell, Pres.; Robert Bailey, Admin.; Robyn Canga, Admin.; Stds.: 615; Bro. Tchrs.: 1; Lay Tchrs.: 43

***Justin-Siena High School Corporation, Inc.** - 4026 Maher St., Napa, CA 94558 t) (707) 255-0950

***Justin-Siena High School Foundation, Inc.** - 4026 Maher St., Napa, CA 94558 t) (707) 255-0950

SANTA ROSA

Cardinal Newman High School - (DIO) (Grades 9-12) 4320 Old Redwood Hwy., Santa Rosa, CA 95403 t) 707-546-6470 info@cardinalnewman.org; norman@cardinalnewman.org cardinalnewman.org Dr. Linda Norman, Pres.; Nicholas Reynolds, Prin.; Rev. John Plass, Chap.; Stds.: 567; Pr. Tchrs.: 1; Sr. Tchrs.: 1; Lay Tchrs.: 43

INSTITUTIONS LOCATED IN DIOCESE

CAMPUS MINISTRY / NEWMAN CENTERS [CAM]

ARCATA

Cal Poly Humboldt Newman Center - 700 Union St., Arcata, CA 95521 t) 707-822-6057 newman@humboldt.edu www.hsunewmancenter.com Rev. Francis Gayam, Pst.; Rev. Fabian Nwokorie, Assoc. Pst.;

PENNGROVE

Newman Center at Sonoma State University - 1798 E. Cotati Ave., Penngrove, CA 94951 c) 707-394-5582 frkeyes@gmail.com www.newmanssu.club Rev. Jeffrey Keyes, Campus Min.;

CATHOLIC CHARITIES [CCH]

SANTA ROSA

Catholic Charities of the Diocese of Santa Rosa - 987 Airway Ct., Santa Rosa, CA 95403; Mailing: P.O. Box 4900, Santa Rosa, CA 95402 t) 707-528-8712; 866-542-5480 (Initial Housing Referrals) info@srcharities.org www.srcharities.org Sharon Vaughn, Chief Admin. Officer; Rebecca Kendall, Chief Devel. Officer; Jennielynn Holmes, CEO; Asstd. Annu.: 10,639; Staff: 240

Coordinated Entry - 987 Airway Ct., Santa Rosa, CA 95403; Mailing: PO Box 4900, Santa Rosa, CA 95402 t) (707) 528-8712 Kathleen Kimpel, Contact;

Family Support Center - 987 Airway Ct., Santa Rosa, CA 95403 t) (707) 528-8712 Kathleen Kimpel, Contact;

Homeless Services Center - 987 Airway Ct., Santa Rosa, CA 95403 t) (707) 528-8712 Kathleen Kimpel, Contact;

Housing Services - 987 Airway Ct., Santa Rosa, CA 95403; Mailing: PO Box 4900, Santa Rosa, CA 95401 t) (707) 528-8712 Kathleen Kimpel, Contact;

Immigration and Resettlement Services - 987 Airway Ct., Santa Rosa, CA 95403; Mailing: P O Box 4900, Santa Rosa, CA 95401 t) (707) 528-8712 Kathleen Kimpel, Contact;

Rainbow House - 987 Airway Ct., Santa Rosa, CA 95403; Mailing: P O Box 4900, Santa Rosa, CA 95401 t) (707) 528-8712 Kathleen Kimpel, Contact;

CEMETERIES [CEM]

PETALUMA

Calvary Catholic - 304 Magnolia Ave., Petaluma, CA 94953; Mailing: P.O. Box 2098, Santa Rosa, CA 95405 t) 707-546-6290 info@dsrcem.org Angela Scheihing, Contact;

SANTA ROSA

Calvary Catholic - 2930 Bennett Valley Rd., Santa Rosa, CA 95404; Mailing: P.O. Box 2098, Santa Rosa, CA 95405 t) 707-546-6290 info@dsrcem.org Angela Scheihing, Contact;

SONOMA

St. Francis Solano - 550 E. Napa St., Sonoma, CA 95476; Mailing: P.O. Box 2098, Santa Rosa, CA 95405 t) 707-546-6290 info@dsrcem.org Angela Scheihing, Contact;

ST. HELENA

Holy Cross - 2121 Spring St., St. Helena, CA 94574; Mailing: P.O. Box 2098, Santa Rosa, CA 95405 t) 707-963-1703 info@dsrcem.org Angela Scheihing, Contact;

CONVENTS, MONASTERIES, AND RESIDENCES FOR WOMEN [CON]

SANTA ROSA

The Marian Sisters of Santa Rosa, MSSR - Mater Dei Convent, 400 Angela Dr, Santa Rosa, CA 95403 t) 707-326-7593 mariansistersjmj@gmail.com www.mariansisters.com Mother Teresa Christe Johnson, M.S.S.R., Supr.; Srs.: 22

Provincialate of Ursuline Nuns - 274 Mockingbird Cir., Santa Rosa, CA 95409 t) 650-755-9897 c) (707) 481-2742; (707) 327-7394 stister2@aol.com; jabramsosu@comcast.net Ursulines of the Roman Union - Western Province. Sr. Shirley Ann Garibaldi, O.S.U., Prov.; Srs.: 13

Ursuline Residence - 274 Mockingbird Cir., Santa Rosa, CA 95409; Mailing: 274 Mockingbird Circle, Santa Rosa, CA 95409 c) (707) 327-7394 jabramsosu@comcast.net Ursuline Western Province Sr. Joanne C Abrams, OSU, Treas.; Srs.: 1

WHITETHORN

Our Lady of the Redwoods Abbey - 18104 Briceland-Thorn Rd., Whitethorn, CA 95589 t) 707-986-7419 kdevico@redwoodsabbey.org www.redwoodsabbey.org Cistercian Nuns of the Strict Observance. Sr. Kathleen De Vico, O.C.S.O., Abbess; Srs.: 10

ENDOWMENTS / FOUNDATIONS / TRUSTS [EFT]

NAPA

Lasallian Christian Brothers Foundation, Inc. - 4401 Redwood Rd., Napa, CA 94558; Mailing: PO Box 3720, Napa, CA 94558 t) 707-252-3800 bromarkfsc@dlis.org Bro. Nick Gonzalez, F.S.C., Chair; Bro. Mark Murphy, F.S.C., CEO;

***Life Legal Defense Foundation** - 1625 Trancas St #4320, Napa, CA 94558; Mailing: P.O. Box 2105, Napa, CA 94558 t) 707-224-6675 info@lldf.org; mary@lldf.org lifelegaldefensefoundation.org/ Mary Riley, COO;

SANTA ROSA

***Angela Merici and John Henry Newman Foundation, Inc.** - 4320 Old Redwood Hwy., Santa Rosa, CA 95403 t) 707-546-6470 norman@cardinalnewman.org For the benefit of Cardinal Newman High School, Santa Rosa, California. Rev. John Plass, Chap.; Dr. Linda Norman, Pres.;

***Catholic Community Foundation** - 985 Airway Ct., Santa Rosa, CA 95403; Mailing: P.O. Box 1297, Santa Rosa, CA 95402 t) 707-566-3344 srcaritasmarie@srdiocese.org Sr. Caritas Marie, M.S.S.R., Dir.;

WINDSOR

Ursuline Sisters Supplemental Care Fund Trust - 9248 Lakewood Dr., Windsor, CA 95492 t) 707-484-7841; 415-586-0680 cvs535@gmail.com; patbyrneduggan@aol.com

HOSPITALS / HEALTH SERVICES [HOS]

EUREKA

St. Joseph Hospital of Eureka - 2700 Dolbeer St., Eureka, CA 95501 t) 949-381-4000 james.watson@stjoe.org www.stjosepheureka.org Bed Capacity: 153; Asstd. Annu.: 180,165; Staff: 1,212

FORTUNA

Redwood Memorial Hospital (St. Joseph Health, Humboldt) - 3300 Renner Dr., Fortuna, CA 95540 t) 949-381-4000 james.watson@stjoe.org www.redwoodmemorial.org Darian Harris, CEO; Bed Capacity: 34; Asstd. Annu.: 50,989; Staff: 211

NAPA

Providence Queen of the Family Medical Center (Providence Queen of the Valley Medical Center) - 1000 Trancas St., Napa, CA 94558 t) 707-252-4411 rachelle.yeates@providence.org www.thequeen.org Terry Anthony Wooten, CEO; Rev. Valentine Ibeh, Chap.; Rev. Frederick K.A. Kutubebi, Chap.; Bed Capacity: 208; Asstd. Annu.: 203,129; Staff: 1,121

PETALUMA

SRM Alliance Hospital Services - 400 N. McDowell Blvd., Petaluma, CA 94954 t) 707-778-1111 james.watson@stjoe.org www.stjoesonoma.org Laureen T Driscoll, Pres.; Bed Capacity: 80; Asstd. Annu.: 52,488; Staff: 348

SANTA ROSA

Providence Santa Rosa Memorial Hospital - 1165 Montgomery Dr., Santa Rosa, CA 95405 t) 949-381-4000 james.watson@stjoe.org www.stjoesonoma.org Rev. Peter Nwanekezie, Chap.; Bed Capacity: 329; Asstd. Annu.: 208,863; Staff: 1,970

MISCELLANEOUS [MIS]

PINOLE

***Maris Stella Institute** - 2644 Appian Way, Unit #206, Pinole, CA 94564; Mailing: P.O. Box 10061, American Canyon, CA 94503 t) 707-704-9025 toveann@marisstellainstitute.org www.marisstellainstitute.org Dr. Tove Ann Catubig Purificacion, Pres.;

SANTA ROSA

Catholic Youth Organization - 985 Airway Ct., Santa Rosa, CA 95403; Mailing: P.O. Box 1297, Santa Rosa, CA 95402-1297 t) 707-566-3300 fjimenez@srdiocese.org www.northbaycyo.org/ Chris Padowan, Pres.;

Pastor of Vietnamese Martyrs Catholic Church of Santa Rosa, A Corporation Sole - 2652 Stony Point Rd., Santa Rosa, CA 95407 t) 707-293-7992 vietcatholicsantarosa@gmail.com Rev. Chinh Nguyen, Admin.;

MONASTERIES AND RESIDENCES FOR PRIESTS AND BROTHERS [MON]

NAPA

De La Salle Institute/Provincial Office - 4401 Redwood Rd., Napa, CA 94558-9708; Mailing: P.O. Box 3720, Napa, CA 94558 t) 707-252-0222 ngonzalez@dlsi.org www.delasalle.org Brothers of the Christian Schools. Bro. Nick Gonzalez, F.S.C., Prov.; Bro. Christopher Brady, F.S.C., Prov. Asst.;

District of San Francisco Christian Brothers Charitable Trust - 4401 Redwood Rd., Napa, CA 94558-9708; Mailing: P.O. Box 3720, Napa, CA 94558 t) (707) 252-0222

Lasallian Education Corporation - 4401 Redwood Rd., Napa, CA 94558-9708; Mailing: P.O. Box 3720, Napa, CA 94558 t) (707) 252-3744

Holy Family Community - 4405 Redwood Rd., Napa, CA 94558-9708 t) 707-252-3713; 707-252-3787 lhaley@dlsi.org www.delasalle.org Brothers of the Christian Schools. Bro. Lawrence Haley, Dir.; Brs.: 18

Provincialate Community - 4403 Redwood Rd., Napa, CA 94558 t) 707-252-0802; 707-252-0222 scampbell@dlsi.org Brothers of the Christian Schools. Bro. Nick Gonzalez, F.S.C., Prov.; Bro. Stanislaus Campbell, F.S.C., Dir.; Brs.: 9

OAKVILLE

Carmelite House of Prayer - 20 Mount Carmel Dr., Oakville, CA 94562; Mailing: PO Box 347, Oakville, CA 94562 t) 707-944-2454 ocdoakville@gmail.com oakvillecarmites.com Discalced Carmelite Fathers Oakville Inc. Rev. Mark Kissner, OCD, Prior; Rev. Matthew Williams, OCD, Subprior; Rev. Donald Kinney, OCD, Sacr. Min.; Rev. Christopher La Rocca, OCD, Sacr. Min.; Rev. Joseph Mary Tran, OCD, Sacr. Min.; Priests: 5

PRESCHOOLS / CHILDCARE CENTERS [PRE]

SONOMA

Hanna Boys Center - 17000 Arnold Dr., Sonoma, CA 95476 t) 707-996-6767 www.hannacenter.org Serving at-risk boys, ages 13 to 18 years, who have a history of adversity and trauma. Cameron Safarloo, CEO; Stds.: 21; Lay Tchrs.: 11

RETREAT HOUSES / RENEWAL CENTERS [RTR]

DUNCAN MILLS

St. Joseph Camp - 22776 Moscow Rd., Duncan Mills, CA 95430-0198; Mailing: P.O. Box 198, Duncan Mills, CA 95430 t) 707-865-0169 (Lodge); 707-865-2135 (Caretaker) jstice@dlsi.org Brothers of the Christian Schools. Bro. Richard Lemberg, F.C.S., Dir.;

NAPA

Christian Brothers Retreat and Conference Center - 4401 Redwood Rd., Napa, CA 94558; Mailing: P.O. Box 3720, Napa, CA 94558 t) 707-252-3810; 707-252-3703; 707-252-3899 confctr@dlsi.org www.christianbrosretreat.com Bro. Nick Gonzalez, F.S.C., Prov.;

OAKVILLE

Carmelite House of Prayer - 20 Mount Carmel Dr., Oakville, CA 94562; Mailing: P.O. Box 347, Oakville, CA 94562 t) 707-944-2454 ocdoakville@gmail.com Rev. Mark Kissner, OCD, Prior; Rev. Matthew Williams, OCD, Subprior; Rev. Donald Kinney, OCD, Sacr. Min.; Rev. Christopher La Rocca, OCD, Sacr. Min.; Rev. Joseph Mary Tran, OCD, Sacr. Min.;

An asterisk (*) denotes an organization that has established tax-exempt status directly with the IRS and is not covered by the USCCB Group Ruling.

Diocese of Savannah

(Dioecesis Savannensis)

MOST REVEREND STEPHEN D. PARKES

Bishop of Savannah; ordained May 23, 1998; appointed Bishop of Savannah July 8, 2020; installed September 23, 2020. Catholic Pastoral Center, 2170 E. Victory Dr., Savannah, GA 31404-3918.

Catholic Pastoral Center, 2170 E. Victory Dr., Savannah, GA 31404-3918. T: 912-201-4100; F: 912-201-4101.
www.diosav.org
communications@diosav.org

Square Miles 37,038.

Established as Diocese of Savannah July 19, 1850. Name changed to Diocese of Savannah-Atlanta Jan. 5, 1937; Redesignated Nov. 8, 1956.

Comprises 90 Counties in the southern part of the State of Georgia.

Patrons of the Diocese: I. St. John the Baptist; II. Our Lady of Perpetual Help. This diocese was solemnly consecrated to the Sacred Heart of Jesus, May 7, 1872, and on Dec. 8, 1943, it was solemnly consecrated to the Immaculate Heart of Mary.

For legal titles of parishes and diocesan institutions, consult the Chancery.

STATISTICAL OVERVIEW

Personnel

Bishop 1
Retired Bishops 1
Priests: Diocesan Active in Diocese 50
Priests: Diocesan Active Outside Diocese 3
Priests: Retired, Sick or Absent 33
Number of Diocesan Priests 86
Religious Priests in Diocese 23
Total Priests in your Diocese 109
Extern Priests in Diocese 19
Ordinations:
Diocesan Priests 2
Transitional Deacons 1
Permanent Deacons 11
Permanent Deacons in Diocese 103
Total Brothers 3
Total Sisters 63

Parishes

Parishes 57
With Resident Pastor:
Resident Diocesan Priests 42
Resident Religious Priests 12
Without Resident Pastor:
Administered by Priests 2
Administered by Deacons 1
Missions 20
Professional Ministry Personnel:
Brothers 3
Sisters 33
Lay Ministers 42

Welfare

Catholic Hospitals 1
Total Assisted 200,000
Special Centers for Social Services 11
Total Assisted 202,009

Educational

Diocesan Students in Other Seminaries 12
Total Seminarians 12
High Schools, Diocesan and Parish 3
Total Students 570
High Schools, Private 3
Total Students 1,039
Elementary Schools, Diocesan and Parish 11
Total Students 3,218
Elementary Schools, Private 1
Total Students 129
Non-residential Schools for the Disabled 1
Total Students 86
Catechesis/Religious Education:
High School Students 973
Elementary Students 4,439
Total Students under Catholic Instruction 10,466
Teachers in Diocese:
Priests 6
Brothers 1
Sisters 5
Lay Teachers 470

Vital Statistics

Receptions into the Church:
Infant Baptism Totals 1,184
Minor Baptism Totals 201
Adult Baptism Totals 125
Received into Full Communion 211
First Communions 1,316
Confirmations 1,213
Marriages:
Catholic 285
Interfaith 102
Total Marriages 387
Deaths 658
Total Catholic Population 80,000
Total Population 3,000,000

LEADERSHIP

Chancellor - t) 912-201-4113 Very Rev. Pablo Migone;
Vicar General - t) 912-201-4126 Very Rev. Daniel F. Firmin;
Chancery - t) 912-201-4100 Very Rev. Daniel F. Firmin, Vicar General;
Safe Environment/Immigration - t) 912-201-4074 Joan B. Altmeyer;
Director of Finance - t) 912-201-4061 Liam J. O'Connor;
Diocesan Tribunal - t) 912-201-4132; 912-201-4133 Very Rev. J. Gerard Schreck;
Judicial Vicar - Very Rev. J. Gerard Schreck;
Tribunal Judges - Very Rev. J. Gerard Schreck; Very Rev. Daniel F. Firmin;
Defender of the Bond - Rev. Andrew Larkin;
Case Assessors & Notaries - Bernadine Rego; Patti Seanor;
Notary - Stephanie Braddy; Eloisa Newman;
Promoter of Justice - Rev. Thomas Healy;
Censor Librorum - Rev. Douglas K. Clark (dclark@diosav.org);
Archivist & Records Manager - t) 912-201-4078 Stephanie M Braddy (sbraddy@diosav.org);
Legal Counsel - t) 912-201-4100 Robert Pace;
Finance Council - Robert W. Schivera, Chair; Very Rev. Daniel F. Firmin; Rev. Stephen Pontzer;
Investment Committee - Paul P. Hinchey, Chair; Jack Markley; Bill Barrett;
Clergy Personnel - Very Rev. Scott Winchel, Chair; Very Rev. Daniel F. Firmin; Very Rev. Pablo Migone;
Human Resources/Director of Operations - t) 912-201-4071 Jo Ann Green, Dir. (jagreen@diosav.org);
Deans -
Albany Deanery - t) 229-439-2302 Very Rev. Raymond G. Levreault;
Augusta Deanery - t) 706-798-1920 Very Rev. Mark N. Van Alstine, Dean;
Columbus Deanery - t) 706-689-5720 Very Rev. Scott Winchel;
Macon Deanery - t) 478-745-1631 Very Rev. John R. Johnson;
Savannah Deanery - t) 912-233-4709 Very Rev. J. Gerard Schreck;
Statesboro Deanery - t) 912-681-6726 Rev. Fredy A. Angel;
Valdosta-Brunswick Deanery - t) 912-265-3249 Very Rev. Timothy P. McKeown;
College of Consultors - Very Rev. Daniel F. Firmin; Very Rev. Pablo Migone; Very Rev. Timothy P. McKeown;
Presbyteral Council - Very Rev. Raymond G. Levreault, Chair; Very Rev. John R. Johnson, Chair (jjohnson@diosav.org); Rev. Christopher Hassel, Secy.;

OFFICES AND DIRECTORS

Campaign for Human Development - t) 912-201-4058 Cynthia Kinnis;
Catholic Relief Services - t) 912-201-4058 Cynthia Kinnis;
Council of Catholic Women - t) 478-442-1850 Kathy Smith;
Delegate for Consecrated Life - t) 443-827-5631 Sr. Nancy Walsh;
Department of Communications - t) 912-201-4051 communications@diosav.org Jillian Parks;
Diocesan Catholic Scouting - t) 912-201-4057 Caroline Ebberwein;
Diocesan Director of Young Adult and Campus Ministry - t) 912-201-4122
Albany State University - t) 229-669-4202 www.newmanconnection.com Terrie Alby, Campus Min.;
Andrew College - Bro. Jason Muhlenkamp, G.H.M., Campus Min.;
Augusta State University - t) 706-863-4956 Rev. Christopher Hassel;
Chaplain, Young Adult and Campus Ministry - College of Coastal Georgia - t) 912-265-3249 Marusol Soler; Laurie Jones;
Columbus State University - t) 706-561-8678 Friar Emanuel Vasconcelos, O.F.M.Conv., Chap.;
Georgia Southern University - t) 912-681-6726 Corey Kieffer, Dir.; Very Rev. John R. Johnson, Chap.;
Georgia Southern University at Armstrong Campus - t) 912-201-4056 Krystyna Swierczwski, Campus Min.; Rev. Patrick May, Chap.;
Mercer University - t) 478-743-1454 Friar Casey Cole;
Savannah College of Art and Design - t) 912-201-4056 Krystyna Swierczwski, Campus Min.; Rev. Andrew Larkin;
Savannah State University - t) 912-201-4056 Krystyna Swierczwski, Campus Min.; Dcn. Hosea Bennett, Chap.;
Valdosta State University - t) 229-561-4456 Lynette Kenworthy;
Diocesan Scout Chairman - Chad Sweeney;
Diocesan Scout Chaplain - t) 229-244-2430 Rev. Jason P. Adams;
Diocesan Worship Commission - t) 912-681-6726 Rev. Douglas K. Clark, Pst. (dclark@diosav.org);
Director of Black Catholic Ministry - t) 912-201-4041 Rev. Robert E. Chaney (af-am-ministry@diosav.org);
Director of Catholic Charities of Savannah - t) 912-201-4058 Cynthia Kinnis;
Director of Catholic Education/Superintendent of Schools - t) 912-201-4120 Very Rev. Kevin O'Keefe, Vicar for Evangelization & Educ. (kokeefe@diosav.org); Carrie Jane Williamson, Supt. (cjwilliamson@diosav.org);
Director of Construction & Properties - t) 912-201-4066 pnott@diosav.org John Grim;
Director of Evangelization - t) 912-201-4122 Very Rev. Kevin O'Keefe (kokeefe@diosav.org);
Director of Family Life - t) 912-201-4068 familylife@diosav.org Jayne Stefanic;
Director of Hispanic Ministry - t) 912-201-4067 Lidia Niederkorn;
Director of Permanent Diaconate - t) 706-855-9893 Dcn. Kelley G. Culver;
Director of Stewardship and Development - t) 912-201-4050 Maureen Coates;
Director of the Catholic Foundation of South Georgia - t) 912-201-4061 Liam J. O'Connor;
Director of Vocations - t) 912-201-4113 Very Rev. Pablo Migone;
Director of Youth & Young Adult Ministry - t) 912-201-4057 Caroline Ebberwein;
Ecumenism and Interreligious Affairs - t) 912-897-5156 Rev. Michael J. Kavanaugh, Dir. (mkavanaug@diosav.org);
Georgia Catholic Conference - t) 440-920-7367 Francis J. Mulcahy, Exec.;
Mission Cooperative Appeal - t) 912-201-4110 Very Rev. Daniel F. Firmin;
Newspaper - t) 912-201-4054 Jillian Parks;
Propagation of the Faith - t) 912-201-4122 Very Rev. Kevin O'Keefe (kokeefe@diosav.org);
Victim Assistance Coordinator - t) 912-201-4071 Brett Murphy-Dawson;

PARISHES, MISSIONS, AND CLERGY

STATE OF GEORGIA

ALBANY

St. Teresa - 421 Edgewood Ln., Albany, GA 31707 t) 229-439-2302; 229-439-2302 x1006 (CRP) stteresasfront@bellsouth.net; stteresasreled@bellsouth.net stteresaschurch.org/ Very Rev. Raymond G. Levreault, Pst.; Dcn. John Johnson; Dcn. Daniel Gillan; Dcn. John C. Dallas; Lori Leach, DRE; Dcn. Michael Leach, DRE; CRP Stds.: 85

St. Teresa School - (Grades PreK-12) 417 Edgewood Ln., Albany, GA 31707-3991 t) 229-436-0134 frontoffice@stteresas.org stteresas.org Susie Hatcher, Prin.; Linda Johnson, Asst. Prin.; Terry McKay, High School Dir.; Stds.: 111; Lay Tchrs.: 14

AMERICUS

St. Mary - 332 S. Lee St., Americus, GA 31709-3916 t) 229-924-3495 stmaryamericus@gmail.com www.stmaryamericus.com/ Rev. Samuel Aniekwe, Admin.; Ron Akerman, DRE; Bernie Bosse, RCIA Coord.; CRP Stds.: 70

AUGUSTA

Church of the Most Holy Trinity - 720 Telfair St, Augusta, GA 30901; Mailing: PO Box 2446, Augusta, GA 30903 t) 706-722-4944 helen@themostholytrinity.org Rev. Jacob N. Almeter, Pst.; Dcn. Elmore J. Butler; Dcn. Keith Liner; Dcn. JJ McKinney; Dcn. Kent Plowman; Dcn. Truong Van; CRP Stds.: 57

Immaculate Conception Catholic School - (Grades PreK-12) 811 Telfair St., Augusta, GA 30901 t) 706-722-9964 principal@icaugusta.org www.icaugusta.org Allison Palfy, Prin.; Stds.: 86; Lay Tchrs.: 12

St. Joseph - 2607 Lumpkin Rd., Augusta, GA 30906-3222 t) 706-798-1920 stjoesaug@aol.com stjoesch.org Very Rev. Mark N. Van Alstine, Pst.; Rev. Christopher Awiliba, Par. Vicar; Rev. InShik Kim (Korea), Korean Community; Dcn. Gregory L. Bernard; Dcn. James Lloyd; Dcn. Tom Valois; Annette Eyrich, DRE; CRP Stds.: 186

St. Mary on the Hill - 1420 Monte Sano Ave., Augusta, GA 30904-5394 t) 706-733-6627 smoth@stmaryonthehill.org www.stmaryonthehill.org Rev. Mark J. Ross, Pst.; Rev. Vernon Knight, Assoc. Pst.; Rev. A. Solomon Kaanan, Par. Vicar; Dcn. Jason Lanham; Dcn. John Leonard; Dcn. Kenneth R. Maleck; Dcn. Don McArdle; Dcn. Jesse Murga; Dcn. Albert J. Sullivan Jr.; CRP Stds.: 323

St. Mary on the Hill School - (Grades K-8) 1220 Monte Sano Ave., Augusta, GA 30904-5394 t) 706-733-6193 smcs@knology.net www.stmaryssaints.org William Todd Shafer, Prin.; Stds.: 497; Lay Tchrs.: 38

Adoration Chapel - 1210 Monte Sano Ave., Augusta, GA 30904-5394 smoth@knology.net

BAINBRIDGE

St. Joseph's - 1207 Randolph St., Bainbridge, GA 39819-0192 t) 229-243-9146 sjcatholichurch@gmail.com stjoebainbridge.diosav.net Rev. Tomas Beroch, Admin.; Rev. Victor M. Canela, S.T., Pst.; CRP Stds.: 80

Church of the Incarnation - 5541 GA-91, Donalsonville, GA 39845; Mailing: 1207 Randolph St., Bainbridge, GA 39819 t) (229) 726-3752 stjoebainbridgediosav.net

BLAKELY

Holy Family - 519 Arlington Ave., Blakely, GA 39823-0425; Mailing: Box 425, Blakely, GA 39823-0425 t) 229-723-3339 hfblakely@outlook.com holyfamilyblakely.diosav.net/ Rev. Michael Kerin, Pst.; Dcn. Scott Watford, Pst. Assoc.; CRP Stds.: 27

St. Luke - 304 Court St., Cuthbert, GA 39840; Mailing: P.O. Box 491, Cuthbert, GA 39840 t) 229-732-5823

BRUNSWICK

St. Francis Xavier - 405 Howe St., Brunswick, GA 31520-7526 t) 912-264-6805 (CRP); 912-265-3249 annbuebel@xavierbrunswick.org Very Rev. Timothy P. McKeown, Pst.; Rev. Esteban Mallar, Vicar; Dcn. Lawrence Guyer; Dcn. Terrence Mermann; Dcn. Chris Sadowski; CRP Stds.: 136

St. Francis Xavier School - (Grades PreK-8) 1121 Union St., Brunswick, GA 31520 t) 912-265-9470 tmermann@sfxcs.org www.sfxcs.org Stds.: 194; Lay Tchrs.: 21

Nativity of Our Lady - 1000 N. Way St., Darien, GA 31305 t) 912-437-4750

Christian Formation Center - 1116 Richmond St.,

Brunswick, GA 31520

CLAXTON

St. Christopher - 400 S. River St., Claxton, GA 30417-2150 t) 912-739-3913 saintchristopher@bellsouth.net www.stchristopherclaxton.com Rev. Vicente Terrazas, Pst.; Rev. Thomas J. Murphy, Par. Admin.; Dcn. James Spacher; CRP Stds.: 58

Holy Cross - 90 W. Bacon St., Pembroke, GA 31321; Mailing: 400 S. River St., Claxton, GA 30417 t) (912) 739-3913 stchristophersecretary@gmail.com

Our Lady of Guadalupe - 3879 S. Berry Rd., Sand Hill, GA 30427; Mailing: 400 S. River St., Claxton, GA 30417 t) (912) 739-3913 stchristophersecretary@gmail.com

St. Jude - 911 N. Veterans Blvd., Glennville, GA 30427 t) (912) 654-1908 stchristophersecretary@gmail.com

COLUMBUS

St. Anne - 2000 Kay Cir., Columbus, GA 31907-3229 t) 706-561-8678 office@stanneweb.com stannecsg.com Very Rev. Scott Winchel, Pst.; Rev. William Cook, Par. Vicar; Dcn. Edgar L. Ensley Jr.; Dcn. Robert Herrmann; Dcn. John R. Quillen; Dolly Vail, DRE; CRP Stds.: 210

St. Anne-Pacelli Catholic School - (Grades PreSchool-12) 2020 Kay Cir., Columbus, GA 31907 t) 706-561-8232 inforequest@sasphs.net beaviking.com Carolyn Brewster, Prin.; Jocelyn Smith, Prin.; Ronie Collins, Pres.; Stds.: 797; Lay Tchrs.: 81

St. Anne Community Outreach - ; Mailing: 1820 Box Rd., Columbus, GA 31907 t) 706-568-1592 hello@stanneoutreach.com; kbyers@stanneoutreach.com www.stannecsg.com/outreach.html Lauren Marquez, Coordinator; Katherine (Katie) Byers, Dir.; Karen Wilson, Admin.; Kathy Gramling, Coordinator;

St. Benedict the Moor Catholic Church - 2930 Thomas St., Columbus, GA 31906-0714; Mailing: 2935 9th St., Columbus, GA 31906-0714 t) 706-323-8300 stbenedict07@knology.net stbenedictthemoorcolumbus.org Rev. Patrick A. Otor, M.S.P.; Gail Buffong, DRE; CRP Stds.: 1

Holy Family - 320 12th St., Columbus, GA 31901 t) 706-323-6908 holyfamily706@bellsouth.net holyfamilycolumbus.com Rev. Benjamin Dallas, Pst.; CRP Stds.: 75

Our Lady of Lourdes - 1953 Torch Hill Rd., Columbus, GA 31903 t) 706-689-5720 secretary@ourladyoflourdesga.org; frbob@ourladyoflourdesga.org www.ourladyoflourdesga.org Rev. Odel Medina, Pst.; Rev. Stephen Giorno, Par. Vicar; CRP Stds.: 125

CORDELE

St. Theresa - 807 Third St. S., Cordele, GA 31015-1705 t) 229-273-3446 churchofthelittleflower@gmail.com Rev. Paulinus Chikelue Okpala, Admin.; CRP Stds.: 17

DOUGLAS

St. Paul's - 4178 U.S. Hwy. 441 S., Douglas, GA 31533-5732 t) 912-384-3560 saintpaul@windstream.net stpaulmissions.org Rev. Paul A. O'Connell, Pst.; Dcn. Ron Milkas; CRP Stds.: 200

St. William - 807 S. Merrimac, Fitzgerald, GA 31750-0801; Mailing: 4178 US Hwy. 441 S, Douglas, GA 31533-5732 t) 229-423-5076 Dcn. William Drexler;

Holy Family - 126 Holy Family Church Rd., Willacoochee, GA 31650; Mailing: 4178 U.S. Hwy. 441 S., Douglas, GA 31535 t) (912) 384-3560

DUBLIN

Immaculate Conception - 1559 U.S. Hwy. 441 N., Dublin, GA 31021 t) 478-272-0266 iccdublin@immaculate-conception-church.net www.immaculate-conception-church.net Rev. Jude Shayo, A.J., Pst.; Rev. John Stephen Ariko, A.J., Par. Vicar; CRP Stds.: 45

St. William - 301 S. Smith St., Sandersville, GA 31082 t) (478) 272-0266

EASTMAN

St. Mark - 1687 Hawkinsville Hwy., Eastman, GA 31023-4241; Mailing: 1559 Hwy 441 N, Dublin, GA 31021 t) 478-272-0266 iccdublin@immaculate-conception-church.net Rev. Jude Shayo, A.J., Pst.; Rev. John Stephen Ariko, A.J., Par. Vicar; CRP Stds.: 6

FORT VALLEY

St. Juliana's Catholic Church - 804 Martin Luther King Jr. Dr., Fort Valley, GA 31030; Mailing: P.O. Box 1022, Fort Valley, GA 31030 t) 478-825-7127 stjulianachurch@outlook.com www.stjulianacc.org Rev. Carlos Eduardo Pinzon, Pst.; Dcn. Kenneth P. Hutnick; CRP Stds.: 70

GROVETOWN

St. Teresa of Avila - 4921 Columbia Rd., Grovetown, GA 30813-5237 t) 706-863-4956; 706-863-0252 (CRP) info@st-teresa.com; ffoffice@st-teresa.com www.st-teresa.com Rev. Walter Y. (Mike) Ingram, Pst.; Rev. Theodore T Agba, Par. Vicar; Rev. Christopher Hassel, Par. Vicar; Rev. Michael E. Roverse, Par. Vicar; Dcn. Ray Adriano; Dcn. Daniel Craig; Dcn. Kerry C. Diver; Dcn. Robert J. Kepshire; Dcn. Joseph S. Soparas; Miriam Martin, DRE; CRP Stds.: 715

HAZLEHURST

Good Shepherd - 259 Baxley Hwy., Hazlehurst, GA 31513; Mailing: P.O. Box 330, Baxley, GA 31515-0330 t) 912-366-0238 goodshepherdsaintrose.com Rev. Rafael A. Estrada, Pst.; CRP Stds.: 100

St. Rose of Lima - 1520 City Circle Rd., Baxley, GA 31513 t) (912) 705-8927

St. Frances of Rome Mission - 1497 12th St. W., Alma, GA 31510 t) (912) 705-8927

HINESVILLE

St. Stephen, First Martyr - 399 Woodland Dr., Hinesville, GA 31313-2719 t) 912-876-4364 ssfmcc399@gmail.com ststephenshinesville.com/ Rev. Adam J. Kasela, Pst.; Dcn. Douglas Delzeith;

JESUP

St. Joseph - 1048 E. Cherry St., Jesup, GA 31546 t) 912-427-9239 stjoejesup@bellsouth.net stjosephsjesup.org Rev. Keith O'Neill, O.F.M.Conv., Admin.; Laura Bradt, DRE; CRP Stds.: 20

KATHLEEN

St. Patrick - 2410 GA Hwy. 127, Kathleen, GA 31047-2820 t) 478-987-4213 saintpat@stpatrickga.org stpatrickga.org/ Rev. Eric R. Filmer, Pst.; Dcn. William Johansen; Dcn. James Roberge, Pst. Assoc.; Dcn. Ralph H. McAtee; CRP Stds.: 120

MACON

Holy Spirit - 4074 Chambers Rd., Macon, GA 31206-4702 t) 478-788-6386; 478-788-9820 hsgirlfriday@gmail.com; friarpriest@gmail.com www.holyspiritmacon.org Rev. Patrick Edwin Tuttle, OFM, Pst.; Friar Casey Cole, In Res.; CRP Stds.: 35

St. Joseph - 830 Poplar St., Macon, GA 31201-2093 t) 478-745-1631 church@st-joseph.cc stjosephmacon.wordpress.com Very Rev. John R. Johnson, Pst.; Rev. Emmanuel Antwi, Par. Vicar; Dcn. Donald R. Coates; Mollie Germann, DRE; CRP Stds.: 114

St. Joseph School - (Grades PreSchool-6) 905 High St., Macon, GA 31201 t) 478-742-0636 amandarogers@sjsmacon.org www.sjsmacon.org Amanda Rogers, Prin.; Stds.: 193; Lay Tchrs.: 24

St. Peter Claver - 131 Ward St., Macon, GA 31204-3193 t) 478-743-1454 bettyemiddlebrooks@yahoo.com www.spcccmacon.com Rev. William McIntyre, O.F.M., Pst.; Rev. Casey Allen Cole, OFM, Par. Vicar; Rev. Rodolfo Ramon-Cabrera, OFM, Par. Vicar; Dcn. James B. Hubbard; Dcn. Reginald Russell; Edgar Cabrera, DRE; Bettye Middlebrooks, DRE; CRP Stds.: 93

St. Peter Claver Catholic School - (Grades PreK-8) 133 Ward St., Macon, GA 31204-3193 t) 478-743-3985 info@spccatholicschool.org www.spccatholicschool.org Sr. Cheryl Ann Hillig, D.C., Prin.; Stds.: 156; Pr. Tchrs.: 1; Sr. Tchrs.: 2; Lay Tchrs.: 15

MCRAE

Holy Redeemer - 17 Telfair Ave., McRae, GA 31055-1625; Mailing: 1559 Hwy 441 N, Dublin, GA 31021 t) 478-272-0266 iccdublin@immaculate-conception-church.net Rev. Jude Shayo, A.J., Pst.; Rev. John Stephen Ariko, A.J., Par. Vicar; CRP Stds.: 10

MONTEZUMA

St. Michael Mission Catholic Church - 718 N. Dooly St., Montezuma, GA 31063; Mailing: 722 N. Dooly St., Montezuma, GA 31063 c) 478-316-0786 stmichaelsmontezuma@gmail.com www.stmichaelsmontezuma.org Rev. Peter Hung Nguyen, Par. Admin.; CRP Stds.: 9

MOULTRIE

Immaculate Conception - 1132 2nd St., S.E., Moultrie, GA 31768 t) 229-985-6550 iccmoultrie.org Rev. Alfonso Gutierrez, Pst.; Dcn. Brian Rollock; Dcn. Philip Wehner; CRP Stds.: 50

St. John Vianney - 425 S. McArthur Dr., Camilla, GA 31730; Mailing: P.O. Box 391, Camilla, GA 31730-0391 t) 229-336-8685 sjvccamilla@gmail.com

PINE MOUNTAIN

Christ the King Church - 6700 GA Hwy. 354, Pine Mountain, GA 31822; Mailing: P.O. Box 899, Pine Mountain, GA 31822 t) 706-663-0090 ctkoffice@ctkpinemountain.net www.christthekingpinemountain.org Rev. Thomas Brian O'Shaughnessy, Pst.; Emily Ellison, DRE; CRP Stds.: 56

PORT WENTWORTH

Our Lady of Lourdes - 501 S. Coastal Hwy, Port Wentworth, GA 31407-4056 t) 912-667-0602 ololchurch@comcast.net ololpw.com Very Rev. Pablo Migone, Pst.; Rev. Carlos Rivero, Par. Vicar; CRP Stds.: 179

Corpus Christi Catholic Church - 1745 Benton Blvd., Savannah, GA 31407; Mailing: P.O. Box 621, Pooler, GA 31322 t) 912-348-6426 poolercatholics@gmail.com www.poolercatholics.com

RAY CITY

St. Anthony of Padua Catholic Church - 2530 Garner Rd., Ray City, GA 31645 t) 229-455-5554 church@anthonyofpaduaga.org www.anthonyofpaduaga.org Rev. Juan Carlos Castillo Mayorga, Pst.; Dcn. Raymond E. Brown; Dcn. Steven Mancuso, DRE; CRP Stds.: 34

RICHMOND HILL

St. Anne - 10550 Ford Ave., Richmond Hill, GA 31324-6551; Mailing: 312 Victors Ct., c/o Rectory, Richmond Hill, GA 31324 t) 912-756-3343; 912-737-0112 www.admin@stannerh.org; frrobert@stannerh.org www.stannerh.org Rev. Dawid A. Kwiatkowski; CRP Stds.: 273

SAVANNAH

Cathedral Basilica of St. John the Baptist - 222 E. Harris St., Savannah, GA 31401-4699 t) 912-233-4709 csjbsav@aol.com; office@savannahcathedral.org savannahcathedral.org Very Rev. J. Gerard Schreck, Rector; Rev. Andrew Larkin, Par. Vicar; Rev. Thomas J. Peyton, In Res.; Dcn. Dewain Smith, DRE; Dcn. Joseph Mullin; Janee Przybyl, DRE; CRP Stds.: 55

St. Benedict the Moor - 441 E. Broad St, Savannah, GA 31401; Mailing: 556 E. Gordon St., Savannah, GA 31401 t) 912-232-7147 stbenedict@bellsouth.net stbenedicttmcc.org Rev. Romanus Obiora Ezeugwu, M.S.P., Pst.; Sharon Carson, DRE; CRP Stds.: 39

St. Frances Xavier Cabrini - 11500 Middleground Rd., Savannah, GA 31419 t) 912-925-4725 sfcc.office@cabrini-sav.org cabrini-sav.org Rev. Gabriel Cummings, Pst.; CRP Stds.: 25

St. James - 8412 Whitfield Ave., Savannah, GA 31406-6198 t) 912-355-1523 bmacaulay@stjamessav.com www.stjamessav.com Very Rev. Daniel F. Firmin, Pst.; Rev. Joey Buencamino, Par. Vicar; Rev. Peter Lanshima, Par. Vicar; Dcn. Louis Santore; CRP Stds.: 45

St. James School - (Grades PreK-8) t) 912-355-3132 srjoan@sjcs-savannahga.org www.stjameschargers.com Sr. Joan Felicia O'Reilly, Prin.; Stds.: 466; Sr. Tchrs.: 2; Lay Tchrs.: 38

Our Lady of Good Hope - 16 Rosenbrook Dr., Savannah, GA 31406 lsantore@stjamessav.com

Most Blessed Sacrament - 1003 E. Victory Dr., Savannah, GA 31405-2499 t) 912-356-6980 parish@mbschurch.org www.mbschurch.org Rev. David A. Koetter, OFM, Pst.; Rev. Nate Swann, Par. Vicar; Dcn. Gerald R. Clark; Dcn. Robert Fritts; CRP Stds.: 32

Most Blessed Sacrament School - (Grades PreK-8) t) 912-356-6987 aswanger@bss-savannah.org bss-savannah.org Lynn Brown, Prin.; Stds.: 458; Lay Tchrs.: 35

Sts. Peter and Paul - 3115 Victory Dr., Savannah, GA 31404-4598 t) 912-354-4014 knguyen@diosav.org cgvnsavannah.org Rev. Kim Son Nguyen, Pst.; Dcn. Hoang Tran; CRP Stds.: 42

St. Peter the Apostle Church - 7020 Concord Rd., Savannah, GA 31410; Mailing: P.O. Box 30859, Savannah, GA 31410 t) 912-897-5156 lwilharm@spacsav.net saintpetertheapostle.com Rev. Michael J. Kavanaugh, Pst.; Dcn. Kevin Knight; Rev. Luis Fonseca, Par. Vicar; CRP Stds.: 55

St. Peter the Apostle Catholic School - (Grades PreK-8) t) 912-897-5224 wkelly@spasav.net school.saintpetertheapostle.com Wynter Kelly, Prin.; Stds.: 241; Sr. Tchrs.: 1; Lay Tchrs.: 20

Resurrection of Our Lord - 112 Fell St., Savannah, GA 31415-1828 t) 912-232-5258 rbrtgen@aol.com resurrection.diosav.net Rev. Robert E. Chaney, Pst.; Dcn. Hosea Bennett; CRP Stds.: 17

Sacred Heart of Jesus - 1707 Bull St., Savannah, GA 31401 t) 912-232-0792 secretary@sacredheartsavannah.org; bookkeeper@sacredheartsavannah.org www.sacredheartsavannah.org Very Rev. Kevin O'Keefe, Pst.; Dcn. Paul Gutting; Dcn. Robert Larcher; Dcn. Mario Rabusin; Veronica Campbell, DRE; CRP Stds.: 131

SPRINGFIELD

St. Boniface Church - 1952 GA Hwy. 21 S., Springfield, GA 31329-5207 t) 912-754-7473 mnguyen@diosav.org; secretary@sbcatholic.com www.sbcatholic.com Rev. Martino Ba Thong Nguyen, Pst.; Dcn. Richard Rafter; CRP Stds.: 115

ST. MARYS

Our Lady Star of the Sea - 106 E. Dillingham St., St. Marys, GA 31558 t) 912-882-4718 office@weareolss.org; religioused@weareolss.org weareolss.org Rev. Mariusz K. Fuks, Pst.; Dcn. Henry Nieves; Dcn. Tim Hughes; Charles Bryant Shepard, DRE; CRP Stds.: 115

St. Francis of Assisi - 700 Kingsland Dr., Folkston, GA 31537; Mailing: 106 E. Dillingham St., Saint Marys, GA 31558 t) 912-496-3219

ST. SIMONS ISLAND

St. William - 2300 Frederica Rd., St. Simons Island, GA 31522-1965 t) 912-638-2647; 912-638-2651 (CRP) stwilliamschurch@comcast.net www.stwill.net Rev. Msgr. Christopher J. Schreck, Pst.; Rev. Jim Holloway, In Res.; Stacey Bristol, Admin.; Kate Hamer, Music Min.; Nancy Power, DRE; CRP Stds.: 99

STATESBORO

St. Matthew - 221 John Paul Ave., Statesboro, GA 30458-5016 t) 912-681-6726 mcannady@saintmatthewsparish.com www.saintmatthewsparish.com Rev. Jason P. Adams, Par. Admin.; Rev. Douglas K. Clark, Pastor Emer.; Dcn. Michael J. McGrath; Dcn. John O'Malley; Dcn. Mark Girardeau; CRP Stds.: 202

SWAINSBORO

Holy Trinity - 928 W. Main St., Swainsboro, GA 30401-5502 t) 478-237-6783 holytrinity.swainsboro@gmail.com Rev. Fredy A. Angel, Pst.; CRP Stds.: 41

Holy Family - 1110 S. Lewis St., Metter, GA 30439; Mailing: P.O. Box 65, Metter, GA 30439 t) 912-685-5811 holyfamily@pineland.net

SYLVANIA

Our Lady of the Assumption - 121 Ridgecrest Dr., Sylvania, GA 30467-1840 t) 912-564-2312 nov45@aol.com; llussier@diosav.org Rev. Louis Lussier, O.S.Cam., Pst.; CRP Stds.: 12

St. Joseph Chapel, Bay Branch. - t) (912) 564-2312

THOMASVILLE

St. Augustine - 211 N. Pinetree Blvd., Thomasville, GA 31792-3973 t) 229-226-3624 staugustinethomasville@gmail.com www.staugustinethomasville.weebly.com Rev. Godfred Boachie-Yiadom, Pst.; Dcn. John Blaha; Dcn. David Wendel; Dcn. Miguel Gutierrez, DRE; CRP Stds.: 95

St. Elizabeth Seton Church - 1500 11th Ave., N.W., Cairo, GA 39828; Mailing: 211 N. Pinetree Blvd., Thomasville, GA 31792 t) (229) 226-3624

TIFTON

Our Divine Saviour - 1205 Love Ave., Tifton, GA 31793-0201; Mailing: 211 E. 12th St., Tifton, GA 31794 t) 229-382-4600 ods@friendlycity.net odsparishtifton.org Rev. Peter Oyenugba, M.S.P., Pst.; Mary McKinnon, DRE; CRP Stds.: 78

St. Ann - 9007 U.S. Hwy. 82 E., Alapaha, GA 31622 t) (229) 382-4600

TYBEE ISLAND

St. Michael's Catholic Church - 801 Butler Ave, Tybee Island, GA 31328-0001; Mailing: 802 Lovell Ave, Tybee Island, GA 31328 t) 912-786-4505 c) (912) 755-1250 (Church Office) office@saintmichaelstybee.org www.saintmichaelstybee.org Rev. Gerald Ragan, Pst.; Madison Salzillo, DRE;

VALDOSTA

St. John the Evangelist - 800 Gornto Rd., Valdosta, GA 31602-1699 t) 229-244-2430 stjohns@stjohnevang.org www.stjohnevang.org Rev. Brian R. LaBurt, Pst.; Rev. Robert A. Phillips, Par. Vicar; Dcn. Columbus Carter; Dcn. Peter Falkenhausen; Dcn. David Lasseter; Dcn. Paul Worth; Susan Kramer, DRE; CRP Stds.: 130

San Jose - 421 W. Marion Ave., Lake Park, GA 31636; Mailing: 800 Gornto Rd., Valdosta, GA 31602 t) (229) 244-2430

St. John Catholic School - (Grades PreK-8) t) 229-244-2556 info@sjcsvaldosta.org Vito Pellitteri, Prin.; Stds.: 153; Lay Tchrs.: 19

VIDALIA

Sacred Heart - 3119 North St. E., Vidalia, GA 30474 t) 912-537-7709 www.sacredheartvidalia.org Rev. Gordian Iwuji, MSP, Pst.; Dcn. Joseph P. Claroni; CRP Stds.: 141

St. Andrew the Apostle - 138 Industrial Blvd., Reidsville, GA 30453; Mailing: 3119 North St. E., Vidalia, GA 30474 t) (912) 537-7709

WARNER ROBINS

Sacred Heart - 300 S. Davis Dr., Ste. 300, Warner Robins, GA 31088 t) 478-923-0124 pastoral.asst@sacredheartwr.com; records@sacredheartwr.com sacredheartwr.org Rev. Stephen J. Pontzer, Pst.; Rev. Carlos Rivero, Par. Vicar; Rev. Msgr. Fred J. Nijem, Pastor Emer.; Dcn. James A. Hunt; Dcn. Robert Perry; Dcn. Ronald Simons; CRP Stds.: 400

Sacred Heart School - (Grades PreK-8) 300 S. Davis Dr., Bldg. 100, Warner Robins, GA 31088 t) 478-923-9668 shsprincipal2016@gmail.com; bquinn@shswr.org www.shswr.org Al Chromy, Prin.; Stds.: 285; Lay Tchrs.: 24

WAYCROSS

St. Joseph's - 2011 Darling Ave., Waycross, GA 31501-1846 t) 912-283-7700 sjcwaycross@att.net Rev. Daniel Ter Melaba (Nigeria), Pst.; Michele Thompson, DRE; CRP Stds.: 81

WAYNESBORO

Sacred Heart - 115 S. Liberty St., Waynesboro, GA 30830-4548; Mailing: P.O. Box 1100, Waynesboro, GA 30830 t) 706-554-2535 sacredheartwaynesboro@yahoo.com Rev. John Wright; Dcn. Brian Goodman; Caroline LaBauve, DRE; CRP Stds.: 30

St. Joan of Arc - 2604 US Hwy. 1 N., Louisville, GA 30434; Mailing: P.O. Box 175, Louisville, GA 30434 t) 478-625-3433 stjoanofarc@yahoo.com

SCHOOLS: PRESCHOOL THRU HIGH SCHOOL

HIGH SCHOOLS

STATE OF GEORGIA

AUGUSTA

Aquinas High School - (DIO) (Grades 9-12) 1920 Highland Ave., Augusta, GA 30904-5305 t) 706-736-5516 mlewis@aquinashigh.org www.aquinashigh.org Very Rev. Mark N. Van Alstine, Chap.; Carrie Jane Williamson, Supt.; Maureen Lewis, Prin.; Stds.: 240; Lay Tchrs.: 16

MACON

Mount de Sales Academy - (PRV) (Grades 6-12) 851 Orange St., Macon, GA 31201; Mailing: 851 Orange St, Macon, GA 31201 t) 478-751-3240 mpdadisman@mountdesales.net www.mountdesales.net Independent school affiliated with the Sisters of Mercy of the Americas. Michael Franklin, Prin.; David Held, Pres.; Stds.: 446; Lay Tchrs.: 41

SAVANNAH

Benedictine Military School - (PRV) 6502 Seawright Dr., Savannah, GA 31406-2752 t) 912-644-7000 barbara.evans@bcsav.net; frank.ziemkiewicz@bcsav.net www.thebc400.com Boys. Rev. Ronald P. Gatman, O.S.B., Campus Min.; Jacob Horne, Prin.; Rev. Frank Ziemkiewicz, OSB, Headmaster; Bro. Matthew Hershey, O.S.B., Teacher; Rev. David Klecker, Teacher; Dcn. Kevin Knight, Teacher; Stds.: 423; Pr. Tchrs.: 5; Bro. Tchrs.: 1; Lay Tchrs.: 42

St. Vincent's Academy - (PRV) (Grades 9-12) 207 E. Liberty St., Savannah, GA 31401-3577 t) 912-236-5508 maryanne.hogan@savga.net; dawn.odom@savga.net www.svaga.net Sisters of Mercy of the Americas and Mercy Education System of the Americas. Dawn Odom, Prin.; Mary Anne Hogan, Pres.; Stds.: 295; Lay Tchrs.: 30

INSTITUTIONS LOCATED IN DIOCESE

CATHOLIC CHARITIES [CCH]

ALBANY

St. Clare's Evangelization-Community Center - 2005 Martin Luther King Dr., Albany, GA 31706-4123; Mailing: P.O. Box 4123, Albany, GA 31706-4123 t) 229-883-2566 centerstclares@gmail.com Tina Appollonio, Dir.; Asstd. Annu.: 23,904; Staff: 2

Neighbors in Need - 2005 Martin Luther King Dr., Albany, GA 31706-3001; Mailing: P.O. Box 4123, Albany, GA 31706-3001 t) 229-883-2872 neighbors-in-need@mediacombb.net Tina Appollonio, Dir.;

AUGUSTA

Catholic Social Services of Augusta - 811 12th St., Augusta, GA 30901-2749 t) 706-364-0208; 706-722-3661 jjrcog@aol.com; director@cssaugusta.com www.cssaugusta.com Sr. Janet Roddy, M.F.I.C., Dir.; Asstd. Annu.: 7,162; Staff: 17

BRUNSWICK

Society of St. Vincent de Paul (Glynn County) - 1217 Newcastle St., Brunswick, GA 31520-7534 c) 908-963-4017 mleckert@me.com Martha Eckert, Pres.; Asstd. Annu.: 10,000; Staff: 100

COLUMBUS

St. Benedict Outreach Program - 2935 Ninth St., Columbus, GA 31906 t) 706-323-8300 bedcas45@yahoo.com stbenedict07@knology.net

Beverly Casimier, Dir.; Asstd. Annu.: 1,720; Staff: 6
Holy Family Social Services Outreach Program - 320 12th St., Columbus, GA 31901-2454 t) 706-322-0098 holyfamily6706@gmail.com holyfamilycolumbus.com Gretchen Whaley-Wong, Dir.;

MACON

Family Advancement Ministries - 538 Orange St., Macon, GA 31201-2073 t) 478-746-9803 grolfes.fam@gmail.com familyadvancementministries.org Social Services; utility/rental assistance and educational support for families with young children. Hispanic support services. Gigi Rolfes, Dir.; Asstd. Annu.: 3,900; Staff: 6

SAVANNAH

Catholic Charities of South Georgia - 2170 E. Victory Dr., Savannah, GA 31404-3918 t) 912-201-4100; 912-201-4058; 912-201-4048 ckinnis@diosav.org; catholiccharities@diosav.org www.diosav.org/offices/catholic-charities Cynthia Kinnis, Dir.; Paola Caudill, Community Navigator Specialist; Staff: 2
Social Apostolate of Savannah - 502 E. Liberty St., Savannah, GA 31401; Mailing: P. O. Box 8703, Savannah, GA 31412 t) 912-233-1877 socialapostolate@comcast.net www.socialapostolate.org Under the umbrella of Catholic Charities of South Georgia Latacia Avila, Dir.; Asstd. Annu.: 5,110; Staff: 5

VALDOSTA

St. Francis Center - CSS - 520 E. Mary St., Valdosta, GA 31601; Mailing: 800 Gornto Rd., Valdosta, GA 31602 t) 229-242-8656 sfc520@att.net Sr. Nuala Mulleady, M.F.I.C., Dir.; Asstd. Annu.: 4,000; Staff: 2

WARNER ROBINS

Sacred Heart Christian Service Center - 136 Northview Ave., Warner Robins, GA 31088; Mailing: 300 S. Davis Dr., Bldg. 300, Warner Robins, GA 31088 t) 478-929-3897 csc@sacredheartwr.com www.sacredheartwr.com Katharine M. Dugas, Dir.; Asstd. Annu.: 2,333; Staff: 2

CEMETERIES [CEM]

SAVANNAH

Savannah Catholic Cemetery - 1720 Wheaton St., Savannah, GA 31404; Mailing: 2170 E. Victory Dr., Savannah, GA 31404 t) 912-201-4100 diosav.org John Grim, Dir.;

CONVENTS, MONASTERIES, AND RESIDENCES FOR WOMEN [CON]

SAVANNAH

Carmelite Monastery - 11 W. Back St., Savannah, GA 31419-3219 t) 912-925-8505; 912-925-8506 olconfidence@yahoo.com carmelofsavannah.org Mother Mary Elizabeth Angline, Prioress; Srs.: 9
Mercy Convent - 11801 McAuley Dr., Savannah, GA 31419-1709 t) 912-925-3800 mshumard@sistersofmercy.org Retired Sisters of Mercy. Maureen Shumard, Admin.; Srs.: 8

ENDOWMENTS / FOUNDATIONS / TRUSTS [EFT]

SAVANNAH

The Catholic Foundation of South Georgia - 2170 E. Victory Dr., Savannah, GA 31404-3918 t) 912-201-4061 loconnor@diosav.org www.diosav.org/catholicfdn-southga Liam J. O'Connor, Admin.; Thomas Kitchin, Chair;
Foundation for Priestly Vocations, Inc. - 1003 E. Victory Dr., Savannah, GA 31405 t) 706-513-4660 bbrannen@diosav.org Rev. Brett A. Brannen, Pres.;

HOSPITALS / HEALTH SERVICES [HOS]

SAVANNAH

St. Joseph's Hospital, Inc. - 11705 Mercy Blvd., Savannah, GA 31419 t) 912-819-3415 beattym@sjchs.org www.sjchs.org Sisters of Mercy, South Central Community Rev. Matthew Ericksen, Chap.; Rev. Rodolfo P. Roxas, Chap.; Rev. Joseph A. Smith, Chap.; Paul P. Hinchey, CEO; Sr. Margaret Beatty, Vice Pres., Mission Svcs.; Bed Capacity: 305; Asstd. Annu.: 120,000; Staff: 1,400

MISCELLANEOUS [MIS]

AUGUSTA

Alleluia Catholic Fellowship - 2110 Richards St., Augusta, GA 30916-6805; Mailing: P.O. Box 6805, Augusta, GA 30916-6805 t) 706-798-1882 danalmeter@hotmail.com www.yeslord.com

FORTSON

Deacons in Ministry, Inc. - 144 Crater Dr., Fortson, GA 31808 t) (706) 243-1944 yahula1@charter.net; pmissions@charter.net eddieensley.com Dcn. Robert Herrmann, Contact;

MONASTERIES AND RESIDENCES FOR PRIESTS AND BROTHERS [MON]

SAVANNAH

The Benedictine Priory - 6502 Seawright Dr., Savannah, GA 31406 t) 912-356-3520 david.klecker@bcsav.net Dependent Priory of St. Vincent Archabbey, Latrobe, PA. Rev. David Klecker, Prior; Rev. Frank Ziemkiewicz, OSB, Headmaster; Rev. John Paul Heiser, OSB, Teacher at BMS; Rev. Ronald P. Gatman, O.S.B., In Res.; Bro. Matthew Hershey, O.S.B., In Res.; Brs.: 1; Priests: 5

An asterisk (*) denotes an organization that has established tax-exempt status directly with the IRS and is not covered by the USCCB Group Ruling.

Diocese of Scranton

(Dioecesis Scrantonensis)

MOST REVEREND JOSEPH C. BAMBERA, D.D., J.C.L.

Bishop of Scranton; ordained November 5, 1983; appointed Bishop of Scranton February 23, 2010; installed April 26, 2010.

Chancery Office: 300 Wyoming Ave., Scranton, PA 18503. T: 570-207-2216; F: 570-207-2236.
www.dioceseofscranton.org

ESTABLISHED MARCH 3, 1868.

Square Miles 8,847.

Comprises the Counties of Luzerne, Lackawanna, Bradford, Susquehanna, Wayne, Tioga, Sullivan, Wyoming, Lycoming, Pike and Monroe in Pennsylvania.

For legal titles of parishes and diocesan institutions, consult the Chancery Office.

STATISTICAL OVERVIEW

Personnel

Bishop....1
Retired Bishops....2
Priests: Diocesan Active in Diocese....87
Priests: Diocesan Active Outside Diocese....4
Priests: Retired, Sick or Absent....101
Number of Diocesan Priests....192
Religious Priests in Diocese....41
Total Priests in your Diocese....233
Extern Priests in Diocese....39
Ordinations:
Transitional Deacons....1
Permanent Deacons....8
Permanent Deacons in Diocese....93
Total Brothers....6
Total Sisters....329

Parishes

Parishes....114
With Resident Pastor:
Resident Diocesan Priests....104
Resident Religious Priests....3
Without Resident Pastor:
Administered by Priests....1
Administered by Deacons....2
Administered by Professed Religious Men....3
Administered by Religious Women....1
Missions....34
Closed Parishes....2

Professional Ministry Personnel:
Sisters....4

Welfare

Catholic Hospitals....2
Total Assisted....97,689
Homes for the Aged....6
Total Assisted....508
Residential Care of Children....1
Total Assisted....155
Day Care Centers....1
Total Assisted....754
Specialized Homes....1
Total Assisted....21
Special Centers for Social Services....16
Total Assisted....99,568
Residential Care of Disabled....2
Total Assisted....18

Educational

Diocesan Students in Other Seminaries....8
Total Seminarians....8
Colleges and Universities....4
Total Students....12,280
High Schools, Diocesan and Parish....4
Total Students....1,083
High Schools, Private....1
Total Students....651
Elementary Schools, Diocesan and Parish....15
Total Students....3,337
Elementary Schools, Private....1
Total Students....67
Catechesis/Religious Education:
High School Students....632
Elementary Students....9,723
Total Students under Catholic Instruction....27,781
Teachers in Diocese:
Priests....3
Sisters....11
Lay Teachers....395

Vital Statistics

Receptions into the Church:
Infant Baptism Totals....1,972
Minor Baptism Totals....134
Adult Baptism Totals....74
Received into Full Communion....66
First Communions....1,797
Confirmations....1,917
Marriages:
Catholic....420
Interfaith....106
Total Marriages....526
Deaths....4,139
Total Catholic Population....317,429
Total Population....1,114,999

LEADERSHIP

Vicar General & Moderator of the Curia - t) 570-207-2269 rev-gerald-shantillo@dioceseofscranton.org; tpetcaugh@dioceseofscranton.org Rev. Gerald W. Shantillo;

Chancery Office - t) 570-207-2216 linda-price@dioceseofscranton.org Linda E. Price, Chancellor;

Regional Episcopal Vicars - Rev. Cyril D. Edwards, Northern Pastoral Region; Rev. Joseph J. Evanko, Southern Pastoral Region; Rev. Richard E. Czachor, Eastern Pastoral Region;

Chancellor - t) 570-207-2216 linda-price@dioceseofscranton.org Linda E. Price;

Diocesan Financial Office - t) 570-207-2237 eileen-giombetti@dioceseofscranton.org Eileen Giombetti, Dir.;

Diocesan Tribunal - t) 570-207-2246 Rev. Jeffrey D. Tudgay, Vicar;

Judicial Vicar & Episcopal Vicar for Canonical Affairs - rev-jeffrey-tudgay@dioceseofscranton.org Rev. Jeffrey D. Tudgay;

Case Manager - t) (570) 207-2246 x1064 judy-myerski@dioceseofscranton.org Judy Myerski, Case Mgr.;

Judges - Rev. Msgr. Patrick J. Pratico; Rev. Brian J.W. Clarke; Rev. Thomas J. Petro;

Defenders of the Bond - Rev. Msgr. Joseph G. Quinn; Rev. Anthony J. Generose; Rev. Eduard Shestak, Defender of the Bond;

Auditor - Rev. Anthony J. Generose, Pst.;

Advocates - Jay Conzemius; Judith Myerski;

Notaries - Judith Myerski; Gayle Stancheski;

Diocesan Finance Council - t) (570) 207-2237 x1028 eileen-giombetti@dioceseofscranton.org Rev. Gerald W. Shantillo, Ex Officio; Eileen Giombetti, Ex Officio; James Bebla;

Diocesan Consultors - t) 570-591-5006 rev-john-polednak@dioceseofscranton.org Rev. Gerald W. Shantillo, Vicar; Rev. John V. Polednak, Vicar; Rev. Jeffrey D. Tudgay;

Deans - t) (570) 591-5006 rev-john-polednak@dioceseofscranton.org Rev. Msgr. Neil J. Van Loon, Scranton Dean; Rev. Seth D. Wasnock, Carbondale Dean; Rev. Msgr. Joseph G. Quinn, Clarks Summit Dean;

Presbyteral Council - t) 570-591-5006 rev-john-polednak@dioceseofscranton.org; gayle-stancheski@dioceseofscranton.org Rev. Msgr. Neil J. Van Loon, Chair; Rev. Kevin M. Miller, Vice Chmn. (apsrolmc@gmail.com); Rev. Mark J. DeCelles, Secy.;

Diocesan Building Commission - t) (570) 558-4310 x1002 (Joe Dunda) jdunda@dioceseofscranton.org Rev. Gerald W. Shantillo, Vicar; Joseph Dunda, Dir.; Eileen Giombetti, CFO;

Episcopal Vicar for Clergy - t) 570-591-5006 rev-john-polednak@dioceseofscranton.org Rev. John V. Polednak;

Diocesan Review Board - t) (570) 207-2269 rev-gerald-shantillo@dioceseofscranton.org Most Rev. Joseph C. Bambera, Bishop; Rev. Gerald W. Shantillo, Vicar Gen.; Mary Beth Pacuska, Victim Assistance Coord. (mary-beth-pacuska@dioceseofscranton.org);

OFFICES AND DIRECTORS

Campus Ministry - t) 570-207-2213 skowalski@dioceseofscranton.org Shannon Kowalski, Dir.;

Catholic Campaign for Human Development - t) 570-207-2213 skowalski@dioceseofscranton.org Shannon Kowalski, Dir.;

Catholic Charismatic Renewal - t) (570) 207-2213 jandres@dioceseofscranton.org Rev. August A. Ricciardi, Spiritual Moderator; Karen McLain, Conference Coord.;

Catholic Relief Services - t) (570) 207-2269 rev-gerald-shantillo@dioceseofscranton.org Rev. Gerald W. Shantillo, Vicar;

Catholic School System Board Members - t) 570-207-2251 kdonohue@dioceseofscranton.org Kristen Donohue, Admin.;

Catholic Social Services - t) 570-207-3808 jmahoney@cssdioceseofscranton.org Joseph Mahoney, Secy.;

Board of Governance - t) (570) 207-3808 jmahoney@dioceseofscranton.org Rev. Gerald W. Shantillo, Vicar Gen.; Dcn. J. Patrick McDonald; Sr. Ann Walsh, I.H.M.;

Catholic Social Services Finance Office - t) 570-822-7118; 570-207-2283 jalu@cssdioceseofscranton.org; jmahoney@dioceseofscranton.org John Alu, Dir., Finance; Gwen Berman, Budget Analyst; Sandra Frazer, Grants & Contracts Billing Specialist;

Immigration Program - t) (570) 207-3808 x1020 jmahoney@cssdioceseofscranton.org Joseph Mahoney, Dir.;

Relief Assistance Program - t) (570) 207-3808 x1020 jmahoney@cssdioceseofscranton.org Joseph Mahoney, Sec., Catholic Human Svcs.;

Cemeteries - t) 570-558-4310 jdunda@dioceseofscranton.org Joseph Dunda, Admin.;

Censor Librorum - t) 570-207-2216 linda-price@dioceseofscranton.org Rev. Charles P. Connor;

Chaplain for the Deaf - t) 570-207-2213 mguarnieri@dioceseofscranton.org Rev. Joseph G. Elston;

Consecrated Life Office - t) 570-591-5002 kkurdziel@dioceseofscranton.org Sr. Kathryn Kurdziel, I.H.M., Dir.;

Coordinator for Ecumenism & Interfaith Relations - t) 570-207-2213 Rev. Msgr. Vincent J. Grimalia, Dir.;

Cursillo Movement - t) 570-457-3412 Rev. Phillip J. Sladicka, Spiritual Adv./Care Srvcs.;

Delegate for Religious - t) 570-591-5002 kkurdziel@dioceseofscranton.org Sr. Kathryn Kurdziel, I.H.M.;

Diocesan Appeal Office - t) 570-207-2250 jim-bebla@dioceseofscranton.org; lmusto@dioceseofscranton.org Luciana Musto, Interim Dir. Devel.; Christopher E. Sheperis, Dir. Devel. Opers.; James Bebla, Diocesan Secy. for Devel.;

Diocesan Grant Writer & Director of Foundation Relations & Special Events - t) (570) 207-2250 x1053 sandra-snyder@dioceseofscranton.org Sandra Snyder;

Diocesan Commission on Ecumenism and Inter-Faith Matters - t) 570-207-2213 Rev. Msgr. Vincent J. Grimalia, Coord.;

Diocesan Historian - t) 570-207-2216 Rev. Charles P. Connor;

Diocesan Office for Clergy Formation - t) (570) 207-1452 msgr-david-bohr@dioceseofscranton.org; rev-alex-roche@dioceseofscranton.org Rev. Msgr. David A. Bohr, Diocesan Sec.; Rev. Alex J. Roche, Dir., Vocations;

Diocesan Office for Communications - t) 800-246-0288; 570-207-2219 edeabill@dioceseofscranton.org; james-brennan@dioceseofscranton.org Eric Deabill, Exec.;

Diocesan Office for Continuing Education for Clergy - t) 570-207-1452 msgr-david-bohr@dioceseofscranton.org Rev. Msgr. David A. Bohr, Dir.;

Diocesan Office of Development - t) 570-207-2250 jim-bebla@dioceseofscranton.org; lmusto@dioceseofscranton.org Luciana Musto, Interim Dir. Devel.; James Bebla, Diocesan Secy. Devel.; Christopher E. Sheperis, Dir., Devel. Opers.;

Diocesan Pro-Life Office - t) 570-207-2213 skowalski@dioceseofscranton.org Shannon Kowalski, Contact;

Diocesan Safe Environment Coordinator - t) 570-207-1453 x1078 emcgrady@dioceseofscranton.org Erin McGrady, Dir.;

Diocesan Secretary for Property & Risk Management - t) 570-558-4310 jdunda@dioceseofscranton.org Joseph Dunda;

Diocesan Television Station-CTV - t) 570-207-2213 edeabill@dioceseofscranton.org Eric Deabill, Exec.; James Brennan, Mgr.;

Diocese of Scranton Catholic Community Foundation - t) 570-207-2250 jim-bebla@dioceseofscranton.org James Bebla, Dir.;

Diocese of Scranton Scholarship Foundation - t) 570-207-2250 jim-bebla@dioceseofscranton.org James Bebla, Dir.;

Hispanic Ministry Outreach - t) 570-207-2213 x1130 (Jose Flores) jflores@dioceseofscranton.org Jose Flores, Coord. Hispanic Ministry; Rev. Jaime Restrepo; Rev. John C. Ruth;

Holy Childhood Association - t) 570-207-2259 rev-brian-jt-clarke@dioceseofscranton.org Rev. Brian J.T. Clarke;

Legion of Mary - t) 570-876-1136; (570) 207-2213 skowalski@dioceseofscranton.org Mary Bolcavage, Pres.;

Liturgical Commission - t) 570-207-2213 david-baloga@dioceseofscranton.org David Baloga, Dir.;

Marriage Encounter - t) 570-207-2213 skowalski@dioceseofscranton.org Shannon Kowalski, Admin.;

Ministry with the Deaf Persons with Disabilities - t) (570) 207-2213 mguarnieri@dioceseofscranton.org Marianne Guarnieri;

Natural Family Planning Coordinator - t) 570-207-2213 skowalski@dioceseofscranton.org Shannon Kowalski;

Newspaper - t) 570-207-2229 eric-deabill@dioceseofscranton.org Eric Deabill, Editor;

Office for Parish Life - t) 570-207-2213 mhallman@dioceseofscranton.org; abecerril@dioceseofscranton.org Dominick Costantino, Mgr., Parish Renewal; Marianne Guarnieri, Dir. Discipleship; David Baloga, Dir. Worship;

Consultant for Parish Pastoral Planning - t) (570) 207-2213 Rev. John M. Lapera;

Consultant for Youth and Campus Ministry - t) (570) 207-2213 skowalski@dioceseofscranton.org Shannon Kowalski, Dir.;

Coordinator for Diocesan Missions and Director for Pontifical Missions - t) 570-207-2259 x1155 rev-brian-jt-clarke@dioceseofscranton.org; tpetcaugh@dioceseofscranton.org Rev. Brian J.T. Clarke;

Coordinator for Ecumenical and Interfaith Relations - t) 570-207-2213 jandres@dioceseofscranton.org Rev. Msgr. Vincent J. Grimalia;

Coordinator for Hispanic Ministry - t) 570-207-2213 x1130 jflores@dioceseofscranton.org Jose Flores;

Coordinator for Lay Ministry Formation/Director of Discipleship - t) (570) 207-2213 mguarnieri@dioceseofscranton.org Marianne Guarnieri, Dir.;

Coordinator for Pilgrimages - t) (570) 207-2213; (570) 675-2121 mhallman@dioceseofscranton.org Rev. Andrew S. Hvozdovic;

Coordinator for RCIA - t) (570) 207-2213 david-baloga@dioceseofscranton.org David Baloga;

Coordinator for Youth/Young Adult Ministry - t) (570) 207-2213 skowalski@dioceseofscranton.org Shannon Kowalski;

D.C.C.M. - t) 570-207-2213 skowalski@dioceseofscranton.org Shannon Kowalski, Admin.; Rev. James E. McGahagan, Chap.;

D.C.C.W. - t) 570-207-2213 skowalski@dioceseofscranton.org Shannon Kowalski, Admin.; Rev. James E. McGahagan, Chap.;

Diocesan Secretary for Parish Life - t) (570) 207-2213 x1148 mhallman@dioceseofscranton.org Mary Clare Hallman;

Director for Community and Family Development - t) (570) 207-2213 mguarnieri@dioceseofscranton.org Marianne Guarnieri, Admin.;

Director for Service and Mission - t) (570) 207-2213 skowalski@dioceseofscranton.org Shannon

Kowalski;

Director for Worship - t) (570) 207-2213 david-baloga@dioceseofscranton.org David Baloga;

Director of Discipleship - t) (570) 207-2213 mguarnieri@dioceseofscranton.org Marianne Guarnieri, Dir.;

Manager, Diocesan Pastoral Center - t) (570) 207-2213 x1157 abecerril@dioceseofscranton.org Ana Becerril, Prog. Coord.;

Formation for Servant Leadership - t) (570) 207-2213 mhallman@dioceseofscranton.org Mary Clare Hallman, Dir.;

Parish Pastoral Planning - t) (570) 207-2213 ann-marie-cawley@dioceseofscranton.org; dcostantino@dioceseofscranton.org Dominick Costantino, Mgr., Parish Renewal; Ann Marie Cawley, Coord., Pastoral Council Devel.;

Permanent Diaconate Office - t) 570-591-5006; 570-207-1452 rev-john-polednak@dioceseofscranton.org; msgr-david-bohr@dioceseofscranton.org Rev. Msgr. David A. Bohr, Dir.; Rev. John V. Polednak, Vicar;

Pilgrimages - t) 570-675-2121 Rev. Andrew S. Hvozdovic, Dir.;

Pontifical Mission Societies - t) 570-207-2259 rev-brian-jt-clarke@dioceseofscranton.org; tpetcaugh@dioceseofscranton.org Rev. Brian J.T. Clarke;

Priests' Purgatorial Society - t) 570-591-5006 rev-john-polednak@dioceseofscranton.org; gayle-stancheski@dioceseofscranton.org Rev. John V. Polednak, Vicar;

Priests' Retirement Advisory Board - t) 570-591-5006 rev-john-polednak@dioceseofscranton.org James R. Burke; Rev. David Cappeloni; Rev. Richard E. Czachor;

Propagation of the Faith - t) 570-207-2259 rev-brian-jt-clarke@dioceseofscranton.org; tpetcaugh@dioceseofscranton.org Rev. Brian J.T. Clarke, Dir.;

Property & Risk Management Office - t) (570) 558-4310 jdunda@dioceseofscranton.org; ed-carlin@dioceseofscranton.org Ed Carlin, Dir.; Michael Fort, Assoc. Dir.; Joseph Dunda, Secy.;

Retirement Fund for Religious - t) 570-207-2269; 570-591-5002 rev-gerald-shantillo@dioceseofscranton.org; kkurdziel@dioceseofscranton.org Rev. Gerald W. Shantillo, Vicar; Sr. Kathryn Kurdziel, I.H.M., Delegate for Rel.;

Schools - t) 570-207-2251 Kristen Donohue, Supt. & Diocesan Secy. of Catholic Educ.; Michelle Long, Asst. Supt. Schools; Michael Slesinski, Asst. Supt.;

Scouts of America - t) 570-207-2213 Rev. Jonathan Kuhar, Chap. (jkuhar@stjnparish.org); Marianne Guarnieri, Dir., Discipleship;

Victim Assistance Coordinator - t) 570-862-7551 Mary Beth Pacuska (mary-beth-pacuska@dioceseofscranton.org);

VIRTUS - t) 570-207-1453 x1078 emcgrady@dioceseofscranton.org Erin McGrady, Safe Environment Coord.;

Vocations - t) 570-207-1452 Rev. Alex J. Roche, Dir.; Rev. Andrew Kurovsky, Asst. Dir., Vocations; Kyra Krzywicki, Vocation Prog. Coord. (kkrzywicki@dioceseofscranton.org);

PARISHES, MISSIONS, AND CLERGY

COMMONWEALTH OF PENNSYLVANIA

St. Andre Bessette Parish - Closed Jan 2022 For sacramental records, contact SS. Peter & Paul, Plains.

ARCHBALD

Christ the King Parish - 429 Church St., Archbald, PA 18403 t) 570-876-1701 www.christthekingpa.org Rev. Brian J.T. Clarke, Pst.; Rev. Michael Amo Gyau, Par. Vicar; CRP Stds.: 90

St. Thomas Aquinas Church - (Worship Site)

St. Mary of Czestochowa Church - 417 Main St., Eynon, PA 18403 (Worship Site)

ASHLEY

St. Leo - 33 Manhattan St., Ashley, PA 18706 t) 570-825-6669 saintlhrc@gmail.com www.stleos-holyrosary.org Rev. Vincent H. Dang, Pst.; CRP Stds.: 81

AVOCA

Queen of the Apostles Parish - 715 Hawthorne St., Avoca, PA 18641 t) 570-457-3412 staff@queenoftheapostles.com Rev. Phillip J. Sladicka, Pst.; Dcn. James A. Rose;

St. Mary's Church - (Worship Site)

BEAR CREEK

St. Elizabeth - 5700 Bear Creek Blvd., Bear Creek, PA 18602; Mailing: P.O. Box 25, Bear Creek, PA 18602 t) 570-472-3061 stelizabethbearcreek@outlook.com churchofstelizabethstmark.org linked with St. Rita's Parish, Gouldsboro Rev. J. Duane Gavitt, Pst.; CRP Stds.: 28

St. Mark -

CANTON

St. Michael (St Johns - St. Michaels Church) - 106 N. Washington St., Canton, PA 17724 t) 570-673-5253 stmichaelscanton.com Rev. Joseph P. Kutch, Pst.; CRP Stds.: 28

St. John Nepomucene - 133 Exchange St., Troy, PA 16947; Mailing: 106 N. Washington St., Canton, PA 17724

St. Aloysius - Green St. & Division Alley, Ralston, PA 17763; Mailing: 106 N. Washington St., Canton, PA 17724

St. Michael Church - 107 N. Washington St., Canton, PA 17724 (Worship Site)

CARBONDALE

Our Lady of Mt. Carmel - 15 Fallbrook St., Carbondale, PA 18407; Mailing: 6 N. Church St., Carbondale, PA 18407 t) 570-282-2991 strose@echoes.net www.olmc.weconnect.com Linked with St. Rose of Lima, Carbondale. Rev. Seth D. Wasnock, Pst.; Rev. Joseph Mosley; Dcn. Patrick J. Massino; Kathryn Yaklic, DRE; CRP Stds.: 30

St. Rose of Lima - 4 N. Church St., Carbondale, PA 18407; Mailing: 6 N. Church St, Carbondale, PA 18407 t) 570-282-2991 strose@echoes.net www.strosecarbondale.weconnect.com Rev. Seth D. Wasnock, Pst.; Rev. Joseph Mosley; Dcn. Patrick J. Massino; Kathryn Yaklic, DRE; CRP Stds.: 89

St. Michael - 46 Midland St., Simpson, PA 18407; Mailing: 6 N. Church St., Carbondale, PA 18407 (Worship Site)

CLARKS GREEN

St. Gregory - 330 N. Abington Rd., Clarks Green, PA 18411 t) 570-587-4808 churchofstgreg@gmail.com Rev. John M. Lapera, Pst.; Dcn. Robert P. Sheils Jr.; CRP Stds.: 308

CLARKS SUMMIT

Our Lady of the Snows - 301 S. State St., Clarks Summit, PA 18411 t) 570-586-1741 info@olsparish.net olsparish.net Rev. Msgr. Joseph G. Quinn, Pst.; Rev. Stephen Asomah, Assoc. Pst.; Dcn. Leo L. Lynn;

St. Benedict -

CONYNGHAM

St. John Bosco - 573 State Rte. 93, Conyngham, PA 18219; Mailing: PO Box 919, Conyngham, PA 18219 t) 570-788-1997 stjb@ptd.net sites.google.com Sacred Heart of Jesus Parish, Weston, is now a worship site for St. John Bosco Parish, Conyngham. Rev. Richard J. Polmounter, Pst.; Rev. Sudhir Toppo, Par. Vicar; Dcn. Maurice J. Cerasaro Jr.; CRP Stds.: 145

CRESCO

Most Holy Trinity Parish - 236 Rte. 390, Cresco, PA 18326 t) 570-595-3100 mht-poconos@outlook.com; bamfinance@gmail.com www.mht-poconos.org Rev. Brian J.W. Clarke, Pst.; Rev. Jaime Restrepo, Assoc. Pst.; Dcn. Alan S. Baranski; Dcn. Jose L. Mendoza;

DALLAS

Gate of Heaven - 40 Machell Ave., Dallas, PA 18612 t) 570-675-2121 x107 parishoffice.goh@goholv.org goholv.org Linked with Our Lady of Victory, Harveys Lake. Rev. Andrew S. Hvozdovic, Pst.; Dcn. Thomas M. Cesarini; Dcn. John Jorda; CRP Stds.: 90

DALTON

Our Lady of the Abingtons - 700 W. Main St., Dalton, PA 18414 t) 570-563-1622 spolachurch@gmail.com www.spolachurch.weebly.com Linked with St. Patrick, Nicholson, and St. Mary of the Lake, Lake Winola Rev. Arbogaste Satoun, Pst.; Rev. John J. Kilpatrick, Pastor Emer.; CRP Stds.: 52

DICKSON CITY

Visitation of the Blessed Virgin Mary - 619 Dundaff St., Dickson City, PA 18519; Mailing: 1090 Carmalt St., Dickson City, PA 18519 t) 570-489-2091 vbvm@comcast.net vbvm.org Rev. Msgr. Patrick J. Pratico, Pst.;

DRUMS

Church of the Good Shepherd - 87 S. Hunter Hwy., Drums, PA 18222 t) 570-788-3141 gsch@ptd.net www.goodshepherd-drums.org Rev. Michael J. Kloton, Pst.; CRP Stds.: 114

DUNMORE

SS. Anthony & Rocco Parish - 303 Smith St., Dunmore, PA 18512 t) (570) 344-1209 office@saintsanthonyandrocco.com Rev. David P. Cappelloni, Pst.;

Religious Teachers Filippini - 118 Kurtz St., Dunmore, PA 18510 t) 570-343-1422

St. Anthony of Padua, Dunmore - 208 Smith St., Dunmore, PA 18512; Mailing: 303 Smith St., Dunmore, PA 18512 www.saintsanthonyandrocco.com (Worship Site) Rev. David Cappelloni, Pst.;

St. Rocco, Dunmore - 122 Kurtz St., Dunmore, PA 18512 (Worship Site)

Our Lady of Mount Carmel Parish - 322 Chestnut St., Dunmore, PA 18512 t) 570-346-7429 info@olmcparish.us sites.google.com/view/dunmmorehome/home Rev. John A. Doris, Pst.; Rev. Kevin P. Mulhern, In Res.; Dcn. Andrew Fazio Sr., Pst. Min./Coord.; Lisa Murphy, CRE; CRP Stds.: 197

Saint Mary of Mount Carmel Elementary School - 325 Chestnut St., Dunmore, PA 18512 t) 570-346-4429 cjslcd@gmail.com Kathleen Hubert, Prin.;

DUPONT

Sacred Heart of Jesus - 215 Lackawanna Ave., Dupont, PA 18641 t) 570-654-3713 shojesuschurch@gmail.com www.sacredheartdupont.com Rev. Thomas J. Petro, Pst.; CRP Stds.: 53

DURYEA

Nativity of Our Lord Parish - 127 Stephenson St., Duryea, PA 18642 t) 570-457-3502 rectory@nativityduryea.org www.nativityduryea.org Rev. Michael M Bryant, Pst.; Dcn. Andre F. Kubacinski; CRP Stds.: 139

Holy Rosary - (Worship Site)

EAST STROUDSBURG

St. John's Church - 5171 Milford Rd., East Stroudsburg, PA 18302 t) 570-223-9144 stjohnchurchmain@gmail.com www.churchofstjohn.com Rev. Gregory A. Reichlen, Pst.; Dcn. Max Francois; CRP Stds.: 150

St. Matthew - 78 Ridgeway St., East Stroudsburg, PA 18301 t) 570-421-2342 rectory@ptd.net www.stmatthewspa.org Rev. Donald J. Williams, Pst.; Rev. Ryan P. Glenn, Assoc. Pst.; Rev. Jaime Restrepo, Assoc. Pst.; Rev. Msgr. John A. Bergamo, Pastor Emer.; Dcn. Luis Rivera; Dcn. Kevin L. Scheirer; CRP Stds.: 289

ELKLAND

St. Thomas the Apostle - 111 First St., Elkland, PA 16920 t) (814) 258-5121 ststhomascatherine@styn.rr.com Linked with Saint Peter's Parish, Wellsboro Rev. Jacek J. Bialkowski, Pst.;

St. Catherine of Siena - 146 Lincoln St., Westfield, PA 16950

EXETER

Saint Barbara Parish - 224 Memorial St., Exeter, PA 18643 t) 570-654-2103 stanthonyexeter@comcast.net Rev. Msgr. John J. Sempa, Pst.; Dcn. William A. Dervinis; Dcn. Walter G. Janoski;

St. Anthony of Padua - (Worship Site)

St. Cecilia - Closed Apr 2022 For sacramental records, contact St. Barbara Parish, Exeter.

FOREST CITY

Ascension Parish - 612 Hudson St., Forest City, PA 18421 t) 570-785-3838 apskdp@nep.net apskdp.org Linked with St. Katharine Drexel Parish, Pleasant Mount. Rev. Binesh Joseph Kanjirakattu, Par. Vicar; Rev. Arun Lakra, Pst.; CRP Stds.: 35

St. Joseph - 741 Delaware St., Forest City, PA 18421 (Worship Site)

FREELAND

Our Lady of the Immaculate Conception - 898 Centre St., Freeland, PA 18224 t) (570) 636-3035 ourladyfreeland@gmail.com Linkded with Good Shepherd Parish, Drums Rev. Rawel Toppo, Par. Vicar; Rev. Michael J. Kloton, Pst.;

FRIENDSVILLE

Saint Brigid Parish - 17 Cottage St., Friendsville, PA 18818; Mailing: PO Box 75, Friendsville, PA 18818 t) 570-553-2288 www.ourparishcommunity.com/ Rev. Kevin M. Miller, Pst.; Dcn. Paul J. Brojack; Dcn. Ronald Maida; CRP Stds.: 50

St. Augustine - 295 Church Rd., Brackney, PA 18812

St. Francis Xavier, Friendsville - 726 Main St., Friendsville, PA 18818 (Worship Site)

GILBERT

Our Lady Queen of Peace - 1402 Rte. 209, Gilbert, PA 18331; Mailing: P.O. Box 38, Brodheadsville, PA 18322 t) 610-681-6137 churchoffice@qopchurch.org www.qopchurch.org Rev. Robert J. Simon, Pst.; Dcn. Robert A. O'Connor Jr.; Dcn. Joseph P. Rodgers; CRP Stds.: 321

GLEN LYON

Corpus Christi - 31 S. Market St., Glen Lyon, PA 18617 (Merging of St. Adalbert, St. Denis & St. Michael's, Glen Lyon & St. Mary's, Wanamie. For inquiries for parish records, contact Corpus Christi.) Rev. Louis T. Kaminski, Pst.;

GOULDSBORO

St. Rita - 512 Main St., Gouldsboro, PA 18424; Mailing: PO Box 537, 512 Main St, Gouldsboro, PA 18424 t) 570-842-4995 strcgouldsboro@gmail.com www.stritaspa.org Rev. J. Duane Gavitt, Pst.; Rev. Frederick J. Riegler, Sacr. Min.;

HANOVER TOWNSHIP

Exaltation of the Holy Cross - 420 Main Rd., Hanover Township, PA 18706-6094 t) 570-823-6242 exhc@aol.com www.exhc.org Linked with St. Robert Bellarmine, Wilkes-Barre. Rev. Richard J. Cirba, Pst.;

HARVEYS LAKE

Our Lady of Victory - 16 Second St., Harveys Lake, PA 18618 t) 570-639-1535 olvhl309@aol.com goholv.org Linked with Gate of Heaven, Dallas. Rev. Andrew S. Hvozdovic, Pst.; Dcn. John Jorda; CRP Stds.: 50

HAWLEY

Blessed Virgin Mary, Queen of Peace - 314 Chestnut Ave., Hawley, PA 18428 t) (570) 226-3183 parishsecretary@queenofpeacehawley.com Rev. Richard W. Beck, Pst.; Dcn. Matthew G. Lorent;

St. Veronica -

St. John Neumann - 705 Rte. 739, Hawley, PA 18428 t) 570-775-6791 sjnfin@ptd.net www.sjneumannchurch.com Linked with St. Ann, Shohola. Rev. Edward J. Casey, Pst.; Dcn. Henry J. Ernst; Dcn. Nicholas Ardito;

Good Shepherd - Rte. 402, Blooming Grove, PA 18428 Rev. Edward Casey, Pst.;

HAZELTON

Queen of Heaven, Hazleton - 750 N. Vine St., Hazelton, PA 18201 t) 570-454-8797 www.queenofheavenolg.com Rev. Anthony J. Generose, Pst.; Rev. Neftali Feliz Sena, Assoc. Pst.; Dcn. Robert A. Roman; CRP Stds.: 98

Our Lady of Grace - (Worship Site)

HAZLETON

Annunciation, Hazleton - 122 S. Wyoming St., Hazleton, PA 18201 t) 570-454-0212 stgabes@ptd.net holyannunciation.com Rev. Mariusz Beczek, O.S.J., Pst.; Rev. Victor Leon, O.S.J., Assoc. Pst.; CRP Stds.: 254

St. Gabriel - (Worship Site)

Church of the Most Precious Blood - 131 E. Fourth St., Hazleton, PA 18201 t) 570-454-8714 mpbhaz@ptd.net mpbhazleton.com Rev. Anthony J. Generose, Pst.; Rev. Neftali Feliz Sena, Assoc. Pst.;

SS. Cyril & Methodius, Hazleton - 604 N. Laurel St., Hazleton, PA 18201; Mailing: P.O. Box 2099, Hazleton, PA 18201 t) 570-454-0881 sjc2@ptd.net Rev. Michael J. Piccola, Pst.;

Holy Rosary - 240 S. Poplar St., Hazleton, PA 18201 t) 570-454-6693 hrosary@ptd.net Rev. Kenneth M. Seegar, Pst.; Rev. Wilfredo Cusicanqui, Assoc. Pst.; Dcn. Vincent M. Oberto; CRP Stds.: 46

HONESDALE

St. John the Evangelist - 414 Church St., Honesdale, PA 18431 t) 570-253-4561 t.parrish.stjohnshonesdale@verizon.net honesdalecatholic.com Rev. William J.P. Langan, Pst.; Dominic Sabi, Asst. Pastor; Anastasia Legg, DRE; CRP Stds.: 134

HUNLOCK CREEK

Our Lady of Mount Carmel - 2011 State Rte. 29, Hunlock Creek, PA 18621-4303 t) 570-477-5040 olmchc@gmail.com olmcsilkworth.com Rev. Brian F. Van Fossen, Pst.; Rev. James R. Nash, Pastor Emer.; Dcn. Eugene Blockus; CRP Stds.: 61

JERMYN

Sacred Hearts of Jesus & Mary, Jermyn - 624 Madison Ave., Jermyn, PA 18433-1697 t) (570) 876-1061 sachmary@echoes.net Rev. John C. Ruth, Pst.; Dcn. Patrick J. Massino;

Sacred Heart of Mary Church - (Worship Site)

JERSEY SHORE

Immaculate Conception of the Blessed Virgin Mary - 118 Kendall Ave., Jersey Shore, PA 17740; Mailing: 5973 Jacks Hollow Rd., Williamsport, PA 17702 t) 570-745-3301 icslloffice@comcast.net Linked with St. Luke, Jersey Shore. Rev. Bert S. Kozen, Pst.;

Mother of the Eucharist - 6100 Jacks Hollow Rd., Williamsport, PA 17702 t) 570-745-3334

JESSUP

Queen of Angels Parish - 320 First Ave., Jessup, PA 18434; Mailing: 605 Church St., Jessup, PA 18434 t) 570-489-2252 stjames-jessup@hotmail.com; queenofangelsparish@gmail.com Rev. Gerard M. McGlone, Pst.; Dcn. Gerard L. Carpenter;

St. Michael - (Worship Site)

KINGSTON

St. Ignatius Loyola, Kingston - 339 N. Maple Ave., Kingston, PA 18704 t) 570-288-6446 officemanager@stignatiuspa.com stignatiuspa.com Rev. Msgr. David L. Tressler, Pst.; Rev. Shawn M. Simchock, Assoc. Pst.; Dcn. Gerard Pernot; CRP Stds.: 146

St. Ann's - t) 570-288-5919 (Worship Site)

LAFLIN

St. Maria Goretti - 42 Redwood Dr., Laflin, PA 18702 t) 570-655-8956 42redwood@comcast.net www.stmariagoretti-laflin.org/ Rev. Alex J. Roche, Pst.; Dcn. Michael S. Imbrogno; Michelle Pinto, DRE; CRP Stds.: 77

LAKE ARIEL

St. Thomas More - 105 Gravity Rd., Lake Ariel, PA 18436; Mailing: P O Box 188, Lake Ariel, PA 18436 t) 570-698-5584 stthomasstmary@echoes.net www.stthomas-stmary.com Rev. Stephen K Bosomafi, Pst.; CRP Stds.: 72

St. Mary -

LAKE WINOLA

St. Mary of the Lake - 1872 Dalton Rd., Lake Winola, PA 18657; Mailing: P.O. Box 1, Lake Winola, PA 18657 t) 570-836-3275; 570-378-2181 saintmaryofthelake@frontier.com nativitystmary.org No longer linked with Tunkhannock. Now linked with Nicholson (St. Patrick) & Dalton (Our Lady of the Abingtons) Rev. Arbogaste Satoun, Pst.; Dcn. Raymond A. Pieretti;

LARKSVILLE

St. John the Baptist - 126 Nesbitt St., Larksville, PA 18651 t) (570) 779-9620 Rev. Gerald J. Gurka, Pst.; Dcn. Frank H. Hine;

LUZERNE

Holy Family - 574 Bennett St., Luzerne, PA 18709 Rev. Jarrod Waugh, C.S.C., Admin.;

MANSFIELD

Holy Child - 240 S. Main St., Mansfield, PA 16933; Mailing: 237 S. Main St., Mansfield, PA 16933 Rev. Bryan B. Wright, Pst.;

St. Mary of Czestochowa Church - 138 St. Mary's St., Blossburg, PA 16912 (Worship Site)

St. Mary - Center St., Tioga, PA 16946

MATAMORAS

St. Joseph - 309 Ave. F, Matamoras, PA 18336 t) 570-491-2618 stjosephchurch@optonline.net Linked with St. Patrick, Milford. Rev. Joseph J. Manarchuck, Pst.;

Holy Family - Cemetery Rd., Mill Rift, PA 18340

MILDRED

Immaculate Heart of Mary Parish - 1 St. Francis Dr., Mildred, PA 18632; Mailing: 101 Churchill St., P.O. Box 307, Dushore, PA 18614-0307 t) 570-928-8865 ihmparish@ptd.net ihmdushore.com Rev. Thomas J. Major, Pst.;

St. Francis Xavier, Overton - (Worship Site)

Sacred Heart, Laporte - (Worship Site)

St. Francis of Assisi - (Worship Site)

St. Francis of Assisi - (Worship Site)

S. Philip and James Church-St. John Neumann Shrine - (Worship Site)

St. Basil the Great - (Worship Site)

MILFORD

St. Patrick - 111 E. High St., Milford, PA 18337; Mailing: P.O. Box W, Milford, PA 18337 linked with St. Joseph, Matamoras. Rev. Joseph J. Manarchuck, Pst.; Dcn. Thomas M. Spataro;

St. Vincent de Paul - 101 St. Vincent Dr., Dingman Township, Milford, PA 18337-9672 t) 570-686-4545 stvoff@ptd.net; svdfrjb@ptd.net stvdepaulchurch.org Rev. John B. Boyle, Pst.; Rev. Msgr. William P. Ward, Pastor Emer.; Rev. Paul M. Mullen, Pastor Emer.; Dcn. Joseph A. LaCorte; JoAnn Fay, Bus. Mgr.; CRP Stds.: 70

MOCANAQUA

St. Mary, Our Lady of Perpetual Help - 150 Main St., Mocanaqua, PA 18655; Mailing: 31 S. Market St., Glen Lyon, PA 18617 t) (570) 736-6372 Rev. Louis T. Kaminski, Pst.;

MONTOURSVILLE

Our Lady of Lourdes - 100 Walnut St., Montoursville, PA 17754; Mailing: 800 Mulberry St., Montoursville, PA 17754 t) 570-368-8598 parishoffice@ourladyoflourdesrcc.org Rev. Michael S. McCormick, Pst.; CRP Stds.: 91

MONTROSE

Holy Name of Mary - 278 S. Main St., Montrose, PA 18801 t) (570) 278-1504 Rev. Philip S. Rayappan, Pst.; CRP Stds.: 22

MOSCOW

St. Catherine of Siena - 220 Church St., Moscow, PA 18444; Mailing: P.O. Box 250, Moscow, PA 18444 t) 570-842-4561 parishoffice@northpoconocatholic.com www.northpoconocatholic.com Rev. Thomas M. Muldowney, Pst.;

MOUNTAIN TOP

St. Jude - 420 S. Mountain Blvd., Mountain Top, PA 18707 t) 570-474-6315 x221 www.stjc.org Linked with Our Lady Help of Christians, Dorrance. Rev. Joseph J. Evanko, Pst.; Rev. Philbert Takyi-Nketiah, Assoc. Pst.; Dcn. James T. Atherton; Dcn. Eugene J. Kovatch; Dcn. Joseph Chimola Jr.;

St. Jude Elementary School - (Grades PreK-8) 422 S.

Mountain Blvd., Mountain Top, PA 18707 t) 570-474-5803 efischer@sjspa.org Sr. Ellen Fischer, S.C.C., Prin.;

MUNCY

Resurrection - 75 Musser Ln., Muncy, PA 17756 t) 570-546-3900 resurrection@windstream.net www.resurrectiononline.net Rev. Sean G. Carpenter, Pst.; Jesse Martin, Pst. Assoc.;

NANTICOKE

Saint Faustina Kowalska Parish - 520 S. Hanover St., Nanticoke, PA 18634-2799 Rev. James R. Nash, Pst.; Rev. Shawn M. Simchock, Assoc. Pst.; Dcn. Florian G. Gyza; Dcn. Thaddeus Wadus;

Holy Trinity Church - (Worship Site)

St. Mary Czestochowa Church - 1030 S. Hanover St., Nanticoke, PA 18634

NICHOLSON

St. Patrick - 205 Main St., Nicholson, PA 18446; Mailing: P.O. Box 409, Nicholson, PA 18446 t) 570-942-6602 spolachurch@gmail.com www.spolachurch.weebly.com Linked with Our Lady of the Abingtons, Dalton. Rev. Arbogaste Satoun, Pst.; Dcn. Paul J. Brojack;

OLD FORGE

Prince of Peace Parish, Old Forge - 123 W. Grace St., Old Forge, PA 18518 t) 570-457-5900 ofparishes@comcast.net Rev. August A. Ricciardi, Pst.; CRP Stds.: 135

St. Mary Church - (Worship Site)

OLYPHANT

Holy Cross Parish - 200 Delaware Ave., Olyphant, PA 18447 t) 570-489-0752 sphg@verizon.net Rev. Scott P. Sterowski, Pst.;

St. Patrick Church - (Worship Site)

PECKVILLE

Sacred Heart of Jesus - 1101 Willow St., Peckville, PA 18452 t) (570) 383-3244 shoffice@shjpeck.org Rev. Andrew Kurovsky, Pst.; Rev. Msgr. Peter P. Madus, Pastor Emer.;

PITTSTON

St. John the Evangelist - 35 William St., Pittston, PA 18640 t) 570-654-0053 angelsofsje@aol.com; joannemchale@stjohnspittston.com www.stjohnspittston.com Rev. Joseph G. Elston, Pst.; Rev. Jackson Pinhero, Assoc. Pst.; Dcn. David E. Marx; Michael Sowa, Youth Min.; JoAnne McHale, DRE;

St. Joseph Marello Parish - 237 William St., Pittston, PA 18640 t) 570-654-6902 office@sjmparish.org Rev. Joseph G. Elston, Pst.; Rev. Jackson Pinheiro, O.S.J., Assoc. Pst.; Brandon Jopling, Pst. Assoc.; Alicia Hintze, DRE;

Our Lady of Mt. Carmel Church - (Worship Site)

Our Lady of the Eucharist Parish - 535 N. Main St., Pittston, PA 18640 t) 570-654-0263 olepittston@gmail.com www.eucharist-pittston.org Rev. Paul A. McDonnell, O.S.J., Sacr. Min.; Sr. Mary Ann Cody, I.H.M., Parish Life Coord.;

St. Mary, Help of Christians Church - (Worship Site)

PLAINS

SS. Peter and Paul - 13 Hudson Rd., Plains, PA 18705 Rev. John C. Lambert, Pst.;

PLEASANT MOUNT

St. Katharine Drexel Parish - 361 Great Bend Tpk., Pleasant Mount, PA 18453; Mailing: 612 Hudson St., Forest City, PA 18421 t) 570-785-3838 apskdp@nep.net apskdp.org Rev. Arun Lakra, Pst.; CRP Stds.: 45

St. James Church -

St. Juliana Church - 2048 Creamton Dr., Rte. 247, Rock Lake, PA 18453

PLYMOUTH

All Saints Parish - 66 Willow St., Plymouth, PA 18651 t) 570-779-5323 allsaints66@comcast.net www.allsaintsplymouth.com Rev. Gerald J. Gurka, Pst.;

Nativity B.V.M. Church - (Worship Site)

POCONO PINES

St. Maximilian Kolbe - 5112 Pocono Crest Rd., Pocono Pines, PA 18350; Mailing: PO Box O, Pocono Pines, PA 18350 t) 570-646-6424 stmaxkolbepoconos.org/ Rev. Paschal Mbagwu;

ROARING BROOK TWP.

St. Eulalia - 214 Blue Shutters Rd., Roaring Brook Twp., PA 18444 t) (570) 842-7656 Rev. David W. Cramer, Pst.; Ellen Dermody, Pst. Assoc.; CRP Stds.: 261

SAYRE

Epiphany Parish - 304 S. Elmer Ave., Sayre, PA 18840 t) 570-888-9641 x2 epiphanyparishoffice304@gmail.com thechurchoftheepiphany.com Rev. Daniel A. Toomey, Pst.; Rev. Shinu Vazhakkoottahil John (India), Par. Vicar; CRP Stds.: 23

Epiphany Elementary School - 627 Stephenson St., Sayre, PA 18840 t) 570-888-5802 kkathleen902@gmail.com Sr. Kathleen Kelly, I.H.M., Prin.;

Our Lady of Perpetual Help - Chapel Hill Rd., Ridgebury, PA 18831

SCOTT TWP.

St. John Vianney - 704 Montdale Rd., Scott Twp., PA 18447 t) 570-254-9502 ccrc402@comcast.net www.stjvp.org Rev. Michael J. Kirwin, Pst.; Dcn. Edwin L. Salva Sr.; JoAnn Wilbur, DRE;

Corpus Christi Church, Scott Twp. -

St. Pius X Church, Royal -

SCRANTON

St. Peter's Cathedral - 315 Wyoming Ave., Scranton, PA 18503 t) 570-344-7231 info@stpeterscathedral.org www.stpeterscathedral.org Most Rev. Joseph C. Bambera, In Res.; Rev. Jeffrey D. Tudgay, Pst.; Rev. Msgr. Dale R. Rupert, Pastor Emer.; Rev. John V. Polednak, In Res.; Rev. Gerald W. Shantillo, In Res.; Dcn. Edward R. Shoener; CRP Stds.: 6

Convent - 333 Wyoming, Scranton, PA 18503

St. Ann's Basilica Parish - 1250 St. Ann St., Scranton, PA 18504 t) 570-347-5166 info@stannsmonasterybasilica.org Rev. Richard Burke, C.P., Pst.; Rev. Sibi Padinjaredath, C.P., Assoc. Pst.; Dcn. Peter Lemoncelli;

Divine Mercy - 312 Davis St., Scranton, PA 18505 t) (570) 344-1724 nkatchur@divinemercyparish.us Restructured with Immaculate Conception, St. John the Baptist, Taylor; St. Mary Czestochowa, Moosic & St. Joseph, Minooka. Rev. Francis L. Pauselli, Pst.;

St. Joseph Church - (Worship Site)

St. Francis of Assisi - c/o 1217 Prospect Ave., Scranton, PA 18505-1716 t) 570-343-6420 Rev. Scott P. Sterowski, Pst.;

Immaculate Conception - 801 Taylor Ave., Scranton, PA 18510 Rev. Patrick J. McLaughlin, Pst.; Dcn. J. Patrick McDonald;

Saint John Neumann Parish - 633 Orchard St., Scranton, PA 18505 t) 570-344-6159 office@stjnparish.org www.stjnparish.org Linked with St. Paul of the Cross Parish, Scranton. Holy Name of Jesus Church, worship site of St. John Neumann was sold. Rev. Jonathan Kuhar, Pst.; Rev. Alfredo Rosario Paulino, Par. Vicar; Dcn. Albert V. Giacometti;

Nativity of Our Lord Church -

St. Lucy's - 949 Scranton St., Scranton, PA 18504 t) 570-347-9421 secretary@stlucy-church.org stlucy-church.org Rev. Samuel J. Ferretti, Pst.; Dcn. Carmine Mendicino, Contact; CRP Stds.: 15

Mary, Mother of God Parish - 316 William St., Scranton, PA 18508 t) 570-342-4881 frcyedwards@gmail.com; mmog.secretary@gmail.com www.marymotherofgodparish.org Rev. Cyril D. Edwards, Pst.; Rev. Martin J. Gaiardo, Pst. Assoc.; Dcn. Jan F. Mroz; Dcn. Joseph Marcellus; Sr. Therese Mary Dougherty, RCIA Coord.;

Holy Rosary Church - (Worship Site)

St. Michael's - 1703 Jackson St., Scranton, PA 18504 t) 570-961-1205 fsspscranton@gmail.com www.stmichaelsrcc.org Rev. Christopher Mahowald, FSSP, Pst.; Rev. Anthony Dorsa, FSSP, Admin. pro tem;

St. Patrick - 1403 Jackson St., Scranton, PA 18504 t) 570-344-2679 stpatrick_scr@yahoo.com Rev. Richard E. Fox, Pst.; CRP Stds.: 68

Scranton, Immaculate Heart of Mary - 1605 Oram St., Scranton, PA 18504

St. Paul - 1510 Penn Ave., Scranton, PA 18509 t) 570-961-1549 info@stpaulscranton.org stpaulscranton.org Rev. Msgr. Neil J. Van Loon, Pst.; Dcn. John Hanni; Rita Cicco, DRE; CRP Stds.: 75

Saint Paul of the Cross, Scranton - 1217 Prospect Ave., Scranton, PA 18505 t) 570-343-6420 sacredhearts@epix.net Linked with St. John Neumann Parish, Scranton Rev. Msgr. Joseph G. Quinn, Pst.; Rev. Jonathan Kuhar, Asst. Pastor;

SS. Peter and Paul - 1309 W. Locust St., Scranton, PA 18504 t) 570-343-7015 secretary.sspp@gmail.com Linked with St. Lucy, Scranton. Rev. Samuel J. Ferretti, Pst.; Dcn. Carmine Mendicino; CRP Stds.: 24

SHAVERTOWN

St. Therese - 64 Davis St., Shavertown, PA 18708 t) 570-696-1144 jpaisley@sttherese-shavertown.com stthereses-shavertown.com Linked with St. Frances Cabrini, Caverton Rev. James J. Paisley, Pst.; CRP Stds.: 322

SHOHOLA

St. Ann's - 125 Richardson Ave., Shohola, PA 18458 t) 570-832-4275 stann@ptd.net; marybajda@gmail.com www.stannshohola.org Linked with St. John Neumann, Lords Valley. Rev. Edward J. Casey, Pst.; Dcn. Joseph Connelly; Mary Bajda, DRE; CRP Stds.: 52

St. Mary of the Assumption -

Sacred Heart of Jesus -

STILLWATER

St. Martha - 260 Bonnieville Rd., Stillwater, PA 17878; Mailing: 150 Main St., Mocanaqua, PA 18655 Rev. Louis T. Kaminski, Pst.;

STROUDSBURG

St. Luke - 818 Main St., Stroudsburg, PA 18360 t) (570) 421-9097 office@churchofsaintluke.org Rev. Michael F. Quinnan, Pst.; Dcn. Thomas W. Hogan Jr.; Dcn. Philip F. Zimich;

SUSQUEHANNA

Most Holy Trinity Parish - 15 E. Church St., Susquehanna, PA 18847 t) (570) 853-4634 jointoffice3@gmail.com Worship sites are: St. John Evg., Susq; St. Lawrence, Great Bend, and St. Martin of Tours, Jackson Rev. Kevin M. Miller, Pst.; Rev. Andrew Amankwaa, Par. Vicar; Dcn. Paul J. Brojack; Dcn. Ronald Maida;

St. John the Evangelist - t) 570-853-4634

St. Lawrence - 380 Franklin St., Great Bend, PA 18821

St. Martin of Tours - 8175 State Rte. 492, Jackson, PA 18825 t) 570-853-4634

Capuchin Sisters of Nazareth St. Joseph Convent - 8175 State Rte. 492, Jackson, PA 18825

SWOYERSVILLE

St. Elizabeth Ann Seton Parish - 116 Hughes St., Swoyersville, PA 18704 t) 570-287-6624 setonpa@aol.com www.setonpa.com Rev. Joseph J. Pisaneschi, Pst.; Dcn. John B. Ziegler; CRP Stds.: 96

TANNERSVILLE

Our Lady of Victory - 327 Cherry Lane Rd., Tannersville, PA 18372; Mailing: P.O. Box 195, Tannersville, PA 18372 t) 570-629-4575 victory2@ptd.net olvchurch.com Rev. Richard E. Czachor, Pst.; CRP Stds.: 155

THROOP

Blessed Sacrament Parish - 215 Rebecca St., Throop, PA 18519 Rev. Scott P. Sterowski, Pst.;

St. Anthony Church - (Worship Site)

TOWANDA

SS. Peter and Paul - 106 Third St., Towanda, PA 18848 t) (570) 265-2113 stppp@yahoo.com Rev. Jose Joseph Kuriappilly, Pst.;

Immaculate Conception -

TUNKHANNOCK

Nativity of Blessed Virgin Mary - 99 E. Tioga St., Tunkhannock, PA 18657-0186; Mailing: P.O. Box 186, Tunkhannock, PA 18657-0186 t) 570-836-3275 saintnativity@gmail.com nativitystmary.org No longer linked with Lake Winola. Now linked with Meshoppen (St. Joachim) Rev. Patrick L. Albert, Pst.; Dcn.

Raymond A. Pieretti;

WAPWALLOPEN

Our Lady Help of Christians - 3529 St. Mary's Rd., (Dorrance), Wapwallopen, PA 18660-1901; Mailing: 3529 St. Mary's Rd., Wapwallopen, PA 18660-1901 t) 570-868-5855 stmarysdorrance@gmail.com www.stmarydorrance.org/ Linked with St. Jude, Mountaintop. Rev. Joseph J. Evanko, Pst.; Rev. Philbert Takyi-Nketiah, Assoc. Pst.;

WAYMART

St. Mary - 242 Carbondale Rd., Waymart, PA 18472; Mailing: P.O. Box 160, Waymart, PA 18472 t) 570-488-6440 stmarysway@echoes.net stmaryswaymart.com Dcn. Edward T. Kelly, Parish Life Coord.; Rev. Joseph S. Sitko, Sacr. Min.;

St. Patrick -

WELLSBORO

St. Peter's - 47 Central Ave., Wellsboro, PA 16901 t) 570-724-3371 stpch@ptd.net www.stpeterswellsboro.org Linked with Elkland (St Thomas the Apostle) Rev. Jacek J. Bialkowski, Pst.;

WEST HAZLETON

Holy Name of Jesus Parish - 213 W. Green St., West Hazleton, PA 18202 t) 570-454-3933 holynameparish@ptd.net Rev. Kenneth M. Seegar, Pst.; Rev. Wilfredo Milan Cusicanqui, Assoc. Pst.; Dcn. Vincent M. Oberto;

Transfiguration Church - (Worship Site)

WEST PITTSTON

Corpus Christi Parish - 605 Luzerne Ave., West Pittston, PA 18643 t) 570-654-2753 ccrectory@corpuschristinepa.com www.corpuschristinepa.com Immaculate Conception West Pittston & Church of the Holy Redeemer Rev. Msgr. John J. Sempa, Pst.; Dcn. James R. Meizanis; CRP Stds.: 120

Holy Redeemer - 2435 State Rte. 92, Falls, PA 18615

WEST WYOMING

Saint Monica Parish - 363 W. 8th St., West Wyoming, PA 18644 Rev. Peter A. Tomczak, Pst.; Dcn. William G. Jenkins;

Our Lady of Sorrows Church, West Wyoming - (Worship Site)

WESTON

Sacred Heart - 554 Main St., Weston, PA 18256; Mailing: P.O. Box A, Weston, PA 18256 A worship site for St. John Bosco Parish, Conyngham Rev. Patrick D. McDowell, Pastor Emer.;

WHITE HAVEN

St. Patrick - 411 Allegheny St., White Haven, PA 18661 t) 570-443-9944 office@stpatrickswhitehaven.org www.stpatrickswhitehaven.org/ Rev. Michael J. Kloton, Admin.; Rev. Peter J. O'Rourke, Sacr. Min.; Rev. Michael Piccola, Priest Moderator; Mary Anne Malone, Parish Life Coord.;

WILKES-BARRE

St. Andrew Parish - 316 Parrish St., Wilkes-Barre, PA 18702 t) 570-823-1948; (570) 822-8330 stbonstpat@verizon.net standrewwilkesbarre.org Rev. Joseph A. Kearney, Sacr. Min.; Rev. James E. McGahagan, Pastor Emer.; Dcn. William F. Behm, Parish Life Coord.; CRP Stds.: 36

St. Patrick Church, Wilkes-Barre - (Worship Site)

St. Nicholas - 226 S. Washington St., Wilkes-Barre, PA 18701-2897 t) (570) 823-7736 stnicholas@stnicholaswb.org Rev. Joseph D. Verespy, Pst.; Rev. Mark J. DeCelles, Asst. Pastor; Rev. Fidel Ticona, C.S.C., Assoc. Pst.; Dcn. Michael Golubiewski; James McDermott, DRE;

Convent - 254 S. Washington St., Wilkes-Barre, PA 18701

Our Lady of Fatima Parish - 134 S. Washington St., Wilkes-Barre, PA 18701; Mailing: P.O. Box 348, Wilkes-Barre, PA 18701 t) (570) 823-4168 olfstmarys@aol.com Rev. Joseph D. Verespy, Pst.; Rev. Mark J. DeCelles, Asst. Pastor; Rev. Fidel Ticona, C.S.C., Asst. Pastor; Dcn. Joseph Sudano; Dcn. Leo R. Thompson;

St. Mary of the Immaculate Conception - (Worship Site)

Our Lady of Hope Parish - 40 Park Ave., Wilkes-Barre, PA 18702 t) 570-824-7832 Rev. John S. Terry, Pst.; Dcn. Joseph F. DeVizia; Rev. Richard G. Ghezzi, In Res.;

Maternity of the Blessed Virgin Mary Church - (Worship Site)

St. Robert Bellarmine Parish - 143 W. Division St., Wilkes-Barre, PA 18706 t) 570-823-3791 x2 stalschurch@staloysiuswb.com www.stalschurchwb.com Linked with Exaltation of the Holy Cross, Hanover Twp. Rev. Richard J. Cirba, Pst.; Dcn. Raymond J. Lenahan;

St. Aloysius Church - (Worship Site)

WILLIAMSPORT

St. Ann - 1220 Northway Rd., Williamsport, PA 17701 t) 570-322-5935 office@stannrcc.org; dre@stannrcc.org www.stannrcc.org Rev. John J. Chmil, Pst.;

St. Boniface - 326 Washington Blvd., Williamsport, PA 17701 t) 570-326-1544 stboniface@comcast.net stbonifacecatholic.com Linked with St. Lawrence, South Williamsport. Rev. Glenn E. McCreary, Pst.; Rev. Robert J. Antonelli, Pst. Assoc.; CRP Stds.: 50

St. Joseph the Worker - 711 W. Edwin St., Williamsport, PA 17701 t) 570-323-9456 office@sjwparish.com sjwparish.com Rev. David W. Bechtel, Pst.; Dcn. Stephen B. Frye; Makenzie Conner, Youth Min.; Caleb Cochran, DRE;

Annunciation Church - 702 W 4th St., Williamsport, PA 17701

St. Lawrence - 821 W. Central Ave., Williamsport, PA 17702; Mailing: 326 Washington Blvd, Williamsport, PA 17701 t) 570-326-1544 stboniface@comcast.net stlawrencecatholic.com Linked with St. Boniface, Williamsport. Rev. Glenn E. McCreary, Pst.; Rev. Robert J. Antonelli, Assoc. Pst.; CRP Stds.: 20

St. Luke - c/o Immaculate Conception, 5973 Jacks Hollow Rd., Williamsport, PA 17702 linked with Immaculate Conception of the Blessed Virgin Mary, Bastress. Rev. Bert S. Kozen, Pst.;

WYALUSING

Our Lady of Perpetual Help Parish - 245 State St., Wyalusing, PA 18853 t) (570) 746-1006 olophparish@gmail.com Linked with Towanda, SS. Peter & Paul; no longer linked with Meshoppen Rev. Edward L. Michelini, Admin.;

St. Joachim Church - Sterling St., Meshoppen, PA 18630

St. Mary of the Assumption Church -

WYOMING

St. Frances Cabrini - 585 Mt. Olivet Rd., Kingston Twp., Wyoming, PA 18644-9333 t) 570-696-3737 sfcbs@comcast.net Linked with St. Therese, Shavertown PA. Rev. James J. Paisley, Pst.;

SCHOOLS: PRESCHOOL THRU HIGH SCHOOL

SCHOOLS

COMMONWEALTH OF PENNSYLVANIA

CLARKS GREEN

Our Lady of Peace Elementary School - (DIO) (Grades PreK-8) 410 N. Abington Rd., Clarks Green, PA 18411 t) 570-587-4152 olpeaceschool@comcast.net Ann D'Arienzo, Prin.; Stds.: 322; Lay Tchrs.: 27

DUNMORE

Saint Mary of Mount Carmel Elementary School - (DIO) (Grades PreK-8) 325 Chestnut St., Dunmore, PA 18512 t) 570-346-4429; 570-346-4560 maryelizabeth.shattin@smmcdunmore.org www.smmcdunmore.org/ Maryelizabeth Shattin, Prin.; Stds.: 174; Lay Tchrs.: 14

DURYEA

Holy Rosary Elementary School - (DIO) (Grades PreK-8) 125 Stephenson St., Duryea, PA 18642 t) 570-457-2553 mskutack@holyrosaryduryea.org Melissa Skutack, Prin.; Stds.: 187; Lay Tchrs.: 14

EAST STROUDSBURG

Notre Dame Elementary School - (DIO) (Grades PreK-6) 60 Spangenburg Ave., East Stroudsburg, PA 18301 t) 570-421-3651 kiblerd@ndelementary.org www.ndelementary.org Sr. Dorothy Kibler, I.H.M., Prin.; Stds.: 198; Sr. Tchrs.: 1; Lay Tchrs.: 11

EXETER

Wyoming Area Catholic Elementary School - (DIO) (Grades PreK-8) 1690 Wyoming Ave., Exeter, PA 18643 t) 570-654-7982; 570-655-8082 erishcoff@wacsh.com wacsh.com Eileen Rishcoff, Prin.; Stds.: 140; Lay Tchrs.: 13

HAZLETON

Holy Family Academy - (DIO) (Grades PreK-8) 601 N. Laurel St., Hazleton, PA 18201 t) 570-455-9431 principal@holyfamilyacademy.info Thomas Kostic, Prin.; Stds.: 186; Lay Tchrs.: 15

JESSUP

La Salle Academy - (DIO) (Grades PreK-8) 309 First Ave., Jessup, PA 18434 t) 570-489-2010 lasalleacademy@lsaelementary.org Ellen M. Murphy, Prin.; Stds.: 211; Lay Tchrs.: 16

KINGSTON

Good Shepherd Academy - (DIO) (Grades PreK-8) 316 N. Maple Ave., Kingston, PA 18704 t) 570-718-4724 jjones@gsapa.org www.gsapa.org/ James A. Jones, Prin.; Stan Pavlick, Vice Principal; Stds.: 408; Sr. Tchrs.: 1; Lay Tchrs.: 28

MOUNTAIN TOP

Saint Jude Elementary School - (DIO) (Grades PreK-8) 422 S. Mountain Blvd., Mountain Top, PA 18707 t) 570-474-5803 efischer@sjspa.org www.sjspa.org Sr. Ellen Fischer, S.C.C., Prin.; Stds.: 270; Sr. Tchrs.: 3; Lay Tchrs.: 14

SAYRE

Epiphany Elementary School - (DIO) (Grades PreK-8) 627 Stevenson St., Sayre, PA 18840 t) 570-888-5802 epiphany-school@hotmail.com; kkathleen902@gmail.com www.epiphany-school.net/ Sr. Kathleen Kelly, I.H.M., Prin.; Stds.: 76; Sr. Tchrs.: 1; Lay Tchrs.: 8

SCRANTON

All Saints Academy - (DIO) (Grades PreK-8) 1425 Jackson St., Scranton, PA 18504 t) 570-343-8114 allsaintsacademy-scranton.org Brittany Haynos-Krupski, Prin.; Stds.: 239; Scholastics: 19; Sr. Tchrs.: 1; Lay Tchrs.: 18

Saint Clare/Saint Paul Elementary School (Main Campus) - (DIO) (Grades 3-8) 1527 Penn Ave., Scranton, PA 18509 t) 570-343-7880; 570-343-4485 kware@scspscranton.org Kara Ware, Prin.; Stds.: 180; Sr. Tchrs.: 1; Lay Tchrs.: 13

Saint Clare/Saint Paul Elementary School (Primary Campus) - (DIO) (Grades PreK-2) 2215 N. Washington Ave., Scranton, PA 18509 t) 570-343-2790 kware@scspscranton.org Kara Ware, Prin.; Stds.: 179; Lay Tchrs.: 13

NativityMiguel Scranton - (PRV) (Grades 5-8) 2300 Adams Ave., Scranton, PA 18509 t) 570-955-5176 abzdick@nmscranton.org Timothy P Casey, Prin.; Ron Prislupski, Pres.; Stds.: 67; Lay Tchrs.: 4

TOWANDA

Saint Agnes Elementary School - (DIO) (Grades PreK-6) 102 Third St., Towanda, PA 18848 t) 570-265-6803 kelly.wilhelm@stagneselem.com; sa123@epix.net www.stagneselem.com Kelly Wilhelm, Prin.; Stds.: 112; Lay Tchrs.: 10

WILKES-BARRE

Saint Nicholas/Saint Mary Elementary School - (DIO) (Grades PreK-8) 242 S. Washington St., Wilkes-Barre, PA 18701 t) 570-823-8089 ctigue@snsmschoolwb.com www.snsmschoolwb.com Christopher Tigue, Prin.; Stds.: 283; Lay Tchrs.: 23

WILLIAMSPORT

Saint John Neumann Regional Academy - (DIO) (Grades PreK-5) 710 Franklin St., Williamsport, PA 17701

t) 570-326-3738; 570-326-7385 amcnamee@sjnra.org Alisia McNamee, Prin.; Stds.: 164; Lay Tchrs.: 10

HIGH SCHOOLS

COMMONWEALTH OF PENNSYLVANIA

DUNMORE

Holy Cross High School - (DIO) (Grades 9-12) 501 E. Drinker St., Dunmore, PA 18512 t) 570-346-7541; 570-346-7542 btolerico@hchspa.org Rev. Cyril D. Edwards, Chap.; Benjamin Tolerico, Prin.; Cathy Chiumento, Vice Principal; Stds.: 330; Lay Tchrs.: 30

EAST STROUDSBURG

Notre Dame Jr./Sr. High School - (DIO) (Grades 7-12) 60 Spangenburg Ave., East Stroudsburg, PA 18301 t) 570-421-0466 principal@ndhigh.org www.ndhigh.org Rev. Ryan Glenn, Chap.; Jeffrey N. Lyons, Prin.; Debra Krogulski, DRE; Stds.: 215; Lay Tchrs.: 24

SCRANTON

***Scranton Preparatory School** - (PRV) (Grades 9-12) 1000 Wyoming Ave., Scranton, PA 18507 t) 570-941-7737 www.scrantonprep.com Private Jesuit Catholic High School. Kristin Cupillari, Prin.; Stds.: 653; Pr. Tchrs.: 3; Lay Tchrs.: 47

WILKES-BARRE

Holy Redeemer High School - (DIO) (Grades 9-12) 159 S. Pennsylvania Blvd., Wilkes-Barre, PA 18701 t) 570-829-2424 ddougherty@holyredeemerhs.org www.holyredeemerhs.org/ Rev. J. Duane Gavitt, Chap.; Doreen Dougherty, Prin.; Cody Opalka, Vice Prin.; Stds.: 452; Sr. Tchrs.: 2; Lay Tchrs.: 39

WILLIAMSPORT

Saint John Neumann Regional Academy High School Campus - (DIO) (Grades 6-12) 901 Penn St., Williamsport, PA 17701 t) 570-323-9953 amcnamee@sjnra.org Rev. Bert S. Kozen, Chap.; Alisia McNamee, Prin.; Eugene Kurzejweski, Admin.; Shawn Moore, DRE; Stds.: 91; Lay Tchrs.: 15

INSTITUTIONS LOCATED IN DIOCESE

CEMETERIES [CEM]

CARVERTON

Mount Olivet - 612 Mt. Olivet Rd., Carverton, PA 18644; Mailing: 300 Wyoming Ave., Scranton, PA 18503 t) 570-696-3636; 570-558-4310 jgabriesheski@dioceseofscranton.org; mmikolosko@dioceseofscranton.org Joseph Dunda, Admin.;

DRUMS

Calvary - Rte. 309, 49 S. Hunter Hwy., Drums, PA 18222; Mailing: P.O. Box 485, Drums, PA 18222 t) 570-788-2150 calvary-cem@dioceseofscranton.org; mfoley@dioceseofscranton.org Joseph Dunda, Admin.;

MONTOURSVILLE

Resurrection - 4323 Lycoming Mall Dr., Montoursville, PA 17754; Mailing: P.O. Box 12, Montoursville, PA 17754 t) 570-368-2727 jdunda@dioceseofscranton.org Joseph Dunda, Admin.;

MOSCOW

St. Catherine - Main St., Rte. 435, Moscow, PA 18444; Mailing: P.O. Box 114, Moscow, PA 18444 t) 570-842-8411 jdunda@dioceseofscranton.org Joseph Dunda, Admin.;

OLD FORGE

Holy Cross - Oak & Keyser Ave., Old Forge, PA 18518 t) 570-347-9251 jdunda@dioceseofscranton.org Dominic Rinaldi, Dir.;

SCRANTON

Cathedral - 1708 Oram St., Scranton, PA 18504; Mailing: 300 Wyoming Ave., Scranton, PA 18503 t) 570-207-2209 cathedral-cem@dioceseofscranton.org; kbeck@dioceseofscranton.org Joseph Dunda, Admin.;

COLLEGES & UNIVERSITIES [COL]

DALLAS

Misericordia University - 301 Lake St., Dallas, PA 18612 t) 570-674-6314 csomers@misericordia.edu www.misericordia.edu Conference for Mercy Higher Education Mid-Atlantic Region Division, Dallas, PA. Dr. Daniel J. Myers, Pres.; Kathleen A. Foley, Vice. Pres.; Rev. Alex J. Roche, Chap.; Susan Helwig, Vice Pres. Instl. Advancement; Barbara Loftus, Vice Pres. Planning, Assessment & Research; Sr. Jean Messaros, R.S.M., Vice Pres. Mission Integration;

SCRANTON

Marywood University - 2300 Adams Ave., Scranton, PA 18509 t) 570-348-6211; (570) 961-4549 (HR) persico@marywood.edu; kapadden@marywood.edu www.marywood.edu Sisters, Servants of the Immaculate Heart of Mary Sr. Mary Persico, I.H.M., Pres.; Dr. Christina A. Clark, Provost; Dr. Jeffrey Johnson, Dean, Liberal Arts and Sciences; Sr. Catherine Luxner, I.H.M., Vice President for Mission Services; William A McDonald, Vice President for Finance and Administration; Ross Novak, Dean of Students; Mary Theresa G. Paterson, Secretary of the University and General Counsel; Robert Piurowski, Vice President for Enrollment Management and Student Services; James J. Sullivan, Dean, Professional Studies; Wendy Yankelitis, Vice President of Operations; Shelby Yeager, Interim Dean, Health and Human Services; Dr. Renee Zehel, Vice President for University Advancement; Stds.: 2,606; Lay Tchrs.: 141; Sr. Tchrs.: 4

The University of Scranton - 800 Linden St., Scranton, PA 18510 t) 570-941-7400 (Main University); 570-941-6245 (Jesuit Business Office) www.scranton.edu Rev. John J. Begley, S.J., Prof.; Rev. Timothy J. Cadigan, S.J., Prof.; Rev. Jack Dennis, S.J., Campus Min.; Rev. James F. Duffy, S.J., Supr.; Rev. Herbert B. Keller, S.J., Prof.; Rev. John J. Levko, S.J., Prof.; Rev. Joseph Marina, S.J, Pres.; Rev. Leonard A. Martin, S.J., Pst.; Rev. Bernard R. McIlhenny, S.J., In Res.; Rev. Ronald H. McKinney, S.J., Prof.; Rev. J. Patrick Mohr, S.J., Prof.; Rev. Eugene A. Nolan, S.J., Admin.; Rev. Angelo Rizzo, S.J., Pres.; Rev. James D. Redington, S.J., Prof.; Rev. Joseph C. Sands, S.J., In Res.; Rev. Daniel Sweeney, S.J., Prof.; Stds.: 4,731; Lay Tchrs.: 412; Pr. Tchrs.: 8

WILKES-BARRE

***King's College** - 133 N. River St., Wilkes-Barre, PA 18711 t) 570-208-5900 www.kings.edu Rev. Thomas P. Looney, C.S.C., Pres.; Rev. Russell K. McDougall, C.S.C., Superior, Holy Cross Community; Rev. Charles J. Kociolek, C.S.C., Chap.; Rev. Daniel J. Issing, C.S.C., Prof.; Bro. James R. Henke, CSC, Camp Min; Bro. Stephen J. LaMendola, C.S.C., Prof.; Rev. Thomas J. O'Hara, C.S.C., Acad Svcs; Bro. John Paige, CSC, In Res.; Rev. Brogan C. Ryan, C.S.C., Dir. Camp. Min.; Rev. Michael B. Wurtz, CSC, Prof.; Daniel T. Cebrick, Registrar; Chris Dearth, Vice. Pres.; Joseph Evan, Provost & Vice Pres. Academic Affairs; Janet Kobylski, CFO; Anitra McShea, Vice. Pres.; Frederick A. Pettit, Vice Pres. Instl. Advancement; Stds.: 2,397; Bro. Tchrs.: 1; Lay Tchrs.: 131; Pr. Tchrs.: 2

CONVENTS, MONASTERIES, AND RESIDENCES FOR WOMEN [CON]

DALLAS

Mercy Center (Convent) - 301 Lake St., Dallas, PA 18612; Mailing: P.O. Box 370, Dallas, PA 18612 t) 570-675-2131 www.mcnu.org Rev. Carmen J. Perry, Chap.; Catrina Flach, Admin.;

Sisters of Mercy of the Americas, Mid-Atlantic Community - 301 Lake St., Dallas, PA 18612-0369; Mailing: P.O. Box 369, Dallas, PA 18612-0369 t) 570-675-2048 ddellaporta@mercymidatlantic.org www.mercymidatlantic.org Sr. Patricia Vetrano, R.S.M., Pres.; Srs.: 75

SCRANTON

Immaculate Heart of Mary Center - 2300 Adams Ave., Scranton, PA 18509 t) 570-342-6850 communications@sistersofihm.org www.sistersofihm.org Sisters, Servants of the Immaculate Heart of Mary. Sr. Kathryn Clauss, I.H.M., Pres.; Srs.: 272

Pascucci Family Our Lady of Peace Residence - 2300 Adams Ave., Scranton, PA 18509 t) 570-346-5423 coughlinj@sistersofihm.org Sr. Jean Coughlin, I.H.M., Admin.; Sr. Mary Kathleen Faliskie, I.H.M., Admin.; Sr. Kate McCarron Sr., Admin.; Mary Theresa Malando, Admin.; Srs.: 85

TUNKHANNOCK

Capuchin Sisters of Nazareth - 215 Wellwood Dr., Tunkhannock, PA 18657 t) 570-836-2737 heather-betts@dioceseofscranton.org Sr. Theresa May, Supr.; Srs.: 5

ENDOWMENTS / FOUNDATIONS / TRUSTS [EFT]

SCRANTON

St. Ann's Foundation - 1239 St. Ann's St., Scranton, PA 18504 t) 570-347-5691 Rev. Richard Burke, C.P., Exec.;

I.H.M. Congregation Charitable Trust - 2300 Adams Ave., Scranton, PA 18509 t) 570-342-6850 jordant@sistersofihm.org Congregation of the Sisters, Servants of the Immaculate Heart of Mary. Sr. Ellen Maroney, I.H.M., Pres.;

Sisters of IHM Foundation - 2300 Adams Ave., Scranton, PA 18509 t) 570-346-5431 bubsera@sistersofihm.org www.sistersofihm.org Sr. Ann Monica Bubser, I.H.M., Exec.;

HOSPITALS / HEALTH SERVICES [HOS]

MUNCY

Muncy Valley Hospital - 215 E. Water St., Muncy, PA 17756 t) 570-546-8282 jacobsta@upmc.edu www.upmc.com/locations/hospitals/muncy Sr. Teresa Ann Jacobs, SCC, Dir.;

WILLIAMSPORT

Divine Providence Hospital of the Sisters of Christian Charity - 1100 Grampian Blvd., Williamsport, PA 17701 t) (570) 326-8000 jacobsta@upmc.edu Sr. Teresa Ann Jacobs, Dir.;

Sisters of Christian Charity Healthcare Corporation - 1100 Grampian Blvd., Williamsport, PA 17701 t) 570-320-7658 tajacobs@scceast.org www.susquehannahealth.org Sr. Teresa Ann Jacobs, S.C.C., Dir.;

MISCELLANEOUS [MIS]

DALLAS

Mercy Consultation Center - 301 Lake St., Dallas, PA 18612-7752; Mailing: P.O. Box 370, Dallas, PA 18612-0370 t) 570-675-2284 mercyconsul3@epix.net Sr. Mary Helen Nugent, RSM, Exec. Dir.;

NANTICOKE

People of God Community of Northeastern PA - 151 Old Newport St., Nanticoke, PA 18634-1300 t) 570-735-2599 jimmyg@epix.net James Gialanella, Pres.;

PITTSTON

The Gabriel House - 13 William St., Pittston, PA 18640 t) 570-602-9796 bkuprionas@csswb.org Transitional housing facility for women and women with young children. Joseph Mahoney, Admin.;

SCRANTON

African Sisters Education Collaborative (ASEC) - Marywood University-Emmanuel Hall, 2300 Adams Ave., Scranton, PA 18509 t) 570-340-6089 executivedirector@asec-sldi.org asec-sldi.org/ Sr. Mary Cecilia Draru, LSMIG, Exec. Dir.;

***Aid to the Church in Russia** - 300 Wyoming Ave., Scranton, PA 18503-1279 t) 570-207-2216 Rev. Thomas M. Muldowney, Dir.;

St. Anthony's Haven - 409-411 Olive St., Scranton, PA 18509 t) 570-342-1295 x204 ghallinan@cssresidential.org Men's & Women's Shelter. Joseph Mahoney, Exec.;

St. James Manor - 600 Wyoming Ave., Scranton, PA 18509 Supportive Housing Program.

Diocesan Cemeteries Office - 300 Wyoming Ave., Scranton, PA 18503 t) 570-558-4310 dominic-rinaldi@dioceseofscranton.org Please contact Joseph Dunda for any cemetery-related questions Dominic Rinaldi, Dir.;

St. Francis of Assisi Kitchen - 500 Penn Ave., Scranton, PA 18509 t) 570-342-5556 jmahoney@dioceseofscranton.org www.stfranciskitchen.com Robert Williams, Exec. Dir.;

Friends of the Poor - 2300 Adams Ave., Scranton, PA 18509 t) 570-340-6086 friendsofthepoor@fotp-ihm.org www.friendsofthepoorscranton.com Emergency Relief for the Poor Meghan Loftus, CEO;

WILKES-BARRE

Project REMAIN - 215 High St., Apt. 100, Wilkes-Barre, PA 18701 t) 570-829-5373 kkurdziel@dioceseofscranton.org Service for the elderly and the needy residents in the High Rises. Sr. Imelda Sherrett, R.S.M., Dir.;

Project Remain Outreach (John B. McGlynn Center) - 72 Midland Ct., Wilkes-Barre, PA 18702 t) 570-824-8891 Outreach to low income families in the housing projects. Sr. Miriam Francis Stadulis, R.S.M., Dir.;

St. Vincent De Paul Kitchen - 39 E. Jackson St., Wilkes-Barre, PA 18701 t) 570-829-7796 amccawley@csswb.org Joseph Mahoney, Exec. Dir.; Mike Cianciotta, Dir.;

MONASTERIES AND RESIDENCES FOR PRIESTS AND BROTHERS [MON]

DUNMORE

Villa St. Joseph - 1600 Green Ridge St., Dunmore, PA 18509 t) 570-343-4791 michelle-brislin@dioceseofscranton.org Rev. Msgr. David A. Bohr, Rector; Rev. John T. Albosta, In Res.; Rev. Eugene R. Carr, In Res.; Rev. William R. Culnane, In Res.; Rev. Msgr. John A. Esseff, In Res.; Rev. Msgr. William J. Feldcamp, In Res.; Rev. Joseph A. Greskiewicz, In Res.; Rev. George A. Jeffrey, In Res.; Rev. Msgr. Joseph P. Kelly, In Res.; Rev. John J. Kilpatrick, In Res.; Rev. Edward P. Lyman, In Res.; Rev. Michael J. Rafferty, In Res.; Most Rev. James C. Timlin, In Res.; Rev. John J. Turi, In Res.; Rev. Msgr. William P. Ward, In Res.; Michelle Brislin, Admin.; Rev. Msgr. John J. Bendik, In Res.; Rev. Michael J. Zipay, In Res.; Priests: 30

LACEYVILLE

Franciscan Missionary Hermits of St. Joseph - 85 Joseph Dr., Laceyville, PA 18623 t) 570-869-2918 Rev. Pio Mandato, F.M.H.J.; Priests: 1

PITTSTON

Holy Spouses Province of the Oblates of St. Joseph - 1880 Hwy. 315, Pittston, PA 18640 t) 570-654-7542 osjseminary@comcast.net Rev. Paul A. McDonnell, O.S.J., Supr.; Priests: 5

S. ABINGTON TWP.

Priestly Fraternity of St. Peter (F.S.S.P.), North American District Headquarters - 450 Venard Rd., S. Abington Twp., PA 18411 t) 570-842-4000 info@fssp.com www.fssp.com Rev. William Lawrence, F.S.S.P., Supr.; Brs.: 185; Priests: 356

SCRANTON

Saint Ann's Passionist Monastery of Scranton PA - 1233 St. Ann St., Scranton, PA 18504 t) 570-347-5691 info@stannsmonasterybasilica.org; erhatigan@cpprov.org stannsmonasterybasilica.org/ Rev. Richard Burke, C.P., Rector; Rev. Robert Carbonneau, C.P., Mem.; Rev. Lee Havey, C.P., Mem.; Rev. Siby John, C.P., Par. Vicar; Rev. Francis Landry, C.P., Mem.; Rev. John Michael Lee, C.P., Mem.; Rev. Thomas McCann, C.P., Mem.; Rev. Micahel Salvagna, C.P., Mem.; Rev. Mark G. Ward, C.P., Mem.; Bro. Andre Mathieu, C.P., Asst. Supr.; Bro. Joseph Rogers, C.P., Mem.; Bro. Daniel Turner, C.P., Mem.; Brs.: 2; Priests: 9

NURSING / REHABILITATION / CONVALESCENCE / ELDERLY CARE [NUR]

ELMHURST TWP.

St. Mary's Villa Nursing Home - 516 St. Mary's Villa Rd., Elmhurst Twp., PA 18444 t) 570-842-7621 lkanarr@stmarysvilla.com Covenant Health Inc., Tewksbury, MA. Linda Kanarr, CEO;

St. Mary's Villa Residence - One Pioneer Pl., Elmhurst Twp., PA 18444 t) 570-842-5274 Covenant Health Inc., Tewksbury, MA Koryn Gallagher, Admin.;

SCRANTON

Home for the Aged, Little Sisters of the Poor, Inc. (Holy Family Residence) - 2500 Adams Ave., Scranton, PA 18509 t) 718-464-1800 provincialbklyn@littlesistersofthepoor.org www.littlesistersofthepoor.org Holy Family Residence is now known as Marywood Heights Little Sisters of the Poor, for tax purposes, list their original entity Sr. Alice Marie Jones, Prov.;

PRESCHOOLS / CHILDCARE CENTERS [PRE]

MOSCOW

St. Catherine Preschool - 220 Church St., Moscow, PA 18444; Mailing: P.O. Box 250, Moscow, PA 18444 t) 570-848-1258 parishoffice@northpoconocatholic.com Lisa Sgobba, Dir.; Stds.: 10; Lay Tchrs.: 3

WILKES-BARRE

Catholic Youth Center - 36 S. Washington St., Wilkes-Barre, PA 18701 t) 570-823-6121 wvcyc@epix.net Mark Soprano, Exec.; Rev. John S. Terry, Dir.; Stds.: 754; Lay Tchrs.: 15

RETREAT HOUSES / RENEWAL CENTERS [RTR]

NANTICOKE

Holy Family Spiritual Renewal Center - 151 Old Newport St., Nanticoke, PA 18634-1300 t) 570-735-2599; 570-735-1068 c) 570-704-9412 mjmhudak@verizon.net Michael J. Hudak, Dir.; Joyce A. Hudak, Mem.;

SEMINARIES [SEM]

PITTSTON

St. Joseph's Oblate Seminary - 1880 Hwy. 315, Pittston, PA 18640 t) 570-654-7542 Rev. Paul A. McDonnell, O.S.J., Rector; Rev. Alvaro de Oliveira Joaquim, O.S.J., Dir.; Rev. John D. Shearer, O.S.J., Dir.; Rev. Joseph D. Sibilano, O.S.J., Dir.; Rev. Raymond Tabon, O.S.J.;

SPECIAL CARE FACILITIES [SPF]

SCRANTON

St. Joseph's Center - 2010 Adams Ave., Scranton, PA 18509 t) 570-342-8379 kkowalchick@stjosephscenter.org www.stjosephscenter.org Sr. Maryalice Jacquinot, I.H.M., Pres.; Bed Capacity: 145; Asstd. Annu.: 155; Staff: 600

Lourdesmont Behavioral Health Services (Good Shepherd Youth & Family Services of NEPA) - 326 Adams Ave., Scranton, PA 18503 t) 570-348-6100; 314-381-3400 tponder@gspmna.org Sr. Dolores Kalina, Treas.;

Archdiocese of Seattle

(Archidioecesis Seattlensis)

MOST REVEREND PAUL D. ETIENNE, D.D., S.T.L.

Archbishop of Seattle; ordained June 27, 1992; appointed Bishop of Cheyenne October 19, 2009; installed December 9, 2009; appointed Archbishop of Anchorage October 4, 2016; installed November 9, 2016; appointed Coadjutor Archbishop of Seattle April 29, 2019; installed June 7, 2019; succeeded to the office of Archbishop September 3, 2019. Chancery Office: 710 9th Ave., Seattle, WA 98104.

Chancery Office: 710 9th Ave., Seattle, WA 98104. T: 206-382-4560
www.seattlearchdiocese.org
info@seattlearch.org

Square Miles 28,731.

Established May 31, 1850. Name Changed to Seattle, September 11, 1907. Created Archdiocese, June 23, 1951.

Comprises the Counties of Clallam, Clark, Cowlitz, Grays Harbor, Island, Jefferson, King, Kitsap, Lewis, Mason, Pacific, Pierce, San Juan, Skagit, Skamania, Snohomish, Thurston, Wahkiakum and Whatcom in the State of Washington.

Legal Title: "Corporation of the Catholic Archbishop of Seattle."

For legal titles of parishes and archdiocesan institutions, consult The Chancery.

Most Reverend Eusebio L. Elizondo, M.SP.S.
Auxiliary Bishop of Seattle; ordained August 18, 1984; appointed Auxiliary Bishop of Seattle and Titular Bishop of Acholla May 12, 2005; ordained June 6, 2005. Office: 710 9th Ave., Seattle, WA 98104. T: 206-274-3112.

Most Reverend Frank R. Schuster
Auxiliary Bishop of Seattle; ordained June 12, 1999; appointed Auxiliary Bishop of Seattle and Titular Bishop of Hirina March 8, 2022; ordained May 3, 2022. Office: 710 9th Ave., Seattle, WA 98104. T: 206-351-9769.

STATISTICAL OVERVIEW

Personnel	
Archbishops	1
Retired Archbishops	1
Auxiliary Bishops	2
Abbots	1
Retired Abbots	1
Priests: Diocesan Active in Diocese	90
Priests: Diocesan Active Outside Diocese	2
Priests: Diocesan in Foreign Missions	1
Priests: Retired, Sick or Absent	78
Number of Diocesan Priests	171
Religious Priests in Diocese	80
Total Priests in your Diocese	251
Extern Priests in Diocese	36
Ordinations:	
Diocesan Priests	3
Transitional Deacons	2
Permanent Deacons in Diocese	114
Total Brothers	8
Total Sisters	292
Parishes	
Parishes	136
With Resident Pastor:	
Resident Diocesan Priests	88
Resident Religious Priests	10
Without Resident Pastor:	
Administered by Priests	31
Administered by Lay People	7
Missions	26
New Parishes Created	2
Closed Parishes	6
Professional Ministry Personnel:	
Sisters	12
Lay Ministers	252
Welfare	
Catholic Hospitals	13
Total Assisted	2,000,000
Health Care Centers	2
Total Assisted	12,500
Homes for the Aged	15
Total Assisted	660
Specialized Homes	12
Total Assisted	405
Special Centers for Social Services	186
Total Assisted	75,886
Educational	
Diocesan Students in Other Seminaries	13
Total Seminarians	13
Colleges and Universities	2
Total Students	8,759
High Schools, Diocesan and Parish	5
Total Students	2,550
High Schools, Private	6
Total Students	3,415
Elementary Schools, Diocesan and Parish	56
Total Students	14,279
Elementary Schools, Private	5
Total Students	918
Catechesis/Religious Education:	
High School Students	4,681
Elementary Students	22,342
Total Students under Catholic Instruction	56,957
Teachers in Diocese:	
Priests	8
Brothers	7
Sisters	31
Lay Teachers	1,903
Vital Statistics	
Receptions into the Church:	
Infant Baptism Totals	1,568
Minor Baptism Totals	272
Adult Baptism Totals	144
Received into Full Communion	243
First Communions	2,556
Confirmations	2,843
Marriages:	
Catholic	240
Interfaith	104
Total Marriages	344
Deaths	835
Total Catholic Population	726,438
Total Population	6,053,656

LEADERSHIP

Chancery Office - t) 206-382-4886
Executive Assistant to Auxiliary Bishop Schuster - t) (253) 839-2320 x207 Mary Lezcano;
Vicar General - t) 206-274-3112 Most Rev. Eusebio L. Elizondo, M.Sp.S.;
Chancellor - t) 206-264-2089 Ben Altenhofen, Chancellor;
Chief Operating Officer - t) 206-382-4882 Caitlin Moulding;
Executive Assistant to the Archbishop - t) 206-382-4525 Angela Kison;
Executive Assistant to Auxiliary Bishop Elizondo - t) 206-274-3112 Fatima Maldonado;
Presbyteral Council - Rev. Chris Cartwright, SJ; Very Rev. Michael Dion; Most Rev. Paul D. Etienne;
College of Consultors - Very Rev. Gary M. Zender; Rev. Tuan Nguyen; Rev. Michael J. McDermott;
Deans -
Eastside - Very Rev. Nicholas F. Wichert, Dean;
North Seattle - Very Rev. William Heric;
Northern - Very Rev. Jeffrey Moore, Dean;
Olympic - Very Rev. Mark M. Kiszelewski, Dean;
Pierce - Very Rev. Gerald Burns, Dean;
Snohomish - Very Rev. Michael Dion, Dean;
South King - Very Rev. Thomas Belleque, Dean;
South Seattle - Very Rev. Matthew T. Oakland, Dean;
South Sound - Very Rev. Paul A. Kaech, Dean;
Southern - Very Rev. Gary F. Lazzeroni, Dean;

OFFICES AND DIRECTORS

Accounting Services - Mary Jo Gillis, Controller; Tom Grechis, Asst. Controller;
Administration and Finance, Office of - t) 206-382-4529 Megan Silvinski, CFO (megan.silvinski@seattlearch.org);
Archives and Records Management - t) 206-382-4352 Seth Dalby, Dir.;
Associated Catholic Cemeteries - t) 206-524-1451 Richard Peterson, Dir.;
Benefits Services - t) (206) 382-4566 Darlenn Sanford, Dir.;
Campaign for Human Development - t) 206-903-4619 Steve Homiak;
Catholic Archdiocese of Seattle Clergy Medical Plan Veba Trust - t) 206-382-2077 Most Rev. Paul D. Etienne; Very Rev. Anthony E. Bawyn, Chair; Darlenn Sanford;
Catholic Relief Services - t) 206-382-4582; 800-869-7028 (Toll Free)
Catholic Youth Organization Athletics - t) 206-274-3128 Kara Stranski, Dir.;
Catholic Youth Organization Camps - t) 425-829-5644 Shaune Randles, Dir.;
Communications, Office of - t) 800-473-5641 (Toll Free); 206-382-4862 Helen McClenehan, Chief Communications Officer;
Magazine "Northwest Catholic" - t) 206-382-4870
Criminal Justice Ministry Services - t) 206-382-4847 Joe Cotton, Dir.;
Faith Formation - t) 800-950-4970 (Toll Free); 206-654-4644 Carlos Carillo, Dir.;
Deacon Services - t) 206-382-1477 Lorrie Conway;
Due Process - Very Rev. Anthony E. Bawyn, Contact;
Hispanic/Latino Ministry Services - t) 206-382-4846; 800-465-6862 x4825 (Toll Free) Edwin Ferrera, Dir.;
Hospital and Healthcare Ministry - t) 206-382-4847 Joe Cotton, Dir.;
Human Resources - t) 206-382-4570; 800-261-4749 (Toll Free) Jeff Pixler, Chief Human Resources Officer;
Inclusion Ministry and Mental Health - t) 206-382-4852 Joe Cotton, Dir.;
Information Technology & Services - t) 206-382-4282 Tom Martin, CIO;
Library Media Center - Lisa Hillyard;
Liturgy - t) 206-654-4652; 800-473-5657 (Toll Free) Corrina Laughlin, Liturgy Consultant; Jennifer Day, Coord.;
Marriage and Family Life - t) 206-382-4864 Dcn. Eric Paige, Dir.;
Multicultural Ministries - t) 800-465-6862 (Toll Free); 206-382-4828 Dcn. Carl Chilo, Dir.;
Office of Catholic Schools - t) 800-473-5651 (Toll Free); 206-382-4861 Nicholas Ford, Supt. (nford@olfatima.org);
Parish Financial Services - Scott Bader, Dir.;
Parish Stewardship - Steve Homiack, Dir.;
Immigration and Refugee - t) 206-382-4847; 800-465-6862 (Toll Free) Chris Koehler, Dir.;
Pastoral Outreach Coordinator - Denise Aubuchon (hotline@seattlearch.org);
Payroll Services Office - t) 206-274-7667 Gloria Ruiz, Payroll Mgr.;
Planned Giving - t) 800-752-5902 (Toll Free); (206) 382-4563
Planning and Mission Effectiveness - t) 206-274-7690 Tim Hunt, Exec.;
Priests' Pension Plan - t) 206-903-4618 Most Rev. Paul D. Etienne; Very Rev. Anthony E. Bawyn, Chair; Steven Treperinas;
Propagation of the Faith, Society for the - t) 206-903-4619 Steve Homiak, Dir.;
Property and Construction Services - Edward Foster, Dir.;
Religious Communities - t) 206-382-4829 Sr. Sharon Park, O.P., Dir.; Sr. Sharon Casey, O.P., Dir.;
Seminarian Services - Rev. Justin Ryan, Dir.;
Stewardship and Development Department - t) 206-382-4563 April Collier, Exec. Dir.;
Vicar for Clergy, Office of - t) 206-382-7317; 800-809-4919 (Toll Free) Very Rev. Gary M. Zender; Nicholas Schoen, Chief of Staff;
Vocations - t) 206-387-4880 Rev. Justin Ryan, Dir.;
Young Adult Ministry - t) 206-382-4963
Youth Ministry - t) 206-274-3175 Kimberly Abadir, Dir.;

ADVISORY BOARDS, COMMISSIONS, COMMITTEES, AND COUNCILS

Archdiocesan Building Commission - t) 206-382-4529 Dennis Lehtinen, Chair;
Archdiocesan Finance Council - t) 206-382-4529 Megan Silvinski, CFO (megan.silvinski@seattlearch.org); Dave Boitano, Chair;
Parish Revolving Fund Commission - t) 206-382-4529 Megan Silvinski, CFO (megan.silvinski@seattlearch.org);

TRIBUNAL

Adjunct Judicial Vicars - Most Rev. Eusebio L. Elizondo, M.Sp.S.; Rev. Paul R. Pluth;
Defenders of the Bond - Karen S. Giffin; Roberta Small; Rev. Robert D. Tuner;
Director - Sr. Carolyn A. Roeber, O.P.;
Judges - Margaret Romano-Hogan; Very Rev. Anthony E. Bawyn; James L. Brooks;
Judicial Vicar - t) 206-382-4830 Very Rev. Anthony E. Bawyn;
Notaries - Christina Machnik; Ligia Mahoney; Noemi Reyes;

PARISHES, MISSIONS, AND CLERGY

STATE OF WASHINGTON

ABERDEEN

St. Mary - 306 E. Third St., Aberdeen, WA 98520 t) 360-532-8300; 360-532-8300 x110 (CRP) stmary@ghcatholic.org Rev. Navykumar Thomas, Par. Vicar; Theresa Wright, Pst. Min./Coord.; Rev. Timothy W. Ilgen, Priest Moderator; Rev. Marcos Villanueva, Parish Priest; Rev. Jaya Kumar Embeti, Par. Vicar;
St. Mary School - (Grades PreSchool-8) 518 N. H St., Aberdeen, WA 98520 t) 360-532-1230 Nicole Franson, Prin.;
St. Paul - ; Mailing: P.O. Box 332, Westport, WA 98585

ANACORTES

St. Mary - 4001 St. Mary's Dr., Anacortes, WA 98221 t) 360-293-2101 admin@stmaryanacortes.org Rev. Mel Strazicich, Pst.; Dcn. Lyle Kendall;

ARLINGTON

Immaculate Conception - 1200 E. Fifth St., Arlington, WA 98223; Mailing: PO Box 69, Arlington, WA 98223 t) 360-435-8565 x13 (CRP); 360-435-8565 kkichlinedre@comcast.net; icc-sjv@comcast.net www.stillycatholic.org Rev. Tyler Y. Johnson, Priest Admin.;
St. John Mary Vianney - 1150 Riddle St., Darrington, WA 98241

AUBURN

Holy Family - 505 17th St., S.E., Auburn, WA 98002 t) 253-833-5130 cbanning@holyfamilyauburn.org Rev. R. Roy C. Baroma, Pst.; Dcn. Richard Werner;
Holy Family School - (Grades PreK-8) t) 253-833-8688 Daniel Hill, Prin.;

BAINBRIDGE ISLAND

St. Cecilia - 1310 Madison Ave. N., Bainbridge Island, WA 98110 t) 206-842-3594 x102 (CRP); 206-842-3594 secretary@saintcparish.org Very Rev. Mark M. Kiszelewski, Pst.;
St. Cecilia School - (Grades PreSchool-8) t) 206-842-2017 info@saintceciliaschool.org www.saintceciliaschool.org Susan Kilbane, Prin.;

BATTLE GROUND

Sacred Heart - 1603 N. Parkway Ave., Battle Ground, WA 98604; Mailing: P.O. Box 38, Battle Ground, WA 98604 t) 360-687-4515 info@sacredheartbg.org; debbie@sacredheartbg.org www.sacredheartbg.org Rev. Nicholas Kayongo, Admin.;
St. Joseph the Worker - 200 W. Jones St., Yacolt, WA 98675 d.wilson@sacredheartbg.org

BELLEVUE

St. Louise - 141 156th Ave., S.E., Bellevue, WA 98007 t) 425-747-4450 x5464 (CRP); 425-747-4450 info@stlouise.org Rev. Joshua T. Nehnevaj, Par. Vicar; Very Rev. Gary M. Zender, Pst.; Dcn. Samuel Basta; Dcn. Cesar Legaria;
St. Louise School - (Grades K-8) 133 156th Ave., S.E., Bellevue, WA 98007 t) 425-746-4220 www.stlouiseschool.org Dan Fitzpatrick, Prin.; Mary Carson, Librn.;
St. Madeleine Sophie - 4400 130th Pl., S.E., Bellevue, WA 98006-2014 t) 425-747-6770 x100; 425-747-6770 x124 (CRP) parishoffice@stmadsophie.org; maggie@stmadsophie.org www.stmadeleine.org Very Rev. Gary M. Zender, Priest Moderator; Dcn. Bruno Bahk; Loretta Sursely, Pst. Min./Coord.; Very Rev. Anthony E. Bawyn, Parish Priest;
St. Madeleine Sophie School - (Grades PreK-8) schooloffice@stmadsophie.org www.smsbellevue.org Dan Sherman, Prin.;
Sacred Heart - 9460 N.E. 14th St., Bellevue, WA 98004 t) 425-454-9536 lpaulsen@sacredheart.org Rev. Kurt Nagel, Pst.; Rev. Joseph Akor, Par. Vicar;
Sacred Heart School - (Grades K-8) 9450 N.E. 14th St., Bellevue, WA 98004 t) 425-451-1773 David Burroughs, Prin.;

BELLINGHAM

Assumption - 2116 Cornwall Ave., Bellingham, WA 98225 t) 360-733-1380 www.assumption.org Dcn. Lawrence Kheriaty; Very Rev. Jeffrey Moore, Pst.;
Assumption School - (Grades PreK-8) t) 360-733-6133 theoffice@school.assumption.org www.school.assumption.org Dan Anderson, Prin.;
Sacred Heart - 1115 14th St., Bellingham, WA 98225 t) 360-734-2850 melissa.johnson@shbham.org Rev. Cody Ross, Priest Admin.; Dcn. Dale Pollard;
Newman Campus Ministry - 714 N. Garden St., Bellingham, WA 98225

BLACK DIAMOND

St. Barbara - 32416 6th Ave., Black Diamond, WA 98010; Mailing: P.O. Box 189, Black Diamond, WA 98010 t) 360-886-2229 office@stbarbarachurch.org Rev. Anthony K. A. Davis, Pst.;

BOTHELL

St. Brendan - 10051 N.E. 195th St., Bothell, WA 98011-2931 t) 425-483-9400 Very Rev. Nicholas F. Wichert, Pst.; Dcn. Leon Garcia-Martinez; Dcn. Armando Medina;

St. Brendan School - (Grades K-8) 10049 N.E. 195th St., Bothell, WA 98011 t) 425-483-8300 secretary@school.saintbrendan.org school.saintbrendan.org Catherine Shumate, Prin.; Joyceanne Michaels, Librn.;

BREMERTON

Holy Trinity - 4215 Pine Rd., N.E., Bremerton, WA 98310; Mailing: P.O. Box 910, Tracyton, WA 98393 t) 360-479-9525 (CRP); 360-377-7674 mail@holytrinitymail.org Rev. Benjamin Bray, Priest Administrator; Dcn. Henry Miner; Dcn. John Amlag;

Our Lady, Star of the Sea - 1513-6th St., Bremerton, WA 98337 t) 360-479-3777 info@starofthesea.net Rev. Dennis Sevilla, Parish Priest; Rev. Derek J. Lappe, Pst.; Dcn. William Hamlin; Dcn. James Johnson;

Our Lady, Star of the Sea School - 1516-5th St., Bremerton, WA 98337 t) 360-373-5162 Jeanette Wolfe, Prin.;

BUCKLEY

St. Aloysius - 211 W. Mason Ave., Buckley, WA 98321 t) 360-829-9958 (CRP); 360-829-6515 office@saint-aloysius-catholic-church.org Rev. Vu Phong Tran, Priest Administrator;

Our Lady of Lourdes -

BURIEN

St. Francis of Assisi - 15226 21st Ave., S.W., Burien, WA 98166; Mailing: P.O. Box 929, Seahurst, WA 98062-0929 t) 206-242-4575 parishoffice@stfoa.org Rev. Richard K. Hayatsu, Pst.;

St. Francis of Assisi School - (Grades K-8) ; Mailing: P.O. Box 870, Seahurst, WA 98062 t) 206-243-5690 Rosemary Leifer, Prin.; Mary DeMarre, Librn.;

BURLINGTON

St. Charles - 935 Peterson Rd., Burlington, WA 98233 t) 360-757-0128 stcharles0burlington-wa.org Rev. Thomas McMichael, Pst.; Rev. Jose Maria Ramirez Briseno, Par. Vicar; Very Rev. Paul A. Magnano; Dcn. Antonio Cavazos;

CAMAS

St. Thomas Aquinas - 324 N.E. Oak, Camas, WA 98607 t) 360-834-2126 x2 (CRP); 360-834-2126 office@stthomascamas.org Rev. Rajasekar Savarimuthu, H.G.N., Priest Administrator;

Our Lady Star of the Sea - ; Mailing: P.O. Box 901, Stevenson, WA 98648 Dcn. William Townsend;

CASTLE ROCK

St. Mary - 120 Powell Rd., Castle Rock, WA 98611-0960; Mailing: 701 26th Ave., Castle Rock, WA 98632 t) 360-274-7404 smcc58@cni.net Rev. Bryan A. Ochs, Pst.; Rev. Michael Barbarossa, Par. Vicar;

CENTRALIA

St. Mary - 225 N Washington Ave, Centralia, WA 98531; Mailing: 157 SW 6th St., Chehalis, WA 98532 t) 360-748-4953 office@wlpcatholic.org Rev. Jorge Flores Molina, Par. Vicar; Rev. Milhton Scarpetta, Pst.; Dcn. Loren Lane; Dcn. Arturo Ramirez;

CHEHALIS

St. Joseph - 682 S.W. Cascade Ave., Chehalis, WA 98532; Mailing: 157 S.W. 6th St., Chehalis, WA 98532 t) 360-748-4953 office@wlpcatholic.org www.wlpcatholic.org Rev. Jorge Flores Molina, Par. Vicar; Rev. Milhton Scarpetta, Pst.; Dcn. Loren Lane; Dcn. Arturo Ramirez;

St. Joseph School - (Grades PreSchool-8) 123 S.W. 6th St., Chehalis, WA 98532 t) 360-748-0961

COVINGTON

St. John the Baptist - 25810 156th Ave., S.E., Covington, WA 98042 t) 253-630-0701 office@sjtbcc.org Rev. William McKee, Pst.;

DES MOINES

St. Philomena - 1790 S. 222nd St., Des Moines, WA 98198 t) 206-824-5582 (CRP); 206-878-8709 parishoffice@stphil.com Rev. Stephen Woodland, Pst.; Dcn. Gerald Graddon; Rev. Gilberto Mora Tapia, Par. Vicar;

St. Philomena School - (Grades K-8) 1815 S. 220th, Des Moines, WA 98198 t) 206-824-4051

DUVALL

Holy Innocents - 26526 N.E. Cherry Valley Rd., Duvall, WA 98019; Mailing: P.O. Box 850, Duvall, WA 98019 t) 425-788-1400 office@holyinn.org Rev. James O. Johnson Jr., Pst.; Rev. Patrick Sherrard, Par. Vicar; Dcn. Mirek Sztajno;

EDMONDS

Holy Rosary - 760 Aloha St., Edmonds, WA 98020-0206; Mailing: P.O. Box 206, Edmonds, WA 98020-0206 t) 425-778-3122 www.holyrosaryedmonds.org Rev. Matthew L. O'Leary; Dcn. Craig Lundberg;

Holy Rosary School - (Grades PreSchool-8) 770 Aloha St., Edmonds, WA 98020; Mailing: P.O. Box 206, Edmonds, WA 98020 t) 425-778-3197 Susan Venable, Prin.; Carlotta Rojas, Librn.;

North American Martyrs Personal Parish - 9924 232nd St. SW, Edmonds, WA 98020; Mailing: 12546 B 5th Ave. N.E., Seattle, WA 98125 t) 206-641-6504 nam@fssp.com www.northamericanmartyrs.org Rev. John Shannon, F.S.S.P., Pst.; Rev. Caleb Insco, FSSP, Par. Vicar;

ELMA

St. Joseph - 501 W. Main St., Elma, WA 98541; Mailing: P.O. Box 3027, Elma, WA 98541 t) 360-482-3190 office.twosaints@gmail.com Rev. Navykumar Thomas, Par. Vicar; Theresa Wright, Pst. Min./Coord.; Rev. Timothy W. Ilgen, Priest Moderator; Rev. Jaya Kumar Embeti, Par. Vicar;

St. John - Broadway and Church St., Montesano, WA 98563

ENUMCLAW

Sacred Heart of Jesus - 1614 Farrelly St., Enumclaw, WA 98022 t) 360-825-3759 brenda@sacredheartenumclaw.org Rev. Anthony K. A. Davis, Admin.; Rev. Clarence Jones, Par. Vicar; Dcn. George Mounce III;

Crystal Mountain, Crystal Mountain Chapel -

EVERETT

St. Mary Magdalen - 8517 7th Ave., S.E., Everett, WA 98208 t) 425-353-1211 Rev. Ronald Gajettan, HGN, Par. Vicar; Rev. Hans M. Olson, Pst.; Dcn. Phuoc Nguyen; Dcn. David P. Alcorta;

St. Mary Magdalen School - (Grades PreK-8) 8615 7th Ave., S.E., Everett, WA 98208 t) 425-353-7559 info@stmarym.org www.stmarym.org Zack Cunningham, Prin.; Laura Mellahan, Librn.;

St. John - 829 3rd St., Mukilteo, WA 98275

Our Lady of Hope - 2501 Hoyt Ave., Everett, WA 98201; Mailing: 2430 Hoyt Ave., Everett, WA 98201 t) 425-349-7014 goldstein@ic-olph.org www.ic-olph.org Rev. Joseph F. Altenhofen, Pst.; Rev. Tuan A. Nguyen, C.Ss.R., Par. Vicar; Dcn. Duane Shireman;

Our Lady of Hope School - (Grades PreSchool-8) 2508 Hoyt Ave., Everett, WA 98201 t) 425-349-7777 Kathy Wartelle, Prin.;

Our Lady of Perpetual Help - 219 Cedar St., Everett, WA 98201 t) (425) 349-7014

FEDERAL WAY

St. Theresa - 3939 S.W. 331st, Federal Way, WA 98023 t) 253-838-5924 linda.demarce@sttheresafw.org Rev. Gilberto Mora Tapia, Par. Vicar; Rev. Jay J. Bonete, Priest Administrator;

St. Vincent De Paul - 30525 8th Ave. S., Federal Way, WA 98003 t) 253-839-2320 info@stvincentparish.org Rev. John P. DePalma, Par. Vicar; Most Rev. Frank Schuster, Pst.; Dcn. Juan Lezcano;

St. Vincent De Paul School - (Grades K-8) 30527 8th Ave. S., Federal Way, WA 98003 t) 253-839-3532 Wanda Stewart, Prin.; Urdene Rickard, Librn.;

FERNDALE

St. Joseph - 5781 Hendrickson Ave., Ferndale, WA 98248 t) 360-384-8818 (CRP); 360-384-3651 administration@stjosephferndale.org Rev. Francis Thumbi, Pst.;

St. Anne -

St. Joachim (Indian Reservation) -

FIFE

St. Martin of Tours - 2303-54th Ave. E., Fife, WA 98424 t) 253-922-6858 (CRP); 253-922-7882 office@stmartinoftoursfife.com stmartinoftoursfife.com Rev. Val Park, Par. Vicar; Rev. Michael Radermacher, Pst.; Dcn. Patrick Kelley;

All Saints at St. Martin of Tours - (Grades K-8) 2323 54th Ave. E., Fife, WA 98424 t) 253-922-5360 www.allsaintspuyallup.org Amy Orm, Prin.;

St. Paul Chong Hasang Personal Parish - 1316 62nd Ave. E., Fife, WA 98424-1312 t) 253-896-4489 Rev. Young-Kwan Kim, Pst.; Rev. Se Ho Lee, Par. Vicar;

FORKS

St. Anne Parish - 511 5th Ave., Forks, WA 98331; Mailing: P.O. Box 2359, Forks, WA 98331 t) 360-374-6405 (CRP); 360-374-9184 stanneforks@centurylink.net Rev. Naresh Gali, Par. Vicar; Dcn. Richard Labrecque, Par. Vicar; Dcn. Daniel Powers; Rev. Randy Guarino, Priest Admin.;

St. Thomas the Apostle -

FRANCES

St. Joseph - 2800 State Hwy. 6, Frances, WA 98577; Mailing: P.O. Box 31, Raymond, WA 98577 t) 360-942-3000 Parish meets at Holy Family Church, Frances Rev. Vinner Raj Simeon Raj, H.G.N., Priest Administrator;

Holy Family - State Hwy. 6, Frances, WA 98572

FRIDAY HARBOR

St. Francis - 425 Price St., Friday Harbor, WA 98250; Mailing: PO Box 1489, Friday Harbor, WA 98250 t) 360-378-2910 stfrancisfh@centurytel.net stfrancissji.org Rev. Albert Arulappan, H.G.N., Priest Administrator;

St. Francis-Eastsound - 956 N. Beach Rd., Eastsound, WA 98245

St. Francis-Lopez Island Community, Center Church - Davis Bay Rd., Lopez Island, WA 98261

GIG HARBOR

St. Nicholas - 3510 Rosedale St. N.W., Gig Harbor, WA 98335-1818 t) 253-851-8850; 253-851-9040 (CRP) office@stnicholascc.org www.stnicholascc.org Dcn. Mikhail S. Alnajjar; Rev. Mark A. Guzman, Pst.;

St. Nicholas School - (Grades PreK-8) 3555 Edwards St., Gig Harbor, WA 98335 t) 253-858-7632 Amy Unruh, Prin.;

HOQUIAM

Our Lady of Good Help - 200 L St., Hoquiam, WA 98550; Mailing: 306 E. 3rd St., Aberdeen, WA 98520 t) 360-532-8300 olgh@ghcatholic.org Rev. Timothy W. Ilgen, Moderator; Rev. Navykumar Thomas, Par. Vicar; Rev. Marcos Villanueva, Par. Vicar; Theresa Wright, Pst. Min./Coord.; Rev. Jaya Kumar Embeti, Par. Vicar;

Our Lady of the Olympics -

ISSAQUAH

St. Joseph - 220 Mt. Park Blvd., S.W., Issaquah, WA 98027; Mailing: P.O. Box 200, Issaquah, WA 98027 t) 425-392-5516 office@sjcissaquah.org Dcn. Patrick Moynihan; Dcn. Brian Freese; Rev. Todd O. Strange, Pst.;

Issaquah Campus - (Grades PreK-4) t) 425-313-9129 Peg Johnston, Prin.;

Snoqualmie Campus - (Grades PreSchool-3) 38645 S.E. Newton St., Snoqualmie, WA 98065 t) 425-888-9130 Peg Johnston, Prin.;

KELSO

Immaculate Heart of Mary - 2200 Allen St., Kelso, WA 98626-5004; Mailing: 2571 Nichols Blvd., Longview, WA 98632 t) 360-423-3650 ihom@cni.net Rev. Bryan A. Ochs, Pst.; Rev. Michael Barbarossa, Par. Vicar;

KENT

Holy Spirit Parish - 327 2nd Ave. S., Kent, WA 98032; Mailing: 310 3rd Ave. S., Kent, WA 98032

t) 253-859-0444 www.holyspiritkent.org Rev. J. Carlos Orozco, Priest Admin.;

KIRKLAND

Holy Family - 7045 120th Ave., N.E., Kirkland, WA 98033 t) 425-822-0295 Rev. Bryan Dolejsi, Pst.;

Holy Family School - (Grades PreSchool-8) 7300 120th Ave., N.E., Kirkland, WA 98033 t) 425-827-0444 www.hfkschool.org Susan Webster, Prin.;

St. John Mary Vianney - 12600 84th Ave., N.E., Kirkland, WA 98034 t) 425-823-0787 mberard@sjvkirkland.org www.sjvkirkland.org Rev. Vu Phong Tran, Pst.;

LA CONNER

St. Paul - 17456 Pioneer Pkwy., La Conner, WA 98257; Mailing: 4001 St. Mary's Dr., Anacortes, WA 98221 t) 360-293-2101 admin@stmaryanacortes.org Rev. Mel Strazicich, Pst.; Dcn. Lyle Kendall;

Sacred Heart - 404 Douglas St., La Conner, WA 98257-0757; Mailing: P.O. Box 757, La Conner, WA 98257-0757 t) 360-466-3967 sacredheartlaconner@gmail.com Rev. Thomas McMichael, Pst.; Rev. Benjamin Bray, Par. Vicar; Very Rev. Paul A. Magnano; Dcn. Antonio Cavazos;

LACEY

Sacred Heart of Jesus - 812 Bowker St., S.E., Lacey, WA 98503-1210; Mailing: P.O. Box 3805, Lacey, WA 98509-3805 t) 360-491-0890 staff@3hearts.org Rev. Clement L. Piruwa, Par. Vicar; Rev. Timothy W. Ilgen, Pst.; Dcn. Terry Barber; Dcn. Rey Ronquillo; Dcn. Ronald San Nicolas;

LAKE STEVENS

Holy Cross Parish - 6915 State Rte. 92, Lake Stevens, WA 98258; Mailing: P.O. Box 746, Lake Stevens, WA 98258 t) 360-691-2636 admin@hcclakestevens.org www.holycrossparish.ws Rev. Joseph DeFolco, Pst.;

LAKEWOOD

St. Frances Cabrini - 5505 108th St., S.W., Lakewood, WA 98499 t) 253-588-2141 Rev. Paul J. Brunet, Pst.; Dcn. George Mounce III;

St. Frances Cabrini School - (Grades PreSchool-8) 5621 108th St., S.W., Lakewood, WA 98499 t) 253-584-3850 Stephanie Van Leuven, Prin.;

St. John Bosco - 10508 112 St., S.W., Lakewood, WA 98498 t) 253-582-1028 Rev. Thomas Tran, Priest Administrator; Dcn. Jeffrey Greer;

Immaculate Conception - Nisqually & Main, Steilacoom, WA 98388

LANGLEY

St. Hubert - 804 3rd St., Langley, WA 98260-0388; Mailing: P.O. Box 388, Langley, WA 98260-0388 t) 360-221-5383 sthubert@whidbey.com Susan Walker, Pst. Min./Coord.; Rev. Joseph DeFolco, Priest Moderator;

LONGVIEW

St. Rose de Viterbo - 701 26th Ave., Longview, WA 98632 t) 360-425-4660 info@strose-longview.org Rev. Bryan A. Ochs, Pst.; Rev. Michael Barbarossa, Par. Vicar; Dcn. Fred Johnson;

St. Rose de Viterbo School - (Grades PreSchool-8) 720 26th Ave., Longview, WA 98632 t) 360-577-6760 www.strose-school.org Chester Novitt, Prin.;

St. Catherine -

LYNDEN

St. Joseph - 205 Twelfth St., Lynden, WA 98264 t) 360-354-2334 info@stjoseph-stpeter.org Rev. Francisco J. Cancino, Pst.;

St. Peter - 6210 Mt. Baker Hwy., Deming, WA 98244

LYNNWOOD

St. Thomas More - 6511-176th St., S.W., Lynnwood, WA 98037 t) 425-743-2929 cathyb@stmp.org www.stmp.org Rev. Stephen Okumu, Pst.;

St. Thomas More School - (Grades PreSchool-8) t) 425-743-4242 Teresa Fewel, Prin.; Tessa Watters, Librn.;

MARYSVILLE

St. Mary - 4200 88th St., N.E., Marysville, WA 98270 t) 360-658-9400 x103 (CRP); 360-653-9400 x104 (CRP); 360-653-9400 stmaryoffice@stmary-stanne.org Rev. Peter Mactutis, Pst.;

St. Anne - 7213 Totem Beach Rd., Tulalip, WA 98271

MERCER ISLAND

St. Monica - 4301 88th Ave., S.E., Mercer Island, WA 98040 t) 206-232-9829 (CRP); 206-232-2900 parishoffice@stmonicami.org Rev. Joseph Akor, Par. Vicar; Rev. Kurt Nagel, Pst.; Dcn. Frank DiGirolamo; Dcn. Larry McDonald;

St. Monica School - (Grades PreK-8) 4320 87th, S.E., Mercer Island, WA 98040 t) 206-232-5432 info@stmonicasea.org stmonicasea.org Marybeth Bohm, Prin.;

MILL CREEK

St. Elizabeth Ann Seton - 3216 180th St., S.E., Mill Creek, WA 98012-6534; Mailing: P.O. Box 12429, Mill Creek, WA 98082-0429 t) 425-481-9358 (CRP); 425-481-0303 Rev. Lucio Villalobos, M.Sp.S., Par. Vicar; Rev. Jose de Jesus Sanchez, M.Sp.S., Par. Vicar; Rev. Miguel Marquez, M.Sp.S., Priest Administrator;

MONROE

St. Mary of the Valley - 601 W. Columbia St., Monroe, WA 98272; Mailing: P.O. Box 279, Monroe, WA 98272-0279 t) 360-794-8945 smvm@stmaryvalley.org Rev. Phillip A. Bloom, Pst.;

MOUNT VERNON

Immaculate Conception - 400 N. 15th St., Mount Vernon, WA 98273 t) 360-336-6622 icc@icc-mv.org Rev. Thomas McMichael, Pst.; Rev. Jose Maria Ramirez Briseno, Par. Vicar; Very Rev. Paul A. Magnano; Dcn. Antonio Cavazos;

Immaculate Conception Regional School - (Grades PreSchool-8) 1321 E. Division St., Mount Vernon, WA 98274 t) 360-428-3912 admissions@icrsweb.org www.icrsweb.org Gwen Rodrigues, Prin.;

MOUNTLAKE TERRACE

St. Pius X - 22301 58th Ave. W., Mountlake Terrace, WA 98043 t) 425-775-7545 stpiusxparish@frontier.com Rev. Roberto Salvidar, M.Sp.S., Par. Vicar; Rev. Cal R. Christiansen, Pst.;

St. Pius X School - (Grades PreSchool-8) 22105 58th W., Mountlake Terrace, WA 98043 t) 425-778-9861 www.stpx.org Clinton Parker, Prin.;

OAK HARBOR

St. Augustine - 185 N. Oak Harbor St., Oak Harbor, WA 98277; Mailing: P.O. Box 1319, Oak Harbor, WA 98277 t) 360-675-2303; 360-675-2303 x25 (CRP) information@staugustineoh.org Rev. Christopher Hoiland, Pst.;

St. Mary - 207 N. Main, Coupeville, WA 98239; Mailing: P.O. Box 1443, Coupeville, WA 98239

OCEAN SHORES

St. Jerome - 15 Patrick Way, Ocean Shores, WA 98569; Mailing: 306 E. Third St., Aberdeen, WA 98520-4007 t) 360-289-2838 stjerome@ghcatholic.org Rev. Navykumar Thomas, Par. Vicar; Theresa Wright, Pst. Min./Coord.; Rev. Timothy W. Ilgen, Priest Moderator; Rev. Jaya Kumar Embeti, Par. Vicar;

OLYMPIA

St. Michael - 1208 11th Ave., S.E., Olympia, WA 98507; Mailing: P.O. Box 766, Olympia, WA 98507 t) 360-754-4667 office@saintmichaelparish.org Rev. Kyle Poje, Par. Vicar; Rev. James E. Lee, Pst.; Dcn. John Bergford; Dcn. Robert Rensel;

St. Michael School - (Grades K-8) 1204 11th Ave., S.E., Olympia, WA 98501 t) 360-754-5131 www.stmikesolympia.org Connor Geraghty, Prin.;

PORT ANGELES

Queen of Angels - 209 W. 11th St., Port Angeles, WA 98362 t) 360-452-2351 qasj@olypen.com Rev. Naresh Gali, Par. Vicar; Dcn. Richard Labrecque; Rev. Randy Guarino, Priest Administrator; Dcn. Stewart Adams; Dcn. Daniel Powers;

Queen of Angels School - (Grades PreSchool-8) 1007 S. Oak, Port Angeles, WA 98362 t) 360-457-6903 www.qofaschool.org Mike Juhas, Prin.; Ceci Kimball, Librn.;

PORT ORCHARD

St. Gabriel - 1150 Mitchell Ave., Port Orchard, WA 98366-4416 t) 360-876-2834 (CRP); 360-876-2762 judyricciardi@stgabrielpo.org Rev. Phuong V. Hoang, Pst.; Dcn. John Ricciardi;

Prince of Peace - N.E. 1171 Sand Hill Rd., Belfair, WA 98528; Mailing: P.O. Box 517, Belfair, WA 98528

PORT TOWNSEND

St. Mary Star of the Sea - 1335 Blaine St., Port Townsend, WA 98368 t) 360-385-1662 (CRP); 360-385-3700 Rev. Peter Adoko-Enchill, Priest Admin.;

POULSBO

St. Olaf - 18943 Caldart Ave., N.E., Poulsbo, WA 98370 t) 360-779-4291 michelleann@stolafschurch.org Rev. David H. Young, Pst.;

St. Peter - 910 South St., Suquamish, WA 98392

PUYALLUP

All Saints - 204 6th Ave., S.W., Puyallup, WA 98371 t) 253-845-7521 allsaints@allsaintsparish.com allsaintsparish.com Rev. Michael Radermacher, Pst.; Rev. Val Park, Par. Vicar; Dcn. Daniel Stamper; Dcn. David Jones, Pst. Assoc.;

All Saints School - (Grades PreSchool-8) 504 2nd St. S.W., Puyallup, WA 98371 t) 253-845-5025; 253-922-5360 www.allsaintspuyallup.org Chris Schlattmann, Prin.;

Holy Disciples - 10425 187th St. E., Puyallup, WA 98374 t) 253-875-6630 info@holydisciples.org Rev. Dominic Chikankheni, Priest Administrator;

Our Lady of Good Counsel - 229 Antonie Ave. N., Eatonville, WA 98328

RAYMOND

St. Lawrence - 1112 Blake St., Raymond, WA 98577; Mailing: P.O. Box 31, Raymond, WA 98577 t) 360-942-3000 Rev. Vinner Raj Simeon Raj, H.G.N., Priest Administrator;

REDMOND

St. Jude - 10526 166th Ave., N.E., Redmond, WA 98052 t) 425-883-7685 kristas@stjude-redmond.org Rev. James O. Johnson Jr., Pst.; Dcn. Reuben D'Sa; Rev. Patrick Sherrard, Par. Vicar;

RENTON

St. Anthony - 416 S. 4th St., Renton, WA 98057; Mailing: 314 S. 4th St., Renton, WA 98057 t) 425-255-3132 info@st-anthony.cc Very Rev. Thomas Belleque, Pst.; Rev. Xavier Sengol Bazil, H.G.N., Par. Vicar; Dcn. Lamar Reed; Dcn. Teodoro Rodriguez;

St. Anthony School - (Grades PreK-8) 336 Shattuck Ave. S., Renton, WA 98057 t) 425-255-0059 cantu@sasr.org www.sasr.org Dcn. Michael Cantu, Prin.;

St. Stephen the Martyr - 13055 S.E. 192nd St., Renton, WA 98058 t) 253-631-1940; 253-631-6175 (CRP) bettymencke@gmail.com Rev. Arulanandam Robert Antony, H.G.N., Par. Vicar; Dcn. Sonny Ungco; Rev. Edward Goodwin White, Pst.; Dcn. Carl Chilo; Dcn. Ike Tarabi;

SAMMAMISH

Mary, Queen of Peace - 1121 228th Ave., S.E., Sammamish, WA 98075 t) 425-391-1178 office@mqp.org Rev. Chad Green, Pst.; Dcn. Marco Alban Galeas; Dcn. Felix Maguire; Dcn. Michael Cantu;

SEATTLE

St. James Cathedral - 804 Ninth Ave., Seattle, WA 98104 t) 206-622-3559 mlaughlin@stjames-cathedral.org www.stjames-cathedral.org/narthex.aspx Very Rev. Michael G. Ryan, Pst.; Rev. Calixto Alex Pablo, Par. Vicar;

St. Ignatius Chapel - 901 12th St., Seattle, WA 98122

St. Alphonsus - 5816 15th Ave., N.W., Seattle, WA 98107 t) 206-784-6464 parishinfo@stalseattle.org Rev. Aloysius G. Ssensamba, Priest Administrator;

St. Alphonsus School - (Grades PreSchool-8) t) 206-782-4363 Matthew Eisenhauer, Prin.;

St. Andrew Kim Personal Parish - 11700 1st Ave., N.E., Seattle, WA 98125-4714 t) 206-362-2278 standrewkim.us@gmail.com Rev. Aloysio Kyeongseok Bang, Pst.; Rev. Leo Yongguk Jeon, Par. Vicar;

St. Anne - 1411 1st Ave. W., Seattle, WA 98119 t) 206-282-0223 info@stanneseattle.org Rev. Colin

Parrish, Pst.;

St. Anne School - (Grades PreSchool-8) 101 W. Lee St., Seattle, WA 98119 t) 206-282-3538 Mary Sherman, Prin.;

Assumption - 6201 33rd Ave. N.E., Seattle, WA 98115 t) 206-522-7674 info@assumptionseattle.com Rev. Oliver Duggan, Pst.;

Assumption School - (Grades PreK-8) 6220 32nd Ave., N.E., Seattle, WA 98115-7233 t) 206-524-7452 Christina Viega McGill, Prin.;

St. Benedict - 1805 N. 49th St., Seattle, WA 98103 t) 206-635-0843 parish@stbens.net www.stbens.net Rev. Marc L. Powell, Par. Vicar; Rev. Dean Mbuzi, Priest Admin.;

St. Benedict School - (Grades PreK-8) 4811 Wallingford Ave. N., Seattle, WA 98103 t) 206-633-3375 Brian Anderson, Prin.; Susan Lisi, Librn.;

St. Bernadette - 1028 SW 128th St., Seattle, WA 98146; Mailing: 861 S.W. 126th St., Seattle, WA 98146 t) 206-242-7370 shellyc@saintbernadette.net Dcn. Vu Do; Rev. John L. Ludvik, Pst.;

St. Bernadette School - (Grades PreK-8) t) 206-244-4934 Carol Diaz Mendoza, Prin.;

Blessed Sacrament - 5041 Ninth Ave., N.E., Seattle, WA 98105 t) 206-547-3020 info@bspwa.org www.blessed-sacrament.org Rev. Dominic Maichrowicz, O.P., Pst.; Rev. Francis Le, O.P., Par. Vicar;

St. Bridget - 4900 N.E. 50th St., Seattle, WA 98105 t) 206-523-8787; 206-523-9760 (CRP) parishoffice@stbridgetchurch.org www.stbridgetchurch.org Very Rev. William Heric, Pst.; Dcn. Angus McDonell;

St. Catherine of Siena - 814 N.E. 85th, Seattle, WA 98115 t) 206-524-8800 Rev. Marc L. Powell, Par. Vicar; Rev. Dean Mbuzi, Priest Admin.;

St. Catherine of Siena School - (Grades PreSchool-8) 8524 8th Ave. N.E., Seattle, WA 98115 t) 206-525-0581 Pamela Schwarz, Prin.;

Christ Our Hope Parish - 1902 2nd Ave., Seattle, WA 98101-1155 t) 206-448-8826 mail@christourhopeseattle.org Very Rev. Michael G. Ryan, Moderator; Deanna Tighe, Pst. Min./Coord.; Rev. Bryan L. Hersey;

Plymouth Congregational Church Chapel - 1217 6th Ave., Seattle, WA 98101

Christ the King - 405 N. 117th St., Seattle, WA 98133 t) 206-362-1545 parish@ckseattle.org Most Rev. Eusebio L. Elizondo, M.Sp.S., Pst.; Rev. Chad Hill, Par. Vicar; Dcn. Joseph Sifferman;

Christ the King School - (Grades PreSchool-8) 415 N. 117th St., Seattle, WA 98133 t) 206-364-6890 Joanne Checchini, Prin.;

St. Edward - 4212 S. Mead St., Seattle, WA 98118 t) 205-722-7888 www.stedwardparish.net Rev. K. Scott Connolly, Pst.; Rev. Armando S. Perez, Assoc. Pst.; Dcn. Asipeli Tuifua;

St. Edward School - (Grades PreK-8) 4200 S. Mead St., Seattle, WA 98118 t) 206-725-1774 Mary Lundeen, Prin.;

St. George - 5306 13th Ave. S., Seattle, WA 98108 t) 206-762-7744 info@stgeorgeparish.com Rev. K. Scott Connolly, Pst.; Rev. Armando S. Perez, Assoc. Pst.; Dcn. Joua Pao Yang; Dcn. Jose DeLeon; Dcn. Asipeli Tuifua;

St. George School - (Grades PreSchool-8) 5117 13th Ave. S., Seattle, WA 98108 t) 206-762-0656 Monica Wingard, Prin.;

Holy Family - 9622 20th Ave., S.W., Seattle, WA 98106 t) 206-767-6220 office@hfseattle.org Rev. Jose M. Alvarez, Pst.; Dcn. Abel Magana;

Holy Family School - (Grades PreSchool-8) 9615 20th Ave., S.W., Seattle, WA 98106 t) 206-767-6640 Larkin Temme, Prin.;

Holy Rosary - 4139 42nd Ave., S.W., Seattle, WA 98116 t) 206-935-8353 x203 (CRP); 206-935-8353 evangelization@holyrosaryseattle.org; parishoffice@holyrosaryseattle.org Very Rev. Matthew T. Oakland, Pst.;

Holy Rosary School - (Grades PreK-8) 4142 42nd Ave., S.W., Seattle, WA 98116 t) 206-937-7255 www.holyrosaryws.org Anna Horton, Prin.; Sue Harris, Librn.;

Immaculate Conception - 820 18th Ave., Seattle, WA 98122 t) 206-322-5970 office@icseattle.org Rev. Richard McCallister, Pst.; Dcn. Joseph Connor;

St. John the Evangelist - 121 N. 80th St., Seattle, WA 98103 t) 206-782-2810 jrudden@stjohnsea.org; parishoffice@stjohnsea.org Rev. Crispin Okoth, Pst.;

St. John School - (Grades PreK-8) 120 N. 79th St., Seattle, WA 98103 t) 206-783-0337 ddamelio@stjohnsea.org www.st-johnsea.org Bernadette O'Leary, Prin.; Merrick Bodmer, Librn.;

St. Joseph - 732 18th Ave. E., Seattle, WA 98112 t) 206-324-2522 Rev. Chris Cartwright, SJ, Pst.; Rev. Matthew T. Pyrc, S.J., Par. Vicar; Dcn. Stephen Wodzanowski;

St. Joseph School - (Grades K-8) 700 18th Ave. E., Seattle, WA 98112 t) 206-329-3260 Patrick Fennessy, Prin.;

St. Patrick - 2702 Broadway E., Seattle, WA 98102 t) (206) 329-2960 office@stpatrickseattle.org Rev. Bryan L. Hersey; Very Rev. Michael G. Ryan, Moderator; Dcn. Dennis Kelly, Pst. Min./Coord.;

St. Margaret of Scotland - 3221 14 Ave W, Seattle, WA 98119 t) 206-282-1804 pastor@st-margaret-church.org st-margaret-church.org Rev. Andrzej Galant, S.Ch., Pst.;

St. Matthew - 1240 N.E. 127th St., Seattle, WA 98125 t) 206-363-6767 office@stmatthewseattle.org Rev. Khanh D. Nguyen, Pst.;

St. Matthew School - (Grades PreK-8) 1230 N.E. 127th St., Seattle, WA 98125 t) 206-362-2785 Karen Herlihy, Prin.;

Our Lady of Fatima - 3218 W. Barrett St., Seattle, WA 98199; Mailing: 3307 W. Dravus St., Seattle, WA 98199 t) 206-352-4586 (CRP); 206-283-1456 lsmith@olfatima.org Rev. Philip H. Raether, Pst.;

Our Lady of Fatima School - (Grades K-8) 3301 W. Dravus St., Seattle, WA 98199 t) 206-283-7031 info@olfatima.org www.school.olfatima.org Nicholas Ford, Prin.; Mollie Overa, Librn.;

Our Lady of Guadalupe - 7000-35th Ave., S.W., Seattle, WA 98126 t) 206-935-0358 parishoffice@olgseattle.org Rev. Kevin F.X. Duggan, Pst.;

Our Lady of Guadalupe School - (Grades PreK-8) 3401 S.W. Myrtle, Seattle, WA 98126 t) 206-935-0651 info@guadalupeâ€'school.org www.guadalupe-school.org Donna Ramos, Prin.; Loretta Kramer, Librn.;

Our Lady of Lourdes - 10243 12th Ave. S., Seattle, WA 98168; Mailing: 4415 S. 140th St., Tukwila, WA 98168 t) 206-735-7598 office.stoll@gmail.com Rev. Joseph Dang Hai Vu, S.D.D., Pst.; Rev. Peter Khoi Anh Doan, S.D.D., Par. Vicar;

Our Lady of Mount Virgin - Closed Jul 2022

Our Lady of the Lake - 8900 35th Ave., N.E., Seattle, WA 98115; Mailing: 3517 N.E. 89th St., Seattle, WA 98115 t) 206-523-6776 tsmith@ollseattle.org Rev. Timothy Clark, Admin.; Dcn. Dennis T. Duffell;

Our Lady of the Lake School - (Grades K-8) 3520 N.E. 89th St., Seattle, WA 98115 t) 206-525-9980 Vince McGovern, Prin.; Deb Werner, Librn.;

St. Paul - 5600 S. Ryan St., Seattle, WA 98178 t) 206-725-2050 Rev. K. Scott Connolly, Pst.; Rev. Armando S. Perez, Assoc. Pst.; Dcn. Jose DeLeon; Dcn. Asipeli Tuifua; Dcn. Joua Pao Yang;

St. Paul School - (Grades PreSchool-8) 10001 57th Ave. S., Seattle, WA 98178 t) 206-725-0780

St. Peter - 2807 15th Ave. S., Seattle, WA 98144 t) 206-324-2290 stpeterseattle@broadstripe.net Dcn. Jose DeLeon; Dcn. Asipeli Tuifua; Rev. K. Scott Connolly, Pst.; Rev. Armando S. Perez, Par. Vicar; Dcn. Joua Pao Yang;

Sacred Heart of Jesus - 205 2nd Ave. N., Seattle, WA 98109 t) 206-284-4680 info@sacredheartseattle.com sacredheartseattle.org/ Rev. Richard Luberti, C.Ss.R., Pst.; Rev. Harry Grile, C.Ss.R., Local Supr.; Bro. Paul Jorns, C.Ss.R., Pastoral Staff; Rev. Tuan Anh Nguyen, C.Ss.R., Vietnamese Ministry; Rev. William M. Cleary, C.Ss.R., In Res.; Rev. Lyle E. Konen, C.Ss.R., In Res.; Rev. Thomas D. Picton, C.Ss.R., In Res.; Rev. Steven Wilson, C.Ss.R., In Res.;

St. Therese - 3416 E. Marion St., Seattle, WA 98122 t) 206-325-2711 office@st-therese.cc Dcn. Gregory McNabb; Rev. Richard McCallister, Pst.;

St. Therese School - (Grades PreK-8) 900-35th Ave., Seattle, WA 98122 t) 206-324-0460 Matthew DeBoer, Prin.;

St. Mary - 611 20th Ave. S., Seattle, WA 98144 t) (206) 324-7100 stmarysparish@hotmail.com www.saintmarysseattle.org Rev. Reynaldo T. Yu; Rev. K. Scott Connolly, Moderator; Olaf Valderrabano, Pst. Min./Coord.;

SEAVIEW

St. Mary - 1310 48th St., Seaview, WA 98644-0274; Mailing: P.O. Box 274, Seaview, WA 98644-0274 t) 360-642-2002 stmaryoffice@stmary-stanne.org Rev. Vinner Raj Simeon Raj, H.G.N., Priest Administrator; Dcn. Dick Wallace;

Station -

SEDRO WOOLLEY

Immaculate Heart of Mary - 719 Ferry St., Sedro Woolley, WA 98284 t) 360-855-0077 iheart@ihm-sw.org Rev. Thomas McMichael, Pst.; Rev. Jose Maria Ramirez Briseno, Par. Vicar; Very Rev. Paul A. Magnano; Dcn. Antonio Cavazos;

St. Catherine - 239 Limestone, Concrete, WA 98237

SEQUIM

St. Joseph - 121 E. Maple St., Sequim, WA 98382; Mailing: P.O. Box 1209, Sequim, WA 98382 t) 360-683-6076 qasj@olypen.com Rev. Naresh Gali, Par. Vicar; Dcn. Stewart Adams; Rev. Randy Guarino, Priest Admin.; Dcn. Rob Lebrecque; Dcn. Daniel Powers;

SHELTON

St. Edward - 601 W. C St., Shelton, WA 98584; Mailing: P.O. Box 758, Shelton, WA 98584 t) 360-426-6134 stedoffice@hctc.com Very Rev. Paul A. Kaech, Pst.;

SHORELINE

St. Luke - 322 N. 175th St., Shoreline, WA 98133 t) 206-546-2451 parishcenter@stlukecp.org Very Rev. Bradley R. Hagelin, Pst.;

St. Luke School - (Grades K-8) 17533 St. Luke Pl. N., Shoreline, WA 98133 t) 206-542-1133 Christopher Sharp, Prin.; Jennifer Feucht, Librn.;

St. Mark - 18033 15th Pl., N.E., Shoreline, WA 98155 t) 206-364-7900 office@saintmarkshoreline.org Rev. Jacob M. Maurer, Pst.; Dcn. Kirk Altenhofen;

St. Mark School - (Grades K-8) t) 206-364-1633 www.stmss.org Kathryn Palmquist-Keck, Prin.;

SNOHOMISH

St. Michael - 1512 Pine Ave., Snohomish, WA 98290 t) 360-568-0821 administrator@stmichaelsnohomish.org Very Rev. Michael Dion, Priest Admin.; Dcn. Pierce Murphy; Dcn. Gene Vanderzanden;

SNOQUALMIE

Our Lady of Sorrows - 39025 S.E. Alpha St., Snoqualmie, WA 98065; Mailing: P.O. Box 909, Snoqualmie, WA 98065 t) 425-888-2974 staff@olos.org Rev. Duc Cong Nguyen, Pst.; Dcn. David Field;

St. Anthony - ; Mailing: P.O. Box 175, Carnation, WA 98014

St. Bernard's Chapel -

STANWOOD

St. Cecilia - 26900 78th Ave., N.W., Stanwood, WA 98292; Mailing: P.O. Box 1002, Stanwood, WA 98292 t) 360-629-4425 (CRP); 360-629-3737 secretary@saintccc.org Rev. Jan Lundberg, O.C.D., Pst.;

SUMNER

St. Andrew - 1401 Valley Ave. E., Sumner, WA 98390 t) 253-863-2253 parishoffice@standrewsumner.org www.standrewsumner.org Very Rev. Gerald Burns, Pst.; Dcn. Eric Paige;

SS. Cosmas and Damian - 213 W. Leber St., Orting, WA 98360; Mailing: P.O. Box 215, Orting, WA 98360

t) 360-893-3154 bulletins@standrewsumner.org

TACOMA

St. Ann - 7025 S. Park Ave., Tacoma, WA 98408 t) 253-472-1360 stanntacoma@gmail.com Rev. Tuan Nguyen, Pst.; Dcn. Theman Pham;

St. John of the Woods - 9903 24th Ave. E., Tacoma, WA 98445 t) 253-537-8551

St. Charles Borromeo - 7112 S. 12th St., Tacoma, WA 98465 t) 253-564-5185; 253-564-5185 x3036 (CRP) parishinfo@stcharlesb.org; jclark@stcharlesb.org www.stcharlesb.org Rev. Dwight P. Lewis, Par. Vicar; Dcn. Mark Shine; Rev. Michael J. McDermott, Pst.;

St. Charles Borromeo School - (Grades PreK-8) Daniel Hill, Prin.; Kim Hart, Librn.;

Holy Cross - 5510 N. 44th St., Tacoma, WA 98407 t) 253-759-3491 (CRP); 253-759-3368 georgina@holycross-tacoma.org Dcn. William Eckert; Rev. David T. Mulholland, Pst.; Rev. Ronald W. Knudsen; Dcn. Steve Cano;

Holy Rosary - Merged Jul 2022 Merged with Pope St. John XXIII Parish, Tacoma.

St. Joseph - 602 S. 34th St., Tacoma, WA 98418 t) 253-472-2489 parish@saintjosephtacoma.org Rev. Timothy P. O'Brien, F.S.S.P., Pst.; Rev. Joseph Loftus, F.S.S.P., Par. Vicar;

St. Leo the Great - 710 S. 13th St., Tacoma, WA 98405 t) 253-272-5136 admin@stleoparish.org Rev. Philip L. Boroughs, S.J., Par. Vicar; Rev. Elias Puentes, S.J., Priest Admin.; Dcn. Tom O'Loughlin;

Our Lady, Queen of Heaven - 14601 A St. S., Tacoma, WA 98444 t) 253-537-3252 kimberlyp@ourladyqueenofheaven.org Rev. Maurice Mamba, Pst.; Dcn. Gary Rose;

St. Patrick - 1123 N. J St., Tacoma, WA 98403; Mailing: 1001 N. J St., Tacoma, WA 98403 t) 253-383-2783 parish@saintpats.org Dcn. Steve Cano; Rev. David T. Mulholland, Pst.; Dcn. William Eckert;

St. Patrick School - (Grades PreK-8) 1112 N. G St., Tacoma, WA 98403 t) 253-272-2297 school@saintpats.org www.saintpats.org Chris Gavin, Prin.;

SS. Peter & Paul - 3422 Portland Ave., Tacoma, WA 98404 t) 253-507-5861 stspeterpaultacoma@comcast.net Rev. Klemens Dabrowski, S.Ch., Pst.;

St. Rita of Cascia - Merged Jul 2022 Merged with St. Ann, Tacoma to form Pope St. John XXIII Parish, Tacoma.

Sacred Heart - 4520 McKinley Ave., Tacoma, WA 98404 t) 253-472-7738 sh-tacoma@live.com Rev. Matthew Holland, Pst.; Rev. Kevin Ballard, S.J., Par. Vicar; Rev. Elias Puentas, S.J., Par. Vicar; Dcn. Mauricio Anaya;

Visitation of the Blessed Virgin Mary - Merged Jul 2022 Merged with St. Ann, Tacoma to form Pope St. John XXIII Parish, Tacoma.

TOLEDO

St. Francis Xavier - 139 Spencer Rd., Toledo, WA 98591 t) 360-864-4126 stfrancis@toledotel.com Rev. Jorge Flores Molina, Par. Vicar; Rev. Milhton Scarpetta, Pst.; Dcn. Loren Lane; Dcn. Arturo Ramirez;

TUKWILA

St. Thomas - 4415 S. 140th St., Tukwila, WA 98168 t) 206-242-8189 (CRP); 206-242-5501 office.stoll@gmail.com Rev. James W. Northrop, Pst.;

Vietnamese Martyrs Personal Parish - 6801 S. 180th St., Tukwila, WA 98188 t) 206-325-5626 vmpadmin@vmpwa.org Rev. Thanh X. Dao, Pst.;

VANCOUVER

Holy Redeemer - 17010 N.E. 9th St., Vancouver, WA 98684; Mailing: P.O. Box 871417, Vancouver, WA 98687-1417 t) 360-885-7780 edb@holyredeemervanc.org Rev. Thomas Nathe, Pst.; Dcn. Scott Aikin;

St. John the Evangelist - 8701 N.E. 119 St., Vancouver, WA 98662 t) 360-573-3325 office@stjohnvancouver.org; saclife@stjohnvancouver.org www.stjohnvancouver.org Dcn. Steven Reeves; Rev. Alfredo M. Velazquez Ramirez, Priest Admin.; Dcn. Adolfo Carbajal;

St. Joseph - 400 S. Andresen Rd., Vancouver, WA 98661; Mailing: 6600 Highland Dr., Vancouver, WA 98661 t) 360-696-4407 carriem@stjoevan.org Dcn. Felix Garcia; Very Rev. Gary F. Lazzeroni, Pst.; Dcn. Thomas Hayward; Dcn. Felix Garcia;

St. Joseph School - (Grades K-8) 6500 Highland Dr., Vancouver, WA 98661 t) 360-696-2586 www.stjoevanschool.org Joe Manning, Prin.;

Our Lady of Lourdes - 4723 N.W. Franklin St., Vancouver, WA 98663 t) 360-695-1366 lisa@ollparish.org; katelyn@ollparish.org Rev. Leonardo Pestano, Priest Admin.; Dcn. Tim Shamrell; Dcn. David L. Robinson;

Our Lady of Lourdes School - (Grades PreSchool-8) 4701 N.W. Franklin St., Vancouver, WA 98663 t) 360-696-2301 Holly Rogers, Prin.;

The Proto-Cathedral of St. James the Greater - 218 W. 12th St., Vancouver, WA 98660 t) 360-693-3052 office@protocathedral.org Rev. Martin Bourke, Pst.;

VASHON

St. John Vianney - 16100 115th Ave., S.W., Vashon, WA 98070; Mailing: P.O. Box 308, Vashon, WA 98070 t) 206-567-4149 vashonsjv@centurytel.net; office@vashonsjv.org www.stjohnvianneyvashon.com Rev. David L. Mayovsky, Pst.;

WOODINVILLE

Saint Teresa of Calcutta - 17856 N.E. Woodinville Duvall Rd., Woodinville, WA 98077 t) 425-806-8096 frschuster@saintteresacalcutta.org www.saintteresacalcutta.org Rev. Ramon Santa Cruz, Pst.;

WOODLAND

St. Philip - 430 Bozarth, Woodland, WA 98674; Mailing: Box 2169, Woodland, WA 98674 t) 360-225-8308 churchoffice@stphilipwoodland.com Rev. Arulanandu David, Priest Administrator;

St. Mary of Guadalupe - 1520 N. 65th Ave., Ridgefield, WA 98642

St. Joseph - 136 S. 4th St., Kalama, WA 98625

YELM

St. Columban - 506 1st St. S., Yelm, WA 98597 t) 360-458-2360 (CRP); 360-458-3031 pat@sc-sp.org Rev. Brian D. Thompson, Priest Admin.;

St. Peter - Sussex & Keithan St., Tenino, WA 98598; Mailing: St. Columban 506 1st St. S., Yelm, WA 98598 t) 360-264-2124 loretta@sc-sp.org

SCHOOLS: PRESCHOOL THRU HIGH SCHOOL

SCHOOLS

STATE OF WASHINGTON

LACEY

Holy Family School - (PRV) (Grades PreSchool-8) 2606 Carpenter Rd., S.E., Lacey, WA 98503; Mailing: P.O. Box 3700, Lacey, WA 98509 t) 360-491-7060 office@holyfamilylacey.com holyfamilylacey.com Samantha Thompson, Prin.;

SEATTLE

Villa Academy - (PRV) (Grades PreK-8) 5001 N.E. 50th St., Seattle, WA 98105 t) 206-524-8885 jmilroy@thevilla.org www.thevilla.org (Coed) Liz Willis, Head of School;

HIGH SCHOOLS

STATE OF WASHINGTON

BELLEVUE

Forest Ridge School of the Sacred Heart - (PRV) (Grades 5-12) 4800 139th Ave., S.E., Bellevue, WA 98006 t) 425-641-0700 mguerin@forestridge.org www.forestridge.org (Girls) Mary Rose Guerin, Headmaster; Stds.: 285; Lay Tchrs.: 44

BURIEN

John F. Kennedy Catholic High School - (DIO) (Grades 9-12) 140 S. 140th St., Burien, WA 98168 t) 206-246-0500 info@kennedyhs.org www.kennedyhs.org (Coed) Matthew Mohs, Prin.; Katie Burns, Vice Prin.; Kristin Kuzmanich, Vice Prin.; Rommel Buenafe, Bus. Mgr.;

EVERETT

Archbishop Thomas J. Murphy High School - (PRV) (Grades 9-12) 12911 39th Ave., S.E., Everett, WA 98208-6159 t) 425-379-6363 www.am-hs.org (Coed) Alicia Mitchell, Prin.; Steve Schmutz, Pres.; Stds.: 440; Lay Tchrs.: 38

LACEY

Pope John Paul II High School - (PRV) 5608 Pacific Ave. S.E., Lacey, WA 98503-1258 t) 360-438-7600 principal@popejp2hs.org www.popejp2hs.org Therese Allin, Prin.; Ronald E. Edwards, Pres.;

SAMMAMISH

Eastside Catholic School - (PRV) 232 228th Ave., S.E., Sammamish, WA 98074 t) 425-295-3000 www.eastsidecatholic.org (Coed) Gil Picciotto, Pres.; Rev. Ryan Aiello, Prin.;

SEATTLE

Bishop Blanchet High School - (DIO) 8200 Wallingford Ave. N., Seattle, WA 98103 t) 206-527-7711 pskinner@bishopblanchet.org www.bishopblanchet.org (Coed) Sam Procopio, Prin.; Antonio DeSapio, Pres.;

Holy Names Academy - (PRV) (Grades 9-12) 728 21st Ave. E., Seattle, WA 98112 t) 206-323-4272 eswift@holynames-sea.org; kdawson@holynames-sea.org www.holynames-sea.org (Girls) Congregation of the Sisters of the Holy Names of Jesus and Mary. Elizabeth Swift, Prin.; Anna Sebree, Librn.; Stds.: 570; Lay Tchrs.: 45

O'Dea High School - (DIO) 802 Terry Ave., Seattle, WA 98104-1238 t) 206-622-6596 jdwalker@odea.org www.odea.org (Boys) James Walker, Prin.;

***Seattle Nativity School** - (PAR) (Grades 6-8) 4200 S. Mead St., Seattle, WA 98118; Mailing: P.O. Box 20730, Seattle, WA 98102 t) 206-494-4708 info@seattlenativity.org; jmcdougall@seattlenativity.org www.seattlenativity.org Rev. Jeff McDougall, S.J., Pres.; Bei Bernal, Prin.; Stds.: 75; Pr. Tchrs.: 1; Lay Tchrs.: 6

Seattle Preparatory School - (PRV) 2400-11th Ave. E., Seattle, WA 98102 t) 206-324-0400 mreid@seaprep.org www.seaprep.org (Coed) Erin Luby, Prin.; Kent Hickey, Pres.; Liz Borgen, Librn.;

TACOMA

Bellarmine Preparatory School - (PRV) 2300 S. Washington, Tacoma, WA 98405 t) 253-752-7701 www.bellarmineprep.org (Coed) Sponsored by the Jesuits West Province of the Society of Jesus. Rev. John D. Fuchs, S.J., Supr.; Rev. Gerard E. Chapdelaine, S.J., Chap.; Cindy Davis, Prin.; Robert Modarelli, Pres.; Rev. Alejandro Baez, In Res.; Rev. Eugene P. Delmore, S.J., In Res.; Rev. Jerry Graham, S.J., In Res.; Rev. Jim Harbaugh, S.J., In Res.; Rev. Peter Henriot, In Res.; Rev. Matthew Holland, In Res.; Rev. Stephen C. Lantry, S.J., In Res.; Rev. Isidro Lepez, In Res.; Rev. Frederick P. Mayovsky, S.J., In Res.; Rev. Joseph O. McGowan, S.J., In Res.; Rev. Robert Niehoff, In Res.; Rev. Alan Yost, In Res.;

VANCOUVER

St. Elizabeth Ann Seton Catholic High School - (PRV) 9000 NE 64th Ave., Vancouver, WA 98665 t) 360-258-1932 Dr. Robert Rusk, Prin.;

INSTITUTIONS LOCATED IN DIOCESE

CAMPUS MINISTRY / NEWMAN CENTERS [CAM]

BELLINGHAM

Western Washington University-Newman Center - 714 A.

N. Garden St., Bellingham, WA 98225 t) 360-410-0218 westerncatholic.org Catholic Campus Ministry. Rev. Cody Ross, Chap.;

LACEY

Saint Martin's University (Lacey) - 5000 Abbey Way., S.E., Lacey, WA 98503-7500 t) 360-412-6155 acarlin@stmartin.edu Campus Ministry. Nick Coffman, Dir.; Rev. Peter Tynan, O.S.B., Chap.;

SEATTLE

Seattle University Campus Ministry - 901 12th Ave., Seattle, WA 98122-1090; Mailing: P.O. Box 222000, Seattle, WA 98122-1090 t) 206-296-6075 campusministry@seattleu.edu www.seattleu.edu/campusministry/ Rev. Vincent Duong, S.J., Campus Min.;

University of Washington, Catholic Newman Center - 4502 20th Ave., N.E., Seattle, WA 98105 t) 206-527-5072 info@uwnewman.org www.uwnewman.org Rev. Marcin Szymanski, O.P., Dir.; Rev. Chrysotom Mijinke, O.P., Assoc. Dir.;

TACOMA

Pacific Lutheran University Catholic Student Ministry - 12180 Park Ave. S., Tacoma, WA 98447 t) 253-531-6900 catholic@plu.edu

University of Puget Sound Catholic Campus Fellowship - 1500 N. Warner St., Tacoma, WA 98416 t) 253-879-3374 ccm@ups.edu

CATHOLIC CHARITIES [CCH]

OLYMPIA

Sunshine House (Providence Health System, WA) - 413 N. Lilly Rd., Olympia, WA 98506-5166 t) 360-493-7900 ed.micas@providence.org www.providence.org

SEATTLE

Archdiocesan Housing Authority (Catholic Housing Services of Western Washington) - 100 23rd Ave. S., Seattle, WA 98144 t) 206-328-5731 info@ccsww.org ccsww.org/ Michael L. Reichert, Pres.; Flo Beaumon, Vice. Pres.; Asstd. Annu.: 4,757; Staff: 250

110 14th Avenue Building - 110 14th Ave., Seattle, WA 98104 t) (206) 325-6451

AHA-Pierce County Association/Norm Fournier Court - 112 127th St. S., Tacoma, WA 98444-5000 t) 253-531-5087

Champion House - 1800 145th Pl., S.E., Bellevue, WA 98007 t) 425-644-4344

Chancery Place Apartments - 910 Marion St., Ste. 105, Seattle, WA 98104 t) 206-343-9415

Dorothy Day House - 106 Bell St., Seattle, WA 98121 t) 206-374-4364

Emmons Apartments - 1010 S. 8th St., Tacoma, WA 98405 t) 253-274-5710

Franciscan Apartments - 15237 21st Ave., S.W., Burien, WA 98166 t) 206-431-8001

Halcyon Foundation - 1200 134th Ave., N.E., Bellevue, WA 98005 t) 425-644-4344

Harrington House - 15980 N.E. 8th St., Bellevue, WA 98008 t) (425) 643-1434

The Inn (Aloha Inn) - 1911 Aurora Ave. N., Seattle, WA 98109 t) (206) 283-6070

Josephinum Apartments - 1902 2nd Ave., Seattle, WA 98101 t) 206-448-8500

Katharine's Place - 3512 S. Juneau St., Seattle, WA 98118 t) 206-722-0717

Kincaid Housing/Kincaid Court Apartments - 6210 Parker Rd. E., Sumner, WA 98390-2645 t) 253-863-8818

La Casa de la Familia Santa - 1809 N. Pearl St., Centralia, WA 98531

La Casa de San Jose - 2419 Continental Pl., Mount Vernon, WA 98273 t) 360-424-3883

La Casa de San Juan Diego II - 125 S. Pekin Rd., Woodland, WA 98674

La Casa de Santa Rosa - 555 Township St., Sedro Woolley, WA 98284

La Casa de San Juan Diego - 125 S. Pekin Rd., Woodland, WA 98674 t) 360-225-9872

La Casa del Padre Miguel - 420 N. LaVenture, Mt. Vernon, WA 98273

Matsusaka Townhomes - 810A S. 13th St., Tacoma, WA 98405 t) 253-593-2120

Maurice G. Elbert House - 16000 N.E. 8th St., Bellevue, WA 98008 t) 425-747-5111

Max Hale Center - 285 5th St., Ste. 1, Bremerton, WA 98337 t) 360-792-2117

Monte Cristo Hotel Apartments - 2929 Hoyt Ave., #111, Everett, WA 98201 t) 425-258-9503

Noel House at Bakhita Gardens - 118 Bell St., Seattle, WA 98121 t) 206-441-3210

Pioneer Court Housing/Pioneer Court Apartments - 507 W. Stewart Ave., #104, Puyallup, WA 98371-9402 t) 253-848-0874

Redmond Elderly Housing Association/Emma McRedmond Manor - 7960 169th Ave., N.E., Redmond, WA 98053 t) 425-869-2424

Renton Family Housing - 1000 Jefferson Ave., N.E., #D102, Renton, WA 98056 t) (425) 793-7060

Rose of Lima at Bakhita Gardens - 118 Bell St., Seattle, WA 98121 t) 206-456-3100

St. Martin's on Westlake - 2008 Westlake Ave., Seattle, WA 98121 t) 206-340-0410

Spruce Park Apartments - 155 21st Ave., Seattle, WA 98122 t) 206-322-0450

Sumner Commons - 6100 154th Ave. Ct. E., Sumner, WA 98390 t) 253-826-5199

Sunrise Court Housing/Sunrise Court Apartments - 110 140th St. S., Tacoma, WA 98444-6931 t) 253-537-2429

Traugott Terrace - 2317 3rd Ave., Seattle, WA 98121 t) 206-267-3023

Tumwater Apartments - 5701 6th Ave., S.W., Tumwater, WA 98501 t) 360-352-4321

Villa San Juan Bautista - 2613 Crooks Hill Rd., Centralia, WA 98531 t) 360-807-6285

Villa San Martin - 2623 Abbotsford Loop, Kelso, WA 98626 t) (360) 575-8300

Villa Santa Maria - 3700 E. College Way, Mount Vernon, WA 98273

Washington Grocery Building - 1133 Railroad Ave., Bellingham, WA 98225 t) 360-738-8234

Wintonia Apartments - 1431 Minor Ave., Seattle, WA 98101 t) 206-467-1878

Woodland Meadows - 130 Hilshire Dr., Woodland, WA 98674 t) (360) 225-0896

Catholic Seafarer's Ministry - 3568 W. Marginal Way, Seattle, WA 98106 t) 206-441-4773 dahra@cscseattle.org (formerly: Catholic Seamen's Club) Rev. Anthony J. Haycock, Chap.;

Sea-Tac Airport - Dcn. Michael Riggio, Dir.;

Providence ElderPlace - 4515 Martin Luther King Jr. Way S., Ste. 100, Seattle, WA 98108 t) 206-320-5325 susan.tuller@providence.org washington.providence.org Susan Tullerq, Dir.;

Providence Regina House - 8201 10th Ave. S., #6, Seattle, WA 98108 t) 206-763-9204

Sojourner Place - 5071 8th Ave., N.E., Seattle, WA 98105 t) 206-545-4200 Sisters of Providence - Mother Joseph Province.

CEMETERIES [CEM]

FEDERAL WAY

Gethsemane Cemetery (Associated Catholic Cemeteries, Inc.) - 37600 Pacific Hwy. S., Federal Way, WA 98003 t) 253-838-2240 richp@mycatholiccemetery.org www.mycatholiccemetery.org Richard Peterson, Pres.;

KENT

St. Patrick Cemetery (Associated Catholic Cemeteries, Inc.) - 20400 Orillia Rd., Kent, WA 98032; Mailing: c/o 37600 Pacific Hwy. S., Federal Way, WA 98003 t) 253-838-2240 richp@mycatholiccemetery.org www.mycatholiccemetery.org Richard Peterson, Pres.;

SEATTLE

Calvary Cemetery (Associated Catholic Cemeteries, Inc.) - 5041 35th Ave., N.E., Seattle, WA 98105 t) 206-522-0996 richp@mycatholiccemetery.org www.mycatholiccemetery.org Richard Peterson, Pres.;

SHORELINE

Holyrood Cemetery (Associated Catholic Cemeteries, Inc.) - 205 N.E. 205th St., Shoreline, WA 98155 t) 206-363-8404 richp@mycatholiccemetery.org www.mycatholiccemetery.org Richard Peterson, Pres.;

COLLEGES & UNIVERSITIES [COL]

LACEY

Saint Martin's University (Order of St. Benedict Master's Comprehensive University) - 5000 Abbey Way, S.E., Lacey, WA 98503 t) 360-491-4700 admissions@stmartin.edu www.stmartin.edu Resident and non-resident students. Roy F. Heynderickx, Pres.; Rt. Rev. Marion (Qui-Thac) Nguyen, Abbot; Rev. Peter Tynan, O.S.B., Campus Min.; Rev. Benedict L. Auer, O.S.B.; Rev. Gerard D. Kirsch, O.S.B.; Rev. Killian Malvey, O.S.B.; Rev. George J. Seidel, O.S.B.; Bro. Aelred Woodard, O.S.B.; Bro. Boniface Lazzari, O.S.B.; Bro. Nicolaus G. Wilson, O.S.B., Treas.; Kathleen Boyle, Provost;

SEATTLE

Seattle University - 901 12th Ave., Seattle, WA 98122-1090 t) 206-296-6000 www.seattleu.edu Eduardo Penalver, Pres.; Rev. Peter B. Ely, S.J., Vice Pres. Mission Ministry; Rev. Arturo Araujo, S.J., Rector; Rev. David Anderson; Rev. Jerry Cobb, S.J.; Rev. Robert Grimm, S.J.; Rev. Patrick J. Howell, S.J.; Rev. Patrick Kelly, S.J.; Rev. David J. Leigh, S.J.; Rev. Thomas R.E. Murphy, S.J.; Rev. Ignatius F. Ohno, S.J.; Rev. Trung Pham, S.J.; Rev. Frank B. Savadera, S.J.; Rev. L. John Topel, S.J.; Rev. Josef V. Venker, S.J.; Rev. Eric J. Watson, S.J.; Bro. James Selinsky;

CONVENTS, MONASTERIES, AND RESIDENCES FOR WOMEN [CON]

BELLEVUE

St. Mary's Residence and Novitiate - 1663 Killarney Way, Bellevue, WA 98004; Mailing: P.O. Box 1763, Bellevue, WA 98009-1763 t) 425-467-5400 afleming@csjp-olp.org www.csjp.org Sr. Andrea Nenzel, Rel. Ord. Ldr.; Srs.: 21

St. Mary's Western U.S. Office for Sisters of St. Joseph of Peace - 1663 Killarney Way, Bellevue, WA 98004; Mailing: PO Box 248, Bellevue, WA 98009-0248 t) 425-467-5403 afleming@csjp-olp.org www.csjp.org Sisters of St. Joseph of Peace. Srs.: 42

KENT

***Lovers of the Holy Cross of Go Vap** - 20013 120th Ave. S.E., Kent, WA 98031-1654 t) 253-592-2541 sotheresa@hotmail.com Sr. Phuong T. Nguyen, LHC, Pres.;

LACEY

St. Placid Priory - 500 College St., N.E., Lacey, WA 98516 t) 360-438-1771 stplacid@stplacid.org; smcdonald@stplacid.org www.stplacid.org Sr. Sharon McDonald, O.S.B., Prioress;

RENTON

Sisters of Providence, Mother Joseph Province - 1801 Lind Ave., S.W., Renton, WA 98057-9016 t) 425-525-3386; 424-525-3999 (Prov. Secy) elinor.alexander@providence.org www.sistersofprovidence.net Sr. Barbara Schamber, SP, Prov.; Srs.: 93

Providence Archives - 4800 37th Ave., S.W., Seattle, WA 98126-2724 t) 206-937-4600 archives@providence.org www.providence.org/phs/archives Loretta Greene, Archivist;

Sisters of Providence Retirement Trust - 1801 Lind Ave., S.W., Renton, WA 98057-9016 t) 425-525-3089 david.neisius@providence.org David Neisius, Treas.;

SEATTLE

St. Joseph's Residence - 4800 37th Ave., S.W., Seattle, WA 98126 t) 206-937-4600 nga.nguyen@providence.org www.sistersofprovidence.net Sr. Hong Nga Nguyen, SP, Spiritual Adv./Care Srvcs.; Srs.: 93

Sisters of St. Joseph of Peace - 1104 21st Ave. E., Seattle, WA 98112 t) 425-467-5403 csjp.org Sr. Andrea Nenzel, Rel. Ord. Ldr.; Srs.: 3

Sisters of St. Joseph of Peace, Our Lady Province, Charitable Trust - 1663 Killarney Way, Bellevue, WA 98009-0248; Mailing: P.O. Box 248, Bellevue, WA

98009-0248 t) 425-467-5400 www.csjp.org

SHAW ISLAND

Our Lady of the Rock Priory - ; Mailing: P.O. Box 425, Shaw Island, WA 98286 t) 360-468-2321 olrmonastery.org (Cloistered) Benedictine Nuns. Rev. Mother Noella Marcellino, O.S.B., Supr.; Srs.: 6

SHORELINE

St. Joseph's Carmelite Monastery (Cloistered) - 2215 N.E. 147th, Shoreline, WA 98155 t) 206-363-7150 seattlecarm@comcast.net seattlecarmel.org Sr. Sean Hennessy, Prioress; Srs.: 11

TACOMA

Sisters of St. Dominic of Tacoma - Tacoma Dominican Center, 935 Fawcett Ave. S., Tacoma, WA 98402 t) 253-272-9688 dominicans@tacomaop.org www.tacomaop.org (Congregation of St. Thomas Aquinas), Sisters of Saint Dominic of Tacoma Charitable Trust - Tacoma Dominican Center, III Order of St. Dominic Sr. Jo Ann Showalter, SP, Pres.; Srs.: 33

Sisters of St. Francis of Philadelphia - Marian House, 6802 47th St. W, Tacoma, WA 98466 t) 253-564-1816 Sr. Karen Pourby, OSF, Secy.; Srs.: 1

ENDOWMENTS / FOUNDATIONS / TRUSTS [EFT]

EVERETT

Providence General Foundation - 916 Pacific Ave., Everett, WA 98201 t) 425-258-7500 Randy Petty, Dir.;

SEATTLE

Catholic Charities Foundation of Western Washington - 100 23rd Ave. S., Seattle, WA 98144-2302 t) 206-328-5707 rosemaryz@ccsww.org Michael Reichert, Pres.;

Fulcrum Foundation - 910 Marion St., Seattle, WA 98104; Mailing: 710 9th Ave., Seattle, WA 98104 t) 206-219-5826 info@fulcrumfoundation.org www.fulcrumfoundation.org Vivian Shannon, Exec.;

HOSPITALS / HEALTH SERVICES [HOS]

CENTRALIA

Providence Centralia Hospital - 914 S. Scheuber Rd., Centralia, WA 98531 t) 360-736-2803 www.providence.org

EVERETT

Providence Regional Medical Center Everett - 1321 Colby Ave., Everett, WA 98201 t) 425-261-2000 washington.providence.org Darren V Redick, CEO; Rev. Kenneth Chukwu, Mgr., Spiritual Health; Barry J. Stueve, Chief Mission Integration Officer;

FEDERAL WAY

St. Francis Hospital of Federal Way - 34515 9th Ave. S. (M.S. 21-01), Federal Way, WA 98003-6761 t) 253-835-8100 (King Co.); 253-944-8100 (Pierce Co.) www.chifranciscan.org Sisters of St. Francis of Philadelphia. Tony McLean, Pres.;

GIG HARBOR

St. Anthony Hospital - 11567 Canterwood Blvd., N.W., Gig Harbor, WA 98332 t) 253-857-1431 Dianna Kielian, Senior Vice Pres. Mission;

LAKEWOOD

St. Clare Hospital - 11315 Bridgeport Way, S.W. (M.S. 41-01), Lakewood, WA 98499 t) 253-985-1711 www.fhshealth.org Sisters of St. Francis of Philadelphia. Syd Bersante, Pres.; Dianna Kielian, Senior Vice Pres., Mission;

OLYMPIA

Providence St. Peter Hospital - c/o Providence Centralia Hospital, 413 Lilly Rd., N.E., Olympia, WA 98506-5166 t) 360-491-9480 Sisters of Providence - Mother Joseph Province Medrice Coluccio, Exec.;

Providence St. Peter Foundation - 413 Lilly Rd., N.E., Olympia, WA 98506-5116 t) 360-493-7980 Nancy Riordan, Dir.;

RENTON

Providence Health & Services - 1801 Lind Ave., S.W., Renton, WA 98057-9016 t) 425-525-3355 cindy.strauss@providence.org

Providence Health & Services - Oregon -

Providence Health & Services - Washington -

Providence Health System - California -

TACOMA

CHI Franciscan Health - 1145 Broadway Plz., Ste. 1200 (MS07-00), Tacoma, WA 98402 t) 253-680-4016 Dianna Kielian, Contact;

St. Joseph Medical Center - 1717 S. J St., Tacoma, WA 98405-2197; Mailing: P.O. Box 2197, Tacoma, WA 98405-2197 t) 253-426-4101 www.chifranciscan.org Sisters of St. Francis of Philadelphia. Rev. Dennis Sevilla; Syd Bersante, Pres.;

VANCOUVER

***PeaceHealth - System Services Center** - 1115 S.E. 164th Ave., Vancouver, WA 98683 t) 360-729-1000 sbrewer@peacehealth.org www.peacehealth.org Liz Dunne, CEO;

PeaceHealth - Peace Island Medical Center - 1117 Spring St., Friday Harbor, WA 98250; Mailing: 1115 S.E. 164th Ave., Dept. 314, Vancouver, WA 98683 t) 360-387-2141

PeaceHealth - Southwest Medical Center - 400 N.E. Mother Joseph Pl., Vancouver, WA 98664; Mailing: 1115 S.E. 164th Ave., Dept. 314, Vancouver, WA 98683 t) 360-514-2000

PeaceHealth - St. John Medical Center - 1615 Delaware St., Longview, WA 98632; Mailing: 1115 S.E. 164th Ave., Dept. 314, Vancouver, WA 98683 t) 360-414-2000 Sisters of St. Joseph of Peace and PeaceHealth.

PeaceHealth - St. Joseph Medical Center - 2901 Squalicum Pkwy., Bellingham, WA 98225; Mailing: 1115 S.E. 164th Ave., Dept. 314, Vancouver, WA 98683 t) 360-734-5400 Sisters of St. Joseph of Peace and PeaceHealth.

PeaceHealth - United General Medical Center - 2000 Hospital Dr., Sedro Woolley, WA 98284; Mailing: 1115 S.E. 164th Ave., Vancouver, WA 98683 t) 360-856-6021

MISCELLANEOUS [MIS]

CENTRALIA

Providence Blanchet House - 1700 Providence Pl., Centralia, WA 98531 t) 360-330-8748

Providence Rossi House - 1700 Providence Pl., Centralia, WA 98531 t) 360-330-8748

FEDERAL WAY

***My Catholic Faith Ministries** - ; Mailing: P.O. Box 24866, Federal Way, WA 98093 t) 888-765-9269 info@mycatholicfaith.org www.mycatholicfaith.org Tom Curran, Exec.;

MOUNT VERNON

Skagit Valley Catholic Churches - 215 N. 15th St., Mount Vernon, WA 98273 t) 360-336-6622 pastor@icc-mv.org www.svcc.us Rev. Martin Bourke, Pst.;

OLYMPIA

Providence St. Francis House - 3415 12th Ave., Olympia, WA 98506 t) 360-493-5700

SEATTLE

Advocacy and Caring for Children - 100 23rd Ave. S., Seattle, WA 98144 t) 206-328-5973 acc@ccsww.org www.advocacyandcaringforchildren.org Helen Santucci, Pres.;

Called To Serve As Christ Campaign Fund - 710 Ninth Ave., Seattle, WA 98114-9919; Mailing: P.O. Box 14964, Seattle, WA 98114

Catholic Community Services of Western Washington - 100 23rd Ave. S., Seattle, WA 98144-2302 t) 206-328-5696 info@ccsww.org www.ccsww.org Michael L. Reichert, Pres.;

Adult Behavioral Health - 403 W. State St., Suite 206, Aberdeen, WA 98520 t) 360-612-3839 ccsww.org/ Mike Curry, Vice. Pres.;

Arrest and Jail Alternatives / Mental Health Field Response - 824 5th Ave., S.E., Olympia, WA 98501 t) (360) 529-7287 Neil Calmjoy, Program Manager;

Bakhita Gardens - 118 Bell St., Seattle, WA 98121 t) (206) 456-3100 Crystal Perine, Prog. Dir.;

Benedict House - 250 S. Cambrian Ave., Bremerton, WA 98312-4102 t) 360-377-6136 ccsww.org/ Mike Curry, Vice. Pres.;

Bertha's Place - 9201 N.E. Vancouver Mall Dr., Vancouver, WA 98622 t) (360) 904-6770

Bertha's Place Too - 7415 N.E. 94th Ave., Vancouver, WA 98662 t) (360) 904-6770

Bob G Shelter - 505 1st Ave. N., Seattle, WA 98109

Bridge Shelter - 1923 3rd Ave., Seattle, WA 98101 t) 206-956-9563 ccsww.org/ Bill Hallerman, Vice. Pres.;

Bridges Village - 1809 E. 31st St., Tacoma, WA 98404 t) (253) 272-1171 x1 ccsww.org/ Mike Curry, Vice. Pres.;

Bunny Wilburn House - 1855 S. Lane St., Seattle, WA 98144 t) (206) 329-5433

Catholic Community Services Long Term Care System - 1323 Yakima Ave., Tacoma, WA 98405-4457 t) 877-870-1582; 253-502-2734 ccsww.org/ Peter Nazzal, Vice Pres. & Long Term Care System Dir.;

Catholic Community Services Northwest Recovery Centers / CCS Recovery Center - Bellingham - 515 Lakeview Dr., Bellingham, WA 98225 t) 360-676-2187 ccsww.org/ Donna Wells, Dir.;

Catholic Community Services Southwest Family Centers & Tahoma Family Center - 1323 S. Yakima Ave., Tacoma, WA 98405-4457 t) 253-383-3697 ccsww.org/ Mike Curry, Dir.;

CCS NW Immigration Services - 300 S. 1st St., Ste. C, Mount Vernon, WA 98273 t) 360-416-7095 ccsww.org/ Will Rice, Vice Pres.;

CCS Recovery Center - Everett - 2610 Wetmore Ave., Everett, WA 98201 t) 425-258-5270 ccsww.org/ Donna Wells, Dir.;

CCS Recovery Center - Marysville - 1227 2nd St., Marysville, WA 98270 t) 360-651-2366 ccsww.org/ Donna Wells, Dir.;

CCS Recovery Center - Skagit - 614 Peterson Rd., Burlington, WA 98233 t) 360-757-0131 ccsww.org/ Donna Wells, Dir.;

Clare's Place - 6200 12th Dr., S.E., Everett, WA 98203 t) (425) 535-4020

Coming Home Program - 1902 2nd Ave., Seattle, WA 98101 t) 206-956-9562 ccsww.org/ Bill Hallerman, Vice. Pres.;

The Community Kitchen - 808 5th St., S.E., Olympia, WA 98507 t) (253) 642-7514 Peter Epperson, Contact;

Cowlitz/Wahkiakum Family Center/Volunteer Services (serving Clark/Skamania Cos.) - 676 26th Ave., Longview, WA 98632-1816 t) 360-577-2200; 844-851-9380 ccsww.org/ Mike Curry, Vice. Pres.;

Counseling Recovery and Wellness (CReW) - 1902 2nd Ave., Seattle, WA 98101 t) 206-956-9570 ccsww.org/ Bill Hallerman, Vice. Pres.;

Devoe Housing - 606 Devoe St., S.E., Olympia, WA 98501

Devoe II Housing - 607 Pattison St., Olympia, WA 98501

Drexel House - 604 Devoe St., SE, Olympia, WA 98501 t) 360-753-3340 x21 ccsww.org/ Mike Curry, Vice. Pres.;

East King County Family Center - 11061 N.E. 2nd St., Bellevue, WA 98004 t) 425-213-1963 ccsww.org/ Bill Hallerman, Vice Pres.;

Everett Children's Mental Health - 2722 Colby Ave., Ste. 610, Everett, WA 98201

Family Behavioral Health System - Aberdeen - 224 E. Wishkah St., Aberdeen, WA 98520 t) 360-532-9050 ccsww.org/ Mary Stone-Smith, Vice Pres.;

Family Behavioral Health System - Bremerton - 5610 Kitsap Way, Ste. 230, Bremerton, WA 98312 t) 360-792-2020; 888-649-6732 ccsww.org/ Mary Stone-Smith, Vice Pres.;

Family Behavioral Health System - Olympia - 1202 Black Lake Blvd., Suite B, Olympia, WA 98502 t) 360-878-8248; 888-322-7156 ccsww.org/ Mary Stone-Smith, Vice Pres.;

Family Behavioral Health System - Oregon - 1904 S.E. Division St., Portland, OR 97202 t) 503-517-8663 ccsww.org/ Mary Stone-Smith, Vice Pres.;

Family Behavioral Health System - St. Patrick's

Tacoma - 1001 N. J St., Tacoma, WA 98403 t) 253-761-3890 ccsww.org/ Mary Stone-Smith, Vice Pres.;
Family Behavioral Health System - Vancouver - 9300 N.E. Oak View Dr., Vancouver, WA 98662 t) 360-567-2211; 800-388-6378 ccsww.org/ Mary Stone-Smith, Vice Pres.;
Family Behavioral Health System - North End Tacoma - 5410 N. 44th St., Tacoma, WA 98407
Family Behavioral Health System - Shelton - 601 W. Franklin St., Ste. T202, Shelton, WA 98554 t) 360-878-8248 ccsww.org/ Mary Stone-Smith, Vice Pres.;
Family Behavioral Health System - Tukwila - 649 Strander Blvd., Ste. E, Tukwila, WA 98188 t) 253-850-2500 ccsww.org/ Mary Stone-Smith, Vice Pres.;
Family Behavioral Health System - Yelm - 715 Yelm Ave. E., Ste. 8, Yelm, WA 98597
Family Behavioral Health - Westside - 7610 40th St., Stes. 200/300/400, University Place, WA 98466 t) 253-830-6242 ccsww.org/ Mary Stone-Smith, Vice. Pres.;
Family Housing Network - 5050 S. Tacoma Way, Tacoma, WA 98409 t) 253-471-5340 ccsww.org/ Mike Curry, Vice. Pres.;
Federal Way Day Center - 33505 13th Pl. S., Ste. D, Federal Way, WA 98003 t) 253-893-7898 ccsww.org/ Bill Hallerman, Vice Pres.;
Feed the Hungry - 410 N. "H" St., Aberdeen, WA 98520
Francis Place - 1122 Cornwall Ave., Bellingham, WA 98225 t) (360) 671-3529
Grays Harbor Family Center - 410 N. H St., Aberdeen, WA 98520-0284 t) 360-637-8563 ccsww.org/ Mike Curry, Vice. Pres.;
Guadalupe Vista - 1305 S. "G" St., Tacoma, WA 98405 t) (253) 272-1171
Holy Rosary Convent - 424 S. 30th St., Tacoma, WA 98405
Holy Rosary Rectory - 512 S. 30th St., Tacoma, WA 98405
Holy Rosary School - 504 S. 30th St., Tacoma, WA 98405
Homeless Adult Services - 702 S. 14th St., Tacoma, WA 98405
Homeless Stability Site - 1423 Puyallup Ave., Tacoma, WA 98421
Hope House - 207 Kentucky St., Bellingham, WA 98225 t) 360-676-2164 ccsww.org/ Will Rice, Vice Pres.;
Hope Village - 1925 Boulevard Rd., S.E., Olympia, WA 98501
International Foster Care Program - 3205 N.E. 78th St., Ste. 103, Vancouver, WA 98685
Issaquah Meals - 11061 N.E. 2nd St., Bellevue, WA 98004
Junction Point - 515 Elliot Ave. W., Seattle, WA 98119
Katherine's House - 1229 W. Smith St., Kent, WA 98035 t) 253-856-7716 ccsww.org/ Bill Hallerman, Vice Pres.;
Kent Community Engagement - 1225 W. Smith St., Kent, WA 98032 t) 253-854-0077 ccsww.org/ Bill Hallerman, Vice. Pres.;
King County Family Centers & Randolph Carter Center - 100 23rd Ave S., Seattle, WA 98144 t) 206-323-6336 ccsww.org/ Bill Hallerman, Vice Pres. & Agency Dir.;
Lee Haven House - 1315 S. 72nd St., Tacoma, WA 98408
Long Term Care Center - Longview - 923 Fir St., Longview, WA 98632-1816 t) 800-925-7186; 360-200-5070 ccsww.org/ Jacquelene Wimbs, Contact;
Long Term Care System - African American Elders Program - Seattle - 100 23rd Ave. S., Seattle, WA 98144
Long Term Care System - Chewelah - N. 106 Second St. E., Chewelah, WA 99114
Long Term Care System - Colville - 251 N. Main St., Ste. C, Colville, WA 99114
Long Term Care System - Moses Lake - 524 E. 3rd Ave., Moses Lake, WA 98837
Long Term Care System - Richland - 124 W. Kennewick Ave., Ste. 6, Richland, WA 99336
Long Term Care System - Seattle - 3210 Beacon Ave. S., Seattle, WA 98144
Long Term Care System - Shelton - 1716 Olympic Hwy. N., Shelton, WA 98584-0947 t) 800-642-8026; 360-427-2230 ccsww.org/ Jennifer Harrell, Contact;
Long Term Care System - Spokane - 222 W. Mission Ave., Ste. 210, Spokane, WA 99201
Long Term Care System - Sunnyside - 1691 Washington Ct., Sunnyside, WA 98944
Long Term Care System - Tumwater - 5109 Capitol Blvd., S.E., Ste. D, Tumwater, WA 98501 t) 800-783-8193 ccsww.org/ Mary Stone-Smith, Vice. Pres.;
Long Term Care System - Wenatchee - 14 N. Mission St., Wenatchee, WA 98801
Long Term Care System - Yakima - 8 E. Washington Ave., Ste. 101, Yakima, WA 98801
Long Term Care System - Vancouver - 14415 S.E. Mill Plain Blvd., #B105, Vancouver, WA 98684-6978 t) 360-213-1023; 360-738-6163 ccsww.org/ Jacquelene Wimbs, Contact;
Long Term Care System - Aberdeen - 218 S. "M" St., Aberdeen, WA 98520-6141 t) 360-637-8784 ccsww.org/ Robin Gibson, Contact;
Long Term Care System - Bellingham - 1742 Iowa St., Bellingham, WA 98229-4702 t) 800-219-0335; 360-758-6163 ccsww.org/ Dave Budd, Contact;
Long Term Care System - Bremerton - 750 Lebo Blvd., Bremerton, WA 98310 t) 800-642-8019; 360-792-2066 ccsww.org/ Dave Budd, Contact;
Long Term Care System - Chehalis - 1570 N. National Ave., Ste. 211, Chehalis, WA 98532-2219 t) 800-642-8021; 360-345-1100 ccsww.org/ Jennifer Harrell, Contact;
Long Term Care System - Everett - 111 S.E. Everett Mall Way, Bldg. A, Everett, WA 98208 t) 800-562-4663; 425-212-9571 ccsww.org/ Dave Budd, Contact;
Long Term Care System - Kent - 835 Central Ave. N., Ste. D-113, Kent, WA 98032 t) 800-722-3479; 253-850-2528 ccsww.org/ Dave Budd, Contact;
Long Term Care System - Lakewood - 5705 Main St., S.W., Lakewood, WA 98499-6508 t) 253-722-5070 ccsww.org/ Jeannette Jordan, Contact;
Long Term Care System - Port Angeles - 701 E. Front St., Port Angeles, WA 98362 t) 360-417-5420; 855-582-2700 ccsww.org/ Dave Budd, Contact;
St. Martin de Porres Shelter - 1561 Alaskan Way S., Seattle, WA 98134 t) 206-323-6341 ccsww.org/ Bill Hallerman, Vice Pres.;
Martina Apartments - 8015 Greenwood Ave. N., Seattle, WA 98103 Kevin Hamel, Program Director;
Matt Talbot Center - 2313 3rd Ave., Seattle, WA 98121 t) (206) 256-9865
Michael's Place - 1307 E. Spring St., Seattle, WA 98122 t) 206-726-5688 ccsww.org/ Bill Hallerman, Vice Pres.;
Monica's Village Place I Programs - 140 23rd Ave. S., Seattle, WA 98144 t) 206-323-7130 ccsww.org/ Bill Hallerman, Vice Pres.;
Native American Men's House - 322 23rd Ave. E., Seattle, WA 98112 t) 206-737-9246 ccsww.org/ Bill Hallerman, Vice Pres.;
Nativity House Apartments - 1411 Yakima Ave., Tacoma, WA 98405
Nativity House Shelter - 702 S. 14th St., Tacoma, WA 98405 t) 253-502-2780 ccsww.org/ Mike Curry, Vice. Pres.;
New Bethlehem Place - 11920 N.E. 80th St., Kirkland, WA 98033 t) 425-679-0354 ccsww.org/ Bill Hallerman, Vice Pres.;
Parke Studios - 1902 2nd Ave., Seattle, WA 98101 t) 206-728-4354 ccsww.org/ Bill Hallerman, Vice. Pres.;
Patrick Place - 4251 Aurora Ave. N., Seattle, WA 98103 t) (206) 737-9253
Phoenix Center - 2329 Rainier Ave. S., Seattle, WA 98144
Pregnancy & Parenting Support - 4250 S. Mead St., Seattle, WA 98118 t) 206-445-5669 ccsww.org/ Bill Hallerman, Vice Pres.;
Puyallup Hotel - 2101 N. Meridian, Puyallup, WA 98372
Quince Street Village - 1211 Quince St., S.E., Olympia, WA 98501
Rita's House - 1229 W. Smith St., Kent, WA 98035 t) 253-883-5271 ccsww.org/ Bill Hallerman, Vice Pres.;
SSVF - 3545 7th Ave., S.W. T-003, Olympia, WA 98502
Sacred Heart Shelter - 232 2nd Ave. S, Kent, WA 98032 t) 206-285-7489 ccsww.org/ Bill Hallerman, Vice Pres.;
Santa Teresita del Nino Jesus - 2427 Holden St., Seattle, WA 98106 t) (206) 767-2005 Holly Irvin, Case Manager;
Sebastian Place - 1925 196th St., S.W., Lynnwood, WA 98036 t) 425-293-0557 ccsww.org/ Will Rice, Vice Pres.;
Skagit County Outreach - 2021 E. College Way, Ste. 206, Mt. Vernon, WA 98273
Skagit Family Center - Children's Mental Health - 614 Peterson Rd., Burlington, WA 98233-3126 t) 360-856-3054 ccsww.org/ Will Rice, Vice Pres.;
Skagit Farmworker Center - 2727 E. College Way, Mount Vernon, WA 98273 t) 360-899-9085 Will Rice, Vice. Pres.;
Skagit WISe - 725 E. Fairhaven Ave., Burlington, WA 98233
Snohomish Family Center - 1918 Everett Ave., Everett, WA 98201-3607 t) 425-257-2111 ccsww.org/ Will Rice, Vice Pres.;
Solanus Casey Center - 804 9th Ave., Seattle, WA 98104 t) 206-223-0907 ccsww.org/ Bill Hallerman, Vice Pres.;
Kent Family Center - 1229 W. Smith St., Kent, WA 98035 t) 253-854-0077 ccsww.org/ Bill Hallerman, Vice Pres.;
South King County Shelters - 1229 W. Smith St., Kent, WA 98035
Spirit Journey - 12794 78th Ave. S., Seattle, WA 98178 t) 425-236-2234 ccsww.org/ Bill Hallerman, Vice Pres.;
Sydney Wilson Homes - 1150 Oakesdale Ave., S.W., Renton, WA 98057 t) (253) 259-6447
Thea Bowman Apartments - 23920 32nd Ave. S., Kent, WA 98032 t) (206) 429-2149
Thurston County Family Center - 604 Devoe St., SE, Olympia, WA 98501 t) 360-753-3340 x25 ccsww.org/ Mike Curry, Vice. Pres.;
Vancouver- Salmon Creek - 10604 N.E. Hwy. 99, Vancouver, WA 98686 t) (360) 644-1631
Village Spirit Center - 140 23rd Ave. S., Seattle, WA 98144 t) 206-328-4470 ccsww.org/ Bill Hallerman, Vice Pres.;
Volunteer Services - 630E. Front St., Ste. D, Port Angeles, WA 98362
Volunteer Services/SSVF/AJA - 3545 7th Ave., S.W., Ste. T-004, Olympia, WA 98502
Whatcom Family Center - Children's Mental Health - 1133 Railroad Ave., Ste. 100, Bellingham, WA 98225-5054 t) 360-676-2164 ccsww.org/ Will Rice, Vice Pres.;
Youth Tutoring Program - 2021 S. Weller St., Seattle, WA 98144 t) 206-328-5719 ccsww.org/ Bill Hallerman, Vice Pres.;

Cursillo Movement - ; Mailing: P.O. Box 68803, Seattle, WA 98168-0803 t) 206-304-0594 Jose Blakely, Dir.;
Edmonds Dominicans, Holy Angels Alumnae Assoc. - 942 N.W. 60th, Seattle, WA 98107 t) 206-782-1181; 206-546-6561

The Food Bank at St. Mary's - 611 20th Ave. S., Seattle, WA 98144 t) 206-324-7100 x21 alison@thefbsm.org

St. Francis House - 169 12th Ave., Seattle, WA 98122 t) 206-621-0945 st.francis@live.com Third Order of St. Francis. Kathleen McKay, Dir.;

***Intercommunity Housing Ferndale** - 2505 3rd Ave., Ste. 204, Seattle, WA 98121 t) 206-838-5700 intercommunity@mercyhousing.org www.mercyhousing.org

***Intercommunity Peace & Justice Center** - 1216 N.E. 65th St., Seattle, WA 98115 t) 206-223-1138 ipjc@ipjc.org www.ipjc.org Patricia Bowman, Exec.;

***L'Arche Noah Sealth of Seattle** - ; Mailing: P.O. Box 22023, Seattle, WA 98122-0023 t) 206-325-9434 info@larcheseattle.org www.larcheseattle.org Very Rev. Michael G. Ryan, Contact;

***Mercy Housing Northwest** - 6930 Martin Luther King Jr. Way S., Seattle, WA 98118; Mailing: 1600 Broadway, Ste. 2000, Denver, CO 80202 t) 303-830-3300 www.mercyhousing.org Joseph Thompson, Pres.;

Sacred Story Institute - 1401 E. Jefferson St., Ste. 405, Seattle, WA 98122 t) 206-302-7630 admin-team@sacredstory.net sacredstory.net Helping individuals and faith communities encounter Christ as the Divine Physician who heals us in body, mind, and spirit. Rev. William M. Watson, S.J., Pres.; Kyle Landers, Treas.;

South Seattle Catholic Schools - 4212 S. Mead, Seattle, WA 98118 t) 206-722-7888

Washington State Catholic Conference - 710 9th Ave., Seattle, WA 98104 t) 206-301-0556 wscc@wacatholics.org www.wacatholics.org/ Mario Villanueva, Exec.;

SNOHOMISH

***Healing the Culture** - 605 2nd St., Ste. 218, Snohomish, WA 98290 t) 360-243-3811 mail@healingtheculture.com Camille Pauley, CEO;

SUMNER

Pierce County Deanery - 1401 Valley Ave. E., Sumner, WA 98390 t) 253-863-2254 admin@piercecountydeanery.org Christine Kolbrick, Admin.; Very Rev. Gerald Burns, Dean;

TACOMA

Catholic Pastoral Care - Hospital Tacoma Ministry - 1401 Valley Ave. E., Tacoma, WA 98390 t) 253-363-2253 Rev. David Gese, Chap.;

YELM

Family Behavioral Health - Yelm - 715 Yelm Ave. E., Ste. 8, Yelm, WA 98597

MONASTERIES AND RESIDENCES FOR PRIESTS AND BROTHERS [MON]

LACEY

St. Martin's Abbey - 5000 Abbey Way, S.E., Lacey, WA 98503-7500 t) 360-491-4700; 360-688-2510 (Abbot) stmartinsabbey.org Order of St. Benedict, University and Novitiate. Rt. Rev. Marion (Qui-Thac) Nguyen, Abbot; Bro. Nicolaus G. Wilson, O.S.B., Prior; Bro. Ramon Newell, O.S.B., Subprior; Rt. Rev. Neal G. Roth, O.S.B., Abbot; Rev. George J. Seidel, O.S.B., Prof.; Rev. Killian Malvey, O.S.B., Prof.; Bro. Boniface Lazzari, O.S.B., Prof.; Rev. Justin D. McCreedy, O.S.B., Mem.; Bro. Edmund Ebbers, O.S.B., Oblate Dir.; Rev. Edward R. Receconi, O.S.B., Mem.; Bro. Aelred Woodard, O.S.B., Mem.; Bro. Bede Nicol, O.S.B., Guestmaster; Rev. Paul M. Weckert, O.S.B., Vocation Dir.; Bro. Luke Devine, O.S.B., Prof.; Rev. Peter Tynan, O.S.B., Campus Min.; Bro. Mark Bonneville, O.S.B., Facilities Mgr.; Bro. Damien-Joseph Brandon Rappuhn, OSB, Asst. Guestmaster; Bro. Pascal-David Lance Greene, Groundskeeper; Bro. Pachomius Patrick Hamor, In Res.; Bro. Therie Jesse Pascua, O.S.B., In Res.; Bro. Simeon Kenjiro Goodson, O.S.B., In Res.; Brs.: 13; Priests: 7

SEATTLE

Arrupe Jesuit Community at Seattle University - 924 E. Cherry St., Seattle, WA 98122-4341 t) 206-296-6340 Rev. David Anderson, In Res.; Rev. Jerry Cobb, S.J., In Res.; Rev. Quentin Dupont, S.J., In Res.; Rev. Peter B. Ely, S.J., In Res.; Rev. Robert Grimm, S.J., In Res.; Rev. Patrick J. Howell, S.J., In Res.; Rev. Patrick Kelly, S.J., In Res.; Rev. David J. Leigh, S.J., In Res.; Rev. Thomas M. Lucas, S.J., In Res.; Rev. Matthew Ma, S.J., In Res.; Rev. Thomas R.E. Murphy, S.J., In Res.; Rev. Colleens Dinladzer Nsame, S.J., In Res.; Rev. Ignatius F. Ohno, S.J., In Res.; Rev. Doug Pduti, S.J., In Res.; Rev. Trung Pham, S.J., In Res.; Rev. Frank B. Savadera, S.J., In Res.; Bro. James Selinsky, In Res.; Lucas Sharma, S.J., In Res.; Rev. Stephen V. Sundborg, S.J., In Res.; Rev. L. John Topel, S.J., In Res.; Rev. James Taiviet Tran, S.J., In Res.; Rev. Patrick J. Twohy, S.J., In Res.; Rev. Josef V. Venker, S.J., In Res.; Rev. Eric J. Watson, S.J., In Res.; Rev. William M. Watson, S.J., In Res.;

Jesuit House, Seattle - 621 17th Ave. E., Seattle, WA 98112 t) 206-324-0329 Rev. Jeff McDougall, S.J., Supr.; Rev. John Whitney, S.J.; Rev. Charles Barnes, S.J., In Res.; Rev. Julian Climaco, In Res.; Rev. James Antonio, S.J., In Res.; Rev. Ryan Rallanka, S.J., In Res.; Rev. John Rashford, S.J., In Res.;

Maryknoll Fathers & Brothers - 958-16th Ave. E., Seattle, WA 98112 t) 206-322-8831 seattle@maryknoll.org www.maryknoll.us Annapatrice Johnson, Dir.;

The Redemptorist Society of Washington - 205 2nd Ave. N., Seattle, WA 98109 t) 206-284-4681 Rev. Harry Grile, C.Ss.R., Local Supr.; Rev. William M. Cleary, C.Ss.R., In Res.; Bro. Paul Jorns, C.Ss.R., Pastoral Staff; Rev. Lyle E. Konen, C.Ss.R., In Res.; Rev. Richard Luberti, C.Ss.R., Pst.; Rev. Tuan Anh Nguyen, C.Ss.R., OLPH Parish, Everett; Rev. Thomas D. Picton, C.Ss.R., In Res.; Rev. Steven Wilson, C.Ss.R., In Res.; Brs.: 1; Priests: 7

NURSING / REHABILITATION / CONVALESCENCE / ELDERLY CARE [NUR]

ISSAQUAH

Providence Marianwood - 3725 Providence Point Dr., S.E., Issaquah, WA 98029 t) 425-391-2800 gennady.calonge@providence.org; maricor.lim@providence.org www.providence.org/locations/wa/marianwood Sisters of Providence Health System. Dr. Maricor Lim, Admin.; Asstd. Annu.: 876; Staff: 175

Providence Marianwood Foundation - t) 425-391-2895 Sr. Anita Butler, S.P., Contact;

SEATTLE

Providence Health and Services - Washington (Providence Mt. St. Vincent) - 4831 35th Ave., S.W., Seattle, WA 98126 t) 206-937-3700 charlene.boyd@providence.org washington.providence.org Sisters of Providence - Mother Joseph Province Charlene Boyd, Admin.;

Providence Mount St. Vincent Foundation - t) 206-938-8994 cscollins@providence.org Pat Welch, Pres.; Molly Swain, Exec.;

***Sterling Senior Housing** - 2505 Third Ave., Ste. 204, Seattle, WA 98121 t) 206-838-5700 Paul Chiocco, Contact;

PRESCHOOLS / CHILDCARE CENTERS [PRE]

SEATTLE

Providence Mount St. Vincent Child Care - 4831 35th Ave., S.W., Seattle, WA 98126-2799 t) 206-938-6784

RETREAT HOUSES / RENEWAL CENTERS [RTR]

FEDERAL WAY

The Archbishop Alex J. Brunett Retreat and Faith Formation Center at the Palisades - 4700 S.W. Dash Point Rd., #100, Federal Way, WA 98023 t) 206-274-3130 palisades@seattlearch.org palisadesretreatcenter.org/ Dcn. Eric Paige, Dir.;

SEATTLE

Camp Don Bosco - 710 9th Ave., Seattle, WA 98104 t) 206-382-4562 cyo@seattlearch.org www.seattlearchdiocese.org/camping

Camp Hamilton - 710 9th Ave., Seattle, WA 98104 t) 206-382-4562 cyo@seattlearch.org www.seattlearchdiocese.org/camping

SPECIAL CARE FACILITIES [SPF]

CHEHALIS

Providence Place - 350 S.E. Washington Ave., Chehalis, WA 98532 t) 360-740-7518

EVERETT

Providence Hospice and Home Care of Snohomish County - 1615 75th St., S.W., Ste. 210, Everett, WA 98203 t) 425-261-4800 Cheryl Cline, Dir.; Mirna Musun, Dir.; Asstd. Annu.: 1,500; Staff: 150

Providence Hospice & Home Care of Snohomish Co. Foundation - t) 425-261-4805 foundation.providence.org/wa/snohomish Mark Johnson, Dir.;

LACEY

Providence Sound HomeCare and Hospice - 4200 6th Ave., S.E., Lacey, WA 98503 t) 800-869-7062; 360-459-8311 www.providence.org Carlos Alaniz, Dir.; Jill Moynihan, Dir.;

OLYMPIA

Providence Mother Joseph Care Center - 3333 Ensign Rd., N.E., Olympia, WA 98506 t) 360-493-4900 www.providence.org Christine Wallace, Chap.; Bed Capacity: 148; Asstd. Annu.: 500; Staff: 210

SEATTLE

Heritage House at The Market - 1533 Western Ave., Seattle, WA 98101 t) 206-382-4119 marika.chadella@providence.org

Providence Mount St. Vincent - 4831 35th Ave. S., Seattle, WA 98126 t) 206-937-3700 charlene.boyd@providence.org www.providence.org/themount Charlene Boyd, Admin.;

Providence Peter Claver House - 7101 38th Ave. S., Seattle, WA 98118 t) 206-721-6265 duong.nguyen@providence.org Duong Nguyen, Dir.;

Providence Vincent House - 1423 First Ave., Seattle, WA 98101 t) 206-682-9307

Diocese of Shreveport

(Dioecesis Sreveportuensis in Louisiana)

MOST REVEREND FRANCIS I. MALONE

Bishop of Shreveport; ordained May 21, 1977; appointed Bishop of Shreveport November 19, 2019; installed January 28, 2020. Chancery Office: 3500 Fairfield Ave., Shreveport, LA 71104.

Chancery Office: 3500 Fairfield Ave., Shreveport, LA 71104. T: 318-868-4441; F: 318-868-4469.
www.dioshpt.org

ESTABLISHED AND CREATED A DIOCESE JUNE 16, 1986.

Comprises the Counties (parishes) of Bienville, Bossier, Caddo, Claiborne, DeSoto, East Carroll, Jackson, Lincoln, Morehouse, Ouachita, Red River, Richland, Sabine, Union, Webster and West Carroll.

For legal titles of parishes and diocesan institutions, consult the Chancery Office.

STATISTICAL OVERVIEW

Personnel

Bishop	1
Priests: Diocesan Active in Diocese	19
Priests: Retired, Sick or Absent	7
Number of Diocesan Priests	26
Religious Priests in Diocese	8
Total Priests in your Diocese	34
Extern Priests in Diocese	4
Ordinations:	
Diocesan Priests	1
Transitional Deacons	2
Permanent Deacons in Diocese	31
Total Sisters	19

Parishes

Parishes	27
With Resident Pastor:	
Resident Diocesan Priests	15
Resident Religious Priests	8
Without Resident Pastor:	
Administered by Priests	4
Missions	10
Pastoral Centers	1
Professional Ministry Personnel:	
Sisters	3
Lay Ministers	6

Welfare

Health Care Centers	3
Total Assisted	438,203

Educational

Diocesan Students in Other Seminaries	4
Total Seminarians	4
High Schools, Diocesan and Parish	2
Total Students	566
Elementary Schools, Diocesan and Parish	4
Total Students	1,760
Catechesis / Religious Education:	
High School Students	264
Elementary Students	1,819
Total Students under Catholic Instruction	4,413
Teachers in Diocese:	
Lay Teachers	178

Vital Statistics

Receptions into the Church:	
Infant Baptism Totals	237
Minor Baptism Totals	29
Adult Baptism Totals	21
Received into Full Communion	66
First Communions	331
Confirmations	317
Marriages:	
Catholic	73
Interfaith	16
Total Marriages	89
Deaths	330
Total Catholic Population	37,986
Total Population	886,376

LEADERSHIP

Vicar General & Moderator of the Curia - t) 318-868-4441 x306 vg@dioshpt.org www.dioshpt.org Very Rev. Matthew T. Long, Vicar;

Vicars Forane - www.dioshpt.org Very Rev. Mark Watson; Very Rev. Keith Garvin (barefootpriest@gmail.com); Very Rev. Michael Thang'wa;

Vicar for Clergy - t) 318-868-4441 rprice@dioshpt.org www.dioshpt.org Very Rev. Rothell Price;

Chancery Office - t) 318-868-4441 chanceryoffice@dioshpt.org www.dioshpt.org Randy G. Tiller, Dir.; Lisa Marcalus, Secy. (chanassistant@dioshpt.org);

Executive Administrative Assistant to the Bishop - t) 318-868-4441 www.dioshpt.org Randy G. Tiller, Dir.;

Chancellor for Personnel and Administration - t) 318-868-4441 www.dioshpt.org Dcn. Michael Straub;

Chancellor for Canonical Affairs - t) 318-868-4441 x304 www.dioshpt.org Very Rev. Peter B. Mangum;

Adjutant Judicial Vicar - www.dioshpt.org Very Rev. Peter B. Mangum;

Ecclesiastical Notary - t) 318-868-4441 vlacour@dioshpt.org www.dioshpt.org Veronica Lacour; Patricia Thomas;

Moderator of the Tribunal - www.dioshpt.org Veronica Lacour;

Judges - www.dioshpt.org Very Rev. Peter B. Mangum; Very Rev. Rothell Price, Moderator of the Curia; Rev. Peter Faulk, Assoc. Judge & Ponems (Diocese of Alexandria);

Defenders of the Bond - www.dioshpt.org Rev. Philip F. Michiels; Rev. James Ferguson;

Promoter of Justice - Rev. James Ferguson;

Advocate - www.dioshpt.org Rev. James Ferguson, (Diocese of Alexandria);

Diocesan Corporate Board of Directors - t) 318-868-4441 x280 www.dioshpt.org Very Rev. Matthew T. Long, Vicar; Dcn. Michael Straub, Chancellor;

College of Consultors - www.dioshpt.org Very Rev. Peter B. Mangum; Very Rev. Rothell Price; Rev. Msgr. Earl V. Provenza;

Presbyteral Council - t) 318-868-4441 www.dioshpt.org Very Rev. Peter B. Mangum; Rev. Joseph Ampatt; Rev. Jerry J. Daigle Jr.;

Ex Officio Members - Very Rev. Matthew T. Long; Very Rev. Rothell Price; Very Rev. Mark Watson;

Finance Council - t) 318-868-4441 x273 www.dioshpt.org Reginald W. Abrams; Charles Allen; Tommy Cockrell;

Ex Officio Members - jbraniff@dioshpt.org Most Rev. Francis I. Malone, Bishop of Shreveport; Very Rev. Matthew T. Long, Vicar; Dcn. Michael Straub, Chancellor;

Priests' Retirement Board - www.dioshpt.org Very Rev. Matthew T. Long, Vicar; Very Rev. Rothell Price, Vicar; Rev. Joseph A. Martina Jr.;

The Catholic Foundation of North-Central Louisiana, Inc. - t) 318-868-4441 www.dioshpt.org

OFFICES AND DIRECTORS

Black Catholic Commission - t) 318-868-4441 x259 rprice@dioshpt.org www.dioshpt.org Very Rev. Rothell Price, Vicar;

Business Affairs - jbraniff@dioshpt.org www.dioshpt.org Jill Braniff, Diocesan Finance Officer;

Campus Ministry - t) 318-868-4441 www.dioshpt.org

Catechesis & Religious Formation - t) 318-868-4441 x302 www.dioshpt.org Delia Barr (dbarr@dioshpt.org);

Catholic Charities - t) 318-865-0200 www.dioshpt.org Meg Goorley, Exec.;

Catholic Relief Services - t) 318-868-4441 x256 www.dioshpt.org Randy G. Tiller, Dir.;

Catholic Scouting - t) 318-868-4441 www.dioshpt.org Dcn. Freeman Ligon; Richard Buchanon, Scouting Chm. (richardbuchanon1956@gmail.com);

Cemeteries - t) 318-868-4441 x256 www.dioshpt.org Randy G. Tiller, Dir.;

Church Vocations - t) 318-868-4441 x261 www.dioshpt.org Very Rev. Peter B. Mangum, Dir.;

Clergy Continuing Formation Director - t) 318-868-4441 x259 rprice@dioshpt.org www.dioshpt.org Very Rev. Rothell Price, Vicar;

Communications - t) 318-868-4441 x260 jwillcox@dioshpt.org www.dioshpt.org John Mark Willcox, Dir.; Kierstin Richter, Publications Editor;

Development - t) 318-868-4441 x260 jwillcox@dioshpt.org; bvice@dioshpt.org www.dioshpt.org John Mark Willcox, Dir.;

Diocesan Publications - t) 318-868-4441 krichter@dioshpt.org www.dioshpt.org Kierstin Richter, Editor;

Director of Facilities, Catholic Center - t) 318-868-4441 x277 ehydro@dioshpt.org www.dioshpt.org Edward Hydro;

Ecumenism and Interreligious Affairs - t) 318-222-2165 www.dioshpt.org Rev. Joseph A. Martina Jr.;

Greco Institute - t) 318-868-4441 pmadden@dioshpt.org www.dioshpt.org

Hispanic Ministry - t) 318-868-4441 x265 www.dioshpt.org Rosalba Quiroz, Dir.; Rev. Aloys Jost, O.F.M., Hispanic Ministry - Eastern Deanery;

Human Resources - Chancellor for Personnel and Administration - t) 318-868-4441 x280 www.dioshpt.org Dcn. Michael Straub, Dir.;

Information Systems Management - t) 318-868-4441 x315 ppillors@dioshpt.org www.dioshpt.org Patricia Pillors, Dir.;

Jail-Prison Ministry - Van Sanders, Contact (saintdismas2@gmail.com);

Permanent Diaconate Program - t) 318-426-7868 bill.kleinpeter@gmail.com www.dioshpt.org Dcn. William L. Kleinpeter, Dir.;

Marriage and Family Life - t) 318-221-5296 www.dioshpt.org Carol Gates (cgates@sjbcathedral.org);

Mission Director - t) 318-868-4441 x306 rtiller@dioshpt.org www.dioshpt.org Very Rev. Matthew T. Long;

Mission Effectiveness - t) 318-868-4441 x256 www.dioshpt.org Randy G. Tiller, Dir.;

Propagation of the Faith - www.dioshpt.org Randy G. Tiller;

Resource Center (Library) - t) 318-868-4441 krhea@dioshpt.org Kate Rhea;

St. Vincent de Paul Society - t) 318-780-7755 Jim Beadles, Contact;

Schools - www.dioshpt.org Sr. Carol Shively, O.S.U., Supt.; Sr. Ann Middlebrooks, S.E.C., Asst. Supt.;

Child Nutrition Program - t) 318-868-4441 sgerman@dioshpt.org Susan German, Prog. Mgr.;

Victim Assistance Coordinator - t) 318-584-2411 Mary Katherine Arcement (mkarcement@gmail.com);

Youth and Young Adult Ministry - t) 318-868-4441

CANONICAL SERVICES

Office of Canonical Affairs - t) 318-868-4441 x304 www.dioshpt.org Very Rev. Rothell Price, Vicar; Veronica Lacour, Contact;

PARISHES, MISSIONS, AND CLERGY

STATE OF LOUISIANA

BASTROP

St. Joseph - 217 Harrington Ave., Bastrop, LA 71220 t) 318-281-4327 sjccbastrop@gmail.com Rev. Michael Thang'wa, F.M.H. (Kenya), Pst.; Dcn. Marc Vereen;

BENTON

St. Jude - 4700 Palmetto Rd., Benton, LA 71006 t) 318-746-2508 dia.finn@stjudebossier.org www.stjudebossier.org Dcn. Burton Ainsworth, Prison Ministry; Rev. Karl J. Daigle, Pst.; Dcn. Steve Lehr; Dcn. Larry Craig Mills; CRP Stds.: 266

BOSSIER CITY

Christ the King - 425 McCormick St., Bossier City, LA 71111-4692 t) 318-221-0238 ctkbossier@christthekingbossier.org christthekingbossier.org Rev. Fidel Mondragon, Pst.; CRP Stds.: 197

Mary, Queen of Peace - 7738 Barksdale Blvd., Bossier City, LA 71112 t) 318-752-5971 mqop.com Rev. James Moran, C.O., Pst.; Dcn. Michael Straub; CRP Stds.: 93

St. George - 3076 Hwy. 155, Coushatta, LA 71019-0937

GRAMBLING

St. Benedict the Black - 471 Main St., Grambling, LA 71245-3088 t) 318-247-6734 Rev. Kevin Joseph Mues, Pst.;

HODGE

St. Lucy - 1100 Second St., Hodge, LA 71247; Mailing: P.O.Box 100, Hodge, LA 71247-0100 t) 318-259-2326 stlucy.hodge@gmail.com stlucyhodge.org Rev. George ThirumangalaM, CMI, Pst.; CRP Stds.: 5

LAKE PROVIDENCE

St. Patrick - 207 Scarborough St., Lake Providence, LA 71254-0351; Mailing: P.O.Box 351, Lake Providence, LA 71254 t) 318-559-2876 stpatrickchurchoffice@gmail.com Rev. Jean Bosco Uwamungu, Pst.; CRP Stds.: 19

MANSFIELD

St. Joseph - 305 Jefferson St., Mansfield, LA 71052; Mailing: P.O Box 760, Mansfield, LA 71052-0760 t) 318-872-1158 stjosephmansfield@dioshpt.org Rev. Mark E. Franklin, Pst.; Dcn. William L. Kleinpeter; CRP Stds.: 58

St. Ann's Chapel - 2260 Hwy. 171, Stonewall, LA 71078

MANY

St. John the Baptist - 1130 E. San Antonio Ave., Many, LA 71449-3226 t) 318-256-5680 office@stjohnmany.org stjohnmany.org Rev. Francis Kamau, F.M.H. (Kenya), Pst.; CRP Stds.: 42

St. Terence - 44847 Hwy 191, Many, LA 71449; Mailing: 1130 E San Antonio Ave, Many, LA 71449

MINDEN

St. Paul - 410 Fincher Rd., Minden, LA 71055; Mailing: P.O.Box 799, Minden, LA 71058-0799 t) 318-377-5364 Rev. Joseph Kallookalam, C.M.I. (India), Pst.; CRP Stds.: 49

Blessed Sacrament - 2688 Military Rd., Ringgold, LA 71068

St. Margaret - 600 E. 2nd St., Homer, LA 71040

MONROE

Jesus the Good Shepherd - 2510 Emerson St., Monroe, LA 71201-2699 t) 318-325-7549 secretary@jgschurch.org www.jgschurch.org Dcn. Tom Deal; Dcn. Christopher Domingue; Rev. Michael Thang'wa, F.M.H. (Kenya), Pst.; CRP Stds.: 135

Jesus the Good Shepherd School - (Grades PreK-6) 900 Good Shepherd Ln., Monroe, LA 71201 t) 318-325-8569 lpatrick@jesusgoodshepherd.org Lisa Patrick, Prin.; Lynda Cookston, Librn.;

Little Flower of Jesus - 600 S. 16th St., Monroe, LA 71201 t) 318-322-1224 hlittleflowerc@comcast.net www.littleflowercatholicchurch.org Rev. Adrian Fischer, O.F.M., Pst.; Dcn. Verdine Williams; Genevieve Armstrong, DRE; CRP Stds.: 15

Little Flower of Jesus School - (Grades PreK- 610 S. 16th St., Monroe, LA 71201 t) 318-322-7379 Day Care Center Deborah S. Marshall, Dir.;

St. Matthew - 121 Jackson St., Monroe, LA 71201 t) 318-323-8878 www.stmatthewmonroe.org Rev. Joseph A. Martina Jr., Pst.; Dcn. Scott Brandle; CRP Stds.: 17

Our Lady of Fatima - 3205 Concordia, Monroe, LA 71211; Mailing: P.O.Box 4136, Monroe, LA 71211-4136 t) 318-325-7595 office@olfmonroe.org www.olfmonroe.org Rev. John Paul Crispin, F.M.H. (Kenya), Pst.; Dcn. William Goss II; CRP Stds.: 22

Our Lady of Fatima School - (Grades PreK-6) 3202

Franklin St., Monroe, LA 71201 t) 318-387-1851 Carynn Wiggins, Prin.;

St. Lawrence - 357 Swartz School Rd., Monroe, LA 71203 t) 318-343-1618 edathinatt@hotmail.com

OAK GROVE

Sacred Heart - 201 Purvis St., Oak Grove, LA 71263; Mailing: P.O.Box 419, Oak Grove, LA 71263 t) 318-428-2683 bwamungu@yahoo.com www.stpatricksacredheart.com Dcn. Daniel LeMoine; Rev. Jean Bosco Uwamungu, Pst.; CRP Stds.: 23

RAYVILLE

Sacred Heart - 716 Francis St., Rayville, LA 71269 t) 318-728-2445 sjccbastrop@gmail.com Rev. Joseph A. Martina Jr., Pst.;

St. Theresa - 640 N. Main St., Delhi, LA 71232; Mailing: 716 Francis St., Rayville, LA 71269 padre_tim@bellsouth.net

RUSTON

St. Thomas Aquinas - 813 Carey Ave., Ruston, LA 71270-4915; Mailing: 810 Carey Ave., Ruston, LA 71270-4915 t) 318-255-2870 stacbulletin@suddenlinkmail.com stthomasaquinasruston.com Rev. Kevin Joseph Mues, Pst.; Dcn. Robert Ransom; Dcn. John J. Serio; CRP Stds.: 144

SHREVEPORT

St. John Berchmans Cathedral - 939 Jordan St., Shreveport, LA 71101-4391 t) 318-221-5296 cgates@sjbcathedral.org www.sjbcathedral.org Dcn. John Basco; Very Rev. Peter B. Mangum, Rector; Rev. Lourdeswamy Dhanraj Narla (India), Par. Vicar; CRP Stds.: 76

St. John Berchmans Cathedral School - (Grades PreK-8) 947 Jordan St., Shreveport, LA 71101 t) 318-221-6005 www.sjbcathedralschool.org

St. Elizabeth Ann Seton - 522 E. Flournoy-Lucas Rd., Shreveport, LA 71115-3802 t) 318-798-1887 office@seasshreveport.com www.seasshreveport.com Dcn. John Lynch; Rev. Richard Norsworthy, Assoc. Pst.; Very Rev. Rothell Price, Pst.; Dcn. Homer Tucker; Dcn. Michael Whitehead; CRP Stds.: 103

Holy Trinity - 315 Marshall St., Shreveport, LA 71101 t) 318-221-5990 gyoungblood@dioshpt.org; dtrombetta@holytrinity-shreveport.com www.holytrinity-shreveport.com Rev. Duane C. Trombetta, Pst.; Gwendolyn Youngblood, Bus. Mgr.;

St. Joseph - 211 Atlantic Ave., Shreveport, LA 71105 t) 318-865-3581 pastor@stjosephchurch.net stjosephchurch.net Rev. Nicholas Duncan, Assoc. Pst.; Dcn. Freeman Ligon; Dcn. Bruce Pistorius; Very Rev. Matthew T. Long, Pst.; CRP Stds.: 154

St. Joseph School - (Grades PreK-8) 1210 Anniston Ave., Shreveport, LA 71105 t) 318-865-3585 Judith McGimsey, Prin.;

St. Mary of the Pines - 1050 Bert Kouns Industrial Loop, Shreveport, LA 71118-3499 t) 318-687-5121 www.stmaryshreveport.org Rev. Mark Andrew Watson, Pst.; Rev. Raney Johnson, Assoc. Pst.; Dcn. Clary Nash; CRP Stds.: 137

Sacred Heart of Jesus - 4736 Lyba St., Shreveport, LA 71149-0467; Mailing: P.O. Box 19467, Shreveport, LA 71149-0467 t) 318-635-2121 mwatson@stmaryshreveport.org

Our Lady of the Blessed Sacrament - 1558 Buena Vista St., Shreveport, LA 71101-2448 t) 318-222-3790 olbschurchsport@gmail.com olbschurchsport.org Dcn. Charles Thomas; Rev. Duane C. Trombetta, Admin.; CRP Stds.: 13

St. Pius X - 4300 N. Market St., Shreveport, LA 71107-2953 t) 318-222-2165 stpiusxsec@bellsouth.net Dcn. Jeff Chapman; Rev. Raney Christopher Johnson, Par. Admin.; CRP Stds.: 30

VIVIAN

St. Clement - 819 N. Pine St., Vivian, LA 71082-3354 t) 318-375-2789 stpiusx@bellsouth.net stclementvivian.org Rev. Raney Christopher Johnson, Pst.; Dcn. Orlando Batongbakal; CRP Stds.: 4

WEST MONROE

St. Paschal - 711 N. 7th St., West Monroe, LA 71291-4211 t) 318-323-1631 office@stpaschalchurch.org stpaschalchurch.org Dcn. Timothy Cotita; Rev. Jerry J. Daigle Jr., Pst.; CRP Stds.: 159

Our Lady of Perpetual Help - 600 Water St., Farmerville, LA 71241 t) (318) 368-9239 Rev. Aloys Jost, O.F.M., Assoc. Pst.;

ZWOLLE

St. Joseph - 307 W. Hammond St., Zwolle, LA 71486; Mailing: PO Box 8, Zwolle, LA 71486 t) 318-645-6155 loveladys@bellsouth.net stjosephzwolle.org Very Rev. Keith Garvin, Pst.; CRP Stds.: 348

St. Ann - 5272 Hwy. 482, Noble, LA 71462

SCHOOLS: PRESCHOOL THRU HIGH SCHOOL

HIGH SCHOOLS

STATE OF LOUISIANA

MONROE

St. Frederick High School - (DIO) (Grades 7-12) 3300 Westminster Ave., Monroe, LA 71201-3299 t) 318-323-9636 warriors@stfrederickhigh.org www.stfrederickhigh.org Dcn. Scott Brandle, Chap.; Carynn Wiggins, Prin.; Stds.: 288; Lay Tchrs.: 24

SHREVEPORT

Loyola College Prep - (DIO) (Grades 9-12) 921 Jordan St., Shreveport, LA 71101-4390 t) 318-221-2675 office@loyolaprep.org www.loyolaprep.org Rev. Raney Christopher Johnson, Chap.; John LeBlanc, Prin.; Stds.: 381; Lay Tchrs.: 36

INSTITUTIONS LOCATED IN DIOCESE

CAMPUS MINISTRY / NEWMAN CENTERS [CAM]

GRAMBLING

Student Center - 471 Main St., Grambling, LA 71245-3088 t) 318-247-6734 stbenedict471@gmail.com Rev. Patrick J. Madden, Sacr. Min.;

MONROE

Catholic Campus Ministry at the University of Louisiana at Monroe - 911 University Ave., Monroe, LA 71211-7250; Mailing: P.O. Box 7250, Monroe, LA 71211-7250 t) 318-343-4897 rquiroz@dioshpt.org (formerly Northeast Louisiana University) Rev. John Paul Crispin, F.M.H., Chap.;

RUSTON

E. Donn Piatt Catholic Student Center at Louisiana Tech University - 600 Thornton St., Ruston, LA 71270-4946 t) 318-251-0793 acts.latech.edu@gmail.com www.stac-acts.com Rev. Kevin Joseph Mues, Campus Min.;

CEMETERIES [CEM]

SHREVEPORT

St. Joseph - 2100 Texas St., Shreveport, LA 71101; Mailing: 3500 Fairfield Ave., Shreveport, LA 71104 t) 318-868-4441 rquiroz@dioshpt.org Rosalba Quiroz, Exec.; Edward Hydro, Contact;

CONVENTS, MONASTERIES, AND RESIDENCES FOR WOMEN [CON]

SHREVEPORT

Motherhouse of the Daughters of the Cross in America - 3500 Fairfield Ave., Shreveport, LA 71104 t) 318-868-4441 jbraniff@dioshpt.org Sr. Lucy Scallan, Supr.; Srs.: 1

ENDOWMENTS / FOUNDATIONS / TRUSTS [EFT]

MONROE

St. Francis Medical Center Foundation, Inc. - 309 Jackson St., Monroe, LA 71201 t) 318-966-7732 Dr. Thomas J Gullatt, Pres.;

HOSPITALS / HEALTH SERVICES [HOS]

COUSHATTA

CHRISTUS Coushatta Health Care Center - 1635 Marvel St., Coushatta, LA 71019 t) 318-932-2000 kim.kelsch@christushealth.org www.christuscoushatta.org CHRISTUS Health Northern Louisiana. Brandon Hillman, Admin.; Thomas Steen Trawick Jr., CEO; Bed Capacity: 25; Asstd. Annu.: 22,138; Staff: 178

MONROE

St. Francis Medical Center, Inc. - 309 Jackson St., Monroe, LA 71210; Mailing: P.O. Box 1901, Monroe, LA 71201 t) 318-966-4000 thomas.gullatt@fmolhs.org; lora.jackson@fmolhs.org www.stfran.com Dr. Thomas J Gullatt, Pres.; Bed Capacity: 328; Asstd. Annu.: 167,587; Staff: 1,800

SHREVEPORT

CHRISTUS Health Northern Louisiana - 1453 E. Bert Kouns Industrial Loop, Shreveport, LA 71105 t) 318-681-5000 kim.kelsch@christushealth.org christushealthsb.org Rev. Stephen Bradley, Chap.; Bradley Harmon, Vice. Pres.; Mary Preziosi, Chap.; Thomas Steen Trawick Jr., CEO; Bed Capacity: 242; Asstd. Annu.: 248,478; Staff: 1,145

MISCELLANEOUS [MIS]

LAKE PROVIDENCE

***LCWR Region V Lake Providence Collaborative Ministries** - 106 Ingram St., Lake Providence, LA 71254 t) 318-559-3747 liturgist44@hotmail.com Tutoring, community organizing, and senior citizen programs. Direct assistance. Assistance with housing challenges.

SHREVEPORT

Magnificat-Nowela Chapter - 7724 Tampa Way, Shreveport, LA 71105; Mailing: P. O. Box 4293, Shreveport, LA 71134 c) 318-564-2672 balistre@bellsouth.net

An asterisk (*) denotes an organization that has established tax-exempt status directly with the IRS and is not covered by the USCCB Group Ruling.

Diocese of Sioux City

(Dioecesis Siopolitana)

MOST REVEREND R. WALKER NICKLESS

Bishop of Sioux City; ordained August 4, 1973; appointed Bishop of Sioux City November 10, 2005; Episcopal ordination January 20, 2006.

Chancery: Administrative Offices, 1821 Jackson St., P.O. Box 3379, Sioux City, IA 51102-3379. T: 712-255-7933; F: 712-233-7598.
www.scdiocese.org
bishopnickless@scdiocese.org

ESTABLISHED JANUARY 15, 1902.

Square Miles 14,518.

Corporate Title: "The Diocese of Sioux City."

Comprises 24 Counties in the northwest part of Iowa, west of Winnebago, Hancock, Wright, Hamilton and Story Counties, and north of Harrison, Shelby, Audubon, Guthrie and Dallas Counties.

For legal titles of parishes and diocesan institutions, consult the Chancery.

STATISTICAL OVERVIEW

Personnel
Bishop 1
Priests: Diocesan Active in Diocese....42
Priests: Diocesan Active Outside Diocese....4
Priests: Retired, Sick or Absent....42
Number of Diocesan Priests....88
Religious Priests in Diocese....2
Total Priests in your Diocese....90
Extern Priests in Diocese....5
Ordinations:
Diocesan Priests....1
Transitional Deacons....1
Permanent Deacons in Diocese....58
Total Sisters....45

Parishes
Parishes....52
With Resident Pastor:
Resident Diocesan Priests....28
Without Resident Pastor:
Administered by Priests....25
Missions....1
New Parishes Created....1
Closed Parishes....9
Professional Ministry Personnel:
Sisters....45

Welfare
Catholic Hospitals....3
Total Assisted....221,055
Homes for the Aged....3
Total Assisted....360
Special Centers for Social Services....6
Total Assisted....3,577

Educational
Diocesan Students in Other Seminaries....8
Total Seminarians....8
Colleges and Universities....1
Total Students....927
High Schools, Diocesan and Parish....7
Total Students....1,348
Elementary Schools, Diocesan and Parish....19
Total Students....4,433
Catechesis/Religious Education:
High School Students....1,552
Elementary Students....4,641
Total Students under Catholic Instruction....12,909
Teachers in Diocese:
Sisters....2
Lay Teachers....476

Vital Statistics
Receptions into the Church:
Infant Baptism Totals....1,095
Minor Baptism Totals....50
Adult Baptism Totals....49
Received into Full Communion....85
First Communions....1,098
Confirmations....1,157
Marriages:
Catholic....173
Interfaith....81
Total Marriages....254
Deaths....1,081
Total Catholic Population....81,402
Total Population....461,541

LEADERSHIP

Vicars General - Very Rev. Bradley C. Pelzel; Rev. Msgr. Kevin C. McCoy;
Moderator of the Curia - Very Rev. Bradley C. Pelzel;
Chancery - t) 712-255-7933 Dcn. Mark Prosser, Contact;
Chancellor - t) 712-233-7514 marks@scdiocese.org Rev. Mark J. Stoll, Chancellor;
Director Pastoral Planning - t) 712-233-7536 Dcn. Mark Prosser;
Diocesan Tribunal - t) 712-233-7533 Very Rev. J. David Esquiliano, Vicar (esquilianod@scdiocese.org); Rev. Michael J. Erpelding; Terri Niedergeses, Secy.;
Judicial Vicar - Very Rev. J. David Esquiliano;
Adjutant Judicial Vicar - Rev. Michael J. Erpelding;
Promoter of Justice - Rev. Mark J. Stoll;
Defenders of the Bond - Rev. Msgr. Kevin C. McCoy; Rev. Msgr. Michael D. Sernett;
Judges - Very Rev. J. David Esquiliano (esquilianod@scdiocese.org); Rev. Michael J. Erpelding; Rev. Msgr. R. Mark Duchaine;
Notary - Terri Niedergeses;
Diocesan Finance Council - Most Rev. R. Walker Nickless, Pres.; Rev. Msgr. Kevin C. McCoy; Randy Kramer, Chair;
Diocesan Legal Counsel - t) 712-277-2373 x20 Kathleen Roe; Jeffrey R. Mohrhauser;
Presbyteral Council - Very Rev. Patrick M. Behm; Very Rev. J. David Esquiliano (esquilianod@scdiocese.org); Very Rev. Andrew J. Galles;
Diocesan Consultors - Very Rev. Patrick M. Behm; Very Rev. J. David Esquiliano (esquilianod@scdiocese.org); Very Rev. Andrew J. Galles;
Deans - Very Rev. Andrew J. Galles; Very Rev. Timothy A. Pick; Very Rev. Daniel C. Guenther, Dean;

OFFICES AND DIRECTORS

Archives - t) 712-233-7525 Cecilia Lopez;
Board of Education - Sue Eldridge; Ted Garringer (tlgarringer@kuemper.org); Christina Peterson (petersonc@bishopgarrigan.org);
Building Commission - Rev. Brent C. Lingle (blingle@stormlakecatholic.com); Very Rev. Andrew J. Galles; Brad Mollet;
Catholic Charities - t) 712-252-4547 info@cathchar.com cathchar.com/ Amy Bloch, Exec. Dir.;
Catholic School Foundation of the Diocese of Sioux City - Carlos Almendarez; Amy Jungers; Jill Book;
Catholic Youth Organization - t) 712-873-3644 schonr@scdiocese.org Rev. Randy L. Schon, Dir.;
Censor Librorum (Vacant) -
Committee for the Continuing Formation of Priests - Rev. Michael J. Cronin, Dir.;
Council of Catholic Women - t) 712-229-2586 Rev. James J. Tigges, Moderator;
Department of Formation and Ministry - t) 712-233-7536 Dcn. Mark Prosser, Dir.; Gracie Ortiz, Dir.; Patty Lansink, Supt.;
Episcopal Representative for Religious - Sr. Mary Day, O.S.F., Secy.;
Monsignor Lafferty Tuition Foundation Board - Sara Bormann (sbormann@stmaryhumboldt.org); Most Rev. R. Walker Nickless; Rev. Msgr. Kevin C. McCoy;
Office of Catholic Education - t) 712-233-7527 Patty Lansink, Supt.;
Office of Communications - t) 712-233-7573 Dawn Prosser, Dir.;
Office of "Lumen Media" - t) 712-255-2550 Dawn Prosser, Editor;
Office of Stewardship and Development - t) (712) 233-7513 John Schmitz, Dir. (johns@scdiocese.org);
Office of Worship - t) 712-233-7534 Very Rev. Andrew J. Galles, Dir.;
Priests' Pension Plan - Board of Trustees - Very Rev. Timothy A. Pick; David Flattery; Rev. Daniel M. Greving;
Priests' Personnel Board - Rev. Craig A. Collison; Very Rev. J. David Esquiliano (esquilianod@scdiocese.org); Rev. Msgr. Kevin C. McCoy;
Propagation of the Faith, Association of the Holy Childhood, Catholic Students' Mission Crusade - t) 712-233-7593 Rev. Mark J. Stoll, Dir.;
Safe Environment Coordinator - t) 712-233-7517 Dr. Dan Ellis (dane@scdiocese.org);
St. Joseph Education Society - t) 712-233-7512 Rev. Bruce A. Lawler; Rev. Msgr. Kevin C. McCoy; Most Rev. R. Walker Nickless;
Victim Assistance Coordinator - t) 866-435-4397 Angie Mack;
Vocations - t) 712-233-7523 Rev. Travis Crotty;

PARISHES, MISSIONS, AND CLERGY

STATE OF IOWA

AKRON

St. Patrick - 650 Dakota St., Akron, IA 51001; Mailing: P.O. Box 317, Akron, IA 51001-0317 t) 712-551-1501 stpatrickakron@gmail.com stpatrickakron.com Rev. Paul Bormann, Pst.; Rev. Cuong Hung Nguyen, Par. Vicar; Dcn. Richard Port; CRP Stds.: 72

ALGONA

Divine Mercy Catholic Parish - 715 E. North St., Algona, IA 50511; Mailing: P.O. Box 633, Algona, IA 50511-0633 t) 515-295-3435 mclouds@dmparish.org my.dmparish.org Rev. Steven J. McLoud, Pst.; Rev. Matthew Solyntjes, Par. Vicar; CRP Stds.: 293

ALTON

St. Mary's - 609 10th St., Alton, IA 51003-8512 t) 712-756-4224 altonstmary@gmail.com pilgrimcluster.org/ Rev. Daniel M. Greving, Pst.; Dcn. Daniel Goebel; CRP Stds.: 25

ANTHON

St. Joseph's - 400 E. Randolph St., Anthon, IA 51004; Mailing: P.O. Box 285, Anthon, IA 51004-0285 t) 712-373-5573 Rev. Randy L. Schon, Pst.; Dcn. Jamie Sitzmann; CRP Stds.: 33

ARCADIA

St. John the Baptist - Merged Jul 2022 Canonical merger with Good Shepherd Parish, Breda. For sacramental records, contact Good Shepherd Parish, Breda.

BOONE

Sacred Heart - 915 12th St., Boone, IA 50036-2245 t) 515-432-1971 parishsecretary@shboone.com www.boonecountycatholics.org Rev. Timothy A. Johnson, Pst.; Dcn. David Brown; CRP Stds.: 204

Friends of Sacred Heart School - bookkeeper@shboone.com

Sacred Heart School - (Grades PreK-8) 1111 Marshall St., Boone, IA 50036-2265 t) 515-432-4124 principal@shboone.com Sue Eldridge, Prin.; Stds.: 98; Lay Tchrs.: 9

BREDA

St. Bernard's - Merged Jul 2022 Canonical merger with Good Shepherd Parish, Breda. For sacramental records, contact Good Shepherd Parish, Breda

Good Shepherd Catholic Parish - 304 N. 2nd St., Breda, IA 51436; Mailing: P.O. Box 39, Breda, IA 51436-0039 t) (712) 673-2582 (Office phone); (712) 673-2351 (Rectory phone) http//gscpcarrollco.org Rev. Terry A. Roder, Pst.; CRP Stds.: 23

Our Lady of Mt. Carmel - Merged Jul 2022 Canonical merger with Good Shepherd Parish, Breda. For sacramental records, contact Good Shepherd Parish, Breda.

CARROLL

St. John Paul II Catholic Parish - 1607 N. West St., Carroll, IA 51401-1498 t) 712-792-0513 (Religious Education); 712-792-9244 (Office) stjp2carroll@gmail.com stjp2carroll.org Rev. Kevin M. Richter, Pst.; Very Rev. Patrick M. Behm, Par. Vicar; Dcn. Tim Murphy, DRE; Dcn. Louis Meiners; Dcn. Dave Prenger; Dcn. Scott Steffen; CRP Stds.: 259

CHEROKEE

Immaculate Conception - 709 W. Cedar St., Cherokee, IA 51012; Mailing: P.O. Box 658, Cherokee, IA 51012-0658 t) 712-225-4606 iccherokee@gmail.com cherokeecountycatholics.org Rev. Daniel J. Rupp, Pst.; Rev. Eugene E. Sitzmann, Pastor Emer.; Dcn. Leroy Rupp; Maylissa Wells, DRE; CRP Stds.: 142

COON RAPIDS

Annunciation - Merged Jul 2022 Canonical merger with St. John Paul II Parish, Carroll. For sacramental records contact St. John Paul II Parish, Carroll.

DANBURY

St. Mary's - 604 Peach St., Danbury, IA 51019; Mailing: 602 Peach St., Danbury, IA 51019 t) 712-364-2718 mccarthyw@scdiocese.org Rev. William A. McCarthy, Pst.; CRP Stds.: 30

DEDHAM

St. Joseph's - Merged Jul 2022 Canonical merger with St. John Paul II Parish, Carroll. For sacramental records, contact St. John Paul II Parish, Carroll.

DENISON

St. Rose of Lima - 916 2nd Ave. S., Denison, IA 51442; Mailing: P.O. Box 280, Denison, IA 51442-0280 t) 712-263-2152 bkdenison@scdiocese.org; croninm@scdiocese.org www.denisoncatholic.com Rev. Michael J. Cronin, Pst.; Rev. Shinoj Jose (India), Par. Vicar; CRP Stds.: 118

St. Rose of Lima School - (Grades PreK-5) 1004 2nd Ave. S., Denison, IA 51442 t) 712-263-5408 astangl@stroseoflimaschools.org www.stroselimacatholic.org/home Angie Stangl, Prin.; Stds.: 125; Lay Tchrs.: 14

EMMETSBURG

Holy Family - 2003 S. Broadway St., Emmetsburg, IA 50536; Mailing: P.O. Box 322, Emmetsburg, IA 50536-0322 t) 712-852-3187 hfp@e-irish.org; bkemmetsburg@scdiocese.org Rev. William A. Schreiber, Pst.; CRP Stds.: 78

Emmetsburg Catholic School - (Grades PreK-8) 1903 Broadway St., Emmetsburg, IA 50536-2267 t) 712-852-3464 kwuebker@e-irish.org; jhyslop@e-irish.org www.emmetsburgcatholic.org Jean Hyslop, Prin.; Stds.: 102; Lay Tchrs.: 8

ESTHERVILLE

St. Patrick's - 903 Central Ave., Estherville, IA 51334; Mailing: P.O. Box 383, Estherville, IA 51334-0383 t) 712-362-5851 stpatssec@outlook.com www.stpatstmary.com Rev. Paul Kelly, Pst.; Dcn. John S. Rudd; Kathy Cornwall, DRE; CRP Stds.: 118

FONDA

Our Lady of Good Counsel - 521 N. Main St., Fonda, IA 50540; Mailing: P.O. Box 339, Fonda, IA 50540-0339 t) 712-288-6480 olgcfonda@gmail.com Rev. Craig A. Collison, Pst.; Dana Erickson, DRE; CRP Stds.: 99

FORT DODGE

Holy Trinity Parish of Webster County - 2506 6th Ave. N., Fort Dodge, IA 50501; Mailing: 2220 4th Ave. N., Fort Dodge, IA 50501 t) 515-955-6077 holytrinityparish@fdcatholic.com www.holytrinitywci.org Mark Steinberg, RCIA Coord.; Rev. Msgr. Kevin C. McCoy, Pst.; Rev. Ross P Caniglia, Par. Vicar; Dcn. Edward Albright; Dcn. Joseph Coleman; Dcn. Rick Salocker; Brenna Peters, DRE; Kate Stucky, Bus. Mgr.; CRP Stds.: 125

GRAETTINGER

Immaculate Conception - 305 N. Cameron Ave., Graettinger, IA 51342; Mailing: P.O. Box 322, Emmetsburg, IA 50536-0322 t) 712-852-3187 hfp@e-irish.org Rev. William A. Schreiber, Pst.; CRP Stds.: 109

GRANVILLE

St. Joseph - 528 Elm St., Granville, IA 51022; Mailing: P.O. Box 127, Granville, IA 51022-0127 t) 712-727-3551 christec@mtcnet.net www.pilgrimcluster.org Rev. Daniel M. Greving, Pst.; Dcn. Daniel Goebel; Diane Rainbolt, DRE; CRP Stds.: 43

HALBUR

St. Augustine's - Merged Jul 2022 Canonical merger with

Good Shepherd Parish, Breda. For sacramental records, contact Good Shepherd Parish, Breda.

HARTLEY

St. Joseph's - 260 N. 4th Ave. W., Hartley, IA 51346; Mailing: P.O. Box 555, Sanborn, IA 51248-0555 c) 507-475-1492 4unioncatholic@gmail.com www.spencersacredheart.com/ Rev. Timothy J. Hogan, Pst.; Megan Wagner, DRE; CRP Stds.: 82

HAWARDEN

St. Mary's - 1125 Ave. L, Hawarden, IA 51023-0271 t) 712-551-1501; 712-551-2526 (parish hall) stmarydre@gohitec.com; stmaryschurch@gohitec.com www.stmaryhawarden.com Rev. Paul Bormann, Pst.; Rev. Cuong Hung Nguyen, Par. Vicar; CRP Stds.: 196

HOLSTEIN

Our Lady of Good Counsel - 517 Mueller St., Holstein, IA 51025; Mailing: P.O. Box 380, Holstein, IA 51025-0380 t) 712-368-4755; 712-225-4606 (Cherokee Office) olgc51025@gmail.com; iccherokee@gmail.com cherokeecountycatholics.org/ Rev. Daniel J. Rupp, Pst.; Rev. Msgr. Kenneth A. Seifried, In Res.; CRP Stds.: 57

HOSPERS

St. Anthony's - 500 Elm St., Hospers, IA 51238; Mailing: P.O. Box 86, Hospers, IA 51238-0086 t) 712-752-8784 stacc@nethtc.net pilgrimcluster.org Rev. Daniel M. Greving, Pst.; Diane Rainbolt, DRE; Dcn. Daniel Goebel; CRP Stds.: 11

HUMBOLDT

St. Mary's - 307 4th St. N., Humboldt, IA 50548-1647 t) 515-332-2856 www.humboldtareacc.org Very Rev. Daniel C. Guenther, Pst.; Dcn. Don Evans; CRP Stds.: 126

St. Mary's School - (Grades PreK-6) 306 3rd St. N., Humboldt, IA 50548-1611 t) 515-332-2134 cedge@stmaryhumboldt.org www.stmaryhumboldt.org Sara Bormann, Prin.; Stds.: 182; Lay Tchrs.: 10

IDA GROVE

Sacred Heart - 800 N. Main St., Ida Grove, IA 51445-1297; Mailing: P.O. Box 203, Ida Grove, IA 51445-0203 t) 712-364-4418 bkidagrove@scdiocese.org Rev. William A. McCarthy, Pst.; Dcn. Mike Stover; CRP Stds.: 107

JEFFERSON

St. Joseph's - 503 N. Chestnut St., Jefferson, IA 50129-1507; Mailing: 501 N. Locust St., Jefferson, IA 50129-1585 t) 515-386-2638 Rev. John J. Gerald (India), Pst.; CRP Stds.: 122

KINGSLEY

St. Michael's - 208 Brandon St., Kingsley, IA 51028; Mailing: P.O. Box 99, Kingsley, IA 51028-0099 t) 712-378-2722; (712) 378-2021 icmoville@wiatel.net; stmichael@wiatel.net westforkcatholiccommunity.org Rev. Randy L. Schon, Pst.; Dcn. Jamie Sitzmann; Megan Thompson, DRE; CRP Stds.: 102

LAKE CITY

St. Mary's - 205 N. Lloyd St., Lake City, IA 51449; Mailing: P.O. Box 131, Lake City, IA 51499-0131 t) 712-464-3395 calhouncatholic.org Rev. Lynn A. Bruch, Pst.; Dcn. Robert Lenz; Sandra Hildreth, DRE; CRP Stds.: 92

LARCHWOOD

St. Mary - 1030 Blaine St., Larchwood, IA 51241; Mailing: P.O. Box 37, Larchwood, IA 51241 t) 712-477-2273 holymarycluster@yahoo.com holymarycluster.com Rev. Sunny Dominic, Pst.; CRP Stds.: 85

LE MARS

All Saints Roman Catholic Church - 605 Plymouth St., N.E., Le Mars, IA 51031-3760 t) 712-546-5223 allsaintslemars.org Rev. Bruce A. Lawler, Pst.; Rev. Douglas M. Klein, Par. Vicar; Dcn. Paul Gengler; Dcn. Richard James Roder; CRP Stds.: 259

All Saints Endowment Fund -

St. Joseph at Ellendale - 23533 CR K22, Ellendale, IA 51038; Mailing: 605 Plymouth St., N.E., Le Mars, IA 51031-3760 t) (712) 546-5223 lawlerb@scdiocese.org

MADRID

St. Malachy's - 405 Gerald St., Madrid, IA 50156; Mailing: 207 Gerald St., Madrid, IA 50156 t) 515-795-2613 (Church); 515-795-2731 (Office) stmalachymadrid@outlook.com; kelley.grothus@gmail.com www.boonecountycatholics.org Rev. Timothy A. Johnson, Pst.; Dcn. Verne Burke; Dcn. David LaMar; CRP Stds.: 204

MANNING

Sacred Heart - 203 Sue St., Manning, IA 51455-1327; Mailing: P.O. Box 280, Denison, IA 51442-0280 t) 712-263-2152 croninm@scdiocese.org; office@denisoncatholic.com www.denisoncatholic.com Rev. Michael J. Cronin, Pst.; Rev. Shinoj Jose (India), Par. Vicar; CRP Stds.: 127

MANSON

St. Thomas - 1100 8th St., Manson, IA 50563; Mailing: P.O. Box 131, Lake City, IA 51449-0131 t) 712-464-3395 www.calhouncatholic.org Rev. Lynn A. Bruch, Pst.; Rev. James A. Bruch, In Res.; Dcn. Robert Lenz; CRP Stds.: 47

MAPLETON

St. Mary's - 703 Heisler St., Mapleton, IA 51034 t) 712-882-1780 mapletonparishcoordinator@gmail.com; bkmapleton@scdiocese.org Rev. William A. McCarthy, Pst.; CRP Stds.: 38

MARCUS

Holy Name - 102 N. Elm St., Marcus, IA 51035; Mailing: P.O. Box 366, Marcus, IA 51035-0366 t) 712-376-2628 pickt@scdiocese.org mostholynameofmary.org/ Very Rev. Timothy A. Pick, Pst.; Dcn. Jerry Bertrand; Dcn. Doug Heeren; CRP Stds.: 101

MILFORD

St. Joseph's - 1305 Okoboji Ave., Milford, IA 51351-1244 t) 712-338-2274 info@stjosephmilford.org www.stjosephmilford.org Rev. Brian C. Hughes, Pst.; Sharon Mayer, DRE; CRP Stds.: 116

MOVILLE

Immaculate Conception - 419 Jones St., Moville, IA 51039; Mailing: P.O. Box 802, Moville, IA 51039-0802 t) 712-873-3644 icmoville@wiatel.net www.westforkcatholiccommunity.org Rev. Randy L. Schon, Pst.; Angela Duffy, DRE; CRP Stds.: 93

ONAWA

St. John - 1009 13th St., Onawa, IA 51040-1508 t) 712-423-1004 (Parish secretary); 712-423-2656 (Pastor's office) secretary@stjohnparishonawa.com www.stjohnonawa.com Rev. Michael J. Erpelding, Pst.; Michelle Rethman, DRE; Dcn. Joseph Scurlock; CRP Stds.: 85

POCAHONTAS

Church of the Resurrection - 11 S.W. 2nd St., Pocahontas, IA 50574; Mailing: 202 W. Elm Ave., Pocahontas, IA 50574-1906 t) 712-335-3242 prparish@gmail.com Rev. Craig A. Collison, Pst.; CRP Stds.: 44

REMSEN

St. Mary's - 121 E. 4th St., Remsen, IA 51050; Mailing: P.O. Box 509, Remsen, IA 51050-0509 t) 712-786-1437 smparish@midlands.net mostholynameofmary.org Very Rev. Timothy A. Pick, Pst.; Dcn. Jerry Bertrand; Dcn. Doug Heeren; CRP Stds.: 285

St. Mary's Schools - (Grades PreSchool-8) 321 Fulton St., Remsen, IA 51050-7749 t) 712-786-1160 phillipsk@rsmschools.org www.rsmschools.org/ Kim Phillips, Prin.; Stds.: 145; Lay Tchrs.: 13

ROCK RAPIDS

Holy Name - 1108 S. Carroll St., Rock Rapids, IA 51246-2060 t) 712-472-3248 holymarycluster@yahoo.com; bkrockrapids@scdiocese.org holymarycluster.com Rev. Sunny Dominic, Pst.; CRP Stds.: 75

ROCK VALLEY

St. Mary's - 1821 14th St., Rock Valley, IA 51247-1212 t) 712-476-2060 smrv@premieronline.net www.stmarysrockvalley.org Rev. Mauro Sanchez, Pst.; CRP Stds.: 140

ROCKWELL CITY

St. Francis of Assisi - 744 Main St., Rockwell City, IA 50579-1344; Mailing: P.O. Box 131, Lake City, IA 51449-0131 t) 712-464-3395 calhouncatholic.org Rev. Lynn A. Bruch, Pst.; Rev. Clair L. Boes, In Res.; Dcn. Robert Lenz; CRP Stds.: 20

SALIX

St. Joseph's - 510 Tipton St., Salix, IA 51052; Mailing: P.O. Box 270, Salix, IA 51052-0270 t) 712-946-5635 (Parish office) secretary@stjoeparishsalix.com www.stjoessalix.com Rev. Michael J. Erpelding, Pst.; Michelle Rethman, DRE; CRP Stds.: 75

SHELDON

St. Patrick's - 310 10th St., Sheldon, IA 51201-1530 t) 712-324-0160 bksheldon@scdiocese.org hwy60catholiccluster.org Rev. Siby Punnoose, Pst.; Paulette Karolczak, DRE; CRP Stds.: 108

St. Patrick's School - (Grades PreK-8) 1020 4th Ave., Sheldon, IA 51201-1520 t) 712-324-3181 jschmalen@stpatrickssheldon.org Jessica Schmalen, Prin.; Stds.: 50; Lay Tchrs.: 8

SIBLEY

St. Andrew's - 708 8th St., Sibley, IA 51249; Mailing: 722 8th Ave., P.O. Box 97, Sibley, IA 51249-0097 t) 712-754-2739 standrewsibley@premieronline.net hwy60catholiccluster.org Rev. Siby Punnoose, Pst.; Christy Funk, DRE; CRP Stds.: 90

SIOUX CENTER

Christ the King - 501 2nd Ave., S.W., Sioux Center, IA 51250-1426 t) 712-722-3011 smrv@premieronline.net www.christthekingsc.org Robyn VanVenrooij, DRE; Rev. Mauro Sanchez, Pst.; CRP Stds.: 195

SIOUX CITY

Cathedral of the Epiphany - 1000 Douglas St., Sioux City, IA 51105-1399 t) 712-255-1637 esquilianod@scdiocese.org www.sccathedral.org Very Rev. J. David Esquiliano, Rector; Very Rev. Andrew J. Galles, Par. Vicar; Rev. Jeremy J. Wind, Par. Vicar; Rev. Travis Crotty, In Res.; Dcn. Bruce Chartier; Dcn. Jorge L. Fernandez; Dcn. David A. Lopez; Dcn. Mark Prosser; Dcn. James H. Sands; CRP Stds.: 309

Holy Cross Catholic Parish - 3012 Jackson St., Sioux City, IA 51104-2742 t) 712-277-2949 frdavid@holycrosssc.org; patty@holycrosssc.org www.holycrosssc.org Very Rev. David A. Hemann, Pst.; Rev. Peter Duc Hung Nguyen, Par. Vicar; Patty Kime, Bus. Mgr.; CRP Stds.: 290

Holy Cross Convent - 2223 Indian Hills Dr., Sioux City, IA 51104-1605 t) 402-992-8533 srgabemarie@hotmail.com www.mbsmissionaries.org Missionary Benedictine Sisters Sr. Gabrielle Marie Oestreich, O.S.B., Supr.;

Mater Dei Catholic Parish - 1212 Morningside Ave., Sioux City, IA 51106 t) 712-276-4821 (Main Line Auto Attendant); 712-226-4320 (Front Office) mdp.priest@materdeisc.org www.materdeisc.org Mater Dei Catholic Parish has 2 locations: 4241 Natalia Way and 1212 Morningside Ave., Sioux City, IA Very Rev. Bradley C. Pelzel, Pst.; Rev. Mark J. Stoll, Par. Vicar; Dcn. Kevin Poss; Dcn. Dennis Brockhaus; Jeff Schoep, Parish Life Coord.; Dcn. Richard James Roder, CRE; CRP Stds.: 328

Sacred Heart - 5010 Military Rd., Sioux City, IA 51103-1564 t) 712-233-1652 www.sacredheartsiouxcity.com Rev. Timothy A. Friedrichsen, Pst.; Mary B Lehr, DRE; CRP Stds.: 85

SPENCER

Sacred Heart - 1111 4th Ave. W., Spencer, IA 51301; Mailing: P.O. Box 817, Spencer, IA 51301-0817 t) 712-262-3047 qtjhz@aol.com www.spencersacredheart.com/ Rev. Timothy J. Hogan, Pst.; Mollie Maurer, DRE; CRP Stds.: 140

Sacred Heart School - (Grades PreK-6) t) 712-262-6428 dfries@spencersacredheart.com Deena Fries, Prin.; Stds.: 180; Lay Tchrs.: 10

SPIRIT LAKE

St. Mary's - 1005 Hill Ave., Spirit Lake, IA 51360; Mailing: P.O. Box 354, Spirit Lake, IA 51360-0354 t) 712-336-1742 smoffice@thelakescatholic.church www.stmarysspiritlake.org Rev. Brian C. Hughes, Pst.; Dcn. Darwin Messerly; CRP Stds.: 147

STORM LAKE

St. Mary's - 300 E. Third St., Storm Lake, IA 50588-2554 t) 712-732-3110 parish@stormlakecatholic.com www.stormlakecatholic.com Rev. Brent C. Lingle, Pst.; Dcn. Mike Higgins; Dcn. Paul M. Kestel; Dcn. Kenny Lindquist; Dcn. Hector Mora; Dcn. Rick Rohr; Kathleen Eckerman, DRE; CRP Stds.: 165

Elementary & High School - (Grades K-12) t) (712) 732-4166 rberg@stmarys-storm.pvt.k12.ia.us Ryan Berg, Prin.; Kate Swanson, Prin.; Stds.: 261; Lay Tchrs.: 25

TEMPLETON

Sacred Heart - Merged Jul 2022 Canonical merger with Good Shepherd Parish, Breda. For sacramental records, contact Good Shepherd Parish, Breda.

VAIL

St. Ann's - 102 5th Ave., Vail, IA 51465; Mailing: P.O. Box 280, Denison, IA 51442-0280 t) 712-263-2152 croninm@scdiocese.org; office@denisoncatholic.com www.denisoncatholic.com Rev. Michael J. Cronin, Pst.; Rev. Shinoj Jose (India), Par. Vicar;

WALL LAKE

St. Joseph's - 102 W. 5th St., Wall Lake, IA 51466; Mailing: P.O. Box 130, Wall Lake, IA 51466-0130 t) 712-662-7240 dillingerj@scdiocese.org; bkwalllake@scdiocese.org Rev. Joseph A. Dillinger, Pst.; Dcn. B. (Butch) Stone; CRP Stds.: 229

WILLEY

St. Mary's - Merged Jul 2022 Canonical merger with St. John Paul II, Carroll. For sacramental records, contact St. John Paul II, Carroll.

SCHOOLS: PRESCHOOL THRU HIGH SCHOOL

SCHOOLS

STATE OF IOWA

ALTON

Spalding Catholic Schools, Inc. - (PAR) (Grades PreK-6) 908 6th Ave., Alton, IA 51003; Mailing: P.O. Box 436, Alton, IA 51003-0436 t) 712-756-4532 (Office); 712-756-4528 (Devel. Dir.) woetken@spaldingcatholic.org; dgoebel@spaldingcatholic.org www.spaldingcatholic.org Serving the parishes of Granville; Alton and Hospers. Rev. Daniel M. Greving, Pres.; Patty Lansink, Prin.; Dcn. Daniel Goebel; Stds.: 46; Lay Tchrs.: 6

CARROLL

Kuemper Catholic School System - (PAR) (Grades PreSchool-12) 116 S. East St., Carroll, IA 51401 t) 712-792-3313 jjsteffes@kuemper.org www.kuemper.org John Steffes, Pres.; Stds.: 1,163; Lay Tchrs.: 77

FORT DODGE

St. Edmond Catholic School, Inc. - (PAR) (Grades PreK-12) 2220 4th Ave. N., Fort Dodge, IA 50501 t) 515-571-5182 gibbm@st-edmond.pvt.k12.is.us www.st-edmond.pvt.k12.ia.us Tabitha Acree, Prin.; Mary Gibb, Pres.; Susan Laufersweiler, Dir.; Stds.: 627; Pr. Tchrs.: 2; Lay Tchrs.: 47

LE MARS

Gehlen Catholic School - (PAR) (Grades PreK-12) 709 Plymouth St., N.E., Le Mars, IA 51031-3701 t) 712-546-4181 lawlerb@scdiocese.org; frtravis@gehlencatholic.org www.gehlencatholic.org Rev. Bruce A. Lawler, Pres.; Rev. Travis Crotty, Par. Vicar; Andrea Loutsch, Prin.; Stds.: 494; Lay Tchrs.: 41

SIOUX CITY

Bishop Heelan Catholic Schools - (PAR) (Grades PreK-12) 50 13th St., Sioux City, IA 51103; Mailing: P.O. Box 1439, Sioux City, IA 51103-1439 t) 712-252-1350 john.flanery@bishopheelan.org www.bishopheelan.org Serving the parishes of Mater Dei, Cathedral, Holy Cross, and Sacred Heart Chris Bork, Prin.; Dr. John Flanery, Pres.; Stds.: 1,564; Pr. Tchrs.: 1; Lay Tchrs.: 154

Sacred Heart - (Grades PreK-12) 5010 Military Rd., Sioux City, IA 51103 t) 712-233-1624 connealyk@bishopheelan.org Kate Connealy, Prin.; Julie Walding, Librn.;

Mater Dei School Immaculate Conception Center - (Grades PreK-12) 3719 Ridge Ave., Sioux City, IA 51106 t) 712-276-6216 fischerm@bishopheelan.org Mary Fischer, Prin.; Vicky Samuelson, Librn.;

Bishop Heelan High School - (Grades PreK-12) 1231 Grandview Blvd., Sioux City, IA 51103 t) 712-252-0573 chris.bork@bishopheelan.org

Holy Cross School-Blessed Sacrament Center - (Grades PreK-12) 3030 Jackson St., Sioux City, IA 51104 t) 712-277-4739 debi.younger@bishopheelan.org

Mater Dei School Nativity Center - (Grades PreK-12) 4243 Natalia Way, Sioux City, IA 51106-4099 t) 712-274-0268 fischerm@bishopheelan.org Mary Fischer, Prin.; Ashley Hanson, Librn.;

St. Michael - (Grades PreK-12) 4105 Harrison, Sioux City, IA 51108 t) 712-239-1090

HIGH SCHOOLS

STATE OF IOWA

ALGONA

Bishop Garrigan Schools - (PAR) (Grades PreSchool-12) 1224 N. McCoy St., Algona, IA 50511 t) 515-295-3521 millerl@bishopgarrigan.org; petersonc@bishopgarrigan.org www.bishopgarrigan.org/ Serving the parishes at Algona, Bancroft, St. Benedict, Bode, Emmetsburg, Humboldt, Livermore, Wesley, West Bend, and Whittemore. Kristie Hough, Prin.; Christina Peterson, Prin.; Lynn Miller, Pres.; Stds.: 450; Lay Tchrs.: 36

REMSEN

St. Mary's High School - (PAR) (Grades 9-12) 523 Madison St., Remsen, IA 51050; Mailing: P.O. Box 500, Remsen, IA 51050-0500 t) 712-786-1433 phillipsk@rsmschools.org www.rsmschools.org Kim Phillips, Prin.; Stds.: 62; Lay Tchrs.: 9

INSTITUTIONS LOCATED IN DIOCESE

CEMETERIES [CEM]

FORT DODGE

Holy Trinity Parish Cemetery Improvement Society - 2220 4th Ave. N., Fort Dodge, IA 50501 t) 515-955-6077 bobh@fdcatholic.com; mccoyk@scdiocese.org Rev. Msgr. Kevin C. McCoy, Contact;

LE MARS

Calvary Cemetery - 605 Plymouth St., N.E., Le Mars, IA 51031-3760 t) 712-546-5223 Steve De Rocher, Admin.;

SIOUX CITY

Calvary Cemetery - 1821 Jackson St., Sioux City, IA 51102; Mailing: P.O. Box 3379, Sioux City, IA 51102-3379 t) 712-233-7511 audreyk@scdiocese.org; bobr@scdiocese.org Very Rev. Bradley C. Pelzel, Vicar;

COLLEGES & UNIVERSITIES [COL]

SIOUX CITY

Briar Cliff University - 3303 Rebecca St., Sioux City, IA 51104-2324 t) 712-279-5321 bernice.metz@briarcliff.edu www.briarcliff.edu Liberal Arts University. Sisters of St. Francis of the Holy Family of Dubuque, Iowa. Patrick Jacobson-Schulte, Pres.; Deidre Engel, Registrar; Stds.: 927; Lay Tchrs.: 68; Sr. Tchrs.: 2

CONVENTS, MONASTERIES, AND RESIDENCES FOR WOMEN [CON]

SIOUX CITY

Monastery of the Discalced Carmelite Nuns - 2901 S. Cecelia St., Sioux City, IA 51106-3256 t) 712-276-1680 carmelitesiouxc@gmail.com www.siouxcitycarmel.org Mother Kateri Marie, O.C.D., Prioress; Srs.: 7

ENDOWMENTS / FOUNDATIONS / TRUSTS [EFT]

ALGONA

Friends of Garrigan High School, Inc. - 1224 N. McCoy St., Algona, IA 50511 t) 515-295-3521; 515-395-3525 laubenthalm@bishopgarrigan.org Lynn Miller, Pres.;

ALTON

Spalding Catholic Schools Foundation, Inc. - 908 6th Ave., Alton, IA 51003; Mailing: P.O. Box 436, Alton, IA 51003-0436 t) 712-756-4532 (Elem.); 712-756-4528 (Devel. Dir.) dgoebel@spaldingcatholic.org www.spaldingcatholic.org Dcn. Daniel Goebel, Secy.;

CARROLL

Kuemper Catholic School Foundation, Inc. - 116 S. East St., Carroll, IA 51401 t) 712-792-3313 cksundrup@kuemper.org www.kuemper.org Alan J Loew, Dir.;

FORT DODGE

Saint Edmond Catholic School Foundation - 2220 4th Ave. N., Fort Dodge, IA 50501 t) 515-955-6077 frkevin@fdcatholic.com; gibbm@st-edmond.pvt.k12.ia.us www.st-edmond.pvt.k12.ia.us Susan Laufersweiler, Dir.; Mary Gibb, Pres.;

Holy Trinity Parish Foundation of Webster County - 2220 4th Ave. N., Fort Dodge, IA 50501 t) 515-955-6077 frkevin@fdcatholic.com Rev. Msgr. Kevin C. McCoy, Contact;

The Marian Home Foundation - 2400 6th Ave. N., Fort Dodge, IA 50501 t) 515-576-1138 ttrotter@marianhome.com Tracy Trotter, Admin.;

SIOUX CITY

The Catholic Schools Foundation of the Diocese of Sioux City - 1821 Jackson St., Sioux City, IA 51105; Mailing: P.O. Box 3379, Sioux City, IA 51102-3379 t) 712-255-7933 lexah@scdiocese.org www.scdiocese.org John Schmitz, Dir.;

Holy Spirit Retirement Home Foundation, Inc. - 1701 W. 25th St., Sioux City, IA 51103 t) 712-252-2726; 712-224-9993 dposs@holyspiritretirementhome.com Kyla Sprakel, Admin.; Most Rev. R. Walker Nickless, Pres.; Deb Poss, Dir.;

Monsignor Lafferty Tuition Foundation - 1821 Jackson St., Sioux City, IA 51105; Mailing: P.O. Box 3379, Sioux City, IA 51102-3379 t) 712-255-7933 pattyl@scdiocese.org scdiocese.org Patty Lansink, Supt.;

STORM LAKE

St. Mary's Foundation of Storm Lake, Iowa - 300 E. 3rd St., Storm Lake, IA 50588 t) 712-732-3110 parish@stormlakecatholic.com; blingle@stormlakecatholic.com www.stormlakecatholic.com Rev. Brent C. Lingle, Pst.;

HOSPITALS / HEALTH SERVICES [HOS]

CARROLL

St. Anthony Regional Hospital - 311 S. Clark St., Carroll, IA 51401; Mailing: P.O. Box 628, Carroll, IA 51401-0628 t) 712-792-3581 aanderson@stanthonyhospital.org www.stanthonyhospital.org Allen K Anderson, Pres.; Bed Capacity: 99; Asstd. Annu.: 77,078; Staff: 750

ESTHERVILLE

Avera Holy Family - 826 N. 8th St., Estherville, IA 51334 t) 712-362-2631 info@avera-holyfamily.org www.averaholyfamily.org Sponsored by Sisters of the

Presentation of the B.V.M. of Aberdeen, S.D., and Benedictine Sisters of Sacred Heart Monastery, Yankton, S.D. Deb Herzberg, Pres.; Bed Capacity: 22; Asstd. Annu.: 42,514; Staff: 143

Holy Family Hospital Foundation - 826 N. 8th St., Estherville, IA 51334 t) (712) 362-2631

SIOUX CITY

MercyOne Siouxland Medical Center - 801 5th St., Sioux City, IA 51101 t) 712-279-2003 hendrikm@mercyhealth.com; hughesb@mercyhealth.com www.mercysiouxcity.com Trinity Health, Catholic Health Ministries Rev. Anthony Nwudah, Chap.; Rev. Augustine Peter, Chap.; Beth Hughes, Pres.; Lea Greathouse, Vice. Pres.; Mary Hendriks, Dir.; Bed Capacity: 464; Asstd. Annu.: 101,463; Staff: 1,141

MISCELLANEOUS [MIS]

CARROLL

Orchard View, Inc. - 421 S. Clark St., Carroll, IA 51401 t) 712-792-2042 aanderson@stanthonyhospital.org www.stanthonyhospital.org

POCAHONTAS

Magnificat - NW Iowa Chapter - 1104 1st Ave., N.W., Pocahontas, IA 50574 t) 712-335-4393 magnificatnwia@gmail.com Julie Storr, Contact;

SIOUX CITY

Queen of Peace Apostolate, Inc. - 2511 33rd St., Sioux City, IA 51108; Mailing: P.O. Box 1707, Sioux City, IA 51102-1707 t) 712-239-8670; 712-239-5835 (Gift Shop) info@trinityheights.com www.trinityheights.com Terry Hegarty, Exec. Dir.; Margie Lancaster, Dir.; Terry Moran, Pres.;

The St. James Fund - 1821 Jackson St., Sioux City, IA 51105; Mailing: P.O. Box 3379, Sioux City, IA 51102-3379 t) (712) 255-7933 x592 An investment corporation to manage investments for entities of the Diocese of Sioux City listed in the OCD.

SPIRIT LAKE

Opus Spiritus Sancti - 1005 Hill Ave., Spirit Lake, IA 51360 t) 712-320-2172 flanagant@scdiocese.org Rev. Thomas J. Flanagan, Dir.;

WEST BEND

Shrine of the Grotto of the Redemption - 208 1st Ave., N.W., West Bend, IA 50597; Mailing: P.O. Box 376, West Bend, IA 50597-0376 t) 515-887-2371 grottocoordinator@gmail.com www.westbendgrotto.com Very Rev. Msgr. Edward M. Girres, Rector; Andrew Milam, Admin.;

NURSING / REHABILITATION / CONVALESCENCE / ELDERLY CARE [NUR]

CARROLL

St. Anthony Nursing Home - 406 E. Anthony St., Carroll, IA 51401 t) 712-794-5291 aanderson@stanthonyhospital.org Allen K Anderson, Pres.; Asstd. Annu.: 79; Staff: 100

FORT DODGE

The Marian Home - 2400 6th Ave. N., Fort Dodge, IA 50501-3542 t) 515-576-1138 ttrotter@marianhome.com www.marianhome.com Tracy Trotter, Admin.; Asstd. Annu.: 131; Staff: 124

SIOUX CITY

Holy Spirit Retirement Home - 1701 W. 25th St., Sioux City, IA 51103 t) 712-252-2726 kylas@holyspiritretirementhome.com www.holyspiritretirementhome.com Rev. Francis S. Makwinja, Chap.; Asstd. Annu.: 150; Staff: 120

An asterisk (*) denotes an organization that has established tax-exempt status directly with the IRS and is not covered by the USCCB Group Ruling.

Diocese of Sioux Falls

(Dioecesis Siouxormensis)

MOST REVEREND DONALD E. DEGROOD

Bishop of Sioux Falls; ordained to priesthood May 31, 1997, Archdiocese of St. Paul/Minneapolis; appointed Bishop of Sioux Falls December 12, 2019; Episcopal ordination February 13, 2020. Chancery Office: 523 N. Duluth Ave., Sioux Falls, SD 57104.

Catholic Chancery Office: 523 N. Duluth Ave., Sioux Falls, SD 57104. T: 605-334-9861; F: 605-334-2092.
sfcatholic.org
cmotz@sfcatholic.org

ESTABLISHED NOVEMBER 12, 1889.

Square Miles 35,091.

Comprises those parts of South Dakota lying east and north of the Missouri River.

For legal titles of parishes and diocesan institutions, consult the Chancery Office.

STATISTICAL OVERVIEW

Personnel
Bishop....1
Priests: Diocesan Active in Diocese....74
Priests: Diocesan Active Outside Diocese....5
Priests: Retired, Sick or Absent....37
Number of Diocesan Priests....116
Religious Priests in Diocese....6
Total Priests in your Diocese....122
Extern Priests in Diocese....1
Ordinations:
Diocesan Priests....3

Parishes
Parishes....120
With Resident Pastor:
Resident Diocesan Priests....66
Resident Religious Priests....2
Without Resident Pastor:
Administered by Priests....49

Welfare
Catholic Hospitals....12
Total Assisted....1,291,769
Health Care Centers....9
Homes for the Aged....3
Total Assisted....96
Special Centers for Social Services....8

Educational
Diocesan Students in Other Seminaries....14
Total Seminarians....14
Colleges and Universities....2
Total Students....1,617
High Schools, Diocesan and Parish....2
Total Students....930
Elementary Schools, Diocesan and Parish....21
Total Students....3,822
Catechesis/Religious Education:
High School Students....2,220
Elementary Students....6,520
Total Students under Catholic Instruction....15,123
Teachers in Diocese:
Priests....4
Lay Teachers....373

Vital Statistics
Receptions into the Church:
Infant Baptism Totals....1,089
Minor Baptism Totals....53
Adult Baptism Totals....50
Received into Full Communion....109
First Communions....1,202
Confirmations....1,032
Marriages:
Catholic....245
Interfaith....148
Total Marriages....393
Deaths....750
Total Catholic Population....105,189
Total Population....630,390

LEADERSHIP

Office of the Bishop - Most Rev. Donald E. DeGrood;
Vicar General - Rev. Andrew Young;
Moderator of the Curia (Vacant) -
Vicar for Clergy (Vacant) -
Catholic Chancery Office - t) 605-334-9861
Chancellor - t) 605-988-3704 Matthew Althoff;
Vice Chancellor - t) 605-988-3745
Vocations - t) 605-988-3772 Rev. Jordan Samson, Dir.;
Deacon Formation - t) 605-988-3715 Dcn. John P. Devlin;
Marriage Tribunal - t) 605-988-3757
Judicial Vicar - Rev. Gregory Tschakert;
Tribunal Judges - Rev. Rodney Farke; Rev. Kenneth J. Koster; Rev. Charles L. Cimpl;
Defender of the Matrimonial Bond - Theresa A. Wyburn;
Matrimonial Tribunal - Heather J. Eichholz, Dir.;
Auditor -
Advocate Ad Casum (Vacant) -
Notary of Matrimonial Tribunal - Emma Murtha, Ecclesiastical Notary;
Safe Environment - Alison Conemac, Coord.;
Financial Administration -
Finance Officer - t) 605-988-3759 Scott A. Johnson;
Information Technology - Dawn Wolf, Dir.;
Human Resources - Twila Roman, Delegate;
Cemeteries and Property Management -
Liturgy, Faith Formation, and Catholic Education -
Office of Discipleship and Evangelization - Rev. Scott Traynor, Vicar;
Marriage, Family and Respect Life - t) 605-988-3776
Master of Ceremonies - Rev. Martin E. Lawrence;
Catholic Schools - t) 605-988-3704
Adult Discipleship & Evangelization - t) 605-988-3770 Christopher Burgwald, Dir.;
Youth Discipleship & Evangelization - t) 605-988-3767 Eric Gallagher, Dir.; Grace Tibbetts, Coord.;
Office of Worship (Vacant) -
Communications and Social Ministries -
The Lourdes Center - t) 605-988-3775 Emily Leedom, Exec. Dir.;
Communications Office - "Bishop's Bulletin" - t) 605-988-3789 Renae Kranz, Editor;
Delegate and Vice Chancellor - t) 605-988-3789
Parish and Diocesan Advancement -
Delegate and President of the Catholic Community Foundation for Eastern South Dakota - t) 605-988-3788 Mark Conzemius, Pres.;
Operations, Catholic Family Sharing Appeal - Tony Menke, COO;
Planned Giving - Cameo Anders, Dir.;
Diocesan Consultors - Rev. Charles L. Cimpl; Rev. James P. Morgan; Rev. Gregory Tschakert;
Consilium Administrationis -
Presbyteral Council - Rev. Terence Anderson; Rev. Thomas Anderson; Rev. Andrew Dickinson;

OFFICES AND DIRECTORS

Apostleship of Prayer -
Building Commission - Matthew Althoff; Scott A. Johnson;
Censor Librorum - Christopher Burgwald;
Clergy Personnel Committee - Rev. Thomas Clement; Rev. Gregory Tschakert; Rev. Paul A. Rutten;
Cursillo - Rev. Rodney Farke;
Diocesan Archivist - Matthew Althoff;
Ecumenical Commission (Vacant) -
Newman Apostolate (Vacant) -
Permanent Diaconate Council -
Propagation of the Faith - Dcn. John P. Devlin; Dcn. Roger R. Heidt;
Search - t) 605-334-9861
Spanish-Speaking Apostolate - Rev. John J. Helmueller;
Teens Encounter Christ - t) 605-334-9861
Victim Assistance Coordinator - t) 800-700-7867

PARISHES, MISSIONS, AND CLERGY

STATE OF SOUTH DAKOTA

ABERDEEN

Saint Mary Parish of Brown County - 409 2nd Ave. NE, Aberdeen, SD 57401-3553 t) 605-229-4422 info@stmaryabr.com stmarysabr.com/ Rev. Mitchell McLaughlin, Vicar; Rev. Michael Thomas Kapperman, Par. Vicar; Rev. Jeffrey Schulte, Par. Vicar; Rev. Andrew Dickinson, Pst.; Dcn. Peter Mehlaff;

Sacred Heart Parish of Brown County - 409 3rd Ave SE, Aberdeen, SD 57401; Mailing: 502 2nd Ave SE, Aberdeen, SD 57401-4468 t) 605-225-7065 sacredheartaberdeen@gmail.com www.sacredheartaberdeen.net Rev. Andrew Dickinson, Pst.; Rev. Jeffrey Schulte, Vicar; Rev. Michael Thomas Kapperman, Par. Vicar; Rev. Mitchell McLaughlin, Par. Vicar; Dcn. Jeff Swank; CRP Stds.: 109

ALEXANDRIA

Saint Mary of Mercy Parish of Hanson County - 220 5th St, Alexandria, SD 57311; Mailing: PO Box 158, Alexandria, SD 57311-0158 t) 605-239-4578 www.mmscatholic.org/ Rev. Robert V. Krantz, Pst.;

ARLINGTON

Saint John The Evangelist Parish of Kingsbury County - 301 S. Main St., Arlington, SD 57212; Mailing: PO Box 15, DeSmet, SD 57231-0015 t) 605-854-3564 catholickingsbury@gmail.com catholicparishesontheprairie.com/ Served from DeSmet. Rev. Richard Baumberger, Pst.;

ARMOUR

Saint Paul the Apostle Parish of Douglas County - 206 1st St., Armour, SD 57313-8800 t) 605-724-2191 stpaul@unitelsd.com www.sfcatholic.org/parishes/st-paul-the-apostle Rev. John J. Helmueller, Pst.;

ARTESIAN

Saint Charles Borromeo Parish of Sanborn County - 541 W. 2nd Ave., Artesian, SD 57314; Mailing: PO Box 266, c/o St. Wilfrid Parish, Woonsocket, SD 57385-0266 t) 605-796-4666 frkevindoyle@sfcatholic.org stwilfridsd.org/st-charles-parish/ Rev. Kevin Doyle, Pst.;

BERESFORD

St. Teresa of Avila Parish of Union County - 901 S. Third St., Beresford, SD 57004; Mailing: P.O. Box 472, Beresford, SD 57004-0472 t) 605-763-2028 office@sdprairiecatholic.org www.sdprairiecatholic.org Rev. David Roehrich, Pst.; CRP Stds.: 80

BIG BEND

Saint Catherine Parish of Hughes County - SD Hwy. 34 & Cut Across Rd. 4 miles S. on W. Bend Rd., Big Bend, SD 57346; Mailing: Box 47, Fort Thompson, SD 57339-0047 t) 605-473-5335 pastteam@gwtc.net Fort Thompson. Rev. Christianus Hendrick, S.C.J., Pst.; Rev. Mark Mastin, SCJ, Assoc. Pst.; Dcn. Steven A. McLaughlin;

BIG STONE CITY

Saint Charles Borromeo Parish of Grant County - 106 3rd Ave., Big Stone City, SD 57216; Mailing: P.O. Box 68, Big Stone City, SD 57216 t) 605-862-8485 bigstone.stcharles@sfcatholic.org Rev. David Garza, Admin.;

BOWDLE

Saint Augustine Parish of Edmunds County - 3023 S. 3rd Ave., Bowdle, SD 57428; Mailing: PO Box 310, Bowdle, SD 57428-0310 t) 605-285-6466 staug@venturecomm.net staugustinebowdle.wordpress.com/ Rev. Darin Schmidt, Pst.;

BRANDON

Risen Savior Parish of Minnehaha County - 301 N. Splitrock Blvd., Brandon, SD 57005-0080; Mailing: PO Box 80, Brandon, SD 57005-0080 t) 605-582-6902 secretary@risensaivorbrandon.com risensaviorbrandon.com Rev. Andrew Young, Pst.;

BRIDGEWATER

Saint Stephen Parish of McCook County - 350 N Juniper St, Bridgewater, SD 57319; Mailing: PO Box 158, Alexandria, SD 57311 t) 605-239-4578 www.mmscatholic.org/ St. Mary of Mercy, Alexandria. Rev. Robert V. Krantz, Pst.;

BRITTON

Saint John de Britto Parish of Marshall County - 812 8th St., Britton, SD 57430; Mailing: P.O. Box 108, Britton, SD 57430-0108 t) 605-448-5379 britton.stjohndebritto@sfcatholic.org Rev. Albert Cizewski, Pst.;

BROOKINGS

Saint Thomas More Parish of Brookings County - 1700 8th St. S., Brookings, SD 57006 t) 605-692-4361 info@stmbrookings.org www.stmbrookings.weebly.org Rev. Terence Anderson, Pst.; CRP Stds.: 376

BRYANT

Saint Mary Parish of Hamlin County - 209 S Broadway, Bryant, SD 57221; Mailing: P.O. Box 15, DeSmet, SD 57231-0015 t) 605-854-9961 catholickingsbury@gmail.com catholicparishesontheprairie.com/ St. Michael, Clark. Rev. Richard Baumberger, Pst.;

CANTON

Saint Dominic Parish of Lincoln County - 800 E. Walnut, Canton, SD 57013 t) 605-764-5640 stdominiccanton@gmail.com; stdominicre@gmail.com www.stdominccanton.org Rev. Martin E. Lawrence, Pst.; CRP Stds.: 64

CENTERVILLE

Good Shepherd Parish of Turner County - 411 Wisconsin, Centerville, SD 57014; Mailing: P.O. Box 472, Beresford, SD 57004-0472 t) 605-763-2028 office@sdprairiecatholic.org sdprairiecatholic.org Rev. David Roehrich, Pst.; CRP Stds.: 36

CHAMBERLAIN

Saint James Parish of Brule County - 400 S. Main St, Chamberlain, SD 57325-1522 t) (605) 734-6729 sjcatholic@midstatesd.net Rev. William Hamak, Pst.; Dcn. Maurice Barrett; Dcn. James Bregel;

CLARK

Saint Michael Parish of Clark County - 112 N. Idaho St., Clark, SD 57225-1423; Mailing: P.O. Box 28, Clark, SD 57225-0028 t) 605-532-3855 office@cfhcatholics.org www.parishesonline.com Rev. Daniel H. Smith, Pst.; Shannon Huber, DRE; CRP Stds.: 75

CLEAR LAKE

Saint Mary Parish of Deuel County - 408 Third St. W., Clear Lake, SD 57226; Mailing: P.O. Box 589, Clear Lake, SD 57226-0589 t) 605-874-2080 triparish@itctel.com Rev. Christopher Hughes, Pst.;

COLMAN

Saint Peter Parish of Moody County - 200 N Allen St, Colman, SD 57017; Mailing: 105 S. Bates St., Flandreau, SD 57028-1809 t) 605-997-2610 www.sodakcatholics.org SS. Simon & Jude, Flandreau. Rev. Melvin T. Kuhn, Pst.; CRP Stds.: 54

COLTON

Saint Joseph the Workman Parish of Minnehaha County - 46408 245th St, Colton, SD 57018; Mailing: P O Box 0, Garretson, SD 57030-0393 t) 605-594-3750 www.stjosephhuntimer.org Rev. Brian Eckrich, Admin.;

DAKOTA DUNES

Saint Teresa of Calcutta of Union County - 995 N. Sioux Point Rd., Dakota Dunes, SD 57049 t) 605-235-1942 www.secatholics.org Rev. Joseph Vogel, Pst.; Rev. Steven Robert Jones, Sacr. Min.; Dcn. Joseph Twidwell Jr.; Julie Eakin, DRE;

DANTE

Assumption of the Blessed Virgin Mary Parish of Charles Mix County - 416 Haines St., Dante, SD 57329; Mailing: P.O. Box 305, Wagner, SD 57380 t) (605) 384-5518 wagner.stjohn@sfcatholic.org Rev. Jim Friedrich, Pst.; CRP Stds.: 58

DE SMET

Saint Thomas Aquinas Parish of Kingsbury - 512 3rd St. SW, De Smet, SD 57231-0015; Mailing: PO Box 15, De Smet, SD 57231-0015 t) 605-854-9961 catholickingsburgy@gmail.com catholicparishesontheprairie.com/ Rev. Richard Baumberger, Pst.;

DELL RAPIDS

Saint Mary Parish of Minnehaha County - 606 E. 8th St., Dell Rapids, SD 57022-1310 t) 605-428-3990 office@stmarydellrapids.org www.stmarydellrapids.org Rev. Shane Stevens, Pst.;

Saint Mary Parish of Minnehaha County School - (Grades PreK-6) 602 E. 6th St., Dell Rapids, SD 57022 t) 605-428-3459 drstmary.org Rev. John Lantsberger, Supt.; Deb Kallhoff, Prin.;

Saint Mary Parish of Minnehaha County School (St. Mary Junior/Senior High School) - (Grades 7-12) 812 State Ave., Dell Rapids, SD 57022 t) 605-428-5591 stmarycatholicschools.org Casey Michel, Prin.;

DIMOCK

Saints Peter and Paul Parish of Hutchinson County - 146 W. 1st St., Dimock, SD 57331-2000; Mailing: PO Box 460, Parkston, SD 57366-0460 t) 605-928-3883 frdavidstevens@sfcatholic.org www.parishesonline.com/ Rev. David Stevens, Pst.;

EDEN

Sacred Heart Parish of Marshall County - 114 S. 2nd St., Eden, SD 57232; Mailing: Box 15, Eden, SD 57232 t) 605-486-4702 sheden@venturecomm.net Rev. Ken Lulf, Pst.;

ELK POINT

Saint Joseph Parish of Union County - 605 E. Main St., Elk Point, SD 57025; Mailing: PO Box 340, Elk Point, SD 57025-0340 t) 605-356-2693 stjoseph@iw.net; stjoseph@secatholics.org www.secatholics.org St. Peter, Jefferson. Rev. Joseph Vogel, Pst.; CRP Stds.: 183

ELKTON

Our Lady of Good Counsel Parish of Brookings County - 202 W. 7th St., Elkton, SD 57026-0337; Mailing: 105 S. Bates, Flandreau, SD 57028 t) 605-997-2610 Flandreau. Rev. Melvin T. Kuhn, Pst.; CRP Stds.: 90

EMERY

Saint Martin Parish of Hanson County - 342 3rd Ave., Emery, SD 57332; Mailing: PO Box 312, Emery, SD 57332 t) 605-239-4578 parishesonline.com St. Mary of Mercy, Alexandria. Rev. Robert V. Krantz, Pst.;

EPIPHANY

Epiphany Parish of Hanson County - 107 Jackson St., Epiphany, SD 57321; Mailing: P.O. Box 100, Howard, SD 57349 t) 605-772-4543 stagatha@alliancecom.net served from St. Agatha, Howard, SD Rev. Chester Murtha, Pst.;

ESTELLINE

Saint Francis de Sales Parish of Hamlin County - 1201 Eva Ave., Estelline, SD 57234; Mailing: P.O. Box 589, Clear Lake, SD 57226 t) 605-874-2080 triparish@itctel.com Rev. Christopher Hughes, Pst.;

EUREKA

Saint Joseph Parish of McPherson County - 602 2nd St., Eureka, SD 57437; Mailing: PO Box 184, Eureka, SD 57437 t) 605-284-5190 stjoseph@valleytel.net; stmicahaels@valleytel.net Herreid. Rev. Michael Griffin, Pst.; Rev. Mark Axtmann, Par. Vicar; CRP Stds.: 31

FAULKTON

Saint Thomas the Apostle Parish of Faulk County - 1013 Court St., Faulkton, SD 57438; Mailing: PO Box 394, Faulkton, SD 57438-0394 t) 605-598-6590 stthomas@venturecomm.net Rev. Randy Phillips, Pst.; Dcn. Arvid Holsing;

FLANDREAU

Saints Simon and Jude Parish of Moody County - 105 S. Bates St., Flandreau, SD 57028 t) 605-997-2610 Rev. Melvin T. Kuhn, Pst.; CRP Stds.: 64

FLORENCE

Blessed Sacrament Parish of Codington County - 803 6th St, Florence, SD 57235; Mailing: PO Box 28, Clark, SD 57225 t) 605-532-3855 office@cfhcatholics.org www.parishesonline.com Rev. Daniel H. Smith, Pst.; Pat Callan, DRE; CRP Stds.: 64

FORT THOMPSON

Saint Joseph Parish of Buffalo County - 817 SD Hwy. 47, Fort Thompson, SD 57339; Mailing: Box 47, Fort Thompson, SD 57339 t) 605-245-2350 pastteam@gwtc.net Rev. Christianus Hendrick, S.C.J., Pst.; Dcn. Steven A. McLaughlin;

GARRETSON

Saint Rose of Lima Parish of Minnehaha County - 705 3rd St., Garretson, SD 57030; Mailing: P O Box 0, Garretson, SD 57030 t) 605-594-3750 Rev. Brian Eckrich, Admin.;

GEDDES

Saint Ann Parish of Charles Mix County - 303 5th St, Geddes, SD 57342; Mailing: P.O. Box 137, Geddes, SD 57342 t) (605) 352-2542 office.stanngeddes@sfcatholic.org Rev. Thomas Clement, Pst.; Dcn. Joseph Tegethoff, DRE; CRP Stds.: 25

GETTYSBURG

Sacred Heart Parish of Potter County - 203 E. Garfield Ave., Gettysburg, SD 57442; Mailing: PO Box 285, Gettysburg, SD 57442 t) 605-765-2161 sacred@venturecomm.net getshc.org Rev. Brian Simon, Pst.;

GRENVILLE

Saint Joseph Parish of Day County - 22 St. Joseph St., Grenville, SD 57239; Mailing: Box 191, Grenville, SD 57239 t) 605-486-4702 sheden@venturecomm.net Rev. Ken Lulf, Pst.;

GROTON

Saint Elizabeth Ann Seton Parish of Brown County - 803 1st St. N., Groton, SD 57445; Mailing: P.O. Box 407, Groton, SD 57445 t) 605-397-2775 seas@nvc.net (formerly St. John the Baptist). Rev. Gregory Tschakert, Pst.;

HARRISBURG

Saint John Paul II Parish of Lincoln County - 220 S. Cliff Ave., Ste. 126, Harrisburg, SD 57032; Mailing: P.O. Box 65, Harrisburg, SD 57032-0065 t) 605-988-3750 office1@jp2sd.org jp2sd.org Rev. Shaun T Haggerty, Pst.; CRP Stds.: 245

HARTFORD

St. George Parish of Minnehaha County - 408 S. Western Ave., St. George Center, Hartford, SD 57033; Mailing: P.O. Box 577, Hartford, SD 57033 t) 605-528-3902 rdissing@stgeorgehartford.com; dre@stgeorgehartford.com www.stgeorgehartford.com Rev. Andrew Thuringer, Par. Admin.; CRP Stds.: 213

HENRY

Saint Henry Parish of Codington County - 605 4th St, Henry, SD 57243; Mailing: P.O. Box 28, Clark, SD 57225 t) 605-532-3855 office@cfhcatholics.org www.parishesonline.com Rev. Daniel H. Smith, Pst.; CRP Stds.: 20

HERREID

Saint Michael Parish of Campbell County - 106 2nd Ave. W., Herreid, SD 57632; Mailing: PO Box 37, Herreid, SD 57632 t) 605-437-2614 www.northernlightscatholics.org Rev. Michael Griffin, Pst.; CRP Stds.: 32

HIGHMORE

Saint Mary Parish of Hyde County - 311 Parker Ave., Highmore, SD 57345; Mailing: Box 457, Highmore, SD 57345 t) 605-852-2733 stmaryshighmore@yahoo.com Rev. Paul Josten, Pst.;

HOVEN

Saint Anthony Parish of Potter County - 546 Main St., Hoven, SD 57450; Mailing: PO Box 339, Bowdle, SD 57428-0339 t) 605-948-2451 stanthony@venturecomm.net Rev. Darin Schmidt, Pst.;

HOWARD

Saint Agatha Parish of Miner County - 202 W. Washington Ave., Howard, SD 57349; Mailing: Box 100, Howard, SD 57349 t) 605-772-4543 stagatha@alliancecom.net; cmurtha@alliancecom.net Rev. Chester Murtha, Pst.;

HUMBOLDT

Saint Ann Parish of Minnehaha County - 409 W. 4th Ave., Humboldt, SD 57035; Mailing: P.O. Box 195, Humboldt, SD 57035 t) (605) 363-3330 rdissing@stgeorgehartford.com www.stgeorgehartford.com Rev. Andrew Thuringer, Par. Admin.; CRP Stds.: 56

HURON

Holy Trinity Parish of Beadle County - 425 21st St., S.W., Huron, SD 57350 t) 605-352-2203 hthuron@hur.midco.net holytrinityhuron.org Rev. Larry Regynski, Pst.; Dcn. William Kappler; Dcn. Roger Puthoff; CRP Stds.: 160

Holy Trinity Parish of Beadle County School - (Grades PreK-6) 425 21st St SW, Huron, SD 57350 t) (605) 352-9344 michelle.schoenfelder@k12.sd.us holytrinity.k12sd.us Michelle Schoenfelder, Prin.;

IDYLWILDE

Saint Boniface Parish of Turner County - 28703 444th Ave., Idylwilde, SD 57043; Mailing: P.O. Box 449, Scotland, SD 57059 t) 605-583-4318 St. George, Scotland. Rev. Mark Lichter, Pst.;

IPSWICH

Holy Cross Parish of Edmunds County - 20 6th St., Ipswich, SD 57451; Mailing: Box 67, Ipswich, SD 57451-0067 t) (605) 971-4556 ipswich.holycross@sfcatholic.org Rev. Timothy Cone, Pst.;

JEFFERSON

Saint Peter Parish of Union County - 402 Main St., Jefferson, SD 57038; Mailing: P.O. Box 188, Jefferson, SD 57038-0188 t) 605-966-5716 stpeters@longlines.com; stpeter@secatholics.org www.secatholics.org Rev. Joseph Vogel, Pst.;

Preschool - 318 Main St, Jefferson, SD 57038; Mailing: P.O. Box 98, Jefferson, SD 57038-0098 t) 605-966-5746 Rev. Melvin T. Kuhn, Contact;

KIMBALL

Saint Margaret Parish of Brule County - 417 S. Elm, Kimball, SD 57355; Mailing: Box 137, Kimball, SD 57355-0137 t) 605-778-6420 smk@sfcatholic.org Rev. William Hamak, Pst.;

Preschool - t) (605) 734-6729

KRANZBURG

Holy Rosary Parish of Codington County - 202 Minnesota Ave., N.E., Kranzburg, SD 57245; Mailing: Box 166, Kranzburg, SD 57245 t) 605-886-9166 Rev. Christopher Hughes, Pst.; CRP Stds.: 83

LAKE ANDES

Saint Mark Parish of Charles Mix County - 251 N. 3rd, Lake Andes, SD 57356; Mailing: 206 1st St., Armour, SD 57313 t) 605-724-2191 stpaul@unitelsd.com Rev. John J. Helmueller, Pst.;

LENNOX

Saint Magdalen Parish of Lincoln County - 417 E. 6th Ave, Lennox, SD 57039; Mailing: Box 136, Lennox, SD 57039 t) 605-647-2187 info@stmagdalenlennox.org stmagdalenlennox.parishesonline.com Rev. Martin E Lawrence, Pst.; Kristine Shaffer, Admin.; Anne Homan, DRE; CRP Stds.: 100

LEOLA

Our Lady of Perpetual Help Parish of McPherson County - 1000 N. Main, Leola, SD 57456; Mailing: PO Box 67, Ipswich, SD 57451-0067 t) (605) 426-6967 leola.olph@sfcatholic.org www.ourladyleola.org Holy Cross, Ipswich. Rev. Timothy Cone, Pst.;

LESTERVILLE

St. John the Baptist Parish of Yankton County - 700 1st St., Lesterville, SD 57040; Mailing: 205 N. Lidice, Tabor, SD 57063 t) 605-463-2336 stwenceslaus@hcinet.net www.stjohnls.org St. Wenceslaus, Tabor. Rev. Mark Lichter, Pst.;

MADISON

Saint Thomas Aquinas Parish of Lake County - 415 N. Van Eps Ave., Madison, SD 57042-2133 t) 605-256-2304 mbeck@sttha.org; dkayser@sttha.org Rev. Anthony Urban, Pst.;

Saint Thomas Aquinas Parish of Lake County School - (Grades PreK-5) 401 N. Van Eps Ave., Madison, SD 57042 t) 605-256-4419 st-thomas.k12.sd.us Cate Luvaas, Prin.;

MARTY

Saint Paul Parish of Charles Mix County - 102 Church Dr., Marty, SD 57361; Mailing: P.O. Box 266, Marty, SD 57361-0266 t) 605-384-3234 stpaulsparish@hcinet.net Rev. Jim Friedrich; CRP Stds.: 22

MELLETTE

All Saints Parish of Spink County - 23 S 1st Ave., Mellette, SD 57461-0046; Mailing: Box 46, Mellette, SD 57461-0046 t) 605-887-3414 mellette.allsaints@sfcatholic.org St. Bernard, Redfield. Rev. John W. Short, Pst.;

MILBANK

Saint Lawrence Parish of Grant County - 113 S. 6th St., Milbank, SD 57252 t) 605-432-9122 stlawrencemilbank@gmail.com www.stlawrencemilbank.org Rev. Gary K. DeRouchey, Pst.; CRP Stds.: 126

Saint Lawrence Parish of Grant County School - (Grades PreK-6) 113 S 6th St, Milbank, SD 57252 t) 605-432-5673 stlawrence.k12.sd.us Brenda Anderson, Prin.;

MILLER

Saint Ann Parish of Hand County - 709 E. 4th St., Miller, SD 57362; Mailing: PO Box 198, Miller, SD 57362 t) 605-853-2207 office@stannmiller.com www.stannmiller.com Rev. Paul Josten, Pst.;

MITCHELL

Holy Family Parish of Davison County - 222 N. Kimball St., Mitchell, SD 57301-3452 t) 605-996-3639 holyfamily@mitchelltelecom.net www.holyfamilymitchell.com Dcn. Joseph Graves; Rev. Cesar Valencia, PES, Pst.;

Holy Spirit Parish of Davison County - 1401 W. Cedar Ave., Mitchell, SD 57301-3853 t) 605-996-7424 secretary@holyspiritmitchell.org www.holyspiritmitchell.org Dcn. Nick Baus; Rev. Cesar Valencia, PES, Pst.;

MOBRIDGE

Saint Joseph Parish of Walworth County - 518 2nd Ave. W., Mobridge, SD 57601-2114 t) 605-845-2100 www.sfcatholic.org/parishes/st-joseph-mobridge/ Rev. Mark A. Axtmann, Par. Vicar; Rev. Michael Griffin, Pst.;

MONTROSE

Saint Patrick Parish of McCook County - 211 S. Church, Montrose, SD 57048; Mailing: P.O. Box 158, Montrose, SD 57048-0158 t) (605) 290-2149 office@stpatrickmontrose.org www.stpatrickmontrose.org Rev. Steven Robert Jones, Pst.;

ONIDA

Saint Pius X Parish of Sully County - 102 6th St., Onida, SD 57564; Mailing: PO Box 13, Onida, SD 57564-0013 t) 605-258-2336 stpiusx@venturecomm.net; stpiusxre@live.com stpiusxonida.org Sacred Heart, Gettysburg. Rev. Brian Simon, Pst.;

PARKER

Saint Christina Parish of Turner County - 380 W. 1st St., Parker, SD 57053; Mailing: PO Box 610, Parker, SD 57053-0610 t) 605-297-4983 stchristina@iw.net www.sfcatholic.org/parishes/st-christina-parker Rev. Tyler Mattson, Pst.;

PARKSTON

Sacred Heart Parish of Hutchinson County - 411 W. Main St., Parkston, SD 57366; Mailing: PO Box 460, Parkston, SD 57366-0460 t) 605-928-3676 sacredheartparkston.org/newweb Rev. David Stevens, Pst.; Dcn. Barry Wagner; CRP Stds.: 149

PIERRE

Saints Peter and Paul Parish of Hughes County - 304 N. Euclid Ave., Pierre, SD 57501; Mailing: 210 E Broadway Ave, Pierre, SD 57501 t) 605-224-2483 sspeterandpaulcatholic@gmail.com www.sspeterpaul.net Rev. J. Joseph Holzhauser, Pst.; CRP Stds.: 144

Saints Peter and Paul Parish of Hughes County School (St. Joseph School) - (Grades K-5) 210 E. Broadway, Pierre, SD 57501 t) 605-224-7185 www.sjspierre.org/ Darlene Braun, Prin.; Stds.: 181; Pr. Tchrs.: 1; Lay Tchrs.: 13

PLANKINTON

Saint John Parish of Aurora County - 308 E. 3rd St., Plankinton, SD 57368; Mailing: PO Box 430, Plankinton, SD 57368-0430 t) 605-942-7125 office@pfcatholics.org www.pfcatholics.org Rev. Terry Weber, Pst.;

PLATTE

Saint Peter the Apostle Parish of Charles Mix County - 321 Ohio Ave., Platte, SD 57369; Mailing: 317 S. Ohio Ave., Platte, SD 57369-2004 t) 605-337-3710 secretary@stpeterplattesd.org stpeterplattesd.parishesonline.com Rev. Thomas Clement, Pst.; Dcn. Joseph Tegethoff;

POLO

Saint Liborius Parish of Hand County - 17985 354th Ave., Polo, SD 57467 t) 605-598-6590 stthomaspastor@venturecomm.net; stliborius@venturecomm.net St. Thomas the Apostle Parish, Faulkton. Rev. Randy Phillips, Pst.;

RAMONA

Saint William of Vercelli Parish of Lake County - 120 W. 3rd St., Ramona, SD 57054; Mailing: PO Box 100, Howard, SD 57349-0100 t) (605) 772-4543 stagatha@alliancecom.net www.sfcatholic.org/parishes/st-william-ramona/ St. Agatha, Howard. Rev. Chester Murtha, Pst.;

REDFIELD

Saint Bernard Parish of Spink County - 217 E. 6th Ave., Redfield, SD 57469-1249 t) 605-472-1482 sbernard@abe.midco.net www.sbernardredfield.org Rev. John W. Short, Pst.; CRP Stds.: 140

REVILLO

Annunciation Parish of Grant County - 301 5th St., Revillo, SD 57259; Mailing: P.O. Box 128, Revillo, SD 57259-0128 t) 605-862-8485 revillo.annunciation@sfcatholic.org www.sfcatholic.org/parishes/annunciation-revillo/ St. Lawrence, Milbank. Rev. David Garza, Admin.;

ROSCOE

Saint Thomas Apostle Parish of Edmunds County - 605 N. Andrew St., Roscoe, SD 57471; Mailing: PO Box 67, Ipswich, SD 57451-0067 t) (605) 971-4556 roscoe.stthomas@sfcatholic.org www.sfcatholic.org/parishes/st-thomas-the-apostle Attended by Ipswich. Rev. Timothy Cone, Par. Admin.;

ROSHOLT

Saint John the Baptist Parish of Roberts County - 218 W. Dakota St., Rosholt, SD 57260; Mailing: PO Box 45, Rosholt, SD 57260-0045 t) 605-537-4583 www.stjohnrosholt.org Rev. Gregory L. Frankman, Pst.;

SALEM

Saint Mary, Help of Christians Parish of McCook County - 240 N. Idaho, Salem, SD 57058; Mailing: P.O. Box 308, Salem, SD 57058 t) 605-425-2600 salem.stmary@sfcatholic.org www.salemcatholic.org Rev. Steven Robert Jones, Pst.;

St. Mary School - (Grades K-8) 205 W. Essex Ave., Salem, SD 57058; Mailing: PO Box 40, Salem, SD 57058 t) 605-425-2607 stmarysschoolsalem.weebly.com Peggy Freidel, Prin.;

SCOTLAND

Saint George Parish of Bon Homme County - 930 3rd St., Scotland, SD 57059; Mailing: Box 449, Scotland, SD 57059 t) 605-583-4318 Rev. Mark Lichter, Pst.;

SELBY

Saint Anthony Parish of Walworth County - 7209 5th Ave., Selby, SD 57472; Mailing: PO Box 231, Selby, SD 57472 t) 605-649-6338 www.northernlightscatholics.org Herreid. Rev. Michael Griffin, Pst.; Rev. Mark A. Axtmann, Par. Vicar; CRP Stds.: 23

SIOUX FALLS

Cathedral of Saint Joseph Parish - 521 Duluth Ave., Sioux Falls, SD 57104 t) 605-336-7390 cathedral@sfcatholic.org Rev. Anthony Klein, Sacr. Min.; Rev. James P. Morgan, Rector; Dcn. Timothy Dickes; Dcn. William Radio;

Christ the King Parish of Minnehaha County - 1501 W. 26th St., Sioux Falls, SD 57105-2698 t) 605-332-5477 office@ctkparish-sf.org www.ctkparish-sf.org/ Rev. Jordan Samson, Pst.; Dcn. James Boorman; Dcn. Peter Cote; CRP Stds.: 40

Holy Spirit Parish of Minnehaha County - 3601 E. Dudley Ln., Sioux Falls, SD 57103-5827 t) 605-371-2320 holyspiritsf@holyspiritsf.org www.holyspiritsf.org Amy Nightingale-Schlup, DRE; Barbara Workman, DRE;

Immaculate Heart of Mary Parish of Minnehaha County - 2109 S. Fifth Ave., Sioux Falls, SD 57105-3199 t) 605-332-6391 stmarysf@midco.net www.stmarysf.org Dcn. Glenn Ridder; Rev. Paul A. Rutten, Pst.;

Saint Katharine Drexel Parish of Minnehaha County - 1800 S. Katie Ave. Suite 1, Sioux Falls, SD 57106 t) 605-275-6870 admin@stkdsfsd.org www.stkdsfsd.org Rev. Thomas Fitzpatrick, Pst.; Dcn. Dennis Seiner;

Saint Lambert Parish of Minnehaha County - 1000 S. Bahnson Ave., Sioux Falls, SD 57103-2939 t) 605-336-8808 stlambertparish@sfcatholic.org www.stlambertparish.org Rev. Paul Stephen King, Pst.; Dcn. Roger R. Heidt; CRP Stds.: 150

Saint Michael Parish of Minnehaha County - 1600 S. Marion Rd., Sioux Falls, SD 57106 t) 605-361-1600 info@stmichaelsfsd.org www.stmichaelsfsd.org Rev. Scott Jeffrey Miller, Par. Vicar; Rev. Thomas Hartman, Pst.; Dcn. John P. Devlin; CRP Stds.: 410

Our Lady of Guadalupe Parish of Minnehaha County - 217 N. Sherman Ave., Sioux Falls, SD 57103-1410 t) 605-338-8126 olgparish@sfcatholic.org www.sfcatholic.org/parishes/our-lady-of-guadalupe Rev. Kristopher Cowles, Pst.;

Saint Therese Parish of Minnehaha County - 901 N. Tahoe Trl., Sioux Falls, SD 57110-5779 t) 605-338-2433 www.sttheresesf.org Rev. Kevin O'Dell, Pst.; Dcn. Thane Barnier;

SISSETON

Saint Kateri Tekakwitha Parish of Roberts County - 619 N. Main Ave., Sisseton, SD 57262; Mailing: 525 E. Chestnut St., Sisseton, SD 57262-1428 t) 605-698-7414 sissetoncath.office@gmail.com www.nesdcatholics.org Rev. Gregory L. Frankman, Pst.;

Saint Peter Parish of Roberts County - 525 E. Chestnut St., Sisseton, SD 57262-1428 t) 605-698-7414 sissetoncath.office@gmail.com www.nesdcatholics.org Rev. Gregory L. Frankman, Pst.;

SPRINGFIELD

Saint Vincent de Paul Parish of Bon Homme County - 1203 Wood St., Springfield, SD 57062; Mailing: PO Box 47, Tyndall, SD 57066-0047 t) 605-589-3504 stleochurch@hcinet.net; pastor@stleotyndall.com www.stleotyndall.com Rev. Joseph Forcelle, Pst.;

STEPHAN

Immaculate Conception Parish of Hyde County - 206 Crow Creek Loop, Stephan, SD 57346-6119 t) (605) 245-2350 pastteam@gwtc.net www.sfcatholic.org/parishes/immaculate-conception Ft. Thompson. Rev. Christianus Hendrick, S.C.J., Pst.; Rev. Mark Mastin, SCJ, Assoc. Pst.; Dcn. Steven A. McLaughlin;

STICKNEY

Saint Mary Parish of Aurora County - 414 Main St., Stickney, SD 57375; Mailing: 308 E. 3rd St., Plankinton, SD 57368-2036 t) 605-942-7125 office@pfcatholics.org www.pfcatholics.org Plankinton. Rev. Terry Weber, Pastor Emer.;

TABOR

Saint Wenceslaus Parish of Bon Homme County - 205 N. Lidice St., Tabor, SD 57063 t) 605-463-2336 office@stwenceslaustabor.org www.stwenceslaustabor.org Rev. Joseph Forcelle, Pst.;

TEA

Saint Nicholas Parish of Lincoln County - 140 W. Brian St., Tea, SD 57064; Mailing: PO Box 116, Tea, SD 57064-0116 t) 605-498-5792 office@stnicholastea.org www.stnicholastea.org Rev. Tyler Mattson, Pst.;

TURTON

Saint Joseph Parish of Spink County - 201 E. Linden St., Turton, SD 57477; Mailing: PO Box 407, Groton, SD

57445-0407 t) (605) 397-2775 seas@nvc.net www.sfcatholic.org/parishes/st-joseph-turton/ Rev. Gregory Tschakert, Pst.;

TYNDALL

Saint Leo The Great Parish of Bon Homme County - 100 E. 20th Ave., Tyndall, SD 57066; Mailing: PO Box 47, Tyndall, SD 57066-0047 t) 605-589-3504 stleochurch@hcinet.net www.stleotyndall.com Rev. Joseph Forcelle, Pst.;

VERMILLION

Saint Agnes Parish of Clay County - 416 S. Walker St., Vermillion, SD 57069-3358 t) 605-624-4478 office@stagnesvermillion.org stagnesvermillion.org/st-agnes-catholic-church Rev. Jerome Ranek, Pst.; Dcn. Dennis Davis;

Saint Agnes Parish of Clay County School - (Grades PreK-5) 909 E. Lewis St., Vermillion, SD 57069 t) 605-624-4144 stagnes.k12.sd.us Darla Hamm, Prin.; Kathy Crowley, Librn.;

WAGNER

Saint John the Baptist Parish of Charles Mix County - 107 High Ave. SW, Wagner, SD 57380; Mailing: PO Box 637, Wagner, SD 57380-0637 t) 605-384-5518 wagner.stjohn@sfcatholic.org www.stjohnthebaptistcatholicchurch.weebly.com Rev. Jim Duane Friedrich, Pst.; CRP Stds.: 60

WAKONDA

Saint Patrick Parish of Clay County - 209 Iowa St., Wakonda, SD 57073-0386; Mailing: PO Box 472, Beresford, SD 57004-0472 t) 605-763-2028 www.sdprairiecatholic.org Rev. David Roehrich, Pst.; CRP Stds.: 29

WATERTOWN

Holy Name of Jesus Parish of Codington County - 1009 Skyline Dr., Watertown, SD 57201-1343 t) 605-886-2628 www.watertownholyname.org Rev. John Fischer, Pst.; CRP Stds.: 199

Immaculate Conception Parish of Codington County - 103 S.E. 3rd St., Watertown, SD 57201 t) 605-886-4049 office@icparishwatertown.org Rev. Richard D. Fox, Pst.;

WAUBAY

Immaculate Conception Parish of Day County - 1045 Main St., Waubay, SD 57273; Mailing: 1101 E. 1st St., Webster, SD 57274-1409 t) 605-345-3447 www.icwaubay.org/home Webster. Rev. Douglas Binsfeld, Pst.;

WEBSTER

Christ the King Parish of Day County - 1101 E. 1st St., Webster, SD 57274-1499 t) 605-345-3447 www.ctkwebster.org Rev. Douglas Binsfeld, Pst.;

WESSINGTON SPRINGS

Saint Joseph Parish of Jerauld County (St. Joseph's Catholic Church of Wessington Springs) - 507 Barrett Ave. N., Wessington Springs, SD 57382; Mailing: PO Box 266, Woonsocket, SD 57385-0266 t) 605-796-4666 www.stjosephsd.org Rev. Kevin Doyle, Pst.; CRP Stds.: 45

WESTPORT

Sacred Heart Parish of Westport - 16 2nd Ave. W., Westport, SD 57481; Mailing: PO Box 87, Westport, SD 57481-0087 t) (605) 229-1011 www.sfcatholic.org/parishes/sacred-heart-westport/ Rev. Andrew Dickinson, Par. Admin.;

WHITE

Saint Paul Parish of Brookings County - 102 W. 5th St., White, SD 57276; Mailing: PO Box 617, White, SD 57276-0617 t) (605) 629-4651 www.sfcatholic.org/parishes/st-paul-white/ Rev. Patrick M. Grode, Pst.;

WHITE LAKE

Saint Peter Parish of Aurora County - 101 S. Ellis St., White Lake, SD 57383; Mailing: PO Box 277, White Lake, SD 57383-0277 t) 605-249-2700 office@pfcatholics.org www.pfcatholics.org Plankinton Rev. Terry Weber, Pst.;

WOONSOCKET

Saint Wilfrid Parish of Sanborn County (St. Wilfrid Church, Woonsocket, SD) - 203 N. 2nd Ave., Woonsocket, SD 57385; Mailing: PO Box 266, Woonsocket, SD 57385-0266 t) 605-796-4666 www.stwilfridsd.org Rev. Kevin Doyle, Pst.; CRP Stds.: 58

YANKTON

Saint Benedict Parish of Yankton County - 1500 St. Benedict Dr., Yankton, SD 57078-6305 t) 605-664-6214 stbenoffice@yanktoncatholic.org www.yanktonsaintbenedict.org Rev. Robert Edward Lacey, Par. Vicar; Rev. Thomas Anderson, Pst.; Dcn. Jack Dahlsied; Dcn. Ronald Kachena;

Sacred Heart Parish of Yankton County - 509 Capitol St., Yankton, SD 57078-4024 t) 605-665-3655 www.yanktonsacredheart.org Rev. Robert Edward Lacey, Par. Vicar; Rev. Thomas Anderson, Pst.;

SCHOOLS: PRESCHOOL THRU HIGH SCHOOL

SCHOOLS

STATE OF SOUTH DAKOTA

ABERDEEN

Aberdeen Catholic Schools Education Office - (PAR) 1400 N. Dakota St., Aberdeen, SD 57401 t) 605-226-2100 vickiehaiar@aberdeenroncalli.org www.aberdeenroncalli.org Tim Weisz, Pres.;

Roncalli High School - 1400 N. Dakota St., Aberdeen, SD 57401 t) 605-225-7440 info@aberdeenroncalli.org Paula Florey, Prin.; Cathy McNeary, Librn.;

Roncalli Elementary School - 501 S.E. 3rd. Ave., Aberdeen, SD 57401 t) 605-229-4100 info@aberdeenroncalli.org Elizabeth Gorski, Prin.; Sandy Andera, Librn.;

Roncalli Primary School - 419 N.E. 1st. Ave., Aberdeen, SD 57401 t) 605-225-3460 info@aberdeenroncalli.org Paula Florey, Prin.; Sandy Andera, Librn.;

CHAMBERLAIN

St. Joseph Indian School - (PRV) 1301 N. Main St., Chamberlain, SD 57325; Mailing: PO Box 89, Chamberlain, SD 57325 t) 605-234-3300 mytrell@stjo.org www.stjo.org Rev. Anthony Kluckman, S.C.J., Chap.; Kathleen Whitebird, Prin.; Mike Tyrell, Pres.; Sharmel Olson, Dir.;

MITCHELL

John Paul II School - (PAR) (Grades PreK-6) 1510 W. Elm Ave., Mitchell, SD 57301 t) 605-996-2365 robin.cahoy@k12sd.us johnpaul2.org Robin Cahoy, Prin.; Jackie Rezac, Librn.;

SIOUX FALLS

Bishop O'Gorman Catholic Schools (Sioux Falls Catholic Schools) - (PAR) (Grades PreK-12) 3100 W. 41st St., Sioux Falls, SD 57105 t) 605-336-6241 kgroos@ogknights.org ogknights.org Rev. Andrew Thuringer, Chap.; Kyle Groos, Pres.; Brenda Mitzel, Dir.;

O'Gorman High School - (Grades PreK-12) 3201 S. Kiwanis Ave., Sioux Falls, SD 57105 t) 605-336-3644 Joan Mahoney, Prin.;

O'Gorman Junior High - (Grades PreK-12) 3201 S Kiwanis Ave, Sioux Falls, SD 57105 t) 605-988-0546 Rev. Tony Klein, Chap.; Wade Charron, Prin.;

St. Mary Elementary - (Grades PreK-12) 2000 S. 4th Ave., Sioux Falls, SD 57105 t) 605-334-9881 Michelle Shields, Prin.;

Christ the King Elementary School - (Grades PreK-12) 1801 S. Lake Ave., Sioux Falls, SD 57105 t) 605-338-5103 Julie Kolbeck, Prin.;

St. Lambert Elementary School - (Grades PreK-12) 1000 S. Bahnson Ave., Sioux Falls, SD 57103 t) 605-338-7042 Colleen Davis, Prin.;

St. Michael Elementary School - (Grades PreK-12) 1610 S. Marion Rd., Sioux Falls, SD 57106 t) 605-361-0021 Lisa Huemoeller, Prin.;

Holy Spirit Elementary - (Grades PreK-12) 4309 S. Bahnson Ave., Sioux Falls, SD 57103 t) 605-371-1481 Regan Manning, Prin.;

St. Katharine Drexel Elementary - (Grades PreK-12) 1800 S. Katie Ave., Ste. 2, Sioux Falls, SD 57106 t) 605-275-6994 Stacy Charron, Prin.;

WATERTOWN

Watertown Catholic School Corporation - (PAR) (Grades PreK-6) 109 3rd St., S.E., Watertown, SD 57201 t) 605-886-3883 carol.dagel@k12.sd.us Carol Dagel, Prin.; Kathy Stewart, Librn.;

YANKTON

Sacred Heart School - (PAR) (Grades PreK-8) 1500 St. Benedict Dr., Ste. 200, Yankton, SD 57078-6884 t) 605-665-5841 laura.m.haberman@k12.sd.us; sherry.rockne@k12.sd.us www.yanktonsacredheartschool.org Laura Haberman, Prin.;

INSTITUTIONS LOCATED IN DIOCESE

CAMPUS MINISTRY / NEWMAN CENTERS [CAM]

ABERDEEN

Saint Thomas Aquinas Newman Center - 310 15th Ave. SE, Aberdeen, SD 57401-7505 t) 605-229-1011 nsunewman@gmail.com www.nsunewman.com Rev. Andrew Dickinson, Pst.; Rev. Mitchell McLaughlin, Par. Vicar;

Northern State University - Megan Schulz, Campus Min.;

BROOKINGS

Pope Pius XII Newman Center - 1321 8th St., Brookings, SD 57006; Mailing: Box 730, Brookings, SD 57006-0730 t) 605-692-9461 catholicjackssecretary@sfcatholic.org www.piusxiinewman.com Rev. Patrick M. Grode, Dir.;

MADISON

Dakota State University - 321 N. Van Eps Ave., Madison, SD 57042 t) 606-256-2304 frscotttraynor@sfcatholic.org Attended by St. Thomas Parish, Madison. Rev. Scott Traynor, Contact;

VERMILLION

Saint Thomas More Newman Center - 320 E. Cherry St., Vermillion, SD 57069-1339 t) 605-624-2697 newmanpc@coyotes.usd.edu www.usdnewman.org/ Rev. John Rutten, Dir.;

University of South Dakota -

CATHOLIC CHARITIES [CCH]

SIOUX FALLS

Magnificat - Sioux Falls, SD Chapter, Inc. - 1804 S. Kiwanis Ave., Sioux Falls, SD 57105 t) (605) 521-5782 Julia Cady, Contact;

CEMETERIES [CEM]

SIOUX FALLS

St. Michael Cemetery - 3001 N. Cliff Ave., Sioux Falls, SD 57104 t) 605-338-3376 djohnson@sfcatholic.org Jeff McCann, Dir.;

COLLEGES & UNIVERSITIES [COL]

ABERDEEN

Presentation College - 1500 N. Main St., Aberdeen, SD 57401 t) 605-225-1634 presidentsoffice@presentation.edu www.presentation.edu Campus also located at Fairmont, MN. Sisters of the Presentation of the B.V.M. Rev. Joseph Sheehan, O.Carm., Chap.; Dr. Paula Langteau, Pres.;

YANKTON

Mount Marty University - 1105 W. 8th St., Yankton, SD 57078 t) 605-668-1545 admissions@mountmarty.edu www.mountmarty.edu Benedictine Sisters of Sacred

Heart Monastery. Rev. Grant Lacey, Chap.; Marcus B. Long, Pres.; Sandra Brown, Librn.; Stds.: 1,252; Lay Tchrs.: 41; Sr. Tchrs.: 3

Mount Marty University-Watertown Location - 1201 Arrow Ave., Watertown, SD 57201; Mailing: P.O. Box 1385, Watertown, SD 57201 t) 605-886-6777 watertown@mountmarty.edu www.mountmarty.edu/watertown/ Benedictine Sisters of Sacred Heart Monastery. Kimberly Bellum, Dir.; Stds.: 99

CONVENTS, MONASTERIES, AND RESIDENCES FOR WOMEN [CON]

ABERDEEN

Presentation Convent - 1500 N. 2nd St., Aberdeen, SD 57401 t) (605) 229-8417 mary.thomas@avera.org www.presentationsisters.org Motherhouse and Novitiate of the Sisters of the Presentation of the B.V.M. Sr. Mary Thomas, PBVM, Pres.; Srs.: 45

ALEXANDRIA

Monastery of Our Mother of Mercy and St. Joseph Discalced Carmelite Nuns - 221 W. 5th St., Alexandria, SD 57311-0067; Mailing: P.O. Box 67, Alexandria, SD 57311-0067 t) 605-239-4382 malthoff@sfcatholic.org Discalced Carmelite Nuns of Alexandria, South Dakota, Inc. Rev. Msgr. Charles Mangan, Chap.; Mother Mary Elias of the Immaculate Conception, O.C.D., Prioress;

MARTY

Motherhouse Oblate Sisters of the Blessed Sacrament - 103 Church Ln., Marty, SD 57361; Mailing: P.O. Box 204, Marty, SD 57361 t) 605-384-3305 osbs@cme.com

MITCHELL

Sisters of St. Francis of Our Lady of Guadalupe - 1417 W. Ash Ave., Mitchell, SD 57301 t) 605-996-1410 sistersofstfrancis@mit.midco.net Private Assn. of the Faithful.

SIOUX FALLS

Perpetual Adoration Sisters of the Blessed Sacrament - 707 W. 4th St., Sioux Falls, SD 57104 t) 605-336-2374 adoratrices@msn.com Sr. Caridad Morales, A.P., Supr.;

WATERTOWN

Mother of God Monastery - 110 28th Ave., S.E., Watertown, SD 57201-8419 t) 605-882-6633 prioress@watertownbenedictines.org watertownbenedictines.org The Benedictine Sisters of Mother of God Monastery Sr. Terri Hoffman, Prioress; Srs.: 40

YANKTON

Monastic Congregation of St. Gertrude, Inc. - 1005 W. 8th St., Yankton, SD 57078 t) (605) 760-0529 (Jeanne Weber, OSB) www.federationofstgertrude.org Sr. Jeanne Weber, OSB, Pres.; Sr. Barbara Lynn Schmitz, OSB, Vice. Pres.;

Sacred Heart Monastery - 1005 W. 8th St., Yankton, SD 57078-3389 t) 605-668-6000 mwentzlaff@yanktonbenedictines.org yanktonbenedictines.org Motherhouse and Novitiate of the Benedictine Sisters. Sr. Maribeth Wentzlaff, O.S.B., Prioress; Srs.: 66

ENDOWMENTS / FOUNDATIONS / TRUSTS [EFT]

ABERDEEN

***Aberdeen Catholic Foundation, Inc.** - 13 S.E. 2nd Ave., Ste. 6, Aberdeen, SD 57401 t) 605-218-0072 david.vetch@acf.network David Vetch, Dir.;

The Presentation Sisters Heritage Trust - 1500 N. 2nd St., Aberdeen, SD 57401 t) 605-229-8419 jklein@presentationsisters.org www.presentationsisters.org Sponsored by: Sisters of the Presentation of the Blessed Virgin Mary of Aberdeen, South Dakota. Sr. Janice Klein, P.B.V.M., Pres.;

MILBANK

Blue Cloud Abbey Retirement Trust - 116 S. Main St., Milbank, SD 57252; Mailing: P.O. Box 1013, Milbank, SD 57252 t) 812-357-6752 mcmullen@tnics.com Rev. John McMullen, O.S.B., Treas.;

Asociacion Benedictina de Coban Resurrection Priory - t) 605-398-9200

MITCHELL

Mitchell Foundation for Catholic Education - 1510 W. Elm Ave., Mitchell, SD 57301 t) 605-999-9127 mfce@mit.midco.net www.mitchellfce.com Nicole Fuhrer, Dir.;

SIOUX FALLS

The Catholic Community Foundation for Eastern South Dakota - 523 N. Duluth Ave., Sioux Falls, SD 57104 t) 605-988-3795 mconzemius@sfcatholic.org www.sfcatholic.org Mark Conzemius, Pres.;

Holy Spirit School Permanent Trust - 3601 E. Dudley Ln., Sioux Falls, SD 57103 t) 605-371-2320 holyspiritsf@holyspiritsf.org Rev. Charles L. Cimpl, Contact;

Little Flower of Jesus School Foundation, Inc. - 901 N. Tahoe Tr., Sioux Falls, SD 57110-5779 t) 605-338-2433 office@sttheresesf.org Rev. Kevin O'Dell, Pst.;

Parish Deposit & Loan Fund Trust - 523 N. Duluth Ave., Sioux Falls, SD 57104-2714 t) 605-334-9861 mbannwar@sfcatholic.org

Pension Plan for Priests of the Diocese of Sioux Falls Trust - 523 N. Duluth Ave., Sioux Falls, SD 57104 t) 605-334-9861 malthoff@sfcatholic.org www.sfcatholic.org Matthew Althoff, Chancellor;

Retired Priests Medical Benefits Plan Trust for the Diocese of Sioux Falls - 523 N. Duluth Ave., Sioux Falls, SD 57104 t) 605-334-9861 malthoff@sfcatholic.org Matthew Althoff, Chancellor;

Sioux Falls Catholic School Foundation - 3100 W. 41st St., Sioux Falls, SD 57105 t) 605-575-3362 mkaten@sfcss.org sfcss.org

WATERTOWN

The Benedictine Sisters Foundation of Watertown - 110 28th Ave., S.E., Watertown, SD 57201 t) 605-882-6633 prioress@dailypost.com watertownbenedictines.org Sr. Terri Hoffman, Prioress;

Holy Name Foundation, Inc. - 1009 Skyline Dr., Watertown, SD 57201 t) 605-886-2628 frmichaelwensing@sfcatholic.org Rev. Michael Wensing, Contact;

Immaculate Conception School Foundation, Inc. - 309 2nd Ave. SE, Watertown, SD 57201-3621 t) (605) 886-4049 office@icparishwatertown.org www.icparishwatertown.org Rev. Richard D. Fox, Pst.;

Retirement Trust - Mother of God Monastery, 110 28th Ave., S.E., Watertown, SD 57201 t) 605-882-6633 prioress@dailypost.com watertownbenedictines.org Sr. Terri Hoffman, Prioress;

YANKTON

Benedictine Health Foundation, Inc. - 1000 W. 4th, Ste. 14, Yankton, SD 57078 t) 605-668-8310 bhf@shhservices.com Frannie Kieffer, Exec.;

Yankton Catholic Community Foundation - 509 Capital St., Yankton, SD 57078 t) 605-665-3655 x3 yccfo@yanktoncatholic.org Kelly Kathol, Dir.;

HOSPITALS / HEALTH SERVICES [HOS]

ABERDEEN

Avera St. Luke's - 305 S. State St., Aberdeen, SD 57401 t) 605-622-5000 daniel.bjerknes@avera.org www.averastlukes.org Sponsored by Sisters of the Presentation of the B.V.M. of Aberdeen, SD, and Benedictine Sisters of Sacred Heart Monastery, Yankton, SD. Daniel Bjerknes, Pres.; Bed Capacity: 60; Asstd. Annu.: 277,836; Staff: 724

Avera St. Luke's (Avera Mother Joseph Manor) - 1002 N. Jay St., Aberdeen, SD 57401 t) 605-622-5850 tom.snyder@avera.org www.avera.org Sponsored by the Sisters of the Presentation of the BVM of Aberdeen, South Dakota, and the Benedictine Sisters of Sacred Heart Monastery, Yankton, SD. Tom Snyder, Admin.;

DE SMET

Avera Queen of Peace (Avera De Smet Memorial Hospital) - 306 S.W. Prairie Ave., De Smet, SD 57231; Mailing: P.O. Box 160, De Smet, SD 57231 t) 605-854-6100 stephanie.reasy@avera.org www.avera.org Sponsored by the Sisters of the Presentation of the BVM of Aberdeen, South Dakota, and the Benedictine Sisters of Sacred Heart Monastery, Yankton, SD. Stephanie Reasy, Admin.; Bed Capacity: 6; Asstd. Annu.: 17,097; Staff: 31

DELL RAPIDS

Avera McKennan (Avera Dells Area Hospital) - 909 N. Iowa Ave., Dell Rapids, SD 57022 t) 605-428-5431 bryan.breitling@avera.org www.avera.org Sponsored by Sisters of the Presentation of the B.V.M. of Aberdeen, S.D., and Benedictine Sisters of Sacred Heart Monastery, Yankton, S.D. Bryan Breitling, Admin.; Bed Capacity: 21; Asstd. Annu.: 24,265; Staff: 62

GETTYSBURG

Avera Gettysburg - 606 E. Garfield, Gettysburg, SD 57442 t) 605-765-2488 kristi.livermont@avera.org avera.org Sponsored by the Sisters of the Presentation of the BVM of Aberdeen, South Dakota, and the Benedictine Sisters of Sacred Heart Monastery, Yankton, SD Kristi Livermont, Admin.; Bed Capacity: 60; Asstd. Annu.: 10,913; Staff: 71

MILBANK

Avera McKennan (Milbank Area Hospital Avera) - 301 Flynn Dr., Milbank, SD 57252; Mailing: PO Box 5045, Sioux Falls, SD 57117-5045 t) 605-432-4538 natalie.gauer@avera.org www.avera.org Sponsored by the Sisters of the Presentation of the BVM of Aberdeen, South Dakota, and the Benedictine Sisters of Sacred Heart Monastery, Yankton, SD. Natalie Gauer, Admin.; Bed Capacity: 25; Asstd. Annu.: 49,765; Staff: 98

MITCHELL

Avera Queen of Peace - 525 N. Foster, Mitchell, SD 57301 t) 605-995-2000 hilary.rockwell@avera.org www.averaqueenofpeace.org Sponsored by Sisters of the Presentation of the B.V.M., Aberdeen, SD, and Benedictine Sisters of Sacred Heart Monastery, Yankton, SD. Dr. Hilary Rockwell, Pres.; Bed Capacity: 50; Asstd. Annu.: 195,294; Staff: 446

Avera Queen of Peace (Avera Brady Health & Rehabilitation, Avera Brady Assisted Living) - 500 S. Ohlman, Mitchell, SD 57301 t) 605-996-7701 julie.hoffman@avera.org www.avera.org Sponsored by Sisters of the Presentation of the B.V.M., Aberdeen, SD, and Benedictine Sisters of Sacred Heart Monastery, Yankton, SD. Julie Hoffmann, Admin.;

PARKSTON

St. Benedict Health Center (Avera St. Benedict Health Center) - 401 W. Glynn Dr., Parkston, SD 57366 t) 605-928-3311 lindsay.weber@avera.org www.averastbenedict.org Sponsored by the Sisters of the Presentation of the BVM of Aberdeen, South Dakota, and the Benedictine Sisters of Sacred Heart Monastery, Yankton, SD. Lindsay Weber, CEO; Bed Capacity: 74; Asstd. Annu.: 39,046; Staff: 143

PIERRE

Avera St. Mary's - 801 E. Sioux Ave., Pierre, SD 57501 t) 605-224-3303 mikel.holland@avera.org www.avera.org Includes: Maryhouse Residential Nursing Facility and Parkwood Retirement Apartments. Dr. Mikel Holland, Pres.; Bed Capacity: 130; Asstd. Annu.: 142,329; Staff: 461

SIOUX FALLS

Avera McKennan - 1325 S. Cliff Ave., Sioux Falls, SD 57117-5045; Mailing: P.O. Box 5045, Sioux Falls, SD 57117-5045 t) 605-322-8000 david.flicek@avera.org www.averamckennan.org Sponsored by Sisters of the Presentation of the B.V.M. of Aberdeen, S.D., and Benedictine Sisters of Sacred Heart Monastery, Yankton, S.D. Rev. David Krogman, Chap.; David Flicek, Pres.; Bed Capacity: 541; Asstd. Annu.: 1,552,451; Staff: 5,516

Avera McKennan (Avera Behavioral Health Center) - 4400 W. 69th St., Sioux Falls, SD 57108 t) 605-322-4005 thomas.otten@avera.org www.avera.org Sponsored by Sisters of the Presentation of the B.V.M. of Aberdeen, S.D. and Benedictine Sisters of Sacred Heart Monastery, Yankton, S.D. Thomas Otten, Vice. Pres.; Bed Capacity: 122; Asstd. Annu.: 117,990; Staff: 271

Avera McKennan (Avera Prince of Peace) - 4513 Prince of Peace, Sioux Falls, SD 57103 t) 605-322-5600 justin.hinker@avera.org www.avera.org Sponsored by the Sisters of the Presentation of the BVM of Aberdeen, South Dakota and the Benedictine Sisters of Sacred Heart Monastery, Yankton, SD. Justin Hinker, Admin.; Bed Capacity: 114; Asstd. Annu.: 346; Staff: 179

TYNDALL

St. Michael's Hospital - 410 W. 16th Ave., Tyndall, SD 57066 t) 605-589-2100 carol.deurmier@avera.org Carol Deurmier, CEO;

WESSINGTON SPRINGS

Avera Queen of Peace (Avera Weskota Memorial Medical Center) - 604 N.E. 1st St., Wessington Springs, SD 57382 t) 605-539-1201 stephanie.reasy@avera.org www.avera.org Sponsored by the Sisters of the Presentation of the BVM of Aberdeen, South Dakota, and the Benedictine Sisters of Sacred Heart Monastery, Yankton, SD. Stephanie Reasy, Admin.; Bed Capacity: 16; Asstd. Annu.: 4,885; Staff: 20

YANKTON

Sacred Heart Health Services (Avera Sacred Heart Hospital) - 501 Summit, Yankton, SD 57078 t) 605-668-8000 douglas.ekeren@avera.org www.avera.org Sponsored by Sisters of the Presentation of the B.V.M. of Aberdeen, SD and Benedictine Sisters of Sacred Heart Monastery, Yankton, SD. Douglas Ekeren, Pres.; Bed Capacity: 75; Asstd. Annu.: 132,850; Staff: 440

Sacred Heart Health Services (Avera Majestic Bluffs) - 2111 W. 11th, Yankton, SD 57078 t) 605-668-8900 karen.westegaard@avera.org Sponsored by the Sisters of the Presentation of the BVM of Aberdeen, South Dakota, and the Benedictine Sisters of Sacred Heart Monastery, Yankton, SD.

MISCELLANEOUS [MIS]

CHAMBERLAIN

Native Hope, Inc. - 112 S. Main St., Chamberlain, SD 57325; Mailing: PO Box 576, Chamberlain, SD 57325 t) 888-999-2108 jennifer.long@nativehope.org Jennifer Long, Contact;

SIOUX FALLS

Avera Health - 3900 W. Avera Dr., Sioux Falls, SD 57108-5721 t) 605-322-4700 contactus@avera.org www.avera.org Sponsored by the Sisters of the Presentation of the B.V.M., Aberdeen, SD, and the Benedictine Sisters of Sacred Heart Monastery, Yankton, SD. Bob Sutton, Pres.;

The Berakhah House - 400 N. Western Ave., Sioux Falls, SD 57104; Mailing: 523 N. Duluth Ave., Sioux Falls, SD 57104 t) 605-334-9861 malthoff@sfcatholic.org Matthew Althoff, Chancellor;

Bishop Dudley Hospitality House - 101 N. Indiana Ave., Sioux Falls, SD 57103 t) 605-809-8418; 605-809-8424 info@bdhh.org www.bdhh.org Madeline Shields, Dir.;

Catholic Member Corporation - 523 N. Duluth Ave., Sioux Falls, SD 57104 t) 605-334-9861 malthoff@sfcatholic.org Matthew Althoff, Chancellor;

Catholic Property Corporation - 523 N. Duluth Ave., Sioux Falls, SD 57104 t) 605-334-9861 malthoff@sfcatholic.org Matthew Althoff, Chancellor;

City of Sioux Falls Catholic Schools Property Corporation - 523 N. Duluth Ave., Sioux Falls, SD 57104 t) 605-988-3759 mbannwar@sfcatholic.org www.sfcatholic.org Matthew Althoff, Chancellor;

Diocese of Sioux Falls Outreach Ministry Property Corporation - 523 N. Duluth Ave., Sioux Falls, SD 57104 t) 605-988-3700 malthoff@sfcatholic.org Most Rev. Donald E. DeGrood, Pres.; Rev. Charles L. Cimpl;

St. Joseph Catholic Housing, Inc. - 523 N. Duluth Ave., Sioux Falls, SD 57104 t) 605-334-9861 mbannwar@sfcatholic.org Matthew Althoff, Chancellor;

St. Matthew Stewardship, Inc. - 523 N. Duluth Ave., Sioux Falls, SD 57104 t) 605-988-3759 mbannwar@sfcatholic.org www.sfcatholic.org Matthew Althoff, Chancellor;

The Sioux Falls Equestrian Order of the Holy Sepulchre of Jerusalem - 523 N. Duluth Ave., Sioux Falls, SD 57104 t) 605-338-0769 caa25@hotmail.com Shawn Cleary, Pres.; Craig Alan Anderson, Secy.; Barbara Anderson, Treas.;

The South Dakota Catholic Physicians Guild - 2809 W. 33rd St., Apt. 8, Sioux Falls, SD 57105-4336 t) 605-335-7883 Dr. David Stevens, Pres.;

WATERTOWN

St. Ann's Corporation - 100 28th Ave., S.E., Watertown, SD 57201 t) 605-886-9177 prioress@dailypost.com Sr. Nancy Zemcuznikov, O.S.B., Admin.;

Benet Place - 100 28th Ave SE, Watertown, SD 57201-8406 t) (605) 886-9177 watertownbenedictines.org/benet-place (Independent Senior Apartments)

Benet Place Assisted Living - 100 28th Ave SE, Watertown, SD 57201-8406 t) (605) 886-9177 benetplace.com

Benedictine Volunteers, Inc. - 110 S.E. 28th Ave. #60, Watertown, SD 57201 t) 605-886-4159 prioress@dailypost.com benedictinevolunteers.com Sr. Terri Hoffman, Prioress;

YANKTON

Benedictine Center, Inc. - 1005 W. 8th, Yankton, SD 57078 t) 605-668-6000 mwentzlaff@mtmc.edu Sr. Maribeth Wentzlaff, O.S.B., Prioress;

The House of Mary Shrine, Inc. - Lewis & Clark Lake, Yankton, SD 57078-0455; Mailing: Box 455, Yankton, SD 57078-0455 t) 605-668-0121 thehouseofmaryshrine@gmail.com Jean Weller, Pres.;

NURSING / REHABILITATION / CONVALESCENCE / ELDERLY CARE [NUR]

EUREKA

Avera St. Luke's (Avera Eureka Health Care Center) - 202 J Ave., Eureka, SD 57437; Mailing: P.O. Box 40, Eureka, SD 57437 t) 605-284-2145 carmen.weber@avera.org www.averastlukes.org Carmen Weber, Admin.; Bed Capacity: 56; Asstd. Annu.: 25; Staff: 45

MILBANK

St. William's Care Center - 103 N. Viola St., Milbank, SD 57252 t) 605-432-5811 hna.rosemary@gmail.com Conducted by Daughters of St. Mary of Providence, Milbank. Sr. Rosemary Bell, DSMP, Dir.;

RETREAT HOUSES / RENEWAL CENTERS [RTR]

IRENE

Broom Tree Retreat and Conference Center - 29827 446th St., Irene, SD 57039 t) 605-263-1040 ksees@sfcatholic.org Kris Sees, Admin.; Rev. Scott S. Traynor, Dir.;

An asterisk (*) denotes an organization that has established tax-exempt status directly with the IRS and is not covered by the USCCB Group Ruling.

Diocese of Spokane

(Dioecesis Spokanensis)

MOST REVEREND THOMAS A. DALY

Bishop of Spokane; ordained May 9, 1987; appointed Auxiliary Bishop of San Jose and Titular Bishop of Tabalta March 16, 2011; Episcopal ordination May 25, 2011; appointed Bishop of Spokane March 12, 2015; installed May 20, 2015.

Chancery: 525 E. Mission Ave., Spokane, WA 99202. T: 509-358-7300; F: 509-358-7302. Mailing Address: P.O. Box 1453, Spokane, WA 99210-1453. chancellor@dioceseofspokane.org

www.dioceseofspokane.org

ESTABLISHED DECEMBER 17, 1913

Square Miles 24,356.

Solemnly consecrated to the Immaculate Heart of Mary on December 8, 1948.

Corporate Title: "The Catholic Bishop of Spokane, a Corporation Sole."

Comprises the following Counties in the State of Washington: Okanogan, Ferry, Stevens, Pend Oreille, Lincoln, Spokane, Adams, Whitman, Franklin, Walla Walla, Columbia, Garfield and Asotin.

For legal titles of parishes and diocesan institutions, consult the Chancery.

STATISTICAL OVERVIEW

Personnel

Bishop....1
Retired Bishops....1
Priests: Diocesan Active in Diocese....42
Priests: Diocesan Active Outside Diocese....2
Priests: Retired, Sick or Absent....31
Number of Diocesan Priests....75
Religious Priests in Diocese....29
Total Priests in your Diocese....104
Extern Priests in Diocese....3
Permanent Deacons in Diocese....46
Total Sisters....81

Parishes

Parishes....80
With Resident Pastor:
Resident Diocesan Priests....35
Resident Religious Priests....4
Without Resident Pastor:
Administered by Priests....41
Missions....3
Pastoral Centers....1
Professional Ministry Personnel:
Sisters....10
Lay Ministers....46

Welfare

Catholic Hospitals....7
Total Assisted....1,421,068
Homes for the Aged....2
Total Assisted....1,005
Residential Care of Children....1
Total Assisted....94
Day Care Centers....1
Total Assisted....260
Specialized Homes....3
Total Assisted....3,035
Special Centers for Social Services....14
Total Assisted....290,235
Residential Care of Disabled....2
Total Assisted....21
Other Institutions....13
Total Assisted....2,441

Educational

Seminaries, Diocesan....1
Students from This Diocese....2
Students from Other Dioceses....12
Diocesan Students in Other Seminaries....7
Total Seminarians....9
Colleges and Universities....1
Total Students....7,295
High Schools, Diocesan and Parish....1
Total Students....84
High Schools, Private....3
Total Students....1,192
Elementary Schools, Diocesan and Parish....14
Total Students....2,263
Catechesis/Religious Education:
High School Students....294
Elementary Students....1,530
Total Students under Catholic Instruction....12,667
Teachers in Diocese:
Priests....12
Sisters....1
Lay Teachers....263

Vital Statistics

Receptions into the Church:
Infant Baptism Totals....916
Minor Baptism Totals....67
Adult Baptism Totals....56
Received into Full Communion....105
First Communions....697
Confirmations....706
Marriages:
Catholic....164
Interfaith....31
Total Marriages....195
Deaths....590
Total Catholic Population....158,534
Total Population....932,550

LEADERSHIP

Chancery - t) 509-358-7300 cmessier@dioceseofspokane.org Carol Messier, Receptionist;

Office of the Bishop - t) 509-358-7305 spotter@dioceseofspokane.org Most Rev. Thomas A. Daly; Very Rev. Darrin Connall, Vicar General (dconnall@dioceseofspokane.org);

Vicar for Finance - t) 509-358-7333 Rev. Victor M. Blazovich, Vicar (vblazovich@dioceseofspokane.org); Rev. Eugene Tracy, Comptroller (etracy@dioceseofspokane.org);

Diocesan Finance Council - Louise Andrews, Mem.; Dan Byrne, Mem.; Mallahan Zach, Mem.;

Vicar for Priests - t) 509-466-0220 Rev. Patrick Kerst, Vicar;

Priest Personnel Board - Rev. Patrick Kerst, Vicar for Priests; Rev. Jeffrey Core, Mem.; Rev. Victor M. Blazovich, Mem.;

Chancellor - t) 509-358-7339 Rev. Msgr. Mark F. Pautler (mpautler@dioceseofspokane.org);

Archivist - t) 509-358-7319 msavelesky@dioceseofspokane.org Rev. Michael Savelesky;

Office of Canonical Services - t) 509-358-7319 tribunal@dioceseofspokane.org Rev. Msgr. Mark F. Pautler, Judicial Vicar (mpautler@dioceseofspokane.org); Rev. Msgr. John Steiner, Defender of the Bond; Fabienne Heacox, Notary;

Censor Librorum - Rev. Michael J. Savelesky;

Presbyteral Council - Most Rev. Thomas A. Daly; Very Rev. Darrin Connall (dconnall@dioceseofspokane.org); Rev. Patrick Kerst;

Deaneries - Rev. Paul Vevik, North Spokane Deanery; Rev. Lucas Ethan Tomson, South Spokane Deanery; Rev. Jeffrey Lewis, East Spokane Deanery;

College of Consultors - Very Rev. Darrin Connall (dconnall@dioceseofspokane.org); Rev. Patrick Kerst; Rev. Victor M. Blazovich (vblazovich@dioceseofspokane.org);

Catholic Foundation of Eastern Washington - t) 509-358-7334 Sr. Mary E. Tracy, S.N.J.M., Exec. Dir. (metracy@dioceseofspokane.org); Samantha Hall, CFO (shall@dioceseofspokane.org);

OFFICES AND DIRECTORS

Office of Human Resources - t) 509-358-7338 Victoria Loveland (vloveland@dioceseofspokane.org); Fabienne Heacox, Asst.;

Office of Education - t) 509-358-7330; 509-358-7335 Katie Rieckers, Dir. Catholic Schools; Sharon Hunt, Assoc. Dir.; Kathy Hicks, Commissioner of Accreditation & School Improvement;

Office of Fiscal Services - t) 509-358-7324 Jim McElroy, Dir. (jmcelroy@dioceseofspokane.org); Hope Smith, Payroll Accountant; Kerry Manzanares, Fund Drive Accountant (kmanzanares@dioceseofspokane.org);

Office of Stewardship & Development - t) 509-358-8000 Chris Kreslins, Dir.; Lindsey Klemmer, Fund Devel. Asst.;

Computer & Technology Services - t) 509-358-7346 Charles Brineman, IT Specialist;

Office of Child and Youth Protection - t) 509-358-4283; 509-358-7319 Duane Schafer, Dir.; Fabienne Heacox, Asst.;

Victim Assistance Coordinator - Victoria Loveland;

Diocesan Review Board - Susan Foster-Dow, Mem.; Janice House, Mem.; John Sheveland, Mem.;

Office of Evangelization - t) 509-358-7314 Brian Kraut, Dir. (bkraut@dioceseofspokane.org);

Respect Life -

Office of Catholic Media - Grant Whitty, Dir. (gwhitty@dioceseofspokane.org);

Social Ministries/Catholic Charities Eastern Washington - t) 509-358-4250 Rob McCann, Pres. (rmccann@ccspokane.org);

Bishop White Seminary - t) 509-313-7100 info@bishopwhitesem.org www.bishopwhitesem.org Very Rev. Daniel J. Barnett, Rector;

Cor Christi (Propaedeutic Year) - t) (509) 313-7100 Very Rev. Daniel J. Barnett, Rector;

Office of Vocations - t) 509-313-7100 vocations@dioceseofspokane.org Rev. Kyle Ratuiste, Dir.;

Immaculate Heart Retreat Center - t) 509-448-1224 ihrc@ihrc.net www.ihrc.net Rick McLean, Exec. Dir.;

Catholic Cemeteries of Spokane DBA Holy Cross Funeral and Cemetery Services - t) 509-467-5496 info@holycrossofspokane.org www.holycrossofspokane.org Rick McLean, Dir.;

Nazareth Guild - t) 509-744-3259 Ben Walker, Exec. Dir.;

Continuing Education of Priests - t) 509-534-2227 ltomson@dioceseofspokane.org Rev. Lucas E. Tomson, Dir.;

Director of Deacons - t) 509-993-4425 Dcn. Kelly Stewart (kstewart@dioceseofspokane.org);

Director of Deacon Formation (Vacant) -

Detention Ministry - t) 509-747-7213 Rev. Miguel Mejia, Coord.;

Charismatic Renewal (Bilingual) - t) 509-747-7213 Rev. Miguel Mejia;

Vietnamese Catholic Community - Our Lady of La Vang Center - t) 509-714-2942 Rev. Vincent Van Dao Nguyen, Chap.;

Catholic Committee on Scouting - Dcn. Daniel Glatt, Chap.; Robert (Bob) Smee, Chair;

Ecumenical Relations - t) 509-358-7300 Most Rev. William S. Skylstad, (Bishop Emeritus) (wskylstad@dioceseofspokane.org);

PARISHES, MISSIONS, AND CLERGY

STATE OF WASHINGTON

BREWSTER

Sacred Heart - 214 S 5th St., Brewster, WA 98812; Mailing: PO Box 548, Brewster, WA 98812 t) 509-689-2931 Rev. Pedro Bautista Peraza, Pst.; Dcn. Jose Aparicio; Dcn. Bonifacio Arebalo; Jessica Garcia, DRE; CRP Stds.: 46

CHENEY

St. Rose of Lima - 460 N. Fifth St., Cheney, WA 99004 t) 509-235-6229; 509-235-6229 (CRP) msine@dioceseofspokane.org stroseoflimacheney.org Rev. David Kuttner, Pst.; CRP Stds.: 9

CHEWELAH

St. Mary of the Rosary - 502 E Main Ave, Chewelah, WA 99109; Mailing: PO Box 26, Chewelah, WA 99109 t) 509-935-8028 sbooth@dioceseofspokane.org chewelahcatholic.org Rev. Kenneth St. Hilaire, Pst.;

CLARKSTON

Holy Family - 1102 Chestnut St., Clarkston, WA 99403 t) 509-758-6102 holyfamily@dioceseofspokane.org hfparish.com Rev. Jeffrey Core, Pst.;

Holy Family School - (Grades K-6) 1002 Chestnut St., Clarkston, WA 99403 t) 509-758-6621 sgehring@holyfamilyclarkston.com Stds.: 144; Lay Tchrs.: 8

Educare Preschool - t) 509-758-2737 Sharon Hunt, Prin.;

COLBERT

St. Joseph - 3720 E. Colbert Rd., Colbert, WA 99005 t) 509-466-4991 office@stjosephcolbert.org stjosephcolbert.org Rev. Thomas Connolly, Pst.; Dcn. Joseph Schroeder; CRP Stds.: 36

COLFAX

St. Patrick - 1018 S. Main St., Colfax, WA 99111 t) 509-397-3921 Rev. Raymond Kalema, Pst.; CRP Stds.: 38

COLTON

St. Gall - 312 Steptoe St., Colton, WA 99113; Mailing: P.O. Box 108, Colton, WA 99113 t) 509-229-3548 stgbcc@gmail.com www.saintbonifaceandsaintgall.org Rev. Paul Heric, Pst.; CRP Stds.: 10

COLVILLE

Immaculate Conception - 320 N. Maple, Colville, WA 99114 t) 509-684-6223 x6; 509-684-6223 (CRP) info@myparishfamily.org www.myparishfamily.org Rev. Kenneth St. Hilaire, Pst.;

CONNELL

St. Vincent - 220 S. Dayton St., Connell, WA 99326; Mailing: P.O. Box 1030, Connell, WA 99326 t) 509-234-2262 stacystvincent@yahoo.com www.stvincentconnell.org Rev. Miguel Gustavo Ruiz-Juarez, Pst.; Enrique Lopez, DRE;

CURLEW

St. Patrick Mission - 9 Church St., Curlew, WA 99118; Mailing: P.O. Box 333, Republic, WA 99166 t) 509-775-3935 ferrycatholic@gmail.com www.myparishfamily.org Mission of Immaculate Conception Republic WA Rev. Kenneth St. Hilaire, Pst.;

CUSICK

Our Lady of Sorrows - 1981 LeClerc Creek Rd., Cusick, WA 99119; Mailing: P.O. Box C, Newport, WA 99156 t) 509-447-4231 pocopastor@gmail.com Rev. Sean Thomson, Pst.;

DAVENPORT

Immaculate Conception - 1310 Adams St., Davenport, WA 99122-9454 t) 509-725-1761 rsemple@dioceseofspokane.org Rev. Sean Thomson, Pst.;

DAYTON

St. Joseph - 112 S. First St., Dayton, WA 99328-0003; Mailing: P.O. Box 0003, Dayton, WA 99328 t) 509-382-2311 stjosephdayton@dioceseofspokane.org www.rcparishes.org Rev. Steven Werner, Pst.; Melissa Gemmell, DRE; CRP Stds.: 3

DEER PARK

St. Mary Presentation - 602 E. 6th St., Deer Park, WA 99006; Mailing: P.O. Box 749, Deer Park, WA 99006 t) 509-276-2948; 509-276-1043 deerpark@dioceseofspokane.org www.stmarypresentationcc.org Rev. Thomas Connolly, Pst.; Dcn. Perry Pearman; Carmen Himenes, RCIA Coord.; CRP Stds.: 22

ELTOPIA

St. Paul the Apostle - 14181 Glade Rd., Eltopia, WA 99330; Mailing: P.O. Box 268, Eltopia, WA 99330 t) 509-297-4371 Rev. Miguel Gustavo Ruiz-Juarez, Pst.; Angie Manterola, DRE;

San Juan Diego (Basin City) - 440 Bailie Blvd., Basin City, WA 99343 t) 509-234-2262 st.paulcatholicchurch1964@gmail.com nfranklincatholic.com

FORD

St. Philip Benizi - 5247 Hubert Rd., Ford, WA 99013; Mailing: Immaculate Conception Parish, 1310 Adam St., Davenport, WA 99122-9454 t) 509-725-1761 rsemple@dioceseofspokane.org Rev. Sean Thomson, Pst.;

FRUITLAND

Our Lady of Lourdes - 6242 West End Rd., Fruitland, WA 99129; Mailing: Immaculate Conception Parish, 1310 Adams St., Davenport, WA 99122-9454 t) 509-725-1761 rsemple@dioceseofspokane.org Rev. Sean Thomson, Pst.;

HARRINGTON

St. Francis of Assisi - 206 Coal Creek Rd., Harrington, WA 99134-0166; Mailing: 1310 Adams St., Davenport, WA 99122-9454 t) 509-725-1761 rsemple@dioceseofspokane.org Rev. Sean Thomson, Pst.;

INCHELIUM

St. Michael's Mission - 21 St. Michael's Way, Inchelium, WA 99138; Mailing: P.O. Box 122, Inchelium, WA 99138 t) 509-720-3815 josephfortier@gmail.com Rev. Joseph Fortier, S.J., Pst.; Rev. Jake Morton, S.J., Pst.; Frances Stensgar, DRE;

IONE

St. Bernard - 302 N. 8th Ave., Ione, WA 99139; Mailing: PO Box 731, Ione, WA 99139 t) 509-447-4231 pocopastor@gmail.com; pocoparishes@gmail.com www.pocoparishes.org Rev. James Peak, Pst.; Erin Kinney, DRE;

KELLER

St. Rose of Lima - ; Mailing: P.O. Box 187, Keller, WA 99140 t) 509-722-4592 josephfortier@gmail.com Rev. Joseph Fortier, S.J., Pst.; Rev. Jake Morton, S.J., Pst.;

KETTLE FALLS

Sacred Heart of Jesus - E. 485 Third Ave., Kettle Falls, WA 99141; Mailing: 320 N. Maple St., Colville, WA 99114 t) 509-684-6223 info@myparishfamily.org www.myparishfamily.org Rev. Kenneth St. Hilaire, Pst.;

LACROSSE

St. Joseph - 308 E. 2nd St., LaCrosse, WA 99143; Mailing: 1018 S. Main St., Colfax, WA 99111 t) 509-397-3921 Rev. Raymond Kalema, Pst.;

MEDICAL LAKE

St. Anne - 708 E. Lake St., Medical Lake, WA 99022; Mailing: PO Box 125, Medical Lake, WA 99022 t) 509-723-1459 llavoie@dioceseofspokane.org Rev. Dale Tuckerman, Admin.; Lara Lavoie, DRE;

METALINE FALLS

St. Joseph - 406 Park St., Metaline Falls, WA 99153; Mailing: PO Box 417, Metaline Falls, WA 99153 t) 509-446-2651 pocopastor@gmail.com; pocoparishes@gmail.com www.pocoparishes.org Rev. James Peak, Pst.; Erin Kinney, DRE;

NESPELEM

Sacred Heart Mission - 209 9th St., Nespelem, WA 99155; Mailing: PO Box 70, Nespelem, WA 99155 t) 509-634-4249 njam52@hotmail.com Rev. Jake Morton, S.J., Pst.; Nancy Armstrong-Montes, DRE; CRP Stds.: 8

NEWPORT

St. Anthony - 612 W. First St., Newport, WA 99156; Mailing: P.O. Box C, Newport, WA 99156 t) 509-447-4231 pocoparishes@gmail.com Rev. James Peak, Pst.; Sasha Tefft, DRE;

NINE MILE FALLS

Our Lady of the Lake - 6122 Hwy 291, Nine Mile Falls, WA 99026; Mailing: P.O. Box 447, Nine Mile Falls, WA 99026 c) (509) 464-9553 (Pastor's phone number) www.olotl.org Rev. Timothy R. Clancy, S.J., Pst.; Dcn. Craig Blomgren; Cindy Blomgren, DRE; CRP Stds.: 15

NORTHPORT

Pure Heart of Mary - 720 W. South Ave., Northport, WA 99157; Mailing: 320 N. Maple St., Colville, WA 99114 t) 509-684-6223 info@myparishfamily.org www.myparishfamily.org Rev. Kenneth St. Hilaire, Pst.;

OAKESDALE

St. Catherine of Alexandria - 4th & Steptoe, Oakesdale, WA 99158; Mailing: c/o Renee Crider, 2732 Trestle Creek Rd, Thornton, WA 99176 t) 509-285-6672 c) 509-981-8598 dkruse@dioceseofspokane.org; reneecrider@gmail.com Very Rev. Daniel J. Barnett, Pst.;

ODESSA

St. Joseph Catholic Parish - Odessa - 208 N. Alder, Odessa, WA 99159; Mailing: PO Box 339, Odessa, WA 99159 t) (509) 659-0437 stagnesritzville@gmail.com Rev. Rory Pitstick, Pst.;

OKANOGAN

Our Lady of the Valley - 2511 N Elmway, Okanogan, WA 98840 t) 509-422-5049 lnsubuga@dioceseofspokane.org okvalleycatholicparishes.org/ Rev. Lutakome Nsubuga, Pst.; Suzanne Craig, DRE;

OMAK

St. Joseph - 530 Jackson St., Omak, WA 98841; Mailing: 323 Edmonds St., Omak, WA 98841 t) 509-826-6401 jedgertonm@gmail.com Rev. Jake Morton, S.J., Pst.;

St. Mary's Mission - 20 Mission Rd., Omak, WA 98841; Mailing: 323 Edmonds St, Omak, WA 98841 t) 509-826-6401 jedgertonm@gmail.com Rev. Jake Morton, S.J., Pst.;

OROVILLE

Immaculate Conception - 1715 Main St., Oroville, WA 98844; Mailing: P.O. Box 308, Oroville, WA 98844 t) 509-476-2110 lnsubuga@dioceseofspokane.org Rev. Lutakome Nsubuga, Pst.; Maria Viveros, DRE; Charlene Stiles, Bus. Mgr.;

OTHELLO

Sacred Heart - 616 E. Juniper St., Othello, WA 99344 t) 509-488-5653 sacredheart@dioceseofspokane.org Rev. Alejandro Zepeda, Pst.; Dcn. Antonio Beraza; Dcn. Joel Pruneda; Dcn. Jesus Rodelo; Geovanny G. Pinzon, DRE;

OTIS ORCHARDS

St. Joseph - 4521 N. Arden Rd., Otis Orchards, WA 99027-9358 t) 509-926-7133 info@stjoeparish.org stjoeparish.org Rev. Jose Luis Millan, Pst.; Gina McCauley, DRE; Dcn. Gonzalo Chalo Martinez; CRP Stds.: 59

PASCO

St. Patrick - 1320 W. Henry St., Pasco, WA 99301 t) 509-547-8841 x119; 509-547-8841 x114 (CRP) llopez@dioceseofspokane.org; raguilera@stpatspasco.org www.stpatspasco.org Rev. Robert D. Turner, Pst.; Raquel Aguilera, DRE; Rev. Jose Jaime Maldonado, Assoc. Pst.; Rev. Rex Familiar, In Res.; Rev. Msgr. Pedro Ramirez, In Res.; Dcn. Robert Kalinowski; Dcn. Gary Franz; Dcn. Victor Ortega; Dcn. Luis Ramos; Dcn. Antonio Rodriguez; Dcn. Abraham Valdovinos; CRP Stds.: 846

St. Patrick School - (Grades K-8) 1016 N. 14th Ave., Pasco, WA 99301 t) 509-547-7261 principal@stpatspasco.org stpatspasco.org/school Arlene Jones, Prin.; Stds.: 150; Lay Tchrs.: 8

POMEROY

Holy Rosary - 634 High St., Pomeroy, WA 99347-9702 t) 509-843-3801 holyrosarypomeroy@dioceseofspokane.org Rev. Steven Werner, Pst.; Cece Meyers, DRE; CRP Stds.: 30

PULLMAN

Sacred Heart - 440 N.E. Ash St., Pullman, WA 99163 t) 509-332-4402 (CRP); 509-332-5312 shpullman@dioceseofspokane.org www.sacredheartpullman.org Rev. Steven L. Dublinski, Pst.; Dcn. James Evermann; Cory Dixon, DRE; CRP Stds.: 49

REARDAN

St. Michael - 455 W. Cottonwood St., Reardan, WA 99029; Mailing: PO Box 125, Medical Lake, WA 99022 t) 509-723-1459 llavoie@dioceseofspokane.org www.westplainscatholicparishes.org Rev. Dale Tuckerman, Admin.; Joanne Schultz, DRE;

REPUBLIC

Immaculate Conception - 261 E. 7th St., Republic, WA 99166; Mailing: PO Box 333, Republic, WA 99166 t) 509-775-3935 ferrycatholic@gmail.com Rev. Kenneth St. Hilaire, Pst.;

RITZVILLE

St. Agnes Catholic Parish - Ritzville - 404 E. Fifth Ave., Ritzville, WA 99169 t) 509-659-0437 stagnesritzville@gmail.com Rev. Rory Pitstick, Admin.;

ROCKFORD

St. Joseph - 138 S. River St., Rockford, WA 99030; Mailing: P.O. Box 54, Rockford, WA 99030 t) 509-928-3210 stmary@dioceseofspokane.org Rev. Robert J. McNeese, Pst.;

ROSALIA

Holy Rosary - 622 N. Plaza Ave., Rosalia, WA 99170; Mailing: P.O. Box 8, Rosalia, WA 99170 c) 509-998-0209 msavelesky@dioceseofspokane.org Rev. Michael J. Savelesky, Pst.;

SPOKANE

Cathedral of Our Lady of Lourdes - 1115 W. Riverside Ave., Spokane, WA 99201 t) 509-358-4290 cberry@dioceseofspokane.org www.spokanecathedral.com Very Rev. Darrin Connall, Pst.; Rev. Andrew O'Leary, Par. Vicar; Rev. Msgr. Robert A. Pearson, In Res.; Rev. Eugene Tracy, In Res.; Dcn. James Kestell, Pst. Assoc.; Dcn. John Ruscheinsky, Pst. Assoc.; Sr. Marie Paschalina, SMMC, DRE;

St. Aloysius - 330 E. Boone Ave., Spokane, WA 99202 t) (509) 313-5896 (Main line.); (509) 313-7009 (CRP) www.stalschurch.org Rev. Tom Lamanna, S.J., Pst.; Michele Lassiter, DRE; CRP Stds.: 102

St. Aloysius School - (Grades K-8) 611 E. Mission Ave., Spokane, WA 99202 t) 509-489-7825 kkelly@stalsschool.org stalsschool.com Angie Krauss, Prin.; Stds.: 310; Lay Tchrs.: 17

Montessori Education Center - t) 509-489-7825 Marta Shollenberger, Dir.;

St. Ann Parish-Spokane - 2120 E. First Ave., Spokane, WA 99202; Mailing: 2116 E. First Ave., Spokane, WA 99202 t) 509-535-3031 info@stannsspokane.org stanncommunityblog.wordpress.com/ Rev. Patrick Baraza, Pst.; Dr. Craig Bartmess, Parish Life Coord.; Jolie Monasterio, DRE;

St. Anthony - 1320 W Montgomery Ave, Spokane, WA 99205; Mailing: 2320 N Cedar St, Spokane, WA 99205 t) 509-327-1162 cberube@dioceseofspokane.org www.stanthonyspokane.org Rev. Brian Sattler, Pst.; Rev. Vincent Van Dao Nguyen, Chap.; Dcn. James Schwarzer; Sr. Consuela Berube, DRE; CRP Stds.: 7

Educare Center - 2315 N. Cedar St., Spokane, WA 99205 t) 509-327-9369 Amber Lynde, Dir.;

Assumption of the Blessed Virgin Mary - 3624 W. Indian Trail Rd., Spokane, WA 99208 t) 509-326-0144 wthomas@dioceseofspokane.org www.assumptionspokane.org Rev. Timothy Hays, Pst.; Dcn. Kelly Stewart; CRP Stds.: 27

Assumption Parish Catholic School - (Grades PreK-8) 3618 W. Indian Trail Rd., Spokane, WA 99208 t) 509-328-1115 tromano@assumptioncatholic.org www.assumptioncatholic.org T.J. Romano, Prin.; Stds.: 192; Lay Tchrs.: 12

St. Augustine - 428 W. 19th Ave., Spokane, WA 99203 t) 509-747-7972 (CRP); 509-747-4421 saintaugustine@dioceseofspokane.org; staugustine@dioceseofspokane.org staugustinespokane.com Rev. Msgr. Brian Mee, Pst.; Dcn. Allen Peterson; Rev. David Kruse, In Res.; Ivana Ackermann, DRE;

St. Charles - 4515 N. Alberta St., Spokane, WA 99205 t) 509-327-9573 esoler@dioceseofspokane.org www.stcharlesspokane.org Rev. Esteban F. Soler, I.V.E., Pst.; Dcn. Roy Buck; CRP Stds.: 2

St. Charles Catholic School - (Grades PreK-8) t) 509-327-9575 principal@stcharlesspokane.org www.school.stcharlesspokane.org/ Heather Schlaich, Prin.; Stds.: 184; Sr. Tchrs.: 1; Lay Tchrs.: 11

St. Francis of Assisi - 1104 W. Heroy Ave., Spokane, WA 99205 t) 509-325-1321 amturney@dioceseofspokane.org Rev. Michael Blackburn, O.F.M., Pst.; Tammie Fabien, DRE;

St. Francis Xavier - 545 E. Providence Ave., Spokane, WA 99207; Mailing: PO Box 7179, Spokane, WA 99207 t) 509-487-6363 office@sfxspokane.org; pastor@sfxspokane.org www.facebook.com/sfxspokane Rev. Richard Semple, Pst.;

St. Joseph - 1503 W. Dean Ave., Spokane, WA 99201 t) 509-328-4841 stjoeondean@aol.com; stjoeondean@dioceseofspokane.org Rev. Brian Sattler, Pst.; Dcn. Harley Salazar; Dcn. Jose Torres; Sr. Consuela Berube, Dir.;

Mary Queen - 3423 E. Carlisle Ave., Spokane, WA 99217-7208 t) 509-483-4384 maryqueen@dioceseofspokane.org Rev. Paul Vevik, Pst.; Dcn. Donald Whitney;

Our Lady of Fatima - 1517 E. 33rd Ave., Spokane, WA 99203 t) 509-747-7213 frontdesk@fatimaspokane.com; mmejia@dioceseofspokane.org www.fatimaspokane.com Rev. Miguel Mejia, Pst.; Rev. Patrick Hartin, Senior Priest;

St. Patrick - 5025 N. Nelson St., Spokane, WA 99217; Mailing: 505 W. St. Thomas More Way, Spokane, WA 99208 t) 509-466-7738 www.stpatrickspokane.org Rev. Richard Semple, Pst.;

St. Peter - 3520 E. 18th Ave., Spokane, WA 99223 t) 509-534-2227 stpeter@dioceseofspokane.org stpeterspokane.org/ Rev. Lucas Ethan Tomson, Pst.; Rev. Michael D. Venneri, Senior Priest; Dcn. Victor Lopez; Dcn. Nick Senger; Michelle Oresky, DRE; CRP Stds.: 7

Sacred Heart - 219 E. Rockwood Blvd., Spokane, WA 99202 t) 509-747-5810 office@shparishspokane.org shparishspokane.org Rev. Victor M. Blazovich, Pst.; Dcn. Brian Ernst; Sr. Gabrielle Marie, DRE; CRP Stds.: 5

St. Thomas More - 505 W. St. Thomas More Way, Spokane, WA 99208 t) 509-466-3811 www.parish.thomasmorespokane.org Rev. Patrick Kerst, Pst.; Dcn. Doug Banks; Dcn. Thomas Heavey; CRP Stds.: 13

St. Thomas More School - (Grades PreK-8) 515 W. St. Thomas More Way, Spokane, WA 99208 t) (509) 466-3811 x313 www.school.thomasmorespokane.org James McCollum, Prin.; Stds.: 243; Lay Tchrs.: 13

SPOKANE VALLEY

St. John Vianney - 503 N. Walnut Rd., Spokane Valley, WA 99206; Mailing: P.O. Box 141125, Spokane Valley, WA 99214-1125 t) 509-926-5428 ksampica@dioceseofspokane.org www.sjvchurch.org Rev. Kevin Oiland, Pst.; CRP Stds.: 146

St. John Vianney Catholic School - (Grades PreK-8) 501 N. Walnut Rd., Spokane, WA 99206 t) 509-926-7987 jolson@sjvspokane.org st.johnvianney.com Dcn. Nick Senger, Contact; Stds.: 120; Lay Tchrs.: 8

St. Mary - 304 S. Adams Rd., Spokane Valley, WA 99216 t) 509-928-3210 stmary@dioceseofspokane.org stmaryspokane.org Rev. Jeffrey Lewis, Pst.; Dcn. Daniel Glatt; Dcn. Mike Miller; Marie Bricher, DRE; CRP Stds.: 88

St. Mary School - (Grades PreK-8) 14601 E. 4th Ave., Spokane, WA 99216 t) 509-924-4300 cweiler@stmarysspokane.org mary.school Ben Walker, Prin.; Stds.: 286; Lay Tchrs.: 16

St. Paschal - 2523 N. Park Rd., Spokane Valley, WA 99214-1125; Mailing: PO Box 141125, Spokane Valley, WA 99214 t) 509-926-5428 ksampica@dioceseofspokane.org sjvchurch.org Rev. Kevin Oiland, Pst.;

Educare Center - t) 509-922-7616

mjpaschall@dioceseofspokane.org Mary Jo Paschall, Dir.;

SPRAGUE

Mary Queen of Heaven - 103 E. Alder St., Sprague, WA 99032; Mailing: P.O. Box 125, Medical Lake, WA 99022 t) 509-723-1459 llavoie@dioceseofspokane.org Rev. Michael L. Ishida, Pst.;

SPRINGDALE

Sacred Heart - 110 S. Main St., Springdale, WA 99173; Mailing: P.O. Box 26, Chewelah, WA 99109 t) 509-935-8028 sbooth@dioceseofspokane.org Rev. Kenneth St. Hilaire, Pst.;

ST. JOHN

Our Lady of Perpetual Help - 403 W. Liberty, St. John, WA 99171; Mailing: P.O. Box 325, St. John, WA 99171 t) 509-397-3921 Rev. Raymond Kalema, Pst.;

TEKOA

Sacred Heart - 822 N. Washington St., Tekoa, WA 99033; Mailing: P.O. Box 957, Tekoa, WA 99033 t) 509-284-3001 dkruse@dioceseofspokane.org Rev. David Gaines;

TONASKET

Holy Rosary - S. Whitcomb Ave. & E. 1st St., Tonasket, WA 98855; Mailing: P.O. Box 308, Oroville, WA 98844 t) 509-476-2110 lnsubuga@dioceseofspokane.org Rev. Lutakome Nsubuga, Pst.; Marta Wisdom, DRE; Charlene Stiles, Bus. Mgr.;

TWISP

St. Genevieve - 403 Burgar St., Twisp, WA 98856; Mailing: PO Box 6, Twisp, WA 98856 t) 509-997-4201 www.methowcatholic.com Rev. Pedro Bautista Peraza, Pst.; Dcn. Bill Wehmeyer; Sarah Salmon, DRE; CRP Stds.: 2

UNIONTOWN

St. Boniface - 205 S. St. Boniface St., Uniontown, WA 99179; Mailing: P.O. Box 108, Colton, WA 99113 t) 509-229-3548 c) 503-599-8437 stgbcc@gmail.com; sdsemler@dioceseofspokane.org www.saintbonifaceandsaintgall.org Rev. Paul Heric, Pst.; CRP Stds.: 10

USK

St. Jude - 111 River Rd., Usk, WA 99180; Mailing: PO Box 385, Usk, WA 99180 t) 509-447-2685 pocopastor@gmail.com www.pocoparishes.org Rev. James Peak, Pst.;

VALLEY

Holy Ghost - 3083 Hemlock St., Valley, WA 99181; Mailing: P.O. Box 26, Chewelah, WA 99109 t) 509-935-8028 mishida@dioceseofspokane.org chewelahcatholic.org Rev. Michael L. Ishida, Pst.;

St. Joseph - 3150 Church Rd., Valley, WA 99181; Mailing: PO Box 26, Chewelah, WA 99109

WAITSBURG

St. Mark - 405 W. 5th St., Waitsburg, WA 99361; Mailing: PO Box 0003, Dayton, WA 99328-0003 t) 509-382-2311 www.rcparishes.org Rev. Steven Werner, Pst.;

WALLA WALLA

Assumption of the Blessed Virgin Mary - 2098 E. Alder St., Walla Walla, WA 99362 t) 509-525-3310 x4 (CRP); 509-525-3310 x2 ffc@wwcatholic.com wwcatholic.org/ Rev. Matthew Nicks, Pst.;

St. Francis of Assisi - 722 W. Alder St., Walla Walla, WA 99362 t) 509-525-3310 x1 stfrancis@wwcatholic.com wwcatholic.org/ Dcn. Jim Barrow; Martha Jimenez, DRE; Rev. Curtis Seidel, Pst.; CRP Stds.: 1

St. Patrick - 408 W. Poplar St., Walla Walla, WA 99362-2831 t) 509-525-3310 x4 (CRP); 509-525-3310 x3 (Tri-Parish) redirector@wwcatholic.com; stpatrick@wwcatholic.com wwcatholic.org/ Rev. Dale Tuckerman, Pst.; Rev. Lourdu Mummadi, S.J. (India), Par. Vicar; Dcn. James Barrow; Dcn. Olegario Reyes; Dcn. Maclobi Robles; Martha Jimenez, DRE; CRP Stds.: 165

WELLPINIT

Sacred Heart - 6156 Ford-Wellpinit Rd, Wellpinit, WA 99040; Mailing: Immaculate Conception Parish, 1310 Adams St, Davenport, WA 99122-9454 t) 509-725-1761 rsemple@dioceseofspokane.org Rev. Sean Thomson, Pst.;

WILBUR

Sacred Heart Catholic Parish - Wilbur - 605 S.W. Alder, Wilbur, WA 99185; Mailing: PO Box 106, Wilbur, WA 99185 t) (509) 659-0437 stagnesritzville@gmail.com Rev. Rory Pitstick, Admin.;

SCHOOLS: PRESCHOOL THRU HIGH SCHOOL

SCHOOLS

STATE OF WASHINGTON

COLTON

Guardian Angel-St. Boniface School - (PAR) (Grades PreK-8) 306 Steptoe St., Colton, WA 99113; Mailing: PO Box 48, Colton, WA 99113 t) 509-229-3579 gasbschool@colton-wa.com gasbschool.org Serving St. Gall and St. Boniface Parishes. Lori Becker, Prin.; Holly Meyer, Librn.; Stds.: 22; Lay Tchrs.: 3

SPOKANE

All Saints Catholic School- Primary Building - (PAR) (Grades K-4) 3510 E. 18th Ave., Spokane, WA 99223 t) 509-534-1098 x215 jlewis@allsaintsspokane.net allsaintsspokane.org Jen Lewis, Prin.; Stds.: 315; Pr. Tchrs.: 2; Lay Tchrs.: 16

All Saints Catholic School - Middle Building - (Grades K-4) 1428 E. 33rd Ave., Spokane, WA 99203 t) 509-624-5712 jlewis@dioceseofspokane.org Serving St. Peter, St. Ann, and Our Lady of Fatima Parishes. Jennifer Lewis, Prin.;

Cataldo Catholic School - (PAR) (Grades PreK-8) 455 W. 18th Ave., Spokane, WA 99203 t) 509-624-8759 office@cataldo.org www.cataldo.org Serving St. Augustine, Sacred Heart, and Cathedral of Our Lady of Lourdes Parishes. Zack Cunningham, Prin.; Sara Raske, Vice Prin.; Stds.: 373; Lay Tchrs.: 25

Trinity School and Educare - (PAR) (Grades PreSchool-8) 2315 N. Cedar, Spokane, WA 99205 t) 509-327-9369 information@trinityspokane.com trinityspokane.org Serving St. Joseph & St. Anthony Catholic Parish - Spokane. Trinity School and Educare Stacie Holcomb, Prin.; Nancy Likarish, Librn.; Stds.: 184; Lay Tchrs.: 8

WALLA WALLA

Assumption Elementary School - (PAR) (Grades PreK-6) 2066 E. Alder St., Walla Walla, WA 99362 t) 509-525-9283 jlesko@wallawallacatholicschools.com; wwcs@thewwcs.com www.wallawallacatholicschools.com Serving Assumption, St. Francis of Assisi, and St. Patrick Parishes. Rev. Matthew Nicks, Pst.; John Lesko, Prin.; Rev. Curtis Seidel, Pres.; Stds.: 190; Pr. Tchrs.: 1; Lay Tchrs.: 13

HIGH SCHOOLS

STATE OF WASHINGTON

PASCO

Tri Cities Prep, A Catholic High School - (PRV) (Grades 9-12) 9612 St. Thomas Dr., Pasco, WA 99301 t) 509-546-2465 blee@tcprep.org; ljacobs@tcprep.org www.tcprep.org Lisa Jacobs, Pres.; Matt Potter, Dean; Stds.: 202; Lay Tchrs.: 14

SPOKANE

***Chesterton Academy of Notre Dame** - (PRV) (Grades 9-12) 2706 E. Queen Ave., Spokane, WA 99217 t) 509-242-3750 chestertonacademynotredame@gmail.com chestertonacademyofnotredame.org/ Rev. Richard Semple, Chap.; Stds.: 96; Lay Tchrs.: 11

Gonzaga Preparatory School - (PRV) (Grades 9-12) E. 1224 Euclid Ave, Spokane, WA 99207 t) 509-483-8511 mdougherty@gprep.com; creopelle@gprep.com www.gprep.com Cindy Reopelle, Prin.; Michael Dougherty, Pres.; Stds.: 807; Pr. Tchrs.: 2; Lay Tchrs.: 65

WALLA WALLA

Walla Walla Catholic School System (DeSales Catholic High School) - (PAR) (Grades PreK-12) 919 E Sumach St., Walla Walla, WA 99362 t) 509-525-3030 desales@thewwcs.com; jlesko@thewwcs.com www.wallawallacatholicschools.com Rev. Matthew Nicks, Pst.; John Lesko, Prin.; Rev. Curtis Seidel, Pres.; Stds.: 293; Pr. Tchrs.: 1; Lay Tchrs.: 15

INSTITUTIONS LOCATED IN DIOCESE

CAMPUS MINISTRY / NEWMAN CENTERS [CAM]

CHENEY

Catholic Newman Center at Eastern Washington University - 837 Elm St., Cheney, WA 99004 t) 509-599-8437 newmanewu@gmail.com www.ewucatholics.org Rev. Paul Heric, Pst.;

PULLMAN

St. Thomas More Catholic Student Center - Washington State University - 820 N.E. B St., Pullman, WA 99163-4025 t) 509-332-6311 catholiccougs@gmail.com www.catholiccougs.org Rev. Paul Heric, Pst.;

CATHOLIC CHARITIES [CCH]

COLVILLE

The Rhodena - 230 S. Wynne, Colville, WA 99114; Mailing: P.O. Box 2253, Spokane, WA 99210-2253 t) 509-459-6183 sharon.budweg@cceasternwa.org www.cceasternwa.org A six unit affordable housing complex for families living in Colville, WA. Glori Houston, Dir.; Asstd. Annu.: 6; Staff: 1

SPOKANE

Catholic Charities of Spokane (Catholic Charities Eastern Washington) - 12 E. Fifth Ave., Spokane, WA 99202; Mailing: P.O. Box 2253, Spokane, WA 99210-2253 t) 509-358-4250 www.cceasternwa.org Robert J. McCann, CEO; Asstd. Annu.: 30,902; Staff: 385

House of Charity - 32 W. Pacific Ave., Spokane, WA 99201; Mailing: P.O. Box 2253, Spokane, WA 99210-2253 t) 509-624-7821 dena.carr@cceasternwa.org www.cceasternwa.org Shelter, sleeping program, services and transitional housing for homeless men and women Dena Carr, Dir.; Asstd. Annu.: 98,330; Staff: 35

WALLA WALLA

Catholic Charities Walla Walla - 408 W. Poplar, Walla Walla, WA 99362; Mailing: P.O. Box 2253, Spokane, WA 99210-2253 t) 509-525-0572 tim.meliah@cceasternwa.org Tim Meliah, Dir.; Asstd. Annu.: 137; Staff: 4

CEMETERIES [CEM]

SPOKANE

Catholic Cemeteries of Spokane - 7200 N. Wall St., Spokane, WA 99208; Mailing: P.O. Box 18006, Spokane, WA 99228 t) 509-467-5496 rickm@holycrossofspokane.org Rick McLean, Dir.;

Holy Cross Funeral and Cemetery Center - 7200 N. Wall St., Spokane, WA 99208; Mailing: P.O. Box 18006, Spokane, WA 99228 t) 509-467-5496 www.holycrossofspokane.org Rick McLean, Dir.;

St. Joseph Funeral and Cemetery Center - 17825 E. Trent Ave., Spokane, WA 99216; Mailing: P.O. Box 18006, Spokane, WA 99228 t) 509-467-5496 info@holycrossofspokane.org www.holycrossofspokane.org Rick McLean, Dir.;

Mary Queen of Peace Funeral and Cemetery Center - 6910 S. Ben Burr Rd., Spokane, WA 99223; Mailing: P.O. Box 18006, Spokane, WA 99228 t) 509-467-5496 info@holycrossofspokane.org www.holycrossofspokane.org Rick McLean, Dir.;

COLLEGES & UNIVERSITIES [COL]

SPOKANE

Gonzaga University - 323 E. Boone Ave., Spokane, WA 99202; Mailing: 502 E. Boone, Spokane, WA 99258 t) 509-313-6076; 509-313-6014 rorholmm@gonzaga.edu; jesuits@gonzaga.edu Jesuit Community at Gonzaga Rev. Thomas Lamanna, SJ, Pst.; Rev. San H Mai, S.J., Assoc. Pst.; Rev. Dan Mai, Campus Min.; Rev. JK Adams, SJ, Educator; Rev. Timothy R. Clancy, S.J.; Rev. Thomas Colgan, S.J.; Rev. Kevin Connell, S.J.; Rev. Michael J. Connolly, S.J.; Rev. Stephen M. Hess, SJ; Rev. Kenneth R. Krall, S.J.; Rev. Stephen R. Kuder, S.J.; Rev. Robert Lyons, S.J.; Rev. Brad Reynolds, S.J.; Rev. Quan Tran, S.J.; Rev. Bryan Pham; Stds.: 7,288; Lay Tchrs.: 459; Pr. Tchrs.: 8

The Ministry Institute (Mater Dei Ministry Institute) - E. 405 Sinto Ave., Spokane, WA 99202-1849 t) 509-313-5765 bartletts@gonzaga.edu (at Gonzaga University) Diane Imes, Admin.; Nathaniel Greene, Pres.; Shonna Bartlett, Dir.;

CONVENTS, MONASTERIES, AND RESIDENCES FOR WOMEN [CON]

NEWPORT

Carmelite Sisters of Mary - 2892 Hwy. 211, Newport, WA 99156 t) 509-292-0978 carmelitesrsofmary@ifiber.tv Sr. Leslie L. Lund, Prioress; Srs.: 2

SPOKANE

Franciscan Monastery of St. Clare - 4419 N. Hawthorne St., Spokane, WA 99205-1399 t) 509-327-4479 stclare800@gmail.com www.calledbyjoy.com Papal Enclosure Novitiate. Poor Clare Nuns Sr. Marcia Kay LaCour, OSC, Abbess; Srs.: 5

Holy Names Foundation - 5915 S. Regal St., Ste. 308, Spokane, WA 99223 t) 503-675-7123 Support for educational activities of Sisters of the Holy Names of Jesus and Mary. Sr. Maureen Delaney, Prov.;

Missionaries of Charity - 5008 N. Lacey St., Spokane, WA 99217 t) 509-487-3963 jsiira@dioceseofspokane.org Sr. Rose Poor, Supr.; Srs.: 3

Sisters of the Holy Names of Jesus and Mary (U.S. Ontario Province) - 5915 S. Regal St., Ste. 308, Spokane, WA 99223 t) 503-675-7123 Vicki Cummings, Treas.; Srs.: 26

ENDOWMENTS / FOUNDATIONS / TRUSTS [EFT]

DAYTON

St. Mark Waitsburg and St. Joseph Dayton Catholic Parish Foundation - 112 S. 1st St., Dayton, WA 99328; Mailing: PO Box 0003, Dayton, WA 99328-0003 t) 509-382-2311 stjosephdayton@dioceseofspokane.org Rev. Steven Werner;

POMEROY

Holy Rosary Catholic Church Foundation of Garfield County - 634 High St., Pomeroy, WA 99347 t) 509-843-3801 holyrosarypomeroy@dioceseofspokane.org Rev. Steven Werner;

SPOKANE

Catholic Charities Foundation - 12 E. Fifth Ave., Spokane, WA 99202; Mailing: P.O. Box 2253, Spokane, WA 99210-2253 t) 509-358-4250 annmarie.byrd@cceasternwa.org Ann Marie Byrd, Dir.;

The Catholic Foundation of Eastern Washington - 525 E. Mission Ave., Spokane, WA 99202; Mailing: P.O. Box 1484, Spokane, WA 99210 t) 509-358-7334 metracy@dioceseofspokane.org www.catholicfoundationspokane.org Sr. Mary E. Tracy, S.N.J.M., Exec.;

HOSPITALS / HEALTH SERVICES [HOS]

CHEWELAH

Providence St. Joseph's Hospital (of Chewelah) (Providence Health & Services-Washington) - 500 E. Webster, Chewelah, WA 99109; Mailing: 982 E. Columbia Ave., Colville, WA 99114 t) 509-935-8211 kelley.robertson@providence.org www.providence.org/stjosephs Ronald G. Rehn, Exec.; Kelly Corcoran, Dir.; Bed Capacity: 25; Asstd. Annu.: 32,064; Staff: 126

COLVILLE

Providence Mount Carmel Hospital (Providence Health & Services-Washington) - 982 E. Columbia Ave., Colville, WA 99114 t) 509-685-5100 kelley.robertson@providence.org www.providence.org/mountcarmel Ronald G. Rehn, Exec.; Kelly Corcoran, Dir.; Bed Capacity: 25; Asstd. Annu.: 88,316; Staff: 290

PASCO

Our Lady of Lourdes Hospital at Pasco - 520 Fourth Ave., Pasco, WA 99301-2568; Mailing: 4600 Edmundson Rd., St. Louis, MO 63134 t) 509-543-2483 Ascension Health, corporate member. Craig Cordola, Executive Vice President & Chief Operating Officer; Thomas VanOsdol, Executive Vice President & Chief Mission Integration Officer; Bed Capacity: 127; Asstd. Annu.: 42,500; Staff: 1,100

SPOKANE

Providence Adult Day Health (Providence Health & Services-Washington) - 6018 N. Astor, Spokane, WA 99208 t) 509-482-2475 oscar.haupt2@providence.org washington.providence.org Purpose: to provide adult day health programs, including rehab & nursing, to the elderly and disabled. Oscar Haupt, Bus. Mgr.; Asstd. Annu.: 15,589; Staff: 20

Providence Holy Family Hospital (Providence Health & Services-Washington) - N. 5633 Lidgerwood St., Spokane, WA 99208 t) 509-482-0111 shmc@providence.org www.holy-family.org Susan Stacey, CEO; Susan Scott, CIO; Bed Capacity: 197; Asstd. Annu.: 196,694; Staff: 1,066

Providence Sacred Heart Medical Center & Children's Hospital (Providence Health & Services-Washington) - W. 101 8th Ave., Spokane, WA 99204 t) 509-474-3040 pshmc.information@providence.org www.shmc.org Susan Stacey, CEO; Bed Capacity: 691; Asstd. Annu.: 632,082; Staff: 3,361

WALLA WALLA

Providence St. Mary Medical Center - 401 W. Poplar, Walla Walla, WA 99362; Mailing: P.O. Box 1477, Walla Walla, WA 99362 t) 509-897-3320 frank.erickson@providence.org www.providence.org/stmary (Part of Providence St. Joseph Health) Sisters of Providence. Reza Kaleel, CEO; Bed Capacity: 99; Asstd. Annu.: 413,823; Staff: 1,476

MISCELLANEOUS [MIS]

DAYTON

Project Timothy: Christian Service Center - 249 E. Main St., Dayton, WA 99328 t) 509-382-2943 tschlachter@hotmail.com projecttimothy.org Sponsored by St. Joseph Catholic Parish - Dayton. Rev. Steven Werner;

St. Vincent de Paul Store - 247 E. Main, Dayton, WA 99328 t) 509-382-4146 jobobpat@hotmail.com Skeeter Reis, Pres.; Bob Patras, Vice. Pres.; Lydia C. Buettner, Treas.;

SPOKANE

Family to Family - 505 W. St. Thomas More Way, Spokane, WA 99208 c) 509-301-1467 ftfguatemala@gmail.com familytofamilyguatemala.com Economic development program in the Guatemalan Highlands Julianne Connell Sachs, Admin.;

Guatemala Commission of the Catholic Diocese of Spokane - 525 E. Mission Ave., Spokane, WA 99202 t) 509-358-7319 bkraut@dioceseofspokane.org Brian Kraut, Contact;

Holy Names Music Center - 3910 W. Custer Dr., Spokane, WA 99224 t) 509-326-9516 music@hnmc.org www.hnmc.org Sponsored by Sisters of the Holy Names, Washington Province. Suzanne Bjork, Admin.;

Kateri Northwest Ministry Institute - 1107 N. Astor St., Spokane, WA 99202; Mailing: P.O. Box 4693, Spokane, WA 99220 t) 509-313-7024 katerinmi@gmail.com; kateri@katerinmi.org www.katerinmi.org Jesuit-affiliated formation development program for Indian Catholic church communities of the Northwest. Jenny Edgren, Admin.; Rev. Michael Fitzpatrick, S.J., Dir.;

***L'Arche Spokane** - 703 E. Nora Ave., Spokane, WA 99207-2455 t) 509-483-0438 info@larcheofspokane.org www.larchespokane.org Homes for adults with developmental disabilities Maurine Barrett, Dir.; Sydney Carrick, Community Coord.; Robin Rohrock, Health Care Coord.;

Nazareth Guild - 12 E. Fifth Ave., Spokane, WA 99202; Mailing: P.O. Box 76, Spokane, WA 99210 t) 509-744-3257; 509-744-3259 dbattaglia@dioceseofspokane.org; alee@dioceseofspokane.org nazarethguild.org Alexandra Lee, Dir.; Debbie Battaglia, Bus. Mgr.;

Our Lady of La Vang Center - 2227 N. Cedar St., Spokane, WA 99205; Mailing: 2320 N Cedar Str., Spokane, WA 99205 t) 509-328-1467 vdao@dioceseofspokane.org Rev. Vincent Van Dao Nguyen, Pst.;

Providence Health Care (Providence Health & Services-Washington) - 101 W. 8th Ave., Mother Gamelin Center, Spokane, WA 99204 t) 509-474-7126 lori.staley@providence.org; patricia.petersen@providence.org An integrated healthcare delivery network made up of: Providence Sacred Heart Medical Center and Children's Hospital, Providence. Elaine Couture, CEO;

Providence Medical Research Center - 105 W. 8th Ave., Ste. 6050W, Spokane, WA 99204 t) 509-474-4345; 509-474-4345 joy.durham@providence.org; lori.staley@providence.org Elaine Couture, CEO;

Sisters of Mary, Mother of the Church - 4624 E. Jamieson Rd., Spokane, WA 99223 t) 509-448-9890 contact@sistersofmarymc.org www.sistersofmarymc.org Mother Kathryn Joseph, SMMC, Supr.;

Summit View - 820 N. Summit Blvd., Spokane, WA 99201; Mailing: P.O. Box 2253, Spokane, WA 99210-2253 t) 509-327-9524 lorraine.brooks@cceasternwa.org www.cceasternwa.org 27 units of housing for families. Glori Houston, Dir.;

SPOKANE VALLEY

Serra Club of Spokane - 4425 S Willow Ln, Spokane Valley, WA 99206; Mailing: P.O. Box 31535, Spokane, WA 99223-3025 t) (509) 468-6774 spokane@serrainternational.org www.serraclubofspokane.com Rev. Kyle Ratuiste, Chap.;

MONASTERIES AND RESIDENCES FOR PRIESTS AND BROTHERS [MON]

SPOKANE

Regis Community - N. 1107 Astor St., Spokane, WA 99202 t) 509-313-6014 rorholmm@gonzaga.edu Bea House Rev. John Murphy, SJ, Pst. Min./Coord.; Rev. John Izzo, SJ, Dir., Ignatian Way Project; Rev. Peter J. Byrne, S.J.; Rev. Robert Erickson; Rev. Joseph Fortier, S.J.; Rev. George (Max) Oliva; Rev. James Torrens; Priests: 7

NURSING / REHABILITATION / CONVALESCENCE / ELDERLY CARE [NUR]

CLARKSTON

Austen Manor - 1222 Chestnut St., Clarkston, WA 99403; Mailing: P.O. Box 2253, Spokane, WA 99210-2253 t) 509-751-9640 austenmanor@cceasternwa.org www.cceasternwa.org Asstd. Annu.: 30; Staff: 2

PULLMAN

Pioneer Square - 220 S.E. Kamiaken St., Pullman, WA 99163; Mailing: P.O. Box 2253, Spokane, WA 99210-2253 t) 509-332-1106 pioneersquare@cceasternwa.org www.cceasternwa.org Glori Houston, Dir.; Asstd. Annu.: 45; Staff: 2

SPOKANE

Cathedral Plaza Apartments - W. 1120 Sprague Ave., Spokane, WA 99201; Mailing: P.O. Box 2253, Spokane, WA 99210-2253 t) 509-747-6777 gary.swartz@cceasternwa.org www.cceasternwa.org Glori Houston, Dir.; Asstd. Annu.: 150; Staff: 3

The Delaney - 242 W. Riverside Ave., Spokane, WA 99201; Mailing: P.O. Box 2253, Spokane, WA 99210-2253 t) 509-747-5081 delaney@cceasternwa.org www.cceasternwa.org Glori Houston, Dir.; Asstd. Annu.: 84; Staff: 3

Fahy Garden Apartments - 1411 W. Dean Ave., Spokane, WA 99201; Mailing: P.O. Box 2253, Spokane, WA 99210-2253 t) 509-326-6759 fahys@cceasternwa.org www.cceasternwa.org Glori Houston, Dir.; Asstd. Annu.: 31; Staff: 2

Fahy West Apartments - W. 1523 Dean Ave., Spokane, WA 99201; Mailing: P.O. Box 2253, Spokane, WA 99210-2253 t) 509-326-6759 fahys@cceasternwa.org www.cceasternwa.org Glori Houston, Dir.; Asstd. Annu.: 55; Staff: 2

The O'Malley Apartments - 707 E. Mission Ave., Spokane, WA 99202; Mailing: P.O. Box 2253, Spokane, WA 99210-2253 t) 509-487-1150 omalley@cceasternwa.org www.cceasternwa.org Glori Houston, Dir.; Asstd. Annu.: 99; Staff: 3

Providence St. Joseph Care Center (Providence Health & Services-Washington) - 17 E. 8th Ave., Spokane, WA 99202 t) 509-474-5678; 509-474-7924 marcia.ross@providence.org (A Non-profit Corporation) Sisters of Providence-Mother Joseph Province. Robert Hellrigel, CEO; Asstd. Annu.: 946; Staff: 185

Rockwood Lane - 221 E. Rockwood Blvd., Spokane, WA 99202; Mailing: P.O. Box 2253, Spokane, WA 99210-2253 t) 509-838-3200 jason.finley@cceasternwa.org www.cceasternwa.org Asstd. Annu.: 106; Staff: 4

Senior Service - Senior Nutrition - 12 E. Fifth Ave., Spokane, WA 99210; Mailing: P.O. Box 2253, Spokane, WA 99210-2253 t) 509-459-6175 tom.carroll@cceasternwa.org www.cceasternwa.org Tom Carroll, Dir.; Asstd. Annu.: 9,340; Staff: 3

WALLA WALLA

Garden Court/Mike Foye - 420 W. Alder St., Walla Walla, WA 99362; Mailing: P.O. Box 2253, Spokane, WA 99210-2253 t) 509-529-4706 glori.houston@cceasternwa.org www.cceasternwa.org Glori Houston, Dir.; Asstd. Annu.: 45; Staff: 2

PRESCHOOLS / CHILDCARE CENTERS [PRE]

SPOKANE

St. Anne's Children and Family Center - 25 W. 5th Ave., Spokane, WA 99204; Mailing: P.O. Box 2253, Spokane, WA 99210-2253 t) 509-232-1111 deitra.miller@cceasternwa.org www.stanneskids.com Dietra Miller, Dir.; Stds.: 153; Lay Tchrs.: 35

Morning Star Boys' Ranch - 4511 S. Glenrose Rd., Spokane, WA 99203; Mailing: PO Box 8087, Spokane, WA 99203 t) 509-448-1202 msbr@msbranch.org morningstarboysranch.org Audrea Marshall, CEO;

RETREAT HOUSES / RENEWAL CENTERS [RTR]

SPOKANE

Immaculate Heart Retreat Center - 6910 S. Ben Burr Rd., Spokane, WA 99223 t) 509-448-1224 ihrc@ihrc.net www.ihrc.net Dcn. John Ruscheinsky, Dir.;

Immaculate Heart Retreat Center Foundation - 6910 S. Ben Burr Rd., Spokane, WA 99223-1819 t) 509-448-1224 ihrc@ihrc.net Dcn. John Ruscheinsky, Dir.;

KAIROS House of Prayer - 1714 W. Stearns Rd., Spokane, WA 99208 t) 509-466-2187 mscole@dioceseofspokane.org Provides a place called to a prayerful, reflective environment for people of all faiths. Spiritual accompaniment is available.

Spiritual Exercises in Everyday Life (SEEL) - 330 E. Boone Ave., Spokane, WA 99202 t) 509-313-5898 seelspokane@gmail.com Jennifer Doolittle, Dir.;

SEMINARIES [SEM]

SPOKANE

Bishop White Seminary - 429 E. Sharp Ave., Spokane, WA 99202 t) 509-313-7100 office@bishopwhitesem.org; tferguson@bishopwhitesem.org www.bishopwhitesem.org Very Rev. Daniel J. Barnett, Rector; Rev. Kyle Ratuiste, Vice Rector & Dean of Men; Rev. John Murphy, SJ, Coordinator of Spiritual Formation; Rev. Jeffrey Lewis, Coordinator of Pastoral Formation; Dr. Michael Tkacz, Coordinator of Intellectual Formation; Most Rev. William S. Skylstad, Spiritual Dir.; Rev. Victor M. Blazovich, Spiritual Dir.; Rev. Michael Kwiatkowski, Spiritual Dir.; Rev. Kenneth St. Hilaire, Spiritual Dir.; Dr. Catherine Tkacz, Formation Consultant; Rev. Patrick Baraza, Extraordinary Confessor; Rev. Patrick Hartin, Extraordinary Confessor; Rev. Lucas E. Tomson, Prof.; Rev. Joachim L. Hien, Extraordinary Confessor; Rev. Paul Vevik, Extraordinary Confessor; Stds.: 14

SPECIAL CARE FACILITIES [SPF]

CHEWELAH

Providence DominiCare - 110 S. 3rd St. E., Chewelah, WA 99109; Mailing: PO Box 1070, Chewelah, WA 99109 t) 509-935-4925 joan.sisco@providence.org washington.providence.org A home care/personal care service in Stevens, Ferry & Pend Oreille Counties. Joan Sisco, Exec.; Asstd. Annu.: 5,500; Staff: 25

SPOKANE

Bernadette Place - 925 N. A St. #2, Spokane, WA 99210-2253; Mailing: P.O. Box 2253, Spokane, WA 99210-2253 t) 509-327-9524 lorraine.brooks@cceasternwa.org www.cceasternwa.org Affordable housing for persons with disabilities and special needs. Robert J. McCann, CEO; Bed Capacity: 9; Asstd. Annu.: 9; Staff: 1

Emilie Court Assisted Living (Providence Health & Services-Washington) - 34 E. 8th Ave., Spokane, WA 99202-1202 t) 509-474-2550 charlene.longworth@providence.org www.emiliecourt.org Charlene Longworth, Admin.; Bed Capacity: 60; Asstd. Annu.: 56; Staff: 28

St. Margaret's Shelter - 101 E. Hartson Ave., Spokane, WA 99210-2253; Mailing: P.O. Box 2253, Spokane, WA 99210-2253 t) 509-624-9788 shannon.boniface@cceasternwa.org www.cceasternwa.org Emergency and transitional shelter for women & children. Shannon Boniface, Dir.; Bed Capacity: 36; Asstd. Annu.: 388; Staff: 26

Transitions - 3128 N. Hemlock, Spokane, WA 99205 t) 509-328-6702; 509-455-4249; 509-496-0396; 509-325-2959; 509-747-9222 info@help4women.org; erice-sauer@help4women.org www.help4women.org Edie A. Rice-Sauer, Exec. Dir.; Bed Capacity: 252; Asstd. Annu.: 1,200; Staff: 45

Home Yard Cottages - 3128 N. Hemlock, Spokane, WA 99205 t) (509) 795-8410

Miryam's House - 3128 N. Hemlock, Spokane, WA 99205 amanning@help4women.com www.help4women.com Transitional housing residential program and supportive services for women in transition.

Transitional Living Center - Housing for homeless women & children.

Transitions Educare - 3128 N. Hemlock, Spokane, WA 99205

Transitions New Leaf Bakery Cafe - 3104 Whistalks Way, Spokane, WA 99204 t) (509) 496-0396 Sarah Lickfold, Dir.;

Women's Hearth - 920 W. 2nd Ave., Spokane, WA 99201 Susan Tyler-Babkirk, Dir.;

Diocese of Springfield-Cape Girardeau

(Dioecesis Campifontis-Capitis Girardeauensis)

MOST REVEREND EDWARD M. RICE

Bishop of Springfield-Cape Girardeau; ordained January 3, 1987; appointed Auxiliary Bishop of Saint Louis and Titular Bishop of Sufes December 1, 2010; ordained January 13, 2011; appointed Bishop of Springfield-Cape Girardeau April 26, 2016; installed June 1, 2016. The Catholic Center, 601 S. Jefferson Ave., Springfield, MO 65806-3143.

Chancery Office: The Catholic Center, 601 S. Jefferson Ave., Springfield, MO 65806-3143. T: 417-866-0841; F: 417-866-1140.

www.dioscg.org

ESTABLISHED AUGUST 24, 1956.

Square Miles 25,719.

Comprises the following Counties in the State of Missouri: Barry, Barton, Bollinger, Butler, Cape Girardeau, Carter, Cedar, Christian, Dade, Dallas, Dent, Douglas, Dunklin, Greene, Howell, Iron, Jasper, Laclede, Lawrence, McDonald, Madison, Mississippi, New Madrid, Newton, Oregon, Ozark, Pemiscot, Polk, Reynolds, Ripley, Scott, Shannon, Stoddard, Stone, Taney, Texas, Wayne, Webster and Wright.

For legal titles of parishes and diocesan institutions, consult The Catholic Center.

STATISTICAL OVERVIEW

Personnel

Bishop	1
Retired Bishops	1
Abbots	1
Retired Abbots	1
Priests: Diocesan Active in Diocese	40
Priests: Diocesan Active Outside Diocese	3
Priests: Retired, Sick or Absent	21
Number of Diocesan Priests	64
Religious Priests in Diocese	55
Total Priests in your Diocese	119
Extern Priests in Diocese	16
Ordinations:	
Diocesan Priests	3
Transitional Deacons	1
Permanent Deacons in Diocese	24
Total Brothers	33
Total Sisters	68

Parishes

Parishes	66
With Resident Pastor:	
Resident Diocesan Priests	37
Resident Religious Priests	7
Without Resident Pastor:	
Administered by Priests	22
Missions	17
Pastoral Centers	1
Professional Ministry Personnel:	
Sisters	14
Lay Ministers	60

Welfare

Catholic Hospitals	10
Total Assisted	810,790
Health Care Centers	350
Total Assisted	974,330
Day Care Centers	2
Total Assisted	33
Specialized Homes	2
Total Assisted	113
Special Centers for Social Services	5
Total Assisted	3,238

Educational

Diocesan Students in Other Seminaries	5
Total Seminarians	5
High Schools, Private	3
Total Students	885
Elementary Schools, Diocesan and Parish	23
Total Students	3,036
Catechesis/Religious Education:	
High School Students	635
Elementary Students	2,134
Total Students under Catholic Instruction	6,695
Teachers in Diocese:	
Priests	6
Sisters	8
Lay Teachers	415

Vital Statistics

Receptions into the Church:	
Infant Baptism Totals	677
Minor Baptism Totals	90
Adult Baptism Totals	83
Received into Full Communion	113
First Communions	700
Confirmations	900
Marriages:	
Catholic	203
Interfaith	64
Total Marriages	267
Deaths	544
Total Catholic Population	61,461
Total Population	1,380,129

LEADERSHIP

Vicar General - Rev. Shoby M. Chettiyath;
Chancery Office - t) 417-866-0841
Chancellor - Dcn. Robert R. Huff;
Vice Chancellor - Rev. Thomas P. Kiefer;

ADMINISTRATION

Catholic Foundation of the Diocese of Springfield-Cape Girardeau - Most Rev. Edward M. Rice, Pres.; Rev. Shoby M. Chettiyath, Vice. Pres.; Janet L. Smith, Secy.;
Development and Properties - Doug Kissinger;
Diocesan Development Fund - Doug Kissinger, Dir. Devel. & Properties; Most Rev. Edward M. Rice; Janet L. Smith;
Finance - Janet L. Smith, Dir.;
Financial Council - Janet L. Smith, Dir.; Doug Kissinger, Dir.; Larry G. Grinstead;
Planned Giving - Doug Kissinger, Coord.;

OFFICES AND DIRECTORS

Campus Ministries - Rev. John (J.) F. Friedel, Dir.; Rev. Bibin Mathew, C.M.F. (bibincmf@gmail.com); Rev. Brian Straus;
***Catholic Charities of Southern Missouri, Inc.** - t) 417-720-4213 ccsomo@ccsomo.org Maura A. Taylor, Exec.;
Diaconate (Permanent) - Rev. Shoby M. Chettiyath; Dcn. Walter L. Biri, Asst. Dir.;
Diocesan Delegates to the Missouri Catholic Conference - Dcn. Mark Kiblinger;
  Public Policy Committee - Dcn. Mark Kiblinger; Richard Russell;
Diocesan Director of Continuing Formation of Clergy - Rev. Rick L. Jones;
Family Ministries - Kim Brayman;
  Diocesan Council on Family Ministries - Rev. John (J.) F. Friedel; Rev. David Baunach; Rev. David N. Coon;
Hispanic Ministries -
Natural Family Planning - Kim Brayman;
Office of Child and Youth Protection - William J. Holtmeyer Jr.;
Office of Worship - Rev. David J. Dohogne, Dir.; Rev. Daniel Belken, Assoc. Dir.;
Priests' Eucharistic League Confraternity of The Most Blessed Sacrament - Rev. Michael V. McDevitt, Dir.;
Rite of Christian Initiation of Adults - Rev. David J. Dohogne, Dir.; Lynn Melendez, Dir.;
Social Ministries, Evangelization, and Formation - Lynn Melendez;
Tribunal - Rev. Thomas P. Kiefer; Rev. Vincent E. Bertrand; Rev. (Timothy M.) MyViet Tran, C.R.M.;
  Adjutant Judicial Vicar - Rev. Vincent E. Bertrand;
  Advocates for the Petitioners -
  Advocates for the Respondent - Rev. Michael V. McDevitt; Rev. Rick L. Jones;
  Auditor - Rev. Shoby M. Chettiyath;
  Defender of the Bond - Rev. Shoby M. Chettiyath;
  Judges - Rev. Vincent E. Bertrand; Rev. Thomas P. Kiefer; Rev. (Timothy M.) MyViet Tran, C.R.M.;
  Judicial Vicar - Rev. Thomas P. Kiefer;
  Moderator - Rev. (Timothy M.) MyViet Tran, C.R.M.;
  Notary - Mary Alice McBain;
  Promoter of Justice - Rev. Michael P. Joyce, C.M.;
Vicar for the Religious - Rev. Shoby M. Chettiyath;
Victim Assistance Coordinators - Denise Essner (deniseessner@yahoo.com); Diana Marie Harold (diana_marie23@yahoo.com);
Vocations-Seminarians - Rev. Scott M. Sunnenberg, Dir.;
Youth Ministry - Lynn Melendez;
  Camp Re-NEW-All - Kim Sellers, Dir.; Eva Rasey; Wayne Verhoff;
  Catholic Scouting - t) 417-883-3440 Rev. Patrick I. Nwokoye, Chap.;

ADVISORY BOARDS, COMMISSIONS, COMMITTEES, AND COUNCILS

Apostolate to the Deaf - t) 573-722-3504 eftinkf@gmail.com Rev. Glenn A. Eftink;
Catholic Relief Services - Dcn. Robert R. Huff;
Cemeteries - Rev. Shoby M. Chettiyath;
Censor - Rev. Allan L. Saunders;
Health Affairs - Rev. Patrick I. Nwokoye;
Missionary Apostolate - Society for the Propagation of the Faith - t) 573-722-3504 Rev. Glenn A. Eftink;
Priests' Mutual Benefit Society - Rev. Allan L. Saunders, Pres.; Rev. John M. Harth, Vice. Pres.; Rev. Shoby M. Chettiyath, Secy.;
Pro-Life Director - Sr. Janine Tran, C.M.R.;
Project Rachel (Post Abortion Ministry) - Kim Brayman, Coord.;

CONSULTATIVE BODIES

Diocesan Consultors - Rev. Shoby M. Chettiyath; Rev. Thomas P. Kiefer; Rev. Allan L. Saunders;
Diocesan Lay Endowment Board - Rev. John (J.) F. Friedel, Chair; Lynn Melendez; Rita Lueckenotte;
Diocesan Pastoral Council - Most Rev. Edward M. Rice;
Diocesan School Board - Dcn. Robert R. Huff, Supt.; Most Rev. Edward M. Rice; Debra Owensby, Secy.;
Presbyteral Council - Rev. Shoby M. Chettiyath; Rev. Rick L. Jones; Rev. Thomas P. Kiefer;

DEANERIES

Deans of Deanery - Rev. Joseph Weidenbenner; Rev. William M. Hodgson; Rev. Scott M. Sunnenberg;

EDUCATION

Catholic Schools - Dcn. Robert R. Huff, Supt.;
Ecumenism - Rev. Patrick I. Nwokoye;
Newspaper, Diocese of Springfield-Cape Girardeau - Leslie A. Eidson, Editor; Debbie Thompson, Circulation & Admin. Asst.;
Office of Communications, Media & Publications - Leslie A. Eidson, Dir.;

ORGANIZATIONS

Charismatic Prayer Groups - Rev. Francisco (Paco) Gordillo Villamil, Dir.;
Cursillo Movement - Rev. William M. Hodgson; Sharon Essner;
  Secretariat for Cursillo - Rev. William M. Hodgson, Chap.; Sharon Essner;
Diocesan Council of Catholic Women (DCCW) - t) 573-262-3210 Rev. Joseph Kelly, Diocesan Spiritual Moderator; Rita Lueckenotte, Dir.;
St. Francis de Sales Association - Rev. Glenn A. Eftink;

PARISHES, MISSIONS, AND CLERGY

STATE OF MISSOURI

ADVANCE

St. Joseph - 33921 State Hwy. 91, Advance, MO 63730; Mailing: P.O. Box 640, Advance, MO 63730 t) 573-722-3504 Rev. Glenn A. Eftink, Pst.; CRP Stds.: 35

AURORA

Holy Trinity - Hwy. 60 & Carnation Rd. (22383 Lawrence 1180), Aurora, MO 65605; Mailing: P.O. Box 533, Aurora, MO 65605 t) 417-678-2403 htcc482@outlook.com Rev. Paul Pudhota, Pst.; CRP Stds.: 58

BENTON

St. Denis - 135 N. Winchester St., Benton, MO 63736; Mailing: P.O. Box 127, Benton, MO 63736 t) 573-545-3864 stdenisparishoffice@yahoo.com saintdenisbenton.weebly.com Rev. Bala Swamy Govindu, Pst.; CRP Stds.: 60
  St. Denis School - (Grades 1-8) 106 N. Winchester, Benton, MO 63736; Mailing: PO Box 189, Benton, MO 63736-0189 t) 573-545-3017 stdenisbenton.eduk12.net Melinda Heisserer, Prin.; Stds.: 93; Lay Tchrs.: 7
St. Lawrence - 1017 State Hwy. A, Benton, MO 63736-8159; Mailing: P.O. Box 247, Benton, MO 63736-8159 t) (573) 545-3317 stlawrencenh@outlook.com splawrencechurchnewhamburg.weebly.com Rev. Bala Govindu, Pst.; CRP Stds.: 114

BILLINGS

St. Joseph - 320 N.W. Washington Ave., Billings, MO 65610; Mailing: PO Box 100, Billings, MO 65610 t) 417-744-2490 stjosephbillinmo@aol.com Rev. Suganthan Selvin, HGN, Pst.; CRP Stds.: 52

BOLIVAR

Sacred Heart - 1405 W. Fair Play St., Bolivar, MO 65613 t) 417-326-5596 sheartbolivar@gmail.com www.sacredheartbolivar.org Rev. Scott M. Sunnenberg, Pst.; CRP Stds.: 48
  St. Catherine of Siena - 100 N. Jefferson, Humansville, MO 65613; Mailing: 1405 W. Fairplay St., Bolivar, MO 65613 t) 417-754-8825

BRANSON

Our Lady of the Lake - 203 Vaughn Dr., Branson, MO 65616 t) 417-334-2928 office@ollbranson.com Rev. John (J.) F. Friedel, Pst.; Rev. Nicholas Newton, Par. Vicar; Dcn. Daniel Vaughn; David Wright, Bus. Mgr.; CRP Stds.: 120

BUFFALO

St. William - 404 S. Locust St., Buffalo, MO 65622; Mailing: P.O. Box 518, Buffalo, MO 65622 t) 417-345-2744 st.william.buffalo@gmail.com Rev. Simon M. Enudu, Pst.; Dcn. Michael Fritz; CRP Stds.: 5

CAMPBELL

St. Teresa - 40694 State Hwy. JJ, Campbell, MO 63933-9148 t) 573-328-4544 stteresa.stann@gmail.com Rev. Victor Anokwute, Pst.; CRP Stds.: 8
  St. Teresa School - (Grades PreK-8) 40648 State Hwy. JJ, Campbell, MO 63933-9148 t) 573-328-4197 stteresaschool54@gmail.com stteresa.eduk12.net Kim Lynn, Prin.; Stds.: 93; Pr. Tchrs.: 1; Lay Tchrs.: 6

CAPE GIRARDEAU

Cathedral of St. Mary of the Annunciation - 615 William St., Cape Girardeau, MO 63703 t) 573-335-9347 smparish@stmarycathedral.net www.stmarycathedral.net Rev. Allan L. Saunders, Pst.; Rev. Daniel Belken, Par. Vicar; Rev. Laurent Okitakatshi, In Res.; Brenda Kuhn, DRE; CRP Stds.: 9
  Cathedral of St. Mary of the Annunciation School - (Grades 1-8) 210 S. Sprigg, Cape Girardeau, MO 63703 t) 573-335-3840 alanbruns@stmarycape.org www.stmarycathedralschool.weeble.com Alan Bruns, Prin.; Stds.: 146; Lay Tchrs.: 16
  Old St. Vincent's - 131 S. Main St., Cape Girardeau, MO 63703; Mailing: 615 William St., Cape Girardeau, MO 63703 t) (573) 335-9347 (Chapel of Ease).
St. Vincent de Paul - 1913 Ritter Dr, Cape Girardeau, MO 63701 t) 573-335-7667 contactus@svparish.com www.svcape.com/ Rev. Rick L. Jones, Pst.; Rev. Alexander Sutachan, Par. Vicar; Dcn. Robert R. Huff; Dcn. Mark Kiblinger; Dcn. Thomas J. Schumer; CRP Stds.: 69
  St. Vincent de Paul School - (Grades PreK-8) 1919 Ritter Dr., Cape Girardeau, MO 63701 t) 573-334-9594 kglastetter@svcape.eduk12.net Kay Glastetter, Prin.; Stds.: 385; Lay Tchrs.: 26

CARTHAGE

St. Ann - 908 Clinton St., Carthage, MO 64836-2832; Mailing: 1156 Grand Ave., Carthage, MO 64836 t) 417-358-1841 stannschurch@sbcglobal.net www.stannscarthage.org/ Rev. Francisco (Paco) Gordillo Villamil, Pst.; Rev. Jose Marino Novoa, CMF, Par. Vicar; Dcn. Jim Walter; CRP Stds.: 56
  St. Ann School - (Grades PreK-6) 1156 Grand, Carthage, MO 64836 t) 417-358-2674 mcortez@stannscarthage.com Mikelle Cortez, Prin.; Stds.: 65; Lay Tchrs.: 6

CARUTHERSVILLE

Sacred Heart - 605 Ward Ave., Caruthersville, MO 63830 t) 573-333-4301 sacredheart63830@outlook.com sacredheart-semo.org/ Rev. Victor Anokwute; Rev. Mark J. Binder; Rev. Dominic Ibok, Pst.;

CASSVILLE

St. Edward - 107 W. 17th St., Cassville, MO 65625; Mailing: PO Box 492, Cassville, MO 65625 t) 417-847-4948 stedwardcassville@gmail.com stewardcatholicchurch.org Rev. William M. Hodgson, Pst.; CRP Stds.: 67

CHAFFEE

St. Ambrose - 418 S. 3rd St., Chaffee, MO 63740 t) 573-887-3953 stambroseparishchaffee@gmail.com www.stambrosechaffee.com/ Rev. Joseph Kelly, Pst.; CRP Stds.: 9

St. Ambrose School - (Grades PreK-8) 419 S. 3rd St., Chaffee, MO 63740 t) 573-887-6711 lenderle@staangels.eduk12.net guardianangel.eduk12.net Laura Enderle, Prin.; Stds.: 70; Lay Tchrs.: 6

CHARLESTON

St. Henry - 304 Court St., Charleston, MO 63834 t) 573-683-2114 connie@sainthenry.org www.sthenrychurch.org/ Rev. David J. Dohogne, Pst.;

St. Henry School - (Grades PreK-8) 306 Court St., Charleston, MO 63834 t) 573-683-6218 principal@sainthenry.org sthenry.eduk12.net/ Amy E. Galemore, Prin.; Stds.: 45; Lay Tchrs.: 6

CONWAY

Sacred Heart - 308 Spruce St., Conway, MO 65632; Mailing: P.O. Box 8, 310 Spruce St, Conway, MO 65632 t) 417-589-6782 sacredheartconwaymo@gmail.com sacredheartconway.org Rev. Simon M. Enudu, Pst.; Dcn. Michael Fritz; Dcn. James Soptick; CRP Stds.: 19

DEXTER

Sacred Heart - 115 E. Market St., Dexter, MO 63841-1732 t) 573-624-7333 dexter.sacred.heart@gmail.com Rev. David N. Coon, Pst.; CRP Stds.: 44

DONIPHAN

St. Benedict - 703 Pine St., Doniphan, MO 63935; Mailing: PO Box 595, Doniphan, MO 63935-0595 t) 573-351-1107 stb1849@windstream.net stbenedictdoniphan.com Rev. Daniel Robles, Pst.; Rev. Samson Dorival, Par. Vicar; CRP Stds.: 12

EL DORADO SPRINGS

St. Elizabeth of Hungary - 609 S. Main, El Dorado Springs, MO 64744 t) 417-876-3216 Rev. Tuan (Bonaventure M.) Van Nguyen, CRM, Par. Admin.; CRP Stds.: 12

St. Peter the Apostle - 222 N. Hwy. J, Stockton, MO 65785; Mailing: P.O. Box 583, Stockton, MO 65785 t) 417-276-5588

FORSYTH

Our Lady of the Ozarks - 951 Swan Valley Dr., Forsyth, MO 65653 t) 417-546-5208 ourladyoftheozarks@gmail.com www.ourladyoftheozarks.com/ Rev. John (J.) F. Friedel, Pst.; Rev. Nicholas Newton, Par. Vicar; Dcn. Daniel Vaughn, Pst. Assoc.; CRP Stds.: 5

FREDERICKTOWN

St. Michael the Archangel - 304 W. Main St., Fredericktown, MO 63645 t) 573-783-2182 stmic@charter.net www.stmichaelfredericktown.com/ Rev. Suresh Samala, Par. Admin.; CRP Stds.: 27

HOUSTON

St. Mark - 118 N. Oak Crest St., Houston, MO 65483; Mailing: 117 E South Oak Crest Dr., Houston, MO 65483 t) 417-967-3589 stmarkhoustonmo@gmail.com Rev. Rayappa Chinnabathini, Pst.; Dcn. Michael Evers; CRP Stds.: 21

St. Vincent de Paul - 12552 Bell Rd., Roby, MO 65557; Mailing: 117 E. S. Oak Crest Dr., Houston, MO 65483

St. John The Baptist - 222 W. Hwy. 32, Licking, MO 65542; Mailing: 117 E. South Oak Crest Dr., Houston, MO 65483

IRONTON

Ste. Marie Du Lac - 350 S. Main St., Ironton, MO 63650 t) 573-546-2611 stmariedu@gmail.com Rev. Emmanuel Konyeaso, Pst.; CRP Stds.: 22

Our Lady of Sorrows - 33733 State Hwy. 21, Lesterville, MO 63654; Mailing: 350 S. Main St., Ironton, MO 63650 t) 573-637-2444 dacypha2003@yahoo.com

JACKSON

Immaculate Conception - 208 S. Hope St., Ste. 101, Jackson, MO 63755 t) 573-243-3182 pastor@icjacksonmo.com www.icjacksonmo.com/ Rev. Randolph G. Tochtrop, Pst.; Dcn. Walter L. Biri; Dcn. Al Stoverink; CRP Stds.: 138

Immaculate Conception School - (Grades PreK-8) 300 S. Hope St., Jackson, MO 63755 t) 573-243-5013 mcampbell@icsjackson.eduk12.net icsjackson.eduk12.net Michele Campbell, Prin.; Stds.: 166; Lay Tchrs.: 14

JOPLIN

St. Mary - 3035 S. Central City Rd., Joplin, MO 64804-8165 t) 417-623-3333 church@stmarysparishjoplin.com stmaryschurchjoplin.com/ Rev. Joseph Weidenbenner, Pst.; Rev. Andrew Williams, Par. Vicar; CRP Stds.: 16

St. Mary School - (Grades PreK-5) 3025 S. Central City Rd., Joplin, MO 64804 t) 417-623-1465 jlown@jacss.org Joanne Lown, Prin.; Stds.: 146; Lay Tchrs.: 16

St. Peter the Apostle - 812 S. Pearl Ave., Joplin, MO 64801-4396 t) 417-623-8643 stpetersjoplin@yahoo.com saintpetertheapostlejoplin.com Rev. Brian Straus, Par. Admin.; CRP Stds.: 37

St. Peter the Apostle School - (Grades 6-8) 931 S. Byers Ave., Joplin, MO 64801-4396 t) 417-624-5605 eyoakam@jacss.org www.jacss.org/ Dr. Emily Yoakam, Prin.; Stds.: 55; Sr. Tchrs.: 1; Lay Tchrs.: 7

KELSO

St. Augustine - 211 S. Messmer, Kelso, MO 63758; Mailing: PO Box 26, Kelso, MO 63758 t) 573-264-4106 (Office); 573-264-4724 (Rectory) office@staugustinekelso.org www.staugustinekelso.org Rev. Tomasz Piotr Wilk, O.S.P.P.E. (Poland), Par. Admin.; CRP Stds.: 211

St. Augustine School - (Grades PreK-8) 231 S. Messmer St., Kelso, MO 63758-0097; Mailing: P.O. Box 97, Kelso, MO 63758-0097 Katie Hendricks, Prin.; Stds.: 187; Lay Tchrs.: 13

KENNETT

St. Cecilia - 1226 College St., Kennett, MO 63857; Mailing: PO Box 306, Kennett, MO 63857-0306 t) 573-388-1951 stceciliakennett@gmail.com Rev. David Baunach, Pst.; CRP Stds.: 130

KIMBERLING CITY

Our Lady of the Cove - 20 Kimberling Blvd., Kimberling City, MO 65686; Mailing: P.O. Box 548, Kimberling City, MO 65686-0548 t) 417-739-4700 ourladyofthecove@yahoo.com www.ourladyofthecove.org/ Rev. William W. Hennecke Jr., Pst.; Dcn. Gregg Erickson; Mary Lippert, DRE; CRP Stds.: 46

LAMAR

The Assumption of the Blessed Virgin Mary - 200 E. 17th St., Lamar, MO 64759 t) 417-682-2492 pteter51@gmail.com Rev. Patrick A. Teter, Pst.; CRP Stds.: 23

LEBANON

St. Francis De Sales - 345 Grand St., Lebanon, MO 65536 t) 417-532-4811 lebanoncatholic@gmail.com Rev. Jose Kumblumkal, CMI, Admin.; CRP Stds.: 28

Bennett Springs, Sportman's Chapel - Bennett Springs State Park, Lebanon, MO 65536; Mailing: 345 Grande Ave., Lebanon, MO 65536-2315

LEOPOLD

St. John - 16784 Main St., Leopold, MO 63760; Mailing: P.O. Box 83, Leopold, MO 63760 t) 573-238-3300 cindythele@hotmail.com www.stjohnchurchleopold.com Rev. Antony Thekkanath, VC, Pst.; CRP Stds.: 144

St. Anthony - 18007 State Hwy. AB, Marble Hill, MO 63764 t) (573) 238-3300

MALDEN

St. Ann - 304 N. Douglass St., Malden, MO 63863; Mailing: C/O St. Teresa Parish, 40694 State Hwy. JJ, Campbell, MO 63933-9148 t) 573-328-4544 stteresa.stann@gmail.com Rev. Victor Anokwute, Pst.; CRP Stds.: 2

MANSFIELD

Immaculate Heart of Mary - 354 N. Roote Ave., Mansfield, MO 65704; Mailing: PO Box 468, Mansfield, MO 65704 t) 417-924-3779; (417) 683-5249 (Ava Rectory number) ihmmansfield@gmail.com; stleoschurchava@gmail.com Rev. Leo Arockiasamy, H.G.N., Pst.; Rev. Thomas Dharelli, HGN, Par. Vicar; Dcn. Joseph Kurtenbach; CRP Stds.: 8

St. Leo the Great - CR 201, Ava, MO 65608; Mailing: R.R. 6 Box 6700, Ava, MO 65608-9678 t) 417-683-5249

St. William - Hwy. 166, Gainesville, MO 65655; Mailing: P.O. Box 367, Gainesville, MO 65655-0367 t) 417-679-4804

MARSHFIELD

Holy Trinity - 515 E. Washington, Marshfield, MO 65706-1865 t) 417-859-2228 holytrinitymarshfield@gmail.com marshfieldcatholic.org/ Rev. Francis Theetla, Pst.; Dcn. Michael Fritz; Dcn. James Soptick; CRP Stds.: 51

MONETT

St. Lawrence - 405 7th St., Monett, MO 65708; Mailing: PO Box 311, Monett, MT 65708-0311 t) 417-235-3286 stlawrence1892@gmail.com stlawbiblestudy.wix.com/ stlawrencemonett Rev. Rahab Isidor, Pst.; CRP Stds.: 172

St. Lawrence School - (Grades PreK-6) 407 7th St., Monett, MO 65708 t) 417-235-3721 twelch@stlawrencecatholicschool.com stlawmonett.eduk12.net/ Tracey Welch, Prin.; Stds.: 80; Sr. Tchrs.: 1; Lay Tchrs.: 5

MOUNT VERNON

St. Susanne - 700 W. Sloan St., Hwy. V W., Mount Vernon, MO 65712; Mailing: P.O. Box 126, Mount Vernon, MO 65712 t) 417-316-9250 stsusanneparish@gmail.com stsusannemountvernonmo.org Rev. Suganthan Selvin, HGN, Pst.; CRP Stds.: 27

MOUNTAIN GROVE

Sacred Heart - 302 E. State St., Mountain Grove, MO 65711 t) 417-926-3803; (417) 683-5249 (Rectory Number) sacredheartmtngrove@gmail.com Rev. Leo Arockiasamy, H.G.N., Admin.; Rev. Thomas Dharelli, HGN, Par. Vicar; Dcn. Joseph Kurtenbach; CRP Stds.: 14

St. Michael - 525 Pine St., Cabool, MO 65689; Mailing: 302 E. State St., Mountain Grove, MO 65711-1759

MOUNTAIN VIEW

St. John Vianney - 808 State Rte. Y, Mountain View, MO 65548 t) (417) 712-6392 sjvmtnview1959@gmail.com Rev. Joseph Stoverink, Admin.;

St. Sylvester - Hwy. 19, Eminence, MO 65466; Mailing: 808 State Rte. Y, Mountain View, MO 65548-7904 t) 417-934-2649 fr.stoverink@gmail.com

NEOSHO

St. Canera - 507 S. Wood St., Neosho, MO 64850; Mailing: 504 S. Washington St., Neosho, MO 64850 t) 417-451-3411 stcanera@sbcglobal.net www.canera.org Rev. Charles Dunn, Pst.; CRP Stds.: 80

Nativity of Our Lord - 227 Sulphur St., Noel, MO 64854; Mailing: P.O. Box 247, Noel, MO 64854-0247 t) 417-475-3144 nativityofourlordnoel@gmail.com

NEW MADRID

Immaculate Conception - 607 Davis St., New Madrid, MO 63869 t) 573-748-5183 icnm1789@gmail.com icnewmadrid.com/ Rev. Victor Anokwute, Admin.; Rev. Mark J. Binder, Sacr. Min.; Dcn. James Darter; CRP Stds.: 53

Immaculate Conception School - (Grades 1-8) 560 Powell, New Madrid, MO 63869 t) 573-748-5123 icsoffice@yahoo.com icssaints.eduk12.net/ Lynette Fowler, Prin.; Stds.: 51; Lay Tchrs.: 5

NIXA

St. Francis of Assisi - 844 S. Gregg Rd., Nixa, MO 65714; Mailing: PO Box 1920, Nixa, MO 65714 t) 417-725-1975 office@stfrancisnixa.org stfrancisnixa.org Rev. Shoby M. Chettiyath, Par. Admin.; Dcn. Gary D. Steffes; CRP Stds.: 70

ORAN

Guardian Angel - 604 Church St., Oran, MO 63771; Mailing: P.O. Box 158, Oran, MO 63771 t) 573-262-3210 kbfarms1@hotmail.com www.gaparish.net/ Rev. Joseph Kelly, Pst.; CRP Stds.: 22

Guardian Angel School - (Grades PreK-8) 514 Church St., Oran, MO 63771; Mailing: PO Box 188, Oran, MO 63771 t) 573-262-3583 kkluesnerga@gmail.com guardianangel.eduk12.net/default Katrina Kluesner, Prin.; Stds.: 61; Lay Tchrs.: 9

OZARK

St. Joseph the Worker - 1796 N. State Hwy. NN, Ozark, MO 65721 t) 417-581-6328 secretary@sjwozark.org sjwozark.org/ Rev. Joji Vincent, O.S.B., Pst.; CRP Stds.: 75

PIEDMONT

St. Catherine of Siena - 109 Piedmont Ave., Piedmont, MO 63957 t) 573-223-4924 stcatherinepiedmont@gmail.com stcatherineofsiena.us Rev. Daniel J. Hirtz, Pst.;

St. George - 205 Ash St., Van Buren, MO 63965; Mailing: 109 Piedmont Ave., Piedmont, MO 63957 t) 573-247-0277

Our Lady of Sorrows - West & Main St., Williamsville, MO 63901; Mailing: 109 Piedmont Ave., Piedmont, MO 63957-1048

PIERCE CITY

St. Mary - 200 Front St., Pierce City, MO 65723 t) 417-476-2827 st_marys@live.com stmaryspcmo.com/ Rev. Matthew J. Rehrauer, Pst.; Martha Randall, DRE; CRP Stds.: 30

St. Mary School - (Grades PreK-8) 202 Front St., Pierce City, MO 65723 t) 417-476-2824 jason.kramer@stmarys-piercecity.org Jason Kramer, Prin.; Stds.: 77; Lay Tchrs.: 6

POPLAR BLUFF

Sacred Heart - 123 N. 8th St., Poplar Bluff, MO 63901; Mailing: 825 Vine St., Poplar Bluff, MO 63901 t) 573-785-9635 shparish@socket.net Rev. Daniel Robles, Pst.; Rev. Samson Dorival, Assoc. Pst.; Dcn. David O. Farris; CRP Stds.: 28

Sacred Heart School - (Grades 1-8) 111 N. 8th St., Poplar Bluff, MO 63901 t) 573-785-5836 robersonconstance0@gmail.com sacredheartpb.eduk12.net Connie Roberson, Prin.; Stds.: 110; Lay Tchrs.: 11

PORTAGEVILLE

St. Eustachius - 210 W. Fourth St., Portageville, MO 63873 t) 573-379-5247 eustachius@sbcglobal.net steustachiusparish.com/ Rev. David Baunach, Pst.; CRP Stds.: 30

St. Eustachius School - (Grades PreK-8) 214 W. Fourth St., Portageville, MO 63873 t) 573-379-3525 steustachiusschool@sbcglobal.net steustachius.eduk12.net/default Patricia Rone, Prin.; Stds.: 82; Lay Tchrs.: 8

PULASKIFIELD

SS. Peter and Paul - 2951 Farm Rd. 2040, Pulaskifield, MO 65708; Mailing: P.O. Box 208, Pierce City, MO 65723-0208 t) 417-205-5765 stspp1892@gmail.com Rev. Paul Pudhota, Admin.; CRP Stds.: 24

SALEM

Sacred Heart - 602 W. Butler, Salem, MO 65560 t) 573-729-4291 sacredheartsalem@gmail.com Rev. Jose Thundathil Antoney, C.M.I., Pst.; CRP Stds.: 22

Christ the King - 16215 Hwy. 72, Bunker, MO 65560; Mailing: 602 W Butler St, Salem, MO 65560 t) (573) 729-4291

Montauk, St. Jude - Hwy. 119, Montauk, MO 65560; Mailing: 602 W. Butler St., Salem, MO 65560 t) (573) 729-4291

SARCOXIE

St. Agnes - 26952 Cherry Rd., Sarcoxie, MO 64862; Mailing: P.O. Box 218, Pierce City, MO 65723-0218 t) 417-476-2827 stagnessp@gmail.com Rev. Matthew J. Rehrauer, Pst.;

SCOTT CITY

St. Joseph - 604 Sycamore St., Scott City, MO 63780; Mailing: 201 S. Messmer, Scott City, MO 63780 t) 573-264-4106 office@staugustinekelso.org www.stjosephsc.org Rev. Tomasz Piotr Wilk, O.S.P.P.E. (Poland), Par. Admin.;

St. Joseph School - (Grades PreK-8) 606 Sycamore, Scott City, MO 63780 t) 573-264-2600 stjoeinsc@charter.net stjoescottcity.eduk12.net Betty Spalding, Prin.; Stds.: 44; Lay Tchrs.: 4

SENECA

St. Mary - 1209 Wyandotte St., Seneca, MO 64865; Mailing: P.O. Box 1169, Seneca, MO 64865 t) 417-776-3786 Rev. Joseph Weidenbenner, Pst.; Rev. Andrew Williams, Par. Vicar; CRP Stds.: 21

SHELL KNOB

Holy Family - 24036 FR 1255, Shell Knob, MO 65747; Mailing: P.O. Box 229, Shell Knob, MO 65747 t) 417-858-2518 catholicchur772@centurytel.net holyfamilyskmo.org Rev. William M. Hodgson, Pst.;

SIKESTON

St. Francis Xavier - 245 W. Front St., Sikeston, MO 63801 t) 573-471-2447 parishoffice@stfxsikeston.org; karen@stfxsikeston.org stfxsikeston.org Rev. Colby J. Elbert, Pst.; CRP Stds.: 17

St. Francis Xavier School - (Grades PreK-8) 106 N. Stoddard, Sikeston, MO 63801 t) 573-471-0841 principal@stfxsikeston.org sfxschool.eduk12.net Barb Tomaszewski, Prin.; Stds.: 83; Lay Tchrs.: 11

SPRINGFIELD

Cathedral of St. Agnes - 533 S. Jefferson Ave., Springfield, MO 65806 t) 417-831-3565 stagnesfrontdesk@gmail.com www.sta-cathedral.org/ Rev. Lewis E. Hejna, Pst.; Rev. (Timothy M.) MyViet Tran, C.R.M., Par. Vicar; Rev. Michael Quang Do, CRM, Chap.; Sr. Elizabeth Ann Weiler, A.S.C., Coord., Care Ministry; CRP Stds.: 77

Cathedral of St. Agnes School - (Grades PreK-8) 531 S. Jefferson Ave., Springfield, MO 65806 t) 417-866-5038 pduda@scspk12.org www.scspk12.org Paige Duda, Prin.; Stds.: 113; Lay Tchrs.: 19

St. Elizabeth Ann Seton - 2200 W. Republic Rd., Springfield, MO 65807 t) 417-887-6472 parishinfo@seaschurch.org www.seaschurch.org Rev. Thomas P. Kiefer, Pst.; CRP Stds.: 242

St. Elizabeth Ann Seton School - (Grades PreK-8) 2200 W Republic Rd, Springfield, MO 65807 t) 417-887-6056 jbailes@scspk12.org www.scspk12.org Joanne Bailes, Prin.; Stds.: 220; Lay Tchrs.: 17

Holy Trinity - 2818 E. Bennett, Springfield, MO 65804 t) 417-883-3440 pliermann@holytrinityspringfield.com www.htscatholic.com/ Rev. Patrick I. Nwokoye, Pst.; CRP Stds.: 69

Immaculate Conception - 3555 S. Fremont, Springfield, MO 65804 t) 417-887-0600 staff@ic-parish.org www.ic-parish.org Rev. Msgr. Thomas E. Reidy, Pst.; Rev. Charles Peirano, Par. Vicar; Dcn. Kevin Carroll; CRP Stds.: 52

Immaculate Conception School - (Grades PreK-8) 3555A S. Fremont, Springfield, MO 65804 t) 417-881-7000 mjohnson@scspk12.org scspk12.org/ Mike Johnson, Prin.; Ashley Harris, Vice Prin.; Stds.: 500; Lay Tchrs.: 29

St. Joseph - 1115 N. Campbell Ave., Springfield, MO 65802 t) 417-865-1112 stjosephspmo@yahoo.com www.stjosephspmo.org Rev. Karl Barmann, OSB, Pst.; Dcn. Mathey F. Fletcher; CRP Stds.: 35

St. Joseph School - (Grades PreK-8) 515 W. Scott, Springfield, MO 65802 t) 417-866-0667 bjohnson@stjosephcatholicacademy.org www.stjosephcatholicacademy.org Angela Stevens, Prin.; Stds.: 71; Lay Tchrs.: 9

Sacred Heart - 1609 N. Summit Ave., Springfield, MO 65803 t) 417-869-3646 pastor.shc.sgf@gmail.com www.sacredheartch.org Rev. Raymond Smith, C.M.F., Pst.; Dcn. James E. Farrar; Rev. Joseph A. Orthel, In Res.; Rev. Bibin Mathew, C.M.F., Sacr. Min.; Bro. Manuel Benavides, CMF, DRE;

VERONA

Sacred Heart - 212 N. 2nd St., Verona, MO 65769; Mailing: P.O. Box 533, Aurora, MO 65605-0533 t) 417-678-2403 htcc482@outlook.com Rev. Rahab Isidor, Pst.; CRP Stds.: 113

WEBB CITY

Sacred Heart - 909 N. Madison Ave., Webb City, MO 64870-0470; Mailing: PO Box 470, Webb City, MO 64870-0470 t) (417) 673-2044 x104 sacredheartsecretary@gmail.com; sacredheartbulletinwc@gmail.com sacredheartwebbcity.org Rev. Francisco (Paco) Gordillo Villamil, Pst.; CRP Stds.: 34

WEST PLAINS

St. Mary - 965 S. Thayer Ave., West Plains, MO 65775; Mailing: PO Box 67, West Plains, MO 65775 t) 417-256-2556 stmarychurchwestplains@gmail.com Rev. Maurice Ejikeme Chukwukere, Pst.; CRP Stds.: 40

Sacred Heart - 3612 Best Cir., Thayer, MO 65791; Mailing: P.O. Box 67, West Plains, MO 65775

St. Joseph - 7077-7199 CR 1940, Pomona, MO 65789; Mailing: 1551 Bill Virdon Blvd., West Plains, MO 65775 t) (417) 256-2556 chuksmaurice2nk@yahoo.com Rev. James J. Unterreiner, Sacr. Min.;

WILLOW SPRINGS

Sacred Heart - 1050 W. Bus Hwy. 60-63, Willow Springs, MO 65793 t) 417-469-2447 sacredheartws1893@gmail.com Rev. Joseph Stoverink, Admin.; CRP Stds.: 3

SCHOOLS: PRESCHOOL THRU HIGH SCHOOL

HIGH SCHOOLS

STATE OF MISSOURI

CAPE GIRARDEAU

Notre Dame Regional High School - (PAR) (Grades 9-12) 265 Notre Dame Dr., Cape Girardeau, MO 63701-8517 t) 573-335-6772 timgarner@notredamecape.org www.notredamehighschool.org Rev. Daniel Belken, Chap.; Rev. Colby J. Elbert, Chap.; Rev. Alexander Sutachan, Chap.; Tim Garner, Prin.; Stds.: 433; Lay Tchrs.: 39

JOPLIN

McAuley Catholic High School - (PAR) (Grades 9-12) 930 S. Pearl Ave., Joplin, MO 64801 t) 417-624-9320 eyoakam@jacss.org www.jacss.org Rev. Brian Straus, Chap.; Rev. Andrew Williams, Chap.; Rev. Joseph Weidenbenner, Chap.; Rev. Francisco (Paco) Gordillo Villamil, Chap.; Dr. Emily Yoakam, Prin.; Stds.: 55; Lay Tchrs.: 11

SPRINGFIELD

Springfield Catholic High School - (PAR) (Grades 9-12) 2340 S. Eastgate, Springfield, MO 65809-2832 t) 417-887-8817 jskahan@scspk12.org www.scspk12.org (Coed) Rev. Allen Kirchner, Chap.; Rev. Charles Peirano, Chap.; Jeanne Skahan, Prin.; Sr. Cecilia Ann Rezac, M.S., Dir.; Stds.: 381; Sr. Tchrs.: 1; Lay Tchrs.: 33

Springfield Catholic School System - (PAR) 2340 S. Eastgate Ave., Springfield, MO 65809-2832

t) 417-865-5567 srceciliaann@scspk12.org www.scspk12.org Sr. Cecilia Ann Rezac, M.S., Dir.;

INSTITUTIONS LOCATED IN DIOCESE

CAMPUS MINISTRY / NEWMAN CENTERS [CAM]

BRANSON

Catholic Campus Ministry - 203 Vaughn Dr., Branson, MO 65616 t) 417-334-2928 jfriedel@dioscg.org ollbranson.com (College of the Ozarks) Rev. John (J.) F. Friedel, Chap.;

CAPE GIRARDEAU

Catholic Campus Ministry Southeast Missouri State University, Newman Center - 902 College Hill, Cape Girardeau, MO 63701-4712; Mailing: 512 N. Pacific St., Cape Girardeau, MO 63701-4712 t) 573-335-3899 deacontom@ccmin.org www.ccmin.org Rev. Laurent Okitakatshi, Chap.; Dcn. Thomas J. Schumer, Dir.;

JOPLIN

Catholic Campus Ministry, Missouri Southern State University - 812 S. Pearl Ave., Joplin, MO 64801 t) 417-623-8643 brianjstraus@gmail.com Rev. Brian Straus, Chap.;

SPRINGFIELD

Catholic Campus Ministry O'Reilly Catholic Student Center, Missouri State University, Drury University, Ozarks Technical Community College - 847 S. Holland, Springfield, MO 65806-3513 t) 417-865-0802 bibincmf@ccm847.org; creichert@ccm847.org www.ccm847.org Rev. Bibin Mathew, C.M.F., Chap.;

CATHOLIC CHARITIES [CCH]

SPRINGFIELD

***Catholic Charities of Southern Missouri, Inc.** - 424 E. Monastery St., Springfield, MO 65807 t) 417-720-4213 info@ccsomo.org www.ccsomo.org Maura A. Taylor, Exec.; Asstd. Annu.: 6,500; Staff: 110

***Consumer Credit Counseling of Springfield, Missouri, Inc.** - 1515 S. Glenstone, Springfield, MO 65804 t) 417-889-7474 mtaylor@ccsomo.org cccsoftheozarks.org/ Maura A. Taylor, Dir.; Asstd. Annu.: 200; Staff: 15

CONVENTS, MONASTERIES, AND RESIDENCES FOR WOMEN [CON]

AVA

Nazareth Hermitage - R.R. 5, Ava, MO 65608; Mailing: Box 1122, Ava, MO 65608 t) 417-683-2401 nazarethhermitage.wordpress.com/ Bro. Joseph Reish, Contact; Srs.: 4

MARIONVILLE

The Society of Our Mother of Peace, Daughters of Our Mother of Peace, Queen of Heaven Solitude - 12494 Hwy. T, Marionville, MO 65705-7121 t) 417-744-2011 qohsmp@gmail.com www.marythefont.org Sr. Dina Marie Egong, SMP, Supr.; Srs.: 4

SPRINGFIELD

Congregation of Mary Queen - 625 S. Jefferson Ave., Springfield, MO 65806 t) 417-869-9842 cmrvocation@hotmail.com www.trinhvuong.org Sr. Pauline Kieu Nguyen, CMR, Supr.; Srs.: 10

Little Portion Franciscans - 2122 W. Village Ter., Springfield, MO 65810 t) 417-766-2220 srcecilia@att.net Sr. Cecilia Bergschneider, OSF, Contact; Srs.: 3

ENDOWMENTS / FOUNDATIONS / TRUSTS [EFT]

JOPLIN

Mercy Health Foundation Joplin - 100 Mercy Way, Joplin, MO 64804-4524 t) 417-208-3609 marynell.ploch@mercy.net Jacquelynn K. Richmond, Contact;

SPRINGFIELD

Mercy Health Foundation Springfield - 3265 S. National Ave. #200, Springfield, MO 65807; Mailing: 3265 S. National Ave., Springfield, MO 65807 t) 417-820-6111 marynell.ploch@mercy.net Jacquelynn K. Richmond, Vice-Pres., Deputy Gen. Counsel;

HOSPITALS / HEALTH SERVICES [HOS]

AURORA

Mercy Hospital Aurora - 500 Porter Ave., Aurora, MO 65605 t) 417-678-7830 marynell.ploch@mercy.net www.mercy.net Suzanne Gamet, Admin.; Bed Capacity: 53; Asstd. Annu.: 37,599; Staff: 176

CAPE GIRARDEAU

***Saint Francis Medical Center** - 211 Saint Francis Dr., Cape Girardeau, MO 63703-8399 t) 573-331-3000 sfmc@sfmc.net www.sfmc.net Owned and operated by a lay board with Diocesan sponsorship. Maryann Reese, CEO; Bed Capacity: 306; Asstd. Annu.: 37,637; Staff: 400

***Saint Francis Foundation** - 211 Saint Francis Dr., Cape Girardeau, MO 63703-8399 t) 573-331-5133 Stacy Huff, Exec. Dir.;

***Saint Francis Healthcare System (formerly known as St. Francis Hospital of Franciscan Sisters)** - 211 Saint Francis Dr., Cape Girardeau, MO 63703 Sr. Kevin Karimi, LSOSF, Supr.; Bed Capacity: 289

CARTHAGE

Mercy Hospital Carthage - 3125 Dr. Russell Smith Way, Carthage, MO 64836 t) 417-358-8121 marynell.ploch@mercy.net www.mercy.net Scott Watson, Admin.; Bed Capacity: 25; Asstd. Annu.: 19,230; Staff: 275

CASSVILLE

Mercy Hospital Cassville - 94 S. Main St., Cassville, MO 65625 t) 417-847-6000 marynell.ploch@mercy.net www.mercy.net Suzanne Gamet, Admin.; Bed Capacity: 18; Asstd. Annu.: 36,543; Staff: 112

LEBANON

***Mercy Hospital Lebanon** - 100 Hospital Dr., Lebanon, MO 65536; Mailing: c/o Mercy Corp Paralegal-Legal Dept., 14528 S. Outer 40 Rd., Ste. 100, Chesterfield, MO 63017 t) 417-533-6100 marynell.ploch@mercy.net www.mercy.net Jacquelynn K. Richmond, Vice-Pres., Deputy Gen. Counsel; Bed Capacity: 58; Asstd. Annu.: 123,207; Staff: 446

MOUNTAIN VIEW

Mercy St. Francis Hospital - 100 W. U.S. Hwy. 60, Mountain View, MO 65548 t) 417-934-7000 marynell.ploch@mercy.net www.mercy.net Daughters of St. Francis of Assisi and Sisters of Mercy (Managed by Mercy Health Springfield Communities) Jacquelynn K. Richmond, Contact; Bed Capacity: 25; Asstd. Annu.: 22,541; Staff: 100

The Sister Cornelia Blasko Foundation, Inc. - 100 W. Hwy. 60, Mountain View, MO 65548; Mailing: P.O. Box 82, Mountain View, MO 65548 t) 417-934-7090 Stephanie Moody, Mgr.;

SPRINGFIELD

Mercy Hospital Springfield - 1235 E. Cherokee St., Springfield, MO 65804 t) 417-820-3612 marynell.ploch@mercy.net www.mercy.net Member of Mercy Health. Jacquelynn K. Richmond, Vice-Pres., Deputy Gen. Counsel; Bed Capacity: 914; Asstd. Annu.: 534,033; Staff: 7,925

MISCELLANEOUS [MIS]

JOPLIN

Mercy Health Southwest Missouri/Kansas Communities - 100 Mercy Way, Joplin, MO 64804-4524 t) 417-781-2727 marynell.ploch@mercy.net Philip Wheeler, Senior Vice Pres., Gen. Counsel;

Mercy Hospital Joplin - 100 Mercy Way, Joplin, MO 64804 t) 417-556-3729 marynell.ploch@mercy.net mercy.net Jacquelynn K. Richmond, Vice-Pres., Deputy Gen. Counsel;

***Mercy Village Joplin, Inc.** - 1148 W. 28th St., Joplin, MO 64804 t) 417-623-7123 www.mercyhousing.org Dee Walsh, COO;

SPRINGFIELD

***Mercy Clinic Springfield Communities** - 1965 S. Fremont St., Ste. 200, Springfield, MO 65804; Mailing: c/o Mercy Corp Paralegal - Legal Dept., 14528 S. Outer 40 Rd., Ste. 100, Chesterfield, MO 63017 t) 417-820-2000 marynell.ploch@mercy.net www.mercy.net Jacquelynn K. Richmond, Contact;

Mercy Health Springfield Communities - 1235 E. Cherokee St., Springfield, MO 65804 t) 417-820-3612 marynell.ploch@mercy.net Philip Wheeler, Senior Vice Pres., Gen. Counsel;

Mercy Research - 1235 E. Cherokee St., Springfield, MO 65804 t) 417-841-0244 marynell.ploch@mercy.net Jacquelynn K. Richmond, Vice-Pres., Deputy Gen. Counsel;

MONASTERIES AND RESIDENCES FOR PRIESTS AND BROTHERS [MON]

AVA

Assumption Abbey (O.Cist) - Rte. 5, Ava, MO 65608; Mailing: Box 1056, Ava, MO 65608 t) 417-683-5110 frmaryalberic@hughes.net www.assumptionabbey.org Very Rev. Basil Nguyen, O.Cist., Supr.; Rt. Rev. Cyprian Harrison, O.C.S.O., Abbot Emeritus; Rev. Alberic Maisog, O.C.S.O.; Rev. Bruno Chi Thien, O.Cist; Bro. Francis Flaherty, O.C.S.O.; Bro. Alphonse Hua; Bro. Ambrose Hung; Bro. Gabriel Nghia; Bro. Joseph Duy Ngo; Brs.: 5; Priests: 4

CARTHAGE

Congregation of the Mother of the Redeemer - 1900 Grand Ave., Carthage, MO 64836; Mailing: P.O. Box 836, Carthage, MO 64836 t) 417-358-7787 cmc@dongcong.net dongcong.us/ Rev. Vincent Thanh Au, CRM, Novice Master; Rev. (Joseph) Thanh Xuan Cao, CRM, Mem.; Rev. Joseph Huy Chuong Doan, In Res.; Rev. (John Bosco M.) Bang Thanh Dao, CRM, Mem.; Rev. Raymond M. Dien Nguyen, CRM, Mem.; Rev. Peter Vien T. Dinh, CRM, Mem.; Rev. (Francis Xavier M.) Tung Cao Do, CRM, Mem.; Rev. Thanh (Philip M.) Do, CRM, Third Asst.; Rev. John M. Hien Duc Tran, CRM, Mem.; Rev. (Thomas M.) Hoc Nguyen, CRM, Mem.; Rev. Francis M. Hung Long Tran, CRM, Secy.; Rev. Albert M. P. Kim Ban, CRM, Mem.; Rev. Simon M. Diem Phuc Le, CRM, Mem.; Rev. (Francis Xavier M.) Tri Van Luong, CRM, Dir., Formation House; Rev. (Timothy M.) MyViet Tran, C.R.M., Fourth Asst.; Rev. (John Damascene M.) Vuong Duc Ngo, CRM, Mem.; Rev. (Dominic M.) Thien Toan Nguyen, CRM, Mem.; Rev. Augustine Trung T. Nguyen, CRM, Mem.; Rev. Khanh (Hilary M.) Hai Nguyen, CRM, Mem.; Rev. Lawrence Hy Nguyen, CRM, Second Asst.; Rev. Luong (Dominic M.) Hoan Nguyen, CRM, First Asst.; Rev. Patrick M. Ngoc Nguyen, CRM, Mem.; Rev. Polycarp M. DucThuan Nguyen, CRM, Treas.; Rev. Raymond Thu M. Nguyen, CRM, Mem.; Rev. Tuan (Andrew M.) Van Nguyen, CRM, Mem.; Rev. Tuan (Bonaventure M.) Van Nguyen, CRM, Mem.; Rev. Andrew M. Nguyen Hong An, CRM, Mem.; Rev. (Benedict M.) Quy Duy Pham, CRM, Mem.; Rev. (Bartholomew M.) Hoa Thai Do, CRM, Mem.; Rev. (Patrick M.) Mac The Tran, CRM, Mem.; Rev. Paul M. Tai Tran, CRM, Prov. Min.; Rev. Peter M. Khuong Tran, CRM, Mem.; Rev. Aloysius M. Tran Liem, CRM, Dir., Mater Dei Bldg.; Rev. (Aloysius M.) Tran Ngoc Thoai, CRM, Mem.; Rev. (Michael M.) Quang Van Do, CRM, Mem.; Rev. Bartholomew M. Van Minh Pham, CRM, Mem.; Rev. Thomas Vu, In Res.; Bro. (Stanislaus M.) An Ngoc Nguyen, CRM, Mem.; Bro. (Barnabas M.) Anh Khai Tran Nguyen, CRM, Mem.; Bro. Stephen M. Chu Du Tran, CRM, Mem.; Bro. (Josaphat M.) Cuong Manh Do, CRM, Mem.; Bro. (John Baptist M.) Duc Hien Nguyen, CRM, Mem.; Bro. (Bernadine M.) Hien Khac Tran, CRM, Mem.; Bro. Matthew M. Kim Vu, CRM, Mem.; Bro. (Justin M.) Ky Tri Nguyen, CRM, Mem.; Bro. Thomas M. Nguyen L. Truong, CRM, Mem.; Bro. (Maximilian M.) Loc the Do, CRM, Mem.; Bro. (Bernard M) Quy Huu Nguyen, CRM, Mem.; Bro. (George M.) Dyllan

Huynh Nguyen, CRM, Mem.; Bro. (John Vianney M.) Huy Duc Nguyen, CRM, Mem.; Bro. (Simon M.) Minh Doanh Ngoc Nguyen, CRM, Mem.; Bro. Anthony M. Dan Huu Nguyen, CRM, Mem.; Bro. Don (Louis de Monfort M.) Quy Nguyen, CRM, Mem.; Bro. James (Juan Diego M.) Son Truong Nguyen, CRM, Mem.; Bro. John Paul II M. Phi Long Nguyen, C.R.M., Mem.; Bro. John XXIII M. Su Giao Nguyen, CRM, Mem.; Bro. Nhan (Matthias M.) Que Nguyen, CRM, Mem.; Bro. Pius Thu T. Nguyen, CRM, Mem.; Bro. Thien (Paul M.) Duy Nguyen, C.R.M., Mem.; Bro. (Titus M.) Si Tien Nguyen, CRM, Mem.; Bro. (Matthew M.) Tan Nhat Pham, CRM, Mem.; Bro. Peter M. Thieu Nguyen, CRM, Mem.; Bro. Joseph M. Tho Pham, CRM, Mem.; Bro. (Sylvester M.) Thuong Quy Lu, CRM, Mem.; Bro. Son (Anthony Padua M.) John Tran, CRM, Mem.; Bro. Michael M. Trung Dan, CRM, Mem.; Bro. John M. Tu Quang Bui, CRM, Mem.; Bro. (Gabriel M.) Thuan Trung Vu, CRM, Mem.; Bro. Justin M. Xuan Binh, CRM, Mem.; Brs.: 31; Priests: 36

Mater Dei Building - 1900 Grand Ave., Carthage, MO 64836 t) (417) 358-7787 (Home for retired priests)

HIGH RIDGE

The Society of Our Mother of Peace, Sons of Our Mother of Peace - Queen of Heaven Solitude - Mary the Font Solitude, 6150 Antire Rd., High Ridge, MO 63049 c) 636-677-3235 smpvocations@gmail.com www.marythefont.org Rev. Placid Guste, S.M.P., Supr.; Rev. John Hansen, SMP, Prov.; Brs.: 1; Priests: 2

SPRINGFIELD

Claretians Missionaries' Residence-Villa Claret - 1530 N. Summit Ave., Springfield, MO 65803 t) 417-869-0075 raysmithiii63@gmail.com www.claretiansusa.org Rev. Raymond Smith, C.M.F., Pst.; Bro. Manuel Benavides, C.M.F., Pst. Assoc.; Rev. Bibin Mathew, C.M.F., Director of Campus Ministry; Priests: 3

PRESCHOOLS / CHILDCARE CENTERS [PRE]

SPRINGFIELD

Queen of Angels Day Care Center - 625 S. Jefferson, Springfield, MO 65806 t) 417-869-9842 queenofangels.abc@gmail.com www.trinhvuong.org Sr. Thu-Hang Martha Nguyen, C.M.R., Dir.; Stds.: 20

RETREAT HOUSES / RENEWAL CENTERS [RTR]

AVA

Assumption Abbey - RR. 5, Ava, MO 65608; Mailing: Box 1056, Ava, MO 65608 t) 417-683-5110 avaguesthouse@hughes.net; frmaryalberic@hughes.net www.assumptionabbey.org (Order of Cistercians of the Common Observance) Very Rev. Basil Nguyen, O.Cist., Supr.;

MARIONVILLE

The Society of Our Mother of Peace, Daughters of Our Mother of Peace, Queen of Heaven Solitude - 12494 Hwy. T, Marionville, MO 65705 t) 417-744-2011 qohsmp@gmail.com www.marythefont.org Sr. Dina Marie Egong, Supr.;

SALEM

Marian Acres - Madonna House - 7626 N. Hwy. 19, Salem, MO 65560 t) 573-729-7693 mhsalemmo@gmail.com www.madonnahouse.org Madonna House fieldhouse in the Missouri Ozarks with guest cottages. Serving local community and open to receive single and married guests religious Patrick Stewart, Dir.;

SEMINARIES [SEM]

AVA

Assumption Novitiate (Trappists) - R.R. 5, Ava, MO 65608-9142; Mailing: Box 1056, Ava, MO 65608-9142 t) 417-683-5110 frmaryalberic@hughes.net assumptionabbey.org Rt. Rev. Cyprian Harrison, O.C.S.O., Abbot; Rev. Alberic Maisog, O.C.S.O., Supr.; Rev. Basil Nguyen, OCist, Supr.;

SHRINES [SHR]

CARTHAGE

Office of the Immaculate Heart of Mary Shrine - 1900 Grand Ave., Carthage, MO 64836 t) 417-358-7787 cmc@dongcong.net www.dongcong.net/khiettam Rev. Francis M. Hung Long Tran, CRM, Contact;

Shrine of Immaculate Heart of Mary - 1900 Grand Ave., Carthage, MO 64836 t) 417-358-8580 heartofmaryshrine@yahoo.com www.dongcong.net/khiettam Rev. Raymond M. Nguyen Dien, C.M.C., Dir.;

SPECIAL CARE FACILITIES [SPF]

SPRINGFIELD

Mercy Hospital Springfield - 1100 E. Montclair, Springfield, MO 65807 t) 417-820-8500 marynell.ploch@mercy.net Skilled Care of Long Term Nursing Home, for the Aged and Chronically Ill. Philip Wheeler, Contact; Bed Capacity: 146; Asstd. Annu.: 24,000; Staff: 256

An asterisk (*) denotes an organization that has established tax-exempt status directly with the IRS and is not covered by the USCCB Group Ruling.

Diocese of Springfield in Illinois

(Dioecesis Campifontis in Illinois)

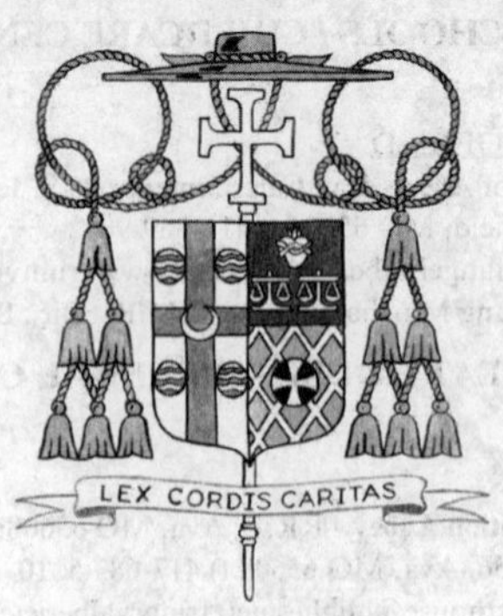

MOST REVEREND THOMAS J. PAPROCKI

Bishop of Springfield in Illinois; ordained May 10, 1978; appointed Auxiliary Bishop of Chicago and Titular Bishop of Vulturara January 24, 2003; consecrated March 19, 2003; installed as ninth Bishop of Springfield in Illinois June 22, 2010. Office: Catholic Pastoral Center, 1615 W. Washington St., Springfield, IL 62702-4757.

Catholic Pastoral Center: 1615 W. Washington St., Springfield, IL 62702-4757. T: 217-698-8500; F: 217-698-0802.

ERECTED JULY 29, 1853.

Square Miles 15,139.

Formerly Diocese of Quincy.

See Transferred to Alton, January 9, 1857. To Springfield, October 26, 1923.

Comprises the following Counties of Illinois: Adams, Bond, Brown, Calhoun, Cass, Christian, Clark, Coles, Crawford, Cumberland, Douglas, Edgar, Effingham, Fayette, Greene, Jasper, Jersey, Macon, Macoupin, Madison, Menard, Montgomery, Morgan, Moultrie, Pike, Sangamon, Scott and Shelby.

For legal titles of parishes and diocesan institutions, consult the Chancery Office.

STATISTICAL OVERVIEW

Personnel

Bishop....1
Priests: Diocesan Active in Diocese....74
Priests: Diocesan Active Outside Diocese....1
Priests: Diocesan in Foreign Missions....1
Priests: Retired, Sick or Absent....28
Number of Diocesan Priests....104
Religious Priests in Diocese....30
Total Priests in your Diocese....134
Extern Priests in Diocese....17
Ordinations:
Diocesan Priests....2
Religious Priests....2
Permanent Deacons....1
Permanent Deacons in Diocese....64
Total Brothers....10
Total Sisters....370

Parishes

Parishes....129
With Resident Pastor:
Resident Diocesan Priests....57
Resident Religious Priests....8
Without Resident Pastor:
Administered by Priests....64
Professional Ministry Personnel:
Brothers....1
Sisters....4
Lay Ministers....114

Welfare

Catholic Hospitals....8
Total Assisted....937,025
Residential Care of Children....1
Total Assisted....57
Day Care Centers....3
Total Assisted....224
Special Centers for Social Services....1
Total Assisted....168,725

Educational

Diocesan Students in Other Seminaries....16
Total Seminarians....16
Colleges and Universities....1
Total Students....1,258
High Schools, Diocesan and Parish....1
Total Students....206
High Schools, Private....6
Total Students....1,967
Elementary Schools, Diocesan and Parish....36
Total Students....4,923
Elementary Schools, Private....1
Total Students....72
Catechesis/Religious Education:
High School Students....672
Elementary Students....4,716
Total Students under Catholic Instruction....13,830
Teachers in Diocese:
Priests....3
Brothers....1
Sisters....2
Lay Teachers....770

Vital Statistics

Receptions into the Church:
Infant Baptism Totals....1,044
Minor Baptism Totals....84
Adult Baptism Totals....65
Received into Full Communion....192
First Communions....1,687
Confirmations....1,944
Marriages:
Catholic....214
Interfaith....102
Total Marriages....316
Deaths....1,338
Total Catholic Population....117,155
Total Population....1,107,081

LEADERSHIP
Bishop's Administrative Team -
Diocesan Curia -
Office of the Bishop - Most Rev. Thomas John Paprocki; Laura Fjelstul, Exec. Sec.; Rev. Dominic J. Rankin, Priest Sec. to the Diocesan Bishop & Master of Ceremonies to Bishop (drankin@dio.org);
Moderator of the Curia/Office of the Vicar General - Rev. Msgr. David J. Hoefler; Teresa Gray, Exec. Sec.; Bro. Anthony Joseph McCoy, F.F.S.C., Assoc. Exec. Sec.;
Chaplain, Courage Apostolate - Rev. James E. Isaacson, S.J.C.;
Commission for Priests' Benefits -
Delegate for Extern Priests - Rev. Msgr. David J. Hoefler;
Delegate for Senior Priests - Rev. Msgr. David L. Peters;
Delegate for Strategy and Logistics - Michael Christie;
Liaison for Prison Ministries - Rev. Daniel L. Willenborg;
Ministry to Priests Team -
Priests' Personnel Board -
Villa Maria Catholic Life Conference and Retreat Center - t) 217-529-2213 www.villa.dio.org Dcn. Gregory Maynerich, Dir.; Sr. M. Catherine Welter, F.S.G.M., House Supvr.;
Department for Canonical and Pastoral Services - Very Rev. Christopher A. House, Dir.;
Canonical Consultant for Priests - Rev. Kevin Michael Laughery;
Chaplain, Catholic Physicians Guild/Catholic Medical Association - Rev. Peter C. Harman; Rev. Christopher A. Trummer;
Chaplain, Equestrian Order of the Holy Sepulchre of Jerusalem - Very Rev. Christopher A. House;
Commission for the Liturgy -
Delegate for Healthcare Professionals - Rev. Peter C. Harman; Rev. Christopher A. Trummer; Dcn. William E. Kessler;
Delegate for Legal Professionals - Rev. Jason P. Stone;
Delegate for Matrimonial Concerns - Rev. Daren J. Zehnle;
Diocesan Ecumenical and Interreligious Officer - Rev. Scott A. Snider;
Office for Divine Worship and the Catechumenate - Rev. Daren J. Zehnle, Dir.; Chelli Branyan, Secy.;
Office for Tribunal Services - Very Rev. Christopher A. House, Judicial Vicar;
Office of the Chancellor and General Counsel - James A. Bock Jr., Chancellor; Katherine Oubre, Vice Chancellor; Sr. M. Consolata Crews, F.S.G.M., Asst. to Chancellor;
Office for Archives and Records Management - Katherine Oubre, Dir.; Phillip (P.J.) Oubre, Asst. Archivist;
Department for Vocational Services - Very Rev. Brian C. Alford, Dir.; Teresa Gray, Exec. Secy.;
Office for the Diaconate - Dcn. David G. Sorrell, Dir.; Dcn. Gregory Maynerich, Assoc. Dir. Ongoing Formation & Ministry;
Office for Vocations - Very Rev. Brian C. Alford, Dir.; Rev. Dominic J. Rankin, Promoter of Vocations; Daniel Heffernan, Prog. Coord.;
Department for Evangelization and Faith Formation Services - Sr. M. Clementia Toalson, F.S.G.M., Dir.;
Black Catholic Commission -
Diocesan Campaign for Justice and Hope - Donna Moore;
Diocesan Campaign for Justice and Hope Allocation Committee -
Diocesan Committee for Hispanic Ministry (Comite Diocesano de Ministerio Hispano) -
Immigration Commission -
Office for Campus Ministry - t) 217-348-0188 Roy Lanham, Dir.;
Office for Catholic Education - Brandi Borries, Supt.; Kyle Holtgrave, Dir.; Lori Casson, Admin. Asst.;
Office for Communications - Andrew Hansen, Dir.;
Office for Ministry and Evangelization - Sr. M. Clementia Toalson, F.S.G.M., Dir.; Donna Moore, Dir. Pro-Life, Missions, & Special Ministries; Cynthia Gallo Callan, Asst.;
Office for Parish Vitality and Mission Advancement - Katie Price, Dir.; Rachel Langdon, Opers. Dir.; Debbie Benz, Stewardship & Communications Dir.;
Foundation for the People of the Roman Catholic Diocese of Springfield in Illinois Advisory Board Members -
Foundation for the People of the Roman Catholic Diocese of Springfield in Illinois Board of Directors -
Department for Financial and Parish Support Services - Stephen Logan, Dir.;
Cemetery Advisory Board -
Commission for Buildings and Property -
Office for Financial Strategy and Planning - Christopher Sommer, CFO;
Deposit and Loan Investment Committee -
Diocesan Health Insurance Program Committee -
Diocese of Springfield in Illinois Deposit and Loan Fund -
Lay Employees' Pension Plan Administrative Committee -
Loan Committee -
Office for Finance Services - Stephen Logan, Dir.; Heather McMillen, Accountant, AR/AP; Christina Maher, Parish Payroll & Reporting;
Office for Information Technology - Dan Gauwitz, Dir.; Cassie Bergschneider, IT Support Specialist;
Office for Insurance and Benefits - Patrick Ketchum, Dir.; Michael Kelly, Assoc. Dir.; Laura Weakley, Financial Svcs. Assoc.;
Office for Property, Buildings and Cemeteries - Gregory Fleck, Dir.; Brad Fisher, Cemetery Svcs.;
Department for Personnel Services - Erin Danaher, Dir.;
Office for Human Resources - Erin Danaher, Dir.; Debbie Maynerich, Admin. Asst.;
Office for Safe Environment - Alison Smith, Dir.; Debbie Maynerich, Admin. Asst.;
Department for Community Services - Steven E. Roach, Exec.;
Corporate Board Directors -
Corporate Board Members -
Office for Catholic Charities - t) 217-523-9201 Steven E. Roach, Exec.; Elaine Perine, Dir.;

ADVISORY BOARDS, COMMISSIONS, COMMITTEES, AND COUNCILS
Bishop's Council -
College of Consultors -
Diocesan Finance Council -
Diocesan Pastoral Council -
Presbyteral Council -

DEANERIES
Vicars Forane -
Alton Deanery - Very Rev. Jeffrey H. Goeckner;
Jerseyville Deanery - Very Rev. Thomas Hagstrom;
Mattoon Deanery - Very Rev. John M. Titus;
Quincy Deanery - Rev. Msgr. Leo Enlow;
Springfield Deanery - Very Rev. Daniel J. Bergbower;

PARISHES, MISSIONS, AND CLERGY

STATE OF ILLINOIS

ALEXANDER
Visitation B.V.M. - 506 Rte. 36, Alexander, IL 62601; Mailing: PO Box 20, New Berlin, IL 62670 t) 217-488-3545 quadparishes@gmail.com www.quadpastoralunit.com Rev. Ron Lorilla, Pst.;

ALTAMONT
St. Clare - 216 N. Ninth St., Altamont, IL 62411 t) 618-483-5346 office@stclarealtamont.dio.org; pastortriparish@yahoo.com Rev. Joseph Havrilka, KCHS, Pst.; Alan Kollmann, DRE; CRP Stds.: 48

ALTON
St. Mary's - 519 E. 4th St., Alton, IL 62002 t) 618-465-4284 laurie@stmarysalton.com www.stmarysalton.com Rev. Benjamin Unachukwu, OMV, Par. Vicar; Rev. Leland Thorpe, OMV, Par. Vicar; Rev. David Beauregard, O.M.V., In Res.; Rev. Paul Kallal, O.M.V., In Res.; Dcn. James Schwartzkopf; Dennis Keller, Music Min.; CRP Stds.: 338
St. Mary's School - (Grades PreSchool-8) 536 E. 3rd St., Alton, IL 62002 t) 618-465-8523; 681-465-9719 www.smsalton.com Beth Hogg, Prin.; Stds.: 217; Sr. Tchrs.: 1; Lay Tchrs.: 16
Middle School - (Grades K-8) 1015 Milton Rd., Alton, IL 62002 t) 618-465-9719 bhogg@smsalton.com Beth Hogg, Prin.; Stds.: 97; Sr. Tchrs.: 1; Lay Tchrs.: 5
Ss. Peter and Paul - 717 State St., Alton, IL 62002 t) 618-465-4221; 618-465-4630 (CRP) ssppchurch717@yahoo.com; clewis@ssppalton.com www.ssppalton.com Rev. William Jeffry Holtman, O.F.S., Pst.; Chrissy Lewis, Bus. Mgr.;

ARCOLA
St. John the Baptist - 204 S. Pine St., Arcola, IL 61910; Mailing: 205 S. Locust Str., P.O. Box 133, Arcola, IL 61910 t) 217-268-3766 Rev. Angel Sierra, Pst.; Maria Miller, DRE; CRP Stds.: 39

ARENZVILLE
St. Fidelis - 601 W. North St., Arenzville, IL 62611; Mailing: 240 E. Myrtle St., Virginia, IL 62691 c) 217-371-4713 Rev. Daren J. Zehnle, Par. Admin.; Dcn. Paul Koch;

ASHLAND
St. Augustine - 320 N. Saratoga, Ashland, IL 62612 t) 217-476-8856 sta@casscomm.com www.staugustineashland.org Rev. Daren J. Zehnle, Pst.; Tanya Wallbaum, DRE; CRP Stds.: 28

ASSUMPTION
Assumption B.V.M. - 301 St. Peter St., Assumption, IL 62510 t) 217-226-3205 (CRP); 217-226-3536 stmarybvm1857@aim.com; stmarybvm1857@aol.com Rev. Pawel Augustyniak, Pst.; Brian Pekovitch, CRE; CRP Stds.: 42

ATHENS
Holy Family - 309 N. Springfield Rd., Athens, IL 62613; Mailing: 711 S. 6th St., Petersburg, IL 62675 t) 217-632-7118 stphf-officeadmin@parish.dio.org hfa.dio.org Rev. Maurice Yonta, Pst.; Dcn. Benedict P. Hoefler;

AUBURN
Holy Cross - 125 E. Washington St., Auburn, IL 62615-0168; Mailing: P.O. Box 168, Auburn, IL 62615 t) 217-438-6222 hcp@royell.org holycrossauburn.com Rev. James Palakudy, S.A.C., Pst.; CRP Stds.: 63
St. Benedict Church - 128 E. Washington St., Auburn, IL 62615

BEARDSTOWN
St. Alexius - 215 W. 5th St., Beardstown, IL 62618; Mailing: 240 E. Myrtle St., Virginia, IL 62691 c) 217-371-4713 staalf4@casscomm.com Rev. Daren J. Zehnle, Par. Admin.; Dcn. Paul Koch; CRP Stds.: 129

BENLD
St. Joseph - 310 W. Central, Benld, IL 62009; Mailing: 304 N. Macoupin, Gillespie, IL 62033 t) 217-839-3456 macoupincatholicchurch.com Rev. Joseph Koyickal, Pst.; Dcn. Dennis W. Baker; Karla Huddlestun, DRE; CRP Stds.: 6

BETHALTO
Our Lady Queen of Peace - 132 Butcher St., Bethalto, IL 62010; Mailing: P.O. Box 100, Bethalto, IL 62010 t) 618-377-6519 church@olqpbethalto.org Rev. Thomas R. Liebler, Pst.; Cindy Stutz, CRE/PSR; CRP Stds.: 21
Our Lady Queen of Peace School - (Grades PreK-8) 618 N. Prairie, Bethalto, IL 62010 t) 618-377-6401 eremis@olqpbethalto.org Steve Menke, Prin.; Stds.:

106; Lay Tchrs.: 8

BETHANY

St. Isidore - 364 CR 2000 N., Bethany, IL 61914; Mailing: 400 N. Whitetail Cir. c/o Our Lady of the Holy Spirit, Mt. Zion, IL 62549 t) 217-864-3467 pastor@mtzolhs.org; secretary@mtzolhs.org www.mtzolhs.org Rev. Jason P. Stone, Pst.;

BRIGHTON

St. Alphonsus - 920 N. Main St., Brighton, IL 62012 t) 618-372-3352 www.sap-brighton.org Rev. William F. Kessler, Pst.; Mary Kate Kinder, CRE; CRP Stds.: 24

BRUSSELS

Blessed Trinity - 111 E. Main St., Brussels, IL 62013-0038; Mailing: P.O. Box 38, Brussels, IL 62013 t) 618-883-2400 skinder@blessedtrinity.dio.org Rev. Don J. Roberts, Pst.; Dcn. Michael B. Hagen; Sarah Kinder, Bus. Mgr.; CRP Stds.: 50

St. Mary School - (Grades 1-8) 105 E. Main, Brussels, IL 62013; Mailing: P O Box 39, Brussels, IL 62013 t) 618-883-2124 Rebecca Lorts, Prin.; Stds.: 39; Lay Tchrs.: 4

CAMP POINT

St. Thomas - 109 E. Spring St., Camp Point, IL 62320; Mailing: P. O. Box 373, Camp Point, IL 62320 t) 217-593-6685 stthomascp@gmail.com www.stthomascp.org Rev. Aaron Kuhn, Pst.; Dcn. Michael P. Ellerman; CRP Stds.: 23

CARLINVILLE

SS. Mary & Joseph - 2010 E. First South St., Carlinville, IL 62626; Mailing: 304 N. Macoupin, Gillespie, IL 62033 t) 217-854-7151 secretaryssmjc@gmail.com www.macoupincatholicchurch.com Rev. Joseph Koyickal, Pst.; CRP Stds.: 81

CARROLLTON

St. John the Evangelist - 414 3rd. St., Carrollton, IL 62016 t) 217-942-3551; 217-942-6814 (CRP) avarble@stjohnscarrollton.org; frcaraj@gmail.com stjohntheevangelistcarrollton.com Rev. Anthony Chowrappa, Pst.; Dcn. Charles Theivagt;

St. John the Evangelist School - (Grades PreK-8) 426 Third St., Carrollton, IL 62016-1319 t) (217) 942-6814 lschnettgoecke@stjohnscarrollton.org st.johntheevangelistcarrollton.com Julie Lake, Prin.; Stds.: 203; Lay Tchrs.: 10

CASEY

St. Charles Borromeo - 300 E. Jefferson St., Casey, IL 62420; Mailing: 414 S. 6th St., Marshall, IL 62441 t) 217-826-2845 stmarysmarshall@hotmail.com mckchurches@weebly.com Rev. Augustine Koomson, Admin.; Jenny Lewis, DRE; CRP Stds.: 6

CHARLESTON

St. Charles Borromeo - 921 E. Madison St., Charleston, IL 61920 t) 217-345-3332 www.saintcharleschurch.org Rev. Joseph Braden Maher, Pst.; Dcn. William Jeffrey Beals; Sarah Fehrenbacher, DRE; CRP Stds.: 80

CHATHAM

St. Joseph the Worker - 700 E. Spruce St., Chatham, IL 62629 t) 217-483-3772 stjos@comcast.net www.stjoschatham.org Rev. Joseph M. Molloy, Pst.; Rev. John H. Nolan, Pastor Emer.; Sr. Judith Pfile, O.P., Pst. Assoc.; CRP Stds.: 141

COLLINSVILLE

SS. Peter and Paul - 207 Vandalia St, Collinsville, IL 62234 t) 618-345-4343 mvojas@saintspeter-paul.org; munfried@saintspeter-paul.org www.saintspeter-paul.org Rev. Michael B. Haag, Pst.; Dcn. James R. Hill; Rev. John P. Beveridge, Pastor Emer.; CRP Stds.: 4

SS. Peter and Paul School - (Grades PreK-8) 210 N. Morrison Ave., Collinsville, IL 62234 t) 618-344-5450 www.sspeter-paulschool.org Julie Buehler, Prin.; Stds.: 163; Lay Tchrs.: 11

DECATUR

Holy Family - 2400 S. Franklin St. Rd., Decatur, IL 62521 t) 217-423-6223 holyfamilychurch1@comcast.net www.decaturholyfamily.com Rev. Mark Tracy, Pst.; CRP Stds.: 43

Holy Family School - (Grades PreK-8) 2400 S. Franklin St., Decatur, IL 62521 t) 217-423-7049 www.hfcschool.org Bryan Kenney, Prin.; Stds.: 243; Lay Tchrs.: 12

Saints James and Patrick Parish - 407 E. Eldorado St., Decatur, IL 62523 t) 217-429-5363 (Office); 217-428-7733 (Office) office@ssjpparish.com www.ssjpparish.org Rev. Christopher J. Comerford, Pst.; Rev. John C. Burnette, Pastor Emer.;

St. Patrick School - (Grades PreK-8) 412 N. Jackson, Decatur, IL 62523 t) 217-423-4351 blackburnn@ssjpparish.com www.decaturstpatrick.org Nicholas Blackburn, Prin.; Stds.: 187; Lay Tchrs.: 14

Our Lady of Lourdes - 3850 Lourdes Dr., Decatur, IL 62526 t) 217-877-4404 mfriedel@dio.org ololchurch.com Rev. Michael Friedel, Pst.; Rev. Richard W. Weltin, Pastor Emer.; CRP Stds.: 40

Our Lady of Lourdes School - (Grades PreK-8) 3950 Lourdes Dr., Decatur, IL 62526 t) 217-877-4408 tbowser@ololschool.com Jennifer Brummer, Prin.; Stds.: 212; Lay Tchrs.: 13

St. Thomas the Apostle - 2155 N. Union St., Decatur, IL 62526; Mailing: 2160 N. Edward St., Decatur, IL 62526 t) 217-877-4146 stthomasdecatur.com Rev. Peter O. Chineke, Par. Admin.; Rev. Msgr. James D. O'Shea, Pastor Emer.; Rev. Richard W. Weltin, Pastor Emer.; Dcn. Kevin Richardson;

DIETERICH

St. Isidore the Farmer Church - 19812 E. 1000th Ave., Dieterich, IL 62424 t) 217-925-5579; 217-925-5788 (CRP) office@stisidore.dio.org; cre@stisidore.dio.org stisidore.weconnect.com Rev. Frank Folino, O.F.M., Pst.; Rosina Esker, DRE; Regina Walker, Bus. Mgr.; CRP Stds.: 255

EDGEWOOD

St. Anne - 408 Broad St., Edgewood, IL 62426; Mailing: 216 N 9th St., Altamont, IL 62411 t) 618-483-5346 office@stclarealtamont.dio.org Rev. T. Joseph Havrilka, Pst.; CRP Stds.: 10

EDWARDSVILLE

St. Boniface - 110 N. Buchanan St., Edwardsville, IL 62025 t) 618-656-6450 stbchurch@st-boniface.com; bdenue@st-boniface.com www.st-boniface.com Very Rev. Jeffrey H. Goeckner, Pst.; Rev. Michael Trummer, Par. Vicar; CRP Stds.: 139

Preschool - 133 N. Fillmore St., Edwardsville, IL 62025 t) 618-692-9315 ndormeier@st-boniface.com Nicole Dormeier, Dir.;

St. Boniface School - (Grades PreK-8) 128 N. Buchanan St., Edwardsville, IL 62025 t) 618-656-6917 stbschool@st-boniface.com Laura Kretzer, Prin.; Stds.: 230; Lay Tchrs.: 12

St. Mary - 1802 Madison Ave., Edwardsville, IL 62025 t) 618-656-4857 office@stmaryedw.org; psr@stmaryedw.org stmaryedw.org Rev. Robert J. Jallas, Pst.; Eva Duncan, PSR Coordinator; CRP Stds.: 65

St. Mary School - (Grades PreK-8) t) 618-656-1230 henkesa@stmaryedw.org Stacy A. Henke, Prin.; Stds.: 217; Lay Tchrs.: 14

EFFINGHAM

St. Anthony of Padua - 101 E. Virginia, Effingham, IL 62401; Mailing: PO Box 764, Effingham, IL 62401 t) 217-347-7129 Rev. Peter C. Harman, Pst.; Rev. Michael Berndt, Par. Vicar; Dcn. Joseph A. Emmerich; CRP Stds.: 20

St. Anthony of Padua School - (Grades PreK-8) 405 N. Second St., Effingham, IL 62401 t) 217-347-0419 vmurphy@stanthony.com stanthony.com Stds.: 510; Lay Tchrs.: 31

St. Anthony of Padua High School - 304 E. Roadway Ave., Effingham, IL 62401 t) 217-342-6969 jsemple@stanthony.com stanthony.com Stds.: 206; Lay Tchrs.: 23

St. Mary Help of Christians - 20057 N. 1525th St., Effingham, IL 62401 t) 217-844-2062 gcstmary@gmail.com; kimgreencreek@consolidated.net Rev. Sunder Ery, Pst.; Eric Thompson, Dir., Faith Formation; CRP Stds.: 62

Sacred Heart - 405 S. Henrietta, Effingham, IL 62401 t) 217-347-7177 shchurch@sheff.org www.sheff.org Rev. Michal Rosa, Pst.; CRP Stds.: 75

Sacred Heart School - (Grades PreSchool-8) 407 S. Henrietta, Effingham, IL 62401 t) 217-342-4060 shschool@sheff.org Angela Sheehan, Prin.; Stds.: 219; Lay Tchrs.: 15

FARMERSVILLE

St. Mary - 310 Nobbie St., Farmersville, IL 62533 t) 217-227-3349 office@stmrm.org www.stmrm.org Rev. Florent Kanga, SAC, Pst.; Marlene Marten, Bus. Mgr.;

FIELDON

St. Mary - 17581 State Hwy. 16, Fieldon, IL 62031; Mailing: 306 N. Washington St., Jerseyville, IL 62052 t) 618-498-3416 hgchurch@gtec.com www.jerseycountycatholicchurches.org Rev. Hyland Smith, Pst.; Dcn. Kenneth Funk; Cathie Ward, DRE; CRP Stds.: 6

FRANKLIN

Sacred Heart of Jesus - 414 Wyatt, Franklin, IL 62638; Mailing: PO Box 20, New Berlin, IL 62670 t) 217-488-3545 quadpastoralunit.com Rev. Ron Lorilla, Pst.; CRP Stds.: 13

GILLESPIE

SS. Simon and Jude - 304 N. Macoupin St., Gillespie, IL 62033 t) 217-839-3456 macoupincatholicchurch.com Rev. Joseph Koyickal, Pst.; Dcn. Dennis W. Baker; Karla Huddlestun, DRE; CRP Stds.: 37

GIRARD

St. Patrick - 745 W. Center St., Girard, IL 62640; Mailing: P.O. Box 105, Girard, IL 62640 c) 217-299-3007 stpat-sec@royell.org; stpat-sec@royell.org www.stpatgirard.com Rev. James Palakudy, S.A.C., Pst.; Terri Joslin, DRE; CRP Stds.: 22

GLEN CARBON

St. Cecilia - St. Cecilia Family Life Center, 155 N. Main St., Glen Carbon, IL 62034-1625 t) 618-288-3200 faithformation@stcparish.org; office@stcparish.org www.stcparish.org Rev. Donald Patrick Gibbons, Pst.; Dcn. Joseph Zagorski; CRP Stds.: 46

GODFREY

St. Ambrose - 820 W. Homer M. Adams Pkwy., Godfrey, IL 62035 t) 618-466-2921 office@saintambroseparish.org www.saintambroseparish.org/ Rev. Steven A. Janoski, Pst.; Dcn. William E. Kessler; Dcn. Jay Wackerly; Dcn. Thomas W. Wilkinson Sr.; Kathy Wittich, Coord., Parish School of Relg.; CRP Stds.: 6

St. Ambrose School - (Grades PreK-8) 822 W. Homer M. Adams Pkwy., Godfrey, IL 62035 t) 618-466-4216 rbaird@stambrosegodfrey.org www.stambrosegodfrey.org Robert Baird, Prin.; Stds.: 247; Lay Tchrs.: 18

GRAFTON

St. Patrick - 11 N. Evans St., Grafton, IL 62037; Mailing: P.O. Box 218, Grafton, IL 62037 t) 618-786-3512 stpatricks@gtec.com Rev. Martin Smith, Pst.;

GRANITE CITY

St. Elizabeth - 2300 Pontoon Rd., Granite City, IL 62040 t) 618-877-3300; 314-266-8387 pastor@stelizabethgc.org; secretary@stelizabethgc.org stelizabethgc.org/ Rev. Alfred Tumwesigye, Pst.; Dcn. Michael Halbrook, Liturgy Dir.; Cathy Cassy, Music Min.; CRP Stds.: 13

St. Elizabeth School - (Grades PreK-8) t) (618) 877-3300 x2001 www.stelizabethgc.org Michelle Williams, Prin.; Stds.: 154; Lay Tchrs.: 10

St. Elizabeth Preschool - t) (618) 877-3300 x2001 mwilliams@stelizabethgc.org stelizabethgc.org Michelle Williams, Prin.;

Holy Family - 2606 Washington Ave., Granite City, IL 62040-4810 t) 618-877-7158 kunfried@holyfamilygc.org holyfamilycatholicgc.org Rev. Stephen A. Thompson, Pst.; Dcn. Neil Wayne Suermann; Nancy Diak, DRE;

Holy Family School - (Grades 1-8) 1900 St. Clair Ave., Granite City, IL 62040 t) 618-877-5500 holyfamsch@yahoo.com holyfamilyhawks.net Brooke Bjorkman, Prin.; Stds.: 142; Lay Tchrs.: 10

GRANTFORK

St. Gertrude - 202 N. Locust St., Grantfork, IL 62249; Mailing: P.O. Box 410, Pierron, IL 62273 t) 618-669-2391 icstn2011@gmail.com www.icstnstg.org Rev. Paul Bonk, Pst.; CRP Stds.: 29

GREENFIELD

St. Michael - 411 Sheffield, Greenfield, IL 62044; Mailing: 414 3rd St., Carrollton, IL 62016 t) 217-368-2176 Rev. Anthony Chowrappa, Pst.; Dcn. Charles Theivagt; Martha Rawe, DRE; CRP Stds.: 6

GREENUP

Christ the King - 110 E. Lincoln Dr., Greenup, IL 62428; Mailing: 414 S. 6th St., Marshall, IL 62441 t) 217-826-2845; 217-923-3523 (CRP) stmarysmarshall@hotmail.com; akoomson@dio.org mckchurches@gmail.com Rev. Augustine Koomson, Admin.; Jenny Lewis, DRE; CRP Stds.: 9

GREENVILLE

St. Lawrence - 512 S. Prairie St., Greenville, IL 62246; Mailing: Po Box 401, Greenville, IL 62246 t) 618-664-9149 (Office); 618-664-3169 (Rectory) Rev. Jeffrey E. Stone, Pst.; Debbie Klincar, DRE; CRP Stds.: 31

HARDIN

St. Francis of Assisi - 304 French St., Hardin, IL 62047; Mailing: PO Box C, Hardin, IL 62047 t) 618-576-2628 gburch@sfacalhoun.com www.sfacalhoun.com Rev. Don J. Roberts, Pst.; Dcn. Mike Hagen Sr.; CRP Stds.: 49

St. Norbert School - (Grades PreK-8) 401 Vineyard St., Hardin, IL 62047; Mailing: P.O. Box 525, Hardin, IL 62047 t) 618-576-2514 stnorbertschool@snswolves.com Stds.: 52; Lay Tchrs.: 5

HIGHLAND

St. Paul - 1412 Ninth St., Highland, IL 62249 t) 618-654-2339 pjakel@stpaulhighland.org www.stpaulhighland.org Rev. Pat G. Jakel, Pst.; Rev. Msgr. David L. Peters, Pastor Emer.; Dcn. David S. Bohnenstiehl; CRP Stds.: 64

St. Paul School - (Grades PreK-8) 1416 Main St., Highland, IL 62249 t) 618-654-7525 htodora@stpaulhighland.org www.stpaulvikings.org Haidee Todora, Prin.; Stds.: 228; Lay Tchrs.: 15

HILLSBORO

St. Agnes - 214 E. Tremont St., Hillsboro, IL 62049; Mailing: P.O. Box 98, Hillsboro, IL 62049 t) 217-532-2631 (CRP); 217-532-5288 agnesone_chris@consolidated.net; stagneshillsboro@ctifiber.com stagneshillsboro.com Rev. Daniel L. Willenborg, Pst.; Dcn. Leland B. Johns; CRP Stds.: 64

HUME

St. Michael - 205 Center St., Hume, IL 61932; Mailing: 206 N. Pine, Villa Grove, IL 61956 t) 217-832-8352; 217-264-4068 (CRP) russellkeske@frontier.com sacredheartandstmicheal.com Rev. Aloysius Okey Ndeanaefo, Pst.; Kim Keske, DRE; CRP Stds.: 4

ILLIOPOLIS

Resurrection Parish (Visitation Parish) - 410 Anne St., Illiopolis, IL 62539; Mailing: P.O. Box 47, Illiopolis, IL 62539 t) 217-486-3851 resurrectionparish1@comcast.net Rev. Fredrick Chima Mbiere (Nigeria), Pst.; Dcn. Andrew Krug; CRP Stds.: 9

JACKSONVILLE

Our Saviour - 500 E. State St., Jacksonville, IL 62650; Mailing: 453 E. State St., Jacksonville, IL 62650 t) 217-245-6184; 217-245-7633 (CRP) office@ospchurch.com; jalexander@jsd117.com www.oursaviourparish.org Rev. Joseph G. Ring, Pst.; Rev. Adam Zawadzki, Par. Vicar; Jill Alexander, PSR Coordinator; CRP Stds.: 58

Our Saviour School - (Grades PreK-8) 455 E. State St., Jacksonville, IL 62650 t) 217-243-8621 svandevelde@oss-shamrocks.com oursaviourshamrocks.com Stephanie VanDeVelde, Prin.; Stds.: 320; Lay Tchrs.: 23

JERSEYVILLE

St. Francis Xavier - 506 S. State St., Jerseyville, IL 62052-0260 t) 618-498-3518 stfrancisxavier@gtec.com jerseycountycatholicchurches.org Rev. Martin Smith, Pst.; Cathie Ward, DRE; CRP Stds.: 11

St. Francis/Holy Ghost School - (Grades PreK-8) 412 S. State St., Jerseyville, IL 62025 t) 618-498-4823 dennis.cramsey@sfhg.org Dr. Dennis Cramsey, Prin.; Stds.: 290; Lay Tchrs.: 28

Holy Ghost - 306 N. Washington St., Jerseyville, IL 62052 t) 618-498-3416 c) 618-791-4461 hgchurch@gtec.com Rev. Hyland Smith, Pst.; Dcn. Kenneth Funk; Cathie Ward, DRE; CRP Stds.: 26

KINCAID

St. Rita - 30 St. Rita Ct., Kincaid, IL 62540; Mailing: P.O. Box 439, Kincaid, IL 62540 t) 217-237-2333 strita1@consolidated.net Rev. Piotr Kosk, Pst.; Cindy Tilley, DRE;

LIBERTY

St. Brigid - 706 N. Main St., Liberty, IL 62347; Mailing: P.O. Box 228, Liberty, IL 62347 t) 217-645-3444 churchbej@gmail.com stbrigidedwardjoseph.weebly.com Rev. Scott A. Snider, Pst.; CRP Stds.: 46

LITCHFIELD

Holy Family - 410 S. State St., Litchfield, IL 62056; Mailing: P. O. Box 8, Litchfield, IL 62056 t) 217-324-2776 holyfamily@consolidated.net www.holyfamilylitchfield.org Formerly St. Mary, founded in 1857 & St. Aloysius founded in 1883. Rev. Daniel L. Willenborg, Pst.; Dcn. Leland B. Johns, DRE; CRP Stds.: 29

LIVINGSTON

Sacred Heart - 188 Livingston Ave., Livingston, IL 62058; Mailing: P.O. Box 458, Livingston, IL 62058 t) 618-637-2211 Very Rev. Thomas Hagstrom, Pst.; Rev. George Radosevich, Pastor Emer.;

MADISON

St. Mary and St. Mark - 1621 10th St., Madison, IL 62060 t) 618-452-5180 stmary.church@ymail.com Rev. Stephen A. Thompson, Pst.; Dcn. Neil Wayne Suermann;

MARINE

St. Elizabeth - 120 N. Windmill St., Marine, IL 62061; Mailing: P.O. Box 457, Marine, IL 62061 t) 618-887-4535 stelizabeth@att.net Rev. Paul A. Habing, Pst.;

MARSHALL

St. Mary - 414 S. Sixth St., Marshall, IL 62441 t) 217-826-2845 stmarysmarshall@hotmail.com; daniellejohnson.smc@gmail.com mckchurches@weebly.com Rev. Augustine Koomson, Admin.; Danielle Johnson, DRE; CRP Stds.: 25

MARYVILLE

Mother of Perpetual Help - 200 N. Lange, Maryville, IL 62062 t) 618-344-6464 secretary@mph.dio.org; bookkeeper@mph.dio.org mph.dio.org Rev. Robert Johnson, Pst.; CRP Stds.: 222

MATTOON

Immaculate Conception - 320 N. 21st St., Mattoon, IL 61938 t) 217-235-0539 icchurchsec@gmail.com www.mattoonimmaculateconception.org Very Rev. John M. Titus, Pst.; Dcn. Eugene V. Uptmor Jr.; CRP Stds.: 40

MEDORA

St. John the Evangelist - 203 N. Main St., Medora, IL 62063; Mailing: 920 N. Main St., Brighton, IL 62012 t) 618-372-3352 www.sap-brighton.org Rev. William F. Kessler, Admin.; Mary Kate Kinder, CRE; CRP Stds.: 4

MENDON

St. Edward - 218 S. State Rd., Mendon, IL 62351; Mailing: P.O. Box 228, Liberty, IL 62347 t) 217-645-3444 churchbej@gmail.com www.stbrigidedwardjoseph.weebly.com Rev. Scott A. Snider, Pst.; CRP Stds.: 37

MONTROSE

St. Rose of Lima - 301 N. Spring Creek Rd., Montrose, IL 62445; Mailing: PO Box 68, Montrose, IL 62445 t) 217-924-4337; (217) 821-0294 (CRP) strosechurch@mmtcnet.com Rev. Dat Hoang, OFM, Pst.; Lisa Probst, DRE; CRP Stds.: 58

MORRISONVILLE

St. Maurice - 706 S.E. 4th St., Morrisonville, IL 62546; Mailing: PO Box 45, Morrisonville, IL 62546 t) 217-526-3363 stmaurice@consolidated.net Rev. Florent Kanga, SAC, Pst.; Debra K Forbes, Bus. Mgr.; CRP Stds.: 20

MOUNT OLIVE

Saint John Paul II - 705 E. Main St., Mount Olive, IL 62069 t) 217-999-4981 bjpii@madisontelco.com Very Rev. Thomas Hagstrom, Pst.; Rev. Larry L. Anschutz, Pastor Emer.; CRP Stds.: 18

MOUNT STERLING

Holy Family - 401 W. North St., Mount Sterling, IL 62353; Mailing: P.O. Box 252, Mount Sterling, IL 62353 t) 217-773-3233 akuhn@dio.org Rev. Aaron Kuhn, Pst.; Dcn. Michael P. Ellerman; CRP Stds.: 7

St. Mary - (Grades PreK-8) 408 W. Washington, Mount Sterling, IL 62353 t) 217-773-2825 tmckeown@smseagle.org www.smseagle.org Melissa Obert, Prin.; Stds.: 125; Lay Tchrs.: 9

MOWEAQUA

St. Frances de Sales - 231 E. Watten, Moweaqua, IL 62550; Mailing: 301 Saint Peter St., Assumption, IL 62510 t) 217-226-3536 stmarybvm1857@aim.com Rev. Pawel Augustyniak, Pst.;

MT. ZION

Our Lady of the Holy Spirit - 400 N. Whitetail Cir., Mt. Zion, IL 62549 t) 217-864-3467 pastor@mtzolhs.org; secretary@mtzolhs.org www.mtzolhs.org Rev. Jason P. Stone, Pst.; CRP Stds.: 35

NEOGA

St. Mary of the Assumption - 690 Walnut Ave., Neoga, IL 62447; Mailing: PO Box 309, Neoga, IL 62447 t) 217-895-2166 stmaryneoga@gmail.com Rev. Sunder Ery, Pst.; Eric Thompson, DRE; CRP Stds.: 6

NEW BERLIN

Sacred Heart of Mary - 404 E. Birch, New Berlin, IL 62670; Mailing: PO Box 20, New Berlin, IL 62670 t) 217-488-3545 quadpastoralunit.com Rev. Ron Lorilla, Pst.; CRP Stds.: 9

NEWTON

St. Thomas the Apostle - 404 W. Jourdan St., Newton, IL 62448; Mailing: P.O. Box 225, Newton, IL 62448 t) 618-783-8741 stthomasnewton.net Rev. R. Dean Probst, Pst.; Rev. Pawel Luczak, Par. Vicar; Pete Pasero, DRE; CRP Stds.: 53

St. Thomas the Apostle School - (Grades K-8) 306 W. Jourdan St., Newton, IL 62448 t) 618-783-3517 jillbierman@stthomassaints.com www.stthomassaints.com Jill Bierman, Prin.; Stds.: 184; Lay Tchrs.: 10

NOKOMIS

St. Louis - 311 S. Elm St., Nokomis, IL 62075-1310 t) 217-563-7146 www.slsk8.org Rev. Michael Joseph Meinhart, Pst.; CRP Stds.: 38

St. Louis School - (Grades PreK-8) 509 E. Union, Nokomis, IL 62075 t) 217-563-7445 www.stlouis-nokomis.k12.il.us Stds.: 63; Lay Tchrs.: 6

OBLONG

Our Lady of Lourdes - 506 W. Missouri St., Oblong, IL 62449; Mailing: 207 E. Walnut St., Robinson, IL 62454 t) 618-544-7526 catholicsofcrawfordcounty@gmail.com Rev. David Beagles, Pst.; Rev. James A. Flach, Pastor Emer.;

OCONEE

Sacred Heart - 201 N. Walnut St., Oconee, IL 62553; Mailing: P.O. Box 45, Oconee, IL 62553 t) 217-539-4325 sacredheartoconee@parish.dio.org Rev. Rodney A. Schwartz, Pst.; CRP Stds.: 23

PANA

St. Patrick - 303 S. Locust St., Pana, IL 62557; Mailing: P O Box 440, Pana, IL 62557 t) 217-562-5396 panastpats@gmail.com Rev. Rodney A. Schwartz, Pst.; CRP Stds.: 15

Sacred Heart - (Grades PreK-8) 3 E. 4th St., Pana, IL 62557 t) 217-562-2425 diese@consolidated.net www.shspana.com Deb Zueck, Prin.; Stds.: 146; Pr. Tchrs.: 1; Lay Tchrs.: 10

PARIS

St. Aloysius - 18925 E. 1350th Rd., Paris, IL 61944; Mailing: P.O. Box 577, Paris, IL 61944 t) 217-466-3355 Rev. Valery Burusu, Admin.;

St. Mary - 528 N. Main St., Paris, IL 61944; Mailing: P. O. Box 577, Paris, IL 61944 t) 217-466-3355 Rev. Valery Burusu, Pst.; CRP Stds.: 10

PETERSBURG

St. Peter - 711 S. 6th St., Petersburg, IL 62675 t) 217-632-7118 stpeter234@sbcglobal.net spp.dio.org Rev. Maurice Yonta, Pst.; Dcn. Roch A. Magerl;

PIERRON

Immaculate Conception - 991 Main St., Pierron, IL 62273; Mailing: P.O. Box 410, Pierron, IL 62273 t) 618-669-2391 immaculateconceptionpierron@parish.dio.org; icstn2011@gmail.com www.icstnstg.org Rev. Paul J. Bonk, Pst.; Mary Jo Luitjohan, DRE; CRP Stds.: 37

PITTSFIELD

St. Mary - 226 E. Adams, Pittsfield, IL 62363 t) 217-285-4321; 217-285-6702 (CRP) religiousedstmarys@gmail.com; stmarymark@gmail.com www.stmaryspittsfield.dio.org Rev. Mark A. Schulte, Pst.; Gloria Heinen, DRE; CRP Stds.: 15

POCAHONTAS

St. Nicholas - 401 E. State St., Pocahontas, IL 62275; Mailing: P.O. Box 410, Pierron, IL 62273 t) 618-669-2391 immaculateconceptionpierron@parish.dio.org; icstn2011@gmail.com www.icstnstg.org Rev. Paul Bonk, Pst.; CRP Stds.: 4

QUINCY

St. Anthony of Padua - 2223 St. Anthony Rd., Quincy, IL 62305 t) 217-222-5996 hglidewell@stdominicquincy.org; secretary@stanthonypadua.org www.stanthonypadua.org Rev. Bernard Thomas Donovan, Pst.; Dcn. Harry L. Cramer; Hope Glidewell, Coord., Family Faith Formation; CRP Stds.: 156

St. Dominic Catholic Elementary School - (Grades PreK-8) 4100 Columbus Rd., Quincy, IL 62305 t) 217-224-0041 www.stdominicquincy.org Carol Frericks, Prin.; Stds.: 188; Lay Tchrs.: 11

Blessed Sacrament - 1119 S. Seventh St., Quincy, IL 62301 t) 217-222-2759; 217-222-2758 (CRP) parishoffice@blessedscs.org www,blessedsacramentqcy.org Rev. Thomas C. Meyer, Pst.; Dcn. Terry Ellerman; Steve Buckman, Music Min.; Ginny Steinkamp, DRE; Linda Ohnemus, Bus. Mgr.; CRP Stds.: 34

Blessed Sacrament School - (Grades PreK-8) 1115 S. 7th, Quincy, IL 62301 t) 217-228-1477 principal@blessedscs.org www.blessedscs.org Lisa Berhorst, Prin.; Stds.: 220; Lay Tchrs.: 13

St. Francis Solanus - 1721 College Ave., Quincy, IL 62301 t) 217-222-2898; 217-222-2898 x108 (CRP) church@stfrancissolanus.com stfrancissolanus.com Rev. Steven M. Arisman, Pst.; Rev. Rafal Pyrchla; Dcn. Wayne R. Zimmerman; Dcn. Dennis Leon Holbrook II; CRP Stds.: 48

St. Francis Solanus School - (Grades PreK-8) 1720 College Ave., Quincy, IL 62301 t) 217-222-4077 school@stfrancissolanus.com www.stfrancissolanus.com Julie Radel, Prin.; Stds.: 256; Lay Tchrs.: 18

St. Joseph - 1435 E. 1500 St., Quincy, IL 62305; Mailing: P.O. Box 228, Liberty, IL 62347 t) 217-434-8442 stjoe@adams.net stsbrigidedwardjoseph.weebly.com Rev. Scott A. Snider, Pst.; CRP Stds.: 18

St. Peter - 2600 Maine St., Quincy, IL 62301 t) 217-222-3155 church@cospq.org www.cospq.org St. Peter Parish of Quincy Illinois Rev. Msgr. Leo J. Enlow, Pst.; Rev. Zachary Samples, Par. Vicar; Dcn. Robert M. Lundberg; Dcn. Jeffrey Wolf; Gina Bergman, DRE; CRP Stds.: 36

St. Peter School - (Grades PreK-8) 2500 Maine St., Quincy, IL 62301 t) 217-223-1120 c.venvertloh@cospq.org www.stpeterschool.com Cindy Venvertloh, Prin.; Stds.: 466; Lay Tchrs.: 27

St. Rose of Lima Parish - 1009 N. 8th St., Quincy, IL 62301 t) 217-222-2511 saintrosequincy@att.net; st-rose-quincy@att.net www.saintrosequincy.org Rev. Karl A. Pikus, F.S.S.P, Pst.; Rev. Arnaud Devillers, In Res.; Rev. Zachary T Edgar, In Res.; CRP Stds.: 29

RAMSEY

St. Joseph - 126 E. Main, Ramsey, IL 62080; Mailing: PO Box 455, Ramsey, IL 62080 t) 618-423-2424 stjramseyil@gmail.com Rev. Seth A. Brown, Pst.; CRP Stds.: 3

RAYMOND

St. Raymond - 306 S. McElroy, Raymond, IL 62560; Mailing: P.O. Box 349, Raymond, IL 62560 t) 217-229-4435 office@stmrm.org; kmarten@stmrm.org www.stmrm.org Rev. Florent Kanga, SAC, Pst.; Marlene Marten, Bus. Mgr.; CRP Stds.: 7

RIVERTON

St. James - 112 N. Sixth St., Riverton, IL 62561-0590; Mailing: P.O. Box 590, Riverton, IL 62561-0590 t) 217-629-7717 stjamesrctry@gcctv.com Rev. Raphael Paul DeMoreno, Pst.;

ROBINSON

St. Elizabeth - 207 E. Walnut St., Robinson, IL 62454 t) 618-544-7526 catholicsofcrawfordcounty@gmail.com www.crawfordcountycatholics.net Rev. David Beagles, Pst.; Rev. James A. Flach, Pastor Emer.; CRP Stds.: 48

ROCHESTER

St. Jude - 633 S. Walnut St., Rochester, IL 62563-0047; Mailing: 633 S. Walnut, P.O. Box 47, Rochester, IL 62563-0047 t) 217-498-9197 cedwards@dio.org; bozanic@stjude.dio.org stjude.dio.org Rev. Charles A. Edwards, Pst.; Dcn. Thomas A. Walker; Dcn. Raymond L. Roth Jr.; Jennifer A. Frericks, DRE; Stacey Harrison, Asst DRE; Michael Spainhour, Music Min.; CRP Stds.: 72

SHELBYVILLE

Immaculate Conception - 1431 State Hwy. 128, Shelbyville, IL 62565; Mailing: P.O. Box 233, Shelbyville, IL 62565 t) 217-774-3434 Rev. Pawel Augustyniak, Pst.; CRP Stds.: 44

SHERMAN

St. John Vianney - 902 Saint John Dr., Sherman, IL 62684; Mailing: P.O. Box 229, Sherman, IL 62684 t) 217-523-3816 ssaladino@sjv.dio.org; parish@sjv.dio.org sjv.dio.org/ Rev. Fredrick Chima Mbiere (Nigeria), Pst.; Rev. Callistus Onumah (Nigeria), In Res.; Dcn. Andrew Krug; Jennifer Grebner, DRE; Stacie Henderson, DRE; CRP Stds.: 68

SHUMWAY

Annunciation - 102 E. Route Hwy. 33, Shumway, IL 62461; Mailing: P.O. Box 96, Shumway, IL 62461 t) (844) 536-6514 stmarysshumway@gmail.com www.stmarysshumway.org Rev. Albert F. Allen, Pst.; CRP Stds.: 50

SIGEL

St. Michael the Archangel - 200 N. Church St., Sigel, IL 62462; Mailing: PO Box 68, Sigel, IL 62462 t) 217-844-3371 sigelstmichaelchurch@gmail.com Rev. Sunder Ery, Pst.; Eric J. Thompson, Dir., Faith Formation;

St. Michael the Archangel School - ; Mailing: P.O. Box 8, Sigel, IL 62462 t) 217-844-2231 n.niemerg@stmichaelsharpshooters.com www.ssmcs.org Nick Niemerg, Prin.; Stds.: 215; Lay Tchrs.: 10

Sacred Heart - 127 County Rd. 100 E., Sigel, IL 62462; Mailing: P. O. Box 68, Sigel, IL 62462 t) 217-844-3371 (office); 217-821-7157 (CRP) c) 217-343-1766 sery@dio.org; ejat.53@yahoo.com Rev. Sunder Ery, Pst.; Eric Thompson, Dir., Faith Formation; CRP Stds.: 53

SPRINGFIELD

Cathedral of the Immaculate Conception - 524 E. Lawrence Ave., Springfield, IL 62703 t) 217-522-3342 info@cathedral.dio.org spicathedral.org/ Very Rev. Brian C. Alford, Rector; Rev. Paul Lesupati, Par. Vicar; Rev. Dominic Rankin, In Res.; Rev. Dominic B. Vahling, In Res.; Dcn. Robert Sgambelluri; Dcn. Irvin (Larry) Smith; CRP Stds.: 16

St. Agnes - 245 N. Amos Ave., Springfield, IL 62702 t) 217-793-1330 office@stagnescatholicparish.org stagnescatholicparish.org Rev. Christopher A. Trummer, Par. Vicar; Cathy Becker, DRE; Rev. Daniel J. Bergbower, Pst.; Dcn. Roy Harley; CRP Stds.: 38

St. Agnes School - (Grades PreK-8) 251 N. Amos Ave., Springfield, IL 62702 t) 217-793-1370 info@stagnescatholicschool.org stagnescatholicschool.org Rachel Cunningham, Prin.; Stds.: 207; Lay Tchrs.: 14

St. Aloysius - 2125 N. 21st St., Springfield, IL 62702 t) 217-544-4554 www.saintaloysius.org Rev. George Philip Nellikunnel, S.A.C., Pst.; Rev. Ramesh Babu Matta, Par. Vicar; Dcn. Jim Dodge;

St. Aloysius School - (Grades PreSchool-8) t) 217-544-4553 angie.daniels@saintaloysius.org saintaloysius.org Denise Reavis, Prin.; Stds.: 131; Lay Tchrs.: 10

Blessed Sacrament - 1725 S. Walnut Ave., Springfield, IL 62704 t) 217-528-7521 mantenan@bsps.org www.bsps.org Rev. Jeffery A. Grant, Pst.; Dcn. Thomas G. Burns; Dcn. David R. Erdmann; CRP Stds.: 30

Blessed Sacrament School - (Grades PreK-8) 748 W. Laurel, Springfield, IL 62704 t) 217-522-7534 hoffmann@bssbruins.org; kuhlman@bssbruins.org www.bssbruins.org Nicole Kuhlman, Prin.; Stds.: 430; Lay Tchrs.: 26

Christ the King - 1930 Barberry Dr., Springfield, IL 62704 t) 217-546-2159 (CRP); 217-546-3527 church@ctkparish.com www.ctkparish.com Very Rev. Christopher A. House, Pst.; Rev. Clinton Honkomp, O.P., Par. Vicar; Rev. Msgr. David S. Lantz, Pastor Emer.; Pamela Fahey, DRE; Dcn. Thomas Scott Keen, RCIA Coord.; CRP Stds.: 19

Christ the King School - (Grades PreK-8) 1920 Barberry Dr., Springfield, IL 62704 selinger@ctkparish.com www.ctkcougars.com Pamela Fahey, Prin.; Stds.: 481; Lay Tchrs.: 26

St. Frances Cabrini - 1020 N. Milton Ave., Springfield, IL 62702 t) 217-522-8555; 217-523-1345 (CRP) parishoffice@stcabrini.dio.org www.stcabrini.dio.org Rev. George Philip Nellikunnel, S.A.C., Pst.; Rev. Ramesh Babu Matta, Par. Vicar; Dcn. James W. Dodge;

St. Joseph - 1345 N. Sixth St., Springfield, IL 62702 t) 217-544-7426 parish@stjoseph.dio.org www.stjoseph.dio.org Rev. Manuel P. Cuizon, Pst.; Dcn. Lawrence H. Day; Sr. Mary Ellen Backes, O.S.U., DRE; CRP Stds.: 9

St. Katharine Drexel - 722 S. 12th St., Springfield, IL 62703 t) 217-523-4501 pastor@kdrexel.org katharinedrexel.com Rev. James E. Isaacson, S.J.C., Pst.; Rev. Brendan Gibson, S.J.C., Assoc. Pst.; Rev. Kevin Mann, S.J.C., Assoc. Pst.; CRP Stds.: 31

Little Flower - 800 Stevenson Dr., Springfield, IL 62703 t) 217-529-1606 pax@littleflowerchurch.net littleflowerchurch.net Rev. Allen M. Kemme, Pst.; Rev. Msgr. John R. Ossola, Pastor Emer.; Rev. Thaddeus Idanosi Adukus, In Res.; CRP Stds.: 14

Little Flower School - (Grades PreK-8) 900 Stevenson Dr., Springfield, IL 62703 t) 217-529-4511 office@little-flower.org little-flower.org William Moredock, Prin.; Stds.: 305; Lay Tchrs.: 27

ST. ELMO

St. Mary - 610 W. Cumberland Rd., St. Elmo, IL 62458; Mailing: 216 N. 9th St., Altamont, IL 62411 t) 618-483-5346 office@stclarealtamont.dio.org Rev. T. Joseph Havrilka, Pst.; CRP Stds.: 1

ST. JACOB

St. James - 503 Washington St., St. Jacob, IL 62281; Mailing: 511 S. Main St., Troy, IL 62294-1812 t) 618-667-6571 www.stjeromeparish.org Rev. Kevin Michael Laughery, Pst.;

STAUNTON

St. Michael the Archangel - 415 E. Main St., Staunton, IL 62088-0240; Mailing: PO Box 240, Staunton, IL 62088 t) 618-635-3140 stmikeof@madisontelco.com www.stmichaelsstaunton.com Very Rev. Thomas Hagstrom, Pst.; Rev. George Radosevich, Pastor Emer.; CRP Stds.: 88

STE. MARIE

St. Mary - 112 W. Embarras St., Ste. Marie, IL 62459; Mailing: P.O. Box 68, Ste. Marie, IL 62459 t) 618-455-3155 stmaryschurch@psbnewton.com Rev. R. Dean Probst, Pst.; Rev. Pawel Luczak, Par. Vicar; Marie Wagner, CRE; CRP Stds.: 52

STONINGTON

Holy Trinity - 308 N. Pine, Stonington, IL 62567; Mailing: P. O. Box 257, Stonington, IL 62567 t) 217-325-3697 holytrinity1879@outlook.com Rev. Piotr Kosk, Pst.; Matt Peabody, CRE/PSR;

SULLIVAN

St. Columcille - 516 W. Jackson St., Sullivan, IL 61951; Mailing: 320 N. 21st St., Mattoon, IL 61938 t) 217-235-0539 st.columcillesullivan@gmail.com st.columcillesullivan.org Very Rev. John M. Titus, Pst.; Rev. John E. Sohm, Pastor Emer.; CRP Stds.: 4

TAYLORVILLE

St. Mary - 116 W. Adams St., Taylorville, IL 62568; Mailing: P.O. Box 470, Taylorville, IL 62568 t) 217-824-8178 Rev. Piotr Kosk, Pst.; Carole Harrison, DRE; CRP Stds.: 32

St. Mary School - (Grades K-6) 422 S. Washington, Taylorville, IL 62568 t) 217-824-6501 jcoady@st-maryschool.com Joanne Coady, Prin.; Stds.: 111; Lay Tchrs.: 7

TEUTOPOLIS

St. Francis of Assisi - 203 E. Main St., Teutopolis, IL 62467-0730; Mailing: P.O. Box 730, Teutopolis, IL 62467-0730 t) 217-961-6477 (CRP); 217-961-6404 sfc@stfrancischurch.com www.stfrancischurch.com Rev. Joseph P. Carlos, O.F.M., Pst.; Rev. Dat Hoang, OFM, Assoc. Pst.; Daniel Williams, Music Min.; Maria Kingery, Youth Min.; Dan Niemerg, DRE; Rev. Dennis Koopman, OFM, Senior Associate Pastor; CRP Stds.: 515

TROY

St. Jerome - 511 S. Main St., Troy, IL 62294 t) 618-667-6571 www.stjeromeparish.org Rev. Kevin Michael Laughery, Pst.; Sr. Linda Mary Delonais, Pst. Assoc.; CRP Stds.: 75

St. John Neumann - (Grades PreK-8) 142 Wilma Dr., Maryville, IL 62062 t) 618-345-7230 office@sjncrusaders.org www.sjncrusaders.org Russell Hart, Prin.; Stds.: 240; Lay Tchrs.: 12

TUSCOLA

Forty Martyrs - 201 E. Van Allen St., Tuscola, IL 61953; Mailing: 110 E. Van Allen St., PO Box 440, Tuscola, IL 61953 t) 217-253-4412 fortymartyrs@gmail.com Rev. Angel Sierra, Pst.; CRP Stds.: 71

VANDALIA

Mother of Dolors - 322 N. Seventh St., Vandalia, IL 62471; Mailing: PO Box 377, Vandalia, IL 62471 t) 618-283-0214 modvandalia@gmail.com motherofdolors.com Rev. Seth A. Brown, Pst.; CRP Stds.: 29

VILLA GROVE

Sacred Heart - 210 N. Pine, Villa Grove, IL 61956; Mailing: 206 N Pine St, Villa Grove, IL 61956 t) 217-832-8352 villagrove.hume@gmail.com sacredheartstmicheal.com Rev. Aloysius Okey Ndeanaefo, Pst.; Michael Stauder, DRE; CRP Stds.: 11

VIRDEN

Sacred Heart - 722 N. Springfield St., Virden, IL 62690 t) 217-965-4545 secretary@sacredheart.dio.org www.sacredheartvirden.com Rev. James Palakudy, S.A.C., Pst.; Dcn. Ricky Joe Schnetzler Sr.; Rebecca Yemm, CRE; CRP Stds.: 28

VIRGINIA

St. Luke - 240 E. Myrtle St., Virginia, IL 62691 c) 217-371-4713 Rev. Daren J. Zehnle, Par. Admin.; Dcn. Dirck Curry; CRP Stds.: 20

WAVERLY

St. Sebastian - 265 E. Elm, Waverly, IL 62692; Mailing: PO Box 20, New Berlin, IL 62670 t) 217-488-3545 quadpastoralunit.com Rev. Ron Lorilla, Pst.; CRP Stds.: 1

WHITE HALL

All Saints - 265 S. Main St., White Hall, IL 62092; Mailing: c/o Linda Keller, 167 Ross St., White Hall, IL 62092 t) 217-942-3551; 217-374-2056 stjohntheevangelistcarrollton.com Rev. Anthony Chowrappa, Pst.; Dcn. Charles Theivagt; Christie Joehl, DRE; CRP Stds.: 13

WINCHESTER

St. Mark - 108 E. Pearl St., Winchester, IL 62694; Mailing: 226 E. Adams, Pittsfield, IL 62363 t) 217-285-4321 stmarymark@gmail.com Rev. Mark A. Schulte, Pst.;

WOOD RIVER

Holy Angels - 345 E. Acton Ave., Wood River, IL 62095 t) 618-254-0679 holyangelswr@yahoo.com www.holyangelsparish.com Rev. Donald L. Wolford, Pst.; CRP Stds.: 21

SCHOOLS: PRESCHOOL THRU HIGH SCHOOL

SCHOOLS

STATE OF ILLINOIS

SPRINGFIELD

Saint Patrick Catholic Grade School - (PRV) (Grades PreK-5) 1800 S. Grand Ave. E., Springfield, IL 62703 t) 217-523-7670 stpatprincipal@st-patrick.org www.st-patrick.org Kristin Cavanagh, Prin.; Lori Reimers, Chair; Stds.: 72; Lay Tchrs.: 5

HIGH SCHOOLS

STATE OF ILLINOIS

ALTON

Marquette Catholic High School - (PRV) (Grades 9-12) 219 E. 4th St., Alton, IL 62002 t) 618-463-0580 scrafton@mychs.org; dwalsh@mymchs.org marquettecatholic.org Timothy James Harmon, Prin.; Stds.: 395; Lay Tchrs.: 35

DECATUR

St. Teresa High School - (PRV) (Grades 9-11) 2710 N. Water St., Decatur, IL 62526 t) 217-875-2431 dalylb@stteresa.org stteresa.org Larry Daly, Prin.; Kenneth C. Hendriksen, Exec.; Stds.: 236; Lay Tchrs.: 18

GLEN CARBON

***Father McGivney Catholic High School** - (PRV) (Grades 9-12) 7190 Bouse Rd., Glen Carbon, IL 62034 t) 618-855-9010 principal@mcgivneygriffins.com; jlombardi@mcgivneygriffins.com www.mcgivneygriffins.com Joseph Lombardi, Prin.; Very Rev. Jeffrey H. Goeckner, Pres.; Stds.: 302; Lay Tchrs.: 20

JACKSONVILLE

Routt Catholic High School - (PRV) 500 E. College Ave., Jacksonville, IL 62650 t) 217-243-8563 dcarie@routtcatholic.com www.routtcatholic.com Dan Carie, Prin.; Stds.: 133; Lay Tchrs.: 12

QUINCY

Quincy Notre Dame High School - (PRV) (Grades 9-12) 1400 S. 11th St., Quincy, IL 62301-7252 t) 217-223-2479 mmcdowell@quincynotredame.org www.quincynotredame.org Mark McDowell, Prin.; Stds.: 401; Lay Tchrs.: 22

SPRINGFIELD

Sacred Heart-Griffin - (PRV) 1200 W. Washington St., Springfield, IL 62702 t) 217-787-1595 rapacz@shg.org www.shg.org Springfield Dominican Sisters. Kara Rapacz, Prin.; Sr. Katherine O'Connor, O.P., Pres.; Rachel Bielby, Librn.; Stds.: 500; Pr. Tchrs.: 1; Lay Tchrs.: 39

INSTITUTIONS LOCATED IN DIOCESE

ASSOCIATIONS [ASN]

CARLINVILLE

Calvary Cemetery Association - 53 White Tail Dr., Carlinville, IL 62626 t) 217-825-8584 jefflink70@gmail.com Jeff Link, Cemetery Mgr.;

New Calvary Cemetery, Carlinville - 53 White Tail Dr., Carlinville, IL 62626

Old Calvary Cemetery, Carlinville -

DECATUR

Calvary Cemetery Association - 407 E. Eldorado St., Decatur, IL 62523 t) 217-429-5363 ccomerford@dio.org Rev. Christopher J. Comerford, Pst.;

Calvary Cemetery, Decatur - jburnette@dio.org

GRANITE CITY

Calvary Cemetery Association - 2606 Washington Ave., Granite City, IL 62040 t) 618-877-7158 sthompson@dio.org Rev. Stephen A. Thompson, Pst.;

Calvary Cemetery, Edwardsville - jholtman@dio.org Rev. William Jeffry Holtman, O.F.S.;

LITCHFIELD

Holy Cross Cemetery Association - ; Mailing: P. O. Box 8, Litchfield, IL 62056 t) 217-324-2776 dwillenborg@dio.org Rev. Daniel L. Willenborg, Cemetery Mgr.;

Holy Cross Cemetery, Litchfield -

MT. STERLIN

Catholic Cemetery Association - 401 W. North St., Mt. Sterlin, IL 62353; Mailing: P. O. Box 252, Mt. Sterling, IL 62353 t) 217-773-3233 akuhn@dio.org Rev. Aaron Kuhn, Pst.;

Mt. Sterling Catholic Cemetery - 401 W. North St., Mt. Sterling, IL 62353; Mailing: P.O. Box 252, Mt. Sterling, IL 62353 Rev. Stephen A. Thompson;

QUINCY

Catholic Cemetery Association - 1730 N. 18th St., Quincy, IL 62301 t) 217-223-3390 qrcca@comcast.net Rev. Msgr. Leo J. Enlow, Cemetery Mgr.;

St. Boniface Cemetery, Quincy - lenlow@dio.org

Calvary Cemetery, Quincy - lenlow@dio.org

St. Peter Cemetery, Quincy - lenlow@dio.org

SPRINGFIELD

Calvary Cemetery Association - 2001 N. 1st St., Springfield, IL 62702 t) 217-523-3726 director@calvary.com Lydia Templin-Collins, Dir.;

CAMPUS MINISTRY / NEWMAN CENTERS [CAM]

CARLINVILLE

Blackburn College Newman Club - 2010 E. 1st South St., Carlinville, IL 62626; Mailing: P.O. Box 647, Carlinville, IL 62626 t) 217-854-7151 Rev. Joseph Koyickal, S.A.C., Chap.;

CHARLESTON

Eastern Illinois University Newman Catholic Center - 500 Roosevelt Ave., Charleston, IL 61920 t) 217-348-0188 newman@eiunewman.org www.eiunewman.org Rev. Joseph Braden Maher, Chap.; Doris Nordin, Campus Min.; Emily Rogers, Campus Min.; Roy Lanham, Dir.; Maureen Smith, Dir. Devel.;

DECATUR

Millikin University Newman Catholic Community - 1184 W. Main St., Decatur, IL 62522; Mailing: 407 E Eldorado St., Decatur, IL 62523 t) 309-846-3949 tprior@millikn.edu www.munewman.org Rev. Michael Trummer, Assoc. Pst.; Rev. Michael Friedel, Chap.; Tom Prior, Campus Min.;

EDWARDSVILLE
Southern Illinois University Edwardsville Catholic Campus Ministry - Cougar Village, Bldg. 531, Apt. 1A, Edwardsville, IL 62025; Mailing: Campus Box 1168, Edwardsville, IL 62026 c) 618-402-3107 roblack@siue.edu www.siuenewmancatholic.com Robin Renee' Black-Rubenstein, Dir.;
JACKSONVILLE
Illinois College Newman Catholic Community - 1101 W. College Ave., Jacksonville, IL 62650; Mailing: 453 E. State St., Jacksonville, IL 62650 t) 217-245-6184 office@ospchurch.com Rev. Joseph G Ring, Chap.;
TEUTOPOLIS
***Newman Connection, Inc.** - 902 W. Main St., Teutopolis, IL 62467 t) 866-815-2034 mniebrugge@newmanconnection.com www.newmanconnection.com Matthew Zerrusen, Pres.; Michele Niebrugge, Treas.; William Zerrusen, Exec.; Rev. Robert Lampitt, Dir.; Rev. Tony Stephens, C.P.M., Dir.;

CATHOLIC CHARITIES [CCH]

ALTON
Madison County Catholic Charities - 3512 McArthur Blvd., Alton, IL 62002 t) 618-462-0634 burton_ccmc@cc.dio.org cc.dio.org Denise Burton, Dir.; Asstd. Annu.: 10,443; Staff: 6
BEARDSTOWN
St. Anne Residence - 309 E. Ninth St., Beardstown, IL 62618 t) 800-745-5194 wessing@cc.dio.org cc.dio.org Steven E. Roach, Exec.; Asstd. Annu.: 23; Staff: 2
CARLINVILLE
Carlinville Catholic Charities - 525 W. Second S., Carlinville, IL 62626 t) 217-854-4511 kelly_cccarl@cc.dio.org cc.dio.org John Kelly, Dir.; Asstd. Annu.: 15,097; Staff: 10
DECATUR
Catholic Charities of Decatur - 247 W. Prairie Ave., Decatur, IL 62523 t) 217-428-3458 fritzgerald_dec@cc.dio.org cc.dio.org Greg Fritzgerald, Dir.; Asstd. Annu.: 33,684; Staff: 21
GRANITE CITY
Madison County Catholic Charities - 1821 Edison Ave., Granite City, IL 62040 t) 618-877-1184 burton_ccmc@cc.dio.org cc.dio.org Denise Burton, Dir.; Asstd. Annu.: 1,680; Staff: 6
MATTOON
Catholic Charities of Coles, Douglas and Edgar Counties - 4217 Dewitt Ave., Mattoon, IL 61938 t) 217-235-0420 honn_matt@cc.dio.org cc.dio.org Amanda Honn, Dir.; Asstd. Annu.: 27,768; Staff: 16
QUINCY
Quincy Catholic Charities - 620 Maine St., Quincy, IL 62301 t) 217-222-0958 williams_qcc@cc.dio.org cc.dio.org Kevin Williams, Dir.; Asstd. Annu.: 16,937; Staff: 11
SPRINGFIELD
Catholic Charities Diocese of Springfield in Illinois - 1625 W. Washington St., Springfield, IL 62702 t) 217-523-9201 drake@cc.dio.org; perine@cc.dio.org Steven E. Roach, Dir.; Asstd. Annu.: 1,224; Staff: 19
Catholic Charities of Springfield - 120 S. 11th St., Springfield, IL 62702 t) 217-523-4551 mcconnell_spfld@cc.dio.org cc.dio.org Patrick McConnell, Dir.; Asstd. Annu.: 166,837; Staff: 24
Crisis Assistance & Advocacy and Holy Family Food Pantry - 120 S. 11th St., Springfield, IL 62702
St. John's Breadline - 430 N. 5th St., Springfield, IL 62702 t) 217-528-6098 sharris_stjb@cc.dio.org
TEUTOPOLIS
Effingham Catholic Charities - 1502 E. Fayette, Teutopolis, IL 62467; Mailing: P.O. Box 1017, Teutopolis, IL 62467 t) 217-857-1458 srcarol_ceff@cc.dio.org cc.dio.org Sr. Carol Beckermann, O.S.F., Dir.; Asstd. Annu.: 55,900; Staff: 16
WOOD RIVER
Society of St. Vincent de Paul (Diocesan Central Council) - 345 E. Acton Ave., Wood River, IL 62095 t) 618-254-0679 mwkwr@aol.com Marie Kladar, Pres.; Asstd. Annu.: 127; Staff: 5

COLLEGES & UNIVERSITIES [COL]

QUINCY
Quincy University Corporation - 1800 College Ave., Quincy, IL 62301 t) 800-688-4295; 217-228-5432; 217-222-8020 admissions@quincy.edu; qualumni@quincy.edu www.quincy.edu Brian Robert McGee, Pres.; Rev. John Doctor, O.F.M., Vice Pres. Mission & Ministry & Univ. Chap.; Tom Oliver, Vice Pres., Enrollment Mgmt.; Teresa Reed, Vice Pres., Academic Affairs; Mark Strieker, Vice Pres., Finance; Bro. Terrence Santiapillai, O.F.M., Librn.; Stds.: 1,258; Lay Tchrs.: 53

CONVENTS, MONASTERIES, AND RESIDENCES FOR WOMEN [CON]

ALTON
St. Francis Convent - 1 Franciscan Way, Alton, IL 62002 t) 618-463-2765 vocations@altonfranciscans.org; secretariat@altonfranciscans.org www.altonfranciscans.org Rev. Stephen T. Sotiroff, Chap.; Mother M. Mediatrix Bexten, F.S.G.M., Prov.; Srs.: 111
Ursuline Convent of the Holy Family of the Ursuline Nuns of the Roman Union - 100 Glenhaven Dr., Alton, IL 62002; Mailing: 353 S. Sappington Rd., St. Louis, MO 63122 t) (314) 821-6884 mbeisiegel40@hotmail.com Sr. Mary B Beisiegel, OSU, Prioress; Srs.: 7
DECATUR
St. Francis Convent - 4145 Sunderland Dr., Decatur, IL 62526 t) 217-877-2278 rmenachery@hsosf-usa.org www.hospitalsisters.org Hospital Sisters of St. Francis-USA, Inc. Sr. Rosily Menachery, Rel. Ord. Ldr.; Srs.: 2
GIRARD
Monastery of Mary the Queen, Dominican Nuns-Order of Preachers - 15635 Greenridge Rd., Girard, IL 62640 t) (217) 627-2023 srannamarie@gmail.com opnunsil.org Sr. Anna Pierre, Prioress; Srs.: 15
SPRINGFIELD
Dominican Sisters of Springfield, Il - 1237 W. Monroe St., Springfield, IL 62704-1680 t) 217-787-0481 sragemma@spdom.org www.springfieldop.org Motherhouse and Novitiate of the Dominican Sisters of Springfield, Illinois. Sr. Rose Miriam Schulte, Vicar; Rev. Michael DeTemple, OP, Chap.; Sr. Ann Clennon, OP, Prioress; Sr. Rebecca Ann Gemma, O.P., Prioress; Srs.: 140
St. Francis Convent - 4849 LaVerna Rd., Springfield, IL 62707 t) 217-522-3386 rmenachery@hsosf-usa.org www.hospitalsisters.org Hospital Sisters of St. Francis-USA, Inc. Sr. Christa Ann Struewing, Rel. Ord. Ldr.; Sr. Maureen O'Connor, O.S.F., Prov.; Srs.: 30
St. Francis Convent - 2717 Arrowhead, Springfield, IL 62702 t) 217-528-6492 rmenachery@hsosf-usa.org www.hospitalsisters.org Hospital Sisters of St. Francis-USA, Inc. Sr. Rosily Menachery, Rel. Ord. Ldr.; Srs.: 2
Hospital Sisters of St. Francis-USA, Inc. - 4849 LaVerna Rd., Springfield, IL 62707 t) 217-522-3386 jschneider@hsosf-usa.org www.hospitalsisters.org Sr. Janice Schneider, Treas.; Srs.: 43
Missionary Sisters of the Sacred Heart of Jesus "Ad Gentes" - 260 N. Amos Ave., Springfield, IL 62702 c) 217-331-4983 ofelia.quiroz@gmail.com adgenteshuamantla.blogspot.com/ Sr. Ofelia Quiroz-Martinez, M.A.G., Supr.; Sr. Ma.Ema Soto Enriquez, MAG, Subprior; Srs.: 2
St. Francis Convent - 2101 Shabbona, Springfield, IL 62702 t) 217-789-4936 moconnor@hsosf-usa.org www.hospitalsisters.org Hospital Sisters of St. Francis-USA, Inc. Sr. Maureen O'Connor, O.S.F., Prov.; Srs.: 2
St. Francis Convent - 52 W. Fairview Ln., Springfield, IL 62711; Mailing: 4849 LaVerna Rd., Springfield, IL 62707 t) 217-522-3386 moconnor@hsosf-usa.org www.hospitalsisters.org Hospital Sisters of St. Francis-USA, Inc. Sr. Maureen O'Connor, O.S.F., Prov.;
Ursuline Convent - 2520 St. James Rd., Springfield, IL 62707 c) (217) 341-5442 www.osucentral.org Sr. Theresa Davey, OSU, Prioress; Srs.: 4

ENDOWMENTS / FOUNDATIONS / TRUSTS [EFT]

SPRINGFIELD
Dominican Sisters of Springfield in Illinois Charitable Trust - Sacred Heart Convent, 1237 W. Monroe, Springfield, IL 62704-1680 t) 217-787-0481 sragemma@spdom.org; mdsolano@spdom.org www.springfieldop.org Dan Anderson, Treas.;
The Foundation for the People of the Roman Catholic Diocese of Springfield in Illinois - 1615 W. Washington St., Springfield, IL 62702 t) 217-698-8500 x121 kprice@dio.org Most Rev. Thomas J. Paprocki;
Hospital Sisters of St. Francis Foundation, Inc. - 4936 LaVerna Rd., Springfield, IL 62794-9456; Mailing: P.O. Box 19456, Springfield, IL 62794-9456 t) 217-523-4747 daniel.mccormack@hshs.org Daniel McCormack, Pres.;

HOSPITALS / HEALTH SERVICES [HOS]

ALTON
OSF HealthCare Saint Anthony's Health Center - 1 Saint Anthony's Way, Alton, IL 62002-0340 t) 618-465-2571 robert.brandfass@osfhealthcare.org www.osfhealthcare.org Two Campuses: OSF Saint Anthony's Health Center and OSF Saint Clare's Hospital Rev. Stephen T. Sotiroff, Chap.; Jerry Rumph, Pres.; Bed Capacity: 140; Asstd. Annu.: 92,575; Staff: 810
DECATUR
St. Mary's Hospital - 1800 E. Lake Shore Dr., Decatur, IL 62521 t) 217-464-2473 amy.bulpitt@hshs.org www.stmarysdecatur.com Rev. Msgr. David J. Hoefler, Vicar; Theresa Rutherford, Pres.; Bed Capacity: 218; Asstd. Annu.: 106,191; Staff: 677
EFFINGHAM
St. Anthony's Memorial Hospital - 503 N. Maple St., Effingham, IL 62401 t) 217-342-2121 saecommunications@hshs.org www.stanthonyshospital.org Rev. Adam Prichard, Chap.; Chad Markham, CEO; Bed Capacity: 133; Asstd. Annu.: 73,498; Staff: 758
GREENVILLE
***HSHS Holy Family Hospital, Inc.** - 200 Healthcare Dr., Greenville, IL 62246 t) 618-690-3401 kelly.sager@hshs.org Rev. Alan Hunter, Chap.; Kelly Sager, CEO; Bed Capacity: 43; Asstd. Annu.: 32,170; Staff: 108
HIGHLAND
HSHS St. Joseph's Hospital - 12866 Troxler Ave., Highland, IL 62249 t) 618-651-2600 amy.bulpitt@hshs.org www.stjosephshighland.org Rev. Pat G. Jakel, Chap.; John A. Ludwig, Pres.; Bed Capacity: 25; Asstd. Annu.: 37,099; Staff: 225
LITCHFIELD
St. Francis Hospital - 1215 Franciscan Dr., Litchfield, IL 62056; Mailing: P.O. Box 1215, Litchfield, IL 62056 t) 217-324-2191 amy.bulpitt@hshs.org www.stfrancis-litchfield.org Jim Timpe, CEO; Bed Capacity: 25; Asstd. Annu.: 42,068; Staff: 237
SHELBYVILLE
***HSHS Good Shepherd Hospital, Inc.** - 200 S. Cedar St., Shelbyville, IL 62565 t) 217-774-3961 Chad Markham, CEO; Bed Capacity: 18; Asstd. Annu.: 7,046; Staff: 75
SPRINGFIELD
St. John's Hospital - 800 E. Carpenter St., Springfield, IL 62769 t) 217-544-6464 www.st-johns.org Damond Boatwright, CEO; Bed Capacity: 368; Asstd. Annu.: 546,378; Staff: 2,587

MISCELLANEOUS [MIS]

MT. ZION
Legion of Mary - 400 N. Whitetail Cir., Mt. Zion, IL 62549-1409; Mailing: C/O Jan Mudd, 925 Woodland Dr., Mt. Zion, IL 62549 t) 217-864-3467 olbssecretary@hotmail.com Janice Mudd, Pres.;
NEW BERLIN
Jubilee Farm, NFP - 6760 Old Jacksonville Rd., New Berlin, IL 62670-6747 t) 217-787-6927

jubilee.farm@comcast.net www.jubileefarm.info Sr. Rose Marie Riley, Dir.; Sr. Sharon Zayac, O.P., Treas.;

QUINCY

Ladies of Charity of Quincy - 510 S. 4th St., Quincy, IL 62301 t) 217-222-6359 locquincy11@yahoo.com Brenda Ehrhardt, Pres.; Kathleen Cecilia Obert, Pres.;

Priestly Fraternity of St. Peter - 1009 N. 8th St., Quincy, IL 62301-1845 t) 217-222-2511 saintrosequincy@att.net; st-rose-quincy@att.net www.saintrosequincy.org Rev. Karl A. Pikus, F.S.S.P, Pst.; Rev. Arnaud Devillers, In Res.;

SPRINGFIELD

Catholic Care Center, Inc. - 1615 W. Washington St., Springfield, IL 62702 t) 217-698-8500 x195 gfleck@dio.org www.dio.org Rev. Msgr. David J. Hoefler, Admin.; Gregory K.J. Fleck, Exec.; Steven E. Roach, Dir.; Chris Sommer, Dir.;

Diocesan Care Management, Inc. - 1615 W. Washington St., Springfield, IL 62702 t) 217-698-8500 x195 gfleck@dio.org www.dio.org Rev. Msgr. David J. Hoefler, Admin.; Chris Sommer, Treas.; Gregory K.J. Fleck, Exec.;

The Evermode Institute - 4875 LaVerna Rd., Springfield, IL 62707 Rev. Ambrose Criste, O.Praem., Exec. Dir.;

St. Francis Catholic Services Corporation - 4875 LaVerna Rd., Springfield, IL 62707 t) (217) 522-3387 x523 Gregory Fleck, Dir.; Charlie O'Malley, Bus. Mgr.;

Hospital Sisters Health System - 4936 LaVerna Rd., Springfield, IL 62794-9456; Mailing: P.O. Box 19456, Springfield, IL 62794-9456 t) 217-523-4747 amy.bulpitt@hshs.org Damond Boatwright, CEO;

Hospital Sisters Mission Outreach Corporation - 4930 LaVerna Rd., Springfield, IL 62705; Mailing: P.O. Box 1665, Springfield, IL 62705-1665 t) 217-525-8843 amy.bulpitt@hshs.org www.mission-outreach.org Damond Boatwright, CEO;

Hospital Sisters Services, Inc. - 4936 LaVerna Rd., Springfield, IL 62794-9456; Mailing: P.O. Box 19456, Springfield, IL 62794-9456 t) 217-523-4747 amy.bulpitt@hshs.org Damond Boatwright, CEO;

***HSHS Medical Group, Inc.** - 3051 Hollis Dr., Springfield, IL 62704 t) 217-523-4747 amy.bulpitt@hshs.org Marc Shelton, Chair;

Leadership Conference of Women Religious - 1237 W. Monroe St., Springfield, IL 62704; Mailing: 5327 S. Ellis Ave., Chicago, IL 60615 c) 312-590-3306 bpawlicki@sinsinawa.org Sr. Betsy Pawlicki, OP, Chairperson;

St. Martin De Porres Center, Inc. - 1725 S. Grand Ave., E., Springfield, IL 62703 t) 217-698-8500 dhoefler@dio.org Rev. Msgr. David J. Hoefler, Vicar General;

***Prairie Cardiovascular Consultants, Ltd.** - 3051 Hollis Dr., Springfield, IL 62704

***Prairie Education and Research Cooperative** - 326 N. 7th St., Springfield, IL 62701 t) 217-523-4747 amy.bulpitt@hshs.org Healthcare Education and Research Marc Shelton, Pres.;

Priests' Purgatorial Society - 1615 W. Washington St., Springfield, IL 62702 t) 217-698-8500 dhoefler@dio.org Catholic Pastoral Center Rev. Msgr. David J. Hoefler, Contact;

***Springfield Developmental Center Ltd.** - 4595 LaVerna Rd., Springfield, IL 62707 t) 217-525-8271 director@spflddevcenter.org; officemanager@spflddevcenter.org Developmental Training Program for Adults with Disabilities. Franciscan Brothers of the Holy Cross. Kathryn Clark, Dir.;

St. Francis Catholic Property Trust - 4875 LaVerna Rd., Springfield, IL 62707 t) (217) 522-3387 x523 Gregory Fleck, Exec. Dir.;

Villa Maria - Catholic Life Center - 1903 E. Lake Shore Dr, Springfield, IL 62712-5514 t) 217-529-2213 villamaria@dio.org; gmaynerich@villa.dio.org villa.dio.org (Retreat and Conference Center) Dcn. Gregory Maynerich, Dir.;

VANDALIA

***Our Sorrowful Mothers Ministry** - 318 N 8th St., Vandalia, IL 62471 c) 618-322-2946 osmm@sbcglobal.net osmm.org Rev. Seth A. Brown, Chap.;

MONASTERIES AND RESIDENCES FOR PRIESTS AND BROTHERS [MON]

MADISON

Canons Regular of Saint Thomas Aquinas - 1621 10th St., Madison, IL 62060 c) 281-677-1510 brmichael@traditionalcanons.org traditionalcanons.org/ Bro. Michael Thomas Connaughton, STA, Prior; Brs.: 2

QUINCY

Holy Cross Friary (Quincy University Friary) - 724 N. 20th St., Quincy, IL 62301 t) 217-223-9920 doctojo@quincy.edu Bro. Terence Santiapillai, O.F.M., Supr.; Rev. John Doctor, O.F.M., Vice. Pres.; Rev. Irenaeus Kimminau, O.F.M., In Res.; Rev. James Wheeler, O.F.M., Sacramental Min.; Rev. Joseph Zimmerman, O.F.M., Sacramental Min.; Albert Merz, Bus. Mgr.; Brs.: 1; Priests: 5

SPRINGFIELD

Franciscan Brothers of the Holy Cross - 2500 Saint James Rd., Springfield, IL 62707-9736 t) 217-528-4757 c) 217-652-1829 br.stephen@franciscanbrothers.net www.franciscanbrothers.net Bro. Stephen Bissler, F.F.S.C., Supr.; Brs.: 5

TEUTOPOLIS

St. Francis Assisi Friary - 203 E. Main St., Teutopolis, IL 62467-0730; Mailing: P.O. Box 730, Teutopolis, IL 62467-0730 t) 217-964-0461 Rev. Joseph P. Carlos, O.F.M., Pst.; Rev. Frank Folino, O.F.M., Pst.; Rev. Dat Hoang, OFM, Vicar; Rev. Dennis Koopman, OFM, Vicar; Priests: 4

PRESCHOOLS / CHILDCARE CENTERS [PRE]

ALTON

Catholic Children's Home - 1400 State St., Alton, IL 62002 t) 618-465-3594 info@catholicchildrenshome.com catholicchildrenshome.com Michael Montez, Admin.; Kim Speidel, Prin.; Steven Roach, Exec.; Stds.: 57; Lay Tchrs.: 5

St. Francis Day Care Center - 710 College Ave., Alton, IL 62002 t) 618-463-2766 saintfrancisdaycare@gmail.com Sr. M. Kateri Hawley, F.S.G.M., Dir.; Stds.: 149; Lay Tchrs.: 24

SEMINARIES [SEM]

GODFREY

Immaculate Heart of Mary Novitiate - 4300 Levis Ln., Godfrey, IL 62035 t) 618-466-0673 frankomi58@icloud.com Rev. Frank Kuczera, Dir.; Bro. George Litiya, OMI, In Res.; Bro. Tchrs.: 1; Pr. Tchrs.: 1

An asterisk (*) denotes an organization that has established tax-exempt status directly with the IRS and is not covered by the USCCB Group Ruling.

Diocese of Springfield in Massachusetts

(Dioecesis Campifontis)

MOST REVEREND WILLIAM D. BYRNE

Bishop of Springfield in Massachusetts; ordained June 25, 1994; appointed Bishop of Springfield in Massachusetts October 14, 2020; consecrated and installed December 14, 2020.

Chancery Office: 76 Elliot St., P.O. Box 1730, Springfield, MA 01102-1730. T: 413-732-3175; F: 413-737-2337.
www.diospringfield.org
mail@diospringfield.org

ESTABLISHED JUNE 14, 1870.

Square Miles 2,822.

Comprises the Counties of Berkshire, Franklin, Hampden and Hampshire in the Commonwealth of Massachusetts.

For legal titles of parishes and diocesan institutions, consult the Chancery Office.

STATISTICAL OVERVIEW

Personnel

Bishop	1
Retired Bishops	1
Priests: Diocesan Active in Diocese	109
Priests: Retired, Sick or Absent	48
Number of Diocesan Priests	157
Religious Priests in Diocese	26
Total Priests in your Diocese	183
Extern Priests in Diocese	4
Permanent Deacons in Diocese	102
Total Brothers	9
Total Sisters	218

Parishes

Parishes	76
With Resident Pastor:	
Resident Diocesan Priests	58
Resident Religious Priests	5
Without Resident Pastor:	
Administered by Priests	11
Administered by Deacons	2
Missions	9
Pastoral Centers	1
New Parishes Created	1
Closed Parishes	2

Welfare

Catholic Hospitals	1
Total Assisted	253,409
Homes for the Aged	5
Total Assisted	867
Day Care Centers	4
Total Assisted	368
Specialized Homes	3
Total Assisted	325
Special Centers for Social Services	4
Total Assisted	67,350

Educational

Diocesan Students in Other Seminaries	2
Total Seminarians	2
Colleges and Universities	1
Total Students	1,275
High Schools, Diocesan and Parish	2
Total Students	500
Elementary Schools, Diocesan and Parish	12
Total Students	2,531
Catechesis / Religious Education:	
High School Students	2,203
Elementary Students	4,197
Total Students under Catholic Instruction	10,708
Teachers in Diocese:	
Priests	1
Sisters	1
Lay Teachers	246

Vital Statistics

Receptions into the Church:	
Infant Baptism Totals	1,077
Minor Baptism Totals	80
Adult Baptism Totals	53
Received into Full Communion	165
First Communions	1,200
Confirmations	1,319
Marriages:	
Catholic	205
Interfaith	27
Total Marriages	232
Deaths	2,916
Total Catholic Population	159,379
Total Population	826,188

LEADERSHIP

Bishop's Office - t) (413) 452-0803 diocesan website: www.diospringfield.org Most Rev. William D. Byrne; Stacy Dibbern;

Notary - t) (413) 452-0803 Stacy Dibbern;

Cabinet (Diocesan) - t) (413) 452-0803 www.diospringfield.org/cabinet

Chancellor and Vicar for Canonical Affairs - t) (413) 452-0802 www.diospringfield.org/office-of-the-chancellors Very Rev. John G. Lessard-Thibodeau;

Chancery Office - t) (413) 452-0802 Very Rev. John G. Lessard-Thibodeau, Chancellor;

College of Consultors - t) (413) 452-0802 www.diospringfield.org/college-of-consultors

Finance Officer - t) (413) 452-0614 Michael Ford;

Judicial Vicar - t) (413) 452-0790 www.diospringfield.org/tribunal-chambers Rev. Msgr. John J. Bonzagni;

Presbyteral Council - list at www.diospringfield.org/presbyteral-council

Deans - list at www.diospringfield.org/viacariate-deanery

Tribunal - t) (413) 452-0790 www.diospringfield.org/tribunal-chambers Rev. Msgr. John J. Bonzagni, Judicial Vicar/Attorney at Law; Very Rev. John G. Lessard-Thibodeau, Adjutant Judicial Vicar; Carmen Martinez, Administrative Asst.;

Notary - t) (413) 452-0790 Carmen Martinez;

Vicar General and Moderator of the Curia - t) (413) 452-0610 Very Rev. Piotr Calik;

Vicars for the Clergy - t) (413) 452-0802 Rev. Msgr. John J. Bonzagni; Rev. Mark S. Stelzer;

OFFICES AND DIRECTORS

Annual Catholic Appeal - t) (413) 452-0670; (413) 452-0838 aca@diospringfield.org Kathleen Harrington; Jonathan Van Beaver;

Apostolate to the Handicapped - t) (413) 532-0713 www.jerichobeca.org Sr. Joan Magnani, S.S.J., Dir.; Rev. John Hurley, Chap.;

Black Catholic Apostolate - t) (413) 563-7518; (413) 781-3656 Marion M. Johnson;

Campaign for Human Development - t) (413) 452-0606 Kathryn Buckley-Brawner;

Catholic Charities Agency - t) (413) 452-0606 Kathryn Buckley-Brawner;

Catholic Communications Corporation - t) (413) 452-0645 Mark Dupont, CEO;

Catholic Latino Ministry - t) (413) 452-0631 Dcn. Pedro Rivera-Moran;

Catholic Relief Services - t) (413) 452-0606 Kathryn Buckley-Brawner;

Cemeteries (Diocesan) - t) (413) 782-4731 www.diospringfieldcemeteries.org Brian Kennedy;

Censor Librorum - t) (413) 566-8843 Rev. Mark S. Stelzer, Librn.;

Clergy Counseling Service - t) (413) 732-3721 Rev. Msgr. George A. Farland;

Communications and Public Relations - Mark Dupont; Carolee McGrath;

Catholic Communications Corporation - Mark Dupont, CEO;

Chalice of Salvation (Televised Mass) - t) (413) 452-0642 Bro. Terrence A. Scanlon, C.P., Exec.;

The Catholic Mirror (Magazine) - t) (413) 452-0636 Dr. Rebecca Drake, Editor;

Real to Reel (Television News Magazine) - t) (413) 452-0648 Sharon Roulier, Producer;

Continuing Education for Priests - t) (413) 265-2575 Rev. Warren J. Savage;

Cori and Virtus Coordinator - t) (413) 452-0662 Paula Denno;

Cursillo Movement - Dcn. Wendell Pennell;

Diocesan Office for Communications - t) (413) 737-4744 Mark Dupont;

iobserve - t) (413) 452-0636 www.iobserve.org Dr. Rebecca Drake, Editor;

Diocesan Website - t) (413) 452-0682 www.diospringfield.org Barbie Bagley, Graphic Artist / Production Asst.;

Education (Diocesan Catholic Schools Office) - t) (413) 452-0830 Maria Wagner, Supt. (m.wagner@diospringfield.org);

Facilities & Maintenance - t) (413) 452-0695 diospringfield.org (facilities & maintenance) Russell Sprague;

Facilities and Maintenance Commission - t) (413) 452-0529 diospringfield.org (facilities & maintenance comm)

Fiscal Affairs - t) (413) 452-0672 Michael Ford, Finance Officer; Jennifer Mallette, Dir. Accounting;

Holy Childhood Association - Very Rev. John G. Lessard-Thibodeau;

Holy Family League of Charity - t) (413) 732-3175

Human Resources - t) (413) 452-0683 Catherine Farr, Dir.; Annette Plourde, Payroll & Benefits Mgr.;

Notary - t) (413) 452-0691 Annette Plourde;

Massachusetts Catholic Conference - t) (413) 732-3175 Most Rev. William D. Byrne; Sr. Annette McDermott, S.S.J.; John Egan;

Ministry to Retired Priests - t) (413) 732-3175 Rev. John A. Roach, Co-Vicar for Retired Priests; Rev. Thomas M. Shea, Co-Vicar for Retired Priests; Susan Wehner, Wellness Coord.;

Ministry to the Deaf - Kay Woods;

Newman Apostolate and Campus Ministry - t) (413) 549-0300 www.newmanumass.org Rev. Gary M. Dailey, Dir.; Rev. John P. McDonagh, Dir.; Rev. Valentine Onyeka Nworah, Chap.;

Office of Divine Worship - t) (413) 452-0839 Rev. William Hamilton, Dir.;

Office of Faith Formation - t) (413) 452-0841 Celeste Labbe, Dir.;

Office of Safe Environment and Victim Assistance - t) (413) 452-0662 Norman Charest, Interim Dir.; Paula Denno, Admin. Asst.;

Office of Social Concerns - t) (413) 452-0662 Norman Charest, Interim Dir.;

Pastoral Ministry - t) (413) 732-3175

Permanent Diaconate - t) (413) 452-0674 www.spflddiaconate.org Dcn. David Picard, Dir.; Josie-Anne Holdsworth, Admin Asst;

Pro-Life Activities (Office of) - t) (413) 732-3175 Rev. Daniel S. Pacholec, Dir.;

Propagation of the Faith - t) (413) 452-0800 Very Rev. John G. Lessard-Thibodeau, Dir.;

Refugee Resettlement Program/Immigration Services - t) (413) 452-0626 Edyta Ras;

Southeast Asian Apostolate - t) (413) 737-4422 Rev. Peter Ha Dinh Dang, Dir.;

Victim Assistance Coordinator - t) (413) 452-0662 Norman Charest, Interim Dir.;

Vocations (Office of) - t) (413) 452-0816 www.myvocation.com Most Rev. William D. Byrne, Dir.; Rev. David M. Darcy, Dir. Seminarians; Rev. Jonathan Reardon, Dir. Recruiting;

Young Adult Ministry (Office of) - t) (413) 452-0677 Joseph Austin, Dir.;

Youth Ministry (Office of) - t) (413) 452-0677 Joseph Austin, Dir.;

ADVISORY BOARDS, COMMISSIONS, COMMITTEES, AND COUNCILS

Commission for the Liturgy - t) (413) 452-0839 Rev. William Hamilton;

Diaconate Formation Board - t) (413) 452-0674 list at www.spflddiaconate.org

Priest Personnel Board - t) (413) 452-0802 www.diospringfield.org/priest-personnel-board

Deacon Council - t) (413) 452-0674 diaconate@diospringfield.org www.spflddiaconate.org

CLERGY AND RELIGIOUS SERVICES

Delegate for the Consecrated Life - t) (413) 452-0656 Rev. Augustine Judd, O.P.;

Wellness Coordinator - t) (413) 452-0697 Rev. John A. Roach; Rev. Thomas M. Shea; Susan Wehner;

ORGANIZATIONS

The Saint Thomas More Society - Dcn. William Kern, Pres.;

TRIBUNAL

Auditors - www.diospringfield.org/tribunal-chambers

Judges - t) (413) 452-0790 Rev. Msgr. John J. Bonzagni; Very Rev. John G. Lessard-Thibodeau; Rev. Msgr. Christopher D. Connelly;

Defender of the Bond - t) (413) 452-0790 Rev. John P. McDonagh; Rev. Michael Pierz;

Instructor Procurator-Advocate - t) (413) 452-0790 Very Rev. John G. Lessard-Thibodeau; Dcn. William F. Kern; Dcn. James Mc Elroy;

Promoter of Justice - t) (413) 452-0790 Very Rev. John G. Lessard-Thibodeau;

Psychological Consultants - t) (413) 452-0790 David Armstrong; Rev. J. Donald R. Lapointe; Rev. Msgr. George A. Farland, CAS Psychology;

PARISHES, MISSIONS, AND CLERGY

COMMONWEALTH OF MASSACHUSETTS

ADAMS

St. John Paul II Parish - 21 Maple St., Adams, MA 01220-0231 t) (413) 743-0577; (413) 749-7142 (Info) p.norman@diospringfield.org www.adamscatholicchurches.org Rev. Paul Norman, Pst.; CRP Stds.: 41

St. Stanislaus Cemetery -

AGAWAM

St. John the Evangelist - 833 Main St., Agawam, MA 01001 t) 413-786-8105 reled@stjohnagawam.org; sje.parishsecretary@gmail.com stjohnagawam.com/ Rev. Michael C. Lillpopp, Pst.; Rev. John Hurley, Par. Vicar; CRP Stds.: 84

In the Beginning Preschool - t) (413) 786-8105 sje.information@gmail.com www.stjohnagawam.com/ pre-school Stds.: 16; Lay Tchrs.: 3

AMHERST

St. Brigid's - 122 N. Pleasant St., Amherst, MA 01004-0424; Mailing: P.O. Box 424, Amherst, MA 01004-0424 t) (413) 256-6181 saintbrigidsamherst@gmail.com www.saintbrigidsamherst.org Rev. Gary M. Dailey, Admin.; CRP Stds.: 53

St. Brigid Cemetery -

BELCHERTOWN

St. Francis of Assisi - 24 Jabish St., Belchertown, MA 01007; Mailing: P.O. Box 612, Belchertown, MA 01007-0612 t) (413) 323-6272 x1 (Office); (413) 323-6272 x3 (Pastor); (413) 323-6272 x2 (CRP) francisatbtown@gmail.com www.stfrancisbelchertown.com Rev. David M. Darcy, Pst.; Melissa Hurst, DRE; Linda Racicot, DRE; CRP Stds.: 140

BRIMFIELD

St. Christopher's - 20 Sturbridge Rd., Rte. 20, Brimfield, MA 01010; Mailing: P.O. Box 387, Brimfield, MA 01010-0387 t) (413) 245-7274 stchrisbrimfield@gmail.com www.stpatstchris.org Rev. John J. Brennan, Pst.; CRP Stds.: 47

CHESHIRE

St. Mary of the Assumption - 159 Church St., Cheshire, MA 01225 t) (413) 743-2110 office@saintmaryscatholic.org www.stmaryscheshire.com Rev. Paul Norman, Pst.; CRP Stds.: 53

CHICOPEE

St. Anne's - 30 College St., Chicopee, MA 01020 t) (413)

533-8038 (Rel Ed); (413) 532-7503 saintanneparishchicopee@gmail.com www.saintanne.us Rev. Dennis Skowera, Pst.; CRP Stds.: 67

St. Anthony of Padua - 56 Saint Anthony St., Chicopee, MA 01013 t) (413) 538-9475; (413) 536-5142 info@stanthonychicopee.com; pastor@stanthonychicopee.com www.stanthonychicopee.com Rev. Jacek Leszczynski, OFMConv., Pst.; Dcn. Lino Sanmiguel; CRP Stds.: 7

Holy Name of Jesus - 94 Springfield St., Chicopee, MA 01013; Mailing: 104 Springfield St., Chicopee, MA 01013 t) (413) 594-8700 holynamechicopee@aol.com www.holynameofjesuschicopee.com Rev. William A. Tourigny, Pst.; Dcn. David Southworth, Parish Mgr.; Isamar Perez, CRE; CRP Stds.: 20

St. Patrick Cemetery - Fuller Rd., Chicopee, MA 01020

Calvary Cemetery - Hampden St., Chicopee, MA 01013

St. Rose de Lima - 600 Grattan St., Chicopee, MA 01020; Mailing: 15 Chapel St., Chicopee, MA 01020 t) (413) 536-4558 frbill@sterose.org www.sterose.org Rev. William A. Tourigny, Pst.; Dcn. Daniel Prats; Dcn. Michael Trznadel; CRP Stds.: 97

St. Joan of Arc - (Grades PreK-8) 587 Grattan St., Chicopee, MA 01020 t) (413) 533-1475 businessoffice@sjachicopee.org www.sjachicopee.org Paula Jenkins, Prin.; Irene Ruel, Librn.; Stds.: 204; Lay Tchrs.: 17

St. Rose Cemetery - t) (413) 536-6298

St. Stanislaus Basilica - 566 Front St., Chicopee, MA 01013; Mailing: 40 Cyman Dr., Chicopee, MA 01013 t) (413) 594-6669 contact@ststansbasilica.org www.ststansbasilica.org Rev. Brad A. Milunski, O.F.M.Conv., Pst.; Rev. John Koziol, O.F.M.Conv., Par. Vicar; Rev. Lucjan Szymanski, Par. Vicar; Dcn. Joseph Peters; Dcn. Michael Pray; Sr. Andrea Ciszewski, FSSJ, DRE; Sr. Agnesa Negru, FMSA, Pst. Min./Coord.; CRP Stds.: 55

St. Stanislaus Basilica School - (Grades PreK-8) 534 Front St., Chicopee, MA 01013 t) (413) 592-5135 ststanis@saintstansschool.org st.stanislaus.mec.edu Sr. Cecelia Haier, F.S.S.J., Prin.; Karen Shea, Prin.; Stds.: 310; Lay Tchrs.: 20

St. Stanislaus Cemetery -

DALTON

St. Agnes - 489 Main St., Dalton, MA 01226 t) (413) 684-1803 (CRP); (413) 684-0125 lstankiewicz@saintagnescc.com; cmalatesta@saintagnescc.com www.saintagnescc.com Rev. Christopher A. Malatesta, Pst.; Dcn. George Morrell; Dcn. Richard Radzick; Lisa Stankiewicz, DRE; CRP Stds.: 117

St. Agnes School - (Grades PreK-8) 30 Carson St., Dalton, MA 01226 t) (413) 684-3143 fmakdisi@saintagnescc.com Fadia Makdisi, Prin.; Stds.: 150; Lay Tchrs.: 10

St. Patrick Chapel - 43 Church St., Hinsdale, MA 01235; Mailing: 489 Main St., Dalton, MA 01226 info@saintagnescc.com

St. Patrick Cemetery -

EAST LONGMEADOW

St. Michael's - 110 Maple St., East Longmeadow, MA 01028; Mailing: 128 Maple St., East Longmeadow, MA 01028 t) (413) 525-4253 stmichaelsparishel@gmail.com www.stmichaelsel.org Rev. Wayne C. Biernat, Pst.; Beth Chase, Pst. Min./Coord.; CRP Stds.: 568

EASTHAMPTON

Our Lady of the Valley - 33 Adams St., Easthampton, MA 01027 t) (413) 527-9778 olveasthampton@gmail.com www.olveasthampton.org Rev. Ryan T. Sliwa, Admin.; CRP Stds.: 185

Our Lady's Child Care Center - (Grades PreK- 35 Pleasant St., Easthampton, MA 01027 t) (413) 527-6133 ourladyccc@charter.net Perri Taylor, Dir.; Stds.: 85; Lay Tchrs.: 17

St. Stanislaus Cemetery -

St. Brigid Cemetery -

FEEDING HILLS

Sacred Heart - 1065 Springfield St., Feeding Hills, MA 01030; Mailing: 1061 Springfield St., Feeding Hills, MA 01030 t) (413) 786-8200 office@sacredheartfeedinghills.org www.sacredheartfeedinghills.org Rev. Steven S. Amo, Pst.; Dcn. Brian Hunt; Lisa Raffia, DRE; CRP Stds.: 147

GRANBY

Immaculate Heart of Mary - 256 State St., Granby, MA 01033 t) (413) 467-9821 parishihmgranby@gmail.com www.ihmparishgranby.org Rev. Michael J. Goodreau, Admin.; CRP Stds.: 45

GREAT BARRINGTON

St. Peter Parish - 213 Main St., Great Barrington, MA 01230; Mailing: 16 Russell St., Great Barrington, MA 01230 t) (413) 528-1157; (413) 274-3443 (Office) st.petergb12@gmail.com Rev. William P. Murphy, Pst.; Dcn. Edward Shaw; CRP Stds.: 41

St. Peter Cemetery -

GREENFIELD

Blessed Trinity Parish - 221 Federal St., Greenfield, MA 01301; Mailing: 14 Beacon St., Greenfield, MA 01301 t) (413) 773-3311 office@blessedtrinitygreenfield.org www.catholiccommunityofgreenfield.org Rev. Michael Pierz, Pst.; Dcn. John Leary; Dcn. George Nolan; CRP Stds.: 54

Calvary Cemetery - Wisdom Way, Greenfield, MA 01301

Blessed Sacrament -

Holy Trinity - 133 Main St., Greenfield, MA 01301

Holy Trinity - 133 Main St., Greenfield, MA 01301-3209; Mailing: 14 Beacon St., Greenfield, MA 01301 t) 413-774-2884 holytrinitygreenfield@gmail.com www.holytrinitychurchgfld.org/ Rev. Michael Pierz, Pst.; Rev. Valentine Onyeka Nworah, Par. Vicar; Dcn. Channing L. Bete Jr.; Dcn. Paul F. DeCarlo; CRP Stds.: 39

HADLEY

Most Holy Redeemer - 120 Russell St., Hadley, MA 01035-0375 t) (413) 584-1326 mhrhadleychurch@gmail.com www.mhrhadley.org Rev. Douglas McGonagle, Pst.; Rev. William Hamilton, In Res.; John Gibbons, DRE; CRP Stds.: 27

Holy Rosary Cemetery - ; Mailing: P.O. Box 375, Hadley, MA 01035

HAMPDEN

Saint Mary's Parish, Hampden - 27 Somers Rd., Hampden, MA 01036 t) (413) 566-8843 Rev. Mark S. Stelzer, Pst.; CRP Stds.: 41

St. Mary Cemetery - www.stmaryshampden.org

HATFIELD

Our Lady of Grace Parish - 15 School St., Hatfield, MA 01038; Mailing: P.O. Box 34, Hatfield, MA 01038 t) (413) 247-9079 ourladyofgracehatfield@yahoo.com Rev. Douglas McGonagle, Pst.; Dcn. Mark Kolasinski, Parish Mgr.; CRP Stds.: 23

Calvary Cemetery - www.ourladyofgracehatfield.com

HAYDENVILLE

Our Lady of the Hills - 173 Main St., Haydenville, MA 01039-9768 t) (413) 268-7212 olothparish@gmail.com Rev. John Gawienowski, Admin.; CRP Stds.: 17

St. Mary Cemetery - www.olothhaydenville.org

HOLYOKE

Blessed Sacrament - 1945 Northampton St., Holyoke, MA 01040 t) (413) 532-0713 blsachol@comcast.net www.blessedsacramentholyoke.org Rev. Robert A. Gentile Jr., Pst.; Rev. Thomas M. Shea, In Res.; Kelly M. O'Connor, DRE; CRP Stds.: 131

Blessed Sacrament School - (Grades K-8) 21 Westfield Rd., Holyoke, MA 01040 t) (413) 536-2236 officebss@comcast.net Sue Heavren, Prin.; Stds.: 177; Lay Tchrs.: 55

Holyoke Soldier's Home Chapel - 110 Cherry St., Holyoke, MA 01040 t) (413) 532-9475 blsachol@comcast.net

St. Jerome - 181 Hampden St., Holyoke, MA 01040; Mailing: 169 Hampden St., Holyoke, MA 01040-4597 t) (413) 532-6381 st-jerome@comcast.net Rev. Francis Eugene Reilly, Pst.; Sr. Catherine Ormond, SSJ, Pst. Min./Coord.; CRP Stds.: 92

St. Jerome Cemetery - Rev. Francis E. Reilly;

Our Lady of the Cross - Holy Cross Ave., Holyoke, MA 01040; Mailing: 15 Maple St., Holyoke, MA 01040 t) (413) 532-5661 parish@ourladyofthecross.com www.ourladyofthecross.com Rev. Albert Scherer, OFM Conv., Pst.; Rev. Gregory Wierzowiecki, OFM Conv (Poland), Par. Vicar; Rev. James McCurry, OFM Conv., In Res.; Rev. Adam Ziolkowski, OFM Conv., In Res.; Rev. Jacek Leszczynski, OFMConv., In Res.; CRP Stds.: 20

Mater Dolorosa School - (Grades PreK-8) 25 Maple St., Holyoke, MA 01040 t) (413) 532-2831 b.brainard@materdolorosaschool.org www.materdolorosaschool.org Stds.: 180; Lay Tchrs.: 13

Mater Dolorosa Cemetery -

HOUSATONIC

Saint Teresa of Calcutta Parish - 1085 Main St., Housatonic, MA 01236; Mailing: P.O. Box 569, Housatonic, MA 01236-0569 t) (413) 274-3443 st.teresa9@gmail.com Rev. William P. Murphy, Pst.; Dcn. Edward Shaw; CRP Stds.: 28

St. Bridget Cemetery -

INDIAN ORCHARD

Immaculate Conception - 25 Parker St., Indian Orchard, MA 01151 t) (413) 543-3627 iccmaoffice@gmail.com www.indian-orchard-immaculate-conception.org Very Rev. Piotr S. Calik, Pst.; CRP Stds.: 27

LEE

St. Mary's - 140 Main St., Lee, MA 01238; Mailing: 40 Academy St., Lee, MA 01238 t) (413) 243-0275 lcsmchurch@gmail.com; stmaryleeccd@gmail.com www.stmarylos.com Rev. Brian F. McGrath, Pst.; Rev. Matthew Barone, Par. Vicar; CRP Stds.: 182

St. Mary's School - (Grades PreK-8) 115 Orchard St., Lee, MA 01238 t) (413) 243-1079 jmasten@stmaryslee.org www.stmaryslee.org Jennifer Masten, Prin.; Paula Salinetti, Librn.; Stds.: 113; Lay Tchrs.: 19

St. Mary of the Lakes - 72 N. Main Rd., Otis, MA 01253 lcsmchurch@gmail.com

Saint Joseph - 11 Elm St., Stockbridge, MA 01262 t) (413) 241-0275 lcsmchurch@gmail.com

St. Joseph Cemetery -

St. Mary Cemetery -

LENOX

St. Ann - 134 Main St., Lenox, MA 01240 t) (413) 637-0157; (413) 637-4027 (CRP) stannlenox@verizon.net www.avptriparish.org Rev. Msgr. John J. Bonzagni, Pst.; Dcn. Daniel Romanello; Dcn. John E. Zick; CRP Stds.: 53

St. Ann Cemetery -

LENOX DALE

St. Vincent de Paul - 29 Crystal St., Lenox Dale, MA 01242-0259; Mailing: P.O. Box 3, Lenox Dale, MA 01242 t) (413) 637-0157 stvincentlenoxdale@gmail.com www.avptriparish.org Rev. Msgr. John J. Bonzagni, Pst.; Dcn. Daniel Romanello; Dcn. John E. Zick;

LONGMEADOW

St. Mary's - 519 Longmeadow St., Longmeadow, MA 01106 t) (413) 567-3124; (413) 567-3420 (CRP) parishoffice@stmarylong.org www.stmarylong.org Rev. Christopher J. Waitekus, Pst.; Dcn. Donald J. Higby; CRP Stds.: 322

St. Mary's School - (Grades PreK-8) 56 Hopkins Pl., Longmeadow, MA 01106 t) (413) 567-0907 jmacdonald@stmaryslongmeadow.org www.stmaryslongmeadow.org Joan MacDonald, Prin.; Stds.: 242; Lay Tchrs.: 18

LUDLOW

Christ the King - 41 Warsaw Ave., Ludlow, MA 01056 t) (413) 583-2630 ctkludlow@gmail.com Rev. Raymond A. Soltys, Pst.; Tom Foye, DRE; CRP Stds.: 61

Saint Elizabeth Parish - 191 Hubbard St., Ludlow, MA 01056; Mailing: 181 Hubbard St., Ludlow, MA 01056 t) (413) 583-4204 (CRP); (413) 583-3467 c) (413) 478-4178 ebarone@stelizabethludlow.org;

lgroux@stelizabethludlow.org www.stelizabethludlow.org Rev. Msgr. Homer P. Gosselin, Pst.; Rev. Norman B. Bolton, In Res.; Dcn. Normand Grondin; Dcn. Thomas Rickson; Dcn. Keith Davies; Leslie A Groux, Bus. Mgr.; Michele Witowski, DRE; CRP Stds.: 182

St. Elizabeth Parish School (St. John the Baptist School) - (Grades PreK-8) 217 Hubbard St., Ludlow, MA 01056 t) (413) 583-8550 sjbsoffice@gmail.com; sjbsprincipal@gmail.com www.sjbludlow.org Shelly Rose, Prin.; Stds.: 194; Lay Tchrs.: 11

Our Lady of Fatima - 438 Winsor St., Ludlow, MA 01056 t) (413) 583-2312; (416) 583-2312 (CRP) fatima7687@charter.net www.ourladyoffatimaparish.org Rev. Pedro de Oliveira, O.F.M. Conv., Pst.; Margarita Rego, DRE; CRP Stds.: 178

MONSON

St. Patrick's - 22 Green St., Monson, MA 01057; Mailing: P.O. Box 473, Monson, MA 01057-0473 t) (413) 267-3622 stpatmon@aol.com www.stpatstchris.org Rev. John J. Brennan, Pst.; Dcn. Gary Doane; Dcn. Bernard Pellissier; CRP Stds.: 42

Bethany Cemetery -

NORTH ADAMS

Saint Elizabeth of Hungary Parish - 70 Marshall St., North Adams, MA 01247 t) (413) 663-5316 stelizabethofhungaryna@gmail.com www.stelizabethofhungaryparish.org Rev. Dariusz P. Wudarski, Pst.; Dcn. George Galli; Connie Therrien, DRE; CRP Stds.: 92

St. Joseph Cemetery -

NORTHAMPTON

Saint Elizabeth Ann Seton - 99 King St., Northampton, MA 01060; Mailing: 87 Beacon St., Florence, MA 01062 t) (413) 584-7310 maryrogers@saintelizabethannseton.net www.saintelizabethannseton.net Rev. Kingsley Ihejirika, Admin.; Mary Rogers, Bus. Mgr.; CRP Stds.: 75

Our Lady of the Annunciation - maryrogers@saintelizabethannseton.net

St. Mary Cemetery -

NORTHFIELD

St. Patrick - 82 Main St., Northfield, MA 01360; Mailing: 80 Main St., Northfield, MA 01360-1022 t) (413) 498-2728 stpats2@msn.com Rev. Thomas Lisowski, Pst.; Dcn. David Culliton, DRE; Kelly Loynd, Bus. Mgr.; CRP Stds.: 5

St. Mary Cemetery -

ORANGE

St. Mary - 19 Congress St., Orange, MA 01364 t) (978) 544-2900 office@stmaryolr.org www.stmaryorange.online Rev. Shaun O'Connor, Pst.; CRP Stds.: 25

PALMER

St. Thomas the Apostle - 1076 Thorndike St., Palmer, MA 01069 t) (413) 283-5091; (413) 283-5651 (CRP) sttompal@comcast.net Rev. Richard M. Turner, Pst.; Carolyn Gibbs, DRE; CRP Stds.: 35

St. Thomas Cemetery -

PITTSFIELD

St. Charles - 89 Briggs Ave., Pittsfield, MA 01201 t) (413) 442-7470 stcharlespittsfield@gmail.com www.stcharlespittsfield.org Rev. Daniel Cymer, Admin.; CRP Stds.: 60

St. Joseph's - 414 North St., Pittsfield, MA 01201 t) (413) 445-5789 michelemadden@berkshire.rr.com; msgrmike@berkshire.rr.com www.stjoepittsfield.com Rev. Msgr. Michael Shershanovich, Pst.; Rev. Robert Miskell, Par. Vicar; Most Rev. Timothy A. McDonnell, In Res.; Dcn. Robert Esposito; CRP Stds.: 78

St. Joseph Mausoleum & Cemetery -

St. Mark's - 400 West St., Pittsfield, MA 01201 t) (413) 447-7510 www.saintmarkspittsfield.org Rev. Christopher Fedoryshyn, Pst.; CRP Stds.: 70

Sacred Heart - 196 Elm St., Pittsfield, MA 01201; Mailing: 56 Newell St., Pittsfield, MA 01201 t) (413) 443-6960 pinkchurch@aol.com www.thepinkchurch.com Rev. Steven G. Montesanti, Pst.; CRP Stds.: 78

RUSSELL

Holy Family Parish - 5 Main St., Russell, MA 01071-0405; Mailing: P.O. Box 405, Russell, MA 01071-0405 t) (413) 862-4418 parish@holyfamilyrussell.org www.holyfamilyrussell.org Rev. Ronald F. Sadlowski, Pst.; Deborah Bogoff, DRE; CRP Stds.: 5

St. Thomas Cemetery - 15 Main St., Russell, MA 01071-0405

SHEFFIELD

Our Lady of the Valley - 99 Maple Ave., Sheffield, MA 01257; Mailing: P.O. Box 515, Sheffield, MA 01257-0515 t) (413) 229-3028 our.lady.valley@gmail.com www.ourolv.org Rev. Frank W. Furman IV; CRP Stds.: 21

Our Lady of the Hills - 70 Beartown Rd., Monterey, MA 01245 our.lady.valley@gmail.com

Our Lady of the Valley Cemetery -

SHELBURNE FALLS

St. Joseph's - 34 Monroe Ave., Shelburne Falls, MA 01370 t) (413) 625-6405 stjosephccsf@gmail.com www.stjosephparishma.com Rev. William H. Lunney, Pst.; Dcn. Thomas Rabbitt; CRP Stds.: 18

St. John the Baptist - Church St., Colrain, MA 01370; Mailing: 34 Monroe Ave., Shelburne Falls, MA 01370 st.josephccsf@comcast.net

St. Christopher - 180 Main Rd., Rte. 2, Shelburne Falls, MA 01370; Mailing: 34 Monroe Ave., Shelburne Falls, MA 01370 stjosephccsf@comcast.net

SOUTH DEERFIELD

Holy Family Parish - 29 Sugarloaf St., South Deerfield, MA 01373 t) (413) 665-3254 holyfamilysd29@gmail.com www.holyfamilysd.org Rev. David Aufiero, Pst.; Dcn. Rodney Patten; CRP Stds.: 30

St. Marks - Delabarre Ave., Conway, MA 01341; Mailing: 29 Sugarloaf St., South Deerfield, MA 01373 holyfamilysd29@gmail.com Rev. David Aufiero;

St. Stanislaus Cemetery - Rev. David Aufiero;

SOUTH HADLEY

St. Patrick's - 30 Main St., South Hadley, MA 01075 t) (413) 532-2850 stpatdre@outlook.com; stpatrickssh@outlook.com www.saintpatrick.cc Rev. James Nolte, Pst.; Dcn. David Bergeron; Kelly M. O'Connor, DRE; CRP Stds.: 105

St. Theresa of Lisieux - 9 E. Parkview Dr., South Hadley, MA 01075-2103 t) (413) 532-3228 x120 (CRP); (413) 532-3228 sttfaithformation@gmail.com www.sttheresaparish.org Rev. Michael J. Twohig, Pst.; Patricia L. Smith, DRE; CRP Stds.: 105

Academy of the Little Flower - t) (413) 896-2535 alittleflower22@gmail.com

SOUTHWICK

Our Lady of the Lake - 224 Sheep Pasture Rd., Southwick, MA 01077; Mailing: P.O. Box 1150, Southwick, MA 01077 t) (413) 569-0161; (413) 569-0162 (Religious Ed) parishoffice@ollsouthwick.org www.ollsouthwick.org Rev. Matthew Guidi, Pst.; Dcn. David Przybylowski; Lynda Daniele, DRE; Rosemarie Ricco, Bus. Mgr.; CRP Stds.: 71

SPRINGFIELD

All Souls - 449 Plainfield St., Springfield, MA 01107; Mailing: 445 Plainfield St., Springfield, MA 01007 t) 413-736-8208 (CRP); 413-736-0076 Rev. Jose Siesquen Flores (Peru), Admin.; Dcn. Angel Delgado; Dcn. Jose Rivera; Gladys Vasquez, DRE;

Blessed Sacrament - 40 Waverly St., Springfield, MA 01107; Mailing: 445 Plainfield St., Springfield, MA 01107 t) 413-736-8208 (CRP); 413-736-2167; 413-736-0076 jssiesquen@hotmail.com; monicaendo78@yahoo.com Rev. Jose Siesquen Flores (Peru), Admin.; Dcn. Angel Delgado; Gladys Vasquez, DRE; CRP Stds.: 151

Cathedral of St. Michael the Archangel - 254 State St., Springfield, MA 01103; Mailing: 260 State St., Springfield, MA 01103 t) (413) 781-3656 stmichaelscathedral@diospringfield.org www.stmichaelscathedralspfld.org Rev. Msgr. Christopher D. Connelly, Rector; Rev. Yerick Mendez, Asst. Rector; Dolly Garzon, Pst. Assoc.; Dcn. Angel Perez; Dcn. Jose Rivera; Lynn Dubreuil, DRE; CRP Stds.: 64

St. Catherine of Siena - 1023 Parker St., Springfield, MA 01129 t) (413) 783-8619 parishoffice@stcatherinespringfield.org Rev. Jeffrey A. Ballou, Pst.; Dcn. John Antaya; Dcn. Jerry Sheehan; Kathy Nemphos, Pst. Min./Coord.; Theresa Hulse, DRE; CRP Stds.: 34

Holy Cross - 221 Plumtree Rd., Springfield, MA 01118 t) 413-783-4111 holy.cross.springfield@gmail.com; hcrectory@gmail.com www.holycrossparish.org Rev. Quynh Dinh Tran, Admin.; Dcn. William Toller; Dcn. Marc Jean Mary; Cathy Daniel, DRE; Sr. Chris Clark, Pst. Min./Coord.; Brian Rucci, Music Min.; Rev. Msgr. David George, In Res.; Rev. Msgr. David Joyce, In Res.; Rev. John F. Tuohey, In Res.; CRP Stds.: 22

Holy Name - 323 Dickinson St., Springfield, MA 01108 t) (413) 733-5823 x123 (CRP); (413) 733-5823 www.holynamespringfieldma.org Rev. Jonathan Reardon, Pst.; Rev. Barrent C. Pease, Par. Vicar; Sr. Melinda Pellerin, S.S.J., Pastoral Min.; Rev. Sinh Trinh, In Res.; CRP Stds.: 40

Mary Mother of Hope Parish - 840 Page Blvd., Springfield, MA 01104 t) (413) 736-1622 (CRP); (413) 739-0546 faithformation@mmohspringfield.org; office@mmohspringfield.org www.mmohspringfield.org Rev. Michael J. Wood Jr., Pst.; Catherine Mary Senecal, DRE; Rev. Donatus Ironuma, In Res.; Rev. Kenneth J. Tatro, In Res.; CRP Stds.: 55

Our Lady of Mt. Carmel - 123 William St., Springfield, MA 01105 t) (413) 204-7789 (CRP); (413) 734-5433 religioused.olmcspfld@gmail.com; mountcarmelrectoryoffice@gmail.com www.olmcspringfield.org Rev. Robert S. White, C.S.S., Pst.; Sr. Elizabeth A. Matuszek, S.S.J., Pst. Assoc.; Rev. Paolo Bagattini, C.S.S., In Res.; CRP Stds.: 71

Our Lady of the Sacred Heart - 407 Boston Rd., Springfield, MA 01109; Mailing: 51 Rosewell St., Springfield, MA 01109 t) (413) 782-8041 olshspringfield@gmail.com www.olshspringfield.org Rev. Ryan Rooney, Pst.; Dcn. Angel Diaz; Rev. Fidelis Lemchi, In Res.; Dorothy Mitchell, DRE; CRP Stds.: 31

St. Patrick's - 1900 Allen St., Springfield, MA 01118-1820 t) (413) 783-6201 stpatspringfield@gmail.com www.saintpatricks-springfield.org Rev. Msgr. Daniel P. Liston, Pst.; Dcn. George Kozach; Helen Laliberte, CRE; Daniel Kane, Music Min.; Judith Smith, Bus. Mgr.; CRP Stds.: 43

St. Paul the Apostle - 235 Dwight Rd., Springfield, MA 01108 t) (413) 737-4422; (413) 391-4470 (CRP) stpaulchurch235@gmail.com Rev. Peter Ha Dinh Dang, Pst.; Rev. Sinh Trinh, Par. Vicar; Dcn. Ly X. Cao; Dcn. Francis D. Rogers; Dcn. Khanh Tran; Mandy Vu, DRE; CRP Stds.: 107

Sacred Heart - 387 Chestnut St., Springfield, MA 01104; Mailing: 395 Chestnut St., Springfield, MA 01104 t) (413) 732-3721 shc395@aol.com Rev. Msgr. George A. Farland, Pst.; Dcn. William Kern; CRP Stds.: 84

THREE RIVERS

Divine Mercy Parish - 2267 Main St., Three Rivers, MA 01080; Mailing: P.O. Box 157, Three Rivers, MA 01080 t) (413) 283-6030 petruspaulus1905@gmail.com churchofdivinemercy.org. Rev. Stefan J. Niemczyk, Pst.; CRP Stds.: 38

St. Peter & Paul Cemetery - www.churchofdivinemercy.org

St. Ann Cemetery - www.churchofdivinemercy.org

TURNERS FALLS

Our Lady of Czestochowa - 84 K St., Turners Falls, MA 01376 t) (413) 863-4748 olczestochowa@gmail.com chroniclesofczestochowa.wordpress.com Rev. Sean O'Mannion, Pst.; CRP Stds.: 63

Our Lady of Czestochowa Cemetery -

Our Lady of Peace - 80 Seventh St., Turners Falls, MA 01376; Mailing: 90 Seventh St., Turners Falls, MA 01376

t) (413) 863-2585 frstan@ourladyofpeacetf.com www.ourladyofpeacetf.org Rev. Stanley J. Aksamit, Pst.; Dcn. Joseph Bucci; Carol Holubecki, DRE; CRP Stds.: 80

Mater Dolorosa Cemetery -

St. Anne Cemetery -

St. Mary Cemetery -

WARE

All Saints - 17 North St., Ware, MA 01082; Mailing: 60 South St., Ware, MA 01082 t) 413-967-4963 allsaintschurch17@gmail.com www.warecatholic.org Rev. Paul Norman, Admin.; Dcn. Gilbert St. George-Sorel; CRP Stds.: 50

Our Lady of Mt. Carmel Cemetery - t) (413) 967-5913 stmaryschurch60@gmail.com Rev. Piotr Pawlus;

St. William Cemetery - t) (413) 967-5913 stmaryschurch60@gmail.com Rev. Piotr Pawlus;

St. Mary's - 60 South St., Ware, MA 01082 t) (413) 967-5913 stmaryschurch60@gmail.com www.warecatholic.org Rev. Piotr Pawlus; Dcn. Gilbert St. George-Sorel; CRP Stds.: 64

St. Mary Cemetery -

WEST SPRINGFIELD

St. Thomas the Apostle - 63 Pine St., West Springfield, MA 01089; Mailing: 47 Pine St., West Springfield, MA 01089 t) (413) 739-4779; (413) 737-8267 (CRP) stthomassecretary@comcast.net; stthomasccd@comcast.net www.stthomaswestspringfield.org Rev. John K. Sheaffer, Pst.; Rev. Stanislaus Achu, Provisional Priest; Dcn. Joseph W. Kielbasa Jr.; Dcn. James H. Marcus; Donna L. Marotto, DRE; CRP Stds.: 279

St. Thomas the Apostle School - (Grades PreK-8) 75 Pine St., West Springfield, MA 01089 t) (413) 739-4131 phottinssj@comcast.net Rev. John K. Sheaffer; Sr. Patricia Hottin, S.S.J., Prin.; Stds.: 188; Sr. Tchrs.: 1; Lay Tchrs.: 25

St. Thomas the Apostle Cemetery - Rev. John K. Sheaffer;

WEST STOCKBRIDGE

St. Patrick's - 30 Albany Rd., West Stockbridge, MA 01266; Mailing: P.O. Box 103, West Stockbridge, MA 01266-0103 t) (413) 232-4427 stpatricksws@verizon.net www.avptriparish.org Rev. Msgr. John J. Bonzagni, Pst.; Dcn. John E. Zick, DRE;

St. Patrick Cemetery -

WESTFIELD

Holy Trinity - 335 Elm St., Westfield, MA 01085 t) (413) 568-1506 htoffice@holytrinitywestfield.com www.holytrinitywestfield.com Polish Rev. Rene Parent, M.S., Pst.; Sharon Czarnecki, DRE; CRP Stds.: 37

St. Mary's - 30 Bartlett St., Westfield, MA 01085 t) (413) 562-5477; (413) 568-1127 (CRP) jbagge@stmsaints.org; lcorriveau@stmsaints.org www.stmarysofwestfield.com Rev. John C. Salatino, Pst.; Rev. Duy Ahn Lee, Par. Vicar; Dcn. Osvaldo Mendez; Dcn. Pedro Rivera-Moran; Joanne Bagge, DRE; Lynne Corriveau, DRE; CRP Stds.: 201

St. Mary Elementary School - (Grades K-8) 35 Bartlett St., Westfield, MA 01085 t) (413) 568-2388 apellan-shea@stmsaints.org www.stmaryofwestfield.com Anne Pellan-Shea, Prin.; Stds.: 185; Lay Tchrs.: 14

St. Mary Pre Kindergarten - 23 Bartlett St., Westfield, MA 01085 t) (413) 568-2388 apellan-shea@stmsaints.org www.stmaryofwestfield.com Anne Pellan-Shea, Prin.; Stds.: 27; Lay Tchrs.: 2

St. Mary Pre-School - (Grades PreSchool- 23 1/2 Bartlett St., Westfield, MA 01085 t) (413) 568-2388 apellan-shea@stmsaints.org Anne Pellan-Shea, Prin.; Stds.: 10; Lay Tchrs.: 1

Our Lady of the Blessed Sacrament - 127 Holyoke Rd., Westfield, MA 01085; Mailing: P.O. Box 489, Westfield, MA 01086-0489 t) (413) 562-3450 olbsoffice@aol.com www.olbswestfield.org Rev. Daniel S. Pacholec, Pst.; Dcn. Andrew Hogan; Mary Federici, Pst. Min./Coord.; Lisa Laferriere, Youth Min.; Dcn. Paul Federici, DRE; CRP Stds.: 105

St. Peter and St. Casimir - 24 State St., Westfield, MA 01085; Mailing: 22 State St., Westfield, MA 01085 t) (413) 568-5421 sspetetcas@comcast.net Rev. Warren J. Savage, Administrator (Pro-Tem); E.Dorthea MacNeil, DRE; CRP Stds.: 20

WILBRAHAM

St. Cecilia's - 42 Main St., Wilbraham, MA 01095; Mailing: 7 Maple St., Wilbraham, MA 01095 t) (413) 596-4232 x101; (413) 596-4232 x113 (CRP) administrator@saintceciliawilbraham.org; cff@saintceciliawilbraham.org www.saintceciliawilbraham.org Rev. John E. Connors, Pst.; Dcn. Andrew Nowicki; Dcn. James Ziemba; Rosemary Oldread, DRE; CRP Stds.: 404

WILLIAMSTOWN

SS. Patrick and Raphael - 63 Southworth St., Williamstown, MA 01267-2414; Mailing: 54 Southworth St., Williamstown, MA 01267 t) (413) 458-4946 x11 saintspatrickandraphael@gmail.com www.williamstowncatholics.org Rev. John P. McDonagh, Pst.; CRP Stds.: 50

SCHOOLS: PRESCHOOL THRU HIGH SCHOOL

SCHOOLS

COMMONWEALTH OF MASSACHUSETTS

ADAMS

St. Stanislaus Kostka School - (DIO) (Grades PreK-8) 108 Summer St., Adams, MA 01220 t) (413) 743-1091 saintstans2014@gmail.com www.ststansadams.org David Orton, Prin.; Stds.: 104; Lay Tchrs.: 9

SPRINGFIELD

Saint Michael's Academy - (PAR) (Grades PreK-8) 153 Eddywood St., Springfield, MA 01118 t) (413) 782-5246 a.obrien@smaspringfield.org www.smaspringfield.org Ann Dougal, Prin.; Stds.: 436; Lay Tchrs.: 27

HIGH SCHOOLS

COMMONWEALTH OF MASSACHUSETTS

SPRINGFIELD

Pope Francis Preparatory School - 99 Wendover Rd., Springfield, MA 01118 t) (833) 999-7673 askus@popefrancisprep.org www.popefrancisprep.org Paul Harrington Jr., Head of School; Cynthia Geiger, Asst. Head of School; Stds.: 396; Lay Tchrs.: 38

WESTFIELD

St. Mary's High School - (DIO) (Grades 9-12) 27 Bartlett St., Westfield, MA 01085 t) (413) 568-5692 businessmanager@stmsaints.org www.stmsaints.org/high-school Matthew Collins, Prin.; Stds.: 104; Lay Tchrs.: 10

INSTITUTIONS LOCATED IN DIOCESE

CAMPUS MINISTRY / NEWMAN CENTERS [CAM]

AMHERST

Amherst College - 38 Woodside Ave., Cadigan Center, Amherst, MA 01002-5000; Mailing: P.O. Box 2277, Amherst, MA 01002 t) 413-542-8489 tlynch@amherst.edu Rev. Warren J. Savage, Sacr. Min.; Dcn. Thomas Lynch, Campus Min.;

University of Massachusetts - 472 N. Pleasant St., Amherst, MA 01002 t) (413) 549-0300 g.dailey@diospringfield.org Rev. Gary Dailey, Dir.; Rev. Robert Miskell, Campus Min.; Dcn. Thomas Lynch, Campus Min.;

CHICOPEE

College of Our Lady of the Elms College - 291 Springfield St., College Center First Fl., BH011, Chicopee, MA 01013 t) (413) 265-2289; (413) 265-2468 kirke@elms.edu; stelzerm@elms.edu www.elms.edu Rev. Mark S. Stelzer, Chap.; Eileen Kirk, Dir.;

LONGMEADOW

Bay Path University - St Mary's Church, 519 Longmeadow St., Longmeadow, MA 01106 t) 413-567-3124 x109 fathercj@stmarylong.org Rev. Christopher J. Waitekus, Pst.;

NORTH ADAMS

Massachusetts College of Liberal Arts - St. Elizabeth of Hungry Parish, 70 Marshall St., North Adams, MA 01247-0868 t) (413) 663-5316 stelizabethbulletin@yahoo.com Served by St. Elizabeth of Hungary, North Adams Rev. Dariusz P. Wudarski, Pst.;

NORTHAMPTON

Smith College - The Smith Center for Religious & Spiritual Life - Helen Hills Hills Chapel, 123 Elm St., Northampton, MA 01062; Mailing: 10 Elm St., Northampton, MA 01063 t) (413) 268-7212 v.nworah@diospringfield.org Rev. Valentine Onyeka Nworah;

PITTSFIELD

Berkshire Community College - St. Mark Parish, 400 West St., Pittsfield, MA 01201 t) 413-447-7510 st.marks.pittsfield@gmail.com Served by St. Mark's Parish Rev. Christopher Fedoryshyn, Pst.;

SOUTH HADLEY

Mount Holyoke College - Office of Spiritual and Religious Life, Eliot House, South Hadley, MA 01075; Mailing: 50 College St., South Hadley, MA 01075 t) (413) 538-2054 ammcderm@mtholyoke.edu; w.savage@mtholyoke.edu Rev. Warren J. Savage, Sacr. Min.; Sr. Annette McDermott, S.S.J., Dean;

SPRINGFIELD

American International College - Campus Outreach, Lee Hall 30, Springfield, MA 01109; Mailing: Diocese of Springfield - Campus Outreach, P.O. Box 1730, Springfield, MA 01102 t) 413-452-0837; 413-205-3090 j.mcdonagh@diospringfield.org Rev. John P. McDonagh, Chap.;

Center for Religious Life - 65 Elliot St., Springfield, MA 01102-1730; Mailing: P.O Box 1730, Springfield, MA 01102-1730 t) (413) 549-0300 newmansecretary@diospringfield.org Rev. Gary Dailey, Dir.;

Newman Apostolates and Campus Ministries - 65 Elliot St., Springfield, MA 01102-1730; Mailing: 54 Southworth St., Sts. Patrick and Raphael Parish, Williamstown, MA 01267 t) (413) 452-0837 c) (413) 531-3610 j.mcdonagh@diospringfield.org Rev. John P. McDonagh, Dir.;

Springfield College Campus Ministry - 263 Alden St., Springfield College Spiritual Life, Springfield, MA 01109-3797 t) (413) 748-3209 mlillpopp@springfield.edu Rev. Michael Lillpopp, Chap.;

Western New England University - 1215 Wilbraham Rd., Germain Campus Center, Room 247, Springfield, MA 01119-2684 t) (413) 782-1628 sheilahanifan@comcast.net Rev. Norman B. Bolton, Sacr. Min.; Sheila Hanifin, Dir.;

WESTFIELD

Westfield State University - 577 Western Ave., Westfield, MA 01086 t) (413) 572-5567; (413) 572-8571 wsavage@westfield.ma.edu; lmcmahon@westfield.ma.edu Albert and Amelia Ferst Interfaith Center Rev. Warren J. Savage, Dir. & Catholic Chap.; Dcn. David Baillargeon, Asst. Catholic Chap.; Dcn. James Conroy, Asst. Catholic Chap.; Colleen Mollica, Campus Min.;

WILLIAMSTOWN

Williams College - 38 Chapin Hall Dr., Paresky Center Rm 205, Williamstown, MA 01267 t) (413) 597-2483 bep3@williams.edu; j.mcdonagh@diospringfield.org Rev. John P. McDonagh, Pst.; Bridget Power, Chap.;

CATHOLIC CHARITIES [CCH]

TURNERS FALLS

Montague Catholic Social Ministries, Inc. - 43 Third St., Turners Falls, MA 01376 t) (413) 863-4804 heather@mcsmcommunity.org; laura@mcsmcommunity.org www.mcsmcommunity.org Purpose: A resource to children and families in the areas of parent education, family literacy, positive conflict resolution, communication skills. Heather Wood, Dir.; Asstd. Annu.: 600; Staff: 9

CEMETERIES [CEM]

HOLYOKE

Calvary Cemetery - Northampton St., Holyoke, MA 01040; Mailing: 63 Lyman St., South Hadley, MA 01075 t) (413) 420-0001; (413) 539-6569 (Garage) w.casagranda@diospringfield.org www.diospringfieldcemeteries.org Brian Kennedy, Dir.;

INDIAN ORCHARD

St. Aloysius Cemetery - 1273 Berkshire Ave., Indian Orchard, MA 01151; Mailing: 1601 State St., Springfield, MA 01109 t) (413) 733-8140; (413) 543-6765 (Garage) w.casagranda@diospringfield.org www.diospringfieldcemeteries.org Brian Kennedy, Dir.;

SOUTH HADLEY

Notre Dame Cemetery - 63 Lyman St., South Hadley, MA 01075 t) (413) 420-0001 w.casagranda@diospringfield.org www.diospringfieldcemeteries.org Brian Kennedy, Dir.;

Precious Blood Cemetery - Willimansett St., South Hadley, MA 01075; Mailing: 63 Lyman St., South Hadley, MA 01075 t) (413) 420-0001 w.casagranda@diospringfield.org www.diospringfieldcemeteries.org Brian Kennedy, Dir.;

St. Rose Cemetery - Rts. 33 & 202, South Hadley, MA 01075; Mailing: 63 Lyman St., South Hadley, MA 01075 t) (413) 420-0001 w.casagranda@diospringfield.org www.diospringfieldcemeteries.org Brian Kennedy, Dir.;

SPRINGFIELD

St. Benedict Cemetery - Liberty St., Springfield, MA 01104; Mailing: 421 Tinkham Rd., Springfield, MA 01129 t) (413) 782-4731 w.casagranda@diospringfield.org www.diospringfieldcemeteries.org Brian Kennedy, Dir.;

Gate of Heaven - 421 Tinkham Rd., Springfield, MA 01129 t) (413) 782-4731; (413) 782-2237 (Garage) goh@diospringfield.org www.diospringfieldcemeteries.org Brian Kennedy, Dir.;

St. Matthew Cemetery - 366 Springfield St., Springfield, MA 01109; Mailing: 421 Tinkham Rd., Springfield, MA 01129 t) (413) 782-4731 w.casagranda@diospringfield.org www.diospringfieldcemeteries.org Brian Kennedy, Dir.;

St. Michael's Cemetery - 1601 State St., Springfield, MA 01109 t) (413) 733-0659; (413) 783-3936 (Garage) w.casagranda@diospringfield.org www.diospringfieldcemeteries.org Brian Kennedy, Dir.;

WESTFIELD

St. Mary Cemetery - 203 Southampton Rd., Westfield, MA 01085 t) (413) 568-7775; (413) 568-7715 (Garage) w.casagranda@diospringfield.org www.diospringfieldcemeteries.org Brian Kennedy, Dir.;

COLLEGES & UNIVERSITIES [COL]

CHICOPEE

College of Our Lady of the Elms - 291 Springfield St., Chicopee, MA 01013 t) (413) 265-6973 breauw@elms.edu; longleyk@elms.edu www.elms.edu Dr. Harry Dumay, Pres.; Walter C. Breau, Vice. Pres.; Katie Longley, Treas.; Anthony Fonseca, Librn.; Stds.: 1,275; Lay Tchrs.: 64; Pr. Tchrs.: 1

CONVENTS, MONASTERIES, AND RESIDENCES FOR WOMEN [CON]

HOLYOKE

Daughters of the Heart of Mary Provincial Residence - 1339 Northampton St., Holyoke, MA 01040-1958 t) (413) 533-6681; (413) 534-4502 (Primary Contact) dhmvocations@gmail.com www.dhm.org Sr. Elizabeth Dodge, DHM, Prov.; Srs.: 28

Franciscan Missionary Sisters of Assisi - Saint Francis Convent - Vice Provincial House and Formation House - 1039 Northampton St., Holyoke, MA 01040-1320 t) (413) 532-8156 fmsausa@comcast.net www.sistersofassisi.org Sr. Monica Partac, S.F.M.A., Vice Provincial Superior; Sr. Anne Mbewe, S.F.M.A., Vice Provincial Vicar; Srs.: 6

Sisters of Providence - 5 Gamelin St., Holyoke, MA 01040 t) (413) 536-7511 kpopko@sisofprov.org www.sisofprov.org Legal Holdings and Titles: Sisters of Providence, Inc., The Hillside at Providence, Inc., Hillside Residence, Inc. Sr. Kathleen Popko, S.P., Pres.; Sr. Mary Caritas Geary, S.P., Vice. Pres.; Sr. Senga Fulton, S.P., Secy.; Srs.: 17

SPRINGFIELD

The Congregation of the Sisters of St. Joseph of Springfield - 577 Carew St., Springfield, MA 01104 t) (413) 536-0853 mail@ssjspringfield.com www.ssjspringfield.org Administrative Offices of the Sisters of St. Joseph of Springfield. Sr. Joan Ryzewicz, Pres.; Sr. Angela Deady, Vice. Pres.; Srs.: 165

TYRINGHAM

Order of the Visitation of Holy Mary - 14 Beach Rd., Tyringham, MA 01264; Mailing: P.O. Box 432, Tryingham, MA 01264 t) (413) 243-3995 vistyr@aol.com www.vistyr.org Sr. Mariam Rose, V.H.M., Supr.; Srs.: 14

WEST SPRINGFIELD

Monastery of the Mother of God, Dominican Nuns (Contemplative) - 1430 Riverdale St., West Springfield, MA 01089-4698 t) (413) 736-3639 monasteryws@comcast.net; srmbursarws@yahoo.com Adoration to the Blessed Sacrament Chapel. Sr. Theresa Marie, Prioress; Sr. Mary of the Immaculate Heart, O.P., Treas.; Srs.: 8

ENDOWMENTS / FOUNDATIONS / TRUSTS [EFT]

CHICOPEE

Elms College Foundation, Inc. - 291 Springfield St., Chicopee, MA 01013 t) (413) 265-2372 longleyk@elms.edu Katie Longley, Treas.;

HOLYOKE

Sisters of Providence Endowment Trust - 5 Gamelin St., Holyoke, MA 01040 t) (413) 536-7511 x2551 kpopko@sisofprov.org Sr. Senga Fulton, S.P., Trustee; Sr. Madeleine Marie Joy, S.P., Trustee; Sr. Kathleen Popko, S.P., Trustee;

Sisters of Providence Retirement and Continuing Care Trust - 5 Gamelin St., Holyoke, MA 01040 t) (413) 536-7511 x2551 kpopko@sisofprov.org Retirement and Continuing Care Trust Sr. Mary Caritas Geary, S.P., Trustee; Sr. Margaret McCleary, SP, Trustee; Sr. Ruth McGoldrick, S.P., Trustee;

SPRINGFIELD

Western Massachusetts Catholic Foundation, Inc. - 65 Elliot St., Springfield, MA 01102-1730; Mailing: P.O. Box 1730, Springfield, MA 01102-1730 t) (413) 452-0838 j.vanbeaver@diospringfield.org www.diospringfield.org

HOSPITALS / HEALTH SERVICES [HOS]

SPRINGFIELD

Trinity Health - Mercy Medical Center (Catholic Health Ministries - Trinity Health, Livonia, MI) - 271 Carew St., Springfield, MA 01102-9012 t) (413) 748-9000 www.trinityhealthofne.org Member of Trinity Health Of New England Regional Health Ministry of Trinity Health, Livonia MI Deborah Bitsoli, Pres.; Robert Roose, Exec.; Grainne Buchanan, Chap.; Julie-Ann Silberman-Bunn, Chap.; Rev. Donatus Ironuma, Chap.; Bed Capacity: 251; Asstd. Annu.: 253,409; Staff: 1,294

Brightside, Inc. - 1233 Main St., Holyoke, MA 01040 t) (413) 827-4244; (413) 539-2480 Private, Nonprofit Agency. Mercy Medical Center, Member of Trinity Health Of New England Regional Health Ministry Gerald Galipeau, Exec. Dir.;

MISCELLANEOUS [MIS]

CHICOPEE

The Friends of the Elms College, Inc. - 291 Springfield St., Chicopee, MA 01013 t) (413) 265-2372 breauw@elms.edu; longleyk@elms.edu Walter C. Breau, Admin.;

Mary's House of Prayer - 202 E. Main St., Chicopee, MA 01020 t) (413) 452-0886 maryshouse@diospringfield.org www.maryshousechicopee.org Rev. J. Donald R. Lapointe, Dir.;

EASTHAMPTON

Bethlehem House, Inc. - 33 Knipfer Ave., Easthampton, MA 01027; Mailing: P.O. Box 1393, Easthampton, MA 01027 t) 413-262-8517; 413-527-2861 bethlehem_house@verizon.net Pamela Hibbard, Dir.;

HOLYOKE

Bureau for Exceptional Children and Adults Inc. - 537 Northampton St., Holyoke, MA 01040; Mailing: P.O. Box 1039, Holyoke, MA 01040 t) (413) 538-7450 linda@jerichobeca.org www.jerichobeca.org Sharon Koehler, Admin.; Sr. Joan Magnani, S.S.J., Pst. Min./Coord.; Linda LaPointe, Dir.;

Marian Center, Inc. - 1365 Northampton St., Holyoke, MA 01040 t) (413) 534-4502 mnajimy@aol.com Sr. Miriam Najimy, D.H.M., Supr.;

Providence Ministries for the Needy, Inc. - 51 Hamilton St., Holyoke, MA 01040 t) (413) 533-5909 jadamczyk@provministries.org www.provministries.org Sponsored by the Sisters of Providence and Sisters of Providence Ministry Corporation of Holyoke, MA. Jennie Rebecca Adamczyk, Exec. Dir.; Sr. Margaret McCleary, SP, Foundress; Sr. Mary Caritas Geary, S.P., Secy.;

Broderick House - 56 Cabot St., Holyoke, MA 01041; Mailing: 51 Hamilton St., Holyoke, MA 01040 t) (413) 533-5909 x2 Sober Home Program Michael Clark, Housing Mgr.;

foodWorks@Kate's Kitchen - 51 Hamilton St., Holyoke, MA 01040 t) (413) 533-5909 x4 Culinary training program for individuals with barriers to employment. Mike Nowak, Contact;

St. Jude's Clothing Center - 56 Cabot St., Holyoke, MA 01040; Mailing: 51 Hamilton St., Holyoke, MA 01040 t) (413) 533-5909 x5 brendal@provministries.org Distributes clothing and household items those in need and hosts a thrift store twice weekly open to the community. Brenda Lamagdeleine, Mgr.;

Kate's Kitchen - 51 Hamilton St., Holyoke, MA 01040 t) 413-533-5909 Community kitchen

Loreto House - 51 Hamilton St., Holyoke, MA 01040 t) (413) 533-5909 x2 MASH (Massachusett Alliance of Sober Housing) Certified sober home assisting men in seeking recovery. Michael Clark, Housing Mgr.;

Margaret's Pantry - 56 Cabot St., Holyoke, MA 01040; Mailing: 51 Hamilton St., Holyoke, MA 01040 t) (413) 533-5909 x8 brendal@provministries.org Provides emergency food to families and individuals. Brenda Lamagdeleine, Pantry Mgr.;

McCleary Manor - 40 Brightside Dr., Holyoke, MA 01041; Mailing: 51 Hamilton St., Holyoke, MA 01040 t) 413-536-9109 Sober Home Program Michael Clark, Housing Mgr.;

Sisters of Providence Ministry Corporation - 5 Gamelin St., Holyoke, MA 01040 t) (413) 536-7511 kpopko@sisofprov.org; jwesolowski@sisofprov.org www.sisofprov.org Genesis Spiritual Life & Conf. Ctr, Inc.; Providence Ministries for the Needy, Inc.; Providence Place, Inc.; Mary's Meadow at Providence Place, Inc. John Wesolowski, CEO; Sr. Senga Fulton, S.P., Secy.; Sr. Mary Caritas Geary, S.P., Vice Pres.; Sr. Kathleen Popko, S.P., Chairperson;

PALMER

Apostolate of the Suffering, Inc. - 1915 Ware St., Palmer, MA 01069-9560 t) 413-283-4529 maryfarm@comcast.net www.sodcvs.org/eng Stasia A.

Bronner, Admin.; Bro. Robert J. Letasz, S.O.D.C., Pres.; Rev. Daniel B. Brunton, Dir.;

SPRINGFIELD

Catholic Latino Ministry - 65 Elliot St., Springfield, MA 01102-1730; Mailing: P.O. Box 1730, Springfield, MA 01102-1730 t) (413) 452-0631 www.diospringfield.org (latino ministry) Dcn. Pedro Rivera-Moran, Dir.;

The Catholic Life Conference of the Diocese of Springfield, MA, Inc. - 65 Elliot St., Springfield, MA 01105

The Friends of the Sisters of St. Joseph of Springfield, Inc. - 577 Carew St., Springfield, MA 01104 t) (413) 536-0853 mail@ssjspringfield.com Sr. Joan Ryzewicz, Pres.;

Trinity Health -Mercy Hospital - 271 Carew St., Springfield, MA 01104 t) (413) 748-9000 janice.hamilton-crawford@trinity-health.org www.mercycares.com Janice Hamilton-Crawford, Admin.;

WEST SPRINGFIELD

Mercy LIFE, Inc. - 200 Hillside Cir., Ste. 1, West Springfield, MA 01089 t) (413) 748-7223 emmanuel.cheo@trinity-health.org www.mercycares.com Emmanuel Cheo, Dir.;

The Hillside at Providence, Inc. - 200 Hillside Cir., West Springfield, MA 01089; Mailing: 5 Gamelin St., Ste. 1, Holyoke, MA 01040 t) (413) 536-7511 x2551 kpopko@sisofprov.org www.sisofprov.org Sr. Kathleen Popko, S.P., Pres.; Sr. Senga Fulton, S.P., Treas.; Sr. Mary Caritas Geary, S.P., Secy.;

Hillside Residence, Inc. - 100 Hillside Cir., West Springfield, MA 01089; Mailing: 5 Gamelin St., Holyoke, MA 01040 t) (413) 409-8420 pattygreene@sisofprov.org Patty Greene, Property Mgr.; John Wesolowski, Treas.;

MONASTERIES AND RESIDENCES FOR PRIESTS AND BROTHERS [MON]

STOCKBRIDGE

Congregation of Marian Fathers of The Immaculate Conception of the Most Blessed Virgin Mary - 2 Prospect Hill Rd., Stockbridge, MA 01262; Mailing: P.O. Box 951, Stockbridge, MA 01262 t) (413) 298-1101 provincial@marian.org; kdossantos@marian.org www.marian.org Very Rev. Christopher Alar, M.I.C., Prov. Supr. & Dir., Assn. of Marian Helpers; Very Rev. Donald Calloway, M.I.C., Vicar Prov.; Rev. Andrew Peter Davy, M.I.C., 2nd Prov. Councilor; Rev. James McCormack, M.I.C., 3rd Prov. Councilor; Rev. Kenneth Dos Santos, M.I.C., 4th Prov. Councilor, Prov. Secy.; Rev. Ronald Lynn McBride, M.I.C., House Supr.; Rev. Matthew Tomeny, MIC, Rector, National Shrine of The Divine Mercy; Rev. Anthony Gramlich, M.I.C., Vice Rector, Shrine Liturgy; Rev. Robert Vennetti, M.I.C., Vice Rector, Events; Bro. Andrew Maczynski, M.I.C., Archivist; Rev. Richard Drabik, M.I.C., In Res.; Rev. Walter Dziordz, M.I.C., In Res.; Rev. Kazimierz Chwalek, M.I.C., In Res.; Rev. Andrzej Gorczyca, M.I.C., In Res.; Rev. Victor Incardona, M.I.C., In Res.; Rev. Jonathan Inskip, M.I.C., In Res.; Rev. Mariusz Jarzabek, M.I.C., In Res.; Rev. David Lord, M.I.C., In Res.; Rev. Gerald Stanley Ornowski, M.I.C., In Res.; Bro. Benancio Bobadilla, M.I.C., In Res.; Bro. John Bryda, M.I.C., In Res.; Bro. Alexander Chung, M.I.C., In Res.; Bro. Mark Fanders, In Res.; Bro. Kenneth Galisa, M.I.C., In Res.; Bro. David Guza, M.I.C., In Res.; Bro. John Luth, M.I.C., In Res.; Bro. Ruben Veloz, M.I.C., In Res.; Paul Capps, Postulant; Alex Luna, Postulant; Phillip Sylvester, Postulant; Brs.: 9; Priests: 41

Provincial Office - 2 Prospect Hill Rd., Stockbridge, MA 01262; Mailing: P.O. Box 951, Stockbridge, MA 01262

Association of Marian Helpers, Marian Helpers Center - 2 Prospect Hill Rd., Stockbridge, MA 01263; Mailing: P.O. Box 951, Stockbridge, MA 01263 t) (413) 298-3691 info@marian.org Kevin Dougherty, Exec. Dir.; Bro. Andrew Maczynski, M.I.C., Editor, Roze Maryi Mag.;

Eucharistic Apostles of the Divine Mercy (EADM) - 2 Prospect Hill Rd., Stockbridge, MA 01262; Mailing: P.O. Box 951, Stockbridge, MA 01262 t) (877) 380-0727 eadm@marian.org www.thedivinemercy.org/eadm (Lay Outreach) Bryan Thatcher, Dir.;

Healthcare Professionals for Divine Mercy - 2 Prospect Hill Rd., Stockbridge, MA 01262; Mailing: P.O. Box 951, Stockbridge, MA 01262 t) (866) 895-3236 hcpfordivinemercy@marian.org www.thedivinemercy.org/healthcare (Lay Outreach) Marie Romagnano, Dir.;

John Paul II Institute of Divine Mercy - 2 Prospect Hill Rd., Stockbridge, MA 01262; Mailing: P.O. Box 951, Stockbridge, MA 01262 t) (866) 895-3236 jpii@marian.org; dme-questions@marian.org www.thedivinemercy.org/jpii Robert Stackpole, Dir.;

Marian Charitable Annuity Trust - 2 Prospect Hill Rd., Stockbridge, MA 01262; Mailing: P.O. Box 951, Stockbridge, MA 01262

Marian Continuing Care Trust - 2 Prospect Hill Rd., Stockbridge, MA 01262; Mailing: P.O. Box 951, Stockbridge, MA 01262

Marian Education and Training Trust - 2 Prospect Hill Rd., Stockbridge, MA 01262; Mailing: P.O. Box 951, Stockbridge, MA 01262

Marian Endowment Trust - 2 Prospect Hill Rd., Stockbridge, MA 01262; Mailing: P.O. Box 951, Stockbridge, MA 01262

Marian Fathers of the Immaculate Conception of the B.V.M., Inc. - 2 Prospect Hill Rd., Stockbridge, MA 01262; Mailing: P.O. Box 951, Stockbridge, MA 01262

Marian Helpers Corporation - 2 Prospect Hill Rd., Stockbridge, MA 01262; Mailing: P.O. Box 951, Stockbridge, MA 01262

Marian Real Estate Trust - 2 Prospect Hill Rd., Stockbridge, MA 01262; Mailing: P.O. Box 951, Stockbridge, MA 01262

Marian Services Corporation - 2 Prospect Hill Rd., Stockbridge, MA 01262; Mailing: P.O. Box 951, Stockbridge, MA 01262

Mother of Mercy Messengers (MOMM) - 2 Prospect Hill Rd., Stockbridge, MA 01262; Mailing: P.O. Box 951, Stockbridge, MA 01262 t) (830) 634-7765 momm@marian.org www.thedivinemercy.org/momm (Lay Outreach) Dave Maroney, Dir.; Joan Maroney, Dir.;

The National Shrine of The Divine Mercy - 2 Prospect Hill Rd., Stockbridge, MA 01262; Mailing: P.O. Box 951, Stockbridge, MA 01262 t) (413) 298-3931 shrine@marian.org www.shrineofdivinemercy.org

National Shrine of the Divine Mercy Corporation - 2 Prospect Hill Rd., Stockbridge, MA 01262; Mailing: P.O. Box 951, Stockbridge, MA 01262

NURSING / REHABILITATION / CONVALESCENCE / ELDERLY CARE [NUR]

HOLYOKE

Beaven Kelly Home - 25 Brightside Dr., Holyoke, MA 01040 t) 413-532-4892 lori.hannah@trinityhealthofne.org www.trinityhealthseniorcommunities.org Lori Hannah, Admin.; Carol Smith, Spiritual Adv./Care Srvcs.; Asstd. Annu.: 75; Staff: 27

Providence Place, Inc. - 5 Gamelin St., Holyoke, MA 01040 t) (413) 534-9700 www.providenceplace.org Senior Independent Living Apartments. Sisters of Providence. Suzie Dickson Moyer, Exec. Dir.; Sr. Kathleen Popko, S.P., Pres.; Sr. Mary Caritas Geary, S.P., Secy.; Sr. Senga Fulton, S.P., Treas.; Asstd. Annu.: 132; Staff: 70

LENOX

Mount Carmel Care Center, Inc. - 320 Pittsfield Rd., Lenox, MA 01240 t) (413) 637-2660 gchamberlin@mcccl.org www.mountcarmelcarecenter.org The Carmelite System Jodi Ouimette, Admin.; Asstd. Annu.: 264; Staff: 77

SPRINGFIELD

St. Luke's Home - 85 Spring St., Springfield, MA 01105 t) (413) 736-5494 barbara.tadeo@trinityhealthofne.org www.trinityhealthseniorcommunities.org Barbara Tadeo, Admin.; Brenda Millar, Dir., Nursing; Asstd. Annu.: 115; Staff: 45

PRESCHOOLS / CHILDCARE CENTERS [PRE]

GOSHEN

Holy Cross Camp Grounds - 108 Cape St., Goshen, MA 01032; Mailing: 489 Main St., Dalton, MA 01226 t) (413) 684-0125 cmalatesta@saintagnescc.com; jbrown@saintagnescc.com www.campholycross.org Rev. Christopher A. Malatesta, Dir.; Stds.: 1,200; Lay Tchrs.: 1

RETREAT HOUSES / RENEWAL CENTERS [RTR]

WESTFIELD

Genesis Spiritual Life and Conference Center, Inc. - 53 Mill St., Westfield, MA 01085 t) (413) 562-3627 genesis@genesisspiritualcenter.org www.genesisspiritualcenter.org Retreats, workshops and spiritual guidance designed to promote health of body, mind and spirit. Anne Chapdelaine, COO;

SPECIAL CARE FACILITIES [SPF]

HOLYOKE

Mary's Meadow at Providence Place, Inc. - 12 Gamelin St., Holyoke, MA 01040; Mailing: c/o Sisters of Providence Ministry Corporation, 5 Gamelin St., Holyoke, MA 01040 t) (413) 420-2500 kpopko@sisofprov.org; patrick.arguin@trinityhealthofne.org www.trinityhealthofne.org Sr. Kathleen Popko, S.P., Pres.; Sr. Mary Caritas Geary, S.P., Secy.; Sr. Senga Fulton, S.P., Treas.; Bed Capacity: 40; Asstd. Annu.: 281; Staff: 82

SPRINGFIELD

Diocesan Office of Child and Youth Protection - 65 Elliot St., Springfield, MA 01102-1730; Mailing: P.O. Box 1730, Springfield, MA 01102-1730 t) (413) 732-3175; (413) 452-0624 reportabuse@diospringfield.org www.diospringfield.org (child-youth-protection) Norman Charest, Interim Director; Asstd. Annu.: 200; Staff: 3

Diocese of Steubenville

(Dioecesis Steubenvicensis)

MOST REVEREND JEFFREY MARC MONFORTON

Bishop of Steubenville; ordained June 25, 1994; appointed Bishop of Steubenville July 3, 2012; installed September 10, 2012. Chancery Office: 422 Washington St., P.O. Box 969, Steubenville, OH 43952-5969.

Chancery Office: 422 Washington St., P.O. Box 969, Steubenville, OH 43952-5969. T: 740-282-3631; F: 740- 282-3327.
www.diosteub.org
bgreer@diosteub.org

ESTABLISHED 1944.

Square Miles 5,913.

Comprises these thirteen Counties in the State of Ohio: Athens, Belmont, Carroll, Gallia, Guernsey, Harrison, Jefferson, Lawrence, Meigs, Morgan, Monroe, Noble and Washington.

For legal titles of parishes and diocesan institutions, consult the Chancery Office.

STATISTICAL OVERVIEW

Personnel
Bishop....1
Retired Bishops....1
Priests: Diocesan Active in Diocese....33
Priests: Diocesan Active Outside Diocese....4
Priests: Retired, Sick or Absent....31
Number of Diocesan Priests....68
Religious Priests in Diocese....28
Total Priests in your Diocese....96
Extern Priests in Diocese....8
Ordinations:
Permanent Deacons....1
Permanent Deacons in Diocese....16
Total Sisters....75

Parishes
Parishes....50
With Resident Pastor:
Resident Diocesan Priests....49
Without Resident Pastor:
Administered by Priests....1
Missions....2
Closed Parishes....1

Professional Ministry Personnel:
Sisters....3
Lay Ministers....8

Welfare
Catholic Hospitals....1
Total Assisted....472,892
Special Centers for Social Services....1
Total Assisted....2,461
Residential Care of Disabled....1
Total Assisted....47

Educational
Diocesan Students in Other Seminaries....5
Total Seminarians....5
Colleges and Universities....1
Total Students....3,656
High Schools, Diocesan and Parish....2
Total Students....295
Elementary Schools, Diocesan and Parish....9
Total Students....1,247
Catechesis/Religious Education:
High School Students....234
Elementary Students....540
Total Students under Catholic Instruction....5,977
Teachers in Diocese:
Sisters....3
Lay Teachers....155

Vital Statistics
Receptions into the Church:
Infant Baptism Totals....221
Minor Baptism Totals....61
Adult Baptism Totals....59
Received into Full Communion....43
First Communions....330
Confirmations....348
Marriages:
Catholic....69
Interfaith....29
Total Marriages....98
Deaths....585
Total Catholic Population....28,339
Total Population....481,411

LEADERSHIP

Vicar General - t) 740-282-3631 Very Rev. James M. Dunfee (jdunfee@diosteub.org);
Executive Secretary to the Bishop - t) 740-282-3631 Deborah Cook, Exec. Secy. (dcook@diosteub.org);
Chancellor - t) 740-282-3631 Very Rev. Bradley W. Greer (bgreer@diosteub.org);

OFFICES AND DIRECTORS

Diocesan Archivist - t) 740-282-3631 Pat Coyle, Diocesan Archivist;
Diocesan Finance Council - Gregory J. Agresta; Thomas H. Hisrich; Susan Tolbert;
Diocesan Finance Office - t) 740-282-3631 Shannon Minch-Hughes, CFO;
Diocesan Tribunal - t) 740-282-3631 wcross@diosteub.org; cbahen@diosteub.org
Auditors - tchillog@diosteub.org; dheusel@diosteub.org Rev. Thomas A. Chillog; Rev. Daniel Heusel;
Defenders of the Bond - gcalovini@diosteub.org; tchillog@diosteub.org Rev. Msgr. Gerald E. Calovini; Rev. Thomas A. Chillog; Rev. Daniel Heusel;
Director of the Tribunal & Notary - t) 740-282-3631 Very Rev. William D. Cross, Dir.; Colleen Bahen, Ecclesiastical Notary;
Judges - t) 740-282-3631 Very Rev. James M. Dunfee; Very Rev. Bradley W. Greer; Rev. Vincent J. Huber;
Judicial Vicar - t) 740-282-3631 Very Rev. William D. Cross;
Notaries - t) 740-282-3631 dheusel@diosteub.org Rev. Daniel Heusel, Notary; Colleen Bahen, Ecclesiastical Notary;

DEANERIES

Campus Ministry - t) 740-592-2711 Rev. Mark A. Moore (mmoore@diosteub.org);
Catholic Rural Life - t) 740-896-3566 dgaydosik@diosteub.org Rev. David L. Gaydosik;
Censores Librorum - t) 740-282-3631 Very Rev. James M. Dunfee (jdunfee@diosteub.org);
Child and Youth Protection - t) 740-282-3631 Very Rev. James M. Dunfee, Contact (jdunfee@diosteub.org);
Child Protection Review Board - Joseph DiPalma; Frank A. Fregiato; Michele Santin;
College of Consultors - Rev. Thomas A. Chillog (tchillog@diosteub.org); Rev. David L. Gaydosik; Rev. Thomas A. Nelson;
Continuing Education of Priests - t) 740-432-7609 phrezo@diosteub.org Very Rev. Paul Hrezo, Coord.;
Deans - Very Rev. William D. Cross, Presentation Deanery (wcross@diosteub.org); Very Rev. Thomas F. Hamm Jr., Nativity of Mary Deanery; Very Rev. Paul E. Hrezo, Visitation Deanery;
Delegate for Religious - t) 740-373-3643 mcampbell@diosteub.org Rev. Msgr. J. Michael Campbell;
Diocesan Building Commission - t) 740-282-3631 syarman@diosteub.org Scott Yarman, Contact; Very Rev. James M. Dunfee (jdunfee@diosteub.org); Louis Almonte;
Diocesan Communications - t) 740-282-3631 dorsatti@diosteub.org Dino Orsatti, Dir.; Matthew DiCenzo, Social Media Coord.;
Diocesan Council of Catholic Women - t) 740-425-2181 (Father David Cornett); 740-695-1617 (Joanne Kolanski) Rev. David Cornett, Moderator; Joanne Kolanski, Pres. (jkolanski51@comcast.net);
Diocesan Director of Cemeteries - t) 740-546-3463 jkolesar@diosteub.org Rev. Msgr. John C. Kolesar;
Diocesan Director of Ecumenism - t) 740-446-0669 thamm@diosteub.org Very Rev. Thomas F. Hamm Jr.;
Diocesan Office of Human Resources - t) 740-282-3631 shughes@diosteub.org Shannon Minch-Hughes, Dir.;
Diocesan Office of Worship - t) 740-282-3631 emaxfield@diosteub.org; cbahen@diosteub.org Rev. Edward A. Maxfield Jr., Dir.; Colleen Bahen, Secy.;
Diocesan/Parish Share Campaign - t) 740-282-3631 Very Rev. James M. Dunfee, Dir. (jdunfee@diosteub.org);
Facilities & Property Management - t) 740-282-3631 syarman@diosteub.org Scott Yarman, Dir.;
Marriage, Family and Respect Life - t) 740-516-9270 Joseph Schmidt, Dir. (jschmidt@diosteub.org);
Office of Catholic Charities and Social Concerns - t) (740) 314-8660 lperdue@diosteub.org; rhawkinberry@diosteub.org Rose Hawkinberry, Dir.; Leah Perdue, Social Svcs. Coord.;
Office of Christian Formation and Schools - t) 740-282-3631 pward@diosteub.org Dcn. Paul Ward, Dir.;
Office of Civil Law - t) 740-282-3631 twilson@diosteub.org Thomas S. Wilson;
Office of Vocations - t) (740) 264-0868 Rev. Joshua Erickson, Dir. (jerickson@diosteub.org); Rev. Nicholas Scott Ward, Asst. Dir. (nward@diosteub.org); Rev. Nicholas Ginnetti, Asst. Dir. (nginnetti@diosteub.org);
Presbyteral Council - Rev. Thomas A. Chillog (tchillog@diosteub.org); Rev. David L. Gaydosik; Rev. Nicholas Ginnetti (nginnetti@diosteub.org);
Priests Personnel Board - Rev. Thomas A. Chillog, Senior Clergy (tchillog@diosteub.org); Rev. David Cornett, Middle Age Clergy; Rev. Nicholas Ginnetti, Younger Clergy (nginnetti@diosteub.org);
Priests' Retirement Board - t) (740) 282-3631 Very Rev. William D. Cross, Chair (wcross@diosteub.org); Rev. John Mucha, Vice Chair; Rev. Thomas A. Chillog (tchillog@diosteub.org);
Propagation of the Faith - t) 740-984-2555 tkozak@diosteub.org Rev. Timothy J. Kozak, Dir.;
Publication, "Steubenville Register" - t) 740-282-3631 dorsatti@diosteub.org Most Rev. Jeffrey M. Monforton, Pres.; Dino Orsatti, Editor;
RCIA - t) 740-446-0669 thamm@diosteub.org Very Rev. Thomas F. Hamm Jr., Dir.;
Sacred Heart Center of Hope - t) (740) 275-4477 Rose Hawkinberry, Mission & Prog. Devel.;
Vicar for Retired Priests - t) 740-635-0408 jmucha@diosteub.org Rev. John Mucha;
Victim Assistance Coordinator - t) 740-282-3631 victimassistance43952@gmail.com Very Rev. James M. Dunfee, Contact (jdunfee@diosteub.org);

PARISHES, MISSIONS, AND CLERGY

STATE OF OHIO

ADENA

St. Casimir Church - 221 Hanna Ave., Adena, OH 43901 t) 740-546-3463; 740-546-4380 (CRP) stcadena@frontier.com; jvucic1@frontier.com Very Rev. William D. Cross, Par. Admin.; Rev. Msgr. John C. Kolesar, Pastor Emer.; Sr. Jeanne Vucic, DRE; CRP Stds.: 7

AMSTERDAM

St. Joseph - 331 N. Main St., Amsterdam, OH 43903; Mailing: 7457 State Rte. 152, Richmond, OH 43944 t) 740-765-4142 jmccoy@diosteub.org Rev. John J. McCoy Jr., Pst.; CRP Stds.: 9

ATHENS

Christ the King University Parish - 141 Mill St., Athens, OH 45701; Mailing: 75 Stewart St., Athens, OH 45701-2925 t) 740-592-2711 wserbonich@athenscatholic.org www.athenscatholic.org Rev. Mark A. Moore, Pst.; Rev. Jeremiah Hahn, Par. Vicar; Dcn. Donald Scott Carson; CRP Stds.: 68

St. Paul Church - 38 N. College St., Athens, OH 45701; Mailing: 75 Stewart St., Athens, OH 45701 t) 740-592-2711 wserbonich@athenscatholic.org www.athenscatholic.org Rev. Mark A. Moore, Pst.; Rev. Jeremiah Hahn, Par. Vicar; Dcn. Donald Scott Carson; CRP Stds.: 68

Guysville, St. John - 75 Stewart St., Athens, OH 45701 mmoore@diosteub.org

BARNESVILLE

Assumption - 306 W. Main St., Barnesville, OH 43713 t) 740-425-2181 assymptionandstmarychurches@yahoo.com; assumptionandstmarychurches@yahoo.com Rev. David Cornett, Pst.; CRP Stds.: 24

St. Mary's - 55699 Marietta St, Barnesville, OH 43713; Mailing: 306 W. Main St., Barnesville, OH 43713 t) 740-425-2181 assumptionandstmarychurches@yahoo.com Rev. David Cornett, Pst.; CRP Stds.: 6

BELLAIRE

St. John - 415 37th St, Bellaire, OH 43906; Mailing: 3745 Tallman Ave., Bellaire, OH 43906 t) 740-676-0051 stjohns3745@comcast.net www.bnspcatholic.org Rev. Daniel Heusel, Pst.; CRP Stds.: 213

BELLE VALLEY

Corpus Christi - 221 Main St., Belle Valley, OH 43717; Mailing: P.O. Box 286, Caldwell, OH 43724 t) 740-732-4129 office@ncccchurches.org www.ncccchurches.org Rev. Thomas A. Nelson, Pst.; CRP Stds.: 6

BEVERLY

St. Bernard - 309 Seventh St., Beverly, OH 45715; Mailing: PO Box 331, Beverly, OH 45715 t) 740-984-2555 stberbev@frontier.org stbernardbeverly.org Rev. Timothy J. Kozak, Pst.; CRP Stds.: 54

BRIDGEPORT

St. Anthony of Padua - 630 Main St., Bridgeport, OH 43912 t) 740-635-0283 bridgeportparishes@comcast.net Rev. John Mucha, Pst.;

St. Joseph - 68210 Neola Ave., Bridgeport, OH 43912 t) 740-635-0408 jmucha@diosteub.org Rev. John Mucha, Pst.;

BUCHTEL

St. Mary of the Hills - Closed Jul 2022

CADIZ

St. Teresa - 143 E. South St., Cadiz, OH 43907 t) 740-942-2211 fkihm@diosteub.org www.harrisoncountycatholicchurches.org Rev. Frederick C. Kihm, Pst.;

CALDWELL

Immaculate Conception - 43700 Fulda Rd., Caldwell, OH 43724; Mailing: P.O. Box 286, Caldwell, OH 43724 t) 740-732-4129 office@ncccchurches.org www.ncccchurches.org Rev. Thomas A. Nelson, Pst.; CRP Stds.: 29

St. Michael - 44935 Carlisle Rd, Caldwell, OH 43724; Mailing: PO Box 286, Caldwell, OH 43724 t) 740-732-4129 office@ncccchurches.org www.ncccchurches.org Rev. Thomas A. Nelson; CRP Stds.: 13

St. Stephen - 1036 Belford St., Caldwell, OH 43724; Mailing: Box 286, Caldwell, OH 43724 t) 740-732-7412 office@ncccchurches.org www.ncccchurches.org Rev. Thomas A. Nelson, Pst.; CRP Stds.: 23

CAMBRIDGE

Christ Our Light Parish - 701 Gomber Ave., Cambridge, OH 43725 t) 740-432-7609 col_office@catholicweb.com; col_dre@catholicweb.com Very Rev. Paul Hrezo, Pst.; Jacob Padden, Parish Life Coord.; Traci Mitchell, DRE; CRP Stds.: 23

St. Benedict School - (Grades PreK-8) 220 N. 7th St., Cambridge, OH 43725 t) 740-432-6751 lynn.padden@omeresa.net www.stbenedictschool.net Jill Lind, Prin.; Stds.: 100; Lay Tchrs.: 10

SS. Peter and Paul - 136 E. High Ave., Lore City, OH 43755 t) 740-685-5582 phrezo@diosteub.org Very Rev. Paul E. Hrezo, Pst.;

CARROLLTON

Our Lady of Mercy - 748 Roswell Rd., S.W., Carrollton, OH 44615; Mailing: P.O. Box 155, Carrollton, OH 44615 t) 330-627-4664 x100; 330-627-4664 (CRP) info@olmcarrollton.org www.olmcarrollton.org Rev. Jonas Shell, Pst.; Jessica Rodgers, DRE; CRP Stds.: 35

CHESAPEAKE

St. Ann - 310 Third Ave., Chesapeake, OH 45619;

Mailing: PO Box 499, Ironton, OH 45638
t) 740-867-4434; (740) 532-0712
stannchurch.weebly.com Rev. Wayne E. Morris, Pst.; Rev. Nicholas Scott Ward, Par. Vicar; CRP Stds.: 4

COLERAIN

St. Frances Cabrini - 72581 Colerain Rd., Colerain, OH 43916; Mailing: St. Mary's Church, 212 W. Main St., Saint Clairsville, OH 43950 t) 740-695-9993 office@stmaryschurchstc.com Rev. Thomas A. Chillog, Pst.; CRP Stds.: 10

DILLONVALE

St. Adalbert - 39 Smithfield St., Dillonvale, OH 43917; Mailing: c/o 221 Hanna Ave., Adena, OH 43901
t) 740-546-3463; 740-769-7858 (CRP)
stcadena@frontier.com; rmzelek@gmail.com Very Rev. William D. Cross, Par. Admin.; Rev. Msgr. John C. Kolesar, Pastor Emer.; James Piazza, DRE; Rosemary Zelek, DRE; CRP Stds.: 7

FREEPORT

St. Matthias Mission - 115 W. Main St., Freeport, OH 43973; Mailing: 143 E. South St., Cadiz, OH 43907
t) 740-942-2211 Rev. Frederick C. Kihm, Pst.;

GALLIPOLIS

St. Louis - 85 State St., Gallipolis, OH 45631
t) 740-446-0669 stlouis85@att.net Very Rev. Thomas F. Hamm Jr., Pst.; CRP Stds.: 18

GLOUSTER

Holy Cross - 31 Republic Ave., Glouster, OH 45732; Mailing: 75 Stewart St, Athens, OH 45701
t) 740-592-2711 skotts@athenscatholic.org; mklim@athenscatholic.org www.athenscatholic.org Rev. Mark A. Moore, Pst.; Rev. Jeremiah Hahn, Vicar; CRP Stds.: 17

HOPEDALE

Sacred Heart - 209 Cross St, Hopedale, OH 43976; Mailing: 143 E South St., Cadiz, OH 43907
t) 740-942-2211 fkihm@diosteub.org www.harrisoncountycatholicchurches.org Rev. Frederick C. Kihm, Pst.; CRP Stds.: 4

IRONTON

St. Joseph Parish - 905 S. Fifth St., Ironton, OH 45638; Mailing: P.O. Box 499, Ironton, OH 45638 t) (740) 532-0712; (740) 532-0561 Rev. Wayne E. Morris; Rev. Nicholas Scott Ward, Par. Vicar; Jane Rudmann, DRE; CRP Stds.: 42

St. Lawrence Parish - 905 S. Fifth St., Ironton, OH 45638-0499; Mailing: P.O. Box 499, Ironton, OH 45638-0499 t) 740-532-0561 Rev. Wayne E. Morris, Pst.; Rev. Nicholas Scott Ward, Par. Vicar; CRP Stds.: 42

St. Lawrence Central Grade School - (Grades PreK-6) 315 S. 6th St., Ironton, OH 45638 t) 740-532-5052 jcm-1@sbcglobal.net irontoncatholicschools.org James Christopher Monte, Prin.; Stds.: 121; Lay Tchrs.: 11

St. Joseph Central High School - (Grades 7-12) 912 S. 6th St., Ironton, OH 45638 t) 740-532-0485 chris.monte@irontoncatholicschools.org irontoncatholicschools.com James Christopher Monte, Prin.; Stds.: 71; Lay Tchrs.: 10

St. Mary - 905 S, Fifth St., Ironton, OH 45638-0499; Mailing: P.O. Box 499, Ironton, OH 45638-0499
t) 740-532-0712 Rev. Wayne E. Morris, Pst.; Rev. Nicholas Scott Ward, Par. Vicar;

LITTLE HOCKING

St. Ambrose - 5080 School House Rd., Little Hocking, OH 45742 t) 740-423-7422 stambroseohio.org Rev. David L. Huffman, Pst.;

LOWELL

Our Lady of Mercy - 5001 Lowell Hill Rd., Lowell, OH 45744 t) 740-896-2207 olm.churchlowell@gmail.com Rev. David L. Gaydosik, Pst.; CRP Stds.: 18

LOWER SALEM

St. Henry - 36575 Church St., Lower Salem, OH 45745; Mailing: 506 Fourth St., Marietta, OH 45750
t) 740-373-3643; 740-896-2207 (Secondary tel) olm.churchlowell@gmail.com www.stmarysmarietta.org/sthenry/ Rev. Msgr. John Michael Campbell, Pst.; Rev. Edward A. Maxfield Jr., Par. Vicar; CRP Stds.: 23

MALVERN

St. Francis Xavier - 125 Carrollton St., Malvern, OH 44644; Mailing: PO Box 275, Minerva, OH 44657
t) 330-868-4498 smstgabriel@frontier.com stgabriel-stfrancis.org Rev. Victor Cinson, Pst.; Fescemyer Michele, DRE; CRP Stds.: 10

MARIETTA

Basilica of St. Mary of the Assumption - 506 Fourth St., Marietta, OH 45750 t) 740-373-3643; 740-373-9815 (CRP) info@stmarysmarietta.org www.stmarysmarietta.org/ Rev. Msgr. John Michael Campbell, Pst.; Rev. Edward A. Maxfield Jr., Par. Vicar; Joseph Schmidt, DRE; CRP Stds.: 60

Basilica of St. Mary of the Assumption School - (Grades PreK-8) 320 Marion St., Marietta, OH 45750 t) 740-374-8181 elizabethtokodi@stmaryscatholic.org stmarys.k12.oh.us Elizabeth Tokodi, Prin.; Stds.: 208; Lay Tchrs.: 13

Marietta College Campus Ministry - t) (740) 373-3643 mcampbell@diosteub.org

St. John the Baptist - 17784 State Rte. 676, Marietta, OH 45750 t) 740-896-3566 stjohnchurchtown@yahoo.com www.stjohnchurchtown.com Rev. David L. Gaydosik, Pst.; CRP Stds.: 20

St. John Central Grade School - (Grades PreK-8) 17654 State Rte. 676, Marietta, OH 45750
t) 740-896-2697 karenpottmeyer@yahoo.com Stds.: 85; Lay Tchrs.: 11

MARTINS FERRY

St. Mary - 20 N. Fourth St., Martins Ferry, OH 43935
t) 740-633-1416 stmarymf@sbcglobal.net Rev. Thomas Marut, Pst.;

St. Mary Central - (Grades PreK-8) 24 N. Fourth St., Martins Ferry, OH 43935 t) 740-633-5424 theresa.young@omeresa.net www.smcmartinsferry.weebly.com Theresa Young, Prin.; Stds.: 101; Lay Tchrs.: 9

MCCONNELSVILLE

St. James - 257 E. Bell Ave., McConnelsville, OH 43756; Mailing: PO Box 331, Beverly, OH 45715
t) 740-984-2555 contact@stjamesmcconnelsville.org stjamesmcconnelsville.org Rev. Timothy J. Kozak, Pst.;

MINERVA

St. Gabriel the Archangel - 400 W. High, Minerva, OH 44657; Mailing: PO Box 275, Minerva, OH 44657
t) 330-868-4498 smstgabriel@frontier.com stgabriel-stfrancis.org Rev. Victor Cinson, Pst.; Fescemyer Michele, DRE; CRP Stds.: 61

MINGO JUNCTION

St. Agnes - 204 St. Clair Ave., Mingo Junction, OH 43938-1047 t) 740-535-1491 offices@stagnesmingo.org; jdunfee@diosteub.org www.stagnesmingo.org Very Rev. James M. Dunfee, Pst.; Dcn. Paul Ward; CRP Stds.: 3

POMEROY

Sacred Heart - 161 Mulberry Ave., Pomeroy, OH 45769; Mailing: 75 Stewart St., Athens, OH 45701
t) 740-592-2711 wserbonich@athenscatholic.org www.athenscatholic.org Sacramental records are at Christ the King University Parish, Athens. Rev. Jeremiah Hahn, Par. Vicar; Rev. Mark A. Moore, Pst.; Dcn. Donald Scott Carson; CRP Stds.: 21

RICHMOND

St. John Fisher - 7457 St. Hwy. 152, Richmond, OH 43944 t) 740-765-4142 jmccoy@diosteub.org Rev. John J. McCoy Jr., Pst.;

SHADYSIDE

St. Mary's - 350 E. 40th St., Shadyside, OH 43947; Mailing: c/o 3745 Tallman Ave, Bellaire, OH 43906
t) 740-676-0051 www.bnspcatholic.org Rev. Daniel Heusel, Pst.; CRP Stds.: 70

ST. CLAIRSVILLE

St. Mary's - 218 W. Main St., St. Clairsville, OH 43950; Mailing: 212 W. Main St., St. Clairsville, OH 43950
t) 740-695-9993; 740-695-2076 office@stmaryschurchstc.com www.stmaryschurchstc.com Dcn. Charles J. Schneider; Rev. Thomas A. Chillog, Pst.; CRP Stds.: 31

St. Mary Central Grade School - (Grades PreK-8) 226 W. Main St., St. Clairsville, OH 43950
t) 740-695-3189 angel.glitch@omeresa.net stmarycentral.com Angelica Glitch, Prin.; Stds.: 117; Lay Tchrs.: 13

STEUBENVILLE

Holy Name Cathedral - 411 S 5th St, Steubenville, OH 43952; Mailing: P.O. Box 908, Steubenville, OH 43952
t) 740-264-6177 totcmailbox@comcast.net triumphofthecross.org Rev. Matthew W.J. Gossett, Pst.; Rev. Nicholas Ginnetti, Par. Vicar; Dcn. Randall Redington; Dcn. Richard G. Adams; CRP Stds.: 13

Holy Family - 2565 Alexander Ave., Steubenville, OH 43952; Mailing: 2608 Hollywood Blvd., Steubenville, OH 43952 t) 740-264-2825 rectory@holyfamilyweb.org www.holyfamilystubenville.com Rev. Msgr. Gerald E. Calovini, Pst.; Rev. Drake McCalister, Assoc. Pst.; Dcn. Edward G. Kovach; Dcn. Stephen F. Miletic; Dcn. Michael Welker; CRP Stds.: 71

St. Peter's - 425 N. 4th St., Steubenville, OH 43952
t) 740-282-7612 office@stpetersteub.com www.stpetersteub.com Very Rev. Timothy J. Huffman, Pst.; Very Rev. Bradley W. Greer, Par. Vicar; Dcn. Thomas F. Maedke; CRP Stds.: 12

Triumph of the Cross - 204 Rosemont Ave, Steubenville, OH 43952; Mailing: P O Box 908, Steubenville, OH 43952 t) 740-264-6177 totcmailbox@comcast.net www.triumphofthecross.org Rev. Matthew W.J. Gossett, Pst.; Rev. Nicholas Ginnetti, Par. Vicar; Dcn. Richard G. Adams; Dcn. Randall Redington; CRP Stds.: 13

TILTONSVILLE

St. Joseph - 204 Mound St., Tiltonsville, OH 43963-0008
t) 740-859-4018 sj-sl@comcast.net stjosephtiltonsville.org Very Rev. William D. Cross, Pst.; Barbara DiCenzo, DRE; CRP Stds.: 20

TORONTO

St. Francis of Assisi - 409 Grant St., Toronto, OH 43964; Mailing: 1225 N. River Ave., Toronto, OH 43964
t) 740-537-4433 sfsjtoronto@sbcglobal.net www.sfsjtoronto.com Rev. Thomas A. Vennitti, Pst.; Dcn. Thomas E. Graham; Judy Koehnlein, DRE;

St. Joseph's - 1225 N. River Ave., Toronto, OH 43964
t) 740-537-4433 sfsjtoronto@sbcglobal.net www.sfsjtoronto.com Rev. Thomas A. Vennitti, Pst.; Dcn. Thomas E. Graham; Judy Koehnlein, DRE; CRP Stds.: 4

WAYNESBURG

St. Mary - 8012 Bachelor Rd, Waynesburg, OH 44688
t) 330-627-4664 info@olmcarrollton.org Rev. Jonas Shell, Pst.; CRP Stds.: 3

WINTERSVILLE

Blessed Sacrament - 852 Main St., Wintersville, OH 43953-3870 t) 740-264-0868 mail@wintersvilleparishes.org www.wintersvilleparishes.org Rev. Michael Gossett, Pst.; Rev. Joshua Erickson, Par. Vicar; Dcn. Mark A. Erste; Dcn. Stephen Frezza; Dcn. Robert Rice; Barbara VanBeveren, DRE; CRP Stds.: 23

Our Lady of Lourdes - 1521 Bantam Ridge Rd., Wintersville, OH 43953; Mailing: 852 Main St., Wintersville, OH 43953 t) 740-264-0868 mail@wintersvilleparishes.org www.wintersvilleparishes.org Rev. Michael Gossett, Pst.; Rev. Joshua Erickson, Par. Vicar; Dcn. Mark A. Erste; Dcn. Stephen Frezza; Dcn. Robert Rice; CRP Stds.: 1

WOODSFIELD

St. John the Baptist - 35560 Miltonsburg-Calais Rd., Woodsfield, OH 43793; Mailing: 334 S. Main St., Woodsfield, OH 43793 t) 740-472-0187 tdavison@diosteub.org; jenshoe77@yahoo.com www.monroecountycatholic.org Rev. Timothy L. Davison, Pst.;

St. Sylvester - 332 S Main St, Woodsfield, OH 43793; Mailing: 334 S Main St, Woodsfield, OH 43793
t) 740-472-0187 tdavison@diosteub.org; jenshoe77@yahoo.com www.monroecountycatholic.org Rev. Timothy L. Davison, Pst.; Schumacher Jill, DRE; CRP Stds.: 2

Central Grade School - (Grades PreSchool-8) 119 Wayne St., Woodsfield, OH 43793 t) 740-472-0321 rguiler@stsylvestercentral.org Robyn Guiler, Prin.; Stds.: 88; Lay Tchrs.: 8

SCHOOLS: PRESCHOOL THRU HIGH SCHOOL

SCHOOLS

STATE OF OHIO

STEUBENVILLE

Bishop John King Mussio Central Elementary School - (PAR) (Grades PreK-5) 100 Etta Ave., Steubenville, OH 43952 t) 740-264-2550 tdanaher@bishopmussio.org www.steubenvillecatholicschools.org Theresa Danaher, Prin.; Stds.: 335; Lay Tchrs.: 21

Bishop John King Mussio Central Junior High School - (DIO) (Grades 6-8) 320 W. View Ave., Ste. 2, Steubenville, OH 43952 t) 740-346-0028 tcostello@steubenvillecatholiccentral.org; cdimichelle@bishopmussio.org www.steubenvillecatholicschools.org Jude Lucas, Prin.; Stds.: 147; Lay Tchrs.: 12

HIGH SCHOOLS

STATE OF OHIO

IRONTON

St. Joseph Central - (PAR) (Grades 7-12) 912 S. Sixth St., Ironton, OH 45638 t) 740-532-0485 chris.monte@irontoncatholicschools.org James Christopher Monte, Prin.; Stds.: 85; Lay Tchrs.: 11

STEUBENVILLE

Catholic Central High School - (DIO) (Grades 9-12) 320 W. View, Steubenville, OH 43952 t) 740-264-5538 tcostello@steubenvillecatholiccentral.org www.steubenvillecatholicschools.org Jude Lucas, Prin.; Stds.: 229; Lay Tchrs.: 17

INSTITUTIONS LOCATED IN DIOCESE

ASSOCIATIONS [ASN]

STEUBENVILLE

Mt. Calvary Cemetery Association - 94 Mt. Calvary Ln., Steubenville, OH 43952 t) 740-264-1331 ldigregory@mountcalvarysteubenville.org Lou DiGregory, Supt.;

CAMPUS MINISTRY / NEWMAN CENTERS [CAM]

ATHENS

Christ the King University Parish - Ohio University - 75 Stewart St., Athens, OH 45701 t) 740-592-2711 mmoore@diosteub.org www.athenscatholic.org Rev. Mark A. Moore, Pst.; Rev. Jeremiah Hahn, Par. Vicar;

Hocking Technical College - 75 Stewart St., Athens, OH 45701 t) 740-592-2711 mmoore@diosteub.org athenscatholic.org Rev. Mark A. Moore, Pst.;

MARIETTA

Marietta College - c/o St. Mary Basilica, 506 Fourth St., Marietta, OH 45750 t) 740-373-3643 www.stmarysmarietta.org Rev. Msgr. John Michael Campbell, Dir.;

ST. CLAIRSVILLE

Ohio University - Eastern - c/o St. Mary's Church, 212 W. Main St., St. Clairsville, OH 43950 t) 740-695-9993 office@stmaryschurchstc.com Rev. Thomas A. Chillog, Contact;

COLLEGES & UNIVERSITIES [COL]

STEUBENVILLE

Franciscan University of Steubenville - 1235 University Blvd., Steubenville, OH 43952 t) 740-283-3771 admissions@franciscan.edu www.franciscan.edu Rev. Shawn Roberson, T.O.R., Chap.; Rev. Daniel Klimek, TOR, Prof.; Rev. Donald S. Frinsko, T.O.R., Prof.; Rev. Nathan Malavolti, T.O.R., Prof.; Rev. Nicholas Polichnowski, Prof.; Rev. Gregory Plow, T.O.R., Pst. Assoc.; Rev. Luke Robertson, TOR, Prof.; Brenan Pergi, COO; Dr. Daniel R. Kempton, Vice. Pres.; Rev. Dave Pivonka, TOR, Pres.; Rev. Jonathan St. Andre, TOR, Vice. Pres.; Rev. Jonathan McElhone, Dir.; Amy Leoni, Librn.; Rev. Brian Cavanaugh, T.O.R., Information Technology Associate; Rev. Dominic Foster, TOR, Counselor; Rev. James Angert, TOR, Pst. Assoc.; Rev. Rufino Corona, TOR, Pst. Assoc.; Rev. Dennis Gang, TOR, Pst. Assoc.; Stds.: 3,656; Lay Tchrs.: 126; Pr. Tchrs.: 5; Sr. Tchrs.: 1; Scholastics: 132

CONVENTS, MONASTERIES, AND RESIDENCES FOR WOMEN [CON]

CARROLLTON

Sisters of Our Lady of Charity of the Good Shepherd - Carrollton, Inc. - 620 Roswell Rd., N.W., Carrollton, OH 44615; Mailing: P.O. Box 340, Carrollton, OH 44615 t) 330-627-1641 x222 cs.provincial@gssweb.org Sr. Veronica Villarreal, RGS, Supr.; Sr. Francisca Aguillon, Prov.; Srs.: 39

Sisters of the Holy Cross OA, Inc. - 164 Apollo Rd. S.E., Carrollton, OH 44615 t) 330-476-7020 c) 234-521-2389 sr.m.genofeva.isser@protonmail.com; office.srsoa.bethany@protonmail.com www.avecrux.org Pontifical Right Institute Sr. Maria Genofeva Helena Isser, SrOA, Supr.; Srs.: 7

TORONTO

Franciscan Sisters Third Order Regular of Penance of the Sorrowful Mother - 369 Little Church Rd., Toronto, OH 43964 t) 740-544-5542 franciscans@torsisters.org www.franciscansisterstor.org Mother Della Marie Doyle, TOR, Rel. Ord. Ldr.; Srs.: 33

ENDOWMENTS / FOUNDATIONS / TRUSTS [EFT]

MUNSONVILLE

Twelve Rivers Foundation (The Language and Catechetical Institute (LCI)) - 221 Aten Rd., Munsonville, NH 03457; Mailing: P.O. Box 4857, Steubenville, OH 43952 c) (740) 284-6160 www.lciaustria.org Bobette Huzovic, Board Member;

HOSPITALS / HEALTH SERVICES [HOS]

STEUBENVILLE

Trinity Health System - Administration, 4000 Johnson Rd., Steubenville, OH 43952 t) 740-264-8360; 740-264-8000 glendaharlan@trinityhealth.com www.trinityhealth.com Glenda Harlan, Administrative Assistant; Bed Capacity: 354; Asstd. Annu.: 472,892; Staff: 2,058

Trinity Health System Foundation - 380 Summit Ave., Steubenville, OH 43952 t) 740-283-7791 cmpoludniak@trinityhealth.com Matthew Grimshaw, COO;

Trinity Medical Center, East - 380 Summit Ave., Steubenville, OH 43952 Matthew Grimshaw, COO;

Trinity Medical Center, West - 4000 Johnson Rd., Steubenville, OH 43952 Matthew Grimshaw, COO; Bed Capacity: 354; Asstd. Annu.: 472,892; Staff: 2,058

MISCELLANEOUS [MIS]

BLOOMINGDALE

***Apostolate for Family Consecration** - 3375 County Rd. 36, Bloomingdale, OH 43910-7903 t) 740-567-7700 info@afc.org www.afc.org Catholic Familyland/John Paul II Holy Family Center Randy A. Christensen, Pres.;

Mount Carmel Hermitage of Ohio, Inc - 1619 Township Rd. 204, Bloomingdale, OH 43910 t) 740-765-5409 dcook@diosteub.org

GALLIPOLIS

RCIA - 85 State St., Gallipolis, OH 45631 t) 740-446-0669 thamm@diosteub.org Very Rev. Thomas F. Hamm Jr., Dir.;

HOPEDALE

***Catholics United for the Faith, Inc.** - 85882 Water Works Rd., Hopedale, OH 43976 t) 740-283-2484 administrativeassistant@cuf.org www.cuf.org International Lay Apostolate Philip Gray, Pres.;

PITTSBURGH

***Vagabond Missions** - 57 21st St., Pittsburgh, PA 15222; Mailing: PO Box 53109, Pittsburgh, PA 15219 t) 724-230-6142 andyl@vagabondmissions.com www.vagabondmissions.com Missionaries serving inner-city teenagers Andy Lesnefsky, Pres.; Kris Frank, Vice. Pres.;

RICHMOND

Boy Scouts - 7457 State Hwy. 152, Richmond, OH 43944 t) 740-765-4142 jmccoy@diosteub.org Rev. John J. McCoy Jr., Dir.;

STEUBENVILLE

Campaign for Human Development - 422 Washington St., Steubenville, OH 43952; Mailing: P.O. Box 969, Steubenville, OH 43952 t) 740-282-3631 x122 rraveaux@diosteub.org www.diosteub.org Rose Raveaux, Dir.;

***Dietrich von Hildebrand Legacy Project** - 1235 University Blvd., Steubenville, OH 43952 t) 740-263-3002 info@hildebrandproject.org www.hildebrandproject.org John Henry Crosby, Pres.;

***Fraternity of Priests, Inc.** - ; Mailing: P.O. Box 442, Steubenville, OH 43952 t) 740-283-4400 contact@fraternityofpriests.org www.fraternityofpriests.org Rev. Volney DeRosia, Chair;

Lay Employees Pension Plan - 422 Washington St., Steubenville, OH 43952; Mailing: P.O. Box 969, Steubenville, OH 43952 t) 740-282-3631 shughes@diosteub.org diosteub.org Shannon Minch-Hughes, Dir.;

Marriage Encounter - 422 Washington St., Steubenville, OH 43952 t) 740-516-9270 jschmidt@diosteub.org Joseph Schmidt, Dir.;

***Mary Seat of Wisdom Classical Community** - 36 Villa Dr., Steubenville, OH 43952 t) 720-635-0857 Karen Reynolds, Contact;

***The Messy Family Project** - 117 S. Hollywood Blvd., #140, Steubenville, OH 43952 t) 740-314-0393 mike@messyfamilyproject.org www.messyfamilyproject.org Michael Hernon, Pres.;

***Pastoral Solutions Institute (CatholicCounselors, CatholicHOM)** - 234 St. Joseph Dr., Steubenville, OH 43952 t) 800-274-4658 gpopcak@catholiccounselors.com www.catholiccounselors.com Providing pastoral counseling, and radio, TV, web and print media resources to Catholics individuals, couples, and families worldwide. Gregory K. Popcak, Pres.;

***St. Paul Center for Biblical Theology** - 1468 Parkview Cir., Steubenville, OH 43952 t) 740-264-9535 www.stpaulcenter.com Emmaus Road Publishing, Emmaus Academic, and the international theological journal Nova et Vetera are programs of the St. Paul Center. Dr. Scott Hahn, Pres.; Ken Baldwin, Dir.;

MONASTERIES AND RESIDENCES FOR PRIESTS AND BROTHERS [MON]

BLOOMINGDALE

Holy Family Hermitage - 1501 Fairplay Rd., Bloomingdale, OH 43910-7971 t) 740-765-4511 dcook@diosteub.org www.camaldolese.org Bro. Charles Albanese; Bro. John Moreno; Rev. Basil Corriere, E.C., Prior; Rev. Stephen Hwang, E.C.; Rev. Aleksander Adamiak; Bro. Solanus Balleza, E.C.; Brs.: 3; Priests: 3

CARROLLTON

Opus Angelorum, Inc. - 164 Apollo Rd., S.E., Carrollton, OH 44615 t) 330-969-9900 frludwig@opusangelorum.org Rev. Ludwig M. Oppl, O.R.C., Pres.; Rev. Wolfgang Seitz, O.R.C., Secy.; Rev. John Eudes Brohl, Treas.; Rev. Matthew Hincks, O.R.C., Dir.; Priests: 4

Order of the Holy Cross, Inc. - 164 Apollo Rd., S.E., Carrollton, OH 44615 t) 330-313-1331 frludwig@opusangelorum.org Rev. Ludwig M. Oppl, O.R.C., Supr.; Rev. John Eudes Brohl; Rev. Matthew Hincks, O.R.C.; Rev. Wolfgang Seitz, O.R.C.; Rev. William Wagner, O.R.C.; Bro. Isaac Yagley, O.R.C.; Bro. Raphael Gotschol; Brs.: 2; Priests: 5

STEUBENVILLE

Diocesan Brotherhood of Immaculate Heart of Mary - 4301 Earl Dr., Unit A6, Steubenville, OH 43953 t) 740-283-2462 dcarroll@diosteub.org Brothers of the Immaculate Heart of Mary Bro. Dominic Carroll, I.H.M., Supr.; Brs.: 3

Holy Spirit Friary - 1235 University Blvd., Steubenville, OH 43952 t) 740-283-6403 www.franciscan.edu Rev. Dave Pivonka, TOR, Pres.; Rev. Brian Cavanaugh, T.O.R.; Rev. Nathan Malavolti, T.O.R.; Rev. Shawn Roberson, T.O.R.; Rev. James Angert, TOR; John Marie Blair, TOR; Rev. Dennis Gang, TOR; Rev. Rufino Corona, TOR; Rev. Dominic Foster, TOR; Rev. Donald S. Frinsko, T.O.R.; Rev. Daniel Klimek, TOR; Rev. Jonathan McElhone; Rev. Gregory Plow, TOR; Rev. Nicholas Polichnowski; Rev. Luke Robertson, TOR; Brs.: 1; Priests: 14

SHRINES [SHR]

IRONTON

Our Lady of Fatima Shrine - 603 County Rd. 1A, Franklin Furnace, Ironton, OH 45638-0499; Mailing: P.O. Box 499, Ironton, OH 45638-0499 t) 740-532-0712 dhuffman@diosteub.org Rev. Wayne E. Morris, Pst.;

SPECIAL CARE FACILITIES [SPF]

CARROLLTON

St. John Villa - 701 Crest St., N.W., Carrollton, OH 44615; Mailing: P.O Box 457, Carrollton, OH 44615 t) 330-627-9789 swilliamson@stjohnsvilla.net stjohnsvilla.net A residential facility for persons with developmental disabilities. Richard Lee Davis, Pres.; Bed Capacity: 55; Asstd. Annu.: 47; Staff: 103

An asterisk (*) denotes an organization that has established tax-exempt status directly with the IRS and is not covered by the USCCB Group Ruling.

Diocese of Stockton

(Dioecesis Stocktoniensis)

MOST REVEREND MYRON J. COTTA

Bishop of Stockton; ordained September 12, 1987; appointed Titular Bishop of Muteci and Auxiliary Bishop of Sacramento January 24, 2014; installed March 25, 2014; appointed Bishop of Stockton January 23, 2018; installed March 15, 2018. Chancery Office, 212 N. San Joaquin St., Stockton, CA 95202

Chancery Office: 212 N. San Joaquin St., Stockton, CA 95202. T: 209-466-0636; F: 209-941-9722.

ESTABLISHED JANUARY 13, 1962

Square Miles 9,938.

Comprises six Counties in the State of California-viz., Alpine, Calaveras, Mono, San Joaquin, Stanislaus and Tuolumne.

Legal Title: The Roman Catholic Bishop of Stockton, a Corporation Sole.

For legal titles of parishes and diocesan institutions, consult the Chancery Office.

STATISTICAL OVERVIEW

Personnel

Bishop 1
Priests: Diocesan Active in Diocese 46
Priests: Diocesan Active Outside Diocese 4
Priests: Retired, Sick or Absent 18
Number of Diocesan Priests 68
Religious Priests in Diocese 14
Total Priests in your Diocese 82
Extern Priests in Diocese 16
Ordinations:
Permanent Deacons 4
Permanent Deacons in Diocese 48
Total Sisters 49

Parishes

Parishes 35
With Resident Pastor:
Resident Diocesan Priests 27
Resident Religious Priests 7
Without Resident Pastor:
Administered by Deacons 1
Missions 14

Professional Ministry Personnel:
Sisters 49
Lay Ministers 75

Welfare

Catholic Hospitals 1
Total Assisted 224,450
Day Care Centers 2
Total Assisted 150
Special Centers for Social Services 1
Total Assisted 93,311

Educational

Diocesan Students in Other Seminaries 8
Total Seminarians 8
High Schools, Diocesan and Parish 2
Total Students 1,208
Elementary Schools, Diocesan and Parish 10
Total Students 2,330
Catechesis / Religious Education:
High School Students 3,436
Elementary Students 10,482
Total Students under Catholic Instruction 17,464

Teachers in Diocese:
Priests 1
Sisters 2
Lay Teachers 202

Vital Statistics

Receptions into the Church:
Infant Baptism Totals 4,885
Minor Baptism Totals 212
Adult Baptism Totals 100
Received into Full Communion 338
First Communions 3,085
Confirmations 2,861
Marriages:
Catholic 582
Interfaith 99
Total Marriages 681
Deaths 1,717
Total Catholic Population 232,547
Total Population 1,458,922

LEADERSHIP

Chancery Office - t) 209-466-0636 www.stocktondiocese.org Most Rev. Myron J. Cotta, Bishop (Bishopcotta@stocktondiocese.org); Rev. William McDonald, Vicar General; Very Rev. John J.M. Foster, Episcopal Vicar for Temporal & Canonical Affairs;

Vicar General - t) 209-466-0636 vicargeneral@stocktondiocese.org www.stocktondiocese.org Rev. William McDonald, Vicar;

Chancellor - t) 209-466-0636 dhollenhorst@stocktondiocese.org Dyan Hollenhorst;

Executive Assistant - t) (209) 466-0636 afranco@stocktondiocese.org Ana Maria Franco, Exec. Asst. to Vicar General & Chancellor;

Vicar for Priests - t) 209-466-0636 vicarforpriests@stocktondiocese.org Rev. Brandon M. Ware, Vicar for Priests (viarforpriests@stocktondiocese.org); Rev. David Dutra, Assoc. Vicar for Priests (ddutra@stocktondiocese.org);

Chief Financial Officer - t) 209-466-0636 dadel@stocktondiocese.org Doug Adel;

Director of Human Resources - t) 209-466-0636 ldillen@stocktondiocese.org Linda Dillen;

Catholic Social Teaching - c) 209-466-0636 Dcn. Michael Wofford (mike.wofford@shs.ca.gov);

Diocesan Tribunal - t) 209-466-0636 judicalvicar@stocktondiocese.org Very Rev. Luis Navarro, Dir. (judicalvicar@stocktondiocese.org);

Judges - t) (209) 466-0636 Elisa Ugarte; Julianne Shanklin; Cherry Clark;

Judicial Vicar - t) 209-466-0636 Very Rev. Luis Navarro;

Moderator - t) 209-466-0636 Very Rev. Luis Navarro;

Vice-Officialis - t) 209-466-0636 Rev. Msgr. Richard Ryan;

Tribunal Personnel - t) 209-466-0636 pcumpian@stocktondiocese.org Pat Cumpian, Admin.; Lourdes Arvizu, Tribunal Asst.;

Defenders of the Bond - Raphael S. Frackiewicz; Elisa Ugarte; Very Rev. Kenneth J. Harder;

Presbyteral Council - t) 209-466-0636 Rev. William McDonald, Vicar; Very Rev. John J.M. Foster, Vicar; Rev. Brandon M. Ware (viarforpriests@stocktondiocese.org);

College of Consultors - t) 209-466-0636 Very Rev. John J.M. Foster; Rev. William McDonald; Rev. Brandon M. Ware (viarforpriests@stocktondiocese.org);

Deans - Rev. Larry Machado, Deanery 1 (lmachado@stocktondiocese.org); Rev. Alvaro H. Delgado, Deanery 2 (adelgado@stocktondiocese.org); Rev. Samuel Woods, Deanery 3;

The Roman Catholic Welfare Corporation of Stockton - t) 209-466-0636 Most Rev. Myron J. Cotta (Bishopcotta@stocktondiocese.org); Very Rev. John J.M. Foster, Vicar; Doug Adel;

Diocesan Building Committee - t) 209-466-0636 Rev. Tom Orlando, Chair (torlando@stocktondiocese.org); Very Rev. John J.M. Foster; Dcn. Greg Yeager;

Diocesan Finance Council - t) (209) 466-0636 Very Rev. John J.M. Foster, Episcopal Vicar for Canonical Affairs; Doug Adel, CFO; Kevin Dougherty;

Personnel Board - t) 209-466-0636 Most Rev. Myron J. Cotta (Bishopcotta@stocktondiocese.org); Rev. William McDonald; Rev. Brandon M. Ware (viarforpriests@stocktondiocese.org);

OFFICES AND DIRECTORS

Apostleship of the Sea - t) 209-607-1450 William Nahorn III, Chap.;

Apostolado Hispano - t) 209-466-0636 dramlo@stocktondiocese.org Digna Ramirez-Lopez, Dir.;

Catholic Charities - t) 209-444-5900 marevalos@ccstockton.org Martha Arevalos, Exec. Dir.;

Catholic Committee on Scouting - t) 209-466-0636 ccc@stocktondiocese.org Helen Hoxie, Dir.;

Catholic Schools Office - t) 209-466-0636 x654 mgraham@stocktondiocese.org Marian Degroot Graham, Dir.; Judee Sani, Curriculum & Instruction Coord.;

Catholic Youth Organization - t) 209-466-0636 cyodirector1@gmail.com Gina Ratto, Dir.;

Cemeteries - t) 209-466-6202 jprieto@sjcemeteries.com Jennifer Prieto, Dir.;

Censor Librorum - Rev. Juan Serna, S.T.L., Dir. (jserna@stocktondiocese.org);

Communications Office - t) 209-466-0636 x659 commsdirector@stocktondiocese.org Erin Haight, Dir.;

Cursillo Movement-English and Spanish - t) 209-608-1307; 209-471-2617 quintanamanuel1955@gmail.com; mercee@hotmail.com Mercy Somera, English Coord.; Manuel Quintana, Spanish Coord.;

Development - t) 209-466-0636 x648 serikson@stocktondiocese.org Stacy Erickson, Dir.;

Ecumenism - t) 209-838-2133 deaconcouple@att.net Dcn. Thomas Ciccarelli (deacontom@stpatricksripon.com);

Engaged Encounter - t) (209) 645-0267 www.stocktonee.com Michael Babowal; Crystal Babowal;

Episcopal Liaison of Catholic Charismatic Renewal - t) (209) 601-4745; (209) 466-0636 Dcn. Leo Canton, English Catholic Charismatic Dir.; Rev. William McDonald, Spanish Catholic Charismatic Dir.;

Family & Respect Life Office - t) 209-466-0636 sbudnik@stocktondiocese.org; rponcini@stocktondiocese.org Dcn. Steve Budnik, Coord., Marriage & Family Life; Robert Poncini, Coord., Life & Dignity;

Filipino Pastoral Ministry - t) 209-483-8930 golanomura@aol.com Gloria Nomura, Coord.;

Hispanic Youth & Young Adult Ministry - t) 209-466-0636 x632 jlopez@stocktondiocese.org

Liturgical Commission - t) 209-466-0636 x637 mschmitz@stocktondiocese.org Michael Schmitz, Dir., Liturgy & Worship;

Executive Committee - Most Rev. Myron J. Cotta, Pres.; Dcn. Jose Reyes, Chair; Michael Schmitz, Mem.;

Members-At-Large - Rev. Jose Salvador Ledesma; Eileen Yeager; David Springer;

Migrant Ministry Team - t) 209-466-0636 jlopez@stocktondiocese.org Jose Lopez-Ceja, Leader; Sr. Alicia Lopez, M.G.Sp.S.; Sr. Lourdes Gonzales, M.G.Sp.S.;

Newman Campus Ministry - t) (209) 669-0473 Rev. Tom Orlando (torlando@stocktondiocese.org);

Office for Deacon Formation - t) 209-466-0636 wbillion@stocktondiocese.org Sr. Wanda Billion, M.S.C., Dir. Dcn. Formation; Dcn. Gregory Yeager, Dir. Deacons;

Office for Seminarians - t) 209-546-7620 cmartinez@stocktondiocese.org Rev. Cesar Martinez, Dir.;

Office for Worship - t) 209-466-0636 x637 mschmitz@stocktondiocese.org Michael Schmitz, Dir., Liturgy & Worship;

Office of Catechumenate - t) 209-466-0636 mschmitz@stocktondiocese.org Michael Schmitz, Dir., Liturgy & Worship;

Office of Evangelization and Faith Formation - t) 209-466-0636 ggayala@stocktondiocese.org Graciela Garza-Ayala, Dir.;

Permanent Diaconate Formation Program - t) 209-466-0636 gyeager@annunciationstockton.org Dcn. Gregory Yeager, Dir.;

Propagation of the Faith - t) 209-466-0636 Dyan Hollenhorst, Chancellor;

School of Ministry - t) 209-466-0636 x631 dbombongan@stocktondiocese.org Dominador Bombongan Jr., Dir.;

Vicar for Religious Women - t) 209-466-0636 wbillion@stocktondiocese.org Sr. Wanda Billion, M.S.C.;

Victim Assistance Coordinator - t) 209-466-0636 Brande Nicole Vargas, Victim Assistance Coord.;

Vocations - t) 209-546-7620 vocations@stocktondiocese.org Rev. Cesar Martinez, Dir.;

CANONICAL SERVICES

Episcopal Vicar For Temporal & Canonical Affairs - t) (209) 466-0636 Very Rev. John J.M. Foster, Episcopal Vicar for Temporal & Canonical Affairs;

PARISHES, MISSIONS, AND CLERGY

STATE OF CALIFORNIA

ANGELS CAMP

St. Patrick Church of Angels Camp (Pastor of) - 820 S. Main St., Angels Camp, CA 95222; Mailing: P.O. Box 576, Angels Camp, CA 95222 t) 209-736-4575 stpatricksparish.ac@gmail.com www.stpatricksangelscamp.com Rev. Johnpaul Pasala, HGN (India), Admin.; Dcn. Jared Hungerford; CRP Stds.: 50

St. Patrick - 619 Sheep Ranch Rd., Murphys, CA 95247 t) 209-728-2854

Our Lady of the Sierra - 1301 Linebaugh Rd., Arnold, CA 95223 t) 209-795-7625 Kathy Soria, Admin.;

St. Ignatius Mission - Poker Flat Community Center, Copperopolis, CA 95228 t) (209) 736-4575 Kathy Soria, Admin.;

CERES

St. Jude Church (Pastor of) - 3824 Mitchell Rd., Ceres, CA 95307-9422 t) 209-537-0516 stjudechurchceres@gmail.com www.stjudeceres.org Rev. Gustavo Quintero V, Pst.; Rev. Alvaro M. Lopez (Colombia), Par. Vicar; Rev. Khoi Pham, Par. Vicar; CRP Stds.: 1,268

Ntra. Senora de Guadalupe - 425 Broadway Ave., Modesto, CA 95351 t) 209-606-6246 silviastjude@gmail.com

HUGHSON

St. Anthony Church of Hughson (Pastor of) - 7820 Fox Rd., Hughson, CA 95326-9309 t) 209-883-4310 liz@stanthony.info; nikki@stanthony.info www.stanthony.info Rev. Chandrasekar Cellian Paulraj (India), Par. Vicar; Nikki Sandoval, DRE; Brenda Mejia, DRE; Rev. Luis Cordeiro (Portugal), Par. Admin.; CRP Stds.: 504

St. Louis - 31201 Floto St., La Grange, CA 95329 t) 209-852-0144 tom@stanthony.info Doris Quinones, Contact;

LATHROP

Our Lady of Guadalupe Church (Pastor of) - 16200 Cambridge Dr., Lathrop, CA 95330 t) 209-858-4466; 209-858-9391 (CRP) guadalupechurchlathrop@gmail.com olgchurchlathrop.com/ Rev. Jose Salvador Ledesma, Parish Admin.; Maria Del Refugio Sifuentes, DRE; CRP Stds.: 421

LINDEN

Holy Cross Church (Pastor of) - 18633 E. Front St., Linden, CA 95236; Mailing: P.O. Box 52, Linden, CA 95236 t) 209-887-4063 (CRP); 209-887-3341 holycrosscatholicchurch@comcast.net; janiceholycross@comcast.net holycrosslinden.org Rev. Bill L. Kraft, Pst.; CRP Stds.: 143

LOCKEFORD

St. Joachim Church of Lockeford (Pastor of) - 13392 Lockeford Ranch Dr., Lockeford, CA 95237; Mailing: P.O. Box 232, Lockeford, CA 95237 t) 209-727-3912;

209-727-0406 (CRP) parish@st-joachim.com; jmccormack@st-joachim.com www.stjoachimlockeford.com Rev. Raju Gudimalla, H.G.N (India), Admin.; Joanna McCormack, DRE; Dcn. Fred Ybarra; CRP Stds.: 200

LODI

St. Anne Church (Pastor of) - 215 W. Walnut St., Lodi, CA 95240; Mailing: P O Box 480, Lodi, CA 95241 t) 209-369-1907 parishoffice@stanneslodi.org www.stanneslodi.org Rev. Robert Oswald, Admin.; Rev. Ronnie Manango, Par. Vicar; Rev. Hung Joseph Nguyen (Vietnam), Par. Vicar; Rev. Brandon M. Ware, In Res.; Dcn. Karl Welsbacher; Dcn. Thomas Driscoll; Dcn. Porfirio Cisneros; Sr. Isabel de la Eucaristia Abril, E.F.M.S., DRE; Sr. Azucena Espinoza, E.F.M.S., DRE; CRP Stds.: 799

St. Anne's School - (Grades K-8) 200 S. Pleasant St., Lodi, CA 95240 t) 209-333-7580 general@stanneslodi.org Elizabeth Mar, Prin.; Stds.: 227; Lay Tchrs.: 10

Mater Ecclesiae - 26500 Sacramento Blvd., Thornton, CA 95686; Mailing: P.O. Box 480, Lodi, CA 95241 t) (209) 369-1907

MAMMOTH LAKES

St. Joseph Church of Mammoth Lakes - 58 Ranch Rd., Mammoth Lakes, CA 93546; Mailing: P.O. Box 372, Mammoth Lakes, CA 93546 t) 760-934-6276 vero.st.josephmammothlakes@gmail.com Rev. Jorge A. Roman, Pst.; Veronica Saray, Pst. Min./Coord.; CRP Stds.: 78

Infant of Prague Mission, Bridgeport - info@mammothcatholicchurch.org mammothcatholicchurch.org

Our Savior of the Mountains Mission, Lee Vining - 85 Mono Lake, Lee Vining, CA 93541 dore@schat.net David Dore, Mission Mgr.;

Our Lady of the Valley Church Mission - 112903 U.S.-395, Coleville, CA 96107 t) (760) 934-6276

MANTECA

St. Anthony Church of Manteca (Pastor of) - 505 E. North St., Manteca, CA 95336 t) 209-823-7197; 209-823-7197 x231 (CRP) mary@st-anthonys.org; laura@st-anthonys.org st-anthonys.org Rev. John Peter Pragasam (India), Pst.; Rev. Madhu Appanapalle, H.G.N. (India), Par. Vicar; Rev. Gilberto Arango, Par. Vicar; Dcn. Ha Nguyen; Dcn. Jeffrey Vierra; Dcn. Fidel Carrillo Jr.; Laura Perez, DRE; CRP Stds.: 364

St. Anthony School - (Grades PreSchool-8) 323 N. Fremont, Manteca, CA 95336 t) 209-823-4513 susie.dickert@sasmanteca.org sasmanteca.org Susan Dickert, Prin.; Stds.: 262; Lay Tchrs.: 10

St. Vincent de Paul Society - ; Mailing: P.O. Box 1644, Manteca, CA 95336 t) 209-823-8099 Gary Rotert, Contact;

St. Anthony School Educational Foundation - 323 N. Fremont, 830 E. Alameda St., Manteca, CA 95336 t) 209-239-4513 susiedickert@sasmanteca.org Susan Dickert, Contact;

MODESTO

Holy Family Church (Pastor of) - 4212 Dale Rd., Modesto, CA 95356 t) 209-545-3553; 209-545-3553 x2 (CRP) frontdesk@holyfamilymodesto.org; assistant@holyfamilymodesto.org holyfamilymodesto.org Rev. Christhudasan Varghese, H.G.N. (India), Par. Admin.; Dcn. Felipe Vallejo; John S. Misiak, Bus. Mgr.; CRP Stds.: 465

Our Lady of San Juan de los Lagos - 4643 Flint Ave., Salida, CA 95368 t) (209) 545-3553

St. Joseph Church of Modesto (Pastor of) - 1813 Oakdale Rd., Modesto, CA 95355 t) 209-551-4973 www.stjmod.com Rev. Samuel G. West, Pst.; Rev. Benny Antoney, O.S.B. (India), Par. Vicar; Rev. Michael Brady, Par. Vicar; Rev. Suresh Babu Ery (India), Par. Vicar; Dcn. Richard Braun; CRP Stds.: 749

Our Lady of Fatima Church (Pastor of) - 505 W. Granger Ave., Modesto, CA 95350 t) 209-524-7421 dspringer@olfmodesto.org Rev. Ernesto Madrigal, Par. Admin.; Rev. Kishor Yerpula, H.G.N. (India), Par. Vicar; Rev. Editho Mascardo, Chap.; Rev. Msgr. Robert J. Silva, In Res.; Dcn. James Johnson; Dcn. Juan Vargas; CRP Stds.: 460

Our Lady of Fatima School - (Grades K-8) 501 W. Granger Ave., Modesto, CA 95350 t) 209-524-4170 Pamela O'Brien, Prin.; Stds.: 180; Lay Tchrs.: 11

The Monsignor William P. Kennedy Education Foundation - 501 W. Granger Ave., Modesto, CA 95350 t) 209-524-4170

St. Stanislaus Church (Pastor of) - 709 J St., Modesto, CA 95354 t) 209-522-6534 (CRP); 209-524-4381 info@ststanscc.org; gsilva@ststanscc.org ststanscc.org Rev. Adrian Ruben Cisneros, Par. Admin.; Rev. Sergio Arcila (Colombia), Par. Vicar; Rev. Sleevaraj Pasala (India), Par. Vicar; Dcn. Jose Reyes; Dcn. Oscar Cervantes; Dcn. Richard Williamsen; Dcn. Juan Carlos Palomar; CRP Stds.: 256

St. Stanislaus School - (Grades PreK-8) 1416 Maze Blvd., Modesto, CA 95351 t) 209-524-9036 principal@ststanscc.org www.ststanscs.org Mercedes Hollcraft, Prin.; Stds.: 233; Lay Tchrs.: 10

NEWMAN

St. Joachim Church of Newman (Pastor of) - 1121 Main St., Newman, CA 95360 t) 209-862-2878; 209-862-3528 office@stjoachimnewman.org; julievelez1125@msn.com www.stjoachimnewman.org/ Rev. Jorge W. Arboleda, Admin.; Dcn. Lance Velez; CRP Stds.: 343

OAKDALE

St. Mary of the Annunciation Church (Pastor of) - 1225 Olive St., Oakdale, CA 95361 t) 209-404-4874 (CRP); 209-581-3822 (CRP); 209-847-2715 x10 abcorissetto@gmail.com; ftinamarie3@aol.com Rev. Matthew O'Donnell, Pst.; Dcn. Jose Rodriguez; Dcn. Dan Paulus; Tina Lucas, DRE; Corinne Rissetto, DRE; CRP Stds.: 345

PATTERSON

Sacred Heart Church of Patterson (Pastor of) - 529 I St., Patterson, CA 95363 t) 209-892-9321; 209-892-6381 (CRP) sheartpatterson@gmail.com; shcreligiousel503@gmail.com Rev. Nhan Tran, C.M. (Vietnam), Parish Admin.; Rev. Luis Ariel Ramirez, C.M. (Colombia), Par. Vicar; Rev. Stephen Gallegos, C.M., In Res.; Angelina Navarro, DRE; CRP Stds.: 642

Sacred Heart School - (Grades PreK-8) 505 M St., Patterson, CA 95363 t) 209-892-3544 principal@shcs-patterson.org www.shcs-patterson.org Theresa Rothstein, Prin.; Stds.: 205; Lay Tchrs.: 13

Immaculate Heart of Mary - 22031 H St., Crows Landing, CA 95313; Mailing: 529 I St., Patterson, CA 95363 t) (209) 892-9321 www.sacredheartpatterson.org Plaugher Norma, Pst. Assoc.;

RIPON

St. Patrick Church of Ripon (Pastor of) - 19399 E St., Rte. 120 Hwy., Ripon, CA 95366 t) 209-838-2133 faithformation@stpatricksripon.com; office@stpatricksripon.com Rev. Kondayya Mocherla, H.G.N. (India), Par. Vicar; Dcn. Thomas Ciccarelli, Parish Life Coord.; Dcn. Juan Estupinan; Dawn Gonzalez, DRE; CRP Stds.: 359

RIVERBANK

St. Frances of Rome Church (Pastor of) - 2827 Topeka St., Riverbank, CA 95367 t) 209-869-2996 lupe.zamora@sfrriverbank.com Rev. Misael Avila, Pst.; Rev. Msgr. Bonifacio Baldonado (Philippines), Assoc. Pst.; Dcn. Librado Ulloa; Guadalupe Zamora, DRE; Betty Huffman, CRE; CRP Stds.: 359

SAN ANDREAS

St. Andrew Church of San Andreas (Pastor of) - 162 Church Hill Rd., San Andreas, CA 95249; Mailing: P.O. Box 550, San Andreas, CA 95249 t) 209-754-3815 standrew-office@comcast.net www.standrewcatholicparish.com Rev. Lonachan W. Arouje (India), Pst.; Dcn. Mark Caruso; Kate Leiga, DRE; CRP Stds.: 15

St. Thomas Aquinas - 8398 Lafayette St., Mokelumne Hill, CA 95245

Our Lady of Fatima - 22581 Hwy. 26, West Point, CA 95255

SONORA

St. Patrick Church of Sonora (Pastor of) - 116 Bradford St., Sonora, CA 95370 t) 209-532-7139 kathy@stpatssonora.org; stpats@stpatssonora.org www.stpatssonora.org Rev. Yesobu Banka (India), Admin.; Dcn. Michael Kubasek; Kathy Casas, DRE; CRP Stds.: 67

Our Lady of Mt. Carmel - 17700 State Hwy. 120, Big Oak Flat, CA 95305; Mailing: 116 Bradford St., Sonora, CA 95370

St. Anne - 22518 Church Ln., Columbia, CA 95310

STOCKTON

Cathedral of the Annunciation (Pastor of) - 400 W. Rose St., Stockton, CA 95204; Mailing: 425 W MAGNOLIA ST, Stockton, CA 95203 t) 209-463-1305 faithformation@annunciationstockton.org; info@annunciationstockton.org annunciationstockton.org Very Rev. John J.M. Foster, Pst.; Rev. Larry Machado, Par. Vicar; Rev. Joseph Son Nguyen, Par. Vicar; Very Rev. Luis Navarro, In Res.; Dcn. Martin Baeza; Dcn. Greg Yeager; Dcn. Armando Moreno; Dcn. Michael Wofford; Liliana Bobadilla, DRE; CRP Stds.: 425

Cathedral of the Annunciation School - (Grades K-8) 1110 N. Lincoln St., Stockton, CA 95203 t) 209-444-4000 jloewen@annunciationsaints.org www.annunciation-school.org Adriana Gonzales, Prin.; Stds.: 236; Lay Tchrs.: 24

St. Bernadette Church (Pastor of) - 2544 Plymouth Rd., Stockton, CA 95204 t) 209-465-3081 stbernstockton@gmail.com; srcatherinediaz@gmail.com www.saintbernadettes.com Rev. Delfin Tumaca, Parish Admin.; Rev. Lawrence M. Guerrero, In Res.; Dcn. Benjamin Joe; CRP Stds.: 167

St. Edward Church (Pastor of) - 731 S. Cardinal Ave., Stockton, CA 95215 t) 209-337-0176 (CRP); 209-466-3020 office@stedwardstockton.family; ccd@stedwardstockton.family stedwardstockton.family Rev. Alvaro H. Delgado, Pst.; Dcn. Jesus Aguilar; Maria Pantoja, DRE; CRP Stds.: 419

St. George Church (Pastor of) - 120 W. Fifth St., Stockton, CA 95206-2695 t) 209-463-3413 Rev. Martin Garcia Marin, Pst.; Rev. Leonardo Del Carmen (Philippines), Par. Vicar; Rev. Alvaro U. Araque (Colombia), In Res.; Dcn. Kevin Amen; Dcn. Juan Espinoza; Linda Reyes, DRE; Marie Lou N. Paulino, Bus. Mgr.; CRP Stds.: 503

St. George REALMS Foundation - 120 W. 5th St., Stockton, CA 95206 t) (209) 463-3413 javascript:;

Good Shepherd - 305 French Camp Rd., French Camp, CA 95231; Mailing: P.O. Box 354, French Camp, CA 95231 t) 209-982-0578 Dcn. Matthew Joseph;

St. Gertrude Church (Pastor of) - 1663 E. Main St., Stockton, CA 95205; Mailing: 1655 E. Main St., Stockton, CA 95205 t) 209-466-0278; 209-969-5345 (CRP) office@stgertrudestockton.com www.stgertrudestockton.com Rev. Nam Kim, P.P.S., Par. Admin.; Dcn. Baltazar Aguirre; Dcn. Louis Juarez; Vicki Brand, DRE; CRP Stds.: 307

St. Linus Church (Pastor of) - 2620 S. B St., Stockton, CA 95206 t) 209-465-1430 linusparish@gmail.com www.linusparish.com Rev. Benjamin Puente (Mexico), Pst.; CRP Stds.: 221

St. Luke Church of Stockton (Pastor of) - 3847 N. Sutter St., Stockton, CA 95204 t) 209-462-0410 (CRP); 209-948-3450 irmamsc@yahoo.com; lrodriguez@stlukestockton.us www.stlukestockton.us Rev. Gustavo Ramirez, SDB (Mexico), Parish Admin.; Rev. Paul Hung Tran, S.D.B. (Vietnam), Par. Vicar; Rev. Marc Rougeau, S.D.B. (Canada), Par. Vicar; Dcn. Joseph Bui; Dcn. Stephen Tran; Dcn. Haet Tansaeng; Sr. Irma Cruz, MSC, RCIA Coord.; CRP Stds.: 270

St. Luke School - (Grades K-8) 4005 N. Sutter St., Stockton, CA 95204 t) 209-464-0801 hbrehm@stlukestockton.com; cohan@stlukestockton.com www.stlukestockton.com Harrison Brehm, Prin.; Stds.: 230; Sr. Tchrs.: 1; Lay Tchrs.: 10

Convent - 230 E. Atlee St., Stockton, CA 95204 info@stlukestockton.us Sr. Angelamaria De Leo, Treas.;

St. Mary of the Assumption Church (Pastor of) - 203 E. Washington St., Stockton, CA 95202 c) 209-490-6790 ourlady1851@gmail.com www.stmaryschurchofstockton.org Rev. Camilo Garcia, Parish Admin.; Rev. Edwin Musico (Philippines), Par. Vicar; Rev. George Okoro (Nigeria), In Res.; Rev. Christian Ezeh (Nigeria), In Res.; Dcn. Leo Canton; Martha Hernandez, DRE; CRP Stds.: 250

St. Michael Church of Stockton (Pastor of) - 5882 N. Ashley Ln., Stockton, CA 95215-9307 t) 209-931-0639; 209-931-6536 office@stmichaelparish.net www.stmichaelparish.net Rev. Msgr. Agustin Gialogo, Pst.; Rev. Msgr. Richard J. Ryan, In Res.; CRP Stds.: 322

Presentation Church (Pastor of) - 1515 W. Benjamin Holt Dr., Stockton, CA 95207; Mailing: 6715 Leesburg Pl., Stockton, CA 95207 t) 209-472-2150 2officemgr@presentationchurch.net www.presentationchurch.net Rev. Mark Wagner, Pst.; Rev. Jose Maghinay (Philippines), Par. Vicar; Rev. William McDonald, Par. Vicar; Dcn. Scott Johnson; Dcn. Francisco Lopez; CRP Stds.: 627

Presentation School - (Grades K-8) 1635 W. Benjamin Holt Dr., Stockton, CA 95207 t) 209-472-2140 office@presentationschool.org; principal@presentationschool.org www.presentationschool.org Maria Amen, Prin.; Nicole Wright, Vice Prin.; Stds.: 247; Lay Tchrs.: 11

TRACY

St. Bernard Church (Pastor of) - 163 W. Eaton Ave., Tracy, CA 95376 t) 209-835-4560 mwhite@st-bernards.org; dgamez@st-bernards.org www.st-bernards.org Rev. David Dutra, Pst.; Rev. Marcelino Marquino Malana, Par. Vicar; Rev. John Hieu Ngo, Par. Vicar; Dcn. Peter Ryza; CRP Stds.: 822

St. Bernard's School - (Grades K-8) 165 W. Eaton Ave., Tracy, CA 95376 t) 209-835-8018 www.st-bernardschool.org Patricia Paredes, Prin.; Stds.: 177; Lay Tchrs.: 11

St. Bernard's Catholic Pre-School and Daycare - 160 W. Beverly Pl., Tracy, CA 95376 t) 209-835-8019 x301 kabelar@st-bernardschool.org st-bernardschool.org Karen Abelar, Dir.;

TURLOCK

Our Lady of the Assumption of the Portuguese Church (Pastor of) - 2602 S. Walnut Rd., Turlock, CA 95380; Mailing: P.O. Box 2030, Turlock, CA 95381 t) 209-634-2222 ahendrex@olassumption.net www.olassumption.net Rev. Manuel F. Sousa, Pst.; Dcn. Edwin Santiago; Dcn. Stephen Valgos; Ashley Hendrex, DRE; CRP Stds.: 320

Pastor of All Saints University Church - 4040 McKenna Dr., Turlock, CA 95382 t) 209-669-0473 ryegor@allsaintscsus.org; mlorenzi@allsaintscsus.org www.allsaintscsus.org Rev. Tom Orlando, Pst.; Dcn. Eric Houghland; Dcn. Lane Menezes; CRP Stds.: 146

Sacred Heart Church of Turlock (Pastor of) - 1200 Lyons Ave., Turlock, CA 95380; Mailing: 1301 Cooper Ave., Turlock, CA 95380 t) 209-634-8578; 209-634-8579 (CRP) leticia.sacredheart@gmail.com shparish.net Rev. J. Patrick Walker, Pst.; Rev. Rolando C. Petronio (Philippines), Assoc. Pst.; Rev. Dante U. Dammay (Philippines), Assoc. Pst.; Rev. Hamilton Suarez (Colombia), Pst. Assoc.; CRP Stds.: 1,226

Sacred Heart School - (Grades K-8) 1225 Cooper Ave., Turlock, CA 95380 t) 209-634-7787 Sara Michelena, Prin.; Stds.: 226; Lay Tchrs.: 10

Preschool - 1250 Cooper Ave., Turlock, CA 95380 t) 209-667-5512 Staci Coelho, Prin.;

TWAIN HARTE

All Saints Church (Pastor of) - 18674 Cherokee Dr., Twain Harte, CA 95383; Mailing: P.O. Box 642, Twain Harte, CA 95383 t) 209-586-3161 parish@allsaintsandsaintjoseph.org; allstsbookkeeper@gmail.com www.allsaintsandsaintjoseph.org Rev. Jeffrey Wilson, Pst.; Dcn. Joseph Gomes; Rev. John E. Fitzgerald, In Res.; Ginger Dugan, Admin.; Dcn. Michael Tippett; Lina Marion, Admin.; CRP Stds.: 16

St. Joseph - 18473 Gardner Ave., Tuolumne, CA 95379 t) (209) 586-3161 Tom Ingalls, Contact;

SCHOOLS: PRESCHOOL THRU HIGH SCHOOL

SCHOOLS

STATE OF CALIFORNIA

STOCKTON

All Saints Academy of Stockton - 144 W. 5th St., Stockton, CA 95206 t) 209-463-1540 njauregui@asastockton.org www.asastockton.org Noehmi Jauregui, Prin.; Stds.: 107; Lay Tchrs.: 7

HIGH SCHOOLS

STATE OF CALIFORNIA

MODESTO

Central Catholic High School - (DIO) (Grades 9-12) 200 S. Carpenter Rd., Modesto, CA 95351 t) 209-524-9611 sawicki@cchsca.org www.cchsca.org Bruce Sawyer, Prin.; Nathaniel Juarez, Vice Prin.; Stds.: 381; Lay Tchrs.: 21

STOCKTON

St. Mary's High School - (DIO) (Grades 9-12) 5648 N. El Dorado St., Stockton, CA 95207; Mailing: P.O. Box 7247, Stockton, CA 95267-0247 t) 209-957-3340 jbrusa@saintmaryshighshool.org; mwright@saintmaryshighschool.org www.saintmaryshighschool.org Michael Wright, Prin.; James Brusa, Pres.; Stds.: 827; Pr. Tchrs.: 1; Sr. Tchrs.: 1; Lay Tchrs.: 50

St. Mary's High School Foundation - 5648 N El Dorado St, Stockton, CA 95207; Mailing: P.O. Box 7247, Stockton, CA 95267-0247 t) (209) 957-0861 jbrusa@saintmaryshighschool.org

INSTITUTIONS LOCATED IN DIOCESE

CATHOLIC CHARITIES [CCH]

MODESTO

The Catholic Social Service Guild - 1833 Covington Way, Modesto, CA 95355 c) (209) 401-4457 cd.bennett60@gmail.com Candrea Jean Bennett, Pres.; Asstd. Annu.: 36,000

STOCKTON

Catholic Charities of the Diocese of Stockton - 1106 N. El Dorado St., Stockton, CA 95202 t) 209-444-5900 marevalos@ccstockton.org; iruelas@ccstockton.org www.ccstockton.org Martha Arevalos, Exec. Dir.; Mark Croce, Bd. Chair; Asstd. Annu.: 31,000; Staff: 100

Catholic Charities ESL/Citizenship Education Program - 1106 N. El Dorado St., Stockton, CA 95202 t) 209-593-6120 iacosta@ccstockton.org English as a Second Language (ESL)/Citizenship classes to help prepare Legal Permanent Residents (LPRs) for Citizenship. Isabel Acosta, ESL Prog. Coord.;

Catholic Charities Services for Seniors & Caregivers - 1106 N. El Dorado St., Stockton, CA 95202 t) 209-444-5931; 209-396-6909 twilliams@ccstockton.org Homemaker (housekeeping), personal care, respite care program, caregiver respite & caregiver chore. Teresa Williams-White, Prog. Mgr.;

Environmental Justice Program (EJ) - 1106 N. El Dorado St., Stockton, CA 95202 t) 209-444-5919 eolivares@ccstockton.org ejstockton.org Serves to engage local parishes in activities to resolve environmental problems, particularly as they affect the poor. Ector Olivares, Prog. Mgr.;

Family Counseling Services - 1106 N. El Dorado St., Stockton, CA 95202; Mailing: P.O. Box 576488, Modesto, CA 95357 t) 209-340-3218; 209-396-6953 eprado@ccstockton.org; cjohnson@ccstockton.org Provides low-cost, short-term counseling services as well as community education workshops and mental health resources and referrals. Rigoberto Lomas, Prog. Mgr.;

Food Bank - 1106 N. El Dorado St., Stockton, CA 95202 t) 209-444-5914; 209-593-6124 aguzman@ccstockton.org Ana Guzman, Prog. Mgr.;

Health Care Access - 1106 N. El Dorado St., Stockton, CA 95202 t) 209-444-5907; 209-444-5940 jgalindo@ccstockton.org Assist adults & children with enrollment for health insurance and utilization of health care benefits. Joanna Galindo, Prog. Mgr.;

Immigration Legal Services - 1106 N. El Dorado St., Stockton, CA 95202 t) 209-444-5910; 209-396-6921 mraya@ccstockton.org Naturalization/citizenship, Green Card renewal/replacement, special case waivers, adjustment of status, family immigration, family petitions, TPS. Maria Raya, Prog. Mgr.;

Mother Lode Senior Services - 88 Bradford St., Sonora, CA 95370 t) 209-532-7632; 209-588-1597 lcampbell@ccstockton.org Ombudsman Program, Legal Advocacy for Seniors Program, Elder Abuse Prevention Program, Older Adult Outreach and Engagement Program. Linda Campbell, Prog. Mgr. & Ombudsman Prog. Coord.;

Multipurpose Senior Service Program (MSSP) - 1106 N. El Dorado St., Stockton, CA 95202 t) 209-444-5931; 209-396-6909 Care management, respite in-home, emergency call device, minor home repair, home safety evaluations, transportation. Teresa Williams-White, Prog. Mgr.;

Nutritional Assistance Service Program - 1106 N. El Dorado St., Stockton, CA 95202 t) (209) 444-5900 aguzman@ccstockton.org Ana Guzman, Prog. Mgr.;

Parenting Education - 1106 N. El Dorado St., Stockton, CA 95202 t) 209-444-5915; 209-444-5927 mperez@ccstockton.org Parenting education classes to assist families through parishes. Maria Perez, Parenting Educ. Coord.;

Stanislaus County Senior Services - 1506 H St., Modesto, CA 95454; Mailing: P.O. Box 576488, Modesto, CA 95357 t) 209-529-3784; 209-444-5919 Homemaker program, long-term care, ombudsman program, senior transportation, social security representative payee program, elder abuse prevention. Casey Armstrong, Prog. Dir.;

VetFam Supportive Services for Veteran Families - 1106 N. El Dorado St., Stockton, CA 95202 t) (209) 444-5935 Nai Sosongkham, Prog. Mgr.;

CEMETERIES [CEM]

ESCALON

St. John's Catholic Cemetery - 17871 S. Carrolton Rd., Escalon, CA 95320; Mailing: P.O. Box 1137, Stockton, CA 95201 t) 209-838-7134 stjohnscatholic@gmail.com Jennifer Prieto, Dir.; Kerri Piacentini, Admin.;

MODESTO

St. Stanislaus Catholic Cemetery - 1141 Scenic Dr., Modesto, CA 95350 t) 209-529-3905 saintstanislaus@sjcemeteries.com Jennifer Prieto, Dir.; Lisa Garcia, Admin.;

STOCKTON

San Joaquin Catholic Cemetery and Mausoleum - 719 E. Harding Way, Stockton, CA 95204; Mailing: P.O. Box 1137, Stockton, CA 95201 t) 209-466-6202 jprieto@sjcemeteries.com Jennifer Prieto, Dir.;

Good Shepherd Catholic Cemetery - 3200 N. Dakota Ave., Modesto, CA 95358 t) (209) 544-1450

CONVENTS, MONASTERIES, AND RESIDENCES FOR WOMEN [CON]

MODESTO

Missionaries Guadalupanas of the Holy Spirit - 3405 Whistler Ave, Modesto, CA 95355 c) (213) 300-1067 Sr. Alicia Lopez, M.G.Sp.S., Contact; Srs.: 2

Sisters of the Cross of the Sacred Heart of Jesus - 1320 Maze Blvd., Modesto, CA 95351 t) 209-526-3525 sistersofthecross.treasurer@rcscj.com; sistersofthecross.mothersuperior@rcscj.com www.sistersofthecross.com Cloistered Convent. Mother Laura Linares, Supr.; Srs.: 8

PATTERSON

Daughters of the Holy Spirit - 624 N. 64th St., Patterson, CA 95363 t) 209-892-3410 lucille1963@gmail.com Sacred Heart Convent. Sr. Lucille Carreau, D.H.S., Assoc. Advisor; Srs.: 2

STOCKTON

Dominican Sisters of San Rafael Convent - 5042 Gadwall Cir., Stockton, CA 95207 t) 209-956-6953 carla.kovack@sanrafaelop.org sanrafaelop.org Sr. Carla Kovack, O.P., Prioress; Srs.: 4

Eucharistic Franciscan Missionary Sisters - 1630 N. Hunter St., Stockton, CA 95204 t) 209-462-3906 c) 209-762-0860 srisabelabril0306@gmail.com efmsla.org Srs.: 3

Sacro Costato Missionary Sisters - St. Luke's Convent, 230 E. Atlee St., Stockton, CA 95204 c) 209-981-0837; (209) 481-2843 mscstockton@comcast.net www.sacrocostato.us Srs.: 4

ENDOWMENTS / FOUNDATIONS / TRUSTS [EFT]

LODI

St. Anne's Endowment - 215 W. Walnut St., Lodi, CA 95240; Mailing: P.O. Box 480, Lodi, CA 95241 t) 209-369-1907 bware@stanneslodi.org Rev. Brandon M. Ware, Pres.;

MODESTO

Central Catholic High School Foundation - 200 Carpenter Rd., Modesto, CA 95351 t) 209-524-6822 paris@cchsca.org www.cchsca.org Joan Hart, Dir.;

Father John C. Silva Education Foundation - 709 J St., Modesto, CA 95354; Mailing: P.O. Box 4304, Modesto, CA 95352 t) 209-524-4381 cbanuelos@aol.com Rev. Adrian Ruben Cisneros, Par. Admin.;

The Monsignor William P. Kennedy Education Foundation - 501 W. Granger Ave., Modesto, CA 95350 t) 209-524-4170 dpringer@olfmodesto.org John Resso, Chair; David Springer, Secy.;

STOCKTON

Bishop Ministry Appeal Trust - 212 N. San Joaquin St., Stockton, CA 95202 t) 209-466-0636 Rev. Brandon M. Ware;

The Bishop's Educational Foundation, Diocese of Stockton - 212 N. San Joaquin St., Stockton, CA 95202-2409 t) 209-466-0636

Church for Tomorrow Fund - 212 N. San Joaquin St., Stockton, CA 95202 t) 209-466-0636

St. Joseph's Foundation of San Joaquin - 1800 N. California St., Stockton, CA 95204 t) 209-467-6347 abby.newton@dignityhealth.org www.supportstjosephshospital.org Julie Eckardt, Vice. Pres.;

TURLOCK

The Father McElligott Sacred Heart School Foundation - 1225 Cooper Ave., Turlock, CA 95350; Mailing: P.O. Box 1254, Turlock, CA 95381 t) (209) 605-6569 shs.development@yahoo.com Jackie Cotta, Exec.;

HOSPITALS / HEALTH SERVICES [HOS]

STOCKTON

St. Joseph's Behavioral Health Center - 2510 N. California St., Stockton, CA 95204 t) 209-461-2000 pam.koerner@commonspirit.org www.stjosephscanhelp.org Sponsored by Catholic Health Care Federation Paul Rains, Pres.; Bed Capacity: 35; Asstd. Annu.: 9,893; Staff: 181

St. Joseph's Medical Center of Stockton - 1800 N. California St., Stockton, CA 95204-9008 t) 209-943-2000 pam.koerner@commonspirit.org www.stjosephscares.org Sponsored by Catholic Health Care Federation. Donald J. Wiley, Pres.; Bed Capacity: 355; Asstd. Annu.: 214,557; Staff: 2,756

MISCELLANEOUS [MIS]

MODESTO

***Mary Mother of God Mission Society** - 1700 McHenry Ave., Ste. 80, Modesto, CA 95350; Mailing: 1736 Milestone Cir., Modesto, CA 95357 t) 209-408-0728 usoffice@vladmission.org www.vladmission.org 501(c)3 nonprofit organization providing spiritual and financial support for the work of the Roman Catholic missionary work in Eastern Russia. Vicky Trevillyan, Dir.;

STOCKTON

Catholic Professional and Business Club - 212 N. San Joaquin St., Stockton, CA 95202-2409 t) 209-466-0636; 209-324-2092 cpbcmodesto@gmail.com

Instituto Fe y Vida (Instituto de Formacion Fe y Vida) - 1737 W. Benjamin Holt Dr., Stockton, CA 95207 t) 209-951-3483 jmatty@feyvida.org; cmcervantes@feyvida.org www.feyvida.org Juan Escarfuller, Exec. Dir.;

St. John Vianney House of Formation - 4101 N. Manchester, Stockton, CA 95207 t) 209-463-1305 cmartinez@stocktondiocese.org Rev. Cesar Martinez, Contact;

San Lorenzo Ruiz De Manila - 1658 Sicily St., Stockton, CA 95206 t) 209-406-6088 Natie R. Banasihan, Pres.;

SEEDS (Assistance for Catholic Education within the Roman Catholic Diocese of Stockton) - 212 N. San Joaquin St., Stockton, CA 95202 t) 209-466-0636 rmoreno@stocktondiocese.org; mgraham@stocktondiocese.org Sherry Leonard, Pres.; Carla Donaldson, Vice. Pres.; Lydia Tinder, Secy.; James Acosta, Treas.;

MONASTERIES AND RESIDENCES FOR PRIESTS AND BROTHERS [MON]

THORNTON

***Monastery of Our Lady of La Vang** - 26952 N. Thornton Rd., Thornton, CA 95686; Mailing: P.O. Box 475, Thornton, CA 95686 t) 209-796-5009 olv.ocist@gmail.com www.lavangusocist.org Sr. Louise Nguyen, Supr.; Srs.: 6

NURSING / REHABILITATION / CONVALESCENCE / ELDERLY CARE [NUR]

STOCKTON

Casa Manana Inn - 3700 N. Sutter St., Stockton, CA 95204 t) 209-466-4046 Senior Housing for those 62 years or older. Melissa Appling, Admin.; Staff: 5

An asterisk (*) denotes an organization that has established tax-exempt status directly with the IRS and is not covered by the USCCB Group Ruling.

Diocese of Superior

(Dioecesis Superiorensis)

MOST REVEREND JAMES P. POWERS

Bishop of Superior; ordained May 20, 1990; appointed Bishop of Superior December 15, 2015; ordained February 18, 2016. Chancery Office: 1201 Hughitt Ave., P.O. Box 969, Superior, WI 54880.

Chancery Office: 1201 Hughitt Ave., Box 969, Superior, WI 54880. T: 715-392-2937; F: 715-395-3149.

ESTABLISHED MAY 3, 1905

Square Miles 15,715.

Comprises the Counties of Ashland, Barron, Bayfield, Burnett, Douglas, Iron, Lincoln, Oneida, Polk, Price, Rusk, Sawyer, St. Croix, Taylor, Vilas and Washburn in the State of Wisconsin.

Incorporated under the laws of the State of Wisconsin as the Diocese of Superior.

For legal titles of parishes and diocesan institutions, consult the Chancery.

STATISTICAL OVERVIEW

Personnel

Bishop....1
Priests: Diocesan Active in Diocese....20
Priests: Diocesan Active Outside Diocese....1
Priests: Retired, Sick or Absent....26
Number of Diocesan Priests....47
Religious Priests in Diocese....1
Total Priests in your Diocese....48
Extern Priests in Diocese....21
Ordinations:
Transitional Deacons....3
Permanent Deacons....4
Permanent Deacons in Diocese....66
Total Sisters....53

Parishes

Parishes....103
With Resident Pastor:
Resident Diocesan Priests....27
Without Resident Pastor:
Administered by Priests....58
Administered by Deacons....14
Administered by Lay People....4
Missions....2
Professional Ministry Personnel:
Sisters....2
Lay Ministers....64

Welfare

Catholic Hospitals....1
Total Assisted....175,000
Homes for the Aged....23
Total Assisted....560
Day Care Centers....1
Total Assisted....65
Special Centers for Social Services....5
Total Assisted....490
Residential Care of Disabled....10
Total Assisted....90
Other Institutions....11
Total Assisted....443

Educational

Diocesan Students in Other Seminaries....6
Total Seminarians....6
Elementary Schools, Diocesan and Parish....14
Total Students....1,907
Catechesis/Religious Education:
High School Students....1,398
Elementary Students....2,123
Total Students under Catholic Instruction....5,434
Teachers in Diocese:
Sisters....3
Lay Teachers....172

Vital Statistics

Receptions into the Church:
Infant Baptism Totals....427
Minor Baptism Totals....39
Adult Baptism Totals....18
Received into Full Communion....53
First Communions....472
Confirmations....441
Marriages:
Catholic....82
Interfaith....37
Total Marriages....119
Deaths....855
Total Catholic Population....53,726
Total Population....456,588

LEADERSHIP

Vicar General - t) 715-394-0209 Very Rev. James F. Tobolski;
Administrative Services Director - t) 715-394-0211 Daniel Blank;
Chancellor - t) (715) 394-0240 Peggy Schoenfuss (pschoenfuss@catholicdos.org);
Secretary to Bishop - t) 715-394-0205 Cindy Gronski;
Office of Ecclesial Ministries & Diocesan Consultation - t) 715-394-0204 Christine Newkirk, Dir.;
Episcopal Vicar for Clergy -
Diocesan Tribunal -
Adjutant Judicial Vicar - Rev. Adam J. Laski;
Defender of the Bond - Rev. Thomas E. Thompson;
Judicial Vicar - Very Rev. James F. Tobolski;
Procurator and Advocate - Patti J. Holt;
Promoter of Justice - Rev. James B. Bissonette;
Vicar for Canonical Affairs - Very Rev. James F. Tobolski;
Diocesan Pastoral Council - Ted Wadzinski, Eastern Deanery; Pam Cira, Eastern Deanery; Kevin Effertz, Southwest Deanery;
Deaneries and Deans - Very Rev. John R. Gerritts, Southwest Deanery; Very Rev. Christopher J. Kemp, East Deanery; Very Rev. James F. Tobolski, Northwest Deanery;
Pastoral Consultors - Rev. Andrew P. Ricci;
Presbyteral Council & Diocesan Consultors - Very Rev. Aloysius Royan Anthony (India) (aloy.royan19@gmail.com); Rev. Papi Reddy Yeruva (India); Very Rev. Christopher J. Kemp, Vice Chm.;
Personnel Placement Board - Very Rev. Aloysius Royan Anthony (India) (aloy.royan19@gmail.com); Very Rev. Patrick J. A. McConnell; Christine Newkirk;

OFFICES AND DIRECTORS

The Bishop George A. Hammes Center - t) 715-234-5044 Chris Hurtubise; Peggy Schoenfuss (pschoenfuss@catholicdos.org);
Bureau of Information - t) 715-394-0211 Daniel Blank, Dir.;
Catholic Boy and Girl Scout Chaplain - t) 715-247-2942 Dcn. Robin Major;
Catholic Charities Bureau - t) 715-394-6617 Alan Rock, Exec.;
Catholic Formation, Department of - t) (715) 234-5044 Chris Hurtubise, Dir. Evangelization & Mission Discipleship; Loree Nauertz, Assoc. Dir. (lnauertz@catholicdos.org);
Catholic Herald, Superior Edition - Anita Draper, Editor (adraper@catholicdos.org);
Catholic Mutual Group - t) 715-394-0222 Matthew Warren (mwarren@catholicmutual);
Catholic Women, Council of - Gail Helmert, Pres. (2019carmelite@gmail.com);
Charismatic Renewal Liaison - t) 715-798-3430 Rev. Dean T. Buttrick (frdean@cheqnet.net);
Diocesan Coordinator of Assistance - t) 715-718-1110 Kathy Drinkwine;
Diocesan Coordinator of Health Affairs -
Diocesan Sisters Council - t) (715) 385-3750 Sr. Elizabeth Amman, O.P. (eaamman@srdominicans.org);
Ecumenical Commission - t) 715-394-0207 Very Rev. James F. Tobolski;
Finance, Department of - t) 715-394-0221 Lawrence French, Dir.;
Holy Childhood Association - t) 715-865-3669 Very Rev. Gregory J. Hopefl, Dir.;
Insurance/Employee Benefits and Payroll, Office of - t) 715-394-0230 Cindy Gronski, Dir.;
Newman Apostolate - Rev. Andrew P. Ricci; Rev. Joseph Stefancin; Gabe Beeksma, UWS Student Rep.;
Office of Worship - t) 715-394-0233 Paul J. Birch;
Parish Accounting, Office of - t) (715) 394-0221 Lawrence French, Dir.;
Permanent Diaconate and Lay Ministry - t) 715-394-0204 Christine Newkirk, Dir.;
Assistant Director of Lay Ministry Outreach Program - t) 715-866-4492 Bluette Puchner;
Director of Diaconal Life - t) 715-394-0235 Dcn. John E. Grek;
Propagation of the Faith - t) 715-865-3669 Very Rev. Gregory J. Hopefl;
Radio and Television - t) 715-394-0211 Daniel Blank, Dir.;
Respect Life Office - Bonita Thom;
St. Pius Priest Fund - Rev. Edwin C. Anderson; Rev. John C. Anderson, Treas.; Rev. David L. Neuschwander, Secy.;
Stewardship and Development, Department of - t) 715-394-0223 Steven P. Tarnowski, Dir.;
Superintendent of Schools - t) 715-234-5044 Peggy Schoenfuss (pschoenfuss@catholicdos.org);
Vocations, Office of - t) 715-394-0234 Rev. John C. Anderson, Team Member; Rev. Adam J. Laski, Team Member; Very Rev. Patrick J. A. McConnell, Team Member;

PARISHES, MISSIONS, AND CLERGY

STATE OF WISCONSIN

ALMENA

Sacred Heart of Jesus Church - 114 Soo Ave., Almena, WI 54805; Mailing: 925 St. Anthony St., P.O. Box 548, Cumberland, WI 54829 t) 715-822-2948 stanthony@actinfaith.net www.actinfaith.net Also serves St. Anthony Abbot, Cumberland & St. Ann, Turtle Lake. Very Rev. John R. Gerritts, Supervising Pst.; Rev. Thomas E. Thompson, Sacr. Min.; Dcn. Steven G. Linton, Parish Life Coord.; Dcn. Stephen Welter; Dcn. Gregory J. Ricci; CRP Stds.: 10

AMERY

St. Joseph - 1050 Keller Ave. N., Amery, WI 54001 t) 715-268-7717 office@stjosephamery.org Also serves Our Lady of the Lakes, Balsam Lake. Rev. Gerald P. Harris, Pst.; CRP Stds.: 90

ASHLAND

Our Lady of the Lake Catholic Community - 106 N. 2nd Ave. E., Ashland, WI 54806 t) 715-682-7620 relform@ourladycc.org; ollcatholicchurch@ourladycc.org www.ourladycc.org Also serves St. Mary, Odanah, St. Peter, Dauby, St. Florian, Ino & SS. Peter & Paul, Moquah. Rev. Jerome D'Souza, Par. Admin.; Dcn. Timothy Mika; Dcn. Clarence L. Campbell; Dcn. Owen T. Gorman; Dcn. John E. Grek; Anna Richardson, DRE; Karen Swanson, Bus. Mgr.; CRP Stds.: 63

Our Lady of the Lake Catholic Community School - (Grades PreK-8) 215 Lake Shore Dr. E., Ashland, WI 54806 t) 715-682-7622 ollschool@ourladycc.org Betty Swiston, Prin.; Stds.: 132; Lay Tchrs.: 11

BALSAM LAKE

Our Lady of the Lakes - 507 W. Main, Balsam Lake, WI 54810; Mailing: P.O. Box 399, Balsam Lake, WI 54810 t) 715-405-2253 ourlady@lakeland.ws www.ourladyofthelakes.ws Also serves St. Joseph, Amery. Joanne Agne, DRE; Rev. Gerald P. Harris, Pst.; CRP Stds.: 50

BARRON

St. Joseph - 827 E. LaSalle Ave., Barron, WI 54812 t) 715-637-3255 sspbandj@outlook.com; patty.sspbandj@outlook.com www.sspbandj.org/ Also serves St. Peter, Cameron, St. Boniface, Chetek, and Assumption of the Blessed Virgin Mary, Strickland. Very Rev. John R. Gerritts, Supervising Pst.; Rev. Chandra Ery (India), Sacr. Min.; Patricia Gerber, Parish Dir.; CRP Stds.: 11

BAYFIELD

Holy Family - 232 N. 1st St., Bayfield, WI 54814; Mailing: P.O. Box 1290, Bayfield, WI 54814 t) 715-779-3316 hfchurch@ncis.net Also serves St. Ann, Cornucopia, St. Joseph (mission), La Pointe, St. Louis, Washburn, St. Francis, Red Cliff. Very Rev. Aloysius Royan Anthony (India), Supervising Pst.; Rev. Rajesh Sagar Sare (India), Sacr. Min.; Dcn. Roger L. Cadotte, Parish Life Coord.; Dcn. Kenneth D. Kasinski;

BIRCHWOOD

St. John Evangelist - 408 S. Main St., Birchwood, WI 54817; Mailing: 111 W. Marshall St., Rice Lake, WI 54868 t) 715-234-2032 clusteroffice@stjosephricelake.org stjosephricelake.org Also serves St. Joseph, Rice Lake, Our Lady of Lourdes, Dobie & Holy Trinity, Haugen. Rev. Edwin C. Anderson, Pst.; Rev. Adam J. Laski, Assoc. Pst.; Dcn. Rod Knight;

BOULDER JUNCTION

St. Anne - 10315 Main St., Boulder Junction, WI 54512; Mailing: P.O. Box 110, Boulder Junction, WI 54512 t) 715-385-2390 stannechurch@centurytel.net www.ncc.weconnect.com Also serves St. Mary, Sayner, and St. Rita, Presque Isle. Rev. Showri Jojappa Pasala (India), Par. Admin.;

BRUCE

St. Mary - 721 N. Second St., Bruce, WI 54819; Mailing: 611 First St. S., Ladysmith, WI 54848 t) 715-532-3051 secretary@ruskcountycatholiccommunity.org; pastor@ruskcountycatholiccommunity.org www.ruskcountycatholiccommunity.org Also serves Our Lady of Sorrows, Ladysmith; St. Francis of Assisi, Flambeau; St. Mary, Hawkins; St. Anthony de Padua, Tony; SS. Peter and Paul, Weyerh Rev. Papi Reddy Yeruva (India), Par. Admin.; Dcn. Thomas E. Fuhrmann; Dcn. Craig J. Voldberg; Dcn. Douglas L. Sorenson; Robert Lecheler, Bus. Mgr.;

BUTTERNUT

Immaculate Conception - 410 Michigan St., Butternut, WI 54514; Mailing: P.O. Box 6, Butternut, WI 54514 t) (715) 769-3644 (CRP); 715-762-4494 icchurchbutternut@plbb.us icbutternut.weebly.com/ Also serves St. Francis of Assisi, Fifield & St. Anthony of Padua, Park Falls. Rev. Shaji Joseph Pazhukkathara, Par. Admin.; Dcn. Chester E. Ball Jr.; Dcn. Robert L. Schienebeck; CRP Stds.: 17

CABLE

St. Ann - 13645 Cty. Hwy. M, Cable, WI 54821-0037; Mailing: P.O. Box 37, Cable, WI 54821-0037 t) (715) 634-2867 (Central Office Number) parish@haywardcatholic.org cablecatholic.org Also serves St. Ignatius, New Post; St. Francis, Reserve; St. Joseph, Hayward; & St. Philip, Stone Lake Rev. David L. Neuschwander, Pst.; Rev. Karunakar Madanu (India), Assoc. Pst.; Dcn. David B. DiSera; Dcn. Brian McCaffery;

CAMERON

St. Peter - 1618 20th St., Cameron, WI 54822; Mailing: 827 E. LaSalle Ave., Barron, WI 54812 t) 715-637-3255 sspbandj@outlook.com; patty.sspandj@outlook.com www.sspbandj.org/ Also serves St. Joseph, Barron, St. Boniface, Chetek, & Assumption of the Blessed Virgin Mary, Strickland. Very Rev. John R. Gerritts, Supervising Pst.; Rev. Chandra Ery (India), Sacr. Min.; Patricia Gerber, Parish Dir.; CRP Stds.: 63

CATAWBA

St. Paul the Apostle - W9485 Hwy. 8, Catawba, WI 54515; Mailing: 655 S. Lake Ave., Phillips, WI 54555 t) 715-339-2222 oln@pctcnet.net Also serves St. Therese of Lisieux, Phillips & St. John the Baptist, Prentice. Rev. Lourduraju Madanu (India), Par. Admin.; CRP Stds.: 18

CHETEK

St. Boniface - 425 S. 3rd St., Chetek, WI 54728; Mailing: 827 E. LaSalle Ave., Barron, WI 54812 t) 715-637-3255 sspbandj@outlook.com www.sspbandj.org/ Also serves St. Joseph, Barron, St. Peter, Cameron & Assumption of the Blessed Virgin Mary, Strickland. Very Rev. John R. Gerritts, Supervising Pst.; Rev. Chandra Ery (India), Sacr. Min.; Patricia Gerber, Parish Dir.; CRP Stds.: 17

CLAM LAKE

St. George - Grant and 2nd St., Clam Lake, WI 54517;

Mailing: P.O. Box 17, Mellen, WI 54546 t) 715-274-3701 mostholyrosary@centurytel.net Summer Chapel. Very Rev. Aloysius Royan Anthony (India), Par. Admin.;

CLEAR LAKE

St. John - 811 4th St., Clear Lake, WI 54005; Mailing: 761 1st St., Glenwood City, WI 54013 t) (715) 554-3836 (FFP Leader); 715-265-7133 (Cluster Office) stjohnbaptist@cltcomm.net www.jbjsaints.com Also serves St. John the Baptist, Glenwood City & St. Bridget, Wilson. Rev. John R. Long, Pst.; CRP Stds.: 15

CORNUCOPIA

St. Ann - 8350 Superior Ave., Cornucopia, WI 54827; Mailing: P.O. Box 311, Cornucopia, WI 54827 t) 715-779-3316 hfchurch@ncis.net Also serves Holy Family, Bayfield, St. Joseph, LaPointe, St. Francis, Red Cliff & St. Louis, Washburn. Very Rev. Aloysius Royan Anthony (India), Supervising Pst.; Rev. Rajesh Sagar Sare (India), Sacr. Min.; Dcn. Roger L. Cadotte, Parish Life Coord.; Dcn. Kenneth D. Kasinski;

CUMBERLAND

St. Anthony Abbot - 925 St. Anthony St., Cumberland, WI 54829; Mailing: P.O. Box 548, Cumberland, WI 54829 t) 715-822-2948; 715-822-8831 stanthony@actinfaith.net www.actinfaith.net/ Also serves Sacred Heart of Jesus, Almena and St. Ann, Turtle Lake. Very Rev. John R. Gerritts, Supervising Pst.; Rev. Thomas E. Thompson, Sacr. Min.; Dcn. Steven G. Linton, Parish Life Coord.; Dcn. Stephen Welter; Dcn. Gregory J. Ricci; Angela Schug, CRE; CRP Stds.: 47

DANBURY

Our Lady of Perpetual Help - 7586 Main St., Danbury, WI 54830; Mailing: P.O. Box 7, Webster, WI 54893 t) 715-866-7321 sjoffice@centurytel.net; sjff@centurytel.net Also serves St. John the Baptist, Webster & Sacred Hearts of Jesus & Mary, Crescent Lake. Very Rev. James F. Tobolski, Supervising Pst.; Rev. Francis Adoboli (Ghana), Par. Admin.; Gwen Nies, DRE; CRP Stds.: 5

EAGLE RIVER

St. Peter the Fisherman - 5001 County Rd. G, Eagle River, WI 54521 t) 715-479-8704; 715-479-8704 x24 (CRP) jen@northernlakescatholics.org; bev@northernlakescatholics.org www.stpeterseagleriver.org Rev. Ronald Serrao, Pst.; Rev. Richard E. Rhinehart, Par. Vicar; Jen Metzger, DRE; CRP Stds.: 58

FIFIELD

St. Francis of Assisi - W7231 Balsam St., Fifield, WI 54524; Mailing: 276 S. 5th Ave., Park Falls, WI 54552 t) 715-762-4494 x113 stanthony75@hotmail.com stfrancisfifield.weebly.com/ Also serves St. Anthony of Padua, Park Falls & Immaculate Conception, Butternut. Rev. Shaji Joseph Pazhukkathara, Par. Admin.; Dcn. Chester E. Ball Jr.; Dcn. Robert L. Schienebeck; CRP Stds.: 1

FOXBORO

St. William - 3095 E. Cty. Rd. B, Foxboro, WI 54836; Mailing: 5601 Tower Ave., Superior, WI 54880 t) 715-394-7919; 715-394-7919 x11 (CRP) secretaryhasw@centurylink.net superiorcatholics.org Also serves Holy Assumption, Superior; Cathedral of Christ the King, Superior; St. Anthony, Superior; St. Anthony, Lake Nebagamon. Rev. Andrew P. Ricci, Pst.; Rev. Anthoni Reddy Yannam (India), Sacr. Min.; Rev. Joji Reddy Boyapati (India), Sacr. Min.;

FREDERIC

St. Dominic - 103 W. Birch St., Frederic, WI 54837; Mailing: P.O. Box 606, Frederic, WI 54837 t) 715-327-8119 stdomfrederic@lakeland.ws; deacon.icsd@gmail.com (Also serves Immaculate Conception, Grantsburg). Very Rev. John R. Gerritts, Supervising Pst.; Rev. Joseph Raj Alluri (India), Sacr. Min.; Dcn. Stanley J. Marczak, Parish Life Coord.; CRP Stds.: 26

GILMAN

SS. Peter and Paul - 315 E. Davlin St., Gilman, WI 54433 t) 715-447-8510 sspp@centurytel.net www.fivesaintscluster.com (Also serves St. Michael, Jump River; St. John the Apostle, Sheldon and St. Stanislaus, Lublin). Rev. Vijay Kumar Madani (India), Par. Admin.; CRP Stds.: 58

GLEASON

St. John the Baptist - N4887 Hwy. 17, Gleason, WI 54435; Mailing: 1708 E. 10th St., Merrill, WI 54452 t) 715-536-2803 kleggett@stfrancismerrill.org Also serves St. Francis Xavier, Merrill. Very Rev. Christopher J. Kemp, Supervising Pst.; Rev. Mariadas Vallabhaneni (India), Sacr. Min.; Dcn. James E. Arndt, Parish Life Coord.;

GLENWOOD CITY

St. John the Baptist - 757 1st St., Glenwood City, WI 54013; Mailing: 761 1st St., Glenwood City, WI 54013 t) 715-265-7331 (CRP); 715-265-7133 ffpnewsgc@gmail.com; stjohnbaptist@cltcomm.net www.jbjsaints.com Also serves St. John in Clear Lake & St. Bridget in Wilson. Rev. John R. Long, Pst.; CRP Stds.: 56

GLIDDEN

Most Precious Blood - 246 Grant St., Glidden, WI 54527; Mailing: P.O. Box 182, Glidden, WI 54527 t) 715-274-3701 mpbchurchglidden@yahoo.com Also serves Most Holy Rosary, Mellen, St. Anthony, Highbridge, St. Anne, Sanborn & St. George, Clam Lake. Very Rev. Aloysius Royan Anthony (India), Par. Admin.; Larry Bay, DRE; Dena Pankratz, DRE; CRP Stds.: 12

GORDON

St. Anthony of Padua - 9718 E. Cty. Rd. Y, Gordon, WI 54838; Mailing: P.O. Box 303, Solon Springs, WI 54873 t) 715-378-4431 stpiusx@centurytel.net stspiusmaryanthony.com Also serves St. Pius X, Solon Springs & St. Mary, Minong. Rev. Balaraju Policetty (India), Par. Admin.;

GRANTSBURG

Immaculate Conception - 411 State Rd. 70, Grantsburg, WI 54840; Mailing: P.O. Box 606, Frederic, WI 54837 t) 715-327-8119 stdomfrederic@lakeland.ws; deacon.icsd@gmail.com sd-ic.org/ Also serves St. Dominic, Frederic. Very Rev. John R. Gerritts, Supervising Pst.; Rev. Joseph Raj Alluri (India), Sacr. Min.; Dcn. Stanley J. Marczak, Parish Life Coord.; CRP Stds.: 36

HAMMOND

Immaculate Conception - 1295 Ridgeway St., Hammond, WI 54015-0018; Mailing: P.O. Box 18, Hammond, WI 54015-0018 t) 715-796-2244 toddedelman@smicparish.org; jackieaune@smicparish.org Also serves St. Bridget, River Falls. Rev. Joseph Stefancin, Par. Admin.; Rev. Joseph Anil Kumar Pasala, SCJ (India), Assoc. Pst.; Dcn. Dan Kohler; Dcn. Joseph F. Paron; Todd Edelman, Bus. Mgr.; CRP Stds.: 260

HARRISON

St. Augustine - Hwys. B & D, Harrison, WI 54487; Mailing: N10090 Cty. Rd. B, Tomahawk, WI 54487 t) 715-453-2561 kathy.staugustinechurch@yahoo.com; dtowle55@gmail.com stmaryschurchtomahawk.com Also serves St. Mary, Tomahawk & St. Francis of Assisi, Pier Willow. Rev. Louis Reddy Maram Reddy (India), Par. Admin.; Dcn. David C. Bablick; Dcn. Russell E. Cabak; Dcn. Clifford Eggett; Dcn. Clarence D. Towle; CRP Stds.: 7

HAUGEN

Holy Trinity - 317 5th St., Haugen, WI 54841; Mailing: 111 W. Marshall St., Rice Lake, WI 54868 t) 715-234-2032 clusteroffice@stjosephricelake.org stjosephricelake.org/ Also serves St. Joseph, Rice Lake, Our Lady of Lourdes, Dobie & St. John the Evangelist, Birchwood. Rev. Edwin C. Anderson, Pst.; Rev. Adam J. Laski, Assoc. Pst.; Dcn. Rod Knight;

HAWKINS

St. Mary of Czestochowa - N7386 Cty. Rd. M, Hawkins, WI 54530; Mailing: 611 First St. S., Ladysmith, WI 54848 t) 715-532-3051 secretary@ruskcountycatholiccommunity.org; pastor@ruskcountycatholiccommunity.org www.ruskcoountycatholiccommunity.org Also serves Our Lady of Sorrows, Ladysmith; St. Mary, Bruce; St. Francis of Assisi, Flambeau; St. Anthony de Padua, Tony; SS. Peter & Paul, Weyerhaeus Rev. Papi Reddy Yeruva (India), Par. Admin.; Dcn. Thomas E. Fuhrmann; Dcn. Douglas L. Sorenson; Dcn. Craig J. Voldberg; Robert Lecheler, Bus. Mgr.;

HAYWARD

St. Joseph's Congregation - 10586 N. Dakota Ave., Hayward, WI 54843; Mailing: P.O. Box 877, Hayward, WI 54843 t) 715-634-2867 parish@haywardcatholic.org www.haywardcatholic.org Also serves St. Ann, Cable; St. Ignatius, New Post; St. Francis Solanus, Reserve; St. Philip, Stone Lake Rev. David L. Neuschwander, Pst.; Rev. Karunakar Madanu (India), Assoc. Pst.; Dcn. David B. DiSera; Dcn. Brian McCaffery; Kevin Sullivan, Dir., Discipleship; Laurel Eyer, DRE; CRP Stds.: 82

HIGHBRIDGE

St. Anthony - 39221 State Hwy. 13, Highbridge, WI 54846; Mailing: P.O. Box 17, Mellen, WI 54546 t) 715-274-3701 mostholyrosary@centurytel.net Also serves Most Holy Rosary, Mellen, Most Precious Blood, Glidden, St. Anne, Sanborn & St. George, Clam Lake. Very Rev. Aloysius Royan Anthony (India), Par. Admin.;

HOLCOMBE

St. Francis of Assisi - W10193 Lehmen Rd., Holcombe, WI 54745; Mailing: 611 First St. So., Ladysmith, WI 54848 t) 715-532-3051 secretary@ruskcountycatholiccommunity.org; pastor@ruskcountycatholiccommunity.org www.ruskcountycatholiccommunity.org Also serves Our Lady of Sorrows, Ladysmith; St. Mary, Bruce; St. Mary of Czestochowa, Hawkins; St. Anthony de Padua, Tony; SS. Peter & Paul, Weyerhaeu Rev. Papi Reddy Yeruva (India), Par. Admin.; Dcn. Thomas E. Fuhrmann; Dcn. Douglas L. Sorenson; Dcn. Craig J. Voldberg; Robert Lecheler, Bus. Mgr.; CRP Stds.: 2

HUDSON

St. Patrick - 1500 Vine St., Hudson, WI 54016 t) 715-381-5120; 715-386-3941 (CRP) church@stpatrickofhudson.org www.stpatrickofhudson.org Very Rev. John R. Gerritts, Pst.; Dcn. Howard Cameron; Dcn. Gregg J. Miller; Dcn. Thomas Kroll; CRP Stds.: 239

St. Patrick School - (Grades PreK-8) 403 St. Croix St., Hudson, WI 54016 t) (715) 381-5120 dbell@stpatrickeducenter.org Dan Bell, Prin.; Stds.: 224; Lay Tchrs.: 20

HURLEY

St. Mary of the Seven Dolors - 404 Iron St., Hurley, WI 54534 t) 715-561-2606 stmaryshurley@gmail.com; stmary7@charter.net stmaryshurley.org Also serves St. Ann, Saxon. Rev. Hrudaya Raju Sunkara (India), Admin.; Leone Sobrack, DRE; CRP Stds.: 61

IRON RIVER

St. Michael - 68105 S. George St., Iron River, WI 54847; Mailing: P.O. Box 97, Iron River, WI 54847 t) 715-372-4756 cathyberube@cheqnet.net; stmichael@cheqnet.net Rev. Andrew P. Ricci, Pst.; Rev. Anthoni Reddy Yannam (India), Sacr. Min.; Dcn. Robert J. Chammings; Dcn. Kevin Feind; Dcn. Arthur Gil de Lamadrid; Dcn. John E. Grek; Cathy Berube, DRE;

JUMP RIVER

St. Michael - Hwy. 73, Jump River, WI 54434; Mailing: 315 E. Davlin St, Gilman, WI 54433 t) 715-447-8510 sspp@centurytel.net www.fivesaintscluster.com Also serves SS. Peter & Paul, Gilman, St. Stanislaus, Lublin & St. John the Apostle, Sheldon. Rev. Vijay Kumar Madani (India), Par. Admin.; CRP Stds.: 1

LA POINTE

St. Joseph - 266 Airport Rd., La Pointe, WI 54850; Mailing: P.O. Box 1290, Bayfield, WI 54814 t) (715) 779-3316 hfchurch@ncis.net (Summer mission only) Dcn. Roger L. Cadotte, Parish Life Coord.; Rev. Rajesh Sagar Sare (India), Sacr. Min.; Dcn. Kenneth D.

Kasinski; Very Rev. Aloysius Royan Anthony (India), Supervising Pastor;

LAC DU FLAMBEAU

St. Anthony of Padua - 650 Old Abe Rd., Lac du Flambeau, WI 54538; Mailing: P.O. Box 38, Lac du Flambeau, WI 54538 t) 715-588-3148 stanthony@frontier.com; souliemdv1@frontier.com www.stpadua.com Also serves Our Lady Queen of Peace, Manitowish Waters, and St. Isaac Jogues & Companions, Mercer. Rev. Maria Joseph Kodiganti (India), Par. Admin.; Dcn. John J. Bardos; Debra Ramsey, DRE; CRP Stds.: 8

LADYSMITH

Our Lady of Sorrows - 120 E. Corbett Ave., Ladysmith, WI 54848; Mailing: 611 First St. S., Ladysmith, WI 54848 t) 715-532-3051 secretary@ruskcountycatholiccommunity.org; pastor@ruskcountycatholiccommunity.org www.ruskcountycatholiccommunity.org Also serves St. Mary of Czestochowa, Hawkins; St. Anthony de Padua, Tony; St. Mary, Bruce; St. Francis of Assisi, Holcombe; SS Peter & Paul, Weyerhaeu Rev. Papi Reddy Yeruva (India), Par. Admin.; Dcn. Thomas E. Fuhrmann; Dcn. Douglas L. Sorenson; Dcn. Craig J. Voldberg; Robert Lecheler, Bus. Mgr.; CRP Stds.: 13

Our Lady of Sorrows School - (Grades PreK-8) 105 E. Washington Ave., Ladysmith, WI 54848 t) 715-532-3232 olsschool@centurytel.net Holly Bacha, Prin.; Stds.: 78; Lay Tchrs.: 9

LAKE NEBAGAMON

St. Anthony Catholic Church - 11648 E. County Rd. B, Lake Nebagamon, WI 54849; Mailing: P.O. Box 397, Lake Nebagamon, WI 54849 t) 715-374-3570 tbrowncre@gmail.com; stanthonyln@gmail.com Also serves St. Anthony, Superior; Cathedral of Christ the King, Superior; Holy Assumption, Superior; St. William, Foxboro. Rev. Andrew P. Ricci, Pst.; Rev. Joji Reddy Boyapati (India), Sacr. Min.; Rev. Anthoni Reddy Yannam (India), Sacr. Min.; Tammy Brown, DRE; CRP Stds.: 47

LAND O'LAKES

St. Albert - 4351 County Rd. B, Land O'Lakes, WI 54540; Mailing: P.O. Box 237, Land O' Lakes, WI 54540 t) (715) 479-8704 (St. Peter's Office #) bev@northernlakescatholics.org saintsalbertandmary.org Also serves St. Mary, Phelps. Rev. Ronald Serrao, Pst.; Rev. Richard E. Rhinehart, Par. Vicar; Dcn. Norman J. Mesun Jr.; CRP Stds.: 21

LUBLIN

St. Stanislaus - W 13381 South St., Lublin, WI 54447; Mailing: 315 E. Davlin St., Gilman, WI 54433 t) 715-447-8510 sspp@centurytel.net www.fivesaintscluster.com Also serves SS. Peter & Paul, Gilman, St. Michael, Jump River & St. John the Apostle, Sheldon. Rev. Vijay Kumar Madani (India), Par. Admin.; CRP Stds.: 5

MANITOWISH WATERS

Our Lady Queen of Peace - 5610 S. Hwy. 51, Manitowish Waters, WI 54545; Mailing: P.O. Box 325, Manitowish Waters, WI 54545 t) 715-543-2274 (CRP); 715-543-8428 queenofpeace@centurytel.net; nanc54545@yahoo.com Also serves St. Anthony of Padua, Lac Du Flambeau & St. Isaac Jogues & Companions, Mercer. Rev. Maria Joseph Kodiganti (India), Par. Admin.; Dcn. John J. Bardos; Nancy Benson, DRE; CRP Stds.: 18

MASON

St. Florian - 19315 Keystone Rd., Mason, WI 54856; Mailing: 106 N. 2nd Ave. E., Ashland, WI 54806 t) 715-682-7620 Also serves Our Lady of the Lake, Ashland; St. Peter, Dauby; St. Mary, Odanah & SS. Peter & Paul, Moquah. Rev. Jerome D'Souza, Par. Admin.; Dcn. Timothy Mika; Dcn. Clarence L. Campbell; Dcn. Owen T. Gorman; Dcn. John E. Grek;

MEDFORD

Our Lady of Perpetual Help - W5409 Whittlesey Ave., Medford, WI 54451; Mailing: P.O. Box 503, Medford, WI 54451 t) 715-748-3366 rspanbauer@holyrosarymedford.org; frpatrick@hrmedford.org hrmedford.org Also serves Our Lady of the Rosary, Medford. Very Rev. Patrick J. A. McConnell, Pst.; Rev. Jayanna Kanna (India), Assoc. Pst.; Dcn. Patrick Gierl; CRP Stds.: 26

Our Lady of the Holy Rosary - 215 S. Washington Ave., Medford, WI 54451; Mailing: P.O. Box 503, Medford, WI 54451 t) 715-748-3336 frpatrick@hrmedford.org; rspanbauer@hrmedford.org hrmedford.org Also serves Our Lady of Perpetual Help, Whittlesey. Very Rev. Patrick J. A. McConnell, Pst.; Rev. Jayanna Kanna (India), Assoc. Pst.; Dcn. Patrick Gierl; CRP Stds.: 265

Our Lady of the Holy Rosary School - (Grades PreK-6) t) (715) 748-3336 x221 principal@hrmedford.org Stds.: 129; Lay Tchrs.: 10

MELLEN

Most Holy Rosary - 203 N. Main St., Mellen, WI 54546; Mailing: P.O. Box 17, Mellen, WI 54546 t) 715-274-3701 mostholyrosary@centurytel.net Also serves St. Anthony, Highbridge; St. Anne, Sanborn; Most Precious Blood, Glidden; St. George, Clam Lake Very Rev. Aloysius Royan Anthony (India), Par. Admin.; Dcn. Timothy Mika; CRP Stds.: 14

MERCER

St. Isaac Jogues and Companions - 2622 W. Garnet St., Mercer, WI 54547; Mailing: 5214 N. Lakeview Ave., Mercer, WI 54547 t) 715-476-2697 stisaacjogues@centurytel.net Rev. Maria Joseph Kodiganti (India), Par. Admin.; Dcn. John J. Bardos;

MERRILL

St. Francis Xavier - 1708 E. 10th St., Merrill, WI 54452 t) 715-536-2803 kleggett@stfrancismerrill.org; jarndt@stfrancismerrill.org Also serves St. John the Baptist, Bloomville. Rev. Mariadas Vallabhaneni (India), Sacr. Min.; Dcn. James E. Arndt, Parish Life Coord.; CRP Stds.: 120

St. Francis School - (Grades PreK-8) t) 715-536-6083 www.stfrancismerrill.org Sonja Doughty, Prin.; Stds.: 123; Lay Tchrs.: 11

MINONG

St. Mary - 506 Main St., Minong, WI 54859; Mailing: P.O. Box 303, Solon Springs, WI 54873 t) 715-378-4431 kathy.stpius@gmail.com; stpiusx@centurytel.net Also serves St. Pius X, Solon Springs & St. Anthony of Padua, Gordon. Rev. Balaraju Policetty (India), Par. Admin.; Kathleen Birtzer, DRE; CRP Stds.: 1

MOQUAH

St. Peter - 23505 Cty. Rd. G, Moquah, WI 55806; Mailing: 106 N. 2nd Ave. E., Ashland, WI 54806 t) 715-682-7620 kswanson@ourladycc.org Also serves Our Lady of the Lake, Ashland, St. Florian, Ino, SS. Peter & Paul, Moquah & St. Mary, Odanah. Rev. Jerome D'Souza, Par. Admin.; Dcn. Timothy Mika; Dcn. Clarence L. Campbell; Dcn. Owen T. Gorman; Dcn. John E. Grek; CRP Stds.: 8

SS. Peter and Paul - 23505 Cty. Rd. G, Moquah, WI 54806; Mailing: 106 N. 2nd Ave. E, Ashland, WI 54806 t) 715-682-7620 Also serves Our Lady of the Lake, Ashland; St. Mary, Odanah; St. Peter, Dauby; St. Florian, Ino. Rev. Jerome D'Souza, Par. Admin.; Dcn. Timothy Mika; Dcn. Clarence L. Campbell; Dcn. Owen T. Gorman; Dcn. John E. Grek; Kathy Huybrecht, DRE; Karen Swanson, Bus. Mgr.; CRP Stds.: 12

NEW POST

St. Ignatius - Lac Courte Oreilles Reservation, County Trunk CC, New Post, WI 54828; Mailing: 13891 W. Mission Rd., Stone Lake, WI 54876 t) 715-865-3669 www.stignatiusnewpost.com Also serves St. Francis Solanus, Reserve; St. Philip, Stone Lake; St. Ann, Cable; St. Joseph, Hayward Rev. David L. Neuschwander, Pst.; Rev. Karunakar Madanu (India), Assoc. Pst.; Dcn. David B. DiSera; Dcn. Brian McCaffery; Sr. Felissa Zander, F.S.P.A.., DRE;

NEW RICHMOND

Immaculate Conception - 151 S. Washington Ave., New Richmond, WI 54017-1523 t) 715-246-4652; 715-246-4652 x228 (CRP) icchurch@ic-church.com www.ic-church.com Also serves St. Patrick, Erin. Rev. John C. Anderson, Pst.; Dcn. Mel (Carmelo) A. Riel; Dcn. Michael J. Germain; Barb Bailey, Bus. Mgr.; Kim Palmer, DRE; Kristin Dittman, CRE; CRP Stds.: 135

St. Mary School - (Grades PreK-8) 257 S. Washington Ave., New Richmond, WI 54017 t) 715-246-2469 principal@st-marysschool.com; saintmry@st-marysschool.com st-marysschool.com Laura Jo Jarchow, Prin.; Stds.: 229; Lay Tchrs.: 15

St. Patrick - 1880 County Rd. G, New Richmond, WI 54017; Mailing: 151 S. Washington Ave., New Richmond, WI 54017 t) 715-248-7205 (CRP); 715-246-4652 threshingtablefarm@frontiernet.net; icchurch@ic-church.com stpatrickserin.com/ Also serves Immaculate Conception, New Richmond. Rev. John C. Anderson, Pst.; Dcn. Mel (Carmelo) A. Riel; Dcn. Michael J. Germain; Jody Lenz, DRE; Kim Palmer, DRE; Barb Bailey, Bus. Mgr.; CRP Stds.: 26

ODANAH

St. Mary - 300 Old Hwy. 2, Odanah, WI 54861; Mailing: 106 N. Second Ave. E., Ashland, WI 54806 t) 715-682-7620 Also serves Our Lady of the Lake, Ashland, St. Peter, Dauby, St. Florian, Ino & SS. Peter & Paul, Moquah. Rev. Jerome D'Souza, Par. Admin.; Dcn. Timothy Mika; Dcn. Clarence L. Campbell; Dcn. Owen T. Gorman; Dcn. John E. Grek; Sr. Roselyn Heil, FSPA, Pst. Assoc.;

OSCEOLA

Assumption of the Blessed Virgin Mary - 265 State Hwy. 35, Osceola, WI 54020; Mailing: P.O. Box 9, Somerset, WI 54025 t) 715-247-3310 deaconlarry@stanne.somerset.org Also serves St. Anne, Somerset & St. Joseph, Osceola. Rev. Joseph Kumar Mayakuntla (India), Sacr. Min.; Rev. Jojappa Madanu (India), Sacr. Min.; Dcn. Lawrence E. Amell, Parish Life Coord.; Dcn. Robin Major; Dcn. Jeffrey Mason; Dcn. Edward C. Colosky; Dcn. Thomas P. Rausch; Very Rev. John R. Gerritts, Supervising Pst.;

St. Joseph - 255 10th Ave., Osceola, WI 54020-0399; Mailing: P.O. Box 399, Osceola, WI 54020 t) 715-294-2243 stjosephchurch@live.com Also serves St. Anne, Somerset & Assumption of the Blessed Virgin Mary, Farmington. Very Rev. John R. Gerritts, Supervising Pst.; Rev. Joseph Kumar Mayakuntla (India), Sacr. Min.; Rev. Jojappa Madanu (India), Sacr. Min.; Dcn. Lawrence E. Amell, Parish Life Coord.; Dcn. Edward C. Colosky; Dcn. Robin Major; Dcn. Richard T. Peterson; Dcn. Thomas P. Rausch; CRP Stds.: 8

PARK FALLS

St. Anthony of Padua - 276 S. 5th Ave., Park Falls, WI 54552 t) 715-762-4494 x2; 715-762-5435 stanthony75@hotmail.com; sapreligion@gmail.com www.stanthonysparkfalls.com/ Also serves Immaculate Conception, Butternut; St. Francis of Assisi, Fifield. Rev. Shaji Joseph Pazhukkathara, Par. Admin.; Dcn. Chester E. Ball Jr.; Dcn. Robert L. Schienebeck; Kathy Rominske, DRE; CRP Stds.: 46

PELICAN LAKE

St. John - Appleton St. & Cty. Hwy. B, Pelican Lake, WI 54463; Mailing: 110 Conro St., Rhinelander, WI 54501 t) 715-362-3169 nativityparish@nativity.me Also serves Nativity of Our Lord, Rhinelander. Very Rev. Christopher J. Kemp, Pst.; Dcn. Richard J. Meier; Michael DeBay, Bus. Mgr.;

PHELPS

St. Mary - 4494 Town Hall Rd., Phelps, WI 54554; Mailing: P.O. Box 237, Land O'Lakes, WI 54540 t) (715) 479-8704 bev@northernlakescatholics.org www.northernlakescatholics.org Rev. Ronald Serrao, Pst.; Rev. Richard E. Rhinehart, Par. Vicar; Dcn. Norman J. Mesun Jr.;

PHILLIPS

St. Therese of Lisieux - 655 S. Lake Ave., Phillips, WI 54555 t) 715-339-2222 sttheresere@gmail.com; oln@pctcnet.net Also serves St. Paul the Apostle, Catawba; St. John the Baptist, Prentice. Rev. Lourduraju Madanu (India), Par. Admin.; Elizabeth Simurdiak, CRE; CRP Stds.: 60

PRENTICE

St. John the Baptist - 935 Town St., Prentice, WI 54556; Mailing: 655 S. Lake Ave., Phillips, WI 54555 t) 715-339-2222 oln@pctcnet.net Also serves St. Therese of Lisieux, Phillips & St. Paul the Apostle, Catawba. Rev. Lourduraju Madanu (India), Par. Admin.; CRP Stds.: 15

PRESQUE ISLE

St. Rita - 11568 Lake St., Presque Isle, WI 54557; Mailing: P.O. Box 110, Boulder Junction, WI 54512 t) 715-385-2390 stannechurch@centurytel.net Also serves St. Anne, Boulder Junction & St. Mary, Sayner. Rev. Showri Jojappa Pasala (India), Par. Admin.;

RADISSON

Sacred Heart - Hwy. 27/70 Marian St., Radisson, WI 54867; Mailing: P.O. Box 216, Winter, WI 54896 t) 715-266-3441 northcentralcluster@hotmail.com Also serves St. Peter, Winter. Rev. Sunil Kumar Thumma (India), Par. Admin.; CRP Stds.: 3

RED CLIFF

St. Francis - Church Rd., Red Cliff, WI 54814; Mailing: P.O. Box 1290, Bayfield, WI 54814 t) 715-779-3316 hfchurch@ncis.net Also serves Holy Family, Bayfield, St. Ann, Cornucopia, St. Joseph, LaPointe & St. Louis, Washburn. Very Rev. Aloysius Royan Anthony (India), Supervising Pst.; Dcn. Roger L. Cadotte, Parish Life Coord.; Rev. Rajesh Sagar Sare (India), Sacr. Min.; Dcn. Kenneth D. Kasinski;

RHINELANDER

Nativity of Our Lord - 110 Conro St., Rhinelander, WI 54501 t) 715-362-3169 nativityparish@nativity.me www.nativityofourlord.net Also serves St. John, Pelican Lake. Very Rev. Christopher J. Kemp, Pst.; Dcn. Richard J. Meier; Barbara Eretto, DRE; Michael DeBay, Bus. Mgr.; CRP Stds.: 81

Nativity of Our Lord School - (Grades PreK-8) 103 E King St., Rhinelander, WI 54501; Mailing: 110 Conro St, Rhinelander, WI 54501 t) 715-362-5588 mnycz@nativity.me nativityofourlord.weconnect.com/school Melanie Nycz, Prin.; Stds.: 171; Lay Tchrs.: 15

RIB LAKE

Good Shepherd Catholic Church - 513 State Rd., Rib Lake, WI 54470; Mailing: P.O. Box 295, Rib Lake, WI 54470 t) 715-427-5259 goodshepherd@newnorth.net www.goodshepherdriblake.org Very Rev. Patrick J. A. McConnell, Pst.; Rev. Jayanna Kanna (India), Assoc. Pst.; Dcn. Patrick Gierl; Mike Bub, DRE; CRP Stds.: 66

RICE LAKE

Assumption of the Blessed Virgin Mary - W16431 Old 14, Rice Lake, WI 54868; Mailing: 827 E. LaSalle Ave., Barron, WI 54812 t) 715-637-3255 sspbandj@outlook.com; patty.sspbandj@outlook.com www.sspbandj.org Also serves St. Joseph, Barron, St. Boniface, Chetek & St. Peter, Cameron. Very Rev. John R. Gerritts, Supervising Pst.; Rev. Chandra Ery (India), Sacr. Min.; Patricia Gerber, Dir.; CRP Stds.: 1

St. Joseph - 111 W. Marshall St., Rice Lake, WI 54868 t) 715-234-2032 clusteroffice@stjosephricelake.org stjosephricelake.org Also serves Holy Trinity, Haugen, Our Lady of Lourdes, Dobie & St. John the Evangelist, Birchwood. Rev. Edwin C. Anderson, Pst.; Rev. Adam J. Laski, Assoc. Pst.; Dcn. Rod Knight; Emily Hagen, Dir.; Krystal Montgomery, DRE; CRP Stds.: 125

St. Joseph School - (Grades PreK-8) 128 W. Humbird St., Rice Lake, WI 54868 t) 715-234-7721 j.mazourek@sjsricelake.org stjoesricelake.com Jerome Van Dyke, Prin.; Stds.: 171; Sr. Tchrs.: 1; Lay Tchrs.: 13

Our Lady of Lourdes - 2411 23rd St., Rice Lake, WI 54868; Mailing: 111 W. Marshall St., Rice Lake, WI 54868 t) 715-234-2032 clusteroffice@stjosephricelake.org stjosephricelake.org Also serves Holy Trinity, Haugen, St. John the Evangelist, Birchwood & St. Joseph, Rice Lake. Rev. Edwin C. Anderson, Pst.; Rev. Adam J. Laski, Assoc. Pst.; Dcn. Rod Knight;

RIVER FALLS

St. Bridget - 211 E. Division St., River Falls, WI 54022; Mailing: P.O. Box 86, River Falls, WI 54022 t) 715-425-1870; 715-425-1879 (CRP) recept@stbparish.com; childrensff@stbparish.com www.saintbridgets.org Also serves Immaculate Conception, Hammond and St Thomas More Newman Center, University of Wisconsin River Falls Rev. Joseph Stefancin, Par. Admin.; Rev. Joseph Anil Kumar Pasala, SCJ (India), Assoc. Pst.; John Hueg, Admin.; Tessa Schuermann, DRE; Diane Wengelski, DRE; Amy Burns, Youth Min.; CRP Stds.: 242

St. Bridget School - (Grades PreK-8) 135 E. Division St., River Falls, WI 54022 t) 715-425-1872 principal@stbparish.com www.saintbridgets.org/school/ Brenda Steward, Prin.; Stds.: 161; Scholastics: 2; Lay Tchrs.: 15

SANBORN

St. Anne - 42070 Cty. Hwy. E, Sanborn, WI 54806; Mailing: P.O. Box 17, Mellen, WI 54546 t) 715-274-3701 mostholyrosary@centurytel.net stannesanborn.faith Also serves Most Holy Rosary, Mellen, Most Precious Blood, Glidden, St. Anthony, Highbridge & St. George, Clam Lake. Very Rev. Aloysius Royan Anthony (India), Par. Admin.;

SARONA

St. Catherine - W5262 Cty. Hwy. D, Sarona, WI 54870; Mailing: 409 Summit St., Spooner, WI 54801 t) 715-635-3105 pj@we3churches.org Also serves St. Francis de Sales, Spooner & St. Joseph, Shell Lake. Rev. Philip J. Juza, Pst.; Dcn. Patrick Haines; Dcn. Joseph J. Wesley; Dcn. James R. Stroede;

SAXON

St. Ann - 14233 N. Church St., Saxon, WI 54559; Mailing: P.O. Box 100, Saxon, WI 54559 t) 715-893-2236 stmary7@charter.net Also serves St. Mary of the Seven Dolors, Hurley. Rev. Hrudaya Raju Sunkara (India), Par. Admin.;

SAYNER

St. Mary - 8705 Cty. Hwy. N., Sayner, WI 54560; Mailing: P.O. Box 110, Boulder Junction, WI 54512-0110 t) 715-385-2390 stannechurch@centurytel.net Also serves St. Anne, Boulder Junction & St. Rita, Presque Isle. Rev. Showri Jojappa Pasala (India), Par. Admin.;

SHELDON

St. John the Apostle - N657 Cty. Rd. V V, Sheldon, WI 54766; Mailing: 315 E. Davlin St., Gilman, WI 54433 t) 715-447-8510 sspp@centurytel.net www.fivesaintscluster.com Also serves SS. Peter & Paul, Gilman, St. Michael, Jump River & St. Stanislaus, Lublin. Rev. Vijay Kumar Madani (India), Par. Admin.; CRP Stds.: 19

SHELL LAKE

St. Joseph - 502 N. 2nd St., Shell Lake, WI 54871; Mailing: 409 Summit St., Spooner, WI 54801 t) 715-635-3105 Also serves St. Francis de Sales, Spooner & St. Catherine, Sarona. Rev. Philip J. Juza, Pst.; Dcn. Patrick Haines; Dcn. Joseph J. Wesley; Dcn. James R. Stroede; CRP Stds.: 3

SOLON SPRINGS

St. Pius X - 11651 S. Business 53, Solon Springs, WI 54873; Mailing: P.O. Box 303, Solon Springs, WI 54873 t) 715-378-4431 jodi.stpius@gmail.com; stpiusx@centurytel.net stspiusmaryanthony.com Also serves St. Anthony of Padua, Gordon; St. Mary, Minong. Rev. Balaraju Policetty (India), Par. Admin.; CRP Stds.: 18

SOMERSET

St. Anne - 141 Church Hill Rd., Somerset, WI 54025; Mailing: P.O. Box 9, Somerset, WI 54025 t) 715-247-3310 rachelm_stanne@somtel.net; bookkeeping@stanne-somerset.org Also serves Assumption of the Blessed Virgin Mary, Farmington & St. Joseph, Osceola. Very Rev. John R. Gerritts, Supervising Pst.; Rev. Jojappa Madanu (India), Sacr. Min.; Rev. Joseph Kumar Mayakuntla (India), Sacr. Min.; Dcn. Lawrence E. Amell, Parish Life Coord.; Dcn. Edward C. Colosky; Dcn. Robin Major; Dcn. Thomas P. Rausch; Dcn. Richard T. Peterson; Rachel McGurran, DRE; CRP Stds.: 133

St. Anne School - (Grades PreK-8) 140 Church Hill Rd., Somerset, WI 54025 t) 715-247-3762 rstanke@stanne-somerset.org Randall Stanke, Prin.; Stds.: 118; Lay Tchrs.: 14

SPOONER

St. Francis De Sales - 409 Summit St., Spooner, WI 54801 t) 715-635-3105 schmidtabbie@gmail.com; pj@we3churches.org Also serves St. Joseph, Shell Lake; St. Catherine, Sarona. Rev. Philip J. Juza, Pst.; Dcn. Patrick Haines; Dcn. Joseph J. Wesley; Dcn. James R. Stroede; Abbie Schmidt, DRE; CRP Stds.: 56

St. Francis De Sales School - (Grades PreK-8) 300 Oak St., Spooner, WI 54801 t) 715-635-2774 sfds@centurytel.net Kathy Kurkiewicz, Prin.; Stds.: 121; Lay Tchrs.: 14

STETSONVILLE

Sacred Heart of Jesus - 322 W. Cty. Hwy. A, Stetsonville, WI 54480 t) 715-678-2395 karleensper@gmail.com; sacredheartchurchstetsonville@gmail.com Very Rev. Patrick J. A. McConnell, Pst.; Rev. Jayanna Kanna (India), Assoc. Pst.; Dcn. Patrick Gierl; Dcn. Joseph F. Roe; CRP Stds.: 10

STONE LAKE

St. Francis of Solanus - 13891 W. Mission Rd., Stone Lake, WI 54876 t) 715-865-3669 www.stfrancismission.org Also serves St. Ignatius, New Post; St. Philip, Stone Lake; St. Ann, Cable; St. Joseph, Hayward Rev. David L. Neuschwander, Pst.; Rev. Karunakar Madanu (India), Assoc. Pst.; Dcn. David B. DiSera; Dcn. Brian McCaffery; CRP Stds.: 6

St. Francis Solanus - (Grades PreK-8) 13885 W. Mission Rd., Stone Lake, WI 54876 t) 715-865-3662 schsis@cheqnet.net Sr. Felissa Zander, F.S.P.A.., Prin.; Stds.: 20; Sr. Tchrs.: 2

St. Philip Catholic Congregation - 5750 N. Frost Ave., Stone Lake, WI 54876; Mailing: 13891 W. Mission Rd., Stone Lake, WI 54876 t) 715-865-3669 Also serves St. Francis Solanus, Reserve; St. Ignatius, New Post; St. Ann, Cable; St. Joseph, Hayward Rev. David L. Neuschwander, Pst.; Rev. Karunakar Madanu (India), Assoc. Pst.; Dcn. David B. DiSera; Dcn. Brian McCaffery; Sr. Felissa Zander, F.S.P.A.., DRE;

SUGAR CAMP

St. Kunegunda of Poland - 6895 Hwy. 17 N., Sugar Camp, WI 54501; Mailing: P.O. Box 8, Three Lakes, WI 54562-0008 t) (715) 479-8704 bev@northernlakescatholics.org www.northernlakescatholics.org Also serves St. Theresa, Three Lakes. Rev. Ronald Serrao, Pst.; Rev. Richard E. Rhinehart, Par. Vicar; Dcn. John McCaughn; Jen Metzger, DRE; CRP Stds.: 28

SUPERIOR

Cathedral of Christ the King - 1410 Baxter Ave., Superior, WI 54880 t) 715-392-8511 margie@superiorcathedral.org; info@superiorcathedral.org www.superiorcatholics.org Also serves St. Anthony, Superior; Holy Assumption, Superior; St. William, Foxboro; St. Anthony, Lake Nebagamon. Rev. Andrew P. Ricci, Rector; Rev. Joji Reddy Boyapati (India), Sacr. Min.; Rev. Anthoni Reddy Yannam (India), Sacr. Min.; Dcn. Arthur Gil de Lamadrid; CRP Stds.: 137

Cathedral School - (Grades PreK-8) 1419 Baxter Ave., Superior, WI 54880 t) 715-392-2976 principal@superiorcathedralschool.org Jaime Samarziya, Prin.; Stds.: 140; Lay Tchrs.: 12

St. Anthony - 4315 E. Third St., Superior, WI 54880 t) 218-590-0757 (CRP); 715-398-3261 tbrowncre@gmail.com; sassecretary1@gmail.com superiorcatholics.org Also serves St. Anthony, Lake Nebagamon; Cathedral of Christ the King, Superior; Holy Assumption, Superior; St. William, Foxboro. Rev. Andrew P. Ricci, Pst.; Rev. Joji Reddy Boyapati (India), Sacr. Min.; Rev. Anthoni Reddy Yannam (India), Sacr. Min.; Dcn. Kevin Feind; CRP Stds.: 37

St. Francis Xavier - 2316 E. 4th St., Superior, WI 54880 t) 715-398-7174 sfx4reled@gmail.com; mary@stfrancisxavier.us Very Rev. James F. Tobolski, Pst.; CRP Stds.: 37

Holy Assumption - 5601 Tower Ave., Superior, WI 54880 t) 715-394-7919; 715-394-7919 x11 (CRP) secretaryhasw@centurylink.net superiorcatholics.org Also serves St. William, Foxboro; Cathedral of Christ the King, Superior; St. Anthony, Superior; St. Anthony, Lake Nebagamon. Rev. Andrew P. Ricci, Pst.; Rev. Anthoni Reddy Yannam (India), Sacr. Min.; Rev. Joji Reddy Boyapati (India), Sacr. Min.; Dcn. Robert J. Chammings;

THREE LAKES

St. Theresa - 6990 Forest St., Three Lakes, WI 54562; Mailing: P.O. Box 8, Three Lakes, WI 54562 t) 715-546-2159; (715) 479-8704 (Cluster Office Number) bev@northernlakescatholics.org Also serves St. Kunegunda of Poland, Sugar Camp. Rev. Ronald Serrao, Pst.; Rev. Richard E. Rhinehart, Par. Vicar; Dcn. John McCaughn; Jen Metzger, DRE; CRP Stds.: 23

TOMAHAWK

St. Mary - 320 E. Washington Ave., Tomahawk, WI 54487 t) 715-453-2878 pastor@smctomahawk.com; smparishoffice@smctomahawk.com stmaryschurchtomahawk.com Also serves St. Francis of Assisi, Pier-Willow & St. Augustine, Harrison. Rev. Louis Reddy Maram Reddy (India), Par. Admin.; Dcn. David C. Bablick; Dcn. Russell E. Cabak; Dcn. Clifford Eggett; Dcn. Clarence D. Towle; CRP Stds.: 53

St. Mary School - (Grades PreK-5) 221 E. Washington Ave., Tomahawk, WI 54487 t) 715-453-3542 smsprincipal@stmarystudents.com www.stmarysschooltomahawk.com/home.html Rita Lee, Prin.; Stds.: 77; Lay Tchrs.: 8

TONY

St. Anthony de Padua - N5333 Maple St., Tony, WI 54563; Mailing: 611 First St. S., Ladysmith, WI 54848 t) 715-532-3051 secretary@ruskcountycatholiccommunity.org; pastor@ruskcountycatholiccommunity.org www.ruskcountycatholiccommunity.org Also St. Mary, Bruce; St. Mary of Czestochowa, Hawkins; St. Francis, Holcombe; Ss. Peter & Paul, Weyerhaeuser; Our Lady of Sorrows, Ladysmith Rev. Papi Reddy Yeruva (India), Par. Admin.; Dcn. Thomas E. Fuhrmann; Dcn. Douglas L. Sorenson; Dcn. Craig J. Voldberg; Robert Lecheler, Bus. Mgr.; CRP Stds.: 12

TRIPOLI

St. Francis of Assisi - 5209 Willow Rd., Tripoli, WI 54564; Mailing: 320 E. Washington Ave., Tomahawk, WI 54487 t) 715-453-2878 pastor@smctomahawk.com; smparishoffice@smctomahawk.com stmaryschurchtomahawk.com Also serves St. Mary, Tomahawk & St. Augustine, Harrison. Rev. Louis Reddy Maram Reddy (India), Par. Admin.; Dcn. David C. Bablick; Dcn. Russell E. Cabak; Dcn. Clifford Eggett; Dcn. Clarence D. Towle;

TURTLE LAKE

St. Ann - 300 Pine St. S., Turtle Lake, WI 54889; Mailing: 925 St. Anthony St., P.O. Box 548, Cumberland, WI 54829 t) 715-822-2948 stanthony@actinfaith.net www.actinfaith.net Also serves St. Anthony, Cumberland & Sacred Heart of Jesus, Almena. Very Rev. John R. Gerritts, Supervising Pst.; Rev. Thomas E. Thompson, Sacr. Min.; Dcn. Stephen Welter; Dcn. Gregory J. Ricci; Dcn. Steven G. Linton, Parish Life Coord.; CRP Stds.: 19

WASHBURN

St. Louis - 217 W. 7th St., Washburn, WI 54891; Mailing: P.O. Box 70, Washburn, WI 54891 t) 715-373-2676 parishoffice@stlouiswashburn.com Also serves Holy Family, Bayfield, St. Ann, Cornucopia, St. Francis, Red Cliff & St. Joseph, LaPointe. Very Rev. Aloysius Royan Anthony (India), Supervising Pst.; Rev. Rajesh Sagar Sare (India), Sacr. Min.; Dcn. Roger L. Cadotte, Parish Life Coord.; Dcn. Kenneth D. Kasinski; Leah Goodness, DRE; CRP Stds.: 23

WEBSTER

St. John the Baptist - 26455 S. Muskey Ave., Webster, WI 54893; Mailing: P.O. Box 7, Webster, WI 54893 t) 715-866-7321 sjff@centurytel.net; sjoffice@centurytel.net Also serves Sacred Hearts of Jesus and Mary, Webster; Our Lady of Perpetual Help, Danbury. Very Rev. James F. Tobolski, Supervising Pst.; Rev. Francis Adoboli (Ghana), Par. Admin.; Gwen Nies, DRE; CRP Stds.: 11

Sacred Hearts of Jesus and Mary - 24680 Cty. Hwy. H, Webster, WI 54893; Mailing: P.O. Box 7, Webster, WI 54893 t) 715-866-7321 sjoffice@centurytel.net; sjff@centurytel.net Also serves St. John the Baptist, Webster & Our Lady of Perpetual Help, Danbury. Very Rev. James F. Tobolski, Supervising Pst.; Rev. Francis Adoboli (Ghana), Par. Admin.; Gwen Nies, DRE; CRP Stds.: 1

WEYERHAEUSER

SS. Peter and Paul - N3729 1st St., Weyerhaeuser, WI 54895; Mailing: 611 First St. S., Ladysmith, WI 54848 t) 715-532-3051 secretary@ruskcountycatholiccommunity.org; pastor@ruskcountycatholiccommunity.org www.ruskcountycatholiccommunity.org Also serves Our Lady of Sorrows, Ladysmith; St. Mary, Bruce; St. Mary of Czestochowa, Hawkins; St. Anthony, Tony; St. Francis, Holcombe. Rev. Papi Reddy Yeruva (India), Par. Admin.; Dcn. Thomas E. Fuhrmann; Dcn. Douglas L. Sorenson; Dcn. Craig J. Voldberg; Robert Lecheler, Bus. Mgr.;

WILSON

St. Bridget - 120 Depot St., Wilson, WI 54027; Mailing: 761 1st St., Glenwood City, WI 54013 t) 715-265-7133 stjohnbaptist@cltcomm.net www.jbjsaints.com Also serves St. John the Baptist, Glenwood City & St. John, Clear Lake. Rev. John R. Long, Pst.;

WINTER

St. Peter - 5106 N. Main St., Winter, WI 54896; Mailing: P.O. Box 216, Winter, WI 54896 t) 715-266-3441 northcentralcluster@hotmail.com Also serves Sacred Heart, Radisson. Rev. Sunil Kumar Thumma (India), Par. Admin.; Dcn. Michael Ryan; CRP Stds.: 3

WOODRUFF

Holy Family - 8950 County Rd. J, Woodruff, WI 54568 t) 715-356-6284 bob.king@holyfamilywoodruff.org; fr.jerry@holyfamilywoodruff.org www.holyfamilywoodruff.org Rev. Gerald A. Hagen, Pst.; Bob King, Admin.; CRP Stds.: 108

INSTITUTIONS LOCATED IN DIOCESE

CAMPUS MINISTRY / NEWMAN CENTERS [CAM]

RIVER FALLS

St. Thomas More Newman Center - 423 E. Cascade Ave, River Falls, WI 54022 t) 715-425-7234 campusminister@uwrfnewman.org uwrfnewman.org Mallory Schneider, Campus Min.; Rev. Joseph Stefancin, Dir.;

SUPERIOR

Newman Catholic Campus Ministry - 801 N. 28th St., Superior, WI 54880 t) 715-392-8511 superiornewmancenter@gmail.com Newman Center Ministry to Young Adults. Brett Jones, Contact;

CATHOLIC CHARITIES [CCH]

AMERY

Apple River, Inc. - 401 Minneapolis Ave. S., Amery, WI 54001; Mailing: 1416 Cumming Ave., Superior, WI 54880 t) 715-925-2015 sgrayson@ccbsuperior.org ccbhousing.org Shannon Grayson, Dir.;

BARRON

Barron County Developmental Services, Inc. - 175 N. Lake St., Barron, WI 54812; Mailing: 1416 Cumming Ave., Superior, WI 54880 t) 715-537-5341 jwacek@ccbsuperior.org www.barroncountydsi.org Joe Wacek, Dir.;

CHETEK

Phoenix Villa, Inc. (Evergreen Apartments) - 707 Tainter St., Chetek, WI 54728; Mailing: 1416 Cumming Ave., Superior, WI 54880 t) 715-925-2015 sgrayson@ccbsuperior.org ccbhousing.org Shannon Grayson, Dir.;

CRANDON

Phoenix Villa, Inc. (Acorn Apartments) - 508 W. Washington, Crandon, WI 54520; Mailing: 1416 Cumming Ave., Superior, WI 54880 t) 715-369-2550 sgrayson@ccbsuperior.org ccbhousing.org Shannon Grayson, Dir.;

DULUTH

Northfield Apartments, Inc. - 2713 W. Superior St., Duluth, MN 55806; Mailing: 1416 Cumming Ave., Superior, WI 54880 t) 715-394-2012 sgrayson@ccbsuperior.org ccbhousing.org Shannon Grayson, Dir.;

HAYWARD

Phoenix Villa, Inc. (Phoenix Villa of Hayward) - 15869 Muriel St., Hayward, WI 54843; Mailing: 1416 Cumming Ave., Superior, WI 54880 t) 715-236-2366 sgrayson@ccbsuperior.org ccbhousing.org Shannon Grayson, Dir.;

MEDFORD

Black River Industries, Inc. - 650 Jensen Dr., Medford, WI 54451; Mailing: 1416 Cumming Ave., Superior, WI 54880 t) 715-748-2950 afallos@ccbsuperior.org www.blackriverindustries.org Amber Fallos, Dir.;

Eastwood Apartments, Inc. - 741-755 Del Rae Ct., Medford, WI 54451; Mailing: 1416 Cumming Ave., Superior, WI 54880 t) 715-748-6962 sgrayson@ccbsuperior.org ccbhousing.org Shannon Grayson, Dir.;

Phoenix Villa, Inc. (Maywood Apartments) - 521 Lemke Ave., Medford, WI 54451; Mailing: 1416 Cumming Ave., Superior, WI 54880 t) 715-369-6962 sgrayson@ccbsuperior.org ccbhousing.org Shannon Grayson, Dir.;

MINONG

Phoenix Villa, Inc. (Acorn Apartments) - 405 2nd St., Minong, WI 54859; Mailing: 1416 Cumming Ave., Superior, WI 54880 t) 715-236-2366 sgrayson@ccbsuperior.org ccbhousing.org Shannon Grayson, Dir.;

PLOVER

Phoenix Villa, Inc. (Maywood Apartments) - 2601 Madison Ave., Plover, WI 54467; Mailing: 1416 Cumming Ave., Superior, WI 54880 t) 715-341-7616 sgrayson@ccbsuperior.org ccbhousing.org Shannon Grayson, Dir.;

RHINELANDER

Phoenix Villa, Inc. (Evergreen Apartments/Timberlane) - 880 E. Timber Dr., Rhinelander, WI 54501; Mailing: 1416 Cumming Ave., Superior, WI 54880 t) 715-369-2550 sgrayson@ccbsuperior.org ccbhousing.org Shannon Grayson, Dir.;

Sumac Trail Apartments, Inc. - 1313 Phillip St., Rhinelander, WI 54501; Mailing: 1416 Cumming Ave., Superior, WI 54880 t) 715-369-2550 sgrayson@ccbsuperior.org ccbhousing.org Shannon Grayson, Dir.;

RICE LAKE

Blue Valley, Inc. - 1310 N. Wisconsin Ave., Rice Lake, WI 54868; Mailing: 1416 Cumming Ave., Superior, WI 54880 t) 715-236-2366 sgrayson@ccbsuperior.org ccbhousing.org Shannon Grayson, Dir.;

Phoenix Villa, Inc. (Phoenix Villa North) - 1305 N. Wisconsin St., Rice Lake, WI 54868; Mailing: 1416 Cumming Ave., Superior, WI 54880 t) 715-236-2366 sgrayson@ccbsuperior.org ccbhousing.org Shannon Grayson, Dir.;

SHELL LAKE

Phoenix Villa, Inc. (Evergreen Apartments) - 797 N. Lake Dr., Shell Lake, WI 54871; Mailing: 1416 Cumming Ave., Superior, WI 54880 t) 715-236-2366 sgrayson@ccbsuperior.org ccbhousing.org Shannon Grayson, Dir.;

SIREN

Diversified Services Center, Inc. - 7649 Tower Rd., Siren, WI 54872; Mailing: 1416 Cumming Ave., Superior, WI 54880 t) 715-349-5724 jwacek@ccbsuperior.org www.dsisiren.com Joe Wacek, Dir.;

Lilac Grove Apartments, Inc. - 24145 1st Ave., Siren, WI 54872; Mailing: 1416 Cumming Ave., Superior, WI 54880 t) 715-925-2015 sgrayson@ccbsuperior.org ccbhousing.org Shannon Grayson, Dir.;

Phoenix Villa, Inc. (Evergreen Apartments/Lakewood) - 24121 Fourth St., Siren, WI 54872; Mailing: 1416 Cumming Ave., Superior, WI 54880 t) 715-925-2015 sgrayson@ccbsuperior.org ccbhousing.org Shannon Grayson, Dir.;

SUPERIOR

Catholic Charities Bureau, Inc. - 1416 Cummings Ave., Superior, WI 54880 t) 715-394-6617 ccbrecep@ccbsuperior.org www.ccbsuperior.org Alan Rock, Exec. Dir.; Asstd. Annu.: 1,842; Staff: 461

Catholic Community Services, Inc. - 1416 Cumming Ave., Superior, WI 54880 t) (715) 394-6617 cthursby@ccbsuperior.org Clint Thursby, Exec.;

Challenge Center A, Inc. (Deer Haven Group Home) - 3105 Cumming Ave., Superior, WI 54880; Mailing: 1416 Cumming Ave., Superior, WI 54880 t) 715-394-2771 mkroll@ccbsuperior.org Mark Kroll, Dir.;

Challenge Center, Inc. - 39 N. 25th St. E., Superior, WI 54880 t) 715-394-2771 mkroll@ccbsuperior.org www.challenge-center.org Mark Kroll, Dir.;

Cypress Group Home - 1415 Cypress, Superior, WI 54880; Mailing: 39 N. 25th St. E., Superior, WI 54880 t) 715-394-2771 mkroll@ccbsuperior.org Mark Kroll, Dir.;

The Dove Agency, Inc. - 1416 Cumming Ave., Superior, WI 54880

The Dove, Inc. - 1416 Cumming Ave., Superior, WI 54880 t) (715) 394-6617

Harborview Group Home - 910 E. 5th St., Superior, WI 54880; Mailing: 39 N. 25th St. E, Superior, WI 54880 t) 715-394-2771 mkroll@ccbsuperior.org Mark Kroll, Dir.;

McKenzie Manor - 3317 N. 21st St., Superior, WI 54880; Mailing: 39 N. 25th St. E., Superior, WI 54880 t) 715-394-2771 mkroll@ccbsuperior.org Mark Kroll, Dir.;

Missouri Gardens Adult Family Home - 2347 Missouri Ave., Superior, WI 54880; Mailing: 39 N. 25th St. E., Superior, WI 54880 t) 715-394-2771 mkroll@ccbsuperior.org Mark Kroll, Dir.;

Mountain View Group Home - 3319 N. 16th St., Superior, WI 54880; Mailing: 39 N. 25th St. E., Superior, WI 54880 t) 715-394-2771 mkroll@ccbsuperior.org Mark Kroll, Dir.;

Northwoods Village, Inc. - 4390 Hackley Cir., Phelps, WI 54554; Mailing: 1416 Cumming Ave., Superior, WI 54880 t) 715-369-2550 sgrayson@ccbsuperior.org Shannon Grayson, Dir.;

Phoenix Villa, Inc. - 1100 Weeks Ave., Superior, WI 54880; Mailing: 1416 Cumming Ave., Superior, WI 54880 t) 715-394-2012 sgrayson@ccbsuperior.org Shannon Grayson, Dir.;

Phoenix Villa of Superior, Inc. (Oakwood Apartments) - 1112 John Ave., Superior, WI 54880; Mailing: 1416 Cumming Ave., Superior, WI 54880 t) 715-394-2012 sgrayson@ccbsuperior.org Shannon Grayson, Dir.;

Phoenix Villa, Inc. (Elmwood Apartments) - 1020 Weeks Ave., Superior, WI 54880; Mailing: 1416 Cumming Ave., Superior, WI 54880 t) 715-394-2012 sgrayson@ccbsuperior.org ccbhousing.org Shannon Grayson, Dir.;

Westbay, Inc. - 1104 John Ave., Superior, WI 54880; Mailing: 1416 Cumming Ave., Superior, WI 54880 t) 715-394-2012 sgrayson@ccbsuperior.org Shannon Grayson, Dir.;

Woodview Family Home - 6001 E. Third St., Superior, WI 54880; Mailing: 39 N 25th St. E, Superior, WI 54880 t) 715-394-2771 mkroll@ccbsuperior.org Mark Kroll, Dir.;

WINTER

Winterhaven Apartments, Inc. - 5038 N. Ellen St., Winter, WI 54896; Mailing: 1416 Cumming Ave., Superior, WI 54880 t) 715-236-2366 sgrayson@ccbsuperior.org ccbhousing.org Shannon Grayson, Dir.;

WISCONSIN RAPIDS

Phoenix Villa, Inc. (Acorn Apartments) - 2721 Tenth St. S., Wisconsin Rapids, WI 54494; Mailing: 1416 Cumming Ave., Superior, WI 54880 t) 715-421-0080 sgrayson@ccbsuperior.org ccbhousing.org Shannon Grayson, Dir.;

CONVENTS, MONASTERIES, AND RESIDENCES FOR WOMEN [CON]

HUDSON

Carmel of the Sacred Heart - 430 Laurel Ave., Hudson, WI 54016 t) 715-386-2156 carmelofthesacredheart@gmail.com www.carmelofthesacredheart.com Sr. Lucia LaMontagne, O.Carm., Prioress; Srs.: 5

LADYSMITH

Servants of Mary - 1000 College Ave. W., Ladysmith, WI 54848; Mailing: P.O. Box 389, Ladysmith, WI 54848-0389 t) 715-532-6153 info@servitesisters.org www.servitesisters.org Mary Bradley Corporation; Pooled Investment Trust of the Servants of Mary, Inc.; Servants of Mary Continuing Care Charitable Trust. Sr. Theresa Sandok, O.S.M., Pres.; Srs.: 26

MERRILL

Sisters of Mercy of the Holy Cross - 1400 O'Day St., Merrill, WI 54452-3417 t) 715-539-1460 Srs.: 20

ENDOWMENTS / FOUNDATIONS / TRUSTS [EFT]

LADYSMITH

Pooled Investment Trust of the Servants of Mary, Inc. - 1000 College Ave. W., Ladysmith, WI 54848; Mailing: P.O. Box 389, Ladysmith, WI 54848-0389 t) 715-532-6153 info@servitesisters.org Sr. Theresa Sandok, O.S.M., Trustee;

Servants of Mary Continuing Care Charitable Trust - 1000 College Ave. W., Ladysmith, WI 54848; Mailing: P.O. Box 389, Ladysmith, WI 54848 t) 750-535-6153 info@servitesisters.org Sr. Theresa Sandok, O.S.M., Trustee;

MERRILL

Sisters of Mercy of the Holy Cross Community Support Charitable Trust - 1400 O'Day St., Merrill, WI 54452-3417 t) 715-539-1460 dmnscsc@gmail.com

RHINELANDER

Headwaters Foundation - 1441 E. Timber Dr., Rhinelander, WI 54501; Mailing: 1416 Cumming Ave., Superior, WI 54880 t) 715-394-6617 mparkes@ccbsuperior.org Maureen Parkes, Dir.;

SUPERIOR

St. Augustine Seminarian Foundation, Inc. - 1201 Hughitt Ave., Superior, WI 54880; Mailing: P.O. Box 969, Superior, WI 54880 t) 715-392-2937 dblank@catholicdos.org Daniel Blank, Admin.;

Challenge Center Foundation Inc. - 1416 Cumming Ave., Superior, WI 54880 t) 715-394-6617 arock@ccbsuperior.org Alan Rock, Exec.;

Superior Retired Priest Health Care Foundation, Inc. - 1201 Hughitt Ave., Superior, WI 54880; Mailing: P.O. Box 969, Superior, WI 54880 t) 715-392-2937 dblank@catholicdos.org Daniel Blank, Admin.;

HOSPITALS / HEALTH SERVICES [HOS]

SUPERIOR

St. Mary's Hospital of Superior - 3500 Tower Ave., Superior, WI 54880 t) 715-817-7014 terrance.jacobson@essentiahealth.org www.essentialhealth.org MaryAnne Korsch, Chap.; Terry R. Jacobson, Admin.; Bed Capacity: 25; Asstd. Annu.: 175,000; Staff: 303

MISCELLANEOUS [MIS]

IRON RIVER

Phoenix Villa, Inc (Phoenix Villa of Iron River) - 62155 Cty. Rd. H, Iron River, WI 54847; Mailing: 1416 Cumming Ave., Superior, WI 54880 t) 715-394-2012 sgrayson@ccbsuperior.org ccbhousing.org Shannon Grayson, Dir.;

LADYSMITH

Mary Bradley Corporation - 1000 College Ave. W., Ladysmith, WI 54848; Mailing: P.O. Box 389, Ladysmith, WI 54848 t) 715-532-6153 info@servitesisters.org Sr. Theresa Sandok, O.S.M., Pres.;

LAKE NEBAGAMON

Phoenix Villa, Inc. (Phoenix Villa of Lake Nebagamon) - 6250 S. Fitch Ave., Lake Nebagamon, WI 54849; Mailing: 1416 Cumming Ave., Superior, WI 54880 t) 715-394-2012 sgrayson@ccbsuperior.org ccbhousing.org Shannon Grayson, Dir.;

LUCK

Mt. Carmel Hermitage of Superior, Wisconsin - 2514 92nd St., Luck, WI 54853 t) 715-472-2570 mountcarmelhermitage@gmail.com Sr. Kristine Haugen, O.C.D.H., Dir.;

MERRILL

Florence Huss Memorial Fund for Bell Tower Residents - 1400 O'Day St., Merrill, WI 54452 t) 715-539-1461 Sr. Linda L. Songy, SCSC, Rel. Ord. Ldr.;

RHINELANDER

Headwaters. Inc. - 1441 E. Timber Dr., Rhinelander, WI 54501; Mailing: 1416 Cumming Ave., Superior, WI 54880 t) 715-369-1337 www.headwatersinc.org

Phoenix Villa, Inc. (Phoenix Villa of Rhinelander) - 1011 Mason St., Rhinelander, WI 54501; Mailing: 1416 Cumming Ave., Superior, WI 54880 t) 715-369-2550 sgrayson@ccbsuperior.org ccbhousing.org Shannon Grayson, Dir.;

WEBSTER

Thomas More Center for Preaching and Prayer, Inc. - 27781 Leef Rd., Webster, WI 54893 t) 715-866-7436 achamplinm@gmail.com www.thomasmorecenter.org Rev. Nicholas W. Punch, O.P., Treas.; Sr. Joan Bukrey, O.S.F., Vice Pres. & Secy.;

NURSING / REHABILITATION / CONVALESCENCE / ELDERLY CARE [NUR]

SUPERIOR

St. Francis Home, Inc. - 1416 Cumming Ave., Superior, WI 54880 t) 715-394-6617 arock@ccbsuperior.org Alan Rock, CEO;

PRESCHOOLS / CHILDCARE CENTERS [PRE]

HUDSON

United Day Care, Inc. (Hudson Community Children's Center) - 824 Fourth St., Hudson, WI 54016; Mailing: 1416 Cumming Ave., Superior, WI 54880 t) 715-386-5912 www.hccc-wi.com Judy Brekke, Dir.;

RETREAT HOUSES / RENEWAL CENTERS [RTR]

ARBOR VITAE

Marywood Franciscan Spirituality Center (FSPA) - 11195 Marywood Cove, Arbor Vitae, WI 54568-9538 t) 715-385-3750 marywood.center@gmail.com www.marywoodsc.org Marywood engages persons seeking greater meaning in life and a deeper relationship with God, self, others and creation. Sr. Elizabeth Amman, O.P., Dir.;

Diocese of Syracuse

(Dioecesis Syracusensis)

MOST REVEREND DOUGLAS J. LUCIA, D.D., J.C.L.

Bishop of Syracuse; ordained May 20, 1989; appointed Bishop of Syracuse June 4, 2019; ordained and installed as Eleventh Bishop of Syracuse, August 8, 2019. Office: 240 E. Onondaga St., Syracuse, NY 13202.

Chancery Office: 240 E. Onondaga St., Syracuse, NY 13202. T: 315-422-7203; F: 315-478-4619. www.syracusediocese.org

ESTABLISHED NOVEMBER 26, 1886

Square Miles 5,749.

Corporate Title: The Roman Catholic Diocese of Syracuse NY.

Comprises the Counties of Broome, Chenango, Cortland, Madison, Oneida, Onondaga and Oswego.

For legal titles of parishes and diocesan institutions, consult the Chancery Office.

STATISTICAL OVERVIEW

Personnel
Bishop....1
Retired Bishops....1
Priests: Diocesan Active in Diocese....77
Priests: Diocesan Active Outside Diocese....3
Priests: Retired, Sick or Absent....74
Number of Diocesan Priests....154
Religious Priests in Diocese....26
Total Priests in your Diocese....180
Extern Priests in Diocese....15
Ordinations:
Transitional Deacons....1
Permanent Deacons....11
Permanent Deacons in Diocese....116
Total Brothers....6
Total Sisters....159

Parishes
Parishes....114
With Resident Pastor:
Resident Diocesan Priests....66
Resident Religious Priests....1
Without Resident Pastor:
Administered by Priests....42
Administered by Deacons....1
Administered by Lay People....5
Missions....15
Professional Ministry Personnel:
Sisters....13
Lay Ministers....12

Welfare
Catholic Hospitals....3
Health Care Centers....1
Homes for the Aged....53
Day Care Centers....18
Specialized Homes....2
Special Centers for Social Services....2
Residential Care of Disabled....14

Educational
Diocesan Students in Other Seminaries....10
Total Seminarians....10
Colleges and Universities....1
Total Students....3,203
High Schools, Diocesan and Parish....4
Total Students....1,117
High Schools, Private....2
Total Students....960
Elementary Schools, Diocesan and Parish....17
Total Students....1,016
Elementary Schools, Private....1
Total Students....70
Catechesis / Religious Education:
High School Students....2,308
Elementary Students....3,786
Total Students under Catholic Instruction....12,470
Teachers in Diocese:
Priests....1
Sisters....1
Lay Teachers....333

Vital Statistics
Receptions into the Church:
Infant Baptism Totals....1,790
Minor Baptism Totals....50
Adult Baptism Totals....53
Received into Full Communion....60
First Communions....1,377
Confirmations....1,457
Marriages:
Catholic....336
Interfaith....114
Total Marriages....450
Deaths....7,732
Total Catholic Population....196,897
Total Population....1,198,000

LEADERSHIP

Vicar General - Rev. John J. Kurgan;
Vicars Forane - Rev. Andrew E. Baranski; Rev. John J. Kurgan; Rev. Sean O'Brien;
Chancery Office - t) 315-422-7203 Danielle Cummings (dcummings@syracusediocese.org);
Chancellor - t) 315-470-1476 Danielle Cummings (dcummings@syracusediocese.org);
Secretary to the Bishop - Julie Hagan;
Board of Diocesan Consultors - Rev. Msgr. Timothy S. Elmer; Rev. John J. Kurgan, Vicar; Rev. Brendan Daniel Foley (bfoley@syrdio.org);
Administration Team - Most Rev. Douglas J. Lucia; Rev. Msgr. James P. Lang; Rev. John D. Manno;
Pastoral Council - t) 315-592-5566 Most Rev. Douglas J. Lucia, Pres.; Kathleen M. Dyer, Exec. Sec.;
Presbyteral Council - Most Rev. Douglas J. Lucia; Rev. John J. Kurgan; Rev. Msgr. Timothy S. Elmer;
Diocesan Pastoral Examiners - Rev. Kevin Corcoran; Rev. John J. Kurgan; Rev. Richard P. Pryor Jr.;
Diocesan Tribunal -
Adjutant Judicial Vicar - Rev. John P. Donovan;
Assistant to the Judicial Vicar - James Salamy;
Associate Judges - Rev. Robert P. Hyde Jr.; Rev. Christopher Seibt; James Salamy;
Case Coordinator/Staff - Julie Hagan;
Defender of the Bond - Rev. Clifford H. Auth;
Judicial Vicar - t) 315-470-1435 Rev. Msgr. Timothy S. Elmer;
Notary of the Tribunal - Julie Hagan;
Promoter of Justice -
Vicar for Administration - t) 315-470-1435 Rev. John J. Kurgan, Vicar;
Director for Community Services - t) 315-424-1800 Michael F. Melara;
Vicar for Parishes - t) 315-470-1437 Rev. Msgr. James P. Lang;
Vicar for Priests - t) 315-470-1460 Rev. John D. Manno;
Vicar for Religious - t) 315-470-1005 Sr. Kathleen Eiffe (keiffe@syrdio.org);

OFFICES AND DIRECTORS

Accounting - t) 315-422-9045 Carol Pieklik;
Administration - t) 315-470-1482 Stephen Breen, CFO; Rev. John J. Kurgan, Vicar;
Adult & Ministerial Formation - t) 315-470-1420 Eileen Ziobrowski, Dir.;
Archives - t) 315-470-1493 Wendy Seabrook;
Asian Apostolate - t) 315-289-7695 Rev. John Baptist Nguyen; Ying Lee;
Benefits - t) 315-422-9091 Rosemary Smith, Admin.;
Boy Scouts/Girl Scouts - t) 315-470-1437 Rev. Msgr. James P. Lang, Chap.;
Building Commission - Most Rev. Douglas J. Lucia; Rev. John J. Kurgan, Vicar; Edward T. King;
Catholic Cemeteries - t) 315-475-4639 Mark Barlow, Dir.;
Catholic Charities - t) 315-424-1800 Michael F. Melara;
Broome County Director - t) 607-729-9166 Lori Accardi, Exec. Dir.;
Chenango County Director - t) 607-334-8244 Robin (Beckwith) Cotter;
Cortland County Director - t) 607-756-5992 Timothy Lockwood;
Oneida and Madison Counties Director - t) 315-724-2158 Jack Callaghan;
Onondaga County Director - Michael F. Melara;
Oswego County Director - t) 315-598-3980 Mary Margaret Pezzella-Pekow;
Catholic Deaf Community - t) 315-470-1463 Michele Murphy;
Catholic Relief Services - t) 315-470-1416 Michael F. Melara;
Catholic School Endowment Fund of the Roman Catholic Diocese of Syracuse - Most Rev. Douglas J. Lucia, Pres.;
Catholic Schools - t) 315-470-1450 William Crist, Supt.; Donald Mills, Asst. Supt.; Rebecca Edsall, Dir.;
Southern Region - t) 607-723-1547
The Catholic Sun - t) 800-333-0571; 315-422-8153 www.sydio.org Dcn. Thomas Cuskey, Editor (tcuskey@syrdio.org);
Catholic Television - t) 315-472-3584 Rick Mossotti, Production Coord.;
Christopher Community - t) 315-414-1821 Justin Rudgick;
Clerical Fund Society of the Roman Catholic Diocese of Syracuse - Most Rev. Douglas J. Lucia, Pres.; Rev. John J. Kurgan, Vicar; Rev. Christopher Seibt;
Deacon Formation - Dcn. Thomas Cuskey (tcuskey@syrdio.org);
Ecumenical Commission - Rev. Jon K. Werner, Dir.;
Facilities Management - Edward T. King;
Family Life/Respect Life Office - t) 315-470-1418 Lisa Hall, Dir.;
Finance Committee - Most Rev. Douglas J. Lucia; Rev. Msgr. Richard M. Kopp; Rev. John J. Kurgan;
Health Care - t) 315-446-0473 Dcn. Dare Dutter, Dir.;
Heritage Campaign - t) 315-472-0203 Beth Lynn Hoey, Dir. (bhoey@syrdio.org);
HOPE Appeal - t) 315-472-0203 Beth Lynn Hoey, Dir. (bhoey@syrdio.org);
Laymen & Laywomen Retreats - t) 315-446-2680 Joan Spector, Dir.;
Liturgy and RCIA - t) 315-470-1420 Rev. Christopher Seibt;
Office of Communications - t) 315-470-1476 Danielle Cummings, Dir. (dcummings@syracusediocese.org);
Parish Services - t) 315-422-9089 Thomas O'Connor, Dir.;
Pastoral Leadership - Sr. Laura Bufano, C.S.J.;
Permanent Diaconate - t) 315-470-1466 Dcn. Robert Fangio, Dir.;
Personal Resource Center - t) 315-470-1462 Rev. Msgr. Neal E. Quartier, Dir.;
Pontifical Mission Societies - t) 315-472-3442 Dcn. Daniel Stevens;
Priest Personnel - t) 315-470-1460 Rev. John D. Manno;
Priests' Personnel Committee - Most Rev. Douglas J. Lucia; Rev. John J. Kurgan, Vicar; Rev. Msgr. James P. Lang, Ex Officio;
Project Rachel - t) 315-424-3737 Lisa Hall, Dir.;
Public Policy - James Salamy;
Child and Family Catechesis - t) 315-470-1431 Andrea Slaven, Dir.;
Eastern Region - t) 315-797-4030 Andrea Slaven, Dir.;
Southern Region - t) 607-348-0746 Andrea Schaffer, Dir.;
Western Region - t) 315-472-6753 Theresa White, Dir.;
Religious Retirement Fund - Sr. Kathleen Eiffe, Vicar (keiffe@syrdio.org); Danielle Cummings (dcummings@syracusediocese.org);
Risk Management - Brian McCauliff;
Ruth Ministry - t) 315-470-1418 Lisa Hall, Dir.;
Safe Environment - Jacqueline Bressette;
Stewardship & Development Office - t) 315-472-0203; 315-472-7902 Beth Lynn Hoey, Dir. (bhoey@syrdio.org);
Syracuse Catholic Press Association, Inc. - t) 800-333-0571; 315-422-8153 Most Rev. Douglas J. Lucia, Pres.; Dcn. Thomas Cuskey, Editor (tcuskey@syrdio.org);
Information Technology - Christopher Garrett, Dir.;
Victim Assistance Coordinator - t) 315-470-1465 Jacqueline Bressette;
Seminarian Formation - t) 315-470-1452 Rev. Joseph O'Connor, Dir.;
Vocation Promotion - t) 315-470-1468 Rev. Jason Hage, Dir.;
Adolescent Catechesis & Discipleship - t) 315-470-1402 Robert Walters, Dir.;

ADVISORY BOARDS, COMMISSIONS, COMMITTEES, AND COUNCILS

Women's Commission - Elizabeth Stewart;

CANONICAL SERVICES

Canonical Affairs - Rev. John P. Donovan;

PARISHES, MISSIONS, AND CLERGY

STATE OF NEW YORK

BAINBRIDGE

St. John the Evangelist - 34 S. Main St., Bainbridge, NY 13733 t) 607-967-4481 stjohnbain@syrdio.org Rev. James P. Serowik, Canonical Pst.; Dcn. Thomas N. Picciano, Admin.; Leslie Tallmadge, DRE; CRP Stds.: 15
St. Agnes - 14 Spring St., Afton, NY 13730; Mailing: 34 S. Main St., Bainbridge, NY 13733

BALDWINSVILLE

St. Augustine - 7333 O'Brien Rd., Baldwinsville, NY 13027 t) 315-638-0864 (CRP); 315-638-0585 www.staugustinesparish.org Rev. Clifford H. Auth, Pst.; Dcn. John Pedrotti; Cathy Mackey, DRE; CRP Stds.: 211
St. Elizabeth Ann Seton - 3494 NY State Rte. 31, Baldwinsville, NY 13027 t) 315-652-4300; 315-652-3900 (CRP) mainoffice@stelizabethbville.org stelizabethbville.org Rev. Joseph O'Connor, Pst.; Dcn. William A. Dotterer; CRP Stds.: 382
St. Mary of the Assumption - 47 Syracuse St., Baldwinsville, NY 13027 t) 315-635-5762 faithformation@stmarysassumption.org; stmarysbville@syrdio.org www.stmarysassumption.org Rev. Clifford H. Auth, Pst.; Dcn. Joseph Casper; Catherine Mackey, DRE; CRP Stds.: 211
St. Mary's Academy - (Grades PreK-6) 49 Syracuse St., Baldwinsville, NY 13027 t) 315-635-3977 svanliew@syrdiocese.org www.stmarysbaldwinsville.com Sarah VanLiew, Prin.; Iveliz Lopez, Librn.;

BINGHAMTON

SS. Cyril and Method - 148 Clinton St., Binghamton, NY 13905 t) 607-724-1372 stcyrilmethodius@syrdio.org www.ht-sscmbinghamton.org Rev. Msgr. John P. Putano, Admin.; Barbara Hill, Pst. Assoc.;
St. Francis of Assisi - 1031 Chenango St., Binghamton, NY 13901-1746 t) 607-722-4388 mkirk@syrdio.org; jcarpenter@syrdio.org www.stfrancisbing.org/ Rev. Timothy J. Taugher, Pst.; Dcn. Steve Blabac; Joseph Carpenter, Admin.; Maria Kirk, DRE; CRP Stds.: 150
Holy Trinity - 346 Prospect St., Binghamton, NY 13905 t) 607-797-1856; 607-724-1372 holytrinitybing@syrdio.org www.ht-sscmbinghamton.org Rev. Msgr. John P. Putano, Admin.; Barbara Hill, Pst. Assoc.;
Saints John & Andrew - 1263 Vestal Ave., Binghamton, NY 13903; Mailing: Parish Office - 7 Livingston St., Binghamton, NY 13903 t) 607-722-0493 stsjohnandrew@syrdio.org www.saintsjohnandandrew.com Rev. Msgr. Michael T. Meagher, Pst.; Rev. Robert J. Sullivan, In Res.; CRP Stds.: 77
St. Mary of the Assumption - 37 Fayette St., Binghamton, NY 13901-2501; Mailing: 15 Doubleday St., Binghamton, NY 13901 t) 607-723-5383 stsmary.paul@gmail.com Rev. Jon Werner, Pst.; CRP Stds.: 13
St. Patrick - 9 Leroy St., Binghamton, NY 13905 t) 607-722-1060 stpatrick@sta-sp.org www.sta-sp.org Linked with St. Thomas Aquinas, Binghamton. Rev. Msgr. John P. Putano, Pst.; Rev. Stephen Nyamweya Ogaro (Kenya), Par. Vicar; Dcn. Adeolu Ademoyo; Dcn. Leslie Distin; Sr. Mary Jane Athieno, L.S.O.S.F., Pst. Assoc.; Jeanne Higgins, DRE; Stewart Higginas,

RCIA Coord.; Karen Gill-Leighton, Youth Min.; Hilary Squier, Music Min.; CRP Stds.: 103

St. Paul - 15 Doubleday St., Binghamton, NY 13901-2501 t) 607-722-6492 stsmary.paul@gmail.com Rev. Jon Werner, Pst.; Sr. Lucia Mugambi, Sacramental Min.; CRP Stds.: 13

St. Thomas Aquinas - One Aquinas St., Binghamton, NY 13905 t) 607-797-4015 stthomasbing@syrdio.org www.sta-sp.org Linked with St. Patrick's, Binghamton. Rev. Msgr. John P. Putano, Pst.; Rev. Stephen Nyamweya Ogaro (Kenya), Par. Vicar; Rev. Paul Machira, In Res.; Dcn. Adeolu Ademoyo; Sr. Theresia Wauuate Mutiso, L.S.O.S.F., Pst. Assoc.; Jeanne Higgins, DRE; Karen Gill-Leighton, Youth Min.; Steven Nanni, Music Min.; CRP Stds.: 40

BOONVILLE

Christ Our Hope Parish - 112 Charles St., Boonville, NY 13309; Mailing: 108 Charles St., Boonville, NY 13309 t) 315-942-4618 christourhoperc@syrdio.org christourhoperc.org Rev. Matthew E. Rawson, Admin.; CRP Stds.: 54

St. Patrick - 11996 River Rd., Forestport, NY 13338

St. Mary of the Snows - State Rt. 28, Otter Lake, NY 13338

BRIDGEPORT

St. Francis of Assisi - 7820 Bridgeport-Minoa Rd., Bridgeport, NY 13030; Mailing: 229 W. Yates St., East Syracuse, NY 13057 t) 315-437-8318 stmarys2@twcny.rr.com Rev. Stephen P. Wirkes, Pst.; Dcn. Dean Brainard; Dcn. Joseph A. Lupia; CRP Stds.: 116

CAMDEN

St. John the Evangelist - 18 Church St., Camden, NY 13316; Mailing: 35 Third St., Camden, NY 13316 c) 315-245-1603; 315-820-4424 (Rectory) stjohncamden@syrdio.org www.stjohncamden.com/ Rev. John F. Hogan Jr., Pst.; Amy Healy, DRE; Glynis Smith, Bus. Mgr.; CRP Stds.: 32

CAMILLUS

St. Joseph - 5600 W. Genesee St., Camillus, NY 13031 t) 315-488-8490 businessmanager@stjosephscamillus.org Rev. Robert P. Hyde Jr., Pst.; Dcn. Nick A. Alvaro; Dcn. Thomas Grigson; CRP Stds.: 370

CANASTOTA

St. Agatha - 329 N. Peterboro St., Canastota, NY 13032; Mailing: Central Office, 121 St. Joseph Pl., Oneida, NY 13421 t) 315-363-3280 soh@syrdio.org www.spiritofhopecatholic.org Rev. Christopher J. Ballard, Pst.; Rev. Nathan W. Brooks, Par. Vicar; Dcn. James M. Chappell; Dcn. David Schiltz; Dcn. Adolph J. Uryniak; CRP Stds.: 32

St. Mary - t) 315-761-4016

St. John -

CAZENOVIA

St. James - 6 Green St., Cazenovia, NY 13035 t) 315-655-3441 stjamesc@stjamescaz.com www.stjamescaz.org Rev. Kevin J. Corcoran, Pst.; Dcn. John Addante; CRP Stds.: 150

CENTRAL SQUARE

Divine Mercy - 592 S. Main St., Central Square, NY 13036 t) 315-676-2898 divinemercy@syrdio.org www.divinemercycny.org Rev. Christopher Seibt, Pst.; Dcn. Mark Berube; CRP Stds.: 74

CHADWICKS

St. Patrick-St. Anthony - 3364 Oneida St., Chadwicks, NY 13319; Mailing: P.O. Box 429, Chadwicks, NY 13319 t) 315-507-2528 kpoupart@syrdio.org stpatricksstanthonys.org Rev. Robert C. Weber, Sacr. Min.; Dcn. James Henck; Katherine Marie Poupart, Parish Life Coord.; CRP Stds.: 102

CHITTENANGO

St. Patrick - 1341 Murray Dr., Chittenango, NY 13037 t) 315-687-6561 (CRP); 315-687-6105 stpatschitt@syrdio.org www.stpatrickschittenango.com Rev. Kevin Corcoran, Pst.; Dcn. John Addante; CRP Stds.: 87

CICERO

Sacred Heart - 8229 Brewerton Rd., Cicero, NY 13039 t) 315-699-2752 sheart@syrdio.org www.sacredheartofcicero.com Rev. John P. Donovan, Pst.; Rev. Amedeo G. Guida, In Res.; Rev. Richard P. Prior Jr., In Res.; Dcn. Brian Lauri; Dcn. Kenneth N. Money; Dcn. Louis Delsole; CRP Stds.: 464

CLARK MILLS

Church of the Annunciation - 7616 E. South St., Clark Mills, NY 13321 t) 315-853-6138 rectory@churchoftheannunciation.org; jnolan@syrdio.org www.churchoftheannunciation.org The Country Pantry (Food Pantry) Rev. Msgr. James P. Lang, Admin.; Rev. Kevin J. Bunger, Pst.; CRP Stds.: 57

CLEVELAND

St. Mary of the Assumption Oratory - 148 State Rte. 49, Cleveland, NY 13042; Mailing: 592 S. Main St., Central Square, NY 13036 t) 315-676-2898 divinemercy@syrdio.org divinemercycny.org Linked with the Mission of St. Bernadette. All records and parish business are conducted via Divine Mercy Parish, Central Square. Rev. Christopher Seibt, Admin.;

CLINTON

St. Mary - 13 Marvin St., Clinton, NY 13323 t) 315-853-6196 (CRP); 315-853-2935 stmarysclinton@syrdio.org Rev. Robert C. Weber; Dcn. John Kopec; Rev. Msgr. James P. Lang, Admin.; CRP Stds.: 151

CORTLAND

St. Anthony of Padua - 50 Pomeroy St., Cortland, NY 13045 t) 607-756-9967 stanthcortland@syrdio.org Rev. Joseph Zareski, Pst.; Rev. Dennis Walker, Par. Vicar; Dcn. Stephen Smith; Dcn. Timothy Stedman; Robert Densmore, DRE; Stephanie Passeriu-Densmore, DRE; CRP Stds.: 31

St. Mary - 46 N. Main St., Cortland, NY 13045; Mailing: 59 N Main St., Cortland, NY 13045 t) 607-756-9967 religiousedk8@gmail.com; stmoffice@centralny.twcbc.com Rev. Joseph Zareski, Pst.; Rev. Dennis Walker, Par. Vicar; Jennifer Fischer, DRE; Dcn. Timothy Stedman; Dcn. Stephen Smith; CRP Stds.: 85

St. Mary School - (Grades PreK-6) 61 N. Main St., Cortland, NY 13045 t) 607-756-5614 dhall@syrdiocese.org Denise Hall, Prin.;

DEPOSIT

St. Joseph - 98 Second St., Deposit, NY 13754; Mailing: 975 NY Rte. 11, Kirkwood, NY 13795 t) 607-775-0086 sebroomecatholics@syrdio.org Rev. James P. Serowik, Canonical Pst.; Barbara Kane, Parish Life Coord.; CRP Stds.: 23

DEWITT

Holy Cross - 4112 E. Genesee St., DeWitt, NY 13214 t) 315-446-0473 julie@holycrossdewitt.org; info@holycrossdewitt.org www.holycrossdewitt.org Rev. John J. Kurgan, Pst.; Rev. Brendan Daniel Foley, Par. Vicar; Dcn. Dare Dutter; Stephen Nepil, DRE; Julie Sheridan, DRE; CRP Stds.: 329

Holy Cross School - (Grades PreK-6) 4200 E. Genesee St., DeWitt, NY 13214 t) 315-446-4890 Stds.: 145

EAST SYRACUSE

St. Matthew - 229 W. Yates St., East Syracuse, NY 13057 t) 315-437-8318 stmatth1@twcny.rr.com Rev. Stephen P. Wirkes, Pst.; Dcn. Dean Brainard; Dcn. Joseph Lupia Jr.; CRP Stds.: 116

ENDICOTT

St. Ambrose - 203 Washington Ave., Endicott, NY 13760 t) 607-754-2330 stambrose@syrdio.org northendicottcatholic.org/home/st-ambrose/ Rev. Kenneth R. Kirkman, Pst.; CRP Stds.: 6

St. Anthony of Padua - 306 Odell Ave., Endicott, NY 13760; Mailing: 906 Jenkins St., Endicott, NY 13760 t) 607-754-4333; 607-429-0041; 607-748-0442 (CRP) stanthendicott@syrdio.org; sherceg@syrdio.org northendicottcatholic.org Rev. Kenneth R. Kirkman, Pst.; Dcn. William Matts; Sally Herceg, DRE; CRP Stds.: 84

St. Anthony's Learning Center - 906 Jenkins St., Endicott, NY 13760 t) 607-748-5184 stanthonytlc@stny.rr.com (Pre-School)

St. Joseph - 207 Hayes Ave., Endicott, NY 13760 t) 607-748-0442 sherceg@syrdio.org; stjoesendicott@syrdio.org northendicottcatholic.org Rev. Kenneth R. Kirkman, Pst.; Dcn. William Matts; Sally Herceg, DRE; CRP Stds.: 58

Our Lady of Good Counsel - 701 W. Main St., Endicott, NY 13760 t) 607-748-7417 x14 tharley-olgc@stny.rr.com olgcendicott.org/ Dcn. Thomas M. Harley, Deacon Admin.; Kathy Hamilton, Youth Min.; Bob Cargil, DRE; CRP Stds.: 150

ENDWELL

Church of the Holy Family - 3600 Phyllis St., Endwell, NY 13760 t) 607-754-1266 churchoftheholyfamily@gmail.com holyfamilyendwell.com Rev. Clarence F. Rumble, Pst.; Dcn. George Phillips Jr.; Dcn. James Tokos; CRP Stds.: 236

FAYETTEVILLE

Immaculate Conception - 400 Salt Springs St., Fayetteville, NY 13066 t) 315-637-9840 (CRP); (315) 637-9846 (Tel/Fax) avoutsinas@syrdio.org; icfayetteville@syrdio.org icfayetteville.org Rev. Thomas J. Ryan, Pst.; Rev. Msgr. Ronald C. Bill, In Res.; Rev. Philip A. Hearn, In Res.; Anne Marie Voutsinas, DRE; CRP Stds.: 379

Immaculate Conception School - (Grades PreK-6) t) (315) 637-3961 efaigle@syrdiocese.org; nferrarone@syrdioese.org Nancy Ferrarone, Prin.;

FULTON

Church of the Holy Trinity - 309 Buffalo St., Fulton, NY 13069 t) 315-598-2118 holytrinityfulton@syrdio.org Rev. Joseph E. Scardella, Pst.; Rev. John Canorro, Pst.; Rev. James A. Schultz, Assoc. Pst.; Dcn. David Sweenie; CRP Stds.: 60

GREENE

Immaculate Conception - 1180 State Hwy. 206, Greene, NY 13778-1193 t) 607-656-9546 immcongreene@syrdio.org iccgreene.com Rev. Msgr. John P. Putano, Admin.; Rev. Paul Machira, Assoc. Pst.; Rev. James P. Serowik, Canonical Pst.; Mary Wentlent, Parish Life Coord.; CRP Stds.: 36

HAMILTON

St. Mary - 16 Wylie St., Hamilton, NY 13346 t) 315-824-2164 route20catholic.org Rev. Jason Hage, Pst.; Dcn. Paul Lehmann; Dcn. Mark Shiner, Campus Min.; Margaret Rhyde, DRE; CRP Stds.: 53

St. Joan of Arc - 6 Brookside Dr., Morrisville, NY 13408; Mailing: 16 Wylie St., Hamilton, NY 13346 t) 315-684-9551 Jessica Tomcho, DRE;

HANNIBAL

Our Lady of the Rosary - 931 Cayuga St., Hannibal, NY 13074; Mailing: 50 E. Mohawk St., Oswego, NY 13126 t) (315) 343-2333 olotrhannibal@syrdio.org Mission of Our Lady of Perpetual Help, Minetto. Rev. John Canorro, Pst.;

HOLLAND PATENT

St. Leo & St. Ann - 7937 Elm St., Holland Patent, NY 13354; Mailing: P.O. Box 185, Holland Patent, NY 13354 t) 315-865-5371 stleos@syrdio.org Rev. Vincent P. Long, Pst.; CRP Stds.: 139

HOMER

St. Margaret - 14 Copeland Ave., Homer, NY 13077 t) 607-749-2542 christine.williams@stmargaret-homer.org; office@stmargaret-homer.org Rev. Joseph Zareski, Pst.; Rev. Dennis Walker, Par. Vicar; Dcn. Dan Reynolds; Rev. Daniel Caughey, Par. Vicar; CRP Stds.: 34

JOHNSON CITY

St. James - 147 Main St., Johnson City, NY 13790 t) 607-729-6147 stjamesjc@syrdio.org stjamesjc.org Rev. Charles Opondo-Owora, Pst.; Dcn. William Fitzpatrick, Pst. Assoc.; Dcn. Edward Blaine, Pst. Assoc.; Carol Hall, Pst. Assoc.; CRP Stds.: 215

JORDAN

St. Patrick - 28 N. Main St., Jordan, NY 13080-0567; Mailing: P.O. Box 567, Jordan, NY 13080 t) 315-689-6240 x114 (Rectory); 315-689-6240 x113 (CRP) stpatsjordan@syrdio.org www.stpatricksjordan.com Rev. John R. DeLorenzo,

Pst.; Mary E. Badger, DRE; CRP Stds.: 34

KIRKWOOD

St. Mary - 975 NY Rte. 11, Kirkwood, NY 13795 t) 607-775-0086 sebroomecatholics@syrdio.org broomecatholics.org/1 Rev. James P. Serowik, Canonical Pst.; Barbara Kane, Parish Life Coord.; CRP Stds.: 46

LAFAYETTE

St. Joseph - 6104 Cherry Valley Rd., Lafayette, NY 13084; Mailing: Box 169, Lafayette, NY 13084 t) 315-677-7735 (CRP); 315-677-3439 stjoeslafayette@syrdio.org Rev. James H. Carey, Admin.; CRP Stds.: 140

LEE CENTER

St. Joseph - 5748 Stokes Lee Center Rd., Lee Center, NY 13363 t) 315-533-6655 stjosephs.leecenter@syrdio.org Rev. Robert L. Kelly, Pst.; Dcn. Edgar A. Doyle Jr.; CRP Stds.: 60

LIVERPOOL

Christ the King - 21 Cherry Tree Cir., Liverpool, NY 13090 t) (315) 652-6591 christtheking@syrdio.org; ctkfaithformation@syrdio.org liverpoolnycatholic.org/ Rev. Zachary K. Miller, Pst.; Dcn. Thomas Cuskey; Dcn. Ralph Jahnige; Dcn. Larry Messina; Dcn. Michael Ruf; Anthony Maio, DRE; CRP Stds.: 48

Epiphany Parish - 425 Beechwood Ave., Liverpool, NY 13088 t) 315-451-5070 info@ihmsjw.org; faithformation@ihmsjw.org www.epiphanyparishliverpool.org/ Rev. Daniel J. O'Hara, Pst.; Rev. Msgr. James P. Lang, In Res.; Sr. Rose Marie Caravaglio, C.S.J., Music Min.; Dcn. Stephen Manzene, Pst. Assoc.; Amy Wojcikowski, DRE; CRP Stds.: 197

Immaculate Heart of Mary -

St. Joseph the Worker - 1001 Tulip St., Liverpool, NY 13088

Immaculate Heart of Mary - 425 Beechwood Ave., Liverpool, NY 13088 t) 315-451-5070 info@ihmsjw.org www.ihmsjw.org Rev. Daniel J. O'Hara, Pst.; Dcn. Stephen Manzene, Pst. Assoc.; Rev. Msgr. James P. Lang, In Res.; Sr. Rose Marie Caravaglio, C.S.J., Music Min.;

St. Joseph the Worker - 1001 Tulip St., Liverpool, NY 13088 t) 315-457-6060 info@ihmsjw.org; jeggert@ihmsjw.org www.ihmsjw.org Rev. Daniel J. O'Hara, Pst.; Dcn. Stephen Manzene, Pst. Assoc.;

Pope John XXIII RC Church - 8290 Soule Rd., Liverpool, NY 13090 t) 315-652-6591 ctkpj23faithformation@syrdio.org; johnxxiii@syrdio.org liverpoolnycatholic.org/ Rev. Zachary K. Miller, Pst.; Dcn. Thomas Cuskey; Dcn. Ralph Jahnige; Dcn. Larry Messina; Dcn. Michael Ruf; Anthony Maio, DRE; CRP Stds.: 148

MAINE

Most Holy Rosary - 2596 Main St., Maine, NY 13802; Mailing: P.O. Box 248, Maine, NY 13802 t) 607-862-3216 mostholyrosary-maineny.org Rev. Clarence F. Rumble, Admin.; Dcn. James Tokos; CRP Stds.: 18

MANLIUS

St. Ann - 104 Academy St., Manlius, NY 13104 t) 315-682-5181 parishoffice@saintannschurch.com saintannschurch.com Rev. Brian E. Lang, Pst.; CRP Stds.: 232

MARCELLUS

St. Francis Xavier - 1 W. Main St., Marcellus, NY 13108; Mailing: P.O. Box 177, Marcellus, NY 13108 t) 315-673-2531 jfalge@syrdio.org Rev. Daniel C. Muscalino, Pst.; Dcn. John Falge; CRP Stds.: 110

MATTYDALE

St. Margaret - 200 Roxboro Rd., Mattydale, NY 13211 t) 315-455-5534 stmargmattydale@syrdio.org Most Rev. Douglas J. Lucia, Admin.; Dcn. David G. Losito; Dcn. Donald R. Whiting; CRP Stds.: 44

MEXICO

St. Anne, Mother of Mary - 3352 Main St., Mexico, NY 13114-0487; Mailing: P.O. Box 487, Mexico, NY 13114-0487 t) 315-963-7182 lbuckley@syrdio.org; stannemexico@syrdio.org stannechristourlight.com St. Anne, Mother of Mary in Mexico. Linked with Christ Our Light, Pulaski. Msgr. Francis Osei-Nyarko, Admin.; Dcn. Terry O'Loughlin; CRP Stds.: 38

MINETTO

Our Lady of Perpetual Help - 2913 State Rte. 48, Minetto, NY 13115; Mailing: 50 E. Mohawk St., Oswego, NY 13126-2724 t) (315) 343-2333 olophminetto@syrdio.org Rev. John Canorro, Pst.;

MINOA

St. Mary - 401 N. Main St., Minoa, NY 13116; Mailing: 229 W. Yates St., East Syracuse, NY 13057 t) 315-656-4220 (CRP); 315-437-8318 cvieau1@gmail.com; stmarys2@twcny.rr.com Rev. Stephen P. Wirkes, Pst.; Dcn. Dean Brainard; Dcn. Joseph A. Lupia, Bus. Mgr.; CRP Stds.: 116

NEW BERLIN

St. Theresa of the Infant Jesus - 24 N. Main St., New Berlin, NY 13411-0780; Mailing: P.O. Box 780, New Berlin, NY 13411-0780 t) 607-847-6851; 607-847-8590 (CRP) carlpat@frontiernet.net; snogaret64@gmail.com Linked Rev. Daniel Caughey, Admin.; CRP Stds.: 15

NEW HARTFORD

St. John the Evangelist - 66 Oxford Rd., New Hartford, NY 13413 t) 315-732-8521 stjohnnh@syrdio.org Rev. Msgr. James P. Lang; Rev. Kevin J. Bunger, Pst.; Dcn. Edward W. Kernan; CRP Stds.: 225

Mary, Mother of Our Savior - 1736 Burrstone Rd., New Hartford, NY 13413 t) 315-724-0402 parishoffice@olrosarynh.org www.olrosarynh.org Formerly Our Lady of the Rosary. Rev. Joseph A. Salerno, Pst.; CRP Stds.: 210

St. Thomas - 150 Clinton Rd., New Hartford, NY 13413 t) 315-735-8381 dsears@syrdio.org Rev. G. David Sears, Pst.;

NEW YORK MILLS

Church of Sacred Heart and St. Mary - 201 Main St., New York Mills, NY 13417 t) 315-316-0506 stmarysnymills@syrdio.org Rev. Arthur Krawczenko (Poland), Pst.; CRP Stds.: 170

NORTH BAY

St. John - 2191 Rte. 49, North Bay, NY 13123; Mailing: P.O. Box 289, North Bay, NY 13123 t) 315-363-3280 soh@syrdio.org www.spiritofhopecatholic.org Oratory of St. Agatha, Canastota. Rev. Christopher J. Ballard, Pst.; Rev. Nathan W. Brooks, Par. Vicar; Dcn. James M. Chappell; Dcn. David Schiltz; Dcn. Adolph J. Uryniak;

NORTH SYRACUSE

St. Rose of Lima - 409 S. Main St., North Syracuse, NY 13212 t) 315-458-0283 strose@syrdio.org strosecny.org Rev. Christopher Celentano, Pst.; Dcn. Nathan Gunn; Dcn. William Wilson; CRP Stds.: 115

Preschool - t) 315-458-6036

St. Rose of Lima School - (Grades PreK-6) 411 S. Main St., North Syracuse, NY 13212 t) 315-458-6036 mcrysler@syrdiocese.org Mary Crysler, Prin.; Stds.: 286; Lay Tchrs.: 17

NORWICH

St. Bartholomew the Apostle - 73 E. Main St., Norwich, NY 13815; Mailing: 30 Pleasant St., Norwich, NY 13815 t) 607-336-2222; 607-336-2215 (Office); 607-337-2200 (CRP) stbarts@syrdio.org www.stbartsnorwich.com Rev. Ralph A. Bove, Pst.; Dcn. Dale Grey; Sr. M. Bartholomew Biviano, C.S.J., DRE; CRP Stds.: 43

St. Paul - 30 Pleasant St., Norwich, NY 13815 t) 607-337-2216 stpaulsnorwich@syrdio.org Rev. Ralph A. Bove, Pst.; Dcn. Dale Grey; Dcn. David Kirsch; Sr. M. Bartholomew Biviano, C.S.J., DRE; CRP Stds.: 32

Holy Family School - (Grades PreK-6) 17 Prospect St., Norwich, NY 13815 t) 607-337-2207 tsorci@syrdiocese.org Thomas Sorci, Prin.;

ONEIDA

St. Joseph - 121 St. Joseph Pl., Oneida, NY 13421 t) 315-363-3280 soh@syrdio.org www.spiritofhopecatholic.org Rev. Christopher J. Ballard, Pst.; Rev. Nathan W. Brooks, Par. Vicar; Dcn. James M. Chappell; Dcn. David Schiltz; Dcn. Adolph J. Uryniak; CRP Stds.: 35

Parish Center - 111 St. Joseph Pl., Oneida, NY 13421

St. Patrick - 347 Main St., Oneida, NY 13421; Mailing: Central Office, 121 St Joseph Pl., Oneida, NY 13421 t) 315-363-3280 soh@syrdio.org spiritofhopecatholic.org Rev. Christopher J. Ballard, Pst.; Rev. Nathan W. Brooks, Par. Vicar; CRP Stds.: 70

St. Patrick School - (Grades PreK-6) 354 Elizabeth St., Oneida, NY 13421 t) 315-363-3620 khealt@syrdiocese.org Kristin Healt, Prin.; Jackie Carll, Librn.;

ORISKANY FALLS

St. Joseph - 229 Main St., Oriskany Falls, NY 13425; Mailing: 199 Stafford Ave S, St. Bernard's Church, Waterville, NY 13480 t) 315-841-4481 route20catholic.org/ Rev. Jason Hage, Pst.; Dcn. Paul Lehmann; Shannon Jones, DRE; Therese Gallagher, Bus. Mgr.; CRP Stds.: 4

OSWEGO

Christ the Good Shepherd - 138 Niagara St., Oswego, NY 13126; Mailing: 50 E. Mohawk St., Oswego, NY 13126 t) 315-343-2333 ctgs@syrdio.org www.christthegoodshepherd.org Rev. John Canorro, Pst.; Rev. John Leo Oduor, Par. Vicar; Rev. John J. Smegelsky, In Res.; Rev. George E. Wurz, In Res.; Dcn. John Lalande II;

St. Joseph - 240 W. First St., Oswego, NY 13126 t) (315) 343-2333 christthegoodshepherd.org

St. Paul - 134 E. Fifth St., Oswego, NY 13126 t) (315) 343-2333

OXFORD

St. Joseph - 3 Scott St., Oxford, NY 13830; Mailing: P.O. Box 352, Oxford, NY 13830 t) 607-843-7021 stjoesoxford@syrdio.org www.stjosephsoxfordny.com/ Rev. Msgr. John P. Putano, Contact; CRP Stds.: 13

New York State Veterans' Home -

PHOENIX

St. Stephen - 469 Main St., Phoenix, NY 13135 t) 315-695-4531 ststephensfaithformation@syrdio.org; ststephenphoenix@syrdio.org www.holytrinityfulton.org Rev. Joseph E. Scardella, Pst.; Dcn. Jeffrey Dean; CRP Stds.: 10

POMPEY

Immaculate Conception - 7386 Academy St., Pompey, NY 13138; Mailing: P.O. Box 79, Pompey, NY 13138 t) 315-677-3061 icpompey@yahoo.com; atchristmas@aol.com icpompey.org Rev. James H. Carey, Admin.; Barbara McKenney, DRE; Ann Christmas, Bus. Mgr.; CRP Stds.: 34

PORT CRANE

St. Joseph - 659 NY Rte. 7-B, Port Crane, NY 13833; Mailing: 975 NY Rte. 11, Kirkwood, NY 13795 t) 607-775-0086 sebroomecatholics@syrdio.org Rev. James P. Serowik, Canonical Pst.; Barbara Kane, Parish Life Coord.; CRP Stds.: 6

PULASKI

Christ Our Light - 23 Niagara St., Pulaski, NY 13142-4425 t) 315-298-5350; 315-298-3863 (Res.) christourlight@syrdio.org; oferguson@syrdio.org stannechristourlight.com Linked with St. Anne, Mother of Mary, Mexico. Msgr. Francis Osei-Nyarko, Admin.; CRP Stds.: 31

ROME

St. John the Baptist - 210 E. Dominick St., Rome, NY 13440 t) 315-337-0990 amhunzinger@yahoo.com; stjohnsrome@syrdio.org Rev. Paul F. Angelicchio, Pst.; Dcn. Michael Gudaitis; Robin Calandra, Youth Min.; Ann Marie Hunzinger, DRE; CRP Stds.: 96

St. Paul - 1807 Bedford St., Rome, NY 13440-2199 t) 315-334-9570 (CRP); 315-336-3082 jstokes@syrdiocese.org; stpaulsrome@syrdio.org Rev. Robert L. Kelly, Pst.; Dcn. Edgar Doyle Jr.; Julianne Stokes, DRE; CRP Stds.: 80

St. Peter's Church - 200 N. James St., Rome, NY 13440 t) 315-336-5072 stpetersrome@syrdio.org stmarysstpeters.com Rev. Sean O'Brien, Pst.; Rev. Bernard Menard, Par. Vicar; Dcn. Nicholas A. Rosher; CRP Stds.: 233

Transfiguration - 210 E. Dominick St., Rome, NY 13440 t) 315-337-0990 transfigurationrome@syrdio.org Rev. Paul F. Angelicchio, Pst.; Dcn. Michael Gudaitis;

SHERBURNE

St. Malachy - 29 E. State St., Sherburne, NY 13460-0722; Mailing: PO Box 722, Sherburne, NY 13460-9788 t) 607-674-9625 stmalachysherburne@gmail.com stmalachysherburne.com Rev. Daniel Caughey, Admin.; CRP Stds.: 3

SHERRILL

St. Helena - 202 Primo Ave., Sherrill, NY 13461; Mailing: Spirit of Hope Catholic Community Central Office, 121 St. Joseph Pl., Oneida, NY 13421 t) 315-363-3280 soh@syrdio.org spiritofhopecatholic.org Rev. Christopher J. Ballard, Pst.; Rev. Nathan W. Brooks, Par. Vicar; Mercedes Genei, DRE; CRP Stds.: 56

SKANEATELES

St. Mary's of the Lake - 81 Jordan St., Skaneateles, NY 13152; Mailing: 10 W. Austin St., Skaneateles, NY 13152 t) 315-685-5083; 315-685-6377 (CRP) stmarysskan@syrdio.org www.stmarysskaneateles.com Rev. Richard B. Dunn, Pst.; CRP Stds.: 174

SOLVAY

St. Marianne Cope Parish - 1001 Woods Rd., Solvay, NY 13209; Mailing: 105 Stanton Ave., Solvay, NY 13209 t) 315-488-3221 stmariannecopeparish@syrdio.org Rev. Joseph J. Clemente, Pst.;

SYRACUSE

The Cathedral of the Immaculate Conception - 259 E. Onondaga St., Syracuse, NY 13202 t) 315-422-4177 cathedral@syrdio.org cathedralsyracuse.org Most Rev. Douglas J. Lucia; Rev. Msgr. Neal E. Quartier, Rector; Dcn. Robert T. Burke; Dcn. Paul Biermann, RCIA Coord.; Sharon Secor, Pst. Assoc.; Rev. William R. Jones, In Res.; Rev. John C. Schopfer, In Res.; CRP Stds.: 61

All Saints - 1342 Lancaster Ave., Syracuse, NY 13210 t) 315-472-9934 Rev. Frederick D. Daley, Pst.; CRP Stds.: 125

St. Anthony of Padua - 1515 Midland Ave., Syracuse, NY 13205; Mailing: C/O Holy Cross Church, 4112 E. Genesee St., DeWitt, NY 13214 t) 315-475-4114 stanthsyr@syrdio.org Rev. John J. Kurgan, Admin.; Rev. Brendan Daniel Foley, Par. Vicar;

Assumption B.V.M. - 812 N. Salina St., Syracuse, NY 13208 t) 315-422-4833 admin@assumptionsyr.org assumptionsyr.org Franciscan Church of the Assumption. Bro. James Moore, OFM Conv, Supr.; Rev. Jude DeAngelo, OFM Conv, Pst.; Friar Nader Ata, O.F.M.Conv., Par. Vicar; Rev. Gerald Waterman, O,F,M.Conv., Campus Min.; Rev. Robert Amrhein, O.F.M.Conv., In Res.; Rev. Steven Frenier, OFM Conv, In Res.; Bro. James Amrhein, O.F.M.Conv., In Res.; Dcn. Philip Slominski; Friar Joseph Krondon, O.F.M.Conv., Dir.; Alexander LaPoint, Dir.; CRP Stds.: 8

Assumption Cemetery Corporation - 2401 Court St., Syracuse, NY 13208 t) 315-454-3841 assump812@aol.com

Basilica of the Sacred Heart - 927 Park Ave., Syracuse, NY 13204 t) 315-422-4086 (CRP); 315-422-2343 shbasilica@syrdio.org www.sacredheartbasilicasyr.org Rev. Andrew E. Baranski, Rector; Dcn. Richard Galloway; Dcn. Frank Timson; Sr. Melanie Jaworski, CSSF, DRE; Dcn. Jeffrey Getman; Dcn. Michael Casey; CRP Stds.: 32

Blessed Sacrament - 3127 James St., Syracuse, NY 13206 t) 315-437-3394 bscoffice@bscstvsyr.org www.bscstvsyr.org/ Rev. Severine Yagaza, Pst.; Dcn. Michael Colabufo; Dcn. Daniel Stevens; Rev. Msgr. Timothy S. Elmer, In Res.; CRP Stds.: 203

Blessed Sacrament School - (Grades PreK-6) 3129 James St., Syracuse, NY 13206 t) 315-463-1261 lcoppola@syrdiocese.org www.blessedsacramentschool.org Lisa Coppola, Prin.;

St. Charles - St. Ann - 501 S. Orchard Rd., Syracuse, NY 13219 t) 315-468-1803 (Office); 315-487-6201 (CRP) tcondon@syrdio.org; stcharles.stanns@gmail.com stcharles-stanns.com Rev. Kevin Maloney, Pst.; Dcn. Anthony J. Paratore; Dcn. Robert Connelly; Sharon P. Guglielmi, Youth Min.; CRP Stds.: 103

St. Daniel - 3004 Court St., Syracuse, NY 13208 t) 315-454-4946 stdaniels@syrdio.org www.stdaniel.com Rev. Thomas I Ward, Pst.; Dcn. Joseph Celentano; CRP Stds.: 30

Church of the Holy Family - 124 Chapel Dr., Syracuse, NY 13219; Mailing: 127 Chapel Dr., Syracuse, NY 13219 t) 315-488-3139 holyfamily@holyfamilysyr.org www.holyfamilysyr.org Rev. John D. Manno, Pst.; Rev. Malachi Clark, Par. Vicar; Rev. Msgr. J. Robert Yeazel, Sacr. Min.; Rev. William Muench, In Res.; Dcn. Robert Fangio; Dcn. Scott Harris; Dcn. Mark Kay; Dcn. Edward Terzolo; CRP Stds.: 245

Holy Family School - (Grades PreK-6) 130 Chapel Dr., Syracuse, NY 13219 t) 315-487-8515 cluczynski@syrdiocese.org www.holyfamilyschoolsyr.org Sr. Christina Marie Luczynski, Prin.;

St. John the Baptist/Holy Trinity - 406 Court St., Syracuse, NY 13208 t) 315-478-0916 nbergeson@syrdio.org www.stjohnthebaptist-holytrinity.com Rev. Daniel M. Caruso, Pst.; Rev. Lester E. Smith, In Res.; CRP Stds.: 16

St. Lucy - 432 Gifford St., Syracuse, NY 13204 t) 315-475-7273 stlucys@syrdio.org Rev. James D. Mathews, Pst.; CRP Stds.: 24

St. Michael & St. Peter - 4791 W. Seneca Tpke., Syracuse, NY 13215; Mailing: 4782 W. Seneca Tpke., Syracuse, NY 13215 t) 315-469-6995 stmichaelstpeter@syrdio.org stmichael-stpeter.org Rev. Michael Galuppi, Pst.; Dcn. Matthew Lumia; CRP Stds.: 166

Most Holy Rosary - 111 Roberts Ave., Syracuse, NY 13207-1397 t) 315-478-5749 mhrsyracuse@syrdio.org Rev. Frederick R. Mannara, Pst.; CRP Stds.: 45

Most Holy Rosary School - (Grades PreK-6) 1031 Bellevue Ave., Syracuse, NY 13207 t) 315-476-6035 slstone@syrdiocese.org www.mhrsyr.org Sherri Stone, Prin.; Sue Limpert, Librn.; Sr. Joan Ottman, I.H.M., Librn.;

Our Lady of Hope - 4845 S. Salina St., Syracuse, NY 13205 t) 315-469-7789 info@ourladyofhopesyr.org ourladyofhopesyr.org Rev. Michael Galuppi, Pst.; CRP Stds.: 30

Onondaga Valley -

Our Lady of Peace - Merged Jan 2023 Merged with St. Cecilia to form St. Marianne Cope.

Our Lady of Pompei/St. Peter - 301 Ash St., Syracuse, NY 13208 t) 315-472-2260 (CRP); 315-422-7163 olopsyracuse@syrdio.org Rev. Daniel M. Caruso, Pst.; Rev. Tuoi (John) V. Nguyen, Chap.; Mary Beth Meade, DRE; CRP Stds.: 91

Our Lady of Pompei/St. Peter School - (Grades PreK-6) 915-917 N. McBride St., Syracuse, NY 13208 t) 315-422-8548 tseymour@syrdiocese.org Tina Seymour, Prin.;

St. Patrick-St. Brigid - 216 N. Lowell Ave., Syracuse, NY 13204 t) 315-475-2185 stpatssyr@syrdio.org Rev. Kevin Maloney, Pst.; Dcn. Anthony J. Paratore; Stephanie De Vito, Music Min.; CRP Stds.: 82

Transfiguration - 740 Teall Ave., Syracuse, NY 13206 t) 315-479-6129 transfigurationsyr@syrdio.org Rev. James A. Schultz, Pst.; Rev. Thomas P. Kobuszewski, Pastor Emer.; Rev. Innocent Onyenagubo (Nigeria), In Res.; Rev. Peter F. Tassini Jr., In Res.; CRP Stds.: 30

St. Vincent de Paul - 342 Vine St., Syracuse, NY 13203 t) 315-479-6689 stvincentsyr@syrdio.org Rev. Severine Yagaza, Pst.; Dcn. Aleu Tong; Dcn. Thomas J. Murphy; CRP Stds.: 32

TABERG

St. Patrick - 9168 Main St., Taberg, NY 13471 t) 315-336-4079 stpatstaberg@syrdio.org Rev. Francis A. Wapen, Pst.; CRP Stds.: 15

TRUXTON

St. Patrick - 3656 Rte. 13, Truxton, NY 13158; Mailing: Box 15, Truxton, NY 13158 t) 607-842-6326 stpatstruxton@syrdio.org Rev. Joseph Zareski, Pst.; Rev. Dennis Walker, Par. Vicar; Rev. Paul J. Alciati, Admin.;

St. Lawrence - 1672 Cortland St., De Ruyter, NY 13052 t) 315-852-6446

TULLY

St. Leo - 10 Onondaga St., Tully, NY 13159; Mailing: P.O. Box 574, Tully, NY 13159 t) 315-696-5092 parish@stleostully.org www.stleostully.org Rev. James H. Carey, Pst.;

UTICA

St. Anthony and St. Agnes Church - 422 Tilden Ave., Utica, NY 13501 t) 315-732-1177 stanthutica@syrdio.org Rev. Mark P. Kaminski, Pst.; Dcn. William Dischiavo; CRP Stds.: 78

Historic Old St. John's Church - 240 Bleecker St., Utica, NY 13501 t) 315-724-6159 stjohnsutica@syrdio.org www.historicoldstjohnschurch.com Rev. Thomas Servatius, Pst.; Rev. Tuoi (John) V. Nguyen, Asian Ministry; Rev. Luis Olguin, Spanish Apostolate; Annette Gape, Pst. Assoc.; CRP Stds.: 48

Parish Center - 520 John St., Utica, NY 13501 t) 315-732-2417

Holy Trinity - 1206 Lincoln Ave., Utica, NY 13502 t) 315-724-7238 holytrinityutica@syrdio.org Dcn. George Spohr; Rev. Canon John E. Mikalajunas, Pst.; Rev. Joseph E. Moskal, Assoc. Pst.; CRP Stds.: 25

Convent - 1218 Lincoln Ave., Utica, NY 13502

St. Joseph and St. Patrick - 702 Columbia St., Utica, NY 13502 t) 315-735-4429; 315-507-2661 sjsputica@syrdio.org; cstaley@syrdio.org www.stjoestpat.org Rev. Thomas R. Servatius, Admin.; Rev. Amedeo G. Guida, Sacr. Min.; Cheryl Staley, DRE; CRP Stds.: 6

St. Mark - 440 Keyes Rd., Utica, NY 13502 t) 315-724-1645 stmarks@syrdio.org stmarkschurchutica.weebly.com Rev. Mark P. Kaminski, Admin.; Dcn. Richard Prusko; Teale LaBarbera, DRE; CRP Stds.: 55

St. Mary of Mt. Carmel/Blessed Sacrament - 648 Jay St., Utica, NY 13501 t) 315-724-3950 (CRP); 315-735-1482 tpanuccio@syrdio.org; aelacqua@sydio.org www.mountcarmelblessedsacrament.com Rev. James M. Cesta, Pst.; Rev. Luis Olguin, In Res.; Anne Elacqua, DRE; Terese Panuccio, DRE; Peter Elacqua, Dir.; Francis Perritano, Editor; CRP Stds.: 148

St. Peter - 422 Coventry Ave., Utica, NY 13502 t) 315-724-6310 stpetersutica@syrdio.org Rev. Thomas R. Servatius, Admin.;

VERNON

Holy Family - 4352 Peterboro St., Vernon, NY 13476; Mailing: 121 St. Joseph Pl., P.O. Box 988, Vernon, NY 13421 t) 315-363-3280 soh@syrdio.org spiritofhopecatholic.org Rev. Christopher J. Ballard, Pst.; Mercedes Genei, DRE; Rev. Nathan W. Brooks, Par. Vicar; CRP Stds.: 60

VERONA

Our Lady of Good Counsel - 5652 E. Main St., Verona, NY 13478; Mailing: P.O. Box 135, Verona, NY 13478 t) 315-363-7696 frcastronovo@gmail.com Latin Mass Rev. Edmund A. Castronovo, Pst.; CRP Stds.: 30

VESTAL

Our Lady of Sorrows - 801 Main St., Vestal, NY 13850; Mailing: P.O. Box 326, Vestal, NY 13851 t) 607-748-8287 office@olsvestal.org www.olsvestal.org Rev. Richard P. Prior Jr., Pst.; Dcn. Edward Blaine; CRP Stds.: 178

St. Vincent de Paul-Blessed Sacrament - 465 Clubhouse Rd., Vestal, NY 13850; Mailing: 165 Clifton Blvd., Vestal, NY 13850 t) 607-722-3988 www.stvbs.org Rev. James P. Serowik, Pst.; Dcn. Gregory Hrostowski; Dcn. Thomas N. Picciano; Dcn. Anthony Miller; CRP Stds.: 108

WATERVILLE

St. Bernard - 199 Stafford Ave., Waterville, NY 13480 t) 315-841-4481 route20catholic@syrdio.org Rev. Jason Hage, Pst.; CRP Stds.: 36

WHITESBORO

St. Paul - 16 Park Ave., Whitesboro, NY 13492 t) 315-736-1124; 315-736-1124 (CRP)

stpauls@stpaulswhitesboro.org; cgodemann@stpaulswhitesboro.org stpaulswhitesboro.org Rev. Thomas P. Durant, Pst.; Dcn. Christopher Engle Sr.; Dcn. Anthony Paparella; Dcn. Robert Stanhope; CRP Stds.: 185

WHITNEY POINT

The Catholic Community of St. Stephen-St. Patrick - 59 Keibel Rd., Whitney Point, NY 13862; Mailing: P.O. Box 711, Whitney Point, NY 13862 t) 607-692-3911 ststephenstpat@syrdio.org ccsssp.com Rev. James P. Serowik, Admin.; Rev. Corey S. Van Kuren, Admin.; CRP Stds.: 21

Our Lady of Perpetual Help - ; Mailing: P.O. Box 310, Cincinnatus, NY 13040

WINDSOR

Our Lady of Lourdes - 594 Kent St., Windsor, NY 13865; Mailing: 975 NY Rt. 11, Kirkwood, NY 13795 t) 607-775-0086 sebroomecatholics@syrdio.org Barbara Kane, Parish Life Coord.; Jennifer Barton, DRE; CRP Stds.: 14

SCHOOLS: PRESCHOOL THRU HIGH SCHOOL

SCHOOLS

STATE OF NEW YORK

BINGHAMTON

St. John the Evangelist - (PAR) (Grades PreK-6) 9 Livingston St., Binghamton, NY 13903 t) 607-723-0703 Jim Abrams, Prin.; Emily Regan, Prin.; Stds.: 171; Lay Tchrs.: 10

ENDICOTT

All Saints Catholic School - (PAR) (Grades PreK-6) 1112 Broad St., Endicott, NY 13760 t) 607-748-7423 wpipher@syrdiocese.org csbcsaints.org/ William Pipher, Prin.; Stds.: 154; Lay Tchrs.: 18

JOHNSON CITY

St. James School - (PAR) (Grades PreK-6) 143 Main St., Johnson City, NY 13790 t) 607-797-5444 Jim Abrams, Prin.; Patrick Monachino, Prin.; Stds.: 132; Lay Tchrs.: 24

OSWEGO

Trinity Catholic School - (PAR) (Grades PreK-6) 115 E. 5th St., Oswego, NY 13126 t) 315-343-6700 Peter Myles, Interim Principal; Barbara Sugar, Prin.; Stds.: 138; Lay Tchrs.: 12

ROME

Rome Catholic School - (PAR) (Grades PreK-6) 800 Cypress St., Rome, NY 13440 t) 315-336-6190 newilson@syrdiocese.org Nancy Wilson, Prin.; Stds.: 138; Lay Tchrs.: 13

UTICA

Notre Dame Elementary School - (PAR) (Grades PreK-6) 11 Barton Ave., Utica, NY 13502 t) 315-732-4374 mrossi@syrdiocese.org notredameelem.org Richard Ambruso, Prin.; Carol Polito, Asst. Principal; Mary Rossi, Prin.; Stds.: 283; Lay Tchrs.: 39

HIGH SCHOOLS

STATE OF NEW YORK

BINGHAMTON

Seton Catholic Central of Broome County - (PAR) 70 Seminary Ave., Binghamton, NY 13905 t) 607-723-5307 Patrick Monachino, Prin.; Kathryn Frech, Librn.; Stds.: 315; Lay Tchrs.: 22

EAST SYRACUSE

Bishop Grimes Jr./Sr. High School - (PAR) (Grades 7-12) 6653 Kirkville Rd., East Syracuse, NY 13057 t) 315-437-0356 pkinne@syrdiocese.org; aheadd@syrdiocese.org www.bishopgrimes.org/ Allyson E. Headd, Prin.; Patrick Kinne, Vice Prin.; Stds.: 270; Lay Tchrs.: 28

SYRACUSE

Bishop Ludden Junior/Senior High School - (PAR) (Grades 7-12) 815 Fay Rd., Syracuse, NY 13219 t) 315-468-2591 michael.mcauliff@syrdiocese.org; sgeorge@syrdiocese.org www.syrdio.org Michael McAuliff, Prin.; Stds.: 264; Lay Tchrs.: 49

Christian Brothers Academy - (PRV) (Grades 7-12) 6245 Randall Rd., Syracuse, NY 13214 t) 315-446-5960 mkeough@cbasyr.org www.cbasyracuse.org Paul Gasparini, Prin.; Matthew Keough, Pres.; Stds.: 730; Sr. Tchrs.: 1; Lay Tchrs.: 53

UTICA

Notre Dame Jr./Sr. High School - (PAR) (Grades 7-12) 2 Notre Dame Ln., Utica, NY 13502 t) 315-724-5118 Roy Kane, Prin.; Richard Ambruso, Prin.; Stds.: 268; Lay Tchrs.: 35

INSTITUTIONS LOCATED IN DIOCESE

CAMPUS MINISTRY / NEWMAN CENTERS [CAM]

CAZENOVIA

Cazenovia College Newman Center - 10 Seminary St., Cazenovia, NY 13035; Mailing: 22 Sullivan St., Cazenovia, NY 13035 t) 315-655-7375 stjyouth@stjamescaz.com www.stjyouth@stjamescaz.com Rev. Kevin Corcoran, Chap.;

CLINTON

Hamilton College Newman Center - 198 College Hill Rd., Clinton, NY 13323 t) 315-859-4129 jcroghan@hamilton.edu Rev. John P. Croghan, Chap.;

CORTLAND

Newman Foundation of Cortland, Inc. at the State University College of New York - 8 Calvert St., Cortland, NY 13045 t) 607-753-6737 twilder@syrdio.org www.cortland.edu/ministry/catholic.html Tricia Wilder, Dir.;

MORRISVILLE

Newman Association at SUNY Morrisville - Mathasis Health Bldg., Morrisville, NY 13408; Mailing: P.O. Box 901, Chaplain's Office, Morrisville, NY 13408 t) 315-684-6201 grafar@morrisville.edu www.morrisville.edu/pages/newman St. Joan of Arc Newman Association at the State University of New York (SUNY) Morrisville Agricultural and Technical College. Rev. Jason Hage, Dir.; Alex Graf, Campus Min.;

OSWEGO

Newman Foundation of Oswego, Inc. - 36 New St., Oswego, NY 13126; Mailing: P.O. Box 207, Oswego, NY 13126 t) 315-312-7222 newctr@oswego.edu www.hallnewmancenter.org Michael Huynh, Dir.;

SYRACUSE

LeMoyne College Campus Ministry - 1419 Salt Springs Rd., Syracuse, NY 13214 t) 315-445-4110 andinotm@lemoyne.edu Thomas Andino, Dir.; Rev. John P. Bucki, S.J., Rector; Rev. William S. Dolan, S.J.;

Syracuse University Catholic Center & St. Thomas More Foundation, Inc. - 110 Walnut Pl., Syracuse, NY 13210 t) 315-443-2600 fwaterma@syr.edu www.sucatholic.org Danielle Drop, Dir.; Rev. Gerald Waterman, O,F,M.Conv., Chap.;

UTICA

Newman Center at SUNY Poly Tech Institute - Newman Community, Utica, NY 13505-8087; Mailing: P.O. Box 8087, Utica, NY 13505-8087 t) 315-792-3284 pdrobin@utica.edu State University of New York (SUNY) Poly Tech Institute Newman Center Dcn. Paul Lehmann, Dir.;

Utica College Newman Center - SUNY Poly Tech & Utica College, Utica, NY 13505-8087; Mailing: P.O. Box 8087, Utica, NY 13505-8087 t) 315-792-3284 pdrobin@utica.edu Dcn. Paul Lehmann, Dir.;

Campus Ministry/Newman Center - Newman Community, Utica, NY 13505-8087; Mailing: P.O. Box 8087, Utica, NY 13505-8087 Dcn. Paul Lehmann, Dir.;

VESTAL

Binghamton University Newman Center - 400 Murray Hill Rd., Vestal, NY 13850 t) 607-798-7202 rcasaleno@syrdio.org Sr. Rose Casaleno, Campus Min.;

CATHOLIC CHARITIES [CCH]

BINGHAMTON

Associated Catholic Charities for Community Development in Broome County - 232 Main St., Binghamton, NY 13905 t) 607-729-9166 www.catholiccharitiesbc.org Lori Accardi, Exec.;

Catholic Charities of Broome County - 232 Main St., Binghamton, NY 13905 t) 607-729-9166 laccardi@ccbc.net www.catholiccharitiesbc.org Lori Accardi, Exec.; Asstd. Annu.: 28,927; Staff: 267

Catholic Charities Office of Social Concerns - Broome County - 232 Main St., Binghamton, NY 13905 t) 607-729-9166 laccardi@ccbc.net www.catholiccharitiesbc.org Lori Accardi, Contact; Asstd. Annu.: 12; Staff: 1

CORTLAND

Catholic Charities of Cortland County - 33-35 Central Ave., Cortland, NY 13045 t) 607-756-5992 info@ccocc.org www.ccocc.org Timothy Lockwood, Exec.; Asstd. Annu.: 3,200; Staff: 50

Case Management Services -

Catholic Charities-STEPS - Supportive teen education-parents services; case management; adolescent group activities. Amanda DeLee, Dir.;

Emergency Assistance - Emergency & basic needs assistance (food pantry, medication, advocacy referral & support; summer lunch program for children).

Residential Services - Adult mental health and substance abuse recovery.

FULTON

Catholic Charities of Oswego Co. - 808 W. Broadway, Fulton, NY 13069 t) 315-598-3980 mmpekow@ccoswego.com www.ccoswego.com Mary-Margaret Pekow, Exec.; Asstd. Annu.: 12,172; Staff: 50

NORWICH

Community Residence Program - 3 O'Hara Dr., Norwich, NY 13815 t) 607-334-8244 rcotter@ccofcc.com Provides housing for mentally ill and intellectually disabled adults. Robin Cotter, Exec.; Asstd. Annu.: 15; Staff: 20

Catholic Charities of Chenango County - jchesbro@ccofcc.com; mcasella@ccofcc.com Jeff Chesebro, Dir.;

The Counseling Program - 3 O'Hara Dr., Norwich, NY 13815 t) 607-334-8244 dsitts@ccofcc.com www.ccofcc.com Provides counseling for children and adults, also specialized counseling for abused children and individuals with developmental disabilities. Robin Cotter, Exec.; Jeff Chesebro, Dir.; Asstd. Annu.: 30; Staff: 1

ONEIDA

Catholic Charities of Oneida - Madison Counties - 248 Main St., Oneida, NY 13421 t) 315-363-5274 vpallozzi@ccharityom.org www.catholiccharitiesom.org Jack Callaghan, Dir.; Asstd. Annu.: 1,716; Staff: 96

Madison County Catholic Charities - 1081 Northside Shopping Ctr., Oneida, NY 13421; Mailing: 1408 Genesee St., Utica, NY 13052 t) 315-363-5274 vpaolozzi@ccharityom.org Jack Callaghan, Dir.; Asstd. Annu.: 1,716; Staff: 96

SYRACUSE

Catholic Charities of Onondaga County - 1654 W. Onondaga St., Syracuse, NY 13204 t) 315-424-1800 info@ccoc.us www.ccoc.us Michael F. Melara, Exec.; Lindsay M. Cronkright, Bus. Mgr.; Asstd. Annu.: 8,467; Staff: 380

Crisis, Stabilization & Capacity Building Services - Crisis Services: emergency services including financial, pantries & relocation services; shelter services for men, women and women with children.

Catholic Charities of the Roman Catholic Diocese of Syracuse - 1654 W. Onondaga St., Syracuse, NY 13204 t) 315-424-1800 www.ccsyrdio.org Michael F. Melara, Exec.; Asstd. Annu.: 1,000; Staff: 1,400

Christopher Community, Inc. - 990 James St., Syracuse, NY 13203 t) 315-424-1821 jrudgick@christopher-community.org www.christopher-community.org Professional management and consultants of housing programs for the elderly, families and special populations. Justin Rudgick, Exec.; Asstd. Annu.: 4,202; Staff: 160

Churchill Manor, Inc. - 750 E. Brighton Ave., Syracuse, NY 13205 t) 315-413-3287 Provides housing for low and moderate income families and individuals. Mary Koenig, Admin.; Asstd. Annu.: 79; Staff: 60

Northside CYO - 527 N. Salina St., Syracuse, NY 13208 t) 315-424-1800 info@ccoc.us Christopher Curry, Admin.; Asstd. Annu.: 1,299; Staff: 48

Vincent House - 514 Seymour St., Syracuse, NY 13204 t) 315-424-1800 info@ccoc.us Christopher Curry, Admin.;

UTICA

Catholic Charities Family & Community Support Services - 1408 Genesee St., Utica, NY 13502 t) 315-724-2158 jcallaghan@ccharityom.org www.catholiccharitiesom.org Jack Callaghan, Admin.; Asstd. Annu.: 10,000; Staff: 120

Catholic Charities of Oneida - Madison Counties - 1408 Genesee St., Utica, NY 13502 t) 315-724-2158 vpaolozzi@ccharityom.org www.catholiccharitiesom.org Victoria Paolozzi, Admin.; Jack Callaghan, Dir.; Asstd. Annu.: 4,700; Staff: 130

CEMETERIES [CEM]

BALDWINSVILLE

Our Lady of Peace Cemetery - 8668 Oswego Rd., Rte. 57, Baldwinsville, NY 13027 t) 315-303-4901 catholiccemeteries@syrdio.org syracusecatholiccemeteries.org Catholic Cemeteries of the Roman Catholic Diocese of Syracuse, Inc. Mark Barlow, Dir.; Tina Smith, Family Svcs. Mgr.; Scott Bivens, Field Lead; Sarah Conklin, Family Svc. Guide;

CLAYVILLE

St. Mary's Cemetery - 2515 Church Rd., Clayville, NY 13322; Mailing: 2407 Oneida St., Utica, NY 13501 t) 315-735-2727 catholiccemeteries@syrdio.org syracusecatholiccemeteries.org Catholic Cemeteries of the Roman Catholic Diocese of Syracuse, Inc. Mark Barlow, Dir.; Brandon Barnes, Opers. Mgr.; Tina Smith, Family Svcs. Mgr.; Kristy Sheldon, Family Svc. Guide; Rikki Walker, Family Svc. Guide;

CORTLAND

St. Mary's Cemetery - 4101 West Rd., Cortland, NY 13045 t) 607-756-8838 catholiccemeteries@syrdio.org syracusecatholiccemeteries.org Catholic Cemeteries of the Roman Catholic Diocese of Syracuse, Inc. Mark Barlow, Dir.; Randy Ramey, Opers. Mgr.; Wayne Moore, Field Lead; Wendy Clinch, Family Svc. Guide; Colin Ramey, Family Svc. Guide;

JOHNSON CITY

Calvary-St. Patrick - 501 Fairview St., Johnson City, NY 13790 t) 607-797-2906 catholiccemeteries@syrdio.org syracusecatholiccemeteries.org Catholic Cemeteries of the Roman Catholic Diocese of Syracuse, Inc. Mark Barlow, Dir.; Randy Ramey, Opers. Mgr.; Colin Ramey, Family Svc. Guide;

OSWEGO

St. Peter & St. Paul - 379 East River Rd., Oswego, NY 13126 t) 315-343-5002 catholiccemeteries@syrdio.org syracusecatholiccemeteries.org Catholic Cemeteries of the Roman Catholic Diocese of Syracuse, Inc. Mark Barlow, Dir.; Dunsmoor Jason, Opers. Mgr.; Tina Smith, Family Svcs. Mgr.; Sarah Conklin, Family Svc. Guide;

SYRACUSE

St. Mary-St. Agnes - 2315 South Ave., Syracuse, NY 13207 t) 315-475-4639 catholiccemeteries@syrdio.org syracusecatholiccemeteries.org Catholic Cemeteries of the Roman Catholic Diocese of Syracuse, Inc. Mark Barlow, Dir.; Jeffery Kraus, Opers. Mgr.; Tina Smith, Family Svcs. Mgr.; Nancy James, Family Svc. Guide; Monica Merritt, Family Svc. Guide;

UTICA

Calvary Cemetery - 2407 Oneida St., Utica, NY 13501 t) 315-735-2727 catholiccemeteries@syrdio.org syracusecatholiccemeteries.org Catholic Cemeteries of the Roman Catholic Diocese of Syracuse, Inc. Mark Barlow, Dir.; Brandon Barnes, Opers. Mgr.; Tina Smith, Family Svcs. Mgr.; Kristy Sheldon, Family Svc. Guide; Rikki Walker, Family Svc. Guide;

Holy Trinity Cemetery - 1500 Champlin Ave., Utica, NY 13502; Mailing: 2407 Oneida St., Utica, NY 13502 t) 315-724-0616 catholiccemeteries@syrdio.org syracusecatholiccemeteries.org Catholic Cemeteries of the Roman Catholic Diocese of Syracuse, Inc. Mark Barlow, Dir.; Brandon Barnes, Opers. Mgr.; Tina Smith, Family Svcs. Mgr.; Kristy Sheldon, Family Svc. Guide; Rikki Walker, Family Svc. Guide;

WHITESBORO

Mount Olivet Cemetery - 70 Wood Rd., Whitesboro, NY 13492; Mailing: 2407 Oneida St., Utica, NY 13501 t) 315-736-4446 catholiccemeteries@syrdio.org syracusecatholiccemeteries.org Catholic Cemeteries of the Roman Catholic Diocese of Syracuse, Inc. Mark Barlow, Dir.; Brandon Barnes, Opers. Mgr.; Tina Smith, Family Svcs. Mgr.; Kristy Sheldon, Family Svc. Guide; Rikki Walker, Family Svc. Guide;

COLLEGES & UNIVERSITIES [COL]

SYRACUSE

Le Moyne College - 1419 Salt Springs Rd., Syracuse, NY 13214-1302 t) 315-445-4100 officeofthepresident@lemoyne.edu www.lemoyne.edu Rev. Donald J. Kirby, S.J., Rector; Linda M. LeMura, Pres.; James Hannan, Provost and Vice. Pres. Academic Affairs; Rev. Patrick D. Rogers, S.J., Vice. Pres. Mission Integration; Stds.: 3,203; Lay Tchrs.: 173; Pr. Tchrs.: 6; Sr. Tchrs.: 1

CONVENTS, MONASTERIES, AND RESIDENCES FOR WOMEN [CON]

BINGHAMTON

Little Sisters of Saint Francis of Assisi Mission - 4 Aquinas St., Binghamton, NY 13905 t) 607-217-7334 lsosfmission12@gmail.com Sr. Teresia Mutiso, L.S.O.S.F., Contact; Srs.: 5

LIVERPOOL

Sisters of St. Francis of the Neumann Communities - 225 Greenfield Pkwy., Suite 208, Liverpool, NY 13088 t) 315-634-7000; 315-422-8652 sisters@sosf.org www.sosf.org Sr. Jeanne Weisbeck, O.S.F., Supr.; Sr. James Peter Ridgeo, O.S.F., Secy.; Sr. Rita Marie Fritzen, O.S.F., Treas.; Sr. Pam Conte, O.S.F., Rel. Ord. Ldr.; Sr. Donna McGartland, O.S.F., Rel. Ord. Ldr.; Srs.: 95

SYRACUSE

Dominican Monastery of the Perpetual Rosary - 802 Court St., Syracuse, NY 13208-1766 t) 315-470-1473 keiffe@syrdio.org www.dominicanmonastery.net Sr. Kathleen Eiffe, Vicar;

WINDSOR

Transfiguration Monastery - 701 NY Rte. 79, Windsor, NY 13865-2700 t) 607-655-2366 transfigurationmonastery@gmail.com www.transfigurationmonastery.org Camaldolese Benedictine Nuns Sr. Sheila Long, O.S.B.Cam., Prioress; Srs.: 3

ENDOWMENTS / FOUNDATIONS / TRUSTS [EFT]

AUBURN

Mercy Housing Development Fund Co., Inc. - Mercy Apartments, 1 Thornton Ave., Auburn, NY 13021; Mailing: 990 James St., Syracuse, NY 13203 t) 315-424-1821 jrudgick@christopher-community.org 40 one-bedroom units for the elderly and handicapped. Christopher Community, Inc., (Managing Agent). Justin Rudgick, Pres.;

BALDWINSVILLE

Smokey Hollow Housing Development Fund Company, Inc. - 100 LaMadre Way, Baldwinsville, NY 13027; Mailing: 990 James St., Syracuse, NY 13203 t) 315-424-1821 jrudgick@christopher-community.org Christopher Community, Inc., (Managing Agent). Justin Rudgick, Pres.;

BREWERTON

Bartell Road Housing Development Fund Co., Inc. - 5500 Miller Rd., Brewerton, NY 13029; Mailing: 990 James St., Syracuse, NY 13203 t) 315-668-9871 jrudgick@christopher-community.org Christopher Community, Inc., (Managing Agent). Justin Rudgick, Pres.;

CANASTOTA

Stoneleigh Housing Development Fund Co., Inc. - Stoneleigh Apartments, 400 Lamb Ave., Canastota, NY 13032; Mailing: 990 James St., Syracuse, NY 13203 jrudgick@christopher-community.org Apartments for elderly and handicapped persons of low income. Justin Rudgick, Pres.;

CICERO

Cicero Housing Development Fund Company Inc. - 8365 Factory St., Sacred Heart Apartments, Cicero, NY 13039; Mailing: 990 James St., Syracuse, NY 13203 t) 315-424-1821 jrudgick@christopher-community.org Justin Rudgick, Pres.;

Sacred Heart Apartments - 990 James St., Syracuse, NY 13203 t) (315) 699-1509 Christopher Community, Inc., (Managing Agent).

DEWITT

Joseph & Elaine Scuderi Foundation - 5786 Widewaters Pkwy., DeWitt, NY 13214; Mailing: P.O. Box 3, DeWitt, NY 13214 t) 315-445-2424 jscuderi@widewaters.com Joseph Scuderi, Contact;

FAYETTEVILLE

Redfield South Housing Development Fund Co., Inc. - Redfield Village Apartments, 380 Salt Springs Rd., Fayetteville, NY 13066; Mailing: 990 James St., Syracuse, NY 13203 t) 315-637-8280 jrudgick@christopher-community.org Christopher Community, Inc., (Managing Agent). Justin Rudgick, Pres.;

HENDERSON

Harbor View Housing Development Fund Co., Inc. - 12541 Harbor View Dr., Henderson, NY 13650; Mailing: 990 James St., Syracuse, NY 13203 t) 315-424-1821 jrudgick@christopher-community.org Justin Rudgick, Pres.;

OSWEGO

St. Luke's Housing Development Fund Co., Inc. - St. Luke's Apartments, 131 W. First St., Oswego, NY 13126; Mailing: 990 James St., Syracuse, NY 13203 t) 315-343-0821 jrudgick@christopher-community.org Apartments for elderly and handicapped persons of low income. Justin Rudgick, Pres.;

ROME

Rome Mall Housing Development Fund Company, Inc. - 146 W. Dominick St., Rome, NY 13440; Mailing: 990 James St., Syracuse, NY 13203 t) 315-424-1821 jrudgick@christopher-community.org Christopher Community, Inc., (Managing Agent). Justin Rudgick, Pres.;

SYRACUSE

Bartell Road Housing Development Co., Inc. - 990 James St., Syracuse, NY 13203 t) 315-424-1821 jrudgick@christopher-community.org (Brewerton); Housing for well elderly. Justin Rudgick, Pres.;

The Foundation of the Roman Catholic Diocese of Syracuse - 240 E. Onondaga St., Syracuse, NY 13202 t) 315-472-0203 bhoey@syrdio.org syracusediocese.org/offices/foundation Beth Lynn Hoey, Dir.;

Grimes Foundation - 240 E. Onondaga St., Syracuse, NY 13202 t) 315-422-7203 sbreen@syrdio.org Most Rev.

Douglas J. Lucia, Pres.; Rev. Msgr. Timothy S. Elmer, Treas.; Rev. John J. Kurgan;

Hawley Winton Housing Development Fund, Inc. - Walter Ludovico Apts., 340 Winton St., Syracuse, NY 13203; Mailing: 990 James St., Syracuse, NY 13203 t) 315-422-0475 jrudgick@christopher-community.org Christopher Community Inc., (Managing Agent). Justin Rudgick, Pres.;

Loretto Apartments Housing Development Fund Co., Inc. - 700 E. Brighton Ave., Syracuse, NY 13205 t) 315-413-3206 jmurray@lorettosystem.org Heather Davis, Contact;

Ludden Housing Development Fund Company, Inc. - Bishop Ludden Apartments, 817 Fay Rd., Syracuse, NY 13219; Mailing: 990 James St., Syracuse, NY 13203 t) 315-424-1821 jrudgick@christopher-community.org Apartments for the elderly & handicapped. Christopher Community Inc. (Managing Agent). Justin Rudgick, Pres.;

Marcellus Apartments Housing Development Fund Company, Inc. - 990 James St., Syracuse, NY 13203 t) 315-424-1821 jrudgick@christopher-community.org Christopher Community, Inc., (Managing Agent). Justin Rudgick, Pres.;

Onondaga County Catholic School Foundation (Western Region Catholic School Foundation) - 240 E. Onondaga St., Syracuse, NY 13202 t) 315-470-1450 wcrist@syrdio.org William Crist, Supt.;

St. Peter's Italian Church Housing Development Fund Co., Inc. Villa Scalabrini Apts. - 825 E. Willow St., Syracuse, NY 13203; Mailing: 990 James St., Syracuse, NY 13203 t) 315-424-1821 jrudgick@christopher-community.org Operation of a nonprofit housing facility for aged, well persons of low income. Justin Rudgick, Pres.;

Pitcher Hill-Christopher Housing Development Fund Co., Inc. - 114 Elbow Rd., Syracuse, NY 13212; Mailing: 990 James St., Syracuse, NY 13203 t) 315-424-1821 pitcherhill@christophercommunity.org; jrudgick@christopher-community.org Apartments for elderly and handicapped persons of low income. Justin Rudgick, Pres.;

Pompei Housing Development Fund Company, Inc. - 143 Mary St., Pompei North Apartments, Syracuse, NY 13208; Mailing: 990 James St., Syracuse, NY 13203 t) 315-424-1821 x636 jrudgick@christopher-community.org Apartments for the elderly & handicapped. Christopher Community, Inc., (Managing Agent). Justin Rudgick, Pres.;

c/o Christopher Community, Inc. - 990 James St., Syracuse, NY 13203 pompeinorth@christopher-community.org

Pond St. Housing Development Fund Co., Inc. - Bishop Harrison Apartments, 300 Pond St., Syracuse, NY 13208; Mailing: 990 James St., Syracuse, NY 13203 t) 315-476-8630 jrudgick@christopher-community.org Apartments for the elderly & handicapped. Christopher Community Inc., (Managing Agent). Justin Rudgick, Pres.;

Roman Catholic Diocese - Bishop Harrison Education Trust - 240 E. Onondaga St., Syracuse, NY 13202 t) 315-470-1472 wcrist@syrdio.org William Crist, Supt.;

The Saint Thomas Aquinas Fund Inc. - 240 E. Onondaga St., Syracuse, NY 13202 t) 315-470-1482 jkurgan@syrdio.org Rev. John J. Kurgan, Vicar;

The Robert L. McDevitt, K.S.G., K.C.H.S. and Catherine H. McDevitt, L.C.H.S. Foundation, Inc. - 240 E. Onondaga St., Syracuse, NY 13202 t) 315-470-1482 jkurgan@syrdio.org Rev. John J. Kurgan, Vicar;

Tyson Place Housing Development Fund Company, Inc. - St. Joseph Manor, 900 Tyson Pl., Syracuse, NY 13206; Mailing: 990 James St., Syracuse, NY 13203 t) 315-424-1821 jrudgick@christopher-community.org Christopher Community, Inc., (Managing Agent). Justin Rudgick, Pres.;

TOWN OF GATES

Steger Housing Development Fund Co., Inc. - St. Jude Apartments, 4075 Lyell Rd., Town of Gates, NY 14606; Mailing: 990 James St., Syracuse, NY 13203 t) 315-424-1821 jrudgick@christopher-community.org 56 apartments for well elderly. Justin Rudgick, Pres.;

UTICA

Catherine St. Housing Development Fund Company, Inc. - 659 Catherine St., Utica, NY 13501; Mailing: 990 James St., Syracuse, NY 13203 t) 315-424-1821 jrudgick@christopher-community.org Christopher Community, Inc., (Managing Agent). Justin Rudgick, Pres.;

The Good News Foundation of Central New York - 10475 Cosby Manor Rd., Utica, NY 13502 t) 315-735-6210 info@thegoodnewscenter.org www.thegoodnewscenter.org Christopher John Spilka, Dir.; Judith Hauck, Exec.;

HOSPITALS / HEALTH SERVICES [HOS]

BINGHAMTON

Our Lady of Lourdes Memorial Hospital, Inc. - 169 Riverside Dr., Binghamton, NY 13905 t) 607-798-5111 sbretscher@ascension.org; kathryn.connerton@ascension.org lourdes.com Susan Bretscher, Exec.; Kathryn Connerton, Pres.; Bed Capacity: 175; Asstd. Annu.: 419,587; Staff: 2,364

SYRACUSE

St. Joseph's Hospital Health Center - 301 Prospect Ave., Syracuse, NY 13203 t) 315-448-5111 marcomm@sjhsyr.org www.sjhsyr.org College for Nurses. Deborah Welch, Contact; Bed Capacity: 451; Asstd. Annu.: 847,399; Staff: 3,976

UTICA

St. Elizabeth Medical Center - 2209 Genesee St., Utica, NY 13501 t) 315-801-8100 www.mvhealth.org College of Nursing. Rev. Arthur Krawczenko, Chap.; Bed Capacity: 202; Asstd. Annu.: 15,400; Staff: 1,860

MISCELLANEOUS [MIS]

BINGHAMTON

Ladies of Charity - 331 Main St., Binghamton, NY 13905; Mailing: PO Box 1133, Binghamton, NY 13902-1133 t) 607-427-8255 isiedlarczyk@stny.rr.com Irene Siedlarczyk, Contact;

Samaritan House - 11 Fayette St., Binghamton, NY 13901 t) 607-724-3969 jimsamhouse@gmail.com James Surdoval, Dir.;

The Robert L. McDevitt, K.S.G., K.C.H.S. and Catherine H. McDevitt, L.C.H.S. Fund of St. Patrick's Catholic Church of Binghamton, N.Y. - 9 Leroy St., Binghamton, NY 13905 t) 607-722-1060 stpatrick@sta-sp.org Rev. Msgr. John P. Putano;

The Robert L. McDevitt, K.S.G., K.C.H.S. and Catherine H. McDevitt, L.C.H.S. Fund of St. Thomas Aquinas Church - 1 Aquinas St., Binghamton, NY 13905 t) 607-797-4015 stthomas@sta-sp.org Rev. Msgr. John P. Putano;

CANASTOTA

Catholic Diocese of Nakuru Mission Office, Inc. - 406 Spencer St., Canastota, NY 13032 t) 315-697-8795 cdnmission@yahoo.com cdnmission.org Rev. Fredrick Mwangi Kooro, Dir.;

ENDWELL

Southern Region Family / Respect Life Ministry - 400 Corey Ave., Endwell, NY 13760 c) 607-727-3039 mklawiter@syrdio.org Kathleen Colligan, Dir.;

FULTON

Catholic Charities Thrift Shop - 808 W. Broadway, Fulton, NY 13069 t) 315-598-3980 hhoefer@ccoswego.com Tim Archer, Contact;

JOHNSON CITY

The Robert L. McDevitt, K.S.G., K.C.H.S. and Catherine H. McDevitt, L.C.H.S. Fund of St. James Church of Lestershire, N.Y. - 147 Main St., Johnson City, NY 13790 t) 607-729-6147 jkurgan@syrdio.org Rev. John J. Kurgan, Vicar;

RICHLAND

Rural & Migrant Ministry of Oswego Co. Inc. - 15 Stewart St., Richland, NY 13144-0192; Mailing: P.O. Box 192, Richland, NY 13144-0192 t) 315-298-1154 rmmoc@yahoo.com Shawn Doyle, Pres.;

SYRACUSE

Saint Andrew Hall - 420 Demong Dr., Syracuse, NY 13214-1499 t) 315-445-3500 standrewhallnovitiate@gmail.com Novitiate of the U.S.A. East Province of the Society of Jesus. Rev. George Witt, S.J., Dir.; Rev. Adam Rosinski, S.J., Asst. Dir.; Rev. Thomas Roach, S.J., Sr. Priest;

***Brady Faith Center, Inc.** - 404 South Ave., Syracuse, NY 13204 t) 315-472-9077 twilliams@bradyfaith.org www.bradyfaithcenter.org Kevin Frank, Exec.; Rev. John C. Schopfer, Dir.;

Child & Family Catechesis - c/o 240 E. Onondaga St., Syracuse, NY 13202 t) 315-472-6753 tmay@syrdio.org Theresa May, Assoc. Dir., Office of Catechesis;

Father Champlin's Guardian Angel Society - 920 N. McBride St., Syracuse, NY 13208; Mailing: 259 E. Onondaga St., Syracuse, NY 13202 t) 315-422-7218 kfedrizzi@guardianangelsoc.org; sarah@guardianangelsoc.org guardianangelsoc.org Sarah Ioele, Exec.; Kathy Fedrizzi, Finance;

Franciscorps, Inc. - ; Mailing: P.O. Box 11166, Syracuse, NY 13218 t) (315) 426-0481 info@franciscorps.org www.franciscorps.org Order of Friars Minor Conventual. Friar Nader Ata, O.F.M.Conv., Chap.;

Jail Ministry of Onondaga County, Inc. - 504 E. Fayette St., Syracuse, NY 13202; Mailing: PO Box 11174, Syracuse, NY 13218 t) 315-860-4528 jailministey@gmail.com www.jailministrysyr.org Keith Ciedlicki, Dir.;

Lasalle Syracuse, Inc. - 6245 Randall Rd., Syracuse, NY 13214; Mailing: 444A Rte. 35 S., Eatontown, NJ 07724 t) 732-380-7926 x103 www.cbasyracuse.org Bro. Joseph Juliano, F.S.C., Secy.;

Mount St. James Corporation - 338 Jamesville Ave., Syracuse, NY 13210; Mailing: 990 James St., Syracuse, NY 13203 t) 315-424-1821 jrudgick@christopher-community.org Apartments for persons of low to moderate income. Justin Rudgick, Pres.;

Office of Family / Respect Life Ministry - 240 E. Onondaga St., Syracuse, NY 13202 t) 315-472-6754 familyrespectlife@syrdio.org www.syrdio.org Lisa Hall, Dir.;

***Our Lady of Lourdes Hospitality - North American Volunteers, Ltd.** - 107 Michaels Ave., Syracuse, NY 13208 t) 315-476-0026 teresa@lourdesvolunteers.org Public Association of the Christian Faithful sharing Marian devotion through the Message of Lourdes with Virtual Pilgrimage. Erika Vincent Watkins, Exec.;

Partners in Franciscan Ministries Inc. - 960 James St., Syracuse, NY 13203 t) 315-634-7086 scrossett@pinfm.org www.sosf.org Sponsored by the Sisters of St. Francis of the Neumann Communities. Susan M. Crossett, Pres.;

Rev. Msgr. J. Robert Yeazel Catholic Education/Vocation Scholarship - c/o Central New York Community Foundation, 431 E. Fayette St., Ste.100, Syracuse, NY 13202 t) 315-422-9538 info@cnycf.org Frank Arkinson, Dir.;

The Syracuse Diocesan Investment Fund, Inc. - 240 E. Onondaga St., Syracuse, NY 13202 t) 315-470-1482 jkurgan@syrdio.org Rev. John J. Kurgan, Vicar; Rev. Msgr. Timothy S. Elmer;

Toomey Residential and Community Services Corp. - 1654 W. Onondaga St., Syracuse, NY 13204 t) 315-424-1845 info@toomeyresidential.org www.toomeyresidential.org/ Tiffany Teeter, Exec.;

UTICA

Christ Child Society of Utica - 140 Hawthorne Ave., Utica, NY 13502 t) 315-797-0748 ckelly140@roadrunner.com Rev. Joseph A. Salerno, Chap.; Cindy Kelly, Pres.;

MONASTERIES AND RESIDENCES FOR PRIESTS AND BROTHERS [MON]

ENDICOTT

Mount St. Francis Hermitage, Inc. - 120 Edson Rd., Endicott, NY 13760; Mailing: P.O. Box 236, Maine, NY 13802 t) 607-754-0001 ffimaine@gmail.com; mountsaintfrancis@gmail.com www.mtstfrancis.com

Friar Jacinto Mary Chapin, Guardian; Rev. John Joseph Mary Cook, F.I., Supr.; Bro. Didacus Cortes, F.I., Vicar; Bro. Cyprian Costello, Secy.; Brs.: 2; Priests: 2

SYRACUSE

Jesuits at LeMoyne, Inc. - 1419 Salt Springs Rd., Jesuit Residence, Syracuse, NY 13214 t) 315-445-4604; 315-445-4605 (Supr.) jesuitres@lemoyne.edu www.lemoyne.edu Rev. William J. Bosch, S.J., Archivist; Rev. James H. Dahlinger, S.J., Prof.; Rev. William S. Dolan, S.J., Prof.; Rev. Jason G Downer, S.J., Campus Min.; Rev. Michael Guzik, Prof.; Rev. Vincent W. Hevern, S.J., Prof.; Rev. Donald J. Kirby, S.J., Supr.; Rev. Frank LaRocca, S.J., Prof.; Rev. Gerard R. McKeon, S.J., Chap.; Rev. Francis J. Nash, S.J., Treas.; Rev. Patrick D. Rogers, S.J., Admin.; Rev. Robert E. Scully, S.J., Prof.; Rev. Louis P. Sogliuzzo, S.J., Pastoral Min./Coord.; Priests: 14

NURSING / REHABILITATION / CONVALESCENCE / ELDERLY CARE [NUR]

OSWEGO

Saint Luke's Health Care Services - 299 E. River Rd., Oswego, NY 13126 t) 315-342-3166 crgill@stlukehs.com www.stlukehs.com Residential Skilled Nursing Facility Catherine R. Gill, Admin.; Asstd. Annu.: 69,000; Staff: 350

SYRACUSE

Bernardine Apartments, Inc. - 417 Churchill Ave., Syracuse, NY 13205 t) 315-469-7786 rmills@lorettosystem.org Rick Mills, Admin.; Asstd. Annu.: 160; Staff: 65

St. Camillus Health & Rehabilitation Center - 813 Fay Rd., Syracuse, NY 13219 t) 315-488-2951 aileen.balitz@st-camillus.org; michael.zingaro@st-camillus.org www.st-camillus.org Michael J Zingaro, CFO; Aileen M. Balitz, Pres.; Asstd. Annu.: 2,700; Staff: 400

Loretto Geriatric Community Residences, Inc. - 5018 S. Salina St., Syracuse, NY 13205 t) 315-413-3287 mgottsch@lorettosystem.org Michele Rita Gottschalk, Dir.; Heather Davis, Contact; Asstd. Annu.: 30; Staff: 30

Residence - 4810 S. Salina St., Syracuse, NY 13205 t) 315-469-8562

Residence - 50 Syracuse St., Baldwinsville, NY 13027 t) 315-635-1647

Loretto Rest Realty Corp. (Loretto Health & Rehabilitation Center) - 700 E. Brighton Ave., Syracuse, NY 13205 t) 315-413-3287 hdavis@lorettosystem.org Jack Pease, Admin.; Asstd. Annu.: 1,000; Staff: 65

Loretto Rest, Inc. - 700 E. Brighton Ave., Syracuse, NY 13205 t) 315-413-3287 hdavis@lorettosystem.org Adult Home. Heather Davis, Contact; Asstd. Annu.: 583; Staff: 65

Loretto and Loretto Apartments Housing Development Fund Co., Inc. - c/o Loretto, 700 E. Brighton Ave., Syracuse, NY 13205 t) 315-469-5570

Providence House Apartments - 1700 W. Onondaga St., Syracuse, NY 13204; Mailing: 990 James St., Syracuse, NY 13203 t) 315-471-8427 jrudgick@christopher-community.org Christopher Community Inc., (Managing Agent). Legal Name: Onondaga Apartments HDFC, Inc. Justin Rudgick, Pres.;

UTICA

St. Joseph Nursing Home - 2535 Genesee St., Utica, NY 13501 t) 315-797-1230 fdeck@stjosephnh.org www.stjosephnh.org Ashley Pease, Contact; Asstd. Annu.: 115; Staff: 170

PRESCHOOLS / CHILDCARE CENTERS [PRE]

BINGHAMTON

Broome County CYO - 86-88 Walnut St., Binghamton, NY 13905 t) 607-584-7800 cyo@ccbc.net Sandra Ohlsen, Dir.;

SKANEATELES

Lourdes Camp - 1150 Ten Mile Point Rd., Skaneateles, NY 13152; Mailing: 1654 W. Onondaga St., Syracuse, NY 13204 t) 315-424-1812 www.lourdescamp.com Greg Vaga, Exec.; Stds.: 1,750; Lay Tchrs.: 50

SYRACUSE

Bishop Foery Foundation - 100 Edmund Ave., Syracuse, NY 13205; Mailing: 1654 W. Onondaga St., Syracuse, NY 13204 t) 315-424-1800 info@ccoc.us www.ccoc.us Christopher Curry, Admin.;

Gingerbread House Preschool & Childcare Center - 3020 Court St., Syracuse, NY 13208 t) 315-471-4198 dave@gingerbreadsyracuse.com David Cole, Dir.; Stds.: 130; Lay Tchrs.: 33

Hawley Youth Organization - 716 Hawley Ave., Syracuse, NY 13203 t) 315-424-1800 info@ccoc.us Christopher Curry, Admin.; Stds.: 300; Lay Tchrs.: 30

UTICA

Camp Nazareth - 1408 Genesee St., Utica, NY 13502 t) 315-801-7015 dgeorge@ccharityom.org Dave George, Contact; Stds.: 171; Lay Tchrs.: 28

Camp Nazareth - 112 Long Lake Rd., Woodgate, NY 13494 t) 315-392-3791 Brad Potter, Dir. Family & Community Support Svcs.;

RETREAT HOUSES / RENEWAL CENTERS [RTR]

ENDICOTT

Mount St. Francis Hermitage, Inc. - 120 Edson Rd., Endicott, NY 13760; Mailing: P.O. Box 236, Maine, NY 13802 t) 607-754-0001 ffimaine@gmail.com; mountsaintfrancis@gmail.com www.mtstfrancis.com Friar Jacinto Mary Chapin, Guardian; Rev. John Joseph Mary Cook, F.I., Supr.; Rev. JoseMaria M. Barbin, F.I., Mem.; Bro. Didacus Cortes, F.I., Vicar; Bro. Cyprian Costello, Secy.;

SYRACUSE

Christ the King Retreat House - 500 Brookford Rd., Syracuse, NY 13224 t) 315-446-2680 ctkretreat@syrdio.org www.ctkretreat.com Syracuse House of Retreats Joan Spector, Dir.; Christopher John Spilka, Dir.;

Spiritual Renewal Center - 1342 Lancaster Ave., Syracuse, NY 13210 t) 315-472-6546 mail@spiritualrenewalcenter.com www.spiritualrenewalcenter.com James Krisher, Dir. Emeritus;

SHRINES [SHR]

OSWEGO

St. Mary's Parish & Shrine - 103 W. Seventh St., Oswego, NY 13126 t) (315) 343-3953 stmarysoswego@syrdio.org Rev. James A. Schultz, Admin.;

SPECIAL CARE FACILITIES [SPF]

SYRACUSE

L'Arche of Syracuse, Inc. - 920 Spencer St., Syracuse, NY 13204 t) 315-479-8088 larche@larchesyracuse.org www.larchesyracuse.org A Christian Community concerned with life sharing between persons with a developmental disability and persons who assist them. John Knechtle, Dir.; Bed Capacity: 16; Asstd. Annu.: 16; Staff: 42

Diocese of Toledo

(Dioecesis Toletana in America)

MOST REVEREND DANIEL E. THOMAS

Bishop of Toledo; ordained May 18, 1985; appointed Titular Bishop of Bardstown and Auxiliary Bishop of Philadelphia June 8, 2006; consecrated July 26, 2006; appointed Bishop of Toledo August 26, 2014; installed October 22, 2014. Chancery: 1933 Spielbusch Ave., Toledo, OH 43604-5360.

Chancery: 1933 Spielbusch Ave., Toledo, OH 43604-5360. T: 419-244-6711; F: 419-244-4791.
www.toledodiocese.org
bishopsoffice@toledodiocese.org

ESTABLISHED APRIL 15, 1910.

Square Miles 8,222.

Comprises the following Counties of northwest Ohio: Williams, Fulton, Lucas, Ottawa, Defiance, Henry, Wood, Sandusky, Erie, Paulding, Putnam, Hancock, Seneca, Huron, Van Wert, Allen, Wyandot, Crawford and Richland.

For legal titles of parishes and diocesan institutions, consult the Chancery.

STATISTICAL OVERVIEW

Personnel
Bishop....1
Priests: Diocesan Active in Diocese....79
Priests: Diocesan Active Outside Diocese....2
Priests: Retired, Sick or Absent....57
Number of Diocesan Priests....138
Religious Priests in Diocese....38
Total Priests in your Diocese....176
Extern Priests in Diocese....5
Ordinations:
Diocesan Priests....1
Religious Priests....1
Transitional Deacons....1
Permanent Deacons in Diocese....177
Total Brothers....4
Total Sisters....400

Parishes
Parishes....122
With Resident Pastor:
Resident Diocesan Priests....77
Resident Religious Priests....7
Without Resident Pastor:
Administered by Priests....4
Administered by Deacons....3
Administered by Religious Women....1
Professional Ministry Personnel:
Sisters....9
Lay Ministers....300

Welfare
Catholic Hospitals....7
Total Assisted....122,754
Homes for the Aged....10
Total Assisted....842
Day Care Centers....1
Total Assisted....1,537
Specialized Homes....2
Total Assisted....176
Special Centers for Social Services....7
Total Assisted....38,836
Residential Care of Disabled....68
Total Assisted....68

Educational
Diocesan Students in Other Seminaries....12
Total Seminarians....12
Colleges and Universities....2
Total Students....2,423
High Schools, Diocesan and Parish....9
Total Students....1,766
High Schools, Private....5
Total Students....2,142
Elementary Schools, Diocesan and Parish....52
Total Students....9,359
Elementary Schools, Private....5
Total Students....725
Catechesis/Religious Education:
High School Students....1,914
Elementary Students....8,820
Total Students under Catholic Instruction....27,161
Teachers in Diocese:
Priests....3
Brothers....6
Sisters....42
Lay Teachers....923

Vital Statistics
Receptions into the Church:
Infant Baptism Totals....1,508
Minor Baptism Totals....652
Adult Baptism Totals....362
Received into Full Communion....257
First Communions....1,937
Confirmations....2,184
Marriages:
Catholic....400
Interfaith....255
Total Marriages....655
Deaths....3,021
Total Catholic Population....316,318
Total Population....1,689,100

LEADERSHIP

Vicar General/Moderator of the Curia - Rev. Msgr. William J. Kubacki (wkubacki@toledodiocese.org);
Tribunal - t) 419-244-6711 Rev. Eric J. Culler (fathericculler@yahoo.com);
Chancellor - t) 419-244-6711 Sr. Rose Marie Timmer, R.S.M. (rmtimmer@toledodiocese.org);

OFFICES AND DIRECTORS

Catholic Cemeteries - t) 419-531-5747 Eric Cerini, Dir. (ecerini@cfcsmission.org);
Cemeteries - t) 419-536-3751; 419-536-3751
Catholic Investment Trust & Deposit and Loan Trust - t) 419-244-6711 Philip Renda (prenda@toledodiocese.org);
Chief Operations/Financial Officer - t) 419-244-6711 Philip Renda (prenda@toledodiocese.org);
Finance - Rene Yuhas Schmidbauer, Controller (rschmidbauer@toledodiocese.org); David Williams, Audit & Compliance Mgr. (dwilliams@toledodiocese.org); Katherine Kellmurray, Parish & Schools Accountant (kkellmurray@toledodiocese.org);
General Counsel - t) 419-244-6711 Thomas Antonini (tantonini@toledodiocese.org);
Human Resources - t) 419-244-6711 Meghan Reed, Dir. (mreed@toledodiocese.org); Patricia Nevolis, Payroll Assoc. (pnevolis@toledodiocese.org);
Information Technology - t) 419-244-6711 Justin Combs, IT Mgr. (jcombs@toledodiocese.org);
Mission Advancement - t) 419-214-4943 Brian Doyle, Officer (bdoyle@toledodiocese.org);
Office of Risk Management - t) 419-244-6711 Thomas Antonini (tantonini@toledodiocese.org);
Pastoral Center Services - Patricia L. Stein, Facilities Mgr.;
Retirement Plan for Lay Employees (RPLE) - t) 800-205-4864 Matthew Hopewell, Plan Admin. (toledodiocese@nyhart.com);
Tax Deferred Savings Program for Employees (403(b)) - t) 800-428-7106 Pamela Haugabrook, Recordkeeper (toledodiocese@nyhart.com);

ADVISORY BOARDS, COMMISSIONS, COMMITTEES, AND COUNCILS

College of Consultors - Rev. Msgr. Kenneth G. Morman, Chair; Rev. Msgr. William J. Kubacki (wkubacki@toledodiocese.org); Rev. Eric J. Culler (fathericculler@yahoo.com);
Deacon Personnel Board - t) 419-244-6711 Rev. Walter R. Oxley, Chair (woxley@toledodiocese.org);
Diocesan Building Commission - t) 419-244-6711 David Williams (dwilliams@toledodiocese.org);
Diocesan Education Council - t) 419-244-6711 Matthew Daniels (mdaniels@toledodiocese.org);
Diocesan Finance Council - t) 419-244-6711 Philip Renda (prenda@toledodiocese.org);
Pastoral Advisory Council - t) 419-244-6711
Presbyteral Council - t) 419-244-6711 Rev. Msgr. Dennis M. Metzger, Dean; Rev. David D. Kidd, Dean; Rev. Walter E. Tuscano, S.A.C., Dean;
Priest Personnel Board - t) 419-244-6711 Rev. Walter R. Oxley, Chair (woxley@toledodiocese.org);

CLERGY AND RELIGIOUS SERVICES

Senior Director/Vicar for Clergy - t) 419-244-6711 Rev. Walter R. Oxley (woxley@toledodiocese.org);
Delegate for Consecrated Life - t) 419-244-6711 Sr. Maria Lin Pacold, R.S.M. (mpacold@toledodiocese.org);
Delegate for Permanent Deacons - t) 419-244-6711 Dcn. Harold Welch (hwelch@toledodiocese.org);
Ecumenical and Interfaith Relations - t) 419-228-7635 Rev. Kent R. Kaufman, Dir. (kkaufman@st-charles.org);
Mission Appeals and Awareness - t) 419-244-6711 Sr. Maria Lin Pacold, R.S.M., Dir. (mpacold@toledodiocese.org);
Office for Diocesan Priestly Vocations - t) 419-244-6711 psmith@toledodiocese.org Rev. Philip A. Smith, Dir.;

COMMUNICATIONS

Senior Director - t) 419-244-6711 Kelly Donaghy (kdonaghy@toledodiocese.org);
Creative Services - t) 419-244-6711 Keith Tarjanyi, Mgr. (ktarjanyi@toledodiocese.org);
Marketing and Production - t) 419-244-6711 Nathan Volker, Sales & Production Specialist (nvolker@toledodiocese.org);
Social Media and Communications - t) 419-244-6711 Annie Lust, Communications & Social Media Specialist (alust@toledodiocese.org);

DEANERIES

Deans - Rev. Nathan Bockrath; Rev. Thomas J. Extejt; Rev. William J. Rose;

EDUCATION

Senior Director - t) 419-244-6711 Matthew Daniels (mdaniels@toledodiocese.org);
Catechetical Formation - t) 419-244-6711 Matthew Daniels, Dir. (mdaniels@toledodiocese.org);
Catholic Schools Office - Jacob Johnson, Dir. (jjohnson@toledodiocese.org); Timothy Mahoney, Curriculum Cons. (tmahoney@toledodiocese.org); Justin Combs, IT Mgr. (jcombs@toledodiocese.org);
Central City Ministry of Toledo (CCMT) - t) 419-244-6711 Matthew Daniels, Dir. (mdaniels@toledodiocese.org);
Homeschool - t) 419-244-6711 Justin Combs (jcombs@toledodiocese.org);

FAMILY LIFE

Senior Director - t) 419-244-6711 Bret Huntebrinker (bhuntebrinker@toledodiocese.org);
Catholic Men's Ministry - t) 419-244-6711 Bret Huntebrinker, Coord. (bhuntebrinker@toledodiocese.org);
Catholic Youth Organization - t) 419-244-6711 Julie Dubielak, Dir. (jdubielak@toledodiocese.org); Jack Jordan, Asst. Dir. (jjordan@toledodiocese.org);
Intercultural Ministries - t) 419-244-6711 Andrea De la Roca, Coord. (adelaroca@toledodiocese.org);
Marriage and Family Life - t) 419-244-6711
Ministry Specialist - Alice Jacobs (ajacobs@toledodiocese.org); Angela Leach, Ministry Asst. (aleach@toledodiocese.org);
Ministry to Catholic Charismatic Renewal (MCCR) - t) 419-691-6686 Steven Toth, Dir. (mccrholyspirit@gmail.com);
Toledo Diocesan Council of Catholic Women (TDCCW) - t) 419-244-6711 Alice Jacobs (ajacobs@toledodiocese.org);

PASTORAL SERVICES

Archives - Sr. Mary Nadine Mathias, S.N.D. (nmathias1@toledodiocese.org);
Child and Youth Protection and Victim Assistance - t) 419-244-4880 Mary Pat Smith (msmith@toledodiocese.org); Kathy Didion, Victim Assistance Coord. (kdidion7@gmail.com);
Office of Conciliation and Arbitration - t) 419-244-6711 Thomas Antonini (tantonini@toledodiocese.org);
Office of Divine Worship - t) 419-244-6711 Rev. David J. Cirata, Dir. (dcirata@toledodiocese.org); Paul J. Monachino, Dir. (pmonachino@toledodiocese.org); Daniel J. Demski, Liturgy Coord. (ddemski@toledodiocese.org);

SOCIAL SERVICES

Senior Director - Rodney O. Schuster (cwheeler@toledodiocese.org);
Catholic Charities - Rodney O. Schuster, Exec. Dir. (cwheeler@toledodiocese.org);
Adult Advocacy Services - t) 419-668-3073 Carol Wheeler;
Care for God's Creation - t) 419-214-4943 Rodney O. Schuster;
Catholic Campaign for Human Development - t) 419-214-4933 Peter Range;
Catholic Club Educational Child Care and Family Center - t) 419-243-7255 Paul Szymanski, Dir.;
Crisis Navigation - Patricia Kemp; Diane Bemiller; Linda Kraft;
Disaster Relief - t) 419-524-0733 Rebecca Owens;
Family Support and Guidance - t) 419-214-4939 Brian Rome, Coord.;
Helping Hands of St. Louis - t) 419-691-0613 sshrewsbery@toledodiocese.org Sue Shrewsbery, Dir.;
H.O.P.E. Food Pantry - t) 419-524-0733 Susan Dyson;
Human Trafficking - t) 419-214-4933 Peter Range;
Immigration - t) 419-214-4943 Rodney O. Schuster;
Jail and Prison Ministry - t) 419-214-4958 Dcn. Ed Irelan, Coord.;
La Posada Family Emergency Shelter - t) 419-244-5931 Jeanelle Addie, Coord.;
Miriam House Huron County Transitional Housing - t) 419-663-6341 Vickie A. Smith, Coord.;
Office for Life and Justice -
Respect Life Ministry - t) 419-214-4933 Peter Range, Coord.;
Permanent Supportive Housing - t) 419-214-4955 Jen Voigt, Coord.;
Project Rachel - t) 419-260-5811 Kerstin Pakka, Coord.;
Rural Life Ministry - t) 419-214-4943 Rodney O. Schuster;

PARISHES, MISSIONS, AND CLERGY

STATE OF OHIO

ARCHBOLD

St. Peter - 614 N. Defiance St., Archbold, OH 43502-1105 t) 419-212-1357 tkunesh66@gmail.com Rev. Stephen L. Stanberry, Pst.; Tami Kunesh, DRE;

ATTICA

Our Lady of Hope - 320 Stump Pike Rd., Attica, OH 44807-9465 t) 419-426-3043 olohbusiness@gmail.com www.ourladyofhopeattica.com Rev. Joseph Panakkal Joseph, S.A.C., Pst.; CRP Stds.: 78

BASCOM

SS. Patrick & Andrew - ; Mailing: P.O. Box 226, Bascom, OH 44809 t) 419-937-2715 patrick2@bright.net Rev. Timothy M. Kummerer, Pst.; Dcn. John F. Walter; Carol Brickner, DRE;

BELLEVUE

St. Gaspar del Bufalo - 16209 E. County Rd. 46, Bellevue, OH 44811-4661 t) 419-483-3231 stgaspar@htmcltd.net (Seneca County.) Rev. Jacob A. Gordon, Pst.;
Immaculate Conception - 231 E. Center St., Bellevue, OH 44811-1404 Rev. Jonathan C. Wight, Pst.;
Immaculate Conception School - (Grades PreK-8) 304 E. Main St., Bellevue, OH 44811-1404 t) 419-483-6066 pgreibel@icbell.org Pamela Griebel, Prin.;

BLUFFTON

St. Mary - 160 N. Spring, Bluffton, OH 45817 t) 419-358-8631 khski7@aol.com; cinkrott@embarqmail.com Rev. John McLoughlin, C.Ss.R., Pst.; Dcn. Michael R. Marcum II; Kelly Honse, DRE;

BOWLING GREEN

St. Aloysius - 150 S. Enterprise St., Bowling Green, OH 43402-0485 t) 419-352-4195 parishoffice@stalbg.org; religioused@stalbg.org www.stalbg.org Rev. Mark E. Davis, Pst.; Dcn. Phillip Avina; Dcn. James Cavera; Jean Bargiel, DRE;

St. Aloysius School - (Grades PreK-8) 148 S. Enterprise, Bowling Green, OH 43402-4738 t) 419-352-8614 principal@stalschoolbg.org Andrea Puhl, Prin.;

St. Thomas More University Parish - 425 Thurstin Ave., Bowling Green, OH 43402-1901 Rev. Jason J. Kahle, Pst.;

BRYAN

St. Patrick - 610 S. Portland St., Bryan, OH 43506-2059 t) 616-633-0994 philipdezern@gmail.com Rev. James E. Halleron, Pst.; Dcn. Steve St. John, Sacr. Min.; Dcn. Thomas F. Dominique; Dcn. Dennis F. Jackson; Philip Dezern, DRE;

St. Patrick School - (Grades PreK-8) t) 419-636-3592 cniese@saintpatrickschoolbryan.org Connie Niese, Prin.;

BUCYRUS

Holy Trinity - 760 Tiffin St., Bucyrus, OH 44820-1551 t) 419-562-1346 llabdite@hotmail.com; htcbucyrus@gmail.com holytrinitybucyrus.org Rev. Paul A. Fahrbach, Pst.; Dcn. Jerome A. Gubernath; Elizabeth Wurm, DRE;

CAREY

Our Lady of Consolation - 315 Clay St., Carey, OH 43316-1498 t) 419-396-1523; 419-396-7107 parishoffice@olcshrine.com; pre@olcshrine.com Basilica and National Shrine of Our Lady of Consolation, Parish & Shrine. Rev. Thomas Merrill, O.F.M.Conv., Pst.; Rev. John Bamman, O.F.M.Conv., Assoc. Pst.; Dcn. James F. Kitzler;

CLOVERDALE

St. Barbara - 160 Main St., Cloverdale, OH 45827; Mailing: P.O. Box 8, Cloverdale, OH 45827 Rev. Jerome A. Schetter, Pst.;

CLYDE

St. Mary - 609 Vine St., Clyde, OH 43410-1537 Rev. Edward J. Schleter;

COLUMBUS GROVE

St. Anthony of Padua - 512 W. Sycamore St., Columbus Grove, OH 45830-1020 judyfhc@yahoo.com Rev. Thomas J. Extejt, Pst.; Judy Schroeder, DRE;

St. Anthony of Padua School - (Grades K-8) 520 W. Sycamore St., Columbus Grove, OH 45830-1020 t) 419-659-2103 giesigl@sa.noacsc.org Scott Hummel, Prin.;

CONTINENTAL

St. John the Baptist - 4893 St. Rte. 634, N, Continental, OH 45831 Rev. Mark Hoying, C.PP.S., Pst.; Rev. Richard Friebel, C.PP.S., Assoc. Pst.;

CRESTLINE

St. Joseph - 331 N. Thoman St., Crestline, OH 44827 t) 419-683-2015 jpalm@stjosephcrestline.org stjosephcrestline.org Rev. Jeffery J. Smith, Pst.;

St. Joseph School - (Grades PreSchool-8) 333 N. Thoman St., Crestline, OH 44827-1445 t) 419-683-1284 dsalvati@stjosephcrestline.org Daniel Salvati, Prin.;

CUSTAR

St. Louis - 22792 Defiance Pike, Custar, OH 43511-9716; Mailing: P.O. Box 125, Custar, OH 43511-9716 t) 419-669-1864 stlouischurch@midohio.twcbc.com Rev. Walter E. Tuscano, S.A.C., Pst.;

St. Louis School - (Grades PreSchool-6) 22776 Defiance Pike, Custar, OH 43511-9716 t) 419-669-1875 stlouis@midohio.twcbc.com Ellie Panning, Admin.;

DEFIANCE

St. Isidore - 05480 Moser Rd., Defiance, OH 43512-9150 t) 419-497-2161 nachoalisongarcia@gmail.com; kb8biq@centurylink.net www.saintisidoreparish.org (Twinned with St. Michael, St. Michael's Ridge.) Rev. Robert J. Kill, Pst.; Dcn. Scott Graham; Alison Garcia, DRE;

St. John the Evangelist - 510 Jackson Ave., Defiance, OH 43512-2189 t) 419-782-7121; 419-782-2776 (CRP) stjohn@stjohndefiance.org; jessicawest@metalink.net www.stjohndefiance.org Rev. Eric L. Mueller, Pst.; Dcn. Mark A. Homier; Dcn. Dominick J. Varano; Jessica West, DRE;

St. Mary - 715 Jefferson Ave., Defiance, OH 43512 Rev. Randy P. Giesige, Pst.; Dcn. Jeff M. Mayer;

St. Michael - 05480 Moser Rd., Defiance, OH 43512-9150 t) 419-497-3122 fabaronitwo@yahoo.com Rev. Robert J. Kill, Pst.; Dcn. Scott Graham;

DELPHOS

St. John the Baptist - 14755 Landeck Rd., Delphos, OH 45833-9438 t) 419-692-0636 sccjoy@yahoo.com; schurch1@woh.rr.com stjohnthebaptistchurchlandeck.org Rev. Dennis G. Walsh, Pst.; Rev. Daniel Parackkukizhakkethil, Assoc. Pst.; Rev. Douglas D. Taylor, Assoc. Pst.; Sr. Immaculata Scarogni, S.C.C., DRE;

St. John the Evangelist - 210 N. Pierce St., Delphos, OH 45833 t) 419-692-1286 (CRP); 419-695-4050 hanf@delphosstjohns.org; dwalsh@delphosstjohns.org delphosstjohnparish.org Rev. Dennis G. Walsh, Pst.; Rev. Scott Perry, Assoc. Pst.; Rev. Vicente Antonio Vera, Assoc. Pst.; Rev. Stephen J. Blum, In Res.; Dcn. David J. Ricker; Dcn. John P. Sheeran;

St. John the Evangelist School - (Grades PreK-6) 110 N. Pierce St., Delphos, OH 45833 t) 419-692-8561 stant@delphosstjohns.org delphosstjohns.org Nathan Stant, Prin.;

St. John the Evangelist High School - 515 E. Second St., Delphos, OH 45833 t) 419-692-5371 lee@delphosstjohns.org Adam Lee, Prin.;

DESHLER

Immaculate Conception - 230 Allendale Ave., Deshler, OH 43516-1103; Mailing: P.O. Box 23, Deshler, OH 43516-1103 Rev. Arthur J. Niewiadomski, Pst.;

EDGERTON

St. Mary - 317 S. Locust St., Edgerton, OH 43517; Mailing: P.O. Box 355, Edgerton, OH 43517 Rev. Daniel E. Borgelt, Pst.; Dcn. Rod Conkle; Dcn. Joseph Timbrook; Karrie Kimpel, DRE;

St. Mary School - (Grades PreSchool-6) 314 S. Locust St., Edgerton, OH 43517 t) 419-298-2531 jtaylor@stmaryedgerton.org www.stmaryedgerton.org Juliana M. Taylor, Prin.;

FAYETTE

Our Lady of Mercy - 409 E. Main St., Fayette, OH 43521-0429; Mailing: P.O. Box 429, Fayette, OH 43521-0429 t) 419-237-2441 ourladyofmercy@frontier.com Rev. Stephen L. Stanberry, Pst.;

FINDLAY

St. Michael the Archangel - 750 Bright Rd., Findlay, OH 45840-2448 t) 419-422-2646 parish@findlaystmichael.org www.findlaystmichael.org Rev. Adam L. Hertzfeld, Pst.; Rev. Peter D. Grodi, Par. Vicar; Dcn. Michael Eier; Dcn. Matthew Kettinger; Dcn. Keith J. Talbert; Dcn. David Gerardi, Parish Life Coord.; CRP Stds.: 388

St. Michael the Archangel School - (Grades PreSchool-8) 723 Sutton Pl., Findlay, OH 45840-6965 t) 419-423-2738 www.findlaystmichaelschool.org Amy Holzwart, Prin.; Stds.: 444; Sr. Tchrs.: 4; Lay Tchrs.: 25

FORT JENNINGS

St. Joseph - 135 N. Water St., Fort Jennings, OH 45844-0068; Mailing: P.O. Box 68, Fort Jennings, OH 45844-0068 t) 419-286-2019 (CRP); 419-286-2132 stjoereled@bright.net; stjoeparishofc@bright.net Rev. Charles Obinwa, Pst.; Dcn. Lawrence Schimmoeller; Rhonda Liebrecht, DRE;

FOSTORIA

St. Wendelin - 323 N. Wood St., Fostoria, OH 44830-0836 shellie.gabel@stwendelin.org Rev. Todd M. Dominique, Pst.; Dcn. David Schiefer; Shellie Gabel, DRE;

St. Wendelin School - (Grades K-12) 533 N. Countryline St., Fostoria, OH 44830-2246 t) 419-435-8144 teresa.kitchen@stwendelin.org Teresa Kitchen, Prin.;

FREMONT

St. Ann - 1021 W. State St., Fremont, OH 43420-2103 Rev. Michael P. Roemmele, Pst.; Rev. Nathan Bockrath, Assoc. Pst.; Dcn. James Heyman;

St. Joseph - 709 Croghan St., Fremont, OH 43420-2482 Rev. Michael P. Roemmele, Pst.; Rev. Nathan Bockrath, Assoc. Pst.; Dcn. Melvin J. Shell;

Sacred Heart - 550 Smith Rd., Fremont, OH 43420-9567 Rev. Krzysztof Kardzis, Pst.; Dcn. Alfredo Diaz;

GALION

St. Joseph - 135 N. Liberty St., Galion, OH 44833-2017 t) 419-468-2884 baker.brittany@sjsaints.org Rev. Paul A. Fahrbach, Pst.; Dcn. Gregory Kirk; Dcn. Alfred Sisson;

St. Joseph School - (Grades PreK-8) 138 N. Liberty St., Galion, OH 44833-2016 t) 419-468-5436 office@sjsaints.org Anissa Tuttle, Prin.; Stds.: 65; Lay Tchrs.: 7

GENOA

Our Lady of Lourdes - 204 Main St., Genoa, OH 43430-1609 t) 419-855-8501 secretary@ourladygenoa.org; religion@sb-oh.org www.ourladygenoa.org Rev. Timothy F. Ferris, Pst.; Dcn. Frank A. Tello;

GIBSONBURG

St. Michael the Archangel Church - 317 E. Madison St., Gibsonburg, OH 43431-1498 t) 419-637-2255; 419-637-9929 (CRP) gburgstmichael@woh.rr.com Rev. Stanislaw Tabor, Admin.;

GLANDORF

St. John the Baptist - 109 N. Main St., Glandorf, OH 45848-0048; Mailing: Box 48, Glandorf, OH 45848-0048 Rev. Anthony Fortman, C.PP.S., Pst.; Rev. Richard Friebel, C.PP.S., Assoc. Pst.; Dcn. Donald W. Inkrott;

GRAND RAPIDS

St. Patrick - 14010 S. River Rd., Grand Rapids, OH 43522-9678 Rev. Walter E. Tuscano, S.A.C., Pst.;

HELENA

St. Mary - 865 State Rte. 635, Helena, OH 43435-9792

HICKSVILLE

St. Michael - 100 Antwerp Dr., Hicksville, OH 43526 t) 419-542-8202; 419-542-8714 saintmichaelhicksville@gmail.com; stmikeccd@gmail.com saintmichaelhicksville.org Rev. Daniel E. Borgelt, Pst.; Dcn. Rod Conkle; Dcn. Joseph Timbrook; Dean Smalley II, DRE;

HOLGATE

St. Mary - 316 Chicago Ave., Holgate, OH 43527-0487; Mailing: P.O. Box 487, Holgate, OH 43527-0487 t) 419-264-3321 smchurch@embarqmail.com Rev. Nicholas J. Cunningham, Pst.; CRP Stds.: 24

HURON

St. Peter - 430 Main St., Huron, OH 44839-1678 Rev. Jeffrey R. McBeth, Pst.;

St. Peter School - (Grades PreK-8) 429 Huron St., Huron, OH 44839-1753 t) 419-433-4640 principal@huronstpeterschool.org Anne Asher, Prin.;

KALIDA

St. Michael - 312 N. Broad St., Kalida, OH 45853-0387; Mailing: P.O. Box 387, Kalida, OH 45853-0387 t) 419-532-3494 Rev. Mark Hoying, C.PP.S., Pst.; Rev. Richard Friebel, C.PP.S., Assoc. Pst.; Dcn. Robert Klausing;

LEIPSIC

St. Mary - 318 State St., Leipsic, OH 45856-1332 Rev. William A. Pifher, Pst.; Dcn. Thomas B. Niese; Dcn. Benjamin R. Valdez;

St. Mary School - (Grades K-8) 129 St. Mary St., Leipsic, OH 45856-1328 t) 419-943-2801 nschroeder@ls.noacsc.org Sr. Carol Ann Mary Smith, S.N.D., Prin.;

LEXINGTON

Resurrection - 2600 Lexington Ave., Lexington, OH 44904-1426 Rev. Nelson G. Beaver, Pst.; Dcn. Thomas R. Dubois;

LIMA

St. Charles Borromeo - 2200 W. Elm, Lima, OH 45805-2697 t) 419-228-7635 burgesse@stcharleslima.org www.stcharleslima.org Rev. Kent R. Kaufman, Pst.; Rev. Thomas Varghese, Assoc. Pst.; Dcn. James S. Bronder;

St. Charles Borromeo School - (Grades PreK-8) 2175 W. Elm St., Lima, OH 45805-2673 t) 419-222-2536 scheidm@sccslima.org sccslima.org Megan Scheid, Prin.;

St. Gerard - 240 W. Robb Ave., Lima, OH 45801-2899; Mailing: 1307 N. Main St., Lima, OH 45801 t) 419-224-3080; 419-224-3080 x230 (CRP) cheryln@sgslima.org; sparker@sgslima.org www.stgerardchurch.org Rev. Michael Sergi, C.Ss.R., Pst.; Rev. Paul Kuzhimannil, C.Ss.R., Assoc. Pst.; Bro. Dan Hall, C.Ss.R., Pst. Assoc.; Shanda Parker, DRE; Marta Truex, Bus. Mgr.; CRP Stds.: 53

St. Gerard School - (Grades PreSchool-8) 1311 N. Main St., Lima, OH 45801-2818 t) 419-222-0431 mtruex@sgslima.org www.sgslima.org Natalie Schoonover, Prin.;

St. John the Evangelist - 222 S. West St., Lima, OH 45801-4842 t) 419-222-5521; 567-242-3089 (CRP) jmstombaugh@wcoil.com; amick@wcoil.com stroselimaohio.org Rev. David M. Ross, Pst.; Dcn. Theodore J. Kaser Jr.; Amanda Mick, DRE;

St. Rose of Lima - 222 S. West St., Lima, OH 45801-4842 t) 419-222-5521; 419-222-2087 (CRP) jmstambaugh@wcoil.com www.stroselimaohio.org Rev. David M. Ross, Pst.; Dcn. Theodore J. Kaser Jr.;

St. Rose of Lima School - (Grades PreK-8) 523 N. West St., Lima, OH 45801-4237 t) 419-223-6361 judyd@srslima.org Donna Judy, Prin.;

MANSFIELD

St. Mary of the Snows - 1630 Ashland, Mansfield, OH 44905-1896 t) 419-589-2114 x507 (CRP); 419-589-2114 x508 (CRP); 419-589-2114 x501 www.mansfieldstmarys.org Rev. John A. Miller, Pst.; Rev. Kevin D. Moebius, Par. Vicar; Rev. Kishore Kottana, Par. Vicar; Jenny Ewing, DRE; Dcn. Allan D. Kopp; Mary Mancha, DRE; CRP Stds.: 29

St. Mary of the Snows School - (Grades PreK-8) sanders.sue@mansfieldstmarymail.org Susan Sanders, Prin.;

St. Peter - 60 S. Mulberry St., Mansfield, OH 44902; Mailing: 104 W. 1st St., Mansfield, OH 44902-2199 t) 419-524-2572 reindl.kristi@myspartans.org www.mansfieldstpeters.org Rev. John A. Miller, Pst.; Rev. Kevin D. Moebius, Par. Vicar; Dcn. John P. Reef;

St. Peter School - (Grades PreK-6) 63 S. Mulberry St., Mansfield, OH 44902-1909 t) 419-524-3351 bauer.madalyn@myspartans.org Madalyn Bauer, Prin.;

St. Peter School - (Grades 7-12) 104 W. First St., Mansfield, OH 44902-2199 t) 419-524-0979 haus.tammy@myspartans.org Michael Wisiniak, Prin.;

MARBLEHEAD

St. Joseph - 822 Barclay St, Marblehead, OH 43440-2118; Mailing: 113 James St, Marblehead, OH 43440-2118 t) 419-798-4177 parish@stjosephm.org; carolann@cros.net stjosephmarblehead.org Rev. James E. Brown, Pst.; Carol Arntz, DRE;

MARTIN

Our Lady of Mt. Carmel - 1105 Elliston Rd., Martin, OH 43445-9601 Rev. Mark J. Herzog, Pst.;

MAUMEE

St. Joseph - 104 W. Broadway, Maumee, OH 43537-2137 t) 419-893-4848 jennifer.drouillard@stjosephmaumee.org Rev. Keith A. Stripe, Pst.; Dcn. Stephen J. Delisle; Dcn. Edgar E. Irelan; Dcn. Joseph Malenfant; Dcn. Dennis Scherger;

St. Joseph School - (Grades PreSchool-8) 112 W. Broadway St., Maumee, OH 43537-2137 t) 419-893-3304 dianna.johnson@stjosephmaumee.org stjosephmaumee.org David Nichols, Prin.;

MILAN

St. Anthony - 145 Center St., Milan, OH 44846-9757; Mailing: P.O. Box 1200, Milan, OH 44846-9757 t) 419-499-4300 Rev. Gilbert Mascarenhas, S.A.C., Pst.; Dcn. David F. Rospert;

MILLER CITY

Holy Family - 201 E. Main Cross St., Miller City, OH 45864; Mailing: P.O. Box 40, Miller City, OH 45864 t) 419-876-3481 snhf@fairpoint.net Rev. Msgr. Charles E. Singler, Pst.; Dcn. Doyle J. Erford;

St. Nicholas - 201 E. Main Cross, Miller City, OH 45864-0040; Mailing: P.O. Box 40, Miller City, OH 45864-0040 dwehri@fairpoint.net Rev. Msgr. Charles E. Singler, Pst.; Dcn. Doyle J. Erford; Deborah Wehri, DRE;

MONROEVILLE

St. Alphonsus Liguori - 66 Chapel St., Monroeville, OH 44847 t) 419-465-4142 st.alphonsus.st.joseph.office@gmail.com; nurse21853@aol.com www.stalphonsus-stjoseph.org Rev. Ronald A. Schock, Pst.; Dcn. Michael L. Wasiniak; Diane Wasiniak, DRE;

St. Joseph - 66 Chapel St., Monroeville, OH 44847 t) 419-512-1713 (CRP); 419-465-4142 nurse21853@aol.com; st.alphonsus.st.joseph.office@gmail.com stalphonsus-stjoseph.org Rev. Ronald A. Schock, Pst.; Dcn. Michael L. Wasiniak; Diane Wasiniak, DRE;

St. Joseph School - (Grades PreK-8) 79 Chapel St., Monroeville, OH 44847 t) 419-465-2625 sjs@msjcs.org www.msjcs.org David McDowell, Prin.;

MONTPELIER

Sacred Heart - 220 S. East Ave., Montpelier, OH 43543-1504 t) 419-485-5914; 419-272-3181 (CRP) michelea@frontier.com; lahf@frontier.com Rev. James E. Halleron, Pst.; Lucinda Held-Faulhaber, DRE;

NAPOLEON

St. Augustine - 210 E. Clinton St., Napoleon, OH 43545-1602 t) 419-592-7656 saintaugustineoffice@gmail.com Rev. J. Douglas Garand, Pst.; Dcn. Jon A. Gottron;

St. Augustine School - (Grades PreK-8) 722 Monroe St., Napoleon, OH 43545-1631 t) 419-592-3641 jim.george@augustinenapoleon.com staugie@henry-net.com Jim George, Prin.;

NEW BAVARIA

Sacred Heart of Jesus - 13779 County Rd. Y, New Bavaria, OH 43548-9738 t) (419) 653-4157 shchurch@metalink.net Rev. Nicholas J. Cunningham, Pst.; CRP Stds.: 95

NEW LONDON

Our Lady of Lourdes - 18 Park Ave., New London, OH 44851 Rev. Douglas D. Taylor, Pst.;

NEW RIEGEL

All Saints - 41 N. Perry St., New Riegel, OH 44853; Mailing: P.O. Box 89, New Riegel, OH 44853 Rev. Timothy M. Kummerer, Pst.; Dcn. John F. Walter;

St. Peter Chapel - 11125 W. Twp. Rd. 96, Alvada, OH 44802

St. Nicholas Chapel - 8981 W. County Rd. 6, Carey, OH 43316

NEW WASHINGTON

St. Bernard - 412 W. Mansfield, New Washington, OH 44854; Mailing: 422 W. Mansfield, New Washington, OH 44854 t) 419-492-2295 stbernard@woh.rr.com; tamiweithman@gmail.com www.stbernardnwo.com/ Rev. Michael J. Diemer, Par. Vicar; Tami Weithman, CRE; CRP Stds.: 92

NORTH BALTIMORE

Holy Family - 115 E. Cherry St., North Baltimore, OH 45872-1134 Rev. Arthur J. Niewiadomski, Pst.;

NORWALK

St. Mary, Mother of the Redeemer - 38 W. League St., Norwalk, OH 44857-1397 Rev. Gilbert Mascarenhas, S.A.C., Pst.; Dcn. Jack Bleile; Dcn. David F. Rospect;

St. Paul - 91 E. Main St., Norwalk, OH 44857-1798 t) 419-668-6044 admin@stpaulchurch.org; katem@stpaulchurch.org www.stpaulchurch.org Rev. Anthony L. Recker, Pst.; Rev. Michael Bialorucki, Assoc. Pst.; Dcn. James A. Reichert; Dcn. David F. Rospert; Jennifer Sanders, Pst. Assoc.; Kathleen R. McKinney, Bus. Mgr.; CRP Stds.: 60

OAK HARBOR

St. Boniface - 215 N. Church St., Oak Harbor, OH 43449-1216 t) 419-898-1389 religion@sb-oh.org; secretary@sb-oh.org www.sb-oh.org Rev. Timothy F. Ferris, Pst.; Dcn. Frank A. Tello;

St. Boniface School - (Grades PreSchool-8) 215 Oak St., Oak Harbor, OH 43449-1227 t) 419-898-1340 school@sb-oh.org; mgreggila@sb-oh.org Millie Greggila, Prin.;

OREGON

St. Ignatius - 212 N. Stadium Rd., Oregon, OH 43616-1536 jmittendorf@stiggys.org Rev. Mark J. Herzog, Pst.; Julie Mittendorf, DRE;

OTTAWA

SS. Peter and Paul - 307 N. Locust St., Ottawa, OH 45875-1495 Rev. Matthew Jozefiak, C.PP.S., Pst.; Rev. Richard Friebel, C.PP.S., Assoc. Pst.; Dcn. James A. Rump;

SS. Peter and Paul School - (Grades K-8) 320 N. Locust St., Ottawa, OH 45875-1496 t) 419-523-3697 nlanwehr@sppsknights.org William Wisher, Prin.;

OTTOVILLE

Immaculate Conception - 211 N. Church St., Ottoville, OH 45876-0296; Mailing: P.O. Box 296, Ottoville, OH 45876-0296 t) 419-453-3513 immac@bright.net Rev. Jerome A. Schetter, Pst.;

PAULDING

Divine Mercy Parish - 417 N. Main St., Paulding, OH 45879-1291 t) 419-399-2576 dre@divinemercycatholic.com; finance@divinemercycatholic.com divinemercycatholic.com Rev. Joseph T. Poggemeyer, Pst.; Dcn. David Jordan; Dcn. David Laker; Dcn. Rosalio M. Martinez; Dcn. Robert Lee Nighswander;

Divine Mercy Parish School - (Grades 1-6) 120 Arturus St., Payne, OH 45880; Mailing: P.O. Box 98, Payne, OH 45880 t) 419-263-2114 principle@dmcschool.com Joseph Linder, Prin.;

PERRYSBURG

Saint John XXIII - 24250 Dixie Hwy., Perrysburg, OH 43551 Rev. Herbert F. Weber, Pst.; Dcn. Thomas Headley;

St. Rose - 215 E. Front St., Perrysburg, OH 43551-2193 t) 419-874-4559 parish@saintroseonline.org saintroseonline.org Rev. Msgr. Charles E. Singler, Pst.; Rev. Kishore Kottana, Par. Vicar; Dcn. Victor DeFilippis; Dcn. Charles W. McDaniel; Dcn. Thomas K. Wray; Charlotte Mariasy, Liturgy Dir.; Robert Hohler, Bus. Mgr.;

St. Rose School - (Grades PreK-8) 217 E. Front St., Perrysburg, OH 43551-2192 t) 419-874-5631 borgelt@saintroseonline.org saintroseonline.org/school Bryon Borgelt, Prin.;

PLYMOUTH

St. Joseph - 117 Sandusky St., Plymouth, OH 44865-1132 Rev. Christopher M. Mileski, Pst.; Dcn. Frederick E. Stockmaster;

PORT CLINTON

Immaculate Conception - 414 Madison St., Port Clinton, OH 43452-1922 Rev. John C. Missler, Pst.; Dcn. Maury A. Hall;

Immaculate Conception School - (Grades PreK-5) 109 W. Fourth St., Port Clinton, OH 43452-1816 t) 419-734-3315 csnyder@portclintonics.net www.portclintonics.net Constance Snyder, Prin.;

PUT-IN-BAY

St. Michael - Chappel St., Put-In-Bay, OH 43456; Mailing: P.O. Box 490, Put-In-Bay, OH 43456 t) 419-285-2741 deaconmike@live.com Rev. Nathan Bockrath; Jimmy McCoy, Pastoral Leader;

Mother of Sorrows - 620 Catawba Ave., Put-In-Bay, OH 43456-0179; Mailing: P.O. Box 179, Put-In-Bay, OH 43456-0179 t) 419-285-2741 deaconmike@live.com Rev. Nathan Bockrath, Chap.;

ROSSFORD

All Saints - 628 Lime City Rd., Rossford, OH 43460 svanhersett@allsaintsrossford.com Rev. Anthony L. Recker, Pst.; Dcn. Gerald E. Galernik; Susan Van Hersett, DRE;

All Saints School - (Grades PreSchool-8) 630 Lime City Rd., Rossford, OH 43460 t) 419-661-2070 tfischer@allsaintscatholic.org www.allsaintscatholic.org Teri Fischer, Prin.;

SANDUSKY

Holy Angels - 428 Tiffin Ave., Sandusky, OH 44870 t) 419-625-3698 mhoyles@sanduskycatholic.org holyangelssandusky.org Rev. Monte J. Hoyles, Pst.; Rev. Christopher Jesudhason, S.A.C., Assoc. Pst.; Rev. Jeffery Walker, Assoc. Pst.;

St. Mary's - 429 Central Ave., Sandusky, OH 44870 t) 419-625-7465 office@stmarysandusky.org Rev. Monte J. Hoyles, Pst.; Rev. Christopher Jesudhason, S.A.C., Assoc. Pst.; Rev. Jeffery Walker, Assoc. Pst.; Dcn. William G. Burch; Dcn. Jeff Claar; Dcn. Philip Dinovo;

SS. Peter and Paul - 510 Columbus Ave., Sandusky, OH 44870-2780 t) 419-625-6655; 419-625-7500 office@stspeterpaul.com peterpaulsandusky.org Rev. Monte J. Hoyles, Pst.; Rev. Christopher Jesudhason, S.A.C., Assoc. Pst.; Rev. Jeffrey Walker, Assoc. Pst.; Dcn. William G. Burch; Dcn. Jeff Claar; Dcn. Philip Dinovo;

SHELBY

Most Pure Heart of Mary - 29 West St., Shelby, OH 44875-1155 Rev. Christopher M. Mileski, Pst.;

Most Pure Heart of Mary School - (Grades PreK-6) 26 West St., Shelby, OH 44875-1148 t) 419-342-2626 kstover@stmaryshelby.org www.stmaryshelby.org Kimberly Stover, Prin.;

Sacred Heart of Jesus - 5742 State Rte. 61 S., Shelby, OH 44875-9080 t) 419-342-2256; 419-683-1697 sacredheartbethlehem.org Sister parish to St. Joseph Catholic Church, Crestline. Rev. Jeffery J. Smith, Pst.;

Sacred Heart of Jesus School - (Grades PreK-8) 5754 State Rte. 61 S., Shelby, OH 44875-9802 lmyers@shelbysacredheart.org Lisa Myers, Prin.;

SPENCERVILLE

St. Patrick - 500 S. Canal St., Spencerville, OH 45887; Mailing: PO Box 63, Spencerville, OH 45887 t) 419-647-6202 stpats45887@gmail.com Rev. Dennis G. Walsh, Pst.; Rev. Scott Perry, Par. Vicar; Rev. Douglas D. Taylor, Par. Vicar;

SWANTON

Holy Trinity - 2649 U.S. Hwy. 20, Swanton, OH 43558-9558 t) 419-644-4014 sroof@htassumption.org; jbartos@htassumption.org www.holytrinityswanton.com/ Very Rev. Michael G. Dandurand, Pst.; Dcn. Robert Gillen; Dcn. Denver Mossing; Sarah Roof, DRE;

Holy Trinity School - (Grades PreK-8) 2639 U.S. Hwy. 20, Swanton, OH 43558-9558 t) 419-644-3971 bkulka@htassumption.org www.holytrinityschool.com Brandon Kulka, Prin.;

St. Richard - 333 Brookside Dr., Swanton, OH 43558-1097 Rev. Adam L. Hertzfeld; Rev. Francis Maridas, Assoc. Pst.;

St. Richard School - (Grades PreK-8) t) 419-826-5041 principal@saintrichard.org Sr. Jean Marie Walczak, S.N.D., Prin.;

SYLVANIA

St. Joseph - 5411 Main St., Sylvania, OH 43560-2177 t) 419-885-2181 (CRP); 419-885-5791 parish@stjoesylvania.org; mbillian@stjoesylvania.org www.stjoesylvania.org Rev. Msgr. Michael Richard Billian, Pst.; Rev. Joseph Mominee, Par. Vicar; Rev. Philip A. Smith, In Res.; Dcn. Anthony J. Pistilli; Dcn. Rick Sasala; Dcn. Paul J. White; Philipp Levering, DRE; Joanne Denyer, Pst. Assoc.; Libby Saxton, Music Min.; Heather Koziarski, Bus. Mgr.; CRP Stds.: 345

St. Joseph School - (Grades PreK-8) t) 419-882-6670 redwards@stjoesylvania.org stjosephschoolsylvania.org Robert Edwards, Prin.;

TIFFIN

St. Joseph - 36 Melmore St., Tiffin, OH 44883-3098 t) 419-447-5848 office@tiffinstjoseph.org tiffinstjoseph.org Rev. Anthony J. Coci; Dcn. David Mileski, Pst. Assoc.; Kristine Wise, Bus. Mgr.; CRP Stds.: 82

St. Mary - 85 S. Sandusky St., Tiffin, OH 44883-2140 t) 419-447-2087 rgaietto@stmarychurch.com; tfry@stmarychurch.com www.stmarychurch.com Rev. Matthew R. Rader, Pst.; Rev. Stanislaw Tabor, Assoc. Pst.; Dcn. Dick Gaietto; Rose Ann Gaietto, DRE;

St. Pius X - 85 S. Sandusky St., Tiffin, OH 44883 t) 419-447-2087 dscherger@stmarychurch.com; torlex@syctelco.com Rev. Gary R. Walters, Pst.; Rev. Anthony J. Coci, Assoc. Pst.; Dcn. John Daniel; Kelli Smith, DRE;

TOLEDO

Our Lady Queen of the Most Holy Rosary Cathedral - 2535 Collingwood Blvd., Toledo, OH 43610 t) 419-244-9575 office@rosarycathedral.org Rev. Msgr. William J. Kubacki, Rector; Dcn. James D. Caruso; Dcn. Brendan Gillen; Dcn. Michael J. Sarra;

SS. Adalbert & Hedwig - 3233 Lagrange St., Toledo, OH 43608-1898 t) 419-241-4179 stadalbert2014@gmail.com ssadalberthedwig.org Rev. Monte J. Hoyles, Admin.; Dcn. Gerald Ignatowski;

St. Catherine of Siena - 4555 N. Haven Ave., Toledo, OH 43612-2350 t) 419-478-9558 pneary@stcatherinetoledo.com Rev. Francis Speier, Pst.; Dcn. Michael R. Learned Sr.; Dcn. Jimmie McCoy; Dcn. Thomas Soper; Michael Salwiesz, DRE; CRP Stds.: 25

St. Catherine of Siena Early Childhood Education Center - 1155 Corbin Rd., Toledo, OH 43612-2366 t) 419-478-9900 ckummer@stcatherineearlyed.org Chris Kummer, Dir.;

St. Charles Borromeo - 1842 Airport Hwy., Toledo, OH 43609-2069 t) 419-535-7077 www.stcharlesstthyacinthtoledo.org/ Rev. Gregory L. Peatee, Pst.;

Christ the King - 4100 Harvest Ln., Toledo, OH 43623-4399 t) 419-475-4348 parish@cktoledo.org www.cktoledo.org Rev. David W. Nuss, Pst.; Dcn. Robert Beisser; CRP Stds.: 102

Christ the King School - (Grades PreK-8) t) 419-475-0909 school@cktoledo.org www.ckschool.org Steve Urbanski, Prin.; Stds.: 406; Lay Tchrs.: 24

St. Clement - 3030 Tremainsville Rd., Toledo, OH 43613-1901 t) 419-472-2111 st.clement08@yahoo.com www.stclementtoledo.com Rev. Francis Speier, Pst.; Dcn. Leroy H. Houghton; Dcn. Ronald G. Peeps; Dcn. Ronald J. Plenzler;

Corpus Christi (University of Toledo) - 2955 Dorr St., Toledo, OH 43607-3023 t) (419) 531-4992 Rev. Jeremy P. Miller, Pst.; Dcn. Justin Moor; CRP Stds.: 4

Epiphany of the Lord Parish - 729 White St., Toledo, OH 43605 t) 419-698-1519 parishoffice@epiphanyofthelord.org www.epiphanyofthelord.org Rev. Eric L. Mueller, Pst.;

Saint Thomas Aquinas Campus - Rev. Gilbert Mascarenhas, S.A.C., Pst.;

Saint Stephen Campus - 1878 Genesee St., Toledo, OH 43605

Sacred Heart of Jesus Campus - 509 Oswald St., Toledo, OH 43605

Gesu - 2049 Parkside Blvd., Toledo, OH 43607-1597 t) 419-531-1421; 419-531-1421 x1101 (CRP) skowronski@gesugreyhoundz.com; toledogesu@gmail.com gesutoledo.org Rev. Martin C. Lukas, O.S.F.S., Pst.; Laurie Skowronski, DRE; Richard Webb, Bus. Mgr.;

Gesu School - (Grades K-8) 2045 Parkside Blvd., Toledo, OH 43607-1555 t) 419-536-5634 gonzales@gesugreyhoundz.com gesutoledo.com Manuel Gonzales, Prin.;

Historic Church of Saint Patrick - 130 Avondale Ave., Toledo, OH 43604 Rev. Msgr. Christopher P. Vasko, Pst.; Dcn. Thomas S. Carone; Dcn. David E. Smith;

St. Hyacinth - 719 Evesham Ave., Toledo, OH 43607 t) 419-535-7077 hyacinth.office@bex.net www.stcharlesstthyacinthtoledo.org/ Rev. Gregory L. Peatee, Pst.;

Immaculate Conception - 434 Western Ave., Toledo, OH 43609-2886 Rev. Msgr. Christopher P. Vasko, Pst.; Rev. Rudi O. Schwarzkopf, O.S.F.S., Pst. Assoc.; Dcn. Thomas S. Carone; Dcn. David E. Smith;

St. Joan of Arc - 5856 Heatherdowns Blvd., Toledo, OH 43614-4570 t) 419-866-6181 kasmus@joanofarc.org www.joanofarc.org Rev. Msgr. Marvin G. Borger, Pst.; Dcn. Gregg Focht; Dcn. Edward Maher; CRP Stds.: 95

St. Joan of Arc School - (Grades PreSchool-8) 5950 Heatherdowns Blvd., Toledo, OH 43614-4500 t) (419) 866-6177 gsattler@school.joanofarc.org; bschmakel@school.joanofarc.org www.joanofarcschool.org Gregory Sattler, Prin.; Stds.: 336; Lay Tchrs.: 23

St. John the Baptist - 5153 Summit St., Toledo, OH 43611-2786 t) 419-726-2034 parishadmin@stjohnpp.com Rev. James Morman, T.O.R., Par. Admin.; CRP Stds.: 23

St. Joseph - 628 Locust St., Toledo, OH 43604; Mailing: 3233 Lagrange St., Toledo, OH 43608 t) 419-261-3928 stjodowntown@gmail.com www.stjosephstoledo.com Rev. David D. Kidd, Pst.; CRP Stds.: 62

Little Flower of Jesus - 5522 Dorr St., Toledo, OH 43615-3612 t) 419-537-6655 parishcenter@littleflowertoledo.org www.littleflowertoledo.org Rev. David W. Nuss, Pst.; Rev. Christopher Hudgin, O.S.F.S., Assoc. Pst.; Dcn. Douglas Bullimore;

St. Martin de Porres - 1119 W. Bancroft St., Toledo, OH 43606 t) 419-241-4544 stmartindeporrestoledo@gmail.com www.stmartindeporres.com CRP Stds.: 12

St. Michael the Archangel - 420 Sandusky St., Toledo, OH 43611-3535 t) 419-726-1947 stmike@bex.net Rev. David J. Cirata, Pst.;

Most Blessed Sacrament - 2240 Castlewood Dr., Toledo, OH 43613 t) 419-473-1161 dklein62@sbcglobal.net Rev. Michael A. Geiger, Pst.; Dcn. Robert Fedynich; Dcn. Harold Welch; Joan Klein, DRE;

Most Blessed Sacrament Parish School - 4255 Bellevue Rd., Toledo, OH 43613 t) 419-472-1121 gsattler@mbsptoledo.org www.mbsptoledo.org Gregory Sattler, Prin.;

Our Lady of Lourdes - 6149 Hill Ave., Toledo, OH 43615-5699 Rev. David R. Bruning, Pst.; Dcn. Gary Thrun;

Our Lady of Perpetual Help - 2255 Central Grove, Toledo, OH 43614-4321 Rev. David L. Ritchie, Pst.; Dcn. Daniel R. Waters;

Our Lady of Perpetual Help School - (Grades PreK-8) t) 419-382-5696 kbonnell@olphtoledo.org Kari Bonnell, Prin.;

St. Patrick of Heatherdowns - 4201 Heatherdowns Blvd., Toledo, OH 43614-3099 rebecca.reamer@toledostpats.org Rev. James R. Sanford, Assoc. Pst.; Dcn. Joel F. Junga; Dcn. David J. Karpanty; Dcn. Joseph H. Kest Jr.; Dcn. Dennis T. Rife; Rebecca Reamer, DRE;

St. Patrick of Heatherdowns School - (Grades PreK-8) t) 419-381-1775 tina.abel@toledostpats.org Tina Abel, Prin.;

SS. Peter and Paul - 738 S. St. Clair St., Toledo, OH 43609-2432 t) 419-283-0884 Rev. Juan Francisco Molina, Pst.; Dcn. Salvador Sanchez;

St. Pius X - 3011 Carskaddon Ave., Toledo, OH 43606-1662 t) 419-535-7672 stpius@buckeye-express.com Rev. David M. Whalen, O.S.F.S., Pst.; Rev. John Lehner, O.S.F.S.;

St. Pius X School - (Grades PreK-8) 2950 Ilger Ave., Toledo, OH 43606-1662 t) 419-535-7688 stpiusx_richardson@nwoca.net Susan Richardson, Prin.;

Regina Coeli - 530 Regina Pkwy., Toledo, OH 43612-3398 Rev. John A. Miller, Pst.; Dcn. James Dudley;

Regina Coeli School - (Grades K-8) 600 Regina Pkwy., Toledo, OH 43612-3399 t) 419-476-0920 dbloomquist@regina-coeli.org Corrine Sharrit, Prin.;

UPPER SANDUSKY

Transfiguration of the Lord - 225 N. Eighth St., Upper Sandusky, OH 43351-1299 Dcn. Kevin Wintersteller; Rev. Antony V. Vattaparambil, O.F.M.Conv., Pst.;

St. Peter Catholic School - (Grades PreK-6) 310 N. 8th St., Upper Sandusky, OH 43351-1144 t) 419-294-1395 panderson@stpetersupper.com Patricia Anderson, Prin.;

St. Mary Chapel - Main St. at State Rte. 639, Upper Sandusky, OH 43351

VAN WERT

St. Mary of the Assumption - 601 Jennings Rd., Van Wert, OH 45891-9702 t) 419-238-3079 Rev. Stanley S. Szybka, Pst.; Dcn. Andrew McMahon;

St. Mary of the Assumption School - (Grades K-6) 611 Jennings Rd., Van Wert, OH 45891-9701 t) 419-238-5186 dmetzger@stmarysvanwert.com Daniel Metzger, Prin.;

VERMILION

St. Mary - 731 Exchange St., Vermilion, OH 44089-1330 Rev. Ronald J. Brickner, Pst.;

St. Mary School - (Grades K-6) 5450 E. Ohio St., Vermilion, OH 44089-1340 t) 440-967-7911 bbialko@stmaryvermilion.org Barbara Bialko, Prin.;

WAKEMAN

St. Mary - 46 E. Main St., Wakeman, OH 44889; Mailing: PO Box 576, Wakeman, OH 44889 t) 440-839-2023 office@stmarywakeman.org www.stmarywakeman.org Rev. Ronald J. Brickner, Pst.;

WALBRIDGE

St. Jerome - 300 Warner St., Walbridge, OH 43465-1142 Rev. Eric P. Schild, Pst.; Dcn. Paul D. Nungester Sr.;

WAUSEON

St. Caspar - 1205 N. Shoop Ave., Wauseon, OH 43567-1828 t) 419-337-2322 ksekula@stcaspar.org www.stcaspar.org Rev. Todd M. Dominique, Pst.; Barbara M. Bonfert, DRE; CRP Stds.: 140

WILLARD

St. Francis Xavier - 25 W. Perry St., Willard, OH 44890-1694 t) 419-935-1149 sfxparishoffice@willard-oh.com Rev. George W. Mahas III, Admin.; Rev. Michael Diemer, M.J.; Dcn. Vincent Foos;

St. Francis Xavier School - (Grades K-6) t) 419-935-4744 mcdowell.donna@sfxwillard.org www.sfxwillard.net Donna McDowell, Prin.;

SCHOOLS: PRESCHOOL THRU HIGH SCHOOL

SCHOOLS

STATE OF OHIO

DEFIANCE

Holy Cross Catholic School of Defiance - (PAR) (Grades PreK-8) 1745 S. Clinton St., Defiance, OH 43512 t) 419-784-2021 principal@defianceholycross.org www.defianceholycross.org Rose A. Reinhart, Prin.;

FREMONT

Bishop Hoffman Catholic School - (Grades K-12) 702 Croghan St., Fremont, OH 43420 t) 419-332-9947 dperin@bishop-hoffman.net Tim Cullen, Supt.;

Sacred Heart Campus - (Grades K-12) 500 Smith Rd., Fremont, OH 43420 t) 419-332-7102 awhitfield@bishop-hoffman.net Teresa Kitchen, Prin.;

Saint Joseph Campus - (Grades K-12) Teresa Kitchen, Prin.;

OREGON

St. Kateri Catholic Schools - (PAR) (Grades PreK-12) 3225 Pickle Rd., Oregon, OH 43616 t) 419-693-0465 gskibinski@cardinalstritch.org www.cardinalstritch.org Melissa Empie, Prin.; Kevin Parkins, Prin.; Rev. Eric P. Schild, Pres.;

SANDUSKY

Sandusky Central Catholic School - (PAR) (Grades PreK-12) 410 W. Jefferson St., Sandusky, OH 44870-2427 t) 419-626-1892 gpalmer@sanduskycc.org www.sanduskycentralcatholicschool.com/ Geoff Palmer, Pres.;

Sandusky Central Catholic School, MS/HS - (Grades PreK-12)

Sandusky Central Catholic School Elementary - (Grades PreK-12) www.sanduskycentralcatholicschool.com

TIFFIN

Calvert Elementary School - (Grades K-8) 357 S. Washington St., Tiffin, OH 44883-2879 t) 419-447-5790 mkaucher@calvertcatholic.org www.calvertcatholic.org Michael J. Kaucher, Pres.;

TOLEDO

St. Benedict School - 5522 Dorr St., Toledo, OH 43615 t) 419-536-1194 mhartman@stbenedicttoledo.org www.stbenedicttoledo.com Martha Hartman, Prin.;

Central City Ministry of Toledo Schools (CCMT) - (Grades K-8) 1933 Spielbusch Ave., Toledo, OH 43604-5360 t) 419-244-6711 mkravetsky@toledodiocese.org A consortium of two Catholic schools joined together: Rosary Cathedral and Queen of Apostles

Queen of Apostles Campus - (DIO) (Grades K-8) 235 Courtland Ave., Toledo, OH 43609-2699 t) 419-241-7829 jweeman@ccmtschool.org Sr. Joselyn Weeman, S.N.D., Prin.;

Rosary Cathedral Campus - (DIO) (Grades K-8) 2535 Collingwood Blvd., Toledo, OH 43610-1400 t) 419-243-4396 lsnyder@ccmtschool.org www.rosarycathedralschool.org Sr. M. Lynda Snyder, S.N.D., Prin.;

WHITEHOUSE

Lial Catholic School - (PRV) (Grades PreK-8) 5700 Davis Rd., Whitehouse, OH 43571-9669 t) 419-877-5167 lcherry@lialschool.org www.lialschool.org Sisters of Notre Dame. Lynn Cherry, Prin.; Stds.: 217; Sr. Tchrs.: 1; Lay Tchrs.: 15

HIGH SCHOOLS

STATE OF OHIO

LIMA

Central Catholic High School - (PAR) 720 S. Cable Rd., Lima, OH 45805 t) 419-222-4276 swilliams@apps.lcchs.edu www.lcchs.edu Stephanie Williams, Prin.; Jennifer Patterson, Campus Min.;

TIFFIN

Calvert High School - (PAR) 152 Madison St., Tiffin, OH 44883-0836 t) 419-447-3844 mkaucher@calvertcatholic.org www.calvertcatholic.org Michael J. Kaucher, Pres.;

TOLEDO

Central Catholic High School - (DIO) 2550 Cherry St., Toledo, OH 43608 t) 419-255-2280 info@centralcatholic.org www.centralcatholic.org Conducted by diocesan priests, sisters and laity. Rev. Matthew R. Rader, Chap.; Kristine Malik, Asst. Prin., Curriculum & Instruction;

St. Francis de Sales School - (PRV) (Grades 7-12) 2323 W. Bancroft St., Toledo, OH 43607-1399 t) 419-531-1618 questions@sfsknights.org www.sfsknights.org School for boys. Oblates of St. Francis de Sales High School, Inc. John Hall, Prin.; Rev. Geoffrey N. Rose, O.S.F.S., Pres.; Stds.: 679; Scholastics: 1; Pr. Tchrs.: 6; Lay Tchrs.: 55

St. John's Jesuit High School and Academy - (PRV) (Grades 6-12) 5901 Airport Hwy., Toledo, OH 43615-7344 t) 419-865-5743 pskeldon@sjjtitans.org; lhoyt@sjjtitans.org www.sjjtitans.org School for boys. USA Midwest Province Mark Mark Swentkofske, Pres.; Christopher Knight, Vice. Pres.; Rev. Brian Lehane, Theology Teacher; Rev. James Sand, English Teacher; Stds.: 743; Pr. Tchrs.: 2; Lay Tchrs.: 56

Notre Dame Academy - (PRV) (Grades 7-12) 3535 W. Sylvania Ave., Toledo, OH 43623-4479 t) 419-475-9359 www.nda.org Girls college preparatory school. Sisters of Notre Dame. Kim Grilliot, Pres.; Stds.: 618; Sr. Tchrs.: 1; Lay Tchrs.: 49

St. Ursula Academy - (PRV) (Grades 6-12) 4025 Indian Rd., Toledo, OH 43606 t) 419-531-1693 mjoseph@toledosua.org www.toledosua.org School for girls. Sponsored by Ursuline Sisters of the Sacred Heart. Nichole Flores, Prin.; Mary Werner, Pres.;

INSTITUTIONS LOCATED IN DIOCESE

ASSOCIATIONS [ASN]

CAREY

Franciscan Mission Association - 322 West St., Carey, OH 43316 t) 419-396-6455 rmallett1@hotmail.com Rev. Raymond Mallett, O.F.M.Conv., Dir.;

CAMPUS MINISTRY / NEWMAN CENTERS [CAM]

BLUFFTON

Bluffton University Campus Ministry - 160 N. Spring St., Bluffton, OH 45817 t) 419-358-8631 cinkrott@embarqmail.com Sr. Carol Inkrott, O.S.F., Campus Min.;

BOWLING GREEN

Bowling Green State University Campus Ministry - 425 Thurstin St., Bowling Green, OH 43402 t) 419-352-7555 theresa@sttomsbg.org; fr.jeffwalker@sttomsbg.org www.sttomsbg.org Attended by St. Thomas More University Parish. Rev. Jeffery Walker, Pst.; Alicia Schmiesing, Campus Min.;

DEFIANCE

Defiance College Catholics on Campus - 701 N. Clinton, Defiance, OH 43512 t) 419-783-2352 baveresch@defiance.edu

FINDLAY

University of Findlay Newman Campus Ministry - 750 Bright Rd., Findlay, OH 45840 t) 419-422-2646 parish@findlaystmichael.org Rev. Peter D. Grodi, Par. Vicar;

TIFFIN

Heidelberg University Newman Campus Ministry - 310 E. Market St., Campus Center 301, Tiffin, OH 44883 t) 419-448-2066 pstark@heidelberg.edu www.heidelberg.edu Sr. Barbara Jean Miller, O.S.F., Campus Min.;

CATHOLIC CHARITIES [CCH]

TOLEDO

Catholic Charitable Ministries Fund - 1933 Spielbusch Ave., Toledo, OH 43604 t) 419-244-6711 wnevolis@toledodiocese.org Walter J. Nevolis, Secy.;

CEMETERIES [CEM]

FREMONT

St. Joseph - t) 419-332-8756

LIMA

Gethsemane -

SANDUSKY

Catholic Cemeteries of Sandusky - 2020 Sanford St., Sandusky, OH 44870 t) 419-625-2673 cc@sanduskycatholic.org Rev. Monte J. Hoyles, Dir.;

TOLEDO

Calvary - 2224 Dorr St., Toledo, OH 43607 t) 419-536-3751 info@cathcemtoledo.org www.cathcemtoledo.org Bob Shenefield, Dir.;

Mount Carmel - 15 E. Manhattan Blvd., Toledo, OH 43608; Mailing: 5725 Hill Ave., Toledo, OH 43615 t) 419-536-3751 info@cathcemtoledo.org Robert Shenefield, Dir.;

Resurrection - 5725 Hill Ave., Toledo, OH 43615 t) 419-531-5747 info@cathcemtoledo.org www.cathcemtoledo.org Bob Shenefield, Dir.;

COLLEGES & UNIVERSITIES [COL]

SYLVANIA

Lourdes University - 6832 Convent Blvd., Sylvania, OH 43560 t) 419-885-3211 tholup@lourdes.edu www.lourdes.edu Sisters of St. Francis of the Congregation of Our Lady of Lourdes, (O.S.F.). Terry Keller, Interim Pres.; Katherine Beutel, Interim Vice Pres., Acad. Affairs; Bryan Barshel, CFO; Michael

McCormick, CIO; Janet Eaton-Smith, Vice Pres., Athletics; Mary Sabin, Vice Pres., Instl. Advancement; Jeffrey Liles, Vice Pres., Enrollment Mgmt.; Sr. Barbara Vano, Vice Pres., Mission & Min.; Alisa Smith, Dean, Student Success; Stds.: 1,226; Lay Tchrs.: 50

Franciscan Theatre and Conference Center of Lourdes University - 6832 Convent Blvd., Sylvania, OH 43560 t) 419-517-8950 kyeager@lourdes.edu Kiley Yeager, Ext. Events Coord.;

TOLEDO

Mercy College of Ohio - 2221 Madison Ave., Toledo, OH 43604 t) 415-251-1313 susan.wajert@mercycollege.edu www.mercycollege.edu Sisters of Mercy of the Americas, Mercy Sisters; Sister of Charity of Montreal, Grey Nuns. Susan C. Wajert, Pres.; Mark Adkins, Vice Pres., Student Affairs; Lori Edgeworth, Vice Pres., Strategic Planning & Enrollment Mgmt.; Stds.: 1,281; Lay Tchrs.: 55

CONVENTS, MONASTERIES, AND RESIDENCES FOR WOMEN [CON]

FREMONT

St. Bernardine Home - 1220 Tiffin St., Fremont, OH 43420 t) 419-332-8208 jking@mercysc.org Sisters of Mercy of the Americas, South Central Community. Rev. Edward J. Schleter, Chap.; James M. King, Admin.; Joanne Kosta, Dir.;

MAUMEE

Sisters of Notre Dame Province Offices - 1656 Henthorne Dr., Ste. 200, Maumee, OH 43537 t) 419-474-5485 Sr. Margaret Mary Gorman, Supr.; Srs.: 143

SYLVANIA

Sisters of St. Francis of the Congregation of Our Lady of Lourdes (Sisters of St. Francis of Sylvania, Ohio) - 6832 Convent Blvd., Sylvania, OH 43560-2897 t) 419-517-8426 jbelt@sistersosf.org www.sistersosf.org Sponsored ministries include Lourdes University, Sylvania Franciscan Ministries and Sisters of St. Francis Foundation Sr. Nancy Linenkugel, O.S.F., CEO; Srs.: 104

TIFFIN

St. Francis Convent - 200 St. Francis Ave., Tiffin, OH 44883-3458 t) 419-447-0435 osftiffin@tiffinfranciscans.org www.tiffinfranciscans.org Motherhouse, Sisters of St. Francis of Tiffin. Srs.: 70

TOLEDO

Monastery of the Visitation - 1745 Parkside Blvd., Toledo, OH 43607-1599 t) 419-536-1343 vhm-superior@toast2.net www.toledovisitation.org Contemplative Order of the Sisters of the Visitation of Toledo, Ohio. Sr. Marie de Sales Kasper, Supr.; Srs.: 16

Notre Dame Academy Convent - 3535 W. Sylvania Ave., Toledo, OH 43623; Mailing: 1656 Henthorne Dr., Ste. 200, Maumee, OH 43537 c) 567-395-2406 awillman@sndusa.org Sisters of Notre Dame. Sr. AliceMarie Willman, S.N.D., Secy.; Srs.: 16

Ursuline Convent of the Sacred Heart - 4045 Indian Rd., Toledo, OH 43606 t) 419-536-9587 ursulines@toledoursulines.org www.toledoursulines.org Sr. Sandra Sherman, O.S.U., Pres.; Srs.: 25

WHITEHOUSE

Lial Residence, Sisters of Notre Dame - 5908 Davis Rd., Whitehouse, OH 43571 t) 419-877-0432 rhug@toledosnd.org Sr. Rosemary Hug, Bus. Mgr.; Srs.: 5

ENDOWMENTS / FOUNDATIONS / TRUSTS [EFT]

DELPHOS

St. John Parish Foundation, Inc. - 201 N. Pierce St., Delphos, OH 45833 t) 419-695-4050 thanf@stjohnpf.com stjohnpf.com Rev. Dennis G. Walsh;

FINDLAY

St. Michael School Educational Foundation - 750 Bright Rd., Findlay, OH 45840 t) 419-422-2646 dcampbell@findlaystmichael.org St. Michael the Archangel School Foundation, St. Michael the Archangel Parish Foundation & St. Michael the Archangel Capital Fund. Dave Seman, Pres.;

LIMA

Lima Central Catholic Educational Foundation - 720 S. Cable Rd., Lima, OH 45805 t) 419-222-4276 kroberts@apps.lcchs.edu Karen Roberts, Dir.;

S.R.H.C. Foundation - 730 W. Market St., Lima, OH 45801-4667 t) 419-226-9775 Timothy Rieger, Exec.;

SANDUSKY

Sandusky Central Catholic Educational Foundation, Inc. - 410 W. Jefferson St., Sandusky, OH 44870 t) 419-626-1892 gpalmer@sanduskycc.org Rev. Joseph R. Steinbauer, Admin.;

SWANTON

St. Richard's School Endowment Foundation - 333 Brookside Dr., Swanton, OH 43558-1097 t) 419-826-2791 ahertzfeld@joanofarc.org saintrichard.org Dcn. Jerry Ziemkiewicz;

SYLVANIA

Sisters of St. Francis Foundation - 6832 Convent Blvd., Sylvania, OH 43560 t) 419-517-8426 jbelt@sistersosf.org Sr. Nancy Linenkugel, O.S.F., Pres.;

TIFFIN

St. Francis Senior Ministries Memorial Foundation, Inc. - 182 St. Francis Ave., Tiffin, OH 44883 t) 419-447-2723 sean.riley@stfrancishome.org www.stfrancistiffin.org Sean Riley, Exec.;

Tiffin Calvert Foundation - 152 Madison St., Tiffin, OH 44883-0836 t) 419-447-3844 eric@engleshook.com Rev. Anthony J. Coci, Chap.; Michael J. Kaucher, Pres.;

TOLEDO

The Diocese of Toledo Cemeteries Perpetual Care Trust - 1933 Spielbusch Ave., Toledo, OH 43604 t) (419) 244-6711 tantonini@toledodiocese.org Thomas Antonini, Contact;

The Diocese of Toledo Health Benefits Trust - 1933 Spielbusch Ave., Toledo, OH 43604 t) (419) 244-6711 tantonini@toledodiocese.org Thomas Antonini, Contact;

The Diocese of Toledo Pre-Need Cemetery Merchandise and Services Trust - 1933 Spielbusch Ave., Toledo, OH 43604

The Diocese of Toledo Properties Trust - 1933 Spielbusch Ave., Toledo, OH 43604 t) (419) 244-6711 tantonini@toledodiocese.org Thomas Antonini, Contact;

The Diocese of Toledo Property and Casualty Trust - 1933 Spielbusch Ave., Toledo, OH 43604 t) (419) 244-6711 tantonini@toledodiocese.org Thomas Antonini, Contact;

Diocese of Toledo Scholarship Fund - 1933 Spielbusch Ave., Toledo, OH 43604

The Diocese of Toledo Catholic Investment Trust - 1933 Spielbusch Ave., Toledo, OH 43604

St. Francis de Sales High School Foundation, Inc. - 2323 W. Bancroft St., Toledo, OH 43607 t) 419-531-1618 jnewman@sfsknights.org sfsknights.org Rev. Joseph Newman, O.S.F.S., Chair;

Saint John's Jesuit High School and Academy Foundation - 5901 Airport Hwy., Toledo, OH 43615 t) 419-865-5743 lhoyt@sjjtitans.org www.sjjtitans.org Michael Savona, Pres.;

Mercy Foundation - 2213 Cherry St., Toledo, OH 43608 t) 419-251-2117 Timothy Koder, Pres.;

Notre Dame Academy Foundation - 3535 Sylvania Ave., Toledo, OH 43623

Sylvania Franciscan Health Foundation - An Affiliate of Catholic Health Initiatives. Sr. Mary Jon Wagner, O.S.F., Supr.;

U.T. Newman Foundation for Student Education and Development - 2955 Dorr St., Toledo, OH 43607-3023 t) 419-531-4992 kwilliams@ccup.org Rev. Msgr. Michael R. Billian;

St. Ursula Academy Foundation, Inc. - 4025 Indian Rd., Toledo, OH 43606 t) 419-531-1693 mjoseph@toledosua.org Mary Werner, Pres.;

Ursuline Convent of the Sacred Heart Foundation, Inc. - 4045 Indian Rd., Toledo, OH 43606 t) 419-536-9587 vmyers@ursulinecenter.org Sr. Sandra J Sherman, OSU, Supr.;

VERMILION

St. Mary's Church Education Endowment Foundation - 731 Exchange St., Vermilion, OH 44089-1330 t) 440-967-8711 parish@stmaryvermilion.org www.stmaryvermilion.org Rev. Ronald J. Brickner;

WILLARD

Mercy Willard Foundation - 1100 Neal Zick Rd., Willard, OH 44890 t) 419-964-5107 mercyweb.org

HOSPITALS / HEALTH SERVICES [HOS]

DEFIANCE

Mercy Health - Defiance Hospital LLC - 1404 E Second St., Defiance, OH 43513 t) 419-782-8444 julie_landoll@mercy.com Dcn. Jeff M. Mayer, Chap.; Bed Capacity: 23; Asstd. Annu.: 10,475; Staff: 327

LIMA

Mercy Health - St. Rita's Medical Center LLC - 730 W. Market St., Lima, OH 45801-4602 t) 419-227-3361; 800-467-0308 admarcum@mercy.com www.stritas.org Rev. Charles Obinwa, Chap.; Ronda Lehman, Pres.; Matthew Etzkorn, Dir.; Amy D. Marcum, Vice Pres. Mission Svcs.; Timothy Rieger, Vice Pres. Finance; Bed Capacity: 367; Asstd. Annu.: 116,181; Staff: 1,900

OREGON

Mercy Health - St. Charles Hospital, LLC - 2600 Navarre Ave., Oregon, OH 43616 t) 419-696-7200 www.mercy.com Craig Albers, Pres.; Bed Capacity: 235; Asstd. Annu.: 38,941; Staff: 919

TIFFIN

Mercy Health - Tiffin Hospital, LLC - 45 St. Lawrence Dr., Tiffin, OH 44883 t) 419-455-7000 www.mercyweb.org Andrew Morgan, Pres.; Julie Landoll, Dir.; Bed Capacity: 45; Asstd. Annu.: 22,479; Staff: 367

TOLEDO

Mercy Health - St. Anne Hospital, LLC - 3404 W. Sylvania Ave., Toledo, OH 43623 t) 419-407-2663 www.mercy.com Andrea Gwyn, Pres.; Bed Capacity: 128; Asstd. Annu.: 53,873; Staff: 663

Mercy Health - St. Vincent Medical Center, LLC - 2213 Cherry St., Toledo, OH 43608-2691 t) 419-251-3232 www.mercyweb.org Affiliated with Mercy Health Partners. Grey Nuns and Sisters of Mercy. Jeffrey Dempsey, Pres.; Bed Capacity: 322; Asstd. Annu.: 92,547; Staff: 2,361

WILLARD

Mercy Health - Willard Hospital, LLC - 1100 Neal Zick Rd., Willard, OH 44890 t) 419-964-5000 www.mercy.com Andrew Morgan, Pres.; Julie Landoll, Dir.; Bed Capacity: 20; Asstd. Annu.: 10,584; Staff: 127

MISCELLANEOUS [MIS]

LIMA

Magnificat of Lima, Ohio - 634 Westerly Dr., Lima, OH 45805 t) 419-230-5045 sharreeb64@gmail.com Sharree Reehling, Dir.;

MONROEVILLE

Our Lady of the Lake Magnificat Inc. - 155 Sandusky St., Monroeville, OH 44847; Mailing: P.O. Box 482, Monroeville, OH 44847 t) 419-465-2691 beddinger155@aol.com huronmagnificat.weebly.com

SYLVANIA

Franciscan Properties, Inc. - 6832 Convent Blvd., Sylvania, OH 43560 t) 419-517-8426 jbelt@sistersosf.org Sr. Julie Myers, O.S.F., Pres.;

Franciscan Shelters-Bethany House - 6832 Convent Blvd., Sylvania, OH 43560 t) 419-727-4948 execdirector@bethanyhousetoledo.org www.bethanyhousetoledo.org

Sophia Center, Inc. - 6832 Convent Blvd., Sylvania, OH 43560 t) 419-882-4529 jbelt@sistersosf.org www.thesophiacenter.org Provides counseling & psychological testing services with a focus on the underserved. Sr. Rachel Marie Nijakowski, O.S.F.S., Dir.;

Sylvania Franciscan Health - 6832 Convent Blvd., Sylvania, OH 43560 t) 419-882-8373 pam.koerner@commonspirit.org www.sylvaniafranciscanhealth.org An Affiliate of CommonSpirit Health Sr. Nancy Linenkugel, O.S.F., Major Supr.;

Sylvania Franciscan Ministries - 6832 Convent Blvd., Sylvania, OH 43560 t) 419-517-8426 jbelt@sistersosf.org Sponsored ministries include Franciscan Properties, Franciscan Shelters, Rosary Care Center and Sophia Center Sr. Sharon Derivan, O.S.F., Pres.;

TIFFIN

Saint Francis Senior Ministries, Inc. - 182 St. Francis Ave., Tiffin, OH 44883 t) 419-447-2723 dawn.snyder@stfrancishome.org www.stfrancistiffin.org Gabriel Stoll, Admin.;

St. Francis Villas, Inc. - 182 St. Francis Ave., Tiffin, OH 44883 t) 419-447-2723 sean.riley@stfrancishome.org www.stfrancistiffin.org Tyler Webb, Chair; Sean Riley, Exec.;

***Franciscan Earth Literacy Center** - 194 St. Francis Ave., Tiffin, OH 44883 t) 419-448-7485 mjohnston@felctiffin.org www.felctiffin.org Mimi Johnston, Admin.;

Friedman Village at Saint Francis, LLC - 175 Saint Francis Ave., Tiffin, OH 44883 t) 419-443-1445 kellie.hartzel@stfrancishome.org Gabriel Stoll, Admin.;

St. Francis Senior Ministries Day Care, Inc. - 182 St. Francis Ave., Tiffin, OH 44883 t) 419-447-2723 sean.riley@stfrancishome.org stfrancistiffin.org Tyler Webb, Chair; Sean Riley, Exec.;

TOLEDO

***Catholic Charities - Diocese of Toledo, Inc.** - 1933 Spielbusch Ave., Toledo, OH 43604 t) 419-244-6711 rschuster@toledodiocese.org www.catholiccharitiesnwo.org Rodney O. Schuster, Exec.;

Catholic Club, The - 1601 Jefferson Ave., Toledo, OH 43604 t) 419-243-7255 info@catholicclub.org www.catholicclub.org Paul Szymanski, Dir.;

Christ Child Society of Toledo - ; Mailing: P.O. Box 352254, Toledo, OH 43635 t) 419-882-1532 christchildsocietytoledo.org Pat Galvin, Pres.; Mary Keener, Secy.; Sandy Arnold, Secy.; Anne Marie Blank, Treas.;

The Diocese of Toledo Cemeteries Corporation - 1933 Spielbusch Ave., Toledo, OH 43604

The Diocese of Toledo Deposit and Loan Trust - 1933 Spielbusch Ave., Toledo, OH 43604

The Diocese of Toledo Management Corporation - 1933 Spielbusch Ave., Toledo, OH 43604

Farley Health Care Corporation - 2200 Jefferson Ave., Toledo, OH 43604 t) 419-251-2889 barry_hudgin@mhsnr.org

Mareda, Inc. - 1931 Scottwood Ave., Ste. 700, Toledo, OH 43620; Mailing: P.O. Box 4719, Toledo, OH 43620 t) 419-242-2300 akott@vmc.org Housing Agency of the Diocese of Toledo. Andy Kott, Exec.;

Mercy Health North, LLC - 2200 Jefferson Ave., Toledo, OH 43604 t) 419-251-0715 dorothy_thum@mercy.com www.mercy.com Robert Baxter, Pres.;

Mercy Health - Life Flight Network LLC - 2409 Cherry St., Toledo, OH 43608 t) 419-251-4290 mh-life-flight-network@mercy.com

Plaza Apartments - 2520 Monroe St., Toledo, OH 43620; Mailing: P.O. Box 4719, Toledo, OH 43620 t) 419-244-1881 akott@vmc.org

MONASTERIES AND RESIDENCES FOR PRIESTS AND BROTHERS [MON]

BELLEVUE

***Mary Lay Center** - 4500 State Rte. 269, Bellevue, OH 44811-8921 t) 419-483-7381 sorrowfulmother@yahoo.com Rev. Scott Kramer, C.PP.S., Dir.; Rev. Harold C. Brown, C.PP.S.; Rev. Yuri (George) J. Kuzara, C.PP.S.; Bro. Terrence Nufer, C.PP.S.;

HOLLAND

St. John's Jesuit High School Jesuit Community - 604 Scenic Cir., Holland, OH 43528 t) 313-231-0915 blehane@jesuits.org Rev. Brian Lehane, Supr.; Rev. James Sand, Teacher; Priests: 2

TOLEDO

Oblate Residences - 1225 Flaire Dr., Toledo, OH 43615; Mailing: 2043 Parkside Blvd., Toledo, OH 43607-1597 t) 419-724-9851 burson@oblates.us Very Rev. John J. Loughran, O.S.F.S., Prov.;

Oblates of St. Francis de Sales - 2323 W. Bancroft St., Toledo, OH 43607; Mailing: P.O. Box 2868, Toledo, OH 43606 t) 419-724-9851 burson@oblates.us www.oblates.org Very Rev. John J. Loughran, O.S.F.S., Prov.; Rev. Ronald W. E. Olszewski, O.S.F.S., Chair; Rev. Geoffrey N. Rose, O.S.F.S., Pres.; Rev. Joseph Newman, O.S.F.S., Vice Pres.; Rev. Roland Calvert, Editor; Rev. John Kasper, O.S.F.S.; Rev. James F. Cryan, O.S.F.S.; Rev. Rudi O. Schwarzkopf, O.S.F.S.; Rev. Alan D. Zobler, O.S.F.S.; Bro. Alfred D. Durant, O.S.F.S.; Brs.: 3; Priests: 33

Provincial Offices - ; Mailing: P. O. Box 2868, Toledo, OH 43606 c) (419) 724-9851 www.oblates.us Rev. David A. Kenehan, OSFS, Rel. Ord. Ldr.; Rev. Michael Newman, OSFS, Prov. Asst.;

Gesu Parish - 2049 Parkside Blvd., Toledo, OH 43607 t) 419-531-1421 gesutoledo@gesutoledo.org gesutoledo.org Rev. Martin C. Lukas, O.S.F.S., Pst.; Rev. Craig Irwin, Assoc. Pst.;

St. Francis de Sales School Faculty House - 2323 W. Bancroft St., Toledo, OH 43607 t) 419-531-1619 mckenna@oblates.us

St. Pius X - 3011 Carskaddon, Toledo, OH 43606 t) 419-535-7672 loughran@oblates.us Rev. Martin C. Lukas, O.S.F.S., Pst.; Rev. Craig Irwin, Assoc. Pst.; Rev. David M. Whalen, O.S.F.S., In Res.;

NURSING / REHABILITATION / CONVALESCENCE / ELDERLY CARE [NUR]

OREGON

CHI Living Communities - 930 S. Wynn Rd., Oregon, OH 43616 t) 567-455-0414 aiffland@chilivingcomm.org www.homeishere.org Prentice Lipsey, Pres. & CEO; Rebecca Hilton, Vice Pres., Mission Integration; Asstd. Annu.: 4,809; Staff: 1,586

The Gardens of St. Francis - 930 S. Wynn Rd., Oregon, OH 43616 t) 419-698-4331 bwebb@chilivingcomm.org An operating unit of CHI Living Communities, a subsidiary of CommonSpirit Health Brandon Webb, Exec. Dir.; Heidi Hoffman, Mission Integration & Spiritual Care;

Sacred Heart Home - 860 Ansonia, Ste. 13D, Oregon, OH 43616 t) 419-214-9551 devoregon@littlesistersofthepoor.org www.littlesistersofthepoor.org Little Sisters of the Poor. Sr. Loraine Maguire, lsp, Admin.;

PERRYSBURG

***St. Clare Commons** - 12469 Five Point Rd., Perrysburg, OH 43551 t) 419-931-0050 smarsh@commonspirit.org www.homeishere.org An operating unit of CHI Living Communities, which is a subsidiary of CommonSpirit Health Sarah Marsh, Admin.; Rebecca Hilton, Vice Pres., Mission Integration; Asstd. Annu.: 267; Staff: 76

SANDUSKY

***The Commons of Providence** - 5000 Providence Dr., Sandusky, OH 44870 t) 419-624-1171 samison@chilivingcomm.org www.homeishere.org An operating unit of CHI Living Communities, which is a subsidiary of CommonSpirit Health Rebecca Hilton, Vice Pres., Mission Integration; Seantell Amison, Admin.; Asstd. Annu.: 136; Staff: 97

Providence Care Center - 2025 Hayes Ave., Sandusky, OH 44870 t) 419-627-2273 jingles@chilivingcomm.org www.homeishere.org An operating unit of CHI Living Communities, which is a subsidiary of CommonSpirit Health John Ingles, Exec. Dir.; Courtney Hurlburt, Chap.; Rebecca Hilton, Vice Pres., Mission Integration; Asstd. Annu.: 420; Staff: 93

SYLVANIA

Rosary Care Center - 6832 Convent Blvd., Sylvania, OH 43560 t) 419-517-8426 jphillips@rosarycare.org Jason Phillips, Admin.; Asstd. Annu.: 122; Staff: 104

TIFFIN

CSJI-Tiffin, Inc. - 182 St. Francis Ave., Tiffin, OH 44883-3491; Mailing: 3450 N. Rock Rd. Ste. 605, Wichita, KS 67226 t) 419-447-2723 kdavis@csjinitiatives.org www.csjinitiatives.org Independent Living, Assisted Living, Long term care home for the aged. Gabriel Stoll, Admin.; Denise Gannon, CEO; Asstd. Annu.: 380; Staff: 229

TOLEDO

Franciscan Care Center - 4111 Holland Sylvania Rd., Toledo, OH 43623-2503 t) 419-882-6582 mdesantis@chilivingcomm.org www.homeishere.org An operating unit of CHI Living Communities, which is a subsidiary of CommonSpirit Health. Marisa DeSantis, Admin.; Asstd. Annu.: 308; Staff: 90

RETREAT HOUSES / RENEWAL CENTERS [RTR]

BELLEVUE

Sorrowful Mother Shrine - 4106 State Rte. 269, Bellevue, OH 44811-9793 t) 419-483-3435 sorrowfulmother@yahoo.com www.sorrowfulmothershrine.org Rev. Scott Kramer, C.PP.S., Rector; Rev. Harold C. Brown, C.PP.S.; Bro. Terrence Nufer, C.PP.S.;

CAREY

Our Lady of Consolation Retreat House - t) 419-396-7970 retreats@olcshrine.com www.olcshrine.com Bro. Tom Hercegovics, OFM Conv., Mgr.;

FREMONT

Our Lady of the Pines Retreat Center - 1250 Tiffin St., Fremont, OH 43420-3562 t) 419-332-6522 olprc@pinesretreat.org; heidiosborne@pinesretreat.org www.pinesretreat.org Sisters of Mercy Heidi Chew Osborne, Exec.;

TIFFIN

St. Francis Spirituality Center - 200 St. Francis Ave., Tiffin, OH 44883-3491 t) 419-443-1485 peace@franciscanretreats.org www.franciscanretreats.org Sisters of St. Francis, Tiffin. Katie Snitker, Admin.;

SHRINES [SHR]

CAREY

Basilica and National Shrine of Our Lady of Consolation - 315 Clay St., Carey, OH 43316 t) 419-396-7107 shrineoffice@olcshrine.com olcshrine.com Rev. Thomas Merrill, O.F.M.Conv., Rector; Rev. John Bamman, O.F.M.Conv., Assoc. Pst.; Rev. Xavier Goulet, O.F.M.Conv., In Res.; Rev. Conrad Sutter, O.F.M.Conv., In Res.;

SPECIAL CARE FACILITIES [SPF]

SANDUSKY

***Providence Residential Community Corporation** - 5055 Providence Dr., Sandusky, OH 44870 t) 419-624-1171 www.homeishere.org An operating unit of CHI Living Communities, which is a subsidiary of CommonSpirit Health. Seantell Amison, Admin.; Rebecca Hilton, Vice Pres., Mission Integration; Bed Capacity: 84; Asstd. Annu.: 119; Staff: 97

TIFFIN

St. Francis Home Inc. - 182 St. Francis Ave., Tiffin, OH 44883 t) 419-447-2723 sean.riley@stfrancishome.org www.stfrancistiffin.org Tyler Webb, Chair; Sean Riley, Exec.;

An asterisk (*) denotes an organization that has established tax-exempt status directly with the IRS and is not covered by the USCCB Group Ruling.

Diocese of Trenton

(Dioecesis Trentonensis)

MOST REVEREND DAVID M. O'CONNELL, C.M., J.C.D., D.D.

Bishop of Trenton; ordained May 29, 1982; appointed Coadjutor Bishop of Trenton June 4, 2010; consecrated July 30, 2010; appointed Tenth Bishop of Trenton December 1, 2010. Office: Chancery/Pastoral Center, 701 Lawrenceville Rd., Trenton, NJ 08648.

Chancery/Pastoral Center: 701 Lawrenceville Rd., Trenton, NJ 08648. T: 609-406-7400; F: 609-406-7412.

ESTABLISHED AUGUST 11, 1881.

Square Miles 2,156.

Legal Corporate Title: "The Diocese of Trenton."

Comprises four Counties in the State of New Jersey: Burlington, Mercer, Monmouth and Ocean.

For legal titles of parishes and diocesan institutions, consult the Chancery Office.

STATISTICAL OVERVIEW

Personnel

Bishop	1
Priests: Diocesan Active in Diocese	132
Priests: Diocesan Active Outside Diocese	5
Priests: Retired, Sick or Absent	78
Number of Diocesan Priests	215
Religious Priests in Diocese	32
Total Priests in your Diocese	247
Extern Priests in Diocese	3
Ordinations:	
Transitional Deacons	1
Permanent Deacons	5
Permanent Deacons in Diocese	188
Total Brothers	21
Total Sisters	39

Parishes

Parishes	97
With Resident Pastor:	
Resident Diocesan Priests	84
Resident Religious Priests	7
Without Resident Pastor:	
Administered by Priests	6
Professional Ministry Personnel:	
Brothers	8
Sisters	20
Lay Ministers	40

Welfare

Catholic Hospitals	1
Total Assisted	71,255
Health Care Centers	2
Total Assisted	1,996
Homes for the Aged	1
Total Assisted	150
Day Care Centers	11
Total Assisted	794
Specialized Homes	4
Total Assisted	1,153
Special Centers for Social Services	85
Total Assisted	300,989
Residential Care of Disabled	20
Total Assisted	111
Other Institutions	207
Total Assisted	4,895

Educational

Diocesan Students in Other Seminaries	12
Total Seminarians	12
Colleges and Universities	1
Total Students	1,962
High Schools, Diocesan and Parish	5
Total Students	3,418
High Schools, Private	6
Total Students	1,727
Elementary Schools, Diocesan and Parish	26
Total Students	8,038
Elementary Schools, Private	4
Total Students	676
Catechesis/Religious Education:	
Elementary Students	32,624
Total Students under Catholic Instruction	48,457
Teachers in Diocese:	
Sisters	7
Lay Teachers	755

Vital Statistics

Receptions into the Church:	
Infant Baptism Totals	5,558
Minor Baptism Totals	321
Adult Baptism Totals	131
Received into Full Communion	79
First Communions	5,292
Confirmations	5,890
Marriages:	
Catholic	1,050
Interfaith	188
Total Marriages	1,238
Deaths	5,621
Total Catholic Population	640,000
Total Population	2,130,044

LEADERSHIP

Chancery/Pastoral Center - t) 609-406-7400
Vicar General and Moderator of the Curia - Rev. Msgr. Thomas N. Gervasio;
Chancellor - Terry Ginther;
Episcopal Vicars - Rev. Edward H. Blanchett; Rev. Msgr. Joseph N. Rosie; Rev. Msgr. Dennis A. Apoldite;
Vicars Forane (Deans) - Rev. Msgr. Sam A. Sirianni; Rev. John P. Bambrick; Rev. Timothy J. Capewell;
Episcopal Master of Ceremonies - Rev. Carlo Calisin, Master of Ceremonies; Rev. Jean Felicien, Secy. to Bishop & Master of Ceremonies;
Executive Administrative Assistant to the Bishop - Grace Magee;
Records Analyst and Archivist - Tanya Taylor-Norwood;
College of Consultors - Rev. Msgr. Edward J. Arnister; Rev. Msgr. Thomas N. Gervasio; Rev. Msgr. Thomas J. Mullelly;
Episcopal Council - Rev. Msgr. Joseph N. Rosie; Rev. Msgr. Thomas N. Gervasio; Rev. Msgr. Thomas J. Mullelly;
Council of Deacons and Vicariate Representatives - Dcn. Gary L. Schmitt; Dcn. Peter F. Downing; Dcn. Tom Wadolowski;
Diocesan Finance Council - Most Rev. David M. O'Connell, C.M., Pres.; A. Kevin Cimei, CFO; Michael J. Castellano, Chair;
Censores Librorum - Rev. John P. Czahur; Rev. Pablo T. Gadenz; Rev. Michael J. Hall;

ADMINISTRATION

Chief Administrative Officer (CAO) - t) 609-403-7208 Joseph Bianchi;
Department of Human Resources - Angela Gitto, Dir.; Erica Armitage, Assoc. Dir. Benefits;
Department of Risk Management - t) 609-403-7189 Joseph Cahill, Dir.;

OFFICES AND DIRECTORS

Director of Vocations - Rev. Jason M. Parzynski, Dir.; Very Rev. Daniel F. Swift, Assoc. Dir. (Father_Dan@smmlparish.org); Rev. Garry Koch, Assoc. Dir.;
Office of Child & Youth Protection - Joseph Bianchi, Exec.; Margaret Dziminski, Assoc. Dir.; William Staub, Assoc. Dir.;
Office of Worship - Rev. Michael J. Hall, Dir.; Carolyn Norbut, Assoc. Dir.;

CANONICAL SERVICES

Office of Canonical Services and the Tribunal - t) 609-406-7411
Judicial Vicar - Rev. Oscar B. Sumanga;
Vice Chancellor - Rev. Jean Felicien, Vice Chancellor for Canonical Services;
Defenders of the Bond - Rev. Peter J. Alindogan (palindo@dioceseoftrenton.org); Dcn. Joseph A. Hannawacker;
Promoter of Justice - Rev. Peter J. Alindogan (palindo@dioceseoftrenton.org);
Tribunal Judges - Rev. Javier A. Diaz; Rev. Msgr. Edward J. Arnister; Rev. Msgr. John K. Dermond;
Secretary of the Tribunal and Notary - Evelyn Aguiar; Roseimelda Moore;

CLERGY AND RELIGIOUS SERVICES

Vicar for Clergy & Consecrated Life, Director of Seminarians - t) 609-403-7181 Rev. Msgr. Thomas J. Mullelly, Vicar;
Ministry of Clergy Personnel - t) 609-403-7181 Rev. Msgr. Thomas J. Mullelly, Vicar;
Ministry of Consecrated Life - t) 609-406-7409

COMMUNICATIONS

Office of Communications & Media - t) 609-403-7188 dotcomm@dioceseoftrenton.org Rayanne Bennett, Exec. Dir. & Diocesan Media Spokesperson (rbenne@dioceseoftrenton.org);
Department of Multimedia Production - t) 609-406-7402 Marianne Hartman, Dir. (mhartm@dioceseoftrenton.org);
Digitial/Social Media Manager - t) 609-403-7137 Rose O'Connor, Digital/Social Media Mgr.;
The Monitor Magazine - t) 609-406-7400 www.trentonmonitor.com Rayanne Bennett, Assoc. Publisher (rbenne@dioceseoftrenton.org); Mary Stadnyk, Assoc. Editor (mstadn@dioceseoftrenton.org);

EDUCATION

Department of Catholic Schools - t) 609-403-7149 Dr. Vincent De Paul Schmidt, Supt.; Bonnie Milecki, Assoc. Dir. Devel. & Oper.; Daniel O'Connell, Assoc. Dir. Curriculum & Instruction;

FINANCE

Chief Fiscal Officer (CFO) - t) 609-406-7440 A. Kevin Cimei;
Construction & Real Estate Commission - t) 609-403-7195 Scot Pirozzi, Chair;
Department of Cemeteries & Operation Services - t) 609-403-7210 Dcn. David O'Connor, Dir.;
St. Mary Cemetery & Mausoleum, Hamilton - t) 609-394-2017 Mary Beth Montgomery, Dir.;
Department of Computer Services - t) 609-403-7166 Anthony DeLorenzo, Dir.;
Department of Development - t) (609) 403-7218 Christine Prete, Dir.;
Department of Finance - t) 609-403-7120 Michael D'Angelo, Dir.;
Department of Property and Construction - t) 609-403-7195 Scot Pirozzi, Dir.;

PASTORAL SERVICES

Office of Pastoral Life and Mission - t) 609-403-7143 Terry Ginther, Exec. Dir.;
Campus Ministries - Terry Ginther, Exec. Dir.;
Aquinas Institute for Catholic Life - t) 609-924-1820 Rev. Zachary Swantek, Chap.;
Bede House - t) 609-771-0543 Rev. Christopher Colavito, Chap.;
Catholic Center - Monmouth University - t) 732-229-9300 Cristina D'Averso Collins, Campus Min.; Rev. Mark Nillo, Chap.;
Rider University Catholic Campus Ministry - t) 609-882-8077 Rev. Leandro B. Dela Cruz, Pst.;
Catholic Scouting - t) 732-458-0220 Rev. Michael A. Santangelo, Chap.;
Department of Catechesis (Catechetics, Sacraments of Initiation, & RCIA) - t) 609-406-7179 Denise Contino, Dir.;
Department of Evangelization & Family Life - Josue Arriola, Dir.; Rachel Hendricks, Respect Life Coord.; Peg Hensler, Assoc. Dir., Marriage & NFP;
Department of Pastoral Planning - t) 609-403-7143 Julianne Nicole Curreri, Data Analyst (jcurreri@DioceseofTrenton.org); Terry Ginther, Dir.;
Department of Youth & Young Adult Ministries - t) 609-403-7140 Daniel Waddington, Dir.;
Hispanic Initiatives - t) 609-403-7138 Sandra Lopez, Coord.;
Jail and Prison Ministries -

SOCIAL SERVICES

Office of Catholic Social Services - t) 609-403-7180 Brenda L. Rascher, Exec. Dir.;
Catholic Campaign for Human Development - t) 609-403-7180 Brenda L. Rascher, Dir.;
Catholic Charities - t) 609-394-5181 Marlene Lao'-Collins, Exec.;
Catholic Relief Services - t) 732-477-0028 Rev. Michael Kennedy, Dir.;
Holy Innocents Society - t) 732-267-3917 Patricia Hertz, Pres.;
Mercer County CYO - t) 609-396-8383 Thomas G. Mladenetz, Exec. (tom@cyomercer.org);
Mount Carmel Guild - t) 609-392-5159 information@mtcarmelguild.org www.mtcarmelguild.org Mary Inkrot, Exec.;
Parish Counseling Services - t) 609-403-7180 Brenda L. Rascher, Dir.;

MISCELLANEOUS / OTHER OFFICES

Charismatic Renewal - t) 732-671-0071 Rev. Jeffrey J. Kegley, Moderator;
Cursillo - t) 732-477-0028 Rev. Edward H. Blanchett, Moderator;
Francis House of Prayer - t) 609-877-0509 Sr. Marcella Springer, S.S.J., Dir. (fhop@verizon.net);
Legion of Mary - Rev. John J. Testa, Chap.;
Upper Room Spiritual Center - t) 732-922-0550 theupper-room.org Sr. Maureen Christensen, R.S.M., Dir.; Sr. Maureen Conroy, R.S.M., Dir.; Sr. Trudy Ahern, S.S.J., Dir. (office@theupper-room.org);

PARISHES, MISSIONS, AND CLERGY

STATE OF NEW JERSEY

ALLENTOWN

St. John - 1282 Yardville-Allentown Rd., Allentown, NJ 08501-1830 t) 609-259-3391 sjbrccre@gmail.com; stjohnallentown@optonline.net stjohnromancatholic.org Very Rev. Michael Wallack, Pst.; Dcn. Philip Clingerman; Dcn. Paul DeGrazia; Dcn. Joseph Hepp; Dcn. Michael V. Scannella; Lauren Walters, DRE; CRP Stds.: 430

ASBURY PARK

The Church of Mother of Mercy, Asbury Park, N.J. - 1212 First Ave., Asbury Park, NJ 07712 t) 732-776-7164 (CRP); 732-775-1056 bchiriboga@momapnj.org; lpopoca@momapnj.org www.momapnj.org Rev. Miguel Virella, S.V.D., Pst.; Rev. Paul Janvier, Assoc. Pst.; Rev. Brandon Mother Hiep Nguyen, S.V.D., Assoc. Pst.; Blanca Chiriboga, DRE; CRP Stds.: 235

Our Lady of Mt. Carmel School - (Grades K-8) First Ave. & Pine St., Asbury Park, NJ 07712 t) 732-775-8989 judeboyce@hotmail.com Sr. Jude Catherine Boyce, S.S.J., Prin.; Stds.: 189; Lay Tchrs.: 10

ATLANTIC HIGHLANDS

The Church of Our Lady of Perpetual Help-Saint Agnes, Atlantic Highlands, N.J. - 103 Center Ave., Atlantic Highlands, NJ 07716 t) 732-291-0272 kpost@olph-sta.org; church@olph-sta.org Rev. Jarlath Quinn, Pst.; Dcn. Robert J. Johnson; Mary McKelvey, DRE; CRP Stds.: 190

BARNEGAT

St. Mary - 747 W. Bay Ave., Barnegat, NJ 08005-0609; Mailing: P.O. Box 609, Barnegat, NJ 08005 t) 609-597-7600 (CRP); 609-698-5531 (Office); 609-597-8289 (Cemetery) donna@stmarybarnegat.com; info@stmarybarnegat.com www.stmarybarnegat.com Rev. Msgr. Kenard J. Tuzeneu, Pst.; Rev. Nestor Chavenia, Par. Vicar; Rev. Walter Andre Quiceno, Par. Vicar; Dcn. Frank Campione; Dcn. Philip Fiore; Dcn. Joseph A. Fiorillo; Dcn. Ronald Haunss; Dcn. Patrick Martin; Dcn. James Petrauskas; Dcn. Joseph A. Vivona; Dcn. Steven A. Wagner; Donna Ann Powers, DRE; CRP Stds.: 863

St. Mary of the Pines - 100 Bishop Ln., Manahawkin, NJ 08050

BAY HEAD

Sacred Heart - 751 Main Ave., Bay Head, NJ 08742 t) 732-899-1398 x1 shrcbh@comcast.net www.sacredheartbyhead.com Rev. Joseph G. Hlubik, Pst.; Rev. Joy T. Chacko, Par. Vicar; John Paglione, DRE; Marta B Barkhausen, Bus. Mgr.; CRP Stds.: 165

BAYVILLE

St. Barnabas - 33 Woodland Rd., Bayville, NJ 08721-0320; Mailing: P.O. Box I, Bayville, NJ 08721-0320 t) 732-269-2208 parishoffice@stbarnabasbayville.com www.stbarnabasbayville.com Rev. Carlos A. Florez, Admin.; Rev. Edward J. Griswold; Dcn. Robert Gay; Dcn. Stanley D. Kendrick; Dcn. Hector Casillas; CRP Stds.: 920

BELMAR

St. Rose - 603 Seventh Ave., Belmar, NJ 07719 t) 732-681-0512 x419 (CRP); 732-681-0512 x415 srdonna@strosebelmar.com; carol@strosebelmar.com strosebelmar.com Rev. Msgr. Edward J. Arnister, Pst.; Rev. Christopher James Dayton, Pst. Assoc.; Dcn. Richard J. Weber; Dcn. Robert Folinus; Sr. Donna D'Alia, DRE;

St. Rose School - (Grades K-8) 605 Sixth Ave., Belmar, NJ 07719 t) 732-681-5555 wroberts@srgs.org Gregory Guito, Prin.; Stds.: 306; Lay Tchrs.: 24

Convent - 610 Eighth Ave., Belmar, NJ 07719

BEVERLY

The Church of Jesus, the Good Shepherd - 805 Warren St., Beverly, NJ 08010 t) 856-461-9343 (CRP); 856-461-0100 m.gimello@jesusthegoodshepherd.org; info@jesusthegoodshepherd.org www.jesusthegoodshepherd.org Rev. Jorge Bedoya, Admin.; Rev. Rafael Esquen, Par. Vicar; Dcn. Richard K. Benner; Dcn. Gary L. Schmitt; Dcn. Eduardo Trani; Maria B. Gimello, DRE; CRP Stds.: 214

St. Joseph Church - (Worship Site)

BORDENTOWN

Parish of Mary, Mother of the Church, Bordentown N.J. - 45 Crosswicks St., Bordentown, NJ 08505 t) 609-291-8281 (CRP); 609-298-0261 mzola@mmotcp.org; calphonse@mmotcp.org www.mmotcp.org Rev. Martin O'Reilly, Pst.; Rev. Cesar R. Anson, Par. Vicar; Dcn. Lawrence W. Finn Sr.; Dcn. Gary T. Richardson; Dcn. Ronald V. Schwoebel; Dcn. Thomas F. Shea; Margaret Zola, DRE; CRP Stds.: 346

BRADLEY BEACH

Parish of St. Teresa of Calcutta, Bradley Beach, N.J. - 501 Brinley Ave., Bradley Beach, NJ 07720 t) 732-774-0456; 732-774-0456 x103 (CRP) saintteresa@stocp.org; faithformation@stocp.nj Rev. Erin Brown, Pst.; Dcn. Richard D. Coscarelli; Dcn. John Kopcak; Carol Freda, DRE; CRP Stds.: 167

BRICK

St. Dominic - 250 Old Squan Rd., Brick, NJ 08724 t) 732-840-1410 bwoodrow@dioceseoftrenton.org; nnahrebne@churchofstdominic.com stdominicsparish.com Rev. Brian P. Woodrow, Pst.; Rev. Michael T. McClane, Par. Vicar; Rev. Marian Kokorzycki, Par. Vicar; Rev. Joseph Gnarackatt, In Res.; Dcn. Damian Ayers; Dcn. Edward Buecker; Marge Moran, DRE; CRP Stds.: 400

St. Dominic School - (Grades PreK-8) t) 732-840-1412 etonkovich@stdomschool.org www.stdomschool.org Elizabeth Tonkovich, Prin.; Stds.: 442; Lay Tchrs.: 35

Epiphany - 615 Thiele Rd., Brick, NJ 08724 t) 732-458-0220 carol@churchofepiphany.org Rev. Michael A. Santangelo, Pst.; Dcn. Louis Commisso; Dcn. Michael Mullarkey; Dcn. Ron Nowak; CRP Stds.: 149

Epiphany Parish Hall - 621 Herbertsville Rd., Brick, NJ 08724

Visitation - 755 Mantoloking Rd., Brick, NJ 08723; Mailing: 730 Lynnwood Ave., Brick, NJ 08723-5397 t) 732-477-0028 info@visitationrcchurch.org www.visitationrcchurch.org Rev. Edward H. Blanchett, Pst.; Rev. Michael Kennedy, Par. Vicar; Dcn. Edward Fischer III; Dcn. Salvatore Vicari; Joanne Martone, DRE; CRP Stds.: 247

BROWNS MILLS

St. Ann - 22 Trenton Rd., Browns Mills, NJ 08015-3236 t) 609-893-3246 stannschurch22@hotmail.com stannschurch.org Rev. Krzysztof Pipa, S.V.D., Admin.; Rev. Pierre Claver Lunimbu, S.V.D., Par. Vicar; Dcn. Michael J. O'Brien; Dcn. Charles D. Raylman; CRP Stds.: 154

Deborah Heart & Lung Center - t) 609-893-6611

Aspen Hills - t) 609-726-7000

BURLINGTON

The Parish of St. Katharine Drexel, Burlington, N.J. - 223 E. Union St., Burlington, NJ 08016 t) 609-386-0163; 609-386-0152; 609-386-1645 x215 (CRP) kdelprato@stkatharinedrexel-nj.org; parish@stkatharinedrexel-nj.org www.stkatharinedrexel-nj.org Rev. Jerome Guld, Pst.; Dcn. Alexander A. Punchello Sr., RCIA Coord.; Dcn. Matthew V. Fung; Dcn. Walter J. Karpecik Jr.; Dcn. Alfred Pennise; Kathleen Del Prato, DRE; CRP Stds.: 171

St. Paul School - (Grades PreK-8) 250 James St., Burlington, NJ 08016 info@stpaulbrl.org stpaulbrl.org William Robbins, Prin.;

CINNAMINSON

St. Charles Borromeo - 2500 Branch Pike, Cinnaminson, NJ 08077; Mailing: P.O. Box 2220, Cinnaminson, NJ 08077 t) 856-829-9119 (DRE); 856-829-3322 mdore@pcscb.com; dkirk@pcscb.com www.scbcinnaminson.com Rev. Daniel E. Kirk, Pst.; Dcn. John Hvizdos; Dcn. Romeo B. Modelo Jr.; Dcn. Carl Sondeen; Michelle Dore, DRE; CRP Stds.: 517

St. Charles Borromeo School - (Grades PreK-8) t) 856-829-2778 mglass@scbpschool.com Kathryn Chesnut, Prin.;

COLTS NECK

St. Mary's - 1 Phalanx Rd., Colts Neck, NJ 07722 t) 732-780-2666 parishoffice@stmaryscoltsneck.org; religioused@stmaryscoltsneck.org www.stmaryscoltsneck.org Rev. Jeffrey E. Lee, Pst.; Julia Cullen, CRE; Rosemarie Farrow, CRE; Andrew J. Macirowski, Pst. Min./Coord.; Edwin Sevillano, Bus. Mgr.; CRP Stds.: 418

DELRAN

The Church of the Resurrection, Delran Township, N.J. - 260 Conrow Rd., Delran, NJ 08075; Mailing: P.O. Box 1099, Delran, NJ 08075 t) 856-461-6555 rich@resurrection2.org; parishoffice@resurrection2.org Rev. John C. Garrett, Pst.; Dcn. William E. Briggs; Dcn. Daniel J. Meehan; Dcn. Dennis J Taylor; Rich Scanlon, DRE; CRP Stds.: 93

EATONTOWN

St. Dorothea - 240 Broad St., Eatontown, NJ 07724 t) 732-542-0148 office@saintdorothea.org www.saintdorothea.org Rev. Michael D. Sullivan, Pst.; Rev. Andres Serna-Ocampo, Par. Vicar; Dcn. John A. Notaro, DRE; Dcn. Ilsoo P. Barng; CRP Stds.: 179

Immaculate Conception - 64 Broad St., Eatontown, NJ 07724 t) 732-389-3830; 732-439-3277 (CRP) eatoncatholic@eatoncatholic.org; hoonheui@optonline.net eatoncatholic.org Rev. Cha Yong (Paul) Lee, Admin.; Hoonhei Lee, DRE;

FAIR HAVEN

Church of the Nativity - 180 Ridge Rd., Fair Haven, NJ 07704 t) 732-741-1714 x10 carolynm@nativitychurchnj.org; claireh@nativitychurchnj.org nativitychurchnj.org Rev. Christopher P. Picollo, Pst.; Dcn. Paul Lang; Dcn. Sean P. Murphy; Claire L. Harbeck, Pst. Assoc.; John Hendrick, Bus. Mgr.; CRP Stds.: 863

FARMINGDALE

St. Catherine of Siena - 31 Asbury Rd., Farmingdale, NJ 07727-3531 t) 732-938-5375 frontoffice@sienachurch.org www.sienachurch.org Rev. Angelito Anarcon, Pst.; Dcn. Daniel C. Sakowski; Laura Randazzo, Bus. Mgr.; Kay Hetherington, DRE; CRP Stds.: 217

FORKED RIVER

St. Pius X - 300 Lacey Rd., Forked River, NJ 08731-3598 t) 609-693-0368 (CRP); 609-693-5107 info@churchofstpius.org; ccraft@churchofstpius.org churchofstpius.org Rev. Richard Basznianin, Pst.; Dcn. Louis (Gino) S. Esposito; Dcn. Philip T. Craft; Dcn. Earl Lombardo; Dcn. Anthony Martucci; Dcn. Tony Repice; Cynthia Craft, DRE; CRP Stds.: 426

FREEHOLD

Co-Cathedral of St. Robert Bellarmine - 61 Georgia Rd., Freehold, NJ 07728 t) 732-462-7429 receptionist@strobert.cc; mrussoniello@strobert.cc www.strobert.cc Rev. Msgr. Sam A. Sirianni, Rector; Rev. Brian T. Butch, Par. Vicar; Dcn. Henry J. Cugini; Dcn. Rolf B. Friedmann; Dcn. John Wedemeyer; Jennifer Elsensohn, Pst. Assoc.; Mark Russoniello, DRE; CRP Stds.: 1,087

St. Rose of Lima - 16 McLean St., Freehold, NJ 07728 t) 732-308-0215 (CRP); 732-462-0859 reled@stroseoflimachurch.org; parish@stroseoflimachurch.org www.stroseoflima.com Rev. James Conover, Pst.; Rev. Jorge Arias, O.P., Assoc. Pst.; Rev. Michael Brizio, I.M.C., Assoc. Pst.; Steven Olson, DRE; CRP Stds.: 672

St. Rose of Lima School - 51 Lincoln Pl., Freehold, NJ 07728 t) 732-462-2646 srpatriciadoyle@stroseoflima.com www.stroseoflimafreehld.com Sr. Patricia Doyle, Prin.;

HAINESPORT

Our Lady Queen of Peace - 1603 Marne Hwy., Hainesport, NJ 08036 t) 609-267-0230 x100 carol@olqponline.org; robyn@olqponline.org ourladyqop.org Rev. Joselito M. Noche, Pst.; Dcn. Lee Zito, Pst. Assoc.; Robyn Modugno, CRE; CRP Stds.: 99

HAMILTON

Our Lady of Sorrows-St. Anthony Parish - 3816 E. State St. Ext., Hamilton, NJ 08619 t) 609-587-4372 mfrancis@ols-sa.org; info@ols-sa.org www.ols-sa.org Rev. Msgr. Thomas N. Gervasio, Pst.; Rev. Pierre Michel Alabre, Assoc. Pst.; Rev. Daniel Gowen, Assoc. Pst.; Dcn. Joseph Jaruszewski; Dcn. Kevin J. O'Boyle; Dcn. Salvatore Petro; Mariyam Iqbal Francis, DRE; CRP Stds.: 220

Hamilton Grove -

Our Lady of Sorrows-St. Anthony Parish School - (Grades PreK-8) 3800 E. State St. Ext., Hamilton, NJ 08619 t) 609-587-4140 mtuohy@olsschool.us olsschool.us Maureen Tuohy, Prin.; Stds.: 191; Lay Tchrs.: 13

St. Raphael-Holy Angels Parish - 3500 S. Broad St., Hamilton, NJ 08610 t) 609-585-0542 (CRP); 609-585-7049 wpalmisano@srhap.org; parishoffice@srhap.org www.srhap.org Rev. Gene P. Daguplo, Pst.; Rev. Stephen Schuler, SVD, In Res.; Dcn. Richard Arcari; Dcn. David C. Colter; Dcn. Gregory J. Costa; Dcn. John Dunn; Dcn. Thomas Lavelle; Dcn. Salvatore Marcello; Dcn. William R. Palmisano, DRE; Dcn. Robert Tharp; Lori Hoos, Dir.; Elaine Welsh, Bus. Mgr.; CRP Stds.: 351

St. Raphael School - (Grades PreK-8) 151 Gropp Ave., Hamilton, NJ 08610 t) 609-585-7733 ann.cwirko@srsnj.org www.srsnj.org Ann M. Cwirko, Prin.;

Robert Wood Johnson University Hospital at Hamilton - One Hamilton Health Pl., Hamilton, NJ 08690

Care One Assisted Living at Hamilton - 1660 Whitehorse-Hamilton Sq. Rd., Hamilton, NJ 08690

Brookdale Hamilton - 1645 Whitehorse-Mercerville Rd., Hamilton, NJ 08619

St. Raphael Church - (Worship Site)

B Well Post Acute Care of Hamilton - 3 Hamilton Health Pl., Hamilton, NJ 08690

HAMILTON SQUARE

St. Gregory the Great - 4620 Nottingham Way, Hamilton Square, NJ 08690 t) 609-587-4877; 609-587-1131 x227 (CRP) webmaster@stgregorythegreatchurch.org; chouck@stgregorythegreat.org www.stgregorythegreatchurch.org Rev. Michael J. Hall, Pst.; Dcn. John A. DiLissio; Dcn. John R. Isaac; Dcn. Paul LaPlante; Dcn. Joseph E. Latini; Dcn. Joseph J. Moore Jr.; Dcn. Andrew A. Sabados Sr.; Sr. Carolyn Houck, M.P.F., DRE; Maureen G Cozzi, Bus. Mgr.; Rev. R. Joy Ballacillo, Par. Vicar; CRP Stds.: 638

St. Gregory the Great Academy - (Grades PreK-8) 4680 Nottingham Way, Hamilton Square, NJ 08690 jbriggs@stgregorythegreat.org; mrivera@stgregorythegreat.org www.stgregorythegreatacademy.org Dr. Jason C.

Briggs, Prin.; Michele L. Rivera, Vice Prin.; Stds.: 469; Sr. Tchrs.: 2; Lay Tchrs.: 30

Convent - 13 Stanley Dr., Robbinsville, NJ 08691

HIGHTSTOWN

St. Anthony of Padua - 251 Franklin St., Hightstown, NJ 08520-3223; Mailing: 156 Maxwell Ave., Hightstown, NJ 08520 t) 609-448-0141; 609-448-0141 x21 (CRP) info@stanthonychurch.org; education@stanthonychurch.org www.stanthony-hightstown.net Rev. Oscar B. Sumanga, Pst.; Viviana Bonilla, DRE; Dcn. Thomas Garvey; CRP Stds.: 441

HOLMDEL

St. Benedict - 165 Bethany Rd., Holmdel, NJ 07733-1699 t) 732-264-4712 x26 (CRP); 732-264-4712 x17 finance@stbenedictnj.org; parishoffice@stbenedictnj.org Rev. Garry Koch, Pst.; Rev. Augusto L. Gamalo, Par. Vicar; Dcn. John L. Clymore; Dcn. Richard L. Morris; Dcn. Raymond R. Pelkowski; Dcn. Paul Remick; Dcn. Stephen G. Scott; Ciro Saverino, Youth Min.; Fran DeMuria, Bus. Mgr.; CRP Stds.: 593

St. Benedict School - (Grades PreK-8) t) 732-264-5578 kdonahue@stbenedictnj.org Kevin Donahue, Prin.; Christine Keeling, Vice Prin.; Stds.: 446; Lay Tchrs.: 26

Church of Saint Catharine - 108 Middletown Rd., Holmdel, NJ 07733; Mailing: P.O. Box 655, Holmdel, NJ 07733 t) 732-842-3963; 732-758-8568 (CRP) parishoffice@stcatharine.net; mangelo@stcatharine.net www.stcatharine.net Rev. Patrick McPartland, Pst.; Dcn. Thomas J. DiCanio; Dcn. Michael Lonie; Michelle Angelo, DRE; CRP Stds.: 626

HOPEWELL

St. Alphonsus - 54 E. Prospect St., Hopewell, NJ 08525 t) 609-737-0122 x820 (CRP); 609-466-0332 parishoffice@stalphonsushopewell.org; llimongello@stjamespennington.org stalphonsushopewell.org Rev. Stephen Sansevere, Pst.; Lisa Limongello, DRE;

HOWELL

St. Veronica - 4215 Hwy. 9 N., Howell, NJ 07731 t) 732-364-4137 (CRP); 732-363-4200 sr.ann@stveronica.com; office@stveronica.com stveronica.com Rev. Peter J. Alindogan, Pst.; Rev. John O. Chang, Assoc. Pst.; Dcn. Charles Daye Jr.; Dcn. John J. Franey; CRP Stds.: 402

Mother Seton Academy - (Grades K-8) 4219 Hwy. 9 N., Howell, NJ 07731 t) 732-364-4130 kblazewicz@msaedu.org Kathleen Blazewicz, Prin.;

Convent - 4217 Hwy. 9 N., Howell, NJ 07731

St. William the Abbot - 2740 Lakewood-Allenwood Rd., Howell, NJ 07731 t) 732-840-3535 stwilliam@optonline.net www.stwilliamtheabbot.com Rev. Thomas F. Maher, Pst.; Dcn. Michael Abatemarco; Dcn. George A. Prevosti Jr.; Dcn. Kevin Smith; Dawn Cappetto, Admin.; CRP Stds.: 336

Geraldine Thompson Nursing Home - 2350 Hospital Rd., Allenwood, NJ 08720

JACKSON

St. Aloysius - 935 Bennetts Mills Rd., Jackson, NJ 08527 t) 732-370-0500; 732-370-1515 (Religious Ed) frbambrick@saintaloysiusonline.org saintaloysiusonline.org Rev. John P. Bambrick, Pst.; Rev. James Smith, Par. Vicar; Dcn. Uku Mannikus; Dcn. Rene Perez; Dcn. Vincent L. Rinaldi; Jennifer Petrillo, DRE; CRP Stds.: 472

Church of St. Monica - 679 W. Veteran's Hwy., Jackson, NJ 08527 t) 732-928-0279; 732-928-4038 (CRP) stmonicanj@yahoo.com; stmonicaccd@yahoo.com www.saintmonica.com Rev. Alexander Enriquez, Pst.; Karen Badach, CRE; Dcn. Christian Knoebel; CRP Stds.: 161

KEANSBURG

St. Ann - 311 Carr Ave., Keansburg, NJ 07734 t) 732-787-5744 (CRP); 732-787-0315 stannkeansburg@gmail.com stannkeansburg.org Rev. Richard C Vila, Pst.; Theresa Kelley, DRE; CRP Stds.: 121

St. Ann Child Care Center - 121 Main St., Keansburg, NJ 07734

Bayshore Senior Health, Education & Recreation Center - 100 Main St., Keansburg, NJ 07734 t) 732-495-2454

***Project Paul** - 211 Carr Ave., Keansburg, NJ 07734

KEYPORT

Parish of Our Lady of Fatima, Keyport, N.J. - 376 Maple Pl., Keyport, NJ 07735 t) 732-264-0304 (CRP); 732-264-0322 nlopez@fatimakeyport.org; abiagianti@fatimakeyport.org www.fatimakeyport.org Rev. Rene Mauricio Pulgarin, Pst.; Dcn. Glen L. Mendonca; Dcn. Donald M. Policastro; Anne Biagianti, Parish Catechetical Leader; CRP Stds.: 177

LAKEHURST

St. John - 619 Chestnut St., Lakehurst, NJ 08733 t) 732-657-2348 (CRP); 732-657-6347 office@stjohnlakehurst.com www.stjohnlakehurst.com/ Rev. James O'Neill, Pst.; Mary Ann Dempkowski, DRE; CRP Stds.: 131

LAKEWOOD

The Parish of Our Lady of Guadalupe - 43 Madison Ave., Lakewood, NJ 08701 t) 732-363-0139 x241 (CRP); 732-363-0139 parish@olglakewood.org; fromprep@olglakewood.org www.olglakewood.org/ Rev. Guilherme A. Andrino, S.V.D., Pst.; Rev. Jan Pastuszczak, SVD, Par. Vicar; Rev. Pelagio Calambia Pateno, S.V.D., Par. Vicar; Dcn. Silverius Galvan; Rev. Pedro L. Bou, S.V.D., In Res.; Dcn. Victor Gomez; Dcn. William Malone; Dcn. James G. McGrath; Dcn. John Cullinane; CRP Stds.: 905

Holy Family Church - 1139 E. County Line Rd., Lakewood, NJ 08701; Mailing: 43 Madison Ave. - Attn: Katie, Lakewood, NJ 08701 smloffice@smlparish.net

LAVALLETTE

The Church of St. Pio of Pietrelcina, Lavallette, N.J. - 103 Washington Ave., Lavallette, NJ 08735 t) 732-793-7291 office@stpioparish.com www.stpioparish.com Rev. Joseph G. Hlubik, Pst.; Rev. Joy T. Chacko, Par. Vicar; Marta B Barkhausen, Bus. Mgr.;

LAWRENCEVILLE

St. Ann - 1253 Lawrenceville Rd., Lawrenceville, NJ 08648 t) 609-882-6491 x106 (Bus. Mgr.); 609-882-1212 (CRP) ldelacruz@churchofsaintann.net; gmacc@churchofsaintann.net churchofsaintann.net Rev. Leandro B. Dela Cruz, Pst.; Dcn. James Scott; Dcn. Frank Golazeski; Gary Maccaroni, Pst. Assoc.; Sr. Pat McGinley, S.S.J., Pst. Assoc.; CRP Stds.: 405

St. Ann School - (Grades PreK-8) 34 Rossa Ave., Lawrenceville, NJ 08648 t) 609-882-8077 dschramke@churchofsaintann.net Salvatore Chiaravalloti, Prin.; Donald Schramke, Bus. Mgr.; Stds.: 219; Lay Tchrs.: 12

LINCROFT

St. Leo the Great - 50 Hurley's Ln., Lincroft, NJ 07738 t) 732-530-0717 (CRP); 732-747-5466 faithformation@stleothegreat.com; parish@stleothegreat.com Rev. John T. Folchetti, Pst.; Dcn. John Senkewicz; Dcn. Richard W. Tucker; Dcn. Edward H. Wilson; Joseph Manzi, Admin.; Gary Arkin, DRE; Paula DeStefano, DRE; CRP Stds.: 634

St. Leo the Great School - (Grades K-8) 550 Newman-Springs Rd., Lincroft, NJ 07738 t) 732-741-3133 saintleothegreatschool.com Cornelius Begley, Prin.; Stds.: 629; Lay Tchrs.: 81

LITTLE EGG HARBOR TWP

St. Theresa - 450 Radio Rd., Little Egg Harbor Twp, NJ 08087 t) 609-296-2504 x224 (CRP); 609-296-2504 info@sttheresa450.org sttheresa450.org Rev. John Large, Pst.; Joana Scmidt, DRE; Cathy Mazanek, Bus. Mgr.; CRP Stds.: 236

LONG BEACH TOWNSHIP

St. Francis of Assisi - 4700 Long Beach Blvd., Long Beach Township, NJ 08008-3926 t) 609-494-8813 fdispigno@stfrancislbi.org www.stfrancisparishlbi.org/ Rev. Francis Di Spigno, O.F.M., Pst.; Rev. Scott Brookbank, O.F.M., Assoc. Pst.; Rev. John Frambes, O.F.M., Assoc. Pst.; Rev. Andrew Reitz, O.F.M., Assoc. Pst.; Dcn. Robert Cunningham; Sr. Patricia McNiff, O.S.F., Pst. Assoc.; Judy Clayton, DRE; Michelle Beck, Liturgy Dir.; CRP Stds.: 215

St. Thomas Aquinas - 2nd & Atlantic, Beach Haven, NJ 08008

St. Clare - 56th & Long Beach Blvd., Loveladies, NJ 08008

St. Thomas of Villanova - 13th & Long Beach Blvd., Surf City, NJ 08008

LONG BRANCH

The Church of Christ the King, Long Branch, N.J. - 380 Division St., Long Branch, NJ 07740 t) 732-222-3216 christthekingparish@comcast.net; mary@cklb.org Rev. Javier A. Diaz, Pst.; Amelia Flego, DRE; CRP Stds.: 214

MANALAPAN

St. Thomas More - 186 Gordons Corner Rd., Manalapan, NJ 07726 t) 732-456-3232 (CRP); 732-446-6661 pat.colontino@moremercy.org; vincenza.magliano@moremercy.org moremercy.org Rev. Juan Daniel Peirano, Pst.; Rev. Msgr. Peter Kochery, In Res.; Dcn. Keith J. Casey; Dcn. Michael Lee Foster; Dcn. Matthew P. Nicosia; Dr. Patricia Colontino, DRE; Vincenza Magliano, Bus. Mgr.; CRP Stds.: 1,011

MANASQUAN

St. Denis - 90 Union Ave., Manasquan, NJ 08736 t) 732-223-1161 (CRP); 732-223-0287 office@stdenisccd.com; st.denis@verizon.net www.churchofstdenis.org Rev. William J. P. Lago, Pst.; Dcn. George R. Kelder Jr.; Dcn. Gary J. Pstrak; Eileen Ziesmer, Pst. Assoc.; CRP Stds.: 548

Our Lady Star of the Sea Chapel - 544 E. Main St., Manasquan, NJ 08736

MAPLE SHADE

Our Lady of Perpetual Help - 236 E. Main St., Maple Shade, NJ 08052 t) 856-667-8850 x107 (CRP); 856-667-8850 x100; 856-667-8850 x102 frwilson@olphparish.com; jklarmann@olphparish.com Rev. Joel R. Wilson, Pst.; Dcn. Fernando Linka; Dcn. Ronald S. Meyers; John Klarmann, DRE; CRP Stds.: 127

MARLBORO

St. Gabriel - 100 N. Main St., Marlboro, NJ 07746 t) 732-946-4487 mmykityshyn@stgabrielsparish.org; info@stgabrielsparish.org Rev. Eugene J. Roberts, Pst.; Rev. Joy T. Chacko, Assoc. Pst.; Dcn. Lester Owens; Dcn. Richard G. Roenbeck; Dcn. Richard Scotti; Mary Mykityshyn, DRE; CRP Stds.: 843

MARLTON

St. Isaac Jogues - 349 Evesboro-Medford Rd., Marlton, NJ 08053 t) 856-797-0999; (856) 235-6555 (CRP) saintisaacs@stisaacjogues.org; rfoffice@stisaacjogues.org www.stisaacjogues.org Rev. Vicente Magdaraog, Par. Vicar; Rev. Phillip C. Pfleger, Pst.; Rev. Michael G. Dunn, Par. Vicar; Dcn. Joseph DeRosa; Dcn. David O'Connor; Sr. Mary Kay Kelley, S.S.J., DRE; CRP Stds.: 220

St. Joan of Arc - 100 Willow Bend Rd., Marlton, NJ 08053 t) 856-983-7575 (CRP); 856-983-0077 x311 theresa.segin@stjoans.org; jessica.donohue@stjoans.org www.stjoans.org Rev. Msgr. Richard D. LaVerghetta, Pst.; Rev. John Michael Patilla, Par. Vicar; Dcn. Jeffrey DeFrehn; Dcn. Barry Tarzy; Jessica Donohue, DRE; CRP Stds.: 826

St. Joan of Arc School - (Grades K-8) 101 Evans Rd., Marlton, NJ 08053 t) 856-983-0774 p.pycik@stjoansk-8.org stjoansk-8.org Sr. Patricia Pycik, S.S.J., Prin.; Stds.: 345; Lay Tchrs.: 23

Convent - 99 Evans Rd., Marlton, NJ 08053

MATAWAN

St. Clement - 172 Freneau Ave., Matawan, NJ 07747 t) 732-566-3616 tsweeney@stclementmatawan.org; admin@stclementmatawan.org www.stclementmatawan.org Rev. Thomas M. Vala, Pst.; Thomas Sweeney, DRE; CRP Stds.: 388

MEDFORD

St. Mary of the Lakes - 40 Jackson Rd., Medford, NJ 08055 t) 609-654-8208 x110 (Office)

skraemer@smlparish.org www.smlparish.org/ Very Rev. Daniel F. Swift, Pst.; Rev. Roy Ballacillo, Assoc. Pst.; Dcn. Richard Lutomski; Linda T Xerri, DRE; CRP Stds.: 437

St. Mary of the Lakes School - (Grades PreK-8) 196 Rte. 70, Medford, NJ 08055 t) 609-654-2546 arash@smlschool.org Amy Rash, Prin.;

St. Vincent DePaul Society-Medford - 1 Jones Rd., Medford, NJ 08055 t) 609-953-0021 James (Jim) Dwyer, Pres.; Joel Martin, Treas.;

MIDDLETOWN

St. Catherine - 110 Bray Ave., Middletown, NJ 07748; Mailing: 130 Bray Ave., Middletown, NJ 07748 t) 732-787-1318 (Office); 732-769-6262 (CRP) stcathek1@aol.com www.stcathek.org Rev. Daniel Hesko, Pst.; Dcn. John G. McGrath; Dcn. John C. Orlando; Carol Ann Mulkeen, DRE; Julia Fehlhaber, Bus. Mgr.; CRP Stds.: 225

St. Mary - 19 Cherry Tree Farm Rd., Middletown, NJ 07748 t) 732-671-0071 pegodun@gmail.com; edonohue@stmarychurchnj.org Rev. Jeffrey J. Kegley, Pst.; Rev. Jordan McConway, Par. Vicar; Rev. Mark Nillo, Par. Vicar; Dcn. Georgi Chemaly; Dcn. Martin K. McMahon; Dcn. Carlo Squicciarini; Margaret Dunne, DRE; CRP Stds.: 1,069

St. Mary School - (Grades PreSchool-8) 538 Church St., Middletown, NJ 07748 t) 732-671-0129 cpalmer@stmaryes.org stmaryes.org Craig Palmer, Prin.;

MILLSTONE TOWNSHIP

St. Joseph - 91 Stillhouse Rd., Millstone Township, NJ 08510 t) 732-792-2270 frmikestjoseph@optonline.net; jeanstjoseph@optonline.net www.stjosephmillstone.org Rev. Michael P. Lang, Pst.; Dcn. Chris Chandonnet; Genevieve Semanchick, CRE; CRP Stds.: 520

MONMOUTH BEACH

Church of the Precious Blood - 72 Riverdale Ave., Monmouth Beach, NJ 07750 t) 732-222-4756 office@churchofthepreciousblood.org www.churchofthepreciousblood.org Rev. Michael D. Sullivan, Pst.; Rev. Andres Serna-Ocampo, Par. Vicar; Dcn. John A. Notaro, DRE; CRP Stds.: 247

MOORESTOWN

Our Lady of Good Counsel - 42 W. Main St., Moorestown, NJ 08057 t) 856-235-7136 (School); 856-235-0181 parish@olgcnj.org www.olgcnj.org Rev. James J. Grogan Sr., Pst.; Brian Kasilowski, Vice Prin.; Rev. John A. Bogacz, Assoc. Pst.; Dcn. John F. Bertagnolli; Dcn. Edward A. Heffernan; Dcn. Thomas F. Kolon; Jim Flanagan, Bus. Mgr.; Cynthia Robinson, DRE; CRP Stds.: 640

Our Lady of Good Counsel School - (Grades PreK-8) 23 W. Prospect St., Moorestown, NJ 08057 t) 856-235-7885 school@olgc.me www.olgc.me Carla Chiarelli, Prin.;

MOUNT HOLLY

Sacred Heart - 260 High St., Mount Holly, NJ 08060-1404 t) 609-267-0209 secretary@parishofsacredheart.org; ministry@parishofsacredheart.org www.parishofsacredheart.org Rev. John P. Czahur, Pst.; Dcn. James Casa; Dcn. John F. Hoefling; Dcn. Charles M. Moscarello; Dcn. Stanley Orkis; Dcn. William Rowley; Barbara Kane, DRE; Mary Verme, RCIA Coord.; CRP Stds.: 281

Sacred Heart School - 250 High St., Mount Holly, NJ 08060 t) 609-267-1728 schooloffice@sacred-heart-school.org www.sacred-heart-school.org Kathryn Besheer, Prin.;

Burlington County Hospital Extended Care Center - t) 609-367-0700

MOUNT LAUREL

St. John Neumann - 560 Walton Ave., Mount Laurel, NJ 08054 t) 856-235-6555 (CRP); 856-235-1330 mike.rocco@sjnmtl.org; sjnreled@gmail.com www.sjnmtl.org Rev. Phillip C. Pfleger, Pst.; Rev. Michael G. Dunn, Assoc. Pst.; Dcn. Joseph Barbara; Dcn. Thomas J. Knowles; Sr. Mary Kay Kelley, S.S.J., DRE; CRP Stds.: 212

NEPTUNE

Holy Innocents - 3455 W. Bangs Ave., Neptune, NJ 07753; Mailing: P.O. Box 806, Neptune, NJ 07754-0806 t) 732-922-4242 x20 parishoffice@holyinnocentschurch.net www.holyinnocentschurch.net Rev. H. Todd Carter, Pst.; Rev. Cesar A. Rubiano, Chap.; Dcn. Robert L. Cerefice; Dcn. John Klincewicz; Fran Burke, CRE; CRP Stds.: 200

PENNINGTON

St. James - 115 E. Delaware Ave., Pennington, NJ 08534 t) 609-730-0122 (CRP); 609-737-0122 parishoffice@stjamespennington.org thecatholiccommunityofhopewellvalley.org/ Rev. Stephen Sansevere, Pst.; Rev. Jean Felicien, Par. Vicar; Rev. Msgr. Thomas J. Mullelly, In Res.; Dcn. Patrick R. Brannigan; Dcn. Richard Currie; Dcn. William Moore Hank; Dcn. Richard J. Hobson; Lisa Limongello, DRE; CRP Stds.: 353

POINT PLEASANT

St. Martha - 3800 Herbertsville Rd., Point Pleasant, NJ 08742 t) 732-295-3630; 732-295-3630 x35 (CRP) business@saintmartha.net; admin@saintmartha.net www.saintmartha.net Rev. David S. Swantek, Pst.; Dcn. John E Barrett; Dcn. Robert Golden; Georgina Kotz, DRE; Nancy A. Dormanski, Bus. Mgr.; CRP Stds.: 267

POINT PLEASANT BEACH

St. Peter's - 406 Forman Ave., Point Pleasant Beach, NJ 08742 t) 732-899-4839 (CRP); 732-892-0049 religioused@saintpetersonline.org; pdeoliveira@dioceseoftrenton.org www.stpetersbytheshore.org Rev. Robert Schlageter, O.F.M.Conv., Pst.; Rev. Nick Rokitka, O.F.M.Conv., Assoc. Pst.; Rev. Brenann Joseph Farleo, O.F.M.Conv., In Res.; Rev. Richard Rossell, O.F.M.Conv., In Res.; CRP Stds.: 248

St. Peter's School - (Grades K-8) 415 Atlantic Ave., Point Pleasant Beach, NJ 08742 t) 732-892-1260 info@stpschool.org www.stpschool.org Tracey Kobrin, Prin.; Stds.: 152; Lay Tchrs.: 10

Convent - 401 Atlantic Ave., Point Pleasant Beach, NJ 08742

PRINCETON

St. Paul - 216 Nassau St., Princeton, NJ 08542 t) 609-924-1743; 609-524-0509 (CRP) mheucke@stpaulsofprinceton.org; lsarubbi@stpaulsofprinceton.org www.stpaulsofprinceton.org Rev. Miguel Valle, Admin.; Rev. Carlo Calisin, Assoc. Pst.; Dcn. Frank Crivello; Dcn. Jim Knipper; Laura Sarubbi, DRE; CRP Stds.: 368

St. Paul School of Princeton - 218 Nassau St., Princeton, NJ 08542 t) 609-921-7587 rkilleen@spsprinceton.org www.spsprinceton.org Ryan Killeen, Prin.;

PRINCETON JCT.

Church of St. David the King - 1 New Village Rd., Princeton Jct., NJ 08550 t) 609-275-7111 x310 (CRP); 609-275-7111 parishoffice@stdavidtheking.com; lff@stdavidtheking.com www.stdavidtheking.com Rev. Timothy J. Capewell, Pst.; Dcn. Thomas Baker; Dcn. Roger Dinella; Nanci Bachman, Dir. Faith Formation; Carol Sullivan, Music Min.; CRP Stds.: 145

RED BANK

St. Anthony Church - 121 Bridge Ave., Red Bank, NJ 07701 t) 732-747-0813 officemgr@stanthonysofredbank.net www.stanthonysofredbank.net Served by the priests and brothers of the Red Bank Oratory of St. Philip Neri (Community-in-Formation). Rev. Alberto W. Tamayo, Pst.; Rev. Nicholas Dolan, Par. Vicar; Bro. Daniel Bower; Bro. Donald J. Ronning Jr.; CRP Stds.: 400

St. James - 94 Broad St., Red Bank, NJ 07701 t) 732-747-6006 (CRP); 732-741-0500 religioused@stjames-redbank.com; saintjames@sjredbank.org www.sjredbank.org Rev. Msgr. Joseph N. Rosie, Pst.; Rev. Daison Areepparampil, Assoc. Pst.; Rev. Vicente Magdaraog, Assoc. Pst.; Dcn. Bryan P. Davis; Fillie Duchaine, DRE; CRP Stds.: 218

Preschool - t) 732-933-1041

St. James Grammar School - (Grades PreK-8) 30 Peters Pl., Red Bank, NJ 07701 t) 732-741-3363 office@mysaintjames.com mysaintjames.com Joann Giordano, Prin.; Catherine Golden, Vice Prin.; Stds.: 475; Lay Tchrs.: 43

Red Bank Catholic High School - 112 Broad St., Red Bank, NJ 07701 t) 732-747-1774 alabat@redbankcatholic.com Robert Abatemarco, Prin.; Stds.: 684; Lay Tchrs.: 63; Sr. Tchrs.: 2

Sisters of Mercy - 25 Drummond Pl., Red Bank, NJ 07701

Riverview Hospital -

RIVERTON

Sacred Heart - 103 Fourth St., Riverton, NJ 08077 t) 856-829-1848 (CRP); 856-829-0090 sacredheartriverton@comcast.net www.shcriverton.org Rev. Charles M. Schwartz, Pst.; Dcn. Robert J. Bednarek; Dcn. Joseph M. Donadieu; Dcn. Kenneth W. Heilig; Dcn. Michael J. Stinsman; Susan Barnett, Music Min.; Bonnie Campbell, CRE; CRP Stds.: 299

RUMSON

Church of the Holy Cross of Sea Bright, NJ - 30 Ward Ave., Rumson, NJ 07760 t) 732-842-0348 webmaster@holycrossrumson.org; skabash@holycrossrumson.org www.holycrossrumson.org Rev. Michael Manning, Pst.; Lori La Plante, Pst. Assoc.; Sally Kabash, DRE; CRP Stds.: 244

Holy Cross School - (Grades PreK-8) 40 Rumson Rd., Rumson, NJ 07760 schooloffice@holycrossrumson.org www.holycrossschoolrumson.org Dr. Mark DeMareo, Prin.;

SEA GIRT

St. Mark - 215 Crescent Pkwy., Sea Girt, NJ 08750 t) 732-449-6364 (CRP); 732-449-6364 rectory@stmarkseagirt.com www.stmarkseagirt.com Rev. Msgr. Sean P. Flynn, Pst.; Rev. Carlos Castilla, Par. Vicar; Diana Zuna, DRE; CRP Stds.: 324

SEASIDE PARK

St. Junipero Serra, Seaside Park - 50 E. St., Seaside Park, NJ 08752; Mailing: Box A, Seaside Park, NJ 08752 t) 732-793-0041 mlorentsen@stjuniperoserra.org www.stjuniperoserra.org Friar Michael Lorentsen, O.F.M.Conv., Pst.; Friar Anthony Kall, O.F.M.Conv., In Res.; Renee Casadonte, DRE; CRP Stds.: 174

SPRING LAKE

St. Catharine-St. Margaret - 215 Essex Ave., Spring Lake, NJ 07762 t) 732-449-5765; 732-449-4424 x305 (CRP) contactus@scsmsl.org scsmsl.org Rev. Damian J. McElroy, Pst.; Rev. Gregg Abadilla, Par. Vicar; Rev. William M. Dunlap, Par. Vicar; Rev. Charles B. Weiser, Par. Vicar; Dcn. Edward Jennings; Dcn. John L. Little; Dcn. Mark McNulty; Tamara Sablom, DRE; Erin Quinn, Bus. Mgr.; CRP Stds.: 328

St. Catharine School - (Grades PreK-8) 301 2nd Ave., Spring Lake, NJ 07762 rdougherty@stcatharineschool.net www.stcatharineschool.net Robert Dougherty, Prin.; Stds.: 308; Sr. Tchrs.: 1; Scholastics: 19; Lay Tchrs.: 19

Convent - 211 Essex Ave., Spring Lake, NJ 07762

St. Margaret Church - 302 Ludlow Ave., Spring Lake, NJ 07762

TABERNACLE

Holy Eucharist - 520 Medford Lakes Rd., Tabernacle, NJ 08088 t) 609-268-8383 x106 (CRP); 609-268-8383 dremaley@holyeucharist.org; hec@holyeucharist.org www.holyeucharist.org Rev. Andrew Jamieson, Pst.; Dcn. Joseph DeLuca; Dcn. Kenneth S. Domzalski; Regan Peiffer, Music Min.; Donna Remaley, DRE; CRP Stds.: 538

TINTON FALLS

St. Anselm - 1028 Wayside Rd., Tinton Falls, NJ 07712 t) 732-493-4411; 732-493-4411 x103 (CRP) stanselm2@gmail.com; franstanselm@gmail.com www.stanselm.com Rev. Eugene B. Vavrick, Pst.; Fran

Burke, DRE; CRP Stds.: 378

TITUSVILLE

St. George - 1370 River Rd., Titusville, NJ 08560; Mailing: P.O. Box 324, Titusville, NJ 08560 t) 609-737-2015 parishoffice@stgeorgetitusville.org www.thecatholiccommunityofhopewellvalley.org The Catholic Community of Hopewell Valley which includes St. George Church. Rev. Stephen Sansevere, Pst.; Rev. Jean Felicien, Par. Vicar; Dcn. Lawrence E. Gallagher; Dcn. Michael J. Riley; Lisa Limongello, DRE; CRP Stds.: 64

TOMS RIVER

St. Joseph - 685 Hooper Ave., Toms River, NJ 08753 t) 732-349-0018; 732-349-0018 x2236 (CRP) parish@stjosephtomsriver.org www.stjosephtomsriver.org Rev. G. Scott Shaffer, Pst.; Rev. Selvam J. Asirvatham, Par. Vicar; Rev. Neiser Cardenas, Par. Vicar; Dcn. Francis J. Babuschak; Dcn. Robert M. Barnes; Dcn. Gerard Luongo; Dcn. Frank J. McKenna; Dcn. Patrick J. Stesner Sr.; Dcn. Michael A. Taylor; Gina Corrao, Music Min.; Catherine Werner, Youth Min.; CRP Stds.: 1,000

St. Joseph School - (Grades K-8) 711 Hooper Ave., Toms River, NJ 08753 t) 732-349-2355 sjgs.nj.k12us.com Madeline Kinloch, Prin.; Stds.: 611; Scholastics: 2; Lay Tchrs.: 34

St. Gertrude - Ocean & Central Aves., Island Heights, NJ 08732 (June-Sept.)

St. Justin - 975 Fischer Blvd., Toms River, NJ 08753 t) 732-270-3797 (CRP); 732-270-3980 mkreder@dioceseoftrenton.org www.stjustin.org Dcn. James L. Campbell; Dcn. Frederick C. Ebenau Sr.; Dcn. James Gillespie; Rev. Mark Kreder, Pst.; Ellen Noble, DRE; CRP Stds.: 419

St. Luke - 1674 Old Freehold Rd., Toms River, NJ 08755 t) 732-286-2222; 732-505-0108 (CRP) kmuzzio@stlukestomsriver.org www.stlukestomsriver.org Rev. Robert S. Grodnicki, Pst.; Dcn. Joseph DeMaria; Dcn. Robert B. Pladek; Kathleen Muzzio, Bus. Mgr.; Teresa Frassetto, CRE; Thomas Hinz, Music Min.; CRP Stds.: 253

St. Maximilian Kolbe - 130 Saint Maximilian Ln., Toms River, NJ 08757 t) 732-914-0300 stmaximiliankolbechurch@gmail.com www.stmaximiliankolbechurch.com Dcn. Thomas Yondolino; Rev. Stephen M. Piga, Pst.; Dcn. Stanley Kwiatek;

TRENTON

St. Mary Cathedral - 151 N. Warren St., Trenton, NJ 08608; Mailing: 149 N. Warren St., Trenton, NJ 08608 t) 609-396-8447 smc.office@smc-trenton.org saintmaryscathedral-trenton.org Rev. Msgr. Joseph L. Roldan, Rector; Rev. Marcin D. Kania, Par. Vicar; Rev. Roberto C Padilla, Par. Vicar; Dcn. Luis Ramos; Dcn. Benito Torres; Ericka Rodriguez, DRE; CRP Stds.: 160

The Church of the Incarnation-St. James - 1545 Pennington Rd., Trenton, NJ 08618 t) 609-882-2860 isjparishoffice@gmail.com www.incarnationstjames.org Rev. Stanley DeBoe, O.S.S.T., Pst.; Dcn. Joseph A. Hannawacker; Dcn. Thomas H. Rivella; Dcn. James A. Alessi; Sr. Lucy Ptak, L.S.I.C., DRE; Ronald W. Kraemer Sr., Bus. Mgr.; CRP Stds.: 47

The Church of the Korean Martyrs - 1130 Brunswick Ave., Trenton, NJ 08638 t) 609-695-6300 ckm6300@gmail.com CRP Stds.: 19

St. Hedwig - 872 Brunswick Ave., Trenton, NJ 08638 t) 609-396-9068 sthedwig@comcast.net Rev. Jacek W. Labinski, Pst.; Dcn. Barry Zadworny; Dorothy Zadworny, DRE; CRP Stds.: 215

St. Joseph - 540 N. Olden Ave., Trenton, NJ 08638 t) 609-218-6834 (CRP); 609-394-5757 erickaro2010@gmail.com; elena@sjctrenton.com Rev. Msgr. Joseph L. Roldan, Pst.; Ericka Rodriguez, DRE; CRP Stds.: 180

Our Lady of the Angels Parish - 19 Bayard St., Trenton, NJ 08611; Mailing: 21-23 Bayard St., Trenton, NJ 08611 t) 609-695-6089 olaparish@olanj.org Rev. Carlos Aguirre, Pst.; Dcn. Guido Mattozzi; CRP Stds.: 350

Parish of the Sacred Heart, Trenton, N.J. - 343 S. Broad St., Trenton, NJ 08608 t) 609-393-2801 x102 reled@trentonsacredheart.org; frdennis@trentonsacredheart.org www.trentonsacredheart.org Rev. Msgr. Dennis A. Apoldite, Pst.; Rev. Charles Muorah, Assoc. Pst.; Mary Tovar, DRE; CRP Stds.: 62

St. Vincent de Paul - 555 Yardville Allentown Rd., Trenton, NJ 08620 t) 609-400-3422 (CRP); 609-585-6470 rectory@svdpnj.org; johanna@svdpnj.org Rev. Stanley Krzyston, Pst.; Rev. Adam Midor, Assoc. Pst.; Rev. Rogatus Mpeka, Assoc. Pst.; Johanna Kraemer, DRE; CRP Stds.: 42

UNION BEACH

Holy Family - 727 Hwy. 36 W., Union Beach, NJ 07735; Mailing: P.O. Box 56, Keyport, NJ 07735 t) 732-264-7043 (CRP); 732-264-1484 hreligioused@verizon.net; hfrccubnj@aol.com www.holyfamily.us Rev. Matthew J. Pfleger, Pst.; Rev. Francis Cheruparambil, V.C., Assoc. Pst.; Dcn. James J. Neubauer; Grace Fagan, Bus. Mgr.; CRP Stds.: 226

WEST END

St. Michael - 800 Ocean Ave., West End, NJ 07740 t) 732-483-0360 x3 (CRP); 732-222-8080 kconnelly@stmichaelnj.com; mvalan@stmichaelnj.com www.stmichaelnj.com Rev. Cyril Johnson (India), Par. Vicar; Kevin Connelly, DRE; Rev. John Butler, Pst.; CRP Stds.: 240

WEST LONG BRANCH

Parish of Our Lady of Hope, West Long Branch, N.J. - 254 Wall St., West Long Branch, NJ 07764 t) 732-222-1424; 732-222-8686 (CRP) etoft@saintjeromeschool.org; stjerome@ladyofhopeparish.org ladyofhopeparish.org Rev. Sheldon Amasa, Pst.; Dcn. Louis E. Jakub; Sr. Elizabeth Toft, M.P.F., DRE; CRP Stds.: 133

St. Jerome School - (Grades PreK-8) 250 Wall St., West Long Branch, NJ 07764 edalessio@filippiniusa.org saintjeromeschool.org Elizabeth Dalessio, Prin.; Stds.: 266; Sr. Tchrs.: 1; Lay Tchrs.: 16

Convent - 250A Wall St., West Long Branch, NJ 07764 t) 732-222-2016 Elizabeth Dalessio, Prin.; Sr. Angelina Pelliccia, Supr.;

WEST TRENTON

Our Lady of Good Counsel - 137 W. Upper Ferry Rd., West Trenton, NJ 08628 t) 609-883-9005 (CRP); 609-882-3277 rectoryoffice@olgcc.net; olgc.re.wt@gmail.com www.olgcc.net Rev. Ariel Robles, Pst.; Brenda O'Callaghan, Dir.; Dcn. Steven K. Szmutko; CRP Stds.: 45

WHITING

Church of St. Elizabeth Ann Seton - 30 Schoolhouse Rd., Whiting, NJ 08759 t) 732-350-5001 parishoffice@easeton.org; ldowning@easeton.org www.seaswhiting.org Rev. Pasquale A. Papalia, Pst.; Rev. Evarist Kabagambe, Par. Vicar; Dcn. Peter F. Downing; Dcn. Kyran J. Purcell; Dcn. Joseph Rider; Dcn. Robert F. Scharen; Linda Quinn, Bus. Mgr.; Lori Downing, DRE; CRP Stds.: 59

WILLINGBORO

Corpus Christi - 63 Sylvan Ln., Willingboro, NJ 08046 t) 609-877-5322 ccnj@mycorpuschristichurch.com www.ccnj.church Rev. John J. Testa, Pst.; Dcn. Michael J. Hagan; CRP Stds.: 40

Convent - 71 Sylvan Ln., Willingboro, NJ 08046

WRIGHTSTOWN

Parish of St. Isidore the Farmer, New Egypt, N.J. - 28 Monmouth Rd., Wrightstown, NJ 08562; Mailing: 76 Evergreen Rd., Parish Office, New Egypt, NJ 08533 t) 609-758-2153; 609-758-3535 (CRP) information@saintisidoreparish.church; cgrant@saintisidoreparish.church saintisidoreparish.church Rev. Robert Holtz, Pst.; Mark Hoeler, Music Min.; Celeste Grant, DRE; Edward G Taddei Jr., Bus. Mgr.; CRP Stds.: 313

SCHOOLS: PRESCHOOL THRU HIGH SCHOOL

SCHOOLS

STATE OF NEW JERSEY

PRINCETON

Princeton Academy of the Sacred Heart - (PRV) (Grades K-8) 1128 Great Rd., Princeton, NJ 08540 t) 609-921-6499 adugan@princetonacademy.org www.princetonacademy.org Boys. Alfred Dugan III, Headmaster; Ellen Dowling, Librn.; Stds.: 180; Lay Tchrs.: 25

Stuart Country Day School of the Sacred Heart - (Grades PreK-12) 1200 Stuart Rd., Princeton, NJ 08540 t) 609-921-2330 admissions@stuartschool.org; pfagin@stuartschool.org stuartschool.org Patty L. Fagin, Headmaster; Stds.: 302; Lay Tchrs.: 59

HIGH SCHOOLS

STATE OF NEW JERSEY

BELMAR

Saint Rose High School - (DIO) (Grades 9-12) 607 Seventh Ave., Belmar, NJ 07719 t) 732-681-2858 jtonero@srhsnj.com www.srhsnj.com John Tonero, Prin.; Stds.: 391; Lay Tchrs.: 41

DELRAN

Holy Cross Preparatory Academy - (PRV) (Grades 9-12) 5035 Rte. 130 S., Delran, NJ 08075 t) 856-461-5400 dmoffa@hcprep.org hcprep.org David Moffa, Prin.; Stds.: 295; Lay Tchrs.: 22

HOLMDEL

St. John Vianney High School - (DIO) (Grades 9-12) 540-A Line Rd., Holmdel, NJ 07733-1697 t) 732-739-0800 kane@sjvhs.org www.sjvhs.org Margaret Kane, Prin.; Richard Lamberson, Vice Prin.; Steven DiMezza, Pres.; Stds.: 847; Lay Tchrs.: 41

LAWRENCEVILLE

Notre Dame High School - (PAR) (Grades 9-12) 601 Lawrence Rd., Lawrenceville, NJ 08648 t) 609-882-7900 duff@ndnj.org www.ndnj.org Joanna Barlow, Prin.; Lisa Lenihan, Vice Prin.; Eleanor MacIsaac, Vice Prin.; Kenneth Jennings, Pres.; Stds.: 892; Lay Tchrs.: 70

LINCROFT

Christian Brothers Academy - (PRV) (Grades 9-12) 850 Newman Springs Rd., Lincroft, NJ 07738 t) 732-747-1959 president@cbalincroftnj.org www.cbalincroftnj.org Sean Nunan, Admin.; Maureen Szablewski, Admin.; Cornelius Begley, Prin.; R. Ross Fales, Pres.; Sylvia McInerney, Librn.; Stds.: 850; Pr. Tchrs.: 1; Bro. Tchrs.: 5; Lay Tchrs.: 75

RED BANK

Red Bank Catholic High School - (PAR) 112 Broad St., Red Bank, NJ 07701 t) 732-747-1774 falcok@redbankcatholic.com www.redbankcatholic.org Karen Falco, Prin.; Robert Abatemarco, Pres.;

TOMS RIVER

Donovan Catholic - (PAR) (Grades 9-12) 711 Hooper Ave., Toms River, NJ 08753 t) 732-349-8801 jkelly@donovancatholic.org www.donovancatholic.org Jillian Kelly, Prin.; Stds.: 591; Scholastics: 2; Lay Tchrs.: 38

TRENTON

Villa Victoria Academy - (PRV) (Grades 6-12) 376 W. Upper Ferry Rd., Trenton, NJ 08628 t) 609-882-1700 srlesley@villavictoria.org; srlillian@villavictoria.org www.villavictoria.org (Girls) Sr. Lesley Draper, M.P.F., Prin.; Sr. Lillian Harrington, Pres.; Stds.: 92; Sr. Tchrs.: 2; Lay Tchrs.: 16

INSTITUTIONS LOCATED IN DIOCESE

CAMPUS MINISTRY / NEWMAN CENTERS [CAM]

PRINCETON

The Aquinas Institute for Catholic Life at Princeton University - 134 Nassau St., Ste. 300, Princeton, NJ 08542 t) 609-924-1820 aquinas@princeton.edu; tuchez@princeton.edu princetoncatholic.org Rev. Zachary Swantek, Chap.;

Bede House, College of New Jersey - 492 Ewingville Rd., Trenton, NJ 08638 t) 609-771-0543 ejb81333@gmail.com Rev. Erin Brown, Chap.;

Catholic Center at Monmouth University - 16 Beechwood Ave., West Long Branch, NJ 07764 t) 732-229-9300 cdaverso@monmouth.edu mucatholic.com Rev. Mark Nillo, Chap.; Cristina D'Averso-Collins, Campus Min.;

Emmaus House, Rider University - 2116 Lawrenceville Rd., Trenton, NJ 08648 t) 609-896-0394 daverso@rider.edu Carlo Calisin, Chap.; Cristina D'Averso-Collins, Campus Min.;

Georgian Court University - 900 Lakewood Ave., Lakewood, NJ 08701 t) 732-364-2200 x600 ksmith@georgian.edu Jeffrey Shaffer, Dir.;

CATHOLIC CHARITIES [CCH]

TRENTON

Catholic Charities - 383 W. State St., Trenton, NJ 08618; Mailing: P.O. Box 1423, Trenton, NJ 08607-1423 t) 609-394-5181 mlaocollins@cctrenton.org catholiccharitiestrenton.org Marlene Lao'-Collins, Exec.; Susan Loughery, Exec.; Debbra Elko, Exec.; Geeta Bhanot, Dir.; Jean Furdella, Dir.; Jennifer Leip, Dir.; Mary Pettrow, Dir.; Joseph Rizziello, Dir.; Arnold Valentin Jr., Dir.; Dr. Lisa Merritt, Exec.; Asstd. Annu.: 11,091; Staff: 591

Behavioral Health Services Burlington County - 25 Ikea Dr., Westampton, NJ 08060 t) 609-267-9339 jrizziello@cctrenton.org

Behavioral Health Services Mercer County - 10 Southard St., Trenton, NJ 08609 t) 609-396-4557 sloughery@cctrenton.org; jrizziello@cctrenton.org

Children & Family Services Mercer County - 55 N. Clinton Ave., Trenton, NJ 08609 t) 609-394-7680 mpettrow@cctrenton.org Services for victims and perpetuators of family violence. Mary Pettrow, Dir.;

Children & Family Services Monmouth/Ocean Counties - 145 Maple Ave., Red Bank, NJ 07701 t) 732-747-9660 mpettrow@cctrenton.org Mary Pettrow, Dir.;

Community Services - 450-460 Veterans Dr., Burlington, NJ 08016 t) 856-764-6940 avalentin@cctrenton.org Arnold Valentin Jr., Dir.;

Community Services (Mercer) - 132 N. Warren St., Trenton, NJ 08608 t) 609-394-8847 avalentin@cctrenton.org Arnold Valentin Jr., Dir.;

Community Services (Ocean) - 200 Monmouth Ave., Lakewood, NJ 08701 t) 732-363-5322 avalentin@cctrenton.org Arnold Valentin Jr., Dir.;

Providence House Domestic Violence Services - 595 Rancocas Rd., Westampton, NJ 08060 t) 856-824-0599 mpettrow@cctrenton.org Services to women and children in danger of physical abuse. Mary Pettrow, Dir.;

Providence House Domestic Violence Services (Ocean) - 88 Schoolhouse Rd., Ste. 1, Whiting, NJ 08759 t) 732-350-2120 mpettrow@cctrenton.org www.catholiccharitiestrenton.org Mary Pettrow, Dir.;

COLLEGES & UNIVERSITIES [COL]

LAKEWOOD

Georgian Court University - 900 Lakewood Ave., Lakewood, NJ 08701-2697 t) 732-987-2200 president@georgian.edu www.georgian.edu Joseph R. Marbach, Pres.; Janice Warner, Provost; Stds.: 1,962; Lay Tchrs.: 95

CONVENTS, MONASTERIES, AND RESIDENCES FOR WOMEN [CON]

ASBURY PARK

Missionaries of Charity - 144 Ridge Ave., Asbury Park, NJ 07712 t) 732-775-1101 michelle@cancungetaways.com Sr. Franslily M.C., Supr.; Srs.: 4

CHESTERFIELD

Monastery of Saint Clare - 150 White Pine Rd., Chesterfield, NJ 08515 t) 609-324-2638 mvarleyosc@verizon.net www.poorclaresofnewjersey.com Srs.: 12

HARVEY CEDARS

Maris Stella Retreat and Conference Center - 7201 Long Beach Blvd., Harvey Cedars, NJ 08008; Mailing: Box 3135, Harvey Cedars, NJ 08008 t) 609-494-1152 mmorleysc@gmail.com Sisters of Charity of St. Elizabeth, Convent Station. Sr. Patricia Dotzauer, S.C., Admin.; Sr. Mary Morley, S.C., Admin.; Srs.: 2

OCEAN

Emmaus House - 5 McKinley Dr., Ocean, NJ 07712 t) 732-493-2516 bernateh@aol.com emmausheartspace.homesteadcloud.com Sr. Margaret Ann Conlon, SC, Admin.; Srs.: 6

TRENTON

Villa Victoria Academy Convent - 376 W. Upper Ferry Rd., Trenton, NJ 08628 t) 609-883-0064 srlillian@villavictoria.org; srlesley@villavictoria.org www.villavictoria.org Religious Teachers Filippini. Sr. Carolyn Houck, M.P.F., In Res.; Srs.: 10

WICKATUNK

Convent of the Sisters of Good Shepherd - 160 Conover Rd., Wickatunk, NJ 07765; Mailing: P.O. Box 300, Wickatunk, NJ 07765 t) 732-946-7877 Sisters of Good Shepherd, Province of New York. Srs.: 5

ENDOWMENTS / FOUNDATIONS / TRUSTS [EFT]

DELRAN

Lancer Fund - c/o Holy Cross Preparatory Academy, 5035 Rte. 130 S., Delran, NJ 08075 t) 609-970-3121 sciortips@verizon.net Peter Sciortino, Contact;

EATONTOWN

Christian Brothers Retirement and Continuing Care Trust - 444A Rte. 35 S., Eatontown, NJ 07724-2200 t) 732-380-7926 froehlich@fscdena.org Bro. Timothy Froehlich, F.S.C., Treas.;

FSC DENA Endowment Trust - 444A Rte. 35 S., Eatontown, NJ 07724-2200 t) 732-380-7926 froehlich@fscdena.org Bro. Timothy Froehlich, F.S.C., Treas.;

FSC DENA Real Estate Trust - 444A Rte. 35 S., Eatontown, NJ 07724-2200 t) 732-380-7926 juliano@fscdena.org Bro. Joseph Juliano, F.S.C., Secy.;

LAWRENCEVILLE

The Foundation of Morris Hall/St. Lawrence, Inc. - 2381 Lawrenceville Rd., Lawrenceville, NJ 08648 t) 609-896-9500 x2215 tboyle@slrc.org www.slrc.org

TRENTON

Diocese of Trenton Charitable Trust for Aged, Infirm and Disabled Priests - 701 Lawrenceville Rd., Trenton, NJ 08648 t) 609-406-7440 kcimei@dioceseoftrenton.org A. Kevin Cimei, Admin.;

Diocese of Trenton Endowment Trust - Catholic Social Services - 701 Lawrenceville Rd., Trenton, NJ 08648 t) 609-406-7440 kcimei@dioceseoftrenton.org A. Kevin Cimei, Admin.;

Diocese of Trenton Endowment Trust - Diocesan Assistance for Parishes - 701 Lawrenceville Rd., Trenton, NJ 08648 t) 609-406-7440 kcimei@dioceseoftrenton.org A. Kevin Cimei, Admin.;

Diocese of Trenton Endowment Trust for Catholic Charities - 701 Lawrenceville Rd., Trenton, NJ 08648 t) 609-406-7440 kcimei@dioceseoftrenton.org A. Kevin Cimei, Admin.;

Diocese of Trenton Endowment Trust for Catholic Education and Religious Formation - 701 Lawrenceville Rd., Trenton, NJ 08648 t) 609-406-7440 kcimei@dioceseoftrenton.org A. Kevin Cimei, Admin.;

Diocese of Trenton Endowment Trust for Seminary and Diaconate Formation - 701 Lawrence Rd., Trenton, NJ 08648 t) 609-406-7440 kcimei@dioceseoftrenton.org A. Kevin Cimei, Admin.;

***Foundation for Student Achievement, Inc.** - 701 Lawrenceville Rd., Trenton, NJ 08648 t) 609-406-7440 kcimei@dioceseoftrenton.org A. Kevin Cimei, Admin.;

HOSPITALS / HEALTH SERVICES [HOS]

TRENTON

St. Francis Medical Center - 601 Hamilton Ave., Trenton, NJ 08629 www.stfrancismedical.com Affiliate of Trinity Health System

MISCELLANEOUS [MIS]

ASBURY PARK

Mercy Center, Inc. - 1106 Main St., Asbury Park, NJ 07712 t) 732-774-9397 kguadagno@mercycenternj.org mercycenternj.org Ministry of the Sisters of Mercy. Kim Guadagno, Dir.;

EATONTOWN

District of Eastern North America Ministry Corporation - 444A Rte. 35 S., Eatontown, NJ 07724-2200 t) 732-380-7926 juliano@fscdena.org Benjamin Ventresca Jr., Chair; Bro. Robert John Schaefer Jr., F.S.C., Pres.; Bro. Timothy Froehlich, F.S.C., Trustee; Bro. Joseph Juliano, F.S.C., Trustee; James Logan, Trustee;

FSC DENA Real Estate Holding Corporation - 444A Rte. 35 S., Eatontown, NJ 07724-2200 t) 732-380-7926 juliano@fscdena.org Bro. Joseph Juliano, F.S.C., Secy.; Bro. Timothy Froehlich, F.S.C., Treas.;

Saint John Baptist De La Salle of New York, Inc. - 444A Rte. 35 S., Eatontown, NJ 07724 t) 732-380-7926 x103 Bro. Joseph Juliano, F.S.C., Secy.;

HAMILTON

***Visitation Home, Inc.** - 2271 Route 33 Suite 105, Hamilton, NJ 08690; Mailing: P.O. Box 11242, Hamilton, NJ 08620 t) 609-585-2151 denise817@optonline.net Denise Reil, Dir.;

LAWRENCEVILLE

***Center for FaithJustice** - 24 Rossa Ave., Lawrenceville, NJ 08648 t) 609-498-6216 speddicord@faithjustice.org faithjustice.org Stephanie J. Peddicord, Pres.;

Morris Hall/St. Lawrence, Inc. - 1 Bishops' Dr., Lawrenceville, NJ 08648-2050 t) 609-896-0006 cdill@morrishall.org www.morrishall.org Caralee Dill, Admin.;

Morris Hall - 1 Bishops Dr., Lawrenceville, NJ 08648 t) (609) 896-0006 x2602

Our Lady of the Rosary Chapel - 1 Bishops' Dr., Lawrenceville, NJ 08648-2050 t) 609-896-0006 info@morrishall.org www.morrishall.org Rev. Angelo Amaral, Chap.;

LINCROFT

Christian Brothers of Lincroft, NJ, Inc. - 854 Newman Springs Rd., Lincroft, NJ 07738-1698 t) 732-747-1959 x128 Bro. Ralph Montedoro, F.S.C., Dir.;

Christian Brothers, St. La Salle Auxiliary - 850 Newman Springs Rd., Lincroft, NJ 07738-1698; Mailing: P.O. Box 238, Lincroft, NJ 07738-1698 t) 732-842-4359 cards@dlsaux.org; donahue@fscdena.org dlsaux.org Bro. Joseph Juliano, F.S.C., Secy.;

LaSalle Lincroft, Inc. - 800 Newman Springs Rd., Lincroft, NJ 07728-0238 t) (732) 380-7926 juliano@fscdena.org

PRINCETON

Opus Dei - Mercer House, 34 Mercer St., Princeton, NJ 08540 t) 609-497-9448 mercerhousepriest@gmail.com www.mercerhouseprinceton.org/ Prelature of the Holy Cross and Opus Dei Rev. Joseph Thomas, Chap.;

TOMS RIVER
Holy Redeemer Visiting Nurse Agency, Inc. - 1228 Rte. 37 W., Toms River, NJ 08755 t) 732-240-2449 pobrien@holyredeemer.com www.holyredeemer.com Patricia O'Brien, Pres.;
TRENTON
New Jersey Catholic Conference - 149 N. Warren St., Trenton, NJ 08608 t) 609-989-1120 info@njcatholic.org www.njcatholic.org His Eminence Joseph Tobin, C.Ss.R., Pres.;

MONASTERIES AND RESIDENCES FOR PRIESTS AND BROTHERS [MON]

EATONTOWN
Brothers of the Christian Schools District of Eastern North America, Inc. (FSC DENA) - 444A Rte. 35 S., Eatontown, NJ 07724-2200 t) 732-380-7926 juliano@fscdena.org www.fscdena.org Bro. Robert John Schaefer Jr., F.S.C., Prov.; Bro. Frank Byrne, F.S.C., Prov. Asst.; Bro. Jules Knight, F.S.C., Prov. Asst.; Bro. Timothy Froehlich, F.S.C., Treas.; Bro. Joseph Juliano, F.S.C., Dir., Admin.; Bro. Robert Wickman, F.S.C., Prov. Del., Min. Governing Bds.; James Logan, Dir., Office for Mission & Min.;
Christian Brothers of Frederick - 444A Rte. 35 S., Eatontown, NJ 07724-2200 t) 732-380-7926 juliano@fscdena.org Bro. Joseph Juliano, F.S.C., Secy.; Bro. Timothy Froehlich, F.S.C., Treas.;
La Salle Provincialate Inc. - 444A Rte. 35 S., Eatontown, NJ 07724-2200 t) 732-380-7926 juliano@fscdena.org Brothers of the Christian Schools. Bro. Joseph Juliano, F.S.C., Secy.;
LINCROFT
De La Salle Hall - 810 Newman Springs Rd., Lincroft, NJ 07738 t) 732-530-9470 lackes@juno.com Brothers Licensed Nursing Home. Bro. Charles Lackes, F.S.C., Dir.; Brs.: 26
TRENTON
Villa Vianney - 2301 Lawrenceville Rd., Trenton, NJ 08648 t) 609-219-0177 tboyle@slrc.org Morris Hall/St. Lawrence, Inc. Rev. Msgr. R. Vincent Gartland, In Res.; Rev. Angelo Amaral, Chap.; Rev. Msgr. Ronald J. Bacovin, In Res.; Rev. Michael J. Burns, In Res.; Rev. Daniel Cahill, In Res.; Rev. Msgr. John K. Dermond, In Res.; Rev. Douglas A Freer, In Res.; Rev. Richard Gallagher, In Res.; Rev. Alejandro Gronifillo, In Res.; Rev. Raymond E. Hughes, In Res.; Rev. Msgr. Casimir H. Ladzinski, In Res.; Rev. Stanley P. Lukaszewski, In Res.; Rev. Brian J. McCormick, In Res.; Rev. Msgr. Joseph R. Punderson, In Res.; Rev. Albert Ricciardelli, In Res.; Rev. Msgr. Hugh F. Ronan, In Res.; Rev. Msgr. Ralph W. Stansley, In Res.; Rev. Msgr. Gregory D. Vaughan, In Res.; Rev. H. Brendan Williams, In Res.; Priests: 29

NURSING / REHABILITATION / CONVALESCENCE / ELDERLY CARE [NUR]

LAWRENCEVILLE
Morris Hall-Saint Lawrence, Inc., St. Mary's Residence & Assisted Living - 1 Bishops' Dr., Lawrenceville, NJ 08648-2050 t) 609-896-0006 www.morrishall.org Toni Rembas, Admin.; Asstd. Annu.: 150; Staff: 40

PRESCHOOLS / CHILDCARE CENTERS [PRE]

LONG BEACH TOWNSHIP
St. Francis of Assisi Day Care Center - 4700 Long Beach Blvd., Long Beach Township, NJ 08008 t) 609-494-8861 wsaunders@stfrancislbi.org stfranciscenterlbi.org Katie Opauski, Dir.; Stds.: 132; Lay Tchrs.: 18

RETREAT HOUSES / RENEWAL CENTERS [RTR]

ALLENTOWN
Francis House of Prayer - 84 Walnford Rd., Allentown, NJ 08501 t) 609-877-0509 fhop@verizon.net www.fhop.org Sr. Marcella Springer, S.S.J., Dir.;
LONG BRANCH
San Alfonso Retreat House - 755 Ocean Ave., Long Branch, NJ 07740; Mailing: P.O. Box 3098, Long Branch, NJ 07740 t) 732-222-2731 info@sanalfonsoretreats.org www.sanalfonsoretreats.org Rev. John Collins, C.Ss.R., Dir.; Rev. Andrew Costello, C.Ss.R, Retreat Staff; Rev. John McGowan, C.Ss.R., Retreat Staff; Rev. Kevin J. O'Neil, C.Ss.R., Retreat Staff; Rev. Edmund Faliskie, C.Ss.R., Retreat Staff; Rev. Eugene Grohe, C.Ss.R., In Res.;
NEPTUNE
The Upper Room Spiritual Center - 3455 W. Bangs Ave. - Bldg. 2, Neptune, NJ 07753 t) 732-922-0550 office@theupper-room.org www.theupper-room.org Sr. Trudy Ahern, S.S.J., Dir.; Sr. Maureen Christensen, R.S.M., Dir.; Sr. Maureen Conroy, R.S.M., Dir.;
SOUTH MANTOLOKING
St. Joseph by the Sea Retreat House - 400 Rte. 35 N., South Mantoloking, NJ 08738 t) 732-892-8494 sjbsea@comcast.net www.sjbsea.org Sr. Brunilda Ramos, M.P.F., Dir.;
TRENTON
Morning Star House of Prayer - 312 W. Upper Ferry Rd., Trenton, NJ 08628 t) 609-882-2766 morningstarh@comcast.net morningstarprayerhouse.org Sr. Josephine Aparo, M.P.F., Dir.;

SPECIAL CARE FACILITIES [SPF]

LAWRENCEVILLE
Morris Hall/Saint Lawrence, Inc. - 2381 Lawrenceville Rd., Lawrenceville, NJ 08648 t) 609-896-9500 tboyle@slrc.org www.slrc.org St. Lawrence Rehabilitation Center. Thomas E. Boyle, CEO; Bed Capacity: 116; Asstd. Annu.: 1,941; Staff: 375
Morris Hall/Saint Lawrence, Inc. - 1 Bishops' Dr., Lawrenceville, NJ 08648-2050 t) 609-896-0006 cdill@morrishall.org www.morrishall.org St. Joseph's Nursing Center, Skilled Nursing Care Facility for the Chronically Ill. Caralee Dill, Admin.; Bed Capacity: 60; Asstd. Annu.: 55; Staff: 40
MorrisHall/Saint Lawrence Inc. - MorrisHall Meadows - t) 609-896-9500 dhanley@slrc.org www.slrc.org Darlene Hanley, CEO;
RED BANK
Collier Group Home - 180 Spring St., Red Bank, NJ 07701 t) 732-842-8337 mkale@collieryouthservices.org www.collieryouthservices.org Sanctuary certified, trauma informed care provided to females ages 14-18. Sponsored by the Sisters of the Good Shepherd. Maureen Kale, Dir.; Bed Capacity: 10; Asstd. Annu.: 13; Staff: 15
Collier House - 386 Maple Pl., Keyport, NJ 07735 t) 732-264-3222
WICKATUNK
Collier Youth Services, Collier School - 160 Conover Rd., Wickatunk, NJ 07765 t) 732-946-4771 info@collieryouthservices.org www.collieryouthservices.org Sr. Deborah M. Drago, L.C.S.W., Exec.; Asstd. Annu.: 200; Staff: 170
Kateri Day Camp - t) 732-946-9694 kstackhouse@collieryouthservices.org www.katericenter.org Children 5-13 years old Karen Stackhouse, Dir.;

An asterisk (*) denotes an organization that has established tax-exempt status directly with the IRS and is not covered by the USCCB Group Ruling.

Diocese of Tucson

(Dioecesis Tucsonensis)

MOST REVEREND EDWARD J. WEISENBURGER

Bishop of Tucson; ordained December 19, 1987; appointed Bishop of Salina February 6, 2012; consecrated and installed Bishop of Salina at Sacred Heart Cathedral May 1, 2012; appointed Bishop of Tucson October 3, 2017; installed as Seventh Bishop of Tucson November 29, 2017. Pastoral Center, 192 S. Stone Ave., Bldg. #2, Tucson, AZ 85701.

Chancery Office: 192 S. Stone Ave., Bldg. #2, Tucson, AZ 85701. Mailing Address: P.O. Box 31, Tucson, AZ 85702. T: 520-838-2500.
www.diocesetucson.org
diocese@diocesetucson.org

ESTABLISHED A VICARIATE-APOSTOLIC 1868.

Square Miles 42,707.

Erected by His Holiness Pope Leo XIII, May 8, 1897.

Comprises the Counties of Cochise, Gila, Greenlee, Graham, La Paz, Pima, Pinal, Santa Cruz and Yuma in the State of Arizona.

For legal titles of parishes and diocesan institutions, consult the Chancery Office.

STATISTICAL OVERVIEW

Personnel
Bishop......1
Auxiliary Bishops......1
Priests: Diocesan Active in Diocese......62
Priests: Diocesan Active Outside Diocese......2
Priests: Retired, Sick or Absent......31
Number of Diocesan Priests......95
Religious Priests in Diocese......69
Total Priests in your Diocese......164
Extern Priests in Diocese......32
Ordinations:
Diocesan Priests......1
Transitional Deacons......5
Permanent Deacons in Diocese......158
Total Brothers......25
Total Sisters......88

Parishes
Parishes......78
With Resident Pastor:
Resident Diocesan Priests......42
Resident Religious Priests......18
Without Resident Pastor:
Administered by Priests......4
Administered by Deacons......1
Missions......34

Welfare
Day Care Centers......1
Total Assisted......9,900
Specialized Homes......2
Total Assisted......500
Special Centers for Social Services......8
Total Assisted......5,500
Residential Care of Disabled......1
Total Assisted......43
Other Institutions......2
Total Assisted......170,100

Educational
Diocesan Students in Other Seminaries......9
Total Seminarians......9
High Schools, Diocesan and Parish......1
Total Students......258
High Schools, Private......5
Total Students......2,184
Elementary Schools, Diocesan and Parish......19
Total Students......3,966
Catechesis / Religious Education:
High School Students......1,795
Elementary Students......6,068
Total Students under Catholic Instruction......14,280
Teachers in Diocese:
Brothers......8
Sisters......20
Lay Teachers......557

Vital Statistics
Receptions into the Church:
Infant Baptism Totals......2,396
Minor Baptism Totals......251
Adult Baptism Totals......166
Received into Full Communion......168
First Communions......2,653
Confirmations......2,142
Marriages:
Catholic......382
Interfaith......47
Total Marriages......429
Deaths......2,504
Total Catholic Population......300,000
Total Population......1,450,000

LEADERSHIP

Bishop - t) 520-838-2500 Most Rev. Edward J. Weisenburger;

Vicar General & Moderator of the Curia - t) 520-838-2500 www.diocesetucson.org Rev. John P. Arnold (jarnold@diocesetucson.org);

Episcopal Vicar for Hispanic Affairs - t) 520-624-7409 stjohnsoffice@netzero.com Rev. Msgr. Raul P. Trevizo, Vicar;

Episcopal Vicar for Retired Priests - t) 480-982-2929 office@stgeorgeaj.com Rev. Msgr. Domencio C. Pinti, Vicar;

Chancellor - t) 520-838-2521 Anne Terry Morales (amorales@diocesetucson.org);

Judicial Vicar - t) 520-838-2516 Rev. Manuel Viera, O.F.M. (mviera@diocesetucson.org);

Vicar for International Priests - t) 520-586-3394 olol@ololparish.org www.ololparish.org Rev. Martin B. Atanga (mbatanga@diocesetucson.org);

Director for Deacons - t) 520-838-2543 Dcn. Richard Valencia, Vicar (valencia@diocesetucson.org);

Chief Financial Officer - t) 520-838-2500 fiscalservices@diocesetucson.org Dcn. Gregory Henderson (ghenderson@diocesetucson.org);

Vicars Forane - t) 520-838-2500 Rev. Michael Martinez, Cochise Vicariate; Rev. Mark J. Long, Pima-Central Vicariate; Rev. Christopher M. Orndorff II, Pima-East Vicariate;

OFFICES AND DIRECTORS

Archives - t) 520-886-5201 www.diocesetucson.org Ana-Elisa Rivera Arredondo, Archivist (archives@diocesetucson.org);

Chancery - t) 520-838-2500 Angelica M. Lozier, Admin. (alozier@diocesetucson.org);

Executive Assistant to Chancellor - t) 520-838-2511 Angelica M. Lozier;

Fiscal and Administrative Services - t) 520-838-2500 fiscalservices@diocesetucson.org Dcn. Gregory Henderson, CFO (ghenderson@diocesetucson.org);

Human Resources - Alicia Corti, Dir.; Martin Presley, Oper. Mgr.;

Information and Technology Department - t) 520-838-2503 Joseph Perdreauville, Network Admin. (jperdreauville@diocesetucson.org);

Moderator of the Curia - t) 520-838-2553 corpmatters@diocesetucson.org Rev. John P. Arnold (jarnold@diocesetucson.org);

Office of Corporate Matters - Rev. John P. Arnold;

Office of Child, Adolescent & Adult Protection - t) 520-838-2513 rserrano@diocesetucson.org Richard M. Serrano, Dir.;

Victim Assistance Coordinator - t) 520-838-2500

Office of the Bishop - t) 520-838-2523 Clara I. Heslinga, Exec. Asst. (cheslinga@diocesetucson.org);

Executive Assistant to Bishop Emeritus - t) 520-838-2510 Sr. Charlotte Anne Swift, O.P.;

Executive Assistant to Bishop of Tucson - t) 520-838-2523 Clara I. Heslinga;

Property and Insurance Services - t) 520-838-2500 propins@diocesetucson.org John C. Shaheen, Dir. (jshaheen@diocesetucson.org); Liz Aguallo, Admin. (eaguallo@diocesetucson.org);

ADVISORY BOARDS, COMMISSIONS, COMMITTEES, AND COUNCILS

Building Committee - t) 520-838-2500 James Ronstadt, Chair; Mike Marum, Vice Chm.; John C. Shaheen, Dir. (jshaheen@diocesetucson.org);

Ecumenical Commission - t) 520-838-2500 Rev. Remigio "Miguel" Mariano, Ecumenical Officer for the Diocese (mmariano@diocesetucson.org);

Renovacion Carismatica Catolica - 111quiroz@comcast.net Luis Quiroz; Lucy Quiroz; Santiago Dorates;

CONSULTATIVE BODIES

College of Consultors - Most Rev. Edward J. Weisenburger; Rev. John P. Arnold (jarnold@diocesetucson.org); Rev. Patrick M. Crino;

Finance Council - t) 520-838-2500 fiscalservices@diocesetucson.org Most Rev. Edward J. Weisenburger, Bishop; Nancy Stephan, Chair; Rev. John P. Arnold (jarnold@diocesetucson.org);

Presbyteral Council - Most Rev. Edward J. Weisenburger, Bishop of Diocese of Tucson; Rev. Christopher M. Orndorff II, Vicar Forane; Rev. Edward F. Lucero, Vicar Forane;

School Board - t) 520-838-2547 Most Rev. Edward J. Weisenburger; Sheri Dahl, Supt. (sdahl@diocesetucson.org); Aida M. Samuel, Pres.;

ORGANIZATIONS

Catholic Cemeteries, Inc. - t) 520-888-0860 info@dotcc.org www.dotcc.org Juventino Solano, Dir.;

All Faiths Cemetery - t) 520-885-9173 Juventino Solano, Exec. Dir.;

Holy Hope Catholic Cemetery -

Catholic Foundation - t) 520-838-2505 www.cathfnd.org Elizabeth Bollinger, Exec. Dir.; Suzanne Hopkins, ACA Oper. Mgr. (svhopkins@diocesetucson.org); Katheryn Hutchinson, Prog. Mgr. Grants (khutchinson@diocesetucson.org);

Catholic Tuition Support Organization - t) 520-838-2571 ctso@ctso-tucson.org www.ctso-tucson.org Gracie Quiroz Marum, CEO (gqmarum@diocesetucson.org); Julieta Gonzalez, Scholarship & Outreach Mgr. (jgonzalez@diocesetucson.org); William Osteen, Corp. Outreach (bosteen@diocesetucson.org);

Cursillo Movement - t) 928-581-0543; 928-782-7516 tucsonyumacursillolaydirector@gmail.com www.tucsoncursillo.org Dcn. David Clark, Spiritual Dir. (chargerclark55@yahoo.com); Alma Clark, Lay Dir.;

Kolbe Society (formerly Detention Ministry) - t) 520-623-0344 Dcn. Michael S. Gutierrez, Dir., Kolbe Society (mikeg@ccs-soaz.org);

Priests' Assurance Corporation - Alicia Corti, Dir.; Anne Terry Morales, Chancellor (amorales@diocesetucson.org); Most Rev. Edward J. Weisenburger, Pres.;

PASTORAL SERVICES

Catholic Schools Department - t) 520-838-2547 Sheri Dahl, Supt. (sdahl@diocesetucson.org); Angelina Schmidt, Asst. Supt. (aschmidt@diocesetucson.org); Lupita Sandoval, School Oper. Mgr.;

Formation - t) 520-838-2545 Sr. Lois J. Paha, O.P., Dir. (lpaha@diocesetucson.org); Bro. Silas Henderson, S.D.S., Seminarian Formation Dir. (silas@jordanministry.org); Ofelia James, Exec. Asst. (ojames@diocesetucson.org);

Office of Evangelization and Hispanic Ministry - t) 520-838-2540 Sr. Gladys Echenique, O.P., Dir. (gechenique@diocesetucson.org);

Permanent Diaconate - Dcn. Richard Valencia, Dir. (valencia@diocesetucson.org);

Associate Vicars - t) 520-838-2500 Dcn. Pat Abiles, Assoc. Dir.; Dcn. Oscar F. Chavez, Assoc. Dir.; Dcn. Joseph Kushner III, Assoc. Dir.;

Priestly Vocations - t) 520-838-2531 vocations@diocesetucson.org Rev. Jorge Farias-Saucedo, Dir.; Rev. John Gonzales, Dir.; Rev. Patrick M. Crino, Dir.;

Propagation of the Faith - t) 520-838-2545 Sr. Lois J. Paha, O.P. (lpaha@diocesetucson.org);

TRIBUNAL

Adjunct Judicial Vicars - t) 520-838-2500 Rev. Arthur J. Espelage, O.F.M. (aespelage@diocesetucson.org); Rev. John P. Arnold (jarnold@diocesetucson.org);

Assessors - t) 520-838-2500 Dcn. Thomas Willis (tomdelia3@msn.com);

Auditors, Notaries, Case Directors - t) 520-838-2500 Diane Coleman, Ecclesiastical Notary; Dcn. Charles A. Gallegos, Notary (cgallegos@diocesetucson.org);

Defenders of the Bond - t) 520-838-2514 mviera@diocesetucson.org Rev. Ariel G. Lustan; Rev. Msgr. John P. Lyons; Rev. Thomas Joseph Fransiscus (tfransiscus@diocesetucson.org);

Judges - t) 520-838-2500 Rev. Manuel Viera, O.F.M. (mviera@diocesetucson.org); Rev. John P. Arnold (jarnold@diocesetucson.org); Rev. Arthur J. Espelage, O.F.M. (aespelage@diocesetucson.org);

Judicial Vicar - t) 520-838-2514 Rev. Manuel Viera, O.F.M. (mviera@diocesetucson.org);

Promoter of Justice - Penal Cases - Rev. Patrick R. Lagges;

MISCELLANEOUS / OTHER OFFICES

St. Gianna Oratory (Latin Rite Oratory) - t) 520-883-4360 stgianna.tucson@institute-christ-king.org www.saintgianna.net Rev. Canon Jonathon Fehrenbacher, I.C.R.S.S. (holyfamilyparishtucson@gmail.com);

Our Lady, Star of the Sea Roman Catholic Parish - Tucson (Quasi-Parish) - t) 520-465-6119 kimpaul405@gmail.com Rev. Yoonsok (Paul) Kim, Pst.;

PARISHES, MISSIONS, AND CLERGY

STATE OF ARIZONA

AJO

Immaculate Conception Roman Catholic Church - Ajo - 101 W. Rocalla Ave., Ajo, AZ 85321; Mailing: P.O. Box 550, Ajo, AZ 85321 t) 520-387-7049 iccajo@hughes.net www.iccajo.net Rev. Peter C. Nwachukwu, Pst.; Carol Johnson, DRE; CRP Stds.: 8

APACHE JUNCTION

Saint George Roman Catholic Parish - Apache Junction - 300 E. 16th Ave., Apache Junction, AZ 85119 t) 480-982-2929 office@stgeorgeaj.com stgeorgeaj.com Rev. Msgr. Domencio C. Pinti, Pst.; Dcn. Bill Jones; Dcn. Paul Rokosz; Christine Ollive, DRE; CRP Stds.: 135

BENSON

The Roman Catholic Parish of Our Lady of Lourdes - Benson - 386 E. 5th St., Benson, AZ 85602; Mailing: P.O. Box 2198, Benson, AZ 85602 t) 520-586-3394 pleichty@diocesetucson.org; matanga@diocesetucson.org www.ololparish.com Rev. Martin B. Atanga, Pst.; Dcn. Richard Valencia; Richard Russell Leichty, DRE; Margaret Zabodyn Leichty, Contact; CRP Stds.: 12

BISBEE

Saint Patrick Roman Catholic Parish - Bisbee - 100 Quality Hill Rd., Bisbee, AZ 85603; Mailing: P.O. Box 164, Bisbee, AZ 85603 t) 520-432-5753 saintpatrick164@gmail.com www.stpatsbisbee.com Rev. Gregory P. Adolf, Pst.; Rev. Amal Sebastiar, M.S.F.S., Sacr. Min.; Dcn. Joseph L. Delgado; Dcn. Guillermo Lugo; Dcn. Tony Underwood; Wanda Leikem, DRE; CRP Stds.: 23

St. Michael - 2090 W. Martinez, Naco, AZ 85620 t) (520) 432-5753 gadolf@diocesetucson.org

CASA GRANDE

Saint Anthony of Padua Roman Catholic Parish - Casa Grande - 201 N. Picacho St., Casa Grande, AZ 85122 t) 520-836-0601 office@stanthonycg.org www.stanthonycg.org Rev. Ariel G. Lustan, Pst.; Rev. Peter Pedrasa, Par. Vicar; Dcn. Alex Coria; Dcn. Steven R. Dimuzio; Dcn. Mark Drost; Dcn. Patrick L. Dugan; Dcn. Dan Hannig; Dcn. Robert Penzenstadler; Dcn. Brian Walsh; CRP Stds.: 237

St. Anthony of Padua School - (Grades PreK-8) 501 E. 2nd St., Casa Grande, AZ 85122 t) 520-836-7247 rlazar@diocesetucson.org www.stanthonycgschool.org Stds.: 169; Lay Tchrs.: 11

CLIFTON

Sacred Heart Roman Catholic Church and St. Mary's Mission - Clifton - 355 Chase Creek Rd., Clifton, AZ 85533; Mailing: P.O. Box 938, Clifton, AZ 85533 t) 928-865-2285; 928-865-3497 (CRP) sacheart@vtc.net greenleecatholic.org Rev. Nathaniel Mma, Pst.; David Esquivel, DRE; CRP Stds.: 16

St. Mary - Third St., Clifton, AZ 85533 t) (928) 865-2285 Martha Baca, DRE;

COOLIDGE

St. James Roman Catholic Parish - Coolidge - 401 W. Wilson Ave., Coolidge, AZ 85128 t) 520-723-3063 secretary@stjamescoolidge.org Rev. Jorge Farias-Saucedo, Admin.; Dcn. Joseph Lyncha; CRP Stds.: 106

DOUGLAS

Immaculate Conception Roman Catholic Parish - Douglas - 928 C Ave., Douglas, AZ 85607; Mailing: P.O. Box 1176, Douglas, AZ 85608 t) 520-364-8494 icchurch@hotmail.com; imac@douglascatholic.org www.douglascatholic.org Rev. Virgilio Tabo Jr., Pst.; Rev. Marco Basulto-Pitol, Par. Vicar; Dcn. Mario Castillo; Dcn. Gabriel Espino; CRP Stds.: 145

Saint Luke Roman Catholic Church - Douglas - 1211 15th St., Douglas, AZ 85607 t) 520-364-4411 mjohn@diocesetucson.org douglascatholic.org Dcn. Mario Castillo; Rev. Virgilio Tabo Jr., Pst.; Rev. Marco Antonio Basulto-Pitol, Par. Vicar; Dcn. Ed Gomez; CRP Stds.: 149

Loretto Central Catholic - (Grades K-8) 1200 14th St., Douglas, AZ 85607 t) 520-364-5754 lorprincipal@lorettoschool.org Sr. Caridad Sandoval, O.C.D., Prin.; Stds.: 207; Lay Tchrs.: 9

ELOY

Saint Helen of the Cross Roman Catholic Church - Eloy - 205 W. 8th St., Eloy, AZ 85131 t) 520-466-7258 vcampa@diocesetucson.org; mcarrasco@diocesetucson.org www.sthelenchurch.com Rev. Marco Carrasco, Pst.; Dcn. Pasqual Abiles Jr.; CRP Stds.: 97

FLORENCE

Assumption of the Blessed Virgin Mary Roman Catholic Parish - Florence - 221 E. 8th St., Florence, AZ 85132; Mailing: P. O. Box 2550, Florence, AZ 85132 t) 520-868-5940 www.assumptionofmary.org Rev. Mark J. Stein, Pst.; Dcn. William Drobick; Dcn. Ernie Trujillo; CRP Stds.: 31

Chapel of the Gila - t) (520) 868-5940 mstein@diocesetucson.org (Historical Site)

Saint Michael the Archangel Roman Catholic Parish - San Tan Valley - 26035 N. Apollo Dr., Florence, AZ 85132 t) 520-723-6570 ccd@stmichaels77.org; pastor@stmichaels77.org www.stmichaels77.org Rev. Dale A. Branson, Pst.; Reajean Porter, DRE; CRP Stds.: 80

GLOBE

Holy Angels Roman Catholic Church - Tucson - 201 S. Broad St., Globe, AZ 85501 t) 928-425-3137 amiranda@diocesetucson.org; holyangelsglobe@gmail.com www.holyangelscatholicchurchglobe.org/ Rev. Albert Miranda, Pst.; CRP Stds.: 17

GREEN VALLEY

Our Lady of the Valley Roman Catholic Parish - Green Valley - 505 N. La Canada Dr., Green Valley, AZ 85614 t) 520-625-4536 olvgv@diocesetucson.org www.olvgv.org Rev. Francisco Maldonado, Pst.; Dcn. Joseph Roinick, Pst. Assoc.; CRP Stds.: 118

HAYDEN

Saint Joseph Roman Catholic Parish - Hayden - 300 Mountain View Dr., Hayden, AZ 85135-1007; Mailing: P.O. Box C, Hayden, AZ 85135-1007 t) 520-356-7223 stjoseph.haden@yahoo.com Rev. George Kunnel, M.S.F.S., Pst.; Kathy Cruz, DRE; CRP Stds.: 73

KEARNY

Infant Jesus of Prague Roman Catholic Parish - Kearny - 501 Victoria Cir., Kearny, AZ 85137; Mailing: P.O. Box 459, Kearny, AZ 85137 t) 520-363-7205 ijp.kearny@yahoo.com Rev. George Kunnel, MSFS (India), Pst.; CRP Stds.: 18

MAMMOTH

Blessed Sacrament Roman Catholic Parish - Mammoth - 122 W. Church Dr., Mammoth, AZ 85618-0220; Mailing: P.O. Box 220, Mammoth, AZ 85618 t) 520-487-2451; 520-487-2182 (CRP) Rev. Bala Kommathoti, Pst.; Helen Ramirez, DRE; CRP Stds.: 60

MARANA

Saint Christopher Roman Catholic Parish - Marana - 12101 W. Moore Rd., Marana, AZ 85653 t) 520-682-3035 reception@stchristophermarana.com www.stchristophermarana.org/ Rev. Edson Elizarraras, Pst.; Dcn. Jorge Munoz; CRP Stds.: 88

MARICOPA

Our Lady of Grace Roman Catholic Parish - Maricopa - 18700 N. St. Gabriel Way, Maricopa, AZ 85138-3228 t) 520-568-4605 amaidman@maricopacatholic.org; information@maricopacatholic.org maricopacatholic.org/ Rev. Jay R. Luczak, Pst.; Rev. Jude Blaise Agada, Par. Vicar; Dcn. Gullermo Castro; Dcn. Roger Maidman; Dcn. Mario Ortega; Dcn. Enrique Padilla; Dcn. Jesus Vasquez; Ann Maidman, DRE; Ann Joy Napolitano, Parish Life Coord.; Edward Talsness, Bus. Mgr.; CRP Stds.: 249

MIAMI

Our Lady of the Blessed Sacrament Roman Catholic Church - Miami - 844 W. Sullivan St., Miami, AZ 85539 t) 928-473-3568 ourladyromancatholic@yahoo.com Rev. Madhu George, Pst.; Lorraine Reves, DRE; CRP Stds.: 68

St. Joseph Chapel - t) (928) 473-3568

St. Theresa Chapel - t) (928) 473-3568

MORENCI

Holy Cross Roman Catholic Church - Morenci - 205 Fairbanks Rd., Morenci, AZ 85540 t) 928-865-3183 holycross@vtc.net Rev. Nathaniel Mma, Pst.; Bertha Morales, DRE; CRP Stds.: 102

NOGALES

Sacred Heart of Jesus Roman Catholic Parish - Nogales - 272 N. Rodriguez St., Nogales, AZ 85621 t) 520-287-9221 shjpoffice@gmail.com sacredheartnogales.com Rev. Marcos Velasquez, Pst.; Dcn. David A. Rojas; Margarita Treto, DRE; CRP Stds.: 209

Sacred Heart of Jesus School - (Grades PreK-8) 207 W. Oak St., Nogales, AZ 85621 t) 520-287-2223 mrothstein@diocesetucson.org sacredheartnogales.org Roxanne Teran, Prin.; Stds.: 191; Lay Tchrs.: 10

San Felipe de Jesus Roman Catholic Parish - Nogales - 1901 N. Jose Gallego Dr., Nogales, AZ 85621; Mailing: P.O. Box 6600, Nogales, AZ 85628 t) 520-761-3100 sanfelipedejesusparish@gmail.com Rev. Jose Manuel Padilla, Pst.; Bertha M Franco, DRE; CRP Stds.: 304

ORACLE

Saint Helen Roman Catholic Parish - Oracle - 66 E. Maplewood St., Oracle, AZ 85623-6148 t) 520-896-2708 sthelensmission@msn.com www.sthelenparishoracle.org Rev. Msgr. Ambrose O. Nwohu, Pst.; Maria Martinez, DRE; CRP Stds.: 20

ORO VALLEY

Saint Mark Roman Catholic Parish - Tucson - 2727 W. Tangerine Rd., Oro Valley, AZ 85742; Mailing: P.O. Box 68650, Tucson, AZ 85737 t) 520-469-7835 office@stmarkov.com; finance@stmarkov.com www.stmarkov.com Rev. John P. Arnold, Pst.; Dcn. Jose Cuestas III; Dcn. Andrew Guarriello; Camryn Conforti, DRE; CRP Stds.: 285

Saint Odilia Roman Catholic Community - Tucson - 7570 N. Paseo del Norte, Oro Valley, AZ 85704 t) 520-297-7272 (CRP); 520-297-7271 susie78@comcast.net; mmariano@diocesetucson.org stodiliaparish.org Rev. Remigio Miguel Mariano, Pst.; Rev. John Ikponko, Par. Vicar; Dcn. Angel Gonzales; Rev. Frank G. Cady, In Res.; Suzanna Chapman, DRE; CRP Stds.: 48

PARKER

Sacred Heart Roman Catholic Parish - Parker - 1101 Joshua Ave., Parker, AZ 85344 t) 928-669-2502 shpp@npgcable.com www.sacredheartparker.org Rev. John Ikponko, Admin.; Dcn. Leonel Bejarano; CRP Stds.: 26

Saint Kateri Tekakwitha Indian Mission - 29070 Mohave Rd., Poston, AZ 85371 t) (928) 669-2502

St. John the Baptist - 70905 Santa Fe, Wendon, AZ 85357 t) (928) 669-2502

Queen of Peace - 5005 Mocking Bird, Quartzite, AZ 85346 t) (928) 669-2502

PATAGONIA

Saint Therese of Lisieux Roman Catholic Parish - Patagonia - 222 Third Ave., Patagonia, AZ 85624; Mailing: P.O. Box 435, Patagonia, AZ 85624 t) 520-394-2954 sttheresa@dakotacom.net stcepatagonia.com/ Rev. Alexander Tigga, M.S.F.S. (India), Pst.; Martha Green, DRE; CRP Stds.: 12

Our Lady of Angels - 22 Los Encinos Dr., Sonoita, AZ 85637 t) (520) 394-2954

PAYSON

Saint Philip the Apostle Roman Catholic Church - Payson - 511 S. St. Phillips St., Payson, AZ 85541-5144 t) 928-474-2392; 928-474-1269 (Religious Ed Direct Line) tquirk@diocesetucson.org; cw2dell@gmail.com catholicpayson.com Rev. Thomas Quirk, Pst.; Dcn. Willard Dwight Capistrant; Dcn. John Lamont Scott; Dcn. William Trudell; Catherine Trudell, DRE; CRP Stds.: 36

PEARCE

Saint Jude Thaddeus Roman Catholic Parish - Pearce Sunsites - 970 N. Hwy. 191, Mile Post 51, Pearce, AZ 85625; Mailing: P.O. Box 328, Pearce, AZ 85625 t) 520-826-3869 msztuk@diocesetucson.org Rev. Martin Bosco Ormin, V.C. (Nigeria), Admin.; Heidi Stemp, DRE; CRP Stds.: 175

St. Francis of Assisi - t) (520) 826-3869 mormin@diocesetucson.org

PIRTLEVILLE

Saint Bernard Roman Catholic Church - Pirtleville - 2308 N. McKinley St., Pirtleville, AZ 85626; Mailing: P. O. Box 3101, Pirtleville, AZ 85626 t) 520-364-4411 (CRP); 520-364-2762 mjohn@diocesetucson.org; st.luke51@yahoo.com www.douglascatholic.org Rev. Virgilio Tabo Jr., Pst.; Rev. Marco Antonio Basulto, Par. Vicar; Dcn. Victor Alvidrez; Dcn. Guadalupe Yanez; Ana Morales, DRE; CRP Stds.: 25

Double Adobe, Our Lady of La Salette - 3879 W. Mission Ln., Double Adobe, AZ 85617 t) (520) 361-2762 vtabo@diocesetucson.org

RIO RICO

Most Holy Nativity of Our Lord Jesus Christ Roman Catholic Parish - Rio Rico - 395 Avenida Coatimundi, Rio Rico, AZ 85648; Mailing: P.O. Box 4024, Rio Rico, AZ 85648 t) 520-281-7414 mostholynativity@qwestoffice.net www.mhnparish.org Rev. Francisco Maldonado, Pst.; Rev. Cayetano Cabrera Duran, Par. Vicar; Dcn. Javier Fierro; Dcn. Francisco Padilla; Dcn. Carl Sadlier; Angela Fragoso, DRE; CRP Stds.: 155

SAFFORD

Saint Rose of Lima Roman Catholic Parish - Safford - 311 S. Central Ave., Safford, AZ 85546-2655; Mailing: P.O. Box 1117, Safford, AZ 85548 t) 928-428-4920; 928-348-4785 (CRP) c) (520) 507-1145 (After Hour / Emergency) st.roselima@gmail.com www.saintroselima-safford.com Dcn. Carlos Vessels; Rev. Nicodemus Shaghel, V.C., Pst.; CRP Stds.: 137

St. Martin de Porres Mission - 50 S. Main, Pima, AZ 85543; Mailing: PO Box 1117, Safford, AZ 85548 t) (928) 428-4920

Newman Center - 3592 W. 4th St., Thatcher, AZ 85552; Mailing: PO Box 1117, Safford, AZ 85548 t) (928) 428-4920

SAHUARITA

Roman Catholic Parish of San Martin De Porres - Sahuarita - 15440 S. Santa Rita Rd., Sahuarita, AZ 85629; Mailing: P.O. Box 65, Sahuarita, AZ 85629 t) 520-625-1154 admin@sanmartinsahuarita.org; pastor@sanmartininsahuarita.org www.sanmartinsahuarita.org Rev. Martin S. Martinez, Pst.; CRP Stds.: 174

SAN CARLOS

St. Charles Roman Catholic Community - San Carlos (San Carlos Apache Community) - 460 San Carlos Ave., San Carlos, AZ 85550; Mailing: P.O. Box 28, San Carlos, AZ 85550 t) 928-475-2210 asteele@diocesetucson.org Rev. John Paul Shea, Pst.;

San Carlos Apache Community School - (Grades K-7) ; Mailing: P.O. Box 339, San Carlos, AZ 85550 t) 928-475-2449 lrussell@diocesetucson.org stcharles@facebook.com Lorraine Russell, Prin.; Stds.: 151; Lay Tchrs.: 11

SAN LUIS

Saint Jude Thaddeus Roman Catholic Parish - San Luis - 984 N. Main St., San Luis, AZ 85349; Mailing: P.O. Box 2888, San Luis, AZ 85349 t) 928-627-8011 sjtparish-sla@hotmail.com Rev. Adolfo Martinez-Escobar, Pst.; Gloria Lastra, DRE; Maria Guadalupe Meza, Bus. Mgr.; CRP Stds.: 264

SAN MANUEL

Saint Bartholomew Roman Catholic Parish - San Manuel - 609 W. Park Pl., San Manuel, AZ 85631 t) 520-385-4156 gloriat527@hotmail.com; mlsanchez@diocesetucson.org Rev. Bala Kommathoti, Pst.; Francis Madrid, DRE; CRP Stds.: 58

SIERRA VISTA

Saint Andrew the Apostle Roman Catholic Parish - Sierra Vista - 800 Taylor Dr., N.W., Sierra Vista, AZ 85635 t) 520-458-2925 bulletin@standrewsv.org www.standrewsv.org Rev. Gregory P. Adolf, Pst.; Rev. Samuel Jandeh, V.C., Par. Vicar; Rev. Robert Neske, Par. Vicar; Dcn. Mike Denton; Dcn. John Joseph Klein; Dcn. Bill Polakowski; Dcn. Lauro A. Teran; Sr. Joellen Kohlmann, DRE; CRP Stds.: 185

Good Shepherd - 2241 N. Good Shepherd Way, Whetstone, AZ 85616 t) (520) 458-2925

Our Lady of the Mountains Roman Catholic Parish - Sierra Vista - 1425 Yaqui St., Sierra Vista, AZ 85650 t) 520-378-2720 dparsons@diocesetucson.org; k.shilson@olmaz.org www.olmaz.org Rev. Michael Martinez, Pst.; Dcn. Kurt Carlson; Dcn. Timothy Krieski; Dcn. Reynaldo Romo; Dcn. Gene Tackett; Kathleen Shilson, DRE; CRP Stds.: 44

All Saints Catholic School - (Grades PreK-8) t) 520-378-7012 schooloffice@ascsaz.org www.ascsaz.org Carmen Rosado, Prin.; Stds.: 99; Lay Tchrs.: 9

SOLOMON

Our Lady of Guadalupe Roman Catholic Parish - Solomon - 2257 S. 1st Ave., Solomon, AZ 85551; Mailing: P.O. Box 147, Solomon, AZ 85551 t) 928-428-0149 olgsolomon@gmail.com Rev. Nicodemus Shaghel, V.C., Pst.; Dcn. Carl Vessels; CRP Stds.: 10

San Jose - 1670 S. Church St., San Jose, AZ 85546 t) (928) 428-0149

SOMERTON

Immaculate Heart of Mary Roman Catholic Parish - Somerton - 310 W. Spring St., Somerton, AZ 85350; Mailing: Po. Box 597, Somerton, AZ 85350 t) 928-627-2918 parishihm@hotmail.com www.ihmsomertonaz.com Rev. Eduardo Lopez-Romo, Pst.; Dcn. Jeff Trujillo; CRP Stds.: 162

SUPERIOR

Saint Francis of Assisi Roman Catholic Parish - Superior - 11 S. Church Ave., Superior, AZ 85173 t) 520-689-2250 info@stfrancissuperior.org www.stfrancissuperior.org Rev. Peter C. Nwachukwu, Pst.; Kathy Zavala, DRE; CRP Stds.: 26

St. Mary's Center - 100 Sunset Dr., Superior, AZ 85173 t) (520) 689-2250

TOMBSTONE

Sacred Heart of Jesus Roman Catholic Parish - Tombstone - 598 E. Safford St., Tombstone, AZ 85638; Mailing: P.O. Box 547, Tombstone, AZ 85638 c) 520-457-3364 sacredheartchurch@powerc.net www.shctombstone.org Rev. Robert Neske, Assoc. Pst.; Rev. Gregory P. Adolf, Pst.; CRP Stds.: 6

TOPAWA

San Solano Missions Roman Catholic Parish - Topawa - Rte. 19 and Topawa Rd., Topawa, AZ 85639-0210; Mailing: P.O. Box 210, Topawa, AZ 85639-0210 t) 520-383-2350 ssmissions@diocesetucson.org (For office and sacramental records pertaining to Tohono O'odham Nation and Mission Churches on the Reservation, please refer to San Solano Missions.) Friar John Gibbons, O.F.M., Pst.; Rev. William J. Minkel, O.F.M., Par. Vicar; Friar Peter Boegel, O.F.M., Guardian; CRP Stds.: 50

TUBAC

Saint Ann's Roman Catholic Parish and Its Missions - Tubac - 11 Calle Iglesias, Tubac, AZ 85646-2911; Mailing: P.O. Box 2911, Tubac, AZ 85629 t) 520-398-2646 stannsparish3@gmail.com stannsparishtubacaz.org/ Rev. Joseph Esson, Pst.; Irma G. Celez, Bus. Mgr.; CRP Stds.: 9

Assumption Chapel - 17 Amado Montosa Rd., Amado, AZ 85640 t) (520) 398-2646

St. Ferdinand - 17140 W. Arivaca Rd., Arivaca, AZ 85645 t) (520) 273-7238

TUCSON

Saint Augustine Cathedral Roman Catholic Parish - Tucson - 192 S. Stone Ave., Tucson, AZ 85701 t) 520-623-6351 office@staugustine.tuccoxmail.com cathedral-staugustine.org Rev. Alan Valencia, Rector; Rev. Ukeyima Emmanuel Adams, Assoc. Pst.; Dcn. Michael S. Gutierrez; Dcn. Salvador Carmona; Dcn. Ricardo M. Pinzon; CRP Stds.: 165

San Cosme - 460 W. Simpson, Tucson, AZ 85701 t) (520) 623-6351

Saint Ambrose Roman Catholic Parish - Tucson - 300 S. Tucson Blvd., Tucson, AZ 85716 t) 520-622-6749 stambrose@stambrosetucson.com; mgonsowski@stambrosetucson.org www.stambroseparishtucson.org Rev. Mark J. Long, Pst.; Dcn. Mark Hohbein; Dcn. Thomas Willis; Marjorie Gonsowski, DRE; CRP Stds.: 20

St. Ambrose Roman Catholic Parish - Tucson School - (Grades PreK-8) 300 S. Tucson Blvd, Tucson, AZ 85716 t) 520-882-8678 officemanager@stambrosetucson.org www.stambrosetucson.org Tanya Duenas, Prin.; Stds.: 212; Lay Tchrs.: 13

Corpus Christi Roman Catholic Parish - Tucson - 300 N. Tanque Verde Loop Rd., Tucson, AZ 85748 t) 520-751-4235 kmontano@cccctucson.org www.cccctucson.org Rev. Christopher M. Orndorff II, Pst.; Rev. Richard M. Kingsley, Pastor Emer.; Dcn. Mark Cesnik; Suzanne Hensel, DRE; Stacey Beste, Youth Min.; Jana Gee, Music Min.; John Salapski, Bus. Mgr.; CRP Stds.: 142

Saint Cyril of Alexandria Roman Catholic Parish - Tucson - 1750 N. Swan Rd., Tucson, AZ 85712; Mailing: 4725 E. Pima St., Tucson, AZ 85712 t) 520-795-1633; 520-881-4240 pastor@stcyril.com; bjenkins@stcyril.com www.stcyrilchurch-tucson.org Rev. Paul Anthony Henson, O. Carm., Pst.; Rev. Edgar Lopez, O.Carm., Par. Vicar; Dcn. Felix Mario Aguirre; Becki Jenkins, DRE; Sally Guerrero, Bus. Mgr.; CRP Stds.: 118

St. Cyril of Alexandria School - (Grades 1-8) 4725 E. Pima St., Tucson, AZ 85712 t) (520) 795-1633 daniellec@stcyril.com Danielle Coleman, Interim Prin.; Stds.: 118; Pr. Tchrs.: 28; Scholastics: 90; Lay Tchrs.: 4

Roman Catholic Church of Saint Elizabeth Ann Seton - Tucson - 8650 N. Shannon Rd., Tucson, AZ 85742 t) 520-297-7357; 520-219-7637 (CRP) church@seastucson.org www.seastucson.org Rev. Edward F. Lucero, Pst.; Rev. James Mascarenhas, M.S.F.S., Par. Vicar; Rev. Richard Rivera Jr., Par. Vicar; Dcn. Richard Kiser; Dcn. Christian Kimminau; Dcn. Mario J. Rodriguez; Dcn. Francis C. Sherlock; Dcn. Jacinto Trevino Jr.; CRP Stds.: 140

St. Elizabeth Ann Seton School - (Grades PreK-8) t) 520-219-7650 npickett@school.seastucson.org; info@school.seastucson.org school.seastucson.org Nicole A. Pickett, Prin.; Gytzel Alatorre, Registrar; Stds.: 305; Lay Tchrs.: 26

Saint Frances Cabrini Roman Catholic Parish - Tucson - 3201 E. Presidio Rd., Tucson, AZ 85716 t) (520) 882-3891 Dcn. Charles A. Gallegos;

Saint Francis de Sales Roman Catholic Parish - Tucson - 1375 S. Camino Seco, Tucson, AZ 85710 t) 520-885-5908 sfds_officemgr@diocesetucson.org www.sfdstucson.org Dcn. Gregory Henderson; Rev. Richard T. Kusugh, Pst.; Dcn. C. Andy Corder; Dcn. Russell Kingery; Dcn. John R. Martin; Dcn. Thai V. Tran; Dcn. Patrick Whaley; Lori McLaughlin, Admin.; Stu Sepulvida, Pst. Assoc.; Terri Gervais, DRE; Maureen Kingery, DRE; David Ahlmeyer, Bus. Mgr.; CRP Stds.: 112

Holy Family Roman Catholic Parish - Tucson - 338 W. University Blvd., Tucson, AZ 85705 t) 520-623-6773 holyfamilyparishtucson@gmail.com; scordova@diocesetucson.org Rev. Canon Jonathon Fehrenbacher, I.C.R.S.S., Admin.;

Saint John the Evangelist Roman Catholic Parish - Tucson - 602 W. Ajo Way, Tucson, AZ 85713 t) 520-624-7409 x100; 520-901-1995 (CRP) llopez@diocesetucson.org; stjohnsoffice@netzero.com www.stjohnevangelisttucson.org Rev. Msgr. Raul P. Trevizo, Pst.; Rev. Robert A. Gonzales, Assoc. Pst.; Dcn. Jose Duarte; Lydia Lopez, DRE; Tom Baca, Bus. Mgr.; CRP Stds.: 396

St. John the Evangelist School - (Grades K-8) 600 W. Ajo Way, Tucson, AZ 85713 t) 520-624-3865 msolorzano@stjohntucson.org www.stjohntucson.org Minh Solorzano, Prin.; Stds.: 385; Lay Tchrs.: 21

Casa San Juan Migrant Center - t) 520-207-8918 casasanjuan@comcast.net www.casasanjuan.org Food pantry, legal services, health services.

Saint Joseph Roman Catholic Parish - Tucson - 215 S. Craycroft Rd., Tucson, AZ 85711 t) 520-747-3100 parish@stjosephtucsonaz.org www.stjosephtucson.org Rev. Robert A. Rodriguez, Pst.; Dcn. Alfonso Gallardo; Dcn. Leon Mazza; Dcn. Teodoro Perez; CRP Stds.: 84

St. Joseph Roman Catholic Parish - Tucson School - (Grades PreK-8) t) 520-747-3060 kvanloan@stjosephtucsonaz.org saintjosephstucson.weebly.com/ Kathy VanLoan, Prin.; Stds.: 240; Lay Tchrs.: 15

Saint Kateri Tekakwitha Roman Catholic Missions Parish - Tucson - 507 W. 29th St., Tucson, AZ 85713 t) 520-622-5363 bl_kateri_tekakwitha@yahoo.com stkateritucson.org Rev. Arokiaraj Varnabas, Pst.; Rev. Charley Piatt, S.T., Par. Vicar; Chris Delsi, CRE; Rosa Galaz, CRE; CRP Stds.: 36

San Martin - 418 W. 39th St., Tucson, AZ 85713 t) (520) 622-5353

Santa Rosa - 2015 N. Calle Central, Tucson, AZ 85705 t) (520) 622-5363

Cristo Rey - t) (520) 622-5363

El Senor de los Milagros - 3410 S. 16th Ave., Tucson, AZ 85713 t) (520) 622-5363

San Ignacio de Loyola - 785 W. Sahuaro, Tucson, AZ 85705 t) (520) 622-5363

San Juan Diego Center - 7465 S. Camino Benem, Tucson, AZ 85757 t) (520) 622-5363

Saint Margaret Mary Alacoque Roman Catholic Parish - Tucson - 801 N. Grande Ave., Tucson, AZ 85745 t) 520-622-0168 religiousedstmargaret@hotmail.com; parishstmargaret@gmail.com www.stmargaretmarytucson.com Rev. Richard T. Awange, C.S.Sp. (Nigeria), Pst.; Dcn. William Carroll III; Dcn. Miguel Lopez; Rosemary Munguia, DRE; Maria Castro, RCIA Coord.; CRP Stds.: 75

Saint Monica Roman Catholic Parish - Tucson - 212 W. Medina Rd., Tucson, AZ 85756 t) 520-294-2694; 520-889-1994 (CRP) santamonicatucson@yahoo.com; gmusumbu@yahoo.com Rev. Gilbert Malu Musumbu, Pst.; Rev. Jose Abraham Guerrero, Par. Vicar; Dcn. Nicolas De La Torre; Dcn. David Vernon Barfuss, Youth Min.; Leonorilda Valenzuela, DRE; Dcn. Ignacio Arvizu, RCIA Coord.; CRP Stds.: 274

Most Holy Trinity Roman Catholic Parish - Tucson - 1300 N. Greasewood Rd., Tucson, AZ 85745 t) 520-884-9021 info@mhtparish.org Rev. Thomas

Tureman, S.D.S., Pst.; Rev. Wilkin Paul, S.D.S., Par. Vicar; Dcn. John Terry; Diana Akroush, DRE; CRP Stds.: 158

Our Lady of Fatima Roman Catholic Parish - Tucson - 1950 W. Irvington Pl., Tucson, AZ 85746 t) 520-883-1717 cdupnik@diocesetucson.org; fatimaintucson@aol.com www.fatimaintucson.org Rev. Viliulfo Valderrama, Pst.; Rev. Simon Ityo, Par. Vicar; Dcn. Anthony Geonnotti; Dcn. Robert Negrette; Dcn. Alejandro Ochoa; CRP Stds.: 93

St. Mary of the Desert - 14319 W. Castro Rd., Tucson, AZ 85736 c) (520) 247-9794 Anthony Geonnotti;

Our Lady of LaVang Roman Catholic Parish - Tucson - 3201 E. Presidio Rd., Tucson, AZ 85716 t) (520) 326-7670 c) 520-241-4152 ftran@diocesetucson.org lavangtucson.com Rev. Francis Dien Tran, CSsR, Pst.; Chau Nguyen, Bus. Mgr.; CRP Stds.: 58

Our Lady Queen of All Saints Roman Catholic Parish - Tucson - 2915 E. 36th St., Tucson, AZ 85713-4041 t) 520-622-8602 olqoas2915@yahoo.com Rev. Bardo Fabian Antunez-Olea, Pst.; Dcn. Armando L. Valenzuela; Carmen Bonillas, DRE; CRP Stds.: 157

Our Lady Star of the Sea Roman Catholic Parish - Tucson - 3820 Sabino Canyon Rd., Tucson, AZ 85710; Mailing: 9331 E. Speedway Blvd., Tucson, AZ 85710 c) 520-490-2289 olss@tucsonkcc.org Rev. Yoonsok Kim, Pst.; Sung Khong, DRE; CRP Stds.: 5

Our Mother of Sorrows Roman Catholic Parish - Tucson - 1800 S. Kolb Rd., Tucson, AZ 85710 t) 520-747-1321 omosparish@omosparish.org; lstehle@omosparish.org www.omosparish.org Rev. Arnold Aurillo, Pst.; Rev. John Juarez Gonzales, Par. Vicar; Rev. Msgr. Thomas Cahalane, Pastor Emer.; Dcn. Adel Abrugena; Dcn. David Caballero; Dcn. Chuck Chajewski; Dcn. Gregory Henderson; Dcn. Hank Krzysik Jr.; Dcn. Eric Maugans; Dcn. Joseph Perotti; Dcn. Scott Thrall; Dcn. Jose Francisco Zamora Arroyo; Laura Stehle, DRE; CRP Stds.: 257

Our Mother of Sorrows School - (Grades PreK-8) t) 520-747-1027 info@omosschool.com www.omosschool.com Shakenya Gholson, Prin.; Stds.: 300; Lay Tchrs.: 19

Saints Peter and Paul Roman Catholic Parish - Tucson - 1946 E. Lee St., Tucson, AZ 85719-4337 t) 520-327-6015 info@sspp-parish.org www.sspp-parish.org Rev. Mario (Ricky) V. Ordonez, Pst.; Rev. Justin Agbir, Par. Vicar; Rev. Rajeev Bobba, Par. Vicar; Rev. Showri Raju Narra, In Res.; Dcn. John K. Ackerley; Dcn. Thomas Campbell; Dcn. Paul N. Duckro; Dcn. Daniel F. Flanagan, DRE; CRP Stds.: 105

Sts. Peter and Paul Roman School - (Grades K-8) 1436 N. Campbell Ave., Tucson, AZ 85719 t) 520-325-2431 info@sspptucson.org www.sspptucson.org Nora Jaramillo, Prin.; Debbie Nielsen, Librn.; Stds.: 349; Lay Tchrs.: 27

Saint Pius X Roman Catholic Parish - Tucson - 1800 N. Camino Pio Decimo, Tucson, AZ 85715 t) 520-885-3573 dlialios@diocesetucson.org; general@stpiusxtucson.org www.stpiusxtucson.org Rev. Dennis Bosse, O.F.M., Pst.; Bro. Andrew Stettler; Dcn. Dennis Ranke; Deanne Lialios, DRE; CRP Stds.: 152

Sacred Heart Roman Catholic Parish - Tucson - 601 E. Ft. Lowell Rd., Tucson, AZ 85705 t) 520-888-1530 x123 (CRP); 520-888-1530 sacredhearttucson@gmail.com www.sacredhearttucson.weconnect.com Dcn. Eugene Fernandez; Rev. Gonzalo J. Villegas, Pst.; Sr. Jerry Brady, S.C., DRE; CRP Stds.: 142

San Xavier Mission Roman Catholic Parish - Tucson - 1950 W. San Xavier Rd., Tucson, AZ 85746 t) 520-294-2624; 520-294-4639 (CRP) criach@diocesetucson.org www.sanxaviermission.org Rev. Alfonso Ponchie Vasquez, O.F.M., Pst.; Rev. Martin Ibarra, O.F.M., In Res.; Rev. Manuel Viera, O.F.M., In Res.; Friar David Paz, O.F.M., In Res.; Sr. Rachel Sena, O.P., DRE; Sr. Carla Riach, F.S.C.C., RCIA Coord.; CRP Stds.: 140

San Xavier Mission Roman Catholic Parish - Tucson School - (Grades K-8) 1980 W. San Xavier Rd., Tucson, AZ 85746 t) 520-294-0628 office@sxmschool.org Maria Vanessa Rothstein, Prin.;

Convent - 1996 W. San Xavier Rd., Tucson, AZ 85746 t) 520-746-4779 Franciscan Sisters of Christian Charity. Rosalyn Muraski, O.S.F., Supr.;

Santa Catalina Roman Catholic Parish - Tucson - 14380 N. Oracle Rd., Tucson, AZ 85739 t) 520-825-9611 office@santacatalinaparish.org; re@santacatalinaparish.org www.santacatalinaparish.org Rev. Huy Vu, C.Ss.R., Par. Admin.; Katharine Lopez, CRE; Dcn. Flavio Sanchez; Dcn. Alfonso De La Riva; CRP Stds.: 32

Santa Cruz Roman Catholic Parish - Tucson - 1220 S. 6th Ave., Tucson, AZ 85713 t) 520-623-3833; 520-882-9687 (CRP) hreyes@diocesetucson.org; mdoe@diocesetucson.org santacruzchurchtucson.com Rev. Stephen Watson, O.C.D., Pst.; Martin Doe, DRE; CRP Stds.: 149

Santa Cruz Roman Catholic Parish - Tucson School - (Grades K-8) 29 W. 22nd St., Tucson, AZ 85713 t) 520-624-2093 aschmidt@santacruzschool.org www.santacruzschool.org Angelina Schmidt, Prin.; Stds.: 150; Lay Tchrs.: 9

Capilla Guadalupe - 401 E. 31st St., Tucson, AZ 85713 t) (520) 623-3833 swatson@diocesetucson.org

Saint Thomas More Roman Catholic Newman Parish - Tucson - 1615 E. 2nd St., Tucson, AZ 85719 t) 520-327-4665 (CRP) manny@uacatholic.org www.uacatholic.org Rev. John Paul Forte, O.P., Pst.; Rev. Emmanuel Taylor, Assoc. Pst.; Rev. Robert Castle, In Res.; Rev. Thomas DeMan, O.P., In Res.; Sr. Lynn Allvin, O.P., Pst. Assoc.; Thomas Booth, Music Min.; Nathan Payne, Music Min.; Manuel Guzman, O.P., Bus. Mgr.; CRP Stds.: 13

Saint Thomas the Apostle Roman Catholic Parish - Tucson - 5150 N. Valley View Rd., Tucson, AZ 85718-6121 t) 520-577-8780 sttomapostle@diocesetucson.org; stareligiousedu@gmail.com www.statucson.org/ Rev. Patrick M. Crino, Pst.; Rev. Callistus Iyorember, Par. Vicar; Rev. Msgr. John P. Lyons, Pastor Emer.; Dcn. Joe G. Cruz Jr.; Dcn. Philip Garcia; Dcn. Edward P. Sheffer, Youth Min.; Robert Weierman, DRE; CRP Stds.: 216

St. Thomas the Apostle School - (Grades PreK-k) t) 520-577-0503 sthomaspreschool@gmail.com saintthomaspreschool.com Michelle Garmon, Prin.; Stds.: 87; Lay Tchrs.: 11

VAIL

Saint Rita in the Desert Roman Catholic Parish - Vail - 13260 E. Colossal Cave Rd., Vail, AZ 85641 t) 520-762-9688 secretary@stritainthedesert.org www.stritainthedesert.org Rev. Alonzo M Garcia, Pst.; Dcn. Ronald J. Desmarais; Beth Green, DRE; Dcn. Daniel Gullotta; CRP Stds.: 131

WELLTON

Saint Joseph the Worker Roman Catholic Parish - Wellton - 8674 S. Ave. 36 E, Wellton, AZ 85356; Mailing: 8674 S. Ave. 36E, Wellton, AZ 85356 t) 928-785-4275 stjoseph157@hotmail.com stjosephwellton.com Rev. Rudolf Ofori, Pst.; Dcn. Wayne L. Preston; Dcn. Benito Rodriguez; Dcn. Alejandro Ortega; Nancy Rodriguez, DRE; CRP Stds.: 40

WILLCOX

Sacred Heart of Jesus Roman Catholic Church - Willcox - 215 W. Maley St., Willcox, AZ 85643 t) 520-384-3432 Rev. Mark J. Stein, Pst.; CRP Stds.: 52

Our Lady of Perpetual Help - t) (520) 384-3432 Rev. Ramonito Celestial;

Our Lady of Guadalupe - 321 E. 4th St., Bowie, AZ 85605 t) 520-847-2557 Rev. Ramonito Celestial;

YUMA

Saint Francis of Assisi Roman Catholic Parish - Yuma - 1815 S. 8th Ave., Yuma, AZ 85364 t) 928-782-1875 admin@stfrancisyuma.com; evillegas@stfrancisyuma.com www.stfrancisyuma.com Rev. Emilio Landeros Chapa, Pst.; Dcn. Rick Hernandez; Dcn. Robert Aguilar; Dcn. Hector Martinez; Dcn. Douglas Nicholls; Dcn. Mark Nixon; Dcn. Gary Pasquinelli; Dcn. Arturo E. Sanchez; Dcn. Todd Taylor; Dcn. Rafael Vidal; Evelia Villegas Nides, RCIA Coord.; Jesus Navarrete, DRE; CRP Stds.: 217

St. Francis of Assisi School - (Grades PreK-8) 700 W. 18th St., Yuma, AZ 85364 t) 928-782-1539 vlopez@diocesetucson.org Veronica Lopez, Prin.; Stds.: 249; Lay Tchrs.: 12

Immaculate Conception & Guadalupe Missions Roman Catholic Parish & Guadalupe Mission - Yuma - 505 S. Ave. B, Yuma, AZ 85364 t) (928) 782-7516 (Parish Office); (928) 783-1324 (CRP); (928) 783-5225 (School Office) brivera@diocesetucson.org; ccdenglish1@outlook.com www.icyuma.com Rev. Manuel Fragoso-Carranza, Pst.; Rev. Timothy Imbya, V.C., Par. Vicar; Rev. Jose Martin Uriarte, Par. Vicar; Rev. Gregory Okafor, In Res.; Dcn. Arnulfo Carbajal; Dcn. Oscar F. Chavez; Dcn. David Clark; Dcn. Javier Domingo Coronado; Dcn. Antonio Gomez; Dcn. Jorge Gonzalez; Dcn. Carlos P. Hernandez, DRE; Dcn. Nieves Hernandez; Dcn. Ernesto Jaramillo; Dcn. Joel Olea; Dcn. David Sampson; Miriam Palencia, DRE; CRP Stds.: 395

Immaculate Conception Roman Catholic Parish & Guadalupe Mission School - (Grades PreK-8) 501 S. Ave. B, Yuma, AZ 85364 t) 928-783-5225 (School Office) icschool@icyuma.com www.icyumaschool.com Maria A. Sullivan, Prin.; Stds.: 241; Lay Tchrs.: 9

Our Lady of Guadalupe - 417 15th Ave., Yuma, AZ 85364; Mailing: 505 South Ave. B, Yuma, AZ 85364 icchurch@icyuma.com Rev. Manuel Fragoso-Carranza, Pst.;

Convent - 500 24th Ave., Yuma, AZ 85364 t) 928-783-5224 icchurch@icyuma.com Sr. Mary Beth Kornely, O.S.F., Supr.;

Saint John Neumann Roman Catholic Church - Yuma - 11545 E. 40th St., Yuma, AZ 85367 t) 928-342-3544 admin@sjnyuma.com www.sjnyuma.com Rev. George Holley, Pst.; Rev. John F. Friel, Pastor Emer.; Dcn. Joe Campbell; Dcn. Jerry A. Conrad; Dcn. Rick Douglas; Dcn. William G. Justice; Dcn. Giuseppe Tollis; Tracy Waters, DRE; CRP Stds.: 185

SCHOOLS: PRESCHOOL THRU HIGH SCHOOL

SCHOOLS

STATE OF ARIZONA

NOGALES

Lourdes Catholic School - (PRV) (Grades PreK-12) 555 E Patagonia Hwy, Nogales, AZ 85628; Mailing: P.O. Box 1865, Nogales, AZ 85628 t) 520-287-5659 highschoolprincipal@lcsnogales.org; elementaryprincipal@lcsnogales.org www.lcsnogales.org Sandra Contreras, Prin.; Rosalinda Perez, Prin.; Sr. Rosa Maria Ruiz, C.F.M.M., Pres.; Stds.: 268; Sr. Tchrs.: 2; Lay Tchrs.: 14

TUCSON

Immaculate Heart Academy - (PRV) (Grades PreSchool-8) 410 E. Magee Rd., Tucson, AZ 85704 t) 520-297-6672 academyoffice@ihschool.org ihschool.org Sr. Veronica Loya, Prin.; Stds.: 155; Lay Tchrs.: 16

HIGH SCHOOLS

STATE OF ARIZONA

TUCSON

St. Augustine Catholic High School - (DIO) (Grades

9-12) 8800 E. 22nd St., Tucson, AZ 85710 t) 520-751-8300 admissions@staugustinehigh.com www.staugustinehigh.com Dr. Barbara Monsegur, Prin.; Dave Keller, Pres.; Stds.: 257; Lay Tchrs.: 29

Immaculate Heart High School - (PRV) (Grades 9-12) 625 E. Magee Rd., Tucson, AZ 85704 t) 520-297-2851 sisteralicemartinez@gmail.com www.ihschool.com Sr. Alice M. Martinez, Prin.; Stds.: 41; Lay Tchrs.: 7

Salpointe Catholic High School - (PRV) (Grades 9-12) 1545 E. Copper St., Tucson, AZ 85719 t) 520-547-5878 ksullivan@salpointe.org www.salpointe.org Carmelite Order. Kay Sullivan, Pres.; Rev. Thomas Butler, O.Carm., In Res.; Rev. William J. Harry, O.Carm., In Res.; Rev. Paul Henson, O.Carm., In Res.; Stds.: 1,260; Pr. Tchrs.: 1; Lay Tchrs.: 97

San Miguel of Tucson Corporation - San Miguel Catholic High School - (PRV) 6601 S. San Fernando Rd., Tucson, AZ 85756 t) 520-294-6403 masond@sanmiguelhigh.org www.sanmiguelcristorey.org Dave Mason, Pres.; Reyna Mendoza, Registrar; Stds.: 322; Bro. Tchrs.: 3; Sr. Tchrs.: 1; Lay Tchrs.: 28

YUMA

Yuma Catholic High School - (PRV) 2100 W. 28th St., Yuma, AZ 85364 t) 928-317-7900 ycinfo@yumacatholic.org yumacatholic.org Rhett Stallworth, Prin.; Louis Pisano, Vice Prin.; Stds.: 497; Sr. Tchrs.: 1; Lay Tchrs.: 29

INSTITUTIONS LOCATED IN DIOCESE

ASSOCIATIONS [ASN]

PAYSON

***RIM Catholic Evangelization Association** - 814 N. Beeline Hwy., Payson, AZ 85541; Mailing: P.O. Box 1635, Payson, AZ 85547 c) 928-277-9851 tmdjfox@msn.com www.kpihradio.com Dcn. Tom Fox, Pres.;

CAMPUS MINISTRY / NEWMAN CENTERS [CAM]

THATCHER

Eastern Arizona College - Newman Center - 3592 W. 4th St., Thatcher, AZ 85552; Mailing: 311 S. Central Ave., Safford, AZ 85546 t) 928-428-4920 stroselima@gmail.com saintroselima-safford.com Rev. Nicodemus Shaghel, V.C., Admin.;

St. Rose of Lima - 311 S. Central Ave., Safford, AZ 85546 t) (928) 428-4920

TUCSON

University of Arizona Newman Center - 1615 E. 2nd St., Tucson, AZ 85719 t) 520-327-4665 newman@uacatholic.org www.uacatholic.org St. Thomas More Newman Center Rev. John Paul Forte, O.P., Pst.; Rev. Emmanuel Taylor, O.P., Par. Vicar; Rev. Nathan Castle, O.P., In Res.; Rev. Thomas DeMan, O.P., In Res.;

CATHOLIC CHARITIES [CCH]

TUCSON

Catholic Community Services of Southern Arizona, Inc. - 140 W. Speedway, Ste. 230, Tucson, AZ 85705 t) 520-623-0344 ccsinfo@ccs-soaz.org www.ccs-soaz.org Maryann Hockstad, Pres.; Marguerite Harmon, CEO; Asstd. Annu.: 150,000; Staff: 450

Social Service Agencies: Pima County - 140 W. Speedway, Ste. 230, Tucson, AZ 85705 t) 520-623-0344 ccsinfo@ccs-soaz.org ccs-soaz.org (Including City of Tucson) Marguerite Harmon, CEO; Asstd. Annu.: 150,000; Staff: 450

Catholic Community Services of Southern Arizona, Inc. - 140 W. Speedway, Ste. 230, Tucson, AZ 85705 t) (520) 623-0344 www.ccs-soaz.org

Catholic Community Services - Sierra Vista - 6049 E. Hwy. 90, Sierra Vista, AZ 85635 t) 520-458-4203

Catholic Community Services - Tucson - 140 W. Speedway, Ste. 130, Tucson, AZ 85705 www.ccs-soaz.org

Catholic Community Services - Yuma - 690 E. 32nd St., Yuma, AZ 85365 t) 928-341-9400 emendez@ccs-westaz.org Eva Mendez-Counts, Dir.;

Community Living Program - 268 W. Adams, Tucson, AZ 85705 t) 520-792-1906 karmenj@clpaz.org Karmen Johnson, Dir.;

Community Outreach Program for the Deaf - 268 W. Adams St., Tucson, AZ 85705 t) 520-792-1906 L'Don Sawyer, Dir.;

Douglas Shelter - 140 W. Speedway, Ste. 230, Tucson, AZ 85705; Mailing: P.O. Box 121, Douglas, AZ 85608 t) 520-364-2465 emendez@ccs-westaz.org Eva Mendez-Counts, Dir.;

Immigration Counseling Service - 140 W. Speedway, Ste. 130, Tucson, AZ 85705 annab@ccs-soaz.org Anna Burke, Dir.;

St. Jeanne Jugan Ministry with Elders - 140 W. Speedway, Ste. 230, Tucson, AZ 85705 t) (520) 623-0344 patsyk@ccs-soaz.org Dcn. Michael S. Gutierrez, Dir.;

Migration and Refugee Services - 140 W. Speedway, Ste. 130, Tucson, AZ 85705 annab@ccs-soaz.org Anna Burke, Dir.;

Pio Decimo Neighborhood Center - 848 S. 7th Ave., Tucson, AZ 85701 t) 520-622-2801 georger@ccs-pio.org George Rushing, Dir.;

Senior Nutrition Services - 5009 E. 29th St., Tucson, AZ 85711 t) 520-624-1562 karam@ccs-soaz.org Kara Melton, Dir.;

Sierra Vista Shelter - 140 W. Speedway, Ste. 230, Tucson, AZ 85705; Mailing: P.O. Box 1961, Sierra Vista, AZ 85636 t) 520-458-9096 emendez@ccs-westaz.org Eva Mendez-Counts, Dir.;

Valley Center for the Deaf - 5025 E. Washington St., Ste. 114, Phoenix, AZ 85034 t) 602-267-1921 cindyw@vcdaz.org Cindy Walsh, Dir.;

CEMETERIES [CEM]

TUCSON

Diocese of Tucson Catholic Cemeteries - 3555 N. Oracle Rd., Tucson, AZ 85705 t) 520-888-0860 info@dotcc.org www.dotcc.org (Sole Corporation) Patrick Lynch, Exec. Dir.;

CONVENTS, MONASTERIES, AND RESIDENCES FOR WOMEN [CON]

DOUGLAS

Loretto Convent - 1200 14th St., Douglas, AZ 85607 t) 522-234-0968 c) 520-227-7319 csandoval@diocesetucson.org; sistertcaridad@lorettoschool.org Sr. Caridad Sandoval, O.C.D., Contact; Srs.: 4

NOGALES

St. Joseph Convent - 405 N. Carondelet Dr., Nogales, AZ 85621-2454 t) 520-287-7139 clmrponce@yahoo.com Sr. Celia Ma. Ponce, C.F.M.M., Supr.; Srs.: 5

Our Lady of Lourdes Convent - 555 E. Patagonia Hwy., Nogales, AZ 85628-1865; Mailing: P.O. Box 1865, Nogales, AZ 85628-1865 t) 520-287-3377 rruiz@diocesetucson.org Sr. Rosa Maria Ruiz, C.F.M.M., Supr.; Srs.: 6

SONOITA

Santa Rita Abbey - 14200 E. Fish Canyon Rd., Sonoita, AZ 85637-6545 t) 520-455-5595 sracommty@gmail.com www.santaritaabbey.org Cistercian Nuns of the Strict Observance, O.C.S.O. Sr. Victoria Murray, O.C.S.O., Prioress; Srs.: 11

TUCSON

St. Ann Convent - 3820 N. Sabino Canyon Rd., Tucson, AZ 85750-6534 t) 520-298-0064; 520-886-1451 stanns@q.com Sr. Luisa Sanchez, I.H.M., Supr.; Srs.: 7

Immaculate Heart Lodge Convent - 410 E. Magee Rd., Tucson, AZ 85704 t) 520-742-5896 sralice@ihschool.org Sr. Alice M. Martinez, Supr.; Srs.: 4

Maria Community - 7818 N. Blue Brick Dr., Tucson, AZ 85743 t) 520-444-8052 irmao@netzero.net Sr. Irma Odabashian, C.S.J., Contact; Srs.: 2

La Paz de Jose Community - 3458 E. Third St., Tucson, AZ 85716 t) 520-795-1974 jbartholomeaux@diocesetucson.org Sr. Jeanne Bartholomeaux, S.C., Contact; Srs.: 2

San Xavier Mission Convent - 1996 W. San Xavier Rd., Tucson, AZ 85746 t) 520-746-4779 Franciscan Sisters of Christian Charity Sr. Carla Riach, O.S.F., Supr.; Srs.: 5

YUMA

Immaculate Conception Convent - 500 S. 24th Ave., Yuma, AZ 85364 t) 928-783-5224 smbkor@hotmail.com Sr. Mary Beth Kornely, O.S.F., Dir.; Srs.: 4

ENDOWMENTS / FOUNDATIONS / TRUSTS [EFT]

HEREFORD

Our Lady of the Sierras Foundation - 10235 S. Twin Oaks Rd., Hereford, AZ 85615; Mailing: P O Box 269, Hereford, AZ 85615 t) 520-378-2950 office@ourladyofthesierras.org www.ourladyofthesierras.org A Marian Shrine Lester Eugene Mundt, Pres.; Charles A Irwin, Vice. Pres.;

TUCSON

Carondelet Foundation Inc. - 2202 N. Forbes Blvd., Exec. Ste., Tucson, AZ 85745-2682; Mailing: 4600 Edmundson Rd., St. Louis, MO 63134 t) 314-733-8000 craig.cordola@ascension.org www.ascension.org Craig Cordola, Exec.;

***Catholic Community Services Foundation** - 140 W. Speedway Blvd., Ste. 230, Tucson, AZ 85705 t) 520-670-0809 development@ccs-soaz.org Sandy Erickson, Contact;

Catholic Foundation for the Diocese of Tucson Stewardship and Charitable Giving - 192-2 S. Stone Ave., Tucson, AZ 85701; Mailing: P.O. Box 31, Tucson, AZ 85702 t) 520-838-2505 khutchinson@diocesetucson.org; ebollinger@diocesetucson.org www.cathfnd.org The official fundraising entity for the Diocese, including its parishes, schools, and ministries. Most Rev. Edward J. Weisenburger, Bishop; Rev. Edward F. Lucero, Moderator; Dcn. Gregory Henderson, CEO, Diocese of Tucson, Ex-Officio; Elizabeth Dorsey Bollinger, Exec. Dir.; Les Orchekowsky, Chair; Kevin Schick, Secy.; Paul Pellegrino, Treas.; Rev. Msgr. Domencio Pinti, Mem.; Rev. Alan Valencia, Mem.; Denis Fitzgibbons, Mem.; Sergio Cardona, Mem.; John Meurant, Mem.; Jeanne Gale, Mem.; Natalie Fernandez Lee, Mem.; Kathy Cuprak, Mem.; Joe Wittmann, Mem.; MaryAnn Wittmann, Mem.;

Parish Pooled Investment Trust - 192 S. Stone Ave., Bldg. #2, Tucson, AZ 85701; Mailing: P.O. Box 31, Tucson, AZ 85702 t) 520-838-2553 cbarrios@diocesetucson.org www.diocesetucson.org Rev. Edward F. Lucero, Moderator; Rev. George Holley, Chair; Dcn. Gregory Henderson, Exec.; Ezzre Robles Diana, Trustee; John Moothart, Trustee; Jimmy Munoz Cano, Trustee; Don Romano, Trustee;

***Salpointe Catholic Education Foundation** - 1545 E. Copper St., Tucson, AZ 85719 t) 520-547-5878 ksullivan@salpointe.org Jennifer Harris, Dir.;

MISCELLANEOUS [MIS]

GOODYEAR

Knights of Columbus - Arizona State Council - 14175 W. Indian School, Ste. B4-626, Goodyear, AZ 85395 t) (602) 326-8511 www.kofc-az.org Luigi Baratta, State Dep.;

HEREFORD

Rachel's Vineyard Retreat Ministries Tucson and Southern Arizona, Inc. - 3107 E. Serritos Ranch Rd., Hereford, AZ 85615; Mailing: P.O. Box 1085, Hereford, AZ 85615 t) 520-743-6777 rachelsvineyardtucson@cox.net www.rachelsvineyardtucson.org Rev. Emilio Landeros Chapa; Rev. Msgr. John J. Cusack; Rev. Robert A. Rodriguez;

MARANA

Christ Child Society of Tucson - 13142 N. Rivercane Loop, Marana, AZ 85658-4031; Mailing: P.O. Box 36212, Tucson, AZ 85740 t) 585-200-9026 c) 520-400-4447 info@christchildtucson.org www.christchildtucson.org Deb Auclair, Pres.;

Retorno (Marriage Retorno) - 12563 N. Summer Wind Dr., Marana, AZ 85658 t) 520-869-9910 awamammen@gmail.com www.marriageretornocpr.org Prayer Retreat for Couples or Marriage Retorno (Couple Prayer Retreat) Rev. Robert Brazaskas;

NOGALES

Kino Border Initiative - 81 N. Terrace Ave., Nogales, AZ 85621; Mailing: P.O. Box 159, Nogales, AZ 85628-0159 t) 520-287-2370 jtorres@kinoborderinitiative.org; jwilliams@kinoborderinitiative.org www.kinoborderinitiative.org Pedro De Velasco, Dir.; Rev. Peter Neeley, S.J., Dir.; Monica Olivas, Dir.; Jorge Torres, Dir.; Joanna Williams, Dir.; Bro. Victor Yanez, Dir.;

TUCSON

Arizona's Catholic Tuition Support Organization (CTSO) - 192 S. Stone Ave., Bldg. 2, Tucson, AZ 85701; Mailing: P.O. Box 31, Tucson, AZ 85702 t) 520-838-2571 gqmarum@diocesetucson.org www.ctso-tucson.org Robert Huber, Pres.; Gracie Quiroz Marum, CEO;

Ascension Arizona - 2202 N. Forbes Blvd., Exec. Ste., Tucson, AZ 85745-2682; Mailing: 4600 Edmundson Rd., St. Louis, MO 63134 t) 314-733-8000 thomas.vanosdol@ascension.org www.ascension.org Thomas VanOsdol, Exec. Vice Pres. & Chief Mission Integration Of.; Craig Cordola, COO;

Casa Maria - 401 E. 26th St., Tucson, AZ 85713 t) 520-624-0312 casamariatucson@yahoo.com casamariatucson.org

Diocese of Tucson Catholic Committee on Scouting - 4165 W Winter Wash Dr, Tucson, AZ 85745; Mailing: P.O. Box 65685, Attn: Joe Reilly, Tucson, AZ 85728 c) 520-982-0982 fjreilly63@gmail.com Rev. Robert A. Rodriguez, Chap.; Joe Reilly, Chair;

The Oratory of St. Gianna - 338 W. University Blvd., Tucson, AZ 85705; Mailing: P.O. Box 87350, Tucson, AZ 85754 t) 520-883-4360 stgianna.tucson@institute-christ-king.org www.institute-christ-king.org/tucson-home Rev. Canon Jonathon Fehrenbacher, I.C.R.S.S., Rector; Rev. Canon Bryan Silvey, I.C.R.S.S., Vice Rector;

Padre Kino Vocations Ministry for the Diocese of Tucson - 192 S. Stone Ave., Bldg. #2, Tucson, AZ 85701; Mailing: P.O. Box 31, Tucson, AZ 85702 t) 520-245-9564 rosiegar@msn.com Rosie Garcia, Pres.; Kenneth Larsen, Vice. Pres.; Bruce Fink, CFO;

***Reachout, Inc.** - 2648 N. Campbell Ave., Tucson, AZ 85719 t) 520-321-4300 info@reachoutwomenscenter.com www.friendsofrwc.life Jeane Breen, Pres.; RJ Saavedra, Dir.;

The Roman Catholic Diocese of Tucson Our Faith, Our Hope, Our Future - 192 S. Stone Ave., Bldg. #2, Tucson, AZ 85702-0031; Mailing: P.O. Box 31, Tucson, AZ 85702-0031 t) 520-838-2554 ghenderson@diocesetucson.org www.diocesetucson.org Rev. Edward F. Lucero, Dir.; Most Rev. Edward J. Weisenburger, Pres.; Dcn. Gregory Henderson, Secy.; Alicia Corti, Dir.; John C. Shaheen, Dir.;

San Miguel Corporate Internship - 6601 S. San Fernando Rd., Tucson, AZ 85756 t) 520-294-6403 millers@sanmiguelhigh.org www.sanmiguelcristorey.org Dave Mason, Pres.; Samantha Miller, Vice. Pres.;

***Society of St. Vincent de Paul** - 829 S. 6th Ave., Tucson, AZ 85701 t) 520-628-7837 inbox@svdptucson.org www.svdptucson.org Maurice P. Blois Jr., Pres.;

***Sr. Jose Women's Center** - 1050 S. Park Ave., Tucson, AZ 85719; Mailing: P.O. Box 1028, Tucson, AZ 85702 t) 520-909-3905; 520-954-3373 execdirector@sisterjose.org sisterjose.org Jean Fedigan, Contact;

The St. Thomas More Society of Southern Arizona - 455 W. Paseo Redondo, Tucson, AZ 85701 t) 520-620-6222 vinzlaw@aol.com Vincent Lacsamana, Contact;

VAIL

Magnificat - Tucson Chapter - 702 E Blue Mesa Pl., Vail, AZ 85641 t) 520-237-7060 tucsonmagnificat@gmail.com A ministry to Catholic women. Pima East Vicariate Chapter. Gloria Roberts, Coord.;

YUMA

St. John Neumann Roman Catholic Church Regional Columbarium - Yuma - 11545 E. 40th St., Yuma, AZ 85367 t) 928-342-3544 admin@sjnyuma.com www.sjnyuma.com Rev. George Holley, Pres.; Juventino Solano, Dir.;

MONASTERIES AND RESIDENCES FOR PRIESTS AND BROTHERS [MON]

TOPAWA

San Francisco Solano Friary - 1 St. Cathrine Mission, San Solano Missions, Topawa, AZ 85639-0210; Mailing: PO Box 210, Topawa, AZ 85639-0210 t) 520-383-2350 pboegel@sbofm.org Friar John Gibbons, O.F.M., Pst.; Rev. William J. Minkel, O.F.M., Par. Vicar; Friar Peter Boegel, O.F.M., Supr.; Brs.: 1; Priests: 2

TUCSON

Carmelite Priory - 1540 E. Glenn St., Tucson, AZ 85719 t) 520-325-1537 phenson@carmelnet.org Our Lady Of Mt. Carmel Priory Rev. Paul Henson, O.Carm., Prior; Rev. Emanuel Franco-Gomez, O.Carm., Treas.; Priests: 6

Jesuit Community of the Vatican Observatory - 2017 E. Lee St., Tucson, AZ 85719 t) 520-795-1694 ccorbally@as.arizona.edu; twilliams@jesuts.org Jesuit Residence. Rev. Christopher Corbally, S.J., Supr.; Rev. Justin Whittington, S.J., Admin.; Bro. Thomas R. Williams, S.J., Treas.; Bro. Guy Consolmagno, S.J., Dir.; Rev. Richard P. Boyle, S.J., Astronomer; Rev. David A. Brown, S.J., Astronomer; Rev. Jean-B Kikwaya Eluo, S.J., Astronomer; Rev. Pavel Gabor, S.J., Astronomer; Rev. Christoforus Bayu Risanto, S.J., Astronomer; Brs.: 2; Priests: 7

***Vatican Observatory Foundation** - 2017 E. Lee St., Tucson, AZ 85719 t) (520) 795-1694 corbally@as.arizona.edu

Vatican Observatory Research Group - Steward Observatory, The University of Arizona, 933 N. Cherry Ave., Tucson, AZ 85721-0065 t) 520-621-6043 vaticanobservatoryrg@gmail.com

Redemptorist Society of Arizona Desert House of Prayer Residence - 7101 W. Picture Rocks Rd., Tucson, AZ 85743 t) 520-744-3400 office@desertrenewal.org desertrenewal.org Rev. Stephen Rehrauer, C.Ss.R., Dir.; Rev. Peter Connolly, C.Ss.R., In Res.; Rev. Ricardo Elford, C.Ss.R., Migrant Min.; Rev. Thomas Fransiscus, C.Ss.R., In Res.; Rev. Patrick Grile, C.Ss.R., Retreat Staff; Rev. Brian Johnson, C.Ss.R., Rector, Our Lady of the Desert; Rev. James E. Shea, C.Ss.R., Retreat Staff; Rev. Huy Vu, C.Ss.R., Admin., Santa Catalina; Priests: 8

San Xavier Mission Friary - 1950 W. San Xavier Rd., Tucson, AZ 85746 t) 520-294-3015 c) 415-341-7374 Rev. Ignatius Harding, O.F.M., In Res.; Friar David Paz, O.F.M., In Res.; Rev. Alfonso Ponchie Vasquez, O.F.M., In Res.; Rev. Manuel Viera, O.F.M., In Res.; Brs.: 2; Priests: 3

Filial Houses - 4110 Jefferson St., Elfrida, AZ 85610; Mailing: P.O. Box 54, Elfrida, AZ 85610 t) 520-361-2419 buerofm@gmail.com Bro. David Buer, O.F.M., Vicar; Friar Hajime Okuhara, O.F.M., In Res.;

RETREAT HOUSES / RENEWAL CENTERS [RTR]

TUCSON

Desert House of Prayer Retreat House - 7101 W. Picture Rocks Rd., Tucson, AZ 85743 t) 520-744-3400 office@desertrenewal.org desertrenewal.org Rev. Stephen Rehrauer, C.Ss.R., Dir.;

Redemptorist Society of Arizona Redemptorist Renewal Center - 7101 W. Picture Rocks Rd., Tucson, AZ 85743 t) 520-744-3400 office@desertrenewal.org www.desertrenewal.org Rev. Stephen Rehrauer, C.Ss.R., Dir.; Rev. Peter Connolly, C.Ss.R., In Res.; Rev. Ricardo Elford, C.Ss.R., Migrant Ministry; Rev. Thomas Fransiscus, C.Ss.R., In Res.; Rev. Patrick Grile, C.Ss.R., Retreat Staff; Rev. Brian Johnson, C.Ss.R., Rector, Our Lady of the Desert; Rev. James E. Shea, C.Ss.R., Retreat Staff; Rev. Huy Vu, C.Ss.R., Administrator, Santa Catalina Parish;

An asterisk (*) denotes an organization that has established tax-exempt status directly with the IRS and is not covered by the USCCB Group Ruling.

Diocese of Tulsa

(Dioecesis Tulsensis)

MOST REVEREND DAVID A. KONDERLA

Bishop of Tulsa; ordained June 3, 1995; appointed Bishop of Tulsa May 13, 2016; installed June 29, 2016. Office: 12300 E. 91st St. S., Broken Arrow, OK 74012.

Chancery Office: 12300 E. 91st St. S., Broken Arrow, OK 74012. Mailing Address: P.O. Box 690240, Tulsa, OK 74169-0240. T: 918-294-1904; F: 918-294-0920.
www.dioceseoftulsa.org
bishop.office@dioceseoftulsa.org

ESTABLISHED FEBRUARY 7, 1973.

Square Miles 26,417.

The Diocese of Tulsa comprises the following 31 Counties: Adair, Atoka, Bryan, Cherokee, Choctaw, Coal, Craig, Creek, Delaware, Haskell, Hughes, Latimer, LeFlore, McCurtain, McIntosh, Mayes, Muskogee, Nowata, Okfuskee, Okmulgee, Osage, Ottawa, Pawnee, Payne, Pittsburg, Pushmataha, Rogers, Sequoyah, Tulsa, Wagoner and Washington.

For legal titles of parishes and institutions, consult the Chancery Office.

STATISTICAL OVERVIEW

Personnel

Bishop	1
Retired Bishops	1
Abbots	1
Priests: Diocesan Active in Diocese	63
Priests: Diocesan Active Outside Diocese	2
Priests: Retired, Sick or Absent	17
Number of Diocesan Priests	82
Religious Priests in Diocese	33
Total Priests in your Diocese	115
Extern Priests in Diocese	15
Ordinations:	
Diocesan Priests	1
Transitional Deacons	1
Permanent Deacons in Diocese	95
Total Brothers	40
Total Sisters	39

Parishes

Parishes	78
With Resident Pastor:	
Resident Diocesan Priests	48
Resident Religious Priests	1
Without Resident Pastor:	
Administered by Priests	29
Missions	2
New Parishes Created	1
Professional Ministry Personnel:	
Sisters	6
Lay Ministers	143

Welfare

Catholic Hospitals	10
Total Assisted	1,147,866
Health Care Centers	1
Total Assisted	274
Specialized Homes	2
Total Assisted	46
Special Centers for Social Services	8
Total Assisted	280,619

Educational

Diocesan Students in Other Seminaries	17
Total Seminarians	17
High Schools, Private	2
Total Students	1,383
Elementary Schools, Diocesan and Parish	9
Total Students	2,173
Elementary Schools, Private	3
Total Students	833
Catechesis/Religious Education:	
High School Students	1,453
Elementary Students	4,008
Total Students under Catholic Instruction	9,867
Teachers in Diocese:	
Priests	3
Sisters	6
Lay Teachers	401

Vital Statistics

Receptions into the Church:	
Infant Baptism Totals	1,162
Minor Baptism Totals	116
Adult Baptism Totals	147
Received into Full Communion	369
First Communions	1,208
Confirmations	1,156
Marriages:	
Catholic	242
Interfaith	63
Total Marriages	305
Deaths	480
Total Catholic Population	57,533
Total Population	1,745,057

LEADERSHIP

Vicar General - Very Rev. Gary Kastl;
Chancery Office - t) 918-294-1904
Chancellor - Dcn. Harrison Garlick;
Finance Office - Thomas Schadle, CFO; Philip J. Creider, Assets Mgr.;
Diocesan Consultors - Very Rev. Gary Kastl; Rev. Jack Gleason; Rev. J. Todd Nance;
Diocesan Marriage Tribunal -
Adjutant Judicial Vicar - Very Rev. Kenneth J. Harder;
Assessor - Rev. Duy Nguyen; Dcn. Larry Schneider;
Auditors - Dcn. Dean Wersel; Dcn. Kevin Malarkey;
Defender of the Bond - Very Rev. Samuel Perez;
Judges - Very Rev. Michael J. Knipe; Very Rev. Kenneth J. Harder; Very Rev. Khiet T. Nguyen;
Judicial Vicar - Very Rev. Michael J. Knipe;
Promoter of Justice - Very Rev. Samuel Perez;
Seminary Board - Very Rev. Gary Kastl; Rev. Michael Pratt, Dir.; Rev. Jack Gleason;

OFFICES AND DIRECTORS

Alcuin Institute for Catholic Culture - t) 918-307-4950 Dr. Richard Meloche, Pres.;
Archivist - t) 918-307-4956 Dr. Joey Spencer;
Calvary Cemetery - t) 918-299-7348 Dcn. John J. Johnson, CEO;
Campus Ministry - t) 918-599-0204 tu-newman@utulsa.edu Rev. David Webb, Chap.; Joshua Carl Funderburk, Devel. Dir. (joshfunderburk5@gmail.com); Gerald Murphy, Faith, Formation & Catechesis;
Catholic Charities of the Diocese of Tulsa - t) 918-949-4673 Dcn. Kevin Sartorious, CEO; Rev. Van Nguyen, Chap.;
Blessed Mother Teresa Dental Center - t) 918-508-7155
Emergency Services - t) 918-508-7127
Helping Center, Muskogee - t) 918-681-6115
Immaculate Conception Helping Center - t) 918-647-2220
Immigration Office - t) 918-508-7103
Madonna House - t) 918-508-7141
Mary Martha Outreach, Bartlesville - t) 918-337-3703
Ministry of Compassion, Broken Arrow - t) 918-258-5276
Pregnancy and Adoption Services - t) 918-508-7142
St. Elizabeth Lodge - t) (918) 508-7141
St. Jude Helping Center - t) 918-423-7707
Sallisaw Helping Center - t) 918-775-6111
Communications & Webmaster - t) 918-307-4933 Adam Minihan, Dir.; Daniel McCay, Media Mgr.;
Council of Catholic Women - mattipalluconi@gmail.com Matti Palluconi;
Diocesan Catholic Committee on Scouting - t) 918-250-8787 Dennis Zvacek;
Ecumenism - t) 918-299-9406 Rev. Leonard Ahanatu (Nigeria);
Faith and Works - t) 918-307-4942 Very Rev. Gary Kastl;
Family Life Office - t) 918-307-4914 Audrey Stubblefield, Coord.;
Hispanic Ministry - t) 918-307-4929 Cristina Contreras, Coord.; Rev. Leonardo Medina, Pastoral Del., Hispanic Ministries for Heavener; Rev. Juan Antonio Hernandez, Pastoral Del., Hispanic Ministries for Claremore;
Human Resources Partner - t) (918) 307-4916 Tim O'Brien;
Magazine "Eastern Oklahoma Catholic" - t) 918-307-4920 Adam Minihan, Editor;
Office of Divine Worship - t) 918-446-8124 Rev. John L. Grant, Dir.;
Office of Permanent Diaconate - t) 918-307-4921 Dcn. Lamar Yarbrough;
Parochial Schools - t) 918-307-4954 catholicschools.office@dioceseoftulsa.org David Dean, Supt.;
Priestly Life and Ministry - t) 918-294-1904 x4900 Very Rev. Bryan Brooks; Very Rev. Gary D. Kastl; Rev. Sean O'Brien;
Prison and Social Ministry - Dcn. Alan G. Mikell, Dir.;
Propagation of the Faith - t) 918-251-4000 Rev. Matthew J. Gerlach, Coord.;
Religious Formation & Education - t) 918-307-4939 Sarah Jameson, Dir.;
Victim Assistance Coordinator - t) 918-307-4919 Donna Eurich;
Vocations - t) 918-307-4936 Rev. Michael Pratt, Dir.; Very Rev. Gary Kastl; Rev. Sean O'Brien;
Young Adult & Campus Ministry & Pro-Life Ministry - t) 918-307-4923 Sarah Jameson;
Youth Ministry - t) 918-307-4907 Sky Creed;

PARISHES, MISSIONS, AND CLERGY

STATE OF OKLAHOMA

ANTLERS

St. Agnes - 503 E. Main, Antlers, OK 74523; Mailing: P.O. Box 206, Antlers, OK 74523 t) 580-326-7300 frtoddnance@gmail.com Rev. J. Todd Nance, Pst.; CRP Stds.: 9

BARTLESVILLE

St. James - 5500 Douglas Ln., Bartlesville, OK 74006 t) 918-335-0844 office_stjms@sbcglobal.net saintjamescatholicparish.org Rev. John O'Neill, Pst.; Rev. Carlos Loaiza, Assoc. Pst.; Dcn. Gerard Rutherford; CRP Stds.: 92

St. John's - 715 S. Johnstone Ave., Bartlesville, OK 74003 t) 918-336-4353; 918-335-0844 (CRP) crebartlesville@gmail.com; bartlesvillecatholicyouth@gmail.com www.stjohn-bartlesville.org Rev. John O'Neill, Pst.; Rev. Carlos Loaiza, Assoc. Pst.; Dcn. Charlie Moomaw; Dcn. Dan Pickett; Carey Auschwitz, DRE; CRP Stds.: 115

St. John's School - (Grades PreK-8) 816 S. Keeler Ave., Bartlesville, OK 74003 t) 918-336-0603 radebaugh@sjcs-ok.org sjcs-ok.org Lexie Radebaugh, Prin.; Stds.: 150; Lay Tchrs.: 14

BIXBY

St. Clement of Rome - 15501 S. Memorial Dr., Bixby, OK 74008 t) 918-366-3166 ereyes@stcbixby.org www.stcbixby.org Rev. Jeffrey S. Polasek, Pst.; Dcn. Jose Guzman; Dcn. Neal Harton; Molly Garrison, DRE; Enilda Reyes de Velazquez, Admin.; Bonnie Griffin, Music Min.; Maria Ester Flores, Youth Min.; CRP Stds.: 178

BROKEN ARROW

St. Anne - 301 S. 9th St., Broken Arrow, OK 74012 t) 918-251-4000 ljones@stanneba.org; frmatt@stanneba.org www.stanneba.org Rev. Matthew J. Gerlach, Pst.; Rev. Daniel Gormley, Assoc. Pst.; Dcn. John Mahon; Dcn. Kevin Malarkey; Dcn. Thomas Moyes; Laura Jones, Dir.; Megan Polly, Contact; CRP Stds.: 221

Church of Saint Benedict - 2200 W. Ithica St., Broken Arrow, OK 74012 t) 918-455-4451 saintben@tulsacoxmail.com www.saintben.com Very Rev. Bryan Brooks, Pst.; Rev. Alessandro Calderoni, Assoc. Pst.; Dcn. Richard Berberet; Dcn. Daniel Brennan; Dcn. Dave Johnson; Dcn. Kevin Stephenson; Dcn. Rick Stookey; Deb Malcom, Youth Min.; Lisa Remmert, DRE; Viviana Suarez, RCIA Coord.; CRP Stds.: 328

Preschool - 2200 W Ithica St, Broken Arrow, OK 74012 t) 918-455-5851 Diana Phillips, Dir.;

CLAREMORE

St. Cecilia - 1304 N Dorothy Ave., Claremore, OK 74017 t) 918-341-2343; 918-341-4238 (CRP) st.cecilia@tulsacoxmail.com www.stceciliaclaremore.com Rev. Sylvanus Amaobi (Nigeria), Pst.; CRP Stds.: 95

COLLINSVILLE

St. Therese Church and Diocesan Eucharistic Shrine of Saint Therese - 1007 N. 19th St., Collinsville, OK 74021 t) 918-371-2704 office@sttheresok.org; education@sttheresok.org www.sttheresok.org Rev. Jose Calvillo, Pst.; Dcn. Peter McLane; Amanda Brillhart, DRE; CRP Stds.: 127

COWETA

St. Vincent de Paul - 15842 S. 297th E. Ave., Coweta, OK 74429; Mailing: P.O. Box 597, Coweta, OK 74429-0597 t) 918-486-4757 svdp1@tulsacoxmail.com stvincentdepaul-coweta.org Rev. Leonard U. Ahanotu, Pst.; CRP Stds.: 23

CUSHING

SS. Peter and Paul - 401 E. Oak St., Cushing, OK 74023; Mailing: P.O. Box 828, Cushing, OK 74023 t) 918-225-0644 cushingcatholicchurch@yahoo.com Rev. Desmond Ibeneme, Pst.; Dcn. Kenneth Longbrake; CRP Stds.: 41

St. Mary - 321 S. Cimarron, Drumright, OK 74030; Mailing: PO Box 828, Cushing, OK 74023

DEWEY

Our Lady of Guadalupe - 400 W. 9th St., Dewey, OK 74029 t) 918-534-3420 c) 918-907-0377 ourladyguadalupe@sbcglobal.net Rev. Leonard H. Higgins, Pst.; Kim Roecker, DRE; Mindy Freeman, Admin.; CRP Stds.: 15

St. Catherine - 217 W. Modoc, Nowata, OK 74048; Mailing: P.O. Box 804, Nowata, OK 74048-0804 t) 918-273-0737

DURANT

St. William - 802 W. University Blvd., Durant, OK 74701-3226 t) 580-924-1989 churchwilliam@sbcglobal.net; fr.carl.kerkemeyer@dioceseoftulsa.org www.stwilliamdurant.com Rev. Carl Kerkemeyer, Pst.; CRP Stds.: 62

St. Patrick Church - 2103 S. Mississippi, Atoka, OK 74525; Mailing: 802 W. University Blvd., Durant, OK 74701-3226 t) (580) 924-1989 (St. William Parish Durant)

FAIRFAX

Sacred Heart - 333 S. 8th St., Fairfax, OK 74637 t) 918-642-5053 Rev. Hrudaya Raj Gade, Pst.; CRP Stds.: 7

Saint Joseph, Cleveland - 421 S. Petit, Hominy, OK 74035 t) 918-358-2333

St. Joseph - Osage & C Ave., Cleveland, OK 74020 t) (918) 358-2333

GROVE

St. Elizabeth - 1653 113th St., N.W., Grove, OK 74344 t) 918-786-9312 frvalleysteliz@boltfiber.net; sfletchersteliz@boltfiber.net stelizabeth-grove.org Rev. Valerian Gonsalves, Pst.; CRP Stds.: 66

HARTSHORNE

Holy Rosary - 912 Cherokee, Hartshorne, OK 74547; Mailing: P.O. Box 389, Hartshorne, OK 74547 t) 918-308-3312 holyrosaryparish1@gmail.com Rev. Leonardo Medina, Pst.; CRP Stds.: 7

HENRYETTA

St. Michael - 1004 W. Gentry St., Henryetta, OK 74437; Mailing: P.O. Box 148, Henryetta, OK 74437 t) 918-652-3445 Rev. Robert Duck, STL, Pst.; Angela Glover, DRE; CRP Stds.: 12

St. Teresa - 8th & Broadway, Okemah, OK 74859 t) (918) 652-3445

HOLDENVILLE

St. Stephen's - 515 E. Hwy., Holdenville, OK 74848 t) 405-379-2512; (918) 652-3445 Rev. Robert Duck, STL, Pst.;

HUGO

Immaculate Conception - 196 Bearden Springs Rd., Hugo, OK 74743; Mailing: P.O Box 99, Hugo, OK 74743 t) 580-326-7300 frtoddnance@gmail.com Rev. J. Todd Nance, Pst.; CRP Stds.: 9

St. Jude - 511 11th St., Boswell, OK 74727; Mailing:

PO Box 99, Hugo, OK 74743 t) (580) 326-7300 Rev. Todd J. Nance, Pst.;

IDABEL

St. Francis De Sales - 13 S.E. Jefferson St., Idabel, OK 74745 t) 580-286-3275 fr.stephen.austin@dioceseoftulsa.org www.stfrancisidabel.org Rev. Stephen E. Austin, Pst.; CRP Stds.: 15

KREBS

St. Joseph's - 290 N.W. Church St., Krebs, OK 74554; Mailing: P.O. Box 621, Krebs, OK 74554 t) 918-423-6695; 918-426-4919 stjosephchurch.krebs@yahoo.com www.stjoseph-krebs.org Rev. Kingsley George-Obilonu, Pst.; Dcn. Bill Anderson; CRP Stds.: 25

St. Paul's - 502 S. 6th St., Eufaula, OK 74432; Mailing: P.O. Box 943, Eufaula, OK 74432 t) 918-689-7345 fr.kingsley.georgeobilonu@dioceseoftulsa.org

LANGLEY

St. Frances of Rome - 13286 Hwy. 28, Langley, OK 74350-0267; Mailing: P.O. Box 267, Langley, OK 74350 t) 918-782-2248 stfrances267@gmail.com Rev. Valentine Ndebilie, Pst.; CRP Stds.: 11

MCALESTER

St. John - 300 E. Washington Ave., McAlester, OK 74501 t) 918-423-0810 mail@stjohn-mcalester.org Rev. Jovita Okonkwo, Pst.; CRP Stds.: 105

MIAMI

Sacred Heart - 2515 N. Main, Miami, OK 74354 t) 918-542-5281 sacredheartmiami.2019@gmail.com; sacredheartfn@gmail.com sacredheartmiami.org Very Rev. Samuel Perez, Pst.; Debbie Jurgensmeyer, Contact; CRP Stds.: 120

MUSKOGEE

Saint Joseph Church - 301 N. Virginia St., Muskogee, OK 74403 t) 918-687-1351 lferguson@stjosephok.com; lcarbone@stjosephok.com www.stjosephok.com Rev. Richard F. Cristler, Pst.; Rev. Robert M. Dye, Assoc. Pst.; Dcn. Edwin Falleur; Dcn. John Hale; Dcn. Carlos Moreno; CRP Stds.: 156

Saint Joseph Church School - (Grades PreK-8) 323 N. Virginia, Muskogee, OK 74403 t) 918-683-1291 chutchens@stjoseph74403.com www.stjoseph74403.com Joanne Myers, Prin.; Julie Rowland, Librn.; Stds.: 74; Lay Tchrs.: 9

OKMULGEE

St. Anthony's - 515 S. Morton Ave., Okmulgee, OK 74447; Mailing: P.O. Box 698, Okmulgee, OK 74447 t) 918-756-4385 saumchurches@gmail.com Rev. Kenneth Harder, Pst.; CRP Stds.: 32

Uganda Martyrs - 808 E. 3rd, Okmulgee, OK 74447 t) (918) 756-4385

OWASSO

St. Henry - 8500 N. Owasso Expwy., Owasso, OK 74055-0181; Mailing: P.O. Box 181, Owasso, OK 74055 t) 918-272-3710; 918-272-3740 (CRP) office@sthenryowasso.org; lvaldez@sthenryowasso.org www.sthenryowasso.org Rev. Matthew G. LaChance, Pst.; Rev. Bala Jayanna Yaddanapalli, Assoc. Pst.; Michael Hall, CRE; CRP Stds.: 331

PAWHUSKA

Immaculate Conception - 1314 N. Lynn Ave., Pawhuska, OK 74056 t) 918-827-1414 Rev. Emmanuel-Lugard Nduka (Nigeria), Pst.; Dcn. Robert Axsom; CRP Stds.: 23

St. Mary - 3rd & Chestnut, Barnsdall, OK 74002; Mailing: 1314 Lynn Ave., Pawhuska, OK 74056 t) 918-287-1414

St. Ann - Gypsy St. & Taylor St., Shidler, OK 74652; Mailing: 1314 Lynn Ave., Pawhuska, OK 74056 t) 918-287-1414

PAWNEE

St. John - 333 S. 8th St., Pawnee, OK 74058; Mailing: P.O. Box 828, Cushing, OK 74023 t) 918-225-0644 Rev. Desmond Ibeneme, Pst.;

POTEAU

Immaculate Conception - 502 N. Bagwell, Poteau, OK 74953; Mailing: P.O. Box 237, Poteau, OK 74953 t) 918-647-3475 imcchurch03@yahoo.com Rev. Sean Obrien, Pst.; David Jones, Bus. Mgr.; CRP Stds.: 62

St. Joseph - 1406 N.W. 7th St., Stigler, OK 74462 t) (918) 647-3475 Rev. Sean O'Brien, Pst.;

St. Elizabeth Seton - 16526 U.S. Hwy. 271, Spiro, OK 74959 t) (918) 647-3475 Rev. Sean O'Brien, Pst.;

PRYOR

St. Mark's - 1507 S. Vann, Pryor, OK 74361; Mailing: P.O. Box 576, Pryor, OK 74362 t) 918-825-4186 stmarkspryor@gmail.com Rev. Valentine Ndebilie, Pst.; Katrina Ballou, DRE; CRP Stds.: 28

SALLISAW

St. Francis Xavier - 2110 N. Dogwood, Sallisaw, OK 74955 t) 918-775-6217 saintfx@sbcglobal.net www.saintfrancisxaviersallisaw.com/ Rev. Lawrence Nwachukwu, Pst.; CRP Stds.: 16

St. John the Evangelist - 32136 Hwy. 82, Cooksom, OK 74427; Mailing: P.O. Box 4, Cookson, OK 74427 t) (918) 775-6217

St. Joseph - 103 Smith St., Webbers Falls, OK 74470; Mailing: P.O. Box 53, Webbers Falls, OK 74470 t) (918) 775-6217

Saint Kateri Tekakwitha - 110840 S. 4760 Rd., Muldrow, OK 74948; Mailing: P.O. Box 17, Roland, OK 74954 t) (918) 775-6217

SAND SPRINGS

St. Patrick's - 204 E. Fourth St., Sand Springs, OK 74063 t) 918-245-5840 stpatrickcatholicchurch@tulsacoxmail.com; bishnik59@gmail.com stpatrickok.wix.com/home Rev. Joe C. Townsend, Pst.; Dcn. Todd Slezak; CRP Stds.: 29

Our Lady of the Lake - 450 Cimarron Dr., Mannford, OK 74044; Mailing: 204 E. 4th St., Sand Springs, OK 74063 t) 918-865-2360

SAPULPA

Sacred Heart - 1777 E. Grayson Ave., Sapulpa, OK 74066 t) 918-224-0944 sacredheart@tulsacoxmail.com www.sacredheartsapulpa.com Rev. Louis C. Obirieze (Nigeria), Pst.; Dcn. Mark Pittman; Dcn. Greg Stice; CRP Stds.: 31

SKIATOOK

Sacred Heart - 109 W. 5th St., Skiatook, OK 74070; Mailing: P.O. Box 878, Skiatook, OK 74070 t) 918-396-1179 shc4luv@yahoo.com (Formerly St. William). Rev. Kenneth Iheanacho (Nigeria), Pst.;

STILLWATER

St. Francis Xavier Catholic Church - 711 N. Country Club Rd., Stillwater, OK 74075 t) 405-372-6886 leah@sfxstillwater.org; sfx@sfxstillwater.org www.sfxstillwater.org Rev. Brian D. O'Brien, Pst.; Rev. Robert Healey, Assoc. Pst.; Dcn. Tom Wallace Cabeen; Dcn. Glenn Collum; Dcn. Bart Brashears; Dcn. Paul Govek; CRP Stds.: 200

St. John the Evangelist Parish and Catholic Student Center - 201 N. Knoblock, Stillwater, OK 74075 t) 405-372-6408 catholicpokes@gmail.com buildingsaints.com/ Rev. Kerry J. Wakulich, Pst.; CRP Stds.: 20

TAHLEQUAH

St. Brigid - 807 Crafton St., Tahlequah, OK 74464 t) 918-456-8388 brigidtahlequah@gmail.com stbrigidtahlequah.com Rev. David Medina, Pst.; Dcn. Roy Don Callison; Dcn. Joseph Faulds; Dcn. Mark Keeley; Carolina Landaverde, CRE; CRP Stds.: 154

San Juan Diego Mission - 23 W. Division St., Stilwell, OK 74960; Mailing: 807 Crafton St., Tahlequah, OK 74464 c) (918) 704-7689 missionsjd@gmail.com Rev. David Medina;

TULSA

Holy Family Cathedral - 122 W. 8th St., Tulsa, OK 74119; Mailing: 820 S. Boulder Ave., Tulsa, OK 74119 t) 918-582-6247 hfc@tulsacathedral.com Very Rev. Gary Kastl, Rector; Rev. Joshua Votruba, Par. Vicar; Rev. Msgr. Gregory A. Gier, Pastor Emer.; Dcn. Thomas Gorman; Dcn. Jerry Mattox; Dcn. John Conro; Dcn. Larry Schneider; Dcn. J. Thomas; CRP Stds.: 50

Holy Family Cathedral School - (Grades PreK-11) 820 S. Boulder Ave., Tulsa, OK 74119 t) (918) 582-6247 school@tulsacathedral.com www.holyfamilycathedralschool.com Dr. Marcel Brown, Headmaster; Patricia Spoerl, Prin.; Stds.: 198; Lay Tchrs.: 17

St. Augustine's - 1728 E. Apache, Tulsa, OK 74110 t) 918-428-3280 saintaugustineparishtulsaok@yahoo.com www.staugustine-tulsa.org Rev. Celestine Obidiegwu, Pst.; Dcn. Steve Litwack; CRP Stds.: 24

St. Bernard of Clairvaux - 4001 E. 101st St., Tulsa, OK 74137 t) 918-299-9406 meellingson@stbernardstulsa.org; emailus@stbernardstulsa.org stbernardstulsa.org Rev. Jack Gleason, Pst.; Rev. Archie Fernandez, Assoc. Pst.; Dcn. Pius Devasahayam; Dcn. Alan Mikell; Dcn. Robert Martin; Dcn. Timothy Sullivan; Dcn. Richard Campbell; Dcn. Vincent Gruel; Sharon Lechtenberg, DRE; Mike Ellingson, Bus. Mgr.; CRP Stds.: 328

Preschool - t) 918-299-9432 tara@stbernardstulsa.org

St. Catherine - 4532 S. 25th West Ave., Tulsa, OK 74107 t) 918-446-8124 church@saint-catherine.org www.saintcatherinechurch.org Rev. John L. Grant, Pst.; Rev. Robert C. Kim (Myanmar), Assoc. Pst.; Dcn. Craig Victor; Dcn. David C. Hamel; CRP Stds.: 133

St. Catherine School - (Grades PreSchool-8) 2515 W. 46th St., Tulsa, OK 74107 t) 918-446-9756 school@saint-catherine.org www.saintcatherineschool.org Michelle Anthamatten, Prin.; Stds.: 160; Pr. Tchrs.: 1; Sr. Tchrs.: 3; Lay Tchrs.: 11

St. Joseph - 302 N. Elm, Bristow, OK 74010; Mailing: P.O. Box 603, Bristow, OK 74010 t) (918) 446-8124 saintjosephbristow@gmail.com www.saintjosephbristow.org Dcn. Tom Loney;

Christ the King - 1520 S. Rockford Ave., Tulsa, OK 74120 t) 918-584-4788 ctkparish@christthekingcatholic.church www.christthekingcatholic.church Very Rev. Elkin Gonzalez, Pst.; Rev. Jon Paul Fincher, Pst. Assoc.; Dcn. John L. Sommer, Bus. Mgr.; Dcn. Michael Loeffler; Dcn. Dean Wersal, RCIA Coord.; Dcn. Harrison Garlick; CRP Stds.: 481

Marquette School - (Grades PreK-8) 1519 S. Quincy, Tulsa, OK 74120 t) 918-584-4631 www.marquetteschool.org Jay Luetkemeyer, Prin.; Tracey Robinson, Vice Prin.; Stds.: 386; Sr. Tchrs.: 1; Lay Tchrs.: 46

Marquette Early Childhood Development Center (ECDC) - (Grades PreK-k) 1528 S. Quincy Ave., Tulsa, OK 74120 t) 918-583-3334 www.marquetteschool.org Pepper McGough, Dir.;

Church of St. Mary - 1347 E. 49th Pl., Tulsa, OK 74105 t) 918-749-1423; 918-749-1423 x108 (CRP) church@churchofsaintmary.com churchofsaintmary.com Rev. Stuart Crevcoure, Pst.; Rev. Vince Fernandez, Assoc. Pst.; Rev. Msgr. Dennis C. Dorney, Pastor Emer.; Dcn. Richard Bender; Dcn. Stephen Craig; Dcn. Gary Gamino; Dcn. Kevin Maloney; CRP Stds.: 148

School of St. Mary - (Grades PreK-8) 1365 E. 49th Pl., Tulsa, OK 74105 t) 918-749-9361 www.schoolofsaintmary.com Lindsay Maricle, Prin.; Peggy Padalino, Librn.; Stds.: 316; Lay Tchrs.: 20

Church of the Madalene - 3188 E. 22nd St., Tulsa, OK 74114 t) 918-744-0023 x18 (CRP); 918-744-0023 theresafyler@gmail.com www.madalenetulsa.org Rev. Desmond Okpogba (Nigeria), Pst.; Dcn. Joseph Fritsch; Dcn. Nelson M. Sousa; CRP Stds.: 38

St. Francis Xavier Church and Diocesan Marian Shrine & Expiatory Temple of Our Lady of Guadalupe - 2434 E. Admiral Blvd., Tulsa, OK 74110 t) 918-592-6770 Rev. Elmer Rodriguez, Pst.; Rev. Juan Angel Grajeda, Assoc. Pst.; Alfredo Marcelo, DRE; CRP Stds.: 500

Instituto Bilingue Guadalupano - t) 918-592-9179 Maria Inez Alcaraz, Dir.;

St. Joseph Church - 14905 E. 21st St., Tulsa, OK 74134 t) 918-438-1380 fr_dovann@yahoo.com www.gxgiusetulsa.net/ Rev. Dovan Nguyen, Pst.; CRP Stds.: 191

St. Monica's - 633 Marshall Pl., Tulsa, OK 74106 t) 918-587-2965 stmonicachurch@aol.com www.stmonica-tulsa.org Rev. Celestine Obidiegwu, Pst.; Dcn. Steve Litwack;

Most Precious Blood Parish - 3029 S. 57th W. Ave., Tulsa, OK 74107 t) 918-615-8404 secretary@mpbptulsa.com www.mpbptulsa.com Parish of St Peter Rev. William Define, F.S.S.P., Pst.; Rev. Elijah Mundattuchundayil, F.S.S.P., Assoc. Pst.; CRP Stds.: 56

SS. Peter and Paul - 1419 N. 67th E. Ave., Tulsa, OK 74115 t) 918-836-2596 churchoffice@peterandpaultulsa.org; mrs.campbell1@gmail.com Rev. Sean T. Donovan, Pst.; Rev. Juan Antonio Hernandez, Assoc. Pst.; Dcn. Erick Bell; Dcn. Thomas Young; Karen Campbell, DRE; CRP Stds.: 137

SS. Peter and Paul School - (Grades PreK-8) 1428 N. 67th E. Ave., Tulsa, OK 74115 t) (918) 836-2165 stspeterandpaul@gmail.com peterandpaultulsa.org Joanne Brown, Prin.; Stds.: 153; Lay Tchrs.: 11

St. Pius X - 1727 S. 75 E. Ave., Tulsa, OK 74112 t) 918-622-4488 parish@spxtulsa.org church.spxtulsa.org Rev. Joshua E. Litwack, Pst.; Rev. David Carvajal Casal, Assoc. Pst.; Dcn. Charles Beard; Dcn. Craig Gunter; Arlene Hausher, DRE; CRP Stds.: 57

St. Pius X School - (Grades PreK-8) 1717 S. 75 E. Ave., Tulsa, OK 74112 t) 918-627-5367 bkrukowski@spxtulsa.org spxtulsa.org Heidi McCoy, Prin.; Therese Iten, Librn.; Stds.: 350; Lay Tchrs.: 27

Resurrection - 4804 S. Fulton, Tulsa, OK 74135 t) 918-663-1907 debbis@cotrtulsa.org; churchoffice@cotrtulsa.org www.resurrection-tulsa.org Very Rev. Michael J. Knipe, Pst.; Dcn. Peter Byrne; Dcn. James Scarpitti; Dcn. Pedro Munoz; Gigi Chavez, DRE; Sergio Chavez, Liturgy Dir.; CRP Stds.: 115

St. Thomas More - 2720 S. 129 E. Ave., Tulsa, OK 74134-2411 t) 918-437-0168 info@stthomasmoretulsa.com; fr.briones@stthomasmoretulsa.com www.stthomasmoretulsa.com Rev. Daniel Campos, Par. Vicar; Dcn. Ernesto Fernandez; Rev. Jose Maria Briones (Mexico), Pst.; Rev. Leonardo Morales, Assoc. Pst.; Dcn. Augusto Pellechia; Dcn. Isidro Saenz; CRP Stds.: 525

VINITA

Holy Ghost - 120 W. Sequoyah Ave., Vinita, OK 74301 t) 918-256-2281 holyghostvinita@gmail.com holyghostvinita.org Rev. Michael E. Cashen, Pst.; Dcn. Anthony Hicks; Stephen Miller, DRE; CRP Stds.: 8

WAGONER

Holy Cross - 708 S.W. 15th St., None, Wagoner, OK 74467; Mailing: P.O. Box 710, None, Wagoner, OK 74477-0710 t) 918-201-5225 fr.leonard.ahanotu@dioceseoftulsa.org; holycrosswagoner@gmail.com holycross-wagoner.org Rev. Leonard U. Ahanotu, Pst.; Dcn. Jim Ruyle; CRP Stds.: 10

WILBURTON

Sacred Heart - 102 Centerpoint Rd., Wilburton, OK 74578 t) 918-465-3996 Rev. Bryan Ketterer, Pst.; Dcn. Clement Bradley;

Holy Trinity - 170564 U.S. Hwy. 271, Clayton, OK 74536; Mailing: P.O. Box 747, Clayton, OK 74536 t) (918) 569-4767

St. Catherine of Siena - 501 2nd St., Talihina, OK 74571; Mailing: P.O. Box 362, Talihina, OK 74571 t) 918-567-2587

SCHOOLS: PRESCHOOL THRU HIGH SCHOOL

SCHOOLS

STATE OF OKLAHOMA

BROKEN ARROW

All Saints Catholic School - (PAR) (Grades PreK-8) 299 S. 9th St., Broken Arrow, OK 74012 t) 918-251-3000 www.allsaintsba.com Suzette Williams, Prin.; Elizabeth Frisillo, Vice Prin.; Laura King, Bus. Mgr.; Stds.: 386; Lay Tchrs.: 30

TULSA

Monte Cassino School - (PRV) (Grades PreK-8) 2206 S. Lewis, Tulsa, OK 74114 t) (918) 746-4146 www.montecassino.org Tracie Kutmas, Interim Head of School; Vicky Adams, Prin.; Janou Farrell, Prin.; Marci Jubelirer, Prin.; Carmen Applegate, Librn.; Carly Carver, Librn.; Stds.: 760; Sr. Tchrs.: 1; Lay Tchrs.: 75

***San Miguel School of Tulsa, Inc.** - (PRV) (Grades 6-8) 2444 E. Admiral Blvd., Tulsa, OK 74110 t) 918-728-7337 rogercarter@sanmigueltulsa.org Roger Carter, Admin.; Stds.: 73; Lay Tchrs.: 7

HIGH SCHOOLS

STATE OF OKLAHOMA

TULSA

Bishop Kelley High School, Inc. - (PAR) (Grades 9-12) 3905 S. Hudson, Tulsa, OK 74135-5699 t) 918-627-3390 sistermaryhanah@bishopkelley.org; ukinzer@bishopkelley.org www.bishopkelley.org Sr. Mary Hanah Doak, R.S.M., Pres.; Rev. Duy Nguyen, Chap.; Jim Franz, Prin.; Jeff Pratt, Vice Prin.; Rick Musto, Bus. Mgr.; Doug Thomas, Admin.; Stds.: 847; Sr. Tchrs.: 1; Lay Tchrs.: 62

Cascia Hall Preparatory School - (PRV) (Grades 6-12) 2520 S. Yorktown Ave., Tulsa, OK 74114 t) 918-746-2600 pwilson@casciahall.com www.casciahall.com Coed College Preparatory School. Augustinians (Order of St. Augustine). Rev. Philip C. Cook, O.S.A., Headmaster; Rev. Stephen Isley, O.S.A., Pst.; Rev. Roland F. Follmann, O.S.A., In Res.; Rev. William A. Hamill, O.S.A., In Res.; Bro. Jack Hibbard, O.S.A., Prior; Shawn Gammill, Upper School Prin.; Todd Goldsmith, Middle School Prin.; Joan O'Brien Hubble, Librn.; Dcn. Michael Loeffler, Dcn, Campus Min.; Stds.: 536; Pr. Tchrs.: 2; Lay Tchrs.: 63

INSTITUTIONS LOCATED IN DIOCESE

ASSOCIATIONS [ASN]

COWETA

Apostolate for the Most Holy Rosary and the Brown Scapular Association - 15842 S. 297th East Ave., Coweta, OK 74429; Mailing: P.O. Box 1041, Coweta, OK 74429 t) (918) 810-3043

CAMPUS MINISTRY / NEWMAN CENTERS [CAM]

STILLWATER

St. John's University Parish and Catholic Student Center - 201 N. Knoblock, Stillwater, OK 74075 t) 405-372-6408 catholicpokes@gmail.com www.stjohn-stillwater.org Rev. Kerry J. Wakulich, Chap.; Cathy Perry, Campus Min.;

TAHLEQUAH

Northeastern State University Catholic Student Organization - 807 Crafton St., Tahlequah, OK 74464 t) 918-456-8388 fr.david.medina@dioceseoftulsa.org; brigidtahlequah@gmail.com Rev. Stuart Crevcoure, Chap.; Savanna Hale, Pres.;

TULSA

St. Philip Neri University Parish - 440 S. Florence Ave, Tulsa, OK 74104 t) 918-599-0204 tu-newman@utulsa.edu www.tu-newman.org Rev. David Michael Webb, Chap.; Gerald Murphy, Campus Min.; Joshua Carl Funderburk, Bus. Mgr.;

CEMETERIES [CEM]

TULSA

Calvary - 9101 S. Harvard, Tulsa, OK 74136 t) 918-299-7348 kimberly.cross@calvarycemetery.org Dcn. John J. Johnson, CEO;

CONVENTS, MONASTERIES, AND RESIDENCES FOR WOMEN [CON]

TULSA

St. Joseph Monastery - 2200 S. Lewis, Tulsa, OK 74114-3100 t) 918-742-4989 sisters@stjosephmonastery.org www.stjosephmonastery.org Congregation of Benedictine Sisters of Sacred Hearts, Inc. Sr. Marie Therese Long, Prioress; Srs.: 12

ENDOWMENTS / FOUNDATIONS / TRUSTS [EFT]

BROKEN ARROW

Catholic Foundation of Eastern Oklahoma, Inc. - 12300 E. 91st St. S., Broken Arrow, OK 74012; Mailing: P.O. Box 690240, Tulsa, OK 74169 t) 918-294-1904 philip.creider@dioceseoftulsa.org Philip J. Creider, Treas.;

Saint Francis of Assisi Tuition Assistance Trust - 12300 E. 91st St. S., Broken Arrow, OK 74012; Mailing: P.O. Box 690240, Tulsa, OK 74169-0240 t) 918-294-1904 Very Rev. Elkin Gonzalez, Vicar;

Saint John Vianney Seminary Trust - 12300 E. 91st St. S., Broken Arrow, OK 74012; Mailing: P.O. Box 690240, Tulsa, OK 74169-0240 t) 918-294-1904 info@dioceseoftulsa.org Rev. Michael Pratt, Contact;

Priest Retirement Trust of the Roman Catholic Diocese of Tulsa - 12300 E. 91st St. S., Broken Arrow, OK 74012; Mailing: P.O. Box 690240, Tulsa, OK 74169-0240 t) 918-294-1904 philip.creider@dioceseoftulsa.org Very Rev. Elkin Gonzalez;

HULBERT

Foundation for the Annunciation Monastery of Clear Creek - 5804 W. Monastery Rd., Hulbert, OK 74441-5698 t) 918-772-2454 abbey@clearcreekmonks.org www.clearcreekmonks.org Rt. Rev. Philip Anderson, O.S.B., Abbot;

MUSKOGEE

St. Joseph School Endowment Trust - 301 N. Virginia, Muskogee, OK 74403 t) 918-687-1351 jmyers@stjosephok.com Rev. Richard F. Cristler, Contact;

TULSA

Bishop Kelley High School Endowment Trust - 3905 S. Hudson Ave., Tulsa, OK 74135 t) 918-627-3390 fr.gary.kastl@dioceseoftulsa.org www.bishopkelley.org Sr. Mary Hanah Doak, R.S.M., Pres.;

St. John Health System Foundation, Inc. - 1923 S. Utica Ave, Tulsa, OK 74104 t) (918) 744-2268 ronald.tremblay@ascension.org www.ascension.org Jeff Nowlin, CEO; Ronald Tremblay, Contact;

HOSPITALS / HEALTH SERVICES [HOS]

BARTLESVILLE

***Jane Phillips Memorial Medical Center** - 3500 E. Frank Phillips Blvd., Bartlesville, OK 74006 t) (918) 744-2268 ronald.tremblay@ascension.org www.ascension.org Jeffrey Dale Nowlin, CEO; Ronald Tremblay, Contact; Bed Capacity: 104; Asstd. Annu.: 83,231; Staff: 552

BROKEN ARROW

St. John Broken Arrow, Inc. (Ascension St John Broken Arrow) - 1000 W. Boise Cir., Broken Arrow, OK 74102 t) (918) 744-2268 ronald.tremblay@ascension.org www.ascension.org Jeff Nowlin, CEO; Ronald Tremblay, Contact; Bed Capacity: 44; Asstd. Annu.: 69,180; Staff: 239

MUSKOGEE

***Saint Francis Hospital Muskogee, Inc.** - 300 Rockefeller Dr., Muskogee, OK 74401 t) 918-684-2555 makeeling@saintfrancis.com Michelle Keeling, Pres.; Bed Capacity: 320; Asstd. Annu.: 94,066; Staff: 844

OWASSO

Owasso Medical Facility, Inc. (St. John Owasso) - 12451 E. 100th St. N., Owasso, OK 74055 t) (918) 744-2268 ronald.tremblay@ascension.org www.ascension.org Jeff Nowlin, CEO; Ronald Tremblay, Contact; Bed Capacity: 36; Asstd. Annu.: 44,744; Staff: 176

TULSA

Saint Francis Hospital - 6161 S. Yale Ave., Tulsa, OK 74136 t) 918-494-2200 tlgrade@saintfrancis.com www.saintfrancis.com Rev. John V. Choorackunnel, C.M.I. (India), Chap.; Rev. Edmond G. Kline, Chap.; Douglas Williams, Pres.; Dr. Cliff A. Robertson, CEO; Bed Capacity: 1,088; Asstd. Annu.: 481,109; Staff: 5,635

Saint Francis Hospital South, LLC - 10501 E. 91st St. S., Tulsa, OK 74133; Mailing: 6161 S. Yale, Tulsa, OK 74136 t) 918-307-6000 tlgrade@saintfrancis.com Todd Schuster, Pres.; Bed Capacity: 110; Asstd. Annu.: 88,159; Staff: 615

St. John Health System, Inc. (Ascension St. John) - 1923 S. Utica, Tulsa, OK 74104 t) (918) 744-2268 ronald.tremblay@ascension.org www.stjohnhealthsystem.com Ronald Tremblay, Contact; Jeffrey Dale Nowlin, CEO; Bed Capacity: 89

St. John Medical Center, Inc. (Ascension St. John Medical Center) - 1923 S. Utica Ave., Tulsa, OK 74104 t) (918) 744-2268 ronald.tremblay@ascension.org stjohnhealthsystem.com Ronald Tremblay, Contact; Jeffrey Dale Nowlin, CEO; Bed Capacity: 503; Asstd. Annu.: 236,923; Staff: 2,371

Laureate Psychiatric Clinic and Hospital, Inc. - 6655 S. Yale, Tulsa, OK 74136 t) 918-481-4000 tlgrade@saintfrancis.com Brandon Keppner, Pres.; Bed Capacity: 90; Asstd. Annu.: 13,393; Staff: 331

VINITA

Saint Francis Hospital Vinita, Inc. - 735 N. Forman, Vinita, OK 74301 t) 918-256-0203 mlculp@saintfrancis.com Todd Schuster, Pres.; Bed Capacity: 50; Asstd. Annu.: 37,061; Staff: 136

MISCELLANEOUS [MIS]

BROKEN ARROW

Veritas Tax School Scholarships, Inc. - 12300 S. 91st St., Broken Arrow, OK 74120 t) (918) 294-1904 Very Rev. Gary Kastl, Dir.;

HULBERT

American Foundation for the Beatification of Empress Zita - 5800 W. Monastery Rd., Hulbert, OK 74441 t) 214-763-7890 empresszitacause@gmail.com Diane Schwind, Pres.;

TULSA

***Saint Francis Health System, Inc.** - 6161 S. Yale Ave., Tulsa, OK 74136 t) 918-494-8452 tlgrade@saintfrancis.com Jake Henry Jr., CEO; Dr. Cliff A. Robertson, CEO;

St. John Auxiliary, Inc. (Ascension St. John Auxiliary) - 1923 S. Utica Ave., Tulsa, OK 74104 t) (918) 744-2268 ronald.tremblay@ascension.org www.ascension.org Jeff Nowlin, CEO; Ronald Tremblay, Contact;

Porta Caeli House Corporation - 2440 N. Harvard Ave., Tulsa, OK 74115; Mailing: PO Box 580460, Tulsa, OK 74158-0460 t) 918-935-2600 ghighberger@portacaeli.org Dcn. Kevin Sartorius, Exec.;

MONASTERIES AND RESIDENCES FOR PRIESTS AND BROTHERS [MON]

HULBERT

Our Lady of the Annunciation of Clear Creek Abbey - 5804 W. Monastery Rd., Hulbert, OK 74441-5698 t) 918-772-2454 abbey@clearcreekmonks.org www.clearcreekmonks.org Rt. Rev. Philip Anderson, O.S.B., Abbot; Rev. Francis Bethel, O.S.B., Prior; Rev. Joshua Morey, O.S.B., Subprior; Rev. Christopher Andrews, O.S.B.; Rev. Mark Bachmann, O.S.B.; Rev. Francis Bales, O.S.B.; Rev. Francis Xavier Brown, O.S.B.; Rev. Lawrence Brown, O.S.B.; Rev. Partrick Carter, O.S.B.; Rev. Christian Felkner, O.S.B.; Rev. Mary David Howells, O.C.S.O.; Rev. Joseph Hudson, O.S.B.; Rev. Vincent Hulot, O.S.B.; Rev. Jose Maria Lagos, O.S.B.; Rev. Philippe Le Bouteiller des Haries, O.S.B.; Rev. James Garrity; Rev. John McFadden; Rev. Peter Miller, O.S.B.; Rev. Robert Nesbit, O.S.B.; Rev. Andrew Norton, O.S.B.; Rev. Matthew Shapiro, O.S.B.; Rev. Ulrich Maria Theuerer, O.S.B.; Rev. James Ullmer, O.S.B.; Rev. Joseph Willett, O.S.B.; Brs.: 40; Priests: 24

An asterisk (*) denotes an organization that has established tax-exempt status directly with the IRS and is not covered by the USCCB Group Ruling.

Diocese of Tyler

(Dioecesis Tylerensis)

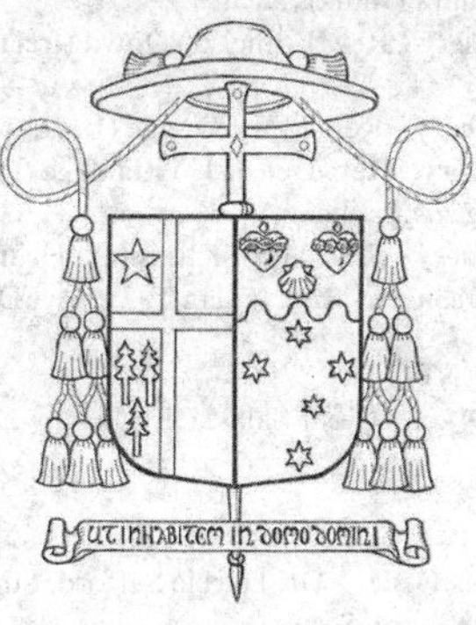

MOST REVEREND JOSEPH E. STRICKLAND

Bishop of Tyler; ordained June 1, 1985; appointed Bishop of Tyler September 29, 2012; ordained November 28, 2012. Chancery: 1015 E.S.E. Loop 323, Tyler, TX 75701-9656.

Chancery: 1015 E.S.E. Loop 323, Tyler, TX 75701-9656. T: 903-534-1077; F: 903-534-1370.

ESTABLISHED DECEMBER 12, 1986.

Square Miles 23,443.

Comprises the following Counties in the State of Texas: Anderson, Angelina, Bowie, Camp, Cass, Cherokee, Delta, Franklin, Freestone, Gregg, Harrison, Henderson, Hopkins, Houston, Lamar, Leon, Madison, Marion, Morris, Nacogdoches, Panola, Rains, Red River, Rusk, Sabine, San Augustine, Shelby, Smith, Titus, Trinity, Upshur, Van Zandt, and Wood.

For legal titles of parishes and diocesan institutions, consult the Chancery Office.

STATISTICAL OVERVIEW

Personnel
Bishop....1
Priests: Diocesan Active in Diocese....60
Priests: Diocesan Active Outside Diocese....9
Priests: Retired, Sick or Absent....18
Number of Diocesan Priests....87
Religious Priests in Diocese....11
Total Priests in your Diocese....98
Extern Priests in Diocese....12
Ordinations:
Diocesan Priests....2
Transitional Deacons....1
Permanent Deacons in Diocese....86
Total Brothers....1
Total Sisters....50

Parishes
Parishes....53
With Resident Pastor:
Resident Diocesan Priests....49
Resident Religious Priests....2
Without Resident Pastor:
Administered by Priests....2
Missions....14
Pastoral Centers....2
New Parishes Created....1
Professional Ministry Personnel:
Brothers....1
Sisters....9
Lay Ministers....14

Welfare
Catholic Hospitals....7
Total Assisted....1,133,526
Special Centers for Social Services....1
Total Assisted....32,000
Other Institutions....10
Total Assisted....25,000

Educational
Diocesan Students in Other Seminaries....18
Total Seminarians....18
High Schools, Diocesan and Parish....3
Total Students....184
Elementary Schools, Diocesan and Parish....4
Total Students....485
Catechesis / Religious Education:
High School Students....773
Elementary Students....5,442
Total Students under Catholic Instruction....6,902
Teachers in Diocese:
Priests....2
Sisters....1
Lay Teachers....66

Vital Statistics
Receptions into the Church:
Infant Baptism Totals....1,705
Minor Baptism Totals....139
Adult Baptism Totals....59
Received into Full Communion....110
First Communions....1,726
Confirmations....1,849
Marriages:
Catholic....276
Interfaith....19
Total Marriages....295
Deaths....436
Total Catholic Population....119,168
Total Population....1,436,247

LEADERSHIP

Bishop - Most Rev. Joseph E. Strickland;
Vicar General - Very Rev. John J. Gomez (Colombia);
Episcopal Vicar for Priests - Rev. Robert H. Lanik;
Chancellor - Peyton Low;
Finance Officer - Dwayne Friesen;

ADVISORY BOARDS, COMMISSIONS, COMMITTEES, AND COUNCILS

College of Consultors - Rev. Guillermo Gabriel-Masonet; Very Rev. John J. Gomez (Colombia); Rev. Victor Hernandez (Colombia);
Finance Council - Neal Slaten, Chair; Dwayne Friesen; Very Rev. John J. Gomez (Colombia);
Presbyteral Council - Rev. James M. Rowland (Ireland), Chair; Rev. Justin Braun, Vice Chmn.; Rev. Jonathon Frels, Secy.;
Permanent Deacon Council - Dcn. Federico Aguilar; Clara Aguilar; Dcn. Fred Arrambidez;
Priest Retirement Board - Rev. Steve Paradis; Rev. James M. Rowland (Ireland); Rev. Jesudoss Thomas (India);
Society for the Propagation of the Faith - Very Rev. John J. Gomez (Colombia);

COMMUNICATIONS

Communications Office - Elizabeth Slaten, Dir.;

DEANERIES

Central Deanery - Rev. James M. Rowland (Ireland), Dean;
East Central Deanery - Msgr. Zacharias S. Kunnakkattuthara (India), Dean;
Northeast Deanery - Rev. Francis O'Dowd (Ireland), Dean;
Northwest Deanery - Rev. Mark Dunne (Ireland), Dean;
Southeast Deanery - Rev. Denzil J. Vithanage, Dean (denzilvithanage@gmail.com);
Southwest Deanery - Rev. Mark Kusmirek, Dean;
West Central Deanery - Rev. Nolan T. Lowry, Dean;

DEVELOPMENT

Development Office - Cesar Salas, Dir.; Danny Elzner; Joana Ruiz;

EDUCATION

Catholic Schools Office - Dr. Darbie Safford, Supt.; Cynthia Cunningham, Secy.;

FAITH FORMATION

Faith Formation Office - Dr. Luke Arredondo, Dir.; Lizabeth Marquez, Secy.;

FAMILY LIFE

Marriage & Family Life Office - Deanna Johnston, Dir.;

FINANCE

Accounting Office - Dwayne Friesen, CFO; D'Andrea Jones; Kristina Wood;

HUMAN RESOURCES

Human Resources Office - Peyton Low, Dir.; Helen Fox, Benefits Coord.;

PASTORAL SERVICES

Prison Ministry Office - Rev. Carlos Piedrahita (Colombia), Dir.; Rev. Timothy J. Kelly (Ireland);

TRIBUNAL

Judicial Vicar - Rev. Lawrence Rasaian (India);
Judges - Rev. Lawrence Rasaian (India); Rev. James M. Rowland (Ireland); Rev. Cristian Casado Carmona (Spain);
Defender of the Bond - Rev. Gavin N. Vaverek;
Promoter of Justice - Very Rev. John J. Gomez (Colombia);
Staff - Delia Campos; Dyana Noriega;

MISCELLANEOUS / OTHER OFFICES

Bishop's Office - Adela Hernandez, Exec. Asst.; Gloria Bustos, Asst.;
Ethics and Integrity Office - Ariseli Lara, Dir.; Veronica Gonzalez, Asst.;
Permanent Deacons Office - Dcn. Fred Arrambidez, Dir.;
Vocations Office - Rev. Justin Braun, Dir.; Rev. Nelson D. Munoz (Colombia), Assoc. Dir.;

PARISHES, MISSIONS, AND CLERGY

STATE OF TEXAS

ATHENS

St. Edward Church - 800 E. Tyler, Athens, TX 75751-2140; Mailing: St. Edwards Education & Ministry Ctr, 1310 S. Palestine, Athens, TX 75751 t) 903-675-2509 x106 pastor@stedwardsparish.org; secretarysteward@gmail.com stedwardsparish.org Rev. Nolan T. Lowry, Pst.; CRP Stds.: 199

ATLANTA

St. Catherine of Siena Church - 309 N. Louise St., Atlanta, TX 75551-2237 t) 903-796-4494 scatlanta1962@gmail.com Rev. George Blasick, C.Ss.R., Admin.; CRP Stds.: 30

BUFFALO

St. Kateri Tekakwitha Church - 208 N. Merrill, Buffalo, TX 75831; Mailing: P.O. Box 878, Buffalo, TX 75831 t) 903-322-3705 stktbuffalotx@gmail.com Rev. Gabriel C. Uzondu (Nigeria), Admin.; CRP Stds.: 118

CANTON

St. Therese - 885 1st Monday Ln., Canton, TX 75103-3676 t) 903-567-4286 sttheresecanton@gmail.com www.sttheresecanton.org Rev. Jesudoss Thomas (India), Pst.; Dcn. James Burkel; Dcn. Jonathan Fadely; Dcn. Larry Edwards; Dcn. Alan Stehsel; CRP Stds.: 127

CARTHAGE

St. William of Vercelli - 4088 N.W. Loop, Carthage, TX 75633-3346 t) 903-693-3766 stwilliamofvercelli@hotmail.com sites.google.com/site/stwilliamofvercellicarthage/ Rev. Steve Paradis, Pst.; Dcn. Juan Gonzalez; Dcn. Lawrence Bate, DRE; CRP Stds.: 32

CENTER

St. Therese of Lisieux - 717 FM 2974, Center, TX 75935-6006 t) 936-598-8458 st.therese.centertx@gmail.com; fathernelson.munoz@yahoo.com Rev. Nelson D. Munoz (Colombia), Pst.; CRP Stds.: 86

Epiphany - 3072 U.S. Hwy. 59 S., Timpson, TX 75975-9350 t) (936) 598-8458

CENTERVILLE

St. Leo the Great - 549 S. Commerce St., Centerville, TX 75833-0356; Mailing: P.O. Box 356, Centerville, TX 75833-0356 t) 903-536-5012 stleocentervilletx@aol.com; caseyfox02@yahoo.com Rev. Joseph Lourdusamy, Pst.; CRP Stds.: 50

St. Thomas More Mission - 1 Ranch Rd., Hilltop Lakes, TX 77871; Mailing: P. O. Box 1745, Hilltop Lakes, TX 77871 t) 936-855-2963 ruth@himecpa.com

CHANDLER

St. Boniface - 318 S. Broad St., Chandler, TX 75758 t) 903-849-3234 frkey2007@yahoo.com Rev. Paul R. Key, Pst.; Rev. Albert Jerome Motte III, Par. Vicar; CRP Stds.: 34

CLARKSVILLE

St. Joseph - 406 E. Broadway St., Clarksville, TX 75426-3110 t) 903-427-5044 stjosephclarksville@gmail.com Rev. Gavin N. Vaverek, Pst.; Rev. Raymundo Garcia, Par. Vicar; CRP Stds.: 25

CROCKETT

St. Francis of the Tejas - 609 N. Fourth St., Crockett, TX 75835-4001 t) 936-544-5338 stfranciscrockett@windstream.net stfranciscrockett.com Rev. Selvaraj Sinnappan, Pst.; CRP Stds.: 75

DAINGERFIELD

Our Lady of Fatima - 1305 Bert St., Daingerfield, TX 75638-9704 t) 903-645-5637 fatima51@windstream.net Rev. Eugene Tillekeratne, S.S.S., Pst.; CRP Stds.: 50

DIBOLL

Our Lady of Guadalupe - 100 Maynard St., Diboll, TX 75941-0310; Mailing: P.O. Box 310, Diboll, TX 75941-0310 t) 936-829-3659; 936-366-2829 (CRP) olg_diboll@hotmail.com; yvttdlcrz@yahoo.com Rev. Luis Fernando Arroyave (Colombia), Pst.; CRP Stds.: 100

EMORY

St. John the Evangelist - 551 E. FM 2795, Emory, TX 75440 t) 903-473-5116 office@stjohnemory.org stjohnemory.org Rev. Michael Ledesma, Admin.; Dcn. Federico Aguilar; Dcn. Marcelino Espinosa; CRP Stds.: 60

St. Celestine - 870 Stadium Dr., Grand Saline, TX 75140; Mailing: P.O. Box 444, Grand Saline, TX 75140 – 0444 t) (903) 962-8177 stcelestine@gmail.com stcelestine.org Rev. Victor Hernandez (Colombia), Pst.; Dcn. William Flores;

FAIRFIELD

St. Bernard of Clairvaux - 630 W. Main St., Fairfield, TX 75840-1418 t) 903-389-4616 stbernardscathchurch@windstream.net Rev. Juan Carlos Sardinas, Pst.; CRP Stds.: 35

St. Mary Mission - 609 Cedar St., Teague, TX 75860-1617; Mailing: 630 W. Main St., Fairfield, TX 75840

FLINT

St. Mary Magdalene Church - 18221 FM 2493, Flint, TX 75762 t) 903-894-7647 general@catholicflint.org www.catholicflint.org Rev. James M. Rowland (Ireland), Pst.; Dcn. Larry Gottschalk; Dcn. Dennis King; CRP Stds.: 191

FRANKSTON

St. Charles Borromeo Catholic Church - 1379 N. Frankston Hwy., Frankston, TX 75763-2112 t) 903-876-3309 c) 936-218-6710 stcharles1379@gmail.com www.stcharlesfrankston.com Rev. Mark Kusmirek, Pst.; CRP Stds.: 18

GILMER

St. Francis of Assisi - 2514 FM 852, Gilmer, TX 75644-0704 t) 903-797-3303 stfrancisgilmer@gmail.com stfrancisgilmertx.org Rev. Hector Arvizu, Admin.; Dcn. Guylan Blasingame; CRP Stds.: 53

GLADEWATER

St. Theresa of the Infant Jesus - 10138 Union Grove Rd., Gladewater, TX 75647-0967 t) 903-845-2306 office@sttheresagladewater.org www.sttheresagladewater.org Rev. Francis O'Dowd (Ireland), Pst.; CRP Stds.: 7

GUN BARREL CITY

St. Jude - 172 Luther Ln., Gun Barrel City, TX 75156 t) 903-887-1452 Rev. John-Mary Sayf Bowlin, Pst.; Dcn. Juan Cazares; Dcn. Richard Sykora; CRP Stds.: 110

HEMPHILL

St. Pius I - 309 Starr St., Hemphill, TX 75948-1925; Mailing: P.O. Box 1925, Hemphill, TX 75948 t) 409-787-4189 sp5566@windstream.net www.stpiushemphill.org Rev. Emmanuel Akpobolokemi (Nigeria), Admin.; Dcn. Kenneth Horn; CRP Stds.: 14

St. Augustine - 621 State Hwy. 21 W., San Augustine, TX 75972; Mailing: P.O. Box 524, San Augustine, TX 75972-0524 t) (936) 275-1514 stpiuscc@gmail.com catholicsanaugustinetx.org/

HENDERSON

St. Jude - 1100 Longview Dr., Henderson, TX 75652 t) 903-657-4398 stjudeshenderson@gmail.com www.facebook.com/stjudehendersontx Rev. Jose J. Kannampuzha, Pst.; Dcn. Lino Huerta; CRP Stds.: 136

HOLLY LAKE RANCH

Holy Spirit - 1612 S. FM 2869, Holly Lake Ranch, TX 75765-7339 t) 903-769-3235 holy.spirit2@yahoo.com www.holyspirithollylake.com Rev. Michael T. Snider, Pst.;

JACKSONVILLE

Our Lady of Sorrows - 1023 Corinth Rd., Jacksonville, TX 75766-3267 t) 903-586-4538

secretary@oloschurch.com oloschurch.com/ Rev. Jayaseelanraj Lucas, Pst.; Rev. Freddy Celano, Assoc. Pst.; Dcn. Juventino Torres; Ana Decious, DRE; CRP Stds.: 249

Our Lady of Guadalupe - 304 FM 235 E., Jacksonville, TX 75766 t) (903) 586-4538

Venerable Antonio Margil-Alto - 498 W. San Antonio St. Hwy. 21, Alto, TX 75925 t) 903-683-1862 Rev. Jorge Dinguis, Admin.;

JEFFERSON

Immaculate Conception - 201 N. Vale St., Jefferson, TX 75657; Mailing: 209 W. Lafayette St., Jefferson, TX 75657 t) 903-665-2869 icccjefferson@sbcglobal.net icccjeffersontx.org Msgr. Zacharias S. Kunnakkattuthara (India), Pst.; Rev. Selvan Melkias, Par. Vicar; Rev. Isaac Oviedo, Par. Vicar; CRP Stds.: 51

Immaculate Conception Catholic Church, Jefferson, TX Foundation - 124 W. Lafayette, Jefferson, TX 75657-2143 t) (903) 665-2869 Tammy Cornett, Chair;

St. Lawrence of Brindisi - 1465 W. Texas Ave., Waskom, TX 75692 t) 903-687-2385 c) (903) 360-6925 slccwaskom@outlook.com stlawrencebrindisiwaskom.org

KILGORE

Christ the King - 1407 Broadway Blvd., Kilgore, TX 75662-3209; Mailing: 1508 Broadway Blvd., Kilgore, TX 75662 t) 903-483-2500 ctkoffice@ctkkilgore.org; frjhenao@ctkkilgore.org www.ctkkilgore.org Rev. John Henao-Lopez, Pst.; Rev. Luis C. Pena, Par. Vicar; Dcn. Isidro Sanchez; Dcn. Alejandro Cisneros; CRP Stds.: 190

Our Lady Queen of Angels - 707 S. Bradford St., Overton, TX 75684 t) (903) 834-0251 overtontxcatholicchurch.wordpress.com Rev. Francis O'Dowd (Ireland), Pst.;

LINDALE

Holy Family - 16314 FM 849, Lindale, TX 75771-1071 t) 903-882-4079 info@holyfamilylindale.org; secretary@holyfamilylindale.org www.holyfamilylindale.org Rev. David P. Bailey, Admin.; CRP Stds.: 36

LONGVIEW

St. Anthony - 508 N. Sixth St., Longview, TX 75601; Mailing: 500 N. Sixth St., Longview, TX 75601 t) 903-758-0116 www.stanthonylongview.org Rev. Jose Luis Vidarte, Pst.; Dcn. Stephen Ondrick; Dcn. Gonzalo Rojas; Dcn. Gregorio Sanchez; Dcn. Manuel Villalobos; CRP Stds.: 107

St. Mary - 2108 Ridgewood Dr., Longview, TX 75605-5121 t) 903-757-5855 parish@stmaryslgv.org www.stmaryslgv.org Rev. Daniel P. Dower, Pst.; Dcn. James Petkovsek; Dcn. Trevor Wells; Dcn. Vincent James Wilson; CRP Stds.: 87

St. Mary School - (Grades PreK-12) 405 Hollybrook Dr., Longview, TX 75605-2464 t) 903-753-1657 admin@stmaryslgv.org www.stmaryslgv.com Darbie Safford, Prin.; Marlena Schuricht, Admin.; Stds.: 178; Pr. Tchrs.: 1; Lay Tchrs.: 25

Our Lady of Grace - 415 Cypress St., Hallsville, TX 75650 t) 903-668-5279 parish_office@ourladyofgracecatholic.org Dcn. William Rhodes; Rev. Roselio Fuentes, Admin.;

St. Matthew Catholic Church - 2800 Pine Tree Rd., Longview, TX 75604; Mailing: 100 Dellbrook Dr., Longview, TX 75604 t) 903-295-3890 churchoffice@stmattlgv.com www.stmattlgv.com Rev. Msgr. Xavier Pappu, Pst.; Dcn. Joseph Bianca; Dcn. John D'Antoni; Dcn. Joel Gonzalez; CRP Stds.: 502

LUFKIN

St. Andrew - 1611 Feagin Dr., Lufkin, TX 75904 t) 936-632-9100 secretary@standrewlufkin.org; admin@standrewlufkin.org www.standrewlufkin.org Rev. Joby C. Thomas, Pst.; Dcn. Jesus Reyes; Dcn. Gary Trevino; CRP Stds.: 100

St. Patrick - 2118 Lowry St., Lufkin, TX 75901-1316 t) 936-634-6833 stpatrickchurchlufkin@yahoo.com; myorojas@gmail.com www.stpatrickslufkin.com Rev. Denzil J. Vithanage, Pst.; Dcn. Martin Aguilar; Dcn. Abelino Cordero; Dcn. Juan Mijares; Dcn. Manuel Ramos; Dcn. Ray Vann; CRP Stds.: 85

St. Patrick School - (Grades PreK-8) 2116 Lowry St., Lufkin, TX 75901 t) 936-634-6719 admin@stpatricklufkin.com www.stpatricklufkin.com Lourdes McKay, Prin.; Stds.: 74; Lay Tchrs.: 12

MADISONVILLE

St. Elizabeth Ann Seton - 100 S. Tammye Ln., Madisonville, TX 77864 t) 936-348-6368 pastorstelizabeth@gmail.com; secretaryseascc@gmail.com www.stelizabethmadisonville.com/ Rev. Guillermo Gabriel-Masonet, Pst.; Dcn. Steven M. Summers; CRP Stds.: 142

MALAKOFF

Mary, Queen of Heaven Church - 2269 Co Rd 1703, Malakoff, TX 75148; Mailing: P.O. Box 508, Malakoff, TX 75148-0508 t) 903-489-2366 mqhchurchmalakoff@gmail.com mqhmalakoff.org/ Rev. Patrick Fenton, Pst.; CRP Stds.: 30

MARSHALL

St. Joseph - 410 N. Alamo Blvd., Marshall, TX 75670-3450 t) 903-935-2536; 903-935-5502 (CRP) saintjosephmarshall@yahoo.com stjosephmarshall.org Msgr. Zacharias S. Kunnakkattuthara (India), Pst.; Rev. Selvan Melkias, Par. Vicar; Rev. Isaac Oviedo, Par. Vicar; Dcn. Magdaleno Aguirre; Dcn. Felipe Pena; Dcn. John Sargent; Dcn. Santiago Suarez; CRP Stds.: 214

San Pedro the Fisherman - 1835 Chaparrall, Hwy. 43, Tatum, TX 75691-0430; Mailing: P.O. Box 430, Tatum, TX 75691-0430 t) 903-947-2454 Rev. Elpidio Lopez, Admin.; Dcn. Jose Mireles;

MINEOLA

St. Peter the Apostle - 203 Meadowbrook Dr., Mineola, TX 75773; Mailing: P.O. Box 1022, Mineola, TX 75773 t) 903-569-3665 stpeter75773@gmail.com www.saintpetermineola.org/ Rev. Lawrence L. Love, Pst.; Dcn. William Faber; CRP Stds.: 115

MOUNT PLEASANT

St. Michael - 1403 E First St., Mount Pleasant, TX 75455-4715 t) 903-572-5227; 903-572-5227 x103 (CRP) office@stmichaelmp.org; emendoza@stmichaelmp.org www.stmichaelmp.org Rev. Ariel Cortes (Colombia), Pst.; Rev. Robert Kenneth Cigainero, Par. Vicar; Dcn. Lorenzo Martinez; CRP Stds.: 255

MOUNT VERNON

Sacred Heart - 406 Texas Hwy. 37 S., Mount Vernon, TX 75457; Mailing: P.O. Box 918, Mount Vernon, TX 75457 t) 903-537-2174 mvtxsacredheart@gmail.com www.sacredheartmountvernontx.com Rev. Mark Dunne (Ireland), Pst.; CRP Stds.: 75

NACOGDOCHES

Sacred Heart - 2508 Appleby Sand Rd., Nacogdoches, TX 75965-3632 t) 936-564-7807 office@sacredheartnac.org www.sacredheartnac.org Rev. George T. Elliott, Pst.; Rev. Jose Marin, Par. Vicar; Rev. Matthew Stehling, Par. Vicar; Dcn. Luis Baca; Dcn. David Darby; Dcn. Pedro Gonzalez; Dcn. Mariano Ibanez; Dcn. Tony Weatherford; CRP Stds.: 450

Our Lady of Lourdes - 1620 CR 353, Chireno, TX 75937; Mailing: 2508 Appleby Sand Rd., Nacogdoches, TX 75965 t) (936) 564-7807 www.catholicnac.org

Immaculate Conception - Moral - 1422 CR 724, Nacogdoches, TX 75964; Mailing: 2508 Appleby Sand Rd., Nacogdoches, TX 75965 t) (936) 564-7807 office@catholicnac.org www.iccmoral.org

Our Lady of Guadalupe - 4401 Old Lufkin Rd., Nacogdoches, TX 75964; Mailing: 2508 Appleby Sand Rd., Nacogdoches, TX 75965 t) (936) 564-7807 www.guadalupenac.org

NEW BOSTON

St. Mary of the Cenacle - 214 W. Magnolia St., New Boston, TX 75570 t) 903-628-2323 stmarycenacle@yahoo.com www.stmarycenacle.org/ Rev. William E. Palmer, Admin.; CRP Stds.: 8

PALESTINE

Sacred Heart - 503 N. Queen St., Palestine, TX 75801-2718 t) 903-729-2463 shpalestine1893@gmail.com www.shpalestine.org Rev. Jonathon Frels, Pst.; Rev. Cristians Zelaya, In Res.; Dcn. Martin Flynn; Dcn. Martin Garcia; Dcn. Daniel Rose; CRP Stds.: 227

PARIS

Our Lady of Victory - 3300 Clarksville St., Paris, TX 75460 t) 903-784-1000; 903-784-1000 x17 (CRP) olv@olvparis.org; faith@olvparis.org olvparis.org Rev. Gavin N. Vaverek, Pst.; Rev. Raymundo Garcia, Par. Vicar; Rev. Martin Ahiaba (Nigeria), In Res.; Dcn. Luis Garza; CRP Stds.: 180

PITTSBURG

Holy Cross - 416 Hill Ave., Pittsburg, TX 75686-1808; Mailing: P.O. Box 846, Pittsburg, TX 75686 t) 903-708-7084 holycrossccpittsburgtx@gmail.com Rev. Juan Carlos Rivera, Pst.; CRP Stds.: 95

RUSK

Sacred Heart of Jesus - 760 S Main St., Rusk, TX 75785 t) (903) 683-1862 Rev. Jorge Dinguis, Pst.;

SULPHUR SPRINGS

St. James - 297 Texas St., Sulphur Springs, TX 75482 t) 903-885-1222 reception@stjamessulphursprings.org stjamessulphursprings.org Rev. Victor Hernandez (Colombia), Pst.; Dcn. Gerald Besze; Dcn. William O'Brien; CRP Stds.: 158

TEXARKANA

Sacred Heart - 4505 Elizabeth St., Texarkana, TX 75503-2998 t) 903-794-4444 mariabsacredheart@gmail.com; shpre4505@aol.com www.sacredhearttxk.org Rev. Justin Braun, Pst.; Rev. Michael J. Adams, Pastor Emer.; Dcn. Larry Benzmiller; Dcn. Craig Lashford; CRP Stds.: 325

TRINITY

Most Holy Trinity - 401 Prospect Dr., Trinity, TX 75862-9801 t) 936-594-6664 mhtc2@windstream.net mhttrinity.org/ Rev. Cesar Betancourt, Admin.; CRP Stds.: 65

TYLER

Cathedral of the Immaculate Conception - 423 S. Broadway, Tyler, TX 75702 t) 903-592-1617 agonzalez@thecathedral.info; pcunningham@thecathedral.info thecathedral.info Rev. Robert H. Lanik, Rector; Rev. Juan Pedro Gonzalez (Mexico), Par. Vicar; Rev. Nicholas Nappier, Par. Vicar; Rev. Justin Wylie, Par. Vicar; Rev. Zachary Dominguez, LC, Pst. Min./Coord.; Dcn. Fred Arrambidez; Dcn. Rufino Cortez; Dcn. Steven Curry; Dcn. Keith Fournier; Dcn. Ramiro Martinez; Dcn. Bill Necessary; Dcn. Hal Williams; CRP Stds.: 141

St. Gregory Cathedral School - (Grades PreK-5) 500 S. College Ave., Tyler, TX 75702 t) 903-595-4109 rperry@bishopgorman.net Michelle Caccitolo, Prin.; Stds.: 192; Sr. Tchrs.: 1; Lay Tchrs.: 21

Sts. Peter & Paul Chapel - 1435 ESE Loop 323, Tyler, TX 75701 t) (903) 592-1617; (903) 592-1617 www.thecathedral.info

St. Gregory Early Learning Center - 500 S. College Ave., Tyler, TX 75702

St. Joseph the Worker Catholic Church - 5075 FM 14, Tyler, TX 75706; Mailing: P.O. Box 4995, Tyler, TX 75712 t) 903-593-5055 latinmasstyler@gmx.com latinmasstyler.org Extraordinary Form parish served by the Priestly Fraternity of Saint Peter. Rev. Joseph Valentine, FSSP, Pst.;

Our Lady of Guadalupe - 922 Old Omen Rd., Tyler, TX 75701-3709 t) 903-593-2006 olgtyler922@gmail.com olgtyler.org Rev. Jesus Rodrigo Arroyave, Pst.; Dcn. Jose Tiscareno; CRP Stds.: 587

St. Peter Claver - 615 W. Cochran St., Tyler, TX 75702 t) 903-595-2612 st.peterclaver@att.net stpeterclavertyler.com Rev. Luis Eduardo Larrea, M.F.E., Pst.; Dcn. Ramon Gonzalez; Bro. Simon L. Nila, Pst. Assoc.; CRP Stds.: 258

WHITEHOUSE

Prince of Peace Catholic Church - 903 E. Main St., Whitehouse, TX 75791 t) 903-871-3230

www.princeofpeacewhitehouse.org Rev. Luke Kalarickal, MSFS, Pst.; Dcn. Clarence Blalock; Dcn. Ruben Natera; CRP Stds.: 72

WILLS POINT

St. Luke - 312 W. O'Neal St., Wills Point, TX 75169 t) 903-873-3862 stlukeoffice75169@gmail.com www.stlukeswillspoint.org Rev. Maria Susai J. Avula, Pst.; Dcn. Edilberto Reyes; CRP Stds.: 75

WINNSBORO

St. Ann Catholic Church - 1010 W. Coke Rd. 515, Winnsboro, TX 75494; Mailing: P.O. Box 733, Winnsboro, TX 75494 t) 903-629-7884 stannwinnsboro@gmail.com Rev. Mani T. Mathai (India), Pst.;

SCHOOLS: PRESCHOOL THRU HIGH SCHOOL

SCHOOLS

STATE OF TEXAS

TYLER

Bishop Thomas K Gorman Catholic School - (PAR) (Grades 6-12) 1405 E SE Loop 323, Tyler, TX 75701 t) 903-561-2424 jkimec@bishopgorman.net bishopgorman.net John Kimec, Prin.; Stds.: 232; Pr. Tchrs.: 1; Lay Tchrs.: 20

HIGH SCHOOLS

STATE OF TEXAS

NACOGDOCHES

St. Boniface Catholic Classical High School - 2508 Appleby Sand Rd., Nacogdoches, TX 75964 t) 936-564-7807 shoey@catholicnac.org www.sacredheartnac.org/ Rev. Matthew Stehling, Prin.; Stds.: 6

INSTITUTIONS LOCATED IN DIOCESE

CAMPUS MINISTRY / NEWMAN CENTERS [CAM]

NACOGDOCHES

St. Mary's Catholic Campus Ministry - 211 E. College St., Nacogdoches, TX 75965 t) 936-564-7807 stmarys@sfacatholic.net www.sfacatholic.net Rev. George T. Elliott, Chap.;

TYLER

John Paul the Great Catholic Campus Ministry - 2603 Old Omen Rd., Tyler, TX 75701 t) 903-266-9110 sdecraene@dioceseoftyler.org Rev. Nicholas Nappier, Chap.;

CATHOLIC CHARITIES [CCH]

TYLER

Catholic Charities - Diocese of Tyler - 202 W. Front St., Tyler, TX 75702; Mailing: P.O. Box 2016, Tyler, TX 75710-2016 t) 903-258-9492 x105 kharry@cctyler.org www.cctyler.org Very Rev. John J. Gomez (Colombia), Pres.; Kathy Shieldes Harry, Exec.; Asstd. Annu.: 32,000; Staff: 6

CONVENTS, MONASTERIES, AND RESIDENCES FOR WOMEN [CON]

LUFKIN

Monastery of the Infant Jesus - 1501 Lotus Ln., Lufkin, TX 75904-2699 t) 936-634-4233 sr.m.m.gyovai@gmail.org; nuns@lufkintxnuns.org www.lufkintxnuns.org Cloistered Dominican Nuns. Sr. Mary Margaret Gyovai, Prioress; Srs.: 22

PARIS

Dominican Sisters of Our Lady of the Rosary of Fatima - 3300 Clarksville St., Paris, TX 75460 t) (903) 784-1000 Sr. Inocencia Olmeda Borges, OP, Supr.; Srs.: 4

RUSK

Daughters of Divine Hope - 1294 CR 2310, Rusk, TX 75785; Mailing: 1910 E.S.E. Loop 323 PMB 240, Tyler, TX 75701 t) 936-554-6120 srsusancatherine@ddhope.org Sr. Susan Catherine Kennedy, Supr.; Srs.: 1

TYLER

Instituto Santa Mariana de Jesus - 2706 Shady Ln., Tyler, TX 75702 t) 903-593-8933 gadelmar85@aol.com www.marianitas.org Sr. Mirna de la Cruz, ISMJ, Supr.; Srs.: 3

ENDOWMENTS / FOUNDATIONS / TRUSTS [EFT]

LONGVIEW

***Longview Catholic School Endowment Fund** - 405 Hollybrook Dr., Longview, TX 75605 t) 903-753-1657 frdower@stmaryslgv.org www.stmaryslgv.org Rev. Daniel P. Dower, Pst.;

LUFKIN

***St. Patrick School Foundation** - 2116 Lowry St., Lufkin, TX 75901 t) 936-634-6719 admin@stpatricklufkin.com www.stpatricklufkin.com Rev. Denzil J. Vithanage, Pst.;

TEXARKANA

CHRISTUS St. Michael Foundation - 2600 St. Michael Dr., Texarkana, TX 75503 t) 903-614-2448 susan.landreaux@christushealth.org www.christusstmichaelfoundation.org Susan Landreaux, Exec. Dir.;

TYLER

***East Texas Catholic Foundation Inc.** - 2094 Three Lakes Pkwy., Tyler, TX 75703 t) 903-630-1401 donderko@etcatholicfoundation.org www.easttexascatholicfoundation.org/ Daniel Onderko, Pres.;

***Tyler Catholic School Foundation** - 1015 E. Southeast Loop 323, Tyler, TX 75703; Mailing: P.O. Box 131175, Tyler, TX 75713 t) 903-526-5988 www.tcsf.net Kara Camp, Pres.;

HOSPITALS / HEALTH SERVICES [HOS]

LUFKIN

***Memorial Health System of East Texas (CHI St. Lukes Health Memorial)** - 1201 W. Frank Ave., Lufkin, TX 75904 Monty Bostwick, CEO;

***Memorial Specialty Hospital (CHI St. Lukes Health Memorial Specialty Hospital)** - 1201 W. Frank Ave., Lufkin, TX 75904

MADISONVILLE

Madison St. Joseph Health Center - ; Mailing: P.O. Box 698, Madisonville, TX 77864 t) 936-348-2631 An Affiliate of Catholic Health Initiatives. Marybeth Murphy, Admin.; Rick Napper, Pres.;

SAN AUGUSTINE

***Memorial Medical Center - San Augustine** - 511 E. Hospital St., San Augustine, TX 75972

SULPHUR SPRINGS

CHRISTUS Mother Frances Hospital Sulphur Springs - 115 Airport Rd., Sulphur Springs, TX 75482 t) 903-885-7671 www.christushealth.org Paul Harvey, Pres.; Bed Capacity: 96; Asstd. Annu.: 87,624; Staff: 377

TEXARKANA

CHRISTUS Health Ark-La-Tex dba CHRISTUS St. Michael Health System - 2600 St. Michael Dr, Texarkana, TX 75503 t) 903-614-1000 lawrence.chellaian@christushealth.org; jason.adams@christushealth.org www.christusstmichael.org Jason M. Adams, Pres.; Bed Capacity: 354; Asstd. Annu.: 261,385; Staff: 1,980

CHRISTUS St. Michael Rehabilitation Hospital - 2400 St. Michael Dr., Texarkana, TX 75503 t) 903-614-4000 Bed Capacity: 50; Asstd. Annu.: 51,823; Staff: 226

TYLER

CHRISTUS Trinity Mother Frances Health System - 800 E. Dawson St., Tyler, TX 75701 t) 903-593-8441 andy.navarro@christushealth.org www.christushealth.org/trinity Chris Glenney, CEO; Jason Proctor, Pres.; Rev. Daniel Oghenerukevwe (Nigeria), Chap.; Bed Capacity: 611; Asstd. Annu.: 732,694; Staff: 3,617

MISCELLANEOUS [MIS]

BIG SANDY

***The Pines Education Group** - 300 White Pine Rd., Big Sandy, TX 75755; Mailing: 14833 Midway Rd., Ste. 210, Addison, TX 75001 t) 214-522-6533; 903-845-5834 registrar@thepines.org Rick Villarreal, Dir.;

TYLER

Catholic Parish and Mission Assistance Program - 1015 E.S.E. Loop 323, Tyler, TX 75701 t) (903) 402-6590 www.catholicpmap.org Pete Weisenberger, Chair; Rev. Robert H. Lanik, Pres.;

St. Philip Institute of Catechesis and Evangelization - 1015 E.S.E. Loop 323, Tyler, TX 75701 t) 903-630-5055 www.stphilipinstitute.org Most Rev. Joseph E. Strickland, Pres.;

Society of St. Vincent de Paul, Immaculate Conception Conference - 410 S. College Ave., Tyler, TX 75702 t) 903-592-0027 tylersvdp@gmail.com www.svdptyler.info/ Michael Allagier, Pres.;

MONASTERIES AND RESIDENCES FOR PRIESTS AND BROTHERS [MON]

PALESTINE

Prayer Mountain Hermitage - 10089 An. Co. Rd. 404, Palestine, TX 75803 t) (903) 549-2950 Sr. Mary Vogel, H.S.S.R., Contact; Priests: 1

An asterisk (*) denotes an organization that has established tax-exempt status directly with the IRS and is not covered by the USCCB Group Ruling.

Diocese of Venice

(Dioecesis Venetiae in Florida)

MOST REVEREND FRANK J. DEWANE

Bishop of Venice; ordained July 16, 1988; appointed Coadjutor Bishop of Venice April 25, 2006; Episcopal ordination July 25, 2006; appointed Second Bishop of Venice January 19, 2007. Res.: 1000 Pinebrook Rd., Venice, FL 34285.

Catholic Center: 1000 Pinebrook Rd., Venice, FL 34285. T: 941-484-9543; F: 941-484-1121.
dioceseofvenice.org
info@dioceseofvenice.org

ESTABLISHED OCTOBER 25, 1984.

Square Miles 9,035.

Comprises the Counties of Charlotte, Collier, DeSoto, Glades, Hardee, Hendry, Highlands, Lee, Manatee and Sarasota in the State of Florida.

For legal titles of parishes and diocesan institutions, consult the Chancellor.

STATISTICAL OVERVIEW

Personnel
Bishop....1
Priests: Diocesan Active in Diocese....72
Priests: Diocesan Active Outside Diocese....8
Priests: Retired, Sick or Absent....27
Number of Diocesan Priests....107
Religious Priests in Diocese....47
Total Priests in your Diocese....154
Extern Priests in Diocese....50
Ordinations:
Diocesan Priests....3
Transitional Deacons....2
Permanent Deacons....1
Permanent Deacons in Diocese....28
Total Brothers....5
Total Sisters....36

Parishes
Parishes....61
With Resident Pastor:
Resident Diocesan Priests....49
Resident Religious Priests....12
Missions....8
Pastoral Centers....2
Professional Ministry Personnel:
Sisters....21
Lay Ministers....110

Welfare
Homes for the Aged....10
Total Assisted....653
Day Care Centers....1
Total Assisted....24
Specialized Homes....4
Total Assisted....90
Special Centers for Social Services....12
Total Assisted....247,465
Other Institutions....17
Total Assisted....791

Educational
Diocesan Students in Other Seminaries....12
Total Seminarians....12
Colleges and Universities....1
Total Students....1,227
High Schools, Diocesan and Parish....4
Total Students....1,884
Elementary Schools, Diocesan and Parish....11
Total Students....3,576
Elementary Schools, Private....1
Total Students....309
Non-residential Schools for the Disabled....1
Total Students....71
Catechesis / Religious Education:
High School Students....3,355
Elementary Students....5,891
Total Students under Catholic Instruction....16,325
Teachers in Diocese:
Priests....2
Sisters....5
Lay Teachers....524

Vital Statistics
Receptions into the Church:
Infant Baptism Totals....2,706
Minor Baptism Totals....342
Adult Baptism Totals....200
Received into Full Communion....361
First Communions....2,329
Confirmations....1,663
Marriages:
Catholic....468
Interfaith....91
Total Marriages....559
Deaths....2,691
Total Catholic Population....242,156
Total Population....2,444,235

LEADERSHIP

Catholic Center - t) 941-484-9543 dioceseofvenice.org/
Office of the Bishop - Most Rev. Frank J. Dewane, Bishop; Marianne Marziano, Secy.; Nancy Lopiccolo, Admin. Asst.;
Vicar General - Very Rev. Msgr. Stephen E. McNamara;
Chancellor - Dr. Volodymyr Smeryk;
Administrative Assistant to the Chancellor - Cheryl Giordano;
College of Consultors - Very Rev. Msgr. Stephen E. McNamara; Very Rev. Jose Gonzales; Rev. George Ratzmann;
Deans -
Central Deanery - Very Rev. Msgr. Stephen E. McNamara, Dean;
Eastern Deanery - Very Rev. Jose Antonio Gonzalez, Dean;
Northern Deanery - Rev. Msgr. Patrick Dubois, Dean;
Southern Deanery - Very Rev. Robert Kantor, Dean;
Presbyteral Council - Most Rev. Frank J. Dewane; Very Rev. Msgr. Stephen E. McNamara; Very Rev. Jose Antonio Gonzalez;
Director for Deacons - Dcn. David Reardon;
Director for Religious -
Continuing Education of Clergy - Rev. George Ratzmann;
Child Protection and Safe Environment Issues -
Victim Assistance Coordinator - t) 941-416-6114 Susan Benton;
Official Archivist - Dr. Volodymyr Smeryk;
Historical Archivist - Cara Smith;
Diocesan Tribunal -
Judicial Vicar - Very Rev. Joseph L. Waters;
Defenders of the Bond - Rev. Anthony Hewitt; Rev. Msgr. Patrick Dubois; Rev. Jaroslaw (Jarek) Sniosek;
Promoter of Justice - Rev. Anthony Hewitt;
Judges - Very Rev. Joseph L. Waters; Rev. Robert T. Dziedziak; Rev. Phillip Schweda;
Ecclesiastical Notary/Case Assessor - Lily Mendez;
Building Department - Joe Rego, Dir.; Jeffrey Higgins, Prog. Mgr.;
Catholic Campaign for Human Development - Dr. Sean Myers;
Catholic Charities of the Diocese of Venice, Inc. - t) 941-488-5581 info@catholiccharitiesdov.org catholiccharitiesdov.org/ Eddie Gloria, CEO; Clint Branam, COO (clint.branam@catholiccharitiesdov.org); Robert Wildermuth, Dir. Finance;
Catholic Relief Services/Operation Rice Bowl - Dr. Sean Myers;
Communications Department - Karen Barry Schwarz, Dir.; Robert Reddy, Media Rels. Coord.;
The Florida Catholic, Venice Edition - t) 941-486-4701 Most Rev. Frank J. Dewane, Publisher; Robert Reddy, Editor;
Stewardship and Development Department - Carla Repollet, Dir.; Robert Jurman, Mgr.;
Diaconate - Dcn. David Reardon, Dir. Diaconate Personnel;
Ecumenical and Interreligious Office - Dcn. Patrick C. Macaulay;
Education - Rev. John Belmonte, S.J., Supt.;
Finance Department - Peter McPartland, Dir.; Deborah Hoagland, Controller; Courtney Hodge, Financial Analyst;
Human Resources - Michelle Grabowski, Dir.; Amanda Dould, Specialist; Lisa Houde, Employee Rels./Benefits Coord.;
Information Technology - Drew Carney, Dir.; Scott Phayre, Sr. Systems Admin.; Andrei Krot, Systems Admin.;
Internal Financial Services - Silvia Fedor, Dir.;
Legal - Joseph A. DiVito, Gen. Counsel;
Parish Accounting Services Department - t) 941-486-4760 Michael Akers, Dir.;
Hispanic, Migrant and Spanish Speaking Apostolate - Rev. Claudio Stewart, I.V.E., Dir.;
Juventud Hispana (Hispanic Youth Outreach) -
Haitian Ministry - Rev. Jean-Marie Fritz Ligonde, Dir.;
Charlotte County - Rev. Tony Chermeil;
Collier County - Rev. Benjamin Casimir; Rev. Jean Kesnel Metellus, C.S.;
Lee County - Rev. Jean-Marie Fritz Ligonde;
Manatee County - Rev. Wilner Durosier;
Outreach to People with HIV/AIDS - t) (941) 366-1886 colleen.mcmenamin@catholiccharitiesdov.org Colleen McMenamin, Dir.;
Office of Worship - Dr. Sean Myers;
Department of Evangelization - James Gontis, Dir.; Carrie Harkey, Coord. Marriage & Family Life;
Charismatic Renewal - Rev. Claudio Stewart, I.V.E., Moderator; Rev. Ananda Anki-Reddy, Spiritual Advisor; Dr. John Gresham, Pres.;
Spanish - Rev. Wilner Durosier, Spiritual Advisor; Rev. Elbano Munoz, Spiritual Advisor;
Family Life Office - Carrie Harkey, Coord.;
Divorced and Separated Ministry - Carrie Harkey;
Youth & Young Adult Outreach - Marthamaria Morales, Dir.;
Peace and Social Justice Department - Dr. Sean Myers, Dir.;
Prison Ministry - Robert Hiniker, Co-Coord.; Joe Mallof, Co-Coord.;
Respect Life Department - Jeanne Berdeaux, Dir.;
Project Rachel - t) 877-908-1212 Sylvia Jimenez, Coord.;
Scouting - Rev. Lawton Lang, Scout Chap.; James Fetterman, Diocesan Scout Coord.; Connie Kantor, Scout Committee Coord.;
Real Estate Department - Dr. Volodymyr Smeryk, Dir.; Shannon Barrows, Coord. Real Estate;
Vocations/Seminarian Formation - Rev. Shawn Roser, Dir.;

ADVISORY BOARDS, COMMISSIONS, COMMITTEES, AND COUNCILS

Audit Committee - Very Rev. Msgr. Stephen E. McNamara, Vicar General; Dr. Volodymyr Smeryk, Chancellor; Stephen W. Buckley;
Diocese of Venice Pension Plan Board of Trustees - Rev. Jerome A. Carosella; Rev. Robert T. Dziedziak; Peter McPartland;
Finance and Investment Committee - Stephen W. Buckley; Kenneth Boehl; Paul J. Von Merveldt;
Investment Advisory Committee - Charles Agles; Brad Campbell; Paul Mostek;
Liturgical Commission - Most Rev. Frank J. Dewane; Rev. Jerome A. Carosella; Dcn. Charles Patrick Macaulay;
Planning and Development Committee - Very Rev. Robert Kantor, Chair; Very Rev. Msgr. Stephen E. McNamara; Dr. Volodymyr Smeryk;
Priest Personnel Board - Very Rev. Msgr. Stephen E. McNamara, Chair; Rev. Robert T. Dziedziak; Very Rev. Robert Kantor;
Real Estate Advisory Board - Dr. Volodymyr Smeryk, Chair; Stephen W. Buckley; Very Rev. Msgr. Stephen E. McNamara;
Review Board - Judith Hughes, Chair; Rev. Steven Clemente; Dcn. David Reardon;

ORGANIZATIONS

Catholic Community Foundation of SW Florida - t) 641-441-1124 ccf@dioceseofvenice.org ccfdioceseofvenice.org/ Michael Morse, Exec. Dir.;
Catholic Lawyers Guild - dioceseofvenice.org
Catholic Medical Association of SWFL - t) 239-849-6908 floridacma.org/ Dr. Stephen E. Hannan;
Courage - Rev. Lawton Lang, Diocesan Coord.;
Cursillo Movement - Rev. Claudio Stewart, I.V.E., Spiritual Dir.; Gabino Garcia, Dir.;
Emmaus Retreat - Rev. Jiobani Batista, Spiritual Dir.; Rev. Luis Hurtado Pacheco, Spiritual Adv./Care Srvcs.;
Equestrian Order of the Holy Sepulchre of Jerusalem - John DeStefano, Diocesan Rep.;
Foundation for the Care of the Migrant Poor - dioceseofvenice.org Robert Woelfel, Secy.;
Knights of Columbus - Very Rev. Robert Kantor, State Chap.; Robert S. Urrutia, State Deputy;
Legion of Mary - t) 941-780-0753 jmp8820@comcast.net dioceseofvenice.org Judy Paleski, Pres., Manasota Curia;
Marriage, Dialogue and Follow-up - Rev. Claudio Stewart, I.V.E., Spiritual Dir.; Irene Reza, Coord.; Jorge Reza, Coord.;
Order of Malta - David Joyce, Area Co-Chair; Maria Joyce, Area Co-Chair;
Padres Madres Orando Por Sus Hijos (PMO) - Rev. Jose del Olmo, Spiritual Advisor; Adriana Sena, Coord.; Carlos Sena, Coord.;
Secretariado Hispano de Cursillos - Rev. Claudio Stewart, I.V.E., Diocesan Spiritual Dir.; Bernabe Sorto, Diocesan Coord.;
Society of St. Vincent de Paul - gcmoerke@gmail.com dioceseofvenice.org Gary C. Moerke, Pres.;
Venice Diocesan Council of Catholic Women - www.vdccw.org/ Josephine Weiss, Pres.; Brenda Dolan, Secy.;

MISCELLANEOUS / OTHER OFFICES

Propagation of the Faith/Mission Cooperative Program - t) (941) 776-9097 missionoffice@dioceseofvenice.org dioceseofvenice.org Rev. Joseph Gates, Dir.;

PARISHES, MISSIONS, AND CLERGY

STATE OF FLORIDA

ARCADIA

St. Paul Parish in Arcadia, Inc. - 1208 E. Oak St., Arcadia, FL 34266 t) 863-494-2611 office@stpaularcadia.org www.stpaularcadia.org/ Rev. Luis Pacheco, Admin.; Rev. Remigious Ssekiranda, Par. Vicar; Sr. Martha Flores, M.H.M.L., DRE; CRP Stds.: 424

AVE MARIA

Ave Maria Parish, Inc. - 5078 Pope John Paul II Blvd, Suite 107, Ave Maria, FL 34142 t) 239-261-5555 craig.k@avemariaparish.org; fr.david@avemariaparish.org www.avemariaparish.org/ Rev. David Vidal, Pst.; Rev. John Andem, Par. Vicar; Dcn. Jeffrey Ball; Dcn. Gary Ingold; Dcn. John Jarvis; Dcn. Thomas Kinnick; Rebecca Hampton, DRE; CRP Stds.: 171
Rhodora J. Donahue Academy of Ave Maria - (Grades PreK-12) 4955 Seton Way, Ave Maria, FL 34142 t) 239-842-3241 office.manager@donahueacademy.org www.donahueacademy.org Dr. Daniel Guernsey, Prin.; Stds.: 375; Lay Tchrs.: 21

AVON PARK

Our Lady of Grace Parish in Avon Park, Inc. - 595 E. Main St., Avon Park, FL 33825 t) 863-453-4757; 863-453-7537 (CRP) betty.heiring@ologap.org ologap.org/home Rev. Ronnie Sison, Pst.; CRP Stds.: 155

BOCA GRANDE

Our Lady of Mercy Parish in Boca Grande, Inc. - 240 Park Ave., Boca Grande, FL 33921; Mailing: P.O. Box 181, Boca Grande, FL 33921 t) 941-964-2254 Rev. Jerome A. Carosella, Pst.;

BOKEELIA

Our Lady of the Miraculous Medal Parish in Bokeelia, Inc. - 12175 Stringfellow Rd., Bokeelia, FL 33922 t) 239-283-0456 office@olmm.org www.miraculousmedalch.org Rev. Jacek Mazur, Pst.; Dcn. William Beck; CRP Stds.: 14

BONITA SPRINGS

St. Leo Parish in Bonita Springs, Inc. - 28290 Beaumont

Rd., Bonita Springs, FL 34134 t) 239-992-0901 www.stleocatholicchurch.org Rev. Jaroslaw (Jarek) Sniosek, Pst.; Rev. David Portorreal, Par. Vicar; CRP Stds.: 234

BRADENTON

St. Joseph Parish in Bradenton, Inc. - 3100 26th St. W., Bradenton, FL 34205; Mailing: 2704 33rd Ave. W., Bradenton, FL 34205 t) 941-756-3732 info@sjcfl.org www.sjcfl.org Rev. Rafal Ligenza, Pst.; Rev. James G. Simko, Par. Vicar; Liliana Ronderos, DRE; CRP Stds.: 94

St. Joseph School - (Grades PreK-8) 2990 26th St. W., Bradenton, FL 34205 t) 941-755-2611 dsuddarth@sjsfl.org sjsfl.org Deborah Suddarth, Prin.; Stds.: 288; Lay Tchrs.: 19

Ss. Peter and Paul the Apostles Parish in Bradenton, Inc. - 2850 75th St. W., Bradenton, FL 34209 t) 941-795-1228 parishoffice@sspeterandpaul.org www.sspeterandpaul.org Rev. Mark L. Heuberger, Pst.; Rev. Arunprakash Paul, Par. Vicar; CRP Stds.: 56

Sacred Heart Parish in Bradenton, Inc. - 1220 15th St. W., Bradenton, FL 34205 t) 941-748-2221; 941-748-2221 x118 (CRP) info@sacredheartbradenton.org www.sacredheartbradenton.org/ Rev. Elbano Munoz, Pst.; Rev. Binu Joseph, Par. Vicar; CRP Stds.: 120

CAPE CORAL

St. Andrew Parish in Cape Coral, Inc. - 2628 Del Prado Blvd. S., Cape Coral, FL 33904 t) 239-574-4545; 239-574-2411 (CRP) cjohnson@standrewrcc.org; rgreen@standrewrcc.org www.standrewrcc.org Cynthia Johnson, DRE; Rev. Eduardo Coll, Pst.; Rev. Ananda Anki-Reddy, Par. Vicar; Rev. Daniel Flens, Par. Vicar; Dcn. Peter Fullen; Dcn. Edison Gibbons; CRP Stds.: 136

St. Andrew School - (Grades PreK-8) 1509 S.E. 27th St., Cape Coral, FL 33904 t) 239-772-3922 kbutler@standrewcs.org www.standrewcs.org David Nelson, Prin.; Bambi Giles, Vice Prin.; Stds.: 436; Lay Tchrs.: 25

St. Katharine Drexel Parish in Cape Coral, Inc. - 1922 S.W. 20th Ave., Cape Coral, FL 33991 t) 239-283-9501; 239-283-0525 (CRP) office@drexelcc.org; giordano@dioceseofvenice.org www.drexelcc.org Rev. Anthonio Jean, Par. Vicar; Rev. Ricky Varner, Pst.; Rose Marie Talbot-Babey, DRE; CRP Stds.: 336

CLEWISTON

St. Margaret Parish in Clewiston, Inc. - 208 N. Deane Duff Ave., Clewiston, FL 33440; Mailing: 318 E. Osceola Ave., Clewiston, FL 33440 t) 863-983-8585 saintmargaretoffice@stmargaretcc.org Rev. Jean Woady Louis, Admin.; Sr. Maria Mercedez Rodriguez Gomez, M.H.M.L., DRE; CRP Stds.: 124

Santa Rosa de Lima Mission - 835 N. Mayoral St., Clewiston, FL 33440 t) (863) 983-8585

ENGLEWOOD

St. Francis of Assisi Parish in Grove City, Inc. - 5265 Placida Rd., Englewood, FL 34224 t) 941-697-4899 giordano@dioceseofvenice.org Rev. Cory A. Mayer, Pst.; Rev. Tony Chermeil, Par. Vicar; Dcn. Robert Godlewsky; CRP Stds.: 95

St. Raphael Parish in Englewood, Inc. - 770 Kilbourne Ave., Englewood, FL 34223 t) 941-474-9595 office@strapheng.org www.strapheng.org Rev. Robert Murphy, Admin.;

FORT MYERS

St. Cecilia Parish in Fort Myers, Inc. - 5632 Sunrise Dr., Fort Myers, FL 33919-1798 t) 239-936-3635 x110 rgarcia@saintcecilias.net www.saintcecilias.org Rev. Paul Gerald Dechant, o.s.f.s., Pst.; Rev. Francis Hanlon, O.S.F.S., Par. Vicar; CRP Stds.: 71

Church of the Resurrection of Our Lord Catholic Parish in Fort Myers, Inc. - 8051 Cypress Lake Dr., Fort Myers, FL 33919; Mailing: 8121 Cypress Lake Dr., Fort Myers, FL 33919 t) 239-481-7171; 239-482-6883 (CRP) deanna@resurrectionch.org; parishoffice@resurrectionch.org resurrectionch.org Very Rev. Msgr. Stephen E. McNamara, Pst.; Rev. Oliver Toner, Assoc. Pst.; Dcn. Michael Esper; Dcn. David Reardon; Deanna Latell, DRE; CRP Stds.: 87

St. Columbkille Parish in Fort Myers, Inc. - 12171 Iona Rd., Fort Myers, FL 33908 t) 239-489-3973 office@stcolumbkille.com Rev. Lorenzo Gonzalez, Pst.; Rev. Jean-Marie Fritz Ligonde, Assoc. Pst.; CRP Stds.: 10

St. Francis Xavier Parish in Fort Myers, Inc. - 2133 Heitman St., Fort Myers, FL 33901; Mailing: P.O. Box 912, Fort Myers, FL 33901 t) 239-334-2161 info@stfrancisfortmyers.org www.stfrancisfm.org Rev. Anthony Hewitt, Pst.; Rev. Augustine Twum Obour, Par. Vicar; CRP Stds.: 65

St. Francis Xavier School - (Grades PreK-8) 2055 Heitman St., Fort Myers, FL 33901 t) 239-334-7707 www.stfrancisfortmyers.org John Gulley, Prin.; Jim Reynolds, Vice Prin.; Stds.: 520; Lay Tchrs.: 31

Jesus the Worker Parish in Fort Myers, Inc. (Jesus Obrero) - 881 Nuna Ave., Fort Myers, FL 33905; Mailing: P.O. Box 50909, Fort Myers, FL 33994 t) 239-693-5333 oficina@jesustheworker.org www.jesustheworker.org Rev. Patrick T. O'Connor, O.S.F.S., Pst.; Rev. Jose Del Olmo, Par. Vicar; Sr. Rosemary Le, F.M.I., DRE; Jose J. Soto, Bus. Mgr.; CRP Stds.: 504

San Jose Mission - 10750 Gladiolus Dr., Fort Myers, FL 33908 t) (239) 693-5333 jesustheworker.org/san-jose-mission

St. John XXIII Catholic Parish in Fort Myers, Inc. - 13060 Palomino Ln., Fort Myers, FL 33912 t) 239-561-2245 info@johnxxiii.net www.johnxxiii.net Rev. Robert D. Tabbert, Pst.; Rev. Simon Dao, C.R.M., Par. Vicar; Rev. Michael Young, Par. Vicar; Dcn. Richard Klish; CRP Stds.: 270

Our Lady of Light Parish in Fort Myers, Inc. - 19680 Cypress View Dr., Fort Myers, FL 33967 t) 239-267-7088 parish-info@ourladyoflight.com www.ourladyoflight.com Rev. Hugh J. McGuigan, O.S.F.S., Pst.; Rev. Anthony Gilborges, O.S.F.S., Assoc. Pst.; Lori Crawford, DRE; CRP Stds.: 259

St. Vincent de Paul Parish in Fort Myers, Inc. - 13031 Palm Beach Blvd., Fort Myers, FL 33905 t) 239-693-0818 contact@stvincentftmyers.org stvincentftmyers.org Rev. Murchadh O'Madagain, Pst.; CRP Stds.: 90

FORT MYERS BEACH

Ascension Parish in Fort Myers Beach, Inc. - 6025 Estero Blvd., Fort Myers Beach, FL 33931 t) 239-463-6754 ascensionfmb@yahoo.com Rev. William Adams, Pst.; Rev. Grzegorz Klich, Par. Vicar;

HOLMES BEACH

St. Bernard Parish in Holmes Beach, Inc. - 248 S. Harbor Dr., Holmes Beach, FL 34217 t) 941-778-4769 office@stbernardcc.org www.stbernardcc.org Rev. Phillip Schweda, Admin.; CRP Stds.: 18

IMMOKALEE

Our Lady of Guadalupe Parish in Immokalee, Inc. - 207 S. 9th St., Immokalee, FL 34142 t) 239-657-2666 office@olguadalupeparish.org Rev. Teofilo Ramirez Moreno, C.S. (Mexico), Admin.; Rev. Jean Kesnel Metellus, C.S., Par. Vicar; CRP Stds.: 568

LABELLE

Our Lady Queen of Heaven Parish in LaBelle, Inc. - 355 S. Bridge St., LaBelle, FL 33935; Mailing: P.O. Box 357, LaBelle, FL 33935 t) 863-675-0030 secretary@olqheaven.org Rev. Jiobani Batista, Pst.; Rev. Juan Carlos Sack, Assoc. Pst.; Angelica Pena, DRE; CRP Stds.: 236

Holy Martyrs Mission - 1722 Crescent Ave., LaBelle, FL 33935; Mailing: 355 S. Bridge St., LaBelle, FL 33935 t) (863) 675-0030 office@olqheaven.org

LAKE PLACID

St. James Catholic Parish in Lake Placid, Inc. - 3380 Placid View Dr., Lake Placid, FL 33852 t) 863-465-3215 lorie.raimondi@stjameschurchlp.org www.stjameschurchlp.org Rev. Vincent L. Clemente, Pst.; Rev. Felix Gonzalez, Par. Vicar; Connie Rollins, DRE; CRP Stds.: 63

Communidad Catolica Hispana Santiago Apostol Mission (Mission of St. James Catholic Parish in Lake Placid, Inc.) - 685 CR 621 E., Lake Placid, FL 33852 t) (863) 465-2470

LAKEWOOD RANCH

Our Lady of the Angels Parish in Lakewood Ranch, Inc. - 12905 SR 70 E., Lakewood Ranch, FL 34202 t) 941-752-6770 parishinfo@olangelscc.org www.olangelscc.org Rev. Sebastian Szczawinski, Admin.; Rev. Shawn Roser, Par. Vicar; CRP Stds.: 371

LEHIGH ACRES

St. Raphael Parish in Lehigh, Inc. - 2514 Lee Blvd., Lehigh Acres, FL 33971 t) 239-369-1831; 239-369-6424 (CRP) parishoffice@saintraphaelccla.org; joseph.allison@saintraphaelccla.org Rev. Michal Szyszka, Admin.; Dcn. Joseph Allison; CRP Stds.: 396

LONGBOAT KEY

St. Mary Star of the Sea Parish in Longboat Key, Inc. - 4280 Gulf of Mexico Dr., Longboat Key, FL 34228 t) 941-383-1255 parishoffice@stmarylbk.org www.stmarylbk.org Rev. Robert T. Dziedziak, Pst.;

MARCO ISLAND

San Marco Parish in Marco Island, Inc. - 851 San Marco Rd., Marco Island, FL 34145 t) 239-394-5181 info@sanmarcochurch.org www.sanmarcochurch.org Rev. Timothy M. Navin, Pst.; Rev. Chuck Ruoff, Par. Vicar; Dcn. John Minicozzi; Arielle Harms, DRE; CRP Stds.: 90

Holy Family Mission - 200 Datura Ave., Everglades City, FL 34139

MOORE HAVEN

St. Joseph the Worker Parish in Moore Haven, Inc. - 24065 U.S. Hwy. 27, Moore Haven, FL 33471; Mailing: P.O. Box 1109, Moore Haven, FL 33471 t) 863-946-0696 office@stjosephtheworkerfl.org Rev. Marcial I. Garcia, Pst.; CRP Stds.: 48

St. Theresa of the Child Jesus Mission - 1027 Chobee Loop, Okeechobee, FL 34974; Mailing: PO Box 1109, Moore Haven, FL 33471 t) (863) 946-0696

NAPLES

St. Agnes Parish in Naples, Inc. - 7775 Vanderbilt Beach Rd., Naples, FL 34120-1641 t) 239-592-1949 info@stagnesnaples.org www.stagnesnaples.org Very Rev. Robert Kantor, Pst.; Rev. Carlos Alberto Encinas, Par. Vicar; Rev. Michael Orsi, Par. Vicar; Rev. Krzysztof Piotrowski, Par. Vicar; Dcn. Hugh Mueller; Dcn. Bill Schultz; Ivy O'Malley, DRE; Dcn. Roberto Landron, Bus. Mgr.; CRP Stds.: 695

St. Ann Catholic Parish in Naples, Inc. a Florida non-profit corporation - 475 Ninth Ave. S., Naples, FL 34102 t) 239-262-4256 faithformation@naplesstann.com; secretary@naplesstann.com www.naplesstann.com Rev. William Davis, Pst.; Rev. Reji Joseph, OSFS, Par. Vicar; Sybil Jean Steuart, DRE; CRP Stds.: 45

St. Ann School - (Grades PreK-8) 542 Eighth Ave. S., Naples, FL 34102 t) 239-262-4110 info@stann.net www.stann.net Michael Buskirk, Prin.; Becky Meinert, Vice Prin.; Stds.: 371; Sr. Tchrs.: 1; Lay Tchrs.: 34

St. Elizabeth Seton Parish in Naples, Inc. - 5260 28th Ave., S.W., Naples, FL 34116 t) 239-455-3900 office@stelizabethseton.org www.stelizabethseton.org/ Dcn. Roberto Landron; Rev. Casey Jones, Pst.; CRP Stds.: 283

St. Elizabeth Seton Catholic School - (Grades PreK-8) 2730 53rd Ter. S.W., Naples, FL 34116 t) 239-455-2262 x309 niebuhr@seseton.org www.saintelizabethseton.com Maria Niebuhr, Prin.; Stds.: 293; Lay Tchrs.: 21

St. Finbarr Parish in Naples, Inc. - 13520 Tamiami Trl. E., Naples, FL 34114-8703 t) 239-417-2084 office@stfinbarr.org stfinbarr.org Rev. Leo Smith, Admin.; Dcn. Alfred J. Mauriello; CRP Stds.: 37

St. John the Evangelist Parish in Naples, Inc. - 625 111th Ave. N., Naples, FL 34108 t) 239-566-8740 info@sjecc.com sjecc.org Rev. Tomasz Zalewski, Pst.; Rev. Nicholas Thompson, Par. Vicar; Rev. Mark Harris, Par. Vicar; Dcn. Harold Brenner; Natalie Campbell, DRE; CRP Stds.: 364

St. Peter the Apostle Parish in Naples, Inc. - 5130 Rattlesnake Hammock Rd., Naples, FL 34113 t) 239-774-3337 business@stpeternaples.com www.stpeternaples.org Rev. Gerard F. Critch, Pst.; Rev. Benjamin Casimir, Par. Vicar; Rev. Franckel Fils-Aime, Par. Vicar; Rev. Wilian Montalvo, Par. Vicar; Dcn. Peter Pavlyshin; Dcn. Willard Passauer; CRP Stds.: 300

St. William Parish in Naples, Inc. - 601 Seagate Dr., Naples, FL 34108; Mailing: 750 Seagate Dr., Naples, FL 34103 t) 239-261-4883 marcy@saintwilliam.org saintwilliam.org Rev. George Ratzmann, Pst.; Rev. Steven Clemente, Par. Vicar; Rev. Mark Schaffner, O.Carm., Par. Vicar; Dcn. Robert Chalhoub; Dcn. Ed O'Connell; CRP Stds.: 105

NORTH FORT MYERS

St. Therese Parish in North Fort Myers, Inc. - 20115 N. Tamiami Tr., North Fort Myers, FL 33903 t) 239-567-2315 barbara.gallagher@sainttheresechurch.net www.sainttheresechurch.net Nelson Perez, DRE; Rev. Jan Antonik, Pst.; CRP Stds.: 9

NORTH PORT

San Pedro Parish in North Port, Inc. - 14380 Tamiami Tr., North Port, FL 34287 t) 941-426-2500; 941-426-2893 (CRP) office@sanpedrocc.org; faithformation@sanpedrocc.org www.sanpedrocc.org/ Rev. Thomas Carzon, O.M.V., Pst.; Rev. Nathan Marzonie, Par. Vicar; CRP Stds.: 127

OSPREY

Our Lady of Mount Carmel Parish in Osprey, Inc. - 425 S. Tamiami Tr., Osprey, FL 34229; Mailing: P.O. Box 1097, Osprey, FL 34229 t) 941-966-0807 ljefferson@olmc-osprey.org www.olmc-osprey.org Rev. Anthony Armstrong, O.Carm., Pst.; Dcn. Thomas Grant; Dcn. Harry Antrim; CRP Stds.: 16

PALMETTO

Holy Cross Parish in Palmetto, Inc. - 505 26th St. W., Palmetto, FL 34221 t) 941-729-3891 afanco@holycrossdov.org holycrossdov.org Rev. Leszek Trojanowski, Par. Vicar; CRP Stds.: 104

PARRISH

St. Frances Xavier Cabrini Parish in Parrish, Inc. - 12001 69th St. E., Parrish, FL 34219 t) 941-776-9097 home@sfxcparrish.com www.sfxcparrish.com Rev. Joseph Gates, Pst.; CRP Stds.: 150

PORT CHARLOTTE

St. Charles Borromeo Parish in Port Charlotte, Inc. - 21505 Augusta Ave., Port Charlotte, FL 33952 t) 941-625-4754 info@stcbc.org stcharlespc.org Rev. John Fitch, Pst.; Rev. Philip J. Scheff, Assoc. Pst.; CRP Stds.: 110

St. Charles Borromeo School - (Grades PreK-8) 21505 Augusta Ave, Port Charlotte, FL 33952 t) 941-625-5533 info@stcbs.org www.stcbs.org Tonya Peters, Prin.; Stds.: 315; Lay Tchrs.: 20

St. Maximilian Kolbe Parish in Port Charlotte, Inc. - 1441 Spear St., Port Charlotte, FL 33948 t) 941-743-6877 parishoffice@stmaxcatholic.org stmaxcatholic.org Rev. Teofilo Useche, Pst.; Rev. Emmanuel Saint-Hilaire, Par. Vicar; Dcn. Joe Plummer; Cindy Kuykendall, DRE; CRP Stds.: 54

San Antonio Parish in Port Charlotte, Inc. - 24445 Rampart Blvd., Port Charlotte, FL 33980 t) 941-624-3799 c) (941) 204-7370 (office manager) barbara@sanantoniorcc.org sanantoniorcc.org Rev. Leo P. Riley, Pst.; CRP Stds.: 26

PUNTA GORDA

Sacred Heart Parish in Punta Gorda, Inc. - 211 W. Charlotte Ave., Punta Gorda, FL 33950-5546 t) 941-639-3957 info@sacredheartfl.org Rev. Jerome P. Kaywell, Pst.; Rev. Mario Kono, Assoc. Pst.; Dcn. George Riegger; Rita Sheridan, DRE; CRP Stds.: 68

SANIBEL

St. Isabel Parish in Sanibel, Inc. - 3559 Sanibel Captiva Rd., Sanibel, FL 33957 t) 239-472-2763 parishoffice@saintisabel.org www.saintisabel.org Rev. Edward Martin, Pst.; Khristy Scheer, Bus. Mgr.; Maria Zoltek, Music Assistant; CRP Stds.: 2

SARASOTA

Christ the King Parish in Sarasota, Inc. - 1900 Meadowood St., Sarasota, FL 34231 t) 941-924-2777 office@christthekingsarasota.org www.christthekingsarasota.org Rev. Christopher Hathaway, F.S.S.P., Pst.; Rev. Vincent Huber, F.S.S.P., Par. Vicar; CRP Stds.: 54

Incarnation Parish in Sarasota, Inc. - 2901 Bee Ridge Rd., Sarasota, FL 34239; Mailing: 2929 Bee Ridge Rd., Sarasota, FL 34239 t) 941-921-6631; 941-924-9566 (CRP) lrusso@incarnationchurch.org; mschorr@incarnationchurch.org www.incarnationchurch.org Rev. Eric Scanlan, Pst.; Rev. James Cogan, Assoc. Pst.; Dcn. Stephen Beck; Dcn. John Crescitelli; Dcn. Kevin McKenny; Dcn. Patrick Palumbo; Molly Schorr, DRE; CRP Stds.: 93

Incarnation School - (Grades PreK-8) 2911 Bee Ridge Rd., Sarasota, FL 34239 t) 941-924-8588 Amy Yager, Prin.; Stds.: 166; Lay Tchrs.: 13

St. Jude Parish in Sarasota, Inc. - 3930 17th St., Sarasota, FL 34235 t) 941-955-3934 frcelestino@stjudeparish.org; janet@stjudesarasota.org www.stjudesarasota.org Rev. Celestino Gutierrez, Pst.; Rev. Robert Tatman, Par. Vicar; Rev. Victor Caviedes, Par. Vicar; Dcn. Humberto R. Alvia; Dcn. Leonardo Pastore; CRP Stds.: 200

St. Martha Parish in Sarasota, Inc. - 200 N. Orange Ave., Sarasota, FL 34236 t) 941-366-4210 x3234 sbrinn@stmartha.org www.stmartha.org Rev. George Suszko, S.A.C., Pst.; Rev. Jan Rykala, Par. Vicar; Rev. Krzysztof Frost, S.A.C., Par. Vicar; Rev. Joseph Toan Du Vu, C.R.M., Par. Vicar & Chap., Our Lady of Lavang Mission; Dcn. John Robert Gaitens; Dcn. William Ladroga; Dcn. R. Patrick Macaulay; Dcn. Vern Smith; Patricia Sileo, DRE; CRP Stds.: 130

St. Martha School - (Grades PreK-8) 4380 Fruitville Rd., Sarasota, FL 34232 t) 941-953-4181 syoung@stmarthaschool.net www.stmarthaschool.net Siobhan Young, Prin.; Stds.: 487; Sr. Tchrs.: 1; Lay Tchrs.: 38

The Vietnam Catholic Community of Our Lady of Lavang Mission -

St. Michael the Archangel Parish in Sarasota, Inc. - 5394 Midnight Pass Rd., Sarasota, FL 34242 t) 941-349-4174 parishoffice@stmichaelssiesta.com www.stmichaelssiesta.com Rev. Michael J. Cannon, Pst.; CRP Stds.: 17

Our Lady Queen of Martyrs Parish in Sarasota, Inc. - 6600 Pennsylvania Ave., Sarasota, FL 34243; Mailing: 833 Magellan Dr., Sarasota, FL 34243-1013 t) 941-755-1826 queenofmartyrs@olqm.net; faithformation@olqm.net www.olqm.net Rev. John N. Hoang, Admin.; Rev. Paul R. D'Angelo, Par. Vicar; Joann R. Deserio, DRE; CRP Stds.: 21

St. Patrick Catholic Parish in Sarasota, Inc. - 7900 Bee Ridge Rd., Sarasota, FL 34241 t) 941-378-1703 kathy@churchofstpatrick.org churchofstpatrick.org Rev. Paul Nguyen, Admin.; Rev. Russell Wright, S.T.L., Par. Vicar; Dcn. Kim Cohen; CRP Stds.: 96

St. Thomas More Parish in Sarasota, Inc. - 2506 Gulf Gate Dr., Sarasota, FL 34231 t) 941-923-1691 info@stthomasmoresrq.org www.stthomasmoresrq.org Rev. Gordon Zanetti, Pst.; Rev. Lawton Lang, Par. Vicar; CRP Stds.: 105

SEBRING

St. Catherine Parish in Sebring, Inc. - 820 Hickory St., Sebring, FL 33870; Mailing: 882 Bay St., Sebring, FL 33870 t) 863-385-0049 frjose@stcathe.org; office@stcathe.org www.stcathe.org Very Rev. Jose Antonio Gonzalez, Pst.; Rev. Pawel Kawalec, Assoc. Pst.; CRP Stds.: 86

St. Catherine School - (Grades PreK-8) 2835 Kenilworth Blvd., Sebring, FL 33870 t) 863-385-7300 higgins@stcatheschool.org www.stcatheschool.org Dr. Christine Higgins, Prin.; Stds.: 186; Lay Tchrs.: 20

VENICE

Epiphany Cathedral Catholic Parish in Venice, Inc. - 310 Sarasota St., Venice, FL 34285 t) 941-484-3505 eccommunications@epiphanycathedral.org www.epiphanycathedral.org Polish Mass Rev. Msgr. Patrick Dubois, Rector; Rev. Jayabalan Raju (India), Par. Vicar; Rev. Alexander W. Pince, Par. Vicar; Dcn. Paul Consbruck; Dcn. James Hanks; Dcn. Scott Little; Dcn. Epimaco Roca Jr.; CRP Stds.: 156

Epiphany Cathedral School - (Grades PreK-8) 316 Sarasota St., Venice, FL 34285 t) 941-488-2215 ecs@ecstigers.com www.ecstigers.com Nicole Loseto, Prin.; Stds.: 235; Lay Tchrs.: 22

Our Lady of Lourdes Parish in Venice, Inc. - 1301 Center Rd., Venice, FL 34292 t) 941-497-2931 office@ollvenice.org www.ollvenice.org Rev. Janusz Jay Jancarz, Pst.; Rev. Saji Ellickal Joseph, Par. Vicar; Dcn. Peter Casamento; Dcn. Dennis McDonald; Elisa Dacey, DRE; CRP Stds.: 157

WAUCHULA

St. Michael Parish in Wauchula, Inc. - 408 Heard Bridge Rd., Wauchula, FL 33873 t) 863-773-4089 x1 michaelwauc@gmail.com; mickey.shames@stmichaelwauchula.org www.stmichaelwauchula.org Rev. Wilner Durosier, Admin.; Rev. Juan Lorenzo, Par. Vicar; Dcn. Ramiro Hernandez; CRP Stds.: 531

Holy Child Mission - 4315 Chester Ave., Bowling Green, FL 33834; Mailing: 408 Heard Bridge Rd., Wauchula, FL 33873 t) (863) 773-4089 x1 parishoffice@stmichaelwauchula.org

SCHOOLS: PRESCHOOL THRU HIGH SCHOOL

SCHOOLS

STATE OF FLORIDA

ARCADIA

Institute for Catholic Studies and Formation, Inc. - (DIO) 10299 S.W. Peace River St., Arcadia, FL 34269-4068 t) 941-766-7334 institute@institute-dov.org institute-dov.org Rev. John Belmonte, S.J., Admin.;

NAPLES

***Royal Palm Academy** - (PRV) (Grades PreK-8) 16100 Livingston Rd., Naples, FL 34110 t) 239-594-9888 jscarafile@royalpalmacademy.org www.royalpalmacademy.org Officially affiliated with the Diocese of Venice through the Florida Catholic Conference Michael Bussman, Head of School; Stds.: 309; Lay Tchrs.: 36

SARASOTA

St. Mary Academy - (DIO) (Grades K-8) 4380 Fruitville Rd., Sarasota, FL 34232-1623 t) 941-366-4010 rreynolds@stmarysarasota.org www.stmarysarasota.org Rebecca Reynolds, Prin.; Stds.: 71; Lay Tchrs.: 11

HIGH SCHOOLS

STATE OF FLORIDA

FORT MYERS

Bishop Verot Catholic High School - (DIO) (Grades 9-12) 5598 Sunrise Dr., Fort Myers, FL 33919 t) 239-274-6700 information@bvhs.org www.bvhs.org Rev. David Portorreal, Chap.; Suzie O'Grady, Prin.; Stds.: 827; Lay Tchrs.: 57

NAPLES

***St. John Neumann Catholic High School, Inc.** - (DIO) (Grades 9-12) 3000 53rd St., S.W., Naples, FL 34116 t) 239-455-3044 proche@sjnceltics.org www.sjnceltics.org Rev. Michael Orsi, Chap.; Sr. Patricia Roche, F.M.A, Prin.; Dr. Donna Noonan, Vice Prin.; Marilyn Fischer, Bus. Mgr.; Stds.: 310; Sr. Tchrs.: 4; Lay Tchrs.: 35

SARASOTA

Cardinal Mooney Catholic High School, Inc. - (DIO) (Grades 9-12) 4171 Fruitville Rd., Sarasota, FL 34232 t) 941-371-4917 bhopper@cmhs-sarasota.org www.cmhs-sarasota.org Rev. Eric Scanlan, Chap.; Ben

Hopper, Prin.; Stds.: 623; Lay Tchrs.: 41

INSTITUTIONS LOCATED IN DIOCESE

CATHOLIC CHARITIES [CCH]

SARASOTA

Bethesda House - HIV/AIDS Ministries - 1670 4th St., Sarasota, FL 34236 t) 941-366-1886; 941-486-4700 (Central Office) colleen.mcmenamin@catholiccharitiesdov.org; helen.rombalski@catholiccharitiesdov.org www.catholiccharitiesdov.org Cristy King, Regional Director; Colleen McMenamin, Dir.; Eduardo Gloria, CEO; Asstd. Annu.: 180; Staff: 2

VENICE

Catholic Charities Housing Sarasota, Inc. - 1000 Pinebrook Rd., Venice, FL 34285 t) 941-486-4700 (Office); 941-484-9543 (Catholic Center) helen.rombalski@catholiccharitiesdov.org; eduardo.gloria@catholiccharitiesdov.org catholiccharitiesdov.org Eduardo Gloria, CEO; Helen Rombalski, Admin.; Asstd. Annu.: 52; Staff: 2

St. Dominic Manor - 1023 Putnam Dr., Sarasota, FL 34232 t) 941-391-5669 (NDC Mgmt.); 942-486-4700 (Central Office) marianmanor@ndcassetmanagement.com Barbara Breault, Mgr.;

St. Monica Residence - 1575 Dr. Martin Luther King Way, Sarasota, FL 34234 t) 941-391-5669; (941) 486-4700 (CC Central Office) marianmanor@ndcassetmanagement.com Barbara Breault, Mgr.;

Catholic Charities of the Diocese of Venice, Inc. - 1000 Pinebrook Rd., Venice, FL 34285 t) 941-486-4700 helen.rombalski@catholiccharititesdov.org; eduardo.gloria@catholiccharitiesdov.org www.catholiccharitiesdov.org Eduardo Gloria, CEO; Clint Branam, COO; Helen Rombalski, Admin.; Asstd. Annu.: 210,115; Staff: 93

African Caribbean American Catholic Center - 3861 Michigan Ave., Fort Myers, FL 33916 t) 239-295-5506 helen.rombalski@catholiccharitiesdov.org Anna Callwood, Prog. Mgr.; Taunya Cola, Case Mgr.;

Casa San Jose - 3900 17th St., Sarasota, FL 34235 t) 941-366-1886; 941-952-1853 colleen.mcmenamin@catholiccharitiesdov.org; marguerite.petit@catholiccharitiesdov.org Colleen McMenamin, Dir.; Cristy King, Rgnl. Dir.; Marguerite Petit, Case Mgr.;

Casa San Juan Bosco II, Inc. - 2358 S.E. Arnold Andrews Ave., Arcadia, FL 34266 t) 863-884-2123; 863-884-2134 casaleasing@ndcassetmanagement.com; casa@ndcassetmanagement.com Clara Alvarez, Prog. Mgr.; Gloria Romero, Rgnl. Dir.;

Casa San Juan Bosco, Inc. - 2358 S.E. Arnold Andrews Ave., Arcadia, FL 34266 t) 863-884-2134 casa@ndcassetmanagement.com; casaleasing@ndcassetmanagement.com catholiccharitiesdov.org Clara Alvarez, Prog. Mgr.; Gloria Romero, Rgnl. Dir.;

Catholic Charities Housing, Diocese of Venice, Inc. - 1000 Pinebrook Rd., Venice, FL 34285 t) (941) 486-4700 helen.rombalski@catholiccharitiesdov.org Eddie Gloria, CEO;

Catholic Charities Immigration Programs - 4235 Michigan Link Ave., Fort Myers, FL 33916 t) (239) 334-4007 x2102; (239) 657-6242 maria.rodriguez@catholiccharitiesdov.org; raquel.ramirez@catholiccharitiesdov.org Raquel Ramirez, Case Worker; Maria Rodriguez, Case Worker;

Catholic Charities Region I - 5055 N. Tamiami Trl., Sarasota, FL 34234 t) 941-355-4680 joan.pierse@catholiccharitiesdov.org; cristy.king@catholiccharitiesdov.org (Sarasota & Manatee Counties) Cristy King, Rgnl. Dir.; Joan Pierse, Office Mgr.;

Catholic Charities Region II - 4235 Michigan Ave. Link, Fort Myers, FL 33916 t) 239-337-4193; 239-334-4007 alex.olivares@catholiccharitiesdov.org; arlene.carratala@catholiccharitiesdov.org (Lee, Henry & Glades Counties) Alex Olivares, Dir.; Arlene Carratala, Admin.;

Catholic Charities Region III - 2210 Santa Barbara Blvd., Naples, FL 34116 t) 239-455-2655 peggy.rodriguez@catholiccharitiesdov.org; esmeralda.alvarado@catholiccharitiesdov.org (Collier County) Peggy Rodriguez, Dir.; Esmeralda Alvarado, Admin.;

Catholic Charities Region IV (Rural Services) - 1210 E. Oak St., Arcadia, FL 34266 t) 863-494-1068 gloria.romero@catholiccharitiesdov.org; jaimira.quesada@catholiccharitiesdov.org (Charlotte, De Soto, Hardee & Highland Counties) Gloria Romero, Dir.; Frantz Sylvestre, Case Mgr.; Jaimira Quesada, Admin.;

Marian Manor, Inc. - 4200 Lister St., Port Charlotte, FL 33980 t) 941-391-5669; (941) 486-4700 helen.rombalski@catholiccharitiesdov.org Barbara Brault, Contact;

New Paradigm of Catholic Charities, Inc. - 5900 Pan American Blvd., Ste. 203, Englewood, FL 34287 t) 941-681-2194 deb.robinson@catholiccharitiesdov.org; nadine.woinoski@catholiccharitiesdov.org Deb Robinson, Housing Mgr.; Nadine Woinoski, Case Mgr.;

St. John II Housing, Inc. - 1000 Pinebrook Rd., Venice, FL 34285 t) 941-486-4700 helen.rombalski@catholiccharitiesdov.org Eduardo Gloria, CEO; Asstd. Annu.: 90; Staff: 2

COLLEGES & UNIVERSITIES [COL]

AVE MARIA

***Ave Maria University** - 5050 Ave Maria Blvd., Ave Maria, FL 34142-9505 t) 239-280-2511; (239) 283-8648 admissions@avemaria.edu www.avemaria.edu Mark Middendorf, Pres.; Stds.: 1,227; Lay Tchrs.: 63; Pr. Tchrs.: 2

CONVENTS, MONASTERIES, AND RESIDENCES FOR WOMEN [CON]

FORT MYERS BEACH

San Damiano Monastery of St. Clare. - 6029 Estero Blvd., Fort Myers Beach, FL 33931-4325 t) 239-463-5599 saintclare@comcast.net www.fmbpoorclare.com Solemn Vows, Papal Enclosure; Poor Clares. Sr. Mary Frances Fortin, O.S.C., Abbess;

NAPLES

Daughters of Mary Help of Christians - 3180 53rd St. S.W., Naples, FL 34116 t) 239-348-2911 naples@salesiansisters.org www.salesiansisters.org Sr. Patricia Roche, F.M.A, Supr.; Srs.: 4

ENDOWMENTS / FOUNDATIONS / TRUSTS [EFT]

SARASOTA

Cardinal Mooney High School Foundation - 4171 Fruitville Rd., Sarasota, FL 34232 t) 941-371-4917 smeryk@dioceseofvenice.org www.cmhs-sarasota.org Dr. Volodymyr Smeryk, Chancellor;

Incarnation School Foundation - 2911 Bee Ridge Rd., Sarasota, FL 34239 t) 941-924-8588 ayager@incarnationschool.edu www.incarnationschool.edu Amy Yager, Prin.;

St. Martha School Foundation - 4380 Fruitville Rd., Sarasota, FL 34232 t) 941-953-4181 kmarshall@stmarthaschool.net www.stmarthaschool.net Rev. George Suszko, S.A.C., Pst.;

VENICE

Catholic Community Foundation of Southwest Florida, Inc. - 1000 Pinebrook Rd., Venice, FL 34285 t) 941-441-1124 ccf@dioceseofvenice.org; morse@dioceseofvenice.org ccfdioceseofvenice.org/ Michael Morse, Exec.;

Catholic Charities Foundation of the Diocese of Venice, Inc. - 1000 Pinebrook Rd., Venice, FL 34285 t) 941-486-4700; 941-484-9543 (Catholic Center) helen.rombalski@catholiccharitiesdov.org; eduardo.gloria@catholiccharitiesdov.org www.ccfdnswfl.org Eduardo Gloria, CEO & Pres.; Helen Rombalski, Admin.;

Diocese of Venice Savings and Loan Trust Fund - 1000 Pinebrook Rd., Venice, FL 34285 t) 941-484-9543 smeryk@dioceseofvenice.org Dr. Volodymyr Smeryk, Contact;

Trinity Trust - 1000 Pinebrook Rd., Venice, FL 34284 t) 941-484-9543 smeryk@dioceseofvenice.org Dr. Volodymyr Smeryk, Contact;

MISCELLANEOUS [MIS]

FORT MYERS

Magnificat-Ft. Myers, FL-Mother of Mercy Chapter of the Diocese of Venice - 5017 Westminster Dr., Fort Myers, FL 33919 t) (239) 826-7475 pegmengle@gmail.com magnificatfortmyers.com/ Peg Mengle, Treas.;

NAPLES

Hope for Haiti, Inc. - 1021 5th Ave. N., Naples, FL 34102 t) 239-434-7183 seline@hopeforhaiti.com www.hopeforhaiti.com Skylar Badenoch, CEO;

OSPREY

Christ Child Society of Sarasota, Inc. - 333 S. Tamiami Trl., Osprey, FL 34229; Mailing: PO Box 306, Osprey, FL 34229 ccssarasota@gmail.com www.christchildsocietyofsarasota.org/about Local affiliate of national non-profit organization whose member-volunteers serve needy children. Loretta Haugh, Interim Pres.;

VENICE

All Saints Catholic Cemetery Inc. - 1000 Pinebrook Rd., Venice, FL 34285 t) 941-484-9543 finance@dioceseofvenice.org Peter McPartland, Treas.;

Casa San Juan Diego Housing, Inc. - 1000 Pinebrook Rd., Venice, FL 34285

CSJD Developer, Inc. - 1000 Pinebrook Rd., Venice, FL 34285

Diocese of Venice in Florida, Inc. - 1000 Pinebrook Rd., Venice, FL 34284 t) 941-484-9543 smeryk@dioceseofvenice.org Dr. Volodymyr Smeryk, Contact;

St. Peter Claver Developer, Inc. - 1000 Pinebrook Rd., Venice, FL 34285

St. Peter Claver Housing, Inc. - 1000 Pinebrook Rd., Venice, FL 34285

San Alfonso Housing, Inc. - 1000 Pinebrook Rd., Venice, FL 34285

Trinity Enterprise Holdings, Inc. - 1000 Pinebrook Rd., Venice, FL 34284 t) 941-484-9543 smeryk@dioceseofvenice.org Dr. Volodymyr Smeryk, Contact;

MONASTERIES AND RESIDENCES FOR PRIESTS AND BROTHERS [MON]

NOKOMIS

Carmel at Mission Valley - 955 Laurel Rd. E., Nokomis, FL 34275-4507 t) 941-412-0678 awocarm@gmail.com Order of Carmelites Inc. Rev. Adrian Wilde, O.Carm., Prior; Rev. Marcel Dube, O.Carm., Mem.; Rev. Joseph Jerome McCarthy, O.Carm., Mem.; Rev. Gregory Klein, O.Carm., Mem.; Priests: 4

SARASOTA

Holy Cross Florida Regional Center - 514 Howard Ct., Sarasota, FL 34236 c) 574-386-0440 lskitzki@sbcglobal.net Holy Cross Brothers residences for retired brothers. Dr. Volodymyr Smeryk, Chair; Bro.

Lawrence Skitzki, Dir.; Brs.: 2

VENICE

Xaverian Brothers - 700 Cadiz, Venice, FL 34285 t) 941-484-9641 smeryk@dioceseofvenice.org www.xaverianbrothers.org Brothers of St. Francis Xavier. Dr. Volodymyr Smeryk, Chancellor;

NURSING / REHABILITATION / CONVALESCENCE / ELDERLY CARE [NUR]

FORT MYERS

St. John XXIII Housing, Inc. - 13251 Apaloosa Ln., Fort Myers, FL 33912 t) 239-561-3535 www.stjohn23villas.com Rev. Robert D. Tabbert, Pres.; Asstd. Annu.: 70; Staff: 3

Villa Francisco - 2140 Cottage St., Fort Myers, FL 33901 t) 239-332-3229 anthony.hewitt@stfrancisfm.org Rev. Anthony Hewitt, Pres.; Asstd. Annu.: 68; Staff: 1

St. Vincent de Paul Housing, Inc. (Villa Vincente) - 13071 Palm Beach Blvd., Fort Myers, FL 33905 t) 239-693-1333 garyb@spm.net www.villavincenteapartments.com Rev. Murchadh O'Madagain, Pres.; Asstd. Annu.: 60; Staff: 1

PALMETTO

Holy Cross Manor, Inc. - 510 26th St. W., Palmetto, FL 34221-5426 t) 941-729-2063 michaelp@spm.net www.liveatholycrossmanor.com Rev. Leszek Trojanowski, Pres.; Asstd. Annu.: 71; Staff: 3

Holy Cross Manor II, Inc. - 540 26th St. W., Palmetto, FL 34221-5425 t) 941-729-2111 michaelp@spm.net www.liveatholycrossmanor2.com Rev. Leszek Trojanowski, Pres.; Asstd. Annu.: 70; Staff: 4

PORT CHARLOTTE

St. Charles Housing I, Inc. (Villa San Carlos) - 2550 Easy St., Port Charlotte, FL 33952 t) 941-624-2266 michaelp@spm.net www.liveatvillasancarlos.com Rev. John Fitch, Pres.; Asstd. Annu.: 52; Staff: 5

St. Charles Housing II, Inc. (Villa San Carlos II) - 22250 Vick St., Port Charlotte, FL 33980-2026 t) 941-624-4404 michaelp@spm.net www.liveatvillasancarlos2.com Rev. John Fitch, Pres.; Asstd. Annu.: 53; Staff: 6

SARASOTA

St. Martha's Housing II, Inc (Casa Santa Marta II) - 800 N. Lemon Ave., Sarasota, FL 34236 t) 941-365-7913 jessicar@spm.net www.casasantamartasarasota.com Rev. George Suszko, S.A.C., Pres.; Asstd. Annu.: 56; Staff: 7

St. Martha's Housing, Inc. (Casa Santa Marta) - 1576 8th St., Sarasota, FL 34236 t) 941-366-4448 jessicar@spm.net www.casasantamartasarasota.com Rev. George Suszko, S.A.C., Pres.; Asstd. Annu.: 78; Staff: 7

VENICE

St. Mark's Housing of Venice, Inc. (Villa San Marco) - 1030 Albee Farm Rd., Venice, FL 34285 t) 941-483-1960 garyb@spm.net www.villasanmarcosapartments.com Rev. Msgr. Patrick Dubois, Pres.; Asstd. Annu.: 83; Staff: 3

RETREAT HOUSES / RENEWAL CENTERS [RTR]

LAKE PLACID

Campo San Jose - 170 S. Sun 'n' Lake Blvd., Lake Placid, FL 33852; Mailing: 882 Bay St., Sebring, FL 33870 t) 863-385-6762 frjose@stcathe.org Very Rev. Jose Antonio Gonzalez, Dir.;

VENICE

Our Lady of Perpetual Help Retreat and Spirituality Center, Inc. - 3989 S. Moon Dr., Venice, FL 34292 t) 941-486-0233 www.olph-retreat.org Rev. Mark Yavarone, O.M.V., Dir.; Rev. Shawn Monahan, O.M.V., Asst. Dir.;

An asterisk (*) denotes an organization that has established tax-exempt status directly with the IRS and is not covered by the USCCB Group Ruling.

Diocese of Victoria in Texas

(Dioecesis Victoriensis in Texia)

MOST REVEREND BRENDAN J. CAHILL, S.T.D.

Bishop of Victoria; ordained May 19, 1990; appointed Third Bishop of Victoria in Texas April 23, 2015; consecrated and installed June 29, 2015. Mailing Address: P.O. Box 4070, Victoria, TX 77903.

Chancery Office: P.O. Box 4070, Victoria, TX 77903. T: 361-573-0828; F: 361-573-5725.

ESTABLISHED AND CREATED A DIOCESE, MAY 29, 1982.

Square Miles 9,609.

Comprises the Counties of Calhoun, DeWitt, Goliad, Jackson, Lavaca, Matagorda, Victoria, Wharton and Colorado; also Fayette County west of the Colorado River in the State of Texas.

Legal Title: Diocese of Victoria in Texas.

For legal titles of parishes and diocesan institutions, consult the Chancery Office.

STATISTICAL OVERVIEW

Personnel

Bishop ... 1
Retired Bishops ... 1
Priests: Diocesan Active in Diocese ... 42
Priests: Diocesan Active Outside Diocese ... 1
Priests: Retired, Sick or Absent ... 10
Number of Diocesan Priests ... 53
Total Priests in your Diocese ... 53
Extern Priests in Diocese ... 14
Ordinations:
Diocesan Priests ... 2
Transitional Deacons ... 2
Permanent Deacons in Diocese ... 48
Total Sisters ... 62

Parishes

Parishes ... 51
With Resident Pastor:
Resident Diocesan Priests ... 40
Without Resident Pastor:
Administered by Priests ... 11
Missions ... 17
New Parishes Created ... 1
Professional Ministry Personnel:
Sisters ... 4
Lay Ministers ... 28

Welfare

Special Centers for Social Services ... 1
Total Assisted ... 478

Educational

Diocesan Students in Other Seminaries ... 10
Total Seminarians ... 10
High Schools, Diocesan and Parish ... 2
Total Students ... 181
High Schools, Private ... 1
Total Students ... 313
Elementary Schools, Diocesan and Parish ... 11
Total Students ... 1,912
Elementary Schools, Private ... 1
Total Students ... 346
Catechesis/Religious Education:
High School Students ... 2,034
Elementary Students ... 3,723
Total Students under Catholic Instruction ... 8,519
Teachers in Diocese:
Sisters ... 9
Lay Teachers ... 226

Vital Statistics

Receptions into the Church:
Infant Baptism Totals ... 899
Minor Baptism Totals ... 116
Adult Baptism Totals ... 43
Received into Full Communion ... 89
First Communions ... 986
Confirmations ... 900
Marriages:
Catholic ... 192
Interfaith ... 63
Total Marriages ... 255
Deaths ... 1,082
Total Catholic Population ... 71,332
Total Population ... 285,475

LEADERSHIP

Chancery Office - t) 361-573-0828 Very Rev. Matthew H. Huehlefeld, Chancellor; Anthony Martinez, CFO (tmartinez@victoriadiocese.org); Rev. Msgr. John C. Peters, Vicar;
Office of Vicar General - t) 361-573-0828 Rev. Msgr. John C. Peters, Vicar;
Office of the Chancellor - chancellor@victoriadiocese.org Very Rev. Matthew H. Huehlefeld, Chancellor;
Office of Vicar for Religious - t) 361-575-2266 Sr. M. Stephana Marbach, I.W.B.S. (srstephana@yahoo.com);
Diocesan Consultors - Rev. Kristopher L. Fuchs (frkristopher@victoriadiocese.org); Very Rev. Matthew H. Huehlefeld, Chancellor; Rev. Msgr. John C. Peters;
Consultors for Pastors - Very Rev. Gregory E. Korenek; Very Rev. Samuel Appiasi; Rev. Edward J. Winkler;
Vicars Forane - Very Rev. Samuel Appiasi; Very Rev. Gabriel Bentil (gabbybentil@hfccvic.org); Very Rev. Bryan Heyer;
Presbyteral Council - Very Rev. Samuel Appiasi, Dean; Rev. Philip Brune, Mem.; Rev. Antonio Perez, Mem.;
Diocesan Tribunal - t) 361-573-0760 Very Rev. Matthew H. Huehlefeld (judicialvicar@victoriadiocese.org);
Judicial Vicar - t) (361) 573-0760 Very Rev. Matthew H. Huehlefeld (judicialvicar@victoriadiocese.org);
Judges - Very Rev. Gregory E. Korenek;
Promoter of Justice - Rev. Gabriel Maison;
Procurator Advocate - Very Rev. Samuel Appiasi; Rev. Michael Rother (mrother@victoriadiocese.org);
Defenders of the Bond - Very Rev. Robert E. Knippenberg;
Auditors - Rev. Philip Brune;
Notaries - Sr. Rosario Resendez; Brenda Ortmann, Secy. (bortmann@victoriadiocese.org);

OFFICES AND DIRECTORS

Building Board - Most Rev. Brendan J. Cahill; Anthony Martinez (tmartinez@victoriadiocese.org); John Gehrke;
Campaign for Human Development and Catholic Relief Services - t) 361-573-5304 Debbie Vanelli, Dir. (dkvanelli@gmail.com);
Catholic Outreach Prison Ministry - t) 361-275-3554 stmchurch@sbcglobal.net Hermes Silva, Dir. (hsilva@victoriadiocese.org);
Council of Catholic Women (DCCW) - Rev. Michael Petering, Mod. (stagnesedna@sbcglobal.net); Janice Ohrt, Chair;
Diaconate Ministry and Life - Dcn. Michael Tankersley, Chair; Dcn. Dennis Kutach, Dir. (deacon@stjcatholicchurch.com);
Diocesan Finance Board - Most Rev. Brendan J. Cahill; Rev. Msgr. John C. Peters; Very Rev. Matthew H. Huehlefeld;
Diocesan Services Appeal - Jeri Joseph, DSA Capital Campaign, Lay & Priest Pension (jjoseph@victoriadiocese.org);
Diocese of Victoria Catholic Committee on Scouting - Gary Rangnow;
Director of Seminarians - Rev. Kristopher L. Fuchs (frkristopher@victoriadiocese.org);
Ecumenical Commission - Rev. Tommy Chen, Dir. (olg@olgulf.org);
The Emmaus Center - Counseling in the Catholic Tradition - t) 361-212-0830 Very Rev. Kirby Hlavaty, Dir. (frkirby@olvcathedral.org);
Lay Pension Board - John McQuillen, Chair; Billy Macha; Kenny French;
Liturgical Commission - Greg Bentz, Dir. (gregbentzmusic@gmail.com);
Missionary Childhood Association - Very Rev. Matthew H. Huehlefeld, Chancellor;
Office of Business and Finance - Barbara Vahalik; Anthony Martinez, CFO (tmartinez@victoriadiocese.org); Zoila Shoemake (zshoemake@victoriadiocese.org);
Office of Catechetical Ministry - Christella Alvarez, Dir. (calvarez@victoriadiocese.org);
Office of Catholic Schools - John Quary, Supt. (jquary@victoriadiocese.org);
Office of Catholic Youth and Young Adult Ministry - Wendy Eggert, Dir. (weggert@victoriadiocese.org); Shannon Thomas, Assoc. Dir. (sthomas@victoriadiocese.org);
Office of Communications/"The Catholic Lighthouse" - lighthouse@victoriadiocese.org Janet Jones, Dir. (jjones@victoriadiocese.org); Regina Matus Janak, Production & Advertising Asst. (janakr@victoriadiocese.org);
Office of Family Evangelization - Aldo Camacho, Dir.; Very Rev. Jacob A. Koether, Vicar;
Office of Human Resources -
Office of Safe Environment - Stephanie Morales, Dir. (smorales@victoriadiocese.org);
Office of Vocations - Rev. Kristopher L. Fuchs, Dir. (frkristopher@victoriadiocese.org);
Pastoral Care and Outreach - t) 361-827-7186 pastoralcare@victoriadiocese.org Shannon Thomas (sthomas@victoriadiocese.org);
Permanent Diaconate Formation - t) 979-253-9616 Dcn. Charles J. Glynn, Dir. (cglynn@victoriadiocese.org);
Priests' Pension Board - Very Rev. Gregory E. Korenek; Very Rev. Roger Hawes; Very Rev. Kirby Hlavaty (frkirby@olvcathedral.org);
Priests' Personnel Board - Very Rev. Samuel Appiasi; Very Rev. Gabriel Bentil (gabbybentil@hfccvic.org); Very Rev. Bryan Heyer;
Respect Life-Pro Life - Very Rev. Gregory E. Korenek;
School Board - Diocesan School Advisory Council (DSAC) - John Quary, Supt. (jquary@victoriadiocese.org);
  Members - Most Rev. Brendan J. Cahill; Anthony Martinez; Michael Seger;
Spiritual Renewal Center - Retreat Center - t) 361-572-0836 x3221; 361-827-7155 x3223 renewalcenter@victoriadiocese.org Matthew Boyle, Dir.;
Vietnamese Apostolate - t) 361-972-2446 Rev. Dominic Trung Nguyen (dtnguyensccr@yahoo.com);

MISCELLANEOUS / OTHER OFFICES

Diocesan Cemeteries - Alice Capelo; Deborah Escalante, Dir. (cemeteries@victoriadiocese.org);
Presidio La Bahia - t) 361-645-3752 Scott McMahon, Dir. (smcmahon.presidiolabahia@gmail.com);

PARISHES, MISSIONS, AND CLERGY

STATE OF TEXAS

ALLEYTON

St. Roch - 1600 Frelsburg Rd., Alleyton, TX 78935 t) 979-732-3460 hannah@saintrochparish.org www.saintrochparish.org Very Rev. Robert E. Knippenberg, Pst.; Dcn. Charles J. Glynn; Dcn. Andrew Joseph Nunmaker III; Dcn. Douglas B. Tromblee; CRP Stds.: 6

BAY CITY

Holy Cross - 2001 Katy Ave., Bay City, TX 77414 t) 979-245-6379 hc3_office@holycrossbaycity.org www.holycrossbaycity.org Rev. Stephen Vacek, Pst.; Dcn. Kevin Gerard Knox; Dcn. Guadalupe Rodriguez; CRP Stds.: 59
  Holy Cross School - (Grades PreK-5) 2001 Katy Ave, Bay City, TX 77414 t) 979-245-5632 lbradford@bcholycrossschool.org bcholycrossschool.org Linda Bradford, Prin.; Stds.: 77; Lay Tchrs.: 11
  Sacred Heart - 13594 State Hwy. 60 S., Wadsworth, TX 77483; Mailing: 2001 Katy Ave., Bay City, TX 77414 t) (979) 245-6379 holycrossbaycity.org
Our Lady of Guadalupe - 1412 12th St., Bay City, TX 77414 t) 979-245-2010 olg2003@sbcglobal.net Rev. Gabriel D. Espinosa, Pst.; Dcn. Joe Ramos; Dcn. Luan Van Tran; CRP Stds.: 128

BLESSING

St. Peter's - 206 Hickory St., Blessing, TX 77419; Mailing: Box 395, Blessing, TX 77419 t) 361-588-6241; 361-588-1156 stpeterblessing@tisd.net www.stpeterblessing.org Rev. Gabriel J. Mensah, Admin.; Lonnie Bullard, DRE; CRP Stds.: 129
  St. Robert - FM Rd. 1468, Markham, TX 77456 t) (361) 588-6241

BLOOMINGTON

St. Patrick's - 13316 State Hwy. 185, Bloomington, TX 77951; Mailing: P. O. Box 2122, Bloomington, TX 77951-2122 t) 361-897-1155 saintpatricks@triplejreal.com; saintpatricks1155@gmail.com saintpatrickschurch.net/ Rev. Peter Oscar Kofi-Amo, Pst.; Dcn. Fred Soto, CRE; Ramona Torres, DRE; Perez Ismael, CRE; CRP Stds.: 76

COLUMBUS

St. Anthony's - 1602 Bowie, Columbus, TX 78934; Mailing: P.O. Box 669, Columbus, TX 78934 t) 979-732-2562 sec.stanthony@gmail.com; lorrainenovosad@gmail.com stanthonycolumbustx.net Rev. Augustine N. Asante, Pst.; Rev. Nelson Gonzalez Nieto, Par. Vicar; Dcn. John William Glueck; Dcn. Bennie Holesovsky; Dcn. Charlie Novosad; Dcn. Charles Russell Theut; Lorraine Novosad, DRE; Kathryn Robinson, Youth Min.; CRP Stds.: 121
  St. Anthony's School - (Grades PreK-8) 635 Bonham St., Columbus, TX 78934 t) 979-732-5505 scollins@stanthonycolumbus.net stanthonycolumbus.net Shanna Collins, Prin.; Stds.: 169; Lay Tchrs.: 9

CUERO

St. Michael - 309 E. Church St., Cuero, TX 77954-2906 t) 361-275-3554 stmchurch@catholiccuero.org; frjacobmendoza@icloud.com www.catholiccuero.org Rev. Jacob Mendoza, Pst.; Rev. Richard Bediako (Ghana), Assoc. Pst.; Dcn. Leo Sharron; CRP Stds.: 104
  St. Michael School - (Grades PreK-6) 309 E Church St, Cuero, TX 77954 t) 361-277-3854; 361-275-8006 jsaenz@stmschoolcuero.org; thiles@stmschoolcuero.org www.stmschoolcuero.org Sandra Stelpflug, Prin.; Stds.: 87; Lay Tchrs.: 9
Our Lady of Guadalupe - 705 W. Broadway, Cuero, TX 77954; Mailing: 309 E. Church St., Cuero, TX 77954 t) 361-275-3554 stmchurch@catholiccuero.org www.catholiccuero.org Part of the Catholic Community of Cuero with St. Michael's Catholic Church Rev. Jacob Mendoza, Pst.; Rev. Richard Bediako (Ghana), Assoc. Pst.;

EAGLE LAKE

Parish of the Nativity - 308 Stevenson St., Eagle Lake, TX 77434; Mailing: P.O. Box 307, Eagle Lake, TX 77434 t) 979-234-2842 nativity1@sbcglobal.net; warobaar@juno.com parishofthenativity.org Rev. Robert F. Guerra, Pst.; Elida Salazar, Parish Catechetical Ldr.; CRP Stds.: 80

EAST BERNARD

Holy Cross - 839 Church St., East Bernard, TX 77435-1325; Mailing: PO Box 1325, East Bernard, TX 77435 t) 979-335-7551 office@eastbernardcatholic.org; faithformation@eastbernardcatholic.org www.eastbernardcatholic.org Very Rev. Charles Elvis Otsiwah, Pst.; Patricia Krenek, DRE; CRP Stds.: 269
  Cemetery Office - t) (979) 335-7551 x5 Very Rev. Charles Elvis Otsiwah, Pst.;

EDNA

St. Agnes - 506 N. Allen, Edna, TX 77957 t) 361-782-3588; 361-782-6171 (CRP) stagnesccd@att.net; stagnesedna@sbcglobal.net Rev. Michael Petering, Pst.; Patricia Kromka, DRE; CRP Stds.: 169

EL CAMPO

St. Andrew - 270 St. Andrew St., El Campo, TX 77437 t) 979-648-2864; 979-541-6413 (CRP) standrew@ykc.com; steph_michell@hotmail.com Rev. Michael Rother, Pst.; Stephanie Garrett, DRE; CRP Stds.: 85

St. Procopius - 814 Elm St., Louise, TX 77455; Mailing: 270 St. Andrew St, El Campo, TX 77437 t) (979) 648-2864

St. John Nepomucene - 1843 County Rd. 469, El Campo, TX 77437 t) 979-543-6985 saintjohnchurch@outlook.com newtaitoncatholic.org Rev. Gabriel Oduro Tawiah, Pst.; Dcn. Patrick Kubala; Dcn. Edward Wendel; Diann Srubar, DRE; CRP Stds.: 76

St. Philip the Apostle - 304 W. Church St., El Campo, TX 77437 t) 979-543-3770; 979-541-9457 (CRP) apostle@stphilipapostle.org; cce@stphilipapostle.org www.stphilipapostle.org Rev. Michael Rother, Pst.; Rev. Samuel Owusu, Par. Vicar; Dcn. Jerome Grahmann; Dcn. Lawrence Hoelscher; Nancy Fenner, DRE; CRP Stds.: 161

St. Philip the Apostle School - (Grades PreK-8) 302 W. Church St., El Campo, TX 77437 t) 979-543-2901 gwene@stphilipschool.org www.stphilipschool.org Gwen Edwards, Prin.; Stds.: 260; Lay Tchrs.: 21

St. Robert Bellarmine - 512 Tegner St., El Campo, TX 77437 t) 979-543-4298 churchoffice@sanrobertochurch.org sanrobertochurch.org Rev. Philip Brune, Pst.; Rev. Anthony Augustine Owusu-Peprah, Par. Vicar; Dcn. Adrian Wayne Canales; Dcn. Margarito Cervantez Jr.; Alicia Gutierrez, Admin.; Joseph Holik, Music Min.; Brandy Flores, Dir.; CRP Stds.: 299

FLATONIA

Assumption of the Blessed Virgin Mary Catholic Church - 821 FM 1295, Flatonia, TX 78941 t) 361-596-4674 st_joe@sbcglobal.net www.stmaryspraha.org Rev. Gabriel Maison, Admin.; CRP Stds.: 9

SS. Cyril and Methodius - 113 Manchester St., Flatonia, TX 78941; Mailing: P.O. Box 186, Flatonia, TX 78941 t) 361-865-3568 sacredheart186@sbcglobal.net shsscm.org Rev. Edward J. Winkler, Pst.; Dcn. Timothy Michael Kozelsky;

Sacred Heart - 516 S. Faires, Flatonia, TX 78941; Mailing: PO Box 186, Flatonia, TX 78941 t) 361-865-3568 sacredheart186@sbcglobal.net shsscm.org Rev. Edward J. Winkler, Pst.; Dcn. Timothy Michael Kozelsky; CRP Stds.: 116

GANADO

Assumption of the B.V.M. - 109 S. Sixth St., Ganado, TX 77962; Mailing: P.O. Box 369, Ganado, TX 77962 t) 361-771-3425 churchoffice@abvmganado.org; pastor@abvmganado.org www.abvmganado.org Very Rev. Gregory E. Korenek, Pst.; Dcn. Kevin Ray Petrash; Joseph Vincent Sablatura, Youth Min.; Dcn. Anthony Hensley; CRP Stds.: 184

GOLIAD

Immaculate Conception - 238 N. Commercial St., Goliad, TX 77963 t) 361-645-3095 office@goliadcatholic.org www.goliadcatholic.org Rev. Ty J. Bazar, Pst.; CRP Stds.: 107

Our Lady of Loreto (Old Franciscan Mission) - 217 U.S. Hwy. 183, Goliad, TX 77963 t) 361-645-3752

HALLETTSVILLE

St. Mary - 1648 FM 340, Hallettsville, TX 77964; Mailing: P.O. Drawer H, Hallettsville, TX 77964 t) 361-798-5888; 361-798-6256 (CRP) rectory@shcatholicchurch.org; rother.carol@gmail.com Rev. Msgr. John C. Peters, Pst.; Rev. James M. Dvorak, Assoc. Pst.; Rev. John Affum, Assoc. Pst.; Carol Rother, DRE; CRP Stds.: 65

Sacred Heart - 400 E. Fifth St., Hallettsville, TX 77964; Mailing: P.O. Box H, Hallettsville, TX 77964 t) 361-798-5888; 361-798-3124 rectory@shcatholicchurch.org; angelamcconnell@shcatholicchurch.org www.shcatholicchurch.org Rev. Msgr. John C. Peters, Pst.; Rev. John Affum, Assoc. Pst.; Rev. James M. Dvorak, Assoc. Pst.; Dcn. Linard Harper; Dcn. Michael Tankersley; Dcn. Joey Targac; Angela McConnell, DRE; CRP Stds.: 246

Sacred Heart School - (Grades PreK-8) 313 S. Texana, Hallettsville, TX 77964 t) 361-798-4251 kevin.haas@shschool.org www.shschool.org Kevin Haas, Prin.; Stds.: 192; Lay Tchrs.: 13

Sacred Heart High School - (Grades 9-12) 313 S. Texana, Hallettsville, TX 77964 t) 361-798-4251 kevin.haas@shschool.org www.shschool.org Kevin Haas, Prin.; Stds.: 98; Lay Tchrs.: 12

HUNGERFORD

St. John the Baptist - 101 Church St., Hungerford, TX 77448; Mailing: P.O. Box 121, Hungerford, TX 77448 t) 979-532-4747 stjohnhungerford@gmail.com Rev. Charles O. Dwomoh, Pst.; Janet Bubela, DRE; CRP Stds.: 61

INEZ

St. Joseph Catholic Church - 17 Church St., Inez, TX 77968; Mailing: PO Box 337, Inez, TX 77968 t) 361-782-3181 stjccd@tisd.net; stjosephchurch@tisd.net stjosephinez.org Rev. Barnabas Kyeah, Admin.; Dcn. Steve Borowicz; CRP Stds.: 148

LA GRANGE

SS. Peter and Paul - 126 Plum Church Rd, La Grange, TX 78945; Mailing: 936 FM 2436, La Grange, TX 78945 t) 979-247-4441 hostynch@cvctx.com www.hostynplumcatholic.org Rev. Felix Twumasi, Admin.; Dcn. John McCourt; CRP Stds.: 27

Queen of the Holy Rosary - 936 FM 2436, La Grange, TX 78945 t) 979-247-4441 hostynch@cvctx.com www.hostynplumcatholic.org Rev. Felix Twumasi, Admin.; Dcn. John McCourt; CRP Stds.: 67

MEYERSVILLE

SS. Peter & Paul - 11220 FM 237, Meyersville, TX 77974 t) 361-275-3868 stspp@gvec.net www.catholiccommunityofcuero.org Rev. Jacob Mendoza, Pst.; Rev. Richard Bediako (Ghana), Par. Vicar; CRP Stds.: 9

St. Aloysius - 19 Catholic Church Ln., Westhoff, TX 77994; Mailing: 11220 FM 237, Meyersville, TX 77974 t) (361) 275-3868 www.catholiccommunityofcuero.org/

MOULTON

St. Joseph's - 601 N. Pecan St., Moulton, TX 77975; Mailing: P.O. Box 399, Moulton, TX 77975 t) 361-596-4674; 361-596-7559 (CRP) st_joe@sbcglobal.net www.stjosephsmoulton.org Rev. Gabriel Maison, Pst.; Dcn. Kenneth Fishbeck; CRP Stds.: 77

NADA

Nativity of the Blessed Virgin Mary - 1261 Old Nada Rd., Nada, TX 77460; Mailing: PO Box 97, Nada, TX 77460 t) 979-758-3218 stmarynadaparish@gmail.com nbvmnada.org Rev. Peter Yeboah-Amanfo, Pst.; Dcn. Dustin Lee Leopold; CRP Stds.: 90

NEW ULM

SS. Peter and Paul - 1031 Church Ln., New Ulm, TX 78950 t) 979-732-3430 www.peterandpaulparish.com Very Rev. Robert E. Knippenberg, Pst.; Dcn. Charles J. Glynn; Dcn. Andrew Joseph Nunmaker III; Dcn. Douglas B. Tromblee; CRP Stds.: 28

PALACIOS

St. Anthony's - 1004 Magnusson, Palacios, TX 77465; Mailing: Box 900, Palacios, TX 77465 t) 361-972-2446 pasaop@yahoo.com; brandigwest@gmail.com Dcn. Michael Vieira; Rev. Eliecer Patino, Admin.; Brandi West, DRE; CRP Stds.: 305

PORT LAVACA

Our Lady of the Gulf - 415 W. Austin St., Port Lavaca, TX 77979 t) 361-552-6140; 361-552-6140 x100 (CRP) olg@olgulf.org; olglindab@hotmail.com www.olgulf.org Rev. Tommy Chen, Pst.; Rev. Richard G. Barfield, Par. Vicar; Dcn. Nazario Hernandez Diaz; Linda Beard, DRE; Tim Dent, Bus. Mgr.; CRP Stds.: 317

Our Lady of the Gulf School - (Grades PreK-8) 301 S. San Antonio St., Port Lavaca, TX 77979; Mailing: 415 W. Austin St., Port Lavaca, TX 77979 t) (361) 552-6140 x6 olgmariners@olgulf.org www.olgmariners.org Theresa Dent, Prin.; Stds.: 104; Sr. Tchrs.: 3; Lay Tchrs.: 7

St. Ann - 709 Lamar, Point Comfort, TX 77978; Mailing: 415 W. Austin St., Port Lavaca, TX 77979 t) (361) 552-6140

St. Joseph - 101 Washington St., Port O'Connor, TX 77982; Mailing: 415 W. Austin St., Port Lavaca, TX 77979 t) (361) 552-6140

St. Patrick - 306 W. Cleveland, Seadrift, TX 77983; Mailing: 415 W. Austin St., Port Lavaca, TX 77979 t) (361) 552-6140

SCHULENBURG

St. John the Baptist - 7745 Mensik Rd., Schulenburg, TX 78956 t) 979-743-3117 office@strosecatholic.org Rev. Jasper Liggio, Pst.; Rev. Chase Goodman, Par. Vicar;

St. Wenceslaus - 9937 FM Rd. 155, La Grange, TX 78945 t) (979) 743-3117 Program is combined with St. Rose - Schulenburg.

St. John the Baptist - 7026 FM 957, Schulenburg, TX 78956; Mailing: P.O. Box H, Hallettsville, TX 77964 t) 361-798-5888; 713-822-3019 (CRP) rectory@shcatholicchurch.org; danadau@cvctx.com www.shcatholicchurch.org Rev. Msgr. John C. Peters, Pst.; Rev. John Affum, Assoc. Pst.; Rev. James M. Dvorak, Assoc. Pst.; Dana Daughtry, DRE; CRP Stds.: 8

Ascension of Our Lord - 11134 FM 957 (Moravia), Hallettsville, TX 77964 t) (361) 798-5888

Nativity of the Blessed Virgin Mary - 2833 FM 2672, Schulenburg, TX 78956-5603 t) 979-743-3117 office@strosecatholic.org Rev. Jasper Liggio, Pst.; Rev. Chase Goodman, Par. Vicar;

St. Rose of Lima - 1010 Lyons Ave., Schulenburg, TX 78956; Mailing: PO Box 310, Schulenburg, TX 78956 t) 979-743-3117 office@strosecatholic.org strosecatholic.org Rev. Jasper Liggio, Pst.; Rev. Chase Goodman, Par. Vicar; CRP Stds.: 137

St. Rose of Lima School - (Grades PreK-8) 405 Black St., Schulenburg, TX 78956 t) 979-743-3080 r.gallia@strosecardinals.org www.strosecardinals.org Rosanne Gallia, Prin.; Stds.: 153; Lay Tchrs.: 12

SHINER

SS. Cyril and Methodius - 306 S. Ave. F, Shiner, TX 77984 t) 361-594-3836 rectory@sscmshiner.org; frbryan@sscmshiner.org www.sscmshiner.org Rev. Michael Odartey-Lamptey (Ghana), Par. Vicar; Very Rev. Bryan Heyer, Pst.; Dcn. Joseph Machacek; Dcn. Michael Henry Morkovsky; Kim Ulcak, Youth Min.; CRP Stds.: 192

St. Ludmila Elementary School - (Grades PreK-8) 424 S. St. Ludmila St., Shiner, TX 77984; Mailing: P.O. Box 725, Shiner, TX 77984 t) 361-594-3843 nyackel@shinercatholicschool.org www.shinercatholicschool.org Neely Yackel, Prin.; Stds.: 187; Sr. Tchrs.: 1; Lay Tchrs.: 13

St. Paul High School - (Grades 9-12) 424 S. St. Ludmila St., Shiner, TX 77984; Mailing: P. O. Box 725, Shiner, TX 77984 t) 361-594-2313 ssiegel@shinercatholicschool.org shinercatholicschool.org Neely Yackel, Pres.; Stds.: 83; Lay Tchrs.: 8; Sr. Tchrs.: 1

SWEET HOME

St. John the Baptist - 13202 FM 531, Sweet Home, TX 77987; Mailing: P.O. Box 201, Sweet Home, TX 77987 t) 361-741-3206 pastor@qpcatholicchurch.com qpcatholicchurch.com Rev. Dominic Antwi-Boasiako, Pst.; CRP Stds.: 15

Queen of Peace - 7273 FM 531, Sweet Home, TX 77987; Mailing: PO Box 201, Sweet Home, TX 77987 t) 361-741-3206 secretary@qpcatholicchurch.com qpcatholicchurch.com Rev. Dominic Antwi-Boasiako, Pst.; Skye Anderle, DRE; CRP Stds.: 85

VANDERBILT

St. John Bosco - 232 Main St., Vanderbilt, TX 77991-0337; Mailing: P. O. Box 337, Vanderbilt, TX 77991 t) 361-284-3361 stjbsttccd@gmail.com Rev. Johnson Owusu-Boateng, Pst.; Emilia Benavides, DRE;

CRP Stds.: 54

St. Theresa - 4612 CR 325, La Salle, TX 77969; Mailing: P.O. Box 337, Vanderbilt, TX 77991 t) (361) 284-3361 (Church Office)

VICTORIA

The Cathedral of Our Lady of Victory - 1309 E. Mesquite Ln., Victoria, TX 77901 t) 361-575-4741; 361-575-8132 (CRP) pbena@olvcathedral.org; ccd@olvcathedral.org www.olvcathedral.org Very Rev. Kirby Hlavaty, Pst.; Rev. Dalton Ervin, Par. Vicar; Dcn. Matthew Wayne Schaefer; Dr. Glenn Hunter, Music Min.; Jennifer Vincent, Pst. Assoc.; Monica Flores, DRE; CRP Stds.: 373

Our Lady of Victory Cathedral School - (Grades PreK-8) 1311 E. Mesquite Ln., Victoria, TX 77901 t) 361-575-5391 jmatias@ourladyvictory.org www.ourladyvictory.org Justin Matias, Prin.; Stds.: 489; Sr. Tchrs.: 1; Lay Tchrs.: 35

Holy Family of Joseph, Mary & Jesus - 704 Mallette Dr., Victoria, TX 77904 t) 361-573-5304; 361-573-5445 (CRP) parish@hfccvic.org www.hfccvic.org Very Rev. Gabriel Bentil, Pst.; Rev. Jonas Kuubeta, Par. Vicar; Dcn. Edward Huse; Debbie Vanelli, Pst. Assoc.; Judy Seiler, Youth Min.; Heather Kallus, DRE; Jeff Williams, Bus. Mgr.; CRP Stds.: 323

St. Mary's - 402 S. Main, Victoria, TX 77902; Mailing: PO Box 2448, Victoria, TX 77902 t) 361-573-4328; 361-578-7724 (CRP) sec@stmvictoria.org; ccd@stmvictoria.org stmvictoria.org Rev. Kristopher L. Fuchs, Pst.; Rev. Tran Dinh, Par. Vicar; Dcn. Jim Koenig; Dcn. Richard Allen Evans; Diana Starnes, DRE; CRP Stds.: 80

Our Lady of Lourdes - 105 N. William St., Victoria, TX 77901 t) 361-575-3813 (Office); 361-485-0501 (Office) marthanlourdes@gmail.com; ollvic@lourdesvictoria.org www.lourdesvictoria.org Rev. Patrick S. Knippenberg, Pst.; Tammy Fikac, DRE; Martha Nichols, DRE; CRP Stds.: 45

Our Lady of Sorrows - 208 W. River St., Victoria, TX 77901 t) 361-575-2293; 361-570-7854 (CRP) abeltran@ourladysorrows.org olsvictoria.org Very Rev. Jacob A. Koether, Pst.; Rev. Parmenio Florez, Par. Vicar; Rev. Peter Nimo, Chap.; Dcn. Larry Koether; Dcn. Edward Molina; Dcn. Frank Steve Tilley; CRP Stds.: 268

Holy Trinity - 2901 Pleasant Green Dr., Victoria, TX 77901 t) (361) 575-2293 Spanish Mission

WEIMAR

St. Michael - 410 N. Center, Weimar, TX 78962; Mailing: P.O. Box 36, Weimar, TX 78962 t) 979-725-6714 irmarerich@gmail.com; stmichaelwei@yahoo.com www.stmichaelweimar.org Rev. Wayne N. Flagg, Pst.; Irma Reich, DRE; CRP Stds.: 110

St. Michael School - (Grades PreK-8) 103 E. N. St., Weimar, TX 78962 t) 979-725-8461 jroeder@stmichaelswords.org Judy Roeder, Prin.; Stds.: 105; Lay Tchrs.: 11

SS. Cyril and Methodius - FM Rd. 1383, Dubina, TX 78962 t) (979) 725-6714

WHARTON

Holy Family - 2011 Briar Ln., Wharton, TX 77488-4470 t) 979-532-3593; 979-532-3747 office@hfwharton.org www.hfwharton.org Very Rev. Samuel Appiasi, Pst.; Dcn. Alvin Matthys; Dcn. Bruce Franklin Turner; Dcn. David Valdez; Vicki Elaine Simper, DRE; CRP Stds.: 120

St. Joseph - 106 Lalla Rookh, Boling, TX 77420; Mailing: 2011 Briar Ln., Wharton, TX 77488 t) (979) 532-3593 Very Rev. Samuel K Appiasi, Pst.;

Our Lady of Mt. Carmel - 506 S. East Ave., Wharton, TX 77488 t) 979-532-3492; 979-532-3215 (CRP) office@olmcwharton.org; religiouseducation@olmcwharton.org olmcwharton.org Rev. Antonio Perez, Admin.; Consuelo Martinez, DRE; CRP Stds.: 60

YOAKUM

St. Joseph - 401 Orth St., Yoakum, TX 77995; Mailing: P.O. Box 734, Yoakum, TX 77995 t) 361-293-3518; 361-293-7572 secretary@stjcatholicchurch.com; faithformation@stjcatholicchurch.com www.stjcatholicchurch.com Very Rev. Matthew H. Huehlefeld, Pst.; Dcn. Dennis Kutach; Jana Guajardo, DRE; CRP Stds.: 227

St. Joseph School - (Grades PreK-8) c/o St. Joseph Parish, 210 Schrimscher St., Yoakum, TX 77995; Mailing: 310 Orth St., Yoakum, TX 77995 t) 361-293-9000 smooney@stjcatholicschool.com www.stjcatholicschool.com Sean Mooney, Prin.; Stds.: 89; Lay Tchrs.: 15

St. Ann - 4162 State Hwy. 111 W., Hochheim, TX 77967 t) (361) 293-3518

YORKTOWN

Holy Cross - 1214 Zorn Rd., Yorktown, TX 78164-1907 t) 361-564-2893 holycross1214@sbcglobal.net; frroger@sbcglobal.net holycrossyorktown.net Very Rev. Roger Hawes, Pst.; Rev. Francis Tam Nguyen III, Par. Vicar; CRP Stds.: 89

San Luis - t) (361) 564-2893

St. Ann's - Hwy. 72 W., Nordheim, TX 78141 t) (361) 564-2893

SCHOOLS: PRESCHOOL THRU HIGH SCHOOL

SCHOOLS

STATE OF TEXAS

VICTORIA

Nazareth Academy Catholic School - (PRV) (Grades PreK-8) 206 W. Convent, Victoria, TX 77901 t) 361-573-6651 lnew@nazarethacademy.org www.nazarethacademy.org Attended from St. Mary's, Our Lady of Lourdes, Our Lady of Victory, Holy Family and Our Lady of Sorrows Churches. Leslie L. New, Prin.; Debbie Michalski, Admin.; Sr. Ann Meletio, I.W.B.S., Bus. Mgr.; Stds.: 346; Sr. Tchrs.: 2; Lay Tchrs.: 25

HIGH SCHOOLS

STATE OF TEXAS

VICTORIA

St. Joseph High School - (PRV) (Grades 9-12) 110 E. Red River St., Victoria, TX 77901 t) 361-573-2446 jgilley@stjflyers.com www.stjflyers.com John Gilley IV, Pres.; Megan Schott, Prin.; John Brouillette, Dean; Stds.: 313; Sr. Tchrs.: 1; Lay Tchrs.: 25

INSTITUTIONS LOCATED IN DIOCESE

CONVENTS, MONASTERIES, AND RESIDENCES FOR WOMEN [CON]

PORT LAVACA

Vietnamese Community - 319 S. Nueces St., Port Lavaca, TX 77979; Mailing: 415 W. Austin St., Port Lavaca, TX 77979 t) 361-552-6140 olg@olgulf.org Sr. Maria Garetti, Supr.; Srs.: 3

VICTORIA

Incarnate Word Convent - 1101 N.E. Water St., Victoria, TX 77901-9233 t) 361-575-2266 skgoike@gmail.com www.iwbsvictoria.org Sr. Geraldine Pavlik, Supr.; Sr. Kathleen M. Goike, Supr.; Srs.: 33

Missionary Catechists of the Sacred Hearts of Jesus and Mary - 203 E. Sabine St., Victoria, TX 77901 t) 361-570-3332 mcbolivia@hotmail.com Immaculate Heart of Mary Province Sr. Rosa Maria Rodriguez Trevino, M.C.S.H, Prov.; Srs.: 8

Sisters of the Incarnate Word and Blessed Sacrament, Victoria, Texas, Inc. - 1101 N.E. Water St., Victoria, TX 77901-9233 t) 361-575-2266 skgoike@gmail.com www.iwbsvictoria.org Sr. Kathleen M. Goike, Supr.; Srs.: 48

ENDOWMENTS / FOUNDATIONS / TRUSTS [EFT]

VICTORIA

Endowment Fund for the Catholic Diocese of Victoria in Texas - 1505 E. Mesquite Ln., Victoria, TX 77901; Mailing: P.O. Box 4070, Victoria, TX 77903 t) 361-573-0828 tmartinez@victoriadiocese.org www.victoriadiocese.org Anthony Martinez, CFO;

Jeanne Chezard De Matel Fund - 1101 N.E. Water St., Victoria, TX 77901-9233 t) 361-575-2266 skgoike@gmail.com www.iwbsvictoria.org Sr. Kathleen M. Goike, Supr.;

Sisters of the Incarnate Word and Blessed Sacrament of Victoria, Texas, Medical and Retirement Trust - 1101 N.E. Water St., Victoria, TX 77901-9233 t) 361-572-9321 iwbsbusofc@yahoo.com Sr. Kathleen M. Goike, Supr.;

MISCELLANEOUS [MIS]

SCHULENBURG

Opus Dei - 934 Holub Rd., Schulenburg, TX 78956-5324 t) 979-743-4642 Rev. Paul D. Kais, Dir.;

VICTORIA

Amor Meus Spirituality Center - 1101 N.E. Water St., Victoria, TX 77901 t) 361-575-7111 amormeuscenter@gmail.com www.amormeusspiritualitycenter.org Sr. Digna M. Vela, Dir.;

Nazareth Academy, Inc. - 206 W. Convent, Victoria, TX 77901 t) 361-573-6651; 361-485-2044 skgoike@gmail.com www.nazarethacademy.org Sr. Kathleen M. Goike, Supr.;

An asterisk (*) denotes an organization that has established tax-exempt status directly with the IRS and is not covered by the USCCB Group Ruling.

Archdiocese of Washington

(Archidioecesis Washingtonensis)

HIS EMINENCE WILTON CARDINAL GREGORY

Archbishop of Washington; ordained May 9, 1973; appointed Auxiliary Bishop of Chicago and Titular Bishop of Oliva October 31, 1983; consecrated December 13, 1983; appointed Bishop of Belleville December 29, 1993; installed February 10, 1994; appointed Archbishop of Atlanta December 9, 2004; installed January 17, 2005; appointed Archbishop of Washington April 4, 2019; installed May 21, 2019; created Cardinal November 28, 2020. Archdiocesan Pastoral Center, 5001 Eastern Ave., Hyattsville, MD 20782-3447. T: 301-853-4500; F: 301-853-5346. Mailing Address: P.O. Box 29260, Washington, DC 20017-0260.

Archdiocesan Pastoral Center: 5001 Eastern Ave., Hyattsville, MD 20782.
Mailing Address: P.O. Box 29260, Washington, DC 20017. T: 301-853-4500; F: 301-853-5346.
chancery@adw.org

Square Miles 2,104.

Established Archdiocese July 22, 1939; Separated from Baltimore November 15, 1947; Became a Metropolitan See October 12, 1965.

Comprises the District of Columbia and Montgomery, Prince George's, St. Mary's, Calvert and Charles Counties in Maryland.

The Province of Washington has as a Suffragan, the Diocese of St. Thomas in the Virgin Islands.

For legal titles of parishes and archdiocesan institutions, consult the Chancery Office.

MOST REVEREND MARIO E. DORSONVILLE, D.D., V.G.
Auxiliary Bishop of Washington; ordained November 23, 1985; appointed Auxiliary Bishop of Washington and Titular Bishop of Kearney March 20, 2015; Episcopal Ordination April 20, 2015. Office: Archdiocesan Pastoral Center, 5001 Eastern Ave., Hyattsville, MD 20782. T: 301-853-4566. Mailing Address: P.O. Box 29260, Washington, DC 20017-0260.

MOST REVEREND ROY E. CAMPBELL, JR., D.D., V.G.
Auxiliary Bishop of Washington; ordained May 26, 2007; appointed Titular Bishop of Ucres and Auxiliary Bishop of Washington March 8, 2017; Episcopal Ordination April 21, 2017. Office: Archdiocesan, Pastoral Center, 5001 Eastern Ave., Hyattsville, MD 20782. T: 301-853-4537; F: 301-853-7698. Mailing Address: P.O. Box 29260, Washington, DC 20017-0260.

MOST REVEREND JUAN ESPOSITO-GARCIA
Auxiliary Bishop of Washington; ordained June 14, 2008; appointed Titular Bishop of Tabla and Auxiliary Bishop of Washington on December 19, 2023; Episcopal Ordination February 21, 2023. Office: Archdiocesan, Pastoral Center, 5001 Eastern Ave., Hyattsville, MD 20782. T: 301-853-4500. Mailing Address: P.O. Box 29260, Washington, DC 20017-0260.

MOST REVEREND EVELIO MENJIVAR-AYALA
Auxiliary Bishop of Washington; ordained May 29, 2004; appointed Titular Bishop of Aëto and Auxiliary Bishop of Washington on December 19, 2023; Episcopal Ordination February 21, 2023. Office: Archdiocesan, Pastoral Center, 5001 Eastern Ave., Hyattsville, MD 20782. T: 301-853-4500. Mailing Address: P.O. Box 29260, Washington, DC 20017-0260.

STATISTICAL OVERVIEW

Personnel
Cardinals....1
Retired Cardinals....1
Auxiliary Bishops....4
Retired Bishops....1
Abbots....1
Priests: Diocesan Active in Diocese....185
Priests: Diocesan Active Outside Diocese....21
Priests: Diocesan in Foreign Missions....3
Priests: Retired, Sick or Absent....68
Number of Diocesan Priests....277
Religious Priests in Diocese....410
Total Priests in your Diocese....687
Extern Priests in Diocese....202
Ordinations:
Diocesan Priests....10
Religious Priests....13
Transitional Deacons....6
Permanent Deacons in Diocese....223
Total Brothers....221
Total Sisters....398

Parishes
Parishes....139
With Resident Pastor:
Resident Diocesan Priests....110
Resident Religious Priests....15
Without Resident Pastor:
Administered by Priests....14
Missions....9
Pastoral Centers....1
Professional Ministry Personnel:
Brothers....3
Sisters....29

Welfare
Catholic Hospitals....3
Total Assisted....423,089
Health Care Centers....71
Total Assisted....1,353,515
Homes for the Aged....30
Total Assisted....2,689
Day Care Centers....13
Total Assisted....729
Specialized Homes....20
Total Assisted....14,529
Special Centers for Social Services....57
Total Assisted....225,780
Residential Care of Disabled....6
Total Assisted....103
Other Institutions....5
Total Assisted....103

Educational
Seminaries, Diocesan....2
Students from This Diocese....37
Students from Other Dioceses....78
Diocesan Students in Other Seminaries....35
Seminaries, Religious....12
Students, Religious....141
Total Seminarians....213
Colleges and Universities....3
Total Students....27,841
High Schools, Diocesan and Parish....2
Total Students....756
High Schools, Private....16
Total Students....9,123
Elementary Schools, Diocesan and Parish....52
Total Students....14,012
Elementary Schools, Private....7
Total Students....2,132
Non-residential Schools for the Disabled....1
Total Students....44
Catechesis/Religious Education:
High School Students....1,235
Elementary Students....13,774
Total Students under Catholic Instruction....69,130
Teachers in Diocese:
Priests....31
Brothers....16
Sisters....28
Lay Teachers....2,131

Vital Statistics
Receptions into the Church:
Infant Baptism Totals....2,796
Minor Baptism Totals....2,225
Adult Baptism Totals....694
Received into Full Communion....474
First Communions....3,906
Confirmations....4,292
Marriages:
Catholic....880
Interfaith....306
Total Marriages....1,186
Deaths....2,700
Total Catholic Population....647,417
Total Population....2,942,809

LEADERSHIP

Archbishop's Office - t) 301-853-5350 His Eminence Wilton Gregory, Archbishop of Washington; Deirdre Schmutz, Exec. Asst. (archbishop@adw.org);

Secretary to the Archbishop - t) 301-853-5350 Rev. Charles A. Cortinovis;

Auxillary Bishops - Most Rev. Roy Edward Campbell Jr.; Most Rev. Mario E. Dorsonville;

Moderator of the Curia - VACANT - t) 301-853-4523

Chief Operating Officer - David Spotanski, COO (spotanskid@adw.org);

Director of Events - t) (301) 853-4561 trillingm@adw.org Michelle Trilling;

Chancellor/Executive Secretary of the Curia - t) 301-853-4523 Terence J. Farrell (chancery@adw.org);

Archives - t) 301-853-5316 archives@adw.org Dr. Stephanie Jacobe, Dir.;

Director for Catechesis - t) 301-853-5368 Sara Blauvelt;

Coordinator of Adult Formation and Hispanic Catechesis - t) 301-853-5384 Kately Javier;

Office of Cultural Diversity and Outreach - t) 301-853-4468 Wendi M. Williams, Exec. Dir.;

Vicars General - Most Rev. Mario E. Dorsonville; Most Rev. Roy Edward Campbell Jr.;

Vice Chancellor - Very Rev. George E. Stuart;

Office of Child Protection and Safe Environment - t) 301-853-5302 Courtney Chase, Exec. Dir. (chasec@adw.org);

Secretariats -

Secretary for Catholic Schools - Kelly A. Branaman;

Secretary for Communications - Paula Gwynn Grant;

Secretary for Ministerial Leadership - Very Rev. Anthony E. Lickteig;

Secretary for Pastoral Ministry and Social Concerns - Dr. Jeannine Marino;

Secretary for Finance and Administration - Liam O'Connor;

General Counsel - t) 301-853-4995 Christopher Anzidei;

CANONICAL SERVICES

Office of Canonical Affairs - t) 301-853-4543 canonical@adw.org

Canonical Services - Very Rev. George E. Stuart, Episcopal Vicar; Melissa Hunsiker, Admin. Asst. (hunsikerm@adw.org);

CLERGY AND RELIGIOUS SERVICES

Secretariat for Ministerial Leadership - t) 301-853-4550 Very Rev. Anthony E. Lickteig (lickteigA@adw.org);

Episcopal Vicar for Clergy - t) 301-853-4550 Very Rev. Anthony E. Lickteig (lickteigA@adw.org);

Continuing Education for Clergy - t) 202-636-9020 Rev. Kevin J. Regan;

Director, Permanent Diaconate - t) 301-853-4583 Dcn. Donald R. Longano;

Assistant Director of Permanent Diaconate Formation - t) 301-853-4582 Dcn. Charles P. Huber;

Office of Consecrated Life - t) 301-853-4576 Sr. Gilmary Kay, R.S.M., Delegate;

Office of Worship - t) 301-853-4549 Rev. T. Joseph Murphy, Dir. (murphyt@adw.org);

Pastoral Care of Priests - t) 301-853-5361 Rev. Msgr. Joseph A. Ranieri, Coord.;

Pope Saint John XXIII Residence for Priests - t) 202-269-7818 Rev. C. Gregory Butta;

Saint John Paul II Seminary - t) 202-636-9020 Rev. Carter H. Griffin, Rector; Rev. Kevin J. Regan, Vice Rector, Dean of Students; Rev. Christopher J. Seith, Dir.;

Saint John Vianney House - t) 301-942-1191

Vocations for Men - Rev. Mark R. Ivany, Dir.; Rev. Robert P. Boxie III, Asst. Dir.; Rev. Mario A. Majano, Asst. Dir.;

COMMUNICATIONS

Carroll Media Company - His Eminence Wilton Gregory, Publisher;

Secretary for Communications - t) 301-853-4516 Paula Gwynn Grant (grantp@adw.org);

Newspaper "The Catholic Standard" - t) 202-281-2412 Mark Zimmermann, Editor (mark@cathstan.org);

Newspaper "El Pregonero" - t) 202-281-2442 Rafael Roncal, Editor (rafael@elpreg.org);

Office of Digital Media - t) 301-853-4484 Jaclyn Lippelmann (lippellmannj@adw.org);

Office of Media and Public Relations - t) 301-853-4516 Patricia Zapor;

Office of Multimedia Production - t) 301-853-4519 Geoffrey Ros;

TV Mass Producer - t) 301-853-4516 John Capobianco;

CONSULTATIVE BODIES

Administrative Board - David Spotanski, COO (spotanskid@adw.org); Liam O'Connor, CFO (oconnorlj@adw.org); Terence J. Farrell (chancery@adw.org);

Archdiocesan College of Consultors - Very Rev. Anthony E. Lickteig (lickteigA@adw.org); Rev. Msgr. Charles V. Antonicelli; Rev. Msgr. William J. English (englishw@aw.org);

Archdiocesan Finance Council - Liam O'Connor (oconnorlj@adw.org); J. Michael Kelly; J. Paul McNamara;

Pastoral Council - Dr. Jeannine Marino (marinoj@adw.org); Yajaira Ortiz-Wilson; Cheryl McLaughlin;

Priest Council - Very Rev. Anthony E. Lickteig (lickteigA@adw.org); Rev. Msgr. Charles V. Antonicelli; Rev. Oscar Astigarraga (fatheroscar@strose.com);

Priest Personnel Board - Very Rev. Anthony E. Lickteig (lickteigA@adw.org); Rev. Thomas M. Kalita (tkalita@adwparish.org); Rev. Msgr. Peter J. Vaghi;

Priest Retirement Board - Rev. Frederick J. Close (closef@adw.org); Rev. Mark F. Hughes (hughesm@adw.org); Rev. Msgr. Salvatore A. Criscuolo (criscuolos@adw.org);

DEANERIES

Deans -

Calvert County - Rev. Michael J. King;

Charles County - Rev. Keith Woods;

District of Columbia -

Northeast, D.C. - Rev. Msgr. Charles E. Pope;

Northwest East, D.C. - Rev. Pawel Sass;

Northwest West, D.C. - Rev. Msgr. James D. Watkins;

Southeast, D.C. - Rev. Raymond H. Moore;

Montgomery County -

Lower Montgomery County - Rev. Joseph A. Calis;

Middle Montgomery County - Rev. Msgr. Charles V. Antonicelli;

Upper-East Montgomery County - Rev. John J. Dillon;

Upper-West Montgomery County - Rev. LeRoy J. Fangmeyer;

Prince George's County -

Lower Prince George's County - Rev. Thomas G. LaHood;

Middle Prince George's County - Rev. Evelio Menjivar-Ayala;

Upper Prince George's County - Rev. Walter J. Tappe;

St. Mary's County - Rev. David W. Beaubien;

DEVELOPMENT

Development - t) (301) 853-5375 Joseph Gillmer, Exec. Dir. (gillmerj@adw.org);

Annual Appeal - t) 301-853-4574 David Cook, Dir. (cookd@adw.org);

Donor Relations and Gift Planning - t) 301-853-4486 Joanne Pipkin, Dir. (pipkinj@adw.org);

Foundation Relations - t) (301) 853-4487 Antonette Bruno, Mgr. (brunoa@adw.org);

Stewardship and Development Services - t) 301-853-5374 Elizabeth Shaughney, Dir. (shaughneye@adw.org);

EDUCATION

Secretary for Catholic Schools and Superintendent of Catholic Schools - t) 301-853-4508 schools@adw.org Kelly A. Branaman;

Associate Superintendent - t) 301-853-5353 schools@adw.org Christian Buchleitner (buchleitnerc@adw.org);

Assistant Superintendent for School Operations and Student Services - t) (301) 853-4569 Anne Dillon (dillona@adw.org);

Assistant Superintendent for Advancement and Marketing - t) (301) 853-4548 Vicky McCann (mccannv@adw.org);

Assistant Superintendent for Catholic Identity and Accreditation - t) (301) 853-4590 Dr. Christina Mendez-Hall (mendezc@adw.org);

Assistant Superintendent for Teaching and Learning - t) (301) 853-4588 Denise Ball (balld@adw.org);

Assistant Superintendent for Research, Planning, and Administrative Technologies - t) (301) 853-4598 Dr. Jeremy McDonald (mcdonaldj@adw.org);

Director for Early Childhood Programs - t) (301) 853-4587 Roshon Casey-Lee (caseyr@adw.org);

Director for Government and Grant Programs - t) (301) 853-5357 Brian Radziwill (radziwillb@adw.org);

Manager for Special Education - t) (301) 853-4458 Margaret Kenney White (kenneym@adw.org);

Director of Counseling Services - t) (301) 853-5354 Ahsley Mickey (mickeya@adw.org);

Director of Curriculum and Instruction - t) (301) 853-4531 Jennifer Monger (mongerj@adw.org);

Funding and Enrollment Coordinator - t) (301) 853-5356 Madelin Fox (foxm@adw.org);

Consortium of Catholic Academies of the Archdiocese of Washington, Inc. - t) 301-853-5340 Dr. Camille Brown Privette (camille.privette@catholicacademies.org);

Board of Education - schools@adw.org Michael Cronin, Pres.;

FACILITIES

General Inquiries - facilitiescontracts@adw.org

Facilities Management & Real Estate - t) (301) 853-4474 Michelle Shelton, Exec. Dir.;

FINANCE

Finance and Management - t) (301) 853-5365 Liam O'Connor, CFO (oconnorlj@adw.org);

Office of Finance - t) (301) 853-5313 Caroline Brillantes-dela Paz, Exec. Dir. of Finance (brillantes-delapazc@adw.org);

Information Technology - t) 301-853-4494 Michael I Wilson, Exec. Dir.;

Parish and School Financial Operations - t) 301-853-5373 Adrienne Willich, Exec. Dir. (willicha@adw.org);

HUMAN RESOURCES

General Questions - archdiocesehr@adw.org

Human Resources - t) (301) 853-4513 Nanette Lowe, Exec. Dir. (lowen@adw.org);

PASTORAL SERVICES

Secretary for Pastoral Ministry and Social Concerns - t) 301-853-4596 Dr. Jeannine Marino (marinoj@adw.org);

Archdiocesan Campus Ministry - t) (301) 853-5308 Amanda Schleimer (schleimera@adw.org);

Assistant Secretary for Pastoral Ministry and Social Concerns/Pastoral Planning - t) 301-853-4466 Deborah McDonald (mcdonald@adw.org);

Boy Scout Chair, Catholic Committee for Boy Scouts - t) 301-251-0359 Chris Murray, Chair (chris.murray3@yahoo.com);

Boy Scouts/Girl Scouts/Camp Fire Boys & Girls - Archdiocesan Chaplain - Catholic Committee on Boy Scouts - t) 301-862-4600 Rev. Charles E. Luckett;

Assistant Secretary for Pastoral Ministry and Social Concerns - Pamela Harris (harrisp@adw.org);

Catholic Charismatic Renewal - t) 202-526-8822 Rev. Frederick J. Close (closef@adw.org);

Catholic Spanish Charismatic Renewal - t) 301-422-8300

Rev. Roberto J. Cortes;
Catholic Youth Organization of Washington DC and the Greater Metropolitan Area - t) (301) 853-4465 Joaquin Trejo, Dir. (trejoj@adw.org); Kevin Donoghue, Pres.; Mary Fava, OYM/CYO Prog. Coord. (favam@adw.org);
Archdiocesan Chaplain - Catholic Committee on Girl Scouts - t) 301-262-0704 Rev. Ronald A. Potts;
Department of Life Issues - t) 301-853-5318 Kathryn Yanik, Dir. (yanikk@adw.org);
Project Rachel Ministry - Maria Tirado, Participant & Outreach Coord.;
Department of Special Needs Ministries - Mary O'Meara, Exec. Dir. (omearam@adw.org); Rachel Chung, Coord. Office for Persons with Disabilities (chungr@adw.org); Laureen Lynch-Ryan, Coord. Office of Deaf Ministry (lynch-ryanl@adw.org);
Office for Ecumenical and Interreligious Affairs - t) 301-853-4421 Rev. Charles A. Cortinovis, Dir. (cortinoviscr@adw.org);
Office for Family Life - t) 301-853-4499 Sally Daniels, Dir. (daniels@adw.org);
Office of Missions - t) 301-853-5388 Maeve Gilheney-Gallagher (gallagherm@adw.org);
Office of Social Concerns/CCHD Diocesan Director/ Catholic Relief Services Liaison - t) 301-853-4567 Ian Mitchell (mitchelli@adw.org);

TRIBUNAL

Tribunal - t) 301-853-4543 tribunal@adw.org
Judicial Vicar - Rev. Msgr. Kevin T. Hart (hartK@adw.org);
Adjutant Judicial Vicars - Rev. Msgr. Charles V. Antonicelli; Rev. Mark E. Tucker;
Metropolitan Judge and Moderator of the Tribunal Chancery - Dr. Sofia Markovich;
Advocates - Dcn. Gary L. Bockweg; Dr. Linda Budney; Dr. Cristina Hip-Flores;
Defenders of the Bond - Very Rev. George E. Stuart; Dr. Jaclyn McEachern;
Judges - Rev. Msgr. Joseph F. Sadusky; Dr. Sofia Markovich;
Promoter of Justice - Very Rev. George E. Stuart;

PARISHES, MISSIONS, AND CLERGY

COMMONWEALTH OF VIRGINIA

MCLEAN

Nativity of the Blessed Virgin (German Mission) - 6330 Linway Ter., McLean, VA 22101-4150 t) 703-356-4473 pfarrer@kathde.org www.kathde.org Rev. Karl Josef Rieger, Pst.;

DISTRICT OF COLUMBIA

WASHINGTON

St. Matthew Cathedral - 1725 Rhode Island Ave., N.W., Washington, DC 20036 t) 202-347-3215 cathstmatt@stmatthewscathedral.org Rev. Msgr. W. Ronald Jameson, Pst.; Rev. Agustin Lopez, Assoc. Pst.; Dcn. Juan Cayrampoma; Dcn. Bartholomew J. Merella; Rev. John Hurley, In Res.; Rev. Conrad Murphy, In Res.; Pamela Erwin, Bus. Mgr.;
St. Ann - 4001 Yuma St., Washington, DC 20016 t) 202-966-6288; 202-363-9524 (CRP) dre@stanndc.org Rev. Msgr. Godfrey T. Mosley, Pst.;
Mission - 4133 Yuma St., N.W., Washington, DC 20016 t) 202-244-2617
Annunciation - 3810 Massachusetts Ave., N.W., Washington, DC 20016-5409; Mailing: 3125 39th St., N.W., Washington, DC 20016 t) 202-362-3323 parish@annunciationdc.org annunciationdc.org Rev. Msgr. Michael J. Mellone, Pst.; Dcn. William T. Maksymiec; Andreja Mezek, DRE;
Annunciation School - 3825 Klingle Pl., N.W., Washington, DC 20016-5434 t) 202-362-1408 info@annunciationschool.net www.annunciationschool.net Nichole Peltier-Lewis, Prin.;
St. Anthony of Padua - 1029 Monroe St., N.E., Washington, DC 20017 t) 202-250-8208 alinder@verizon.net; stanthony.dc@adwparish.org Rev. Frederick J. Close, Pst.; Rev. Joseph D. Kirkconnell; Rev. Sean Paul Fleming; Rev. Bruno Maurel (France); Arthur Linder, DRE;
St. Anthony School - 3400 Lawrence St., N.E., Washington, DC 20017 t) 202-526-4657 www.stanthonyschooldc.org Michael R. Thomasian, Prin.;
St. Augustine - 1419 V St., N.W., Washington, DC 20009 t) 202-265-1470 Rev. Patrick A. Smith, Pst.; Rev. Paul John T. Camiring, Assoc. Pst.;
St. Augustine School - 1421 V St., N.W., Washington, DC 20009 t) 202-667-2608 Donna Edwards, Prin.;
St. Benedict the Moor - 320 21st St., N.E., Washington, DC 20002 t) 202-397-3895 Rev. Andrew B. Gonzalo, Pst.;
St. Blaise - 4835 Macarthur Blvd., N.W., Washington, DC 20007 t) 202-255-0856; 202-492-9088 (CRP) hrkmisija.svblaz@gmail.com (Croatian Pastoral Mission) Rev. Maurus Dolcic, T.O.R., Pst.;
Blessed Sacrament, Shrine of the Most - 3630 Quesada St., N.W., Washington, DC 20015-2538 t) 202-966-6575; 202-449-3989 (CRP) mbalch@blessedsacramentdc.org Rev. Ronald A. Potts, Pst.; Rev. Percival L. D'Silva, Assoc. Pst.; Rev. Alexander B. Scott, Assoc. Pst.; Dcn. Donald Mays; Dcn. Kenneth Angell; Michelle Balch, DRE;
Blessed Sacrament School, Shrine of the Most - 5841 Chevy Chase Pkwy., N.W., Washington, DC 20015-2599 t) 202-966-6682 www.bsstoday.org Christopher Kelly, Prin.;
Church of St. Louis - 4125 Garrison St., N.W., Washington, DC 20016 t) 202-537-0709 frenchparish@saintlouisdefrance.us www.saintlouisdefrance.us (Paroisse St. Louis de France-French-speaking Catholic Parish of Washington) Rev. Pierre Henri Montagne, Pst.;
Church of the Assumption of the Blessed Virgin Mary - 3411 Martin Luther King Jr. Ave., S.E., Washington, DC 20032-1597 t) 202-561-4178 info@assumptiondc.org Rev. Gregory William Shaffer, Pst.; Shelah Gray, DRE;
St. Dominic Church & Priory - 630 E St., S.W., Washington, DC 20024 t) 202-554-7863 office@stdominicchurch.org stdominicchurch.org Rev. Jacob Restrick, O.P., Prior; Rev. Hyacinth Cordell, O.P., Pst.; Rev. Luke Clark, O.P., In Res.; Rev. John Paul Kern, O.P., In Res.; Rev. Gerard Lessard, O.P., In Res.; Rev. Carl Louis Mason, O.P., In Res.; Rev. J. Andrew Nicolicchia, O.P., In Res.; Rev. Gabriel O'Donnell, O.P., In Res.; Rev. Matthew Rzeczkowski, O.P., In Res.; Rev. Antoninus Samy, O.P., In Res.; Rev. Bede Shipps, O.P., In Res.; Rev. Paul Clarke, O.P., In Res.; Rev. Bill Garrott, O.P., In Res.; Rev. Kenneth Andrew Hofer, O.P., In Res.; Rev. Keliher Norbert, O.P., In Res.; Rev. John Mark Solitario, O.P., In Res.; Rev. Jonah Teller, O.P., In Res.; Rev. Anthony VanBerkum, O.P., In Res.; Bro. Patrick Foley, O.P., In Res.; Bro. Albert Dempsey, O.P., In Res.; Bro. Eprhem Reese, O.P., In Res.; Bro. Ambrose Arralde, O.P., In Res.; Bro. Justin Bolger, O.P., In Res.; Bro. Irenaeus Dunlevy, O.P., In Res.;
Epiphany - 2712 Dumbarton St., N.W., Washington, DC 20007 t) 202-965-1610 epiphanygeorgetown@gmail.com www.georgetownepiphany.org Rev. Stefan Megyery, Admin.; Sr. Martina Koh, L.S.H.F., DRE;
St. Francis de Sales - 2021 Rhode Island Ave., N.E., Washington, DC 20018 t) 202-529-7451 office@stfds.org stfds.org Rev. Brian P. Sanderfoot, Pst.; Rev. Henry Slevin, In Res.;
St. Francis Xavier - 2800 Pennsylvania Ave., S.E., Washington, DC 20020 t) 202-582-5021 sfxdcparish@gmail.com Rev. Mark A. Cusick, Admin.;
St. Gabriel - 26 Grant Cir., N.W., Washington, DC 20011 t) 202-726-9092; 202-726-9212 (CRP) Rev. Avelino A. Gonzalez, Pst.; Dcn. Roberto Salgado; Rev. Tesfamariam Baraki, In Res.;
Holy Comforter - St. Cyprian - 1357 E. Capitol St., S.E., Washington, DC 20003 t) 202-546-1885 hcscstaff@hcscchurch.org www.hcscchurch.org Rev. Msgr. Charles E. Pope, Pst.; Dcn. Ralph Cyrus; Rev. F. Michael Bryant, In Res.; Rev. Araia Ghiday Ghebray, In Res.; Thomas Valayathil, In Res.; Shirley Austin, DRE;
Holy Name - 920 11th St., N.E., Washington, DC 20002 t) 202-397-2525 Rev. Michael W. Briese, Pst.; Rev. Francis M. Walsh, In Res.;
Holy Redeemer - 206 New York Ave., N.W., Washington, DC 20001 t) 202-347-7510 Rev. David Bava, Pst.;
Holy Rosary - 595 Third St., N.W., Washington, DC 20001-2703 t) 202-638-0165 casaitaldc@gmail.com www.holyrosarychurchdc.org Rev. Sergio Dall'Agnese, C.S., Pst.; CRP Stds.: 28
Holy Trinity - 3513 N St NW, Washington, DC 20007 t) 202-337-2840 kgillespie@trinity.org; communications@trinity.org www.trinity.org Rev. C. Kevin Gillespie, S.J., Pst.; Rev. Patrick Earl, SJ, Assoc. Pst.; Rev. Benjamin Hawley, SJ, Assoc. Pst.; Rev. William J. Kelley, S.J., Assoc. Pst.; CRP Stds.: 439
Holy Trinity School - (Grades PreK-8) 1325 36th St NW, Washington, DC 20007 t) 202-337-2339 principal@htsdc.org htsdc.org Kevin McShane, Prin.; Stds.: 332
Immaculate Conception - 1315 8th St., N.W., Washington, DC 20001 t) 202-332-8888 mstafford@immaculateconceptionchurchdc.org www.immaculateconceptionchurchdc.org/ Rev. Charles M. Gallagher, Pst.;
Incarnation - 880 Eastern Ave., N.E., Washington, DC 20019 t) 202-396-0942 incarnationpastor@comcast.net incarnationdc.org Rev. Stephen Sohe, SSJ, Pst.; Dcn. Joseph E. Bell; Dcn. William Mike Greenfield;
St. Joseph's on Capitol Hill - 313 Second St., N.E., Washington, DC 20002 t) 202-547-1223 stjosephsdc@st-josephs.org www.stjosephsdc.org Rev. William H. Gurnee III, Pst.; Rev. Christopher T. Begg, Prof.; Rev. Eugene Hemrick; Dcn. Gary L. Bockweg; CRP Stds.: 37
Kidane-Mehret Ge'ez Rite Catholic Church - 1001 Lawrence St., N.E., Washington, DC 20017; Mailing: P.O. Box 29616, Washington, DC 20017 t) 202-756-2756 Rev. Araia Ghiday Ghebray, Pst.;
St. Luke - 4925 E. Capitol St., S.E., Washington, DC 20019-5202 t) 202-584-8322 Rev. Cornelius K. Ejiogu, Pst.; Rev. Denis Mandamuna, In Res.;
St. Martin of Tours - 1908 N. Capitol St., Washington, DC 20002 t) 202-232-1144 mjkelley@verizon.net www.stmartinsdc.org Rev. Michael J. Kelley, Pst.;
St. Mary, Mother of God - 727 Fifth St., N.W., Washington, DC 20001 t) 202-289-7771 stmarys20001@gmail.com www.saintmarymotherofgod.org Rev. Vincent John DeRosa, Admin.;
Nativity - 6000 Georgia Ave., N.W., Washington, DC 20011 t) 202-726-6262 Rev. Blake Evans-Campos, Pst.; Rev. William L. Montgomery, In Res.; Rev. Mark E. Tucker, In Res.;
Our Lady of Perpetual Help - 1600 Morris Rd., S.E., Washington, DC 20020-6312 t) 202-678-4999 info@olphsedc.com www.olphsedc.com Rev. Michael Leon Thompson, S.S.J., Pst.; Rev. Kingsley Ogbuji, S.S.J., Par. Vicar; Dcn. Thomas Jones; Dcn. Timothy E. Tilghman; Cynthia Battle, DRE;
Our Lady of Victory - 4835 MacArthur Blvd., N.W., Washington, DC 20007 t) 202-337-4835; 202-337-4835 x14 (CRP) olvparishsec@gmail.com; frandrewgonzalo@gmail.com Rev. Andrew Gonzalo, Pst.; Rev. Leo D. Lefebure, In Res.;
Our Lady of Victory School - 4755 Whitehaven Pkwy.,

N.W., Washington, DC 20007 t) 202-337-1421 olvschooldc.org Sheila Martinez, Prin.;

Our Lady Queen of Peace - 3800 Ely Pl., S.E., Washington, DC 20019 t) 202-582-8600; 202-581-4986 (CRP) Rev. Pawel Sass, Pst.; Dcn. Alfred Miller;

Convent - 3740 Ely Pl., S.E., Washington, DC 20019 t) 202-581-4963

Our Lady Queen of the Americas (Parroquia Nuestra Senora Reina de las Americas) - 2200 California St., N.W., Washington, DC 20008 t) 202-332-8838; 202-332-8838 x225 (CRP) adiaz201olqa@gmail.com; lcifuentes225olqa@gmail.com www.ourladyqueenoftheamericasdc.org/ Rev. Alejandro Diaz, Pst.; Dcn. Jorge W. Vargas;

St. Patrick - 619 Tenth St., N.W., Washington, DC 20001-4587 t) 202-347-2713 Rev. Msgr. Salvatore A. Criscuolo, Pst.; Rev. Frederick H. MacIntyre, In Res.; Rev. Roderick D. McKee, In Res.; Rev. Fabrizio Meroni, P.I.M.E., In Res.; Robert Quinlan, DRE; Ronald Stolk, Dir.;

St. Peter - 313 Second St., S.E., Washington, DC 20003 t) 202-547-1430 rectory@saintpetersdc.org; dre@saintpetersdc.org saintpetersdc.org Rev. Daniel B. Carson, Pst.; Rev. Brendan Glasgow, Par. Vicar; Rev. Msgr. Joseph F. Sadusky, In Res.; Julie Penndorf, DRE; CRP Stds.: 156

St. Peter School - (Grades PreK-8) 422 Third St., S.E., Washington, DC 20003 t) 202-544-1618 info@stpeterschooldc.org stpeterschooldc.org Karen Clay, Prin.; Stds.: 223; Sr. Tchrs.: 1; Scholastics: 1; Lay Tchrs.: 24

Shrine of the Sacred Heart - 3211 Sacred Heart Way, N.W., Washington, DC 20010 t) 202-234-8000; 202-234-8002; 202-667-2446 (CRP) shdc.office@gmail.com Rev. Emilio Biosca, O.F.M.Cap., Pst.; Rev. Diogo Escudero, O.F.M.Cap., Par. Vicar; Rev. Orlando Reyes, O.F.M.Cap., Par. Vicar; Rev. Armand Blanc, O.F.M.Cap., Pst. Min./Coord.; Rev. Tage A. Danielson, O.F.M.Cap., Pst. Min./Coord.; Rev. James P. Froehlich, O.F.M.Cap., Formation Faculty; Rev. Luc Philogene, O.F.M.Cap., In Res.; CRP Stds.: 572

Shrine of the Sacred Heart School - -8) 1625 Park Rd., N.W., Washington, DC 20010 t) 202-265-4828 beverly.bonilla@catholicacademies.org Elise Heil, Prin.;

St. Stephen Martyr - 2436 Pennsylvania Ave., N.W., Washington, DC 20037 t) 202-785-0982 Rev. Msgr. Paul Dudziak, Pst.; Rev. Klaus J. Sirianni, Assoc. Pst.;

St. Teresa of Avila - 1401 V St., S.E., Washington, DC 20020-5692 t) 202-678-3709 Rev. Msgr. Raymond G. East, Pst.; Dcn. William J. Hawkins;

St. Thomas Apostle - 2665 Woodley Rd., N.W., Washington, DC 20008 t) 202-234-1488 Rev. Richard A. Mullins, Pst.; Dcn. William C. Boesman;

St. Thomas More - 4275 4th St., S.E., Washington, DC 20032 t) 202-562-0431 stmchurch@comcast.net Rev. Raymond H. Moore, Pst.;

St. Thomas More - (Grades PreK-8) t) 202-561-1189 Gearld Smith, Prin.;

St. Vincent De Paul - 14 M St., S.E., Washington, DC 20003-3511 t) 202-488-1354 Rev. Andrew B. Gonzalo;

STATE OF MARYLAND

AVENUE

Holy Angels - 21340 Colton Point Rd., Avenue, MD 20609-2422 t) 301-769-3332 Very Rev. Anthony E. Lickteig, Pst.; Dcn. Joseph W. Lloyd Jr.;

BARNESVILLE

St. Mary Church and Shrine of Our Lady of Fatima - 18230 Barnesville Rd., Barnesville, MD 20838; Mailing: P.O. Box 67, Barnesville, MD 20838 t) 301-972-8660 stmarysb@yahoo.com www.stmaryonline.com Rev. Kevin P. O'Reilly, Pst.; Dcn. David Cahoon; Liz Smith, DRE; CRP Stds.: 87

BELTSVILLE

St. Joseph - 11007 Montgomery Rd., Beltsville, MD 20705 t) 301-937-7183 reled@stjos.org www.stjos.org Rev. Msgr. Karl A. Chimiak, Pst.; Rev. Joseph F. Wimmer, O.S.A., In Res.; Dcn. Chris Schwartz;

St. Joseph School - 11011 Montgomery Rd., Beltsville, MD 20705 t) 301-937-7154 schooloffice@stjos.org

BENEDICT

St. Francis de Sales - 7185 Benedict Ave., Benedict, MD 20612-0306; Mailing: P.O. Box 306, Benedict, MD 20612-0306 t) 301-274-3416; 301-870-4991; 301-274-0904 (CRP) religioused@stfrancisdesalescc.org Rev. Kevin M. Cusick, Pst.;

BETHESDA

St. Bartholomew - 6900 River Rd., Bethesda, MD 20817; Mailing: 6902 River Rd., Bethesda, MD 20817 t) 301-229-7933; 301-229-3431 (CRP) parishsecretary@stbartholomew.org www.stbartholomew.org Rev. Mark Leo Smith, Pst.; Rev. Oscar Astigarraga, Par. Vicar; Rev. Msgr. John J. Enzler, In Res.; Cathy Mills, DRE; CRP Stds.: 131

St. Bartholomew School - (Grades PreK-8) t) 301-229-5586 admissions@stbartholomew.org www.school.stbartholomew.org Frank English, Prin.;

St. Jane Frances de Chantal - 9601 Old Georgetown Rd., Bethesda, MD 20814; Mailing: 9701 Old Georgetown Rd, Bethesda, MD 20814-1795 t) 301-530-1550; 301-530-1640 (CRP) seton.center@stjanedechantal.org; parish.office@stjanedechantal.org www.stjanedechantal.org Rev. Samuel C. Giese, Pst.; Rev. Jeremy Hammond, Par. Vicar; James Caulfield, DRE;

St. Jane Frances de Chantal School - -8) 9525 Old Georgetown Rd., Bethesda, MD 20814 t) 301-530-1221 ehamilton@dechantal.org www.dechantal.org Betsy Hamilton, Prin.;

Little Flower - 5607 Massachusetts Ave., Bethesda, MD 20816 t) 301-320-4538; 301-320-5833 (CRP) thompsonr@lfschool.org; pwhitty@lfparish.org www.lfparish.org Rev. Msgr. Peter J. Vaghi, Pst.; Rev. Patrick S. Lewis, Assoc. Pst.; Rev. Stephen Giulietti, In Res.; Very Rev. George E. Stuart, In Res.; Sr. Roberta Thompson, S.N.J.M., DRE;

Little Flower School - 5601 Massachusetts Ave., Bethesda, MD 20816 t) 301-320-3273 rrynn@lfschool.org lfschool.org

Our Lady of Lourdes - 7500 Pearl St., Bethesda, MD 20814 t) 301-654-1287; 301-654-5954 (CRP) sgolden@ololrcc.org www.lourdesbethesda.net Rev. Robert E. Walsh, Pst.; Rev. James Morrison, Par. Vicar;

Our Lady of Lourdes School - t) 301-654-5376 www.bethesda-lourdes.org Patricia K. McGann, Prin.;

BOWIE

Ascension - 12700 Lanham-Severn Rd., Bowie, MD 20720 t) 301-262-2227 office@ascensionbowie.org ascensionbowie.org Rev. Timothy G. Daniel, Pst.; CRP Stds.: 50

St. Edward - 1940 Mitchellville Rd., Bowie, MD 20716; Mailing: 16304 Pond Meadow Ln., Bowie, MD 20716-1863 t) 301-249-9199 office@stedwardbowie.com www.stedwardbowie.com Rev. Scott S. Holmer, Pst.; Dcn. David Barnes; Dcn. J. Christopher Garner; Dcn. Bartholomew J. Merella; CRP Stds.: 90

St. Pius X - 14720 Annapolis Rd., Bowie, MD 20715; Mailing: 3300 Moreland Pl., Bowie, MD 20715 t) 301-262-2141; 301-262-3644 (CRP) office@spxbowie.org spxbowie.org Rev. Michael T. Jones, Pst.; Anne Brennan, DRE;

St. Pius X Regional School - 14710 Annapolis Rd., Bowie, MD 20715 t) 301-262-0203

Sacred Heart - 16501 Annapolis Rd., Bowie, MD 20715 t) 301-262-0704; 301-262-1221 (CRP) ccdsacredheart@gmail.com; parishoffice@sacredheartbowie.org www.sacredheartbowie.org Rev. Ronald A. Potts, Pst.; Rev. Michael A. Russo, Par. Vicar; Dcn. Dan D. Abeyta; Dcn. Robert P. Seith; CRP Stds.: 211

BRANDYWINE

St. Michael's - 17510 Horsehead Rd., Brandywine, MD 20613 t) 301-888-1498 (CRP); 240-681-3551 secretary@stmichaelbaden.org stmichaelbaden.org Rev. Martin E. Flum, Pst.;

St. Dominic's - 22400 Aquasco Rd., Aquasco, MD 20608; Mailing: 17510 Horsehead Rd., Brandywine, MD 20613

BRYANTOWN

St. Mary - 13715 Notre Dame Pl., Bryantown, MD 20617-2224 t) 301-870-2220; 301-274-3187; 301-274-3800 (CRP) Rev. Rory T. Conley, Pst.; Dcn. Eugene Burroughs; Dcn. Daniel E. Ford; Dcn. Henry Middleton;

St. Mary School - 13735 Notre Dame Pl., Bryantown, MD 20617 t) 301-932-6883

BURTONSVILLE

Resurrection Parish - 3315 Greencastle Rd., Burtonsville, MD 20866 t) 301-288-4664 Rev. Jeffrey M. Defayette, Pst.; Rev. William M. Brailsford, In Res.;

BUSHWOOD

Sacred Heart - 23080 Maddox Rd., Bushwood, MD 20618; Mailing: P.O. Box 37, Bushwood, MD 20618 t) 301-769-3100 Very Rev. Anthony E. Lickteig, Pst.;

CAMP SPRINGS

St. Philip the Apostle - 5416 Henderson Way, Camp Springs, MD 20746 t) 301-423-4244 st.philipparish@comcast.net Rev. Edward Anthony Hegnauer, Pst.;

St. Philip the Apostle School - 5414 Henderson Way, Camp Springs, MD 20746 t) 301-423-4740 principal@stphiliptheapostlemd.org; officemanager@stphiliptheapostlemd.org www.stphiliptheapostlemd.org/ Stephen Lamont, Prin.;

CHAPTICO

Our Lady of the Wayside - 37575 Chaptico Rd., Chaptico, MD 20621-0097; Mailing: P.O. Box 97, Chaptico, MD 20621-0097 t) 301-884-3165 Rev. Charles M. Gallagher, Pst.;

Mother Catherine Spalding Tri Parish School - c/o Our Lady of the Wayside Parish, 37575 Chaptico Rd., Chaptico, MD 20621-0097

CHARLOTTE HALL

St. Mary - 11555 St. Mary's Church Rd., Charlotte Hall, MD 20622 t) 301-934-8825 stmarycatholicchurchnewportmd@gmail.com www.stmarychurchnewport.org/ Rev. Matthew J. Fish, Pst.; Mary Ellen Heinze, DRE; CRP Stds.: 31

CHEVERLY

St. Ambrose - 3107 63rd Ave., Cheverly, MD 20785; Mailing: 6301 Jason St., Cheverly, MD 20785 t) (301) 773-9300 (Phone calls only); (301) 773-9301 (Phone calls only) ambroserectory@gmail.com; ambrosepst@gmail.com sacheverly.org Rev. Alejandro Diaz, Pst.; CRP Stds.: 274

St. Ambrose School - (Grades PreK-8) 6310 Jason St., Cheverly, MD 20785 t) 301-773-0223 saschevwebmaster@gmail.com Taylor Baker, Prin.;

CHILLUM

St. John Baptist de la Salle - 5706 Sargent Rd., Chillum, MD 20782 t) 301-559-3636; 301-559-3637 (CRP) Rev. Diego Ruiz, I.V.E., Pst.;

CLINTON

Church of St. John the Evangelist - 8908 Old Branch Ave., Clinton, MD 20735 t) 301-868-1070; 301-868-3026 (CRP) st.johnchurch01@gmail.com Rev. Jaime B. Hernandez, Pst.;

Church of St. John the Evangelist School - (Grades PreK-8) 8912 Old Branch Ave., Clinton, MD 20735 t) 301-868-2010 principal@saintjohnsschool.org saintjohnsschool.org

St. Mary's Church of Piscataway - 13401 Piscataway Rd., Clinton, MD 20735-4564; Mailing: 13405 Piscataway Rd, Clinton, MD 20735-4564 t) 301-292-0527 parish@stmaryspiscataway.org www.saintmaryspiscataway.net/ Rev. Samuel Isaac Plummer, Pst.; Dcn. George Ames; Dcn. Stephen McKimmie;

St. Mary's Church of Piscataway School - (Grades PreK-8) 13407 Piscataway Rd., Clinton, MD 20735-4564 t) 301-292-2522 school@smsp.school www.stmaryspiscataway.org Lynsie K. Reavis, Prin.;

COLLEGE PARK

Holy Redeemer - 4902 Berwyn Rd., College Park, MD 20740 t) 301-474-3920 beth.berard@holy-redeemer.org; parish@holy-redeemer.org Rev. Mark Leo Smith, Pst.; Rev. Andrew Clyne, Assoc. Pst.; Rev. Jonathan A. Berard, DRE;

Holy Redeemer School - (Grades PreK-8) t) 301-474-3993 school@holy-redeemer.org www.holy-redeemer.org Maria Bovich, Prin.;

DAMASCUS

St. Paul - 9240 Damascus Rd., Damascus, MD 20872 t) 301-253-2027; 301-253-5941 (CRP) pastor@stpauldamascus.org; info@stpauldamascus.org stpauldamascus.org/ Rev. Msgr. Edward J. Filardi, Pst.; Dcn. Maury Huguley Jr.; Dcn. Donald Mays; Dcn. David Terrar; CRP Stds.: 199

DARNESTOWN

Our Lady of the Visitation - 14139 Seneca Rd., Darnestown, MD 20874 t) 301-948-5536 parishoffice@olvp.org www.olvp.org Rev. Gregory W. Shaffer, Pst.; Dcn. Thaddeus A. Dmuchowski; CRP Stds.: 167

DERWOOD

St. Francis of Assisi - 6701 Muncaster Mill Rd., Derwood, MD 20855 t) 301-840-1407; 301-258-9193 (CRP) sanderson@sfadw.org; dzezzo@sfadw.org www.sfadw.org Rev. John J. Dillon, Pst.; Dcn. James J. Datovech; Dcn. Wilberto Garcia; Dcn. James McCann; Susan Anderson, DRE;

FORESTVILLE

Church of the Holy Spirit - 1717 Ritchie Rd., Forestville, MD 20747 t) 301-336-3707 holyspirit.md@adw.org adw.org/parishes/holy-spirit-church-of-the/ Rev. Everett Pearson, Admin.; Rev. Michael P Edathil, Assoc. Pst.; Rev. Jeffrey F. Samaha, In Res.;

Mt. Calvary - 6700 Marlboro Pike, Forestville, MD 20747 t) 301-735-5532; 301-735-5262 x17 (CRP) caziegler7@yahoo.com; mtcalvary.md@adw.org mountcalvarycatholicchurch.org Rev. Everett Pearson, Pst.; Dcn. Lawrence Miles; Cathy Ziegler, DRE;

FORT WASHINGTON

St. Ignatius - 2315 Brinkley Rd., Fort Washington, MD 20744 t) 301-567-4740; 301-567-6546 (CRP) Rev. G. Paul Herbert, Pst.;

GAITHERSBURG

St. John Neumann - 8900 Lochaven Dr., Gaithersburg, MD 20882-4460 t) 301-977-7990 info@saintjohnneumann.org www.saintjohnneumann.org Rev. Joseph E. Rogers, Pst.; Dcn. Carlo Caraballo; Dcn. Eugene Cummins; Dcn. Michael W. Davy;

St. Martin of Tours - 201 S. Frederick Ave., Gaithersburg, MD 20877 t) 301-990-3203; 301-990-2556 (CRP) parish@stmartinsweb.org; faithformation@stmartinsweb.org Rev. David G. Wells, Admin.; Rev. Jonathan Santiago Vanegas Calderon, Par. Vicar; Rev. Tony A. D'Souza, Par. Vicar; Dcn. Lawrence Bell; Dcn. Mauricio O. Rivas; Dcn. William A. Vita Jr.; Josh Moldiz, DRE;

St Martin of Tours School - (Grades PreK-8) 115 S. Frederick Ave., Gaithersburg, MD 20877 t) 301-990-2441 office@smsmd.org www.smsmd.org Stephen Lamont, Prin.;

St. Rose of Lima - 11701 Clopper Rd., Gaithersburg, MD 20878-1024 t) 301-948-7545 strose@strose.com www.strose-parish.org Rev. Agustin Mateo-Ayala, Pst.; Rev. Emanuel Lucero, Par. Vicar; Dcn. Frank Avenilla; Dcn. Mario F. Moreno; Dcn. Leo F. Schneider; Christine Jeffrey, DRE; Susan Joseph, DRE; Ivonne Salazar, DRE;

GARRETT PARK

Holy Cross - 4900 Strathmore Ave., Garrett Park, MD 20896; Mailing: P.O. Box 249, Garrett Park, MD 20896 t) 301-942-1020; 301-942-8790 (CRP) ilagan@hcrosschurch.org; parishsecretary@hcrosschurch.org www.hcrosschurch.org Rev. Robert P. Buchmeier, Pst.; Rev. Joseph F. Perkins; Dcn. Robert Hubbard; Dcn. Robert W. Stout III; Michelle Ilagan, DRE;

Holy Cross School - (Grades PreK-8) t) 301-949-0053 office@hcross.org www.hcross.org Lisa Maio Kane, Prin.;

GERMANTOWN

Mother Seton Parish - 19951 Father Hurley Blvd., Germantown, MD 20874 t) 301-924-3838; 301-444-3496 (CRP); 301-444-3495 (CRP) motherannseton@gmail.com Rev. LeRoy J. Fangmeyer, Pst.; Rev. Philip Ilg, Par. Vicar; Rev. Louis J. Faust; Dcn. Francis W. Bendel; Dcn. Fidencio Gonzalez; Dcn. Stephen M. Maselko;

GREAT MILLS

Holy Face - 20408 Point Lookout Rd., Great Mills, MD 20634 t) 301-994-0525 Rev. Jaroslaw S. Gamrot, Pst.; Dcn. Paul A. Bielewicz, Pst. Assoc.; Laura Lang, DRE;

Little Flower - 20410 Point Lookout Rd., Great Mills, MD 20634 t) 301-994-0404

GREENBELT

Saint Hugh of Grenoble - 135 Crescent Rd., Greenbelt, MD 20770 t) 301-474-4322 shreligiousedd4@gmail.com; sthughoffice@gmail.com Rev. Walter J. Tappe, Pst.;

HILLCREST HEIGHTS

Holy Family - 2210 Callaway St., Hillcrest Heights, MD 20748 t) 301-894-2222 Rev. Kevin J. Regan, Pst.;

Holy Family School - 2200 Callaway St., Hillcrest Heights, MD 20748 t) 301-894-2323

HOLLYWOOD

St. John Francis Regis - 43950 St. John's Rd., Hollywood, MD 20636 t) 301-373-2281 rolon@sjchollywood.org; haydenp@sjchollywood.org Rev. Raymond F. Schmidt, Pst.; Dcn. Ammon S. Ripple; Rev. Eamon Dignan, In Res.; Richard Olon, DRE;

St. John Francis Regis School - -8) t) 301-373-2142 office@sjshollywood.org www.sjshollywood.org Susan McDonough, Prin.;

HUNTINGTOWN

Jesus the Divine Word Parish - 885 Cox Rd., Huntingtown, MD 20639 t) 410-414-8304 office@jesusdivineword.org; religioused@jesusdivineword.org www.jesusdivineword.org Rev. John T. Dakes, Pst.; Dcn. Ronald J. Burns; Tracey Smith, Youth Min.; Karen Burns, DRE;

HYATTSVILLE

St. Jerome - 5205 43rd Ave., Hyattsville, MD 20781 t) 301-927-6684 religioused@stjeromes.org; ajstjerome@hotmail.com Rev. Scott R. Hahn, Pst.; Rev. Isadore Dixon, In Res.; Rev. Charles Edeh, In Res.; Dcn. Neal T. Conway;

St. Jerome School - (Grades PreK-8) 5207 42nd Pl., Hyattsville, MD 20781 t) 301-277-4568 dflynn@stjeromes.org Daniel Flynn, Prin.;

Convent - 5300 43rd Ave., Hyattsville, MD 20781 t) 301-864-2016

Child Center - t) 301-699-1314

St. Mark - 7501 Adelphi Rd., Hyattsville, MD 20783 t) 301-422-8300; 301-422-7822 (CRP) religioused@stmarkhyattsville.org Rev. Roberto J. Cortes, Pst.; Rev. Gustavo Perez, Assoc. Pst.; Rev. Paul Sullins, Assoc. Pst.; Dcn. Jose Renato Molina; Dcn. Curtis Turner; Most Rev. Michael W. Fisher, In Res.; Steward Benalcazar, DRE;

INDIAN HEAD

St. Mary Star of the Sea - 30 Mattingly Ave., Indian Head, MD 20640 t) 301-753-9177; 301-743-5770 parish@staroftheseaindianhead.org www.staroftheseaindianhead.org Rev. Brian Alick Coelho, Admin.;

KENSINGTON

Holy Redeemer - 9705 Summit Ave., Kensington, MD 20895 t) 301-942-2333; 301-942-2333 x200 (CRP) Rev. Mark F. Hughes, Pst.; Rev. Ryan I. Pineda, Par. Vicar; Rev. Mark E. Tucker, Par. Vicar; Marylou McDonald, DRE;

Holy Redeemer School - 9715 Summit Ave., Kensington, MD 20895 t) 301-942-3701 hrs-ken.org Colleen Ryan, Prin.;

LA PLATA

Sacred Heart - 201 St. Mary's Ave., La Plata, MD 20646; Mailing: P.O. Box 1390, La Plata, MD 20646 t) 301-934-2261; 301-934-3386 (CRP) Rev. Lawrence C. Swink, Pst.; Rev. Martin E. Flum, Assoc. Pst.; Dcn. Anthony Barrasso; Dcn. Albert E. Graham Jr.; Dcn. Walter G. Rourke;

Archbishop Neale School - (Grades PreK-8) 104 Port Tobacco Rd., La Plata, MD 20646 t) 301-934-9595 office@archbishopnealeschool.org www.archbishopnealeschool.org Linda Bourne, Prin.;

LANDOVER HILLS

St. Mary's Catholic Church - 7401 Buchanan St., Landover Hills, MD 20784-2323 t) 301-577-8844 Rev. Richard K. Gancayco, Pst.; Dcn. Stephen M. Robinson;

St. Mary's Catholic Church School - 7207 Annapolis Rd., Landover Hills, MD 20784 t) 301-577-0031 admin.stmarys@comcast.net stmaryslh.org Christian Buchleitner, Prin.;

Syro-Malankara Mission - 7401 Buchanan St., Landover Hills, MD 20784-9998 t) 301-577-8844 Rev. Mathai Mannoorvadakkethil, Pst.;

LANHAM

St. Matthias Apostle - 9475 Annapolis Rd., Lanham, MD 20706-3020 t) 301-459-4814; 301-459-4814 x205 (CRP) Rev. John H. Kennealy, Pst.; Rev. Canice Enyiaka, In Res.; Dcn. Alton Davis;

Hughes Center - www.stmatthias.org

St. Matthias Apostle School - 9473 Annapolis Rd., Lanham, MD 20706-3020 t) 301-577-9412 www.stmatthias.org Patricia Schratz, Prin.;

LARGO

St. Joseph - 2020 St. Joseph Dr., Largo, MD 20774 t) 301-773-4838; 301-773-2480 (CRP) Most Rev. Roy Edward Campbell, Pst.; Dcn. Alton Davis;

LAUREL

St. Mary - 114 St. Mary's Pl., Laurel, MD 20707 t) 301-725-3080; 301-490-8770 (CRP) Rev. Msgr. Michael J. Mellone, Pst.; Rev. Phillip Ilg, Assoc. Pst.; Dcn. Robert L. Gignilliat; Dcn. Brandon B. Justice; Dcn. Perfecto Santiago; Gina Iampieri, Music Min.; Jennifer Juzwiak, DRE;

St. Mary School - 106 St. Mary's Pl., Laurel, MD 20707 t) 301-498-1433 www.stmaryofthemill.org Alisha Jordan, Prin.;

St. Nicholas - 8603 Contee Rd., Laurel, MD 20708 t) (301) 490-5116; 301-490-5116 x109 (Dir. of Faith Formation) st.nicholaschurch@verizon.net www.stnicholaslaurel.org Rev. Timothy K. Baer, Pst.; CRP Stds.: 65

LEONARDTOWN

St. Aloysius - 22800 Washington St., Leonardtown, MD 20650; Mailing: P.O. Box 310, Leonardtown, MD 20650 t) 301-475-8064 lwathen@saintaloysiuschurch.org Rev. David W. Beaubien, Pst.;

Father Andrew White, S.J. - -8) 22850 Washington St., Leonardtown, MD 20650; Mailing: P.O. Box 1756, Leonardtown, MD 20650 t) 301-475-9795 fradwh@verizon.net www.fatherandrewwhite.org Heather Francisco, Prin.;

St. Francis Xavier - 21370 Newtowne Neck Rd., Leonardtown, MD 20650 t) 301-475-9885 sfxparishoffice1662@gmail.com stfrancisxavierchurch.org Rev. Robert G. Maro, Pst.; Dcn. William J. Nickerson; Paula McLeod, DRE;

Our Lady's - 41348 Medley's Neck Rd., Leonardtown, MD 20650 t) 301-475-8403 olcmedleysneck@gmail.com ourladyschurch.org Rev. John Tung Nguyen, Pst.;

LEXINGTON PARK

Immaculate Heart of Mary - 22375 Three Notch Rd., Lexington Park, MD 20653-2017 t) 301-863-8144; 301-863-8793 (CRP) office@ihmrcc.org; cff@ihmrcc.org www.ihmrcc.org Rev. Marco Federico Schad, Pst.; Rev. Edward Anthony Hegnauer, Par. Vicar; Dcn. Michael J. Crowe; Dcn. Juan Carlos Ortiz; Damaritza Ortiz, CRE; Jacinta Thompson, Bus. Mgr.; Virgen Torres, CRE; CRP Stds.: 84

MECHANICSVILLE

Immaculate Conception - 28297 Old Village Rd., Mechanicsville, MD 20659; Mailing: P.O. Box 166, Mechanicsville, MD 20659 t) 301-884-3123; 240-249-6010 immaculateconception.md@adw.org; deacon.kyte@gmail.com icchurchmd.org Rev. Michael E. Tietjen, Pst.; Dcn. William L. Kyte; CRP Stds.: 98

MITCHELLVILLE

Holy Family - 12010 Woodmore Rd., Mitchellville, MD 20721 t) 301-249-2266; 301-249-1167 (CRP) holyfamilyadmin@msn.com holyfamilywoodmore.com Rev. Joseph A. Jenkins, Pst.;

MORGANZA

St. Joseph - 29119 Point Lookout Rd., Morganza, MD 20660; Mailing: P.O. Box 175, Morganza, MD 20660 t) 301-475-3293 sjcmorganza@gmail.com www.stjosephmorganza.org Rev. Andrew Francis Royals, Pst.; Dcn. James A. Somerville;

MOUNT RAINIER

St. James - 3628 Rhode Island Ave., Mount Rainier, MD 20712 t) 301-927-0567 st.jamescatholicchurch@gmail.com Rev. Pablo Bonello, I.V.E., Pst.; Rev. Nathaniel Dreyer, I.V.E., Assoc. Pst.; Rev. Javier Ibarra, I.V.E., In Res.; Sr. Maria de San Juan de los Lagos Vargas, S.S.V.M., DRE;

NEWBURG

Holy Ghost - 15848 Rock Point Rd., Newburg, MD 20664 t) 301-259-2515 Rev. Gregory S. Coan, Pst.; Dcn. Walter G. Rourke;

St. Francis de Sales - 13675 Furbush Rd., Rock Point, MD 20682

NORTH BEACH

St. Anthony's - 8900 Bay Ave., North Beach, MD 20714; Mailing: P.O. Box 660, North Beach, MD 20714 t) 443-646-5721; 443-646-5722; 443-646-5724 (CRP) Rev. James M. Stack, Pst.; Dcn. Francis E. Baker Jr.; Dcn. Eric B. Mueller; Deborah Wheeler, DRE;

OLNEY

St. Andrew Kim - 17615 Old Baltimore Rd., Olney, MD 20832 t) 301-275-3734

St. Peter - 2900 Olney-Sandy Spring Rd., Olney, MD 20832 t) 301-924-3774; 301-570-4952 (CRP) info@stpetersolney.org Rev. Thomas M. Kalita, Pst.; Rev. Ryan I. Pineda, Par. Vicar; Dcn. Chang Choi; Dcn. Thomas Cioffi; Dcn. Rory P. Crawford; Dcn. Vincent J. Wolfinger; Cindy Dixon, DRE;

St. Peter School - t) 301-774-9112 school@stpetersolney.org Mary Elizabeth Whelan, Prin.;

OWINGS

Jesus the Good Shepherd - 1601 W. Mt. Harmony Rd., Owings, MD 20736 t) 410-257-3810 (CRP); 410-257-3810 secretary@ccjgs.org; community@ccjgs.org ccjgs.org Rev. Michael J. King, Pst.; Dcn. Paul Fagan; Maggie Gorman, DRE; Pam Huseman, Bus. Mgr.; Katie Evans, Dir.; CRP Stds.: 430

Cardinal Hickey Academy - (Grades PreK-8) t) 410-286-0404 office@cardinalhickeyacademy.org www.cardinalhickeyacademy.org (Regional) Jennifer Griffith, Prin.;

OXON HILL

St. Columba - 7804 Livingston Rd., Oxon Hill, MD 20745 t) 301-567-5506; 301-567-6113 (CRP) Rev. Gary T. Villanueva, Pst.; Dcn. Leandro Y. Espinosa; Dcn. Robert C. Villanueva;

St. Columba School - (Grades PreK-8) 7800 Livingston Rd., Oxon Hill, MD 20745 t) 301-567-6212 schooloffice@stccatholic.org www.stccatholic.org Katrina Fernandez, Prin.;

POMFRET

St. Joseph - 4590 St. Joseph Way, Pomfret, MD 20675 t) 301-539-3903 stjoeoffice@comcast.net; stjoeformation@comcast.net www.stjoepomfret.weconnect.com Rev. Harry J. Stokes, Pst.; Dcn. John R. Barnes; Dcn. James M. Tittinger; CRP Stds.: 54

POOLESVILLE

Our Lady of the Presentation - 17220 Tom Fox Ave., Poolesville, MD 20837; Mailing: P.O. Box 428, Poolesville, MD 20837 t) 301-349-2045 parishoffice@olpresentationmd.org www.olpresentationmd.org Rev. Justin A. Huber, Pst.; Maria Villarrubia, DRE;

PORT TOBACCO

St. Catherine of Alexandria - 7865 Port Tobacco Rd., Port Tobacco, MD 20677; Mailing: 7640 Port Tobacco Rd., Port Tobacco, MD 20677 t) 301-934-9630 stcatherine-alexandria.md@adw.org www.stcsti.org Rev. Aaron M. Qureshi, Pst.;

St. Ignatius - 8855 Chapel Point Rd., Port Tobacco, MD 20677 t) 301-934-8245 cliffordt@adw.org; ignatiusreligion@gmail.com www.chapelpoint.org Rev. Thomas F. Clifford, S.J., Pst.; CRP Stds.: 63

St. Ignatius Loyola - 6455 Port Tobacco Rd., Port Tobacco, MD 20677; Mailing: P.O. Box 278, Port Tobacco, MD 20677 t) 301-934-9630 admin.stcatherine-alexandria.md@adw.org www.stignatiusmd.org Rev. Kenneth J. Gill, Pst.;

POTOMAC

Our Lady of Mercy - 9200 Kentsdale Dr., Potomac, MD 20854 t) 301-365-1415 church@olom.org www.olom.org Rev. Msgr. Charles V. Antonicelli, Pst.; Rev. Joseph Cwik, Pst. Assoc.; CRP Stds.: 142

Our Lady of Mercy School - (Grades PreK-8) 9222 Kentsdale Dr., Potomac, MD 20854 t) 301-365-4477 schooloffice@olom.org www.schoololom.org Christine Green, Prin.; Jason Knecht, Vice Prin.; Stds.: 220; Lay Tchrs.: 21

PRINCE FREDERICK

St. John Vianney - 105 Vianney Ln., Prince Frederick, MD 20678-4123 t) 410-535-0223; 410-535-4395 (CRP) office@sjvchurch.net; ccd@sjvchurch.net www.sjvchurch.net Rev. Joseph B. Pierce, Pst.; Kimberly Stack, DRE; CRP Stds.: 164

RIDGE

St. Michael - 16566 Three Notch Rd., Ridge, MD 20680; Mailing: P.O. Box 429, Ridge, MD 20680 t) 301-872-4321 church.stmichaels@md.metrocast.net saintmichaelscatholicchurch.org Rev. Peter M. Giovanoni, Pst.;

St. Michael School - 16560 Three Notch Rd., Ridge, MD 20680; Mailing: P.O. Box 259, Ridge, MD 20680 t) 301-872-5454 principal@saint-michaels-school.org Lila Ridgell Hofmeister, Prin.;

RIVERDALE

Our Lady of Fatima Parish - 5700 St. Bernard's Dr., Riverdale, MD 20737 t) 301-277-1000 bernard.fatimachurch@gmail.com; teresadluna@gmail.com Rev. Jefferson Bariviera, C.S., Pst.; Rev. Lino Garcia, C.S., Assoc. Pst.; Teresa Luna, DRE;

RIVERDALE PARK

St. Bernard - 5700 St. Bernard Dr., Riverdale Park, MD 20737-2102 t) 301-277-1000 bernard.fatimachurch@gmail.com; teresadluna@gmail.com Rev. Jefferson Bariviera, C.S., Pst.; Rev. Lino Garcia, C.S., Assoc. Pst.; Dcn. Desmond Yorke; Teresa Luna, DRE;

ROCKVILLE

St. Elizabeth - 917 Montrose Rd., Rockville, MD 20852 t) 301-881-1380 Rev. Msgr. John F. Macfarlane, Pst.; Rev. Jacob C. George, Assoc. Pst.;

St. Elizabeth School - (Grades PreK-8) t) 301-881-1824

St. Mary - 520 Veirs Mill Rd., Rockville, MD 20852 t) 301-424-5550; 301-762-8750 (CRP) oysterc@adw.org; stmaryrockville@yahoo.com www.stmarysrockville.org Rev. Msgr. Robert G. Amey, Pst.; Rev. James Glasgow, Par. Vicar; Rev. M. Valentine Keveny, In Res.; Dcn. Louis Brune III; Dcn. Daniel Kostka; Catherine Gallerizzo Oyster, DRE; Olivia Crosby, RCIA Coord.; CRP Stds.: 325

St. Mary School - (Grades PreK-8) 600 Veirs Mill Rd., Rockville, MD 20852 t) 301-762-4179 stmaryschoolrockville.org Debra Eisel, Prin.;

Our Lady of China Pastoral Mission - 1001 Grandin Ave., Rockville, MD 20851

St. Patrick - 4101 Norbeck Rd., Rockville, MD 20853 t) 301-924-2284; 301-929-9314 (CRP) saintpatrickreled@gmail.com; parishoffice@stpatrickadw.org www.stpatricksmd.org Rev. Msgr. Charles J. Parry, Pst.; Rev. Martino I. Choi, Par. Vicar; Dcn. James T. Nalls; Dcn. David J. Suley; Jane Baily, DRE;

St. Raphael - 1592 Kimblewick Rd., Rockville, MD 20854; Mailing: 1513 Dunster Rd., Rockville, MD 20854 t) 301-762-2143 www.straphaels.org Rev. Michael A. Salah, Pst.; Rev. Christian Huebner, Par. Vicar; Rev. Thomas G. Morrow, In Res.; Dcn. Jose R. Carbonell; Dcn. Frank Salatto; Dcn. Richard Meyer; Mary Beaudoin, DRE;

Shrine of St. Jude - 12701 Veirs Mill Rd., Rockville, MD 20853 t) 301-946-8200; 301-949-2336 (CRP) Rev. Paul D. Lee, Pst.; Rev. Kenneth J. Gill, Assoc. Pst.; Rev. John Tung Nguyen, Assoc. Pst.; Rev. Daniele Rebeggiani, Assoc. Pst.; Dcn. Donald Mays; Dcn. Nicholas E. Scholz;

Shrine of St. Jude School - 4820 Walbridge St., Rockville, MD 20853 t) 301-946-7888 stjudemain@yahoo.com www.stjudesschool.org

SEAT PLEASANT

St. Margaret - 408 Addison Rd. S., Seat Pleasant, MD 20743 t) 301-336-3345; 301-336-3344 (CRP) Rev. Michael P. Moran, S.M.A., Pst.; Rev. David Reid, SS.CC., Assoc. Pst.; Rev. Fintan Sheeran, SS.CC., Assoc. Pst.; Rev. Austin Charles Ochu, S.M.A. (Nigeria), Chap.; Dcn. Samuel Miror;

SILVER SPRING

St. Andrew Apostle - 11600 Kemp Mill Rd., Silver Spring, MD 20902 t) 301-649-3700 saabulletins@yahoo.com; faith.formation@standrewapostle.org www.standrewapostle.org/ Mision San Andres Rev. John H. Kennealy, Pst.; Rev. Blake Evans-Campos, Assoc. Pst.; Rev. Msgr. Kevin T. Hart, In Res.; Dcn. Stephen D. O'Neill; CRP Stds.: 336

St. Andrew Apostle School - 11602 Kemp Mill Rd., Silver Spring, MD 20902 t) 301-649-3555 standrew20902@yahoo.com school.standrewapostle.org/ Susan M. Sheehan, Prin.; Stds.: 383; Lay Tchrs.: 32

Mision San Andres - 12247 Georgia Ave., Silver Spring, MD 20902 t) 301-202-9496 sacerdote@misionsanandres.org

St. Bernadette - 70 University Blvd., E., Silver Spring, MD 20901 t) 301-593-0357 parish@stbernadetteschurch.org silverspringcatholic.com Rev. Msgr. K. Bartholomew Smith, Pst.; Rev. Michael P. Novajosky, In Res.; Rev. Peter Santandreu, In Res.; CRP Stds.: 102

St. Camillus - 1600 St. Camillus Dr., Silver Spring, MD 20903 t) 301-434-8400; 301-434-2111 (CRP) faithformation@stcamilluschurch.org stcamilluschurch.org Rev. Jean-Marie Kabango, O.F.M., Assoc. Pst.; Dcn. Peter Barbernitz; William Pineda, DRE;

St. Francis International School - (Grades K-8) 1500 St. Camillus Dr., Silver Spring, MD 20903 t) 301-434-2344 tharkleroad@sfismd.org www.saintfrancisinternational.org Tobias A. Harkleroad, Prin.;

Catholic Community of Langley Park - 1408 Merrimac Dr., Langley Park, MD 20787 t) 301-328-5105

Christ the King - 2300 East-West Hwy., Silver Spring, MD 20910 t) 301-495-2306 Rev. Rodolfo A. Salinas, Admin.; Dcn. Stephen Mitchell;

St. John the Baptist - 12319 New Hampshire Ave., Silver Spring, MD 20904 t) 301-622-1122 dre@sjbssparish.org; secretary@sjbssparish.org www.sjbssparish.org Rev. Y. David Brault, Pst.; Rev. Nathanael Peter Anderson, Assoc. Pst.; Dcn. Edward J. McCormack; Dcn. James J. Gorman;

St. John the Baptist School - (Grades PreK-8) t) 301-622-3076 brian.blomquist@sjbsilverspring.org www.sjbsilverspring.org/school Brian Blomquist, Prin.;

St. John the Evangelist - 10103 Georgia Ave., Silver

Spring, MD 20902 t) 301-681-7663; 301-681-7634 (CRP) hardingr@sjeparish.org; office@sjeparish.org www.sjeparish.org Rev. Joseph A. Calis, Pst.; Rev. Jan Pietryga, Par. Vicar; Dcn. Alan Jeeves; Sr. Roberta Harding, I.H.M., DRE;

St. John the Evangelist School - 10201 Woodland Dr., Silver Spring, MD 20902 t) 301-681-7656 office@sjte.org www.sjte.org Margaret Durney, Prin.;

St. Michael - 824 Pershing Dr., Silver Spring, MD 20910 t) 301-589-1155; 301-587-2395 (CRP) stmichaelreled@yahoo.com Rev. Msgr. Eddie E. Tolentino, Pst.; Rev. Alberto Biondi, Assoc. Pst.; Rev. Saulo S. Vicente, Assoc. Pst.; Dcn. Ronald Ealey, Dir.; Dcn. Stephen B. Frye; Dcn. Carlos E. Hernandez;

Our Lady of Grace - 15661 Norbeck Blvd., Silver Spring, MD 20906 Rev. James D. Boccabella, Pst.; Rev. Michael Murray, In Res.; Dcn. William J. Heineman;

Our Lady of Vietnam - 11812 New Hampshire Ave., Silver Spring, MD 20904 t) 301-622-4895 info@olvn-dc.org www.olvn-dc.org Rev. Paul Tam X. Tran, Pst.; Dcn. Nguyen Thanh Nguyen;

Our Lady Queen of Poland and Saint Maximilian Kolbe - 9700 Rosensteel Ave., Silver Spring, MD 20910 t) 301-589-1857 Rev. Jan Fiedurek, T.Chr, Pst.;

SOLOMONS

Our Lady Star of the Sea - 50 Alexander Ln., Solomons, MD 20688; Mailing: P.O. Box 560, Solomons, MD 20688 t) 410-326-3535 olstar-sea.md@adw.org; youthministry@olss.org Rev. Msgr. Michael Wilson, Pst.; Dcn. Anton J. Geisz; Dcn. Chad Martin; Joanne Pensenstadler, DRE;

Our Lady Star of the Sea School - (Grades PreK-8) 90 Alexander Ln., Solomons, MD 20688 t) 410-326-3171 olssschool@comcast.net Mary Bartsch, Prin.;

ST. INIGOES

St. Peter Claver - ; Mailing: P.O. Box 240, St. Inigoes, MD 20684 t) 301-872-5460 Rev. Scott Woods, Pst.;

ST. MARY'S CITY

St. Cecilia - 47950 Mattapany Rd., St. Mary's City, MD 20686; Mailing: P.O. Box 429, St. Mary's City, MD 20686 t) 301-862-4600 stcecilia@md.metrocast.net Rev. Lawrence C. Swink, Pst.;

SUITLAND

St. Bernardine of Siena - 2400 Brooks Dr., Suitland, MD 20746-1101 t) 301-736-0707 www.stbernardineparish.com Rev. Jose Raul DeLeon, In Res.;

TAKOMA PARK

Our Lady of Sorrows - 1006 Larch Ave., Takoma Park, MD 20912 t) 301-891-3500; 301-891-2033 (CRP) Rev. Raymond J. Wadas, Pst.; Rev. Mario A. Majano, Assoc. Pst.; Dcn. Patrick L. Brown; Dcn. Trinidad Soc;

UPPER MARLBORO

Saint Mary of the Assumption - 14908 Main St., Upper Marlboro, MD 20772 t) 301-627-3255 parish@stmaryum.org www.stmaryum.org Rev. Thomas G. LaHood, Pst.; Dcn. Frank Klco; Dcn. Thomas Molineaux; Shirley Byrd, DRE; Regina Piazza, DRE;

Saint Mary of the Assumption School - (Grades PreK-8) 4610 Largo Rd., Upper Marlboro, MD 20772 t) 301-627-4170 tcampbell@stmaryum.org Steven Showalter, Prin.;

Most Holy Rosary - 11704 Duley Station Rd., Upper Marlboro, MD 20772 t) 301-856-3880 mostholyrosary@outlook.com mostholyrosarychur.wixsite.com/website Rev. Rodolfo A. Salinas, Pst.;

VALLEY LEE

St. George - 19199 St. George Church Rd., Valley Lee, MD 20692 t) 301-994-0607; 301-994-0737 (CRP) secretary@stgeorgercc.org; kim.browne@stgeorgercc.org www.stgeorgercc.org Rev. Paul Dean Nguyen, Pst.; Dcn. Joel P. Carpenter; Kimberley Browne, DRE;

St. George's Island, St. Francis Xavier - 16370 Thomas Rd., Piney Point, MD 20674; Mailing: 19199 St. George's Church Rd., Valley Lee, MD 20692

WALDORF

Our Lady Help of Christians - 100 Village St., Waldorf, MD 20602-2183 t) 301-645-7112 olhc@verizon.net www.olhoc.org Rev. Alain Colliou, Pst.; Rev. Jan Pietryga, Par. Vicar; Dcn. Richard F. Dubicki; Dcn. William T. Scott; Sr. Rosario A. Salazar, M.C.S.T., CRE;

St. Peter - 3320 St. Peter's Dr., Waldorf, MD 20601 t) 301-843-8916 parishsecretary@stpeterswaldorf.org Dcn. Robert L. Martin; Rev. Keith A. Woods, Pst.; Rev. Msgr. Oliver W. McGready, In Res.; Alice Culbreth, DRE;

St. Peter School - 3310 St. Peter's Dr., Waldorf, MD 20601 t) 301-843-1955 J.R. West, Prin.;

WHEATON

St. Catherine Laboure - 11801 Claridge Rd., Wheaton, MD 20902 t) 301-946-3636; 301-946-3010 (CRP); 301-946-1606 (CRP) sclredirector@gmail.com Rev. Francisco E. Aguirre, Pst.; Rev. Alberto Biondi, Par. Vicar; Dcn. Raymond L. Chaput; Dcn. Rafael G. Pagan; Dcn. G. Stephane Philogene; Dcn. Bartolo Serafini;

SCHOOLS: PRESCHOOL THRU HIGH SCHOOL

SCHOOLS

DISTRICT OF COLUMBIA

WASHINGTON

***The Washington School for Girls** - (PRV) 1901 Mississippi Ave., S.E., Ste. 203, Washington, DC 20020 t) 202-678-1113 breaves@wsgdc.org; srockwell@wsgdc.org www.washingtonschoolforgirls.org All-scholarship independent Catholic school. Beth Reaves, Pres.;

STATE OF MARYLAND

BETHESDA

The Woods Academy - (PRV) 6801 Greentree Rd., Bethesda, MD 20817 t) 301-365-3080 jpowers@woodsacademy.org www.woodsacademy.org Katya Pilong, Librn.;

DARNESTOWN

Mary of Nazareth Roman Catholic Elementary School - (DIO) (Grades PreK-8) 14131 Seneca Rd., Darnestown, MD 20874 t) 301-869-0940 mfriel@maryofnazareth.org; mwray@maryofnazareth.org www.maryofnazareth.org Michael J. Friel, Prin.; Dr. Raymond Fecteau, Canonical Admin.;

GAITHERSBURG

Emmanuel, Inc (Mother of God School) - (PRV) (Grades PreK-8) 20501 Goshen Rd., Gaithersburg, MD 20879 t) 301-990-2088 mog@mogschool.com www.mogschool.com Authentically Catholic and academically excellent, forming students and families to bear the light of Christ to the world. Melissa Sloan, Prin.; William Hall Miller, Pres.; Stds.: 246; Lay Tchrs.: 20

POTOMAC

The Heights School - (PRV) 10400 Seven Locks Rd., Potomac, MD 20854 t) 301-365-4300 adevicente@heights.edu www.heights.edu Private, Independent, Spiritual Formation and Religious Education provided by the Prelature of Opus Dei. Rev. Diego Daza, Chap.; Joseph Cardenas, Dean; James Nelson, Librn.;

HIGH SCHOOLS

DISTRICT OF COLUMBIA

WASHINGTON

St. Anselm's Abbey School, Inc - (PRV) (Grades 6-12) 4501 S. Dakota Ave., N.E., Washington, DC 20017-2795 t) 202-269-2350 jcorrigan@saintanselms.org www.saintanselms.org College preparatory. Separate subsidiary corporation of The Benedictine Foundation at Washington, DC (St. Anselm's Abbey). Rev. Anthony E. Giampietro, C.S.B., Pres.; John Corrigan, Headmaster; Rev. Samuel Springuel, O.S.B., Chap.; Stds.: 233; Pr. Tchrs.: 3; Lay Tchrs.: 55

Archbishop Carroll High School - (PAR) 4300 Harewood Rd., N.E., Washington, DC 20017 t) 202-529-0900 ipuryear@achsdc.org www.achsdc.org (Coed) Rev. Jordan Kelly, O.S.P.; Rev. John Mudd; Elana Gilmore, Prin.; Larry Savoy, Pres.;

Georgetown Visitation Preparatory School, Inc. - (PRV) (Grades 9-12) 1524 35th St., N.W., Washington, DC 20007 t) 202-337-3350 barbara.edmondson@visi.org www.visi.org Leonor Ponzio, Prin.; Barbara Edmondson, Headmaster; Elizabeth Burke, Librn.; Stds.: 508; Lay Tchrs.: 75

Gonzaga College High School - (PRV) 19 Eye St., N.W., Washington, DC 20001 t) 202-336-7100 info@gonzaga.org www.gonzaga.org Society of Jesus, Maryland Province. Rev. Stephen W. Planning, S.J., Pres.; Thomas K. Every II, Headmaster; Rev. Gasper F. LoBiondo, S.J., In Res.; Rev. Gerald V. O'Connor, S.J., In Res.;

St. John's College High School, Brothers of the Christian Schools - (PRV) (Grades 9-12) 2607 Military Rd., N.W., Washington, DC 20015 t) 202-363-2316 stjohnschs@stjohnschs.org stjohnschs.org Christopher Themistos, Prin.; Jeffrey Mancabelli, Pres.;

***San Miguel School** - (PRV) 7705 Georgia Ave., N.W., Washington, DC 20012 t) 202-232-8345 Bro. Francis Eells, F.S.C., Prin.; Martha W. Kendall, Exec.;

STATE OF MARYLAND

BETHESDA

Mater Dei School, Inc. - (PRV) 9600 Seven Locks Rd., Bethesda, MD 20817 t) 301-365-2700; 301-365-2701 Edward N. Williams, Headmaster; Christopher S. Abell, Pres.;

Stone Ridge School of the Sacred Heart - (PRV) 9101 Rockville Pike, Bethesda, MD 20814 t) 301-657-4322 ckarrels@stoneridgeschool.org www.stoneridgeschool.org Religious of the Sacred Heart. Carla Bosco, Librn.;

BLADENSBURG

Elizabeth Seton High School - (PRV) 5715 Emerson St., Bladensburg, MD 20710-1844 t) 301-864-4532 lgrillo@setonhs.org www.setonhs.org Lisa Grillo, Pres.; Vanessa Cooke, Prin.; Nancy Hernick, Dir.; Stds.: 528; Scholastics: 34; Lay Tchrs.: 40

FORESTVILLE

Bishop McNamara High School - (PRV) (Grades 9-12) 6800 Marlboro Pike, Forestville, MD 20747 t) 301-735-8401 john.barnhardt@bmhs.org www.bmhs.org (Coed) Congregation of Holy Cross. Dr. John Barnhardt, Pres.; Dian Carter, Prin.; Stds.: 867; Bro. Tchrs.: 1; Lay Tchrs.: 79

HYATTSVILLE

DeMatha Catholic High School - (PRV) (Grades 9-12) 4313 Madison St., Hyattsville, MD 20781 t) 240-764-2200 tpaolucci@dematha.org; mkerley@dematha.org www.dematha.org Boys. Conducted by the Order of the Most Holy Trinity, Province of the Immaculate Heart of Mary. Daniel J. McMahon, Prin.; Rev. James R. Day, O.SS.T., Pres.;

KENSINGTON

The Academy of the Holy Cross, Inc. - (PRV) (Grades 9-12) 4920 Strathmore Ave., Kensington, MD 20895 t) 301-942-2100 schooloffice@academyoftheholycross.org academyoftheholycross.org John Sullivan, Prin.; Kathleen Ryan Prebble, Pres.; Stds.: 400; Lay Tchrs.: 34

LAUREL

St. Vincent Pallotti High School - (PRV) 113 St. Mary's Pl., Laurel, MD 20707 t) 301-725-3228 admissions@pallottihs.org www.pallottihs.org Pallottine Missionary Sisters of the Catholic Apostolate. Jeffrey A. Palumbo, Pres.;

LEONARDTOWN

St. Mary's Ryken High School - (PRV) (Grades 9-12) 22600 Camp Calvert Rd., Leonardtown, MD 20650 t) 301-475-2814 rwood@smrhs.org www.smrhs.org Sponsored by the Xaverian Brothers. Catherine Bowes, Prin.; Rick Wood, Pres.; Stds.: 641; Lay Tchrs.: 64

NORTH BETHESDA

Georgetown Preparatory School - (PRV) (Grades 9-12) 10900 Rockville Pike, North Bethesda, MD 20852 t) 301-493-5000 www.gprep.org Jesuit Community; Society of Jesus. Rev. James Van Dyke, SJ, Pres.; Rev. David A. Sauter, S.J., Supr.; John Glennon, Headmaster; Stds.: 496; Lay Tchrs.: 57

OLNEY

Our Lady of Good Counsel High School - (PRV) (Grades 9-12) 17301 Old Vic Blvd., Olney, MD 20832 t) 240-283-3200 tcampbell@olgchs.org olgchs.org Xaverian Brothers sponsored high school Rev. Thomas Lavin, O.F.M., Chap.; Thomas Campbell, Prin.; Amelia Davis, Librn.; Stefanie Morgan-Davis, CFO; Stds.: 1,280; Pr. Tchrs.: 1; Lay Tchrs.: 117

POTOMAC

Connelly School of the Holy Child - (PRV) (Grades 6-12) 9029 Bradley Blvd., Potomac, MD 20854 t) 301-365-0955 www.holychild.org College Preparatory for Girls. Sisters of the Holy Child Jesus. Julie Burke, Dean; Shannon Gomez, Headmaster; Claire Drummond, Librn.;

TAKOMA PARK

Don Bosco Cristo Rey High School of the Archdiocese of Washington - 1010 Larch Ave., Takoma Park, MD 29012; Mailing: P.O. Box 56481, Washington, DC 20040-6481 t) 301-891-4750 eblanco@dbcr.org www.dbcr.org Elias Blanco, Prin.; Mark K Shriver, Pres.;

INSTITUTIONS LOCATED IN DIOCESE

ASSOCIATIONS [ASN]

FORT WASHINGTON

Archdiocesan Association of Ladies of Charity - 12706 Parkton St., Fort Washington, MD 20744; Mailing: P.O. Box 10038, Washington, DC 20018 t) 301-292-9315 Individual charity work; supports various other agencies, food banks, child care centers and pregnancy aid centers. Viola Johnson-Robinson, Pres.;

WASHINGTON

Association of Catholic Colleges and Universities - One Dupont Cir. N.W., Ste. 650, Washington, DC 20036 t) 202-457-0650 accu@accunet.org www.accunet.org Rev. Dennis H. Holtschneider, CM, Pres.;

Association of Jesuit Colleges and Universities - One Dupont Cir., N.W., Ste. 405, Washington, DC 20036 t) 202-862-9893 info@ajcunet.edu www.ajcunet.edu National voluntary organization that serves its member institutions and associate members. Rev. Michael Garanzini, S.J., Pres.;

The Catholic Biblical Association of America - 431 Caldwell Hall, 620 Michigan Ave., NE, Washington, DC 20064 t) 202-319-5519 cba-office@cua.edu www.catholicbiblical.org Archie T. Wright, Dir.;

Roundtable Association of Catholic Diocesan Social Action Directors - ; Mailing: P.O. Box 96503, #81001, Washington, DC 20090 t) 202-854-8806 coordinator@catholicroundtable.org www.catholicroundtable.org Kevin Fitzpatrick, Chair;

Sovereign Military Order of Malta-Federal Association - 1730 M St., N.W., Ste. 403, Washington, DC 20036 t) 202-331-2494 info@orderofmalta-federal.org www.orderofmaltafederal.org Dcn. Michael J. Stankewicz, Exec.;

CAMPUS MINISTRY / NEWMAN CENTERS [CAM]

WASHINGTON

Archdiocesan Campus Ministry - Kay Spiritual Life Center, 4400 Massachusetts Ave., N.W., Washington, DC 20016-8010

American University Catholic Community - t) 202-885-3327 Rev. Ivan Pertine, Chap.; Rev. Joseph Piper, Chap.;

Gallaudet University Catholic Community - 800 Florida Ave., N.E., Washington, DC 20002 t) (301) 200-5430 (VP) Rev. Min Seo Park, Chap.;

Gallaudet University Catholic Community - 7202 Buchanan St., Landover Hills, MD 20784 t) 301-459-7467; 301-459-7464

George Washington University Newman Center - 2210 F St., N.W., Washington, DC 20037 t) 202-676-6855 www.gwcatholics.org Rev. Benjamin Petty, Chap.; Rachel Grabowski, Campus Min.;

Howard University Newman Center - 818 Newman Center, Washington, DC 20059 t) (202) 238-2447 Rev. Robert P. Boxie III, Chap.;

St. Mary's College Campus Ministry - 47950 Mattapany Rd., St. Mary's City, MD 20686; Mailing: P.O. Box 429, St. Mary's City, MD 20686 t) 301-862-4600 Maryrose Depperschmidt, Campus Min.; Rev. Larry Swink, Chap.;

University of Maryland Catholic Student Center - 4141 Guilford Dr., College Park, MD 20740 t) 301-864-6223 catholicterps@catholicterps.org www.catholicterps.org Rev. Conrad Murphy; Matthew Aujero, Campus Min.; MJ Richard, Campus Min.; Ann Gradowski, Admin.;

CATHOLIC CHARITIES [CCH]

LANDOVER

SHARE Food Network - 3222 Hubbard Rd., Landover, MD 20785-2005 t) 301-864-3115 jaynee.acevedo@cc-dc.org Jaynee Acevedo, Dir.;

ROCKVILLE

Rollingcrest Commons, Inc. - 11400 Rockville Pike, Rockville, MD 20852 t) 301-493-6000 info@victoryhousing.org Leila Finucane, Pres.;

WASHINGTON

Catholic Charities of the Archdiocese of Washington, Inc. - 924 G St., N.W., Washington, DC 20001 t) 202-772-4300 john.enzler@cc-dc.org catholiccharitiesdc.org Rev. Msgr. John Enzler, Pres.;

Anchor Mental Health Association/Division of Adult and Family Clinical Services - 1001 Lawrence St., N.E., Washington, DC 20017; Mailing: P.O. Box 29058, Washington, DC 20017 t) 202-635-5940 denise.capaci@cc-dc.org www.catholiccharitiesdc.org

CCS Housing, Inc. -

Division of Catholic Charities Enterprises, Employment and Education - 1001 Lawrence St., N.E., Anacostia, Washington, DC 20017 t) 202-635-5970 scott.lewis@cc-dc.org Scott Lewis, Contact;

Division of Children's Services - lovannia.dofat-avent@cc-dc.org www.catholiccharitiesdc.org Lovannia Dofat-Avent, Contact;

Division of Housing and Support Service - 1001 Lawrence St., N.E., Anacostia, Washington, DC 20017 t) 202-481-1435 amanda.chesney@cc-dc.org www.catholiccharitiesdc.org Amanda Chesney, Dir.;

Montgomery County Family Center - 12247 Georgia Ave., Silver Spring, MD 20902 t) 301-933-3164 faye.frempong@cc-dc.org Faye Frempong, Contact;

Southeast Family Center - 220 Highview Pl., S.E., Washington, DC 20032 t) 202-574-3442 peggy.lawrence@cc-dc.org Peggy Lawrence, Contact;

The Catholic Charities Foundation of the Archdiocese of Washington - Tara Arras, Exec.;

CEMETERIES [CEM]

CLINTON

Resurrection Cemetery - 8000 Woodyard Rd., Clinton, MD 20735; Mailing: P.O. Box 151, Clinton, MD 20735 t) 301-868-5141 res@ccaw.org www.ccaw.org Marcus Robinson, Bus. Mgr.;

GERMANTOWN

All Souls Cemetery - 11401 Brink Rd., Germantown, MD 20876 t) 301-428-1995 asc@ccaw.org www.ccaw.org Andrew Gauvin, Bus. Mgr.;

MECHANICSVILLE

St. Mary's Queen of Peace Cemetery - 38888 Dr. Johnson Rd., Mechanicsville, MD 20659; Mailing: P.O. Box 497, Mechanicsville, MD 20659 t) 301-475-5005 qop1@ccaw.org www.ccaw.org Juli A. Tolson, Bus. Mgr.;

SILVER SPRING

The Catholic Cemeteries of the Archdiocese of Washington, Inc. - 13801 Georgia Ave., Silver Spring, MD 20906 t) 301-871-1300 llm@ccaw.org www.ccaw.org Lilliam L Machado, Pres. & CEO;

Gate of Heaven Cemetery - 13801 Georgia Ave., Silver Spring, MD 20906 t) 301-871-6500 goh@ccaw.org www.ccaw.org Melissa Baughman, Bus. Mgr.;

WASHINGTON

Mount Olivet Cemetery & St. Mary's Cemetery - 1300 Bladensburg Rd., N.E., Washington, DC 20002 t) 202-399-3000 mto@ccaw.org www.ccaw.org Cheryl Tyiska, Bus. Mgr.;

COLLEGES & UNIVERSITIES [COL]

WASHINGTON

***Catholic University of America, The** - Nugent Hall/ Executive Offices, 620 Michigan Ave., N.E., Washington, DC 20064 t) 202-319-5000 webmaster@cua.edu www.catholic.edu His Eminence Wilton Cardinal Gregory, Chancellor; His Eminence Blase J. Cupich, Trustee; His Eminence Daniel N. DiNardo, Trustee; His Eminence Timothy Cardinal Dolan, Trustee; His Eminence Sean Cardinal O'Malley, O.F.M.Cap., Trustee; His Eminence Joseph Tobin, C.Ss.R., Trustee; Most Rev. Samuel J. Aquila, Trustee; Most Rev. John O. Barres, Trustee; Most Rev. Michael F. Burbidge, Trustee; Most Rev. Daniel E. Flores, Trustee; Most Rev. Jose H. Gomez, Trustee; Most Rev. Joseph E. Kurtz, Trustee; Most Rev. William E. Lori, Trustee; Rev. Msgr. Michael G. Clay, Prof.; Rev. Msgr. Kevin W. Irwin, Prof.; Rev. Msgr. Ronny E. Jenkins, Dean; Rev. Msgr. Stephen J. Rossetti, Prof.; Rev. Msgr. Robert S. Sokolowski, Prof.; Rev. Msgr. Walter R. Rossi, Trustee; Rev. Msgr. Peter J. Vaghi, Trustee; Rev. Msgr. John Wippel, Prof.; Rev. Stefanos Alexopoulos, Prof.; Rev. Regis Armstrong, O.F.M.Cap., Emer. Prof.; Rev. John P. Beal, Prof.; Rev. Christopher T. Begg, Prof.; Rev. James Brent, O.P., Prof.; Rev. Ignacio de Ribera Martin, D.C.J.M., Prof.; Rev. Jude DeAngelo, O.F.M.Conv., Chap.; Rev. John P. Galvin, Prof.; Rev. John P. Heil, S.S.D., Prof.; Rev. Nicholas E. Lombardo, O.P., Prof.; Rev. Gerald D. McBrearity, P.S.S., Rector; Rev. Mark Morozowich, S.E.O.D., Dean; Rev. Raymond C. O'Brien, Prof.; Rev. Dominic F. Serra, Prof.; Rev. Raymond Studzinski, O.S.B., Prof.; Rev. Paul Sullins, Prof.; Rev. David D. Thayer, P.S.S., Lecturer; Rev. Michael G. Witczak, Prof.; John H. Garvey, Pres.;

***Georgetown University** - 37th and O Sts., N.W., Washington, DC 20057 t) 202-687-0100 gucomm@georgetown.edu www.georgetown.edu John J. DeGioia, Pres.; Rev. Matthew E. Carnes, S.J.; Rev. Drew Christiansen, S.J.; Rev. David J. Collins, S.J.; Rev. Christopher J. Duffy, S.J.; Rev. James F. Duffy, S.J.; Rev. Stephen M. Fields, S.J.; Rev. Kevin T. FitzGerald, S.J.; Rev. David Hollenbach, S.J.; Rev. John P. Langan, S.J.; Rev. Joseph E. Lingan, S.J.; Rev. Daniel A. Madigan, S.J. (Australia); Rev. William C. McFadden, S.J.; Rev. Dennis L. McNamara, S.J.; Rev. G. Ronald Murphy, S.J.; Rev. John W. O'Malley, S.J.; Rev. Ladislas Orsy, S.J.; Rev. Paul K. Rourke, S.J.; Rev. Christopher W. Steck, S.J.;

Edmund A. Walsh School of Foreign Service - Joel Hellman, Dean;

Georgetown College - Chester Gillis, Dean;
Graduate School of Arts & Sciences - Norberto M. Graywacz, Dean;
Joseph Mark Lauinger Library - Artemis G. Kirk, Librn.;
Law Center - 600 New Jersey Ave., N.W., Washington, DC 20001 William M. Treanor, Vice Pres., Dean of the Law Center & Prof. of Law;
McCourt School of Public Policy - 37th St. & O St., N.W., Washington, DC 20057 Edward Montgomery, Dean;
Office of Advancement - 2115 Wisconsin Ave., N.W., Ste. 500, Washington, DC 20057 t) 202-687-4111
Office of Institutional Diversity, Equity & Affirmative Action - 37th St. & O St., N.W., Washington, DC 20057 t) 202-687-4798
Robert Emmett McDonough School of Business - Rohan Williamson, Dean;
School of Continuing Studies - Kelly J. Otter, Dean;
School of Medicine - 3900 Reservoir Rd., N.W., Washington, DC 20007 Edward B. Healton, Exec Vice Pres., Health Sciences & Exec. Dean, School of Medicine;
School of Nursing & Health Studies - 3700 Reservoir Rd., N.W., Washington, DC 20007 Patricia Cloonan, Dean;
Trinity College - 125 Michigan Ave., N.E., Washington, DC 20017 t) 202-884-9000 pauleya@trinitydc.edu www.trinitydc.edu Sisters of Notre Dame de Namur. Patricia A. McGuire, Pres.; Robert Preston, Vice Pres. Academic Affairs;

CONVENTS, MONASTERIES, AND RESIDENCES FOR WOMEN [CON]

ANACOSTIA
Missionaries of Charity (Contemplatives) - 1244 V St., S.E., Anacostia, DC 20020-7016 t) 202-889-6100 Sr. M. Dorothy Bly, M.C., Supr.;
CLINTON
The Missionary Catechists of St. Therese of the Infant Jesus, Inc. - 8914 Old Branch Ave., Clinton, MD 20735 t) 301-839-7751 mcstusa@yahoo.com Sr. Helen B. Sumander, M.C.S.T., Pres.;
Religious Sisters of Mercy of Alma, MI - 6100 Wolverton Ln., Clinton, MD 20735 t) 301-297-5617 saintandrews@rsmofalma.org www.rsmofalma.org St. Andrew Home of Mercy Sr. Mary Christine Cremin, Contact;
HYATTSVILLE
Sisters of St. Francis of the Neumann Communities - 3916 Queensbury Rd., Hyattsville, MD 20782 t) 240-603-9933; 301-779-1642 jebert@sosf.org www.sosf.org Sr. Marie Joette Ebert, O.S.F., Contact;
KENSINGTON
Congregation of the Sisters of the Holy Cross - St. Angela Hall, 4910 Strathmore Ave., Kensington, MD 20895 t) 574-284-5625 rkeck@cscsisters.org Sisters of the Holy Cross, Inc. Sr. Kathleen Moroney, C.S.C., Treas.;
LA PLATA
Discalced Carmelites of Maryland, Inc. - 5678 Mt. Carmel Rd., La Plata, MD 20646-3625 t) 301-934-1654 purchases@carmelofporttobacco.com; contact@carmelofporttobacco.com www.carmelofporttobacco.com Sr. Virginia O'Connor, Prioress; Sr. Marie Penland, Treas.;
LAUREL
Pallotti Convent - 404 Eighth St., Laurel, MD 20707 t) 301-725-1717 Sr. Bernadette Peterson, S.A.C., Supr.; Sr. M. Karen Lester, S.A.C., Dir.;
POTOMAC
Little Sisters of the Holy Family - 13529 Magruder Farm Ct., Potomac, MD 20854 t) 301-947-1955 Sr. Domina Son, L.S.H.F., Supr.;
RIVERDALE
Carmelite Sister of Charity - Vedruna - 5410 56th Pl., #101, Riverdale, MD 20737 t) 301-277-2963 maureenfoltz@hotmail.com www.vedruna.org Sr. Maureen Foltz, C.C.V., Admin.;
SILVER SPRING
The Daughters of Mary Immaculate, Inc. - 13004 Marlow Farm Dr., Silver Spring, MD 20904 t) 301-288-7663 thuyliendmi@gmail.com Sr. Thuy-Lien Doan, Pres.; Srs.: 5
Sisters of Charity of St. Charles Borromeo - 11320 Classical Ln., Silver Spring, MD 20901 t) 301-681-9665
Sisters of Mercy of the Americas - Institute Administrative Offices - 8403 Colesville Rd., Ste. 400, Silver Spring, MD 20910 t) 301-587-0423 www.sistersofmercy.org Legal Holdings: Sisters of Mercy of the Americas, Inc., Mercy Ministry Cor; Sisters of Mercy Operating Trust, Sisters of Mercy Fund for Ministry. Sr. Patricia McDermott, R.S.M., Pres.; Sr. Pat Flynn, RSM, Vice. Pres.; Srs.: 2,044
Sisters of the Good Shepherd - 504 Hexton Hill Rd., Silver Spring, MD 20904-3300 c) (314) 397-9436 (Antonia M. Ponder) www.sistersofthegoodshepherd.com Antonia Ponder, COO; Srs.: 3
Sisters of the Holy Names (S.N.J.M.) - 9603 Flower Ave., Silver Spring, MD 20901 t) 301-587-1717 kksnjm@gmail.com www.snjmusontario.org
Sisters of the Holy Names - 519 Varnum St., N.W., Washington, DC 20011 t) 202-829-8671
Sisters of the Holy Names - 9212 Glenville Rd., Silver Spring, MD 20901 t) 301-445-0309
Sisters of the Holy Names - 3200 39th St., N.W., Washington, DC 20016 t) 202-362-1464
Sisters of the Holy Names - 12007 Bernard Dr., Silver Spring, MD 20902 t) 301-942-0701
UPPER MARLBORO
***SSVM Missions, Inc.** - 1714 Crain Hwy., Upper Marlboro, MD 20774 t) 301-627-5337 nov.kateritekakwitha@servidoras.org Sr. Mary Mother of the Crucified, S.S.V.M., Novitiate Supr.;
WASHINGTON
Carmelite Sisters of Charity, Vedruna - 1222 Monroe St., N.E., Washington, DC 20017 t) 202-832-2114 maureenfoltz@hotmail.com; carmenmsoto@hotmail.com www.vedruna.org Sr. Maureen Foltz, C.C.V., Admin.; Sr. Carmen M Soto, ccv, Supr.; Sr. Maria Dolores Mairlot, C.C.V., Secy.; Delfina Castro, Treas.; Srs.: 5
St. Cecilia Congregation - 721 Lawrence St., N.E., Washington, DC 20017 t) 202-525-2223 Sr. Mary Juliana Cox, O.P., Supr.;
Franciscan Sisters of Atonement - 4000 Harewood Rd., N.E., Washington, DC 20017 t) 202-529-1111 washretreat@juno.com www.graymoor.org Sr. Josephine Dullaghan, Dir.;
Georgetown Visitation Monastery - 1500 35th St., N.W., Washington, DC 20007 t) (202) 558-7975 mary.siegel@visi.org www.gvmonastery.org Mother Anne Francis Ng'ang'a, Supr.; Srs.: 13
Institute of Our Lady of Mount Carmel - 4415 8th St., N.E., Washington, DC 20017 t) 202-526-5106
Missionaries of Charity - 3310 Wheeler Rd., S.E., Washington, DC 20032 t) 202-562-6890 Sr. Mary Clovis, M.C., Supr.;
Missionaries of Charity, Gift of Peace Convent - 2800 Otis St., N.E., Washington, DC 20018 t) 202-269-3313 Sr. M. Lisseria, M.C., Supr.;
North American Delegation, Carmelites of Charity, Vedruna - 1222 Monroe St., N.E., Washington, DC 20017 t) 301-277-2963; 202-832-2114 maureenfoltz@hotmail.com; carmenmsoto@hotmail.com www.vedruna.org Sr. Maureen Foltz, C.C.V., Admin.;
Oblates Sisters of the Most Holy Eucharist - 2907 Ellicott Ter., N.W., Washington, DC 20008 t) 202-244-7714 oblatesdc@hotmail.com Sr. Margarita Jaime, O.S.S.E., Supr.;
Poor Clares of Perpetual Adoration - 1150 Varnum St., N.E., Washington, DC 20017-2699 t) 202-526-6808 ourprayer4u@poorclareswdc.org www.poorclareswdc.org Cloistered Monastery of Perpetual Adoration.
Religious of Jesus and Mary, Inc. - 821 Varnum St., N.E., Washington, DC 20017-2144 t) 202-526-3203 Sr. Margaret Perron, R.J.M., Pres.; Sr. Anne Magner, Secy.; Srs.: 57
Religious of Jesus and Mary - 6709 41st Ave., University Park, MD 20782 t) 301-779-0662
Religious of Jesus and Mary - 4602 Clemson Rd., College Park, MD 20740 t) 301-699-3931 Sr. Rita Ricker, RJM, Treas.;
Religious of Jesus and Mary - 3521 13th St., N.W., Washington, DC 20010 t) 202-265-8812 Sr. Mary Bourdon, RJM, Treas.;
Religious of the Sacred Heart - 1215 Perry St., N.E., Washington, DC 20017 t) 202-832-0071 Oakview Community. Sr. Fleisa Garcia, Contact;
Rosary House of Studies-Dominican Sisters of The Presentation - 1201 Monroe St., N.E., Washington, DC 20017 t) 202-529-1768 rosaryhouseop@gmail.com
***Servants of the Lord and Virgin of Matara, Inc.** - 28 15th St., S.E., Washington, DC 20003 t) 202-543-2064 m.immaculate@servidoras.org www.ssvmusa.org Mother Mary of the Immaculate Conception, SSVM, Prov.;
Sisters of the Holy Child Jesus - 1033 Newton St., N.E., Washington, DC 20017 t) 202-526-6832 www.shcj.org Novitiate Community Carroll Juliano, Prov.; Srs.: 4
WASHINGTON D
Lovers of the Holy Cross of Hanoi, Inc. - ; Mailing: P.O. Box 32004, Washington, DC 20007 t) 832-758-7096 lhchnhk@gmail.com Sr. Thu Thi Do, L.H.C., Supr.;

ENDOWMENTS / FOUNDATIONS / TRUSTS [EFT]

BELTSVILLE
The Bethlehem University Foundation, Inc. - 6001 Ammendale Rd., Ste. 200, Beltsville, MD 20705; Mailing: P.O. Box 555, Beltsville, MD 20704-0355 t) 240-241-4381 info@bufusa.org bufusa.org John L Schlageter, Exec.;
HYATTSVILLE
St. Ann's Donor Trust - 4901 Eastern Ave., Hyattsville, MD 20782 t) 301-559-5500 srmaryb@stanns.org Sr. Mary Bader, D.C., CEO;
Catholic Education Foundation of the Archdiocese of Washington, Inc. - 5001 Eastern Ave., N.E., Hyattsville, MD 20782
MOUNT RAINIER
IVE Real Estate Trust - 3706 Rhode Island Ave., Mount Rainier, MD 20712 t) 347-491-8123 prov.immaculate.conception@ive.org Rev. Alberto Barattero, Pres.;
ROCKVILLE
Rosaria Communities Foundation, Inc. - 15400 Calhoun Dr., Ste. 125, Rockville, MD 20855 t) 301-279-2020
SILVER SPRING
***St. Luke Institute Foundation** - 8380 Colesville Rd., Ste. 300, Silver Spring, MD 20910-6264 t) 301-445-7970 getinfo@sli.org Rev. David Songy, O.F.M.Cap., Pres.;
Sisters of Mercy Fund for Infirmed, Disabled, or Elderly Sisters Trust - 8403 Colesville Rd., Ste. 400, Silver Spring, MD 20910 t) 301-587-0423 Sr. Judith Frikker, RSM, Trustee;
Sisters of Mercy Fund for Ministry Trust - 8403 Colesville Rd., Ste. 400, Silver Spring, MD 20910 t) 301-587-0423 Sr. Anne Marie Miller, RSM, Trustee;
Sisters of Mercy Operating Trust - 8403 Colesville Rd., Ste. 400, Silver Spring, MD 20910 t) 301-587-0423 Sr. Patricia McDermott, R.S.M., Trustee;
Sisters of Mercy Real Estate Trust - 8403 Colesville Rd., Ste. 400, Silver Spring, MD 20910 t) (301) 587-0423 Sr. Aine O'Connor, RSM, Trustee;
WASHINGTON
St. Anselm's Abbey School Donor Trust - 4501 S. Dakota Ave., N.E., Washington, DC 20017-2795 t) 202-281-1645 mcommins@saintanselms.org Trust holding funds for the benefit of St. Anselm's Abbey School, Inc. Mark Commins, Admin.;
Christ Our Hope Foundation, Inc. - ; Mailing: P.O. Box 29260, Washington, DC 20017
Friends of John Paul II Foundation - 3885 Harewood

Rd., N.E., Washington, DC 20017 t) 703-501-6152 virginiaegg@cox.net jp2friends.org Rev. James McCormack, MIC, Supr.; Raymond Glembocki, Treas.;

Gregorian University Foundation - 3220 N St., NW #201, Washington, DC 20007 t) 202-333-1551 mmcfarland@gregorianfoundation.org; info@gregorianfoundation.org www.gregorianfoundation.org Rev. Michael C. McFarland, S.J., Pres.; Rev. William L George, S.J., Senior Advisor;

Holy Family Hospital of Bethlehem Foundation - 2000 P St., N.W., Ste. 310, Washington, DC 20036 t) 202-785-0801 michele.bowe@icloud.com www.birthplaceofhope.org Michele Burke Bowe, CEO;

ICEL Foundation - 1100 Connecticut Ave., N.W., Ste. 710, Washington, DC 20036 t) 202-347-0800 admin@eliturgy.org www.icelweb.org Edmund Yates, Admin.;

Jesuit Health Trust - 1726 New Hampshire Ave., NW, Washington, DC 20009 t) 202-462-0400 jccutreasurer@jesuits.org Rev. Sean D. Michaelson, S.J., Treas.;

St. Joseph Trust - 1326 Quincy St., N.E., Washington, DC 20017 t) 202-543-1179 economia.usa@servidoras.org Sr. Mary of the Immaculate Conception Ambrogio, Pres.;

NAC Humility Street Foundation - c/o Pontifical North American College, 3211 Fourth St., N.E., Washington, DC 20017 t) 202-541-5411 pnacdc@pnac.org Most Rev. Austin Vetter, Pres.;

Order of Malta Lourdes Endowment Trust - c/o SMOM-Federal Assn., 1730 M St., N.W., Ste. 403, Washington, DC 20036 t) 202-331-2494 info@orderofmalta-federal.org Dcn. Michael J. Stankewicz, Exec.;

Pope John Paul II Cultural Foundation, Inc. - 3900 Harewood Rd., N.E., Washington, DC 20017 t) 202-635-5407

RJM Endowment and Continuing Care Trust - 821 Varnum St., N.E., Washington, DC 20017 t) 202-526-3203 Sr. Anne Magner, Trustee; Sr. Margaret Perron, R.J.M., Trustee;

RJM Real Estate Trust - 821 Varnum St., N.E., Washington, DC 20017 t) 202-526-3203 Sr. Anne Magner, Trustee; Sr. Margaret Perron, R.J.M., Trustee;

S.N.D.B.C. Charitable Trust - 125 Michigan Ave., N.E., Washington, DC 20017-1004 t) 202-884-9750 sndbcunit@aol.com www.sndden.org/ Sr. Helen Bellew, SNDdeN, Trustee; Sr. Elizabeth Smoyer, S.N.D.de.N., Trustee; Sr. Virginia West, SNDdeN, Trustee;

Sisters of the Visitation of Georgetown Charitable Assets Trust - 1500 35th St., N.W., Washington, DC 20007 t) (202) 558-7975 msiegel@visi.org Mother Anne Francis Ng'ang'a, Supr.;

Sisters of the Visitation of Georgetown Continuing Care Trust - 1500 35th St., N.W., Washington, DC 20007 t) (202) 558-7975 msiegel@visi.org Mother Anne Francis Ng'ang'a;

Sisters of the Visitation of Georgetown Preparatory School Endowment Trust - 1500 35th St., N.W., Washington, DC 20007 t) 202-337-3350 barbara.edmondson@visi.org Mother Anne Francis Ng'ang'a;

HOSPITALS / HEALTH SERVICES [HOS]

SILVER SPRING

***Holy Cross Health, Inc.** - 1500 Forest Glen Rd., Silver Spring, MD 20910 t) 301-754-7000; 301-754-7715 tyler.pickrel@holycrosshealth.org www.holycrosshealth.org A member of Trinity Health which is sponsored by Catholic Health Ministries. Rev. Casmir Onyegwara; Norvell Coots, Pres.; Steven Fowler, Exec.;

WASHINGTON

Medstar Georgetown University Hospital - 3800 Reservoir Rd., N.W., Washington, DC 20007 t) 202-444-3030 thomas.j.devaney@gunet.georgetown.edu www.georgetownuniversityhospital.org Rev. John O. Ekeocha, Chap.; Rev. Albert Shuyaka, Chap.; Michael C. Sachtleben, Pres.; Dcn. Thomas J. Devaney, Dir.;

Providence Health Services, Inc. - 1150 Varnum St., N.E., Washington, DC 20017; Mailing: 4600 Edmundson Rd., St. Louis, MO 63134 t) 314-733-8000 craig.cordola@ascension.org www.ascension.org Ambulatory-Outpatient Care, Promote Wellness and Carry Out Educational Activities and Scientific Research. Parent Entity is Providence Hospital. Craig Cordola, Exec.; Asstd. Annu.: 56,282; Staff: 76

Providence Hospital - 1150 Varnum St., N.E., Washington, DC 20017; Mailing: 4600 Edmundson Rd., St. Louis, MO 63134 t) 314-733-8000 craig.cordola@ascension.org www.ascension.org Daughters of Charity of St. Vincent de Paul. Craig Cordola, CEO; Asstd. Annu.: 12,322; Staff: 82

Providence Health Foundation - 1150 Varnum St., N.E., Washington, DC 20017; Mailing: 4600 Edmundson Rd., St. Louis, MO 63134 t) 202-269-7776 www.providencehealthfoundation.org

MISCELLANEOUS [MIS]

BELTSVILLE

The Saint LaSalle Auxiliary - 6001 Ammendale Rd., Beltsville, MD 20705-1202 t) 301-210-7443; 732-980-7926 x103 juliano@fscdena.org Development Office for the Christian Brothers of the Baltimore Province. Bro. Joseph Juliano, F.S.C., Secy.;

BERLIN

Holy Name Society - 141 Nottingham Ln., Berlin, MD 21811-1663 t) 443-614-5411 joelatchford@gmail.com Joseph Latchford, Vice Pres., Region XIV;

BETHESDA

***Alliance for Communities in Action, Inc.** - 5403 Waneta Rd., Bethesda, MD 20816-2131 t) 301-229-0351 richard@allact.org Dcn. Richard Schopfer, Pres.; Juan Claudio Devincenti, Vice Pres.;

Missionaries of the Kingship of Christ - 5223 River Rd. #5030, Bethesda, MD 20816 t) 917-327-0255 susanlark2@aol.com www.simkc.org A Franciscan Secular Institute of Pontifical Right. Rev. Dominic Monn, O.F.M.;

Priestly Fraternity of the Missionaries of St. Charles Borromeo, Inc. - 7600 Carter Ct., Bethesda, MD 20817 t) 301-983-4624; 617-290-9127 a.lopez@sancarlo.org; s.zamagni@sancarlo.org sancarlo.org/ Rev. Roberto Amoruso, F.S.C.B., Prof.; Rev. Antonio Lopez, F.S.C.B., Prof.; Rev. Jose Medina, F.S.C.B., Prof.; Rev. Stefano Zamagni, FSCB, Treas.; Rev. Tommaso Badiani, FSCB, In Res.;

BOWIE

Sodality Union - 3300 Moreland Pl., Bowie, MD 20715 t) 301-262-2141 Cindy Perry, Pres.; Rev. Lawrence C. Swink, Spiritual Dir. & Mod.;

BROOKEVILLE

Divine Mercy Chapel - 19109 Georgia Ave., Brookeville, MD 20833; Mailing: 3885 Harewood Rd., N.E., Washington, DC 20017-1504 t) 202-526-8884 marian.scholasticate.office@gmail.com www.marian.org Congregation of Marian Fathers of the Immaculate Conception of the B. V. M., Inc. Rev. James McCormack, M.I.C., Supr.;

CHARLOTTE HALL

Serra Club of Southern Maryland - 10548 Wicomoco Ridge Rd., Charlotte Hall, MD 20622 Walter Rourke, Pres.;

CHILLUM

IVE Higher Studies, Inc. - 5706 Sargent Rd., Chillum, MD 20782 t) 301-559-3636 Doing Business as Fides et Ratio Institute Christine Miola, Contact;

FORT WASHINGTON

Birhen Ng Antipolo, USA, Inc. - 8504 Oxon Hill Rd., Fort Washington, MD 20744 t) 301-567-4914 www.antipolo.us Eddie D. Caparas, Pres.;

GAITHERSBURG

Legion of Christ King, Inc. - 25 Cedar Ave., Gaithersburg, MD 20877

Serra Club of Washington, D.C. - 422 Sanders Ln., Gaithersburg, MD 20877 t) 301-670-1069 Cindy Selby, Pres.;

GLEN ECHO

The John Carroll Society - ; Mailing: P.O. Box 454, Glen Echo, MD 20812 t) 301-654-4399 johncarrollsociety1951@gmail.com www.johncarrollsociety.org Rev. Msgr. Peter J. Vaghi, Chap.; Andrew N. Cook, Pres.;

HYATTSVILLE

Carroll Media Company - 5001 Eastern Ave., N.E., Hyattsville, MD 20782

Faith House - 4903 Eastern Ave., Hyattsville, MD 20782 t) 301-559-5500 peggy.gatewood@stanns.org Sr. Mary Bader, D.C., CEO;

Forward in Faith, Inc. - 5001 Eastern Ave., N.E., Hyattsville, MD 20782

KENSINGTON

Inter Mirifica - 2812 Jutland Rd., Kensington, MD 20895 t) 301-949-4840 jdhoconnell@comcast.net Religious publications. John O'Connell, Contact;

St. John Vianney House - 4214 Saul Rd., Kensington, MD 20895 t) 301-942-1191 yaom@adw.org Mary Ruth Yao, Admin.;

LANDOVER HILLS

Archdiocese of Washington, Department of Special Needs Ministries - 7202 Buchanan, Landover Hills, MD 20784 t) 301-459-7464 specialneedsministry@adw.org Rev. Frank A. Wright, S.M.A., Chap.;

Catholic Youth Organization of Washington, D.C. and Metropolitan Area, Inc. - 7202 Buchanan St., Landover Hills, MD 20784

LANHAM

***Asian Relief, Inc.** - 4200 Parliament Pl., Ste. 240, Lanham, MD 20706 dba World Villages for Children of the Sisters of Mary ("World Villages").

MCLEAN

German Speaking Catholic Mission, Washington DC - 6330 Linway Ter., McLean, VA 22101-4150 t) 703-356-4473 kontakt@kathde.org; pfarrer@kathde.org www.kathde.org Rev. Karl Josef Rieger, Pst.;

MOUNT RAINIER

***Dominican Fathers & Brothers, Province of Nigeria** - 4504 21st St., Mount Rainier, MD 20712; Mailing: P. O. Box 5087, W Hyattsville, MD 20782 t) 301-927-0387 rayezeop@yahoo.com www.dominicans.org.ng/ Rev. Raymond Nwabueze, O.P., Dir.;

POTOMAC

Potomac Pastoral Center Inc. - 10211 Norton Rd., Potomac, MD 20854 t) (770) 828-4950 fformolo@legionaries.org Rev. Frank Formolo, Secy.;

ROCKVILLE

Archdiocesan Council of Catholic Women - 520 Veirs Mill Rd., Rockville, MD 20852 t) 301-424-5550 archdioceseccw@gmail.com www.councilofcatholicwomen-adw.com/ Carol-Ann Parker, Pres.; Rev. Msgr. Robert G. Amey, Dir.;

Avondale Park Apartments, Inc. - c/o Victory Housing, 11400 Rockville Pike, Ste. 505, Rockville, MD 20852 t) 301-493-6000 info@victoryhousing.org www.victoryhousing.org Leila Finucane, Pres.;

National Christ Child Society, Inc. - 6110 Executive Blvd., Ste. 504, Rockville, MD 20852 t) 301-881-2490 office@nationalchristchild.org; mlynch@nationalchristchild.org www.nationalchristchild.org A national nonprofit organization with 44 affiliate chapters consisting of nearly 6,000 member volunteers serving under-resourced children. Moira Lynch, Exec.;

Rosaria Communities in Colesville, Inc. - 15400 Calhoun Dr., Ste. 125, Rockville, MD 20855 t) 301-279-2020 tom@jrwinc.com Thomas Welch Jr., Pres.;

Rosaria Communities in Gaithersburg, Inc. - 15400 Calhoun Dr., Ste. 125, Rockville, MD 20855 t) 301-279-2020 tom@jrwinc.com Thomas Welch Jr., Pres.;

Rosaria Communities in Montgomery County, Inc. - 15400 Calhoun Dr., Ste. 125, Rockville, MD 20855

Rosaria Communities in Olney, Inc. - 15400 Calhoun Dr.,

Ste. 125, Rockville, MD 20855 t) 301-279-2020 tom@jrwinc.com Thomas Welch Jr., Pres.;
Rosaria Communities in Silver Spring, Inc. - 15400 Calhoun Dr., Ste. 125, Rockville, MD 20855 t) 301-279-2020 tom@jrwinc.com Thomas Welch Jr., Pres.;
Victory Court, Inc. - 11400 Rockville Pike, Ste. 505, Rockville, MD 20852 t) 301-493-6000 info@victoryhousing.org Leila Finucane, Pres.;
Victory Crest, Inc. - 11400 Rockville Pike, Ste. 505, Rockville, MD 20852 t) 301-493-6000 info@victoryhousing.org www.victoryhousing.org Leila Finucane, Pres.;
Victory Lakeside, Inc. - 11400 Rockville Pike, Ste. 505, Rockville, MD 20852 t) 301-493-6000 info@victoryhousing.org Leila Finucane, Pres.;
Victory Oaks, Inc. - 11400 Rockville Pike, Ste. 505, Rockville, MD 20852 t) 301-493-6000 info@victoryhousing.org Leila Finucane, Pres.;

SILVER SPRING

Archdiocesan Council of Washington - 12447 Georgia Ave., Silver Spring, MD 20902; Mailing: 5804 Sherier Pl., N.W., Anacostia, Washington, DC 20016 t) 202-362-0403 svdpadccwash@gmail.com Ann Barbagallo, Pres.; Tommye Grant, Pres.;
The Blue Army, Archdiocese of Washington Division - ; Mailing: P.O. Box 4934, Silver Spring, MD 20914 t) 301-595-1770 www.bluearmy.com/washingtondc/ World Apostolate of Fatima Rev. Thomas G. Morrow, Spiritual Adv./Care Srvcs.; Mary Ann Hanson, Pres.;
Conference for Mercy Higher Education - 8403 Colesville Rd., Ste. 400, Silver Spring, MD 20910 t) 301-273-9736 jcavallo@sistersofmercy.org www.mercyhighered.org Dr. Julia Cavallo, Dir.;
***Friends in Solidarity, Inc.** - 8737 Colesville Rd., Ste. 610, Silver Spring, MD 20910 c) 734-731-3726 info@solidarityfriends.org www.solidarityfriends.org USA partner to Solidarity with South Sudan Sr. Joan Mumaw, Pres.;
Leadership Conference of Women Religious in the U.S.A. - 8737 Colesville Rd., Ste. 610, Silver Spring, MD 20910 t) 301-588-4955 director@lcwr.org www.lcwr.org Sr. Elise Garcia, OP, Pres.; Sr. Jayne Helmlinger, CSJ, Pres.; Sr. Mary Jane Herb, IHM, Pres.; Sr. Catherine Sheehan, DW, Secy.; Sr. Maureen O'Connor, OSF, Treas.; Sr. Carol Zinn, SSJ, Exec.;
Lumen Catechetical Consultants, Inc. - 10018 Woodland Dr., Silver Spring, MD 20902; Mailing: P.O. Box 1761, Silver Spring, MD 20915 t) 301-593-1066; 800-473-7980 lumen@lifeaftersunday.com lifeaftersunday.com Provides Consulting & Production Services to Catholic Organizations; Assists in Development and Production of Catechetical Materials in Various Media. John M. Capobianco, Pres.;
Mercy Education System of the Americas - 8403 Colesville Rd., Ste. 400, Silver Spring, MD 20910 t) 301-273-9775 mesa@sistersofmercy.org www.mercyedu.org An international Mercy education system organized under the Institute of the Sisters of Mercy of the Americas. Sr. Lisa Griffith, RSM, Exec. Dir.;
Mercy Real Estate Holding Corporation - 8403 Colesville Rd., Ste. 400, Silver Spring, MD 20910 t) (301) 587-0423 Sr. Judith Frikker, RSM, Pres.;
MIA-USA Fundraising Inc. - 8403 Colesville Rd., Ste. 400, Silver Spring, MD 20910-6264 t) 301-587-0423 www.sistersofmercy.org Sr. Patricia McDermott, R.S.M., Pres.;
Missionary Cenacle Family - 9001 New Hampshire Ave., Ste. 300, Silver Spring, MD 20903-3626 t) 301-434-0092 secgen@trinitymissions.org Bro. Steven Vesely, S.T., Secy.;
Sisters of Mercy of the Americas CCASA Community, Inc. - 8403 Colesville Rd., Ste. 400, Silver Spring, MD 20910 t) 301-587-0423 www.sistersofmercy.org Sr. Anne Marie Miller, RSM, Pres.;
***Society of St. Vincent de Paul** - 12447 Georgia Ave., Silver Spring, MD 20902 t) 301-942-1110 Tommye Grant, Pres.;
Office of Archdiocesan Council -
St. Vincent de Paul Society -
Support Our Aging Religious, Inc. (SOAR!) - 8484 Georgia Ave., Ste. 300, Silver Spring, MD 20910; Mailing: PO Box 96409, Washington, DC 20090-6409 t) 202-529-7627 info@soar-usa.org www.soar-usa.org Sr. Kathleen Lunsmann, I.H.M., Pres.; Elizabeth Goral-Makowski, Dir.; Stephanie Marcantonio, Trustee;
U.S. Good Shepherd Conference, a Corporation - 504 Hexton Hill Rd., Silver Spring, MD 20904 c) (314) 397-9436 (Antonia M. Ponder COO) tponder@gspmna.org This entity is used for charitable purposes for the work of the three U.S. Provinces of the Sisters of the Good Shepherd Antonia Ponder, COO;

TAKOMA PARK

Don Bosco Cristo Rey Work-Study of the Archdiocese of Washington - 1010 Larch Ave., Takoma Park, MD 20912; Mailing: P.O. Box 56481, Washington, DC 20040-6481 t) 301-891-4750 achapa@dbcr.org www.dbcr.org Mark K Shriver, Pres.; Ana Chapa, Exec.;

UPPER MARLBORO

Irish Apostolate USA, Inc. - 14406 Old Mill Rd., Upper Marlboro, MD 20772; Mailing: 5340 Geary Blvd., Ste. 206, San Francisco, CA 94121 t) 415-752-6006 nationaloffice@usairish.org; coordinator@usairish.org www.usairish.org Rev. Brendan McBride, Pres.; Rev. Daniel Finn, Treas.;

WALDORF

***Black Leadership and Christ's Kingdom Society** - 3325 Martha Pl., Waldorf, MD 20601; Mailing: P.O. Box 410, Waldorf, MD 20604-0410 t) 301-888-2566 bodyofchristfarm@yahoo.com Patricia E Coyle, Pres.;

WASHINGTON

***Africa Faith and Justice Network, Inc.** - 3025 4th St, N.E., FL 2, Washington, DC 20017 t) 202-817-3670 director@afjn.org; info@afjn.org www.afjn.org Sr. Nkechi Iwuoha, P.H.JC., Chair; Dr. Steven Nabieu Rogers, Exec. Dir.;
African Conference of Catholic Clergy & Religious in the United States, Inc. - St. Joseph Seminary, 1200 Varnum St., N.E., Washington, DC 20017 t) 202-460-5019 www.acccrus.org Rev. Xavier Edet, S.S.J., Chapt. Pres.; Rev. Ebuka Mbanude, Secy.;
***Asian and Pacific Catholic Network** - 913 Hamilton St., N.E., Washington, DC 20011
***Bethlehem House** - 1401 Lawrence St., N.E., Washington, DC 20017 t) 202-526-3222
CARA, Center for Applied Research in the Apostolate - 2300 Wisconsin Ave., N.W., Ste. 400 A, Washington, DC 20007 t) 202-687-8080 cara@georgetown.edu cara.georgetown.edu Rev. Thomas P. Gaunt, S.J., Exec.;
Caritas Christi - 5410 Connecticut Ave., N.W. #506, Washington, DC 20015-2821 t) 202-363-2839 A Secular Institute of Pontifical Right.
Carmelite Institute of North America - 1600 Webster St., N.E., Washington, DC 20017 t) 202-526-1221 www.carmelstream.org Rev. Steven Payne, O.C.D., Pres.; Matlock Edith, Dir.;
***Catholic Climate Covenant** - 415 Michigan Ave., N.E., Ste. 260, Washington, DC 20017 t) 202-756-5545 info@catholicclimatecovenant.org catholicclimatecovenant.org Daniel Misleh, Exec. Dir.;
***Catholic Labor Network** - Georgetown University, Washington, DC 20057
***Catholic Mobilizing Network** - 415 Michigan Ave., N.E., Ste. 210, Washington, DC 20017 t) 202-541-5290 info@catholicsmobilizing.org; jeff@catholicsmobilizing.org www.catholicsmobilizing.org Ending the death penalty. Promoting restorative justice. Krisanne Vaillancourt Murphy, Exec.;
Center of Concern - 1627 K St., N.W., 11th Fl., Washington, DC 20006-1710 t) 202-635-2757 coc@coc.org www.coc.org Lester A. Myers, Pres.;
Religious of Mary Immaculate (Centro Maria) - 650 Jackson St., N.E., Washington, DC 20017-1424 t) 202-635-1697 sr.incharge@centromariadc.org; rmi@centromariadc.org www.centromariadc.org Residence for young students and working women (18-29). Sr. Ruby Sampang, RMI, Supr.;
Christ Child Society of Washington, DC, Inc. - 5101 Wisconsin Ave., N.W., Ste. 102, Washington, DC 20016 t) 202-966-9250 info@christchilddc.org www.christchilddc.org Nonprofit, women's volunteer organization serving children. Kathleen Curtin, Exec.;
Christian Brothers Conference - 415 Michigan Ave., N.E., Ste. 300, Washington, DC 20017-4501 t) 202-529-0047 tsouthard@cbconf.org; jlindsay@cbconf.org www.lasallian.info Serving: Regional Conference of Christian Brothers; Huether Lasallian Conference. Thomas Southard, CEO;
Communio: International Catholic Review - ; Mailing: P.O. Box 4557, Washington, DC 20017 t) 202-526-0251 communio@aol.com www.communio-icr.com David L. Schindler, Editor;
Community of Christ - 1003 Kearney St., N.E., Washington, DC 20017 t) 202-832-9710; 202-797-8806 frjohn@some.org A Private Association Community of Archdiocesan Right for Priests, Lay Men and Lay Women. Rev. John E. Adams;
Consortium of Catholic Academies of the Archdiocese of Washington, Inc. - 415 Michigan Ave., N.E., Ste. 110, Washington, DC 20017
Council for Research in Values and Philosophy - The Catholic University of America, Gibbons Hall B20, Washington, DC 20064 t) 202-319-6089 c) 202-213-9644; 202-526-2578 cua-rvp@cua.edu; barbieri@cua.edu www.crvp.org William Barbieri Jr., Chair; Yeping Hu, Dir.;
Crusaders of Mary - 3706 15th St., N.E., Washington, DC 20017
Diocesan Laborer Priests - 3706 15th St., N.E., Washington, DC 20017 t) 202-832-4217
DISC Diocesan Information Systems Conference - 1250 Connecticut Ave., N.W., Ste. 700, Washington, DC 20036 t) 512-949-2555 president@discinfo.org discinfo.org Jeffrey Hardy, Pres.; Marcus Madsen, Vice. Pres.; Michael Irish, Secy.; Matthew Dolan, Treas.;
Equestrian Order of the Holy Sepulchre of Jerusalem - Middle Atlantic Lieutenancy U.S.A. - 1400 Quincy St., N.E., Washington, DC 20017; Mailing: P.O. Box 29480, Washington, DC 20017 t) 202-526-4217 secretary@midatlanticeohs.com www.midatlanticeohs.com/ Valencia Yvonne Camp, Exec.;
***The Father McKenna Center, Inc.** - 900 N. Capitol St., N.W., Washington, DC 20001; Mailing: 19 Eye St., N.W., Washington, DC 20001-1425 t) 202-842-1112 kcox@fathermckennacenter.org www.fathermckennacenter.org Food pantry and homeless services for men. Kimberly Cox, Pres.;
Fellowship of Catholic Scholars - Curley Hall, 620 Michigan Ave., N.E., Washington, DC 20064; Mailing: Fellowship of Catholic Scholars, Administrative Office, P.O. Box 7632, Springfield, OR 97475-1100 c) 203-589-8082 aegcsb@gmail.com; services@catholicscholars.org www.catholicscholars.org Rev. Anthony E. Giampietro, C.S.B., Pres.; Dr. Grattan Brown, Vice. Pres.;
***Sts. Francis and Alphonsus Corporation** - 4036 Alabama Ave., S.E., Washington, DC 20020; Mailing: P.O. Box 10316, Washington, DC 20020 t) 202-678-5898 asimplehouse@gmail.com Clark Massey, Dir.;
Franciscan Mission Service of North America - 415 Michigan Ave., N.E., Ste. 104, Washington, DC 20017 t) 202-832-1762 info@franciscanmissionservice.org www.franciscanmissionservice.org Liz Hughes, Dir.;
Friends of Lasallian Volunteers, Inc. - 415 Michigan Ave., N.E., Ste. 300, Washington, DC 20017 t) 202-529-0047 kswain@cbconf.org lasallianvolunteers.org Kathleen Swain, Dir.;
***Friends of the Benedictines in the Holy Land, Inc.** - 2715 Jenifer St., N.W., Washington, DC 20015 c) 202-207-8705 jsheridany@gmail.com fbhl.us Dr. Robin Darling Young, Prof.;
***The Friends of the Ethiopian Catholic University of St.**

Thomas Aquinas - c/o Holy Rosary Church, 595 Third St., N.W., Washington, DC 20001

Gift of Peace House - 2800 Otis St., N.E., Washington, DC 20018 t) 202-269-3313

***Imago Dei, Inc.** - 4393 Embassy Park Dr., N.W., Washington, DC 20016 t) 301-905-8700 stsash@aol.com imagodei-tob.org Suzanne Shaffer, Chair;

Jesuit Conference, Inc. - 1726 New Hampshire Ave., NW, Washington, DC 20009 t) 202-462-0400 skrudys@jesuits.org www.jesuits.org Rev. Brian G. Paulson, S.J., Pres.; Rev. Sean D. Michaelson, S.J.;

Jesuit Missions, Inc. - 1726 New Hampshire Ave., NW, Washington, DC 20009 t) 202-462-0400 jmiexecdir@jesuits.org Rev. Sean D. Michaelson, S.J., Exec.;

Jesuit Refugee Service - 1627 K St., N.W., Ste. 1100, Washington, DC 20006 t) 202-462-5200 giulia.mcpherson@jrsusa.org www.jrsusa.org Giulia McPherson, Dir.;

Jesuit Schools Network - 1726 New Hampshire Ave., NW, Washington, DC 20009 t) 202-667-3888 jccuseced@jesuits.org jesuitschoolsnetwork.org Rev. Robert E. Reiser, S.J., Exec. Dir.; Iliana M. Brown, Opers. Officer;

Jesuit Social and International Ministries-National Office - 1726 New Hampshire Ave., NW, Washington, DC 20009 t) 202-462-0400 www.jesuits.org Rev. Ted Penton, Secy.;

***John Paul II Shrine & Institute, Inc.** - 3900 Harewood Rd., N.E., Washington, DC 20017 t) 202-635-5400 visitorservices@jp2shrine.org www.jp2shrine.org Patrick Kelly, Exec.; Maxime Nogier, Dir.;

Kidane-Mehret Ge'ez Rite Ethiopian Catholic Church - 415 Michigan Ave., N.E., Ste. 65, Washington, DC 20017; Mailing: P.O. Box 29616, Washington, DC 20017 t) 202-756-2756 kmgeezrite@aol.com www.catholic-forum.com Rev. Abayneh Franswa Gebremichael, Rev, Dir.;

***Knights of St. Jerome, Inc.** - ; Mailing: P.O. Box 29260, Chancellor, Washington, DC 20017 Bobby Gant, Pres.;

***The Leonine Forum, Inc.** - 1501 K St., Ste. 175, Washington, DC 20005 t) 202-783-2062 mitch.boersma@leonineforum.org www.leonineforum.org Mitch Boerma, Contact;

***Magis Americas, Inc.** - 1726 New Hampshire Ave NW, Washington, DC 20009 t) 301-246-0325 (Exec. Dir.); 301-246-2034 (Main line) n.radomski@magisamericas.org; info@magisamericas.org www.magisamericas.org Nate Radomski, Exec.;

Mount Carmel House - 471 G Pl., N.W., Washington, DC 20001 t) 202-289-6315 Transitional Housing for Women.

National Black Sisters' Conference - 1200 Varnum St., N.E., Washington, DC 20017-2740 t) 202-529-9250 tthenationalblacksistersconfer@verizon.net www.nbsc68.com Sr. Roberta Fulton, S.S.M.N., Pres.;

National Eucharistic Congress, Inc. - 3211 4th St., N.E., Washington, DC 20017

National Institute for the Family - 1200 Varnum St., N.E., Ste. 54, Washington, DC 20017-2796 t) 202-302-1339; 202-557-4468 (alternate) dconroy@comcast.net Research and development with leadership formation programs for family & intergenerational ministry and parish team formation. Rev. Donald B. Conroy, Chair; John Przypysz, Exec.; Lauri Przypysz, Exec.;

Oblate Missionary Society, Inc. - 391 Michigan Ave., N.E., Washington, DC 20017 t) 202-529-4505; 202-529-4572 province@omiusa.org Rev. Louis Studer, O.M.I., Prov.; Rev. David Uribe, OMI, Dir.;

Paulist Evangelization Ministries - 1200 Varnum St., N.E., Washington, DC 20017-1102 t) 202-832-5022 admin@pemdc.org; lwilliams@pemdc.org www.pemdc.org Rev. Francis P. DeSiano, C.S.P., Pres.;

Pax Romana/Catholic Movement for Intellectual and Cultural Affairs-USA - 1025 Connecticut Ave., NW, Ste. 1000, Washington, DC 20036 t) 202-239-0074 pax-romana-cmica-usa@comcast.net www.pax-romana-cmica-usa.org Edward Joe Holland, Pres.;

Prelature of the Holy Cross and Opus Dei - 2301 Wyoming Ave., N.W., Washington, DC 20008 t) 202-234-1567 alvarojdevicente@gmail.com www.opusdei.org Rev. Joe Landauer, Chap.; Rev. Charles Trullols, Chap.; Rev. Salvador S. Vahi, Chap.;

Tenley Study Center - 4300 Garrison St., N.W., Washington, DC 20016 t) 202-362-2419 Rev. Javier Bujalance; Rev. Diego Daza;

Queen of Peace House - 3310 Wheeler Rd., S.E., Washington, DC 20032 Sr. Maria Bernadette, M.C., Supr.;

RJM Ministry Corporation - 821 Varnum St., N.E., Washington, DC 20017 t) 202-526-3203 Sr. Margaret Perron, R.J.M., Pres.; Sr. Anne Magner, Secy.;

***Salt and Light Catholic Media (USA), Inc.** - 3001 Fourth St., N.E., Washington, DC 20017

Serra Club of Downtown Washington - 4409 Westover Pl., N.W., Washington, DC 20016; Mailing: 6313 Hunting Ridge Ln., McLean, VA 22101 t) 202-362-2477; 703-821-0449 cathcap@aol.com Alice Middleton, Pres.; Gerrald Giblin, Vice. Pres.;

Sisters of Notre Dame de Namur Base Communities, Inc. - 125 Michigan Ave., N.E., Washington, DC 20017-1004 t) 202-884-9750 sndbcunit@aol.com www.sndden.org/ Sr. Elizabeth Smoyer, S.N.D.de.N., Canonical Liaison;

Spanish Catholic Center - ; Mailing: P.O. Box 11450, Washington, DC 20008-0650 t) 202-939-2437 infoscc@yahoo.com www.centrocatolicohispano.org Rev. Donald F. Lippert, O.F.M.Cap;

Adult Clinic - 1015 University Blvd. E., Silver Spring, MD 20903 t) 301-434-8381 Langley Park Office.

Dental Clinic - 1618 Monroe St., N.W., Washington, DC 20010 t) 202-939-2423 Mt. Pleasant Branch.

Gaithersburg Branch - 117 N. Frederick Ave., Gaithersburg, MD 20877 t) 301-417-9113

Immigration Services - 1618 Monroe St., N.W., Washington, DC 20010 t) 202-939-2420 Mt. Pleasant Branch.

Langley Park Office - 1015 University Blvd. E., Silver Spring, MD 20903 t) 301-431-3773

Medical Clinic - 1618 Monroe St., N.W., Washington, DC 20010 t) 202-939-2400 Mt. Pleasant Branch.

Medical Clinic - 1015 University Blvd. E., Silver Spring, MD 20903 t) 301-929-0207 Langley Park Office.

Mt. Pleasant Branch - 1618 Monroe St., N.W., Washington, DC 20010

Pediatric Clinic - 1015 University Blvd. E., Silver Spring, MD 20903 t) 301-434-3999 Langley Park Office.

Piney Branch Office - 8545 Piney Branch Rd., Silver Spring, MD 20901

Social Services - 1618 Monroe St., N.W., Washington, DC 20010 t) 202-939-2414 Mt. Pleasant Branch.

Social, Employment & Immigration Services - 1015 University Blvd. E., Silver Spring, MD 20903 t) 301-587-0582 Langley Park Office.

Social, Employment & Immigration Services - 117 N. Frederick Ave., Gaithersburg, MD 20903 t) 301-417-9113

Theological Studies, Inc. - 3700 O St., N.W., Georgetown University Dept of Theology, Washington, DC 20057-1135 t) 202-687-9294 c) 202-494-9221 editortheologicalstudies@gmail.com www.theologicalstudies.net Rev. Christopher W. Steck, S.J., Editor; Dawn Sjurset, Bus. Mgr.;

US Province of the Religious of Jesus and Mary, Inc. - 821 Varnum St., N.E., Washington, DC 20017 t) 202-526-3203 Sr. Margaret Perron, R.J.M., Prov.; Sr. Anne Magner, Secy.;

Victory Youth Center - 4275 4th St., S.E., Washington, DC 20032; Mailing: 5001 Eastern Ave, Hyattsville, MD 20782 t) 202-562-7590 fosterd@adw.org www.merrickcenter.org Darren Foster, Dir.;

Visitation Monasteries, Inc. - 1500 35th St., N.W., Washington, DC 20007

The Washington Cursillo Movement - 6312 2nd St., N.W., Washington, DC 20011 t) 202-330-7227 Jacquelyn DeMesme-Gray, Dir.; Rev. William E. Foley, Dir.;

***Washington Jesuit Academy** - 900 Varnum St., N.E., Washington, DC 20017 t) 202-832-7679 wwhitaker@wjacademy.org www.wjacademy.org William B. Whitaker, Pres.;

***Workers of St. Joseph** - 5542 Friendship Station, Washington, DC 20017 t) 301-399-2480 tony_s1@verizon.net

WEST HYATTSVILLE

Catholic Apostolate Center, Inc. - 2009 Van Buren St., West Hyattsville, MD 20782; Mailing: P.O. Box 4556, Washington, DC 20017 t) 301-448-1880 director@catholicapostolatecenter.org www.catholicapostolatecenter.org Rev. Frank S. Donio, S.A.C., Dir.;

MONASTERIES AND RESIDENCES FOR PRIESTS AND BROTHERS [MON]

ADELPHI

Father Judge Missionary Cenacle - 1733 Metzerott Rd., Adelphi, MD 20783 t) 301-439-3171 secgen@trinitymissions.org www.trinitymissions.org Senior Ministry Residence. Bro. Steven Vesely, S.T., Dir.; Bro. Jordan Baxter, S.T.; Rev. Rudy Breunig, S.T.; Bro. William Coombs, S.T.; Rev. Anselm Deehr, S.T.; Rev. Edwin Dill, S.T.; Rev. Stephen T. Ernst, S.T.; Rev. Joseph Keenan; Bro. Richard McCann, S.T.; Rev. Daniel McLaughlin, S.T.; Rev. Louis Murphy, S.T.; Rev. James O'Bryan, S.T.; Rev. Walter O'Donnell, S.T.; Bro. Loughlan Sofield, S.T., In Res.; Rev. Victor Seidel, S.T.; Rev. Gary M. Banks, S.T., In Res.; Rev. Ralph Frisch, In Res.; Bro. Howard F. Piller, S.T., In Res.; Rev. Conrad Schmitt, In Res.;

CHILLUM

Institute of the Incarnate Word - 5706 Sargent Rd., Chillum, MD 20782 t) 301-773-3635 c) 507-720-5616 prov.immaculate.conception@ive.org iveamerica.org Rev. Alberto Barattero, Prov.; Rev. Pablo Bonello, I.V.E., Prov. Asst.; Brs.: 7; Priests: 50

MOUNT RAINIER

Dominican Province of Saint Joseph the Worker: Nigeria and Ghana, Inc. - 4504 21st St., Mount Rainier, MD 20712

POTOMAC

Legionaries of Christ - 10211 Norton Rd., Potomac, MD 20854 t) 248-431-0117 dpajerski@legionaries.org Rev. Daniel Pajerski, L.C., Supr.; Rev. Vito Crincoli, L.C., Mem.; Rev. Peter Hopkins, L.C., Mem.; Rev. Vinh Pham, L.C., Mem.; Rev. Robert Presutti, L.C., Mem.; Rev. Michael Sliney, L.C., Mem.; Rev. John Sweeney, L.C., Mem.;

RIVERDALE

Holy Spirit Missionary Cenacle - 5809 Riverdale Rd., Riverdale, MD 20737 t) 301-277-7442 hfpiller@gmail.com Bro. Howard F. Piller, S.T., Supr.; Rev. Gary M. Banks, S.T., In Res.; Rev. Stephen Giorno, S.T., In Res.; Rev. Sidney H. Griffith, S.T., In Res.; Rev. J. Roberto Mena, S.T., In Res.; Bro. David Sommer, S.T., In Res.;

SILVER SPRING

Missionary Servants of the Most Holy Trinity - 9001 New Hampshire Ave., Ste. 300, Silver Spring, MD 20903-3626 t) 301-434-0092 secgen@trinitymissions.org www.trinitymissions.org Trinity Missions Rev. Michael K. Barth, S.T., Rel. Ord. Ldr.; Rev. Dieudonne Nsom Nsom Kindong Jr., S.T., Secy.; Brs.: 37; Priests: 77

WASHINGTON

St. Anselm's Abbey - 4501 S. Dakota Ave., N.E., Washington, DC 20017 t) 202-269-2300 jwiseman@saintanselms.org www.stanselms.org Benedictine Foundation at Washington, DC, Order of St. Benedict. Rt. Rev. James A. Wiseman, O.S.B., Abbot; Rev. Philip Simo, O.S.B., Prior; Rev. Joseph Jensen, O.S.B.; Rev. Michael Hall, O.S.B.; Rev. Christopher Wyvill, O.S.B.; Rev. Peter Weigand, O.S.B.; Rev. Paul McKane; Rev. Boniface von Nell, O.S.B.; Rev. Gabriel Myers, O.S.B.; Bro. Dunstan Robidoux,

O.S.B.; Bro. Matthew Nylund, O.S.B.; Bro. Ignacio Gonzalez, O.S.B.; Rev. Samuel Springuel, O.S.B., Novice Master; Bro. Cyprian Morales, O.S.B.; Brs.: 4; Priests: 10

Center for Assisted Living - 630 E St., S.W., Washington, DC 20024-2503 t) 202-488-4188 Dominican Fathers and Brothers. Rev. Carl Louis Mason, O.P., Dir.;

Commissariat of the Holy Land, Franciscan Monastery - Mount St. Sepulchre - 1400 Quincy St., N.E., Washington, DC 20017 t) 202-526-6800 x887 commissary@myfranciscan.com; mail@myfranciscan.com www.myfranciscan.org Rev. David Grenier, OFM, Commissary; Rev. Ramzi Sidawi, OFM, Vice Commissary; Brs.: 5; Priests: 13

Franciscan Monastery USA Inc. - 1400 Quincy St., N.E., Washington, DC 20017 t) 202-526-6800 mail@myfranciscan.com myfranciscan.org Rev. Ramzi Sidawi, OFM, Guardian and Vice-Commissary; Friar Thomas Courtney, O.F.M.; Rev. James Gardiner, S.A.; Friar Gregory Giannoni, O.F.M.; Rev. Romuald Green, O.F.M.; Rev. David Grenier, OFM, Vicar and Commissary; Bro. Jude Lustyk, O.F.M.; Friar Simon McKay, O.F.M.; Rev. Benjamin Owusu, OFM; Friar Michael Raum, OFM; Rev. Salvador Rosas Flores, OFM; Rev. Ambrose K. Phillips, T.O.R.; Rev. Jacob Mathew Smith, O.F.M.; Rev. Kevin Treston, O.F.M.; Rev. David Wathen, O.F.M.; Friar Maximilian Wojciechowski, O.F.M.; Rev. Manuel Ybarra, O.F.M.; Brs.: 5; Priests: 13

The Jesuit Community at Georgetown University - 3700 O St., N.W. Wolfington Hll, Washington, DC 20057-1200; Mailing: PO Box 571200, Washington, DC 20057 t) 202-687-4000 sr368@georgetown.edu www.georgetown.edu/jesuitcommunity Rev. Ronald J. Anton, S.J., Supr.; Rev. Stephen W. Planning, S.J., Treas.; Rev. Mark Bosco, S.J., Exec.; Rev. Thomas J. Buckley, S.J., Spiritual Adv./Care Srvcs.; Rev. Matthew E. Carnes, S.J., Prof.; Rev. Thomas F. Clifford, S.J., Pst.; Rev. David J. Collins, S.J., Prof.; Rev. James R. Conroy, S.J., Chap.; Rev. Quentin Dupont, S.J., Prof.; Rev. Patrick Earl, SJ, Par. Vicar; Rev. Stephen M. Fields, S.J., Prof.; Rev. Peter Folan, S.J., Prof.; Rev. Philip A. Ganir, S.J., Mem.; Rev. Michael Garanzini, S.J., Pres.; Rev. Thomas P. Gaunt, S.J., Admin.; Rev. William George, SJ, Mem.; Rev. C. Kevin Gillespie, S.J., Pst.; Rev. Gael Giraud, S.J., Prof.; Rev. Benjamin Hawley, SJ, Par. Vicar; Rev. Jerome T. Hayes, S.J., Chap.; Rev. Otto H. Hentz, S.J., Prof.; Rev. David Hollenbach, S.J., Prof.; Rev. William J. Kelley, S.J., Assoc. Pst.; Rev. Robert McChesney, S.J., Chap.; Rev. Brian O. McDermott, S.J., Admin.; Rev. Michael C. McFarland, S.J., Pres.; Rev. Gerard J. McGlone, S.J., Prof.; Rev. Dennis L. McNamara, S.J., Prof.; Rev. G. Ronald Murphy, S.J., Prof.; Rev. Richard Nichols, S.J., Chap.; Rev. William A. Ryan, Mem.; Rev. Raimundo Salas, S.J., Mem.; Rev. David A. Sauter, S.J., Chap.; Rev. Gregory A. Schenden, S.J., Dir.; Rev. Armel Setubi, S.J., Mem.; Rev. James Matthew Shea, S.J., Chap.; Rev. Myles Sheehan, SJ, Prof.; Rev. Lawrence C. Smith, S.J., Assoc. Pst.; Rev. Christopher W. Steck, S.J., Prof.; Rev. Vincent L. Strand, S.J., Prof.; Rev. Stephen V. Sundborg, S.J., Admin.; Rev. James Van Dyke, SJ, Pres.; Rev. Christopher Wagner, SJ, Prof.; Priests: 45

The Jesuit Community of St. Aloysius Gonzaga - 19 I St., N.W., At Gonzaga College High School, Washington, DC 20001 t) 202-336-7186 llundin@jesuits.net; hgeib@gonzaga.org Rev. Taroh Amede, S.J. (Chad), Admin.; Rev. Ricardo Avila, S.J., Prof.; Rev. Augustine E. Ekeno, S.J (Kenya), In Res.; Rev. Thomas Michael Gavin, S.J., Sacr. Min.; Rev. Harry F. Geib, S.J., Rector; Rev. Mark F. Horak, S.J., Prof.; Rev. Timothy Kesicki, S.J., In Res.; Rev. Michael J. Lamanna, S.J., In Res.; Rev. Joseph E. Lingan, S.J., Pres.; Rev. Sean D. Michaelson, S.J., Prov. Asst.; Rev. Rodrigue Bamenga Ntungu, S.J., In Res.; Rev. Brian G. Paulson, S.J., Pres.; Rev. Edward Penton, S.J., Admin.; Rev. Thomas J. Reese, S.J., In Res.; Rev. Robert E. Reiser, S.J., Exec.; Bro. Lawrence Lundin, S.J., Bus. Mgr.; Brs.: 1; Priests: 15

Leonard Neale House - 1726 New Hampshire Ave., N.W., Washington, DC 20009 Rev. Timothy Kesicki, S.J., Pres.; Rev. Michael J. Sheeran, S.J., Pres.; Rev. Sean D. Michaelson, S.J., Exec.; Rev. William H. Muller, S.J., Exec.; Rev. David A. Godleski, S.J.; Rev. Joseph A. Koczera, S.J.; Rev. Thomas J. Reese, S.J.; Bro. Michael E. Breault, S.J., Dir.;

St. Louis Friary - 831 Varnum St., N.E., Washington, DC 20017-2144 t) 202-734-3610 House of Post-Novitiate Formation for Franciscan Friars, T.O.R., Province of the Most Sacred Heart of Jesus. Rev. Patrick Whittle, Dir. Formation & Post-Novitiate Formation; Rev. Vincent Yeager, Dir. Vocations & Postulants;

Marist Center (The Marist Finance Center of the Atlanta Province of the Society of Mary, Marist Fathers and Brothers) - 4408 8th St., N.E., Washington, DC 20017-2298 t) 202-529-4800 randyh@maristsociety.org Society of Mary (Marist) (S.M.); Marist Society, Inc.; Marist Society (DC) Rev. John Beckley, S.M., Sr. Rel.; Rev. John Bolduc, S.M., Pst.; Rev. Richard K. Colbert, S.M., Sr. Rel.; Rev. Ronald DesRosiers, Sr. Rel.; Rev. Albert DiIanni, S.M., Sr. Rel.; Rev. Joseph Fenton, S.M., Chap.; Rev. Joseph M. Fleury, S.M., Chap.; Rev. Paul Frechette, S.M., Par. Vicar; Rev. Philip S. Gage, S.M., Sr. Rel.; Rev. John David Galvin, S.M., Sr. Rel.; Rev. Walter L. Gaudreau, S.M., Dir.; Rev. Juan Gonzalez, S.M., On Sabbatical; Rev. Andre L. Gosselin, S.M., Sr. Rel.; Rev. Joel R. Grissom, S.M., Chap.; Rev. Paul Hachey, S.M., On Assignment, Australia; Rev. John H. Harhager, S.M., Rel. Ord. Ldr.; Rev. Joseph C. Hindelang, S.M., Prov.; Rev. Souvenir Jean-Paul, S.M., Chap.; Rev. James B. McCafferty, S.M., Sr. Rel.; Rev. Joseph M. Pusateri, S.M., Sr. Rel.; Rev. Howard C. Smith, S.M., Sr. Rel.; Rev. George Szal, S.M., Chap.; Rev. Kenneth Thibodeau, S.M., Sr. Rel.; Rev. H. Joseph Wilhelm, S.M., Sr. Rel.; Bro. Leonard Haley, S.M., Sr. Rel.; Bro. Roy Madigan, S.M., Chap.; Bro. Richard McKenna, S.M., Sr. Rel.; Brs.: 3; Priests: 26

Missionaries of La Salette Corporation - 1243 Monroe St., N.E., Washington, DC 20017 t) 202-526-8070 mlsprovinceoffice@gmail.com www.lasalette.org Rev. Brian Schloth, M.S., Dir.; Priests: 1

Missionary Oblates of Mary Immaculate - 391 Michigan Ave., N.E., Washington, DC 20017-1516 t) 202-529-4505 province@omiusa.org www.omiusa.org Rev. Thomas Coughlin, O.M.I., Supr.; Rev. Louis Studer, O.M.I., Prov.; Rev. James Chambers, O.M.I., Treas.; Rev. Arthur Flores, O.M.I., Vicar Prov. & Dir., Personnel; Rev. Seamus P. Finn, O.M.I., Dir., USA JPIC & OIP FCI Investing; Rev. Leopoldo Perez, Dir., Church in Latin America; Rev. David Uribe, OMI, Dir., OMSI; Rev. Rocky Grimard, O.M.I., Asst. Treas.; Rev. Warren Brown, O.M.I., Gen. Councilor; Rev. Raymond Cook, O.M.I., Prov. Councilor; Rev. Mark Dean, OMI, Prov. Councilor; Rev. Emmanuel Mulenga, OMI, Prov. Councilor; Rev. Jose Antonio Ponce, O.M.I., Prov. Councilor; Rev. James Brobst, O.M.I., Rome; Rev. Rufus Whitley, O.M.I., Legal Admin.; Brs.: 25; Priests: 191

Oblate Annuity Trust - 391 Michigan Ave., N.E., Washington, DC 20017-1516 t) (202) 529-4505

Oblate Continuing Care Trust - 391 Michigan Ave., N.E., Washington, DC 20017-1516 t) (202) 529-4505

Oblate Education and Formation Trust - 391 Michigan Ave., N.E., Washington, DC 20017-1516 t) (202) 529-4505

Oblate Endowment Trust - 391 Michigan Ave., N.E., Washington, DC 20017-1516 t) (202) 529-4505

Oblate Patrimony Trust - 391 Michigan Ave., N.E., Washington, DC 20017-1516 t) (202) 529-4505

Oblate Real Estate Trust - 391 Michigan Ave, NE, Washington, DC 20017 t) (202) 529-4505

Oblate Service Corporation - 391 Michigan Ave., N.E., Washington, DC 20017-1516 t) (202) 529-4505

Oblate Service Trust - 391 Michigan Ave., N.E., Washington, DC 20017-1516 t) (202) 529-4505

Oblate Shrines and Renewal Centers, Inc. - 391 Michigan Ave., N.E., Washington, DC 20017-1516 t) (202) 529-4505

Oblate Title Holding Corporation - 391 Michigan Ave., N.E., Washington, DC 20017-1516 t) (202) 529-4505

Provincial Offices of the United States Province of the Missionary Oblates of Mary Immaculate - 391 Michigan Ave., N.E., Washington, DC 20017-1516 t) (202) 529-4505 Missionary Oblates of Mary Immaculate Eastern Province

The United States Province of the Missionary Oblates of Mary Immaculate, Inc. - 391 Michigan Ave., N.E., Washington, DC 20017-1516 t) (202) 529-4505

Oblate Community - 391 Michigan Ave., N.E., Washington, DC 20017-1516 t) 202-529-4505 province@omiusa.org www.omiusa.org Missionary Oblates of Mary Immaculate Rev. Bevil Bramwell, O.M.I., Prof.; Rev. James Brobst, O.M.I., Gen. Councilor, Rome; Rev. Patrick Casey, Juneau, AK; Rev. James Chambers, O.M.I., Treas.; Rev. Thomas Coughlin, O.M.I., Supr.; Rev. Arthur Craig, O.M.I., Phoenix, AZ; Rev. Karl Davis, O.M.I., New Haven, CT; Rev. Seamus P. Finn, O.M.I., Mem.; Rev. Arthur Flores, O.M.I., Vicar; Rev. Rocky Grimard, O.M.I., Asst. Treas.; Rev. Roger Hallee, O.M.I., Cuba; Rev. Nick Harding, OMI, Cuba; Rev. George Kirwin, O.M.I., Mem.; Rev. Daniel LeBlanc, O.M.I., New York, NY; Rev. Raymond A. Lebrun, O.M.I., Dir.; Rev. William Mason, O.M.I., Buffalo, NY; Rev. Leopoldo Perez, In Res.; Rev. Michael Powell, O.M.I., Chicago, IL; Rev. Andrew Small, O.M.I., Attached; Rome; Rev. Louis Studer, O.M.I., Prov.; Rev. Louis Villarreal, O.M.I., Turnersville, NJ; Rev. Rufus Whitley, O.M.I., Dir.; Priests: 19

Piarist Fathers, Province of the U.S.A. and Puerto Rico - 1339 Monroe St., N.E., Washington, DC 20017 t) 202-529-7734 piaristfl@bellsouth.net www.piarist.info Rev. Fernando Negro, Sch.P., Prov.; Rev. Emilio Sotomayor, Sch.P., Provincial Asst.; Rev. Luis Cruz, Sch.P., Prov. Asst.; Rev. John Callan, Sch.P., Provincial Treas.; Brs.: 1; Priests: 40

Society of Missionaries of Africa - 1624 21st St., N.W., Washington, DC 20009-1003 t) 202-232-5154 usasuperior@mafrdc.org www.missionariesofafrica.org USA Sector Rev. Barthelemy Bazemo, M.Afr., Supr.; Rev. David J. Goergen, M.Afr., Secy.; Rev. Komi Sedomo (Antonio) Koffi, Treas.; Rev. Robert C. McGovern, M.Afr.; Bro. James M. Heintz, M.Afr.; Brs.: 1; Priests: 4

Society of the Divine Word/Divine Word House - 832 Varnum St., N.E., Washington, DC 20017 t) 202-635-7810 Rev. Dominikus Boak, S.V.D.; Rev. Georges Kintiba, S.V.D.; Bro. Brian McLauchlin, S.V.D.; Rev. Binh Thanh Nguyen, S.V.D.;

NURSING / REHABILITATION / CONVALESCENCE / ELDERLY CARE [NUR]

BELTSVILLE

Ammendale Normal Institute of Prince George's County-La Salle Hall - 6001 Ammendale Rd., Beltsville, MD 20705 t) 301-210-7443 x13 Residence for retired and convalescent Brothers of the Christian Schools. Bro. Richard Buccina, F.S.C., Dir.; Asstd. Annu.: 19; Staff: 3

HYATTSVILLE

Sacred Heart Home Inc. - 5805 Queens Chapel Rd., Hyattsville, MD 20782 t) 301-277-6500 sistervacha@sacredhearthome.org www.sacredhearthome.org Sister Servants of Mary Immaculate. Rev. Emett Schuler, O.F.M.Cap., Chap.; Sr. Waclawa Kludziak, Admin.; Asstd. Annu.: 44; Staff: 60

ROCKVILLE

Palmer Park Seniors Housing, Inc. - c/o Victory Housing, Inc., 11400 Rockville Pike, Ste. 505, Rockville, MD 20852 t) 301-493-6000 info@victoryhousing.org www.victoryhousing.org Leila Finucane, Pres.;

Takoma Tower, Inc. - c/o Victory Housing, Inc., 11400 Rockville Pike, Ste. 505, Rockville, MD 20852 t) 301-493-6000 info@victoryhousing.org www.victoryhousing.org Leila Finucane, Pres.;

Victory Housing, Inc. - 11400 Rockville Pike, Ste. 505, Rockville, MD 20852 t) 301-493-6000 ecreskoff@victoryhousing.org www.victoryhousing.org Leila Finucane, Pres.;

Andrew Kim House, Inc. - 2100 Olney Sandy-Spring Rd., Olney, MD 20832; Mailing: 11400 Rockville Pike, Ste. 505, Rockville, MD 20852 t) 301-260-2500 manager435@habitatamerica.com www.victoryhousing.org/ilkim.html

Avondale Park Apartments, Inc. - 4915 Eastern Ave., Hyattsville, MD 20782; Mailing: 11400 Rockville Pike, Rockville, MD 20852 t) 301-853-7787 manager418@habitatamerica.com

Bartholomew House, Inc. - 6904 River Rd., Bethesda, MD 20817; Mailing: 11400 Rockville Pike Ste. 505, Rockville, MD 20852 t) 301-320-6151 bartholomew@victoryhousing.org www.victoryhousing.org/albartholomew.html Joseph Hanle, Dir.;

Byron House, Inc. - 9210 Kentsdale Dr., Potomac, MD 20854; Mailing: 11400 Rockville Pike, Ste. 505, Rockville, MD 20852 t) 301-469-9400 byron@victoryhousing.org www.victoryhousing.org/albyron.html Pearl Botchway, Dir.;

Cambridge Apartments, Inc. - 676 Houston Ave., Takoma Park, MD 20912; Mailing: 11400 Rockville Pike, Ste. 505, Rockville, MD 20852 t) 301-585-3750 manager413@habitatamerica.com www.victoryhousing.org/wfcambridge.html

Cheval Court, Inc. - 2611 Luana Dr., Forestville, MD 20747; Mailing: 11400 Rockville Pike, Ste. 505, Rockville, MD 20852 t) 301-736-0685 manager419@habitatamerica.com www.victoryhousing.org/ilcheval.html

Grace House, Inc. - Victory Housing, Inc., 11400 Rockville Pike, Ste. 505, Rockville, MD 20852 info@victoryhousing.org

Malta House, Inc. - 4916-18 LaSalle Rd., Hyattsville, MD 20782-3302; Mailing: 11400 Rockville Pike, Ste. 505, Rockville, MD 20852 t) 301-699-8600 malta@victoryhousing.org www.victoryhousing.org/almalta.html Elisabeth Orchard, Dir.;

Manor Apartments, Inc. - 4907 Eastern Ave., Hyattsville, MD 20782; Mailing: 11400 Rockville Pike, Ste. 505, Rockville, MD 20852 t) 301-853-2900 manager417@habitatamerica.com www.victoryhousing.org/ilmanor.html

Marian Assisted Living, Inc. - 19109 Georgia Ave., Brookeville, MD 20833; Mailing: 11400 Rockville Pike, Ste. 505, Rockville, MD 20852 t) 301-570-3190 marian@victoryhousing.org www.victoryhousing.org/almarian.html Marcy Hunter, Dir.;

Palmer Park Seniors Housing, Inc. - 7801 Barlowe Rd., Palmer Park, MD 20785; Mailing: 11400 Rockville Pike, Ste..505, Rockville, MD 20852 t) 301-341-4995 manager405@habitatamerica.com www.victoryhousing.org/ilpalmer.html

Parkfair Associates, LLC - 1611 Park Rd., N.W., Washington, DC 20010; Mailing: 11400 Rockville Pike, Ste. 505, Rockville, MD 20852 t) 202-986-1600 manager319@habitatamerica.com www.victoryhousing.org/wfparkfair.html

Raphael, Inc. - 1515 Dunster Rd., Rockville, MD 20854; Mailing: 11400 Rockville Pike, Ste. 505, Rockville, MD 20852 t) 301-217-9116 raphael@victoryhousing.org www.victoryhousing.org/alraphael.html Nellia Kaiyo, Dir.;

Takoma Tower, Inc. - 7051 Carroll Ave., Takoma Park, MD 20912 t) 301-270-1858 manager412@habitatamerica.com

Trinity Terrace, Inc. - 6001 Fisher Rd., Temple Hills, MD 20748; Mailing: 11400 Rockville Pike, Ste. 505, Rockville, MD 20852 t) 301-630-7717 manager402@habitatamerica.com www.victoryhousing.org/iltrinity.html

Victory Crest, Inc. - 6100 Sargent Rd., Hyattsville, MD 20782; Mailing: 11400 Rockville Pike, Ste. 505, Rockville, MD 20852 t) 301-559-3891 egibson@hrehllc.com www.victoryhousing.org/ilvcrest.html

Victory Forest, L.P. - 10000 Brunswick Ave., Silver Spring, MD 20910; Mailing: 11400 Rockville Pike, Ste. 505, Rockville, MD 20852 t) 301-589-4030 manager406@habitatamerica.com www.victoryhousing.org/ilvforest.html

Victory Heights, Inc. - 1369 Irving St., N.W., Washington, DC 20010; Mailing: 11400 Rockville Pike, Ste. 505, Rockville, MD 20852 t) 202-939-1431 manager320@habitatamerica.com www.victoryhousing.org/ilvheights.html

Victory Terrace, Inc. - 9440 Newbridge Dr., Potomac, MD 20854; Mailing: 11400 Rockville Pike, Ste. 505, Rockville, MD 20852 t) 301-983-9600 manager401@habitatamerica.com

Winslow House, Inc. - 666 Houston Ave., Takoma Park, MD 20912; Mailing: 11400 Rockville Pike, Ste. 505, Rockville, MD 20852 t) 301-585-3750 manager413@habitatamerica.com www.victoryhousing.org/wfwinslow.html

Winslow House, Inc. - c/o Victory Housing, Inc., 11400 Rockville Pike, Ste. 505, Rockville, MD 20852 t) 301-493-6000 info@victoryhousing.org www.victoryhousing.org Leila Finucane, Pres.;

WASHINGTON

Cardinal O'Boyle Residence for Priests - 1150 Varnum St., N.E., Washington, DC 20017-0206; Mailing: P.O. Box 29206, Washington, DC 20017-0206 t) 202-359-1593; 202-269-7810 (Rector) c.butta0181@yahoo.com Rev. C. Gregory Butta, Dir.; Rev. Donald Brice, In Res.; Rev. Thomas A. Kane, In Res.; Rev. Gerard A. Trancone, In Res.;

Carroll Manor d/b/a Ascension Living Carroll Manor - 725 Buchanan St. NE, Washington, DC 20017-2180 t) 314-292-9308 ahscm-mission@ascension.org www.ascensionliving.org/ Ryan Endsley, COO; Asstd. Annu.: 435; Staff: 177

Little Sisters of the Poor of Washington, D.C., Inc. - 4200 Harewood Rd., N.E., Washington, DC 20017-1554 t) 202-269-1831 washington@littlesistersofthepoor.org www.littlesistersofthepoorwashingtondc.org Sr. Mary Michael Nickles, L.S.P., Supr.;

PRESCHOOLS / CHILDCARE CENTERS [PRE]

HYATTSVILLE

St. Ann's Center for Children, Youth and Families - 4901 Eastern Ave., Hyattsville, MD 20782 t) 301-559-5500 donations@stanns.org www.stanns.org Supportive housing programs for pregnant and parenting mothers and their children; day care center. Sr. Mary Bader, D.C., CEO;

ROCK POINT

Camp St. Charles, Inc. - 15375 Stella Maris Dr., Rock Point, MD 20664; Mailing: P.O. Box 99, Issue, MD 20645 t) 240-372-9437; 301-934-8799 csclaurahall@gmail.com; director@campstcharles.org www.campstcharles.org Summer Camp and Retreat Center Laura Hall, Dir.; Stds.: 700; Lay Tchrs.: 2

WASHINGTON

Victory Youth Centers, Inc. - Mary Virginia Merrick Center, 4275 4th St SE, Washington, DC 20017; Mailing: Victory Youth Center c/o ADW, P.O. Box 29260, Washington, DC 20017 t) 202-562-7590 c) 202-412-8952 fosterd@adw.org Darren Foster, Dir.;

RETREAT HOUSES / RENEWAL CENTERS [RTR]

BETHESDA

Alpha Omega, Inc. (Our Lady of Bethesda) - Our Lady of Bethesda Retreat Center, 7007 Bradley Blvd., Bethesda, MD 20817 t) 301-365-0612 info@ourladyofbethesda.org www.ourladyofbethesda.org Retreats, marriage preparation & enrichment. Rev. Daniel Pajerski, L.C., Dir.; Rev. Frank Formolo, Secy.;

FAULKNER

Loyola Retreat House - 9270 Loyola Retreat Rd., Faulkner, MD 20632; Mailing: P.O. Box 9, Faulkner, MD 20632 t) 301-392-0800 director@loyolaretreat.org; reservations@loyolaretreat.org www.loyolaonthepotomac.com Jim Palmer, Dir.; Rev. Paul J. McCarren, S.J., Spiritual Dir.; Rev. William Rakowicz, S.J., Spiritual Dir.;

ROCKVILLE

St. Michael Center for Spiritual Renewal, Inc. - 5904 Hubbard Dr., Rockville, MD 20852

UPPER MARLBORO

Our Lady of Mattaponi Youth Retreat and Conference Center - 11000 Mattaponi Rd., Upper Marlboro, MD 20772 t) 301-952-9074 mattaponi@adw.org

WASHINGTON

Catholic Information Center - 1501 K St., N.W., Ste. 175, Washington, DC 20005-1401 t) 202-783-2062 director@cicdc.org www.cicdc.org Rev. Charles Trullols, Dir.;

Madonna House - 220 C St., N.E., Washington, DC 20002 t) 202-547-0177 madonnahousedc@gmail.com www.madonnahouse.org Shatzi Luisa Duffy, Dir.; Andorra Simone Howard, Mem.; Elizabeth Holmes, Staff;

Washington Retreat House, Inc. - 4000 Harewood Rd., N.E., Washington, DC 20017 t) 202-529-1111 washretreat@juno.com www.graymoor.org Franciscan Sisters of the Atonement. Sr. Josephine Dullaghan, Dir.;

SEMINARIES [SEM]

HYATTSVILLE

Redemptoris Mater Archdiocesan Missionary Seminary - 4900 Lasalle Rd., Hyattsville, MD 20782 t) 301-277-4960 seminary@rmwashington.org www.rmwashington.org Rev. Jose Matias Diaz, Rector; Rev. Saulo S. Vicente, Vice Rector; Rev. Rafael Barberi de Carvalho, Spiritual Dir.; Stds.: 26

SILVER SPRING

St. Bonaventure Friary - 10400 Lorain Ave., Silver Spring, MD 20901 t) 301-593-3018 saintbonaventurefriary@gmail.com Rev. Michael Zielke, O.F.M.Conv., Dir.; Very Rev. Jacob Carazo, O.F.M. Conv., Assoc. Dir.; Rev. John Burkhard, O.F.M.Conv., In Res.; Stds.: 7

Holy Family Seminary - 401 Randolph Rd., Silver Spring, MD 20904-4138; Mailing: P.O. Box 4138, Silver Spring, MD 20904-4138 t) 301-622-1184 holyfamilyseminary@gmail.com www.holyfamilyseminary.com (Retreat House) Sons of the Holy Family Rev. Ronald Carrillo, S.F.; Rev. Luis Picazo, S.F.; Most Rev. Francisco Gonzalez, S.F., In Res.;

Holy Name College - 1650 St. Camillus Dr., Silver Spring, MD 20903 t) 301-434-3400; 646-473-0265 wliss@hnpfriar.org; mharlan@hnp.org Residence for Postulancy for the Order of Friars Minor Rev. Gino Correa, O.F.M., Dir.; Rev. Charles Miller, O.F.M., In Res.; Rev. Russel Murray, O.F.M., Chap.; Rev. Rommel Perez, O.F.M., In Res.; Bro. Tom Carroll, O.F.M., In Res.; Bro. Ed Demyanovich, O.F.M., In Res.; Bro. Walter Liss, O.F.M., Guardian; Bro. David W. Schlatter, O.F.M., Chap.; Stds.: 2; Pr. Tchrs.: 2

Salvatorian Community - 1700 Briggs Chaney Rd., Silver Spring, MD 20905-5527 t) 301-370-2471 glenwillis@verizon.net www.sds.org Society of the Divine Savior/Salvatorians; Camp St. Charles. Rev. Julian Guzman, S.D.S.; Rev. Richard Maloney, S.D.S.; Bro. Sean McLaughlin, S.D.S.; Rev. Eliot Nitz, S.D.S.; Rev. Roman Stadtmueller, S.D.S.; Rev. Glen Willis, S.D.S.; Bro. Roger Nelson, S.D.S., Vicar;

WASHINGTON

Atonement Seminary-Franciscan Friars of the Atonement - 5207 Colorado Ave., N.W., Washington, DC 20011 t) 202-722-0461 Rev. C. Donald Howard, S.A.; Rev. Dennis Polanco, S.A., Dir.;

Deshairs Community-Oblates of St. Francis de Sales Residence - 1621 Otis St., N.E., Washington, DC 20018-2321 t) 202-529-1926 Rev. John W. Crossin, O.S.F.S.; Rev. Richard DeLillio, O.S.F.S.;

Diocesan Laborer Priests, House of Studies - 3706 15th

St., N.E., Washington, DC 20017 t) 202-832-4217 info@solinstitutedc.com www.solinstitutedc.com Rev. Ovidio Pecharroman, Dir.; Rev. Victor Salomon;

Discalced Carmelite Friars, Inc. - 2131 Lincoln Rd., N.E., Washington, DC 20002-1199 t) 202-832-6622 brpaquette@aol.com; mossytangle@hotmail.com ics publications.org ICS Publications Institute of Carmelite Studies Rev. Emmanuel Betasso, O.C.D., Mem.; Rev. Marc Foley, O.C.D., Prior; Rev. John Sullivan, O.C.D., Mem.; Rev. Eugene C. Wehner, O.C.D., Mem.; Rev. Salvatore Sciurba, O.C.D., Mem.; Bro. Bryan Paquette, O.C.D., Mem.; Bro. Robert Sentman, Mem.; Rev. Steven Payne, O.C.D., Mem.; Bro. Michael Stoeghauer, Mem.; Pr. Tchrs.: 1

Dominican House of Studies - 487 Michigan Ave., N.E., Washington, DC 20017 t) 202-529-5300 www.dhspriory.org (Pontifical Faculty of the Immaculate Conception; Dominican College; Dominican College Library; Dominican Friars, Priory of the Immaculate Conception) Very Rev. Gregory Schnakenberg, O.P., Prior; Very Rev. Jacob Thomas Petri, O.P., Pres., Pontifical Faculty of the Immaculate Conception; Rev. Christopher Antoninus Niemiec, O.P., Procurator/Economic Admin.; Rev. Sebastian White, O.P., Student Master; Editor (Magnificat); Rev. Dominic Langevin, O.P., Vice Pres. & Academic Dean, Pontifical Faculty of the Immaculate Conception; Rev. Bonaventure Chapman, O.P., Asst. Student Master; Rev. David Dominic Legge, O.P., Dir., Thomistic Institute; Rev. John Martin Ruiz, O.P., Librn.; Rev. Jeremy Aquinas Gilbeau, O.P., Chap.; Rev. Frassati Davis, O.P., Chap.; Rev. Hugh Vincent Dyer, O.P., Chap.; Rev. Joseph Hagan, O.P., Chap.; Rev. Brian Chrzastek, O.P., Prof.; Rev. Guy Albert Trudel, O.P., Prof.; Rev. Jordan Joseph Schmidt, O.P., Subprior; Rev. Basil Burr Cole, O.P., Prof.; Rev. Gabriel O'Donnell, O.P., Prof.; Rev. Stephen Desmond Ryan, O.P., Prof.; Rev. Nicholas E. Lombardo, O.P., Prof.; Rev. James Brent, O.P., Prof.; Rev. Michael D. O'Connor, O.P., Prof.; Rev. Reginald Lynch, O.P., Prof.; Rev. Ambrose Little, O.P., Prof.; Rev. Cajetan Cuddy, O.P., Prof.; Rev. Michael O'Connor, O.P., Prof.; Rev. Michael J. McCormack, O.P., Mem.; Rev. Patrick Mary Briscoe, O.P., Mem.; Rev. Raphael Christianson, O.P., In Res.; Rev. Joseph Tongchun Chen, O.P. (Taiwan), In Res.; Rev. John Baptist Ssmugabe, O.P. (Uganda), In Res.; Rev. Thomas Aquinas Pickett, O.P., In Res.; Rev. Francis Xinfei Wu, O.P. (Taiwan), In Res.; Stds.: 93; Lay Tchrs.: 2; Pr. Tchrs.: 18

St. Francis Friary-Capuchin College - 4121 Harewood Rd., N.E., Washington, DC 20017-1593 t) 202-529-2188 joekusnir@capuchin.com Rev. Gregory J. Brown, O.F.M.Cap., Pst. Min./Coord.; Rev. Timothy Durairaj, O.F.M.Cap. (India), Student; Rev. William Gillum, O.F.M.Cap., Spiritual Dir.; Rev. Daniel Mindling, O.F.M.Cap., Faculty & Formation Team; Rev. German Quiñones Tirú, O.F.M.Cap., Pst. Min./Coord.; Rev. Emett Schuler, O.F.M.Cap., Chap.; Rev. Brian Stacy, O.F.M.Cap., Dir., Post Novitiate Formation; Rev. Qiang (Keon) Tu, O.F.M.Cap., Student; Rev. Abihlash Varghese, O.F.M.Cap. (Ethiopia), Student; Rev. Thomas Weinandy, O.F.M.Cap., Theological Writer; Bro. Collin Brown, O.F.M.Cap., Student; Bro. Michael Herlihey, O.F.M.Cap., Student; Bro. Robert Herrick, O.F.M.Cap., Liturgy Dir.; Bro. Luke (Don Gun) Kim, O.F.M.Cap., Student; Bro. Michael Meza, O.F.M.Cap., Dir., Solanus Casey Prog.; Stds.: 6; Pr. Tchrs.: 1

Saint John Paul II Seminary - 145 Taylor St., N.E., Washington, DC 20017 t) 202-636-9020 jp2seminary@adw.org www.dcpriest.org Rev. Mark R. Ivany, Dir.; Rev. Carter H. Griffin, Rector; Rev. Msgr. Robert J. Panke, Rector;

Josephite Pastoral Center - 1200 Varnum St., N.E., Washington, DC 20017 t) 202-526-9270; 202-526-9271 ssjpastrcntr@aol.com Maria M. Lannon, Admin.; Rev. James E. McLinden, S.S.J., Dir.;

St. Joseph's Seminary - 1200 Varnum St., N.E., Washington, DC 20017 t) 202-526-4231; 202-526-4229 (Student) St. Joseph's Society of the Sacred Heart-Josephite Fathers & Brothers. Most Rev. John Ricard, Supr.; Rev. Nixon Mullah, S.S.J, Rector; Rev. Leo Udeagu, S.S.J., Rector; Rev. Godwin Akpan, S.S.J, In Res.; Rev. Joseph Ssemakula, In Res.;

Marian Fathers Scholasticate and Novitiate - 3885 Harewood Rd., N.E., Washington, DC 20017 t) 202-526-8884 marian.scholasticate.office@gmail.com www.marian.org Marian Fathers of the Immaculate Conception of the B.V.M., Inc. Rev. James McCormack, M.I.C., Supr.; Rev. Matthew Holladay, MIC, In Res.; Rev. David Smith, MIC, Treas.; Stds.: 9; Pr. Tchrs.: 2; Scholastics: 5

Marist College, Provincialate of the Marist Society in the USA - 815 Varnum St., N.E., Washington, DC 20017 t) 202-529-2821 randyh@maristsociety.org www.societyofmaryusa.org Society of Mary (Marists) (S.M.) Rev. Timothy G. Keating, S.M., Rector; Rev. Joseph C. Hindelang, S.M., Prov.; Bro. Randy T. Hoover, S.M., Admin.;

Maryknoll Fathers and Brothers - 1233 10th St., N.W., Washington, DC 20001 t) 202-450-3756 www.maryknoll.org Rev. David J. Schwinghamer, M.M.; Bro. Wm. Timothy Raible, M.M., Dir.;

Maryknoll Office of Global Concerns - 200 New York Ave., N.W., Washington, DC 20001 t) 202-832-1780 ogc@maryknoll.org Gerry Lee, Dir.;

Oblates of St. Francis de Sales - 1409 Kearney St., N.E., Washington, DC 20017 t) 202-269-2014 jextejt@gmail.com www.oblates.org Rev. John W. Crossin, O.S.F.S.; James Cummins, Pastoral Min./Coord.; Rev. John I. Extejt, O.S.F.S., Supr.;

Paulist Washington Community - 3001 4th St., NE, Washington, DC 20017 t) 202-832-6262 paulistsdc@gmail.com Paulist Fathers. Rev. Gregory Apparcel, Supr.; Rev. Michael Kallock, Dir.; Rev. John E. Lynch, C.S.P.; Rev. Ronald G. Roberson, C.S.P.; Rev. Francis P. DeSiano, C.S.P.; Stds.: 7

Queen of Pious Schools, Inc. - 1339 Monroe St., N.E., Washington, DC 20017-2510 t) 202-529-7734 queenofpiousschools@gmail.com Rev. Andrew C. Buechele, Sch.P., Rector; Rev. Fernando Negro, Sch.P., Prov.; Rev. John Callan, Sch.P., Secy.;

Theological College of the Catholic University of America - 401 Michigan Ave., N.E., Washington, DC 20017 t) 202-756-4900 www.theologicalcollege.org Sulpician Fathers. Rev. Dominic G. Ciriaco, Rector; Rev. Chris Arockiaraj, P.S.S., Vice Rector & Dir., Pastoral Formation; Rev. James McKearney, P.S.S., Dir., Music & Formation Faculty; Rev. Robert J. Cro, P.S.S., Formation Faculty; Rev. James P. Froehlich, O.F.M.Cap., Formation Faculty; Rev. Jaime Robledo, P.S.S., Formation Faculty; Dcn. Edward J. McCormack, Formation Faculty; Stds.: 55; Pr. Tchrs.: 7

Whitefriars Hall - 1600 Webster St., N.E., Washington, DC 20017 t) 202-526-1221 nwillemsen@carmelnet.org Rev. Rolf Willemsen, O.Carm., Prior; Rev. Nicholas Dustin Blackwell, O.Carm., In Res.; Rev. Craig Morrison, O.Carm.; Rev. Elias O'Brien, O.Carm.; Bro. Daryl Moresco, O.Carm., In Res.; Rev. Raimundo Luis, O.Carm., In Res.; Rev. Dimas Alexander Pele Alu, O.Carm., Mem.; Rev. Dionisius Aditya, O.Carm. (Indonesia), Mem.; Rev. Charles Setiawan (Indonesia), Mem.; Bro. David McGinnis, O.Carm., Treas.; Stds.: 17; Pr. Tchrs.: 1; Sr. Tchrs.: 1

The Carmelitana Library - Patricia O'Callagan, Librn.;

WEST HYATTSVILLE

Pallottine Seminary at Green Hill - 2009 Van Buren St., West Hyattsville, MD 20782-1761; Mailing: P.O. Box 5399, West Hyattsville, MD 20782 t) 301-422-3777 frfrank@sacapostles.org Society of the Catholic Apostolate. Rev. Frank S. Donio, S.A.C., Rector; Rev. Louis F. Micca, S.A.C., In Res.;

SHRINES [SHR]

WASHINGTON

Basilica of the National Shrine of the Immaculate Conception - 400 Michigan Ave., N.E., Washington, DC 20017-1566 t) 202-526-8300 info@nationalshrine.com www.nationalshrine.com Rev. Msgr. Walter R. Rossi, Rector; Rev. Ismael (Mel) N. Ayala, Liturgy Dir.; Rev. Msgr. Vito A. Buonanno, Dir. Pilgrimages; Rev. Raymond A. Lebrun, O.M.I., Spiritual Dir.;

Basilica of the National Shrine of the Immaculate Conception - 400 Michigan Ave., N.E., Washington, DC 20017-1566 t) 202-526-8300 info@nationalshrine.com www.nationalshrine.com Rev. Msgr. Walter R. Rossi, Rector; Rev. Msgr. Vito A. Buonanno, Dir.; Rev. Raymond A. Lebrun, O.M.I., Dir.; Rev. Michael D. Weston, Dir.;

Rosary Shrine of St. Jude - St. Dominic's Church, 630 E. St., S.W., Washington, DC 20024-2598; Mailing: 141 E. 65th St., New York, NY 10065 t) 212-595-3664 df@dominicanfriars.org Dominican Fathers and Brothers. Rev. Gabriel Gillen, O.P., Dir.;

SPECIAL CARE FACILITIES [SPF]

SILVER SPRING

Saint Luke Institute, Inc. - 8380 Colesville Rd., Ste. 300, Silver Spring, MD 20910-6264 t) 301-445-7970 getinfo@sli.org www.sli.org Education, candidate assessment, intensive behavioral and spiritual health treatment services for clergy & religious; outpatient services for laity. Marianne Durgavich, Admin.; Rev. David Songy, O.F.M.Cap., Pres.;

WASHINGTON

Lt. Joseph P. Kennedy, Jr., Institute - 801 Buchanan St., N.E., Washington, DC 20017 A private, nonprofit organization providing education, training and employment. Dcn. Richard C. Birkel, Pres.;

Adult Learning & Employment Services - t) 202-529-0500

Community Living Partnership -

Family & Personal Support Services - t) 301-251-2860

Kennedy Education - t) 202-529-7600 Includes Kennedy School, Outreach Program to Catholic Schools & Inclusion 2000.

Diocese of Wheeling-Charleston

(Dioecesis Vhelingensis Carolopolitanus)

MOST REVEREND MARK E. BRENNAN

Bishop of Wheeling-Charleston; ordained May 15, 1976; appointed Titular Bishop of Rusibisir and Auxiliary Bishop of Baltimore December 5, 2016; installed January 19, 2017; appointed Bishop of Wheeling-Charleston July 23, 2019; installed August 22, 2019. 1311 Byron St., Wheeling, WV 26003.

Chancery Office: 1311 Byron St., P.O. Box 230, Wheeling, WV 26003. T: 304-233-0880; F: 304-233-0890.
www.dwc.org
ccarter@dwc.org

Square Miles 24,041.

Established as Diocese of Wheeling July 19, 1850; Redesignated Diocese of Wheeling-Charleston October 4, 1974.

Comprises the entire State of West Virginia.

For legal titles of parishes and diocesan institutions, consult the Chancery Office.

STATISTICAL OVERVIEW

Personnel

Bishop....1
Retired Bishops....1
Priests: Diocesan Active in Diocese....45
Priests: Retired, Sick or Absent....26
Number of Diocesan Priests....71
Religious Priests in Diocese....33
Total Priests in your Diocese....104
Extern Priests in Diocese....32
Permanent Deacons in Diocese....48
Total Brothers....5
Total Sisters....78

Parishes

Parishes....92
With Resident Pastor:
Resident Diocesan Priests....52
Resident Religious Priests....18
Without Resident Pastor:
Administered by Priests....22
Missions....20
Professional Ministry Personnel:
Sisters....11
Lay Ministers....20

Welfare

Catholic Hospitals....1
Total Assisted....752,023
Day Care Centers....1
Total Assisted....95
Specialized Homes....1
Total Assisted....14
Special Centers for Social Services....14
Total Assisted....6,306

Educational

Diocesan Students in Other Seminaries....9
Total Seminarians....9
Colleges and Universities....1
Total Students....700
High Schools, Diocesan and Parish....6
Total Students....818
Elementary Schools, Diocesan and Parish....18
Total Students....3,604
Catechesis/Religious Education:
High School Students....337
Elementary Students....2,482
Total Students under Catholic Instruction....7,950
Teachers in Diocese:
Sisters....2
Lay Teachers....339

Vital Statistics

Receptions into the Church:
Infant Baptism Totals....478
Minor Baptism Totals....89
Adult Baptism Totals....90
Received into Full Communion....163
First Communions....593
Confirmations....651
Marriages:
Catholic....123
Interfaith....64
Total Marriages....187
Deaths....849
Total Catholic Population....64,231
Total Population....1,775,156

LEADERSHIP

Vicar General and Moderator of the Curia - t) 304-233-0880 jpeterson@dwc.org Rev. Msgr. Joseph L. Peterson, Vicar;

Director of Diocesan Administrative Services - t) 304-233-0880 x263 bminor@dwc.org Bryan E. Minor;

Chancery Office - t) 304-233-0880 Chad R. Carter, Chancellor;

Chancellor - t) 304-233-0880 x260 ccarter@dwc.org Chad R. Carter;

Diocesan Tribunal - t) 304-233-0880 jaugustine@dwc.org Very Rev. Joseph Mandokkara Augustine, Judicial Vicar;

Judicial Vicar - t) 304-233-0880 jaugustine@dwc.org Very Rev. Joseph Mandokkara Augustine;

- **Defender of Bond -** Dcn. Dennis W. Nesser; Rev. Narisetti Sateesh, H.G.N.;
- **Judges -** Very Rev. Joseph Mandokkara Augustine; Dcn. Dennis W. Nesser; Rev. Msgr. Kevin Michael Quirk;
- **Promoter of Justice -** Rev. Msgr. Kevin Michael Quirk;

Diocesan Consultors - t) 304-233-0880 Rev. Carlos L. Melocoton Jr. (stlukepastor@comcast.net); Rev. Msgr. Eugene S. Ostrowski; Rev. Msgr. Joseph L. Peterson;

Delegate for Consecrated Life - t) 304-233-0880 mgomez@dwc.org Sr. Martha Teresa Gomez, R.G.S., Delegate for Consecrated Life;

Episcopal Vicar for Clergy - t) 304-233-0880 Very Rev. Dennis R. Schuelkens Jr.;

Vicars Forane - t) 304-233-0880 Very Rev. Sebastian Embrayil Devasya (sdevasya@dwc.org); Very Rev. Timothy J. Grassi; Very Rev. Donald X. Higgs;

Finance Council - t) 304-233-0880 Most Rev. Mark E. Brennan; Rev. Msgr. Eugene S. Ostrowski; Chad R. Carter;

Diocesan Financial Administrator/Chief Financial Officer - t) 304-233-0880 phenry@dwc.org Patrick Henry, CFO;

OFFICES AND DIRECTORS

Apostleship of Prayer -

Archivists - t) 304-233-0880 x325 jgilot@dwc.org Jon-Erik Gilot, Archivist; Chad R. Carter, Chancellor;

Associate Superintendent for Accreditation and Technology - t) 304-233-0880 x208 jhornyak@dwc.org Jennifer L. Hornyak, Asst. Supt.;

Behavioral Counseling and Ministry - t) 304-233-0880 x472 rpark@dwc.org Rev. Robert G. Park, Dir.;

Buildings and Properties - t) 304-233-0880 x293 jreardon@dwc.org John Reardon, Dir.;

Catholic Charismatic Renewal - t) 304-229-5014 deaconbrian@stleo.com Dcn. Ben Brian Crim, Liaison;

Catholic Committee on Scouting - t) (304) 463-4488 Daniel A. Maul, Mem.; Mark Enders, Chair; Richard E. Fauss;

Catholic Conference of West Virginia - t) (304) 230-1581 Matthew R. Bowles, Exec. Dir.;

Catholic University of America, Friends of the - t) 304-233-0880

(CCWVa) Catholic Charities West Virginia - t) 304-905-9860 Beth Zarate, CEO;

- **(CCWVa) Advancement Office -** t) (304) 905-9860 John Catone, CAO;
- **(CCWVa) Child and Adult Care Food Program -** t) 304-230-1280 Jane Rose, Dir.;
- **(CCWVa) Child Care Resource Center -** t) (304) 232-1603 Brittany Lucci, Dir.;
- **(CCWVa) HomeCare Services -** t) (304) 905-9860 Ed Murray, Prog. Coord.;
- **(CCWVa) WV Birth to Three Region One -** t) 304-214-5775 Wendy Miller, Dir.;

Cemeteries - t) 304-242-0460 dbreiding@dwc.org Dcn. Doug Breiding;

Censor Librorum - Very Rev. Joseph Mandokkara Augustine;

Computer Information Systems - t) 304-233-0880 Richard A. Harrold, Dir.; David Hanes, Technology Network Engineer; Nicholas Gulisek, Website Devel. (ngulisek@dwc.org);

Curriculum and Instruction - t) 304-233-0880 x359 tradinsky@dwc.org Troy Radinsky, Dir.;

Department of Catholic Schools - t) 304-233-0880 mdeschaine@dwc.org Mary Ann Deschaine, Supt.;

- **Schools, Superintendent of -** t) 304-233-0880 Mary Ann Deschaine, Supt.;

Diaconate Executive Committee - t) 304-233-0880 Very Rev. Dennis R. Schuelkens Jr., Ex-Offiicio; Dcn. John W. Yaquinta, Chair; Dcn. Doug Breiding, Mem.;

Diocesan and Foreign Missions, Office of - t) 304-233-0880 ccarter@dwc.org Chad R. Carter, Dir.;

Diocesan (Home) Missions - t) 304-233-0880 ccarter@dwc.org Chad R. Carter, Dir.;

Diocesan Newspaper: "The Catholic Spirit" - t) 304-233-0880 x347 crowan@dwc.org Colleen Rowan, Editor;

Diocesan Spokesperson - t) 304-233-0880 Tim Bishop (tbishop@dwc.org);

Ecumenism, Office of - t) 304-720-8313 rgodwin@dwc.org Dcn. Raymond G. Godwin, Ecumenical Officer;

Evangelization and Catechesis, Office of - t) 304-233-0880 dmaul@dwc.org Daniel A. Maul, Dir.;

Finance Office - t) 304-233-0880 phenry@dwc.org Patrick Henry, CFO; Michael Deemer, Assoc. CFO (mdeemer@dwc.org); Frank Bonacci, Controller;

Holy Childhood Association - t) 304-233-0880 ccarter@dwc.org Chad R. Carter, Dir.;

Human Resources, Office of - t) 304-233-0880 x253 Michael Walsh, Dir.;

Justice and Life, Office of - t) (304) 233-0880

Migration and Refugee Services - Martinsburg, Office of - t) 304-267-3071 Nicole Annan, Assoc. Immigration Attorney;

Migration and Refugee Services - Morgantown - t) 304-343-1036 Kellie Rogers, Mng. Attorney/ Dir. Refugee Resettlement & Immigration;

Office of Worship and Sacraments - t) 304-233-0880 x288 bkime@dwc.org Bernadette McMasters Kime, Dir.;

- **Diocesan Liturgical Commission -** t) (304) 233-0880 Bernadette McMasters Kime;

Permanent Diaconate Formation - t) 304-233-0880 Very Rev. Dennis R. Schuelkens Jr., Dir.;

Presbyteral Council - t) 304-233-0880 Most Rev. Mark E. Brennan; Rev. Msgr. Eugene S. Ostrowski; Very Rev. Dennis R. Schuelkens Jr.;

Priests' Health and Retirement Association - t) 304-233-0880 Very Rev. Dennis R. Schuelkens Jr., Vice. Pres.; Rev. Msgr. Frederick P. Annie, Mem. (fannie@dwc.org); Very Rev. John S. Ledford, Mem.;

Prison Ministry, Office of - t) 304-472-1217 Rev. William J. Kuchinsky, Supvr.; Dcn. John W. Sarraga, Dir.; Dcn. Rue C. Thompson Jr., Dir.;

- **Federal Facilities -** t) 304-472-1217 Rev. William J. Kuchinsky, Supvr.; Dcn. John W. Sarraga, Dir.;
- **State Facilities -** t) 304-472-1217 Rev. William J. Kuchinsky, Supvr.; Dcn. Rue C. Thompson Jr., Dir.;

Propagation of the Faith, Pontifical Society for - t) 304-233-0880 x260 ccarter@dwc.org Chad R. Carter, Dir.;

Safe Environment, Office of - t) 304-233-0880 x458 sgoudy@dwc.org Sharon K. Goudy, Coord.;

Social Ministries Office - t) (304) 233-0880 x289 Kathy Barton, Dir.;

Stewardship and Development, Office of - t) 304-233-0880 kbenson@dwc.org; hsforza@dwc.org Kristen Benson, Dir.; Heidi Sforza, Dir.;

Victim Assistance Coordinator - t) 304-242-6988 Dr. Patricia M. Bailey;

Vocations, Office of - t) 304-233-0880 x442 wvpriests.org/ Rev. Brian J. Crenwelge, Dir.; Ross Semler, Office Mgr.;

PARISHES, MISSIONS, AND CLERGY

STATE OF WEST VIRGINIA

BARTOW

St. Mark the Evangelist Mission - Catholic Church Rd., Bartow, WV 24954 t) 304-799-6778 pastor@pocahontascatholic.org pocahontascatholic.org See St. John Neumann, Marlinton. Rev. Arthur Bufogle Jr., Pst.;

BECKLEY

St. Francis De Sales - 614 S. Oakwood Ave., Beckley, WV 25801 t) 304-256-3594 (Rectory); 304-253-3695 (Parish); 304-255-4694 (CRP) church@stfrancis-wv.org stfrancis-wv.org/ Rev. Leonard A. Smith, Pst.; Dcn. Harry K. Evans; Dcn. John F. Ziolkowski; CRP Stds.: 207

- **St. Francis de Sales School** - (Grades PreK-8) 622 S. Oakwood Ave., Beckley, WV 25801 t) 304-252-4087 sfschool@suddenlinkmail.com Mary Grace Peck, Prin.; Stds.: 196; Scholastics: 17; Lay Tchrs.: 17

BENWOOD

St. John - 622 Main St., Benwood, WV 26031; Mailing: c/o St. Alphonsus Parish, 2111 Market St., Wheeling, WV 26003 t) 304-232-6455 offices@saintsjamesandjohn.org Very Rev. John S. Ledford, Pst.; Rev. Doney Chacko, R.C.J., Par. Vicar; CRP Stds.: 10

BERKELEY SPRINGS

St. Vincent de Paul - 67 Liberty St., Berkeley Springs, WV 25411; Mailing: P.O. Box 634, Berkeley Springs, WV 25411-0634 t) 304-258-1311 parishoffice@stvindepaulwv.com stvincentdepaulcatholicchurchbs.com Rev. J. Michael O. Lecias, Admin.; CRP Stds.: 30

BLUEFIELD

Sacred Heart - 1003 Wyoming St., Bluefield, WV 24701; Mailing: P.O. Box 608, Bluefield, WV 24701-0608 t) 304-327-5623 khickman@sacredheartblfd.org; julia@sacredheartblfd.org www.sacredheartblfd.org Very Rev. Sebastian Embrayil Devasya, Pst.; Julia Harrison, Pst. Assoc.; CRP Stds.: 33

BOOMER

St. Anthony's Shrine - 2764 Midland Tr., Rte. 60, Boomer, WV 25031; Mailing: c/o Immaculate Conception Parish, P.O. Box 65, Montgomery, WV 25136-0065 t) 304-442-2101 ic_sa@frontier.com See Immaculate Conception, Montgomery. Rev. Dominikus Baok, S.V.D., Admin.;

BRIDGEPORT

All Saints - 317 E. Main St., Bridgeport, WV 26330-1750 t) 304-842-2283 allsaintswv@gmail.com allsaintsbridgeport.com Rev. Walter M. Jagela, Pst.; CRP Stds.: 124

BUCKHANNON

Holy Rosary - 35 Franklin St., Buckhannon, WV 26201; Mailing: 34 Franklin St., Buckhannon, WV 26201-0848 t) 304-472-3414 hrp2306buc@dwc.org holyrosarywv.org Rev. Edward Tetteh, SVD, Admin.; Rev. John Hue Tran, S.V.D., In Res.; Dcn. Rue C. Thompson Jr.; CRP Stds.: 40

CAMDEN

St. Boniface - 9140 U.S. Hwy. 33W, Camden, WV 26338-8256 t) 304-269-1767 saintbonifacechurch@yahoo.com Rev. Gary P. Naegele, Pst.;

- **St. Clare in St. Clara, WV** - 2531 Little Buck Run Rd, New Milton, WV 26411; Mailing: 9140 U.S. Hwy. 33W, Camden, WV 26338-8256

CHAPMANVILLE

St. Barbara - 33 Sawmill Rd., Chapmanville, WV 25508; Mailing: P.O. Box 467, c/o St. Mary Queen of Heaven Parish, Madison, WV 25130 t) 304-369-4538; (304) 855-7962 nbuchlein@dwc.org See St. Mary Queen of Heaven, Madison. Rev. Neil R. Buchlein, Pst.;

CHARLES TOWN

St. James - 49 Crosswinds Dr., Charles Town, WV 25414 t) 304-725-5558 parsec@stjameswv.org www.stjameswv.org Very Rev. Timothy J. Grassi, Pst.; Dcn. David E. Galvin, Pst. Assoc.; Dcn. James T. Munuhe; Dcn. Luis A. Pagano; Gary Penkala, Pst. Assoc.; CRP Stds.: 233

St. Peter - 110 Church St., Harpers Ferry, WV 25425 stjp2011ct@dwc.org

CHARLESTON

Basilica of the Co-Cathedral of the Sacred Heart - 1032 Virginia St. E., Charleston, WV 25301; Mailing: 1114 Virginia St., E., Charleston, WV 25301-2407 t) 304-342-8175 sacredheart@shccwv.us Most Rev. Mark E. Brennan, Pst.; Very Rev. Donald X. Higgs, Rector; CRP Stds.: 21

Basilica of the Co-Cathedral of the Sacred Heart School - 1035 Quarrier St. E., Charleston, WV 25301 t) 304-346-5491 adavis@sacredheartgradeschool.org shgs.us Anne Davis, Prin.; Stds.: 289; Scholastics: 26; Lay Tchrs.: 26

St. Agnes - 49th St. and Staunton Ave., S.E., Charleston, WV 25304; Mailing: 4807 Staunton Ave., S.E., Charleston, WV 25304-1951 t) 304-925-2836 stap1101char@dwc.org; st.agneswv@gmail.com Rev. Jose Manuel Escalante, Pst.;

St. Anthony - 1000 Sixth St., Charleston, WV 25302 t) 304-342-2716 secretary@stanthonywv.com www.stanthonywv.com Rev. Thomas K. Kalapurackal, Pst.; Rev. Charles I. Anemelu, In Res.; Jennifer Burdette, DRE; Dcn. David Wuletich; CRP Stds.: 3

CHESTER

Sacred Heart - 424 4th St., Chester, WV 26034-0313; Mailing: 418 4th St., Chester, WV 26034-0313 t) 304-387-0198 shp2226ches@dwc.org; sacredheart1925@comcast.net sacredheartchester.org Rev. William K. Matheny Jr., Pst.; Robert Glass, DRE; CRP Stds.: 65

CLARKSBURG

Immaculate Conception - 126 E. Pike St., Clarksburg, WV 26301; Mailing: 150 S. Maple Ave., Clarksburg, WV 26301 t) 304-622-8243 icchurchclarksburg@gmail.com icclarksburg.com Very Rev. Casey B. Mahone, Pst.; CRP Stds.: 69

St. James the Apostle - Pride Ave. & N. 21st St., Clarksburg, WV 26301; Mailing: 2107 Pride Ave., Clarksburg, WV 26301-1819 t) 304-622-1668 stjamesparishclarksburg@gmail.com www.stjamesparishclarksburg.org Rev. B.K. Akila Gayan Rodrigo, T.O.R., Pst.; Rev. Christopher Turner, Assoc. Pst.; CRP Stds.: 44

COALTON

St. Patrick - 200 Church St., Coalton, WV 26257; Mailing: P.O. Box 99, Coalton, WV 26257-0099 t) 304-636-0546 joconnor@dwc.org Rev. James O'Connor, Pst.; Dcn. Raymond G. Godwin; Dcn. John W. Sarraga;

DUNBAR

Christ the King - 1504 Grosscup Ave., Dunbar, WV 25064; Mailing: P.O. Box 339, c/o Holy Trinity Parish, Nitro, WV 25143-0339 t) 304-755-0791 nitrocatholic@aol.com Rev. John Chapin Engler Jr., Pst.; Dcn. Dennis W. Nesser; CRP Stds.: 2

ELIZABETH

St. Elizabeth of Hungary - 24 Butternut St., Elizabeth, WV 26143 t) 681-236-2700 rprechtl@dwc.org See Holy Redeemer, Spencer. Rev. Ronald G. Prechtl, Pst.;

ELKINS

St. Brendan - 181 St. Brendan Way, Elkins, WV 26241 t) 304-636-0546 stbrendanchurch.elkinswv@gmail.com stbrendanwv.weebly.com Rev. James O'Connor, Pst.; Dcn. Raymond G. Godwin; Dcn. John W. Sarraga; CRP Stds.: 22

St. John Bosco - Rte. 1, Huttonsville, WV 26273-9737; Mailing: Box 9D, Huttonsville, WV 26273-9737 joconnor@dwc.org

ELKVIEW

Our Lady of the Hills - 100 Jackson Dr., Elkview, WV 25071; Mailing: 1000 6th St., c/o St. Anthony Catholic Church, Charleston, WV 25302 t) 304-342-2716 secretary@stanthonywv.com www.ourladyofthehills.com Rev. Thomas K. Kalapurackal, Pst.; CRP Stds.: 11

FAIRMONT

St. Anthony - 1660 Mary Lou Retton Dr., Fairmont, WV 26554 t) 304-363-1328 parishoffice@sahswv.org www.sahswv.org Rev. Romeo Bacalso, S.V.D., Pst.; CRP Stds.: 21

Immaculate Conception - 329 Maryland Ave., Fairmont, WV 26554; Mailing: 406 Alta Vista Ave., Fairmont, WV 26554 t) 304-363-5796 church@icfairmont.com www.icfairmont.com Rev. Kishore Babu Varaparla, H.G.N. (India), Admin.; Sr. Stella Cronauer, C.S.J., Pst. Assoc.; CRP Stds.: 40

St. Peter the Fisherman - Corner of Jackson and Madison St., Fairmont, WV 26554; Mailing: 407 Jackson St., Fairmont, WV 26554-2941 t) 304-363-7434 churchoffice@thefisherman.org www.thefisherman.org Very Rev. Joseph M. Konikattil, Pst.; Dcn. David P. Lester; CRP Stds.: 7

FARMINGTON

St. Peter - 1304 Mill St., Farmington, WV 26571; Mailing: 204 Furbee Ave., Mannington, WV 26582-1399 t) 304-986-2321 stpatstpete@comcast.net Rev. Binu Emmanuel, C.S.T., Admin.; Diane Aloi, DRE; CRP Stds.: 2

FOLLANSBEE

St. Anthony - 1017 Jefferson St., Follansbee, WV 26037-1334 t) 304-527-2286 stanthonychurch@comcast.net Rev. L.J. Asantha Jude Perera, T.O.R., Pst.; CRP Stds.: 20

FORT ASHBY

Annunciation of Our Lord - 8819 Frankfort Hwy., Fort Ashby, WV 26719; Mailing: P.O. Box 1560, Fort Ashby, WV 26719-1560 t) 304-298-3392 annunciationchurch@atlanticbbn.net aoolsa.org Rev. Daniel Price, Pst.; CRP Stds.: 17

FRANKLIN

St. Elizabeth Ann Seton - 167 Walnut St., Franklin, WV 26807; Mailing: P.O. Box 890, Franklin, WV 26807 t) 304-358-7012 jpisano@dwc.org Rev. Joseph Daniel Pisano, Pst.; Dcn. John E. Windett; CRP Stds.: 4

GASSAWAY

St. Thomas - 624 Kanawha St., Gassaway, WV 26624-1208 t) 304-364-5895 stthomasgassaway@gmail.com Rev. Thien Duc Nguyen, S.V.D., Pst.; CRP Stds.: 12

GLEN DALE

St. Jude - 710 Jefferson Ave., Glen Dale, WV 26038-0147; Mailing: P.O. Box 147, Glen Dale, WV 26038-0147 t) 304-845-2646 x1 stjp1066gd@dwc.org www.stjudewv.com Very Rev. John S. Ledford, Pst.; CRP Stds.: 12

GLENVILLE

Good Shepherd - 701 Mineral Rd., Glenville, WV 26351-1310 t) 304-462-7130 goodshepherdglenville@gmail.com Rev. Gary P. Naegele, Pst.;

GRAFTON

St. Augustine - 17 W. Washington St., Grafton, WV 26354 t) 304-265-3861 staugustinegrafton@comcast.net Rev. Babu Joseph Elamturuthil, Pst.;

HEDGESVILLE

St. Bernadette Catholic Church - 113 W. Main St., Hedgesville, WV 25427; Mailing: P.O. Box 11, Hedgesville, WV 25247 t) 304-754-7830 office@stbernadettewv.org stbernadettewv.org Rev. Aloysius N Boh, Admin.; CRP Stds.: 41

HINTON

St. Patrick - 309 -2nd Ave., Hinton, WV 25951-0008; Mailing: 309 2nd Ave., Hinton, WV 25951 t) 304-466-3966 stpathintonwv@yahoo.com; psychedinwv@yahoo.com www.stpatrickhintonwv.org Rev. Chinh Quang Joseph Tran, S.V.D., Admin.; Dcn. J. Peter Minogue; Cam Pulliam, DRE;

St. Colman - (Irish Mountain, WV)

HUNTINGTON

St. Joseph Parish - 1304 6th Ave., Huntington, WV 25708; Mailing: P.O. Box 369, Huntington, WV 25708 t) 304-525-5202 dborgmeyer@dwc.org www.stjoeshuntington.org Rev. Msgr. Dean G. Borgmeyer, Pst.; CRP Stds.: 20

St. Joseph Catholic School - (Grades PreK-8) 1326 Sixth Ave., Huntington, WV 25701 t) 304-522-2644 ctempleton@stjosephgs.org www.stjosephgs.org Dr. Carol Templeton, Prin.; Stds.: 340; Scholastics: 26; Lay Tchrs.: 26

Our Lady of Fatima - 545 Norway Ave., Huntington, WV 25705 t) 304-525-0866 church@olofatima.org www.ourfatimafamily.com Rev. Tijo George, M.C.B.S., Pst.; Rev. Pradeep Kumar, H.G.N., Par. Vicar; CRP Stds.: 13

Our Lady of Fatima School - 535 Norway Ave., Huntington, WV 25705 t) 304-523-2861 moconnor@olofatima.org Micah OConnor, Prin.; Stds.: 90; Scholastics: 14; Lay Tchrs.: 14

St. Peter Claver - 828 - 15th St., Huntington, WV 25701; Mailing: P.O. Box 326, Huntington, WV 25708 t) 304-523-7311 spchwv@gmail.com www.spcwv.com Rev. Shaji Jacob Thomas (India), Admin.; CRP Stds.: 10

Sacred Heart - 2015 Adams Ave., Huntington, WV 25704-1419 t) 304-429-4318 shcchwv@gmail.com shcchwv.com Rev. Shaji Jacob Thomas (India), Pst.; CRP Stds.: 19

HURRICANE

Catholic Church of the Ascension - 905 Hickory Mill Rd., Hurricane, WV 25526 t) 304-562-5816 aperkins@ascensionhurricane.org Rev. Vincent Ezhanikatt Joseph (India), Pst.; CRP Stds.: 93

INWOOD

St. Leo - 2109 Sulphur Springs Rd., Inwood, WV 25428; Mailing: P.O. Box 93, Inwood, WV 25428-0093 t) 304-229-8945 aobiudu@dwc.org; secretary@stleo.com www.stleo.com Rev. Alfred U. Obiudu (Nigeria), Pst.; Dcn. Ben Brian Crim; CRP Stds.: 54

KEYSER

Assumption - 34 James St., Keyser, WV 26726-2721 t) 304-788-2488 acckwv@gmail.com assumptionkeyserwv.org Dcn. Lawrence V. Hammel; Rev. Thomas A. Sebastian, C.S.T., Pst.; CRP Stds.: 65

KINGWOOD

St. Sebastian - 324 E. Main St., Kingwood, WV 26537; Mailing: 322 E. Main St., Kingwood, WV 26537-1237 t) 304-329-1519 prestoncountycatholic@gmail.com www.prestoncountycatholic.org Rev. Dominic Athishu, Admin.; CRP Stds.: 39

LOGAN

St. Francis of Assisi - 561 Main St., Logan, WV 25601-3899 t) 304-752-3017 stfrancislogan@gmail.com Rev. Biju Paul Parampil, Admin.; Connie Bazzilla, Pst. Assoc.;

LUBECK

St. Monica Mission - 1942 Harris Hwy., Lubeck, WV 26181; Mailing: c/o St. Francis Xavier, 609 Market St., Parkersburg, WV 26101-5144 t) 304-422-6786 jrice@dwc.org Rev. John Rice, Pst.;

MADISON

St. Mary Queen of Heaven - 51 Madison Ave., Madison, WV 25130; Mailing: P.O. Box 467, Madison, WV 25130-0467 t) 304-369-4538 nbuchlein@dwc.org Rev. Neil R. Buchlein, Pst.; CRP Stds.: 1

St. Joseph the Worker - State Rte. 3, Whitesville, WV 25209 t) (304) 854-2997

MANNINGTON

St. Patrick - 204 Furbee Ave., Mannington, WV 26582-1399 t) 304-986-2321 stpatstpete@comcast.net Rev. Binu Emmanuel, C.S.T., Admin.; Stephanie Tomana, DRE; CRP Stds.: 6

MARLINTON

St. John Neumann - 714 - 10th Ave., Marlinton, WV 24954-1314 t) 304-799-6778 pastor@pocahontascatholic.org pocahontascatholic.org Rev. Arthur Bufogle Jr., Pst.;

MARTINSBURG

St. Joseph's - 225 S. Queen St., Martinsburg, WV 25401;

Mailing: 336 S. Queen St., Martinsburg, WV 25401 t) 304-267-4893 office@stjosephwv.org www.stjosephwv.org Rev. Thomas R. Gallagher, Pst.; Rev. Manuel T. Gelido, Assoc. Pst.; Dcn. Luis A. Pagano; Dcn. Marcus C. Pressl; CRP Stds.: 101

St. Joseph's School - (Grades PreK-8) 110 E. Stephen St., Martinsburg, WV 25401 t) 304-267-6447 info@sjswv.org www.sjswv.org Maria Byrd, Prin.; Stds.: 326; Lay Tchrs.: 27

MASONTOWN

St. Zita Mission - 33 Maple St., Masontown, WV 26542; Mailing: c/o St. Sebastian Church, 322 E. Main St., Kingwood, WV 26537-1237 t) 304-329-1519 prestoncountycatholic@yahoo.com www.prestoncountycatholic@gmail.com See St. Sebastian, Kingwood. Rev. Dominic Athishu, Admin.;

MAYSEL

Risen Lord Mission - 67 Wallback Rd., Maysel, WV 25133 t) 304-587-4740 risenlordchurch@gmail.com Rev. Thien Duc Nguyen, S.V.D., Pst.;

MCMECHEN

St. James - 326 Logan St., McMechen, WV 26040; Mailing: 2111 Market St., c/o St. Alphonsus Parish, Wheeling, WV 26003 t) 304-232-1227 offices@saintjamesandjohn.org Very Rev. John S. Ledford, Pst.; Rev. Doney Chacko, R.C.J., Par. Vicar;

MONONGAH

Holy Spirit - 687 Maple Ter., Monongah, WV 26554-1116 t) 304-534-3020 parishoffice@sahswv.org sahswv.org Rev. Romeo Bacalso, S.V.D.; CRP Stds.: 24

MONTGOMERY

Immaculate Conception - 708 First Ave., Montgomery, WV 25136; Mailing: P.O. Box 65, Montgomery, WV 25136-0065 t) 304-442-2101 ic_sa@frontier.com Rev. Dominikus Baok, S.V.D., Admin.; Dcn. John Divita; CRP Stds.: 4

MOOREFIELD

Epiphany of the Lord - 2029 State Rd. 55, Moorefield, WV 26836 t) 304-434-2547 ephiphanyrc@hardynet.com Rev. Joseph Daniel Pisano, Pst.; CRP Stds.: 7

MORGANTOWN

St. Francis de Sales Catholic Church - 1 Guthrie Ln., Morgantown, WV 26508-4837 t) 304-296-5353 stfrancisdesalesparish.com/ Formerly The New St. Theresa & St. Elizabeth Ann Seton. Rev. Msgr. Anthony Cincinnati, Pst.; Dcn. Pierce Murphy, Pst. Assoc.; Sr. Nancy White, C.S.J., Pst. Assoc.; CRP Stds.: 130

St. John University - 1481 University Ave., Morgantown, WV 26505-5598 t) 304-296-8231 stjup1656morg@dwc.org; info@mountaineercatholic.com www.mountaineercatholic.com Rev. Brian J. Crenwelge, Pst.; Rev. Phillip R. Szabo, Par. Vicar; Dcn. Joseph J. Prentiss; John Lojewski, DRE; CRP Stds.: 29

St. Luke the Evangelist - 19 Jo Glen Dr., Morgantown, WV 26508-4434 t) 304-594-2353 st.luke.secretary@comcast.net; stlukeschurch@comcast.net stlukemorgantown.com/ Rev. Biju T. Devassy, Pst.; CRP Stds.: 69

St. Mary - 3346 University Ave., Morgantown, WV 26505 t) 304-599-3747 www.stmarystarcity.com Rev. John P. McDonough, Pst.; Sr. Rachel Blais, S.C., Dir., St. Ursula Food Pantry & Outreach; CRP Stds.: 111

MOUNDSVILLE

St. Francis Xavier - 7th St. & Jefferson Ave., Moundsville, WV 26041; Mailing: 912 - 7th St., Moundsville, WV 26041-2106 t) 304-845-1593 sfxmoundsville@comcast.net sfxmoundsville.org Mary Helen Marling, DRE; Rev. That Son Ngoc Nguyen, Pst.; CRP Stds.: 13

NEW CUMBERLAND

Immaculate Conception - 1016 Ridge Ave., New Cumberland, WV 26047-0666 t) 304-564-5068 icp2236nc@dwc.org immaculateconceptionnc.org/ Rev. William K. Matheny Jr., Pst.; Beth Ann Dicks, DRE; CRP Stds.: 9

NEW MARTINSVILLE

St. Vincent de Paul - 21 Rosary Rd., New Martinsville, WV 26155-1602 t) 304-455-4615 office@svdpnm.org; stvdpp2116nm@dwc.org Rev. Msgr. Kevin Michael Quirk, Pst.; CRP Stds.: 13

NITRO

Holy Trinity - 2219 - 22nd St., Nitro, WV 25143; Mailing: P.O. Box 339, Nitro, WV 25143-0339 t) 304-755-0791 nitrocatholic@aol.com triparishwv.org Rev. John Chapin Engler Jr., Pst.; CRP Stds.: 8

St. Patrick - 207 Jefferson St., Bancroft, WV 25011; Mailing: c/o Holy Trinity Parish, P.O. Box 339, Nitro, WV 25143 t) 304-586-3485

OAK HILL

SS. Peter and Paul - 129 Elmore St., Oak Hill, WV 25901-2628 t) 304-465-5445 ssppp1216oh@dwc.org Rev. Jojan Joseph, C.S.T., Pst.; CRP Stds.: 12

SS. Peter and Paul School - 123 Elmore St., Oak Hill, WV 25901-2628 t) 304-465-5045 nmucho@ssppcatholic.org Natasha Mucho-Seay, Prin.; Stds.: 59; Scholastics: 6; Lay Tchrs.: 6

ONA

St. Stephen - 2491 James River Tpke., Ona, WV 25545; Mailing: 651 Hollow Rd., Ona, WV 25545 t) 304-743-3234 ststephens@suddenlinkmail.com www.ststephens1.com Rev. Tijo George, M.C.B.S., Pst.; Rev. Pradeep Kumar, H.G.N., Assoc. Pst.; CRP Stds.: 15

PADEN CITY

Mater Dolorosa - 302 E. Main St., Paden City, WV 26159-1736; Mailing: 21 Rosary Rd., c/o St. Vincent dePaul Church, New Martinsville, WV 26155 t) 304-455-4615 office@svdpnm.org Rev. Msgr. Kevin Michael Quirk, Pst.; CRP Stds.: 3

PARKERSBURG

St. Francis Xavier - 532 Market St, Parkersburg, WV 26101; Mailing: 609 Market St., Parkersburg, WV 26101 t) 304-422-6786 stxoffice@stx-pburg.org www.stx-pburg.org Rev. John Rice, Pst.; CRP Stds.: 26

St. Margaret Mary - 2438 Dudley Ave., Parkersburg, WV 26101 t) 304-428-1262 stmmpsr@suddenlinkmail.com; jvallelonga@dwc.org stmmdwc.org Very Rev. J. Stephen Vallelonga, Pst.; Dcn. John F. Maher; Dcn. George B. Showalter; Dcn. Stephen E. Wharton; CRP Stds.: 18

PARSONS

Our Lady of Mercy Mission - 221 Water St., Parsons, WV 26287; Mailing: P.O. Box 300, Thomas, WV 26292 t) 304-463-4488 father@sttsite.com sttsite.com See St. Thomas, Thomas. Rev. Martin Smay, Admin.;

PENNSBORO

Christ Our Hope Mission - 108 W Penn Ave., Pennsboro, WV 26415; Mailing: 310 Washington St., c/o St. John Parish, St. Marys, WV 26170 t) 304-684-7669 cohp2111harr@dwc.org; stjohnsm@suddenlinkmail.com cohwv.org/ Rev. Shinto Mathew (India), Admin.;

PETERSBURG

St. Mary, Petersburg - 4 Grant St., Petersburg, WV 26847; Mailing: 5 Pierpont St., Petersburg, WV 26847-1633 t) 304-257-1057 smcc@frontiernet.net Rev. Joseph Daniel Pisano, Pst.; CRP Stds.: 12

PHILIPPI

St. Elizabeth Parish - College Hill, Philippi, WV 26416; Mailing: 104 Canter St., Philippi, WV 26416-8383 t) 304-457-2641 Rev. Babu Joseph Elamturuthil; Sam Santilli, DRE;

POINT PLEASANT

Sacred Heart Mission - 2222 Jackson Ave., Point Pleasant, WV 25550-2004; Mailing: 600 Crooks Ave., c/o St. Matthew Parish, Ravenswood, WV 26164 t) 304-273-2175 (Ravenswood Parish) stmatthewravens@gmail.com Rev. Penumaka Manikyalarao, H.G.N., Pst.;

St. Joseph - 580 Pomeroy St., Mason, WV 25260

POWHATAN

Sacred Heart - 35508 Coal Heritage Rd., Rte. 52, Powhatan, WV 24877; Mailing: 111 Virginia Ave., Welch, WV 24801 t) 304-436-2014 shp1311pow@dwc.org stpeterwelch.org/sacred-heart-powhatan/ Rev. Binny Thomas Mulackal, Admin.;

PRINCETON

Sacred Heart - 507 Harrison St., Princeton, WV 24740-3198; Mailing: P.O. Box 1310, Princeton, WV 24740-1310 t) 304-425-3664 church@sacredheartprinceton.org; lwyatt@sacredheartprinceton.org www.sacredheartprinceton.org Very Rev. Sebastian Embrayil Devasya, Pst.; CRP Stds.: 37

Campus Ministry, Concord College - 301 Vermillion St., Athens, WV 24712; Mailing: P.O. Box 447, Athens, WV 24712 t) 304-320-6037 pkrause@dwc.org Paul Krause, Campus Min.;

PROCTOR

St. Joseph - 64 Frohnapfel Ln., Proctor, WV 26055; Mailing: 21 Rosary Rd., c/o St. Vincent de Paul, New Martinsville, WV 26155 t) 304-455-4615 stvdpp2116nm@dwc.org Rev. Msgr. Kevin Michael Quirk, Pst.; Cindy Fox, DRE;

RAINELLE

Sacred Heart - 109 13th St., Rainelle, WV 25962; Mailing: c/o St. Patrick Parish, 309 2nd Ave., Hinton, WV 25951 t) 304-438-8687 psychedinwv@yahoo.com; stpathintonwv@yahoo.com See St. Patrick, Hinton. Rev. Chinh Quang Joseph Tran, S.V.D., Admin.; Dcn. J. Peter Minogue;

RAVENSWOOD

St. Matthew - 400 Kaiser Ave., Ravenswood, WV 26164; Mailing: 600 Crooks Ave., Ravenswood, WV 26164-1312 t) 304-273-2175 stmatthewravens@gmail.com sites.google.com/site/stmattheworg/ Rev. Penumaka Manikyalarao, H.G.N., Pst.; CRP Stds.: 18

RICHWOOD

Holy Family - 4 Maple St., Richwood, WV 26261-1318 t) 304-846-2873 hfp1241rich@dwc.org Rev. Quy Ngoc Dang, S.V.D., Pst.;

RIDGELEY

St. Anthony - 176 Main St., Ridgeley, WV 26753; Mailing: P.O. Box 1560, Fort Ashby, WV 26719-1560 t) 304-298-3392 annunciationchurch@atlanticbbn.net Rev. Daniel Price, Pst.; CRP Stds.: 5

ROMNEY

Our Lady of Grace - 299 School St., Romney, WV 26757 t) 304-822-5561 ourladyofgraceromneywv.org Rev. Thomas A. Sebastian, C.S.T., Pst.; Dcn. Lawrence V. Hammel; CRP Stds.: 5

RONCEVERTE

St. Catherine of Siena - 407 Walnut St., Ronceverte, WV 24970; Mailing: c/o 40798 Midland Trail E., White Sulphur Springs, WV 24986 t) 304-536-1813 stborromeo@frontier.com stcatherinewv.org Rev. James C. Conyers, Pst.; Dcn. Robert A. Holliday; Dcn. William B. Strange Jr.;

The Immaculate Conception of the Blessed Virgin Mary - c/o 325 W. Main St., White Sulphur Springs, WV 24986

St. Louis, King of France - 322 Court St. S., Lewisburg, WV 24901

SALEM

Sacred Heart Mission - 53 Sacred Heart Ln., Salem, WV 26426; Mailing: 2107 Pride Ave., c/o St. James the Apostle, Clarksburg, WV 26301-1819 t) 304-782-2277; 304-622-1668 arodrigo@dwc.org www.stjamesparishclarksburg.org Rev. B.K. Akila Gayan Rodrigo, T.O.R., Pst.; Rev. Christopher Turner, Assoc. Pst.;

SHEPHERDSTOWN

St. Agnes - 200 S. Duke St., Shepherdstown, WV 25443; Mailing: P.O. Box 1603, Shepherdstown, WV 25443-1603 t) 304-876-6436 stagnesshepherdstown.org/ Rev. Andrew M. Switzer, Pst.; CRP Stds.: 51

SHINNSTON

St. Ann Catholic Church - 610 Pike St., Shinnston, WV 26431; Mailing: 43 Mahlon St., Shinnston, WV 26431 t) 304-592-2733 stannshinnston@aol.com www.stannshinnston.com Rev. B.K. Akila Gayan Rodrigo, T.O.R., Pst.; Rev. Christopher Turner, Assoc. Pst.; Marianne Strugarek, DRE; CRP Stds.: 12

SISTERSVILLE

Holy Rosary Mission - 519 Main St., Sistersville, WV 26175-1405; Mailing: c/o St. Vincent dePaul Church, 21 Rosary Rd., New Martinsville, WV 26155 t) 304-455-4615 office@svdpnm.org; stvdpp2116nm@dwc.org Rev. Msgr. Kevin Michael Quirk, Pst.;

SOUTH CHARLESTON

Blessed Sacrament - 305 E St., South Charleston, WV 25303-1597; Mailing: P.O. Box 18427, South Charleston, WV 25303 t) 304-744-5523 www.blessedsacramentwv.org Rev. Paul J. Wharton, Pst.;

SPENCER

Holy Redeemer - 602 Parkersburg Rd., Spencer, WV 25276-1024 t) 304-927-2013 hrp2141spen@dwc.org; rprechtl@dwc.org Rev. Ronald G. Prechtl, Pst.; CRP Stds.: 3

ST. ALBANS

St. Francis of Assisi - 1023 Sixth Ave., St. Albans, WV 25177 t) 304-727-3033 parish@stfranciswv.org www.stfranciswv.org Rev. Sojan Xavier (India), Admin.; CRP Stds.: 20

St. Francis of Assisi School - (Grades PreK-5) 525 Holley St., St. Albans, WV 25177 t) 304-727-5690 sfswv@yahoo.com sfswv.com Theresa O'Leary, Prin.; Stds.: 171; Scholastics: 7; Lay Tchrs.: 7

ST. MARYS

St. John - 310 Washington St., St. Marys, WV 26170 t) 304-684-7669 stjohnsm@suddenlinkmail.com; stjp2126stm@dwc.org stjohncatholic.org Rev. Shinto Mathew (India), Admin.;

St. Joseph - 108 W. Penn Ave., Pennsboro, WV 26415 t) (304) 684-7669

STONEWOOD

Our Lady of Perpetual Help - 8092 3rd St., Stonewood, WV 26301 t) 304-623-2334 info@olphwv.com www.olphwv.com/ Rev. Sraven Kumar Reddimasu, Pst.; Dcn. John W. Yaquinta; CRP Stds.: 39

SUMMERSVILLE

St. John the Evangelist - 1704 Webster Rd., Summersville, WV 26651-1096 t) 304-872-2554 stjohnsummersville@gmail.com Rev. Rene F. Gerona, S.V.D., Pst.; CRP Stds.: 30

TERRA ALTA

St. Edward the Confessor Mission - 1204 E. State Ave., Terra Alta, WV 26764; Mailing: 322 E. Main St., c/o St. Sebastian Parish Office, Kingwood, WV 26537-1237 t) 304-329-1519 www.prestoncountycatholic.org See St. Sebastian, Kingwood. Rev. Dominic Athishu, Admin.;

THOMAS

St. Thomas Aquinas - 316 Brown St., Thomas, WV 26292-0300; Mailing: P.O. Box 300, Thomas, WV 26292-0300 t) 304-463-4488 father@sttsite.com; msmay@dwc.org sttsite.com Rev. Martin Smay, Admin.;

TRIADELPHIA

Our Lady of Seven Dolors Mission - Chapel Hill Rd., Triadelphia, WV 26059 t) 304-547-5342 See St. Vincent de Paul, Wheeling. Rev. Jeeson Venattu Stephan, Pst.;

VIENNA

St. Michael - 55th St. & Grand Central Ave., Vienna, WV 26105; Mailing: 213 55th St., Vienna, WV 26105-2007 t) 304-295-6109; 304-295-6648 (Rectory) stmoffices@yahoo.com www.stmichaelvienna.com Rev. John R. Gallagher, Pst.; CRP Stds.: 21

WEBSTER SPRINGS

St. Anne - 160 McGraw Ave., Webster Springs, WV 26288 t) 304-847-5512 stap1526ws@dwc.org Rev. Quy Ngoc Dang, S.V.D., Pst.; Dcn. Raymond G. Godwin; CRP Stds.: 3

WEIRTON

St. Joseph the Worker - 229 California Ave., Weirton, WV 26062-3790 t) 304-723-2054 stjosephtheworker229@yahoo.com stjoeweirton.org Very Rev. Dennis R. Schuelkens Jr., Pst.; Dcn. Vincent P. Olenick; CRP Stds.: 58

St. Joseph the Worker Grade School - 151 Michael Ave., Weirton, WV 26062 t) 304-723-1970 r.fuscardo@weirtonstjoseph.net Recheal Fuscardo, Prin.; Stds.: 185; Scholastics: 14; Lay Tchrs.: 14

St. Paul - 140 Walnut St., Weirton, WV 26062-4521 t) 304-748-6710; 304-748-4118 stpaulschurch@comcast.net stpaulcommunity.net Rev. Binu Sebastian, M.C.B.S., Pst.; CRP Stds.: 15

St. Paul School - t) 304-748-5225 info@weirtonstpaul.org weirtonstpauls.org James Lesho, Prin.; Stds.: 132; Scholastics: 14; Lay Tchrs.: 14

Sacred Heart of Mary - 200 Preston Ave., Weirton, WV 26062 t) 304-723-7175 shmp@sacredheartweirton.org sacredheartweirton.org Very Rev. Dennis R. Schuelkens Jr., Pst.; Dcn. Vincent P. Olenick; Rev. Anthony Thurston, Assoc. Pst.; CRP Stds.: 1

WELCH

St. Peter - 111 Virginia Ave., Welch, WV 24801-2424 t) 304-436-2014 stpp1331wel@dwc.org; stpeterwelch@gmail.com stpeterwelch.org Rev. Binny Thomas Mulackal, Admin.;

WELLSBURG

St. John the Evangelist - 1300 Charles St., Wellsburg, WV 26070-1408 t) 304-737-0429 stjohn1300@comcast.net www.stjohnwellsburgwv.com/ Rev. Justin M. Golna, Admin.; CRP Stds.: 8

WESTON

St. Patrick - 210 Center Ave., Weston, WV 26452-2029 t) 304-269-3048 secretary@spchurchweston.net www.spchurchweston.org Rev. Douglas A. Ondeck, Pst.; CRP Stds.: 10

St. Patrick's School - 224 Center Ave., Weston, WV 26452 t) 304-269-5547 st.pats@stpatswv.org stpatswv.org Stds.: 83; Scholastics: 3; Lay Tchrs.: 3

Loveberry, St. Bernard - 1820 Loveberry Run Rd., Weston, WV 26452; Mailing: 210 Center Ave., c/o St. Bernard Chapel, Weston, WV 2645

Roanoke, St. Bridget - Goosepen Rd., Roanoke, WV 26447; Mailing: 210 Center Ave., c/o St. Bridget Chapel, Weston, WV 26452-2029 dondeck@dwc.org

WHEELING

Cathedral of St. Joseph - 13th and Eoff Sts., Wheeling, WV 26003-0051; Mailing: 1218 Eoff St., Wheeling, WV 26003 t) 304-233-4121 cathedralofstjosephwheeling@dwc.org; dfahey@dwc.org www.saintjosephcathedral.com Most Rev. Mark E. Brennan, Pst.; Rev. Narisetti Sateesh, H.G.N., Assoc. Pst.; Rev. Robert G. Park, In Res.; Dcn. Doug Breiding; CRP Stds.: 3

St. Alphonsus - 2111 Market St., Wheeling, WV 26003-3827 t) 304-232-4353 saintalphonsuswheeling@gmail.com Rev. Nye Wiley, Par. Vicar; Dcn. George E. Smoulder; CRP Stds.: 7

Corpus Christi - 1518 Warwood Ave., Wheeling, WV 26003-7197; Mailing: 1508 Warwood Ave., Wheeling, WV 26003 t) 304-277-2911 ptempleton@dwc.org; office@corpuschristiwheeling.org corpuschristiwheeling.org/ Rev. Paul Mundumoozhikkaranirappel, C.S.T., Pst.; CRP Stds.: 7

Corpus Christi School - (Grades PreK-8) 1512 Warwood Ave., Wheeling, WV 26003 t) 304-277-1220 swall@ccwheeling.net Shannon Wall, Prin.; Stds.: 86; Scholastics: 14; Lay Tchrs.: 14

St. Michael - 1225 National Rd., Wheeling, WV 26003-5791 t) 304-242-1560 stmikes@stmikesparish.org stmikesparish.org Rev. Carlos L. Melocoton Jr., Pst.; CRP Stds.: 58

St. Michael School - 1221 National Rd., Wheeling, WV 26003 t) 304-242-3966 mrsburge@smpswv.org Kim Burge, Prin.; Stds.: 278; Scholastics: 21; Lay Tchrs.: 21

Our Lady of Peace - 690 Mt. Olivet Rd., Wheeling, WV 26003 t) 304-242-6579; 304-242-6575 (Rectory) www.olpwv.org Very Rev. Joseph Mandokkara Augustine, Pst.; CRP Stds.: 211

Our Lady of Peace School - t) 304-242-1383 mkerr@olpschool.org Maureen Kerr, Prin.; Stds.: 220; Scholastics: 18; Lay Tchrs.: 18

St. Vincent de Paul - 2244 Marshall Ave., Wheeling, WV 26003-7440 t) 304-242-0406 info@saintvincentparish.org www.saintvincentparish.org Rev. Jeeson Venattu Stephan, Pst.; CRP Stds.: 20

St. Vincent de Paul School - 127 Key Ave., Wheeling, WV 26003 t) 304-242-5844 Jarett Kuhns, Prin.; Stds.: 130; Scholastics: 19; Lay Tchrs.: 19

WHITE SULPHUR SPRINGS

St. Charles Borromeo - 40798 Midland Trail E., White Sulphur Springs, WV 24986 t) 304-536-1813 stborromeo@frontier.com stcharlesborromeowv.org Rev. James C. Conyers, Pst.; Dcn. Robert A. Holliday; Dcn. William B. Strange Jr.; CRP Stds.: 2

St. John - State Rtes. 3 & 311, Sweet Springs, WV 24941; Mailing: 325 W. Main St., c/o St. Charles Borromeo, White Sulphur Springs, WV 24986 t) (304) 536-1813

WILLIAMSON

Sacred Heart - 160 W. Fourth Ave., Williamson, WV 25661 t) 304-235-3027 www.sacredheartwilliamson.com Rev. Biju Paul Parampil, Admin.; CRP Stds.: 14

SCHOOLS: PRESCHOOL THRU HIGH SCHOOL

SCHOOLS

STATE OF WEST VIRGINIA

CLARKSBURG

St. Mary's Central Grade School - 107 E. Pike St., Clarksburg, WV 26301 t) 304-622-9831 lcavallo@stmaryswv.org Loria Cavallo, Prin.; Stds.: 110; Scholastics: 10; Lay Tchrs.: 10

FAIRMONT

Fairmont Catholic Grade School - (DIO) (Grades K-8) 416 Madison St., Fairmont, WV 26554 t) 304-363-5313 dburnside@fairmontcatholic.com Diane Burnside, Prin.; Stds.: 132; Sr. Tchrs.: 2; Lay Tchrs.: 12

MORGANTOWN

St. Francis de Sales Central Catholic School - (PAR) (Grades PreK-8) 41 Guthrie Ln., Morgantown, WV 26508 t) 304-291-5070 amoore@stfrancismorgantown.com www.stfrancismorgantown.com Arthur Moore, Prin.; Stds.: 396; Scholastics: 32; Lay Tchrs.: 32

PARKERSBURG

Parkersburg Catholic Elementary School - (PAR) (Grades PreK-6) 810 Juliana St., Parkersburg, WV 26101 t) 304-422-6694 pces@pchs1.com pceswv.org Very Rev. J. Stephen Vallelonga, Pst.; Amanda Weatherwax, Prin.; Stds.: 74; Scholastics: 12; Lay Tchrs.: 12

HIGH SCHOOLS

STATE OF WEST VIRGINIA

CHARLESTON

Charleston Catholic High School - (PAR) (Grades 6-12) 1033 Virginia St. E., Charleston, WV 25301 t) 304-342-8415 cchschar@dwc.org www.charlestoncatholic-crw.org Colleen Hoyer, Prin.; Stds.: 367; Scholastics: 38; Lay Tchrs.: 38

CLARKSBURG

Notre Dame High School - (PAR) (Grades 7-12) 127 E. Pike St., Clarksburg, WV 26301 t) 304-623-1026 klight@notredamewv.org Kelly Light, Prin.; Stds.: 124; Scholastics: 20; Lay Tchrs.: 20

HUNTINGTON

St. Joseph Central Catholic High School - (PAR) 600 13th St., Huntington, WV 25701 t) 304-525-5096 carol.templeton@stjosephhs.org www.stjosephhs.org Dr. Carol Templeton, Prin.; Stds.: 91; Scholastics: 13; Lay Tchrs.: 13

PARKERSBURG
Parkersburg Catholic Junior-Senior High School - (PAR) (Grades 7-12) 3201 Fairview Ave., Parkersburg, WV 26104 t) 304-485-6341 pchs@pchs1.com pchs1.com Michael DeRose, Prin.; Rev. John Rice, Chap.; Stds.: 77; Scholastics: 18; Lay Tchrs.: 18

WEIRTON
Madonna High School - (PAR) 150 Michael Way, Weirton, WV 26062 t) 304-723-0545 prujak@weirtonmadonna.org www.weirtonmadonna.org Very Rev. Dennis R. Schuelkens Jr., Pst.; Philip Rujak, Prin.; Stds.: 113; Lay Tchrs.: 10

WHEELING
Central Catholic High School - (PAR) 75-14th St., Wheeling, WV 26003 t) 304-233-1660 wheelingcentral@cchsknights.org www.cchsknights.org Rev. Paul Mundumoozhikkaranirappel, C.S.T.; Rev. Nye Wiley, Chap.; Rebecca Sancomb, Prin.; Stds.: 268; Scholastics: 29; Lay Tchrs.: 29

INSTITUTIONS LOCATED IN DIOCESE

CAMPUS MINISTRY / NEWMAN CENTERS [CAM]

ATHENS
Concord University Newman Center - 301 Vermillion St., Athens, WV 24712; Mailing: P.O. Box 447, Athens, WV 24712 t) 304-320-6037 deacondon@sacredheartblfd.org See Sacred Heart, Princeton. Paul Krause, Campus Min.;

BUCKHANNON
West Virginia Wesleyan College Newman Center - 34 Franklin St., Buckhannon, WV 26201-0848 t) 304-472-3414 hrp2306buc@dwc.org Rev. Edward Tetteh, SVD, Chap.;

CHARLESTON
St. John Paul II Catholic Campus Ministry Center - 310-26th St., Charleston, WV 25304 t) 304-342-9940 uccatholoic@gmail.com Rev. Jose Manuel Escalante, Chap.; Matthew Benincosa, Campus Min.;

FAIRMONT
Fairmont State University Newman Center - 1200 College Park, Fairmont, WV 26554 t) (304) 534-8093 Rev. Binu Emmanuel, C.S.T., Chap.; Daniel Thele, Campus Min.;

HUNTINGTON
Marshall Catholic Newman Center - 1609 Fifth Ave., Huntington, WV 25703 t) 304-525-4618 nchancey@dwc.org www.marshallcatholic.com Nicholas Chancey, Campus Min.;

PHILIPPI
Alderson-Broaddus College Newman Center - Newman Center, College Hill, 104 Canter St., Philippi, WV 26416 t) 304-457-2641 joconnor@dwc.org Rev. James O'Connor;

SHEPHERDSTOWN
Good Shepherd Catholic Campus Ministry Center - 101 W. High St., Shepherdstown, WV 25443; Mailing: P.O. Box 1163, Shepherdstown, WV 25443 t) 304-876-0231 kadidden@frontiernet.net Maggie Moran, Campus Min.;

WEST LIBERTY
West Liberty State College, St. Thomas Aquinas Campus Ministry - 483 Van Meter Way, West Liberty, WV 26074; Mailing: P.O. Box 230, Wheeling, WV 26003 t) 304-780-0616 scarter@dwc.org Shirley Carter, Campus Min.; Rev. L.J. Asantha Jude Perera, T.O.R., Chap.;

CATHOLIC CHARITIES [CCH]

KERMIT
A.B.L.E. Families, Inc. - 100 Lincoln St., Kermit, WV 25674; Mailing: P.O. Box 1249, Kermit, WV 25674 t) 304-393-4987 mspaulding@ablefamilies.org www.ablefamilies.org Marlene Spaulding, Exec.; Asstd. Annu.: 565; Staff: 13

WHEELING
Catholic Charities Neighborhood Center - 125 18th St., Wheeling, WV 26003-0713 t) 304-232-7157 Jessica Klinger, Coordinator;

CEMETERIES [CEM]

WHEELING
Mount Calvary - 1685 National Rd., Wheeling, WV 26003-5599 t) 304-242-0460 dbreiding@dwc.org Dcn. Doug Breiding, Dir.;

COLLEGES & UNIVERSITIES [COL]

CHARLES TOWN
Catholic Distance University - 300 S. George St., Charles Town, WV 25414 t) 304-724-5000; 888-254-4238 cdu@cdu.edu www.cdu.edu Most Rev. Timothy Broglio, Chancellor; Dr. Peter Brown, Dean; Marianne Mount, Pres.; Stds.: 592; Lay Tchrs.: 5; Pr. Tchrs.: 1

WHEELING
Wheeling University - 316 Washington Ave., Wheeling, WV 26003-6243 t) 304-243-2000 president@wju.edu www.wheeling.edu Ginny Favede, Pres.; Stds.: 1,304

CONVENTS, MONASTERIES, AND RESIDENCES FOR WOMEN [CON]

WHEELING
Sisters of Our Lady of Charity of the Good Shepherd Central South U.S. Province (Sisters of Our Lady of Charity of the Good Shepherd - Wheeling, Inc.) - 155 Edgington Ln., Wheeling, WV 26003; Mailing: 620 Roswell Rd., S.W., P.O. Box 340, Carrollton, OH 44615 t) 304-242-1093 carol.pregno@gssweb.org Sr. Carol Pregno, R.G.S., Supr.; Srs.: 2

Wheeling Center, Congregation of St. Joseph - 137 Mount St. Joseph Rd., Wheeling, WV 26003-1799 t) 304-232-8160 pwarbritton@csjoseph.org www.csjoseph.org Attended by Wheeling Jesuit University. Sr. Kathleen Brazda, C.S.J., Pres.; Rose Mathes, Community Life Coord.; Srs.: 42

ENDOWMENTS / FOUNDATIONS / TRUSTS [EFT]

PARKERSBURG
Parkersburg Catholic Schools Foundation, Inc. - 3201 Fairview Ave., Parkersburg, WV 26104-2111 t) 304-428-7528 pcsf@pchs1.com pchs1.com John Golebiewski, Exec.;

Sisters Health Foundation - 4420 Rosemar Ctr., Ste. 204, Parkersburg, WV 26104-4440; Mailing: P.O. Box 4440, Parkersburg, WV 26104-4440 t) 304-424-6080 rsteffen@sistershealthfdn.org www.sistershealthfdn.org Renee L. Steffen, Exec. Dir.; Sr. Molly Bauer, C.S.J., Sr. Prog. Officer; Sheiron Sanchez, Prog. Officer;

WHEELING
***Clarence L. Christ Trust** - 1311 Byron St., Wheeling, WV 26003; Mailing: P.O. Box 230, Wheeling, WV 26003 t) 304-233-0880 ccarter@dwc.org Chad R. Carter, Chancellor;

John S. Thoner Family Charitable Trust - 1311 Byron St., Wheeling, WV 26003; Mailing: P.O. Box 230, Wheeling, WV 26003 t) 304-233-0880 ccarter@dwc.org Chad R. Carter, Chancellor;

Medical Park Foundation - One Medical Park, Wheeling, WV 26003 t) 304-243-2969 jmurdy@wheelinghospital.org James Murdy, CFO;

***Michael Christ Trust** - 1311 Byron St., Wheeling, WV 26003; Mailing: P.O. Box 230, Wheeling, WV 26003 t) 304-233-0880 ccarter@dwc.org Chad R. Carter, Chancellor;

Retirement Trust Agreement of the Priests' Health and Retirement Association - 1311 Byron St., Wheeling, WV 26003; Mailing: P.O. Box 230, Wheeling, WV 26003 t) 304-233-0880 ccarter@dwc.org Chad R. Carter, Chancellor;

The Sisters of St. Joseph Health & Wellness Foundation - 137 Mount St. Joseph Rd., Wheeling, WV 26003-1799 t) 304-233-4500; 304-232-8160 x148 ecollins@ssjhwf.org www.ssjhealthandwellnessfoundation.org Elizabeth Collins, Exec. Dir.;

Sisters of St. Joseph of Wheeling Foundation, Inc. - 137 Mount St. Joseph Rd., Wheeling, WV 26003-1799 t) 304-232-8160 pwarbritton@csjoseph.org www.csjoseph.org Sr. Patricia Warbritton, Treas.;

West Virginia Catholic Foundation - 1311 Byron St., Wheeling, WV 26003; Mailing: P.O. Box 230, Wheeling, WV 26003 t) 304-233-0880 bminor@dwc.org wvcf.dwc.org Bryan E. Minor, Exec.;

Wheeling Hospital Foundation, Inc. - 1 Medical Pk., Wheeling, WV 26003 t) 304-243-3000; 304-598-4943 jessica.alsop@wvumedicine.org; douglas.coffman@wvumedicine.org Jessica Alsop, Contact;

HOSPITALS / HEALTH SERVICES [HOS]

WHEELING
Continuous Care Center Wheeling Hospital - 236 Hullihen Pl., Wheeling, WV 26003; Mailing: P.O. Box 6316, Wheeling, WV 26003 t) 304-243-3800 crtarr@wheelinghospital.org www.wheelinghospital.org Skilled & intermediate care. Christy Tarr, Admin.; Bed Capacity: 144; Asstd. Annu.: 561; Staff: 160

Wheeling Hospital - 1 Medical Pk., Wheeling, WV 26003 t) 304-243-3000 jmurdy@wheelinghospital.org www.wheelinghospital.com Douglass E. Harrison, CEO; Rev. Michael O. Nwokocha, Chap.; Rev. Cyprian C. Osuegbu, Chap.; Sr. Mary Ann Rosenbaum, C.S.J., Dir., Pastoral Care; Dcn. Paul C. Lim, Vice Pres., Mission Integration; Bed Capacity: 446; Asstd. Annu.: 752,023; Staff: 3,369

MISCELLANEOUS [MIS]

ALDERSON
***Bethlehem Farm, Inc.** - 572 Bethlehem Farm Ln., Alderson, WV 24910; Mailing: P.O. Box 415, Talcott, WV 24981 t) 304-445-7143 eric.fitts@bethlehemfarm.net www.bethlehemfarm.net Intentional Catholic community offering service-retreat experiences, low-income home repair, and teaching of sustainable practices. Eric Fitts, Dir.;

CAMERON
St. Martin of Tours Chapel - 1 Fitzgerald Ave., Cameron, WV 26033; Mailing: c/o St. Francis Xavier Church, 912-7th St., Moundsville, WV 26041 t) 304-845-1593 sfxmoundsville@comcast.net Rev. That Son Ngoc Nguyen, Pst.;

GARY
Our Lady of Victory Chapel - 81 Miracle Mountain Rd, Gary, WV 24836; Mailing: c/o 111 Virginia Ave., Welch, WV 24801 t) 304-436-2014 stpeterwelch.org/our-lady-of-victory/ Rev. Binny Thomas Mulackal, Admin.;

HUNTINGTON
Pallottine Health Services, Inc. - 2900 First Ave., Huntington, WV 25702 t) 304-526-8915 sister.diane@st-marys.org www.st-marys.org Sponsored by the Pallottine Missionary Sisters. Michael G. Sellards, CEO; Sr. Mary Grace Barile, S.A.C., Pres.; Sr. M. Diane Bushee, S.A.C., Contact;

HUTTONSVILLE
Mary Help of Christians Pastoral Center - 39 Catholic Conference Center, Huttonsville, WV 26273 t) 304-335-2165; 304-233-0880 x260 (Chancellor) ccarter@dwc.org www.bishophodges.org Pastoral Center is currently closed to public. Chad R. Carter, Chancellor;

MAN
St. Edmund - 106 N. Bridge St., Man, WV 25635 t) 304-583-2476 bparampil@dwc.org Karen Arons, DRE; Rev. Biju Paul Parampil, Admin.;

MORGANTOWN
Morgantown Magnificat Chapter of the Diocese of Wheeling-Charleston - 229 Fountain View, Morgantown, WV 26505 t) 304-319-2747 hearingservices1@comcast.net

PICKENS

Sacred Heart Chapel - 35 Franklin St., Pickens, WV 26230; Mailing: 34 Franklin St., c/o Holy Rosary Parish, Buckhannon, WV 26201 t) 304-472-3414 etetteh@dwc.org Rev. Edward Tetteh, SVD, Admin.;

PINEVILLE

Holy Cross Chapel - 595 Appalachian Hwy., Pineville, WV 24874; Mailing: c/o 111 Virginia Ave., Welch, WV 24801 t) 304-436-2014 (Office); (304) 732-6199 stpeterwelch.org/holy-cross-mission/ Rev. Binny Thomas Mulackal, Admin.;

SALEM

***Nazareth Farm, Inc.** - 665 Nazareth Farm Rd., Salem, WV 26426-6180 t) 304-782-2742 director.nazfarm@gmail.com nazarethfarm.org Allyson Petry, Exec. Dir.;

SNOWSHOE

St. Bernard - 10 Snowshoe Dr., Snowshoe, WV 26209 t) 304-799-6778 pastor@pocahontascatholic.org pocahontascatholic.org Rev. Arthur Bufogle Jr., Pst.;

WHEELING

Daily Living Ministries, Inc. - 1311 Byron St., Wheeling, WV 26003; Mailing: P.O. Box 339, Nitro, WV 25143 t) 304-860-0007 Rev. John Chapin Engler Jr., Pres.;

St. John's Home for Children - 141 Key Ave., Wheeling, WV 26003-7412 t) 304-242-5633 office@stjohnshome.net www.stjohnshomeforchildren.org Julie Cunningham, Exec. Dir.;

St. Joseph Center - 137 Mount St. Joseph Rd., Wheeling, WV 26003-1799 t) 304-232-8160 atroiani@csjoseph.org; pwarbritton@csjoseph.org www.csjoseph.org Congregation of St. Joseph. Anna Marie Troiani, Exec. Dir.;

St. Joseph Health Initiative, Inc. - 137 Mount St. Joseph Rd., Wheeling, WV 26003-1799 t) 304-232-8160 pwarbritton@csjoseph.org Sr. Marguerite O'Brien, C.S.J., Pres.;

NURSING / REHABILITATION / CONVALESCENCE / ELDERLY CARE [NUR]

WHEELING

Good Shepherd Nursing Home LC - 159 Edgington Ln., Wheeling, WV 26003 t) 304-242-1093 good.shepherd@comcast.net Rev. Joel Grissom, S.M., Chap.; Donald R. Kirsch, Admin.; Asstd. Annu.: 267; Staff: 258

Mount St. Joseph, Inc. - 137 Mount St. Joseph Rd., Wheeling, WV 26003-1799 t) 304-232-8160 Assisted living facility. Cindy Albert, Admin.; Asstd. Annu.: 24; Staff: 24

Welty Home for the Aged, Inc. - 83 Edgington Ln., Wheeling, WV 26003-6261 t) 304-242-2300 Most Rev. Mark E. Brennan, Pres.; William J. Yaeger Jr., Treas.; Rev. Msgr. Eugene S. Ostrowski, Vice. Pres.; Lawrence Bandi, Trustee; Asstd. Annu.: 224; Staff: 53

Welty Home LC - 21 Washington Ave., Wheeling, WV 26003 t) (304) 242-5233 Randy Forzano, Admin.;

Welty Retirement Apartments LC (The Clara Welty Apartments LC) - 1276 National Rd., Wheeling, WV 26003 t) 304-242-5820

PRESCHOOLS / CHILDCARE CENTERS [PRE]

HUTTONSVILLE

Camp Carlo - 225 Catholic Conference Center, Huttonsville, WV 26273; Mailing: 39 Catholic Conference Center, Huttonsville, WV 26273 t) 304-335-2130 (In Season); 304-233-0880 (Off Season) dmaul@dwc.org Diocesan Children's Camp. Dcn. Raymond G. Godwin, Dir.;

WHEELING

Holy Family Child Care & Development Center, Inc. - 161 Edgington Ln., Wheeling, WV 26003 t) 304-242-5222 director@holyfamilychildcarecenter.com www.holyfamilychildcarecenter.com Paula McIntyre, Exec.; Stds.: 60; Lay Tchrs.: 12

RETREAT HOUSES / RENEWAL CENTERS [RTR]

CHARLESTON

Saint John XXIII Pastoral Center - 100 Hodges Rd., Charleston, WV 25314 t) 304-342-0507 johnxxiiiguestservices@dwc.org johnxxiiipc.org Geraldine Wright, Dir.;

KEARNEYSVILLE

Priest Field Pastoral Center - 4030 Middleway Pike, Kearneysville, WV 25430 t) 304-725-5558 skersey@stjameswv.org www.priestfield.org Very Rev. Timothy J. Grassi, Pst.; Susan Kersey, Retreat Coord.;

An asterisk (*) denotes an organization that has established tax-exempt status directly with the IRS and is not covered by the USCCB Group Ruling.

Diocese of Wichita

(Dioecesis Wichitensis)

MOST REVEREND CARL ALAN KEMME

Bishop of Wichita; ordained May 10, 1986; appointed Bishop of Wichita February 20, 2014; installed May 1, 2014. Chancery: 424 N. Broadway, Wichita, KS 67202.

The Chancery: 424 N. Broadway, Wichita, KS 67202. T: 316-269-3900; F: 316-269-3902.
www.CatholicDioceseOfWichita.org

ESTABLISHED AUGUST 2, 1887.

Square Miles 20,021.

New boundaries established by Apostolic Letters dated May 19, 1951. Bounded on the west by the west lines of Rice, Reno, Kingman and Harper counties, south by Oklahoma, east by Missouri, and north by the north lines of Bourbon, Allen, Woodson, Greenwood, Morris, Marion, McPherson and Rice Counties in Kansas.

For legal titles of parishes and diocesan institutions, consult the Chancery Office.

STATISTICAL OVERVIEW

Personnel

Bishop 1
Priests: Diocesan Active in Diocese 100
Priests: Diocesan Active Outside Diocese 7
Priests: Retired, Sick or Absent 23
Number of Diocesan Priests 130
Religious Priests in Diocese 3
Total Priests in your Diocese 133
Extern Priests in Diocese 5
Ordinations:
Diocesan Priests 3
Permanent Deacons in Diocese 5
Total Sisters 169

Parishes

Parishes 90
With Resident Pastor:
Resident Diocesan Priests 62
Resident Religious Priests 2
Without Resident Pastor:
Administered by Priests 26
Professional Ministry Personnel:
Sisters 13
Lay Ministers 44

Welfare

Catholic Hospitals 5
Total Assisted 592,605
Homes for the Aged 9
Total Assisted 2,353
Specialized Homes 1
Total Assisted 363
Special Centers for Social Services 1
Total Assisted 174
Other Institutions 1
Total Assisted 437

Educational

Students from This Diocese 29
Diocesan Students in Other Seminaries 15
Total Seminarians 44
Colleges and Universities 1
Total Students 2,883
High Schools, Diocesan and Parish 4
Total Students 2,265
Elementary Schools, Diocesan and Parish 34
Total Students 5,776
Catechesis/Religious Education:
High School Students 1,004
Elementary Students 4,317
Total Students under Catholic Instruction 16,289
Teachers in Diocese:
Priests 3
Sisters 13
Lay Teachers 694

Vital Statistics

Receptions into the Church:
Infant Baptism Totals 1,611
Minor Baptism Totals 281
Adult Baptism Totals 234
Received into Full Communion 256
First Communions 1,054
Confirmations 2,902
Marriages:
Catholic 322
Interfaith 140
Total Marriages 462
Deaths 1,054
Total Catholic Population 108,484
Total Population 996,805

LEADERSHIP

Chancery Office - t) 316-269-3900
Vicar General - Rev. David J. Lies;
Moderator of the Diocesan Curia - Rev. David J. Lies;
Vicar for Clergy - Rev. Patrick G. York;
Chancellor - azizj@catholicdioceseofwichita.org Rev. Brian D. Nelson (nelsonb@catholicdioceseofwichita.org);
College of Consultors - t) 316-269-3900 Most Rev. Carl A. Kemme, Bishop (winslowt@catholicdioceseofwichita.org); Rev. David J. Lies, Vicar; Rev. Patrick G. York;
Presbyteral Council - Rev. James J. Billinger; Rev. Bernard X. Gorges; Rev. David J. Lies;
Tribunal - t) 316-269-3960 martinc@catholicdioceseofwichita.org Rev. Brian D Nelson (nelsonb@catholicdioceseofwichita.org);
Adjutant Judicial Vicar - t) 316-269-3900 martinc@catholicdioceseofwichita.org Rev. Michael E. Nolan;
Judicial Vicar - t) 316-269-3900 Rev. Brian D Nelson;
Promoter of Justice - Rev. Stuart M. Smeltzer;
Judges - Rev. John V. Hotze; Rev. John F. Jirak (jjirak@magdalenwichita.com); Rev. Michael E. Nolan;
Defenders of the Bond - Rev. Stuart M. Smeltzer; Rev. Patrick R. Reilley;
Notaries - Cheryl Martin; Tracy Winslow;
Ongoing Formation of the Clergy Committee - Rev. Darrin May; Ryan Purcell (Purcellr@catholicdioceseofwichita.org); Rev. Gabriel Greer (greerg@catholicdioceseofwichita.org);

OFFICES AND DIRECTORS

Building Commission - t) 316-269-3900 Bryan R. Coulter (bryan.coulter@catholicdioceseofwichita.org); Michael W. Wescott (westcottm@catholicdioceseofwichita.org); Rev. David J. Lies, Chair;
Catholic Charities - t) 316-264-8344 wglick@catholiccharitieswichita.org Wendy Glick, Exec.;
Catholic Diocese of Wichita - t) 316-269-3900 winslowt@catholicdioceseofwichita.org Most Rev. Carl A. Kemme;
Catholic School Office - t) 316-269-3950 cso@catholicdioceseofwichita.org Janet Eaton, Supt. (supt@catholicdioceseofwichita.org);
Cemeteries - t) 316-722-1971 markm@catholicdioceseofwichita.org Mark Miller, Dir.;
Communications Office - t) 316-269-3921 Matt Vainer, Dir.;
Cursillo (English language) - Rev. Jacob K. Carlin, Coord.;
Cursillo (Spanish language) - t) 316-518-4683 Rev. Jacob K. Carlin, Coord.;
Development and Planned Giving Office - t) 316-269-3917 Michael W. Wescott, Dir. (westcottm@catholicdioceseofwichita.org); Connor Meier, Giving Coord. (Meierc@catholicdioceseofwichita.org);
Evangelization + Discipleship + Stewardship Office - Rev. John F. Jirak, Vicar, Evangelization, Discipleship, Stewardship (jjirak@magdalenwichita.com); Rev. Jose Machado, Facilitator, Evangelization, Stewardship, & Discipleship for Hispanics (frmachado@gmail.com); Audrey Ronnfeldt, Dir., Office of Stewardship (ronnfeldta@catholicdioceseofwichita.org);
Father Kapaun Guild - hotzej@catholicdioceseofwichita.org Scott Carter, Prog. Coord. (carters@catholicdioceseofwichita.org);
Finance and Administrative Services Office - Bryan R. Coulter, Dir. (bryan.coulter@catholicdioceseofwichita.org); Wes Etheredge, Controller (etheredgew@catholicdioceseofwichita.org);
Finance Council - Most Rev. Carl A. Kemme; Rev. David J. Lies; Bryan R. Coulter (bryan.coulter@catholicdioceseofwichita.org);
Health Affairs - Diocesan Liaison - Rev. Patrick G. York; Rev. John Lanzrath (frjohn@stjohneldorado.com);
Hispanic Ministry Office - t) 316-269-3919 Danny Krug, Dir. (krugd@catholicdioceseofwichita.org);
Human Resource Office - t) 316-269-3900 Therese Seiler, Dir. (seilert@catholicdioceseofwichita.org); Randy Phelps, Personnel/Benefits Coord. (phelpsr@catholicdioceseofwichita.org);
Legion of Mary - t) 316-744-0167 Rev. Chris Martin, Chap.;
Lord's Diner - t) 316-266-4966 www.thelordsdiner.org Emily Thome, Dir. (Janh@thelordsdiner.org);
Ministry with Persons with Disabilities Office - t) 316-269-3900 jacobsj@catholicdioceseofwichita.org Myra Jacobs, Dir.;
Mission Formator - t) 316-269-3900 Janice Aziz, Prog. Coord.;
Newspaper: "The Catholic Advance" - t) 316-269-3921 Christopher M. Riggs, Editor;
Office of Faith Formation - t) 316-269-3940 Anthony Keiser, Dir. (keisera@catholicdioceseofwichita.org); David Purcell, Prog. Coord., Youth & Young Adult (purcelld@catholicdioceseofwichita.org); David Walker, Prog. Coord., High School & Young Adult (walker@catholicdioceseofwichita.org);
Office of Marriage and Family Life - t) 316-685-5240 Jake Samour, Dir. (samourj@catholicdioceseofwichita.org); Becky Knapp, Prog. Coord. Natural Family Planning (knappb@catholicdioceseofwichita.org); Sharon Witzell, Ministry to Seniors, Prog. Coord. (witzells@catholicdioceseofwichita.org);
Engaged Encounter - Becky Knapp, Coord.; Robert Knapp, Coord.;
Marriage Encounter - t) 620-480-0288 Jake Samour, Dir., Office of Marriage & Family Life;
Respect Life and Social Justice Office - t) 316-269-3900 Bonnie Toombs, Dir.;
St. Dismas Ministry to the Incarcerated - t) 316-744-0167 Brant Baca, Prog. Coord.;
Retreats - t) 316-744-0167 Rev. Darrin May;
Rural Life Ministry - Bonnie Toombs;
Safe Environment Program - Therese Seiler, Dir. (seilert@catholicdioceseofwichita.org);
Spiritual Life Center - Rev. Darrin May;
Victim Assistance Coordinator - t) 316-440-1733 Stephanie Nemechek (nemecheks@catholicdioceseofwichita.org);
Vocations - Rev. Chad Arnold, Dir.;
Wichita Catholic Secondary Schools - t) 316-269-3950 Janet Eaton (supt@catholicdioceseofwichita.org);
Worship Office - Rev. Gabriel Greer, Dir. (greerg@catholicdioceseofwichita.org); Rev. Michael E. Nolan, Coord., Rite of Christian Initiation of Adults; Sr. John Patrick Beckius, Coord. (beckiusj@catholicdioceseofwichita.org);

PARISHES, MISSIONS, AND CLERGY

STATE OF KANSAS

ANDALE

St. Joseph - 318 Rush Ave., Andale, KS 67001; Mailing: P.O. Box 8, Andale, KS 67001 t) 316-444-2196 office@stjosephandale.com www.stjosephandale.com Rev. Daryl Befort, Pst.; Mary Jo Hieger, DRE; CRP Stds.: 278

ANDOVER

St. Vincent de Paul - 123 N. Andover Rd., Andover, KS 67002 t) 316-733-1423 kathleen@svdpks.org; susan@svdpks.org svdpks.org Rev. Kenneth S. Van Haverbeke, Pst.; Teresa Marshall-Patterson, RCIA Coord.; CRP Stds.: 89

ARKANSAS CITY

Sacred Heart - 326 S. B St., Arkansas City, KS 67005; Mailing: 302 S. B St., Arkansas City, KS 67005 t) 620-442-0566 parish@sacredheartarkcity.org www.sacredheartac.com Rev. Samuel R. Brand, Pst.; CRP Stds.: 32

Sacred Heart School - (Grades PreK-5) 312 S. B St., Arkansas City, KS 67005 t) 620-442-6550 abutler@sacredheartarkcity.org Adam Butler, Prin.; Jamie Larson, Librn.;

ARMA

St. Joseph - 310 W. South St., Arma, KS 66712; Mailing: P.O. Box 948, Arma, KS 66712 t) 620-347-4525 stjoseph@ckt.net Rev. Michael A. Klag, Pst.;

AUGUSTA

St. James the Greater - 1012 Belmont Ave., Augusta, KS 67010 t) 316-775-2155 vknebler@saintjamesaugusta.com saintjamesaugusta.com Rev. Philip John (P.J.) Voegeli Jr., Pst.; Kathi Martinez, DRE; CRP Stds.: 67

St. James School - (Grades PreK-8) 1010 Belmont Ave., Augusta, KS 67010 t) 316-775-5721 wbecker@saintjamesaugusta.org Stephanie Rziha, Prin.;

BAXTER SPRINGS

St. Joseph - 324 E. 12th St., Baxter Springs, KS 66713; Mailing: 115 W. Walnut, Columbus, KS 66725 t) 620-429-2639 ckcocatholics@live.com www.ckcocatholics.org Rev. Jeremy S. Huser, Pst.; CRP Stds.: 2

BUSHTON

Holy Name of Jesus - 296 3rd Rd., Bushton, KS 67427; Mailing: 415 Saint Francis St., Lyons, KS 67554 t) 620-257-3503 parishoffice@stpaulslyons.com Rev. Michael G. Brungardt, Pst.;

CALDWELL

St. Martin of Tours - 428 N. Main, Caldwell, KS 67022; Mailing: P.O. Box 289, Caldwell, KS 67022 t) 620-845-6763 stmartinscaldwell@gmail.com stmartincaldwell.org/ Rev. Thomas M. Hoisington, Pst.; CRP Stds.: 18

CANEY

Sacred Heart - 301 N. Hooker, Caney, KS 67333; Mailing: P.O. Box 276, Moline, KS 67353 t) 620-879-2883 (CRP); 620-647-3577 bailadores33@yahoo.com; deceejoy@yahoo.com Rev. Robert K Spencer, Pst.; Joy Freisberg, DRE; CRP Stds.: 10

CHANUTE

St. Patrick - 424 S. Central, Chanute, KS 66720 t) 620-431-3165 jbetzen@stpatrickchanute.org Rev. John D. Betzen, Pst.; CRP Stds.: 57

St. Patrick School - (Grades PreK-5) 409 S. Malcolm, Chanute, KS 66720 t) 620-431-4020 mdurand@stpatrickchanute.org stpatrickchanute.org/school Mary Durand, Prin.;

CHENEY

St. Rose - 4813 N.E. 150 Ave., Cheney, KS 67025; Mailing: P.O. Box 528, Mount Hope, KS 67025 t) 316-500-1940 frdanieljduling@gmail.com; stroseoflimamtvernon@gmail.com www.strosemtvernon.com Rev. Daniel J. Duling, Pst.; Tammie Hopper, DRE; CRP Stds.: 135

CHERRYVALE

St. Francis Xavier - 202 S. Liberty St., Cherryvale, KS 67335 t) 620-331-1789 standrewindp@sbcglobal.net Rev. Zachary G.B. Pinaire, Pst.;

COFFEYVILLE

Holy Name - 408 Willow St., Coffeyville, KS 67337 t) 620-251-0475; 620-251-0480 (CRP) d.howard878@gmail.com www.holynamecoffeyville.org Rev. James M. Schibi, Pst.; Brian Sherwood, Parish Life Coord.; CRP Stds.: 25

Holy Name School - (Grades PreK-7) 406 Willow St., Coffeyville, KS 67337 schooloffice@holyname.kscoxmail.com Lisa Payne, Prin.;

COLUMBUS

St. Rose - 115 W. Walnut St., Columbus, KS 66725 t) 620-429-2639 ckcocatholics@live.com www.ckcocatholics.org Rev. Jeremy S. Huser, Pst.; Regina Jameson, DRE; CRP Stds.: 25

COLWICH

St. Mark - 19230 W. 29th St. N., Colwich, KS 67030 t) 316-796-1604 secretary@stmarkks.org; mbina@stmarkks.org stmarkks.org Rev. Brian D. Nelson, Pst.; Molly Bina, DRE; CRP Stds.: 143

Sacred Heart - 311 S. Fifth St., Colwich, KS 67030; Mailing: P.O. Box 578, Colwich, KS 67030-0578 t) 316-796-1224 office@sacredheartcolwich.org; fryork@sacredheartcolwich.org www.sacredheartcolwich.org Rev. Patrick G. York, Pst.; Jillian Linnebur, Parish Life Coord.; Lindsay Durler, DRE; CRP Stds.: 85

CONWAY SPRINGS

St. Joseph - 217 N. Sixth St., Conway Springs, KS 67031 t) 620-456-2276 sjcs@juno.com; parish@stjoecs.org stjoecs.org/ Rev. Kyle Dugan, Pst.; CRP Stds.: 89

St. Joseph School - (Grades K-6) 218 N. 5th St., Conway Springs, KS 67031 t) 620-456-2270 arnold@stjoecs.org stjoecs.org/school Joel Arnold, Prin.;

COUNCIL GROVE

St. Rose of Lima - 300 Spencer St., Council Grove, KS 66846 t) 620-767-6412; 620-528-3797 (CRP) rosalima@cgtelco.net; julieg@satelephone.com www.stanthonystrose.org/ Rev. Andrew J. Seiler, Pst.; Julie Galloway, DRE; CRP Stds.: 40

CUNNINGHAM

Sacred Heart - 404 E. First St., Cunningham, KS 67035; Mailing: 8035 S.W. 160th Ave., Cunningham, KS 67112 t) 620-246-5370 judicis20@yahoo.com; rigor20@icloud.com Rev. Roger S. Lumbre, Pst.; Megan Osner, DRE; CRP Stds.: 68

DERBY

St. Mary - 2300 E. Meadowlark Rd., Derby, KS 67037 t) 316-788-5525; 316-788-3151 (CRP) kbrennan@stmarysderby.com; religiousEd@stmarysderby.com stmarysderby.com Rev. Joseph A. Eckberg, Pst.; Catherine Wilson, DRE; CRP Stds.: 49

St. Mary Catholic School - (Grades PreK-8) 2306 E. Meadowlark Rd., Derby, KS 67037 alesley@stmarysderby.com Richard Montgomery, Prin.; Jean Schif, Librn.;

EL DORADO

St. John the Evangelist - 302 N. Denver Ave., El Dorado, KS 67042 t) 316-321-4796 mail@stjohneldorado.com; frjohn@stjohneldorado.com www.stjohneldorado.com Rev. John P. Lanzrath, Pst.; Lynda Cope, DRE; CRP Stds.: 97

ERIE

St. Ambrose - 519 N. Main, Erie, KS 66733; Mailing: P.O. Box 216, St. Paul, KS 66771 t) 620-449-2224 saintfrancis66771@gmail.com www.stfrancis-stambrose.org Rev. Theodore Khin, Pst.;

EUREKA

Sacred Heart - 514 N. Elm St., Eureka, KS 67045 t) 620-583-7100 sheureka67045@gmail.com Rev. Nicholaus L Jurgensmeyer, Pst.; CRP Stds.: 17

FORT SCOTT

Mary Queen of Angels - 714 S. Eddy St., Fort Scott, KS 66701-2506; Mailing: 705 S. Holbrook, Fort Scott, KS 66701 t) 620-223-4340 mqa@mqaftscott.com; michaudjennifer@gmail.com www.mqaftscott.com/ Rev. Yancey Q. Burgess, Pst.; CRP Stds.: 45

Mary Queen of Angels School - (Grades PreK-5) 702 S. Eddy St., Fort Scott, KS 66701-2506 t) 620-223-6060 sms@smsftscott.com smsftscott.com Josh Regan, Prin.; Jill Gorman, Librn.;

FREDONIA

Sacred Heart - 1223 Madison St., Fredonia, KS 66736; Mailing: 428 N. 12th St., Fredonia, KS 66736 t) 620-378-3658 sacredheart.fkb@gmail.com Rev. Stuart M. Smeltzer, Admin.; CRP Stds.: 24

FRONTENAC

Sacred Heart - 100 S. Cherokee St., Frontenac, KS 66763 t) 620-231-7747 monawachter46@gmail.com; sacredheart66763@gmail.com sacredheartfrontenac.com Rev. Joshua R. Evans, Pst.; CRP Stds.: 87

GALENA

St. Patrick - 307 Galena Ave., Galena, KS 66739; Mailing: 115 W. Walnut, Columbus, KS 66725 t) 620-429-2639 ckcocatholics@live.com www.ckcocatholics.org Rev. Jeremy S. Huser, Pst.; CRP Stds.: 5

GARDEN PLAIN

St. Anthony - 607 N. Main, Garden Plain, KS 67050; Mailing: 616 Biermann St., P.O. Box 275, Garden Plain, KS 67050 t) 316-531-2252 office@stanthonygardenplain.com; jpuetz@stanthonygardenplain.com www.stanthonygardenplain.com Rev. H. Jay Setter, Pst.; Julie Puetz, DRE; CRP Stds.: 285

Immaculate Conception (St. Mary, Aleppo) - 25741 W. 13th N., Garden Plain, KS 67050; Mailing: P.O. Box 275, Garden Plain, KS 67050 t) 316-531-2662 office@stanthonygardenplain.com www.stanthonygardenplain.com Rev. H. Jay Setter, Pst.; Rev. Jason W. Borkenhagen, Asst. Pastor;

GIRARD

St. Michael - 106 N. Western St., Girard, KS 66743 t) 620-724-8717 Rev. Michael A. Klag, Pst.; CRP Stds.: 55

GODDARD

Church of the Holy Spirit - 18218 W. Hwy. 54, Goddard, KS 67052 t) 316-794-3496 parish@holyspiritwichita.com; rkerschen@holyspiritwichita.com www.holyspiritwichita.com Rev. Matthew D. Marney, Pst.; Rita Kerschen, DRE (P); CRP Stds.: 35

Holy Spirit School - (Grades PreSchool-8) t) 316-794-8139 kbright@holyspiritwichita.com www.holyspiritwichita.com/school Kelly Bright, Prin.;

HALSTEAD

Sacred Heart Parish - 419 Poplar, Halstead, KS 67056 t) 316-830-2818 office@sacredhearthalstead.com; jrootfamily@yahoo.com www.sacredhearthalstead.com Rev. Andrew E. Heiman, Pst.; Stacy Root, DRE; Carrie A Bridges, Bus. Mgr.; CRP Stds.: 50

HAMILTON

St. John - Township Rd. 91, Hamilton, KS 66853; Mailing: 514 N. Elm St., Eureka, KS 67045 t) 620-583-7100 sheureka67045@gmail.com greenwoodcountycatholicchurches.org/ Rev. Nicholaus L Jurgensmeyer, Pst.; CRP Stds.: 2

HARPER

St. Joan of Arc - 1023 W. Main St., Harper, KS 67058; Mailing: P.O. Box 218, Harper, KS 67058 t) 620-896-7886 stjoanofarcharper@gmail.com Rev. Babu Pinninti, Pst.; CRP Stds.: 65

Sacred Heart, Anthony - 121 S. Madison Ave., Anthony, KS 67003

Immaculate Conception - 102 Ashman St., Danville, KS 67036

St. Patrick -

HAYSVILLE

St. Cecilia - 1830 W. Grand, Haysville, KS 67060 t) 316-524-7801; 316-522-0461 (CRP) church@stceciliahaysville.org www.stceciliahaysville.org Rev. Patrick S. Kotrba, Pst.; Marcia Miller, DRE; CRP Stds.: 60

St. Cecilia School - (Grades K-8) 1912 W. Grand, Haysville, KS 67060 mbowmaker@stceciliahaysville.org Charlene Laramore, Prin.; Jane Betzen, Librn.;

HUMBOLDT

St. Joseph - 514 Central, Humboldt, KS 66748; Mailing: 424 S. Central Ave., Chanute, KS 66720 t) 620-431-3165 jbetzen@stpatrickchanute.org Rev. John D. Betzen, Pst.; CRP Stds.: 16

HUTCHINSON

Church of the Holy Cross - 2631 Independence Rd., Hutchinson, KS 67502 t) 620-665-5163; 620-665-6168 (CRP) rectory@holycross-hutch.com; doohl@holycross-hutch.com Rev. Aaron Spexarth, Pst.; Rev. Kirk Matthew Glazier, Assoc. Pst.; Rev. Will Stuever, Assoc. Pst.; Dcn. Hap Ramsey; Kim Griffith, DRE; CRP Stds.: 68

Holy Cross School - (Grades PreK-6) 2633 Independence Rd., Hutchinson, KS 67502 holycross-hutch.com/school Amy Wagoner, Prin.;

St. Teresa - 211 E. Fifth Ave., Hutchinson, KS 67501; Mailing: 2631 Independence Rd., Hutchinson, KS 67502-8417 t) 620-662-7812 stteresahutchinson@gmail.com www.saintteresahutchinson.com Rev. Michael J. Maybrier, Pst.; Steve Dechant, DRE; CRP Stds.: 23

INDEPENDENCE

St. Andrew - 210 N. Fourth St., Independence, KS 67301 t) 620-331-1789; (620) 331-2870 (St. Andrew School) standrewindp@gmail.com www.standrewindependence.com Rev. Zachary G.B. Pinaire, Pst.; CRP Stds.: 21

St. Andrew School - (Grades PreK-8) 215 N. Park Blvd., Independence, KS 67310 t) 620-331-2870 school@standrewindependence.com standrewindependence.com/school Becky Brown, Prin.;

IOLA

St. John - 310 S. Jefferson Ave., Iola, KS 66749 t) 620-365-2277; 620-365-3454 susan@stjohnstjoseph.com; dmigueldep@gmail.com Rev. David Michael, Pst.; David Roos, DRE; CRP Stds.: 33

St. Martin - 1368 Xylan Rd. KS 66761, Piqua, KS 66761

KINGMAN

St. Patrick - 638 Ave. D W., Kingman, KS 67068 t) 620-532-5440 office@stpatskingman.org stpatskingman.org Rev. Andrew J Walsh, Pst.; CRP Stds.: 77

St. Patrick School - (Grades PreK-8) 630 Ave. D W., Kingman, KS 67068 t) 620-532-2791 eharmon@stpatskingman.org stpatskingman.org/school Eva Harmon, Prin.; Mary Meng, Librn.;

LINDSBORG

St. Bridget of Sweden - 206 W. Swennson, Lindsborg, KS 67456; Mailing: 520 E. Northview, McPherson, KS 67460 t) 620-241-0821 office@stjosephmcpherson.com stjosephmcpherson.com Rev. Benjamin D. Shockey, Pst.; Amber Pracht, DRE; CRP Stds.: 20

LITTLE RIVER

Holy Trinity - 455 Harrison St., Little River, KS 67457; Mailing: P. O. Box 32, Little River, KS 67457 t) 620-665-5163; 620-897-6443 grasser@lrmutual.com; rectory@holycross-hutch.com Rev. Aaron Spexarth, Pst.; Rev. Edmond G. Kline, Assoc. Pst.; Shayla Grasser, DRE;

LYONS

St. Paul - 1205 S. Douglas Ave., Lyons, KS 67554; Mailing: 415 Saint Francis St., Lyons, KS 67554 t) 620-257-3503 parishoffice@stpaulslyons.com stpaulslyons.com/ Rev. Michael G. Brungardt, Pst.; CRP Stds.: 80

MADISON

St. Teresa of Avila - 1002 S. 4th St., Madison, KS 66860; Mailing: 514 N. Elm St., Eureka, KS 67045 t) 620-583-7100 sheureka67045@gmail.com greenwoodcountycatholicchurches.org/ Rev. Nicholaus L Jurgensmeyer, Pst.; CRP Stds.: 4

MARION

Holy Family - 415 N. Cedar St., Marion, KS 66861 t) 620-382-3369 hfpmarion@yahoo.com hfpmc.org Rev. Brian D. Bebak, Pst.; CRP Stds.: 114

St. Patrick - 201 W. 8th St., Florence, KS 66851

St. Mark -

St. John Nepomucene - 2744 Remington, Pilsen, KS 66861

Holy Redeemer Church - 426 Main, Tampa, KS 67483

MCPHERSON

St. Joseph - 520 E. Northview, McPherson, KS 67460 t) 620-241-0821 lharger@stjosephmcpherson.com; office@stjosephmcpherson.com www.stjosephmcpherson.com Rev. Benjamin D. Shockey, Pst.; Linda Harger, DRE; CRP Stds.: 66

St. Joseph School - (Grades PreK-6) t) 620-241-3913 school@stjosephmcpherson.com stjosephmcpherson.com/school Peggy Bahr, Prin.;

MOLINE

St. Mary's - 320 N. Main, Moline, KS 67353-0276; Mailing: Box 276, Moline, KS 67353-0276 t) 620-647-3577 bailadores33@yahoo.com; drugstore@sktc.net Rev. Robert K Spencer, Pst.; Julie Perkins, DRE; CRP Stds.: 24

MOUNT HOPE

St. Joseph - 13015 E. Maple Grove Rd., Mount Hope, KS 67108 t) 316-444-2210 www.stjosephost.com Rev. Bernard X Gorges, Pst.;

St. Joseph Catholic School - Ost - (Grades PreK-8) 12917 E. Maple Grove Rd., Mount Hope, KS 67108 t) 316-444-2548 ehohl@stjoeost.com Erin Hohl, Prin.;

MULVANE

St. Michael the Archangel - 525 E. Main St., Mulvane, KS 67110 t) 316-777-4221 stmichaelmulvane@sbcglobal.net; dre@stmichaelmulvane.org Rev. John V. Hotze, Pst.; Joanne Nesmith, DRE; CRP Stds.: 130

MURDOCK

St. Louis - 9800 N.E. 20th St., Murdock, KS 67111; Mailing: P.O. Box 528, Cheney, KS 67025 t) 316-500-1940 frdanieljduling@gmail.com www.stlouiswaterloo.com Rev. Daniel J. Duling, Pst.;

NASHVILLE

St. Leo the Great - 8035 S.W. 160 Ave., Nashville, KS 67112 t) 620-246-5370 judicis20@yahoo.com; rigor20@icloud.com Rev. Roger S. Lumbre, Pst.; CRP Stds.: 20

NEODESHA

St. Ignatius - 801 N. 8th, Neodesha, KS 66757; Mailing: P.O. Box 186, Neodesha, KS 66757 t) 620-325-5215 stignatiusneodesha@gmail.com Rev. Stuart M. Smeltzer, Admin.; CRP Stds.: 24

NEWTON

St. Mary - 106 E. Eighth St., Newton, KS 67114 t) 316-282-0459 parish@stmarynewton.org; mando3232@gmail.com www.stmarynewton.org Rev. Nicholas A. Voelker, Pst.; Rev. Maximilian K Biltz, Par. Vicar; Mandy Casey, DRE; CRP Stds.: 41

St. Mary School - (Grades PreK-8) 101 E. 9th St., Newton, KS 67114 t) 316-282-1974 nsteiner@smcsnewton.org smcsnewton.org/school Natalie Steiner, Prin.;

Our Lady of Guadalupe - 421 S. Ash St., Newton, KS 67114 t) 316-283-3499 olgnewton@gmail.com www.olgnewton.com Rev. Jorge Lopez, Pst.; CRP Stds.: 52

OSWEGO

Mother of God - 1105 4th St., Oswego, KS 67356 t) 620-795-2262 mogoswego@gmail.com; goldieunderwood2208@gmail.com Rev. Larry Parker, Admin.; Pam Overman, DRE; CRP Stds.: 39

OXFORD

St. Mary's - 608 N. Sumner, Oxford, KS 67119; Mailing: 412 E. 8th Ave., Winfield, KS 67156 t) 620-221-3610 frschuckman@gmail.com Rev. Kenneth J. Schuckman, Pst.;

PARSONS

St. Patrick - 1807 Stevens Ave., Parsons, KS 67357 t) 620-421-6762 rectory@stpatricksparsons.org stpatricksparsons.org Rev. Curtis L. Robertson, Pst.; Marena Kirkpatrick, DRE; CRP Stds.: 54

St. Patrick Catholic School - (Grades PreK-8) 1831 Stevens Ave., Parsons, KS 67357 t) 620-421-0710 school@stpatricksparsons.org stpatricksparsons.org/school Autumn Carson, Prin.; Stds.: 95; Lay Tchrs.: 10

PITTSBURG

Our Lady of Lourdes - 109 E. 9th St., Pittsburg, KS 66762; Mailing: P.O. Box 214, Pittsburg, KS 66762 t) 620-231-2135 ourladyoflourdes@ollsmc.com; parishsecretary@ollsmc.com www.ollsmc.com Rev. Jerome J. Spexarth, Pst.; Rev. Andrew Labenz, Par. Vicar; Rev. Chris Rumback, Par. Vicar; Rosario Del Pilar Mendez, DRE; CRP Stds.: 67

St. Mary's Elementary School - (Grades PreK-6) 301 E. 9th St., Pittsburg, KS 66762 t) 620-231-6941 smeschool@ollsmc.com Nancy Hicks, Prin.; Terri Tener, Librn.;

St. Mary's Colgan High School - 212 E. 9th St., Pittsburg,, KS 66762 t) 620-231-4690 smcjhhs@ollsmc.com www.ollsmc.com/school/ David Stephenson, Prin.; Beverly Mitchelson, Librn.;

SCAMMON

St. Bridget's - 406 N. Keith, Scammon, KS 66773; Mailing: 115 W. Walnut, Columbus, KS 66725 t) 620-429-2639; 620-479-2601 ckcocatholics@live.com www.ckcocatholics.org Rev. Jeremy S. Huser, Pst.; CRP Stds.: 20

SEDAN

St. Robert Bellarmine - 407 S. Montgomery, Sedan, KS 67361; Mailing: 320 N. Main, P.O. Box 276, Moline, KS 67353-0276 t) 620-647-3577; 620-725-3812 (CRP) bailadores33@yahoo.com Rev. Robert K Spencer, Pst.; CRP Stds.: 3

SOUTH HUTCHINSON

Our Lady of Guadalupe - 612 S. Maple, South Hutchinson, KS 67505-2099 t) 620-662-6443 office@olghutch.com olghutch.com/ Rev. Eric M. Weldon, Pst.; Jim Hoover, DRE; CRP Stds.: 182

SPIVEY

St. Peter - 10044 S.W. 90 St., Spivey, KS 67142; Mailing: 8035 S.W. 160th Ave., Nashville, KS 67112 t) 620-246-5370 judicis20@yahoo.com; rigor20@icloud.com Rev. Roger S. Lumbre, Pst.; CRP Stds.: 4

ST. PAUL

St. Francis - 208 Washington St., St. Paul, KS 66771-0216; Mailing: P.O. Box 216, St. Paul, KS 66771 t) 620-449-2224 saintfrancis66771@gmail.com www.stfrancis-stambrose.org Rev. Theodore Khin, Pst.; CRP Stds.: 103

STRONG CITY

St. Anthony of Padua - 602 Cottonwood, Strong City, KS 66869 t) 620-767-6412; 620-273-8617 (CRP) rosalima@cgtelco.net www.stanthonystrose.org/ Rev. Andrew J. Seiler, Pst.; Julie Puetz, DRE; CRP Stds.: 65

VIOLA

St. John - 18630 W. 71st St., Viola, KS 67149 t) 620-545-7171 faithformation@stjohnsclonmel.org; mhalstead@stjohnsclonmel.org www.stjohnsclonmel.org Rev. Joseph Tatro, Pst.; Cassi FitzGerald, Admin.; Madelyn Halstead, Admin.; Deborah Tamburro, Admin.; CRP Stds.: 90

WELLINGTON

St. Anthony/St. Rose - 210 N. B St., Wellington, KS 67152; Mailing: 217 N. C St., Wellington, KS 67152 t) 620-326-3480 (CRP); 620-326-2522 stanthony@sutv.com www.stanthonychurchwellington.org Rev. Michael J. Maybrier, Pst.; CRP Stds.: 58

WICHITA

Cathedral of the Immaculate Conception - 430 N. Broadway St., Wichita, KS 67202 t) 316-263-6574 parish@wichitacathedral.com www.wichitacathedral.com Rev. Adam J. Keiter, Rector; Rev. Todd Shepherd, Par. Vicar; Maribel Benedict, DRE; CRP Stds.: 240

All Saints - 3205 E. Grand St., Wichita, KS 67218 t) 316-682-1415 bschwartz@allsaintswichita.com; snettleton@allsaintswichita.com www.allsaintswichita.com Rev. Hien Paul Nguyen, Pst.; Sandra Nettleton, DRE;

All Saints School - (Grades PreK-8) 3313 E. Grand, Wichita, KS 67218 t) 316-682-6021 schoolinfo@allsaintswichita.com www.allsaintswichita.com/school Joyce Frederiksen, Prin.;

St. Anne - 2801 S. Seneca, Wichita, KS 67217-2399 t) 316-522-2383 church@stannewichita.org; alucero@stannewichita.org www.stannewichita.org Rev. David Marstall, Pst.; Rev. Clay Kimbro, Par. Vicar; Amanda Lucero, DRE; CRP Stds.: 126

St. Anne School - (Grades K-8) 1121 W. Regal St., Wichita, KS 67217-2399 t) 316-522-6131 school@stannewichita.org Gerry Hamilton, Prin.;

St. Anthony - 1214 E. 2nd St. N., Wichita, KS 67214 t) 316-269-4101 fr.bennguyen@gmail.com; fr.bennguyen@gmail.com www.stanthonywichita.com Rev. Benjamin N. Nguyen, Pst.; Khoa V Tran, PCL (V); CRP Stds.: 6

St. Catherine of Siena - 3642 N. Ridge Rd., Wichita, KS 67205 t) 316-425-0595 clista@saintcatherinewichita.com; fatherdan@saintcatherinewichita.com www.saintcatherinewichita.com Rev. Daniel J. Spexarth, Pst.; CRP Stds.: 250

St. Catherine of Siena Catholic School - (Grades PreK-8) 3660 N. Ridge Rd., Wichita, KS 67205 t) 316-719-2917 school@saintcatherinewichita.com saintcatherinewichita.com/school Jeremy Barr, Prin.; Andrea Iseman, Librn.;

Christ the King - 4411 Maple Ave., Wichita, KS 67209 t) 316-943-4353 rwinter@ctkwichita.org; cdutton@ctkwichita.org ctkwichita.org Rev. Devin T. Burns, Pst.; Robyn Winter, DRE; CRP Stds.: 23

Christ the King School - (Grades PreK-8) 4501 Maple Ave., Wichita, KS 67209 t) 316-943-0111 school@ctkwichita.org Mary Jo Evans, Prin.;

Church of Blessed Sacrament - 124 N. Roosevelt St., Wichita, KS 67208 t) 316-682-4557; 316-684-3752 (CRP) parish@blessedsacramentwichita.com blessedsacramentwichita.com Rev. Luke Downing, Par. Vicar; Rev. Matthew Siegman, Par. Admin.; CRP Stds.: 74

Blessed Sacrament School - (Grades PreK-8) 125 N. Quentin, Wichita, KS 67208 mhittner@blessedsacramentwichita.com blessedsacramentwichita.com/school Dan Dester, Prin.; Pam Loyle, Librn.;

Church of the Magdalen - 12626 E. 21st St. N., Wichita, KS 67206 t) 316-634-2315 info@magdalenwichita.com www.magdalenwichita.com Rev. John F. Jirak, Pst.; Rev. Michael L. Kerschen, Par. Vicar; Rev. Seth Arnold, Par. Vicar; Dcn. Jeff Jacobs; CRP Stds.: 160

Magdalen School - (Grades PreK-8) 2221 N. 127th St. E, Wichita, KS 67226 t) 316-634-1572 school@magdalenwichita.com; kschmitz@magdalenwichita.com www.magdalenwichita.com/school Kristin Schmitz, Prin.;

Church of the Resurrection - 4910 N. Woodlawn, Wichita, KS 67220 t) 316-744-2776 church@resurrectionwichita.com; chutfles@resurrectionwichita.com www.resurrectionwichita.com Rev. Michael Schemm, Pst.; Cindy Hutfles, DRE; CRP Stds.: 34

Resurrection School - (Grades PreK-8) 4900 N. Woodlawn, Wichita, KS 67220 t) 316-744-3576 school@resurrectionwichita.com resurrectionwichita.com/school Kori Heiman, Prin.;

St. Elizabeth Ann Seton - 645 N. 119th St. W., Wichita, KS 67235 t) 316-721-1686 church@seaswichita.com; bbalza@seaswichita.com Rev. Sherman A. Orr, Pst.; CRP Stds.: 115

St. Elizabeth Ann Seton School - (Grades PreK-8) t) 316-721-5693 school@seaswichita.com www.seaswichita.com/school David Charles, Prin.; Vicki Munsinger, Librn.;

St. Francis of Assisi - 861 N. Socora, Wichita, KS 67212 t) 316-722-4404 sfac@stfranciswichita.com www.stfranciswichita.com Rev. C. Jarrod Lies, Pst.; Rev. Luke Downing, Par. Vicar; Rev. Andrew Meng, Par. Vicar; Rev. Edmund M Herzog, In Res.; CRP Stds.: 602

St. Francis of Assisi School - (Grades PreK-8) 853 N. Socora, Wichita, KS 67212 t) 316-722-5171 school@stfranciswichita.com Mary Carter, Prin.; Ashley Wescott, Librn.;

Holy Savior - 3000 E. 13th St. N., Wichita, KS 67214 t) 316-682-8712 church@holy-savior.org holy-savior.org Rev. James J. Billinger, Pst.; Andrea Penelton, Parish Life Coord.; CRP Stds.: 35

Holy Savior School - (Grades PreK-8) t) 316-684-2141 school@holy-savior.org Philip Stutey, Prin.; Delia Shropshire, Pres.;

St. Joseph - 132 S. Millwood Ave., Wichita, KS 67213 t) 316-261-5800 saintjosephwichita@gmail.com stjosephwichita.com/ Rev. John Lanzrath, Pst.; Rev. Andrew Bergkamp, Par. Vicar; Kenneth Blaschke, DRE; CRP Stds.: 6

St. Joseph School - (Grades PreK-8) 139 S. Millwood Ave., Wichita, KS 67213 t) 316-261-5801 jcooke@stjosephwichita.com www.stjosephwichita.com/school Ellen Albert, Prin.;

St. Jude - 3030 Amidon Ave., Wichita, KS 67204 t) 316-838-1963 sjoffice@stjudewichita.org stjudewichita.org Rev. John P. Fogliasso, Pst.; Nicole Donohue, DRE; CRP Stds.: 42

St. Jude School - (Grades PreK-8) t) 316-838-0800 school@stjudewichita.org stjudewichita.org/school Robert Lyall, Prin.;

St. Margaret Mary - 2701 S. Pattie St., Wichita, KS 67216 t) 316-262-1821; 316-267-4911 (School); 316-201-4354 (Office) parish@smmwichita.com; school@smmwichita.com smmwichita.com/ Rev. Ned J. Blick, Pst.; Rev. Garett Burns, Vicar; CRP Stds.: 207

St. Margaret Mary School - (Grades PreK-8) 2635 S. Pattie St., Wichita, KS 67216 smmwichita.com/school Theresa Lam, Prin.; Lisa Hinson, Librn.;

Our Lady of Perpetual Help - 2351 N. Market St., Wichita, KS 67219 t) 316-838-8373; 316-838-5750 (CRP) olphwichitaks@gmail.com; olphwichita@gmail.com olphwichitaks.com Rev. Marco A DeLoera, Pst.; Rev. Juan G. Garza, Par. Vicar; CRP Stds.: 200

Parish Center - 2409 N. Market St., Wichita, KS 67219

St. Patrick - 2007 Arkansas Ave., Wichita, KS 67203 t) 316-262-4683 stpatrickchurch@stpatswichita.org stpatswichita.org Rev. James F. Weldon, Pst.; Rev. Hayden Charles, Par. Vicar; CRP Stds.: 254

St. Patrick School - (Grades PreK-8) 2023 Arkansas Ave., Wichita, KS 67203 t) 316-262-4071 stpatswichita.org/school Brandon Relph, Prin.;

Convent - 2045 Arkansas Ave., Wichita, KS 67203 t) 316-267-0021 Sr. Rosa Linda Lopez, Supr.;

St. Paul Parish - 1810 N. Roosevelt, Wichita, KS 67208 t) 316-684-6896 stpaul@stpauluniversityparish.com www.stpauluniversityparish.com Rev. Andrew K. Hoffman, Pst.;

St. Peter the Apostle - 11000 Southwest Blvd., Wichita, KS 67215 t) 316-522-4728 psecretary@stpeterschulte.com www.stpeterschulte.com Rev. Bernard X. Gorges, Pst.; CRP Stds.: 400

St. Peter the Apostle School - (Grades PreK-8) 11010 Southwest Blvd., Wichita, KS 67215 t) 316-524-6585 school@stpeterschulte.com stpeterschulte.com/school Brenda Hickok, Prin.;

St. Thomas Aquinas - 1321 Stratford Ln., Wichita, KS 67206 t) 316-683-6569 church@stthomaswichita.com www.stthomaswichita.com Rev. Matthew C. McGinness, Pst.; Rev. Andrew Dellasega, Par. Vicar; CRP Stds.: 84

St. Thomas Aquinas School - (Grades PreK-8) 1215 Stratford Ln., Wichita, KS 67206 t) 316-684-9201 school@stthomaswichita.com stthomaswichita.com/school Stephanie Warren, Prin.;

WINFIELD

Holy Name - 412 E. Eighth Ave., Winfield, KS 67156 t) 620-221-3610; 620-221-0230 amolander@holynamewinfield.org; frschuckman@gmail.com holynamewinfield.org Rev. Clay Kimbro, Pst.; Sr. Charlotte Brungardt, DRE; CRP Stds.: 37

Holy Name School - (Grades PreK-6) 700 Fuller St., Winfield, KS 67156 school@holynamewinfield.org; kporter@holynamewinfield.org Kim Porter, Prin.;

YATES CENTER

St. Joseph - 105 E. Bell St., Yates Center, KS 66783; Mailing: 310 S. Jefferson Ave., Iola, KS 66749 t) 620-365-2277 susan@stjohnstjoseph.com Rev. David Michael, Pst.; Leon Weber, DRE; Mary Weber, DRE; CRP Stds.: 35

ZENDA

St. John - 109 N. Ada St., Zenda, KS 67159; Mailing: 8035 S.W. 160th Ave., Nashville, KS 67112 t) 620-246-5370 judicis20@yahoo.com; rigor20@icloud.com Rev. Roger S. Lumbre, Pst.; CRP Stds.: 8

SCHOOLS: PRESCHOOL THRU HIGH SCHOOL

HIGH SCHOOLS

STATE OF KANSAS

HUTCHINSON

Trinity Catholic High School - (PAR) (Grades 7-12) 1400 E. 17th St., Hutchinson, KS 67502 t) 620-662-5800 rsnyder@trinity-hutch.com www.trinity-hutch.com Rev. Will Stuever, Chap.; Nancy McElgunn, Librn.; Stds.: 211; Sr. Tchrs.: 3; Lay Tchrs.: 16

WICHITA

Bishop Carroll Catholic High School - (PAR) (Grades 9-12) 8101 W. Central, Wichita, KS 67212 t) 316-722-2390 nielsenleticia@bcchs.org www.bcchs.org Rev. Edmund M Herzog, Chap.; Vanessa Harshberger, Prin.; Leticia C. Nielsen, Pres.; Stds.: 1,147; Pr. Tchrs.: 2; Sr. Tchrs.: 3; Lay Tchrs.: 66

Kapaun Mt. Carmel Catholic High School - (DIO) (Grades 9-12) 8506 E. Central, Wichita, KS 67206 t) 316-634-0315 rknapp@kapaun.org www.kapaun.org Robert Knapp, Pres.; Christopher Bloomer, Prin.; Rev. Curtis D.L. Hecker, Chap.; Stds.: 907; Pr. Tchrs.: 1; Sr. Tchrs.: 2; Lay Tchrs.: 65

INSTITUTIONS LOCATED IN DIOCESE

CAMPUS MINISTRY / NEWMAN CENTERS [CAM]

PITTSBURG

St. Pius X Catholic Student Center (Pittsburg State University) - 301A E. Cleveland, Pittsburg, KS 66762 t) 620-235-1138 frderek@catholicgorillas.org; spx@catholicgorillas.org catholicgorillas.org Rev. Derek Thome;

WICHITA

St. Paul Catholic Student Center - 1810 N. Roosevelt, Wichita, KS 67208 t) 316-684-6896 stpaul@stpauluniversityparish.com www.stpauluniversityparish.com Rev. Andrew K. Hoffman, Pst.;

CATHOLIC CHARITIES [CCH]

WICHITA

Catholic Charities, Inc. - Diocese of Wichita - 437 N. Topeka St., Wichita, KS 67202-2413 t) 316-264-8344 comms@catholiccharitieswichita.org www.catholiccharitieswichita.org Traci Kennedy, CEO; Asstd. Annu.: 15,000; Staff: 121

Adult Day Services - 2235 W. 37th St. N., Wichita, KS 67204 t) 316-942-2008

St. Anthony Family Shelter - 256 N. Ohio, Wichita, KS 67214 t) 316-264-7233

Cana Counseling - 439 N. McLean, Ste. 101, Wichita, KS 67203 t) 316-263-6941

Foster Grandparent Program - 437 N. Topeka St., Wichita, KS 67202 t) (316) 264-8344 x1210

Harbor House - ; Mailing: P.O. Box 3759, Wichita, KS 67201 t) 316-263-6000

Immigration Services - 437 N Topeka St, Wichita, KS 67202 t) 316-264-0282 www.catholiccharitieswichita.org

Our Daily Bread Food Pantry - 2825 S. Hillside, Wichita, KS 67216

Southeast Kansas Services - Pittsburg - 417 N. Broadway, Ste. B, Pittsburg, KS 66762 t) 620-235-0633

***Center of Hope, Inc.** - 1100 E. 1st St. N., Wichita, KS 67214-3905 t) 316-267-3999 george@centerofhopeinc.org www.centerofhopeinc.org Homelessness prevention sponsored by Adorers of the Blood of Christ. George Dinkel, CEO; Asstd. Annu.: 9,162; Staff: 4

COLLEGES & UNIVERSITIES [COL]

WICHITA

Newman University - 3100 McCormick St., Wichita, KS 67213-2008 t) 316-942-4291 dodoshg@newmanu.edu www.newmanu.edu Founded by Sisters of Adorers of the Blood of Christ; accredited by the Higher Learning Commission. Rev. Adam E. Grelinger, Chap.; Rev. Joseph M. Gile, Dean; Dr. Kathleen S. Jagger, Pres.; Steve Hamersky, Librn.; Stds.: 2,883; Lay Tchrs.: 79; Pr. Tchrs.: 2

CONVENTS, MONASTERIES, AND RESIDENCES FOR WOMEN [CON]

COLWICH

Sisters of the Immaculate Heart of Mary of Wichita, Inc. (I.H.M.) - 3550 N. 167th St. W., Colwich, KS 67030 t) 316-722-9316; 316-722-9778 ihmmail@sistersihmofwichita.org www.sistersihmofwichita.org Mother Mary Magdalene O'Halloran, I.H.M., Supr.; Srs.: 31

WICHITA

Adorers of the Blood of Christ U.S. Region - Wichita Center, 1165 Southwest Blvd., Wichita, KS 67213 t) 316-942-2201 schumerf@adorers.org; rawlingsd@adorers.org www.adorers.org Rev. Thomas Welk, C.P.P.S., Chap.; Sr. Diana Rawlings, A.S.C., Dir.; Sr. Fran Schumer, A.S.C., Dir.; Srs.: 41

Dominican Sisters of Peace - 201 S. Millwood, Wichita, KS 67213 t) 316-267-4551 patricia.twohill@oppeace.org Sr. Patricia Twohill, O.P., Prioress;

Medical Sisters of St. Joseph-United States Foundation - 3435 E. Funston, Wichita, KS 67218 t) 316-686-4746 josmy61@yahoo.com.au Sr. Laly Josmy George, Supr.; Srs.: 3

Wichita Center, Congregation of the Sisters of St. Joseph - 3700 E. Lincoln, Wichita, KS 67218-2099 t) 316-686-7171 pwarbritton@csjoseph.org www.csjoseph.org Rev. Joseph M. Gile, Chap.; Sr. Pam Young, C.S.J., Pst. Min./Coord.; Srs.: 61

ENDOWMENTS / FOUNDATIONS / TRUSTS [EFT]

WICHITA

Guadalupe Health Foundation - 940 S. St. Francis, Wichita, KS 67211 t) 316-264-6464 x213 amiller@guadalupeclinic.com guadalupeclinic.com Supports, assists & promotes the interests and welfare of programs and activities providing health care services to the poor. J. V. Johnston, Exec.;

Holy Family Special Needs Foundation - 424 N. Broadway, Wichita, KS 67202 t) 316-269-3900 jacobsm@catholicdioceseofwichita.org Myra Jacobs, Dir.;

Priests' Retirement and Education Fund of Wichita - 424

N. Broadway, Wichita, KS 67202 t) 316-269-3900 bryan.coulter@catholicdioceseofwichita.org Rev. Chad Arnold, Pres.;

Via Christi Foundation, Inc. - 3600 E. Harry, 3rd Fl., Wichita, KS 67218 t) (316) 858-4921 tracey.biles@ascension.org viachristi.org\foundation Kevin Strecker, CEO; Tracey Biles, Contact;

HOSPITALS / HEALTH SERVICES [HOS]

COLUMBUS

Mercy Hospital Columbus - 220 N. Pennsylvania Ave., Columbus, KS 66725 t) 620-429-2545 angella.saporito@mercy.net Julie Mercer, Chap.; Bed Capacity: 25; Asstd. Annu.: 8,600; Staff: 61

PITTSBURG

Ascension Via Christi Hospital Pittsburg, Inc. - 1 Mt. Carmel Way, Pittsburg, KS 66762 t) (316) 858-4921 tracey.biles@ascension.org www.viachristi.org Kevin Strecker, CEO; Tracey Biles, Contact; Bed Capacity: 89; Asstd. Annu.: 164,178; Staff: 423

WICHITA

Ascension Via Christi Hospital St. Teresa, Inc. - 14800 W. St. Teresa, Wichita, KS 67235 t) (316) 858-4921 tracey.biles@ascension.org www.ascension.org Tracey Biles, Contact; Kevin Strecker, CEO; Bed Capacity: 35; Asstd. Annu.: 40,740; Staff: 171

Ascension Via Christi Hospitals Wichita, Inc. - 929 N. St. Francis, Wichita, KS 67214 t) (316) 858-4921 tracey.biles@ascension.org www.viachristi.org Kevin Strecker, CEO; Tracey Biles, Contact; Bed Capacity: 671; Asstd. Annu.: 285,886; Staff: 2,859

Via Christi Hospital St. Francis - 929 N. St. Francis, Wichita, KS 67214 www.ascension.org

Via Christi Hospital St. Joseph - 3600 E. Harry, Wichita, KS 67218 www.ascension.org

Ascension Via Christi Rehabilitation Hospital, Inc. - 1151 N. Rock Rd., Wichita, KS 67206 t) (316) 858-4921 tracey.biles@ascension.org www.ascension.org Tracey Biles, Contact; Kevin Strecker, CEO; Bed Capacity: 30; Asstd. Annu.: 93,201; Staff: 105

MISCELLANEOUS [MIS]

BEL AIRE

Priests Retirement Center - 6900 E. 45th St. N., Bel Aire, KS 67226 t) 316-744-2020 bryan.coulter@catholicdioceseofwichita.org; jirakh@catholicdioceseofwichita.org Cindy LaFleur, Admin.; Priests: 14

ST. LOUIS

Leaven International Corporation - 4233 Sulphur Ave., St. Louis, MO 63109 t) 314-351-6294 woodruffm@adorers.org www.adorers.org A charitable organization of the Adorers of the Blood of Christ. Sr. Michelle Woodruff, Treas.;

WICHITA

Ascension Via Christi Health, Inc. - 929 N St Francis, Wichita, KS 67214 t) (316) 858-4921 tracey.biles@ascension.org www.viachristi.org Subsidiary of Ascension Health & sponsored by the congregations of Ascension Health. Kevin Strecker, CEO; Tracey Biles, Contact;

Ascension Via Christi Health Partners, Inc. - 929 N. St. Francis, Wichita, KS 67214 t) (316) 858-4921 tracey.biles@ascension.org www.viachristi.org Kevin Strecker, CEO; Tracey Biles, Contact;

***Ascension Via Christi Property Services, Inc.** - 1100 N. St. Francis Ave., Ste. 240, Wichita, KS 67214; Mailing: 8200 E. Thorn Dr., Wichita, KS 67226 t) (316) 858-4921 tracey.biles@ascension.org www.viachristi.org Kevin Strecker, CEO; Tracey Biles, Contact;

***Casting Net Ministries, Inc.** - 1117 Hazelwood, Wichita, KS 67212; Mailing: P.O. Box 656, Colwich, KS 67030 t) 800-217-5710 info@castingnetsministries.com www.castingnetsministries.com Apostolate for the New Evangelization. Tony Brandt, Pres.; Chris Stewart, COO;

MDM Hearts & Hands, Inc. - 1165 Southwest Blvd., Wichita, KS 67213 t) 316-942-2201 welsbys@adorers.org www.adorers.org Sr. Susan Welsby, A.S.C., Admin.;

***Support for Catholic Schools, Inc** - 424 N. Broadway, Wichita, KS 67202 t) 316-269-3900 wescottm@catholicdioceseofwichita.org Mike Wescott, Dir.;

Wichita Women's Initiative Network - 510 E. 3rd St., N., Wichita, KS 67202 t) 316-262-3960 win@wichitawin.org www.wichitawin.org Amber Beck, Contact;

NURSING / REHABILITATION / CONVALESCENCE / ELDERLY CARE [NUR]

BEL AIRE

Catholic Care Center, Inc. - 6700 E. 45th St. N., Bel Aire, KS 67226 t) 316-744-2020 cindy.lafleur@catholiccarecenter.org catholiccarecenter.org Rev. Chris Martin, Chap.; Cindy LaFleur, Exec.; Sr. Agnes Weber, Dir., Mission Integration; Asstd. Annu.: 806; Staff: 266

Shepherd's Crossing - t) 316-210-4225

MULVANE

Villa Maria, Inc. - 116 S. Central Ave., Mulvane, KS 67110 t) 316-777-1129 schumerf@adorers.org www.villamariainc.org Rev. John V. Hotze, Chap.; Asstd. Annu.: 140; Staff: 90

Maria Court Assisted Living - 633 E. Main, Mulvane, KS 67110 t) 316-777-9917 pam.darnell@villamariainc.com Pam Darnall, Dir.;

PITTSBURG

Via Christi Village Pittsburg, Inc. (Ascension Living Via Christi Village Pittsburg) - 1502 E. Centennial, Pittsburg, KS 66762 t) 314-292-9308 ahscm-mission@ascension.org www.ascensionliving.org Ryan Endsley, COO; Asstd. Annu.: 247; Staff: 99

WICHITA

Caritas Center, Inc. - 1400 S. Sheridan St., Wichita, KS 67213 t) 316-942-2201 roughtons@adorers.org www.adorers.org Sue Roughton, Admin.; Asstd. Annu.: 18; Staff: 59

Cornerstone Assisted Living, Inc. - 1240 N. Broadmoor, Wichita, KS 67211 t) 314-292-9308 ahscm-mission@ascension.org www.ascensionliving.org/ Ryan Endsley, COO; Asstd. Annu.: 52; Staff: 29

Ascension Living Via Christi Village Ridge (Cornerstone Assisted Living, Inc.) - 3636 N. Ridge Rd., Wichita, KS 67205 t) (314) 292-9308

Mount St. Mary, Inc. - 3700 E. Lincoln, Wichita, KS 67218 t) 316-686-7171 mrajewski@csjinitiatives.org Michael Rajewski, Admin.; Asstd. Annu.: 71; Staff: 71

Sheridan Village, Inc. - 1051 S. Bluffview, Wichita, KS 67218 t) 316-681-1172 sheridanvillage@keymgmtsites.com; kdavis@csjinitiatives.org www.keymgmt.com HUD low-income senior housing. Denise Gannon, CEO; Asstd. Annu.: 80; Staff: 3

Via Christi Village Georgetown, Inc. (Ascension Living Via Christi Village Georgetown) - 1655 S. Georgetown, Wichita, KS 67218 t) 314-292-9308 ahscm-mission@ascension.org www.ascensionliving.org/ Ryan Endsley, COO; Asstd. Annu.: 156; Staff: 17

Via Christi Village McLean, Inc. (Ascension Living Via Christi Village McLean) - 777 N. McLean Blvd., Wichita, KS 67203 t) 314-292-9308 ahscm-mission@ascension.org www.ascensionliving.org/ Ryan Endsley, COO; Asstd. Annu.: 255; Staff: 74

SPECIAL CARE FACILITIES [SPF]

WICHITA

Guadalupe Clinic, Inc. - 940 S. St. Francis, Wichita, KS 67211 t) 316-264-6464 x205 jv@guadalupeclinic.com www.guadalupeclinic.org Healthcare clinics serving the uninsured working poor and poor under the poverty line. J. V. Johnston, CEO; Asstd. Annu.: 7,900; Staff: 26

Via Christi Healthcare Outreach Program for Elders, Inc. (HOPE) (Ascension Living HOPE) - 2622 W. Central, Ste. 101, Wichita, KS 67203 t) 314-292-9308 ahscm-mission@ascension.org www.ascensionliving.org/ Program of All-Inclusive Care for the Elderly (PACE). Ryan Endsley, COO; Bed Capacity: 300; Asstd. Annu.: 363; Staff: 134

Via Christi Villages, Inc. - 2622 W. Central, Ste. 200, Wichita, KS 67203 t) 314-292-9308 ahscm-mission@ascension.org www.ascensionliving.org/ Ryan Endsley, COO;

An asterisk (*) denotes an organization that has established tax-exempt status directly with the IRS and is not covered by the USCCB Group Ruling.

Diocese of Wilmington

(Dioecesis Wilmingtoniensis)

MOST REVEREND WILLIAM EDWARD KOENIG, D.D.

Bishop of Wilmington; ordained May 14 1983; appointed Bishop of Wilmington April 30, 2021; Episcopal ordination and installation: July 13, 2021. Chancery: 1925 Delaware Ave., P.O. Box 2030, Wilmington, DE 19899. T: 302-573-3100; F: 302-573-6836. Email: trubini@cdow.org.

Chancery Office: P.O. Box 2030, Wilmington, DE 19899-2030. T: 302-573-3100; F: 302-573-6836.
www.cdow.org
chancery@cdow.org

ESTABLISHED MARCH 3, 1868.

Square Miles Delaware 1,932; Maryland 3,375; Total 5,307.

Comprises the State of Delaware and the Counties of Caroline, Cecil, Dorchester, Kent, Queen Anne's, Somerset, Talbot, Wicomico and Worcester in Maryland.

For legal titles of parishes and diocesan institutions, consult the Chancery Office.

STATISTICAL OVERVIEW

Personnel

Bishop	1
Retired Bishops	1
Priests: Diocesan Active in Diocese	53
Priests: Diocesan Active Outside Diocese	2
Priests: Retired, Sick or Absent	40
Number of Diocesan Priests	95
Religious Priests in Diocese	52
Total Priests in your Diocese	147
Extern Priests in Diocese	22
Ordinations:	
Diocesan Priests	1
Transitional Deacons	1
Permanent Deacons in Diocese	121
Total Brothers	6
Total Sisters	138

Parishes

Parishes	56
With Resident Pastor:	
Resident Diocesan Priests	46
Resident Religious Priests	4
Without Resident Pastor:	
Administered by Priests	6
Missions	18

Welfare

Catholic Hospitals	1
Total Assisted	139,113
Health Care Centers	2
Total Assisted	323
Homes for the Aged	8
Total Assisted	500
Day Care Centers	3
Total Assisted	108
Specialized Homes	1
Total Assisted	15
Special Centers for Social Services	4
Total Assisted	108,195

Educational

Diocesan Students in Other Seminaries	9
Total Seminarians	9
High Schools, Diocesan and Parish	4
Total Students	1,553
High Schools, Private	4
Total Students	1,648
Elementary Schools, Diocesan and Parish	18
Total Students	4,930
Elementary Schools, Private	6
Total Students	752
Catechesis/Religious Education:	
High School Students	339
Elementary Students	4,992
Total Students under Catholic Instruction	14,223
Teachers in Diocese:	
Priests	7
Sisters	6
Lay Teachers	820

Vital Statistics

Receptions into the Church:	
Infant Baptism Totals	1,522
Minor Baptism Totals	166
Adult Baptism Totals	53
Received into Full Communion	87
First Communions	1,459
Confirmations	1,377
Marriages:	
Catholic	278
Interfaith	91
Total Marriages	369
Deaths	1,786
Total Catholic Population	246,120
Total Population	1,509,022

LEADERSHIP

Bishop - Most Rev. William E. Koenig;
Vicar General and Moderator of the Curia - Rev. Msgr. Steven P. Hurley;
Judicial Vicar - Very Rev. Joseph W. McQuaide IV;
Vicar for Clergy - Very Rev. Glenn M. Evers, V.C.;
Chancellor - Very Rev. Joseph W. McQuaide IV;

ADMINISTRATION

Office of the Bishop - t) 302-573-3146 bishop@cdow.org Most Rev. William E. Koenig, Bishop of Wilmington;
Office of the Vicar General - t) 302-573-3118 scook@cdow.org Rev. Msgr. Steven P. Hurley, Vicar Gen. & Moderator of the Curia;
Catholic Cemeteries - t) 302-656-3323 Scott Hudson, Exec. Dir.;
Information Technology - t) 302-573-3122 Nancy Moore, Dir.;
Office of Safe Environments and Survivors Assistance Coordinator - t) 302-295-0668 Michael D. Connelly, Dir.;
Office of the Vicar for Clergy - t) 302-573-3114 Very Rev. Glenn M. Evers, V.C., Vicar For Clergy;
Coordinator of Institutional Chaplains - t) 302-573-3144 Very Rev. Glenn M. Evers, V.C.;
Office of the Permanent Diaconate - t) 302-573-2390 Dcn. Philip Belt, Dir.;
Office of Priestly and Religious Vocations and Seminarians and Newly Ordained - t) 302-573-3113 Rev. Norman P. Carroll, Vocation Dir.; Rev. Richard Jasper, Assoc. Vocation Dir.;
Office of the Chancellor - t) 302-573-3100 chancery@cdow.org Very Rev. Joseph W. McQuaide IV, Chancellor & Judicial Vicar;
Archives - t) 302-655-0597 archives@cdow.org Susan Kirk Ryan, Archivist;
Censor of Books - Very Rev. James S. Lentini;
Mission Office - t) 302-573-3100 Very Rev. Joseph W. McQuaide IV, Dir., Society for the Propagation of the Faith & the Holy Childhood;
Office of Worship - t) 302-573-3137 Rev. Michael A. Preston, Dir.;

OFFICES AND DIRECTORS

Catholic Cemeteries, Inc. - t) 302-656-3323 Most Rev. William E. Koenig, Pres.; Scott Hudson, Secy.; Joseph P. Corsini, Treas.;
Catholic Charities, Inc. - t) 302-655-9624 Xavier DeCaire, Vice. Pres.; Frederick "Fritz" Jones, Secy.; Joseph P. Corsini, Treas.;
Catholic Diocese of Wilmington, Inc. - t) 302-573-3118 Most Rev. William E. Koenig, Pres.; Rev. Msgr. Steven P. Hurley, Vice. Pres.; Very Rev. Joseph W. McQuaide IV, Secy.;
Catholic Ministry to the Elderly, Inc. - t) 302-573-3118 Most Rev. William E. Koenig, Pres.; Susan D'Alonzo Ament, Vice. Pres.; James Dugar, Secy.;
Catholic Press of Wilmington, Inc. - t) 302-573-3118 Most Rev. William E. Koenig, Pres.; Rev. Msgr. Steven P. Hurley, Vice Pres. & Secy.; Joseph P. Corsini, Treas.;
Catholic Youth Organization, Inc. - t) 302-573-3118 Most Rev. William E. Koenig, Pres.; Rev. Msgr. Steven P. Hurley, Vice. Pres.; Dr. Louis DeAngelo, Secy.;
Children's Home, Inc. - t) 302-655-9624 Most Rev. William E. Koenig, Pres.; Xavier DeCaire, Vice. Pres.; Frederick "Fritz" Jones, Secy.;
Delegate for Religious - t) 302-573-3124 Sr. Ann David Strohminger, O.S.F. (religious@cdow.org);
Diocese of Wilmington Schools, Inc. - t) 302-573-3118 Most Rev. William E. Koenig, Pres.; Rev. Msgr. Steven P. Hurley, Vice. Pres.; Dr. Louis DeAngelo, Secy.;
Office for Cultural Ministries - t) (302) 573-3100 gevers@cdow.org Very Rev. Glenn M. Evers, V.C., Dir.;
Office of Hispanic Ministry - t) 302-731-2200 Rev. Carlos Ochoa, Coord.;
Korean Catholic Community - t) 302-998-7609 Very Rev. Glenn M. Evers, V.C., Dir., Office for Cultural Ministries; Rev. Yong Kook Silvio Woo, Pst. Min./Coord.; Lawrence Chi Young Kim, Korean Catholic Community Parish Coord.;
Ministry For Black Catholics - t) 302-573-3104 Brenda Burns, Dir.;
Native American Ministry - t) 302-573-3100 Very Rev. Glenn M. Evers, V.C.;
Seton Villa, Inc. - t) 302-655-9624 Frederick "Fritz" Jones, Secy.;
Siena Hall, Inc. - t) 302-655-9624 Frederick "Fritz" Jones, Secy.;

ADVISORY BOARDS, COMMISSIONS, COMMITTEES, AND COUNCILS

Catholic Diocese Foundation - t) 302-573-3105 Joseph P. Corsini, Exec. Dir.;
College of Consultors - Very Rev. Roger F. DiBuo; Rev. Charles C. Dillingham; Very Rev. John B. Gabage;
Diocesan Building Committee - t) 302-573-3118 Rev. Msgr. Steven P. Hurley, Bishop's Rep.; Romeo Aquino, Chair; Rev. Msgr. Charles L. Brown III, Clergy;
Diocesan Religious Education Board - t) 302-573-3130 Dr. MaryAnn Wallen, Ex-officio;
Diocesan School Board - t) 302-573-3133 Dr. Louis DeAngelo, Ex-officio;
Due Process Commission - Very Rev. Joseph W. McQuaide IV, Clerk of the Commission;
Finance Council - t) 302-573-3105 Most Rev. William E. Koenig, Ex-officio; Rev. Msgr. Steven P. Hurley, Vice. Pres.; Joseph P. Corsini, Secy.;
Pastoral Council - t) 302-573-3100 Very Rev. Joseph W. McQuaide IV;
Priests' Continuing Formation Committee - t) 410-822-2344 Rev. James Nash, Chair;
Priests' Council - Most Rev. William E. Koenig, Ex-officio; Rev. Msgr. Steven P. Hurley, Vicar General; Very Rev. Joseph W. McQuaide IV, Chancellor & Judicial Vicar;
Priests' Personnel Board - Very Rev. Glenn M. Evers, V.C., Dir.; Very Rev. Roger F. DiBuo; Rev. Msgr. John P. Hopkins;
Public Policy Committee - t) 302-573-3118 Rev. Msgr. Steven P. Hurley;

CATHOLIC CHARITIES

Catholic Charities - t) 302-655-9624 Frederick "Fritz" Jones, Exec. Dir.;

COMMUNICATIONS

Secretary - Robert G. Krebs, Dir.;
Office of Public Relations and Media - t) 302-573-3116 Robert G. Krebs, Dir.;
The Dialog, Catholic Press - t) 302-573-3109 (Newsroom); 302-573-3112 (Advertising) news@thedialog.org www.thedialog.org Most Rev. William E. Koenig, Publisher; Joseph P. Owens, Editor/ Mgr. (jowens@thedialog.org);

DEANERIES

City Deanery - Very Rev. Roger F. DiBuo, Dean;
Brandywine Hundred Deanery - Very Rev. James T. Kirk Jr., Dean;
Central New Castle Deanery - Very Rev. Joseph J. Piekarski, Dean;
Eastern Shore Deanery - Very Rev. John B. Gabage, Dean;
Iron Hill Deanery - Rev. Edward F. Ogden, O.S.F.S., Dean;
Ocean Deanery - Very Rev. John T. Solomon, Dean;
Silver Lake Deanery - Very Rev. James S. Lentini, Dean;

DEVELOPMENT

Secretary - t) 302-573-3121 Sheila O'Hagan McGirl, Dir. (smcgirl@cdow.org);
Faith and Charity Appeal - t) 302-573-3121 Sheila O'Hagan McGirl, Dir. (smcgirl@cdow.org);

EDUCATION

Secretary - Dr. Louis DeAngelo;
Catholic Schools Office - t) 302-573-3133 Dr. Louis DeAngelo, Supt.; Carol Ripken, Asst. Supt.;
Catholic Youth and Young Adult Ministry - t) 302-658-3800 catholicyouth@cdow.org www.cdowcym.org Daniel Pin, Dir.; Very Rev. Joseph W. McQuaide IV, Chap.; Aaron Frye, Athletic Coord.;
Catholic Campus Ministry - t) 302-368-4728 Rev. Timothy M. McIntire, O.S.F.S.; Dr. William Hamant, Dir.;
Catholic Scouting Program - dpin@cdow.org Robert Murray, Chair, Catholic Com. for Boy Scouts; Dcn. Thomas E. Watts Sr., Boy Scout Chap.; Joan Pryzwara, Chair, Catholic Com. for Girl Scouts;
Religious Education - t) 302-573-3130 Dr. MaryAnn Wallen, Dir.;
Education Ministry for Persons With Special Needs - Debbie Ciafre, Coord. Spec. Rel. Educ.;
Office for Marriage and Family Life - t) 302-295-0684 Dr. MaryAnn Wallen, Dir.;
Respect Life Office -

FINANCE

Secretary and Chief Financial Officer - t) 302-573-3105 Joseph P. Corsini, Dir.;

HUMAN RESOURCES

Secretary - t) 302-573-3126 humanresources@cdow.org Kelly Anne Donahue, Dir.;

ORGANIZATIONS

***Birthright of Delaware -** t) 302-656-7080 birthrightofdel@verizon.net www.birthright.org/wilmington Tinisha Brown, Dir.;
Delawareans United for Education - t) 302-573-3118 Rev. Msgr. Steven P. Hurley;
Maryland Catholic Conference - t) 302-573-3118; 410-269-1155 Jennifer Kraska, Exec. Dir.;
Regina Coeli Society -
World Wide Marriage Encounter - t) (302) 220-9833 applications@wwme-delmar.org wwme.org Barney Bellard, Contact; Kathy Bellard, Contact;

TRIBUNAL

Tribunal Chancery - t) 302-573-3107 tribunal@cdow.org Very Rev. Joseph W. McQuaide IV, Judicial Vicar; Elaine Atz, Sec. & Ecclesiastical Notary;
Judicial Vicar - Very Rev. Joseph W. McQuaide IV;
Judges - Rev. Msgr. George J. Brubaker, Tribunal Judge; Rev. Michael C. Connolly, O.S.F.S., Tribunal Judge; Rt. Rev. James B. Herring, O.Praem., Tribunal Judge;
Defender of the Bond - Sr. Patricia Smith, O.S.F.;

MISCELLANEOUS / OTHER OFFICES

Catholic Charismatic Renewal - Rev. Thomas A. Flowers, Diocesan Liaison; Demetrio Ortega, Hispanic Lay Dir.;
Catholic Relief Services - t) 302-328-3431 Rev. Msgr. George J. Brubaker, Dir.;
Cursillo Movement - Glem Olivares, Lay Dir. (saintpaulrectory@gmail.com); Dcn. Eliezer Soto, Spiritual Adv./Care Srvcs. (rectory@olfnewcastle.com);
Diocese of Wilmington - Diocesan Vocations Guild - t) 302-573-3113 Rev. Norman P. Carroll, Chap.; Francis Woerner, Pres. (francissfo2003@gmail.com);
Liaison for Ecumenical & Inter-Religious Dialog - Very Rev. Roger F. DiBuo, Liaison;
Marian Devotions - Rev. Brian S. Lewis, Dir.;
St. Thomas More Society - t) 302-573-3100 Nick Caggiano, Pres.; Peter Sweeney, Pres.-Elect; Very Rev. Glenn M. Evers, V.C., Chap.;

PARISHES, MISSIONS, AND CLERGY

STATE OF DELAWARE

BEAR

St. Elizabeth Ann Seton - 345 Bear-Christiana Rd., Bear, DE 19701-1048 t) 302-322-6430 office@setonparish.net www.setonparish.net Rev. Norman P. Carroll, Pst.; Dcn. William Kibler; Dcn. Cruz Rodriguez; Dcn. Jose A. Sanchez; Olga Matias, DRE; CRP Stds.: 179

BETHANY BEACH

St. Ann - 691 Garfield Ave., Bethany Beach, DE 19930 t) 302-539-6449 office@stannsbethany.org www.stannbb.org Rev. John P. Klevence, K.H.S., Pst.; Rev. Joseph Dovari, Assoc. Pst.; Dcn. Dennis Hayden; Dcn. Michael J. Malecki; Dcn. Fred Mauser; Belkis Stallings, DRE; CRP Stds.: 79

Our Lady of Guadalupe - 35318 Church Rd., Frankford, DE 19945; Mailing: 691 Garfield Pkwy., Bethany Beach, DE 19930 stannbb.org

CLAYMONT

Holy Rosary - 3200 Philadelphia Pike, Claymont, DE 19703 t) 302-798-2904 office@hrparish.com www.hrparish.com Rev. John J. Gayton, Pst.; Dcn. Jose Perez; Rev. Leonard J. Kempski, In Res.; CRP Stds.: 192

DELAWARE CITY

St. Paul - 209 Washington St., Delaware City, DE 19706-0544; Mailing: P O Box 544, Delaware City, DE 19706-0544 t) 302-834-4321 stpaulsdecity@verizon.net www.stpaulsrcchurch.org Rev. Msgr. George J. Brubaker, Pst.; Dcn. Charles Schauber Sr.; Linda Michel, Co-CRE; Patricia Walker, Co-CRE;

DOVER

Holy Cross - 631 S. State St., Dover, DE 19901 t) 302-674-5787 secretary@holycrossdover.org; mdornberger@holycrossdover.org www.holycrossdover.org Very Rev. James S. Lentini, Pst.; Rev. Brennan H. Ferris, Assoc. Pst.; Dcn. Philip Belt; Dcn. John Harvey; Dcn. Richard Kosior; Dcn. Robert McMullen; Dcn. Vincent Pisano; Rev. Msgr. Daniel J. McGlynn, In Res.; CRP Stds.: 178

Holy Cross School - (Grades PreK-8) t) (302) 674-5782 elementary@holycrossdover.org holycrossdover.org/school Linda Pollitt, Prin.; Stds.: 339; Lay Tchrs.: 23

GEORGETOWN

St. Michael the Archangel - 202 Edward St., Georgetown, DE 19947 t) 302-856-6451 info@smammop.com www.smammop.com Rev. Robert E. Coine, Pst.; Rev. Timothy J. Brady, Par. Vicar; Rev. Idelmo Mego Diaz, Par. Vicar; Dcn. Kenneth J. Hall; Yeny Perez, DRE; CRP Stds.: 303

Mary Mother of Peace - 30839 Mt. Joy Rd. at Rte. 24, Millsboro, DE 19966; Mailing: 202 Edward St., Millsboro, DE 19966 t) (302) 856-6451

HOCKESSIN

St. Mary of the Assumption - 7200 Lancaster Pike, Hockessin, DE 19707 t) 302-239-7100 office@smachurch.com www.smachurch.com Rev. Charles C. Dillingham, Pst.; Rev. David F. Murphy, Assoc. Pst.; Dcn. Larry Brecht; Dcn. John Giacci; Dcn. Joseph W. Jackson Sr.; Dcn. Joseph M. LoPorto; Dcn. Larry Morris; Cindy Krebs, DRE; CRP Stds.: 348

LEWES

St. Jude the Apostle - 152 Tulip Dr., Lewes, DE 19958 t) 302-644-7300; 302-644-7413 office@stjudelewes.org www.stjudelewes.org Rev. Brian S. Lewis, Pst.; Rev. Jones Kukatla, Assoc. Pst.; Dcn. Al Barros; Dcn. Howard C. League; Dcn. Martin J. Barrett; Dcn. Joseph Cilia Jr.; Dcn. William McGann; Dcn. Barry Taylor; Michael McShane, DRE; CRP Stds.: 234

MIDDLETOWN

St. Joseph - 319 E. Main St., Middletown, DE 19709; Mailing: 371 E. Main St., Middletown, DE 19709 t) 302-378-5800 office@stjosephmiddletown.com www.stjosephmiddletown.com/ Sacramental records 1790-1964 at Diocesan Archives. Rev. Mark A. Kelleher, Pst.; Rev. Bruce T. Anderson, Assoc. Pst.; Dcn. Michael A. Boyd Sr.; Dcn. David Feaster II; CRP Stds.: 347

St. Rose of Lima - 301 Lock St., Chesapeake City, MD 21915 office@st.josephmiddletown.com www.stjosephmiddletown.com

St. Francis Xavier-Old Bohemia - 1064 Church Rd., Warwick, MD 21912 office@st.josephmiddletown.com www.stjosephmiddletown.com

MILFORD

St. John the Apostle - 506 Seabury Ave., Milford, DE 19963-2217 t) 302-422-5123 stjohn@stjohnsmilford.com; admin@stjohnsmilford.com www.stjohnsmilford.com Rev. Anthony Giamello, Pst.; Rev. Jones Kukatla, Assoc. Pst.; Dcn. Philip Gonzalez; Dcn. Scott J. Landis; Dcn. John G. Molitor; Dcn. Guillermo Nick Vasquez; Judy Purcell, DRE; CRP Stds.: 90

St. Bernadette - 109 Dixon, Harrington, DE 19952 t) 302-398-8269 stb@stjohnsmilford.com www.stbernadettesharrington.com

NEW CASTLE

Holy Spirit - 12 Winder Rd., New Castle, DE 19720; Mailing: 521 Harmony St., New Castle, DE 19720 t) 302-658-1069 holyspiritde@gmail.com www.holyspirtchurchde.org Rev. Timothy M. Nolan, Pst.; Dcn. Thomas G. Halko; Dcn. Patrick Johnston; Dcn. Christopher Moran; Dcn. P. Michael Olliver; CRP Stds.: 80

Our Lady of Fatima - 801 N. Dupont Blvd., New Castle, DE 19720 t) 302-328-3431 fatimachurch@aol.com www.olfnewcastle.com Rev. Msgr. George J. Brubaker, Pst.; Dcn. James I. Kledzik; Dcn. Eliezer Soto; Pattie Riccio, CRE;

St. Peter the Apostle - 521 Harmony St., New Castle, DE 19720 t) 302-328-2335 parish@stpeternewcastle.org www.stpeternc.org Rev. Timothy M. Nolan, Pst.; Dcn. Christopher Moran; Dcn. Thomas G. Halko; Dcn. Patrick Johnston; Dcn. P. Michael Olliver;

St. Peter the Apostle School - (Grades PreK-8) 515 Harmony St., New Castle, DE 19720 t) 302-328-1191 info@saintpeternewcastle.org Carlo Testa, Prin.; Stds.: 139; Lay Tchrs.: 19

NEWARK

Holy Family - 15 Gender Rd., Newark, DE 19713 t) 302-368-4665; 302-368-8976 (CRP) parish@holyfamilynewark.org www.holyfamilynewark.org Rev. Msgr. David F. Kelley, Pst.; Dcn. Darrell J. LaShomb; Dcn. Joseph P. Roach; Mare Draper, DRE; CRP Stds.: 78

St. John the Baptist-Holy Angels - 82 Possum Park Rd., Newark, DE 19711 t) 302-731-2200; 302-731-2209 (CRP) aahar@holyangels.net; hare@holyangels.net www.stjohn-holyangels.com Rev. Carlos Ochoa, Pst.; Rev. Christopher Hanley, Assoc. Pst.; Mary Alberici, DRE; CRP Stds.: 532

Holy Angels School - (Grades PreK-8) t) 302-731-2210 memuir@holyangelsschool.org www.holyangelsschool.org Dr. Mary Elizabeth Muir, Prin.; Stds.: 348; Lay Tchrs.: 28

St. Margaret of Scotland - 2431 Frazer Rd., Newark, DE 19702 t) 302-834-0225 parishoffice@margaretofscotland.org www.margaretofscotland.org Rev. Edward F. Ogden, O.S.F.S., Pst.; Dcn. Thomas E. Watts; Madeline Romano, Dir., Faith Formation; CRP Stds.: 193

St. Thomas More Oratory - 45 Lovett Ave., Newark, DE 19711 t) 302-368-4728 udcatholic@gmail.com www.udcatholic.org Rev. Timothy M. McIntire, O.S.F.S., Pst.; Dr. William Hamant, Dir., Campus Min. & Catechesis;

REHOBOTH BEACH

St. Edmond - 403 King Charles Ave., Rehoboth Beach, DE 19971; Mailing: P.O. Box 646, Rehoboth Beach, DE 19971 t) 302-227-4550 serbde@comcast.net www.stedmond.org Rev. William T. Cocco, Pst.; Rev. Mano Salla, Assoc. Pst.; Dcn. James J. Cadigan; Dcn. David S. McDowell; Dcn. Philip Ricker; Dcn. James M. Walls; Marie Kopf, DRE; CRP Stds.: 173

SEAFORD

Our Lady of Lourdes Church, Inc. - 528 E. Stein Hwy., Seaford, DE 19973-0719 t) 302-629-3591 parishoffice@ollseaford.org www.ollseaford.org Rev. Steven B. Giuliano, Pst.; Dcn. Nicholas Donofrio; Dcn. James M. Mueller; Debra Depta, DRE; CRP Stds.: 135

SMYRNA

St. Polycarp - 55 Ransom Ln., Smyrna, DE 19977 t) 302-653-8279 office@saintpolycarp.org www.saintpolycarp.org Rev. James D. Hreha, Pst.; Dcn. Francis Weber Jr.; Erica Taylor, DRE; CRP Stds.: 100

WILMINGTON

Cathedral of St. Peter - 500 N. West St., Wilmington, DE 19801; Mailing: c/o St. Patrick, 1414 King St., Wilmington, DE 19801 t) 302-654-5920 office@downtowncatholic.com www.downtowncatholic.com Very Rev. Joseph W. McQuaide IV, Rector; Rev. Christopher M. Markellos, O.Praem., Assoc. Pst.;

St. Peter's Cathedral School - (Grades PreK-8) 310 W. 6th St., Wilmington, DE 19801 t) 302-655-5234 principal@stpetercathedralschool.org www.stpetercathedralschool.org Jane Manley, Prin.; Stds.: 84; Sr. Tchrs.: 2; Lay Tchrs.: 10

St. Ann - 2013 Gilpin Ave., Wilmington, DE 19806 t) 302-654-5519 stannschurch@stannwilmington.com www.stannwilmington.com Rev. John J. Mink, Pst.; Rev. Richard Jasper, Assoc. Pst.; Dcn. Matthew F. Boyer; Patricia Walker, DRE; CRP Stds.: 47

St. Ann School - (Grades PreK-8) 2006 Shallcross Ave., Wilmington, DE 19806 t) 302-652-6567 rcasey@thesaintannschool.org www.thesaintannschool.org Rachel Casey, Prin.; Stds.: 230; Lay Tchrs.: 24

St. Anthony of Padua - 901 N. DuPont St., Wilmington, DE 19805 t) 302-421-3700 parish@stanthonynet.org www.sapde.org Rev. Mark J. Wrightson, O.S.F.S., Pst.; Rev. Sleeva R. Kala, O.S.F.S., Assoc. Pst.; Rev. Francis J. Rinaldi, O.S.F.S., In Res.; Patty Roach, CRE;

St. Anthony of Padua School - (Grades PreK-8) 1715 W. 9th St., Wilmington, DE 19805 t) 302-421-3743 office@stanthonynet.org www.sapgs.org Judith Jakotowicz White, Prin.; Stds.: 198; Lay Tchrs.: 31

Padua Academy - (Grades 9-12) 905 N. Broom St., Wilmington, DE 19806 t) 302-421-3739 info@paduaacademy.org www.paduaacademy.org Dr. Mary McClory, Prin.; Stds.: 440; Lay Tchrs.: 41

St. Anthony's Education Fund, Inc. - t) (302) 421-3700 x207 Ray Ianni, Dir.;

St. Catherine of Siena - 2503 Centerville Rd., Wilmington, DE 19808 t) 302-633-4900 stcathwilm@comcast.net www.scswilmde.org Rev. John M. Hynes, Pst.; Dcn. Gianni Chicco; Dcn. John J. Falkowski; Yolanda Torres-Ward, CRE; CRP Stds.: 180

Church of the Holy Child - 2500 Naamans Rd., Wilmington, DE 19810 t) 302-475-6486 mcarrier@chcparish.org www.chcparish.org Rev. Michael J. Carrier, K.H.S., Pst.; Dcn. William J. Johnston Jr.; Sr. Ann Hughes, S.S.J., Pst. Assoc.; Margie Fiorella, DRE; Kevin Mucchetti, Music Min.; CRP Stds.: 107

Corpus Christi - 905 New Rd., Elsmere, Wilmington, DE 19805; Mailing: c/o St. Matthew, 901 E. Newport Pike, Wilmington, DE 19804 t) 302-994-2922 secretary@corpuschristide.com www.ccparishwilmington.org Rev. Michael P. Darcy, K.H.S., Pst.; Dcn. David M. DeGhetto; Dcn. Sean Sudler; Debbie Ciafre, CRE; CRP Stds.: 15

Convent -

St. Elizabeth - 809 S. Broom St., Wilmington, DE 19805-4296 t) 302-652-3626 office@steparish.org www.steparish.org Very Rev. Roger F. DiBuo, Pst.; Dcn. Walter E. Ferris Jr.; Dcn. Kenneth Pulliam Sr.; CRP Stds.: 51

St. Elizabeth School - (Grades PreK-8) 1500 Cedar

St., Wilmington, DE 19805-4249 t) 302-656-3369 contact@steschools.org www.steschools.org Joseph Petruzzeli, Pres.; Dr. Tracey Rush, Prin.; Stds.: 270; Pr. Tchrs.: 1; Lay Tchrs.: 29

St. Elizabeth High School - (Grades 9-12) 1500 Cedar St., Wilmington, DE 19805 t) 302-656-3369 contact@steschools.org www.steschools.org Joseph Petruzzeli, Prin.; Stds.: 179; Lay Tchrs.: 31

St. Hedwig - 408 S. Harrison St., Wilmington, DE 19805 t) 302-594-1400 sthedwigchurch@comcast.net www.sthedwigde.org Rev. Andrew Molewski, Pst.; Rev. Julian Kaczowka, S.Chr., Assoc. Pst.; Dcn. Raymond R. Zolandz Jr.; Roweena Rego, DRE;

St. Helena - 602 Philadelphia Pike, Wilmington, DE 19809 t) 302-764-0325 x106 parishinfo@sainthelenas.org www.sainthelenas.org Rev. Msgr. Stanley J. Russell, Pst.; Rev. Edward J. Fahey, In Res.; Hummy Pennell, DRE; CRP Stds.: 67

Convent - 610 Philadelphia Pike, Wilmington, DE 19809 parishinfo@sthelenas.org www.sthelenas.org

Immaculate Heart of Mary - 4701 Weldin Rd., Liftwood, Wilmington, DE 19803 t) 302-764-0357 parishoffice@ihm.org www.ihm.org Rev. Robert A. Wozniak, Pst.; Rev. William D. Melnick, In Res.; Dcn. Frank C. Conway; Claire D. DaSalla, CRE; Rita McDowell, Pst. Assoc.; CRP Stds.: 146

Immaculate Heart of Mary School - (Grades PreK-8) 1000 Shipley Rd., Wilmington, DE 19803 t) 302-764-0977 office@ihm.org ihm.org/ihm_school Tina Morroni, Prin.; Kathy Ifkovits, Vice Prin.; Stds.: 460; Lay Tchrs.: 29

St. John the Beloved - 907 Milltown Rd., Sherwood Park, Wilmington, DE 19808 t) 302-999-0211 parish@sjbde.org www.sjbde.org Very Rev. Joseph J. Piekarski, Pst.; Rev. Michael A. Preston, Assoc. Pst.; Dcn. Thomas A. Bailey; Dcn. Mark A. Fontana; Dcn. Stephen W Oldiges; Susan Murray, DRE; CRP Stds.: 221

St. John the Beloved School - (Grades PreK-8) 905 Milltown Rd., Wilmington, DE 19808 t) 302-998-5525 sjtbschooloffice@sjbdel.org www.sjbdel.org Richard D. Hart, Prin.; Stds.: 528; Lay Tchrs.: 28

St. Joseph on the Brandywine - 10 Old Church Rd., Wilmington, DE 19807 t) 302-658-7017 fharkins@stjosephonthebrandywine.org www.stjosephonthebrandywine.org Rev. Msgr. John P. Hopkins, Pst.; Dcn. Austin A. Lobo; Dcn. Michael J. Stankewicz; Jessie Curtin, DRE; CRP Stds.: 90

St. Joseph's R.C. Church of Wilmington, Inc. - 1012 N. French St., Wilmington, DE 19801 t) 302-658-4535 parishsecretary@stjosephfrenchst.org www.stjosephfrenchst.org Very Rev. Glenn M. Evers, V.C., Pst.; Dcn. Robert J. Cousar Jr.;

St. Mary Magdalen - 7 Sharpley Rd., Wilmington, DE 19803 t) 302-652-6800 stephanie.casey@smmchurch.org smmchurch.org Very Rev. James T. Kirk Jr., Pst.; Dcn. Howard S. Eck Jr.; Dcn. Justin C. Pollio; Karin Yasik, DRE; CRP Stds.: 148

St. Mary Magdalen School - (Grades PreK-8) 9 Sharpley Rd., Wilmington, DE 19803 t) 302-656-2745 info@smmschoolde.com www.smmschoolde.com Patrick Tiernan, Prin.; Stds.: 541; Lay Tchrs.: 44

St. Mary of the Immaculate Conception - Sixth & Pine Sts., Wilmington, DE 19801; Mailing: 1414 King St., Wilmington, DE 19801 t) 302-652-0743 office@downtowncatholic.com www.downtowncatholic.com Very Rev. Joseph W. McQuaide IV, Pst.; Rev. Christopher M. Markellos, Assoc. Pst.; Dcn. Anthony J. Gallo;

St. Matthew - 901 E. Newport Pike, Wilmington, DE 19804; Mailing: 1013 E. Newport Pike, Wilmington, DE 19805 t) 302-633-5850 secretary@stmatthewsde.com www.stmatthewsde.com Rev. Michael P. Darcy, K.H.S., Pst.; Dcn. William A. Kaper; Dcn. Sean Sudler; Dcn. Michael T. Wilber;

Parish of the Resurrection - 3000 Videre Dr., Skyline Ridge, Wilmington, DE 19808 t) 302-368-0146 office@resurrectionde.org www.resurrectionde.org Rev. Msgr. David F. Kelley, Pst.; Anne D'Ascoli, CRE; CRP Stds.: 51

St. Patrick - 1414 King St., Wilmington, DE 19801 t) 302-652-0743 office@downtowncatholic.com www.downtowncatholic.com Very Rev. Joseph W. McQuaide IV, Pst.; Rev. Christopher M. Markellos, Assoc. Pst.; Dcn. Anthony J. Gallo; Maria Dempsey, Parish Office Admin.;

St. Paul's - 1010 W. 4th St., Wilmington, DE 19805 t) 302-655-6596 saintpaulrectory@gmail.com www.stpaulchurchde.org Rev. John E. Olson, Pst.; Rev. Anthony M. Pileggi, In Res.; Damaris Hernandez, CRE;

St. Thomas the Apostle - 301 N. Bancroft Pkwy., Wilmington, DE 19805 t) 302-658-5131 rectory@sainttom.org www.sainttom.org Rev. Msgr. Steven P. Hurley, Pst.; Dcn. Francis (Frank) A. Quinlan;

STATE OF MARYLAND

BERLIN

St. John Neumann Roman Catholic Church - 11211 Beauchamp Rd., Berlin, MD 21811 t) 410-208-2956 parishoffice@stjnrcc.com www.stjohnneumannrcc.com Rev. Joseph M.P.R. Cocucci, K.H.S., Pst.; Dcn. David Kolesky; Dcn. Charles A. Weschler; Jamey Sturgill, CRE; CRP Stds.: 51

CAMBRIDGE

St. Mary Refuge of Sinners - 1515 Glasgow St., Cambridge, MD 21613; Mailing: 2000 Hambrooks Blvd., Cambridge, MD 21613 t) 410-228-4770 stmarys@comcast.net www.stmaryscambridge.org Rev. Stephen C. Lonek, Pst.; Rosemary Robbins, DRE; CRP Stds.: 53

St. Mary, Star of the Sea - 917 Hoopers Island Rd., Church Creek, MD 21622 t) (410) 228-4770 www.stmarycambridge.org

CENTREVILLE

Our Mother of Sorrows - 303 Chesterfield Ave., Centreville, MD 21617; Mailing: 301 Homewood Ave., Centrevlle, MD 21617 t) 410-758-0143 mosparish@verizon.net www.sorrowsparish.org Rev. Clemens D. Manista Jr., Pst.; Dcn. Robert A. Wilson; Yvette Baggs, DRE; CRP Stds.: 79

St. Peter - 5319 Ocean Gateway, Queenstown, MD 21658 t) (410) 758-0143

CHESTER

St. Christopher - 1861 Harbor Dr., Chester, MD 21619 t) 410-643-6220 parishoffices@stchristopherski.org www.stchristopherski.org Very Rev. John B. Gabage, Pst.; Dcn. Francis X. Hesson; Katherine Sukley, DRE; CRP Stds.: 235

CHESTERTOWN

Sacred Heart - 508 High St., Chestertown, MD 21620 t) 410-778-3160 rdavis@sacredparish.org; religioused@sacredparish.org www.sacredparish.org Rev. Patrick D. Bergquist, O.Praem., Pst.; Dcn. John L. Davis; Cherylin Bennek, CRE; CRP Stds.: 23

St. John - 5521 Catholic Ave., Rock Hall, MD 21661; Mailing: 508 High St., c/o Sacred Heart, Chestertown, MD 21620 t) (410) 778-3160

EASTON

SS. Peter and Paul - 1210 S. Washington St., Easton, MD 21601; Mailing: 1214 S. Washington St., Easton, MD 21601 t) 410-822-2344; 410-822-2251 x108 (Finance Office) parishoffice@ssppeaston.org; lhaas@ssppeaston.org www.ssppeaston.org Rev. James Nash, Pst.; Rev. Michael A. Angeloni, Assoc. Pst.; Rev. Ofonmbuk (Oscar) Ekwere, Assoc. Pst.; Dcn. Stephen Gunther; Dcn. Bradley D. Taylor; Linda Steinmiller, DRE; CRP Stds.: 127

SS. Peter and Paul School - (Grades PreK-8) 900 High St., Easton, MD 21601 sconnolly@ssppeaston.org www.es.ssppeaston.org Sherrie Connolly, Prin.; Stds.: 407; Lay Tchrs.: 34

SS. Peter and Paul High School - (Grades 9-12) 1212 S. Washington St., Easton, MD 21601 t) 410-822-2275 dmorton@ssppeaston.org www.hs.ssppeaston.org James Nemeth, Prin.; Stds.: 187; Lay Tchrs.: 23

St. Joseph - 13209 Church Ln., Cordova, MD 21625 t) (410) 822-2344

St. Michael - 109 Lincoln Ave., St. Michaels, MD 21663 t) (410) 822-2344

ELKTON

Immaculate Conception - 455 Bow St., Elkton, MD 21921 t) 410-398-1100 iccoffice455@gmail.com www.iccparish.weconnect.com/ Rev. James R. Yeakel, O.S.F.S., Pst.; Rev. Gerald Dunne, O.S.F.S., Assoc. Pst.; Dcn. Benjamin G.M. Feril; Dcn. Roberto Ortiz; Dcn. Michael Truman; Vickie Eichler, CRE; CRP Stds.: 89

St. Jude - 928 Turkey Point Rd., North East, MD 21901

GALENA

St. Dennis - 153 N. Main St., Galena, MD 21635; Mailing: P.O. Box 249, Galena, MD 21635 t) 410-648-5145 stdennischurchoffice@gmail.com www.stdennischurch.org Rev. James D. Hreha, Pst.; Rev. Ofonmbuk (Oscar) Ekwere, Pastoral Min., Hispanic Min.; Jennifer Hinton, DRE; CRP Stds.: 40

MARYDEL

Immaculate Conception - 522 Main St., Marydel, MD 21649; Mailing: P.O. Box 399, Marydel, MD 21649 t) 410-482-7687; 410-482-8939 (CRP) dre@iccmarydel.org www.iccmarydel.org Very Rev. James S. Lentini, Pst.; Rev. Brennan H. Ferris, Assoc. Pst.; Dcn. Sherman Mitchell III; Alicia Poppiti, DRE; CRP Stds.: 93

OCEAN CITY

St. Luke-St. Andrew - 9903 Coastal Hwy., Ocean City, MD 21842; Mailing: 14401 Sinepuxent Ave., Ocean City, MD 21842 t) 410-250-0300 stluke@stlukeoc.com www.stlukeoc.com Rev. Paul F. Jennings Jr., Pst.; Rev. John A. Lunness, Assoc. Pst.; Rev. Lance S. Martin, Assoc. Pst.; Dcn. John (Jack) Ames; Dcn. Joseph Carraro; Dcn. Robert J. McNulty Jr.; Kim Zarif, CRE; CRP Stds.: 35

St. Andrew - 14401 Sinepuxent Ave., Ocean City, MD 21842 stlukeoc.com

St. Mary, Star of the Sea - 200 S. Baltimore Ave., Ocean City, MD 21842-4106; Mailing: St. Mary Star of the Sea Parish, 1705 Philadelphia Ave., Ocean City, MD 21842 t) 410-289-0652 office@stmaryholysavior.com www.stmaryholysaviorocmd.com Very Rev. John T. Solomon, Pst.; Rita Danhardt, DRE; CRP Stds.: 112

Holy Savior - 1705 Philadelphia Ave., Ocean City, MD 21842 t) (410) 289-0652 www.stmarystaroftheseaocmd.com

PERRYVILLE

Church of the Good Shepherd - 810 Aiken Ave., Perryville, MD 21903 t) 410-642-6534 x10 gsparish@goodshephrd.org www.goodshepherdcecilmd.org Rev. Jay R. McKee, Pst.; Dcn. Robinson A. Collado; Dcn. Matthew L. Raymond; Dcn. Luke E. Yackley; Jean Marie Sepka, DRE; CRP Stds.: 52

Good Shepherd Catholic School - (Grades PreK-8) 800 Aiken Ave., Perryville, MD 21903 t) 410-642-6265 info@goodshepherdschool.net www.goodshepherdschool.net Sinead Boyd, Prin.; Stds.: 86; Lay Tchrs.: 13

St. Teresa - 162 N. Main St., Port Deposit, MD 21904; Mailing: c/o Church of the Good Shepherd, 810 Aiken Ave., Perryville, MD 21903 goodshepherdcecilmd.org

St. Patrick - 287 Pleasant Grove Rd., Conowingo, MD 21918 (Inactive)

St. Agnes - 150 S. Queen St., Rising Sun, MD 21911

POCOMOKE CITY

Holy Name of Jesus - 1913 Old Virginia Rd., Pocomoke City, MD 21851; Mailing: PO Box 179, Pocomoke, MD 21851 t) 410-957-1215 hnj7@hotmail.com Rev. Daniel Staniskis, Pst.; Lynn Lang, DRE;

St. Elizabeth - 8734 Old Westover Rd., Westover, MD 21871 t) (410) 957-1215

RIDGELY

St. Benedict - 408 Central Ave., Ridgely, MD 21660;

Mailing: P.O. Box 459, Ridgely, MD 21660 t) 410-634-2253 parishoffice@beparish.com www.beparish.com Rev. Christopher R. Coffey, Pst.; Dcn. Harold D. Jopp Jr.; Dcn. William G. Nickum; Dcn. Adam M. Perza; Maureen Duggan-Cassidy, DRE; CRP Stds.: 82

St. Elizabeth of Hungary - 106 S. First St., Denton, MD 21629 t) (410) 634-2253

SALISBURY

St. Francis De Sales - 535 Riverside Dr., Salisbury, MD 21801; Mailing: 514 Camden Ave., Salisbury, MD 21801 t) 410-742-6443 parish@visitstfrancis.org www.visitstfrancis.org Rev. Christopher W. LaBarge, Pst.; Rev. Idongesit A. Etim, Assoc. Pst.; Rev. John A. Lunness, Assoc. Pst.; Rev. Edward M. Aigner Jr., In Res.; Rev. Raymond F. Weisman, In Res.; Dcn. Bruce Abresch; Dcn. Axel Blanco; Dcn. William M. Folger; Dcn. Don Q. Geaga; Janet Hastings, DRE; CRP Stds.: 125

St. Francis De Sales School - (Grades PreK-8) 500 Camden Ave., Salisbury, MD 21801 t) 410-749-9907 dtraum@sfdscs.org stfrancisdesales.net Debra Traum, Prin.; Stds.: 257; Lay Tchrs.: 14

Holy Redeemer - Bi-State Blvd. at Chestnut St., Delmar, MD 21875

SECRETARY

Our Lady of Good Counsel - 109 Willow St., Secretary, MD 21664; Mailing: P.O. Box 279, Secretary, MD 21664 t) 410-943-4300 c) 443-521-2981 olgc25@yahoo.com www.ourladyofgoodcounselchurch.com Rev. Stephen C. Lonek, Pst.; Denise Tomey, DRE; CRP Stds.: 30

SCHOOLS: PRESCHOOL THRU HIGH SCHOOL

SCHOOLS

STATE OF DELAWARE

BEAR

***Aquinas Academy** - (PRV) (Grades K-12) 2370 Red Lion Rd., Bear, DE 19701 t) 302-838-9601 jack.moore@aquinasacademy.net www.aquinasacademy.net John J. Moore, Prin.; Stds.: 85; Lay Tchrs.: 15

NEWARK

Christ the Teacher Catholic School - (DIO) (Grades PreK-8) 2451 Frazer Rd., Newark, DE 19702 t) 302-838-8850 klee@christtheteacher.org www.cttcs.org Kathy Lee, Prin.; Stds.: 602; Lay Tchrs.: 32

WILMINGTON

Saint Edmond's Academy - (PRV) (Grades PreK-8) 2120 Veale Rd., Wilmington, DE 19810 t) 302-475-5370 dmaiorano@stedmondsacademy.org; mreichert@stedmondsacademy.org stedmondsacademy.org Domenic J. Maiorano, Head of School; Dr. Michael C. Reichert, Prin.; Bridgid Rubio, Registrar; Karen Smith, Bus. Mgr.; Stds.: 154; Lay Tchrs.: 32

Saint Mark's High School - (DIO) (Grades 9-12) 2501 Pike Creek Rd., Wilmington, DE 19808 t) 302-738-3300 bmoore@stmarkshs.net www.stmarkshs.net Thomas Fertal, Pres.; Diane Casey, Prin.; Francis Corrigan, Vice Prin.; Maureen Roach, Vice Prin.; Stds.: 768; Lay Tchrs.: 44

Nativity Preparatory School - (PRV) (Grades 5-8) 1515 Linden St., Wilmington, DE 19805 t) 302-777-1015 info@nativitywilmington.org www.nativitywilmington.org Boys. Brian Ray, Pres.; Shaquona Meyers, Prin.; Stds.: 42; Lay Tchrs.: 12

Salesianum School - (PRV) (Grades 9-12) 1801 N. Broom St., Wilmington, DE 19802 t) 302-654-2495 principal@salesianum.org www.salesianum.org Rev. J. Christian Beretta, O.S.F.S., Prin.; Rev. Joseph G. Morrissey, O.S.F.S., School Admin.; Rev. Patrick Kifolo, O.S.F.S., Campus Min.; Rev. Brian D. Zumbrum, O.S.F.S., Chap.; Bro. Daniel P. Wisniewski, O.S.F.S., Supr.; Thomas Kardish, Pres.; Nicholas Grant, Campus Min.; Rev. Joseph Chorpenning, O.S.F.S., In Res.; Rev. Sean P. Connery, O.S.F.S., In Res.; Rev. Michael C. Connolly, O.S.F.S., In Res.; Rev. Richard DeLillio, O.S.F.S., In Res.; Rev. Edward Fitzpatrick, O.S.F.S., In Res.; Rev. William J. Keech, O.S.F.S., In Res.; Rev. Robert Mancini, O.S.F.S., In Res.; Rev. Thomas J. McGee, O.S.F.S., In Res.; Rev. Francis J. Pileggi, O.S.F.S., In Res.; Rev. Alexander T. Pocetto, O.S.F.S., In Res.; Jonathan Dick, O.S.F.S., In Res.; Stds.: 861; Pr. Tchrs.: 1; Lay Tchrs.: 81

Ursuline Academy of Wilmington, DE, Inc. - (PRV) (Grades PreSchool-12) 1106 Pennsylvania Ave., Wilmington, DE 19806 t) 302-658-7158 info@ursuline.org www.ursuline.org Trisha Medeiros, Pres.; Samantha Varano, Early Childhood & Lower School Prin.; Ann Phillips, Middle School Prin.; Jeffrey Danilak, Upper School Prin.; Stds.: 431; Lay Tchrs.: 34

STATE OF MARYLAND

BERLIN

Most Blessed Sacrament Catholic School - (DIO) (Grades PreK-8) 11242 Racetrack Rd., Berlin, MD 21811 t) 410-208-1600 mostblessedss@yahoo.com mostblessedsacramentschool.com Trinette Stilman, Prin.; Stds.: 254; Lay Tchrs.: 25

CHILDS

Mount Aviat Academy - (PRV) (Grades PreK-8) 399 Childs Rd., Childs, MD 21916 t) 410-398-2206 school@mountaviat.org; principal@mountaviat.org www.mountaviat.org Oblate Sisters of St. Francis de Sales. Sr. John Elizabeth Callaghan, O.S.F.S., Prin.; Sr. Anne Elizabeth Eder, O.S.F.S., Bus. Mgr.; Stds.: 233; Sr. Tchrs.: 4; Lay Tchrs.: 12

HIGH SCHOOLS

STATE OF DELAWARE

CLAYMONT

Archmere Academy - (PRV) (Grades 9-12) 3600 Philadelphia Pike, Claymont, DE 19703 t) 302-798-6632 generale-mailbox@archmereacademy.com www.archmereacademy.com Rev. Joseph P. McLaughlin, O.Praem., Chap.; Katie Eissler Thiel, Prin.; Michael Marinelli, Headmaster; Rosemary Conway-Bauer, Librn.; Stds.: 530; Lay Tchrs.: 91

INSTITUTIONS LOCATED IN DIOCESE

CAMPUS MINISTRY / NEWMAN CENTERS [CAM]

NEWARK

Catholic Campus Ministry, University of Delaware - St. Thomas More Oratory, 45 Lovett Ave., Newark, DE 19711 t) 302-368-4728 william@udcatholic.org www.udcatholic.org Rev. Timothy M. McIntire, O.S.F.S., Pst.; Dr. William Hamant, Dir. Campus Ministry and Catechesis;

SALISBURY

Salisbury University - 211 W. College Ave., Salisbury, MD 21801 t) (410) 572-4675 www.ccmsalisbury.org Liza Alvarado, Campus Min.;

University of Maryland Eastern Shore - 211 W. College Ave., Salisbury, MD 21801 t) (410) 572-4675 www.ccmsalisbury.org Liza Alvarado, Campus Min.;

WILMINGTON

Washington College - 1626 N. Union St., c/o Dan Pin, Catholic Diocese of Wilmington, Wilmington, DE 19806 t) (302) 658-3800 Daniel Pin, Dir., Office for Catholic Youth, Young Adult & Family Min.;

CATHOLIC CHARITIES [CCH]

WILMINGTON

Catholic Charities, Inc. - 2601 W. 4th St., Wilmington, DE 19805-0610 t) 302-655-9624 sstephenson@ccwilm.org www.ccwilm.org Fritz Jones, Exec. Dir., Catholic Charities; Asstd. Annu.: 15,000; Staff: 97

Casa San Francisco - 127 Broad St., Milton, DE 19968; Mailing: Catholic Charities, 2601 W. 4th St., Wilmington, DE 19805 t) 302-684-8694 casa@ccwilm.org

Seton Center - 30632 Hampden Ave., Princess Anne, MD 21853; Mailing: P.O. Box 401, Princess Anne, MD 21853 t) 410-651-9608 setoncenter@ccwilm.org

Addiction and Substance Abuse Counseling - 2601 W. 4th St., Wilmington, DE 19805-0610 t) 302-655-4624 sstephenson@cdow.org Addiction & substance abuse counseling. Fritz Jones, Exec. Dir.;

Kent County Office - 2099 S. DuPont Hwy., Dover, DE 19901; Mailing: Catholic Charities, 2601 W. 4th St., Wilmington, DE 19805 t) 302-674-1600 substanceabuse@ccwilm.org

New Castle County Office - 2601 W. 4th St., Wilmington, DE 19805-0610 t) 302-655-9624 substanceabuse@ccwilm.org

Sussex County Office - 406 S. Bedford St., Ste. 9, Georgetown, DE 19947; Mailing: Catholic Charities, 2601 W. 4th St., Wilmington, DE 19805 t) 302-856-9578 substanceabuse@ccwilm.org

Basic Needs Program - 2601 W. 4th St., Wilmington, DE 19805 t) 302-655-9624 sstephenson@ccwilm.org Basic needs program. Fritz Jones, Exec. Dir.;

Eastern Shore Office - 30632 Hampden Ave., Princess Anne, MD 21853; Mailing: Catholic Charities, 2601 W. 4th St., Wilmington, DE 19805 t) 410-651-9608 basicneeds@ccwilm.org

Kent County Office - 2099 S. DuPont Hwy., Dover, DE 19901; Mailing: Catholic Charities, 2601 W. 4th St., Wilmington, DE 19805 t) 302-674-4016 basicneeds@ccwilm.org

New Castle County Office - 2601 W. 4th St., Wilmington, DE 19805 basicneeds@ccwilm.org

Sussex County Office - 406 S. Bedford St., Ste. 9, Georgetown, DE 19947; Mailing: Catholic Charities, 2601 W. 4th St., Wilmington, DE 19805 t) 302-856-9578 basicneeds@ccwilm.org

Behavioral Health Services - 2601 W. 4th St., Wilmington, DE 19805 t) 302-655-9624 sstephenson@ccwilm.org Behavioral health services. Fritz Jones, Exec. Dir.;

Eastern Shore Office - 30632 Hampden Ave., Princess Anne, MD 21853; Mailing: Catholic Charities, 2601 W. 4th St., Wilmington, DE 19805 t) 410-651-9608 counseling@ccwilm.org

Kent County Office - 2099 S. DuPont Hwy., Dover, DE 19901; Mailing: Catholic Charities, 2601 W. 4th St., Wilmington, DE 19805 t) 302-674-1600 counseling@ccwilm.org

New Castle County Office - 2601 W. 4th St., Wilmington, DE 19805 counseling@ccwilm.org

Sussex County Office - 406 S. Bedford St., Ste. 9, Georgetown, DE 19947; Mailing: Catholic Charities, Inc., 2601 W. 4th St., Wilmington, DE 19805 t) 302-856-9578 counseling@ccwilm.org

CACFP (Child & Adult Care Food Program) - 2601 W. 4th St., Wilmington, DE 19805-0610 t) 302-655-9624 sstephenson@ccwilm.org Child & adult care food program. Fritz Jones, Exec. Dir.;

Kent County Office - 2099 S. DuPont Hwy., Dover, DE 19901; Mailing: Catholic Charities, 2601 W. 4th St., Wilmington, DE 19805 t) 302-674-1600 cacfp@ccwilm.org

New Castle County Office - 2601 W. 4th St., Wilmington, DE 19805 cacfp@ccwilm.org

Sussex County Office - 406 S. Bedford St., Ste. 9, Georgetown, DE 19947; Mailing: Catholic Charities,

Inc., 2601 W. 4th St., Wilmington, DE 19804 t) 302-856-9578 cacfp@ccwilm.org

Delaware Energy Assistance Program - 2601 W. 4th St., Wilmington, DE 19805-0610 t) 302-654-9295 energy@ccwilm.org Delaware energy assistance program. Fritz Jones, Exec. Dir.;

Kent County Office - 2099 S. DuPont Hwy., Dover, DE 19901; Mailing: Catholic Charities, 2601 W. 4th St., Wilmington, DE 19805 t) 302-674-1782 sstephenson@ccwilm.org

New Castle County Office - 2601 W. 4th St., Wilmington, DE 19805-0610 sstephenson@ccwilm.org

Sussex County Office - 406 S. Bedford St., Ste. 9, Georgetown, DE 19947; Mailing: Catholic Charities, 2601 W. 4th St., Wilmington, DE 19805 t) 302-856-6310 sstephenson@ccwilm.org

HIV Services - 2601 W. 4th St., Wilmington, DE 19805 t) 302-655-9624 sstephenson@ccwilm.org Fritz Jones, Exec. Dir.;

New Castle County Office - 2601 W. 4th St., Wilmington, DE 19805 hivservices@ccwilm.org Paula Savini, Contact;

Immigration & Refugee Services - 2601 W. 4th St., Wilmington, DE 19805 t) 302-655-9624 sstephenson@ccwilm.org Immigration & refugee services. Fritz Jones, Exec. Dir.;

Eastern Shore Office - 30632 Hampden Ave., Princess Anne, MD 21853; Mailing: Catholic Charities, 2601 W. 4th St., Wilmington, DE 19805 t) 410-651-9608 immigration@ccwilm.org

Kent County Office - 2099 S. DuPont Hwy., Dover, DE 19901; Mailing: Catholic Charities, 2601 W. 4th St., Wilmington, DE 19805 t) 302-674-1600 immigration@ccwilm.org

New Castle County Office - 2601 W. 4th St., Wilmington, DE 19805 immigration@ccwilm.org

Sussex County Office - 406 S. Bedford St., Ste. 9, Georgetown, DE 19947; Mailing: 2601 W. 4th St., Wilmington, DE 19805 t) 302-856-9578 immigration@ccwilm.org

Residential Services - 2601 W. 4th St., Wilmington, DE 19805 t) 302-655-9624 sstephenson@ccwilm.org Fritz Jones, Exec. Dir.;

Bayard House, Maternity Services, Pregnancy Counseling - 300 Bayard Ave., Wilmington, DE 19805; Mailing: Catholic Charities, 2601 W. 4th St., Wilmington, DE 19805 t) 302-654-1184 bayardhouse@ccwilm.org www.ccwilm.org/bayard-house/

Seton Villa, Inc. - 2601 W. 4th St., Wilmington, DE 19805 t) 302-655-9624 communityrelations@ccwilm.org www.cdow.org Fritz Jones, Exec. Dir.;

CEMETERIES [CEM]

DAGSBORO

Gate of Heaven Cemetery - 32112 Vines Creek Rd., Dagsboro, DE 19939 t) 302-732-3690 nhoopes@cathcemde.org www.cdow.org/cemeteries Nicholas Hoopes, Supt.; Scott Hudson, Exec. Dir.;

WILMINGTON

Catholic Cemeteries, Inc. - 2400 Lancaster Ave., Wilmington, DE 19805 t) (302) 656-3323 shudson@cathcemde.org; staylor@cathcemde.org Scott Hudson, Exec. Dir.; Steve Taylor, Finance Mgr.;

All Saints Cemetery - 6001 Kirkwood Hwy., Wilmington, DE 19808 t) 302-737-2524 shudson@cathcemde.com www.cathcemde.com/cemeteries Scott Hudson, Dir.;

Cathedral Cemetery - 2400 Lancaster Ave., Wilmington, DE 19805 t) 302-656-3323 shudson@cathcemde.org www.cathcemde.com/cemeteries Scott Hudson, Dir.;

CONVENTS, MONASTERIES, AND RESIDENCES FOR WOMEN [CON]

CHILDS

Oblate Sisters of St. Francis de Sales, Inc. - 399 Childs Rd., Childs, MD 21916 t) 410-398-3699 oblatesisters@mountaviat.org www.oblatesisters.org Sr. Anne Elizabeth Eder, O.S.F.S., Supr.; Srs.: 11

Aviat Foundation Endowment Trust - 399 Childs Rd., Childs, MD 21916 t) 410-398-2206 x211 principal@mountaviat.org

Villa Aviat, Inc. - 399 Childs Rd., Childs, MD 21916 t) (410) 398-8063

NEW CASTLE

Caterina Benincasa Dominican Monastery, Inc. - 6 Church Dr., New Castle, DE 19720 t) 302-654-1206 hscathchurch@aol.com Rev. Timothy M. Nolan;

NEWARK

St. Benedict - 25 Gender Rd., Newark, DE 19713 t) (410) 829-0754 bantry65@yahoo.com www.osbridgely.com/ Benedictine Sisters of Newark, DE. Sr. Catherine Godfrey, Prioress; Srs.: 12

St. Gertrude's Monastery, Motherhouse and Novitiate of the Sisters of St. Benedict - 25 Gender Rd., Newark, DE 19713 t) (410) 829-0754 bantry65@yahoo.com www.ridgelybenedictines.org Benedictine Sisters of Saint Gertrude. Sr. Catherine Godfrey, OSB, Prioress; Srs.: 12

PRINCESS ANNE

St. Joseph Novitiate - 10572 Anderson Rd., Princess Anne, MD 21853 c) (410) 430-6554 (Sr. Marilyn) lsjm@comcast.net thejosephhouse.org Sr. Marilyn Bouchard, L.S.J.M., Supr. Gen.; Srs.: 4

SALISBURY

Joseph House, Little Sisters of Jesus & Mary - 411 N. Poplar Hill Ave., Salisbury, MD 21801; Mailing: P.O. Box 1755, Salisbury, MD 21802 t) 410-543-1645 lsjm@comcast.net www.thejosephhouse.org Sr. Marilyn Bouchard, L.S.J.M., Supr. Gen.; Sr. Constance R. Ladd, L.S.J.M., Vicar; Srs.: 3

WILMINGTON

Monastery of St. Veronica Giuliani - 816 Jefferson St., Wilmington, DE 19801 t) 302-654-8727 capuchinpoorc@comcast.net capuchinpoorclaresdelaware.org Capuchin Poor Clare Nuns of Delaware. Rev. Francis Sariego, O.F.M.Cap., Chap.; Mother Maria de La Luz Solorio, O.S.C.Cap., Abbess; Srs.: 11

Ursuline Academy Inc., The - 1104 Pennsylvania Ave., Wilmington, DE 19806; Mailing: 1338 North Ave., New Rochelle, NY 10804 t) 914-712-0060 x130 maureen.welch@osueast.org osueast.otg Sr. Maureen Welch, Pres.;

ENDOWMENTS / FOUNDATIONS / TRUSTS [EFT]

CLAYMONT

The Archmere Fund - 3600 Philadelphia Pike, Claymont, DE 19703 t) 302-798-6632 x702 lcarney@archmereacademy.com John F. Cirillo III, Treas.;

TUCKAHOE

***Saint Pio Foundation, Inc.** - 24 Depot Sq., Tuckahoe, NY 10707 t) 203-416-1471 info@saintpiofoundation.org www.saintpiofoundation.org Luciano Lamonarca, Pres.;

WILMINGTON

Nativity Preparatory School of Wilmington Trust - 1515 Linden St., Wilmington, DE 19805 t) (302) 777-1015 bray@nativitywilmington.org www.nativitywilmington.org Rev. Joseph G. Morrissey, O.S.F.S., Treas.; Brian Ray, Pres.;

Salesianum School Endowment Trust I - 1801 N. Broom St., Wilmington, DE 19802 t) 302-654-2495 jmorrissey@salesianum.org Rev. Joseph G Morrissey, O.S.F.S., Treas.;

Salesianum School Endowment Trust II - 1801 N. Broom St., Wilmington, DE 19802 t) 302-654-2495 jmorrissey@salesianum.org Rev. Joseph G Morrissey, O.S.F.S., Treas.;

HOSPITALS / HEALTH SERVICES [HOS]

WILMINGTON

Saint Francis Hospital, Inc. - 701 N. Clayton St., Wilmington, DE 19805-0500 t) 302-421-4100 edward.lis@trinity-health.org www.stfrancishealthcare.org Part of Trinity Health System. James L. Woodward, Interim Pres.; Edward Lis, Mission Leader; Bed Capacity: 395; Asstd. Annu.: 139,113; Staff: 1,029

MISCELLANEOUS [MIS]

NEWARK

Our Lady of Grace Home, Inc. - 2300 Mary Angela Way, Newark, DE 19713-2682 t) (302) 643-3026 smaquinas@feliciansisters.org www.ourladyofgracevillage.org/ Affordable housing operating as Our Lady of Grace Village; managed by Felician Services. Sr. Aquinas Szott, Pres., Our Lady of Grace Village; Jean Jacobson, Sr. Min. Advisor, Our Lady of Grace Village;

Secular Order of Discalced Carmelites - 15 Gender Rd., c/o Holy Family Church, Newark, DE 19713 c) (302) 252-8784 blizzard.2000@yahoo.com www.ocdswashprov.org Dan Petillo, Formation Dir.; Bro. Bryan Paquette, O.C.D., Spiritual Dir.;

SEAFORD

Secular Order of Discalced Carmelites - c/o Our Lady of Lourdes, 528 E. Stein Hwy., Seaford, DE 19973 t) (301) 855-1190 thur21156@aol.com www.ocdswashprov.org (Community of Mary) Diane Mary Theresa Householder, Pres.; Bro. Bryan Paquette, O.C.D., Spiritual Dir.;

WILMINGTON

Brisson Fund - 2200 Kentmere Pkwy., Wilmington, DE 19806 t) 302-656-8529 ghoffman@oblates.org Rev. John Kolodziej, O.S.F.S., Pres.;

Catholic Diocese Foundation, Inc. - 1925 Delaware Ave., Wilmington, DE 19808; Mailing: P.O. Box 2030, Wilmington, DE 19899 t) (302) 573-3100 www.cdow.org Joseph P. Corsini, Exec. Dir.;

Catholic Diocese of Wilmington, Inc. - 1925 Delaware Ave., Wilmington, DE 19806; Mailing: P.O. Box 2030, Wilmington, DE 19899 t) (302) 573-3100 www.cdow.org Very Rev. Joseph W. McQuaide IV, Secy.;

Catholic Ministry to the Elderly, Inc. - 1925 Delaware Ave., Wilmington, DE 19806; Mailing: P.O. Box 2030, Wilmington, DE 19899 t) (302) 573-3100 www.cdow.org Rev. Msgr. Steven P. Hurley, Vice President;

Catholic Press of Wilmington, Inc. - 1925 Delaware Ave., Wilmington, DE 19806; Mailing: P.O. Box 2030, Wilmington, DE 19899 t) (302) 573-3100 www.cdow.org Most Rev. William E. Koenig, Pres.; Rev. Msgr. Steven P. Hurley, Vice. Pres.;

Catholic Youth Organization, Inc. - 1925 Delaware Ave., Wilmington, DE 19806; Mailing: P.O. Box 2030, Wilmington, DE 19899 t) (302) 658-3800 catholicyouth@cdow.org www.cdowcym.org Rev. Msgr. Steven P. Hurley, Vice. Pres.; Daniel Pin, Dir., Office for Catholic Youth, Young Adult & Family Min.;

Children's Home, Inc. - 1925 Delaware Ave., Wilmington, DE 19806; Mailing: P.O. Box 2030, Wilmington, DE 19899 t) (302) 655-9624 www.cdow.org Frederick "Fritz" Jones, Secy.;

Diocese of Wilmington Schools, Inc. - 1626 N. Union St., Wilmington, DE 19899; Mailing: P.O. Box 2030, Wilmington, DE 19899 t) (302) 573-3133 www.cdow.org Dr. Louis DeAngelo, Supt.; Rev. Msgr. Steven P. Hurley, Vice. Pres.;

Mid-Atlantic Catholic Schools Consortium - 1626 N. Union St., Wilmington, DE 19806 t) (302) 573-3133 Dr. Louis DeAngelo, Admin.;

Oblate Development Fund - 2200 Kentmere Pkwy., Wilmington, DE 19806 t) 302-656-8529 ghoffman@oblates.org Rev. John Kolodziej, O.S.F.S., Pres.;

OSFS Endowment Trust - 2200 Kentmere Pkwy., Wilmington, DE 19806 t) 302-656-8529 ghoffman@oblates.org Rev. Michael S. Murray, O.S.F.S., Trustee;

OSFS Real Estate Holding Corporation - 2200 Kentmere Pkwy., Wilmington, DE 19806 t) 302-656-8529 ghoffman@oblates.org Rev. John Kolodziej, O.S.F.S., Pres.;

OSFS Real Estate Trust - 2200 Kentmere Pkwy.,

Wilmington, DE 19806 t) 302-656-8529 ghoffman@oblates.org Rev. John Kolodziej, O.S.F.S., Trustee;
OSFS Service Corporation - 2200 Kentmere Pkwy., Wilmington, DE 19806 t) 302-656-8529 ghoffman@oblates.org Rev. John Kolodziej, O.S.F.S., Dir.;
Sacred Heart Oratory, Inc. - 917 N. Madison St., Wilmington, DE 19801 t) (302) 428-3658 srsarina@ministryofcaring.org www.sacredheartoratory.org A center for evangelization. Sacramental records 1874-1948 at Diocesan Archives. Rev. Ronald Giannone, O.F.M.Cap., Pst.; Sr. Sarina Gurram, CSA, Supr.;
Secular Franciscan Order - 2508 Oakfield Ln., Wilmington, DE 19810; Mailing: 2508 Oakfield Lane, Wilmington, DE 19810 t) 302-478-6593 carisio@yahoo.com San Damiano Fraternity Justin Carisio, Chap.;
Siena Hall, Inc. - 1925 Delaware Ave., Wilmington, DE 19806; Mailing: P.O. Box 2030, Wilmington, DE 19899 t) (302) 655-9624 www.cdow.org Frederick "Fritz" Jones, Secy.;

MONASTERIES AND RESIDENCES FOR PRIESTS AND BROTHERS [MON]

CHILDS
Oblates of St. Francis De Sales - 1120 Blue Ball Rd., Childs, MD 21916-0043; Mailing: PO Box 43, Childs, MD 21916 t) 410-398-3040 ghoffman@oblates.org www.oblates.org Rev. Paul Colloton, O.S.F.S., Supr.; Brs.: 4; Priests: 24
Retirement and Assisted Care Facility - 1120 Blue Ball Rd., Childs, MD 21916-0043; Mailing: P.O. Box 43, Childs, MD 21916 t) (410) 398-3040 Rev. Robert D. Ashenbrenner, O.S.F.S., In Res.; Rev. Francis J. Blood, O.S.F.S., In Res.; Rev. John W. Brennan, O.S.F.S., In Res.; Rev. Cornelius F. Kilty, O.S.F.S., In Res.; Rev. Mark S. Mealey, O.S.F.S., In Res.; Rev. John M. Mokluk, O.S.F.S., In Res.; Rev. William Nessel, O.S.F.S., In Res.; Rev. R. Douglas Smith, O.S.F.S., In Res.; Rev. John P. Spellman, O.S.F.S., In Res.; Rev. Thomas J. Tucker, O.S.F.S., In Res.; Rev. Joseph E. Tustin, O.S.F.S., In Res.; Rev. Joseph Zuschmidt, O.S.F.S., In Res.; Bro. Robert M. Carter, O.S.F.S., In Res.; Bro. Joseph H. Hayden, O.S.F.S., In Res.;
MIDDLETOWN
Immaculate Conception Priory of the Canons Regular of Premontre - 1269 Bayview Rd., Middletown, DE 19709 t) 302-449-1840 x31 info@icpbayview.org Norbertine Fathers of Delaware, Inc. Rt. Rev. James B. Herring, O.Praem., Prior; Friar William Trader, O.Praem., Subprior; Rev. Edward Smith, O.Praem., Treas.; Rev. James D. Bagnato, O.Praem.; Rev. Jeffrey T. Cesarone, O.Praem.; Rev. David Driesch, O.Praem.; Bro. Jhon Lemos, O.Praem.; Brs.: 1; Priests: 6
Norbertine Fathers of Delaware, Inc. - 1269 Bayview Rd., Middletown, DE 19709 t) 302-449-1840 info@icpbayview.org icpbayview.org Rt. Rev. James B. Herring, O.Praem., Prior; Friar William Trader, O.Praem., Subprior; Brs.: 1; Priests: 6
WILMINGTON
Capuchin Franciscan Friars, St. Francis of Assisi Friary - 1901 Prior Rd., Wilmington, DE 19809-1315 t) 302-798-1454 c) 302-893-7035 frafrancesco@msn.com Friar Francisco Arredondo, Vicar; Rev. Francis Sariego, O.F.M.Cap., Supr.; Rev. Cyprian Rosen, O.F.M.Cap., Friar; Priests: 3
De Sales Spirituality Services - 2200 Kentmere Pkwy., Wilmington, DE 19806 t) 302-383-3585 mmurray@oblates.org www.oblates.org/dss Rev. Michael S. Murray, O.S.F.S., Dir.; Priests: 1
St. Felix Friary - 119 N. Jackson St., Wilmington, DE 19805-3670 t) 302-652-5523 mail@ministryofcaring.org Rev. Ronald Giannone, O.F.M.Cap.; Rev. Udayameena V. Gude, O.F.M.Cap.; Priests: 2
OSFS Wilmington-Philadelphia Province, Inc. - 2200 Kentmere Pkwy., Wilmington, DE 19806 t) 302-656-8529 ghoffman@oblates.org Rev. John Kolodziej, O.S.F.S., Pres.;
Wilmington-Philadelphia Province of the Oblates of St. Francis de Sales - 2200 Kentmere Pkwy., Wilmington, DE 19806 t) 302-656-8529 ghoffman@oblates.org www.oblates.org Rev. Barry R. Strong, O.S.F.S., Supr.; Rev. John Kolodziej, O.S.F.S., Prov.; Rev. Francis W. Danella, O.S.F.S., Gen. Councilor; Rev. Michael C. Vannicola, O.S.F.S., Prov. Asst.; Rev. Robert L. Bazzoli, O.S.F.S., Treas.; Rev. Marc Gherardi, O.S.F.S.; Rev. William R. Gore, O.S.F.S.; Rev. John W. Lyle, O.S.F.S.; Bro. Harry Schneider, O.S.F.S.; Brs.: 1; Priests: 8

NURSING / REHABILITATION / CONVALESCENCE / ELDERLY CARE [NUR]

NEWARK
Jeanne Jugan Residence - 185 Salem Church Rd., Newark, DE 19713 t) 302-368-5886 msnewark@littlesistersofthepoor.org www.littlesistersofthepoordelaware.org Conducted by the Little Sisters of the Poor. Sr. Mary Michael Nickels, Mother Superior; Asstd. Annu.: 50; Staff: 112
Marydale Retirement Village - 135 Jeandell Dr., Newark, DE 19713 t) 302-368-2784 marydale@ccwilm.org www.ccwilm.org/marydale-retirement-village/ Apartments for elderly. Catherine P. Weaver, Admin.; Asstd. Annu.: 114; Staff: 5
WILMINGTON
The Antonian - 1701 W. 10th St., Wilmington, DE 19805 t) 302-421-3758 antonian@stanthonycenter.org; antonian1@comcast.net Congregate housing for the elderly. Debra Wirt, Dir.; Shaun Russell, Office Manager; Asstd. Annu.: 136; Staff: 6

RETREAT HOUSES / RENEWAL CENTERS [RTR]

GALENA
Oblate Sisters of St. Francis de Sales - 13828 Duck Hollow Rd., Galena, MD 21635; Mailing: 399 Childs Rd., Childs, MD 21916 t) 410-398-3699 oblatesisters@mountaviat.org www.oblatesisters.org Sr. Anne Elizabeth Eder, O.S.F.S., Supr.;
WILMINGTON
***Jesus House** - 2501 Milltown Rd., Wilmington, DE 19808 t) 302-995-6859 jesus.house.de@gmail.com www.jesushousecenter.org Angela Malmgren, Pres.;

SPECIAL CARE FACILITIES [SPF]

WILMINGTON
LIFE at St. Francis Healthcare, Inc. - 1072 Justison St., Wilmington, DE 19801 t) 302-660-3351 kirha.rodriguez@trinity-health.org www.trinityhealthpace.org This is a program for all-inclusive care including outpatient & home care visit care. Amy L. Milligan, Exec. Dir.; Asstd. Annu.: 282; Staff: 90
Ministry of Caring, Inc. - 115 E. 14th St, Wilmington, DE 19801-3209 t) 302-652-5523 mail@ministryofcaring.org www.ministryofcaring.org Annie Halverson, Dir.;
Andrisani Building - 1803 W. 6th St., Wilmington, DE 19805; Mailing: 115 E. 14th St., Wilmington, DE 19801-3209 t) 302-428-3702 jbates@ministryofcaring.org John Bates, Dir.;
Angela Merici House - 1105 W. 8th St., Wilmington, DE 19806-4605 t) 302-655-4817 ahalverson@ministryofcaring.org Residence for Sisters of St. Francis. Sr. Bernadette McGoldrick, O.S.F., Admin.;
Benedictine Park - 731 W. 9th St., Wilmington, DE 19801; Mailing: 115 E. 14th St., Wilmington, DE 19801-3209 t) (302) 652-5523 ahalverson@ministryofcaring.org Bro. Ronald Giannone, O.F.M.Cap., Dir.;
Bethany House - 601 N. Jackson St., Wilmington, DE 19805-3241 t) 302-656-8391 krobinson@ministryofcaring.org Permanent housing for women with special needs. Audrey Roberts, Res. Mgr.;
Bethany House II - 615 N. Jackson St., Wilmington, DE 19805 t) 302-652-1266 ahalverson@ministryofcaring.org Khadija Robinson, Dir.;
Child Care Center - 221 N. Jackson St., Wilmington, DE 19805-3649 t) 302-652-8992 pannane@ministryofcaring.org Child care for homeless children, from infancy to 4 years old. Paulette Annane, Dir.;
St. Clare Medical Outreach - 7th & Clayton Sts., Wilmington, DE 19805-3156 t) 302-575-8218 ebrown@che-east.org Mobile medical van which provides health services for the poor.
Emmanuel Dining Room, East - 226 N. Walnut St., Wilmington, DE 19801-3934 t) 302-652-2577 dsmith@ministryofcaring.org
Emmanuel Dining Room, South - 500 Rogers Rd., New Castle, DE 19720 t) 302-622-4555 srkodonnell@ministryofcaring.org
Emmanuel Dining Room, West - 121 N. Jackson St., Wilmington, DE 19805-3670 t) 302-652-3228 frmeena@ministryofcaring.org Rev. Udayameena V. Gude, O.F.M.Cap., Dir.;
St. Francis Transitional Residence - 103-107 N. Jackson St., Wilmington, DE 19805-3648 c) 302-747-0218 ahalverson@ministryofcaring.org Transitional living for women and children. Andrea Brooks, In Res. Mgr.;
Francis X. Norton Center - 917 N. Madison St., Wilmington, DE 19801 t) 302-594-9455 bbradley@ministryofcaring.org Multigenerational community center. William Bradley, Exec. Chef;
Guardian Angel Child Care - 1000 Wilson St., Wilmington, DE 19801-3432 t) 302-428-3620 srkathleen@ministryofcaring.org Sr. Pollard Kathleen, Site Mgr.;
House of Joseph I - 1328 W. 3rd St., Wilmington, DE 19805 t) 302-652-0904 dmurphy@ministryofcaring.org Shelter for homeless employable men who are seeking employment. Dion Murphy, Prog. Mgr.;
House of Joseph II - 9 W. 18th St., Wilmington, DE 19802-4833 t) 302-594-9473 aedwards@ministryofcaring.org Hospice for people with AIDS. Ashley Edwards, Prog. Dir.;
House of Joseph Transitional Residence - 704 West St., Wilmington, DE 19801-1523 t) 302-652-0904 Transitional residence for employable, formerly homeless persons. Dion Murphy, Dir.;
Il Bambino - 903 N. Madison St., Wilmington, DE 19801 t) 302-594-9449 pannane@ministryofcaring.org Infant day care program. Paulette Annane, Dir.;
Job Placement Center - 1100 Lancaster Ave., Wilmington, DE 19805-4009 t) 302-652-5522 msullivan@ministryofcaring.org Employment agency to assist the poor. Michael Sullivan, Dir.;
St. John Paul II Convent - 111 N. Jackson St., Wilmington, DE 19805 t) (302) 652-5523 Residence for Sisters of Christ the Light. John Bates, Dep. Dir. Prog. Svcs.;
Josephine Bakhita Convent - 401 Washington St., Wilmington, DE 19801 t) 302-691-3010 sragnes@ministryofcaring.org Residence for Sisters of the Order of St. Clare. Sr. Agnes Mathew Kanlyamkandathil, Supr.;
Margaret Nusbaum House - 207 S. Van Buren St., Wilmington, DE 19805 t) 302-652-8532 ahalverson@ministryofcaring.org Khadija Robinson, Dir.;
Maria Lorenza Longo House - 822 Jefferson St., Wilmington, DE 19801 t) 302-420-7781 ahalverson@ministryofcaring.org Transitional residence for families. Khadija Robinson, Dir.;
Mary Mother of Hope House I - 1103 W. 8th St., Wilmington, DE 19806 t) 302-652-8532 ahalverson@ministryofcaring.org Emergency shelter for homeless women. Khadija Robinson, Dir.;

Mary Mother of Hope House II - 121 N. Jackson St., Wilmington, DE 19805-3670 t) 302-652-1935 tmaldonado@ministryofcaring.org Emergency shelter for women with children. Trudy Maldonado, Program Manager;

Mary Mother of Hope House III - 515 N. Broom St., Wilmington, DE 19805-3114 t) 302-652-0970 jjohnson@ministryofcaring.org Emergency shelter for women with children. Jamie Johnson, Site Mgr.;

Mary Mother of Hope House Permanent Housing - 818-820 Jefferson St., Wilmington, DE 19801-1432; Mailing: Ministry of Caring, Inc., 115 E. 14th St., Wilmington, DE 19801 t) 302-594-9448 ahalverson@ministryofcaring.org Transitional residence for single women. Khadija Robinson, Dir.;

Ministry of Caring - 115 E. 14th St, Wilmington, DE 19801-3209 t) (302) 652-5523 ahalverson@ministryofcaring.org ministryofcaring.org Mayor James Baker, Pres.; Rev. Ronald Giannone, O.F.M.Cap., Exec.;

Ministry of Caring Distribution Center - 1410 N. Claymont St., Wilmington, DE 19802-5227; Mailing: Ministry of Caring, Inc., 115 E. 14th St., Wilmington, DE 19801 t) 302-652-0969 rradcliff@ministryofcaring.org Robert Radcliff, Dir.;

Ministry of Caring Guild - 506 N. Church St., Wilmington, DE 19801-4812; Mailing: Ministry of Caring, Inc., 115 E. 14th St., Wilmington, DE 19801 t) (302) 652-5523 Janet Killian, Pres.;

Nazareth House I - 106 N. Broom St., Wilmington, DE 19805-4241; Mailing: Ministry of Caring, 115 E. 14th St., Wilmington, DE 19801 c) 302-275-9379 tmaldonado@ministryofcaring.org Trudy Maldonado, Site Mgr.;

Nazareth House II - 898 Linden St., Wilmington, DE 19805-4423 c) (302) 652-5523 Transitional residence for families. Trudy Maldonado, Site Mgr.;

Nazareth Long Term Housing - 203 N. Jackson St., Wilmington, DE 19805-3649 t) (302) 652-5523 jbates@ministryofcaring.org Long term housing. John Bates, Dir.;

Nazareth Long Term Housing - 807 W. 6th St., Wilmington, DE 19805 t) (302) 652-5523 jbates@ministryofcaring.org John Bates, Dir.;

Nazareth Long Term Housing - 207 S. Van Buren St., Wilmington, DE 19805 t) (302) 652-5523 jbates@ministryofcaring.org Transitional residence for families. John Bates, Dir.;

Nazareth Long Term Housing - 109-1/2 & 111 N. Jackson St., Wilmington, DE 19805; Mailing: Ministry Caring Inc., 115 E. 14th St., Wilmington, DE 19801 t) (302) 652-5523 Transitional residence for families. John Bates, Dir.;

Padre Pio House - 213 N. Jackson St., Wilmington, DE 19805; Mailing: Ministry of Caring, Inc., 115 E. 14th St., Wilmington, DE 19801 t) 302-658-6123 Permanent housing for men with special needs. Dion Murphy, Prog. Dir.;

Pierre Toussaint Dental Office - 830 Spruce St., Wilmington, DE 19801-4205 t) 302-652-8947 mvu@ministryofcaring.org Dental office for the homeless. Myhanh Vu, Dir.;

Sacred Heart Convent - 700 W. 9th St., Wilmington, DE 19801 t) (302) 652-5523 srsarina@ministryofcaring.org Residence for the Sisters of the Sacred Heart of Jesus. Sr. Sarina Gurram, CSA, Supr.;

Sacred Heart Permanent Housing - 917 N. Madison St., Wilmington, DE 19801 t) 302-652-8532 ahalverson@ministryofcaring.org Dion Murphy, Dir.;

Samaritan Outreach - 1410 N. Claymont St., Wilmington, DE 19802-5227 t) 302-594-9476 jbates@ministryofcaring.org Social outreach for the homeless. John Bates, Dir.;

***Mother Teresa House, Inc.** - 829 N. Church St., Wilmington, DE 19801; Mailing: Ministry of Caring, Inc., 115 E. 14th St., Wilmington, DE 19801 t) 302-540-6544 rmosley@ministryofcaring.org Renee Mosley, Dir.; Bed Capacity: 6; Asstd. Annu.: 9; Staff: 1

***Sacred Heart Village II, Inc.** - 625 E. 10th St., Wilmington, DE 19801; Mailing: 115 E. 14th St., Wilmington, DE 19801 t) 302-300-3771 pkerezsi@sacredheartvillage2.org www.sacredheartvillage2.org/ Pat Kerezsi, Dir.; Bro. Ronald Giannone, O.F.M.Cap., Exec.; Asstd. Annu.: 27; Staff: 10

An asterisk (*) denotes an organization that has established tax-exempt status directly with the IRS and is not covered by the USCCB Group Ruling.

Diocese of Winona-Rochester

(Dioecesis Vinonaensis-Roffensis)

MOST REVEREND ROBERT E. BARRON, D.D., S.T.D.

Bishop of Winona-Rochester; ordained May 24, 1986; appointed Auxiliary Bishop of the Archdiocese of Los Angeles and Titular See of Macriana in Mauritania July 21, 2015; ordained September 8, 2015; appointed Bishop of Winona-Rochester June 2, 2022; installed July 29, 2022.

Pastoral Center: 55 W. Sanborn St., P.O. Box 588, Winona, MN 55987. T: 507-454-4643; F: 507-454-8106.
www.dowr.org
diocese@dowr.org

ESTABLISHED NOVEMBER 26, 1889. RENAMED DIOCESE OF WINONA-ROCHESTER JANUARY 23, 2018.

Square Miles 12,282.

Comprises the Counties of Winona, Wabasha, Olmsted, Dodge, Steele, Waseca, Blue Earth, Watonwan, Cottonwood, Murray, Pipestone, Rock, Nobles, Jackson, Faribault, Martin, Freeborn, Mower, Fillmore and Houston in the State of Minnesota.

For legal titles of parishes and diocesan institutions, consult the Pastoral Center.

STATISTICAL OVERVIEW

Personnel

Bishop	1
Retired Bishops	2
Priests: Diocesan Active in Diocese	44
Priests: Diocesan Active Outside Diocese	3
Priests: Retired, Sick or Absent	30
Number of Diocesan Priests	77
Religious Priests in Diocese	6
Total Priests in your Diocese	83
Extern Priests in Diocese	17
Ordinations:	
Diocesan Priests	1
Permanent Deacons in Diocese	37
Total Brothers	13
Total Sisters	175

Parishes

Parishes	98
With Resident Pastor:	
Resident Diocesan Priests	41
Resident Religious Priests	2
Without Resident Pastor:	
Administered by Priests	55
Closed Parishes	6
Professional Ministry Personnel:	
Sisters	4
Lay Ministers	40

Welfare

Homes for the Aged	4
Total Assisted	1,325
Day Care Centers	1
Total Assisted	60
Special Centers for Social Services	6
Total Assisted	3,626

Educational

Seminaries, Diocesan	1
Students from This Diocese	10
Students from Other Dioceses	48
Diocesan Students in Other Seminaries	10
Seminaries, Religious	1
Students, Religious	24
Total Seminarians	44
Colleges and Universities	1
Total Students	848
High Schools, Diocesan and Parish	4
Total Students	780
Elementary Schools, Diocesan and Parish	19
Total Students	3,852
Catechesis/Religious Education:	
High School Students	2,586
Elementary Students	4,200
Total Students under Catholic Instruction	12,310
Teachers in Diocese:	
Priests	3
Sisters	4
Lay Teachers	416

Vital Statistics

Receptions into the Church:	
Infant Baptism Totals	1,163
Minor Baptism Totals	47
Adult Baptism Totals	18
Received into Full Communion	87
First Communions	1,177
Confirmations	1,057
Marriages:	
Catholic	151
Interfaith	70
Total Marriages	221
Deaths	944
Total Catholic Population	114,255
Total Population	607,741

OFFICES AND DIRECTORS

Vicar General - t) 507-858-1267 vicargeneral@dowr.org Very Rev. William D. Thompson;

Chancellor - t) (507) 858-1260 jcooper@dowr.org Jenna Cooper;

Archives - t) 507-858-1267

Vicar for Clergy - t) 507-452-4770 mmcnea@dowr.org Very Rev. Mark C. McNea;

Assistant Vicar for Clergy - t) 507-288-5528 pschuster@dowr.org Rev. Peter L. Schuster;

Co-Vicars for Senior Priests - Very Rev. James D. Russell; Very Rev. Donald J. Schmitz;

Finance & Administration - t) 507-858-1241 finance@dowr.org; accounting@dowr.org Andrew D. Brannon, COO & CFO;

Diocesan Self-Insurance Plan - t) 507-454-6452 rchristianson@catholicmutual.org Ryan Christenson;

Moderator of the Curia - t) 507-858-1267 curiamoderator@dowr.org Very Rev. William D. Thompson;

Catholic Cemeteries - t) 507-858-1247 ldose@dowr.org Lawrence J. Dose, Dir.;

Catholic Schools - t) 507-858-1269 catholicschools@dowr.org Marsha Stenzel, Supt.;

Communications - t) 507-858-1273 communications@dowr.org Peter Martin, Dir.;

Divine Worship - t) 507-858-1254 parens@dowr.org Very Rev. Patrick O. Arens, Dir.;

Hispanic Ministry - t) 507-433-1888 rsilva@dowr.org Very Rev. Raul I. Silva, Vicar;

Human Resources - t) 507-858-1250 dfricke@dowr.org; benefits@dowr.org David Fricke, Dir.;

Lay Formation and RCIA - t) 507-858-1270 tgraff@dowr.org Todd Graff, Dir.;

Life, Marriage and Family - t) 507-858-1273 pmartin@dowr.org Peter Martin, Dir.;

Courage / EnCourage - Rev. Andrew P. Vogel, Chap.;

Missionary Discipleship - t) 507-858-1277 swindley@dowr.org Dr. Susan Windley-Daoust, Dir.;

Pastoral Planning - t) 507-858-1267 vicargeneral@dowr.org Very Rev. William D. Thompson, Dir.;

Permanent Diaconate - t) 507-858-1266 pdiaconate@dowr.org Dcn. John F. Hust, Dir.;

Propagation of the Faith - t) 507-858-1244 spof@dowr.org Rev. Timothy E. Biren, Dir.;

Safe Environment - t) 507-858-1244 safeenvironment@dowr.org Mary Hamann, Prog. Mgr.;

Victim Assistance - t) 507-454-2270 x255

Vocations - t) 507-858-1266 jkern@dowr.org Rev. Jason L. Kern, Dir.;

Young Adults - t) 507-858-1258 alofy@dowr.org Aaron Lofy, Dir.;

Youth Ministry and Faith Formation - t) 507-858-1272 dpetricka@dowr.org Dana Petricka, Dir.;

Pathways TEC (Together Encounter Christ) - tec@dowr.org Monica Anderson, Coord.;

Scouting - t) 507-234-6244 bmulligan@dowr.org Rev. Brian M. Mulligan, Chap.;

ADVISORY BOARDS, COMMISSIONS, COMMITTEES, AND COUNCILS

Civil Corporation Board - Very Rev. William D. Thompson, Vice. Pres.; Jenna Cooper, Secy.; Andrew D. Brannon, Treas.;

Clergy Personnel Committee -

Ex Officio - Very Rev. William D. Thompson; Very Rev. Mark C. McNea; Rev. Peter L. Schuster;

Deans - Very Rev. Gregory G. Havel; Rev. Msgr. Gerald C. Kosse; Very Rev. Thomas A. Loomis;

Other Members - Rev. Jason L. Kern; Rev. Martin T. Schaefer; Very Rev. Raul I. Silva;

College of Consultors - Rev. Glenn K. Frerichs; Very Rev. Mark C. McNea; Rev. James C. Berning;

Commission on Sacred Liturgy - Very Rev. Patrick O. Arens; Rev. Timothy J. Hall; Sebastian Modarelli;

Finance Council - James Anderson; Michael Brinkman; Bro. Louis De Thomasis, F.S.C.;

Incardination Board -

Ex Officio - Very Rev. William D. Thompson; Very Rev. Mark C. McNea; Rev. Peter L. Schuster;

Deacon - Dcn. John Kluczny;

Other Members - Very Rev. Michael J. Cronin; Very Rev. Patrick O. Arens; Rev. John M. Sauer;

Ministerial Standards Board -

Chair - Mitchell Moore;

Ex Officio - Mary Hamann;

Consultative Members - Thomas Braun; Very Rev. Michael J. Cronin;

Other Members - Nelle Moriarty; Kenneth Reed; Don Carlson;

Presbyteral Council -

Ex Officio - Very Rev. William D. Thompson; Very Rev. Mark C. McNea; Rev. Peter L. Schuster;

Appointed Members - Rev. Martin T. Schaefer; Very Rev. Raul I. Silva;

Elected At-Large Representatives - Rev. The Hoang; Rev. Swaminatha R. Pothireddy;

Elected Deanery Representatives -

Austin/Albert Lea Deanery - Rev. Kurt P. Farrell;

Mankato Deanery - Rev. Andrew J. Beerman;

Rochester Deanery - Rev. Timothy E. Biren;

Winona Deanery - Rev. John L. Evans II;

Worthington Deanery - Rev. Jonathan Joseph Fasnacht;

Elected Senior Representative - Rev. Joseph P. Pete;

Priests' Pension Board -

Ex Officio - Very Rev. William D. Thompson; Very Rev. Mark C. McNea; Andrew D. Brannon;

Elected Representatives - Rev. Gregory W. Parrott; Rev. Edward F. McGrath; Rev. Robert J. Schneider;

Appointed Members - Thomas Crowley; Daniel Kutzke; Tim Scanlon;

CATHOLIC CHARITIES

Catholic Charities - t) 507-454-2270 www.ccsomn.org Shanna Harris, Exec. Dir. (sharris@ccsomn.org);

Catholic Charities Board - Dean Beckman, Chair (dbeckman@smumn.edu);

Regional Offices -

Albert Lea - t) 507-377-3664

Austin - t) 507-433-9120

Mankato - t) 507-387-5586

Owatonna - t) 507-455-2008

Rochester - t) 507-287-2047

Winona - t) 507-454-2270

Active Aging Programs - t) 507-454-2270 Sue Degallier, Dir. (sdegallier@ccsomn.org);

Family and Individual Counseling - t) 507-387-5586 Kristine Madsen, Dir. (kmadsen@ccsomn.org);

Adult Advocacy Program - t) 507-454-2270 Michael Hanratty, Dir. (mhanratty@ccsomn.org);

Housing Programs - t) 507-454-2270 Audrey Rivenburg, Dir. (arivenburg@ccsomn.org);

Parish Social Ministry - t) 507-384-5770 Isaac Landsteiner, Dir. (ilandsteiner@ccsomn.org);

Pregnancy, Parenting & Adoption Program - t) 507-287-2047 Sarah Vetter, Dir. (svetter@ccsomn.org);

Refugee Resettlement - t) 507-287-2047 John Meyers, Dir. (jmeyers@ccsomn.org);

DEANERIES

Deans -

Austin/Albert Lea Deanery - Very Rev. Marreddy Pothireddy;

Mankato Deanery - Very Rev. Gregory G. Havel;

Rochester Deanery - Very Rev. Thomas A. Loomis;

Winona Deanery - Very Rev. Mark C. McNea;

Worthington Deanery - Rev. Msgr. Gerald C. Kosse;

ORGANIZATIONS

Council of Catholic Women - wdccw@dowr.org Eleanore Jones, Pres.; Rev. Msgr. Gerald C. Kosse, Spiritual Advisor;

TRIBUNAL

Tribunal - t) 507-454-4643 tribunal@dowr.org Jenna Cooper, Coord.;

Judicial Vicar - Very Rev. Michael J. Cronin;

Associate Judges - Rev. Glenn K. Frerichs; Rev. Msgr. R. Paul Heiting; Jenna Cooper;

Defenders of the Bond - Very Rev. Timothy Ferguson; Theresa Wyburn; Rev. John Griffiths;

Promoter of Justice - Very Rev. Timothy Ferguson; Sr. Victoria Vondenberger;

Ecclesiastical Notary - Julie Wright;

Experts - Dr. Annette Krutsch;

MISCELLANEOUS / OTHER OFFICES

Censor Librorum - Rev. Timothy J. Hall;

Ecumenism - t) 507-452-5656 frmike@stmaryswinona.org Very Rev. Michael J. Cronin, Ecumenical Officer;

Rural Life - t) 507-483-2317 richardmcolletti@gmail.com Rev. Msgr. Richard M. Colletti, Chap.;

PARISHES, MISSIONS, AND CLERGY

STATE OF MINNESOTA

ADAMS

St. John's - 10343 640th Ave., Adams, MN 55909; Mailing: 412 W. Main St., P.O. Box 352, Adams, MN 55909 t) 507-582-3321 office@sacredheartadams.org Rev. Antony Arokiyam, Pst.; CRP Stds.: 11

Sacred Heart - 412 W. Main St., Adams, MN 55909; Mailing: P.O. Box 352, Adams, MN 55909 t) 507-582-3321 Rev. Antony Arokiyam, Pst.; CRP Stds.: 32

Sacred Heart School - (Grades K-8) 11 5th St., S.W., Adams, MN 55909; Mailing: P.O. Box 249, Adams, MN 55909 t) 507-582-3120 www.sacredheartadams.org Darlene Boe, Prin.; Stds.: 103; Lay Tchrs.: 10

ADRIAN

St. Adrian - 512 Maine Ave., Adrian, MN 56110-0475; Mailing: P.O. Box 475, Adrian, MN 56110-0475 t) 507-483-2317 stadriancluster@hotmail.com Rev. Msgr. Richard M. Colletti, Pst.; CRP Stds.: 91

ALBERT LEA

St. James - 308 E. Fountain St., Albert Lea, MN 56007 t) 507-373-0603 office@sttheo.org Clustered with St. Theodore, Albert Lea. Rev. Kurt P. Farrell, Pst.;

St. Theodore - 315 E. Clark St., Albert Lea, MN 56007-2456; Mailing: 308 E. Fountain St., Albert Lea, MN 56007 t) 507-373-0603 office@sttheo.org www.sttheo.org Rev. Kurt P. Farrell, Pst.; CRP Stds.: 165

AUSTIN

St. Augustine's - 405 Fourth St. N.W., Austin, MN 55912-1599 t) 507-437-4537 fathersteffes.ae@gmail.com www.staugustinestedward.org Rev. James P. Steffes, Pst.; Dcn. Richard Aho; Dcn. John Kluczny; CRP Stds.: 85

St. Edward's - 2000 Oakland Ave. W., Austin, MN 55912-1599; Mailing: 405 N.W. Fourth St., Austin, MN 55912-3091 t) 507-437-4537 fathersteffes.ae@gmail.com www.staugustinestedward.org Rev. James P. Steffes, Pst.; Dcn. Richard Aho; Dcn. John Kluczny; CRP Stds.: 30

Queen of Angels - 1001 Oakland Ave. E., Austin, MN 55912-3896 t) 507-433-1888; 507-433-8474 (Spanish) fatherraul@queenofangels.church www.queenofangels.church Very Rev. Raul I. Silva, Pst.; Dcn. David Blake; CRP Stds.: 92

BLOOMING PRAIRIE

St. Columbanus - 114 E. Main St., Blooming Prairie, MN 55917-1427 t) 507-583-2784 columbanusbp@gmail.com www.stcolumbanuschurch.org/ Rev. William M. Becker, Pst.; CRP Stds.: 48

BLUE EARTH

SS. Peter and Paul's - 214 S. Holland, Blue Earth, MN 56013-1331 t) 507-526-5626 www.sspeterpaulmary.org Rev. Andrew J. Beerman, Pst.; Rev. Gregory W. Parrott, Par. Vicar; Dcn. Steven Landsteiner; CRP Stds.: 100

BREWSTER

Sacred Heart - 516 10th St., Brewster, MN 56119; Mailing: P.O. Box 187, Brewster, MN 56119 t) 507-842-5584 sacreds@centurytel.net Rev. Pratap Reddy Salibindla, O.F.M. (India), Pst.; CRP Stds.: 26

BROWNSVILLE

St. Patrick's - 302 N. 7th St., Brownsville, MN 55919; Mailing: P.O. Box 77, Brownsville, MN 55919 t) (507) 725-3804; (507) 482-6818 stpatricks@acegroup.cc www.stpatrickschurchbrownsvillemn.org Rev. Matthew R. Wagner, Pst.; Dcn. Robert Yerhot; CRP Stds.: 17

BYRON

Christ the King - 202 Fourth St., N.W., Byron, MN 55920-1000; Mailing: P.O. Box 1000, Byron, MN 55920 t) 507-775-6455 jenniferckhf@gmail.com www.christkingholyfamily.org Rev. John Lugala Lasuba, Pst.; CRP Stds.: 120

CALEDONIA

St. Mary - 453 S. Pine St., Caledonia, MN 55921-0406; Mailing: P.O. Box 406, Caledonia, MN 55921-0406 t) 507-725-3804 stmaryschurch@acegroup.cc www.churchofstmary.net Rev. Matthew Wagner, Pst.; Dcn. Robert Yerhot; CRP Stds.: 96

St. Mary School - (Grades PreK-8) 308 E. South St., Caledonia, MN 55921 t) 507-725-3355 stmarysschool@acegroup.cc Rebecca Stutzman, Prin.; Stds.: 140; Lay Tchrs.: 12

CANTON

Assumption - 207 N. May, Canton, MN 55939; Mailing: 405 Bench St., S.W., Chatfield, MN 55923 t) 507-886-2393; 508-867-3922 (Main Office) nativity@harmonytel.net; parishcenter.hfc@gmail.com www.holyfamilyclustermn.org Rev. Edward F. McGrath, Pst.; Dcn. Terrence Smith;

CHATFIELD

St. Mary - 323 Twiford St., S.W., Chatfield, MN 55923; Mailing: 405 Bench St., S.W., Chatfield, MN 55923 t) 507-867-3922 parishcenter.hfc@gmail.com www.holyfamilyclustermn.org Rev. Edward F. McGrath, Pst.; Rev. Glenn K. Frerichs, In Res.; Dcn. Terrence Smith; CRP Stds.: 50

CURRIE

Immaculate Heart of Mary - 501 Mill St., Currie, MN 56123; Mailing: 1374 225th Ave. Currie, M, Currie, MN 56123 t) 507-763-3545 radold1940@gmail.com Rev. Msgr. R. Paul Heiting, Pst.; CRP Stds.: 42

DAKOTA

Holy Cross - Merged Feb 2022 Merged with Crucifixion, La Crescent.

DODGE CENTER

St. John Baptist de La Salle - 20 Second St., N.E., Dodge Center, MN 55927-0310; Mailing: P.O. Box 310, Dodge Center, MN 55927 t) 507-374-6830 office@dodgecatholic.org Rev. John Lugala Lasuba, Pst.; CRP Stds.: 34

EASTON

Our Lady of Mount Carmel - 27 Main St., Easton, MN 56025; Mailing: P.O. Box 8, Easton, MN 56025 t) 507-787-2303 olmc@bevcomm.net www.olmcstcstjb.org Very Rev. Gregory G. Havel, Pst.; Dcn. Eugene Paul; CRP Stds.: 11

ELBA

St. Aloysius - Merged Feb 2022 Merged with St. Charles Borromeo, St. Charles.

EYOTA

Holy Redeemer - 22 E. 2nd St., Eyota, MN 55934; Mailing: 1900 E. 6th St., St. Charles, MN 55972-1426 t) 507-932-3294 administrator@redeemersaints.org www.redeemersaints.org Rev. Timothy E. Biren, Pst.; Dcn. John LaValla; CRP Stds.: 74

FAIRMONT

Holy Family - 2481 50th St., Fairmont, MN 56031; Mailing: 901 S. Prairie Ave., Fairmont, MN 56031 t) 507-235-5535 admin@fmcatholic.org www.sjvhf.org Rev. Andrew J. Beerman, Pst.; Rev. Gregory W. Parrott, Par. Vicar; Dcn. Steven Landsteiner; CRP Stds.: 14

St. John Vianney - 901 S. Prairie Ave., Fairmont, MN 56031-3023 t) 507-235-5535 admin@fmcatholic.org www.sjvhf.org Rev. Andrew J. Beerman, Pst.; Rev. Gregory W. Parrott, Par. Vicar; Dcn. Steven Landsteiner; CRP Stds.: 130

St. John Vianney School - (Grades PreK-6) 911 S. Prairie Ave., Fairmont, MN 56031 t) 507-235-5304 sstriemer@sjvschool.net www.sjvschool.net Sarah Striemer, Prin.; Stds.: 90; Lay Tchrs.: 8

FULDA

St. Gabriel's - 309 Lake Ave. W., Fulda, MN 56131-9402 t) 507-425-2369 stgab2369@gmail.com www.triparishcfw.org Rev. Msgr. R. Paul Heiting, Pst.; CRP Stds.: 73

GOOD THUNDER

St. Joseph - 130 N. Ewing St., Good Thunder, MN 56037; Mailing: P.O. Box 305, Mapleton, MN 56065 t) 507-524-3127 sjsmst@gmail.com www.sjsmst.org Rev. Andrew P. Vogel, Pst.; CRP Stds.: 32

GRAND MEADOW

St. Finbarr's - 504 1st St., S.W., Grand Meadow, MN 55936; Mailing: P.O. Box 374, Grand Meadow, MN 55936 t) 507-754-5190; 507-346-7565 triparishsecretary@gmail.com www.tri-parish.net Rev. Marreddy Pothireddy, Pst.; CRP Stds.: 55

HARMONY

Nativity of the Blessed Virgin Mary - 640 First Ave., S.W., Harmony, MN 55939-0596 t) 507-867-3922 nativity@harmonytel.net; parishcenter.hfc@gmail.com www.holyfamilyclustermn.org Rev. Edward F. McGrath, Pst.; Dcn. Terrence Smith;

HAYFIELD

Sacred Heart - 150 2nd St., N.E., Hayfield, MN 55940; Mailing: P.O. Box 27, Hayfield, MN 55940 t) 507-477-2256 sacredhearthayfield@gofast.am Rev. William M. Becker, Pst.; CRP Stds.: 27

HERON LAKE

Sacred Heart - 321 9th St., Heron Lake, MN 56137; Mailing: P.O. Box 377, Heron Lake, MN 56137-0377 t) 507-793-2357 hlsacredheart@gmail.com www.sacredheartheronlake.org Rev. Pratap Reddy Salibindla, O.F.M. (India), Pst.; CRP Stds.: 43

HOKAH

St. Peter's - 34 Main St., Hokah, MN 55941; Mailing: P.O. Box 357, 34 Main St., Hokah, MN 55941 t) (507) 894-4375 secretary@stpetershokah.org www.stpetershokah.org Rev. John L. Evans II, Pst.; CRP Stds.: 1

St. Peter's School - (Grades PreK-8) t) 507-894-4375 principal@stpetershokah.org www.stpetershokah.org/school Doug Harpenau, Prin.; Stds.: 50; Lay Tchrs.: 5

IONA

St. Columba's - 451 McDonnell Ave., Iona, MN 56141; Mailing: 2747 29th St., Slayton, MN 56172 t) 507-836-8030 office@acmcatholic.org www.acmcatholic.org Rev. Thien Van Nguyen, Pst.; CRP Stds.: 22

JACKSON

Good Shepherd - 311 N. Sverdrup Ave., Jackson, MN 56143-1329; Mailing: P.O. Box 65, Jackson, MN 56143-1329 t) 507-407-2944 goodshepherd@triparishcommunity.org Rev. Jonathan Joseph Fasnacht, Pst.; CRP Stds.: 51

JANESVILLE

St. Ann - 313 W. 2nd St., Janesville, MN 56048-0218; Mailing: P.O. Box 218, Janesville, MN 56048-0218 t) 507-234-6244 stann.triparish@gmail.com www.stannjan.com Rev. Brian Mulligan, Pst.; CRP Stds.: 98

KASSON

Holy Family - 1904 N. Mantorville Ave., Kasson, MN 55944; Mailing: P.O. Box 171, Kasson, MN 55944 t) 507-634-7520 jenniferckhf@gmail.com www.christkingholyfamily.org Rev. John Lugala Lasuba, Pst.; CRP Stds.: 113

KELLOGG

St. Agnes - 135 W. Glasgow Ave., Kellogg, MN 55945; Mailing: 117 3rd St. W., Wabasha, MN 55981-1201 t) 651-565-3931 office@felixagnes.org www.wabashakelloggparishes.org Rev. Prince Raja, Pst.; Dcn. John F. Hust; CRP Stds.: 4

Immaculate Conception - 22032 County Rd. 18, Kellogg, MN 55945; Mailing: c/o St. Joachim Church, 900 W. Broadway, Plainview, MN 55964 t) 507-534-3321 stjoachimchurch@hotmail.com; immaculateconception55945@gmail.com www.saintjoachimchurch.org Rev. Msgr. Thomas P. Melvin, Pst.; Dcn. John DeStazio; Dcn. Scott Schwalbe; CRP Stds.: 54

LA CRESCENT

The Church of the Crucifixion - 415 S. Second St., La Crescent, MN 55947-1326; Mailing: 423 S. Second St., La Crescent, MN 55947 t) 507-895-4720 cruxch@acegroup.cc www.cruxcifixionschool.org Rev. John L. Evans II, Pst.; Dcn. Gerald Trocinski; CRP Stds.: 128

Crucifixion Catholic School - (Grades PreK-6) 420 S. 2nd St., La Crescent, MN 55947 t) 507-895-4402 www.crucifixionschool.org Doug Harpenau, Prin.; Stds.: 134; Lay Tchrs.: 8

LAKE CITY

St. Mary's of the Lake - 419 W. Lyon Ave., Lake City, MN 55041-1649 t) 651-345-4134 stmaryslakecity@gmail.com www.stmarysandstpatricksmn.org Rev. Matthew J. Fasnacht, Pst.; Dcn. David Dose; CRP Stds.: 109

LAKE CRYSTAL

Holy Family - 211 N. Hunt St., Lake Crystal, MN 56055; Mailing: 423 W. 7th St., Mankato, MN 56001 t) 507-388-3766 office@sjwhf.org www.sjwhf.org Rev. Timothy T. Reker, Pst.; CRP Stds.: 49

LAKE WILSON

St. Mary - 320 Paul Ave., Lake Wilson, MN 56151; Mailing: 2747 29th St., Slayton, MN 56172 t) 507-836-8030 office@acmcatholic.org www.acmcatholic.org Rev. Thien Van Nguyen, Pst.; CRP Stds.: 21

LAKEFIELD

St. Joseph - 410 Broadway Ave., Lakefield, MN 56150; Mailing: P.O. Box 517, Lakefield, MN 56150 t) 507-847-2504; 507-407-2944 sjcc@triparishcommunity.org; goodshepherd@triparishcommunity.org Rev. Jonathan Joseph Fasnacht, Pst.; CRP Stds.: 61

LANESBORO

St. Patrick - 200 Ridgeview Ln., Lanesboro, MN 55949; Mailing: 405 Bench St. SW, Chatfield, MN 55923 t) 507-867-3922 parishcenter.hfc@gmail.com www.holyfamilyclustermn.org Clustered with St. Mary, Chatfield. Rev. Edward F. McGrath, Pst.; Dcn. Terrence Smith;

LEROY

St. Patrick's - 436 W. Main St., LeRoy, MN 55951-0310 t) 507-346-7565 triparishsecretary@gmail.com www.tri-parish.net Rev. Marreddy Pothireddy, Pst.; CRP Stds.: 18

LEWISTON

St. Rose of Lima - 180 S. Fremont St., Lewiston, MN 55952; Mailing: P.O. Box 402, Lewiston, MN 55952 t) 507-523-2428 strose@hbci.com www.st-rose.org Rev. Chinnappa Pothireddy, Pst.; CRP Stds.: 105

LISMORE

St. Anthony's - 310 3rd Ave., Lismore, MN 56155; Mailing: P.O. Box 475, Adrian, MN 56110 t) 507-483-2317 stadriancluster@hotmail.com www.stadriancluster.org Rev. Msgr. Richard M. Colletti, Pst.; CRP Stds.: 21

LUVERNE

St. Catherine's - 203 E. Brown St, Luverne, MN 56156-1599 t) 507-283-8502; (507) 283-8071 (Faith

Formation) www.stscl.org Rev. Msgr. Gerald C. Kosse, Pst.; Dcn. Kevin Paul Aaker; CRP Stds.: 174

LYLE

Queen of Peace - 301-399 3rd St., Lyle, MN 55953; Mailing: 412 W. Main St., P.O. Box 352, Adams, MN 55909 t) 507-582-3321 office@sacredheartadams.org Rev. Antony Arokiyam, Pst.; CRP Stds.: 15

MABEL

St. Olaf - 114 N. Locust St., Mabel, MN 55954; Mailing: P.O. Box 8, Mabel, MN 55954 t) 507-493-5268 stolafcatholic@gmail.com Rev. Edward F. McGrath, Pst.; Dcn. Terrence Smith; CRP Stds.: 24

MADELIA

St. Mary - 212 First St., N.E., Madelia, MN 56062-1702 t) 507-642-8305 www.maryjamesschool.org Rev. Timothy J. Hall, Pst.; CRP Stds.: 38

St. Mary School - (Grades PreK-6) 223 First St., N.E., Madelia, MN 56062 t) 507-642-3324 madeliacatholicschool@gmail.com Jennifer Slater, Prin.; Stds.: 69; Lay Tchrs.: 6

Noah's Ark Child Care Center - 223 N.E. First St., Madelia, MN 56062 t) 507-642-3626 noahsarkmadelia@gmail.com Sarah Pfeffer, Dir.;

MADISON LAKE

All Saints - 601 4th St., Madison Lake, MN 56063; Mailing: P.O. Box 217, Madison Lake, MN 56063-0217 t) 507-243-3319 asoffice@hickorytech.net www.as-ic.org Rev. Robert J. Schneider, Pst.; CRP Stds.: 117

MANKATO

St. John the Baptist - 632 S. Broad St., Mankato, MN 56001-3890 t) 507-625-3131 stjohnch@stjohnsmankato.net www.stjohnscatholicchurch.com Rev. John M. Kunz, Pst.; Dcn. Christopher Walchuk; CRP Stds.: 160

St. Joseph the Worker - 423 W. 7th St., Mankato, MN 56001-2131 t) 507-388-3766 office@sjwhf.org www.sjwhf.org Rev. Timothy T. Reker, Pst.; CRP Stds.: 106

SS. Peter and Paul Catholic Church - 105 N. Fifth St., Mankato, MN 56001-5371 t) 507-388-2995 office@sspeterandpaul.com www.sspeterandpaul.com Rev. Andrew Whiting, IVE, Pst.; Rev. Javier Ibarra, I.V.E., Par. Vicar; Rev. Kevin Stolt, Par. Vicar; Dcn. Frank Cesario; Dcn. Preston Doyle; CRP Stds.: 171

Mother Theodor Convent - 104 N. 5th St., Mankato, MN 56001 t) 507-388-8088 Servants of the Lord and the Virgin of Matara. Mother Faith O'Connor, Local Supr.;

St. Thomas More Catholic Newman Center Parish of Mankato, Minnesota - Minnesota State Univ., 1502 Warren St., Mankato, MN 56001; Mailing: P.O. Box 4222, Mankato, MN 56003 t) 507-387-4154 frapvogel@gmail.com; betsy.landsteiner@mnsu.edu www.catholicmavs.org Rev. Andrew P. Vogel, Pst.;

MAPLETON

St. Teresa Church - 102 Central Ave. N., Mapleton, MN 56065; Mailing: P.O. Box 305, Mapleton, MN 56065 t) 507-524-3127 sjsmst@gmail.com www.sjsmst.org Rev. Andrew P. Vogel, Pst.; CRP Stds.: 63

MAZEPPA

SS. Peter and Paul - 222 First Ave. S., Mazeppa, MN 55956; Mailing: P.O. Box 224, Mazeppa, MN 55956 t) 507-843-3885 bookkeeper@sspnp.com; parishadmin@sspnp.com www.sspeterandpaulmazeppa.org Rev. John M. Sauer, Pst.; Dcn. Paul Tschann; Dcn. Michael Zaccariello; Rev. Shawn J. Haremza, Sacr. Min.; CRP Stds.: 110

MEDFORD

Christ the King - 205 N.W. Second Ave., Medford, MN 55049; Mailing: P.O. Box 120, Medford, MN 55049-0120 t) 507-451-4845 parishoffice@stjosephowatonna.org Rev. James Starasinich, Pst.; Rev. Dharmendra Pasala (India), Par. Vicar; CRP Stds.: 61

MILLVILLE

St. Patrick of West Albany - 30932 Hwy. 60, Millville, MN 55957; Mailing: 419 W. Lyon Ave., Lake City, MN 55041 t) 651-345-4134; 651-345-2439 c) (507) 273-1983 dddose49@gmail.com www.stpatrickswestalbany.org Rev. Matthew J. Fasnacht, Pst.; Dcn. David Dose; CRP Stds.: 46

MINNEISKA

St. Mary's - Merged Dec 2022 Merged with St. Agnes, Kellogg.

MINNESOTA CITY

St. Paul's - 132 Anderson St., Minnesota City, MN 55959; Mailing: 1303 W Broadway, Winona, MN 55987 t) (507) 452-5656 stmarys@stmaryswinona.org Very Rev. Michael J. Cronin, Pst.; Dcn. William Keiper;

MINNESOTA LAKE

St. John the Baptist - 100 Park St. N., Minnesota Lake, MN 56068; Mailing: P.O. Box 158, Minnesota Lake, MN 56068 t) 507-462-3636 stjb@bevcomm.net www.olmcstcstjb.org Very Rev. Gregory G. Havel, Pst.; Dcn. Eugene Paul; CRP Stds.: 9

NEW RICHLAND

All Saints - 307 1st St., S.W., New Richland, MN 56072; Mailing: 313 W. 2nd St., P.O. Box 218, Janesville, MN 56048 t) 507-234-6244 stann.triparish@gmail.com www.stannjan.com Rev. Brian Mulligan, Pst.; CRP Stds.: 20

OWATONNA

Holy Trinity - 9946 S.E. 24th Ave., Owatonna, MN 55060 t) 507-583-2784 monij_13@hotmail.com www.litomysl.webs.com/ Rev. William M. Becker, Pst.; CRP Stds.: 114

St. Joseph - 512 S. Elm Ave., Owatonna, MN 55060-3399 t) 507-451-4845 parishoffice@stjosephowatonna.org Rev. James Starasinich, Pst.; Rev. Dharmendra Pasala (India), Par. Vicar; CRP Stds.: 158

Church of the Sacred Heart - 810 S. Cedar Ave., Owatonna, MN 55060-3297 t) 507-451-1588 office@sacredheartowatonna.org www.sacredheartowatonna.org Rev. Swaminatha R. Pothireddy, Pst.; Rev. Dharmendra Pasala (India), Par. Vicar; Dcn. Scot Berkley; Dcn. Placido Zavala; CRP Stds.: 158

PIPESTONE

St. Leo - 415 S. Hiawatha Ave., Pipestone, MN 56164-1557; Mailing: P.O. Box 36, Pipestone, MN 56164-0036 t) 507-825-3152 www.stscl.org Rev. Msgr. Gerald C. Kosse, Pst.; Dcn. Kevin Paul Aaker; CRP Stds.: 133

Noah's Ark Preschool - t) (507) 825-3152 Amy VandenBosch, Dir.;

St. Joseph - Merged Feb 2022 Merged with St. Leo, Pipestone.

St. Martin - Merged Feb 2022 Merged with St. Leo, Pipestone.

PLAINVIEW

St. Joachim's - 900 W. Broadway, Plainview, MN 55964 t) 507-534-3321 jspeedling@saintjoachimchurch.org www.saintjoachimchurch.org Rev. Msgr. Thomas P. Melvin, Pst.; Dcn. John DeStazio; Dcn. Scott Schwalbe; CRP Stds.: 248

PRESTON

St. Columban - 408 Preston St., N.W., Preston, MN 55965; Mailing: 405 Bench St., S.W., Chatfield, MN 55923 t) 507-867-3922 parishcenter.hfc@gmail.com www.holyfamilyclustermn.org Rev. Edward F. McGrath, Pst.; Dcn. Terrence Smith; CRP Stds.: 35

ROCHESTER

St. Bridget's - 2123 County Rd. 16, S.E., Rochester, MN 55904; Mailing: 116 4th Ave., S.E., Stewartville, MN 55976 t) 507-533-8257 office@sbsbparishes.org www.sbsbparishes.org Very Rev. Thomas A. Loomis, Par. Admin.; Rev. Kevin Connolly, Sacr. Min.;

Co-Cathedral of St. John the Evangelist - 11 4th Ave., S.W., Rochester, MN 55902-3098 t) 507-288-7372 stjohn@sj.org www.sj.org Rev. Msgr. Gerald A. Mahon, Rector; Dcn. Randy Horlocker; Dcn. Gerald Freetly; CRP Stds.: 164

St. Francis of Assisi - 1114 3rd St., S.E., Rochester, MN 55904-7293 t) 507-288-7313 parishadmin@stfrancis-church.org www.stfrancis-church.org Rev. James C. Berning, Pst.; Rev. Luis Vargas, Par. Vicar; CRP Stds.: 172

Holy Spirit - 5455 50th Ave., N.W., Rochester, MN 55901 t) 507-280-0638 hspirit@holyspiritrochester.org www.holyspiritrochester.org Very Rev. Thomas A. Loomis, Pst.; Dcn. Joseph Weigel; Dcn. Christopher Orlowski; CRP Stds.: 154

Pax Christi - 4135 18th Ave., N.W., Rochester, MN 55901-0460 t) 507-282-8542 bvelez@paxchristichurch.org www.paxchristichurch.org Rev. John M. Sauer, Pst.; Rev. Michael Churchill, Par. Vicar; Dcn. Michael Zaccariello; CRP Stds.: 250

St. Pius X - 1315 12th Ave., N.W., Rochester, MN 55901-1744 t) 507-288-8238 church@piusx.org www.piusx.org Rev. Russell G. Scepaniak, Pst.; Dcn. Patrick Fagan; CRP Stds.: 50

Resurrection - 1600 11th Ave., S.E., Rochester, MN 55904-5499 t) 507-288-5528 pastor@rescathroch.org; officemgr@rescathroch.org www.rescathroch.org Rev. Peter L. Schuster, Pst.; Rev. Shawn J. Haremza, Par. Vicar; Dcn. Robert Miller; CRP Stds.: 141

ROLLINGSTONE

Holy Trinity - 83 Main St., Rollingstone, MN 55969-9759; Mailing: P.O. Box 402, Lewiston, MN 55952 t) (507) 523-2428 www.htpm.us Rev. Chinnappa Pothireddy, Pst.; CRP Stds.: 16

ROSE CREEK

St. Peter's - 300 Maple St., S.W., Rose Creek, MN 55970; Mailing: 412 W. Main St., P.O. Box 352, Adams, MN 55909 t) 507-582-3321 'office@sacredheartadams.org Rev. Antony Arokiyam, Pst.; CRP Stds.: 23

RUSHFORD

St. Joseph - 103 N. Mill St., Rushford, MN 55971; Mailing: P.O. Box 577, Rushford, MN 55971 t) (507) 523-2428 stjosephr@hbci.com Rev. Chinnappa Pothireddy, Pst.; CRP Stds.: 30

SHERBURN

St. Luke's - 303 S. Lake St., Sherburn, MN 56171; Mailing: P.O. Box 669, Sherburn, MN 56171 t) 507-407-2944 goodshepherd@triparishcommunity.org Rev. Jonathan Joseph Fasnacht, Pst.; CRP Stds.: 12

SLAYTON

St. Ann's - 2747 29th St., Slayton, MN 56172-1485 t) 507-836-8030 office@acmcatholic.org www.acmcatholic.org Rev. Thien Van Nguyen, Pst.; CRP Stds.: 77

SPRING VALLEY

St. Ignatius - 213 W. Franklin St., Spring Valley, MN 55975-1312 t) 507-346-7565 triparishsecretary@gmail.com www.tri-parish.net Rev. Marreddy Pothireddy, Pst.; CRP Stds.: 25

ST. CHARLES

St. Charles Borromeo - 1900 E. 6th St., St. Charles, MN 55972-1426 t) 507-932-3294 administrator@redeemersaints.org www.redeemersaints.org Rev. Timothy E. Biren, Pst.; Dcn. John LaValla; CRP Stds.: 214

ST. CLAIR

Immaculate Conception - 101 Church St., St. Clair, MN 56080; Mailing: P.O. Box 217, Madison Lake, MN 56063 t) (507) 243-3319 icoffice@hickorytech.net www.as-ic.org Rev. Robert J. Schneider, Pst.; CRP Stds.: 97

ST. JAMES

St. James - 707 4th St. S., St. James, MN 56081-1808 t) 507-375-3542 www.maryjamesschool.org Rev. Timothy J. Hall, Pst.; CRP Stds.: 151

STEWARTVILLE

St. Bernard's - 116 Fourth Ave., S.E., Stewartville, MN 55976 t) 507-533-8257 office@sbsbparishes.org www.sbsbparishes.org Very Rev. Thomas A. Loomis, Par. Admin.; Rev. Kevin Connolly, Sacr. Min.; CRP Stds.: 188

VERNON CENTER

St. Matthew - 200 Kendall St., Vernon Center, MN 56090; Mailing: P.O. Box 305, Mapleton, MN 56065-0305 t) 507-524-3127 sjsmst@gmail.com www.sjsmst.org Rev. Andrew P. Vogel, Pst.; CRP Stds.: 16

WABASHA
St. Felix - 117 W. Third St., Wabasha, MN 55981-1201 t) 651-565-3931 office@felixagnes.org www.wabashakelloggparishes.org Rev. Prince Raja, Pst.; Dcn. John F. Hust; CRP Stds.: 38

St. Felix School - (Grades PreK-6) 130 E. 3rd St., Wabasha, MN 55981 t) 651-565-4446 esonnek@stfelixschool.org www.stfelixschool.org Eric Sonnek, Prin.; Stds.: 99; Lay Tchrs.: 9

WALDORF
St. Joseph - 225 3rd Ave. N., Waldorf, MN 56091; Mailing: P.O. Box 218, Janesville, MN 56048-0218 t) 507-234-6244 stann.triparish@gmail.com www.stannjan.com Rev. Brian Mulligan, Pst.;

WASECA
Sacred Heart - 111 Fourth St., N.W., Waseca, MN 56093-2413 t) 507-835-1222 kjuarez@sacredheartwaseca.org; shfinancewaseca@gmail.com www.sacredheartwaseca.org Rev. The Hoang, Pst.; CRP Stds.: 101

Sacred Heart School - (Grades K-4) 308 W. Elm Ave., Waseca, MN 56093 t) 507-835-2780 Chris Dahle, Prin.; LeAnn Dahle, Prin.; Stds.: 102; Lay Tchrs.: 8

Sacred Heart Montessori - 308 W. Elm St., Waseca, MN 56093 t) 507-835-2780 Kathy Petracek, Dir.; LeAnn Dahle, Dir.;

WELLS
St. Casimir's - 320 Second Ave., S.W., Wells, MN 56097-1399 t) 507-553-5391 scasimir@bevcomm.net www.olmcstcstjb.org Very Rev. Gregory G. Havel, Pst.; Dcn. Eugene Paul; CRP Stds.: 64

St. Casimir's School - (Grades PreK-6) 300 2nd Ave., S.W., Wells, MN 56097 t) 507-553-5822 casimir@bevcomm.net www.stcasimirsschool.net Diane Edwards, Prin.; Stds.: 59; Lay Tchrs.: 6

WESTBROOK
St. Anthony's - 1153 1st Ave., Westbrook, MN 56183; Mailing: P.O. Box 278, Westbrook, MN 56183 t) 507-425-2369 (St. Gabriel); 507-274-5946 (St. Anthony) stanthonys@centurytel.net www.triparishcfw.org Rev. Msgr. R. Paul Heiting, Pst.; CRP Stds.: 18

WILMONT
Our Lady of Good Counsel - 605 4th Ave., Wilmont, MN 56185; Mailing: P.O. Box 475, Wilmont, MN 56185 t) 507-483-2317 stadriancluster@hotmail.com www.stadriancluster.org Rev. Msgr. Richard M. Colletti, Pst.; CRP Stds.: 51

WINDOM
St. Francis Xavier Church - 532 17th St., Windom, MN 56101; Mailing: P.O. Box 39, Windom, MN 56101 t) 507-831-1985 stfxavier@windomnet.com www.sfxwindom.org Rev. Pratap Reddy Salibindla, O.F.M. (India), Pst.; CRP Stds.: 53

WINNEBAGO
St. Mary's - 40 1st St., N.E., Winnebago, MN 56098; Mailing: 214 S. Holland, Blue Earth, MN 56013 t) 507-526-5626 www.sspeterpaulmary.org Rev. Andrew J. Beerman, Pst.; Rev. Gregory W. Parrott, Par. Vicar; Dcn. Steven Landsteiner; CRP Stds.: 10

WINONA
Cathedral of the Sacred Heart - 360 Main St., Winona, MN 55987-3299 t) 507-452-4770 info@cathedralwinona.org www.cascwinona.org Very Rev. Mark C. McNea, Rector; Dcn. James Welch; Tanya Diggins, Liturgy Dir.; Anna Therneau, DRE; CRP Stds.: 27

Basilica of St. Stanislaus - 625 E. Fourth St., Winona, MN 55987-4297 t) 507-452-5430 ststans@hbci.com www.ssk-sjn.weconnect.com/ Very Rev. Patrick O. Arens, Rector; Dcn. Justin Green; CRP Stds.: 71

St. Casimir - 626 W. Broadway, Winona, MN 55987-2721; Mailing: 360 Main St., Winona, MN 55987 t) 507-452-4770 info@cathedralwinona.org Very Rev. Mark C. McNea, Pst.; Dcn. James Welch; Anna Therneau, DRE; CRP Stds.: 5

Immaculate Conception - Merged Mar 2022 Merged with St. Rose of Lima, Lewiston.

St. John Nepomucene - 558 E. Broadway, Winona, MN 55987; Mailing: 625 E. Fourth St., Winona, MN 55987-4297 t) 507-452-5430 ststans@hbci.com www.ssk-sjn.weconnect.com Very Rev. Patrick O. Arens, Pst.; Dcn. Justin Green; CRP Stds.: 7

St. Mary's - 1303 W. Broadway St, Winona, MN 55987-2395 t) 507-452-5656 stmarys@stmaryswinona.org www.stmaryswinona.org/ Very Rev. Michael J. Cronin, Pst.; Dcn. William Keiper, Pst. Assoc.; CRP Stds.: 39

WORTHINGTON
St. Mary's - 1215 Seventh Ave., Worthington, MN 56187-2297 t) 507-376-6005 stmaryschurchworthington@gmail.com www.stmarysworthington.org/ Rev. James F. Callahan, Pst.; Rev. Miguel E. Proanos, Par. Vicar; Dcn. Vernon Behrends; CRP Stds.: 209

St. Mary's School - (Grades PreSchool-8) 1206 8th Ave., Worthington, MN 56187 t) 507-376-5236 jackie.probst@smswgtn.org www.smswgtn.org Jackie Probst, Prin.; Stds.: 134; Lay Tchrs.: 9

SCHOOLS: PRESCHOOL THRU HIGH SCHOOL

SCHOOLS

STATE OF MINNESOTA

ALBERT LEA
St. Theodore Elementary School - (PAR) (Grades PreK-5) 323 E. Clark St., Albert Lea, MN 56007 t) 507-373-9657 samundson@sttheoschool.org www.sttheo.org Susan Amundson, Prin.; Stds.: 89; Lay Tchrs.: 5

AUSTIN
Pacelli Catholic Schools - (PAR) (Grades PreK-12) 311 4th St., N.W., Austin, MN 55912 t) 507-437-3278 admin@pacellischools.org www.pacellischools.org Kane Jason Malo, Prin.; Stds.: 341; Lay Tchrs.: 21

MANKATO
Loyola Catholic School (Mankato Area Catholic School) - (PAR) (Grades PreK-12) 145 Good Counsel Dr., Mankato, MN 56001-3146 t) 507-388-0600 croesler@loyolacatholicschool.org www.loyolacatholicschool.org Dr. Claudia Roesler, Head of School; Stds.: 578; Lay Tchrs.: 42

OWATONNA
St. Mary's School - (PAR) (Grades PreK-8) 730 S. Cedar Ave., Owatonna, MN 55060 t) 507-446-2300 jswanson@stmarys-owatonna.org www.stmarys-owatonna.org Stacey Ginskey, Dean; Jen Swanson, Prin.; Stds.: 330; Lay Tchrs.: 22

ROCHESTER
Rochester Catholic Schools - (PAR) (Grades PreK-12) 1710 Industrial Dr. NW, Rochester, MN 55901 t) 507-424-1817 www.rcsmn.org Annemarie Vega, Pres.; Stds.: 1,346; Lay Tchrs.: 104

St. Francis of Assisi School - (Grades PreK-12) 318 11th Ave., S.E., Rochester, MN 55904 t) 507-288-4816 apoterucha@rcsmn.org Andrew Poterucha, Prin.; Stds.: 402; Lay Tchrs.: 24

St. Pius X School - (Grades PreK-12) 1205 12th Ave., N.W., Rochester, MN 55901 t) 507-282-5161 djenson@rcsmn.org Dave Jenson, Prin.; Stds.: 181; Lay Tchrs.: 11

Lourdes High School - (Grades PreK-12) 2800 19th St., N.W., Rochester, MN 55901 t) 507-289-3991 mspring@rcsmn.org Mary Spring, Prin.; Stds.: 335; Lay Tchrs.: 32

Holy Spirit School - (Grades PreK-12) 5455 50th Ave., N.W., Rochester, MN 55901 t) 507-288-8818 aheimer@rcsmn.org Amy Heimer, Prin.; Stds.: 242; Lay Tchrs.: 15

Co-Cathedral of St John the Evangelist School - (Grades PreK-12) 424 W. Center St., Rochester, MN 55902 t) (507) 282-5248 Matt Langsdale, Prin.; Stds.: 186; Lay Tchrs.: 11

WINONA
Cotter Schools - (PRV) (Grades K-12) 1115 W. Broadway Ave., Winona, MN 55987 t) 507-453-5000 communications@cotterschools.org www.cotterschools.org Mary Eileen Fitch, Pres.; David Forney, Prin.; Pam Kimber, Bus. Mgr.; Marisa Corcoran, Campus Min.; Stds.: 886; Sr. Tchrs.: 1; Lay Tchrs.: 59

Winona Area Catholic Schools - (PAR) (Grades PreSchool-k) 602 E. 5th St., Winona, MN 55987 t) 507-452-3766 pbowlin@cotterschools.org Patrick Bowlin, Prin.;

W.A.C.S. - St. Mary Educare - (Grades PreSchool-k) 1315 W. Broadway Ave., Winona, MN 55987 t) 507-452-2890 cnichols@wacs1.org www.cotterschools.org/ (Educare at 16 months) Christine Nichols, Dir.; Stds.: 124; Lay Tchrs.: 10

INSTITUTIONS LOCATED IN DIOCESE

ASSOCIATIONS [ASN]

ROCHESTER
Diocese of Winona-Rochester Guild of the Catholic Medical Association - 200 First St., S.W., Rochester, MN 55905 t) 507-266-3412 lane.john@mayo.edu Diocesan association of Catholic health care providers; affiliated with the Catholic Medical Association. Dr. John I. Lane, Pres.;

The Roman Catholic Pontifical Lay Association Memores Domini - 6006 Woodridge Ct., N.E., Rochester, MN 55906 t) 507-202-2017 smodarelli@sj.org www.comunioneliberazione.org Sebastian Modarelli, Head of the House;

CAMPUS MINISTRY / NEWMAN CENTERS [CAM]

WINONA
St. Thomas Aquinas Newman Center - 475 Huff St., Winona, MN 55987 t) 507-452-2781 newmanwsu@gmail.com Aaron Lofy, Dir.;

CATHOLIC CHARITIES [CCH]

WINONA
Catholic Charities of the Diocese of Winona-Rochester - 111 Market St., Ste. 2, Winona, MN 55987 t) (507) 454-2270 info@ccsomn.org www.ccsomn.org Shanna Harris, Exec. Dir.; Asstd. Annu.: 3,626; Staff: 72

CEMETERIES [CEM]

AUSTIN
Calvary Cemetery - 1803 4th Ave., S.W., Austin, MN 55912; Mailing: 1001 E. Oakland Ave., Austin, MN 55912 t) 507-433-1888 bookkeeping@queenofangels.church Dan Ball, Chair; Very Rev. Raul I. Silva, Dir.; Rev. James P. Steffes, Dir.;

MANKATO
Calvary Cemetery Association - 200 Goodyear Ave., Mankato, MN 56001; Mailing: P.O. Box 4143, Mankato, MN 56002 t) 507-995-1010; 507-388-3766 x125 gbarnette@sjwhf.org www.calvarymankato.wordpress.com Terry Miller, Supt.; Rev. Timothy Reker, Canonical Admin.;

OWATONNA
Sacred Heart Cemetery - 2150 S. Cedar Ave., Owatonna, MN 55060-3399; Mailing: 512 S. Elm Ave., Owatonna, MN 55060-3399 t) 507-451-4845 iketen@charter.net; tomkubista@charter.net Tomas Kubista, Pres.;

ROCHESTER
Calvary Cemetery of Rochester, Minnesota - 500 11th

Ave., N.E., Rochester, MN 55906; Mailing: 1700 N. Broadway, Ste. 154, Rochester, MN 55906 c) 507-273-0140 calvarydirector@gmail.com www.calvarycemeteryrochester.wordpress.com Steven Flynn, Dir.;

WINONA

Saint Mary's Cemetery of Winona, MN - 1333 Homer Rd., Winona, MN 55987 t) 507-452-2769 office@smcofwinona.org www.smcofwinona.org Julie A. Koehler, Supt.;

COLLEGES & UNIVERSITIES [COL]

WINONA

Saint Mary's University of Minnesota - 700 Terrace Hts., Winona, MN 55987-1399 t) 507-457-1700 admission@smumn.edu www.smumn.edu (Coed) DeLaSalle Christian Brothers. Rev. James P. Burns, I.V.D., Pres.; Stds.: 848; Lay Tchrs.: 82

CONVENTS, MONASTERIES, AND RESIDENCES FOR WOMEN [CON]

HOUSTON

Hermits of St. Mary of Carmel, (H.S.M.C.) - 33005 Stinson Ridge Rd., Houston, MN 55943-4033 t) 507-896-2125 www.hsmcmn.com Carmelite eremitical community of diocesan right. Sr. Helen Lee, Prioress; Srs.: 4

MANKATO

School Sisters of Notre Dame - 170 Good Counsel Dr., Mankato, MN 56001-3138; Mailing: 320 Ripa Ave., St. Louis, MO 63125 t) 507-389-4200 mhummert@ssndcp.org www.ssnd.org Central Pacific Province. Sr. Debra Marie Sciano, SSND, Prov.; Srs.: 12

ROCHESTER

Franciscan Poor Clare Nuns - 1001 14th St., N.W., Ste. 200, Rochester, MN 55901 t) 507-282-7441 executive.assistant@rochesterfranciscan.org www.stclaresrochester.org Sr. Ramona Miller, Superior Administrator; Srs.: 9

Sisters of St. Francis of the Third Order Regular of the Congregation of Our Lady of Lourdes - Assisi Heights Admin. Ctr., 1001 14th St., N.W., Ste. 100, Rochester, MN 55901 t) 507-282-7441 executive.assistant@rochesterfranciscan.org www.rochesterfranciscan.org Academy of Our Lady of Lourdes Sr. Tierney Trueman, Pres.; Srs.: 138

WINONA

Immaculate Heart Convent, Religious Sisters of Mercy - 700 Terrace Heights #63, Winona, MN 55987 t) 507-474-6939 rsmwinona@gmail.com www.rsmofalma.org Sr. Mary Andrea Lesko, RSM, Supr.; Srs.: 4

ENDOWMENTS / FOUNDATIONS / TRUSTS [EFT]

ALBERT LEA

St. Theodore Catholic School Endowment - 308 E. Fountain St., Albert Lea, MN 56007-2456 t) 507-373-0603 office@sttheo.org www.sttheo.org Rev. Kurt P. Farrell, Contact;

ROCHESTER

St. Francis Catholic Church Endowment Fund, Inc. - 1114 3rd St., S.E., Rochester, MN 55904

WINONA

Catholic Foundation of Southern Minnesota - 750 Terrace Hts., Ste. 105, Winona, MN 55987; Mailing: P.O. Box 30098, Winona, MN 55987 t) 507-858-1275 mherman@catholicfsmn.org www.catholicfsmn.org Monica Herman, Exec. Dir.;

Catholic Schools Foundation of Winona - 1115 W. Broadway Ave., Winona, MN 55987 t) 507-453-5000 x5116 dguzzo@cotterschools.org www.cotterschools.org Mike Hansen, Pres.;

Vision 2020 Education Foundation - 1115 W. Broadway, Winona, MN 55987 t) (507) 453-5017 mefitch@cotterschools.org Mary Eileen Fitch, Pres.;

MISCELLANEOUS [MIS]

ROCHESTER

Seeds of Wisdom in South Sudan - 11 Fourth Ave., S.W., Rochester, MN 55902 t) 507-288-7372 info@sowsouthsudan.org www.sowsouthsudan.org Steven Deick, Pres.;

***St. James Coffee** - 4156 18th Ave., N.W., Rochester, MN 55901 t) 507-281-3559 info@stjamescoffee.com www.stjamescoffee.com Katherine Letellier, Pres.; Melissa Scaccio, Bus. Mgr.;

ST. JAMES

SSVM Formation Program - 707 4th St. S., St. James, MN 56081

WINONA

Lasallian Educational and Research Initiatives - 702 Terrace Hts., Winona, MN 55987 t) 800-533-8095; 507-457-7900 smpress@smp.org; chunger@smp.org www.smp.org John M. Vitek, Pres.;

MONASTERIES AND RESIDENCES FOR PRIESTS AND BROTHERS [MON]

AUSTIN

Annunciation Hermitage, North American Province of St. Elias, Carmelites - 1009 Oakland Ave. E., Austin, MN 55912 t) 507-437-4015 annunciationhermitage@q.com Rev. Jon H. Moore, O.Carm., Prior; Brs.: 1; Priests: 2

WINONA

De La Salle Christian Brothers Residence - 736 Terrace Hts., Winona, MN 55987; Mailing: 700 Terrace Hts. #24, Winona, MN 55987 c) 630-460-5753 carrfr44@gmail.com Bro. Francis August Carr, FSC, Local Supr.; Brs.: 10

NURSING / REHABILITATION / CONVALESCENCE / ELDERLY CARE [NUR]

AUSTIN

Sacred Heart Care Center, Inc. - 1200 Twelfth St., S.W., Austin, MN 55912 t) 507-433-1808 lborris@sacredhcc.org www.sacredhcc.org Laura Sue Borris, Admin.; Asstd. Annu.: 320; Staff: 150

OWATONNA

Benedictine Living Communities Owatonna - 2255 30th St., N.W., Owatonna, MN 55060

ROCHESTER

Madonna Meadows of Rochester (Benedictine Living Community, Rochester) - 3035 Salem Meadows Dr., S.W., Rochester, MN 55902 t) 507-252-5400 www.benedictineliving.org/rochester-mn/ Assisted living facility of the Benedictine Health System and Sisters of St. Scholastica Monastery. Molly Wendroth, Admin.; Asstd. Annu.: 90; Staff: 66

Madonna Towers of Rochester, Inc. (Benedictine Living Community, Rochester) - 4001 19th Ave., N.W., Rochester, MN 55901 t) 507-288-3911 www.benedictineliving.org/rochester-mn/ Independent, assisted and nursing care facility; T. Emil Gauthier Memory Care. Subsidiary of Benedictine Health System. Molly Wendroth, Admin.; Asstd. Annu.: 500; Staff: 197

WINONA

Saint Anne of Winona (Benedictine Living Community, Winona) - 1347 W. Broadway, Winona, MN 55987 t) 507-454-3621 carol.ehlinger@benedictineliving.org www.benedictineliving.org/winona-mn/ Subsidiary of Benedictine Health System, sponsored by the Sisters of St. Scholastica Monastery. Carol Ehlinger, Exec. Dir.; Asstd. Annu.: 475; Staff: 208

St. Anne of Winona Benedictine Adult Day Center - 1455 W. Broadway, Winona, MN 55987 t) (507) 457-3810 tammy.ross@benedictineliving.org Tammy Ross, Dir.;

St. Anne of Winona Callista Court (Benedictine-Callista Court) - 1455 W. Broadway, Winona, MN 55987 t) 507-457-0280 katherine.johnson@benedictineliving.org Assisted living for seniors. Subsidiary of Benedictine Health Systems, sponsored by the Sisters of St. Scholastica Monastery. Katherine Johnson, Dir.;

St. Anne of Winona Training Center (Benedictine-Saint Anne Training Center) - 902 E. Second St., Winona, MN 55987 t) 507-474-4980 kimberly.nahrgang@benedictineliving.org Kimberly Nahrgang, Contact;

SEMINARIES [SEM]

MANKATO

IVE Formation Program, Inc. - 512 E. Mulberry St., Mankato, MN 56001 t) 507-387-2565 javieribarra@ive.org www.iveminorseminary.com Rev. Javier Ibarra, I.V.E., Rector; Stds.: 24; Lay Tchrs.: 4; Pr. Tchrs.: 3; Sr. Tchrs.: 3

WINONA

Immaculate Heart of Mary Seminary - 750 Terrace Hts., Winona, MN 55987-1320 t) 507-205-9237 info@ihmseminary.org www.ihmseminary.org Affiliated with Saint Mary's University of MN. Rev. Robert S. Horihan, Rector; Rev. Martin T. Schaefer, Vice Rector & Dean, Formation; Rev. Jeffrey L. Dobbs, Dir., Spiritual Life; Rev. Jason L. Kern, Vocations Dir.; Stds.: 58

An asterisk (*) denotes an organization that has established tax-exempt status directly with the IRS and is not covered by the USCCB Group Ruling.

Diocese of Worcester

(Dioecesis Wigorniensis)

MOST REVEREND ROBERT J. MCMANUS

Bishop of Worcester; ordained May 27, 1978; appointed Auxiliary Bishop of Providence and Titular Bishop of Allegheny December 1, 1998; consecrated February 22, 1999; appointed Bishop of Worcester March 9, 2004; installed May 14, 2004. Chancery Office: 49 Elm St., Worcester, MA 01609

Chancery Office: 49 Elm St., Worcester, MA 01609. T: 508-791-7171; F: 508-754-2768.
www.worcesterdiocese.org

ESTABLISHED JANUARY 14, 1950.

Square Miles 1,532.

Comprises the County of Worcester in the State of Massachusetts.

For legal titles of parishes and diocesan institutions, consult the Chancery Office.

STATISTICAL OVERVIEW

Personnel
Bishop....1
Retired Bishops....1
Abbots....3
Retired Abbots....1
Priests: Diocesan Active in Diocese....113
Priests: Diocesan Active Outside Diocese....5
Priests: Retired, Sick or Absent....46
Number of Diocesan Priests....164
Religious Priests in Diocese....58
Total Priests in your Diocese....222
Extern Priests in Diocese....3
Ordinations:
Diocesan Priests....7
Religious Priests....1
Transitional Deacons....2
Permanent Deacons in Diocese....107
Total Brothers....54
Total Sisters....166

Parishes
Parishes....91
With Resident Pastor:
Resident Diocesan Priests....84
Resident Religious Priests....2
Without Resident Pastor:
Administered by Priests....7
Missions....3
Pastoral Centers....2
New Parishes Created....2
Closed Parishes....7
Professional Ministry Personnel:
Sisters....4
Lay Ministers....83

Welfare
Catholic Hospitals....1
Total Assisted....250,000
Health Care Centers....3
Total Assisted....8,900
Homes for the Aged....4
Total Assisted....270
Day Care Centers....1
Total Assisted....1,400
Specialized Homes....5
Total Assisted....178
Special Centers for Social Services....6
Total Assisted....46,615

Educational
Diocesan Students in Other Seminaries....22
Total Seminarians....22
Colleges and Universities....3
Total Students....6,800
High Schools, Diocesan and Parish....1
Total Students....426
High Schools, Private....5
Total Students....1,534
Elementary Schools, Diocesan and Parish....13
Total Students....2,870
Elementary Schools, Private....4
Total Students....433
Catechesis/Religious Education:
High School Students....2,692
Elementary Students....7,089
Total Students under Catholic Instruction....21,866
Teachers in Diocese:
Priests....12
Brothers....4
Sisters....10
Lay Teachers....1,203

Vital Statistics
Receptions into the Church:
Infant Baptism Totals....1,652
Minor Baptism Totals....112
Adult Baptism Totals....153
Received into Full Communion....98
First Communions....1,452
Confirmations....1,419
Marriages:
Catholic....246
Interfaith....24
Total Marriages....270
Deaths....2,686
Total Catholic Population....266,700
Total Population....862,111

LEADERSHIP

Vicar General & Moderator of the Curia - t) 508-929-4346 Rev. Richard F. Reidy (rreidy@worcesterdiocese.org);

Chancellor - t) 508-929-4313 Raymond L. Delisle (rdelisle@worcesterdiocese.org);

Diocesan Director of Fiscal Affairs - t) 508-929-4335 pschasel@worcesterdiocese.org Marybeth Gilmore (mgilmore@worcesterdiocese.org);

Diocesan Tribunal - t) 508-791-7171 Rev. Msgr. F. Stephen Pedone;

Advocates - Rev. Michael A. DiGeronimo; Rev. William F. Sanders; Rev. Terence T. Kilcoyne;

Associate Judicial Vicar - t) 508-791-7171 Rev. Paul T. O'Connell;

Defenders of the Bond - t) 508-791-7171 Rev. Juan David Echavarria, Defender of the Bond; Rev. Richard F. Reidy; Rev. Msgr. Anthony S. Czarnecki;

Judges - t) 508-791-7171 Rev. Msgr. F. Stephen Pedone; Rev. Paul T. O'Connell; Rev. David W. Masello;

Judicial Vicar and Vicar for Canonical Affairs - fpedone@worcesterdiocese.org Rev. Msgr. F. Stephen Pedone;

Notary - Eileen Charbonneau;

Promoter of Justice - Sr. Mary Lou Walsh, S.N.D.;

Psychologist - Kathleen Kelley;

Secretary to the Tribunal - t) 508-929-4354 echarbonneau@worcesterdiocese.org Eileen Charbonneau;

Diocesan College of Consultors - Rev. Msgr. Thomas J. Sullivan; Rev. H. Edward Chalmers; Rev. Richard F. Reidy (rreidy@worcesterdiocese.org);

Deans - Rev. Msgr. Francis J. Scollen, Area I; Rev. Richard W. Polek, Dean Area II; Rev. Msgr. Thomas J. Sullivan, Area III;

Director of Priest Personnel - c) 508-340-5788 fatherjamesmazzone@gmail.com Rev. James S. Mazzone, Dir.;

OFFICES AND DIRECTORS

The Adopt-A-Student Endowment Trust - David Perda;

Archivist - t) 508-929-4346 Raymond L. Delisle, Chancellor (rdelisle@worcesterdiocese.org);

Campus Ministry (Vacant) -

Communication Ministry - t) 508-791-7171 Raymond L. Delisle, Dir. (rdelisle@worcesterdiocese.org); Stephen Kaufman, TV Ministry Production Mgr.; Margaret M. Russell, Editor;

Newspaper - t) 508-757-6387 editor@catholicfreepress.org; advertising@catholicfreepress.org www.catholicfreepress.org Margaret M. Russell, Editor; Raymond L. Delisle, Communications Dir.;

Director of Catholic Relief Services - Rev. Richard F. Reidy, Dir. (rreidy@worcesterdiocese.org);

Diocesan Cemeteries Office - t) 508-757-7415 James F. Brasco (JamesB@stjcemetery.com);

Diocesan Hispanic/Latino Apostolate - t) 508-981-9414 Rev. Hugo Cano, Dir.;

Diocesan Scouts - t) 508-929-4360 Timothy Messenger, Dir.; Rev. Donato Infante III, Chap.;

Director of Priest Personnel - t) 978-368-0366 Rev. James S. Mazzone, Dir.;

Episcopal Liaison to Religious - Sr. Paula Kelleher, S.S.J., Interim Liaison;

Ethnic Ministries -

African Ministry - t) 508-929-1329 Rev. Enoch Kyeremateng, Chap.;

Brazilian Ministry - t) 508-752-6364 Rev. Cleber de Paula; Rev. Dario Acevedo, Chap.;

Haitian Apostolate of the Diocese of Worcester -

Hispanic/Latino Ministry - Rev. Hugo Cano;

Annunciation Parish - Rev. Thiago Ibiapina;

Holy Trinity - t) 978-534-5258 Rev. Jose A. Rodriguez, Chap.; Sr. Yalile Ruiz, R.O.D.A., Chap.;

Our Lady of Providence - t) 508-755-3820 Rev. William E. Reiser, S.J.; Sr. Susana Miranda, X.M.M.; Dcn. Gilberto Javier-Altmonte;

St. Francis of Assisi - t) 978-342-9651 Rev. Angel R. Matos; Yesenia Quinones;

St. Joan of Arc - t) 508-852-3232 Rev. Wilmar Ramos, Admin.; Sr. Andrea Avellaneda, R.O.D.A.;

St. John, Guardian of Our Lady - t) 978-368-0366 Rev. Julio R. Granados;

St. John Paul II - t) 508-765-0394 Rev. Carlos Ardila; Sr. Rosita Campos, R.O.D.A.; Dcn. Juan J. Guzman;

St. Louis - t) 508-943-0240 Rev. Javier Julio; Noelia Rivera;

St. Luke - t) 508-366-5502 Rev. Diego A. Buritica, Pst.; Rev. William E. Reiser, S.J.; Sr. Yalile Ruiz, R.O.D.A.;

St. Mary of the Assumption - t) 508-473-2000 Rev. Peter Joyce; Rev. Victor A. Sierra;

St. Paul - t) 508-754-3195 Rev. Hugo Cano, Pst.; Rev. Juan Parra; Dcn. Francisco Escobar;

St. Peter - t) 508-752-4674 Rev. Dario Acevedo; Dcn. George Estremera;

Polish Ministry - t) 508-943-0467

Portuguese Ministry - t) 508-473-2000 Rev. Dario Acevedo;

Vietnamese Ministry - t) 508-752-1825 Rev. Tam M. Bui;

Finance Office - t) 508-791-7171 Marybeth Gilmore, CFO (mgilmore@worcesterdiocese.org);

Office for Divine Worship - t) 508-798-0417 ofworship@worcesterdiocese.org Rev. Msgr. James P. Moroney, Dir.; Elizabeth Marcil, Assoc. Dir.; Rev. Alfredo Raul Porras, Assoc. Dir.;

Office of Marriage and Family - t) 508-929-4311 Allison LeDoux, Dir.;

Office of Ongoing Priestly Formation - t) 508-393-2223 Rev. Ronald Falco, Dir.;

Permanent Diaconate - t) 508-929-4332 Dcn. William A. Bilow Jr., Dir.;

Presbyteral Council - t) 508-791-7171 Rev. Msgr. Francis J. Scollen; Rev. Richard W. Polek; Rev. Msgr. Thomas J. Sullivan;

Propagation of the Faith - t) 508-929-4335 Kathleen Barrett, Secy.;

Religious Education Office - t) 508-929-4303 Elizabeth Marcil, Diocesan D.R.E.;

Respect Life - t) 508-929-4311 aledoux@worcesterdiocese.org Allison LeDoux;

School Department - t) 508-929-4320 dperda@worcesterdiocese.org David Perda, Supt.;

Stewardship and Development Office - t) 508-929-4368 Michael Gillespie, Dir.;

Tri-Conference Retirement Fund for Religious - Michael Gillespie, Diocesan Coord.;

Victim Assistance Coordinator - t) 508-929-4363 Judith Audette (jaudette@worcesterdiocese.org);

Vocations Office - t) 508-630-4473 director@worcestervocations.com Rev. Donato Infante III, Dir.;

Holy Name of Jesus House of Studies - t) 508-630-4473 Rev. Donato Infante III, Dir.;

Youth and Young Adult Ministry - t) 508-929-4360 Timothy Messenger, Dir.;

ADVISORY BOARDS, COMMISSIONS, COMMITTEES, AND COUNCILS

Diocesan Building Commission - Nathan Schroeder (nschroeder@worcesterdiocese.org); Stephen Sycks (ssycks@worcesterdiocese.org); Rev. Charles F. Monroe, Chair;

Diocesan Finance Committee - Richard Fournier, Chair;

Priests' Personnel Board - t) 978-368-0366 Rev. James S. Mazzone, Dir.;

St. Paul Catholic Schools Consortium - t) 508-929-4320 Patricia M. Halpin, Chair;

Worcester Diocesan Commission for Women -

CLERGY AND RELIGIOUS SERVICES

Clergy Benefit Plan - t) 508-459-9195 admin@clergybenefitplan.org Rev. Charles F. Monroe, Pres.; Rev. Edward D. Niccolls, Treas.; Mary Lou Verla, Admin.;

Minister to Priests - t) 508-755-5291 Rev. Richard F. Trainor;

Ministry to Retired Priests - t) 508-868-9239 Sr. Mary Ann Bartell, C.S.E.;

DEVELOPMENT

The Annual Partners in Charity Appeal - t) 508-929-4368 development@worcesterdiocese.org Michael Gillespie;

FINANCE

Diocesan Expansion Fund - Marybeth Gilmore (mgilmore@worcesterdiocese.org); Stephen Sycks (ssycks@worcesterdiocese.org); Peter J. Dawson, Chair;

SOCIAL SERVICES

Catholic Charities - t) 508-798-0191 tmcmahon@ccworc.org Timothy McMahon, Exec.;

St. Vincent dePaul Society - t) (508) 556-0559 svdpworcestercouncil37@gmail.com Rev. William E. Champlin, Chap. (wechamplin@msn.com); Susan Trevaloni, Pres.;

Ctrl. Worcester County Dist. Coun. - Colleen Resca, Pres.;

No. Worcester County Dist. Coun. - Elaine Murphy, Pres.;

So. Worcester County Dist. Coun. - Patricia Nedoroscik, Pres.;

Urban Missionaries of Our Lady of Hope - t) 508-831-7455 Dcn. Walter F. Doyle;

SPIRITUAL LIFE

Black Catholics: African American - t) 508-752-4674 Rev. Msgr. Francis J. Scollen, Contact;

Charismatic Renewal, Office of - t) (508) 366-5502 Rev. Diego A. Buritica, Liaison (frdiegoburitica@gmail.com);

Cursillo - t) 978-534-7284 Rev. Donald C. Ouellette, Dir.;

PARISHES, MISSIONS, AND CLERGY

COMMONWEALTH OF MASSACHUSETTS

ASHBURNHAM

St. Denis - 85 Main St., Ashburnham, MA 01430 t) 978-827-5806; 978-827-4892 (CRP) stdenisre@comcast.net; stdenis@comcast.net www.saintdenisashburnham.com Rev. Kevin F. Hartford, Admin.; Dcn. Richard DesJardins; Kim Brown, DRE;

ATHOL

St. Francis - 101 Main St., Athol, MA 01331; Mailing: 192 School St., Athol, MA 01331 t) 978-249-2738; (978) 249-7690 Rev. Mateus Monteiro De Souza, Pst.; Dcn. Bryan A. Lagimoniere; CRP Stds.: 1

Our Lady Immaculate - 192 School St., Athol, MA 01331-2399 t) 978-249-7690 (CRP); 978-249-2738 www.nqcatholic.com Rev. Mateus Monteiro De Souza, Pst.; Dcn. Bryan A. Lagimoniere; CRP Stds.: 44

AUBURN

St. Joseph's - 194 Oxford St. N., Auburn, MA 01501-1529 t) 508-832-2074; 508-832-6683 (CRP) stjoesreledaub@gmail.com; stjoes01501@gmail.com Rev. Paul M. Bomba, Pst.; Lisa Wass, DRE; CRP Stds.: 43

North American Martyrs - 8 Wyoma Dr., Auburn, MA 01501 t) 508-798-8779; 508-798-0612 (CRP) szammarelli@namartyrsauburn.org www.namartyrsauburn.org Rev. Frederick D. Fraini III, Pst.; Lisa Marie Burkitt, DRE; CRP Stds.: 188

BALDWINVILLE

St. Vincent De Paul - 1 Forest St., Baldwinville, MA 01436; Mailing: PO Box 14, 18 Pleasant St., Baldwinville, MA 01436 t) 978-939-8851; 978-939-8290 (CRP) stvindepaul05@aol.com saintvincentcatholicchurch.com Rev. Francis A. Roberge, Pst.; Dcn. James A. Connor; Jennifer McNeaney, DRE; CRP Stds.: 24

BERLIN

St. Joseph the Good Provider - 52 West St., Berlin, MA 01503-0284; Mailing: Box 284, Berlin, MA 01503-0284 t) 978-838-9922 stjoe9922@charter.net stjosephberlin.org Rev. Thomas M. Tokarz, Pst.; Mary Jo Kriz, DRE; CRP Stds.: 45

BLACKSTONE

Divine Mercy Parish - 48 St. Paul St., Blackstone, MA 01504 t) (508) 883-6726 info@divinemercyparishma.org divinemercyparishma.org Rev. John L. Larochelle, Pst.;

St. Paul - Merged Jul 2022 Merged with St. Augustine and St. Theresa to form Divine Mercy, Blackstone.

St. Theresa - Merged Jul 2022 Merged with St. Augustine and St. Paul to form Divine Mercy Parish, Blackstone.

BOYLSTON

St. Mary of the Hills - 630 Cross St., Boylston, MA 01505; Mailing: 620 Cross St., Boylston, MA 01505 t) 508-869-6771 secretary@saintmaryofthehills.com www.saintmaryofthehills.com Rev. Juan David Echavarria, Pst.; Dcn. Richard C. Martino; Anne Dowen, DRE;

CHARLTON

St. Joseph's - 10 H. Putnam Rd. Ext., Charlton, MA 01507; Mailing: P.O. Box 338, Charlton City, MA 01508 t) 508-248-7862 stjoecharlton@aol.com stjosephscharlton.com Rev. Robert A. Grattaroti, Pst.; Dcn. Steve Miller; Dcn. William Shea; Sr. Agnes Patricia, DRE; CRP Stds.: 198

CLINTON

St. John the Guardian of Our Lady - 80 Union St., Clinton, MA 01510 t) 978-368-0366 stjohnclintonma@gmail.com www.stjohnsclinton.org Rev. James S. Mazzone, Pst.; Rev. Julio R. Granados, Assoc. Pst.;

DOUGLAS

St. Denis - 23 Manchaug St., Douglas, MA 01516 t) 508-476-2002 nanorberg@saintdenischurch.com; pstewart@saintdenischurch.com www.saintdenischurch.com Rev. Nelson Rivera, Pst.; Dcn. Patrick W. Stewart; CRP Stds.: 120

DUDLEY

St. Andrew Bobola - 54 W. Main St., Dudley, MA 01571 t) 508-943-5633 rectory@standrewbobola.net Rev. Krzysztof Korcz, Pst.; CRP Stds.: 20

St. Anthony - 22/24 Dudley Hill Rd., Dudley, MA 01571 t) 508-949-0335 stanthonyofpaduareled@gmail.com; stanthonypaduadudley@gmail.com www.stanthony-dudley.org Rev. Daniel E. Moreno, Pst.; Dcn. William White; Mary Plante, DRE; CRP Stds.: 65

EAST BROOKFIELD

St. John the Baptist - 121 Blaine Ave., East Brookfield, MA 01515 t) 508-867-3738 stjohnseb01515@verizon.net www.stjohnsebma.org Rev. Joseph Rice, Admin.; Rev. Donald C. Ouellette, Assoc. Pst.; Mary Gershman, DRE; CRP Stds.: 26

FISKDALE

St. Anne and St. Patrick - 16 Church St., Fiskdale, MA 01518 t) 508-347-7338; 508-347-9353 (CRP) stannestpatpastor@gmail.com; reledof@gmail.com stannestpatrickparish.com Rev. Alex Castro, A.A., Pst.; Rev. John Franck, A.A., Assoc. Pst.; Rev. Luc Martel, A.A., Assoc. Pst.; Dcn. Keith Caplette; Dcn. Dominick F. DeMartino; Dcn. Wesley Stevens; CRP Stds.: 121

FITCHBURG

St. Anthony of Padua - 84 Salem St., Fitchburg, MA 01420 t) 978-342-4706 church.office@stanthonyfitchburg.net www.stanthonyfitchburg.net Rev. Juan Ramirez, Pst.; Dcn. Salvatore Tantillo; CRP Stds.: 16

St. Bernard Parish at St. Camillus de Lellis - 333 Mechanic St., Fitchburg, MA 01420 t) 978-342-7921; 978-343-7459 stbernardfitch@verizon.net saintbernardparish.net/ Rev. Joseph M. Dolan, Pst.; Dcn. Benjamin A. Nogueira; Dcn. John J. Aliskevicz; Dcn. Steven P. Gendron; Susan Saari, DRE; CRP Stds.: 65

St. Bernard Elementary School - (Grades PreK-8) 254 Summer St., Fitchburg, MA 01420 t) 978-342-1948 dwright@stbernardselementary.org stbernardselementary.org Deborah Wright, Prin.; Stds.: 258; Lay Tchrs.: 16

St. Francis of Assisi - 81 Sheridan, Fitchburg, MA 01420; Mailing: 63 Sheridan, Fitchburg, MA 01420 t) 978-342-9651; 978-342-3521 (CRP) pastor-@saintfrancis-fitchburg.com; yquinones08@aol.com saintfrancis-fitchburg.com Rev. Angel R. Matos, Pst.; Yesenia Quinones, DRE; CRP Stds.: 73

St. Joseph's - 49 Woodland St., Fitchburg, MA 01420 t) 978-345-7997 stj2010@verizon.net stjosephfitchburg.org Rev. Dario Acevedo, Admin.; Maureen Beauvais, DRE;

GARDNER

Annunciation Parish - 135 Nichols St., Gardner, MA 01440 t) 978-632-0253 religioused@annunciationgardner.org; office@annunciationgardner.org www.annunciationgardner.org Rev. Thiago Ibiapina; Rev. Stephen E. Lundrigan, Pst.; Dcn. Stanley H. Baczewski; Maura L. Sweeney, DRE; CRP Stds.: 76

Holy Family Academy - (Grades PreK-8) 99 Nichols St., Gardner, MA 01440 t) 978-632-8656 ahardersen@holyfamilyacademyma.org www.holyfamilyacademyma.org Colette Goguen, Prin.; Stds.: 174; Lay Tchrs.: 11

GILBERTVILLE

St. Aloysius - 58 Church St., Gilbertville, MA 01031-0542; Mailing: P.O. Box 542, Gilbertville, MA 01031-0542 t) 413-477-6493 st.aloysius@verizon.net Lorretta DiPietro, DRE; CRP Stds.: 6

St. Augustine - 98 Church Ln., Wheelwright, MA 01094

GRAFTON

St. Philip - Merged Jul 2022 Merged with St. Mary and St. James to form Our Lady of Hope, North Grafton.

HARVARD

Holy Trinity - 15 Still River Rd., Harvard, MA 01451; Mailing: PO Box 746, Harvard, MA 01451 t) 978-456-3563 htpboltonharvard@aol.com Rev. Terence T. Kilcoyne, Pst.; CRP Stds.: 165

HOPEDALE

Sacred Heart of Jesus - 187 Hopedale St., Hopedale, MA 01747 t) 508-473-1900 parishoffice@sacredhearthopedale.org www.sacredhearthopedale.org Rev. William C. Konicki, Pst.; CRP Stds.: 127

JEFFERSON

St. Mary - 114 Princeton St., Jefferson, MA 01522; Mailing: P.O. Box 2200, Jefferson, MA 01522 t) 508-829-4508; 508-829-6758 (CRP) stmaryreled@charterinternet.com; stmaryjeff@stmaryjeff.com Rev. Timothy M. Brewer, Pst.; CRP Stds.: 545

LANCASTER

Immaculate Conception - 28 Packard St., Lancaster, MA 01523; Mailing: P.O. Box 95, Lancaster, MA 01523 t) 978-365-6582 iconception@comcast.net Rev. Thomas H. Hultquist, Pst.; Dcn. William A. Bilow Jr.; Eileen Erickson, Admin.; CRP Stds.: 67

LEICESTER

St. Aloysius-St. Jude - 491 Pleasant St., Leicester, MA 01524 t) 508-892-8296 aloysius-jude@charter.net www.saintaloysiusjude.org Rev. John M. Lizewski, Pst.; Kevin D Mathieu, Music Min.;

St. Joseph-St. Pius X Parish - 761 Main St., Leicester, MA 01524 t) 508-892-0660 (CRP); 508-859-8083 stjosephstpiusx759@gmail.com Rev. Robert A. Loftus, Pst.; CRP Stds.: 71

LEOMINSTER

St. Anna - 199 Lancaster St., Leominster, MA 01453 t) 978-537-5293 stanna9@comcast.net stannaparish.org/ Rev. Carlos Ruiz, Pst.; Dcn. James E. Graves; CRP Stds.: 91

St. Anna School - (Grades PreK-8) 213 Lancaster St, Leominster, MA 01453 t) 978-534-4770 principal@stannaleom.org www.stannaschool.org Renee Legendre, Prin.; Stds.: 230; Scholastics: 27; Lay Tchrs.: 12

St. Cecilia - 170 Mechanic St., Leominster, MA 01453 t) 978-537-6541; 978-537-4673 (CRP) office@stceciliachurch.net www.stceciliachurch.net Rev. Msgr. James P. Moroney, Pst.; Rev. Paul Shaunessey, S.J., Par. Vicar; Rev. Leo-Paul J. LeBlanc, In Res.; Dcn. Robert Connor Jr.; CRP Stds.: 60

Holy Family of Nazareth - 750 Union St., Leominster, MA 01453 t) 978-537-3016 churchonhill@aol.com holyfamilyofnazareth.org Rev. Jose A. Rodriguez, Pst.; Jessica Smith, DRE; CRP Stds.: 123

St. Leo - 108 Main St., Leominster, MA 01453 t) 978-537-7257; 978-537-1194 (CRP) stleoparish@verizon.net stleosparish.org Rev. William E. Champlin, Pst.; CRP Stds.: 20

St. Leo School - (Grades PreK-8) 120 Main St., Leominster, MA 01453 t) 978-537-1007 nancy.pierce@st-leoschool.org www.st-leoschool.com Nancy Pierce, Prin.; Stds.: 249; Lay Tchrs.: 17

Our Lady of the Lake - 1400 Main St., Leominster, MA 01453 t) 978-342-2978 www.ourladylake.org Rev. Michael Broderick, Pst.; CRP Stds.: 160

LINWOOD

Good Shepherd - Merged Jul 2022 Merged with St. Mary, Uxbridge.

LUNENBURG

St. Boniface - 817 Massachusetts Ave., Lunenburg, MA 01462 t) 978-582-4008 stbonifaceparish@verizon.net www.stboniface-lunenburg.org Rev. Charles Omolo, Admin.; Lucia Marcil, DRE; CRP Stds.: 110

MILFORD

St. Mary of the Assumption - 17 Winter St., Milford, MA 01757 t) 508-473-2000; 508-478-7440 (CRP) frpeter@stmarymilford.org www.stmarymilford.org (Portuguese and Brazilian) Rev. Peter Joyce, Pst.; Rev. Victor A. Sierra, Par. Vicar; Dcn. David F. Vaillancourt; Kathy Moran, DRE; CRP Stds.: 412

Sacred Heart of Jesus - 5 E. Main St., Milford, MA 01757 t) 508-634-5435; 508-478-0139 (Religious Educ) ccdoffice@sacredheartmilford.org; office@sacredheartmilford.org www.sacredheartmilford.org Rev. Richard A. Scioli, C.S.S., Pst.; Rev. Gregory J. Hoppough, C.S.S., In Res.; Robert William Blake Jr., Music Min.; Amy Donahue, DRE; Andrew Tomaski, DRE; CRP Stds.: 200

MILLBURY

Assumption - 12 Waters St., Millbury, MA 01527; Mailing: 59 Main St., Millbury, MA 01527 t) 508-865-2657; 508-865-6624; 508-865-5404 julie.olson@assumption-cs.org Rev. Daniel R. Mulcahy Jr., Pst.; Dcn. Ronald B. Buron; Deborah Blicharz, Pst. Assoc.; Gregory Bernard, DRE; CRP Stds.: 55

Assumption School - (Grades PreK-8) 17 Grove St., Millbury, MA 01527 assumption-cs.org Julie Olson, Prin.;

St. Brigid - 59 Main St., Millbury, MA 01527 t) 508-865-6624 www.stbrigidparish.org/ Rev. Daniel R. Mulcahy Jr., Pst.; Dcn. Ronald B. Buron; Deborah Blicharz, Pst. Assoc.; Gregory Bernard, DRE; CRP Stds.: 124

MILLVILLE

St. Augustine - Merged Jul 2022 Merged with St. Theresa and St. Paul to form Divine Mercy Parish, Blackstone.

NORTH BROOKFIELD

St. Joseph - 28 Mt. Pleasant St., North Brookfield, MA 01535 t) 508-867-6811 saintjosephrectory@verizon.net www.stjosephsnbma.org Rev. Joseph Rice, Admin.; Rev. Donald C. Ouellette, Assoc. Pst.; Lynne Losurdo, DRE; CRP Stds.: 38

NORTH GRAFTON

St. Mary - Merged Jul 2022 Merged with St. Philip and St. James to form Our Lady of Hope, North Grafton.

Our Lady of Hope Parish Grafton - 17 Waterville St., North Grafton, MA 01536 t) (508) 839-3993 ourladyofhopegrafton.org Rev. Anthony Mpagi, Pst.; Dcn. Timothy Cross;

St. James Church - 89 Main St., South Grafton, MA 01560

St. Philip Church - 12 West St., Grafton, MA 01519

NORTH OXFORD

St. Ann - 652 Main St., North Oxford, MA 01537; Mailing: P.O. Box 488, North Oxford, MA 01537 t) 508-987-8892 www.stannschurch.us Rev. Michael J. Roy, Pst.; Rev. James J. Boulette, Assoc. Pst.; CRP Stds.: 26

NORTHBORO

St. Bernadette - 266 Main St., Northboro, MA 01532 t) 508-393-2838; 508-393-7445 (CRP) office@stb-parish.net stb-parish.org Rev. Ronald Falco, Pst.; Virginia Boland, DRE; CRP Stds.: 82

St. Bernadette School - (Grades PreK-8) t) 508-351-9905 principal@stb-school.org www.stb-school.org Deborah O'Neil, Prin.; Mary Bardellini, Librn.; Stds.: 371; Lay Tchrs.: 39

St. Rose of Lima - 244 W. Main St., Northboro, MA 01532; Mailing: P.O. Box 685, Northboro, MA 01532 t) 508-393-2413 lmcgarvey@saintroseoflima.com saintroseoflima.com/ Rev. Juan Escudero, Pst.; Theresa Fugardi, Pst. Assoc.; Susan McGoldrick, DRE; CRP Stds.: 273

NORTHBRIDGE

St. Peter - 39 Church Ave., Northbridge, MA 01534; Mailing: PO Box 446, Northbridge, MA 01534-0446 t) 508-234-2156 (Parish Office); (508) 234-6355 (Religious Ed Office) parishoffice@stpeterrockdale.org www.stpeterrockdale.org Rev. Michael N. Lavallee, Pst.; CRP Stds.: 35

OTTER RIVER

St. Martin Mission - 248 State Rd., Otter River, MA 01436 t) 978-939-5588 info@saintmartinchurch.org saintmartinchurch.org Rev. Patrick Ssekyole, Pst.;

OXFORD

St. Roch - 334 Main St., Oxford, MA 01540 t) 508-987-8987; 508-987-2382 (Rel Ed) strochrectory@gmail.com www.strochoxford.com Rev. Michael J. Roy, Pst.; Rev. James J. Boulette, Assoc. Pst.; Dcn. Paul R. Connelly; CRP Stds.: 49

PAXTON

St. Columba - 10 Richards Ave., Paxton, MA 01612 t) (508) 755-0408 (CRP); (508) 755-0601 stcolumba@charter.net Rev. David Cotter, Pst.; CRP Stds.: 108

PETERSHAM

St. Peter - 18 North St., Petersham, MA 01366; Mailing: 192 School St., Athol, MA 01331 t) 978-249-7690 (CRP); 978-249-2738 Rev. Mateus Monteiro De Souza, Pst.; Dcn. Bryan A. Lagimoniere; CRP Stds.: 2

PRINCETON

Prince of Peace - 5 Worcester Rd., Princeton, MA 01541; Mailing: P O Box 305, Princeton, MA 01541 t) 508-464-2871 princeofpeace@verizon.net princeofpeacema.org Rev. H. Edward Chalmers, Pst.; Sharon Bushway, DRE; CRP Stds.: 30

RUTLAND

St. Patrick - 258 Main St., Rutland, MA 01543; Mailing: Box 939, Rutland, MA 01543 t) 508-886-4309 (Rectory); 508-886-4984 (Parish Center/Offices) das@stpatricksrutland.org stpatricksrutland.org/ Rev. James Boland, Pst.; Dcn. Pierre G.L. Gemme; Dcn. Brian Stidsen; Christine Mulry, DRE; Jean Urbanowski, DRE; CRP Stds.: 248

SHREWSBURY

St. Anne - 130 Boston Tpke., Shrewsbury, MA 01545 t) 508-757-5154; 508-752-5040 (CRP) rectory@stannesparish.org stannesparish.org Rev. Walter J. Riley, Pst.; Rev. Paul T. O'Connell, In Res.; Rev. Enoch Kyeremateng, In Res.; Dcn. Peter Ryan; Tracy Flynn, DRE; Eleanor Smith, Pst. Assoc.; CRP Stds.: 100

St. Mary's - 640 Main St., Shrewsbury, MA 01545; Mailing: 20 Summer St., Shrewsbury, MA 01545 t) 508-845-6341; 508-845-6341 (CRP) michael.rose@stmarysparish.org www.stmarysparish.org Rev. Msgr. Michael F. Rose, Pst.; Rev. Jose Carvajal, Assoc. Pst.; CRP Stds.: 459

St. Mary's School - (Grades PreK-8) 16 Summer St., Shrewsbury, MA 01545 t) 508-842-1601 principal@stmarysparish.org school.stmarysparish.org Stds.: 202; Lay Tchrs.: 13

SOUTH BARRE

St. Francis of Assisi Parish - 398 Vernon Ave., South Barre, MA 01074; Mailing: P.O. Box 186, South Barre, MA 01074-0186 t) 978-355-2228 barrestfrancisparish@gmail.com www.saintfrancisofassisiparish.com Rev. James B. Callahan, Pst.; Dcn. Scott Colley; CRP Stds.: 44

SOUTH GRAFTON

St. James - Merged Jul 2022 Merged with St. Philip and St. Mary to form Our Lady of Hope, North Grafton.

SOUTHBOROUGH

St. Anne - 20 Boston Rd., Southborough, MA 01772 t) 508-485-0141 stanne403@stannesouthborough.org www.stannesouthborough.org Rev. Albert Irudayasamy, Pst.; CRP Stds.: 93

St. Matthew - 26 Highland St., Southborough, MA 01772; Mailing: 105 Southville Rd, Southborough, MA 01772-1936 t) 508-485-2285; 508-229-2429 (CRP) office@stmatthewsb.org Rev. James B. Flynn, Pst.; Amy Comcowich, DRE; CRP Stds.: 363

SOUTHBRIDGE

Saint John Paul II - 279 Hamilton St., Southbridge, MA 01550 t) 508-765-3704 (CRP); 508-765-3701 maddieb.stjp2@gmail.com Rev. Kenneth Cardinale, Pst.; Rev. Carlos Ardila, Assoc. Pst.; Dcn. Juan Guzman; CRP Stds.: 165

SPENCER

Mary, Queen of the Rosary - 46 Maple St., Spencer, MA 01562 t) 508-885-3111 maryqueen@mqrparish.org www.maryqueenoftherosary.org Rev. William Schipper, Pst.; Kelly Sullivan, DRE; CRP Stds.: 83

STERLING

St. Richard of Chichester - 4 Bridge St., Sterling, MA 01564; Mailing: PO Box 657, Sterling, MA 01564 t) 978-422-8881; 978-422-8921 (CRP) strichardreled@comcast.net; strichardsterling@comcast.net strichardsterling.org Rev. Juan-Sebastian Sanchez Guzman, Pst.; Kathleen Majikas, Admin.; Susan Gallivan, DRE; CRP Stds.: 132

SUTTON

St. Mark - 356 Boston Rd., Sutton, MA 01590 t) 508-865-3860 st-mark-office@verizon.net Rev. Michael A. DiGeronimo, Pst.; Dcn. Daniel Lavoie; Kathleen Huggins, Pst. Min./Coord.; Lisa M. DeHaan, Youth Min.; CRP Stds.: 103

TEMPLETON

Holy Cross - 25 Lake Ave., Templeton, MA 01468 t) 978-632-2121 hcchurchet@comcast.net Rev. Patrick Ssekyole, Pst.; Dcn. Dennis J. Cormier; CRP Stds.: 31

St. Martin - 247 State Rd., Otter River, MA 01436 t) 978-939-5588

UPTON

St. Gabriel the Archangel - 151 Mendon St., Upton, MA 01568 t) 508-603-1430 info@stgabrielma.org www.stgabrielma.org Rev. Laurence V. Brault, Pst.; Rev. V. Sagar Gundiga, Assoc. Pst.; Simone Caron, DRE; CRP Stds.: 243

UXBRIDGE

St. Mary's - 77 Mendon St., Uxbridge, MA 01569 t) 508-278-2226; 508-278-3777 (CRP) fathernick@stmaryuxbridge.org; sleighton@stmaryuxbridge.org www.stmaryuxbridge.org Rev. Nicholas Desimone, Pst.; Dcn. John Dugan; CRP Stds.: 111

WARREN

St. Paul - 1050 Main St., Warren, MA 01083-1027; Mailing: P.O. Box 1027, Warren, MA 01083 t) (508) 929-4345 ststanoffice@gmail.com warrenmass.org Rev. Richard F. Reidy, Admin.; Rev. Edward M. Ryan, Sacr. Min.;

WEBSTER

St. Joseph Basilica - 53 Whitcomb St., Webster, MA 01570 t) 508-943-0467 rectory@saintjosephbasilica.com www.saintjosephbasilica.com Rev. Grzegorz Chodkowski, Pst.; Rev. Anthony S. Kazarnowicz, Assoc. Pst.; Elizabeth Sabaj, CRE; CRP Stds.: 61

St. Joseph School - (Grades PreK-8) 47 Whitcomb St., Webster, MA 01570 t) 508-943-0378 principal@sjs-webster.com; secretary@sjs-webster.com www.sjs-webster.com Beth Boudreau, Prin.; Stds.: 198; Sr. Tchrs.: 1; Lay Tchrs.: 10

St. Louis - 14 Lake St., Webster, MA 01570; Mailing: 15 Lake St., Webster, MA 01570 t) 508-943-0240; 508-943-0817 (CRP) saintlouischurch@verizon.net stlouischurchwebster.org Rev. Javier Julio, Admin.; Dcn. Peter J. Motyka; Teresa Cacciapouti, CRE; CRP Stds.: 68

Sacred Heart of Jesus - 18 E. Main St., Webster, MA 01570 t) 508-943-3140 office@sacredheartwebster.org Rev. Adam R. Reid, Pst.; Dcn. Paul J. Lesieur; Nancy Kudzal, Admin.; CRP Stds.: 37

WEST BOYLSTON

Our Lady of Good Counsel - 111 Worcester St., West Boylston, MA 01583 t) 508-835-3606; 508-835-6336 (CRP) r.crouse@goodcounselma.com; t.king@goodcounselma.com www.goodcounselma.com Rev. Steven M. Labaire, Pst.; Rev. Adriano Lessa Natalino, C.Ss.R., In Res.; Dcn. Martin Beck; Dcn. Scott Camilleri; Kevin O'Connell, DRE; CRP Stds.: 76

WEST BROOKFIELD

Our Lady of the Sacred Heart - 10 Milk St., West Brookfield, MA 01585-0563; Mailing: P.O. Box 563, West Brookfield, MA 01585-0563 t) 508-867-6469; 508-867-4460 (CRP) rectory@sacredheartwb.com www.ourladyofthesacredheart.org. Rev. Joseph Rice, Admin.; Rev. Donald C. Ouellette, Assoc. Pst.; CRP Stds.: 61

WEST WARREN

St. Stanislaus - 2270 Main St., West Warren, MA 01092-0723; Mailing: PO Box 1027, Warren, MA 01083 t) (508) 929-4345 ststanoffice@gmail.com warrenmass.org Rev. Richard F. Reidy, Admin.; Rev. Edward M. Ryan, Sacr. Min.;

WESTBOROUGH

St. Luke the Evangelist - 70 W. Main St., Westborough, MA 01581 t) 508-366-5502; 508-366-8509 religiouseducation@stlukes-parish.org; office@stlukes-parish.org www.stlukes-parish.org Rev. Diego A. Buritica, Pst.; Julie Basque, Pst. Assoc.; CRP Stds.: 404

WESTMINSTER

St. Edward the Confessor - 10 Church St., Westminster, MA 01473 t) 978-874-2362; 978-874-1559 (CRP) office@stedwardconf.org; reled@stedwardconf.org stedwardconf.org/ Rev. Juan G. Herrera, Pst.; Dcn. Malcolm Colgate; CRP Stds.: 108

WHITINSVILLE

St. Patrick - 1 Cross St., Whitinsville, MA 01588; Mailing: 7 East St., P.O. Box 60, Whitinsville, MA 01588 t) 508-234-5656; 508-234-3511 (CRP) frtomasz@mystpatricks.com www.mystpatricks.com Rev. Tomasz J. Borkowski, Pst.; Dcn. Christopher R. Finan; Aileen Lemoine, DRE; CRP Stds.: 180

WINCHENDON

Immaculate Heart of Mary - 52 Spruce St., Winchendon, MA 01475 t) 508-297-0280 renee@heartofmary.net; pastor@heartofmary.net heartofmary.net Rev. Henry Ramirez, Admin.; Dcn. Mark J. Carrier; CRP Stds.: 20

WORCESTER

St. Paul Cathedral - 15 Chatham St., 15 Chatham St., Worcester, MA 01609; Mailing: 38 High St., Worcester, MA 01609 t) 508-799-4193; 508-755-1414 (CRP) cathedralofsaintpaul@gmail.com; rel.edu.stpaulcathedral@gmail.com www.cathedralofsaintpaul.net Rev. Juan Parra, Assoc. Pst.; Dcn. Francisco Escobar; Dcn. Colin Novick; Dcn. Anthony J. Xatse; CRP Stds.: 222

St. Andrew the Apostle - 5 Spaulding St., Worcester, MA 01603; Mailing: St. Peter Parish, 931 Main St., Worcester, MA 01610 t) 508-752-4674 stpeters_standrewsparishes@verizon.net Now a mission of St. Peter, Worcester. Rev. Msgr. Francis J. Scollen, Pst.;

Blessed Sacrament - 551 Pleasant St., Worcester, MA 01602 t) 508-755-5291 blessedsacrament@charter.net blessedsacrament.us Rev. Thomas Landry, Pst.; Rev. Andres A. Araque, In Res.; Joseph A. Marcotte, In Res.; CRP Stds.: 52

Christ the King - 1052 Pleasant St., Worcester, MA 01602 t) 508-754-5361 tsullivan5@mac.com ctkworc.org Rev. Msgr. Thomas J. Sullivan, Pst.; Rev. Richard F. Reidy, In Res.; Anne Thompson, DRE; CRP Stds.: 107

St. Christopher - 950 W. Boylston St., Worcester, MA 01606 t) 508-853-1492; 508-853-3302 (CRP) religioused@stchristopherparishworcester.org; parish@stchristopherparishworcester.org www.stchristopherworcester.org Rev. Stanley F. Krutcik, Pst.; Dcn. Van X. Nguyen; Kim Fitzpatrick, DRE; Clesson Dupuis, Bus. Mgr.; CRP Stds.: 14

St. George - 40 Brattle St., Worcester, MA 01606 t) 508-853-0183 office@saintgeorgesparish.org www.saintgeorgesparish.org Rev. Edward D. Niccolls, Pst.; Rev. Miguel Pagan, Assoc. Pst.; Dcn. Paul T. Audette; Sarah Kelly, DRE; CRP Stds.: 121

Holy Family Parish - 41 Hamilton St., Worcester, MA 01604; Mailing: 20 Hamilton St., Worcester, MA 01604 t) 508-754-6722 ndsj@holyfamilyparishworcester.org www.holyfamilyparishworcester.org Rev. Msgr. Robert K. Johnson, Pst.; Rev. Cleber de Paula, Assoc. Pst.; Dcn. Israel Fernandez; Dcn. Alex M. Garcia; Dcn. Franklin Lizardo; Dcn. Paul Reuter; Karla Rueter, DRE; Lucia Falco, Music Min.; CRP Stds.: 107

Immaculate Conception - 353 Grove St., Worcester, MA 01605 t) 508-754-8419 icworc@live.com www.icworc.com Rev. Edwin Montana, Admin.; Dcn. Kevin Deignan; Dcn. Frank B. Myska Jr.; CRP Stds.: 42

St. Joan of Arc - 570 Lincoln St., Worcester, MA 01605 t) 508-852-3232 stjoan570@hotmail.com mystjoanofarc.org Rev. Wilmar Ramos, Admin.; Dcn. Samuel Morrison; Sr. Ines Almeida, R.O.D.A., Pst. Assoc.; Sr. Andrea Avellaneda, O.D.L., Pst. Assoc.;

St. John's - 44 Temple St., Worcester, MA 01604 t) 508-756-7165 stjohnsworc@gmail.com www.stjohnsworcester.org Rev. John F. Madden, Pst.; Rev. Jean Robert Brice, Pst. Assoc.; Dcn. Eduardas Meilus; Dianne Gustowski, DRE; Donna Mastrovito, DRE; CRP Stds.: 93

Our Lady of Mt. Carmel and Our Lady of Loreto Parish - 37 Massasoit Rd., Worcester, MA 01604 t) 508-753-5001 lisaolmc@gmail.com www.mtcarmel.ws Rev. Msgr. F. Stephen Pedone, Pst.; Dcn. Gerald Montiverdi; Dcn. Donald Pegg; CRP Stds.: 31

Our Lady of Czestochowa - 34 Ward St., Worcester, MA 01610 t) 508-755-5959 rectory@olcworcester.com www.olcworcester.com Rev. Richard W. Polek, Pst.; Rev. Tomasz Gora, Assoc. Pst.; Rev. Edward Michalski, In Res.; CRP Stds.: 34

Our Lady of Lourdes (Roman Catholic Bishop of Worcester, Corporation Sole) - 1290 Grafton St., Worcester, MA 01604 t) 508-757-0789 ladyoflourdes1290@gmail.com ololma.org Rev. Brian P. O'Toole, Pst.; Rev. Francis J. Roach, In Res.; CRP Stds.: 16

Our Lady of Providence Parish - 228 Lincoln St., Worcester, MA 01605; Mailing: 236 Lincoln St., Worcester, MA 01605 t) 508-755-3820 religioused@olpworcester.org; parish@olpworcester.org www.olpworcester.org St. Bernard's Church Rev. Jonathan J. Slavinskas, Pst.; Dcn. Gilberto Javier-Almonte; Sr. Susi Miranda, DRE; CRP Stds.: 44

Our Lady of the Angels - 1222 Main St., Worcester, MA 01603 t) 508-791-0951 sallard@ourladyofangels.org; admin@ourladyofangels.org Rev. Mark Rainville, Pst.; Rev. Terrence Dougherty, O.C.D., In Res.; CRP Stds.: 40

Our Lady of the Angels School - (Grades PreK-8) 1220 Main St., Rear, Worcester, MA 01603 t) 508-752-5609 doreen.albert@ourladyoftheangels.us www.ourladyoftheangels.us Doreen J. Albert, Prin.;

Our Lady of the Rosary - 23 Fales St., Worcester, MA 01606 t) 508-853-1640; 508-852-5474 (CRP) olrparish1@gmail.com olr.weconnect.com Rev. Patrick J. Hawthorne, Pst.; Sr. Irene Moran, M.P.V., DRE; CRP Stds.: 48

Father Riley Center - Emerson Rd., Worcester, MA 01606

Our Lady of Vilna - 151 Sterling St., Worcester, MA 01610; Mailing: 153 Sterling St., Ste. 2, Worcester, MA 01610 t) 508-752-1825 chatambui@yahoo.com Rev. Peter Tam Bui, Pst.; Rev. Son Anh Nguyen, In Res.; Dcn. Quat Van Tran; CRP Stds.: 92

St. Peter - 931 Main St., Worcester, MA 01610; Mailing: 929 Main St., Worcester, MA 01610 t) 508-752-4674; 508-752-0797 (CRP) stpeters_standrewsparishes@verizon.net stpeters-standrews.com Rev. Msgr. Francis J. Scollen, Pst.; Dcn. Robert F. Dio; Dcn. George Estremera; Dcn. Peter Quy Nguyen; CRP Stds.: 185

St. Andrew the Apostle Mission - Spaulding St., Worcester, MA 01603

Sacred Heart of Jesus-St. Catherine of Sweden - 596 Cambridge St., Worcester, MA 01610 t) 508-752-1608 sacredheartstcatherines@gmail.com shscparish.com Rev. Eric K. Asante, Admin.; CRP Stds.: 12

St. Stephen's - 357 Grafton St., Worcester, MA 01604; Mailing: 20 Hamilton St, Worcester, MA 01604 t) 508-755-3165 ststephenchurch2@verizon.net www.ststephenworcester.org Rev. Msgr. Robert K. Johnson, Pst.; Dcn. Israel Fernandez; Dcn. Alex M. Garcia; Dcn. Franklin Lizardo; Dcn. Paul Rueter; Karla Rueter, DRE; Lucia Falco, Music Min.; CRP Stds.: 54

SCHOOLS: PRESCHOOL THRU HIGH SCHOOL

SCHOOLS

COMMONWEALTH OF MASSACHUSETTS

SOUTHBRIDGE

Trinity Catholic Academy - (PAR) (Grades PreK-8) 11 Pine St., Southbridge, MA 01550 t) 508-765-5991 angela.symock@tca11.com trinitycatholicacademy.org Angela Symock, Prin.; Stds.: 123; Lay Tchrs.: 11

UXBRIDGE

Our Lady of the Valley Regional School - (PAR) (Grades PreK-8) 75 Mendon St., Uxbridge, MA 01569 t) 508-278-5851 ed.reynolds@worcesterdiocesek12.org www.ourladyofthevalleyregional.com Edward M. Reynolds, Prin.; Stds.: 210; Lay Tchrs.: 15

WEBSTER

All Saints Academy of Webster, Massachussetts, Inc. - (PAR) (Grades PreK-8) 48 Negus St., Webster, MA 01570 t) 508-943-0257 headofschool@allsaintswebster.org allsaintswebster.org Joan E Matys, Prin.; Stds.: 202; Lay Tchrs.: 14

WORCESTER

St. Peter's Central Catholic Elementary School - (DIO) 865 Main St., Worcester, MA 01610 t) 508-791-6496 meg.kursonis@stpetercc.com www.stpetercentralcatholic.com Stds.: 350; Lay Tchrs.: 24

Venerini Academy - (PRV) (Grades PreK-8) 27 Edward St., Worcester, MA 01605 t) 508-753-3210 admin@veneriniacademy.com www.veneriniacademy.com Beth Chase, Prin.; Stds.: 240; Sr. Tchrs.: 1; Lay Tchrs.: 26

HIGH SCHOOLS

COMMONWEALTH OF MASSACHUSETTS

FITCHBURG

St. Bernard's High School, Inc. - (PRV) (Grades 9-12) 45 Harvard St., Fitchburg, MA 01420 t) 978-342-3212 landerson@stbernardshighschool.org stbernardshighschool.org Linda Anderson, Prin.; Stds.: 196; Lay Tchrs.: 19

LANCASTER

Trivium School - (PRV) (Grades 7-12) 471 Langen Rd., Lancaster, MA 01523; Mailing: P.O. Box 597, South Lancaster, MA 01561 t) 978-365-4795 office@triviumschool.com triviumschool.com William M. Schmitt, Headmaster; Stds.: 101; Bro. Tchrs.: 1; Lay Tchrs.: 5

SHREWSBURY

St. John's High School - (PRV) (Grades 7-12) 378 Main St., Shrewsbury, MA 01545 t) 508-842-8934 mgranados@stjohnshigh.org; azequeira@stjohnshigh.org www.stjohnshigh.org Xaverian Brothers Alex Zequeira, Headmaster; Margaret Granados, Prin.; David Curtis, Admin.; Jennifer Hanson, Librn.; Stds.: 937; Pr. Tchrs.: 1; Lay Tchrs.: 80

STILL RIVER

Immaculate Heart of Mary School - (PRV) (Grades 1-12) 282 Still River Rd., Still River, MA 01467; Mailing: P.O. Box 1000, Harvard, MA 01451 t) 978-456-8877 x202 smmarie@immaculateheartschool.org www.immaculateheartschool.org Slaves of the Immaculate Heart of Mary of St. Benedict Center, Inc. Bro. Thomas Augustine, M.I.C.M., Prin.; Stds.: 135; Bro. Tchrs.: 3; Sr. Tchrs.: 8

WORCESTER

Notre Dame Academy - (PRV) (Grades 7-12) 425 Salisbury St., Worcester, MA 01609 t) 508-757-6200 jobrien@nda-worc.org www.nda-worc.org A private day school for girls. Marilyn Tencza, Prin.; Stds.: 266; Lay Tchrs.: 30

St. Paul Diocesan Jr./Sr. High School - (DIO) (Grades 7-12) 144 Granite St., Worcester, MA 01604 t) 508-852-5555; 508-753-6371 mclark@saintpaulknights.org; mandrysick@saintpaulknights.org www.saintpaulknights.org Michael Clark, Headmaster; Stds.: 450; Lay Tchrs.: 30

INSTITUTIONS LOCATED IN DIOCESE

CAMPUS MINISTRY / NEWMAN CENTERS [CAM]

FITCHBURG

Fitchburg State College (Fitchburg) - 333 Mechanic St., Fitchburg, MA 01420 t) 978-342-7921 Rev. Anthony Mpagi, Chap.;

PAXTON

Anna Maria College - Office of Campus Ministry, 50 Sunset Ln., Paxton, MA 01612-1198 t) 508-849-3205 campusministry@annamaria.edu www.annamaria.edu Rev. David Cotter, Chap.; Dcn. John Franchi;

WORCESTER

Assumption University - 500 Salisbury St., Worcester, MA 01609 t) 508-767-7419 sbousquet@assumption.edu www.assumption.edu Bro. Hugo Ballesteros, A.A., Chap.; Scott Brill, Campus Min.; Bro. Daniele Caglioni, A.A., Campus Min.; Nicholas Coccoma, Campus Min.; Rachel Dean, Campus Min.; Daniel Payne, Campus Min.; Dcn. Paul F.X. Covino, Dir.;

Clark University - 930 Main St., Worcester, MA 01610 t) 508-793-7737 Rev. Msgr. Francis J. Scollen, Chap.;

Holy Cross College - 11 College St., Worcester, MA

01610; Mailing: P.O. Box 16A, Worcester, MA 01610 t) 508-793-2448 mkearns@holycross.edu Marybeth Kearns-Barrett, Dir.;
Worcester Polytechnic Institute - Religious Center at WPI, 19 Schussler Rd., Worcester, MA 01609 t) 508-981-9414 alejitcocano@gmail.com
Worcester State College - Campus Ministry Center, 17 Candlewood St., Worcester, MA 01602; Mailing: 1052 Pleasant St., Attn: Msgr. Sullivan, Worcester, MA 01602 t) 508-929-8017 Rev. Msgr. Thomas J. Sullivan, Chap.;

CATHOLIC CHARITIES [CCH]

WORCESTER
Catholic Charities - 10 Hammond St., Worcester, MA 01610-1513 t) 508-798-0191 smacmajor@ccworc.org www.ccworc.org Timothy McMahon, Dir.;
Blackstone Valley/Greater Milford Area Office - 200 Main St., Milford, MA 01757 t) 508-234-3800 Danishka Valdes, Admin.;
Blackstone Valley/Greater Milford Area Office - 126 Main St., Rm. 6, Milford, MA 01757 t) 508-478-9632 Noreen Landry, Admin.;
Crozier House - A Half-Way House for Substance Abusing Men. Scott Eaton, Admin.;
Family & Community Services - Marie Kudron, Admin.;
Homecare Program - 12 Riverbend St., Athol, MA 01331-2520 t) 978-249-4563 Heather MacDonald, Admin.;
Literacy, Citizenship & Immigration - Madelyn Hennessy, Admin.;
Mercy Centre (Developmental Disabilities) - 25 W. Chester St., Worcester, MA 01605-1136 t) 508-852-7165 Day Program and Employment Training for Adults with Developmental Disabilities. Margaret Buzzell, Admin.;
North County Area Office - 196 Mechanic St., Leominster, MA 01453 t) 978-840-0696 Maritza Cedeno, Admin.;
Senior Employment Service - Susan Maedler, Admin.;
Southbridge Area Office - 79 Elm St., Southbridge, MA 01550-2601 t) 508-765-5936 Marie Kudron, Admin.;
Youville House Shelter for Homeless Families - 4 Caroline, Worcester, MA 01604-4500 t) 508-753-3084 Gail Flynn, Admin.;
Pernet Family Health Service - 237 Millbury St., Worcester, MA 01610 t) 508-755-1228 sdooley@pernetfamilyhealth.org pernetfamilyhealth.org Mission of the Little Sisters of the Assumption. Sheilah Dooley, Exec.; Asstd. Annu.: 8,553; Staff: 26

CEMETERIES [CEM]

WORCESTER
St. John's Cemetery - 260 Cambridge St., Worcester, MA 01603 t) 508-757-7415 michelem@stjcemetery.com; jamesb@stjcemetery.com worcesterdiocese.org/st-john-cemetery James F. Brasco, Dir.;
Saint Anne Cemetery - Arnold Rd., Sturbridge, MA 01518
Saint Brigid Cemetery - West St., Millbury, MA 01527
Calvary Cemetery - 191 Vine St., Athol, MA 01331
Calvary Cemetery - Oxford Ave., Dudley, MA 01571 t) (508) 757-7415
Saint George Cemetery - Paige Hill, Southbridge, MA 01550
Gethsemane Cemetery - Fielding Way, Athol, MA 01331
Saint Mary Cemetery - Main St., Holden, MA 01520 rackerman@stjcemetery.com
New Notre Dame Cemetery - Woodstock Rd., Southbridge, MA 01550 t) (508) 757-7415
Notre Dame Cemetery - 162 Webster St., Worcester, MA 01603 t) 508-753-7692
Old Notre Dame Cemetery - Charlton St., Southbridge, MA 01550
Saint Philip Cemetery - Millbury St., Grafton, MA 01519
Sacred Heart Cemetery - Worcester Rd., Webster, MA 01570
Sacred Heart Cemetery - W. Main St., West Brookfield, MA 01585

COLLEGES & UNIVERSITIES [COL]

PAXTON
Anna Maria College - 50 Sunset Ln., Paxton, MA 01612 t) 508-849-3300 toliver@annamaria.edu www.annamaria.edu A Coed Catholic College. Sisters of St. Anne. Barbara Zawalich, Registrar; Mary Lou Retelle, Pres.; Tricia Oliver, Dir.; Jan Wilbur, Librn.;
WORCESTER
Assumption University - 500 Salisbury St., Worcester, MA 01609 t) 508-767-7321 presoffice@assumption.edu www.assumption.edu Liberal arts institution sponsored by the Augustinians of the Assumption. Dr. Francesco C. Cesareo, Pres.; Dr. Deborah Cady Melzer, Vice Pres., Student Affairs; Dr. Conway Campbell, Vice Pres., Student Success; Rev. Richard E. Lamoureux, A.A, Vice Pres., Mission; Dr. Gregory Weiner, Vice Pres., Acad. Affairs & Provost; Peter Wells, Vice Pres., Fin. & Admin.;
College of the Holy Cross, Inc. - 1 College St., Office of Communications, Worcester, MA 01610 t) 508-793-2011 rblackwe@holycross.edu www.holycross.edu Rev. Philip L. Boroughs, S.J., Pres.; Karen Reilly, Dir.;

CONVENTS, MONASTERIES, AND RESIDENCES FOR WOMEN [CON]

CHARLTON
Carmelite Sisters of the Eucharist of Worcester, MA - 188 Old Worcester Rd., Charlton, MA 01507 t) 508-248-2936 sisteragnespatricia@yahoo.com Sr. Mary Ann Bartell, C.S.E., Admin.;
LEOMINSTER
The Sisters of the Presentation of the Blessed Virgin Mary, New Windsor, NY - 99 Church St., Leominster, MA 01453 t) 978-537-7108 pbvmadministration@hvc.rr.com www.sistersofthepresentation.org Sr. Mary Anne Seliga, P.B.V.M., Admin.; Sr. Patricia Anastasio, P.B.V.M., Pres.;
Sisters of the Presentation of the B.V. Mary -
NORTHBORO
Xaverian Missionary Society of Mary, Inc. - 266 Main St., Northboro, MA 01532-1626 t) 508-757-0514 xaverian.missionaries.us@gmail.com saveriane.it/en/ Sr. Laura Canali, Supr.; Srs.: 206
PETERSHAM
St. Scholastica Priory - 271 N. Main St., Petersham, MA 01366-9503; Mailing: P.O. Box 606, Petersham, MA 01366-0606 t) 978-724-3213; 978-724-3217 sspriory@aol.com www.stscholasticapriory.org Benedictine Nuns (Cloistered). Mother Mary Elizabeth Kloss, O.S.B., Prioress; Sr. Mary Angela Kloss, O.S.B., Sub Prioress; Srs.: 12
STILL RIVER
Sisters of Saint Benedict Center, Slaves of the Immaculate Heart of Mary Inc. - 254 Still River Rd., Still River, MA 01467; Mailing: P.O. Box 22, Still River, MA 01467 t) 978-456-8017 micm@verizon.net Sr. Cecilia Cannon, Prioress;
WEBSTER
St. Joseph Convent - 5 Maynard St., Webster, MA 01570-2425 t) 508-943-2228 cssfwebster@feliciansisters.org www.feliciansistersna.org Srs.: 2
WORCESTER
Little Franciscans of Mary - 12 Jones St., Apt. 1, Worcester, MA 01604 t) 508-755-0878 Sr. Adrienne Lamoureux, P.F.M., Treas.;
Little Sisters of the Assumption, Pernet Family Health Service, Inc. - 137 Endicott St., Worcester, MA 01610 t) 914-299-3036 jeanmccorm1@littlesisters.org www.pernetfamilyhealth.org Home-based nursing and family health agency. Sr. Jean McCormick, Contact;
Religious Oblates to Divine Love - 50 Moore Ave., Worcester, MA 01602-1820 Sr. Rosita Campos, R.O.D.A., Supr.;
Religious Venerini Sisters - 23 Edward St., Worcester, MA 01605 t) 508-754-1020 www.religiousvenerinisisters.org Sr. Carmen Capriole, Prov.; Srs.: 11
Sisters of St. Joseph, S.S.J. - 101 Chadwick St., D22, Worcester, MA 01605 t) 508-852-1659

ENDOWMENTS / FOUNDATIONS / TRUSTS [EFT]

WORCESTER
Monsignor Thomas Griffin Foundation - 49 Elm St., Worcester, MA 01609 t) 508-929-4339 pschasel@worcesterdiocese.org Paul G. Schasel, Contact;

HOSPITALS / HEALTH SERVICES [HOS]

WHITINSVILLE
St. Camillus Nursing Home Inc. - 447 Hill St., Whitinsville, MA 01588 t) 508-234-7306 William Graves, Admin.; Bro. Thomas Farrell, O.S.Cam., Dir.;
WORCESTER
Notre Dame Health Care Center, Inc. - 559 Plantation St., Worcester, MA 01605 t) 508-852-3011 klaganelli@notredamehealthcare.org www.notredamehealthcare.org Karen Laganelli, CEO;

MISCELLANEOUS [MIS]

AUBURN
Kateri Tekakwitha Development, Inc. - 8 Wyoma Dr., Auburn, MA 01501 t) 508-798-8779 namartyrs01501@gmail.com
Kateri Tekakwitha Housing Corp. - 8 Wyoma Dr., Auburn, MA 01501 t) 508-798-8779
LANCASTER
Community of St. John - 465 Langen Rd., Lancaster, MA 01523 t) 978-368-8291 wschmitt@triviumschool.com William M. Schmitt, Contact;
PETERSHAM
St. Mary and St. Scholastica Church, Inc. - 271 N. Main St., Petersham, MA 01366-0606; Mailing: P.O. Box 606, Petersham, MA 01366-0606 t) 978-724-3213; 978-724-3350 srgemmameade@gmail.com; vincent@stmarysmonastery.org Rev. Gregory Phillips, O.S.B., Pres.; Mother Mary Elizabeth Kloss, O.S.B., Vice. Pres.;
WHITINSVILLE
St. Camillus Institute, Inc. - 497 Hill St., Whitinsville, MA 01588 t) 508-266-1045 Order of the Servants of the Sick (St. Camillus).
WORCESTER
Catholic Restoration Apostolate - 123 Summer St., Worcester, MA 01608 t) 508-363-5545 peterbeaulieu@verizon.net Rev. Msgr. Peter R. Beaulieu, Chap.;
The Charlton Charitable Corporation, Inc. - 49 Elm St., Worcester, MA 01609 t) 508-791-7171
Dismas House of Massachusetts - ; Mailing: P.O. Box 30125, Worcester, MA 01603 t) 508-799-9389 cmdismashouse@aol.com www.dismashouse.org Transitional services for those leaving prison. Colleen Hilferty, Dir.; David McMahon, Dir.;
The Guild of Our Lady of Providence - 49 Elm St., Worcester, MA 01609 t) 508-791-7171
Mendon Charitable Corporation, Inc. - 49 Elm St., Worcester, MA 01609 t) 508-791-7171 pschasel@worcesterdiocese.org
Visitation House - 119 Endicott St., Worcester, MA 01606; Mailing: P.O. Box 60115, Worcester, MA 01606 t) 508-798-0762 evelindquist@visitationhouse.org Transitional home for homeless pregnant women in crisis. Eve Lindquist, Exec.;

MONASTERIES AND RESIDENCES FOR PRIESTS AND BROTHERS [MON]

PETERSHAM
St. Mary's Monastery - 271 N. Main St., Petersham, MA

01366; Mailing: P.O. Box 345, Petersham, MA 01366 t) 978-724-3350 monks@stmarysmonastery.org www.stmarysmonastery.org Rev. Gregory Phillips, O.S.B., Supr.;

SHREWSBURY

Xaverian Brothers - 378 Main St., Shrewsbury, MA 01545 t) 508-845-1878 pfeeney@stjohnshigh.org Bro. William Cushing, CFX, Mem.; Bro. Paul Feeney, C.F.X., Mem.; Brs.: 2

SPENCER

St. Joseph's Abbey (Cistercian Abbey of Spencer, Inc., Cistercian Order of the Strict Observance (Trappists)) - St Joseph's Abbey, 167 N. Spencer Rd., Spencer, MA 01562-1233 t) 508-885-8700 monks@spencerabbey.org www.spencerabbey.org Rt. Rev. Vincent Rogers, Abbot; Rev. Dominic Whedbee, O.C.S.O., Prior; Rev. Damian Carr, O.C.S.O., Abbot Emeritus; Rev. Gabriel Bertoniere, O.C.S.O.; Rev. William Dingwall, O.C.S.O.; Rev. Aquinas Keane, O.C.S.O.; Rev. Isaac Keeley, O.C.S.O.; Rev. Eugene Lacasse, O.C.S.O.; Rev. Simeon Leiva-Merikakis, O.C.S.O.; Rev. Aidan (Arthur H.) Logan, O.C.S.O.; Rev. Francis Rodriguez, O.C.S.O.; Rev. Peter Schmidt, O.C.S.O.; Rev. Timothy Scott, O.C.S.O.; Rev. James Palmigiano, O.C.S.O., Vocations Dir.; Rev. Luke Truhan, O.C.S.O., Novice Dir.; Rev. Emmanuel Morinelli, O.C.S.O., Music Dir.; Rev. Kevin Hunt, O.C.S.O., Chap.; Rev. David Lavich, O.C.S.O., Chap.;

STILL RIVER

Benedictine Monks, St. Benedict Abbey - 252 Still River Rd., Still River, MA 01467; Mailing: P O Box 67, Still River, MA 01467 t) 978-456-3221 abbey@abbey.org; frjamesosb@outlook.com www.abbey.org (Harvard) Rt. Rev. Marc Crilly, O.S.B., Abbot; Rev. James Doran, O.S.B., Prior; Rev. Peter Connelly, O.S.B.; Rev. Anthony Kloss, O.S.B.; Rev. Augustine Senz, O.S.B.; Brs.: 3; Priests: 5

WORCESTER

Assumptionists (Augustinians of the Assumption) - 50 Old English Rd., Worcester, MA 01609 t) 508-754-6276 vtgdinh@gmail.com www.assumption.us Rev. Dihn Vo Tran Gia, AA, Supr.; Bro. Richard Gagnon, A.A., Treas.; Rev. Aidan M. Furlong, A.A., Mem.; Bro. Paul Henry, A.A., Mem.; Rev. Donat R. Lamothe, A.A., Mem.; Rev. Norman Meiklejohn, A.A., Mem.; Brs.: 2; Priests: 4

Augustinians of the Assumption at Assumption University - Emmanuel House, 512 Salisbury St., Worcester, MA 01609-1326 t) 508-767-7523 rcorrive@assumption.edu www.assumption.us Assumption College in now Assumption University Rev. Roger R. Corriveau, A.A., Supr.; Rev. Richard E. Lamoureux, A.A, Vice. Pres.; Rev. Ai Nguyen Chi, AA, Prof.; Bro. Daniele Caglioni, A.A., Campus Min.; Bro. Ryan Carlsen, A.A., Mem.; Rev. Michel Mbusa Kalumba, AA, Mem.; Rev. Pacifique Kambale Tsongo, AA, Mem.; Brs.: 2; Priests: 5

Jesuits of the Holy Cross, Inc. - 1 College St., Worcester, MA 01610 t) 508-793-2427 ciampi@holycross.edu www.holycross.edu/index.html Rev. Thomas D. McMurray, S.J., Chap.; Rev. Philip L. Boroughs, S.J.; Rev. William F. Campbell, S.J.; Rev. William A. Clark, S.J.; Rev. Michael F. Ford, S.J.; Rev. John F. Gavin, S.J.; Rev. Paul F. Harman, S.J.; Rev. James M. Hayes, S.J.; Rev. Vincent A. Lapomarda, S.J.; Rev. Earle L. Markey, S.J.; Rev. Janez Percic, S.J.; Rev. John P. Reboli, S.J.; Rev. William E. Reiser, S.J.; Rev. Michael J. Rogers, S.J.; Rev. Kevin Spinale, S.J.; Rev. William E. Stempsey, S.J.; Rev. James R. Stormes, S.J.; Rev. Edward J. Vodoklys, S.J.;

NURSING / REHABILITATION / CONVALESCENCE / ELDERLY CARE [NUR]

LEOMINSTER

Presentation Health Care Center - 99 Church St., Leominster, MA 01453-3147 t) 978-537-7856 srmaureenrn@verizon.net Rest home for aged and/or infirmed sisters at Presentation Convent. Sr. Patricia Anastasio, P.B.V.M., Pres.;

SPENCER

St. Joseph's Abbey Resident Care Facility, Inc. - 167 N. Spencer Rd., Spencer, MA 01562-1233 t) 508-885-8702 aelredmarrah@yahoo.com www.spencerabbey.org Bro. Aelred Marrah, O.C.S.O., Admin.; Asstd. Annu.: 15; Staff: 19

WORCESTER

Notre Dame du Lac - 555 Plantation St., Worcester, MA 01605 t) 508-852-5800 klaganelli@notredamehealthcare.org www.notredamehealthcare.org Karen Laganelli, Exec.;

PRESCHOOLS / CHILDCARE CENTERS [PRE]

WORCESTER

The Guild of St. Agnes - 405 Grove St., Worcester, MA 01605 t) 508-755-2238 swood016@aol.com www.guildofstagnes.org Family day care program for infants, toddlers, preschoolers & school-age children aged 4 weeks-12 years. Edward Madaus, Exec.;

Guild of St. Agnes - 19 Harvard St., Worcester, MA 01609 t) 508-755-2238 emadaus@aol.com www.guildofstagnes.org Edward Madaus, CEO;

RETREAT HOUSES / RENEWAL CENTERS [RTR]

SPENCER

St. Joseph Abbey - 167 N. Spencer Rd., Spencer, MA 01562-1233 t) 508-885-8710 retreats@spencerabbey.org www.spencerabbey.org Guest & retreat house. Rev. Emmanuel Morinelli, O.C.S.O.;

Mary House, Inc. - 186 N. Spencer Rd. (Rte. 31), Spencer, MA 01562; Mailing: P.O. Box 20, Spencer, MA 01562 t) 508-885-5450 maryhousespencer@netzero.com maryhousespencer.com House of prayer and contemplation. Joyce Thomasmeyer, Pres.;

STILL RIVER

Benedictine Monks, St. Benedict Abbey - 252 Still River Rd., Still River, MA 01467 t) 978-456-3221 www.abbey.org (See separate listing under Monasteries and Residences for Priests and Brothers). Rt. Rev. Marc Crilly, O.S.B., Abbot; Rev. James Doran, O.S.B., Prior;

SPECIAL CARE FACILITIES [SPF]

CHARLTON

Ministry to Retired Priests - 188 Old Worcester Rd., Charlton, MA 01507 t) 508-868-9239 Sr. Mary Ann Bartell, C.S.E., Dir.;

An asterisk (*) denotes an organization that has established tax-exempt status directly with the IRS and is not covered by the USCCB Group Ruling.

Diocese of Yakima

(Dioecesis Yakimensis)

MOST REVEREND JOSEPH J. TYSON

Bishop of Yakima; ordained June 10, 1989; appointed Auxiliary Bishop of Seattle and Titular Bishop of Migirpa May 12, 2005; ordained June 6, 2005; appointed Bishop of Yakima April 12, 2011; installed May 31, 2011.

Pastoral Office (Chancery): 101 S. 12th Ave., Yakima, WA 98902. T: 509-965-7117; F: 509-966-8334. info@yakimadiocese.net

ESTABLISHED JUNE 23, 1951.

Square Miles 17,787.

Comprises the following Counties in the State of Washington: Benton, Chelan, Douglas, Grant, Kittitas, Klickitat and Yakima.

Legal Title: Corporation of the Catholic Bishop of Yakima.

For legal titles of parishes and diocesan institutions, consult the Pastoral Office.

STATISTICAL OVERVIEW

Personnel

Bishop	1
Retired Bishops	1
Priests: Diocesan Active in Diocese	48
Priests: Diocesan Active Outside Diocese	1
Priests: Retired, Sick or Absent	20
Number of Diocesan Priests	69
Religious Priests in Diocese	1
Total Priests in your Diocese	70
Extern Priests in Diocese	1
Ordinations:	
Diocesan Priests	1
Permanent Deacons	1
Permanent Deacons in Diocese	46
Total Sisters	18

Parishes

Parishes	39
With Resident Pastor:	
Resident Diocesan Priests	39
Missions	3

Professional Ministry Personnel:	
Sisters	2
Lay Ministers	4

Welfare

Homes for the Aged	1
Total Assisted	47
Day Care Centers	1
Total Assisted	188
Special Centers for Social Services	4
Total Assisted	56,452

Educational

Diocesan Students in Other Seminaries	6
Total Seminarians	6
High Schools, Private	1
Total Students	225
Elementary Schools, Diocesan and Parish	6
Total Students	1,569
Catechesis/Religious Education:	
High School Students	2,505
Elementary Students	3,294
Total Students under Catholic Instruction	7,599
Teachers in Diocese:	
Sisters	3
Lay Teachers	145

Vital Statistics

Receptions into the Church:	
Infant Baptism Totals	2,147
Minor Baptism Totals	258
Adult Baptism Totals	83
Received into Full Communion	265
First Communions	1,478
Confirmations	1,492
Marriages:	
Catholic	291
Interfaith	26
Total Marriages	317
Deaths	517
Total Catholic Population	176,126
Total Population	751,808

LEADERSHIP

Pastoral Office (Chancery) - t) 509-965-7117 info@yakimadiocese.net
Vicar General - Rev. Msgr. John A. Ecker;
Episcopal Vicar - Rev. Msgr. Robert M. Siler;
Vicar for Priests - Very Rev. Felipe Pulido;
Moderator of the Curia - Rev. Msgr. Robert M. Siler;
Chancellor - Rev. Msgr. Robert M. Siler;
Vice Chancellor for Personnel & Policies - Diana E. Aparicio-Sosa;
Office of Canonical Concerns - t) 509-965-7123
Adjutant Judicial Vicar - Rev. David J. Jimenez Alvarez;
Advocates -
Defenders of the Bond - Rev. Msgr. Thomas C. Champoux; Rev. Salomon Covarrubias Pina; Very Rev. Michael Brzezowski;
Judges - Very Rev. Michael J. Ibach; Very Rev. Michael E. Brzezowski; Very Rev. Jose De Jesus Mariscal;
Judicial Vicar - Very Rev. Michael J. Ibach, Vicar;
Notaries - M. Guadalupe Flores; Eileen M. Walker;
Diocesan Consultors - Very Rev. Osmar R. Aguirre (oaguirre@stjoewen.org); Very Rev. Jaime H. Chacon; Rev. Msgr. John A. Ecker;

OFFICES AND DIRECTORS

Adults with Developmental Disabilities - t) 509-965-4642 Michele Wall;
Calvary Cemetery - t) 509-457-8462 Rev. Darell J. Mitchell;
Campaign for Human Development - Darlene Darnell;
Catholic Charities - t) 509-965-7100 Darlene Darnell, Pres.;
Charismatic Renewal, English -
Charismatic Renewal, Spanish - Very Rev. Jaime H. Chacon;
Cornerstone Ministry - Dcn. Mikhail Alnajjar (dmikhail925@gmail.com);
Cursillo, English - t) 509-946-2264 Dcn. Dan Sisk, Dir.; Dcn. Kerry Turley, Spiritual Dir.;
Spanish - Dcn. Frank Martinez, Dir.; Teodoro Flores, Dir.;
CYO - t) 509-965-3382 Don Erickson;
Development Office/Stewardship - t) 509-965-7117 Alma Benitez, Dir.;
Diocesan Catholic Committee on Scouting - Dcn. William A. Dronen, Chap.;
Director of Planned Giving - t) 509-965-7117 Alma Benitez;
Ecumenical Liaison - t) 509-575-3713 Rev. Msgr. John A. Ecker;
Engaged Encounter - t) 509-627-1076 Frank Becker; Tracy Becker;
Registration Coordinators - Paul Ackerman; Pegi Ackerman;
Home Schooling - Dcn. Duane Berger, Chap.; Jonella Leadon;
Marriage Encounter - Rev. Salomon Covarrubias Pina;
English Coordinators - Frank Becker; Tracy Becker;
Registration Coordinators - Paul Ackerman; Pegi Ackerman;
Spanish Coordinators - Benjamin Reyes; Maria Reyes;
Ministry & Education Center -
Deacon Council - Dcn. Indalecio Gonzalez; Dcn. William Mich; Dcn. Robert J. Schrom;
Deacon Formation - Very Rev. Osmar R. Aguirre; Dcn. Robert J. Schrom, Assoc. Dir.;
Hispanic Ministries/Hispanic Ministry Formation Director - Very Rev. Jaime H. Chacon, Vicar;
Permanent Diaconate Liaison with Bishop Joseph Tyson - t) 509-346-9464 Dcn. Robert J. Schrom;
Religious Education and Hispanic Catechesis - Very Rev. Jaime H. Chacon;
Youth/Young Adult Director - Marcus Ayers;
Youth/Young Adult Hispanic Ministry - Rev. Jose M. Herrera;
Native American Ministries -
Presbyteral Council Executive Committee - Most Rev. Joseph J. Tyson; Rev. Msgr. John A. Ecker; Rev. Msgr. Robert M. Siler;
Press (Central Washington Catholic) - Rev. Msgr. Robert M. Siler;
St. Joseph Mission at the Ahtanum - t) 509-965-7117 Valeria Flores, Administrative Asst. (valeria.flores@yakimadiocese.net);
St. Vincent de Paul Society - t) 509-946-1675 Rev. Msgr. Thomas C. Champoux, Dir.;
Serra Club - t) 509-452-6907 Dcn. Timmothy Wauzynski; Dick Krema;
Victim Assistance Coordinator - t) 888-276-4490 Leanne Labissoniere;
Vocations - Very Rev. Felipe Pulido;

PARISHES, MISSIONS, AND CLERGY

STATE OF WASHINGTON

BENTON CITY

St. Frances Xavier Cabrini - 1000 Horne Dr., Benton City, WA 99320; Mailing: P.O. Box 179, Benton City, WA 99320 t) 509-588-3636 stfrancisxbc@yakimadiocese.org Rev. Msgr. Thomas C. Champoux, Admin.; Rev. Juan Manuel Flores, Pst.; Rev. John C. Vogl, Assoc. Pst.; Dcn. German Gonzalez; Dcn. Jose Luis Ochoa; CRP Stds.: 75

CHELAN

St. Anne's - 1910 Tacoma Ave., Chelan, WA 98816-1089 t) 509-682-2433 chelanchurch@gmail.com Rev. David J. Jimenez Alvarez, Pst.;

St. Francis de Sales - 315 N. Cedar St., Chelan, WA 98816; Mailing: 215 W. Allen Ave., Chelan, WA 98816-9622 t) 509-682-2433 chelanoffice@gmail.com www.saintfrancischelan.org/ Rev. David J. Jimenez Alvarez, Pst.; CRP Stds.: 20

St. Mary - Mansfield Blvd. & 2nd, Mansfield, WA 98830

CLE ELUM

St. John the Baptist - 303 W. 2nd St., Cle Elum, WA 98922; Mailing: P.O. Box 630, Cle Elum, WA 98922-0630 t) 509-674-2531 icsjbparishes.org Rev. Francisco Higuera, Pst.; Dcn. James Joseph Johnson; CRP Stds.: 22

COWICHE

St. Juan Diego - 15800 Summitview Rd., Cowiche, WA 98923 t) 509-678-4164 stjuandiego@yakimadiocese.org (Formerly known as St. Peter the Apostle). Very Rev. Brooks F. Beaulaurier, Pst.; Sr. Blanca Brizeida Jimenez-Espino, DRE; CRP Stds.: 121

EAST WENATCHEE

Holy Apostles - 1315 8th St., N.E., East Wenatchee, WA 98802 t) 509-884-5444 Very Rev. Argemiro Orozco, Pst.; Rev. Seamus Kerr, Assoc. Pst.; Dcn. John Blackburn; Dcn. Jorge Calderilla; Dcn. Thomas Richtsmeier; CRP Stds.: 287

St. Joseph Parish - 101 Poplar St., Waterville, WA 98858 t) 509-745-8205 janetchapin@hotmail.com

ELLENSBURG

St. Andrew's - 401 S. Willow St., Ellensburg, WA 98926 t) 509-962-9819 standrewparish@yahoo.com; standrewparishre@yahoo.com st-andrewsparish.org/ Very Rev. Alejandro Trejo-Estrada, Pst.; CRP Stds.: 156

EPHRATA

St. Rose of Lima - 323 D St., S.W., Ephrata, WA 98823; Mailing: 560 Nat Washington Way, Ephrata, WA 98823 t) 509-754-3640 strose@nwi.net; strosesecretary@nwi.net Rev. Jose M. Herrera, Pst.; CRP Stds.: 134

St. Rose of Lima School - (Grades PreK-6) 520 Nat Washington Way, Ephrata, WA 98823 t) 509-754-4901 info@saintroseschool.org Stefanie Bafus, Prin.; Stephanie Moore, Librn.; Stds.: 125; Lay Tchrs.: 6

GOLDENDALE

Holy Trinity - 210 S. Schuster St., Goldendale, WA 98620 t) 509-773-4516 Rev. William Byron, Pst.; CRP Stds.: 33

GRAND COULEE

St. Henry's - 590 W. Grand Coulee Ave., Grand Coulee, WA 99133; Mailing: PO Box 519, Waterville, WA 98858 t) 509-745-8205 st.josephinfo@icloud.com; stjosephinfo@icloud.com Rev. Teodulo G. Taneo, Pst.;

Holy Angels - McEntee & Douglas Sts., Coulee City, WA 99133

GRANDVIEW

Blessed Sacrament - 1201 Missouri, Grandview, WA 98930 t) 509-882-1657; 509-882-1721 (CRP) blessedsacrament@yakimadiocese.org; blsreligioused@gmail.com www.blessedsacramentgrandview.org Rev. Jesus Alatorre, Pst.; CRP Stds.: 210

GRANGER

Our Lady of Guadalupe - 608 Granger Ave., Granger, WA 98932; Mailing: P.O. Box 308, Granger, WA 98932 t) 509-854-2164 (CRP); 509-854-1181 ourladyofguadalupeparish1966@gmail.com Rev. Tomas Vidal, Pst.;

KENNEWICK

Holy Spirit - 7409 W. Clearwater, Kennewick, WA 99336; Mailing: 7411 W. Clearwater Ave., Ste. A, Kennewick, WA 99336 t) 509-735-8558; 509-735-8559 (CRP) office@holyspiritkennewick.org; pat@holyspiritkennewick.org www.holyspiritkennewick.org Very Rev. Michael Brzezowski, Pst.; Rev. Msgr. Perron J. Auve, In Res.; Rev. John G. O'Shea, In Res.; Dcn. Ken Ellis; Dcn. Mike Gaulke; Dcn. Eric Shaber; Pat Moore, DRE; CRP Stds.: 145

St Joseph Parish - 520 S. Garfield St., Kennewick, WA 99336 t) 509-586-3820 parish.office@stjoseph-kennewick.org; pastor@stjoseph-kennewick.org stjoseph-kennewick.org/ Very Rev. Felipe Pulido, Pst.; Very Rev. Cesar Izquierdo, Par. Vicar; Very Rev. Lawrence Reilly, In Res.; Rev. Ricardo Keolker, In Res.; Dcn. Herman Farias; Dcn. Juan Garcia; Dcn. William Mich; Dcn. Edilberto Sanchez; Dcn. Gustavo Valdivia; CRP Stds.: 467

St. Joseph's School - (Grades PreK-8) 901 W. 4th Ave., Kennewick, WA 99336 t) 509-586-0481 pkelly@sjske.org; secretary@sjske.org www.sjske.org Perry Kelly, Prin.; Stds.: 306; Lay Tchrs.: 18

MABTON

Immaculate Conception - 4th & Adams, Mabton, WA 98935; Mailing: P.O. Box 275, Mabton, WA 98935 t) 509-882-1657; 509-854-1181 (CRP) Rev. Tomas Vidal, Pst.; CRP Stds.: 95

MATTAWA

Our Lady of the Desert - 301 8th St., Mattawa, WA 99349; Mailing: PO Box 1185, Mattawa, WA 99349 t) 509-932-5424 ourladyofthedesertparish.org Rev. Lalo Barragan, Pst.; CRP Stds.: 245

MOSES LAKE

Our Lady of Fatima - 200 N. Dale Rd., Moses Lake, WA 98837 t) 509-765-6729 Rev. Dan Dufner, Pst.; Rev. Edwin Lozada, Pst.; Dcn. Armando Escamilla; Dcn. Mark Krcma; CRP Stds.: 123

Parish Center - 210 N. Dale Rd., Moses Lake, WA 98837 administrator@olf.church

Queen of All Saints - c/o 200 N. Dale Rd., Moses Lake, WA 98837 t) 509-346-2730 Rev. Jorge Granados, Assoc. Pst.; Dcn. George Legg; Dcn. Robert J. Schrom; CRP Stds.: 145

MOXEE

Holy Rosary - 201 N. Iler, Moxee, WA 98936; Mailing: P O Box 279, Moxee, WA 98936 t) 509-453-4061 holyrosary29@gmail.com www.holyrosarymoxee.org Very Rev. Jaime H. Chacon, Pst.; CRP Stds.: 190

NACHES

St. John - 206 Moxee Ave., Naches, WA 98937; Mailing: P.O. Box 128, Naches, WA 98937-0128 t) 509-653-2534 Very Rev. Brooks F. Beaulaurier, Pst.; CRP Stds.: 9

PESHASTIN

Our Lady of the Assumption Parish - 9500 Jeske Rd., Peshastin, WA 98847 t) 509-548-5119 olassumption@nwi.net Dcn. William A. Dronen; Very Rev. Miguel Gonzalez, Pst.; Dcn. Jorge Calderilla; CRP Stds.: 123

PROSSER

Sacred Heart - 1905 Highland Dr., Prosser, WA 99350 t) 509-786-1783 sacredheart1905@gmail.com www.prossersacredheart.com/ Rev. Francisco Gutierrez, Pst.; Dcn. Terry Wentz; CRP Stds.: 205

QUINCY

St. Pius X - 805 N. Central Ave., Quincy, WA 98848; Mailing: P.O. Box 308, Quincy, WA 98848 t) 509-787-2622 stpiusxquincy.com Rev. Gerardo Cisneros, Admin.; Ana Espinoza, DRE; Debbie Graaff, DRE; CRP Stds.: 304

RICHLAND

Christ the King - 1111 Stevens Dr., Richland, WA 99354 t) 509-946-1675; 509-946-1154 (CRP) bulletin@ckparish.org www.ckparish.org Rev. Msgr. Thomas C. Champoux, Pst.; Rev. Edgar Quiroga Ceballos, Par. Vicar; Rev. Juan Flores, Par. Vicar; Rev. Vandennis Nguyen, In Res.; Dcn. Doroteo Collado; Dcn. Alfredo Jocson; Dcn. Ross Ronish; Carrie Fetto, DRE; CRP Stds.: 382

Christ the King Catholic School - (Grades PreK-8) 1122 Long Ave., Richland, WA 99354 t) 509-946-6158 kpeugh@ckschool.net www.ckschoolrichland.org Kris Peugh, Prin.; Stds.: 476; Lay Tchrs.: 26

ROSLYN

Immaculate Conception - 211 N. B St., Roslyn, WA 98941; Mailing: P.O. Box 630, Cle Elum, WA 98922-0630 t) 509-674-2531 www.icsjbparishes.org Very Rev. Francisco Higuera, Pst.; Dcn. James Joseph Johnson; CRP Stds.: 7

ROYAL CITY

St. Michael the Archangel - 145 Daisy St., N.W., Royal City, WA 99357; Mailing: P.O. Box 340, Royal City, WA 99357 t) 509-346-2730; 509-346-2236 (CRP) Rev. Jorge Granados, Pst.; Dcn. Robert J. Schrom; CRP Stds.: 153

SELAH

Our Lady of Lourdes - 1107 W. Fremont Ave., Selah, WA 98942 t) 509-697-4633 Rev. Richard D. Sedlacek, Pst.; CRP Stds.: 95

SUNNYSIDE

St Joseph Parish Sunnyside - 907 S. 6th St., Sunnyside, WA 98944 t) 509-837-2243 www.saintjosephsunnyside.org Rev. Rogelio Gutierrez, Pst.; Dcn. Kerry Turley; CRP Stds.: 304

TOPPENISH

St. Aloysius - 213 N. Beech St., Toppenish, WA 98948 t) 508-865-4725; 509-865-4725 (CRP) st.aloysius47@gmail.com Rev. Felix Rodriguez, Pst.; Dcn. Peter Fadich; CRP Stds.: 235

Religious Education Center - 214 N. Beech St., Toppenish, WA 98948

WAPATO

St. Peter Claver - 509 S. Satus Ave., Wapato, WA 98951 t) 509-877-2813 drestpclaver@gmail.com; stpclaver@gmail.com stpeterclaver.blogspot.com/ Rev. Roleto Amoy, Pst.; Dcn. Genaro Ramos; Leticia Rios, DRE; CRP Stds.: 139

WATERVILLE

St. Joseph's - 101 E. Poplar St., Waterville, WA 98858; Mailing: P.O. Box 519, Waterville, WA 98858 t) 509-745-8205 teody_0423@yahoo.com Rev. Teodulo G. Taneo, Pst.;

WENATCHEE

St. Joseph's - 625 S. Elliott St., Wenatchee, WA 98801 t) 509-662-4569 stjosephwen.org Very Rev. Osmar R. Aguirre, Pst.; Rev. Eduardo Chavez, Pst.; Dcn. Gregory Haberman; Dcn. Robert Hulligan II; Dcn. Robert Turner; Dcn. Carlos Luna; Dcn. Gene Ockinga; CRP Stds.: 377

St. Joseph's School - (Grades PreK-5) 600 St. Joseph Pl., Wenatchee, WA 98801 t) 509-663-2644 stjosephschoolwenatchee@yakimadiocese.org www.saintjosephcatholicschool.org Lisa Martinez, Prin.; Stds.: 144; Lay Tchrs.: 8

WHITE SALMON

St. Joseph - 240 N.W. Washington, White Salmon, WA 98672; Mailing: P.O. Box 2049, White Salmon, WA 98672 t) 509-493-2828 stjosephws@yakimadiocese.org stjosephwhitesalmon.org Rev. Salomon Covarrubias-Pina, Pst.; CRP Stds.: 142

WHITE SWAN

St. Mary's - 360 Signal Peak Rd. (UPS), White Swan, WA 98952-0417; Mailing: P.O. Box 417, White Swan, WA 98952 t) 509-874-2436 kurt.hadley@yakimadiocese.org Very Rev. Kurt Hadley, Pst.; Dcn. Andy Gonzalez; CRP Stds.: 71

YAKIMA

St. Paul Cathedral - 15 S. 12th Ave., Yakima, WA 98902 t) 509-575-3713 stpaulyakima.org Rev. Msgr. John A. Ecker, Pst.; Rev. Jesus Mariscal, Pst. Assoc.; Emma Mendoza, DRE; CRP Stds.: 100

Catholic Young Adult Center - 810 S. 16th Ave., Yakima, WA 98902 t) 314-330-7634

Holy Family - 5315 Tieton Dr., Yakima, WA 98908 t) 509-966-0830 Rev. Cesar Vega Mendoza, Pst.; Very Rev. Michael J. Ibach, Par. Vicar; Rev. Daniel O. Steele, Par. Vicar; Dcn. John Cornell; Dcn. James Kramper; CRP Stds.: 297

Christ the Teacher Catholic School - (Grades PreK-8) 5508 W. Chestnut Ave., Yakima, WA 98908 t) 509-575-5604 hremillard@ctcsyakima.org ctcsyakima.org Cody Lamb, Prin.; Stds.: 229; Lay Tchrs.: 25

Holy Redeemer - 1707 S. 3rd Ave., Yakima, WA 98902 t) 509-248-2241 Very Rev. Kurt Hadley, Pst.; Dcn. Duane Berger; CRP Stds.: 196

St. Joseph Parish - 212 N. 4th St., Yakima, WA 98901-2426 t) 509-248-1911 stjosephyakima.com Rev. Mauricio Munoz, Pst.; Rev. Michael Kelly, Assoc. Pst.; Rev. Bill Vogel, S.J., Assoc. Pst.; Dcn. Nestor Chavez; CRP Stds.: 167

St. Joseph/Marquette - (Grades PreK-8) 202 N. 4th St., Yakima, WA 98901 t) 509-575-5557 gpleger@sjmms.org Gregg Pleger, Prin.; Stds.: 355; Lay Tchrs.: 27

ZILLAH

Resurrection - 704 Schooley Rd., Zillah, WA 98953-0567; Mailing: P.O. Box 567, Zillah, WA 98953-0567 t) 509-829-5433 Rev. Jacob W. Davis, Pst.; Rev. William Vogel, S.J., Pst.; CRP Stds.: 49

SCHOOLS: PRESCHOOL THRU HIGH SCHOOL

HIGH SCHOOLS

STATE OF WASHINGTON

UNION GAP

La Salle High School of Yakima - (PAR) 3000 Lightning Way, Union Gap, WA 98903 t) 509-225-2900 rsoptich@lasalleyakima.org www.lasalleyakima.com Ted Kanelopoulos, Prin.; Stds.: 224

INSTITUTIONS LOCATED IN DIOCESE

ASSOCIATIONS [ASN]

TOPPENISH

Association of Catholic Sisters for Educational Opportunities for the Poor - 109 N. E St., Toppenish, WA 98948 t) 509-865-3836 ross_k@heritage.edu Sr. Kathleen Ross, S.N.J.M., Pres.;

CAMPUS MINISTRY / NEWMAN CENTERS [CAM]

ELLENSBURG

Catholic Campus Ministry at Central Washington University - 706 N. Sprague St., Ellensburg, WA 98926 t) 509-925-3043 marcus.ayers@yakimadiocese.org www.cwucatholics.com/ Marcus Ayers, Dir.;

CATHOLIC CHARITIES [CCH]

EAST WENATCHEE

Holy Apostles Parish - 1315 N.E. 8th St., East Wenatchee, WA 98801 t) 509-884-5444; 509-884-0681; 509-886-7624 www.holyapostlesew.net Very Rev. Argemiro Orozco; Lee Gale, Pres.;

KENNEWICK

St. Joseph Parish Conference - 520 S. Garfield St., Kennewick, WA 99336 t) 509-586-3820 parish.office@stjoseph-kennewick.org St. Vincent de Paul Rev. V. Felipe Pulido, Pst.;

RICHLAND

Catholic Charities Serving Central Washington - 2139 Van Giesen, Richland, WA 99354 t) 509-946-4645 ddarnell@catholiccharitiescw.org www.catholiccharitiescw.org Darlene Darnell, Pres.;

Christ the King Parish Conference - 1111 Stevens Dr., Richland, WA 99354 t) 509-946-1675 lori@ckparish.org www.ckparish.org Rev. Msgr. Thomas C. Champoux, Pst.; Asstd. Annu.: 200; Staff: 28

WENATCHEE

Catholic Charities Serving Central Washington - 145 S. Worthen St., Wenatchee, WA 98801 t) 509-662-6761 ddarnell@catholiccharitiescw.org www.catholiccharitiescw.org Darlene Darnell, Pres.;

St. Joseph Parish Conference, St. Vincent de Paul - 625 S. Elliott Ave., Wenatchee, WA 98801 t) 509-667-7837 svdp.wenatcheeconference@gmail.com Very Rev. Osmar R. Aguirre, Pst.;

YAKIMA

Carroll Children's Center - 5301 Tieton Dr., Ste. C, Yakima, WA 98908 t) 509-965-7104 ddarnell@catholiccharitiescw.org Asstd. Annu.: 188; Staff: 75

Catholic Charities of the Diocese of Yakima - 5301 Tieton Dr., Ste. C, Yakima, WA 98908 t) 509-965-7100 ddarnell@catholiccharitiescw.org www.catholiccharitiescw.org Darlene Darnell, CEO; Manuel Villafan, COO; Paul Palmer, CFO; Asstd. Annu.: 40,631; Staff: 387

Catholic Charities of the Diocese of Yakima - Moses Lake - 1019 W. Broadway, Moses Lake, WA 98837 t) 509-765-1875

Catholic Charities of the Diocese of Yakima - Richland - 2139 Van Giesen, Richland, WA 99354 t) 509-946-4645

Catholic Charities of the Diocese of Yakima - Wenatchee - 145 S. Worthen St., Wenatchee, WA 98801 t) 509-662-6761

St. Vincent Centers - Union Gap - 2629 Main St., Union Gap, WA 98903 t) 509-457-5111

St. Paul's Parish Conference - 15 S. 12th Ave., Yakima, WA 98902 t) 509-575-3713 stpaul@wolfenet.com Greg Vavricka, Pres.; Patty Schumm, Secy.; Jeffrey Arkills, Treas.; Asstd. Annu.: 250; Staff: 3

COLLEGES & UNIVERSITIES [COL]

TOPPENISH

***Heritage University** - 3240 Fort Rd., Toppenish, WA 98948 t) 509-865-8600 ross_k@heritage.edu www.heritage.edu Interdenominational university with an independent Board. Andrew Sund, Pres.; Sr. Kathleen Ross, S.N.J.M., Pres. Emeritus & Prof.; Stds.:

1,000; Lay Tchrs.: 58; Sr. Tchrs.: 1

ENDOWMENTS / FOUNDATIONS / TRUSTS [EFT]

UNION GAP

La Salle Foundation of Yakima - 3000 Lightning Way, Union Gap, WA 98903 t) 509-225-2990 snelson@lasalleyakima.org www.lasalleyakima.com Ted Kanelopulos, Pres.;

YAKIMA

***Central Washington Catholic Foundation** - 5301 Tieton Dr., Ste. F, Yakima, WA 98908-3479 t) 509-972-3732 info@cwcatholicfoundation.org www.cwcatholicfoundation.org Nicole Franson, Dir.;

Irrevocable Priest Retirement Trust for the Diocese of Yakima - 101 S. 12th Ave., Yakima, WA 98902; Mailing: P.O. Box 2189, Yakima, WA 98907 t) 509-965-7117 sue.schoolcraft@yakimadiocese.net Susan Schoolcraft, CFO;

Irrevocable Seminarian Education Trust for the Diocese of Yakima - 101 S. 12th Ave., Yakima, WA 98902; Mailing: P.O. Box 2189, Yakima, WA 98907 t) 509-965-7117 sue.schoolcraft@yakimadiocese.net Susan Schoolcraft, CFO;

MISCELLANEOUS [MIS]

UNION GAP

St. Vincent Centers - 2629 Main St., Union Gap, WA 98903 t) 509-457-5111 ddarnell@catholiccharitiescw.org www.catholiccharitiescw.org Paul Palmer, Admin.; Darlene Darnell, Pres.;

YAKIMA

***Catholic Charities Housing Services, Diocese of Yakima** - 5301 Tieton Dr., Ste. G, Yakima, WA 98908-3479 t) 509-853-2800 bketcham@catholiccharitiescw.org www.catholiccharitiescw.org Darlene Darnell, Pres.;

Diocese of Yakima Capital Revolving Program - 101 S. 12th Ave., Yakima, WA 98902; Mailing: P.O. Box 2189, Yakima, WA 98907 t) 509-965-7117 sue.schoolcraft@yakimadiocese.net Susan Schoolcraft, CFO;

ZILLAH

Catholics In Action - ; Mailing: P.O. Box 673, Zillah, WA 98953 t) 509-790-7696 yakimacatholicradio@gmail.com Richard Sevigny, Pres.;

NURSING / REHABILITATION / CONVALESCENCE / ELDERLY CARE [NUR]

YAKIMA

***The Gamelin Association-Providence House** - 312 N. 4th St., Yakima, WA 98901 t) 509-452-5017 isidro.renteria@providence.org providence.org Low income housing for elderly & disabled 18 & older. Isidro Renteria, Dir.; Johnny Cox, Vice Pres., Providence Min.; Barbara Schamber, Secy., Providence House; Anita Butler, Treas., Providence House; Asstd. Annu.: 47; Staff: 2

An asterisk (*) denotes an organization that has established tax-exempt status directly with the IRS and is not covered by the USCCB Group Ruling.

Diocese of Youngstown

(Dioecesis Youngstoniensis)

MOST REVEREND DAVID J. BONNAR

Bishop of Youngstown; ordained July 23, 1988; appointed Bishop of Youngstown November 17, 2020; episcopal ordination January 12, 2021. Chancery Office,144 W. Wood St., Youngstown, OH 44503.

Chancery Office: 144 W. Wood St., Youngstown, OH 44503. T: 330-744-8451; F: 330-742-6448; F: 330-744-2848.
www.doy.org
chancery@doy.org

ESTABLISHED MAY 15, 1943.

Square Miles 3,404.

Canonically Erected July 22, 1943.

Comprises six Counties in the northeastern part of the State of Ohio, namely, Ashtabula, Columbiana, Mahoning, Portage, Stark and Trumbull Counties.

For legal titles of parishes and diocesan institutions, consult the Chancery Office.

STATISTICAL OVERVIEW

Personnel
Bishop....1
Priests: Diocesan Active in Diocese....60
Priests: Diocesan Active Outside Diocese....2
Priests: Retired, Sick or Absent....48
Number of Diocesan Priests....110
Religious Priests in Diocese....15
Total Priests in your Diocese....125
Extern Priests in Diocese....3
Ordinations:
Diocesan Priests....1
Transitional Deacons....4
Permanent Deacons in Diocese....80
Total Brothers....9
Total Sisters....147

Parishes
Parishes....84
With Resident Pastor:
Resident Diocesan Priests....44
Resident Religious Priests....2
Without Resident Pastor:
Administered by Priests....29
Administered by Deacons....1
Administered by Religious Women....1
Administered by Lay People....3
Missions....1
Closed Parishes....2
Professional Ministry Personnel:
Sisters....12
Lay Ministers....222

Welfare
Catholic Hospitals....4
Total Assisted....662,258
Health Care Centers....1
Total Assisted....52,651
Homes for the Aged....5
Total Assisted....567
Day Care Centers....7
Total Assisted....425
Special Centers for Social Services....1
Total Assisted....320

Educational
Diocesan Students in Other Seminaries....14
Total Seminarians....14
Colleges and Universities....1
Total Students....2,320
High Schools, Diocesan and Parish....6
Total Students....1,626
Elementary Schools, Diocesan and Parish....21
Total Students....4,416
Elementary Schools, Private....1
Total Students....159
Catechesis / Religious Education:
High School Students....1,412
Elementary Students....7,829
Total Students under Catholic Instruction....17,776
Teachers in Diocese:
Sisters....2
Lay Teachers....388

Vital Statistics
Receptions into the Church:
Infant Baptism Totals....979
Minor Baptism Totals....45
Adult Baptism Totals....74
Received into Full Communion....153
First Communions....1,102
Confirmations....1,075
Marriages:
Catholic....255
Interfaith....89
Total Marriages....344
Deaths....2,169
Total Catholic Population....124,206
Total Population....961,625

LEADERSHIP

Vicar General & Moderator of the Curia - Very Rev. Msgr. Robert J. Siffrin, Vicar General & Moderator of the Curia; Very Rev. Msgr. John A. Zuraw, Vicar General;
Chancellor - Joan Lawson, Chancellor;
College of Consultors - Very Rev. Msgr. Robert J. Siffrin; Very Rev. Michael D. Balash; Very Rev. Martin Celuch;
Presbyteral Council - Rev. Shawn Conoboy, Chair (sconoboy@youngstowndiocese.org);
Finance Council - Pat Kelly; Very Rev. Msgr. Robert J. Siffrin; Jerry M. Bryan;
Diocesan Pastoral Council - Very Rev. Msgr. John A. Zuraw;
Development/Stewardship - Rev. John-Michael Lavelle;
Ecumenism - t) 330-562-8519 Rev. Shawn Conoboy (sconoboy@youngstowndiocese.org);
Office of Missionary Discipleship - Rev. John-Michael Lavelle;
Office of Propagation of the Faith and Missions - Rev. Edward R. Brienz, Dir.;
Scouting, Diocesan Office - Rev. Leo J. Wehrlin (lwehrlin@youngstowndiocese.org);

OFFICES AND DIRECTORS

Department of Canonical Services - t) 330-744-8451 Very Rev. Martin Celuch, Dir.;
Matrimonial Dispensations - Very Rev. Martin Celuch;
Office of Conciliation - Very Rev. Martin Celuch;
Tribunal - Very Rev. Martin Celuch;
Adjutant Judicial Vicar - Rev. Msgr. Michael J. Cariglio Jr.;
Advocates - Vicki Kidd; Linda Tedde;
Defenders of the Bond - Very Rev. Msgr. John A. Zuraw;
Judges - Very Rev. Martin Celuch; Rev. Msgr. Michael J. Cariglio Jr.; Rev. Msgr. William J. Connell;
Judicial Vicar - Very Rev. Martin Celuch;
Notary - Regina Yakimoff; Carolyn Wooten;
Promoter of Justice - Very Rev. Msgr. John A. Zuraw;

CATHOLIC CHARITIES

Catholic Charities Bureau - Rachel Hrbolich;
Department of Catholic Charities Services - Rachel Hrbolich;
Office of Social Action - Robert (R.J.) Mangan;
Office of Social Services - Rachel Hrbolich, Pres.;
Criminal Justice Ministry - Robert (R.J.) Mangan;
Hispanic Ministry - Rev. Brian C. Smith (bsmith@youngstowndiocese.org);

CLERGY AND RELIGIOUS SERVICES

Department of Clergy and Religious Services - Very Rev. Michael D. Balash;
Office of Clergy Services - Very Rev. Michael D. Balash;
Office of Continuing Education and Formation of Priests - Very Rev. Michael D. Balash;
Office of Permanent Diaconate - Dcn. Michael A. Kocjancic, Dir.;
Office of Religious - Sr. Joyce Candidi, O.S.H.J., Dir.;
Diocesan Conference of Religious - Sr. Joyce Candidi, O.S.H.J., Dir.;
Office of Vocations - Rev. Chad Johnson (cjohnson@youngstowndiocese.org);

COMMUNICATIONS

Communications - Justin Huyck (justin@stmichaelcanton.org);
Public-Media Relations - Justin Huyck, Dir. (justin@stmichaelcanton.org);
"The Catholic Exponent", Diocesan Media - t) 330-744-5251 Most Rev. David J. Bonnar;
Catholic Television Network of Youngstown (CTNY) - t) (330) 744-8451 Bob Gavalier, Gen. Mgr.;

FINANCE

Department of Financial Services - Patrick A. Kelly, CFO;
Office of Finance - Patrick A. Kelly, CFO; Christine Jickess, Dir., Accounting & Financial Reporting;
Office of Information Systems Services - Matthew Pecchia, Dir.;

PASTORAL SERVICES

Office of Campus Ministry - t) 330-678-0240 Carmen Roebke, Dir.;
Hiram College - t) 330-527-4105
University Parish Newman Center (Kent State) - Rev. Chad Johnson;
Walsh University - t) 330-490-7341 Ben Walther, Dir.;
Youngstown State University - t) 330-747-9202 Rev. Nobert Keliher, O.P., Dir.;
Office of Catholic Schools - Mary Fiala, Supt.; James King, Assoc. Supt.;
The Catholic Diocese of Youngstown Educational Fund, Inc. - Mary Fiala, Supt.;
Office of Faith Formation and Lay Ecclesial Ministry - Barbara Walko, Diocesan D.R.E.; Margie Hynes;
Council for Catechesis - Nicholas Perkoski, Chair;
Diocesan Lay Ecclesial Ministry Board - Barbara Walko;
Office of Pro-Life, Marriage & Family Ministry - David R. Schmidt, Dir.;
Office of Worship - Very Rev. Michael D. Balash, Dir.;
Office of Youth and Young Adult Ministry - Rev. Ryan A. Furlong, Dir. (rfurlong@youngstowndiocese.org);
Pastoral and Educational Services - Very Rev. Msgr. John A. Zuraw, Dir.;

MISCELLANEOUS / OTHER OFFICES

Catholic Women, Diocesan Council of - t) 330-875-4635 Rev. Joseph W. Witmer, Spiritual Advisor;
Charismatic Prayer Group - t) 330-332-0336 Rev. Robert R. Edwards, Dir.;
Disabled Services - Very Rev. Msgr. Robert J. Siffrin;
Deaf and Hearing Impaired - t) 330-744-8451 Very Rev. Msgr. Robert J. Siffrin;
Physically and Developmentally - t) (330) 744-8451 Very Rev. Msgr. Robert J. Siffrin, Chap.;
Victim Assistance Coordinator - t) 330-718-1388 Dominic Colucy, Safe Envrionment Coord.;

PARISHES, MISSIONS, AND CLERGY

STATE OF OHIO

ALLIANCE

St. Joseph - 427 E. Broadway, Alliance, OH 44601 t) 330-821-5760 mzeni@youngstowndiocese.org www.stjoseph-alliance.org Rev. G. David Weikart, Pst.; Matthew Zeni, DRE; CRP Stds.: 25

St. Joseph - 12055 Easton St., N.E., Alliance, OH 44601; Mailing: P.O. Box 219, Maximo, OH 44650-0219 t) 330-823-7809 parish524@youngstowndiocese.org www.facebook.com/st.joseph.maximo Rev. G. David Weikart, Pst.; Roger Herstine, DRE; CRP Stds.: 35

Regina Coeli (Queen of Heaven) - 663 Fernwood Blvd., Alliance, OH 44601-2728 t) 330-821-5880 parish502@youngstowndiocese.org; abenedetti@youngstowndiocese.org reginacoeliparish.com/ Rev. G. David Weikart, Pst.; Amy Benedetti-Dyke, DRE; CRP Stds.: 39

Regina Coeli School - (Grades PreK-5) 733 Fernwood Blvd., Alliance, OH 44601-2730 t) 330-829-9239 rcelem@youngstowndiocese.org rcsjalliance.com Mario Calandros, Prin.; Monica Ketler, Librn.; Stds.: 79; Lay Tchrs.: 9

ANDOVER

Our Lady of Hope - 481 S. Main St., Andover, OH 44003-0669; Mailing: P.O. Box 669, Andover, OH 44003-0669 t) 440-293-6218 secretary@andoverkinsmanparishes.org andoverkinsmanparishes.org Rev. John Ettinger, Pst.; CRP Stds.: 10

St. Patrick - 6397 State Rte. 87, Kinsman, OH 44428 t) (440) 293-6218 (Worship Site).

Our Lady of Victory - (Worship Site)

ASHTABULA

Our Lady of Peace Parish - 3312 Lake Ave., Ashtabula, OH 44004 t) 440-992-0330 ourladyofpeace@olopparish.org olopash.org Rev. Raymond J. Thomas, Pst.; Dcn. Richard Johnson; CRP Stds.: 30

Mother of Sorrows - 1500 W. 6th St., Ashtabula, OH 44004-3310 (Worship Site)

Our Lady of Mt. Carmel - 1200 E. 21st St., Ashtabula, OH 44004 (Worship Site)

St. Joseph Church - 3400 Lake Ave., Ashtabula, OH 44004 (Worship Site)

AURORA

Our Lady of Perpetual Help - 342 S. Chillicothe Rd., Aurora, OH 44202-7814 t) 330-562-8519 parish401@youngstowndiocese.org www.olphaurora.org Rev. Shawn Conoboy, Pst.; Jeff Botos, Pst. Assoc.; Margaret Ann Clapp, DRE; CRP Stds.: 210

AUSTINTOWN

Immaculate Heart of Mary - 4490 Norquest Blvd., Austintown, OH 44515 t) 330-793-9988 parish113@youngstowndiocese.org; secty4490@zoominternet.net www.ihm-parish.com Rev. Gregory F. Fedor, Pst.; Nicholas Moliterno, DRE; CRP Stds.: 65

St. Joseph - 4545 New Rd., Austintown, OH 44515 t) 330-792-1919 austjoseph@zoominternet.net stjosephaustintown.org Rev. Gregory F. Fedor, Pst.; Jim Merhaut, Pst. Assoc.; Linda Landers, DRE; CRP Stds.: 90

BOARDMAN

St. Charles Borromeo - 7345 Westview Dr., Boardman, OH 44512 t) 330-758-8063 (CRP); 330-758-2325 office@stcharlesbdm.org Very Rev. Msgr. Msgr. John Zuraw, Pst.; Rev. Matthew Hummerickhouse, Par. Vicar; Dcn. Michael A. Kocjancic, Pst. Assoc.; Dcn. Paul Lisko, Pst. Assoc.; Natalie Wardle, Youth Min.; JoAnn Drummond, DRE; CRP Stds.: 290

St. Charles Borromeo School - (Grades K-8) 7325 Westview Dr., Boardman, OH 44512 t) 330-758-6689 stcharleselem@youngstowndiocese.org Teresa Yarger, Prin.; Stds.: 257; Lay Tchrs.: 16

St. Luke - 5235 South Ave., Boardman, OH 44512 t) 330-782-9783 parish115@youngstowndiocese.org www.saintluke-parish.org Very Rev. Msgr. John A. Zuraw, Pst.; Sr. Mary Alyce Koval, O.S.U., Pst. Assoc.; Rev. Matthew Humerickhouse, Par. Vicar; Dcn. Robert T. Redig; CRP Stds.: 56

CAMPBELL

Christ the Good Shepherd Parish - 159 Reed Ave., Campbell, OH 44405; Mailing: 159 W Rayen Ave., Youngstown, OH 44503 t) 330-743-2955 parish129@youngstowndiocese.org; ctgsparish633@gmail.com Rev. Matthew Zwilling, Admin.; Dcn. Ronald J. Bunofsky; Dcn. John Rentas;

CANAL FULTON

SS. Philip and James - 412 High St., Canal Fulton, OH 44614 t) 330-268-3227 (CRP); 330-854-2332 bjprosise@sssnet.com; sspj@sssnet.com spjcanalfulton.com Rev. Kevin McCaffrey, Pst.; Jackie Prosise, DRE; CRP Stds.: 36

SS. Philip and James School - (Grades PreSchool-8) 532 High St., Canal Fulton, OH 44614 t) 330-854-2823 sspandjsecretary@youngstowndiocese.org www.saintsphilipandjames.org Lisa Montgomery, Prin.; Stds.: 72; Lay Tchrs.: 11

CANFIELD

St. Michael - 300 N. Broad St., Canfield, OH 44406 t) 330-533-6839; 330-533-5275 (CRP) info@saintmichaelparish.net www.stmichaelcanfield.org Rev. John-Michael Lavelle, Pst.; Marcy Fessler, DRE; Maureen Hall, Pst. Assoc.; CRP Stds.: 276

CANTON

St. Anthony/All Saints Parish - 1530 11th St., S.E., Canton, OH 44707 t) 330-452-9539 office@stanthonycanton.org www.stanthonyallsaintscanton.org Hispanic Ministry, Catechesis of the Good Shepherd Rev. Thomas P. Kraszewski, Pst.; Dcn. Alfredo Aguierre; Sr. Karen Lindenberger, Hispanic Min. Coord.; Maggie Connor-Spitale, DRE; Cristina Hernandez, Youth Min.; Michele Higham, Music Min.; CRP Stds.: 67

Basilica of Saint John the Baptist - 627 McKinley Ave., N.W., Canton, OH 44703 t) 330-454-8044 x201 musicatthebasilica@gmail.com; jsheridan@youngstowndiocese.org www.stjohncanton.com Very Rev. John E. Sheridan, Rector; Dcn. Michael T. Seaman; CRP Stds.: 10

Christ the Servant Parish - 833 39th St., N.W., Canton, OH 44709 t) 330-492-0757 christtheservantparish@gmail.com christtheservantparish.org Rev. Scott Kopp, Pst.; Rev. Msgr. Lewis F. Gaetano, Pastor Emer.; Dcn. Thomas Mierzwa, Bus. Mgr.; Rita Kingsbury, DRE; CRP Stds.: 42

Our Lady of Peace School - (Grades K-5) 1001 39th St., N.W., Canton, OH 44709 t) 330-492-0622 olopelem@youngstowndiocese.org Lenora Krueger, Librn.; Stds.: 213; Lay Tchrs.: 16

Our Lady of Peace Church - (Worship Site)

St. Joan of Arc - 4940 Tuscarawas St. W., Canton, OH 44708-5012 t) 330-477-2972 (CRP); 330-477-6796 secretary@sjacanton.com; parish511@youngstowndiocese.org www.sjacanton.com Rev. Brian James Cline, Pst.; Rev. Donald E. King, In Res.; Sarah Knight, CRE; Richard Hull, Pst. Min./Coord.; Jon M. Simsic, Music Min.; Phil J. Salasek, Bus. Mgr.; CRP Stds.: 40

St. Joan of Arc School - (Grades PreK-8) 120 Bordner Ave., S.W., Canton, OH 44710 Daniel Mitchell, Prin.; Stds.: 263; Lay Tchrs.: 14

St. Joseph - 2427 W. Tuscarawas St., Canton, OH 44708 t) 330-454-2144 (CRP); 330-453-2526 (Rectory) stjosephcanton@catholicweb.com; stjoereled@catholicweb.com stjosephcanton.org Rev. Brian James Cline, Pst.; Rev. Edward L. Beneleit, In Res.; Rev. Msgr. Frank A. Carfagna, Pastor Emer.; Dcn. Wilbur J. Bagley; Sarah Knight, CRE; Richard Hull, Pst. Min./Coord.; Jon M. Simsic, Music Min.; Phil J. Salasek, Bus. Mgr.; CRP Stds.: 18

Little Flower Catholic Church - 2040 Diamond St. NE, Canton, OH 44721-1709 t) 330-494-2759 chenyk@youngstowndiocese.org Rev. Canon Christopher Henyk, Pst.; CRP Stds.: 101

St. Mary/St. Benedict Parish - 1602 Market Ave. S., Canton, OH 44707 t) 330-453-2110 stmarystbenedict2011@gmail.com www.stmary-stbenedict.com Rev. Thomas P. Kraszewski, Canonical Pastor; Dcn. Randolph Smith, DRE; Lee Ann Smith, Youth Min.; Judy Cerny, Music Min.; Diane Snyder, Music Min.; Janella Mazzocca, Music Min.; CRP Stds.: 35

St. Mary of the Immaculate Conception - (Worship Site)

St. Benedict - 2207 3rd St., S.E., Canton, OH 44707 (Worship Site)

St. Michael the Archangel - 3430 St. Michael Blvd., N.W., Attn: Bruce Gordon, Canton, OH 44718 t) 330-492-3119 bruce@stmichaelcanton.org www.stmichaelcanton.org Rev. Benson Claret Okpara, Pst.; Rev. Connor Hetzel, Par. Vicar; Dcn. Philip Tischler; Dcn. Peter P. Pohl; Dcn. Mark J. Fuller; Sr. Carolyn Capuano, HM, Pst. Assoc.; Roberta Muoio, Pst. Assoc.; Julie Sutton, DRE; Jeff Fricker, Dir., Music Min.; Kayla Brent, Music Min.; Rachel Shumar, Youth Min.; Bruce Gordon, Bus. Mgr.; CRP Stds.: 167

St. Michael the Archangel School - (Grades PreK-8) 3430 St Michael Blvd NW, Canton, OH 44718 t) 330-492-2657 stmichaelelem@youngstowndiocese.org www.smscanton.org/ Claire Gatti, Prin.; Stds.: 407; Lay Tchrs.: 31

St. Peter - 726 Cleveland Ave NW, Canton, OH 44702 t) 330-453-8493 stpetersoffice@youngstowndiocese.org www.stpetercanton.org Very Rev. John E. Sheridan, Pst.; CRP Stds.: 19

COLUMBIANA

St. Jude - 180 Seventh St., Columbiana, OH 44408 t) 330-482-2351; 330-482-2888 (CRP) mburkey@ololstj.org www.ololstj.org Rev. David M. Misbrener, Pst.; Janette Koewacich, DRE; CRP Stds.: 106

CONNEAUT

Corpus Christi Parish - 744 Mill St., Conneaut, OH 44030 t) 440-599-8570 stmsfc@hotmail.com www.corpuschristiparishconneaut.org Rev. Raymond J. Thomas, Pst.; Rev. Philip Miller, Sacr. Min.; Dcn. Nicholas Iarocci; Nicholas Perkoski, Pst. Assoc.; CRP Stds.: 68

CORTLAND

St. Robert Bellarmine Parish - 4659 Niles-Cortland Rd., N.E., Cortland, OH 44410 t) 330-637-4886 strbchurch@aol.com www.strobertcortland.org Rev. Carl Kish, Pst.; Dcn. Robert Green; CRP Stds.: 135

EAST LIVERPOOL

Holy Trinity Parish - 512 Monroe St., East Liverpool, OH 43920 t) 330-385-7131 ccdholytrinity@gmail.com; parish303@youngstowndiocese.org www.holytrinityelo.org Rev. Leo J. Wehrlin, Pst.; Robert Barto, DRE; Kristin Smith, Treas.; CRP Stds.: 42

St. Aloysius Church - 235 W. 5th St., East Liverpool, OH 43920

EAST PALESTINE

Our Lady of Lourdes - 210 E Main, East Palestine, OH 44413; Mailing: 180 Seventh St., Columbiana, OH 44408 t) 330-426-9346; 330-482-2351 (CRP) burkeymary@comcast.net; jkoewacich.ololstj@gmail.com www.ololstj.org Rev. David M. Misbrener, Pst.; Janette Koewacich, DRE; CRP Stds.: 106

GARRETTSVILLE

St. Ambrose - 10692 Freedom St., Garrettsville, OH 44231 t) 330-527-4105 parish402@youngstowndiocese.org www.stambroseonline.com Rev. Shawn Conoboy, Pst.; CRP Stds.: 26

GENEVA

Assumption B.V.M. - 30 Lockwood St, Geneva, OH 44041 t) 440-466-3427 bk208@youngstowndiocese.org assumptionchurchoh.org Rev. Daniel Finnerty, Pst.; CRP Stds.: 88

GIRARD

St. Rose of Lima Parish - 48 E. Main St., Girard, OH 44420 t) 330-545-4351 parish603@youngstowndiocese.org; strose@neo.rr.com strosegirard.com/ Rev. Jordan Kelly, OP, Pst.; Dcn. Paul Milligan; Jeannine Frederick, DRE; Pat Finn, Bus. Mgr.; CRP Stds.: 150

St. Rose School - (Grades PreSchool-8) 61 E. Main St., Girard, OH 44420 t) 330-545-1163 stroseelem@youngstowndiocese.org saintrosecatholicschool.com/ Anthony Catale, Prin.; Stds.: 235; Lay Tchrs.: 18

Sunny Days Day Care Center - 61 E Main St., Girard, OH 44420 t) 330-545-1490 sunnydayscc@att.net Jennifer Pasvanis, Dir.;

HANOVERTON

St. Philip Neri - 11328 Gavers Rd., Hanoverton, OH 44423; Mailing: 271 W. Chestnut St, Lisbon, OH 44432 t) 330-424-7648 www.stphilipneo.org Rev. Stephen M. Wassie, Pst.;

HUBBARD

St. Patrick - 357 N. Main St., Hubbard, OH 44425; Mailing: 225 N. Main St., Hubbard, OH 44425 t) 330-534-1928 parish406@youngstowndiocese.org; cccm113@aol.com stpatshub.org Rev. Michael Swierz, Pst.; Sr. Bernadine Janci, S.N.D., Pst. Assoc.; Dcn. Robert Friedman, Pst. Assoc.; Dcn. John Bartos; Dcn. Michael Medvec; CRP Stds.: 285

JEFFERSON

St. Joseph Calasanctius - 32 E. Jefferson St., Jefferson, OH 44047 t) 440-576-3651 faithformation@jeffersoncatholic.com; saintjoseph@jeffersoncatholic.com www.jeffersoncatholic.com Rev. John Ettinger, Pst.; Dcn. Michael Gardner; Lindsay Fuentes, DRE; CRP Stds.: 40

KENT

St. Patrick's - 313 N. Depeyster St., Kent, OH 44240 t) 330-673-5849 rpentello@youngstowndiocese.org www.stpatrickkent.org Rev. Richard J. Pentello, Pst.; Dcn. Timothy DeFrange; Dcn. Michael W. Stabilla; CRP Stds.: 110

St. Patrick's School - (Grades K-8) 127 Portage St., Kent, OH 44240 t) 330-673-7232 stpatelemkent@youngstowndiocese.org www.stpatskent.org Howard Mancini, Prin.; Stds.: 201; Lay Tchrs.: 17

University Parish Newman Center - 1424 Horning Rd., Kent, OH 44240 t) 330-678-0240 croebke@kent.edu; parish415@youngstowndiocese.org kentnewmancenterparish.org Rev. Richard J. Pentello, Pst.; Rev. Chad Johnson, Par. Vicar; Dcn. Timothy DeFrange; Dcn. Michael W. Stabilla; Veronica Victoria, Campus Min.; Carmen Roebke, Pst. Assoc.; Dr. John Roebke, Music Min.; CRP Stds.: 44

KINGSVILLE

St. Andrew Bobola - 3700 State Rte. 193, Kingsville, OH 44048 t) 440-224-0987 st.andrew@windstream.net www.stjoseph-standrew.com Rev. Raymond J. Thomas, Pst.; Rev. Philip Miller, Sacr. Min.; Dcn. Nicholas Iarocci; Nicholas Perkoski, Pst. Assoc.; CRP Stds.: 18

KINSMAN

St. Patrick - Merged Mar 2022 Merged with Our Lady of Victory, Andover to form Our Lady of Hope, Andover.

LAKE MILTON

Our Lady of the Lakes Parish, St. Catherine Church - 1254 Grandview Rd., Lake Milton, OH 44429; Mailing: 50 Rosemont Rd., North Jackson, OH 44451 t) 330-538-2602 ourladyofthelakes@att.net ourladyotl.org Rev. David W. Merzweiler, Pst.; CRP Stds.: 8

LEETONIA

St. Patrick - 167 W. Main St., Leetonia, OH 44431 t) 330-427-6577 Rev. Peter M. Polando, Pst.; Dcn. Lawrence Parks;

LISBON

St. George - 271 W. Chestnut St., Lisbon, OH 44432 t) 330-424-7648 Rev. Stephen M. Wassie, Pst.; CRP Stds.: 5

St. Agatha - 13523 Washington St. at State Rte. 518, Lisbon, OH 44432; Mailing: 271 W. Chestnut St, Lisbon, OH 44432

LOUISVILLE

St. Louis - 300 N. Chapel St., Louisville, OH 44641 t) 330-875-1658 parish520@youngstowndiocese.org; officemanager@saintlouiscc.org Rev. Thomas Cebula, Admin.; Mario Calandros, DRE; Stacey Hackney; CRP Stds.: 52

Sacred Heart of Mary - 8277 Nickelplate Ave., N.E., Louisville, OH 44641 t) 330-875-2827 office@shmparish.org Rev. Thomas Cebula, Admin.; Mario Calandros, DRE;

LOWELLVILLE

Our Lady of the Holy Rosary - 131 E. Wood St., Lowellville, OH 44436 t) 330-536-6436 parish132@youngstowndiocese.org Very Rev. Martin Celuch, Admin.; CRP Stds.: 52

MANTUA
St. Joseph - 11045 St. Joseph Blvd., Mantua, OH 44255 t) 330-274-2253; 330-274-2268 (CRP) phaney@stjosephmantua.com; parishoffice@stjosephmantua.com www.stjosephmantua.com Rev. Shawn Conoboy, Pst.; Dcn. Gerolome P. Scopilliti; Margaret Haney, DRE; CRP Stds.: 40
MASSILLON
St. Barbara - 2813 Lincoln Way, N.W., Massillon, OH 44647 t) 330-833-6898 amy.davis@youngstowndiocese.org; mmankowski@youngstowndiocese.org www.saintbarbaraparish.com Rev. Canon Matthew Mankowski, Pst.; Amy Davis, DRE; Daniel Bressi, Bus. Mgr.; Kevin Kutz, Music Min.; CRP Stds.: 86
St. Joseph - 322 Third St., S.E., Massillon, OH 44646 t) (330) 833-4907 (Office) bit.ly/stjosephsmassillon Rev. Canon Maciej Mankowski, Pst.; CRP Stds.: 83
Saint Mary - 206 Cherry Rd., N.E., Massillon, OH 44646; Mailing: 2809 Lincoln Way W., Massillon, OH 44647 t) (330) 833-6898 www.stmarymassillon.com/ Rev. Canon Maciej Mankowski, Pst.; Dcn. Steven A. Wyles; CRP Stds.: 73
St. Mary School - (Grades PreK-8) 640 First St., N.E., Massillon, OH 44646 t) 330-832-9355 stmaryelem@youngstowndiocese.org www.stmarymassillon.org Dr. Lucia Heddleson, Prin.; Stds.: 212; Lay Tchrs.: 13
MCDONALD
Our Lady of Perpetual Help - 618 Ohio Ave., McDonald, OH 44437 t) 330-530-1111 olphparish618@aol.com Rev. Edward R. Brienz, Admin.; Heidi Smith, DRE; CRP Stds.: 37
MINERAL RIDGE
St. Mary - 3504 Main St., Mineral Ridge, OH 44440 t) 330-565-2449 (CRP); 330-652-7761 kdcheryl@aol.com; parish608@youngstowndiocese.org Rev. Richard Murphy, Pst.; Dcn. Frank Marino; Cheryl Basista, CRE; CRP Stds.: 36
MOGADORE
St. Joseph - 2643 Waterloo Rd., Mogadore, OH 44260 t) 330-628-9941 sandy@stjosephrandolph.org www.stjosephrandolph.org Rev. Zachary Coulter, Pst.; CRP Stds.: 9
St. Joseph School - (Grades PreK-8) 2617 Waterloo Rd., Mogadore, OH 44260 t) 330-628-9555 stjoeelemmogadore@youngstowndiocese.org sjsrandolph.org Stds.: 199; Lay Tchrs.: 10
NAVARRE
Holy Family Parish - 216 Wooster St., N.E., Navarre, OH 44662 t) 330-879-5900 office@holyfamilyparishnavarre.org; pcondello@youngstowndiocese.org holyfamilyparishnavarre.org Rev. Canon Matthew Mankowski, Pst.; Rev. Edward L. Beneleit, Sacr. Min.; Rev. Thomas G. Bishop, Sacr. Min.; Pattie Condello, Diocesan Pastoral Associate; CRP Stds.: 45
St. Clement Church - (Worship Site)
St. Therese Church - 512 Wabash Ave., S., Brewster, OH 44613 (Worship Site)
NEW MIDDLETOWN
St. Paul the Apostle - 10143 Main St., New Middletown, OH 44442; Mailing: P.O. Box 515, New Middletown, OH 44442 t) 330-542-3466 albert.pompeo@gmail.com; parish133@youngstowndiocese.org Rev. Stephen Zeigler, Pst.; Albert Pompeo, DRE; CRP Stds.: 129
NEWTON FALLS
St. Mary and St. Joseph Parish - 131 Quarry St., Newton Falls, OH 44444; Mailing: 120 Maple Dr., Newton Falls, OH 44444 t) 330-872-5742 parish609@youngstowndiocese.org; parishssmaryjoseph@yahoo.com www.stmarystjosephparish.com Rev. David W. Merzweiler, Pst.;
NILES
Our Lady of Mount Carmel Parish - 381 Robbins Ave., Niles, OH 44446 t) 330-652-5825 parish611@youngstowndiocese.org Very Rev. Michael D. Balash; CRP Stds.: 63
St. Stephen - 129 W. Park Ave., Niles, OH 44446 t) 330-652-4396 churchofsaintstephen@yahoo.com www.ststephenchurchniles.com Rev. Richard Murphy, Pst.; Dcn. Frank Marino; CRP Stds.: 26
NORTH CANTON
St. Paul - St. Paul Church, 241 S. Main St., North Canton, OH 44720 t) 330-499-2201; 330-499-2201 x109 (CRP) info@stpaulncanton.org; dmay@stpaulncanton.org www.stpaulncanton.org Rev. John Keehner, Pst.; Rev. Simon Mino, Par. Vicar; Rev. Msgr. James A. Clarke, Pastor Emer.; Rev. James E. McKarns, Pastor Emer.; Dcn. William Lambert; Dcn. Edward Laubacher; Dcn. Ron Reolfi; Dcn. Dennis Ross; Dustine May, DRE; CRP Stds.: 240
St. Paul School - (Grades PreK-8) 303 S. Main St., North Canton, OH 44720 t) 330-494-0223 stpaulelemncanton@youngstowndiocese.org spsnorthcanton.com Amie Hale, Prin.; Kathy Yackshaw, Librn.; Stds.: 300; Lay Tchrs.: 20
NORTH JACKSON
Our Lady of the Lakes Parish, St. James Church - 50 Rosemont Rd., North Jackson, OH 44451 t) 330-538-2602 ourladyofthelakes@att.net ourladyotl.org Rev. David W. Merzweiler, Pst.; CRP Stds.: 8
ORWELL
St. Mary - 103 N. Maple St., Orwell, OH 44076 t) 440-437-6262 parish210@youngstowndiocese.org; stmaryofc@fairpoint.net Rev. David I. Bridling, Pst.; Sr. Barbara Morscher, DRE; CRP Stds.: 36
POLAND
Holy Family - 2729 Center Rd., Poland, OH 44514 t) 330-757-1545 holy_family@sbcglobal.net; parish135@youngstowndiocese.org www.holyfamilypoland.org Very Rev. Martin Celuch, Pst.; Dcn. Ray Hatala; Dcn. Andrew McDonald; CRP Stds.: 438
Holy Family School - (Grades PreK-8) 2731 Center Rd., Poland, OH 44514 t) 330-757-3713 hfelem@youngstowndiocese.org hfspoland.org Laura Parise, Prin.; Stds.: 238; Lay Tchrs.: 13
RAVENNA
Immaculate Conception - 409 W. Main St., Ravenna, OH 44266 t) (330) 296-6434 parish406@youngstowndiocese.org Rev. William B. Kraynak, Pst.; Dcn. Christopher L. Germak, Pst. Assoc.; Eileen Edwards, DRE; CRP Stds.: 16
ROCK CREEK
Sacred Heart - 3049 SR 45, Rock Creek, OH 44084; Mailing: P.O. Box 310, Rock Creek, OH 44084 t) 440-563-3010 (Office); 440-563-5255 (Church) parish211@youngstowndiocese.org Sr. Barbara Morscher, S.N.D., DRE; CRP Stds.: 5
ROOTSTOWN
St. Peter of the Fields - 3487 Old Forge Rd., Rootstown, OH 44272 t) 330-325-7543 st.peterschurch.rootstown@gmail.com www.stsjosephpeter.org Rev. Zachary Coulter, Pst.; CRP Stds.: 50
SALEM
St. Paul - 935 E. State St., Salem, OH 44460 t) 330-332-0336; 330-337-3019 (CRP) pfitch@stpaulsalem.org stpaulsalem.org Rev. Peter M. Polando, Pst.; Margaret Fitch, DRE; CRP Stds.: 72
St. Paul School - (Grades PreK-6) 925 E. State St., Salem, OH 44460 t) 330-337-3451 stpaulelemsalem@youngstowndiocese.org www.stpaul.k12.oh.us Dr. Jacqueline Mumford, Prin.; Stds.: 134; Lay Tchrs.: 10
SEBRING
St. Ann - 323 S. 15th St., Sebring, OH 44672 t) 330-938-2033 stannchurchsebring@gmail.com stannchurchsebring.org Rev. G. David Weikart, Pst.; Dcn. Ralph Chase; Dcn. Gregory J. Wood, Admin.; Rebecca Szekely, DRE;
STREETSBORO
St. Joan of Arc - 8894 State Rte. 14, Streetsboro, OH 44241 t) 330-626-3424 parish409@youngstowndiocese.org www.sjoa-church.org Rev. Christopher Luoni, Pst.;
STRUTHERS
Christ Our Savior Parish - 764 5th St., Struthers, OH 44471 t) 330-755-6245 (CRP); 330-755-9819 bsafranski@youngstowndiocese.org; cosparishstruthers@gmail.com www.cosparish.org Rev. Philip E. Rogers, Pst.; Dr. Benjamin Safranski, DRE;
Saint Nicholas School - (Grades K-8) 762 5th St., Struthers, OH 44471-1702 t) 330-755-2128 stnickelem@youngstowndiocese.org Pat Fletcher, Librn.; Stds.: 164; Lay Tchrs.: 12
St. Nicholas Church - t) (330) 755-9819 (Worship Site)
Holy Trinity Church - 250 N. Bridge St., Struthers, OH 44471 (Worship Site)
SUMMITVILLE
St. John - 16017 Smith Rd., Summitville, OH 43692; Mailing: 271 W. Chestnut St, Lisbon, OH 44432 t) 330-424-7648 bk307@youngstowndiocese.org Rev. Stephen M. Wassie, Pst.; CRP Stds.: 51
UNIONTOWN
Holy Spirit - 2952 Edison St. NW, Uniontown, OH 44685 t) 330-699-4500 cathykasza@holyspiritunoh.org; anneweeks@holyspiritunoh.org holyspiritunoh.org/ Rev. John E. Keehner, Pst.; Rev. Simon Mino, Par. Vicar; Anne Weeks, Pst. Assoc.; Cathy Kasza, CRE; CRP Stds.: 84
VIENNA
Queen of the Holy Rosary - 291 Scoville Dr., Vienna, OH 44473 t) 330-856-4204 qhrvienna@gmail.com qhrparish.org/ Served by the Priestly Fraternity of St. Peter Rev. Joshua Houck, FSSP, Temporary Admin.; Rev. John Fongemie, F.S.S.P., On Leave; CRP Stds.: 54
St. Thomas the Apostle Parish - 4453 Warren-Sharon Rd., Vienna, OH 44473; Mailing: P.O. Box 148, Vienna, OH 44473 t) 330-394-2461 theapostlethomas@aol.com theapostlethomas.com Rev. Ryan A. Furlong; CRP Stds.: 75
WARREN
Blessed Sacrament - 3020 Reeves Rd., N.E., Warren, OH 44483 t) 330-372-2215 info@warrencatholic.org www.warrencatholic.org Rev. Christopher Cicero, Pst.; Rev. Thomas C. Eisweirth, Pastor Emer.; CRP Stds.: 69
St. Elizabeth Ann Seton Parish - 2532 Burton St. S.E., Warren, OH 44484 t) 330-393-9766 seton@warrencatholic.org www.seaswarrenohio.org Rev. Christopher Cicero, Pst.; Dcn. Edward Kleese; Dcn. Joseph P. Toth; Dcn. Robert Simmerly;
SS. Cyril and Methodius Church - (Worship Site)
St. James Church - (Worship Site)
Saint Mary Saint Joseph Parish - 232 Seneca St., N.E., Warren, OH 44481 t) 330-393-8721 parish619@youngstowndiocese.org stmarywarren.org Rev. Frantisek Katrinak, Pst.; Sam Trina, Music Min.; CRP Stds.: 21
St. Joseph Church - 420 North St., N.W., Warren, OH 44483 (Worship Site)
St. William - 5411 Mahoning Ave., N.W., Warren, OH 44483 t) 330-847-8677 ctimko@stwilliamchampion.org; parishoffice@stwilliamchampion.org www.stwilliamchampion.org Very Rev. Michael D. Balash, Pst.; Dcn. Robert Mintus; Carol Timko, DRE; CRP Stds.: 40
WAYNESBURG
St. James - 400 W. Lisbon St., Waynesburg, OH 44688 t) 330-866-9449 st.jamescp@yahoo.com Rev. Joseph Zamary, Pst.; Dcn. Dave Kenney; CRP Stds.: 35
St. James School - (Grades PreK-6) 400 W. Wilson St., Waynesburg, OH 44688 t) 330-866-9556 stjameselem@youngstowndiocese.org sjswaynesburg.org Sandie Fusillo, Prin.; Stds.: 87; Sr. Tchrs.: 2; Lay Tchrs.: 7
YOUNGSTOWN
Saint Angela Merici Parish - 397 S. Jackson St., Youngstown, OH 44506 t) 330-747-6080 sharon@stangelayoungstown.org www.stangelayoungstown.org Rev. Kevin Peters, Pst.; Dcn. William Bone; Sr. Elisa Bonano, O.S.F., Pst. Assoc.; Diana Hancharenko, Pst. Assoc.; Dr. Linda

Miller, DRE; Shannon Pecchia, Youth Min.; Sharon Kent, Bus. Mgr.; CRP Stds.: 32

St. Angela Merici - t) 330-747-6090 natalie@stangelayoungstown.org (Worship Site)

Basilica of Our Lady of Mount Carmel - St. Anthony of Padua Parish - 343 Via Mt. Carmel, Youngstown, OH 44505 t) 330-743-3508 (CRP); 330-743-4144 office@olmcsta.com; olmcreligiousedoffice@gmail.com www.olmcsta.com Rev. Msgr. Michael J. Cariglio Jr., Pst.; Dcn. Anthony Falasca; Dcn. Mark Izzo; Nick Mattiussi, Music Min.; Therese Ivanisin, CRE; Leanna Pipala, CRE; CRP Stds.: 78

St. Anthony - 1125 Turin Ave., Youngstown, OH 44510 (Worship Site)

Our Lady of Mt. Carmel Basilica - St. Anthony of Padua - (Worship Site)

St. Brendan - 2800 Oakwood Ave., Youngstown, OH 44509 t) 330-792-3875 x12 (CRP); 330-792-3875 parish103@youngstowndiocese.org; office@stbrendanyo.org Rev. Steven J. Agostino, Admin.;

St. Christine - 3165 S. Schenley Ave., Youngstown, OH 44511 t) 330-792-3829 parish105@youngstowndiocese.org; parishoffice@stchristine.org www.stchristine.org Rev. John Jerek, Pst.; Dcn. Mark Kiraly; Dcn. Ronald Layko; Jamie Miller, DRE; CRP Stds.: 170

St. Christine School - (Grades K-8) 3125 S. Schenley Ave., Youngstown, OH 44511 t) 330-792-4544 stchristine@youngstowndiocese.org Cara Pribula, Prin.; Stds.: 303; Lay Tchrs.: 24

St. Columba Parish - 154 W. Wood St., Youngstown, OH 44503; Mailing: 159 W. Rayen Ave., Youngstown, OH 44503-1033 t) 330-744-5233 mreed@youngstowndiocese.org; info@stcolumbacathedral.org www.stcolumbacathedral.org Very Rev. Msgr. Robert J. Siffrin, Rector; Rev. Matthew Zwilling, Pst. Assoc.; Dcn. Sylvester Frazzini; Dcn. Michel Puhalla; Sr. Martha Reed, DRE; Ralph Holtzhauser, Music Min.; CRP Stds.: 36

St. Dominic - 77 E. Lucius Ave., Youngstown, OH 44507 t) 330-783-1900 parish107@youngstowndiocese.org; office@saintdominic.org saintdominic.org Rev. Vincent DeLucia, O.P., Pst.; Rev. Bernard Confer, O.P., Par. Vicar; Rev. Nicholas Ingham, O.P., Par. Vicar; Rev. Carlos Quijano, O.P., Par. Vicar; Rev. Norbert Keliher, Campus Min.; Rev. Louis Bertrand Lemoine, Campus Min.; CRP Stds.: 66

St. Edward - 240 Tod Ln., Youngstown, OH 44504 t) 330-743-2308 rsiffrin@youngstowndiocese.org Very Rev. Msgr. Robert J. Siffrin, Admin.; Rev. Matthew Zwilling, Par. Vicar; Dcn. Sylvester Frazzini; Dcn. Michael Puhala; Dcn. James Smith; CRP Stds.: 47

Holy Apostles Parish - 854 Wilson Ave., Youngstown, OH 44506 t) 330-743-1905 holyapostlesparishyoungstown@gmail.com www.hapyoungs.town Rev. Joseph S. Rudjak, Pst.; CRP Stds.: 8

SS. Peter and Paul - 421 Covington St., Youngstown, OH 44510 (Worship Site)

St. Stephen of Hungary Church - (Worship Site)

Our Lady of Sorrows Parish - 915 Cornell St., Youngstown, OH 44502 t) 330-788-5082 ourlady915@gmail.com www.ourlady915.org Rev. John Jerek, Pst.;

St. Matthias Church - t) (330) 788-5082 (Worship Site)

St. Patrick - 1420 Oak Hill Ave., Youngstown, OH 44507 t) 330-743-1109 stpatricks@neo.rr.com stpatsyoungstown.com Rev. Kevin Peters, Pst.; CRP Stds.: 45

SCHOOLS: PRESCHOOL THRU HIGH SCHOOL

SCHOOLS

STATE OF OHIO

ASHTABULA

Saint John School - (PAR) (Grades PreK-12) 7911 Depot Rd., Ashtabula, OH 44004 t) 440-997-5531 mburke@sjheralds.org; splescia@sjheralds.org www.sjheralds.org Sr. Maureen Burke, S.N.D., Pres.; Scott Plescia, Prin.; Millicent Zullo, Vice Prin.; Stds.: 545; Sr. Tchrs.: 1; Lay Tchrs.: 40

LOUISVILLE

Holy Cross Academy - (PRV) (Grades PreK-8) 2121 Reno Dr., Louisville, OH 44541 t) 330-875-1631 dgravo@youngstowndiocese.org www.starkcountycatholicschools.org Daniel Gravo, Pres.; Stds.: 1,200; Lay Tchrs.: 200

WARREN

John F. Kennedy Catholic School - (PAR) (Grades PreK-12) 2550 Central Pkwy., S.E., Warren, OH 44483 t) 330-372-2375 jkenneally@youngstowndiocese.org warrenjfk.com Allyse Consiglio, Prin.; Jacquelyn Venzeio, Prin.; Joseph Kenneally, Pres.; Joyce Cahill, Bus. Mgr.; Stds.: 379; Lay Tchrs.: 16

Lower Campus - (Grades PreK-12) 3000 Reeves Rd., N.E., Warren, OH 44483 jfkelem@youngstowndiocese.org Jackie Venzio, Prin.;

Upper Campus - (Grades PreK-12) 2550 Central Pkwy., S.E., Warren, OH 44484 t) 330-369-1804 jkenneally@warrenjfk.com www.warrenjfk.com Tina McCue, Dir.;

YOUNGSTOWN

St. Joseph the Provider Catholic School - (PRV) (Grades K-8) 1145 Turin St., Youngstown, OH 44510 t) 330-259-0353 stjoetheproelem@youngstowndiocese.org stjosephtheprovider.com Rev. Michael Swierz, Pres.; Cheryl Jablonski, Prin.; Sr. Bernadine Janci, S.N.D., Campus Min.; Sr. Charlotte Italiano, O.S.U., Dir.; Stds.: 159; Pr. Tchrs.: 1; Lay Tchrs.: 12

HIGH SCHOOLS

STATE OF OHIO

CANTON

Central Catholic High School - (DIO) (Grades 9-12) 4824 Tuscarawas St. W., Canton, OH 44708-5118 t) 330-478-2131 doates@youngstowndiocese.org www.cchsweb.com Rev. Donald E. King, Pres.; David M. Oates, Prin.; Noelle Waltenbaugh, Vice Prin.; Dcn. Randolph Smith, Campus Min.; Stds.: 310; Lay Tchrs.: 24

LOUISVILLE

St. Thomas Aquinas High School & Middle School - (PAR) 2121 Reno Dr., N.E., Louisville, OH 44641 t) 330-875-1631 tneary@youngstowndiocese.org www.stahs.org Rev. Donald E. King, Pres.; Timothy Neary, Prin.; Stds.: 173; Lay Tchrs.: 9

YOUNGSTOWN

Cardinal Mooney High School - (DIO) (Grades 9-12) 2545 Erie St., Youngstown, OH 44507 t) 330-788-5007 nbeyer@cardinalmooney.com www.cardinalmooney.com Nick Beyer, Pres.; Stds.: 325; Lay Tchrs.: 23

Ursuline High School - (DIO) (Grades 9-12) 750 Wick Ave., Youngstown, OH 44505 t) 330-744-4563 ursulinehigh@youngstowndiocese.org www.ursuline.com Matthew Sammartino, Prin.; Rev. Richard Murphy, Pres.; Stds.: 500; Pr. Tchrs.: 1; Lay Tchrs.: 41

INSTITUTIONS LOCATED IN DIOCESE

CAMPUS MINISTRY / NEWMAN CENTERS [CAM]

KENT

Kent State University Newman Center - 1424 Horning Rd., Kent, OH 44240 t) 330-678-0240 parish415@youngstowndiocese.org www.kentnewmancenterparish.org Rev. Richard J. Pentello, Pst.; Carmen Roebke, Pst. Assoc.; Veronica Victoria, Campus Min.; Dr. John Roebke, Dir.;

YOUNGSTOWN

St. John Henry Newman Center at Youngstown State University aka YSU Newman Center - 254 Madison Ave, Youngstown, OH 44504-1627 t) 330-747-9202 office@catholicpenguins.org www.catholicpenguins.org Rev. Norbert Keliher, Chap.; Carly Koewacich, Secy.;

CATHOLIC CHARITIES [CCH]

ASHTABULA

Catholic Charities of Ashtabula County - 4200 Park Ave., 3rd Floor, Ashtabula, OH 44004 t) 440-992-2121 info@doyccac.org; jillv@doyccac.org www.doyccac.org Jill Valentic, Exec.; Asstd. Annu.: 8,000; Staff: 20

RAVENNA

Catholic Charities Serving Portage and Stark Counties - 206 W. Main St., Ravenna, OH 44266 t) 330-297-7745 info@catholiccharitiesps.org; rick.squier@catholiccharitiesps.org Rick Squier, Exec.; Asstd. Annu.: 10,200; Staff: 18

YOUNGSTOWN

Catholic Charities Regional Agency - 319 W. Rayen Ave., Youngstown, OH 44502 t) 330-744-3320 nvoitus@ccregional.org ccdoy.org Social services for families, homeless, seniors, domestic violence victims, returning citizens and low income. Nancy Voitus, Exec.; Asstd. Annu.: 18,105; Staff: 47

Diocese of Youngstown Catholic Charities Corporation - 144 W. Wood. St., Youngstown, OH 44503 t) 330-744-8451 rhrbolich@youngstowndiocese.org www.ccdoy.org Rachel Hrbolich, Pres.;

CEMETERIES [CEM]

CORTLAND

All Souls - 3823 Hoagland Blackstub Rd., Cortland, OH 44410 t) 330-637-2761 cblasko@cfcsmission.org (The Catholic Cemeteries of the Diocese of Youngstown Inc.) Christa Blasko, Dir.;

MASSILLON

Calvary - 3469 Lincoln Way E., Massillon, OH 44646 t) 330-832-1866 cblasko@cfcsmission.org; btully@youngstowndiocese.org (The Catholic Cemeteries of the Diocese of Youngstown Inc.) Christa Blasko, Dir.; Becky Tully, Location Mgr.;

YOUNGSTOWN

Calvary - 248 S. Belle Vista Ave., Youngstown, OH 44509 t) 330-792-4721 cblasko@cfcsmission.org; rheald@youngstowndiocese.org www.cfcsyoungstown.org (The Catholic Cemeteries of the Diocese of Youngstown Inc.) Christa Blasko, Dir.; Patrick A. Kelly, CFO; Rachael Shinol, Location Mgr.;

Catholic Cemeteries of the Diocese of Youngstown, Inc. - 144 W. Wood St., Youngstown, OH 44503 t) 330-744-8451 pkelly@youngstowndiocese.org Christa Blasko, Dir.;

Resurrection - 300 N. Raccoon Rd., Youngstown, OH 44515 t) 330-799-1900 cblasko@cfcsmission.org (The Catholic Cemeteries of the Diocese of Youngstown Inc.) Christa Blasko, Dir.; Rachael Shinol, Location Mgr.;

COLLEGES & UNIVERSITIES [COL]

NORTH CANTON

Walsh University - 2020 E. Maple St., North Canton, OH 44720-3396 t) 330-490-7090 admissions@walsh.edu; cscheetz@walsh.edu www.walsh.edu (Coed) Brothers of Christian Instruction. Dr. Tim Collins, Pres.; Rev. Louis

Bertrand Lemoine, O.P., Chap.; Stds.: 2,320; Lay Tchrs.: 93; Pr. Tchrs.: 2

CONVENTS, MONASTERIES, AND RESIDENCES FOR WOMEN [CON]

CANFIELD

Ursuline Sisters of Youngstown - 4280 Shields Rd., Canfield, OH 44406 t) 330-792-7636 mmc4250@gmail.com www.theursulines.org Sr. Mary McCormick, O.S.U., Supr.; Brigid M. Kennedy, CEO; Srs.: 28

Beatitude House - 238 Tod Ln., Youngstown, OH 44504; Mailing: Ursuline Sisters Mission, 4280 Shields Rd., Canfield, OH 44406 t) (330) 744-3147 info@beatitudehouse.com www.beatitudehouse.com Programs for disadvantaged women and children.

Ursuline Center - 4280 Shields Rd., Canfield, OH 44406 t) 330-799-4941; (330) 793-0434 www.ursulinesistersmission.org Outreach and resources primarily for the poor, Ursuline Sisters HIV/AIDS Ministry, Comprehensive Care Center.

Ursuline Sisters Mission - 4280 Shields Rd., Canfield, OH 44406 t) (330) 792-7636 x318; (330) 793-0434 www.ursulinesistersmission.org Direct services including Immigrant Outreach, Ursuline Sisters Scholars, Ursuline Preschool & Kindergarten.

Ursuline Sisters Senior Living - 4260 Shields Rd., Canfield, OH 44406 t) (330) 792-7636 peggyeicher@gmail.com ursulinesisterssseniorliving.org Senior living community for lay people. Peggy Eicher, Dir.;

CANTON

Congregation of the Divine Spirit - 2700 Harvard Ave., N.W., Canton, OH 44709; Mailing: 2700 Harvard Ave. NW, Canton, OH 44709 t) (330) 453-8526 adsum409@neohio.twcbc.com www.sempercaritas.org Sr. Michele Beauseigneur, Supr.; Srs.: 18

Sancta Clara Monastery - 4200 N. Market Ave., Canton, OH 44714 t) 330-492-1171 pcpacanton4200@gmail.com www.poorclares.org Poor Clares of Perpetual Adoration. Srs.: 11

HUBBARD

Oblate Sisters of the Sacred Heart of Jesus Institute, Villa Maria Teresa - 50 Warner Rd., Hubbard, OH 44425 t) 330-759-9329 vmtoblate@aol.com; jcoblate@aol.com www.oblatesistersofshj.com Novitiate and American Headquarters of Oblate Sisters of the Sacred Heart of Jesus. Sr. Joyce Candidi, O.S.H.J., Supr.; Srs.: 17

VIENNA

The Missionary Sisters of St. Francis of Assisi - 333 Scoville Dr., Vienna, OH 44473 t) (330) 240-1017 vocations.mssf@gmail.com www.dominusvobiscum.org Mother Mary Francis, Supr.; Srs.: 2

ENDOWMENTS / FOUNDATIONS / TRUSTS [EFT]

CANTON

Mercy Development Foundation - 1320 Mercy Dr., N.W., Canton, OH 44708 t) 330-489-1421 Thomas Turner, Pres.;

LOUISVILLE

St. Thomas Aquinas High School Endowment Fund - 2121 Reno Dr., N.E., Louisville, OH 44641 t) 330-875-1631 bmoeglin@youngstowndiocese.org www.stahs.org Rev. Donald E. King;

YOUNGSTOWN

Declaration of Trust of Trumbull - Dept. of Educ., 144 W. Wood St., Youngstown, OH 44503 t) 330-744-8451 mfiala@youngstowndiocese.org County Catholic School Endowment Fund. Joan Lawson, Chancellor;

Roman Catholic Diocese of Youngstown Foundation - 144 W. Wood St., Youngstown, OH 44503 t) 330-744-8451 pkelly@youngstowndiocese.org Patrick A. Kelly, Treas.;

HOSPITALS / HEALTH SERVICES [HOS]

BOARDMAN

Mercy Health Youngstown LLC (St. Elizabeth Boardman Hospital) - 8401 Market St., Boardman, OH 44512 t) 330-729-2929 Eugenia L. Aubel, Pres.; Bed Capacity: 220; Asstd. Annu.: 73,366; Staff: 1,062

CANTON

***Mercy Medical Center (1908)** - 1320 Mercy Dr., N.W., Canton, OH 44708 t) 330-489-1011 www.cantonmercy.org Thomas Strauss, CEO; Bed Capacity: 390; Asstd. Annu.: 394,054; Staff: 2,447

GIRARD

Mercy Health Youngstown LLC - 979 Tibbetts-Wick Rd., Ste. A, Girard, OH 44420 t) 330-480-3776 Mercy Health Home Care - Youngstown, dba Mercy Health Home Infusion - Youngstown; dba Mercy Health Home Medical Equipment - Youngstown John Luellen, Pres.;

WARREN

Mercy Health Youngstown LLC (St. Joseph Warren Hospital) - 667 Eastland Ave., S.E., Warren, OH 44484 t) 330-841-4000 www.mercy.com Martin Tursky, Pres.; Bed Capacity: 147; Asstd. Annu.: 87,113; Staff: 855

YOUNGSTOWN

Mercy Health Youngstown LLC (St. Elizabeth Youngstown Hospital) - 1044 Belmont Ave., Youngstown, OH 44501-1790; Mailing: Box 1790, Youngstown, OH 44501-1790 t) 330-746-7211 www.mercy.com/youngstown Kathy Harley, Pres.; Bed Capacity: 409; Asstd. Annu.: 107,725; Staff: 2,167

MISCELLANEOUS [MIS]

CANFIELD

Society of St. Paul (Alba House Communications) - 9531 Akron-Canfield Rd., Canfield, OH 44406; Mailing: P.O. Box 595, Canfield, OH 44406 t) 330-533-5503 provincialoffice@stpauls.us; ssp_canfield@stpauls.us www.stpaulsusa.com Pious Society of St Paul Bro. Dominic Calabro, S.S.P., Supr.; Bro. Marco Bulgarelli, SSP, Treas.; Bro. Augustine Condon, SSP, Mem.; Bro. Edward Donaher, SSP, Mem.; Bro. Joseph Dubois, SSP, Mem.; Bro. John Naranjo, S.S.P., Mem.; Rev. Matthew Roehrig, S.S.P., Mem.; Bro. Tim Joshua Seidl Douglas, Mem.; Rev. Anthony Warren, SSP, Mem.; Bro. Aloysius Milella, S.S.P., Mem.;

CANTON

Catholic Migrant Farmworker Network, Inc. - 701 Walnut Ave., N.E., Canton, OH 44702 t) 402-213-6428 zeusariza.1958@gmail.com; teresitakontos@gmail.com Ricardo Ariza, Pres.; Teresita Kontos, Vice Pres./Coord. Migrant Min.;

Early Childhood Resource Center - 1718 Cleveland Ave., N.W., Canton, OH 44703 t) 330-491-3272 shasselman@ecresourcecenter.org www.sistersofcharityhealth.org Scott Hasselman, Dir.;

YOUNGSTOWN

The Catholic Exponent - 144 W. Wood St., Youngstown, OH 44501-6787; Mailing: P.O. Box 6787, Youngstown, OH 44501-6787 t) 330-744-5251 exponent@youngstowndiocese.org www.cathexpo.org Pete Sheehan, Editor;

Conference of Slovak Clergy - 144 W. Wood St., Youngstown, OH 44503 t) 330-744-8451 rsiffrin@youngstowndiocese.org www.doy.org Founded 1985, incorporated 2000. It associates bishops, priests and deacons of Slovak ancestry in the U.S. preparing for ordained ministry. Very Rev. Msgr. Robert J. Siffrin, Chair; Very Rev. Martin Celuch, Secy.; Rev. Thomas A. Nasta, Vice Chairman;

The Diocese of Youngstown Scholarship Granting Organization - 144 W. Wood St., Youngstown, OH 44503 t) (330) 744-8451 Mary Fiala, Pres.;

First Friday Club of Greater Youngstown - ; Mailing: P.O. Box 11146, Youngstown, OH 44511 t) 330-720-4498 meblegal@aol.com www.firstfridayclubofgreateryoungstown.org Monthly luncheon speaker series Very Rev. Msgr. John A. Zuraw;

Lake to River Telecommunications Corporation - 144 W. Wood St., Youngstown, OH 44503 t) 330-744-8451 pkelly@youngstowndiocese.org Patrick A. Kelly, Treas.;

Midwest Canon Law Society - 141 W. Rayen Ave., Youngstown, OH 44503 t) 330-744-8451 mceluch@youngstowndiocese.org Very Rev. Martin Celuch, Pst.;

The Roman Catholic Diocese of Youngstown Annual Bishop's Appeal - 144 W. Wood St., Youngstown, OH 44503 t) 330-744-8451 pkelly@youngstowndiocese.org www.doy.org Patrick A. Kelly, Treas.;

Roman Catholic Diocese of Youngstown Property Corporation - 144 W. Wood St., Youngstown, OH 44503 t) 330-744-8451 pkelly@youngstowndiocese.org Patrick A. Kelly, Treas.;

MONASTERIES AND RESIDENCES FOR PRIESTS AND BROTHERS [MON]

YOUNGSTOWN

Mt. Alverna Friary - 517 S. Belle Vista Ave., Youngstown, OH 44509 t) 330-799-1888 Franciscan Friars Rev. Vit Fiala, O.F.M., Dir.; Rev. Jules Wong, O.F.M., Mem.; Priests: 2

NURSING / REHABILITATION / CONVALESCENCE / ELDERLY CARE [NUR]

AUSTINTOWN

Humility House - 755 Ohltown Rd., Austintown, OH 44515 t) 330-505-0144 Melessa Scattino, Exec. Dir.; Asstd. Annu.: 84; Staff: 98

CANTON

House of Loreto - 2812 Harvard Ave., N.W., Canton, OH 44709 t) 330-453-8137 loreto1955@neohio.twcbc.com www.sempercaritas.org/ministry-to-the-aged Congregation of the Divine Spirit. Sr. Janet Harold, C.D.S., Admin.; Sr. Marilee Heuer, C.D.S., Admin.; Sr. Michele Beauseigneur, Supr.; Asstd. Annu.: 40; Staff: 40

HUBBARD

Villa Maria Teresa - 50 Warner Rd., Hubbard, OH 44425 t) 330-759-9329 vmtoblate@aol.com www.oblatesistersofshj.com Retired Priests' Residence. Sr. Joyce Candidi, O.S.H.J., Supr.; Asstd. Annu.: 3; Staff: 2

LOUISVILLE

Emmaus House - 1515 California Ave., Louisville, OH 44641-8708 t) 330-875-4635 joewitmer@juno.com Retired Priests' Residence. Rev. Joseph W. Witmer, Admin.; Asstd. Annu.: 6; Staff: 3

St. Joseph Care Center (St. Joseph Senior Living) - 2308 Reno Dr., Louisville, OH 44641 t) 330-875-5562 info@stjsl.org www.saintjosephseniorliving.org Skilled Nursing and Rehabilitation, Assisted Living, Memory Support, Senior Retirement Apartments (The Alsatian) Brian Harbert, CFO; Asstd. Annu.: 350; Staff: 175

NORTH LIMA

The Assumption Village, Humility Health Center (Nursing Care) - 9800 Market St., North Lima, OH 44452 t) 330-549-0740 Sisters of the Humility of Mary.Member: Mercy Health, Skilled Nursing Unit with Subacute Care Program, Special Care Unit Melessa Scattino, Exec.; Asstd. Annu.: 168; Staff: 186

PRESCHOOLS / CHILDCARE CENTERS [PRE]

HUBBARD

Villa Maria Teresa Daycare and Kindergarten - 50 Warner Rd., Hubbard, OH 44425 t) 330-759-7383 jcoblate@aol.com; vmtoblate@aol.com www.oblatesisterofshj.com Sr. Vittoria Nisi, Prin.; Stds.: 65; Lay Tchrs.: 2

SHRINES [SHR]

MASSILLON

National Shrine of St. Dymphna - 206 Cherry Rd., N.E., Massillon, OH 44646 t) 330-833-8478 stdymphnashrinemassillon@gmail.com www.natlshrinestdymphna.org Rev. Canon Matthew Mankowski, Rector;

SPECIAL CARE FACILITIES [SPF]

NORTH LIMA

The Assumption Village, Marian Living Center (Assisted

Living Facility) - 9802 Market St., North Lima, OH 44452 t) 330-549-2434 Member of Mercy Health (Assisted Living Facility). Sponsorship: Sisters of the Humility of Mary. Melessa Scattino, Exec. Dir.; Bed Capacity: 48; Asstd. Annu.: 168; Staff: 16

POLAND

Hospice of the Valley, Hospice House - 9803 Sharrott Rd., Poland, OH 44514 t) 330-549-5850 www.hospiceofthevalley.com Liz McGarry, Dir.; Bed Capacity: 16; Asstd. Annu.: 52,651; Staff: 96

An asterisk (*) denotes an organization that has established tax-exempt status directly with the IRS and is not covered by the USCCB Group Ruling.

Apostolate to Hungarians

MOST REVEREND FERENC CSERHATI, S.T.D.

Titular Bishop of Centuria, Auxiliary to Esztergom-Budapest, especially entrusted with the coordination of the pastoral service of Hungarians abroad; ordained April 18, 1971 in Alba Julia; appointed June 15, 2007; consecrated in Esztergom August 15, 2007.
Res.: MKPK, Kulfoldi Magyar Lelkipasztori Szolgalat, Papnovelde utca 5-7, Budapest, H-1053. T: 36-1-266-4515; F: 36-1-266-4515; cserhati@katolikus.hu.

ESTABLISHED MAY 20, 1983.

The Apostolate of the Bishop of Hungarians living outside of Hungary extends territorially to all the Hungarian communities existing outside of Hungary. The main purpose of the Apostolate is to give spiritual assistance to them through and in cooperation with the local ordinary and pastors.

LEADERSHIP

Delegate in North America—t) 313-842-1133
Rev. Barnabas G. Kiss, O.F.M. (holycross1905@att.net)

ORGANIZATIONS

American Hungarian Catholic Priests' Association—(USA) t) 313-842-1133
Rev. Barnabas G. Kiss, O.F.M. (holycross1905@att.net)

Hungaran Priests' Association in Canada—
Rev. Barnabas G. Kiss, O.F.M., Pres. (holycross1905@att.net); Rev. Tamas G. Forrai, S.J., Secy. (forrai.tamas@gmail.com)

STATISTICS

Most personnel and institutions are under the jurisdiction of their local ordinaries.

An asterisk (*) denotes an organization that has established tax-exempt status directly with the IRS and is not covered by the USCCB Group Ruling.

Apostolate For Lithuanian Catholics

Living Outside Lithuania

ARCHBISHOP LIONGINAS VIRBALAS, S.J.

Delegate of the Lithuanian Bishops Conference; appointed January 26, 2023 to coordinate the pastoral care of Lithuanian Catholics living in the Diaspora.

Office: S. Skapo g. 4, LT-01122 Vilnius, Lithuania T: (+370-5) 212 54 55; virbalas@sielovada.org

ESTABLISHED JUNE 1, 1984.

The Apostolate for Lithuanian Catholics, extends worldwide to all Lithuanian communities existing outside Lithuania. Fifty percent of them in the U.S.A.

The purpose of the apostolate is to give spiritual assistance to them in cooperation with the local ordinaries and pastors.

LEADERSHIP

Office of General Counsel—t) 312-346-5275
Saulius V. Kuprys (svkuprys@gmail.com)

CLERGY AND RELIGIOUS SERVICES

Lithuanian Franciscan Province of St. Casimir—
t) 416-533-0621 Rev. Jonas Sileika, O.F.M., Delegate

Lithuanian Jesuits—t) 630-257-5613
Rev. Vaidas Lukosevicius, S.J., Pst.

Marian Province of Mary Mother of Mercy—
t) 413-298-3691
Rev. Kazimierz Chwalek, M.I.C., Prov.

Poor Sisters of Jesus Crucified and the Sorrowful Mother—t) 508-588-5070
Sr. Geraldine Nevaras, Dir.

Sisters of St. Casimir—t) 773-776-1324

Sisters of St. Francis—t) 412-882-9911
Sr. Joanne Brazinski, O.S.F., Supr.

Sisters of the Immaculate Conception of the Blessed Virgin Mary—t) 860-928-7955
Sr. Igne Marijosiute, Prov.

COMMUNICATIONS

Publications—Draugas (Chicago, IL); Draugas News (Chicago, IL); Lithuanian Catholic Press Society; Lithuanian Heritage (Chicago, IL); Teviskes Aidai (Adelaide, Australia); Teviskes Ziburiai (Toronto, Ontario, Canada)

EDUCATION

Pontifical Lithuanian College of St. Casimir—
t) 06-70-26-774
Rev. Audrius Arstikaitis, Rector

ORGANIZATIONS

Lithuanian American R. Catholic Federation—
Dana Rugienius, Pres.

Lithuanian R. Catholic Priests' League of America—
t) 773-776-4600
Rev. Jaunius Kelpsas (Lithuania), Pres.

Lithuanian Roman Catholic Priests' League of America—

Lithuanian R. Catholic Priests' League of Canada—
t) 416-533-0621 Rev. Jonas Sileika, O.F.M., Pres.;
Rev. Nerijus Smerauskas (Lithuania), Pres.

SOCIAL SERVICES

***Lithuanian R. Catholic Religious Aid, Inc.**—
t) 718-326-5202 info@lcraid.org
Jurate Zukauskiene, Exec.

Lithuanian Roman Catholic Charities, Inc.—

INSTITUTIONS LOCATED IN DIOCESE

CATHOLIC CHARITIES [CCH]

CHICAGO

Lithuanian Roman Catholic Charities—
4545 W. 63rd St., Chicago, IL 60629
t) 773-585-9500 administracija@draugas.org
Linas Sidrys, Pres.
Asstd. Annu.: 20; Staff: 1

CEMETERIES [CEM]

CHICAGO

St. Casimir Lithuanian—
4401 W. 111th St., Chicago, IL 60655

ENDOWMENTS / FOUNDATIONS /TRUSTS [EFT]

CHICAGO

Catholic Action Fund—

MISCELLANEOUS [MIS]

CHICAGO

Jesuit Lithuanian Center—

***Lithuanian Catholic Press Society**—
4545 W. 63rd St., Chicago, IL 60629
t) 773-585-9500 administracija@draugas.org
Vytas Stanevicius, Chair

Matulaitis Institute—

PUTNAM

American Lithuanian Catholic Archives—
37 Mary Crest Dr., Putnam, CT 06260
Mirga Girniuviene, Archivist

NURSING / REHABILITATION / CONVALESCENCE / ELDERLY CARE [NUR]

LEMONT

Holy Family Villa—

PUTNAM

Matulaitis Nursing Home—
10 Thurber Rd., Putnam, CT 06260
t) 860-928-7976

PRESCHOOLS / CHILDCARE CENTERS [PRE]

MANCHESTER

Lithuanian American R. Catholic Federation Youth Camp—
15100 Austin Rd., Manchester, MI 48158;
Mailing: 10 Algonquin Rd., Clarendon Hills, IL 60514
t) 773-307-9777 danarugienius@gmail.com
dainava.org
Danute Rugienius, Pres.
Stds.: 300; Lay Tchrs.: 30

STATISTICS

Most personnel and institutions are under the jurisdiction of their local ordinaries.

An asterisk (*) denotes an organization that has established tax-exempt status directly with the IRS and is not covered by the USCCB Group Ruling.

Prelature of the Holy Cross and Opus Dei

(Praelatura Sanctae Crucis et Operis Dei)

REVEREND MONSIGNOR FERNANDO OCARIZ, Ph.D., S.T.D.

Prelate of the Prelature of the Holy Cross and Opus Dei; ordained August 15, 1971; appointed January 23, 2017. Mailing Address: Viale Bruno Buozzi, 73, Rome, 00197.

PRELATURE OF OPUS DEI

Erected by the Apostolic Constitution, "Ut sit," on November 28, 1982 by Pope John Paul II.

Opus Dei was founded on October 2, 1928 by Saint Josemaria Escriva, to spread in all sectors of society a profound awareness of the universal call to sanctity in ordinary life and, more specifically, in the exercise of one's work.

LEADERSHIP

Curia of the Prelature—info@opusdei.org

Prelate—Rev. Msgr. Fernando Ocariz

Auxiliary Vicar—Rev. Msgr. Mariano Fazio

Vicar General—Rev. Msgr. Antoni Pujals

Regional Vicar for the United States—t) 646-742-2700
Very Rev. Javier del Castillo

Vicar for the Central United States—t) 773-283-5800
Very Rev. Peter V. Armenio

Vicar for California—t) 323-930-2844
Very Rev. Luke J. Mata

Regional Vicar for Puerto Rico—t) 787-781-9123
Rev. Msgr. Justiniano Garcia Arias

CLERGY AND RELIGIOUS SERVICES

CHAPLAINS FOR THE UNITED STATES

STATE OF NEW YORK

NEW YORK CITY - MURRAY HILL
t) 646-742-2700
Rev. Msgr. Thomas G. Bohlin, Chap.; Rev. Joseph Keefe, Chap.; Rev. John C. Agnew, Chap.

NEW YORK CITY - RIVERSIDE
t) 212-222-3285
Rev. Robert A. Connor, Chap.; Rev. Timothy J. Uhen, Chap.

NEW ROCHELLE
t) 914-235-0199
Rev. Bradley K. Arturi, Chap.; Rev. Michael J. Manz, Chap.

DISTRICT OF COLUMBIA

WASHINGTON - KALORAMA
t) 202-234-1567
Rev. Joseph P. Ruisanchez, Chap.; Rev. Rene J. Schatteman, Chap.; Rev. Charles Trullols, Chap.

WASHINGTON - TENLEYTOWN
t) 202-362-2419
Rev. Diego Daza, Chap.; Rev. Salvador Vahi, Chap.

STATE OF MASSACHUSETTS

CAMBRIDGE
t) 617-354-3204
Rev. Jeffrey Langan, Chap.

NEWTON - CHESTNUT HILL
t) 617-738-7348
Rev. David J. Cavanagh, Chap.; Rev. George A. Crafts, Chap.; Rev. John Grieco, Chap.

STATE OF NEW JERSEY

PRINCETON
t) 609-497-9448
Rev. Joseph P. Thomas, Chap.

SOUTH ORANGE
t) 973-763-8397
Rev. Henry Bocala, Chap.

STATE OF PENNSYLVANIA

PITTSBURGH
t) 412-683-8448
Rev. Joseph P. Landauer, Chap.; Rev. Martin John Miller, Chap.

STATE OF FLORIDA

MIAMI
t) 305-551-7956
Rev. Oscar Regojo, Chap.; Rev. William Shaughnessy, Chap.; Rev. Juan R. Velez, Chap.

DELRAY BEACH
t) 516-498-1249
Rev. Oscar Regojo, Chap.

STATE OF RHODE ISLAND

PROVIDENCE
t) 401-272-7834
Rev. George A. Crafts, Chap.

STATE OF ILLINOIS

CHICAGO - SAUGANASH
t) 312-283-5800
Very Rev. Pedro Pablo Arriagada, Chap.; Rev. John Paul Mitchell, Chap.; Rev. Leo Austin, Chap.

CHICAGO - ROGERS PARK
t) 773-465-3468
Rev. G. Barry Cole, Chap.; Rev. Deogracias Rosales, Chap.

CHICAGO - BUCKTOWN
t) 773-292-5450
Rev. Steven Brock, Chap.; Rev. Juan Diego Ibañez, Chap.; Rev. John R. Waiss, Chap.

DARIEN
t) 630-541-8769
Rev. Derek Esclanda, Chap.; Rev. Charles R. Ferrer, Chap.

URBANA
t) 217-367-6650
Rev. G. Barry Cole, Chap.; Rev. John Paul Mitchell, Chap.

STATE OF INDIANA

SOUTH BEND
t) 574-232-0550
Rev. Martin Joseph Miller, Chap.

STATE OF MISSOURI

KIRKWOOD
t) 314-821-1608
Rev. Gregory J. Coyne, Chap.; Rev. Michael E. Giesler, Chap.

STATE OF WISCONSIN

BROOKFIELD
t) 414-784-1523
Rev. Eduardo Castillo, Chap.; Rev. John C. Kubeck, Chap.

STATE OF CALIFORNIA

LOS ANGELES
t) 323-930-2844
Rev. John R. Meyer, Chap.; Rev. Mark Mannion, Chap.; Rev. Victor G. Cortes, Chap.

BERKELEY
t) 415-327-1675
Rev. Msgr. James A. Kelly, Chap.; Rev. Javier Bujalance, Chap.

MENLO PARK
t) 650-327-1675
Rev. Edward G. Maristany, Chap.; Rev. Torlach Delargy, Chap.

STATE OF TEXAS

HOUSTON - RICE VILLAGE
t) 770-523-4351
Rev. Msgr. Javier Garcia de Cardenas, Chap.; Rev. Francisco Vera, Chap.; Rev. John J. Alvarez, Chap.

HOUSTON - MEMORIAL PARK
t) 713-534-1976
Rev. Paul D. Kais, Chap.; Rev. Christopher Schmitt, Chap.

IRVING
t) 214-650-0064
Rev. Jerome L. Jung, Chap.; Rev. Michael Fagan, Chap.

SAN ANTONIO
t) 210-732-3065
Rev. Msgr. Javier Garcia de Cardenas, Chap.

STATE OF VIRGINIA

RESTON
t) 703-689-3433
Rev. Gerald Kolf, Chap.; Rev. Malcolm M. Kennedy, Chap.; Rev. Lawrence A. Kutz, Chap.

PUERTO RICO

GUAYNABO
t) 787-781-9123
Rev. Martin Llambias, Chap.; Rev. Juan Jose Salinas, Chap.; Rev. Andres Eiroa, Chap.

SAN JUAN
t) 787-759-6193
Rev. Juan Ignacio Ballesteros, Chap.; Rev. Jaime Bermudez, Chap.

PONCE
t) 787-844-2661
Rev. Javier Bernaola, Chap.; Rev. Alejandro Zubieta, Chap.

MAYAGUEZ
t) 787-833-6461

Holy Protection of Mary Byzantine Catholic Eparchy of Phoenix

(VACANT SEE)

Chancery Office: 8131 N. 16th St., Phoenix, AZ 85020. T:602-861-9778; F: 602-861-9796.
www.ephx.org
msgrmcauliffe@ephx.org

ESTABLISHED DECEMBER 3, 1981.

Established in 1981 as the Byzantine Catholic Eparchy of Van Nuys. The name was changed to Holy Protection of Mary Byzantine Catholic Eparchy of Phoenix on February 10, 2010 by the Holy See.

Embraces all Catholics of the Byzantine-Ruthenian Church in the States of California, Oregon, Washington, Idaho, Nevada, Arizona, Utah, Wyoming, Montana, Colorado, New Mexico, Alaska and Hawaii.

Principal Patron-Holy Protection of the Mother of God (Pokrov).

Legal Titles: Byzantine Catholic Bishop of Phoenix, An Arizona Non-profit Corporation

For Legal Titles of Eparchial and Parish Institutions, please consult the Chancellor.

Most Reverend Thomas J. Olmsted, J.C.D.
Apostolic Administrator, Sede Vacante Bishop of Phoenix; ordained July 2, 1973; appointed Coadjutor Bishop of Wichita February 16, 1999; appointed Bishop of Wichita October 4, 2001; appointed Bishop of Phoenix November 25, 2003; installed December 20, 2003. Office: 8131 N. 16th St., Phoenix, AZ 85020.

STATISTICAL OVERVIEW

Personnel

Retired Bishops	1
Abbots	1
Priests: Diocesan Active in Diocese	19
Priests: Diocesan Active Outside Diocese	3
Priests: Retired, Sick or Absent	7
Number of Diocesan Priests	29
Religious Priests in Diocese	1
Total Priests in your Diocese	30
Extern Priests in Diocese	2
Ordinations:	
Diocesan Priests	2
Transitional Deacons	1
Permanent Deacons in Diocese	13
Total Brothers	4

Parishes

Parishes	19
With Resident Pastor:	
Resident Diocesan Priests	18
Resident Religious Priests	1
Missions	1

Welfare

Educational

Diocesan Students in Other Seminaries	3
Total Seminarians	3
Catechesis / Religious Education:	
High School Students	72
Elementary Students	228
Total Students under Catholic Instruction	303

Vital Statistics

Receptions into the Church:	
Infant Baptism Totals	62
Minor Baptism Totals	7
Adult Baptism Totals	17
First Communions	85
Confirmations	94
Marriages:	
Catholic	20
Interfaith	1
Total Marriages	21
Deaths	38
Total Catholic Population	2,424

LEADERSHIP

Chancery Office - t) 602-861-9778 msgrmcauliffe@ephx.org
Protosyncellus (Vicar General) - Very Rev. Diodoro Mendoza (frmendoza@ephx.org);
Chancellor - Rev. Msgr. Kevin W. McAuliffe (msgrmcauliffe@ephx.org);
College of Consultors - Most Rev. Kurt Burnette; Rt. Rev. Stephen G. Washko; Rt. Rev. Joseph Stanichar;
Finance Officer - Patricia Henderson (patriciah@ephx.org);
Finance Council - Most Rev. Kurt Burnette; Patricia Henderson; Very Rev. Diodoro Mendoza;
Eparchial Appeal - Patricia Henderson (patriciah@ephx.org);
Presbyteral Council -
Secretary for the Presbyteral Council & The College of Consultors - Rev. Michael S. Bezruchka;

OFFICES AND DIRECTORS

Building and Sacred Arts Commission - Rt. Rev. Stephen G. Washko; Dcn. John Montalvo III; Very Rev. Diodoro Mendoza (frmendoza@ephx.org);
Censor - Rt. Rev. Joseph Stanichar; Rev. David M. Petras; Rev. Andrew Summerson;
Director of Ecumenical Affairs - Rt. Rev. Stephen G. Washko;
Ecclesiatical Notaries - Very Rev. Diodoro Mendoza (frmendoza@ephx.org); Teresa Blanc;
Financial Stewardship Committee -
Intereparchial Evangelization Commission - Very Rev. Michael O'Loughlin;
Intereparchial Liturgical Commission - Rev. Robert M. Pipta;
Intereparchial Music Commission - Rev. Michael S. Bezruchka;
Intereparchial Religious Education Commission - Rev. Nathan Simeon Adams; Rev. Daniel Dozier;
Intereparchial Youth Commission - Dcn. Jonathan Deane; Rev. Artur Bubnevych;
Pension Committee - Most Rev. Kurt Burnette; Rev. James Barrand; Subdeacon Stephen Melancon;
Personnel Board - Most Rev. Kurt Burnette; Very Rev. Michael Mandelas; Rt. Rev. Mitred Archpriest Stephen Washko;
Pro-Life Coordinators - prolife@ephx.org Kenneth Roberts; Rebecca Roberts;
Safe Environment Coordinator - safeenvironment@ephx.org Subdeacon Paul F. Kilroy (sdcnkilroy@ephx.org);
Victim Advocate and Assistance Coordinator - Dcn. Michael Hanafin (vac@ephx.org);
Vocation Review Board - Most Rev. Kurt Burnette; Rev. Michael Mandelas; Rev. James Bankston;
Vocations Office - Rev. Michael Mandelas, Dir.;

COMMUNICATIONS

Eparchial Website - Marcus Cabrera (cabrera@ephx.org); Cole Harter;
Magazine - Vacant -
Public Relations Liaison - publicrelations@ephx.org John Surmay;
Social Media - Cole Harter;

TRIBUNAL

Eparchial Tribunal - t) 602-861-9778 Rev. Msgr. Kevin W. McAuliffe; Teresa Blanc;
Adjutant Judicial Vicar (Vacant) -
Auditors/Advocates - Dcn. John Montalvo III; Teresa Blanc;
Defender of the Bond - Rev. Nelson Libera;
Judge - Rev. Msgr. Kevin W. McAuliffe;
Judicial Vicar - Rev. Msgr. Kevin W. McAuliffe;
Notaries - Very Rev. Diodoro Mendoza; Teresa Blanc;
Promoter of Justice - Rev. Nelson Libera;
Secretary - Teresa Blanc;

PARISHES, MISSIONS, AND CLERGY

STATE OF ALASKA

ANCHORAGE

Saint Nicholas of Myra - 2200 Arctic Blvd., Anchorage, AK 99503-1909 t) 907-277-6731 frwargacki@ephx.org www.ak-byz-cath.org Rev. Joseph Wargacki, Pst.;
Blessed Theodore Romzha Mission - 1201 Bogard Rd., Wasilla, AK 99654

STATE OF ARIZONA

GILBERT

St. Thomas the Apostle - 19 W. Bruce Ave., Gilbert, AZ 85233; Mailing: P.O. Box 667, Gilbert, AZ 85299-0667 t) 480-497-6726 saint.thomas.pastor@gmail.com www.stabcc.org Rev. Adam Lowe, Admin.; Dcn. Michael Sullivan; CRP Stds.: 22

LAS VEGAS

***Our Lady of Wisdom Italo-Greek** - 2120 Lindell Rd., Las Vegas, AZ 89146-0387; Mailing: 2120 S. Lindell, Rd., Las Vegas, NV 89146 t) 702-873-5101 ourladyofwisdomitalogreek@gmail.com www.ourladyofwisdom.net Rev. Nathan Daniel Adams, Admin.; CRP Stds.: 20

PHOENIX

St. Stephen Cathedral - 8141 N. 16th St., Frnt., Phoenix, AZ 85020-3999 t) 602-943-5379 rector@ephx.org; dcndanovich@ephx.org www.stsbcc.org Very Rev. Diodoro Mendoza, Rector; Dcn. James Danovich; Dcn. Michael Hanafin; Dcn. John Montalvo III; CRP Stds.: 10
St. Stephen Convent - 8141 N. 16th St., #27, Phoenix, AZ 85020 t) 602-944-5121

TUCSON

St. Melany - 1212 N. Sahuara Ave., Tucson, AZ 85712-5018 t) 520-886-4225 frrankin@ephx.org; stmelany@msn.com Rev. Robert Rankin, Pst.; Dcn. Thomas Campbell, Campus Min.; Dcn. Joseph Kushner, Campus Min.; CRP Stds.: 31

STATE OF CALIFORNIA

ANAHEIM

Annunciation - 995 N. West St., Anaheim, CA 92801-4305 t) 714-533-6292 abcc72069@gmail.com; bethgath@gmail.com www.annunciationbyzantine.org Rt. Rev. Stephen G. Washko, Pst.; Dcn. Gregory M Gath; CRP Stds.: 15

FONTANA

St. Nicholas - 9112 Oleander Ave., Fontana, CA 92335-5599 t) 909-822-9917 st.nicholas.fontana@gmail.com stnicholasfontana.org Stephen George Washko, Admin.;

LOS GATOS

St. Basil the Great - 14263 Mulberry Dr., Los Gatos, CA 95032-1208 t) 408-871-0919 frhernandez@ephx.org Rev. Anthony Hernandez, Pst.; Dcn. Craig Anderson;

SACRAMENTO

St. Philip the Apostle - 3866 65th St., Sacramento, CA 95820-2033 t) 916-452-1888 frandrews@ephx.org stphilipofsacramento.wordpress.com/ Rev. Christopher Andrews, O.S.B., Admin.;

SAN DIEGO

Holy Angels - 2235 Galahad Rd., San Diego, CA 92123-3931 t) 858-277-2511 pastorhasd@gmail.com www.holyangelssandiego.com Rev. James Patrick Bankston, Admin.; Dcn. Jonathan Andrew Deane; CRP Stds.: 27

SAN LUIS OBISPO

Saint Anne - 222 E. Foothill Blvd., San Luis Obispo, CA 93405-1540 t) 805-543-8883 stanneslo@gmail.com; frbezruchka@ephx.org www.stanneslo.org Rev. Michael S. Bezruchka, Pst.; CRP Stds.: 26

SHERMAN OAKS

St. Mary Proto-Cathedral - 5329 Sepulveda Blvd., Sherman Oaks, CA 91411-3441 t) 818-905-5511 froloughlin@ephx.org; admin@byzantinela.com byzantinela.com Rev. Michael O'Loughlin, Pst.;

STATE OF COLORADO

DENVER

Holy Protection of the Mother of God - 1201 S. Elizabeth St., Denver, CO 80210 t) (720) 910-3084 pastor@holyprotection.org www.holyprotection.org Rev. Joel Barstad, Par. Admin.; Dcn. Basil Ryan Balke;

STATE OF NEVADA

LAS VEGAS

St. Gabriel the Archangel - 2250 E. Maule Ave., Las Vegas, NV 89119-4607 t) 702-361-2431 frgomori@ephx.org stgabrielbyzantinecatholicchurch.org Rev. Marcus Gomori, Pst.;
St. Gabriel Littlest Angels Catholic Preschool - (Grades PreK- t) 702-361-5531 Teri De La Torre, Dir.;

STATE OF NEW MEXICO

ALBUQUERQUE

Our Lady of Perpetual Help - 1837 Alvarado Dr., N.E., Albuquerque, NM 87110 t) 505-256-1539; 505-268-2877 frbubnevych@ephx.org; abbaolph@gmail.com www.olphnm.org Rev. Artur Bubnevych, Pst.; Rev. Christopher L. Zugger, In Res.; CRP Stds.: 46

STATE OF OREGON

PORTLAND

St. Irene Byzantine Catholic Church - 4630 N. Maryland Ave., Portland, OR 97217 t) 503-281-6744 stirenebcc@gmail.com www.saintirene.org Rev. Vasyl Mutka, Pst.; CRP Stds.: 2

STATE OF WASHINGTON

OLYMPIA

St. George Byzantine Catholic Church - 9730 Yelm Hwy., S.E., Olympia, WA 98513 t) 360-459-8373 stgeorgeolympia@outlook.com saintgeorgeolympia.org Rev. Daniel Dozier, Admin.; CRP Stds.: 40

SEATTLE

St. John Chrysostom - 1305 S. Lander St., Seattle, WA 98144-5038 t) 206-329-9219 frmandelas@ephx.org stjohnchrysostom.org/ Rev. Michael Mandelas, Pst.; CRP Stds.: 46
Whatcom, Skagit & Island Outreach - St. Charles R.C. Church, 935 Peterson Rd., Burlington, WA 98233

SPOKANE VALLEY

SS. Cyril & Methodius - 4315 N. Evergreen Rd., Spokane Valley, WA 99216; Mailing: P.O. Box 15314, Spokane Valley, WA 99215-5314 t) 509-922-4527 frobrien@ephx.org Rev. William O'Brien, Pst.; CRP Stds.: 30

INSTITUTIONS LOCATED IN DIOCESE

ENDOWMENTS / FOUNDATIONS / TRUSTS [EFT]

FONTANA

Saint Nicholas, Fontana Charitable Trust - 9112 Oleander Ave., Fontana, CA 92335-5527; Mailing: 8131 N. 16th St., Pheonix, AZ 85020 t) 602-861-9778 chancellor@ephx.org Diodoro Mendoza, Chancellor;

PHOENIX

Saint Anne, San Luis Obispo Charitable Trust - 8131 N. 16th St., Phoenix, AZ 85020 t) 602-861-9778 chancellor@ephx.org Diodoro Mendoza, Dir.;
Annunciation, Anaheim Charitable Trust - 8131 N. 16th St., Phoenix, AZ 85020 t) 602-861-9778 chancellor@ephx.org Diodoro Mendoza, Chancellor;

Saint Basil, Los Gatos Charitable Trust - 8131 N. 16th St., Phoenix, AZ 85020 t) 602-861-9778 chancellor@ephx.org Diodoro Mendoza, Chancellor;
Saints Cyril and Methodius, Spokane Charitable Trust - 8131 N. 16th St., Phoenix, AZ 85020 t) 602-861-9778 chancellor@ephx.org Diodoro Mendoza, Chancellor;
Saint Gabriel, Las Vegas Charitable Trust - 8131 N. 16th St., Phoenix, AZ 85020 t) 602-861-9778 chancellor@ephx.org Diodoro Mendoza, Chancellor;
Saint George, Olympia Charitable Trust - 8131 N. 16th St., Phoenix, AZ 85020 t) 602-861-9778 chancellor@ephx.org Diodoro Mendoza, Chancellor;
Holy Angels, San Diego Charitable Trust - 8131 N. 16th St., Phoenix, AZ 85020 t) 602-861-9778 chancellor@ephx.org Very Rev. Diodoro Mendoza, Chancellor;
Holy Protection of Mary Foundation - 8131 N. 16th St., Phoenix, AZ 85020 t) 602-861-9778 chancellor@ephx.org Diodoro Mendoza, Chancellor;
Holy Protection, Denver Charitable Trust - 8131 N. 16th St., Phoenix, AZ 85020 t) 602-861-9778 chancellor@ephx.org Diodoro Mendoza, Chancellor;
Saint Irene, Portland Charitable Trust - 8131 N. 16th St., Phoenix, AZ 85020 t) 602-861-9778 chancellor@ephx.org Diodoro Mendoza, Chancellor;
Saint John, Seattle Charitable Trust - 8131 N. 16th St., Phoenix, AZ 85020 t) 602-861-9778 chancellor@ephx.org Diodoro Mendoza, Chancellor;
Saint Mary, Sherman Oaks Charitable Trust - 8131 N. 16th St., Phoenix, AZ 85020 t) 602-861-9778 chancellor@ephx.org Diodoro Mendoza, Chancellor;
Saint Melany, Tucson Charitable Trust - 8131 N. 16th St., Phoenix, AZ 85020 t) 602-861-9778 chancellor@ephx.org Diodoro Mendoza, Chancellor;
Saint Nicholas, Anchorage Charitable Trust - 8131 N. 16th St., Phoenix, AZ 85020 t) 602-861-9778 chancellor@ephx.org Diodoro Mendoza, Chancellor;
Our Lady of Perpetual Help, Albuquerque Charitable Trust - 8131 N. 16th St., Phoenix, AZ 85020 t) 602-861-9778 chancellor@ephx.org Diodoro Mendoza, Chancellor;
Saint Philip, Sacramento Charitable Trust - 8131 N. 16th St., Phoenix, AZ 85020 t) 602-861-9778 chancellor@ephx.org Diodoro Mendoza, Chancellor;
Saint Stephen, Phoenix Charitable Trust - 8131 N. 16th St., Phoenix, AZ 85020 t) 602-943-5379 rectorss@ephx.org Diodoro Mendoza, Rector;
Saint Thomas, Gilbert Charitable Trust - 8131 N. 16th St., Phoenix, AZ 85020 t) 602-861-9778 chancellor@ephx.org Diodoro Mendoza, Chancellor;

MISCELLANEOUS [MIS]

PHOENIX

Holy Protection of Mary Byzantine Catholic Bishop of Phoenix - 8131 N. 16th St., Phoenix, AZ 85020 t) 602-861-9778 eparch@ephx.org ephx.org Most Rev. John Pazak, Bishop;
Holy Protection of Mary Byzantine Catholic Eparchy of Phoenix - 8131 N. 16th St., Phoenix, AZ 85020 t) 602-861-9778 chancellor@ephx.org ephx.org Byzantine Catholic Eparchy of Phoenix Rev. Msgr. Kevin W. McAuliffe;
Holy Protection of Mary Facilities Corporation - 8131 N. 16th St., Phoenix, AZ 85020 t) 602-861-9778 chancellor@ephx.org Rev. Msgr. Kevin W. McAuliffe, In Res.;

MONASTERIES AND RESIDENCES FOR PRIESTS AND BROTHERS [MON]

CALIMESA

Byzantine Brothers of St. Francis - 9443 Sharondale Rd., Calimesa, CA 92320-2017 t) 951-850-9625 brmike_7@msn.com Bro. John Gray, B.B.S.F., Supr.; Brs.: 1

NURSING / REHABILITATION / CONVALESCENCE / ELDERLY CARE [NUR]

PHOENIX

St. Stephen Senior Citizen Apartments - 8141 N. 16th St., Phoenix, AZ 85020 t) 602-943-5379 frmendoza@ephx.org Very Rev. Diodoro Mendoza, Rector; Asstd. Annu.: 25; Staff: 1

An asterisk (*) denotes an organization that has established tax-exempt status directly with the IRS and is not covered by the USCCB Group Ruling.

Eparchy of Newton (Melkite-Greek Catholic)

MOST REVEREND FRANÇOIS BEYROUTI, Ph.D., D.D.

Eparchial Bishop of Newton; Ordained October 4, 1998; Appointed 6th Eparchial Bishop of Newton August 20, 2022; Consecrated Bishop October 12, 2022; Enthroned October 19, 2022. Mailing Address: 3 VFW Pkwy., West Roxbury, MA 02132.

Chancery: 3 Veterans of Foreign Wars Pkwy., West Roxbury, MA 02132. T: 617-323-9922
www.melkite.org

Established as an Apostolic Exarchate January 10, 1966.

Elevated to Eparchy, June 28, 1976; Serves the faithful of the Melkite Greek Catholic Church in the United States.

For legal titles of parishes and institutions, consult the Chancery Office.

STATISTICAL OVERVIEW

Personnel

Bishop	1
Retired Bishops	1
Priests: Diocesan Active in Diocese	44
Priests: Diocesan Active Outside Diocese	9
Priests: Retired, Sick or Absent	22
Number of Diocesan Priests	75
Religious Priests in Diocese	13
Total Priests in your Diocese	88
Ordinations:	
Diocesan Priests	4
Transitional Deacons	4
Permanent Deacons in Diocese	44
Total Brothers	1
Total Sisters	2

Parishes

Parishes	50
With Resident Pastor:	
Resident Diocesan Priests	43
Resident Religious Priests	5
Without Resident Pastor:	
Administered by Priests	5
Administered by Deacons	2
Missions	8
Professional Ministry Personnel:	
Brothers	1
Sisters	2

Educational

Diocesan Students in Other Seminaries	2
Total Seminarians	2
Catechesis / Religious Education:	
High School Students	205
Elementary Students	630
Total Students under Catholic Instruction	837
Teachers in Diocese:	
Priests	3

Vital Statistics

Receptions into the Church:	
Infant Baptism Totals	637
Adult Baptism Totals	122
Received into Full Communion	87
First Communions	759
Confirmations	759
Marriages:	
Catholic	236
Interfaith	51
Total Marriages	287
Deaths	624
Total Catholic Population	35,000

ADMINISTRATION

Chancery Office - t) 617-323-9922
Protosyncellus - t) (617) 323-5242 graczka@alumni.nd.edu bostonmelkite.org Rt. Rev. Philip Raczka;
Chancellor - t) 617-323-9922 x207 chancellor@melkite.org Very Rev. James Koury;
Eparchial Tribunal - t) 205-533-1996 Rt. Rev. Michael K. Skrocki;
Judicial Vicar - Rt. Rev. Michael K. Skrocki;
Judges - Rt. Rev. Michael K. Skrocki; Michael Souckar;
Defender of the Bond and Promoter of Justice - Rt. Rev. Joseph S. Haggar;
Notaries - Very Rev. James Koury; Ben Cafeo;
Chief Finance Officer - t) 973-785-2433 Dcn. Robert Shalhoub;
Protopresbyters - Rt. Rev. Alexei Smith; Rt. Rev. Michel Cheble; Rev. Justin Rose, Southeast;

COMMUNICATIONS

Office of Communications - Doreen Pierson;
Sophia Magazine -
Sophia Press - t) (617) 323-9922 www.melkite.org Saideh Dagher;

CONSULTATIVE BODIES

College of Eparchial Consultors - Rt. Rev. John Azar; Rt. Rev. Philip Raczka; Rt. Rev. Michael K. Skrocki;
Diocese of Newton for the Melkites in the USA, Inc., a Massachusetts Corporation - Most Rev. Francois Beyrouti; Rt. Rev. Philip Raczka; Very Rev. James Koury;
Finance Council - Most Rev. Francois Beyrouti; Very Rev. James Koury; George Mussali;
Legal Consultant - Karim Kaspar;
Presbyteral Council - Rt. Rev. James K. Babcock; Rt. Rev. Damon Geiger; Rev. Bryan McNeil (Brymc56@comcast.net);

PASTORAL SERVICES

Shepherd's Care Associated Charities - t) 617-323-9922 x207 Very Rev. James Koury;
Liturgical Arts -
MAYA (Melkite Assoc. of Young Adults) - t) (305) 546-6049; (205) 542-9947 jnjadon@gmail.com; mariebaroody@gmail.com usmaya.org Marie Baroody; Juliana Jadon;
NAMW (National Assoc. of Melkite Women) - Susan Elek (elek70@comcast.net);
NAMY (National Assoc. of Melkite Youth) - Very Rev. Archpriest Thomas P. Steinmetz;
Office of Evangelization & Catechesis - Rev. Hezekias Carnazzo;
Order of St. Nicholas - t) 617-323-9922 George Mussali; Dr. Sherine Rabbat;
Victim Assistance Coordinator - Liza Sarrouf;
Vocations Office - t) (210) 628-9778 c) (210) 929-5585 vocations@melkite.org melkite.org Rev. John Mefrige, Dir. (frjohnmefrige@gmail.com);

PARISHES, MISSIONS, AND CLERGY

COMMONWEALTH OF MASSACHUSETTS

LAWRENCE

St. Joseph - 241 Hampshire St., Lawrence, MA 01841 t) 978-682-8152; 978-685-9734 lawrencestjoseph@gmail.com; zjlayous@gmail.com Rev. Ziad Layous, Pst.; Dcn. John Fleshman; Dcn. Michael Macoul;

WEST ROXBURY

Annunciation Cathedral Melkite Catholic Church Inc. - 7 V.F.W. Pkwy., West Roxbury, MA 02132 t) 617-323-5242 melkitecathedral@gmail.com www.bostonmelkite.org Rt. Rev. Philip Raczka, Rector; Rev. Deacon Elias (Richard) Bailey; Dcn. John Moses; Rev. Deacon Ibrahim Zeinieh; CRP Stds.: 35

WORCESTER

Our Lady of Perpetual Help - 256 Hamilton St., Worcester, MA 01604 t) 508-752-4174 olphmelkite@gmail.com Rev. Bryan McNeil, Pst.;

COMMONWEALTH OF PENNSYLVANIA

ALLENTOWN

Our Lady of Mercy Melkite Mission - 501 Ridge Ave., Allentown, PA 18102 c) 484-747-7006 vico113@hotmail.com Rev. Victor Hanna, Admin.;

SCRANTON

St. Joseph Catholic Church, Inc. - 130 St. Francis Cabrini Ave., Scranton, PA 18504 t) 570-343-6092 stjosephscranton@gmail.com www.melkitescranton.org Rev. Christopher Manuele, Pst.; CRP Stds.: 30

COMMONWEALTH OF VIRGINIA

MCLEAN

Holy Transfiguration - 8501 Lewinsville Rd., McLean, VA 22102 t) 703-734-9566 office@holytransfiguration.org holytransfiguration.org Rt. Rev. Mark E. Melone, Pst.; Rev. Elias Dorham, Assoc. Pst.; Rev. David Baroody, Assoc. Pst.; Rev. Ephrem Handal, Assoc. Pst.; Rev. Peter Wingerter, Assoc. Pst.; Dcn. Steven Rosenzweig; Dcn. David Black; Dcn. Joseph Olt; CRP Stds.: 85

STATE OF ALABAMA

BIRMINGHAM

St. George Church - 425 Sixteenth Ave. S., Birmingham, AL 35205 t) 205-252-5788 parishadmin@stgeorgebham.com Rev. Justin Rose, Pst.; Rev. Deacon Andrew Baroody; Rev. Deacon Seraphim Ritchey;

STATE OF ARIZONA

PHOENIX

St. John of the Desert Melkite Catholic Church - 3718 E. Greenway Rd., Phoenix, AZ 85032 t) 602-787-4787 frpeter@typicon.com; frzyad@icloud.com www.stjohnofthedesert.com Very Rev. Peter Boutros, Pst.; Rev. Zyad Abyad, Assoc. Pst.; Dcn. Marion Rimmer; CRP Stds.: 32

STATE OF CALIFORNIA

COVINA

Annunciation Melkite Catholic Church Inc. - 381 W. Center St., Covina, CA 91723; Mailing: 170 E. College St., P.O. Box 4872, Covina, CA 91723 t) (626) 359-3976 (CRP) c) (626) 893-0302 annunciationmission@gmail.com Rev. George Sayegh, Admin.; CRP Stds.: 20

EL SEGUNDO

St. Paul - 538 Concord St., El Segundo, CA 90245 t) 310-322-1892 Rt. Rev. Alexei Smith, Admin.;

NORTH HOLLYWOOD

St. Anne Melkite Co-Cathedral - 11211 Moorpark St., North Hollywood, CA 91602; Mailing: 11245 Rye St., North Hollywood, CA 91602 t) 818-761-2035 office@stannecathedral.org www.melkitesinlosangeles.org Rev. Dimitrios Saliba, BCO (Lebanon), Pst.; Rev. Deacon Thom O'Malley; Rev. George Sayegh; Dcn. Estephanos Helo; Dcn. George Karout; Dcn. Tareq Nasrallah;

PLACENTIA

Holy Cross - 451 W. Madison Ave., Placentia, CA 92870 t) 714-985-1710 office@holycrossmelkite.org; fbeyrouti@gmail.com Melkite Catholic Parish in Orange County, California. Rev. Oliver Black, Admin.; Dcn. Elias Kashou;

SACRAMENTO

St. George Melkite Church Inc. - 9501 Folsom Blvd., Sacramento, CA 95827; Mailing: P.O. Box 660425, Sacramento, CA 95866 t) 916-920-2900 fatherhezekias@gmail.com www.stgeorgemelkite.org Rev. Hezekias Carnazzo, Pst.;

SAN BERNARDINO

St. Philip - 923 W. Congress St., San Bernardino, CA 92410 c) 909-289-2098 comeandsee@earthlink.net Rev. Paul (Adham) Fallouh, Pst.; Protodeacon Stephen Ghandour; Dcn. Michael Mobley; Dcn. Jacob Pesta;

SAN DIEGO

St. Jacob Melkite Catholic Church, Inc. - 2235 Galahad Rd., San Diego, CA 92123; Mailing: P.O. Box 231328, San Diego, CA 92193 t) 619-333-2772 www.stjacobmelkite.org Services at Holy Angels Church, San Diego. Rev. Shaun S. Brown, Admin.; CRP Stds.: 13

SAN JOSE

St. Elias - 14263 Mulberry Dr., San Jose, CA 95032; Mailing: 7644 Langley Canyon Rd., Prunedale, CA 93907 c) 831-229-8350 steliasmelkite@gmail.com steliasmelkite.org Rev. Sebastian A. Carnazzo, Admin.;

TEMECULA

Virgin Mary Mission - 42030 Avenida Alvarado, Ste. A, Temecula, CA 92590; Mailing: P.O. Box 1679, Temecula, CA 92590 t) 909-289-2098 info@virginmarymgcc.com virginmarymgcc.com Rev. Paul (Adham) Fallouh, Pst.; Protodeacon Habib Khasho; Rt. Rev. Archmandrite James Babcock, Chap.;

STATE OF CONNECTICUT

DANBURY

St. Ann - 181 Clapboard Ridge Rd., Danbury, CT 06811 t) 203-743-5119 pastor@saintann.org Rev. Thomas Davis, Pst.; Dcn. Nicholas Bourjaili;

WATERFORD

St. Ann - 41 Cross Rd., Waterford, CT 06385 t) 860-442-2211 abounadennis@gmail.com Rev. Dennis J. McCarthy, Pst.; CRP Stds.: 7

STATE OF FLORIDA

DELRAY BEACH

St. Nicholas - 5715 Lake Ida Rd., Delray Beach, FL 33484 t) 561-499-3161; 305-794-5716 parish@stnicholasmelkite.org; melkite126@bellsouth.com Rt. Rev. Exarch Gabriel Ghanoum, B.S.O., Pst.; Protodeacon Magdi Negm;

MIAMI

St. Jude - 126 S.E. 15th Rd., Miami, FL 33129-1207 t) 305-856-1500 p.ezzat@yahoo.com; office@stjudemiami.org stjudemiami.org Rev. Ezzat Bathouche, Pst.; Protodeacon Magdi Negm; Dcn. Dorotheos Rose;

STATE OF GEORGIA

ATLANTA

St. John Chrysostom Melkite Church, Inc. - 1428 Ponce de Leon Ave., N.E., Atlanta, GA 30307 t) 404-373-9522 contact@stjohnmelkite.org stjohnmelkite.org Dcn. Elie Hanna, Admin.; Dcn. Sami Jajeh, Admin.;

AUGUSTA

St. Ignatios of Antioch - 1003 Merry St., Augusta, GA 30904 t) 706-364-6219 abounamike@aol.com; stignatiosmelkite@gmail.com melkitechurch.wixsite.com Rt. Rev. Michael K. Skrocki, Pst.;

STATE OF ILLINOIS

NORTHLAKE

St. John the Baptist - 200 E. North Ave., Northlake, IL 60164 t) 858-280-6131 stjohnthebaptistchicago@hotmail.com Rev. Rezkallah Samaan, Pst.; Dcn. Fadi Rafidi; Protodeacon Antoine Shehata;

STATE OF MICHIGAN

LANSING

St. Joseph - 725 W. Mt. Hope Ave., Lansing, MI 48910; Mailing: 921 Westover Cir., Lansing, MI 48917 t) 517-575-6264 stjosephlansing@gmail.com Rev. Alexei Woltornist, Admin.; CRP Stds.: 14

PLYMOUTH

St. Michael - 585 N. Mill St., Plymouth, MI 48170 c) 734-589-9394 abouna24elie@gmail.com; stmichaelmelkite@gmail.com Rev. Elie Eid, Admin.;

WARREN
Our Lady of Redemption - 29293 Lorraine Ave., Warren, MI 48093 t) 586-751-6017 info@olormelkite.org www.olormelkite.org Rt. Rev. Michel Cheble, Pst.; Dcn. David Herr; Rev. Deacon Rick Trabulsy;

STATE OF NEW HAMPSHIRE

MANCHESTER
Our Lady of the Cedars - 140 Mitchell St., Manchester, NH 03103 t) 603-623-8944 oloc.church@comcast.net Very Rev. Archpriest Thomas P. Steinmetz, Pst.; Dcn. John Fleshman;

STATE OF NEW JERSEY

CLIFFSIDE PARK
St. Demetrius - 184 Cliff St., Cliffside Park, NJ 07010 t) 973-256-7217 antoin_2008@outlook.com; acs090102@msn.com Rev. Choukri Sabbagh, Admin.;

WOODLAND PARK
St. Ann - 802 Rifle Camp Rd., Woodland Park, NJ 07424 t) 973-785-4144 Rt. Rev. Kenneth Sherman, Pst.; Dcn. Roland Basinski; Archdeacon Edward Bsarany; Dcn. Robert Shalhoub;

STATE OF NEW YORK

BROOKLYN
Church of the Virgin Mary - 216 Eighth Ave., Brooklyn, NY 11215 t) 718-788-5454 cvm@melkitesofnyc.net www.churchofthevirginmary.net Rev. Antoine Rizk, B.S.O., Pst.; Dcn. Nagi Youssef; CRP Stds.: 20

ROCHESTER
St. Nicholas - 1492 Spencerport Rd., Rochester, NY 14606 t) 585-426-4218 stnicholasrochester@gmail.com saintnicholas.cc Rev. Michael Copenhagen, Admin.; Dcn. Edmond Elhilow; Dcn. Terry Hyland; Dcn. Elias Sarkis; CRP Stds.: 20

UTICA
St. Basil - 901 Sherman Dr., Utica, NY 13501 t) 315-732-4662 stbasilsutica@gmail.com stbasilutica.org Rev. Thomas Moses, Admin.;

YONKERS
Christ the Savior Church - 491 Palisade Ave., Yonkers, NY 10703 t) 914-963-6680 christ.savior1@gmail.com Rev. Musil Kamil Shihadeh, Pst.; Protodeacon Saleem Naber; CRP Stds.: 10

STATE OF OHIO

AKRON
St. Joseph - 927 N. Portage Path, Akron, OH 44303 t) 330-400-4882 office@stjosephakron.org Rt. Rev. Eugene Mitchell, B.S.O., Pst.; Dcn. Dennis Jebber; CRP Stds.: 5

BROOKLYN
St. Elias Melkite Church, Inc. - 8023 Memphis Ave., Brooklyn, OH 44144 t) 216-661-1155 sainteliasmelkitechurch@gmail.com steliasmelkitechurch.org Rev. George Haddad, Pst.; CRP Stds.: 15

COLUMBUS
Holy Resurrection - 4611 Glenmawr Ave., Columbus, OH 43224; Mailing: 8148 Wildflower Ln., Westerville, OH 43081 t) 614-396-8821 c) 614-783-0042 columbus.melkite@gmail.com Rev. Ignatius Harrington, Pst.;

STATE OF RHODE ISLAND

LINCOLN
St. Basil the Great - 15 Skyview Dr., Lincoln, RI 02865; Mailing: 111 Cross St., Central Falls, RI 02863 t) 514-224-1664 emkardouh@gmail.com Rev. Ephrem Kardouh, BSO, Pst.; Rev. Deacon Gilbert Altongy; Rev. Deacon Edmond Raheb; Rt. Rev. Joseph S. Haggar, In Res.;

STATE OF TEXAS

HOUSTON
St. Barbara the Great - Martyr Mission - 5402 Acorn St., Houston, TX 77092; Mailing: 16802 Bonnie Sean Dr., Spring, TX 77379 c) 832-846-5720 f_mimass@hotmail.com www.stbarbaramelkite.com Rev. Fadi Al Mimass, Pst.;

STATE OF WASHINGTON

SEATTLE
St. Joseph Mission - 1240 N.E. 127th St., Seattle, WA 98125; Mailing: 17112 44th Ave. W., #B101, Lynnwood, WA 98037 c) 425-679-2892 samirabulail@gmail.com Rev. Samir Abu-Lail, Pst.;

STATE OF WISCONSIN

MILWAUKEE
St. George's Syrian Congregation - 1617 W. State St., Milwaukee, WI 53233 t) 414-342-1543 info@byzantinemilwaukee.com byzantinemilwaukee.com Archimandrite Paul G. Frechette, Pst.;

INSTITUTIONS LOCATED IN DIOCESE

CONVENTS, MONASTERIES, AND RESIDENCES FOR WOMEN [CON]

DANBURY
Community of The Mother of God of Tenderness - 79 Golden Hill Rd., Danbury, CT 06811-4631 t) 203-794-1486 maryanns333@sbcglobal.net Sr. Mary Ann Socha, C.M.G.T., Pres.; Srs.: 2

MONASTERIES AND RESIDENCES FOR PRIESTS AND BROTHERS [MON]

METHUEN
Monastery of St. Basil the Great - 30 East St., Methuen, MA 01844 t) 978-683-2471 stbasil@comcast.net Rev. Ibrahim El Haddad, B.S.O. (Lebanon), Supr.;

An asterisk (*) denotes an organization that has established tax-exempt status directly with the IRS and is not covered by the USCCB Group Ruling.

Diocese of Our Lady of Deliverance

Eparchia Nostrae Dominae Liberationis Novarcensis Syrorum

MOST REVEREND MAR BARNABA YOUSIF HABASH

Second Bishop of Our Lady of Deliverance; ordained priest August 31, 1975; ordained Bishop June 11, 2010; installed Bishop of Our Lady of Deliverance Syriac Catholic Diocese in the United States and Canada July 31, 2010. Mailing and Residential Address: 25600 Drake Rd., Farmington Hills, MI 48335. T: 248-987-6143; F: 248-987-6176.

Chancery Office: 25600 Drake Rd., Farmington Hills, MI 48335. T: 248-987-6143; F: 248-987-6176.
www.syriaccatholic.us
marbarnaba@yahoo.com
syriac_chancery@yahoo.com

DIOCESE ESTABLISHED NOVEMBER 6, 1995.

Comprises the United States.

STATISTICAL OVERVIEW

Personnel

Bishop	1
Priests: Diocesan Active in Diocese	12
Priests: Retired, Sick or Absent	1
Number of Diocesan Priests	13
Total Priests in your Diocese	13

Parishes

Parishes	10
With Resident Pastor:	
Resident Diocesan Priests	9
Missions	6

Educational

Catechesis / Religious Education:	
High School Students	142
Elementary Students	356
Total Students under Catholic Instruction	498

Vital Statistics

Receptions into the Church:	
Infant Baptism Totals	180
First Communions	148
Confirmations	180
Marriages:	
Catholic	78
Total Marriages	78
Deaths	31
Total Catholic Population	10,392

LEADERSHIP

Chancery -

Chancellor - Rev. Luke A. Edelen, O.S.B. (syriac_chancery@yahoo.com);

Episcopal Vicar - t) 904-240-8527 Chorbishop Caesar Russo, Vicar (qaisarrusso@gmail.com);

Officialis - Rev. Luke A. Edelen, O.S.B. (syriac_chancery@yahoo.com);

PARISHES, MISSIONS, AND CLERGY

COMMONWEALTH OF MASSACHUSETTS

WORCESTER

St. Ignatius of Antioch Syriac Catholic Mission - 551 Pleasant St., Worcester, MA 01602 c) 201-978-0316 syriac_chancery@yahoo.com Rev. Luke A. Edelen, O.S.B., Chancellor;

STATE OF ARIZONA

PHOENIX

Saints Behnam and Sarah Mission - 11001 N. 40th St., Phoenix, AZ 85028 c) 818-318-5858 raad_muoshe@yahoo.com Rev. Aphram Mushe, Admin.;

St. Joseph - (Worship Site)

STATE OF CALIFORNIA

EL CAJON

Saint Joseph Mission - 1101 S. Mollison Ave., El Cajon, CA 92020 t) 619-440-5555 msgrhannashaikh@yahoo.com Rev. Msgr. Emad Hanna Al-Shaikh, Pst.;

St. Luis Rey R.C. Church - (Worship Site)

Our Mother of Perpetual Help Church - 1101 S. Mollison Ave., El Cajon, CA 92020 t) 619-440-5555 syriaccatholicchurchsd@gmail.com Rev. Msgr. Emad Hanna Al-Shaikh, Pst.;

NORTH HOLLYWOOD

Jesus Sacred Heart Church - 10837 Collins St., North Hollywood, CA 91601-2009 c) 904-536-7509 talatpastor@gmail.com Rev. Talat Yazji I, Pst.; George Ibrahim Maida, Youth Min.;

STATE OF FLORIDA

JACKSONVILLE

Saint Ephrem Syriac Church - 4650 Kernan Blvd., S., Jacksonville, FL 32224 c) 586-868-3023 qaisarrusso@gmail.com; faditechnolojy@yahoo.com Rev. Msgr. Caesar Russo, Admin.; Rev. Fadi Matlob, Par. Vicar; Dcn. Joseph Al-Saigh;

Our Lady of Peace Syriac Catholic Church Incorporated - 5854 University Blvd. W., Jacksonville, FL 32216 c) 904-597-3875 ourladyofpeace2012@gmail.com Rev. Nimatullah Muneam Butrus, Admin.;

STATE OF MICHIGAN

FARMINGTON HILLS

Saint Toma Church - 25600 Drake Rd., Farmington Hills, MI 48335 c) 248-567-9699 haddadmuntaser@gmail.com Rev. Muntaser Haddad, Rector;

LANSING

St. Isaac of Nineveh Syriac Catholic Church - 1314 Ballard St., Lansing, MI 48906 c) 248-818-2886 habashsafaa@gmail.com Rev. Msgr. Safaa Habash, Pst.;

TROY

Christ the King Church - 2300 John R. Rd., Troy, MI 48083 t) 248-835-1035 ch.christtheking@gmail.com Rev. Rabee Habash, Pst.; Rev. Yousif Sheto, Par. Vicar;

STATE OF NEW JERSEY

BAYONNE

Our Lady of Deliverance Parish - 21 E. 23rd St., Bayonne, NJ 07002-4678 c) 818-913-8156 olodeliverance@gmail.com Rev. Andrwos Habash, Pst.;

St. Michael Byzantine Cathedral Chapel - 415 Lackawanna Ave., Woodland Park, NJ 07424 (Worship Site)

INSTITUTIONS LOCATED IN DIOCESE

MISCELLANEOUS [MIS]

SHELBURNE

Institute for Ancient and Threatened Christianity, Inc. - 145 Pine Haven Shores Rd., Shelburne, VT 05482 c) 207-475-2581 smrasche@gmail.com Stephen Rosche, Exec.;

An asterisk (*) denotes an organization that has established tax-exempt status directly with the IRS and is not covered by the USCCB Group Ruling.

Eparchy of Our Lady of Lebanon of Los Angeles

MOST REVEREND A. ELIAS ZAIDAN

Bishop of the Eparchy of Our Lady of Lebanon of Los Angeles; ordained July 20, 1986; appointed Bishop of Our Lady of Lebanon of Los Angeles July 10, 2013; consecrated September 28, 2013.

Pastoral Center: 1021 S. 10th St., St. Louis, MO 63104. T: 314-231-1021; F: 314-231-1316
www.eparchy.org
info@eparchy.org

Comprises the States of Ohio, West Virginia, Illinois, Alabama, Michigan, Minnesota, Missouri, Texas, Utah, Arizona, Nevada, Oregon, California, Alaska, Hawaii, Indiana, Kentucky, Tennessee, Mississippi, Wisconsin, Iowa, Arkansas, Louisiana, North Dakota, South Dakota, Kansas, Oklahoma, Nebraska, Montana, Wyoming, Colorado, New Mexico, Idaho and Washington.

STATISTICAL OVERVIEW

Personnel

Bishop	1
Priests: Diocesan Active in Diocese	31
Priests: Diocesan Active Outside Diocese	1
Priests: Retired, Sick or Absent	8
Number of Diocesan Priests	40
Religious Priests in Diocese	21
Total Priests in your Diocese	61
Extern Priests in Diocese	6
Ordinations:	
Diocesan Priests	2
Religious Priests	2
Transitional Deacons	3
Permanent Deacons	1
Permanent Deacons in Diocese	24

Parishes

Parishes	34
With Resident Pastor:	
Resident Diocesan Priests	26
Resident Religious Priests	10
Missions	9
Professional Ministry Personnel:	
Brothers	7
Sisters	9

Welfare

Homes for the Aged	1
Total Assisted	100
Day Care Centers	1
Total Assisted	8,400

Educational

Diocesan Students in Other Seminaries	6
Students, Religious	8
Total Seminarians	14
Catechesis / Religious Education:	
High School Students	385
Elementary Students	1,054
Total Students under Catholic Instruction	1,453

Vital Statistics

Receptions into the Church:	
Infant Baptism Totals	518
Minor Baptism Totals	34
Adult Baptism Totals	9
Received into Full Communion	118
First Communions	368
Confirmations	367
Marriages:	
Catholic	146
Interfaith	29
Total Marriages	175
Deaths	210
Total Catholic Population	35,802

LEADERSHIP

Pastoral Center - t) 314-231-1021 Rev. Albert Constantine, Chancellor; Jamileh Koury, Chief Fiscal Officer; Rev. John Paul Kimes, Canonical Vicar;
College of Consultors - Chorbishop Anthony Spinosa; Chorbishop Donald Sawyer; Chorbishop Sharbel Maroun;
Commission for Lebanon & The Middle East - Rev. Toufic M. Nasr;
Protosyncellus - Chorbishop Sharbel Maroun;
Tribunal -
Assessor - t) 818-626-9193 Rev. Albert Constantine, Chancellor; Ivette Jackson, Secy.;
Defender of the Bond - Rev. Anthony Alle;
Judicial Vicar - Rev. John Caronan;
Moderator of the Tribunal - Most Rev. A. Elias Zaidan;
Notaries - Ivette Jackson; Jamileh Koury;
Procurator/Advocate - Rev. Ramsine Hage-Moussa, Petitioner; Rev. Elias Sleiman, M.L.M., Respondent;
Promoter of Justice - Rev. John Caronan;
Personal Secretary - Rev. Milad T. Yaghi, M.L.M.;

OFFICES AND DIRECTORS

Archivist - c) 918-688-2161 Randa Hakim;
Board of Pastors - t) 818-626-9193 Chorbishop Donald Sawyer; Chorbishop Sharbel Maroun; Rev. Milad T. Yaghi, M.L.M.;
Caritas Lebanon - t) 210-288-5512 Rev. John Nahal, M.L.M.;
Catholic Schools Assistance Fund Lebanon - Rev. Charles H. Khachan, M.L.M.;
Continuing Education for Clergy - Rev. Armando Elkhoury;
Eparchial Newsletter Consulter - Rev. Pierre Bassil;
Eparchial Pastoral Council -
Eparchial Stewardship - John Kurey;
Inter-Eparchial History Committee - Rev. George Hajj;
Legal Counsel Board - Rev. Albert Constantine; Richard Karam, Attorney;
Liturgical Music Commission - Chorbishop Alfred Badawi;
Master of Ceremonies - Rev. Milad T. Yaghi, M.L.M.;
Noursat - Chorbishop Sharbel Maroun;
Office for Immigration - Ivette Jackson;
Office of Caregivers - Chorbishop Donald Sawyer;
Office of Communications - Ivette Jackson;
Office of Evangelization & Outreach - Chorbishop Sharbel Maroun;
Office of Inter-faith/Ecumenical Affairs - Rev. Msgr. Antoine Bakh;
Office of Liturgy - Rev. Michael Shami;
Office of Ministries - Rev. Patrick Kassab (patrickkassab@outlook.com);
Office of Our Lady of Lebanon Seminary Alumni - Rev. George Hajj;
Office of Priestly Vocations - Chorbishop Donald Sawyer;
Office of Protection of Minors - t) 310-435-3493 Rev. Elias Sleiman, M.L.M., Dir.;
Chairman of the Review Board - Joe Petro;
Program Coordinator - Susie Hage;
Victim Assistance Coordinator - Laura Kahwaji;
Office of Religious Education - Sr. Martha Mechleb;
Office of Young Adult Ministry - Rev. Tony Massad;
Office of Youth Ministries - Rev. Edward Hanna, M.L.M.;
Order of St. Sharbel - Rev. Msgr. Peter Azar, Spiritual Adv./Care Srvcs.; James Abdo, Pres.; Mary Milton, Vice. Pres.;
Personnel Board - Chorbishop Anthony Spinosa; Chorbishop Donald Sawyer; Chorbishop Sharbel Maroun;
Presbyteral Council - Rev. John Nahal, Ex-Officio; Rev. Elias Sleiman, M.L.M., Ex Officio; Rev. Tony Massad, Elected;
Priests' Retirement Fund - Chorbishop Faouzi Elia; Chorbishop Anthony Spinosa; Rev. Jibran BouMerhi;
Pro-Life & Family Life Office - Alberto Tohme; Lynn Tohme;
Project Roots - Rev. Charles H. Khachan, M.L.M.;
Protopresbyters - Chorbishop Anthony Spinosa, Midwest Region; Rev. Elias Sleiman, M.L.M., Southwest Region; Chorbishop Donald Sawyer, Southern Region;
Spiritual Director for the National Apostolate of Maronites - Rev. Albert Constantine;
Technology - Rev. John Nahal;
Vicar for Clergy - Rev. Msgr. Donald J. Sawyer (dsawyer@grandecom.net);

COMMUNICATIONS

Eparchial App and Facebook - Ivette Jackson;
Eparchial Newsletter - t) 804-762-4301 Chorbishop John Faris (john.jd@gmail.com); Rev. Pierre Bassil, Consultor;

FACILITIES

Office of Building Oversight - Chorbishop Faouzi Elia;
Properties Owned -
Father Tobia Retirement Home -
Maronite Catholic Pastoral Center -
Residence House -

PARISHES, MISSIONS, AND CLERGY

STATE OF ALABAMA

BIRMINGHAM

St. Elias Maronite Catholic Church - 836 Eighth St. S., Birmingham, AL 35205-4567 t) 205-251-5057 info@stelias.org www.stelias.org Rev. Peter John Zogbi, Admin.; Chorbishop Richard D. Saad, Pastor Emer.; Rev. Jean-Maroun El Helou (Lebanon), In Res.; Beverly Kimes, DRE;

STATE OF ARIZONA

PHOENIX

St. Joseph Maronite Catholic Church - 5406 E. Virginia Ave., Phoenix, AZ 85008 t) 602-667-3280 stjosephmaronitechurch@gmail.com www.stjosephphoenix.org Rev. Wissam Akiki, Pst.; Manal Akiki, DRE; CRP Stds.: 86

STATE OF CALIFORNIA

CARMICHAEL

Our Lady of the Rosary Mission - 6811 Fair Oaks Blvd., Carmichael, CA 95608 t) 916-483-6691; 916-546-8973 mccsacramento@gmail.com; frghattas@gmail.com www.maronite-sac.org Rev. Ghattas Khoury, Pst.; CRP Stds.: 3

EL CAJON

St. Ephrem Maronite Catholic Church - 750 Medford St., El Cajon, CA 92020 t) 619-337-1350; 619-508-5401 (CRP) ghosn@att.net; stephrem@sbcglobal.net www.stephremchurch.com/ Rev. Toufic M. Nasr, Pst.; Dcn. George Geagea; Dcn. Georges Ghosn; CRP Stds.: 30

LOS ANGELES

Our Lady of Mt. Lebanon-St. Peter Maronite Catholic Cathedral - 333 S. San Vicente Blvd., Los Angeles, CA 90048 t) 310-275-6634 ourladymtlebanon@yahoo.com; olmlcathedral@yahoo.com Most Rev. Abdallah E. Zaidan; Rev. Elias Sleiman, M.L.M., Rector; Rev. Etienne Hanna, Assoc. Pst.; Dcn. Emile Abboud; Dcn. Mikael Zaarour; CRP Stds.: 41

MILLBRAE

Our Lady of Lebanon Maronite Catholic Church - 600 El Camino Real, Millbrae, CA 94030 t) 650-741-6342 ourladyol.sf@gmail.com www.olol-sf.org Rev. Rami Razzouk, Pst.; Dcn. Tony Boukhalil, Liturgy Dir.; CRP Stds.: 35

ORANGE

St. John Maron Maronite Catholic Church - 300 S. Flower St., Orange, CA 92868 t) 714-940-0009 fr.bakh@johnmaron.org stjohnmaronchurch.org Rev. Msgr. Antoine Bakh, Pst.; Rev. Wadih Kaldawi, Assoc. Pst.; Subdeacon Joseph Waked; Subdeacon Charles Doche; Sr. Martha Mechleb, Rel. Ord. Ldr.; CRP Stds.: 90

RIVERSIDE

St. Joseph Maronite Catholic Mission - 3870 Castleman St., Riverside, CA 92503 t) 951-406-1406 stjosephmcc2017@gmail.com Rev. Fadi Bazouzi, Pst.; CRP Stds.: 50

SIMI VALLEY

Saints Peter and Paul Maronite Catholic Church - 1059 Ashland Ave., Simi Valley, CA 93065 t) 929-620-7095 sppmaronite@gmail.com; abdasfeir@hotmail.com www.sppmission.org Rev. Abda Sfeir, Pst.; Dcn. Tayar Dib; CRP Stds.: 13

STOCKTON

St. Sharbel Maronite Catholic Mission - 4981 E. Eight Mile Rd., Stockton, CA 95212 c) 602-680-8749 stockston.st.sharbel@gmail.com Rev. Ghattas Khoury, Admin.;

WEST COVINA

St. Jude Maronite Catholic Church - 1437 W. Badillo St., West Covina, CA 91790 t) 626-962-0222 Rev. Ramsine Hage-Moussa, Pst.; Subdeacon Pierre El-Khoury; Subdeacon George Haddad; CRP Stds.: 75

STATE OF COLORADO

LAKEWOOD

St. Rafka Maronite Catholic Church - 2301 Wadsworth Blvd., Lakewood, CO 80214 t) 720-833-0354 strafkalkwd@outlook.com strafkadenver.org Rev. Andre Mehanna, Pst.; Rev. El-Badaoui Habib, Admin.; Mike Dunn, Bus. Mgr.; CRP Stds.: 2

STATE OF ILLINOIS

LOMBARD

Our Lady of Lebanon Maronite Catholic Church - 950 N. Grace St., Lombard, IL 60148 t) 630-932-9640 frpierre@gmail.com; ollofficechicago@gmail.com www.ollchicago.org Rev. Pierre El Khoury, M.L.M., Pst.; Subdeacon Thomas Podraza; Subdeacon George Romanos, Sacr. Min.; CRP Stds.: 68
Maronite Religious Education -

PEORIA

St. Sharbel Maronite Catholic Church - 2914 W. Scenic Dr., Peoria, IL 61615 t) 309-688-5555 stsharbell@gmail.com Chorbishop Faouzi Elia, Pst.; Rev. Bechara Awada, Assoc. Pst.; Subdeacon George Romanos; Dcn. George Geagea; CRP Stds.: 17

STATE OF MICHIGAN

CLINTON TOWNSHIP

St. Sharbel Maronite Catholic Church - 43888 Hayes Rd., Clinton Township, MI 48038 t) 586-630-0002 c) (586) 899-4189 stsharbelmichigan@gmail.com www.stsharbelmichigan Chorbishop Alfred Badawi, Pst.; Staci Saker, DRE; Dcn. Michael Magyar; CRP Stds.: 143

DETROIT

St. Maron Maronite Catholic Church - 11466 Kercheval St., Detroit, MI 48214 t) 313-824-0196 saintmarondetroit@gmail.com www.saintmarondetroit.org Rev. Roby Zibara, Pst.;

FLINT

Our Lady of Lebanon Maronite Catholic Church - 4133 Calkins Rd., Flint, MI 48532 t) 810-733-1259; 810-732-2370 olol-flint@outlook.com www.ololmi.org Rev. Pierre Bassil, Pst.; Subdeacon Earl Matte; Dcn. Joseph Pavlovich; Dcn. Martin J. Rachid; CRP Stds.: 35

LIVONIA

St. Rafka Maronite Catholic Church - 32765 Lyndon St., Livonia, MI 48154 t) 734-525-2828 st.rafkachurch@gmail.com www.saintrafkamichigan.com Rev. Rodrigue

Constantin, Pst.; Alice Bodagh, DRE; CRP Stds.: 68

STATE OF MINNESOTA

MENDOTA HEIGHTS

Holy Family Maronite Catholic Church - 1960 Lexington Ave. S., Mendota Heights, MN 55118 t) 651-291-1116 emanuelng@hotmail.com www.holyfamilymaronitechurch.org Rev. Emmanuel Makhle-Ghorr, Pst.; CRP Stds.: 4

MINNEAPOLIS

St. Maron Maronite Catholic Church - 602 University Ave., N.E., Minneapolis, MN 55413 t) (612) 379-2758 c) 612-876-2133 www.stmaron.com Chorbishop Sharbel Maroun, Pst.; Jaonnie Moses, DRE; CRP Stds.: 67

STATE OF MISSOURI

CRESTWOOD

St. Raymond - St. Elizabeth Maronite Catholic Church - 1420 S. Sappington Rd., Crestwood, MO 63126 t) 314-968-0760 steeliz@sbcglobal.net www.stelizabethhungary.org Rev. John Nahal, M.L.M., Pst.; Rev. Patrick Kassab, Assoc. Pst.; Dcn. William G. Meister; CRP Stds.: 30

ST. LOUIS

St. Raymond Maronite Catholic Cathedral - 931 Lebanon Dr., St. Louis, MO 63104 t) 314-621-0056 rector@straymond-mc.org Rev. John Nahal, M.L.M., Rector; Rev. Patrick Kassab, Assoc. Pst.; Dcn. Anthony Simon; Subdeacon David Wahby; CRP Stds.: 30

STATE OF NEVADA

LAS VEGAS

St. Sharbel Maronite Catholic Mission - 10325 Rancho Destino Rd., Las Vegas, NV 89183 t) 702-616-6902 stsharbel.lv@gmail.com www.stsharbellasvegas.org Rev. Nadim Abou Zeid, M.L.M., Admin.; CRP Stds.: 39

STATE OF OHIO

CINCINNATI

St. Anthony of Padua Maronite Catholic Church - 2530 Victory Pkwy., Cincinnati, OH 45206 t) 513-961-0120 saintanthonycincinnati@gmail.com www.staparish.org Rev. George Hajj, Pst.; Subdeacon Donald George; Subdeacon Tom Simon; CRP Stds.: 15

COLUMBUS

Our Lady of Lebanon Maronite Catholic Mission - 893 Hamlet, Columbus, OH 43201-3536 t) 818-620-0100 Most Rev. A. Elias Zaidan, Contact;

DAYTON

Saint Ignatius of Antioch Maronite Catholic Church - 50 Nutt Rd., Dayton, OH 45458 t) 937-428-0372 info@stiparish.org stiparish.org Rev. Jean Paul Khoury, Pst.; Laura Thomas, DRE; William Thomas, DRE;

FAIRLAWN

Our Lady of the Cedars of Mt. Lebanon Maronite Catholic Church - 507 S. Cleveland-Massillon Rd., Fairlawn, OH 44333-3019 t) 330-666-3598 ourladyofthecedarschurch@gmail.com www.ourladyofthecedarschurch.org Rev. Ronald W. Eid, Pst.; Subdeacon Paul Boulos; Dcn. Tom Maroon; Dcn. Robert Foster; CRP Stds.: 40

INDEPENDENCE

St. Maron Maronite Catholic Church - 7800 Brookside Rd., Independence, OH 44131 t) 216-520-5081 saintmaroncleveland@gmail.com www.saintmaron-clev.org Rev. Elias Yazbeck, Admin.; Subdeacon Georges Faddoul; Subdeacon Ghazi Faddoul; Subdeacon Lattouf Lattouf; Dcn. George M. Khoury; Elias Kanaan, DRE; CRP Stds.: 45

YOUNGSTOWN

St. Maron Maronite Catholic Church - 1555 S. Meridian Rd., Youngstown, OH 44511-1199 t) 330-792-2371; 330-538-9822 (CRP) srjinane@hotmail.com; parishoffice@stmaronyoungstown.org www.stmaronyoungstown.org Rev. Tony Massad, Pst.; Rev. Jacques Kik, Assoc. Pst.; Subdeacon Albert Dohar; Subdeacon James Essad; Dcn. William George; Sr. Jinane Farah, DRE; CRP Stds.: 40

STATE OF OKLAHOMA

NORMAN

Our Lady of Lebanon Maronite Mission - 500 Alameda, Norman, OK 73071 t) 405-321-3097 pmarienabil@gmail.com Rev. Nabil Mouannes, Admin.; CRP Stds.: 4

TULSA

St. Therese of the Child Jesus Maronite Catholic Church - 8315 S. 107th Ave., E., Tulsa, OK 74133 t) 918-872-7400 marwanabinadder@gmail.com saintherese.org Rev. Marnan Abinader, M.L.M., Pst.; CRP Stds.: 3

STATE OF OREGON

PORTLAND

Saint Sharbel Maronite Catholic Church - 1804 S.E. 16th Ave., Portland, OR 97214 t) 503-231-3853 n.redmond@comcast.net; stsharbelpdx@gmail.com Rev. Christopher Faber, Pst.; Nadia Redmond, DRE; CRP Stds.: 12

STATE OF TENNESSEE

LEBANON

St. Sharbel Maronite Catholic Mission Inc. - 479 Centerville Rd., Lebanon, TN 37087 c) (615) 281-0256 stsharbeltn@gmail.com Nadine Choufani, Admin.;

STATE OF TEXAS

AUSTIN

Our Lady's Maronite Parish - 1320 E. 51st St., Austin, TX 78723 t) 512-458-3693 email@ourladysmaronite.org www.ourladysmaronite.org Rev. Msgr. Donald J. Sawyer, Pst.; Dcn. Michael Cunningham; Dcn. Guy Helou;

EL PASO

St. Sharbel Maronite Catholic Mission - 851 Thorn Ave., El Paso, TX 79912 t) 915-234-2303 stsharbelelpaso@gmail.com www.stsharbelelpaso.org Rev. Mikhael Chady Jalkh, Pst.; CRP Stds.: 16

HOUSTON

Our Lady of the Cedars Maronite Catholic Church - 11935 Bellfort Village Dr., Houston, TX 77031 t) 281-568-6800 parish@olchouston.org www.ourladyofthecedars.net Rev. Milad T. Yaghi, M.L.M., Pst.; Rev. Edward Hanna, M.L.M., Assoc. Pst.; Susan Hage, DRE; CRP Stds.: 206

LEWISVILLE

Our Lady of Lebanon Maronite Catholic Church - 719 University Pl., Lewisville, TX 75067 t) 972-436-7617; 817-491-0763 (CRP) smarincel001@tx.rr.com; ladyofl719@gmail.com ourladylebanon.com Rev. Assaad El Basha, M.L.M., Pst.; Sue Marincel, DRE; CRP Stds.: 78

SAN ANTONIO

St. George Maronite Catholic Church - 6070 Babcock Rd., San Antonio, TX 78240 t) 210-690-9569 www.stgeorgesa.org Rev. Charles H. Khachan, M.L.M., Pst.; Rev. Mhanna Joseph Kallas, M.L.M, Assoc. Pst.; Subdeacon Joseph Harb; Subdeacon Dustin Raymond; Subdeacon Ernest Karam; Dcn. Chris Pond; CRP Stds.: 45

STATE OF UTAH

MURRAY

Saint Jude Maronite Catholic Church - 4893 Wasatch St., Murray, UT 84107 t) 801-268-2820 saintjudemaronite@gmail.com; fatherjoubran@hotmail.com Rev. Jibran BouMerhi, Pst.; Subdeacon Athony Allam; CRP Stds.: 5

STATE OF WEST VIRGINIA

WHEELING

Our Lady of Lebanon Maronite Catholic Church - 2216 Eoff St., Wheeling, WV 26003 t) 304-233-1688 www.ololwv.com Rev. Msgr. Bakhos Chidiac, Pst.; Lou Khoury, DRE;

STATE OF WISCONSIN

UNION GROVE

Saint Sharbel Maronite Catholic Mission of Milwaukee Inc. - 1501 172nd Ave., Union Grove, WI 53182 c) (805) 402-5060 abouna@saintsharbelmission.com www.saintsharbelmission.com Rev. Joe Daccache, Pst.; CRP Stds.: 2

INSTITUTIONS LOCATED IN DIOCESE

CONVENTS, MONASTERIES, AND RESIDENCES FOR WOMEN [CON]

NORTH JACKSON

Antonine Maronite Sisters of Youngstown, Inc. - 2691 N. Lipkey Rd., North Jackson, OH 44451 t) 330-538-9822 anto9srs@aol.com www.antoninesisters.com Sr. Samia Abou-Shakra, AS, Supr.; Srs.: 5

Antonine Sisters Adult Day Care, Inc. - 2675 N. Lipkey Rd., North Jackson, OH 44451 t) (330) 538-9822 www.antoninevillage.org Sr. Marie Madeleine Iskandar, MMI, Dir.;

Antonine Therapy Center - 2675 N. Lipkey Rd., North Jackson, OH 44451 t) (330) 538-9822 Sr. Kawsar Choufani, AS, Dir.;

Antonine Village - 2675 N. Lipkey Rd., North Jackson, OH 44451 www.antoninevillage.org

ENDOWMENTS / FOUNDATIONS / TRUSTS [EFT]

LOS ANGELES

Maronite Catholic Foundation, a California Nonprofit Religious Corp - 333 San Vincente Blvd., Los Angeles, CA 90048 t) 310-275-6634 bishop@eparchy.org Most Rev. Abdallah E. Zaidan, Chair; Bourjois Abboud, Vice. Pres.; Edward Salem, Secy.; Jay Abdo, Treas.;

SANTA ANA

Lebanese Hospital Geitaoui Foundation - 18791 Winnwood Ln., Santa Ana, CA 92705 c) 657-262-8316 Sr. Martha Mechleb, Contact;

Maronite Endowment for the Poor - 18791 Winnwood Ln., Santa Ana, CA 92705 c) 657-262-8316 marthamechleb@hotmail.com Sr. Martha Mechleb, Contact;

ST. LOUIS

Catholic School Assistance Fund - 1021 S. 10th St., St. Louis, MO 63104 t) 314-231-1021 www.eparchy.org Most Rev. A. Elias Zaidan;

Eparchial Endowments - 1021 S. 10th St., St. Louis, MO 63104 t) 314-231-1021 Most Rev. A. Elias Zaidan, Chair;

The Eparchy of Our Lady of Lebanon of LA Order of St. Sharbel Trust - 1021 S. 10th St., St. Louis, MO 63104 t) 818-626-9193 jamileh@eparchy.org Most Rev. Abdallah E. Zaidan, CEO;

St. Ephrem Maronite Cath Ch El Cajon Real Estate Trust - 1021 S. 10th St., St. Louis, MO 63104 t) 314-231-1021 Most Rev. A. Elias Zaidan;

St. George Maronite Catholic Church-San Antonio Real Estate Trust - 1021 S. 10th St., St. Louis, MO 63104 t) 314-231-1021 Most Rev. A. Elias Zaidan, Trustee;

Holy Family Maronite Catholic Church-St. Paul, MN Real Estate Trust - 1021 S. 10th St., St. Louis, MO 63104 t) 314-231-1021 jamileh@eparchy.org Most Rev. A. Elias Zaidan;

St. John Maron Maronite Catholic Church-Orange Real Estate Trust - 1021 S. 10th St., St. Louis, MO 63104 t) 314-231-1021 Most Rev. A. Elias Zaidan;

St. Joseph Maronite Catholic Church-Phoenix Real Estate Trust - 1021 S. 10th St., St. Louis, MO 63104 t) 314-231-1021 Most Rev. A. Elias Zaidan;

St. Jude Maronite Catholic Church-W. Covina Real Estate Trust - 1021 S. 10th St., St. Louis, MO 63104 t) 314-231-1021 Most Rev. A. Elias Zaidan;

St. Maron Maronite Cath Ch- Minneapolis Real Estate Trust - 1021 S. 10th St., St. Louis, MO 63104 t) 314-231-1021 Most Rev. A. Elias Zaidan;

Our Lady of Lebanon Maronite Catholic Church-Lewisville Real Estate Trust - 1021 S. 10th St., St. Louis,

MO 63104 t) 314-231-1021 Most Rev. A. Elias Zaidan;
Our Lady of Lebanon Maronite Mission-Norman Real Estate Trust - 1021 S. 10th St., St. Louis, MO 63104 t) 314-231-1021 Most Rev. A. Elias Zaidan;
Our Lady of Mt. Lebanon-St. Peter Maronite Catholic Cathedral-LA Real Estate Trust - 1021 S. 10th St., St. Louis, MO 63104 t) 314-231-1021 Most Rev. A. Elias Zaidan;
Our Lady of the Cedar Maronite Catholic Church-Houston Real Estate Trust - 1021 S. 10th St., St. Louis, MO 63104 t) 314-231-1021 Most Rev. A. Elias Zaidan;
Our Lady of the Rosary Maronite Cath Mission-Carmichael Real Estate Trust - 1021 S. 10th St., St. Louis, MO 63104 t) 314-231-1021 Most Rev. A. Elias Zaidan;
Our Lady's Maronite Catholic Church-Austin Real Estate Trust - 1021 S. 10th St., St. Louis, MO 63104 t) 314-231-1021 Most Rev. A. Elias Zaidan;
Saint Peter and Paul Maronite Catholic Mission Simi Valley Real Estate Trust - 1021 S. 10th St., St. Louis, MO 63104 t) 314-231-1021 Most Rev. A. Elias Zaidan;
Priest's Retirement Fund - 1021 S. 10th St., St. Louis, MO 63104 t) 314-231-1021 www.eparchy.org Jamileh Koury, Contact;
St. Rafka Maronite Catholic Church-Lakewood, CO Real Estate Trust - 1021 S. 10th St., St. Louis, MO 63104 t) 314-231-1021 Most Rev. A. Elias Zaidan, Contact;
St. Rafka Maronite Cath Ch-Livonia Real Estate Trust - 1021 S. 10th St., St. Louis, MO 63104 t) 314-231-1021 Most Rev. A. Elias Zaidan;
St. Raymond Maronite Catholic Cathedral - Real Estate Trust - 1021 S. 10th St., St. Louis, MO 63104 t) 314-231-1021 Most Rev. A. Elias Zaidan;
St. Sharbel Manonite Catholic Mission - El Paso Real Estate Trust - 1021 S. 10th St., St. Louis, MO 63104 t) 314-231-1021 Most Rev. A. Elias Zaidan;
St. Sharbel Maronite Catholic Church - Michigan Real Estate Trust - 1021 S. 10th St., St. Louis, MO 63104 t) 314-231-1021 Most Rev. A. Elias Zaidan;
St. Sharbel Maronite Catholic Church - Portland Real Estate Trust - 1021 S. 10th St., St. Louis, MO 63104 t) 314-231-1021 Most Rev. A. Elias Zaidan;
St. Sharbel Maronite Catholic Mission - Las Vegas Real Estate Trust - 1021 S. 10th St., St. Louis, MO 63104 t) 314-231-1021 Most Rev. A. Elias Zaidan;

MISCELLANEOUS [MIS]

LOS ANGELES

The Congregation of Maronite Lebanese Missionaries - 333 S. San Vicente Blvd., Los Angeles, CA 90048 t) 310-275-6634 Rev. Elias Sleiman, M.L.M., Supr.;

ST. LOUIS

Bishop's Charities - 1021 S. 10th St., St. Louis, MO 63104 t) 314-231-1021 Most Rev. A. Elias Zaidan, Chair;
Caritas Lebanon - 1021 S. 10th St., St. Louis, MO 63104 t) 314-231-1021 Rev. John Nahal, M.L.M., Contact;
LEAF USA, Inc. - 1021 S. 10th St., St. Louis, MO 63104 t) 314-231-1021 Most Rev. A. Elias Zaidan, Contact;
Maronite Heritage Institute - 1021 S. 10th St., St. Louis, MO 63104 t) 314-231-1021 mdenny@usamaronite.org Jamileh Koury, Bus. Mgr.;
Maronite Outreach - 1021 S. 10th St., St. Louis, MO 63104 t) 314-231-1021 info@maroniteoutreach.org www.maroniteoutreach.org Most Rev. A. Elias Zaidan, Chair;
Maronite Youth Organization - 1021 S. 10th St., St. Louis, MO 63104 t) 314-231-0121 hanna_edward@hotmail.com Rev. Edward Hanna, M.L.M., Dir.;

YOUNGSTOWN

National Maronite Young Adult Organization - National MYA - 1555 S. Meridian Rd., Youngstown, OH 44511 c) 810-691-7055 nationalmya@gmail.com www.maroniteyoungadults.org Rev. Tony Massad, Dir.; Sr. Therese Marie Touma, Dir.;

MONASTERIES AND RESIDENCES FOR PRIESTS AND BROTHERS [MON]

ANN ARBOR

Maronite Order of the Blessed Virgin Mary - 4405 Earhart Rd., Ann Arbor, MI 48105 t) 734-662-4822 pilotjohnny@hotmail.com Rev. Roger Chekri, Dir.; Rev. Nabil Habchi, O.M.M., Treas.; Rev. Paul Tarabay, O.M.M., Secy.; Toni Jabbour, Secy.; Priests: 4

BEAVERTON

Oblates of Jesus, Mary & Joseph - 3880 N.W. 171 Pl., Beaverton, OR 97006; Mailing: P.O. Box 13723, Portland, OR 97213 t) 503-690-4425 maronitemonks@gmail.com maronitemonastery.com Maronite Monks of Jesus, Mary and Joseph Rev. W. Jonathan Decker, M.M.J.M.J., Abbot; Rev. Anthony J. Alles, M.M.J.M.J., Prior; Rev. John Michael Morgan, M.M.J.M.J., Subprior; Dcn. Daniel Harris, M.M.J.M.J.; Dcn. Raphael Lefevre, M.M.J.M.J.; Brs.: 5; Priests: 3
Sacred Heart Maronite Monastery - 3880 N.W. 171 Pl., Beaverton, OR 97006; Mailing: P.O. Box 13723, Portland, OR 97213 t) 503-690-4425 maronitemonks@gmail.com maronitemonastery.com Maronite Monks of Jesus, Mary and Joseph Monastery of Jesus, Mary and Joseph Rev. W. Jonathan Decker, M.M.J.M.J., Abbot; Rev. Anthony J. Alles, M.M.J.M.J., Prior; Rev. John Michael Morgan, M.M.J.M.J., Subprior; Dcn. Daniel Harris, M.M.J.M.J.; Dcn. Raphael Lefevre, M.M.J.M.J.; Brs.: 2; Priests: 3

HOUSTON

The Congregation of Maronite Lebanese Missionaries - 11935 Bellfort Village, Our Lady of the Cedars, Houston, TX 77031 t) 281-568-6800 frmilad@usa.com Rev. Charles H. Khachan, M.L.M., Pst.; Rev. Elias Sleiman, M.L.M., Supr.; Rev. Assaad El Basha, M.L.M.; Rev. Pierre El Khoury, M.L.M.; Rev. Ramsine Hage-Moussa, M.L.M.; Rev. Edward Hanna, M.L.M.; Rev. Marwan Abi Nader, M.L.M.; Rev. Milad T. Yaghi, M.L.M.; Rev. Nadim Abou Zeid, M.L.M.; Rev. ElBadaoui Habib; Rev. Etienne Hanna; Rev. Mhanna Joseph Kallas, M.L.M; Priests: 13

NORTH JACKSON

Father Tobia Retirement Home - 2759 N. Lipkey Rd., North Jackson, OH 44451 t) 330-538-3351 office@ourladyoflebanonshrine.com www.ourladyoflebanonshrine.com Chorbishop Anthony Spinosa, Rector; Priests: 1

SHRINES [SHR]

NORTH JACKSON

Basilica & National Shrine of Our Lady of Lebanon - 2759 N. Lipkey Rd., North Jackson, OH 44451 t) 330-538-3351 office@ourladyoflebanonshrine.com www.ourladyoflebanonshrine.com Chorbishop Anthony Spinosa, Rector;

An asterisk (*) denotes an organization that has established tax-exempt status directly with the IRS and is not covered by the USCCB Group Ruling.

Armenian Catholic Eparchy of Our Lady of Nareg in the United States of America and Canada

MOST REVEREND MIKAEL ANTOINE MOURADIAN, I.C.P.B.

Bishop of the Armenian Catholic Eparchy of Our Lady of Nareg; ordained October 24, 1987; appointed Eparch of Our Lady of Nareg May 21, 2011; consecrated July 31, 2011; installed October 2, 2011. Chancery: 1510 E. Mountain St., Glendale, CA 91207-1226.

Chancery & Vicar General Office: 1510 E. Mountain St., Glendale, CA 91207-1226. T: 818-243-8400; F: 818-243-0095.

www.ourladyofnareg.org

Established as an Apostolic Exarchate July 3, 1981; elevated to an Eparchy on September 12, 2005.

Comprises the entire United States and Canada.

Legal Title: Armenian Catholic Eparchy of Our Lady of Nareg in the United States and Canada.

STATISTICAL OVERVIEW

Personnel

Bishop	1
Priests: Diocesan Active in Diocese	4
Number of Diocesan Priests	4
Religious Priests in Diocese	5
Total Priests in your Diocese	9
Permanent Deacons in Diocese	2
Total Sisters	7

Parishes

Parishes	9
With Resident Pastor:	
Resident Diocesan Priests	4
Resident Religious Priests	4
Without Resident Pastor:	
Administered by Priests	1
Missions	3
Professional Ministry Personnel:	
Sisters	7

Educational

High Schools, Diocesan and Parish	1
Total Students	314
Elementary Schools, Private	4
Total Students	632
Catechesis / Religious Education:	
High School Students	34
Elementary Students	76
Total Students under Catholic Instruction	1,056
Teachers in Diocese:	
Priests	1
Sisters	2
Lay Teachers	146

Vital Statistics

Receptions into the Church:	
Infant Baptism Totals	128
Minor Baptism Totals	40
First Communions	94
Confirmations	168
Marriages:	
Catholic	58
Interfaith	23
Total Marriages	81
Deaths	62
Total Catholic Population	51,000

LEADERSHIP

Chancery & Vicar General Office - t) 818-243-8400
Vicar General - Rev. Georges Zabarian;
Business Chancellor - t) (818) 243-8400 www.ourladyofnareg.org/ Msgr. Parsegh Manuel Baghdassarian, Chancellor;

COMMUNICATIONS

Newspaper Diocesan Bulletins -
The Eternal Flame - t) 818-243-8400
Verelk - t) 818-243-8400

PARISHES, MISSIONS, AND CLERGY

COMMONWEALTH OF MASSACHUSETTS

BELMONT

Holy Cross - 200 Lexington St., Belmont, MA 02478 t) (617) 489-2280 Most Rev. Mikael Antoine Mouradian, I.C.P.B., Admin.; Dcn. M.J. Connolly; CRP Stds.: 4

COMMONWEALTH OF PENNSYLVANIA

WYNNEWOOD

St. Mark's Armenian Catholic - 400 Haverford Rd., Wynnewood, PA 19096-2699 t) 610-896-7789 armcathphil@gmail.com Rev. Asadur Minasian, Pst.;

STATE OF CALIFORNIA

GLENDALE

St. Gregory Armenian Catholic Cathedral - 1510 E. Mountain St., Glendale, CA 91207-1226 t) (818) 243-8400 www.stgregoryarmenian.org Msgr. Parsegh Manuel Baghdassarian, Pst.; Rev. Levon Joulian Estefan, Assoc. Pst.;

LOS ANGELES

Our Lady Queen of Martyrs - 1327 Pleasant Ave., Los Angeles, CA 90033-2328 c) (610) 739-8195 Rev. Armenag Bedrossian, Pst.;

STATE OF MICHIGAN

FARMINGTON HILLS

St. Vartan's - 34080 Edmonton St., Farmington Hills, MI 48335 t) (248) 877-3718 Msgr. Andon Atamian, Pst.;

STATE OF NEW JERSEY

LITTLE FALLS

St. Ann's Armenian Catholic Church - 155 Long Hill Rd., Little Falls, NJ 07424-2318 t) 973-890-0447 shacc01@gmail.com Rev. George Kalousieh, Pst.;

Sacred Heart - 155 Long Hill Rd., Little Falls, NJ 07424-2318 t) 973-890-0447 shacc01@gmail.com Rev. George Kalousieh, Pst.; Rev. Richard Shackil, Pst. Assoc.; CRP Stds.: 17

SCHOOLS: PRESCHOOL THRU HIGH SCHOOL

SCHOOLS

COMMONWEALTH OF PENNSYLVANIA

RADNOR

Armenian Sisters Academy - 440 Upper Gulph Rd., Radnor, PA 19087-4699 t) 610-687-4100 asaphila.org/ Sr. Emma Moussayan, Prin.; Stds.: 150; Sr. Tchrs.: 1; Lay Tchrs.: 21

STATE OF CALIFORNIA

MONTROSE

Armenian Sisters Academy Preschool - (PRV) 2361 Florencita Dr., Montrose, CA 91020-1817 t) 818-249-8783 www.asapreschool.org Karin Bilavian, Dir.;

INSTITUTIONS LOCATED IN DIOCESE

MISCELLANEOUS [MIS]

MONTROSE

Armenian Sisters of the Immaculate Conception - 2361 Florencita Dr., Montrose, CA 91020-1817 t) 818-249-7493 Sr. Lucia Al-Haik, Contact;

RADNOR

Armenian Sisters of the Immaculate Conception - 440 Upper Gulph Rd., Radnor, PA 19087-4699 t) 610-687-4100; 610-688-9360 sisteremma@asaphila.org www.asaphila.org Sr. Emma Moussayan, Supr.;

An asterisk (*) denotes an organization that has established tax-exempt status directly with the IRS and is not covered by the USCCB Group Ruling.

Byzantine Catholic Eparchy of Parma of the Ruthenians

MOST REVEREND MILAN LACH, S.J.

Bishop of Parma; ordained July 1, 2001; appointed Auxiliary Bishop of Presov, Slovakia and Titular Bishop of Ostracine April 19, 2013; ordained June 1, 2013; appointed Apostolic Administrator of Parma June 24, 2017; installed July 21, 2017; Succeeded to See June 1, 2018; installed June 30, 2018.

Chancery Office: 5000 Rockside Rd., Ste. 310, Independence, OH 44131. T: 216-741-8773; F: 216-741-9356.
www.parma.org

ESTABLISHED FEBRUARY 21, 1969.

Embraces all Byzantine Ruthenian Rite Catholics in the States of Illinois, Indiana, Iowa, Kansas, Michigan, Minnesota, Missouri, Nebraska, North Dakota, South Dakota and Wisconsin. Also the entire State of Ohio excluding the Counties of Ashtabula, Trumbull, Mahoning, Columbiana, Carroll, Harrison, Guernsey, Noble, Morgan, Athens, Meigs, Gallia and Lawrence.

For legal titles of parishes and diocesan institutions, consult the Chancery Office.

STATISTICAL OVERVIEW

Personnel

Bishop	1
Retired Bishops	1
Priests: Diocesan Active in Diocese	15
Priests: Diocesan Active Outside Diocese	2
Priests: Retired, Sick or Absent	15
Number of Diocesan Priests	32
Religious Priests in Diocese	2
Total Priests in your Diocese	34
Extern Priests in Diocese	10
Permanent Deacons in Diocese	15

Parishes

Parishes	24
With Resident Pastor:	
Resident Diocesan Priests	8
Without Resident Pastor:	
Administered by Priests	16
Missions	1
Pastoral Centers	3
Closed Parishes	2

Welfare

Day Care Centers	1
Total Assisted	18
Special Centers for Social Services	1
Total Assisted	60

Educational

Elementary Schools, Diocesan and Parish	1
Total Students	156
Catechesis/Religious Education:	
High School Students	78
Elementary Students	269
Total Students under Catholic Instruction	503
Teachers in Diocese:	
Lay Teachers	14

Vital Statistics

Receptions into the Church:	
Infant Baptism Totals	46
Minor Baptism Totals	4
Adult Baptism Totals	4
Received into Full Communion	27
First Communions	51
Confirmations	55
Marriages:	
Catholic	19
Interfaith	1
Total Marriages	20
Deaths	89
Total Catholic Population	4,309

LEADERSHIP

Chancery Office - t) 216-741-8773
Protosyncellus -
Chancellor - Rev. Gary Yanus;
Eparchial Finance Council - Most Rev. Milan Lach, S.J.; Mitred Archpriest Marek Visnovsky; Martin Kopmeyer;
Protopresbyter for Great Lakes Region - Rev. Mychail Rozmarynowycz;
Protopresbyter for Midwest Region - Very Rev. Thomas Loya;
Protopresbyter for Ohio Region - Rev. Robert Jager (Slovakia) (bobjager@hotmail.com);
Presbyteral Council - Mitred Archpriest Marek Visnovsky; Very Rev. Thomas Loya; Rev. Charles Strebler;
Finance Officer - Martin Kopmeyer, CFO;
Eparchial Consultors - Mitred Archpriest Marek Visnovsky; Rev. Charles Strebler; Very Rev. Thomas Loya;
Protopresbyters - Rev. Robert Jager (Slovakia) (bobjager@hotmail.com); Very Rev. Thomas Loya; Rev. Mychail Rozmarynowycz;
Vicar Judicialis - Rev. Charles Strebler;
Judges - Vincet M. Gardiner; Lynette Tait;
Defender of the Bond - Rev. A. Jonathan Zingales;
Promoter of Justice - Rev. Richard Bona;
Notary - Rev. Richard Bona; Lee Ann Calvert;
Eparchial Censor - Rev. Robert Jager (Slovakia);

ADVISORY BOARDS, COMMISSIONS, COMMITTEES, AND COUNCILS

Building Commission - Nick Lizanich, Chair; Mark Papke; Frank Tombazzi;
Eparchial Shrine of Our Lady of Mariapoch - Most Rev. Milan Lach, S.J.; Mother Theodora Strohmeyer, Admin.;
Office of Vocations - Rev. Robert Jager (Slovakia);
Office of Youth Ministry - Rev. Lukas Mitro (Slovakia);
Pre-Cana Office - Very Rev. Thomas Loya;
Priest's Pension Board - Mitred Archpriest Marek Visnovsky; Martin Kopmeyer; Rev. Bryan R. Eyman;
Respect Life Office - Very Rev. Thomas Loya;
Safe Environment Review Board - Rev. Richard Bona; Sharon DiLauro Petrus; Mitred Archpriest Marek Visnovsky;
Safe Environment - Rita Basalla;
Seminary Education Formation Board - Rita Basalla; Rev. Miron Kerul-Kmec; Dcn. John Petrus;
Victim Assistance Coordinator - Sharon DiLauro Petrus;

PARISHES, MISSIONS, AND CLERGY

STATE OF ILLINOIS

HOMER GLEN

Annunciation Byzantine Catholic Church - 14610 S. Will-Cook Rd., Homer Glen, IL 60491-9212 t) 708-645-0241 annuncbyzchurch@aol.com www.byzantinecatholic.com Very Rev. Thomas Loya, Pst.; Dcn. John Evancho; Dcn. J. Timothy Tkach; CRP Stds.: 54

STATE OF INDIANA

INDIANAPOLIS

St. Athanasius Church - 1117 S. Blaine Ave., Indianapolis, IN 46221-1110 t) 317-632-4157 pastor@saindy.com www.saindy.com Rev. Mykhaylo Shkyndya, Admin.; CRP Stds.: 9

MERRILLVILLE

St. Michael - 557 W. 57th Ave., Merrillville, IN 46410-2540 t) 219-980-0600; 219-980-9074 stmichaelmerrillville@parma.org www.stmichaelbyz.org Rev. Michal Bucko, Admin.; CRP Stds.: 9

MUNSTER

Saint Nicholas - 8103 Columbia Ave., Munster, IN 46321-1802 t) 219-838-9380 skoplinka21@gmail.com Rev. Steven Koplinka, Pst.; CRP Stds.: 10

WHITING

Assumption of the Blessed Virgin (St. Mary Byzantine Catholic Church) - 2011 Clark St., Whiting, IN 46394-2023 t) 219-659-0277 stmarywhiting@parma.org stmarywhiting.org Rev. Andrew Summerson, Admin.; CRP Stds.: 16

STATE OF MICHIGAN

ALLEN PARK

St. Stephen - 4141 Laurence Ave., Allen Park, MI 48101-3049 t) 313-382-5901 ststephen@parma.org saintstephenbyzantine.church Rev. John Russell, Admin.; Dcn. Lawrence Hendricks; CRP Stds.: 9

BAY CITY

Saint George - 204 N. Van Buren St., Bay City, MI 48706-6519 t) 810-659-4887 stgeorgebyz@gmail.com Rev. James J. Batcha, Admin.; CRP Stds.: 8

CLINTON TOWNSHIP

St. Nicholas - 23300 King Dr., Clinton Township, MI 48035 t) 586-791-1052 stnicksbyzantine@yahoo.com www.stnicksdetroit.com Rev. Mykhailo Solianyk (Ukraine), Admin.; CRP Stds.: 11

FLUSHING

St. Michael - 2333 N. Elms Rd., Flushing, MI 48433-9426 t) 810-659-4887 stmichaelbyz@gmail.com Rev. James J. Batcha, Pst.; CRP Stds.: 14

LIVONIA

Sacred Heart - 29125 W. Six-Mile Rd., Livonia, MI 48152-3661 t) 734-522-3166 fatherjosmarquis@currently.com www.shbyzantine.com Rev. Joseph Marquis, Pst.; CRP Stds.: 11

STERLING HEIGHTS

St. Basil - 4700 Metropolitan Pkwy., Sterling Heights, MI 48310-3905 t) 586-268-1082 mrozmar05@aol.com www.stbasilbyz.com Rev. Mychail Rozmarynowycz, Pst.; Dcn. Paul Latcha; CRP Stds.: 17

STATE OF MINNESOTA

MINNEAPOLIS

St. John the Baptist - 2205 Third St., N.E., Minneapolis, MN 55418-3422; Mailing: 2215 3rd St., N.E., Minneapolis, MN 55418 t) 612-789-6252 stjohnminneapolis@comcast.net www.byzantinemn.org Rev. Cyril Farmer, Pst.;

STATE OF MISSOURI

ST. LOUIS

St. Louis Mission - 7100 Virginia Ave., St. Louis, MO 63111 t) 314-434-1312 x5 stlouis@parma.org www.stlouis.byzcath.org Rev. Joseph A. Weber, Admin.; Rev. Paul Niemann, Pst. Assoc.; Rev. James D. Theby, Pst. Assoc.; Rev. Steven Hawkes-Teeples, S.J., Pst. Assoc.; Rev. James Michael Deshotels, S.J., Pst. Assoc.; CRP Stds.: 15

SUGAR CREEK

St. Luke, Byzantine Catholic Parish - 11413 Chicago St., Sugar Creek, MO 64054 c) 816-231-7100 stlukebyz@gmail.com byzantinekc.org/ Rev. Michael Lee, Admin.; Dcn. Nicholas Szilagye;

STATE OF OHIO

BARBERTON

St. Nicholas - 1051 E. Robinson St., Barberton, OH 44203-3852 t) 330-753-2031 stnickbyz@gmail.com www.stnickbyz.com Rev. Miron Kerul-Kmec, Pst.; Dcn. Robert Cripps; CRP Stds.: 54

BRECKSVILLE

St. Joseph - 8111 Brecksville, Brecksville, OH 44141-1204 t) 440-526-1818 stjoseph@parma.org; frmvisnovsky@parma.org www.stjoebyz.com Rev. Vasyl Kupar (Ukraine), Par. Vicar; Mitred Archpriest Marek Visnovsky, Admin.; Dcn. William Fredrick; CRP Stds.: 9

BRUNSWICK

St. Emilian - 1231 Substation Rd., Brunswick, OH 44212-0843 t) 330-225-9857 st.emilianbyzantine@gmail.com www.stemilian.com Rev. Peter Boksay (Hungary), Admin.; Dcn. John Petrus;

CLEVELAND

Dormition of the Theotoko - 4600 State Rd., Cleveland, OH 44109 t) 216-741-7979 marekvisnovsky@yahoo.com www.stmarybyz.com Mitred Archpriest Marek Visnovsky, Pst.; Dcn. Gregory Loya; Dcn. Joseph Hnat; CRP Stds.: 12

St. Mary School - (Grades K-8) t) 216-749-7980 basalla4@att.net Rita Basalla, Prin.; Stds.: 156; Lay Tchrs.: 14

Holy Spirit - 5500 W. 54th St., Parma, OH 44129-2274 t) (440) 884-8452 contactus@holyspiritbyzantine.org holyspiritbyzantine.org

St. John the Baptist - 1900 Carlton Rd., Parma, OH 44134-3129 t) (216) 661-8658 frmvisnovsky@parma.org

COLUMBUS

St. John Chrysostom - 5858 Cleveland Ave., Columbus, OH 43231-2862 t) 614-882-7578 stjohnbyz@hotmail.com www.byzantinecolumbus.com Rev. Robert Jager (Slovakia), Pst.; Dcn. Jeffrey Martin; CRP Stds.: 39

EUCLID

Holy Resurrection Church - 532 Lloyd Rd., Euclid, OH 44132 t) 216-732-7292 holyresurrection@parma.org www.holyresurrectionbyz.org Rev. Lukas Mitro (Slovakia), Admin.; CRP Stds.: 30

Holy Transfiguration Church - 5768 Andrews Rd., Mentor-on-the-Lake, OH 44060 (Worship Site)

St. Stephen Church - (Worship Site)

FAIRVIEW PARK

St. Mary Magdalene - 5390 W. 220th St., Fairview Park, OH 44126-2968 t) 440-734-4644 stmmbyzantinechurch@gmail.com www.stmarymagdalenebyzantine.org Rev. Bryan R. Eyman, Pst.; Dcn. Daniel Surniak; CRP Stds.: 11

LORAIN

St. Nicholas - 2711 W. 40th St., Lorain, OH 44053-2252 t) 440-282-7525 info@stnicks.org; pastor@stnicks.org www.stnicks.org Rev. Andrew Nagrant, Admin.; CRP Stds.: 7

MARBLEHEAD

St. Mary - 506 E. Main St., Marblehead, OH 43440-2232 t) 419-967-7398 stmarymarblehead@parma.org stmarymarblehead.com Rev. Joseph Repko, Pst.;

OREGON

St. Michael the Archangel - 4001 Navarre Ave., Oregon, OH 43616 t) 419-691-6222 jrprussell@gmail.com Rev. Robert Stash, Admin.; Dcn. James Sofalvi; CRP Stds.: 2

SOLON

St. John the Baptist - 36125 Aurora Rd., Solon, OH 44139-3841 t) 440-248-0417; 440-218-4096 (CRP) chancery@parma.org Mitred Archpriest Marek Visnovsky, Admin.;

INSTITUTIONS LOCATED IN DIOCESE

CONVENTS, MONASTERIES, AND RESIDENCES FOR WOMEN [CON]

BURTON

Christ the Bridegroom Monastery - 17485 Mumford Rd., Burton, OH 44021 t) 440-834-0290 christthebridegroom@gmail.com www.christthebridegroom.org Mother Theodora Strohmeyer, Supr.; Srs.: 7

NORTH ROYALTON

Motherhouse and Novitiate - 6688 Cady Rd., North

Royalton, OH 44133 t) 216-741-8773 chancery@parma.org Most Rev. Milan Lach, S.J., Jurisdiction;

ENDOWMENTS / FOUNDATIONS / TRUSTS [EFT]

INDEPENDENCE

Byzantine Catholic Eparchy of Parma Foundation, Inc. - 5000 Rockside Rd., Ste. 310, Independence, OH 44131 t) 216-299-5303 Marty Kopmeyer, Treas.;

The Parishes Together Fund of the Byzantine Catholic Eparchy of Parma - 5000 Rockside Rd., Ste. 310, Independence, OH 44131 t) 216-741-8773 x1221 mkopmeyer@parma.org Marty Kopmeyer, Contact;

MISCELLANEOUS [MIS]

FAIRBORN

St. Barbara Prayer Community - St. John Bosco Chapel, 3650 Colonel Glenn Hwy., Fairborn, OH 45324; Mailing: 2306 Polo Park Dr., Dayton, OH 45439 t) (602) 622-6310 Rev. Milan Kasperek, Admin.;

MUSCATINE

Byzantine Catholic Outreach of Iowa - 1506 Isett Ave., Muscatine, IA 52761 t) (833) 690-1299 (Toll Free); (708) 645-0241 iowaoutreach@parma.org www.byzantineiowa.org Very Rev. Thomas Loya, Admin.;

PARMA

St. Mary Hospitality House - 5500 W. 54th St., Parma, OH 44129 t) 440-884-8452 contactus@holyspiritbyzantine.org Dcn. Robert Cripps, Admin.;

RALSTON

Byzantine Catholic Outreach of Omaha & Lincoln - 7857 Lakeview St., Ralston, NE 68127; Mailing: 22520 Mount Michael Rd., c/o Mount Michael Abbey, Elkhorn, NE 68022 t) (708) 645-0241 omahabyzantine@gmail.com www.omahabyzantine.com Very Rev. Thomas Loya, Admin.;

SHRINES [SHR]

BURTON

Shrine of Mariapoch - 17486 Mumford Rd., Burton, OH 44021; Mailing: 5000 Rockside Rd., Ste. 310, Independence, OH 44131 t) (216) 741-8773 x1221 www.shrineofmariapoch.com Dcn. William Fredrick, Admin.;

An asterisk (*) denotes an organization that has established tax-exempt status directly with the IRS and is not covered by the USCCB Group Ruling.

Byzantine Catholic Eparchy of Passaic

MOST REVEREND KURT BURNETTE, D.D., J.C.L.

Bishop of Passaic; ordained April 26, 1989; appointed Bishop of Passaic October 29, 2013; ordained and enthroned December 4, 2013.
Office: 445 Lackawanna Ave., Woodland Park, NJ 07424.

Chancery Office: 445 Lackawanna Ave., Woodland Park, NJ 07424. T: 973-890-7777; F: 973-890-7175.
www.eparchyofpassaic.com
bishop@eparchyofpassaic.com

ESTABLISHED JULY 31, 1963.

Embraces all Catholics of the Byzantine-Ruthenian Rite in the States of New Jersey, Connecticut, Florida, Georgia, Maryland, New York, North Carolina, South Carolina, Virginia and all Eastern Pennsylvania within the western boundaries of the Counties of Franklin, Juniata, Lycoming, Mifflin, Union and Tioga.

For legal titles of parishes and diocesan institutions, consult the Chancery Office.

STATISTICAL OVERVIEW

Personnel

Bishop	1
Priests: Diocesan Active in Diocese	49
Priests: Diocesan Active Outside Diocese	3
Priests: Retired, Sick or Absent	17
Number of Diocesan Priests	69
Religious Priests in Diocese	2
Total Priests in your Diocese	71
Extern Priests in Diocese	16
Permanent Deacons in Diocese	28
Total Sisters	12

Parishes

Parishes	83
With Resident Pastor:	
Resident Diocesan Priests	54
Resident Religious Priests	1
Without Resident Pastor:	
Administered by Priests	27
Administered by Deacons	1
Missions	3

Educational

Diocesan Students in Other Seminaries	2
Total Seminarians	2
Catechesis/Religious Education:	
High School Students	60
Elementary Students	350
Total Students under Catholic Instruction	412
Teachers in Diocese:	
Priests	1

Vital Statistics

Receptions into the Church:	
Infant Baptism Totals	95
Minor Baptism Totals	10
Adult Baptism Totals	5
Received into Full Communion	10
First Communions	85
Confirmations	90
Marriages:	
Catholic	30
Interfaith	8
Total Marriages	38
Deaths	300
Total Catholic Population	8,200

LEADERSHIP

Chancery Office - t) 973-890-7777

Syncellates and Protopresbyterates -

Central Pennsylvania Syncellate - Very Rev. Edward J. Higgins;

Mid-Pennsylvania Protopresbyterate - t) 570-544-2074 Very Rev. Gregory J. Noga;

South Pennsylvania Protopresbyterate - t) 215-334-5129 Very Rev. Andriy Kovach;

Syncellus - t) 610-867-2322 Very Rev. Edward J. Higgins;

Middle States Syncellate - Very Rev. John G. Basarab;

Middle States Protopresbyterate - t) 703-573-3986 Very Rev. Alex Shuter;

Syncellus - t) 703-573-3986 Very Rev. John G. Basarab;

New Jersey Syncellate - Very Rev. John S. Custer;

Central New Jersey Protopresbyterate - Very Rev. Francis J. Rella;

Northern New Jersey Protopresbyterate - t) 973-777-2553 Very Rev. John S. Custer;

Syncellus - t) 973-777-2553 Very Rev. John S. Custer;

New York-New England Syncellate - Very Rev. Nicholas A. Daddona;

New York/New England Protopresbyterate - Very Rev. Ronald J. Hatton;

Syncellus - Very Rev. Nicholas A. Daddona;

Southern States Syncellate - Very Rev. Robert Evancho;

Southern States Protopresbyterate - t) 407-351-0133 Rev. Salvatore A. Pignato, Protopresbyter;

Syncellus - t) 727-323-4022 Very Rev. Robert Evancho;

Susquehanna Valley Syncellate - Rev. Michael Kerestes;

Northern Pennsylvania/Northern New York Protopresbyterate - t) 570-457-3042 Very Rev. Eduard Shestak;

Syncellus - t) 570-822-6028 Rev. Michael Kerestes;

Wyoming Valley Protopresbyterate - t) 570-595-3265 Very Rev. Michael J. Salnicky;

Protosyncellus - Rt. Rev. Mitred Archpriest James Hayer;

Vicar for Clergy - Very Rev. Nicholas A. Daddona;

Chancellor - Lori Albanese (chancellor@eparchyofpassaic.com);

Eparchial Finance Officer/Controller/CFO - Rev. Deacon Robert Shalhoub;

Eparchial Finance Council - Rt. Rev. Mitred Archpriest James Hayer; Rev. Deacon Robert Shalhoub; Stephen Kowalski;

Eparchial College of Consultors - Very Rev. John G. Basarab; Very Rev. John S. Custer; Very Rev. Nicholas A. Daddona;

Presbyteral Council - Rev. James Badeaux; Rev. Sergij Deiak; Rev. Salvatore A. Pignato;

Eparchial Tribunal - t) 973-890-7777

Adjutant Judicial Vicar - Very Rev. Andriy Kovach;

Defenders of the Bond - Very Rev. Andriy Kovach;

Judges - Rev. Msgr. Robert Senetsky;

Judicial Vicar - Very Rev. Eduard Shestak;

Notaries - Very Rev. Gregory J. Noga; Maureen French;

Promoter of Justice - Very Rev. Ronald Barusefski;

Vocations - Rev. Michael Kerestes;

ADVISORY BOARDS, COMMISSIONS, COMMITTEES, AND COUNCILS

Building and Liturgical Arts Commission - Rt. Rev. Mitred Archpriest James Hayer, Chair; Rev. Peter J. Hosak; Rev. Michael G. Popson;

Cemeteries Commission - Rt. Rev. Mitred Archpriest James Hayer; Rev. Robert W. Lozinski, C.S.C.; Very Rev. John S. Custer;

Clergy Continued Education - Very Rev. John S. Custer;

Commission for Ecumenism - Very Rev. Edward J. Higgins;

Communications and Telecommunications - Rt. Rev. Mitred Archpriest James Hayer;

Deacons Diaconate Formation Program - Very Rev. Nicholas A. Daddona; Dcn. Lawrence Foran;

Eparchial Cultural Archives Commission - Very Rev. John S. Custer, Chair; Rev. Joseph Bertha; Rt. Rev. Mitred Archpriest James Hayer;

Eparchial Historian (vacant) -

Eparchial Music Commission - Elias Zareva, Member & Rep.; Joseph K. Ferenchick, Member & Rep.;

Eparchial Newspaper - t) 973-890-7794 Rev. James Badeaux, Editor; Very Rev. Ronald J. Hatton, Assoc. Editor; Rev. Lewis Rabayda, Layout Editor;

Evangelization - Rev. Joseph Bertha, Chair; Very Rev. John S. Custer; Very Rev. John G. Basarab;

Family Life (vacant) -

Office for Eastern Christian Formation (formerly: Office of Religious Education) - Rev. Vasyl Chepelskyy (Ukraine);

PENSION Board - Very Rev. Ronald Barusefski; Rev. Vincent M. Brady; Rev. Edward G. Cimbala;

Respect Life - Rev. G. Scott Boghossian;

Safe Environment Program - Rev. David J. Baratelli, Coord. (fr.dave.ewr@juno.com);

Victim Assistance Coordinator - Maureen Daddona;

Saint Nicholas Shrine - Carpathian Village - t) 570-595-3265 Very Rev. Michael J. Salnicky, Dir.;

MISCELLANEOUS / OTHER OFFICES

Eastern Catholic Associates - t) 973-890-7777 Most Rev. Kurt Burnette;

PARISHES, MISSIONS, AND CLERGY

COMMONWEALTH OF PENNSYLVANIA

ALLENTOWN

St. Michael - 156 Green St., Allentown, PA 18102; Mailing: 1140 Johnston Dr., Bethlehem, PA 18017 t) 610-867-2322 schnauzerfred@aol.com Administered from SS Peter & Paul, Bethlehem, PA. Very Rev. Edward J. Higgins, Admin.;

BEAVER MEADOWS

St. Mary's - c/o 119 Berwick St., Beaver Meadows, PA 18216; Mailing: P.O. Box 206, Beaver Meadows, PA 18216 t) 570-455-1442 Administered from SS. Peter and Paul, Beaver Meadows, PA Rev. Vasyl Chepelskyy (Ukraine), Admin.;

SS. Peter and Paul - 119 Berwick St., Beaver Meadows, PA 18216; Mailing: P.O. Box 206, Beaver Meadows, PA 18216 t) 570-455-1442 Rev. Vasyl Chepelskyy (Ukraine), Pst.;

BETHLEHEM

SS. Peter and Paul - 1140 Johnston Dr., Bethlehem, PA 18017 t) 610-867-2322 schnauzerfred@aol.com saintspeterpaulbethlehempa.org Very Rev. Edward J. Higgins, Pst.; CRP Stds.: 17

BROCKTON

St. Mary's - 230 Green St., Brockton, PA 17925; Mailing: 621 W. Mahanoy St., Mahanoy City, PA 17948 t) 570-773-2631 jimc12@ptd.net Administered from St. Mary's, Mahanoy City, PA. Rev. James Carroll, O.F.M., Admin.; CRP Stds.: 1

COATESVILLE

St. Mary's - 88 Gap Rd., Coatesville, PA 19320; Mailing: 203 Jacob St., Mont Clare, PA 19453 t) 610-933-2819 pastor@stmichaelbyzantine.org www.bvmdormition.org Administered from St. Michael, Mont Clare, PA. Andriy Kovach, Admin.;

DUNMORE

St. Michael - 511 E. Drinker St., Dunmore, PA 18512 t) 570-344-2521 rwlcsc18505@aol.com Rev. Robert W. Lozinski, C.S.C., Pst.; CRP Stds.: 9

FOREST CITY

St. John the Baptist - 306 Susquehanna St., Forest City, PA 18421; Mailing: 313 1st Ave, Jessup, PA 18434 t) 570-489-2353 holyghostjessup@yahoo.com Administered from Holy Ghost, Jessup, PA Rev. John J. Cigan, Admin.; CRP Stds.: 2

FREELAND

St. Mary's - 643 Fern St., Freeland, PA 18224 t) 570-636-0700 frscottb@gmail.com Rev. G. Scott Boghossian, Pst.;

HARRISBURG

St. Ann - 5408 Locust Ln., Harrisburg, PA 17109 t) 717-652-1415 stann@stannbyz.org www.stannbyz.org Rev. Taras Lovska, Admin.; CRP Stds.: 39

HAZLETON

St. John the Baptist Church - 5 E. 20th St., Hazleton, PA 18201 t) 570-454-1142 stjohnbyz18201@gmail.com www.facebook.com/stjohnbyz.hazleton/ Rev. Yevhenii Hradil, Par. Vicar; Dcn. Lawrence Foran; Very Rev. Gregory J. Noga, Admin.; Monica Washko, DRE; CRP Stds.: 6

St. Mary's - 227 E. Beech St., Hazleton, PA 18201 t) 570-455-3232 Rev. Yevhenii Hradil, Par. Vicar;

JESSUP

Holy Ghost - 313 First Ave., Jessup, PA 18434 t) 570-489-2353 holyghostjessup@yahoo.com www.holyghostjessup.weebly.com Rev. John J. Cigan, Pst.; Joyce Covaleski, DRE; CRP Stds.: 6

KINGSTON

St. Mary's - 321 Chestnut Ave., Kingston, PA 18704 t) 570-287-0282 saintmarykingston@yahoo.com Rev. Mykhaylo Prodanets, Pst.; CRP Stds.: 8

LANSFORD

St. John the Baptist - 116 E. Bertsch St., Lansford, PA 18232 t) 570-645-2640 sjpastor@ptd.net www.stjohnsbyzantinecatholicchurch.org Rev. Gregory Hosler, Admin.;

LEVITTOWN

Our Lady of Perpetual Help - 1773 Woodbourne Rd., Levittown, PA 19057; Mailing: PO Box 777, Levittown, PA 19058 t) 215-968-8707 pastorolph@gmail.com www.olphbyzpa.org Rev. Paul R. Varchola West, Admin.; CRP Stds.: 16

MAHANOY CITY

St. Mary's - 621 W. Mahanoy Ave., Mahanoy City, PA 17948 t) 570-773-2631 jimc12@ptd.net Rev. James Carroll, O.F.M., Pst.; CRP Stds.: 10

MCADOO

St. Michael - 17 E. Blaine St., McAdoo, PA 18237 t) 570-929-1062 gtrccollies@ptd.net Rev. Gregory Hosler, Pst.;

MINERSVILLE

St. Mary's - c/o 107 S. 4th St., Minersville, PA 17954 t) 570-544-2074 tvrgjn@outlook.com Administered from SS. Peter and Paul, Minersville, PA. Very Rev. Gregory J. Noga, Admin.;

SS. Peter and Paul - 107 S. Fourth St., Minersville, PA 17954 t) 570-544-2074 tvrgjn@outlook.com www.sspeterandpaulminersville.com Very Rev. Gregory J. Noga, Pst.; CRP Stds.: 8

MONT CLARE

St. Michael - 203 Jacob St., Mont Clare, PA 19453 t) 610-933-2819 pastor@stmichaelbyzantine.org stmichaelbyzantine.org/ Dcn. John Harden; Andriy Kovach, Admin.; CRP Stds.: 21

NESQUEHONING

St. Mary's - 141 W. High St., Nesquehoning, PA 18240 t) 570-645-2640 sjpastor@ptd.net Administered from St. John the Baptist, Lansford, PA. Rev. Vasyl Chepelskyy (Ukraine), Admin.;

OLD FORGE

St. Mary's - c/o 140 Church St., Old Forge, PA 18518 t) 570-457-3042 Administered from St. Nicholas, Old Forge, PA Very Rev. Eduard Shestak, Admin.;

St. Nicholas - 140 Church St., Old Forge, PA 18518 t) 570-457-3042 Very Rev. Eduard Shestak, Admin.;

PALMERTON

SS. Peter and Paul - 142 Lafayette Ave., Palmerton, PA

18071; Mailing: 1140 Johnston Dr., Bethlehem, PA 18017 t) 610-867-2322 schnauzerfred@aol.com Administered from SS Peter & Paul, Bethlehem, PA Very Rev. Edward J. Higgins, Admin.;

PHILADELPHIA

Holy Ghost - 2310 S. 24th St., Philadelphia, PA 19145-3207 t) 215-334-5129 holyghostphila.byzcath.org/ Very Rev. Andriy Kovach, Admin.;

Holy Trinity - 6801 N. 10th St., Philadelphia, PA 19126-2906; Mailing: P.O. Box 777, Levittown, PA 19058 t) (215) 968-8707 pastorolph@gmail.com www.olphbyzpa.org Administered from Our Lady of Perpetual Help, Levittown, PA. Rev. Paul R. Varchola West, Admin.; CRP Stds.: 2

PITTSTON

St. Michael - 205 N. Main St., Pittston, PA 18640 t) 570-654-4564 gfire3363@gmail.com; lawrencejworlinsky@gmail.com Rev. Andrii Dumnych, Assoc. Pst.; Dcn. Lawrence Worlinsky, Admin.; CRP Stds.: 7

St. Nicholas - c/o 205 N. Main St., Pittston, PA 18640; Mailing: 205 N. Main St., Pittston, PA 18640 t) 570-654-4564 lawrencejworlinsky@gmail.com Administered from St. Michael, Pittston, PA Dcn. Lawrence Worlinsky, Admin.; Rev. Andrii Dumnych, Pst. Assoc.; CRP Stds.: 12

POCONO SUMMIT

St. Nicholas - 2121 Commerce St., Pocono Summit, PA 18346; Mailing: PO Box 515, Pocono Summit, PA 18346-0515 t) 570-839-8090; 570-595-3265; 570-650-3252 stnicpoc@earthlink.net stnicpoc.org Very Rev. Michael J. Salnicky, Pst.; CRP Stds.: 3

POTTSTOWN

St. John's Greek Catholic Church Pottstown PA - 301 Cherry St., Pottstown, PA 19464 t) 610-326-1877 stjohnbyzcathchurch@gmail.com Rev. Nicholas DeProspero, Pst.; CRP Stds.: 22

SCRANTON

St. John the Baptist - c/o 310 Mifflin Ave., Scranton, PA 18503 t) 570-342-8429 revleonardmartinsj@hotmail.com Administered from St. Mary's, Scranton, PA. Rev. Leonard A. Martin, S.J., Admin.;

St. Mary's - 310 Mifflin Ave., Scranton, PA 18503 t) 570-342-8429 revleonardmartinsj@hotmail.com Rev. Leonard A. Martin, S.J., Pst.;

WILKES-BARRE

St. John's - 526 Church St., Wilkes-Barre, PA 18702 t) 570-825-4338 saintmarykingston@yahoo.com Administered from St. Mary's, Kingston, PA. Rev. Mykhaylo Prodanets, Admin.;

St. Mary's - 695 N. Main St., Wilkes-Barre, PA 18705 t) 570-822-6028 secretary@stmarywb.com www.stmarywb.com Rev. Michael Kerestes, Pst.;

COMMONWEALTH OF VIRGINIA

ANNANDALE

Epiphany of Our Lord - 3410 Woodburn Rd., Annandale, VA 22003 t) 703-573-3986; 703-573-1042 (CRP) epiphanyva@aol.com; epiphanyofourlord3420@gmail.com www.eolbcc.com Epiphany Mission, 9301 Warfield Road, Gaithersburg, MD 20882 Very Rev. John G. Basarab, Pst.; Dcn. Elmer Pekarik; Dcn. Peter Turko, DRE; CRP Stds.: 21

WILLIAMSBURG

Ascension of Our Lord - 114 Palace Ln., Williamsburg, VA 23185; Mailing: P.O. Box 5096, Williamsburg, VA 23185 t) 757-220-8098 pastor@ascensionva.org ascensionva.org Very Rev. Alex Shuter, Pst.; CRP Stds.: 7

Our Lady of Perpetual Help - 216 S. Parliament Dr., Virginia Beach, VA 23462

STATE OF CONNECTICUT

DANBURY

Saint Nicholas Byzantine Catholic Church - 13 Pembroke Rd., Danbury, CT 06811 t) 203-743-1106 stnicholasdanbury@icloud.com stnicholasdanbury.org Very Rev. Ronald J. Hatton, Pst.; Dcn. Stephen R. Russo; Ann Devine, DRE; CRP Stds.: 6

MERIDEN

St. Nicholas Greek Catholic Church - 89 Summer St, Meriden, CT 06450; Mailing: 13 Pembroke Rd, Danbury, CT 06811 t) 860-229-2531; 203-377-5967 stnick.holytrinity@gmail.com Very Rev. Ronald J. Hatton, Admin.;

NEW BRITAIN

Holy Trinity Greek Catholic Church - 121 Beaver St., New Britain, CT 06051 t) 860-229-2531 saintnicholasdanbury@gmail.com; hryhoriylozinskyy@gmail.com www.stnick.holytrinity@gmail.com Very Rev. Ronald J. Hatton, Admin.;

TRUMBULL

St. John the Baptist - 100 St. John's Dr., Trumbull, CT 06611 t) 203-377-5967 stjohntrumbull@gmail.com www.stjohntrumbull.org Rev. Hryhoriy Lozinskyy, Admin.; CRP Stds.: 16

STATE OF FLORIDA

COCONUT CREEK

Our Lady of the Sign - 7311 Lyons Rd., Coconut Creek, FL 33073 t) 954-429-0056 ourladyofthesign.org/ Rev. Michael Kane, Pst.;

FORT PIERCE

SS. Cyril and Methodius - 1002 Bahama Ave., Fort Pierce, FL 34982 t) 772-595-1021 cmchurchoffice@gmail.com www.fortpiercebyzantine.com/ Rev. Frank A. Hanincik, Pst.;

MIAMI

St. Basil - 1475 N.E. 199 St., Miami, FL 33179; Mailing: P.O. Box 11011, Fort Lauderdale, FL 33339 t) 786-320-5125 secretary.stbasil@gmail.com stbasilbyzantinecatholicchurch.org Rev. Salvatore A. Pignato, Admin.;

NEW PORT RICHEY

St. Anne's - 7120 Massachusetts Ave, New Port Richey, FL 34653 t) 727-849-1190 olexiynebesnyk@gmail.com stannesbyzantine.com Rev. Oleksiy Nebesnyk, Admin.; CRP Stds.: 5

NORTH FORT MYERS

All Saints Byzantine Catholic - 10291 Bayshore Rd., North Fort Myers, FL 33917 t) 239-599-4023 allsaintsbyzantine@gmail.com www.allsaintsbyzantine.com Very Rev. Steven Galuschik, Admin.;

ORLANDO

St. Nicholas of Myra - 5135 W. Sand Lake Rd., Orlando, FL 32819 t) 407-351-0133 stnicholascatholicchurch@cfl.rr.com orlandobyzantine.com Rev. Salvatore A. Pignato, Pst.; CRP Stds.: 17

ORMOND BEACH

Holy Dormition - 17 Buckskin Ln., Ormond Beach, FL 32174 t) 407-351-0133 stnicholascatholicchurch@cfl.rr.com Administered from St. Nicholas of Myra, Orlando, FL. Rev. Vincent M. Brady, In Res.; Rev. Salvatore A. Pignato, Admin.;

ST. PETERSBURG

St. Therese - 4265 13th Ave. N., St. Petersburg, FL 33713 t) 727-323-4022 sconven1@tampabay.rr.com Very Rev. Robert Evancho, Pst.; CRP Stds.: 11

STATE OF GEORGIA

ROSWELL

Epiphany of Our Lord Byzantine Catholic Church - 2030 Old Alabama Rd., Roswell, GA 30076 t) 770-993-0973 epiphanybyz.org Rev. Lewis Rabayda, Admin.; Dcn. James Smith; Dcn. John Reed; Karen Madrigal, DRE; CRP Stds.: 14

STATE OF MARYLAND

ARBUTUS

Patronage of the Mother of God - 1260 Stevens Ave., Arbutus, MD 21227 t) 410-247-4936 c) 410-703-5099 lisaguba@sprintmail.com patronagechurch.com Rev. Sergij Deiak, Admin.; Lisa Guba, DRE;

St. Ann's - 1525 Oak Hill Ave., Hagerstown, MD 21742 t) 301-797-5847 www.patronagechurch.com Joseph Repasi, Contact;

BELTSVILLE

St. Gregory of Nyssa - 12420 Old Gunpowder Rd. Spur, Beltsville, MD 20705 t) 301-953-9323 info@stgregoryofnyssa.net stgregoryofnyssa.net Rev. Sergij Deiak, Admin.; Dcn. William Szewczyk;

STATE OF NEW JERSEY

BAYONNE

St. John the Baptist - 15 E. 26th St., Bayonne, NJ 07002 t) 201-339-1840 info@stjohnbayonne.org stjohnbayonne.org Rev. Joseph Bertha, Admin.;

CARTERET

St. Elias - 42 Cooke Ave., Carteret, NJ 07008 t) 732-541-5213 vitalgugle@gmail.com Rev. Vitaliy Pukhayev, Admin.;

DUNELLEN

St. Nicholas - 121 Madison Ave., Dunellen, NJ 08812 t) 732-968-3337; 908-725-0615 stnicholasdunellen@gmail.com Rev. James Badeaux, Admin.;

EAST BRUNSWICK

Nativity of Our Lord - 700 Old Bridge Tpke., East Brunswick, NJ 08816 c) 570-507-4483 korostil.00@mail.ru Rev. Iaroslav Korostil (Ukraine), Pst.;

FLANDERS

Holy Wisdom - 197 Emmans Rd., Flanders, NJ 07836; Mailing: 96 1st St., Passaic, NJ 07055 t) 973-777-2553 holywisdomnj@gmail.com Administered from St. Michael Cathedral, Passaic, NJ. Very Rev. John S. Custer, Admin.; CRP Stds.: 1

HILLSBOROUGH

St. Mary's - 1900 Brooks Blvd., Hillsborough, NJ 08844 t) 908-725-0615 pastor@stmaryhillsboroughnj.org www.stmaryhillsboroughnj.org Rev. James Badeaux, Pst.; Dcn. Alexander Kubik; Julie Klikus, DRE; CRP Stds.: 60

JERSEY CITY

St. Mary's - 231 Pacific Ave., Jersey City, NJ 07304 t) 201-333-2975 info@stmaryjerseycity.org stmaryjerseycity.org Administered from St. John the Baptist, Bayonne, NJ. Rev. Joseph Bertha, Admin.;

LINDEN

St. George the Great Martyr - 417 McCandless St., Linden, NJ 07036 t) 908-486-6500 stgeorgelinden@gmail.com stgeorgelinden.com Rev. Vitaliy Pukayev (Ukraine), Admin.;

MAHWAH

Holy Spirit - 104 Church St., Mahwah, NJ 07430; Mailing: 768 North St., White Plains, NY 10605 t) 973-777-2553; 201-529-3269 (CRP); 914-681-0659 (St. Nicholas of Myra, White Plains) holyspiritmahwah@gmail.com holyspiritmahwah.com Administered from St. Nicholas of Myra in White Plains, NY Rev. Ihor Vorontsov, Admin.;

NEW BRUNSWICK

St. Joseph - 30 High St., New Brunswick, NJ 08901 t) 732-545-1686 sspeterpaul1969@gmail.com Rev. Mykhaylo Kravchuk (Ukraine), Admin.;

NEWARK

St. George - 214 Warwick St., Newark, NJ 07105 t) 973-589-7202 fr.dave.ewr@juno.com Rev. David J. Baratelli, Admin.;

PASSAIC

St. Michael Cathedral - 96 First St., Passaic, NJ 07055 t) 973-777-2553 passaiccathedral@gmail.com stmichaelsarchangel.org St Michaels Greek Rite Catholic Church Very Rev. John S. Custer, Pst.; CRP Stds.: 12

St. Michael's Cathedral Chapel - 445 Lackawanna Ave., Woodland Park, NJ 07424

PERTH AMBOY

St. Michael - 401 Hall Ave., Perth Amboy, NJ 08861; Mailing: P.O. Box 1297, Perth Amboy, NJ 08862-1297 t) 732-862-0792 www.facebook.com/ stmichaelsperthamboy/ Rev. Martin Vavrak (Slovakia), Pst.; CRP Stds.: 19

St. Nicholas - 320 Washington St., Perth Amboy, NJ

08861; Mailing: P.O. Box 1030, Perth Amboy, NJ 08862-1030 t) 732-442-0418 stnicholaspa@gmail.com www.facebook.com/saintnicholasperthamboy (Administered to by St. Michael, Perth Amboy) Rev. Martin Vavrak (Slovakia), Admin.;

PHILLIPSBURG

SS. Peter and Paul - 723 S. Main St., Phillipsburg, NJ 08865; Mailing: 1140 Johnston Dr., Bethlehem, PA 18017 t) 610-867-2322 schnauzerfred@aol.com saintspeterpaulbethlehempa.org Administered from SS Peter & Paul, Bethlehem PA Very Rev. Edward J. Higgins, Admin.;

RAHWAY

St. Thomas the Apostle - 1410 Church St., Rahway, NJ 07065 t) 732-382-5300 stthomasbyz@aol.com www.stthomastheapostle.org Rt. Rev. Mitred Archpriest James Hayer, Pst.; Rev. Thomas Shubeck, Par. Vicar; CRP Stds.: 12

ROEBLING

St. Nicholas - 191 Norman Ave., Roebling, NJ 08554 t) 609-447-0688 stnicholasbyzcatholic@gmail.com stnicholasroebling.org/ Administered from St. Mary's, Trenton, NJ. Rev. Yuriy Oros, Admin.;

SOMERSET

Saints Peter and Paul Byzantine Catholic Church - 285 Hamilton St., Somerset, NJ 08873 t) 732-545-5500 sspeterpaul1969@gmail.com Administered by St. Joseph Catholic Church (Byzantine Rite), New Brunswick, NJ Rev. Mykhaylo Kravchuk (Ukraine), Pst.;

TOMS RIVER

Our Lady of Perpetual Help - 1937 Church Rd., Toms River, NJ 08753 t) 732-255-6272 francis.rella@olphtr.org olphtr.org/ Very Rev. Francis J. Rella, Pst.;

TRENTON

St. Mary - 335 Adeline St., Trenton, NJ 08611; Mailing: 191 Norman Ave, Roebling, NJ 08554 t) 609-394-5004 stmarybyzcatholic@gmail.com stmarybyzcatholictrenton.org/ Rev. Yuriy Oros, Admin.;

STATE OF NEW YORK

BINGHAMTON

Holy Spirit - 360 Clinton St., Binghamton, NY 13905 t) 607-203-1151 administratorhsppbyzcathny@stny.rr.com www.facebook.com/groups/717045149323204/ Rev. Deacon Richard Terza, Admin.;

ENDICOTT

SS. Peter and Paul's - 106 N Rogers Ave., Endicott, NY 13760; Mailing: c/o 360 Clinton St., Binghamton, NY 13905 t) 607-203-1151 administratorhsppbyzcathny@stny.rr.com www.facebook.com/groups/717045149323204/ Administered from Holy Spirit, Binghamton, NY Rev. Deacon Richard Terza, Admin.;

NEW YORK

Greek Rite Catholic Church of Exaltation of Holy Cross (and) Exaltation of the Holy Cross Byzantine Catholic Church - 323 E 82nd St., New York, NY 10028; Mailing: 246 E. 15th St., New York, NY 10003 t) 212-677-0516 fredcimbala@gmail.com Administered from St. Mary's, New York, NY Rev. Edward G. Cimbala, Admin.;

St. Mary's - 246 E. 15th St., New York, NY 10003 t) 212-677-0516 fredcimbala@gmail.com stmarybccnyc.org Rev. Edward G. Cimbala, Pst.;

SS. Peter and Paul - c/o 246 E. 15th St., New York, NY 10003 t) 212-677-0516 pastorsaintmary@gmail.com Administered from St. Mary's, New York, NY Rev. Robert J. Hospodar, Admin.;

OLEAN

St. Mary's - 718 Fountain St., Olean, NY 14760; Mailing: 445 Lackawanna Ave, Woodland Park, NJ 07424 t) 973-890-7777 (Administered to by St. Mary, Scranton, PA) Rev. Leonard A. Martin, S.J., Admin.;

PEEKSKILL

Saints Peter and Paul's Byzantine Catholic Church - 705 Shenandoah Ave., Peekskill, NY 10566 t) 914-737-8249 robsen@aol.com Rev. Msgr. Robert Senetsky, Pastor Emer.; Very Rev. Ronald J. Hatton, Admin.; Rev. Msgr. Robert Senetsky, Parish Life Coord.;

SMITHTOWN

Byzantine Catholic Church of the Resurrection - 38 Mayflower Ave., Smithtown, NY 11787 c) 631-759-6083 resurrectionsmithtown@gmail.com Rev. Vladyslav Budash, Admin.; CRP Stds.: 13

WESTBURY

St. Andrew the Apostle - 275 Ellison Ave., Westbury, NY 11590; Mailing: P.O. Box 684, Westbury, NY 11590 c) 516-404-1162; 516-457-5617 fathernick0417@gmail.com Very Rev. Nicholas A. Daddona, Pst.; CRP Stds.: 4

WHITE PLAINS

St. Nicholas of Myra - 768 North St., White Plains, NY 10605 t) 914-681-0659 frvorontsov@gmail.com www.stnicholas.life Rev. Ihor Vorontsov, Admin.;

STATE OF NORTH CAROLINA

CARY

Saints Cyril and Methodius Byzantine Catholic Church - 2510 Piney Plains Rd., Cary, NC 27518 t) 919-239-4877 sscyrilmethodius@gmail.com www.sscyrilmethodius.org Rev. Vasyl Sokolovych, Admin.; Lance Morgan, CFO; CRP Stds.: 37

STATE OF SOUTH CAROLINA

CONWAY

Blessed Basil Hopko Byzantine Catholic Mission - 3059 South Carolina Hwy. 90, Conway, SC 29526; Mailing: St Nicholas Byzantine Church, 768 North St, White Plains, NY 10605 t) 410-247-4936 frvorontsov@gmail.com Rev. Ihor Vorontsov, Admin.;

INSTITUTIONS LOCATED IN DIOCESE

CONVENTS, MONASTERIES, AND RESIDENCES FOR WOMEN [CON]

SUGARLOAF

Holy Annunciation Monastery - 403 W. County Rd., Sugarloaf, PA 18249 t) 570-788-1205 marija@ptd.net www.byzantinediscalcedcarmelites.com Discalced Carmelite Nuns of the Byzantine Rite. Sr. Marija Shields, Abbess; Srs.: 12

WILKES-BARRE

Sisters of Saint Basil The Great Saint Mary of the Assumption Convent - 522 Madison St., Wilkes-Barre, PA 18705 t) 570-824-3973 srreginaosbm@verizon.net Sr. Regina Adams, Supr.; Srs.: 2

ENDOWMENTS / FOUNDATIONS / TRUSTS [EFT]

NEW YORK

Maria Theresa Foundation, Inc. - 246 E. 15th St, New York, NY 10003 t) 727-323-4022 revancho@tampabay.rr.com Very Rev. Robert Evancho, Contact;

MISCELLANEOUS [MIS]

WOODLAND PARK

Eastern Catholic Associates - 445 Lackawanna Ave., Woodland Park, NJ 07424 t) 973-890-7777 bishop@eparchyofpassaic.com Most Rev. Kurt Burnette, Pres.;

God with Us Publications - ndaddona@eparchyofpassaic.com

SHRINES [SHR]

CRESCO

Carpathian Village - 802 Snow Hill Rd., Cresco, PA 18326 t) 570-595-3265 c) 570-650-3252 carpathianvillage@earthlink.net Very Rev. Michael J. Salnicky, Dir.;

An asterisk (*) denotes an organization that has established tax-exempt status directly with the IRS and is not covered by the USCCB Group Ruling.

Metropolitan Archeparchy of Philadelphia Ukrainian

MOST REVEREND BORYS ANDRIJ GUDZIAK

Archbishop of Philadelphia Ukrainian; ordained November 26, 1998; appointed Titular Bishop of Carcabia and Apostolic Exarch of France (Ukrainian); ordained August 26, 2012; installed Apostolic Exarch of France (Ukrainian) December 2, 2012; appointed Saint Vladimir-Le-Grand de Paris (Ukrainian) January 19, 2013; appointed Philadelphia Ukrainian February 18, 2019; installed June 4, 2019.

Chancery Office: 810 N. Franklin St., Philadelphia, PA 19123-2097. T: 215-627-0143; F: 215-627-0377.
ukrmet@ukrcap.org

ESTABLISHED MAY 28, 1913.

The jurisdiction of the Metropolitan Archdiocese of Philadelphia includes the District of Columbia, the States of Virginia, Maryland, Delaware, New Jersey and eastern Pennsylvania to the eastern boundaries of the following Counties: Potter, Clinton, Center, Mifflin, Huntington and Fulton. With regard to persons, his subjects are all Catholics of the Byzantine Rite: 1. Who immigrated to this country from Galicia, Bucovina and other Ukrainian provinces; 2. Who descend from such persons (can. 755); 3. Women married to men referable to 1. and 2. if they comply with can. 98, n. 4; 4. Who in accordance with can. 98, n. 3 changed their Rite; 5. Converts to the Catholic Church of the Byzantine Rite; 6. And in fact all other Catholics of the Byzantine Rite who are attached to parishes subject to the jurisdiction of the Archbishop.

For legal titles of parishes and archdiocesan institutions, consult the Chancery Office.

STATISTICAL OVERVIEW

Personnel
Archbishops....1
Retired Archbishops....1
Retired Bishops....1
Abbots....1
Priests: Diocesan Active in Diocese....38
Priests: Diocesan Active Outside Diocese....1
Priests: Retired, Sick or Absent....6
Number of Diocesan Priests....45
Religious Priests in Diocese....3
Total Priests in your Diocese....48
Extern Priests in Diocese....6
Ordinations:
Transitional Deacons....1
Permanent Deacons in Diocese....6
Total Sisters....42

Parishes
Parishes....62
With Resident Pastor:
Resident Diocesan Priests....42
Resident Religious Priests....1
Without Resident Pastor:
Administered by Priests....19
Missions....1
Closed Parishes....1
Professional Ministry Personnel:
Lay Ministers....3

Welfare
Homes for the Aged....2
Total Assisted....340

Educational
Seminaries, Diocesan....1
Diocesan Students in Other Seminaries....2
Total Seminarians....2
Colleges and Universities....1
Total Students....578
Elementary Schools, Diocesan and Parish....3
Total Students....426
Catechesis/Religious Education:
High School Students....99
Elementary Students....610
Total Students under Catholic Instruction....1,715
Teachers in Diocese:
Priests....1
Sisters....7
Lay Teachers....37

Vital Statistics
Receptions into the Church:
Infant Baptism Totals....265
Minor Baptism Totals....5
Received into Full Communion....69
First Communions....187
Confirmations....238
Marriages:
Catholic....55
Interfaith....7
Total Marriages....62
Deaths....292
Total Catholic Population....12,180

LEADERSHIP

Chancery Office - t) 215-627-0143 ukrmet@ukrcap.org; pwaslo@ukrcap.org Rev. Msgr. Peter D. Waslo, Chancellor; Sofia Zacharczuk, Secy.;
Protosyncellus - t) 215-627-0143 x136 Rev. Msgr. Peter D. Waslo;
Chancellor - t) 215-627-0143 x136 pwaslo@ukrcap.org Rev. Msgr. Peter D. Waslo;
Secretary - t) 215-627-0143 x131 ukrmet@ukrcap.org Sofia Zacharczuk;
College of Archeparchial Consultors - Rev. Mark Fesniak; Very Rev. Robert J. Hitchens; Rev. Taras Svirchuk, C.Ss.R.;
Presbyteral Council - Msgr. Peter D. Waslo; Rev. Ihor Bloshchynskyy; Very Rev. Robert J. Hitchens;
Archeparchial Corporation - John Drozd, Treas.; Very Rev. Robert J. Hitchens, Secy.;
Archdiocesan Tribunal - t) 215-627-0143 Rev. Mykola Ivanov, Vicar;
Judicial Vicar - t) 215-370-6463; 570-648-5932 Rev. Mykola Ivanov;
Judge - t) 215-627-0143 x136 Msgr. Peter D. Waslo;
Promoter of Justice -
Auditor - Very Rev. Nestor Iwasiw; Rev. Roman Svirdan;
Defender of the Bond - Rev. Ruslan Romanyuk;
Notary - Sofia Zacharczuk;
Director of Evangelization -
Archeparchial Finance Council - Msgr. Peter D. Waslo; John Drozd; Leonard Mazur;
Financial Officer - t) 215-627-0143 phillyfinance@ukrcap.org John Drozd, Dir.; Ihor Kovaliv, Assoc. Dir.;
Protopresbyters (Deans) - Rev. Mark Fesniak, Dean; Very Rev. Volodymyr Klanichka, Philadelphia; Very Rev. Nestor Iwasiw, North Anthracite;

ADMINISTRATION

Archeparchy of Philadelphia - Rev. Ruslan Boroviy (Ukraine), Vice Chancellor (Borovij@gmail.com);

OFFICES AND DIRECTORS

Apostolate -
Archeparchial Museum - t) 215-627-3389 tofmuseum@ukrcap.org Sr. Timothea Konyu, M.S.M.G., Dir.;
Archeparchial Seminary Advisory and Admissions Board - Very Rev. Robert J. Hitchens; Very Rev. Nestor Iwasiw;
Byzantine Church Supplies - t) 215-627-0660 Myroslava Demkiv;
Cemeteries - t) 215-627-0143 ikovaliv@ukrcap.org Ihor Kovaliv, Dir.;
Censor -
Deacon Formation -
Department of Religious Education - ukrcatecheticaloffice@ukrcap.org
Director of Communications - communications@ukrcap.org Mariana Karapinka, Dir. (mariana.karapinka@ucu.edu.ua); Rev. D.George Worschak, Assoc. Dir. (usalemko@ukrcap.org);
Director of Development - t) 215-627-0143 smclaughlin@ukrcap.org Sean McLaughlin;
Ecumenical Relations -
Insurance Commission - John Drozd; John Kurey;
Office of Vocations - t) 215-627-0143 vocations@ukrcap.org Rev. Volodymyr Radko (France);
Priests Beneficial Fund - Rev. Msgr. Peter D. Waslo; Rev. Ivan Demkiv; Rev. Archpriest Michael Hutsko;
Pro-Life and Family Ministry - Very Rev. Taras Lonchyna;
Victim Assistance Coordinator - t) 845-709-0769 ukrchildprotection@ukrcap.org Sean McLaughlin, Dir.; Helen Chaykowsky, Chair; Sr. Natalia Stoczanyn, S.S.M.I., Contact;
The Way - Online Newspaper - t) 215-627-0143 x123 theway@ukrarcheparchy.us www.ukrarcheparchy.us Mariana Karapinka, Editor (mariana.karapinka@ucu.edu.ua); Rev. D. George Worschak, Asst. Editor;
Youth Ministry (Vacant) - Rev. Ostap Mykytchyn (Ukraine), Youth Min.;

SOCIAL SERVICES

Social Services - t) (215) 627-0143 x131 Marta Rubel;

PARISHES, MISSIONS, AND CLERGY

COMMONWEALTH OF PENNSYLVANIA

BERWICK

SS. Cyril and Methodius - 706 N. Warren St., Berwick, PA 18603 t) 570-752-3172 sscmuccpa2@gmail.com www.sscyrilandmethodius.net Rev. Roman Petryshak (Ukraine), Pst.;

BETHLEHEM

St. Josaphat's - 1826 Kenmore Ave., Bethlehem, PA 18018-3305 t) 610-865-2521 www.stjosaphatbethlehem.org Rev. Paul J. Makar, Pst.; CRP Stds.: 20

BRIDGEPORT

SS. Peter and Paul - 519 Union Ave., Bridgeport, PA 19405; Mailing: P.O. Box 126, Bridgeport, PA 19405 t) 610-272-7035 rppopivchak@aol.com Rev. Msgr. Ronald P. Popivchak, Pst.; George Maxim, DRE; CRP Stds.: 65

BRISTOL

St. Mary's - 2026 Bath Rd., Bristol, PA 19007 t) 215-788-7117 stmarychurch2@yahoo.com Rev. Ivan Demkiv, Pst.; CRP Stds.: 11

CENTRALIA

Assumption of B.V.M. - N. Paxton St., Centralia, PA 17927; Mailing: 131 N. Beech St., Mount Carmel, PA 17851 t) 570-339-0650 stsppmc@ptd.net Mt. Carmel. Rev. Archpriest Michael Hutsko, Admin.;

EDWARDSVILLE

St. Vladimir's - Closed Jun 2022

FRACKVILLE

St. Michael's - 335 W. Oak St., Frackville, PA 17931; Mailing: 243 S. Middle St., Frackville, PA 17931 t) 570-874-1101 ssjohnmikefrack12@ptd.net Dcn. Paul Mark Spotts; Rev. Petro Zvarych, Pst.; CRP Stds.: 18

GLEN LYON

St. Nicholas - 153 E. Main St., Glen Lyon, PA 18617 t) 570-752-3172 stnicholasgl@gmail.com Ss Cyril and Methodius, Berwick, PA Rev. Roman Petryshak (Ukraine), Pst.;

HAZLETON

St. Michael's - 74 N. Laurel St., Hazleton, PA 18201 t) 570-455-0643 Rev. Roman Oliinyk, Pst.; CRP Stds.: 6

JENKINTOWN

St. Michael the Archangel - 1013 Fox Chase Rd., Jenkintown, PA 19046 t) 215-576-5827 parish@mykhailivka.org Rev. Wasyl Kharuk, Pst.; Rev. Ostap Mykytchyn, Par. Vicar; CRP Stds.: 35

LANSDALE

Presentation of Our Lord - 1564 Allentown Rd., Lansdale, PA 19446; Mailing: 1545 Easton Rd., Warrington, PA 18976 t) 215-343-0779 mykolaivan1977@yahoo.com presentationukrainiancc.com Rev. Mykola Ivanov, Admin.; CRP Stds.: 8

MAIZEVILLE

St. John the Baptist - 1408 Main St., Maizeville, PA 17934; Mailing: 243 S. Middle St., Frackville, PA 17931 t) 570-874-1101 ssjohnmikefrack12@ptd.net St. Michael, Frackville. Rev. Petro Zvarych, Admin.;

MARION HEIGHTS

Patronage of the Mother of God - 145 E. Melrose St., Marion Heights, PA 17832; Mailing: 303 N. Shamokin St., Shamokin, PA 17872 t) 570-373-3441; 570-648-5932 transfigurationshamokin@gmail.com Transfiguration, Shamokin. Rev. Archpriest Michael Hutsko, Admin.;

MCADOO

St. Mary's - 210 W. Blaine St., McAdoo, PA 18237 t) 570-929-7058 Rev. Roman Oliinyk, Admin.; CRP Stds.: 5

MELROSE PARK

Annunciation of the B.V.M. - 1206 Valley Rd., Melrose Park, PA 19027-3035 t) 215-635-1627 a.b.v.m@verizon.net Rev. Ihor Bloshchynskyy, Pst.; CRP Stds.: 1

MIDDLEPORT

Nativity of B.V.M. - Kaska St., Middleport, PA 17953; Mailing: St. Nicholas Rectory, 415 N. Front St., Minersville, PA 17954 t) 570-544-4581 church@stnickpa.com www.facebook.com/nativitybvm.middleport.pa/ Rev. Mark Michael Fesniak, Pst.; Christine Palko, Trustee; CRP Stds.: 1

MINERSVILLE

St. Nicholas - 415 N. Front St., Minersville, PA 17954 t) 570-544-4581 c) 570-205-2053 sisternatalya@gmail.com; church@stnickpa.com www.facebook.com/stnickschurchminersvillepa/ Rev. Mark Michael Fesniak, Pst.; Sr. Natalia Stoczanyn, S.S.M.I., DRE; Sr. Zenovia Chmilar, S.S.M.I., Teacher/ CCD Instructor; CRP Stds.: 10

St. Nicholas School - (Grades PreK-8) 515 N. Front St., Minersville, PA 17954 t) 570-544-2800 snsoffice@ptd.net www.snsminersville.com Susan Miller, Prin.; Stds.: 119; Pr. Tchrs.: 1; Sr. Tchrs.: 2; Lay Tchrs.: 11

MOUNT CARMEL

SS. Peter and Paul - 131 N. Beech St., Mount Carmel, PA 17851 t) 570-339-0650 stsppmc@ptd.net Rev. Archpriest Michael Hutsko, Pst.; Christine Bogner, DRE; CRP Stds.: 5

NANTICOKE

Transfiguration of Our Lord - 240 Center St., Nanticoke, PA 18634 t) 570-735-2262 transfigurationucc@comcast.net transfigurationucc.org/ Rev. Walter Pasicznyk, Pst.; CRP Stds.: 2

NORTHAMPTON

St. John the Baptist - 1343 Newport Ave., Northampton, PA 18067 t) 610-262-4104 stjohn1900@rcn.com Rev. Wasyl Bunik, Pst.; CRP Stds.: 15

OLYPHANT

St. Cyril's Church - 137 River St., Olyphant, PA 18447; Mailing: 135 River St., Olyphant, PA 18447 t) 570-291-4451 sscyrilandmethodius@comcast.net stcyrils.weconnect.com Very Rev. Nestor Iwasiw, Pst.; Patrick Marcinko III, Music Min.; Sandra Berta, DRE; CRP Stds.: 16

PALMERTON

St. Vladimir's - 101 Lehigh Ave., Palmerton, PA 18071 t) 610-826-2359 stvlad@ptd.net Rev. Wasyl Bunik, Pst.;

PHILADELPHIA

Immaculate Conception of Blessed Virgin Mary, Cathedral - 830 N. Franklin St., Philadelphia, PA 19123; Mailing: 819 N. 8th St., Philadelphia, PA 19123 t) 215-922-2845 cathedralonfranklin@comcast.net www.ukrcathedral.com Very Rev. Roman Pitula, Rector; CRP Stds.: 3

Christ the King Ukrainian Catholic Church - 1629 W. Cayuga St., Philadelphia, PA 19140 t) 215-455-2416 ctkucc@aol.com Rev. Yaroslav Kurpel, Pst.;

St. Nicholas Ukrainian Catholic Church - 871 N. 24th St., Philadelphia, PA 19130 t) 267-237-6037 snukrcc@aol.com saintnicholas.us/ Ukrainian Rev. Ruslan Borovyi (Ukraine), Admin.;

PHOENIXVILLE

SS. Peter and Paul - 301 Fairview St., Phoenixville, PA 19460; Mailing: 472 Emmett St., Phoenixville, PA 19460 t) 610-933-7801 sspeterandpaulukr@gmail.com www.sspeterandpaulukr.com Very Rev. Ihor Royik, Pst.;

PLYMOUTH

SS. Peter and Paul - 20 Nottingham St., Plymouth, PA 18651; Mailing: P.O. Box 60, Plymouth, PA 18651

t) 570-779-3323 sspeterandpaulucc@gmail.com sspeterandpaulucc.org Rev. Walter Pasicznyk, Pst.; CRP Stds.: 5

POTTSTOWN

St. Michael's - 425 W. Walnut St., Pottstown, PA 19464 t) 610-933-7801 stmichaelthearchangel@outlook.com Served by SS. Peter & Paul Church, Phoenixville, PA. Very Rev. Ihor Royik, Pst.; CRP Stds.: 5

READING

Nativity of Blessed Virgin Mary - 501 Summit Ave., Reading, PA 19611 t) 610-376-0586 nativitybvmchurch@gmail.com ukrainianchurchreadingpa.com Rev. Roman Sverdan, Pst.; Debbie Marco, DRE; CRP Stds.: 9

St. Andrew the Apostle - 1834 Lititz Pike, Lancaster, PA 17601 t) 267-303-8041 st_andrew_church@outlook.com Rev. Roman Svirdan;

SAINT CLAIR

St. Nicholas - 105 N. Morris St., Saint Clair, PA 17970; Mailing: 114 S. Chestnut St., Shenandoah, PA 17976 t) 570-462-0809 St. Michael, Shenandoah. Rev. Msgr. Myron Grabowsky, Admin.;

SAYRE

Ascension of Our Lord - 108 N. Higgins Ave., Sayre, PA 18840; Mailing: 410 E. McCanns Blvd., Elmira Heights, NY 14903 t) (570) 888-1060 auccs@stny.rr.com Served by Priest from St. Nicholas Ukrainian Catholic Church, Elmira Heights NY. Rev. Teodor Czabala (Ukraine), Pst.;

SCRANTON

St. Vladimir's - 430 N. Seventh Ave., Scranton, PA 18503 t) 570-342-7023 myronyukm@yahoo.com Rev. Myron Myronyuk (Ukraine), Pst.;

SHAMOKIN

Transfiguration of Our Lord - 303 N. Shamokin St., Shamokin, PA 17872-5460 t) 570-648-5932 transfigurationshamokin@gmail.com transfigurationukrainiancatholicchurch.com Dcn. Theodore Spotts; Most Rev. Andriy Rabiy, Admin.; CRP Stds.: 6

SHENANDOAH

St. Michael's - 114 S. Chestnut St., Shenandoah, PA 17976 t) 570-462-0809 stmichaelfirst.com Rev. Msgr. Myron Grabowsky, Pst.; Alice Blacznik, DRE;

SIMPSON

SS. Peter and Paul - 43 Rittenhouse St., Simpson, PA 18407; Mailing: PO Box 124, Simpson, PA 18407 t) 570-282-0331 Attended to from Ss. Cyril and Methodius Ukrainian Catholic Church, Olyphant, PA Very Rev. Nestor Iwasiw, Pst.;

SWARTHMORE

Holy Myrrh-Bearers Ukrainian Catholic Church - 900 Fairview Rd., Swarthmore, PA 19081 t) 610-544-1215 hmbchurch@verizon.net Very Rev. Archpriest Daniel Troyan, Pst.;

WARRINGTON

St. Anne's - 1545 Easton Rd., Warrington, PA 18976 t) 215-343-0779 mykolaivan1977@yahoo.com Rev. Mykola Ivanov, Pst.; CRP Stds.: 12

WEST EASTON

Holy Ghost - 315 Fourth St., West Easton, PA 18042 t) 610-252-4266 pastor@holyghostucc.com; parochialvicar@holyghostucc.com www.holyghostucc.com Rev. Yaroslav Lukavenko (Ukraine), Par. Vicar; Bohdana Sidlar, Trustee; Rev. Paul J. Makar, Pst.; Theodore Veresink, Trustee; CRP Stds.: 9

WILKES-BARRE

SS. Peter and Paul - 635 N. River St., Wilkes-Barre, PA 18705 t) 570-823-1821 sspeterandpaulwb.org/ Rev. Myron Myronyuk (Ukraine), Admin.;

COMMONWEALTH OF VIRGINIA

FRONT ROYAL

Saints Joachim and Anna Ukrainian Catholic Church - 1396 Linden St., Front Royal, VA 22630 t) 540-551-3591 c) 202-262-5040 ssjoachimandannaucc@gmail.com www.ssjoachimandanna.org Rev. Andrii Chornopyskii (Ukraine), Par. Vicar; Very Rev. Robert J. Hitchens, Pst.;

MANASSAS

Annunciation of the Blessed Virgin Mary - 6719 Token Valley Rd., Manassas, VA 20112 t) 703-791-6635 alexanderd715@aol.com www.stmarysbyz.com Rev. Alexander Dumenko (Ukraine), Pst.; Helen Troy, Treas.; CRP Stds.: 5

DISTRICT OF COLUMBIA

WASHINGTON

Ukrainian Catholic National Shrine of the Holy Family - 4250 Harewood Rd. NE, Washington, DC 20017-1511 t) 202-526-3737 ucnsholyfamily@gmail.com www.ucns-holyfamily.org Rev. Andrii Chornopyskii (Ukraine), Par. Vicar; Very Rev. Robert J. Hitchens, Admin.;

STATE OF DELAWARE

WILMINGTON

St. Nicholas - 801 Lea Blvd., Wilmington, DE 19802 t) 302-762-5511 stnicholas2@verizon.net www.stnicholaschurchde.org Very Rev. Volodymyr Klanichka, Pst.;

STATE OF MARYLAND

BALTIMORE

St. Michael's - 2401 Eastern Ave., Baltimore, MD 21224 t) 410-675-7557 tserkva@yahoo.com Rev. Vasyl Sivinskyi, Admin.;

SS. Peter and Paul - 1506 Church St., Baltimore, MD 21226; Mailing: 2401 Eastern Ave., Baltimore, MD 21224 t) 410-675-7557 tserkva@yahoo.com St. Michael's, Baltimore, MD Rev. Vasyl Sivinskyi, Admin.;

CHESAPEAKE CITY

St. Basil the Great - 231 Basil Ave., Chesapeake City, MD 21915; Mailing: P.O Box 624, Chesapeake City, MD 21195 t) 302-762-5511 stnicholas2@verizon.net Very Rev. Volodymyr Klanichka, Admin.;

SILVER SPRING

Holy Trinity - 16631 New Hampshire Ave., Silver Spring, MD 20905-3919 t) 301-421-1739 alexanderd715@aol.com Rev. Alexander Dumenko (Ukraine), Pst.; CRP Stds.: 3

STATE OF NEW JERSEY

BAYONNE

Assumption B.V.M. - 30 E. 25th St., Bayonne, NJ 07002; Mailing: 30 Bentley Ave., Jersey City, NJ 07304 t) 201-432-3122 vputera@yahoo.com SS. Peter and Paul, Jersey City, NJ Rev. Vasyl Putera, Pst.;

CARTERET

St. Mary's - 719 Roosevelt Ave., Carteret, NJ 07008 t) 732-366-2156 neokozak@msn.com; vladykavasyl@yahoo.com stmaryscarteret.org Rev. Vasyl Vladyka, Pst.;

CHERRY HILL

St. Michael's - 675 Cooper Landing Rd., Cherry Hill, NJ 08002 t) 856-482-0938 stmichaelscherryhill@gmail.com Rev. Evhen Moniuk, Pst.; CRP Stds.: 8

ELIZABETH

St. Vladimir's - 309 Grier Ave., Elizabeth, NJ 07202-3310 t) 908-352-8823 ourstvladimir@gmail.com stvladimirnj.com Rev. Ruslan Romanyuk, Pst.; CRP Stds.: 8

GREAT MEADOWS

St. Nicholas - 335 Rte. 46, Great Meadows, NJ 07838; Mailing: P.O. Box 162, Great Meadows, NJ 07838 t) 908-799-3386 stnicholasgm@gmail.com www.stnicknj.org Rev. Volodymyr Kostyuk (Ukraine), Admin.;

HILLSBOROUGH

St. Michael's - 1700 Brooks Blvd., Hillsborough, NJ 08844 t) 908-526-9195 stmichaelucc@yahoo.com Rev. Orest Kunderevych, Pst.;

HILLSIDE

Immaculate Conception - Bloy St. & Liberty Ave., Hillside, NJ 07205; Mailing: 719 Roosevelt Ave., Carteret, NJ 07008 t) 732-366-2156 icukrainiancatholic@yahoo.com byzcath.org/immaculateconception Rev. Vasyl Vladyka, Pst.; Joseph Shatynski, DRE; CRP Stds.: 8

JERSEY CITY

SS. Peter and Paul - 549 Bergen Ave., Jersey City, NJ 07304; Mailing: 30 Bentley Ave., Jersey City, NJ 07304 t) 201-432-3122 vputera@yahoo.com Rev. Vasyl Putera, Pst.;

MILLVILLE

St. Nicholas - 801 Carmel Rd., Millville, NJ 08332 t) 856-825-4826 stnicholasmilleville@gmail.com Attended from St. Michael's in Cherry Hill, NJ Rev. Evhen Moniuk, Admin.;

NEW BRUNSWICK

Nativity of B.V.M. - 80 Livingston Ave., New Brunswick, NJ 08901 t) 732-246-1516 nativitybvmucc@yahoo.com nbvmchurch.com St. Michael, Hillsborough, NJ. Rev. Orest Kunderevych, Pst.;

NEWARK

St. John the Baptist - 719 Sanford Ave., Newark, NJ 07106 t) 973-371-1356 stjohn-nj@outlook.com www.stjohn-nj.com/ Rev. Taras Svirchuk, C.Ss.R., Pst.; Rev. Ihor Kolisnyk, Assoc. Pst.;

PASSAIC

St. Nicholas - 217 President St., Passaic, NJ 07055; Mailing: 60 Holdsworth Court, Passaic, NJ 07055 t) 973-471-9727 stnicholasucc@gmail.com www.stnicholasucc.org Rev. Andriy Dudkevych, Pst.; Sr. Cecilia Sworin, S.S.M.I., DRE; CRP Stds.: 30

St. Nicholas School - (Grades PreK-8) 223 President St., Passaic, NJ 07055; Mailing: 60 Holdsworth Ct., Passaic, NJ 07055 t) 973-779-0249 snucs.news@gmail.com www.stnicholaschool.com/ Sr. Kathleen Hutsko, SSMI, Prin.; Stds.: 130; Sr. Tchrs.: 2; Lay Tchrs.: 15

PERTH AMBOY

Assumption of B.V.M. - 684 Alta Vista Pl., Perth Amboy, NJ 08861 t) 732-826-8721 (CRP); 732-826-0767 acsschooloffice@gmail.com; assumptionchurch@verizon.net www.assumptioncatholicchurch.net Rev. Ivan Turyk, Pst.; Dcn. Paul Makar; CRP Stds.: 14

Assumption of B.V.M. School - (Grades 1-8) 380 Meredith St, Perth Amboy, NJ 08861-2765 t) (732) 826-8721; (732) 826-8721 assumptioncatholicschool.net Lissette Shumny, Prin.; Stds.: 177; Sr. Tchrs.: 3; Lay Tchrs.: 11

RAMSEY

St. Paul - 79 Cherry Ln., Ramsey, NJ 07446 c) (215) 869-8027 stpaulukrchurch@gmail.com Rev. Volodymyr Kostyuk (Ukraine), Admin.;

TOMS RIVER

St. Stephen's - 1344 White Oak Bottom Rd., Toms River, NJ 08755 t) 732-505-6053 pastor@ststephenchurch.us www.ststephenchurch.us Rev. Volodymyr Popyk, Pst.; CRP Stds.: 12

TRENTON

St. Josaphat's - 1195 Deutz Ave., Trenton, NJ 08611-3239 t) 609-695-3771 tarlonch@gmail.com ukrcathchurchnj.com Rev. Taras R. Lonchyna, Pst.; CRP Stds.: 45

WHIPPANY

St. John the Baptist - 60 N. Jefferson Rd., Whippany, NJ 07981 t) 973-887-3616 stjohnukrcc@gmail.com sjucc.com Rev. Stepan Bilyk, Pst.; CRP Stds.: 202

INSTITUTIONS LOCATED IN DIOCESE

CEMETERIES [CEM]

LANGHORNE

Mother of Sorrows - 2618-2637 Village Rd., Langhorne, PA 19047; Mailing: 810 N. Franklin St., Philadelphia, PA 19123 t) 215-627-0143 ukrmet@ukrcap.org; phillyfinance@ukrcap.org Ihor Kovaliv, Admin.;

COLLEGES & UNIVERSITIES [COL]

JENKINTOWN

***Manor College** - 700 Fox Chase Rd., Jenkintown, PA 19046 t) 215-885-2360 kilmer@manor.edu www.manor.edu Dr. Jonathan Peri, Pres.; Richard Jutkiewicz, Librn.; Katharina Kilmer, Contact; Stds.: 578; Lay Tchrs.: 23

CONVENTS, MONASTERIES, AND RESIDENCES FOR WOMEN [CON]

FOX CHASE MANOR

Provincial Motherhouse of the Sisters of St. Basil the Great - 710 Fox Chase Rd., Fox Chase Manor, PA 19046 t) 215-379-3998 province@stbasils.com www.stbasils.com Rev. John Ciurpita, Chap.; Joann Sosler, Prov.; Sr. Dorothy Ann Busowski, Prov. Asst.; Sr. Clement Bartholomew, Provincial Councilor; Sr. Teodora Kopyn, Provincial Councilor; Sr. Lydia Anna Sawka, Provincial Secretary; Srs.: 26

PHILADELPHIA

Missionary Sisters of Mother of God, Inc. - 711 N. Franklin St., Philadelphia, PA 19123 t) 215-627-7808 msmgnuns@gmail.com msmgnuns.com Mother Maria Kelly, Supr.; Srs.: 6

Sacred Heart Convent - 160 W. Carpenter Ln., Philadelphia, PA 19119 t) 215-843-2266 Sr. Jiss Maria, Contact; Srs.: 2

MISCELLANEOUS [MIS]

JENKINTOWN

The Basileiad Library/Manor College - 700 Fox Chase Rd., Jenkintown, PA 19046 t) 215-885-2360 library@manor.edu manor.edu/academics/library/ Richard Jutkiewicz, Librn.;

PHILADELPHIA

Archieparchial Museum and Educational Center - 810 N. Franklin St., Philadelphia, PA 19123 t) 215-627-3389 tofmuseum@ukcap.org Sr. Timothea Konyu, MSMG, Dir.;

MONASTERIES AND RESIDENCES FOR PRIESTS AND BROTHERS [MON]

WASHINGTON

Monastery of the Holy Cross - 1302 Quincy St., N.E., Washington, DC 20017-2614 t) 202-832-8519 abbotdc@aol.com Rev. Archmandrite Joseph (Richard) Lee, Abbot; Priests: 1

NURSING / REHABILITATION / CONVALESCENCE / ELDERLY CARE [NUR]

PHILADELPHIA

Ascension Manor, Inc. - 911 N. Franklin St., Philadelphia, PA 19123 t) 215-922-1116 john@ascensionmanor.org www.ascensionmanor.org Most Rev. Borys Gudziak, Pres.; Andrew Fylypowych, Dir.; Most Rev. Andriy Rabiy, Dir.; John Siwak, Manager; Asstd. Annu.: 340; Staff: 11

Ascension Manor I - 911N. Franklin St., Philadelphia, PA 19123 t) (215) 922-1116

Ascension Manor II - 970 N. 7th St., Philadelphia, PA 19123 t) 215-923-3907

RETREAT HOUSES / RENEWAL CENTERS [RTR]

FOX CHASE MANOR

Basilian Spirituality Center - 710 Fox Chase Rd., Fox Chase Manor, PA 19046 t) 215-780-1227 basilcenter@stbasils.com www.stbasils.com Joann Sosler, Prov.; Sr. Dorothy Ann Busowski, O.S.B.M., Prov. Asst.;

SEMINARIES [SEM]

WASHINGTON

St. Josaphat Seminary - 201 Taylor St., N.E., Washington, DC 20017 t) 202-529-1177 stjosaphatseminary@gmail.com www.sjucs.org Very Rev. Robert J. Hitchens, Rector; Stds.: 1; Pr. Tchrs.: 1

An asterisk (*) denotes an organization that has established tax-exempt status directly with the IRS and is not covered by the USCCB Group Ruling.

Metropolitan Archeparchy of Pittsburgh, Byzantine

MOST REVEREND WILLIAM C. SKURLA

Metropolitan Archbishop of Pittsburgh; ordained November 1, 1993; appointed Bishop of Van Nuys February 19, 2002; ordained April 23, 2002; appointed Bishop of Passaic December 6, 2007; enthroned January 29, 2008; appointed Metropolitan Archbishop of Pittsburgh January 19, 2012; enthroned April 18, 2012. Chancery: 66 Riverview Ave., Pittsburgh, PA 15214.

Chancery: 66 Riverview Ave., Pittsburgh, PA 15214. T: 412-231-4000; F: 412-231-1697. secretary@archpitt.org

ESTABLISHED FEBRUARY 25, 1924.

Raised to Archeparchy February 21, 1969.

Embraces all Byzantine Ruthenian Rite Catholics in that part of the State of Pennsylvania west of the western boundaries of the Counties of Tioga, Lycoming, Union, Mifflin, Juniata and Franklin. In the State of Ohio, the Counties of Ashtabula, Athens, Belmont, Carroll, Columbiana, Gallia, Guernsey, Harrison, Jefferson, Lawrence, Mahoning, Meigs, Morrow, Morgan, Noble, Trumbull and Washington and also the States of Alabama, Arkansas, Kentucky, Louisiana, Mississippi, Oklahoma, Tennessee, Texas and West Virginia.

For legal titles of parishes and diocesan institutions, consult the Chancery.

STATISTICAL OVERVIEW

Personnel
Archbishops....1
Retired Abbots....1
Priests: Diocesan Active in Diocese....35
Priests: Diocesan Active Outside Diocese....2
Priests: Retired, Sick or Absent....9
Number of Diocesan Priests....46
Religious Priests in Diocese....2
Total Priests in your Diocese....48
Extern Priests in Diocese....11
Ordinations:
Diocesan Priests....1
Permanent Deacons in Diocese....24
Total Brothers....1
Total Sisters....32

Parishes
Parishes....71
With Resident Pastor:
Resident Diocesan Priests....36
Resident Religious Priests....2
Without Resident Pastor:
Administered by Priests....30
Administered by Deacons....2
Completely vacant....1
Missions....1
Pastoral Centers....5
Closed Parishes....2
Professional Ministry Personnel:
Sisters....2

Welfare
Health Care Centers....1
Total Assisted....115
Homes for the Aged....1
Total Assisted....42

Educational
Seminaries, Diocesan....1
Students from This Diocese....6
Students from Other Dioceses....4
Total Seminarians....6
Catechesis/Religious Education:
High School Students....85
Elementary Students....338
Total Students under Catholic Instruction....429

Vital Statistics
Receptions into the Church:
Infant Baptism Totals....81
Minor Baptism Totals....19
Adult Baptism Totals....3
Received into Full Communion....19
First Communions....135
Confirmations....138
Marriages:
Catholic....22
Interfaith....16
Total Marriages....38
Deaths....247
Total Catholic Population....19,195

LEADERSHIP
Chancery - t) 412-231-4000 secretary@archpitt.org
Presbyteral Council - Very Rev. Andrew J. Deskevich; Rev. Kevin E. Marks; Rev. Paul-Alexander Shutt OSB, O.S.B.;
Protosyncellus - Very Rev. Andrew J. Deskevich;
Chancellor - Very Rev. Vasyl Polyak;
Vicar for Canonical Services - Rev. Valerian M. Michlik;
Finance Council - Most Rev. William C. Skurla; Very Rev. Andrew J. Deskevich; Dcn. Robert J. Shalhoub;
Consultors - Very Rev. Andrew J. Deskevich; Very Rev. James A. Spontak; Rev. Mykhaylo Farynets;
Protopresbyters - Very Rev. James A. Spontak, Johnstown; Very Rev. David A. Bosnich, North Central; Very Rev. Frank A. Firko, Greater Pittsburgh;
Finance Officer - Dcn. Robert J. Shalhoub;
Tribunal -
Judicial Vicars - Rev. Valerian M. Michlik; Jay Conzemsus; Rev. Dennis P. Yurochko;
Notary -
Secretary - Sr. Elaine Kisinko, O.S.B.M.;

OFFICES AND DIRECTORS
Archieparchial Choir - Darlene Fejka, Dir.;
Archieparchial Newspaper - David Mayernik Jr., Editor;
Byzantine Catholic Seminary Press - t) 412-322-8307 order@byzantineseminarypress.com Patricia Bovee, Dir.;
Communications - David Mayernik Jr.; Very Rev. Andrew J. Deskevich, Asst. Dir. Media;
Diaconate Program - t) 412-321-8383 Very Rev. Robert M. Pipta, Dir.;
Evangelization, Mission Activity and Ecumenism - Rev. Robert F. Oravetz, Dir.;
Office of Religious Education - t) 412-322-8773 Sr. Marion Dobos, O.S.B., Dir.;
Priests' Pension Board - Most Rev. William C. Skurla; Very Rev. Andrew J. Deskevich; Dcn. Robert J. Shalhoub, Finance Officer;
Revitalization and Renewal Commission - Very Rev. Andrew J. Deskevich; Helen Kennedy; Dcn. Dennis M. Prestash;
Safe Environment Coordinator - t) 724-438-8644 Sr. Joanne Lickvar, O.S.B.M.;
Victim Assistance Coordinator - c) 724-504-9588 Courtney Minerd;
Vocations - t) 330-755-4831 Rev. Kevin E. Marks, Dir.;

PARISHES, MISSIONS, AND CLERGY

COMMONWEALTH OF PENNSYLVANIA

ALIQUIPPA
St. George the Great Martyr - 1001 Clinton St., Aliquippa, PA 15001-3903 t) 724-375-2742 stmarybyzantine@verizon.net stgeorgebyzantinecatholicchurch.org/ Rev. Geoffrey Mackey, Admin.; CRP Stds.: 3

AMBRIDGE
St. Mary's - 624 Park Rd., Ambridge, PA 15003 t) 724-266-2030 stmarybyzantine@verizon.net Rev. Geoffrey Mackey, Pst.; Dcn. Thomas J. Klacik; CRP Stds.: 2

AVELLA
St. John the Baptist - 176 Cross Creek Rd., Avella, PA 15312; Mailing: P.O. Box 565, Avella, PA 15312 c) (817) 271-0968 stjohnavellabyz@gmail.com Rev. Brian Norrell, Admin.; CRP Stds.: 2

BEAVER
Saint Nicholas Chapel - 5400 Tuscarawas Rd., Beaver, PA 15009-9513 t) 724-266-2030 rupp.william@gmail.com www.gcuusa.com/snc.htm Attended by St. Mary's Ambridge Very Rev. Andrew J. Deskevich, Contact;

BEAVERDALE
St. Mary's - 214 Stewart St., Beaverdale, PA 15921; Mailing: P.O. Box 610, Beaverdale, PA 15921 t) 814-736-9780 james_armand_spontak@verizon.net Sts. Peter and Paul, Portage. Dcn. Daniel F. Perich; Very Rev. James A. Spontak, Admin.;

BRADDOCK
SS. Peter and Paul - 431 George St., Braddock, PA 15104; Mailing: 4200 Homestead-Duquesne Rd., Munhall, PA 15120 t) 412-461-1712 stspeterpaulbc@gmail.com stspeterpaulbcc.com/ Rev. Vitalii Stashkevych, Admin.;

BRADENVILLE
St. Mary's - 112 St. Mary's Way, Bradenville, PA 15620-1017 t) 724-537-5839 archpitt@aol.com Rev. Athanasius C. Cherry, O.S.B., Admin.; CRP Stds.: 10

BROWNSVILLE
St. Nicholas - 302 Third Ave., Brownsville, PA 15417 t) 724-785-7573 frchris53@gmail.com Rev. Christopher R. Burke, Pst.;

CANONSBURG
St. Michael - 166 E. College St., Canonsburg, PA 15317 t) 724-745-7117 frj455@outlook.com saintmichaelscanonsburg.org Very Rev. R. Joseph Raptosh, Pst.; Dcn. Lance D. Weakland;

CHARLEROI
Holy Ghost - 828 Meadow Ave., Charleroi, PA 15022 t) 724-379-9751 stmichaelstmary@comcast.net Rev. Stephen J. Wahal, Admin.;

CLAIRTON
Ascension of Our Lord - 318 Park Ave., Clairton, PA 15025 t) 412-233-7422 ivan.mina.phd@gmail.com Rev. John L. Mina, Pst.; CRP Stds.: 8

CLARENCE
Dormition of the Mother of God - 104 Byzantine Ln., Clarence, PA 16829-0304; Mailing: P.O. Box 2, Hawk Run, PA 16840 t) 814-387-4161; 814-342-4315 c) 724-388-6176 stjohns024@comcast.net; golden15739@gmail.com www.archpitt.org Hawk Run, PA. St. John the Baptist Byzantine Catholic Parish. State College, PA. Byzantine Catholic Community. Dcn. John A. Custaney; Rev. James A. Ragan, Sacr. Min.;

CLYMER
St. Anne - 360 Franklin St., Clymer, PA 15728 t) 814-938-4244 stmaryandstanne@gmail.com www.byzantinechurches.org Rev. Wesley M. Mash, Admin.;

CONEMAUGH
Holy Trinity - 217 Fourth St., Conemaugh, PA 15909 t) 814-535-5231 byzbob@aol.com Rev. Robert F. Oravetz, Pst.;

DONORA
St. Michael - 511 Murray Ave., Donora, PA 15033 t) 724-379-9751 stmichaelstmary@comcast.net Rev. Stephen J. Wahal, Admin.;

DU BOIS
Nativity of the Mother of God - 200 McCullough St., Du Bois, PA 15801 t) 814-371-4911; 814-371-4276 (CRP) vasylbanyk@gmail.com Rev. Vasyl Banyk, Admin.; Dcn. Paul M. Boboige;
All Generations -

DUNLO
SS. Peter and Paul - Roberts St., Dunlo, PA 15930; Mailing: P.O. Box 610, Beaverdale, PA 15921-0610 t) 814-736-9780 james_armand_spontak@verizon.net Sts. Peter and Paul, Portage Very Rev. James A. Spontak, Pst.;

DUQUESNE
SS. Peter and Paul - 701 Foster Ave., Duquesne, PA 15110 t) 412-466-3578 saintspeterpaulduq@comcast.net www.facebook.com/peterpaulduquesne Rev. David S Abernethy, Admin.; Dcn. Sean Petrisko;

ERIE
SS. Peter and Paul - 3415 Wallace St., Erie, PA 16504 t) 814-825-8140 eriecountybyzantines@verizon.net Rev. John J. Mihalco, Pst.; Andrew Pushchak, DRE; CRP Stds.: 12

ERNEST
St. Jude Thaddeus - 330 Main St., Ernest, PA 15739; Mailing: P.O. Box 130, Ernest, PA 15739 t) 724-465-6738 vasylradar@gmail.com www.stjudebyzantinecatholic.org/ SS Peter and Paul, Punxsutawney. Rev. Vasyl Kadar, Admin.;

GIBSONIA
St. Andrew the Apostle - 235 Logan Rd., Gibsonia, PA 15044 t) (724) 625-1160 (Office) standrewbcchurch@gmail.com Rev. Radko Blichar, Admin.; Dcn. Larry Hruska;

GIRARD
SS. Cyril and Methodius - 1022 Tilden Ave., Girard, PA 16417 t) 814-774-3281 jjmihalco@gmail.com Sts. Peter and Paul, Erie. Rev. John J. Mihalco, Admin.;

GREENSBURG
St. Nicholas of Myra - 624 E. Pittsburgh St., Greensburg, PA 15601 t) 724-837-0295 archpitt@aol.com Rev. Regis J. Dusecina, Pst.;

HANNASTOWN
St. Mary's - Pollins Ave., Hannastown, PA 15635; Mailing: 624 E. Pittsburgh St., Greensburg, PA 15601 t) 724-837-0295 archpitt@aol.com St. Nicholas of Myra, Greensburg. Rev. Regis Dusecina, Admin.;

HAWK RUN
St. John the Baptist - 24 Fulton St., Hawk Run, PA 16840; Mailing: P.O. Box 2, Hawk Run, PA 16840 t) 814-342-4315 c) 724-388-6176 stjohns024@comcast.net; golden15739@gmail.com www.archpitt.org Clarence, PA. Dormition of the Mother of God Byzantine Catholic Parish. State College, PA. Byzantine Catholic Community. Dcn. Dennis M. Prestash, Par. Admin.; Rev. James A. Ragan, Sacr. Min.; CRP Stds.: 13

HERMINIE
St. Mary's - 5 Second St., Herminie, PA 15637 t) 724-446-5570 Rev. Vasyl Yakubych, Admin.;

HERMITAGE
St. Michael - 2230 Highland Rd., Hermitage, PA 16148 t) 724-981-6680 kevmarks630@gmail.com; stmichaelhermitage2230@gmail.com www.stmichaelbyzhermitage.com Rev. Kevin E. Marks, Pst.; William Dzuricsko, DRE; CRP Stds.: 10

HOMER CITY
St. Mary's Holy Protection - 279 Yellow Creek St., Homer City, PA 15748 t) 724-479-2206 saintmaryandsaintanne@gmail.com Rev. Wesley M. Mash, Pst.;

JEROME
SS. Peter and Paul - 139 Phillips St., Jerome, PA 15937; Mailing: 803 Somerset Ave., Windber, PA 15963 t) 814-467-7309 irusyn21@gmail.com Rev. Ivan Rusyn, Admin.;

JOHNSTOWN
St. Mary's - 411 Power St., Johnstown, PA 15906 t) 814-535-4132 stmarys@atlanticbb.net Rev. Msgr. Raymond A. Balta, Pst.;

LATROBE
St. Mary - 4480 State Route 981, Latrobe, PA 15650 t) 724-423-3673 st.marytrauger@gmail.com www.stmarybyzantinecatholic.org Rev. Paul-Alexander Shutt OSB, O.S.B., Pst.; CRP Stds.: 3

LEISENRING
St. Stephen - 3120 W. Crawford Ave., Leisenring, PA 15455; Mailing: P.O. Box 128, Leisenring, PA 15455 t) 724-628-6611 fatherbotsko@gmail.com Rev. Jerome G. Botsko, Admin.;

LYNDORA
St. John the Baptist - 105 Kohler Ave., Lyndora, PA 16045 t) 724-287-5000 radko.blichar@gmail.com www.stjohnbyzlyn.com Rev. Radko Blichar, Admin.; Dcn. Paul Simko; CRP Stds.: 12

MCKEES ROCKS
Holy Ghost - 225 Olivia St., McKees Rocks, PA 15136 t) 412-771-3324 steve@puluka.com; secretary225@verizon.net www.holyghost-byzantinecatholic.org Very Rev. Frank A. Firko, Pst.; Steven Puluka, DRE; CRP Stds.: 9

MCKEESPORT

St. Nicholas - 410 Sixth St., McKeesport, PA 15132 t) 412-664-9131 stnickmck@gmail.com Rev. Donald J. Voss, Pst.;

MONESSEN

Assumption of the Blessed Virgin - 125 McKee Ave., Monessen, PA 15062 t) 724-379-9751 stmichaelstmary@comcast.net St. Michael, Donora. Rev. Stephen J. Wahal, Admin.; Dcn. John M. Hanchin; CRP Stds.: 3

MONROEVILLE

Church of the Resurrection - 455 Center Rd., Monroeville, PA 15146 t) 412-372-8650 cotr455@gmail.com Rev. Donald McChesney Bolls, Pst.; CRP Stds.: 7

MUNHALL

St. John the Baptist Cathedral - 210 Greentree Rd., Munhall, PA 15120 t) 412-461-0944 stjohnsbyzantinecathedral@gmail.com Very Rev. Andrew J. Deskevich, Rector; CRP Stds.: 8

St. Elias - 4200 Homestead-Duquesne Rd., Munhall, PA 15120 t) 412-461-1712 steliasbcc@gmail.com steliasmunhallpa.weebly.com/ Rev. Vitalii Stashkevych, Admin.; CRP Stds.: 4

NANTY-GLO

St. Nicholas - 1191 Second St., Nanty-Glo, PA 15943 t) 814-535-5231 byzbob@aol.com Holy Trinity, Conemaugh. Rev. Robert F. Oravetz, Admin.;

NEW SALEM

St. Mary's - 12 Center St. Ext., New Salem, PA 15468; Mailing: P.O. Box 487, New Salem, PA 15468 t) 724-245-7188 frchris53@gmail.com St. Nicholas, Brownsville. Rev. Christopher R. Burke, Admin.;

NORTH HUNTINGDON

St. Stephen's - 90 Bethel Rd., North Huntingdon, PA 15642 t) 724-863-6776 ststephennh@outlook.com www.ststephensbyzcath.org Rev. Vasyl Yakubych, Pst.;

NORTHERN CAMBRIA

St. John the Baptist - 719 Chestnut Ave., Northern Cambria, PA 15714-1459 t) 814-674-5552 n.cambriabyzcath@gmail.com www.ncambriabyzcath.org Rev. Roman Andriitso, Admin.;

PATTON

SS. Peter and Paul - 516 Palmer Ave., Patton, PA 16668 t) 814-674-5552 pattonbyzcath@gmail.com www.pattonbyzcath.org St. John, Northern Cambria. Rev. Roman Andriitso, Admin.; Dcn. Raymond J Zadzilko;

PERRYOPOLIS

St. Nicholas - 102 Railroad St., Perryopolis, PA 15473 t) 724-887-5072 olegseremchuk@gmail.com Rev. Oleh Seremchuk, Pst.; CRP Stds.: 4

PITTSBURGH

Holy Ghost - 1437 Superior Ave., Pittsburgh, PA 15212 t) 412-771-3324 secretary225@verizon.net Filial Parish of Holy Ghost, McKees Rocks. Very Rev. Frank A. Firko, Admin.; Dcn. Michael E. Meaders; CRP Stds.: 1

Holy Spirit - 4815 Fifth Ave., Pittsburgh, PA 15213 t) 412-687-1220 holyspiritinformation@gmail.com www.holyspiritchurchpgh.org Rev. Michael David Kunitz, Admin.; CRP Stds.: 6

St. John Chrysostom - 506 Saline St., Pittsburgh, PA 15207 t) 412-421-9243 stjohnchrysostom@comcast.net sjcbcc.com Rev. Miron Kerul-Kmec, Admin.;

St. John the Baptist - 1720 Jane St., Pittsburgh, PA 15203 t) 412-431-1090 stjohnbaptist@comcast.net Rev. Miron Kerul-Kmec, Admin.;

St. Pius X - 2336 Brownsville Rd., Pittsburgh, PA 15210 t) 412-881-8344 Rev. Michael David Kunitz, Admin.;

PORTAGE

SS. Peter and Paul - 143 Church Rd., Portage, PA 15946 t) 814-736-9780 james_armand_spontak@verizon.net www.byzantinecatholic.net Very Rev. James A. Spontak, Pst.; CRP Stds.: 11

PUNXSUTAWNEY

SS. Peter and Paul - 714 Sutton St., Punxsutawney, PA 15767 t) 814-938-6564 peter_and_paul@verizon.net Rev. Vasyl Kadar, Admin.; Dcn. Steven F. White; CRP Stds.: 2

SCOTTDALE

St. John the Baptist - 525 Porter Ave., Scottdale, PA 15683 t) 724-887-5072 st.johnsbyz@zoominternet.net Rev. Oleh Seremchuk, Admin.; CRP Stds.: 9

SHEFFIELD

St. Michael - 407 School St., Sheffield, PA 16347; Mailing: P.O. Box 471, Sheffield, PA 16347 t) 814-968-5478 larocheud@westpa.net Very Rev. David A. Bosnich, Pst.;

STATE COLLEGE

State College PA Byzantine Catholic Community - 1606 Norma St., State College, PA 16801; Mailing: P.O. Box 2, Hawk Run, PA 16840 t) 814-342-4315 c) 724-388-6176 stjohns024@comcast.net; golden15739@gmail.com Hawk Run, PA. St. John the Baptist Byzantine Catholic Parish. Clarence, PA. Dormition of the Mother of God Byzantine Catholic Parish. Dcn. Dennis M. Prestash, Admin.; Rev. James A. Ragan, Sacr. Min.;

SYKESVILLE

Holy Trinity - 104 Shaffer St., Sykesville, PA 15865 t) 814-894-5440 holytrinitysykesville@gmail.com Rev. Vasyl Banyk, Admin.; Dcn. Lucas M. Crawford; CRP Stds.: 48

TARENTUM

Sts. Peter and Paul - 339 E. 10th Ave., Tarentum, PA 15084-1003 t) 724-224-3026 tarentumbyzcath@gmail.com www.tarentumbyzcath.org Very Rev. Vasyl Polyak, Pst.; CRP Stds.: 10

UNIONTOWN

St. John the Baptist - 185 E. Main St., Uniontown, PA 15401 t) 724-438-6027 stjohnthebaptistuniontown@gmail.com Very Rev. Vasyl Symyon, Pst.; CRP Stds.: 12

UPPER ST. CLAIR

St. Gregory Nazianzus - 2005 Mohawk Rd., Upper St. Clair, PA 15241 t) 412-835-7800 stgregoryusc@aol.com stgregoryusc.org Rev. Valerian M. Michlik, Pst.; Dcn. Timothy J Corbett; Dcn. Michael E. George; CRP Stds.: 43

WALL

Holy Trinity - 472 Wall Ave., Wall, PA 15148 t) 412-372-8650 fatherdonbolls@gmail.com Church of the Resurrection, Monroeville. Rev. Donald McChesney Bolls, Admin.;

WINDBER

St. Mary (Dormition) Church - 803 Somerset St., Windber, PA 15963 t) 814-467-7309 irusyn21@gmail.com www.stmaryswindber.com/home.html Rev. Ivan Rusyn, Admin.; CRP Stds.: 7

STATE OF LOUISIANA

NEW ORLEANS

St. Nicholas of Myra Byzantine Catholic Mission - 2435 S. Carrollton Ave., New Orleans, LA 70118; Mailing: 4680 W. Main St., Houma, LA 70360-4916 t) 504-861-0806 c) (985) 232-6841 (Also receive Text Message) stnicholasnola@yahoo.com www.archpitt.org/place/neworleansla-2/ Byzantine Ruthenian Church Recension Rev. Nile C. Gross, Assoc. Pst.; Dcn. Gregory A. Haddad, Admin.; Rev. John Mefrige, Assoc. Pst.;

STATE OF OHIO

BOARDMAN

Infant Jesus of Prague - 7754 S. Ave., Boardman, OH 44512 t) 330-758-6019 farynec@gmail.com infantjesusbyz.org Rev. Mykhaylo Farynets, Pst.; CRP Stds.: 10

CAMPBELL

St. Michael - 463 Robinson Rd., Campbell, OH 44405; Mailing: Box 426, Campbell, OH 44405 t) 330-755-4831 kevmarks@hotmail.com; stmichaelcampbell100@gmail.com www.stmichaelbyzcampbell.org Rev. Kevin E. Marks, Pst.; CRP Stds.: 20

MINGO JUNCTION

St. John the Baptist - 207 Standard St., Mingo Junction, OH 43938 t) 740-535-0271 revfrjohn@sbcglobal.net served from St. Joseph, Toronto. Rev. John J. Kapitan Jr., O.F.M., Admin.;

PLEASANT CITY

St. Michael the Archangel - 408 Walnut St., Pleasant City, OH 43772 t) 330-832-1270 romkat206@yahoo.com Attended from St. Mary, Massillon, OH. Rev. A. Edward Gretchko, Pst.;

TORONTO

St. Joseph - 814 N. Fifth St., Toronto, OH 43964 t) 740-537-1026 revfrjohn@sbcglobal.net Rev. John J. Kapitan Jr., O.F.M., Pst.;

WARREN

SS. Peter and Paul's - 180 Belvedere Ave., N.E., Warren, OH 44483 t) 330-372-1875 sppbyzchurch@gmail.com sppbyzantinecatholic.org Rev. William J. Rupp, Admin.; CRP Stds.: 8

YOUNGSTOWN

Assumption of the Blessed Virgin - 356 S. Belle Vista, Youngstown, OH 44509 t) 330-799-8163; 330-792-1578 (Secretary) stmarysyoungstown@att.net; maddsinger@sbcglobal.net Very Rev. Richard I. Lambert, Pst.; CRP Stds.: 3

St. Nicholas - 1898 Wilson Ave., Youngstown, OH 44506; Mailing: 3801 Shady Run Rd, Youngstown, OH 44502 t) 330-743-0419 stnick9000@aol.com Infant Jesus of Prague, Boardman. Rev. Mykhaylo Farynets, Admin.;

STATE OF TEXAS

HOUSTON

St. John Chrysostom - 5402 Acorn St., Houston, TX 77092-4255 t) 713-681-3580 pastor@stjohnchrysostom.com www.stjohnchrysostom.com Dcn. Andrew F. Veres; Rev. Thomas Wells, Pst.; CRP Stds.: 31

IRVING

St. Basil the Great - 1118 E. Union Bower Rd., Irving, TX 75061 t) 972-438-5644 eliasdfw@gmail.com stbasilsinirving.org Very Rev. Elias L. Rafaj, Pst.; CRP Stds.: 65

STATE OF WEST VIRGINIA

MORGANTOWN

St. Mary Holy Protection - 2115 Listravia Ave., Morgantown, WV 26505 t) 304-296-2455 jfraseriv@gmail.com Rev. James Fraser IV, Admin.;

WEIRTON

St. Mary's - 3116 Elm St., Weirton, WV 26062 t) 304-748-2780 c) (817) 271-0968 stmaryweirton@gmail.com Rev. Brian Norrell, Admin.; CRP Stds.: 12

INSTITUTIONS LOCATED IN DIOCESE

CONVENTS, MONASTERIES, AND RESIDENCES FOR WOMEN [CON]

ALIQUIPPA

St. George Convent - 1000 Clinton St., Aliquippa, PA 15001 t) 724-378-0238 pastor@stgeorgebyzantinecatholicchurch.org Sr. Mary Virginia Ermany, Admin.; Srs.: 1

UNIONTOWN

Monastery and Novitiate of the Sisters of St. Basil the Great - 500 W. Main St., Uniontown, PA 15401; Mailing: P.O. Box 878, Uniontown, PA 15401 t) 724-438-8644 osbmolph@verizon.net www.sistersofstbasil.org Sr. Susan Sisko, OSBM, Prov.; Rev. Jerome G. Botsko, Chap.; Srs.: 29

WARREN

Queen of Heaven Monastery - 169 Kenmore Ave. N.E., #302, Warren, OH 44483 t) 330-856-1813 www.benedictinebyzantine.org Sr. Barbara Pavlik, Admin.; Srs.: 2

ENDOWMENTS / FOUNDATIONS / TRUSTS [EFT]

PITTSBURGH

Eastern Catholic Benefit Trust - 66 Riverview Ave., Pittsburgh, PA 15214 t) 412-231-4000 secretary@archpitt.org Most Rev. William C. Skurla, Pres.;

MONASTERIES AND RESIDENCES FOR PRIESTS AND BROTHERS [MON]

PITTSBURGH

Holy Trinity Monastery - c/o 66 Riverview Avenue, Pittsburgh, PA 15214; Mailing: P.O. Box 990, Butler, PA 16003-0990 t) 724-996-0472 proto@archpitt.org Rt. Rev. Leo R. Schlosser; Bro. Michael Zetzer; Brs.: 1; Priests: 1

NURSING / REHABILITATION / CONVALESCENCE / ELDERLY CARE [NUR]

UNIONTOWN

Mt. Macrina Manor - 520 W. Main St., Uniontown, PA 15401-2602 t) 724-437-1400 info@mtmacrinamanor.com www.mtmacrinamanor.com Caroline Bercosky, Admin.; Asstd. Annu.: 115; Staff: 177

WARREN

Infant of Prague Manor - 169 Kenmore, N.E., Warren, OH 44483 t) 330-372-4700 praguemanor@gmail.com Independent senior housing. Rev. William J. Rupp, Admin.; Susan Gresley, Bus. Mgr.; Staff: 2

RETREAT HOUSES / RENEWAL CENTERS [RTR]

UNIONTOWN

Mt. St. Macrina House of Prayer - 510 W. Main St., Uniontown, PA 15401-0878; Mailing: P.O. Box 878, Uniontown, PA 15401-0878 t) 724-438-7149 hpmsm@verizon.net www.sistersofstbasil.org Sr. Carol Petrasovich, O.S.B.M., Dir.;

SEMINARIES [SEM]

PITTSBURGH

Byzantine Catholic Seminary of SS. Cyril and Methodius - 3605 Perrysville Ave., Pittsburgh, PA 15214-2229 t) 412-321-8383 rector@bcs.edu www.bcs.edu Very Rev. Robert M. Pipta, Rector; Very Rev. Ronald Barusefski, Campus Min.; Rev. Ivan Chirovsky, Spiritual Adv./Care Srvcs.; Rev. Christiaan Kappes, Dean; Sr. Marion Dobos, O.S.B., Pastoral Min.; Sandra A. Collins, Librn.; Carol Przyborski, Registrar; Stds.: 10; Lay Tchrs.: 3; Pr. Tchrs.: 5

An asterisk (*) denotes an organization that has established tax-exempt status directly with the IRS and is not covered by the USCCB Group Ruling.

Romanian Catholic Diocese of Saint George in Canton

MOST REVEREND JOHN MICHAEL BOTEAN, D.D.

Bishop for the Romanian Catholic Diocese of Canton; ordained May 18, 1986; appointed Bishop for the Romanian Catholic Diocese of Canton July 15, 1996; Episcopal Ordination August 24, 1996. Res.: 1325 Skyway St., N.E., Canton, OH 44721. T: 330-493-9355; F: 330-493-9963.

Chancery: 1121 44th St., N.E., Canton, OH 44714-1297. T: 330-493-9355; F: 330-493-9963.
www.romaniancatholic.org
ovim@rcdcanton.org

Elevated from Apostolic Exarchate for Romanian Byzantine to the Rank of an Eparchy (Diocese) March 26, 1987.
The Jurisdiction of the Romanian Catholic Diocese of Canton extends territorially to all of the United States and Canada.

Legal Title: The Romanian Catholic Diocese of Canton.

STATISTICAL OVERVIEW

Personnel

Bishop	1
Abbots	1
Retired Abbots	1
Priests: Diocesan Active in Diocese	13
Priests: Diocesan Active Outside Diocese	2
Priests: Retired, Sick or Absent	8
Number of Diocesan Priests	23
Religious Priests in Diocese	2
Total Priests in your Diocese	25
Extern Priests in Diocese	6
Ordinations:	
Religious Priests	1
Transitional Deacons	2
Permanent Deacons in Diocese	5
Total Brothers	6
Total Sisters	4

Parishes

Parishes	12
With Resident Pastor:	
Resident Diocesan Priests	9
Resident Religious Priests	1
Without Resident Pastor:	
Administered by Priests	1
Administered by Lay People	1
Missions	4
Closed Parishes	2
Professional Ministry Personnel:	
Lay Ministers	4

Educational

Catechesis/Religious Education:	
High School Students	13
Elementary Students	28
Total Students under Catholic Instruction	41

Vital Statistics

Receptions into the Church:	
Infant Baptism Totals	25
Minor Baptism Totals	2
Received into Full Communion	11
First Communions	16
Confirmations	21
Marriages:	
Catholic	5
Interfaith	4
Total Marriages	9
Deaths	16
Total Catholic Population	5,000

LEADERSHIP

Vicar General (Protosyncellus) - Very Rev. Iuliu-Vasile Muntean;
Chancery -
Chancellor and Moderator of the Curia - t) 330-875-4032 Very Rev. Ovidiu Ioan Marginean;
Vice Chancellor - Dcn. Remus Anghel Orian;

OFFICES AND DIRECTORS

Assistant to the Economos for Risk Management - Dcn. George Wendt;
Child Protection Office Director and Safe Environment Coordinator - Julie Shocksnider, Dir. (julies@rcdcanton.org);
College of Consultors - Very Rev. Ovidiu Ioan Marginean; Very Rev. Iuliu-Vasile Muntean; Rev. Sergiu Cornea;
Communications - Raul Botha;
Diocesan Secretary - Ann Fosnaught (annf@rcdcanton.org);
Director of Vocations - Very Rev. Iuliu-Vasile Muntean;
Economos - Very Rev. Ovidiu Ioan Marginean;
Finance Council - Most Rev. John Michael Botean; Very Rev. Iuliu-Vasile Muntean; Very Rev. Ovidiu Ioan Marginean;
Office to Aid the Church in Romania - Very Rev. Michael Moisin, Coord.;
Presbyteral Council - Most Rev. John Michael Botean; Very Rev. Iuliu-Vasile Muntean; Rt. Rev. Archmandrite Nicholas Zachariadis;
Protopresbyters: Deans & Deaneries in US -
Aurora Deanery - Rev. Calin Tamiian;
Canton Deanery - Very Rev. Ovidiu Ioan Marginean;
Trenton Deanery - Very Rev. George David;
Tribunal of the Eparchy -
Judicial Vicar - Rev. Francis J. Marini;
Vicar for Clergy (Vacant) -
Vicar for Theological Affairs - Sr. Theresa Koernke, I.H.M.;
Victim Assistance Coordinator - Ann Fosnaught (annf@rcdcanton.org);
Victim Assistance Resource - Grete Antonia Heatherly;

PARISHES, MISSIONS, AND CLERGY

COMMONWEALTH OF MASSACHUSETTS

ROCKPORT

Romanian Catholic Mission of Boston - 3 Norwood Ave., Rockport, MA 01966 t) 617-216-4980 mmoisin1@aol.com Very Rev. Michael Moisin, Admin.;

COMMONWEALTH OF PENNSYLVANIA

MCKEESPORT

St. Mary - 318 26th St., McKeesport, PA 15132-7014 t) 412-673-5552 dmpandullo@comcast.net Donna Pandullo, Lay coordinator;

STATE OF CALIFORNIA

SHERMAN OAKS

Presentation of Mary Romanian Catholic Church - 5329 Sepulveda Blvd., Sherman Oaks, CA 91411 t) 617-615-2352 fr.adrianrosca@gmail.com Rev. Adrian V. Rosca, Pst.;

TUSTIN

St. John the Baptist Romanian Catholic Mission - 16791 E. Main St., Tustin, CA 92780 c) 805-765-0761 ctamaiian@hotmail.com Very Rev. Calin Tamaiian, Dean;

STATE OF ILLINOIS

AURORA

St. George - 720 Rural St., Aurora, IL 60505 t) 630-851-4002 fpeterson@marmion.org saintgeorgeaurora.org Dcn. Paul Crawford; Dcn. George Dzuricsko; Rev. Frederick Peterson, O.S.B., Pst.;

St. Michael - 609 N. Lincoln Ave., Aurora, IL 60505-2112 c) 330-809-2500 remuso@rcdcanton.org www.stmichaelromanianchurch.org/ Rev. Remus Anghel Orian, Admin.;

CHICAGO

Ss. Peter and Paul Church - 3107 W Fullerton Ave, Chicago, IL 60647-2809; Mailing: 1472 Burr Oak Circle, Aurora, IL 60506 c) 630-205-4806 slcornea@aol.com Rev. Sergiu Cornea, Pst.;

STATE OF INDIANA

EAST CHICAGO

St. Nicholas - Closed Jan 2022

STATE OF MICHIGAN

DEARBORN

St. Mary - 823 S. Military St., Dearborn, MI 48124-2109 t) 313-451-1143 stmdearborn@gmail.com Rev. Cristian Laslo, Admin.;

DETROIT

St. John the Baptist - 2371 Woodstock Dr., Detroit, MI 48203-1060 c) 248-688-6605 constantinhadarag@gmail.com Rev. Constantin Hadarag, Admin.;

STATE OF NEW JERSEY

ROEBLING

St. Mary - 180 Alden Ave., Roebling, NJ 08554-1125; Mailing: 238 Adeline St., Trenton, NJ 08611-2420 t) 609-695-6093 frgeorgedavid46@gmail.com St. Basil, Trenton. Very Rev. George David, Pst.;

TRENTON

St. Basil - 238 Adeline St., Trenton, NJ 08611-2420 t) 609-695-6093 frgeorgedavid46@gmail.com Very Rev. George David, Pst.;

STATE OF NEW YORK

ASTORIA

St. Mary Romanian Catholic Mission - 31-12 30th St., Astoria, NY 11101; Mailing: 11814 83rd Ave., Apt. 2F, Kew Gardens, NY 11415-1309 c) 347-935-5378 rtitonea@gmail.com Rev. Radu Titonea, Admin.;

STATE OF OHIO

ALLIANCE

St. Theodore - 820 Linden Ave., Alliance, OH 44601; Mailing: 1121 44th St NE, Canton, OH 44714 t) 330-493-9355 iulium@rcdcanton.org Under Diocesan Administration. Very Rev. Iuliu-Vasile Muntean, Admin.;

CANTON

St. George Cathedral - 1123 44th St., N.E., Canton, OH 44714-1297 t) 330-492-8413 annf@rcdcanton.org; ovim@rcdcanton.org stgeorgeoh.org Very Rev. Ovidiu Ioan Marginean, Rector; Carol Popa, DRE; Emily Stoffer, DRE; James Dershaw, Music Min.; William Galida, Music Min.; Nancy Maciag, Music Min.;
Bishop's Residence - 1325 Skyway St., N.E., Canton, OH 44721

CHESTERLAND

Most Holy Trinity - 8549 Mayfield Rd., Chesterland, OH 44026-2625 t) 440-729-7636 georgew@rcdcanton.org www.mhtohio.org/ Rev. George Wendt, Pst.;

CLEVELAND

St. Helena - 1367 W. 65th St., Cleveland, OH 44102-2109 t) 216-651-0965 mihaltanu@yahoo.com Rev. Petru Stinea, Pst.; Carmen Stinea, DRE;

INSTITUTIONS LOCATED IN DIOCESE

MONASTERIES AND RESIDENCES FOR PRIESTS AND BROTHERS [MON]

OLYMPIA

Holy Theophany Monastery - 10220 66th Ave., S.E., Olympia, WA 98513-9207 t) 360-491-8233 htheophany@earthlink.net www.holytheophanymonastery.org

ST. NAZIANZ

Holy Resurrection Monastery - 300 S. 2nd Ave., St. Nazianz, WI 54232; Mailing: P.O. Box 276, St. Nazianz, WI 54232 t) 920-881-4009 monks@hrmonline.org www.hrmonline.org Rev. Archmandrite Seoirse (Tomas) Murray, Admin.; Rt. Rev. Archmandrite Nicholas Zachariadis, Abbot; Brs.: 4; Priests: 3

An asterisk (*) denotes an organization that has established tax-exempt status directly with the IRS and is not covered by the USCCB Group Ruling.

Ukrainian Catholic Diocese of St. Josaphat in Parma

MOST REVEREND BOHDAN JOHN DANYLO

Bishop of St. Josaphat in Parma; ordained October 1, 1996; appointed Bishop of St. Josaphat in Parma August 7, 2014; ordained and installed November 4, 2014. Chancery: 5720 State Rd., P.O. Box 347180, Parma, OH 44134-7180.

Chancery: 5720 State Rd., P.O. Box 347180,Parma, OH 44134-7180. T: 440-888-1522; F: 440-888-3477.
info@stjosaphateparchy.com

ESTABLISHED DECEMBER 3, 1983

The jurisdiction of the Bishop of St. Josaphat in Parma extends territorially through all the States of Ohio, Mississippi, West Virginia, Kentucky, Tennessee, Alabama, Georgia, North Carolina, South Carolina, Florida and western Pennsylvania. With regards to persons, his subjects are Catholics of the Byzantine Ukrainian Rite: 1. Who immigrated to this country from Galicia, Bucovina and other Ukrainian provinces; 2. Who descend from such persons (Can. 755); 3. Women married to men referable to 1 and 2, if they comply with (Can. 98, n.4); 4. Who in accordance with (Can. 98, n.3) changed their Rite; 5. Converts to the Catholic Church of the Byzantine Ukrainian Rite; 6. And in fact, all other Catholics of the Byzantine Ukrainian Rite who are attached to p arishes subject to the jurisdiction of the Bishop of St. Josaphat in Parma.

For legal titles of parishes and diocesan institutions, consult the Chancery.

STATISTICAL OVERVIEW

Personnel

Bishop	1
Priests: Diocesan Active in Diocese	30
Priests: Diocesan Active Outside Diocese	4
Priests: Retired, Sick or Absent	16
Number of Diocesan Priests	50
Total Priests in your Diocese	50
Permanent Deacons in Diocese	20
Total Brothers	2
Total Sisters	2

Parishes

Parishes	38
With Resident Pastor:	
Resident Diocesan Priests	26
Without Resident Pastor:	
Administered by Priests	12
Missions	9
Professional Ministry Personnel:	
Brothers	2
Sisters	2
Lay Ministers	1

Welfare

Other Institutions	3
Total Assisted	176

Educational

Catechesis/Religious Education:	
High School Students	142
Elementary Students	322
Total Students under Catholic Instruction	464

Vital Statistics

Receptions into the Church:	
Infant Baptism Totals	98
Adult Baptism Totals	3
Received into Full Communion	11
First Communions	69
Confirmations	101
Marriages:	
Catholic	23
Interfaith	4
Total Marriages	27
Deaths	130
Total Catholic Population	11,110

LEADERSHIP

Chancery - t) 440-888-1522 info@stjosaphateparchy.com Most Rev. Bohdan John Danylo; Yevhen Gulenko;

Chancellor/Financial Officer - Rev. Canon Steven Paliwoda (stevenpaliwoda@yahoo.com);

Vicar General - Very Rev. Archpriest Michael Polosky (sspandpchurch@gmail.com);

Consultors - Rev. Canon Steven Paliwoda (stevenpaliwoda@yahoo.com); Very Rev. Archpriest Michael Polosky (sspandpchurch@gmail.com); Rev. Canon Andrew Hanovsky (ahanowsky@gmail.com);

Eparchial Corporation - Most Rev. Bohdan John Danylo, Pres.; Rev. Canon Steven Paliwoda, Secy. (stevenpaliwoda@yahoo.com); Very Rev. Archpriest Michael Polosky (sspandpchurch@gmail.com);

Administrative Council - Most Rev. Bohdan John Danylo; Rev. Canon Steven Paliwoda (stevenpaliwoda@yahoo.com); Rev. Ihor Kasiyan (pastor@standrewucc.org);

Vicar for Clergy - Very Rev. Archpriest Volodymyr Hrytsyuk (rectorstjosaphat@gmail.com);

Vicar for Religious - Rev. Canon Steven Paliwoda (stevenpaliwoda@yahoo.com);

OFFICES AND DIRECTORS

Acolyte Confraternity - Dcn. Myron Spak; Joseph Levy;

Arbitration Board - Very Rev. Archpriest Volodymyr Hrytsyuk (rectorstjosaphat@gmail.com); Very Rev. Archpriest Andrii Romankiv (aromankiv@yahoo.com);

Child Protection - Rev. Lubomir Zhybak (zhybak@hotmail.com);

Eparchial Convention - Most Rev. Bohdan John Danylo;

Examiner of Clergy - Very Rev. Archpriest Michael Polosky (sspandpchurch@gmail.com);

Family and Sanctity of Life - Bro. Dale Sefcik, B.H.S.; Bro. David Robert, B.H.S.;

Lay Ministries - Sr. Ann Laszok, O.S.B.M.; Sr. Olga Marie Faryna, O.S.B.M.;

League of Ukrainian Catholics - Rev. Gregory Madeya (greggorio2@aol.com);

Liturgical Commission - Most Rev. Bohdan John Danylo; Rev. Ivan Chirovsky; Rev. Joseph Matlak (jmcmatlak@gmail.com);

Permanent Deacon Program - Dcn. Myron Spak; Dcn. Christopher Bellock (cbellock@verizon.net);

Personnel Board - Rev. Ihor Kasiyan (pastor@standrewucc.org); Very Rev. Archpriest Michael Polosky (sspandpchurch@gmail.com); Very Rev. Archpriest Volodymyr Hrytsyuk, Chair (rectorstjosaphat@gmail.com);

Presbyteral Council - Most Rev. Bohdan John Danylo; Rev. Canon Steven Paliwoda (stevenpaliwoda@yahoo.com); Very Rev. Archpriest Michael Polosky (sspandpchurch@gmail.com);

Presbyters - Rt. Rev. Archmandrite George Appleyard (gappleyard@zoominternet.net); Rev. Richard Armstrong (rarmstrong@dioknox.org); Rev. Anthony Balistreri (abalistreri@comcast.net);

Priests' Continuing Education - Most Rev. Bohdan John Danylo;

Protopresbyteries -

- **Central Protopresbytery -** t) 724-266-2262 Very Rev. Archpriest Michael Polosky;
- **Eastern Protopresbytery -** t) 724-266-2262 Very Rev. Archpriest Michael Polosky;
- **Mid-Atlantic Protopresbytery -** t) 919-779-7246 Very Rev. Archpriest Mark Shuey;
- **Southern Protopresbytery -** t) 786-606-6120 Very Rev. Archpriest Andrii Romankiv;
- **Western Protopresbytery -** t) 216-401-0004 Rev. Canon Andrew Hanovsky;

Religious Education - Rev. Kevin Bezner (kevin.bezner@gmail.com);

St. Josaphat Sacerdotal Society - Most Rev. Bohdan John Danylo, Ex Officio; Rev. Canon Steven Paliwoda, Ex Officio (stevenpaliwoda@yahoo.com); Rev. Canon Andrew Hanovsky, Secy. (ahanowsky@gmail.com);

Vocations - Rev. Vsevolod Shevchuk, Dir.;

Youth Ministries - Rev. Lubomir Zhybak (zhybak@hotmail.com);

PARISHES, MISSIONS, AND CLERGY

COMMONWEALTH OF PENNSYLVANIA

ALIQUIPPA

Ss. Peter and Paul - 2001 Main St., Aliquippa, PA 15001 t) 724-266-2262 sspandpchurch@gmail.com Served from St. Peter & Paul, Ambridge. Very Rev. Archpriest Michael Polosky, Pst.; Rev. Canon Philip Bumbar, In Res.;

ALTOONA

Immaculate Conception - 2024 20th St., Altoona, PA 16601 t) 814-378-7688 c) 814-762-9846 thelittlewaybodyandsoul@gmail.com; jpd4448@gmail.com Served by Ramey, Pa. Rev. James Davidson, Admin.;

AMBRIDGE

Ss. Peter and Paul - 404 6th St., Ambridge, PA 15003 t) 724-266-2262 sspandpchurch@gmail.com www.sspeter-paul.com Very Rev. Archpriest Michael Polosky, Pst.; Rev. Canon Walter Wysochansky, In Res.; CRP Stds.: 52

Convent - 542 Melrose Ave., Ambridge, PA 15003 Sisters of St. Basil the Great.

ARNOLD

St. Vladimir - 1601 Kenneth Ave., Arnold, PA 15068 c) 412-770-4915 yaro1973@libero.it Rev. Yaroslav Koval, Pst.;

CARNEGIE

Holy Trinity Ukrainian Catholic Church - 730 Washington Ave., Carnegie, PA 15106 t) 412-279-4652 holytrinitycarnegie@gmail.com www.htucc.com Rev. John Smereka; Rev. Jason Charron, Pst.; Dcn. Myron Spak; CRP Stds.: 12

FORD CITY

Patronage of the Mother of God - 514 Ninth St., Ford City, PA 16226 t) 724-763-1203; 724-763-1948 (Church Hall) jdgribik@windstream.net Rev. John Gribik, Pst.; CRP Stds.: 10

JEANNETTE

St. Demetrius - 1015 Gaskill Ave., Jeannette, PA 15644-3307 c) 412-672-0923 greggorio2@aol.com Rev. Gregory Madeya, Pst.;

JOHNSTOWN

St. John the Baptist - 606 Maple Ave., Johnstown, PA 15901 t) 814-535-2634 c) 814-762-9846 thelittlewaybodyandsoul@gmail.com; jpd4448@gmail.com Rev. James Davidson, Admin.; CRP Stds.: 2

LATROBE

Assumption of the Blessed Virgin Mary - 4827 Rt. 982, Latrobe, PA 15650 c) 724-622-2607 Very Rev. Archpriest Michael Polosky, Admin.;

LYNDORA

St. Michael - 610 Hansen Ave., Lyndora, PA 16045-1325 t) 724-283-0363 (Office); 724-283-6230 (Rectory) stmikeschurch@zoominternet.net Very Rev. Archpriest Douglas Lorance, Pst.;

MCKEES ROCKS

St. John the Baptist - 204 Olivia St., McKees Rocks, PA 15136 t) 412-331-5605 revingvar@yahoo.com Very Rev. Archpriest Ihor Hohosha, Pst.; CRP Stds.: 2

MCKEESPORT

St. John the Baptist - 1907 Eden Park Blvd., McKeesport, PA 15132 c) 412-672-0923 greggorio2@aol.com Rev. Gregory Madeya, Pst.;

NEW ALEXANDRIA

Nativity of the Mother of God - Shersburg Rd., New Alexandria, PA 15670 t) 412-537-6450; 412-770-4915 yaro1973@libero.it Assumption of B.V.M., Latrobe Rev. Yaroslav Koval, Admin.;

NORTHERN CAMBRIA

Immaculate Conception (St. Mary's Ukrainian Catholic Church) - 3711 Campbell Ave., Northern Cambria, PA 15714 t) 814-948-9193 icbvm@yahoo.com Rev. Andriy Kelt, Admin.; CRP Stds.: 2

PITTSBURGH

St. George - 3455 California Ave., Pittsburgh, PA 15212 t) 412-766-8801 saintgeorgepghs@yahoo.com Very Rev. Archpriest Ihor Hohosha, Pst.; CRP Stds.: 9

St. John the Baptist - 109 S. Seventh St., Pittsburgh, PA 15203 t) 412-431-2531 stjohnucc@comcast.net Rev. Yaroslav Koval, Pst.; Irene Borodycia, DRE;

RAMEY

Annunciation of the Mother of God - 22 Bentz St., Ramey, PA 16671; Mailing: P.O. Box 205, Ramey, PA 16671 t) 814-378-7688 c) 814-762-9846 thelittlewaybodyandsoul@gmail.com; jpd4448@gmail.com Rev. James Davidson, Admin.; Anne Janocko, DRE; CRP Stds.: 7

REVLOC

Protection Blessed Virgin Mary - 560 Cambria Ave., Revloc, PA 15948; Mailing: P.O. Box 194, Revloc, PA 15948 t) 814-948-9193 keltandriy@yahoo.com; protectionofthebvm@verizon.net protectionofthebvm.org Dcn. Anthony Dragani; Dcn. Christopher Bellock; Rev. Andriy Kelt, Admin.; CRP Stds.: 6

WEST LEECHBURG

St. Michael - Main St., West Leechburg, PA 15656; Mailing: 514 9th St., Ford City, PA 16226 t) 724-763-1203 jdgribik@windstream.net Ford City, PA Rev. John Gribik, Pst.;

STATE OF FLORIDA

APOPKA

Protection of the Mother of God - 245 Lake McCoy Dr., Apopka, FL 32712 t) 407-927-6586 kuzminskyi.ugcc.if@gmail.com Dcn. Richard Wilhelm; Rev. Roman Kuzminskyi, Admin.; CRP Stds.: 15

BROOKSVILLE

St. Andrew - 8064 Weeping Willow St., Brooksville, FL 34613 t) 352-596-2433 zenonkouts@gmail.com Rev. Michael Kouts, Pst.;

MIAMI

Assumption of the Blessed Virgin Mary - 39 NW 57 Ct., Miami, FL 33126; Mailing: 11000 SW 128th St., Miami, FL 33176 t) 786-592-1563 ukrainianmiami@gmail.com ukrainianmiami.org/uk/ Very Rev. Archpriest Andrii Romankiv, Pst.;

NORTH PORT

Presentation of the Most Holy Mother of God (St. Mary's) - 1078 N. Biscayne Dr., North Port, FL 34291 t) 941-426-7931 kasiyand93@yahoo.com Rev. Dmytro Kasiyan, Pst.; CRP Stds.: 7

ST. PETERSBURG

Epiphany of Our Lord - 434 90th Ave. N., St. Petersburg, FL 33702 t) 727-576-1001 bbarytskyy@gmail.com www.epiphanyukrch.com/ Rev. Bohdan Barytskyy, Admin.;

STATE OF GEORGIA

CONYERS

Protection of the Mother of God - 2880 Hwy. 138, N.E., Conyers, GA 30013 t) 770-760-1111 parish@mogchurch.com motherofgodatlanta.com Rev. Volodymyr Petrytsya, Admin.;

MARTINEZ

St. John the Theologian Ukrainian Catholic Mission - 634 Furys Ferry Rd., Martinez, GA 30907 t) (919) 349-8704 rfmark@nc.rr.com Very Rev. Archpriest Mark Shuey, Admin.; CRP Stds.: 2

STATE OF NORTH CAROLINA

CARY

St. Nicholas Mission - Merged Sep 2022 Merged with SS. Volodymyr and Olha Mission, Garner to form St. Sophia Ukrainian Catholic Church.

CHARLOTTE

St. Basil the Great - 1400 Suther Rd., Charlotte, NC 28213 t) (980) 785-2764 stbasilcharlotte@gmail.com stbasil.weebly.com Dcn. Matthew Hanes; Rev. Joseph Matlak, Admin.; CRP Stds.: 12

St. John the Baptist Mission - 7702 Pineville Matthews Rd., Charlotte, NC 28226; Mailing: 8455 Sunnydale Dr, Brecksville, OH 44141-1516 c) 440-503-9685 michael1kulick@gmail.com Rev. Michael Kulick, Admin.; CRP Stds.: 12

GARNER

St. Sophia Ukrainian Catholic Church - 8312 White Oak Rd., Garner, NC 27529 t) (919) 376-8099 mail.stsophiaugcc@gmail.com stsophiaugcc.com Very Rev. Archpriest Mark Shuey, Admin.;

St. Nicholas Mission - 2510 Piney Plains Rd., Cary, NC 27518 t) (919) 779-7246 rfmark@nc.rr.com www.saintnicholasraleigh.org

SS. Volodymyr and Olha Mission - Merged Sep 2022 Merged with St. Nicholas Mission, Cary to form St. Sophia Ukrainian Catholic Church.

STATE OF OHIO

AKRON

Holy Ghost - 1859 Carter Ave., Akron, OH 44301 t) 330-724-8277 pastor@hgucc.org www.hgucc.org Very Rev. Archpriest Vsevolod Shevchuk, Admin.; Maria Griffiths, DRE; CRP Stds.: 8

AUSTINTOWN

St. Anne - 4310 Kirk Rd., Austintown, OH 44511 t) 330-744-5820 yngholytrinity@att.net www.stanneucc.com Rev. Lubomir Zhybak, Admin.;

CLEVELAND

Ss. Peter and Paul - 2280 W. 7th St., Cleveland, OH 44113 t) 216-861-2176 c) 216-401-0004 motherchurch2008@gmail.com Rev. Canon Andrew Hanovsky, Pst.;

LORAIN

St. John the Baptist - 3038 Charleston Ave., Lorain, OH 44055-2164 t) 440-277-7114 stevenpaliwoda@yahoo.com Rev. Canon Steven Paliwoda, Pst.; CRP Stds.: 2

PARMA

St. Josaphat Cathedral - 5720 State Rd., Parma, OH 44134-2536 t) 440-886-2108 rectorstjosaphat@gmail.com; officestjosaphat@gmail.com www.stjosaphatcathedral.com Archdeacon Jeffrey Smolilo; Very Rev. Archpriest Volodymyr Hrytsyuk, Rector; Rev. Sviatoslav Ditchuk, Par. Vicar; CRP Stds.: 12

St. Andrew - 7700 Hoertz Rd., Parma, OH 44134-6404 t) 440-843-9149 pastor@standrewucc.org www.standrewucc.org Rev. Ihor Kasiyan, Pst.; Wira Gernaga, DRE; CRP Stds.: 15

Pokrova Ukrainian Catholic Parish - 6812 Broadview Rd., Parma, OH 44134 t) 216-524-0918 mykhaylodrozdovsky@gmail.com pokrova-church.com Rev. Mykhaylo Drozdovsky, Pst.; CRP Stds.: 60

ROSSFORD

St. Michael - 135 Walnut St., Rossford, OH 43460-1248; Mailing: 133 Walnut St., Rossford, OH 43460-1248 t) 419-666-3770 Dcn. Trevor Fernandes; Rev. Canon Steven Paliwoda, Admin.;

SOLON

Protection of the Blessed Virgin Mary - 27275 Aurora Rd., Solon, OH 44139-1804 t) 330-689-9072 pastor@hgucc.org Rev. Vsevolod Shevchuk, Admin.;

YOUNGSTOWN

Holy Trinity - 526 W. Rayen Ave., Youngstown, OH 44502-1124 t) 330-744-5820 (Office/Rectory); 330-746-9528 (Social Hall) yngholytrinity@att.net www.holytrinityucc.com Rev. Lubomir Zhybak, Admin.; Protodeacon Donald Billy;

STATE OF SOUTH CAROLINA

BLYTHEWOOD

Holy Cross Mission - 306 N. Pines Rd., Blythewood, SC 29016; Mailing: 1400 Suther Rd., Charlotte, NC 28213 t) (980) 785-2764 colabyzantinecatholic@gmail.com colabyzcatholic.weebly.com Rev. Joseph Matlak, Admin.;

GREER

Dormition of the Mother of God Mission - 1215 SC-14, Greer, SC 29650; Mailing: 1400 Suther Rd., Charlotte, NC 28213 t) 980-785-2764 dormitiongreenville@gmail.com dormition.weebly.com Rev. Joseph Matlak, Admin.;

STATE OF TENNESSEE

KNOXVILLE

St. Thomas the Apostle Mission - 2304 Ault Rd., Knoxville, TN 37914 t) 865-621-8499 rfmark@nc.rr.com Rev. Kevin Bezner, Admin.;

NASHVILLE

St. Nicholas Mission - 1219 Second Ave. S., Nashville, TN 37210 c) (704) 907-3875 rarmstrong@dioknox.org Rev. Kevin Bezner, Admin.;

STATE OF WEST VIRGINIA

WHEELING

Our Lady of Perpetual Help - 4136 Jacob St., Wheeling, WV 26003 t) 304-232-2168 holytrinitycarnegie@gmail.com Served by Holy Trinity, Carnegie. Rev. Jason Charron, Pst.;

INSTITUTIONS LOCATED IN DIOCESE

CONVENTS, MONASTERIES, AND RESIDENCES FOR WOMEN [CON]

AMBRIDGE

Ss. Peter & Paul Convent - 542 Melrose Ave., Ambridge, PA 15003 t) 724-266-5578 Sisters of St. Basil the Great. Most Rev. Bohdan John Danylo, Contact; Srs.: 2

MONASTERIES AND RESIDENCES FOR PRIESTS AND BROTHERS [MON]

BROOKLYN

Holy Spirit Monastery - 4150 Rabbit Run, Brooklyn, OH 44144 t) 216-741-3653 brotherdalebhs@gmail.com Bro. David Robert, B.H.S.; Bro. Dale Sefcik, B.H.S.; Brs.: 2

NURSING / REHABILITATION / CONVALESCENCE / ELDERLY CARE [NUR]

PARMA

Shevchenko Manor - 5620 W. 24th St., Parma, OH 44134-2751 t) 216-459-1440 j.joycejr@retireehousing.com Asstd. Annu.: 82; Staff: 3

PITTSBURGH

St. George's Close - 3505 Mexico St. at Chidel St., Pittsburgh, PA 15212 t) 412-766-8802 j.joycejr@retireehousing.com Asstd. Annu.: 39; Staff: 3

Sheptytsky Arms - 3503 Mexico St., Pittsburgh, PA 15212 t) 412-766-8802 j.joycejr@retireehousing.com Asstd. Annu.: 54; Staff: 3

Eparchy of St. Maron of Brooklyn

MOST REVEREND GREGORY J. MANSOUR

Bishop of Saint Maron of Brooklyn; ordained September 18, 1982; appointed Bishop of Saint Maron of Brooklyn January 10, 2004; consecrated March 2, 2004; installed April 27, 2004. Chancery: 109 Remsen St., Brooklyn, NY 11201.

Chancery Office: 109 Remsen St., Brooklyn, NY 11201. T: 718-237-9913; F: 718-243-0444.
chancerystmaron@verizon.net
www.stmaron.org

Established as an Apostolic Exarchate January 10, 1966; Elevated to a Diocese November 11, 1971.

The jurisdiction of the Diocese extends to all the Maronite Catholics in New York, New Jersey, Pennsylvania, Florida, Georgia, North Carolina, South Carolina, Delaware, Virginia, District of Columbia, Maine, New Hampshire, Vermont, Massachusetts, Rhode Island, Connecticut and Maryland.

For legal titles of parishes and diocesan institutions, consult the Chancery Office.

STATISTICAL OVERVIEW

Personnel
Bishop....1
Abbots....1
Priests: Diocesan Active in Diocese....37
Priests: Retired, Sick or Absent....18
Number of Diocesan Priests....55
Religious Priests in Diocese....14
Total Priests in your Diocese....69
Extern Priests in Diocese....13
Ordinations:
Diocesan Priests....2
Permanent Deacons....2
Permanent Deacons in Diocese....24
Total Brothers....8
Total Sisters....3

Parishes
Parishes....41
With Resident Pastor:
Resident Diocesan Priests....39
Resident Religious Priests....2
Missions....4

Welfare
Day Care Centers....1
Total Assisted....54

Educational
Seminaries, Diocesan....1
Students from This Diocese....4
Students from Other Dioceses....4
Total Seminarians....4
Catechesis/Religious Education:
High School Students....437
Elementary Students....1,032
Total Students under Catholic Instruction....1,473

Vital Statistics
Receptions into the Church:
Infant Baptism Totals....428
Minor Baptism Totals....18
Adult Baptism Totals....15
Received into Full Communion....17
First Communions....327
Confirmations....503
Marriages:
Catholic....115
Interfaith....28
Total Marriages....143
Deaths....244
Total Catholic Population....26,378

LEADERSHIP

The Chancery - t) 718-237-9913 chancerystmaron@verizon.net

Protosyncellus (Vicar General) - Chorbishop Michael G. Thomas (chancerystmaron@verizon.net);

Chancellor - Chorbishop Michael G. Thomas (chancerystmaron@verizon.net);

Tribunal of the Eparchy of Saint Maron of Brooklyn - t) 570-207-2246 maronitetribunal@aol.com

Tribunal - t) (570) 207-2246 x1065

Advocates - Rev. Msgr. Nevin J. Klinger; Rev. Msgr. Joseph G. Quinn; Rev. Tanios Kozhaya Akoury;

Defenders of the Bond - Rev. Anthony J. Generose; Rev. James J. Walsh;

Judges - Chorbishop Michael G. Thomas; Chorbishop John D. Faris; Rev. Msgr. Francis J. Marini;

Judicial Vicar - t) 570-207-2246 x1065 maronitetribunal@aol.com Rev. Msgr. Francis J. Marini;

Notary - Judith Myerski;

Promoter of Justice - Rev. William J. King;

OFFICES AND DIRECTORS

Archivist - chancerystmaron@verizon.net Rev. Michael Barone, Archivist;

Board of Pastors - Rev. Tony Akoury; Rev. Msgr. James A. Root; Rev. Bassam M. Saade;

Child and Youth Protection Coordinator - t) 917-825-3777 vivakchildprotection@gmail.com Vivian Akel;

College of Consultors - Rev. Msgr. Peter Fahed Azar; Rev. Dominique Hanna (cathrectory@verizon.net); Rev. Msgr. James A. Root;

Family and Sanctity of Life - familyandsanctityoflife777@gmail.com Linda George;

Finance Council - Chorbishop Michael G. Thomas (chancerystmaron@verizon.net); Tony Richa, CFO; Edward Massoud;

General Counsel - c) (202) 230-4316 jlschlageter@gmail.com John Schlageter, General Counsel;

Immigration Office - Chorbishop Michael G. Thomas (chancerystmaron@verizon.net);

Lebanon Commission - Chorbishop Seely Beggiani, Chair (seebeggiani@comcast.net);

Ministries (Permanent Deacons and Subdeacons) - t) 508-817-6121 Rev. Jack Morrison (aboonajack@aol.com);

National Apostolate of Maronites National Office - t) (914) 964-3070 Rose Sahyoun, Dir.;

Presbyteral Council - Rev. Msgr. James A. Root, Ex Officio; Rev. Msgr. George M. Sebaali, Ex Officio; Rev. Tony Akoury, Ex Officio;

Priests' Ministry - maroniteseminary@comcast.net Rev. Msgr. Peter Fahed Azar, Dir.;

Protopresbyters (Deans) - Rev. Msgr. James A. Root, New England Region; Rev. Claude W. Franklin Jr., Mid-Atlantic West Region; Rev. Dominique Hanna, Mid-Atlantic East Region (cathrectory@verizon.net);

Religious Education - t) 617-522-0225 pastor@ourladyofthecedars.org Rev. Msgr. Georges Y. El-Khalli, Diocesan D.R.E.; Sr. Marla Lucas, Asst. Diocesan D.R.E.;

Stewardship - t) (718) 237-9913 johnkurey@yahoo.com John Kurey, Dir.;

Victim Assistance Coordinator - t) 617-327-1317 Rosanne Solomon (rosannesolomon@hotmail.com);

Vocations - t) 718-624-7228 Rev. Dominique Hanna (cathrectory@verizon.net);

Young Adult Ministry - t) 508-965-6945 Sr. Therese Maria Touma (srtherese2010@gmail.com);

Youth Ministry Office - t) (315) 732-6018 saintlouisgonzaga@gmail.com Rev. Boutros El Hachem, Dir.;

PARISHES, MISSIONS, AND CLERGY

COMMONWEALTH OF MASSACHUSETTS

BROCKTON

St. Theresa - 343 N Main St, Brockton, MA 02301; Mailing: PO Box 2567, Brockton, MA 02305-2567 t) 508-586-1428 rectory@sttheresabrockton.org; rectory@sttheresabrockton.org www.sttheresabrockton.org Rev. Joseph Abisaad, Admin.; Subdeacon Alexander McKinnon, DRE; CRP Stds.: 14

FALL RIVER

St. Anthony of the Desert - 300 N. Eastern Ave., Fall River, MA 02723 t) 508-672-7653 saotd@verizon.net sao.church/ Rev. Msgr. James A. Root, Pst.; Dcn. Brian Dunn; Dcn. Donald P. Massoud; Dcn. Andre Nasser; Samia Yamin-Brownell, DRE; CRP Stds.: 32

JAMAICA PLAIN

Our Lady of the Cedars of Lebanon Maronite Catholic Church - 61 Rockwood St., Jamaica Plain, MA 02130 t) 617-522-0225; 617-522-0025 pastor@ourldayofthecedars.org; pastor@ourladyofthecedars.org www.ourladyofhecedars.org Rev. Msgr. Georges Y. El-Khalli, Pst.; Randa Yazbeck, DRE; CRP Stds.: 42

LAWRENCE

Saint Anthony Maronite Catholic Church, Inc. - 145 Amesbury St., Lawrence, MA 01841 t) 978-685-7233 rectory@stanthonylawrence.org; ccd@stanthonylawrence.org www.stanthonylawrence.org Rev. Edgard (Neemtallah) Oneissy; Rev. Elie Mikhael, Pst.; Dcn. Nadim Daou; Dcn. James Demers; Dcn. David Leard; Subdeacon Antoine Nammour; Susan Veilleux, DRE; CRP Stds.: 120

NEW BEDFORD

Our Lady of Purgatory - 11 Franklin St., New Bedford, MA 02740 t) 508-996-8934 ourladyofpurgatory@gmail.com www.ourladyofpurgatory.org Rev. Vincent Farhat, Pst.; Dcn. Jean E. Mattar, DRE; CRP Stds.: 12

SPRINGFIELD

St. Anthony - 375 Island Pond Rd., Springfield, MA 01118-1002; Mailing: 419 Island Pond Rd., Springfield, MA 01118-1002 t) 413-732-0589 stanthony419@comcast.net www.saintanthonyschurch.org Rev. Bassam M. Saade, Pst.; Dcn. Enzo DiGiacomo; Dcn. Norman Hannoush; CRP Stds.: 10

WORCESTER

Our Lady of Mercy - 341 June St., Worcester, MA 01602-2845 t) 508-752-4287 ourladymercymaroniteworcester@gmail.com www.ourladyofmercymaronite.org Rev. Alexander Joseph, Pst.; Tarek E. Zoghby, DRE; CRP Stds.: 7

COMMONWEALTH OF PENNSYLVANIA

ALLENTOWN

Saints Joachim and Anne Maronite Catholic Church, Inc. - 1065 Fullerton Ave., Allentown, PA 18102 t) (845) 689-4468 georgearrouk@hotmail.com Rev. Georges Arrouk, Admin.; CRP Stds.: 12

BADEN

Saint Teresa of Calcutta Maronite Mission - 375 Linmore Ave., Baden, PA 15005 t) 724-732-4064 stteresamaronite@gmail.com www.stteresamaronite.org Rev. Antoine Kairouz, Admin.; Subdeacon Vincent Michael, DRE; CRP Stds.: 8

EASTON

Our Lady of Lebanon - 55 S. Fourth St., Easton, PA 18042; Mailing: 54 S. 4th St., Easton, PA 18042 t) 610-252-5275 ololchurch@yahoo.com www.ololeaston.org Dcn. Anthony P. Koury; Rev. Youssef Keikati, Admin.; Sr. Lilia Domingo, DRE; CRP Stds.: 4

NEW CASTLE

St. John the Baptist - 2 W. Reynolds St., New Castle, PA 16101 t) 724-658-0787 stjohnmaronite@hotmail.com www.stjohnmaronite.org Rev. Hanna Karam, Pst.; Dcn. Richard E. Stone; Lori Doran, DRE; Subdeacon Andrew Demko; CRP Stds.: 15

NEWTOWN SQUARE

Saint Sharbel Maronite Catholic Church - 3679 Providence Rd., Newtown Square, PA 19073-3006 t) 610-353-5952 pastor@stsharbelpa.org www.stsharbelpa.org Rev. Joseph Daiif, Admin.; CRP Stds.: 25

PHILADELPHIA

St. Maron - 1013 Ellsworth St., Philadelphia, PA 19147 t) 215-389-2000 saintmaronphiladelphia@hotmail.com www.saintmaron.org Rev. Fadi (Andrawos) El Tabchi, Pst.; Janah Szewczyk, DRE; CRP Stds.: 35

PITTSBURGH

Our Lady of Victory - 1000 Tropical Ave., Pittsburgh, PA 15216 t) 412-278-0841 office@olovpittsburgh.org www.olovpittsburgh.org Rev. Samir Chebli, Pst.; Lori Evans, DRE; Dcn. Bahige Alchoufete; CRP Stds.: 28

SCRANTON

St. Ann - 1320 Price St., Scranton, PA 18504-3336 t) 570-344-2129 www.saintannmaronite.com Rev. Antoun Youssef, Admin.; Jennifer Cawley Iorio, DRE; Subdeacon Said J. Douaihy; Subdeacon Robert Rade; CRP Stds.: 7

UNIONTOWN

St. George - 6 Lebanon Ter., Uniontown, PA 15401-3011 t) 724-437-5589 info@stgeorgeuniontown.org www.stgeorgeuniontown.org Rev. Aaron J. Sandbothe, Pst.; Subdeacon Thomas R. George; Subdeacon Mallard George; Subdeacon Charles D. Machesky; Subdeacon Charles Maronite Michael; CRP Stds.: 25

WILKES-BARRE

St. Anthony & St. George - 323 Park Ave., Wilkes-Barre, PA 18702 t) 570-824-3599 stanthonystgeorge@gmail.com www.stanthonystgeorge.org Rev. Adib Salameh, Pst.; CRP Stds.: 22

COMMONWEALTH OF VIRGINIA

GLEN ALLEN

Saint Anthony Maronite Catholic Church - 4611 Sadler Rd., Glen Allen, VA 23060 t) 804-270-7234 stanthonymaronitechurch@gmail.com www.stanthonymaronitechurch.org Chorbishop John D. Faris, Pst.; Rev. Butros (Peter) Frangie, Par. Vicar; Subdeacon Michael Maynes; Subdeacon Tony Y. Saad; Catherine George, Pst. Min./Coord.; Amanda S. Walton, DRE; CRP Stds.: 135

ROANOKE

St. Elias - 4730 Cove Rd., N.W., Roanoke, VA 24017 t) 540-562-0012 secretary@steliaschurch.org; fr@steliaschurch.org www.steliaschurch.org Rev. George Zina, Pst.; CRP Stds.: 30

DISTRICT OF COLUMBIA

WASHINGTON

Our Lady of Lebanon Maronite Church - 7142 Alaska Ave., N.W., Washington, DC 20012; Mailing: 7237 15th Place NW, Washington, DC 20012 t) 202-291-5153 www.ololdc.org Rev. Msgr. George M. Sebaali, Pst.; Dcn. Michel Touma; CRP Stds.: 45

STATE OF CONNECTICUT

DANBURY

St. Anthony - 17 Granville Ave., Danbury, CT 06810 t) 203-744-3372 parish@stanthonydanbury.com www.stanthonydanbury.com Rev. Naji Kiwan, Pst.; Debbie Urban, DRE; Subdeacon George Jabbour; Subdeacon Randall Michael; CRP Stds.: 27

TORRINGTON

St. Maron Maronite Catholic Church - 613 Main St., Torrington, CT 06790 t) 860-489-9015 stmaronchurchtorrinton@gmail.com www.stmaronchurch.org Dcn. Steven Marcus; CRP Stds.: 5

WATERBURY

Our Lady of Lebanon - 8 E. Mountain Rd., Waterbury, CT 06706 t) 203-753-6633 ourladywaterbury@gmail.com Rev. Joseph Khoueiry, Pst.; Dcn. Camille Atallah; CRP Stds.: 7

STATE OF FLORIDA

FORT LAUDERDALE

Heart of Jesus Catholic Church - 1800 N.E. 6th Ct., Fort Lauderdale, FL 33304 t) 954-522-3939 heartofjesusfll@gmail.com www.heartofjesus.org Chorbishop Michael G. Thomas, Pst.; Dcn. John Jarvis; CRP Stds.: 30

JACKSONVILLE

St. Maron Maronite - 7032 Bowden Rd., Jacksonville, FL 32216 t) 904-448-0203 stmaronjax@comcast.net www.stmaronjax.com Rev. Raymond Khallouf, Pst.; Dcn. Elias Shami; Christine El Hajj, DRE; CRP Stds.: 35

MIAMI

Our Lady of Lebanon - 2055 Coral Way, Miami, FL 33145 t) 305-856-7449 www.ololmiami.org Rev. Manuel Bassam Rahmeh, Pst.; Rev. Michael Marie Charchaflian, Vicar; Subdeacon Joseph Lahoud; CRP Stds.: 55

ORLANDO

St. Jude - 5555 Dr. Phillips Blvd., Orlando, FL 32819 t) 407-363-7405 www.saintjudechurch.org Rev. Elie Abi Chedid, Pst.; CRP Stds.: 50

TAMPA

Mission of Sts. Peter & Paul - 6201 Sheldon Rd., Tampa, FL 33615 t) (508) 542-3243 peterpaultampa@gmail.com www.peterpaultampa.com Rev. Fadi Rouhana, Admin.; Christine Rathgeber, DRE; CRP Stds.: 50

TEQUESTA

Mary Mother of the Light Maronite Catholic Church - 46 Willow Rd., Tequesta, FL 33469 t) 561-427-1331 mmolchurch@gmail.com www.marymotherofthelight.com/ Maronite Catholic Parish & Pre-School Rev. Gary George, Admin.; Michelle Azzi, DRE; Subdeacon Dennis Somerville; Subdeacon Elias Azzi; CRP Stds.: 22

STATE OF GEORGIA

SANDY SPRINGS

St. Joseph's Maronite Church - 6025 Glenridge Dr., Sandy Springs, GA 30328 t) 404-525-2504 sjmcc@sjmcc.org; info@sjmcc.org www.sjmcc.org Rev. Tony Akoury, Pst.; Subdeacon David Nasser; Dcn. Robert Calabrese; Ghada Osta, DRE; CRP Stds.: 20

STATE OF MAINE

WATERVILLE

St. Joseph - 3 Appleton St., Waterville, ME 04901 t) 207-872-8515 stjoesinmaine@yahoo.com www.sjmaronite.org Rev. James Doran, Pst.; Subdeacon Stephen Crate, DRE; CRP Stds.: 9

STATE OF NEW HAMPSHIRE

DOVER

St. George - 15 Chapel St., Dover, NH 03820-2210; Mailing: P.O. Box 2210, Dover, NH 03821-2210 t) 603-740-4287 stgeorgedover@outlook.com www.stgeorgemaronite.org Rev. Jebrael Moussallem, Admin.; CRP Stds.: 1

STATE OF NEW JERSEY

PLEASANTVILLE

Our Lady Star of the East - 25 W. Black Horse Pike, Pleasantville, NJ 08232 t) 609-241-8109 olsechurch@gmail.com www.olsechurch.org Rev. Kamil Alchouefati, Pst.; Subdeacon Fahid Nammour; CRP Stds.: 42

SOMERSET

Saint Sharbel Maronite Catholic Church - 7 Reeve St., Somerset, NJ 08873 t) 732-828-2055 yamarsharbel@gmail.com www.saintsharbelnj.org Rev. Simon El-hajj, Pst.; Dcn. Joseph Chebli; Christine Zeinoun, DRE; CRP Stds.: 79

STATE OF NEW YORK

BROOKLYN

Cathedral of Our Lady of Lebanon - 113 Remsen St., Brooklyn, NY 11201 t) 718-624-7228 cathrectory@verizon.net ololc.org Rev. Dominique Hanna, Rector; Norma Haddad, DRE; Subdeacon Adonis El-Asmar; Subdeacon Norbert Vogl; CRP Stds.: 55

OLEAN

St. Joseph Maronite Catholic Church - 1102 Walnut St., Olean, NY 14760 t) 716-379-8436 x10; 716-379-8436 (CRP) office@stjosepholean.com www.stjosepholean.org Rev. Claude W. Franklin Jr., Pst.; CRP Stds.: 5

SLEEPY HOLLOW

Saint John Paul II - 199 N. Broadway, Sleepy Hollow, NY 10591 t) 914-631-0446 jpiimc.ny@gmail.com www.johnpaul2parish.org Rev. Dany Abi-Akar, Pst.; Subdeacon Bchara Sherfan; CRP Stds.: 32

UTICA

St. Louis Gonzaga - 520 Rutger St., Utica, NY 13501 t) 315-732-6019 saintlouisgonzaga@gmail.com www.saintlouisgonzaga.org Rev. Boutros El Hachem, Pst.; Dcn. Peter M. Hobaica; Dcn. Paul A. Salamy; CRP Stds.: 23

WATERVLIET

St. Ann - 1919 3rd Ave., Watervliet, NY 12189 t) 518-272-6073 stannmaronitechurch@gmail.com www.stann1905.com Rev. Alaa Issa, Pst.; Dcn. Richard Thornton; CRP Stds.: 13

WILLIAMSVILLE

St. John Maron - 2040 Wehrle Dr., Williamsville, NY 14221-7041 t) 716-634-0669 stjmaron@gmail.com www.stjohnmaron.org Rev. Elie G. Kairouz, Pst.; Deborah Tartick, DRE; Rev. Elias Khalil Adwan, Assoc. Pst.; CRP Stds.: 61

STATE OF NORTH CAROLINA

FAYETTEVILLE

St. Michael the Archangel - 806 Arsenal Ave., Fayetteville, NC 28305 t) 910-484-1531 stmikemcc@embarqmail.com www.stmichaelsmaronite.net Rev. Paul Damien, Pst.; CRP Stds.: 40

RALEIGH

Saint Sharbel Maronite Catholic Church - 600 Mt. Vernon Church Rd., Raleigh, NC 27614 t) 919-917-7597 c) 202-531-7441 abouna@saintsharbelchurch.org www.saintsharbelchurch.org Rev. Robert Farah, Admin.; Maribel Rizk, DRE; Subdeacon Claude Shiver Jr.; CRP Stds.: 30

WAXHAW

Saint Stephen Maronite Catholic Church - 4116 Waxhaw-Marvin Rd, Waxhaw, NC 28173; Mailing: P.O. Box 49021, Charlotte, NC 28277 t) 704-412-1016 c) 412-853-8494 saintstephenmaronitechurch@gmail.com www.ststephenmaronite.org Rev. Rodolph Wakim, Admin.;

STATE OF RHODE ISLAND

CRANSTON

St. George - 1493 Cranston St., Cranston, RI 02920 t) 401-723-8444 stgeorgeri1@gmail.com www.stgeorgeri.com Rev. Antoine Saab, Pst.; Janelle Khoury, DRE; Dcn. Farid Zaarour; CRP Stds.: 12

STATE OF SOUTH CAROLINA

GREER

St. Rafka Maronite Mission - 1215 S. Hwy. 14, Greer, SC 29650 t) 864-469-9119 saintrafkagreenville@gmail.com; secretary@saintrafka.org www.saintrafka.org Rev. Toni Gerges Jabbour, OMM (Lebanon), Par. Vicar; Rev. Bartholomew Leon, Admin.; CRP Stds.: 6

INSTITUTIONS LOCATED IN DIOCESE

CONVENTS, MONASTERIES, AND RESIDENCES FOR WOMEN [CON]

DARTMOUTH

Servants of Christ the Light - 856 Tucker Rd., Dartmouth, MA 02747-3531 t) 508-996-1753 sister@maroniteservants.org www.maroniteservants.org Sr. Marla Lucas, Supr.; Srs.: 3

ENDOWMENTS / FOUNDATIONS / TRUSTS [EFT]

BROOKLYN

Bishops Retirement Trust Fund - 109 Remsen St., Brooklyn, NY 11201 t) 718-237-9913 chancerystmaron@verizon.net Chorbishop Michael G. Thomas, Chancellor;

Disability Fund Trust - 109 Remsen St., Brooklyn, NY 11201 t) 718-237-9913 Chorbishop Michael G. Thomas, Chancellor;

Endowment Fund Trust - 109 Remsen St., Brooklyn, NY 11201 t) 718-237-9913 Chorbishop Michael G. Thomas, Chancellor;

Order of St. Sharbel Trust Fund - 109 Remsen St., Brooklyn, NY 11201 t) (718) 237-9913 chancerystmaron@verizon.net James Abdo, Pres.; Charlene Hiffa, Vice. Pres.;

Priest Retirement Trust Fund - 109 Remsen St., Brooklyn, NY 11201 t) 718-237-9913 chancerystmaron@verizon.net Chorbishop Michael G. Thomas, Chancellor;

Seminary Endowment Trust - 109 Remsen St., Brooklyn, NY 11201 t) 718-237-9913 Chorbishop Michael G. Thomas, Chancellor;

SOMERSET

Saint Sharbel Maronite Catholic Church Endowment Trust - 7 Reeve St., Somerset, NJ 08873 t) (732) 828-2055 yamarsharbel@gmail.com Rev. Simon Elhajj, Trustee;

GLEN ALLEN

Saint Anthony Maronite Scholarship Endowed Trust Agreement - 4611 Sadler Rd., Glen Allen, VA 23060 t) (804) 270-7234 saintanthonymaronitechurch@gmail.com Chorbishop John D. Faris, Trustee;

Saint Maron Publications - 4611 Sadler Rd., Glen Allen, VA 23060 t) (804) 346-1160 stmaronpublications@gmail.com Chorbishop John D. Faris, Dir.;

MISCELLANEOUS [MIS]

BROOKLYN

Tele Lumiere and Noursat USA - 109 Remsen St., Brooklyn, NY 11201 t) 718-237-9913 chancerystmaron@verizon.net Chorbishop Michael G. Thomas, Chancellor;

CANFIELD

National Apostolate of Maronites - 2110 Redwood Pl., Canfield, OH 44406 t) (914) 964-3070 info@namnews.org Rose Sahyoun, Exec. Dir.;

MONASTERIES AND RESIDENCES FOR PRIESTS AND BROTHERS [MON]

BROOKLYN

Bishop's Residence - 8070 Harbor View Ter., Brooklyn, NY 11209 t) 718-237-9913 chancerystmaron@verizon.net Chorbishop Michael G. Thomas, Chancellor;

PETERSHAM

Maronite Monks of Adoration - Most Holy Trinity Monastery - 67 Dugway Rd., Petersham, MA 01366-9725 t) 978-724-3347 mhtmcontact@maronitemonks.org www.maronitemonks.org Rt. Rev. Patrick Kokorian,

M.M.A., Abbot; Rev. Maron Henricks, M.M.A., Prior; Rev. Giles R. Goyette, M.M.A., Priest; Bro. Ephrem Martin, M.M.A., Subdeacon; Rev. Michael Gilmary Cermak, M.M.A., Vocations Director; Rev. Louis Marie Dauphinais, M.M.A., Priest; Rev. Elias Havel, M.M.A., Priest; Rev. Robert Nortz, M.M.A., Treas.; Rev. Ignatius Dec, M.M.A., Priest; Bro. John Baptist Livingston, M.M.A., Subdeacon; Bro. Bernard Choupin, M.M.A., Brother; Bro. Paul Hoover, M.M.A., Brother; Rev. Bernardo Vargas-Castro, M.M.A., Priest; Rev. Raphael Maria Magee, M.M.A., Priest; Bro. Matthew Zaloum, M.M.A., Brother; Bro. Solanus Joseph Rodriguez, M.M.A., Brother; Bro. Felix Maria Taylor, M.M.A., Brother; Bro. Theophilus O'Connell, M.M.A., Brother; Brs.: 8; Priests: 10

SEMINARIES [SEM]

WASHINGTON

Our Lady of Lebanon Maronite Seminary - 7164 Alaska Ave., N.W., Washington, DC 20012 t) 202-723-8831 maroniteseminary@comcast.net www.maroniteseminary.org Rev. Msgr. Peter Fahed Azar, Rector; Rev. Armando Elkhourey, Vice Rector; Stds.: 9; Pr. Tchrs.: 2

An asterisk (*) denotes an organization that has established tax-exempt status directly with the IRS and is not covered by the USCCB Group Ruling.

St. Nicholas Diocese in Chicago for Ukrainians

MOST REVEREND BENEDICT ALEKSIYCHUK, M.S.U.

Bishop of St. Nicholas in Chicago; ordained March 29, 1992; appointed Bishop of St. Nicholas of Chicago April 20, 2017; installed June 29, 2017. Office: 2245 W. Rice St., Chicago, IL 60622.

Chancery Office: 2245 W. Rice St., IL 60622. T: 773-276-5080; F: 773-276-6799
info@esnucc.org
chicagougcc.org

Comprises all of the United States west of the western borders of Ohio, Kentucky, Tennessee and Mississippi.

For legal titles of parishes and diocesan institutions, consult the Chancery Office.

STATISTICAL OVERVIEW

Personnel

Bishop	1
Abbots	2
Priests: Diocesan Active in Diocese	51
Priests: Diocesan Active Outside Diocese	1
Priests: Retired, Sick or Absent	9
Number of Diocesan Priests	61
Total Priests in your Diocese	61
Extern Priests in Diocese	8
Permanent Deacons in Diocese	12
Total Brothers	10
Total Sisters	5

Parishes

Parishes	41
With Resident Pastor:	
Resident Diocesan Priests	37
Without Resident Pastor:	
Administered by Priests	4
Administered by Professed Religious Men	1
Missions	6

Educational

Elementary Schools, Diocesan and Parish	2
Total Students	424
Catechesis / Religious Education:	
High School Students	34
Elementary Students	68
Total Students under Catholic Instruction	526
Teachers in Diocese:	
Priests	4
Lay Teachers	36

Vital Statistics

Receptions into the Church:	
Infant Baptism Totals	225
First Communions	225
Confirmations	225
Marriages:	
Catholic	42
Total Marriages	42
Deaths	164
Total Catholic Population	18,000

LEADERSHIP
Chancery Office - t) 773-276-5080 info@esnucc.org
Protosyncellus - Rev. Richard Janowicz;
Chancellor - Very Rev. Serhiy Kovalchuk;
Vice Chancellor -

OFFICES AND DIRECTORS
Chief Financial Officer and Eparchial Financial Manager - t) 773-276-5080 Anna Szalewa Shaleva (finances@esnucc.org);
College of Eparchial Consultors - Rev. Richard Janowicz; Very Rev. Serhiy Kovalchuk; Rev. Abraham Miller;
Diocesan Consultors - Rev. Richard Janowicz; Very Rev. Serhiy Kovalchuk; Rev. Abraham Miller;
New Star - Eparchial Newspaper - Rev. Roman Bobesiuk, Editor; Rev. John P. Lucas, English Editor;
Office for Protection of Children and Youth - George Matwyshyn, Dir. (child-protection@esnucc.org);
Presbyteral Council - Rev. Richard Janowicz; Very Rev. Serhiy Kovalchuk; Archpriest Yaroslav Mendyuk;
Protopresbyteries (Deans) - Rev. Ivan Shkumbatyuk, Protopresbyter; Rev. Richard Janowicz, Protopresbyter; Archpriest Yaroslav Mendyuk, Dean;
Eparchial Censor -
Eparchial Office of Religious Education & Catechesis - Rev. Roman Artymovych;
Stewardship and Development Office - t) 773-276-9500 capitalcampaign@esnucc.org Mariya Kokor;
Task Force for a Safe Environment -
Tribunal -

PARISHES, MISSIONS, AND CLERGY

STATE OF ARIZONA

PHOENIX
Dormition of the Mother of God - 3730 W. Maryland Ave., Phoenix, AZ 85019 t) 602-973-3667 dmofgod@cox.net; dmofgod@aol.com www.ukrainianchurch.org Very Rev. Hugo C. Soutus, Pst.;

TUCSON
St. Michael Ukrainian Greco-Catholic Church - 715 W Vanover Rd., Tucson, AZ 85705-4137; Mailing: 420 E Deer's Rest Place, Tucson, AZ 85704-6939 t) 520-298-4967 stmichaeltucson@gmail.com www.stmichaeltucson.org Dcn. David Maciborski; Rev. Nicholas Kostyk, Admin.;

STATE OF CALIFORNIA

CITRUS HEIGHTS
Holy Wisdom - 6520 Van Maren Ln., Citrus Heights, CA 95621; Mailing: 1324 La Sierra Dr., Sacramento, CA 95864 t) 916-387-5037 ux7bvasil@gmail.com holywisdomsacramento.org Rev. Vasyl Miziuk, Admin.;

LA MESA
St. John the Baptizer - 4400 Palm Ave., La Mesa, CA 91941; Mailing: P. O. Box 3116, La Mesa, CA 91941 t) 619-697-5085 c) 917-224-0904 yuriisas70@gmail.com www.stjohnthebaptizer.org Rev. Yurii Sas, Pst.;

LOS ANGELES
Nativity of B.V.M. - 5154 De Longpre Ave, Los Angeles, CA 90027 t) 323-663-6307 c) 773-934-3685 ikoshyk@gmail.com; info@ukrainiancatholicla.com www.ukrainiancatholicla.com Rev. Ihor Koshyk, Pst.;

SACRAMENTO
St. Andrew the Apostle - 7001 Florin Rd., Sacramento, CA 95828 c) 916-387-5037 ux7bvasil@gmail.com www.ukrainianparish.com Rev. Vasyl Miziuk, Admin.;

SAN FRANCISCO
Immaculate Conception Catholic Church - 215 Silliman, San Francisco, CA 94134 t) 415-763-9587 petrodyachok1967@gmail.com Rev. Petro Dyachok, Admin.;
St. Volodymyr - 445 Washington St., Santa Clara, CA 95050

SANTA CLARA
St. Volodymyr Ukrainian Catholic Mission - 445 Washington Ave., Santa Clara, CA 95050 t) 408-248-1462 st_volodymyr_ucc@att.net stvolodymyrucc.org Immaculate Conception, San Francisco. Rev. Petro Dyachok, Admin.;

STATE OF COLORADO

DENVER
Transfiguration of Our Lord - 4118 Shoshone St., Denver, CO 80211 t) 313-515-4114 info@transfiguratondenver.org www.transfigurationdenver.org Rev. Valeriy Kandyuk, Admin.;

STATE OF ILLINOIS

CHICAGO
St. Nicholas Ukrainian Catholic Cathedral - 835 N. Oakley Blvd., Chicago, IL 60622-4811; Mailing: 2245 W. Rice St., Chicago, IL 60622-4858 t) 773-276-4537 office@stnicholaschicago.org www.stnicholaschicago.org Rev. Serhiy Kovalchuk, Admin.; Rev. Roman Bobesiuk, Assoc. Pst.; Rev. Ihor Khomytskyy, Pst. Assoc.; CRP Stds.: 30
St. Nicholas Cathedral School - (Grades PreK-8) 2200 W. Rice St., Chicago, IL 60622-4811 t) 773-384-7243 admin@stnickschicago.org www.stnicholascathedralschool.org Anna Cirilli, Prin.; Stds.: 200; Lay Tchrs.: 12
St. Joseph - 5000 N. Cumberland Ave., Chicago, IL 60656 t) 773-625-4805 stjosephucc@gmail.com stjosephukr.com Rev. Mykola Buryadnyk, Pst.; Rev. Bohdan Nalysnyk, Assoc. Pst.; Rev. Andriy Delisandru, Assoc. Pst.; Dcn. Marko Krutiak;
St. Michael's - 12211 S. Parnell Ave., Chicago, IL 60628 c) 773-291-0168 znamiboh@aol.com Rev. John P. Lucas, In Res.;
SS. Volodymyr and Olha - 739 N. Oakley Blvd, Chicago, IL 60612; Mailing: 2245 W. Superior St., Chicago, IL 60612 t) 312-829-5209 stsvo@comcast.net Rev. Oleh Kryvokulsky, Pst.; Rev. Roman Artymovych, Assoc. Pst.; Rev. Stepan Kostiuk, Assoc. Pst.; Rev. Ivan Krotec, Pastor Emer.;

MADISON
St. Mary's Greek Catholic Church - 1310 Iowa St., Madison, IL 62060; Mailing: 1312 Iowa St., Madison, IL 62060 t) 314-303-2892 ewlogu52@yahoo.com Dcn. Eugene Logusch, Admin.;

PALATINE
Immaculate Conception Ukrainian Catholic Church - 116 E. Illinois Ave., Palatine, IL 60067; Mailing: 745 S. Benton St., Palatine, IL 60067 t) 847-991-0820 frmykhailo@att.net icshrine.org/ Mitred Archpriest Mykhailo Kuzma, Pst.; Archpriest Yaroslav Mendyuk, Assoc. Pst.;

PALOS PARK
Nativity of B.V.M. - 8530 W. 131 St., Palos Park, IL 60464 t) 708-361-8876; 708-361-8857 c) 917-675-0821 nativityukrainian@sbcglobal.net; rilnicki@hotmail.com Rev. Roman Theodosious Ilnicki, O.B.S.M, Pst.; Patricia Kuzmak, DRE;

STATE OF INDIANA

MISHAWAKA
St. Michael - 712 E. Lawrence St., Mishawaka, IN 46544 t) 574-703-7229 c) 312-838-0103 hudzanusa@hotmail.com Rev. Volodymyr Hudzan, Admin.;

MUNSTER
St. Josaphat - 8624 White Oak Ave., Munster, IN 46321 t) 219-923-0984 st.josaphat@comcast.net www.stjosaphatugcc.org Rev. Volodymyr Kushnir, Pst.;

STATE OF KANSAS

LAWRENCE
Holy Apostles (New Martyrs Ukrainian Greek Catholic Mission) - 1301 Vermont St., Lawrence, KS 66044 t) 816-516-4351 c) 785-220-3322 nikolaibr93@yahoo.com Dcn. Randolph Brown, Admin.;

STATE OF MICHIGAN

DEARBORN
St. Michael's - 6340 Chase Rd., Dearborn, MI 48126 t) 313-582-1424 c) 313-580-4412 wruchgy@gmail.com stmichaelarchangel.org Rev. Canon Wayne J. Ruchgy, Pst.;

DEARBORN HEIGHTS
Our Lady of Perpetual Help - 26667 Joy Rd., Dearborn Heights, MI 48127; Mailing: 26606 Ann Arbor Trail, Dearborn Heights, MI 48127 t) 313-278-0470 olphukr@gmail.com Rev. Volodymyr Petriv, Pst.; CRP Stds.: 2

DETROIT
St. John the Baptist - 3877 Clippert St., Detroit, MI 48210 t) 701-495-8583 dumychmyroslav@yahoo.com Ukrainian Divine Liturgy Rev. Myroslav Dumych, Admin.;

FLINT
St. Vladimir's Ukrainian Catholic Church - 3464 W. Pasadena, Flint, MI 48504; Mailing: 3850 Dwight Dr., Warren, MI 48092 t) 810-394-3091 rybbog@yahoo.com Liturgical services are in Ukrainian and English Rev. Bogdan Rybchuk (Ukraine), Pst.;

GRAND RAPIDS
St. Michael the Archangel Ukrainian Greek Catholic Church - 154 Gold Ave. N.W., Grand Rapids, MI 49504 c) 773-969-1181 (Pastor); 616-363-2972 (Asst.) o.romanif@gmail.com; ejh498@juno.com stmichaelgrandrapids.org Rev. Roman Fedchyk (Ukraine), Admin.;

HAMTRAMCK
Immaculate Conception Ukrainian Catholic Church - 11700 McDougall St., Hamtramck, MI 48212 t) (313) 893-1710 frdanieltchai@gmail.com www.icchurchosbm.com Rev. Daniel Schaicoski, O.S.B.M., Supr.; CRP Stds.: 360
Immaculate Conception Ukrainian Catholic Schools Association - (Grades K-8) 29500 Westbrook, Warren, MI 48093 t) 586-574-2480 frdanieltchai@aol.com icschools.org/ Mary Ann Gruda, Prin.; Stds.: 360; Pr. Tchrs.: 1; Scholastics: 22; Lay Tchrs.: 22
Immaculate Conception Endowment Fund Inc. - c) (586) 907-8552 Lauro Schaicoski, Admin.;

WARREN
St. Josaphat - 26401 St. Josaphat Dr., Warren, MI 48091 t) 586-755-1740 c) 516-650-3615 (Fr. Dorosh, OSBM); 313-610-1764 (Fr. Hykavy, OSBM); 586-945-9003 (CRP) stjucch@aol.com; emilianeuropeusa@gmail.com www.stjoschurch.com St. Josaphat Banquet Centre Rev. Emilian Dorosh, Pst.; Rev. Roman Hykavy, OSBM, Assoc. Pst.;

STATE OF MINNESOTA

MINNEAPOLIS
St. Constantine - 515 University Ave. NE, Minneapolis, MN 55413-1944 t) 612-379-2394 stconstantineucc@gmail.com www.stconstantine.org St. Constantine Ukrainian Catholic Church, St. Constantine Ruthenian Greek Catholic Church Rev. Ivan Shkumbatyuk, Pst.;

STATE OF MISSOURI

ST. JOSEPH
St. Joseph's - 526 Virginia, St. Joseph, MO 64546; Mailing: 1513 Martha St., Omaha, NE 68108 t) 916-387-5037 o.petro.kozar@gmail.com Rev. Petro Kozar, Admin.;

ST. LOUIS
St. Mary's Assumption Ukrainian Catholic Church - 11363 Oak Branch Dr., St. Louis, MO 63128; Mailing: P.O. Box 4172, Chesterfield, MO 63006 t) 314-487-1786 c) 314-303-2893 ewlogu52@yahoo.com Served by Chicago. Dcn. Eugene Logusch, Admin.;

STATE OF NEBRASKA

LINCOLN

St. George's - 3330 N. 13th St., Lincoln, NE 68521; Mailing: 1513 Martha St., Omaha, NE 68108 t) 916-387-5037 o.petro.kozar@gmail.com Rev. Petro Kozar, Admin.;

OMAHA

Assumption of B.V.M. - 1513 Martha St., Omaha, NE 68108 t) 916-387-5037 kozar@gmail.com Rev. Petro Kozar, Admin.;

St. Joseph - 526 Virginia St., St. Joseph, MO 64504

STATE OF NORTH DAKOTA

BELFIELD

St. Demetrius - 2123 Hwy. 85 SW, Belfield, ND 58622; Mailing: 12897 20th St. S.W., Belfield, ND 58622 t) 701-575-4281 martinenagy@gmail.com www.saint-demetrius.com Rev. Martin Nagy, Admin.;

St. John the Baptist - 305 6th St. NE, Belfield, ND 58622; Mailing: 12897 20th St SW, Belfield, ND 58622 t) 701-575-4993 martinenagy@gmail.com Rev. Martin Nagy, Admin.;

WILTON

SS. Peter and Paul - 106 N. 7th St., Wilton, ND 58579; Mailing: P.O. Box 275, Wilton, ND 58579 t) 701-734-6464 rya@midco.net Rev. George L. Pruys, Admin.;

St. Michael - 812 N. Main St., Minot, ND 58703

STATE OF OREGON

SPRINGFIELD

Nativity of the Mother of God Byzantine Catholic Church - 704 Aspen St., Springfield, OR 97477 t) 541-726-7309 rjano@aol.com www.nativityukr.org Rev. Richard Janowicz, Pst.;

STATE OF TEXAS

HOUSTON

Protection of the Mother of God - 9102 Meadowshire St., Houston, TX 77037 t) 281-447-2749 frmdovzhuk@att.net pokrova.org Rev. Mykola Dovzhuk, Pst.;

THE COLONY

St. Sophia Ukrainian Catholic Church - 5600 N. Colony Blvd., The Colony, TX 75056-1927 t) 972-370-4700 frpavlo@stsophiaukrainian.cc www.stsophiaukrainian.cc Rev. Pavlo Popov, Admin.; Rev. Frank Avant, In Res.; Dcn. John Novocilsky; Dcn. Kostiantyn Popov; CRP Stds.: 15

STATE OF WASHINGTON

SEATTLE

Our Lady of Zarvanycia - 5321 17th Ave., S., Seattle, WA 98108 t) 206-762-1055 olzarv@gmail.com www.ukrchurch.org Rev. Abraham Miller, Pst.; Oresta Rzhyskij, DRE;

STATE OF WISCONSIN

MILWAUKEE

St. Michaels - 1025 S. 11th St., Milwaukee, WI 53204 t) 414-672-5616 stmichaelsukr@gmail.com stmichaelsukr.org/ Rev. Vasyl Savchyn, Pst.;

INSTITUTIONS LOCATED IN DIOCESE

ENDOWMENTS / FOUNDATIONS / TRUSTS [EFT]

CHICAGO

***Ukrainian Catholic Education Foundation (Ukrainian Catholic University Foundation)** - 2247 W. Chicago Ave., Chicago, IL 60622 t) 773-235-8462 jsolimini@ucufoundation.org; matuszak@ucufoundation.org www.ucufoundation.org Joseph Solimini, COO;

MISCELLANEOUS [MIS]

FLAGSTAFF

Metropolitan Andrey Sheptytsky Institute of Eastern Christian Studies - 2401 W. Rte. 66, Unit 86, Flagstaff, AZ 86001 t) 480-217-8505; 416-926-7133 (Main office) sheptytsky@utoronto.ca www.sheptytskyinstitute.ca Metropolitan Andrey Sheptytsky Institute Foundation holds and manages the endowments for the Institute. Both operate in the USA and Canada Rev. Alexander Michael Laschuk (Canada), Exec. Dir.; Rev. Andrew Summerson, Prof.; Archpriest Peter Galadza (Canada), Professor Emeritus; Mitred Archpriest Andriy Chirovsky, Founder;

MONASTERIES AND RESIDENCES FOR PRIESTS AND BROTHERS [MON]

EAGLE HARBOR

Holy Protection Monastery - 6559 State Hwy. M26, Eagle Harbor, MI 49950 t) 906-289-4484 holyprotectionmonastery@protonmail.com societystjohn.com Society of Saint John, Inc. Rev. Ambrose Nemeth, Abbot; Brs.: 3; Priests: 1

REDWOOD VALLEY

Holy Transfiguration Monastery - 17001 Tomki Rd., Redwood Valley, CA 95470; Mailing: P.O. Box 217, Redwood Valley, CA 95470 t) 707-485-1122 fatherd@earthlink.com www.monksofmttabor.com Monks of Mount Tabor. Very Rev. Damien Higgins, Admin.;

An asterisk (*) denotes an organization that has established tax-exempt status directly with the IRS and is not covered by the USCCB Group Ruling.

Eparchy of St. Peter the Apostle (Chaldean)

MOST REVEREND EMANUEL HANA SHALETA

Second Bishop-Eparch of the Eparchy of Saint Peter the Apostle-Chaldean; ordained May 31, 1984; appointed Chaldean Bishop January 15, 2015; consecrated Bishop February 6, 2015 in Baghdad, Iraq; appointed second Eparch to the Eparchy of St. Peter the Apostle-Chaldean Catholic Diocese of America August 9, 2017; installed August 29, 2017. Office: 1627 Jamacha Way, El Cajon, CA 92019.

Chancery Office: 1627 Jamacha Way, CA 92019. T: 619-579-7997; F: 619-588-8281. stpeterdiocese@gmail.com

ESTABLISHED JULY 25, 2002.

The Jurisdiction of the Eparchy extends territorially to all Western States in the United States of America inclusive. With regards to persons, its subjects are all Catholics of the Chaldean or Assyrian Ancestry: (1) Who immigrated to this country from the Middle East, especially from Iraq and Iran; (2) Who descends from such persons (can. 755); (3) Women married to men referable to (1) & (2) if they comply with can. 98, n.4; (4) Who in accordance with can. 98, n. 3, changed their Rite; (5) converts to the Catholic Church of the Chaldean Rite; (6) And in fact, all other Catholics of the Chaldean Rite who are attached to the parishes subject to the jurisdiction of the Eparch. For legal titles of parishes and diocesan institutions, consult the Chancery Office.

Legal Title: The Chaldean Catholic Diocese of St. Peter the Apostle.

STATISTICAL OVERVIEW

Personnel
Bishop 1
Retired Bishops 1
Abbots 1
Priests: Diocesan Active in Diocese 22
Priests: Retired, Sick or Absent 3
Number of Diocesan Priests 25
Religious Priests in Diocese 1
Total Priests in your Diocese 26
Ordinations:
Diocesan Priests 1
Transitional Deacons 2
Permanent Deacons in Diocese 16
Total Brothers 6
Total Sisters 8

Parishes
Parishes 13
With Resident Pastor:
Resident Diocesan Priests 13
Missions 2

Welfare
Homes for the Aged 1

Educational
Seminaries, Diocesan 1
Students from This Diocese 3
Total Seminarians 3
Total Students under Catholic Instruction 3

Vital Statistics
Receptions into the Church:
Infant Baptism Totals 491
First Communions 521
Confirmations 492
Marriages:
Catholic 148
Total Marriages 148
Deaths 205
Total Catholic Population 46,800

LEADERSHIP
Chancery Office - t) 619-579-7997
Vicar General - t) 619-444-9911 Rev. Msgr. Archdeacon Sabri A. Kejbo, Vicar (st.michaels@cox.net);
Office of Diocesan Chancellor - Monica Yousif, Chancellor;
Chancellor - Rev. Simon Esshaki;
Judicial Officer - Rev. Ankido Sipo;

OFFICES AND DIRECTORS
Chaldean Social Services -
Child Protection Review Board - Rev. Simon Esshaki;
Diocesan Advisory Council - Samir Salem;
Director of Finance - Diocesan Board -
Director of Religious Education - Rev. Andrew Younan;
Rector of Seminary of Mar Abba - Rev. Andrew Younan;

PARISHES, MISSIONS, AND CLERGY

STATE OF ARIZONA

SCOTTSDALE
Mar Auraha Chaldean Catholic Parish (The Chaldean Catholic Church of Arizona Corporation) - 6816 E. Cactus Rd., Scottsdale, AZ 85254 t) 480-905-1545 macatholicchurch@gmail.com Rev. Felix Shabi, Pst.; Rev. Royal Hannosh, Assoc. Pst.;
The Chaldean Catholic Church of Arizona Corporation -
Holy Family Mission - 3847 W. Bluefield Ave., Glendale, AZ 85305 Polly Sesi, DRE;
Holy Cross Chaldean Mission - 19 W. Bruce Ave., Gilbert, AZ 85233
Holy Family Chaldean Catholic Mission - 12225 N. 68th St., Scottsdale, AZ 85254

STATE OF CALIFORNIA

CAMPBELL
Assyrian Chaldean Catholic Church California Corporation - 109 N. First St., Campbell, CA 95008 t) 619-579-7997 stpeterdiocese@gmail.com Rev. Joseph Kachappilly, Pst.;
St. Mary Assyrian-Chaldean Parish (Assyrian Chaldean Catholic Church California Corporation) - 109 N. First St., Campbell, CA 95008 c) 408-318-8303 frbarota@gmail.com Rev. Michael Barota, Pst.;
Assyrian Chaldean Catholic Church California Corporation -

CERES
St. Matthew's Assyrian-Chaldean Catholic Church - 3005 6th St., Ceres, CA 95307 t) 209-541-1660 joekachappilly@hotmail.com Rev. Peter Patros, Pst.;

EL CAJON
***St. Peter Chaldean Cathedral** - 1627 Jamacha Way, El Cajon, CA 92019 t) 619-447-8876 (CRP); 619-579-7913 christine1627@hotmail.com Most Rev. Emanuel Hana Shaleta; Rev. Michael J. Bazzi, Assoc. Pst.; Rev. Andrew Younan, Assoc. Pst.; Rev. Daniel Shaba, Assoc. Pst.;
St. Michael Chaldean Catholic Church - 799 E. Washington Ave., El Cajon, CA 92020 t) 619-444-9911 st.michaels@cox.net Rev. Simon Esshaki, Pst.;

NORTH HOLLYWOOD
St. Paul Assyrian-Chaldean Catholic Parish - 6628 Alcove Ave., North Hollywood, CA 91605 t) 619-579-7997 stpeterdiocese@gmail.com Rev. Michael Barota, Pst.;

ORANGEVALE
Our Lady of Perpetual Help Chaldean Catholic Church - 7625 Hazel Ave., Orangevale, CA 95662 t) 209-668-4500 mansoor.mikhael@yahoo.com Tom Simon, DRE; Rev. Lucian Ayoub, Pst.;

SANTA ANA
St. George Chaldean Catholic Church - 4807 W. McFadden, Santa Ana, CA 92704 t) 619-579-7997 lucianayoub@yahoo.com Rev. Roni Schamoun, Pst.;

TURLOCK
St. Thomas Assyrian-Chaldean Parish - 2901 N. Berkeley Ave., Turlock, CA 95380 c) 209-535-6555 joekachappilly@hotmail.com Rev. Peter Patros, Pst.;
Chaldean Sisters - 2937 N. Berkeley Ave., Turlock, CA 95380
St. Thomas Retirement Center - t) 209-634-7252

STATE OF NEVADA

LAS VEGAS
St. Barbara Chaldean Catholic Church - 4514 Meadows Ln., Las Vegas, NV 89107; Mailing: 1900 N. Torrey Pines Dr. #209, Las Vegas, NV 89108 t) 702-542-3390 stbarbarachaldeanchurch@gmail.com www.saintbarbarachurch.com Rewayda Coda, DRE; Rev. Mazin Hanna Al-Botany, Pst.;

INSTITUTIONS LOCATED IN DIOCESE

CONVENTS, MONASTERIES, AND RESIDENCES FOR WOMEN [CON]

EL CAJON
Chaldean Sisters - 1591 Jamacha Way, El Cajon, CA 92019 t) 619-447-4842 info@goodsamretirement1.org Sr. Alexandra Matti, Dir.;

MISCELLANEOUS [MIS]

EL CAJON
Chaldean Media Center - 1627 Jamacha Way, El Cajon, CA 92019 t) 619-590-9028 infokaldu@gmail.com kaldaya.net Rev. Daniel Shaba, Dir.;
Good Samaritan Retirement Center - 1515 Jamacha Way, El Cajon, CA 92019 t) 619-590-1515 info@goodsamretirement1.org www.goodsamretirement.org Sr. Alexandra Matti, Exec.;

MONASTERIES AND RESIDENCES FOR PRIESTS AND BROTHERS [MON]

EL CAJON
Sons of the Covenant Monastery - 1111 N. Pepper Dr., El Cajon, CA 92021 c) 619-454-2686 frankidosipo@gmail.com Ankido Sipo, Admin.;

SEMINARIES [SEM]

EL CAJON
Seminary of Mar Abba the Great - 1400 Monument Hill Rd., El Cajon, CA 92020 c) 619-550-6868 simon.esshaki@gmail.com www.marabba.org Rev. Simon Esshaki, Rector;

An asterisk (*) denotes an organization that has established tax-exempt status directly with the IRS and is not covered by the USCCB Group Ruling.

Eparchy of Saint Thomas the Apostle (Chaldean)

MOST REVEREND FRANCIS Y. KALABAT

Second Bishop-Eparch of the Eparchy of Saint Thomas the Apostle-Chaldean Catholic Diocese of America; ordained July 4, 1995; appointed second Bishop-Eparch to the Eparchy of Saint Thomas the Apostle-Chaldean Catholic Diocese of America May 3, 2014; ordained and installed June 14, 2014 in Southfield, Michigan. Res.: 25603 Berg Rd., Southfield, MI 48033.

Chancery Office: 25603 Berg Rd., Southfield, MI 48033. T: 248-351-0440; F: 248-351-0443. office@chaldeanchurch.org

Exarchate Erected January 26, 1982. Elevated to the Rank of Eparchy September 14, 1985.

The Jurisdiction of the Eparchy extends territorially to all Eastern States in the United States of America inclusive. With regard to persons, its subjects are all Catholics of the Chaldean or Assyrian Ancestry: (1) Who immigrated to this country from the Middle East, especially from Iraq and Iran; (2) Who descends from such persons (can. 755); (3) Women married to men referable to (1) & (2) if they comply with can. 98, n. 4; (4) Who in accordance with can. 98, n. 3., changed their Rite; (5) Converts to the Catholic Church of the Chaldean Rite; (6) And in fact, all other Catholics of the Chaldean Rite who are attached to the parishes subject to the jurisdiction of the Eparch.

For legal titles of parishes and diocesan institutions, consult the Chancery Office.

STATISTICAL OVERVIEW

Personnel

Bishop	1
Retired Bishops	1
Priests: Diocesan Active in Diocese	22
Priests: Diocesan in Foreign Missions	1
Priests: Retired, Sick or Absent	4
Number of Diocesan Priests	27
Religious Priests in Diocese	1
Total Priests in your Diocese	28
Extern Priests in Diocese	2
Permanent Deacons in Diocese	1
Total Sisters	14

Parishes

Parishes	12
With Resident Pastor:	
Resident Diocesan Priests	10
Resident Religious Priests	1
Without Resident Pastor:	
Administered by Priests	1
Administered by Deacons	1
Missions	3
Pastoral Centers	1

Welfare

Homes for the Aged	2

Educational

Diocesan Students in Other Seminaries	14
Total Seminarians	14
Total Students under Catholic Instruction	14

Vital Statistics

Receptions into the Church:	
Infant Baptism Totals	1,242
Adult Baptism Totals	10
First Communions	1,063
Confirmations	1,252
Marriages:	
Catholic	483
Interfaith	65
Total Marriages	548
Deaths	336
Total Catholic Population	180,000

LEADERSHIP

Chancery Office - t) 248-351-0440 office@chaldeanchurch.org www.chaldeanchurch.org Most Rev. Francis Y. Kalabat; Most Rev. Ibrahim N. Ibrahim;

Vicar General - t) 586-254-7221 Rev. Fawaz Kako, Vicar;

Judicial Vicar - Rev. Pierre Konja, Vicar;

Presbyteral Council - Rev. Fawaz Kako; Rev. Bryan Kassa; Rev. Pierre Konja;

OFFICES AND DIRECTORS

Diocesan Corporation-The Chaldean Catholic Church of U.S.A. - Most Rev. Francis Y. Kalabat, Pres.; Vincent Jarbow, Treas.; Rev. Pierre Konja, Secy.;

Eparchial College of Consultors - Rev. Manuel Y. Boji; Rev. Msgr. Zouhair T. Kejbou; Rev. Rudy Zoma;

Eparchial Tribunal (Vacant) -

Office of Safety Environment - t) 248-351-0440 Johnathon Francis, Dir.; Janan Senawi, Victim Assistance Advocate;

COMMUNICATIONS

Chaldean Voice Radio Program - t) 248-353-1083 www.chaldeanvoice.org

MISCELLANEOUS / OTHER OFFICES

Chaldean Manor Housing for Elders - t) 248-355-9491

Chaldean Home of Sterling Heights - t) 586-884-6560

Our Lady of the Fields Camp & Retreat Center - t) 810-822-2226; 800-822-2226 (Toll Free)

PARISHES, MISSIONS, AND CLERGY

STATE OF ILLINOIS

CHICAGO

St. Ephrem's Chaldean Catholic Church - 2537 W. Bryn Mawr Ave., Chicago, IL 60659-4996 t) 773-506-9957 (CRP); 773-888-7984 st.ephremchaldeancatholicchurch@yahoo.com Rev. Hermiz Haddad, Admin.;

NORTHBROOK

Mart Mariam Chaldean Catholic Church - 2700 Willow Rd., Northbrook, IL 60062 t) 630-847-0149 martmariamchurch@gmail.com Rev. Ayad Hanna, Pst.; Rev. Rodney Abasso, Par. Vicar;

STATE OF MICHIGAN

FARMINGTON HILLS

Holy Cross Chaldean Catholic Church - 32500 Middlebelt Rd., Farmington Hills, MI 48334 t) 248-626-0285; 248-626-5055 holycrosschaldeancc@gmail.com Rev. Msgr. Zouhair Toma Keijbou, Pst.; Rev. Andrew Seba, Par. Vicar;

GRAND BLANC

St. Paul Caldean Catholic Church - 5150 E. Maple Ave., Grand Blanc, MI 48439 t) 810-820-8450 st.paulccc@comcast.net Rev. Muhanned Al-Tawil, Pst.;

OAK PARK

Mar Addai Chaldean Parish - Mar Addai Chaldean Catholic Chruch, 24010 Coolidge Hwy., Oak Park, MI 48237 t) 248-547-4648 office@chaldeanchurch.org Rev. Stephen H. Kallabat, In Res.;

SHELBY TWP.

St. George Chaldean Catholic Church - 45700 Dequinder Rd., Shelby Twp., MI 48317 t) 586-254-7221 saintgeorgechaldeanchurch@gmail.com Rev. Fawaz Kako, Pst.; Rev. John Jaddou, Par. Vicar; Rev. Kevin Yono, Par. Vicar;

SOUTHFIELD

Our Lady of Chaldeans Cathedral, Mother of God Chaldean Parish - 25585 Berg Rd., Southfield, MI 48033 t) 248-356-0565; 248-356-2448 (CRP) ourladyofthechaldeans@gmail.com Rev. Perrin Atisha, Par. Vicar; Rev. Bryan Kassa, Admin.; Rev. Sanharib Youkhanna, Par. Vicar; Most Rev. Francis Y. Kalabat, Bishop of the Diocese;

STERLING HEIGHTS

Holy Martyrs Chaldean Catholic Church - 43700 Merrill Rd., Sterling Heights, MI 48314 t) 586-803-3114 secretary@holymartyrsccc.org Rev. Selwan Taponi, Pst.; Rev. Marcus Shammami, Par. Vicar;

TROY

St. Joseph Chaldean Parish - 2442 E. Big Beaver Rd., Troy, MI 48083 t) 248-528-3676 saintjosephccc@gmail.com Rev. Sameem Balius, Pst.; Rev. Fadi Gorgies, Par. Vicar; Rev. Patrick Setto, Par. Vicar;

WARREN

Our Lady of Perpetual Help Chaldean Catholic Church - 11200 E. 12 Mile Rd., Warren, MI 48093 t) 586-804-2114 olphmission@gmail.com Rev. Rudy Zoma, Pst.;

Sacred Heart Chaldean Parish - 30590 Dequindre Rd., Warren, MI 48092 t) 586-313-5809; 248-548-0066 (CRP) sacredheartchurch310@gmail.com Rev. Fadi Philip, Pst.;

WEST BLOOMFIELD

St. Thomas Chaldean Catholic Parish - 6900 Maple Rd., West Bloomfield, MI 48322 t) 248-788-2460; 248-306-6004 (CRP) stthomaschaldeanchurch@gmail.com Rev. Pierre Konja, Pst.; Rev. Wisam Matti, Par. Vicar; Rev. Matthew Zetouna, Par. Vicar;

INSTITUTIONS LOCATED IN DIOCESE

CONVENTS, MONASTERIES, AND RESIDENCES FOR WOMEN [CON]

CHICAGO

Daughters of Mary Our Lady of the Immaculate Conception Order - Chaldean Sisters, Daughter of Mary Immaculate Chicago Convent, 2908 W. Morse, Chicago, IL 60645 t) 773-338-8832 chaldean.sisters@gmail.com Sr. Agnes Odisho, Prioress;

FARMINGTON

Daughters of Mary Our Lady of the Immaculate Conception Order - 24900 Middlebelt, Farmington, MI 48336 t) 248-615-2951 chaldean.sisters@gmail.com Sr. Benynia Shikwana, Supr.; Srs.: 14

MISCELLANEOUS [MIS]

BLOOMFIELD TOWNSHIP

St. Ephrem Re-Evangelization Center - 4875 Maple Rd., Bloomfield Township, MI 48301 t) 248-538-9903 info@ecrc.us www.ecrc.us Candace Rabban, Dir.;

Martoma Productions - 4875 Maple Rd., Bloomfield Township, MI 48301 t) 248-538-9903 info@ecrc.us Candace Rabban, Dir.;

NURSING / REHABILITATION / CONVALESCENCE / ELDERLY CARE [NUR]

SOUTHFIELD

Chaldean Manor - 25775 Berg Rd., Southfield, MI 48033 t) 248-355-9491 lubnaseba@gmail.com Vincent Jarbow, Bus. Mgr.; Asstd. Annu.: 100; Staff: 2

STERLING HEIGHTS

Chaldean Home of Sterling Heights - 43700 Merrill Rd., Sterling Heights, MI 48314 t) (248) 351-0440 Vincent Jarbow, CFO; Asstd. Annu.: 130; Staff: 3

RETREAT HOUSES / RENEWAL CENTERS [RTR]

BRIGHTON

Our Lady of the Fields Camp and Retreat Center L3C - 1391 Kellogg Rd., Brighton, MI 48114 t) (248) 351-0440 Vincent Jarbow, Contact;

An asterisk (*) denotes an organization that has established tax-exempt status directly with the IRS and is not covered by the USCCB Group Ruling.

St. Thomas Syro-Malabar Catholic Diocese of Chicago

MOST REVEREND JOY ALAPPATT

Bishop of St. Thomas Syro-Malabar Catholic Diocese of Chicago; ordained December 31, 1981; appointed Bishop of St. Thomas Syro-Malabar Catholic Diocese of Chicago July 3, 2022; Episcopal Ordination September 27, 2014. Office: 372 S. Prairie Ave., Elmhurst, IL 60126-4020. T: 630-279-1386; T: 630-279-1383; Cell: 201-951-1701; bishop@syromail.com.

Diocesan Office: 372 S. Prairie Ave., IL 60126-4020. T: 630-279-1386; T: 630-279-1383. curia@syromail.com

ESTABLISHED MARCH 13, 2001.

Comprises all of the United States.

STATISTICAL OVERVIEW

Personnel

Bishop	1
Retired Bishops	1
Priests: Diocesan Active in Diocese	60
Priests: Diocesan Active Outside Diocese	1
Priests: Retired, Sick or Absent	1
Number of Diocesan Priests	62
Religious Priests in Diocese	23
Total Priests in your Diocese	85
Ordinations:	
Diocesan Priests	1
Transitional Deacons	1
Total Brothers	6
Total Sisters	184

Parishes

Parishes	50
With Resident Pastor:	
Resident Diocesan Priests	44
Resident Religious Priests	7
Missions	34

Welfare

Day Care Centers	1

Educational

Diocesan Students in Other Seminaries	9
Total Seminarians	9
Catechesis/Religious Education:	
High School Students	3,164
Elementary Students	5,456
Total Students under Catholic Instruction	8,629
Teachers in Diocese:	
Lay Teachers	8

Vital Statistics

Receptions into the Church:	
Infant Baptism Totals	455
Minor Baptism Totals	4
Adult Baptism Totals	3
Received into Full Communion	133
First Communions	769
Confirmations	457
Marriages:	
Catholic	234
Interfaith	15
Total Marriages	249
Deaths	100
Total Catholic Population	53,779

LEADERSHIP

Diocesan Office - t) 630-279-1383; 630-279-1386 chancellor@syromail.com

Vicar Generals (Syncellus) - Very Rev. Thomas Kadukappillil (India), Vicar (kadukappilly@yahoo.com); Rev. Msgr. Thomas Mulavanal, Vicar (tmulavan@gmail.com);

Chancellor & Secretary to Bishop - t) 630-279-1383 chancellor@syromail.com Rev. George Danavelil;

Finance Officer - Procurator - t) 630-279-1386 procurator@syromail.com Rev. Kurian N. Varghese;

ADMINISTRATION

Curia Secretarial Staff - secretary@syromail.com Gina Gallo, Secy.;

Eparchial Consultors - Very Rev. Thomas Kadukappillil (India) (kadukappilly@yahoo.com); Rev. Msgr. Thomas Mulavanal (tmulavan@gmail.com); Rev. George Danavelil;

OFFICES AND DIRECTORS

Director of Religious Education - c) 630-286-3767 (Fr. George) Rev. George Danavelil, Diocesan D.R.E.; Rev. Joby Joseph, Assoc. Dir. (frjoby@smchicago.org); Tinson Thomas, Secy.;

Office for Formation and Vocations - c) 919-749-7175 Rev. Paul Chalissery;

Victim Assistance Coordinators - t) 620-279-1383 Thomas Moolayil, Exec. Dir.; Dr. Paul Cherian, Chair; Jacqualine Harock, Admin. (compliance@syromail.com);

Youth and Family Apostolate - c) 919-749-7175 (Fr. Paul); 914-648-8369 (Fr. Kevin) Rev. Paul Chalissery, Dir.; Rev. Kevin Mundackal, Dir.;

MISCELLANEOUS / OTHER OFFICES

Mar Thoma Sleeha Cathedral - t) 708-544-7250

PARISHES, MISSIONS, AND CLERGY

COMMONWEALTH OF KENTUCKY

COLUMBUS

St. Mary Syro-Malabar Catholic Mission Columbus, OH - 893 Hamlet St., Columbus, KY 43201; Mailing: 107 N. Walnut St., CYNTHIANA, KY 41031 c) 859-866-9345 smchurchinfo@gmail.com; nibyk@yahoo.com www.columbuschurch.org Services held at: Sacred Heart Catholic Church, 893 Hamlet St, Columbus, OH Rev. Niby Kannai, Dir.; CRP Stds.: 29

LOUISVILLE

Divine Mercy Syro-Malabar Catholic Mission Louisville, Kentucky - 3926 Poplar Level Rd., Louisville, KY 40213 c) 502-322-4282 syromalabarlouisville@gmail.com www.syromalabarlouisville.org Services held at: Holy Family Catholic Church, Louisville, KY. Rev. George Munjanattu, O.F.M.Conv, Pst.; CRP Stds.: 26

COMMONWEALTH OF MASSACHUSETTS

FRAMINGHAM

St. Thomas the Apostle Syro-Malabar Catholic Church (Boston) - 41 Brook St., Framingham, MA 01701 t) 508-532-8620 parishoffice@smcboston.org www.smcboston.org Rev. Stephen Kanippillil, M.C.B .S., Pst.; CRP Stds.: 106

COMMONWEALTH OF PENNSYLVANIA

FEASTERVILLE

St. John Neumann Syro-Malabar Knanaya Catholic Mission of Greater Philadelphia - 1900 Meadow Brook Rd., Feasterville, PA 19053 c) 281-818-6518 frbins@gmail.com Services held at: Our Lady of Fathima Catholic Church Rev. Bins Jose Chethalil, Dir.; CRP Stds.: 47

PHILADELPHIA

St. Thomas Syro-Malabar Catholic Church (Philadelphia) - 608 Welsh Rd., Philadelphia, PA 19115 t) 215-464-4008 c) 215-459-6310 jakester174@gmail.com; vicar.stsmccphila@gmail.com www.syromalabarphila.org Rev. Kuriakose Kumbakeel, Pst.; CRP Stds.: 228

PITTSBURGH

St. Mary Syro-Malabar Catholic Mission Pittsburgh, PA - 1607 Greentree Rd., Pittsburgh, PA 15220; Mailing: 418 4th St., Chester, VA 26034 c) 304-780-2110 syromalabarpittsburgh@gmail.com; jstephan@dwc.org www.syromalabarpittsburgh.org Services held at St Simon & Jude Church, 1607 Greentree Rd, Pittsburgh, PA Rev. Jeeson V. Stephan, MCBS, Dir.; CRP Stds.: 46

COMMONWEALTH OF VIRGINIA

CHANTILLY

St. Jude Syro-Malabar Catholic Church, Northern Virginia of St. Thomas Syro-Malabar Catholic Diocese - 4219 Lafayette Center Dr., Chantilly, VA 20151 c) 630-822-1905 nvasyromalabar@gmail.com; tansdb@yahoo.com stjudenva.org Rev. Nicholas Thalakkottur Anthony, S.D.B., Pst.; CRP Stds.: 181

NORTH CHESTERFIELD

St. Alphonsa Syro-Malabar Catholic Church, Richmond, VA of St. Thomas Syro-Malabar Catholic Diocese of Chicago - 9841 W. Providence Rd., North Chesterfield, VA 23236; Mailing: 9841 West Providence RD, N Chesterfield, Richmond, VA 23236 c) 202-975-3020 st.alphonsarichmond@gmail.com; shanoymannathara@gmail.com stalphonsamissionva.org Rev. Shanoy John (India), Pst.; CRP Stds.: 80

STATE OF ARIZONA

PHOENIX

Holy Family Syro-Malabar Catholic Church (Phoenix) - 3221 N. 24th St., Phoenix, AZ 85016 t) 623-328-5784 info@syromalabraz.org; pastor.holyfamily20@gmail.com www.syromalabaraz.org Rev. Dels Alex, Pst.; CRP Stds.: 152

STATE OF CALIFORNIA

FAIRFIELD

St. John Paul II Syro-Malabar Knanaya Catholic Mission, Sacramento - 1070 N. Texas St., Fairfield, CA 94533 c) (872) 806-5013 regiachant@gmail.com Services held at St. Paul Catholic Church, 8720 Florin Road, Sacramento, CA Rev. Regimon Thandassery Chandy, Vicar; CRP Stds.: 16

LIVERMORE

St. Teresa of Calcutta Syro-Malabar Catholic Church, San Francisco, California of St. Thomas Syro-Malabar Catholic Diocese of Chicago - 678 Enos Way, Livermore, CA 94551; Mailing: 1137 Hibiscus Way, Livermore, CA 94551 c) (630) 706-0358 missiondirector@stteresasyromalabar.org www.stteresasyromalabar.org/ Services held at St Bartholomew's Episcopal Church, 678 Enos Way, Livermore, CA Rev. Sijo Tharakunnel Scaria, Pst.; CRP Stds.: 149

MILPITAS

St. Thomas Syro-Malabar Catholic Church of San Francisco (Indian) - 200 N. Abbott Ave., Milpitas, CA 95035 t) 408-219-6508 (CRP); 408-471-7261 vipin.jose.p@gmail.com; vicar@syromalabarsf.org www.syromalabarsf.org Rev. Ligory Johnson Kattiakaran, Pst.; Vipin Jose, DRE; CRP Stds.: 247

St. Thomas Preschool - 200 N Abbott Ave, Milpitas, CA 95035 t) 408-946-0190 efronlorenztigas@gmail.com (2-4 yr. olds) Tigas Efren, Prin.;

MONTEBELLO

St. Pius X Syro-Malabar Knanaya Catholic Church - 124 N. 5th St., Montebello, CA 90640 t) 909-268-7939 c) 210-630-2295 skmudakodil@gmail.com; piusxla@yahoo.com knanayaregion.us/losangeles Rev. Siju Kuriakose Mudakodil, Pst.; CRP Stds.: 45

SACRAMENTO

Infant Jesus Syro Malabar Catholic Church, Sacramento, CA of St. Thomas Syro Malabar Catholic Diocese of Chicago - 6200 McMahon Dr., Sacramento, CA 95824 c) 267-616-2951 vicar@infantjesussacramento.org; rubanjt@yahoo.com infantjesussacramento.org Rev. Ruban Thannickal, Pst.; CRP Stds.: 145

SAN FERNANDO

St. Alphonsa Syro-Malabar Catholic Church of Los Angeles - 215 N. Macneil St., San Fernando, CA 91340 t) 818-365-5522 c) 213-804-9997; 754-366-6765 alphonsa.angeles@gmail.com syromalabarla.org/ Rev. Sebastian Valiyaparampil, Pst.; CRP Stds.: 117

Bl. Chavara Syro-Malabar Catholic Mission (Bakersfield) - 11342 Laurel Canyon Blvd., San Fernando, CA 91340 t) 818-365-5522 c) 754-366-6765 alphonsa.angeles@gmail.com Services at: St. John's Lutheran Church,4500 Buena Vista Rd, Bakersfield, CA 93311 Rev. Sebastian Valiyaparampil, Pst.; CRP Stds.: 15

SAN JOSE

St. Mary's Syro-Malabar Knanaya Catholic Church of San Jose - 324 Gloria Ave., San Jose, CA 95127; Mailing: 3450 E. Hills Dr., San Jose, CA 95127 t) 408-836-5804 (CRP); 408-770-3282 sajipinarkayil@gmail.com; jkurian1568@gmail.com sanjoseknanayachurch.com Rev. Saji Kurian Pinarkayil, Pst.; CRP Stds.: 113

SANTA ANA

St. Thomas Apostle Syro-Malabar Catholic Church (Santa Ana) - 5021 W. 16th St., Santa Ana, CA 92703 t) 714-530-2900; 714-399-6785 (CRP) pastor@stthomassyromalabarca.org; nixon.philip@gmail.com www.stthomassyromalabar.com Rev. Mathews Kurian Munjanath, Pst.; CRP Stds.: 145

STATE OF COLORADO

DENVER

St. Thomas Syro-Malabar Catholic Mission, Denver, CO, Inc. of St. Thomas Syro-Malabar Catholic Diocese of Chicago - 3554 Humboldt St., Denver, CO 80205 jobcap@gmail.com Services held at: Annunciation Catholic Church, 3601 Humboldt St, Denver, CO Rev. Job Arakkaparambil, OFM Cap. (India), Pst.; Navya Davis Joshy, DRE; CRP Stds.: 36

STATE OF CONNECTICUT

STAMFORD

Our Lady of the Assumption Syro-Malabar Catholic Church Norwalk, CT Inc. - 274 Strawberry Hill Ave, Stamford, CT 06902 c) 203-451-0017 jamesvc88@gmail.com Services held at: St. Ladislaus Roman Catholic Church, 25 Cliff St, Norwalk, CT Pavan John Antony, DRE; Rev. James Vattakunnel, V.C., Dir.; CRP Stds.: 18

WEST HARTFORD

St. Thomas Syro-Malabar Catholic Church, West Hartford, CT, Inc. of St. Thomas Syro-Malabar Catholic Diocese of Chicago - 30 Echo Ln., West Hartford, CT 06107 t) 860-325-2383 c) 203-233-9321 frjpullikattil@gmail.com; contact@syromalabarct.org syromalabarct.org Rev. Joseph Pullikattil, Pst.; Baby Mathew, DRE; CRP Stds.: 58

STATE OF FLORIDA

BRANDON

Sacred Heart Syro-Malabar Knanaya Catholic Church, Tampa - 3920 S. Kings Ave., Brandon, FL 33511 c) 914-673-6956 (Pastor); 813-751-4504 (Office); (352) 584-2524 (Kishore trustee) tampaknanayamission@gmail.com; joseadoppillil@gmail.com www.shkcctampa.com Rev. Joby Puchakattil Baby (India), Assoc. Pst.; Rev. Joseph Mathew Adoppillil (India), Pst.; CRP Stds.: 200

CORAL SPRINGS

St. George Syro-Malabar Catholic Mission, Miami FL - 217 NW 95th Terrace, Coral Springs, FL 33071 c) 630-202-2989 jthachara@gmail.com; thomaspulickal@gmail.com Services held at St

Catherine of Siena Church, 9200 SW 107th Ave Miami, FL 33176 Rev. John Thomas (Thachara), Dir.;
Our Lady of Health Syro-Malabar Catholic Church, Coral Springs, FL, Inc. of St. Thomas Syro-Malabar Catholic Diocese of Chicago - 201 N. University Dr., Coral Springs, FL 33071; Mailing: 217 NW 95th Terrace, Coral Springs, FL 33071 t) 786-382-9501 c) 630-202-2989 jthachara@gmail.com; olhcatholicchurch@gmail.com olhchurch.org Rev. John Thomas (Thachara), Vicar; CRP Stds.: 307

FORT LAUDERDALE

St. Jude Syro-Malabar Knanaya Catholic Parish of South Florida - 1105 N.W. 6th Ave., Fort Lauderdale, FL 33311 t) 954-530-3335 c) 972-302-5652 (CRP); 872-305-1345 stjudemiamikna@hotmail.com; jsauriamakel@gmail.com miamikna.com Rev. Joseph Chirappurathu, Pst.; CRP Stds.: 72

JACKSONVILLE

St. Mary's Syro-Malabar Catholic Mission, Jacksonville, FL, Inc. of St. Thomas Syro-Malabar Catholic Diocese of Chicago - 2575 Riverside Ave., #1, Jacksonville, FL 32204; Mailing: 1606 Blanding Blvd., Middleburg, FL 32068 t) 904-480-9664 c) 904-440-4140 stmarysjax@gmail.com; reena7uk1@rediffmail.com stmaryssyromalabarjax.org Services held at St. Ephrem Syriac Catholic Church, 4650 Kernan Blvd. S., Jacksonville, FL 32224. Rev. Jaisemon Xaviour(Punnolikunnel), Dir.; CRP Stds.: 38

ORLANDO

St. Stephen's Knanaya Catholic Mission Orlando, Inc. - 14801 Sussex Dr., Orlando, FL 32826; Mailing: 3920 S. King Ave., Brandon, FL 33511 c) 407-970-9037 (Jimmy Trustee); (224) 766-5831 (Pastor); (321) 960-7940 (luke Trustee) jjpuchukandathil@gmail.com; orlandoknanayachurch@gmail.com Rev. Joby Poochakkattil Baby (India), Pst.; CRP Stds.: 45

SANFORD

St. Mary's Syro-Malabar Catholic Church (Orlando) - 2581 Sanford Ave., Sanford, FL 32773 t) 407-463-9492 c) 346-270-0262 michaelnaijumon@yahoo.com; syromalabarchorlando@gmail.com www.stmarysmcc.com Rev. Siby Sebastian, MST, Pst.; Rev. Benoy Joseph, DRE; CRP Stds.: 219

SEFFNER

St. Joseph Syro-Malabar Catholic Church (Tampa) - 5501 Williams Rd., Seffner, FL 33584 t) 813-621-1451 c) 813-323-0306 vicar@sjsmcc.church; secretary@sjsmcc.church www.sjsmcc.church Rev. Rijo Cheerakathil, Vicar; CRP Stds.: 189

STATE OF GEORGIA

LOGANVILLE

St. Alphonsa Syro-Malabar Catholic Church, Atlanta - 4561 Rosebud Rd., Loganville, GA 30052 t) 404-921-1267 c) 630-901-5724 vicar@stalphonsacatholicchurch.org www.stalphonsacatholicchurch.org Rev. Vinod Madathiparambil George, Pst.; Gijo V George, DRE; CRP Stds.: 188
Holy Family Syro-Malabar Knanaya Catholic Church (Atlanta) - 3885 Rosebud Rd., Loganville, GA 30052 t) 706-207-9043 c) 773-934-1644 hfchurchatlanta@gmail.com Rev. Boby Vattampurath, Pst.; CRP Stds.: 61
St John Paul 2 Syro Malabar Catholic Church Inc. - 4599 Rosebud Rd., Loganville, GA 30052 c) 630-901-5724 vicar@sjp2smc.church Rev. Vinod Madathiparambil George, Pst.; CRP Stds.: 142

STATE OF ILLINOIS

BELLWOOD

Mar Thoma Sleeha Cathedral (Chicago) - 5000 St. Charles Rd., Bellwood, IL 60104 t) 708-544-7250 (Parish Landline) c) 908-235-8449 (Pastor); (951) 219-7646 (Asst Pastor); 262-612-0494 (DRE) kadukappilly@yahoo.com; srlindam@smchicago.org www.smchicago.org Very Rev. Thomas Kadukappillil (India), Pst.; Rev. Joby Joseph, Assoc. Pst.; Sr. Linda Moolechalil, CMC, DRE; CRP Stds.: 682

MAYWOOD

Sacred Heart Knanaya Catholic Parish, Chicago - 611 Maple St., Maywood, IL 60153; Mailing: 3935 N. Melvina Ave., Chicago, IL 60634 c) 773-412-6254 mutholath2000@gmail.com www.shkcparish.us Rev. Abraham Mutholathu Jacob, Pst.; Zachariah Abraham Chelakal, DRE; CRP Stds.: 214

MORTON GROVE

St. Mary's Syro-Malabar Knanaya Catholic Parish (Morton Grove) - 7800 W. Lyons St., Morton Grove, IL 60053 t) 310-709-5111 tmulavan@gmail.com www.smkcparish.us Rev. Msgr. Thomas Mulavanal, Pst.; Rev. Kochuparambil Lijo, Assoc. Pst.; Saji Pootrukayil, DRE; CRP Stds.: 432

STATE OF MARYLAND

GAITHERSBURG

Our Lady of Perpetual Help Syro-Malabar Catholic Parish of Greater Washington Inc. of St. Thomas Syro Malabar Diocese of Chicago - 20533 Zion Rd., Gaithersburg, MD 20882 t) 410-639-5275 c) 630-880-8520 roymoolechalil@gmail.com syromalabargw.org Rev. Roy Varkey Moolachalil, Pst.; CRP Stds.: 56

HALETHORPE

St. Alphonsa Syro-Malabar Catholic Church Baltimore - 5709 Oakland Rd., Halethorpe, MD 21227 t) 410-247-0240 c) 832-614-6654 stalphonsabaltimore@gmail.com www.stalphonsachurch.org Rev. Wilson Antony, Pst.; CRP Stds.: 117

STATE OF MICHIGAN

BERKLEY

St. Mary's Syro-Malabar Knanaya Catholic Church of Detroit - 3238 Royal Ave., Berkley, MI 48072 t) 630-400-7162 c) 619-307-3390 detroitknanayamission@gmail.com; jemy15@hotmail.it www.stmarysknanayacatholicchurchdetroit.org Rev. Joseph Jemy Puthuseril, Pst.; Biju Thomas, DRE; CRP Stds.: 49

SOUTHFIELD

St. Thomas Syro-Malabar Catholic Church, Detroit - 17235 Mt. Vernon St., Southfield, MI 48075 t) 248-552-6620 secretary.stmcc@gmail.com; dtvicar@gmail.com www.syromalabardetroit.org Rev. Justin Ouseph Puthussery, Pst.; CRP Stds.: 180

STATE OF MINNESOTA

MINNEAPOLIS

St. Paul Knanaya Catholic Mission, Minnesota - 629 2nd St., NE, Minneapolis, MN 55413-1905 c) 773-412-6254; 651-399-5928 muthalath2000@gmail.com; frbijm@gmail.com www.knanayaregion.us/minnesota.html Services held at St Boniface Church,629 2nd St NE Minneapolis, MN 55413 Rev. Abraham Mutholathu Jacob, Pst.; Rev. Biju Mathew Pattasseril, Assoc. Pst.;

RICHFIELD

St. Alphonsa Syro-Malabar Catholic Church Minnesota - 7540 Penn Ave, Richfield, MN 55423; Mailing: 7540 Penn Ave., Richfield, MN 55423 t) 952-473-4771 (CRP) syromalabarmn@yahoo.com; srsanctaezhani@gmail.com www.stalphonsamn.org Services held at: St Richard's Catholic Church,7540 Penn Ave S, Minneapolis, MN 55423 Rev. Antony Skaria, C.F.I.C., Dir.; Sr. Sancta Ezhani, DRE; CRP Stds.: 49

STATE OF NEVADA

HENDERSON

St. Mother Teresa of Calcutta Syro-Malabar Catholic Church - 240 S. Cholla St., Henderson, NV 89015 c) (317) 965-9892 motherteresalv@outlook.com motherteresalv.org Rev. George Joseph Nangachiveettil, Pst.; CRP Stds.: 27

LAS VEGAS

St. Stephen's Syro-Malabar Knanaya Catholic Mission, Las Vegas - 2461 E. Flamingo Rd., Las Vegas, NV 89121; Mailing: 124 N 5th St, Montebello, CA 90640 c) 210-630-2295 skmudakodil@gmail.com Services held at: St. Viator Catholic Church, 2461 E Flamingo Rd, Las Vegas, NV Rev. Siju Kuriakose Mudakodil, Dir.;

STATE OF NEW JERSEY

CARTERET

Christ the King Knanaya Catholic Church of New Jersey - 67 Fitch St, Carteret, NJ 07008; Mailing: 1900 Meadowbrook Rd., Feasterville, PA 19053 t) 281-818-6518 frbins@gmail.com; lumonlukose@gmail.com Rev. Bins Jose Chethalil, Pst.; CRP Stds.: 46

HAMMONTON

Holy Trinity Syro-Malabar Catholic Church, Delaware, Inc. of St. Thomas Syro-Malabar Catholic Diocese of Chicago - 250 S. Rte. 73, Hammonton, NJ 08037 c) (630) 261-5865 (Pastor); (302) 463-5666 (Sunday School Principal) vicar@holytrinityde.org; daeykripa@gmail.com Services held at: St. Elizabeth Ann Seton Catholic Church, 345 Bear Christiana Rd., Bear, DE, 19701. Rev. Varghese George, MST (India), Pst.; Mathew George, DRE; CRP Stds.: 40
St. Jude Syro-Malabar Catholic Church, South Jersey of St. Thomas Syro-Malabar Catholic Diocese of Chicago, Inc. - 250 S. Rte. 73, Hammonton, NJ 08037 t) 609-878-3878 c) (630) 261-5865 (Pastor); 215-360-6380 (Prin.) vicar@stjudesyromalabarsj.com; daeykripa@gmail.com www.stjudesyromalabarsj.com Rev. Varghese George, MST (India), Pst.; John Varghese, Prin.; CRP Stds.: 39

PATERSON

St. George Syro-Malabar Catholic Church - 408 Getty Ave., Paterson, NJ 07503 c) 630-828-4003; (201) 681-5703 trustees.sgsmccpaterson@gmail.com wp.sgsmccpaterson.com/ Rev. Thomas Mangattu Mathai, VC, Pst.; CRP Stds.: 206

SOMERSET

St. Thomas Syro-Malabar Catholic Church Inc. (East Millstone) - 510 Elizabeth Ave., Somerset, NJ 08873; Mailing: 508 Elizabeth Ave, Somerset, NJ 08873 t) 848-216-3363; 732-873-1620; 732-570-9024 (CRP) c) 334-427-5921 trustee@stthomassyronj.org; mineshjo@yahoo.com www.stthomassyronj.org Rev. Antony Xavier Pullukattu, Pst.; Minesh Joseph, CRE; CRP Stds.: 318

STATE OF NEW YORK

BRONX

St. Thomas Syro-Malabar Catholic Mission Westchester, New York of St. Thomas Syro-Malabar Catholic Diocese of Chicago - 820 E 221 St., Bronx, NY 10476; Mailing: 810 E. 221st St., Bronx, NY 10467 t) 718-944-4747 c) 248-794-4343 gelambasseril@gmail.com; stsmcmissionwestchester@gmail.com Rev. George Elambasseril, Pst.;
St. Thomas Syro-Malabar Catholic Church (Bronx) - 810 E. 221 St., Bronx, NY 10467 t) 718-944-4747 c) 646-523-3710 stsmccbronx810@gmail.com; gelambasseril@gmail.com www.stsmcc.org Rev. George Elambasseril, Pst.; CRP Stds.: 120

BROOKLYN

St. Thomas Syro-Malabar Catholic Mission, Brooklyn, New York, Inc. - 2978 Ocean Pkwy., Brooklyn, NY 11235; Mailing: 90 Brooklake Rd., Florham Park, NJ 07932 t) 718-266-1612 c) 347-729-2203 shijuchittatt@gmail.com Services held at Guardian Angel Roman Catholic Church, 2978 Ocean Pkwy, Brooklyn, NY. Rev. Shiju Chittattukara, S.D.V., Dir.;

BUCHANAN

St. Joseph Syro-Malabar Catholic Mission Hudson Valley, New York of St. Thomas Syro-Malabar Catholic Diocese of Chicago - 3094 Albany Post Rd., Buchanan, NY 10511; Mailing: 608 Isham St., New York, NY 10034 t) 914-645-4134 c) 917-345-2610 bvandanath@gmail.com; rmenolickal@gmail.com www.stjosephsyrohvny.org Services held at: St. Christopher And St. Patrick Parish, 3094 Albany Post Rd, Buchanan, NY 10511 Rev. Royson Menolickal Antony, O.F.M.Cap., Dir.; CRP Stds.: 64

HAVERSTRAW

St. Mary's Syro-Malabar Knanaya Catholic Church,

Rockland, NY - 46 Conklin Ave, Haverstraw, NY 10927 t) 845-786-2610 c) 773-943-2290 st.mary's.kccr@gmail.com; tharayilbibyachan@gmail.com Rev. Bipy Mathew Tharayil (India), Pst.; CRP Stds.: 39

HEMPSTEAD

Brooklyn Queens Long Island Knanaya Catholic Mission Inc. (St. Stephen's Knanaya Catholic Forane Church) - 384 Clinton St., Hempstead, NY 11550 t) 917-853-4759 c) 847-322-9503 josetharackal@yahoo.com; joseph3112@yahoo.com ststephensknanayaforanechurchnewyork.org Rev. Joseph Tharackal, Pst.; Lissy Vattakalam, DRE; CRP Stds.: 94

OLD BETHPAGE

St. Mary Syro Malabar, Old Bethpage, New York - 926 Round Swamp Rd., Old Bethpage, NY 11804 t) 516-454-7550 c) 215-808-4052 trustees@stmaryssyromalabar.org; johnmelepuram@gmail.com www.stmaryssyromalabar.org Rev. John P Melepuram, Pst.; CRP Stds.: 277

STATEN ISLAND

Blessed Kunjachan Syro-Malabar Catholic Mission, Staten Island, NY - 463 Tompkins Ave, Staten Island, NY 10305; Mailing: P. O. Box 140171, Staten Island, NY 10314 t) 718-207-5445 smcmission@gmail.com; sojuvarghesett@hotmail.com www.facebook.com/smcmission Services held at: St. Joseph Catholic Church, Staten Island, NY. Rev. Soju Thekkineth, Dir.;

WESLEY HILLS

Holy Family Syro-Malabar Catholic Church, Rockland, New York, Inc. of St. Thomas Syro Malabar Diocese of Chicago - 5 Willow Tree Rd., Wesley Hills, NY 10952 t) 845-694-8435 c) 845-499-4176 ambadan9@yahoo.com syromalabarrockland.org Rev. Raphael Ambadan Ouseph, Pst.; Ronny Muricken, DRE; CRP Stds.: 134

YONKERS

St. Joseph's Syro-Malabar Knanaya Catholic Mission of Westchester, NY - 670 Yonkers Ave., Yonkers, NY 10704 c) 773-943-2290 tharayilbibyachan@gmail.com Rev. Bipy Mathew Tharayil (India), Pst.;

STATE OF NORTH CAROLINA

APEX

Lourdes Matha Syro-Malabar Catholic Church, Raleigh/ Durham, North Carolina of St. Thomas Malabar Catholic Diocese of Chicago - 1400 Vision Dr., Apex, NC 27523; Mailing: 103 Holmhurst Ct, Cary, NC 27519 t) 919-439-0305; 919-360-6955 (CRP) c) 407-900-4999 vicar@lourdesmatha.org; trustees@lourdesmatha.org www.lourdesmatha.org Rev. Kuriakose Chacko Vadana, M.S.T., Pst.; Biju Thomas, DRE; CRP Stds.: 208

CHARLOTTE

St. Mary's Syro-Malabar Catholic Church Charlotte, North Carolina, Inc. of St. Thomas Syro-Malabar Catholic Diocese of Chicago - 715 E. Arrowood Rd., Charlotte, NC 28217; Mailing: 8008 Bronze Pike Dr., Charlotte, NC 28273 t) (630) 706-0358 c) (813) 318-2186 smsmcc.clt@gmail.com; vicarstmarysclt@gmail.com stmarysyroclt.org/ Rev. Rajeev Valiyaveettil Philip, Pst.; CRP Stds.: 101

STATE OF OHIO

CINCINNATI

St. Chavara Syro-Malabar Catholic Church - Cincinnati - 7600 Winton Rd., Cincinnati, OH 45224; Mailing: 401 Berry St., Dayton, KY 41074-1139 t) 224-666-5607 events.stchavara@gmail.com www.stchavaracincinnati.org Services held at St. Vivian Catholic Church, Cincinnati, OH Rev. Roshan Varghese, Pst.; CRP Stds.: 26

CLEVELAND

St. Raphel Syro-Malabar Mission Cleveland, OH - 12503 Buckingham Ave., (Shaker Blvd. & E. 126th St.), Cleveland, OH 44120; Mailing: 372 S. Prairie Ave., Elmhurst, IL 60126 t) 630-279-1383 x202 syromalabarcleveland@gmail.com syromalabarccc.org Services held at: Our Lady of Peace, 126th St., Shaker Blvd.-12503 Buckingham Ave., Cleveland, OH 44120. Rev. George Danavelil, Dir.;

STATE OF OKLAHOMA

OKLAHOMA CITY

Holy Family Syro-Malabar Catholic Church Oklahoma - 3901 SW 29th St, Oklahoma City, OK 73101; Mailing: P.O. Box 32180, Oklahoma, OK 73123 t) 405-474-4647 (CRP); 405-677-7976 c) 918-829-5115 paulkodakarakaran@hotmail.com; oksyromalabarchurch@yahoo.com holyfamilyok.org Rev. Paul Kodakarakaran (India), Pst.; CRP Stds.: 31

STATE OF TENNESSEE

NASHVILLE

St. Teresa of Calcutta Syro-Malabar Mission, Nashville, TN - 1227 Seventh Ave., Nashville, TN 37208; Mailing: 372 S. Prairie, Elmhurst, IL 60126 c) (931) 652-3663 regimsfs@gmail.com www.syromalabarnashville.com Services held at: Assumption Catholic Church, Nashville, TN. Rev. Regi Augustine Narikunnel, Pst.; CRP Stds.: 37

STATE OF TEXAS

COPPELL

St. Alphons Syro Malabar Catholic Church (Coppell) - 200 S. Heartz Rd., Coppell, TX 75019; Mailing: P.O. Box 1862, Coppell, TX 75019 c) (816) 529-5052 (secretary); (469) 771-7900 (trustee); (972) 602-5166 (Trustee) stalfonsa1@gmail.com; jacobchristy@gmail.com www.saintalphonsachurch.org Rev. Jacob Christy Parambukattil, Pst.; CRP Stds.: 644

EDINBURG

Divine Mercy Syro-Malabar Catholic Church (Edinburg), Texas - 300 W. Cano St., Edinburg, TX 78539; Mailing: 321 W. Mahl St., Edinburg, TX 78539 t) 956-380-1363 c) (956) 207-5820 (Secy); 956-566-8005 (Pastor); 779-240-0976 (Pastor) divinemercymalabar@gmail.com; vicar@divinemercyedinburg.org www.divinemercyedinburg.org Rev. Antony Pittappillil, Pst.; CRP Stds.: 81

FARMERS BRANCH

Christ the King Syro-Malabar Knanaya Catholic Church DFW - 13565 Webb Chapel Rd., Farmers Branch, TX 75234; Mailing: 13416 Onyx Ln., Farmers Branch, TX 75234 c) (630) 828-4513 ctkknachurch@gmail.com; pastor@christthekingknanaya.org christthekingknanaya.org Rev. Abraham Kalarickal Chacko, Pst.; Joseph Elakodikal, DRE; CRP Stds.: 245

GARLAND

St. Thomas the Apostle Syro-Malabar Forane Catholic Church, Dallas/Garland, Texas - 4922 Rosehill Rd., Garland, TX 75043; Mailing: 1118 Dandelion Dr., Garland, TX 75043 t) (972) 240-1100 vicar@syromalabarchurchdallas.org; trustee@syromalabarchurchdallas.org www.syromalabarchurchdallas.org Rev. James Nirappel, Pst.; CRP Stds.: 309

MANOR

St. Alphonsa Syro-Malabar Catholic Church, Austin, Texas, Inc. of St. Thomas Syro-Malabar Catholic Diocese of Chicago - 8701 Burleson Manor Rd., Manor, TX 78653; Mailing: P O Box 307, Manor, TX 78653 t) 512-718-6405; 512-272-4005; (512) 293-6953 antogalapat@yahoo.com; trustees@stalphonsaaustin.com stalphonsaaustin.com Rev. George Antoo Alappat, Pst.; CRP Stds.: 180

MISSOURI CITY

St. Joseph Syro-Malabar Catholic Church - 211 Present St., Missouri City, TX 77489 t) 281-969-7236; 832-980-7730 (CRP) c) 916-803-5307 asst.vicar@sjsmcc.org; ccdcoordinator@sjsmcc.org www.stjosephhouston.org Rev. Johnykutty George, Pst.; Rev. Melvin M. Paul, Par. Vicar; Jose Mathew, DRE; CRP Stds.: 706

St. Chavara Syro-Malabar Catholic Mission - 19740 Candle Creek Dr., Spring, TX 77388; Mailing: 211 Present St., Missouri City, TX 77489 (Worship Site)

St. Mary's Syro-Malabar Knanaya Catholic Church of Houston - 6400 W. Fuqua St., Missouri City, TX 77489, Missouri City, TX 77489-2826; Mailing: 2303 Brett Ct., Missouri City, TX 77459 t) 281-957-5264; 708-953-1912 hkcmission@gmail.com; stmaryshouston@outlook.com stmarysknanayacatholicchurchhouston.com Our parish was established in 1995 as a mission. Ever since we conducted Holy Mass every Sunday. We bought the current church (building) in 2011. Rev. Suni Thomas Padinjarekkara, Vicar; Rev. Joseph Thachara (India), Assoc. Pst.; CRP Stds.: 431

PEARLAND

St. Mary's Syro-Malabar Catholic Church - 1610 O'Day Rd., Pearland, TX 77581 t) 713-315-7787 c) 919-600-9412 vicar@stmaryspearland.org; trustees@stmaryspearland.org www.stmaryspearland.org Rev. Jobimon Joseph Chelakunnel, MCBS, Pst.; CRP Stds.: 275

SAN ANTONIO

St. Anthony Syro-Malabar Knanaya Catholic Church (San Antonio) - 9347 Oakland Rd., San Antonio, TX 78240 t) 773-934-1644 c) 210-723-8243 stanthonyprayforus@gmail.com; bijok2000@yahoo.com knanayaregion.us/san_antonio.html Rev. Boby Thomas, Pst.; CRP Stds.: 40

St. Thomas Syro-Malabar Catholic Church of San Antonio - 8333 Braun Rd., San Antonio, TX 78254; Mailing: 15519 Luna Ridge, Helotes, TX 78023 c) 210-749-7076 frgeorgecgeorge@gmail.com syromalabarsa.org Rev. George C. George, Pst.; Sr. Beena Mathew, DRE; CRP Stds.: 42

STATE OF WASHINGTON

KIRLAND

Holy Family Syro-Malabar Catholic Mission, Seattle, Washington of St. Thomas Syro-Malabar Diocese of Chicago - 8512 122nd Ave., N.E., Suite 227, Kirland, WA 98033 c) (551) 482-6369 smcseattle.trustees@gmail.com holyfamilyseattle.org/ Services held at Christ the King Lutheran Church, 3730 148th Ave SE, Bellevue, WA 98006. Rev. James Joseph, S.D.B., Pst.; CRP Stds.: 122

STATE OF WISCONSIN

MILWAUKEE

St. Antony Syro Malabar Catholic Mission - 9525 W. Bluemound Rd., Milwaukee, WI 53226 t) 414-244-9875 st.antonymke@gmail.com stantonysyromalabar.org/ Services held at: St. Therese Catholic Church, 9525 W Bluemound Rd, Milwaukee, WI Rev. Mathai Pallurathil Chacko, Dir.; Stephen Paul, DRE; CRP Stds.: 25

INSTITUTIONS LOCATED IN DIOCESE

CONVENTS, MONASTERIES, AND RESIDENCES FOR WOMEN [CON]

BERWYN

Daughters of St. Thomas Congregation - 2319 Clarence Ave., Berwyn, IL 60402 t) 708-739-2194 dsttexas2010@gmail.com dstsisters.org Sr. Christy Jose, Supr.; Srs.: 3

BRANDON

Visitation Congregation of North America - Tampa - 601 Valle Vista Dr., Brandon, FL 33511 t) 813-322-3711; 813-278-0708 svmtampa@yahoo.com Sr. Meera Parayil Sr., SVM, Supr.; Srs.: 3

ELMHURST

Sisters of Saint Clare Inc. - 382 W. Avery St., Elmhurst, IL 60126 t) 813-324-6067 c) 773-756-6588 mparavara@yahoo.com Sr. Mary Paravara, S.S.C., Supr.; Srs.: 2

JACKSONVILLE

Sacred Heart Congregation of the Syro-Malabar Catholic

Church USA Inc. - 6814 Larkin Rd., Jacksonville, FL 32211 c) (904) 947-1239 Sr. Roselit Madappallil, SH, Supr.; Srs.: 4

MARGATE

Sisters of The Adoration Corporation - 3172 N.W. 72nd Ave., Margate, FL 33063 t) 954-826-4964 elsa.joseph08@gmail.com Sr. Elsa Idiyakunnel Sr., S.A.B.S., Supr.; Srs.: 16

MISSOURI CITY

St. Joseph Convent - 2123 Kottayam Dr., Missouri City, TX 77489 t) 832-679-3702 c) (832) 679-3724 Sr. Reji Philip, S.J.C., Supr.; Sr. Joicy Joseph, SJC, Secy.; Sr. Josia (Jossy) Lukose, SJC, Treas.; Srs.: 4

MORTON GROVE

Visitation Convent - 7801 W. Maple St., Morton Grove, IL 60053 t) 847-324-9480 svminchicago@yahoo.com Sr. Jeseena Manaalel, SVM, Supr.; Sr. Rajamma Thomas, Secy.; Sr. Sanija Kunjirakattu, SVM, Treas.; Srs.: 3

OAK LAWN

Congregation of the Mother of Carmel - 9310 S. 55th Ct., Oak Lawn, IL 60453 t) 708-422-0280; (219) 316-2235 c) 708-949-2786 cmcusa16@gmail.com; srjyothimacmc@gmail.com Sr. Alice Navya, Rel. Ord. Ldr.; Sr. Jyothi Maria, C.M.C., Supr.; Srs.: 48

PUTNAM

Sisters of St. Martha - 441 Church St., Putnam, CT 06260 t) 860-963-1119; (959) 929-8776 Sr. Jessy Joseph, Supr.; Srs.: 13

SAN ANTONIO

Missionary Sisters of Mary Immaculate - 8735 Sarasota Woods, San Antonio, TX 78250 t) 210-647-2947 msmi2usa@yahoo.com Other location: 1903 Rochester Ave, Edinburgh, TX 78539, Superior: Sr. Licy George Sr. Beena Mathew, Supr.; Srs.: 2

STAFFORD

Missionary Sisters of Mary Immaculate - 630 Easy Jet Dr., Stafford, TX 77477 t) 281-499-0030; 346-400-6106 msmisisters@hotmail.com Sr. Betsy M.S.M.I., Supr.; Srs.: 4

MISCELLANEOUS [MIS]

GLENVIEW

Missionary Society of St. Thomas the Apostle, M.S.T. - 2909 Central Rd., Glenview, IL 60025-4047 t) 847-904-2306 c) 630-670-6899 mstinusa2005@gmail.com; shajit91@gmail.com Rev. Antony Thundathil, Dir.;

PLANT CITY

Vincentian House, Divine Mercy Prayer House - 2905 S. Frontage Rd., Plant City, FL 33566 t) 813-567-1226 divinefl12@gmail.com www.divinefl.org Rev. Baiju Antony Poovathumoottil, Admin.;

WASHINGTON

Vincentian House & Divine Prayer Center - 426 Rte. 57 W., Washington, NJ 07882 t) 908-835-9989 dmhcnj@gmail.com Rev. Thomas Sunil Aenekatt, V.C., Dir.;

MONASTERIES AND RESIDENCES FOR PRIESTS AND BROTHERS [MON]

BENSENVILLE

Vincentian House - 1027 Twin Oaks St., Bensenville, IL 60106 t) 630-422-5236 vcsjprovince@gmail.com www.vincentianssjp.com Vincentian Congregation Rev. Johnus S. Cherunilath, V.C.; Rev. Jose Edayadiyil, VC, Supr.; Rev. Joseph J. Arackal, V.C., Mission Co-op Coordinator; Priests: 6

An asterisk (*) denotes an organization that has established tax-exempt status directly with the IRS and is not covered by the USCCB Group Ruling.

Ukrainian Catholic Diocese of Stamford

MOST REVEREND PAUL PATRICK CHOMNYCKY, O.S.B.M.

Bishop of Stamford; ordained October 1, 1988; appointed Apostolic Exarch of Great Britain, Faithful of Eastern Rite & Titular Bishop of Buffada April 5, 2002; ordained June 11, 2002; appointed Bishop of Stamford for Ukrainians January 3, 2006; installed February 20, 2006. Office: 161 Glenbrook Rd., Stamford, CT 06902-3019.

Chancery Office: 161 Glenbrook Rd., Stamford, CT 06902-3019. T: 203-324-7698; F: 203-357-7681. stamfordeparchy@optonline.net

ESTABLISHED AUGUST 8, 1956.

The jurisdiction of the Bishop of Stamford extends territorially throughout all of New York State and the New England States. With regard to persons, his subjects are all members of the Ukrainian Catholic Church (Byzantine Rite), irrespective of where they received Baptism.

For legal titles of parishes and diocesan institutions, consult the Chancery Office.

STATISTICAL OVERVIEW

Personnel

Bishop	1
Retired Bishops	1
Priests: Diocesan Active in Diocese	55
Priests: Diocesan Active Outside Diocese	3
Priests: Retired, Sick or Absent	3
Number of Diocesan Priests	61
Religious Priests in Diocese	10
Total Priests in your Diocese	71
Ordinations:	
Permanent Deacons	5
Permanent Deacons in Diocese	13
Total Brothers	1
Total Sisters	33

Parishes

Parishes	51
With Resident Pastor:	
Resident Diocesan Priests	48
Resident Religious Priests	3
Missions	2

Educational

Seminaries, Diocesan	1
Students from This Diocese	4
Diocesan Students in Other Seminaries	2
Total Seminarians	6
High Schools, Diocesan and Parish	1
Total Students	131
Catechesis / Religious Education:	
High School Students	251
Elementary Students	987
Total Students under Catholic Instruction	1,375

Vital Statistics

Receptions into the Church:	
Infant Baptism Totals	271
Minor Baptism Totals	1
Adult Baptism Totals	3
Received into Full Communion	2
First Communions	193
Confirmations	275
Marriages:	
Catholic	43
Interfaith	10
Total Marriages	53
Deaths	323
Total Catholic Population	15,837

LEADERSHIP

Chancery Office - t) 203-324-7698 stamfordeparchy@optonline.net www.stamforddio.org
Vicar General - Archpriest Ihor Midzak;
Econome - Dcn. Stephen A. Wisnowski;
Chancellor & Archivist - Very Rev. Archpriest Kiril Angelov (kire.angelov@gmail.com);
Vice Chancellor - Rev. Taras Chaparin;
Chancery Secretary - Oksana Dragan;
Notary Public - Oksana Dragan;
Diocesan Consultors - Very Rev. Archpriest Kiril Angelov (kire.angelov@gmail.com); Rev. Archpriest Ivan Kaszczak; Rev. Paul Luniw;
Diocesan Tribunal - t) 203-324-7698
Defender of the Bond - Nataliya Pistun;
Judge - Rev. Msgr. Martin Canavan;
Judicial Vicar - Rev. Paul Luniw;
Notary - Very Rev. Archpriest Kiril Angelov;
Diocesan Protopresbyters (Deans) - Rev. Archpriest Ivan Kaszczak; Rev. Kiril Manolev; Rev. Peter Shyshka;
Presbyteral Council - Most Rev. Paul P. Chomnycky, O.S.B.M.; Archpriest Ihor Midzak; Very Rev. Archpriest Kiril Angelov (kire.angelov@gmail.com);
Pastoral Planning Council - Most Rev. Paul P. Chomnycky, O.S.B.M.; Archpriest Ihor Midzak; Very Rev. Archpriest Kiril Angelov (kire.angelov@gmail.com);

OFFICES AND DIRECTORS

Administrative Council - Very Rev. Archpriest Kiril Angelov (kire.angelov@gmail.com); Rev. Zbigniew Canon Brzezicki; Most Rev. Paul P. Chomnycky, O.S.B.M.;
Apostleship of Prayer - Rev. Olvian Popovici;
Catechetics - Rev. Vasile Colopelnic;
Cemeteries - t) 845-496-5506 Most Rev. Paul P. Chomnycky, O.S.B.M., Pres.; Rev. Yaroslaw Kostyk, Exec.; Very Rev. Archpriest Kiril Angelov (kire.angelov@gmail.com);
Censor - Rev. Archpriest Edward Canon Young; Rev. Archpriest Ivan Kaszczak;
Chaplain to the Ukrainian American Youth Association - Archpriest Ihor Midzak, Chap.;
Chaplain to the Ukrainian Scouts Plast Organization - Rev. Archpriest Ivan Kaszczak, Chap.;
Communications - Rev. Taras Chaparin (thesower@optonline.net);
Development Office - Nataliya Pistun;
Diaconate, Permanent - Rev. Cyril Manolev;
Diocesan Charities and Missions - Most Rev. Paul P. Chomnycky, O.S.B.M.; Stefan Tinyszin;
Director of Religious Education for Ukrainian Heritage Schools - Very Rev. Bohdan Tymchyshyn;
Ecumenical Commission - Most Rev. Paul P. Chomnycky, O.S.B.M.; Most Rev. Basil H. Losten; Very Rev. Archpriest Kiril Angelov (kire.angelov@gmail.com);
Educational Institutions - Most Rev. Paul P. Chomnycky, O.S.B.M.; Rev. James Morris; Rev. Peter Shyshka, Supt.;
Family Life - Nataliya Pistun;
Holy Name Societies - Rev. Bohdan Hedz;
League of Ukrainian Catholics - Rev. Marijan Procyk, Dir.;
Liturgical Commission - Rev. Bohdan Tymchyshyn; Rev. Archpriest Roman Malyarchuk;
Missionaries, Diocesan - Sr. Natalya Stoczanyn, S.S.M.I.;
Office of Safe Environment - Rev. Peter Shyshka; Rev. Cyril Manolev;
Personnel Board - Most Rev. Paul P. Chomnycky, O.S.B.M.; Archpriest Ihor Midzak; Rev. Michael Bundz;
Press, Diocesan: "The Sower" - Rev. Taras Chaparin, Editor (thesower@optonline.net); Rev. Vasyl S. Behay, Editor;
Priests' Benevolent Association - Rev. Mikhail Myshchuk;
Religious Communities, Vicar - Rev. Basil Salkovski, O.S.B.M.;
Religious Education - Rev. Vasile Colopelnic;
Sodalities, B.V.M. - Rev. Ilya Bronovskyy, O.S.B.M.;
Ukrainian Museum and Library of Stamford, Inc. - t) 203-327-7899 Lubow Wolynetz, Cur., Librarian & Archivist; Rt. Rev. Mitred Msgr. John Terlecky, Librn.; Nataliia Kyrych;
Vocations - Rev. Bohdan Tymchyshyn;
Youth Apostolate - Sr. Eliane Ilnitski, S.S.M.I.;
Youth-For-Christ Association - Sr. Eliane Ilnitski, S.S.M.I.;

PARISHES, MISSIONS, AND CLERGY

COMMONWEALTH OF MASSACHUSETTS

FALL RIVER

St. John-the-Baptist - 339 Center St., Fall River, MA 02724 t) 401-762-2733 mdosyak@gmail.com Woonsocket, RI. Rev. Mykhaylo Dosyak, Pst.;

JAMAICA PLAIN

Christ the King - 146 Forest Hills St., Jamaica Plain, MA 02130 t) 617-522-9720 yaroslavnalysnyk@aol.com www.christ-the-king-ucc.org Archpriest Yaroslav P Nalysnyk, Pst.;
Saturday Ukrainian School -

LUDLOW

SS. Peter and Paul - 45 Newbury St., Ludlow, MA 01056 t) 413-583-2140 63krip@cua.edu Rev. Andriy Krip, Admin.;

SALEM

St. John the Baptist - 124 Bridge St., Salem, MA 01970-0206; Mailing: P.O. Box 206, Salem, MA 01970 t) 978-745-3151; 978-594-8360 c) 781-632-5182 stjnsalem624@gmail.com www.saintjohnsukr.com Rev. James Morris, Admin.;

SOUTH DEERFIELD

Holy Ghost - 44 Sugarloaf St., South Deerfield, MA 01373 t) 413-583-2140 63krip@cua.edu www.dhsparish.com Rev. Andriy Krip, Admin.;

STATE OF CONNECTICUT

ANSONIA

SS. Peter and Paul - 105 Clifton Ave., Ansonia, CT 06401 t) 203-734-3055 (CRP); 203-734-3895 younge8073@aol.com www.stsppucc.org Rev. Archpriest Edward Canon Young, Pst.; Audrey Sokol, DRE; CRP Stds.: 11

BRIDGEPORT

Protection of B.V.M. - 457 Noble Ave., Bridgeport, CT 06608; Mailing: 255 Barnum Ave., Bridgeport, CT 06608 t) 203-367-5054 pokrova@optimum.net www.pokrovact.com Rev. Ivan Mazuryk, Pst.; CRP Stds.: 7

COLCHESTER

St. Mary Dormition - 178 Linwood Ave., Colchester, CT 06415 c) 860-537-2069 cyril_manolev@yahoo.com Rev. Kiril Manolev, Pst.;

GLASTONBURY

St. John the Baptist - 26 New London Tpke., Glastonbury, CT 06033 c) 860-537-2069 cyril_manolev@yahoo.com St. Mary Dormition, Colchester. Rev. Kiril Manolev, Pst.;

HARTFORD

St. Michael - 125 Wethersfield Ave., Hartford, CT 06114; Mailing: 135 Wethersfield Ave., Hartford, CT 06114 t) 860-525-7823 st_michael@comcast.net Rev. Pawlo Martyniuk, Pst.; CRP Stds.: 156
Saturday Ukrainian School - (Grades K-11) c/o St. Michael Parish, 125 Wethersfield Ave., Hartford, CT 06114 c) (860) 990-9957 Stds.: 156

NEW BRITAIN

St. Josaphat - 303 Eddy Glover Blvd., New Britain, CT 06053 t) 860-225-7340 bereza.stephan@yahoo.com Rev. Stepan Bereza, Pst.;

NEW HAVEN

Saint Michael the Archangel Ukrainian Catholic Church - 569 George St., New Haven, CT 06511 t) 203-865-0388 stmichaels@snet.net stmichaelukrainian.org Rev. Iura Godenciuc, Pst.; CRP Stds.: 14
St. Michaels Ukrainian Heritage School - c/o St. Michael Parish, 569 George St., New Haven, CT 06511

STAMFORD

St. Vladimir Cathedral - 24 Wenzel Ter., Stamford, CT 06902 t) 203-324-0242 stvladimircath@optonline.net Archpriest Ihor Midzak, Rector; CRP Stds.: 6

TERRYVILLE

St. Michael - 35 Allen St., Terryville, CT 06786 t) 860-583-7588 stmichaels@comcast.net Rev. Paul Luniw, Pst.; Kristine Meinert, DRE; CRP Stds.: 15

WILLIMANTIC

Protection of B.V.M. - 70 Oak St., Willimantic, CT 06226 c) 860-423-5031 ivanbilyk7@gmail.com Rev. Ivan Bilyk, Pst.;

STATE OF NEW HAMPSHIRE

MANCHESTER

Protection of B.V.M. - 54 Walnut St., Manchester, NH 03104 c) (603) 793-9513 pbvm.manchester.nh@gmail.com pbvmnh.org/ Celebration of Divine Liturgy in both Ukrainian and English. Rev. Ihor Papka, Pst.; CRP Stds.: 3

STATE OF NEW YORK

AMSTERDAM

St. Nicholas - 24 Pulaski St., Amsterdam, NY 12010 t) 518-842-8731 mkos61@hotmail.com Rev. Marian Kostyk, Pst.;
St. Nicholas - 24 Pulaski St., Amsterdam, NY 12010 t) 518-842-8731 mkos61@hotmail.com Rev. Marian Kostyk, Pst.;

AUBURN

SS. Peter and Paul - 136 Washington St., Auburn, NY 13021 t) 315-252-5573 vasylcolopelnic@yahoo.com; peterpaulucc@gmail.com peterandpaulukr.com Rev. Vasile Colopelnic, Pst.; CRP Stds.: 11

BRONX

St. Mary Protectress - 1745 Washington Ave., Bronx, NY 10457 c) 917-499-7862 petrush@verizon.net Rev. Lawrence Lawryniuk, O.S.B.M., Pst.;

BROOKLYN

Holy Ghost - 161 N. 5th St., Brooklyn, NY 11211; Mailing: 160 N. 5th St., Brooklyn, NY 11211 t) 718-782-9592 tykhovytch@aol.com Rev. Ivan Tyhovych, Pst.;
St. Nicholas - 256 19th St., Brooklyn, NY 11215; Mailing: 261 19th St., Brooklyn, NY 11215 t) 718-369-4301 rmalyarchuk@yahoo.com Archpriest Roman Malyarchuk, Pst.;

BUFFALO

St. Nicholas - 308 Fillmore Ave., Buffalo, NY 14206 t) 716-852-7566 stnbuffalo@gmail.com www.stnbuffalo.com Rev. Marijan Procyk, Pst.; Rev. Robert Moreno, Par. Vicar; Elaine P. Nowadly, DRE; CRP Stds.: 25

CAMPBELL HALL

St. Andrew's - 141 Sarah Wells Tr., Campbell Hall, NY 10916 t) 845-496-5506; 845-496-4156 yaroslav_01@yahoo.com www.holyspirit-saintandrew.org Very Rev. Yaroslav Kostyk, Admin.; CRP Stds.: 4
St. Volodymyr - 141 Sarah Wells Trl., Campbell Hall, NY 10916; Mailing: P.O. Box 108, Glen Spey, NY 12737 t) 845-496-5506; 845-496-5506 yaroslav_01@yahoo.com Very Rev. Yaroslav Kostyk, Admin.;

COHOES

SS. Peter and Paul - 198 Ontario St., Cohoes, NY 12047 t) 518-237-0535 am3168@verizon.net Rev. Canon

Vladimir Marusceac, Pst.;

ELMIRA HEIGHTS

St. Nicholas - 410 E. McCanns Blvd., Elmira Heights, NY 14903 t) 607-734-1221; 607-734-2232 (Annex Building) snucceh@stny.rr.com Rev. Teodor Czabala (Ukraine), Pst.;

FRESH MEADOWS

Annunciation of the B.V.M. - 48-26 171st St., Fresh Meadows, NY 11365 t) 718-939-4116 bvm@netzero.net Rev. Zbigniew Canon Brzezicki, Pst.;

HEMPSTEAD

Saint Vladimir Ukrainian Catholic Church - 718 Front St., Hempstead, NY 11550; Mailing: 709 Front St., Hempstead, NY 11550 t) 516-481-7717 stvladimir@optonline.net Rev. Wasyl Hrynkiw, Pst.; CRP Stds.: 11

Parish Center - 226 Uniondale Ave., Uniondale, NY 11553

Saturday Ukrainian School - (Grades 1-12) c/o St. Vladimir Parish, 709 Front St., Hempstead, NY 11550

HUDSON

St. Nicholas - 206-209 Union St., Hudson, NY 12534 t) 518-828-5226 saintnicholas1922@gmail.com Rev. Janusz Jedrychowski, Pst.; CRP Stds.: 7

HUNTER

St. John the Baptist - Rte. 23A, Hunter, NY 12442; Mailing: P.O. Box 284, Hunter, NY 12442 t) 518-263-3862 info@holytrinityny.org ukrainianmountaintop.org Rev. Archpriest Ivan Kaszczak, Pst.;

JOHNSON CITY

Sacred Heart Ukrainian Catholic Church - 230 Ukrainian Hill Rd., Johnson City, NY 13790 t) 607-797-6293; 607-797-6294 shucc@stny.rr.com www.sacredheartucc.org Rev. Teodor Czabala (Ukraine), Pst.;

KENMORE

St. John the Baptist - 3275 Elmwood Ave., Kenmore, NY 14217 t) 716-873-5011 stjohnparishk@gmail.com Rev. Mykola Drofych, Pst.;

KERHONKSON

Holy Trinity Ukrainian Catholic Church - 211 Foordmore Rd., Kerhonkson, NY 12446-2914 t) 845-626-2864; 845-626-2864 info@holytrinityny.org www.holytrinityny.org Rev. Archpriest Ivan Kaszczak, Pst.;

LACKAWANNA

Our Lady of Perpetual Help - 1182 Ridge Rd., Lackawanna, NY 14218 t) 716-823-6182 olphuchurch@aol.com Rev. Andriy Kasiyan, Pst.; CRP Stds.: 2

LANCASTER

St. Basil - 3657 Walden Ave., Lancaster, NY 14086; Mailing: 1182 Ridge Rd., Lackawanna, NY 14218 t) 716-823-6182 olphuchurch@aol.com Rev. Andriy Kasiyan, Pst.; Dcn. David Wik;

LINDENHURST

Holy Family - 225 N. 4th St., Lindenhurst, NY 11757 t) 631-225-1168 olvianpopovici@yahoo.com Rev. Olvian Popovici, Pst.; CRP Stds.: 27

LONG ISLAND CITY

Holy Cross - 31-12 30th St., Long Island City, NY 11106 t) 718-932-4060 hcukicc@yahoo.com Rev. Mario Dacechen, O.S.B.M., Pst.; Rev. Bernard Joseph Panczuk, O.S.B.M, Assoc. Pst.;

MT. KISCO

Holy Protection of the Mother of God - 2 Green St., Mt. Kisco, NY 10549; Mailing: 161 Glenbrook Rd., Stamford, CT 06902 t) 203-324-7698 holyprotectionm@optonline.net www.pokrovany.com Rev. Taras Chaparin, Admin.; Elizabeth Gardasz, DRE; CRP Stds.: 6

NEW YORK

St. George - 30 E. 7th St., New York, NY 10003 t) 212-674-1615 osbmnyc@gmail.com stgeorgechurch.us Rev. Oleksiy Horobets, Assoc. Pst.; Rev. Cyril Iszezuck, O.S.B.M., Assoc. Pst.; Rev. Yoan Lubiv, O.S.B.M., Assoc. Pst.; Rev. Peter Shyshka, Assoc. Pst.; Methodius Soroka, OSBM; Rev. Elias Bronovskyy, OSBM, Admin.; Josaphat Oribka, OSBM, Mem.;

St. George School - (Grades PreK-12) 215 E. Sixth St., New York, NY 10003 t) 212-473-3323 stasiw@sga.nyc saintgeorgeacademy.net Andrew Stasiw, Prin.;

St. George High School - 215 E. 6th St., New York, NY 10003 t) 212-473-3323 saintgeorgeacademy.net Rev. Emilian Dorosh, Admin.; Andrew Stasiw, Prin.;

OZONE PARK

St. Mary Protectress - 97-06 87th St., Ozone Park, NY 11416 t) 718-845-5366 stmarysozpk@aol.com Rev. Vasile Tivadar, Admin.;

Blessed Nicholas Chernetsky - Rev. Vasile Tivadar, Admin.;

RIVERHEAD

St. John the Baptist - 820 Pond View Rd., Riverhead, NY 11901 t) 631-727-2766 info@sjbucc.org www.sjbucc.org Rev. Bohdan Hedz, Pst.; CRP Stds.: 4

ROCHESTER

St. Josaphat - 940 E. Ridge Rd., Rochester, NY 14621 t) 585-467-6457 rstjosap@rochester.rr.com www.stjosaphats.org Mitred Archpriest Philip Weiner, Pst.; Rev. Vasyl Kadylo, Par. Vicar; Protodeacon A Stephen Wisnowski; CRP Stds.: 15

Ukrainian Catholic Church of Epiphany - 202 Carter St., Rochester, NY 14621 t) 585-266-4036 ukr.epiphany@yahoo.com Very Rev. Roman Sydorovych, Dean; CRP Stds.: 39

ROME

St. Michael - Closed May 2022 For sacramental records, contact St. Volodymyr, Utica.

SPRING VALLEY

St. Peter & Paul Ukrainian Catholic Church - 43 Collins Ave., Spring Valley, NY 10977; Mailing: 39 Collins Ave., Spring Valley, NY 10977 t) 845-356-1634 jmterlecky@aol.com Rt. Rev. Mitred Msgr. John Terlecky, Pst.; CRP Stds.: 5

STATEN ISLAND

Holy Trinity - 288 Vanderbilt Ave., Staten Island, NY 10304 t) 718-442-2555 frvasile@aol.com Rev. Vasile Godenciuc, Pst.; CRP Stds.: 10

SYRACUSE

St. John the Baptist - 207 Tompkins St., Syracuse, NY 13204 t) 315-478-5109 stjbuccsyracuse@gmail.com www.stjohnbaptistucc.com/ Rt. Rev. Mitred Archpriest Mihai Dubovici, Pst.; CRP Stds.: 10

TROY

Protection of B.V.M. - 459 Second St., Troy, NY 12180 t) 518-273-6752 office@cerkva.com St. Nicholas Watervilet. Rev. Mikhail Myshchuk, Pst.;

UTICA

St. Volodymyr the Great - 4 Cottage Pl., Utica, NY 13502; Mailing: 296 Genessee St., Utica, NY 13502 t) 315-735-5138 stvolodymyrucc@gmail.com www.stvolodymyrutica.com Rev. Michael Bundz, Pst.;

WATERVLIET

St. Nicholas Ukrainian Catholic Church - 2410 4th Ave., Watervliet, NY 12189 t) 518-273-6752 office@cerkva.com www.cerkva.com Rev. Mikhail Myshchuk, Pst.; Dcn. Thomas Gutch;

YONKERS

St. Michael - 21 Shonnard Pl., Yonkers, NY 10703 t) 914-963-0209 stmichaelsukrainian@gmail.com stmichaelsukrainian.com Very Rev. Archpriest Kiril Angelov, Pst.; Rev. Vasyl S. Behay, Assoc. Pst.; Elizabeth Gardasz, DRE; CRP Stds.: 70

STATE OF RHODE ISLAND

WOONSOCKET

St. Michael - 394 Blackstone St., Woonsocket, RI 02895 t) 401-762-2733 st.michaelucc@verizon.net www.stmichaelsri.org/ Rev. Mykhaylo Dosyak, Pst.;

INSTITUTIONS LOCATED IN DIOCESE

CONVENTS, MONASTERIES, AND RESIDENCES FOR WOMEN [CON]

SLOATSBURG

Sister Servants of Mary Immaculate, Inc. - 150 Sisters Servants Ln., 9 Emmanuel Dr., Sloatsburg, NY 10974-0009; Mailing: P.O. Box 9, Sloatsburg, NY 10974-0009 t) 845-753-2840 ssminy@aol.com; srkath25@gmail.com www.ssmi-us.org Sr. Kathleen Hutsko, S.S.M.I., Prov.; Srs.: 14

MISCELLANEOUS [MIS]

NEWARK

Mary Theotokos Center Inc. - 572 Lake Rd., Newark, VT 05871 t) 802-467-3009 marytheotokosvt@comcast.net www.marytheotokosvt@comcast.net Retreat Center

STAMFORD

Institute of Catechists of the Heart of Jesus - 161 Glenbrook Rd., Stamford, CT 06902 c) 203-998-8400 ukrcathsem@optonline.net Sr. Elvira Julek, Rel. Ord. Ldr.;

MONASTERIES AND RESIDENCES FOR PRIESTS AND BROTHERS [MON]

LOCUST VALLEY

Provincialate of the Basilian Order of St. Josaphat - 29 Peacock Ln., Locust Valley, NY 11560 t) 516-609-3262 c) 708-925-3841 salkovskiv@aol.com; osbminusa@gmail.com Order of St. Basil the Great Rev. Varcilio Basil Salkovski, O.S.B.M., Prov.; Brs.: 1; Priests: 17

NURSING / REHABILITATION / CONVALESCENCE / ELDERLY CARE [NUR]

SLOATSBURG

St. Joseph's Adult Care Home, Inc. - 125 Sisters Servants Ln., Sloatsburg, NY 10974-0008 t) 845-753-2555 srmicheley75@aol.com Sr. Michele Yakymovitch, S.S.M.I., Admin.;

SEMINARIES [SEM]

GLEN COVE

Basilian Fathers Novitiate of the Order of St. Basil the Great (St. Josaphat Monastery) - 1 E. Beach Dr., Glen Cove, NY 11542 t) 516-671-0545 osbminusa@gmail.com; stjosaphats.monastery@gmail.com www.stjmny.org Dcn. Andrew Kornelyuk, OSBM, Vicar; Rev. Philip Patrick Sandrick, OSBM, Supr.;

STAMFORD

Ukrainian Catholic Seminary Inc. St. Basil College - Seminary - 195 Glenbrook Rd., Stamford, CT 06902-3099 t) 203-324-4578 ukrcathsem@gmail.com stbasilseminary.com Archpriest Bohdan Tymchyshyn, Rector; Rev. Raphael Strontsitskyy, Spiritual Adv./Care Srvcs.; Most Rev. Paul P. Chomnycky, O.S.B.M., Chair; Stds.: 5

SPECIAL CARE FACILITIES [SPF]

SLOATSBURG

St. Mary's Villa Spiritual, Cultural & Educational Center - 150 Sisters Servants Ln., Sloatsburg, NY 10974-0009; Mailing: P.O. Box 9, Sloatsburg, NY 10974-0009 t) 845-753-5100 srkath25@gmail.com Sr. Kathleen Hutsko, S.S.M.I., Admin.; Bed Capacity: 48; Asstd. Annu.: 120; Staff: 12

An asterisk (*) denotes an organization that has established tax-exempt status directly with the IRS and is not covered by the USCCB Group Ruling.

St. Mary, Queen of Peace, Syro-Malankara Catholic Eparchy in USA and Canada

MOST REVEREND PHILIPOS MAR STEPHANOS

Bishop of the Syro-Malankara Catholic Eparchy in USA and Canada; ordained April 27, 1979; consecrated Bishop March 13, 2010; installed Bishop of the Eparchy in USA and Canada October 28, 2017. Chancery Office & Res.: 1500 DePaul St., Elmont, NY 11003. T: 516-233-1656; F: 516-616-0727.

Chancery Office: 1500 De Paul St., Elmont, NY 11003. T: 516-233-1656; F: 516-616-0727.

ESTABLISHED JULY 14, 2010

The jurisdiction of the Eparchy is all Syro-Malankara Catholics in the United States of America and Canada.

STATISTICAL OVERVIEW

Personnel

Bishop	1
Priests: Diocesan Active in Diocese	5
Number of Diocesan Priests	5
Total Priests in your Diocese	5
Extern Priests in Diocese	16
Total Sisters	29

Parishes

Parishes	12
With Resident Pastor:	
Resident Diocesan Priests	11
Without Resident Pastor:	
Administered by Priests	1
Missions	5
Pastoral Centers	1

Educational

Diocesan Students in Other Seminaries	1
Total Seminarians	1
Catechesis / Religious Education:	
High School Students	173
Elementary Students	234
Total Students under Catholic Instruction	408

Vital Statistics

Receptions into the Church:	
Infant Baptism Totals	28
Adult Baptism Totals	1
Received into Full Communion	14
First Communions	35
Confirmations	31
Marriages:	
Catholic	15
Interfaith	13
Total Marriages	28
Deaths	10
Total Catholic Population	11,000

ADMINISTRATION

Leadership - Rt. Rev. Msgr. Augustine Mangalath Abraham (mangalathfr@gmail.com); Very Rev. Msgr. Gigi Philip; Very Rev. Saji G. Mukkoot, Chancellor;

Chancellor - Very Rev. Saji G. Mukkoot;

Chief Vicar General - c) (203) 444-8542 Rt. Rev. Msgr. Augustine Mangalath Abraham;

Finance Officer - c) (203) 444-8542 Rt. Rev. Msgr. Augustine Mangalath Abraham;

Judicial Vicar - Rev. George Oonnoony;

Secretary - Rev. Thomas Ayyaneth, Secy. to the Bishop; Rev. Jobin Thomas, Secy. to the Curia;

Vicar General - Very Rev. Msgr. Gigi Philip;

OFFICES AND DIRECTORS

Diocesan Apostolates and Directors -

Bible Apostolate Director - Rev. Abraham Thomas, Dir.;

Ecumenism and MCA Director - Rev. Binny Philip;

Faith Formation (Catechism) Director - Rev. Liju Thomas;

Family Apostolate Director - Rev. Michael Philipose Edathil, Dir.;

Fathers' Forum Director - Rev. John Kuriakose;

Liturgy Director - Rev. Abraham Lukose;

Mothers' Forum Director - Rev. Babu Madathilparambil;

Seminary Formation Director - Very Rev. Saji G. Mukkoot;

Vocation Promotion Director - Rev. Jobin Thomas;

Youth Apostolate Director - Rev. Jerry Mathew, Dir.;

ADVISORY BOARDS, COMMISSIONS, COMMITTEES, AND COUNCILS

Councils -

Council for Planning and Development - Most Rev. Philipos Mar Stephanos, Pres.; Rt. Rev. Msgr. Augustine Mangalath Abraham; Very Rev. Msgr. Gigi Philip;

Planning and Development - Rt. Rev. Msgr. Augustine Mangalath Abraham, Chief Vicar Gen.; Very Rev. Msgr. Gigi Philip, Vicar; Very Rev. Saji G. Mukkoot, Chancellor;

Council for the Promotion of Culture and Heritage - Very Rev. Saji G. Mukkoot, Pres.;

Promotion of Culture and Heritage - Philip John Ravi; Thomas Abraham; Rajan Kakkanattu;

Finance Council - Most Rev. Philipos Mar Stephanos, Pres.; Rt. Rev. Msgr. Augustine Mangalath Abraham, CFO; Rev. Jobin Thomas;

Finance Council - Rt. Rev. Msgr. Augustine Mangalath Abraham, Finance Officer; Rev. Jobin Thomas, Secy.; Reji Jose;

Pastoral Council - Most Rev. Philipos Mar Stephanos, Pres.; Very Rev. Saji G. Mukkoot, Chancellor; Sunil Chacko, Secy.;

Elected Members - Raju Vincent; Theresa Thomas; John Thomas (Appukuttan);

Ex Officio Members - Rt. Rev. Msgr. Augustine Mangalath Abraham, Chief Vicar Gen.; Very Rev. Msgr. Gigi Philip, Vicar; Saji Keekkadan, PRO;

Nominated Members - Binu Abraham; Aloysius John; Geevarghese Thankachan;

North Region Members - Christina George; Francis Thazhamon; Philip Thuruthy;

East Region Members - Thomas Abraham; Simon John; Geevarghese Mathew;

South Region Members - Renjan Abraham; Philip John (Biju); Binu Varghese;

West Region Members - Cheru John; James Koodal; Jimmy Kulangara;

Youth Members - Samson Zachariah; John Ettikkalayil; Tessy Philip;

Priests - Heads of Apostolates - Rev. Michael Philipose Edathil; Rev. Jerry Mathew; Rev. Jobin Thomas;

Representatives of Religious Orders - Rev. Francis Assisi, O.I.C.; Sr. Arpitha Chakkalakal, S.I.C.; Sr. Jovina D.M.;

Vicariates - Rev. Babu Madathilparambil; Rev. Thomas Ayyaneth; Rev. Binny Philip;

Presbyteral Council - Most Rev. Philipos Mar Stephanos, Pres.; Rt. Rev. Msgr. Augustine Mangalath Abraham; Rev. Abraham Thomas, Secy.;

Elected Members - Rev. Pathrose Panuvel; Rev. Thomas Ayyaneth; Rev. Michael Philipose Edathil;

Ex Officio Members - Rt. Rev. Msgr. Peter Kochery; Very Rev. Msgr. Gigi Philip; Very Rev. Saji G. Mukkoot, Chancellor;

Eastern - Rev. Babu Madathilparambil; Rev. Liju Thomas; Rev. Jobin Thomas;

North Region - Rev. Abraham Lukose; Rev. Praneesh Anchanithadathil; Rev. John Kuriakose;

West Region - Rev. Aji Varghese; Rev. Binny Philip; Rev. Biju Varghese;

South Region - Rev. Sam John; Rev. Jerry Mathew; Rev. Santhosh Thomas;

COMMUNICATIONS

Eparchy Webteam - Most Rev. Philipos Mar Stephanos, Pres.; Rt. Rev. Msgr. Augustine Mangalath Abraham, Vice. Pres. (mangalathfr@gmail.com);

Public Relations Office - Rev. Thomas Ayyaneth, Dir.; Saji Keekkadan, PRO;

TRIBUNAL

Tribunal - Rev. George Oonnoony;

Defender of the Bond - Very Rev. Saji G. Mukkoot;

Judicial Vicar - Rev. George Oonnoony;

Notary - Rev. Thomas Ayyaneth;

Office - Rev. Jobin Thomas;

Promoter of Justice - Rev. Abraham Thomas;

MISCELLANEOUS / OTHER OFFICES

Malankara Catholic Children's League - Rev. Jobin Thomas;

PARISHES, MISSIONS, AND CLERGY

COMMONWEALTH OF MASSACHUSETTS

WALTHAM

Boston Syro-Malankara Mission - 920 Trapelo Rd., c/o Our Lady Comforter of the Afflicted Parish, Waltham, MA 02452; Mailing: 872 Farmington Ave., West Hartford, CT 06119 t) 781-799-7535 Rev. Sam John, Admin.;

COMMONWEALTH OF PENNSYLVANIA

BENSALEM

St. Jude Malankara Catholic Church - 1200 Park Ave., Bensalem, PA 19020 c) 773-754-9638 tochacko123@gmail.com Rev. Babu Madathilparambil, Pst.; Very Rev. Saji G. Mukkoot, Pst. Min./Coord.; CRP Stds.: 71

STATE OF CALIFORNIA

NORTH HOLLYWOOD

St. Mary's Malankara Catholic Church - 6153 Cahuenga Blvd., North Hollywood, CA 91606 c) 215-971-0639 edailakattu@yahoo.co.in Rev. Daniel Edailakatt, Rector; CRP Stds.: 5

SARATOGA

St. Jude Malankara Catholic Church - 13716 Saratoga Ave., Saratoga, CA 95070; Mailing: 3815 Elston Dr., San Bruno, CA 94066 c) 215-971-0639; 650-355-5291 (Secy.) bvarghese@mccna.org; matkulangara@hotmail.com stjudemission.org Rev. Biju Varghese, Par. Vicar; CRP Stds.: 12

STATE OF FLORIDA

FORT LAUDERDALE

St. Mary's Malankara Catholic Church - 2512 Barbara Dr., Fort Lauderdale, FL 33316 t) 516-428-6909 frantonyvayali@gmail.com Rev. Santhosh Thomas, Pst.; CRP Stds.: 12

STATE OF GEORGIA

LAWRENCEVILLE

Atlanta Syro-Malankara Catholic Mission - c/o 1486 Duluth Hwy., Lawrenceville, GA 30043 t) (917) 673-5318 mukkudan@yahoo.com Very Rev. Saji G. Mukkoot, Admin.;

STATE OF ILLINOIS

EVANSTON

St. Mary's Malankara Catholic Church - 1208 Ashland Ave., Evanston, IL 60202 c) 586-690-3610 frjerrymathew@gmail.com Rev. Jerry Mathew, Pst.; CRP Stds.: 44

STATE OF MARYLAND

FORESTVILLE

St. Mary's Malankara Catholic Church - 1717 Ritchie Rd., Forestville, MD 20747 c) 240-532-2170 pastor@stmarysdc.org stmarysdc.org/ Rev. Michael Philipose Edathil, Pst.; CRP Stds.: 22

STATE OF MICHIGAN

WARREN

St. Joseph's Malankara Catholic Church - 25130 Lorraine Ave., Warren, MI 48089 c) 586-690-2072 patrosefr@gmail.com Rev. Pathrose Panuvel, Pst.; CRP Stds.: 8

STATE OF NEW JERSEY

ELIZABETH

St. Thomas Malankara Catholic Church - 11 Delaware St., Elizabeth, NJ 07206 c) 732-446-6311 frkochery@gmail.com Rev. Msgr. Peter Kochery, Pst.; Rev. Jobin Thomas, Par. Vicar; CRP Stds.: 19

STATE OF NEW YORK

ALBANY

Syro-Malankara Catholic Mission - 207 Main St., Albany, NY 12201; Mailing: 1500 DePaul St., Elmont, NY 11003 c) (203) 444-8542 Very Rev. Saji G. Mukkoot, Parish Life Coord.;

BLAUVELT

St. Peter's Malankara Catholic Church - 614 Western Hwy. S., Blauvelt, NY 10913 c) 203-444-8542 mangalathfr@gmail.com Rev. Msgr. Augustine Abraham Mangalath, Pst.; CRP Stds.: 31

ELMONT

St. Vincent de Paul Malankara Catholic Cathedral - 1500 DePaul St., Elmont, NY 11003 c) 516-303-5056 nobyaj@gmail.com Rev. Thomas Ayyaneth, Rector; CRP Stds.: 79

Syro-Malankara Catholic Mission, Phoenix, AZ - c/o 1500 Depaul St., Elmont, NY 11003 t) 480-452-5576 c) (917) 673-5318 Very Rev. Saji G. Mukkoot, Admin.;

YONKERS

St. Mary's Malankara Catholic Church - 18 Trinity St., Yonkers, NY 10701 c) 914-218-0758 lijuthundy@gmail.com Rev. Liju Thomas, Pst.; CRP Stds.: 18

STATE OF TEXAS

MESQUITE

St. Mary's Malankara Catholic Church - 2650 E. Scyene Rd., Mesquite, TX 75181 t) 214-563-0376 c) 469-705-8052 frvavoly@gmail.com Rev. Abraham Thomas, Pst.; CRP Stds.: 31

STAFFORD

St. Peter's Malankara Catholic Church - 3135 5th St., Stafford, TX 77477 c) 281-886-2013 frbinnyphilip@gmail.com spmcc.org Rev. Binny Philip, Pst.; CRP Stds.: 65

INSTITUTIONS LOCATED IN DIOCESE

CONVENTS, MONASTERIES, AND RESIDENCES FOR WOMEN [CON]

BOWIE

Daughters of Mary Convent (The Congregation of the Daughters of Mary, Inc.) - 12200 Rustic Hill Dr., Bowie, MD 20715 c) (202) 394-1030 dmcbowiewashington@gmail.com Sr. Divya George, D.M., Supr.; Srs.: 3

ELKINS PARK

Bethany Convent - 8381 Glen Rd., Elkins Park, PA 16027 t) 267-248-6394 bethanysrsphila@gmail.com Sr. Arpitha Chakkalakal, S.I.C., Supr.; Srs.: 2

GREENSBURG

Daughters of Mary Convent (The Congregation of the Daughters of Mary, Inc.) - 685 Angela Dr., Greensburg, PA 15601 c) 724-216-3375; 724-877-9050 dmcstanne@gmail.com Sr. Amala Jose, D.M., Supr.; Srs.: 2

LIVONIA

Daughters of Mary Convent (The Congregation of the Daughters of Mary, Inc.) - 33315 Broadmoor Ct., Livonia, MI 48154 t) (734) 353-5354 dmclivonia@gmail.com Sr. Litty Maria, D.M., Supr.; Srs.: 4

MONROVIA

Daughters of Mary Convent (The Congregation of the Daughters of Mary, Inc.) - 340 Norumbega Dr., Monrovia, CA 91016 t) 626-988-7461 dmlivonia@gmail.com Sr. Paul Maria, D.M., Supr.; Srs.: 2

MORTON GROVE

Bethany Convent - 7910 Arcadia St., Morton Grove, IL 60053 t) 847-972-1104 bethany@chicagomalankara.org Sr. Slooso Mannikkarottu, S.I.C., Supr.; Srs.: 3

NEW HYDE PARK

Bethany Convent - 1653 Highland Ave., New Hyde Park, NY 11040 t) 516-358-4597 usbethany@gmail.com Sr. Kanchana S.I.C., Supr.; Srs.: 3

YONKERS

Daughters of Mary Convent (The Congregation of the Daughters of Mary, Inc.) - 15 Trinity St., Yonkers, NY 10701 t) 914-207-6854 c) 646-919-7036 dmcityisland@optimum.net Sr. Savidha D.M., Supr.; Sr. Agnes Jose, D.M., Secy.; Srs.: 2

Daughters of Mary Convent (The Congregation of the Daughters of Mary, Inc.) - 45 Verona Ave., Yonkers, NY 10710 t) 914-202-9255 madonadmsisters@gmail.com Sr. Jovina D.M., Supr.; Srs.: 5

An asterisk (*) denotes an organization that has established tax-exempt status directly with the IRS and is not covered by the USCCB Group Ruling.

Archdiocese of Agana

MOST REVEREND MICHAEL J. BYRNES

Archbishop of Agana; ordained May 25, 1996; appointed Auxiliary Bishop of Detroit and Titular Bishop of Eguga March 22, 2011; consecrated May 5, 2011; appointed Coadjutor Archbishop of Agana October 31, 2016; installed November 30, 2016; Succeeded to See April 4, 2019. Chancery Office: 196 Cuesta San Ramon, Ste. B, Hagatna, GU 96910.

Chancery Office: 196 Cuesta San Ramon, Ste. B, Hagatna, GU 96910. T: 671-472-6116; T: 671-472-6573; T: 671-562-0000; F: 671-477-3519.

Erected by Pope Pius X, March 1, 1911 and Committed to the Order of Friars Minor Capuchin. Extended to all the Marianas Islands, July 4, 1946, Wake Island, June 14, 1948. Elevated to a Diocese, October 14, 1965, as a Suffragan of San Francisco. Elevated to Metropolitan Archdiocese, May 20, 1984 with a Suffragan See, Diocese of Caroline-Marshalls and Diocese of Chalan Kanoa (subsequently added January 13, 1985). Member of CEPAC Conference. Member of Federation of Catholic Bishops Conference of Oceania. Observer to NCCBUSCC Conference.

Guam is a Territory of the U.S.A. by Act of the U.S. Congress July 21, 1949.

Legal Title: Archbishop of Agana, a Corporation Sole.

STATISTICAL OVERVIEW

Personnel

Archbishops....1
Priests: Diocesan Active in Diocese....27
Priests: Retired, Sick or Absent....13
Number of Diocesan Priests....40
Religious Priests in Diocese....10
Total Priests in your Diocese....50
Permanent Deacons in Diocese....19
Total Brothers....3
Total Sisters....45

Parishes

Parishes....26
With Resident Pastor:
Resident Diocesan Priests....21
Resident Religious Priests....4
Without Resident Pastor:
Administered by Priests....6
Pastoral Centers....26

Welfare

Homes for the Aged....1
Total Assisted....40
Day Care Centers....3
Total Assisted....399
Specialized Homes....1
Total Assisted....55
Special Centers for Social Services....1
Total Assisted....14,100

Educational

High Schools, Diocesan and Parish....3
Total Students....1,025
Elementary Schools, Diocesan and Parish....9
Total Students....2,175
Catechesis / Religious Education:
High School Students....695
Elementary Students....881
Total Students under Catholic Instruction....4,776
Teachers in Diocese:
Sisters....5
Lay Teachers....398

Vital Statistics

Receptions into the Church:
Infant Baptism Totals....1,083
Minor Baptism Totals....72
Adult Baptism Totals....15
Received into Full Communion....42
First Communions....873
Confirmations....820
Marriages:
Catholic....128
Interfaith....10
Total Marriages....138
Deaths....919
Total Catholic Population....144,656
Total Population....170,184

LEADERSHIP

Delegate for Abuse and Clergy Misconduct - jalvarez@archagana.org Rev. Jonathan Alvarez;
Delegate for Women Religious - aperez@aolg.edu.gu Sr. Mary Angela Perez, R.S.M.;
Director of Communications - tony.diaz@archagana.org Antonio Diaz;
Director of Faith Formation - rkidd@archagana.org Rev. Richard Meno Kidd (vocations@archagana.org);
Chancellor - t) (671) 562-0021 jshimizu@archagana.org archagana.org Jennise T. Shimizu, Chancellor;
Judicial Vicar - cvila@archagana.org Rev. Carlos S. Vila, Judicial Vicar;
Finance Officer - t) 671-562-0064 Josephine G. Villanueva (jvillanueva@archagana.org);
Superintendent of Catholic Education - superintendent@archagana.org Rev. Jeffrey C. San Nicolas, Interim Supt. (vicargeneral@archagana.org);
Vicar for Clergy - vicarforclergy@archagana.org Rev. Michael Crisostomo, Vicar for Clergy;
Vicar General - t) (671) 562-0040 rconvocar@archagana.org archagana.org Very Rev. Romeo Duetao Convocar;

ADMINISTRATION

Chancery Office - t) 671-472-6116; 671-472-6573; 671-562-0000 archagana.org
Human Resources - t) (671) 562-0021 jshimizu@archagana.org
Office of the Archbishop - t) 671-562-0076 Elizabeth A. Weisenberger, Admin. Asst. to Archbishop (lweisenberger@archagana.org);
Office of Communications - tony.diaz@archagana.org archagana.org Antonio Diaz, Dir.;
Office of Delegate for Abuse and Clergy Misconduct - jalvarez@archagana.org Rev. Jonathan Alvarez;
Office of Finance - Almira Balagtas, Accounting Supvr. (abalagtas@archagana.org);
Office of the Vicar for Clergy - vicarforclergy@archagana.org Rev. Michael Crisostomo, Vicar for Clergy;
Office of the Vicar General - t) (671) 562-0063 abarber@archagana.org Angela Barber, Admin. Asst.;
Canonical Records - Luz Oberiano, Archives Asst. (luz.oberiano@archagana.org); June P. Ungacta, Archives & Records (jungacta@archagana.org);
Office of Catholic Education - Rev. Jeffrey C. San Nicolas, Interim Supt. (vicargeneral@archagana.org); Rosie Quitugua, Admin. Asst.;

ADVISORY BOARDS, COMMISSIONS, COMMITTEES, AND COUNCILS

Archdiocesan Liturgical Commission - Rev. Paul A.M. Gofigan, Chair; Rev. Jonathan Alvarez; Rev. Michael Crisostomo;

COMMUNICATIONS

Catholic Educational Radio (KOLG) The Light 90.9 - t) 671-475-4448 kolg.guam@gmail.com Rev. Michael Crisostomo, Exec.;

CONSULTATIVE BODIES

Archdiocesan College of Consultors - Rev. Joseph Anore (jbanore2015@outlook.com); Rev. Romeo (Romy) D. Convocar; Rev. Michael Crisostomo;
Archdiocesan Presbyteral Council - Rev. Joseph Anore, Chair (jbanore2015@outlook.com); Rev. Patrick Castro, O.F.M.Cap.; Rev. Romeo (Romy) D. Convocar;
Archdiocesan Finance Council - Ricardo (Rick) C. Duenas, Chair; Christopher Felix; Michael Flynn Jr.;

FAITH FORMATION

Office of Faith Formation - rkidd@archagana.org Rev. Richard Meno Kidd, Dir. (vocations@archagana.org);

FAMILY LIFE

Catholic Pro-Life Committee - t) 671-472-4569 Patricia (Pat) Perry, Chair; Sharon O'Mallan, Chair;
Couples for Christ - t) 671-487-1298 Rev. Paul A.M. Gofigan, Spiritual Adv./Care Srvcs.; Greg Calvo (calvogreg49@gmail.com);
Marriage Encounter - David Duenas (president@bbmcs.org); Liza Duenas; Rev. Jeffrey C. San Nicolas, Presenting Pastor (vicargeneral@archagana.org);
Natural Family Planning Program - tricia.tenorio@archagana.org

ORGANIZATIONS

Alee Shelter - Family Violence & Child Abuse and Neglect - t) 671-648-4673 (Hotline); 671-648-5888 Paula P. Siguenza, Prog. Mgr. (paula.perez@catholicsocialserviceguam.org);
Association of Diocesan Clergy of the Archdiocese of Agana (ADCAA) - Rev. Danilo (Dan) C. Bien; Rev. Manuel (Jun) Trenchera Jr.; Rev. Romeo (Romy) D. Convocar;
Catholic Charities of the Archdiocese of Agana/Catholic Social Services - t) 671-635-1406; 671-635-1441; 671-635-1442 info@cssguam.org www.catholicsocialserviceguam.org Diana B. Calvo, Exec.; Ronald B. Carandang, Deputy Dir.;
Gentle Refuge Crisis Pregnancy Center/Project Rachael - gentlerefuge@yahoo.com
Pontifical Holy Childhood Association & Pontifical Society for the Propagation of the Faith - t) 671-472-6573; 671-472-6116 Rev. Michael Crisostomo, Contact;
St. Anthony's Catholic Church - Faith-Based Program Project - t) 671-646-8044 Rev. Michael Crisostomo, Dir.; Roxanne Aguon, Prog. Coord.;
St. Dominic's Senior Care Home - t) 671-632-9370; 671-632-9379; 671-632-9378; 671-632-9372 info@stdominicsguam.org Sr. Maria Teresita Velez Manaloto, O.P., Admin.;

PASTORAL SERVICES

The Catholic Cemeteries of Guam, Inc. - t) 671-477-9329 catholiccemeteries.aoa@gmail.com Owen B.P. Bollinger, Admin.;
Director for the Ministry and Life of Permanent Deacons - Dcn. Leonard John Stohr (deaconlen@hotmail.com);
Director of Vocations - t) 671-477-7256 Rev. Richard Meno Kidd (vocations@archagana.org);

SOCIAL SERVICES

Safe Environment Office - Coordinator - t) 671-562-0029 safeenvironment@archagana.org Tricia L.T. Tenorio;
Victim Assistance Hotline - t) 671-562-0039
Ministry to the Homeless - t) 671-472-4569 ministrytothehomeless@gmail.com Rev. Michael Crisostomo, Exec.;
Ministry to the Homeless Thrift Shop - t) 671-472-4569 ministrytothehomeless@gmail.com Rev. Michael Crisostomo, Exec.;

SPIRITUAL LIFE

Office of Youth and Campus Ministries - rpangan@archagana.org Rev. Honorio Pangan, Dir.;

TRIBUNAL

Metropolitan Tribunal -
Adjunct Judge - Rev. Francis Demers, O.M.I.;
Advocate/Auditor - Rev. Romeo (Romy) D. Convocar;
Associate Judges - Rev. Julius Paul Factora, O.P.; Rev. Danilo Ramiro Flores; Rev. Joeffrey B. Catuiran;
Defender of the Bond - Rev. Jonathan Alvarez;
Ecclesiastical Notary - Rev. Felixberto Leon Guerrero, O.F.M.Cap.;
Judicial Vicar - Rev. Carlos S. Vila;
Promoter of Justice - Rev. Jose G. Villagomez, O.F.M.Cap.;

MISCELLANEOUS / OTHER OFFICES

Catholic Daughters of the Americas -
Court Maria Rainan Y Familia #2450 - t) 671-888-1540 Louise Rivera, Regent; Lorraine Rivera, Vice Regent;
Court Santa Barbara #2055 - t) 671-632-2899 Evangeline M. Cepeda, Regent; Nadine Cepeda, Vice Regent;
Our Lady of Camarin Court #2047 - t) 671-477-7929 Priscilla S.N. Muna, Regent; Sr. Mary Stephen Torres, R.S.M., Vice Regent;
Confraternity of Christian Mothers - t) 671-989-9732; 671-562-0000; 671-472-6116 palemike@yahoo.com Rev. Felixberto Leon Guerrero, O.F.M.Cap., Spiritual Dir.; Leila San Nicolas, Pres.; Carmelita Paet, Vice. Pres.;
Divine Mercy Apostolate - t) 671-483-9464 mercydiv@yahoo.com Rev. Joel de los Reyes, Contact;
El Shaddai, DWXI, PPFI, Fellowship Guam, USA, Guam Chapter - t) 671-632-5659 Rev. Danilo (Dan) C. Bien, Spiritual Dir.; Virginia Guanlao, Coord.;
Equestrian Order of the Holy Sepulcher of Jerusalem - t) 671-472-6201; 671-477-1842 Rev. Msgr. James L.G. Benavente, Contact;
Guam Cursillo Movement - t) 671-483-9464 Rev. Joel de los Reyes, Dir. (dreyes@guam.net); Maria S.T. Perez, Pres. (scm.perez@gmail.com);
Knights of Columbus Guam State Council - t) 617-888-2621 Rev. Joseph English, O.F.M.Cap., Chap.; Bobby O. Pelkey, State Deputy (bobpelkey55@gmail.com);
Latin Mass Community - t) 671-472-6339 Rev. Eric Forbes, O.F.M.Cap., Contact;
Legion of Mary, Guam Comitum - Rev. Danilo (Dan) C. Bien, Spiritual Dir.; Imelda Zimara, Guam Conitium (melzimara@yahoo.com);
Malojloj Retreat Center - t) 671-828-8454 malojlojretreatcenter@gmail.com Rev. Gerardo (Gerry) N. Hernandez, Contact; Jesse Perez, Asst. Oper. Mgr.;
Neo Catechumenal Way - t) 671-472-1729; 671-472-6201 Rev. Antonino Caminiti, Presbyter;
Nuestra Senora de la Paz y Buen Viaje Parish - t) 671-734-3723
Our Lady of Guadalupe Parish - t) 671-565-2160
Our Lady of Lourdes Parish -
Our Lady of Mt. Carmel Parish - t) 671-565-2136 Rev. Jose Alberto Rodriguez, Presbyter;
San Dimas & Our Lady of the Rosary Parish - t) 671-828-8056 Rev. Julius B. Akinyemi, Presbyter;
St. Padre Pio Fraternity - Secular Franciscans Order - t) 671-472-6339 Rev. Patrick Castro, O.F.M.Cap., Spiritual Asst.; Violet Manibusan, Min. (violet@netpci.com);
Secular Franciscans (Third Order) - Rev. Jose G. Villagomez, O.F.M.Cap.; Rev. Eric Forbes, O.F.M.Cap.; Teresita R. Sablan, Minister;

PARISHES, MISSIONS, AND CLERGY

TERRITORY OF GUAM

AGANA

Dulce Nombre de Maria Cathedral - Basilica - 207 Archbishop Felixberto C. Flores St., Agana, GU 96910 t) 671-472-6201; 671-477-1842 info@aganacathedral.org Most Rev. Michael J. Byrnes, Archbishop; Rev. Msgr. James Leon Guerrero Benavente, Pst.; Rev. William Mamangun, Par. Vicar; Rev. Thomas B. McGrath, S.J., Par. Vicar; Dcn. Stephen Martinez; Dcn. Augusto (Gus) F. Cepeda; Dcn. John Dierking; CRP Stds.: 139

AGANA HEIGHTS

Our Lady of the Blessed Sacrament - 135 Chalan Kapuchino, Agana Heights, GU 96910 t) 671-472-6246 olbsaganaheights@gmail.com Rev. Andre Eduvala, O.F.M.Cap., Pst.; Sylvia T. Calvo, DRE; Christine M. Chargualaf, DRE; CRP Stds.: 53

ASAN

Nino Perdido Y Sagrada Familia - 141 Nino Perdido Dr.,

Asan, GU 96910; Mailing: P.O. Box 45, Hagatna, GU 96932 t) 671-477-2211 jlcabana22@yahoo.com; frjonalvarez@yahoo.com Rev. Jonathan Alvarez, Pst.; CRP Stds.: 19

BARRIGADA

San Vicente Ferrer and San Roke - 229 San Roque Dr., Barrigada, GU 96913 t) 671-734-4573 sanvicentechurch@gmail.com Rev. Joel de los Reyes, Pst.; Rev. Francesco S. Asproni, In Res.; Dcn. Larry Claros, DRE; CRP Stds.: 75

DEDEDO

St. Andrew Kim - St. Andrew Kim Rd. Harmon, Dededo, GU 96929; Mailing: P.O. Box 1555, Agana, GU 96932 t) 671-637-4148 (Office); 671-637-1116 (Rectory); 671-483-8200 (CRP) philips97@hanmail.net; bimok67@hanmail.net www.guam.catb.kr Under the Jurisdiction of Santa Barbara Parish, Dededo. Rev. Jae Heon Song, Admin.; CRP Stds.: 24

Santa Barbara - 330 Iglesia Cir., Dededo, GU 96929 t) 671-632-5659 santabarbaraguam@gmail.com Dcn. Alfred Ray; Rev. Dan Bien, Pst.; Rev. Francis X. Hezel, S.J., Par. Vicar; Rev. Michael Vincent Jucutan, Par. Vicar; Dcn. Joe Gumataotao; Dcn. Romeo Hernandez; CRP Stds.: 108

HÅGAT

Our Lady of Mount Carmel - 157 S. Eugenio St, Hågat, GU 96915; Mailing: P.O. Box 8353, Agat, GU 96928 t) 671-565-2136 Rev. Jose Alberto Rodriguez, Pst.; CRP Stds.: 149

Santa Ana Chapel - Lot No. 306-4-2, Agat, GU 96928

HAGATNA

Nuestra Senora de la Paz y Buen Viaje - ; Mailing: P.O. Box EC, Hagatna, GU 96932 t) 671-734-4223 (CRP); 671-734-3723 Rev. Carlos S. Vila, Admin.; CRP Stds.: 27

HUMÅTAK

San Dionisio - San Dionisio Dr., Humåtak, GU 96915; Mailing: P.O. Box 6099, Merizo, GU 96915 t) 671-828-8056 Rev. Harold Colorado Prieto, Admin.; CRP Stds.: 6

INARAJAN

St. Joseph - St. Joseph Church, Building #719 Pale Duenas St., Inarajan, GU 96917; Mailing: P.O. Box 170022, Inarajan, Inarajan, GU 96917 t) 671-828-8102 stjoseph_guest@outlook.com Rev. Joseph Anore, Admin.; CRP Stds.: 47

San Isidro - 131 San Isidro St., Inarajan, GU 96915; Mailing: HC 1 Box 17083, Inarajan, GU 96915 t) 671-828-8454 sanisidromalojloj@gmail.com Rev. Gerardo (Gerry) N. Hernandez, Pst.; CRP Stds.: 18

MAINA

Our Lady of the Purification - 220 Maria Candelaria Rd., Maina, GU 96910; Mailing: 196 Cuesta San Ramon, Ste. B, Hagatna, GU 96910 t) 671-477-7256 mainacatholicchurch@gmail.com Rev. Junee Valencia, Admin.;

MALESSO

San Dimas and Our Lady of the Rosary - 329 Chalan Canton Tasi, Malesso, GU 96915; Mailing: P.O. Box 6099, Merizo, GU 96916 t) 671-828-8056 Rev. Harold Colorado Prieto, Admin.; CRP Stds.: 24

MANGILAO

Santa Teresita Catholic Church - 192 Vietnam Veterans Hwy., Mangilao, GU 96913 t) 671-689-6231 (CRP); 671-734-2100; 671-734-2171 missionsupport@archspm.org; santateresitaguam@gmail.com Dcn. George Quitugua; Rev. Joseph English, O.F.M.Cap., Pst.; Dcn. Huan Hosei; CRP Stds.: 250

MONGMONG

Nuestra Senora de las Aguas - 139 Roy T. Damian St., Mongmong, GU 96927; Mailing: P.O. Box 163, Hagatna, GU 96932 t) 671-477-6754 nsdlaguas@guam.net Dcn. Louis J. Rama; Rev. Manuel (Jun) Trenchera Jr., Pst.; CRP Stds.: 23

ORDOT

San Juan Bautista - 107A Judge Sablan St., Ordot, GU 96910; Mailing: P.O. Box 49, Hagatna, GU 96932 t) 671-472-8341 Rev. Antonino Caminiti, Pst.; CRP Stds.: 29

PITI

Assumption of Our Lady - 314 Assumption Dr., Piti, GU 96915 t) 671-472-2272 assumptionpitichurch@gmail.com Rev. Danilo B. Trajano, Pst.; CRP Stds.: 12

SANTA RITA

Our Lady of Guadalupe - 708 Bishop Olano St., Santa Rita, GU 96915; Mailing: P.O. Box 7355, Agat, GU 96928 t) 671-565-2160 ologsr@gmail.com Dcn. John Fernandez; Rev. Richard Meno Kidd, Pst.; CRP Stds.: 74

SINAJANA

St. Jude Thaddeus - 122 Bien Avenida, Sinajana, GU 96910 t) 671-475-6530 stjudeguam@gmail.com Rev. Patrick Castro, O.F.M.Cap., Pst.; Cynthia Eclavea, DRE; CRP Stds.: 48

TALO'FO'FO'

San Miguel - 138 San Miguel St., Talo'fo'fo', GU 96915-3606 t) 671-789-1069 sanmiguelguam@gmail.com Rev. Danilo D. Ferrandiz, Par. Admin.; CRP Stds.: 55

TAMUNING

St. Anthony and St. Victor - 507 Chalan San Antonio, Tamuning, GU 96913 t) 671-646-8044; 671-646-7181 pastor@stanthonyguam.org www.stanthonyguam.org Rev. Michael Crisostomo, Pst.; Rev. Honorio Pangan, Par. Vicar; Rev. Edwin Bushu, In Res.; Rev. Jeffrey C. San Nicolas, In Res.; CRP Stds.: 68

TOTO

Immaculate Heart of Mary (Toto Church) - Immaculate Heart of Mary Church, 225 Aragon St., Toto, GU 96910 t) 671-477-9118 ihom@yahoo.com ihomguam.com Chuukese Community Rev. Val Gabriel Roa Rodriguez, Pst.; Dcn. Rene Dela Cruz; Dcn. Anthony Leon Guerrero; Dcn. Elias Itoy Ruda; CRP Stds.: 110

TUMON

Blessed Diego Luis de San Vitores Church - 884 Pale' San Vitores Rd., Tumon, GU 96913-4013 t) 671-646-5649 blsdiego@yahoo.com Rev. Romeo (Romy) D. Convocar, Pst.; CRP Stds.: 23

YIGO

Our Lady of Lourdes - 153 Chalan Pale Ramon Lagu, Unit A, Yigo, GU 96929 t) 671-653-1102 (CRP); 671-653-2584 ourlady@teleguam.net Dcn. Greg Calvo; Dcn. David Richards; Dcn. Leonard Stohr; Rev. Paul A.M. Gofigan, Pst.; Veronica Lizama, DRE; Femelyne Wesolowski, DRE; CRP Stds.: 66

YONA

San Francisco de Asis - 1404 N. Canton Tasi, Yona, GU 96915; Mailing: 135 Chalan Kapuchino, Agana Heights, GU 96910 t) 671-789-1492 (CRP); 671-789-1491 stfrancisyona@gmail.com Rev. Felixberto Leon Guerrero, OFM Cap., Pst.; Sharon O'Mallan, DRE; CRP Stds.: 136

SCHOOLS: PRESCHOOL THRU HIGH SCHOOL

SCHOOLS

TERRITORY OF GUAM

DEDEDO

Santa Barbara Catholic School - (PAR) (Grades PreK-8) 274 W. Santa Barbara Ave., Ste. A., Dededo, GU 96929-5378 t) 671-632-5578 info@sbcs.edu.gu www.sbcs.edu.gu Sr. Maria Rosario Gaite, R.S.M., Prin.; Stds.: 347; Sr. Tchrs.: 1; Lay Tchrs.: 29

HAGAT

Our Lady of Mount Carmel Catholic School - (PAR) 32A Calle Delos Marteres, Hagat, GU 96915; Mailing: P.O. Box 7830, Agat, GU 96928 t) 671-565-3822; 671-565-5128 office@mcs51.com Krystal Agustin, Prin.; Michael F. Phillips, Chair; Stds.: 256; Lay Tchrs.: 19

SINAJANA

Bishop Baumgartner Memorial Catholic School - (DIO) (Grades K-8) 281 Calle Angel Flores St., Sinajana, GU 96910 t) 671-472-6670 principal@bbmcs.org Lila Lujan, Prin.; David Duenas, Pres.; Stds.: 445; Scholastics: 35; Lay Tchrs.: 35

TAMUNING

Saint Anthony Catholic School - (PAR) 529 Chalan San Antonio, Tamuning, GU 96913 t) 671-647-1140 angie.susuico@sacsguam.com www.sacsguam.org Rev. Michael Crisostomo, Admin.; Angie Susuico, Admin.; Maricon Reyes, Admin.; Stds.: 400; Lay Tchrs.: 37

YIGO

Dominican Catholic School - 114 Chalan Pale Ramon-Lagu Rte. 1, Yigo, GU 96929 t) 671-653-3021 admin@dcsguam.com; dcdcordot@gmail.com www.dcsguam.com Sr. Esperanza H. Seguban, O.P., Prin.; Sr. Antonia Balagtas Egar, O.P., Prioress; Sr. Victoria Cambronero, O.P., Treas.; Stds.: 108; Sr. Tchrs.: 4; Lay Tchrs.: 13

YONA

St. Francis School - (PAR) 1426 N. Chalan Kanton Tasi, Yona, GU 96915; Mailing: P.O. Box 21297, GMF, GU 96921 t) 671-789-1270; 671-789-1351 admin@sfcscrusaders.com www.sfsguam.com Lisa Baza-Cruz, Prin.; Anthony Quitugua, Vice Prin.; Stds.: 178; Lay Tchrs.: 16

HIGH SCHOOLS

TERRITORY OF GUAM

AGANA

Academy of Our Lady of Guam - (DIO) (Grades 9-12) 233 W. Archbishop Felixberto C. Flores St., Agana, GU 96910 t) 671-477-8203 acad@aolg.edu.gu www.aolg.edu.gu Iris D. Gaza, Prin.; Dr. Rita Duenas, Pres.; Stds.: 291; Sr. Tchrs.: 1; Lay Tchrs.: 24

CHALAN PAGO

Father Duenas Memorial School - (DIO) 119 Dueñas Ln., Chalan Pago, GU 96910; Mailing: P.O. Box FD, Hagatna, GU 96932 t) 671-734-2261; 671-734-2263 fdms@fatherduenas.com www.fatherduenas.com Ismael Perez, Prin.; Dante Perez, Librn.; N. Oscar Miyashita, Endowment Chairman; Stds.: 411; Scholastics: 1; Pr. Tchrs.: 1; Lay Tchrs.: 31

TALO'FO'FO'

Notre Dame High School, Inc. - (PRV) (Grades 9-12) 480 S. San Miguel St., Talo'fo'fo', GU 96915-3540 t) 671-789-1676; 671-789-1745 info@ndhsguam.com ndhsguam.com Nicole Manahan, Prin.; Sr. Jean Ann Crisostomo, S.S.N.D., Pres.; Stds.: 317; Lay Tchrs.: 23

INSTITUTIONS LOCATED IN DIOCESE

CATHOLIC CHARITIES [CCH]

BARRIGADA

Catholic Social Service of Guam - 234 U.S. Army Juan C. Fejeran St., Barrigada, GU 96913-1407 t) 671-635-1442; 671-635-1406 info@cssguam.org www.catholicsocialserviceguam.org Diana B. Calvo, Dir.; Paula P. Siguenza, Deputy Director; Asstd. Annu.: 6,115; Staff: 162

Alee I Shelter for Abused Spouses & Children - 234A U.S. Army Juan G. Fejeran St., Barrigada, GU 96913 t) 671-648-5888 alee@catholicsocialserviceguam.org Leinanimatsu Naholowaa, Program Manager;

Alee II Shelter for Abused Children - 234A U.S. Army Juan G. Fejeran St., Barrigada, GU 96913 t) 671-648-5888 alee@catholicsocialserviceguam.org Leinanimatsu Naholowaa, Program Manager;

Community Habilitation Program - 234A U.S. Army

Juan G. Fejeran St., Barrigada, GU 96913 t) 671-472-8598 PeterJohn Camacho, Prog. Mgr.;
Emergency Food Bank - 234A U.S. Army Juan G. Fejeran St., Barrigada, GU 96913 t) 671-635-1424 md@cssguam.org
Federal Grant (St. Anthony Church -STOP Violence Against Women) - 507 Chalan San Antonio, Tamuning, GU 96913 t) 671-646-8044 www.stanthonyguam.org St. Anthony's Church Faith-Based Program. Rev. Michael Crisostomo, Dir.;
Finger Printing - 234A U.S. Army Juan G. Fejeran St., Barrigada, GU 96913 t) 671-635-1441 dianacalvo@cssguam.org
Guma San Jose - 234A U.S. Army Juan G. Fejeran St., Barrigada, GU 96913 t) 671-633-2955 gumasanjose@catholicsocialserviceguam.org
Guma Serenidad - 234A U.S. Army Juan C. Fejeran St., Barrigada, GU 96913 t) 671-632-8853 epatague@cssguam.org Edward Patague, Acting Program Manager;
Housing Program - 234A U.S. Army Juan C. Fejeran St., Barrigada, GU 96913 blainefchargualaf@gmail.com Blaine F Chargualaf, Program Manager;
Karidat Shelter for Adults - 234A U.S. Army Juan G. Fejeran St., Barrigada, GU 96913 t) 671-635-1404 karidat@cssguam.org
Monthly Rummage Sale - 234A U.S. Army Juan C. Fejeran St., Barrigada, GU 96913 t) 671-635-1441 Joseph Diaz, Program Manager;
Msgr. David I.A. Quitugua Foundation - 234A U.S. Army Juan G. Fejeran St., Barrigada, GU 96913 t) 671-635-1441 dianacalvo@cssguam.org
Respite Care - 234A U.S. Army Juan C. Fejeran St., Barrigada, GU 96913 t) 671-635-1418 respite@cssguam.org
Support Services - 234A U.S. Army Juan G. Fejeran St., Barrigada, GU 96913 t) 671-635-1441 dianacalvo@cssguam.org
Thrift Shop - 234A U.S. Army Juan G. Fejeran St., Barrigada, GU 96913 jsdbonita@yahoo.com Joseph Diaz, Program Manager;

CONVENTS, MONASTERIES, AND RESIDENCES FOR WOMEN [CON]

BARRIGADA
Religious Missionaries of St. Dominic - 350 N. Sabana Dr., Barrigada Heights, Barrigada, GU 96913 t) 671-632-7104; 671-632-9370 (Nursing Home) sehsop@yahoo.com; info@stdominicsguam.org www.stdominicsguam.org Sr. Esperanza H. Seguban, O.P., Prov. Asst.; Srs.: 16

DEDEDO
Santa Barbara Convent - 274 B. W. Santa Barbara Ave., Dededo, GU 96929 t) 671-632-2384 bibamercy70@gmail.com Institute of the Sisters of Mercy of the Americas, South Central Community on Guam. Sr. Marian Therese Arroyo, R.S.M., Admin.; Srs.: 2

HAGATNA
Cathedral Mercy Convent - 221 Archbishop F. C. Flores St., Hagatna, GU 96910-5102 t) 671-477-9291 aperez@mercysc.org Sr. Mary Emiline Artero, R.S.M., Contact; Srs.: 3
Mercedarian Missionaries of Berriz - 161 Sunset Dr., Apt. A, Hagatna, GU 96910-6451 t) 671-477-8303 mmbguam@yahoo.com www.mmberriz.com Sr. Anotia Addy, M.M.B., Representative Mission of Micronesia; Srs.; 5

MANGILAO
Tai Mercy Convent and Formation House - 164 Sabanan Magas Rd., Mangilao, GU 96913; Mailing: P.O. Box 22865 GMF, Barrigada, GU 96921-2865 t) 671-734-3312 bibamercy70@gmail.com sistersofmercyguam.org Institute of the Sisters of Mercy of the Americas, South Central Community on Guam, Professed Sisters in various Apostolates. Sr. Marian Therese Arroyo, R.S.M., Admin.; Srs.: 8

TALO'FO'FO'
S.S.N.D. Notre Dame Center - 480 S. San Miguel St., Talo'fo'fo', GU 96915-3540 t) 671-789-0501 francineperez41@gmail.com Sr. Mary Francine Perez, SSND, Contact; Srs.: 7

TAMUNING
Mercy Action Marianas, Ltd. (MAML) (Institute of the Sisters of Mercy of the Americas, South Central Community on Guam) - 211 Fr. San Vitores St., Tamuning, GU 96913 t) 671-649-7561 marroyo@mercysc.org sistersofmercyguam.org Sr. Marian Therese Arroyo, R.S.M., Sister Life Minister - Administrator; Srs.: 2
Mercy Heights Convent - 211 Fr. San Vitores St., Tamuning, GU 96913 t) 671-646-7246 marroyo@mercysc.org sistersofmercyguam.org Sr. Marian Therese Arroyo, R.S.M., Admin.; Srs.: 16

MISCELLANEOUS [MIS]

AGANA HEIGHTS
Secular Franciscans - 135 Chalan Kapuchino, Agana Heights, GU 96910 t) 671-472-6339 rosebaker50@gmail.com Maria Rosario B. Baker, Minister; Rev. Patrick Castro, O.F.M.Cap., Spiritual Assistant;

MONASTERIES AND RESIDENCES FOR PRIESTS AND BROTHERS [MON]

AGANA HEIGHTS
St. Fidelis Friary - 135 Chalan Kapuchino, Agana Heights, GU 96910 t) 671-472-6339 capuchin@netpci.com Headquarters of Capuchin Friars (Provincial Custody, Star of the Sea). Rev. Andre Eduvala, O.F.M.Cap., Pst.; Rev. Joseph English, O.F.M.Cap., Pst.; Rev. Eric Forbes, O.F.M.Cap., Pst.; Rev. Felixberto Leon Guerrero, O.F.M.Cap., Pst.; Rev. Jose G. Villagomez, O.F.M.Cap., Pst.; Bro. Jason Chargualaf, Brother; Rev. Patrick Castro, O.F.M.Cap., Custos; Brs.: 8; Priests: 7

TAMUNING
Society of Jesus Micronesia - 153 Linda Way, Tamuning, GU 96913; Mailing: P.O. Box 315244, Tamuning, GU 96931 t) 671-649-0073 c) (670) 286-5000; 671-929-6753 ueamicfjsuperior@jesuits.org; fhezel@jesuits.org Rev. Edward J. Quinnan, S.J., Supr.; Rev. Francis X. Hezel, S.J., Par. Vicar; Rev. Thomas B. McGrath, S.J., Par. Vicar; Priests: 2

NURSING / REHABILITATION / CONVALESCENCE / ELDERLY CARE [NUR]

BARRIGADA HEIGHTS
Saint Dominic's Senior Care Home - 350 N. Sabana Dr., Barrigada Heights, GU 96913-1262 t) 671-632-9370; 671-632-9378; 671-632-7104; 671-632-9379 stdom@teleguam.net; info@stdominicsguam.org www.stdominicsguam.org Sr. Maria Teresita Velez Manaloto, O.P., Admin.; Sr. Bernadita Delos Reyes, O.P., Treas.; Sr. Ursula Antazo Apacionado, O.P., Local Superior; Asstd. Annu.: 40; Staff: 59

PRESCHOOLS / CHILDCARE CENTERS [PRE]

AGANA
Dominican Child Development Center - ; Mailing: P.O. Box 5668, Agana, GU 96932 t) 671-477-7228; 671-472-1524 avegamotin@gmail.com Sr. Eva P. Gamotin, Prin.; Sr. Versamin Calamiong, Prioress; Stds.: 117; Lay Tchrs.: 9

MANGILAO
Infant of Prague Nursery and Kindergarten, Inc. (Institute of the Sisters of the Mercy of the Americas, South Central Community on Guam) - 164 Sabanan Magas Rd., Mangilao, GU 96913 t) 671-734-2785 iopmercy18@gmail.com Sr. Erencia Saipweirik, Prin.; Stds.: 24; Lay Tchrs.: 2

TAMUNING
Mercy Heights Nursery and Kindergarten, Inc. - 211 Fr. San Vitores St., Tamuning, GU 96913 t) 671-646-1185 mhcnk211@gmail.com Belen Defant, Prin.; Stds.: 142; Lay Tchrs.: 17

Diocese of Arecibo, Puerto Rico

(Dioecesis Arecibensis)

MOST REVEREND ALBERTO ARTURO FIGUEROA MORALES

Bishop of Arecibo; ordained June 2, 1990; appointed Titular Bishop of Phelbes and Auxiliary Bishop of San Juan, P.R. November 19, 2019; ordained December 27, 2019; appointed Bishop of Arecibo September 14, 2022; installed October 17, 2022.

The Chancery: 206 Dr. Salas St., P.O. Box 616, Arecibo, PR 00613. T: 787-878-3180; T: 787-878-3110; F: 787-880-2661.
arecibo@diocesisdearecibo.org

ESTABLISHED APRIL 30, 1960.

Square Miles 833.

Comprises the mid-northern part of the Island.

STATISTICAL OVERVIEW

Personnel
Bishop 1
Retired Bishops 1
Priests: Diocesan Active in Diocese 51
Priests: Diocesan Active Outside Diocese 10
Priests: Retired, Sick or Absent 12
Number of Diocesan Priests 73
Religious Priests in Diocese 29
Total Priests in your Diocese 102
Ordinations:
Transitional Deacons 2
Permanent Deacons 3
Permanent Deacons in Diocese 54
Total Brothers 4
Total Sisters 145

Parishes
Parishes 58
With Resident Pastor:
Resident Diocesan Priests 43
Resident Religious Priests 13
Without Resident Pastor:
Administered by Priests 2
Missions 232
Pastoral Centers 1

Welfare
Homes for the Aged 2
Total Assisted 48
Residential Care of Children 2
Total Assisted 36
Specialized Homes 1
Total Assisted 18
Special Centers for Social Services 1
Total Assisted 25
Other Institutions 1
Total Assisted 796

Educational
Diocesan Students in Other Seminaries 5
Total Seminarians 5
Colleges and Universities 1
Total Students 1,648
High Schools, Diocesan and Parish 7
Total Students 843
High Schools, Private 6
Total Students 901
Elementary Schools, Diocesan and Parish 7
Total Students 1,274
Elementary Schools, Private 6
Total Students 1,535
Total Students under Catholic Instruction 6,206
Teachers in Diocese:
Sisters 6
Lay Teachers 313

Vital Statistics
Receptions into the Church:
Infant Baptism Totals 1,091
Minor Baptism Totals 140
Adult Baptism Totals 31
First Communions 1249
Confirmations 1,362
Marriages:
Catholic 253
Interfaith 13
Total Marriages 266
Deaths 1,701
Total Catholic Population 307,903
Total Population 549,827

LEADERSHIP

Chancery Office - t) 787-878-3110; 787-878-3180 jorgemorales@obispado.org Lyanne M. Ruiz Ramos, Secy.;

Secretary to the Bishop - t) 787-878-3180 h.anama@obispado.org Sr. Ana Maria Granados;

Vicar General - t) 787-878-3180 pluismsemv@yahoo.com Rev. Luis A. Colon Rivera, S.E.M.V., Vicar;

Secretary and Receptionist - t) 787-878-3180 wcordero@obispado.org Waleska Cordero;

Economic Administrator - t) 787-878-3180 Antonio Perez Lopez;

Economic Administrator Assistant - t) 787-878-3180 admin@obispado.org Mariluna Roman (mroman@obispado.org); Kathy Paulino Collazo (kathypaulino@obispado.org);

Chancellor - t) 787-878-3180; 787-878-3110 Rev. Jorge Yamil Morales Rivera, Chancellor;

Diocesan Tribunal of Arecibo - Rev. Ramon Olivencia Velez, Vicar;

Adjutant Judges - t) 787-816-5614 lsrivera@obispado.org Rev. Jorge Yamil Morales Rivera; Rev. Lisimaco Hincapie Ramirez; Rev. Jorge Luis Virella Vazquez;

Advocate - t) 787-816-5614 lsrivera@obispado.org Rev. Oscar Chacon Gonzalez, O.SS.T.;

Defenders of the Bond - t) 787-816-5614 lsrivera@obispado.org Rev. Alberto Diaz Colon; Rev. Hector I. Flores Gonzalez;

Notary - t) 787-816-5614 lsrivera@obispado.org Luz S. Rivera Velazquez, Secy.; Itza I. Roa Cuevas, Secy.;

Promoter of Justice - Rev. Hector I. Flores Gonzalez;

Secretary -

Vicar of Diocesan Pastoral Affairs - t) 787-878-3180 ajimenez@obispado.org Rev. Adrian N. Jimenez Ortiz;

Secretary -

Comision Diocesana Catequesis - t) 787-878-8401 catequesis_arecibo@hotmail.com Olvidalia Fernandez;

Departamento de Catequesis - t) 787-878-8401 catequesis_arecibo@hotmail.com Liliam Gonzalez Guzman;

Patrimonio Eclesial - t) 787-878-3180 Lyanne M. Ruiz Ramos, Secy.;

Consejo Episcopal - t) 787-878-3180 arecibo@obispado.org Most Rev. Daniel Fernandez Torres; Rev. Luis A. Colon Rivera, S.E.M.V.; Rev. Adrian Jimenez Ortiz;

Diocesan Consultors - t) 787-878-3180 arecibo@obispado.org Rev. P. Jesus Monreal Pujante, O.Carm.; Rev. Luis A. Colon Rivera, S.E.M.V.; Rev. Victor Rojas Rodriguez;

Priest's Senate (Consejo Presbiteral) - t) 787-878-3180 arecibo@obispado.org Most Rev. Daniel Fernandez Torres; Rev. Luis A. Colon Rivera, S.E.M.V.; Rev. Ramon Olivencia Velez;

OFFICES AND DIRECTORS

Ayuda Social Movimiento Juan XXIII - t) 787-881-7141 retirosanjuan23@gmail.com www.ayudasocialjuanxxiii.org Eduviges Rivera Cheveres, Pres. (reduviges5@gmail.com);

Caballeros de Colon - c) 787-510-9142 betan62@gmail.com Edgard Quiñonez Morales;

Cursillos de Cristiandad - t) 787-650-6665 Nelson Morales (cayitosg@hotmail.com);

Director of Communications Media - c) 787-309-9777 vm2@obispado.org Vivian Maldonado;

Director of Youth - t) 787-855-8743 panal2000@yahoo.com Rev. Elmon M. Hernandez Fana;

Encuentro Matrimonial - t) 787-640-4593; 787-317-8576 Manuel Robles (merobles22@gmail.com); Carmen Ruiz (carmenceci22@gmail.com);

Equipos de Nuestra Senora - t) 787-607-6636; 787-901-1117 mlopezdefranqui@hotmail.com Manuel Franqui Perez; Marisol López Cuevas;

Hospital Chaplains - t) 787-878-1149 (Cathedral San Felipe); 787-878-1822 (San Martín de Porres, Arecibo) chatedralarecibo@hotmail.com; sanmartinarecibo@gmail.com Rev. Adrian N. Jimenez Ortiz, Chap.; Rev. Josue Efraín Colon Claudio, Chap.;

Pavia Hospital - Rev. Josue Efrain Colon Claudio, Chap.;

Susoni Hospital - Dcn. Javier Rodriguez Figueroa, Coord. Capellania; Rev. Adrian N. Jimenez Ortiz, Chap.; Rev. Fernando Morell;

Instituto San Jose, Corp. - t) 787-400-0127 institutosanjose2018@gmail.com Cesar Augusto Serrano Zuluaga, Dir.;

Legion of Mary - t) 787-880-7414 Lucy Salvat; Rev. Victor Rojas Rodriguez;

Movimiento Familia de Jesus - t) 787-366-1446; 787-366-1420 lillian_freddy@yahoo.com Wilfredo Mercado; Lillian Mercado;

Pastoral Familiar - t) 787-883-4875 pbrorojasvictor@hotmail.com Rev. Victor Rojas Rodriguez, Dir.;

Pastoral Vocational Program - t) 787-878-3180 arecibo@obispado.org Rev. Jorge Yamil Morales Rivera;

Programs -

Renovacion Carismatica - t) 787-235-0434 Eliezer Maldonado (maldonadoe1307@yahoo.com);

Retreat House, Centro Diocesano Mons. Mendez - t) 787-878-3110 Antonio Perez Lopez, Admin.;

Seminario San Jose College Seminary - t) 34-948-144-023 ssjnavarra@gmail.com Rev. Eduardo Torres Moreno, Admin.;

Seminary Board and Vocation Program - t) 787-878-3180 arecibo@obispado.org Most Rev. Daniel Fernandez (daniel@obispado.org); Rev. Luis A. Colon Rivera, S.E.M.V.; Rev. Victor Rojas Rodriguez;

Servicios Administrativos Perpetuo Socorro - t) 787-878-3180 colegiosdiocesanos@obispado.org Antonio Perez, Dir.; Kenneth Pagan Lafontaine, Admin.;

Sociedad de El Santo Nombre - t) 787-390-7364 Maritza Cordova (rodzlz@yahoo.com);

Sociedad San Vincente de Paul (Vincentinos) - t) 787-854-2858 manaticm@yahoo.com Jose Luis Colon Rodriguez, Pres.;

Superintendent of Schools - t) 787-878-1095; 787-880-0111 educa@supesca.org Dcn. Juan A. Valdes;

Vocations - t) 787-878-3110 arecibo@obispado.org Rev. Jorge Yamil Morales Rivera;

CATHOLIC CHARITIES

Oficina para la Promocion y el Desarrollo Humano, Inc. - t) 787-817-6951 opdhinc@gmail.com www.opdh.org Angelica M. Flores, Dir. (aflores.opdh@gmail.com); Maribel Rodriguez; Sylma Cuevas, Psychology Asst.;

PARISHES, MISSIONS, AND CLERGY

COMMONWEALTH OF PUERTO RICO

ÁNGELES

Our Lady of Angels - Carr. 111 Ramal 602 Km 1.3, Bo. Ángeles, Ángeles, PR 00611; Mailing: P.O. Box 98, Angeles, PR 00611-0098 t) (787) 680-1828 ofiparr12@gmail.com Rev. Miguel Jose Velez Nieves, Par. Admin.; Dcn. Ferdinand Reyes Sisco; Magali Vargas Ocasio, DRE; CRP Stds.: 25

Chapel Sagrada Familia - Las Vegas, Bo. Ángeles, Ángeles, PR 00611

Chapel Nuestra Senora de la Monserrate - Santa Isabel, Ángeles, PR 00611

Chapel San Jose - El Corcho, Bo. Ángeles, Ángeles, PR 00611

ARECIBO

Cathedral of San Felipe Apostol - 60 Ave. José de Diego, Arecibo, PR 00612; Mailing: P.O. Box 577, Arecibo, PR 00612 t) 787-878-1149; 787-879-2759 chatedralarecibo@hotmail.com Rev. Adrian N. Jimenez Ortiz, Rector; Rev. Fernando Morell Dominguez, In Res.; Dcn. Daniel Galindez Torres; Dcn. Juan A. Valdes Lazo; Madeline Lorenzo, DRE; CRP Stds.: 36

Chapel San Juan Apostol - Víbora- Islote III, Arecibo, PR 00612 t) (787) 878-1149 Rev. Adrian N. Jimenez Ortiz, Pst.;

Chapel Santa Maria Reina - Boan- Islote, Arecibo, PR 00612 t) (787) 878-1149 Rev. Adrian N. Jimenez Ortiz, Pst.;

Chapel Sagrada Familia - Islote II, Arecibo, PR 00612 t) (787) 878-1149 Rev. Adrian N. Jimenez Ortiz, Pst.;

Chapel Ermita del Carmen - Islote I, Arecibo, PR 00612 t) (787) 878-1149 Rev. Adrian N. Jimenez Ortiz, Pst.;

Church of Christ the King - Carr. 651 Km 5.9, Sector La Pra, Bo. Dominguito, Arecibo, PR 00612; Mailing: P.O. Box 1932, Arecibo, PR 00613-1932 t) (939) 814-1019 cristoreydom20@gmail.com Rev. Oran de Jesús Ramirez López, Pst.; Marisel Torres, DRE; CRP Stds.: 40

Chapel Maria Auxiliadora - Bo. Hato Arriba, Arecibo, PR 00613

Church of Sagrado Corazon de Jesus - Ave. San Luis #566, Arecibo, PR 00612; Mailing: Ave. San Luis #570, Arecibo, PR 00612 t) 787-878-4910 sagradocorazon_arecibo@yahoo.com Rev. Jorge L. Virella Vazquez, Pst.; Luisa Villenas, DRE; CRP Stds.: 57

Chapel Inmaculada Concepcion - Bo. Obrero, Arecibo, PR 00612 t) (787) 878-4910

Colegio San Felipe - (Grades PreK-12) Ave. San Luis #566, Arecibo, PR 00612; Mailing: P.O. Box 673, Arecibo, PR 00613 t) (787) 878-3532 csf@sanfelipeedu.org Diana Vidot Nuñez, Prin.; Antonio Perez Lopez, Dir.; Stds.: 501; Lay Tchrs.: 37

Church of San Martin de Porres - Urb. University Gardens Calle Almácigo F-12 A, Arecibo, PR 00612; Mailing: P.O. Box 142142, Arecibo, PR 00614-2142 t) (787) 878-1822 sanmartinarecibo@gmail.com Rev. Josue Efrain Colon Claudio, Pst.; Dcn. Angel Guillermo Santos Santos; Nayda Alvarez, DRE; CRP Stds.: 42

Chapel San Jose Obrero - Víctor Rojas II, Arecibo, PR 00612 Rev. Josue Efraín Colon Claudio, Pst.;

Church of Santa Cecilia - Carr. #10 Int. 636 Km 80.2, Bo. Tanamá, Sector La Planta, Arecibo, PR 00612; Mailing: HC-04 Box 13674, Arecibo, PR 00612 t) (787) 879-3364 santaceciliavm@gmail.com Rev. Jesús Antonio Rodriguez Muniz, Pst.; Dcn. Freddy Serrano Agueda; Gladys Santana, DRE; CRP Stds.: 45

Chapel San Jose - Calichosa, Arecibo, PR 00612 Rev. Jesús Antonio Rodriguez Muniz, Pst.;

Chapel La Milagrosa - La Guinea, Arecibo, PR 00612 Rev. Jesús Antonio Rodriguez Muniz, Pst.;

Chapel San Martin de Porres - Los Caños, Arecibo, PR 00612 Rev. Jesús Antonio Rodriguez Muniz, Pst.;

Chapel Santisimo Sacramento - Bo. Rio Arriba, Arecibo, PR 00612 Previously the Santísimo Sacramento parish which was suppressed Rev. Jesús Antonio Rodriguez Muniz, Pst.;

Chapel San Pascual - Sector Jobos, Arecibo, PR 00612 Rev. Jesús Antonio Rodriguez Muniz, Pst.;

Church of Santa Teresita - Carr. 492 Km 4.4 Bo. Hato Abajo, Arecibo, PR 00613; Mailing: P.O. Box 9242, Cotto Station, Arecibo, PR 00613-9242 t) (787) 878-7015 parroquiasantateresitaarecibo@gmail.com Rev. Miguel Mercado Rivera, Pst.; Dcn. Angel Rafael Betancourt Garcia, Admin.; Misty Gonzalez, DRE;

Chapel La Milagrosa - Bo. Barrancas, Arecibo, PR 00613 Rev. Miguel Mercado, Pst.;

Chapel La Providencia - Bo. Hato Arriba, Arecibo, PR 00613 Rev. Miguel Mercado;

Nuestra Senora del Carmen - Ave. Francisco Jiménez #985, Urb. Víctor Rojas I, Arecibo, PR 00612; Mailing: P.O. Box 9949, Cotto Station, Arecibo, PR 00612 t) 787-817-5062 parrnsaredelcarmen@gmail.com Rev. Ernest Jr. Cruz Córdova, Pst.; Dcn. Javier Rodriguez Figueroa; Dcn. Miguel Alejandro Rodriguez Soto; Ramonita Gonzalez, DRE; CRP Stds.: 33

Colegio La Milagrosa - (Grades PreK-12) Urb. Zeno Gandía, Ave. 987 Francisco Jiménez González, Arecibo, PR 00612-3877 t) 787-878-0341; 787-879-4912 hogarcolegiolamilagrosa@yahoo.com; administracion@hclmpr.com hogarcolegiolamilagrosa.com Sr. Carmen G. Alayón, Admin.; Tamara Medina, Dir.; Stds.: 227; Lay Tchrs.: 26

Chapel San Francisco de Asis - Rodríguez Olmo, Arecibo, PR 00612 t) (787) 817-5062

Chapel San Antonio de Padua - Abra San Francisco, Arecibo, PR 00612 t) (787) 817-5062

Our Lady of Hope - Parcelas Cienegueta Carr. 626 Km 0.1, Bo. Esperanza, Arecibo, PR 00612; Mailing: P.O. Box 489, Arecibo, PR 00613-0489 t) (787) 881-0097 Rev. Rafael Nuño Gorbea, Pst.; Arisbel Rivera, DRE; CRP Stds.: 31

Chapel Sagrado Corazon - Canta Gallo, Bo. Esperanza, Arecibo, PR 00613

Chapel San Rafael Arcangel - Bo. Plan Bonito, Arecibo, PR 00613

San Juan Bosco - Jardines de Arecibo, Calle R-Y-26, Arecibo, PR 00614; Mailing: P.O. Box 142457, Arecibo, PR 00614-2457 t) (787) 879-2069 psjblee@gmail.com Rev. Jorge A. Paredes Beltran, Pst.; Iris A Perez, DRE; CRP Stds.: 72

Colegio San Juan Bosco - (Grades PreK-12) Urbanizacion Jardines de Arecibo, Calle R-Y-26, Arecibo, PR 00612; Mailing: Apartado 142457, Arecibo, PR 00614 t) 787-879-1070 colegiosanjuanboscoare@gmail.com Janice Despiau, Prin.; Antonio Perez Lopez, Dir.; Stds.: 313; Lay Tchrs.: 27

Chapel La Dolorosa - Las Canelas, Arecibo, PR 00614

Santa Ana - Carr. #2 R. 662 Km 10.2, Bo. Santana, Arecibo, PR 00612; Mailing: P.O. Box 318, Arecibo, PR 00613-0318 t) 787-881-6005 santaanaarecibo@gmail.com Rev. Jorge L. Ruiz Rivera, Pst.; Lourdes Córdova, DRE; CRP Stds.: 55

Chapel Santuario Cristo de los Milagros - Factor, Arecibo, PR 00613 t) (787) 881-6005 Rev. Jorge L. Ruiz Rivera, Pst.;

Chapel Nuestra Senora del Carmen - Factor II, Arecibo, PR 00612 t) (787) 881-6005 Rev. Jorge L. Ruiz, Pst.;

BAJADERO

La Milagrosa - Carr. 638 Km 5.0, Bo. Miraflores, Bajadero, PR 00616; Mailing: P.O. Box 204, Bajadero, PR 00616-0204 t) (787) 650-3420 la_milagrosa_are@hotmail.com Rev. Carlos Guillermo Monroig Colón, Pst.; Dcn. Jose Enrique Valentin Mercado; Lourdes Serrano, DRE; CRP Stds.: 80

Chapel San Judas Tadeo - Carreras, Bajadero, PR 00616

Chapel Inmaculada Concepcion - Arenalejos, Bajadero, PR 00616

Chapel Nuestra Senora del Carmen - Biáfara, Bajadero, PR 00616

Chapel Nuestra Senora Madre de la Providencia - Domingo Ruiz, Bajadero, PR 00616

BARCELONETA

Church of Our Lady of Mt. Carmel - Calle Georgetti #47, Barceloneta, PR 00617; Mailing: P.O. Box 136, Barceloneta, PR 00617-0136 t) (787) 846-5625 sradelcarmen@gmail.com (Ntra. Sra. del Carmen) Rev. Roberto Vega Caraballo, Pst.; Dcn. Jose L. Castro Reyes; Sonia N. Rodriguez, DRE; CRP Stds.: 71

Chapel San Antonio de Padua - Bo. Palmas Altas, Barceloneta, PR 00617 Rev. Roberto Vega, Pst.;

Chapel Nuestra Senora del Mar - Bo. Punta Palmas, Barceloneta, PR 00617 Rev. Roberto Vega, Pst.;

Chapel Nuestra Senora de Fatima - Garrochales, Barceloneta, PR 00617 Rev. Roberto Vega, Pst.;

Our Lady of Victory - Carr. #2 Km 0.1, Sector Cruce Dávila, Barceloneta, PR 00617; Mailing: P.O. Box 2020 PMB 125, Barceloneta, PR 00617-2020 t) (787) 654-0452 ntrasradelavictoria@yahoo.com Rev. Wiktor Tarnawski, Pst.; Dcn. Edwin Pagan Belen, Admin.; Maina Torres, DRE; CRP Stds.: 43

Academia Ntra. Sra. de Fatima - (Grades PreK-12) Calle Georgetti, Edificio Rafael Balserio, Barceloneta, PR 00616; Mailing: P.O. Box 469, Bajadero, PR 00616 t) 787-623-4566; (787) 372-5881 academiafatima@yahoo.com academiafatima.com Ángeles Carrión, Dir.; Stds.: 227; Lay Tchrs.: 26

Chapel Inmaculado Corazon de Maria - Quebrada, Barceloneta, PR 00617 Rev. Wiktor Tarnawski, Pst.;

Chapel San Jose Obrero - Parcelas Imbery, Barceloneta, PR 00617 Rev. Wiktor Tarnawski, Pst.;

Chapel Nuestra Senora de Fatima - Parcelas Tiburón, Barceloneta, PR 00617 Rev. Wiktor Tarnawski, Pst.;

Chapel San Juan Bautista - Palenque, Barceloneta, PR 00617 Rev. Wiktor Tarnawski, Pst.;

CAMUY

St. Joseph - Calle Infanzón Rivera #5, Camuy, PR 00627; Mailing: P.O. Box 414, Camuy, PR 00627 t) 787-898-1234 parroquiasanjosecamuy@yahoo.es Rev. Hector I. Flores Gonzalez, Pst.; Rev. Reinaldo I. Davila Lopez, Par. Vicar; Dcn. Edwin J. Martinez Hernandez; Dcn. Eduardo Rivera Santana; Elizabeth Maldonado, DRE; CRP Stds.: 123

Chapel La Milagrosa - Sector Parcelas, Bo. Puente, Camuy, PR 00627 t) (787) 898-1234 parroquiasanjosecamuy@yahoo.com Rev. Hector I. Flores Gonzalez, Pst.;

Chapel Espiritu Santo - Bo. Abra Honda, Camuy, PR 00627 t) (787) 898-1234 parroquiasanjosecamuy@yahoo.com Rev. Hector I. Flores Gonzalez, Pst.;

Chapel Nuestra Senora del Rosario - Sector Pica, Bo. Puente, Camuy, PR 00627 t) (787) 898-1234 parroquiasanjosecamuy@yahoo.com Rev. Hector I. Flores Gonzalez, Pst.;

Chapel Nuestra Senora de la Monserrate - Bo. Membrillo, Camuy, PR 00627 t) (787) 898-1234 parroquiasanjosecamuy@yahoo.com Rev. Hector I. Flores Gonzalez, Pst.;

Chapel Sagrado Corazon - Sector Zarza, Bo. Puente, Camuy, PR 00627 t) (787) 898-1234 parroquiasanjosecamuy@yahoo.com Rev. Hector I. Flores Gonzalez, Pst.;

Chapel Inmaculada Concepcion - Bo. Zanja, Camuy, PR 00627 t) (787) 898-1234 parroquiasanjosecamuy@yahoo.com Rev. Hector I. Flores Gonzalez, Pst.;

Our Lady of Asumption - Carr. 486 Km 1.4, Bo. Quebrada, Camuy, PR 00627; Mailing: HC-02 Box 8047, Camuy, PR 00627-9122 t) (787) 403-8937 parroquia.laasuncion@yahoo.com Rev. Marco Antonio Cepeda Contreras, M.N.M, Pst.; Dcn. Felipe López Echevarría; Maria Santiago, DRE; CRP Stds.: 60

Chapel Perpetuo Socorro - Cibao Ocasio, Camuy, PR 00627

Chapel Sagrado Corazon - Callejones, Camuy, PR 00627

Chapel San Pablo de la Cruz - Callejones II, Camuy, PR 00627

Our Lady of Monserrate - Carr. 453 Km 5.5 Sector Soller, Bo. Cibao, Camuy, PR 00627; Mailing: HC-03 Box 16512, Bo. Cibao, Soller, Quebradillas, PR 00678-9820 t) (787) 680-8947 parroquialamonserratesoller@gmail.com Rev. Candido Maldonado Orozco, M.N.M., Par. Admin.; Dcn. Israel Rodriguez Diaz; Maribeth Crespo Tirado, DRE; CRP Stds.: 62

Chapel Santa Ana - Bo. Cibao, San Sebastián, PR 00685

Chapel San Antonio de Padua - Bo. Aibonito, Sector Beltrán, San Sebastián, PR 00685

Chapel Santa Cruz - Bo. Planas I, Isabela, PR 00662

Chapel Nuestra Senora del Carmen - Bo. Piletas, Lares, PR 00669

Chapel Nuestra Senora del Rosario - Bo. Planas II, Isabela, PR 00662

Chapel Nuestra Senora de Fatima - Bo. Guajataca, Quebradillas, PR 00678

Our Lady of the Miraculous Medal - Carr. 483 Km 4.1, Camuy, PR 00627; Mailing: HC-06 Box 65240, Camuy, PR 00627-9039 t) (787) 898-5825 santuariolamilagrosa@gmail.com (El Calvario) Rev. Eric Hernandez Figueroa, M.N.M, Pst.; Dcn. Carlos Noel Vangas Perez; Libertad Muñiz, DRE; CRP Stds.: 144

Chapel Sagrado Corazon - Bo. Puertos, Camuy, PR 00627 Rev. Eric Hernandez Figueroa, M.N.M, Pst.;

Chapel Nuestra Senora del Carmen - Sector Parcelas, Bo. Camuy Arriba, Camuy, PR 00627 Rev. Eric Hernandez Figueroa, M.N.M, Pst.;

Chapel Cristo Rey - Bo. Ciénagas, Camuy, PR 00627 Rev. Eric Hernandez Figueroa, M.N.M, Pst.;

Chapel Santiago Apostol - Bo. Planas, Isabela, PR 00662 Rev. Eric Hernandez Figueroa, M.N.M, Pst.;

Chapel Sagrado Corazon de Jesus - Sector El Maní, Bo. Planas, Isabela, PR 00662 Rev. Eric Hernandez Figueroa, M.N.M, Pst.;

CIALES

Holy Rosary - Calle Palmer Frente a la Plaza Pública, Ciales, PR 00638; Mailing: P.O. Box 26, Ciales, PR 00638 t) (787) 691-4518 pnsrdeciales@gmail.com Rev. Jorge R. Betancourt Ramirez, O.Carm., Pst.; Rev. Felix A. Rivera Rivera, O.Carm., Par. Vicar; Rev. Rubén Darío Rodríguez Ramos, O. Carm., Par. Vicar; Dcn. Ruben Zayas Miranda; Mayra Berrios, DRE; CRP Stds.: 218

Colegio Nuestra Senora del Rosario - (Grades PreK-12) Calle José de Diego #19, Ciales, PR 00638; Mailing: P.O. Box 1334, Ciales, PR 00638 t) 787-871-2222 cnsrc@rosarioencialesedu.org Alexandra Torres, Prin.; Antonio Perez Lopez, Dir.; Stds.: 135; Lay Tchrs.: 18

Chapel San Jose - Toro Negro, Ciales, PR 00638 Rev. Jorge R. Betancourt, O.Carm., Pst.;

Chapel Inmaculado Corazon de Maria - Bo. Cialitos, Ciales, PR 00638 Rev. Jorge R. Betancourt, O.Carm., Pst.;

Chapel San Antonio - Lomas, Ciales, PR 00638 Rev. Jorge R. Betancourt, O.Carm., Pst.;

Chapel Maternidad Divina de Maria - Parcelas María, Ciales, PR 00638 Rev. Jorge R. Betancourt, O.Carm., Pst.;

Chapel Sagrado Corazon - Cumbre, Ciales, PR 00638 Rev. Jorge R. Betancourt, O.Carm., Pst.;

Chapel Buen Pastor - Cialitos Portón, Ciales, PR 00638 Rev. Jorge R. Betancourt, O.Carm., Pst.;

Chapel San Elias - Bo. Pozas, Ciales, PR 00638 Rev. Jorge R. Betancourt, O.Carm., Pst.;

Chapel San Ignacio - Bo. Pesas, Ciales, PR 00638 Rev. Jorge R. Betancourt, O.Carm., Pst.;

Chapel Santa Clara - Bo. Jaguas, Ciales, PR 00638 Rev. Jorge R. Betancourt, O.Carm., Pst.;

Chapel Divino Nino Jesus - Bo. Casitas, Ciales, PR 00638 Rev. Jorge R. Betancourt, O.Carm., Pst.;

Ntra. Sra. Madre del Redentor - Carr. 146 Km 14.5, Bo. Frontón, Ciales, PR 00638; Mailing: P.O. Box 1181, Ciales, PR 00638-1181 t) (939) 451-7601 pnsmadredelredentor@gmail.com Rev. Roy Negron Martinez, Par. Admin.; Carmen I. Pagan, DRE; CRP Stds.: 34

Chapel Divina Providencia - Cordillera 5, Ciales, PR 00638 Rev. Roy F. Martinez Negron, Par. Admin.;

Chapel Sagrada Familia - Cordillera 7, Ciales, PR 00638 Rev. Roy F. Martinez Negron, Par. Admin.;

Chapel Perpetuo Socorro - Sabana, Ciales, PR 00638 Rev. Roy F. Martinez Negron, Par. Admin.;

Chapel San Jose - Yunes, Ciales, PR 00638 Rev. Roy F. Martinez Negron, Par. Admin.;

COROZAL

Christ the King - Carr. 807 Km 5.6 Interior, Bo. Palos Blancos, Sector Tato López, Corozal, PR 00783; Mailing: P.O. Box 1091, Corozal, PR 00783-1091 t) (787) 859-7313 parroquia_cristo_rey@yahoo.com Rev. German Valverde, Pst.; Dcn. Oscar Torres Sachez; Luz E. Fontanez, DRE; CRP Stds.: 163

Chapel Nuestra Senora del Perpetuo Socorro - Cuchillas, Corozal, PR 00783

Chapel Santa Teresita - Palos Blancos, Sector La

Riviera, Corozal, PR 00783

Holy Family - Calle Bon #13, Plaza de Recreo, Corozal, PR 00783; Mailing: P.O. Box 474, Corozal, PR 00783-0474 t) (787) 859-2595 psfcor@yahoo.com Rev. Lisimaco Hincapie Ramirez, Pst.; Rev. Mario Elias Blanes, Par. Vicar; Dcn. Rafael Ramos Guzman; Maria M. Diaz, DRE; CRP Stds.: 222

Colegio Sagrada Familia - (Grades PreK-12) Urbanización Sobrino Calle Carmelo Aponte #38, Corozal, PR 00783; Mailing: P.O. Box 769, Corozal, PR 00783 t) 787-859-2420 csfacademico.ofic@hotmail.com Sr. María Salvador Miranda Vázquez, Dir.; Ángel L. Adorno, Vice Prin.; Stds.: 610; Sr. Tchrs.: 2; Lay Tchrs.: 32

Chapel Nuestra Senora del Carmen - Cibuco, Corozal, PR 00783 Rev. Lisimaco Hincapie Ramirez, Pst.;

Chapel San Vicente de Paul - Palmarejo, Corozal, PR 00783 Rev. Lisimaco Hincapie Ramirez;

Chapel Santa Teresita del Nino Jesus - Dos Bocas, Corozal, PR 00783 Rev. Lisimaco Hincapie Ramirez, Pst.;

Chapel Nuestra Senora del Perpetuo Socorro - Urb. Silvia, Corozal, PR 00783 Rev. Lisimaco Hincapie Ramirez;

Chapel San Jose - Abras, Corozal, PR 00783 Rev. Lisimaco Hincapie Ramirez;

La Milagrosa - Carr. 801 Km 0.5, Bo. Palmarito, Corozal, PR 00783; Mailing: HC-06 Box 13976, Corozal, PR 00783-9803 t) (939) 276-5936 lamilagrosa33@gmail.com Rev. Angel M. Santos Santos, Pst.; Evelyn Rivera Rivera, DRE; CRP Stds.: 203

Chapel Nuestra Senora del Carmen - Radio Oro, Corozal, PR 00783

Chapel Nuestra Senora de Fatima - Maná, Coral, PR 00783 t) (939) 576-5936

Chapel Nuestra Senora de la Divina Providencia - Quebrada Fría, Corozal, PR 00783

Chapel Cristo Rey - Magueyes, Corozal, PR 00783

Our Lady of the Seven Sorrows - Carr. 568 Km 19.0 Int., Calle P. Luis Esparza, Bo. Padilla, Corozal, PR 00783; Mailing: HC-05 Box 10955, Corozal, PR 00783-9550 t) (787) 600-7019 parroquia7dolores@yahoo.com Rev. Kenneth D. Moore Irizarry, Pst.; Dcn. Javier Cancel Rodriguez; Dcn. Adalberto Ortiz Miranda; Carmen M. Rivera, DRE; CRP Stds.: 117

Chapel Perpetuo Socorro - Bo. Cienegueta, Vega Alta, PR 00692 Rev. Kenneth Daniel Moore Irizarry, Pst.;

Chapel San Martin de Porres - Sector Hormigas 1, Bo. Padilla Ermita, Corozal, PR 00783 Rev. Kenneth Daniel Moore Irizarry, Pst.;

Chapel San Rafael Arcangel - Bo. Padilla Ermita, Corozal, PR 00783 Rev. Kenneth Daniel Moore Irizarry, Pst.;

FLORIDA

Our Lady of Mercy - Calle Muñoz Rivera #2, Florida, PR 00650; Mailing: P.O. Box 1184, Florida, PR 00650-1184 t) (939) 440-0126 parroquialamercedfloridapr@gmail.com Rev. Roy F. Martinez Negron, Pst.; Dcn. Carlos R. Santa Perez; Viviana Bruno, DRE; CRP Stds.: 36

Chapel Nuestra Senora del Carmen - Bo. Monte Bello, Manatí, PR 00674 parroquilamercedfloridapr@gmail.com

Chapel Santa Rosa de Lima - Bo. Pajonal, Florida, PR 00650 parroquilamercedfloridapr@gmail.com

Chapel San Pablo - Sector La Fuente, Florida, PR 00650 parroquilamercedfloridapr@gmail.com

HATILLO

Our Lady of Guadalupe - Carr. 129 Km 9.3 Int. Calle P. Anibal Reyes, Bo. Campo Alegre, Hatillo, PR 00659; Mailing: P.O. Box 1131, Arecibo, PR 00613-1131 t) (787) 898-8035 Rev. Rene A. Colon Rivera, S.E.M.V., Pst.; Rev. Luis Roberto Banchs Plaza, S.E.M.V., Assoc. Pst.; Rev. Luis A. Colon Rivera, S.E.M.V., Assoc. Pst.; Rev. Luis Antonio David Mendez Acevedo, S.E.M.V., Assoc. Pst.; Michelle Hernandez, DRE; CRP Stds.: 119

Chapel Santa Rosa de Lima - Bo. Pajuil, Hatillo, PR 00659 Rev. Rene A. Colon Rivera, S.E.M.V., Pst.;

Chapel San Jose - Sector La Paloma, Bo. Naranjito, Hatillo, PR 00659 Rev. Rene A. Colon Rivera, S.E.M.V., Pst.;

Chapel Inmaculada Concepcion - Bo. Buena Vista, Hatillo, PR 00659 Rev. Rene A. Colon Rivera, S.E.M.V., Pst.;

Our Lady of Mt. Carmel - Calle PH Hernández #61, Hatillo, PR 00659; Mailing: P.O. Box 2, Hatillo, PR 00659 t) (787) 898-5300 parrnscarmen@gmail.com Rev. Ramon V. Olivencia Velez, Pst.; Dcn. Luis E. Jimenez Velez; Dcn. Felix O. Mendez Feliciano; Maria Perez, DRE; CRP Stds.: 106

Colegio Nuestra Senora del Carmen - (Grades PreK-12) Ave. Dr. Susoni #168, Hatillo, PR 00659; Mailing: P.O. Box 937, Hatillo, PR 00659 t) 787-898-2800 rserran0.cnsc@gmail.com Wilmari Colón, Prin.; Antonio Perez Lopez, Dir.; Stds.: 352; Sr. Tchrs.: 1; Lay Tchrs.: 23

Chapel San Pio X - Sector Lechuga, Bo. Capáez, Hatillo, PR 00659 Rev. Ramon V. Olivencia Velez, Pst.;

Chapel Sagrado Corazon de Jesus - Bo. Carrizales, Hatillo, PR 00659 Rev. Ramon V. Olivencia Velez, Pst.;

Chapel Sagrada Familia - Sector Palma Gorda, Bo. Corcovado, Hatillo, PR 00659 Rev. Ramon V. Olivencia Velez, Pst.;

Chapel Nuestra Senora del Perpetuo Socorro - Bo. Capáez, Hatillo, PR 00659 Rev. Ramon V. Olivencia Velez, Pst.;

Chapel Santa Rosa de Lima - Bo. Santa Rosa, Hatillo, PR 00659 Rev. Ramon V. Olivencia Velez, Pst.;

Perpetual Help - Carr. 134 Km 11.8, Bo. Bayaney, Hatillo, PR 00659; Mailing: P.O. Box 69001 PMB 393, Hatillo, PR 00659 t) (787) 898-7771 perpetuo.socorro393@gmail.com Rev. Patricio Antonio Gallego Cifuentes, Par. Admin.; Dcn. Eladio Candelario Rios, Admin.; Jeanette Rivera, DRE; CRP Stds.: 65

Chapel Cristo Rey - Bo. Aibonito, Hatillo, PR 00659

Chapel Sagrado Corazon - Sector Berrocal, Hatillo, PR 00659

Chapel Nuestra Senora de la Providencia - Sector Cantera, Hatillo, PR 00659

Chapel Nuestra Senora de la Milagrosa - Sector Sonadora, Hatillo, PR 00659 Rev. Patricio Antonio Gallego Cifuentes, Par. Admin.;

Chapel Nuestra Senora del Carmen - Sector Mariposa, Hatillo, PR 00659

ISABELA

St. Anthony - Calle Corchado #81, Isabela, PR 00662; Mailing: P.O. Box 525, Isabela, PR 00662 t) (787) 872-0126 sanantoniotrinitariosisabela@gmail.com Rev. Willmar A. Guiral Cadavid, O.SS.T, Pst.; Rev. Wilfredo Echevarria Lopez, O.SS.T, Par. Vicar; Dcn. Teodoro Gonzalez Serrano; Dcn. Jose A. Vargas Gonzalez; Yziz Anazagasty, DRE; CRP Stds.: 144

Chapel Buen Pastor - Bo. Jobos, Isabela, PR 00662

Chapel Espiritu Santo - Bo. Guayabos, Isabela, PR 00662

Chapel La Monserrate - Bo. Arenales, Isabela, PR 00662

Chapel Sagrado Corazon - Sector Los Pinos, Isabela, PR 00662

Chapel Santisima Trinidad - Urb. Medina, Isabela, PR 00662

Chapel San Martin de Porres - Bo. Coto, Isabela, PR 00662

Chapel Cristo Salvador - Sector Capiro, Bo. Galateo Alto, Isabela, PR 00662

Chapel Nuestra Senora de la Providencia - Sector Vendrell, Isabela, PR 00662 Rev. Willmar A. Guiral Cadavid, O.SS.T, Pst.;

Chapel Virgen del Rosario - Sector El Salto, Isabela, PR 00662

Chapel Santa Rosa de Lima - Sector La Curva, Isabela, PR 00662

Our Lady of Mount Carmel - Carr. 446 Km 15.5, Bo. Llanadas, Isabela, PR 00662; Mailing: P.O. Box 1555, Isabela, PR 00662-1555 t) (787) 872-5550 delcarmenisabela@gmail.com Rev. Jorge Iván Mantilla Ramírez, O.SS.T., Par. Admin.; Yanira Roman, DRE; CRP Stds.: 51

Chapel Santos Inocentes - Sector Poncito, Bo. Llanadas, Isabela, PR 00662

Chapel La Milagrosa - Bo. Galateo Bajo, Isabela, PR 00662

Chapel San Juan de Mata - Sector La Tuna, Bo. Coto, Isabela, PR 00662

Chapel La Encarnacion - Bo. Galateo Alto, Isabela, PR 00662

LARES

St. Joseph - Calle Gándara #8, Lares, PR 00669; Mailing: P.O. Box 103, Lares, PR 00669-0103 t) (787) 897-2067 parroquia.san.jose.lares@gmail.com Rev. Luis Javier Rivera Rivera, Pst.; Rev. Edgardo Javier Aviles Rosa, Par. Vicar; Dcn. Arstides Arce Gonzalez; Dcn. Alexander Santiago Martinez; Mayra Cardona, DRE; CRP Stds.: 201

Chapel Nuestra Senora de la Divina Providencia - Bo. Espino, Parcelas Tabonuco, Lares, PR 00669 Rev. Luis J. Rivera, Pst.;

Chapel San Carlos - Bo. Piletas, Lares, PR 00669 Rev. Luis J. Rivera, Pst.;

Chapel La Pasion - Bo. Callejones, Lares, PR 00669 Rev. Luis J. Rivera, Pst.;

Chapel La Milagrosa - Bo. Piletas Arce, Lares, PR 00669 Rev. Luis J. Rivera, Pst.;

Chapel La Resurreccion - Sector Seburuquillo, Lares, PR 00669 Rev. Luis J. Rivera, Pst.;

St. Judas Tadeos - Carr. 128 Int. 129 Km 12.08, Bo. Buenos Aires, Sector La América, Lares, PR 00669; Mailing: P.O. Box 1109, Lares, PR 00669-1109 t) (787) 897-3540 Rev. Angel L. Soto Maldonado, Pst.; Maria Santiago, DRE; CRP Stds.: 72

Chapel Nuestra Senora de los Dolores - Bo. Pezuela, Sector La Vega, Lares, PR 00669 Rev. Angel L. Soto Maldonado, Pst.;

Chapel Sagrada Familia - Bo. Buenos Aires, Lares, PR 00669 Rev. Angel L. Soto Maldonado, Pst.;

Chapel Nuestra Senora del Perpetuo Socorro - Sector Palmarllano, Bo. Lares, Lares, PR 00669 Rev. Angel L. Soto Maldonado, Pst.;

Chapel San Antonio de Padua - Sector La Matilde, Lares, PR 00669 (Suppressed) Rev. Angel L. Soto Maldonado, Pst.;

MANATI

La Candelaria - 2 Calle Padial, Manati, PR 00674 t) (787) 854-2013 lacandelariaysanmatias@yahoo.com Rev. Carlos Eduardo Granados Penagos, Pst.; Luz Delia Santos, DRE; CRP Stds.: 32

Colegio De La Inmaculada Concepcion - (Grades PreK-12) Carr. #2 Km. 49.6, Manati, PR 00674; Mailing: P.O. Box 3400, Manatí, PR 00674 t) 787-854-2079; (787) 854-5265 cicmanati@outlook.com Sr. María Dolores Vicens, Admin.; Sr. Rosalina Santiago, Prin.; Hilda M. Crespo, Assoc. Dir.; Stds.: 480; Sr. Tchrs.: 2; Lay Tchrs.: 37

Chapel Sagrado Corazon - Bo. Cortés, Manati, PR 00674

Chapel Espiritu Santo - Bo. La Ceiba, Manati, PR 00674

Chapel Nuestra Senora del Perpetuo Socorro - Bo. Pugnado, Manati, PR 00674

Chapel La Milagrosa - Villa Amalia, Manati, PR 00674

Chapel Nuestra Senora de la Monserrate - Sector Polvorín, Manati, PR 00674

Nuestra Senora del Mar - Carr. 685 Km 5.0, Bo. Boquillas, Manati, PR 00674; Mailing: P.O. Box 1183, Manati, PR 00674-1183 t) (787) 854-5388 Rev. Roberto C. Gerena Lopez, Pst.; Dcn. Jorge Jimenez Sanchez; Jacqueline Maisonet, DRE; CRP Stds.: 45

Chapel La Milagrosa - Sector Cantito, Manati, PR 00674

Chapel Santa Rosa de Lima - Tierras Nuevas, Manati, PR 00674

Chapel Nuestra Senora de Lourdes - Sector Laguna,

Manati, PR 00674

Our Savior - Urb. San Salvador Calle Ángel Ramos B-32, Manati, PR 00674; Mailing: P.O. Box 465, Manati, PR 00674 t) (787) 884-3664 parroquia.elsalvador@yahoo.com Rev. Melquiades Rojas Rodriguez, Pst.; Dcn. Jose A. Morales Hernaiz; Dcn. Eddie J. Perez Gonzalez; Dcn. Ezequiel Rivera Burgos; Lourdes Robles, DRE; CRP Stds.: 47

Colegio Marista El Salvador - (Grades PreK-12) Carr. #2 K.m. 45.5, Bo. coto Norte, Sector M. Champagnat, Manatí, PR 00674; Mailing: P.O. Box 856, Manati, PR 00764 t) 787-854-1075; 787-854-2485 oficinamaristamanati@live.com; oficina@maristamanati.org Bro. Edgardo López, Pres.; Ángel García, Dir.; Stds.: 567; Lay Tchrs.: 46

Chapel San Jose - San José, Manati, PR 00674 Rev. Melquiades Rojas Rodriguez, Pst.;

Chapel San Martin de Porres - Bo. Guayaney, Manati, PR 00674 Rev. Melquiades Rojas Rodriguez, Pst.;

Sagrada Familia - Carr. 670 K.m. 1.5, Villa Evangelina, Manati, PR 00674; Mailing: P.O. Box 704, Manati, PR 00674 t) (787) 854-2858 manaticm@yahoo.com Rev. Marion Poncette, C.M., Pst.; Dcn. Jose Escudero Gines; Olga Rivera, DRE; CRP Stds.: 42

Chapel San Judas Tadeo - Parcelas Marquez, Manati, PR 00674

Chapel La Monserrate - Sector Palo Alto, Manati, PR 00674

Chapel La Milagrosa - Sector Polvorín, Manati, PR 00674

MOROVIS

Nuestra Senora del Carmen - Calle El Carmen #12, Morovis, PR 00687; Mailing: P.O. Box 428, Morovis, PR 00687-0428 t) (787) 862-2620 rivera-1025-@hotmail.com Rev. Jesús Monreal Pujante, O. Carm, Pst.; Rev. Salvador Rodrigo Gil, O.Carm, Par. Vicar; Rev. Tomás Ciscar Nadal, O. Carm., Par. Vicar; Rev. Pablo Roberto De la Cruz, O. Carm., Par. Vicar; Rev. Hector Manuel Garcia Morales, O.Carm, Par. Vicar; Dcn. Luis Quintín Colón Ortiz; Dcn. Jaime Rivera Estela; Alberto Gutierrez, DRE; CRP Stds.: 452

Chapel San Jose - Jobos, Morovis, PR 00687

Chapel Nuestra Senora del Carmen - Perchas, Morovis, PR 00687

Chapel Nuestra Senora del Carmen - Buena Vista, Morovis, PR 00687

Chapel Nuestra Senora del Carmen - Pastos, Morovis, PR 00687

Chapel Nuestra Senora del Rosario - San Lorenzo, Morovis, PR 00687

Chapel Reina de la Paz - Cuchillas, Morovis, PR 00687

Chapel Segrado Corazon - Cuchillas, Bo. Pimiento, Morovis, PR 00687

Chapel La Milagrosa - Rio Grande, Morovis, PR 00687

Chapel San Judas Tadeo - Vaga I, Morovis, PR 00687

Chapel San Miguel Arcangel - Unibón, Morovis, PR 00687

Chapel Sagrada Familia - Patrón, Morovis, PR 00687

St. Paul Apostle - Carr. 155 Ramal 633 Km 4.3, Bo. Barahona, Morovis, PR 00687; Mailing: P.O. Box 537, Morovis, PR 00687-0537 t) (787) 862-3445 parroquiasanpabloapostol22@gmail.com Rev. Diego De La Texera Rojas, Pst.; Dcn. Manuel Alberto Rodriguez Santiago; Dcn. Rumar Rolón Narvaez; Carmen Melendez, DRE; CRP Stds.: 184

Chapel Divino Nino Jesus de Praga - Bo. Fránquez Centro, Morovis, PR 00687 Rev. Diego Francisco De La Texera Rojas, Pst.;

Chapel Senor de los Milagros - Bo. Torrecillas, Morovis, PR 00687 Rev. Diego Francisco De La Texera Rojas, Pst.;

Chapel Nuestra Senora de La Providencia - Bo. Fránquez Carr., Morovis, PR 00687 Rev. Diego Francisco De La Texera Rojas, Pst.;

OROCOVIS

Our Lady of Fatima - Carr. 566 Km 0.2, Sector Puente Doble, Bo. Saltos, Orocovis, PR 00720; Mailing: P.O. Box 2118, Orocovis, PR 00720-2118 t) (787) 867-3277 fatimaorocovis@hotmail.com Rev. Tomas Santos Rodriguez, Pst.; Dcn. Victor Rosario Marquez; Wanda Rodriguez, DRE; CRP Stds.: 136

Chapel Santo Cristo de la Salud - Bermejales, Orocovis, PR 00720 Rev. Tomas Santos, Pst.;

Chapel San Martin de Porres - Miraflores, Orocovis, PR 00720 Rev. Tomas Santos, Pst.;

Chapel Virgen de los Dolores - Bo. Bauta, Orocovis, PR 00720 Rev. Tomas Santos, Pst.;

Chapel Nuestra Senora del Perpetuo Socorro - Damián Arriba, Orocovis, PR 00720 Rev. Tomas Santos, Pst.;

Chapel Espiritu Santo - Bo. Pellejas, Orocovis, PR 00720 t) (787) 867-2210 Rev. Tomas Santos, Pst.;

San Juan Bautista - Calle Ramos Antonini #1, Orocovis, PR 00720; Mailing: P.O. Box 2114, Orocovis, PR 00720-2114 t) (787) 867-2210 parroquiaorocovis@yahoo.com Rev. Luis Alberto Reyes Paulino, Pst.; Rev. Adan Luis Marrero Berrios, S.D.B., Par. Vicar; Rev. Emilio Jose Torres Germoso, S.D.B., Par. Vicar; Dcn. Eugenio Soto Santiago, DRE;

Colegio San Juan Bautista - (Grades PreK-12) Carr. 157 Km. 23.7 Interior, Bo. Barros, Orocovis, PR 00720; Mailing: P.O. Box 1877, Orocovis, PR 00720 t) 787-867-2295 colegio.sanjuanbautista.58@gmail.com Zaida Perez, Prin.; Sr. Araceli Reyes, Dir.; Stds.: 320; Sr. Tchrs.: 1; Lay Tchrs.: 20

Chapel Santos Angeles Custodios - Bo. Sabana Abajo, Orocovis, PR 00720

Chapel El Divino Nino - Sector Las Marianas, Orocovis, PR 00720

Chapel Espiritu Santo - Bo. Damián, Orocovis, PR 00720

Chapel Nuestra Senora de Guadalupe - Bo. Barros, Orocovis, PR 00720

Chapel Santa Clara - Bo. Botijas 2, Orocovis, PR 00720

Chapel Cristo Resucitado - Bo. Botijas 1, Orocovis, PR 00720

Chapel Sagrado Corazon - Bo. Mata de Caña, Orocovis, PR 00720

Chapel Nuestra Senora de la Providencia - Sector Bajuras, Orocovis, PR 00720

Chapel San Juan Bosco - Bo. Gato, Orocovis, PR 00720

Chapel Virgen del Carmen - Sector Montebello, Orocovis, PR 00720

Chapel San Pablo Apostol - Sector Puente - Alturas, Orocovis, PR 00720

QUEBRADILLAS

Santuario Diocesano Virgen del Perpetuo Socorro - Carr. 484 Km 0.6, Bo. Cocos, Quebradillas, PR 00678; Mailing: P.O. Box 1569, Quebradillas, PR 00678-1569 t) (787) 895-3033 pscjcocos@gmail.com Rev. Martin Jose Sadaba Sarobe, Pst.; María Núñez, DRE; Dcn. Jose Ignacio Pagan Franqui; CRP Stds.: 127

Chapel San Miguel Arcangel - Bo. San Antonio, Quebradillas, PR 00678 Rev. Martin Jose Sadaba Sarobe, Pst.;

Chapel Madre Dolorosa - Sector El Verde, Bo. Cocos, Quebradillas, PR 00678 Rev. Martin Jose Sadaba Sarobe, Pst.;

Chapel Nuestra Senora del Perpetuo Socorro - Sector Yeguada, Bo. San José, Quebradillas, PR 00678 Rev. Martin Jose Sadaba Sarobe, Pst.;

San Raphael - Calle San Carlos #110, Quebradillas, PR 00678; Mailing: P.O. Box 57, Quebradillas, PR 00678-0057 t) (787) 895-3463 sanrafael1828@gmail.com Rev. Gabriel Alonso Sanchez, Pst.; Rev. Carmelo Urarte Aberasturi, Vicar; Dcn. Wilfredo López Mora; Dcn. Efrain Muniz Perez; Dcn. Nathaniel Roman Nieves; Luis Nieves, DRE; CRP Stds.: 198

Colegio San Rafael - (Grades PreK-12) Calle Lamela #213, Quebradillas, PR 00678 t) 787-895-2280 csrque@gmail.com Iris Y. Santiago, Prin.; Antonio Perez Lopez, Dir.; Stds.: 480; Lay Tchrs.: 36

Chapel Nuestra Senora de Guadalupe - Sector Las Talas, Bo. Cacao, Quebradillas, PR 00678

Chapel San Jose - Bo. San José, Quebradillas, PR 00678

Chapel Nuestra Senora del Perpetuo Socorro - Bo. Charcas, Quebradillas, PR 00678

Chapel Santa Cruz - Sector Las Chivas, Bo. Cacao, Quebradillas, PR 00678

Chapel Nuestra Senora de la Monserrate - Bo. San Antonio, Quebradillas, PR 00678

Chapel San Antonio - Bo. San Antonio, Quebradillas, PR 00678

Chapel Nuestra Senora del Carmen - Sector Quebrada Mala, Bo. Terranova, Quebradillas, PR 00678

Chapel La Milagrosa - Bo. Cacao, Quebradillas, PR 00678

SABANA HOYOS

Inmaculado Corazon de Maria - Carr. 639 Km 4.0 Sector Allende, Sabana Hoyos, PR 00688; Mailing: P.O. Box 1282, Sabana Hoyos, PR 00688-1282 t) (787) 879-8191 Rev. Victor Sanchez Velez, Pst.; Dcn. Kevin D. Hernandez Rivera; Hairy Guzman, DRE; CRP Stds.: 32

Chapel San Jose - Arrozal, Sabana Hoyos, PR 00688

Chapel San Isidro - Asomante, Sabana Hoyos, PR 00688

Chapel Sagrado Corazon - Sector Carolina, Sabana Hoyos, PR 00688

Chapel San Francisco de Asis - Bo. Arrozal, Sector Los Muertos, Sabana Hoyos, PR 00688

Nuestra Senora de Fatima - Carr. 2 Int., Carr. 639 Km 0.7, Sector Candelaria, Bo. Sabana Hoyos, Arecibo, Sabana Hoyos, PR 00688; Mailing: P.O. Box 667, Sabana Hoyos, PR 00688-0667 t) (787) 881-8274 parr.fatima.ar@gmail.com Rev. Juan Carlos Cotto Soto, C.M.V., Pst.; Rev. Fabio Gatti Florian, C.M.V., Par. Vicar; Rev. Juan Ramón Ramos Medina, C.M.V., Par. Vicar; Bro. Sergio Maramgon; Ivelisse Cornier, DRE; CRP Stds.: 70

Chapel Inmaculada Concepcion - Sector El Espino, Sabana Hoyos, PR 00688

Chapel La Milagrosa - Bo. Garrochales, Sector San Luis, Sabana Hoyos, PR 00688

Chapel San Francisco de Asis - Bo. Garrochales, Sabana Hoyos, PR 00688

Chapel Nuestra Senora del Carmen - Bo. Ballajá, Sabana Hoyos, PR 00688

UTUADO

Nuestra Senora del Monte Carmelo - Carr. 613 Km 0.2, Bo. Caonillas, Utuado, PR 00641; Mailing: HC-01 Box 4179, Utuado, PR 00641 t) (787) 527-1996 pmontecarmelo81@gmail.com Rev. William Martinez Pastoriza, Par. Admin.; Idhem Heredia Perez, DRE; CRP Stds.: 18

Chapel San Antonio de Padua - Mameyes, Utuado, PR 00641

Chapel La Milagrosa - Bo. Don Alonso, Utuado, PR 00641

Chapel San Salvador - Tetuán I y II, Utuado, PR 00641

Chapel Sagrado Corazon - Tetuán III, Utuado, PR 00641

Our Lady of Sorrows - Carr. 111 Km 8.9, Bo. Caguana, Utuado, PR 00641; Mailing: P.O. Box 2525 CMB-73, Utuado, PR 00641-2525 t) (787) 933-4746 ofiparr08@gmail.com Rev. Miguel Jose Velez Nieves, Par. Admin.; Dcn. Antonio Rodríguez; Brenda L. Beauchamp, DRE; CRP Stds.: 33

Chapel Nuestra Senora de la Monserrate - Sector Jácanas, Bo. Caguana, Utuado, PR 00641

Chapel Cristo Rey - Sector Cayuco, Bo. Caguana, Utuado, PR 00641

Chapel San Martin de Porres - Bo. Roncador, Utuado, PR 00641

San Miguel Arcangel - Calle Barceló #8, Utuado, PR 00641; Mailing: PO Box 10, Utuado, PR 00641-0010 t) (939) 814-1205; (939) 814-1206 sanmiguelutuado@outlook.com www.yosoycapuchino.com Rev. Jose F Irizarry Santana, ofm Cap., Pst.; Rev. Edward Maldonado Plaza, OFM Cap., Priest; Friar Cadelin Prosper, O.F.M.Cap. (Haiti),

Priest; Dcn. Pedro Antonio Collazo Cruz; Dcn. Nelson Perez Martinez; Elda Maldonado Medina, DRE; Sr. Juanita Torres, DRE; CRP Stds.: 117

Chapel San Fidel - Bo. Arenas Sector Puente Blanco, Carr. PR-123, Utuado, PR 00641 Rev. Jose F. Irizarry Santana, Pst.;

Chapel Nuestra Senora del Perpetuo Socorro - Bo. Sabana Grande Sector La Sanchez, Carr. PR-511, Utuado, PR 00641 Rev. Jose F. Irizarry Santana, Pst.;

Chapel San Jose - Bo. Río Abajo Sector Adrian Torres, Carr. 123, Utuado, PR 00641 Rev. Jose F. Irizarry Santana, Pst.;

Chapel San Martin de Porres - Bo. Arenas Sector La Capilla, Carr. PR-523, Utuado, PR 00641 Rev. Jose F. Irizarry Santana;

San Pedro y San Pablo - Bo. Paso Palmas, Carr. 140 Km 15.7, Utuado, PR 00641; Mailing: P.O. Box 1878, Utuado, PR 00641-1878 t) (787) 567-3144 p.sanpedroysanpabloutuado@gmail.com Rev. Elvin A. Irizarry Roman, Pst.; Dcn. Milton Diaz Negrón; Evelyn Roman Marin, DRE; CRP Stds.: 33

Chapel La Milagrosa - Sector La Pica, Bo. Consejo, Utuado, PR 00641

Chapel San Jose - Bo. Consejo, Utuado, PR 00641

Chapel San Francisco de Asis - Bo. Las Palmas, Utuado, PR 00641

Chapel La Providencia - Bo. Viví Abajo, Utuado, PR 00641

Chapel Inmaculada Concepcion - Bo. Viví Arriba, Utuado, PR 00641

VEGA ALTA

Immaculate Conception of Blessed Virgin Mary - Calle Georgetti #42, Vega Alta, PR 00692; Mailing: P.O. Box 775, Vega Alta, PR 00692-0775 t) (787) 883-4875 parroquialainmaculada@yahoo.com Rev. Victor Rojas Rodriguez, Pst.; Dcn. Enrique Laureano Molina; Zulimar Nevarez, DRE; CRP Stds.: 68

Chapel Inmaculado Corazon de Maria - Bo. Candelaria, Vega Alta, PR 00692 Rev. Victor Rojas Rodriguez, Pst.;

Chapel Santa Ana - Bo. Bajura, Vega Alta, PR 00692 Rev. Victor Rojas Rodriguez, Pst.;

Chapel Nuestra Senora de Lourdes - Bo. Pámpanos, Vega Alta, PR 00692 Rev. Victor Rojas Rodriguez, Pst.;

Chapel Sagrado Corazon de Jesus - Bo. Maricao, Vega Alta, PR 00692 Rev. Victor Rojas Rodriguez, Pst.;

Our Lady of Mt. Carmel - Calle Camelia #48 Sector Carmelita, Bo. Sabana, Vega Alta, PR 00692; Mailing: P.O. Box 1417, Vega Baja, PR 00694-1417 t) (787) 654-7891 parroquiacarmelitavg@gmail.com Rev. Osvaldo Perez Gonzalez, C.S.Sp., Pst.; Virginia Gaetan, DRE; CRP Stds.: 44

Chapel Nuestra Senora de Guadalupe - Sector Santa Rosa, Bo. Sabana, Vega Alta, PR 00692

Chapel La Milagrosa - Bo. Pueblo Nuevo, Vega Baja, PR 00694

Chapel San Judas Tadeo - Bo. Sabana Hoyos, Vega Alta, PR 00692

Santa Ana - Urb. Santa Ana, Calle 3 H-9, Vega Alta, PR 00692; Mailing: P.O. Box 2105, Vega Alta, PR 00692-2105 t) (787) 883-2502 santaanap49@gmail.com Rev. Wilson Saldaña Sarmiento, Par. Admin.; Dcn. Wilbert F. Davila Cortes, Admin.; Maria Bruno, DRE; CRP Stds.: 54

Chapel Nuestra Senora del Carmen - Bo. Espinosa, Sector Fortuna, Vega Alta, PR 00692 t) (787) 883-2505

VEGA BAJA

The Blessed Trinity - Carr. 160 Km 8.6, Bo. Almirante Sur, Vega Baja, PR 00694; Mailing: P.O. Box 58, Almirante Sur Station, Vega Baja, PR 00694-0058 t) (787) 855-8743 panal2000@yahoo.com Rev. Elmon M. Hernandez Fana, Pst.; Dorian Sinigaglia, DRE; CRP Stds.: 48

Chapel Sagrada Familia - Almirante Norte, Vega Baja, PR 00694

Chapel Nuestra Senora de la Providencia - Sector Patrón II, Bo. Unibón, Morovis, PR 00687

Holy Rosary - Calle Betances #36, Vega Baja, PR 00694; Mailing: P.O. Box 1388, Vega Baja, PR 00694-1388 t) (787) 858-2969 pnsrosario@hotmail.com Rev. Jorge Yamil Morales Rivera, Pst.; Dcn. Ángel González Arce; Dcn. William Mirada; Maria Otero Figueroa, DRE; CRP Stds.: 23

Colegio Nuestra Senora del Rosario - (Grades PreK-12) Carr. 686 Km. 17.2 Zona Industrial, Bo. Cabo Caribe, Vega Baja, PR 00694; Mailing: P.O. Box 1457, Vega Baja, PR 00694 t) 787-858-4111 cnsrvbpr@gmail.com; maldonadocnsr@gmail.com Janice Cintrón, Prin.; Antonio Perez Lopez, Dir.; Stds.: 193; Lay Tchrs.: 22

Chapel San Jose - Bo. Arenales, Vega Baja, PR 00694

Chapel La Milagrosa - Bo. La Trocha, Vega Baja, PR 00694 t) (787) 585-2969

Chapel Nuestra Senora de Fatima - Almirante, Vega Baja, PR 00694

Ntra. Sra. de la Providencia - Ave. Guarico Calle Providencia #1, Urb. Jardines de Vega Baja, Vega Baja, PR 00694; Mailing: P.O. Box 4056, Vega Baja, PR 00694-4056 t) (787) 654-8676 pnsprovidencia@gmail.com Rev. Angel R. Diaz Marrero, Pst.; Dcn. Jose Antonio Rivera Vega; Dcn. Waldemar Vives Rodriguez; Maria Adorno, DRE; CRP Stds.: 66

Chapel San Jose - Brisas de Tortuguero, Vega Baja, PR 00694 Rev. Angel Diaz Marrero, Pst.;

Chapel San Pedro Apostol - Vega Baja Lakes, Vega Baja, PR 00694 Rev. Angel Diaz Marrero, Pst.;

Our Lady of Carmen-Playa - Ave. Júpiter, Bda. Sandín, Carr. 6686 Calle Marte #79, Vega Baja, PR 00694; Mailing: P.O. Box 4095, Vega Baja, PR 00694-4095 t) (787) 807-8390 p.nuestrasenoradelcarmen@outlook.com Rev. Freddo Lesly Andre, Pst.; Maria E. Melendez, DRE; CRP Stds.: 36

Chapel San Judas Tadeo - Los Naranjos, Bo. Cabo Caribe, Vega Baja, PR 00694 Rev. Fredo Lesly Andre, Pst.;

Chapel Divino Nino Jesus - San Demetrio, Bo. Puerto Nuevo, Vega Baja, PR 00694 Rev. Fredo Lesly Andre, Pst.;

Our Lady of Lourdes - Calle R Esquina Q, Urb. Alturas de Vega Baja, Vega Baja, PR 00694; Mailing: P.O. Box 4414, Vega Baja, PR 00694-4414 t) (787) 855-4942 parroquianslourdesv@gmail.com Rev. Juan Rolando González González, Pst.; Dcn. Luis Collazo Rodriguez; Maria I. Ortiz, DRE; CRP Stds.: 83

Chapel Santa Rosa de Lima - Bo. Rio Abajo, Vega Baja, PR 00694

Chapel San Juan Bautista - Bo. Quebrada Arenas, Vega Baja, PR 00694

Chapel San Francisco de Asis - Bo. Las Granjas, Vega Baja, PR 00694

Parroquia de San Martin de Porres - Calle Parque A-2 #5, Parcelas Amadeo, Vega Baja, PR 00694; Mailing: P.O. Box 254, Vega Baja, PR 00694-0254 t) (787) 654-9501 s_an_martin@yahoo.com Rev. David Rivas Rivera, Pst.; Aida Rodriguez, DRE; CRP Stds.: 23

Chapel San Jose - Bo. Pugnado Adentro, Vega Baja, PR 00694 Rev. David Rivas Rivera, Pst.;

Chapel St. Anthony de Padua - Villa Colombo, Bo. Algarrobo, Vega Baja, PR 00694 Rev. David Rivas Rivera, Pst.;

Chapel Sagrado Corazon - Comunidad de Panaini, Bo. Algarrobo, Vega Baja, PR 00694 Rev. David Rivas Rivera, Pst.;

Perpetuo Socorro - Carr. 690 Km 5.6, Bo. Breñas, Vega Baja, PR 00694; Mailing: P.O. Box 1997, Vega Baja, PR 00694 t) (787) 883-5776 pquiu@yahoo.com Rev. Luis Ángel Vazquez Santos, Pst.; Irma Castro, DRE; CRP Stds.: 32

Chapel San Vicente de Paul - Bo. Sabana, Vega Baja, PR 00694

Chapel Nuestra Senora del Carmen - Bo. Cerro Gordo, Vega Baja, PR 00694

SCHOOLS: PRESCHOOL THRU HIGH SCHOOL

SCHOOLS

COMMONWEALTH OF PUERTO RICO

ARECIBO

Pontificia Universidad Catolica de Puerto Rico, Recinto de Arecibo - Carr. 662 km. 2.3, Bo. Santana, Arecibo, PR 00613; Mailing: P.O. Box 144045, Arecibo, PR 00614-4045 t) 787-881-1212 info@pucpr.edu www.pucpr.edu Edwin Hernandez Vera, Chancellor; Rev. Luis A. Mendez, Chap.; Yazdel Martinez Colon, Dean; Luz C. Rivera Correa, Librn.; Stds.: 1,296

INSTITUTIONS LOCATED IN DIOCESE

MISCELLANEOUS [MIS]

ARECIBO

Hogar Infantil Santa Teresita del Nino Jesus, Inc. - Carr. 492 Km 4.3, Bo. Hato Abajo, Sector Iglesias, Arecibo, PR 00614; Mailing: P.O. Box 140057, Arecibo, PR 00614 t) 787-817-6651; 787-650-7731 hogarsantateresita@hotmail.com Melva Arvelo Mangual, Dir.;

Oficina para la Promocion y el Desarrollo Humano, Inc. - Carr. 651 Km 2.1, Bo. Juncos, Arecibo, PR 00612; Mailing: P.O. Box 353, Arecibo, PR 00613 t) 787-817-6951; 787-817-6954; 787-817-6955 opdhinc@gmail.com; aflores.opdh@gmail.com www.opdh.org Angelica M. Flores Figueroa, Dir.;

CAMUY

Hogar de Ninas Fray Luis Amigo - Carr. 453 K.m 4.4, Bo. Piedra Gorda, Camuy, PR 00627; Mailing: HC-06 Box 65162, Camuy, PR 00627 t) 787-544-6671 c) 787-356-2634 hogarfrayluiscamuy@gmail.com Sr. Maria L. Padin Rivera, H.T.C., Admin.; Sr. Eulalia Hernandez Roman, H.T.C., Dir.;

UTUADO

Fondita Santa Marta - 8 Calle Barceló, Utuado, PR 00641; Mailing: PO Box 10, Utuado, PR 00641 t) 787-894-2696 fonditasantamarta@gmail.com www.yosoycapuchino.com Rev. Jose F Irizarry Santana, ofm Cap., Dir.; Ruben Gonzalez, Admin.;

NURSING / REHABILITATION / CONVALESCENCE / ELDERLY CARE [NUR]

ARECIBO

Hogar Sta. Maria Eufrasia - Carr. Est. 651-10, Sector Junco, Arecibo, PR 00612; Mailing: P.O. Box 1909, Arecibo, PR 00613 t) 787-878-5166 eufrasia86@gmail.com www.hogareufrasia.org House for pregnant teens. Sr. Marta Villalobos, Admin.; Raquel Gonzalez Bravo, Dir.; Asstd. Annu.: 18; Staff: 14

San Rafael Geriatric Center - #49 Calle Cervantes, Arecibo, PR 00612-4558 t) 787-878-3813 asilosanrafael@gmail.com Sr. Juanita Flores, H.C., Dir.; Asstd. Annu.: 24; Staff: 25

LARES

Hogar Envejecientes Irma Fe Pol Mendez, Inc. - Calle Pedro Albizu Campo #52, Lares, PR 00669; Mailing: P.O. Box 1185, Lares, PR 00669 t) 787-897-6090 hogarirmafe@yahoo.com www.hogarirmafepol.org Sr. Lizanett Aleman Orozco, H.J., Dir.; Sr. Margoth Quinteros, H.J., Admin.; Asstd. Annu.: 24; Staff: 22

An asterisk (*) denotes an organization that has established tax-exempt status directly with the IRS and is not covered by the USCCB Group Ruling.

Diocese of Caguas, Puerto Rico

(Dioecesis Caguana)

MOST REVEREND EUSEBIO RAMOS MORALES

Bishop of Caguas; ordained June 3, 1983; appointed Bishop of Fajardo-Humacao March 11, 2008; consecrated May 31, 2008; appointed Bishop of Caguas February 2, 2017; installed February 26, 2017.

www.diocesisdecaguaspr.org
diocesisdecaguas@gmail.com

ESTABLISHED NOVEMBER 1964.

Square Miles 737.

Comprises east and southeast portion of Puerto Rico.

Patroness of the Diocese: Maria, Madre de la Iglesia, November 12, 1988.

STATISTICAL OVERVIEW

Personnel

Bishop	1
Retired Bishops	1
Priests: Diocesan Active in Diocese	43
Priests: Diocesan Active Outside Diocese	5
Priests: Retired, Sick or Absent	4
Number of Diocesan Priests	52
Religious Priests in Diocese	17
Total Priests in your Diocese	69
Extern Priests in Diocese	1
Ordinations:	
Diocesan Priests	2
Permanent Deacons in Diocese	85

Parishes

Parishes	34
With Resident Pastor:	
Resident Diocesan Priests	30
Resident Religious Priests	4

Educational

Seminaries, Diocesan	1
Students from This Diocese	5
Students from Other Dioceses	5
Total Seminarians	5
High Schools, Diocesan and Parish	4
Total Students	1,934
Elementary Schools, Diocesan and Parish	4
Total Students	1,307
Total Students under Catholic Instruction	3,246
Teachers in Diocese:	
Sisters	2
Lay Teachers	233

Vital Statistics

Receptions into the Church:	
Infant Baptism Totals	580
Minor Baptism Totals	499
Adult Baptism Totals	124
First Communions	1,179
Confirmations	1,172
Marriages:	
Catholic	212
Interfaith	78
Total Marriages	290
Deaths	373
Total Catholic Population	305,000
Total Population	523,806

LEADERSHIP

Vicar General - t) (787) 747-5885 diocesisdecaguas@gmail.com Rev. Juan Luis Negrón;

Sec. Chancellor - t) 787-747-5885 cancilleriacaguas@gmail.com Rev. Israel Ramos Cintron;

Sec. Vice Chancellor - t) (787) 747-5885 Rev. Angel Molina;

Diocesan Consultors - Rev. Felix Nunez; Rev. Carlos J. Vazquez; Rev. Orlando de Jesus;

Diocesan Tribunal of Caguas - t) (787) 286-8595 tribunaldiocesano@hotmail.com Rev. Luis A Alicea; Rev. Felix Nunez; Rev. Angel Molina;

Board of Diocesan Government - Rev. Juan Luis Negrón; Rev. Luis A Alicea; Rev. Reinaldo Estrada;

Priests Senate - Rev. Antonio Cartagena; Rev. Angel Molina; Rev. Felix Nunez;

OFFICES AND DIRECTORS

Building Commission (Vacant) -

Catechetical Vicar - Rev. Rafael Hernández;

Catholic Charities (Vacant) -

Catholic School Consultors - t) 787-743-1171 Sr. Iris Rivera;

Catholic Social Action (Vacant) -

Catholic Youth - t) (787) 747-5885 diocesisdecaguas@gmail.com Natalia M García-Jiménez;

Comisiones Diocesanas -

Espiritualidad Comunitaria - t) 787-746-2669 Herminia Fonseca;

Formacion Diac. Permanentes - Rev. Ricardo Santin;

Misiones - Dcn. Humberto Martinez;

Pastoral Familiar - t) (787) 747-5885 diocesisdecaguas@gmail.com Rev. Roberto Gómez-Cuadrado;

Pastoral Nec. Especiales (Vacant) -

Pastoral Penitenciaria - t) 787-263-0976 D. Anibal Gonzalez;

Pastoral Preadolescentes -

Pastoral Social - t) (787) 747-5885 diocesisdecaguas@gmail.com Rev. Yamil A. Velazquez;

Commission of Permanent Deacons - Dcn. Carlos Lugo;

Communication Office - t) 787-747-5885 Rev. Feliciano Rodriguez;

Economic Administrator - t) 787-747-5885 Rev. Reinaldo Estrada;

Hospitals - Rev. Juan J. Colon;

Legion of Mary - Isabelo Huertas;

Liturgical Consultor - t) 787-747-5885 x222 Rev. Ricardo Santin;

Master of Ceremonies - t) 787-747-5885

Pastoral Vicar - t) 787-286-0075 x245 diocesisdecaguas@gmail.com Rev. Jose R. Figueroa; Angel David Montes-Reyes;

Planning Vicar (Vacant) -

Red de Esperanza y Solidaridad (REDES) - t) 787-747-5767 Magaly Millán; Sr. Maria Jesus Mompo;

Schools - t) 787-743-1171

School Superintendent - t) (787) 743-1171 Sr. Iris Rivera;

Vincentian Society - Carmencita Colon;

Vocations - t) 787-747-5885 Rev. Felix Nunez;

ORGANIZATIONS

Movimientos y Organizaciones Diocesanas -

Apostolado de la Cruz - t) 787-736-5312 Ana Acevedo;

Caballeros de Colon - t) 787-746-4747 Jose Soto Carmona;

Camino Neo Catecumenal - Domingo Vega;

Cursillos de Cristiandad - t) 787-734-7068 Felipe Sanchez Ramos;

Equipo Ntra. Sra. - t) 787-206-7744 Israel Rosado Y Joan Ruiz;

Equipos Ntra. Sra. - Guillermo Torres; Milagros Ortiz;

Hijas Catolicas - Gloria M. Benitez de Sola;

Hnos. Cheos - t) 787-382-8986 Jose Ortiz;

Juan XXIII - t) 787-747-3748 Carlos De Jesús;

La Piedra que Cristo Edifico en Mi - Regino Vazquez;

Legion de Maria - Maria C. Cotto;

Misioneros Padre Nuestro - Ramon L. Ramos;

Renovacion Carismatica - Noel Morales Rodriguez;

Schoenstatt - t) 787-722-3941 Jose N. Bracero;

Sociedad del Santo Nombre - Victor Cotto;

Talleres de Oracion y Vida - t) 787-745-4123 Petronila Ruiz;

Vicentinos - t) 787-747-6546 Carmencita Colon;

PARISHES, MISSIONS, AND CLERGY

COMMONWEALTH OF PUERTO RICO

AGUAS BUENAS

Church of Tres Santos Reyes - 4 Munoz Rivera St., Aguas Buenas, PR 00703; Mailing: P.O. Box 1, Aguas Buenas, PR 00703 t) 787-732-2741 parroquialostressantosreyes@yahoo.com Redemptorist Fathers. Rev. Angel López-Sanchez, C.Ss.R., Vicar; Rev. Sergio Del Carmen-Espinoza, C.Ss.R., Pst.; Rev. Gerardo Hernandez, C.Ss.R., Pst.; Rev. Edgar Luis Torres-Santos, C.Ss.R., Vicar; Dcn. Julio Resto; Dcn. Pedro Montanez; Dcn. Ramon Rosa;

Bo. Sumidero, Ntra. Sra. del Perpetuo Socorro -

Sector Las Corujas del Barrio Sumidero, Buen Pastor -

Bo. Sonadora, Sagrado Corazon -

Bo. Jagueyes Abajo, San Jose -

Bo. Jagueyes Quintas, Santisimo Redentor -

Bo. Caguitas, Madre del Perpetuo Socorro -

Bo. Caguitas, Sector La Brusca, Ntra. del Rosario -

Parcelas Santa Clara, Santa Clara -

Espiritu Santo - ; Mailing: P.O. Box 40, Aguas Buenas, PR 00703 t) 787-732-1270 iglesanto1991@gmail.com Rev. Melvin Montanez; Dcn. Jose Cotto-Cotto; Dcn. Domingo Falcon;

Carr. 156, Santa Teresita -

Bo. Mulitas Alvelo, De Todos los Santos -

Bo. Mulitas Tiza, San Gerardo Mayela -

Bo. Juan Ascencio, San Alfonso -

AIBONITO

Church of St. Joseph - ; Mailing: Box 2038, Aibonito, PR 00705 t) 787-735-4856 (CRP); 787-735-3741 parrsanjose@yahoo.com Rev. Miguel A. de Angel; Rev. Libardo Rodriguez; Dcn. Juan E. Colon; Dcn. Angel Manuel Santiago-Santiago; Dcn. Carlos Lugo; Dcn. Luis Ortiz-Burgos; Dcn. Pedro Rivera-Ayala; Dcn. Rafael Torres-Delgado; Dcn. Humberto Martinez;

Bo. Algarrobo - t) 787-735-5032

Bo. Asomante (Cuadritos), Ntra. Sra. del Carmen (1959) - t) 787-735-1811

Bo. Asomante (Abejas), Inmaculada Concepcion (1965) - t) 787-735-6455

Bo. Pasto, Ntra. Sra. de Guadalupe (1970) - t) 787-735-6977

Ntra. Sra. de la Providencia (1982) - t) 787-735-3072

Bo. Rabanal (Parcelas), Ntra. Sra. de Fatima (1972) - t) 787-735-0395

Ext. San Luis, Ntra. Sra. del Carmen (1986) - t) 787-735-7189

La Plata, La Milagrosa (1986) - t) 787-735-4038

Llanos, Sector El Juicio - t) 787-735-1973

La Sierra, San Judas Tadeo - t) 787-735-2835

BARRANQUITAS

Church of St. Anthony of Padua - ; Mailing: P.O. Box 1099, Barranquitas, PR 00794 t) 787-857-3585 p_barranquitas@hotmail.com Rev. Roberto Gomez, Pst.; Rev. Oscar Rivera, Vicar; Rev. Jaime A. Rodriguez, S.S.S.; Dcn. Candido Torres; Dcn. Carlos Colón-Bernardi; Dcn. Jose L. Nunez; Dcn. Jose Luis Zayas; Dcn. Visitación Santana-Rivera;

San Francisco de Asis -

Bo. Mana, Virgen del Carmen -

Bo. Canabon, Virgen de la Providencia -

Bo. Helechal, San Jose Obrero -

Bo. Quebrada Grande, Nuestra Sra. de la Monserrate -

Bo. Palo Hincado, Virgen del Perpetuo Socorro -

Bo. Lajitas, Ntra. Sra. del Pilar -

Sector La Torre, Santa Cruz -

Bo. Helechal, San Martin de Porres -

CAGUAS

Catedral Dulce Nombre de Jesus - 44 Betances St., Caguas, PR 00725; Mailing: Box 665, Caguas, PR 00726 t) 787-743-4311; 787-743-2927 catedraldecaguas@yahoo.com catedraldecaguas.org Rev. Juan Luis Negron, Rector; Rev. Boris Espinosa; Rev. Juan J. Colon; Dcn. Bruno Dueno; Dcn. Enrique Santiago; CRP Stds.: 685

Ntra. Sra. Perpetuo Socorro - 24 Aguayo St., Caguas, PR 00726

San Gerardo - 221 B St., B-14, Jardines de Caguas, PR 00726

San Vicente de Paul -

La Sagrada Familia - 1004 P St., Caguas, PR 00725

Divino Nino - ; Mailing: P.O. Box 9416, Caguas, PR 00726 t) 787-746-1450 psantuariodivinonino@gmail.com Rev. Rafael Hernández-Ortiz; Dcn. José A. Méndez-Ortiz; Dcn. Rafael Quiles-Rodríguez; Dcn. Moise's Vargas;

San Francisco Javier - t) 787-286-0440

El Salvador - HC 03 Buzon 38888, Caguas, PR 00725-9723 t) 787-747-0091 pelsalvador1@gmail.com Rev. Pastor Arroyabe; Dcn. Antonio Rosario; Dcn. Pablo Gonzalez; Dcn. Rafael Torres;

Bo. San Salvador, Cristo Rey -

Sector Anon, San Alfonso -

Sector Hato, Ntra. Sra. del Carmen -

Inmaculado Corazon de Maria - Bo. Rio Cañas, HC-05, Caguas, PR 00725-9228; Mailing: Box 56764, Caguas, PR 00725-9228 t) 787-747-6336 inmaculadocorazoncmf@gmail.com Rev. Jose Daniel De Jesus, CMF, Vicar; Rev. Jairo A. Perez, CMF, Vicar; Rev. Carmelo Luciano-Gonzalez, cmf, Pst.; Dcn. Rafael Pagan;

Bo. La Barra, Cristo Rey -

San Antonio -

Bo. La Mesa, Ntra. Sra. Providencia -

Bo. Quebrada Arenas, San Felipe -

Guasabara, Sta. Teresa del Nino Jesus -

Maria Madre de la Iglesia - Calle Juan M. Morales D-23 Urb Valle Tolima, Caguas, PR 00725 t) 787-258-4481 pmariamadredelaiglesia@gmail.com Rev. Ramón Santana-Figueroa; Dcn. Jorge Quinonez-Hernandez;

Bo. Canabon, Maria Reina -

Las Carolinas, Ntra. Sra. del Carmen -

Parroquia Nuestra Senora de la Providencia - Urb. Villa del Carmen, Caguas, PR 00726; Mailing: P.O. Box 6318, Caguas, PR 00726 t) 787-743-8200 providenciasinfronteras@hotmail.com Dcn. Leonardo Matos; Rev. Reinaldo Estrada, Pst.; Dcn. Ruben Villodas;

Urb. Mariolga -

Caserio Publico -

Los Flamboyanes -

Rio Verde -

Villa Carmen -

Villa del Rey I -

Residencial San Carlos -

Residencial San Alfonso -

Parroquia Nuestra Senora del Perpetuo Socorro - Calle 2, A-13, Villa Nueva, Caguas, PR 00725 t) 787-744-1420 vpsocorro@hotmail.com Rev. Antonio Cartagena; Dcn. Carlos Alfonso Muniz-Gonzalez; Dcn. Juan José Rivera-Ortiz;

San Patricio -

San Judas Tadeo -

Sagrado Corazon -
Ntra. Sra. del Carmen -
Sagrado Corazon de Jesus - HC 04, Bo. Beatriz, Caguas, PR 00725; Mailing: Box 45078, Caguas, PR 00725 t) 787-747-5170 pscj1963@yahoo.com Rev. Roberto Solivan; Dcn. Víctor Lebrón-Jiménez;
Bo. Beatriz, Cristo Rey -
San Martin -
San Jose - Coral St., Villa Blanca, Caguas, PR 00726; Mailing: P.O. Box 1749, Caguas, PR 00726 t) 787-743-5889 sanjose.caguas@gmail.com (Discalced Carmelites from Spain) Rev. Fernando Sanchez, O.C.D., Pst.; Dcn. Roberto Berrios-Berrios;
San Jose School - ; Mailing: P.O. Box 1101, Caguas, PR 00726 t) 787-743-2032 csje-sec@csje-sec.org www.csje-sec.org Sr. Nelly O. Rodriguez, C.M., Prin.;
San Jose High School - Coral St., Villa Blanca, Caguas, PR 00726 t) 787-744-8993 webmaster_csjs@yahoo.com Brenda Figueroa de Soler, Prin.;
Nuestra Senora del Rosario - Boi Bairoa La 25, Caguas, PR 00725
San Juan Apostol y Evangelista - Apt. 459, Ave. Bairoa, Caguas, PR 00726 t) 787-744-6359 sjabairoa@gmail.com Rev. Jorge D. Cardona; Dcn. Damaso Roche; Dcn. Jose L. Santiago; Dcn. Ruben Huertas;
San Pablo Apostol - Kennedy U-32-B Urb. Jose Mercado, Caguas, PR 00725 t) 787-743-3546 sanpabloapostol.caguas@gmail.com Rev. Pedro Ortiz; Dcn. Jose R. Rivera; Dcn. Luis F. Laporte-Torres;
Bo. Tomas de Castro I, Ntra. Sra. de Guadalupe -
Bo. Tomas de Castro II, Santa Rose de Lima -
Sector Ramal, San Martin de Porres -
Sector Buenos Aires, San Juan Bautista y Santa Ines -
Sector RM5, Ntra. Sra. de la Monserrate -
San Pedro Apostol - Urb. Bonneville, Caguas, PR 00726; Mailing: P.O. Box 8878, Caguas, PR 00726 t) 787-744-2036 sanpedroap@gmail.com Rev. José O. Camacho-Torres; Dcn. Benjamin Lopez-Molina;
Santisima Trinidad - ; Mailing: P.O. Box 9630, Caguas, PR 00726-9630 t) 787-747-6967 pstcaguaspr@yahoo.com Rev. Orlando de Jesus Gomez; Dcn. Héctor Santos-Reyes; Dcn. Alex Vazquez-Baez;
Santisimo Sacramento - Calle Caney A-11, Caguax, Caguas, PR 00725 t) 787-745-5165 pss.caguax@gmail.com Blessed Sacrament Fathers. Rev. Luis A Alicea, Pst.; Rev. Juan Javier Pena Berrios; Dcn. Luis Lopez;
Urb. Caguas Norte, San Antonio de Padua -
Ntra. Sra. de Guadalupe - 5th St., Caguas, PR 00725

CAYEY

Nuestra Senora de la Asuncion - ; Mailing: P.O. Box 372887, Cayey, PR 00737-2887 t) 787-738-2763 asuncion.cayey@gmail.com Rev. Feliciano Rodriguez; Rev. Luis Rivera, Vicar; Dcn. Edgardo Rivera; Dcn. Jose E. Melendez; Dcn. Lino Ortiz-Tapia; Dcn. Rafael Santos;
Bo. Jajome, Sagrado Corazon de Jesus -
Bo. Pasto Viejo, Ntra. Sra. del Carmen -
Bo. Toita, Ntra. Sra. de la Merced -
Res. Brisas de Cayey, San Ramon Nonato -
Bo. Maton Arriba, Santa Teresita del Nino Jesus -
Nuestra Senora de la Merced - ; Mailing: P.O. Box 1840, Cayey, PR 00737 t) 787-738-3872 mercedario_montellano@hotmail.com Rev. Wilfredo Riveros, Pst.; Rev. Jules Roger-Ndzana, O. de M.; Dcn. Gilberto Meléndez-Montes;
Bo. Vegas, San Ramon Nonato -
Bo. Culebras, Ntra. Sra. del Carmen -
Bo. Farallon, San Pedro Nolasco -
San Pedro Armengol (La Plata) -
San Esteban Protomartir - Bo. Guavate, 22601 Sector Nieves, Cayey, PR 00736-9522 t) 787-747-4555 p.sanesteban@gmail.com Rev. Encarnacion Nieves; Dcn. Anibal Gonzalez Vazquez;
Bo. Borinquen Pradera, Nuestra Senora del Carmen -
Bo. Guavate, San Jose de la Montana -

CIDRA

Nuestra Senora de Fatima - ; Mailing: Box 214, Cidra, PR 00739 t) 787-739-0633 iglesiafatima@hotmail.es Rev. Miguel Claudio; Dcn. Jose E. Melendez; Dcn. Samuel Rodriguez; Dcn. Israel Santiago;
Bo. Toita, Sagrado Corazon de Jesus -
Bo. Salto, San Vicente -
Bo. Honduras, Perpetuo Socorro -
Bo. Rabanal, Jesus Salvador -
Bo. Parcelas, La Milagrosa -
Bo. Salto, Nuestra Senora de la Providencia -
Bo. Salto, Santa Teresita -
Santo Cristo de Los Milagros -
Nuestra Senora del Carmen - ; Mailing: P.O. Box 359, Cidra, PR 00739 t) 787-739-2406 Dcn. Jose Nelson Garcia; Rev. Ricardo Santin; Rev. Karlogs Lopez, Assoc. Pst.; Rev. Juan Antonio Blanco-Rivera; Dcn. Angel Alberto Perez Arroyo; Dcn. Felipe Flores;
Centro Plaza Municipal -
Bo. Rio Abajo, Madre del Salvador -
Urb. Treasure Valley, La Milagrosa -
Bo. Bayamon-Centenejas I, La Inmaculada -
Bo. Montellano, Santa Teresa del Nino Jesus -
Bo. Bayamon-Certenejas II, Perpetuo Socorro -
Bo. Bayamon-Juan del Valle, Nuestra Senora del Rosario -
Bo. Arena-Santa Clara, San Joaquin -
Bo. Ceiba-Hevia, Nuestra Senora del Rosario -
Bo. Arenas, Nuestra Senora de la Providencia -
Bo. Ceiba, Cristo Rey -
Bo. Bayamon-San Jose, San Jose -
Bo. Rincon, San Francisco de Asis -
Bo. Sud, La Milagrosa -
Bo. Sud, San Pablo -

COMERIO

San Andres Apostol - ; Mailing: HC 02 Box 5840, Comerio, PR 00782 t) 787-875-5424 Rev. Raul Morales, Pst.; Dcn. Florencio Mercado; Dcn. Optaciano Rivera Ortiz; Dcn. José A. Hernández-Rivera;
Bo. Palomas, Comerio, San Jose -
Bo. Quebradillas, Barranquitas, Corazon de Jesus -
Bo. Cedro Arriba, Naranjito, San Antonio de Padua -
Bo. Quebradillas, Barranquitas, Inmaculada Concepcion y Santa Cruz -
Bo. Cedro Arriba, Naranjito, Santuario Maria Auxiliadora -
Santo Cristo de la Salud - ; Mailing: P.O. Box 1139, Comerio, PR 00782 t) 787-875-4525 stocristo@coqui.net Rev. Angel L. Cintron; Rev. Yean Reyes; Dcn. Heriberto Santos-Vazquez; Dcn. Jorge Luis Cabrera-Rivera; Dcn. José A. Flores-Colón;
Bo. Sabana, Nuestra Senora del Santisimo Rosario -
Bo. Rio Hondo, Nuestra Senora de Fatima -
Bo. Palomas, Santa Cecilia -
Bo. Cedrito, Virgen de la Providencia -
Bo. Rio Hondo-Sector Las Parcelas, San Pablo -
Bo. Pinas Arriba, Nuestra Senora del Carmen -
Bo. Naranjo-Sector Las Parcelas, San Antonio de Padua -
Bo. Vega Redonda, San Francisco de Asis -
Bo. Cejas, Santa Rosa de Lima -
Bo. Dona Elena, San Martin de Porres -
Rio Hondo II, Maria Madre de la Iglesia -

GURABO

San Jose - 7 Santiago Iglesias St., Gurabo, PR 00778; Mailing: P.O. Box 733, Gurabo, PR 00778 t) 787-737-2656 parroquiasan@hotmail.com Dcn. Juan Alberto Ortiz-Cordero; Rev. Jose R. Figueroa; Dcn. Jose Velazquez;
Bo. Jagual, Sagrado Corazon de Jesus -
Bo. Jaguas Llano, Virgen del Carmen -
Bo. Santa Rita, Santa Rita -
La Milagrosa - Bo. Hato Nuevo, Gurabo, PR 00778
Bo. Celada, Santa Francisca Javier Cabrini -
Bo. Hato Nuevo, La Milagrosa -
Bo. Jaguas Loma, San Miguel -
Bo. Mamey II, Ntra. Sra. del Carmen -

JUNCOS

Inmaculada Concepcion - Calle Almodóvar #18, Juncos, PR 00777; Mailing: P.O. Box 1728, Juncos, PR 00777 t) 787-734-2431 parroquiajuncosuno@gmail.com Rev. Angel Molina; Dcn. Avelino Perez; Dcn. César F. Bautista-Castillo; Dcn. Francisco Gonzalez; Dcn. Rafael Delgado-Rodriguez;
Bo. Canta Gallo, Cristo Redentor -
Bo. Ceiba Sur, Sagrado Corazon -
Bo. Valenciano Sector Amigo, Espiritu Santo -
Bo. Ceiba Norte, Cristo Rey -
Bo. Valenciano Arriba, San Juan Bautista -
Bo. Ceiba Norte Sector Chinos, Buen Pastor -
Bo. Pinas, Santa Cruz -
Bo. Lirios, San Jose -
Bo. Canta Gallo Secto Reparto Valenciano, Maria Madre de la Iglesia -
Santisima Trinidad -

LAS PIEDRAS

Inmaculada Concepcion - ; Mailing: Box 324, Las Piedras, PR 00771 t) 787-733-8325 (CRP); 787-733-2381 inmaculadaconcepcionpr@gmail.com Rev. Yamil A. Velazquez; Dcn. Antonio Diaz; Dcn. Domingo Figueroa; Dcn. Jose Lozada; Dcn. Jose O. Rosario;
Bo. Montones I, Perpetuo Socorro -
Bo. Tejas Asomante, Nuestra Senora de la Providencia -
Bo. La Fermina, Jesus de Nazaret -
Bo. Montones IV, Santa Teresa del Nino Jesus -
Bo. Montones II, San Juan Bautista -
Mission -
San Juan Bautista - HC 02 Buzon 4467, Las Piedras, PR 00771 t) 787-733-0986 Rev. Kevin Cintron Gonzalez; Dcn. Josue Diaz-Miranda;
Finca Roig, San Juan Bautista -
Bo. Boqueron, La Sagrada Familia -
Bo. Pena Pobre, Sagrado Corazon -
Bo. Rio Blanco, La Milagrosa -
Bo. Mango, San Francisco Javier -
Bo. Pasto Seco, El Buen Pastor -

MAUNABO

San Isidro Labrador - ; Mailing: P.O. Box 248, Maunabo, PR 00707 t) 787-861-5526 parroquiasanisidromaunabo@gmail.com Rev. Angel Colon; Dcn. Frank R. Serrano-Torres; Dcn. Andres Camacho;
Nuestra Senora del Carmen -
Bo. Calzada, Nuestra Senora de la Providencia -
Bo. Matuyas, Nuestra Senora de la Candelaria -
Bo. Palo Seco, San Judas Tadeo -
Bo. Emajaguas, San Antonio de Padua -
Mission -
Mission -
Ntra. Sra. del Rosario de Fatima -
Mission -
Mission -
Mission -

NARANJITO

San Miguel Arcangel - Centro Parroquial, Naranjito, PR 00719; Mailing: P.O. Box 68, Naranjito, PR 00719 t) 787-869-2840 sanmiguel.parroquia@yahoo.com Rev. Jose A Ortiz, Pst.; Rev. Felix Nunez; Dcn. Gerardo Rodriguez; Dcn. Ramón Luis Torres-Miranda; Dcn. Samuel Velazquez;
Bo. Nuevo, Santa Rosa de Lima -
Bo. Lomas Centro, Virgen del Carmen -
Bo. Anones, La Milagrosa -
Bo. Lomas Valles, San Judas Tadeo -
Bo. Guadiana, La Monserrate -
Bo. Achiote, Sagrado Corazon -
Bo. Nuevo Parcelas, San Vicente de Paul -
Bo. Cedro Abajo, San Jose -

SAN LORENZO

Nuestra Senora de la Mercedes - Munoz Rivera 55, San Lorenzo, PR 00754; Mailing: Apartado 1280, San Lorenzo, PR 00754 t) 787-736-2571 nsdelasmercedes@gmail.com Rev. Felipe Santiago, C.Ss.R., Pst.; Rev. Hector Garcia-Flores, C.Ss.R., Assoc. Pst.; Rev. Antonio Hernandez, C.Ss.R., Assoc. Pst.; Rev. Andres Spacht, C.Ss.R., Assoc. Pst.; Dcn. Gaspar Laureano; Dcn. Javier Lebron; Dcn. Ramon

Rojas;

Bo. Jagual, Nuestra Senora del Carmen -
Bo. Quemados, Nuestra Senora del Perpetuo Socorro -
Bo. Cerro Gordo Abajo, Cristo Redentor -
Bo. Quebrada, Jesus Maestro -
Bo. Florida, Santa Monica -
Bda. Roosevelt, Nuestra Senora del Carmen -
Bo. Hato Km. 6, Nuestra Senora del Perpetuo Socorro -
Bo. Cerro Gordo Arriba, Inmaculada Concepcion -
Bo. Lorenzo del Valle, Inmaculado Corazon de Maria -
Bo. Santa Clara, San Gerardo -
Urb. Los Flamboyanes, Bo. Florida, Nuestra Senora de Lourdes -

Sagrado Corazon de Jesus y 12 Apostoles - ; Mailing: HC 30 Box 32716, San Lorenzo, PR 00754-9726 t) 787-715-6947 corazon12apostoles@hotmail.com Rev. Israel Ramos Cintron; Rev. Jonathan Perez; Dcn. Efrain del Valle;

San Francisco de Asis -
Santa Rosa de Lima -
San Jose -
Ntra. Sra. del Rosario -
Maria Madre de la Iglesia -
San Pedro -
Santa Teresita del Nino Jesus -

YABUCOA

Santos Angeles Cutodios - Degetau St. #2, Yabucoa, PR 00767; Mailing: Box 7, Yabucoa, PR 00767 t) 787-893-3347 iglesiastoangelescustodios@gmail.com Rev. Baltazar Nunez; Rev. David Diaz, Vicar; Rev. Jose Luis Betancourt; Dcn. Felix C. Andino-Vazquez; Dcn. Luis M. Surrillo-Andino; Dcn. Ruben Ramos; Dcn. Bienvenido Abreu;

Bo. Rosa Sanchez, Santa Rosa de Lima -
Bo. Jacanas Granjas, San Juan Evangelista -
Bo. Jac. Piedra Blanca, Sagrado Corazon -
Bo. Tejas Piedra Azul, Sta. Maria Reina Paz -
Bo. Martorell, Santa Teresita del Nino Jesus -
Bo. Tejas, Ntra. Sra. de la Divina Providencia -
Bo. Playita Cuesta, San Bernardo -
Bo. Playita Arriba, San Antonio de Padua -
Bo. Playita Parcelas, Virgen Milagrosa -
Bo. Quebradillas, Ntra. Sra. del Carmen -
Bo. Guayabota, La Sagrada Familia -
Bo. Calabazas Arriba, San Jose -
Bo. Quebrada Grande, San Benito -
Bo. Playa Guayanes, Ntra. Sra. del Carmen -
Bo. Aguacate, Ntra. Sra. del Perpetuo Socorro -
Bo. Jagueyes, Inmaculada Concepcion -
Bo. Ingenio, Santisima Trinidad -
Bo. Camino Nuevo, San Jeronimo -
Bo. Jacanas Sur, Divino de Jesus y Beato Diego -
Bo. Tejas - Valerio, Corpus Christi, Caguas, PR 00725

Camino Nuevo, El Guano, San Esteban -
Jacanas, Piedra Blanca, Sagrado Corazon de Jesus -
Limones, Campo Alegre, San Francisco de Asis -

SCHOOLS: PRESCHOOL THRU HIGH SCHOOL

SCHOOLS

COMMONWEALTH OF PUERTO RICO

AGUAS BUENAS

Academia San Alfonso - (PAR) (Grades PreK-9) Pio Rechani St., Aguas Buenas, PR 00703; Mailing: P.O. Box 97, Aguas Buenas, PR 00703 t) 787-732-8288 asaalfonso@gmail.com Rev. P. Miguel Garcia, C.Ss.R.; Nydia Velazquez, Prin.;

CAGUAS

Academia Cristo de los Milagros - (DIO) ; Mailing: Box 7618, Caguas, PR 00726-7618 t) 787-743-3131; 787-743-4242; 787-743-4855 cristo@acmpr.net Yolanda Flores, Prin.; Yanira Flores, Prin.; Nilda Aponte, Librn.;

Colegio Catolico Notre Dame - (PRV) (Grades PreK-4) Ave. Troche Esquina Calle Troche, Caguas, PR 00726; Mailing: P.O. Box 937, Caguas, PR 00726 t) 787-743-2385; 787-743-2524; 787-743-3693 principal@ccndpr.com; asuntosacademicos@ccndpr.com www.ccnd.org Luz Rodriguez, Prin.; Jose J. Grillo, Dir.; Stds.: 314; Pr. Tchrs.: 1; Lay Tchrs.: 34

Colegio Catolico Notre Dame Superior - (PRV) (Grades 5-12) Ave. Troche #34, Caguas, PR 00725; Mailing: Box 937, Caguas, PR 00726 t) 787-743-3693; 787-743-5501; 787-653-0834 principal@ccndpr.com; asuntosacademicos@ccndpr.com www.ccnd.org Jose J. Grillo, Prin.; Gildo Jesús Peña Garcia, Associate Principal; Wilfredo Ocasio, Associate Principal; Stds.: 1,084; Pr. Tchrs.: 1; Lay Tchrs.: 85

Colegio San Juan Apostol y Evangelista - (PRV) ; Mailing: P.O. Box 459, Caguas, PR 00726-0459 t) 787-743-8266; 787-747-4302; 787-744-6359 sjabairoa@gmail.com Wilma Roman, Admin.; Marie Lozano, Prin.; Rev. Antonio Cartagena Veguilla, Dir.; Teresa Cruz Ortiz, Librn.; Natalia Hernandez, Librn.;

CAYEY

Colegio Nuestra Senora de la Merced - (PRV) ; Mailing: P.O. Box 372678, Cayey, PR 00736 t) 787-738-3438 lamercedcayey@yahoo.com; administracion@colegio-lamerced.org (Nuestra Senora de la Asuncion Parish) Laura Ortiz, Prin.; Nancy Diaz Morales, Dir.; Maricarmen Lopez, Librn.;

INSTITUTIONS LOCATED IN DIOCESE

CONVENTS, MONASTERIES, AND RESIDENCES FOR WOMEN [CON]

CIDRA

Santa Clara Monastery - ; Mailing: P.O. Box 725, Cidra, PR 00739-0725 t) 787-732-5771 Hermanas Clarisas

MISCELLANEOUS [MIS]

CAGUAS

Diocesan Tribunal of Caguas - ; Mailing: P.O. Box 9779, Caguas, PR 00726 t) 787-286-8595 tribunaldiocesano@hotmail.com Rev. Luis A Alicea, Vicar; Rev. Felix Nunez; Rev. Orlando de Jesus Gomez, Mem.; Dcn. Ramon Rojas, Mem.; Rev. Ricardo Santin, Mem.;

Hnas. Hijas de Santa Maria de la Ternura - Calle Naranjito 220, Bo. Boringuen Parcelas Viejas, Caguas, PR 00726; Mailing: P.O. Box 5097, Caguas, PR 00726 t) 787-653-5813 Sr. Sonia Maria La Luz, H.S.M.T., Prioress;

Instituto Secular de Ntra. Sra. de la Altagracia - Calle 13, L23. Urb. Delgado, Caguas, PR 00725 t) 787-744-3628

Movimiento Juan XXIII - ; Mailing: P.O. Box 7229, Caguas, PR 00726 t) 787-747-3748 Rev. Karlogs Lopez; Rev. Hipolito Torres;

NARANJITO

Seminario Pablo VI - Theological - HC 72, Naranjito, PR 00719; Mailing: Box 376625, Naranjito, PR 00719 Rev. Felix Nunez, Rector;

Casa del Apostol San Andres - Rev. Carlos J. Vazquez;

MONASTERIES AND RESIDENCES FOR PRIESTS AND BROTHERS [MON]

AIBONITO

Casa Salesiana de Retiros - ; Mailing: P.O. Box 2019, Aibonito, PR 00705 t) 787-735-2486 sdbaibon@coqui.net Rev. Lorenzo Ruiz-Victoria, SDB, Vicar; Mario A. Leonardo, SDB, Admin.; Juan Martinez, SDB, Dir.;

CAGUAS

Misioneros Hijos del Inmaculado Corazon de Maria (Claretianos) - Bo. Rio Cañas, HC-05, Caguas, PR 00725-9233; Mailing: Box 57564, Caguas, PR 00725-9233 t) 787-747-6336 jvicente@coqui.net; jvmsg@hotmail.com Rev. Jose Daniel De Jesus, CMF, Vicar; Rev. Jairo A. Perez, CMF, Vicar; Rev. Carmelo Luciano-Gonzalez, cmf, Pst.;

RETREAT HOUSES / RENEWAL CENTERS [RTR]

AGUAS BUENAS

Casa Cristo Redentor - ; Mailing: P.O. Box 8, Aguas Buenas, PR 00703-0008 t) 787-732-5161 pdamian@coqui.net Rev. Gerardo Hernandez, C.Ss.R., Pst.; Rev. Edgar Luis Torres-Santos, CSsR, Pst.;

AIBONITO

Casa Manresa - ; Mailing: P.O. Box 1319, Aibonito, PR 00705 t) 787-735-8016; 787-735-8017 manresa@caribe.net www.casamanresaaibonito.org Rev. Miguel A. de Angel;

JUNCOS

Casa Cursillos de Cristiandad of Caguas - Salida de Juncos Carr. 919, Juncos, PR 00777; Mailing: P.O. Box 1762, Juncos, PR 00777 t) 787-734-7068 (Lay Corp. of Cursillistas)

SAN LORENZO

Casa Charlie Rodriguez - ; Mailing: P.O. Box 1190, San Lorenzo, PR 00754 t) 787-736-5750 santuariopr@gmail.com www.santuariopr.org Rev. Baltazar Nunez, Rector;

SHRINES [SHR]

SAN LORENZO

Diocesan Shrine Our Lady of Mount Carmel - ; Mailing: HC 30 Box 36876, San Lorenzo, PR 00754 t) 787-736-5750 santuariopr@gmail.com www.santuariopr.org Rev. Jonathan Perez, Rector; Dcn. Luis Zayas-Carrasquillo; Dcn. Efrain del Valle;

Diocese of the Caroline Islands

MOST REVEREND JULIO ANGKEL, D.D.

Bishop of Caroline Islands; ordained December 3, 1983; appointed Coadjutor Bishop of Caroline Islands November 18, 2017; consecrated Bishop February 4, 2018; Succeeded as Bishop of the Diocese of the Caroline Islands February 2, 2020. P.O. Box 939, Weno, Chuuk, FM 96942.

Chancery Office: P.O. Box 939, Weno, Chuuk, FM 96942. T: 691-330-2399.

Square Miles Ocean 1,725,000.

Vicariate of the Caroline Islands erected December 10, 1905 and committed to the Order of Friars Minor Capuchin, extended to the Mariana Islands March 1, 1911. Vicariate of the Marianas and Caroline and Marshall Islands erected May 4, 1923 and committed to the Society of Jesus. Marianas Islands separated July 4, 1946. Diocese of the Caroline-Marshalls created February 3, 1980. The Marshalls made a separate Prefecture Apostolic August 15, 1993, and the Diocese renamed "Diocese of the Caroline Islands."

Civilly it includes the four Federated States of Micronesia (Chuuk, Kosrae, Pohnpei and Yap) and the Republic of Palau.

STATISTICAL OVERVIEW

Personnel

Bishop	1
Priests: Diocesan Active in Diocese	14
Priests: Retired, Sick or Absent	1
Number of Diocesan Priests	15
Religious Priests in Diocese	7
Total Priests in your Diocese	22
Ordinations:	
Religious Priests	1
Permanent Deacons in Diocese	67
Total Brothers	1
Total Sisters	12

Parishes

Parishes	28
With Resident Pastor:	
Resident Diocesan Priests	12
Resident Religious Priests	4
Without Resident Pastor:	
Administered by Deacons	12
Administered by Lay People	1
Missions	1
Professional Ministry Personnel:	
Brothers	1
Sisters	1

Educational

Seminaries, Diocesan	1
Students from This Diocese	4
Diocesan Students in Other Seminaries	9
Total Seminarians	13
High Schools, Diocesan and Parish	6
Total Students	700
High Schools, Private	2
Total Students	357
Elementary Schools, Diocesan and Parish	4
Total Students	675
Catechesis/Religious Education:	
High School Students	1,000
Total Students under Catholic Instruction	2,745
Teachers in Diocese:	
Priests	1
Sisters	10
Lay Teachers	102

Vital Statistics

Receptions into the Church:	
Infant Baptism Totals	1,286
First Communions	594
Confirmations	565
Marriages:	
Catholic	262
Interfaith	32
Total Marriages	294
Total Catholic Population	77,733
Total Population	120,815

LEADERSHIP

Chancery Office - t) 691-330-2399

Vicar General - dioceseofthecarolineislands@gmail.com Rev. Kelly Yalmadau, Vicar;

Chancellor - c) (691) 926-9597 kenu16@gmail.com Rev. Kenneth Urumolug, S.J., Chancellor (ken16@yahoo.com);

Diocesan Consultors - Rev. Rusk Saburo (ruskaburo@yahoo.com); Rev. Kenneth Urumolug, S.J. (ken16@yahoo.com); Rev. Kelly Yalmadau;

Finance Committee - Emmanuel Mori; Jenelyn Perez; Fabian Nimea;

Episcopal Vicars -

Chuuk - t) 691-330-8293 rosend278@yahoo.com Rev. Rosendo Rudolf;

Palau - Rev. Rusk Saburo;

Pohnpei-Kosrae - t) 691-320-4661 kenu16@gmail.com Rev. Kenneth Urumolug, S.J.;

Yap - t) 691-350-2265 batarichsj@gmail.com Rev. Richard McAuliff, S.J.;

Diocesan Tribunal -

Adjunct Judge - t) (691) 330-2399 dioceseofthecarolineislands@gmail.com Rev. Kelly Yalmadau (Micronesia);

Defenders of the Bond - Rev. Rusk Saburo;

Judicial Vicar - t) 691-350-2265 dioceseofthecarolineislands@gmail.com Rev. Kelly Yalmadau, Vicar;

Notary - Miriam Chin;

Vocations - Rev. Florentinus Akkin;

PARISHES, MISSIONS, AND CLERGY

FEDERATED STATES OF MICRONESIA

CHUUK

Immaculate Heart of Mary Cathedral - ; Mailing: P.O. Box 250, Chuuk, FM 96942 t) 691-330-2313 sisamkaster@gmail.com Dcn. Marselo Ludwig; Dcn. Redley Noporu; Dcn. Yostaro Noporu; Dcn. Adarino Pete; Dcn. Anchelino Rosokow; Rev. Kaster Sisam, Rector; Rev. Fernando Titus, Assoc. Pst.;

St. Cecilia School - (Grades K-8) ; Mailing: P.O. Box 850, Chuuk, FM 96942 t) 691-330-4362

St. Anthony's - ; Mailing: P.O. Box 250, Chuuk, FM 96942 t) 691-330-2399 flonorthwest@gmail.com Dcn. Basiente Atan; Dcn. Rinder Fidel; Dcn. Joseph Kasian Jr.; Dcn. Tobias Soram; Rev. Florentinus Akkin, Pst.;

Assumption of the Blessed Virgin Mary - ; Mailing: P.O. Box 939, Chuuk, FM 96942 t) 691-330-2399 edmond.ludwick@yahoo.com Dcn. Sakuruta Berminar; Dcn. Edmond Isac; Dcn. Faustino Katsuta; Dcn. Seferino Kuan; Dcn. Hauk Paul; Dcn. Krispino Raphael; Dcn. Roke Rokop; Dcn. John Soichy; Dcn. Hauk Tonis; Dcn. Kirisos Victus; Dcn. Gabriel Ykuda; Rev. Edmond Ludwick, Pst.;

St. Francis Assisi - ; Mailing: P.O. Box 939, Chuuk, FM 96942 t) 691-330-2399 rosend278@yahoo.com Dcn. Benry Bernard; Dcn. Innocent Fred; Dcn. John Fritz; Dcn. Rosenino Joseph; Dcn. Tionisio Moses; Dcn. Julian Ranu; Dcn. Kanda Rousan; Dcn. Aldon Ruben; Dcn. Kerno Sam; Dcn. Manen Souleng; Dcn. Diophil Binak Wasan; Rev. Julio Angkel, Pst.;

Hall Islands Parish - ; Mailing: P.O. Box 939, Chuuk, FM 96942 t) 691-330-2399 Rev. Rosendo Rudolf, Pst.; Dcn. Kawaichy James, Admin.;

Holy Cross Parish - ; Mailing: P.O. Box 939, Chuuk, FM 96942 t) 691-330-2399 seren_paw@yahoo.com Rev. Dominic Theodor, Pst.; Dcn. Tarsisio Atty; Dcn. Atitor Edmond; Dcn. Josuah Hilario; Dcn. Kapier Kepwe; Dcn. Terencio Lorenso; Dcn. Freddy Mailos; Dcn. Simon Soien Muety; Dcn. Kantaro Nethon; Dcn. Yulian Nethon; Dcn. Iowan Nimas; Dcn. Henery Nimeisa; Dcn. Kantino Nimeisa; Dcn. Peter Ori; Dcn. Suchan Stephen; Dcn. Joseph Suda;

Holy Family Parish - ; Mailing: P.O. Box 120, Chuuk, FM 96942 t) 691-339-2456 bishopangkel@gmail.com Dcn. Jimmy Emilio; Dcn. Rikarto Fabian; Dcn. Sandy Frank; Dcn. Kandy Koichy; Dcn. Steve Marcus; Dcn. Alfred Ray; Most Rev. Julio Angkel, Pst.;

Mortlock Parish - ; Mailing: P.O. Box 939, Chuuk, FM 96942 t) 691-330-2399 asamo@mail.fm Dcn. Soichy Buliche; Rev. Rosendo Rudolf, Pst.;

Pattiw Parish - ; Mailing: P.O. Box 939, Chuuk, FM 96942 Dcn. Mariano Easu; Dcn. Julio Naich;

Sacred Heart Parish - ; Mailing: P.O. Box 250, Chuuk, FM 96942 t) 691-330-2313 ferntitus@gmail.com Dcn. Anthonio Anthonio; Dcn. Joe Commor; Dcn. Tom Edgar; Dcn. Benisio Joseph; Dcn. Henry Michael; Dcn. Gregorio Nedelec; Rev. Fernando Titus, Pst.;

Weito Parish - ; Mailing: P.O. Box 939, Chuuk, FM 96942 t) 691-330-2313 flonorthwest@gmail.com Dcn. Christino Afeiluk; Rev. Florentinus Akkin, Pst.;

COLONIA, YAP

St. Ignatius - ; Mailing: P.O. Box A, Colonia, Yap, FM 96943 t) 691-350-2265 kyalmadau@yahoo.com Dcn. John Talugmai; Dcn. Xavier Yarofaliyong;

St. Joseph - ; Mailing: P.O. Box A, Colonia, Yap, FM 96943 t) 691-350-2598 batarichsj@gmail.com Dcn. Francis Genong; Rev. Masco S. Sinaga, S.J., Pst.;

St. Mary's - ; Mailing: P.O. Box A, Colonia, Yap, FM 96943 t) 691-350-2265 kyalmadau@yahoo.com Dcn. Charles Flanning; Rev. Moses Tashibelit, Assoc. Pst.; Rev. Cuthbert Yiftheg, Assoc. Pst.;

St. Mary School - t) 691-350-2269 Rufino Xavier, Prin.;

Queen of Heaven - ; Mailing: P.O. Box A, Colonia, Yap, FM 96943 t) 691-350-7273 kyalmadau@yahool.com

KOLONIA, POHNPEI

St. Augustine - ; Mailing: P.O. Box 160, Kolonia, Pohnpei, FM 96941 t) 691-920-7313 fredmartin01@gmail.com Dcn. Adelino Lorens; Dcn. Fred Martin, Admin.;

St. Barnabas - ; Mailing: P.O. Box 160, Kolonia, Pohnpei, FM 96942 t) 691-320-1505 Dcn. Michael Sardis; Dcn. Innocensio Elias, Admin.;

Christ the King - ; Mailing: P.O. Box 2056, Kolonia, Pohnpei, FM 96941 t) 691-320-3744 Dcn. Sosua Dungken; Fabian Nimea, Admin.;

Immaculate Heart of Mary - ; Mailing: P.O. Box 160, Kolonia, Pohnpei, FM 96941 t) 691-320-2244 Dcn. Patrick Paul; Dcn. Luciano Iowanis, Admin.;

St. Joseph - ; Mailing: P.O. Box 671, Kolonia, Pohnpei, FM 96941 t) 691-320-6025; 691-320-3699 Dcn. Henry Donre, Admin.;

Our Lady of Mercy - ; Mailing: P.O. Box 160, Kolonia, Pohnpei, FM 96941 t) 691-320-2557 araceleyberley@gmail.com Dcn. Burdenciol Andreas; Dcn. Augustine Damarlane; Dcn. Edgar Martin; Dcn. Berley Arecely, Admin.;

Pohnpei Catholic School - (Grades K-9) ; Mailing: P.O. Box 1650, Kolonia, Pohnpei, FM 96941 t) 691-320-2556 Bernadita Benavente Helstrom, Prin.;

St. Paul - ; Mailing: P.O. Box 160, Kolonia, Pohnpei, FM 96941 t) 691-320-5822; 691-320-3615 Rev. Robert Ifamilik, Pst.; Dcn. William Ioanis, Admin.;

St. Peter's - ; Mailing: P.O. Box 160, Kolonia, Pohnpei, FM 96941 t) 691-320-4667 Dcn. Bellarmine Ioanis; Dcn. Mikel Dano, Admin.;

Sacred Heart - ; Mailing: P.O. Box 160, Kolonia, Pohnpei, FM 96941 t) 691-320-3200; 691-320-1957 Dcn. Ioanis Tihpen; Dcn. Casiano Nennis, Admin.;

St. Ignatius -

St. John -

REPUBLIC OF PALAU

KOROR

St. John Baptist - ; Mailing: P.O. Box 128, Koror, PW 96940 t) 680-488-1758 rusksaburo@gmail.com

Sacred Heart - ; Mailing: P.O. Box 148, Koror, PW 96940 t) 680-488-1758 rusksaburo@gmail.com Rev. Rusk R. Saburo, Pst.;

Maris Stella - (Grades K-8) ; Mailing: P.O. Box 787, Koror, PW 96940 t) 680-488-2436 Lorenza Olkeriil, Prin.;

Mission - Ngcheangl, PW -

Mission - Sonsorol, PW -

St. Thomas the Apostle - ; Mailing: P.O. Box 128, Koror, PW 96940 t) 680-488-2392

SCHOOLS: PRESCHOOL THRU HIGH SCHOOL

HIGH SCHOOLS

FEDERATED STATES OF MICRONESIA

CHUUK

Saramen Chuuk Academy - (PAR) ; Mailing: P.O. Box 662, Chuuk, FM 96942 t) 691-330-4442 wayneolap@gmail.com Wayne Olap, Prin.;

Xavier High School - (PAR) ; Mailing: P.O. Box 220, Chuuk, FM 96942 t) 691-330-4266 xhsmicronesia@mail.fm Martin K. Carl, Prin.; Rev. Dennis Baker, S.J., Dir.;

POHNPEI

Our Lady of Mercy Catholic High School - (PAR) ; Mailing: P.O. Box 73, Pohnpei, FM 96941 t) 691-320-2888 knamio@gmail.com Sr. Krista Namio, M.M.B., Prin.;

YAP

Yap Catholic High School - ; Mailing: P.O. Box 950, Yap, FM 96943 t) 691-350-8390 Michael Wieneck, Prin.; Rev. Robert Richard McAuliff, S.J., Dir.;

REPUBLIC OF PALAU

KOROR

Mindszenty High School - (PAR) ; Mailing: P.O. Box 69, Koror, PW 96940 t) 680-488-2437 batarichsj@gmail.com Rev. Robert Richard McAuliff, S.J., Prin.;

INSTITUTIONS LOCATED IN DIOCESE

COLLEGES & UNIVERSITIES [COL]

CHUUK

Caroline College and Pastoral Institute - ; Mailing: P.O. Box 462, Chuuk, FM 96942 t) 691-330-8293 rosend278@yahoo.com Working in collaboration with Chaminade University of Honolulu through online courses (distance education). Rev. Rosendo Rudolf, Pres.; Emmanuel Mori, Dir.;

CONVENTS, MONASTERIES, AND RESIDENCES FOR WOMEN [CON]

AWAK, POHNPEI

Sisters of Marie Auxiliatrice - ; Mailing: P.O. Box 1375, Awak, Pohnpei, FM 96942 t) 691-320-2626 eliaschristina12@yahoo.com

KOLONIA, POHNPEI

Mercedarian Missionaries of Berriz - ; Mailing: P.O. Box 73, Kolonia, Pohnpei, FM 96941 t) 691-320-2558 knamio@gmail.com Sr. Antonina Malsol, M.M.B., Contact;

KOROR

Mercedarian Missionaries of Berriz - ; Mailing: P.O. Box 56, Koror, PW 96940 t) 680-488-2272 Sr. Connie Kinosta, M.M.B., Contact;

WENO, CHUUK

Mercedarian Missionaries of Berriz - ; Mailing: P.O. Box

67, Weno, Chuuk, FM 96942 t) 691-330-4587 globilmmb@yahoo.com Sr. Gloria Billimont, M.M.B., Contact;

MISCELLANEOUS [MIS]

CHUUK

Micronesian Seminar Library - 1 Xavier Cir., Chuuk, FM 96942-0220; Mailing: P.O. Box 220, Chuuk, FM 96942-0220 t) 691-330-4266 Velpa Veloso, Admin.;

MONASTERIES AND RESIDENCES FOR PRIESTS AND BROTHERS [MON]

CHUUK

Jesuit Community of Micronesia - 1 Xavier Cir., Chuuk, FM 96942-0220; Mailing: P.O. Box 220, Chuuk, FM 96942-0220 c) (917) 214-6290 ueamicfjsuperior@jesuits.org Rev. David L. Andrus, S.J., Pst. Min./Coord.; Rev. Matthew J. Cassidy, S.J., Supr.; Rev. Thomas Todd Kenny, S.J., Pres.; Tomas Becket Pramudita, S.J., Teacher; Benicdiktus Juliar, S.J., Teacher; Brs.: 2; Priests: 5

St. John Vianney Formation House - ; Mailing: P.O. Box 939, Chuuk, FM 96942 t) 691-330-3364 revjulioangkel@gmail.com Rev. David Lewis; Most Rev. Julio Angkel, Dir.;

KOLONIA

Jesuit Community of Pohnpei - Vicariate Office, Kolonia, FM 96941; Mailing: P.O. Box 160, Kolonia, Pohnpei, FM 96941 t) 691-320-2317 kenu16@gmail.com; dandrus@jesuits.org Rev. Kenneth Urumolug, S.J., Vicar; Rev. David Andrus, S.J., Sacr. Min.; Priests: 2

KOLONIA, POHNPEI

Vicariate Residence - ; Mailing: P.O. Box 160, Kolonia, Pohnpei, FM 96941 t) 691-320-2557 Rev. Robert Ifamilik;

KOROR

Jesuit Community of Palau, Manresa Jesuit House - Sacred Heart Parish, Main Rd., Koror, PW 96940; Mailing: P.O. Box 128, Koror, PW 96940 t) (680) 488-2392 (Landline for Manresa) domtyl@riccimac.org; ueamicfjsuperior@jesuits.org Rev. Arthur F. Leger, S.J. (Fiji), Assoc. Pst.; Rev. Dominique Tyl, S.J., Sacr. Min.; Rev. Edward J. Quinnan, S.J., Supr.; Priests: 3

Vicariate Residence - ; Mailing: P.O. Box 128, Koror, PW 96940 t) 680-488-2226 rusksaburo@gmail.com Rev. Rusk R. Saburo;

TUNNUK, CHUUK

Vicariate Residence - ; Mailing: P.O. Box 250, Tunnuk, Chuuk, FM 96942 t) 691-330-2313 sisamkaster@gmail.com Rev. Rosendo Rudolf; Rev. Kaster Sisam; Rev. Fernando Titus;

YAP

Jesuit Community of Yap - Yap Catholic High School, Yap, FM 96943; Mailing: P.O. Box 1009, Yap, FM 96943 t) 691-350-2148 rmcauliff@jesuits.org Rev. Robert Richard McAuliff, S.J., Vicar; Priests: 1

Vicariate Residence - ; Mailing: P.O. Box "A", Yap, FM 96943 t) 691-350-2265 kyalmadau@yahoo.com Rev. Moses Tashibelit; Rev. Kelly Yalmadau; Rev. Cuthbert Yiftheg;

An asterisk (*) denotes an organization that has established tax-exempt status directly with the IRS and is not covered by the USCCB Group Ruling.

Diocese of Chalan Kanoa

(Dioecesis Vialenbensis)

MOST REVEREND RYAN P. JIMENEZ

Bishop of Chalan Kanoa; ordained priest June 8, 2003 by Most Rev. Tomas A. Camacho; appointed Apostolic Administrator December 28, 2010 by his Holiness Pope Benedict XVI; appointed Bishop of Chalan Kanoa June 24, 2016; installed August 14, 2016.

Mailing Address: P.O. Box 500745 CK, Saipan, MP 96950. T: 670-234-3000; F: 670-234-3002.
bishop@rcdck.org
www.rcdck.org

ESTABLISHED NOVEMBER 8, 1984.

Square Miles 184.

Corporate Title: "Bishop of Chalan Kanoa, a Corporation Sole." Comprises the Mariana Island chain except for Guam, known legally as the Commonwealth of the Northern Mariana Islands.

For legal titles of parishes and diocesan institutions, consult the Diocesan Curia.

STATISTICAL OVERVIEW

Personnel
Bishop....1
Priests: Diocesan Active in Diocese....8
Number of Diocesan Priests....8
Religious Priests in Diocese....5
Total Priests in your Diocese....13
Extern Priests in Diocese....6

Parishes
Parishes....13
With Resident Pastor:
Resident Diocesan Priests....9
Resident Religious Priests....4
Professional Ministry Personnel:
Sisters....3
Lay Ministers....6

Welfare
Special Centers for Social Services....1
Total Assisted....1,000

Educational
High Schools, Diocesan and Parish....1
Total Students....180
Elementary Schools, Diocesan and Parish....1
Total Students....420
Total Students under Catholic Instruction....600
Teachers in Diocese:
Lay Teachers....44

Vital Statistics
Receptions into the Church:
Infant Baptism Totals....325
Adult Baptism Totals....54
Received into Full Communion....3
First Communions....263
Confirmations....235
Marriages:
Catholic....101
Interfaith....2
Total Marriages....103
Deaths....213
Total Catholic Population....33,000
Total Population....48,000

LEADERSHIP

Vicar General - Rev. Charlito A. Borja, Vicar;
Vicar for Clergy - Rev. Charlito A. Borja, Vicar;
Vicar for Religious Women - Rev. Michael D. Linden, S.J., Vicar;
Vicar for Lay Personnel - Rev. Michael D. Linden, S.J., Vicar;
Chancellor - Sr. Narcisa Penaredonda, S.J.B.P.;
Diocesan Internal Auditor - Bettina Lynette G. Terlaje;
Personnel Officer - Rev. Michael D. Linden, S.J.;
Director of Religious Education - Sr. Saturnina Caccam, S.J.B.P.;
Diocesan Legal Counsel - Jesus C. Borja;
Superintendent of Catholic Schools -

ADMINISTRATION

Finance Officer - Sherwin Pasillos;
Official Chamorro Translator, Bishop's Community Liaison - Rita C. Guerrero;
Assistant Accountant - Ruth Torrecampo;
Archivist Librarian -

ADVISORY BOARDS, COMMISSIONS, COMMITTEES, AND COUNCILS

Commission on Evangelization - Rev. Michael D. Linden, S.J., Chair; Gary Orpiano; Dcn. Thomas Schweiger;
Commission on Heritage Cultural of the Church - Most Rev. Ryan Jimenez, Chair;
Commission on Marriage and Family Life - Rev. Jason Granado, Coord.; Gonzalo Pangelinan; Linda Pangelinan;
Commission on Ministerial Development - Rev. Charlito A. Borja;
Commission on Social Justice and Outreach - Rev. Michael D. Linden, S.J.; Laurie Ogumoro; Galvin S. Deleon Guerrero;
Commission on Vocations - Rev. Anthony O. Aguason, Chair; Sr. Narcisa Penaredonda, S.J.B.P.; John Terlaje;
Commission on Worship - Margaret C. Dela Cruz, Chair; Rev. Harold Funa; Rev. Isaac M. Ayuyu;
Diocesan Youth Commission - Rev. Jason G. Downer, S.J., Dir.; Sr. Emma Lusterio, S.J.B.P., Asst. Youth Dir.;
Korean Catholic Church -
Kristo Rai Parish - Frances Sablan, Kristo Rai; Eloise Lopez;
Mount Carmel Parish - Gerald De Guzman;
San Francisco de Borja Parish, Rota - Tito T. Hocog;
San Isidro Parish, Rota -
San Jose Parish - Ariel Lapuz;
San Jose Parish, Tinian - Don Kristoffer J. Sarmiento;
San Jude Parish - Dcn. Antonio Yarobwemal; Sam Santos; Tiava To'omata;
San Roque Parish - Olive Aninon; Ryan Gabuel;
San Vicente Parish - Sr. Emma Lusterio, S.J.B.P., Asst. Dir.; Don Taisacan; Molena MacDuff;
Santa Remedios Parish - Julie Ann Loong;
Faith Formation Committee - Sr. Saturnina Caccam, S.J.B.P., DRE; Sr. MaryAnn Hartmann, M.M.B.; Esther S. Fleming;
Health Ministry - Glorybel O. Tan;
Media Ministries - Rommell Buenaflor;

CONSULTATIVE BODIES

Diocesan Finance Council - Rose Soledad; Martha Camacho; Michael S. Sablan;
Presbyteral Council - Most Rev. Ryan Jimenez; Rev. Charlito A. Borja; Rev. Albert Pellazar, O.A.R.;

FAITH FORMATION

Children of God the Father, Inc. - Roxanne Aranda Ada, Pres.; Rev. Jesse T. Reyes, Dir. (palijessetreyes@gmail.com);
Confraternity of Christian Mothers - Soledad Babauta Sasamoto, Pres.; Rev. Albert Pellazar, O.A.R., Spiritual Adv./Care Srvcs.;
Couples for Christ - Ogie Pagcaliwagan;
Divine Mercy - Rev. Jesse T. Reyes, Dir. (palijessetreyes@gmail.com);
El Shaddai Movement - Rev. Anthony O. Aguason, Spiritual Dir.; Gary Orpiano, Leader;
Eucharistic Adoration Society - Most Rev. Ryan Jimenez; Rev. Jason Granado; Rev. Isidro T. Ogumoro (anniol2000@yahoo.com);
Legion of Mary - Rev. Neil Bullos, O.A.R., Dir.;
Kristo Rai Parish - Mother Refuge of Sinners, Praesidium - Rosanna Gamier, Pres.;
Our Lady of Mount Carmel Cathedral - Mary, Mediatrix of All Grace Praesidium - Lourdes Leong, Pres.;
San Antonio Parish - Mother of Perpetual Help Praesidium - Ofelia Pangilinan, Pres.;
San Roque Parish - Mother of Divine Love Praesidium - Richard Cano, Pres.;
Santa Remedios Parish - Nuestra Sra. Bithen Delos Remedios Praesidium - Julie Cunanan, Pres.;
Light & Salt Catholic Charismatic Community - Cely Zamora, Head Servant; Rev. Charlito A. Borja, Dir.;
Marriage Encounter - Gonzalo Pangelinan; Linda Pangelinan;
Representatives from Church Organizations & Movements -
Neocatechumenal Way - Frank Peredo; Olivia Peredo;
Simbang Gabi Group - Nanette Delos Santos, Pres.;

ORGANIZATIONS

Eskuelan San Francisco de Borja School, Inc. (Rota) - Kary John Ramos, Chair; Carmen H. Atalig, Admin.;
Karidat, Inc. - Laurie Ogumoro, Exec.; Josephine T. Sablan, Pres.; Marcie M. Tomokane, Secy.;
Mount Carmel School, Inc. (Saipan) - t) 670-235-1251; 670-234-6184 president.mcs@pticom.com Vicente M. Babauta Jr., Chair; Galvin S. Deleon Guerrero, Pres.; Carmen S. Taimanao, Prin.;

PASTORAL SERVICES

Hospital Chaplaincy (Saipan) -
Mt. Carmel Catholic Cemetery - Rev. Jason Granado, Chair; Dcn. Jeffrey Tenorio Camacho; Doris S. Nuique;
Police and Fire Departments Chaplaincy -
Prison Chaplaincy - Dcn. Rosiky Bernardino Camacho; Dcn. Thomas Schweiger;

TRIBUNAL

Judicial Vicar - Rev. Carlos Vila;
Tribunal Judge -
Defender of the Bond - Rev. Jonathan Alvarez;
Tribunal Auditor -
Notary - Rita C. Guerrero;

PARISHES, MISSIONS, AND CLERGY

COMMONWEATH OF NORTHERN MARIANA ISLANDS

ROTA

San Francisco de Borja Parish - Songsong, Rota, MP 96951; Mailing: P.O. Box 542, Rota, MP 96951 t) 670-532-3522 c) 670-287-0131 bronelsonplohimon@yahoo.com www.rcdck.org Rev. Nelson S. Plohimon, OAR (Philippines), Admin.; Rev. Jayferson Baldelovar, O.A.R. (Philippines), Par. Vicar; CRP Stds.: 27

San Isidro Parish - Sinapalo, Rota, MP 96951; Mailing: P.O. Box 590, Rota, MP 96951 t) 670-532-3522 c) (670) 287-0130 bronelsonplohimon@yahoo.com www.rcdck.org (Sinapalo) Rev. Nelson S. Plohimon, OAR (Philippines), Admin.; Rev. Jayferson Baldelovar, O.A.R., Par. Vicar; CRP Stds.: 98

SAIPAN

Cathedral of Our Lady of Mt. Carmel - Beach Rd., Chalan Kanoa, Saipan, MP 96950; Mailing: P.O. Box 500745, Saipan, MP 96950 t) 670-234-3000 x100 bishop@rcdck.org; ryansaipan@gmail.com www.rcdck.org Most Rev. Ryan Jimenez; Rev. Rey Rosal, Rector; Dcn. Rosiky Bernadino Flores Camacho; CRP Stds.: 140

Korean Catholic Church of Saipan - Knights St., Chalan Kanoa, Saipan, MP 96950; Mailing: P.O. Box 500541, Saipan, MP 96950 t) (670) 235-1449 Rev. Kim (John) Hyeyeon (Korea), Pst.;

Kristo Rai Parish - Beach Rd., Garapan, Saipan, MP 96950; Mailing: P.O. Box 500745, Saipan, MP 96950 t) 670-233-2700 sansantiagu@gmail.com www.rcdck.org Rev. James Balajadia, Admin.; CRP Stds.: 170

Maturana House of Prayer -

Navy Hill, Commonwealth Health Center Chapel -

San Antonio Parish - San Antonio St., San Antonio, Saipan, MP 96950; Mailing: P.O. Box 500745, Saipan, MP 96950 t) 670-235-4515 armancrm@gmail.com www.rcdck.org Rev. Arman Hagos, C.R.M. (Philippines), Admin.; Dcn. Estanislao K. Benavente; CRP Stds.: 112

San Jose Chapel - ; Mailing: PO Box 500745 CK, Saipan, MP 96950

San Jose Parish - Apengagh Ave., San Jose, Saipan, MP 96950; Mailing: P.O. Box 500745, Saipan, MP 96950 t) 670-234-6991 frjasongranado@gmail.com www.rcdck.org Rev. Jason Granado, Pst.; Dcn. Rosiky Bernadino Flores Camacho; CRP Stds.: 99

San Jude Parish - Chalan Msgr. Martinez Rd., Koblerville, Saipan, MP 96950; Mailing: P.O. Box 500745, Saipan, MP 96950 t) (670) 288-0008 c) (670) 788-6358 melvincrm@yahoo.com www.rcdck.org Rev. Melvin Ilagan Avilla, C.R.M. (Philippines), Admin.; Dcn. Antonio Yarobwemal; CRP Stds.: 77

San Roque Parish - Mamate Loop, San Roque, Saipan, MP 96950; Mailing: P.O. Box 500745, Saipan, MP 96950 t) 670-322-2404 c) (670) 285-3000 anniol2000@yahoo.com www.rcdck.org Rev. Isidro T. Ogumoro, Admin.; Dcn. Thomas Schweiger; CRP Stds.: 39

San Vicente Parish - Isa Dr., San Vicente, Saipan, MP 96950; Mailing: P.O. Box 500745, Saipan, MP 96950 t) 670-235-8208 c) (670) 483-7254 palijessetreyes@gmail.com www.rcdck.org Rev. Jesse T. Reyes, Pst.; CRP Stds.: 67

Our Lady of the Most Holy Rosary -

Santa Remedios Parish - Santa Remedio Dr., Tanapag, Saipan, MP 96950; Mailing: P.O. Box 500745, Saipan, MP 96950 t) 670-322-2404 sansantiagu@gmail.com www.rcdck.org Rev. James Balajadia, Admin.; Dcn. Jeffrey Tenorio Camacho; CRP Stds.: 32

Santa Soledad Mission Parish - Kagman, Saipan, MP 96950; Mailing: P.O. Box 500745, Saipan, MP 96950 t) (670) 256-4568 c) (670) 287-2664 charlieborja@hotmail.com www.rcdck.org Rev. Charlito A. Borja, Pst.; CRP Stds.: 61

TINIAN

San Jose - ; Mailing: P.O. Box 131, Tinian, MP 96952 t) 670-433-3000 c) 670-788-4201 aguasonanthony@gmail.com www.rcdck.org Rev. Anthony O. Aguason, Pst.; CRP Stds.: 68

INSTITUTIONS LOCATED IN DIOCESE

CONVENTS, MONASTERIES, AND RESIDENCES FOR WOMEN [CON]

SAIPAN

MMB Maturana Community - Navy Hill, Saipan, MP 96950; Mailing: P.O. Box 501178-CK, Saipan, MP 96950 t) 670-322-9713 ramaruimmb@yahoo.com www.mmberriz.com Sr. Martha Ramarui, MMB, Maturana Community Coordinator; Srs.: 9

Pastorelle Sisters Convent (San Antonio Parish) - San Antonio, Saipan, MP 96950; Mailing: P.O. Box 500745, Saipan, MP 96950 t) 670-234-1213; 670-234-6177 x100 srcynthiaangalot@gmail.com en.pastorelle.online/ Sr. Emma Lusterio, S.J.B.P., Pst. Assoc.; Sr. Cynthia Angalot, S.J.B.P., Pst. Assoc.; Sr. Adoracion Manuel, S.J.B.P., DRE; Srs.: 3

An asterisk (*) denotes an organization that has established tax-exempt status directly with the IRS and is not covered by the USCCB Group Ruling.

Diocese of Fajardo-Humacao, Puerto Rico

(Dioecesis Faiardensis-Humacaensi)

MOST REVEREND LUIS F. MIRANDA RIVERA, O. CARM.

Bishop of Fajardo-Humacao; ordained September 14, 1984; appointed Bishop of Fajardo-Humacao May 16, 2020; consecrated August 15, 2020. Bishop House: Calle 3, Final, K. m 0.7 Urbanizacion Bermudez, Fajardo, PR 00738.

Bishop House: Calle 3, Final, K. m 0.7 Urbanizacion Bermudez, Fajardo, PR 00738. Mailing Address: Apartado 888, Fajardo, PR 00738.
T: 787-801-5700; T: 787-801-5800.
cancilleriadfh@gmail.com

ESTABLISHED JUNE 1, 2008

Comprises southeast municipalies of Puerto Rico: Humacao, Naguabo; east municipalies of Puerto Rico: Ceiba, Fajardo, Luquillo, northeast municipalies of Puerto Rico Rio Grande, Loiza, Canovanas and the Islands Municipalies of Culebra and Vieques.

Patroness of the Diocese: Nuestra Senora del Carmen and Santiago Apostol (official)

STATISTICAL OVERVIEW

Personnel
Bishop........1
Abbots........1
Priests: Diocesan Active in Diocese........16
Priests: Diocesan Active Outside Diocese........2
Number of Diocesan Priests........18
Religious Priests in Diocese........10
Total Priests in your Diocese........28
Extern Priests in Diocese........1
Ordinations:
Diocesan Priests........1
Transitional Deacons........1
Permanent Deacons in Diocese........30
Total Brothers........3
Total Sisters........12

Parishes
Parishes........22
With Resident Pastor:
Resident Diocesan Priests........16
Resident Religious Priests........6

Welfare
Residential Care of Children........1
Total Assisted........20

Educational
Diocesan Students in Other Seminaries........9
Total Seminarians........9
Colleges and Universities........5
Total Students........1,180
High Schools, Diocesan and Parish........4
Total Students........439
High Schools, Private........1
Total Students........86
Elementary Schools, Diocesan and Parish........4
Total Students........536
Elementary Schools, Private........1
Total Students........95
Catechesis/Religious Education:
High School Students........250
Elementary Students........358
Total Students under Catholic Instruction........2,953

Teachers in Diocese:
Priests........1
Brothers........4
Sisters........4
Lay Teachers........106

Vital Statistics
Receptions into the Church:
Infant Baptism Totals........136
Minor Baptism Totals........31
Adult Baptism Totals........33
First Communions........169
Confirmations........297
Marriages:
Catholic........65
Interfaith........2
Total Marriages........67
Deaths........343
Total Catholic Population........85,353
Total Population........298,567

LEADERSHIP

Vicar General - Rev. Jose Colon, Vicar;
Sec. Chancellor - Rev. Hector M Rodriguez, Chancellor (secobdfh@gmail.com);
Judicial Vicar - Rev. Luis Norberto Correa, Vicar (ncorrea78@yahoo.com);
Episcopal Vicar (Mission Loiza) - Rev. Rocendo Herrera, S.T.;
Episcopal Vicar (Mission Fajardo) - Rev. Peter Francis Okih, C.S.Sp., Vicar;
Episcopal Vicar (Mission Humacao) - Rev. Victor Santiago Mateo, S.T., Vicar;

OFFICES AND DIRECTORS

Director Caritas (DFH) - Rev. Floyd Mercado Vidro;
Economic Administrator - Rev. Roberto Medina Radesco;
Education Vicar - Rev. Jose A. Rivera Maldonado, Vicar (rivermal23@hotmail.com);
Master of Ceremonies - Rev. Hector M. Rodriquez Villanueva;
Pastoral Vicar - Rev. Floyd Mercado Vidro, Vicar;
Spiritual Director Catequesis Familiar Integral - Rev. Oscar A. Sanchez Lopez, CRE;
Supervisora de Catequesis Familiar Integral - Myriam Caballero, Contact;
Vicar for Deacons - Rev. Adrian Alicea Padilla, Vicar;
Vocations Director - Rev. Juan Antonio Figueroa, Vicar (jafb_55@hotmail.com);

CLERGY AND RELIGIOUS SERVICES

Vicario para la Vida Consagrada - Rev. Francis Okih Peter, Vicar;

COMMUNICATIONS

Comisión de Comunicaciones - Rev. Hector M Rodriguez, Contact (secobdfh@gmail.com);

ORGANIZATIONS

Diocesan Movements y Organizations -
Caballeros de Colon - Justino Cruz;
Cursillos de Cristiandad - Johnny Morales; Jose Marrero;
Emaus -
Juan XXIII - Hector Carino;
Legion de Maria - Aida Jimenez;
Renovacion Carismatica - Lucy Figueroa; Nilda Velazquez;

PARISHES, MISSIONS, AND CLERGY

COMMONWEALTH OF PUERTO RICO

CANOVANAS

Nuestra Senora del Pilar - ; Mailing: P.O. Box 10000-PMB 320, Canovanas, PR 00729 t) 787-886-3307; 787-957-7818 parroquiaelpilar20@gmail.com Rev. Jose A. Rivera Maldonado, Pst.; Dcn. Pedro Castro; Dcn. Jose R. Rivera;
Nuestra Senora del Pilar School - 3 Luis Hernaiz St., Canovanas, PR 00729 t) 787-876-3002 tribunaldfh@gmail.com Iris del Valle Jimenez, Dir.;
San Francisco Javier - Bo. Camabalache, Canovanas, PR 00729
Resurreccion del Senor - Carr. 188, Km 2.0 San Isidro, Canovanas, PR 00729; Mailing: P.O. Box 896, Canovanas, PR 00729 t) 787-876-9900 theresurrectionpr@hotmail.com Rev. Canice Chukwuemeka Njoku, C.S.Sp., Pst.; Dcn. Pedro Flores Torres; Dcn. Wilfredo Luis; Migdalia Pizarro, DRE;
Ntra. Sra. de la Providencia -
Sagrado Corazon de Jesus - RR 186 Km. 7, Bo. Cubuy, Canovanas, PR 00729-0014; Mailing: PMB 20147, P.O. Box 35000, Canovànas, PR 00729 t) 787-876-1355 pscj_canovanas@yahoo.com; pscj_canovanas@hotmail.com Dcn. Angel Jesus Rodriguez; Rev. Vicente Pasqualetto, S.T., Admin.;
La Milagrosa - Bo. Cuatrocientas, Canovanas, PR 00729
San Pedro Apostol - Bo. Lomas, Canovanas, PR 00729
San Jose - Carr. 185 Km 5.3 Bo. Campo Rico, Canovanas, PR 00729-9736; Mailing: HC-02 Box 6502, Canóvans, PR 00729-9736 t) 787-876-7167 psanjosecr@gmail.com Dcn. Felipe A. Rivera Estremera; Dcn. Pedro Rivera; Rev. Luis Manuel Ruiz Lebron, Pst.;
Ntra. Sra. de la Asuncion - Carr. 957 Km. 6.8, Palma Sola, Canovanas, PR 00729
Ntra. Sra. del Carmen - Carr. 185 Km. 5.3, Alturas de Campo Rico, Canovanas, PR 00729
Santa Maria Madre de Dios - Urb. Loiza Valley, Calle Girasol E189, Canovanas, PR 00729 t) 787-876-0827 pstamariamadrededios@gmail.com Rev. Frederic Kabran, Pst.; Dcn. Jose L. Casaigne;
Capilla Cristo Salvador - Sector Pueblo Indio, Canovanas, PR 00729
Iglesia Santa Maria Madre De Dios - Carr. 8874-Bo. La Central, Canovanas, PR 00729 pstmariamadrededios@gmail.com Most Rev. Luis F. Miranda, O.Carm.;

CEIBA

San Antonio de Padua - 561 Escolastico Lopez St., Ceiba, PR 00735; Mailing: P.O. Box 77, Ceiba, PR 00735 c) 787-885-2530 psadp@hotmail.com Dcn. Jose Pomales; Rev. Roberto Medina, Pst.; Dcn. Rafael Pagan;
Sagrado Corazon de Jesus - Parcelas Aguas Claras, Ceiba, PR 00735
Ntra. Sra. del Perpetuo Socorro - Bo. Rio Abajo, Ceiba, PR 00735
Ntra. Sra. de Fatima - Bo. Daguao, Ceiba, PR 00735

CULEBRA

Nuestra Senora del Carmen - Calle Ntra. Sra. del Carmen, Culebra, PR 00775; Mailing: P.O. Box 236, Culebra, PR 00775 c) 939-496-2727 martin.cssr@hotmail.com Rev. Martin Garcia, Pst.;

FAJARDO

Cathedral Santiago Apostol - 16 Garrido Morales St., Fajardo, PR 00738; Mailing: P.O. Box 806, Fajardo, PR 00738 t) 787-863-2365 catedralsantiagodfh@gmail.com Rev. Hector M. Rodriquez Villanueva, Rector; Dcn. Ruben Borgos; Dcn. Jesus Ramos; Rev. Julio Vera, Par. Vicar;
Bo. Florencio, Santa Elena -
Bo. Quebrada Vueltas, Perpetuo Socorro -
La Milagrosa, Santa Isidra -
Madre del Salvador, Bo. Paraiso -
Santisimo Redentor - Urb. Monte Brisas, Calle C-V-19, Fajardo, PR 00738 t) 787-863-5227 santisimoredentorpr@gmail.com Dcn. Luis A. Cordero; Rev. Luis Norberto Correa, Pst.;
Puerto Real, Ntra. Sra. de Carmen - Calle Union 393 Int. Fajardo, Fajardo, PR 00738
Sardinera, San Juan Bautista - Carr. 987 Km. 2 H3 Bo. Sardinera, Fajardo, PR 00738
Fajardo Gardens, Maria, Madre de la Providencia - 10 C-5 Urb. Quinta Extension de Monte Brisas, Fajardo, PR 00738

HUMACAO

Concathedral Dulce Nombre de Jesus - 5 Font Martelo St., Humacao, PR 00791; Mailing: Box 9087, Humacao, PR 00791 t) 787-852-0868 victor.vrsmst@gmail.com Dcn. Hector Velazquez Velazquez; Rev. Victor Santiago Mateo, S.T., Rector; Dcn. Pablo J. Colon Ojeda; Rev. Henry Guerra, Par. Vicar; Dcn. Hector Noel Gonzalez;
San Agustin - Carr. 927 Km 0 Hm. 6 Parcela 74 Bo. Anton Ruiz, Humacao, PR 00792; Mailing: P.O. Box 9087, Humacao, PR 00792
San Jose - Carr. 198 R 922 Km 1 Hm 1 Bo. Coto Mabu, Humacao, PR 00792; Mailing: P.O. Box 9087, Humacao, PR 00792
Nuestra Senora de Fatima - Carr. 3 R 925 Km. 0 Hm. 2 Calle Girasol Esquina Orquidea Bo. Junquito, Humacao, PR 00792; Mailing: P.O. Box 9087, Humacao, PR 00792
Nuestra Senora de la Providencia - Carr. 910 Km. 0.80 Bo. Catano Sector Los Flechas, Humacao, PR 00792; Mailing: P.O. Box 9087, Humacao, PR 00792
Perpetuo Socorro - Carr. 3 R 923 Km. 1 9 ML Bo. Buena Vista, Humacao, PR 00792; Mailing: P.O. Box 9087, Humacao, PR 00792
Inmaculada Concepcion - Urbanizacion Villa Calle 13 E 1, Humacao, PR 00792; Mailing: P.O. Box 9087, Humacao, PR 00792
San Pedro y San Pablo - Caserio Antonio Roig, Humacao, PR 00792; Mailing: P.O. Box 9087, Humacao, PR 00792
La Sagrada Familia Parish - 3 Executive Office Dr., Humacao, PR 00791 t) 787-719-5269 lasagradafamiliapdm@hotmail.com www.facebook.com Rev. Floyd Mercado Vidro, Pst.; Dcn. Frankie Lasanta-Gonzalez; Dcn. Jose Cruz Nevarez; Dcn. Andres Velazquez;
Nuestra Señora de la Candelaria - Bo. Candelero Arriba, Humacao, PR 00791
Santa Teresita del Niño Jesus - Bo. Candelero Abajo, Parcelas Aniceto Cruz, Humacao, PR 00791
Maria Auxiliadora - Bo. Candelero Abajo, Parcelas Martinez, Humacao, PR 00791
Maria Reina de la Paz - Urb. Villa Universitaria, Calle 4 A-20, Humacao, PR 00791 t) 787-850-3081 mariareinadelapazhumacao@gmail.com Rev. Eduardo del Rivero, Par. Vicar; Dcn. Emilio Colon Cosme; Dcn. Roberto Velazquez; Rev. Jose Colon, Pst.;
Sagrado Corazon de Jesus - Carr. #3R. 909 K.6 h.3 Int., Bo Mariana III, Humacao, PR 00791
San Martin de Porres - Bo. Patagonia Num. 128, Ave. Tejas, Humacao, PR 00791
Buen Pastor - Carr. #3 R.908 K. 8. h.7 Int. RO22, Bo. Mariana II, Humacao, PR 00791
Cristo Rey - Carr. #189 R.914 K.1, Asturianas RL 26052, Humacao, PR 00791
Santa Rosa de Lima - Carr. #3 R909 K3 h.3 Int., Bo. Mariana 1, Humacao, PR 00791
Casa de Oracion Espiritu Santo - Carr. 908 Bo. Tejas, Humacao, PR 00791

LOIZA

Espiritu Santo y San Patricio - ; Mailing: Box 504, Loiza, PR 00772-0504 t) 787-886-1539 Dcn. Marcos Penalosa Lacen; Dcn. Roberto Ferris; Dcn. Santiago Acosta Osorio; Rev. Rocendo Herrera, S.T., Pst.;
Santa Rosa de Lima - Bo. Pinones, Loiza, PR 00772
Ntra. Sra. del Perpetuo Socorro - Bo. La Torre, Loiza, PR 00772
Santisima Trinidad - Bo. Mediana Baja, Loiza, PR 00772
San Antonio - Bo. Las Cuevas, Loiza, PR 00772
Ntra. Sra. de Fatima - Villa Canona, Loiza, PR 00772
San Rafael - Villa Alvarez, Loiza, PR 00772
Santiago Apostol, El Mayor - ; Mailing: P.O. Box 118, Loiza, PR 00772-0118 t) 787-961-3904 parroquiasantiagoapostolloiza@gmail.com Rev. Rocendo Herrera, S.T., Pst.; Dcn. Pedro Recci;
Ntra. Sra. Perpetuo Socorro - Parcelas Suarez, Loiza, PR 00772
La Milagrosa - Bo. El Jobos, Loiza, PR 00772
La Providencia - Bo. Mini Mine, Loiza, PR 00772
Ntra. Sra. De Fatima - Parcelas Vieques, Loiza, PR 00772

LUQUILLO

Maria, Madre del Redentor - ; Mailing: P.O. Box 591, Luquillo, PR 00773-0591 c) 787-534-7923 Rev. Saint-Louis Ulrick, O. Carm., Admin.; Dcn. Luis A. Cordero; Dcn. Jose M. Lopez Alverio;
Ntra. Sra. del Carmen - Carr. 983 K.2 H.0, Luquillo, PR 00773
Ntra. Sra. Milagrosa - Carr. 983 K.6 H.3, Luquillo, PR 00773
San Vicente de Paul - Carr. 3H 43 H.9, Luquillo, PR 00773
Ntra. Sra. del Perpetuo Socorro - Carr. 984 K.2 H.2,

Luquillo, PR 00773
San Jose - ; Mailing: P.O. Box 493, Luquillo, PR 00773-0493 t) 787-889-2590 psanjosepr@gmail.com Rev. Francis Okih Peter, Pst.; Rev. Innocent Madu, Par. Vicar; Dcn. Albert Gutierrez;
San Judas - Bo. Mata de Platano, Luquillo, PR 00773
Ntra. Sra. del Cobre - Parcelas Fortuna, Luquillo, PR 00773
NAGUABO
Nuestra Senora del Rosario - Calle Juan R. Garzot n. 12, Naguabo, PR 00718; Mailing: Box 665, Naguabo, PR 00718 c) 787-874-2235 parrvrosario@hotmail.com Dcn. Rafael Garcia Pizarro; Dcn. Angel Jesus Rodriguez; Rev. Alien Illiotes, Pst.; Rev. Juan Carlos Neira, Par. Vicar;
Nuestra Senora del Perpetuo Socorro -
Nuestra Senora de la Altagracia -
Nuestra Senora de Fatima - Bo. Duque, Naguabo, PR 00718
Bo. Florida, Nuestra Senora del Perpetuo Socorro -
Nuestra Senora del Carmen Playa (Hucares) - Bo. Maizales, Naguabo, PR 00718
Nuestra Senora de la Providencia - Bo. Mariana, Naguabo, PR 00718
Santa Rosa de Lima - Bo. Sandiago 4 Lima, Naguabo, PR 00718
Mission - Barrio Rio Sector Brazo Seco, Naguabo -
Mission - Capilla Beato Carlos Manuel Rodriguez, Sector La Fe, Naguabo -
PALMER
Cristo Rey - Palmer, Rio Gande, Palmer, PR 00721-0382; Mailing: P.O. Box 382, Palmer, PR 00721-0382 t) 787-887-3552 sendero137@aol.com Dcn. Fernando Marrero; Rev. Oscar A. Sanchez Lopez, Admin.;
La Milagrosa - Parcela 69 Hato Rio Grande, Bo. Carola, PR 00721
Ntra. Sra. de la Providencia - Bloque S-1 #7, Palmer, PR 00721
PUNTA SANTIAGO
Nuestra Senora del Carmen - Calle Marina 33, Punta Santiago, PR 00741; Mailing: P.O. Box 91, Punta Santiago, PR 00741 t) 939-232-4612 delcarmenpuntasantiago@gmail.com Dcn. Angel M. Rodriguez Cedeno; Rev. Jose Colon Otero, Pst.; Rev. Juan Antonio Figueroa, Par. Vicar;
Bo. Pasto Viejo, Sector El Batey, Nuestra Senora del Perpetuo Socorro - t) 787-852-4421
RIO GRANDE
Nuestra Senora del Carmen - Calle del Carmen #9, Rio Grande, PR 00745; Mailing: Apartado 845, Rio Grande, PR 00745 t) 787-887-2365 delcarmen_9@yahoo.com Dcn. Vidal Diaz; Rev. Adrian Alicea Padilla, Pst.; Dcn. Julio Alejandro Olivo;
Nuestra Senora del Carmen School - Calle 14 Urb. Alturas de Rio Grande, Apartado 1389, Rio Grande, PR 00745; Mailing: P.O. Box 818, Rio Grande, PR 00745 t) 787-887-4099 cnscrg@yahoo.com Myrtha Perez, Prin.;
Nuestra Senora de Fatima - Bo. El Verde, Rio Grande, PR 00745
Ntra. Sra. de Guadalupe - Jardines de Rio Grande, Rio Grande, PR 00745
San Pedro - Bo. Bartolo, Rio Grande, PR 00745
La Milagrosa - Calle 14, Alturas de Rio Grande, Rio Grande, PR 00745
Sagrado Corazon de Jesus - Coco Beach, Rio Grande, PR 00745
San Francisco de Asis - Carr. 958, Km. 2.6, Bo. Malpica, Rio Grande, PR 00745-1449; Mailing: P.O. Box 1449, Rio Grande, PR 00745 t) 787-657-5872 p_sanfcodeasis@hotmail.com; sanfcodeasis71@gmail.com Dcn. Jose Rios; Rev. Antonio Marrero Aballe, Pst.;
VIEQUES
Santiago Apostol e Inmaculada Concepcion - 442 Lebrum St., Vieques, PR 00765 c) 787-405-5664 padreabreu@gmail.com Rev. Leonidas Abreu Ortiz, Pst.;
Sagrado Corazon de Jesus -
Nuestra Senora de Lourdes -
Nuestra Senora del Perpetuo Socorro -
Virgen del Carmen -
Nuestra Senora de Fatima -

SCHOOLS: PRESCHOOL THRU HIGH SCHOOL

SCHOOLS

COMMONWEALTH OF PUERTO RICO

CANOVANAS
College of Our Lady of Pilar - (Grades PreK-12) Calle Luis Hernaiz #3 Esquina Muñoz Rivera, Canovanas, PR 00729; Mailing: Apartado 1615, Canovanas, PR 00729 t) 787-876-3002 cnspilar2010@gmail.com Alberto Rosario Diaz, Prin.; Iris del Valle Jimenez, Dir.;
HUMACAO
Colegio Nuestra Senora del Perpetuo Socorro de Humacao, Inc. - (PRV) (Grades K-12) Carr. 908, Km. 2.0, Ave. Tejas, Humacao, PR 00792; Mailing: P.O. Box 9107, Humacao, PR 00792 t) 787-852-0845 c) (787) 903-0043 (Emergency Phone) miperpetuosocorro.com Michelle N. Arroyo, Dir.; Sr. Isabel Vila, Librn.; Stds.: 202; Scholastics: 18; Lay Tchrs.: 18
Colegio San Antonio Abad - (PRV) ; Mailing: P.O. Box 729, Humacao, PR 00792 t) 787-852-1616 csaa.hermits@gmail.com (Benedictines) Gabriela Resto, Headmaster; Rt. Rev. Oscar Rivera, O.S.B., Dir.; Brunilda Ruiz, Librn.; Stds.: 337; Bro. Tchrs.: 1; Lay Tchrs.: 34
Colegio San Benito - (PRV) ; Mailing: P.O. Box 728, Humacao, PR 00792 t) 787-852-1365 www.csb.edu.pr Hermanas Benedictinas. Sr. Carmen Davila, O.S.B., Admin.; Sr. Mary Ruth Santana, O.S.B., Dir.;
RIO GRANDE
Colegio Nuestra Senora del Carmen - (DIO) (Grades PreK-12) Alturas de Rio Grande,Calle 14 Main, Apartado 1389, Rio Grande, PR 00745; Mailing: P.O. Box 1389, Rio Grande, PR 00745 t) 787-882-4825 director@colegiodelcarmen.org; principal@colegiodelcarmen.org Rev. Hector M Rodriguez, Dir.; Mother Isabel Maria Fejervary, Prin.;

INSTITUTIONS LOCATED IN DIOCESE

MONASTERIES AND RESIDENCES FOR PRIESTS AND BROTHERS [MON]

HUMACAO
San Antonio Abad Abbey of the Order of St. Benedict - Carretera 908 Km 2.2 Barrio Tejas, Humacao, PR 00792; Mailing: P O Box 729, Humacao, PR 00792 t) 787-852-1616 c) 787-372-7065 oscarmonje1950@yahoo.com; csaa.hermits@gmail.com csaapr.com/abadia/ Benedictine Monks-Order of St. Benedict, Humacao, Puerto Rico Rt. Rev. Oscar Rivera, O.S.B., Abbot; Rev. Rafael Perez, O.S.B., Prior; Rev. Ignacio Aguirre, O.S.B.; Bro. Aristedes Pacheco, Subprior; Bro. Felix Neussendorfer; Bro. Randolph Perkins; Rev. Jaime Reyes, O.S.B.; Brs.: 3; Priests: 4
LOIZA
Siervos Misioneros de la Santisima Trinidad - San Patricio Loiza, Loiza, PR 00772; Mailing: P.O. Box 118, Loiza, PR 00772 t) 787-564-0319 victor.vrsmst@gmail.com Rev. Victor Santiago Mateo, S.T., Contact;

PRESCHOOLS / CHILDCARE CENTERS [PRE]

LUQUILLO
Divine Child Jesus Children's Home of the Hermanas Hijas del Corazon Misericordioso de Maria - Calle Angel Gutierrez #68, Luquillo, PR 00773; Mailing: P.O. Box 1413, Luquillo, PR 00773 t) 787-889-6033 convento1973@yahoo.com hogarinfantildivinoninojesus.org Rev. Hector M Rodriguez, Contact;

SPECIAL CARE FACILITIES [SPF]

LOIZA
Hogar Teresa Toda - Calle 5-A, R-14, Villa De Loiza, Loiza, PR 00729; Mailing: P.O. Box 868, Canovanas, PR 00729 t) 787-886-2060 hogaresteresatoda@yahoo.com www.hogaresteresatoda.org (For Girls) Sr. Norma Matar, Dir.;

An asterisk (*) denotes an organization that has established tax-exempt status directly with the IRS and is not covered by the USCCB Group Ruling.

Prefecture Apostolic of the Marshall Islands

REVEREND MONSIGNOR ARIEL GALIDO, M.S.C.

Third Prefect Apostolic of the Marshall Islands; ordained June 9, 2004; appointed June 28, 2017. Res.: Cathedral of the Assumption, Uliga, P.O. Box 8, Majuro, MH 96960.

Mailing Address: Assumption, Uliga, Majuro, P.O. Box 8, Majuro, MH 96960. Tel: 692-625-6675; Tel: 692-625-8307
rmi.prefecture93@gmail.com

Square Miles 186,000.

Total Population (est.) 58,791

Prefecture Apostolic of the Marshall Islands divided from the Diocese of the Carolines-Marshall Islands and erected on August 15, 1993 and committed to the Society of Jesus, New York Province; and on January 6, 2008 committed to the Missionaries of the Sacred Heart. Area is that of the Republic of the Marshall Islands which is related by Compact of Free Association to the United States.

STATISTICAL OVERVIEW

Personnel
Religious Priests in Diocese....6
Total Priests in your Diocese....6
Permanent Deacons in Diocese....3
Total Sisters....7

Parishes
Parishes....4
With Resident Pastor:
Resident Religious Priests....4
Missions....9
Pastoral Centers....1
Professional Ministry Personnel:
Sisters....7
Lay Ministers....70

Educational
High Schools, Diocesan and Parish....1
Total Students....146
Elementary Schools, Diocesan and Parish....3
Total Students....357
Catechesis / Religious Education:
High School Students....55
Elementary Students....407
Total Students under Catholic Instruction....965
Teachers in Diocese:
Sisters....4
Lay Teachers....2

Vital Statistics
Receptions into the Church:
Infant Baptism Totals....71
Minor Baptism Totals....38
Adult Baptism Totals....2
Received into Full Communion....5
First Communions....76
Confirmations....16
Marriages:
Catholic....4
Interfaith....5
Total Marriages....9
Deaths....26
Total Catholic Population....5,176
Total Population....58,413

LEADERSHIP

Prefecture Consultors - Rev. Tatieru Ewenteang, M.S.C.; Rev. Johanis Kilmas, M.S.C.; Rev. Rolando Cuasito, M.S.C.;
Religious Formation Ministry Coordinator - Dcn. Alfred Capelle;
Catholic Education Ministry Coordinator - Sr. Christel Beckmann, M.S.C.;
Pastoral and Social Ministry Coordinator - Sr. Kairaman Tekitanga, F.D.N.S.C.;
Finance Committee - Alan Fowler; Dennis Momotaro;
Catechists Coordinators - t) 692-625-6307 Rosita Capelle; Daisy de Brum;
Vocations - Rev. Rolando Cuasito, M.S.C.;

PARISHES, MISSIONS, AND CLERGY

REPUBLIC OF MARSHALL ISLANDS

EBEYE

Queen of Peace - Queen of Peace Road, Ebeye, MH 96970; Mailing: P.O. Box 5065, Ebeye, MH 96970 t) 692-329-3828 lcuasito69@gmail.com Rev. Rolando Cuasito, M.S.C., Pst.; CRP Stds.: 143

Queen of Peace Elementary School - (Grades K-8) ; Mailing: c/o Queen of Peace Parish, P.O. Box 5818, Ebeye, MH 96970 t) 692-329-3150 jessica.calep@gmail.com Jessica Calep, Prin.; Amenta Jorbwuj, Librn.;

Fr. Hacker High School - c/o Queen of Peace Parish, Ebeye, Kwajalein, MH 96970 t) 692-329-3150 jessica.calep@gmail.com Jessica Calep, Prin.; Brenda Loeak, Librn.;

Santo - t) 692-329-3826 cuasito69@gmail.com (St. Leonard) Jessica Calep, Prin.;

Guguugue - c/o Queen of Peace Parish, Ebeye, Kwajalein, MH 96970 t) 692-625-3826 cuasito69@gmail.com (St. Thomas)

JALUIT

Sacred Heart of Jesus - Sacred Heart Rd., Jaluit, MH 96960; Mailing: P.O. Box 8, Jabor, Jaluit, MH 96960 c) 692-456-1416 londonmsc163@gmail.com Rev. Johanis Kilmas, M.S.C., Pst.; Sr. Lumine Beckmann, M.S.C., Pastoral Coord.; CRP Stds.: 58

St. Joseph Elementary School - (Grades K-8) c) 692-456-1426; 692-545-1315 Sweeter Kalous, Prin.;

KWAJALEIN

Blessed Sacrament - Blessed Sacrament Rd., Kwajalein, MH 96970; Mailing: P.O. Box 171, Kwajalein Atoll, MH 96970 t) 805-355-3505; 805-355-4536 pulpit3speaker@yahoo.com Rev. James Ludwikoski, Pst.;

LIKIEP

Holy Rosary - Holy Rosary Road, Likiep, MH 96960; Mailing: P.O. Box 8, Likiep, MH 96960 c) 692-455-8923 123kiaman@gmail.com Rev. Tokabwebwe Kaiman, M.S.C., Pst.; CRP Stds.: 20

MAJURO

Cathedral of the Assumption - Uliga Village, Majuro, MH 96960; Mailing: P.O. Box 8, Majuro, MH 96960 t) 692-625-8307 rmi.prefecture93@gmail.com Rev. Msgr. Ariel A. Galido, M.S.C., Admin.; CRP Stds.: 240

Assumption Elementary School - (Grades K-8) Uliga Main Rd., Majuro, MH 96960; Mailing: P.O. Box 3146, Majuro, MH 96960 t) 692-625-3795 victoria.capelle85@gmail.com Victoria Langidrik, Prin.; Biram Stege, Prin.;

Assumption High School - Uliga Main Rd., Majuro, MH 96960; Mailing: P.O. Box 3146, Majuro, MH 96960 t) 692-625-3795 victoria.capelle85@gmail.com Luisa Kamenio, Prin.; Biram Stege, Prin.; Erica Block, Librn.;

St. Francis Xavier - 524P+3V, Ajeltake, Laura Village, Majuro Atoll, MH 96960 c) 692-456-6373 (St. Francis Xavier)

Outer Island Missions - c/o Assumption Parish, Uliga Village, Majuro, MH 96960; Mailing: P.O. Box 8, Majuro, MH 96960-0008 t) 692-625-6675; 692-625-8375 rmi.prefecture93@gmail.com Rev. Msgr. Ariel A. Galido, M.S.C., Pst.; CRP Stds.: 30

Arno - c) 692-456-6373 (St. Paul)

Ailinglaplap: Buoj - t) 692-625-8307 (Immaculate Heart of Mary)

Wotje - ; Mailing: P.O Box 8, Majuro, MH 96960 c) 692-456-6373 (St. Thomas)

Ailinglaplap: Woja - c) 692-456-6373 (St. James)

Namdrik - c) 692-456-6373 Our Lady of the Sacred Heart

INSTITUTIONS LOCATED IN DIOCESE

MISCELLANEOUS [MIS]

MAJURO

Catholic Pastoral Center: Ajeltake - c/o Assumption Parish, Uliga Village, Majuro, MH 96960; Mailing: P.O. Box 8, Majuro, MH 96960 c) 692-456-6373 rmi.prefecture93@gmail.com Marciana Jorju, Contact; Rev. Msgr. Ariel A. Galido, M.S.C., Admin.;

An asterisk (*) denotes an organization that has established tax-exempt status directly with the IRS and is not covered by the USCCB Group Ruling.

Diocese of Mayaguez, Puerto Rico

(Dioecesis Maiaguezensis)

MOST REVEREND ANGEL LUIS RIOS MATOS, J.C.D.

Bishop of Mayaguez; ordained August 1, 2020; Mailing Address: P.O. Box 2272, Mayaguez, PR 00681.

Erected by the Bull "Qui arcano Dei" on March 1, 1976, by Pope Paul VI.

Comprises a portion of the southwest of the Island.

STATISTICAL OVERVIEW

Personnel
Bishop....1
Retired Bishops....1
Priests: Diocesan Active in Diocese....48
Priests: Diocesan Active Outside Diocese....2
Priests: Retired, Sick or Absent....3
Number of Diocesan Priests....53
Religious Priests in Diocese....12
Total Priests in your Diocese....65
Extern Priests in Diocese....3
Ordinations:
Diocesan Priests....1
Religious Priests....1
Transitional Deacons....1
Permanent Deacons....3
Permanent Deacons in Diocese....57
Total Brothers....1
Total Sisters....80

Parishes
Parishes....31
With Resident Pastor:
Resident Diocesan Priests....25
Resident Religious Priests....6
Missions....156
Pastoral Centers....1

Professional Ministry Personnel:
Brothers....1
Sisters....83
Lay Ministers....717

Welfare
Catholic Hospitals....1
Total Assisted....10,186
Homes for the Aged....1
Total Assisted....115
Day Care Centers....9
Total Assisted....360
Specialized Homes....2
Total Assisted....157
Special Centers for Social Services....1
Total Assisted....7,775

Educational
Diocesan Students in Other Seminaries....17
Total Seminarians....17
Colleges and Universities....1
Total Students....790
High Schools, Diocesan and Parish....7
Total Students....844
High Schools, Private....1
Total Students....388
Elementary Schools, Diocesan and Parish....7
Total Students....722
Elementary Schools, Private....1
Total Students....103
Catechesis/Religious Education:
High School Students....89
Elementary Students....580
Total Students under Catholic Instruction....3,533
Teachers in Diocese:
Sisters....2
Lay Teachers....171

Vital Statistics
Receptions into the Church:
Infant Baptism Totals....922
Minor Baptism Totals....117
Adult Baptism Totals....46
Received into Full Communion....7
First Communions....1,498
Confirmations....745
Marriages:
Catholic....189
Interfaith....12
Total Marriages....201
Deaths....1,161
Total Catholic Population....268,698
Total Population....447,830

LEADERSHIP

Vicar General - Rev. Msgr. Gonzalo Diaz;

Episcopal Vicars -

For Diocesan Administration - Rev. Msgr. Rogelio Mur, O.Carm.;

For Pastoral - Rev. Msgr. Ramon E. Albino;

Matrimonio y Familia - Rev. Msgr. Humberto Lopez Bonilla;

Chancery Office - t) 787-833-5411 Rev. Eric Ivan Garcia-Concepcion, Chancellor;

Diocesan Consultors - Rev. Msgr. Gonzalo Diaz Hernandez; Rev. Angel Luis Rios Matos; Rev. Ramon Emilio Albino Guzman;

Diocesan Board of Administration - Rev. Msgr. Gonzalo Diaz Hernandez; Rev. Msgr. Rogelio Mur, O.Carm.; Pedro J. Rivera;

Administrator - Alberto Rodriguez;

Censor Librorum -

Parish Priests Consultors - Rev. Msgr. Gonzalo Diaz Hernandez; Rev. Rogelio Mur Aguilar, O.Carm.;

OFFICES AND DIRECTORS

Caritas - Rev. Orlando Rosas Muniz, Dir. (sscdmaya@gmail.com);

Catechetics - Sr. Miriam Nieves, O.P.;

Communications Media - Rev. Edgardo Acosta Ocasio;

Cursillos de Cristiandad - Dcn. Carlos Valentin Vale;

Development and Planification - Rev. Msgr. Rogelio Mur, O.Carm.;

Holy Childhood (Vacant) -

Legion of Mary (Vacant) -

Religious Consultor -

Religious Coordinator -

Seasonal Head Start Program - t) 787-892-3800 Myrna Carrero, Dir.;

Superintendent of Schools - Ivette Rodriguez;

Vocations - Rev. Delroy Thomas; Rev. Daniel Enrique Hernandez Velez; Rev. Wilson Montes Rodriguez;

Youth Apostolate - Rev. Jose Gustavo Torres;

PARISHES, MISSIONS, AND CLERGY

COMMONWEALTH OF PUERTO RICO

AGUADA

St. Francis of Assisi - ; Mailing: P.O. Box 608, Aguada, PR 00602 t) 787-868-2630 fr_felo@hotmail.com Rev. Jose R Cepeda, OSA, Pst.; Rev. Felipe Fernandez, Par. Vicar; Rev. Elvi J Restituyo, OSA, Par. Vicar; Dcn. Gerardo Caban; Dcn. Dionisio Jimenez; Dcn. Gregorio Ruiz; Dcn. Wilfredo Valle; Dcn. Hector Vargas;

Hermanas de la Caridad del Cardenal Sancha - Calle Jose Hernandez, Aguada, PR 00602; Mailing: Box 1136, Aguada, PR 00602 t) 787-868-8257

San Jose -

Santa Rita -

Santa Monica -

Santo Tomas de Villanueva -

San Augustin -

Perpetuo Socorro -

Ntra. Madre de la Consolacion -

Ntra. Sra. de Altagracia -

San Pablo -

Asuncion de Maria -

Buen Consejo -

Perpetuo Socorro -

Ntra. Sra. del Carmen -

Ntra. Sra. de las Mercedes -

Inmaculada Concepcion -

Sagrada Familia -

Sgdo. Corazon de Jesus -

Ntra. Sra. del Carmen -

El Buen Pastor -

Ntra. Sra. Reina de la Paz -

Centro de Espiritualidad, Madre de la Consolacion -

Santuario Protomártires de la Inmaculada Concepción - Carr. 115, Int. 442; 1162 Bo. Espinar, Aguada, PR 00602; Mailing: Buzon 1162 Bo. Espinar, Aguada, PR 00602 t) 787-891-2989 secretaria@yosoycapuchino.com www.yosoycapuchino.com Rev. Jose A Cruz-Collazo, ofm Cap., Pst.; Rev. Gastin Delys, ofm Cap., Priest; Rev. Samuel De Jesus Plancencia-Puntiel, OFM Cap. (Dominican Republic), Priest; Dcn. Dereck Molinary; Raquel Lopez-Jimenez, Accountant;

El Buen Pastor - Carr. 111 Km 1 #9 Int. Bo. Palmar, Aguada, PR 00602; Mailing: Buzón 1162 Bo. Espinar, Aguada, PR 00602

Sagrado Corazon de Jesus - Bo. Tablonar, 113 Carr. 439 Km 0.9 Calle Dalia, Comunidad las Flores, Aguada, PR 00602; Mailing: Buzón 1162 Bo. Espinar, Aguada, PR 00602

Nuestra Senora del Carmen - Bo. Victoria, Ave. Victoria, Aguada, PR 00602

AGUADILLA

St. Charles Borromeo - Aguadilla Pueblo, Aguadilla, PR 00605-0238; Mailing: P.O. Box 238, Aguadilla, PR 00605-0238 t) 787-891-0575 p.sancarlos1@gmail.com Rev. Delroy E. Thomas, Pst.; Rev. Tomas Galarza Figueroa, Vicar; Dcn. Herminio Blas; Dcn. Jose Castro; Dcn. Jose Chaparro; Dcn. Benjamin Echevarria; Dcn. Victor Morales;

St. Charles Borromeo School - c/o St. Charles Borromeo Parish, Aguadilla, PR 00605-0238 Irma Corrno, Prin.;

Convent - Calle José de Diego #18, Aguadilla, PR 00605 t) 787-882-7027 diazlo13@yahoo.com Sr. Lourdes Diaz, Supr.;

Convent - Calle Mercado 110, Aguadilla, PR 00605 t) 787-891-7496

Bo. Corrales, Our Lady of Perpetual Help - Bo. Corrales, Calle Esmeralda Esq. Calle Tanzanita, Aguadilla, PR 00605

Caimital Alto, St. John Baptist - Calle Las Rosas, Aguadilla, PR 00605

Esteves, Our Lady of Rosary - Comunidad Esteves, Aguadilla, PR 00605

Bda. Caban, Holy Family - Calle El Parque, Aguadilla, PR 00605

La Milagrosa - Urb. Marbella, Calle 1 Num. 379, Aguadilla, PR 00603 c) 787-891-7014 ramon.albino@diocesisdemayaguez.org Rev. Alberto I Gonzalez (Puerto Rico), Vicar; Rev. Msgr. Ramon E. Albino, Pst.; Dcn. Milton Concepcion; Dcn. Felipe Perez; Dcn. Heriberto Garcia; Dcn. Tadeo Jimenez; CRP Stds.: 168

Educational Service Corpus Christi School - c/o La Milagrosa Parish, Urb. Marbella, Calle 1 Num. 379, Aguadilla, PR 00603

Our Lady of Victory - Borinquen, Aguadilla, PR 00605

Our Lady of Fatima - Bo. Camaseyes, Aguadilla, PR 0065

San Judas Tadeo - Playuelas, Aguadilla, PR 00605

ANASCO

St. Anthony Abbot - #47 Calle 65 Infanteria, Anasco, PR 00610 t) 787-826-2215 murcarmelita@gmail.com Rev. Tomas Ciscar, O.Carm., Pst.; Rev. Ruben Dario Rodriguez, Par. Vicar; Dcn. Ramón Echevarria; Dcn. Juan Hernandez; Dcn. Jose A. Rivera; Dcn. Victor M Rosado; Dcn. Edwin Vega;

LaSalle - c/o St. Anthony Abbot Parish, Anasco, PR 00610; Mailing: P.O. Box 392, Anasco, PR 00610 t) 787-826-6071 Emma Mayens, Dir.;

Chapel of Our Lady of Perpetual Help - Bo. Miraflores Carr 109 Km 10.5, Anasco, PR 00610

Our Lady of Carmel - Bo. Playa Calle Reina de la Flores esq. Calle Orquidea, Anasco, PR 00610

St. Lawrence Martyr - Bo. Espino Carr 109 Km 5.1, Anasco, PR 00610

La Immaculade - Bo. Piñales Arriba Carr 411 Km 10.5 Bo. Atalaya, Anasco, PR 00610

La Providencia - Bo. Carreras Carr. 109 Km 2.3, Anasco, PR 00610

Our Lady of Monserrat - Bo. Cerro Gordo Camino Reyes Magos Carr 405 Km 3.7 Interior, Anasco, PR 00610

St. Rita - Bo. Marías Calle Luis Muñoz Marín al final, Anasco, PR 00610

Cristo Redentor - Bo. Ovejas Carr 430 Km 1.5 Ramal 4430, Anasco, PR 00610

BOQUERON

Parroquia San Jose, Custodio de la Sagrada Familia - Apt. 238, Boqueron, PR 00622 t) 787-940-6385 coriesu@gmail.com Rev. Edward Acevedo, Pst.; Dcn. Ricardo Camacho; Dcn. Isidro de Jesus; Dcn. Eddie Vargas;

Nuestra Senora de Fatima - Bo. Betances, Cabo Rojo, PR 00623 t) 787-357-7079

Santa Rita de Casia - Las Palmas, Cabo Rojo, PR 00623

Cristo Rey - El Corozo, Cabo Rojo, PR 00623

CABO ROJO

St. Michael - ; Mailing: Box 625, Cabo Rojo, PR 00623 t) 787-851-1283 wil_montes@hotmail.com Dcn. Luis A. Lopez; Dcn. Oscar Rivera; Dcn. Nelson Seda; Rev. Wilson Montes Rodriguez, Pst.; Rev. Juan R Gonzalez, Par. Vicar;

San Agustin - c/o St. Michael Parish, Cabo Rojo, PR 00623; Mailing: P.O. Box 625, Cabo Rojo, PR 00623 t) 787-851-1950 colegiosanagustin@hotmail.com Sr. Raymond Perez, Prin.; Raquel Alvarengua, Dir.;

Our Lady of Mt. Carmel -

St. John the Baptist -

Our Lady of Good Counsel -

St. Jude Thaddeus -

St. Martin de Porres -

Ntra. Sra. de la Providencia -

Hnas. de Nazaret - Urb. Margarita Calle Baldorioty #2, Cabo Rojo, PR 00623 t) 787-550-4575

HORMIGUEROS

El Salvador - ; Mailing: Box 567, Hormigueros, PR 00660 t) 787-834-1993 granadososcarma@gmail.com Rev. Oscar Granados, Admin.; Rev. Julio Angel Vera Gonzalez, Par. Vicar; Dcn. Roberto Aleman; Dcn. Jorge Lopez;

Valle Hermoso Arriba, San Judas Tadeo - Valle Hermoso Arriba, Hormigueros, PR 00660

Parcelas S. Romualdo, Sta. Teresita - Parcelas San Romualdo, Hormigueros, PR 00660

Unas. Misioneras Dominicas del Rosario - Urb. Valle Hermoso Calle Bucare SU 55, Hormigueros, PR 00660 t) 787-935-7048; 787-407-2311

Shrine of Our Lady of Monserrate - ; Mailing: Box 24, Hormigueros, PR 00660 t) 787-849-2260 mryl_40@yahoo.com Rev. Msgr. Gonzalo Diaz Hernandez, Pst.; Most Rev. Luis A Jusino, Par. Vicar; Dcn. Gilberto H. Rodriguez; Dcn. Jaime Rodriguez;

Convent - ; Mailing: Box 185, Hormigueros, PR 00660 t) 787-849-2055

Sagrado Corazon de Jesus - Bo. Lavadero, Hormigueros, PR 00660

Ntra. Sra. de la Paz - Bo. Jaguitas, Hormigueros, PR 00660

La Asuncion - Carr. Nueva, Hormigueros, PR 00660

San Martin de Porres - Bo. Hoya Grande, Hormigueros, PR 00660

Santa Rosa de Lima - Bo. El Hoyo, Hormigueros, PR 00660

LAJAS

De la Merced Parish - Calle Violeta #113, Lajas, PR 00667-1063; Mailing: P.O. Box 1023, Lajas, PR 00667-1063 t) 787-899-1910 padreurianperez@gmail.com Rev. Urian J. Perez Zapata, Admin.; Rev. Jose L Ocasio, Vicar; Dcn. Andres Almanzar;

Ntra. Sra. de la Monserrate - Carr. 101 Ramal 303 K.2.4, Bo. Maguayo, PR 00667

San Pedro - Carr. 304 Calle Principal, Bo. Parguera, PR 00667

Ntra. Sra. de Monserrate - Carr. 116 Parcellas Cuesta Blanca #264, Bo. Cuesta Blanca, PR 00667

Ntra. Sra. del Carmen - Carr. 324 Km 5.6, Bo. Salinas,

PR 00667

Ntra. Sra. del Perpetuo Socorro - Carr. 306, Bo. Paris, PR 00667

Our Lady of the Purification - ; Mailing: Box 425, Lajas, PR 00667 t) 787-899-1911 lacandelaria.lajas@gmail.com Rev. Angel Ortiz Velez, Pst.; Rev. Juan Chavajay, Par. Vicar;

St. Louis Academy Sisters of St. Joseph - c/o Our Lady of the Purification Parish, Lajas, PR 00667; Mailing: P.O. Box 425, Lajas, PR 00667 t) 787-899-4080 (Brooklyn) Sr. Teresita Alicea, C.S.J., Prin.;

La Providencia - t) 787-899-5180

Sagrado Corazon de Jesus - Parcelas #201, Bo. La Plata, PR 00667

Ntra. Sra. del Perpetuo Socorro - Carr. 118 Km 0, Bo. Lajas Arriba (La Tea), PR 00667

San Pablo - Parcelas #48, Bo. Lajas Arriba (Parcelas), PR 00667

Santa Rosa de Lima - Comunidad Sta. Rosa #35, Bo. Parcelas Santa Rosa, PR 00667

San Judas Tadeo - Parcelas #172, Bo. Parcelas Palmarejo, PR 00667

San Juan Bautista - Parcela #80, Bo. Palmarejo II, PR 00667

Santa Rosa de Lima -

LAS MARIAS

Immaculate Heart of Mary - ; Mailing: Box 126, Las Marias, PR 00670 t) 787-827-3300 javieraquinoflorenciani@gmail.com Rev. Javier Aquino, Admin.; Dcn. Robertyo Cruz;

San Jose - Carr. 406, Km. 3.9, Anones, PR 00607

La Milagrosa - Carr. 124, R. 370, Km. 6.8 Int Buena Vista, Buena Vista, PR 00670

Ntra. Sra. de Fatima - Buena Vista, Las Marias, PR 00670

MARICAO

St. John the Baptist - ; Mailing: Box 453, Maricao, PR 00606 t) 787-436-4488 bosques.eric7@gmail.com Rev. Eric J Bosques, Admin.; Dcn. Jose R. Martinez;

Sagrado Corazon - Bo Bucarabones, Maricao, PR 00606

Santa Rosa - Indiera Fria, Maricao, PR 00606

Montoso, Immaculado Corazon de Maria - Bo. Montoso, Maricao, PR 00606 t) 787-838-2272 Sr. Angeles Marie Pacheco, O.P., Supr.;

MAYAGUEZ

Cathedral of Our Lady of Purification - ; Mailing: P.O. Box 220, Mayaguez, PR 00681-0220 t) 787-832-4441 hlopez1962@gmail.com Dcn. Eddie O. Perez; Dcn. Edwin Ramos; Dcn. Israel Valentin; Rev. Alexander Crespo (Venezuela), Vicar; Rev. Msgr. Humberto Lopez Bonilla, Rector; Rev. Paulino Mazuelos, Assoc. Pst.;

Maria Socorro de los Cristianos - Bo. Leguisamo, Mayaguez, PR 00680

Santa Ana - Quebrada Grande, Mayaguez, PR 00680

Ascension - 363 Calle Broadway Este Bo. Salud, Mayaguez, PR 00681 t) 787-832-0766 ascensionmay1968@gmail.com Rev. Luis A Mojica, Pst.; Dcn. Gilberto Martinez; Dcn. Samuel S. Collazo;

St. Teresita - Bo. El Limón Carr. 105 Km 105. Km 7.7, Mayaguez, PR 00681

Our Lady of Perpetual Help - Bo. Las Vegas Carr. 105 Km 16.0, Mayaguez, PR 00681

Ntra. Sra. de la Providencia (Rep. Masias) - Reparto Macías Carr. 105 Km 9.1 Int, Mayaguez, PR 00681

Church de El Buen Pastor - Urb. Mayaguez Ter., 5000 Calle San Gerardo, Mayaguez, PR 00682-6627 t) 787-833-8800 eigarcia@outlook.com; parroquiabuenpastormayaguez@gmail.com Rev. Eric I Garcia, Pst.; Rev. Gerardo E Caraballo, Par. Vicar; Dcn. Carlos F Padilla;

El Cristo de Los Milagros - 1116 Calle Perpetuo Socorro, Bo. Algarrobo, Mayaguez, PR 00682 t) 787-265-5936

Sta. Teresita - Parcelas Soledad, Mayaguez, PR 00682

Church of the Resurrection - Balboa 285, Mayaguez, PR 00680 t) 787-831-6180 laresurreciondelsenor@gmail.com Dcn. Jose Luis Rodriguez; Rev. Milton Morales Villarrubia, Pst.; CRP Stds.: 9

Consumo, Jesus Redentor -

Rio Canas, Nuestra Senora del Perpetuo Socorro -

Barrio Quemado, Nuestra Senora del Carmen -

Nuestra Senora de Fatima - Parcelas Castillo C-2, Mayaguez, PR 00682 t) 787-833-0794 sanbenitoabad5@hotmail.com Rev. Omar Yanez, Pst.; Dcn. Roberto Aleman;

Cristo Rey - Andalucia St., Sultana, Mayaguez, PR 00680

Espiritu Santo - Sagitario St., Villa del Oeste, Sabalos, Mayaguez, PR 00680

Corpus Christi - Urb. Vista Verde, Mayaguez, PR 00680

Our Lady of Mt. Carmel - ; Mailing: Box 3166, Mayaguez, PR 00681 t) 787-652-4999 parroquiaelcarmenmayaguez@hotmail.com Rev. William Saltar Arocho, S.F.M., Pst.; Dcn. Roberto Candelaria; Dcn. Rafael A Quiñones; Dcn. Jose Valentin Sanabria;

Infant of Prague - Mani, Mayaguez, PR 00680

Perpetuo Socorro - La Mora, Mayaguez, PR 00680

Sacred Heart - Marina Sta., Mayaguez, PR 00681-3626; Mailing: P.O. Box 3626, Mayaguez, PR 00681-3626 t) 787-831-3940 parroquiasagradocorazonmaya@gmail.com Rev. Moises Rios, Pst.; Rev. Renel Ramirez, Par. Vicar; Dcn. Julio Carreras; Dcn. Pedro Gonzalez; Dcn. Josue C Martinez;

St. Benedict - c/o Sacred Heart Parish, Mayaguez, PR 00681-3626 Nadia Lugo, Prin.; Ivette Rodriguez, Prin.;

San Jose - Rosario, Mayaguez, PR 00681

San Carlos y San Antonio - Rio Hondo, Mayaguez, PR 00681

La Milagrosa - Bo. Malezas, Mayaguez, PR 00681

San Vicente - Ave. Guanajibo, No. 401, Mayaguez, PR 00680 t) 787-832-8874 mondemry@yahoo.fr Rev. Emmery Mondesir (Haiti), Pst.;

Santa Teresita - Principe St., 203 Bo. Colombia, Mayaguez, PR 00680 t) 787-806-0881 gaspar2003@hotmail.com Dcn. Carlos J. Mercado; Rev. Edgar A. Carlo Rodriguez, Pst.;

MOCA

Our Lady of Monserrate - ; Mailing: P.O. Box 435, Moca, PR 00716 t) 787-877-2765 parroquialamonserrate@gmail.com Rev. Angel Ortiz (Puerto Rico); Rev. Enrique Cordero, Par. Vicar; Rev. David Perez, Par. Vicar; Dcn. Efrain Acevedo; Rev. Renel Ramirez, Vicar; Dcn. Miguel Acevedo; Dcn. German Colon; Dcn. Edwin Hernandez; Dcn. Domingo Lorenzo; Dcn. Gumersindo Sosa; CRP Stds.: 156

San Judas Tadeo - Bo. Plata, Moca, PR 00676

Espiritu Santo - Bo. Voladoras, Moca, PR 00676

Sagrada Familia - Bo. Voladoras, Moca, PR 00676

Sagrado Corazon de Jesus - Bo. Naranjo, Moca, PR 00676

Santos Guillermo Abad y San Mateo - Bo. Cuchilla - Lassalle, Moca, PR 00676

Inmaculado Corazon de Maria - Bo Cuchillas Cordero, Moca, PR 00676

Virgen del Perpetuo Socorro - Bo. Sierra, Moca, PR 00676

Cristo Rey - Bo. Cuchillas - Loperena, Moca, PR 00676

Virgen de la Monserrate - Bo Cuchillas Cordero, Moca, PR 00676

Virgen de la Providencia - Bo. Rocha Magueyes, Moca, PR 00676

San Pedro Apostol - Bo. Rocha Sect Lassalle, Moca, PR 00676

Virgen del Rosario - Bo. Capa Barreto, Moca, PR 00676

Corpus Christi - Bo Capa - osque, Moca, PR 00676

El Buen Pastor - Bo. Cerro Gordo, Moca, PR 00676

San Martin de Porres - Bo. Aceituna, Moca, PR 00676

RINCON

St. Rose of Lima - ; Mailing: Box 128, Rincon, PR 00677 t) 787-823-2650 padrejoseg2012@yahoo.com Rev. Jose Gustavo Torres, Pst.; Rev. Rafael A Mendez, Assoc. Pst.; Rev. Angel Roman Ramos, Par. Vicar; Dcn. Gilberto Medina Agron; Dcn. Isaac Candelaria; Dcn. George Mercado; Dcn. Juan Ventura;

Santa Rosa - Bo. Calvache, Rincón, PR 00677

El Cristo de la Reconciliacion - Bo. Atalaya, Rincón, PR 00677

La Milagrosa - Bo. Corcega, Rincón, PR 00677

Sagrado Corazon de Jesus - Bo. Cruces, Rincón, PR 00677

Nuestra Senora del Carmen - Bo. Puntas, Rincón, PR 00677

San Jose - Bo. Jaguey, Rincón, PR 00677

La Virgin de Guadalupe - Bo. Río Grande, Rincón, PR 00677

ROSARIO

Our Lady of Rosary - ; Mailing: Box 692, Rosario, PR 00636 t) 787-832-3533 a.luisrp@gmail.com Rev. Angel L Rivera, Admin.;

Nuestra Senora del Rosario - Rosario Poblado, Rosario, PR 00636

La Monseirate - Bo. Rosario Peñón, Rosario, PR 00636

La Milagrosa - Bo. Rosario Alto, Rosario, PR 00636

SABANA GRANDE

Church of San Isidro - Sabana Grande Pueblo, Sabana Grande, PR 00637; Mailing: Box 817, Sabana Grande, PR 00637 t) 787-873-4475 sanisidropr@yahoo.com Rev. Edgardo Acosta, Pst.; Rev. Edgardo López, Par. Vicar; Rev. Angel Valle, Par. Vicar; Dcn. Milton Ortiz;

Convent - t) 787-873-2750

Cristo Rey - Carr. 368, R. 367, Km. 2.0, El Papayo, PR 00637

La Resurreccion - Carr. 121, Calle Azucena, Susua, PR 00637

Sagrado Corazon de Jesus - Calle Roble #44, Carr. 121, Km. 5.0, Bo. Maginas, PR 00637

San Jose - Carr. 121, Km 4.1, Bo. La Pica, PR 00637

San Francisco de Asis - Carr. 369, Km. 1.4, Bo. Cerro Gordo, PR 00637

Ntra. Sra. de Fatima - Carr. 328, Km. 3.6, Bo. Guaras, PR 00637

Santa Catalina de Siena - Carr. 388, Km. 5.9, Interior, Bo. La Torre, PR 00637

Santa Ana - Carr. 114, R. 363, Km. 2.4, Bo. La Maquina, PR 00637

Ntra. Sra. del Rosario - Carr. 120, Km. 6, Bo. Santana Pichel, PR 00637

La Virgen Milagrosa - Carr. 364, Km. 7, Interior, Bo. El Hoyo, PR 00637

San Judas Tadeo - Carr. 117, Km. 10.7, Bo. Rayo Plata, PR 00637

Sta. Lucia - Carr. 120, Km. 3.1, Bo. Sta. Ana Moreno, PR 00637

Divino Nino Jesus - Carr. 102, Km. 38.1, Interior, Bo. Rayo, Sect. David Mendez, Sabana Grande, PR 00637

SAN ANTONIO

San Jose Obrero - ; Mailing: P.O. Box 787, San Antonio, PR 00690-0787 t) 787-891-2449 parrroquiasjo2017@outlook.com Dcn. Carlos Valentin; Rev. Miguel Cruz (Cuba), Admin.;

La Providencia - Bo. Guerrero, Poblado San Antonio, PR 00690

Los Santos Reyes - Bo. Ramey-Maleza, Poblado San Antonio, PR 00690

SAN GERMAN

Iglesia Diocesana de La Inmaculada Concepcion Hospital La Concepcion - Apt. 285, San German, PR 00683 t) 787-892-1860 leonides.soto@diocesisdemayaguez.org Rev. Angel Leonides Soto, Pst.;

St. Rose of Lima - ; Mailing: Box 364, San German, PR 00683 t) 787-892-1276 diocesismayaguez@yahoo.es Rev. Abdon Atienza, O.S.A., Pst.; Rev. Saturnino Juan Vega, Par. Vicar;

Ntra. Sra. de la Consolacion - Bo. Guama, San

Germán, PR 00623
Perpetuo Socorro - Bo. Minillas Carr., San Germán, PR 00623
Santa Rita - Bo. Retiro Tea, San Germán, PR 00623
Santa Monica - Bo. Minillas Valle, San Germán, PR 00623
St. Martin de Porres - Bo. Cain, San Germán, PR 00623

San German de Auxerre - ; Mailing: Box 305, San German, PR 00683 t) 787-892-1027 secretariaparroquiadesangerman@gmail.com Rev. Daniel Enrique Hernandez Velez, Pst.; Rev. Edwin Lugo-Silva, Vicar; Dcn. Rafael Velez Torres;
Chapel of St. Augustin - Duey, San Germán, PR 00683
Chapel of St. Joseph - Hoconuco, San Germán, PR 00623
Gruta de Lourdes - Bo. Maresua, San Germán, PR 00623
Our Lady of Fatima - Bo. Cotuy, San Germán, PR 00623
San Judas Tadeo - Bo. Sabana Eneas, San Germán, PR 00623

SAN SEBASTIAN

San Sebastian Martir - ; Mailing: P.O. Box 801, San Sebastian, PR 00685 t) 787-896-1028 parroquiass@gmail.com Rev. Marcelino Arocho, Pst.; Rev. Nomar J Calero, Par. Vicar; Rev. Dennys W Cruz, Par. Vicar; Rev. Julio A Echevarria, Par. Vicar; Rev. Christopher L Gonzalez, Par. Vicar; Dcn. Luis A. Arocho; Dcn. Adalberto Colon; Dcn. Nestor Gonzalez; Dcn. Bernardino Medina; Dcn. Victor Torres;
San Sebastian Martir - c/o San Sebastian Martir Parish, San Sebastian, PR 00685 t) 787-896-5728 Administrated by the Passionist Sisters "Hijas de la Pasion" Nia K. Mendez, Prin.;
Cristo Rey -
La Pasion del Senor -
San Gabriel de la Dolorosa -
La Immaculada Concepcion -
Santa Teresita del Nino Jesus -
Ntra. Sra. del Carmen -
San Judas Tadeo -
San Patricio -
San Pablo de la Cruz -
Ntra. Sra. de Fatima -
Sagrado Corazon de Jesus -
San Jose Obrero -
Santa Cruz -
Espiritu Santo -
Cristo Resucitado -
Ntra. Sra. de La Providencia -
Sagrada Familia -
Hnas. Hijas de la pasion y Maria Dolorosa - ; Mailing: P.O. Box 3132, San Sebastian, PR 00685 c) 787-847-8669 albericisecundaria@gmail.com

INSTITUTIONS LOCATED IN DIOCESE

COLLEGES & UNIVERSITIES [COL]

ANASCO

De La Salle Catholic College - Apt. 61, Anasco, PR 00610 t) 787-826-6071 secmayaguez@yahoo.com Emma Mayens, Dir.;

AQUADILLA

Corpus Christi College - Apt. 4021, Aquadilla, PR 00605-4021 t) 787-882-8433 colegiocorpuschristi@yahoo.com Rev. Msgr. Ramon E. Albino; Esmeralda Perez, Prin.;

MOCA

Nuestra Senora de la Monserrate College - Calle Blanca E. Chico #201, Moca, PR 00676; Mailing: Apartado 435, Moca, PR 00676 t) 787-877-5444 colegiolamonserrate@yahoo.com www.iglesialamonserrate.org Damaris Gonzalez, Prin.; Rev. Jorge Luis Caro Morales, Dir.;

CONVENTS, MONASTERIES, AND RESIDENCES FOR WOMEN [CON]

MAYAGUEZ

Convent of the Servants of Mary - Hostos Ave., 401, Mayaguez, PR 00680 t) 787-832-0391 siervas125maya@gmail.com Sr. Aurea Fernandez, Supr.; Sr. Rosaura Morales Rivera, Otro;

HOSPITALS / HEALTH SERVICES [HOS]

SAN GERMÁN

Hospital of the Immaculate Conception - Hospital de la Concepción, San Germán, PR 00683; Mailing: Box 285, San German, PR 00683 t) 787-892-1860 ecrespo@hospitalconcepcion.org www.hospconcepcion.com Rev. Angel Leonides Soto, Chap.; Edgar Crespo, Admin.; Bed Capacity: 187; Asstd. Annu.: 10,893; Staff: 667

MISCELLANEOUS [MIS]

HORMIGUEROS

Residence for the Aged, San Jose - Valle Hermoso, Hormigueros, PR 00660 t) 787-832-4243 hogarsanjose25@yahoo.es Sr. Margarita Ramirez, Supr.;

MAYAGUEZ

Comunidad Belen - Carr. 354 Km 7.9 Int. Bo. Leguizamo, Mayaguez, PR 00681; Mailing: P.O. Box 2938, Mayaguez, PR 00681 t) 787-832-2203 william-sfm@hotmail.com

Opus Dei (Prelature of the Holy Cross and Opus Dei) - 69 Orquideas St., Ensanche Martinez, Mayaguez, PR 00680 t) 787-833-6461 diocesismayaguez@yahoo.es Rev. Javier Bernaola;

SAN GERMAN

Egida de la Concepcion - Calle Variante #1, San German, PR 00683 t) 787-892-6620 aegidadelaconcepcion@yahoo.com Alicia Espada, Dir.;

An asterisk (*) denotes an organization that has established tax-exempt status directly with the IRS and is not covered by the USCCB Group Ruling.

Diocese of Ponce, Puerto Rico

(Dioecesis Poncensis)

MOST REVEREND RUBEN ANTONIO GONZALEZ MEDINA, CMF

Bishop of Ponce; ordained February 9, 1975; appointed Bishop of Caguas December 12, 2000; consecrated February 4, 2001; appointed Bishop of Ponce December 22, 2015; installed January 31, 2016. Mailing Address: Bishop's House, P.O. Box 801246, Coto Laurel, PR 00780-1246.

ESTABLISHED NOVEMBER 21, 1924.

Square Miles 830.

Comprises the south portion of the Island of Puerto Rico and is in the Ecclesiastical Province of Puerto Rico.

STATISTICAL OVERVIEW

Personnel

Bishop 1
Retired Bishops 1
Priests: Diocesan Active in Diocese 42
Priests: Diocesan Active Outside Diocese 3
Priests: Retired, Sick or Absent 18
Number of Diocesan Priests 63
Religious Priests in Diocese 30
Total Priests in your Diocese 93
Extern Priests in Diocese 1
Ordinations:
Diocesan Priests 2
Permanent Deacons in Diocese 85
Total Sisters 147

Parishes

Parishes 43
With Resident Pastor:
Resident Diocesan Priests 31
Resident Religious Priests 8
Without Resident Pastor:
Administered by Priests 4
Pastoral Centers 1
Professional Ministry Personnel:
Sisters 4

Welfare

Homes for the Aged 2
Total Assisted 122
Day Care Centers 3
Total Assisted 35
Specialized Homes 2
Total Assisted 35
Special Centers for Social Services 4
Total Assisted 5,744
Residential Care of Disabled 1
Total Assisted 245

Educational

Seminaries, Diocesan 1
Students from This Diocese 6
Students from Other Dioceses 22
Seminaries, Religious 1
Students, Religious 4
Total Seminarians 10
Colleges and Universities 1
Total Students 7,697
High Schools, Diocesan and Parish 11
Total Students 1,310
High Schools, Private 5
Total Students 526
Elementary Schools, Diocesan and Parish 12
Total Students 2,747
Elementary Schools, Private 5
Total Students 1,010
Catechesis / Religious Education:
High School Students 179
Elementary Students 4,476
Total Students under Catholic Instruction 17,955
Teachers in Diocese:
Priests 15
Brothers 1
Sisters 8
Lay Teachers 698

Vital Statistics

Receptions into the Church:
Infant Baptism Totals 1,913
Minor Baptism Totals 137
Adult Baptism Totals 45
First Communions 1,497
Confirmations 1,374
Marriages:
Catholic 269
Interfaith 12
Total Marriages 281
Deaths 1,500
Total Catholic Population 351,913
Total Population 469,684

LEADERSHIP

Administrator - t) (787) 840-3332 administracion@diocesisdeponce.org Teresa Aponte Rivera, Economa;
Vicar General - t) 787-840-3332 ramireztorresgeral17@gmail.com Rev. Gerardo Ramirez Torres;
Pro-Vicar General (Vacant) -
Chancellor - t) 787-848-5265 cancilleria@diocesisdeponce.org Rev. Christopher C. de Herrera Sandoval, O.S.;
Notary - t) 787-840-3332 nancy.mendez@diocesisdeponce.org Nancy Ivonne Mendez Garcia;
Vice-Chancellor - t) 787-848-5265 cancilleria@diocesisdeponce.org Alejandra Marie Rivera Rivera;
Episcopal Vicar for Diocesan Administration -
Episcopal Vicar of the Central Zone - t) (787) 913-0083 vicariacentro@diocesisdeponce.org Rev. Orlando Lugo Perez, Episcopal Vicar (santisimosacramentoponce@gmail.com);
Episcopal Vicar of the West Zone - Rev. Segismundo Cintron Orengo (pcintron@gmail.com);
Episcopal Vicar of the Eastern Zone - Rev. Victor Manuel Hernandez Velazquez (vhernandez112475@gmail.com);
Episcopal Vicar for Pastoral Coordination - t) 787-840-3332 vicariapastoral@diocesisdeponce.org Rev. Carlos Manuel Grullon Capellan;
Episcopal Vicar for Family Pastoral - t) 787-848-2030 parr.virgendelcarmen@gmail.com Rev. Manuel Santiago Hernandez;
Episcopal Vicar for Social Pastoral - t) 787-848-3313 collazo25@aol.com Rev. Carlos A. Collazo Santiago;
Episcopal Vicar for Institutes of Consecrated Life and Societies of Apostolic Life - c) (787) 445-7341 Rev. José Vicente Martínez-Santos Gallego, CMF, Pst.;
Coordinator of the Education Commission - c) 787-640-3981 jalop311@gmail.com Rev. Jose Antonio Lopez Vega;
Coordinator of the Sick - t) (787) 390-6587 josecvo@hotmail.com Rev. Jose Carlos Vargas Oliveras;
Clergy Permanent Formation Commission - t) (787) 600-4621 sotoomi@yahoo.com Rev. Omar Omi Soto Torres; Rev. Gerardo Ramirez Torres;
Diocesan Priest Consultors - Rev. Gerardo Ramirez Torres; Rev. Msgr. Elias S. Morales Rodriguez; Rev. Carlos M. Grullon Capellan;
Diocesan Board of Administration - Jeanette Soto Vega; Jorge Alexis Torres Montes; Jaime Banchs Pieretti;
Censores Librorum - Rev. Adalin Rivera;
Tribunal Diocesano de Ponce - t) 787-843-4630 tribunalinterdiocesanopr@gmail.com Rev. Juan Jose Saliva Gonzalez, Patrono;
Associate Judicial Vicar - t) 787-824-2215 c) 787-974-6098 carlosmanuel.gc@gmail.com Rev. Carlos Manuel Grullon Capellan;
Auditors - Dcn. Joseph Burgos Roca; Eva Charisse Cruz Morel;
Judges - Rev. Omar Omi Soto Torres; Rev. Manuel A. Santiago Hernandez; Rev. Oscar A. Chacon Gonzalez, O.SS.T.;
Judicial Vicar - t) 787-843-4630 Rev. Msgr. Elias S. Morales Rodriguez;
Moderator - t) 787-290-7887 oficinaobispoponcepr@gmail.com Most Rev. Ruben Antonio Gonzalez Medina, C.M.F.;
Notary - Maria de los Angeles Raldiris Aponte; Maria Victoria Santiago Rivera;

OFFICES AND DIRECTORS

Adoracion Nocturna - c) 787-640-3981 jalop311@gmail.com Rev. Jose Antonio Lopez Vega;
Boy Scouts of America - t) 787-298-5757 buffalo_pr@hotmail.com Anibal Diaz Colon;
Caballeros de Colon (Knights of Columbus) - c) 787-646-4825 gonzo.3033@gmail.com Fernando Gonzalez Cordero;
Camino Neocatacumenal - Julio Alvarez (julioybeli@gmail.com);
Capellanes de la Policia - c) 787-317-6885; 787-375-4885; 787-579-8060 Rev. Segismundo Cintron Orengo (pcintron@gmail.com); Rev. Juan Jose Saliva Gonzalez (saliva_60@hotmail.com); Rev. Samuel Santiago De Jesus (sammystgo50@yahoo.com);
Centro Catequistico Diocesano - t) 787-842-9178 centrocatequisticoponce@yahoo.com; centrocatequisticoponce@gmail.com Sr. Cristina Morales Rivas, O.P.;
Centro Diocesano De Pastoral San Juan Diego - t) 787-301-0018 cedipa1965@gmail.com Rev. Ovidio Perez Perez, Admin.;
Centro Diocesano Pro-Vida (Pro-Life Center) - t) 787-848-2030 parr.virgendelcarmen@gmail.com Rev. Manuel A. Santiago Hernandez;
Cofradia Diocesana del Sagrado Corazon - t) 787-843-6409 rosie_santiago@hotmail.com Rosie Santiago;
Cofradia Virgen Dolorosa - t) 787-840-0695 jpenanic@gmail.com Juanita Pena Nicolao;
Comision Liturgica - t) 787-842-0069 parroquialamerced@gmail.com Rev. Ovidio Perez Perez, Coord.;
Comunidad Carismatica de la Visitacion y de la Eucaristia - c) 787-231-4498 cortiluna@hotmail.com Carmen I. Ortiz Luna;
Comunidad Jesus Resucitado - c) 939-452-0104; 787-901-1189 mercac@hotmail.com; lizette.guzman.cruz@gmail.com Lisette Guzman; Carlos Mercado;
Comunidades de Oracion y Reflexion Biblica - t) 787-843-8207 Gilda Cruz Batiz (cruzgilda72@gmail.com);
Comunion y Liberacion - t) 787-473-0897 wadar3@gmail.com Wadi Adames Roman;
Cursillos de Cristiandad - t) 787-840-3332 ramireztorresgeral17@gmail.com Rev. Gerardo Ramirez Torres;
Ecumenism - t) 787-840-3332 jrorengo@gmail.com Rev. Msgr. Juan Rodriguez Orengo;
Equipo de Nuestra Senora - t) 787-828-6350; 787-828-0874 ntrasramonserratejayuya@hotmail.com Rev. Deacon Carlos Orama, D.P.;
Equipo de Nuestra Senora - c) (939) 397-7592 (Sra. Sylvia Trinta); (787) 692-8770 (Sr. Roberto Espada) sylviatrintats@yahoo.com; espadita13@gmail.com
Estudios Peregrinos en la Fe - t) 787-677-8723 Gloria Rodriguez De Banchs (glo67@hotmail.com);
Grupo de la Divina Misericordia - t) 787-259-1752 n.faustina@gmail.com Naida Costa;
Hijas Catolicas de America (Catholic Daughters of America) - t) 787-415-7259 Silvia Vazquez Rios, Regente (silviavazquezr@yahoo.com);
Hijas de Maria - Rev. Msgr. Juan Rodriguez Orengo, Dir. Espiritual;
Instituto de Orientacion Familiar - t) 787-651-3932; 787-567-5708 Rev. Manuel A. Santiago Hernandez; Salvador Ocasio; Dcn. Arnaldo Lopez;
Ministerio de Evangelizacion Catolico de la Diocesis de Ponce - t) 787-315-0082 c) 787-630-6099 Carlos Melendez;
Ministerio Emaus - c) 787-678-4814 (Varones); 787-432-9912 (Mujeres) abigailalvaradorivera@gmail.com Herenio Correa; Lucelenia Criado Maldonado (lcriadomldo@outlook.com);
Movimiento Familia de Jesus - t) 787-632-1275 Jose Lucas Rodriguez (joselucasr@gmail.com);
Movimiento Juan XXIII - c) 787-448-9422 movimientojnxxiiiponce@gmail.com Abraham Velez Acevedo;
Movimiento Schoenstatt - c) 939-645-8616 William Rosaly; Migdalia Torres;
Oficina de Medios de Comunicacion Social - t) 787-843-1548 omecosponce@gmail.com Sr. Lizandra Rosa Pagan, O.P., Dir.;
Orden Ecuestre del Santo Sepulcro - t) 787-380-8391 Jose Frontera Agenjo (jose_frontera@pucpr.edu);
Orden Franciscana Seglar - t) 787-842-3137 pstponce@gmail.com
Pastoral Carcelaria - t) 787-840-3332 ramireztorresgeral17@gmail.com Rev. Gerardo Ramirez Torres;
Pastoral de la Salud - Hospitales - t) (787) 390-6587 josecvo@hotmail.com Rev. Jose Carlos Vargas Oliveras;
Pastoral Juvenil - c) 787-314-3569; 787-709-5947 pjdponce@gmail.com Rev. Javier Vega Graniela; Christian De Hoyos Reyes, Coord.;
Pastoral Vocacional - t) 787-848-4380 seminarioreginacleri@gmail.com Rev. Msgr. Elias S. Morales Rodriguez, Rector; Rev. Juan Carlos Rivera Medina, Dir. Espiritual;
Propagation of the Faith - t) 787-848-5265
Renovacion Carismatica Catolica (Catholic Charismatic Renewal) - t) 787-486-4660 tule@jritc.com Noelma Cintron (rcc.ponce@yahoo.com);
Sacred Music Commission (Vacant) -
Siervos de Cristo Vivo - c) 787-637-5792 casasanfranciscodeasis@hotmail.com; jamspr@hotmail.com Julio M. Acevedo Santiago, Dir.;
Sociedad del Santo Nombre (Holy Name Society) - t) 787-240-9204 w_romero47@icloud.com Wanda Vazquez, Contact;
Superintendencia de Escuelas Catolicas - t) 787-848-4020 superintendencia_ponce@yahoo.com Dr. Justina Ocasio Landron;
Talleres de Oracion y Vida - t) (787) 432-8280 Hiram Navarro, Mem. (hiram.navarro@upr.edu);
Vigilance for the Faith - t) 787-840-3332 oficinaobispoponcepr@gmail.com Most Rev. Ruben Antonio Gonzalez Medina, C.M.F.;

COMMUNICATIONS

Catolica Radio - t) 787-844-8809 Manuel Vega Gonzalez, Dir.;
Television Station - Catholic TV - Channel 14 - t) 787-841-2000 Ivan Falto, Dir. (cifalto@pucpr.edu);

PARISHES, MISSIONS, AND CLERGY

COMMONWEALTH OF PUERTO RICO

ADJUNTAS

San Joaquin y Santa Ana - 14 Calle Rius Rivera, Adjuntas, PR 00601 t) 787-829-3145 parroquiasanjoaquinysantaana@hotmail.com Rev. Federico Avila Piña, Sch. P., Pst.; Rev. Nelson Henao Rincón, Sch. P., Par. Vicar; Dcn. Edgardo Rivera Garcia; Dcn. Edwin Portalatin Padua; Dcn. Jose M. Maldonado Plaza; Dcn. Efrain Bernard Sierra; Dcn. Wilfredo Torres Maldonado; Dcn. Radames Marcucci; Maria N. Perez Albarran, CRE; CRP Stds.: 101
Academia San Joaquin - (Grades K-12) 12 Calle Primo Delgado, Adjuntas, PR 00601 t) 787-829-3040 acasjoaquin@yahoo.com Rev. Nelson Henao Rincon, Sch. P., Dir.; Mari H. Rivera Hernandez, Prin.; Stds.: 159; Pr. Tchrs.: 1; Lay Tchrs.: 19
San Francisco - Bo. Garzas, Adjuntas, PR 00601; Mailing: 14 Calle Rius Rivera, San Joaquin y Santa Ana, Adjuntas, PR 00601 t) (787) 829-2145
Sta. Ana - Bo. Vegas Arriba, Adjuntas, PR 00601; Mailing: 14 Calle Rius Rivera, San Joaquin y Santa Ana, Adjuntas, PR 00601 t) (787) 829-3145
Santa Teresita - Bo. Tres de Jayuya, Adjuntas, PR 00601; Mailing: 14 Calle Rius Rivera, San Joaquin y Santa Ana, Adjuntas, PR 00601 t) (787) 829-3145
Santa Rosa - Bo. Pellejas, Adjuntas, PR 00601; Mailing: 14 Calle Rius Rivera, San Joaquin y Santa

Ana, Adjuntas, PR 00601 t) (787) 829-3145

Virgen del Carmen - Bo. Yahuecas, Adjuntas, PR 00601; Mailing: 14 Calle Rius Rivera, San Joaquin y Santa Ana, Adjuntas, PR 00601 t) (787) 829-3145

Sagrado Corazon - Bo. Tanama, Adjuntas, PR 00601; Mailing: 14 Calle Rius Rivera, San Joaquin y Santa Ana, Adjuntas, PR 00601 t) (787) 829-3145

San Antonio - Bo. Guilarte, Adjuntas, PR 00601; Mailing: 14 Calle Rius Rivera, San Joaquin y Santa Ana, Adjuntas, PR 00601 t) (787) 829-3145

La Milagrosa - Bo. Vegas Abajo, Adjuntas, PR 00601; Mailing: 14 Calle Rius Rivera, San Joaquin y Santa Ana, Adjuntas, PR 00601 t) (787) 829-3145

Nuestra Senora de Fatima - Bo. Limani, Adjuntas, PR 00601; Mailing: 14 Calle Rius Rivera, San Joaquin y Santa Ana, Adjuntas, PR 00601 t) (787) 829-3145

AGUIRRE

Sagrado Corazon de Jesus - Bo. Coqui, Carr. #3 Km 157, Aguirre, PR 00704; Mailing: P.O. Box 260, Aguirre, PR 00704-0260 t) 787-696-1224 (CRP); 787-696-1238 corazonsagradosalinas@gmail.com Rev. Orlando Rivera Soto, Pst.; Lucinel Cartagena, Coord.; CRP Stds.: 53

San Judas - Bo. Las Mareas, Aguirre, PR 00704 t) (787) 696-1224

San Martin de Porres - Bo. San Felipe, Aguirre, PR 00704 t) (787) 696-1224

La Milagrosa - El Poblado, Aguirre, PR 00704 t) (787) 696-1224

ARROYO

Nuestra Senora del Carmen - 18 General Brook, Arroyo, PR 00714; Mailing: P.O. Box 388, Arroyo, PR 00714 t) 787-839-3465 parroquiadelcarmen5@gmail.com Rev. Juan Alberto Torres Reyes, Pst.; Dcn. Esteban Rivera; Dcn. Jacinto Rodriguez; Carmen Cabrera, CRE; Iris Y. Rosario, CRE; CRP Stds.: 112

Ntra. Sra. del Carmen - Bo. Pitahaya Carr. 3 Km 43, Arroyo, PR 00714 t) (787) 839-3465

La Milagrosa - Carr. 3 Bda. Marin, Arroyo, PR 00714 t) (787) 839-3465

San Jose - Sector Palmarejo, Carr. 3 Km 6 H3, Arroyo, PR 00714 t) (787) 839-3465

Ntra. Sra. de Fatima - Bo. Palmas Parcela 526, Arroyo, PR 00714 t) (787) 839-3465

San Martin - Sector Santa Clara, Carr. 3, Arroyo, PR 00714 t) (787) 839-3465

CASTANER

Nuestra Senora de la Medalla Milagrosa - Carr. 135 Km 4.3, Castaner, PR 00631; Mailing: P.O. Box 1006, Castaner, PR 00631 t) (939) 238-6047 lamilagrosacastaner@gmail.com Rev. Ramon J. Arellano Devia, Pst.; Angelica M. Lopez, CRE; Dcn. Wilfredo Torres Maldonado; Dcn. William Ramos Rivera; CRP Stds.: 22

Virgen de la Medalla Milagrosa - Bo. Bartolo, Lares, PR 00669; Mailing: Parroquia Nuestra Senora de la Medalla Milagrosa, Castaner, PR 00631 c) (939) 238-6047

La Virgen de Fatima - Bo. Mirasol, Castaner, PR 00669; Mailing: Parroquia Nuestra Senora de la Medalla Milagrosa, Castaner, PR 00631 c) (939) 238-6047

COAMO

San Antonio de Padua - 545 Carr. 14 Hec 2, Km 26, Bo. Los Llanos, Coamo, PR 00769; Mailing: P.O. Box 2227, Coamo, PR 00769 t) 787-803-4801 ps.antonio@hotmail.com Rev. Ferdinand Cruz Cruz, Pst.; Dimaraly Santiago Torres, CRE; CRP Stds.: 103

San Martin - Bo. Las Flores, Coamo, PR 00769 t) (787) 803-4801

Nuestra Senora de Lourdes - Bo. Rio Jueyes, Coamo, PR 00769 t) (787) 803-4801

San Blas de Illescas - 3 Calle Obispo Salamanca, Plaza Mayor, Coamo, PR 00769; Mailing: P.O. Box 196, Coamo, PR 00769 t) (787) 379-8711 psblas@hotmail.com Rev. Julio A. Rolon Torres, Pst.; Friar Silvestre Gomez Rueda, O.P., Par. Vicar; Dcn. Alfredo Rivera Cardona; Dcn. Angel R. Morales Colon; Dcn. Angel A. Negron Ortiz; Dcn. Jaime Ortiz Diaz; Nilda Violeta Espada, CRE; Benigno Colón, CRE; CRP Stds.: 297

Colegio Nuestra Senora de la Valvanera - (Grades PreK-12) 53 Calle Jose I. Quinton, Coamo, PR 00769; Mailing: Apartado 1903, Coamo, PR 00769 t) 787-825-1145 colegio-valvanerapr@hotmail.com Odaliz Torres Torres, Prin.; Stds.: 363; Pr. Tchrs.: 1; Lay Tchrs.: 27

Inmaculado Corazon de Maria - Bo. Palmarejo, Coamo, PR 00769

Cristo Rey - Bo. Pulguillas, Coamo, PR 00769

Nuestra Senora del Carmen - Bo. Hayales, Coamo, PR 00769

Virgen Milagrosa - Bo. Descalabrado, Coamo, PR 00769

Santa Catalina - Bo. Verdum, Coamo, PR 00769

Santiago Apostol - Bo. Cilantro, Coamo, PR 00769

Virgen Milagrosa - Bo. Pedro Garcia, Coamo, PR 00769

Santa Ana - Bo. Santa Ana, Coamo, PR 00769

San Diego - Bo. San Diego, Coamo, PR 00769

Sagrada Familia - Bo. Emanueli, Coamo, PR 00769

Nuestra Senora de la Providencia - Bo. Melendez, Coamo, PR 00769

Nuestra Senora de Fatima - Bo. Cuyon, Coamo, PR 00769

Sagrado Corazon - Bo. Coamo Arriba, Coamo, PR 00769

ENSENADA

Sagrado Corazon de Jesus - 19 Ave. Los Veteranos Principal, Ensenada, PR 00647; Mailing: P.O. Box 179, Ensenada, PR 00647 t) 787-821-2857 pscjesusensenada@gmail.com Rev. Eliud Aponte Rivera, Pst.; Dcn. Wallis S. Sanchez; Eduvigis Gonzalez, CRE; CRP Stds.: 30

Nuestra Senora de la Divina Providencia - Bo. Salinas Providencia, Ensenada, PR 00647 t) (787) 821-2857

Nuestra Senora de la Monserrate - Bo. Fuig, Ensenada, PR 00647 t) (787) 821-2857

Nuestra Senora del Rosario - Bo. Guaypao, Ensenada, PR 00647 t) (787) 821-2857

GUANICA

San Antonio Abad - 21 Calle San Miguel, Guanica, PR 00653; Mailing: P.O. Box 804, Guanica, PR 00653 t) 787-821-2147 santonioabadguanica@gmail.com Rev. Eliud Aponte Rivera, Pst.; Lillybette Cancel, CRE; CRP Stds.: 51

Cristo Rey - Bo. Belgica, Guanica, PR 00653 t) (787) 821-2147

Nuestra Senora del Rosario - Bo. Santa Juanita, Guanica, PR 00653 t) (787) 821-2147

San Judas - Bo. La Luna, Guanica, PR 00653 t) (787) 821-2147

Nuestra Senora de Fatima - Bo. Laguna, Guanica, PR 00653 t) (787) 821-2147

La Providencia - Bda. Esperanza, Guanica, PR 00653 t) (787) 821-2147

GUAYAMA

San Antonio de Padua - 5 Calle Parmel, Guayama, PR 00784; Mailing: P.O. Box 2820, Guayama, PR 00785-2820 t) 787-864-4100 sanantonioguayama@yahoo.com Rev. Hipolito Vicens Vicens, C.Ss.R., Pst.; Rev. Jose J. Rached Herrera, C.Ss.R., Supr.; Rev. Philip Patrick Andrews Neenan, C.Ss.R., Par. Vicar; Rev. Hector L. Colon Ferrer, C.Ss.R., Par. Vicar; Dcn. Francisco Carrasquillo Castro; Dcn. Genaro Rivera Alicea; Maria C. Arroyo, CRE; CRP Stds.: 415

Colegio Catolico San Antonio - (Grades K-12) Calle Vicente Palés # 3 Este, Guayama, PR 00784; Mailing: Apartado 2189, Guayama, PR 00785-2189 t) 787-864-2062 ccsaguayama@gmail.com www.ccsapr.org Dr. Jeffrey Quiñones Gonzalez, Dir.; Myrta Bermudez Reyes, Prin.; Stds.: 129; Lay Tchrs.: 21

Nuestra Senora del Perpetuo Socorro - Bo. Caimital, Guayama, PR 00784; Mailing: Parroquia San Antonio de Padua, P.O. Box 2820, Guayama, PR 00785-2820 t) (787) 864-4100

San Gerardo Mayela - Bo. Palmas, Guayama, PR 00784; Mailing: Parroquia San Antonio de Padua, P.O. Box 2820, Guayama, PR 00785-2820 t) (787) 864-4100

Nuestra Senora del Carmen - Bo. Pueblito del Carmen, Guayama, PR 00784; Mailing: Parroquia San Antonio de Padua, P.O Box 2820, Guayama, PR 00785-2820 t) (787) 864-4100

Cristo Rey - Bo. Olimpo, Guayama, PR 00784; Mailing: Parroquia San Antonio de Padua, P.O. Box 2820, Guayama, PR 00785-2820 t) (787) 864-4100

La Candelaria - Bo. Corazon, Guayama, PR 00784; Mailing: Parroquia San Antonio de Padua, P.O. Box 2820, Guayama, PR 00785-2820 t) (787) 864-4100

Sagrado Corazon de Jesus - Bo. Guamani, Guayama, PR 00784; Mailing: Parroquia San Antonio de Padua, P.O. Box 2820, Guayama, PR 00785-2820 t) (787) 864-4100

San Martin de Porres - Bo. Carite, Guayama, PR 00784; Mailing: Parroquia San Antonio de Padua, P.O. Box 2820, Guayama, PR 00785-2820 t) (787) 864-4100

San Jose Obrero - Bo. Branderi, Guayama, PR 00784; Mailing: Parroquia San Antonio de Padua, P.O. Box 2820, Guayama, PR 00785-2820 t) (787) 864-4100

Santos Apostoles Pedro y Pablo - Carr. # 3 Km. 150.0, Guayama, PR 00784; Mailing: P.O. Box 837, Guayama, PR 00785-0837 t) 787-866-1781 parroquiapedroypablo@yahoo.es Rev. Jesus Alberto Rangel Calderon, Pst.; Dcn. Rene Antonetty Giraud; Claribed Cruz Camacho, CRE; CRP Stds.: 40

GUAYANILLA

Inmaculada Concepcion - Calle Concepcion, Guayanilla, PR 00656; Mailing: P.O. Box 560573, Guayanilla, PR 00656-0573 t) 787-835-3035 inmaculada.guayanilla@gmail.com Rev. Melvin Diaz Aponte, Pst.; Rev. Adalin Rivera Saez, Par. Vicar; Dcn. Miguel A. Sepulveda Lopez; CRP Stds.: 63

Colegio Inmaculada Concepcion - (Grades PreK-12) 1 Calle Padre Napoleon Fruscoloni, Guayanilla, PR 00656; Mailing: Apartado 560573, Guayanilla, PR 00656-0573 t) 787-835-2230 cic_guayanilla@gmail.com Carmen A. Rodriguez Echevarria, Prin.; Stds.: 220; Pr. Tchrs.: 1; Lay Tchrs.: 18

Nuestra Senora del Carmen - Bo. Sierra Baja, Guayanilla, PR 00656; Mailing: P.O. Box 560573, Parroquia Inmaculada Concepcion, Guayanilla, PR 00656 t) (787) 835-3035

Perpetuo Socorro - Bo. Magas Arriba, Guayanilla, PR 00656; Mailing: Parroquia Inmaculada Concepcion, P.O. Box 560573, Guayanilla, PR 00656 t) (787) 835-3035

San Francisco de Asis - Bo. Quebradas, Guayanilla, PR 00656; Mailing; Parroquia Inmaculada Concepcion, P.O. Box 560573, Guayanilla, PR 00656 t) (787) 835-3035

San Juan Bosco - Bo. Indios, Guayanilla, PR 00656; Mailing: P.O. Box 560573, Parroquia Inmaculada Concepcion, Guayanilla, PR 00656 t) (787) 835-3035

La Monserrate - Bo. Consejo Alto, Guayanilla, PR 00656; Mailing: Parroquia Inmaculada Concepcion, P.O. Box 560573, Guayanilla, PR 00656 t) (787) 835-3035

Virgen de Fatima - Bo. Macana Rio, Guayanilla, PR 00656; Mailing: Parroquia Inmaculada Concepcion, P.O. Box 560573, Guayanilla, PR 00656 t) (787) 835-3035

Nuestra Senora La Milagrosa - Quebrada Honda, Guayanilla, PR 00656; Mailing: Parroquia Inmaculada Concepcion, P.O. Box 560573, Guayanilla, PR 00656 t) (787) 835-3035

San Martin de Porres - Bo. Macana Parcelas, Guayanilla, PR 00656; Mailing: Parroquia Inmaculada Concepcion, P.O. Box 560573, Guayanilla, PR 00656 t) (787) 835-3035

Nuestra Senora del Carmen - Bo. La Playa, Guayanilla, PR 00656; Mailing: Parroquia Inmaculada Concepcion, P.O. Box 560573,

Guayanilla, PR 00656-0573 t) (787) 835-3035

San Martin de Porres - Bo. Consejo Bajo, Guayanilla, PR 00656; Mailing: Parroquia Inmaculada Concepcion, P.O. Box 560573, Guayanilla, PR 00656 t) (787) 835-3035

San Jose - Bo. Jagua Tuna, Guayanilla, PR 00656; Mailing: Parroquia Inmaculada Concepcion, P.O. Box 560573, Guayanilla, PR 00656 t) (787) 835-3035

La Milagrosa - Bo. Verdun, Guayanilla, PR 00656; Mailing: Parroquia Inmaculada Concepcion, P.O. Box 560573, Guayanilla, PR 00656 t) (787) 835-3035

JAYUYA

Nuestra Senora de la Monserrate - 13 Calle Figueras, Jayuya, PR 00664 t) 787-828-6350 ntrasramonserratejayuya@hotmail.com Rev. Gerardo Ramirez Torres, Pst.; Rev. Jaime Silva González, Par. Vicar; Dcn. Dalvin Orama de Jesus; Dcn. Carlos Orama Torres; Dcn. Luis Rosario Colon; Dcn. Jose A. Perez Santos; Carmen D. Orama Burgos, CRE; CRP Stds.: 170

Cristo Rey - Bo. Collores, Jayuya, PR 00664; Mailing: 13 Calle Figueras, Nuestra Senora de la Monserrate, Jayuya, PR 00664 t) (787) 828-6350 parroquiajayuya@hotmail.com

San Jorge - Bo. Coabey, Jayuya, PR 00664; Mailing: 13 Calle Figueras, Nuestra Senora de la Monserrate, Jayuya, PR 00664 t) (787) 828-6350 parroquiajayuya@hotmail.com

La Milagrosa - Bo. Canalizo, Jayuya, PR 00664; Mailing: 13 Calle Figueras, Nuestra Senora de la Monserrate, Jayuya, PR 00664 t) (787) 828-6350 parroquiajayuya@hotmail.com

Buen Pastor - Bo. Gripinas, Jayuya, PR 00664; Mailing: 13 Calle Figueras, Nuestra Senora de la Monserrate, Jayuya, PR 00664 t) (787) 828-6350 parroquiajayuya@hotmail.com

Santa Cecilia - Bo. Zama, Jayuya, PR 00664; Mailing: 13 Calle Figueras, Nuestra Senora de la Monserrate, Jayuya, PR 00664 t) (787) 828-6350 parroquiajayuya@hotmail.com

Ntra. Sra. de la Divina Providencia - Bo. Hoyo Planes, Jayuya, PR 00664; Mailing: 13 Calle Figueras, Nuestra Senora de la Monserrate, Jayuya, PR 00664 t) (787) 828-6350 parroquiajayuya@hotmail.com

San Antonio de Padua - Bo. Mameyes, Jayuya, PR 00664; Mailing: 13 Calle Figueras, Nuestra Senora de la Monserrate, Jayuaya, PR 00664 t) (787) 828-6350 parroquiajayuya@hotmail.com

San Francisco - Bo. Saliente, Jayuya, PR 00664; Mailing: 13 Calle Figueras, Nuestra Senora de la Monserrate, Jayuaya, PR 00664 t) (787) 828-6350 parroquiajayuya@hotmail.com

San Juan Evangelista - Bo. Puerto Plata, Jayuya, PR 00664; Mailing: 13 Calle Figueras, Nuestra Senora de la Monserrate, Jayuya, PR 00664 t) (787) 828-6350 parroquiajayuya@hotmail.com

San Patricio - Bo. La Pica, Jayuya, PR 00664; Mailing: 13 Calle Figueras, Nuestra Senora de la Monserrate, Jayuya, PR 00664 t) (787) 828-6350 parroquiajayuya@hotmail.com

JUANA DIAZ

Nuestra Senora de Lourdes - 105 Calle del Parque, Bo. Aguilita, Juana Diaz, PR 00795; Mailing: P.O. Box 1824, Juana Diaz, PR 00795 t) 787-837-1097 vhernandez112475@gmail.com Rev. Victor Manuel Hernandez Velazquez, Pst.; Rosa A. Green, CRE; Dcn. Cirilo Carmona Cruz; Dcn. Jaime Velez; CRP Stds.: 99

San Pedro Nolasco - Bo. La cuarta, Juana Diaz, PR 00795 t) (787) 837-1097

San Ramon Nonato - Plaza Roman Baldorioty de Castro, Calle Munoz Rivera, Juana Diaz, PR 00795; Mailing: P.O. Box 1426, Juana Diaz, PR 00795 t) 787-412-8584; 787-412-8588 parroquiasanramonnonatus@gmail.com Rev. Pedro J. Guzman Quintana, Pst.; Rev. Juan Jose Saliva Gonzalez, Par. Vicar; Dcn. Orlando Pagan Figueroa; Dcn. William Santiago Figueroa; Dcn. Norberto Santiago Negron; Maria Isabel Martinez, CRE; CRP Stds.: 260

San Judas - Sector Rio Canas Abajo, Juana Diaz, PR 00795 t) (787) 412-8584

Ntra. Sra. de Fatima - Bo. Jacaguas, Juana Diaz, PR 00795 t) (787) 412-8584

La Milagrosa - Bo. Collores, Juana Diaz, PR 00795 t) (787) 412-8584

Santiago Apostol - Bo. Collores, Sector Las Margaritas, Juana Diaz, PR 00795 t) (787) 412-8584

Nuestra Senora del Rosario - Bo. Guayabal, Juana Diaz, PR 00795 t) (787) 412-8584 Rev. Pedro J. Guzman Quintana;

San Ramon - Bo. Cayabo, Juana Diaz, PR 00795 t) (787) 412-8584

La Merced - Bo. Rio Cana Arriba, Juana Diaz, PR 00795 t) (787) 412-8584

La Merced - Sector Cuatro Calles, Juana Diaz, PR 00795 t) (787) 412-8584

Santa Teresita del Nino Jesus - Carr. 1 Km 117.8, Juana Diaz, PR 00795; Mailing: P.O. Box 1620, Juana Diaz, PR 00795-1620 t) (787) 260-8940 santateresitajd@gmail.com Rev. Carmelo J. Serrano Figueroa, Admin.; Vivian Roche, CRE; Carmen Rodriguez, CRE; CRP Stds.: 41

San Martin de Porres - Bo. Singapur, Juana Diaz, PR 00795 (Singapur)

Divina Misericordia (Piedra Aguza) - Bo. Piedra Aguza, Juana Diaz, PR 00795

OROCOVIS

Nuestra Senora de la Divina Providencia - Bo. Cacao, Carr. 157 Km. 2.2, Orocovis, PR 00720; Mailing: HC 01 Box 3471, Villalba, PR 00766 t) 787-923-2516 divinaproproro19@yahoo.com Rev. Nicolas Perez Lopez (Nicaragua), Pst.; Elsa Rivera Rivera, CRE; CRP Stds.: 94

Nuestra Senora del Carmen - Bo. Alturita, Carr. 157, Orocovis, PR 00720 t) (787) 923-2516

Inmaculada Concepcion - Bo. Cacao Hacienda, Carr. 157, Orocovis, PR 00766 t) (787) 923-2516

Nino Jesus de Praga - Bo. El Frio, Carr. 143, Orocovis, PR 00720 t) (787) 923-2516

Nuestra Senora del Rosario - Bo. Bauta, Carr. 590, Orocovis, PR 00720 t) (787) 923-2516 divinaproro19@yahoo.com

Nuestra Senora del Pilar - Bo. Damian Abajo, Carr. 157, Orocovis, PR 00720 t) (787) 923-2516 divinaproro19@yahoo.com

Nuestra Senora de la Monserrate - Bo. Pozas de Ciales, Carr. 615, Orocovis, PR 00720 t) (787) 923-2516

Nuestra Senora del Perpetuo Socorro - Bo. Ala de la Piedra, Carr. 149, Orocovis, PR 00720 t) (787) 923-2516

PATILLAS

Inmaculado Corazon de Maria - 1 Calle Cristo, Patillas, PR 00723; Mailing: P.O. Box 635, Patillas, PR 00723 t) 787-839-5333 parroquia_patillas@yahoo.com Rev. Francisco Santiago Torres, Pst.; Rev. George Antonio Torres Santos, Par. Vicar; Dcn. Ruben Pabon Gonzalez; Dcn. Hector Luis Pagan Morales; Dcn. Juan Francisco Rodriguez Rivera; Rosaura Cruz, CRE; Maria del C de Leon, CRE; CRP Stds.: 233

Perpetuo Socorro - Bo. Marin Alto, Patillas, PR 00723 t) (787) 839-5333

Nuestra Senora de la Candelaria - Bo. Guardarraya, Patillas, PR 00723 t) (787) 839-5333

Santo Cristo de la Salud - Bo. Guardarraya, Patillas, PR 00723 t) (787) 839-5333

Nuestra Senora del Carmen - Bo. Jacaboa, Patillas, PR 00723 t) (787) 839-5333

Cristo Rey - Bo. El Bajo, Patillas, PR 00723 t) (787) 839-5333

Ntra. Sra. de la Providencia - Bo. Providencia, Patillas, PR 00723 t) (787) 839-5333

Santa Rosa de Lima - Bo. Los Pollos, Patillas, PR 00723 t) (787) 839-5333

San Juan Evangelista - Bo. Marin Bajo, Patillas, PR 00723 t) (787) 839-5333

San Guillermo - Bo. El Real, Patillas, PR 00723 t) (787) 839-5333

Nuestra Senora del Carmen - Bo. Jagual, Patillas, PR 00723 t) (787) 839-5333

PENUELAS

Sagrado Corazon de Jesus - Bo. Tallaboa Encarnacion, Carr. 127 Sector El Pueblito, Penuelas, PR 00624; Mailing: HC 03 Box 13063, Penuelas, PR 00624 t) 787-836-1164 parroquiatallaboa@gmail.com Rev. Segismundo Cintron Orengo, Pst.; Ruth N. Montalvo, CRE; CRP Stds.: 44

Inmaculado Corazon de Maria - Bo. Tallaboa Poniente, Sector Juncos, Penuelas, PR 00624 t) (787) 836-1164

San Jose - 603 Calle Doctor Loyola, Penuelas, PR 00624; Mailing: P.O. Box 25, Penuelas, PR 00624 t) 787-836-0167 parroquiasanjose1038@gmail.com Rev. Manuel E. Salgado Benitez, O.SS.T., Admin.; Dcn. Jose E. Gelpi Ortiz; Dcn. Joaquin Massoller Santiago; Dcn. Glidden Perez Diaz; Dcn. Jose Torres Santiago; Coralys Garcia, CRE; CRP Stds.: 77

La Milagrosa - Bo. El Rucio, Carr. #132 R 391 Km 5 Sect. Pueblito, Penuelas, PR 00624 t) 787-836-1038

San Antonio de Padua - Bo. El Alto, Carr. #132 K-16 H 9, Bo. El Alto - Penuelas, PR 00624 t) 787-836-1038

Ntra. Sra. de Fatima - Bo. Macana, Carr. #131 Km 5 Sect. La Vega, Penuelas, PR 00624 t) 787-836-1038

Santa Ana - Bo. Tallaboa Alta, Carr. #132 Km 14.7, Penuelas, PR 00624 t) 787-836-1038

Santa Cruz - Sect. Felipe Quinones Barreal, Carr. #132 Rte. 386 Km 6 H-7, Penuelas, PR 00624 t) 787-836-1038

Ntra. Sra. del Carmen - Bo. Santo Domingo, Carr. #132 Km 7 H 9, Penuelas, PR 00624 t) 787-836-1038

San Judas Tadeo - Bo. Coto el Mato, Carr. #132, Penuelas, PR 00624 t) 787-836-1038

San Martin de Porres - 996 Comunidad Caracoles III, Penuelas, PR 00624 t) 787-836-1038

Divino Nino - Bo. Tallaboa Alta III, Penuelas, PR 00624 t) 787-836-1038

PONCE

Catedral Nuestra Senora de Guadalupe - Plaza las Delicias, Calle Unión, Ponce, PR 00730; Mailing: P.O. Box 32210, Ponce, PR 00732-2210 t) 787-507-0134 poncecatedral@gmail.com Wanda M. Quiñones, CRE; Rev. Gilberto Rodriguez Ferra, Admin.; Dcn. Carlos Juan Rodriguez Sanchez; CRP Stds.: 45

Nuestra Senora de la Medalla Milagrosa - Bo. Tibes, Sector Jácanas, Ponce, PR 00731 t) (787) 507-0134

Maria Inmaculada - Bo. Tibes, Sector Pastillo, Ponce, PR 00731 t) (787) 507-0134

Corazon de Jesus - Bo. Sabanetas, Ponce, PR 00716; Mailing: P.O. Box 577, Mercedita, PR 00715-0577 t) 787-298-4524 corazondejesusponce@gmail.com Rev. Msgr. Roberto Garcia Blay, Pst.; Dcn. Rafael Castro Belen; Dcn. Reinaldo Rivera; Juanita de la Torre, CRE; CRP Stds.: 76

Cristo Rey - Urb. La Rambla, 2933 Calle Valladolid, Ponce, PR 00730-4011 t) 787-843-3028 cristoreyponce2933@hotmail.com Rev. Jose Antonio Lopez Vega, Pst.; Dcn. Juan Altori Vargas; Dcn. Eduardo A. Dosal Lines; Dcn. Jose Plaud Medina; Dcn. Manuel Roman Perez; Dcn. Anibal Rosario Rodriguez; Maria Enid Gonzalez, CRE; CRP Stds.: 61

Santa Teresita - Urb. Santa Teresita, Calle Santa Luisa, Ponce, PR 00730; Mailing: Urb. La Rambla, 2933 Calle Valladolid, Ponce, PR 00730-4011 t) (787) 843-3028

Nino Jesus de Praga - Bo. Rio Chiquito, Ponce, PR 00730; Mailing: Urb. La Rambla, 2933 Calle Valladolid, Ponce, PR 00730-4011 t) (787) 843-3028

El Buen Pastor - Urb. Jardines del Caribe, Calle 40-NN25, Ponce, PR 00728-2675; Mailing: P.O. Box 7612, Ponce, PR 00732-7612 t) 787-843-6202 pastorbonuspr@gmail.com Rev. José Carlos Vargas Oliveras, Pst.; Dcn. Edgardo Muniz Rivera; Dcn. Rafael D. Ruiz Irizarry; Jocelyn Collazo, CRE; CRP Stds.: 62

La Milagrosa - Bo. Quebrado del Agua, Calle 5 #69, Ponce, PR 00731 t) (787) 843-6202 Rev. Jose Carlos Vargas Oliveras, Pst.;

La Resurreccion - Urb. Glenview Gardens, E-9 Final, Ponce, PR 00730; Mailing: PMB-98, P.O. Box 780, Mercedita, PR 00715 t) 787-842-7167 p.laresurreccion@outlook.com Rev. Winston R. Mendez Silvagnoli, Pst.; Rev. Sergio Alfonso Larios Martinez, O.SS.T., Par. Vicar; Dcn. Jose A. Rosario Colon; Marilyn Maldonado, CRE; CRP Stds.: 62

Inmaculado Corazon de Maria - Bo. La Yuca, Ponce, PR 00730; Mailing: Parroquia La Resurreccion, PMB 98 P.O. Box 780, Mercedita, PR 00715 t) (787) 842-7167

Nuestra Senora de la Monserrate - Bo. El Collado, Ponce, PR 00730; Mailing: Parroquia La Resurreccion, PMB 98 P.O. Box 780, Ponce, PR 00715 t) (787) 842-7167

San Lucas - Bo. Las Vallas, Ponce, PR 00730; Mailing: Parroquia La Resurreccion, PMB 98 P.O. Box 780, Mercedita, PR 00715 t) (787) 842-7167

San Jose - Bo. El Paraiso, Ponce, PR 00730; Mailing: PMB 98 P.O. Box 780, Parroquia La Resurreccion, Mercedita, PR 00715 t) (787) 842-7167

Nuestra Senora del Carmen - Bo. Carmelita, Ponce, PR 00730; Mailing: Parroquia La Resurreccion, PMB 98 P.O. Box 780, Mercedita, PR 00715 t) (787) 842-7167

Nuestra Senora de la Medalla Milagrosa - 2 Calle Guadalupe, Ponce, PR 00730-3110 t) 787-842-3188 parmilagrosa@gmail.com Rev. Socrate Laupe Dorvil, C.M. (Haiti), Pst.; Rev. Gregoire Joseph, C.M. (Haiti), Par. Vicar; Dcn. Carlos Juan Ramos Torres; Dcn. Hector Luis Santiago; Dcn. Ramon L. Vazquez; Mirna Martinez, CRE; CRP Stds.: 212

Colegio La Milagrosa - (Grades PreK-12) 9 Calle Guadalupe, Ponce, PR 00730 t) 787-842-6349 lamilagrosaponce@gmail.com Liz Marie Santiago Rivera, Prin.; Stds.: 417; Pr. Tchrs.: 2; Lay Tchrs.: 25

Nuestra Senora de la Merced - 4632 Calle Luna, Ponce, PR 00717-2000; Mailing: P.O. Box 32216, Ponce, PR 00732-2216 t) 787-842-0069 parroquialamerced@gmail.com Rev. Ovidio Perez Perez, Pst.; Dcn. Emerito Lopez Cosme; CRP Stds.: 37

Nuestra Senora del Carmen - 12 Ave. Padre Noel, Ponce, PR 00716 t) 787-842-5018 pdelcarmenplayaponce@gmail.com Rev. Salvador Salgado Pabón, cmf, Pst.; Rev. Luis Enrique Ortiz Alvarez, cmf, Par. Vicar; Rev. Jose Vicente Martinez Santos Gallego, cmf, Par. Vicar; Dcn. Jose Rivera Saez; Damaris Rosado, CRE; CRP Stds.: 50

San Martin de Porres - Constancia Ave., Ponce, PR 00716; Mailing: Parroquia Nuestra Senora del Carmen, P.O. Box 7760, Ponce, PR 00732-7760 t) (787) 842-5018

Santa Marta - Bo. Salistral, c/o Santa Marta #8, Ponce, PR 00732; Mailing: Parroquia Nuestra Senora del Carmen, P.O. Box 7760, Ponce, PR 00732-7760 t) (787) 842-5018

Nuestra Senora del Carmen - Carr. 14, Ponce, PR 00780; Mailing: P.O. Box 800187, Coto Laurel, PR 00780-0187 t) 787-848-2030 parr.virgendelcarmen@gmail.com Rev. Manuel A. Santiago Hernandez, Pst.; Dcn. Luis Arnaldo Lopez Quirindongo; Carmen Rivera Perez, CRE; CRP Stds.: 95

Santa Maria Virgen - Bo. Hoyos, Ponce, PR 00780; Mailing: Parroquia Nuestra Senora del Carmen, P.O. Box 800187, Coto Laurel, PR 00780-0187 t) (787) 848-2030

Sagrado Corazon de Jesus - Bo. Las Raices, Carr. 511 K. 15, Ponce, PR 00780; Mailing: Parroquia Nuestra Senora del Carmen, P.O. Box 800187, Coto Laurel, PR 00780-0187 t) (787) 848-2030

San Mateo - Bo. Real Anon Abajo, Ponce, PR 00780; Mailing: Parroquia Nuestra Senora del Carmen, P.O. Box 800187, Coto Laurel, PR 00780-0187 t) (787) 848-2030

San Martin de Porres - Bo. Real Anon Arriba, Ponce, PR 00780; Mailing: Parroquia Nuestra Senora del Carmen, P.O. Box 800187, Coto Laurel, PR 00780-0187 t) (787) 848-2030

Parroquia San Judas Tadeo - Urb. Constancia, 2518 Calle Conquista, Ponce, PR 00717-2223; Mailing: P.O. Box 7046, Ponce, PR 00732-7046 t) 787-843-0572 psjudasponce@hotmail.com Rev. Pabel Amaury Alba Hernandez, O. de M., Pst.; Rev. Angel Cuadrado Calvo, O.de.M., Par. Vicar; Rev. Javier Errecalde Conte, O. de M.; Dcn. Antonio Victor Fabre Torres; Emma Baez Lopez, CRE; CRP Stds.: 31

Colegio Mercedario San Judas Tadeo - (Grades PreK-12) Urb. Constancia, 2518 Calle Eureka, Ponce, PR 00717 t) 787-844-2610 colmer@colegiosanjudastadeo.org Carmen Mendez Rios, Dir.; Edwin Rivas Cartagena, Prin.; Rev. Pabel Alba Hernandez, O. de M., Spiritual Director; Stds.: 614; Lay Tchrs.: 41

San Conrado - 3167 Ave. Roosevelt, Ponce, PR 00717; Mailing: P.O. Box 7362, Ponce, PR 00732 t) 787-843-0560 psconrado@gmail.com Rev. Javier Vega Graniela, Admin.; Rev. Msgr. Juan Rodriguez Orengo, Pst.; Carmen Noemi Gonzalez, CRE; CRP Stds.: 27

Colegio San Conrado - (Grades PreK-12) 3167 Ave. Franklin Roosevelt, Ponce, PR 00717-0268; Mailing: PO Box 7111, Ponce, PR 00732 t) 787-843-1405; 787-842-2293 superior@colegiosanconrado.com; biblioteca@colegiosanconrado.com Sr. Nildred Rodriguez, C.S.J., Prin.; Stds.: 276; Pr. Tchrs.: 1; Sr. Tchrs.: 1; Lay Tchrs.: 19

San Jose - Urb. San Jose, 416 Calle Beato Francisco Palau, Ponce, PR 00728; Mailing: P.O. Box 8414, Ponce, PR 00732 t) 787-437-0126 psanjoseponce@gmail.com Rev. Msgr. Juan Rodriguez Orengo, Pst.; Dcn. Benjamin Pagan Diaz; Dcn. David Rodriguez Rivera; Leonor Morales, CRE; Maria V. Castro, CRE; CRP Stds.: 36

San Jose Obrero - Parcelas El Tuque, 632 Calle Ernesto Ramos Antonini, Ponce, PR 00728; Mailing: P.O. Box 8027, Ponce, PR 00732-8027 t) 787-843-9072 psjoseobrero@yahoo.com Rev. Jose Diego Rodriguez Martino, Pst.; Dcn. Vicente Aponte Arroyo; Nelly Y. Feliciano, CRE; CRP Stds.: 45

Ntra. Sra. del Pilar - Urb. Punto Oro, 616 M #7, Ponce, PR 00728; Mailing: Parroquia San Jose Obrero, P.O. Box 8027, Ponce, PR 00732 t) (787) 843-9072

Cristo de la Misericordia - Nueva Vida, Calle J D-9, Ponce, PR 00728; Mailing: Parroquia San Jose Obrero, P.O. Box 8027, Ponce, PR 00732 t) (787) 843-9072; (787) 843-9072

Inmaculado Corazon de Maria - Brisas del Caribe, Calle Lorencita Ferre, Ponce, PR 00728; Mailing: Parroquia San Jose Obrero, P.O. Box 8027, Ponce, PR 00732 t) (787) 843-9072

Ntra. Sra. de la Medalla Milagrosa - Punta Diamante, Ponce, PR 00728 t) (787) 843-9072 (Encargada - Hermanas Dominicas de Fatima)

San Vicente de Paul - 67 Paseo La Cantera, Ponce, PR 00730-3026 t) 787-843-1976 parroquiasanvicentedepaulponce@gmail.com Rev. Athas S. Emile Dormil, C.M., Pst.; Dcn. Jorge Almodovar Capielo; Modesta Guzman, CRE; CRP Stds.: 22

San Vicente - Bo. Rio Chiquito, Ponce, PR 00730; Mailing: 67 Paseo La Cantera, San Vicente de Paul, Ponce, PR 00730-3026 t) (787) 843-1976

Santos Reyes - Bo. La Mocha, Ponce, PR 00730; Mailing: 67 Paseo La Cantera, San Vicente de Paul, Ponce, PR 00730 t) (787) 843-1976

Santa Luisa - Bo. Nuevo Mameyes, Ponce, PR 00730; Mailing: 67 Paseo La Cantera, San Vicente de Paul, Ponce, PR 00730-3026 t) (787) 843-1976

La Inmaculada - Sector San Patricio, Ponce, PR 00730; Mailing: Parroquia San Vicente de Paul, Ponce, PR 00730-3026 t) (787) 843-1976

Santa Maria Reina - 1290 Ave. Munoz Rivera, Ponce, PR 00717; Mailing: P.O. Box 32101, Ponce, PR 00732-2101 t) 787-848-3313 santamariareinaponce@gmail.com Rev. Carlos A. Collazo Santiago, Pst.; Dcn. David Ramos Torres; Dcn. Jaime Martinez Addarich Martinez Addarich; Dcn. Angel R. Mendez Molina; Rebecca E. Roman Morales, CRE; CRP Stds.: 14

Academia Santa Maria Reina - (Grades PreK-12) Calle Interior Reparto Universitario, Ponce, PR 00732; Mailing: P.O. Box 32225, Ponce, PR 00732-2225 t) 787-842-1164 directorescolarasmr@gmail.com; principal@asmrpr.com Juan M. Colón Rodriguez, Prin.; Stds.: 310; Pr. Tchrs.: 1; Lay Tchrs.: 22

Santa Teresita del Nino Jesus - 342 Calle Victoria, Ponce, PR 00730; Mailing: PO Box 7244, Ponce, PR 00732-7244 t) 787-842-3137 pstponce@gmail.com Rev. Ramón Jaime Casellas Rivera, O.F.M. Cap., Pst.; Rev. Roberto Martinez Rivera, OFM Cap, Guardian; Dcn. Ildefonso Gonzalez Plaza; Dcn. Casildo Rodriguez; Zaida C. Velez Ayala, CRE; CRP Stds.: 30

Santisima Trinidad - 985 Ave. Ponce de Leon, Urb. Las Delicias I, Ponce, PR 00728; Mailing: P.O. Box 8226, Ponce, PR 00732-8226 t) 787-842-6073 psantisimatrinidadponce@outlook.com Rev. Carlos Alonso Torres Hernandez, O.SS.T., Pst.; Rev. Oscar Alexander Chacon Gonzalez, O.SS.T., Par. Vicar; Dcn. Jose Rodriguez Mendez; Dcn. Francisco Lugo Santiago; Dcn. Nestor Rentas; Brunilda Sierra, CRE; CRP Stds.: 126

San Juan de Mata - Bo. Magueyes, Ponce, PR 00728 t) (787) 842-6073

San Andres - Bo. Guaraguao, Ponce, PR 00732 t) (787) 842-6073

Santa Ana - Bo. Guaraguao Arriba, Ponce, PR 00732 t) (787) 842-6073

Ntra. Sra. Fatima - Bo. Marueno, Sector Jaguas, Ponce, PR 00732 t) (787) 842-6073

San Antonio de Padua - Parcelas de Marueno, Ponce, PR 00732 t) (787) 842-6073

Ntra. Sra. del Rosario - El Madrigal, Ponce, PR 00730 t) (787) 842-6073

Inmaculada - Bo. Pastillo, Ponce, PR 00732 t) (787) 842-6073

Cristo Rey - Bo. Corral Viejo, Ponce, PR 00732 t) (787) 842-6073

San Miguel de los Santos - Urb. Las Delicias, Ponce, PR 00728 t) (787) 842-6073

Santisimo Sacramento - Urb. Vista del Mar, 2238 Calle Marlin, Ponce, PR 00716-0834; Mailing: P.O. Box 32212, Ponce, PR 00732 t) 787-843-0245 santisimosacramentoponce@gmail.com Rev. Orlando Lugo Perez, Pst.; Ady Colon Diaz, CRE; CRP Stds.: 78

SALINAS

Nuestra Senora de la Monserrate - 3 Calle Miguel Ten, Salinas, PR 00751; Mailing: P.O. Box 1172, Salinas, PR 00751 t) 787-824-2215 parroquia_salinas@yahoo.com Rev. Carlos Manuel Grullon Capellan, Pst.; Rev. Samuel Santiago De Jesus, Par. Vicar; Dcn. Jose Luis Rodriguez Collazo; Dcn. Jose Francisco Martinez Munoz; Jenny Antonnetty, CRE; CRP Stds.: 151

San Jose - Bo. Plena, Salinas, PR 00751 t) (787) 824-2215

Santa Ana - Bo. Coco, Salinas, PR 00751 t) (787) 824-2215

Espiritu Santo - Parcelas Vazquez, Salinas, PR 00751 t) (787) 824-2215

Virgen del Carmen - Bo. Las Palmas, Salinas, PR 00751 t) (787) 824-2215

Santa Marta - Bo. Naranjo, Salinas, PR 00751 t) (787) 824-2215

Inmaculada Concepcion - Bo. Las Ochenta, Salinas, PR 00751 t) (787) 824-2215

Virgen Milagrosa - Bo. Playita, Salinas, PR 00751 t) (787) 824-2215

Virgen del Carmen - Bo. Playa, Salinas, PR 00751 t) (787) 824-2215

Perpetuo Socorro - Bo. Sabana Llana, Salinas, PR 00751 t) (787) 824-2215

SANTA ISABEL

Parroquia Santiago Apostol - 2 Calle Hostos, Santa Isabel, PR 00757; Mailing: P.O. Box 137, Santa Isabel, PR 00757 t) 787-845-2450 parroquiasantiagoapostol2017@outlook.com; angel4225@hotmail.com Rev. Angel M. Sanchez

Hernandez, Pst.; Dcn. Jose Manuel Rivera Colon; Karimarie Diaz Rentas, CRE; Shirly Ortiz Zayas, CRE; CRP Stds.: 137

San Patricio - Bo. Playita Cortada, Santa Isabel, PR 00757 t) (787) 845-2450

Virgen del Rosario - Bo. Penuelas, Santa Isabel, PR 00757 t) (787) 845-2450

Virgen del Perpetuo Socorro - Bo. Paso Seco, Santa Isabel, PR 00757 t) (787) 845-2450

Nuestra Senora de la Monserrate - Bo. Ollas, Santa Isabel, PR 00757 t) (787) 845-2450

San Ignacio de Loyola - Bo. Jauca, Santa Isabel, PR 00757 t) (787) 845-2450

Ntra. Sra. del Carmen - Bo. Playa, Santa Isabel, PR 00757 t) (787) 845-2450

VILLALBA

Nuestra Senora del Carmen - Calle Munoz Rivera, Villalba, PR 00766; Mailing: P.O. Box 432, Villalba, PR 00766 t) 787-847-0695 parroquianscarmenvillalba@gmail.com Rev. Jose Rafael Alvarado De Jesus, Pst.; Rev. Pedro Faustino Echeverria Murillo, Par. Vicar; Rev. Alberto Melendez Vazquez, Par. Vicar; Dcn. Jaime Luis Rivera Rivera; Dcn. Javier Gonzalez Rosado; Dcn. Jose A. Pagan Rivera; Lucy Gonzalez, CRE; Esther Ocasio, CRE; CRP Stds.: 570

Colegio Nuestra Senora del Carmen - (Grades PreK-8) #1 Calle Walter Mc Jones, Villalba, PR 00766; Mailing: PO Box 1033, Villalba, PR 00766 t) 787-847-2875 colegiodevillalba@gmail.com Maria E. Maldonado Maldonado, Prin.; Rev. Jose Rafael Alvarado de Jesus, Dir.; Yomari Barrios, Pastoral Coordinator; Stds.: 192; Pr. Tchrs.: 1; Lay Tchrs.: 17

Sagrado Corazon - Bo. Romero, Villalba, PR 00766; Mailing: Parroquia Nuestra Senora del Carmen, P.O. Box 432, Villalba, PR 00766-0432 t) (787) 847-0695 Rev. Jose Rafael Alvarado de Jesus, Pst.;

Nuestra Senora del Carmen - Bo. Vista Alegre, Carr. 151 Km 3.3, Villalba, PR 00766; Mailing: Parroquia Nuestra Senora del Carmen, P.O. Box 432, Villalba, PR 00766 t) (787) 847-0695 Rev. Jose Rafael Alvarado de Jesus, Pst.;

Santisima Trinidad - Bo. Mogote, Villalba, PR 00766 t) (787) 847-0695 Rev. Jose Rafael Alvarado de Jesus, Pst.;

Espiritu Santo - Bo. Cerro Gordo, Villalba, PR 00766; Mailing: Parroquia Nuestra Senora del Carmen, P.O. Box 432, Villalba, PR 00766 t) (787) 847-0695 Rev. Jose Rafael Alvarado de Jesus, Pst.;

La Milagrosa - Jagueyes Arriba, Carr. 149 R 513 Km 1.7, Villalba, PR 00766; Mailing: Parroquia Nuestra Senora del Carmen, P.O. Box 432, Villalba, PR 00766 t) (787) 847-0695 Rev. Jose Rafael Alvarado de Jesus, Pst.;

San Pedro - Bo. Corillo, Villalba, PR 00766; Mailing: Parroquia Nuestra Senora del Carmen, P.O. Box 432, Villalba, PR 00766 t) (787) 847-0695 Rev. Jose Rafael Alvarado de Jesus, Pst.;

San Pablo - Bo. Palmarejo, Carr. 149 Km. 46.6, Villalba, PR 00766; Mailing: Parroquia Nuestra Senora del Carmen, P.O. Box 432, Villalba, PR 00766 t) (787) 847-0695 Rev. Jose Rafael Alvarado de Jesus;

Santisimo Sacramento - Bo. Higuero, Villalba, PR 00766; Mailing: Parroquia Nuestra Senora del Carmen, P.O. Box 432, Villalba, PR 00766 t) (787) 847-0695 Rev. Jose Rafael Alvarado de Jesus, Pst.;

Jesus Crucificado - Bo. Camarones Arriba, Villalba, PR 00766; Mailing: Parroquia Nuestra Senora del Carmen, P.O. Box 432, Villalba, PR 00766 t) (787) 847-0695 Rev. Jose Rafael Alvarado de Jesus, Pst.;

Cristo de la Salud - Bo. Sierrita Caonillas, Villalba, PR 00766; Mailing: Parroquia Nuestra Senora del Carmen, P.O. Box 432, Villalba, PR 00766 t) (787) 847-0695 Rev. Jose Rafael Alvarado de Jesus, Pst.;

Santa Cecilia - Bo. El Semil, Villalba, PR 00766; Mailing: Parroquia Nuestra Senora del Carmen, P.O. Box 432, Villalba, PR 00766 t) (787) 847-0695 Rev. Jose Rafael Alvarado de Jesus;

La Providencia - Carr. 150 Parc. 33, Bo. Hatillo, PR 00766; Mailing: Parroquia Nuestra Senora del carmen, P.O. Box 432, Villalba, PR 00766 t) (787) 847-0695 Rev. Jose Rafael Alvarado de Jesus, Pst.;

San Antonio - Bo. Camarones, Villalba, PR 00766; Mailing: Parroquia Nuestra Senora del Carmen, P.O. Box 432, Villalba, PR 00766 t) (787) 847-0695 Rev. Jose Rafael Alvarado de Jesus, Pst.;

Vigen Dolorosa - Bo. El Limon, Carr. 151 Km. 8.3, Villalba, PR 00766; Mailing: Parroquia Nuestra Senora del Carmen, P.O. Box 432, Villalba, PR 00766 t) (787) 847-0695 Rev. Jose Rafael Alvarado de Jesus;

Ntra. Sra. del Carmen - Bo. Dajaos, Carr. 151 R 559 Km. 2.0, Villalba, PR 00766; Mailing: Parroquia Nuestra Senora del Carmen, P.O. Box 432, Villalba, PR 00766 t) (787) 847-0695 Rev. Jose Rafael Alvarado de Jesus, Pst.;

San Francisco de Asis - Bo. La Sierrita de Vacas, Villalba, PR 00766; Mailing: Parroquia Nuestra Senora del Carmen, P.O. Box 432, Villalba, PR 00766 t) (787) 847-0695 Rev. Jose Rafael Alvarado de Jesus, Pst.;

La Milagrosa - Bo. El Pino, Villalba, PR 00766; Mailing: Parroquia Nuestra Senora del Carmen, P.O. Box 432, Villalba, PR 00766 t) 787-847-0691

San Juan Evangelista - Bo. Aceituna Chichon, Villalba, PR 00766; Mailing: Parroquia Nuestra Senora del Carmen, P.O. Box 432, Villalba, PR 00766 t) (787) 847-0695 Rev. Jose Rafael Alvarado de Jesus, Pst.;

YAUCO

Nuestra Senora del Rosario - 11 Calle Comercio, Yauco, PR 00698; Mailing: Parroquia Nuestra Senora del Rosario, P.O. Box 46, Yauco, PR 00698 t) 787-856-1222 rosariodm014@gmail.com Rev. Rafael Gonzalez Padro, O.P., Admin.; Dcn. Carlos Alberto Rodriguez Villanueva, O.P.; Dcn. David Fuentes Rivera; Dcn. Luis M. Jusino Cintron; Dcn. Ramon Santiago Ortiz; Dcn. Jesus Vazquez Orengo; Maria Colón, CRE; CRP Stds.: 222

Colegio Santisimo Rosario - (Grades PreK-12) Calle Dr. A. Gatel #15, Yauco, PR 00698; Mailing: P.O. Box 26, Yauco, PR 00698 t) 787-856-1001 santisimorosariodeyauco@gmail.com Elaine Vega, Prin.; Stds.: 188; Pr. Tchrs.: 1; Lay Tchrs.: 20

Nuestra Senora del Carmen - Bo. Duey, Yauco, PR 00698 t) (787) 856-1222

Santiago Apostol - Bo. Barinas, Yauco, PR 00698 t) (787) 856-1222

Nuestra Senora del Perpetuo Socorro - Bo. Cambalache, Yauco, PR 00698 t) (787) 856-1222

Nuestra Senora de la Monserrate - Bo. Carrizales, Yauco, PR 00698 t) (787) 856-1222

Santa Lucia - Bo. Sierra Alta, Yauco, PR 00698 t) (787) 856-1222

San Antonio - Bo. Naranjo, Yauco, PR 00698 t) (787) 856-1222

San Antonio de Padua - Bo. Diego Hernandez, Yauco, PR 00698 t) (787) 856-1222

Sagrado Corazon de Jesus - Bo. Quebradas, Yauco, PR 00698 t) (787) 856-1222

La Milagrosa - Bo. Mogotes, Yauco, PR 00698 t) (787) 856-1222

San Vicente de Paul y San Alvaro de Cordoba - Bo. Jacana, Yauco, PR 00698 t) (787) 856-1222

San Martin de Porres - Barrio Las Palomas, 9 Calle 1, Yauco, PR 00698; Mailing: Parroquia San Martin de Porres, P.O. Box 2005, Yauco, PR 00698 t) 787-856-7905 parroquiasanmartin2019@gmail.com Rev. Raymond L. Rivera Sepulveda, Pst.; Elizabeth Santiago Morales, CRE; CRP Stds.: 11

Nuestra Senora de la Providencia - Bo. Las Joyas, Yauco, PR 00698 t) 787-856-7403

San Francisco de Asis - Bo. Magueyes, Yauco, PR 00698 t) (787) 856-7403

Santo Domingo de Guzman - Urb. Costa Sur, Calle Padre Alfredo Varina, Yauco, PR 00698; Mailing: Parroquia Santo Domingo de Guzman, P.O. Box 3036, Yauco, PR 00698-3036 t) 787-856-8212 psdomingoyauco@gmail.com Rev. Victor Rene Sanchez Muniz, Pst.; Dcn. Reinaldo Sanchez Caraballo; Nydia Perez Figueroa, CRE; CRP Stds.: 150

Sagrado Corazon - Bo. Collores, Yauco, PR 00698 t) (787) 856-8212 Rev. Victor Rene Sanchez Muniz;

Santa Teresita - Bo. Las Vegas, Yauco, PR 00698 t) (787) 856-8212 Rev. Victor Rene Sanchez Muniz;

San Jose - Bo. Lluberas, Yauco, PR 00698 t) (787) 856-8212 Rev. Victor Rene Sanchez Muniz;

Nuestra Senora de Fatima - Bo. Algarrobos, Yauco, PR 00698 t) (787) 856-8212 Rev. Victor Rene Sanchez Muniz;

San Martin de Porres - Bo. Almacigo Bajo, Yauco, PR 00698 t) (787) 856-8212 Rev. Victor Rene Sanchez Muniz;

San Juan Macias - Bo. Almacigo Alto, Yauco, PR 00698 t) (787) 856-8212 Rev. Victor Rene Sanchez Muniz;

Nuestra Senora de la Monserrate - Bo. Rio Loco, Yauco, PR 00698 t) (787) 856-8212 Rev. Victor Rene Sanchez Muniz;

Santa Rosa de Lima - Bo. El Cafetal, Yauco, PR 00698 t) (787) 856-8212 Rev. Victor Rene Sanchez Muniz, Pst.;

SCHOOLS: PRESCHOOL THRU HIGH SCHOOL

SCHOOLS

COMMONWEALTH OF PUERTO RICO

PONCE

Academia Cristo Rey Inc. - (PRV) (Grades PreK-12) Urb. La Rambla, 3011 Calle San Judas, Ponce, PR 00730-4091; Mailing: Ave. Tito Castro 609, Ste. 102 PMB 361, Ponce, PR 00716-3222 t) 787-843-0766; (787) 219-5505 principal@academiacristorey.net Gicela Bonilla Rodriguez, Prin.; Kim Fausto Ramos, Principal Assistant; Rev. Jose Antonio Lopez Vega, Spiritual Director; Felicita Torres Vargas, Pastoral Coordinator; Stds.: 662; Sr. Tchrs.: 1; Lay Tchrs.: 43

Centro San Francisco - (PRV) (Grades PreK-12) Bo. Tamarindo, 105 Calle Tamal, Ponce, PR 00732; Mailing: PO Box 10479, Ponce, PR 00732 t) 787-987-8001; (787) 913-1928 centrosanfrancisco@gmail.com Dr. Sonia Pagan Figueroa, Dir.; Maria de los Angeles Piris Grau, Prin.; Stds.: 141; Lay Tchrs.: 27

Colegio Del Sagrado Corazon De Jesus de Ponce, Inc. - (PRV) (Grades PreSchool-12) Urb. Ext. Alhambra, 2511 Calle Obispado, Ponce, PR 00716 t) 787-843-4718; 787-842-0339 info@sagradoponce.org www.sagradoponce.org Rev. Gerardo Ramirez Torres, Spiritual Dir.; Dr. Maria Serrano Guilló, Dir.; Juan Sanchez Medina, Dir.; Diana Muñoz, Pst. Min./Coord.; Stds.: 766; Lay Tchrs.: 58

Colegio El Ave Maria - (PAR) (Grades PreK-12) 4506 Dr. Luis Bartolomei, Carr. 132, Reparto Valle Alegre, Ponce, PR 00728-3151 t) 787-284-2453 colegioelavemaria@yahoo.com Sr. Milagros Pizarro Nieves, Dir.; Sr. Maria Magali Vazquez Alvarez, Sub-Dir. & Pastoral Coord.; Stds.: 257; Sr. Tchrs.: 4; Lay Tchrs.: 20

Colegio Ponceno - (PRV) (Grades PreSchool-12) Carr. 14, Km 6.3 Bo. Cerrillos, Ponce, PR 00717; Mailing: 1900 Carr. 14, Coto Laurel, PR 00780-2147 t) 787-848-2525 oficina@copin.net www.copin.net Day school, Preparatory for college, Bilingual: Spanish & English Rev. Luis Alberto Cruz Baerga, Sch. P., Dir.; Rev. Pedro De Jesús Rivas Guardado, Sch. P., Spiritual Dir.; Glorian Clavell Acosta, Prin.; William Guzman, Prin. Asst.; Marines Castillo, Pst. Min./Coord.; Stds.: 575; Pr. Tchrs.: 2; Lay Tchrs.: 45

Sagrada Familia de Nazaret - (PRV) (Grades K-12) 1270

Ave. Hostos, Esq. Calle Ramon Power, Ponce, PR 00717-0928 t) 787-842-3208 csfnazaret@gmail.com Dr. Maribel Gómez Cruz, Dir.; Keysla Borges, Pastoral Coord.; Stds.: 29; Lay Tchrs.: 8

INSTITUTIONS LOCATED IN DIOCESE

ASSOCIATIONS [ASN]

PONCE

Pontifical Catholic University of Puerto Rico Service Association (PCUSA) - 2250 Blvd. Luis A. Ferré, Ste. 516, Ponce, PR 00717-9997 t) 787-841-2000 x1893 avelez@pucpr.edu Dr. Ashley L. Velez Toro, Exec.;

COLLEGES & UNIVERSITIES [COL]

PONCE

The Pontifical Catholic University of Puerto Rico - 2250 Blvd. Luis A. Ferre Aguayo, Ste. 564, Ponce, PR 00717-9997 t) 787-841-2000 x1303 fcortes@pucpr.edu www.pucpr.edu Dr. Jorge I. Velez Arocho, Pres.; Most Rev. Ruben Antonio Gonzalez Medina, C.M.F., Bishop & Chancellor; Dr. Frank Jimmy Sierra Cortes, Interim Rector, PUCPR-Mayagüez; Dr. Edwin Hernandez Vera, Rector, PUCPR-Arecibo; Dr. Felix Cortes Morales, Vice Pres., Planning & Devel.; Jose Frontera Agenjo, Vice Pres., Admin.; Dr. Myriam Lopez Velazquez, Vice Pres., Students; Dr. Leandro A. Colon Alicea, Vice Pres., Academics; Luis V. Badillo Lozano, Dean, School of Architecture; Ana Baez Rodriguez, Dean, College of Education; Dr. Alma Santiago Cortes, Dean, School of Science; Dr. Fernando Moreno Orama, Dean, Law School; Rev. Juan Luis Negron Delgado, Dean, College of Arts & Humanitites; Dr. Ilia Rosario Nieves, Dean, College of Behavioral Sciences & Community Affairs; Dr. David Zayas Montalvo, Dean, College of Bus. Admin.; Stds.: 7,697; Bro. Tchrs.: 1; Lay Tchrs.: 248; Pr. Tchrs.: 4; Sr. Tchrs.: 1

CONVENTS, MONASTERIES, AND RESIDENCES FOR WOMEN [CON]

GUANICA

Hermanas Dominicas de Nuestra Señora del Rosario de Fátima - Carr. 326 Km 2.6, Guanica, PR 00653; Mailing: P.O. Box 62, Yauco, PR 00698-0062 t) (787) 856-4330 c) 787-458-8426 secretariageneralfatima@gmail.com; prioragenetal.guanica@gmail.com Sr. Margarita Mangual Colon, O.P., Prioress; Sr. Maria Judith Maldonado Lazu, O.P., Secy. Gen.; Srs.: 53

PONCE

Religiosas del Apostolado del Sagrado Corazon de Jesus - Bo. Pampanos, Ramal 2, Ponce, PR 00732; Mailing: P.O. Box 8300, Ponce, PR 00732-8300 t) 787-842-4340; 787-853-0041 coquira03@yahoo.es See School Section for related school. Sr. Zonia Gamito, Supr.; Sr. Aurea Fuentes Reyes, R.A., Regl. Delegate & Supr.; Srs.: 12

Colegio Nuestra Senora del Perpetuo Socorro - Bo. Coqui, Carr. 3 km 150.6, Salinas, PR 00704; Mailing: Bo. Coqui, Aguirre, PR 00704 t) 787-853-2270 cpscoqui@gmail.com; coquira@yahoo.es Rev. Orlando Rivera Soto, Spiritual Dir.; Sr. Aurea E. Fuentes Reyes, R.A.D., Dir.; Wilmar Colon Ortiz, Prin.; Stds.: 295; Sr. Tchrs.: 1; Lay Tchrs.: 20

Siervas de María Ministras de los Enfermos - Urb. La Rambla, 1703 Calle Siervas de Maria, Ponce, PR 00730-4027 t) 787-842-2336 siervasponce@gmail.com Sr. Marilyn Hernandez Colon, Supr.; Srs.: 26

Siervas Misioneras de la Santisima Trinidad - Ave. Padre Noel 30, Ponce, PR 00716; Mailing: P.O. Box 7282, Ponce, PR 00732-7282 t) 787-844-1627 milva_msbt@yahoo.com www.msbt.org Sr. Mildred Vazquez Rivera, M.S.B.T., Supr.; Srs.: 3

MISCELLANEOUS [MIS]

JUANA DIAZ

Santuario de Schoenstatt - 14 Calle Padre Kentenich, Juana Diaz, PR 00795; Mailing: P.O. Box 800371, Coto Laurel, PR 00780-0371 t) 787-526-6362 santuariojuanadiaz@gmail.com Rev. Antonio Portalatin, Rector; Ida Ramos Maldonado, Admin.;

PENUELAS

Congregacion Misionera de San Juan Evangelista - Carr. 385 Km 0.7, Penuelas, PR 00624; Mailing: P.O. Box 118, Penuelas, PR 00624 t) 787-836-1512 hermanoscheos@yahoo.com Jose Ortiz Zayas, Pres.; Luz E. Torres Perez, Vice. Pres.; Luz Selenia Rivera Velazquez, Secy.; Luis M. Hernandez Ramos, Treas.;

PONCE

Institucion Magdalena Aulina - Operarias Parroquiales - Urb. Vistas del Mar, 2315 Calle Azabache, Ponce, PR 00716; Mailing: P.O. Box 801051, Coto Laurel, PR 00780 t) 787-218-7868 c) 939-640-7578 celismarrero@hotmail.com (Secular Institute) Ana Celis Marrero Fernandez, Dir.;

Memores Domini - 2250 Blvd. Luis A. Ferre, Ponce, PR 00717; Mailing: P.O. Box 32197, Ponce, PR 00732-2197 t) 787-515-6464 gzaffaroni@pucpr.edu Zaffaroni Giuseppe, Contact;

Oblates of Wisdom - Bo. Canitas, Carr. Estatal 504, Ponce, PR 00730; Mailing: P.O. Box 801246, Coto Laurel, PR 00780-1246 t) 787-605-1195 p.christopher1997@gmail.com www.rtforum.org Rev. Christopher De Herrera Sandoval, O.S., Chancellor;

Prelatura de la Santa Cruz y Opus Dei - Urb. Alhambra, 1814 Calle Alcazar, Ponce, PR 00716-3829 t) 787-844-2661 pricoinf@coqui.net opusdei.org.pr Rev. Javier Bernaola Hortigüela, Dir.; Rev. Francisco Alejandro Zubieta Peniche, Contact;

YAUCO

Instituto Especial para el Desarrollo Integral del Individuo, la Familia y la Communidad, Inc. - 66 Calle Madre Dominga, Yauco, PR 00968; Mailing: P.O. Box 1241, Yauco, PR 00968-1241 t) 787-856-1573; (787) 856-3798 instyco@coqui.net Sr. Mariangel Acevedo Nicasio, O.P., Dir.;

NURSING / REHABILITATION / CONVALESCENCE / ELDERLY CARE [NUR]

PONCE

Misioneras de la Caridad - El Tuque, 683 Ramos Antonini, Ponce, PR 00728; Mailing: P.O. Box 32177, Ponce, PR 00732-2177 t) 787-841-5443 psjoseobrero@yahoo.com (Hogar Inmaculado Corazon de Maria) Sr. Mary Vazhakala Anthony, M.C., Supr.; Asstd. Annu.: 14; Staff: 9

Residencia Santa Marta - Calle 4 de Julio Final Serro Betania, Sector Sabanetas, Ponce, PR 00715; Mailing: P.O. Box 242, Mercedita, PR 00715-0242 t) 787-840-7575 rsmarta2012@yahoo.com Home for aged & infirm. Sr. Gladys Rosario Gomez, Supr.; Asstd. Annu.: 108; Staff: 73

SEMINARIES [SEM]

PONCE

Seminario Mayor Interdiocesano Maria, Madre de la Divina Providencia - 32 Calle Cristina, Ponce, PR 00730; Mailing: P.O. Box 32110, Ponce, PR 00732-2110 t) 787-812-3024 seminarioreginacleri@gmail.com www.reginacleri.com Rev. Msgr. Elias S. Morales Rodriguez, Rector; Rev. Omar Omi Soto Torres, Vice Rector; Rev. Juan Carlos Rivera Medina, Admin.; Stds.: 28; Bro. Tchrs.: 1; Lay Tchrs.: 8; Pr. Tchrs.: 4

SPECIAL CARE FACILITIES [SPF]

ADJUNTAS

Instituto Santa Ana - Carr. 5516, KM 0.2, Sector El Desvio, Adjuntas, PR 00601; Mailing: P.O. Box 554, Adjuntas, PR 00601 t) 787-829-2504 isahogar@gmail.com institutosantaana.com Sr. Ismaela Castro, Dir.;

PONCE

Centro Madre Dominga, Casa Belen - Calle Castillo #3, Ponce, PR 00730 t) 787-290-3627 madredominga@gmail.com Sr. Amarilis Rosario Santos, O.P., Dir.; Ana Celis Marrero Fernandez, Clinical Psychologist;

Centros Sor Isolina Ferre, Inc. - 4903 Calle Roberto Collado Final, Ponce, PR 00716-1350; Mailing: P.O. Box 7313, Ponce, PR 00732-7313 t) 787-842-0000 info@csifpr.org centrossorisolinaferre.org Non-profit organization dedicated to community revitalization. Sr. Celia Gandia, Dir., Lighthouse of Hope; Jose Morales, Mgr., Tabaiba Education; Erick Rivera, Mgr., Prevention Prog.; Jasmin Rodriguez, Suprv., TANF Prog.; Asstd. Annu.: 2,856; Staff: 259

An asterisk (*) denotes an organization that has established tax-exempt status directly with the IRS and is not covered by the USCCB Group Ruling.

Diocese of St. Thomas in the Virgin Islands

MOST REVEREND JEROME FEUDJIO

Bishop of St. Thomas in the Virgin Islands; ordained September 29, 1990; appointed Bishop of St. Thomas in the Virgin Islands March 2, 2021; installed April 17, 2021.

Chancery Office: P.O. Box 301825, Charlotte Amalie, VI 00803. T: 340-774-3166; F: 340-774-5816.
www.catholicvi.com
vichancery@gmail.com

ESTABLISHED AS PRELATURE OF VI, JULY 23, 1960.

Established as Diocese of St. Thomas in the Virgin Islands April 20, 1977.

Comprises the Islands of St. Thomas, St. Croix, St. John and Water Island.

STATISTICAL OVERVIEW

Personnel

Bishop	1
Retired Bishops	1
Priests: Diocesan Active in Diocese	14
Priests: Diocesan Active Outside Diocese	5
Priests: Retired, Sick or Absent	3
Number of Diocesan Priests	22
Religious Priests in Diocese	3
Total Priests in your Diocese	25
Extern Priests in Diocese	8
Ordinations:	
Religious Priests	1
Permanent Deacons in Diocese	27
Total Sisters	5

Parishes

Parishes	9
With Resident Pastor:	
Resident Diocesan Priests	9
Resident Religious Priests	1
Missions	2

Welfare

Specialized Homes	2
Total Assisted	58
Special Centers for Social Services	2
Total Assisted	107,817

Educational

Diocesan Students in Other Seminaries	2
Total Seminarians	2
High Schools, Diocesan and Parish	2
Total Students	180
Elementary Schools, Diocesan and Parish	2
Total Students	191
Catechesis / Religious Education:	
High School Students	18
Elementary Students	150
Total Students under Catholic Instruction	541
Teachers in Diocese:	
Sisters	3
Lay Teachers	35

Vital Statistics

Receptions into the Church:	
Infant Baptism Totals	63
Minor Baptism Totals	6
Adult Baptism Totals	8
Received into Full Communion	9
First Communions	45
Confirmations	54
Marriages:	
Catholic	16
Interfaith	3
Total Marriages	19
Deaths	132
Total Catholic Population	30,000
Total Population	110,000

LEADERSHIP

Chancery Office - t) 340-774-3166 vichancery@gmail.com Most Rev. Jerome Feudjio, Bishop;

Vicar General - t) 340-773-7564 Rev. Patrick Edward Lynch, C.Ss.R., Vicar (holycrossstx@gmail.com);

Vicar for Clergy and Religious - Most Rev. Jerome Feudjio;

Chancellor - Rev. Julio Cesar Faes (Argentina), Vice Chancellor (cathedralvi@gmail.com); Rev. Robert Kenfack (Cameroon) (vichancery@gmail.com);

Fiscal Officer - warrentbush@gmail.com Warren Bush, CFO;

OFFICES AND DIRECTORS

Catholic Charities of the Virgin Islands, Inc. - t) 340-777-8518 info@catholiccharitiesvi.org Andrea Shillingford, Exec.;

Shelters for the Homeless - t) 340-777-5001 Andrea Shillingford, Exec.;

Communications - t) (340) 774-3166; (340) 778-0484 Rev. Julio Cesar Faes (Argentina) (cathedralvi@gmail.com); Rev. Louis Kemayou;

Caribbean Catholic Network (CCN) - t) 340-778-0484 stannbarrenspot@gmail.com Rev. Louis Kemayou;

Catholic Islander - t) 340-774-3166 thecatholicislander@gmail.com Dcn. Denis Griffith, Editor-St. Croix; Bernadette Patrick, Editor-Chancery Office;

Catholic Television Network (CTN) - t) (340) 423-6824 catholicdiocesestt@gmail.com Clovis Tangkwale;

Family Life - Rev. Julio Cesar Faes (Argentina) (cathedralvi@gmail.com);

Hispanic Ministry - Rev. Julio Cesar Faes (Argentina) (cathedralvi@gmail.com);

Prison Ministry - t) 340-773-7564 Rev. Yacob Fopa Lonfo (Cameroon) (holycrossstx@gmail.com);

Vocations - Most Rev. Jerome Feudjio;

Youth Ministry - t) 340-772-0138 saintpatrickusvi@gmail.com Rev. Touchard G. Tignoua (Cameroon), Dir.;

PARISHES, MISSIONS, AND CLERGY

THE U.S. VIRGIN ISLANDS

CHARLOTTE AMALIE

Cathedral of SS. Peter and Paul - 2322 Kronprindsens Gade, 22 Kronprindsens Gade, Charlotte Amalie, VI 00802; Mailing: P.O. Box 301767, Charlotte Amalie, VI 00803 t) 340-774-0201; 340-693-9735 cathedralvi@gmail.com www.cathedralvi.org Rev. Modeste Digwou (Cameroon), Admin.; Rev. Serapio Lopez Cruz (Mexico), Par. Vicar; Rev. Julio Cesar Faes (Argentina), Par. Vicar; Rev. Andrew Paul Lesko, Par. Vicar; Dcn. Wilfredo Acosta; Dcn. Clement Daniel; Dcn. Frank Kearney; Dcn. Jose Vasquez; Sr. Sylverine Fola, DRE; Sr. Adele Gatsi, DRE; CRP Stds.: 17

Sts. Peter and Paul School - (Grades 1-12) 12-17 Kronprindsens Gade, St. Thomas, VI 00802; Mailing: P.O. Box 301706, St. Thomas, VI 00803 t) 340-774-5662; 340-774-2199 info@spps.edu.vi sppcsvi.com Marie Jules-Daniel, Prin.; Stds.: 130; Sr. Tchrs.: 2; Lay Tchrs.: 15

Chapel of St. Anne - Altona 42, Carenage, VI 00803; Mailing: P.O. Box 306810, Carenage, VI 00803 t) 340-714-1101 chapelvi@gmail.com Rev. Boniface-Blanchard M. Twaibu, Pst.;

Daughters of the Holy Family - 31A Prindcesse Gade, St. Thomas, VI 00803 t) (340) 774-0201 x23 adeletsaguegat@hotmail.com

Our Lady of Perpetual Help - Estate Elizabeth #8i, Charlotte Amalie, VI 00803; Mailing: P.O. Box 304983, Charlotte Amalie, VI 00803 t) 340-774-0885 olphmafolie@gmail.com Rev. John K. Mark, Pst.; Dcn. Bernard Gibs; Keya Chongasing Garner, Bus. Mgr.; CRP Stds.: 23

CHRISTIANSTED

Church of the Holy Cross - 2182 Queen St., Christiansted, VI 00820 t) 340-773-7564 www.hccstx.org Dcn. David Capriola; Dcn. Vincent Colianni; Dcn. Reynold Modeste; Dcn. Benjamin Parrilla; Rev. E. Patrick Lynch, C.Ss.R., Pst.; Rev. Yacob Fopa Lonfo, Assoc. Pst.; Dcn. David Capriola; CRP Stds.: 20

St. Mary's - (Grades PreK-8) 2184 Queen St., Christiansted, VI 00820-4848 t) 340-773-0117 officeatstmarys@gmail.com Edna Thomas, Prin.; Stds.: 89; Lay Tchrs.: 11

Sacred Heart Chapel - Lyndon B Johnson Gardens, Christiansted, VI 00820 t) (340) 773-7564 Rev. Patrick Edward Lynch, C.Ss.R., Pst.;

Missionaries of Charity - 55 Queen St., Christiansted, VI 00820; Mailing: P.O. Box 3058, Christiansted, VI 00821 t) 340-473-7055 Sr. Arwind Indwar, M.C., Supr.;

FREDERIKSTED

Church of St. Joseph - #1 Mount Pleasant, Frederiksted, VI 00840; Mailing: P.O. Box 2150, Kingshill, VI 00851-2150 t) 340-692-2005 stjoseph1973@yahoo.com www.saintjosephvi.com Rev. Andrea Filippucci, Pst.; Rev. Victor Luna Vitug II, Par. Vicar; Dcn. Hector Arroyo; Dcn. James Verhoff;

Sacred Heart Society - t) (340) 692-2005

Church of St. Patrick - 416 Custom House St., Frederiksted, VI 00840 t) 340-772-0138 c) (340) 514-3050 saintpatrickusvi.org Very Rev. Cyprian Tatah Ferdzefer, Pst.; Rev. Touchard G. Tignoua (Cameroon), Assoc. Pst.; Dcn. Emith Fludd; Dcn. Melford Murray; Nereida C. Washington, DRE; Alvin M. Milligan, Music Min.; CRP Stds.: 7

Church of St. Patrick School - (Grades PreK-8) 406 Custom House St., Frederiksted, St. Croix, VI 00840; Mailing: 16 Custom House St., St. Croix, VI 00840 t) 340-772-5052 sps1866@yahoo.com Lydia P Davis, Prin.; Stds.: 66; Sr. Tchrs.: 1; Scholastics: 58; Lay Tchrs.: 9

KINGSHILL

St. Ann's Roman Catholic Congregation, Inc - 42 Barrenspot Hill, Kingshill, VI 00850; Mailing: P.O. Box 1160, Kingshill, VI 00851-1160 t) 340-778-0484 stannbarrenspot@gmail.com www.catholicvi.com/stann/ Rev. Louis Kemayou, Pst.; Dcn. Denis Griffith; Patricia Browne, DRE; CRP Stds.: 49

Chaplaincy - Herbert Grigg Home for the Aged, Kingshill, VI 00851 t) 340-778-0708

Our Lady of Barrenspot Hill - No. 42 Barrenspot, Kingshill, VI 00850

ST. JOHN

Our Lady of Mt. Carmel Parish - 5AB Cruz Bay, St. John, VI 00830; Mailing: P.O. Box 241, St. John, VI 00831 t) 340-643-7097 (CRP); 340-776-6339 magdalene6054@gmail.com; olmc@hotmail.com olmcvi.org Rev. Anthony Abraham, Pst.; Dcn. Evan Doway; Dcn. Michael A. Jackson Sr.; Dcn. Peter C. Laurencin; Dcn. Cassius Mathurin; Maggie Metor, DRE; CRP Stds.: 36

ST. THOMAS

Holy Family Parish - 213 Anna's Retreat, St. Thomas, VI 00802; Mailing: P.O. Box 502218, St. Thomas, VI 00805 t) 340-775-1650 holyfamilyusvi@gmail.com www.holyfamilystt.com Rev. Robert Kenfack Ngnintedem (Cameroon), Pst.; Rev. Kerly Francois, Par. Vicar; CRP Stds.: 25

SCHOOLS: PRESCHOOL THRU HIGH SCHOOL

HIGH SCHOOLS

THE U.S. VIRGIN ISLANDS

ST. CROIX

St. Joseph High School - (PAR) (Grades 9-12) 3 Mt. Pleasant, Rte. 2, Frederiksted, St. Croix, VI 00840 t) (340) 692-2455 smiranda@stjosephhighschool.vi Sandra N. Maynard, Prin.; Stds.: 50

INSTITUTIONS LOCATED IN DIOCESE

MISCELLANEOUS [MIS]

CHARLOTTE AMALIE

Miscellaneous Organizations - 29A-30A Prindsesse Gade, The Catholic Chancery, Charlotte Amalie, VI 00802; Mailing: P.O. Box 301825, St. Thomas, VI 00803-1825 t) 340-774-3166 vichancery@gmail.com www.catholicvi.com Most Rev. Jerome Feudjio, Bishop; Most Rev. Herbert A. Bevard, Bishop Emeritus; Rev. Kerly Francois, Haitian Min.; Rev. Louis Kemayou, Communications Coord.; Rev. Robert Kenfack (Cameroon), Chancellor; Rev. Andrew Paul Lesko, Diocesan Coord., Svc. of Charities; Rev. Yacob Fopa Lonfo, Vocations Office; Rev. Patrick Edward Lynch, C.Ss.R., Vicar; Rev. John Kennedy Mark, Dir., Office for Worship & Diaconate Prog.; Marie Pascale Duplan, Coord., Child Protection Prog.; Rev. Touchard Goula Tignoua (Cameroon), Diocesan Coord., Youth Min.;

St. Ann's Stewards of Christ - 42 Barrenspot, Kingshill, VI 00851; Mailing: P.O. Box 1160, Kingshill, VI 00851 t) 340-277-1002 stannbarrenspot@gmail.com Phillip Payne, Pres.;

Catholic Charismatic Renewal - #5 AB Cruz Bay, St. John, VI 00830; Mailing: P.O. Box 241, St. John, VI 00831 t) 340-776-6339 olmc@hotmail.com Rev. Anthony Abraham, Dir.;

Catholic Charities of the Virgin Islands, Inc. - 68 Kronprindsens Gade, The Catholic Chancery, Charlotte Amalie, VI 00801; Mailing: P.O. Box 10736, St. Thomas, VI 00801-0736 t) 340-777-8518 info@catholiccharitiesvi.org Andrea Shillingford, Exec.;

Catholic Daughters of the Americas - 2322 Kronprindsens Gade, Charlotte Amalie, VI 00802; Mailing: P.O. Box 301767, St. Thomas, VI 00803 t) 340-777-6778 c) 340-643-9461 cathedralvi@gmail.com Carole Nelthropp, Dir.;

Children of Mary - 213 Estate Anna's Retreat, Holy Family Church, St. Thomas, VI 00805; Mailing: P.O. Box 502218, St. Thomas, VI 00805-2218 t) 340-775-1351 holyfamilyusvi@gmail.com

Cursillo Movement - St. Joseph Church, Kingshill, VI 00851-2150; Mailing: P.O. Box 2150, Kingshill, VI 00851-2150 t) 340-692-2005 stjoseph1973@yahoo.com

Fraternity Our Lady of the Angels - St. Ann Church, Kingshill, VI 00851-1160; Mailing: P.O. Box 1160, Kingshill, VI 00851-1160 t) 340-778-0484 stannbarrenspot@gmail.com Third Order Franciscans.

Hispanic Ministry - 45 A Queen St., Christiansted, St. Croix, VI 00820 t) 340-773-7564 holycrossstx@gmail.com catholicvi.com Dcn. David Capriola, Dir.;

Hispanic Ministry - 20-21A Kronprindsens Gade, St. Thomas, VI 00803; Mailing: P.O. Box 301767, St. Thomas, VI 00803 t) 340-774-0201 cathedralvi@gmail.com Rev. Julio Cesar Faes (Argentina);

St. Joseph Workers - 213 Estate Anna's Retreat, St.

Thomas, VI 00805; Mailing: P.O. Box 502218, Holy Family Church, St. Thomas, VI 00805-2218 t) 340-775-2890; 340-775-1351 holyfamilyusvi@gmail.com Orville Rouse, Pres.;
Knights of Columbus Council 6187 - 2322 Kronprindsens Gade, Charlotte Amalie, VI 00802; Mailing: P.O. Box 301767, St. Thomas, VI 00803-1767 t) 340-626-4139 alridlockhart@gmail.com
Knights of Columbus Council 6482 - Sunny Isle, St. Croix, VI 00823-6185; Mailing: P.O. Box 6185, St. Croix, VI 00823-6185 t) 340-643-2353 c) 340-277-1106 royzech@gmail.com Dr. Roy Arcamo, Contact; Delano King, Contact;
Legion of Mary - 5AB Cruz Bay, St. John, VI 00831; Mailing: P.O. Box 241, St. John, VI 00831 t) 340-227-0168 grandmuff1010@gmail.com (St. John) Janice Mathurin, Pres.;
Legion of Mary, Curia Immaculate Conception - ; Mailing: P.O. Box 503302, St. Thomas, VI 00805 t) 340-774-0743 olphmafolie@gmail.com Timothy Olive, Pres.;
Legion of Mary, Holy Family Church, St. Thomas, Presidium Mary, Mystic Rose - ; Mailing: P.O. Box 502218, St. Thomas, VI 00805 t) 340-775-3503 holyfamilyusvi@gmail.com Eubald Rene, Pres.;
Legion of Mary, OLPH Morning Star Praesidium - ; Mailing: P.O. Box 304983, St. Thomas, VI 00803 t) 340-774-0885 olphmafolie@gmail.com Timothy Olive, Pres.;
Legion of Mary, Spanish Community, Presidium Maria, Arca de la Alianza - ; Mailing: P.O. Box 8421, St. Thomas, VI 00801 t) 340-774-0201 cathedralvi@gmail.com Marina Salem, Pres.;
Lumen 2000/Caribbean Region - 42 Barrenspot, Kingshill, VI 00851; Mailing: P.O. Box 1160, Kingshill, VI 00851-1160 t) 340-778-0484 stannbarrenspot@gmail.com Rev. Louis Kemayou, Dir.;
Magnificat Ministry For Women - 2322 Kronprindsens Gade, Main St., Charlotte Amalie, St. Thomas, VI 00802 t) 340-774-0201 cathedralvi@gmail.com www.cathedralvi.org Bernadette Patrick, Contact;
Magnificat Ministry For Women - St. John - 5AB Cruz Bay, St. John, VI 00831; Mailing: P.O. Box 241, St. John, VI 00831 t) 340-643-7097 magdalene6054@gmail.com
Neocatecumenal Way - #1 Mt. Pleasant, Frederiksted, St. Croix, VI 00851; Mailing: P. O. Box 2150, St. Joseph Church, Kingshill, VI 00851-2150 t) 340-692-2005 stjoseph1973@yahoo.com Dcn. Conrad Williams, Contact;
Sacred Heart Society - 416 Custom House St., Frederiksted, VI 00840 t) 340-772-3042 saintpatrickusvi@gmail.com www.saintpatrickusvi.org Julia Pankey, Pres.;
Sacred Heart Society - ; Mailing: P.O. Box 301767, St. Thomas, VI 00803 t) 340-774-0201
Sacred Heart Society - 42 Barrenspot, Kingshill, VI 00851; Mailing: P.O. Box 1160, Kingshill, VI 00851 t) 340-778-0484 stannbarrenspot@gmail.com Clara Xavier, Dir.;
Secular Franciscans - #5 -D Upper Love, Kingshill, VI 00851; Mailing: P.O. Box 1847, Kingshill, VI 00851-1847 t) 340-778-5773
Secular Order Discalced Carmelites - 42 Barrenspot, Kingshill, St. Croix, VI 00851; Mailing: P.O. Box 1160, St. Ann Church, Kingshill, VI 00851-1160 t) 340-778-2083 stannbarrenspot@gmail.com Kathleen Mark, Pres.;
Sons of Mary and Joseph - OLPH - ; Mailing: P.O. Box 304983, St. Thomas, VI 00803 t) 340-774-0885 olphmafolie@gmail.com Rev. John K. Mark, Pst.;
St. Vincent de Paul Society and Young Vincentians - 213 Estate Anna's Retreat, Holy Family Church, St. Thomas, VI 00805; Mailing: P.O. Box 502218, Holy Family Church, St. Thomas, VI 00805-2218 t) 340-775-1650 holyfamilyusvi@gmail.com Alma Wells, Pres.;
Wednesday Prayer Group - OLPH - ; Mailing: P.O. Box 304983, St. Thomas, VI 00803 t) 340-774-0885

An asterisk (*) denotes an organization that has established tax-exempt status directly with the IRS and is not covered by the USCCB Group Ruling.

Diocese of Samoa-Pago Pago

MOST REVEREND PETER H. BROWN, C.SS.R.

Bishop of Samoa-Pago Pago; ordained December 19, 1981; appointed Bishop of Samoa-Pago Pago May 31, 2013; installed August 22, 2013.

CREATED A DIOCESE NOVEMBER, 1982.

The Diocese of Samoa-Pago Pago includes the islands of Tutuila; Swains; Manu'a Is., Ofu, Olosega & Ta'u; Aunu'u and Rose Island.

MOST REVEREND KOLIO ETUALE
Coadjutor Bishop of Samoa-Pago Pago; ordained March 29, 2003; appointed Coadjutor Bishop of Samoa-Pago Pago August 4, 2022; installed November 4, 2022.

STATISTICAL OVERVIEW

Personnel

Bishop	2
Priests: Diocesan Active in Diocese	15
Priests: Diocesan Active Outside Diocese	1
Priests: Retired, Sick or Absent	1
Number of Diocesan Priests	17
Total Priests in your Diocese	17
Extern Priests in Diocese	2
Permanent Deacons in Diocese	12
Total Sisters	2

Parishes

Parishes	18
With Resident Pastor:	
Resident Diocesan Priests	16
Resident Religious Priests	3
Missions	3

Welfare

Catholic Hospitals	1
Total Assisted	40
Health Care Centers	1
Total Assisted	25
Homes for the Aged	1
Total Assisted	34
Residential Care of Children	1
Total Assisted	2
Day Care Centers	1
Total Assisted	61
Specialized Homes	1
Total Assisted	20
Special Centers for Social Services	1
Total Assisted	15

Educational

Students from This Diocese	2
Total Seminarians	2
High Schools, Private	1
Total Students	350
Elementary Schools, Private	2
Total Students	515
Catechesis/Religious Education:	
High School Students	2,100
Elementary Students	1,506
Total Students under Catholic Instruction	4,473
Teachers in Diocese:	
Priests	4
Lay Teachers	80

Vital Statistics

Receptions into the Church:	
Infant Baptism Totals	51
Minor Baptism Totals	40
Adult Baptism Totals	15
Received into Full Communion	160
First Communions	205
Confirmations	349
Marriages:	
Catholic	1
Interfaith	1
Total Marriages	2
Deaths	105
Total Catholic Population	26,047
Total Population	45,835

LEADERSHIP

Vicar General of Diocese - Rev. Msgr. Etuale Lealofi, Vicar; Rev. Msgr. Viane Etuale (fatherve@blueskynet.as);
Chancellor - Rev. Iosefo V. Tupuola;
Diocesan Consultors - Most Rev. Peter H. Brown, C.Ss.R.; Rev. Msgr. Viane Etuale (fatherve@blueskynet.as); Rev. Iosefo V. Tupuola;

OFFICES AND DIRECTORS

Children of Mary - Khymoriah Isaia, Pres.; Frances Nautu, Vice. Pres.; Etevise Esekio, Treas.;
Diocesan Pastoral Council - Faiivae Iuli Godinet, Pres.; Paolo Sivia, Vice. Pres.; Tasileta Teo, Secy.;
Director of Propagation of the Faith - Rev. Etuale To'alepai;
Director of Vocations - Rev. Kolio Etuale;
Divine Mercy - Nancy Matamua, Pres.; Muaau M., Vice. Pres.; Mary Putuga, Secy.;
Fatuoaiga Multipurpose Cultural and Pastoral Center - Rev. Msgr. Viane Etuale (fatherve@blueskynet.as); Rev. Kelemete L. Pua'auli; Rev. Kolio Etuale;
Hospital Chaplain - Rev. Faitau Lemautu;
Matrimonial Tribunal - Rev. Iosefo V. Tupuola; Most Rev. Peter H. Brown, C.Ss.R., Pres.; Rev. Kolio Etuale;
Adjunct Judicial Vicars - Rev. Msgr. Etuale Lealofi; Rev. Msgr. Viane Etuale;
Defender of the Bond (Vacant) -
Ecclesiastical Notary - Rev. Iosefo V. Tupuola;
Judge - Rev. Msgr. Viane Etuale;
Judicial Vicar - Most Rev. Peter H. Brown, C.Ss.R., Vicar;
Tribunal Administrator (Vacant) -
Port Chaplain - Rev. Jeudiel Galvo; Rev. Setefano T. Luamanu;
Prison Chaplain - Dcn. Chaira Uiagalelei;
Rosary Society - Ioana Atamai, Pres.; Mata'u Atafau, Vice. Pres.; Siniva Letufufuga, Secy.;
Sacred Heart Society - Annie Fuavai, Pres.; Suni Felise, Vice. Pres.; Joanne Kimoto, Secy.;
St. Anne Society - Kalala Kaio, Pres.; Telefina Nautu, Vice. Pres.; Fia Malae, Secy.;
Vicar for Diocesan Youth - Rev. Asalemo Asalemo Jr., Vicar;
Women's Organization - Nina Taufetee, Pres.; Luana Tafano, Vice. Pres.; Tina Mataafa, Secy.;
Youth - Aigkin Ieremia, Pres.;

PARISHES, MISSIONS, AND CLERGY

TERRITORY OF AMERICAN SAMOA

PAGO PAGO

Co-Cathedral of St. Joseph the Worker - ; Mailing: P.O. Box AA, Pago Pago, AS 96799 t) 684-633-1483 iosefo.vaitele@gmail.com; schmidtpale@gmail.com Rev. Teofilo Pale Schmidt, Pst.; Rev. Faitau Lemautu, Assoc. Pst.; Ierenimo Laupapa, DRE; Tomasi Ta'avili, DRE;
Utulei Mission -
Faga'alu Mission -
Cathedral of the Holy Family - ; Mailing: P.O. Box 3594, Pago Pago, AS 96799-3594 t) 684-699-1446; 684-699-2209 (CRP) iosefovaitele@gmail.com; maurice.lolesio@gmail.com Most Rev. Peter H. Brown, C.Ss.R.; Rev. Iosefo V. Tupuola, Chancellor; Rev. Jeudiel Galvo, Assoc. Pst.; Rev. Msgr. Etuale Lealofi, Assoc. Pst.; Rev. Setefano Tuisea, Assoc. Pst.; Dcn. Filipo Toilolo; Dcn. Chaira Uiagalelei;
Mary, Star of the Sea -
Christ the King - ; Mailing: P.O. Box 5408, Pago Pago, AS 96799 t) 684-688-5765 c) 684-733-0735 iosefo.vaitele@gmail.com; maurice.lolesio@gmail.com Rev. Tagaloa Tatino, Pst.;
Christ the King - ; Mailing: P.O. Box 596, Pago Pago, AS 96799 t) 684-688-1965 tausagaese@gmail.com Rev. Sagato Tavete, Pst.;
Christ the King - ; Mailing: P.O. Box 596, Pago Pago, AS 96799 t) 684-699-4465 iosefo.vaitele@gmail.com; maurice.lolesio@gmail.com Rev. Asalemo Asalemo Jr., Pst.; Iosefo Vitaliano;
Church of St. Peter and Paul - ; Mailing: P.O. Box 985, Pago Pago, AS 96799 t) 684-644-5581; 684-644-4697 (CRP) iosefo.vaitele@gmail.com; petinasiliako2010@hotmail.com Rev. Petelo Siliako, Pst.; Dcn. Setefano Lesa;
Church of the Holy Cross - ; Mailing: P.O. Box 1206, Pago Pago, AS 96799 t) 684-688-7663 nfklp33@yahoo.com Dcn. Nua Sipiliano; Dcn. Vaipuna Tia; Rev. Kelemete L. Pua'auli, Pst.; Dcn. Laloasi Seui; Rev. Andrew Wilson, Pst. Assoc.; Joseph Stowers, DRE;
Church of the Immaculate Conception - ; Mailing: P.O. Box 398, Pago Pago, AS 96799 t) 684-644-5512 fatherve@blueskynet.as; fatherve@blueskynet.com Rev. Msgr. Viane Etuale, Pst.; Rev. Salesi Moimoi, Assoc. Pst.; Dcn. Lino Auva'a; Ioane Matafeo, DRE; Tumaai Solimalo, F.K., DRE;
Afono Mission -
Lepua Mission -
St. Joseph the Worker Futiga - ; Mailing: P.O. Box 596, Pago Pago, AS 96799 t) 684-688-7765; 684-699-7572 ketuale@yahoo.com Rev. Kolio Etuale, Pst.; Dcn. Alefosio Uelese;
Our Lady of Fatima - ; Mailing: P.O. Box 4052, Pago Pago, AS 96799 t) 684-644-5826 fatherve@blueskynet.as Rev. Msgr. Viane Etuale, Pst.; Aukusitine Paniani, DRE; Moe Sagote, DRE;
Our Lady of the Rosary Parish - ; Mailing: P.O. Box 596, Pago Pago, AS 96799 t) 684-688-5765 c) 684-733-0735 samoa_143@yahoo.com Rev. Tagaloa Tatino, Pst.; Siutulei Bell, DRE;
St. Paul - ; Mailing: P.O. Box 2004, Pago Pago, AS 96799 t) 684-699-7572 ketuale@yahoo.com Rev. Kolio Etuale, Pst.; Dcn. Malaki Timu; Dcn. Iosefo Toilolo; Visesio Tulua, DRE;
Faleniu Mission -
Sts. Peter & Paul - ; Mailing: P.O. Box 7286, Pago Pago, AS 96799 t) 684-688-7236 nfklp33@yahoo.com (Asili) Rev. Kelemete L. Pua'auli, Pst.; Rev. Andrew Wilson, Assoc. Pst.; Silipa Afoa, DRE;
Amaluia Mission -
St. Peter Chanel Parish Fagasa - ; Mailing: P.O. Box 596, Pago Pago, AS 96799 c) 684-733-8774 iosefo.vaitele@gmail.com Rev. Eneliko Auva'a, Pst.; Malu Tuiafiso, DRE;
St. Peter Chanel-Sa'ilele - ; Mailing: P.O. Box 596, Pago Pago, AS 96799 t) 684-622-7512 iosefo_vaitele@gmail.com Rev. Petelo Siliako, Pst.; Faleagafulu Filipo, DRE;
Masefau Mission -
Faga'itua Mission -
Sacred Heart of Jesus - ; Mailing: P.O. Box 4175, Pago Pago, AS 96799 t) 684-622-7145 frpioafu@gmail.com Rev. Pio Gamig Afu, Pst.; Toni Tavite Lolesio, DRE; Lui Polu, DRE; Paulo Sagato, DRE;
Aoa Mission -
Amouli Mission -
Sacred Heart of Jesus Parish - ; Mailing: P.O. Box 596, Pago Pago, AS 96799 t) 684-688-1965 c) 684-733-6323 kelelp68@gmail.com Rev. Kelemete L. Puaauli, Pst.; Malaki Aunoa, DRE;
Sacred Heart Parish-Pago Pago - ; Mailing: P.O. Box 596, Pago Pago, AS 96799 t) 684-644-4034 c) 684-256-7257 iosefo.vaitele@gmail.com Rev. Etuale Toalepai, Pst.; Rev. Michael Vito, Assoc. Pst.; Sauleoge Aigofie;

SCHOOLS: PRESCHOOL THRU HIGH SCHOOL

SCHOOLS

TERRITORY OF AMERICAN SAMOA

LEONE

St. Theresa - (DIO) (Grades 1-8) Malaeloa, Leone, AS 96799-0596; Mailing: P.O. Box 596, Leone, AS 96799-0596 t) 684-688-1105; 684-688-1114 (Other) st.theresa1105@gmail.com Rev. Kolio Etuale, Chap.; Sr. Soana Taliauli, Spiritual Adv./Care Srvcs.;

LEPUA

Marist St. Francis - (DIO) (Grades 1-8) Fatuoaiga, Lepua, AS 96799-0429; Mailing: P.O. Box 429, Lepua, AS 96799-0429 t) 684-644-1784 palepasmsm@gmail.com Sr. Palepa Aukusitino, Prin.;

HIGH SCHOOLS

TERRITORY OF AMERICAN SAMOA

LEPUAPUA

Faasao Marist High School - (DIO) ; Mailing: P.O. Box 729, Lepuapua, AS 96799 t) 684-688-7731 iosefo.vaitele@gmail.com; ocesecretary@gmail.com fmhs411.weebly.com Lentoy Matagi, Prin.; Fausia Leiato, Vice Prin.; Jeanette L. Alvarez, Dir.;

INSTITUTIONS LOCATED IN DIOCESE

CATHOLIC CHARITIES [CCH]

PAGO PAGO

Catholic Social Services, Inc. - Fatuoaiga St., Tafuna, Pago Pago, AS 96799; Mailing: P.O. Box 596, Pago Pago, AS 96799 t) 684-699-5683 ntagaloa.css@blueskynet.as Nancy Lolenese-Tagaloa, Exec. Dir.; Elena Ioane, Victim's Advocate; Asstd. Annu.: 225; Staff: 2

MISCELLANEOUS [MIS]

PAGO PAGO

Diocesan Eucharistic League - ; Mailing: P.O. Box 596, Pago Pago, AS 96799 t) 684-699-1402 teri_684@yahoo.com; maurice.lolesio@gmail.com Teuila Love, Pres.; Theresa D. Silao, Secy.;

PRESCHOOLS / CHILDCARE CENTERS [PRE]

PAGO PAGO

Mary The Mother Montessori Early Education Center - Lepua, Pago Pago, AS 96799; Mailing: P.O. Box 596, Pago Pago, AS 96799 t) 684-644-1311 ocesecretary@gmail.com; iosefo.vaitele@gmail.com Dr. Lina Scanlan, Prin.;

SPECIAL CARE FACILITIES [SPF]

PAGO PAGO

Hope House - ; Mailing: P.O. Box 596, Pago Pago, AS 96799 t) 684-699-2101 mccutchankathryn@gmail.com Kathryn McCutchan, Admin.;

Archdiocese of San Juan, Puerto Rico

(Sancti Joannis Portoricensis)

MOST REVEREND ROBERTO O. GONZALEZ NIEVES, O.F.M.

Archbishop of San Juan; ordained May 8, 1977; appointed Titular Bishop of Ursona and Auxiliary Bishop of Boston July 19, 1988; consecrated October 3, 1988; appointed Coadjutor Bishop of Corpus Christi May 16, 1995; transferred to Corpus Christi June 26, 1995; succeeded to See April 1, 1997; appointed Archbishop of San Juan March 26, 1999; installed May 8, 1999.

Chancery Office: P.O. Box 9021967, San Juan, PR 00902-1967. T: 787-727-7373; F: 787-726-8280.

ERECTED AUGUST 8, 1511.

Square Miles 245.

Erected an Archdiocese April 30, 1960.

Comprises the northeast portion of the Island of Puerto Rico, with a Total Population of 1,229,117

STATISTICAL OVERVIEW

Personnel

Archbishops	1
Abbots	1
Priests: Diocesan Active in Diocese	112
Priests: Diocesan Active Outside Diocese	2
Priests: Retired, Sick or Absent	25
Number of Diocesan Priests	139
Religious Priests in Diocese	134
Total Priests in your Diocese	273
Extern Priests in Diocese	8
Permanent Deacons in Diocese	197
Total Brothers	18
Total Sisters	386

Parishes

Parishes	142
With Resident Pastor:	
Resident Diocesan Priests	56
Resident Religious Priests	47
Without Resident Pastor:	
Administered by Priests	37
Administered by Deacons	2
Administered by Lay People	1
Missions	143

Welfare

Catholic Hospitals	11
Total Assisted	35,450
Health Care Centers	9
Total Assisted	8,512
Homes for the Aged	18
Total Assisted	40,150
Residential Care of Children	8
Total Assisted	6,425
Day Care Centers	1
Total Assisted	1,200
Specialized Homes	10
Total Assisted	21,000
Special Centers for Social Services	23
Total Assisted	198,635
Residential Care of Disabled	2
Total Assisted	2,000
Other Institutions	4
Total Assisted	415

Educational

Seminaries, Diocesan	1
Students from This Diocese	7
Diocesan Students in Other Seminaries	7
Total Seminarians	14
Colleges and Universities	2
Total Students	6,895
High Schools, Diocesan and Parish	1
Total Students	303
High Schools, Private	6
Total Students	2,181
Elementary Schools, Diocesan and Parish	15
Total Students	5,112
Elementary Schools, Private	26
Total Students	9,459
Non-residential Schools for the Disabled	1
Total Students	113
Total Students under Catholic Instruction	24,077
Teachers in Diocese:	
Brothers	18
Sisters	150
Lay Teachers	1,685

Vital Statistics

Receptions into the Church:	
Infant Baptism Totals	1,386
Minor Baptism Totals	1,567
First Communions	2,785
Confirmations	2,041
Marriages:	
Catholic	1,386
Interfaith	42
Total Marriages	1,428
Deaths	250
Total Catholic Population	636,318
Total Population	991,318

LEADERSHIP

Episcopal Moderator -

for Administration of Temporalities - Rev. Tomas Gonzalez-Gonzalez;

for Education - www.escueloscatolicos-sj.org

for Geographic-Pastoral Zones - Rev. Benjamin Antonio Perez Cruz; Rev. Carlos Ruben Algarin Lopez, O.S.A.; Rev. Angel Pagan Torres;

for Pastoral Affairs - Rev. Rodney Algarin Rosado;

Chancery Office - www.arqsj.org

Chancery Affairs - t) 787-977-0672 Lucia Guzman Orta;

Vice Chancellor - Rev. Anibal Rafael Torres-Ortiz;

Metropolitan Curia -

Adjunct Vicars - Vacant -

Defenders of the Bond - Rev. Walter Salomon Gomez-Baca; Maria del Rosario Rincon-Becerra;

Executive Assistant to the Archbishop - Samuel Soto-Alonso;

Instructors - Rev. Ernesto Gonzalez-Gonzalez; Rev. Pedro Luis Reyes-Lebron; Dcn. Ramon Guzman;

Judges - Abraham Morales Berrios; Luis Vazquez-Marin; Rev. Rafael Garcia-Molina;

Judicial Vicar - Rev. Jorge Luis Saenz-Ramos;

Justice Promoter - Rev. Jose Miguel Cedeno;

Lawyers - Orlando Duran; Joan Marie Rodriguez-Veve;

Moderator - Rev. Tomas Gonzalez-Gonzalez;

Secretary to the Archbishop - Rev. Alfonso Guzman-Alfaro, O.F.M.;

Diocesan Consultors - Rev. Tomas Gonzalez-Gonzalez; Rev. Msgr. Leonardo J. Rodriguez-Jimenes; Rev. Msgr. Jose Emilio Cummings-Espada (cquintana@perpetuo.org);

Censor Librorum - Rev. Msgr. Fernando B. Felices Sanchez;

Vicar for Education - Vacant -

Vicar for Pastoral Affairs - Rev. Rodney Algarin-Rosado;

Vicar for Priests - Friar Gerardo Antonio Vargas Cruz, O.F.M., Vicar;

Vicar for the Seminaries - Rev. Jaime Luis Ortiz-Cruz, Vicar;

Vicar for Vocations - Rev. Carlos Rafael Santiago-Ramirez;

Vicar for Youth - Rev. Raul Ivan Galarza-Roldan;

Vicar of Catechesis Affairs - Rev. Agapito Antonio Ramos-Valdes, M.SS.CC.;

Vicar of Cultural Affairs - Rev. Msgr. Efrain Rodriguez-Otero, Vicar;

Vicar of Development - Rev. Tomas Gonzalez-Gonzalez;

Pro-Synodal Examiner (Vacant) -

Vicar of Economic Affairs (Vacant) -

Interim Delegate of Economic Affairs - Sandra Rodriguez;

Vicar of Ecumenism - Rev. William Torres-Pagan;

Vicar of Family Affairs - Rev. Phillip Nunez-Carrion, Vicar;

Vicar of Religious - Rev. Alfonso Guzman-Alfaro, O.F.M.;

Vicar of Social Communication (Vacant) -

Auxiliary Vicar of Social Communication (Vacant) -

Vicar of Sports -

Examinatores Cleri (Vacant) -

OFFICES AND DIRECTORS

Angelica Cofradia De Nuestra Senora De Belen - Else Zayas Leon, Interim Butler; Rev. Benjamin Antonio Perez Cruz, Spiritual Adv./Care Srvcs. (virgendebelenpr@gmail.com);

Archdiocesan Historical Archive - t) 787-977-1447 Else Zayas Leon;

Asociacion De Profesionales Catolicos - Jose Varela, Committee Coord.; Lelis Rodriguez (asocprofesionalescatolicos@gmail.com);

Boy Scouts (Vacant) -

Caritas of Puerto Rico - Rev. Enrique Manuel Camacho-Monserrate, Exec. (ssc@arqsj.org);

Carmelite Third Order - t) 787-726-2631 Rev. Hector Luis Cruz-Santiago, O.Carm.;

Casa San Clemente -

Psychological and Pastoral Counseling - t) 787-723-6915

Catechetics - Rev. Agapito Antonio Vargas, M.SS.CC.;

Catechetics Center - Sr. Mercedes Cadenas, H.M.; Sr. Lissette Aviles, O.P.; Sr. Isabel Soto, M.SS.S.;

Catholic Charismatic Renewal - Rev. Jose Angel Rodriguez Reyes;

Catholic Charities - Rev. Enrique Manuel Camacho-Monserrate (ssc@arqsj.org);

Catholic Daughters of America - t) 787-872-6831 Irma Bonilla;

Spiritual Director - Rev. Msgr. Wilfredo Pena-Moredo, Spiritual Adv./Care Srvcs.;

Centro Apostolado De La Cruz - t) 787-637-7475 Maricarmen Rivera, Coord., Urb. Braulio Dueno;

Clergy Social Security (Prevision Social del Clero) - t) 787-728-1650 Raymond Rivera, Pres.; Rev. Jorge Ernesto Torres Rivera, Treas.;

Cofradia De Los Santos Angeles De La Guarda - Maria T. Pagan, Pres. (obrasantosangeles@aol.com);

Cofradia De Nuestra Senora De La Soledad Y Santo Entierro - Maria del Carmen Velez Pabon, Butler; Rev. Benjamin Antonio Perez Cruz, Spiritual Adv./Care Srvcs. (soledadysantoentierropr@gmail.com);

Cofradia Peregrinos De Tierra Santa - t) 787-308-0822 Miguel Torres Soto;

Commission for Sacred Liturgy and Popular Piety - Rev. Msgr. Leonardo J. Rodriguez-Jimenes;

Subcommission for Ministries - Rev. Msgr. Leonardo J. Rodriguez-Jimenes;

Subcommission for Popular Piety (Vacant) -

Subcommission for Sacred Art - t) 787-763-9154 Rev. Msgr. Leonardo J. Rodriguez-Jimenes;

Subcommission for Sacred Music - Rev. Miguel Angel Trinidad-Fonseca;

Comunidad De Vida Cristiana - t) 787-379-5649 Luis E. Marina (lemarini@gmail.com);

Consecratio Mundi - t) 787-203-1058 Migdalia Rojas, Pres.;

Consejo De Accion Social Arquidiocesano - t) 787-308-2212 Hector Bousson;

Cursillos De Cristiandad - Enrique Rivera, Dir.; Rev. Tomas Gonzalez-Gonzalez;

El Visitante - t) 787-728-3710 Most Rev. Ruben Gonzalez-Medina, C.M.F., Pres.; Rev. Efrain Zabala, Editor; Enrique Lopez;

Encuentro Catolico de Novios - Esperanza Miranda Diaz, Natl. Coord.; Dcn. Luis Alvarez Suria;

Equipo De Retiros "A Los Pies De Jesus" - t) 787-964-0104 Jose Gonzalez, Coord.;

Escuela De Evangelizacion - Virgen Milagros Rivera Colon, Contact;

Focolares - Dcn. Jose Hernandez, Dir. (josehernandezjorge23@gmail.com); Diana Rivera;

Franciscan Third Order (Secular Franciscan Order) - t) 787-752-7363 Awilda Vasquez, Natl. Min.;

Grupo Devocion Divina Misericordia - Vacant -

Grupo Misioneros De Amor Y Fe - t) 787-397-1612 Jose A. Mendez, Coord. y Fundador (jamisionerosdeamoryfe@gmail.com);

Grupo Reina De La Paz - t) 787-644-8256 Ivette Pacheco, Pres.;

Grupos De Retiros -

Grupo de Retiros Paz y Bien - t) 787-784-5579 Sr. Osvaldo Roman, Dir.;

Grupos Para La Juventud -

Consejo Arquidiocesano De Pastoral Juvenil - t) 787-671-8251; 787-789-0090 coarqpaj@gmail.com Rev. Raul Ivan Galarza-Roldan, Vicar;

Grupo Juvenil Damasco - t) 787-530-5062 Olga Reboredo, Dir.;

Hermandad Ntra. Sra. de la Caridad - t) 787-720-2361 Angel Pinera, Dir.; Rev. Msgr. Mario Guijarro, Dir.;

Holy Childhood Association - Rev. Jose Orlando Camacho-Torres, C.S.Sp.;

Holy Name Society - Jose E. Rodriguez-Delgado, Dir. (joseeliasrodz@yahoo.com);

Immigrant Aid - t) 787-727-7373

ISTEPA - t) 787-200-6891 Rev. Msgr. Francisco Medina-Santos; Rev. Anibal Rafael Torres-Ortiz, Rector;

Juventud Mariana Vicentina (JMV) - t) 787-727-3963 Janet Rodriguez, Dir.; Sr. Milagros Olivencia, H.C., Archdiocesan Rep., Hospital Auxilio Mutuo (jmvpr@yahoo.com);

Knights of Columbus - Vacant -

La Mujer Por La Familia Catolica En Puerto Rico - t) 787-723-1620 Teruca Rullan, Pres.;

Legion of Mary - t) 787-203-1058 daliaredd@gmail.com Migdalia Rojas, Pres.;

Maranatha House of Prayer - t) 787-759-7734 Rev. Baudilio Guzman, S.J., Dir.; Silvia Saavedra de Badia, Dir. (cmaranatha@gmail.com);

Marriage Encounter - t) 787-963-0247; 787-525-6332 Felix Y Lucy Santana (lucylufalmodovar@gmail.com);

Master of Ceremonies to the Archbishop - Luis Dacosta-De Jesus;

Ministerio Anawin - t) 787-608-1290 Jorge E. Capote (sinsonte67@hotmail.com);

Movimiento De Schoenstatt - t) 787-759-8604 Mario Sanchez; Nancy Sanchez (aprendizdemago@hotmail.com);

Movimiento Juan XXIII - Angel L. Rios, Pres. (libreria_atenas@hotmail.com);

Neocatecumenal Way - t) 787-985-1329 Julio Alvarez, Dir.;

Nocturnal Adoration - Angel Pagan, Pres. (pagandiazangel@gmail.com); Ismael Suarez, Secy.; Ramon Mendez, Santa Maria de Cana;

Spiritual Director - Rev. Ricardo Hernandez Morales;

Our Lady of Providence Cofraterny - cofradia.nsmdprovidencia@gmail.com Hector Balvanera Alfaro, Butler; Rev. Ernesto Gonzalez-Gonzalez, Spiritual Adv./Care Srvcs.;

Padre Nuestro - t) 787-368-3810 Elimelec Valentin, Pres. (elimelec_v@hotmail.com);

Pius Union of the Clergy (Vacant) -

Police Chaplains - Rev. Msgr. Baudilio Merino Merino (Spain); Rev. Msgr. Valeriano Miguelez (Spain); Dcn. Jose Pena Gonzalez;

Pre Cana Conferences (Vacant) -

Pro-Life Center (Human Life International) (Vacant) -

Pro-Life Pharmacists International - Sandra Fabregas, Dir.;

Propagation of the Faith - Rev. Jose Orlando Camacho-Torres, C.S.Sp.;

Radio Stations - Alan Corales, Dir.;

Renovacion Conyugal (Fundacion Fernando Martinez Calle, Inc.) - t) 787-766-7363; 787-751-6001 inf@renovacioncoyugalpr.org Rev. Jorge Ambert, S.J., Dir. (ambertsj@aol.com);

Retiro Reencuentro Familiar - t) 787-797-4500 (Office); 787-797-4288 (Retreat House) Alberto Rosa;

San Juan Bautista Regional Seminary - t) 787-273-8090 seminario.mayor@yahoo.com Rev. Jaime Luis Ortiz-Cruz, Vicar;

San Juan International Airport Chapel - t) 787-487-3731 Dcn. Eduardo Gonzalez;

Secretariado Sagrado Corazon - t) 787-781-6295 Ana M. Bonet, Pres.;

Spiritual Director - Rev. Benjamin Antonio Perez Cruz, Spiritual Adv./Care Srvcs.;

Serra Club (Vacant) -

Servicios Pastorales Paules - t) 787-728-0670 Rev. Santiago Arribas, C.M., Dir.;

Sociedad San Vicente De Paul - t) 787-321-9586 William Rodriguez (wrm940@yahoo.com);

Society for the Protection of Children - Most Rev. Roberto O. Gonzalez-Nieves, O.F.M.;

Superintendent of Schools - Ana Cortes;

Talleres De Oracion y Vida P. Larranaga - t) 787-240-6318 Ana Maria de Orbeta (adeorbeta@yahoo.com);

Television Station - t) 787-276-1300 Luis Quinonez Mora, Gen. Mgr.;

Tourism and Apostleship of the Sea -

Casamar (Vacant) -
Union Eucaristica Reparadora (UNER) - t) 787-789-6660 Esther Vargas; Dollie Morales; Mariza Belarana;
United Against Hunger (Unidos Contra El Hambre) - t) 787-300-4959 uch@arqsj.org Dcn. Jose Aguilera (aguilera57@yahoo.com);
UPR Catholic Student Center - t) 787-767-3348 Rev. Rafael Rodriguez, S.J.;
Vocations Promoter - t) 787-706-9455; 787-273-8090 Rev. Edwin Albeiro Londono Zuluaga; Rev. Carlos Rafael Santiago Ramirez; Rev. Fernando Rafael Colon-Gutierrez;
World Apostolate of Fatima - Rev. Msgr. Fernando B. Felices-Sanchez, Spiritual Dir. (alfatima@coqui.net);
Youth Ministries (Vacant) -

PARISHES, MISSIONS, AND CLERGY

COMMONWEALTH OF PUERTO RICO

BAYAMON

Ascension del Senor - Urb. Rexville, Calle 31 Final, Bayamon, PR 00957; Mailing: P.O. Box 3367, Bayamon, PR 00958-3367 t) 787-799-6120; 787-380-0626 (CRP) trinita@prtc.net Rev. Dairo Hernando Arboleda Ibarra, O.S.S.T., Pst.; Dcn. Luis A Perez;
Catalina de Siena - Urb. Hnas Davila, Q-3 Calle 10, Bayamon, PR 00959 t) 787-785-2381 psantacatalina@gmail.com Rev. Msgr. Alberto Lopez Figueroa, Pst.;
Espiritu Santo - Bella Vista Gardens, Y-300 Calle 24, Bayamon, PR 00957; Mailing: Urb. Bella Vista Gardens, Y-300 Calle 24, Bayamon, PR 00957 t) 787-222-0935 espiritusantobayamon@gmail.com Rev. Sergio Jeair Pereira, O.S.S.T. (Colombia), Pst.; Dcn. Angel Acevedo-Denis; Dcn. Pablo Gonzalez Rosario;
Invencion de la Santa Cruz - 12 Degetau St., Bayamon, PR 00961 t) 787-785-2134 parr.delasantacruz@gmail.com Rev. James Spahn, OP, Pst.; Dcn. William Rodriguez Serrano;
La Resurreccion del Senor - Urb. Royal Town, F-1 Calle 12, Bayamon, PR 00956 c) 939-579-7100 resurreccionroyaltown@gmail.com Dcn. Nicanor Mercado; Rev. Edwin A. Cruz Garcia, Pst.; Dcn. Jose M. Rosario Rivera;
Ntra. Sra. de la Monserrate - Bo. Santa Olaya, Carr. 829 Km 6.2, Bayamon, PR 00956; Mailing: P.O. Box 3948, Bayamon, PR 00958-3948 t) 787-797-7340 lamonserrate.bayamonpr@gmail.com Friar Reynaldo Rivera, O.S.A., Pst.; Friar Antonio Then de la Cruz, O.S.A., Pst.;
  Cristo Rey - Bo. Guaraguao, Sector La Morenita, Bayamon, PR 00957
  Santa Monica - Bo. Guaraguao, Sector Pena, Bayamon, PR 00619
  Ntra. Sra. de la Esperanda - Carr. 8829, Km. 1.5, Bo. Dajaos Sector El Chicharo, Bayamon, PR 00956
Ntra. Sra. de los Dolores - Urb. Alturas de Flamboyan, Bloque DD 25 Calle 18, Bayamon, PR 00957 t) 787-786-7494 (CRP); 787-786-9999 jarsorc1968@hotmail.com Rev. Jorge Alberto Ramirez Sanchez, C.O.R.C., Admin.; Dcn. Francisco Rodriguez Rodriguez;
Ntra. Sra. del Rosario - Carr. 816, Km 5.6, Bo. Nuevo, Bayamon, PR 00958; Mailing: P.O. Box 3917, Bayamon, PR 00958-3917 t) 787-730-6000; 787-221-7878 mojicapaezabel@yahoo.com Rev. Abelardo Mojica Paez, Pst.; Dcn. Enrique Resto-Vargas; Dcn. Hector Reyes Nieves;
  San Juan Bautista -
  Jesus Maestro -
  La Providencia -
Nuestra Senora de la Milagrosa - Carr. 864 Interseccion 80, Bo. Hato Tejas, Bayamon, PR 00960; Mailing: P.O. Box 2104, Bayamon, PR 00960-2104 t) 787-785-6620 parroquialamilagrosa@hotmail.com Rev. Emmanuel Toledo Ramirez, Pst.;
Nuestra Senora del Perpetuo Socorro - Comerio St. No. 190, Bayamon, PR 00956 t) 787-636-1062 frayrafael@dominicospr.com Friar Rafael Gonzalez Padro, O.P., Pst.; Dcn. Ramon L. Ramos; Dcn. Miguel Velez;
Nuestra Senora del Rosario - Urb. Villa Espana, Calle Zaragoza, Bloque, B No. 34, Esq. Calle Vizcaya, Bayamon, PR 00961 t) 939-460-4799 parroquiadelrosario.090@gmail.com Rev. Anibal Rafael Torres-Ortiz, Pst.; Dcn. Norman Aponte; Dcn. Antonio Colon Rivera;
Sagrada Familia - Extension Forrest Hills, Calle Valparaiso Esq Calle Caracas, Bayamon, PR 00959; Mailing: P.O. Box 8478, Bayamon, PR 00960-8478 t) 787-798-2010 parroquiasagradafamilia.bayamon@gmail.com parroquiasagradafamiliabayamon.wordexpress.com Rev. Edwin Hernandez-Ralat, P.B.R.O., Pst.; Dcn. Juan Gabriel Cintron; Dcn. Luis Antonio Colton-Rosa; Dcn. Higinio Santiago Santos;
San Agustin - Urb. Lomas Verdes, Calle Duende Blq. 2E # 21, Bayamon, PR 00956; Mailing: P.O. Box 4263, Bayamon Gardens Sta., Bayamon, PR 00958-4263 t) 787-785-8611 bayamonsanagustin@hotmail.com Friar Antonio Then de la Cruz, O.S.A., Pst.; Dcn. Alberto Enrique Irizarry Caro; Dcn. Cristobal Rivera; Dcn. Juan Alberto Rosario Nieves;
  San Martin de Porres - Calle 1 Bo. Juan Sanchez, Bayamon, PR 00959
  Ntra. Sra. del Buen Consejo - Villas de San Agustin, Bayamon, PR 00959
San Antonio Maria Claret - Urb. Bayamon Gardens, Ave. Castiglione D-24, Bayamon, PR 00957; Mailing: P.O. Box 3292, Bayamon Gardens Sta., Bayamon, PR 00958-3292 t) 787-797-3337 parroquiaclaretbayamon@gmail.com Rev. Demuel Tavarez, CMF, Pst.;
San Jose - Urb. Forest View, Dakar, F-169, Bayamon, PR 00956 t) 787-785-6675 sanjose_claret@yahoo.com Rev. Hector Cuadrado, C.M.F., Pst.; Rev. Tomas Cabello Miguelez, CMF, Assoc. Pst.; Rev. Jose Nieto, C.M.F., Assoc. Pst.;
  Academia Claret - Dakar, F-169, Forest View, c/o San Jose Parish, Bayamon, PR 00956 t) 787-787-6685; 787-786-7976 Nilda Rivera Miranda, Prin.;
San Juan Bautista de la Salle - Estancias de Rio Hondo St. 1ra. Secc., A-19 Rio Cialitos, Bayamon, PR 00961 t) 787-787-9567 plasallepr@gmail.com Rev. Francisco Jose Rodriguez Genao, M.SS.CC., Pst.; Rev. Antonio Romero Iglesias, MM.SS.CC., Assoc. Pst.; Dcn. Francisco Ortiz; Dcn. Jose Vega;
San Miguel Arcangel - Urb. Jardines de Caparra, Calle A-B 32, Bayamon, PR 00959; Mailing: P.O. Box 1714, San Juan, PR 00936-1714 t) 787-222-4720 luismarrerop@yahoo.com Rev. Luis Marrero Padilla, Pst.;
  San Miguel - Bda. San Miguel, Guaynabo, PR 00657
Santa Elena - Urb. Santa Elena, Calle 6 A-14, Bayamon, PR 00957; Mailing: P.O. Box 366, Bayamon, PR 00960-0366 t) 787-230-2204 jorgesaenz_ramos@hotmail.com Dcn. Ruben Gonzalez Reyes;
Santa Maria - Urb. Cana, Calle 24 #II-1, Bayamon, PR 00957 t) 787-797-7248; 787-797-8230 psantamariacmf@gmail.com Dcn. Rafael Araya; Dcn. Jose Ramon Cruz; Rev. Norberto Padilla Cruz, C.M.F., Pst.; Rev. Jose Nunez, C.M.F. (Spain), Assoc. Pst.; Dcn. Jose Velez;
  San Gerardo Mayela - Bo. Buena Vista, Bayamon, PR 00957
  Sagrado Corazon - Bo. Cerro Gordo, Bayamon, PR 00956
Santa Rita de Casia - Urb. Santa Juanita, NS-8 Ave., Hostos, Bayamon, PR 00956-5102 t) 787-786-3971 santaritapr@hotmail.com Friar Carlos Cordero, O.S.A., Pst.; Friar Benigno Palomo Casares, O.S.A., Par. Vicar; Dcn. Ramon L. Rivera; Dcn. Noel Vasquez;
  San Jose - Carr. 831, Bo. Minillas, Bayamon, PR 00619
  Ntra. Sra. Del Carmen - Calle Reno P-54, Urb. Vista Bella, Bayamon, PR 00619
  Sagrado Corazon De Jesus - Calle Palestina D, Z-10, Bayamon, PR 00619
Santa Rosa de Lima - Urb. Santa Rosa, 28-9, Calle 12, Bayamon, PR 00959 t) 787-798-2300 bayamonsantarosa@gmail.com asantarosabay.wix.com/academia Rev. Carlos Ruben Algarin, Pst.;
  Santa Rosa de Lima School - Urb. Santa Rosa, Ave. Main, Bayamon, PR 00959 t) 787-798-2829; 787-798-2539 Lorrie M. Cuevas Torres, Prin.;
Santa Teresa de Jesus - Urb. Santa Teresita, F-10 Calle 12, Bayamon, PR 00960; Mailing: P.O. Box 9204, Bayamon, PR 00960-9204 t) 787-269-6749 parsteresa@gmail.com Dcn. Jimmy Martinez Perez; Rev. Carlos Rafael Santiago Ramirez, Pst.;
  San Martin de Porres - Rio Plantation Urb., Bayamon, PR 00961
  Convento Missioneras de La Caridad - t) 787-269-0207
Santiago Apostol - Urb. Sierra Bayamon, 23-17 Calle 23, Bayamon, PR 00961-4418 t) 787-288-1966 p.sanapostol@yahoo.com Dcn. Angel Pabon; Rev. Agapito Antonio Ramos-Valdes, M.SS.CC., Pst.;
  Santiago Apostol School - c/o Santiago Apostol Parish, Urb. Sierra Bayamon, 23-17 Calle 23, Bayamon, PR 00961-4418 t) 787-786-9179 Neyda Perez-Hernandez, Prin.;
Santo Domingo de Guzman - Ext. La Milagrosa, Calle 2 # 200, Bayamon, PR 00959; Mailing: P.O. Box 4188, Bayamon, PR 00960-4188 c) 787-636-1062 cancilleria2018@arqsj.org Friar Rafael Gonzalez Padro, O.P., Pst.; Dcn. Ruben Gonzalez; Dcn. Hector Negron;
Santo Domingo de Guzman - Urb. Van Scoy, Calle Principal Esq. Calle 3 Oeste, Bayamon, PR 00957; Mailing: P.O. Box 3342, Bayamon, PR 00958-3342 t) 787-797-5510 padrefrancisco@hotmail.com Dcn. Virgilio Andino; Dcn. Ramon L. Ramos; Rev. Edwin A. Cruz Garcia, Pst.;
  Santisima Trinidad - Carretera 167 Km. 10, Bo. Ortiz, PR 00953
  Ntra. Sra. de la Providencia - Urb. Los Dominicos, Bayamon, PR 00958
  Carlos Manuel Rodriguez - Urb. Los Palacios, Toa Alta, PR 00954

CAROLINA

Cristo Rey - Urb. Parque Ecuestre, Calle Dulce Sueño U-8, Carolina, PR 00987; Mailing: P.O. Box 1215, Carolina, PR 00986-1215 t) 787-752-9939 parroquiacristorey92@gmail.com Rev. Rafael De Jesus Gonzalez Ayala, Pst.;
  San Francisco de Asis - Entre las calles Tinajero y Dulce Sueno, Parque Encuestre, PR 00985
  Maria Auxiliadora - Carr. 857 Km 3.6, Bo. Canovanillas, PR 00987
  Divino Nino Jesus - Urb. Ciudad Jardin y Colobos Park, Bo. Cambute, PR 00987
  Cristo Rey - Bo. Carruzos, San Juan, PR 00901
Epifania del Senor - Calle Calais 425, Ext. El Comandante, Carolina, PR 00982 t) 787-752-1149 parroquia.epifania@yahoo.com Rev. Grzegorz Okarma, C.S.M.A., Pst.;
Inmaculada Concepcion - Urb. Valle Arriba Heights, Calle Almendro A-15, Carolina, PR 00983; Mailing: P.O. Box 3562, Carolina, PR 00984-3562 t) 787-276-1527 pinmacconc@gmail.com Rev. Tomas Felipe Chacon-Mora, Pst.; Dcn. Miguel A. Roman Maldonado;
Ntra. Sra. de Fatima - Carr. 853 Km 13.6, Bo. Cedros, Carolina, PR 00985; Mailing: HC 03 Box 12076, Bo. Cedros, Carolina, PR 00985 t) 787-750-2168 nsdefatima853@yahoo.com Rev. Victor Manuel Llenas-Urenas, Pst.; Dcn. Eduardo Betancourt Medero; Dcn. Orlando Rodriguez Melendez;
  Ntra. Sra. del Carmen - Carr. 853, Km 8.0, Carolina, PR 00987
  Santa Teresa de Jesus - Bo. Carr. 853, Km 5.0,

Carolina, PR 00987

Ntra. Sra. del Carmen - Urb. Lomas de Carolina, Calle Monte Membrillo K-8, Carolina, PR 00987; Mailing: P.O. Box 299, Carolina, PR 00986-0299 t) 787-757-5729 parroquiadelcarmen132@yahoo.com Rev. Jesus Mario Gonzalez Zapata, Pst.; Dcn. Cesar Avila; Dcn. Ernie Diaz; Dcn. Jose Luis Rosa Diaz;

Ntra. Sra. Reina de la Paz - Urb. Sabana Gardens, Calle 6 Final, Carolina, PR 00984; Mailing: P.O. Box 3688, Carolina, PR 00984-6388 t) 787-946-5873 parroquiareinadelapaz@yahoo.com Rev. Tomas Felipe Chacon-Mora, Pst.; Dcn. Euripides Lugo;

Divino Nino Jesus -

Ntra. Sra. Reina de Los Angeles - Urb. Los Angeles, 29 Calle Lira, Carolina, PR 00979-1659 t) 787-791-2594 reinadelosangeles29@gmail.com Rev. Carmelo Soto-Tanon, Pst.; Dcn. Vicente Nieves De Leon;

Nuestra Senora de la Piedad - 1001 Marginal Baldorioty de Castro, Ext. Villamar A B-1, Carolina, PR 00979; Mailing: P.O. Box 79520, Carolina, PR 00984 t) 787-726-2880 lapiedadcp@gmail.com Rev. Carlos Luis Rodriguez Hernandez, CP, Pst.;

Nuestra Senora de la Piedad School - c/o Nuestra Senora de la Piedad Parish, Carolina, PR 00984 t) 787-727-7585 (H.S.); 787-727-2460 (Elem.) Lizette Matos, Prin.; Rev. Florencio Landa, C.P. (Spain), Dir.;

San Andres - Urb. Country Club (4 Ta. Ext.), MF-15 Calle 482, Carolina, PR 00982 t) 787-769-7076 padrefelo66@hotmail.com Dcn. Gilberto Mejias; Rev. Rafael Mendez-Hernandez, P.B.R.O., Pst.;

San Felipe Apostol - Urb. Villa Carolina 4ta Ext., Calle 419 Blq 165 #3, Carolina, PR 00984; Mailing: P.O. Box 1494, Carolina, PR 00984-1494 t) 787-762-6250 parroquiasanfelipe@yahoo.com Dcn. Manuel Correa Cruz; Rev. Rodney Algarin-Rosado, Pst.; Dcn. Jose Jaramillo;

San Fernando - Calle Munoz Rivera, S 5 Int., Carolina, PR 00986; Mailing: P.O. Box 128, Carolina, PR 00986-0128 t) 787-769-0170 sanfernandoreydelacarolina@gmail.com Dcn. Presbitero Rivera; Rev. Msgr. Efrain Rodriguez-Otero, Pst.; Dcn. Santiago Diaz Rosa; Dcn. Richard Rodriguez De Jesus;

San Francisco de Asis - Urb. Metropolis, 0-31-A Calle 224, Carolina, PR 00987 t) 787-998-8331 parsanfa@gmail.com Rev. Frank de la Rosa Peguero (Dominican Republic), Pst.; Dcn. Joseph Raymond Vizcarrondo Perez;

San Juan de Dios - Urb. Jardines de Borinquen, Calle Canaria R-9, Carolina, PR 00985; Mailing: P.O. Box 3179, Carolina, PR 00984-3179 t) 787-757-5060 parroq89@gmail.com Dcn. Jose Otero Lugo; Rev. Rodney Algarin, Pst.; Dcn. Juan Munet;

La Sagrada Familia - C. Progreso A-79A, Villa Esperanza, PR 00985

San Valentin - Urb. Rolling Hills, 128 Calle San Luis, Carolina, PR 00988; Mailing: P.O. Box 9382, Carolina, PR 00988-9382 t) 787-750-5277 parroquiasanvalentin083@gmail.com Rev. Natividad Acevedo Vizcaya, Pst.; Dcn. Jose A. Pappaterra;

San Antonio - Urb. San Anton, Calle Ortiz Esq. Quercado, Carolina, PR 00987

Santa Clara de Asis - Urb. Villa Fontana, JL-456 Via 14, Carolina, PR 00983 t) 787-768-1708 parroquiasantaclara1@yahoo.com Rev. Luis S. Olmo, O.F.M. (Spain), Pst.;

San Francisco de Asis -

Santa Gema Galgani Parish Sanctuary - Ave. Galicia Final, Carolina, PR 00983; Mailing: PO Box 2789, Carolina, PR 00984-2789 t) 787-769-5663 andyrrpassio@gmail.com Rev. Anibal Rodriguez, C.P., Pst.; Rev. Javier Montalvo-Aviles, C.P., Par. Vicar;

Santa Gema Galgani Parish Sanctuary School - c/o Santa Gema Galgani Parish Sanctuary, Carolina, PR 00984-2789; Mailing: P.O. Box 2789, Carolina, PR 00984-2789 t) 787-768-3082; 787-757-2505 Sr. Maria Rafaela Ojeda, Dir.;

Santisima Trinidad - Ave. Campo Rico PA-16, 3ra Ext. Urb. Country Club, Carolina, PR 00982 t) 939-204-7404 santisimatrinidad.carolina@gmail.com Rev. William Torres Pagan, Pst.; Dcn. Ibrahim Suarez;

Santo Cristo de la Agonia - Urb. Eduardo J Saldaña, La Ceramica, Calle Roble C29, Carolina, PR 00983; Mailing: P.O. Box 5108, Carolina, PR 00984-5108 t) 787-768-0374 cancilleria2018@arqsj.org Dcn. Miguel A. Marrero-Nieves; Rev. Ivan Luis Huertas Colon, Pst.; Dcn. Antonio Hernandez;

Ntra. Sra. de la Esperanza - Sabana Abajo, Carolina, PR 00982

Santo Cristo de los Milagros - Urb. Villa Carolina, 3ra Ext., Ave. Sanchez Castaño Blq. 122 #42-A, Carolina, PR 00985; Mailing: P.O. Box 834, Carolina, PR 00986-0834 t) 787-636-0317 oficina@pscmpr.org Dcn. Jorge Rivera; Rev. Msgr. Nestor Yulfo-Hoffman, Pst.; Dcn. Manuel Reyes Matos;

CATANO

Nuestra Senora del Carmen - Calle Tren #42, Catano, PR 00963; Mailing: P.O. Box 427, Catano, PR 00963-0427 t) 787-788-0099 parroquiadelcarmencatano@gmail.com Dcn. Angel Oquendo; Rev. Jose Gabriel Corazon Lopez, Pst.;

San Martin de Porres - Urb. Bayview, Catano, PR 00962

San Jose Obrero -

San Francisco de Sales - Urb. Las Vegas, BB-108 Ave. Flor del Valle, Catano, PR 00963; Mailing: P.O. Box 567, Catano, PR 00963-8163 t) 787-788-5036 24sanfranciscodesales@gmail.com Rev. Edwin Albeiro Londono Zuluaga, Pst.;

Santo Domingo De Guzman -

Maria Auxiliadora - Urb. Vistas Del Morro, Catano, PR 00962

San Judas Tadeo (Santuario) - Parcelas Bo. Palmas, Catano, PR 00962

Immaculada Concepcion -

CONDADO, SAN JUAN

Stella Maris - 69 Cervantes St., Condado, San Juan, PR 00907-1947 t) 787-723-2240 parroquia_stellamaris@yahoo.com Rev. Msgr. Antonio Jose Vazquez Colon, Pst.; Dcn. Gilberto Recio Gomez; Rev. Enrique Manuel Camacho-Monserrate, In Res.;

DORADO

Ntra. Sra. de La Salud - Bo. Higuillar, Sector San Antonio, 210 Calle Principal, Dorado, PR 00646; Mailing: P.O. Box 470, Dorado, PR 00646-0470 t) 787-626-4849 pntrasradelasalud@gmail.com Rev. Angel Pagan Torres, Pst.; Dcn. Luis Antonio Alayon-Legrand;

San Antonio de Padua - 184 Calle Norte, Dorado, PR 00646; Mailing: P.O. Box 602, Dorado, PR 00646-0602 t) 787-278-1416 saintantny@coqui.net Dcn. Jose E. Colon; Dcn. Jose C. Diaz; Rev. Jose Angel Rodriguez Reyes, Pst.; Dcn. Jose Del Rio; Dcn. Benito Lugo;

Christ of Reconciliation - Urb. Martorell, Paseo Del Cristo Lot #8, Dorado, PR 00646 t) 787-278-1154

San Martin de Porres - Calle Principal Bo. Mameyal, Dorado, PR 00646

GUAYNABO

Buen Pastor - Urb. Apolo QQIA Calle Acropolis, Guaynabo, PR 00969-5014 t) 787-789-2837 elbuenpastorparroquia@gmail.com www.elbuenpastorguaynabo.net Rev. Jesus Garcia Rodriguez (Venezuela), Pst.;

Corazon de Jesus - Sonadora Km 4.3, Guaynabo, PR 00971-0225; Mailing: HC-01 Box 5735, Guaynabo, PR 00971-5735 t) 787-789-5421 corazondejesuspr@gmail.com Rev. Phillip Nuñez Carrion, Pst.; Dcn. Fernando Figueroa Carrillo;

San Juan Bosco - Bo. Mamey 1, Aguada, PR 00602

Sagrada Familia - Bo. Sonadora, Villa Jalena, Bo. Sonadora, PR 00971

Cristo Salvador - Los Filtros Centro Comunal, Rio Bayamon, Guaynabo, PR 00969; Mailing: PMB 464, P.O. Box 7891, Guaynabo, PR 00970-7891 t) 787-720-6596 cristosalvador08@hotmail.com Rev. Luis Felipe Rodriguez Garnica, Pst.; Dcn. Victor Veguilla Colon;

Divino Nino Jesus - Urb. Lomas del Sol, Calle Principal #54, Guaynabo, PR 00960; Mailing: PBM 143, HC-01, Box 29030, Caguas, PR 00725 t) 787-720-0203 rlamas1951@gmail.com Rev. Rodolfo Lamas, Pst.;

San Rafael Arcangel - Bo. Camarones, Carr. #20, Guaynabo, PR 00970

Jesus Nazareno - Bo. Mamey, Guaynabo, PR 00970

El Buen Pastor - Carr. #1, Guaynabo, PR 00970 t) 787-798-9596

Ntra. Sra. de la Paz - Bo. Quebrada Arenas, Guaynabo, PR 00971

Maria Madre de la Misericordia - Ave. Santa Ana. #150, Guaynabo, PR 00969 t) 787-789-0090 oficina@pmariamm.org Rev. Msgr. Leonardo J. Rodriguez-Jimenes, Pst.; Rev. Emmanuel Toledo Ramirez, Par. Vicar; Dcn. Ivan Llado-Gonzalez; Dcn. Ricardo Lopez Rios;

Maria Madre de Mi Senor - Bo. Tortugo, Carr. 873 #1904, Guaynabo, PR 00969; Mailing: Urb. Santa Clara, F-3 Calle Roble Blanco, Guaynabo, PR 00969 t) 787-400-0707 madredemisenor@gmail.com Rev. Jairo Enrique Granados-Benavides, Pst.; Rev. Leandro Antonio Blandon Rojas, Vicar; Dcn. Fernando Figueroa Carrillo;

Ntra. Sra. del Carmen - Bo. Frailes Llanos, Sector Los Baez, Guaynabo, PR 00657

Nuestra Senora de Belen - Urb. San Patricio, K6 Jacinto Galib, Guaynabo, PR 00968; Mailing: PMB 707 Box 7891, Guaynabo, PR 00970-7891 t) 787-793-2485 parroquiabelenpr@gmail.com

Nuestra Senora de la Paz - Carr. 833 Km 3 Hm 7, #12, Guaynabo, PR 00971; Mailing: PMB 774, P.O. Box 7891, Guaynabo, PR 00970-7891 t) 787-287-5714 nuestrasenoradelapaz152@gmail.com Rev. Jairo Enrique Granados-Benavides, Pst.; Dcn. Jose M. Castillo; Dcn. Porfirio Franco; Dcn. William Manzano;

Ntra. Sra. de la Divina Providencia - Cantagallo, Guaynabo, PR 00971

Espiritu Santo - Bo. Sta. Rosa I, Guaynabo, PR 00971 t) 787-287-2335

Inmaculada Concepcion - Bo. Camarones Centro, Guaynabo, PR 00971

San Jose Obrero - Bo. Sta. Rosa II, Guaynabo, PR 00971

Sagrados Corazones - Urb. Ponce de Leon, 208 Ave. Esmeralda, Guaynabo, PR 00969 t) 787-720-6151 sagradoscorazonespr@gmail.com Rev. Victor Hugo Mira Alvarez, SS.CC., Pst.; Rev. Luis Enrique Leon Aguirre, SS.CC., Assoc. Pst.; Dcn. Ivan E. Dominguez; Dcn. Ulpiano Rivera;

Virgen de la Paz - Bda. Cruz Melendez, Guaynabo, PR 00969

San Jose - Villa Caparra, 215 Carr. #2, Guaynabo, PR 00966-0915 t) 787-781-1155 psanjose48@gmail.com Rev. Ricardo Hernandez Morales, Pst.;

San Jose School - Villa Caparra, 215 #2, Guaynabo (Villa Caparra), PR 00966-1915 t) 787-781-1212 Sr. John Christian, Prin.; Emma Morales Hernandez, Prin.;

San Juan Evangelista - Urb. Torrimar, J-5 Calle Church Hill, Guaynabo, PR 00966 t) 787-783-3522 psanjuanevangelista@gmail.com Rev. Walter S. Gomez-Baca, Pst.; Dcn. Isidro Garcia; Dcn. Sauniel Rondon; Dcn. Miguel De La Sota;

San Juan Evangelista School - c/o San Juan Evangelista Parish, San Juan, PR 00922-0151; Mailing: P.O. Box 10151, San Juan, PR 00922-0151 t) 787-781-5325

San Francisco de Asis - Carr. 19, La Marina, PR 00966

San Pedro Martir de Verona - Guaynabo Centro, Calle Tapia 5, Guaynabo, PR 00969; Mailing: P.O. Box 32, Guaynabo, PR 00970-0032 t) 787-720-2361 parroquiasanpedromartir@gmail.com Rev. Msgr. Mario A. Guijarro de Corzo (Cuba), Pst.; Dcn. Gregory A. Guijarro; Dcn. Carlos Rivera Martinez; Dcn. Jose E. Morales-Rodriguez; Dcn. Angel Loyola Zayas;

San Pedro Martir de Verona School - Alpierre St. Final, Urb. Colimar, Guaynabo, PR 00970-2560; Mailing: P.O. Box 2560, Guaynabo, PR 00970-2560

t) 787-720-2219 Leonardo L. Cuadros, Prin.;

Santa Rosa de Lima - 16 Parque St., Bo. Amelia, Guaynabo, PR 00965 t) 787-781-5855 joseguaipo123@gmail.com Rev. Jose Gregorio Guaipo, Pst.; Dcn. Miguel Torres;

La Milagrosa -

HATO REY

Espiritu Santo - Urb. Floral Park, Calle Ruiz Belvis 75, Hato Rey, PR 00919; Mailing: P.O. Box 190259, San Juan, PR 00919-0259 t) 787-754-0570 director@colespiritusanto.com Rev. Msgr. Valeriano Miguelez (Spain), Pst.;

Espiritu Santo School - ; Mailing: P.O. Box 191715, San Juan, PR 00917 t) 787-754-0490; 787-754-0555

LEVITTOWN

Santisima Trinidad - Ave. Dominicos, Levittown, PR 00950; Mailing: Apt. 50378, Levittown Sta., Toa Baja, PR 00950-0378 t) 787-784-2889 beristain@prtc.net Rev. Jaime Luis Ortiz, Pst.; Dcn. Eusebio Jaca; Dcn. Edwin Negron Rivera;

PUERTO NUEVO

San Pablo - Duero St., No. 370, Urb. Villa Borinquen, Puerto Nuevo, PR 00920 t) 787-507-3234 fmedinasantos@gmail.com Rev. Msgr. Francisco Medina Santos, Pst.;

Ntra. Sra. de la Caridad - Del Cobre Borinquen Towers, San Juan, PR 00920

RIO PIEDRAS

Nuestra Senora de la Providencia - Urb. San Gerardo, 1730 Santa Agueda St., Rio Piedras, PR 00926 t) 787-765-6240 academialaprovidencia@gmail.com Rev. Msgr. Carlos Quintana Puente, Pst.; Dcn. Ricardo Martinez; Dcn. Wilfredo Rodriguez;

Nuestra Senora de la Providencia School - Carr. #176, Km. 2.7, Calle Santa Agueda 1733, Urb. San Gerardo, Rio Piedras, PR 00926 t) 787-767-6552; 787-767-6755 Yolanda I. Martinez, Prin.;

Santismo Sacramento - Urb. Matienzo Cintron, 500 Jerusalem St., Rio Piedras, PR 00923 t) 787-764-3438 rogersalazarvalero@yahoo.com Rev. Rogelio Salazar-Valero (Mexico), Pst.; Dcn. Tomas Febo Rodriguez;

SAN JUAN

Asuncion de La Virgen - Urb. Antonsanti, Calle Calve No. 1484, San Juan, PR 00927 t) 787-250-6771 100.asuncion@gmail.com Rev. Fernando Rafael Colon Gutierrez, Pst.; Dcn. George Enchautegui Ramos;

Catedral de San Juan Bautista - 151 Cristo St., San Juan, PR 00902; Mailing: P.O. Box 9022145, San Juan, PR 00902-2145 t) 787-722-0861 catedral1521@gmail.com www.catedralsanjuanbautista.org (Nuestra Sra. de los Remedios). Rev. Benjamin Antonio Perez Cruz, Rector; Rev. Ernesto Gonzalez Gonzalez, Par. Vicar; Dcn. Benjamin Antonio Ramos; Dcn. Angel Antonio Nieves Colon; Dcn. Louis J. Marin Mingarro; Dcn. Roberto Gonzalez Rosado;

Santo Cristo -

San Jose - t) 787-725-7501

Santa Ana -

Corpus Christi - Urb. Club Manor, Calle Jose Abad 1224, San Juan, PR 00924 t) 787-757-5821 jjjffquintero23@gmail.com Rev. Jose Maria Solano-Uribe (Colombia), Pst.; Dcn. Luis Fernando Amador; Dcn. Tomas Febo; Dcn. Juan Minier; Dcn. Jose Perez;

Santo Domingo de Guzman - Carr. 849 Km 8.7, Sector Santo Domingo, PR 00924

Cristo Redentor - Urb. El Paraiso, 140 Calle Ganges, San Juan, PR 00926-2928 t) 787-946-1999 pangelciappi@me.com Rev. Angel L. Ciappi-Azcorra, Pst.; Dcn. Jose Baez;

Cristo Rey - Urb. Los Maestros, 789 Calle Jaime Drew, San Juan, PR 00923 t) 787-767-3289 parroquiacristorey2014@outlook.com Dcn. Victor Reyes; Rev. Msgr. Manuel Garcia-Perez, Pst.; Dcn. Miguel Roman Del Valle;

Francisca Javiera Cabrini - 1564 Encarnacion St., San Juan, PR 00920 t) 787-783-7447 parroquiamadrecabrini@yahoo.com (Mother Cabrini) Rev. Msgr. Francisco Medina-Santos, Pst.; Dcn. Pedro Juan Baez;

Inmaculado Corazon de Maria - Urb. Santiago Iglesias, #1740 Calle Rodriguez Vera, San Juan, PR 00921-3625 t) 787-782-0245 corazondemaria1704@hotmail.com inmaculadocorazon.tripod.com Rev. Luis Alejandro Mora Duarte, SS.CC., Pst.; Dcn. Benjamin Antonio Ramos Rivera; Dcn. Israel Suarez; Dcn. Pablo Manuel Davila De Jesus;

Capilla - Residencial San Fernando, 1564 Calle Encarnacion, San Juan, PR 00920

Ntra. Sra. del Camino, Metropolitan Hospital -

Jesus Maestro - Urb. Rio Piedras Heights, 1725 Segre, San Juan, PR 00926-3246 t) 787-763-8291 oficina@parroquiajm.org Rev. Jean Rolex, CM, Pst.; Rev. Manuel Aznar, CM, Vicar;

Jesus Nazareno - Calle Guadiana #1666, Urb. El Cerezal, San Juan, PR 00926

Jesus Mediador - Urb. Country Club, 1000 Calle Demetrio O'Daly, San Juan, PR 00924 t) 787-752-2410 parroquiajesusmediador@yahoo.com Dcn. Edwin Rivera; Dcn. Santiago Roman Ramirez; Rev. Jan Krol, C.S.M.A., Pst.; Dcn. Candido Martinez; Dcn. Ramon L. Rivera Rivera;

Maria Auxiliadora - Calle Constitucion Esq. Santa Elena, Cantera, San Juan, PR 00915; Mailing: P.O. Box 14367, San Juan, PR 00916-4367 t) 787-727-5346 24mariaauxiliadora24@gmail.com Rev. Nicolas Navarro Quintana, SDB, Pst.; Rev. Andres Rivera, SDB, Pst.; Rev. Jorge Santiago, SDB, Pst.; Bro. Jose Cabo;

Sagrado Corazon -

Nra. Sra. del Altagracia -

Santisima Trinidad - Ave. Borinquen Final, San Juan, PR 00908

Maria Madre de La Iglesia - Urb. Villa Nevarez, 1120 Calle 5, San Juan, PR 00927-5131 t) 787-765-0600 parrmmiglesia@yahoo.com Rev. Fernando Rafael Colon Gutierrez, Pst.; Dcn. George Enchautegui Ramos;

Maria Reina del Mundo - Calle Nemesio R. Canales Final, San Juan, PR 00918; Mailing: G.P.O. Box 3828, San Juan, PR 00936-3828 t) 787-781-0303 pmariareinadelmundo@gmail.com Rev. Jose Antonio Santiago, Pst.;

Ntra. Sra. de Fatima - Urb. Baldrich, Ave. Munoz Rivera 608, San Juan, PR 00919; Mailing: P.O. Box 190396, San Juan, PR 00919-0396 t) 787-753-6334 pnsdefatima@yahoo.com Rev. Elias Lorenzana Fernandez, O.de.M. (Spain), Pst.; Rev. Jesus Saez Castrillo, Par. Vicar; Rev. Ramon Conde Ocampo, O.de.M., In Res.; Dcn. Gilberto Ramos-Pesquera;

La Merced - ; Mailing: P.O. Box 364048, San Juan, PR 00936-4048 t) 787-765-7342; 787-754-1162 Rosa M. Figueroa, Prin.;

Egida del Maestro -

Ntra. Sra. de Guadalupe - Urb. Puerto Nuevo, 1 N.E. Calle 19, San Juan, PR 00921; Mailing: P.O. Box 364125, San Juan, PR 00936-4125 t) 787-782-0016 pguadalp@coqui.net Rev. Jose Antonio Santiago, Vicar;

Ntra. Sra. de Guadalupe School - c/o Ntra. Sra. de Guadalupe Parish, San Juan, PR 00936-4125; Mailing: G.P.O. Box 364125, San Juan, PR 00936-4125 t) 787-782-0330 Genevieve Zayas, Prin.;

Ntra. Sra. de la Caridad del Cobre - Urb. Buena Vista, Calle 5, No. 124, San Juan, PR 00917; Mailing: P.O. Box 194649, San Juan, PR 00919-4649 t) 787-777-8696 pfeedie@yahoo.com; lbriosotex@yahoo.com Rev. Patrick Celestine;

Sma. Trinidad - Calle Buenos Aires, No. 25, Parada 27, Hato Rey, PR 00919

Ntra. Sra. de la Medalla Milagrosa - Urb. Perez Moris, 209 Calle Mayaguez, San Juan, PR 00917-5147 t) 787-751-2335 lamilagrosahatorey@hotmail.com Rev. Carlos Verdia Nay, Pst.;

Ntra. Sra. de la Monserrate - Ave. Manuel Fernandez Juncos, 1058, San Juan, PR 00908; Mailing: P.O. Box 13726, San Juan, PR 00908-3726 t) 787-722-3134 lamonserratesanturce@gmail.com Friar Jose Aridio Taveras De Leon, O.S.A., Pst.;

Santa Ana -

Nuestra Senora de la Altagracia - Urb. Villa Prades, Calle Felipe Gutierrez #672, San Juan, PR 00924; Mailing: Apt. 29493, San Juan, PR 00929-0493 t) 787-451-5927; 787-590-2022; 787-764-0614 (CRP) altagraciapr04@yahoo.com Rev. Eugenio Francisco Gomez Sr., Pst.; Dcn. Jorge Camacho; Dcn. Hector Rivera; Dcn. Freddie Acevedo Toledo;

Nuestra Senora de la Esperanza - Urb. Hipodromo, Calle Republica 864, San Juan, PR 00910; Mailing: P.O. Box 8532, Fernandez Juncos Sta., San Juan, PR 00910-8532 t) 787-723-5998 virgenmariadelaesperanza@gmail.com Rev. Miguel Rivera-Borges, Pst.; Dcn. Alfredo Serrano Rivera;

Ntra. Sra. de la Providencia - Bda. Figueroa, San Juan, PR 00907

Nuestra Senora de la Merced - Urb. Roosevelt, Calle Pedro Espada 430, San Juan, PR 00918; Mailing: P.O. Box 364133, San Juan, PR 00936-4133 t) 787-763-3657 lamercedhr@yahoo.com Rev. Jesus Saez, O M, Pst.; Dcn. Roberto Irizarry Brignoni;

Nuestra Senora de la Providencia - 219 Aponte St., San Juan, PR 00912 t) 787-692-7507 cancilleria2019@arqsj.org Rev. Olin Pierre Louis, Pst.;

Nuestra Senora de Lourdes - Villa Palmeras, Esq. Calle Colton 288, Ave Gilberto Monroig, San Juan, PR 00915; Mailing: P.O. Box 14452, Bo. Obrero Sta., San Juan, PR 00916-4452 t) 787-726-4643 lourdes.villapalmeras@gmail.com Rev. Manuel Duprey, Pst.;

Nuestra Senora de Lourdes - Urb. El Comandante, 1173 Calle Alejo Cruzado, San Juan, PR 00924 t) 787-752-3716 parrlourdescomandante@aol.com Rev. Grzegorz Okarma, CSMA, Pst.;

Nuestra Senora del Carmen - Ave. Borinquen, Esq. Calle Tapia 609, Bo. Obrero, San Juan, PR 00916; Mailing: P.O. Box 7275, San Juan, PR 00916-7275 t) 787-727-0737 pnsdelcarmenbo@gmail.com Rev. Jose Miguel Cedeño Velez, Pst.; Dcn. Jose Gabriel Corazon De Jesus;

San Martin de Porres - Calle Tito Rodriguez #719, Bo. Obrero, PR 00916

Capilla Sagrado Corazon - Universidad del Sagrado Corazon, San Juan, PR 00916

Nuestra Senora del Pilar - Plaza de Recreo, Rio Piedras, San Juan, PR 00928; Mailing: Box 21134, San Juan, PR 00928-1134 t) 787-692-0452 sfm@coqui.net Rev. Carlos Gonzalez Santiago, S.F.M., Pst.; Rev. Oscar Granados del Valle, SFM, Par. Vicar; Friar Samuel Perez Martell, S.F.M., In Res.; Friar Sergio Ramirez, S.F.M., In Res.; Friar Emanuel Reyes, S.F.M., In Res.; Friar Joshua Torres, S.F.M., In Res.;

Santa Teresita de Nino Jesus - Calle, Tanque #37, Bda. Venezuela, Rio Piedras, PR 00925

Hogar Crea - Barriada Venezuela, San Juan, PR 00901 t) 787-751-5640

Resurreccion del Senor - Calle 31, S.O. #797, Urb. Las Lomas, San Juan, PR 00921-1205 t) 787-792-5939 cancilleria2019@arqsj.org Dcn. Jose M. Sanchez; Rev. Leonardo Rodriguez-Ochoa, Pst.;

Sagrada Familia - Parcelas Hill Brothers, Calle 7 #112 Ave. 65 Inf., San Juan, PR 00929; Mailing: P.O. Box 29311, San Juan, PR 00929-9311 t) 787-767-1723 padrerafaelgarcia@gmail.com Rev. Rafael Garcia-Molina, Pst.;

Sagrado Corazon de Jesus - Calle Oxford 251, Esq. Howard Urb. University Gardens, San Juan, PR 00927 t) 787-765-4798 info@psagradocorazon.org Rev. Antonio Hiciano, C.M., Pst.; Rev. Ignacio Alonso, C.M., Assoc. Pst.; Rev. Anulfo del Rosario Sosa, CM, Assoc. Pst.;

Sagrado Corazon de Jesus School - Esq. Iteramericana y Palma Real, Urb. University Gardens, Rio Piedras, PR 00927-4826 t) 787-765-9430 Mary Andreen, O.S.F., Prin.;

Sagrado Corazon de Jesus - Ave. Ponce de Leon, Parada 19, San Juan, PR 00910; Mailing: F. Juncos Sta., Box 8312, San Juan, PR 00910-8312 t) 787-722-0235 cancilleria2019@arqsj.org Rev. Miguel Rivera-Borges,

Pst.;

San Agustin - Ave. Constitucion 265, Puerto de Tierra, San Juan, PR 00902; Mailing: P.O. Box 9024108, San Juan, PR 00902-4108 t) 787-722-4289 sanagustiniglesia@yahoo.com Rev. Esteban De la Rosa-Martinez, C.Ss.R., Pst.; Rev. Damian Wall, C.Ss.R., In Res.;

Colegio San Agustin - 255 Constitution Ave., San Juan, PR 00902-4078; Mailing: Box 9024078, San Juan, PR 00902-4078 t) 787-722-4544 Marie Benitez Alonso, Prin.;

San Antonio de Padua - Calle Arzuaga # 218, San Juan, PR 00925; Mailing: P.O. Box 21350, San Juan, PR 00928-1350 t) 787-765-0606 sanantoniopr@gmail.com Friar Ramon Hiram Negron Cruz, O.F.M.Cap., Supr.; Friar Roberto Colon Ortiz, O.F.M.Cap., Pst.; Friar Gamalier Martinez, O.F.M.Cap., Par. Vicar;

Nuestra Senora del Buen Consejo - Calle De Diego, San Juan, PR 00928

San Francisco de Asis - 301 San Francisco St., Viejo San Juan, San Juan, PR 00902; Mailing: Box 9024231, San Juan, PR 00902-4231 t) 787-724-1131 secretaria@yosoycapuchino.com www.yosoycapuchino.com Friar Jose David Maldonado Rivas, O.F.M.Cap., Pst.; Friar Moises Villalta, O.F.M.Cap. (El Salvador), Par. Vicar; Rev. Ramon Lopez-Lopez, O.F.M.Cap., In Res.;

Capilla San Conrado - Bo. La Perla, San Juan, PR 00902 t) (787) 724-1131

San Francisco de Monte Alvernia - Calle 10, #15 Ext. San Agustin, San Juan, PR 00926 t) 787-200-5305 perezjuansilva@gmail.com Rev. Anibal Rosario Mercado, O.F.M.Cap., Pst.; Dcn. Juan Bautista Perez Silva;

San Francisco Javier - Urb. Fair View, Calle 19, G46., San Juan, PR 00926 t) 787-761-2115 oficina@sanfj.com Rev. Raul Ivan Galarza, Pst.; Dcn. Luis Alvarez Suria; Dcn. Jose Hernandez; Dcn. Raul A. Perez Gonzalez;

San Ignacio de Loyola - Urb. Santa Maria, 1904 Calle Narciso, San Juan, PR 00927-6706 t) 787-751-7512 parroquiasanignaciopr@hotmail.com Rev. Timothy Howe, S.J., Pres.; Rev. Anthony Borrow, S.J., Pst.; Rev. Ronald Gonzales, S.J., Pst.; Rev. Baudilio Guzman, S.J., Par. Vicar; Rev. Sean O'Sullivan, S.J., Par. Vicar; Rev. Samuel Wilson, S.J., Par. Vicar; Rev. Jorge Ambert, S.J., In Res.; Rev. Fabian Rodriguez Rodriguez, S.J., In Res.; Rev. Jose Alejandro Ruiz Andujo, S.J., In Res.; Rev. Mario A. Torres, S.J., In Res.; Rev. Andres Val-Serra, S.J., In Res.; Rev. Alfredo Guzman, S.J., DRE; Dcn. Carmelo Rivera;

Academia San Ignacio de Loyola - 1908 Calle Narciso, Rio Piedras, PR 00936 t) 787-765-8190 Glorimar Soegaard, Prin.;

Cond. Jardines de San Francisco -

San Jorge - Calle San Jorge 157, Santurce, San Juan, PR 00914; Mailing: P.O. Box 6427, Loiza Sta, San Juan, PR 00914-6427 t) 787-724-7780 sanjorgeparroquiapr@gmail.com Rev. Pedro L. Reyes-Lebron, Pst.; Rev. Jose Antonio Landrau Roman, Vicar;

San Jose Obrero - Calle Belmonte 470, San Juan, PR 00923 t) 787-767-1448 royersalazarvalero@yahoo.com Rev. Rogelio Salazar-Valero (Mexico), Pst.;

San Juan Bosco - Villa Palmeras, Calle Lutz 368, San Juan, PR 00915; Mailing: P.O. Box 14125, Barrio Obrero Sta., San Juan, PR 00916-4125 c) 939-287-4186 cancilleria2018@arqsj.org Rev. Jorge L. Gonzalez, S.D.B., Pst.;

La Milagrosa - Villa Palmeras, C. Lutz 300 Final, Santurce, PR 00915 t) 787-728-2175

Ntra. Sra. del Rosario - Fajardo St., San Juan, PR 00915

San Martin de Porres - Union St. #58, Playita, PR 00915

San Juan de La Cruz - Urb. Los Paseos, 120 Blvd. de la Fuente, San Juan, PR 00926 t) 787-283-9983 parroquiasanjuandelacruz@live.com Rev. Jose Juan Cardona Diaz, Pst.; Dcn. Jorge Colon Velez; Dcn. Luis Francisco Hernandez; Dcn. Omar Santamarina;

San Juan M. Vianney - Urb. Garcia Calle, Calle A-12, San Juan, PR 00932 t) 787-980-8515 cancilleria2018@arqsj.org (Santo Cura de Ars) Rev. Gerardo Enrique Oliveras, Pst.; Dcn. Manuel Andino;

La Milagrosa - Urb. Hillside Calle 2 I 14, San Juan, PR 00926

Cristo del Perdon - Parcelas Canejas, Bo. Caimito Bajo, San Juan, PR 00901

Dulce Nombre de Maria - Bo. Dulce, Caimito Bajo, San Juan, PR 00901

Ntra. Sra. del Carmen - Calle Fidalgo, Sector Corea, Bo. Caimito Bajo, San Juan, PR 00901

San Lucas - Urb. El Senorial, Calle Pio Baroja 380, San Juan, PR 00926 t) 787-761-5476 psanlucas.evangelista@gmail.com Rev. Ramon Orlando Tirado, Pst.;

San Luis Gonzaga - Urb. Villa Andalucia, Calle Ronda A-17, San Juan, PR 00926 t) 787-761-9438 parroquiasanluisgonzaga1965@gmail.com Rev. Victor Modesto Torres-Cesneros (Panama), Pst.;

San Luis Rey - Urb. Reparto Metropolitano, 869 Calle 43 S.E., Ste. #65, San Juan, PR 00921 t) 787-767-6235 psanluisrey869@gmail.com Dcn. Carlos J. Amador-Hernandez; Rev. Marco Antonio Rivera-Perez, Pst.; Dcn. Fernando M. Padilla Nazario;

San Mateo - Calle San Mateo, Esq. San Jorge, San Juan, PR 00912; Mailing: P.O. Box 6081, San Juan, PR 00914-6081 t) 787-722-4158 parroquiasanmateo1773@gmail.com Rev. Olin Pierre Louis, Pst.;

San Vicente de Paul - 160 Ave. Fernandez Juncos, Parada 24, San Juan, PR 00910; Mailing: P.O. Box 19118, San Juan, PR 00910-0118 t) 787-727-3963 parroquiasanturce@hotmail.com Rev. Misser Louis, C.M, Pst.;

San Vicente de Paul School - 709 Bolivar St., San Juan, PR 00910; Mailing: Box 8699, San Juan, PR 00910 t) 787-727-4273 Emilio Roldan, Prin.;

Santa Bernardita Soubirous - Urb. Country Club, Calle Espioncela y Torcaza, San Juan, PR 00929; Mailing: P.O. Box 29826, 65 Infanteria Sta., San Juan, PR 00929-9826 t) 787-762-0375; 787-257-7643; 787-762-2010 santabernarditapr@yahoo.com www.parroquiasantabernardita.org Dcn. Ernesto Rivera Negron; Rev. Msgr. Wilfredo Pena-Moredo, Pst.;

Santa Catalina Laboure - Carr. 842 Km 3.6, Bo. Caimito, San Juan, PR 00926; Mailing: P.M.B. 507, 267 Calle Sierra Morena, San Juan, PR 00926-5583 t) 787-720-0303 eusebiocfernandez@yahoo.com Rev. Eusebio C. Fernandez Salazar (Colombia), Pst.;

Medalla Milagrosa - Bo. Los Romeros, San Juan, PR 00926-5636

San Pablo - Carr. 842, San Juan, PR 00926

Santa Cecilia - Urb. Riveras de Cupey, Ave. Ceciliana #600, San Juan, PR 00926; Mailing: Urb. Crown Hill, El Señorial Mail Sta., PMB 333, San Juan, PR 00926-0333 t) 787-755-8670 danilo.martinezduarte@gmail.com Rev. Danilo Martinez, Pst.;

Capilla San Agustin - Carr. 844, Cupey Bajo, San Juan, PR 00926

Santa Luisa de Marillac - Urb. La Cumbre Ave., Emiliano Pol, San Juan, PR 00926; Mailing: PMB 17, 267 Calle Sierra Morena, San Juan, PR 00926-5583 t) 787-720-3150 parroquiasantaluisademarillac2@gmail.com Rev. Tomas Gonzalez-Gonzalez, Pst.; Dcn. Francisco Colon; Dcn. Eddie Lopez Alonso;

Santa Maria de Los Angeles - Urb. La Riviera, Ave. De Diego 930, San Juan, PR 00922; Mailing: Box 10716, Caparra Heights Sta., San Juan, PR 00922-0716 t) 787-792-2640 parroquiasantamaria@yahoo.com Rev. Marco Antonio Rivera-Perez, Pst.;

Santa Rosa de Lima - Urb. Venus Gardens, 1765 Calle Lesbos, San Juan, PR 00926-4843 t) 787-761-6586 santarosadelimapr@yahoo.com santarosadelimapr.blogspot.com Rev. Carlos Perez Toro, Pst.; Dcn. Pedro Costa; Dcn. Jose Febres Maeso; Dcn. Edwin Rodriguez;

Santa Teresa de Jesus Jornet - Carr. 176, Km 10.0, Camino Los Gonzalez, Cupey Alto, San Juan, PR 00926; Mailing: El Senorial Mail Sta., P.O. Box 415, San Juan, PR 00926-0415 t) 787-230-0273 brandopr62@gmail.com Rev. Giovanni Perez Berrios, Pst.; Dcn. Martin Cuevas;

San Martin de Porres - Camino El Mudo. Cupey, Alto, San Juan, PR 00926 t) 787-748-2978

Ntra. Sra. de la Salud - Camino Guayabos Carr. 176, Km. 9.5, Cupey, Alto, San Juan, PR 00926 t) 787-748-2978

Parroquia Santa Teresa de Jesus Jornet - Camino Los Gonzalez, Km. 5.3, San Juan, PR 00926

Santa Teresita del Nino Jesus - 2059 Calle Loiza, Santurce, San Juan, PR 00914; Mailing: P.O. Box 6065, Loiza Sta., San Juan, PR 00914-6065 t) 787-727-0030 cancilleria2019@arqsj.org Rev. Jorge Maria Rivera Maldonado, O.Carm., Par. Vicar; Friar Hector Luis Cruz Santiago, O.Carm., Assoc. Pst.; Rev. Jose Maldonado Vazquez, O.Carm., In Res.;

Sagrada Familia - Residencial, Luis Llorens Torres, PR 00913 t) 809-726-0570

Santisimo Salvador - Urb. Villa Capri, Niza St., 575, San Juan, PR 00924 t) 787-761-3314 parroquiadelsalvador@gmail.com Rev. Nicolas Zunun, SCH.p, Pst.; Rev. Manuel Civeles Villanueva, SchP, Vicar; Rev. Juan L. Cabrerizo, Sch.P. (Spain), Assoc. Pst.; Dcn. Luis O. del Rio; Dcn. Luis A. Medina;

Calasanz - Ave. Montecarlo, Esq. Z, Urb. Montecarlo, San Juan, PR 00929-0067; Mailing: P.O. Box 29067, San Juan, PR 00929-0067 t) 787-750-2500 Glenda Laureano, Prin.; Ana Celia Santos, Prin.;

Ntra. Sra. Reina de la Paz - Calle #1 Esq. C-8 Urb. Berwind States, Rio Piedras, PR 00924

San Jose de Calasanz - Calle #23 408, Parc. Hills Brothers, Rio Piedras, PR 00924

Santos Pedro y Pablo los Apostoles - Urb. Jardines de Berwind, Calle 1 Lote K, San Juan, PR 00929; Mailing: P.O. Box 30666, San Juan, PR 00929-1666 t) 787-226-7616 padrerafaelgarcia@gmail.com Rev. Rafael Garcia-Molina, Pst.;

<u>SANTURCE</u>

Ntra. Sra. del Perpetuo Socorro - Calle Marti 704, Miramar, Santurce, PR 00907-3227 t) 787-721-1015 cancilleria2019@arqsj.org Rev. Msgr. Jose Emilio Cummings-Espada, Pst.;

Ntra. Sra. del Perpetuo Socorro School - t) 787-724-1447; 787-721-4540 Angel Cintron, Prin.;

<u>TOA ALTA</u>

Ntra. Sra. de la Providencia - Bo. Pinas Carr. 861 Km 5.2, Toa Alta, PR 00954; Mailing: P.O. Box 3836, Bayamon Gardens Sta., Bayamon, PR 00958-3836 t) 787-224-2235 info@parroquialaprovidencia.org www.parroquialaprovidencia.org Dcn. Federico Diaz; Rev. Cesar Edgardo Santos Romero, Admin.;

Ntra. Sra. de Fatima - Sector Rincon, Bo. Pinas, PR 00953

La Resurreccion - Villa del Rio, Bo. Pinas, PR 00953

Ntra. Sra. del Carmen - Sector del 7, San Juan, PR 00901

Sagrada Familia - Villa Juventud, Bo. Pinas, PR 00953

San Ricardo - Bo. Pinas, Toa Alta, PR 00954

Nuestra Senora de la Medalla Milagrosa - Bo. Quebrada Cruz, Parcelas Viejas , Carr. 824 Km 3.8, Toa Alta, PR 00953; Mailing: P.O. Box 335, Toa Alta, PR 00954-0335 t) 787-870-4090 milagrosatoaalta@gmail.com Rev. Joaquin Mayorga-Fonseca, Pst.; Dcn. German Hernandez Pagan; Dcn. Francisco Villamil;

Nuestra Senora del Carmen - Sector El Cuco, Bo. Quebrada Cruz, Toa Alta, PR 00953

San Esteban, Protomartir - Frente Urb. Montesol, Ave. Hato Tejas Esq. 861 Km 4.0, Toa Alta, PR 00953; Mailing: P.O. Box 3729, Bayamon, PR 00958-3729 t) 787-799-2925 parroquiasanesteban@prtc.net Dcn. Rafael Morales Figueroa; Dcn. Jose Ramon Perez-Bracero; Dcn. Emerito Ventura Ruiz; Rev. Hernan Berdugo-Sanjuan, Pst.;

Capilla Cristo Rey - Sector La Cuerda, Bo. Bucarabones, Toa Alta, PR 00953

San Fernando Rey - Calle Jose De Diego #10, Toa Alta, PR 00954; Mailing: P.O. Box 63, Toa Alta, PR 00954-0063 t) 787-870-2585 fdo8702585@coqui.net Dcn. Felipe Collazo; Dcn. Pablo Irene; Dcn. Jose Narvaez; Rev. Eddie Rivera-Marzan, Pst.;

San Antonio - Rio Lajas, Dorado, PR 00646

San Jose - Bo. Rio Lajas, Sector Jazmin Carr. 823, Toa Alta, PR 00954; Mailing: P.O. Box 777, Toa Alta, PR 00954-0777 t) 787-693-4493 parroquiasanjose694@gmail.com Dcn. Luis R. Nieves Marrero; Rev. Gerard Mugabi, A.J., Pst.;

Ntra. Sra. del Camino - Bo. Espinosa, Carr. #2, Dorado, PR 00646

Santa Teresita -

Sagrada Familia - Sector Marzan, Bo. Rio Lajas, Toa Alta, PR 00758

Sagrado Corazon - Sector Los Mudos, Bo. Quebrada Arenas, Toa Alta, PR 00758

San Judas Tadeo - Bo. Galateo Centro, Carr. 804, K0.4, Toa Alta, PR 00953; Mailing: P.O. Box 1006, Toa Alta, PR 00954-1006 t) 787-430-8670 sanjudastadeo_toaalta@hotmail.com Rev. Pius Wesonga, A.J., Pst.; Dcn. Jose Mojica-Torres;

San Martin de Porres -

Santa Teresa De Jesus - Bo. Quebrada Cruz, Toa Alta, PR 00758

TOA BAJA

Espiritu Santo - Urb. Levittown, Paseo Damisela 1453, Toa Baja, PR 00949; Mailing: P.O. Box 50272, Levittown Sta., Toa Baja, PR 00950-0272 t) 787-784-4805 parroqespiritusanto072@gmail.com Dcn. Jose Aguilera; Dcn. Martin Estrada; Dcn. Guillermo M. Vaello Perez; Dcn. Manuel Sanchez; Rev. Milton Agustin Rivera-Vigo, Pst.;

Ntra. Sra. del Carmen - Calle Carmen, Bo. Palo Seco, Toa Baja, PR 00649

Ntra. Sra. de la Candelaria - Bo. Pajaro Carr. 863 Km 0.5, Toa Baja, PR 00949; Mailing: P.O. Box 892, Toa Baja, PR 00951-0892 t) 787-251-0503 cancilleria2019@arqsj.org Rev. Jose Dario Martinez Tobon (Colombia), Pst.; Dcn. Victor Manuel Charriez; Dcn. Anselmo Miranda Mercado; Dcn. Roberto Ortiz;

Cristo Rey - Calle 10, Bo. Bucarabones, Toa Alta, PR 00758

Santa Maria La Mayor - Carr. #2 R.063, Bo. Macun, Bo. Macun, PR 00759

Santisima Trinidad - Urb. Las Colinas, Toa Baja, PR 00759

Buen Pastor - Urb. Sta. Maria, Toa Baja, PR 00759

Nuestra Senora de Covadonga - Urb. Covadonga, Calle Clarin 100, Toa Baja, PR 00949; Mailing: P.O. Box 9076, Bayamon, PR 00960 t) 787-251-6466 p.covadonga@gmail.com Dcn. Efrain Narvaez; Rev. Jairo Salazar Castano, Pst.;

Ntra. Sra. de Lourdes - Bo. Candelaria Arenas, Toa Baja, PR 00759

San Martin de Porres - Bo. Kennedy, Toa Baja, PR 00759

San Jose Obrero - Sabana Seca, Carr. 866, Km 3.6, Toa Baja, PR 00952; Mailing: Box 173, Sabana Seca, PR 00952-0173 t) 787-784-1400 josantpe@hotmail.com Dcn. Ramon L. Colon-Hernandez; Friar Gerardo Antonio Vargas Cruz, O.F.M., Par. Vicar; Rev. Alfonso Guzman-Alfaro, O.F.M., In Res.; Rev. Santos Perez Castillo, O.F.M., Supr.;

Ntra. Sra. del Carmen - Carr. 2-R 866 K4 H4 Int., Los Bravos, Sabana Seca, PR 00949

San Martin de Porres - Carr. 816 PAR 1034, Villa Marisol, Sabana Seca, PR 00949

San Pedro Apostol - Las Flores 47, Toa Baja, PR 00949; Mailing: P.O. Box 513, Toa Baja, PR 00951-0513 t) 787-794-1327 psanpedroapostol.parroquia98@gmail.com Rev. Calixto Soto Silvera (Colombia), Pst.; Dcn. Joaquin Rivera Vazquez;

Santa Teresita - Calle Quintero, Toa Baja, PR 00949

Ntra. Sra. de Guadalupe - Calle Crisantemo, Parcela 137-A, Toa Baja, PR 00950

San Jose - Calle San Jose #303, San Juan, PR 00901

TRUJILLO ALTO

Exaltacion de la Santa Cruz - Calle J. G. Diaz 515, Trujillo Alto, PR 00977; Mailing: Box 1808, Trujillo Alto, PR 00977-1808 t) 787-761-0570 santacruzpr@yahoo.com Dcn. Alfredo Aponte; Dcn. Domingo Vargas; Rev. Carlos Alberto Contreras Tribaldo, Pst.;

Gruta de Lourdes - Bo. Cuevas Carr. 876 Km 1.7, Trujillo Alto, PR 00976; Mailing: P.O. Box 1081, Trujillo Alto, PR 00977-1081 t) 787-761-0571 grutadelourdes1925@yahoo.com lagrutadelourdes.org Dcn. Pablo Torres; Rev. Msgr. Fernando Benicio Felices Sanchez, Pst.;

Maria Llena de Gracia - Urb. Rincon Espanol, Calle 1 Esq 4, Trujillo Alto, PR 00977; Mailing: P.O. Box 1618, Trujillo Alto, PR 00977-1618 t) 787-945-5289 jmcdno@gmail.com Rev. Raul Ivan Galarza Roldan, Pst.;

San Bartolome - Urb. Ciudad Universitaria, X-1 Calle 16, Trujillo Alto, PR 00976 t) 787-755-0120 parr.sanbartolome@yahoo.com Dcn. Angel L. Davila Casado; Dcn. Victor Vega Laureano; Rev. Rafael Delgado-Diaz, O.P., Admin.;

San Francisco de Asis - Comunidad Ramon T. Colon, Calle 2 # 32 Qda. Negrito, Trujillo Alto, PR 00976; Mailing: P.O. Box 1316, Trujillo Alto, PR 00977-1316 t) 787-755-5661 josevolquez27@yahoo.es Rev. Luis Amaury Jose Volques, CRL, Pst.; Dcn. Alfredo Aponte; Dcn. William Rios; Dcn. Hector Rivera;

Espiritu Santo - Bo. Kennedy Hills, Carr. 181 Km 10, San Juan, PR 00907

San Jose de la Montana - Carr. #181 R-851, Bo. Sabana, PR 00965

La Inmaculada Concepcion - Bo. Talanco, Carr. #181 R-852, San Juan, PR 00907

San Judas Tadeo - Urb. El Conquistador, Calle 7 Esq. 8, Trujillo Alto, PR 00977; Mailing: Apt. 1535, Trujillo Alto, PR 00977-1535 t) 787-755-5993 ivanbsa@hotmail.com Dcn. Marcos Arcay-Garcia; Rev. Ivan R. Serrano-Rivera, Pst.; Dcn. Vicente LaSanta Arroyo;

Madre del Divino Pastor - Carr. 844 Km. 0.2, Parcelas Carraizo, Trujillo Alto, PR 00760

Virgen del Carmen - Carr. 175, Bo. Carraizo Alto, Trujillo Alto, PR 00760

San Pio X - Bo. Saint Just, Carr. 848 Km 1.4, Trujillo Alto, PR 00978; Mailing: P.O. Box 631, Saint Just, PR 00978-0631 t) 787-761-5040 alpiox2010@yahoo.com Rev. Ismael Fernandez-Torres, O.P., Pst.; Dcn. Rolando Flores Rivera; Dcn. Martin Rosado;

Ntra. Sra. del Rosario - Calle Lirio, Esq. Orquidea, Urb. Round Hill, Rio Piedras, PR 00923

SCHOOLS: PRESCHOOL THRU HIGH SCHOOL

SCHOOLS

COMMONWEALTH OF PUERTO RICO

BAYAMON

Casa Mision Claret - (PAR) Bo. Buena Vista, Bayamon, PR 00956; Mailing: R.R. 12, Box 10131, Bo. Buena Vista, Bayamon, PR 00956 t) 787-797-8230 faustocmf@hotmail.com (Claretians) Rev. Hector Cuadrado, C.M.F., Moderator; Rev. Norberto Padilla Cruz, C.M.F., Pst.; Rev. Jose Vicente Martinez-Santos, C.M.F., Pst.; Rev. Toribio Nicolas Garcia-Lora, C.M.F., Par. Vicar; Rev. Jose Nieto, C.M.F., Par. Vicar; Rev. Luis Enrique Ortiz Alvarez, C.M.F., Par. Vicar; Rev. Tomas Cabello Miguelez, C.M.F., Assoc. Pst.; Rev. Fausto Cruz Rosa, C.M.F., Assoc. Pst.; Rev. Jose Felix Nuñez, C.M.F., Assoc. Pst.; Rev. Vicente Peñalba, C.M.F., Assoc. Pst.; Rev. Salvador Salgado Pabon, C.M.F., Assoc. Pst.;

Colegio Beato Carlos Manuel Rodriguez - (PAR) 3000 Jazmin, Urb. Lomas Verdes, Bayamon, PR 00956; Mailing: P.O. Box 4225, Bayamon, PR 00958 t) 787-798-5260; 787-798-1548; 787-798-2329 pjmartinez@colegiobeato.org www.cbcmr-bay.org Luisa M. Morales, Prin.; Pedro J. Martinez, Dir.; Jaime Solivan, Librn.;

Colegio Ntra. Sra. del Rosario - (PAR) Calle 5, AA-7, Rep. Valencia, Bayamon, PR 00659 t) 787-798-5100 cnsr2003@cnsr.hotmail.com Elba I. Soto, Prin.; Sr. Ma. Ana Jimenez Maldonado, O.P., Dir.;

Colegio Santa Rosa - (PAR) Urb. Santa Rosa, Calle 12 Blq 28 #9, Bayamon, PR 00960 t) 787-798-2829 santarosacuevas@gmail.com www.asantarosa.wordpress.org Neymi A. Aponte, Prin.; Nilsa Gonzales, Prin.; Rev. Virgilio Martinez (Spain), Dir.;

CAROLINA

Colegio Maria Auxiliadora - (PAR) (Grades PreK-12) Urb. Villa Carolina, 3ra Ext. Ave., Sanchez Castaño, Blq. 122 #42A, Carolina, PR 00986-7770; Mailing: Box 7770, Carolina, PR 00986-7770 t) 787-768-6924 info@auxiliadorapr.net auxiliadorapr.net Rev. Msgr. Nestor Yulfo-Hoffman, Dir.;

Colegio Santa Gema - (Grades PreK-12) 100 Galicia Ave., Vistamar, Carolina, PR 00983; Mailing: P.O. Box 2789, Carolina, PR 00984-2789 t) 787-768-3082 santagema@gmail.com www.csgpr.org Rev. Anibal Rodriguez, C.P., Dir.; Wanda Sanchez, Librn.;

CATANO

Prenoviciado Salesiano - (PAR) Ave. Flor Del Valle, Bloque BB #108, Urb. Las Vegas, Catano, PR 00962; Mailing: P.O. Box 567, Catano, PR 00963-8163 t) 787-275-1921 sanfasal@coqui.net Don Bosco Salesians. Rev. Adan Marrero, S.D.B.;

GUAYNABO

Colegio Marista - (PRV) (Grades PreK-12) Alturas de Torrimar #6 Calle Marcelino Champagnat, Guaynabo, PR 00969-3251 t) 787-720-2186; 787-720-2187 secretaria@maristasguaynabo.org www.maristasguaynabo.org Marist Brothers. Annabel Correa, Prin.; Bro. Luis Carlos Gutierrez, F.M.S., Pres.;

Colegio San Pedro Martir - Urb. Colimar, Calle Alpierre Final, Guaynabo, PR 00969; Mailing: P.O. Box 2560, Guaynabo, PR 00970-2560 t) 787-720-2219 colegiosanpedrom@yahoo.com Leonardo L. Cuadros, Prin.; Rev. Msgr. Mario Guijarro, Dir.;

Preescolar San Juan Evangelista - (Grades PreSchool-Urb. Torrimar, JA-5 Calle Church Hill, Guaynabo, PR 00966-3109 t) 787-781-5325 info@pesje.org www.pesje.org Isamari Rivera Ortiz, Prin.; Rev. Walter S. Gomez-Baca, Dir.;

HATO REY

Colegio Nuestra Senora de La Merced - Calle Sargento Luis Medina #374, Hato Rey, PR 00936; Mailing: P.O. Box 364048, San Juan, PR 00936-4048 t) 787-754-1162 directorlamerced@gmail.com www.colegiolamercedpr.com Rev. Pavel Alba Hernandez, O.de.M., Admin.; Rev. Elias Lorenzana Fernandez, O.de.M. (Spain), DRE; Cinthia Piovanetti, Dir.; Vanessa Zayas, Prin.;

PUERTO NUEVO

San Gabriel School For The Deaf - Prolongacion Calle 19, N.E., Puerto Nuevo, PR 00920; Mailing: P.O. Box 360347, San Juan, PR 00936-0347 t) 787-783-3455 Sr. Amparo Blasco, Dir.;

RIO PIEDRAS

Colegio Mater Salvatoris - Carr. 8838 Km 4.8 de Rio Piedras Caguas, Rio Piedras, PR 00926-9690; Mailing: R.R. 37 Box 3080, San Juan, PR 00926-9601 t) 787-765-0130 puertorico.colegio@matersalvatoris.org sanjuan.matersalvatoris.org/

Colegio Nuestra Senora de la Providencia - (PAR) Ave. San Ignacio #1358, Urb. Altamesa, Rio Piedras, PR 00921; Mailing: P.O. Box 11610, San Juan, PR 00922-1610 t) 787-781-7506; 787-782-6344 zegri@coqui.net www.colegiolaprovidencia.org (Girls) Mercedarian Sisters. Sr. Lourdes Martinez, Prin.;

SABANA SECA

Post-Noviciado San Jose Obrero - (PAR) Carr. 866 Km. 3.4, Sabana Seca, Sabana Seca, PR 00952; Mailing: P.O. Box 173, Sabana Seca, PR 00952-0173 t) 787-795-3141 (Franciscans) Rev. Eddie Caro, O.F.M., Rector;

SAN JUAN

Academia Maria Reina - Urb. College Park, Glasgow #1879, San Juan, PR 00921-4899 t) 787-764-0690 amrjcb@yahoo.com Girls. Rita Hernandez, Prin.; Sr. Judith Burchyns, C.S.J., Pres.; Lucila Aponte, Librn.;

Academia Perpetuo Socorro - (PAR) (Grades PreK-12) 704 Calle Jose Marta, San Juan, PR 00907-3227 t) 787-721-4540 (H.S.); 787-724-1447 (Elem.) perpetuo@perpetuo.org www.perpetuo.org Sarita Vazquez, Prin.; Rev. Msgr. Jose Emilio Cummings-Espada, Dir.;

Academia San Ignacio de Loyola - (PAR) (Grades PreK-6) Urb. Santa Maria, 1908 Calle Narciso, San Juan, PR 00927-6716 t) 787-765-8190 academia@asiloyola.org www.asiloyola.org Glorimar Soegaard, Prin.;

Colegio Angeles Custodios - (PAR) Urb. San Jose #13 Calle Sicilia, San Juan, PR 00923 t) 787-763-3829 angelescustodios1954@gmail.com Rev. Rogelio Salazar-Valero (Mexico), Chap.; Luis Roberto Rivera Cepeda, Prin.; Sr. Maria Aranzazu Labak, Dir.;

Colegio Calasanz - (PAR) Montecarlo Ave., San Juan, PR 00929-0067; Mailing: P.O. Box 29067, San Juan, PR 00929-0067 t) 787-750-2500 calasanzpr@cc-rpi.org Glenda Laureano, Prin.; Ana Celia Santos, Prin.; Rev. Cecilio LaCruz, Sch.P. (Spain), DRE; Rev. Juan L. Cabrerizo, Sch.P. (Spain), Dir.;

Colegio de La Inmaculada - (PRV) (Grades PreK-12) 1711 Ponce de Leon Ave., San Juan, PR 00909-1997 t) 787-727-6673 inmaculadasanturce@yahoo.com www.inmaculadasanturce.com Ana Matos, Prin.; Sr. Luz Mary Arzuaga Sr., Dir.; Maria Acosta Perez, Librn.;

Colegio Espiritu Santo - (PAR) Pachin Marin Esq. Suiza St., San Juan, PR 00917; Mailing: P.O. Box 191715, San Juan, PR 00917-1715 t) 787-754-0490 ces@colespiritusanto.com; hv@colespiritusanto.com Elena Rivera, Prin.; Milagros Zurkowsky, Prin.; Rev. Msgr. Valeriano Miguelez (Spain), Dir.; Olga D. Torres, Librn.;

Colegio Lourdes - (PRV) 87 Mayaguez St., San Juan, PR 00917; Mailing: P.O. Box 190847, San Juan, PR 00919-0847 t) 787-767-6106; 787-756-5436 clourdes@coqui.net; clourdes@colegiolourdespr.org colegiolourdes.net Isamari Cruz, Prin.; Sr. Anabelle Flores, O.P., Prin.; Sr. Maria Milagros Velez, O.P., Dir.;

Colegio Maria Auxiliadora - (PAR) 2273 Eduardo Conde, San Juan, PR 00915 t) 787-726-8288 smmmfma@hotmail.com Sr. Magna M. Martinez, F.M.A., Prin.; Elba Varela, Librn.;

Colegio Nuestra Senora de Guadalupe - (Grades PreK-12) 19 N.E. St. #1, Puerto Nuevo, San Juan, PR 00920; Mailing: P.O. Box 364125, San Juan, PR 00936-4125 t) 787-782-0330 colegioguadalupano@yahoo.com www.colegioguadalupe.org Genevieve Zayas, Prin.; Rev. Neil Macaulay, O.M.I. (Canada), Dir.; Jackeline Wys, Librn.;

Colegio Nuestra Senora Del Carmen - (PAR) Carr. 181, Marginal 877, San Juan, PR 00926; Mailing: R.R. 2 Box 15, San Juan, PR 00926 t) 787-761-8010 melisea@coqui.net Sr. Elizabeth Andino, Prin.; Liliana Santiago, Prin.; Lissette Torres, Prin.; Sr. Arlyn Medina Vazquez, Dir.;

Colegio Sagrada Familia - (PAR) Urb. Llorens Torres #2059, Calle Loiza, San Juan, PR 00913 t) 787-726-1742 cancilleria2019@arqsj.org Ines Y. Elias, Prin.; Rev. Luis Miranda, O.Carm., Dir.; Vanessa Valdes, Dir.;

Colegio Sagrado Corazon de Jesus - (PAR) (Grades PreK-8) 251 Calle Oxford Esq. Howard, Urb. University Gardens, San Juan, PR 00927-4826 t) 787-765-4798 info@psagradocorazon.org Rev. Jose Matinez Santos Sr., Pst. Min./Coord.; Rev. Anulfo Del Rosario, C.M. (Dominican Republic), Dir.; Milagros Lugo, Librn.;

Colegio San Antonio - (PAR) (Grades PreSchool-12) Calle Arzuaga Esq. Barbosa, San Juan, PR 00925; Mailing: PO Box 21350, San Juan, PR 00928-1350 t) 787-764-0090 secretaria@yosoycapuchino.com www.yosoycapuchino.com Friar Ramon Hiram Negron, O.F.M.Cap., Pres.; Marlene Feliu, Prin.; Katherine Gibbs, Prin.; Jozairaf Asad, Dir.; Stds.: 630; Scholastics: 10; Lay Tchrs.: 80

Colegio San Ignacio de Loyola - (PAR) Urb. Santa Maria, 1940 Calle Sauco, San Juan, PR 00927-6718 t) 787-294-4302 csi@sanignacio.org; contralorpri@gmail.com www.colegiosanignacio.org Compania de Jesus en Puerto Rico, Inc. Rev. Timothy Howe, S.J., Pres.; Rev. Flavio I. Bravo, S.J.; Rev. Baudilio Guzman, S.J., Chap.;

Colegio San Jose - (PRV) (Grades 6-12) Calle los Marianistas Esq. La Paz, San Juan, PR 00925; Mailing: P.O. Box 21300, San Juan, PR 00928-1300 t) 787-751-8177 fgonzalez@csj-rpi.org www.csj-rpi.org Bro. Francisco T. Gonzalez, S.M., Dir.;

Colegio San Juan Bosco - (PAR) Carpenter Rd., Constitucion Santos Elena, San Juan, PR 00915; Mailing: P.O. Box 14367, San Juan, PR 00916-4367 t) 787-726-1995 lizpr2000@yahoo.com Rev. Hiriam Santiago, S.B.D., Dir.;

Colegio San Vicente de Paul - 709 Bolivar St., San Juan, PR 00910; Mailing: P.O. Box 8699, Fernandez Juncos Sta., San Juan, PR 00910-8699 t) 787-727-4273 administrator@csvp-sj.org www.csvp-sj.org Operated by: Congregacion de la Mision de San Vincente de Paul, Inc. (Padres Paules) Rev. Manuel Aznar, CM, Dir.; Emilio Roldan, Prin.; Marina Perez, Librn.;

Nuestra Senora de Belen - (PAR) ; Mailing: P.O. Box 10845, San Juan, PR 00922-0845 t) 787-792-3115 colegiobelen11@yahoo.com Ivette Cabrera, Academic Dir.; Ana Yepez, Associate Dir.;

Nuestra Senora de la Altagracia - (PAR) (Grades PreK-12) Urb. Villa Prades, Calle Felipe Gutierrez 672, San Juan, PR 00924; Mailing: P.O. Box 29493, San Juan, PR 00929-0493 t) 787-763-7755 altagraciapr04@yahoo.com Sr. Marta Gonzalez, Prin.;

San Jorge - (PAR) 1701 Colon St., San Juan, PR 00911-2041 t) 787-722-3182 sanjorge@iname.com Maritza Rosario, Prin.; Rev. Pedro L. Reyes-Lebron, Dir.; Vanesa Valdes, Dir.;

TRUJILLO ALTO

Academia Santa Maria del Camino - (Grades PreSchool-8) Carr. 658, 8860, Trujillo Alto, PR 00987 t) 787-752-6555 cancilleria2019@arqsj.org Margarita Montesinos Ortiz, Prin.; Sr. Lucy del Blanco, O.S.R., Dir.; Myrna Lee Roman Miro, Librn.;

Santa Cruz - (PAR) Dr. Fernandez St., #203, Trujillo Alto, PR 00977; Mailing: P.O. Box 1809, Trujillo Alto, PR 00977-1809 t) 787-761-1100 Ana L. Monzon de Matos, Prin.; Rev. Carlos Alberto Contreras Tribaldo, Dir.;

COLLEGES & UNIVERSITIES [COL]

BAYAMON

ISTEPA (Instituto Superior de Teologia y Pastoral - Luis Cardenal Aponte Martinez) - Ext. Forest Hills, Calle Valparaíso, Esq. Caracas, Bayamon, PR 00959; Mailing: P.O. Box 9021967, San Juan, PR 00902-1967 t) 787-200-6891 mdjr7566@gmail.com For lay ministers & deacons Rev. Msgr. Francisco Medina Santos, Rector; Rev. Anibal Rafael Torres-Ortiz, Rector;

Universidad Central de Bayamon, Inc. - Ave. Zaya Verde, Bo. Hato Tejas, Bayamon, PR 00960-1725; Mailing: P.O. Box 1725, Bayamon State, PR 00960-1725 t) (787) 786-3030 avalentin@ucb.edu.pr ucb.edu.pr Friar Rafael Gonzalez Padro, O.P., Pres.; Friar Jose Santiago Roman, O.P., Dir.; Rev. Dennys Cruz Cuevas, C.P., Prof.; Rev. Alfonso Guzman-Alfaro, O.F.M., Prof.; Rev. Ricardo Santin-Flores, P.B.R.O., Prof.; Rev. Willmar Guiral Cadavid, O.S.S.T., Prof.; Rafael Vazquez Cruz, Pres.; Angel Valentin-Roman, Vice. Pres.;

SANTURCE

Universidad del Sagrado Corazón - Calle Rosales Esq. San Antonio, Parada 26 1/2, Santurce, PR 00914; Mailing: P.O. Box 12383, San Juan, PR 00914-0383 t) (787) 727-7033 gilberto.marxuach@sagrado.edu www.sagrado.edu Most Rev. Roberto O. Gonzalez-Nieves, O.F.M.; Stds.: 4,224; Lay Tchrs.: 31; Pr. Tchrs.: 1

CONVENTS, MONASTERIES, AND

INSTITUTIONS LOCATED IN DIOCESE

RESIDENCES FOR WOMEN [CON]

BAYAMON

Convento Ntra. Sra. del Rosario - ; Mailing: P.O. Box 1968, Bayamon, PR 00960 t) 787-785-6542; 787-786-4508 dominicospr.com (Dominicans)

ENDOWMENTS / FOUNDATIONS / TRUSTS [EFT]

SAN JUAN

Renovacion Conyugal (Fundacion Fernando Martinez) - 573 Calle Alverio, San Juan, PR 00918 t) 787-751-6001 renovacionpr@yahoo.com geocities.com/renovacionpr Rev. Jorge Ambert, S.J., Dir.;

HOSPITALS / HEALTH SERVICES [HOS]

BAYAMON

Hospital Hermanos Melendez - ; Mailing: P.O. Box 306, Bayamon, PR 00960-0306 t) 787-785-6542

Hospital Hima San Pablo - ; Mailing: P.O. Box 236, San Juan, PR 00959-0236 t) 787-620-4747; 787-620-4762 Rev. Jorge Saenz, Chap.;

Hospital Matilde Brenes - ; Mailing: P.O. Box 2957, Bayamon, PR 00960-2957 t) 787-785-2381

Hospital Universitario - Ave. Laurell, Bayamon, PR 00956 t) 787-785-8611 Ramon Ruiz Arnau, Dir.;

CAROLINA

Hospital de la Universidad de Puerto Rico, Dr. Federico Trilla - ; Mailing: P.O. Box 6021, Carolina, PR 00984 t) 787-757-1800 dmaldonado@hospitalupr.org hospitalupr.org Rev. Frank de la Rosa, Chap.;

HATO REY

Hospital Auxilio Mutuo - Ave. Ponce de Leon, Hato Rey, PR 00919; Mailing: P.O. Box 1277, San Juan, PR 00919 t) 787-758-2000 x3070 www.auxiliomutuo.com Rev. Francisco J. Marrodan, C.M. (Spain), Chap.;

Hospital Pavia - Ave. Ponce de Leon, Hato Rey, PR 00917; Mailing: P.O. Box 190828, San Juan, PR 00919-0828 t) 787-754-0570 Rev. Msgr. Valeriano Miguelez (Spain);

RIO PIEDRAS

Hospital del Maestro - Calle Flamboyanes #218, Hyde Park, Rio Piedras, PR 00929 t) 787-763-8383 Rev. Jose Francisco Quintero-Angueira;

Hospital San Francisco - ; Mailing: P.O. Box 29025, San Juan, PR 00929-0025 t) 787-765-0606

SAN JUAN

Doctors' Community Hospital - 1395 Calle San Rafael, San Juan, PR 00909; Mailing: P.O. Box 11338, San Juan, PR 00910 t) 787-999-7620 echevarria@dchpr.com Rev. Miguel Rivera Borges, S.D.B., Chap.;

Hospital San Juan Capestrano - Carr. 877 Km 1.6, Camino Las Lomas Capuccino, San Juan, PR 00926; Mailing: RR2 Box 11, San Juan, PR 00926 t) 787-625-2900 laura.vargas@uhsinc.com sjcapestrano.com Laura Vargas, Contact;

San Jorge's Children Hospital - Calle San Jorge 258, San Juan, PR 00912; Mailing: P.O. Box 6308, San Juan, PR 00914-6308 t) 787-727-1000 cruz.vivaldi@sanjorgechildrenshospital.com www.sanjorgechildrenshospital.com Rev. Olin Pierre

Louis, Chap.;
VA Medical Center - 10 Calle Casia, San Juan, PR 00921-3200 t) 787-641-7582; 787-641-7575 hrd198254@yahoo.com Rev. Hector Diaz Estrada, Chap.;
SANTURCE
Hospital Pavia - ; Mailing: P.O. Box 11137, San Juan, PR 00910-1137 t) 787-727-3963 Vincentian Fathers.

MISCELLANEOUS [MIS]

GUAYNABO
Opus Dei - Urb. Villa Caparra, #35 Calle A, Guaynabo, PR 00966-2211 t) 787-783-6206 info@opusdei.org.pr www.opusdei.org.pr Rev. Ramon Alvarez Infiesta, Pst.; Rev. Gonzalo Diaz, Pst.; Rev. Juan Ignacio Ballesteros, Vicar; Rev. Jaime Bermudez, Vicar; Rev. Andres Eiroa, Vicar; Rev. Msgr. Justiniano Garcia Arias, Vicar; Rev. Juan Jose Salinas, Vicar;
SAN JUAN
Caritas de Puerto Rico, Inc. - 201 San Jorge St., San Juan, PR 00910-0812; Mailing: P.O. Box 8812, San Juan, PR 00910-0812 t) 787-300-4953 x1156; 787-727-7373 x1153; 787-300-4953 x1108 info@caritas.pr caritas.pr Rev. Enrique Manuel Camacho-Monserrate;
Casa San Clemente - 257 Ave. de la Constitucion, Puerta De Tierra, San Juan, PR 00901; Mailing: P.O. Box 9066315, San Juan, PR 00902-3545 t) 787-723-6915 cancilleria2019@arqsj.org Counseling svcs. Domingo G. Perez, Exec.; Rev. Terence Damian Wall, C.Ss.R., Exec.;
Centro Sor Isolina Ferre - ; Mailing: Box 9511, San Juan, PR 00926 t) 787-731-5700 lurema@coqui.net; lortiz@csifpr.org (Social Improvement of the Poor).
Centro Universitario Catolico - 10 Mariana Bracetti St., San Juan, PR 00925-2201 t) 787-763-5432; 787-767-3348 elcuc2003@hotmail.com www.administracion@centrouniversitariocatolics.org Rev. Rafael Rodriguez, S.J., Dir.;
Hogar de Ninas de Cupey, Inc. - Carr. 176 Km. 4.2 Bo. Cupey Alto, San Juan, PR 00926; Mailing: P.O. Box 20667, San Juan, PR 00928-0667 t) 787-761-2805 info@hogardeninasdecupez.org hogardeninasdecupez.org
Hogar Del Buen Pastor - Constitucion #250, Puerta de Tierra, San Juan, PR 00901; Mailing: P.O. Box 9066547, San Juan, PR 00906-6547 t) 787-721-8579 hopastor@coqui.net (Homeless Shelter)
Hogar Padre Venard, Inc. - 305 Calle San Francisco, San Juan, PR 00901; Mailing: P.O. Box 9020274, San Juan, PR 00902-0274 t) 787-724-1131 secretaria@yosoycapuchino.com www.yosoycapuchino.com Friar Ramon Hiram Negron Cruz, O.F.M.Cap., Pres.; Friar Moises Villalta, O.F.M.Cap. (El Salvador), Dir.;
Paulinas Multimedia - Calle Arzuaga #164, San Juan, PR 00925-3322 t) 787-764-4885; 787-765-4390 libecria@paulinaspr.com www.paulinaspr.com Catholic Publications Sr. Milagrosa Miranda Rivera, F.S.P., Supr.;
R. R. Siervas de Maria Ministras de los Enfermos - 1 Calle Fortaleza, San Juan, PR 00901-1501 t) 787-723-4558; 787-724-2228 siervasmsj@coqui.net Sr. Aurea Fernandez Fontan, M.S.J., Supr.;
Santa Ana Chapel - Calle Tetuan 203, San Juan, PR 00902; Mailing: P.O. Box 9022145, San Juan, PR 00902 t) 787-722-0861 catedralsj1521@gmail.com Perpetual Adoration Rev. Benjamin Antonio Perez Cruz, Rector;
Servicios Pastorales Paules - 1650 Fernández Juncos, Santurce, San Juan, PR 00910; Mailing: P.O. Box 19118, San Juan, PR 00910-9118 t) 787-728-0670 centrosp@onelinkpr.net Catholic Publications Rev. Santiago Arribas, C.M., Dir.;
SANTURCE
Corporacion La Fondita De Jesus - Calle Monserrate 704, PDA 16 1/2, Santurce, PR 00909; Mailing: P.O. Box 19384, San Juan, PR 00910-1384 t) 787-724-4051; 787-725-0660 cartas@lafonditadejesus.org Supportive svcs & housing Socorro Rivera Rosa, Exec.;

MONASTERIES AND RESIDENCES FOR PRIESTS AND BROTHERS [MON]

RIO PIEDRAS
Fraternidad Santa Maria de Los Angeles - Carr. 877 Km. 1 Hm 6, Rio Piedras, PR 00936; Mailing: Apt. 29882, San Juan, PR 00929-0882 t) (787) 761-8410; (787) 764-3090 secretaria@yosoycapuchino.com www.yosoycapuchino.com Retreat House and House of Friars Friar Luis Oscar Padilla Cruz, O.F.M.Cap., Supr.; Friar Gabriel Juarbe-Perez, O.F.M.Cap., Admin.; Bro. Jaime Perez Munoz, O.F.M.Cap., In Res.; Friar Jose Antonio Villaran, O.F.M.Cap., In Res.;
SAN JUAN
The Capuchin Formation Trust of Puerto Rico - ; Mailing: P.O. Box 21350, San Juan, PR 00928-1350 t) 787-764-6090 secretaria.capuchinospr@gmail.com www.capuchinospr.org Rev. Roberto Martinez, O.F.M.Cap.;
Compania de Jesus en Puerto Rico, Inc - 1940 Calle Sauco, San Juan, PR 00927-6718 t) 787-758-1717 x1721 academia@asiloyola.org www.asiloyola.org Rev. Flavio I. Bravo, S.J.; Rev. Baudilio Guzman, S.J., Supr.;
The Custody of Saint John the Baptist, Puerto Rico, of the Order Friars Minor Capuchin - 216 Arzuaga St., San Juan, PR 00925; Mailing: P.O. Box 21350, San Juan, PR 00928-1350 t) 787-764-3090 secretaria@yosoycapuchino.com www.yosoycapuchino.com Friar Ramon Hiram Negron, O.F.M.Cap., Supr.; Rt. Rev. Economos Fray Roberto Colón, O.F.M.Cap., Treas.; Rev. Jose A. Cruz Collazo, O.F.M.Cap., First Counselor; Rev. Jose Fernando Irizarry-Santana, O.F.M.Cap., Second Counselor; Friar Gamalier Martinez, O.F.M.Cap., Vocational Coord.; Brs.: 4; Priests: 20
Capuchin Health and Retirement Trust of Puerto Rico - 216 Arzuaga St, San Juan, PR 00925; Mailing: P.O. Box 21350, San Juan, PR 00928-1350 t) (787) 764-3090 Asociacion Frailes Capuchinos, Inc. Friar Ramon Hiram Negron Cruz, O.F.M.Cap., Pres.;
San Antonio de Padua School - 216 Arzuaga St., San Juan, PR 00925; Mailing: P.O. Box 21350, San Juan, PR 00928-1350 t) 787-764-0090 Friar Ramon Hiram Negron Cruz, O.F.M.Cap., Pres.; Stds.: 630; Scholastics: 10; Lay Tchrs.: 80
Fraternidad San Antonio - 216 Calle Arzuaga, San Juan, PR 00925; Mailing: P.O. Box 25177, San Juan, PR 00928 t) (787) 764-3090 secretaria@yosoycapuchino.com www.yosoycapuchino.com Fraternity - House of Friars Friar Ramon Hiram Negron Cruz, O.F.M.Cap., Supr.; Friar Roberto Colon Ortiz, O.F.M.Cap., Treas.; Friar Pedro Juan Silva_Bisbal, OFM Cap, Priest; Friar Gamalier Martinez, O.F.M.Cap., Priest;
TRUJILLO ALTO
Carmelite Monastery of St. Joseph - Camino Los Barros, Trujillo Alto, PR 00977; Mailing: P.O. Box 568, Trujillo Alto, PR 00977-0568 t) 787-761-9548 mcsjose@prtc.net (Monasterio Carmelita De San Jose) Sr. Madre Ines Maria Carmona Ortiz, O.Carm, Prioress;

NURSING / REHABILITATION / CONVALESCENCE / ELDERLY CARE [NUR]

SAN JUAN
Hermanitas de los Ancianos Desamparados Hogar Santa Teresa Jornet de Cupey Inc. - Rd. 199 Km 14.3 Las Cumbres Ave., Cupey, San Juan, PR 00926; Mailing: 181 Calle Teresa Jornet, San Juan, PR 00926-7542 t) 787-761-5805 jornet@prtc.net Sister of the Poor. Sr. Yolanda Cueto, Mother Superior; Asstd. Annu.: 150; Staff: 58

SEMINARIES [SEM]

SAN JUAN
Seminario Mayor Arquidiocesano - Ave. De Diego No. 930, Urb. La Riviera, San Juan, PR 00921; Mailing: Apdo. 11714, Rio Piedras, PR 00922-1714 t) 787-273-8090; 787-706-9455 seminario.mayor@yahoo.com; vocacioncsarq@yahoo.com (Diocesan) Samuel Velasquez, Rector;

SPECIAL CARE FACILITIES [SPF]

BAYAMON
Hogar Del Nino "El Ave Maria Corp." - Carretera 861, km 2.0, Bo. Pajaros Americanos, Bayamon, PR 00957; Mailing: PMB 239-A, P.O. Box 607071, Bayamon, PR 00960-7071 t) 787-797-2382; 787-279-3003 hogaresavemariainc@hotmail.com Home for abused children. Sr. Florencia Santos, Dir.;
Hogar Escuela Sor Maria Rafaela - Carr. 871, Km 1.0, Bo. El Volcan, Hato Tejas, Bayamon, PR 00961; Mailing: P.O. Box 3024, Bayamon, PR 00960 t) 787-785-9517; 787-785-1125 hogar.sormaria@gmail.com Home for girls. Sr. Nelida Gonzalez, Dir.;
Hogar Fatima - Ave. Santa Juanita Final, Camino Esteban Cruz, Bayamon, PR 00961; Mailing: P.O. Box 4228, Bayamon Garden Sta., Bayamon, PR 00958-4228 t) 787-787-2580 fatima001@prtc.net www.osrhogarfatimainc.com (Girls) Sr. Maria Saez, Dir.;
DORADO
Santuario del Espiritu Santo-Congregacion del Espiritu Santo - ; Mailing: PO Box 187, Dorado, PR 00646-0187 t) 787-796-2798 espiritanospr@gmail.com www.espiritanos.com Rev. Jonas Rivera-Martinez, C.S.Sp., Rector; Rev. Jose Orlando Camacho-Torres, C.S.Sp., Admin.;
PUERTA DE TIERRA
Asylum For The Aged and Infirm - Stop 5, Edif. 205, Puerta De Tierra, PR 00906-6571 t) 787-722-1331; 787-723-2419; 787-724-3574 htas.sanjuanprovidencia@gmail.com (Hogar de Ntra. Sra. de la Providencia) Sisters of the Poor. Rev. Esteban Antonio De La Rosa, Chap.; Dr. Blanca Bravo, Mother Superior;
SAN JUAN
Casa de Ninos Manuel Fernandez Juncos - Calle Villa Verde Esq. Refugio, Pda 11, Miramar, San Juan, PR 00902; Mailing: P.O. Box 9020163, San Juan, PR 00902-0163 t) 787-724-2904; 787-725-6328 cnmfj2016@outlook.com www.casadeninomfj.org Home for orphans and abused boys. Rev. Pablo Julio Osario Carmona; Friar Darwing Duarte Miranda, T.C., Admin.; Bro. Jorge Fiscal, T.C., Pastoral svcs; Bro. Jose Ramirez, T.C., Pastoral svcs;
Casa La Providencia - 200 Calle Norzagaray, San Juan, PR 00901-1122; Mailing: P.O. Box 9020614, San Juan, PR 00902-0614 t) 787-725-5358 casalaprovidencia@hotmail.com Drug Addicted Women Sr. Adela Dominguez, Dir.;
Centro Medico de P.R. - Calle 10 #1030, Puerto Nuevo, Apt. 347, San Juan, PR 00920 t) 787-763-7272 Rev. Hector Diaz; Dcn. Andres Figueroa; Rev. Francisco J. Marrodan, C.M. (Spain); Rev. Msgr. Valeriano Miguelez (Spain); Dcn. Jose R. Rivera; Rev. Jorge Saenz; Rev. Msgr. Antonio Jose Vazquez Colon; Rev. Francisco Arana (Spain), Chap.; Rev. Marcos Rivera-Perez, Chap.; Rev. Fabian Rodriguez Rodriguez, S.J., Chap.; Rev. Pedro Luis Zaballa, Chap.;
Centro Santa Luisa - Carr. 842, Camino Los Romero, Km 1.5, Bo. Caimito, San Juan, PR 00926; Mailing: RR 6 Box 9492, San Juan, PR 00926-9492 t) 787-720-2764 centrosantaluisa@yahoo.com (Services for the Elderly) Sr. Altagracia Rosario, H.C., Dir.;
Hogar Carmelitano - Calle Julian Bengoechea Final, San Juan, PR 00924 t) 787-769-6510; 787-769-3110 maribellemejias@gmail.com Julian Bengochea Final (Elderly Retirement Hospice) Carmelite Sisters (Spain). Sr. Maribelle Mejias Muniz, Admin.;
Hogares Rafaela Ibarra - Urb.San Jose 432 Calle Torrelaguna, San Juan, PR 00923; Mailing: 432 Calle Torrelaguna, San Juan, PR 00923-1773 t) 787-763-1204 hrafaelaybarra@gmail.com www.hogaresrafaelaybarra.com (Orphan or Abused Girls) Sr. Elena Crespo, Dir.;

SANTURCE

Politecnico Amigo - Calle Refugio #960, Pda II, Santurce, PR 00940; Mailing: P.O. Box 13204, San Juan, PR 00908 t) 787-725-2059 peosoriocarmona@gmail.com Home for dropout schoolboys. Rev. Pablo Osorio, T.C., Dir.;

TOA ALTA

Hogar Santisima Trinidad - Lote A y Lote B, km 7.0, Bo Mucarabones, Carr. 861, Toa Alta, PR 00954; Mailing: PMB 326-A, P.O. Box 607071, Bayamon, PR 00960-7071 t) 787-799-6208 hstrinita@gmail.com Drug addiction rehabilitation home. Rev. Pedro Gorena, O.SS.T. (Spain);

TOA BAJA

Hogar Divino Nino Jesus - Carr. 854, Km. 3.5, Toa Baja, PR 00949; Mailing: P.O. Box 2464, Toa Baja, PR 00951-2662 t) 787-794-0020 divinoninojesus@yahoo.es Detox and Tx Residencial. Julio Pacheco, Dir.;

An asterisk (*) denotes an organization that has established tax-exempt status directly with the IRS and is not covered by the USCCB Group Ruling.

Index for Religious Institutes of Men

Religious Order Initials for Men

A.A. Assumptionists [0130]
B.G.S. Little Brothers of the Good Shepherd [0580]
B.H.S. Brothers of the Holy Spirit-Cleveland [0645]
B.S.O. Basilian Salvatorian Fathers [0190]
C.C. Companions of the Cross [0385]
C.F.A. Alexian Brothers [0120]
C.F.C. Congregation of Christian Brothers [0310]
C.F.P. Brothers of the Poor of St. Francis [0460]
C.F.R. Franciscan Friars of the Renewal [0535]
C.F.X. Brothers of St. Francis Xavier [1350]
C.I.C.M. Missionhurst Congregation of the Immaculate Heart of Mary [0860]
C.J. Josephite Fathers [0710]
C.J.M. Congregation of Jesus and Mary [0450]
C.M. Congregation of the Mission [1330]
C.R.M. Congregation of Mother of the Redeemer [0865]
C.M.F. Claretian Missionaries [0360]
C.M.I. Carmelites of Mary Immaculate [0275]
C.M.L.M. The Congregation of Maronite Lebanese Missionaries [0785]
C.M.M. Congregation of Mariannhill Missionaries, Mariannhill Fathers & Brothers [0750]
C.O. Oratorians [0950]
C.P. Congregation of the Passion [1000]
C.P.M. Congregation of the Fathers of Mercy [0820]
C.PP.S. Society of the Precious Blood [1060]
C.R. Congregation of the Resurrection [1080]
C.R. Theatine Fathers [1300]
C.R.L. Canons Regular of the Lateran [0250]
C.R.M. Adorno Fathers [0100]
C.R.S. Somascan Fathers [1250]
C.R.S.P. Clerics Regular of St. Paul [0160]
C.S. Missionaries of St. Charles-Scalabrinians [1210]
C.S.B. Basilian Fathers [0170]
C.S.C. Brothers of the Congregation of Holy Cross [0600]
C.S.C. Priests of the Congregation of Holy Cross [0610]
C.S.J. Congregation of St. Joseph [1150]
C.S.P. Paulist Fathers [1030]
C.S.P.X. Brothers of Saint Pius X [1180]
C.S.S. Stigmatine Fathers and Brothers [1280]
C.S.Sp. Congregation of the Holy Spirit [0650]
C.Ss.R. Redemptorist Fathers [1070]
C.S.V. Clerics of St. Viator [1320]
Er. Cam. Camaldolese Hermits of the Congregation of MonteCorona [0230]
F.C. Brothers of Charity [0290]
F.D.P. Sons of Divine Providence [0410]
F.F.I. Franciscan Friars of the Immaculate [0533]
F.F.S.C. Franciscan Brothers of the Holy Cross [0510]
F.I.C. Brothers of Christian Instruction [0320]
F.M.M. Brothers of Mercy [0810]
F.M.M. Missionary Fraternity of Mary [0855]
F.M.S. The Marist Brothers [0770]
F.M.S.I. Sons of Mary Missionary Society [1270]
F.S.C. Brothers of the Christian Schools [0330]
F.S.C.B. Priestly Fraternity of the Missionaries of St. Charles Borromeo [1205]
F.S.E. Brothers of the Holy Eucharist [0620]
F.S.P. Brothers of St. Patrick [1160]
F.S.R. Brothers of the Congregation of Our Lady of the Holy Rosary [0960]
F.S.S.P. Priestly Fraternity of St. Peter [1065]
F.SS.R. Congregation of the Sons of the Most Holy Redeemer [1145]
G.H.M. The Glenmary Home Missioners [0570]
H.G.N. Heralds of Good News [0585]
I.C. Institute of Charity [0300]
I.C. Institute of Christ the King - Sovereign Priest [0305]
I.H.M. Brothers of the Immaculate Heart of Mary [0680]
I.M.C. Consolata Missionaries [0390]
I.V.E. Institute of the Incarnate Word [0685]
L.B.S.F. Little Brothers of Saint Francis [1144]
L.C. Legionaries of Christ [0730]
M.Afr. Missionaries of Africa [0850]
M.C.C.J. Comboni Missionaries of the Heart of Jesus (Verona) [0380]
M.H.M. Mill Hill Missionaries [0830]
M.I. Camillian Fathers and Brothers [0240]
M.I.C. Congregation of Marians of the Immaculate Conception [0740]
M.J. Missionaries of Jesus, Inc. [0852]
M.M. Maryknoll [0800]
M.M.A. Maronite Monks of Adoration [0790]
M.S. The Missionaries of Our Lady of La Salette [0720]
M.S.A. Society of the Missionaries of the Holy Apostles [0590]
M.S.C. Missionaries of the Sacred Heart [1110]
M.S.F. Congregation of the Missionaries of the Holy Family [0630]
M.S.F.S. Missionaries of St. Francis de Sales [0485]
M.S.P. Missionary Society of St. Paul of Nigeria [0854]
M.Sp.S. Missionaries of the Holy Spirit [0660]
M.S.S. Missionaries of the Blessed Sacrament [0825]
M.SS.CC. Missionaries of the Sacred Hearts of Jesus and Mary [1120]
O.A.R. Order of Augustinian Recollects [0150]
O.Carm. Carmelite Fathers and Brothers [0270]
O.Cart. Order of Carthusians [0280]
O.C.D. Discalced Carmelite Friars [0260]
O.Cist. Cistercian Abbey [0340]
O.C.S.O. The Cistercian Order of the Strict Observance (Trappists) [0350]
O.de.M. Order of Our Lady of Mercy [0970]
O.F.M. Franciscan Friars [0520]
O.F.M.Cap. The Capuchin Franciscan Friars [0470]
O.F.M.Conv. Conventual Franciscans [0480]
O.H. Hospitaller Brothers of St. John of God [0670]
O.M. Minim Fathers [0835]
O.M.I. Oblates of Mary Immaculate [0910]
O.M.M. Maronite Order of the Blessed Virgin Mary [0782]
O.M.V. Oblates of the Virgin Mary [0940]
O.P. Order of Preachers (Dominicans) [0430]
O.Praem. Canons Regular of Premontre [0900]
O.S.A. The Augustinians [0140]
O.S.B. Benedictine Monks [0200]
O S.B.M. Order of St. Basil the Great [0180]
O.S.C. Canons Regular of the Order of the Holy Cross [0400]
O.S.F. Congregation of the Religious Brothers of the Third Order Regular of St. Francis [0490]
O.S.F. Franciscan Brothers of the Third Order Regular [0515]
O.S.F. Franciscan Missionary Brothers of the Sacred Heart of Jesus [0540]
O.S.F.S. Oblates of St. Francis de Sales [0920]
O.S.J. Oblates of St. Joseph [0930]
O.S.M. Servites [1240]
O.S.P.P.E. Pauline Fathers [1010]
O.Ss.S. Brigittine Monks [0895]
O.SS.T. Order of the Most Holy Trinity [1310]
P.I.M.E. Pontifical Institute for Foreign Missions, Inc. [1050]
P.S.S. Society of the Priests of Saint Sulpice [1290]
R.C.J. Rogationist Fathers [1090]
S.A. Franciscan Friars of the Atonement [0530]
S.A.C. Society of the Catholic Apostolate [0990]
S.C. Brothers of the Sacred Heart [1100]
S.C. Servants of Charity [1220]
S.Ch. Society of Christ [1260]
Sch.P. Piarist Fathers [1040]
S.C.J. Congregation of the Priests of the Sacred Heart [1130]
S.D.B. Salesians of Don Bosco [1190]
S.D.S. Society of the Divine Savior [1200]
S.D.V. Vocationist Fathers [1340]
S.F. Sons of the Holy Family [0640]
S.J. Jesuit Fathers and Brothers [0690]
S.M. Society of Mary (Marianists) [0760]
S.M. Marist Fathers [0780]
S.M.A. Society of African Missions [0110]
S.M.M. Montfort Missionaries [0870]
S.O.L.T. Society of Our Lady of the Most Holy Trinity [0975]
s.P. Servants of the Paraclete [1230]
S.P.S. St. Patrick's Missionary Society [1170]
S.S.C. Society of St. Columban [0370]
S.S.C.C. Congregation of the Sacred Hearts of Jesus and Mary [1140]
S.S.E. Society of Saint Edmund [0440]
S.S.J. St. Joseph's Society of the Sacred Heart [0700]
S.S.P. Pauline Fathers and Brothers [1020]
S.S.S. Congregation of the Blessed Sacrament [0220]
S.T. Missionary Servants of the Most Holy Trinity [0840]
S.V.D. Society of the Divine Word [0420]
S.X. Xaverian Missionary Fathers [1360]
T.O.R. Third Order Regular of Saint Francis [0560]
V.C. Vincentian Congregation (India) [1335]

Religious Institutes of Men

The Conference of Major Superiors of Men of the United States, Inc.—7300 Hanover Dr., Suite 304, Greenbelt, MD 20770. Tel: 301-588-4030; Fax: 240-650-3697. Website: www.cmsm.org. Very Rev. Jeffrey Kirch, C.PP.S., Pres.; Rt. Rev. James Herring, O.Praem., Vice Pres.; Very Rev. Christopher Fadok, O.P., Sec. & Treas. A canonical conference of the major superiors of religious communities and institutes of men for the purpose of promoting the spiritual and apostolic welfare of priests and brothers.

[0100] (C.R.M.)—ADORNO FATHERS

(Clerics Regular Minor)

General Motherhouse: Via Tribuna di Campitelli 6A, 00186 Rome, Italy. Very Rev. Teodoro O. Kalaw, C.R.M., Supr. Gen.

U.S. Foundation (1936): St. Michael's Seminary, 575 Darlington Ave., Ramsey, NJ 07446. Tel: 201-327-7375; Fax: 201-327-8131. Email: adornofathers1588@gmail.com. Rev. Jason S. Caganap, C.R.M., J.C.L., Delegation Supr. of the U.S. - Philippines Delgation of the Adorno Fathers.

Priests 20; Brothers 8

Represented in the Archdiocese of Newark and in the Diocese of Charleston. Also in Italy, Germany, India, Democratic Republic of Congo, Kenya, Tanzania and the Philippines.

[0110] (S.M.A.)—SOCIETY OF AFRICAN MISSIONS

(Societas Missionum ad Afros)

Founded Dec. 8, 1856 with the approval of Pope Pius IX. A clerical society of apostolic life.

Generalate: Via della Nocetta 111, 00164, Rome, Italy, Rev. Antonio Porcellato, S.M.A., Supr. Gen.; Rev. Francois de Paul Houngue, S.M.A., Vicar Gen.; Rev. Francis Rozario, S.M.A., Gen. Councilor; Rev. Krzystof Pachut, S.M.A., Gen. Councilor.

American Province (1941): 23 Bliss Ave., Tenafly, NJ 07670. Tel: 201-567-0450; Fax: 201-541-1280. Very Rev. Ranees A. Rayappan, S.M.A., Prov. Supr.; Rev. Dermot Roache, S.M.A., Vice Prov.; Rev. Richard A. Mwisheni, S.M.A., Councilor.

Legal Title: Society of African Missions, Inc. NJ.

Priests 14; Lay Associate in Permanent Commitment: 1; Priest Associates: 1

Represented in the Archdioceses of Boston, Newark and Washington.

[0120] (C.F.A.)—ALEXIAN BROTHERS

(Congregatio Fratrum Cellitarum seu Alexianorum)

Generalate: Signal Mountain, TN 37377. Tel: 423-886-2969. Bro. Lawrence Krueger, C.F.A., Supr. Gen.; Bro. Dermot O'Leary, C.F.A., Asst. Supr. Gen., Knock Ireland; Bro. Nikolaus Hahn, C.F.A., Gen. Councilor, Aachen, Germany; Bro. John of God Oblina, C.F.A., Gen. Councilor Davao City, Philippines.

General Motherhouse: Congregation of Alexian Brothers, 198 James Blvd., Signal Mountain, TN 37377. Tel: 423-886-2969.

United States Province: 600 Alexian Way, Elk Grove Village, IL 60007. Tel: 847-264-8701; Fax: 847-264-8679. Email: Daniel.McCormick@Alexian.net. Councilors: Bro. Daniel McCormick, C.F.A., Prov.; Bro. Richard Lowe, C.F.A., Asst. Prov.; Bro. Thomas Klein, C.F.A.; Bro. Warren Longo, C.F.A.

Professed Brothers 27

Properties owned or sponsored: Novitiate 1; Wellness Center (Davao City, Philippines) 1

Represented in the Archdioceses of Chicago and Milwaukee and in the Diocese of Knoxville. Also in Davao City, Philippines and Györ, Hungary.

[0130] (A.A.)—ASSUMPTIONISTS

(Augustinians of the Assumption)

General House: via San Pio V, 55, 00165, Rome, Italy, Very Rev. Benoît Grière, A.A., Supr. Gen.

Province of North America (1946): 330 Market St., Brighton, MA 02135. Tel: 617-783-0400. Rev. Dennis M. Gallagher, A.A., Prov. Supr. Councilors: Rev. Peter Precourt, A.A; Rev. Chi Ai Nguyen, A.A.; Rev. Alex Castro, A.A., Treas.

Priests 37; Brothers 11; Parishes 5; Shrines: 1; Colleges 1; Formation Centers 4; Residences: 9

Represented in the Archdiocese of Boston and in the Diocese of Worcester. Also in Philippines, Kenya, Mexico, Tanzania, Italy and Canada.

[0140] (O.S.A.)—THE AUGUSTINIANS

(Ordo Sancti Augustini)

Founded in 1244, first American foundation 1796.

Generalate: Curia Generalizia Agostiniana, Via Paolo VI # 25, 00193, Rome, Italy, Tel: 011-39-06-68-00-61; Fax: 011-39-06-68-00-6299. Most Rev. Alejandro Moral Anton, O.S.A., Prior Gen.; Very Rev. Joseph L. Farrell, O.S.A., Vicar Gen.; Very Rev. Robert P. Hagan, O.S.A., Prior Prov.; Rev. Aldo R. Potencio, O.S.A., Province Sec. & Treas.

Province of St. Thomas of Villanova (1796): Provincial Offices: St. Augustine Friary, 214 Ashwood Rd., P.O. Box 340, Villanova, PA 19085-0340. Tel: 610-527-3330; Fax: 610-520-0618. Counselors: Rev. Raymond F. Dlugos, O.S.A; Rev. Robert J. Guessetto, O.S.A.; Rev. James D. Paradis, O.S.A.; Rev. Luis A. Vera, O.S.A.; Rev. Joseph L. Narog, O.S.A.; Rev. Kevin M. DePrinzio, O.S.A.; Paul Ashton, Abuse Prevention & Educ. Coord.; Rev. Joseph Narog, O.S.A., Dir. Vocations; Bro. Richard Ekmann, O.S.A., Province Archivist; Rev. John E. Deegan, O.S.A., Dir. Justice & Peace.

Legal Title: The Brothers of the Order of Hermits of Saint Augustine (The Brothers of the Order of Hermits of St. Augustine, a corporation in the state of Pennsylvania 1804).

Professed Friars: 119; Ordained Priests: 110; Brothers: 8; Students of Theology: 2; Pre-Theology Students: 2; Parishes (U.S.): 7; Parishes (Japan): 4; Major Seminaries 1; Colleges 1; Universities: 1; Preparatory Schools 2; Foreign Missions (Peru): 1

Represented in the Archdioceses of Boston, New York and Philadelphia and in the Dioceses of Albany and Camden. Also in Czech Republic, Italy, Japan and Peru.

Province of Our Mother of Good Counsel (Order of St. Augustine) (1941): Augustinian Province Offices, 10161 S. Longwood Dr., Chicago, IL 60643. Tel: 872-265-1100; Fax: 773-614-5863. Email: secretary@midwestaugustinians.org; Web: www.MidwestAugustinians.org. Very Rev. Anthony B. Pizzo. O.S.A., Prior Prov.; Bro. Nicholas J. Mullarkey, O.S.A., Prov. Sec.; Rev. James R. Halstead, O.S.A., Prov. Treas.

Fathers 54; Bishops 2; Professed Brothers 13; Parishes 6; High Schools 3; Residences: 2

Represented in the Archdioceses of Chicago and Philadelphia and in the Dioceses of Gary, Green Bay, Joliet, Lexington and Tulsa. Also in Mexico, Peru, Toronto and Vancouver.

The Province of St. Augustine in California: 3180 University Ave., Ste. 255, San Diego, CA 92104-2045. Tel: 619-235-0247. Email: osa-west@sbcglobal.net. Very Rev. Gary E. Sanders, O.S.A., Prov. Counselors: Rev. Maxime Villeneuve, O.S.A., Sec.; Rev. Carlos Medina, O.S.A; Rev. Barnaby Johns, O.S.A; Rev. Kirk Davis, O.S.A.

Priests 26; Deacons 4; Brothers 7; Parishes 3; High Schools 2; Orphanages: 1

Legal Holdings or Titles: St. Augustine High School, San Diego, CA; Monica House, San Diego, CA; Tierra del Sol, Boulevard, CA; St. Rita House, San Francisco, CA; Villanova Preparatory School, Ojai, CA; Austin House, San Diego, CA.

Represented in the Archdioceses of Chicago, Los Angeles, San Francisco and Portland in Oregon and in the Diocese of San Diego.

Augustinian Monastery: 611 Cedar Ave., Richland, NJ 08350-0279. Tel: 856-697-2600; Fax: 856-285-7108. Rev. Francis X. Devlin, O.S.A., Prior; Rev. Robert Murray, O.S.A., Pres.; Rev. Anthony Burrascano, O.S.A., Asst. to Pres. for Mission & Ministry; Rev. Stephen Curry, O.S.A., Treas., Dir. of 8th Grade Program.

Represented in the Archdiocese of Philadelphia and in the Diocese of Camden.

Region U.S.A. (1993): Our Lady of Guadalupe Church (1927), 3648 S/Sgt. Lucian Adam (61st), Port Arthur, TX 77642-6403. Tel: 409-962-6777. Rev. Urbano Sáenz Ramirez, O.S.A.; Rev. Jacob James Mado, O.S.A.

Fathers 2

Represented in the Diocese of Beaumont.

[0150] (O.A.R.)—ORDER OF AUGUSTINIAN RECOLLECTS

(Ordo Augustinianorum Recollectorum)

General Motherhouse: Viale dell' Astronomia, 27, asella Postale 10760, 00144, Rome, Italy, Very Rev. Miguel Miro, O.A.R., Prior Gen.

Province of St. Augustine (1943): Augustinian Recollects, 29 Ridgeway Ave., West Orange, NJ 07052-3297. Tel: 973-731-0616; Fax: 973-731-1033. Rev. J. Michael Rafferty, O.A.R., Prior Prov.; Rev. Marlon Beof, O.A.R., 1st Councilor & Vicar; Rev. Fredric Abiera, O.A.R., 2nd Councilor; Rev. Gerard Cosgayon, O.A.R., 3rd Councilor; Rev. Charles Huse, O.A.R., 4th Councilor.

Bishops 1; Priests 32; Brothers 2; Professed Clerics: 1; Permanent Deacons 3.

Represented in the Archdioceses of Los Angeles, Newark and New York and in the Diocese of Orange. Also in Mexico.

Province of St. Nicholas of Tolentine (U.S.A. Delegation): 3021 Frutas Ave., El Paso, TX 79905. Rev. Jesus M. Mena, O.A.R., Prov. Delegate.

Priests 18; Brothers 1

Represented in the Archdiocese of Newark and in the Dioceses of El Paso and Las Cruces.

[0160] (C.R.S.P.)—CLERICS REGULAR OF ST. PAUL

(Barnabite Fathers)

(Ordo Clericorum Regularium Sancti Pauli)

Founded in Milan, Italy in 1533. First foundation in the United States in 1952 in Buffalo, NY.

General Motherhouse: Historical Motherhouse: Church of St. Barnabas, Milan, since 1545. Via Giacomo Medici, 15, 00153 Rome, Italy, Most Rev. Francisco M. Silva, C.R.S.P., Supr. Gen.

North American Province: 981 Swann Rd., P.O. Box 167, Youngstown, NY 14174-0167. Tel: 716-754-7489. Very Rev. Peter M. Calabrese, C.R.S.P., Prov. Supr.

Legal Title: Order of Barnabite Fathers, Inc.

Priests 10

Fathers staff and serve: Parishes; Marian Shrine.

Properties Owned or Sponsored: Our Lady of Fatima Shrine, NY; St. Anthony M. Zaccaria Seminary, Youngstown, NY.

Represented in the Dioceses of Buffalo, and San Diego. Also in Hamilton, Ontario, Canada.

[0170] (C.S.B.)—BASILIAN FATHERS

(Congregatio Presbyterorum a St. Basilio)

General Curia: Cardinal Flahiff Basilian Centre, 95 St. Joseph St., M5S 3C2, Toronto, Tel: 416-921-6674; Fax: 416-920-3413. Email: katulski@basilian.org. Very Rev. Kevin J. Storey, C.S.B., Supr. Gen.; Rev. David Katulski, C.S.B., Vicar Gen.; Rev. Morgan Rice, C.S.B., Gen. Councilor.

U.S. Headquarters: Catholic Central High School, 27225 Wixom Rd., Novi, MI 48374. Rev. Dennis Noelke, C.S.B., Gen. Councilor.

[0180] (O.S.B.M.)—ORDER OF ST. BASIL THE GREAT

(Ordo Sancti Basilii Magni)

General Superior "Protoarchimandrita": Via San Giosafat 8, (Aventino), 00153, Rome, Italy, Very Rev. Robert Roman Leseiko, O.S.B.M.

American Province (1948): 29 Peacock Ln., Locust Valley, NY 11560. Tel: 516-609-3262; Cell: 708-925-3841; Fax: 516-609-3264. Very Rev. Varcilio Basil Salkovski, O.S.B.M., Prov. Superior.

Fathers 17; Brothers 2; Deacons 1; Parishes 5; Community Houses 8; Novitiates 1; Monasteries: 3; Retreat Houses 1; Libraries: 1

Represented in the Archdiocese of Chicago and Diocese of Stamford.

[0190] (B.S.O.)—BASILIAN SALVATORIAN FATHERS

General Motherhouse: Holy Savior Monastery, Saida, Lebanon, Archimandrite Tony Dib, B.S.O., Supr. Gen.

American Headquarters: Basilian Salvatorian Fathers, 30 East St., Methuen, MA 01844. Rev. Ibrahim El Haddad, B.S.O., Local Supr.; Rev. Lawrence Tumminelli, B.S.O., Gen. Economos; Rt. Rev. Archimandrite Martin A. Hyatt, B.S.O; Rev. Antoine Rizk, B.S.O., Regl. Supr.

Fathers in American Region: 8

Novitiate and House of Studies: St. Basils Seminary; Methuen, MA: 4

Parishes Canada 4; U.S.A. 4.

Represented in the Archdioceses of Boston and Miami and in the Dioceses of Cleveland and Eparchy of Newton.

[0200] (O.S.B.)—BENEDICTINE MONKS

(Ordo Sancti Benedicti)

American Cassinese Congregation of the Order of Saint Benedict (Established by Pope Pius IX, August 24, 1855.) 230 Mendham Rd., Morristown, NJ 07960. Tel & Fax: 973-538-3763; Web: www.amcass.org; Email: president@amcass.org. Rt. Rev. Jonathan R. Licari, O.S.B., Abbot Pres.; Rt. Rev. Marion Nguyen, O.S.B., Second Councilor, St. Martin's Abbey, Lacey, WA; Very Rev. Edward Mazick, O.S.B., Third Councilor, St. Vincent Archabbey, Latrobe, PA; Rev. Elias Correa-Torres, O.S.B., Mary Help of Christians Abbey, Belmont, NC, Fourth Councilor; Rev. Michael Patella, O.S.B., St. John's Abbey, Collegeville, MN, Exec. Sec.; Rev. Geraldo Gonzalez y Lima, O.S.B., Procurator Gen., Sant'Anselmo, Rome, Italy.

Bishops: 3; Total Priests: 382; Deacons: 7; Solemnly Professed Brothers: 194; Junior Professed Brothers: 50; Novices: 18; Claustral Oblates: 3; Total Membership: 657.

Represented in Archdioceses of Kansas City; Newark, Oklahoma City, Seattle and in the Dioceses of Birmingham, Bismarck, Charlotte, Cleveland, Fajardo-Humacao, Greensburg, Joliet, Manchester, Paterson, Peoria, Pueblo, Richmond, Savannah, St. Cloud and St. Petersburg.

The Abbeys and Priories belonging to this Congregation are as follows:

Saint Vincent Archabbey: 300 Fraser Purchase Rd., Latrobe, PA 15650-2690. Tel: 724-532-6600. Rt. Rev. Martin de Porres Bartel, O.S.B., Archabbot; Very Rev. Killian Loch, O.S.B., Prior; Bro. Anthony Kirsch, O.S.B., Subprior.

Legal Title: The Benedictine Society of Westmoreland County; Saint Vincent College Corporation; The Wimmer Corporation; The Saint Vincent Cemetery Corporation.

Priests 102; Deacons 5; Solemn Professed Choir-Monks: 34; Junior Professed Monks: 12; Choir Novices 3

Represented in the Archdiocese of Baltimore and in the Dioceses of Altoona-Johnstown, Erie, Greensburg, Harrisburg, Pittsburgh, Richmond, Savannah and Wheeling-Charleston.

American Cassinese Congregations

St. John's Abbey: 2900 Abbey Plaza, P.O. Box 2015, Collegeville, MN 56321-2015. Tel: 320-363-2546; Fax: 320-363-3082. Rt. Rev. John Klassen, O.S.B., Abbot; Very Rev. Eric Hollas, O.S.B., Prior; Bro. Simon-Hòa Phan, O.S.B., Subprior.

Fathers 64; Professed Brothers 37; Deacons 1; Oblates: 1; Abbeys: 1; Parishes 11; Chaplaincies 4; Schools of Theology: 1; Universities: 1; High Schools 1; Novitiates 1; Publishing Houses 1

Monastery founded in 1856 and raised to an Abbey in 1866.

Legal Holdings: Saint John's Seminary; Saint John's Preparatory School; Saint John's Abbey; Liturgical Press. Sponsored Apostolate: Saint John's University.

Represented in the Archdiocese of St. Paul and Minneapolis and in the Dioceses of St. Cloud and San Bernardino.

St. Benedict's Abbey: 1020 N. Second St., Atchison, KS 66002-1499. Tel: 913-367-7853; Fax: 913-367-6230. Rt. Rev. James R. Albers, O.S.B., Abbot; Rt. Rev. Barnabas Senecal, O.S.B.; Bro. Leven Harton, O.S.B., Prior; Rev. Jay Kythe, O.S.B., Subprior.

Fathers 29; Brothers 13; Abbeys: 1; Parishes 6; Missions: 1; Chaplaincies 3; Colleges 1; High Schools 1

Founded in 1857 and raised to an Abbey in 1876.

Represented in the Archdiocese of Kansas City in Kansas. Also in Brazil.

St. Mary's Abbey: Delbarton, 230 Mendham Rd., Morristown, NJ 07960. Tel: 973-538-3235; Fax: 973-538-7109; Web: www.osbmonks.org. Rt. Rev. Jonathan Licari, O.S.B., Abbot Admin.; Very Rev. Edward Seton Fittin, O.S.B., Prior; Rev. John Hesketh, O.S.B., Subprior.

Priests 15; Brothers 3; Juniors 1; Preparatory Schools 1; Retreat Centers 1

Monastery founded in 1857 and raised to an Abbey in 1884.

Represented in the Diocese of Paterson.

Belmont Abbey: 100 Belmont-Mount Holly Rd., Belmont, NC 28012-1802. Tel: 704-461-6675; Fax: 704-461-6242. Rt. Rev. Placid D. Solari, O.S.B., Abbot; Very Rev. Christopher Kirchgessner, O.S.B., Prior; Rev. Elias Correa-Torres, O.S.B., Subprior.

Legal Title: Southern Benedictine Society of North Carolina, Incorporated.

Priests 5; Brothers 9

Monastery founded in 1876, raised to an Abbey in 1884 and erected into an Abbey Nullius in 1910; Abbey Nullius suppressed January 1, 1977 and incorporated into Diocese of Charlotte.

Properties owned or sponsored: Belmont Abbey College, Belmont, NC.

St. Bernard Abbey (1891): Cullman, AL 35055. Tel: 256-734-8291; Fax: 256-734-3885. Rt. Rev. Marcus Voss, O.S.B., Abbot; Very Rev. Francis Reque, O.S.B., Prior; Rev. Linus Klucaritis, O.S.B., Subprior.

Legal Title: Benedictine Society of Alabama, Inc.

Priests 10; Brothers 14

Represented in the Archdiocese of Mobile and in the Diocese of Birmingham.

St. Procopius Abbey: 5601 College Rd., Lisle, IL 60532. Tel: 630-969-6410; Fax: 630-969-6426; Web: www.procopius.org. Rt. Rev. Austin G. Murphy, O.S.B., Abbot; Very Ven. Guy Jelinek, O.S.B., Prior & Business Mgr; Rev. James Flint, O.S.B., Subprior, Treas. & Procurator.

Priests 13; Brothers 6

Monastery founded in 1885 and raised to an Abbey in 1894.

Legal Holdings or Titles: Benedictine University, Lisle, IL; Benet Academy, Lisle, IL; Benedictine Chinese Mission, Lisle, IL; Slav Mission, Lisle, IL; St. Procopius Abbey Endowment, Lisle, IL.

Represented in the Diocese of Joliet.

St. Gregory's Abbey: 1900 W. MacArthur St., Shawnee, OK 74804. Tel: 405-878-5491; Fax: 405-878-5189. Rt. Rev. Lawrence Stasyszen, O.S.B., Abbot; Rt. Rev. Adrian Vorderlandwehr, O.S.B., Resigned Abbot & Treas.; Very Rev. Boniface T. Copelin, O.S.B., Prior; Rt. Rev. Martin Lugo, O.S.B, Resigned Abbot; Rev. Joachim Spexarth, O.S.B., Subprior.

Legal Titles: Benedictine Fathers of Sacred Heart Mission, Inc.; Endowment Foundation, Inc., Shawnee, OK; Saint Gregory's Abbey Benefit Trust.

Priests 12; Brothers 7; Military Installations: 3

Monastery founded in 1875 and raised to an Abbey in 1896.

Ministries in 1 Parish; 2 Military installations; 1 Catholic hospital.

Represented in the Archdiocese of Oklahoma City.

Properties owned or sponsored: Mabee-Gerrer Museum of Art, Shawnee, OK.

Saint Leo Abbey: 33601 SR 52, P.O. Box 2350, Saint Leo, FL 33574. Tel: 352-588-8624; Fax: 352-588-5217; Email: abbey@saintleo.edu; Web: www.saintleoabbey.org. Rt. Rev. Isaac Camacho, O.S.B., Abbot; Very Rev. Lucias Amarillas, Prior.

Legal Title: Order of St. Benedict of Florida, Inc. Fathers 7; Brothers 5. Founded in 1889 and raised to an Abbey in 1902.

Represented in the Diocese of St. Petersburg.

Assumption Abbey: P.O. Box A, Richardton, ND 58652.Tel: 701-974-3315. Rt. Rev. Daniel Maloney, O.S.B., Abbot; Very Ven. Michael Taffe, O.S.B., Prior; Rev. Jacob Deiss, O.S.B., Subprior.

Priests 16; Brothers 20

Founded in 1893 and raised to an Abbey in 1903.

Represented in the Dioceses of Bismarck, Cheyenne and Fargo. Also in Colombia

Properties owned or sponsored: Abbey; Dependent Priory; Parishes 2; Chaplaincies 5; Indian Mission.

St. Bede Abbey: 24 W. U.S. Hwy. 6, Peru, IL 61354. Tel: 815-223-3140. Rt. Rev. Michael Calhoun, O.S.B., Abbot; Very Rev. Dominic M. Garramone, O.S.B., Prior; Rev. Dominic M. Garramone, O.S.B., Subprior.

Legal Title: The Benedictine Society of Saint Bede.

Priests 8; Brothers 5

Monastery founded in 1891 and raised to an Abbey in 1910.

Represented in the Diocese of Peoria. Properties owned or sponsored: Parishes 1 & St. Bede Academy.

St. Martin's Abbey: 5000 Abbey Way S.E., Lacey, WA 98503-7500. Rt. Rev. Marion Nguyen, O.S.B; Rt. Rev. Adrian Parcher, O.S.B., Resigned Abbot; Very Ven. Nicolaus Wilson, O.S.B., Prior; Bro. Ramon Newell, O.S.B., Subprior.

Priests 8; Brothers 9

Monastery founded in 1895 and raised to an Abbey in 1914.

Legal Holdings or Titles: St. Martin's Abbey; St. Martin's University.

Represented in the Archdiocese of Seattle.

Holy Cross Abbey: 2951 E. Hwy. 50, Canon City, CO 81212. Tel: 719-275-8631. Rev. Maurice C. Haefling, O.S.B., Vicar Admin.; Rt. Rev. Kenneth C. Hein, O.S.B., Retired Abbot.

Fathers 2; Oblates: 1

Founded in 1886 and raised to an Abbey in 1925.

Represented in the Archdiocese of Denver and in the Diocese of Pueblo.

St. Anselm Abbey: 100 St. Anselm Dr., Manchester, NH 03102-1310. Tel: 603-641-7652; Fax: 603-641-7267. Rt. Rev. Mark A. Cooper, O.S.B., Abbot; Rt. Rev. Matthew K. Leavy, O.S.B., 4th Abbot; Most Rev. Joseph John Gerry, O.S.B., 3rd Abbot, Tenth Bishop of Portland, ME; Very Rev. Augustine Kelly, O.S.B., Prior; Rev. Benet Phillips, O.S.B., Subprior.

Legal Title: Order of Saint Benedict of New Hampshire.

Bishops 1; Abbots: 2; Fathers 18; Brothers 9.

Monastery founded in 1889 and raised to an Abbey in 1927.

Represented in the Archdiocese of San Francisco and in the Diocese of Manchester.

St. Andrew Abbey: 10510 Buckeye Rd., Cleveland, OH 44104. Tel: 216-721-5300. Rt. Rev. Gary Hoover, O.S.B., Abbot; Very Ven. Peter Ancell, O.S.B., Prior; Rev. Michael Brunovsky, O.S.B., Subprior.

Bishops 1; Abbots: 3; Priests 15; Brothers 5; Abbeys: 1; Parishes 1; High Schools 1; Chaplaincies 1

Founded in 1922 and raised to an Abbey in 1934.

Legal Holdings or Titles: Benedictine Order of Cleveland; Benedictine High School.

Represented in the Diocese of Cleveland.

Newark Abbey: 528 Dr. Martin Luther King, Jr. Blvd., Newark, NJ 07102. Tel: 973-643-4800; Fax: 973-643- 6922. Rt. Rev. Augustine J. Curley, O.S.B., Abbot; Very Rev. Albert Holtz, O.S.B., Prior; Bro. Patrick Winbush, O.S.B., Subprior.

Priests 10; Brothers 5; Novices 1; Abbeys: 1; Public Oratory: 1; Preparatory High Schools 1

Priory founded 1857; Abbey in 1884; title transferred from Newark to Morristown, N.J. in 1956; became Abbey again in 1968 and known as Newark Abbey under the patronage of the Immaculate Conception.

Legal Holding: St. Benedict Preparatory School, Newark, NJ.

Represented in the Archdiocese of Newark.

Benedictine Priory: 6502 Seawright Dr., Savannah, GA 31406. Tel: 912-356-3520; Fax: 912-356-3527. Very Rev. David Klecker, O.S.B., Prior.

Priests 5; Brothers 2; High Schools 1

Founded 1902, dependent priory of St. Vincent Archabbey, Latrobe, PA.

Represented in the Diocese of Savannah.

Woodside Priory: 302 Portola Rd., Portola Valley, CA 94028. Tel: 650-851-8220. Very Rev. Martin J. Mager, O.S.B., Supr.

Legal Title: Benedictine Fathers of the Priory, Inc.

Priests 3; High Schools 1; Middle Schools 1

Founded in 1956, erected as Conventual Priory 1958, became a dependent Priory upon St. Anselm's Abbey, Manchester, NH, 1976.

Represented in the Archdiocese of San Francisco.

Abadia de San Antonio Abad: P.O. Box 729, Humacao, PR 00792. Tel: 787-852-1616; Tel: 787-852-1766; Fax: 787-852-1920. Rt. Rev. Oscar Rivera, O.S.B., Abbot; Very Rev. Rafael Quiñones, O.S.B., Prior; Bro. Aristedes Pacheco, Subprior.

Priests 4; Brothers 4

Monastery founded in 1947 and became an Abbey in 1984.

Mary Mother of the Church Abbey: 12829 River Rd., Richmond, VA 23238-7206. Tel: 804-784-3508; Fax: 804-708-5064. Rt. Rev. Placid D. Solari, O.S.B., Admin.; Very Rev. John Mary Lugemwa, O.S.B., Prior.

Priests 2; Brothers 3; Abbeys: 1; Chaplaincies 3; High Schools 1 Community founded in 1911 and became an Abbey in 1989.

Legal Holdings: Benedictine High School of Richmond; Mary Mother of the Church Abbey

Represented in the Diocese of Richmond.

Mount Saviour Monastery: 231 Monastery Rd., Pine City, NY 14871-9787. Tel: 607-734-1688; Fax: 607-734-1689; Email: info@msaviour.org. Bro. John Thompson, O.S.B., Prior Admin.

Professed Monks 10; Simply Professed Monks 1; Novices 1.

Monastery founded in 1950, raised to Independent Priory 1957.
Represented in the Diocese of Rochester.

Swiss-American Congregation

The Abbeys and Priories belonging to this Federation are as follows:

St. Meinrad Archabbey: No. 100 Hill Dr., Saint Meinrad, IN 47577. Tel: 812-357-6611; Fax: 812-357-6551. Email: secretary@saintmeinrad.edu; Web: www.saintmeinrad.org. Rt. Rev. Kurt Stasiak, O.S.B., Archabbot; Rev. Bede Cisco, O.S.B., Prior; Rev. Joseph Cox, O.S.B., Subprior; Rt. Rev. Lambert Reilly, O.S.B., Resigned Archabbot.
Priests 45; Brothers 22; Parishes 6; Schools of Theology: 1; Chaplaincies 2
Founded 1854; raised to an Abbey in 1870.
Represented in the Archdioceses of Indianapolis, San Francisco, and Washington and in the Dioceses of Belleville, Evansville, Venice, Lafayette in Indiana and Owensboro.

Conception Abbey: 37174 State Hwy. VV, Conception, MO 64433. Tel: 660-944-3100; Fax: 660-944-2800. Rt. Rev. Benedict Neenan, O.S.B., Abbot; Bro. Jonathan Clark, O.S.B., Prior; Bro. Thomas Sullivan, O.S.B., Subprior; Most Rev. Jerome Hanus, O.S.B., Retired Archbishop.
Legal Title: Conception Abbey, Inc.
Archbishops 1; Fathers 36; Brothers 17; Parishes 9; Seminary College: 1; Chaplaincies 3
Founded December 8, 1873; Abbey April 5, 1881.
Represented in the Archdioceses of Milwaukee, Oklahoma City and Omaha and in the Dioceses of Kansas City-St. Joseph and Springfield-Cape Girardeau.

Mount Michael Abbey: 22520 Mount Michael Rd., Elkhorn, NE 68022-3400. Tel: 402-289-2541; Fax: 402-289-4539. Email: business@mountmichael.org. Rt. Rev. Michael Liebl, O.S.B., Abbot; Rev. Louis Sojka, O.S.B., Prior.
Fathers 7; Brothers 7
Legal Holdings & Titles: Mount Michael Benedictine Abbey; Mount Michael Benedictine School; Mount Michael Foundation.
Monks serve and staff: Parishes 1.
Represented in the Archdiocese of Omaha and in the Diocese of Pueblo.

Subiaco Abbey: Subiaco, AR 72865. Tel: 479-934-1000; Fax: 479-934-4328. Email: abbot@subi.org. Rt. Rev. Elijah Owens, O.S.B., Abbot; Rev. Richard Walz, O.S.B., Prior; Bro. Adrian Strobel, O.S.B., Subprior; Rt. Rev. Leonard Wangler, O.S.B., Resigned Abbot; Rt. Rev. Jerome Kodell, O.S.B., Resigned Abbot.
Fathers 12; Perpetually Professed Brothers 19; Temporarily Professed Brothers 2
Properties staffed or sponsored: Parishes 5; High School 1.
Represented in the Diocese of Little Rock.

St. Joseph Abbey: Saint Benedict, LA 70457. Tel: 985-892-1800; Fax: 985-867-2270. Vocations Email: frephrem@sjasc.edu. Web: www.saintjosephabbey.com. Rt. Rev. Justin Brown, O.S.B., Abbot; Bro. Brian Harrington, O.S.B., Prior; Rev. Augustine Foley, Subprior.
Fathers 16; Brothers 9; Parishes 1; Seminary College: 1
Legal Holdings: St. Joseph Seminary College, St. Benedict, LA.
Represented in the Archdiocese of New Orleans.

Mt. Angel Abbey: 1 Abbey Dr., Saint Benedict, OR 97373. Tel: 503-845-3030. Email: abbotsec@mtangel.edu. Rt. Rev. Jeremy Driscoll, O.S.B., Abbot; Very Rev. Vincent Trujillo, O.S.B., Prior; Rev. William Hammelman, O.S.B., Subprior.
Finally Professed Monks (Priests): 25; Finally Professed Monks (Brothers): 17; Temporarily Professed Monks (Brothers): 8
Founded on Oct. 30, 1882, from Engelberg in Switzerland and raised to an Abbey on March 24, 1904.

Marmion Abbey: 850 Butterfield Rd., Aurora, IL 60502. Tel: 630-897-7215. Rt. Rev. John Brahill, O.S.B., Abbot; Very Rev. Michael Burrows, O.S.B., Prior; Rev. Joel Rippinger, O.S.B., Subprior; Rt. Rev. Vincent Bataille, O.S.B., Abbot Emeritus.
Priests 18; Brothers 3
Founded as Dependent Priory of St. Meinrad's Abbey, June 20, 1943; Abbey since March 21, 1947.
Represented in the Diocese of Rockford. Also in Quetzaltenango, Guatemala.
Properties staffed or sponsored: Parishes 1; High Schools 1.

St. Benedict's Abbey: 12605 224th Ave., Benet Lake, WI 53102-1000. Tel: 262-396-4311; Fax: 262-396-4365; Email: macario@benetlake.org. Rt. Rev. Edmund J. Boyce, O.S.B., Abbot Resigned and Treas.; Rev. Macario Martinez, O.S.B., Supr.; Rev. Daniel Petsche, O.S.B., Asst. Supr.
Legal Titles: Benedictine Monks, Inc.; St Benedict's Home Missionary Society.
Priests 3; Brothers 1
Monastery founded in 1945 and raised to an Abbey in 1952; became dependent priory of Conception Abbey in 2014.
Represented in the Archdiocese of Milwaukee.

Glastonbury Abbey: 16 Hull St., Hingham, MA 02043. Tel: 781-749-2155; Fax: 781-749-6236. Rt. Rev. Thomas O'Connor, Abbot; Bro. Daniel Walters, O.S.B., Prior.
Monks in Solemn Vows 8; Temporary Vows 2.
Represented in the Archdiocese of Boston.

Prince of Peace Abbey: 650 Benet Hill Rd., Oceanside, CA 92058. Mailing address: P.O. Box 3470, Oceanside, CA 92051. Tel: 760-967-4200; Email: princeabby@aol.com. Email: princeabby@aol.com; dearmonks@gmail.com; Web: www.princeofpeaceabbey.blogspot.com. Rt. Rev. Sharbel Ewen, O.S.B., Abbot; Bro. Raphael Meyer, O.S.B., Prior.
Priests 7; Brothers 14

St. Benedict Abbey: 252 Still River Rd., Still River, MA 01467. Tel: 978-456-3221; Fax: 978-456-8181; Email: saintbenedict@abbey.org. Web: www.abbey.org. Mailing address: P.O. Box 778, Harvard, MA 01451. Rt. Rev. Marc Crilly, O.S.B., Abbot; Very Rev. James Doran, O.S.B., Prior.
Priests 5; Brothers 2
Represented in the Diocese of Worcester.

Ascension Monastery: 541 East 100 South, Jerome, ID 83338. Tel: 208-324-2377. Very Rev. Boniface Lautz, O.S.B., Prior; Rev. Hugh Feiss, O.S.B., Subprior.
Priests 6; Brothers 3.

Congregation of St. Ottilien for Foreign Missions

St. Paul's Abbey: 289 U.S. Hwy. 206 S., P.O. Box 7, Newton, NJ 07860-0007. Tel: 973-383-2470; Fax: 973-383-5782. Rt. Rev. Joel P. Macul, O.S.B., Abbot Emeritus; Rt. Rev. Justin E. Dzikowicz, O.S.B., Resigned Abbot; Very Rev. Samuel Kim, O.S.B., Prior.
Solemnly Professed Monks: 10; Priests 4
(Benedictine Missionaries)
Monastery established March 15, 1924; elevated to an Abbey June 9, 1947.
Represented in the Diocese of Paterson.

Christ the King Priory (1985) - Benedictine Mission House (1935): Benedictine Mission House was founded in 1935 and raised to the rank of Priory in 1985. P.O. Box 528, Schuyler, NE 68661. Tel: 402-352-2177; Fax: 402-352-2176. Rev. Anastasius Reiser, O.S.B., Prior; Rev. Adam Patras, O.S.B., Subprior; Rev. Thomas Andrew Hillenbrand, O.S.B.; Rev. Volker Futter, O.S.B; Rev. Thomas Leitner, O.S.B; Rev. Jacques Missihoun, O.S.B.; Rev. Paul L. Kasun, O.S.B.
Fathers 7; Brothers 3
Represented in the Archdiocese of Omaha.

Congregation of the Annunciation

St. Andrew's Abbey: P.O. Box 40, Valyermo, CA 93563. Tel: 661-944-2178. Rev. Damien Toilolo, O.S.B., Abbot; Rev. Joseph Brennan, O.S.B., Prior.
Monks in Solemn Vows 18
Represented in the Archdiocese of Los Angeles.

Camaldolese Benedictine Congregation (Congregatio Camaldulensis Ordinis Sancti Benedicti)

U.S. Foundation (1958): New Camaldoli Hermitage, 62475 Hwy. 1, Big Sur, CA 93920. Tel: 831-667-2456. Email: monks@contemplation.com. Rev. Cyprian Consiglio, O.S.B.Cam., Prior; Rev. Thomas Matus, O.S.B.Cam.; Rev. Isaiah Teichert, O.S.B.Cam.; Rev. Raniero Hoffman, O.S.B.Cam.; Rev. Zacchaeus Naegle, O.S.B.Cam.; Rev. Ignatius Tully, O.S.B.Cam.
Fathers 6; Professed Brothers 4; Professed Monks (including priests): 10.
Represented in the Dioceses of Monterey and Oakland.

English Benedictine Congregation

St. Anselm's Abbey: 4501 S. Dakota Ave., N.E., Washington, DC 20017. Tel: 202-269-2300; Fax: 202-269-2312. Email: abbot@stanselms.org. Rt. Rev. James Wiseman, O.S.B., Abbot.
Legal Title: Benedictine Foundation at Washington DC.
Professed Monks: 13

Abbey of St. Gregory the Great: 285 Cory's Ln., Portsmouth, RI 02871. Tel: 401-683-2000; Fax: 401-682-1750. Rt. Rev. Michael Brunner, O.S.B., Abott.
Choir Religious: 12

Abbey of St. Mary and St. Louis: 500 S. Mason Rd., Saint Louis, MO 63141-8500. Tel: 314-434-3690; Fax: 314-434-0795. Rt. Rev. Gregory Mohrman, O.S.B.
Solemnly Professed Monks: 24; Priests 20; Oblates: 1
Founded as a dependent Priory 1955, granted independence 1973, raised to status of Abbey 1989.

Sylvestrine Benedictine Congregation (Monachorum Silvestrinorum, O.S.B.)

Foundations in the U.S. (1910): Saint Benedict Priory, 2711 E. Drahner Rd., Oxford, MI 48370. Tel: 248-628-2249. Rev. Damien Gjonaj, O.S.B., Conventual Prior.
Brothers 4; Priests 6; Regular Oblates: 2
Represented in the Archdiocese of Detroit and in the Diocese of Paterson.

Olivetan Benedictines (Congregatio Sanctae Mariae Montis Oliveti Ordinis Sancti Benedicti)

General Motherhouse: St. Sylvester Monastery, Fabriano, Italy, Very Rev. Michael Kelly, O.S.B., Abbot Gen.

Our Lady of Guadalupe Abbey: P.O. Box 1080, Pecos, NM 87552-1080. Tel: 505-757-6415. Email: guestmaster@pecomonastery.org. Rev. Aidan Gore, O.S.B., Abbot; Bro. James Marron.
Priests 2; Brothers 5
Represented in the Archdiocese of Santa Fe.

Benedictine Monastery of Hawaii: 67-290 Farrington Hwy., P.O. Box 490, Waialua, HI 96791. Tel: 808-637-7887; Fax: 808-637-8601; Email: monastery@hawaiibenedictines.org; Web: www.hawaiibenedictines.org. Rev. David Barfknecht, O.S.B., Supr.
Legal Title: Mary, Spouse of the Holy Spirit Monastery.
Priests 2

Subiaco Benedictine Congregation

Monastery of Christ in the Desert (1964): Abiquiu, NM 87510. Tel: 575-613-4233. Rt. Rev. Christian Leisy, O.S.B., Abbot.
Monks: 55
Independent 1983; Abbey 1996.
Represented in the Archdiocese of Santa Fe. Also in Mexico.

***Benedictine Monastery of Thien Tam:** 13055 S.E. CR 4271, Kerens, TX 75144. Tel: 903-229-2034. Rev. Paulavang Luu Vuong, O.S.B., Subprior.

Saint Mary's Monastery: P.O. Box 345, Petersham, MA 01366. Tel: 978-724-3350. Rev. Dom Gregory Phillips, O.S.B., Supr.
Monks: 8
Dependent Monastery 1987.
Represented in the Diocese of Worcester.

Subiaco Cassinese Benedictine Congregation

Monastery of the Holy Cross: 3111 S. Aberdeen St., Chicago, IL 60608-6503. Tel: 773-927-7424; Fax: 773-927-5734; Email: fatheredwardglanzmann@gmail.com; Web: www.chicagomonk.org. Rev. Peter Funk, O.S.B., Prior.
Monastery established in the Diocese of Crookston, MN in 1988 and transferred to the Archdiocese of Chicago in 1991. With the incorporation of the Cassinese Congregation of the OSB, established in 1408, into the Subiaco Congregation of the OSB, established by Pope Pius in 1867, the Subiaco Cassinese Benedictine Congregation was established by Pope Benedict XVI on February 7, 2013.

Solesmes Congregation

Benedictine Monks, Solesmes Congregation: Our Lady of Clear Creek Abbey, 5804 W. Monastery Rd., Hulbert, OK 74441. Tel: 918-772-2454; Fax: 918-772-1044; Email: abbey@clearcreekmonks.org; Web: www.clearcreekmonks.org. Rt. Rev. Philip Anderson, O.S.B., Abbot.
Legal Title: Foundation for the Annunciation Monastery of Clear Creek.

Outside the Congregation

Weston Priory (1952): 58 Priory Hill Rd., Weston, VT 05161. Tel: 802-824-5409; Fax: 802-824-3573. Email: brothers@westonpriory.org. Very Rev. Richard Iaquinto, O.S.B., Prior.
Founded in 1952 and established as a Conventual Priory July 18, 1968 under the jurisdiction of the Abbot Primate.

Legal Title: The Benedictine Foundation of the State of Vermont, Inc.
Monks: 11
Represented in the Diocese of Burlington.

[0220] (S.S.S.)—CONGREGATION OF THE BLESSED SACRAMENT

(Congregatio Sanctissimi Sacramenti)

Generalate: 46 Via Giovanni Battista de Rossi, 00161, Rome, Italy, Very Rev. Eugenio Barbosa Martins, S.S.S., General Supr.

Province of St. Ann (1931): 5384 Wilson Mills Rd., Cleveland, OH 44143. Tel: 440-442-6311. Rev. John Keenan, S.S.S., Provincial Supr.; Rev. Robert Stark, S.S.S., Consultor & Prov. Treas.; Rev. Thomas Smithson, S.S.S., Consultor.
Priests 19; Permanent Deacons 1; Brothers 6
Properties staffed or owned: Parishes 5; Community Houses 6.
Represented in the Archdioceses of Galveston-Houston, New York and San Antonio and in the Dioceses of Cleveland and St. Petersburg.

[0230] (ER. CAM.)—CAMALDOLESE HERMITS OF THE CONGREGATION OF MONTE CORONA

(Eremitae Camaldulenses Congregationis Montis Coronae)

General Motherhouse: Sacro Eremo Tuscolano, Via Tuscolo 45, 00078 Monte Porzio Catone, Rome, Italy, Rt. Rev. Elias Castillo, Er.Cam., Father Major.

U.S. Foundation (1959): Holy Family Hermitage, 1501 Fairplay Rd., Bloomingdale, OH 43910-7971. Tel: 740-765-4511. Email: dcook@diosteub.org. Very Rev. Basil Corriere, Er.Cam., Prior.
Hermit Priests 3; Professed 4; Novice 1; Donate 1.
Represented in the Diocese of Steubenville.

[0240] (M.I.)—CAMILLIAN FATHERS AND BROTHERS OR ORDER OF ST. CAMILLUS

(Ministers of the Infirm)

General Motherhouse: Casa Generalizia, Ministri degli Infermi, Piazza della Maddalena 53, 00186, Rome, Italy; Rev. Pedro Celso Tramontin, M.I., Gen. Superior & Gen. Vicar; Rev. Gianfranco Lunardon, M.I. Consultor Gen.; Bro. Paul Kabore, M.I., Consultor Gen.; Rev. Medard Aboue, M.I., Consultor Gen.; Rev. Baby Ellickal, M.I.

U.S.A. Camillian (1921): Delegation of Brazilian Prov., 10101 W. Wisconsin Ave., Wauwatosa, WI 53226. Tel: 414-259-4744. Rev. Pedro Tramontin, M.I., Delegate.
Fathers 14; Professed Brothers 1
Legal Titles: St. Camillus Health Center Inc., Wauwatosa, WI; St. Camillus Health System, Wauwatosa, WI; San Camillo, Inc., Wauwatosa, WI; St. Camillus Ministries Inc., Wauwatosa, WI; St. Camillus Communities Inc., Wauwatosa, WI; Order of St. Camillus Foundation, Wauwatosa, WI.
Represented in the Archdiocese of Milwaukee and in the Dioceses of Savannah and Pittsburgh.

[0250] (C.R.L.)—CANONS REGULAR OF THE LATERAN

(Ordo Canonicorum Regularium S. Augustini Congregations Ss. Salvatoris Lateranensis)

General House: Curia Generalizia dei Canonicio Regolari Lateranensi, Piazza S. Pietro in Vincoli, 4A, 00184, Roma, Italy.

United States: Canons Regular of the Lateran, 130 Beekman Ave., Sleepy Hollow, NY 10591. Tel: 914-631-0720. Rev. Rumando Peralta, C.R.L., Supr.
Priests 5
Represented in the Archdiocese of New York.

[0260] (O.C.D.)—DISCALCED CARMELITE FRIARS

(Ordo Carmelitarum Discalceatorum)

Founded Mt. Carmel, Palestine in the 13th Century.

Generalate: Carmelitani Scalzi, Corso d'Italia, 38, 00198, Rome, Italy. Very Rev. Saverio Cannistra, O.C.D., Supr. Gen.

California-Arizona Province (1983): 926 E. Highland Ave., P.O. Box 8700, Redlands, CA 92375. Tel: 909-793-0424; Fax: 909-335-1304. Rev. Stephen Watson, O.C.D., Prov.
Legal Title: Discalced Carmelite Province of California.
Fathers 34; Brothers 3; Students: 3
Represented in the Archdioceses of Los Angeles, Portland in Oregon and Seattle and in the Dioceses of San Jose, San Bernardino, Santa Rosa and Tucson. Also in Uganda.
Properties owned, staffed or sponsored: Parishes 3; Retreat House; Novitiate; House of Studies; House of Prayer; Institute of Spirituality.

Province of St. Therese of Oklahoma (1935): Provincial House, 906 Kentucky Ave., San Antonio, TX 78201. Tel: 201-865-0142. Email: provincial@carmelitefriarsocd.com; executivedirector@carmelitedriarsocd.com. Rev. Luis J. Castaneda, O.C.D., Prov.
Fathers 14; Brothers 1
Represented in the Archdioceses of Oklahoma City and San Antonio and in the Dioceses of Dallas and Little Rock.
Properties staffed or sponsored: Parishes 3; Community Houses 1; Novitiate 1.

Washington Province of the Immaculate Heart of Mary (1947): Discalced Carmelites-Prov. Office, 1233 S. 45th St., Milwaukee, WI 53214-3693. Tel: 414-672-7212; Fax: 414-672-3138. Very Rev. Michael Berry, O.C.D., Prov.
Fathers 52; Brothers 9; Professed Brothers 20; Novices 10; Postulants: 7
Represented in the Archdioceses of Boston, Milwaukee and Washington. Also in Kenya and the Philippines.
Properties owned or sponsored: Community Houses 7.

Washington Province Discalced Carmelite Secular Order, Inc. (2021): OCDS Main Office, 166 Foster St., Brighton, MA 02135. Tel: 617-851-8584. Email: ocdsmainoffice@gmail.com. Rev. Leonard Copeland, O.C.D., Prov. Delegate; Loretta L. Gallagher, O.C.D.S., Admin.

Polish Province of the Holy Spirit, Poland (1949): Monastery of Our Lady of Mt. Carmel, 1628 Ridge Rd., Munster, IN 46321. Tel: 219-838-7111; Fax: 219-838-7214; Email: carmelmunster@yahoo.com. Rev. Franciszek Czaicki, O.C.D., Prior.
Priests 7; Brothers 1
Represented in the Diocese of Gary.

[0270] (O.CARM.)—CARMELITE FATHERS & BROTHERS

(Ordo Fratrum Beatissimae Virginis Mariae de Monte Carmelo)

General Curia: Via Giovanni Lanza, 138, 00184, Rome, Italy. Most Rev. Mícéal O'Neill, O.Carm., Prior Gen.

Province of the Most Pure Heart of Mary (1864): Carmelite Provincial Office, 1317 Frontage Rd., Darien, IL 60561. Tel: 630-971-0050; Fax: 630-971-0195. Email: areynolds@carmelnet.org. Very Rev. Carl J. Markelz, O.Carm., Prior Prov.; Very Rev. David McEnvoy, O.Carm., Vice Prior Prov.; Rev. Elias O'Brien, O.Carm., Treas. Councilors: Bro. Daryl Moresco, O.Carm.; Rev. Gregory Houck, O.Carm.; Rev. Luis Jesús Paz Acosta, O.Carm.; Rev. Rolf Nepomuck Willemsen, O.Carm.; Rev. Thomas Schrader, O.Carm., Dir. Little Flower Society; Rev. Joseph O'Brien, O.Carm., Dir.-Carmelite Mission Office; Very Rev. Carl J. Markelz, O.Carm., Delegate to Lay Carmelites.
Priests 124; Clerics: 3; Pre-Novitiates 25; Novices 4; Brothers 40
Ministries in 20 Parishes.
Properties owned: Spiritual Centers 2; High Schools 5; Community Houses 20; House of Study 5; Shrine 2.
Represented in the Archdioceses of Chicago, Kansas City in Kansas, Los Angeles, Newark, Philadelphia, San Francisco and Washington and in the Dioceses of Joliet, Phoenix, Sacramento, Tucson and Venice. Also in Australia, Canada, Italy, El Salvador, Peru, Mexico and Honduras.

Province of the Most Pure Heart of Mary: St. Therese Priory, 75 E. Mariposa St., Phoenix, AZ 85012-1631. Rev. James Mueller, O.Carm; Rev. Kevin Lafey, O.Carm.; Rev. Ronald Oakham, O.Carm.; Bro. Eric Bell, O.Carm.

Province of St. Elias (1931): P.O. Box 3079, Middletown, NY 10940-0890. Tel: 845-344-2223; Fax: 845-344-2210. Email: wward@carmelites.com. Very Rev. Mario Esposito, O.Carm., Prov.
Fathers 60; Deacons 1; Brothers 6; Novices 6; Pre-Novices 6; Professed Students: 19; Members: 98
Legal Holdings or Titles: The Missionary Society of Our Lady of Mt. Carmel of the State of New York; The Carmelite Fathers, Inc. of New York; Carmelite Fathers, Inc. of the Commonwealth of Massachusetts; Mt. Carmel Hermitage; Order of Carmelites of Palm Beach, Inc.; National Shrine of Our Lady of Mount Carmel, Inc.
Represented in the Archdioceses of New York, Newark and Washington and in the Dioceses of Albany, Greensburg, Palm Beach, Rochester, Sioux Falls and Winona-Rochester. Also in Trinidad & Vietnam.
Properties staffed, owned or sponsored: Parishes 6; Priories 16; Houses of Study 1; Novitiates 2; Hermitages 2; Shrines 1.

Pre-Novitiate: St. Eliseus Priory, 324 Jersey St., Harrison, NJ 07029-1704. Tel: 973-485-7233; Fax: 973-485-7244. Rev. Joseph Nguyen Do, O.Carm., Prior; Very Rev. Mario Esposito, O.Carm, Dir.; Bro. Robert Bathe, O.Carm.
Priests 2; Brothers 1; Pre-Novices 2

Mt. Carmel Hermitage: 244 Baileys Rd., Bolivar, PA 15923-9668. Tel: 724-238-0423; Fax: 724-238-0423. Email: wward@carmelites.com. Bro. Robert Ryba, O.Carm.
Brothers 1
Founded in 1970, became dependent upon St. Elias Province in 1995.
Represented in the Diocese of Greensburg.

Carmelite Hermitage of the Blessed Virgin Mary (O.Carm): 8249 de Montreville Tr. N., Lake Elmo, MN 55042-9545. Tel: 651-779-7351; Fax: 651-779-7351; Email: carmelbvm@gmail.com; Web: www.carmelitehermitage.org. Rev. John M. Burns, O.Carm., Prior; Rev. Peter Peach, O.Carm.; Rev. Elijah Schwab, O.Carm.
Fathers 3; Brothers 6

[0275] (C.M.I.)—CARMELITES OF MARY IMMACULATE

(Congregatio Fratrum Carmelitarum B.V. Mariae Immaculatae)

Founded by Saint Kuriakose Elias Chavara and Companions at Mannanam, Kerala, India in 1831.

Generalate: CMI Generalate Chavara Hills, P.B. No. 3105, Kakkanad P.O., 682030, Kochi, India, Tel: 91-484-288-1816; Fax: 91-484-288-1811. Rev. Thomas Chathamparambil, C.M.I., Prior Gen.

North American Headquarters: 862 Manhattan Ave., Brooklyn, NY 11222. Tel: 718-383-3339; Email: cmiusa@hotmail.com. Rev. Sebastian Augustine, C.M.I., Delegate Superior.
Legal Title: Carmelites of Mary Immaculate, Inc.
Priests in U.S. & Canada: 110
Ministries in Parishes; Hospitals; Universities; Prisons; Syro-Malabar Catholics.
Represented in the Archdioceses of Boston, Los Angeles, Louisville, Miami, New York and Philadelphia and in the Dioceses of Alexandria, Austin, Baker, Beaumont, Biloxi, Brooklyn, Camden, Charleston, Covington, Joliet, Knoxville, Lafayette, Lake Charles, Metuchen, Nashville, Orlando, Rockville Center, Sacramento, Sioux Falls, St. Augustine, St. Paul & Minneapolis, Salina, San Angelo, Shreveport and Tulsa. Also in Canada.

Carmelites of Mary Immaculate, St. Joseph Province Kottayam: 11730 Old St. Augustine Rd., Jacksonville, FL 32258. Tel: 386-503-0957; Email: cmiktminc@gmail.com. Rev. Sebastian K. George, C.M.I., Provincial Coord.
Legal Title: Carmelites of Mary Immaculate Florida Inc.
Priests: 18

[0280] (O.CART.)—ORDER OF CARTHUSIANS

(Ordo Cartusianorum)

Motherhouse: Grande Chartreuse, St. Pierre de Chartreuse (Isere), France, Rev. Francois Marie Velut, O.Cart., Supr. Gen.

U.S. Charterhouse of the Transfiguration (1951): Carthusian Monastery, 1084 Ave Maria Way, Arlington, VT 05250. Tel: 802-362-2550; Fax: 802-362-3584; Email: carthusians_in_america@chartreuse.info; Web: www.chartreux.org; Web: transfiguration.chartreux.org. Rev. Lorenzo Maria T. De La Rosa Jr., O.Cart., Prior.
Total in Community: 15
Legal Titles: Carthusian Foundation in America, Inc.; Carthusian Foundation, Association Fraternelle Romande.
Represented in the Diocese of Burlington.

[0290] (F.C.)—BROTHERS OF CHARITY

(Congregatio Fratrum Caritate)

General Motherhouse (1807): Via G.B. Pagano 35, 00167, Rome, Italy. Bro. Rene Stockman, F.C., Supr. Gen.

American District (1963): Region of Our Lady of Charity, 7720 Doe Ln., Glenside, PA 19038. Bro. John Fitzgerald, F.C., Provincial Supr. for Province of the Americas.
Represented in the Archdioceses of Philadelphia and Washington.

[0300] (I.C.)—INSTITUTE OF CHARITY

(Rosminians Institutum Charitatis)

General Motherhouse: Collegio Rosmini Via Porta, Latina 17, Rome, Italy, Very Rev. Vito Nardin, I.C., Supr. Gen.

U.S. Foundation (1877): 11565 66th Ave. N., Seminole, FL 33772. Email: frickpilger@sairf.com. Rev. Rick Pilger, I.C.

Fathers in the U.S: 8; Parishes 3

Represented in the Diocese of St. Petersburg.

[0305] (I.C.)—INSTITUTE OF CHRIST THE KING-SOVEREIGN PRIEST

(Institutum Christi Regis Summi Sacerdotis)

General Motherhouse and House of Formation: Villa Martelli, Via di Gricigliano 52, 50065, Sieci, Italy, Rev. Msgr. Gilles Wach, Prior Gen.

U.S. Mailing Address: Institute of Christ the King-Sovereign Priest, 6415 S. Woodlawn Ave., Chicago, IL 60637.

American Headquarters: Shrine of Christ the King Sovereign Priest, 6415 S. Woodlawn Ave., Chicago, IL 60637. Tel: 773-363-7409; Fax: 773-363-7824; Email: info@institute-christ-king.org. Rev. Msgr. R. Michael Schmitz, Vicar Gen.; Rev. Matthew L. Talarico, Prov. Supr.; Rev. Luke Zignego, Vice-Rector; Rev. James Hoogerwerf, Bursar; Rev. David Le, Sec.

[0310] (C.F.C.)—EDMUND RICE CHRISTIAN BROTHERS NORTH AMERICA CONGREGATION OF CHRISTIAN BROTHERS

Founded in Ireland in 1802. First foundation in the United States in 1906.

Edmund Rice Christian Brothers North America, a province of the Congregation of Christian Brothers (1906): 260 Wilmot Rd., New Rochelle, NY 10804-1526. Tel: 914-636-6194; Fax: 914-636-0021. Email: gmd@cbinstitute.org; pezawot@hotmail.com. Bro. Peter E. Zawot, C.F.C., Prov. Leader; Bro. Peter O'Loughlin, C.F.C., Deputy Prov. Leader. Councilors: Bro. Sean Moffett, C.F.C.; Bro. Michael Segvich, C.F.C.; Bro. Edward Bergeron, C.F.C.

Legal Title: The Christian Brothers' Institute; Christian Brothers of Ireland, Inc.; Mount Sion Community, Inc.

Brothers 150

Represented in the Archdioceses of Boston, Chicago, Detroit, Miami, New York, Newark and Seattle in the Dioceses of Brownsville, Honolulu, Monterey, Providence, Rochester and St. Petersburg. Also in Canada, Latin America, West Indies, Peru, Argentina, and Uruguay.

Ministries: Colleges 1; High Schools 15; Grade Schools 3; House of Formation 1; Care Center 1; Retreat Center 1; Outreach Ministries 8.

Development Office: The Christian Brothers Foundation, dba Edmund Rice Christian Brothers Foundation, 260 Wilmot Rd., New Rochelle, NY 10804. Tel: 914-636-1035. Bro. Peter Zawot, C.F.C., Pres. Email: pezawot@hotmail.com. Georganne Dotto, Dir. of Finance. Email: gmd@cbinstitute.org. Kevin Brewer, Development Dir. Email: kbrewer@cbfoundation.org.

[0320] (F.I.C.)—BROTHERS OF CHRISTIAN INSTRUCTION

(La Mennais Brothers)

(Institutum Fratrum Instructionis Christianae)

General Motherhouse: Casa Generalizia, Via della Divina Provvidenza, 44, 00166, Rome, Italy, Tel: 39-06-66-41-56-18; Fax: 39-06-45-44-35-92. Bro. Herve Zamor, Supr. Gen.

LaMennais - North American Province American Delegation (2016): P.O. Box 159, Alfred, ME 04002. Tel: 207-324-1017, Ext. 3. Bro. Daniel Caron, Prov. Delegate

Brothers 10; Retirement community 1

Represented in the Dioceses of Portland (In Maine) and Youngstown.

[0330] (F.S.C.)—BROTHERS OF THE CHRISTIAN SCHOOLS

(Fratres Scholarum Christianarum)

General Motherhouse: Casa Generalizia, Via Aurelia 476, CP 9099 00100, Rome, Italy, Web: www.lasalle.org. Bro. Robert Schieler, F.S.C., Supr. Gen.; Bro. Jorge Gallardo de Alba, F.S.C., Vicar Gen.

Christian Brothers Conference: 415 Michigan Ave., N.E., Ste. 300, Washington, DC 20017-4501.Tel: 202-529-0047; Fax: 202-529-0775. Bro. Timothy Coldwell, F.S.C., Gen. Councilor; Mr. James G. Lindsay, Dir. of Administration.

Legal Title: Christian Brothers Major Superiors, Inc.

Organizations and programs served by this office: Regional Conference of Christian Brothers; Lasallian Volunteers; Huether Lasallian Conference; Buttimer Institute of Lasallian Studies; Brother John Johnston Institute of Contemporary Lasallian Practice; Lasallian Social Justice Institute; Lasallian Education Council.

Organizations associated with this office: Christian Brothers Major Superiors.

Institutions owned and/or sponsored: Bethlehem University of the Holy Land; Sangre de Cristo Center, Santa Fe, NM; Christian Brothers Services, Romeoville, IL.

Brothers of the Christian Schools (Midwest Province): 7650 S. County Line Rd., Burr Ridge, IL 60527-7959. Tel: 630-323-3725; Fax: 630-323-3779; Email: jsaurbier@cbmidwest.org. Bro. Michael Fehrenbach, F.S.C., Visitor; Bro. Chris Englert, F.S.C., Aux. Visitor; Bro. Joseph Saurbier, F.S.C., Dir. Admin. & Operations; Mr. Anthony Chimera, Dir. Development; Dr. Scott Kier, Supt., Lasallian Educ.

Brothers 101

Legal Titles: The Christian Brothers of the Midwest, Inc.; The Christian Brothers of Illinois; Brothers of the Christian Schools of the St. Louis District; The Christian Brothers of Minnesota.

Represented in the Archdioceses of Chicago, Cincinnati, Milwaukee, St. Louis and St. Paul-Minneapolis and the Dioceses of Helena, Joliet, Kansas City-St. Joseph, Memphis, Omaha and Winona-Rochester.

Properties owned, staffed or sponsored: Communities 24; Universities 3; High Schools 11; Middle Schools 3; Elementary Schools 1; Retreat Houses 4; Publishing Houses 1.

Province of San Francisco New Orleans (1868): Brothers of the Christian Schools Provincial Office, P.O. Box 3720, Napa, CA 94558-0372. Tel: 707-252-0222. Bro. Nick Gonzalez, F.S.C., Prov.

Brothers 92

Represented in the Archdioceses of Denver, Los Angeles, New Orleans, Portland in Oregon, San Francisco and Santa Fe and the Dioceses of El Paso, Oakland, Orange, Sacramento, Santa Rosa, Tucson and Yakima. Also in Ethiopia, Rome and Thailand.

Legal Holdings or Titles: NOSF, Inc.; St. La Salle Auxiliary; Brothers of the Christian Schools of Lafayette Retirement Trust; Christian Brothers Charitable Trust; Magnolia Lafayette, Inc.; Lasallian Education Corporation; Lasallian Christian Brothers Foundation, Inc.; De La Salle Institute.

Properties owned, staffed or sponsored: Colleges 1; High Schools 18; Middle and Elementary Schools 3; Community Houses 14; Retreat & Conference Centers 2.

District of Eastern North America: 444A Rte. 35 S., Eatontown, NJ 07724-2200. Tel: 732-380-7926; Fax: 732-380-7937. Email: info@fscdena.org; Web: www.fscdena.org. Bro. Robert Schaefer, F.S.C., Visitor/ Prov. & Pres.; Bro. Frank Byrne, F.S.C., Auxiliary; Bro. Jules Knight, F.S.C., Asst. Visitor; Bro. Joseph Juliano, F.S.C., Dir. Admin. & Sec.; Bro. Timothy J. Froehlich, F.S.C., Dir. Finance & Treas.; Mr. Benjamin Ventresca, Jr., Prov. Delegate for Ministry Governing Boards; Mr. James Logan, Dir. Office for Mission & Ministry; Ms. H. Carroll Bennett, Admin. Asst.; Mr. Philip De Rita, Dir. Communications & Public Rels.; Bro. Edward Shields, F.S.C., Dir. of Vocations; Mrs. Janice Shea, Personal Asst. to the Brother Visitor; Mr. Patrick Donahue, Dir. Advancement.

Legal Titles: Brothers of the Christian Schools, District of Eastern North America, Inc. (d/b/a: FSC DENA); Brothers of the Christian Schools, Long Island-New England Province; Christian Brothers of Frederick, Inc.; La Salle Provincialate, Inc.; Ammendale Normal Institute of Prince George's County, Inc.

Brothers 207

Represented in the Archdioceses of Baltimore, Detroit, Miami, New York, Philadelphia and Washington and in the Dioceses of Albany, Brooklyn, Buffalo, Camden, Palm Beach, Pittsburgh, Providence, Rockville Centre, San Juan, Syracuse and Trenton. Also in Canada.

[0340] (O.CIST.)—CISTERCIAN ABBEY

(Ordo Cisterciensis)

Headquarters: Piazza del Tempio di Diana, 14 I-00153, Rome, Italy, Rt. Rev. Mauro-Giuseppe Lepori, O.Cist., Abbot Gen.

Cistercian Monastery: Our Lady of Dallas, 3550 Cistercian Rd., Irving, TX 75039. Tel: 972-438-2044. Email: fr-peter@cistercian.org. Rt. Rev. Peter Verhalen, O.Cist., Abbot; Rev. Paul McCormick, O.Cist., Prior; Rev. Thomas Esposito, O.Cist., Subprior.

Priests 21; Deacon 1; Junior Monk: 1; Novice: 1

Institutions Staffed: Universities 1; Preparatory School 1; Novitiate 1.

Properties owned: Abbey and Preparatory School.

Represented in the Dioceses of Dallas.

Cistercian Monastery of Our Lady of Fatima: 564 Walton Ave., Mount Laurel, NJ 08054. Tel: 856-235-1330. Rev. Lino S. Parente, O.Cist., Prior; Rev. Maurizio Nicoletti, O.Cist.; Rev. Awte Weldu, O.Cist.; Rev. Musie Tesfayohannes.

Established in 1961 as a dependent Monastery of the Congregation of Casamari (Italy).

Property owned: Fatima House and the Monastery.

Our Lady of Sacramento Monastery: P.O. Box 99, 14080 Leary Rd., Walnut Grove, CA 95690. Tel: 916-776-1356; Fax: 916-776-1921. Rev. Dominic Hung Tran, O.Cist., Abbot; Rev. Nicolas Thanh Quang Le, O.Cist., Prior; Rev. Leo Tiên Van Nguyen, O.Cist., SubPrior.

Established in Sacramento in 2004.

Represented in the Diocese of Sacramento. Also in Vietnam.

[0350] (O.C.S.O.)—THE CISTERCIAN ORDER OF THE STRICT OBSERVANCE (TRAPPISTS)

(Ordo Cisterciensium Strictioris Observantiae)

Generalate: Casa Generalizia O.C.S.O., 33 Viale Africa, 00144, Rome, Italy, Rt. Rev. Dom Bernardus Peeters, O.C.S.O., Abbot Gen.

Abbey of Gethsemani (1848): No. 3642 Monks Rd., Trappist, KY 40051. Tel: 502-549-3117. Email: vocations@monks.org; Web: www.monks.org. Rt. Rev. Elias Dietz, O.C.S.O., Abbot.

Priests 12; Brothers 24

Abbey of Our Lady of New Melleray (1849): 6632 Melleray Cir., Peosta, IA 52068. Tel: 563-588-2319. Vocation Director Email: vocationdirector@newmelleray.org. Rt. Rev. Brendan Freeman, O.C.S.O., Supr.; Rev. Ephrem Poppish, O.C.S.O., Prior; Bro. Paul Andrew Tanner, O.C.S.O., Subprior; Rev. Stephen Verbest, O.C.S.O., Novice Master.

Priests 10; Professed Monks: 22

St. Joseph's Abbey (1825): 167 N. Spencer Rd., Spencer, MA 01562-1233. Tel: 508-885-8700; Fax: 508-885-8701. Rt. Rev. Vincent Rogers, O.C.S.O., Abbot.

Legal Title: Cistercian Abbey of Spencer, Inc.

Total in Community: 50; Priests 19; Solemnly Professed 44; Novices 6

Monastery of the Holy Spirit, Inc. (1944): 2625 Hwy. 212, S.W., Conyers, GA 30094. Tel: 770-483-8705; Fax: 770-760-0989. Rev. Francis Michael Stiteler, O.C.S.O., Abbot.

Priests 13; Professed Monks: 37

Represented in the Archdiocese of Atlanta.

Abbey of Our Lady of Guadalupe (1948): 9200 N.E. Abbey Rd., Carlton, OR 97111-9504. Tel: 503-852-7174; Fax: 503-852-7748. Rt. Rev. Peter McCarthy, O.C.S.O., Abbot; Rev. Dominique-Savio Nelson, O.C.S.O., Prior; Bro. Chris Balent, O.C.S.O., Subprior.

Solemnly Professed 16; Junior 1; Priests 6

Abbey of the Genesee (1951): 3258 River Rd., Piffard, NY 14533. Tel: 585-243-0660. Email: frgerarddsouza@gmail.com. Rev. Gerard D'Souza, O.C.S.O., Abbot; Rt. Rev. John Denburger, O.C.S.O., Abbot Emeritus & Prior; Rev. Isaac Slater, O.C.S.O., Novice Master.

Solemnly Professed 22; Professed Priests 8

Mepkin Abbey (1949): 1098 Mepkin Abbey Rd., Moncks Corner, SC 29461. Tel: 843-761-8509; Fax: 843-761-6719. Rev. Kevin V. Walsh, O.C.S.O., Novice Master & Prior; Rt. Rev. Stan Gumula, O.S.C.O., Abbot; Bro. John Corrigan, O.C.S.O., Business Mgr.

Priests 7; Monks in Community: 16

Abbey of Our Lady of the Holy Cross (1950): 901 Cool Spring Ln., Berryville, VA 22611-2700. Tel: 540-955-4536; Fax: 540-955-1356. Email: information@hcava.org. Rt. Rev. Joseph Wittstock, O.C.S.O., Abbot; Bro. Efrain Sosa, O.C.S.O., Prior & Vocation Dir.

Legal Title: Community of Cistercians of the Strict Observance, Inc.

Solemnly Professed 8; Priests 3

Assumption Abbey: Rte. 5, Box 1056, Ava, MO 65608. Tel: 417-683-5110; Fax: 417-683-5658. Rt. Rev. Alberic

Maisog, O.C.S.O., Supr.; Rt. Rev. Cyprian Harrison, O.C.S.O., Abbot (Retired).

Priests 2; Professed 1

Abbey of New Clairvaux (1955): Trappist-Cistercian Abbey, Box 80, 26240 7th St., Vina, CA 96092. Tel: 530-839-2161. Email: monks@newclairvaux.org. Rt. Rev. Paul Mark Schwan, O.C.S.O., Abbot.

Legal Title: Abbey of New Clairvaux, Inc.

Solemn Vows 15; Novices 4

St. Benedict's Monastery (1956): 1012 Monastery Rd., Snowmass, CO 81654. Tel: 970-279-4400. Rev. Charles Albanese, O.C.S.O., Abbot; Bro. Raymond Roberts, O.C.S.O., Prior; Rev. Edward Hoffman, O.C.S.O., Subprior.

Professed Monks: 7

[0360] (C.M.F.)—CLARETIAN MISSIONARIES

(Missionary Sons of the Immaculate Heart of Mary)

(Congregatio Missionariorum Filiorum Immaculati Cordis Beatae Mariae Virginis.)

General Headquarters: Via Sacro Cuore di Maria 5, Rome, Italy, Very Rev. Mathew Vattamattam, C.M.F., Supr. Gen.

Claretian Missionaries U.S.A. - Canada Province: Claretian Missionaries Headquarters, 205 W. Monroe St., 7th Fl., Chicago, IL 60606. Tel: 312-236-7782; Fax: 312-236-7230. Very Rev. Rosendo Urrabazo, C.F.M., Prov. Supr.; Rev. Thomas McGann, C.M.F., Treas. & Consultor; Rev. Jose Sanchez, C.M.F., Consultor; Rev. Paul Keller, C.M.F., Consultor; Rev. Fernando Ferrera, C.M.F., Consultor.

Fathers 90; Brothers 9; Students 4

Legal Holdings or Titles: Claret Center, Chicago, IL; Claretian Volunteer Program, Chicago, IL; Claretian Associates, Chicago, IL; Claretians, Inc.; St. Jude League, Inc.; Claretian Missionaries - Western Province, Inc.; Dominguez Seminary, Inc., Compton, CA.

Represented in the Archdioceses of Atlanta, Chicago, Los Angeles, Newark and San Antonio and in the Dioceses of Fresno, Metuchen, Phoenix and Springfield-Cape Girardeau. Also in Canada.

[0370] (S.S.C.)—SOCIETY OF ST. COLUMBAN

(Societas Sancti Columbani pro missionibus ad Exteros)

Central Administration (1918): Missionary Society of St. Columban, No 3 and 4 Ma Yau Tong Village, Po Lam Rd., Tseung Kwan, Hong Kong, Very Rev. Timothy Mulroy, S.S.C., Supr. Gen.

Members: 331

Region in the United States: Society of St. Columban, 1902 N. Calhoun St., St. Columbans, NE 68056. Tel: 402-291-1920. Rev. Gerald Chris Saenz, S.S.C., Dir.; Rev. William Morton, Vice Dir. Council: Rev. Albert Utzig, S.S.C.; Rev. John Brannigan, S.S.C.

Fathers 40; Lay Missionaries 1.

Legal Titles: St. Columban's Foreign Mission Society; The Columban Fathers; Missionary Society of St. Columban.

Represented in the Archdioceses of Los Angeles, Omaha and Washington and in the Dioceses of Buffalo, El Paso, Orange, Providence, San Bernardino, San Diego and Springfield, MA.

[0380] (M.C.C.J.)—COMBONI MISSIONARIES OF THE HEART OF JESUS

(Verona Fathers) Missionarii Comboniani Cordis Jesu) (A Pontifical World Missionary Congregation Of Priests And Brothers)

Founded by Saint Daniel Comboni in 1867, First foundation in the United States in 1939.

General Motherhouse: Missionari Comboniani, Via Luigi Lilio 80, 00142, Rome, Italy, Very Rev. Tesfaye Tadesse Gebresilasie, M.C.C.J., Supr. Gen.

North American Province (1950): Comboni Mission Center, 1318 Nagel Rd., Cincinnati, OH 45255-3120. Tel: 513-474-4997; Fax: 513-474-0382; Email: info@ComboniMissionaries.org; Web: www.ComboniMissionaries.org. Rev. John M. Converset, M.C.C.J., Prov.; Rev. Ruffino Ezama, M.C.C.J., Mission Office Dir.

Legal Title: Comboni Missionaries of the Heart of Jesus, Inc.

Priests 26; Home Mission Parishes 4; Mission Centers 3

Represented in the Archdioceses of Chicago, Cincinnati, Los Angeles and Newark and Diocese of San Bernardino.

[0385] (C.C.)—COMPANIONS OF THE CROSS

Visitation House: 17330 Quincy Street, Detroit, MI 48221. Tel: 866-885-8824. Rev. Rick Jaworski, C.C., Local Supr.

[0390] (I.M.C.)—CONSOLATA MISSIONARIES

(Institutum Missionum a Consolata)

General Motherhouse: Viale delle Mura Aurelie 11, Rome, Italy, Very Rev. Stefano Camerlengo, Supr. Gen.

Headquarters in the U.S.: 2624 Rte. 27, North Brunswick, NJ 08902. Mailing Address: P.O. Box 5550, Somerset, NJ 08875-5550. Tel: 732-297-9191. Email: cimcrao@aol.com. Rev. Paolo Fedrigoni, I.M.C., Supr.

Legal Title: Consolata Society for Foreign Missions.

Priests 8

Properties owned: Mission Community House 1.

Represented in the Dioceses of Metuchen and San Bernardino.

[0400] (O.S.C.)—CANONS REGULAR OF THE ORDER OF THE HOLY CROSS

(Crosier Fathers and Brothers)

Canonici Regulares Ordinis Sanctae Crucis (Cruciferi) Generalate: Generalatus Ordinis S. Crucis, Via del Velabro 19, 00186, Rome, Italy, Very Rev. Laurentius Tarpin, O.S.C., Master Gen.

United States National Headquarters: Conventual Priory of the Holy Cross, 717 E. Southern Ave., Phoenix, AZ 85040-3142. Tel: 602-443-7100; Email: crosier@crosier.org. Rev. Thomas A. Enneking, O.S.C., Conventual Prior; Councilors: Bro. Jeffrey Breer, O.S.C.; Rev. Kermit Holl, O.S.C.; Rev. Glen Lewandowski, O.S.C.

Fathers 28; Brothers 12

Legal Titles: Crosier Fathers and Brothers Province, Inc.; Canons Regular of the Order of the Holy Cross.

Represented in the Dioceses of Phoenix and St. Cloud.

Properties owned, sponsored or staffed: Houses 2; Novitiates 1; Parishes 5.

[0410] (F.D.P.)—SONS OF DIVINE PROVIDENCE

(Filiorum Divinae Providentiae)

General Motherhouse: Via Etruria 6, 00183, Rome, Italy, Very Rev. Flavio Peloso, F.D.P., Supr. Gen. Founded in 1893 by St. Luis Orione.

Missionary Delegation-Our Lady Mother of the Church-U.S. Foundation: 150 Orient Ave., East Boston, MA 02128. Tel: 617-569-8792; Fax: 617-569-8701. Very Rev. Tarcisio Vieira, F.D.P., Supr. Gen.; Rev. Oreste Ferrari, F.D.P.

Priests 5

Properties staffed or owned: Parishes 1; Nursing Homes 1; Shrines 1.

Represented in the Archdiocese of Boston.

[0420] (S.V.D.)—SOCIETY OF THE DIVINE WORD

(Societatis Verbi Divini)

General Motherhouse: Collegio del Verbo Divino, Via dei Verbiti 1, 00154, Rome, Italy. Very Rev. Paulus Budi Kleden, S.V.D., Supr. Gen.

Founded 1875, in Steyl, Netherlands; First U.S.A. province erected in 1897 with Headquarters at St. Mary's Mission House (Divine Word Seminary) Techny, Illinois; later separating into four provinces. In 1985 the Eastern and Northern Provinces combined.

Chicago Province (1985): Province of Saint Joseph Freinademetz, S.V.D. Province Center, 1985 Waukegan Rd., P.O. Box 6038, Techny, IL 60082-6038. Tel: 847-272-2700; Fax: 847-412-9505. Very Rev. Quang Duc Dinh, S.V.D., Prov.; Rev. Carlos Macatangga, S.V.D., Vice Prov.; Rev. Matheus Bitin Ro, S.V.D., Provincial Treas.

Legal Titles: Society of the Divine Word; Divine Word Funds, Inc.; Techny Towers Conference and Retreat Center; Blessed Arnold Charitable Trust; DWTCRE Charitable Trust; S.V.D. Funds, Inc.

Priests 142; Brothers 24; Theologians 33; Brothers in Temporary Vows 3; Novices 6.

Properties owned: Theologate; College; 2 Retreat Houses; House of Studies; Conference Center; 1 Retirement Houses.

Represented in the Archdioceses of Boston, Chicago, Cincinnati, Detroit, Dubuque, Indianapolis, Milwaukee, St. Louis and Washington and in the Dioceses of Camden, Fort Wayne-South Bend, Gary, Memphis, Omaha, Sioux City, Trenton and Wheeling-Charleston. Also in Canada and Caribbean.

Eastern Province: Amalgamated with Northern Province. See Chicago Province.

Divine Word Missionaries: 1835 Waukegan Rd., P.O. Box 6099, Techny, IL 60082-6099.Tel; 847-272-7600. Email: hebner@svdmissions.org. Bro. Dan Holman, S.V.D., Pres.

Divine Word Missionaries is within the territory of the Chicago Province but assists members of all three United States S.V.D. Provinces serving overseas and reports directly to Rome regarding its international fundraising activities.

Legal Titles: Divine Word Missionaries, Inc.; S.V.D. Catholic Universities.

Southern Province: Southern Province of St. Augustine, 204 Ruella St., Bay Saint Louis, MS 39520. Tel: 228-467-4322; Tel: 228-467-3815; Email: ussprovincial@gmail.com. Rev. Michael Somers, S.V.D., Prov.; Rev. Augustine Wall, S.V.D., Vice Prov.; Rev. George Gormley, S.V.D., Treas.

Fathers 61; Brothers 3; Parishes 34; Mission Stations: 10; Elementary Schools 3

Address applications for Retreats and Missions to: Rev. Joseph Dang, S.V.D.

Represented in the Archdioceses of Galveston-Houston, Mobile and New Orleans and in the Dioceses of Baton Rouge, Beaumont, Biloxi, Jackson, Lafayette (LA), Little Rock, St. Petersburg and Pensacola-Tallahassee.

Western Province (1964): Province of St. Therese of the Child Jesus, 11316 Cypress Ave, Riverside, CA 92505. Tel: 951-687-7600; Fax: 951-687-3158. Very Rev. Soney Sebastian, S.V.D., Prov.; Rev. Alan Jenkins, S.V.D., Vice Prov.; Rev. Pavol Sochulak, S.V.D., Prov. Treas.

Fathers 63; Brothers 2

Represented in the Archdioceses of Los Angeles and San Francisco and in the Dioceses of Oakland, Orange, San Bernardino and San Diego.

Properties staffed, sponsored or owned: Parishes 18; Hospitals 1; Prisons 1; Retreat Centers 1.

[0430] (O.P.)—ORDER OF PREACHERS

(Dominicans Fratres Sacri Ordinis Praedicatorum)

Generalitia: Convento Santa Sabina, Piazza Pietro d'Illiria, Aventino 00153, Rome, Italy, Most Rev. Gerard Timoner, O.P., 87th Master of the Order; Very Rev. Christopher Eggleton, O.P., Socius for the United States Provs. & Vietnamese Vicariate; Very Rev. Benjamin Earl, O.P., Procurator Gen.

Province of St. Joseph-Eastern Dominican Province (1805): Dominican Provincial Offices, 141 E. 65th St., New York, NY 10065-6618. Tel: 212-737-5757; Fax: 212-409-8811. Email: provincial.secretary@opeast.org; socius@opeast.org. Very Rev. Albert Duggan, O.P., Vicar of the Prov. & Socius; Rev. John Chrysostom Kozlowski, O.P., Vicar Prov. for Administration; Bro. Martin Davis, O.P., Econ. Admin.; Rev. Gregory Schnakenberg, O.P., Archivist; Rev. John Baptist Ku, O.P., Dir. Continuing Formation; Rev. Mario Calabrese, O.P., Dir., Vocations; Rev. David C. Adilletta, O.P, Mission Sec.; Rev. Thomas More Garrett, O.P., Promoter of Catholic Social Teaching; Rev. John Devaney, O.P., Promoter, Holy Name Society; Rev. Paul Marich, O.P., Promoter, Confraternity of the Most Holy Rosary; Rev. John Paul Kern, O.P., Vicar Prov. for Advancement; Rev. Thomas Petri, O.P., Pres., Pontifical Faculty of the Immaculate Conception (Washington, D.C.); Rev. Simon Teller, O.P., Promoter, Angelic Warfare Confraternity.

Professed 306; Solemnly Professed 262; Simply Professed 44; Priests 236; Novices 12; (Arch)Bishops 3; Cooperator Brothers 8.

Corporate Title: Dominican Fathers Province of St. Joseph, Inc.

Legal Titles: Benefit Trust for Retirement Housing and Funeral Plan of the Dominican Fathers, Province of St. Joseph; Retirement Plan and Pension Plan; Dominican Fathers, Province of St. Joseph; Dominican Friars' Guilds, Inc.; Deserving Poor Boys Priesthood Association, Inc.; St. Jude Dominican Missions, Inc.; St. Martin de Porres Guild, Inc.; Dominican Foreign Missions; Handicapped Children's Fund, Peru; Rosary Shrine of St. Jude, (Washington, DC); Rosary Apostolate; Dominican Foundation of Dominican Friars, Province of St. Joseph, Inc.

Represented in the Archdioceses of Baltimore, Boston, Chicago, Cincinnati, Galveston-Houston, Hartford, Los Angeles, Louisville, New York, Newark, Philadelphia, San Juan, St. Paul Minneapolis and Washington and in the Dioceses of Brooklyn, Charlotte, Columbus, Fort Wayne-South Bend, Honolulu, Manchester,

Oakland, Providence, Richmond, Rockville Centre, Springfield (MA), Venice and Youngstown. Properties owned, staffed or sponsored: Priories 12; Houses 7; Parishes 18; Campus Ministries 9; Colleges 1; Houses of Study 2; Novitiates 1; Mission Abroad 1; Health Care Ministry 1.

Province of the Most Holy Name of Jesus-Western Dominican Province (1912): 5877 Birch Ct., Oakland, CA 94618-1626. Tel: 510-658-8722; Fax: 510-658-1061; Email: WDP@opwest.org. Very Rev. Christopher Fadok, O.P., Prov.; U.S. Religious serving in Latin America: Rev. Timothy Conlan, O.P.; Rev. Bartholomew de la Torre, O.P. Rev. Martin de Porres Walsh; Rev. David Bello, O.P.

Legal Title: Province of the Holy Name, Inc.

Fathers 110; Brothers 4; Professed Clerics: 20; Novices 5; Parishes 8; Newman Centers/Personal Parishes 7; Retreat Houses 1; Houses of Study: 1; Novitiates 1

Represented in the Archdioceses of Anchorage-Juneau, Los Angeles, Portland in Oregon, San Francisco, and Seattle and in the Dioceses of Fall River, Las Vegas, Oakland, Providence, Sacramento, Salt Lake City, San Jose and Tucson. Also in Germany, Guatemala, Italy, Mexico and Switzerland.

Province of St. Albert the Great-Central Dominican Province (1939): 1910 S. Ashland Ave., Chicago, IL 60608. Tel: 312-243-0011; Fax: 312-829-8471. Email: office@opcentral.org. Rev. James V. Marchionda, O.P., Prov.; Rev. Donald J. Goergen, O.P., Socius, Vicar Prov.; Rev. Andrew Carl Wisdom, O.P., Dir., Society Vocational Support & Vicar, Mission Advancement; Rev. Samuel P. Hakeem, O.P., Promoter, Vocations; Rev. Kevin Stephens, O.P., Regent; Rev. Michail P. Ford, O.P., Dir., Shrine of St. Jude; Rev. Gerald L. Stookey, O.P., Dir. St. Dominic Mission Society.

Professed Members 146; Priests 115; Brothers 9; Students 10; Special Status 7; Novices 5.

Legal Titles: Dominicans, Province of St. Albert the Great, U.S.A.; Shrine of St. Jude Thaddeus, Inc.; Society for Vocational Support, Inc.; St. Dominic Mission Society; The Bolivian Trust of the Dominicans, Office for Mission Advancement.

Represented in the Archdioceses of Chicago, Denver, Detroit, Indianapolis, St. Louis, St. Paul and Minneapolis and Santa Fe and in the Dioceses of Grand Rapids, Lafayette in Indiana, Madison, Ponce, San Juan, Springfield in Illinois and Superior.

Properties owned, staffed or sponsored: Parishes 10; Convents 7; Houses 6; Houses of Studies 1; Novitiate 1; High Schools 3.

Southern Dominican Province of St. Martin de Porres (1979): 1611 Mirabeau Ave., New Orleans, LA 70122; Mailing Address: P.O. Box 8129, New Orleans, LA 70182. Tel: 504-837-2129; Fax: 504-837-6604. Email: provassistant@opsouth.org. Rev. Roberto Merced, O.P., Prov.; Rev. Jorge Rátiva, O.P., Socius; Rev. Augustine DeArmond, O.P., Syndic; Rev. Scott O'Brien, O.P., Promoter for Permanent Formation; Rev. Wayne Cavalier, O.P., Regent of Studies; Rev. Carl Joseph Paustian, O.P., Dir. of Vocations; Rev. Juan Torres, Dir. of Devel.

Fathers 67; Professed Clerics 4; Brothers 2; Deacons 2; Novices 5

Legal Holdings or Titles: Southern Dominican Foundation; Retirement and Community Support Plan, Southern Dominican Province, U.S.A.; Shrine of St. Martin de Porres.

Represented in the Archdioceses of Atlanta, Galveston-Houston, Miami, New Orleans, San Antonio and St. Louis and in the Dioceses of Baton Rouge, Dallas, Fort Worth, Lubbock and Memphis.

Properties owned, staffed or sponsored: Parishes 8; Priories 4; Houses 6; Shrines 1; Provincial Offices 1.

[0440] (S.S.E.)—SOCIETY OF SAINT EDMUND

(Societas Sancti Edmundi)

General Motherhouse: Edmundite Generalate, One Winooski Park, Box 270, Colchester, VT 05439. Tel: 802-654-3400; Fax: 802-654-3409. Email: sse@sse.org; Web: www.sse.org. Very Rev. David G. Cray, S.S.E., Supr. Gen. Councilors: Rev. Rev. Brian J. Cummings, S.S.E; Rev. David J. Theroux, S.S.E; Rev. Marcel R. Rainville, S.S.E.; Rev. Stanley Deresienski, S.S.E.

Legal Title: Society of St. Edmund, Inc.; Fathers of St. Edmund, Southern Missions, Inc.

Fathers 16; Brothers 3

Represented in the Archdiocese of Mobile and in the Dioceses of Burlington and Norwich.

Properties owned, staffed or sponsored: Parishes 4; College 1; Shrine 1; Edmundite Missions.

[0450] (C.J.M.)—THE EUDISTS-CONGREGATION OF JESUS AND MARY

Founded in 1643 by St. John Eudes in Caen, France as a Society of Apostolic Life.

General Motherhouse: Via dei Querceti, 15, 00184, Rome, Italy, Rev. Jean-Michel Amouriaux, C.J.M., Supr. Gen. 744 Sonrisa St., Solana Beach, CA 92075. Rev. William Rowland, C.J.M., Regl. Supr.

Priests 10; Seminarians: 1

Represented in the Dioceses of Buffalo, Fresno and San Diego.

[0460] (C.F.P.)—BROTHERS OF THE POOR OF ST. FRANCIS

(Congregatio Fratrum Pauperum)

Motherhouse: Aachen, Germany, Bro. Lukas Junemann, C.F.P., Min. Gen.

U.S.A. Community of St. Joseph: P.O. Box 30359, Cincinnati, OH 45230-0359. Tel: 513-924-0111; Fax: 513-321-3777. Email: Hibrothers@fuse.net. Bro. Edward Kesler, C.F.P., U.S.A Community Min.

Professed Brothers 12

Brothers serve and staff: Brothers' Special Mission: Care and education of youth; elementary & secondary education; pastoral ministry.

Represented in the Archdioceses of Cincinnati and Newark and in the Dioceses of Covington, Davenport, Las Cruces and Little Rock.

[0470] (O.F.M.CAP.)—THE CAPUCHIN FRANCISCAN FRIARS

(Ordo Fratrum Minorum Capuccinorum)

Generalate: Curia Generale dei Cappuccini, Via Piemonte 70, 00187, Rome, Italy, Web: www.ofmcap.org. Bro. Roberto Genuin, O.F.M.Cap., Gen. Min.

Province of St. Joseph (1857): Calvary Province, 1820 Mt. Elliott St., Detroit, MI 48207-3485. Tel: 313-579-2100; Fax: 313-579-2275. Rev. Steven Kropp, O.F.M.Cap., Prov. Vicar; Rev. Mark Joseph Costello, O.F.M.Cap., Prov. Min.; Rev. William Hugo, Councilor; Rev. Tien Dinh, Councilor; Rev. Zoilo Garibay, Councilor; Rev. John Celichowski, Dir. Continuing Education; Rev. Roach Gaspar, Dir. Post Novitiate Min.; Rev. Michael Joseph Groark, Dir. Preaching and Evangelization; Rev. Jerome Schroeder, O.F.M.Cap., Secular Franciscan; Rev. George Kooran, O.F.M. Cap., Dir. Solanus Guild; Ms. Junia Yasenov, Archivist; Rev. Robert Wotypka, Corp. Resp. Agent; Rev. Vito Martinez, Dir. Communications; Ms. Diane Simpkins, Corp. Sec./Treas.; Ms. Debi Piontkowski, Admin. Asst.; Mr. Jeff Parrish, Dir., Prov. Ministries & Dir., Human Resources; Ms. Amy Peterson, Dir., Office of Pastoral Care & Conciliation; Mr. Tim Hinkle, Dir. Public Rels.; Ms. Debra Van Ermen, Dir. Wellness; Rev. Edward Foley, O.F.M.Cap., Vice Postulator Cause of Bl. Solanus Casey.

Legal Title: Province of St. Joseph of the Capuchin Order, Inc.

Priests 84; Perpetually Professed Lay Friars: 28

Parishes, Hospitals, Nursing Homes, Prisons, Retreat Centers, Soup Kitchens; Direct Services to the Poor; Educational Institutions; Home and Foreign Missions.

Represented in the Archdioceses of Chicago, Detroit, Los Angeles and Milwaukee and in the Dioceses of Great Falls-Billings, Green Bay, La Crosse, Marquette Saginaw and Tucson. Also in the Apostolic Vicariate of Northern Arabia and in the Diocese of Panama.

Province of St. Augustine (1873): Provincial Office, 220 37th St., Pittsburgh, PA 15201. Tel: 412-682-6011; Fax: 412-682-0506. Very Rev. Thomas Betz, O.F.M.Cap., Prov. Min.; Rev. John Pfannenstiel, O.F.M.Cap., Coord. of Missions. U.S. Religious serving in Papua New Guinea (Custody of St. Michael Archangel) of Papua, New Guinea and Solomon Islands): Most. Rev. Donald Francis Lippert, O.F.M.Cap., Bishop of Diocese of Mendi; Rev. Colman Studeny, O.F.M.Cap.; Bro. Raymond Ronan, O.F.M.Cap.; Rev. Roshan Anthonypillai, O.F.M.Cap.; Rev. Albert Carver, O.F.M.Cap.; Bro. Thomas Choi, O.F.M.Cap. U.S. Serving in Puerto Rico (Custody of St. John the Baptist): Rev. Mario Mastrangelo, O.F.M.Cap.; Rev. Manuel M. Avilés, O.F.M.Cap.; Rev. Moisés Villalta, O.F.M.Cap.; Rev. Juan Antonio Ortiz, O.F.M.Cap.

Cardinals: 1; Bishops 1; Priests 109; Brothers 38; Professed in Formation: 26; Novices 6; Postulants: 20

Legal Titles: Province of St. Augustine of the Capuchin Order; Headquarters of Capuchin Franciscan Volunteer Corps., Inc.; Augustine Province of the Capuchin Order; National Headquarters of Archconfraternity of Christian Mothers; Mission Office of Seraphic Mass Association; Secular Franciscan Order of St. Augustine, Province; Capuchin Friars Sick and Elderly Trust Fund; St. Fidelis, Inc.; Capuchin Friars Formation and Education Trust Fund.

Represented in the Archdioceses of Baltimore, Philadelphia and Washington and in the Dioceses of Altoona-Johnstown, Cleveland, Greensburg, Harrisburg and Pittsburgh. Also in Papua, New Guinea and Puerto Rico.

Properties owned, staffed or sponsored: Parishes 19; Formation Houses 1; Friaries 16; Postulancy Houses 1; Hospital Chaplains 7; Missions 2.

The Province of St. Mary of the Capuchin Order: St. Conrad Friary, 30 Gedney Park Dr., White Plains, NY 10605-3599. Tel: 914-761-3008; Fax: 914-948-6429. Email: smpcomcap2@capuchin.org. Very Rev. Michael J. Greco, O.F.M.Cap., Prov. Min.; Very Rev. Robert J. Abbatiello, O.F.M.Cap., Vicar Prov. Min.; Councilors: Bro. Lake A. Herman, O.F.M.Cap.; Bro. James M. Peterson, O.F.M.Cap.; Rev. Salvatore Cordaro, O.F.M.Cap.

Legal Title: The Province of St. Mary of the Capuchin Order.

Bishops 2; Priests 97; Permanent Deacons 1; Professed Lay Brothers 24; Temporary Professed Friars 4.

Represented in the Archdioceses of Agaña, Boston and New York and in the Dioceses of Bridgeport, Brooklyn, Burlington, Norwich, Portland (In Maine), Rochester, and Rockville Centre. Also in Japan.

Properties staffed or sponsored: Parishes 9; Chaplaincies 20; Novitiate 1.

Development Office: Sacred Heart Friary, 110 Shonnard Pl., Yonkers, New York, NY 10703.

Province of the Sacred Stigmata of St. Francis: Our Lady Guadalupe Friary, 319 - 36th St., P.O. Box 809, Union City, NJ 07087. Tel: 201-865-0611. Email: StigmataProvince@capuchinfriars.org. Rev. Remo DiSalvatore, OFM Cap, Prov. Min.; Rev. Robert Williams, OFM Cap, Prov. Vicar. Councilors: Rev. Francisco Arredondo, OFM Cap; Rev. Robert Perez, OFM Cap; Rev. Martin Schratz, OFM Cap; Bro. Rudolph Pieretti, OFM Cap, Prov. Sec.

Priests 15; Brothers 14; Parishes 3; Friaries 7; Retreat Houses 1

Represented in the Archdioceses of Atlanta, Miami, Newark and New York and in the Diocese of Wilmington.

Our Lady of Angels, Western America Province: 1345 Cortez Ave., Burlingame, CA 94010. Email: finance@olacapuchins.org. Very Rev. Joseph Seraphin Dederick, O.F.M.Cap., Prov.; Rev. Miguel Angel Ortiz, O.F.M.Cap., Dir.-Foreign Missions, Sec. Councilors: Rev. Hai Minh Ho, O.F.M.Cap., Vicar; Rev. Christopher Michael Iwancio, O.F.M.Cap; Bro. Tran Vu, O.F.M.Cap; Rev. Hung Nguyen, O.F.M.Cap.

Priests 30; Brothers 6; Brothers in Formation 3; Postulants 3.

Ministries in Parishes, High Schools, Novitiates, Chaplaincies, House of Study, Retreats, Foreign Missions, Campus Ministry, Prison Chaplaincy and Hospital Chaplaincy.

Represented in the Archdioceses of Los Angeles and San Francisco and in the Diocese of Oakland. Also in Mexico.

Province of SS. Stanislaus and Adalbert (1948): St. Stanislaus Friary, 2 Manor Dr., Oak Ridge, NJ 07438. Tel: 973-697-7757. Rev. Lukasz Wozniak, O.F.M.Cap., Prov. Min. Email: prow.ofmcap@post.pl; Rev. Tomasz Wronski, O.F.M.Cap., Sec.; Email: kuria.ofmcap@post.pl; Rev. Zdzislaw Tokarczyk, O.F.M.Cap., Financial Dir. Email: ekonom.ofmcap.post.pl; Deacon Jerzy Krzyskow, Admin. Email: jkrzyskow@yahoo.com.

Fathers 4

Represented in the Dioceses of Metuchen and Paterson.

Custody of Our Lady of Guadalupe: Capuchin Franciscan Friars of Texas, 2911 Lapsley St., Dallas, TX 75212. Tel: 214-377-7643; Fax: 214-637-2454. Fathers 4

Members serve and staff: Parishes 2; Cursillo Centers 1.

Represented in the Dioceses of Dallas and Fort Worth.

Province of Mid-America (1977): 3613 Wyandot St., Denver, CO 80211-2950. Tel: 303-477-5436; Fax: 303- 477-6925; Email: contact@capuchins.org; Web: www.capuchins.org. Bro. Mark Schenk, O.F.M.Cap., Prov. Min.; Rev. Bill Kraus, O.F.M.Cap., Prov. Vicar;

Rev. Sojan Parappilly, O.F.M.Cap., Second Councillor & Treas.; Rev. Jason Moore, O.F.M.Cap., Third Councilor; Rev. Joseph Elder, O.F.M.Cap., Fourth Councilor; Bro. Joseph Quinlan, O.F.M.Cap., Corp. Sec.; Rev. Blaine Burkey, O.F.M.Cap., Archivist & Communications; Rev. Joseph Mary Elder, O.F.M.Cap., Vocations.

Bishops 2; Priests 37; Transitional Deacons 4; Lay Brothers 10; Temporarily Professed Brothers 7; Novices 2; Postulants 3

Legal Titles: Capuchin Province of Mid-America, Inc.

Represented in the Archdioceses of Denver, Kansas City in Kansas and San Antonio and in the Dioceses of Colorado Springs, Kansas City-St. Joseph, Pueblo, and Salina.

Custody of St. John the Baptist (1905): Custody Offices, 216 Arzuaga St., P.O. Box 21350, San Juan, PR 00928-1350. Tel: 787-764-3090; Fax: 866-234-1781; Email: Secretaria@yosoycapuchino.com; Web: www.yosoycapuchino.org. Friar Ramón H. Negrón-Cruz, O.F.M.Cap., Custos; Friar José A. Cruz-Collazo, O.F.M.Cap., First Councilor; Friar José F. Irizarry-Santana, O.F.M.Cap., Second Councilor; Friar Roberto Colón Ortiz, O.F.M.Cap., Bursar of the Custody and Spiritual Director of Asociación Misionera Capuchina, Inc.

Friars 25; Post Novices 3

Legal Titles: Asociación de Frailes Capuchinos, Inc.; Asociación Misionera Capuchina. Inc.; Capuchin Formation Trust of Puerto Rico; Capuchin Health and Retirement Trust of Puerto Rico; San Antonio de Rio Piedras, Inc.; Centro Capuchinos, Inc. Monasterio San Miguel de Utuado, Inc.; Caridades Capuchinas, Inc.; Casa Divina Pastora de Barranquitas, Inc.; Colegio San Antonio de Padua, Inc.

Represented in the Archdiocese of San Juan and in the Dioceses of Arecibo, Caguas, Mayagüez and Ponce.

Properties owned, staffed and sponsored: Formation Fraternities 3; Parishes 5; Retreat Centers 1; Friaries 7; Schools 1.

[0480] (O.F.M.CONV.)—CONVENTUAL FRANCISCANS

(Friars Minor Conventual)

(Ordo Fratrum Minorum S. Francisci Conventualium)

Our Lady of the Angels Province, Inc. (2014): Provincial House, 12300 Folly Quarter Rd., Ellicott City, MD 21042-1419. Tel: 410-531-1400; Fax: 410-531-4881. Email: provsec2@olaprovince.org. Rev. Michael Heine, O.F.M.Conv., Min. Prov.; Rev. Gary Johnson, O.F.M.Conv., Vicar Prov.; Bro. Nicholas Romeo, O.F.M.Conv. Prov. Sec.

Priests 127; Brothers in Solemn Vows 24; Clerics in Temporary Vows 7; Novices 2; Friaries 28

Legal Titles: St. Francis High School of Athol Springs, NY, Inc.; The Father Justin Rosary Hour, Inc.; Franciscan Fathers Minor Conventuals of Buffalo, NY, Inc.; The Franciscan Center, Inc.; St. Anthony of Padua Province, Franciscan Fathers Minor Conventual, U.S.A., Inc.; Order of Friars Minor Conventual, Inc.; Conventual Franciscan Friars, St. Anthony of Padua Province, Franciscan Mission Association, Inc.; Franciscan Fathers Minor Conventual, St. Anthony of Padua Province U.S.A., MA. Inc.; Franciscan Friars, St. Anthony of Padua Province, Education Fund, Inc.; Franciscan Friars, St. Anthony of Padua Province, Fund for the Aged and Infirm, Inc.; Franciscan Minor Conventuals of Maryland, of Ellicott City, MD, Inc.; The Franciscan Fathers, Minor Conventuals of St. Stanislaus Church of Baltimore City, MD, Inc.; St. Francis of Assisi Community, Inc.; Order of Friars Minor Conventual, St. Anthony of Padua Province, U.S.A., Inc.; St. Stanislaus Cemetery, Inc.; Anthony Corps, Inc.; Fr. Justin Ministry Fund, Inc.; Carrollton Hall Inc.; Order Minor Conventuals, Inc.

Represented in the Archdioceses of Atlanta, Baltimore, Boston, Hartford and Washington, DC and in the Dioceses of Albany, Altoona-Johnstown, Bridgeport, Brooklyn, Buffalo, Harrisburg, Norwich, Palm Beach, Paterson, Raleigh, Springfield in Massachusetts, Syracuse and Trenton. Also in Canada.

Apostolates owned, staffed or sponsored: Novitiates 1; Houses of Study 1; Parishes 28; Campus Ministries 4; High Schools 2; Sisters' Chaplaincies 1; Hospital-Nursing Home Chaplaincies 3; Apostolates; Healing Ministry; Preaching Apostolate; Foreign Missions 3; Youth Ministry; Post-Formation House.

St. Bonaventure Province (1939): 6107 N. Kenmore Ave., Chicago, IL 60660-2797. Tel: 773-274-7681; Fax: 773-274-9751. Email: provsec@franciscancommunity.org. Definitors: Rev. Paul Joseph Langevin, O.F.M. Conv., Min. Prov.; Rev. James Ciaramitaro, O.F.M. Conv., Vicar; Bro. Joseph Schenk, O.F.M. Conv., Sec.; Rev. Alejandro Lopez, O.F.M. Conv.; Rev. Robert Cook, O.F.M. Conv.; Rev. Arturo Felix, O.F.M.Conv.; Rev. Paul Schneider, O.F.M. Conv., Treas.; Rev. Alejandro Lopez, O.F.M. Conv., Vocation Dir.

Priests 30; Brothers 15; Seminarians 1; In Formation 4.

Legal Titles: Conventual Franciscans of St. Bonaventure Province; Franciscan Friars Educational Corp.; Conventual Franciscan Friars of Marytown; Shrine of St. Maximilian Kolbe; St. Hedwig Cemetery and Mausoleum; The Conventual Franciscans of Saint Bonaventure Province Charitable Continuing Care Trust Fund.

Represented in the Archdioceses of Chicago, Detroit and Milwaukee and in the Diocese of Peoria. Also in Australia.

Properties owned or sponsored: Parishes 12; Marian Center/Shrine/Retreat House; House of Formation; Cemetery.

Province of Our Lady of Consolation (1926): 101 Anthony Dr., Mount Saint Francis, IN 47146. Tel: 812-923-8444. Very Rev. Martin Day, O.F.M., Prov.; Friar Mario L. Serrano, O.F.M.Conv., Prov. Sec.

Priests 48; Brothers 11; Permanent Deacons 1; Professed Clerics: 4; Houses of Formation: 1; Retreat Renewal Centers 3; Missions: 3; Chaplaincies 5

Mission Advancement Office (Development Office): 103 St. Francis Blvd., Mount Saint Francis, IN 47146. Tel: 812-923-5250.

Province of St. Joseph of Cupertino (1981): St. Joseph of Cupertino, 19697 Redwood Rd., Castro Valley, CA 94546-3456. Phone: 510-582-7333; Fax: 510-225-2510. Very Rev. Victor P. Abegg, O.F.M.Conv., Min. Prov.; Very Rev. Jacob Carazo, O.F.M.Conv., Vicar Prov.; Bro. James M. Reiter, O.F.M.Conv., Definitor & Sec.; Rev. Paul Gawlowski, O.F.M.Conv., Definitor; Rev. Thomas Czeck, O.F.M.Conv., Definitor; Rev. John Heinz, O.F.M.Conv., Treas.

Legal Title: Conventual Franciscans of California, Inc.

Priests 27; Brothers (includes seminarians) 17; Total 44.

Represented in the Archdioceses of Los Angeles and in the Dioceses of Fresno, Las Vegas, Monterey, Oakland and Vietnam.

Properties owned, staffed or sponsored: Parishes 5; Chaplaincies 4; Houses of Formation 1.

[0485] (M.S.F.S.)—MISSIONARIES OF ST. FRANCIS DE SALES

(Missionariorum Sancti Francisci Salesii)

Founded in Annecy, France 1838. Ministering in the United States from 1969 and established as a Vice Province on July 3, 2013.

MSFS - Generalate - Rome: Missionari de S. Francesco di Sales, Via delle Testuggini, 21, I-00143, Roma, Italy.

MSFS Provincial House: 3887 Rosebud Rd., Loganville, GA 30052-4656. Tel: 470-268-4069. Email: viceprovincialusamsfs@gmail.com; msfsinc2011@hotmail.com; Web: www.fransaliansusa.org. Rev. Anthony Bonela, M.S.F.S., Prov.

Fathers within the U.S. Province: 19; Fathers from Provinces outside U.S.: 61; Parishes: 70.

Properties owned: Fransalian House, Loganville, GA.

Represented in the the Archdiocese of Los Angeles and San Antonio and in the Dioceses of Dallas, Raleigh and Santa Rosa.

Wellspring: Fransalian Center for Spirituality, P.O. Box 440, Whitehouse, TX 75791.

Legal Title: Missionaries of St. Francis de Sales, Inc

Fathers 19; Fathers from Provinces Outside U.S: 61. Properties Staffed: Religious Houses 3; Parishes 45; Convents 1.

Properties Owned: MSFS Provincial House, Loganville-Atlanta, GA; Villa Luyet, Snellville, GA; "Wellspring", Fransalian Center for Spirituality, Whitehouse, TX.

Represented in the Archdioceses of Atlanta, Chicago, Detroit, Galveston-Houston, Kansas City in Kansas, New York and St. Louis and in the Dioceses of Alexandria, Allentown, Cleveland, Dodge City, Harrisburg, Houma-Thibodaux, Kalamazoo, Knoxville, Lansing, La Crosse, Nashville, St. Augustine, St. Thomas Syro-Malabar, Toledo, Tucson, Tyler and Wichita.

[0490] (O.S.F.)—CONGREGATION OF THE RELIGIOUS BROTHERS OF THE THIRD ORDER REGULAR OF ST. FRANCIS

(Franciscan Brothers of Brooklyn)

Generalate (1858): St. Francis Monastery, 135 Remsen St., Brooklyn, NY 11201-4212. Tel: 718-858-8217; Fax: 718-858-8306. Bro. Gabriel O'Brien, O.S.F., Supr. Gen. Councilors: Bro. Damian Novello, O.S.F; Bro. David Anthony Migliorino, O.S.F; Bro. Joshua DiMauro, O.S.F; Bro. Richard Contino, O.S.F.

Brothers 54

Legal Titles and Holdings: St. Francis Monastery; Franciscan Brothers' Generalate; Franciscan Brothers, Inc., Brooklyn, NY; Mount Alvernia, Inc.; St. Francis Center, Inc., Rockville Centre, NY.

Ministries in the field of Education at all levels; Pastoral Ministries, Social Services; Spirituality Centers.

Represented in the Dioceses of Brooklyn, Paterson, Rockville Centre and Springfield-Cape Girardeau.

[0510] (F.F.S.C.)—FRANCISCAN BROTHERS OF THE HOLY CROSS

Generalate: St. Josefshaus, 53547 Hausen-Wied, Germany, Bro. John Francis Tyrell, F.F.S.C., Supr. Gen.

American Region (1924): 2500 St. James Rd., Springfield, IL 62707. Tel: 217-528-4757; Fax: 217-528-4824. Bro. Stephen Bissler, F.F.S.C., Pres./Supr.

Brothers 8

Represented in the Archdiocese of St. Louis and in the Diocese of Springfield in Illinois.

Properties owned, staffed or sponsored: Home for Mentally Handicapped; Adult Training Center for Mentally Handicapped.

[0515] (O.S.F.)—FRANCISCAN BROTHERS OF THE THIRD ORDER REGULAR

Generalate: Franciscan Brothers' Generalate, Mountbellew, Ireland. United States Region: 4522 Gainsborough Ave., Los Angeles, CA 90027. Tel: 213-216-2218. Bro. Hilarion O'Connor, O.S.F., Regl. Supr.

Brothers 6

Ministries in the field of secondary education.

Represented in the Archdiocese of Los Angeles.

[0520] (O.F.M.)—FRANCISCAN FRIARS

(Ordinis Fratrum Minorum)

General Headquarters: Curia Generalizia dei Frati Minori, Via S. Maria Mediatrice, 25, 00165, Rome, Italy. Most Rev. Massimo Fusarelli, O.F.M., Min. Gen.; Rev. Jimmy Zammit, O.F.M., English-Speaking General Definitor.

Order of Friars Minor: English Speaking Conference, 5831 Saranac St., Cincinnati, OH 45224-3034. Tel: 513-541-0488. Rev. Pat McCloskey, O.F.M., Exec. Sec.; Very Rev. Thomas Nairn, O.F.M., Pres.

Includes: Order of Friars Minor Provinces 11; Custodies 2: of the United States, Canada, England, Ireland, Lithuania and Malta.

Province of St. John the Baptist (1844): 1615 Vine St., Cincinnati, OH 45202-6400. Tel: 513-721-4700; Fax: 513-421-9672. Rev. Jeffrey Scheeler, O.F.M., Prov. Min.; Rev. Luis Aponte-Merced, O.F.M., Vocation Dir.; Rev. Manuel Viera, O.F.M., Prov. Canonist. Councilors: Rev. Mark Soehner, O.F.M.; Bro. Vincent Delorenzo, O.F.M.; Rev. Page Polk, O.F.M.; Bro. Alexander Krate, O.F.M., Prov. Sec.; Rev. Kenan Freson, O.F.M., Prov. Liaison to Sponsored Ministries; Rev. Maynard Tetreault, O.F.M., Bldg. Coord.; Rev. Patrick McCloskey, O.F.M., Dir. Continuing Educ./Formation; Bro. Scott Obrecht, O.F.M. Dir. Office of Peace, Justice & Integrity of Creation; Bro. Vincent Delorenzo, O.F.M., Dir. Franciscan Mission Office; Rev. Daniel J. Anderson, O.F.M., Prov. Sec.; Bro. Juniper Crouch, O.F.M., Prov. Spiritual Asst. for Secular Order; Rev. Frank J. Jasper, O.F.M., Prov. Vicar & Treas.; Mr. David O'Brien, CFO; Rev. John Bok, O.F.M., Co-Dir.-Friar Works/Franciscan Mission & Ministry; Ms. Colleen Cushard, Co-Dir. Friar Works/Franciscan Mission & Ministry; Ms. Toni Cashnelli, Dir.-Office of Communications; Mr. Ronald Cooper, Prov. Archivist.

Priests 90; Temporary Professed 2; Novices 1; Brothers 47

Represented in the Archdioceses of Chicago, Cincinnati, Detroit, Galveston-Houston, Indianapolis, Military Services, Milwaukee, New Orleans, Santa Fe and Washington and in the Dioceses of Allentown, Lafayette, Pittsburgh, Shreveport, Springfield-Cape Girardeau, St. Petersburg, Tucson and Venice.

Province of The Sacred Heart (1858): 3140 Meramec St., Saint Louis, MO 63118. Tel: 314-353-3421. Email: provsec@thefriars.org. Very Rev. Thomas Nairn, O.F.M., Prov. Min.; Very Rev. John Eaton, O.F.M., Prov. Vicar; Rev. James Lause, O.F.M., Sec. of the Province; Rev. Michael Hill, O.F.M., Prov. Treas.; Bro. Joseph Rogenski, Prov. Promoter of the Missions, Commissary of the Holy Land, Secretariat Missionary Evangelization. Councilors: Rev. Gerald Bleem, O.F.M.; Rev. William Burton, O.F.M.; Bro. Doug Collins, O.F.M.; Rev. Duc Pham, O.F.M.; Rev. Dennis Schafer, O.F.M.; Bro. Michael Ward, O.F.M.

Bishops 1; Solemnly Professed Priests 116; Brothers 43; Novices 2

Legal Titles: Franciscan Fathers of the State of Missouri; Franciscan Fathers of the State of Illinois; Franciscan Press; Franciscan Tertiary Province of the Sacred Heart, Incorporated; Mayslake Village; Franciscan Mayslake Village; Cloister Courts; Employees of the Franciscan Orders; St. Germain Friary.

Represented in the Archdioceses of Chicago, Indianapolis, St. Louis and San Antonio and the Dioceses of Belleville, Cleveland, Fairbanks, Gaylord, Green Bay, Joliet, Shreveport, Springfield in Illinois and Superior.

Properties owned, sponsored or staffed: Friaries 21; Parishes 21; Missions 5; Chaplains 6; Chaplaincies for Religious 5; Formation Houses 2; Novitiates 1; Colleges 1; High Schools 1.

Province of the Assumption of the Blessed Virgin Mary, Inc. (1887): Provincial Office, 9230 W. Highland Park Ave., Franklin, WI 53132. Tel: 414-525-9253; Fax: 414-525-9289; Email: jgannonofm@thefranciscans.net; Web: www.franciscan-friars.org. Rev. James Gannon, O.F.M., Prov. Min.; Rev. Joachim Studwell, O.F.M., Vicar Prov. Provincial Councilors: Rev. John Cella, O.F.M.; Bro. Craig Wilking, O.F.M.; Rev. Edward Tlucek, O.F.M. Prov. Secretary; Rev. John Cella, O.F.M., Prov. Bursar, Dir. of Evangelization; Rev. Jerome J. Wolbert, O.F.M., Prov. Spiritual Asst. of Secular Franciscan Order; Rev. Jerome J. Wolbert, O.F.M., Prov. Spiritual Asst. of Secular Franciscan Order; Bro. Craig Wilking, O.F.M., Dir. Franciscan Missionary Union.

Priests 50; Professed Brothers 21

Legal Holdings or Titles: Queen of Peace Friary, Burlington, WI; San Damiano, La Crosse, WI; Our Lady of Lourdes Friary, Cedar Lake, IN; St. Francis of Assisi School, Greenwood, MS; Francis and Clare Friary, Franklin, WI; Franciscan Pilgrimage Programs, Inc., Franklin, WI; Holy Name Friary, Chicago, IL; St. Francis of Assisi Friary, Greenwood, MS; Assumption BVM Friary, Pulaski, WI; Junipero Serra Friary, McAllen, TX.

Properties owned or staffed: Parishes 10; Friaries 6.

Represented in the Archdioceses of Chicago, Milwaukee and Pittsburgh Byzantine and in the Dioceses of Brownsville, Gary, Green Bay, Parma, Passaic.

Province of Our Lady of Guadalupe (1985): The Curia, 1204 Stinson St., S.W., Albuquerque, NM 87121-3440. Tel: 505-831-9199; Fax: 505-831-9577. Email: ofmprovsec@aol.com. Very Rev. Jack Clark Robinson, O.F.M., Min. Prov.; Rev. Carlos Martinez, O.F.M., Vicar Prov. & Sec. Formation; Rev. Ron Walters, O.F.M. Treas.; Rev. Erasmo Romero, O.F.M., Vocation Dir.; Councilors: Rev. Gerald Steinmetz, O.F.M.; Rev. Dale Jamison, O.F.M.; Rev. Patrick Schafer, O.F.M.; Bro. Efren Quintero, O.F.M., Sec., Province Notary.

Priests 29; Brothers 15

Legal Titles: The Province of Our Lady of Guadalupe of the Order of Friars Minor, Inc.

Represented in the Archdioceses of San Antonio and Santa Fe and in the Dioceses of Gallup and Las Cruces.

Franciscan Friars - Holy Name Province (1901): 129 W. 31st. St., 2nd Fl., New York, NY 10001-3403. Tel: 646-473-0265; Fax: 800-420-1078; Email: hnp@hnp.org. Provincial Administration: Very Rev. Kevin J. Mullen, O.F.M., Prov. Minister; Rev. Lawrence J. Hayes, O.F.M., Prov. Vicar; Bro. Michael J. Harlan, O.F.M., Prov. Sec.; Rev. Dennis M. Wilson, O.F.M., Prov. Treas. Provincial Councilors: Rev. Thomas Gallagher, O.F.M.; Bro. Walter Liss, O.F.M.; Rev. Erick Lopez. O.F.M.; Rev. David Convertino, O.F.M.; Bro. Frederick C. Dilger, O.F.M.; Bro. Robert M. Frazzetta, O.F.M. Other Administrative Offices: Bro. Basil J. Valente, O.F.M., Dir. Vocations; Rev. David I. Convertino, O.F.M, Dir. Office of Devel., St. Anthony's Guild, Natl. Shrines of St. Anthony & St. Jude & Dir. Franciscan Missionary Union; Bro. Paul O'Keeffe, O.F.M., Moderator of Missionary Evangelization; Rev. John J. Coughlin, O.F.M., Canonical Counsel; Rev. Gene B. Pistacchio, O.F.M., Spiritual Asst., Secular Franciscan Order (OFS); Rev. Thomas R. Hartle, O.F.M., Spiritual Asst., Poor Clares; Ms. Jocelyn Thomas, Dir. Office of Communications.

Priests 198; Brothers 54; Temporary Professed Brothers 14; Temporary Professed Clerics: 4; Temporary Professed Novices 4; Permanent Deacons 3

Solemn Profession: Archbishops 1; Priests 198; Brothers 54; Permanent Deacons 3; Temporary Profession: Brothers 14; Clerics 4; Novices 4.

Represented in the Archdioceses of Atlanta, Boston, Chicago, Hartford, Los Angeles, Newark, New York, Philadelphia, San Juan and Washington and in the Dioceses of Albany, Arlington, Buffalo, Charleston, Charlotte, Fall River, Orlando, Paterson, Raleigh, Savannah, St. Petersburg, Trenton and Wilmington. Also in Archdiocese of Lima, Peru.

Properties owned or sponsored: Province Parishes 22; Missions 1; University 1; Colleges 1; Community Houses-Residences 28; Houses of Formation 1; Shrine Churches 2; Campus Ministry 4.

Province of St. Barbara (1915): The Franciscan Friars of California (1900), 1500 34th Ave., Oakland, CA 94601. Tel: 510-536-3722; Fax: 510-536-3970. Very Rev. David Gaa, O.F.M., Prov. Min.; Rev. Martin Ibarra, O.F.M., Vicar Prov. Definitors: Rev. Joe Schwab, O.F.M.; Rev. Bill Minkel, O.F.M.; Rev. Dan Lackie, O.F.M.; Rev. Anthony Garibaldi, O.F.M.; Rev. Garrett Galvin, O.F.M.; Rev. John Gibbons, O.F.M.; Rev. Tom West, O.F.M., Prov. Sec.

Priests 71; Solemnly Professed Lay Brothers 40; Simply Professed Brothers 6; Novices 1

Legal Titles: Franciscan Friars of California; Franciscan Friars of Arizona; Franciscan Friars of Oregon.

Represented in the Archdioceses of Los Angeles and San Francisco and in the Dioceses of Monterey, Oakland, Phoenix, San Diego, Spokane and Tucson.

Province of the Immaculate Conception (Friars Minor of the Order of St. Francis): 125 Thompson St., New York, NY 10012. Tel: 212-674-4388. Email: Internos@icprovince.org; Rev. Robert M. Campagna, O.F.M., Minister Prov.; Rev. Patrick D. Boyle, O.F.M. Vicar Prov. Definitors: Rev. Richard Martignetti, O.F.M., Ave Maria, Florida; Rev. Joseph Lorenzo, O.F.M., Padua Friary, New York, NY; Bro. Vincent DePaul Ciaravino, O.F.M., Padua Friary, New York, NY; Rev. Orlando Ruiz, O.F.M., Our Lady of Peace Friary, Brooklyn, NY; Rev. Antonio Riccio, O.F.M., Convento San Francesco, Rome, Italy; Rev. Joseph F. Lorenzo, O.F.M., Secretary of the Province; Rev. Vit Fiala, O.F.M., SFO Prov. Spiritual Asst., Mount Alverna Friary, Youngstown, OH; Fr. Patrick Boyle, O.F.M., Promoter of the Franciscan Missions; Rev. Robert M. Campagna, O.F.M., Pious League of St. Anthony; Ms. Madeline Bonnici, Exec. Dir. Franciscan Mission Associates, 274-280 W. Lincoln Ave., Mount Vernon, NY 10550.

Fathers 71; Bishops 3; Brothers 16; Permanent Deacons 1; Friars in Formation 14.

Properties owned or staffed: Parishes 17; Residences 16.

Represented in the Archdioceses of Boston, Hartford and New York and in the Dioceses of Albany, Brooklyn, Manchester and Youngstown. Also in Central America, Toronto and Italy.

Commissariat of The Holy Cross (1912): 14246 Main St., P.O. Box 608, Lemont, IL 60439. Tel: 630-257-2494; Fax: 630-257-2359. Rev. Metod Ogorevc, O.F.M., Pres. Councilors: Rev. Bernard Karmanocky, O.F.M.; Rev. Krizolog Cimerman, O.F.M.; Rev. Christian Gostecnik, O.F.M.

Fathers 3; Monasteries: 1; Retreat Houses 1; Mission Centers 1

Legal Titles: The Slovene Franciscan Fathers, Order of Friars Minor, Commissariat of the Holy Cross, Lemont, IL; St. Mary's Retreat House, Lemont, IL. Represented in the Archdioceses of Chicago and New York and in the Diocese of Altoona-Johnstown.

Franciscan Friars: Mt. Alverna Friary, 517 S. Belle Vista Ave., Youngstown, OH 44509. Tel: 330-799-1888. Rev. Jules Wong, O.F.M.; Rev. Vit Fiala, O.F.M., Dir. & Guardian; Rev. Richard Martignetti, O.F.M.; Rev. Dennis Arambasick, O.F.M.

Represented in the Diocese of Youngstown.

Croatian Franciscan Custody of the Holy Family of U.S. & Canada (1926): 4851 S. Drexel Blvd., Chicago, IL 60615-1703. Tel: 773-536-0552; Fax: 773-536-2094; Email: chicagoofm@gmail.com; Web: crofranciscans.com. Rev. Joe Grbes, O.F.M., Custos. Councilors: Rev. Nikola Pasalic, O.F.M.; Rev. Drazan Boras, O.F.M.; Rev. Miro Grubisic, O.F.M.; Rev. Marko Puljic, O.F.M.

Fathers 23; Friaries 1; Parishes 7; Missions in Canada 6

Represented in the Archdioceses of Chicago, Milwaukee, New York and St. Louis as well as Military Chaplaincy. Also in Canada.

Lithuanian Franciscan Province of St. Casimir: 28 Beach Ave., P.O. Box 980, Kennebunkport, ME 04046-0980. Tel: 207-967-2011; Fax: 207-967-0423; Email: jonasbac@gmail.com; Web: www.framon.net. Rev. Aurelijus Gricius, O.F.M., Guardian; Rev. John J. Bacevicius, O.F.M., Friar; Rev. Raimundas Bukauskas, O.F.M., Treas. of Friary, Vicar, Assistant Delegate of Province in North America Delegate of St. Casimir's Prov.; Rev. Andrew R. Bisson, O.F.M., Friar.

Legal Title: Society of the Franciscan Fathers of Greene, Maine.

Fathers 4

Properties owned or sponsored: Friaries 2; Parishes 1; Summer Camps 1; Guest House 1.

Represented in the Diocese of Portland (In Maine). Also in Toronto, Canada.

U.S. Foundation (1940): Province of the Holy Gospel Roger Bacon College, 2400 Marr St., El Paso, TX 79903. Rev. Flavio Alberto Hernandez, O.F.M.

Priests 2; Lay Brother 1.

Represented in the Diocese of El Paso.

Franciscan Monastery: 1400 Quincy St., N.E., Washington, DC 20017. Tel: 202-526-6800; Fax: 202-529-9889; Email: secretariatU.S.A.@myfrancsican.com; Web: www.myfranciscan.com. Rev. Larry Dunham, O.F.M., Commissary and Guardian; Friar Christopher Coppock, O.F.M.; Friar Thomas Courtney, O.F.M.; Friar Gregory Giannoni, O.F.M.; Friar Michael Raum, O.F.M.; Friar Simon McKay, O.F.M.; Rev. Kevin Treston, O.F.M.; Rev. David Wathen, O.F.M., Dir. Holy Land Pilgrimage; Friar Maximilian Wojciechowski, O.F.M.; Rev. Manuel Ybarra, O.F.M.; Rev Benjamin Owusu, O.F.M.; Friar-Deacon John Sebastian, O.F.M., Sec. to the Commissary/Guardian, Vicar and Vice Commissary; Rev. Gregory F. Friedman, O.F.M., Editor Holy Land Review; Rev. James Gardiner, S.A.; Rev Charles Smiech, O.F.M.; Rev Michael Cusato, O.F.M.; Rev. Romuald Green, O.F.M.; Friar Jude Lustyk, O.F.M.

Priests 10; Brothers 7; Permanent Deacons 1; Solemnly Professed 18

Represented in the Archdiocese of Washington.

Academy of American Franciscan History: 4050 Mission Ave., Oceanside, CA 92057. Dr. Jeffrey M. Burns, Dir. Email: acadafh@fst.edu.

Legal Title: Academy of American Franciscan History.

[0530] (S.A.)—FRANCISCAN FRIARS OF THE ATONEMENT

(Societas Adunationis T.O.R.)

Motherhouse: St. Paul Friary, New York Office of the Minister General PO Box 300, Garrison, NY 10524-0300. Tel: 845-424-2113; Fax: 845-424-2166. Email: csharon@atonementfriars.org.

Priests 35; Professed Brothers 19; Friaries 15; Parishes (U.S. & Canada): 2; Overseas Ministries (England, Italy & Japan): 3; Ecumenical Institute: 1; Pastoral Center: 1; Retreat & Conference Center: 1; Rehabilitation Center for Alcoholics: 1; Shelter for Homeless Men: 1; Correctional Facility Chaplaincies 1

Legal Titles: St. Christopher's Inn; St. James Friary; St. Paul Friary; St. Francis of Assisi Novitiate; Friars of the Atonement, Inc.; Friars of the Atonement (Canada), Inc.; Graymoor Village, Inc.; Union That Nothing Be Lost, Inc.; Paul Wattson Human Resources, Inc.

Represented in the Archdioceses of Boston, New York and Washington and in the Dioceses of Albany and Raleigh.

[0533] (F.F.I.)—FRANCISCAN FRIARS OF THE IMMACULATE

General Motherhouse: Founded 1990. Benevento, Italy.

American Motherhouse: Marian Friary of Our Lady of Guadalupe, 199 Colonel Brown Rd., Griswold, CT 06351. Tel: 860-376-6840. Rev. Ignatius Manfredonia, F.I., General Delegate Supr.; Rev. Josemaria Barbin, Local Guardian Supr.

Legal Title: Marian Friary of Our Lady of Guadalupe.

Represented in the Archdiocese of Indianapolis and in the Dioceses of Fall River, Norwich and Syracuse.

[0535] (C.F.R.)—FRANCISCAN FRIARS OF THE RENEWAL

Our Lady of the Angels: 427 E. 155th St., Bronx, NY 10455. Tel: 718-993-3405. Rev. Pierre Toussaint Guiteau, C.F.R., Local Servant; Bro. Seraphim Pio Baalbaki, C.F.R., Local Vicar; Rev. Stan Fortuna, C.F.R.; Bro. Maximilian Stelmachowski, C.F.R.; Bro. Pio Maria Hoffman, C.F.R.; Bro. John Francis Thomson, C.F.R.; Bro. Joseph Pio Young, C.F.R.; Bro. Francis Xavier Danos, C.F.R.

General Offices: 421 East 155th St., Bronx, NY 10455. Tel: 718-402-8255; Email: CFROffice@franciscanfriars.com. Rev. John Paul Ouellette, C.F.R., Gen. Servant; Rev. John Anthony Boughton, C.F.R., Gen. Vicar; Councilors: Rev. Agostino Torres, C.F.R.; Rev. Emmanuel Mansford, C.F.R.; Rev. Francis Mary Roaldi, C.F.R.; Bro. Joachim J. Bellavance, C.F.R.; Bro. Peter Marie Westall, C.F.R., Gen. Steward; Bro. Maximilian Mary Stelmachowski, C.F.R, Gen. Sec.

Legal Titles: The Community of the Franciscan Friars of the Renewal

Represented in the Archdioceses of Chicago, Newark, New York and Santa Fe and in the Diocese of Paterson. Also in England, Ireland, Northern Ireland, Nicaragua and Honduras.

St. Crispin Friary: 420 E. 156th St., Bronx, NY 10455. Tel: 718-665-2441; Fax: 718-292-2432. Rev. John Anthony Boughton, C.F.R., Local Servant; Rev. Ignatius Shin, C.F.R., Local Vicar; Rev. John Paul Ouellette, C.F.R.; Rev. Giles Barrie, C.F.R.; Rev. James Atkins, C.F.R.; Bro. Damien Novak, C.F.R.; Bro. Jan Cyril Vanek, C.F.R.; Rev. Terrence Messer, C.F.R; Rev. Malachy Napier, C.F.R.

St. Joseph Friary: 523 W. 142nd St., New York, NY 10041. Tel: 212-234-9089; Fax: 212-234-8871. Vocation Office: 212-281-4355. Rev. Innocent Montgomery, C.F.R., Local Servant and Postulant Dir.; Rev. Mark-Mary Ames, C.F.R., Local Vicar; Rev. Angelus Montgomery, C.F.R., Vocation Dir.; Rev. Glenn Sudano, C.F.R.; Bro. Peter Marie Westall, C.F.R.; Rev. Gabriel Mary Bakkar, C.F.R.; Bro. Angelo LeFever, C.F.R.; Rev. Mark-Mary Ames, C.F.R.; Bro. Kolbe Blashock, C.F.R.; Bro. Mariano Ravazzano, C.F.R.; Bro. Paul Jones, C.F.R., Postulants.

St. Leopold Friary: 259 Nepperhan Ave., Yonkers, NY 10701. Tel: 914-965-8143; Fax: 914-709-8986. Rev. John-Mary Johannssen, C.F.R., Local Servant; Rev. Joseph Michael Fino, C.F.R., Local Vicar; Rev. Fidelis Moscinski, C.F.R.; Rev. Luke Mary Fletcher, C.F.R.; Rev. Conrad Osterhout, C.F.R.; Rev. Lawrence Schroedel, C.F.R.; Bro. Pius Gagne, C.F.R.; Bro. Michaelangelo Best, C.F.R.; Bro. François Fontanié, C.F.R.; Bro. Lawrence Johnson, C.F.R.

Most Blessed Sacrament Friary: 375 13th Ave., Newark, NJ 07103. Tel: 973-622-6622; Fax: 973-624-8998. Rev. Stephen Dufrene, C.F.R., Local Servant; Rev. Francis Mary Roaldi, C.F.R., Local Vicar; Rev. Sebastian Kajko, C.F.R.; Rev. Raphaël Chilou, C.F.R.; Bro. André Manders, C.F.R.; Bro. Simeon Synoski, C.F.R.; Bro. Zachary Indovino, C.F.R., Novices.

St. Michael Friary: 190 Butler St., Paterson, NJ 07524. Tel: 973-345-7082; 973-345-7081. Bro. Shawn O'Connor, C.F.R., Local Servant; Bro. Joachim Bellavance, C.F.R., Local Vicar; Rev. Herald Brock, C.F.R.; Rev. Mariusz Koch, C.F.R.; Rev. Emmanuel Mansford, C.F.R.; Rev. Agustino Torres, C.F.R.; Bro. Dominic Ruiz, C.F.R.; Bro. Michael Kearney, C.F.R.

St. Juan Diego Friary: 404 San Mateo Blvd., N.E., Albuquerque, NM 87108. Tel: 505-990-3001; Fax: 505-990-0187. Rev. Roch Greiner, C.F.R., Local Servant; Rev. Juan Diego Sutherland, C.F.R., Local Vicar; Rev. Leo Fisher, C.F.R.; Rev. Juan Diego Sutherland, C.F.R.; Bro. Gerard Kanapes, C.F.R.; Bro. Teresiano Madrigal, C.F.R.

[0540] (O.S.F.)—FRANCISCAN MISSIONARY BROTHERS OF THE SACRED HEART OF JESUS

(Fratres Missionarii sti Francisci de Sso. Corde Jesu)

Motherhouse (1927): Our Lady of Angels Monastery, 265 Saint Joseph Hills Rd., Pacific, MO 63069. Tel: 636-938-5361. Email: shrine1olc@aol.com. Mailing Address: Box 181, Eureka, MO 63025. Bro. John A. Spila, O.S.F., Dir. Gen.

Brothers 3

Legal Holdings or Titles: The Black Madonna Shrine and Grottos (Our Lady of Czestochowa).

Represented in the Archdiocese of St. Louis.

[0560] (T.O.R.)—THIRD ORDER REGULAR OF SAINT FRANCIS

(Tertius Ordo Regularis de Poenitentia)

General Motherhouse: SS. Cosmas and Damian, Via dei Fori Imperiali, 1, Rome, Italy. Very Rev. Amando Trujillo Cano, T.O.R.; Rev. Sean Sheridan, T.O.R., Vicar Gen. Councilors: Rev. Thomas Kochuchira, T.O.R., 1st Councilor; Rev. Calogero Favata, T.O.R., 2nd Councilor; Rev. Danjel Gornik , T.O.R., 3rd Councilor; Rev. Gregory Vajiro Silva, T.O.R., 4th Councilor.

Province of the Most Sacred Heart of Jesus (1910): Provincial Office, P.O. Box 137, Loretto, PA 15940. Tel: 814-419-8890; Fax: 814-472-8992. Very Rev. Joseph J. Lehman, T.O.R., Min. Prov.; Rev. Jonathan St. André, T.O.R., Vicar Prov.; Councilors: Rev. David Pivonka, T.O.R.; Rev. Patrick Whittle, T.O.R.; Rev. Nathan Malavolti, T.O.R.; Rev. Thomas Stabile, T.O.R.

Legal Title: Province of the Most Sacred Heart of Jesus, Third Order Regular of Saint Francis (U.S.A.), Loretto, PA.

Fathers 76; Professed Clerics: 7; Brothers 14

Ministries in Parishes; Universities and Colleges; High Schools; Chaplaincies; Houses of Study 1; Novitiates 1; Laymen's Retreat League.

Represented in the Archdiocese of Washington and in the Dioceses of Altoona-Johnstown, Arlington, Camden, Fort Worth, Pittsburgh, St. Petersburg, Steubenville and Trenton.

Province of the Immaculate Conception: Office of Minister Provincial, P.O. Box 659, Hollidaysburg, PA 16648-0659. Tel: 814-696-3321; Fax: 814-695-1611. Very Rev. Frank A. Scornaienchi, T.O.R., Min. Prov.; Councilors: Rev. J. Patrick Quinn, T.O.R.; Rev. Christopher Panagoplos, T.O.R.; Rev. Ambrose K. Phillips, T.O.R.

Legal Title: Third Order Regular of St. Francis, Province of the Immaculate Conception (U.S.A.).

Priests 19; Brothers 1

Represented in the Archdiocese of Washington and in the Dioceses of Altoona-Johnstown, Orlando and Steubenville.

U.S.A. Franciscan Vice Province of Our Lady of Guadalupe - T.O.R: 301 Jefferson Ave., Waco, TX 76701. Very Rev. Florencio Rodriguez, T.O.R.; Very Rev. Jose Eduardo Jazo, T.O.R.; Very Rev. Miguel Gonzalez, T.O.R.; Very Rev. Rogue Ocampo Lopez, T.O.R.; Very Rev. Juan Diego Lopez Perez, T.O.R.

Fathers 5

Represented in the Diocese of Austin.

[0570] (G.H.M.)—THE GLENMARY HOME MISSIONERS

(Societas Missionariorum Domesticorum Americas)
(The Home Missioners of America)

General Headquarters: P.O. Box 465618, Cincinnati, OH 45246. Tel: 513-874-8900; Web: www.glenmary.org. Rev. Daniel Dorsey, G.H.M., Pres.; Rev. R. Aaron Wessman, G.H.M., 1st Vice Pres.; Bro. Larry Johnson, G.H.M., 2nd Vice Pres.; Ms. Charlotte Carpenter, Treas.; Mrs. Chris Phelps, Development; Rev. Dominic R. Duggins, House Dir.; Bro. David Henley, G.H.M., Dir.-Vocation Office.

House of Formation: Glenmary House of Studies, 12484 E. State Rd 62, St. Meinrad, IN 47577. Tel: 812-357-2090. Rev. Bruce C. Brylinski, G.H.M., Dir. Candidacy; Rev. Tom Kirkendoll, G.H.M., Co-Dir. Novices; Rev. Dan Dorsey, G.H.M., Dir., Formation; Lorraine Vancamp, Dir. Dept. of Pastoral Ministers & Pastoral Svcs.; Joseph Grosek, Dir. Volunteer Programs, P.O. Box 69, Rutledge, TN 37861

Fathers 36; Brothers 16; Seminarians: 8; Brothers in Training: 1; Aspirants: 3

Represented in the Archdioceses of Cincinnati and Indianapolis and in the Dioceses of Covington, Jackson, Knoxville, Nashville, Raleigh and Savannah.

Properties owned, sponsored or staffed: Missions & Ministries 40; Houses of Study 1; Volunteer Center.

[0585] (H.G.N.)—HERALDS OF GOOD NEWS

Founded on Oct. 14, 1984 at Eluru, Andhra Pradesh, India. A Clerical Missionary Society of Apostolic Life of Pontifical Right serving various dioceses in Asia, Africa, America, Australia, & Europe.

Generalate: Heralds of Good News: R.S. Post, W.G. Dt., Eluru, Andhra Pradesh - 534005, India. Tel: 91-88-12-235973; Fax: 91-88-12-230256.

U.S. Address: Heralds of Good News, 204 North Main St., Leitchfield, KY 42754. Tel: 270-231-5312 Legal Representative: Rev. Sinoj Pynadath, H.G.N.

Legal Title: Heralds of Good News Missionary Society, Inc.

Priests in the U.S.: 148

Represented in the Archdioceses of Denver, Indianapolis, Portland in Oregon, San Antonio and Seattle and in the Dioceses of Altoona Johnstown, Baton Rouge, Biloxi, Burlington, Columbus, Corpus Christi, Evansville, Fargo, Fort Worth, Great Falls-Billings, Jackson, Lafayette, Lake Charles, Las Cruces, Lubbock, Manchester, Mobile, Ogdensburg, Owensboro, Pensacola-Tallahassee, Portland (ME), Providence, Pueblo, Rochester, Salina, San Bernardino, Santa Rosa, Scranton, Springfield, Springfield-Cape Girardeau, Stockton, & Wheeling-Charleston.

[0590] (M.S.A.)—SOCIETY OF THE MISSIONARIES OF THE HOLY APOSTLES

General Administration: Society of the Missionaries of the Holy Apostles, 8594 rue Berri, H2P 2G4, Montreal, Canada, Tel: 514-387-2222; Fax: 514-387-0863. Very Rev. Luis A. Luna, M.S.A., Supr. Gen. Animator.

Society of Missionaries of Holy Apostles: Provincial Administration Headquarters, 22 Prospect Hill Rd., Cromwell, CT 06416. Tel: 860-316-5926. Very Rev. Edward Przygocki, M.S.A., Prov. Animator.

Priests 28; Brothers 3

Represented in the Archdioceses of Los Angeles and Washington and in the Diocese of Norwich. Also in Vietnam.

Properties owned, staffed or sponsored: Holy Apostles College and Seminary; Hospital Chaplaincies; House of Formation.

[0600] (C.S.C.)—BROTHERS OF THE CONGREGATION OF HOLY CROSS

(Congregatio A Sancta Cruce)

Generalate: Congregazione di Santa Croce, Via Framura 85, 00168, Rome, Italy, Tel: 011-39-06-612-962-10; Fax: 011-39-06-614-7547. Bro. Paul Bednarczyk, C.S.C., Supr. Gen.; Rev. Emmanuel Kallarackal, C.S.C., Vicar & 1st Asst.; Bro. Prodip Placid Gomes, C.S.C., 2nd Asst.; Rev. Andrew Gawrych, C.S.C., 3rd Asst.; Bro. Bertrand Nee Wayoe, C.S.C., 4th Asst.; Rev. Vijai Amritharaj, C.S.C., 5th Asst.; Bro. Jonathan Beebe, C.S.C., 6th Asst.

Midwest Province of the Brothers of Holy Cross (1841): 54515 State Rd. 933 N., P.O. Box 460, Notre Dame, IN 46556. Tel: 574-631-4000; Fax: 574-631-2999. Email: spalmer@brothersofholycross.com. Web: www.brothersofholycross.com. Bro. Kenneth Haders, C.S.C., Prov. Supr.; Bro. Robert Lavelle, C.S.C., Asst. Prov. & Vicar; Bro. James Spooner, C.S.C., Sec., Steward & Treas.; Councilors: Bro. Lewis T. Brazil, C.S.C.; Bro. James Van Dyke, C.S.C.; Bro. Christopher Torrijas, C.S.C; Bro. John Affum, C.S.C.; Bro. Robert Livernois, C.S.C.

Legal Title: Notre Dame, Ind. Brothers of Holy Cross, Inc.

Professed Brothers 126

Properties owned, staffed or sponsored: Community Houses 3; Colleges 1; High Schools 6; Scholasticates 1; Foreign Mission Schools 5.

Represented in the Archdioceses of Chicago, Indianapolis, Portland in Oregon and San Antonio and in the Dioceses of Cleveland, Fort Wayne-South Bend, Gary and Venice. Also in Ghana, Chile, Kenya, Peru, Bangladesh and Canada.

Congregation of Holy Cross, Moreau Province: Brother John Baptist Province Center, 1101 St. Edwards Dr., Austin, TX 78704. Tel: 512-442-7856. Email: MoreauProvinceOffices@gmail.com. Bro. Thomas Dziekan, C.S.C., Prov. Supr.; Bro. Donald Blauvelt, C.S.C., Asst. Prov.; Bro. Richard Critz, C.S.C., Sec.; Bro. Harold Ehlinger, C.S.C., Steward. Councilors: Bro. Stephen LaMendola, C.S.C.; Bro. Michael Winslow, C.S.C.

Legal Title: Congregation of Holy Cross Moreau Province, Inc.

Professed Brothers 95; Temporarily Professed 11

Represented in the Archdioceses of Hartford, Los Angeles, New Orleans, San Antonio and Washington and in the Dioceses of Albany, Austin, Brooklyn, Oakland, San Jose and Wilmington.

Properties owned, staffed or sponsored: High Schools 10; Middle Schools 1; Schools Foreign Mission Schools 5.

[0610] (C.S.C.)—PRIESTS OF THE CONGREGATION OF HOLY CROSS

(Congregatio a Sancta Cruce)

Generalate: Curia Generalizia di Santa Croce, Via Framura 85, 00168, Rome, Italy. Bro. Paul P. Bednarczyk, C.S.C., Supr. Gen.; Rev. Emmanuel

Kallarackal, C.S.C., First Asst. & Vicar; Bro. Prodip Placid Gomes, C.S.C., Second Asst. & Sec.; Rev. Andrew M. Gawrych, C.S.C., Third Asst. & Procurator Gen.; Bro. Bertrand Nee Wayoe, C.S.C., Fourth Asst.; Rev. Vijai Amirtharaj, C.S.C., Fifth Asst.; Bro. Jonathan Beebe, C.S.C., Sixth Asst.; Rev. John J. Ryan, C.S.C., Gen. Steward; Bro. Ronnie Lenno Farias Silva, Admin. Asst; Rev. John E. Conley, C.S.C., Archivist.

Congregation of Holy Cross, United States Province: Provincial Admin. Office, 54515 State Rd. 933 N., P.O. Box 1064, Notre Dame, IN 46556-1064. Tel: 574-631-6196.

Res: Provincial House, 1304 E. Jefferson Blvd., South Bend, IN 46617. Rev. William M. Lies, C.S.C., Prov. Supr.; Rev. Peter A. Jarret, C.S.C., First Asst. Prov. & Vicar; Rev. E. William Beauchamp, C.S.C., Sec. & Steward; Provincial Councilors: Rev. Austin I. Collins, C.S.C.; Rev. John F. Denning, C.S.C.; Rev. John J. Dougherty, C.S.C.; Rev. Gregory P. Haake, C.S.C.; Rev. Daniel J. Issing, C.S.C., Rev. Charles F. McCoy, C.S.C., Bro. Donald J. Stabrowski, C.S.C.

Legal Title: Congregation of Holy Cross, United States Province, Inc.; Priests of Holy Cross, Indiana Province, Inc.; Congregation of Holy Cross, Eastern Province, Inc.; Congregation of Holy Cross, Southern Province, Inc.; Priests of Holy Cross in Oregon, Inc.

Fathers 245; Professed Clerics: 1; Temporary Professed Clerics: 23; Novices 7; Candidates 6; Professed Brothers 17.

Represented in the Archdioceses of Atlanta, Los Angeles, New Orleans, New York and Portland in Oregon and in the Dioceses of Albany, Austin, Bridgeport, Burlington, Cleveland, Charleston, Colorado Springs, Fall River, Fort Wayne-South Bend, Kalamazoo, Oakland, Orlando, Palm Beach, Paterson, Pensacola-Tallahassee, Peoria, Phoenix, San Jose and Scranton.

Properties owned, sponsored or staffed: College Seminary; Theological Seminary; Novitiate; André House of Arizona; Holy Cross Family Ministries; Mission Center; Casa Santa Cruz; Christopher Lodge; Provincial House; Postulate; Universities 4; Parishes 28; Chaplaincies 21; Publishing House.

Holy Cross Association: Box 771, Notre Dame, IN 46556. Tel: 574-631-6022; Fax: 574-631-9390. Email: blohr@holycrossusa.org; association@holycrossusa.org. Brian Lohr, Dir.

[0620] (F.S.E.)—BROTHERS OF THE HOLY EUCHARIST

Founded in the United States 1957.

General Motherhouse and Novitiate: P.O. Box 25, Plaucheville, LA 71362. Tel: 318-922-3630. Bro. Augustine Kozdroj, F.S.E., Supr. Gen.

Represented in the Diocese of Alexandria.

[0630] (M.S.F.)—CONGREGATION OF THE MISSIONARIES OF THE HOLY FAMILY

(Congregatio Missionariorum a Sacra Familia)

General Motherhouse: Via Odoardo Beccari, 41, Rome 00154 Italy. Tel: 011-39-0657-250639; Fax: 011-39-0657-55192. Very Rev. Augustinus Purnama, M.S.F., Supr. Gen.

MSF Center: Provincialate U.S.A. of the Missionaries of the Holy Family, Office, 3014 Oregon Ave., Saint Louis, MO 63118. Tel: 314-577-6300; Fax: 314-577-6301. Vocations Email: Vocations@MSF-America.org; Provincial Superior Email: MSF@MSF-America.org. Rev. Philip Sosa, M.S.F., Prov. Supr.

Fathers 14; Brothers 1

Ministries in House of Study 1; Parishes 5.

Represented in the Archdioceses of St. Louis and San Antonio and in the Diocese of Brownsville. Also in Canada.

MSF Provincial Residence: 3582 Pearson Pointe Ct., Saint Louis, MO 63139. Tel: 314-416-0299. Email: psosa@msf-america.org.

[0640] (S.F.)—SONS OF THE HOLY FAMILY

(Congregatio Filiorum Sacrae Familiae)

General Motherhouse: Entenza 301, 08029, Barcelona, Spain, Very Rev. Jesus Diaz, S.F., Gen. Supr.

U.S. Foundation Sons of the Holy Family (1920): Holy Family Seminary, 401 Randolph Rd., P.O. Box 4138, Silver Spring, MD 20914-4138. Tel: 301-622-1184. Very Rev. Luis Picazo, S.F., Delegate Supr.

Fathers 12

Represented in the Archdioceses of Santa Fe and Washington.

[0645] (B.H.S.)—BROTHERS OF THE HOLY SPIRIT - CLEVELAND

General Motherhouse: Holy Spirit Monastery, 4150 Rabbit Run Dr., Brooklyn, OH 44144. Tel: 216-741-3653; Email: brotherdale@catholicweb.com. Bro. Dale Sefcik, B.H.S., Supr.; Bro. David Robert, B.H.S., Community Councilor.

Legal Title: Brothers of the Holy Spirit Cleveland.

Represented in the Ukrainian Catholic Diocese of St. Josaphat in Parma.

[0650] (C.S.SP.)—CONGREGATION OF THE HOLY SPIRIT

(Congregation of the Holy Spirit under the protection of the Immaculate Heart of Mary, Spiritans)

(Congregatio Sancti Spiritus sub tutela Immaculati Cordis Beatissimae Virginis Mariae)

Generalate: Clivo di Cinna 195, 00136, Rome, Italy, Very Rev. Alain Mayama, C.S.Sp.

Province of the United States (1872): 6230 Brush Run Rd., Bethel Park, PA 15102. Tel: 412-831-0302; Fax: 412-831-0970. Very Rev. Donald J. McEachin, C.S.Sp., Prov. Supr. Councilors: Rev. John Sawicki, C.S.Sp., Prov. Treas. & Councilor; Rev. Daniel Abba, C.S.Sp; Rev. Binh Quach, C.S.Sp; Rev. Benoit Mukamba, C.S.Sp; Rev. William Christy, C.S.Sp.

Fathers in the U.S: 72; Professed Brothers 1; Scholastics: 1; Lay Spiritans: 11

Legal Holdings: Archconfraternity of the Holy Ghost; Provincial Residence; Duquesne University, Laval House; Holy Ghost Preparatory School; The Spiritan Center.

Represented in the Archdioceses of Baltimore, Chicago, Cincinnati, Detroit, Galveston-Houston, Miami, New York and Philadelphia and in the Dioceses of Arlington, Baton Rouge, Little Rock, Phoenix, Pittsburgh, Providence, San Bernardino and San Diego. Also in Puerto Rico and the Dominican Republic.

Properties owned, sponsored or staffed: Parishes 19; Retirement Residences 1; Training Centers 1; Spiritan Residence, Houston; Properties in Mexico.

Holy Ghost Fathers of Ireland (1971): 99-15 Rockaway Beach Blvd., Rockaway Park, NY 11694. Tel: 718-672-4848; Fax: 718-457-4055. Rev. Joseph Glynn, C.S.Sp., Prov. Delegate U.S.A. Councilors: Very Rev. Thomas Basquel, C.S.Sp; Rev. Diarmuid C. Casey, C.S.Sp; Rev. Brendan Hally, C.S.Sp.

Fathers 11

Represented in the Archdioceses of Boston and San Francisco and in the Dioceses of Brooklyn, Metuchen and St. Augustine.

[0660] (M.SP.S.)—MISSIONARIES OF THE HOLY SPIRIT

General Motherhouse: Av. Universidad 1702 04010, Mexico, D.F., Mexico, Tel: 5-658-74-33; Tel: 5-658-7851. Very Rev. José Luis Loyola, M.Sp.S., Supr. Gen.

Provincial House (Christ the Priest Province): 2512 S.E. Monroe St., Milwaukie, OR 97222, P.O. Box 22387, Milwaukie, OR 97269. Tel: 503-324-2492; Fax: 503-324-2493. Email: secretary@mspscpp.org. Rev. Pedro Arteaga, M.Sp.S., Prov. Supr. Council Members: Rev. Mario Rodriguez, M.Sp.S., Vicar; Rev. Alexandro Rubio, M.Sp.S., Vicar; Rev. Joel Quezada, M.Sp.S.; Rev. Juan J. Gonzalez, M.Sp.S., Prov. Treas.; Rev. Jose Ugalde, M.Sp.S., Prov. Treas.

Priests 28; Professed 7; Parishes 4; Houses of Study: 1; Postulancy 1; Theologates 1

Represented in the Archdioceses of Los Angeles, Portland in Oregon, San Antonio and Seattle.

[0670] (O.H.)—HOSPITALLER BROTHERS OF ST. JOHN OF GOD

General Motherhouse: Hospitaller Brothers of St. John of God, Order founded by St. John of God at Granada, Spain, in 1537, via della Nocetta 263, 00164, Rome, Italy, Rev. Jesus Etayo, Prior General.

American Province of Our Lady Queen of Angels (1970): Villa Maria Provincial Curia, 2425 S. Western Ave., Los Angeles, CA 90018. Tel: 323-734-0233; Fax: 323-731-5987; Email: usaprov-office@sbcglobal.net. Bro. Stephen de la Rosa, O.H., Prov.; Bro. Ignatius Sudol, O.H., Prov. Sec.; Bro. Michael Bassemier, O.H., Prov. Treas.; Bro. Pablo Lopez, O.H., Councilor; Bro. Edward Francis McEnroe, O.H., Councilor.

Brothers 12; Solemnly Professed 12; Priests: 2

Legal Holdings: St. John of God Retirement and Care Center, Los Angeles, CA; St. Joseph Health and Retirement Center, Ojai, CA; St. John of God HealthCare Services, Victorville, CA.

Represented in the Archdiocese of Los Angeles and in the Diocese of San Bernardino.

Province of the Good Shepherd in North America: Hospitaller Brothers of St. John of God, 114 W. Washington St., P.O. Box 736, Momence, IL 60954. Mission Advancement and Stewardship Office Email: development@sjog-na.org; Finance and Corporate Office Email: Judy@sjog-na.org. Bro. David Lynch, O.H., Prov.; Bro. Thomas Osorio, O.H., Sec. Gen.; Bro. Nicholas Foran, O.H., Councilor; Bro. Gary Hill, O.H., Councilor; Bro. Richard MacPhee, O.H., Treas. Gen.

Provincial Curia: 84 Grant St., P.O. Box 1003, Hamilton, ON L8N 2X7 Canada. Tel: 416-203-2711. Email: eileen@goodshepherd.ca.

Brothers 20; Solemnly Professed 19; Temporary Professed 1; Oblate 1; Priests 4.

Sponsorships: Properties owned and/or sponsored: temporary shelters for marginalized men and women 14; shelter for battered women & children 6; residence for persons with AIDS 1; palliative care 1; rehabilitation 2; medical clinic 1; special needs education 1.

Legal Holdings and Titles: Caritas Deus, Inc.; Camillus House Inc.; Camillus Health Concern Inc.; Charity Unlimited; BGS Charitable Trust; Brother Mathias Barrett, Inc. of Illinois; Brothers of the Good Shepherd of Florida, Inc.; The Brothers of the Good Shepherd; Good Shepherd Center Inc.; Little Brothers of the Good Shepherd, Inc.; Villa Mathias, Inc.; Brother Keily Place, Inc.; Brownsville Housing Inc.; Charity Unlimited of Florida, Inc.; Hospitaller Order of St. John of God; St. John of God Community Services; Hospitaller Order of St. John of God Province of the Good Shepherd in North America, Inc.; Charity Unlimited Foundation, Inc.; Emmaus Place, Inc.; Good Shepherd Villas, Inc.; Labre Place, Inc.; Somerville Residence, Inc.; New Camillus House Campus, Inc.; Brother Mathias Barrett, Inc.

Represented in the Archdioceses Miami and Santa Fe and in the Dioceses of Camden and Joliet.

[0680] I.H.M.—BROTHERS OF THE IMMACULATE HEART OF MARY

General Motherhouse (1948): 4301 Earl Dr., Apt. A6, Steubenville, OH 43953. Tel: 740-283-2462. Bro. Dominic Carroll, I.H.M., Supr. Gen.; Bro. Patrick Geary, I.H.M., Novice Master & Vocation Dir.

Professed Brothers 3; Pastoral Associates 1.

Ministries in: Novitiate; CCD Center.

Represented in the Diocese of Steubenville.

[0685] I.V.E.—INSTITUTE OF THE INCARNATE WORD

General House: Via Filippo da Segni, 4, Segni (RM) Italy 00037. Tel: 0039-0697 66068. General Procura, Via Arnaldo Di Colonia, 9 Acilia (RM) 00126 Italy. Tel: 39-06-591-5896; Fax: 39-06-454-33003

Provincial House: Province of the Immaculate Conception of the Institute of the Incarnate Word, 5706 Sargent Rd., Chillum, MD 20782. Tel: 301-773-3635; Fax: 301-710-6505; Email: prov.immaculate.conception@ive.org; Web: www.iveamerica.org. Rev. Alberto Barattero, I.V.E., Provincial Supr.

Fathers 53; Brothers 9; Students in Houses of Formation 48; Students in High School Seminary 26.

Represented in the Archdioceses of Baltimore, Chicago, New York, Philadelphia and Washington, DC and in the Dioceses of Columbus, Dallas, Fall River, Phoenix, San Jose and Winona-Rochester. Also in Canada, Guyana, Bahrain and Mexico.

Provincial House: 5706 Sargent Rd., Chillum, MD 20782. Tel: 301-773-3635; Fax: 301-701-6505.

[0690] S.J.—JESUIT FATHERS AND BROTHERS

(Societas Jesu)

Generalate: Borgo S. Spirito 4, 00193, Rome, Italy, Rev. Arturo Sosa, S.J., Gen.; Rev. Antoine Kerhuel, S.J., Sec.; Rev. Douglas W. Marcouiller, S.J., U.S. Asst.

Jesuit Conference: The Society of Jesus in Canada and the United States, 1726 New Hampshire Ave., N.W., Washington, DC 20009. Tel: 202-462-0400; Fax: 202-328-9212. Very Rev. Brian Paulson, S.J., Pres.; Rev. Sean D. Michaelson, S.J., Socius & Treas.

U.S.A. East Province of the Society of Jesus (2020): 39 E. 83rd St., New York, NY 10028; Tel: 212-774-5500; Fax: 212- 794-1036. 8600 LaSalle Rd., Ste. 620, Towson, MD 21286; Tel. 443-921-1310; Fax: 443-871-0994. P.O. Box 456, Weston, MA 02493; Tel: 617-607-2800; Fax: 617-607-2888. Rev. Joseph M. O'Keefe, S.J., Prov.; Rev. John J. Hanwell, S.J.,

Socius; Rev. Richard A. McGowan, S.J., Treas.; Rev. Philip A. Florio, S.J., Vocations Dir.; Rev. John C. Wronski, S.J., Asst. for Formation; Rev. George M. Witt, S.J., Novice Dir.; Rev. Thomas Benz, S.J., Asst., International Ministries and Safeguarding; Rev. Joseph P. Parkes, S.J., Asst. Secondary Education; Mr. Nicholas Napolitano, Asst. Ecology & Justice; Rev. Michael F. Tunney, S.J., Asst., Higher Educ.

Legal Title: The USA East Province of the Society of Jesus, Inc.

Fathers 533; Scholastics: 44; Brothers 21.

Represented in the Archdioceses of Atlanta, Baltimore, Boston, Chicago, Newark, New Orleans, New York, Philadelphia, St. Louis, Seattle and Washington and in the Dioceses of Albany, Allentown, Baton Rouge, Bridgeport, Brooklyn, Buffalo, Charlotte, Honolulu, Manchester, Oakland, Paterson, Portland (in Maine), Rapid City, Raleigh, Richmond, Rochester, Rockville Centre, San Diego, San Jose, Scranton, Spokane, Syracuse, Wheeling-Charleston and Worcester. Also in Guam, the Caroline Islands, Chalan Kanoa and the Prefecture Apostolic of Marshall Islands, Philippines, and West Africa - Nigeria & Ghana.

Properties owned, sponsored or staffed: Colleges and Universities 11; Houses of Retreats: 5; Houses of Study: 1; Novitiates: 1; Parishes 17; Residences: 39; Secondary and Pre-Secondary Schools 26.

Maryland Province of the Society of Jesus (1833): 8600 LaSalle Rd., Ste. 620, Towson, MD 21286.

Legal Title: Corporation of the Roman Catholic Clergymen, Maryland. (See U.S.A. East Province of the Society of Jesus in the Archdiocese of New York.)

U.S.A. Northeast Province (1943): 39 E. 83rd St., New York, NY 10028.

Legal Title: The New York Province of the Society of Jesus, New York, NY. (See U.S.A. East Province of the Society of Jesus in the Archdiocese of New York)

U.S.A. Northeast Province (1926): P.O. Box 456, Weston, MA 02493.

Legal Title: The Society of Jesus of New England. (See U.S.A. East Province of the Society of Jesus, Archdiocese of New York)

U.S. Central and Southern Province, Society of Jesus: Province Offices, 4511 W. Pine Blvd., Saint Louis, MO 63108-2191. Tel: 314-361-7765; Fax: 314-230-9739. Email: UCSSocius@jesuits.org. Rev. Thomas P. Greene, S.J., Prov.; Rev. Francis W. Huete, S.J., Socius; Rev. J. Daniel Daly, S.J., Treas.; Rev. John F. Armstrong, S.J. Province Sec.; Rev. Hung T. Pham, S.J., Asst. for Formation; Rev. Michael D. Dooley, S.J., Dir. Vocations; Dr. Ronald W. Rebore, Asst. for Secondary & Pre-Secondary Education; Dr. David P. Miros, Archivist; Rev. Ronald J. Boudreaux, S.J., Asst. for Pastoral & Spiritual Ministries; Ms. Therese Meyerhoff, Asst. for Communications; Rev. Brian J. Christopher, S.J., Asst. Social & Intl. Ministries; Ms. Paula Parrish, Asst. for Advancement; Ms. Eileen Croghan, Asst. for Healthcare; Ms. Mary Baudouin, Asst. for Justice and Ecology; Dr. Thomas E. Reynolds, Asst. for Higher Education.

Fathers 261; Students in Major Seminary 37; Novices 12; Brothers 16

U.S. Central and Southern Province, Society of Jesus. Ministries in Parishes; Universities; High Schools; Middle Schools; Novitiate; First Studies House; Curia; Retreat Houses.

Represented in the Archdioceses of Denver, Galveston-Houston, Miami, Mobile, New Orleans and St. Louis and in the Dioceses of Baton Rouge, Colorado Springs, Dallas, El Paso, Ft. Worth, Kansas City-St. Joseph, Lafayette and St. Petersburg. Also in Belize and Puerto Rico.

USA West Province, Society of Jesus (2017): 3215 S.E. 45th Ave, P.O. Box 86010, Portland, OR 97286-0010. Tel: 503-226-6977. Los Gatos Office: 300 College Ave., P.O. Box 519, Los Gatos, CA 95031-0519. Tel: 408-884-1600. Email: uweprovince@jesuits.org. Very Rev. Scott R. Santarosa, S.J., Prov.; Rev. Michael C. Gilson, S.J., Socius; Rev. John D. Martin, S.J., Treas.; Rev. Alfred E. Naucke, S.J., Province Sec.; Mr. Tim Caslin, Asst for Secondary & Pre-Secondary Educ.; Rev. Anthony E. Sholander, S.J., Delegate for Formation; Rev. Christopher T. Nguyen, S.J., Dir. Vocations; Rev. Robert L. Niehoff, S.J., Asst. for Higher Educ.; Rev. Ignatius F. Ohno, S.J., Delegate for Senior Jesuits; Rev. Theodore E. Gabrielli, S.J., Asst. for Intl. Min.; Ms, Siobhán T. Lawlor, Asst. for Advancement & Communications; Bro. Daniel J. Peterson, S.J., Prov. Archivist; Rev. Michael S. Bayard, S.J., Asst for Mission Integration & Liason to Social Ministries; Rev. Christopher S. Weekly, Asst., Parish & Social Ministries; Ms. Annie Fox, Asst. for Social Ministry Organizing; Mr. Arnie J. Shafer, Asst. for Health Care; Ms. Sheila Yrure, Exec. Dir. of Business Operations and Admin.

Legal Titles: USA West Province, Society of Jesus; Society of Jesus, Oregon Province, Portland, OR; The Pioneer Educational Society, Spokane, WA; Montana Catholic Missions, SJ; The Society of Jesus, Alaska; Jesuit Seminary Association; California Jesuit Missionaries; Our Lady of the Oaks dba Jesuit Retreat Center of the Sierra.

Fathers: 388; Brothers: 23; Scholastics: 54; Scholastic Novice: 8.

Represented in the Archdioceses of Los Angeles, Portland in Oregon, San Francisco and Seattle, and in the Dioceses of Baker, Boise, Fairbanks, Fresno, Great Falls-Billings, Helena, Oakland, Orange, Phoenix, Sacramento, San Diego, San Jose, Spokane, Tucson, and Yakima.

Properties owned, sponsored or staffed: Parishes 18; Universities 5; High Schools 11; Middle Schools 2; Novitiates 1, Retreat Centers 2.

U.S.A. Midwest Province of the Society of Jesus (S.J.) (2011): (Canonical Title) 1010 N. Hooker St., Chicago, IL 60642. Tel: 773-975-6363; Fax: 773-975-0230. Very Rev. Brian G. Paulson, S.J., Prov.; Rev. Glen J. Chun, S.J., Socius; Rev. Albert J. DiUlio, S.J., Prov. Treas.

Legal Titles: U.S.A. Midwest Province of the Society of Jesus; Chicago Province of the Society of Jesus; Detroit Province of the Society of Jesus; U.S.A. Midwest Province of the Society of Jesus Apostolic Works Trust; U.S.A. Midwest Province of the Society of Jesus Aged and Infirmed Trust; U.S.A. Midwest Province of the Society of Jesus Formation Trust; U.S.A. Midwest Province of the Society of Jesus Foundation Trust; U.S.A. Midwest Province of the Society of Jesus St. Ignatius Trust; Jesuit International Missions; Jesuit Seminary Association; Bellarmine Jesuit Retreat House; Colombiere Center, Clarkston, MI; Loyola University Chicago; St. Ignatius College Prep, Chicago.

Priests 378; Brothers 27; Scholastics: 79

Represented in the Archdioceses of Atlanta, Baltimore, Boston, Chicago, Cincinnati, Denver, Detroit, Indianapolis, Los Angeles, Louisville, Military Services, Mobile, Milwaukee, New Orleans, New York, Omaha, San Antonio, San Francisco, Seattle, St. Louis, St. Paul and Minneapolis and Washington and in the Dioceses of Austin, Brooklyn, Charlotte, Cleveland, Columbus, Covington, Des Moines, Fort Wayne-South Bend, Gaylord, Green Bay, Honolulu, Joliet, Lafayette in Indiana, Lansing, Lexington, Oakland, Rapid City, Saginaw, San Jose, St. Petersburg, Toledo and Winona. Also in Canada.

Properties Sponsored: Parishes 12; Universities 6; High Schools 15; Retreat Houses 7.

Oregon Province - Society of Jesus (1932): 3215 S.E. 45th Ave, P.O. Box 86010, Portland, OR 97286-0010. Tel: 503-226-6977. Email: uweprovince@jesuits.org. Rev. Scott Santarosa, S.J., Prov.; Rev. John D. Martin, S.J., Treas.; Rev. Michael C. Gilson, S.J., Socius.

U.S. Address: 12725 S.W. 6th St., Miami, FL 33184. Tel: 786-621-4594; Fax: 305-554-0017. Email: agarciasj@belenjesuit.org. Rev. Javier Vidal, S.J., Prov.; Rev. Alberto Garcia, S.J., Miami Regl. Supr.

Fathers 91; Scholastics: 26; Brothers 7

Represented in the Archdiocese of Miami. Also in Santo Domingo.

Properties owned, staffed or sponsored: High Schools Loyola in Dominican Republic, Belen Jesuit Prep in Miami; Novitiate 1; House of Retreat 3 in Santo Domingo; Casa Manresa in Miami; Residences 2

Puerto Rico Province - Society of Jesus (1987): Urb.Santa Maria, 1940 Calle Sauco, San Juan, PR 00927-6718. Tel: 787-294-4301; Fax: 787-294-4302. Rev. Mario A. Torres, S.J., Regl. Supr.; Rev. John F. Talbot, S.J., Exec. Asst., Regl. Supr.; Rev. Alvaro Velez, S.J., Auditor.

Bishop: 1; Fathers 19; Scholastics: 6

Represented in the Archdioceses of Miami, Omaha and San Juan and in the Diocese of Mayaguez.

Properties owned, sponsored or staffed: Parishes 2; High Schools 1; Residences 3; Campus Ministry Centers 1.

[0700] (S.S.J.)—ST. JOSEPH'S SOCIETY OF THE SACRED HEART

(The Josephites)

(Societas Sancti Joseph SSmi Cordis)

Central House Administration: 1097-C West Lake Ave., Baltimore, MD 21210. Tel: 410-727-3386; Fax: 410-727-1006; Email: josephite1@aol.com; Web: www.josephites.org. Most. Rev. John H. Ricard, S.S.J., Supr. Gen.

Fathers 52; Brothers 4; Deacons 3; Seminarians: 13.

Legal Titles: St. Joseph's Society of the Sacred Heart, Inc.; St. Joseph Manor Foundation, Inc.; The Josephite Retirement and Disability Benefits Trust; The Josephite Seminarian Education Trust.

Represented in the Archdioceses of Baltimore, Galveston-Houston, Los Angeles, Mobile, New Orleans and Washington and in the Dioceses of Arlington, Baton Rouge, Biloxi, Birmingham, Jackson and Lafayette (LA). Also in Nigeria.

Properties owned, staffed or sponsored: Parishes 36; Elementary Schools 5; High School; House of Study; Major Seminary; Novitiate; Nigerian Formation House.

[0710] (C.J.)—JOSEPHITE FATHERS

(Institutum Josephitarum Gerardimontensium)

General Motherhouse: Geraardsbergen (Ghent), Belgium, Rev. Jacob Beya, C.J., Supr. Gen.

U.S. Foundation: St. Joseph Seminary, Provincialate and Novitiate, 180 Patterson Rd., Santa Maria, CA 93455. Tel: 805-937-5378; Fax: 805-937-5759. Email: tlane11564@aol.com. Rev. Ludo DeClippel, C.J., Prov. Supr.

Fathers 8; Brothers 2

Ministry to Parishes; Academic Education.

Represented in the Archdiocese of Los Angeles.

[0720] (M.S.)—THE MISSIONARIES OF OUR LADY OF LA SALETTE

(Congregatio Missionariorum Vulgo "De la Salette")

General House: Piazza Madonna Della Salette 3, 00152, Rome, Italy, Very Rev. Silvano Marisa, M.S., Supr. Gen.

American Region was established in 1892; Canonically erected 1934; Divided into other Provinces in 1945, 1958, 1967 and restructured into one Province in 2000.

Province of Mary, Mother of the Americas (2000): 915 Maple Ave., Hartford, CT 06114-2330. Tel: 860-956-8870. Very Rev. William Kaliyadan, M.S., Prov. Supr.; Rev. Roland Nadeau, M.S., Prov. Vicar; Rev. Ronald Foshage, M.S., Councilor.

Legal Title: Missionaries of LaSalette Corp.; MLS Religious Trust.

Priests 67; Brothers 18; Oblates: 3

Represented in the Archdioceses of Atlanta, Boston, Galveston-Houston Hartford, Milwaukee, St. Louis and Washington and in the Dioceses of Albany, Beaumont, Fall River, Lake Charles, Manchester, Norwich, Orlando, Raleigh, Springfield in Massachusetts and Worcester.

[0730] (L.C.)—LEGIONARIES OF CHRIST

Founded in Mexico in 1941, first foundation in United States 1965.

General Headquarters: Via Aurelia 677, Rome, Italy, Tel: 011-39-06-664-991; Fax: 011-39-06-6649-9372. Very Rev. John Connor, L.C., Gen. Dir.

North American Headquarters: 30 Mansell Ct., Ste. 103, Roswell, GA 30076. Tel: 770-828-4950; Fax: 678-782-8173. Rev. Shawn Aaron, L.C., Territorial Dir.; Rev. William Martin Connor, L.C., Natl. Vocation Dir.; Rev Timothy Walsh, L.C., Rector.

Priests 140; Religious: 60; Novices 9

Represented in the Archdioceses of Atlanta, Chicago, Cincinnati, Detroit, Galveston-Houston, Hartford, Los Angeles, New Orleans, New York, Philadelphia and Washington and in the Dioceses of Dallas, Gary, Madison, Manchester, Providence, San Jose and Raleigh.

[0740] (M.I.C.)—CONGREGATION OF MARIANS OF THE IMMACULATE CONCEPTION

(Congregatio Clericorum Marianorum ab Immaculata Conceptione Beatissimae Virginis Mariae)

General Motherhouse: Via Corsica 1, 00198, Rome, Italy, Tel: 011-39-06-853-703-1; Fax: 011-39-06-853-703-22. Web: padrimariani.org. Very Rev. Andrzej Pakula, M.I.C., Gen. Supr.; General Councilors: Very Rev. Joseph Roesch, M.I.C.; Rev. Jovanete Vieira, M.I.C.; Rev. Zbigniew Pilat, M.I.C.; Rev. Wojciech Jasinski, M.I.C.

Marian Fathers of the Immaculate Conception of the B.V.M., 2 Prospect Hill Rd., Stockbridge, MA 01262.

Blessed Virgin Mary, Mother of Mercy Province: 2 Prospect Hill Rd., Stockbridge, MA 01262-0951. Tel: 413-298-3931; Fax: 413-298-0207; Email: provincial@

marian.org; Web: www.marian.org; Web: www.thedivinemercy.org. Very Rev. Kazimierz Chwalek, M.I.C., Prov. Supr. Provincial Councilors: Very Rev. Donald Calloway, M.I.C.; Rev. Andrew Davy, M.I.C.; Rev. James McCormack, M.I.C.; Rev. Kenneth Dos Santos, M.I.C.

Fathers 45; Brothers 10; Seminarians 20; Novices 3; Postulants 3

Legal Holdings: Marian Fathers of the Immaculate Conception of the B.V.M., Inc., 2 Prospect Hill Rd., Stockbridge, MA 01262; Congregation of Marians of the Immaculate Conception; Congregation of Marian Fathers of the Immaculate Conception of the Most Blessed Virgin Mary; Association of Marian Helpers; Marian Service Corporation; Marian Helpers Corporation; Eucharistic Apostles of the Divine Mercy (EADM); John Paul II Institute of Divine Mercy; Marian Helpers Center; Marian House of Studies; Marian Scholasticate; Marianapolis Preparatory School; Mother of Mercy Messengers (MOMM); National Shrine of the Divine Mercy; National Shrine of the Divine Mercy Gift Shop.

Represented in the Archdioceses of Chicago, Milwaukee and Washington and in the Dioceses of Joliet, Norwich, Springfield in Massachusetts and Steubenville. Also in Argentina: Archdiocese of Rosario and the Diocese of Avellaneda.

Sponsorships: Properties owned, staffed or sponsored: 7 Religious Houses; 1 Residence; 5 Parishes; 1 Grade School. Within the Argentine Vicariate 2 Religious Houses; 2 Parishes; 2 Grade Schools; 2 High Schools; 1 Residence.

[0750] (C.M.M.)—CONGREGATION OF MARIANNHILL MISSIONARIES, MARIANNHILL FATHERS AND BROTHERS

(Congregatio Missionariorum de Mariannhill)

Generalate: Via S. Giovanni Eudes 91, 00163, Rome, Italy, Very Rev. Michael Mass, C.M.M., Supr. Gen. American-Canadian Province (1938): Our Lady of Grace Monastery, 23715 Ann Arbor Tr., Dearborn Heights, MI 48127-1449. Tel: 313-561-7140; Fax: 313-561-9486. Rev. Raymond Lucasinsky, C.M.M., House Leader; Rev. Thomas Szura, C.M.M., American District Supr. & Procurator.

Fathers 7; Brothers 1

Represented in the Archdiocese of Detroit.

[0760] (S.M.)—SOCIETY OF MARY

(Marianists)

(Societas Mariae–Marianistae)

General Motherhouse: Via Latina 22, 00179, Rome, Italy, Very Rev. André-Joseph Fétis, S.M., Supr. Gen.

The Province of Cincinnati (1849); Province of the Pacific (1948); Province of St. Louis (1908) and the Province of New York (1961) have merged July 1, 2002 to form the Marianist Province of the United States.

Marianist Province of the United States (Society of Mary) (2002): 4425 W. Pine, Saint Louis, MO 63108-2301. Tel: 314-533-1207; Fax: 314-533-0778. Rev. Oscar Vasquez, S.M., Prov.; Bro. Bernard J. Ploeger, S.M., Asst. Prov. Councilors: Rev. Timothy Kenney S.M.; Bro. Joseph Markel, S.M.; Bro. Jesse O'Neill, S.M.; Bro. Charles Johnson, S.M.; Rev. Charles Stander, S.M.

Fathers 64; Brothers 144; Perpetual Professed 207; Temporarily Professed 1

Legal Titles and Holdings - Properties owned: Marianist Provincial Office, St. Louis, MO; St. Mary's University, San Antonio, TX; Central Catholic Marianist High School, San Antonio, TX; Tecaboca: Marianist Center for Spiritual Renewal, Mountain Home, TX; Chaminade College Preparatory, St. Louis, MO; St. John Vianney High School, St. Louis, MO; Marianist Retreat & Conference Center, Eureka, MO; Marianist Communities, St. Louis; Mount St. John; Bergamo Center; University of Dayton; Chaminade-Julienne High School; Marianist Mission, Dayton OH; Governor's Island, Huntsville, OH; Marianist Communities in: Cincinnati, OH; Dayton, OH; Marianist Family Retreat Center, Cape May Point, NJ; Marianist Community Residences, Hollywood, FL; Chaminade/Madonna High School, Hollywood, FL; Colegio San Jose, Rio Piedras, PR; Chaminade University, Honolulu, HI; St. Louis School, Honolulu, HI; Marianist Center, Honolulu, HI; Marianist Communities, Honolulu, HI; National Archives, San Antonio, TX.

Members serve and staff: Parishes; Universities, High Schools, Middle Schools and Elementary Schools; Retreat Houses; Apostolic Centers; Missions in Africa, India & Mexico.

Represented in the Archdioceses of Cincinnati, Indianapolis, Los Angeles, Miami, Philadelphia, St. Louis, San Antonio, San Francisco and San Juan and in the Dioceses of Camden, Cleveland, Honolulu, Pittsburgh, Orange and San Jose. Also in Ireland.

Province of Meribah (1976): Marianist Provincial Residence, 240 Emory Rd., Mineola, NY 11501. Tel: 516-742-5555 ext 589. Bro. Timothy S. Driscoll, S.M., Prov. & Asst. for Education; Rev. Thomas A. Cardone, S.M., Asst. Prov. & Asst. for Rel. Life; Bro. James W. Conway, S.M., Asst. for Temporalities. Councilors: Bro. Thomas J. Cleary, S.M.; Rev. Daniel Griffin, S.M.

Legal Holdings: Chaminade High School, Mineola, NY; Kellenberg Memorial High School, Uniondale, NY; Marianist Residence, Accord, NY.

[0770] (F.M.S.)—THE MARIST BROTHERS

(Fratres Maristae a Scholis)

Generalate: Rome, Italy, Rev. Bro. Ernesto Sanchez, F.M.S., Supr. Gen.; Rev. Bro. Luis Carlos Guittierez, F.M.S., Vicar Gen.

Province of the United States of America (2003): Provincial Office, 70-20 Juno St., Forest Hills, NY 11375. Tel: 718-480-1306; Fax: 718-881-7888. Email: patmcnam@aol.com. Bro. Hugh Turley, F.M.S., Co-Dir. Devel.; Mrs. Paulette Karas, Co-Dir. Devel.; Mr. Frank Pellegrino, C.F.O.; Bro. Patrick McNamara, F.M.S., Prov.; Bro. Daniel O'Riordan, F.M.S., Asst. Prov.; Bro. Thomas Schady, F.M.S., Dir. Schools.

Brothers 130

Legal Titles: Marist Brothers of the Schools, Inc.; The Marist Brothers.

Represented in the Archdioceses of Boston, Chicago, Miami, Newark, New Orleans and New York and in the Dioceses of Albany, Brooklyn, Brownsville, Laredo, Rockville Centre and Wheeling-Charleston.

Properties owned, staffed or sponsored; High Schools 15; Community Houses 31; Junior High Schools 2.

[0780] (S.M.)—MARIST FATHERS

(Societas Mariae)

General Motherhouse: via Alessandro Poerio 63, 00152, Rome, Italy, Very Rev. John Larsen, S.M., Supr. Gen.; Rev. John Harhager, S.M., Treas. Gen.

The first Marist foundation in the United States was in 1863, St. Michael's in Convent, Louisiana. The first Marist Province in the United States was established in 1889 under the name of American Province. This Province was subdivided in 1924 into the Washington Province and the Boston Province; On January 1, 1962, the San Francisco Province was established. On January 1, 2000 the San Francisco and Washington Provinces merged. On September 8, 2000 the merged entity became officially known as the Atlanta Province. The Boston Province continues as a separate province.

Atlanta Province (2000): P.O. Box 888263, Atlanta, GA 30356. Tel: 770-451-1316. Very Rev. Joseph Hindelang, S.M., Prov. Rev. Timothy G. Keating, S.M., Prov. Treas., Prov. Council & Promoter of Marist Laity; Rev. Walter Gaudreau, S.M., Mission Promoter; Rev. Francis J. Kissel, S.M., Archivist; Bro. Randy T. Hoover, S.M., Prov. Council; Rev. William Rowland, S.M., Vicar & Prov. Council; Rev. Kevin Duggan, S.M., Prov. Council.

Fathers 33; Brothers 5

Legal Holdings & Titles: Marist Society, Inc.; Marist College and Marist Center, Washington, DC; Marist Society of GA; Marist School, Atlanta, GA; Marist Society of OH; Marist Society of LA; Marist Society of PA.

Properties owned, sponsored or staffed: Community Houses 8; Parishes 5; Seminaries/Houses of Study 1; High School 1.

Represented in the Archdioceses of Atlanta, Los Angeles, Military Services, U.S.A., New York, San Francisco, St. Paul-Minneapolis and Washington and in the Dioceses of Brownsville, Savannah, St. Petersburg and Wheeling-Charleston.

Boston Province (Marist Fathers) (1924): Marist Fathers of Boston, Colin House, 13 Isabella St., Boston, MA 02116-5216; Tel: 617-426-4448. Very Rev. Joseph Hindelang, S.M., Provincial; Rev. Philip Parent, S.M., Prov. Dir. of Third Order of Mary; Rev. William Rowland, S.M., Vicar & Prov. Council; Bro. Randy T. Hoover, S.M., Prov. Council; Rev. Timothy G. Keating, S.M., Prov. Council & Prov. Treas; Rev. Kevin J. Duggan, S.M., Prov. Council; Rev. Philip Parent, S.M., Dir. Lourdes Center.

Legal Titles: Marist Fathers of Boston; Marist Fathers of Detroit, Inc.; Marist Fathers of New York; Senior Religious Trust of Marist Fathers of Boston.

Fathers: 24; Brothers: 2

Properties owned, sponsored or staffed: Community Houses 3; High Schools 1.

Represented in the Archdioceses of Boston and Detroit, and in the Diocese of Brooklyn.

[0782] (O.M.M.)—MARONITE ORDER OF THE BLESSED VIRGIN MARY

Maronite Order of the Blessed Virgin Mary: 4405 Earhart Rd., Ann Arbor, MI 48105. Tel: 734-662-4822; Fax: 734-662-4822. Email: abounapilot@hotmail.com. Rev. John Tayar, O.M.M., Supr.; Rev. Paul Tarabay, O.M.M.; Rev. Joseph Khalil, O.M.M.

[0785] (C.M.L.M.)—THE CONGREGATION OF MARONITE LEBANESE MISSIONARIES

Founded at the Monastery of Kreim-Ghosta (Mountain of Lebanon), in the year 1865. Established in the United States March of 1991: Agreement between Archbishop Zayek of the Diocese of St. Maron and the Congregation to serve the parishes of San Antonio, Dallas and Houston.

U.S. Headquarters: Our Lady of the Cedars Maronite Church, 11935 Bellfort Village, Houston, TX 77031. Tel: 281-568-6800; Fax: 281-564-6961. Rev. Elias Sleiman, M.L.M., Supr.

Bishops 4; Priests 98; Seminarians: 16; Postulants: 2; Novices 5

Represented in the Dioceses of Our Lady of Lebanon and the Eparchy of St. Maron.

333 S. San Vicente Blvd., Los Angeles, CA 90048. Tel: 310-275-6634; Fax: 310-858-0856.

[0790] (M.M.A.)—MARONITE MONKS OF ADORATION

Most Holy Trinity Monastery 67 Dugway Rd., Petersham, MA 01366-9725. Tel: 978-724-3347. Web: www.maronitemonks.org. Rt. Rev. Patrick Kokorian, M.M.A., Abbot; Very Rev. Maron Hendricks, M.M.A., Prior.

Priests 10; Brothers 8; Monks in Community 18

[0800] (M.M.)—MARYKNOLL

(Catholic Foreign Mission Society of America, Inc.)

U.S. Foundation (1911): Maryknoll Society Center & Admin. Offices, P.O. Box 303, Maryknoll, NY 10545-0303. Tel: 914-941-7590; Fax: 914-944-3600. Email: mklcouncil@maryknoll.org. Rev. Lance P. Nadeau, M.M., Supr. Gen. & Pres.; Rev. James M. Lynch, M.M., Vicar Gen. & Vice Pres.; Rev. Juan M. Zuñiga, M.M., Sec. Gen.; Rev. Timothy O. Kilkelly, M.M., Asst. Gen.

Legal Title: Catholic Foreign Mission Society of America, Incorporated; Maryknoll Society Center, Maryknoll, NY 10545.

Houses in Archdioceses and Dioceses:

Chicago: Maryknoll Fathers and Brothers, 5128 S. Hyde Park Blvd., Chicago, IL 60615-4217. Tel: 773-288-3143; Tel: 773-493-3367; Fax: 773-493-3427; Email: chicago@maryknoll.org; Web: www.maryknollsociety.org. Rev. Russell J. Feldmeier, M.M., Rector; Bro. Mark Gruenke, M.M.

San Jose: Maryknoll Residence, 23000 Cristo Rey Dr., Los Altos, CA 94024-7425. Tel: 650-386-4342; Fax: 650-386-4377.

Seattle: Maryknoll Fathers and Brothers, 958 16th Ave., E., Seattle, WA 98112. Tel: 206-322-8831; Fax: 206-324-6909. Anna Johnson, House Dir.; Priests in Res.: Rev. Robert Wynne, M.M.; Rev. Edward Shellito, M.M.

[0810] (F.M.M.A.)—BROTHERS OF MERCY OF MARY HELP OF CHRISTIANS

General Motherhouse: 54292 Trier, Germany, Bro. Benedikt Molitor, F.M.M.A., Supr. Gen.

American House (Convent): 4540 Ransom Rd., Clarence, NY 14031. Tel: 716-759-7205, ext. 203; Bro. Kenneth Thomas, F.M.M.A., House Supr.; Assistants: Bro. Edward Lewis, F.M.M.A.; Bro. Matthias Moeller, F.M.M.A.

Brothers 6

Legal Holdings or Titles: Brothers of Mercy Nursing Home Co., Inc.; Brothers of Mercy Housing Co., Inc.; Brothers of Mercy Sacred Heart Home, Inc.

Represented in the Diocese of Buffalo.

[0820] (C.P.M.)—CONGREGATION OF THE FATHERS OF MERCY

(Congregatio Presbyterorum a Misericordia)

Generalate and Novitiate (1808): 806 Shaker Museum Rd., Auburn, KY 42206. Tel: 270-542-4146; Email frandycpm@gmail.com; Web: www.fathersofmercy.com. Very Rev. David Wilton, C.P.M.,

Supr. Gen.; Rev. Wade Menezes, C.P.M., Asst. Gen.; Rev. Joseph Aytona, C.P.M., Consultor; Rev. Anthony M. Stephens, C.P.M., Consultor; Rev. Joel Rogers, C.P.M., Consultor; Rev. Allan A. Cravalho, C.P.M., Sec. Gen.; Rev. Ricardo N. Pineda, C.P.M., Treas. Gen.

Priests 27; Students 6

Represented in the Archdioceses of Louisville and Cincinnati and in the Dioceses of Columbus, Green Bay, Lexington and Owensboro.

[0825] (M.S.S.)—MISSIONARIES OF THE BLESSED SACRAMENT

(Missionary Priests of the Blessed Sacrament)

Regional Headquarters: 2290 Galloway Rd., B7, Bensalem, PA 19020. Tel: 215-244-9211; Fax: 215-244-9211. Rev. Victor P. Warkulwiz, M.S.S., Supr.

Fathers 1

Ministries in Special Apostolate: Promotion of perpetual Eucharistic adoration.

Represented in the Archdiocese of Philadelphia.

[0830] (M.H.M.)—MILL HILL MISSIONARIES

(St. Joseph's Missionary Society)

International Headquarters: St. Joseph's Missionary Society, 6 Colby Gardens, Maidenhead SL6 7GZ, United Kingdom. Web: www.millhillmissionaries.co.uk. Very Rev.Michael Cocoran, M.H.M., Gen. Supr.

American Headquarters: Mill Hill Missionaries, 222 W. Hartsdale Ave., Hartsdale, NY 10530-1667. Tel: 914-682-0645; Fax: 914-682-0862; Email: wklaver@millhillusa.org. Rev. Willem Klaver, MHM Society Rep.

Legal Title: Mill Hill Fathers, Inc.

Fathers 8

Represented in the Archdiocese of New York and in the Diocese of Phoenix.

[0835] (O.M.)—MINIM FATHERS

General Motherhouse: Piazza San Francesco di Paola, 10 00184, Rome, Italy, Tel: 011-39-6-4882613; Fax: 011-39-6-4882613. Very Rev. Gregorio Colatorti, O.M., Supr. Gen.

North American Delegation (1970): 3431 Portola Ave., Los Angeles, CA 90032. Tel: 323-223-1101. Rev. Mario Pisano, O.M., Delegate Gen.

Legal Title: Minim Fathers.

Priests 4

Represented in the Archdiocese of Los Angeles.

[0840] (S.T.)—MISSIONARY SERVANTS OF THE MOST HOLY TRINITY

(Missionarii Servi Sanctissimae Trinitatis)
(Trinity Missions)

Generalate-Missionary Servants of the Most Holy Trinity: 9001 New Hampshire Ave., Ste. 300, Silver Spring, MD 20903-3626. Tel: 301-434-0092; Fax: 301-434-0255. Email: generalate@trinitymissions.org. Very Rev. Michael K. Barth, S.T., Gen. Custodian; Rev. Rafael Pisso, S.T., Vicar Gen.; Rev. Dieudonne Nsom Kindong, S.T., Sec. Gen.; Rev. Francisco Gomez, S.T., Treas. Gen.; General Councilors: Rev. Jesus Ramirez, S.T.; Bro. Raul Mejia, S.T.; Rev. Guy Wilson, S.T.

Legal Title: Missionary Servants of the Most Holy Trinity (aka) Trinity Missions; Missionary Servants Charitable Trust; Father Judge Charitable Trust.

Priests 80; Brothers 14; Student Brothers 4; Novices 4; Candidates 10; Deacons 2.

Ministry in the following areas: Missionary Cenacles; Parishes; Missions; Stations and Specialized Apostolates; Lay Apostolate Secretariat; Counseling Centers; Hospitals and Rest Home Chaplains; AA Programs; Protective Institutions; Prison Chaplains; Community Centers.

Properties owned and or sponsored: Generalate, Silver Spring, MD; Parish, rectory and school, Holy Trinity, AL; School Buildings, Camden, MS; St. Joseph Shrine, Stirling, NJ; Former minor seminary building, Monroe, VA; Residences: Senior Ministry Residence, Adelphi, MD.

Represented in the Archdioceses of Baltimore, Chicago, Los Angeles, Mobile and Washington and in the Dioceses of Jackson, Knoxville, Paterson, San Bernardino, Savannah and Tucson. Also in Colombia, Costa Rica, Haiti, Honduras, Mexico and Puerto Rico.

[0850] (M.AFR.)—SOCIETY OF MISSIONARIES OF AFRICA

(Societas Missionariorum Africae)

Generalate: 269 via Aurelia, I-00165, Rome, Italy, Rev. Stanley Lubungo, M.Afr., Supr. Gen.

U.S.A. Sector of the Province of the Americas: 1624 21st. St., N.W., Washington, DC 20009-1003. Tel: 202-232-5154. Rev. George Markwell, M.Afr.; Bro. James Heintz, M.Afr.; Rev. Thomas Reilly, M.Afr.; Rev. Jean-Claude Robitaille, M.Afr., Coord.; Rev. Joseph Elmo Hebert, M.Afr.; Rev. Robert C. McGovern, M.Afr.; Rev. Barthelemy Bazemo, M.Afr., Delegate Supr. & Coord.; Rev. David J. Goergen, M.Afr., Sec.; Rev. Komi Sedomo Koffi (Antonio), M.Afr., Treas.; Rev. Bartholomew Mrosso, M.Afr.; Rev. William Curran, M.Afr.; Rev. Cristobal G. Padilla, M.Afr.; Rev. Erick Baldras Vega, M.Afr.

Priests 14; Brothers 1

Represented in the Archdiocese of Washington and in the Dioceses of Brooklyn and St. Petersburg.

[0852] M.J.—MISSIONARIES OF JESUS, INC.

Founded in Philippines.

Rev. Melanio Viuya Jr., M.J., Treas., Sec. & Mission Dir. 435 S. Occidental Blvd., Los Angeles, CA 90057. Tel: 213-389-8439, ext 15; Fax: 213-389-1951. Email: info.missionariesofjesus@gmail.com; Web: www.missionariesofjesus.com. Rev. Euginius Canete, M.J., Gen. Supr.; Rev. Manuel Gacad, M.J., Vicar Gen.; Rev. Crespo Lape, M.J.; Rev. Freddie Pinuela, M.J.; Rev. Manuel Gacad, M.J. Mission Team, Precious Blood Church, 435 S. Occidental Blvd., Los Angeles, CA 90057. Tel: 213-389-8439. Rev. Benedicto Lagarde, M.J.; Rev. Melchor Villero, M.J. Mission Team, St. Anne Church, Coconut Palm St., Penitas, TX. Rev. Joseph Guerrero, M.J.; Rev. Gregorio Domilies, M.J. Mission Team, Missionaries of Jesus, Matamoros, Tamaulipas, Mexico.

Priests 43; Brothers 1; Seminarians: 26

In the United States, work in parish ministry and work with migrants in Guatemala, Papua New Guinea and in the Philippines, work with tribal minorities and non-Christians.

[0854] (M.S.P.)—MISSIONARY SOCIETY OF ST. PAUL OF NIGERIA

Generalate: P.O. Box 23, Abuja, Nigeria. Very Rev. Callistus Isara, M.S.P., Supr. Gen.

U.S. Region: Missionary Society of St. Paul, Inc., 3607 Meriburr Ln., Houston, TX 77021. Mailing Address: P.O. Box 300145, Houston, TX 77230-0145. Tel: 713-842-6090; 713-747-1722; Fax: 713-741-0245; Web: www.mspfathers.org; www.mspfathers.org/americas. Very Rev. Ambrose Akinwande, M.S.P., Regl. Supr.

Legal Title: Missionary Society of St. Paul, Inc., Houston, TX.

Universal Number of Priests 284; Priests in U.S. 56

Ministries in Parishes; Education; Social Justice; Hospitals; Evangelism.

Represented in the Archdioceses of Baltimore, Chicago, Detroit, Galveston-Houston, New York and San Antonio and the Dioceses of Austin, Baton Rouge, Beaumont, Birmingham, Charlotte, Dodge City, Great Falls-Billings, Las Vegas, Savannah and St. Petersburg.

[0860] (C.I.C.M.)—MISSIONHURST CONGREGATION OF THE IMMACULATE HEART OF MARY

(Congregatio Immaculati Cordis Mariae)

Foreign and Home missions.

Generalate: Casa Generalizia C.I.C.M., Via S. Giovanni Eudes, 95, 00163, Rome, Italy, Very Rev. Charles Phukuta Khonde, CICM, Supr. Gen.

U.S. Province (1946): Missionhurst, 4651 25th St. N., Arlington, VA 22207. Tel: 703-528-3800; Fax: 703-528-5355. Very Rev. Celso Tabalanza, CICM, Prov. Sup.

Legal Title: American I.H.M. Province, Inc.; Immaculate Heart Missions, Inc.; Missionhurst, Inc.

Fathers 32; Brothers 1; Seminarians 2

Ministries in Parishes; Poverty Awareness Ministry; Hospital Pastoral Work; Justice, Peace & Integrity of Creation.

Represented in the Archdiocese of San Antonio and in the Dioceses of Arlington and Raleigh.

[0865] (C.R.M.)—CONGREGATION OF THE MOTHER OF THE REDEEMER

Founded in the United States 1975.

U.S. Assumption Province: Congregation of the Mother of the Redeemer, 1900 Grand Ave., Carthage, MO 64836- 3500. Tel: 417-358-7787; Fax: 417-358-9508; Email: cmc@dongcong.net. Rev. Paul Tai V. Tran, C.R.M., Prov. Supr.

Priests 72; Brothers 32

Represented in the Diocese of Springfield-Cape Girardeau.

[0870] (S.M.M.)—MONTFORT MISSIONARIES

(Missionaries of the Company of Mary)
(Societas Mariae Montfortana)

Generalate: Viale Dei Monfortani 65, 00135, Rome, Italy, Very Rev. Luiz Augusto Stefano, S.M.M.

United States Province (1948): Montfort Missionaries, 26 S. Saxon Ave., Bay Shore, NY 11706. Tel: 917-921-6814. Very Rev. Thomas D. Poth, S.M.M. Counselors: Rev. Donald LaSalle, S.M.M.; Rev. Francis Pizzarelli, S.M.M.; Rev. Alonso Lazo, S.M.M.; Rev. Gerald Fitzsimmons, S.M.M., Dir. of Child Protection; Rev. Matthew Considine, S.M.M., Finance.

Legal Title: Missionaries of the Company of Mary.

Fathers 21; Community Houses 4

Represented in the Archdioceses of Hartford and St. Louis and in the Diocese of Rockville Centre. Also in Nicaragua.

[0895] (O.SS.S.)—BRIGITTINE MONKS

(The Order of the Most Holy Savior)

Priory of Our Lady of Consolation: 23300 Walker Ln., Amity, OR 97101. Tel: 503-835-8080; Fax: 503-835-9662; Email: monks@brigittine.org; Web: www.Brigittine.org. Bro. Bernard Ner Suguitan, O.Ss.S., Prior.

Professed Monks 5

Represented in the Archdiocese of Portland in Oregon.

[0900] (O.PRAEM.)—CANONS REGULAR OF PREMONTRE

(Norbertines, Order of St. Norbert, Premonstratensians)

(Ordo Canonicorum Regularium Praemonstratensium)

Founded in France in the 12th century. First foundation in the United States in 1893.

Most Rev. Thomas A. Handgratinger, O.Praem., Abbot Gen.

Norbertine Generalate: 27 Viale Giotto, 00153, Rome, Italy, Tel: 011-39-06-571-766-1; Tel: 571-766-212; Fax: 011-39-06-57-80906.

United States: St. Norbert Abbey, 1016 N. Broadway, De Pere, WI 54115-2697. Tel: 920-337-4300; Fax: 920-337-4328. Email: communications@norbertines.org. Rt. Rev. Dane J. Radecki, O.Praem., Abbot; Rt. Rev. Gary J. Neville, O.Praem., Abbot Emeritus; Rt. Rev. Thomas DeWane, O.Praem., Abbot Emeritus; Rt. Rev. Jerome G. Tremel, O.Praem., Abbot Emeritus; Very Rev. Bradley R. Vanden Branden, O.Praem., Prior; Rev. Michael J. Brennan, O.Praem., Vocation Coord.; Re. John P. Kastenholz, O.Praem. Sec. Treas.; Rev. David M. Komatz, O.Praem. Dir. of Formation, St. Norbert Abbey.

Legal Title: The Premonstratensian Fathers; NORBERT & CO., a nominee of The Premonstratensian Fathers; Norbertine Fathers; St. Norbert Abbey, Inc.; The Walnut Markets, Inc.; Los Amigos del Peru, Inc.; Norbertine Generalate, Inc.

Fathers 41; Brothers 3; Novices 5

Properties owned, staffed or sponsored: House of Studies 1; Colleges 1; Parishes 6.

Represented in the Archdiocese of Chicago and in the Dioceses of Green Bay and Jackson.

Daylesford Abbey: Norbertine Fathers and Brothers, 220 S. Valley Rd., Paoli, PA 19301-1911. Tel: 610-647-2530; Fax: 610-651-0219. Rt. Rev. Domenic A. Rossi, O.Praem., Abbot & Vocation Dir. Email: drossi@daylesford.org; Rt. Rev. Richard J. Antonucci, O.Praem., Abbot Emeritus; Rt. Rev. Ronald J. Rossi, O.Praem., Abbot Emeritus; Very Rev. John C. Zagarella, O.Praem., Prior, Email: jzagarella@daylesford.org; Rev. Joseph A. Serano, O.Praem., Treas.

Legal Title: Daylesford Abbey; Norbertine Fathers, Inc.

Fathers 22; Seminarians 1.

Properties Owned, Staffed or Sponsored: Chaplaincies 2; Parishes 1

Represented in the Archdiocese of Philadelphia.

St. Michael's Abbey: 19292 El Toro Rd., Silverado, CA 92676. Tel: 949-858-0222; Fax: 949-858-4583. Rt. Rev. Eugene J. Hayes, O.Praem., Abbot; Very Rev. Chrysostom A. Baer, O.Praem., Prior.

Legal Title: The Norbertine Fathers of Orange, Inc.

Priests 50; Brothers 1; Juniors: 25; Postulants: 3; Novices 5

Properties owned: St. Michael's Preparatory School, Silverado, CA; Summer Camp, Silverado, CA; Abbey, Silverado, CA.

Represented in the Archdiocese of Los Angeles and in the Diocese of Orange.

[0910] (O.M.I.)—OBLATES OF MARY IMMACULATE

General Administration: Casa Generalizia OMI, Via Aurelia 290 I, 00165, Roma, Italy, Most Rev. Luis Ignacio Rois Alonso, O.M.I., Supr. Gen.; Very Rev. Antoni Bochm, O.M.I., Vicar Gen.

United States Province (1999): Missionary Oblates of Mary Immaculate, Provincial Admin. Office, 391 Michigan Ave., N.E., Washington, DC 20017-1516. Tel: 202-529-4505; Fax: 202-529-4572. Rev. Louis Studer, O.M.I. Prov. Councilors: Rev. Raymond Cook, O.M.I.; Rev. Mark Dean, O.M.I.; Rev. Arthur Flores, O.M.I.; Rev. Emmanuel Mulenga, O.M.I.; Rev. José Antonio Ponce Diaz, O.M.I.

Fathers 190; Brothers 16; Scholastics 12

Ministries in Retreat Centers, Shrines, Parishes, Chaplaincies, Religious Residences and Houses and Retirement Centers.

Represented in the Archdioceses of Boston, Chicago, Galveston-Houston, Los Angeles, New Orleans, New York, St. Paul and Minneapolis, San Antonio and Washington and in the Dioceses of Belleville, Brownsville, Buffalo, Corpus Christi, Crookston, Duluth, Anchorage-Juneau, Laredo, Oakland, San Diego and Springfield in Illinois. Also in Brazil, Hong Kong, Mexico, Peru, Rome and Zambia.

[0920] (O.S.F.S.)—OBLATES OF ST. FRANCIS DE SALES

(Congregatio Oblatorum Sancti Francisci Salesii)

General Motherhouse: Via Dandolo 49, Rome, Italy, In July 1966, the American Province was renamed the Wilmington/Philadelphia Province, and the Toledo/Detroit Province was canonically established.

Wilmington-Philadelphia Province (1906): 2200 Kentmere Pkwy., Wilmington, DE 19806. Very Rev. John Kolodziej, O.S.F.S., Prov.; Very Rev. Michael Vannicola, O.S.F.S., Asst. Prov.; Provincial Councilors: Very Rev. Michael Murray, O.S.F.S.; Very Rev. Michael Vannicola, O.S.F.S.; Very Rev. Joseph Camfellone, O.S.F.S.; Bro. Daniel Wisniewski, O.S.F.S. Provincial Staff: Rev. Timothy McIntire, O.S.F.S., Dir. Assoc.; Rev. Robert Mazzoci, O.S.F.S., Dir. Prov. Admin. & Devel.; Rev. Michael J. McCue, O.S.F.S., Dir., De Sales Svc. Works; Rev. John E. McGee, O.S.F.S., Coord. Provincial Special Events. Chapter of the Whole; Rev. Joseph G. Morrissey, Mission Procurator, O.S.F.S.

Fathers 100; Brothers 7; Post-Novitiates 1

Properties owned, staffed or sponsored: Parishes 23; Universities 1; Houses of Study 1; Novitiates 1; High Schools 3; Chaplaincies 8; Foreign Missions 1; Middle Schools 1.

Represented in the Archdioceses of Boston, Military Services, Philadelphia and Washington and in the Dioceses of Allentown, Arlington, Camden, Charlotte, Lansing, Raleigh, Toledo, Venice and Wilmington. Also in Monaco.

Toledo-Detroit Province (1966): 2323 W. Bancroft St., Toledo, OH 43607. Tel: 419-724-9851; Tel: 734-657-7225. Very Rev. John J. Loughran, O.S.F.S., Prov.; Rev. Michael E. Newman, O.S.F.S., Asst. Prov. & Councilor; Rev. Ronald W. Olszewski, O.S.F.S., Treas.; Rev. John Kasper, O.S.F.S., Councilor; Rev. David Kenehan, O.S.F.S., Councilor.

Legal Title: Oblates of St. Francis de Sales, Inc.

Priests 34; Brothers 6; Scholastics: 2; Novices: 2

Ministries in Parishes; Schools; Chaplaincies; Missionaries; Senior Citizens Residence.

Properties owned, staffed or sponsored: Provincialate, Toledo, OH; St. Francis de Sales High School, Toledo, OH; Oblate Residence, Toledo, OH; Brisson Hall, Washington, DC; Salesian Studios, Buffalo, NY.

Represented in the Archdioceses of Detroit and Washington and in the Dioceses of Allentown, Arlington, Buffalo, Erie, Lansing, Oakland, Saginaw, Stockton, Toledo. Also in Mexico.

[0930] (O.S.J.)—OBLATES OF ST. JOSEPH

(Congregatio Oblatorum S. Joseph)

Founded in Italy in 1878. Founder: Saint Joseph Marello (1844-1895). Cause of Beatification introduced May 28, 1948; Beatified 1993; Canonized 2001. First foundation in U.S. in 1929.

Motherhouse: Corso Alfieri 384, Asti, Italy, General House: Via Boccea 364, Rome, Italy. Rev. Jan Pelczarski, O.S.J., Supr. Gen.; Very Rev. John Attulli, O.S.J., Vicar Gen.; Very Rev. Giocondo Bronzini, O.S.J., Procurator Gen.

Oblates of St. Joseph USA Province: 544 W. Cliff Dr., Santa Cruz, CA 95060. Tel: 831-457-1868; Fax: 831-457-1617. Very Rev. Matthew D. Spencer, O.S.J., Prov.

Priests 23; Brothers 2; Parishes 5; Shrine 1; Chapel 1; Community Houses 3; Novitiate 1; Youth Center 1.

Properties owned: St. Joseph's Oblate Religious House, Pittston, PA; Oblates Provincial Campus, Santa Cruz, CA; Mount St. Joseph, Loomis, CA.

Represented in the Dioceses of Fresno, Monterey, Sacramento and Scranton.

[0940] (O.M.V.)—OBLATES OF THE VIRGIN MARY

(Congregation of the Oblates of the Virgin Mary)
(Congregatio Oblatorum Beatae Mariae Virginis)

Generalate: Viale XXX Aprile, 00153, Rome, Italy, Very Rev. Luis Costantino, O.M.V., Rector Major.

St. Ignatius Province: 2 Ipswich St., Boston, MA 02215-3607. Tel: 617-536-4141; Web: www.omvusa.org. Email: office@omvusa.org. Very Rev. James Walther, O.M.V., Prov.

Priests in U.S. 44; Brothers 2

Ministries in Parishes; Hospital and Prison Chaplaincies; Retreats & Parish Missions; Novitiate; Community Houses; College Seminary; Shrine Chaplaincies.

Legal Holdings: St. Clement's Eucharistic Shrine, Boston, MA; St. Joseph House, Milton, MA; St. Ignatius Province of the Oblates of the Virgin Mary, Inc., Boston, MA.

Represented in the Archdioceses of Boston, Denver, and Los Angeles and in the Diocese Springfield in Illinois and Venice. Also in Cebu and Antipolo, Philippines.

[0950] (C.O.)—ORATORIANS

(Confederatio Oratorii S. Philippi Nerii)

A Confederation of Autonomous Houses first founded in Rome, 1575.

General Confederation: Via Di Parione, 33, 1-00186, Rome, Italy, Tel: (39) 06-689-25-37. Email: rhoratory@comporium.net. Rev. Michele Nicolis, C.O., Procurator Gen.; Rev. Marco Gullien, C.O., Delegate of the Holy See, Toronto, Canada.

The Oratory of Rock Hill: P.O. Box 11586, Rock Hill, SC 29731. Tel: 803-327-2097. Very Rev. Dr. Joseph F. Pearce, C.O., Provost.

Fathers 7; Brothers 2; Novices 2.

Represented in the Diocese of Charleston.

The Oratorian Community of Monterey: P.O. Box 1688, Monterey, CA 93942. Tel: 831-373-0476. Very Rev. Peter C. Sanders, Provost. & Major Supr.; Rev. Thomas A. Kieffer, Vicar & Sec.

Total in Community: 2

Oratorian Foundation Inc., Arizona, Yarnell, AZ 85362. An outreach of the Oratorian Community in Monterey.

Represented in the Diocese of Monterey.

The Pittsburgh Oratory: Congregation of the Oratory of St. Philip Neri, 4450 Bayard St., Pittsburgh, PA 15213-1506. Tel: 412-681-3181. Email: info@pittsburghoratory.org. The Very Rev. Michael J. Darcy, C.O., Provost; Rev. Joshua M. Kibler, C.O., Vice-Provost; Rev. Stephen W. Lowery, C.O., Campus Min.; Rev. Peter J. Gruber, C.O., Dir. Campus Ministry; Rev. Reed Frey, C.O., Campus Min.; Rev. Thomas Skamai, C.O., Campus Min.; Bro. Leo Dornan, C.O.; Bro. Kurt Kessler, C.O.

Fathers 6; Brothers 2

Represented in the Diocese of Pittsburgh.

The Oratory of Pharr: P.O. Box 1698, Pharr, TX 78577-1630. Tel: 956-843-8217; Fax: 956-843-2946. Very Rev. Leo Francis Daniels, C.O., Provost; Rev. Mario Alberto Aviles, C.O., Treas., Procurator Gen. & Sec.; Rev. Jose Encarnacion Losoya, C.O., Vicar; Rev. Jose Juan Ortiz, C.O.

Ministries in Parish work; Services to the poor; promotion of Mexican-American cultural services; Education at all levels; Spanish language communities.

Properties owned: Casa Maria of the Oratory, Pharr, TX; Oratory Academy-Academia Oratoriana, Pharr; TX; Oratory Athenaeum For University Preparation; Pharr Oratory of St. Philip Neri of Pontifical Right.

Represented in the Diocese of Brownsville. Also in Mexico.

Secular Oratory, Lay institute Founded by St. Philip Neri. Principal Work; Federacion Mexicana del Oratorio de San Felipe Neri, American Office, The Oratory, Rte. 4 Box 118, Pharr, TX 78577. The Pharr Oratory is a member of the Mexican Federation of Oratories and at present serves as the American office of all eleven houses.

The Oratory of St. Philip Neri: 64 Middagh St., Brooklyn, NY 11201. Tel: 718-875-2096. Very Rev. Anthony Andreassi, C.O., Provost; Rev. Dennis M. Corrado, C.O; Rev. Mark J. Lane, C.O; Rev. Michael J. Callaghan, C.O; Rev. Mark Paul Amatrucola, C.O.; Bro. James Simon, C.O.

Fathers 5; Brothers 1

The Raritan Congregation of the Oratory of St. Philip Neri: 45 Anderson St., Raritan, NJ 08869. Tel: 732-725-1008; Email: oratorians@raritanoratory.org; Web: www.raritanoratory.org. Very Rev. Jeffrey M. Calia, C.O., Provost; Rev. Peter R. Cebulka, C.O., Vicar; Rev. Thomas A. Odorizzi, C.O., Treas. & Sec.; Rev. Kevin Patrick Kelly, C.O.; Rev. John Fredy Triana Beltran, C.O.; Bro. Steven J. Bolton, C.O.

Priests 5; Seminarians 1

[0960] (F.S.R.)—BROTHERS OF THE CONGREGATION OF OUR LADY OF THE HOLY ROSARY

Founded in the United States in 1957.

General Motherhouse and Novitiate: 232 Sunnyside Dr., Reno, NV 89503-3510. Tel: 775-747-4441. Email: bros-reno@charter.net. Bro. Matthew Cunningham, F.S.R., Supr.; Bro. Philip Napolitano, F.S.R., Asst. Supr.

Brothers 3

Ministries in the field of Education and Pastoral Ministry.

Represented in the Diocese of Reno.

[0970] (O.DE.M)—ORDER OF OUR LADY OF MERCY

(Mercedarians Friars)

(Ordo de Beatae Mariae Virginis de Mercede)

Founded in Barcelona, Spain on August 10, 1218.

Generalate: Curia Generalizia dei PP Mercedari, Via Monte Carmelo 3 00166, Rome, Italy, Most Rev. Juan Carlos Saavedra Lucho, O.de.M., Master Gen.

U.S.A. Provincial Headquarters: Vicariate of Mary, Co-Redemptress, 6398 Drexel Rd., Philadelphia, PA 19151. Tel: 215-473-1669. Rev. Michael R. Rock, O.de.M., Vicar Prov.

Priests 19; Brothers 5

Ministries in Parishes, education, hospital and prison chaplaincies, retreats; Newman campus chaplaincies; mission word.

Properties owned: Monastery of Our Lady of Mercy, Philadelphia, PA; Saint Peter Nolasco Residence, St. Petersburg, FL.

Represented in the Archdiocese of Philadelphia and San Juan and in the Dioceses of Buffalo, Cleveland, St. Augustine and St. Petersburg. Also in South India.

[0975] (S.O.L.T.)—SOCIETY OF OUR LADY OF THE MOST HOLY TRINITY

International Headquarters: Our Lady of Corpus Christi, 1200 Lantana St., Corpus Christi, TX 78407. Tel: 361-289-9095; Fax: 361-289-0088. Rev. Peter Marsalek, S.O.L.T., Gen. Priest Servant; Very Rev. Anthony Blount, S.O.L.T., Vicar Servant; Rev. Fausto Rodel C. Malanyaon, S.O.L.T., 2nd Asst.

Regional Headquarters (American Region): Our Lady of Corpus Christi, 1200 Lantana St., Corpus Christi, TX 78007. Tel: 361-387-8090; Fax: 361-387-3818. Rev. Jerome Drolshagen, S.O.L.T., Regl. Supr.; Rev. Dennis Walsh, S.O.L.T., 1st Asst.; Rev. Mark Wendling, S.O.L.T., 2nd Asst., Vocation Dir.

Priests 82; Brothers 5; Permanent Deacons 1; Seminarians: 5

Pastoral Ministries: Parish Work, Migrant Ministries, Native Americans, Marian Shrine, Hospital Chaplaincies, Prison Chaplaincies, Military Chaplaincy, Retreat Houses, Schools, Nursing Homes, Youth Work, Marian Shrines and specialized ministries. Community Houses. Houses of the Sick and Infirm. Houses of Formation: Novitiate and House of Studies.

Represented in the Archdioceses of Atlanta, Detroit, Santa Fe and in the Dioceses of Corpus Christi, Fargo, Kansas City-St. Joseph, Paterson, Phoenix, Portland (In Maine) and Pueblo.

[0990] (S.A.C.)—SOCIETY OF THE CATHOLIC APOSTOLATE

(Pallottines)

Generalate: Pallottines, Piazza S.V. Pallotti 204 00186, Rome, Italy,

Irish Province (1909): Mother of Divine Love Province, Pallotine Fathers, Sandyford Rd., Dundrum, Dublin 16, Ireland, Rev. Liam McClarey, S.A.C., Prov.

Province of the Immaculate Conception (Eastern) (1953): 204 Raymond Ave., P.O. Box 979, South Orange, NJ 07079. Tel: 201-943-0972. Email: frpeter@

nj.rr.com. Very Rev. Peter T. Sticco, S.A.C., Prov.; Rev. Frank Donio, S.A.C., Vicar Prov. Consultors: Bro. James Beamesderfer, S.A.C., Sec.; Rev. Frank Amato, S.A.C., Bursar; Rev. Bernard P. Carman, S.A.C.

Fathers 12; Professed Brothers 2

Properties owned, sponsored or staffed: Parishes 2; Seminary; High School; Novitiate; St. Jude Shrine, Pallottine Center for Apostolic Causes.

Represented in the Archdioceses of Baltimore, Newark and Washington and in the Diocese of Camden.

Mother of God Province (1946): Pallottine Fathers and Brothers, Inc., 5424 W. Blue Mound Rd., Milwaukee, WI 53208. Tel: 414-259-0688; Fax: 414-258-9314. Email: pallotti.milw@pallottines.org; Vocations Email: vocationspall@gmail.com. Very Rev. Davies Edassery, S.A.C., Prov.; Bro. James Scarpace, S.A.C., Consultor; Rev. Joseph Dominic, S.A.C., 1st Consultor.

Fathers 16; Brothers 1; Parishes 12

Ministries in Parishes; Retreat House; High School.

Represented in the Archdiocese of Milwaukee and in the Diocese of Springfield in Illinois.

U.S. Delegature (Irish Province): 3352 4th St., P.O. Box 249, Wyandotte, MI 48192. Rev. Michael O'Sullivan, S.A.C., Prov. Delegate; Rev. Brendan McCarrick, S.A.C., Mission Dir.

Fathers 7; Brothers 1; Parishes 4; Missions 3.

Represented in the Archdiocese of Detroit and in the Diocese of Fort Worth.

Mother of Divine Love Province (1909): The Pallottine Fathers, Sandyford Rd., Dundrum, Dublin 16, Ireland. Rev. Jeremiah Murphy Sac, Prov.

U.S. Foundation: Our Lady of Mt. Carmel Shrine and Church, 448 E. 116th, New York, NY 10029. Tel: 212-534-0681.

Fathers 7; Parishes 3.

Represented in the Archdiocese of New York and in the Dioceses of Albany and Pensacola-Tallahassee.

Infant Jesus Delegature of Annunciation Province: Mission House and Infant Jesus Shrine, 3452 Niagara Falls Blvd., North Tonawanda, NY 14120-0563. Rev. Slawomir Siok, S.A.C., Supr. & Prov. Delegate.

Priests 15

Represented in the Archdiocese of New York and in the Dioceses of Brooklyn, Buffalo, Columbus and Venice.

[1000] (C.P.)—CONGREGATION OF THE PASSION

(Congregatio Passionis Jesu Christi)

Founded in Italy in 1720 by St. Paul of the Cross. First foundation in the United States in 1852.

Generalate: SS. Giovani e Paolo Monastery, Rome 00184, Italy. Most Rev. Joachim Rego, C.P., Supr. Gen.

St. Paul of the Cross Province (Eastern): Passionist Provincial Office, 111 South Ridge St., Ste. 302, Rye Brook, NY 10573. Very Rev. James O'Shea, C.P., Prov.; Very Rev. Salvatore Enzo Del Brocco, C.P., 1st Consultor; Very Rev. James Price, C.P., 2nd Consultor; Very Rev. William Murphy, C.P., 3rd Consultor; Very Rev. Hugo Esparza-Perez, C.P., 4th Consultor; Rev. David Monaco, C.P., Treas.

Legal Title: St. Paul's Benevolent, Educational and Missionary Institute; Passionist Missions, Inc.; Passionist Missionaries, Inc.

Bishops 1; Fathers 87; Brothers 16; Confrater 1; Novices 2.

Properties owned, sponsored or staffed: Parishes 11; Monasteries 4; Retreat Houses 5; Schools 3; Residence 4; Houses of Study 1.

Represented in the Archdioceses of Atlanta, Chicago, Hartford, New York, San Francisco, Santa Fe and San Juan and in the Dioceses of Arecibo, Brooklyn, Palm Beach, Pittsburgh, Raleigh, St. Louis, Scranton, and Springfield in Massachusetts. Also in Canada, Haiti and Jamaica.

Holy Cross Province (Western): Passionist Provincial Office, 660 Busse Highway, Park Ridge, IL 60068. Tel: 847-518-8844. Rev. Joseph Moons, C.P., Prov. Consultors: Rev. David Colhour, C.P., Consultor; Rev. James Strommer, C.P., Prov. Consultor; Rev. Philip Paxton, C.P., Consultor; Rev. Alfredo Ocampo, C.P., Consultor.

Legal Title: The Congregation of the Passion, Holy Cross Province.

Fathers 31; Brothers 6; Deacons 1

Properties owned or sponsored: Passionist Provincial Office; St. Vincent Strambi Passionist Community, Chicago, IL; Retreat Centers 4.

Represented in the Archdioceses of Chicago, Detroit, Galveston-Houston, Los Angeles and Louisville and in the Dioceses of Birmingham and Sacramento.

[1010] (O.S.P.P.E.)—PAULINE FATHERS

(Ordo Sancti Pauli Primi Eremitae)

Founded in Hungary in the 13th Century. First foundation in the United States in 1953.

General Motherhouse: Ojcowie Paulini - Jasna Gora, ul. Kordeckiego 2 42-225, Czestochowa, Poland, Email: osppe@jasnagora.pl. Rev. Arnold Chrapkowski, O.S.P.P.E., Gen. Supr.

American Provincial Motherhouse (1984): Shrine of Our Lady of Czestochowa, Pauline Fathers Monastery, Beacon Hill, P.O. Box 2049, 654 Ferry Rd., Doylestown, PA 18901. Tel: 215-345-0600; Fax: 215-348-2148; Email: info@czestochowa.us; Web: www.czestochowa.us. Rev. Tadeusz Lizinczyk, O.S.P.P.E., Prov.; Rev. Krzysztof Drybka, O.S.P.P.E., Prior; Rev. Edward Raymond Volz, O.S.P.P.E., Shrine Dir.

Priests in U.S: 25; Brothers 5

Represented in the Archdioceses of Chicago, New York and Philadelphia and in the Dioceses of Buffalo, Greensburg, Orlando and Norwich.

[1020] (S.S.P.)—PAULINE FATHERS AND BROTHERS

(Society of St. Paul for the Apostolate of Communications)

Corporate Name: Pious Society of St. Paul

General Motherhouse: Via Alessandro Severo, 58 00145, Rome, Italy, Very Rev. Valdir DeCastro, S.S.P., Supr. Gen.; Very Rev. Vito Fracchiolla, S.S.P., Vicar Gen.

United States Province (1932): Pious Society of St. Paul, 2187 Victory Blvd., Staten Island, NY 10314. Tel: 718-761-0047. Rev. Tony Bautista, S.S.P., Personal Delegate of the Superior General; Bro. Marco Bulgarelli, S.S.P., Sec.

Legal Title: Pious Society of St. Paul, Inc.

Priests 4; Brothers 9

Represented in the Archdioceses of Chicago and New York and in the Diocese of Youngstown.

Los Angeles Province: 112 S. Herbert Ave., Los Angeles, CA 90063. Tel: 323-269-5010; Fax: 323-268-4583. Rev. Marco Antonio Vences, S.S.P., Supr.; Rev. Francisco M. Rosas Zevada, S.S.P; Rev. Tomas Martinez, S.S.P.

Priests 5

Miami Province: Society of St. Paul, 8455 S.W. 2nd St., Miami, FL 33144. Tel: 305-480-5377; Web: www.sanpablomia.com. Rev. Arnulfo Gomez, S.S.P., Supr.; Bro. Salvador Ramirez, M.S.S.P., Admin.

Priests 3

[1030] (C.S.P.)—PAULIST FATHERS

(Societas Missionaria a S. Paulo Apostolo)

Paulist Fathers Generalate (1858): 415 W. 59th St., New York, NY 10019. Tel: 212-757-8072. Very Rev. René I. Constanza, C.S.P.

Legal Titles: Missionary Society of St. Paul the Apostle in the State of New York; The Missionary Society of St. Paul the Apostle in the State of California; Missionary Society of St. Paul the Apostle in Massachusetts; Paulist Productions; Paulist Pictures; Paulist Religious Property Trust; Paulist Press; Paulist Mission Trust; Paulist Foundation, Inc.

Fathers 96; Students in Major Seminary: 6

Sponsored Ministries: Paulist Evangelization Ministries; Paulist Reconciliation Ministries; Paulist Ecumenical and Interfaith Relations.

Represented in the Archdioceses of Boston, Chicago, Los Angeles, Newark, New York, San Francisco and Washington and in the Dioceses of Albany, Austin, Brooklyn, Grand Rapids, Knoxville, Oakland and Palm Beach. Also in Rome.

[1040] (SCH.P.)—PIARIST FATHERS

(Ordo Clericorum Regularum Pauperum Matris Dei Scholarum Piarum)

General Motherhouse: San Pantaleo, Piazza De Massimi, 00186, 4, Rome, Italy, Very Rev. Pedro Aguado, Sch.P., Supr. Gen.

Province of the United States of America and Puerto Rico (2011): 1339 Monroe St., N.E., Washington, DC 20017-2510. Tel: 202-529-7734; Tel: 787-309-5520; Fax: 954-771-8060; Email: fernandonegroschp@gmail.com; Web: www.piarist.info. Very Rev. Fernando Negro, Sch.P., Prov. Supr.

Bishops 1; Priests 35; Deacons 2; Professed Seminarians: 13; Pre-Novices 4.

Legal Titles and Holdings: Piarist Fathers-U.S.A. Province, Inc., Washington, DC; Piarist Fathers, Inc.; Order of the Pious Schools, Inc., Washington, DC; Piarist Fathers House of Studies, Washington, DC; Piarist Fathers, Queen of Pious Schools, Inc., Washington, D.C.; The Piarist School, Martin, KY; Piarist Fathers Residence, Prestonsburg, KY; Devon Preparatory School, Devon, PA; Calasanzian Fathers, New York, NY; Casa Calasanz, Miami, FL; Colegio Calasanz, San Juan, PR; Santisimo Salvador, San Juan, PR.

Represented in the Archdioceses of Miami, New York, Philadelphia, San Juan and Washington and in the Dioceses of Lexington and Ponce.

New York-Puerto Rico Vice Province: 1900 Road 14, Coto Laurel, PR 00780-2147. Tel: 787-309-5520; Fax: 954-776-8060. Very Rev. Fernando Negro, Sch.P., Prov. Supr.

Bishops 1; Priests 15; Deacons 1; Pre-Novices 1; Houses 5; House of Formation 2; Parishes 3; High Schools 3; Elementary Schools 3.

Represented in the Archdioceses of New York and San Juan and in the Diocese of Ponce. Also Calasanzian Fathers and Padres Escolapios de P.R.

Piarist Fathers Californias Vice Province, 3940 Perry St., Los Angeles, CA 90063-1174. Tel: 424-208-4223; Fax: 323-266-4907. Rev. Hilario Flores, Sch.P., Vice Prov. Email: hilof@yahoo.com. Rev. John Callan, Sch.P. Email: jgcallan@bellsouth.net. Tel: 954-552-9048.

Priests 18; Brothers 1; Seminarians: 7

Properties owned, staffed or sponsored: Parishes 7; Grammar Schools 2; High School 1; Houses of Formation 2.

Represented in the Archdiocese of Los Angeles and in the Diocese of San Diego.

[1050] (PIME)—PONTIFICAL INSTITUTE FOR FOREIGN MISSIONS, INC.

General Motherhouse: Via Monte Rosa 81, 20149, Milan, Italy, Very Rev. Ferruccio Brambillasca, PIME, Supr. Gen.

U.S. Delegation: 17330 Quincy Ave., Detroit, MI 48221. Tel: 313-342-4066; Fax: 313-342-6816. Email: secretary@pimeusa.org. Rev. Kenneth Mazur, PIME, U.S. Supr. & Pres.

Fathers 10

Legal Titles and Holdings: PIME Missionaries - PIME Mission Center; PIME College Community, Detroit, MI; PIME Missionaries

Mission Houses 1.

Represented in the Archdioceses of Boston, Detroit and New York.

[1060] (C.PP.S.)—SOCIETY OF THE PRECIOUS BLOOD

(Congregatio Missionariorum Pretiosissimi Sanguinis Domini Nostri Jesu Christi)

General Motherhouse: Viale di Porta Ardeatina 66, I-00154 Rome, Italy, Very Rev. Emanuele Lupi, C.PP.S., Moderator Gen.

Cincinnati Province: 431 E. Second St., Dayton, OH 45402. Tel: 937-228-9263; Email: prodirsec@cpps-preciousblood.org.

Kansas City Province: 2130 Saint Gaspar Way, Liberty, MO 64069-0339. Tel: 816-781-4344; Fax: 816-781-3639. Email: prodirsec@preciousbloodkc.org.

Atlantic Province: Society of the Precious Blood, Atlantic Province, 1261 Highland Ave., Rochester, NY 14620. Tel: 585-244-2692.

United States Province: 431 E. Second St., Dayton, OH 45402. Tel: 937-228-9263; Email: prodirsec@cppspreciousblood.org. Very Rev. Jeffrey S. Kirch, C.PP.S, Prov. Dir. Provincial Council: Rev. Joseph Nassal, C.PP.S.; Rev. Benjamin Berinti, C.PP.S.; Rev. Ron Will, C.PP.S.; Bro. Daryl Charron, C.PP.S., Rev. William Nordenbrock, C.PP.S., Prov. Sec./Treas.

Bishops 1, Fathers 100; Brothers 18; Students in Major Seminaries 1

Ministries in Parishes; Missions; Chaplaincies; Shrine; Education; Retreat Preaching; Community Houses; Mission Houses; Precious Blood Ministry of Reconciliation.

Represented in the Archdioceses of Chicago, Cincinnati, Indianapolis, Kansas City, Milwaukee, and San Francisco and in the Dioceses of Cleveland, Columbus, Davenport, Detroit, Des Moines, Fort Wayne-South Bend, Gary, Joliet in Illinois, Kansas City-St. Joseph, Lafayette-in-Indiana, Orlando, Oakland, Phoenix, San Angelo, Toledo and Wichita.

Provincial House: 13313 Niagara Pkwy., L2G 0P8, Niagara Falls, Canada, Tel: 905-382-1118. Email: rpwiecek@aol.com. Rev. John A. Colacino, C.PP.S., Vice Prov.

Priests in the U.S: 4

Represented in the Archdioceses of Boston and San Francisco and in the Dioceses of Albany, Oakland, Orlando and Rochester. Also in Canada.

[1065] (F.S.S.P.)—PRIESTLY FRATERNITY OF ST. PETER

Founded in Switzerland in 1988. First foundation in United States in 1991.

General House: Fraternitas Sacerdotalis Sancti Petri, Maison St. Pierre Canisius, Chemin du Schoenberg 8, CH-1700 Fribourg, Switzerland, Tel: 41-26-488-0037; Fax: 41-26-488-0038. Very Rev. Andrzej Komorowski, F.S.S.P., Supr. Gen.

International Seminary: Priesterseminar Sankt Petrus, Kirchstrasse 16, D-88145, Opfenbach-Wigratzbad, Germany, Tel: 49-8385 9221 0; Fax: 49-8385 9221 33. Rev. Vincent Ribeton, F.S.S.P., Rector.

U.S. Headquarters: Priestly Fraternity of St. Peter-North American Provincial Headquarters, 450 Venard Rd., South Abington Township, PA 18411. Email: info@fssp.com; Tel: 570-842-4000; Fax: 570-319-9770. Very Rev. William Lawrence, F.S.S.P., Prov. Supr.; Rev. Matthew Vierno, F.S.S.P., Prov. Sec.; Rev. Gregory Pendergraft, F.S.S.P., Prov. Bursar; Rev. Zachary Akers, F.S.S.P., Dir.-Devel.

House of Formation: Our Lady of Guadalupe Seminary, 7880 W. Denton Rd., P.O. Box 147, Denton, NE 68339. Tel: 402-797-7700; Fax: 402-797-7705; Email: seminary@fsspolgs.org; Web: www.fsspolgs.org. Very Rev. Josef Bisig, F.S.S.P., Rector; Rev. Robert Ferguson, F.S.S.P; Rev. Joseph Lee, F.S.S.P; Rev. Gregory Eichman, F.S.S.P; Rev. Charles Ryan, F.S.S.P; Rev. Rhone Lillard, F.S.S.P; Rev. Benoit Guichard, F.S.S.P.; Rev. Anthony Uy, F.S.S.P.

Priests 8; Seminarians 75

Properties owned or sponsored: Houses 41.

Represented in the Archdioceses of Atlanta, Baltimore, Cincinnati, Denver, Galveston-Houston, Indianapolis, Kansas City, Los Angeles, Oklahoma City, Omaha, St. Paul-Minneapolis and Seattle and in the Dioceses of Allentown, Boise, Colorado Springs, Dallas, El Paso, Fort Wayne-South Bend, Fort Worth, Fresno, Harrisburg, Joliet, Lexington, Lincoln, Little Rock, Manchester, Orlando, Paterson, Phoenix, Rapid City, Richmond, Sacramento, San Diego, Scranton, Springfield (IL), Tulsa, Tyler, Venice and Youngstown. Also Canada.

[1070] (C.Ss.R.)—REDEMPTORIST FATHERS

(Congregatio Sanctissimi Redemptoris-Redemptorist)

Generalate: Sant' Alfonso, Via Merulana 31. C.P. 2458 I-00100, Rome, Italy, Rev. Michael Brehl, C.Ss.R., Supr. Gen.; Rev. Alberto Eseverri, C.Ss.R., Vicar Gen.; Rev. John C. Vargas, C.Ss.R., Procurator.

Province of Baltimore (1850): Provincial Residence, 3112 7th St., N.E., Washington, DC 20017. Tel: 202-529-4410; Fax: 718-306-6014. Email: secprovince@redemptorists.net. Very Rev. Paul J. Borowski, C.Ss.R., Prov. Supr.; Rev. Gerard J. Knapp, C.Ss.R., Prov. Vicar; Rev. Matthew Allman, C.Ss.R.; Rev. Henry Sattler, C.Ss.R., Sec. & Treas.; Rev. Gerard Knapp, C.Ss.R., Rector.

Bishops 2; Priests 130; Brothers 9; Postulants 2; Students in Vows 3

Properties owned, staffed or sponsored: Parishes 21; Residences 4; Retreat Houses 2; Community Houses 27.

Represented in the Dioceses of Charleston, Charlotte, and Orlando.

Redemptorist Office for Mission Advancement: 107 Duke of Gloucester St., Annapolis, MD 21401-2526. Tel: 410-990-1680; Tel: 877-876-7662.

The Redemptorists Denver Province (1996): Redemptorist Provincial Offices, 1633 N. Cleveland Ave., Chicago, IL 60614. Tel: 312-248-8894; Fax: 312-248-8852. Email: provincial@redemptorists-denver.org; Web: www.redemptoristsdenver.org. Very Rev. Kevin Zubel, C.Ss.R., Prov. Supr.; Rev. Aaron Meszaros, C.Ss.R., Prov. Vicar; Rev. Anthony Nguyen, C.Ss.R., Prov. Consultor; Rev. Gregory May, C.Ss.R., Treas.; Rev. John Steingraeber, C.Ss.R., Asst. Treas.

Cardinal 1; Priests 111; Permanent Deacons 2; Brothers 17; Seminarians 4.

Legal Titles: The Redemptorists/Denver Province; The Redemptorists of Denver, Colorado; The Redemptorists of Greeley, Colorado, Inc.; Redemptorist Fathers (Idaho); Redemptorists Society of Oregon; The Society of the Redemptorists of the City Grand Rapids, Michigan; The Redemptorists of Nebraska; Redemptorists of Hamtramck; The Redemptorist Fathers of Hennepin County; Redemptorist Fathers (St. Louis); The Redemptorist Fathers of Kansas City, Missouri; The Redemptorists of Blessed Sacrament; The Redemptorist Fathers of Chicago; Redemptorist Society of Alaska; The Redemptorist Society of Arizona; The Redemptorists Society of Washington; Palisades Retreat Association, A School of Christian Living; The Redemptorist Community of Wichita, Kansas, Inc.; Society of the Redemptorist Fathers of Wichita, Kansas; Redemptorist Fathers of St. Alphonsus Parish of Chicago; Redemptorist Fathers of Iowa; Redemptorists of Berkeley; Redemptorists of Oakland; Redemptorists of Whittier; The Redemptorists of Glenview, Illinois; Redemptorist Fathers, d/b/a Liguori Publications; Holy Redeemer Center; Redemptorist Society of California; Redemptorist Theology Residence; Redemptorist Hispanic Ministry, Inc.; Liguori Mission House/Redemptorists; St. Clement Health Care Center; St. John Neumann House; Our Mother of Perpetual Help Retreat House of Oconomowoc, Wisc. Inc., d/b/a/ Redemptorist Retreat Center; Redemptorist Social Services Center, Inc.; Redemptorists of Mattese; Redemptorist Fathers of Bellaire, Texas; The Redemptorists/San Antonio; The Society of Redemptorists; Redemptorist Vice-Provincialate of New Orleans; Redemptorist Fathers of Baton Rouge, Inc.; The Redemptorists of the South Endowment Fund, Inc.; The Redemptorist Education and Formation Foundation, Inc.; Redemptorists of Tennessee; Redemptorist Vietnamese Ministry; Redemptorists of Mississippi; Redemptorists of Greenwood; North American Redemptorist Theology Residence; Redemptorist Vice Province Initiative; Redemptorist Apostolic Works.

Properties owned, sponsored or staffed: Parishes 14; Retreat Houses 2; National Shrine 1; Community Houses 15.

Represented in the Archdioceses of Chicago, Galveston-Houston, Los Angeles, Milwaukee, New Orleans, San Antonio, St. Louis, St. Paul-Minneapolis and Seattle and in the Dioceses of Baton Rouge, Grand Rapids, Kansas City-St. Joseph and Tucson. Also in Foreign Missions.

Manaus Vice-Province: Redentoristas, Caixa Postal 217, 69011-970 Manaus-AM, Amazonas, Brazil, Very Rev. José Amarildo Luciano da Silva, C.Ss.R., Vice Prov. Supr.

Vice Province of Nigeria: Sts. Michael, Raphael & Gabriel Church, P.O. Box 541, Satellite Town, Lagos State, Nigeria, Very Rev. Michael Chukwuyem Emerue, C.Ss.R., Vice Prov. Supr.

[1080] (C.R.)—CONGREGATION OF THE RESURRECTION

(Congregatio a Resurrectione Domini Nostri Jesu Christi)

Generalate: Via San Sebastianello 11 00187, Rome, Italy, Very Rev. Paul Voisin, C.R. Supr. Gen.

U.S.A. Province: 3601 N. California Ave., Chicago, IL 60618-4602. Tel: 773-463-7506. Very Rev. Steven Bartczyszyn, C.R., Prov. Supr.; Very Rev. Steve Thoma, C.R., Vicar Prov. Supr. Councilors: Rev. Jerzy Zieba, C.R.; Rev. Tomasz Wojciechowski, C.R.; Rev. Joseph Glab, C.R.

Fathers 42; Brothers 3

Ministries in Parishes; Missions; High School; Chaplaincies; University.

Represented in the Archdioceses of Chicago, Los Angeles, Louisville, Mobile and St. Louis and in the Dioceses of Belleville, Joliet, Kalamazoo, Rockford and San Bernardino.

Seminary House: 4252 W. Pine Blvd., Saint Louis, MO 63108. Tel: 314-652-8814. Rev. Gary Hogan, C.R., Rector.

[1090] (R.C.J.)—ROGATIONIST FATHERS

(Congregatio Rogationis-a-Corde-Jesu)

Generalate: via Tuscolana 167 00182, Rome, Italy, Very Rev. Bruno Rampazzo, R.C.J., Supr. Gen.

U.S.A. Delegation: 2688 S. Newmark Ave., P.O. Box 37, Sanger, CA 93657. Tel: 559-875-5808; Tel: 559-875-2025; Fax: 559-875-2618. Rev. Antonio Fiorenza, R.C.J., Delegation Supr.

U.S. Foundations: St. Mary's Church, 828 O St., P.O. Box 335, Sanger, CA 93657. Tel: 559-875-2025. Rev. John Bruno, R.C.J; Rev. Rene Panlasigui, R.C.J.; Rev. Edwin Manio, R.C.J.

St. Elisabeth Church, 6635 Tobias Ave., Van Nuys, CA 91405. Tel: 818-779-1756. Rev. Antonio Fiorenza, R.C.J.; Rev. Shinto Sebastian, R.C.J.; Rev. Dileep Sebastian, R.C.J.; Rev. Mark Destura, R.C.J.; Bro. Eduardo Rodriguez.

Legal Title: Congregation of Rogationists, Inc.

Priests 4

Ministries in Parishes; Vocation Center; Formation House; Social Service Center.

Represented in the Archdiocese of Los Angeles and in the Diocese of Fresno.

[1100] (S.C.)—BROTHERS OF THE SACRED HEART

(Societas Fratrum Sacris Cordis)

Founded in Lyon, France in 1821 by Rev. André Coindre.First foundation in the United States in Mobile, AL in 1847.

Generalate: Piazza del Sacro Cuore, No. 3, 00151, Rome, Italy, Bro. Mark Hilton, S.C., Supr. Gen.

Provincial Office: 4600 Elysian Fields Ave., New Orleans, LA 70122. Tel: 504-301-4758; Fax: 504-301-4843. Bro. Ronald Hingle, S.C., Prov. Supr.; Prov. Councilors: Bro. Barry Landry, S.C.; Bro. Ivy LeBlanc, S.C., Treas.; Bro. Clifford King, S.C., Sec.; Bro. Michael Migacz, S.C., Vocation Dir.; Mission Procurator: Bro. Henry Gaither, S.C.

Legal Title: The Province of the United States of the Brothers of the Sacred Heart, Inc., (a Delaware Corporation); Brothers of the Sacred Heart of New England, Inc.; Brothers of the Sacred Heart of New Orleans, Inc.; Brothers of the Sacred Heart of New Jersey/New York, Inc.; Brothers of the Sacred Heart Foundation, Inc.; Father André Coindre Charitable Trust; The Charles Lwanga Charitable Trust, 4600 Elysian Fields Ave., New Orleans, LA 70122. Tel: 504-301-4758; Fax: 504-301-4843; Email: Bileblancsc@gmail.com. Bro. Ivy LeBlanc, S.C., Exec. Dir.

Brothers 112; Novice 1; Ordained Brothers 4

Brothers of the Sacred Heart Foreign Missions: 4600 Elysian Fields Ave., New Orleans, LA 70122. Tel: 504-301-4758; Fax: 504-301-4843. Bro. Ronald Hingle, S.C., Prov. Supr.; Bro. Henry Gaither, S.C., Mission Procurator.

Brothers in Eastern and Southern Africa: 45; Brothers in Philippines: 18; Brothers in Mozambique: 11.

The Brothers of the Sacred Heart have mission schools and other establishments in 30 countries around the world, including the following with historical ties to the U.S.: Kenya, Lesotho, Mozambique, Philippines, Uganda, Zambia and Zimbabwe.

[1110] (M.S.C.)—MISSIONARIES OF THE SACRED HEART

(Societas Missionarii Sacratissimi Cordis Jesu)

General Motherhouse: Via Asmara 11 00199, Rome, Italy, Very Rev. Mark McDonald, M.S.C., Supr. Gen.

United States Province (1939): 305 S. Lake St., P.O. Box 270, Aurora, IL 60507. Tel: 630-892-8400; Tel: 630-892-2371; Fax: 630-892-1678. Web: www.misacor-usa.org. Very Rev. Richard Kennedy, M.S.C., Prov. Supr.; Rev. Stephen Boland, M.S.C., Treas. Religious Serving in Colombia: Very Rev. Hugo Londono, M.S.C., Section Supr.; Very Rev. German Barona Monsalve, M.S.C.; Rev. Tito Abdenago Medina Mora, M.S.C.; Rev. Favio Castro Andino, M.S.C.; Rev. Dario Moreno Endiso, M.S.C.; Rev. Miguel Henry Piamba, M.S.C., Rev. Jairo Alexander Palacios, M.S.C.; Rev. Juan Romero, M.S.C.; Bro. Geovany Quintero, M.S.C.; Bro. Diego Lagos, M.S.C.; Bro. Raul Perez, M.S.C.; Bro. Antonio Posadas, M.S.C.; Bro. Guillermo Aza, M.S.C.; Bro. Ricardo Perdomo, M.S.C.; Bro. Cristian Puliche, M.S.C. Religious Serving in Rome, Italy: Rev. Michael Miller, M.S.C.; Religious Serving in Fiji Islands: Bro. Warren Perrotto, M.S,C.

Legal Title: Society of the Missionaries of the Sacred Heart.

Fathers 42; Brothers 9; Professed Students: 4

Properties owned, staffed or sponsored: Residential Houses 3; Parishes 15; Chaplaincies 1.

Represented in the Archdioceses of Chicago and Philadelphia and in the Dioceses of Allentown, Ogdensburg, Pensacola-Tallahassee, Rockford and San Bernardino. Also in Colombia and Italy.

U.S. Section of the Irish Province for California and Southern States: Sectional Hqtrs, 123 W. Laurel, San Antonio, TX 78212-4667. Tel: 210-226-5514; Fax: 210-226-5725. Sectional Leadership Team Rev. Kevin Shanahan, M.S.C., Supr.; Rev. William Collins, M.S.C.; Rev. Michael Fitzgibbon, M.S.C.

Priests 11

Represented in the Archdiocese of San Antonio and in the Dioceses of Austin and Charleston.

[1120] (M.SS.CC.)—MISSIONARIES OF THE SACRED HEARTS OF JESUS AND MARY

(Missionarii a Sacris Cordibus Jesus et Mariae)

Founded in Italy in 1833.

General Motherhouse: Via dei Falegnami 23, Rome, Italy, Very Rev. Luigi Toscano, M.SS.CC., Supr. Gen.

American Headquarters: 2249 Shore Rd., Linwood, NJ 08221. Tel: 609-927-5600; Fax: 609-927-5262. Email: msscusa@aol.com. Rev. Frederick Clement, M.SS.CC; Rev. John Perdue, M.SS.CC; Rev. Damian Anumba, M.SS.CC; Rev. Prashanth Lobo, M.SS.CC; Bro. David Graber, M.SS.CC.

Legal Title: Missionaries of the Sacred Heart of Jesus and Mary.

Priests 9; Brothers 2

Represented in the Dioceses of Camden and Harrisburg.

[1130] (S.C.J.)—CONGREGATION OF THE PRIESTS OF THE SACRED HEART

(Priests of the Sacred Heart)

(Congregazione Dei Sacredoti Del a Cuore di Gesu)

General Motherhouse: Curia Generale, S.C.J., Via Casale S. Pio V, 20 00165, Rome, Italy, Very Rev. Carlos Luis Suarez Codorniú, S.C.J., Supr. Gen.

United States Province (1933): Provincialate Offices, P.O. Box 289, Hales Corners, WI 53130-0289. Tel: 414-425-6910. Email: provsec@usprovince.org. Very Rev. Vien Nguyen, S.C.J., Prov. Supr.

Bishops 1; Priests 56; Clerics 6; Brothers 13; Deacons 1.

Represented in the Archdioceses of Galveston-Houston and Milwaukee and in the Dioceses of Jackson, Rapid City, St. Petersburg and Sioux Falls.

[1140] (SS.CC.)—CONGREGATION OF THE SACRED HEARTS OF JESUS AND MARY

(Congregatio Sacrorum Cordium)

General Motherhouse: Casa Generalizia-Padri Dei Sacri Cuori-Via, Rivarone 85 00166, Rome, Italy, Very Rev. Alberto Toutin Cataldo, SS.CC., Supr. Gen.

Legal Title: Congregation of the Sacred Hearts of Jesus and Mary.

United States Province: Provincial Administration Office, Box 111, Fairhaven, MA 02719- 0111. Tel: 508-993-2442; Fax: 508-996-5499.

Provincial House: Box 1365, Kaneohe, Oahu, HI 96744. Tel: 808-247-5035; Fax: 808-235-8849. Rev. Lane Akiona, SS.CC., Prov. Supr.; Rev. Robert Charlton, SS.CC., Vicar; Councilors: Rev. Stephen Banjare, SS.CC.; Rev. Richard Danyluk, SS.CC.; Rev. Edward Popish, SS.CC.

Priests 37; Brothers 8

Properties owned or staffed: Parishes 12; Community Houses 4; Houses of Formation 2.

Represented in Dioceses of Brownsville, Fall River and Honolulu.

U.S. West Region of the U.S. Province: Congregation of the Sacred Hearts of Jesus and Mary, 2150 Damien Ave., La Verne, CA 91750. Tel: 909-593-5441; Fax: 909-593-3971. Rev. Richard J. Danyluk, SS.CC., Regional Supr.

Priests 17

Ministries in the field of Religious and Academic Education; Parishes; Chaplaincies.

Represented in the Archdiocese of Los Angeles and in the Dioceses of Orange and San Bernardino.

[1145] (F.SS.R.)—CONGREGATION OF THE SONS OF THE MOST HOLY REDEEMER

Motherhouse: Golgotha Monastery Island, Papa Stronsay, KW172AR Orkney Isles, Scotland.

U.S. Headquarters: 72 Redshale Ln., Forsyth, MT 59327. Tel: 406-557-2444; Email: fr.yousef@the-sons.org. Rev. Michael Mary Sim, F.SS.R., Rector Major. Rev. Yousef Marie Abdel-Ahad, F.SS.R., Rector.

Legal Title: Transalpine Redemptorist Inc.

Represented in the Diocese of Great-Falls Billings. Also in Scotland and New Zealand.

[1150] (C.S.J.)—CONGREGATION OF ST. JOSEPH

(Congregatio Sancti Joseph)

Founded in Turin, Italy in 1873. First foundation in United States in 1951.

General Motherhouse: Via Belvedere Montello 77, 00166, Rome, Italy, Rev. Mario Aldegani, C.S.J., Supr. Gen.

U.S. and Mexico Vice Province: St. Leonard House, 4076 Case Rd., Avon, OH 44011. Tel: 440-934-6270. Rev. Roberto Landa, C.S.J., Prov. Supr.

Priests 21; Brothers 1; Scholastics: 15

Properties owned, staffed or sponsored: Parishes 5; High Schools 1; Youth Retreat Center.

Properties owned: St. Leonard House, Avon, OH.

Represented in the Archdiocese of Los Angeles and in the Diocese of Cleveland. Also in Mexico.

[1160] (F.S.P.)—BROTHERS OF ST. PATRICK

(Patrician Brothers)

Founded in Ireland 1808 by Bishop Daniel Delaney.

U.S. Foundation (1948): St. Patrick's Novitiate, 7820 Bolsa Ave., Midway City, CA 92655. Tel: 714-897-8181. Email: brophilip5@yahoo.com. Bro. Philip Shepler, F.S.P., Pres.

Brothers 5

Represented in the Archdiocese of Los Angeles and in the Diocese of Orange.

[1170] (S.P.S.)—ST. PATRICK'S MISSIONARY SOCIETY

(St. Patrick Fathers)

Founded March 17, 1932 with the approval of Pope Pius XI. A Pontifical Society of secular priests devoted entirely to the missionary needs of the Church.

International Headquarters: St. Patrick's, Kiltegan, Wicklow, Ireland, Rev. Richard Filima, S.P.S., Society Leader; Rev. Sean Cremin, S.P.S., Asst. Society Leader; Rev. Raphael Mwenda, S.P.S., Society Councilor; Rev. Peter Esekon, S.P.S., Society Councilor; Rev. Michael Madigan, S.P.S., Society Leader U.S.

Total number of Priests 288; Priests in the U.S: 3

U.S. Foundations (1965): St. Patrick Fathers (1968), 8422 W. Windsor Ave., Chicago, IL 60656-4252. Tel: 773-887-4741. Rev. Michael Moore, S.P.S.; Rev. Michael Madigan, S.P.S.

Legal Titles: St. Patrick's Missionary Society; St. Patrick's Fathers, Guilds & Associates.

[1180] (C.S.P.X.)—BROTHERS OF SAINT PIUS X

Founded in the United States in 1952.

Motherhouse: P.O. Box 284, Spring Valley, WI 54767. Tel: 715-778-4999. Bro. Michael Mandernach, Dir. Ministries in the field of Religious and Academic Education; Health Care; Community services and Administration.

Represented in the Diocese of La Crosse.

[1190] (S.D.B.)—SALESIANS OF DON BOSCO

(Societas Sancti Francisci Salesii)

Generalate: Salesiani Don Bosco, via Della Pisana, 1111, C.P. 18333, 00163 Roma-Bravetta, Italy. Very Rev. Angel Fernandez Artime, Rector Major.

Province of St. Philip the Apostle (1902): 148 Main St., New Rochelle, NY 10801. Tel: 914-636-4225. Very Rev. Steve Shafran, S.D.B., Prov.; Very Rev. Timothy Zak, S.D.B., Vice Prov.; Rev. Dennis Donovan, S.D.B., Prov. Economer & Councilor; Rev. John Serio, S.D.B.. Schools Councilor; Rev. Abraham Feliciano, S.D.B., Dir. of Youth Ministry & Councilor; Rev. David Moreno, S.D.B., Prov. Sec.; Rev. Michael Pace, S.D.B., Councilor.

Legal Title: Salesian Society, Province of St. Philip the Apostle, Inc.

Fathers 119; Professed Clerics: 15; Students in Major Seminaries 6; Coadjutor-Brothers 27

Ministries in: Parishes; High Schools; Boys and Girls Clubs; Camps; Shrine; Retreat Center.

Represented in the Archdioceses of Boston, Chicago, Newark, New Orleans, New York and Washington and in the Dioceses of Palm Beach and St. Petersburg. Also in Canada.

San Francisco Province (1926): Salesian Society - San Francisco, 1100 Franklin St., San Francisco, CA 94109. Tel: 415-441-7144; Fax: 415-441-7155. Email: suosec@salesiansf.org. Rev. Melchor Trinidad, S.D.B., Prov.; Rev. John T. Itzaina, S.D.B. Vice. Prov. Councilors: Rev. Tho Bui, S.D.B., Treas.; Rev. Fabian Cardenas, S.D.B.; Bro. Alphonse Vu, S.D.B.

Priests 58; Professed Brothers 16; Seminarians: 7

Ministries in Parishes; High Schools; Retreat House; Youth Centers.

Represented in the Archdioceses of Los Angeles and San Francisco and in the Dioceses of Laredo, Monterey, Oakland and Stockton.

House of Formation: De Sales Hall, 13856 Bellflower Blvd., Bellflower, CA 90706. Tel: 562-925-1973.

[1200] (S.D.S.)—SOCIETY OF THE DIVINE SAVIOR

(Salvatorian Fathers and Brothers)

(Salvatorians - Societas Divini Salvatoris)

Very Rev. Milton Zonta, S.D.S., Supr. Gen.

U.S.A. Province (1892): Salvatorian Provincial Offices, 1735 N. Hi Mount Blvd., Milwaukee, WI 53208-1720. Tel: 414-258-1735; Fax: 414-258-1934. Email: sds@salvatorians.com. Very Rev. Jeffrey Wocken, S.D.S., Prov.; Rev. Peter Schuessler, S.D.S., Vicar & Dir. Formation. Consultors: Rev. Raúl Gómez-Ruiz, S.D.S.; Rev. Paul Portland, S.D.S.; Bro. Silas Henderson, S.D.S.; Rev. Patric Nikolas, S.D.S.

Fathers 48; Brothers 14; Clerics 1

Legal Titles: Society of the Divine Savior; Society of the Divine Savior Ongoing Community Support Trust; Camp St. Charles, Inc.; Lay Salvatorians Inc.; Salvatorian Institute of Philosophy and Theology Inc.; Jordan Ministry Team, Inc.

Properties owned, staffed or sponsored: Parishes, Hospitals, Schools 10; Houses of Study and Formation 2.

Represented in the Archdioceses of Indianapolis, Miami, Milwaukee and Washington, DC and in the Dioceses of Arlington, Birmingham, Bismarck, Bridgeport, Brooklyn, Oakland, Orlando, Phoenix, Sacramento, St. Petersburg, Tucson, Venice and Wilmington.

[1205] F.S.C.B.—PRIESTLY FRATERNITY OF THE MISSIONARIES OF ST. CHARLES BORROMEO

(Sacerdotalis Fraternitas Missionarium a Sancti Carolo Borromeo)

General Motherhouse: Via Boccea 761, 00166, Rome, Italy, Rev. Paolo Sottopietra, F.S.C.B., Supr. Gen.; Rev. Emmanuele Silanos, F.S.C.B., Gen. Vicar; Rev. Giovani Fasani, F.S.C.B., Gen. Sec.

North American Regional Delegation: Priestly Fraternity of the Missionaries of St. Charles Borromeo, Inc., 7600 Carter Court, Bethesda, MD 20817. Tel: 301-983-4624; Web: www.sancarlo.org. Rev. Antonio Lopez, F.S.C.B., Regl. Delegate; Rev. Stefano Zamagni, F.S.C.B., Contact Person; Rev. Jose Medina, F.S.C.B; Rev. Luca Brancolini, F.S.C.B; Rev. Michael Carvill, F.S.C.B; Rev. Accursio Ciaccio, F.S.C.B; Rev. Roberto Amoruso, F.S.C.B; Rev. Pietro Rossotti, F.S.C.B; Rev. Jose Maria Cortes, F.S.C.B; Rev. Tommaso Badiani, F.S.C.B.; Rev. Emanuele Fadini, F.S.C.B.; Rev. Matteo Invernizzi, F.S.C.B.; Rev. John Roderick, F.S.C.B.; Rev. Michele Benetti, F.S.C.B.; Rev. Paolo Cumin, F.S.C.B.; Rev. Luis Miguel Hernandez, F.S.C.B.; Rev. Paolo Di Gennaro, F.S.C.B.; Rev. Ettore Ferrario, F.S.C.B.; Rev. Stefano Colombo, F.S.C.B.

Legal Title: Priestly Fraternity of the Missionaries of St. Charles Borromeo, Inc.

Priests 18

Properties owned: House of Formation 1; Parishes staffed: 3

Represented in the Archdioceses of Boston, Denver, St. Paul and Washington.

[1210] (C.S.)—MISSIONARIES OF ST. CHARLES-SCALABRINIANS

(Congregatio Missionariorum A Sancto Carolo)

General Motherhouse: Via Ulisse Seni 2, 00153, Rome, Italy, Very Rev. Leonir Mario Chiarello, C.S., Supr. Gen.

Province of St. Charles Borromeo (188): Scalabrinians Provincial Curia, 27 Carmine St., New York, NY 10014-4423. Tel: 212-675-3993; Fax: 646-998-4625; Email: scbprovince@gmail.com. Rev. Angelo Plodari, C.S., Pres. & Prov. Supr.; Rev. Jesus E. Salinas Hernandez, C.S., Vice Pres. & Vicar Prov.; Rev. Ezio Marchetto, C.S., Bursar; Councilors: Rev. Edison A. Osorio Agudelo, C.S.; Rev. Rubens Sylvain, C.S.

Legal Title: The Pious Society of the Missionaries of St. Charles Borromeo, Inc.

Fathers 89

Properties staffed or owned: Parishes 24; Missions 9; Homes for Aged 2; Seminaries 5; Retreat House 1; Center for Migrants 4; Scalabrini International Migration Network (SIMN); Center for Migration Studies (CMS).

Represented in the Archdioceses of Atlanta, Boston, Miami, New York and Washington and in the Dioceses of Brooklyn, Orlando, Palm Beach, Providence and Venice. Also in Eastern Canada, Colombia, Ecuador, Dominican Republic, Haiti and Venezuela.

Province of St. John Baptist (1906): Missionaries of St. Charles - Fathers of St. Charles, 546 N. East Ave., Oak Park, IL 60302. Tel: 708-386-4430. Email: SJBProvince@comcast.net. Rev. Miguel Alvarez, C.S., Prov. Supr.

Fathers 75; Brothers 2

Legal Titles: Fathers of Saint Charles; Scalabrinian Community Support Corp.; Scalabrinian Community Formation Corp.

Ministries in 14 Parishes; 1 Homes for the Aged; 3 Missions; 4 Seminaries; 7 Centers for Migrants and Refugees; 2 Diocesan office for Hispanic Ministry.

Represented in the Archdioceses of Chicago, Galveston-Houston, Kansas City in Kansas and Los Angeles and in the Dioceses of Dallas, Kansas City-St. Joseph, San Diego and San Jose. Also in Canada, El Salvador, Guatemala and Mexico.

[1220] (SDC)—SERVANTS OF CHARITY

(Guanellians)

(Congregatio Servorum a Charitate)

General Motherhouse: Vicolo Clementi 41, Rome, Italy, Very Rev. Alfonso Crippa, SdC, Supr. Gen.

U.S. Headquarters: Servants of Charity, 118 Taunton Ave., East Providence, RI 02914. Rev. Satheesh Alphonse Caniton, SdC, Prov. Counselor & U.S. Rep.; Rev. Ronald Jesiah, SdC Prov., Divine Providence Province.

Legal Title: Pious Union of St. Joseph.

Priests 13

Publication: Now And At The Hour.

Ministry for the suffering and dying: Residences for persons with Intellectual disabilities 1; Parishes 2; Chaplaincies 2.

Represented in the Archdioceses of Chicago and Philadelphia and in the Dioceses of Lansing and Providence.

[1230] (S.P.)—SERVANTS OF THE PARACLETE

Generalate: 6476 Eime Rd., Dittmer, MO 63023. Tel: 636-274-5226. Web: www.servantsoftheparaclete.org. Rev. Raffaele Talmelli, s.P., Vicar Gen. acting as Supreme Moderator; Rev. Nguyen Van Thac, s.P., Treas. Gen.; Rev. Isaac Yiadom Boakye, s.P., Sec. Gen.; Rev. Jacob Bempah Owusu, s.P., Asst. for Apostolate.

Legal Titles: Servants of the Paraclete: A New Mexico Corporation; Servants of the Paraclete, A Missouri Corporation; Servants of the Paraclete Foundation.

Represented in the Archdioceses of St. Louis and Santa Fe.

U.S. Motherhouse (1952): Servants of the Paraclete, 6476 Eime Rd., Dittmer, MO 63023. Tel: 636-274-5226. Email: praff@gmail.com. Rev. Raffaele Talmelli, s.P.

[1240] (O.S.M.)—SERVITES

(Order of Friar Servants of Mary)

(Ordo Fratrum Servorum Beatae Virginis Mariae)

Generalate: Curia Generalizia dei Servi di Maria, Convento San Marcello Piazza San Marcello al Corso, 5, 00187, Rome, Italy,

Servite Friars (1999): United States of America Province Servite Provincial Center, 3121 W. Jackson Blvd., Chicago, IL 60612-2729. Tel: 773-533-0360; Fax: 773-533-8307. Very Rev. Eugene M. Smith, O.S.M., Prior Prov.; Rev. Donald M. Siple, O.S.M., Asst. Prov., Province Vocation and Formation Dir.; Rev. Joseph M. Chamblain, O.S.M., Prov. Councilor; Bro. Arnaldo M. Sanchez, O.S.M., Prov. Councilor, Corp. Sec. & Treas.; Rev. Joseph M. Cheah, O.S.M., Prov. Councilor; Rev. Paul M. Gins, O.S.M., Prov. Archivist; Rev. Leonardus M. Hambur, O.S.M., Rector, National Sanctuary of Our Sorrowful Mother, Portland, OR; Mr. Eddie Murphy, Province Vocation Team; Mr. James Forester, Province Development Dir.; Rev. Christopher M. Krymski, O.S.M., Co-Dir.; Rev. John M. Fontana, Co-Dir., Natl. Shrine of St. Peregrine, O.S.M., Chicago, IL.; Rev. Dennis M. Kritz, O.S.M., Prov. Min. to the Servite Secular Order.

Priests 43; Professed Brothers 3; Temporary Professed Students 4

Legal Titles: The Order of Friar Servants of Mary United States of America Province, Inc., 3121 W. Jackson Blvd., Chicago, IL, Tel: 773-533-0360; Fax: 773-533-8307; Charitable Trust of the Order of Friar Servants of Mary-United States of America Province, Inc., 3121 W. Jackson Blvd., Chicago, IL 60612-2729, Tel: 773-533-0360; Fax: 773-533-8307; Servite High School, Anaheim, CA, A California Corporation, 1952 W. La Palma Ave., Anaheim, CA 92801, Tel: 714-774-7575; Fax: 714-774-1404.

Properties Owned, Staffed and Sponsored: Parishes 2 owned, 5 staffed; High Schools 2; Shrines 3; Residences 14; Missions 3.

Represented in the Archdioceses of Chicago, Denver, Hartford, Portland in Oregon and in the Diocese of Orange. Also in Australia and South Africa.

[1250] (C.R.S.)—SOMASCAN FATHERS

(Clericorum Regularium Somaschensium)

(Order of St. Jerome Aemilian)

General Motherhouse: Via Casal Morena, 8 00040, Morena - Rome, Italy. Rev. Jose Antonio Nieto Sepulveda, C.R.S., Father Gen.

U.S. Foundation: Pine Haven Boys Center, 133 River Rd., P.O. Box 162, Suncook, NH 03275. Tel: 603-485-7141. Email: info@pinehavenboyscenter.org. Rev. Remo Zanatta, C.R.S., Major Supr.

Priests 9

Represented in the Archdiocese of Galveston-Houston and in the Diocese of Manchester.

[1260] (S.CH.)—SOCIETY OF CHRIST

(Societas Christi Pro Emigrantibus Polonis)

General Motherhouse: 60-962 Poznan Ulica Panny Marii 4, Poland, Very Rev. Ryszard Glowacki, S.Ch., Supr. Gen.; Rev. Matthew John Gardzinski, S.Ch., Procurator Gen Via Pier Ruggero Piccio 55/B, Rome, Italy, 00136.

American-Canadian Province: Provincial House, 786 W. Sunset Ave., Lombard, IL 60148. Tel: 630-424-0401; Fax: 630-424-0409. Email: schprov@aol.com. Rev. Pawel Bandurski, S.Ch., Prov.; Rev. Andrzej Totzke, S.Ch., Vice Prov.; Rev. Zygmunt Ostrwoski, S.Ch., Treas.

Priests 55; Seminarians: 4

Represented in the Archdioceses of Atlanta; Baltimore, Boston, Chicago, Denver, Detroit, Galveston - Houston, Los Angeles, Miami, Milwaukee, New York, Portland in Oregon, St. Paul-Minneapolis, St. Louis, San Francisco, Seattle and Washington and in the Dioceses of Dallas, Joliet, Las Vegas, Phoenix, San Diego and San Jose. Also in Canada.

[1270] (F.M.S.I.)—SONS OF MARY MISSIONARY SOCIETY

(Sons of Mary, Health of the Sick)

(Filii Mariae Salutis Infirmorum)

General Headquarters: 567 Salem End Rd., Framingham, MA 01702-5599. Tel: 508-879-6711; Email: sonskevin@gmail.com; Web: www.sonsofmary.com.ph. Bro. Kevin Courtney, F.M.S.I., Coord.; Bro. John Coss, F.M.S.I., Councilor; Rev. Robert Rivard, F.M.S.I., Councilor.

Professed 5

Represented in the Archdiocese of Boston. Also in the Philippines.

[1280] (C.S.S.)—STIGMATINE FATHERS AND BROTHERS

(Congregation of the Sacred Stigmata)

General Motherhouse: Via Mazzarino No. 16, Rome, Italy, Very Rev. Rubens Sodrè Miranda, C.S.S.

North American Province (1940): 554 Lexington St., Waltham, MA 02452. Tel: 413-734-5433; Fax: 413-731-0680. Very Rev. Robert S. White, C.S.S., Prov. Supr.

Legal Title: Stigmatine Fathers & Brothers, Inc.

Priests 6

Properties owned, staffed or sponsored: Parishes 2.

Represented in the Archdiocese of Boston and in the Dioceses of Springfield in Massachusetts and Worcester.

[1290] (P.S.S.)—SOCIETY OF THE PRIESTS OF SAINT SULPICE

(Societas Presbyterorum a S. Sulpitio)

General Motherhouse: 6 rue du Regard, Paris 75006, France, Very Rev. Shayne E.M. Craig, P.S.S., Supr. Gen.

U.S. Provincial House: 5408 Roland Ave., Baltimore, MD 21210. Tel: 410-323-5070; Fax: 410-433-6524. Very Rev. Daniel F. Moore, P.S.S., Prov.; Carleen P. Kramer, Exec. Asst. to Prov.; Rev. Anthony J. Pogorelc, P.S.S., Prov. Sec. and Dir., Initial Formation; Rev. Paul A. Maillet, P.S.S., Prov. Treas.; Rev. Martin J. Burnham, Dir. of Discernment & Admissions.

Legal Title: The Associated Sulpicians of the United States, Inc.

Fathers 58

Represented in the Archdioceses of Baltimore, San Antonio and Washington and in the Diocese of Stockton. Also in Paris, France; Maynooth, Ireland & Rome, Italy. African Region: Lusaka, Zambia, Kachebere, Malawi and Gaborone, Botswana.

[1300] (C.R.)—THEATINE FATHERS

(Ordo Clericorum Regularium vulgo Theatinorum)

General Curia: Sant'Andrea della Valle, Piazza Vidoni, 6 00186, Roma, Italia, Very Rev. Salvador Rodea-Gonzalez, C.R., Theat. Supr. Gen. Tel: +39 066 861339.

U.S. Headquarters: Our Lady of Purity Province, St. Andrew Avelino Seminary, 1050 S. Birch St., Denver, CO 80246. Tel: 303-757-4280. Email: 1906.ccrr@gmail.com. Very Rev. Heriberto Torres, C.R., Prov. Supr.

Priests 19; Deacons 2; Clerics 8; Novices 2; Postulants 3.

Parishes 4; House of Formation 1; Provincial House 1.

Represented in the Archdiocese of Denver and in the Dioceses of Columbus and Pueblo. Also in Guadalajara.

[1310] (O.SS.T.)—THE ORDER OF THE MOST HOLY TRINITY AND OF THE CAPTIVES

(Holy Trinity Fathers, Inc.)

(Ordo Sanctissimae Trinitatis; The Trinitarians)

Founded in France in 1198 by St. John de Matha for the ransom of Christian slaves. First settlement in the United States in 1911.

General Curia: Piazza Sonnino, 44 00153, Rome, Italy, Most Rev. Luigi Buccarello, O.SS.T., Min. Gen.

U.S.A. Province (1950): Province of the Immaculate Heart of Mary, P.O. Box 1828, Sykesville, MD 21784-1820. Tel: 410-486-5171. Very Rev. William J. Sullivan, O.SS.T., Min.; Rev. Santhosh George, O.SS.T., Vicar Prov. & Councilor; Rev. Victor J. Scocco, O.SS.T., Councilor; Rev. Stanley W. DeBoe, O.SS.T., Councilor; Rev. Thomas H. Dymowski, O.SS.T., Councilor & Prov. Sec.; Rev. Kurt J. Klismet, O.SS.T., Prov. Treas.

Trinitarian Communities in the U.S: 8; Fathers 20; Brothers 3

Ministries in 6 parishes; College Faculty; DeMatha Catholic High School, Hyatttsville, MD; Senior Health Care Chaplaincies; Philippine Foundation; Mission for Persecuted Christians.

Properties owned: Holy Trinity Monastery, Sykesville, MD; Domus Trinitatis, San Antonio, TX.

Represented in the Archdioceses of Baltimore, Miami and San Antonio and in the Dioceses of Las Vegas and Trenton.

[1320] (C.S.V.)—CLERICS OF ST. VIATOR

(Congregatio Clericorum Sancti Viatoris)

General Motherhouse: Centre Louis Querbes, 3, rue Louis-Querbes, 69390, Vourles, France, Very Rev. Robert M. Egan, C.S.V., Supr. Gen.

Province of Chicago (1882): 1212 E. Euclid Ave., Arlington Heights, IL 60004. Tel: 847-398-1354. Very Rev. Mark R. Francis, C.S.V., Prov.; Rev. Richard A. Rinn, C.S.V., Asst. Prov.; Rev. Thomas R. von Behren, C.S.V., Prov. Treas.; Bro. Michael T. Gosch, C.S.V., Councilor; Rev. Edgar O. Suárez, C.S.V., Councilor.

Fathers 41; Brothers 17

Properties owned, staffed or sponsored: Parishes 6; High Schools 7; Formation Houses 3.

Represented in the Archdiocese of Chicago and in the Dioceses of Joliet, Las Vegas, Peoria, Rockford, San Bernardino and Tuscon. Also in Colombia and France.

[1330] (C.M.)—CONGREGATION OF THE MISSION

(Vincentians)

(Congregatio Missionis Sti. Vincentii a Paulo)

Founded in France in 1625. First foundation in the United States in 1818.

General Motherhouse: Curia Generalizia, Via dei Capasso, 30 00164, Roma, Italy, Very Rev. Tomaz Mavric, C.M., Supr. Gen.; Rev. Paul Parackal, C.M., Econome Gen.

Eastern Province of the U.S.A. (1888): St. Vincent's Seminary, 500 E. Chelten Ave., Philadelphia, PA 19144. Tel: 215-713-2400; Fax: 215-844-2085. Very Rev. Stephen M. Grozio, C.M., Prov.; Rev. Thomas F. McKenna, C.M., Asst. Prov.; Rev. Elmer Bauer III, C.M., Prov. Treas.; Mr. Allen Andrews, Exec. Dir. Finance. Consultors: Rev. Gregory P. Cozzubbo, C.M.; Rev. Aidan R. Rooney, C.M.; Rev. Bernard M. Tracey, C.M.

Legal Title: Congregation of the Mission of St. Vincent de Paul in Germantown, Inc.

Priests 87; Brothers 5; College Seminarians: 18

Properties owned, sponsored or staffed: Parishes 8; Missions in Republic of Panama 5; Universities 2; Novitiates 2.

Represented in the Archdioceses of Baltimore, New York and Philadelphia and in the Dioceses of Allentown, Brooklyn, Buffalo, Charleston, Charlotte, and Rockville Centre. Also in Panama.

Western Province of the U.S.A. (1888): 3701 Forest Park Ave, St. Louis, MO 63108. Tel: 314-344-1184; Fax:

314-344-2989. Very Rev. Patrick J. McDevitt, C.M., Prov.; Rev. Thomas E. Esselman, C.M., Asst. Prov.

Legal Title: Congregation of the Mission Western Province (The Vincentians); Congregation of the Mission Western Province, Texas; Congregation of the Mission Western Province, Louisiana; Congregation of the Mission Western Province, California.

Priests 125; Brothers 14; Permanent Deacons 1

Serving in 17 U.S. (Arch)Dioceses; Universities; Foreign Mission Stations; Houses of Apostolic Activity; Parishes; Home Mission Parishes; Seminaries; Retreat/Evangelization Centers.

Represented in the Archdioceses of Anchorage-Juneau, Chicago, Kansas City in Kansas, Los Angeles, Milwaukee, New Orleans, Saint Louis and San Antonio and in the Dioceses of Dallas, Evansville, Gallup, Phoenix, San Jose and Stockton. Also in France, Ireland and Kenya.

The New England Province of the Vincentian Fathers (1975): DePaul Vincentian Provincial Residence, 234 Keeney St., Manchester, CT 06040-7048. Tel: 860-643-2828; Fax: 860-533-9462. Very Rev. Grzegorz Marek Sadowski, C.M., Prov.

Fathers 17

Legal Title: New England Province of the Congregation of the Mission, Inc.; Charitable Trust of the New England Province of the Congregation of the Mission.

Represented in the Archdiocese of Hartford and in the Dioceses of Brooklyn and Manchester.

American Italian Branch (Naples, Italy) (1922): Our Lady of Pompei Church, 3600 Claremont St., Baltimore, MD 21224. Tel: 410-675-7790. Rev. Luigi Esposito, Supr.

Represented in the Archdiocese of Baltimore.

[1335] (V.C.)—VINCENTIAN CONGREGATION

(Vincentians)

Founded by Rev. Fr. Varkey Kattarath at Thottakom, Kerala, India in 1904.

Generalate: Vincentian Generalate, P.O. Box No. 2250 - Edappally Kochi 682 024, Kerala, India, Very Rev. John Kandathinkara, V.C., Supr. Gen.

St. Joseph Province: Vincentian Provincial House, S.H. Mount P.O. Kottayam 686 006, Kerala, India, Tel: 481-256-3559. Very Rev. Mathew Kakkattupillil, V.C., Prov. Supr.

North American Headquarters: Vincentian House, 1027 Twin Oaks St., Bensenville, IL 60106. Tel: 630-422-5236. Email: vcsjprovince@gmail.com. Rev. Joseph Perumpanani, V.C., Reg. Coord.; Rev. Joseph J. Arackal, V.C., Mission Coop Coord.; Rev. Jose Edayadiyil, V.C., Mission Procurator.

Fathers 6

Represented in the Dioceses of St. Cloud and St. Thomas Syro-Malabar Catholic Diocese of Chicago.

[1340] (S.D.V.)—VOCATIONIST FATHERS

(The Society of Divine Vocations)

Generali: Via Cortina D'Ampezzo, 140 00135, Rome, Italy, Tel: 011 39 06 33 12725; Fax: 011 39 06 33 12758. Rev. Antonio Rafael do Nascimento, S.D.V., Supr. Gen.

USA Quasi Province - American Headquarters: 90 Brooklake Rd., Florham Park, NJ 07932. Tel: 973-966-6262; Fax: 973-845-2996. Rev. Michael Reardon, S.D.V., Fr. Prov. Email: frmichaelsdv@gmail.com.

[1350] (C.F.X.)—BROTHERS OF ST. FRANCIS XAVIER

(Congregatio Fratrum Xaverianorum)

Generalate - Xaverian Brothers 4409 Frederick Ave., Baltimore, MD 21229. Tel: 410-644-0034; Fax: 410-644-2762. Email: development@xaverianbrothers.org. Bro. Daniel Skala, C.F.X., Gen. Supr.; Bro. Patrick Fumbisha Kakusu, C.F.X., Vicar; Bro. Dominique Omedjunga Olondo, C.F.X.; Bro. Brian Davis, C.F.X.; Bro. Lawrence Harvey, C.F.X., Gen. Councilors; Bro. Arthur Caliman, C.F.X., Treas.; Bro. Paul Murray, C.F.X., Leadership Team; Dr. Patrick J. Slattery, Exec. Dir. Xaverian Brothers Sponsored Schools; Mr. Benjamin Horgan, Dir. of Formation, X.B.S.S.; Mrs. Stephanie Stricker, Development Assoc.; Josh Kinney, Dir. Communications.

Brothers 200

Legal Titles: Xaverian Brothers U.S.A. Inc.; Xaverian Brothers Massachusetts, Inc.; Isidore Charitable Trust; Paul van Gerwen Religious & Charitable Trust.

Ministries in the field of: Religious and Academic Education at all levels; Diocesan Offices; Pastoral Ministry; Mission Schools; Communities; Houses and House of Formation.

Represented in the Archdioceses of Baltimore, Boston, Louisville and Washington and in the Dioceses of Brooklyn, Norwich, Richmond, Syracuse, Venice and Worcester. Also in Bolivia, Belgium, Congo, England, Haiti, Kenya and Lithuania.

[1360] (S.X.)—XAVERIAN MISSIONARY FATHERS

(Saint Francis Xavier Foreign Mission Society)

(Pia Societas Sancti Francisci Xaverii pro Exteris Missionibus)

General Motherhouse: Istituto Saveriano Missioni Estere, Viale Vaticano 40 00165, Rome, Italy, Very Rev. Fernando Garcia Rodriguez, S.X., Supr. Gen.

U.S. Delegation: Xaverian Missionary Fathers, 12 Helene Ct.,Wayne, NJ 07470. Tel: 973-942-2975; Fax: 973-942-5012. Emails: wayne@xaverianmissionaries.org. Very Rev. Mark Marangone, S.X., Delegate Supr.

Fathers 13

Mission House 1; Houses of Formation 2.

Represented in the Archdioceses of Boston and Milwaukee and in the Diocese of Paterson.

Index for Religious Institutes of Women

(The initial D or P indicates Diocesan or Pontifical Jurisdiction.)

Religious Order Initials for Women

A.B.S. Auxiliaries of the Blessed Sacrament []
A.C.J. Handmaids of the Sacred Heart of Jesus [1870]
A.D. Sisters of the Lamb of God [2260]
A.I.M. Association of Mary Immaculate []
A.N.G. A New Genesis []
A.P. Nuns of Perpetual Adoration of Blessed Sacrament [3190]
A.P.B. Adorers of the Precious Blood [0110]
A.P.G. Sisters of Perpetual Adoration [3195]
A.R. Handmaids of Reparation of the Sacred Heart of Jesus [1880]
A.R. Augustinian Recollects []
A.S.C. Adorers of the Blood of Christ [0100]
A.S.C.J. Apostles of the Sacred Heart of Jesus [0130]
B.C. Notre Dame du Bon Conseil (Quebec) []
Bethl. Bethlemita, Daughter of the Sacred Heart of Jesus [0910]
B.V.M. Sisters of Charity of Blessed Virgin Mary [0430]
B.V.M.C. Blessed Virgin Missionaries of Carmel []
C.a.Ch. Carmelite Sisters of Charity [0340]
Carmel.D.C.J. Carmelite Sisters of the Divine Heart of Jesus [0360]
C.B.S. Congregation of Bon Secours [0270]
C.C. Carmel Community [0310]
C.C.V.I. Sisters of Charity of Incarnate Word [0460]
CCVI Sisters of Charity of Incarnate Word (Houston, TX) [0470]
C.C.W. Carmelite Community of the Word [0315]
C.D.P. Sisters of Divine Providence [0990]
C.D.P. Sisters of Divine Providence of Melbourne, Kentucky [1000]
C.D.P. Sisters of Divine Providence of San Antonio, TX [1010]
C.D.P. Capuchin Sisters (Spain) []
C.D.S. Congregation of Divine Spirit [1040]
C.F.M.M. Minim Daughters of Mary Immaculate [2675]
C.F.P. Feminine Congregation of the Passion []
C.F.P. Mexican Passionist Sisters []
C.G.S. Contemplatives of Good Shepherd [1830]
C.H.F. Sisters of Holy Faith [1940]
C H.M. Congregation of Humility of Mary [2100]
C.H.S. Community of the Holy Spirit [2020]
C.I.C. Sisters of Immaculate Conception [2120]
C.I.J. Congregation of Infant Jesus [2230]
C.J.C. Poor Sisters of Jesus Crucified and Sorrowful Mother [3240]
C.K. School Sisters of Christ the King []
C.L.H.C. Congregation of Our Lady Help of the Clergy [3090]
C.M.C. Congregation of Mother of Carmel []
C.M.R. Congregation of Mary, Queen [0397]
C.M.S. Comboni Missionary Sisters [0690]
C.M.S. Cashel Mercy Sisters [2515]
C.M.S.T. Missionary Carmelites of St. Teresa [0390]
C.N.D. Congregation De Notre Dame [2980]
C.O.C. Companions of Christ []
C.P. Religious of the Passion of Jesus Christ [3170]
C.P. Sisters of the Cross and Passion [3180]
C.P.C. Capuchin Poor Clares []
C.P.C. St. Clare Capuchin Sisters []
C.P.P.S. Sisters of the Precious Blood Dayton, Ohio [3260]
C.P.P.S. Sisters of the Most Precious Blood, (O'Fallon, MO) [3270]
C.P.S. Missionary Sisters of the Precious Blood [2850]
C.R. Sisters of the Resurrection [3480]
C.S. Company of the Savior [0710]
C.S. The Christian Sisters (Pious Union) []
C.S.A. Sisters of Charity of St. Augustine [0580]
C.S.A. Sisters of St. Agnes [3710]
C.S.A. Albertine Sisters (Krakow, Poland) []
C.S.A.C. Sisters of the Catholic Apostolate (Pallottine) [3140]
C.S.B. Congregation of St. Brigid [3735]
C.S.C. Congregation of Sisters of Holy Cross [1920]
C.S.J. Congregation of the Daughters of Jesus [0830]
C.S.C. Sisters of Holy Cross [1930]
C.S.C. Sisters of Holy Cross and Seven Dolors []
C.S.E. Carmelite Sisters of the Eucharist []
C.S.F.N. Sisters of Holy Family of Nazareth [1970]
C.S.J. Hermanas Carmelitas de San Jose [1895]
C.S.J. Sisters of St. Joseph [3830]
C.S.J. Sisters of St. Joseph (Boston, Brighton) [3830-01]
C.S.J. Sisters of St. Joseph (Orange) [3830-03]
C.S.J. Sisters of St. Joseph (Rockville Centre, Brentwood) [3830-05]
C.S.J. Sisters of St. Joseph (Pittsburgh, Baden) [3830-13]
C.S.J. Sisters of St. Joseph (Salina, Concordia) [3830-15]
C.S.J. Sisters of St. Joseph (Wichita) [3830-18]
C.S.J. Congregation of the Sisters of St. Joseph [3832]
C.S.J. Sisters of St. Joseph of Carondelet [3840]
C.S.J. Sisters of St. Joseph of Chambery [3850]
C.S.J. Sisters of St. Joseph (Lyons, France) [3870]
C.S.J. Sisters of St. Joseph of Medaille [3880]
C.S.JB. Sisters of St. John the Baptist [3820]
C.S.J.P. Sisters of St. Joseph of Peace [3890]
C.S.M. Sisters of St. Martha of Antigonish N.S. [3937]
C.S.N. Congregation of Sisters of Nazareth [3242]
C.S.R. Sisters of Holy Redeemer [2000]
C.S.S.F. Felician Sisters [1170]
C.S.S.T. Carmelite Sisters of St. Teresa []
C.S.T. Carmelite Sisters of St. Therese of Infant Jesus [0380]
C.V.D. Sisters of Bethany [0250]
C.V.I. Congregation of Incarnate Word and Blessed Sacrament [2190]
C.V.I. Religious of the Incarnate Word [3449]
D.C. Daughters of Charity of St. Vincent de Paul [0760]
D.C.M. Diocesan Carmelites of Maine []
D.C.P.B. Daughters of Charity of Most Precious Blood [0740]
D.D.L. Daughters of Divine Love [0793]
D.H.M. Daughters of Heart of Mary [0810]
D.H.S. Daughters of the Holy Spirit [0820]
D.L.F. Daughters of Our Lady of Fatima []
D.L.J.C. Disciples of the Lord Jesus Christ [0965]
D.M. Daughters of Mary of the Immaculate Conception [0860]
D.M. Daughters of Our Lady of Mercy [0890]
D.M.I. Daughters of Mary Immaculate [0855]
D.M.J. Daughters of Mary and Joseph [0880]
D.M.M.M. Daughters of Mary Mother of Mercy [0885]
D.O.M. Daughters of Mercy (Croatian) []
D.S.F. Daughters of St. Francis of Assisi [0920]
D.S.M.P. Daughters of St. Mary of Providence [0940]
D.S.T. Daughters of St. Thomas Congregation [4035]
D.W. Daughters of Wisdom [0960]
E.F.M.S. Eucharistic Franciscan Missionary Sisters [1150]
E.I.N. Servants of the Immaculate Child Mary [3615]
E.M.S. Eucharistic Missionary Society []
F.A.S. Franciscan Apostolic Sisters []
F.C. Daughters of the Cross of Liege [0780]
F.C.J. Society of Sisters Faithful Companions of Jesus [4048]
F.C.S.C.J. Daughters of Charity of the Sacred Heart of Jesus [0750]
F.D.C. Daughters of Divine Charity [0790]
Fd.CC. Canossian Daughters of Charity [0730]
F.D.L.P. Daughters of Providence []
F.D.N.S.C. Daughters of Our Lady of the Sacred Heart [0900]
F.D.P. Daughters of Divine Providence [0800]
F.D.Z. Daughters of Divine Zeal [0795]
F.H.I.C. Franciscan Hospitaller Sisters of the Immaculate Conception [1270]
F.H.M. Franciscan Handmaids of the Most Pure Heart of Mary [1260]
F.H.M. Franciscan Sisters Daughters of Mercy [1235]
F.L.G. Franciscan Sisters of Our Lady of Grace []
F.M.A. Daughters of Mary Help of Christians [0850]
F.M.I. Congregation of the Daughters of Mary Immaculate (Marianist Sisters) [0870]
F.M.I. Franciscan Sisters of Mary Immaculate of the Third Order of St. Francis of Assisi [1500]
F.M.I.J. Franciscan Missionaries of theInfant Jesus [1365]
F.M.M. The Franciscan Missionaries of Mary [1370]
F.M.S.A. Franciscan Missionary Sisters for Africa [1320]
F.M.S.C. Franciscan Missionary Sisters of the Sacred Heart [1400]
F.M.S.J. Mill Hill Sisters [1410]
F.M.S.R. Daughters of Our Lady of Holy Rosary [0895]
F.N.S.S.C. Franciscan Sisters of Our Lady of the Sacred Heart []
F.S.E. Franciscan Sisters of the Eucharist, Inc. [1250]
F.S.G.M. Sisters of St. Francis of the Martyr St. George [1600]
F.S.J. Religious Daughters of St. Joseph [0930]
F.S.M. Franciscan Sisters of Mary [1415]
F.S.O.L. Franciscan Sisters of Our Lady []
F.S.P. Pious Society Daughters of St. Paul [0950]
F.S.P. Franciscan Sisters of Peace [1425]
F.S.P.A. Congregation of the Sisters of the Third Order of St. Francis of Perpetual Adoration [1780]
F.S.R. Franciscan Sisters of Ringwood [1420]
F.S.S.C. Franciscan Sisters of St. Clare (Pious Union) []
F.S.S.E. Franciscan Sisters of St. Elizabeth [1460]
F.S.S.J. Franciscan Sisters of St. Joseph [1470]
F S.S.M. Franciscan Sisters of the Sorrowful Mother []
F.S.Sp.J. Franciscan Sisters of the Spirit of Jesus []
G.H.M.S. Home Mission Sisters of America (Glenmary) [2080]
G.N.S.H. Grey Nuns of the Sacred Heart [1840]
H.B.S. Hermanas Contemplativas del Buen Pastor []
H.C.G. Hermanas Catequistas Guadalupanas [1900]
H.F.deS.J. Franciscan Sisters of St. Joseph (Mexico City) []
H.F.S.J. Franciscan Sisters of St. Joseph [1480]
H.G.S. Congregation de Hermanas Guadalupanas de la Salle []
H.H.C.J. Congregation of the Handmaids ofthe Holy Child Jesus [1855]
H.H.S. Society of Helpers [1890]
H.J. Hermanas Josefinas [1910]
H.J.D. Las Hermanas de Juan Diego []
H.L.M.C. Handmaids Of Our Lady of Mount Carmel (Carmelite Sisters) [1857]
H.M. Sisters of the Humility of Mary [2110]
H.M.C. Hermits of Mount Carmel []
H.M.S.S. Mercedarian Sisters of the Blessed Sacrament [2590]
H.M.S.S. Religious Sisters of the Apostolate of the Blessed Sacrament [3370]
H.O.Carm. Hermits of Our Lady of Mt. Carmel []
H.P.B. Congregation of the Handmaids of the Precious Blood [1860]
H.R.F. Sisters of the Holy Rosary of Fatima (Mexico) []
H.S.H. Handmaids of the Sacred Heart of Pohang []
H.S.M. Hermit Sisters of Mary []
H.Sp.S. Daughters of the Holy Spirit Nazareth of the Good Shepherd []
H.S.S. Hermanas del Servicio Social []
H.S.S.R. Hermit Sisters of Romuald []
H.T. Handmaids of the Most Holy Trinity []
H.V.M. Sisters, Home Visitors of Mary [2090]
I.B.V.M. Institute of the Blessed Virgin Mary (Loretto Sisters) [2370]
I.B.V.M. Institute of the Blessed Virgin Mary (Loretto Sisters) [2380]
I.C. Vietnamese Sisters Incarnational Consecration []
I.C.M. Missionary Sisters of the Immaculate Heart of Mary [2750]
I.C.M. Sisters of Incarnation-Consecration-Mission [2187]
I.H.M.M. Sisters of the Immaculate Heart of Mary at Mirinae [2182]
I.H.M. Sisters of the Immaculate Heart of Mary Mother of Christ [2183]
I.H.M. Sisters Servants of the Immaculate Heart of Mary [2150]
I.H.M. Sisters Servants of the Immaculate Heart of Mary [2160]
I.H.M. Sisters Servants of the Immaculate Heart of Mary [2170]
I.H.M. Sisters Servants of the Immaculate Heart of Mary [2180]
I.H.M. The California Institute of the Sisters of the Most Holy and Immaculate Heart of the Blessed Virgin Mary [2930]
I.H.M. Sisters of the Immaculate Heart of Mary of Wichita [2185]
I.J. Sisters of the Infant Jesus [2240]
I.M. Sisters of Charity of the Infant Mary []
I.S.S.M. Secular Institute of Schoenstatt Sisters of Mary []
I.W.B.S. Sisters of the Incarnate Word and Blessed Sacrament [2200]

I.W.B.S. Congregation of the Incarnate Word and Blessed Sacrament [2205]
J.S.O.P. Dominican Oblates of Jesus (Spain) []
L.B. Ladies of Bethany []
L.C.M. Sisters of the Little Company of Mary [2270]
L.H.C.N.T. Lovers of the Holy Cross Nha Trang [2385]
L.H.C. Lovers of the Holy Cross Sisters [2375]
L.H.C. Lovers of the Holy Cross Sisters [2390]
L.H.C. Lovers of the Holy Cross Sisters [2392]
L.H.C. Quinhon Missionary Sisters of the Holy Cross [2397]
L.M.S.C. Little Missionary Sisters of Charity [2290]
L.S. Lasallian Sisters (Vietnam) []
L.S.A. Little Sisters of the Assumption [2310]
L.S.G. Little Sisters of the Gospel (France) [2315]
L.S.I.C. Little Servant Sisters of the Immaculate Conception [2300]
L.S.J. Little Sisters of Jesus [2330]
L.S.J.M. Little Sisters of Jesus and Mary [2331]
L.S.O.S.F. Little Sisters of St. Francis of Assisi [2335]
L.S.P. Little Sisters of the Poor [2340]
M.C. Consolata Missionary Sisters [0720]
M.C. Missionaries of Charity [2710]
M.C. Poor Clare Missionary Sisters [2840]
M.C.D.P. Missionary Catechists of Divine Providence, San Antonio, TX [2690]
M.Ch.R. Missionary Sisters of Christ the King for Polonia [2715]
M.C.M. Cordi Marian Sisters [0725]
M.C.P. Missioneras Catequestas de los Pobres []
M.C.S. Missionary Sisters of the Sacred Side []
M.C.S.J.M. Congregation of Missionary Catechists of the Sacred Heart of Jesus and Mary []
M.D. Mothers of the Helpless [2920]
M.D.P.V.M. Missionary Daughters of the Most Pure Virgin Mary [2717]
M.E. Missionary Ecumenical (Rome) []
M.C.S.H. Missionary Catechists of the Sacred Hearts of Jesus and Mary [2700]
M.E.S.S.T. Eucharistic Missionaries of the Most Holy Trinity []
M.E.S.T. Eucharistic Missionaries of St. Theresa (Mexico) []
M.F.I.C. Missionary Franciscan Sisters of the Immaculate Conception [1360]
M.F.P. Franciscan Missionaries Our Lady of Peace []
M.G.Sp.S. Missionaries Guadalupanas of the Holy Spirit [1845]
M.H.S. Sisters of the Most Holy Sacrament [2940]
M.H.S.H. Mission Helpers of the Sacred Heart [2720]
M.I.C. Missionary Sisters of the Immaculate Conception (Canada) []
M.J. Missionary Sisters of Jesus []
M.J.M.J. Missionaries of Jesus, Mary and Joseph [2770]
M.M. Maryknoll Sisters of St. Dominic [2470]
M.M.B. Mercedarian Missionaries of Berriz [2510]
M.M.D. Servite Missionary Sisters of the Sorrowful Mother []
M.M.M. Medical Missionaries of Mary [2480]
M.M.S. Medical Mission Sisters [2490]
M.O.M. Missionary Sisters of Our Lady of Mercy [2830]
M.P.F. Religious Teachers Filippini [3430]
M.P.H. Missionary Sisters of Our Lady of Perpetual Help []
M.P.S. Misioneras del Perpetual Socorro []
M.P.S. Missionary Sisters of Our Lady of Perpetual Help []
M.P.V. Religious Venerini Sisters [4180]
M.R. Marianist Sisters []
M.S. Marian Sisters of the Diocese of Lincoln [2400]
M.S.B.A.V. Monastic Sisters of Bethlehem and of the Assumption of the Virgin [2910]
M.S.B.T. Missionary Servants of the Most Blessed Trinity [2790]
M.S.C. Congregation of the Marianites of the Holy Cross [2410]
M.S.C. Missionary Sisters of the Most Sacred Heart of Jesus of Hiltrup [2800]
M.S.C. Missionary Sisters of the Sacred Heart [2860]
M.S.C.Gpe. Missionaries of the Sacred Heart of Jesus and of Our Lady of Guadalupe [2865]
M.S.C.K. Missionary Sisters of Christ the King [2715]
M.S.E. Missionary Sisters of the Eucharist [2725]
M.S.F. Missionary Sisters of the Holy Family []
M.S.H.F. Missionary Sisters of the Holy Family (Poland) []
M.S.H.R. Missionary Sisters of the Holy Rosary [2730]
M.S.J. Medical Sisters of St. Joseph [2500]
M.S.K.C.P. Missionary Sisters of Christ the King of Polonia []
M.S.M.G. Missionary Sisters of Mother of God [2810]
M.S.O.L.A. Missionary Sisters of Our Lady of Africa [2820]
M.S.S.A. Missionary Servants of St. Anthony [2890]
M.S.C.S. Missionary Sisters of St. Charles Borromeo [2900]
M.S.S.J. Missionary Servants of St. Joseph (Spain) []
M.S.Sp. Mission Sisters of the Holy Spirit [2740]
M.SS.S. Missionary Sisters of the Most Blessed Sacrament [2780]
M.T.G. Adorers of the Holy Cross [4155]
M.V.Z. Sisters of Charity of St. Vincent de Paul of Zagreb [0630]
M.X.Y. The Yarumal Foreign Mission Institute (Colombia) []
N.D. Notre Dame Sisters [2960]
C.N.D. Congregation of Notre-Dame of Montreal [2955]
N.D.S. Congregation of Notre Dame de Sion [2950]
O.A.R. Augustinian Recollect Sisters []
O.B.T. Sisters Oblates to the Blessed Trinity [3020]
O.C.A. Carmelite Vietnamese of Our Lady of Mt. Carmel. []
O.Carm. Calced Carmelites [0300]
O.Carm. Carmelite Nuns of the Ancient Observance [0320]
O.Carm. Carmelite Sisters for Aged and Infirm [0330]
O.Carm. Carmelite Sisters (Corpus Christi) [0350]
O.Carm. Congregation of Our Lady of Mt. Carmel [0400]
O.Carm. Institute of the Sisters of Our Lady of Mt. Carmel [0410]
O.C.D. Carmelite Sisters of the Most Sacred Heart of Los Angeles [0370]
O.C.D. Discalced Carmelite Nuns [0420]
O.C.D. Carmelitas del Sagrado Corazon []
O.Cist. Cistercian Nuns [0680]
O.C.S.O. Cistercian Nuns of the Strict Observance [0670]
O.D.N. Company of Mary [0700]
O.L.C. Sisters of Our Lady of Charity [3071]
O.L.C. Sisters of Our Lady of Charity [3073]
O.L.G. Sisters of Our Lady of the Garden []
O.L.L. Sisters of Our Lady of Lourdes []
O.L.M. Sisters of Charity of Our Lady of Mercy [0510]
O.L.S. Sisters of Our Lady of Sorrows [3120]
O.L.V.M. Our Lady of Victory Missionary Sisters [3130]
O.M.M.I. Oblate Missionaries of Mary Immaculate []
O.P. Collaborative Dominican Novitiate Dominican Sisters [1070]
O.P. The Congregation of the Dominican Sisters of Our Lady of the Springs of Bridgeport CT [1025]
O.P. Dominican Contemplative Nuns (Cloistered) [1050]
O.P. Dominican Contemplative Sisters (Cloistered) [1060]
O.P. Dominican Sisters (Sinsinawa, WI) [1070-03]
O.P. Dominican Sisters (San Rafael, CA) [1070-04]
M.V.S. Sisters of the Immaculate Conception of the Blessed Virgin Mary (Lithuanian) [2140]
O.P. Dominican Sisters (Amityville, NY) [1070-05]
O.P. Dominican Sisters (Newburgh, NY) [1070-06]
O.P. Dominican Sisters (Nashville, TN) [1070-07]
O.P. Dominican Sisters (Racine, WI) [1070-09]
O.P. Dominican Sisters (Springfield, IL) [1070-10]
O.P. Dominican Sisters (Sparkill, NY) [1070-11]
O.P. Dominican Sisters (Fremont, CA) [1070-12]
O.P. Dominican Sisters (Adrian, MI) [1070-13]
O.P. Dominican Sisters (Grand Rapids, MI) [1070-14]
O.P. Dominican Sisters (Blauvelt, NY) [1070-15]
O.P. Dominican Sisters (Ossining, NY) [1070-16]
O.P. Dominican Sisters (Caldwell, NJ) [1070-18]
O.P. Dominican Sisters (Houston, TX) [1070-19]
O.P. Dominican Sisters (Tacoma, WA) [1070-20]
O.P. Dominican Sisters (Edmonds, WA) [1070-21]
O.P. Dominican Sisters (Fall River, MA) [1070-22]
O.P. Dominican Sisters (Hawthorne, NY) [1070-23]
O P. Dominican Sisters (Saratoga, CA) [1070-25]
O.P. Dominican Sisters (Justice, IL) [1070-27]
O.P. Dominican Sisters (Spokane, WA) [1070-29]
O.P. Dominican Sisters of Oakford [1070-30]
O.P. Marian Society of Dominican Catechists [1090]
O.P. Dominican Sisters of Charity of the Presentation of the Blessed Virgin [1100]
O.P. Dominican Sisters of Hope [1105]
O.P. Dominican Sisters of Our Lady of the Rosary and of Saint Catherine of Siena, Cabra [1110]
O.P. Dominican Sisters of Peace [1115]
O.P. The Dominican Sisters of St. Cecilia of Nashville, Tennessee [1117]
O.P. Dominican Sisters of the Roman Congregation [1120]
O.P. Dominican Rural Missionaries [1130]
O.P. Dominican Sisters of Carondelet []
O.P. Religious Missionaries of St. Dominic (Spanish Prov.) [1145]
O.P. Dominican Sisters of Mt. Thabor []
O.P. Dominican Sisters of Our Lady of the Most Holy Rosary []
O.P. Dominican Sisters (Vietnam) []
O.P. Dominican Contemplative Sisters []
O.P. Dominican Sisters (Colombia) []
O.P. Dominican Sisters (Ecuador) []
O.P. Hermanas Dominicanas de la Doctrine Cristiana []
O.P. The Dominican Sisters of St. Cecilia of Nashville, Tennessee []
O.S.A. Augustinian Nuns of Contemplative Life [0160]
O.S.A. Congregation of Augustinian Sisters Servants of Jesus and Mary [2145]
O.S.A. Sisters of St. Rita [4010]
O.S.A. Sisters of St. Augustine []
O.S.A. Augustinian Sisters of Our Lady of Consolation []
O.S.B. Benedictine Nuns of the Congregation of Solesmes [0170]
O.S.B. Benedictine Nuns of the Primitive Observance [0180]
O.S.B. Benedictine Nuns [0190]
O.S.B. Benedictine Sisters [0200]
O.S.B. Missionary Benedictine Sisters [0210]
O.S.B. Congregation of the Benedictine Sisters of Perpetual Adoration of Pontifical Jurisdiction [0220]
O.S.B. Benedictine Sisters of Pontifical Jurisdiction [0230]
O.S.B. Benedictine Nuns [0233]
O.S.B. Benedictines of Mary, Queen of Apostles [0237]
O.S.B. Olivetan Benedictine Sisters [0240]
O.S.B. Congregation of Jesus Crucified [2250]
O.S.B. Benedictine Congregation of Our Lady of Monte []
O.S.B. Benedictine Sisters of Sacred Heart []
O.S.B. Contemplative Sisters of St. Benedict []
O.S.B. Benedictine Sisters of Liberty []
O.S.B. Congregation of the Benedictine Sisters of the Sacred Heart []
O.S.B.Cam. Camaldolese Benedictine Sisters [0235]
O.S.B.M. Sisters of the Order of St. Basil the Great [3730]
O.S.B.S. Oblate Sisters of the Blessed Sacrament [3010]
O.S.C.P.C.C. Order of St. Clare Poor Clare Colettines [3760]
O.S.C. Sisters of St. Clare [3770]
O.S.C.Cap. Capuchin Poor Clares [3765]
O.S.F. Franciscan Sisters of Allegany New York [1180]
O.S.F. The Franciscan Sisters of Baltimore [1200]
O.S.F. Franciscan Sisters of Chicago [1210]
O.S.F. Franciscan Sisters of Christian Charity [1230]
O.S.F. Franciscan Sisters, Daughters of the Sacred Hearts of Jesus and Mary [1240]
O.S.F. Franciscan Sisters of the Immaculate Conception [1280]
O.S.F. Franciscan Sisters of the Immaculate Conception and St. Joseph for the Dying [1300]
O S.F. Franciscan Sisters of Little Falls, Minnesota [1310]
O.S.F. Franciscan Missionary Sisters of the Immaculate Conception [1350]
O.S.F. Franciscan Missionaries of Our Lady [1380]
O.S.F. Franciscan Missionary Sisters of Our Lady of Sorrows [1390]
O.S.F. Franciscan Sisters of Our Lady of Perpetual Help [1430]
O.S.F. Franciscan Sisters of the Sacred Heart [1450]
O.S.F. Franciscan Sisters of St. Paul, MN [1485]
O.S.F. Sisters of the Third Franciscan Order [1490]
O.S.F. St. Francis Mission Community [1505]
O.S.F. Sisters of St. Francis [1510]

O.S.F. Sisters of St. Francis of the Congregation of Our Lady of Lourdes, Sylvania, Ohio [1530]
O.S.F. Sisters of Saint Francis, Clinton, Iowa [1540]
O.S.F. Sisters of St. Francis of the Holy Cross [1550]
O.S.F. Sisters of St. Francis of the Holy Eucharist [1560]
O.S.F. Sisters of St. Francis of the Holy Family [1570]
O.S.F. Sisters of St. Francis of the Immaculate Conception [1580]
O.S.F. Sisters of St. Francis of the Immaculate Heart of Mary (Hankinson, North Dakota) [1590]
O.S.F. Sisters of Saint Francis of Millvale, Pennsylvania [1620]
O.S.F. Sisters of St. Francis of Penance and Christian Charity [1630]
O.S.F. Sisters of St. Francis of Perpetual Adoration [1640]
O.S.F. Sisters of St. Francis of the Neumann Communities [1805]
O.S.F. The Sisters of St. Francis of Philadelphia [1650]
O.S.F. Sisters of Saint Francis of the Providence of God [1660]
O.S.F. Sisters of St. Francis of Savannah, MO [1670]
O.S.F. School Sisters of St. Francis [1680]
O.S.F. School Sisters of the Third Order of St. Francis (Pittsburgh, PA) [1690]
O.S.F. School Sisters of the Third Order of St. Francis (Panhandle, TX) [1695]
O S F. The Sisters of St. Francis of Assisi [1705]
O.S.F. Congregation of the Third Order of St. Francis of Mary Immaculate (Joliet, IL) [1710]
O.S.F. Sisters of the Third Order Regular of St. Francis of the Congregation of Our Lady of Lourdes [1720]
O.S.F. Congregation of the Sisters of the Third Order of St. Francis (Oldenburg, IN) [1730]
O.S.F. Sisters of the Third Order of St. Francis of Penance and Charity [1760]
O.S.F. Sisters of the Third Order of St. Francis (Peoria, IL) [1770]
O.S.F. Sisters of St. Francis of the Third Order Regular (Williamsville, New York) [1800]
O.S.F. Bernardine Sisters of the Third Order of St. Francis [1810]
O.S.F. Hospital Sisters of the Third Order of St. Francis [1820]
O.S.F. Servants of the Holy Infancy of Jesus [1980]
O.S.F. Consolation Sisters (Highland, CA) []
O.S.F. Franciscan Sisters of Christ the Divine Teacher []
O.S.F. St. Francis Mission Community []
O.S.F.S. Oblate Sisters of St. Francis de Sales [3060]
O.S.H.J. Oblate Sisters of the Sacred Heart of Jesus [3050]
O.S.M. Mantellate Sisters, Servants of Mary of Blue Island [3570]
O.S.M. Mantellate Sisters, Servants of Mary of Plainfield [3572]
O.S.M. Servants of Mary [3580]
O.S.M. Servants of Mary (Servite Sisters) [3590]
O.S.M. Oblates of St. Martha []
O.S.P. Oblate Sisters of Providence [3040]
O.S.S. Sacramentine Nuns [3490]
O.SS.R. Order of the Most Holy Redeemer [2010]
O.SS.R. Oblates of the Most Holy Redeemer [3030]
O.SS.S. The Brigittine Sisters [0280]
O.SS.T. Sisters of the Most Holy Trinity [2060]
O.S.U. Ursuline Nuns (Roman Union) [4110]
O.S.U. Ursuline Nuns of the Congregation of Paris (St. Martin, OH) [4120]
O.S.U. Ursuline Nuns of the Congregation of Paris (Cincinnati, OH) [4120-01]
O.S.U. Ursuline Nuns of the Congregation of Paris (Louisville, KY) [4120-03]
O.S.U. Ursuline Nuns of the Congregation of Paris (Cleveland, OH) [4120-04]
O.S.U. Ursuline Nuns of the Congregation of Paris (Owensboro, KY) [4120-05]
O.S.U. Ursuline Nuns of the Congregation of Paris (Toledo, OH) [4120-06]
O.S.U. Ursuline Nuns of the Congregation of Paris (Youngstown, OH) [4120-07]
O.S.U. Ursuline Sisters of the Congregation of Tildonk, Belgium [4130]
O.S.U. Irish Ursuline Union [4150]
P.B.V.M. Presentation of the Blessed Virgin Mary Sisters [3280]
P.B.V.M. Sisters of the Presentation of the B.V.M. [3320]
P B.V.M. Union of the Sisters of the Presentation of the Blessed Virgin Mary [3330]
P.C.C. Poor Clare of Our Lady of Guadalupe [3761]
P.C.I. Pax Christi Institute []
P.C.J. Sisters of the Poor Child Jesus [3220]
P.C.P.A. Poor Clares of Perpetual Adoration [3210]
P.C.M. Preachers of Christ and Mary [3255]
P.D.D.M. Pious Disciples of the Divine Master [0980]
P.F.M. Franciscans of Mary [2280]
P.H.J.C. Poor Handmaids of Jesus Christ [3230]
P.M. Sisters of the Presentation of Mary [3310]
P.O.S.C. Little Workers of the Sacred Heart [2345]
P.S.S.F. The Little Sisters of the Holy Family [2320]
P.S.S.J. Poor Sisters of St. Joseph [3250]
P.V.M.I. The Parish Visitors of Mary Immaculate [3160]
R.A. Religious of the Apostolate of the Sacred Heart [3380]
R.A. Religious of the Assumption [3390]
R.A. Antonine Sisters []
R.A.D. Sisters of the Love of God []
R.C. Congregation of Our Lady of Retreat in the Cenacle [3110]
R.C.D. Sisters of Our Lady of Christian Doctrine [3080]
R.C.E. Religious of Christian Education [3410]
R.C.S.C.J. Sisters of the Cross of the Sacred Heart of Jesus (Mexico) []
R.D.C. Sisters of the Divine Compassion [0970]
R.F. Sisters of St. Philip Neri Missionary Teachers []
R.F.R. Sisters of Our Lady of Refuge []
R.G.S.- The Sisters of the Good C.G.S Shepherd [1830]
R.H.S.J. Religious Hospitallers of Saint Joseph [3440]
R.J.M. Religious of Jesus and Mary [3450]
R.M. Marianitas []
R.M.I. Claretian Missionary Sisters [0685]
R.M.I. Religious of Mary Immaculate [3460]
R.M.M. Mercedarian Sisters []
R.O.D.A. Sisters Oblates to Divine Love []
R.O.L.C. Our Lady of Charity of Refuge [3072]
R.S.C. Religious Sisters of Charity [3400]
R.S.C.J. Society of the Sacred Heart [4070]
R.S.H.M. Religious of the Sacred Heart of Mary [3465]
R.S.J. Religious of St. Joseph of Australia []
R.S.M. Religious Sisters of Mercy of Alma, Michigan [2519]
R.S.M. Sisters of Mercy [2520]
R.S.M. Sisters of Mercy of Ardagh & Clonmacnois [2523]
R.S.M. Sisters of Mercy (Galway) [2535]
R.S.M. Sisters of Mercy [2540]
R.S.M. Sisters of Mercy (Sligo) [2549]
R.S.M. Sisters of Mercy [2550]
R.S.M. Sisters of Mercy of the Americas [2575]
R.S.M. Sisters of Mercy (Ballyshannon, Ireland) []
R.S.M. Sisters of Mercy (Mayo, Ireland) []
R.S.M. Sisters of Mercy of Mississippi, Inc. []
R.S.M. Diocesan Sisters of Mercy of Portland [2655]
R.S.M. Diocesan Sisters of Mercy []
R.S.R. Congregation of Our Lady of the Holy Rosary [3100]
R.T. Theatine Sisters of the Immaculate Conception []
R.V.M. Religious of the Blessed Virgin Mary []
S.A. Franciscan Sisters of the Atonement [1190]
S.A.A. Sisters Auxillaries of the Apostolate [0140]
S.A.B. Sisters of St. Anne Bangalone []
S.A.C. Sisters of the Guardian Angel [1850]
S.A.C. Pallottine Missionary Sisters Queen of Apostles Prov [3150]
S.A.S.V. Sisters of the Assumption [0150]
S.B.S. The Sisters of the Blessed Sacrament for Indians and Colored People [0260]
S.B.S. Sisters of the Blessed Sacrament [3135]
S.C. Sisters of Charity of Cincinnati, Ohio [0440]
S.C. Sisters of Charity of Seton Hill, Greensburg, PA [0570]
S.C. Sisters of St. Elizabeth, Convent Station [0590]
S.C. Sisters of Charity of St. Vincent de Paul, Halifax [0640]
S.C. Sisters of Charity of St. Vincent de Paul, New York [0650]
S.C.C. Sisters of Christian Charity [0660]
Sch.P. Sisters of the Pious Schools [3200]
S.C.I.C. Sisters of Charity of the Immaculate Conception of Ivrea [0450]
S.C.I.M. Servants of the Immaculate Heart of Mary [3550]
S.C.K. Sisters of Christ the King []
S.C.L. Sisters of Charity of Leavenworth, Kansas [0480]
S.C.M.C. Sisters of Charity of Our Lady, Mother of the Church [0530]
S.C.M.M. Sisters of Charity of Our Lady Mother of Mercy [0520]
S.C.M.M. Medical Mission Sisters [2490]
S.C.N. Sisters of Charity of Nazareth [0500]
S.C.O. Sisters of Charity of Ottawa (Grey Nuns of the Cross) [0540]
S.C.Q. Sisters of Charity of Quebec (Grey Nuns) [0560]
S.C.R.H. Sisters of Charity of Rolling Hills S.C.S.C. Sisters of Mercy of the Holy Cross [2630]
S.C.S.J.A. Sisters of Charity of St. Joan Antida [0600]
S.C.S.L. Sisters of Charity of St. Louis [0620]
S.C.V. Sisters of Charity of St. Vincent de Paul of Suwon [0655]
S.deM. Sisters Servants of Mary [3600]
S.deP. Sister Servants of the Poor []
S.D.R. Sisters of the Divine Redeemer [1020]
S.D.S. Sisters of the Divine Saviour [1030]
S.D.S.H. Sisters of the Society Devoted to the Sacred Heart [4050]
S.D.V. Vocationist Sisters [4210]
S.E. Sisters of Emanuel []
S.E.C. Sisters of the Eucharistic Covenant []
S.F.C.C. Sisters for Christian Community [3469]
S.F.M.A. Franciscan Missionary Sisters of Assisi [1330]
S.F.P. Franciscan Sisters of the Poor [1440]
S.G.M. Sisters of Charity of Montreal (Grey Nuns) [0490]
S.G.S. Hermanas del Buen Pastor []
S.H.C.J. Society of the Holy Child Jesus [4060]
S.H.F. Sisters of the Holy Family [1960]
S.H.J.M. Sisters of the Sacred Hearts of Jesus and Mary [3680]
S.H.S. Sisters of the Holy Spirit [2040]
S.H.Sp. Sisters of the Holy Spirit and Mary Immaculate [2050]
S.I.M. Missionaries of the Kingship of Christ []
S.I.W. Sisters of the Incarnate Word and the Blessed Sacrament [2210]
S.J. Servants of Jesus [3560]
S.J.A. Sisters of Ste. Jeanne D'Arc [3815]
S.J.B. Sisters of St. John Bosco (Taylor, TX) []
S.J.C. Sisters of St. Joseph of Cluny [3860]
S.J.S. Servants of the Blessed Sacrament [3499]
S.J.S. Sisters of Jesus the Savior [2245]
S.J.S.M. Sisters of St. Joseph of St. Mark [3910]
S.J.W. Sisters of St. Joseph the Worker [3920]
S.L. Sisters of Loretto at the Foot of the Cross [2360]
S.L.T. Pious Society of Our Lady of the Most Holy Trinity []
S.L.W. Sisters of the Living Word [2350]
S.M. Sisters of Mercy [2516]
S.M. Sisters of Mercy [2518]
S.M. Sisters of Mercy [2570]
S.M. Misericordia Sisters [2680]
S.M. Sisters Servants of Mary [3600]
S.M. Sisters of Mercy (Loughrea, Ireland) []
S.M. Sisters of Mercy of Tralee []
S.M.G. Poor Servants of the Mother of God [3640]
S.M.I. Sisters of Mary Immaculate [2440]
S.M.I. Sisters of Mary Immaculate of Nyeri [2445]
S.M.I.C. Missionary Sisters of the Immaculate Conception of the Mother of God [2760]
S.M.M.G. Sisters of Mary, Mother of God []
S.M.M.I. Sisters Minor of the Mary Immaculate [2677]
S.M.M.I. Salesian Missionaries of Mary Immaculate [3468]
S.M.M.S. Society of Mary Missionary Sisters []
S.M.P. Sisters of Mary of the Presentation [2450]
S.M.P. Daughters of Our Mother of Peace []
S.M.P. Society of Our Mother of Peace []
S.M.R. Society of Mary Reparatrix [2460]
S.M.S.H. Sisters of Saint Marthe (of St. Hyacinthe) [3940]
S.M.S.M. Marist Missionary Sisters [2420]

S.N.D. Sisters of Notre Dame of the United States....[2990]
S.N.D.deN. Sisters of Notre Dame de Namur............[3000]
S.N.J.M. Sisters of the Holy Names of Jesus and Mary ....[1990]
S.O.L.M. Sisters of Our Lady of Mercy........................[2670]
S.O.L.P.H. Sisters of Our Lady of Perpetual Help............[]
S.O.L.T. Sisters of the Society of Our Lady of the Most Holy Trinity........[3105]
S.P. Sisters of Providence........[3340]
S.P. Sisters of Providence........[3350]
S.P. Sisters of Providence of Saint Mary-of-the-Woods, IN ....[3360]
S.P.C. Sisters of St. Paul of Chartres........[3980]
S.R. Sisters of Reparation of the Sacred Wounds of Jesus ....[3475]
S.R.C.M. Sisters of Reparation of the Congregation of Mary ....[3470]
S.S.A. Sisters of St. Ann........[3718]
S.S.A. Sisters of St. Anne........[3720]
S.S.C. Missionary Sisters of St. Columban........[2880]
S.S.C. Society of the Sisters of the Church........[]
SS.CC. Congregation of the Sacred Hearts and of Perpetual Adoration........[3690]
S.S.Ch. Sisters of St. Chretienne........[3750]
S.S.C.J. Servants of the Most Sacred Heart of Jesus ....[3630]
S.S.C.J. Sisters of the Sacred Heart of Jesus of Saint Jacut ....[3670]
S.S.C.K. Congregation of Sister Servants of Christ the King........[3510]
S.S.C.M. Servants of the Holy Heart of Mary........[3520]
SS.C.M. Sisters of Saints Cyril and Methodius........[3780]
S.S.D. Institute of the Sisters of St. Dorothy........[3790]
S.S.E. Sisters of St. Elizabeth........[3800]
S.S.F. Congregation of the Sisters of the Holy Family ....[1950]
S.S.F.C.R. School Sisters of St. Francis of Christ O.S.F. the King........[1520]
S.S.H. Sisters Servants of the Most Sacred Heart........[]
S.S.H.J. Sisters of the Sacred Heart of Jesus........[3658]
S.S.H.J.P. Servants of the Sacred Heart of Jesus and of the Poor........[3660]
S.S.J. Servants of St. Joseph........[3595]
S.S.J. Sisters of St. Joseph (Buffalo)........[3830-06]
S.S.J. Sisters of St. Joseph (Burlington)........[3830-07]
S.S.J. Sisters of St. Joseph (Erie)........[3830-09]
S.S.J. Sisters of St. Joseph (Kalamazoo, Nazareth) ....[3830-11]
S.S.J. Sisters of St. Joseph (Ogdensburg)........[3830-12]
S.S.J. Sisters of St. Joseph (Rochester)........[3830-14]
S.S.J. Sisters of St. Joseph, (Springfield, MA)........[3830-16]
S.S.J. Sisters of St. Joseph (Wheeling, Eng)........[3830-17]
S.S.J. Sisters of Saint Joseph of Chestnut Hill, Philadelphia........[3893]
S.S.J. Sisters of St. Joseph of St. Augustine, Florida ....[3900]
S.S.J.C. Sisters of St. Joseph Benedict Cottolengo........[]
S.S.J.-T.O.S.F. Sisters of St. Joseph of the Third Order of St. Francis........[3930]
S.S.L. Congregation of the Sisters of St. Louis, Juilly-Monaghan........[3935]
S.S.LOG. Seton Sisters of Our Lady of Guadalupe, Tucson........[]
S.S.M. Sisters of the Sorrowful Mother (Third Order of St. Francis)........[4100]
S.S.M.I. Sisters Servants of Mary Immaculate........[3510]
S.S.M.I. Sisters Servants of Mary Immaculate........[3610]
S.S.M.I. Sisters Servants of Mary Immaculate........[3620]
S.S.M.N. Sisters of Saint Mary of Namur........[3950]
S.S.M.O. Sisters of St. Mary of Oregon........[3960]
S.S.N.D. School Sisters of Notre Dame........[2970]
S.S.P.C. Missionary Sisters of St. Peter Claver........[3990]
S.Sp.S. Missionary Sisters Servants of the Holy Spirit........[3530]
S.Sp.S.- Sister Servants of the Holy Spirit deA.P. of Perpetual Adoration........[3540]
S.S.S. Servants of the Blessed Sacrament........[3500]
S.S.S. Sisters of Social Service of Los Angeles, Inc. ...[4080]
S.S.S. Sisters of Social Service of Buffalo, Inc.........[4090]
S.S.S.F. School Sisters of St. Francis........[1680]
S.S.T.V. Congregation of Sisters of St. Thomas of Villanova ....[4030]
S.S.V.M Servants of the Lord and Virgin of Matara, Inc. ....[3625]
S.T.J. Society of St. Teresa of Jesus........[4020]
S.U. Society of St. Ursula........[4040]
S.U.S.C. Sisters of the Holy Union........[2070]
S.V. Sisters of Life........[2265]
S.V.M. Sisters of the Visitation of the Congregation of the Immaculate Heart of Mary........[4200]
V.D.C. Verbum Dei Community........[]
V.D.M.F. Verbum Dei Missionary Fraternity.........[4140]
V.H.M. Visitation Nuns........[4190]
V.S. Vestiarski Sisters........[]
V.S.C. Vincentian Sisters of Charity........[4160]
V.S.C. Vincentian Sisters of Charity........[4170]
X.M.M. Xaverian Missionary Society of Mary, Inc.....[4230]
X.S. Catholic Mission Sisters of St. Francis Xavier....[3810]

Religious Institutes of Women

Leadership of Women Religious in the United States of America—National Office: 8737 Colesville Rd., Suite 610, Silver Spring, MD 20910. Tel: 301-588-4955; Fax: 301-587-4575; Website: www.lcwr.org. Sr. Rebecca Ann Gemma, O.P., Pres.; Sr. Maureen Geary, O.P., Pres.-Elect; Sr. Mary Jane Herb, I.H.M., Past Pres.; Sr. Maureen O'Connor, O.S.F., Treas.; Sr. Carol Zinn, C.S.J., Exec. Dir. Council of Major Superiors of Women Religious in the United States of America—415 Michigan Ave., N.E., Ste. 420, P.O. Box 4467, Washington, DC 20017-0467. Tel: 202-832- 2575; Fax: 202-832-6325; Website: cmswr.org. Mother Anna Grace Neenan, O.P., Chairperson; Sr. Anne Catherine Burleigh, O.P. Asst. Chairperson; Mother Margaret Mary Waldron, C.K., Sec.; Sr. Judith Ann Duvall, O.S.F., Treas.; Sr. Mary Bendyna, O.P., Exec. Dir.

(The initial (D) or (P) indicates Diocesan or Pontifical Jurisdiction.)

[0100] (A.S.C.)—ADORERS OF THE BLOOD OF CHRIST (P)

Founded in Acuto, Italy, in 1834. First foundation in the United States in 1870.

General Motherhouse: Via Beata Maria De Mattias 10, Rome, Italy, 00183. Sr. Nadia Coppa, A.S.C., Supr. Gen.

Regional Offices - United States Region: Adorers of the Blood of Christ, 4233 Sulphur Ave., Saint Louis, MO 63109. Tel: 314-351-6294; Fax: 314-351-6789. Sr. Vicki Bergkamp, A.S.C., Regl. Leader.

Professed Sisters: 166.

Properties owned and/or sponsored: Villa Maria, Mulvane, KS; Newman University, Wichita, KS; St. Anne's Retirement Community, Inc.; De Matias Residence; St. Anne's Independent Living Retirement Village, Columbia PA.

Legal Title: Adorers of the Blood of Christ.

Sisters serve and staff: Colleges; Secondary & Elementary Schools; Special & Religious Education; Hospitals; Pastoral Care; Nursing Homes; Administration in Religious Orders & Parishes; Prayer Ministry; Retreat Ministry; Social Service; Pastoral & Chaplaincy Ministry; Prison & Minority Ministries; Ministry to the Homeless; Diocesan Offices; Home Nursing; Foreign Missions.

Represented in the Archdioceses of Kansas City in Kansas, St. Louis, San Antonio and Washington and in the Dioceses of Belleville, El Paso, Harrisburg, Kansas City-St. Joseph, Lincoln, Springfield-Cape Girardeau, Springfield in Illinois, Wilmington, Wichita and Youngstown. Also in Korea and Rome.

Ruma Center (1876): 2 Pioneer Ln., Red Bud, IL 62278. Tel: 618-282-3848.

Wichita Center (1929): 1165 Southwest Blvd., Wichita, KS 67213-1394. Tel: 316-942-2201.

Columbia Center (1925): 3954 Columbia Ave., Columbia, PA 17512-9714. Tel: 717-285-4536.

[0110] (A.P.B.)—THE SISTERS ADORERS OF THE PRECIOUS BLOOD (P) (Cloistered Contemplative Order)

American Federation: Consisting of Four Autonomous Monasteries: 400 Pratt St., Watertown, NY 13601-4238. Tel: 315-788-1669. Sr. Joan Milot, A.P.B., Pres. American Federation.

Professed Sisters: 44; Novices: 2; Postulants: 1.

Represented in the Dioceses of Brooklyn, Manchester, Ogdensburg and Portland (In Maine).

New York: 5400 Ft. Hamilton Pkwy., Brooklyn, NY 11219. Tel: 718-438-6371.

New Hampshire: 700 Bridge St., Manchester, NH 03104. Tel: 603-623-4264.

New York: 400 Pratt St., Watertown, NY 13601. Tel: 718-788-1669. Professed Sisters: 6.

Maine: 166 State St., Portland, ME 04101. Tel: 207-774-0861.

[0130] (A.S.C.J.)—APOSTLES OF THE SACRED HEART OF JESUS (P)

Founded in Italy in 1894. First Foundation in United States 1902.

General Motherhouse: Apostole del Sacro Cuore di Gesu, Via Germano Sommeiller 38, Rome, Italy, 00185. Mother Miriam Sobrinha Cunha, A.S.C.J., Supr. Gen.; Sr. Susana de Jesus Fadel, Sec.

U.S. Provincial Motherhouse: Mount Sacred Heart, 295 Benham St., Hamden, CT 06514. Tel: 203-248-4225; Fax: 203-230-8341; Email: secretary@ascjus.org.

Professed Sisters: 103.

Properties owned and/or sponsored: Mount Sacred Heart College for Sisters; Sacred Heart Academy; Sacred Heart Manor; Sacred Heart on the Lake; Apostles of the Sacred Heart of Jesus, New York, Inc.; Clelian Adult Day Center, Hamden, CT; Cor Jesu Academy, St. Louis, MO; Sacred Heart Villa Nursery, St. Louis, MO; Clelian Heights School for Exceptional Children, Greensburg, PA; Sacred Heart Private School, Bronx, NY; Mary, Mother of the Church Convent, Hamden, CT; Mount Sacred Heart Provincialate Convent, Hamden, CT; Sr. Antonine Signorelli Formation House, Hamden, CT; Sacred Heart Academy Convent, Hamden, CT; Sacred Heart Manor Convent, Hamden, CT; Cor Jesu Academy Convent, St. Louis, MO; Clelian House Convent, St. Louis, MO; Clelian Heights Convent, Greensburg, PA.

Legal Title: Corporation Name: Apostles of the Sacred Heart of Jesus, Incorporated.

Ministry in the fields of Education, Health Care, Parishes, Adult Day Care, Pastoral Ministry and Immigrant Services.

Represented in the Archdioceses of Hartford, New York and St. Louis and in the Dioceses of Bridgeport, Greensburg, Norwich and Pensacola-Tallahassee. Also in Rome, Sicily and Ireland.

Clelian House Convent: 5324 Wilson Ave., St. Louis, MO 63110.

Cor Jesu Academy Convent: 10230 Gravois Rd., St. Louis, MO 63123.

Sacred Heart Villa Convent: 2108 Macklind Ave., St. Louis, MO 63110.

[0150] (S.A.S.V.)—SISTERS OF THE ASSUMPTION (P)

Founded in Saint-Gregoire, P.Q., Canada in 1853. First foundation in the United States in 1891.

General Motherhouse: Nicolet, Canada Sr. Muriel Lemoine, S.A.S.V., Congregational Leader.

United States Region: 316 Lincoln St., Worcester, MA 01605. Tel: 508-856-9383. Sr. Lorraine Normand, S.A.S.V., Regl. Treas.

Total in Region and Professed: 48.

Ministry in all levels of education.

Missions in Japan, Brazil and Ecuador.

Represented in the Archdiocese of Boston and in the Dioceses of Fall River, Portland (In Maine), Providence, Springfield in Massachusetts and Worcester.

[0160] (O.S.A.)—AUGUSTINIAN NUNS OF CONTEMPLATIVE LIFE (P)

Augustinian Contemplative Nuns: Mother of Good Counsel Convent, 440 N. Marley Rd., New Lenox, IL 60451. Email: augustiniannuns@sbcglobal.net; Sr. Mary Grace Kuppe, O.S.A., Prioress.

Total in Community: 4.

Legal Title: Augustinian Cloistered Nuns, Inc.

Represented in the Diocese of Joliet.

[0170] (O.S.B.)—BENEDICTINE NUNS OF THE CONGREGATION OF SOLESMES (P)

Order originated in Italy, c.529. Congregation of Solesmes formed in France in 1837.

U.S. Establishment (1981): Monastery of the Immaculate Heart of Mary, 4103 VT Rte. 100, Westfield, VT 05874. Tel: 802-744-6525; Fax: 802-744-6236. Email: monastery@ihmwestfield.com. Rev. Mother Benedict McLaughlin, O.S.B., Prioress.

Total in Congregation: 882; Total in Community: 16.

Represented in the Diocese of Burlington.

[0180] (O.S.B.)—BENEDICTINE NUNS OF THE PRIMITIVE OBSERVANCE (P)

First founded in Italy in about c.529. First United States establishment in 1948.

Abbey of Regina Laudis: 273 Flanders Rd., Bethlehem, CT 06751. Tel: 203-266-7727. Rt. Rev. Mother Lucia Kuppens, Abbess.

Professed Nuns: 28; Sisters in First Vows: 1; Novices: 2; Postulants: 2.

[0190] (O.S.B.)—BENEDICTINE NUNS (P)

First founded in Italy in c.529. Founded in the United States in 1931 from St. Walburg Abbey, Eichstatt, Bavaria, Germany.

The Sisters of St. Benedict of Westmoreland County: St. Emma Monastery, 1001 Harvey Ave., Greensburg, PA 15601-1491. Tel: 724-834-3060; Fax: 724-834-5772; Email: benedictinenuns@stemma.org. Mother Mary Anne Noll, O.S.B., Prioress.

Professed Nuns: 9.

Ministry in Monastic Life; Benedictine hospitality extended through adjacent St. Emma Retreat House; Monastic Guest House.

Represented in the Diocese of Greensburg.

Benedictine Nuns: Abbey of St. Walburga, 1029 Benedictine Way, Virginia Dale, CO 80536. Tel: 970-472-0612; Email: abbey@walburga.org. Mother Maria Michael Newe, O.S.B., Abbess; Mother Maria-Thomas Beil, O.S.B., Retired Abbess.

Sisters: 19; Postulants: 2; Claustral Oblates: 2.

Represented in the Archdiocese of Denver.

[0210] (O.S.B.)—MISSIONARY BENEDICTINE SISTERS (P)

The Congregation of Missionary Benedictine Sisters is of Pontifical Jurisdiction. Its Constitutions were approved by Rome on June 25, 1934; Revised approval June 29, 1983.

Generalate: Rome, Italy.

Priory House and Novitiate: Immaculata Monastery (1923), 300 N. 18th St., Norfolk, NE 68701-3622. Tel: 402-371-3438; Fax: 402-371-0127. Sr. Roseann Ocken, O.S.B., Prioress.

Professed Sisters: 36.

Legal Holdings or Titles: Missionary Benedictine Sisters, Inc., Norfolk, NE; Hildegard House, Creighton, NE.

Ministry in the fields of Retreat; Education; Health; Outreach Services with Hispanics and Elderly.

Represented in the Archdiocese of Omaha.

[0220] (O.S.B.)—CONGREGATION OF THE BENEDICTINE SISTERS OF PERPETUAL ADORATION OF PONTIFICAL JURISDICTION (P)

Founded from Maria Rickenbach, Switzerland in 1874 with first monastery at Clyde, MO. Congregation erected by decree of the Holy See on June 16, 1936.

General Motherhouse: Benedictine Convent of Perpetual Adoration, 31970 State Hwy. P, Clyde, MO 64432. Tel: 660-944-2221; Fax: 660-944-2133; Email sister@benedictinesisters.org; Web: benedictinesisters.org. Sr. Dawn Annette Mills, Prioress Gen.

Total in Congregation: 46.

Ministry in Monastic/Contemplative/Eucharistic Apostolate of Prayer; Liturgy of the Hours four times daily in Choir; Contemplative Prayer and Monastic Atmosphere Shared with Others; Editing and Publishing Bimonthly Magazine: Spirit & Life; Production and Distribution of Altar Breads; Correspondence.

Represented in the Diocese of Kansas City-St. Joseph.

[0230] (O.S.B.)—BENEDICTINE SISTERS OF PONTIFICAL JURISDICTION (P)

(I) The Monastic Congregation of St. Scholastica

Erected by Decree of the Holy See, February 25, 1922, with final approbation by Decree of June 10, 1930. Sixteen Monasteries in the United States and one in Mexico. Total number in the Federation 473. Sr. Lynn Marie McKenzie, O.S.B., Federation Pres., residing at: Sacred Heart Monastery, 916 Convent Rd., N.E., Cullman, AL 35055. Tel: 256-615-6115.

Benedictine Sisters of Baltimore, Inc: Emmanuel Monastery, 2229 W. Joppa Rd., Lutherville Timonium, MD 21093. Tel: 410-821-5792; Fax: 410-296-9560; Email: bensrs@emmanuelosb.org; Web: www.emmanuelosb.org.

Total in Community: 11.

Ministry in Retreats and Spiritual Direction; Justice Ministry; Social Services; Hospital Service Ministry; Music/Music Therapy.

Represented in the Archdiocese of Baltimore.

Benedictine Sisters of the Byzantine Rite (1969): Queen of Heaven Monastery, 169 Kenmore Ave., N.E., #302, Warren, OH 44483. Tel: 330-856-1813. Sr. Barbara Pavlik, O.S.B., Admin.

Professed Sisters: 2.

Ministry in Religious Education; Pastoral Ministry; Administration.

Represented in the Archdiocese of Pittsburgh Byzantine Rite.

Mount St. Scholastica Inc. (1863): Motherhouse of the Sisters of St. Benedict, 801 South 8th St., Atchison, KS 66002-2724. Tel: 913-360-6200; Fax: 913-360-6190. Vocation Director Email: vocation@mountosb.org. Web: www.mountosb.org. Sr. Esther Fangman, O.S.B., Prioress.

Professed Sisters: 91; Novice: 1.

Legal Holdings: Dooley Center, Inc.; Mount St. Scholastica, Inc., Atchison, KS.

Ministry in the field of Academic Education at all levels; Counseling; Retreats; Spirituality Center; Spiritual Direction; Social Services; Hospitality; Pastoral Ministry; Ministry to women of all ages; Missionary Work in Brazil.

Represented in the Archdiocese of Kansas City in Kansas and in the Diocese of Kansas City-St. Joseph. Also in Brazil.

Benedictine Sisters of Erie (1856): Mount St. Benedict Monastery, 6101 East Lake Rd., Erie, PA 16511. Tel: 814-899-0614; Fax: 814-898-4004. Sr. Anne Wambach, O.S.B., Prioress.

Total in Congregation: 92; Final Profession: 85; First Profession: 4; Postulants: 3.

Properties owned and/or sponsored: Mount Saint Benedict Monastery; Glinodo Center; St. Benedict Education Center; Benet Center; 6 Community Houses; St. Benedict Community Center.

Sisters serve and staff: Elementary Schools; Colleges; Day Care Centers; Residence for Elderly and Handicapped; Nat'l Mission Office; Social Services; Diocesan Offices; Pastoral Ministry; Publications & Communications; Religious Education.

Represented in the Dioceses of Cleveland and Erie.

Benedictine Sisters of Chicago O.S.B. (1861): St. Scholastica Monastery, 7430 N. Ridge Blvd., Chicago, IL 60645. Tel: 773-764-2413; Email: prioress@osbchicago.org. Sr. Judith Murphy, O.S.B., Prioress; Sr. Virginia Jung, Community Archivist.

Professed Sisters: 23.

Properties owned and/or sponsored: St. Scholastica Monastery, Chicago, IL.

Sisters serve and staff: Parish Ministry; Religious Education; Spiritual Direction; Shelter Ministry; Community Center Work; Social Service & Pastoral Counseling; Massage Therapy; Group Facilitation; Immigrant Support; Interfaith Ministry; University Chaplaincy, Pre-School.

Represented in the Archdioceses of Chicago and New Orleans and in the Diocese of Pueblo.

Benedictine Sisters of the Sacred Heart O.S.B. (1895): Sacred Heart Monastery, 1910 Maple Ave., Lisle, IL 60532-2164. Tel: 630-725-6000. Sr. Mary Bratrsovsky, O.S.B., Prioress.

Professed Sisters: 21.

Legal Title: Benedictine Sisters of the Sacred Heart Charitable Trust.

Sisters serve and staff: Villa St. Benedict; Religious and Social Education; Pastoral Ministry; Diocesan and Parish Liturgical Director.

Represented in the Diocese of Joliet.

Benedictine Sisters of Elizabeth, NJ O.S.B. (1868): St. Walburga Monastery, 851 N. Broad St., Elizabeth, NJ 07208. Tel: 908-352-4278. Sr. Mariette Thérèse Bernier, O.S.B., Prioress; Sr. Marcia Lammerding, O.S.B., Sub Prioress.

Professed Sisters: 22.

Legal Holdings and Titles: Benedictine Academy, Elizabeth, NJ.

Represented in the Archdioceses of Newark and New York.

Benedictine Sisters of Pittsburgh, PA O.S.B. (1870): St. Benedict Monastery, 3526 Bakerstown Rd., Bakerstown, PA 15007-9705. Tel: 724-502-2600; Fax: 724-502-2601; Email: osbpgh@osbpgh.org; Web: www.osbpgh.org. Sr. Karen R. Brink, O.S.B., Prioress.

Professed Sisters: 34.

Ministry in the field of Education at all levels; Religious; Pastoral Ministry; Social Service; Art Education; Outreach with Poor.

Represented in the Diocese of Pittsburgh.

Benedictine Sisters O.S.B. (1879): St. Joseph Monastery, 2200 S. Lewis, Tulsa, OK 74114-3100. Tel: 918-742-4989; Fax: 918-744-1374; Email: mtlong@stjosephmonastery.org. Sr. Marie Therese Long, O.S.B., Prioress.

Sisters: 14; Professed Sisters: 13.

Legal Holdings and Titles: Congregation of the Benedictine Sisters of the Sacred Hearts; Monte Cassino School.

Ministry in the field of Academic Education; Catechetics; Hospitality – Directed Retreats; Spiritual Direction; Religious Education & Religious Formation.

Represented in the Diocese of Tulsa.

Benedictine Sisters of Pontifical Jurisdiction O.S.B. (1857): St. Gertrude Monastery, 14259 Benedictine Ln., Ridgely, MD 21660-1434. Tel: 410-634-2497. Sr. Jacquelyn Ernster, O.S.B., Admin.

Professed Sisters: 15.

Legal Holdings & Titles: St. Benedict, Wilmington, DE.

Ministry in Special Schools; Ministry to the poor and homeless.

Represented in the Diocese of Wilmington.

St. Walburg Monastery of Benedictine Sisters of Covington, KY O.S.B. (1859): St. Walburg Monastery, 2500 Amsterdam Rd., Villa Hills, KY 41017-5316. Tel: 859-331-6324; Fax: 859-331-2136. Sr. Aileen Bankemper, O.S.B., Prioress; Sr. Deborah Harmeling, O.S.B., Community Archivist.

Professed Sisters: 29.

Legal Titles and Holdings: Villa Madonna Montessori School; Villa Madonna Academy.

Sisters serve and staff: Diocesan Offices; Pastoral and Social Ministry; High School.

Represented in the Dioceses of Covington and Pueblo.

Benedictine Sisters of Cullman, AL (1902): Sacred Heart Monastery, 916 Convent Rd., Cullman, AL 35055. Tel: 256-734-4622; Fax: 256-255-0048. Sr. Lynn Elisabeth Meadows, O.S.B., Prioress; Sr. Thérèse Haydel, O.S.B., Community Archivist.

Professed Sisters: 32.

Properties owned and/or sponsored: Benedictine Sisters Retreat Center; Sacred Heart Monastery of Cullman, AL Foundation.

Sisters serve and staff: Education; Parish Ministry; Retreat Centers; Rural Health Center (Doctor); Law.

Represented in the Diocese of Birmingham.

Benedictine Sisters of Virginia O.S.B. (1868): St. Benedict Monastery, 9535 Linton Hall Rd., Bristow, VA 20136-1217. Tel: 703-361-0106. Email: jburley@osbva.org. Sr. Joanna Burley, O.S.B., Prioress.

Total Professed Sisters: 27.

Legal Holdings and Titles: Benedictine Sisters of Virginia, Inc.; Linton Hall School; Benedictine Pastoral Center; Benedictine Counseling Services, Bristow, VA; B.E.A.C.O.N., Bristow, VA.

Represented in the Dioceses of Arlington and Richmond.

Benedictine Sisters (1911): (Congregation of Benedictine Sisters), 216 W. Highland Dr., Boerne, TX 78006. Tel: 830-816-8504; Fax: 830-249-1365. Email: sahrosb@gvtc.com. Sr. Bernadine Reyes, O.S.B., Prioress.

Total in Community: 13.

Properties owned and/or sponsored: St. Scholastica Monastery; Benedictine Sisters Charitable Trust Fund; Benedictine Sisters Charitable Trust Two; Omega Retreat Center; The Health and Wholeness Center.

Represented in the Archdiocese of San Antonio and in the Diocese of Laredo.

Benedictine Sisters of St. Lucy's Priory Inc. O.S.B. (1956): St. Lucy's Priory, 19045 E. Sierra Madre Ave., Glendora, CA 91741. Tel: 626-335-1682; Email: stlucysebrown@aol.com. Sr. Elizabeth Brown, O.S.B., Prioress.

Professed Sisters: 4.

Legal Holdings: St. Lucy's Priory High School.

Sisters serve and staff: all levels of Academic Education; Pastoral Ministry.

Represented in the Archdiocese of Los Angeles and in the Diocese of San Bernardino.

Benedictine Sisters of Florida (1889): Holy Name Monastery, P.O. Box 2450, St. Leo, FL 33574-2450. Tel: 352-588-8320; Fax: 352-588-8319. Email: holyname@saintleo.edu. Sr. Roberta Bailey, O.S.B., Prioress; Sr. Roberta Bailey, O.S.B., Archivist.

Professed Sisters: 12.

Represented in the Diocese of St. Petersburg.

Sisters of St. Benedict (1963): Benet Hill Monastery Motherhouse, 3190 Benet Ln., Colorado Springs, CO 80921-1509. Tel: 719-633-0655; Fax: 719-471-0403. Sr. Clare Carr, O.S.B., Prioress; Sr. S. Margaret Meaney, O.S.B., Community Archivist.

Total in Community: 27.

Properties owned and/or sponsored: Benet Hill Monastery and Ministry Center.

Represented in the Archdiocese of Denver and in the Diocese of Colorado Springs.

Benedictine Sisters O.S.B. (1989): Queen of Angels Monastery, 23615 N.E. 100th St., Liberty, MO 64068. Tel: 816-750-4618; Fax: 816-750-4620; Web: www.libertybenedictinesisters.org. Sr. Agnes Helgenberger, O.S.B., Prioress.

Professed Sisters: 6.

Ministry in Companioning; food for the hungry; prison ministry; thrift stores; Religious education and retreats; Nursing.

Represented in the Diocese of Kansas City-St. Joseph.

Erected by Decree of the Apostolic See on April 14, 1937, with final approbation by Decree of April 4, 1950.

(II) The Monastic Congregation of St. Gertrude:

Office: Sacred Heart Monastery (1880), 1005 W. 8th St., Yankton, SD 57078-3389. Tel: 605-668-6000; Fax: 605-668-6153. Email: jweber@yanktonbenedictines.org. Sr. Jeanne Weber, O.S.B., Federation Pres.

Total in Federation: 429.

Twelve member monasteries from this Federation as follows:

Monastery of St. Gertrude (1882): 465 Keuterville Rd., Cottonwood, ID 83522-5183. Tel: 208-962-3224; Fax: 208-962-7212. Email: kjordan@stgertrudes.org. Sr. Mary Forman, O.S.B., Prioress; Rev. Meinrad Schallberger, O.S.B., Chap.

Professed Sisters: 32.

Legal Title: Idaho Corporation of Benedictine Sisters.

Sisters serve in Parish Ministry; Health Care; Retreat Ministry; Social Work; Counseling; St. Gertrude's Museum, Spirit Center Retreat House.

Represented in the Archdioceses of Los Angeles and Seattle and in the Dioceses of Boise and Spokane.

Sisters of St. Benedict of Crookston O.S.B: Mount St. Benedict Monastery (1919): 620 E. Summit Ave., Crookston, MN 56716-2713. Tel: 218-281-3441; Fax: 218-281-6966. Email: crxbenedictines@gmail.com. Sr. Jane Becker, O.S.B., Admin.

Professed Sisters: 27.

Represented in the Dioceses of Brownsville and Crookston.

Benedictine Sisters O.S.B. (1867): Monastery Immaculate Conception, 802 E. 10th St., Ferdinand, IN 47532-9239. Tel: 812-367-1411; Fax: 812-367-2313. Sr. Anita Louise Lowe, O.S.B., Prioress.

Perpetually Professed Sisters: 110; Exclaustration: 2; Peru: 7. Total: 118.

Legal Title: Sisters of St. Benedict of Ferdinand, IND, Inc.

Sponsorships: Benet Hall.

Sisters serve and staff: on all levels of Academic Education; Religious Education; Parish Ministry; Hospitals; Public Health-Social Service Agencies; Diocesan Offices; Foreign Missions; Latino Ministries; Hospitality Center; Spirituality Ministry; Community Ministry; Psychology and Counseling Agencies.

Represented in the Archdiocese of Indianapolis and Louisville and in the Diocese of Evansville. Also in Peru.

Benedictine Sisters, O.S.B. of St. Scholastica Monastery (1879): St. Scholastica Monastery, 1315 S. Albert Pike, P.O. Box 3849, Fort Smith, AR 72913. Tel: 479-783-4147; Fax: 479-782-4352; Email: email@stscho.org. Sr. Kimberly Rose Prohaska, O.S.B., Prioress. Email: monastery@stscho.org; kimberly@stscho.org; prioress@stscho.org.

Professed Sisters: 24; Novice 1.

Ministry: Retreat Ministry; House of Prayer; Teaching, Spiritual Direction; University/Marketing, Parish Ministry and sponsor education for orphans in Guatemala.

Benedictine Sisters of Mt. Angel, Oregon (1882): Queen of Angels Monastery, 840 S. Main St., Mount Angel, OR 97362-9527. Tel: 503-845-6141; Fax: 503845-6585; Email: info@benedictine-srs.org; Web: www.benedictine-srs.org. Sr. Jane Hibbard, SNJM, Pastoral Admin.

Legal Title: Benedictine Sisters of Mt. Angel, Oregon

Professed Sisters: 20.

Ministry: Shalom at the Monastery Retreat Ministry, Mt. Angel, OR.

Sisters serve: Seminary; Retreat and Prayer Ministry; Spiritual Direction; Ministry to homeless and poor; parish ministry.

Represented in the Archdiocese of Portland in Oregon.

Benedictine Convent of St. Martin (1889): St. Martin Monastery, 1851 City Spring Rd., Rapid City, SD 57702-9613. Tel: 605-343-8011; Fax: 605-399-2723. Email: jennifer.kehrwald@gmail.com. Sr. Jennifer Kehrwald, Admin.

Professed Sisters: 12.
Ministry in the fields of Retreat and Spiritual Direction.
Represented in the Diocese of Rapid City.

Sisters of St. Benedict of Beech Grove, Ind., Inc. (1956): Our Lady of Grace Monastery, 1402 Southern Ave., Beech Grove, IN 46107-1197. Tel: 317-787-3287; Fax: 317-780-2368. Email: prioress@benedictine.com. Sr. Julie Sewell, O.S.B., Prioress.
Professed Sisters: 46.
Legal Titles: Sisters of St. Benedict of Beech Grove, Ind., Inc.; Charitable Trust of the Monastery of Our Lady of Grace, Sisters of the Order of St. Benedict.
Ministry in Education; Retreat Center; Religious Education.
Represented in the Archdioceses of Cincinnati and Indianapolis.
Properties owned and sponsored: Our Lady of Grace Monastery; Benedict Inn Retreat and Conference Center; Regina Retreat.

Benedictine Sisters of Richardton, O.S.B. (1916): Sacred Heart Monastery (1916), 2441 10th Ave. West, Dickinson, ND 58601. Tel: 701-456-1900; Fax: 701-456-1919. Email: prioress@sacredheartmonastery.com. Sr. Paula Larson, O.S.B., Prioress.
Professed Sisters: 15.
Legal Titles or Holdings: Benedictine Sponsorship Board, Inc.; Sacred Heart Benedictine Foundation; Pia Tegler Benedictine Foundation.
Ministry in the fields of Chaplaincy and Health Care.
Represented in the Diocese of Bismarck.

The Benedictine Sisters of Mother of God Monastery O.S.B: Mother of God Monastery (1961): 110 28th Ave., S.E., Watertown, SD 57201-8418. Tel: 605-882-6600; Fax: 605-882-6658. Sr. Terri Hoffman, Prioress. Email: prioress@watertownbenedictines.org.
Perpetual Vows: 42
Legal Titles: The Benedictine Sisters of Mother of God Monastery, Watertown, SD; St. Ann's Corporation (includes Benet Place), Watertown, SD; Retirement Trust, Watertown, SD.
Sisters serve: Retreat Center; Spiritual Direction Ministry; Hispanic Ministries and Congregate Housing for Elderly.
Represented in the Archdiocese of St. Paul-Minneapolis and in the Diocese of Sioux Falls.

St. Benedict's Monastery (1912): 225 Masters Ave., Winnipeg, Canada, R4A 2A1. Tel: 204-794-1943. Email: stbensmon@gmail.com. Sr. Dorothy Levandosky, O.S.B., Admin.
Professed Sisters: 12.
Ministry in Prayer and Spiritual Direction.
Represented in Canada.

Benedictine Convent of the Sacred Heart: Sacred Heart Monastery (1880), 1005 W. 8th St., Yankton, SD 57078-3389. Tel: 605-668-6000; Fax: 605-668-6153. Sr. Maribeth Wentzlaff, O.S.B., Prioress.
Professed Sisters: 67.
Sisters serve and staff: in Health Care Institutions; Academic Education; Parish Ministry; Pastoral Care; Counseling, Religious Education & Administration; Spiritual Direction and Retreat Work.
Represented in the Archdiocese of Omaha and in the Dioceses of Sioux City & Sioux Falls.

Benedictine Sisters of Nanaimo: House of Bread Monastery (1993), 2329 Arbot Rd., Nanaimo, Canada, V9R 6S8. Tel: 250-753-1763. Email: houseofbread@shaw.ca. Sr. Barbara Rinehart, O.S.B., Prioress.
Professed Sisters: 7.
Corporate Ministry: Hospitality
Sisters serve: Prayer Ministry.
Represented in Canada.

(III): The Federation of St. Benedict: 104 Chapel Ln., St. Joseph, MN 56374-0220. Tel: 320-363-7004; Fax: 320-363-7130. Sr. Kerry O'Reilly, O.S.B., Pres. & Contact Person. Email: koreilly@csbsju.edu. Total number of Sisters in Federation: 358.
Legal Title: Federation of St. Benedict.
Erected by decree of the Holy See March 24, 1947.
Ten monasteries form this Federation; in addition to the seven American monasteries listed, three autonomous monasteries exist: Japan, St. Benedict's Monastery (1985) Muroran, Hokkaido; Taiwan, St. Benedict Monastery (1988) Tanshui, Taipei; Bahamas, Saint Martin Monastery (1994) Nassau.

Sisters of the Order of Saint Benedict-O.S.B. (1857): Monasterio Santa Escolastica, Apartado 8526, Humacao, Puerto Rico Tel: 787-852-4222; Fax: 787-850-5279. Sr. Angela Berrios, O.S.B. Sisters: 10; Novices: 1.
Legal Title: Sisters of the Order of Saint Benedict, Inc.
Ministry in the field of Education at all levels; Parish Ministry.
Represented in the Diocese of Caguas.

Sisters of the Order of Saint Benedict O.S.B. (1857): St. Benedict's Monastery-Motherhouse and Novitiate, 104 Chapel Ln., St. Joseph, MN 56374-0220. Tel: 320-363-7100. Sr. Susan Rudolph, O.S.B., Prioress; Sr. Patricia Kennedy, O.S.B., Archivist.
Total Sisters in Congregation: 159.
Legal Title: Sisters of the Order of Saint Benedict, St. Joseph, MN.
Ministry in the field of Education at all levels; Hospitals; Nursing Homes; Individual Apostolates; Parish Ministry; Social Work; Spirituality and Retreat Counseling; Pastoral Ministry.
Represented in the Archdioceses of St. Paul-Minneapolis and in the Diocese of St. Cloud.

Sisters of St. Benedict - St. Scholastica Monastery O.S.B. (1892): 1001 Kenwood Ave., Duluth, MN 55811. Tel: 218-723-6555. Sr. Beverly Raway, O.S.B., Prioress; Sr. Luce Marie Dionne, O.S.B., Archivist.
Total in Community: 51.
Ministry in the field of Academic Education; Religious Education; Residence for Elderly; Nursing Homes; Hospitals; Pastoral Care; Peace and Justice; Retreat Center.
Properties owned and/or sponsored: Benedictine Sisters Benevolent Association, McCabe Renewal Center, Duluth, MN; The College of St. Scholastica; Benedictine Health System; St. Mary's Medical Center, Duluth, MN; Benedictine Living Communities, Inc., Duluth, MN: Benedictine Living Center of Garrison, Garrison, ND; Benedictine Health System Foundation, Duluth, MN; Benedictine Living Communities, Inc., dba St. Gabriel's Community, Bismarck, ND; Prince of Peace Care Center & Evergreen Place, Ellendale, ND; St. Benedict's Health Center & Benedict's Court, Dickinson, ND; Benedictine Living Community of Wahpeton, Wahpeton, ND; St. Rose Care Center & Rosewood Court, LaMoure, ND; Polinsky Rehabilitation Center, Duluth, MN; St. Joseph's Medical Center, Brainerd, MN; St. Mary's Regional Health Center, Detroit Lakes, MN; St. Francis Regional Medical Center, Shakopee, MN; St. Mary's Hospital & Clinics, Cottonwood, ID; St. Gertrude's Health Rehabilitation and Center, Shakopee, MN; The Gardens at St. Gertrude's Shakopee, MN; St. Mary's Hospital, Superior, WI; St. Anne of Winona and Callista Court, Winona, MN; Villa St. Benedict, Lisle, IL; Villa St. Vincent, Crookston, MN, Benedictine Care Centers: Benedictine Health Center at Innsbruck, New Brighton, MN; Benedictine Living Community of St. Peter, St. Peter, MN; Madonna Meadows of Rochester, Rochester, MN; Madonna Towers of Rochester, Inc., Rochester, MN; Living Community of St. Joseph, St. Joseph, MO; Benedictine Senior Living at Steeple Pointe, Osseo, MN; Benedictine Health Center of Minneapolis, Minneapolis, MN; Holy Trinity Hospital, Graceville, MN; Graceville Health Center Clinic, Graceville, MN; Grace Home, Graceville, MN; Grace Village, Graceville, MN; Catholic Residential Services, Inc.; Benedictine Living Community of Wausau, Wausau, WI; Benedictine Living Community of LaCrosse, LaCrosse, WI; Bridges Care Center DBA Benedictine Living Community of Ada, Ada, MN; Benedictine Health Center DBA Benedictine Living Community, Duluth, MN.
Represented in the Archdioceses of Chicago and St. Paul-Minneapolis, and in the Dioceses of Bismarck, Boise, Crookston, Duluth, Fargo, Joliet, Kansas City-St. Joseph; LaCrosse, New Ulm, Peoria, Phoenix, St. Cloud, Superior and Winona-Rochester.

Sisters of St. Benedict O.S.B. (1874): St. Mary Monastery, 2200 88th Ave., W., Rock Island, IL 61201-7649. Tel: 309-283-2100; Fax: 309-283-2200; Email: benedictines@smmsisters.org. Sr. Susan Hutchens, O.S.B., Prioress; Sr. Marilyn Roman, Archivist.
Total in Community: 19.
Ministry in the field of Religious and Academic Education; Pastoral Care; Retreat Ministry; Prison Ministry.
Represented in the Diocese of Peoria.

Benedictine Sisters of the Annunciation, B.M.V. (1947): Annunciation Monastery, 7520 University Dr., Bismarck, ND 58504-9619. Tel: 701-255-1520. Sr. Nicole Kunze, O.S.B., Prioress.
Professed Sisters: 39.
Ministry in Hospitals; Parish Ministry and Catechetical Work; Education, Health Care and Spiritual Direction and Social Services.
Represented in the Diocese of Bismarck.

Sisters of St. Benedict (1948): St. Paul's Monastery, 2675 Benet Rd., St. Paul, MN 55109. Tel: 651-777-8181; Fax: 651-773-5124. Email: info@stpaulsmonastery.org. Sr. Catherine Nehotte, O.S.B., Prioress.
Professed Sisters: 20; Benedictine Associates 2.
Sisters serve and staff: Schools; Long term care facilities; Administration; Ministries to women and children; Retreat Ministries; Parish Ministry; Social Service and various other apostolic work.
Represented in the Archdiocese of St. Paul-Minneapolis.

Sisters of St. Benedict O.S.B. (1952): St. Placid Priory, 500 College St., NE, Lacey, WA 98516. Tel: 360-438-1771; Email: stplacid@stplacid.org. Sr. Sharon McDonald, O.S.B., Prioress.
Professed Sisters: 12.
Sisters serve in the field of Education; Spirituality and Pastoral Care.
Represented in the Archdioceses of Portland in Oregon and Seattle in Washington.

[0233] (O.S.B.)—BENEDICTINE NUNS (P)
Subiaco Congregation

St. Scholastica Priory, Benedictine Nuns (Cloistered): 271 N. Main St., Box 606, Petersham, MA 01366-0606. Tel: 978-724-3213. Email: sspriory@aol.com. Very Rev. Mother Mary Elizabeth Kloss, O.S.B., Prioress; Sr. Mary Angela Kloss, O.S.B., Sub-Prioress.
Junior Professed: 3.

[0235] (O.S.B.)—BENEDICTINE SISTERS (P)

Camaldolese Benedictines

Transfiguration Monastery: 701 NY Rte. 79, Windsor, NY 13865. Tel: 607-655-2366. Email: transfigurationmonastery@gmail.com. Sr. Sheila Long, O.S.B., Prioress.
Professed Nuns: 4.
Ministry in Monastic life and Benedictine hospitality.
Represented in the Diocese of Syracuse.

[0237] (O.S.B.)—BENEDICTINES OF MARY, QUEEN OF APOSTLES (D)

Established in the Diocese of Kansas City-St. Joseph in 2006.
Abbey of Our Lady of Ephesus: 8005 N.W. 316th St., Gower, MO 64454. Tel.: 816-424-3194; Mother Cecilia Snell, O.S.B., Abbess.
Total in Community: 57.
Ministries: Contemplation; Retreat House for Priests.
Represented in the Dioceses of Kansas City-St. Joseph and Springfield-Cape Girardeau.

[0240] (O.S.B.)—OLIVETAN BENEDICTINE SISTERS (D)

Established in the Diocese of Little Rock in 1887.

Motherhouse and Novitiate (1887): Holy Angels Convent, P.O. Drawer 1209, Jonesboro, AR 72403-1209. Tel: 870-935-5810; Fax: 870-935-4210. Mother Mary Clare Bezner, O.S.B., Prioress.
Professed Sisters: 27.
Properties owned and/or sponsored: St. Bernards Healthcare, Inc., Jonesboro, AR; St. Bernards Development Foundation, Inc., Jonesboro, AR.
Sisters serve and staff: Healthcare Ministries; Grammar Schools; Diocesan Ministries; Religious Education; Parish Services; Hispanic Center.
Represented in the Dioceses of Fort Worth and Little Rock.

[0250] (C.V.D.)—SISTERS OF BETHANY (P)

Founded in El Salvador in 1928.

General Motherhouse: Instituto Bethania, Santa Tecla, El Salvador Madre Adriana Maria Giraldo, Supr. Gen.; Mother Foundress Dolores de Maria Zea.

U.S. Address (1949): Bethany House, 850 N. Hobart Blvd., Los Angeles, CA 90029. Tel: 323-665-6937. Sr. Leticia Gomez, C.V.D., Supr.
Professed Sisters: 10.
Ministry in Parish Work, Residence.
Represented in the Archdiocese of Los Angeles.

[0260] (S.B.S.)—THE SISTERS OF THE BLESSED SACRAMENT FOR INDIANS AND COLORED PEOPLE (P)

Founded in the United States in 1891.

General Motherhouse: Four Neshaminy Interplex Dr., Suite 205, Trevose, PA 19053. Tel: 215-244-8174. Development Email: sbsdevelop1@verizon.net; schmidtsl@aol.com. Sr. Stephanie Henry, S.B.S., Pres.
Professed Sisters: 62.

Sisters serve and staff in the field of Education on all levels; Catechetical Schools; Adult Education and Social Service; Evangelization Center.
Represented in the Archdioceses of Cleveland, New Orleans, Philadelphia and Santa Fe and in the Dioceses of Gallup, Nashville, Richmond and Savannah.

[0270] (C.B.S.)—CONGREGATION OF BON SECOURS (P)

Founded in France in 1824. First foundation in the United States in 1881.
United States: Provincial House and Novitiate, 1525 Marriottsville Rd., Marriottsville, MD 21104. Tel: 410-442-3113; Fax: 410-442-1394. Provincial Offices Email: cbsoffice@bonsecoursusa.org. Vocation Office Email: CBSVocations@cbsusa.org. Sr. Fran Gorsuch, C.B.S., U.S.A. Leader; Sr. Elaine Davia, C.B.S., Congregation Leader; Sr. Rose Marie Jasinski, C.B.S.
Total Sisters in U.S.: 19.
Congregation of Bon Secours, C.B.S., Provincial House: 5912 Monument Avenue, Richmond, VA 23226.
Total Sisters in Order: 200.
Ministry in Healthcare.
Sisters own and operate: Retreat & Conference Center. Member of UNANIMA International, Inc.
Represented in the Archdioceses of Baltimore and in the Dioceses of Charleston and Richmond.

[0280] (O.SS.S.)—THE BRIGITTINE SISTERS (P)

Founded in Sweden in the 14th century.
Motherhouse: Rome, Italy.
Convent in U.S.A. (1957): Convent of St. Birgitta, 4 Runkenhage Rd., Darien, CT 06820. Tel: 203-655-1068; Fax: 203-655-3496; Email: conventsb@optonline.net. Sr. M. Renzy Sebastian, O.SS.S., Supr.
Professed Sisters: 7.
Legal Title: Order of the Most Holy Savior of St. Bridget.
Monastic tradition, Semi cloister.
Represented in the Diocese of Bridgeport.

[0300] (O.CARM.)—CALCED CARMELITES (P)

Carmelite Nuns of the Ancient Observance, Strictly Cloistered, belonging in the Second Order of Carmel.
Founded in Naples, Italy in 1536. First foundation in the United States in 1931.
Carmelite Monastery of St. Therese: Little Flower of Jesus and St. M. Magdalen De Pazzi, St. Therese's Valley, 3551 Lanark Rd., Coopersburg, PA 18036-9324. Web: www.carmelite-nuns.com. Mother Mary Gertrude, O.Carm., Prioress.
Professed Sisters: 6.
Legal Title: The Carmelite Sisters of St. Therese's Valley, Inc.
Represented in the Dioceses of Allentown, Fargo, San Angelo and Superior.

[0315] (C.C.W.)—CARMELITE COMMUNITY OF THE WORD (D)

Motherhouse & Novitiate: Incarnation Center (1971), 394 Bem Rd., Gallitzin, PA 16641. Fax: 814-886-7115. Sr. Marilyn Welch, C.C.W., Admin. Gen.
Total in Community: 13.
Ministries in Diocesan Administration; the field of Religious and Academic Education at all levels; Pastoral Care, Institutionalized, Elderly, Family Life Support Groups and the Poor; Parish Ministry; Mission activity in Appalachia & Haiti.
Represented in the Diocese of Altoona-Johnstown.

[0320] (O.CARM.)—CARMELITE NUNS OF THE ANCIENT OBSERVANCE (P)

Carmelite Nuns of the Ancient Observance
Strictly Cloistered, belonging to the Second Order of Carmel. Founded in Guelder, Holland, in 1453. First foundation in the United States in 1930.
Carmel of Mary (1954): 17765 78th St., S.E., Wahpeton, ND 58075. Tel: 701-642-2360. Email: carmelwahpeton@gmail.com. Mother Madonna of the Assumption, O.Carm., Prioress.
Total in Community: 10.
Represented in the Diocese of Fargo.
Monastery of Our Lady of Grace (1989): 6202 CR 339, Christoval, TX 76935-3023. Tel: 325-853-1722; Web: carmelnet.org/christoval/christoval.htm. Sr. Mary Grace, O.Carm., Sister Responsible.
Professed Sisters: 4; Novices: 1.
Represented in the Diocese of San Angelo.
Carmel of the Sacred Heart (1963): 430 Laurel Ave., Hudson, WI 54016. Tel: 715-386-2156. Email: carmelofthesacredheart@gmail.com. Sr. Lucia LaMontagne, O.Carm., Prioress & Archivist.
Professed Sisters: 4; Postulant: 1.
Legal Title: Carmelite Nuns of the Diocese of Superior, Inc.
Represented in the Diocese of Superior.

[0330] (O.CARM.)—CARMELITE SISTERS FOR THE AGED AND INFIRM (P)

Founded in 1929 in New York, Foundress: Venerable Mary Angeline Teresa McCrory, O.Carm.
Motherhouse and Novitiate: St. Teresa's Motherhouse and Novitiate, 600 Woods Rd., Avila on the Hudson, Germantown, NY 12526. Email: smrc@stmhcs.org. Mother Mary Rose, O.Carm., Prioress Gen.; Sr. M. Richard Carmel O.Carm., Sec. Gen.
Professed Sisters: 122.
Sponsored Works: Carmelite System Inc., Germantown, NY; Carmel Terrace, Framingham, MA; St. Patrick's Home, Bronx, NY; St. Margaret Hall, Cincinnati, OH; Carmel Manor, Fort Thomas, KY; Kahl Home for the Aged, Davenport, IA; St. Patrick's Manor, Framingham, MA; Marian Manor, South Boston, MA; St. Patrick's Residence, Naperville, IL; Lourdes - Noreen McKeen Residence, West Palm Beach, FL; Mother Angeline McCrory Manor, Columbus, OH; Avila Institute of Gerontology Inc, Germantown, NY; Our Lady's Manor, Dublin, Ireland; Mount Carmel Care Center, Lenox, MA; The Villas at St. Therese, Columbus, OH; D'Youville Life and Wellness Center, Lowell, MA.
Represented in the Archdioceses of Boston, Cincinnati and New York and in the Dioceses of Albany, Altoona-Johnstown, Brooklyn, Columbus, Covington, Davenport, Joliet, Palm Beach and Springfield in Massachusetts.

[0350] (O.CARM.)—CARMELITE SISTERS (CORPUS CHRISTI) (P)

First foundation in the United States in 1920.
General Motherhouse: Mt. St. Benedict, Tunapuna, Trinidad, West Indies Sr. Petronilla Joseph, O.Carm., Prioress Gen.
U.S. Address: Mount Carmel Home-Keen's Memorial, 412 W. 18th, Kearney, NE 68847. Tel: 308-237-2287; Tel: 308-293-6149. Sr. Mary Florence Blavet, O.Carm., Prioress.
Professed Sisters Worldwide: 65; Professed Sisters in U.S.: 2.
Ministry in Home and foreign missions; Academic and Religious Education; Social Work; Catechetics; Youth Ministry.
Represented in the Dioceses of Grand Island and Providence.

[0360] (CARMEL D.C.J.)—CARMELITE SISTERS OF THE DIVINE HEART OF JESUS (P)

Founded in Germany in 1891. First Convent in the United States in 1912.
General Motherhouse: Sittard, Netherlands Antilles Mother Karla Marija, Supr. Gen.
Northern Province: 1230 Kavanaugh Pl., Milwaukee, WI 53213. Tel: 414-453-4040; Fax: 414-453-6503. Email: carmeldcjnorth@gmail.com. Sr. Maria Giuseppe, Prov. Supr.; Sr. M. Immaculata, Wauwatosa Supr.
South Central Province: 10341 Manchester Rd., St. Louis, MO 63122. Tel: 314-965-7616. Sr. Anna Maria, Prov. Supr.
Professed Sisters Worldwide: 337; Total Sisters in U.S.: 49; Novices: 10; Postulants: 5.
The Sisters serve in 43 Homes worldwide and minister to Homes for Children, Youth, Home for the Aged, Day Nurseries & Persons with Intellectual & Developmental Disabilities.
Represented in the Archdioceses of Milwaukee, St. Louis and in the Dioceses of Gary, Grand Rapids and Owensboro.

[0370] (O.C.D.)—CARMELITE SISTERS OF THE MOST SACRED HEART OF LOS ANGELES (P)

General Motherhouse & Novitiate: Carmelite Sisters of the Most Sacred Heart of Los Angeles, 920 E. Alhambra Rd., Alhambra, CA 91801. Tel: 626-289-1353. Email: gensecretary@carmelitesistersocd.com. Mother Gloria Therese Laven, O.C.D., Supr. Gen.
Total in Community: 120.
Legal Titles: Carmelite Sisters of the Most Sacred Heart of Los Angeles; Carmelite Sisters of the Most Sacred Heart of Los Angeles Education, Inc.; Sacred Heart Retreat House, Inc.; Little Flower Center; dba Little Flower Missionary House; Avila Gardens, Inc.; Santa Teresita, Inc.; Marycrest Manor, Inc.; Mount Carmel Health Ministries, Inc.; Flos Carmeli Formation Centers, Inc.; Carmelite Sisters Foundation, Inc.
The sisters serve and staff: Religious and academic education; healthcare centers; skilled nursing facilities for the care of the aged; retreat houses; ministry to the elderly, sick and convalescents; evangelization centers and ministry to the youth.
Represented in the Archdioceses of Denver, Los Angeles and Miami.

[0380] (C.S.T.)—CARMELITE SISTERS OF ST. THERESE OF THE INFANT JESUS (D)

Founded in the United States in 1917 at Bentley, OK.
General Motherhouse: 7501 W. Britton Rd., #140, Oklahoma City, OK 73132. Tel: 405-837-7068. Sr. Barbara Joseph Foley, Gen. Supr.
Total in Community: 13.
Legal Title: Carmelite Sisters of St. Therese of the Infant Jesus.
Ministry in the field of Academic Education; Religious Education, Serving the Poor and Parish Ministry.
Represented in the Archdiocese of Oklahoma City.

[0390] (C.M.S.T.)—MISSIONARY CARMELITES OF ST. TERESA (P)

Founded in Mexico City in 1903.
General Motherhouse: Fresno No. 150, Col. Santa Maria la Ribera, 06400, Mexico, D.F., Mexico Sr. Maria Margarita Molina, Supr. Gen.
U.S. Holy Family Province (1983): 9826 Marek Dr., Houston, TX 77038. Tel: 281-445-5520. Sr. Margarita Castro, Prov. Supr.
Professed Sisters: 47.
Ministry in Pastoral; Hispanic Ministry and Retreats.
Represented in the Archdiocese of Galveston-Houston and in the Dioceses of Beaumont and Little Rock.

[0397] (C.M.R.)—CONGREGATION OF MARY, QUEEN (P)

Began in Vietnam by Bishop Pierre Lambert de la Motte in 1670. Canonically established as a religious institute on September 14, 1953. First foundation in the United States, Springfield, Missouri, 1979.
U.S. Regional House: 625 S. Jefferson Ave., Springfield, MO 65806. Tel: 417-869-9842; Fax: 417-832-0852. Sr. Pauline Nguyen, C.M.R., Regl. Supr.
Professed Sisters: 23.
Legal Title: Congregation of Mary Queen, American Region.
Represented in the Archdiocese of St. Louis and in the Dioceses of Dallas, Kansas City-St. Joseph and Springfield-Cape Girardeau.

[0400] (O.CARM.)—CONGREGATION OF OUR LADY OF MOUNT CARMEL (P)

Founded in France in 1824. First foundation in the United States in 1833.
Generalate: 62284 Fish Hatchery Rd., P.O. Box 476, Lacombe, LA 70445. Tel: 504-524-2398; Tel: 985-882-7577; Fax: 504-524-5011. Sr. Lawrence Habetz, O.Carm., Pres.; Sr. Sheila Undang, O.Carm., Vice Pres. & Sec.; Sr. Therese Gregoire, O.Carm., Treas. & Archivist.
Professed Sisters: 76.
Sponsorships: Carmelite Ministries, Inc./Cub Corner Preschool; Carmelite NGO, New Orleans, LA.
Ministry in the field of Education on all levels; Hospitals; Social Service; Religious Education; Pastoral Ministry and Retreat Work; Prison Education Ministry; Child Care.
Represented in the Archdiocese of New Orleans and in the Dioceses of Houma-Thibodaux, Joliet in Illinois and Lafayette (LA). Also in the Philippines and Timor-Leste.

[0405] (C.M.C.) CONGREGATION OF THE MOTHER OF CARMEL

Founded February 13, 1866.
9310 S. 55th Court, Oak Lawn, IL 606043.
Motherhouse: Aluva, Kerala, India. Sr. Alphonse, Supr.
Sisters U.S.A.: 45; Sisters Abroad: 6,350
Ministries: Education; Healing; Pastoral Care.
Represented in the Archdioceses of Chicago, Milwaukee and Philadelphia and in the Dioceses of Baton Rouge, Oakland, Gary and Tyler.

[0410] (O.CARM.)—INSTITUTE OF THE SISTERS OF OUR LADY OF MOUNT CARMEL (P)

Istituto delle Suore di Nostra Signora del Carmelo Founded in Italy in 1854. First foundation in the United States, 1947.

General Motherhouse: Istituto di Nostra Signora del Carmelo, Via dei Baglioni 10, Rome, Italy. U.S. Headquarters: Carmelite Sisters, 5 Wheatland St., Peabody, MA 01960. Tel: 978-531-4733. Sr. Kathleen A. Bettencourt, I.N.S.C., Supr.

Professed Sisters: 16.

Ministry in Holy Childhood Nursery; Kindergarten; Preschools; Daycare Centers

Represented in the Archdioceses of Boston and Washington and in the Diocese of St. Augustine.

[0420] (O.C.D.)—DISCALCED CARMELITE NUNS (P)

Founded in Spain in 1562. First foundation in the United States in 1790 in Charles County, Maryland; later this monastery was moved to Baltimore. The Monasteries listed here are strictly contemplative and belong to the Order of Discalced Carmelites.

Carmelite Monastery (1790): 1318 Dulaney Valley Rd., Baltimore, MD 21286. Tel: 410-823-7415; Email: info@baltimorecarmel.org; Web: www.baltimorecarmel.org. Sr. Colette Ackerman, O.C.D., Prioress.

Professed Sisters: 17; Novices: 1.

Legal Title: Carmelite Sisters of Baltimore.

Carmel of St. Joseph (1863): 9150 Clayton Rd., St. Louis, MO 63124. Tel: 314-993-6899; Fax: 314-993-4346; Email: prioress@stlouiscarmel.org; Web: www.stlouiscarmel.com. Mother Mary Joseph, O.C.D., Prioress.

Professed Cloistered Nuns: 12; Temporary Professed: 2; Novices: 1; Postulants: 1.

Monastery of St. Joseph and St. Teresa (1877): Discalced Carmelite Nuns, 73530 River Rd., Covington, LA 70435-2206. Tel: 985-898-0923; Email: covingtoncarmel@yahoo.com; Web: www.covingtoncarmel.org. Sr. Edith Turpin, O.C.D., Prioress.

Solemnly Professed: 6; Junior Professed: 3.

Carmelite Monastery of Boston (1890): Cloistered, Discalced Carmelite Nuns - O.C.D.61 Mt. Pleasant Ave., Boston, MA 02119. Tel: 617-442-1411; Fax: 617-442-0203; Email: carmelitesofboston@gmail.com; Web: www.carmelitesofboston.org. Sr. Bernadette Therese Huang, O.C.D., Prioress.

Professed: 8; Postulant: 1.

Monastery of the Most Holy Trinity: Discalced Carmelite Nuns, 29190 SW 209 Ave., Homestead, FL 33030. Tel: 305-558-7122. Mother Teresa Lucía del Inmaculado Corazón, O.C.D., Prioress.

Total in Community: 11.

Legal Title: Discalced Carmelite Nuns, Inc.

Carmelite Monastery (1902): 1400 66th Ave., Philadelphia, PA 19126. Tel: 215-424-6143. Mother Pia of Jesus Crucified, O.C.D., Prioress.

Monastery of Our Lady of Mt. Carmel (1907): 361 Highland Blvd., Brooklyn, NY 11207. Tel: 718-235-0035; Fax: 718-235-0542; Email: carmelofbrooklyn@gmail.com. Mother Ana Maria, O.C.D.

Monastery of Our Lady of Mt. Carmel and St. Joseph: 361 Highland Blvd., Brooklyn, NY 11207. Tel: 718-235-0035; Fax: 718-235-0542; Email: carmelofbrooklyn@gmail.com. Mother Ana Maria, O.C.D., Prioress.

Total in Community: 10.

Carmelite Monastery of the Infant Jesus (1908): 1000 Lincoln St., Santa Clara, CA 95050. Tel: 408-296-8412. Sr. Emmanuel of Bethlehem, O.C.D., Prioress.

Sisters Solemn Vows: 12.

St. Joseph's Carmelite Monastery (1908): 2215 N.E. 147th, Shoreline, WA 98155. Tel: 206-363-7150; Fax: 206-365-7335. Sr. Maria Valla, O.C.D., Prioress.

Professed Sisters: 12.

Legal Title: Carmelite Monastery of Seattle.

Carmel of the Queen of Heaven (Formerly known as Regina Coeli Monastery) (1911): 841 13th Ave. N., Clinton, IA 52732-5115. Tel: 563-285-8387. Email: carmelitesistersqh@gmail.com. Sr. JonFe De Torres, O.C.D., Local Supr.

Professed Sisters: 5.

Discalced Carmelite Nuns (1930): Monastery of Mary Immaculate and St. Joseph, 3115 Lexington Rd., Louisville, KY 40206. Tel: 502-896-3958; Fax: 502-896-3958. Mother John-Baptist, O.C.D., Prioress; Sr. Katherine, O.C.D., Archivist.

Solemnly Professed Sisters: 8.

Legal Title: Carmelite Monastery of Louisville, Inc.

Order of Discalced Carmelites O.C.D. (1913): Carmel of St. Teresa of Los Angeles, Inc., 215 E. Alhambra Rd., Alhambra, CA 91801. Tel: 626-282-2387; Fax: 626-282-0144; Email: teresacarm1913@gmail.com. Mother Brenda Marie Schroeder, O.C.D., Prioress.

Total in Community: 13.

Discalced Carmelite Nuns (1916): Monastery of Our Lady of Guadalupe, 4300 Mount Carmel Dr. N.E., Ada (Parnell), MI 49301. Tel: 616-691-7764. Email: carmelada@copper.net or carmelparnell@mymailstation.com; Web: www.carmelitenuns.org. Mother Mary Angela, O.C.D., Prioress.

Professed Nuns: 7; Novices: 2.

Discalced Carmelite Nuns (2000): Carmelite Monastery, 89 Hiddenbrooke Dr., Beacon, NY 12508-2230. Tel: 845-831-5572; Fax: 845-831-5579; Email: carmelitesbeacon@gmail.com; Web: www.carmelitesbeacon. org. Sr. Marjorie Robinson, O.C.D., Prioress. Email: srmarjorie@gmail.com

Total in Community: 11.

Discalced Carmelite Monastery of St. Therese of the Child Jesus (1920): 75 Carmel Rd., Buffalo, NY 14214. Tel: 716-837-6499. Mother Teresa of Jesus, O.C.D., Prioress.

Cloistered Professed Sisters: 9; Extern Professed Sister: 1; Novices: 4; Postulants: 2; Aspirants: 2.

Monastery of Discalced Carmelites (1922): 22143 Main St., P.O. Box 260, Oldenburg, IN 47036-0260. Tel: 812-212-5901. Sr. Jean Alice McGoff, O.C.D., Prioress.

Contemplative Professed Nuns: 4.

Legal Title: Monastery of the Resurrection, Discalced Carmelites, Sisters of Our Lady of Mount Carmel Carmelite Monastery, Carmelites of Indianapolis.

Carmel of the Holy Family (1923): 2541 Arlington Rd., Cleveland Heights, OH 44118. Tel: 216-321-6568; Email: barb.carmel@gmail.com. Sr. Barbara Losh, O.C.D., Supr.

Contemplative Professed Nuns: 7.

Discalced Carmelites of the Order of Our Lady of Mount Carmel O.C.D. (1925): Monastery of Our Lady and St. Therese, 27601 Hwy. 1, Carmel, CA 93923. Tel: 831-624-3043; Fax: 831-624-5495; Email: carmelitesofcarmelca@gmail.com; Web: carmelite sistersbythesea.org. Mother Teresita of the Holy Face, O.C.D., Prioress.

Professed Sisters: 11.

Legal Title: Carmelite Monastery of Carmel, California, Inc.

Discalced Carmelites O.C.D. (1926): Monastery of the Most Blessed Virgin Mary of Mount Carmel, 189 Madison Ave., Morristown, NJ 07960. Mother Therese, O.C.D., Prioress.

Professed Sisters: 14; Novices: 4.

Order of Discalced Carmelites O.C.D. (1926): Carmelite Monastery of San Diego, 5158 Hawley Blvd., San Diego, CA 92116-1934. Tel: 619-280-5424. Email: srmomsd@outlook.com. Sr. Joanna Baker, O.C.D., Prioress.

Professed Nuns: 14.

Monastery of St. Therese of the Child Jesus (1926): 35750 Moravian Dr., Clinton Township, MI 48035-2138. Tel: 586-790-7255. Mother Mary Elizabeth, O.C.D., Prioress.

Professed Nuns: 10; Sisters in Temporary Vows: 2; Transfer Candidate: 1.

Carmel of St. Therese of Lisieux, Inc. (1927): Discalced Carmelite Nuns, 2101 Manor Dr., P.O. Box 57, Loretto, PA 15940-0057. Tel: 814-472-8620; Email: lorettocarmel@hotmail.com; Web: www.lorettocarmel.org. Mother John of the Cross, O.C.D., Prioress.

Solemn Professed Nuns: 8; Junior Professed: 2; Aspirant: 2.

Discalced Carmelite Nuns O.C.D. (1928): Carmelite Monastery of Cristo Rey, 721 Parker Ave., San Francisco, CA 94118-4227. Tel: 415-387-2640. Email: prioress@cmcrnuns.org.

Total in Community: 13.

Carmelite Nuns of Dallas: Monastery of Discalced Carmelites (1928), 600 Flowers Ave., Dallas, TX 75211. Rev. Mother Juanita Marie, O.C.D., Prioress.

Professed Nuns: 16.

Discalced Carmelite Nuns (1930): Monastery of Our Lady and St. Joseph, 1931 W. Jefferson Rd., Pittsford, NY 14534. Tel: 585-427-7094. Email: ocdrochester@gmail.com; Web: www.carmelitesofrochester.org. Mother Therese Marie of Jesus Crucified, O.C.D., Prioress.

Professed Nuns with Solemn Vows: 13; Aspirants: 2.

Legal Title: Carmelite Monastery of Rochester.

Monastery of Discalced Carmelites O.C.D. (1930): Monastery of Our Lady of Mount Carmel and St. Therese of the Child Jesus, 25 Watson Ave., Barrington, RI 02806. Tel: 401-245-3421. Email: barringtoncarmel@fullchannel.net. Sr. Susan Lumb, O.C.D., Prioress.

Total in Community: 12.

Discalced Carmelite Nuns O.C.D. (1934): Monastery of the Infant Jesus of Prague and Our Lady of Guadalupe, 6301 Culebra Rd., San Antonio, TX 78238-4909. Tel: 210-680-1834. Mother Therese Leonard, O.C.D., Prioress.

Total in Community: 8.

Carmel of the Holy Family and St. Therese (1935): 6981 Teresian Way, P.O. Box 4210, Georgetown, CA 95634. Tel: 530-333-1617; Email: georgetown2004@juno.com; Web: www.carmelitemonastery.org. Mother Mary Bethany, Prioress.

Total in Community: 13.

Discalced Carmelite Nuns O.C.D. (1936): Monastery of Mary, Mother of Grace, 1250 Carmel Dr., Lafayette, LA 70501. Tel: 337-232-4651; Fax: 337-232-3540;. Email: lafayettecarmelites@gmail.com. Mother Mary John Billeaud, O.C.D., Prioress; Rev. Ken Broussard, J.C.L., Chap.

Total in Community: 16; Solemn Professed: 11; Junior Professed: 1; Postulants: 1; Externs in Perpetual Vows: 2.

Discalced Carmelite Nuns O.C.D. (1939): Carmel of St. Joseph, 2370 Morgan Rd., N.E., Piedmont, OK 73078. Email: vocation@okcarmel.org. Sr. Donna Ross, O.C.D., Prioress.

Total in Community: 8.

Discalced Carmelite Nuns of Milwaukee O.C.D. (1940): Carmel of the Mother of God, W267 N2517 Carmelite Rd., Pewaukee, WI 53072-4528. Tel: 262-691-0336; Email: pewaukeecarmel@aol.com. Sr. Mary Agnes Kramer, O.C.D., Prioress; Rev. Jude Peters, O.C.D., Chap.

Professed Sisters: 7.

Discalced Carmelite Nuns of Alexandria, South Dakota, Inc. O.C.D: Monastery of Our Mother of Mercy and St. Joseph, 221 5th St. W., P.O. Box 67, Alexandria, SD 57311-0067. Tel: 605-239-4382. Mother Mary Elias of the Immaculate Conception, Prioress.

Total in Community: 6.

Carmelite Monastery (1943): 716 Dauphin Island Pkwy., Mobile, AL 36606. Tel: 251-471-3991; 251-401-1223; Email: bradbmb55@gmail.com; Carmelmobile.viet@gmail.com; Web: www.carmelmobileal.com. Mother M. Catherine of the Cross, Prioress.

Solemnly Professed Nuns: 10; Perpetually Professed Externs: 2; Novice: 1.

Discalced Carmelite Monastery (1945): 49 Mount Carmel Rd., Santa Fe, NM 87505-0352. Tel: 505-983-7232. Mother Mary Louise, O.C.D., Prioress.

Total in Community: 9.

Discalced Carmelite Monastery (1946): 275 Pleasant St., Concord, NH 03301-2590. Tel: 603-225-5791. Sr. Claudette Blais, O.C.D., Prioress.

Solemnly Professed Nuns: 9; Perpetually Professed Sisters: 1.

Sisters of Our Lady of Mount Carmel of Terre Haute: Carmelite Monastery, 59 Allendale, Terre Haute, IN 47802-4751. Tel: 812-299-1410; Fax: 812-299-5820; Email: carmelth@heartsawake.org; Web: www.heartsawake.org. Mother Mary Joseph Nguyen, O.C.D., Prioress.

Professed Nuns: 13; Temporary Professed: 2.

The Discalced Carmelite Nuns of Colorado (1947): Carmel of the Holy Spirit, 6138 S. Gallup St., Littleton, CO 80120-2702. Tel: 303-798-4176. Mother Mary of Jesus, D.C., Prioress.

Order of Discalced Carmelites O.C.D. (1949): Carmel of Mary Immaculate and St. Mary Magdalen, 26 Harmony School Rd., Flemington, NJ 08822. Email: friendsofcarmelnj@gmail.com. Mother Mary Elizabeth, O.C.D., Prioress.

Professed: 9; Total in Community: 11.

Discalced Carmelite Nuns O.C.D. (1950): Monastery of the Infant Jesus of Prague, 3501 Silver Lake Rd., Traverse City, MI 49684-8949. Tel: 231-946-4960; Email: nuns@carmeltraversecity.org; Web: carmeloftraversecity.org. Mother Mary of Jesus, O.C.D., Prioress.

Solemnly Professed: 4; Sisters in Formation: 3.

Discalced Carmelite Nuns O.C.D. (1951): Monastery of the Holy Cross, N4028 N. Hwy. U.S. 2, P.O. Box 397, Iron Mountain, MI 49801. Tel: 906-774-0561; Fax: 906-774-0561. Mother Maria of Jesus, O.C.D., Prioress.

Total in Community: 19.

Discalced Carmelite Nuns O.C.D: Monastery of the Holy Name of Jesus, 6100 Pepper Rd., Denmark, WI 54208. Tel: 920-863-5055; Email: mttabor@holyname carmel.org. Mother Mary Elizabeth, O.C.D., Prioress.

Discalced Carmelite Nuns O.C.D. (1950): Discalced Carmelite Nuns, 7201 W. 32nd St., Little Rock, AR 72204-4716. Tel: 501-565-5121. Email: Lrcarmel@comcast.net. Sr. Lucia N. Ellender, O.C.D., Prioress.

Professed Sisters: 10; First professed: 2.

Legal Title: Discalced Carmelite Nuns aka Carmel of St. Teresa of Jesus.

Discalced Carmelite Nuns O.C.D. (1951): Monastery of Our Lady of Mount Carmel and The Little Flower, 2155 Terry Rd., Jackson, MS 39204. Tel: 601-373-1460. Email: jacksoncarmelites@gmail.com. Sr. Mary Jane Agonoy, O.C.D., Prioress.

Professed Nuns: 6.

Carmel of the Immaculate Heart of Mary (1952): 5714 Holladay Blvd., Salt Lake City, UT 84121-1599. Tel: 801-277-6075. Mother Margaret Mary Miller, O.C.D., Prioress; Sr. Therese Bui, O.C.D., Archivist.

Solemn Vows: 9.

Discalced Carmelite Nuns of St. Paul (1952): Carmel of Our Lady of Divine Providence, 8251 Demontreville Trail N., Lake Elmo, MN 55042-9547. Tel: 651-777-3882. Email: carmelbvm@gmail.com. Mother Marie-Ange of the Eucharistic Heart, O.C.D., Prioress.

Professed Sisters: 13; Novice: 1; Postulants: 3.

Discalced Carmelite Nuns O.C.D. (1953): 1 Maria Hall Dr., Danville, PA 17821. Tel: 570-275-4682; Fax: 570-275-4684. Sr. Angela Pikus, O.C.D., Prioress.

Professed Sisters: 6.

Sisters of Our Lady of Mount Carmel: 1950 La Fond Dr., Reno, NV 89509-3099. Tel: 775-323-3236; Fax: 775-322-1532; Email: renocarmel@carmelofreno.net; Web: www.carmelofreno.com. Sr. Susan Weber, O.C.D., Prioress.

Professed Nuns: 11.

Carmel of Maria Regina O.C.D. (1957): 87609 Green Hill Rd., Eugene, OR 97402. Tel: 541-345-8649; Fax: 541-345-4857. Sr. Elizabeth Mary, O.C.D., Prioress & Community Archivist.

Total in Community: 7.

Monastery of the Holy Family (1957): 510 E. Gore Rd., Erie, PA 16509.

Discalced Carmelite Nuns (1958): 11 W. Back St., Savannah, GA 31419-3219. Tel: 912-925-8505. Sr. Mary Elizabeth Angaine, Prioress.

Total in Community: 8; Professed Nuns: 5.

Monastery of the Most Holy Trinity (1958): 5801 Mt. Carmel Dr., Arlington, TX 76017. Tel: 817-468-1781. Email: supcarmel@aol.com. Mother Anne Teresa Kulinski, O.C.D., Prioress.

Total in Community: 12.

Discalced Carmelite Nuns O.C.D. (1958): Discalced Carmelite Nuns of New Caney, Texas, 1100 Parthenon Pl., New Caney, TX 77357-3276. Email: carmelnewcaney@gmail.com. Sr. Angel Teresa Sweeney, O.C.D., Prioress; Sr. Mary Ann Harrison, O.C.D., 1st Council Sister.

Total in Community: 8.

Legal Title: Discalced Carmelite Nuns of New Caney, TX.

Monastery of Discalced Carmelites (1959): 949 N. River Rd., Des Plaines, IL 60016. Tel: 847-298-4241; Fax: 847-298-4242. Mother Marie Benedicta of the Cross, Prioress.

Total in Community: 19.

Order of Discalced Carmelites O.C.D. (1958): Carmel of St. Therese, 15 Mt. Carmel Rd., Danvers, MA 01923-3796. Tel: 978-774-3008. Sr. Michael of Christ the King, O.C.D., Prioress.

Legal Title: Discalced Carmelite Nuns of Danvers.

Discalced Carmelite Nuns O.C.D. (1960): Monastery of The Sacred Heart and St. Joseph, 1106 Swifts Highway, Jefferson City, MO 65109. Tel: 573-636-3430. Mother Marie Therese, O.C.D., Prioress.

Solemnly Professed Nuns: 4.

Carmel of the Assumption (1961): 5206 Center Dr., Latrobe, PA 15650-5204. Tel: 724-539-1056. Email: contact@latrobecarmel.org. Sr. Marie Elizabeth, O.C.D., Prioress.

Professed Sisters: 9.

Discalced Carmelite Nuns, Inc. (1962): Our Lady of the Incarnation Monastery, 2901 S. Cecelia St., Sioux City, IA 51106-3299. Tel: 712-276-1680. Email: carmelitesiouxc@gmail.com. Mother Joseph of Jesus, O.C.D., Prioress.

Total in Community: 8.

Carmelite Monastery of the Mother of God (1965): 530 Blackstone Dr., San Rafael, CA 94903. Tel: 415-479-6872; Fax: 415-491-4964; Email: sram@motherofgodcarmel.org. Sr. Anna Marie Vanni, O.C.D., Prioress.

Total in Community: 6.

Carmel of the Holy Trinity: 6301 Pali Hwy., Kaneohe, HI 96744-5224. Tel: 808-261-6542; 808-466-5486. Sr. Mary Elizabeth of the Trinity, O.C.D., Mother Prioress. Email: carith89@outlook.com.

Total in Community: 8.

Discalced Carmelite Nuns of the Byzantine Rite (1980): Holy Annunciation Monastery, 403 W. County Rd., Sugarloaf, PA 18249. Tel: 570-788-1205; Fax: 570-788-3329. Mother Maria of the Holy Spirit, O.C.D., Prioress.

Professed Nuns: 11; Novices: 1.

Represented in the Diocese of Passaic.

Discalced Carmelites of Maryland, Inc: Carmel of Port Tobacco (1976), 5678 Mt. Carmel Rd., La Plata, MD 20646-3625. Email: contact@carmelofporttobacco.com. Mother Marie Bernardina, O.C.D., Prioress.

Solemn Professed: 9; Novices: 1.

[0430] (B.V.M.)—SISTERS OF CHARITY OF THE BLESSED VIRGIN MARY (P)

Founded in America in 1833.

BVM Center: Mount Carmel, 1100 Carmel Dr., Dubuque, IA 52003-7991. Tel: 563-588-2351; Web: www.bvmsisters.org. Sr. LaDonna Manternach, B.V.M., Pres.

Total in Congregation: 221.

Sisters serve and staff: in the field of Academic Education on all levels; Religious Education; Chaplaincies; Pastoral Care and Parish Ministry; Campus Ministry; Social Work; Social Justice/Advocacies.

Represented in the Archdioceses of Chicago, Detroit, Dubuque, Los Angeles, Milwaukee, Portland in Oregon, St. Louis and St. Paul-Minneapolis and in the Dioceses of Davenport, Des Moines, Fort Wayne-South Bend, Kansas City-St. Joseph, Madison, Memphis, Ogdensburg, Peoria, Phoenix, San Jose, Santa Rosa, Springfield-Cape Girardeau and Venice. Also in Ecuador, Freeport and Ghana.

[0440] (S.C.)—SISTERS OF CHARITY OF CINCINNATI, OHIO (P)

Founded by Saint Elizabeth Ann Seton, Emmitsburg, MD, 1809. The Cincinnati Community became independent in 1852, Papal approval in 1939.

General Motherhouse (1852): Mount St. Joseph, 5900 Delhi Rd., Mount Saint Joseph, OH 45051. Tel: 513-347-5300; Fax: 513-347-5228. Email: pat.hayden@srcharitycinti.org. Web: www.srcharitycinti.org. Sr. Patricia Hayden, S.C., Pres.

Professed Sisters: 203.

Legal Title: Sisters of Charity, Cincinnati, OH.

Sisters serve and staff: Colleges; Secondary and Elementary Schools; Parishes; Healthcare; Senior Care Services; Social Services; Congregational Services; Retreat Center; Spiritual Direction.

Represented in the Archdioceses of Cincinnati, Denver, Detroit, New Orleans, New York, Santa Fe and Washington and in the Dioceses of Brownsville, Cleveland, El Paso, Helena, Lansing, Las Cruces, Pueblo, Saginaw and Venice.

[0450] (S.C.I.C.)—SISTERS OF CHARITY OF THE IMMACULATE CONCEPTION OF IVREA (P)

Founded in Italy in the 18th Century. First foundation in the United States in 1961.

General Motherhouse: Via della Renella 85, Rome, Italy. Tel: 011-39-06-581-8145. Sr. Raffaella Giudici, Supr. Gen.

Total in Congregation: 583.

U.S. Foundation (1961): Immaculate Virgin of Miracles Convent, 268 Prittstown Rd., Mount Pleasant, PA 15666. Tel: 724-887-6753. Sr. Angelina Grimoldi, S.C.I.C., Reg. Supr. Tel: 724-887-6753. Email: office@vernamontessorischool.org.

Professed Sisters in the U.S.: 8.

Properties owned and/or sponsored: Verna Montessori Children's House, Elementary School & Middle School; Immaculate Virgin of Miracles Convent, Mt. Pleasant, PA.

Sisters serve and staff: Kindergarten and Elementary Schools and Middle School; Parish Services; Religious Education; Pastoral Ministry.

Represented in the Diocese of Greensburg.

[0460] (C.C.V.I.)—CONGREGATION OF THE SISTERS OF CHARITY OF THE INCARNATE WORD (P)

Founded in 1869 at San Antonio, Texas.

Generalate: 4503 Broadway, San Antonio, TX 78209-6209. Tel: 210-828-2224; Fax: 210-828-9741. Sr. Yolanda Tarango, C.C.V.I., Congregational Leader.

Universal total in Congregation: 216; U.S. Sisters: 103.

Properties owned and/or sponsored: Universities 1; High Schools 3; Hospitals (co-sponsored) 27; Temporary shelters for homeless women & children 2; Retirement Centers 1; Services for the Elderly 1.

Ministry in the field of Education at all levels; Hospitals and Health Service Agencies; Nursing Homes; Pastoral Ministries; Diocesan Offices; Social Service Agencies.

Represented in the Archdioceses of St. Louis, and San Antonio and in the Dioceses of Corpus Christi, Dallas, El Paso, Grand Rapids, Jefferson City, Joliet, Springfield-Cape Girardeau and Victoria. Also in Chile, Columbia, Ireland, Mexico and Peru.

[0470] (CCVI)—CONGREGATION OF THE SISTERS OF CHARITY OF THE INCARNATE WORD, HOUSTON, TEXAS (P)

Founded in the United States in 1866, St. Mary's Infirmary Galveston, TX.

Motherhouse: Villa de Matel, 6510 Lawndale St., P.O. Box 230969, Houston, TX 77223-0969. Tel: 713-928-6053; Fax: 713-928-8148. Sr. Celeste Trahan, CCVI, Congregational Leader. Email: ctrahan@ccvi-vdm.org; vacuna@ccvi-vdm.org; Sr. Ethel Puno, Gen. Sec. Email: epuno@ccvi-vdm.org. 6510 Lawndale St., Houston, TX 77023. Sr. Celeste Trahan, Supr.

Total in Congregation: 116.

Legal Titles: Incarnate Word Religious and Charitable Trust; The Congregation of the Sisters of Charity of the Incarnate Word, Houston, Texas; The Claude Marie Dubuis Religious and Charitable Trust.

Sisters serve in: Hospitals; Homes for the Aged; Elementary and Secondary Schools; Literacy; Social Services; Retreat Centers, Spirituality and Vocation Formation.

Represented in the Archdioceses of Galveston-Houston and St. Louis and in the Dioceses of Austin, Lake Charles, San Bernardino and Tyler. Also in Guatemala, Ireland, Kenya, Mexico and El Salvador.

[0480] (S.C.L.)—SISTERS OF CHARITY OF LEAVENWORTH, KANSAS (P)

Founded in the United States in 1858.

Community Offices and Motherhouse: 4200 S. 4th St., Leavenworth, KS 66048-5054. Tel: 913-682-7500; Fax: 913-364-5401. Sr. Eileen Haynes, S.C.L., Community Dir.; Tonya Crawford, Archivist.

Total in Community: 163.

Sisters minister in the areas of Care of Creation; Diocesan Offices (Parish Pastoral Ministry, Adult Formation, Liturgy, Music Ministry); Education (Campus Ministry, Elementary, College, Nursing, Religious); Healthcare (Hospitals, Clinics, Health Services Agencies); Missions (Latin America); Social Services (Counseling, Foster Care); Social Justice (Immigrant, Prisoners, Housing); Spiritual Direction.

Properties owned and sponsored: University of Saint Mary, Leavenworth, KS; Cristo Rey Kansas City High School, KCMO.

Represented in the Archdioceses of Denver, Kansas City in Kansas and St. Louis and in the Dioceses of Bismarck, Cheyenne, Grand Island, Great Falls-Billings, Kansas City-St. Joseph and Oakland. Also in Canada and Peru.

[0490] (S.G.M.)—SISTERS OF CHARITY OF MONTREAL (P) (Grey Nuns)

Founded in 1737 by Saint Marguerite d'Youville at Montreal, Canada. First foundation in the United States in 1855.

Generalate: General Administration, 138 Rue Saint-Pierre, Montreal, Canada, H2Y 2L7. Tel: 514-842-9411; Web: www.sgm.qc.ca. Sr. Aurore Larkin, S.G.M., Congregational Leader.

St. Joseph Area U.S.A.: Area Administration-SGM,10 Pelham Rd., Ste. 1000, Lexington, MA 02421-8499. Tel: 781-674-7407; Emailo: srjeanneepoor@verizon.net. Sr. Jeanne Poor, S.G.M., Area Coord.

Total in Community: 13.

Legal Title: The Grey Nuns Charities, Inc.

Ministry in retreat ministry, social justice, congregational governance & administration, pastoral care and prayer ministry, ESL tutoring and food preparation for the poor.

Represented in the Archdiocese of Boston.

[0500] (S.C.N.)—SISTERS OF CHARITY OF NAZARETH (P)

Founded in the United States in 1812.

SCN Center: P.O. Box 172, Nazareth, KY 40048. Tel: 502-348-1555; Fax: 502-348-1502. Email: info@nazareth.org. Sr. Sangeeta Ayithamattam, S.C.N., Pres. Sr. Jackulin Jesu, S.C.N., Vice Pres.; Sr. Adeline Fehribach, S.C.N., Vice Pres.

Total in Congregation: 472.

Legal Title: Nazareth Literary & Benevolent Institution.

Properties owned or sponsored: Nazareth Retreat Center, Nazareth, NY; Camp Maria, Leonardtown, MD; Nazareth Villages Inc., Nazareth Villages II, Inc., Nazareth, KY; Nazareth Home, Inc., Louisville, KY; Vincentian Collaborative System, Pittsburgh, PA; Vincentian Home, Inc., Pittsburgh, PA; Vincentian de Marillac, Pittsburgh, PA; Vincentian Collaborative System Rehabilitation Services, Pittsburgh, PA; Vincentian Child Development Center, Pittsburgh, PA.

Nazareth Office: P.O. Box 187, Nazareth, KY 40048. Tel: 502-331-4072; Fax: 502-331-4073. Email: info@nazareth.org. Sr. Barbara Flores, SCN, Prov.; Sr. Michelle Grgurich, SCN, Vice Prov.; Sr. Camille Panich, S.C.N., Vice Prov.

Sisters serve and staff: in the field of Academic Education; Social Services; Parish Ministry; Archdiocesan Offices; Health Care Institutions; Retreat Centers; Retirement Centers.

Represented in the Archdioceses of Boston, Chicago, Indianapolis and Louisville and in the Dioceses of Charleston, Cleveland, Columbus, Greensburg, Knoxville, Memphis and Pittsburgh. Also in Belize, Botswana, India, Kenya and Nepal.

Patna Province: SCN Provincial House, E. Boring Canal Rd., KSV Raman Ln., GPO Box 219, Patna, Bihar, India, 800 001. Tel: 011-91-6122-559-221. Sr. Latika Kottuppallil, S.C.N., Prov.; Sr. Basanti Lakra, S.C.N., Vice Prov.; Sr. Suchita Kulla, S.C.N., Vice Prov.

Bangalore Province: Nazareth Convent, Hosur Main Rd., Chandapura PO, Bangalore, India 560 099. Tel: 011-91-7259-307-105, Sr. Mary Margaret Nirmala, S.C.N., Prov.; Sr. Vijaya Chalil, S.C.N., Vice Prov.

[0510] (O.L.M.)—SISTERS OF CHARITY OF OUR LADY OF MERCY (D)

Founded in Charleston, South Carolina in 1829.

Generalate and Motherhouse: Sisters of Charity of Our Lady of Mercy, 424 Fort Johnson Rd., Charleston, SC 29412. Tel: 843-795-2866; Fax: 843-795-6083 Email: smjritter@gmail.com.

Mailing Address: P.O. Box 12410, Charleston, SC 29422. Sr. Mary Joseph Ritter, O.L.M., Gen. Supr.

Total in Community: 12.

Properties owned and/or sponsored: Motherhouse, May Forest, Charleston, SC.

Legal Title: Sisters of Charity of Our Lady of Mercy. Sisters serve and staff: Parishes; Social Services.

Represented in the Diocese of Charleston.

[0520] (S.C.M.M.)—SISTERS OF CHARITY OF OUR LADY, MOTHER OF MERCY (P)

Founded in Holland 1832. First foundation in the United States in 1874.

General Motherhouse: Den Bosch, The Netherlands

Universal total in Congregation: 379.

SCMM Provincial Center: 32 Tuttle Pl., East Haven, CT 06512. Tel: 203-469-7872. Email: scmm@comcast.net. Sr. Mary Ellen Ryley, S.C.M.M., Regional Coord.

Total in Community: 6.

Represented in the Archdioceses of Chicago and Hartford.

[0530] (S.C.M.C.)—SISTERS OF CHARITY OF OUR LADY, MOTHER OF THE CHURCH (P)

First foundation in the United States in 1970.

General Motherhouse: Baltic, CT 06330. Tel: 860-822-8241; Fax: 860-822-9842. Email: motherhouse@sistersofcharity.com. Mother M. Marie Julie Saegaert, S.C.M.C., Supr. Gen.

Professed Sisters: 45.

Properties owned, staffed or sponsored: High Schools 1; Nursing Home 1; Elementary Schools 5; Catechetical Schools 7; Shelters for the Homeless 1; Hispanic Ministry 1; Educational Tutoring Centers 1; Assisted Living, CBRF 1.

Represented in the Dioceses of Madison and Norwich.

[0540] (S.C.O.)—SISTERS OF CHARITY OF OTTAWA (P) (Grey Nuns of the Cross)

Founded in Ottawa, Canada, in 1845. First foundation in the United States in 1857.

General Motherhouse: 27 Bruyere St., Ottawa, Canada, K1N 5C9. Sr. Rachelle Watier, S.C.O., Gen. Supr.

Total number of Sisters in Congregation based in Ottawa: 413: U.S.: 9.

American Province (1950): St. Joseph, 977 Varnum Ave., Lowell, MA 01854-1913. Tel: 978-454-4364; Fax: 978-569-1027. Sr. Prescille Malo, S.C.O., Prov. Supr.; Sr. Pauline Leblanc, S.C.O., Archivist.

Professed U.S. Sisters: 9.

Properties owned and/or sponsored: Bachand Hall, Lowell, MA; St. Joseph Residence, Lowell, MA.

Legal Title: Sisters of Charity of Ottawa.

Sisters staff: Pastoral Ministries; Apostolate of Aging.

Represented in the Archdiocese of Boston.

[0565] (S.C.R.H.)—SISTERS OF CHARITY OF ROLLING HILLS (D)

Founded in Los Angeles, CA in 1964.

General Motherhouse & U.S. House: 28600 Palos Verdes Dr. E., Rancho Palos Verdes, CA 90275. Tel: 310-831-4104. Email: srtsharp@gmail.com. Sr. Tracey Sharp, S.C.R.H., Supr.

Sisters: 6.

Legal Title: Sisters of Charity of Rolling Hills. Ministries: Service to those in need, supported through ministry in Catholic institutions according to the talents of each sister.

Represented in the Archdiocese of Los Angeles.

[0570] (S.C.)—SISTERS OF CHARITY OF SETON HILL, U.S. PROVINCE, GREENSBURG, PENNSYLVANIA (P)

Founded in the United States in 1870.

Administrative Offices U.S. Province: DePaul Center, 144 DePaul Center Rd., Greensburg, PA 15601. Tel: 724-836-0406; Fax: 724-836-8280; Email: ejohnston@scsh.org; Web: www.scsh.org. Sr. Mary Norbert Long, S.C., Prov. Supr.

Motherhouse: Caritas Christi, 129 DePaul Center Rd., Greensburg, PA 15601. Tel: 724-853-7948; Fax: 724-838-1512.

Total Sisters in U.S. Province: 110.

Generalate: Sisters of Charity of Seton Hill, 7005 Baptist Rd., Bethel Park, PA 15102-3905. Tel: 412-831-1242; Fax: 412-831-2184; Email: cblazina@scsh.org. Web: www.sistersofcharityofsetonhillgeneralate.org. Sr. Jane Ann Cherubin, S.C., Gen. Supr.

Total in Community: 304.

[0580] (C.S.A.)—SISTERS OF CHARITY OF ST. AUGUSTINE (D)

Founded in Cleveland, Ohio in 1851.

Motherhouse: Mount Augustine, 5232 Broadview Rd., Richfield, OH 44286. Email: sisters@srsofcharity.org. Sr. Judith Ann Karam, C.S.A., Congregational Leader; Sr. Mary Denis Maher, C.S.A., Archivist.

Total in Congregation: 28.

Properties owned and sponsored: CSA Health System Ministries (PJP), Cleveland, OH; Sisters of Charity of St. Augustine Health System Inc., Cleveland OH; Mercy Medical Center, Inc., Canton OH; Regina Health Center, Richfield, OH; Sisters of Charity Foundation of Cleveland; Sisters of Charity Foundation of Canton; Sisters of Charity Foundation of South Carolina; St. Vincent Charity Medical Center; Healthy Learners, Columbia, SC; Early Childhood Resource Center, Canton, OH; Light of Hearts Villa, Bedford, OH.

Represented in the Dioceses of Charleston, Cleveland, Lexington and Youngstown.

[0590] (S.C.)—SISTERS OF CHARITY OF SAINT ELIZABETH, CONVENT STATION (P)

Founded in Newark, New Jersey in 1859.

General Motherhouse: Convent of St. Elizabeth Administration Building, P.O. Box 476, Convent Station, NJ 07961-0476. Tel: 973-290-5000; Tel: 973-290-5450; Fax: 973-290-5434. Sr. Maureen Shaughnessy, S.C., Gen. Supr.; Sr. Noreen Neary, Archivist; Blessed Miriam Teresa, League of Prayer.

Total Enrollment: 228.

Properties and Legal Titles: Sisters of Charity of Saint Elizabeth Academy of Saint Elizabeth, Convent Station, NJ; Saint Vincent Academy, Newark, NJ; Josephine's Place, Elizabeth, NJ.

Sisters serve and staff: Academies; High Schools; Elementary Schools; Hospitals; C.C.D.; Parish Work; Social Work; Health Services; College of Saint Elizabeth.

Represented in the Archdioceses of Chicago, Hartford and Newark and in the Dioceses of Charlotte, Fall River, Metuchen, Palm Beach, Paterson, Raleigh, Trenton and Tucson. Also in Haiti, Central America and San Salvador.

[0600] (S.C.S.J.A.)—SISTERS OF CHARITY OF ST. JOAN ANTIDA (P)

Founded in France in 1799 by Saint Joan Antida Thouret. First foundation in the U.S. 1932.

General Motherhouse: Suore della Carita di Santa Giovanna Antida, Via S. Maria in Cosmedin #5, Rome, Italy, 00153. Sr. Maria Rosa Muscarella, Supr. Gen.

North American Province (1976): Regina Mundi Provincial House, 8560 N. 76th Pl., Milwaukee, WI 53223. Tel: 414-354-9233; Fax: 414-355-6463. Email: sisters@scsja.org. Sr. Theresa Rozga, S.C.S.J.A., Prov.

Total in Congregation: 19.

Ministry in schools; neighborhood services and parishes. Properties owned and sponsored: St. Joan Antida High School, Inc.; St. Joan Antida High School Foundation, Ltd.

Represented in the Archdiocese of Milwaukee.

[0620] (S.C.S.L.)—SISTERS OF CHARITY OF ST. LOUIS (P)

Founded in France in 1803. First foundation in the United States in 1910.

Generalate: 5169 Avenue MacDonald, Montreal, Canada, H3X 2V9. Sr. Alberte Piche, Supr. Gen.

Universal total in Congregation: 425.

American Sector: 4907 S. Catherine St., Apt. 107, Platts-burgh, NY 12901. Tel: 518-802-0331; Email: srbernadetted @gmail.com. Sr. Bernadette Ducharme, Local Supr./Prov. Delegate.

Total in Community: 3.

Represented in the Diocese of Ogdensburg.

[0640] (S.C.)—SISTERS OF CHARITY OF ST. VINCENT DE PAUL, HALIFAX (P)

Founded by Saint Elizabeth Ann Seton, Emmitsburg, Maryland in 1809. Congregation at Halifax became independent in 1856, Papal approved in 1908.

Sisters of Charity Centre: 215 Seton Rd., Halifax, Canada, B3M 0C9. Tel: 914-261-4292; Fax: 902-457-3506. Sr. Margaret Mary Fitzpatrick, S.C., Congregational Leader.

Total in Congregation: 205.

Legal Title: Sisters of Charity (Halifax).

Commonwealth of Massachusetts: Boston Office, 125 Oakland St., Wellesley Hills, MA 02481-5338. Tel: 781-997-1100; Fax: 781-997-1358. Sr. Mary Anne Foster, S.C., Congregational Councillor Tel: 617-372-4395.

Legal Titles: Sisters of Charity (Halifax) Supporting Corporation, 125 Oakland St. Wellesley Hills, MA 02481-5338. Phone: 781-997-1110; Fax: 781-237-8152. Sr. Margaret Mary Fitzpatrick, Congregational Leader; Sisters of Charity (Halifax) Corporate Mission, Inc., 125 Oakland St. Wellesley Hills, MA 02481-5338. Tel: 781-997-1100; Fax: 781-997-1358. Sr. Margaret Mary Fitzpatrick, Congregational Leader.

Mount St. Vincent Retirement Community: 125 Oakland St., Wellesley Hills, MA 02481-5338. Tel: 781-997-1110; Fax: 781-237-8152; Tel: 781-997-1165; Fax: 781-237-8152.

Legal Titles and Holdings: Marillac Residence, Inc., Wellesley Hills, MA; Elizabeth Seton Residence, Inc., Wellesley Hills, MA.

State of NY: Sisters of Charity (Halifax), New York Office, 84-32 63 Ave., Middle Village, NY 11379. Tel: 718-639-9295; Fax: 718-651-5645; Email: scnyoffice@aol.com. Sr. Joan Dawber, Congregational Councillor. Tel: 718-570-2866.

Ministering in education at all levels; parish ministry; spiritual direction/retreats; social services; pastoral ministry; administration.

Represented in the Archdioceses of Boston and New York and in the Dioceses of Brooklyn and Rockville Centre. Also in Canada, Bermuda and Peru.

[0650] (S.C.)—SISTERS OF CHARITY OF ST. VINCENT DE PAUL OF NEW YORK (D)

Founded in Emmitsburg, Maryland in 1809 by Saint Elizabeth Ann Seton.

General Motherhouse: Sisters of Charity Center, 6301 Riverdale Ave., Bronx, NY 10471-1093. Tel: 718-549-9200; Fax: 718-884-3013. Email: megan@scny.org. Sr. Donna Dodge, Pres.

Total in Congregation: 158.

Sisters serve and staff: Colleges; Elementary Schools; House of Prayer; Supportive Housing for low income Elderly; Residence for Senior and Invalid Sisters; Mental Health Divisions, Rest House for Community use; Outreach for Homeless; Parish Pastoral Ministry; Advocacy Programs; Outreach Pastoral Ministry; Spirituality Programs.

Represented in the Archdiocese of New York. Also in Guatemala.

[0655] (S.C.V.)—CONGREGATION OF SISTERS OF CHARITY OF ST. VINCENT DE PAUL

Motherhouse is located in Suwon, Korea.

The sisters provide service to the poor, caring for the sick poor, elderly, mentally disabled, single mothers, dying people, prisoners, and refugees from North Korea. Sr. Biatrix M. Hyang Sook Han, S.C., Supr.

Total Members: 230.

Motherhouse & Generalate: 93-1 Jungbu-daero Paldal-gu Suwon-si, Gyeonggi-do 16247 South Korea. Tel: 031-241-2151.

U.S. Address (1996): St. Anna's Home, 13901 E. Quincy Ave., Aurora, CO 80015. Tel: 303-627-2986; Fax: 720-379-6308; Email: st.annashome@hotmail.com.

Total Sisters in U.S.: 3.

Represented in the Archdiocese of Denver.

[0660] (S.C.C.)—SISTERS OF CHRISTIAN CHARITY (P)

Daughters of the Blessed Virgin Mary of the Immaculate Conception

Founded in Germany in 1849. First foundation in the United States in 1873.

Generalate: Haus Mallinckrodt Mallinckrodt Str. 5 D-33098 Paderborn, Germany Tel: 011-495251-68324-20. Sr. Maria del Rosario Castro, Supr. Gen.

Universal total in Congregation: 329.

North American Eastern Province (1927): Mallinckrodt Convent Div. of North American Province, 350 Bernardsville Rd., Mendham, NJ 07945. Tel: 973-543-6528. Sr. Joann Marie Aumand, S.C.C., Prov. Supr.; Sr. Mary Perpetua Rehle, S.C.C., Archivist.

Professed Sisters: 143.

Ministry in Academic Education; Retreat House; Catechetical Centers; Religion Coordinators; Health care, Parish Ministry and Chaplains.

Sponsored work: Villa Pauline, Retreat House, Mendham, NJ; Divine Providence Hospital, Williamsport, PA; Muncy Valley Hospital, Muncy, PA; Holy Spirit Hospital, Camp Hill, PA; Passaic Neighborhood Center, Paterson, NJ; Nativity Miguel School, Scranton, PA; ACS College, Denville, NJ.

Represented in the Archdioceses of Chicago, Newark, New Orleans, New York and Philadelphia and in the Dioceses of Allentown, Camden, Harrisburg, Metuchen, Paterson, Scranton and Toledo.

Also in West Virgina.

North American Western Region: Sisters of Christian Charity - Daughters of the Blessed Virgin Mary of the Immaculate Conception, 2041 Elmwood Ave., Wilmette, IL 60091-1431. Tel: 847-920-9341; Fax: 847-920-9346. Sr. Juliana Miska, S.C.C., Regl. Supr.; Sr. Anastasia Sanford, Archivist.

Professed Sisters: 25.

Ministry in Religious Education; Pastoral Ministry; Prayer Ministry; Ministry of Presence to the Poor, Hospital Chaplaincy and Multi-Cultural.

Properties owned Maria Immaculata Convent; Sacred Heart Convent, Wilmette, IL; the Josephinum Convent and Josephinum Academy of the Sacred Heart, Chicago, IL.

Represented in the Archdiocese of Chicago and the Diocese of Scranton.

[0670] (O.C.S.O.)—CISTERCIAN NUNS OF THE STRICT OBSERVANCE (P)

Founded at Citeaux, France, in 1098. First foundation in the United States in 1949.

Generalate: Viale Africa 33, Rome, Italy, 00144. Total Universal Number of Nuns in Order: estimated 1,800. Contemplative and Monastic.

U.S. Establishments:

Mount St. Mary's Abbey: 300 Arnold St., Wrentham, MA 02093-1799. Tel: 508-528-1282; Fax: 508-528-5360. Email: secretary@msmabbey.org. Mother Sofia Millican, O.C.S.O., Abbess.

Total in Community: 38.

Represented in the Archdiocese of Boston.

Our Lady of the Mississippi Abbey: 8400 Abbey Hill Rd., Dubuque, IA 52003. Tel: 563-582-2595; Fax: 563-582-5511. Rev. Mother Rebecca Stramoski, O.C.S.O., Abbess.

Total in Community: 20.

Legal Title: Trappistine Nuns, Inc.; Iowa Cistercians of the Strict Observance.

Represented in the Archdiocese of Dubuque.

Santa Rita Abbey: 14200 E. Fish Canyon Rd., Sonoita, AZ 85637-6545. Tel: 520-455-5595. Email: sracommty@gmail.com. Mother Victoria Murray, O.C.S.O., Prioress.

Total in Community: 11.

Legal Title: Cistercian Nuns of the Strict Observance.

Represented in the Diocese of Tucson.

Our Lady of the Redwoods Abbey: 18104 Briceland Thorn Rd., Whitethorn, CA 95589. Tel: 707-986-7419; Email: vocationdirector@redwoodsabbey.org; Web: www.redwoodsabbey.org. Sr. Kathy DeVico, O.C.S.O., Abbess.

Total in Community: 10.

Represented in the Diocese of Santa Rosa.

Our Lady of the Angels Monastery: 3365 Monastery Dr., Crozet, VA 22932. Tel: 434-823-1452; Fax: 434-823-6379. Email: sisters@olamonastery.org. Mother Kathy Ullrich, O.C.S.O., Prioress.

Legal Title: Cistercian Nuns of the Strict Observance in Virginia, Inc.

Represented in the Diocese of Richmond.

[0680] (O.CIST.)—CISTERCIAN NUNS (P)

Founded in 1098 at Citeaux, France. It is composed of monks and nuns in independent houses. The Swiss abbey Frauenthal founded Valley of Our Lady Monastery in 1956. The community will be relocating in late 2023.

Generalate: Piazza del Tempio di Diana, 14, Rome, Italy, 00153. Rt. Rev. Mauro-Giuseppe Lepori, O.Cist., Abbot Gen.

U.S.: Valley of Our Lady Monastery, E11096 Yanke Dr., Prairie Du Sac, WI 53578-9737. Tel: 608-643-3520. Email: cisterciannuns@valleyofourlady.org. Rev. Mother Anne Marie Joerger, O. Cist., Prioress.

Total in Community: 23.

[0685] (R.M.I.)—CLARETIAN MISSIONARY SISTERS (P)

Religious of Mary Immaculate Claretian Missionary Sisters

Founded in Santiago de Cuba, August 25, 1855. Established in the United States in 1956.

Generalate: Via Calandelli 12, Rome, Italy, 00153. Soledad Galeron, Supr. Gen.

U.S. Delegation: 7080 S.W. 99 Ave., Miami, FL 33173. Sr. Ondina Cortes, R.M.I.

Sisters in the World: 600; Sisters in Florida: 11.

Legal Title: Claretian Missionary Sisters of Florida, Inc.

Ministry in Religious Education; Theological Formation in Pastoral Institutes, Seminaries and Universities; Social Ministries; Parish and Diocesan Ministries.

Represented in the Archdiocese of Miami and in the Dioceses of Palm Beach and St. Augustine.

[0690] (C.M.S.)—COMBONI MISSIONARY SISTERS (P)

Founded in Italy in 1872. An international congregation of 1,105 sisters serving in the mission fields of Africa, America, Europe, the Middle East and Sri Lanka. First United States foundation in 1950.

Generalate: Rome, Italy. Sr. Luigia Coccia, C.M.S., Supr. Gen.

American Headquarters: 1307 Lakeside Ave., Henrico, VA 23228-4710. Tel: 804-262-8827; Email: usacomboni.deleg@gmail.com; Web: www.combonimissionarysistersusa.org. Sr. Olga Estela Sanchez Caro, C.M.S., Delegate Supr.

Legal Titles & Holdings: Provincial House, Comboni Missionary Sisters, Inc., Richmond, VA.

Represented in the Archdioceses of Baltimore and San Antonio and in the Diocese of Richmond.

[0700] (O.D.N.)—COMPANY OF MARY, OUR LADY (P)

Founded in Bordeaux, France, April 7, 1607, by St. Jeanne de Lestonnac. First foundation in the United States in 1926, in Douglas, Arizona.

General Motherhouse: Rome, Italy. Sr. Maria Rita Calvo, O.D.N., Gen. Supr.

Universal total in Congregation: 1306.

U.S. Regional Office (1926): Company of Mary Regional Offices, 16791 E. Main St., Tustin, CA 92780. Tel: 714-541-3125. Sr. Liliana Franco, O.D.N., Prov. Supr.; Sr. Leticia Salazar, O.D.N., Pres. of Corporation; Sr. Kathy Schneider, O.D.N., Archivist.

Professed: 30.

Properties owned and/or sponsored: St. Jeanne De Lestonnac School, Tustin, CA; St. Jeanne de Lestonnac School, Temecula, CA; St. Joseph Residence for Women, Los Angeles, CA; Vina de Lestonnac Ministry Center Retreat, Temecula, CA; Lestonnac Residence for Women, Tustin, CA; Lestonnac Retreat Center, Tustin, CA.

Sisters serve and staff: Pre-Schools; Kindergartens; Elementary & High Schools; Faith Formation Centers; Residences & Retreat Centers.

Represented in the Archdiocese of Los Angeles and in the Dioceses of Orange and San Bernardino.

[0710] (C.S.)—SISTERS OF THE COMPANY OF THE SAVIOR (D)

Founded in Spain in 1952. First United States foundation in 1962.

General Motherhouse: Tapia de Casariego 19, Madrid, Spain, 28023. Mother Mercedes Diez de Angulo, C.S., Supr. Gen.

U.S. Foundation: 914 Newfield Ave., Stamford, CT 06605. Tel: 203-368-1875. Email: stamford@ciasalvador.org. Sr. Maria Alguacil, C.S., Supr.

Apostolate: Education.

Professed Sisters: 68; Juniors: 30; Novices: 14.

Represented in the Diocese of Bridgeport.

[0715] CONSECRATED WOMEN OF REGNUM CHRISTI NA (P)

Founded in 1969.

General Headquarters: Via Corrado Barbagallo 20, Castel Di Guido, Rome, Italy. Nancy Nohrden, Gen. Dir.

North American Headquarters: 951 Peachtree Pkwy., Cumming, GA 30041. Tel: 214-562-2565. Kathleen Murphy, Territorial Dir.

Members: 73 U.S.; 497 Worldwide.

Members serve in the areas of Catechesis, Education, Pastoral Work with Children, Youth and Families, Evangelization and Works of Charity.

Represented in the Archdioceses of Atlanta, Chicago, Cincinnati, Detroit, Galveston-Houston, New Orleans and Washington and the Dioceses of Dallas and Providence.

[0720] (M.C.)—CONSOLATA MISSIONARY SISTERS (P)

Founded in Italy in 1910. First foundation in the United States in 1954.

Motherhouse: Istituto Suore Missionarie della Consolata, Via Umilta 745, Nepi, VT, Italy, 01036. Mother Simona Brambilla, M.C., Supr. Gen.

Universal total in Congregation: 500.

Represented in the Dioceses of Birmingham, Grand Rapids and Phoenix.

U.S. Headquarters: Consolata Missionary Sisters, 6801 Belmont Rd., P.O. Box 371, Belmont, MI 49306. Tel: 616-361-2072; Fax: 616-361-2072; Email: reusamc@consolatasisters.org. Sr. Rosa Rosito, M.C., Contact Person.

Total in Community: 10.

Sisters serve and staff: Catechetical and Pastoral Work; Apostolate among Minorities; Elementary Schools and Pastoral Ministries.

[0725] (M.C-M.)—CORDI-MARIAN MISSIONARY SISTERS CONGREGATION (P)

Founded in Mexico City in 1921. First United States foundation in 1926.

General Motherhouse: Apdo. Postal #1109, Toluca, Mexico, 50091. Sr. Maria Cibrian, M.C.M., Supr. Gen.

U.S. Delegation House: 11624 Culebra Rd., Apt. 501, San Antonio, TX 78253. Tel: 210-798-8220, ext. 15 or 16; Fax: 210-798-8225. Sr. M. Teresa Cruz, Del. Supr.

Total in Congregation: 83; Total number in U.S. community: 24.

Properties owned and/or sponsored: Cordi-Marian Villa Retreat Center and Provincial House, San Antonio, TX; Formation House, San Antonio, TX; 10 other properties in Mexico; 5 schools; 2 houses of formation; 2 elderly residences; 2 bookstores; 2 houses of administration.

Ministry in Catechetical Centers; Pastoral Ministry Programs; Retreat Center; Social Service; Ministry to Hispanics; Bereavement Program.

Represented in the Archdiocese of San Antonio and in the Diocese of Springfield-Cape Girardeau. Also in Mexico and Central America.

[0730] (FdCC)—CANOSSIAN DAUGHTERS OF CHARITY (P)

Canossian Sisters

Founded in Verona, Italy in 1808.

General Motherhouse: Via della Stazione di Ottavia 70, Rome, Italy, 00135.

U.S. Provincial House: Cristo Rey-Canossian Sisters, 5625 Isleta Blvd., S.W., Albuquerque, NM 87105. Tel: 505-873-2854. Email: canossiansrs@yahoo.com. Sr. Anna Maria Serafini, F.D.C.C., Prov. Leader.

Sisters in U.S.: 31.

Ministry in Evangelization; Integral Promotion of the Person; Parish Pastoral Ministry; Pastoral Care of the Sick; Intermediate Care Facility for Developmentally Disabled Children; Lay Volunteer Program; Pastoral Outreach to Incarcerated; Education.

Represented in the Archdioceses of San Francisco and Santa Fe and in the Diocese of Sacramento. Also in Canada and Mexico.

[0740] (D.C.P.B.)—DAUGHTERS OFCHARITY OF THE MOST PRECIOUS BLOOD

Founded in Pagani, Italy in 1872. First foundation in United States in 1908.

Generalate: Via Vigna Fabbri 45, Rome, Italy. Sr. Alfonsa Bove, Mother Gen.

U.S. Address: Daughters of Charity of the Most Precious Blood, 1482 North Ave., Bridgeport, CT 06604. Tel: 203-334-7000. Sr. Rosamma Joseph, Supr.

Total in Community: 16; Number of Communities: 3. Represented in the Dioceses of Albany, Bridgeport and Paterson.

[0750] (F.C.S.C.J.)—DAUGHTERS OF THE CHARITY OF THE SACRED HEART OF JESUS (P)

First founded in France at La Salle de Vihiers in 1823. First founded in the United States at Newport, Vermont in October 1905.

Generalate: Etampes, France

General Motherhouse: La Salle de Vihiers, France Sr. Maria Andree Huveke, F.C.S.C.J., Supr. Gen.

U.S. Address: Daughters of the Charity of the Sacred Heart of Jesus (1949), 226 Grove St., Littleton, NH 03561. Tel: 603-444-5346; Fax: 603-444-5348. Sr. Juanita Durgin, F.C.S.C.J., Del.

Total number in Province: 17.

Sisters serve and staff: Spiritual Directors; Pastoral Ministry; Foreign Missions.

Represented in the Archdiocese of Boston and in the Dioceses of Fall River, Manchester and Ogdensburg. Also in Rutland.

[0760] (D.C.)—DAUGHTERS OF CHARITY OF ST. VINCENT DE PAUL (P)

Founded in France in 1633. First foundation in the United States in 1809 by Saint Elizabeth Ann Seton, Emmitsburg, MD.

General Motherhouse: Paris, France Sr. Françoise Petit, D.C., Supr. Gen.

Province of St. Louise (2011): 4330 Olive St., St. Louis, MO 63108-2622. Tel: 314-533-4770; Fax: 314-561-4676. Email: tom.beck@doc.org. Web: www.daughtersofcharity.org. Sr. Catherine Mary Norris, D.C., Prov.

Total in Community: 348.

Legal Title: Daughters of Charity, Inc.; Daughters of Charity Ministries, Inc.

Sisters serve and staff: Religious and Academic Education at all levels; Medical Clinics; Hospitals; Nursing Homes; Ministries to Persons who are Victims of Human Trafficking; Child Care Centers; Social Service Centers; Catholic Charities; Parish Ministries; Outreach Centers; Hispanic Ministry; Hospice; Peace and Justice; (Arch)Diocesan Offices; Emergency Relief Centers; Spiritual Direction; Retreats; Campus Ministry; Prison Ministry; Shelters for the Homeless; Immigration Ministries; Climate Resilence and Sustainability; Vocation Ministry.

Represented in the Archdioceses of Baltimore, Chicago, Detroit, Mobile, New Orleans, New York, Philadelphia, St. Louis, San Antonio and Washington and in the Dioceses of Albany, Belleville, Brownsville, Buffalo, Charleston, El Paso, Evansville, Jackson, Little Rock, Savannah, Syracuse and Wilmington. Also in Canada.

Province of the West (Los Altos Hills) (1969): Seton Provincialate, 26000 Altamont Rd., Los Altos Hills, CA 94022-4317. Tel: 650-941-4490; Fax: 650-949-8883. Web: www.daughtersofcharity.com. Sr. Christina Maggi, DC Prov.

Total in Community: 87.

Properties owned and/or sponsored: Healthcare: Villa Siena, Mountain View, CA; Education: De Marillac Academy, San Francisco, CA; Mother of Sorrows School, Los Angeles, CA; Our Lady of the Miraculous Medal School, Montebello, CA; Our Lady of the Rosary of Talpa School, Los Angeles, CA; Our Lady of the Visitacion School, San Francisco, CA; Sacred Heart Cathedral Preparatory, San Francisco, CA; St. Elizabeth Seton School, Palo Alto, CA; St. Patrick School, San Jose, CA; St. Vincent de Paul School, Phoenix, CA; St. Vincent School, Los Angeles, CA; Social Ministries: Give Me a Chance, Inc., Ogden, UT; Hotel Dieu, Los Angeles, CA; Life Sharing Center, Inc. dba St. Jude Food Bank, Tuba City, AZ; Maryvale, Rosemead, CA; Mount St. Joseph-St. Elizabeth, San Francisco, CA; Rosalie Rendu, Inc., East Palo Alto, CA; St. Vincent's Institution, Santa Barbara, CA; St. Vincent's Senior Citizen Nutrition Program, Los Angeles, CA; Other: Daughters of Charity Ministry Service Corps, Los Altos Hills, CA; Ministry Services of the Daughters of Charity of St. Vincent de Paul, Los Altos Hills, CA; GRACE, Inc., Pasadena, CA; Villa Siena Foundation, Mountain View, CA; Vincentian Marian Youth, Los Altos Hills, CA; Vincentian Service Corps West, Daly City, CA; St. Louise Resource Services, Los Angeles, CA.

Represented in the Archdioceses of Anchorage-Juneau, Los Angeles and San Francisco and in the Dioceses of Gallup, Phoenix, Salt Lake City and San Jose.

[0790] (F.D.C.)—DAUGHTERS OF DIVINE CHARITY (P)

Founded in Austria on November 21, 1868 by Mother Franziska Lechner. First founded in the United States on October 8, 1913, in New York City.

General Motherhouse: Vienna, Austria

Generalate: Grottaferrata, Rome, Italy.

Holy Family Province (2012): Provincialate: 850 Hylan Blvd., Staten Island, NY 10305-2021. Tel: 718-720-7365; Fax: 718-727-5701; Email: smcoffeltfdc@hotmail.com; Web: www.daughtersofdivinecharity.org. Sr. Mary Coffelt, F.D.C., Prov. Supr.

Professed Sisters: 31.

Properties owned and/or sponsored: St. Mary's Residence, NY; St. Joseph Hill Academy, Staten Island, NY; Leonora Hall and Francesca Residence, Akron, OH.

Legal Title: Congregation of the Daughters of Divine Charity, Inc.

Ministry in Education; Residence for Women; CCD; Youth Ministry; Care of the Elderly; Spiritual Direction; Retreat Work; Pastoral Care.

Represented in the Archdiocese of New York and in the Dioceses of Cleveland and San Diego.

[0793] (D.D.L.)—DAUGHTERS OF DIVINE LOVE (P)

Founded in Ukpor, Nigeria in 1969. First United States Foundation in 1990.

General House: Fifth Avenue, P.O. Box 546, Enugu, Nigeria Tel: 042-559071; Tel: 042-551742. Rev. Mother Anastasia Dike, D.D.L., Mother Gen.

Professed Sisters in Congregation: 962.

U.S. Regional House: 133 N. Prater Ave., Northlake, IL 60164. Tel & Fax: 708-223-0262; Email: ddloveus@aol.com. Sr. Mary Olivia Agbakoba, D.D.L., Reg. Supr.

Professed Sisters in U.S.: 68.

Ministry in the field of Administration; Religious and Academic Education at all levels; Special Education; Health Services; Parish and Diocesan Services; Retreat Work; Social Work.

Represented in the Archdioceses of Chicago, Galveston-Houston, Newark, and Washington and in the Dioceses of Austin, Brooklyn, Brownsville, Lexington, Little Rock, Pueblo, Rockford and Syracuse.

[0795] (F.D.Z.)—DAUGHTERS OF DIVINE ZEAL (P)

Founded in Messina, Italy in 1887 by Saint Hannibal Maria DiFrancia. First foundation in the United States in 1951.

Generalate: Figlie Del Divino Zelo, Circonvallazione Appia 144, Rome, Italy, 00179. Mother M. Teolinda Salemi, F.D.Z., Supr. Gen.

Universal total in Congregation: 1000.

U.S. Headquarters: Hannibal House Spiritual Center, 1526 Hill Rd., Reading, PA 19602. Tel: 610-375-1738; Tel: 610-375-9072; Fax: 610-374-0369; Email: srdivinezeal@hotmail.com. Sr. Marietta Castellano, F.D.Z., Supr.

Total in Community: 3.

Ministry in the field of Religious and Academic Education; Parish and Youth Ministry; Retreat, Vocation, Prayer and Apostolate.

Represented in the Diocese of Allentown.

[0810] (D.H.M.)—DAUGHTERS OF THE HEART OF MARY (P)

Founded in France in 1790. First United States foundation in 1851.

Generalate: 39 rue Notre Dame des Champs, Paris, France, 75006.

Provincialate: 1339 Northampton St., Holyoke, MA 01040-1958. Tel: 413-532-7406; Fax: 413-533-4217. Email: dhmvocations@gmail.com. Sr. Elizabeth Dodge, D.H.M., Prov.

Professed Sisters U.S.A.: 30.

Properties owned or sponsored: Marian Center, Holyoke, MA; Maryhill, St. Paul, MN; Ephpheta Center, Chicago, IL; Nardin Academy, Buffalo, NY; Heart of Mary Center, St. Louis, MO; St. Joseph's School for the Deaf, Bronx, NY.

Represented in the Archdioceses of Chicago, Newark, New York, St. Louis and St. Paul-Minneapolis and in the Diocese of Springfield in Massachusetts.

[0820] (D.H.S.)—DAUGHTERS OF THE HOLY SPIRIT

Founded in France in 1706. First foundation in the U.S. in 1902.

Generalate: Congregation des Filles du Saint Esprit, 15 Boulevard Sebastopol, B.P. 50148, Rennes Cedex 3, France, 35101. Sr. Ann Almodovar, F.S.E., Supr. Gen.

General Motherhouse: Maison-mere des Filles du Saint Esprit, 20 rue des Capucins BP 4538, Saint-Brieuc Cedex 2, France, 22045.

Administrative Offices: Daughters of the Holy Spirit, Inc., P.O. Box 419, 508B Pomfret St., Putnam, CT 06260. Tel: 860-928-0891. Sr. Gertrude Lanouette, D.H.S., Prov.

Total in Community: 45.

Ministry in the field of Education; Home Health Care and Hospital Support; Various Social and Pastoral Ministries of Service.

Represented in the Archdioceses of Hartford and in the Dioceses of Norwich, Sacramento and Stockton.

[0850] (F.M.A.)—DAUGHTERS OF MARY HELP OF CHRISTIANS (P)

Salesian Sisters of St. John Bosco

Founded in Mornese, Italy, in 1872. First foundation in the U.S. in 1908 at Paterson, NJ.

General Motherhouse: Via Ateneo Salesiano, 81, 00139, Rome, Italy. Very Rev. Mother Chiara Cazzuola, F.M.A., Mother Gen.

Universal total in Congregation: 11,265.

Province of St. Joseph: Provincial House, 655 Belmont Ave., Haledon, NJ 07508-2301. Tel: 973-790-7963. Sr. Joanne Holloman, F.M.A., Prov.

Total in Community: 116.

Properties owned and/or sponsored: St. Joseph Provincial Center, Haledon, NJ; Mary Help of Christians Academy, North Haledon, NJ; Sacred Heart Center, Newton, NJ; Villa Madonna School-Salesian Sisters of Tampa, Inc., Tampa, FL; Sacred Heart Novitiate, Newton, NJ.

Legal Title: Missionary Society of the Salesian Sisters, Inc.; Salesian Sisters of Tampa, Inc.

Ministry in the field of academic and religious education at all levels; Youth Ministry; Retreat and Family Ministry.

Represented in the Archdioceses of Miami, Newark, New Orleans and New York and in the Dioceses of Paterson, Columbus, St. Petersburg and Venice.

Province of Mary Immaculate: FMA Provincial House, 6019 Buena Vista, San Antonio, TX 78237. Tel: 210-432-0090; Fax: 210-432-4016. Sr. Rosann Ruiz, F.M.A., Prov.

Total in Community: 82.

Properties owned and/or sponsored: FMA Provincial House & St. John Bosco School, San Antonio, TX; Mary Help of Christians School, Laredo, TX; Salesian Sisters School - Salesian Sisters: MHC Youth Center, Inc., Corralitos, CA; Salesian Sisters Convent, Colorado Springs, Co; Formation House, Bellflower, CA.

Legal Title: Institute of the Daughters of Mary Help of Christians - Salesian Sisters of St. John Bosco, San Antonio, TX.

Ministry in Education; Youth Ministry; Religious Education and Outreach to the Poor.

Represented in the Archdioceses of Los Angeles, New Orleans, San Antonio and San Francisco and in the Dioceses of Austin, Colorado Springs, Laredo, Monterey and Baker.

[0855] (D.M.I.)—THE DAUGHTERS OF MARY IMMACULATE (D)

Founded in Viet Nam in 1920 by the French missionary Bishop Eugène Marie Joseph Allys. First foundation in the U.S. in 2003.

Motherhouse: 32 Kim Long, Hue City, Viet Nam.

U.S. Regional House: 13004 Marlow Farm Drive, Silver Spring, MD 20904. Tel: 301-288-7663. Email: thuyliendmi@gmail.com. Sr. Thuy-Lien Thi Doan, Local Supr. and Pres.

Total in Viet Nam Community: 485; Total in U.S. Community: 12.

Convents: 12500 Patterson Ave., Richmond, VA 23238; 13004 Marlow Farm Dr., Silver Spring, MD 20904. Sr. Matta Nguyen Hoang Vy Chinh, Supr.

Perpetually Professed: 405; Temporarily Professed: 60; Novices: 37; Postulants: 17; Aspirants: 68

Legal Title: The Daughters of Mary Immaculate, Inc.

Ministry in the fields of Education, Pastoral Ministry, Faith Formation, Childcare services and Socio-charitable works.

Represented in the Archdiocese of Washington and in the Diocese of Richmond.

[0860] (D.M.)—DAUGHTERS OF MARY OF THE IMMACULATE CONCEPTION (P)

Founded in New Britain in 1904.

Daughters of Mary General: 314 Osgood Ave., New Britain, CT 06053. Tel: 860-225-9406. Mother Mary Jennifer, Supr. Gen.

Total in Community: 21.

Properties owned and/or sponsored: St. Lucian's Home, New Britain, CT; Monsignor Bojnowski Manor, New Britain, CT; Motherhouse and Novitiate Comples, New Britain, CT; St. Joseph's Home, NY; St. Agnes Residence, NY; Our Lady's Guild House, Boston, MA; Sancta Maria Nursing Facility, Cambridge MA; Marian Heights; Prudence Crandall; Mary Immaculate; Miriam House.

Legal Title: Congregation of the Daughters of Mary of the Immaculate Conception, Inc.

Ministry in the field of Education; Home for the Aged; Homes for Working Girls and Students; Skilled Care.

Represented in the Archdioceses of Boston, Hartford and New York.

[0870] (F.M.I.)—CONGREGATION OF THE DAUGHTERS OF MARY IMMACULATE (P)

Marianist Sisters

Founded in France in 1816.

Motherhouse: Rome, Italy. Mother Susanna Kim, Supr. Gen.

U.S. Foundation (1949): Marianist Sisters Residence, 235 W. Ligustrum Dr., San Antonio, TX 78228. Tel: 210-433-5501; Email: provincialfmiusa@gmail.com. Sr. Gretchen Trautman, F.M.I., Prov. Supr.

Total in Community: 14.

Properties owned and/or sponsored: Marianist Sisters Residence, San Antonio, TX; Marianist Sisters Communities, Dayton OH.

Represented in the Archdioceses of Cincinnati and San Antonio.

[0880] (D.M.J.)—DAUGHTERS OF MARY AND JOSEPH (P)

Founded in Belgium in 1817. First U.S. Foundation in 1926.

Generalate: 65 Iona Rd., Glasnevin, Dublin 9, Ireland, 9. Sr. Helen Lane, Supr. Gen.

Regionalate & Novitiate: 5300 Crest Rd., Rancho Palos Verdes, CA 90275-5004. Tel: 310-377-9968; Fax: 310-541-5967. Sr. Linda Webb, D.M.J., Regl. Supr.; Sr. Teresa Groth, Vocation Dir.; Sr. Pascazia Kinkuhaire, Formation Contact.

Professed Sisters: 34.

Legal Title: Daughters of Mary and Joseph in California. Sisters staff: Grammar Schools, Parish Ministry; Health Ministry; Retreat Work.

Represented in the Archdioceses of Los Angeles and San Francisco.

[0885] (D.M.M.M.)—DAUGHTERS OF MARY MOTHER OF MERCY (P)

Founded in Umuahia, Abia State, Nigeria.

Motherhouse: Umuahia, Nigeria

U.S. Regional House: St. Teresa of Avila Parish Convent, 109-26 130th St., South Ozone Park, NY 11420. Tel: 718-843-1364; Email: dmmmusacanadareg@gmail.com.

Total in U.S.: 190; Universal total in Congregation: 1025.

Ministry in the fields of teaching, medical, pastoral, orphanages & motherless babies homes, social.

[0890] (D.M.)—DAUGHTERS OF OUR LADY OF MERCY (P)

Founded in Italy in 1837 by Saint Mary Joseph Rossello. First foundation in the United States in 1919.

Generalate: Via Monte Grappa, No. 7, Savona, Italy Rev. Mother Angela Maria Vieria Santos, Supr. Gen.

Provincialate: Villa Rossello, 1009 Main Rd., Newfield, NJ 08344. Tel: 856-697-2983. Email: daughtersofmercy@gmail.com. Sr. M. Ambrogina Aldeni, Prov. Supr., Email: sambrogina@gmail.com.

Total in Community: 24.

Legal Holdings: Our Lady of Mercy Academy, Newfield, NJ; Misericordia Nursing & Rehabilitation Center, York, PA.

Ministry in the field of Education; Health Services; Skilled Nursing Center; Pastoral Counseling, C.C.D. and Parish Work. Represented in the Dioceses of Camden and Harrisburg. Also in Haiti.

[0895] (F.M.S.R.)—DAUGHTERS OF OUR LADY OF THE HOLY ROSARY (P)

Founded in 1946 in Trung Linh, Bui Chu, North Vietnam by Bishop Dominic Maria Ho Ngoc Can. First foundation in the United States in 1967.

Sr. M. Rose Loan Vu, F.M.S.R.

U.S. Provincial Office: Queen of Peace Province, 1492 Moss St., New Orleans, LA 70119-2904. Email: fmsrusaprovince@yahoo.com. Sr. M. Gemma Thu-Mai Nguyen, F.M.S.R., Prov. Supr.

Total in Community: 60.

Properties owned and/or sponsored: Six residences. Ministry in the field of Education; Health Services; Pastoral Ministry.

Represented in the Archdioceses of New Orleans and Oklahoma City and in the Dioceses of Baton Rouge, Houma-Thibodaux, Biloxi and Little Rock.

[0900] (F.D.N.S.C.)—DAUGHTERS OF OUR LADY OF THE SACRED HEART (P)

Founded in France in 1874.

Motherhouse: Via Casale S. Pio V, 37, Rome, Italy 00165. Sr. Marife Mendoza, F.D.N.S.C., Supr. Gen.

U.S. Foundation (1955): St. Francis de Sales Convent, 424 E. Browning Rd., Bellmawr, NJ 08031. Tel: 856-931-8973; Fax: 856-931-7018.

Professed Sisters in the U.S.: 7.

Represented in the Diocese of Camden.

[0910] (BETHL.)—BETHLEMITA, DAUGHTER OF THE SACRED HEART OF JESUS (P)

Founded in Guatemala in 1861. First foundation in the United States in Dallas, TX.

Motherhouse: Bogota, Colombia

U.S. Foundation: St. Joseph Residence, Inc., 330 W. Pembroke Ave., Dallas, TX 75208. Tel: 214-948-3597. Sr. Carolina Sanchez Botero, Admin.

Professed Sisters: 4.

Represented in the Diocese of Dallas.

[0920] (D.S.F.)—CONGREGATION OF THE DAUGHTERS OF ST. FRANCIS OF ASSISI

Founded in Hungary, 1894. First foundation in the United States in 1946.

Motherhouse: American Region: St. Joseph's Convent, 507 N. Prairie St., Lacon, IL 61540. Tel: 309-246-2175. Sr. Loretta Matas, D.S.F., Pres.

Professed Sisters: 12.

Legal Title: Congregation of the Daughters of St. Francis of Assisi.

Represented in the Dioceses of Peoria and Springfield-Cape Girardeau.

[0940] (D.S.M.P.)—DAUGHTERS OF ST. MARY OF PROVIDENCE (P)

Founded in Italy in 1881. First foundation in the United States in 1913.

Generalate: Rome, Italy. Sr. Neuza M. Giordani, D.S.M.P., Mother Vicar.

Provincialate: Daughters of St. Mary of Providence Immaculate Conception Province, 4200 N. Austin Ave., Chicago, IL 60634. Tel: 773-205-1313. Sr. Rita Butler, Prov.

Professed Sisters: 56.

Represented in the Archdioceses of Chicago and Philadelphia and in the Dioceses of Lansing, New Ulm, Sioux Falls and Syracuse.

[0950] (F.S.P.)—PIOUS SOCIETY DAUGHTERS OF ST. PAUL (P)

Missionary Sisters of the Media of Communications

Founded in Alba, Piedmont, Italy, on June 15, 1915. First founded in the United States on June 28, 1932, in New York.

General Motherhouse: Rome, Italy. Sr. Anna Caiazza, Supr. Gen.

Universal total in Congregation: 1,915.

Provincial House, Novitiate, Publishing House: 50 St. Paul's Ave., Jamaica Plain, MA 02130. Tel: 617-522-8911. Sr. Patricia Mary Maresca, Local Supr.; Sr. Donald Maria Lynch, F.S.P., Prov. Supr.

Total in Community: 131.

Properties owned and/or sponsored: Pauline Book and Media Centers, found in 9 locations throughout the U.S.; Provincialate, Boston, MA; St. Thecla Retreat House, Billerica, MA.

Legal Title: Daughters of St. Paul, Inc.; Daughters of St. Paul Community Foundation Inc., Daughters of St. Paul Religious Trust.

Represented in the Archdioceses of Boston, Los Angeles, Miami, New Orleans, New York, St. Louis, and San Francisco and in the Diocese of Arlington. Also in Canada.

[0960] (D.W.)—DAUGHTERS OF WISDOM (P)

Founded in France in 1703. First foundation in the United States in 1904.

Motherhouse: St. Laurent-sur-Sevre, Vendee, France. Congregational Headquarters located in Paris, France.

U.S. Province (1949): Provincial House, 385 Ocean Ave., Islip, NY 11751-4600. Tel: 631-277-2660; Fax: 631-277-3274. Email: dwadministration@daughtersofwisdom.com; Sr. Catherine Sheehan, D.W., Prov. Leader.

Professed Sisters: 52.

Properties owned and/or sponsored: Wisdom House Center for Spirituality, Litchfield, CT; Our Lady of Perpetual Help Convent (Retirement Home for Sisters), Sound Beach, NY; Provincial Office & House, Islip, NY.

Ministries in Education; Spirituality and Health.

Represented in the Archdioceses of Hartford and Washington and in the Dioceses of Brooklyn, Charleston, Omaha, Portland (In Maine), Richmond, Rockville Centre, St. Augustine and St. Petersburg.

[0965] (D.L.J.C.)—DISCIPLES OF THE LORD JESUS CHRIST (P)

Founded in the United States in 1972.

Motherhouse: P.O. Box 64, Prayer Town, TX 79010. Tel: 806-534-2312; Fax: 806-534-2223; Email: sistersdljc@gmail.com; Web: www.dljc.org. Mother Lucy Lukasiewicz, D.L.J.C., Supr. Gen.

Total in Community: 42.

Legal Holdings and Titles: Prayertown Emmanuel Retreat House, Prayer Town, TX.

Ministry in Retreat Work and Evangelization

Represented in the Archdiocese of Santa Fe and in the Dioceses of Amarillo and Pittsburgh. Also in Mexico.

[0970] (R.D.C.)—SISTERS OF THE DIVINE COMPASSION (D)

Founded in the United States in 1886.

R.D.C. Administrative Offices, 52 N. Broadway, White Plains, NY 10603. Tel: 914-798-1300; Fax: 914-949-5169. Sr. Laura Donovan, R.D.C., Pres.

Total in Community: 54.

Legal Holdings and Titles: Academy of Our Lady of Good Counsel High School and Elementary School, White Plains, NY; Preston High School, Bronx, NY; Residence, Hampton Bays, NY.

Ministry in Preschool, Elementary, Secondary, Religious Education; Adult Education; Special Education; Pastoral Ministry; Retreat Work and Spiritual Direction; Counseling; Social Services; Health Services; Administration and Business Services.

Represented in the Archdiocese of New York.

[0980] (P.D.D.M.)—PIOUS DISCIPLES OF THE DIVINE MASTER (P)

Founded in 1924. First foundation in the United States in 1948.

General Motherhouse: Rome, Italy. Sr. M. Micaela Monetti, Supr. Gen.

Universal total in Congregation: 1300.

U.S. Headquarters: 43 West St., Boston, MA 02111. Tel: 617-482-0978. Sr. M. Kathryn Williams, Reg. Supr.

Total number in Region: 32.

Ministry is a Three Dimensional Mission: Eucharistic, Priestly, Liturgical.

Represented in the Archdioceses of Boston and Los Angeles and in the Diocese of Fresno.

[0990] (C.D.P.)—SISTERS OF DIVINE PROVIDENCE (P)

Founded in Germany in 1851. First foundation in the United States in 1876; incorporation granted September 17, 1881.

Amended and restated articles of incorporation on December 28, 2001.

General Motherhouse: Mother of Providence Convent, 12 Christopher St., Wakefield, RI 02879. Tel: 401-782-1785; Fax: 401-782-6967. Sr. Barbara McMullen, Gen. Supr.

Marie de la Roche Province (2001): Providence Heights, 9000 Babcock Blvd., Allison Park, PA 15101. Tel: 412-931-5241; Fax: 412-635-5416. Email: srohm@cdpsisters.org. Sr. Michele Bisbey, C.D.P., Prov. Supr.; Sr. Mary Michael McCulla, C.D.P., Area Asst.-Kingston, MA; Sr. Ann Pairn, C.D.P., Area Asst.-St. Louis, MO.

Total in Community: 147.

Ministry in the fields of Education; Social Services; Pastoral Ministry; and Health Care Services.

Properties owned and sponsored: La Roche University, Pittsburgh, PA; Providence Heights Alpha School, Allison Park, PA; Kearns Spirituality Center, Allison Park, PA; Providence Connections, Inc.; Providence Family Support Center, Pittsburgh, PA; Sisters of Divine Providence of Allegheny County, Allison Park, PA; Sisters of Divine Providence Charitable Trust, Allison Park, PA; Room at the Inn, Bridgeton, MO; Sacred Heart School System, Kingston, MA; Congregation of the Sisters of Divine Providence, Kingston, MA; Sisters of Divine Providence of Missouri, Bridgeton, MO, La Posada Providencia, San Benito, TX.

Represented in the Archdioceses of Boston, Detroit, Mobile, St. Louis and San Juan and in the Dioceses of Arecibo, Belleville, Nashville, Orlando, Pittsburgh, Providence, Raleigh, Springfield in Illinois and Wheeling-Charleston.

[1000] (C.D.P.)—CONGREGATION OF DIVINE PROVIDENCE, MELBOURNE, KENTUCKY (P)

Founded in France in 1762. First foundation in the United States in 1889.

General Motherhouse: St. Jean de Bassel, Fenetrange, France, 57930. Sr. Susan Baumann, Supr. Gen.

American Provincial House (1889): St. Anne Convent, 5300 St. Anne Dr., Melbourne, KY 41059. Tel: 859-441-0679. Sr. Barbara Rohe, C.D.P., Prov. Supr.

Total number in Province: 74.

Ministry in the field of Academic Education at all levels; Religious Education & Pastoral Ministry; Health & Social Services.

Represented in the Archdioceses of Cincinnati and Boston and in the Dioceses of Covington, Lexington, Mobile and Rapid City.

[1010] (C.D.P.)—CONGREGATION OF DIVINE PROVIDENCE, SAN ANTONIO, TEXAS (P)

Founded in France in 1762. First foundation in the United States in 1866.

The Generalate: 515 S.W. 24th St., San Antonio, TX 78207. Tel: 210-434-1866; Fax: 210-568-1050. Sr. Pearl Ceasar, C.D.P., Supr. Gen.; Sr. Charlotte Kitowski, Archivist; Sr. Patricia Regan, C.D.P., Treas. Councilors: Sr. Anita Brenek, C.D.P.; Sr. Lourdes Leal, C.D.P.; Sr. Mary Bordelon, C.D.P.

Novitiate and Formation: Formation/Vocation Office, 515 S.W. 24th St., San Antonio, TX 78207. Tel: 210-587-1135.

Properties owned and/or sponsored: Our Lady of the Lake Retirement Center, San Antonio, TX; Moye Center, Castroville, TX.

Legal Titles & Holdings: Congregation of Divine Providence, Inc.; Providence Trust, San Antonio, TX.

Ministry in all levels of Education; Catechetical Centers; Diocesan Offices; Retreat Houses; Spiritual Direction-Counseling; Pastoral; Social Work; Chaplaincies in Public Institutions; Administration and Campus Ministry.

Represented in the Archdioceses of Galveston-Houston, Pittsburgh, San Antonio, and St. Louis and in the Dioceses of Austin, Fort Worth, San Angelo, Beaumont, San Jose and Lake Charles. Also in Mexico.

[1020] (S.D.R.)—SISTERS OF THE DIVINE REDEEMER (P)

Founded in 1849 at Niederbronn, France. First foundation in the United States on October 3, 1912 at McKeesport.

Generalate: Generalat der Kongregation der Schwestern vom Göttlichen Erlöser, Bürgerspitalgasse 6/17 7000 Eisenstadt, Austria. Tel: 011-43-2682-22711. Sr. Johanna Vogl, Supr. Gen.

American Region (1912): Sisters of the Divine Redeemer Motherhouse, 999 Rock Run Rd., Elizabeth, PA 15037-2613. Tel: 412-751-8600; Fax: 412-751-0355. Email: sdrarusa@gmail.com. Web: www.divine-redeemer-sisters.org. Sr. M. Monica Kosztolnyik, Archivist & Regl. Vicar; Sr. M. Alojziana Spišáková, S.D.R., Regl. Supr.

Total number in Province: 12.

Legal Titles and Holdings: Sisters of the Divine Redeemer Charitable Trust; Divine Redeemer Health Care Ministries Corp., Elizabeth, PA.

Ministry in the fields of education & music education.

Represented in the Diocese of Pittsburgh.

[1030] (S.D.S.)—SISTERS OF THE DIVINE SAVIOR

Founded in Tivoli, Italy in 1888. First foundation in the United States in 1895.

General Motherhouse: Viale delle Mura Gianicolensi 67, Rome, Italy. Sr. Maria Yaneth Moreno, Gen. Supr.

North American Province: Sisters of the Divine Savior, 4311 N. 100th St., Milwaukee, WI 53222-1393. Tel: 414-466-0810; Fax: 414-466-4335. Sr. Jean Schafer, S.D.S., Prov. Supr.; Sr. Mary Jo Stoffel, S.D.S., Archivist.

Total number in U.S. community: 45.

Ministry in all levels of Education; Pastoral and Social Services; Health Care; and Homes for the Aged.

Properties owned or sponsored: Divine Savior Holy Angels High School, Milwaukee, WI.

Represented in the Archdiocese of Milwaukee and in the Dioceses of Green Bay, Madison and Sioux Falls.

[1040] (C.D.S.)—CONGREGATION OF THE DIVINE SPIRIT (D)

First foundation in Erie, Pennsylvania in 1956.

Motherhouse: 2700 Harvard Ave., N.W., Canton, OH 44709. Sr. Michele Beauseigneur, Supr. Gen.

Membership: 18.

Sisters serve and staff: Parochial Schools; CCD Activities; Home for Aged.

Represented in the Diocese of Youngstown.

[1050] (O.P.)—DOMINICAN CONTEMPLATIVE NUNS (P)

(The Nuns of the Order of Preachers)

Founded in France in 1206. Founded in 1889. Nuns of the Order of Preachers. Papal cloister.

Nuns of the Order of Preachers O.P: Corpus Christi Monastery, 1230 Lafayette Ave., Bronx, NY 10474. Tel: 718-328-6996; Fax: 718-328-1974. Sr. Mary Catharine of Jesus Perry, O.P., Prioress.

Solemnly Professed: 13; Novices: 1.

Monastery of the Blessed Sacrament: Nuns of the Order of Preachers, 29575 Middlebelt Rd., Farmington Hills, MI 48334-2311. Tel: 248-626-8321; Tel: 248-626-8253; Fax: 248-626-8724. Sr. Mary Peter, O.P., Prioress.

Cloistered Sisters: 18; Extern Sisters: 4.

Nuns of the Order of Preachers (Cloistered Dominican Nuns, Perpetual Adoration)

Monastery of the Angels: Cloistered Dominican Nuns, 1977 Carmen Ave., Los Angeles, CA 90068. Tel: 323-466-2186. Email: laopnuns@monasteryoftheangels.org; Web: www.monasteryoftheangels.org. Sr. Maria Christine, O.P., Prioress.

Sisters: 10.

Legal Title: The Monastery of the Angels.

Monastery of the Angels: Karachi, Pakistan. Sr. Mary Martin, O.P., Prioress.

Sisters: 12.

Queen of Angels Monastery: Bocaue, Bulacan, Philippines. Sr. Mary Lourdes, O.P., Prioress.

Sisters: 14.

Corpus Christi Monastery: 215 Oak Grove Ave., Menlo Park, CA 94025-3272. Tel: 650-322-1801; Fax: 650-322-6816. Sr. Mary Isabel, O.P., Prioress.

Cloistered Total Number in Community: 14.

Dominican Nuns O.P: Monastery of the Mother of God, 1430 Riverdale St., West Springfield, MA 01089-4698. Tel: 413-736-3639; Fax: 413-736-0850. Emails: monasteryws@comcast.net; srmbursarws@yahoo.com. Sr. Theresa Marie, O.P., Prioress.

Total in Community: 8.

Dominican Contemplative Nuns O.P.: Monastery of Our Lady of the Rosary, 2734 Seminary Rd., Heath, OH 43056-9339. Tel: 740-928-0637; Fax: 844-304-9968. Email: bursar@opnuns.org. Web: opnuns.org. Sr. Mary Dominic, O.P., Prioress.

Religious: 12.

Legal Title: Dominican Nuns of the Perpetual Rosary.

Monastery of Our Lady of Grace: 11 Race Hill Rd., Guilford, CT 06437-1099. Tel: 203-457-0599. Sr. Maria of the Angels, O.P., Prioress.

Total in Community: 27.

Legal Title: Dominican Nuns of North Guilford, CT Inc.

Monastery of the Infant Jesus: Dominican Contemplative Nuns, 1501 Lotus Ln., Lufkin, TX 75904. Tel: 936-634-4233; Fax: 936-634-2156. Sr. Mary Margaret, O.P., Prioress.

Professed: 19.

Monastery of Our Lady of the Rosary (Rosary Shrine): 543 Springfield Ave., Summit, NJ 07901. Tel: 908-273-1228. Email: info@summitdominicans.org. Sr. Joseph Maria, O.P., Prioress.

Solemnly Professed: 13; Temporary Professed: 3; Novices: 2; Postulants: 1.

The Dominican Nuns/Saint Dominic's Monastery (Contemplative): 2636 Monastery Rd., Linden, VA 22642. Email: monastery@lindenopnuns.org. Sr. Mary Fidelis, O.P., Prioress.

Nuns: 12.

The Dominican Nuns of the Perpetual Rosary (Cloistered-Contemplative): Monastery of the Immaculate Heart of Mary, 1834 Lititz Pike, Lancaster, PA 17601-6585. Tel: 717-569-2104; Fax: 717-569-1598; Email: monlanc@aol.com. Sr. Mary Veronica, O.P., Prioress.

Solemnly Professed: 6.

Dominican Monastery of the Perpetual Rosary: 802 Court St., Syracuse, NY 13208. Tel: 315-471-6762. Sr. Bernadette Marie, O.P., Prioress.

Total in Community: 11.

Dominican Monastery of St. Jude: 143 County Rd. 20 E., P.O. Box 170, Marbury, AL 36051-0170. Tel: 205-755-1322; Fax: 205-755-9847; Email: stjudemonastery@aol.com; Web: www.marburydominicannuns.org. Mother Mary of the Precious Blood, O.P., Prioress.

Solemnly Professed Nuns: 7; Aspirant: 1.

[1060] (O.P.)—DOMINICAN CONTEMPLATIVE SISTERS (D)
Cloistered Contemplative

Founded in Calais, France in 1880.

Monastery of the Dominican Sisters of the Perpetual Rosary (Cloistered): 3980 W. Kimberly Ave., Greenfield, WI 53221-4553. Tel: 414-258-0579; Email: mjoannahastings@gmail.com; Web: www.dsopr.org. Mother Joanna Hastings, O.P., Prioress.

Professed Sisters: 4.

[1070] (O.P.)—COLLABORATIVE DOMINICAN NOVITIATE DOMINICAN SISTERS (P)

There are seventeen Congregations of the Dominican Sisters in the United States, plus the Maryknoll Sisters of St. Dominic who collaborate in the Collaborative Dominican Novitiate. The Dominican collaborating Congregations are contained within the list of General Motherhouses. If the Congregation is known under a more familiar name, that name is given under the name of the Congregation.

4950 S. Ellis Ave., Chicago, IL 60615-2708. Tel: 517-270-9293.

[1070-03]—SINSINAWA DOMINICAN CONGREGATION OF THE MOST HOLY ROSARY (P)

Generalate: Sinsinawa Dominican Congregation of the Most Holy Rosary, 585 County Rd. Z, Sinsinawa, WI 53824-9701. Tel: 608-748-4411. Communication Office Email: communication@sinsinawa.org. Sr. Antoinette Harris, O.P., Prioress of the Congregation; Cassandra Vazquez, Archivist.

Total in Community: 284.

Ministry in a variety of cultures in Preaching & Evangelization; Elementary, Secondary and Higher Education; Medical, Legal and Social Services; Adult and Religious Education; Diocesan and Parish Administration, Spiritual Direction and Counseling; Rural, Migrant Services; Writing Research.

Properties owned or Institutions sponsored: Sinsinawa Dominicans, Inc., Dominican University, River Forest, IL; Sinsinawa Housing, Inc., (Academy Apartments), Sinsinawa, WI; Bethlehem Academy, Faribault, MN; Dominican High School, Whitefish Bay, WI; Trinity High School, River Forest, IL; Dominican Motherhouse, Sinsinawa, WI; Edgewood Campus School; Edgewood High School; Edgewood College, Madison, WI.

Represented in the Archdioceses of Atlanta, Chicago, Denver, Dubuque, Los Angeles, Miami, Milwaukee, Mobile, Omaha, St. Louis, St. Paul-Minneapolis, San Francisco, Seattle and Washington and in the Dioceses of Austin, Cheyenne, Dallas, Great Falls-Billings, Green Bay, Helena, Joliet, La Crosse, Madison, Oakland, Orlando, Palm Beach, Pensacola-Tallahassee, Rockford, San Jose, St. Augustine, St. Petersburg, Spokane, and Winona-Rochester. Also in Bolivia and Trinidad.

[1070-04]—CONGREGATION OF THE MOST HOLY NAME (P)

Generalate: Dominican Sisters of San Rafael, 1520 Grand Ave., San Rafael, CA 94901. Tel: 415-453-8303; Fax: 415-453-8367. Email: info@sanrafaelop.org. Sr. Carla Kovack, O.P.

Total in Community: 57.

Legal Holdings and Titles: San Domenico School, San Anselmo, CA; Santa Sabina Retreat Center, San Rafael, CA; St. Rose Corporation, San Francisco, CA; Sisters of St. Dominic, Congregation of the Most Holy Name, San Rafael, CA; Mission Holding Corporation, San Rafael, CA.

Represented in the Archdiocese of San Francisco and in the Dioceses of Oakland, Santa Rosa and Stockton.

[1070-05]—CONGREGATION OF THE HOLY CROSS (D)

General Motherhouse: Queen of the Rosary Mother house, 555 Albany Ave., Amityville, NY 11701. Tel: 631-842-6000; Fax: 631-842-0240. Email: sistersop@amityop.org. Sr. Peggy McVetty, O.P., Prioress; Sr. Margaret Kavanagh, O.P., Archivist; Sr. Patricia Koehler, O.P., Treas.

Total in Community: 292.

Legal Title: The Sisters of the Order of Saint Dominic.

Sisters are engaged in the ministry of Education at all levels; Adult and Continuing Education; Homes for the Aged; Residence for Senior Citizens; Chaplaincy; Advocacy; Communications; Shelters; Pastoral Services; Prison Ministry; Ministry to AIDS Victims; Environmental Education Ministry.

Represented in the Archdioceses of Newark and New York and in the Dioceses of Albany, Brooklyn, Providence, Rockville Centre and Trenton. Also in Puerto Rico.

[1070-07]—CONGREGATION OF ST. CECILIA (P)

General Motherhouse: St. Cecilia Convent, 801 Dominican Dr., Nashville, TN 37228-1905. Tel: 615-256-5486. Vocation Office Email: vocation@op-tn.org. Advancement Office Email: diradvance@op-tn.org. Mother Anna Grace Neenan, O.P., Prioress Gen.; Sr. Lucia Marie Siemering, O.P., Archivist and Sec. Gen. Email: slmsiemering@op-tn.org.

Professed Sisters in Community: 276; Apostolic Novices: 9; Canonical Novices: 12; Postulants: 18.

Ministry in the field of Academic Education at all levels. Legal Holdings and Titles: Aquinas College, Nashville, TN.

Represented in the Archdioceses of Atlanta, Baltimore, Cincinnati, Denver, Galveston-Houston, Gaylord, Louisville, St. Louis, St. Paul-Minneapolis, Seattle and Washington and in the Dioceses of Arlington, Birmingham, Charleston, Dallas, Joliet in Illinois, Knoxville, Lafayette in Indiana, Memphis, Nashville, Phoenix, Providence and Richmond. Also in Australia, Canada, Ireland, Italy, Scotland, and The Netherlands.

[1070-09]—CONGREGATION OF ST. CATHERINE OF SIENA (P)

General Motherhouse: Convent of St. Catherine, 5635 Erie St., Racine, WI 53402-1900. Tel: 262-639-4100; Fax: 262-639-9702. Sr. Maryann McMahon, O.P., Pres.; Sr. Shirley Kubat, Archivist.

Total in Community: 121.

Legal Holdings and Titles: Sisters of St. Dominic, Racine, WI; St. Catherine's High School of Racine, Inc., Racine, WI; Racine Dominican Ministries, Inc., Racine, WI; HOPES Center of Racine, Inc.; Siena Retreat Center, Inc.; Eco-Justice Center, Inc.; Senior Companion Program, Inc.; Dominicans at Siena on the Lake, Inc.

Properties sponsored: Sisters of St. Dominic, Racine, WI; Catherine Marian Housing, Inc.

Sisters minister in the areas of Higher and Music Cultural Education; Adult Education; Religious Education; Administration; Parish and Pastoral Ministry; Prison Ministry; Social Justice; Social Services, Hospital and Health Services; Writing Research; Hospital Chaplains; Retreats-Prayer Programs; Community Services.

Represented in the Archdioceses of Detroit, Milwaukee, St. Louis and Santa Fe and in the Dioceses of Grand Rapids, Green Bay, Las Vegas, Madison and Yakima.

[1070-10]—DOMINICAN SISTERS OF SPRINGFIELD, ILLINOIS (P)

General Motherhouse: Sacred Heart Convent, 1237 W. Monroe St., Springfield, IL 62704-1680. Tel: 217-787-0481; Fax: 217-787-8169. Sr. Rebecca Ann Gemma, O.P., Prioress Gen.; Maira Herrara, Archivist.

Total in Community: 140.

Legal Holdings or Titles: Dominican Sisters of Springfield, Illinois, Inc., Dominican Sisters of Springfield in Illinois Charitable Trust, Springfield, IL; Jubilee Farm, NFP, Springfield, IL; Dominican Literacy Center, Aurora, IL; Dominican Literacy Center, Chicago, IL; Marian Catholic High School, Chicago Heights, IL; Rosary High School, Aurora, IL; Sacred Heart-Griffin High School, Springfield, IL.

Ministry in Elementary, Secondary Schools and Universities, Religious & Academic Education; Learning Centers; Hospitals, Nursing Homes, Congregation's Infirmary and Retirement Center; Retreat, Renewal & Ecological Center; Administrative Positions in Parishes and Archdiocesan Office; Parish Liturgist/Musician & Pastoral Associates; Justice Advocacy; Social Services; Foreign Missions.

Represented in the Archdiocese of Chicago and Dubuque and in the Dioceses of Belleville, Jackson, Joliet, Peoria, Rapid City, Rockford, and Springfield in Illinois. Also in Peru.

[1070-11]—CONGREGATION OF OUR LADY OF THE ROSARY (D)

General Motherhouse and Novitiate: Dominican Convent of Our Lady of the Rosary, 175 Rte. 340, Sparkill, NY 10976. Tel: 845-359-4088. Sr. Irene Ellis, O.P., Prioress.

Total in Community: 207.

Legal Title: Dominican Convent of Our Lady of the Rosary.

Ministry in High Schools and Elementary Schools; Adult Education/Literacy; Parishes; Pastoral; Colleges; Housing and Community Centers; Foreign Missions; Substance Abuse Recovery.

Properties sponsored: Albertus Magnus High School, Bardonia, NY; One to One Learning Inc., Nyack, NY; Dowling Housing Corp., Sparkill, NY.

Represented in the Archdioceses of Chicago, New York and St. Louis and in the Dioceses of Brooklyn, Great Falls-Billings, Jefferson City, Rockville Centre, San Diego and Trenton.

[1070-12]—CONGREGATION OF THE QUEEN OF THE HOLY ROSARY (P)

General Motherhouse: Dominican Convent, 43326 Mission Cir., Fremont, CA 94539. Tel: 510-657-2468. Sr. Celeste Marie Botello, Congregational Prioress; Sr. Pauline Bouton, Congregational Sec.

Professed: 138.

Legal Title: Dominican Sisters of Mission San Jose, a Corporation, Queen of the Holy Rosary College, a Corporation, St. Catherine's Academy, a Corporation, Anaheim, CA; Immaculate Conception Academy, a Corporation, San Francisco, CA; Flintridge Sacred Heart Academy, a Corporation, La Canada-Flintridge, CA; Pia Backes Support Trust, Fremont, CA; Dominican Sisters Foundation, a corporation Dominican Sisters Vision of Hope.

The Community is engaged in the Preaching Mission of St. Dominic through ministry in education at all levels, pastoral services, social justice, communications, health services, Congregational services, and full time study.

Represented in the Archdioceses of Los Angeles, San Francisco and in the Dioceses of Oakland, Orange, San Bernardino and San Jose. Also in Mexico.

[1070-13]—CONGREGATION OF THE MOST HOLY ROSARY (P)

General Motherhouse: 1257 E. Siena Heights Dr., Adrian, MI 49221. Tel: 517-266-3400; Fax: 517-266-3545. Sr. Elise D. García, O.P., Prioress.

Total in Congregation: 432.

Legal Holdings or Titles: Camilla Madden Charitable Trust, Adrian, MI; Adrian Dominican Sisters Office of Development, Adrian, MI; Dominican Life Center, Adrian, MI; Regina Dominican High School, Wilmette, IL; Rosarian Academy, West Palm Beach, FL; Siena Heights University, Adrian, MI; Weber Retreat Center, Adrian, MI.

Sisters minister in the areas of Formal Education - as administrators, teachers and consultants at elementary, secondary, college, state and diocesan levels; Pastoral Ministry - parishes, hospitals and campuses; Religious Education - coordinators and teachers; Social Services - case workers, administrators, counselors, therapists, consultants, care-givers for elderly and staff for retirement centers; Health Services administrators, nurses, therapists, doctors, physician assistants, psychologists, technologists and dietitians; Business Services - directors, accountants, secretaries, administrative assistants, typists, bookkeepers, office managers, office staff, drivers and housekeeping staff; Spiritual Direction - retreat work, formation, congregation leadership and as diocesan vicars for Religious; Social Justice - coordinators, staff and community organizers; other ministries including research, law, science, public relations, art, communications and full-time study.

Represented in the Archdioceses of Atlanta, Chicago, Detroit, Galveston-Houston, Indianapolis, Louisville, Miami, New Orleans, New York, St. Louis, and Seattle and the Dioceses of Arlington, Burlington, Charleston, Cleveland, Fort Wayne-South Bend, Gaylord, Green Bay, Joliet, Las Vegas, Lansing, Marquette, Monterey, Oakland, Orlando, Palm Beach, Providence, Rockford,

Rockville Centre, Saginaw, San Diego, St. Cloud, Tucson and Venice. Also in Dominican Republic, Mexico, Norway and Philippines.

Mission Chapters (2022):

Adrian Crossroads Mission Chapter: 1257 Siena Heights Dr., Adrian, MI 49221. Tel: 517-266-4242. Sr. Peggy Coyne, O.P., Chapter Prioress.

Catherine Siena Mission Chapter: 10024 S. Central Park Ave., Chicago, IL 60655. Tel: 773-253-3822. Sr. Mary Margaret Priniski, O.P., Chapter Prioress; Sr. Mary Jane Lubinski, O.P., Mission Prioress; Sr. Mary Soher, O.P., Mission Prioress.

Holy Rosary Mission Chapter: 1257 E. Siena Heights Dr., Adrian, MI 49221. Tel: 517-266-4107. Sr. Judith Friedel, O.P., Chapter Prioress; Sr. Sharon Spanbauer, O.P., Mission Prioress.

Our Lady of Remedies Mission Chapter: Dominican Sisters Sindalan City of San Fernando, Pampanga Philippines. Tel: 0116309338699004. Sr. Maria Yolanda G. Manapsal, O.P., Chapter Prioress.

[1070-14]—CONGREGATION OF OUR LADY OF THE SACRED HEART (P)

General Motherhouse: Marywood, 111 Lakeside Dr., NE, Grand Rapids, MI 49503-3811. Tel: 616-459-2910. Sr. Sandra Delgado, O.P., Prioress; Sr. Mary Navarre, O.P., Archivist.

Total in Community: 148.

Legal Holdings or Titles: Sisters of the Order of St. Dominic of Grand Rapids; Marywood Academy; Sisters of St. Dominic of the Congregation of Our Lady of the Sacred Heart Charitable Trust.

Sisters are involved in Academic and Religious Education; Liturgy; Pastoral Ministry and Administration; Spirituality Centers; Health Care; Congregational Services; Social Work; ESL; Foreign Missions; Justice Advocacy.

Represented in the Archdioceses of Chicago, Detroit, Santa Fe and Washington, DC, and in the Dioceses of Colorado Springs, Fort Wayne-South Bend, Gaylord, Grand Rapids, Helena, Kalamazoo, Lansing, Rapid City, Saginaw and Superior. Also in Peru.

[1070-15]—CONGREGATION OF SAINT DOMINIC (D)

General Motherhouse: Sisters of Saint Dominic of Blauvelt, 496 Western Hwy., Blauvelt, NY 10913-2097. Tel: 845-359-5600; Fax: 845-359-5773. Sr. Michaela Connolly, O.P., Prioress.

Total in Community: 85.

Sisters serve and staff: Elementary; Higher Education; Special Education; Pastoral Care; Parish Ministry; Neighborhood Services; Services to Migrants; Services to Chemically Dependent.

Represented in the Archdioceses of Newark and New York and in the Dioceses of Orlando, Providence, Trenton and Venice.

[1070-18]—SISTERS OF ST. DOMINIC OF THE AMERICAN CONGREGATION OF THE SACRED HEART OF JESUS (D)

Dominican Motherhouse: 1 Ryerson Ave., Caldwell, NJ 07006. Tel: 973-403-3331; Fax: 973-228-9611. Email: dominicans@caldwellop.org. Sr. Luella Ramm, O.P., Prioress; Sr. Elaine Keenan, O.P., Archivist; Sr. Marie Mueller, O.P., Contact Person. Email: mmueller@caldwellop.org.

Total in Community: 92.

Properties owned and/or sponsored: Caldwell University, Caldwell, NJ; Mount Saint Dominic Academy, Caldwell, NJ; St. Dominic Academy, Jersey City, NJ; Lacordaire Academy, Upper Montclair, NJ.

Legal Title: Sisters of St. Dominic of Caldwell, NJ, Inc. Ministry in Education at all levels; Pastoral Ministry; Health and Human Services.

Represented in the Archdioceses of Newark and Portland in Oregon and in the Dioceses of Metuchen, Norwich, St. Augustine and Trenton.

[1070-19]—DOMINICAN SISTERS OF HOUSTON, TEXAS (CONGREGATION OF THE SACRED HEART) (P)

General Motherhouse & Novitiate: Dominican Sisters, 6501 Almeda Rd., Houston, TX 77021. Tel: 713-747-3310; Fax: 713-747-4707. Sr. Donna M. Pollard, O.P., Prioress.

Total in Community: 49.

Legal Title: Dominican Sisters of Houston, Texas, Inc. (aka Sacred Heart Convent of Houston).

Ministry in the field of Academic Education at all levels and parish Ministry.

Properties owned and sponsored: St. Agnes Academy, St. Agnes Academy Foundation, St. Pius X High School, St. Pius X High School Foundation, Inc., The Sacred Heart Convent Retirement Trust.

Represented in the Archdioceses of Galveston-Houston and Los Angeles and in the Dioceses of Beaumont and Tyler. Also in Guatemala.

[1070-20]—CONGREGATION OF ST. THOMAS AQUINAS (P)

Motherhouse: Tacoma Dominican Center, 935 Fawcett Ave. S., Tacoma, WA 98402-5605. Tel: 253-272-9688; Fax: 253-272-8790. Sr. Jo Ann Showalter, S.P., Pontifical Commissary.

Total in Community: 33.

Legal Holdings and Titles: Sisters of St. Dominic, Tacoma Dominican Center.

Ministry in a variety of missions.

Represented in the Archdiocese of Seattle and in the Dioceses of Oakland and Yakima.

[1070-23]—DOMINICAN SISTERS, CONGREGATION OF ST. ROSE OF LIMA (P)

General Motherhouse: Rosary Hill Home, 600 Linda Ave., Hawthorne, NY 10532. Tel: 914-769-0114. Vocation Email: vocationdirector@hawthorne-dominicans.org.

Mother Marie Edward, O.P., Supr. Gen.

Total in Community: 47.

The work of these sisters is confined entirely to the incurable cancerous poor.

Represented in the Archdioceses of Atlanta, New York and Philadelphia.

[1070-25]—DOMINICAN SISTERS OF ST. CATHERINE OF SIENA (P)

Motherhouse: 14735 Aloha Ave., Saratoga, CA 95070. Tel: 414-807-3456. Rev. Scott Wallenfelsz, S.D.S., Pontifical Commissary.

Total in Community: 3.

Legal Title: Dominican Sisters of St. Catherine of Siena, Inc.

Represented in the Diocese of San Jose.

[1070-27]—DOMINICAN SISTERS, IMMACULATE CONCEPTION PROVINCE (D)

Provincial House: 9000 W. 81st St., Justice, IL 60458. Tel: 708-458-3040. Mother M. Natalie, O.P., Vicar Prov.; Mother Helena Cempa, O.P., Prov.

Total in Community: 31.

Represented in the Archdioceses of Chicago and Milwaukee and in the Dioceses of Columbus and Little Rock. Also in Canada.

[1070-30]—DOMINICAN SISTERS OF OAKFORD (P)

U.S. Regional Center: Dominican Sisters of Oakford, Regional Office, 22320 Foothill Boulevard, Suite 322, Hayward, CA 94541. Tel: 510-398-8112; Fax: 510-274-5025. Sr. Mary de Crus Nolan, O.P., Regl. Prioress.

Total in Community: 14.

Ministries in Teaching, Spiritual Direction; Counseling; Parish Work; Adult Education; Community Outreach; Social Work, Chaplaincy and Nursing.

Represented in the Dioceses of Oakland and Tucson.

[1100] (O.P.)—DOMINICAN SISTERS OF CHARITY OF THE PRESENTATION OF THE BLESSED VIRGIN (P)

Founded in France in 1696. First foundation in the United States in 1905.

Motherhouse: 15 Quai Portillon, Tours Cedex 2, France, 37081.

Universal total in Congregation: 1986.

Provincial House: 3012 Elm St., Dighton, MA 02715. Tel: 508-669-5425; Tel: 508-669-5433; Tel: 508-669-5023. Email: domsrs@presentation-op-usa.org. Sr. Marta Ines Toro, O.P., Major Supr.

Total number in Province: 32.

Ministry in Hospitals; Homes for the Aged; Dispensaries; Education; Pastoral Ministry; Human Promotions through work.

Represented in the Archdiocese of Washington and in the Dioceses of Brownsville and Fall River. Also in Honduras and 33 other countries.

[1105] (O.P.)—DOMINICAN SISTERS OF HOPE INC. (P)

Founded July 20, 1995, as a merging of three former Congregations: Dominican Sisters of the Congregation of the Most Holy Rosary of Newburgh, NY; Dominican Sisters of the Sick Poor of Ossining, NY and Congregation of Catherine of Siena of Fall River, MA.

General Administrative Offices: Dominican Sisters of Hope, 299 N. Highland Ave., Ossining, NY 10562. Tel: 914-941-4420; Fax: 914-941-1125. Sr. Catherine McDonnell, O.P., Prioress.

Total in Community: 117.

Legal Titles and Holdings: Sisters of St. Dominic Charitable Trust; Dominicare, Inc., Ossining, NY. Ministry in Religious & Academic Education at all levels; health, social, community and pastoral services; Parish service, counseling, retreats and spiritual direction.

Represented in the Archdioceses of Cincinnati, Hartford, Los Angeles, Newark, New York and San Juan and in the Dioceses of Albany, Bridgeport, Camden, Fall River, Manchester, Metuchen, Ogdensburg, Orlando, Paterson, Providence, Richmond, Trenton and Venice.

[1110] (O.P.)—DOMINICAN SISTERS OF OUR LADY OF THE ROSARY AND OF SAINT CATHERINE OF SIENA, CABRA (P)

Founded in Ireland in 1644.

General Motherhouse: Cabra, Dublin 7, Ireland Region of Louisiana established in 1978.

Regional House: Dominican Sisters, Cabra: 3524 DeSaix Blvd., New Orleans, LA 70119. Tel: 504-267-7867.

Total number in local community: 3.

Ministry in Academic and Religious Education; Parish Ministry; Neighborhood Social Service Agency; Prison Ministry; Adult Education.

Represented in the Archdiocese of New Orleans.

[1115] (O.P.)—DOMINICAN SISTERS OF PEACE (P)

Generalate: 2320 Airport Dr., Columbus, OH 43219-2098. Tel: 614-416-1900; Fax: 614-252-7435. Email: info@oppeace.org. Sr. Patricia Twohill, O.P., Prioress.

Total in Community: 370.

Legal Title: Dominican Sisters of Peace, Inc.

Properties Owned and/or Sponsored: Albertus Magnus College, New Haven, CT; Cedar Park Place, Great Bend, KS; Clausen Manor, Waterford, MI; Crown Point Ecology Center, Bath, OH; Dominican Academy, New York, NY; Fox Manor, Waterford, MI; Heartland Center for Spirituality, Great Bend, KS; Heartland Farm, Pawnee Rock, KS; Lourdes Nursing Home & Rehabilitation Center, Waterford, MI; Martin de Porres Center, Columbus, OH Mendelson Assisted Living Home, Waterford, MI; Mohun Health Care Center, Columbus, OH; Ohio Dominican University, Columbus, OH; Our Lady of the Elms School, Akron, OH; Peace Center, New Orleans, LA; St. Agnes Academy-St. Dominic School, Memphis, TN; St. Catharine Farm, St. Catharine, KY; St. Mary's Dominican High School, New Orleans, LA; St. Rose Spirituality House, Waterford, MI; Sansbury Care Center, St. Catharine, KY Shepherd's Corner, Blacklick, OH; Dominican Learning Center, Columbus, OH; Siena Learning Center, New Britain, CT; Springs Learning Center, New Haven, CT; Dominican Retreat and Conference Center, Schenectady, NY.

Ministry in Diocesan Offices; the field of Academic Education at all levels; Religious Education; Adult Education Programs; Congregational Infirmary; Art and Ecological/Environment; Hospitals; Care of the Elderly; Parish Ministry; Pastoral Care; Justice and Peace Ministry; Retreat Centers and Spiritual Programs; Foreign Missions; Counseling and Canon Law Ministry; Campus Ministry; Social Work; Health Care Ministries; Ministry to Minorities; Housing.

Represented in the Archdioceses of Boston, Chicago, Denver, Detroit, Hartford, Louisville, New Orleans, New York, Philadelphia, San Antonio and Santa Fe and in the Dioceses of Albany, Brooklyn, Cleveland, Columbus, Dodge City, Fort Wayne-South Bend, Great Falls-Billings, Lansing, Memphis, Orlando, Pittsburgh, Sacramento, Steubenville, Tucson, Wichita and Youngstown. Also in Peru and Nigeria.

[1117] (O.P.)—THE DOMINICAN SISTERS OF ST. CECILIA OF NASHVILLE, TENNESSEE (P)

Order founded in 1216. Congregation founded in 1860.

Motherhouse: 801 Dominican Dr., Nashville, TN 37228. Sr. Anna Grace Neenan, O.P.

Total Sisters: 314.

Ministry in Education

Represented in the Diocese of Nashville.

[1120] (O.P.)—DOMINICAN SISTERS OF THE ROMAN CONGREGATION

Founded in France in 1621. First United States foundation in 1904 in Lewiston, Maine.

General Motherhouse: Rome, Italy. Sr. Ysabel Barroso, Prioress Gen. Universal total in Congregation: 310.

U.S. Vicarial Office: 61 Lisbon Rd., Sabattus, ME 04280-4209. Tel: 207-782-3535; Fax: 207-375-2694. Email: moniquebelanger22@gmail.com. Sr. Monique Belanger, O.P., Vicarial Prioress.

Total in Vicariate Community: 9.

Properties owned and/or sponsored: Retreat House; Residence 1.

Ministry in the field of Religious & Academic Education; Adult Education; Indian Reservation; Pastoral Ministry; Health Care; Social Work; Ministry to the poor through the Loaves and Fishes Program in Sabattus, ME.

Represented in the Archdioceses of Chicago and New York and in the Dioceses of Gallup and Portland (In Maine).

[1125] (O.P.)—DOMINICAN SISTERS OF OUR LADY OF THE SPRINGS OF BRIDGEPORT (D)

Founded April 2, 2009 in Bridgeport CT.

Motherhouse: Dominican House, 124 Bugg Hill Rd., Monroe, CT 06468. Tel: 203-880-4455. Sr. Mary Elizabeth Donohue, O.P., Prioress.

Total in Congregation: 19.

Legal Title: Dominican Sisters of Our Lady of the Springs of Bridgeport, Inc.

[1145] (O.P.)—RELIGIOUS MISSIONARIES OF ST. DOMINIC, INC. (P)

General Motherhouse: Via di Val Cannuta 138, Rome, Italy, 00166. Tel: 39-06-66-37-521; Email: dominicas.roma@libero.it. Sr. Elvira Diez, O.P., Prioress Gen.

U.S. Delegation Office: 2237 Waldron Rd., Corpus Christi, TX 78418. Tel: 361-937-5978; Fax: 361-939-0890. Sr. Esperanza H. Seguban, O.P., Delegate of the Gen.

Total in Congregation: 667; Sisters in the U.S.: 20.

Represented in the Archdiocese of Los Angeles and in the Diocese of Corpus Christi.

[1150] (E.F.M.S.)—EUCHARISTIC FRANCISCAN MISSIONARY SISTERS (D)

Founded in Mexico in 1943. Mother Maria Gemma de Jesus Aranda, Foundress.

Motherhouse: Our Lady's Convent, 943 S. Soto St., Los Angeles, CA 90023. Tel: 323-264-6556.

1421 Cota Ave., Torrance, CA 90501. Tel: 310-328-6725. Mother Angelica Orozco, E.F.M.S., Supr. Gen.; Sr. Bernadette de la Santa Faz, E.F.M.S., Gen. Sec.

Total in Community: 25.

Legal Title: Eucharistic Franciscan Missionary Sisters of Los Angeles.

Sisters serve and staff: The field of Education; Missionary Activities; Catechetics; Social Work; Diocesan and Administration offices.

Represented in the Archdiocese of Los Angeles and in the Dioceses of Stockton and Tyler.

[1170] (C.S.S.F.)—FELICIAN SISTERS (P) (Congregation of Sisters of St. Felix of Cantalice, of the III Order of St. Francis)

Founded in Poland in 1855. First foundation in the United States in Polonia, Wisconsin in 1874.

Total in North America, Our Lady of Hope Province: 416.

General Motherhouse: Via del Casaletto 540, Rome, Italy, 00151. Sr. Danat Marie Brysch, C.S.S.F., Min. Gen.

Presentation of the B.V.M. Convent (1874): 36800 Schoolcraft Rd., Livonia, MI 48150-1172. Tel: 734-591-1730; Fax: 734-591-1710; Web: www.feliciansistersna.org. Sr. Judith Marie Kubicki, C.S.S.F., Prov. Min.

Professed Sisters: 54.

Properties owned and/or sponsored: Madonna University; Montessori Center of Our Lady, Livonia, MI; St. Mary Mercy Hospital, Livonia, MI; The Felician Sisters Child Care Centers, Inc., Livonia, MI; Maryville Center, Holly, MI; Angela Hospice Home Care and Inpatient Facility, Marian Professional Building, Livonia, MI; Marywood Nursing Care Center; Inpatient Facility, Marian Professional Bldg.; Marybrook Manor Assisted Living.

Ministry in the field of Academic Education at all levels; CCD Programs; Pastoral Ministry Programs; DRE Offices; Hospital; Health Care Nursing Homes; Assisted Living; Hospice Inpatient and Home Care Program; Day Care Centers; Retreat Centers; Senior Clergy Residence; Child Care Centers.

Represented in the Archdiocese of Detroit and in the Diocese of Lansing.

Immaculate Heart of Mary Convent (1900): 600 Doat St., Buffalo, NY 14211. Tel: 716-892-4141; Fax: 716-892-4177; Web: www.feliciansistersna.org. Sr. Judith Marie Kubicki, C.S.S.F., Prov. Min.; Sr. Mary Kenneth Mondrala, C.S.S.F., Community Archivist.

Professed Sisters: 78.

Properties owned and/or sponsored: Villa Maria College of Buffalo.

Ministry in Education on all levels; Religious Education Programs; Outreach Centers; Parish Ministries; Social Services; Prison Ministries; Campus Ministries; Diocesan Office.

Represented in the Archdioceses of Los Angeles and New York and in the Dioceses of Buffalo and Syracuse. Also in Italy.

Mother of Good Counsel Convent (1910): 3800 W. Peterson Ave., Chicago, IL 60659. Tel: 773-463-3020; Web: www.feliciansistersna.org. Sr. Judith Marie Kubicki, C.S.S.F., Prov. Min.

Professed Sisters: 86.

Ministry in the field of Academic and Religious Education at all levels; Homes for Aged; Independent Living for the Elderly; Assisted Living for the Elderly; Pastoral Ministry; Social Workers; Family Therapists; Day Care Centers; Hospitals; Infirmary for Sisters.

Represented in the Archdioceses of Chicago and Milwaukee and in the Dioceses of Belleville and Green Bay.

Immaculate Conception Convent (1913): 260 S Main St., Lodi, NJ 07644-2196. Tel: 973-473-7447; Fax: 973-473-7126; Web: www.feliciansistersna.org. Sr. Judith Marie Kubicki, C.S.S.F., Prov. Min.; Sr. Mary Catherine Ryzewicz, C.S.S.F., Treas.

Professed Sisters: 64.

Properties sponsored: Immaculate Conception High School; Felician University; Felician University Day Care Center; Felician School for Exceptional Children, Lodi, NJ; St. Ignatius Nursing & Rehab Center.

Sisters serve and staff: Colleges; High Schools; Elementary Schools; Home for Aged; Infirmary for Sisters; Day Care Center; School for Exceptional Children; Religious Education; Parish Ministries.

Represented in the Archdioceses of Newark and Philadelphia and in the Diocese of Metuchen.

Our Lady of the Sacred Heart Convent (1921): 1500 Woodcrest Ave., Coraopolis, PA 15108. Tel: 412-264-2890; Fax: 412-264-7047; Web: www.feliciansistersna.org. Sr. Judith Marie Kubicki, C.S.S.F., Prov. Min.

Professed Sisters: 35.

Legal Holdings and Titles: Felician Sisters of Pennsylvania; Our Lady of the Sacred Heart High School.

Ministry in the field of Academic Education at all levels; Religious Education; CCD Centers; Youth and Pastoral Ministry; Home for Mentally Challenged Children & Adults; Infirmary and Home for Aged.

Represented in the Dioceses of Charleston, Greensburg and Pittsburgh.

Our Lady of the Angels Convent (1932): 1315 Enfield St., Enfield, CT 06082-4929. Tel: 860-745-7791; Fax: 860-741-0819; Web: www.feliciansistersna.org. Sr. Judith Marie Kubicki, C.S.S.F., Prov. Min.

Professed Sisters: 31.

Ministry in the field of Religious and Academic Education; Pastoral Ministry; Social Services; Healthcare. Properties owned and sponsored: Enfield Montessori School; St. Francis Residence, Enfield, CT.

Represented in the Archdiocese of Hartford and in the Dioceses of Manchester, Portland (In Maine), Providence and Worcester.

Assumption of the B.V.M. Convent (1953): 4106 Pico Norte, N.E., Rio Rancho, NM 87124-1021. Web: www.feliciansistersna.org. Sr. Judith Marie Kubicki, C.S.S.F., Prov. Min.

Professed Sisters: 17.

Legal Titles and Holdings: Felician Sisters of the Southwest, Inc.; St. Felix Pantry Inc. Sisters serve and staff: High Schools; Elementary Schools; Religious Education Centers & Classes; Health Care; Pastoral Care; Food & Clothing Pantry; Youth Ministry; Adult Education; Social Work.

Represented in the Archdioceses of Los Angeles, San Antonio and Santa Fe and in the Dioceses of Laredo and Las Cruces.

[1180] (O.S.F.)—FRANCISCAN SISTERS OF ALLEGANY, NEW YORK (P)

Founded in the United States in 1859.

General Motherhouse (1859): St. Elizabeth Motherhouse, 115 E. Main St., Allegany, NY 14706. Tel: 716-373-0200; Fax: 716-372-5774. Sr. Margaret Magee, O.S.F., Congregational Min.; Laura Whitford, Mission Society Pres.

Total in Community: 169.

Legal Titles and Holdings: Franciscan Sisters of Allegany, NY, Inc.; Canticle Farm, Inc., Allegany, NY; St. Elizabeth Mission Society, Inc., Allegany, NY; Dr. Lyle F. Renodin Foundation, Inc., Allegany, NY; Franciscan Center of Tampa, FL, Inc., Tampa, FL; The Dwelling Place of NY Inc., NY.

Ministry to Evangelization at all levels of Education; Health Care; Social Services; Pastoral; Spiritual Ministries and Social Advocacy.

Represented in the Archdioceses of Boston, New York and Philadelphia and in the Dioceses of Buffalo, Camden, Metuchen, Palm Beach, St. Petersburg, Springfield, Syracuse and Trenton. Also in Bolivia, Brazil, Jamaica and Mozambique.

Jamaica: Immaculate Conception Convent, 152 Constant Spring Rd., Box 1654, Kingston, Jamaica Tel: 876-925-6888. Sr. Maureen Clare Hall, O.S.F., Local Min.

Brazil Region: Convento Mae Admiravel, C.P. 322, 75001-970 Anapolis, Goias, Brazil Tel: 011-55-62-33333803. Sr. Goianira Silva, O.S.F., Regl. Min.

Publication: Zeal.

[1190] (S.A.)—FRANCISCAN SISTERS OF THE ATONEMENT (P)

Founded in the United States in 1898.

Motherhouse: St. Francis Convent-Graymoor, 41 Old Highland Tpke., Garrison, NY 10524. Tel: 845-424-3625; Fax: 845-424-3298. Web: www.graymoor.org. Sr. Mary Patricia Galvin, S.A., Min. Gen.; Sr. Denise Robillard, S.A., Sec. Gen. Email: secretarygeneral@graymoor.org; Tel: 845-230-8235.

Total in Community: 79.

Properties owned and/or sponsored: St. Francis Convent-Complex, Garrison, NY; Mother Lurana House, Garrison, NY; Washington Retreat House, Washington, D.C.

Represented in the Archdioceses of New York and Washington, D.C. and in the Dioceses of Lansing and Trenton. Also in Canada, Italy, Japan and the Philippines.

[1210] (O.S.F.)—FRANCISCAN SISTERS OF CHICAGO (P)

Founded in Chicago, Illinois in 1894 by Mother Mary Theresa (Josephine Dudzik) Venerable Servant of God.

General Motherhouse: Our Lady of Victory Convent, 11400 Theresa Dr., Lemont, IL 60439-2728. Tel: 630-243-3600; Fax: 630-243-3601; Email: bbajuscik@chicagofrancicans.com; jduckett@chicagofranciscans.com. Sr. M. Bernadette Bajuscik, O.S.F., Gen. Min.

Total in Community: 17.

Properties owned and/or sponsored: Addolorata Villa, Wheeling, IL; St. Joseph Village of Chicago, Inc., Chicago, IL; Marian Village, Homer Glen, IL; Mount Alverna Village, Parma, OH; Franciscan Village, Lemont, IL; St. Francis House of Prayer, Lemont, IL; Our Lady of Victory Convent, Lemont, IL; St. Jude House, Crown Point, IN; The Village at Victory Lakes, Lindenhurst, IL; University Place, West Lafayette, IN; St. Joseph Senior Housing; *Franciscan Sisters of Chicago Service Corp. DBA/Franciscan Ministries Sponsored by Franciscan Sisters of Chicago, Lemont, IL.

Represented in the Archdiocese of Chicago and in the Dioceses of Cleveland, Gary, Joliet and Lafayette in Indiana.

[1230] (O.S.F.)—FRANCISCAN SISTERS OF CHRISTIAN CHARITY (P)

Founded in the United States in 1869.

Motherhouse: Holy Family Convent, 2409 S. Alverno Rd., Manitowoc, WI 54220. Tel: 920-682-7728; Fax: 920-682-4195. Email: snatalie@fscc-calledtobe.org. Sr. Natalie Binversie, Community Dir.; Sr. Caritas Strodthoff, Community Archivist.

Total in Community: 177.

Properties owned or sponsored: Holy Family Convent, Manitowoc, WI; Holy Family Convent of Franciscan Sisters of Christian Charity, Inc., Manitowoc, WI; Holy Family Memorial, Inc., Manitowoc, WI; The Retirement Trust of the Franciscan Sisters of Christian Charity, Manitowoc, WI; St. Paul Home and St. Paul Villa (St. Paul Elder Services, Inc.) Kaukauna, WI; Franciscan Sisters of Christian Charity Sponsored Ministries Inc., Manitowoc, WI; Holy Family Conservatory of Music, Manitowoc, WI; Chiara Convent, Manitowoc, WI; St. Francis Convent, Manitowoc, WI; Franciscan Care Services dba St. Francis Memorial Hospital, West Point, NE; St. Joseph Elder Services, Inc.: St. Joseph's Hillside and St. Joseph's Retirement Community, West Point, NE; Genesis HealthCare System, Zanesville, OH; Genesis Hospital, Zanesville, OH.

Represented in the Archdioceses of Omaha and in the Dioceses of Columbus, Green Bay, Marquette, Phoenix, Steubenville, Lincoln and Tucson.

[1235] (F.H.M.)—FRANCISCAN SISTERS DAUGHTERS OF MERCY (P)

Franciscanas Hijas de la Misericordia

Founded in Pina, Mallorca, Spain in 1856. First U.S. establishment in 1962.

General Motherhouse: Calle El Nectar, 18, Madrid, Spain, 28022. Sr. Alicia Garcia Lazaro, Supr. Gen.

Universal total in Congregation: 262.

U.S. Regional and House of Formation: 1207 Montopolis Dr., Austin, TX 78741. Sr. Rose Moreno, F.H.M., Reg. Delegate.

Professed Sisters: 6.

Ministry in Catechetical work; Pastoral work; Kindergarten.

Represented in the Diocese of Austin.

St. Francis Convent: 612 N. 3rd St., Waco, TX 76701.

[1240] (O.S.F.)—FRANCISCAN SISTERS, DAUGHTERS OF THE SACRED HEARTS OF JESUS AND MARY (P)

Founded in Germany in 1860. First foundation in the United States in 1872.

Generalate: Via di S. Alessio 24, Rome, Italy, 00153. Sr. Magdalena Schmitz, Gen. Dir.

Universal total in Congregation: 522.

St. Clare Region (1877): Convent of Our Lady of the Angels, Motherhouse and Novitiate, P.O. Box 667, Wheaton, IL 60187. Tel: 630-909-6600. Sr. Melanie Paradis, O.S.F., Reg. Dir.

Total number in Region: 35.

Legal Holdings and Titles: Wheaton Franciscan Sisters Corporation, Wheaton, IL.

Sisters serve, sponsor and staff: Spirituality Center; Corporate Offices; Spiritual Direction.

Represented in the Diocese of Joliet. Also in Italy.

[1250] (F.S.E.)—FRANCISCAN SISTERS OF THE EUCHARIST, INC.

Founded December 2, 1973.

Motherhouse: 405 Allen Ave., Meriden, CT 06451. Tel: 203-237-0841. Team Members: Mother Miriam Seiferman, Mother Gen.; Mother Barbara Johnson, F.S.E., Vicar Gen.; Mother Suzanne Gross, F.S.E.; Mother Mary Richards, F.S.E.; Mother Raffaella Petrini, F.S.E.; Mother Clare Hunter, F.S.E. Total in Community: 81.

Legal Title: Franciscan Sisters of the Eucharist, Inc. Schools and programs operated under: Franciscan Life Center Network, Incorporated and Franciscan Family Care Center, Incorporated.

Represented in the Archdioceses of Hartford and Portland in Oregon and in the Dioceses of Arlington, Boise, Burlington, Grand Rapids and Palm Beach. Also in Canada, Israel, Italy and Latin Patriarchate of Jerusalem.

Generalate: Meriden, CT 06451. Tel: 203-237-0841.

[1260] (F.H.M.)—FRANCISCAN HANDMAIDS OF THE MOST PURE HEART OF MARY (D)

Founded in the United States in 1916.

Administrative Center: Most Pure Heart of Mary. Mailing Address: 1175 East 223rd St., Bronx, NY 10466. Tel: 212-289-5655. Email: handmaidsofmary@aol.com. Sr. Vincent Marie Wilson, F.H.M., Congregation Min.

Altar Bread Distribution: 63 Bayside Ln., Staten Island, NY 10309. Tel: 347-852-2306.

Franciscan Handmaids/St. Edward Food Pantry, 6581 Hylan Blvd., Staten Island, NY 10309. Tel: 718-984-1625. Email: st.edwardfoodpantry@gmail.com.

Total in community: 31

Properties owned and/or sponsored: St. Edward Food Pantry; Franciscan Handmaids of Mary Convent; Franciscan Handmaids of Mary Administrative Center.

Ministry in the field of Education, Pastoral Work, Integrative Health, School & Parish Catechesis; Family & Youth Empowerment (Rural Poverty Alleviation Apostolate) & Social Service.

Represented in the Archdiocese of New York. Also in Nigeria and St. Croix, V.I.

[1270] (F.H.I.C.)—FRANCISCAN HOSPITALLER SISTERS OF THE IMMACULATE CONCEPTION (P)

Founded in Portugal in 1871.

General Motherhouse: Linda-a-Pastora, Portugal. Sr. Shirley Ninfa Fernandes, Supr. Gen.

U.S. Foundation (1960): St. Joseph Novitiate, 300 S. 17th St., San Jose, CA 95112-2245. Tel: 408-998-2896; Fax: 408-998-3407. Sr. Mary Augustine, F.H.I.C., Regl. Supr., 1441 Berkeley Dr., Los Banos, CA 93635. Tel: 209-827-8942; Fax: 209-827-8989. Email: del.olpcal@confhic.org.

Total in Community: 15.

Sisters serve and staff: Parishes; Residential care and Skilled Nursing; Social Work.

Represented in the Dioceses of Fresno and San Jose.

[1300] (O.S.F.)—FRANCISCAN SISTERS OF THE IMMACULATE CONCEPTION AND ST. JOSEPH FOR THE DYING (D)

Founded in the United States in December, 1919 at San Carlos Parish, Monterey, California.

General Motherhouse: Ave Maria Convent, 1249 Josselyn Canyon Rd, Monterey, CA 93940. Tel: 831-373-1216.

Legal Holding: Ave Maria Convalescent Hospital, Monterey, CA.

Represented in the Diocese of Monterey.

[1310] (O.S.F.)—FRANCISCAN SISTERS OF LITTLE FALLS, MINNESOTA (P)

Founded in the United States in 1891.

General Motherhouse: 116 8th Ave. S.E., Little Falls, MN 56345. Tel: 320-632-2981. Email: info@fslf.org. Sr. Carol Schmit, O.S.F., Community Min./Pres.

Total in Community: 89.

Ministry in Home Health Care; Hospice Care; religious education; parish ministry; liturgical music ministry; music center; health and wellness center; retreat ministry; counseling; spiritual direction; social service; ministry to the poor; ministry to the migrants; art therapist; Hispanic Ministry; pastoral ministry.

Properties owned or sponsored: St. Francis Music Center; Franciscan Life Center.

Represented in the Archdioceses of Milwaukee, St. Paul-Minneapolis, and San Francisco and in the Dioceses of Brownsville, Oakland and St. Cloud. Also in Mexico.

[1320] (F.M.S.A.)—FRANCISCAN MISSIONARY SISTERS FOR AFRICA (P)

Generalate: Franciscan Missionary Sisters for Africa, 34a Gilford Rd., Sandymount, Dublin 4, DO4 FN79 Ireland. Tel: 011-353-1-2838376; Fax: 011-353-1-2602049.

American Headquarters: 38 Wiley Rd., Belmont, MA 02478. Tel: 617-415-6944. Email: marymfisher9@gmail.com. Sr. Mary Fisher, FMSA.

Total in Community: 4.

Represented in the Archdiocese of Boston.

[1330] (S.F.M.A.)—FRANCISCAN MISSIONARY SISTERS OF ASSISI (P)

General Motherhouse: Via San Francesco, 13, Assisi, Italy, 06081. Sr. Francesca Farina, Mother Gen.

U.S. Vice Province (1961): St. Francis Convent/Vice Provincial House and Formation House, 1039 Northampton St., Holyoke, MA 01040. Tel: 413-532-8156. Sr. Monica Partac, S.F.M.A., Vice Prov. Supr.

Total in Community: 12.

Represented in the Archdiocese of New York and in the Diocese of Springfield in Massachusetts.

[1350] (O.S.F.)—FRANCISCAN SISTERS OF THE IMMACULATE CONCEPTION (P)

Founded in Mexico in 1874. First foundation in the United States in 1926.

Provincial House: 13367 Borden Ave., Unit A, Sylmar, CA 91342-2804. Tel: 818-364-5557; Tel: 818-364-5558; Fax: 818-362-7536; Email: provstclare@outlook.com. Sr. Catalina Avila, O.S.F., Prov. Supr.; Sr. Yolanda Yanez, O.S.F., Community Archivist.

Total in Community: 91.

Legal Holdings and Titles: Franciscan Missionary Sisters of the Immaculate Conception, Inc.; Poverello of Assisi Retreat House, San Fernando, CA; St. Francis Home, Santa Ana, CA; Mother Gertrude Balcazar Home, San Fernando, CA; Provincialate, Sylmar, CA; St. Clare Convent, Sylmar, CA; Proverello of Assisi Preschool, Sylmar, CA; Novitiate, Sheerwood Forest, CA.

Ministry in the field of Education and Religious Education to Children and Adults; Health Care in Hospitals and Residential Care Facilities for Elderly.

Represented in the Archdiocese of Los Angeles and in the Dioceses of Gallup and Orange in California. Also in Mexico.

House of Formation: 11306 Laurel Canyon Blvd., San Fernando, CA 91340.

Novitiate: 8619 Louise Ave., Sherwood Forest, CA 91325-3417. Tel: 818-709-7523.

[1360] (M.F.I.C.)—MISSIONARY FRANCISCAN SISTERS OF THE IMMACULATE CONCEPTION (P)

Founded in the United States in 1873 in Belle Prairie, Minnesota.

General Motherhouse: Sydney, Australia. Sr. Pauline Robinson, M.F.I.C., Gen. Min.

Provincialate: Immaculate Conception Province, 790 Centre St., Newton, MA 02458-2530. Tel: 617-527-1004; Fax: 617-527-2528. Sr. Jeanette Gaudet, M.F.I.C., Prov.

Total number in Province: 56.

Represented in the Archdioceses of Boston, Newark and New York and in the Dioceses of Fall River, Providence, Savannah and Syracuse. Also in Ireland.

[1365] (F.M.I.J.)—FRANCISCAN MISSIONARY SISTERS OF THE INFANT JESUS (P)

Founded in Aquila, Italy in 1879 by Sr. Maria Giuseppa Micarelli. First foundation in the United States in 1961.

Generalate: Piazza Nicoloso da Recco 13, Rome, Italy, 00154. Tel: 6-575-8358. Mother Lilia Agnese Contini, F.M.I.J., Supr. Gen.

U.S. Delegation and Novitiate: 1215 Kresson Rd., Cherry Hill, NJ 08003. Tel: 856-428-8834; Fax: 856-428-5599; Email: fmijusdel@yahoo.com. Sr. Jerilyn Einstein, F.M.I.J., Delegate Supr.

Professed Sisters: 11.

Ministries of Evangelization; Education; Social Pastoral Services; Retreat Ministry.

Represented in the Dioceses of Camden.

[1370] (F.M.M.)—THE FRANCISCAN MISSIONARIES OF MARY (P)

Founded in India in 1877. First foundation in the United States in 1903.

General Motherhouse: 12 via Giusti, Rome, Italy. Sr. Francoise Massy, F.M.M., Supr. Gen.

Franciscan Missionaries of Mary-U.S. Province (1920): 3305 Wallace Ave., Bronx, NY 10467-6599. Tel: 718-547-4693; Fax: 718-325-5102; Email: nmfmm@aol.com; Web: www.fmmusa.org. Sr. Noreen Murray, F.M.M., Prov.

Total in Province: 64.

Ministry in Educational Projects among Minority Group of Immigrants; Cardiac and General Hospital; General Pediatric Hospital with Rehabilitation Specialty; Chaplaincy; Retreat Work; Catechetics; Mission Animation & Formation; Home Visiting & Community Development.

Represented in the Archdioceses of Boston, Chicago and New York and in the Dioceses of El Paso, Las Cruces, Providence and Rockville Centre.

[1380] (O.S.F.)—FRANCISCAN MISSIONARIES OF OUR LADY (P)

Founded in Calais, France in 1854. First U.S. foundation in Monroe, LA 1911.

Generalate: Paris, France

Provincial and Novitiate House: Maryville Convent, 4200 Essen Ln., Baton Rouge, LA 70809. Tel: 225-922-7443; Fax: 225-922-7497; Email: barbara.arceneaux@fmolhs.org.

Total in Community: 13.

Properties owned and sponsored: Our Lady of the Lake Regional Medical Center, Baton Rouge, LA; Ollie Steele Burden Manor, Inc., Baton Rouge, LA; Our Lady of Lourdes Regional Medical Center, Lafayette, LA; St. Francis Medical Center, Monroe, LA; FMOL Health System, Inc., Baton Rouge, LA; Haiti Mission, Inc., Baton Rouge, LA; St. Elizabeth Hospital, Gonzales, LA., Franciscan Health & Wellness; Our Lady of the Angels Hospital, Bogalusa, LA.

Represented in the Dioceses of Baton Rouge, Lafayette (LA) and Shreveport.

[1390] (O.S.F.)—FRANCISCAN MISSIONARY SISTERS OF OUR LADY OF SORROWS (D)

Founded in Hunan China in 1939. First United States foundation in 1950.

Community Headquarters: Our Lady of Peace Retreat House, 3600 S.W. 170th Ave., Beaverton, OR 97003-4467. Tel: 503-649-7127; Fax: 503-259-9507. Sr. Anne Marie Warren, O.S.F., Supr. Gen.

Total in Community: 41.

Legal Titles and Holdings: Our Lady of Peace Retreat, Beaverton, OR; St. Clare Retreat House, Soquel, CA.

Ministry in religious and academic education; retreat houses, group homes and foreign missions.

Represented in the Archdiocese of Portland in Oregon and in the Diocese of Monterey.

[1400] (F.M.S.C.)—FRANCISCAN MISSIONARY SISTERS OF THE SACRED HEART (P)

Founded in Italy in 1861. First foundation in the U.S. in New York City (1865).

General Motherhouse: Rome, Italy. Sr. Paola Dotto, F.M.S.C., Supr. Gen.

St. Francis Province (1869): Mt. St. Francis, 250 South St., Peekskill, NY 10566. Tel: 914-737-5409; Fax: 914-736-9614. Vocations email: sajfmsc@mail.com. Sr. Laura Morgan, F.M.S.C., Prov. Supr.

Universal total in Congregation: 660; Total in United States Province: 25.

Legal Title: Missionary Sisters of the Third Order of St. Francis.

Ministry in Religious and Academic Education; Health Care for Retired Sisters; Pastoral Ministry.

Represented in the Archdioceses of Newark and New York and in Diocese of Paterson, NJ.

[1410] (F.M.S.J.)—MILL HILL SISTERS (P)

Franciscan Missionaries of St. Joseph

Founded in 1883. First United States foundation in 1952.

Generalate: St. Joseph's Convent, 150 Greenleach Ln., Worsley, Manchester, England, M28 2TS. Sr. Maureen Murphy, F.M.S.J., Community Leader.

American Headquarters: Franciscan House, 703 Derzee Ct., Delmar, NY 12054. Tel: 518-512-4362. Sr. Judith Dever, F.M.S.J., Admin.

Total in Community: 2.

Legal Title: Mill Hill Sisters - New York Charitable Trust.

Represented in the Diocese of Albany.

[1415] (F.S.M.)—FRANCISCAN SISTERS OF MARY (P)

Founded in the United States in 1872.

Administrative Offices & Novitiate: Franciscan Sisters of Mary, 3221 McKelvey Rd., Ste. 107, Bridgeton, MO 63044-2551. Tel: 314-768-1824; Fax: 314-768-1880. Email: info@fsmonline.org. Sr. Judith Bell, F.S.M., Pres.

Total in Community: 49.

[1425] (F.S.P.)—FRANCISCAN SISTERS OF PEACE (D)

Sisters of St. Francis of Peace: Congregation Center, 20 Ridge St., Haverstraw, NY 10927-1115. Tel: 845-942-2527; Fax: 845-429-8141. Email: ddeyoung@fspnet.org. Sr. Helen Wacker, F.S.P., Congregation Min.

Total in Community: 37.

Legal Titles and Holdings: Cortlandt Manor, NY; Congregation Center, Haverstraw, NY.

Ministry in Administration & Administrative Services; Catechetical; Evangelization.

Represented in the Archdioceses of Newark and New York and in the Dioceses of Paterson and Tucson.

[1430] (O.S.F.)—FRANCISCAN SISTERS OF OUR LADY OF PERPETUAL HELP (P)

Founded in the United States in 1901.

Motherhouse and Novitiate: Franciscan Sisters of Our Lady of Perpetual Help, 335 S. Kirkwood Rd., St. Louis, MO 63122. Tel: 314-965-3700; Fax: 314-965-3710. Email: info@fsolph.org. Sr. Renita Brummer, O.S.F., Supr. Gen.

Total in Community: 72.

Legal Holdings and Titles: Tau Center, Kirkwood, MO; Perpetual Help Retirement Corporation, St. Louis, MO. Ministry in Education; Faith Formation; Parish Ministries; Retreat and Program Directors; Not for Profit Administration; Hospital Ministry.

Represented in the Archdioceses of Chicago, Cincinnati, Omaha, St. Louis, and Washington, DC and in the Dioceses of Austin, Belleville, Fort Wayne, Kansas City, Las Cruces, Rockford, St. Petersburg, Shreveport, Springfield (IL) and Toledo.

[1440] (S.F.P.)—FRANCISCAN SISTERS OF THE POOR (P)

Founded in Aachen, Germany in 1845. First foundation in the United States in 1858.

Congregational Office: 505 8th Ave., Ste. 900, New York, NY 10018. Tel: 718-643-1945; Fax: 212-808-0096. Sr. Licia Mazzia, S.F.P., Congregational Min. Total in Community: 102.

U.S. Area: 60 Compton Rd., Cincinnati, OH 45215. Tel: 513-761-9040; Fax: 513-761-6703; Email: office@franciscansistersofthepoor.org; Web: www.franciscansistersofthepoor.org; Sr. Marilyn Trowbridge, S.F.P., Congregational Councilor & Contact Person; Sr. Ann Cecile Albers, S.F.P., Community Min.

Sisters in Archdiocese: 37.

Congregation sponsors: Franciscan Sisters of the Poor Foundation, Inc., New York, NY; Franciscan Ministries, Inc., Cincinnati, OH.

Represented in the Archdioceses of Cincinnati and New York. Also in Brazil, Italy, Philippines and Senegal.

[1450] (O.S.F.)—FRANCISCAN SISTERS OF THE SACRED HEART (P)

Congregation of the Franciscan Sisters of the Sacred Heart. Founded in Germany 1866. Established in the United States in 1876.

Motherhouse, Novitiate, Postulancy & Portiuncula Center for Prayer: St. Francis Woods, 9201 W. St. Francis Rd., Frankfort, IL 60423-8330. Tel: 815-469-4895; Fax: 815-464-3809. Sr. Joyce Shanabarger, O.S.F., Gen. Supr.

Total in Community: 56.

Legal Title: An Association of Franciscan Sisters of the Sacred Heart; Legal Titles for Franciscan Foundation.

Sisters sponsor: Portiuncula Center for Prayer, Frankfort, IL.

Sisters serve in: Academic Institutions; Religious Education Centers; Neighborhood Health Care Centers; Foreign Mission Centers; Diocesan Offices; Retreat Centers; Home Health Agencies, Hospitals, Nursing and Retirement Homes; Parish & Youth Ministry; Liturgical Ministry; Social Work.

Represented in the Archdioceses of Chicago and Los Angeles and in the Dioceses of Fort Wayne-South Bend and Joliet. Also in Brazil.

[1460] (F.S.S.E.)—FRANCISCAN SISTERS OF ST. ELIZABETH (P)

(Suore Franciscane Elisabettine)

First founded in Naples, Italy, 1865. Founded in the United States in Newark, New Jersey in 1919.

General Motherhouse: Via Marsico Nuovo 35, Rome, Italy. Mother Clara Capaso, Supr. Gen.

Delegate House: 499 Park Rd., Parsippany, NJ 07054. Tel: 973-539-3797. Mother Lilly Perapadan, Delegate Gen.

Total number in the U.S.: 52; Total in Community: 300.

Ministry in Day Nurseries; Mission Houses; Elementary Schools and Montessori Schools.

Sister Serve Christ in the person of the poor in Schools & Day Nursery Schools; Catechetical Instruction; Hospitals; Homes for the Poor, Aged and Disabled.

Represented in the Archdiocese of Newark and in the Dioceses of Paterson and St. Petersburg. Also in India, Indonesia, Italy, Panama, Philippines and Africa.

[1470] (F.S.S.J.)—FRANCISCAN SISTERS OF ST. JOSEPH OF HAMBURG, NY (P)

Founded in the United States in 1897.

Congregational office: Franciscan Sisters of St. Joseph, Immaculate Conception Convent, 5229 S. Park Ave., Hamburg, NY 14075. Tel: 716-649-1205; Fax: 716-202-4940. Email: adminassist@fssj.org. Sr. Marcia Ann Fiutko, F.S.S.J., Gen. Min.

Total in Community: 38.

Properties owned and/or sponsored: Immaculata Academy, Hamburg, NY.

Ministry in Education; Health Care; Parish Ministries; Social Services.

Represented in the Archdioceses of Baltimore and in the Dioceses of Buffalo and Springfield in Massachusetts.

[1485] (O.S.F.)—FRANCISCAN SISTERS OF ST. PAUL, MN (P)

Franciscan Sisters of the Blessed Virgin Mary of the Holy Angels (Beatae Mariae Virginis Angelorum)

Founded in Germany in 1863. First foundation in the United States in St. Paul in 1923.

General Motherhouse (1863): St. Marienhaus, Waldbreitbach, bei Neuwied, Rhine, Germany Sr. Edith-Maria Schug, O.S.F., Supr. Gen.

Universal total in Congregation: 333.

U.S. Foundation: 225 Frank St. #144, St. Paul, MN 55106. Tel: 654-495-1922. Sr. Mary Lucy Scheffler, O.S.F.

Total in Community: 4.

Represented in the Archdiocese of St. Paul-Minneapolis.

[1500] (F.M.I.)—FRANCISCAN SISTERS OF MARY IMMACULATE OF THE THIRD ORDER OF ST. FRANCIS OF ASSISI (P)

Founded in Switzerland in the 16th Century. First founded in the United States on Aug. 15, 1932 at Amarillo, Texas.

General House: Carrera 81 C No. 24B-20, Barrio Modelia, Bogota, Colombia Sr. Nilka Judith Cerezo Rodríguez, F.M.I., Supr. Gen.

Universal total in Congregation: 495.

St. Francis Convent and Novitiate (1964): St. Francis Convent (1932), 4301 N.E. 18th Ave., Amarillo, TX 79107-7220. Tel: 806-383-5769; Fax: 806-383-6545. Email: animationst.francis@outlook.com.

Total in Community: 19.

Represented in the Archdiocese of Los Angeles and in the Dioceses of Amarillo, Kansas City-St. Joseph and Venice.

[1505] (O.S.F.)—ST. FRANCIS MISSION COMMUNITY (P)

Established in 1981 in the United States of America in Amarillo, Texas, as an autonomous province of the Franciscan Sisters of Mary Immaculate.

General Motherhouse: Our Lady of the Angels Convent, 8202 CR 7700, Wolfforth, TX 79382. Tel: 806-863-4904. Sr. Mary Jane Alaniz, O.S.F., Prov. Min.

Professed Sisters: 18.

Ministry in the field of Religious and Academic Education at all levels; Parish Work; Pastoral Care in Hospitals.

Properties owned: St. Francis Convent, Lubbock, TX; 43 acres of real estate.

Represented in the Dioceses of Lubbock and San Angelo.

[1520] (S.S.F.C.R.-O.S.F.)—SCHOOL SISTERS OF ST. FRANCIS OF CHRIST THE KING (D)

Founded in Maribor, Slovenia in 1869 by Sr. Margareta Pucher. First house in the United States at Kansas City, Kansas, in 1909. U.S. Province established in 1922.

Generalate: Grottaferrata, Italy Sr. M. Klara Šimunović, Supr. Gen.

Universal total in Congregation: 830.

North American Provincial House: 13900 Main St., Lemont, IL 60439. Tel: 630-257-7495. Email: lemont.province@ssfcr.org. Sr. Therese Ann Quigney, SSFCR, Prov. Supr. U.S.A.

Total in Community: 24.

Ministry in Education, Care for Seniors, Parish Ministry; Retreat Ministry.

Properties owned and sponsored: Mount Assisi Convent, Lemont, IL; Mount Assisi [Academy building] Center; Our Lady of Angels House of Prayer, Lemont, IL.

Represented in the Archdiocese of Chicago and in the Diocese of Joliet.

[1530] (O.S.F.)—SISTERS OF ST. FRANCIS OF THE CONGREGATION OF OUR LADY OF LOURDES, SYLVANIA, OHIO (P)

Founded in the United States in 1916 at Sylvania, Ohio. Foundation from Rochester, Minnesota.

General Motherhouse: Convent, 6832 Convent Blvd., Sylvania, OH 43560-2897. Tel: 419-824-3618; Fax: 419-824-3700; Email: lstout@sistersosf.org; Web: www.sistersosf.org. Sr. Mary Jon Wagner, O.S.F., Congregational Min.

Total number in the Congregation: 117.

Ministry in the field of Religious and Academic Education at all levels; Healthcare; Communications; Media Producing; Counseling; Parish Ministries; Retreat Center; Social Services; Administration.

Properties sponsored and owned: Lourdes University, Sylvania, OH.

Sponsored Ministries: Sisters of St. Francis Foundation, Sylvania, OH; Sylvania Franciscan Ministries, Sylvania, OH, including: Rosary Care Center, Sylvania, OH; Franciscan Properties, Sylvania, OH; Franciscan Shelters DBA Bethany House, Toledo, OH; Sophia Center, Sylvania, OH.

Represented in the Archdioceses of Detroit and St. Paul-Minneapolis and in the Dioceses of Austin, Biloxi, Cleveland, Fort Wayne-South Bend, Nashville, St. Cloud, and Toledo.

[1540] (O.S.F.)—SISTERS OF SAINT FRANCIS, CLINTON, IOWA (P)

Founded in the United States in 1866.

General Motherhouse: Administrative Center, 843 13th Ave. N., Clinton, IA 52732-5115. Tel: 563-242-7611; Fax: 563-243-0007; Email: office@clintonfranciscans.com. Sr. Janice Cebula, O.S.F., Pres.

Ministry in the field of Education; Pastoral Ministry; Religious Education; Spiritual Direction; Social Justice & Peace Advocacy; Prayer Ministry; Ministry to those who are impoverished or disabled.

Properties and Legal Holdings: Sisters of St. Francis, Clinton, Iowa, Charitable Trust; The Canticle, Clinton, IA.

Represented in the Archdioceses of Chicago and in the Dioceses of Davenport, Portland, Rockford, San Diego and Sioux City.

[1550] (O.S.F.)—SISTERS OF ST. FRANCIS OF THE HOLY CROSS (P)

Founded in Wisconsin in 1881.

Motherhouse: St. Francis Convent, 3110 Nicolet Dr., Green Bay, WI 54311-7212. Tel: 920-468-1828; Fax: 920-468-1207. Sr. Rose Jochmann, O.S.F., Pres.

Total in Community: 43.

Legal Title: Sisters of St. Francis of the Holy Cross, Inc.

Ministries in the following areas: Education; Pastoral Ministry and Religious Education; Ministry to the Elderly; Retreat Work.

Represented in the Diocese of Green Bay.

[1560] (O.S.F.)—SISTERS OF ST. FRANCIS OF THE HOLY EUCHARIST (D)

Founded in Grimmenstein, Switzerland in 1378. First foundation in the United States in 1892.

Motherhouse, Novitiate and Prayer Center: St. Francis Convent, 2100 N. Noland Rd., Independence, MO 64050. Tel: 816-252-1673; Fax: 816-252-5574. Email: boulch2100@gmail.com. Sr. M. Connie Boulch, O.S.F., Sister Servant; Sr. M. Sharon Giemza, O.S.F., Vicar.

Total in Community: 13.

Legal Titles: Franciscan Prayer Center, Independence, MO; Sisters of St. Francis of the Holy Eucharist Foundation, Independence, MO.

Ministry in the following areas: Education at all levels; Retreat; Evangelization; Pastoral; Foreign Mission Relief.

Represented in the Diocese of Kansas City-St. Joseph.

[1570] (O.S.F.)—SISTERS OF ST. FRANCIS OF THE HOLY FAMILY (P)

Founded in Germany in 1864. First foundation in the United States in 1875.

Motherhouse and Novitiate: Mount St. Francis, 3390 Windsor Ave., Dubuque, IA 52001-1311. Tel: 563-583-9786; Fax: 563-583-3250. Sr. Kathy Knipper, O.S.F., Pres.; Sr. Maxine Lavell, O.S.F., Community Archivist.

Total in Community: 159.

Ministry in the following areas: Academic and Religious Education at all levels; Spirituality and Parish Ministry; Health-Pastoral Care; Caregiving; Social Service-Social Justice and Peace; Hispanic and Immigrant Outreach; Counseling; Communication/Resource Centers; Clerical Work Business; Administration; International Missions.

Properties owned and sponsored: Shalom Spirituality Center, Dubuque, IA; Sisters of St. Francis of the Holy Family Charitable Trust, Dubuque, IA.

Represented in the Archdioceses of Chicago, Detroit and Dubuque and in the Dioceses of Birmingham, El Paso, Green Bay, Jackson, Madison, Phoenix, Sioux City and Springfield-Cape Girardeau.

[1580] (O.S.F.)—SISTERS OF ST. FRANCIS OF THE IMMACULATE CONCEPTION (D)

Founded in the United States in 1891.

Motherhouse: Immaculate Conception Convent, 2408 W. Heading Ave., West Peoria, IL 61604-5096. Tel: 309-674-6168. Sr. Kathleen Ann Mourisse, Pres.; Sr. Mary Louise Hynd, Archivist.

Total in Community: 28.

Properties owned: Immaculate Conception Convent, Peoria, IL; St. Joseph's Home of Springfield in Illinois.

Represented in the Dioceses of Peoria and Springfield in Illinois.

[1590] (O.S.F.)—FRANCISCAN SISTERS OF DILLIGEN, HANKINSON, NORTH DAKOTA (P)

Founded in 1241 in Bavaria. First founded in the United States in 1913 at Collegeville, Minnesota.

General Motherhouse: Dillingen, Germany Sr. Roswitha Heinrich, Supr. Gen.

Province of Hankinson (1928): Franciscan Sisters of Dillingen Provincial House, 102 6th St., S.E., P.O. Box 447, Hankinson, ND 58041-0447. Tel: 701-242-7195. Email: dillingenfranciscansusa@rrt.net; Vocation Director Email: ndfranciscan@yahoo.com. Sr. Donna M. Welder, O.S.F., Prov. Supr.

Professed Sisters: 15.

Legal Holdings or Titles: St. Gerard's Community of Care, Hankinson, ND; St. Anne's Guest Home, Grand Forks, ND.

Ministry in the field of Religious and Academic Education; Health Care in long term care facilities; Elementary School; Retreat Center and Spiritual Direction.

Represented in the Diocese of Fargo.

[1600] (F.S.G.M.)—SISTERS OF ST. FRANCIS OF THE MARTYR ST. GEORGE (P)

Founded in Thuine, Germany. First United States foundation in 1923.

General Motherhouse: Thuine, Germany Mother Maria Cordis Reiker, F.S.G.M., Supr. Gen.

Provincial Motherhouse: St. Francis Convent and Novitiate, 1 Franciscan Way, Alton, IL 62002. Tel: 618-463-2750; Tel: 618-463-2755. Secretary Email: secretariat@altonfranciscans.org. Mother M. Mediatrix Bexten, Prov. Supr.

Total: 1100; Total in American Province: 138.

Properties owned and sponsored: St. Francis Day Care Center, Alton, IL; Mother of Good Counsel Home, St. Louis, MO.

Sisters serve and staff: Hospitals; Skilled Nursing Facility; Foreign Missions; Day Care Center; Retirement Homes for the Aged; Grade & High Schools; University; Retirement Homes for Priests; Archdiocesan & Diocesan Offices.

Represented in the Archdioceses of Kansas City in Kansas and St. Louis and in the Dioceses of Lincoln, Peoria, Rockford, Springfield in Illinois, Steubenville and Tulsa. Also in Brazil and Cuba.

[1630] (O.S.F.)—SISTERS OF ST. FRANCIS OF PENANCE AND CHRISTIAN CHARITY (P)

Founded in Holland in 1835. First foundation in the United States in 1874.

General Motherhouse: Rome, Italy. Sr. Rita Cammack, O.S.F., Gen. Min.

Universal total in Congregation: 1256.

Holy Name Province (1928): Sisters of St. Francis, 4421 Lower River Rd., Stella Niagara, NY 14144. Tel: 716-754-4311; Fax: 716-754-7657. Sr. Jo-Anne Grabowski, O.S.F., Prov. Min.

Total in Community: 91.

Legal Holdings: Stella Niagara Education Park, Stella Niagara, NY; Buffalo Academy of the Sacred Heart, Buffalo, NY; Francis Center, Niagara Falls, NY; Sisters of St. Francis of Holy Name Province, Inc., Stella Niagara, NY; Center of Renewal, Stella Niagara, NY.

Ministry in the field of Academic Education at all levels; Foreign Mission Work; Health and Hospital Care; Social Work; Pastoral Ministry.

Represented in the Archdioceses of Miami and Omaha and in the Dioceses of Buffalo, Columbus, Palm Beach, Trenton, and Wheeling-Charleston.

Sacred Heart Community (1939): 5314 Columbine Rd, Denver, CO 80221. Tel: 303-458-6270; Fax: 303-477-4105; Web: www.franciscanway.org. Sr. Susan Artone-Fricke, O.S.F., Community Min.

Total in Community: 18.

Legal Holdings or Titles: Casa Chiara, Denver, CO; Marian Residence for aged, infirm sisters, Alliance, NE; Sisters of St. Francis, Denver, Colorado.

Ministry in the following areas: Prayer; Spirituality; Human and pastoral services; Education; Advocacy for peace, justice, social and environmental concerns; General, administrative support services.

St. Francis Province (1939): 1330 Brewster Ave., P.O. Box 1028, Redwood City, CA 94062-1312. Tel: 650-369-1725; Fax: 650-369-0845. Email: provincialcouncil-SFP@franciscanway.org. Sr. Mary Litell, O.S.F., Prov. Min.

Total in Community: 48.

Legal Title: Sisters of St. Francis - Mount Alverno.

Ministry in the following areas: Diocesan Offices; Parish Ministry; Pastoral Ministry; Service Agencies; Advocacy.

Represented in the Archdioceses of Los Angeles and San Francisco and in the Dioceses of Oakland and Sacramento.

[1640] (O.S.F.)—SISTERS OF ST. FRANCIS OF PERPETUAL ADORATION (P)

Founded in Germany in 1863. First foundation in the United States in 1875.

Generalate: Olpe, Westfalen, Germany Sr. Magdalena Krol, Supr. Gen.

Universal total in Congregation: 303.

Province of the Immaculate Heart of Mary (1875): Provincial House and Novitiate, St. Francis Convent, P.O. Box 766, Mishawaka, IN 46546-0766. Tel: 574-259-5427. Sr. M. Angela Mellady, O.S.F., Prov.

Total in Community: 97.

Ministry in the field of Academic Education at all levels; Health Care in Hospitals; Ecclesial Ministry at parish and diocesan level.

Properties owned: Sisters of St. Francis of Perpetual Adoration, Inc.; St. Francis Convent, Mishawaka, IN; University of Saint Francis, Inc., Fort Wayne, IN; Franciscan Alliance, Inc., Franciscan Alliance Corporate Office, Mishawaka, IN, owns the following: Franciscan Health Crown Point; Franciscan Health Michigan City; Franciscan Health Crawfordsville; Franciscan Health Lafayette East; Franciscan Health Lafayette Central; Franciscan Health Rensselaer; Franciscan Health Indianapolis; Franciscan Health Mooresville; Franciscan Health Carmel; Franciscan Health Chicago Heights; Franciscan Health Olympia Fields; Franciscan Health Dyer; Franciscan Health Munster; Franciscan Alliance Information Services, Beech Grove, IN.

Represented in the Archdioceses of Chicago and Indianapolis and in the Dioceses of Fort Wayne-South Bend, Gary and Lafayette in Indiana.

Province of St. Joseph (March 19, 1932): Provincial House Mt. St. Francis, 7665 Assisi Heights, Colorado Springs, CO 80919. Tel: 719-598-5486. Sr. Marietta Spenner, O.S.F., Prov.

Professed Sisters: 30.

Ministry in Homes for the Aged; Parish/Pastoral Ministry; Peace & Justice; Social Ministries; Retreat Centers.

Represented in the Diocese of Colorado Springs.

[1650] (O.S.F.)—THE SISTERS OF ST. FRANCIS OF PHILADELPHIA (P)

Founded in the United States in 1855.

Congregational Motherhouse: Our Lady of Angels Convent, 609 S. Convent Rd., Aston, PA 19014. Tel: 610-459-4125. Email: congregationalrecords@osfphila.org. Sr. Theresa Firenze, O.S.F., Congregational Min.; Sr. Celeste Crine, O.S.F., Asst. Congregational Min.; Sr. Karen Pourby, O.S.F., Congregational Sec.; Sr. Helen Jacobson, O.S.F., Archivist.

Total in Community: 326.

Ministry in Health Care; Eldercare; Academic and Religious Education at all Levels; Specialized Education; Parish Ministry; Social Services; Family Centers; Renewal Centers; Diocesan Offices; Retreat Ministry; National Organizations.

Properties owned: Sisters of St. Francis, Sea Isle City, NJ; Marion House, Tacoma, WA; Neumann University, Aston, PA; Assisi House, Aston, PA; Portiuncula Convent, Aston, PA; San Damiano Convent; The Catholic High School of Baltimore, Baltimore, MD; Anna Bachmann House, Aston, PA; Sisters of St. Francis, Wilmington, DE; Sisters of St. Francis of Philadelphia, St. Clare Renewal Center, Aston, PA; Sisters of St. Francis of Philadelphia; Convents in Aston, PA: 609 S. Convent Rd., 607 S. Convent Rd., 6 Red Hill Rd.

Represented in the Archdioceses of Baltimore, Newark, Philadelphia, Portland in Oregon, Seattle, and Washington and in the Dioceses of Allentown, Camden, Charlotte, Cheyenne, Fairbanks, Harrisburg, Newark, Oakland, Paterson, Pensacola-Tallahassee, San Diego, Spokane, Trenton, Wilmington and Worcester. Also in Ireland and Kenya.

[1660] (O.S.F.)—SISTERS OF SAINT FRANCIS OF THE PROVIDENCE OF GOD

Founded in Pittsburgh in 1922.

5802 Curry Rd., Pittsburgh, PA 15236-3522. Tel: 412-882-9911; Fax: 412-386-8191. Sr. Janet Gardner, O.S.F., United States Area Min.

U.S. Professed: 15; Total: 51.

Generalate: Sao Paulo, Brazil. Sr. Rute Guimaraes, Gen. Min.

Ministries in Pastoral, Spiritual, Social Services; Education and Pastoral Ministry in Brazil.

Sponsored Ministry: Franciscan Child Day Care Center.

Represented in the Diocese of Pittsburgh. Also in Brazil.

[1670] (O.S.F.)—SISTERS OF ST. FRANCIS OF SAVANNAH, MO (P)

Founded in Austria in 1850. Founded in the United States, August 22, 1922.

Provincial House and Novitiate: 908 Franciscan Way, Box 488, Savannah, MO 64485-0488. Tel: 816-324-3179; Fax: 816-324-7264. Email: scm@osfsav.org. Web: www.sistersofstfrancis.org. Sr. Christine Martin, O.S.F., Prov. Supr.

Total in Community: 6.

Legal Holdings and Titles: Sisters of St. Francis of Savannah, Inc.; Maintenance and Custodial Care Trust of the Franciscan Sisters of Savannah. Also serve in Rural Ministry; Justice Advocacy; Religious Education; Food Pantry.

Represented in the Diocese of Kansas City-St. Joseph.

[1680] (O.S.F.)—SCHOOL SISTERS OF ST. FRANCIS (P)

Founded in the United States in 1874.

General Motherhouse: 1501 S. Layton Blvd., Milwaukee, WI 53215. Tel: 414-808-3779; Fax: 414-944-6060. Email: cryan@sssf.org. Sr. Mary Diez, O.S.F., Pres.; Sr. Tresa Abraham Kizhakeparambil, O.S.F., Vice Pres.; Sr. Barbara Kraemer, O.S.F., Vice Pres.; Sr. Lucy Kalapurackel, O.S.F., Vice Pres.; Sr. Catherine M. Ryan, O.S.F., Treas.

Total in Congregation: 594; Total in U.S.: 302.

Properties owned and/or sponsored: St. Joseph Convent, Milwaukee, WI; School Sisters of St. Francis, Inc.

U.S. Province: 1515 S. Layton Blvd., Milwaukee, WI 53215. Tel: 414-384-1515. Provincial Team: Sr. Kathleen O'Brien, O.S.F.; Sr. Mary C. Schneider, O.S.F.; Sr. Kathleen Braum, O.S.F.

Properties owned and sponsored: Alverno College, Milwaukee, WI; Clement Manor, Inc., Greenfield, WI; Maryhill Manor, Niagara, WI; Our Lady of the Angels Convent, Greenfield, WI; New Cassel, Omaha, NE; Clare Towers, Milwaukee, WI; St. Clare Management, Inc., Milwaukee, WI; Sacred Heart, Milwaukee, WI; Telos, Inc., Milwaukee, WI.

Sisters serve and staff: Colleges, High Schools, Grade Schools, Adult and Special Education; Diocesan Offices; Hospitals and Nursing Homes; Retreat and Spiritual Direction; Social Ministries; Psychotherapy; Health Care; Religious Education; Pastoral Ministry; Retirement Homes; Legal Services; Food Service; Visual Arts; Graphic Arts; RCIA Program, Music & Liturgy.

Represented in the Archdioceses of Chicago, Dubuque, Milwaukee, Omaha and St. Paul-Minneapolis and in the Dioceses of Charlotte, El Paso, Grand Island, Jackson, Joliet, Lincoln, Madison, Nashville, Phoenix, Rockford, San Bernardino, Superior and Tucson.

[1690] (O.S.F.)—SCHOOL SISTERS OF THE THIRD ORDER REGULAR OF ST. FRANCIS UNITED STATES PROVINCE (PITTSBURGH, PA) (P)

Founded in Austria in 1843. First foundation in the U.S. in 1913.

Generalate: Via Nicolo Piccolomini 27, 00165, Rome, Italy. Sr. Frances Marie Duncan, O.S.F., Gen. Min.

Novitiate: St. Francis Convent, 395 Bridle Path Rd., Bethlehem, PA 18017. Tel: 610-866-2597.

Provincial Offices: 4900 Perry Highway, Suite 201, Pittsburgh, PA 15229. Tel: 412-761-2855; Fax: 412-761-0290. Emails: msgriccia@schoolsistersosf.org.com; administrationusa@schoolsistersosf.org. Sr. Marian Sgriccia, O.S.F., Prov. Min. Tel: 412-761-2855.

Total in Community: 60.

Legal Title: School Sisters of the Third Order Regular of St. Francis.

Ministry in the following areas: the field of academic education at all levels; Religious Education; Pastoral Ministry; Pastoral Associate; Mission Work; Social Ministry; Evangelization and Catechesis, Retreat Ministry.

Represented in the Archdioceses of San Antonio and in the Dioceses of Allentown, Erie, Metuchen, Pittsburgh and San Angelo. Also in Italy.

[1695] (O.S.F.)—SCHOOL SISTERS OF THE THIRD ORDER OF ST. FRANCIS (PANHANDLE, TEXAS) (P)

Founded in Austria, 1723; The Vienna Foundation in 1845. First founded in the United States in 1931.

Motherhouse: Vienna, Austria

Generalate American Center and Novitiate: 119 Franciscan Way, P.O. Box 906, Panhandle, TX 79068. Tel: 806-537-3182. Email: schsrs@gmail.com. Sr. Mary Michael Huseman, O.S.F., Regl. Supr.

Total number in U.S.: 14.

Ministry in the following areas: Catholic Schools; Faith Formation; Evangelization of youth, young adults and families.

Represented in the Diocese of Amarillo.

[1705] (O.S.F.)—THE SISTERS OF ST. FRANCIS OF ASSISI (P) (Sisters of Penance and Charity)

Founded in the United States in 1849.

General Motherhouse: St. Francis Convent, 3221 S. Lake Dr., Saint Francis, WI 53235-3702. Tel: 414-744-1160; Fax: 414-744-7193; Email: administration@lakeosfs.org; Web: www.lakeosfs.org. Sr. Diana De Bruin, O.S.F., Dir.

Total in Community: 128.

Legal Titles: The Sisters of St. Francis of Assisi, Inc.; The Ongoing Community Support Trust of the Sisters of St. Francis, Inc.; Sisters of St. Francis of Assisi of New Mexico.

Corporate Ministries: St. Elizabeth School, Inc., Baltimore, MD; Franciscan Center, Inc., Baltimore, MD; St. Ann Center for Intergenerational Care, Inc., Milwaukee, WI; St. Francis Convent, Inc., Saint Francis, WI; Cardinal Stritch University, Inc., Milwaukee, WI; St. Coletta of Wisconsin, Inc., Jefferson, WI; St. Coletta of Wisconsin Charitable Foundation, Inc., St. Coletta's of Illinois, Tinley Park, IL; St. Coletta's of Illinois Foundation, Inc., Tinley Park, IL; Cardinal Cushing Centers, Inc., Hanover, MA; Cardinal Cushing Centers, Inc., Braintree St. Coletta School, Braintree, MA. Services to the Elderly: Canticle Court, Inc.; Juniper Court, Inc.; Canticle and Juniper Courts Foundation, Inc., Saint Francis, WI.

Represented in the Archdioceses of Baltimore, Boston, Dubuque, Milwaukee, San Antonio and Santa Fe and in the Dioceses of Brownsville, Ft. Wayne/South Bend, Madison and Superior. Also in Taiwan.

[1710] (O.S.F.)—CONGREGATION OF THE THIRD ORDER OF ST. FRANCIS OF MARY IMMACULATE, JOLIET, IL (P)

Founded in the United States, Joliet, Illinois, in 1865.

Central Administration Offices: 1433 Essington Rd., Joliet, IL 60435-2873. Tel: 815-725-8735. Sr. Jeanne Bessette, O.S.F., Pres.

Total in Community: 118.

Legal Titles: Congregation of the Third Order of St. Francis of Mary Immaculate, Joliet, IL; Retirement Plan Trust of the Congregation of the Third Order of St. Francis of Mary Immaculate, Joliet, IL.

Sponsored Institutions: Joliet Catholic Academy, Our Lady of Angels Retirement Home, University of St. Francis.

Ministry in the following areas: School and Adult Education; Retirement Home; House of Prayer. Also engaged in Religious Education; Social Services; Spiritual Direction; Nursing and Health Services; Hospital and Parish Ministry; Prison Ministry; Hispanic Ministry; Senior Housing.

Represented in the Archdioceses of Boston, Chicago, Cincinnati, Denver, Detroit, Milwaukee, New York and in the Dioceses of Cleveland, Colorado Springs, Columbus, Joliet, Peoria, Phoenix, St. Cloud, Springfield in Illinois, Superior, Tucson and Youngstown. Also in Brazil.

[1720] (O.S.F.)—SISTERS OF THE THIRD ORDER REGULAR OF ST. FRANCIS OF THE CONGREGATION OF OUR LADY OF LOURDES (P)

Founded in the United States in 1877.

Administration Center: Assisi Heights, 1001 14th St., N.W., Ste 100, Rochester, MN 55901. Tel: 507-282-7441; Fax: 507-282-7762. Email: executive.assistant@rochesterfranciscan.org. Sr. Tierney Trueman, O.S.F., Congregational Min. & Pres. Tel: 507-529-3533.

Total in Community: 137.

Ministry in the following areas: Education Services; Pastoral Concerns Development; Religious Life Development; Spiritual Life Development; Community Life Development; Social Concerns Development; Business Services; Health Care Services; Support Services.

Properties owned and sponsored: Assisi Heights, Rochester, MN.

Represented in the Archdioceses of Chicago, Denver, St. Paul-Minneapolis, Santa Fe and in the Dioceses of El Paso, Great Falls-Billings, Joliet, New Ulm, Rapid City, St. Cloud, San Bernardino, San Diego, Springfield-Cape Girardeau and Winona-Rochester. Also in Colombia.

[1730] (O.S.F.)—CONGREGATION OF THE SISTERS OF THE THIRD ORDER OF ST. FRANCIS, OLDENBURG, IN (P)

Founded in U.S., Oldenburg, Indiana in 1851.

General Motherhouse and Novitiate: Convent of the Immaculate Conception, P.O. Box 100, Oldenburg, IN 47036. Tel: 812-934-2475. Sr. Christa Franzer, O.S.F., Congregational Min.

Total in Community: 138.

Properties owned and/or sponsored: Marian University, Indianapolis, IN; Oldenburg Academy, Oldenburg, IN.

Sisters serve & staff: Liberal Arts University, High Schools, Elementary Schools; Navajo, Indian Missions; Religious Education Centers; Hospital & Parish Ministry; Apostolate of Aging; Retreat & Counseling Ministry; Justice & Peace Office; Clerical Staff; Social Services.

Represented in the Archdioceses of Cincinnati, Indianapolis and St. Louis and in the Dioceses of Evansville, Gallup, Great Falls-Billings, Lexington, and Springfield in Illinois.

[1760] (O.S.F.)—SISTERS OF THE THIRD ORDER OF ST. FRANCIS OF PENANCE AND OF CHARITY (P)

Founded in Tiffin, Ohio in 1869.

General Motherhouse: St. Francis Convent, 200 St. Francis Ave., Tiffin, OH 44883. Tel: 419-447-0435; Fax: 419-447-1612. Sr. Sara Aldridge, O.S.F., Community Min.

Total in Community: 71.

Legal Title: Sisters of St. Francis of Tiffin, OH. Ministry in the following areas: Ministry to the Aged; Parish Ministry; Retreat and Renewal Centers; Health Care; Health-Pastoral Care; Administration; Social Justice Outreach; Education.

Properties owned or sponsored: St. Francis Spirituality Center (SFSC); Franciscan Earth Literacy Center, 194 St. Francis Ave. Tiffin, 44883.

Represented in the Dioceses of Lexington, Owensboro, Toledo, and Youngstown.

[1770] (O.S.F.)—THE SISTERS OF THE THIRD ORDER OF ST. FRANCIS (EAST PEORIA, ILLINOIS) (P)

Founded in the United States in 1877.

Motherhouse: 1175 St. Francis Ln., East Peoria, IL 61611-1299. Tel: 309-699-7215. Sr. Judith Ann Duvall, O.S.F., Major Supr.

Total in Community: 22.

Properties owned and sponsored: Saint Francis Medical Center, Peoria, IL; St. Joseph Medical Center, Bloomington, IL; St. Mary Medical Center, Galesburg, IL; St. James-John W. Albrecht Medical Center, Pontiac, IL; Saint Anthony Medical Center, Rockford, IL; St. Francis Hospital, Escanaba, MI; OSF Healthcare System, Peoria, IL; OSF Healthcare Foundation, Peoria, IL; Motherhouse, East Peoria, IL; Holy Family Medical Center, Monmouth, IL; OSF Saint Elizabeth Medical Center, Ottawa, IL; OSF Saint Anthony Health Center, Alton, IL; OSF Saint Luke Medial Center, Kewanee, IL.

Represented in the Dioceses of Marquette, Peoria, Rockford and Springfield.

[1780] (F.S.P.A.)—CONGREGATION OF THE SISTERS OF THIRD ORDER OF ST. FRANCIS OF PERPETUAL ADORATION (P) (Franciscan Sisters of Perpetual Adoration)

Founded in the United States in 1849.

Generalate - Motherhouse and Novitiate: St. Rose Convent, 912 Market St., La Crosse, WI 54601-4782. Tel: 608-782-5610; Fax: 608-782-6301. Email: fspa@fspa.org. Sr. Eileen McKenzie, F.S.P.A., Pres.; Sr. Mary Ann Gschwind, F.S.P.A., Archivist.

Total in Congregation: 164.

Properties owned and sponsored: St. Rose Convent, La Crosse, WI; Villa St. Joseph, La Crosse, WI; Franciscan Spirituality Center, La Crosse; Prairiewoods Franciscan Spirituality Center, Hiawatha, IA; Marywood Franciscan Spirituality Center, Arbor Vitae, WI.

Represented in the Archdioceses of Agana, Chicago, Dubuque, Philadelphia, Portland in Oregon, Seattle and St. Paul-Minneapolis and in the Dioceses of Colorado Springs, Des Moines, Dodge City, Gallup, Green Bay, Jackson, La Crosse, Savannah, Sioux City, Spokane and Superior. Also in Canada.

[1805] O.S.F.—SISTERS OF ST. FRANCIS OF THE NEUMANN COMMUNITIES (P)

Congregation Offices (1860): 225 Greenfield Pkwy., Ste. 208, Liverpool, NY 13288. Tel: 315-634-7000; Fax: 315-634-7023; Email: sisters@sosf.org; Web: www.sosf.org.

Total in Community: 284.

Ministry in academic education; hospitals; religious education & pastoral ministry; home for the dying; child day care; diocesan offices; social services; day nurseries; parishes.

Sponsored ministries: Gingerbread House Day Care & Preschool, Syracuse, NY; Francis House, Syracuse, NY; St. Francis Healthcare System, Honolulu, HI; Portiuncula Foundation, Millvale, PA; Mt. Alvernia Day Care & Learning Center, Millvale, PA.

Properties owned: Sisters of St. Francis campus in Honolulu, HI.

Represented in the Archdioceses of Newark, New York and Washington and in the Dioceses of Buffalo, Charleston, El Paso, Greensburg, Honolulu, Joliet, Lubbock, Orlando, Pittsburgh, Scranton, St. Petersburg and Syracuse. Also in Peru.

[1810] (O.S.F.)—BERNARDINE FRANCISCAN SISTERS (P)

Founded in the United States in 1894.

Congregational Leadership Offices: 450 St. Bernardine St., Reading, PA 19607-1737. Tel: 484-334-6976; Fax: 484-334-6977; Email: Robertaann@bfranciscan.org. Sr. John Ann Proach, O.S.F., Congregational Min.

Total in Community: 201.

Total number in the United States: 120.

Ministry in the field of academic education at all levels -preschool to college; religious education of children & adults; health & home care; retreat work; social work.

Represented in the Archdioceses of Detroit, Philadelphia and in the Dioceses of Allentown, Bridgeport, Richmond, and Saginaw. Also in Brazil, Dominican Republic, Liberia and Mozambique.

[1820] (O.S.F.)—HOSPITAL SISTERS OF THE THIRD ORDER REGULAR OF ST. FRANCIS (P)

Founded in Germany in 1844. First foundation in the United States in 1875.

General Motherhouse: Muenster, Westphalia, Germany. Sr. Margarete Ulager, O.S.F., Gen. Supr.

American Province (1875): St. Francis Convent, Motherhouse and Novitiate, Box 19431, Springfield, IL 62794. Tel: 217-522-3386. Sr. Maureen O'Connor, O.S.F., Prov. Supr.; Sr. Rosily Menachery, O.S.F., Prov. Councilor/Sec. & Contact Person.

Total in Community: 42.

Legal Title: Hospital Sisters of St. Francis-USA, Inc.

Properties owned or sponsored: Residences 4; St. Francis Convent, Motherhouse, Novitiate, Springfield, IL.

Sisters are engaged in the Ministry of Prayer; Hospitals; Social Ministries; Pastoral Ministries and Retreat and Spiritual Direction Ministries.

Hospital Sisters Ministries: Represented in the Archdiocese of Milwaukee and in the Dioceses of Belleville, Green Bay, La Crosse, and Springfield in Illinois.

[1830] (R.G.S.)—THE SISTERS OF THE GOOD SHEPHERD (P)

Congregation of Our Lady of Charity of the Good Shepherd Founded in France in 1835. First foundation in the United States in Louisville, KY, 1842.

Generalate for the Provinces: Suore del Buon Pastore, via Raffaello Sardiello 20, Rome, Italy, 00165. Sr. Ellen Kelly, Supr. Gen.

Province of Mid-North America (2000): Province Center, 7654 Natural Bridge Rd., St. Louis, MO 63121. Tel: 314-381-3400; Fax: 314-381-7102. Sr. Madeleine Munday, R.G.S., Prov.

Professed Apostolic Sisters: 79; Contemplative Sisters: 17.

Legal Title: Sisters of the Good Shepherd Province of Mid-North America; Pelletier Trust, a Charitable Trust of the Sisters of the Good Shepherd; Sisters of the Good Shepherd Province of Mid-North America Foundation.

Properties owned and staffed: Sisters of the Good Shepherd of Detroit aka Vista Maria, Dearborn Heights, MI; CORA Services, Inc., Philadelphia, PA; Good Shepherd Corporation d.b.a. Good Shepherd Neighborhood House, Mediation Program, Philadelphia, PA; Good Shepherd Services, Atlanta, GA; Gracenter, San Francisco, CA; House of the Good Shepherd of Memphis dba DeNeuville Learning Center, Memphis, TN; Good Shepherd Provincialate, St. Louis, MO.

Represented in the Archdioceses of Atlanta, Cincinnati, Detroit, Los Angeles, Louisville, Omaha, Portland in Oregon, Philadelphia, St. Louis, St. Paul-Minneapolis, San Francisco and Washington and in the Diocese of Scranton.

Province of New York (1857): Sisters of the Good Shepherd, 25-30 21st. Ave., Astoria, NY 11105. Tel: 718-278-1155; Fax: 718-278-1158. Sr. Maureen McGowan, Province Leader.

Professed Apostolic Sisters: 35; Professed Contemplative Sisters: 10.

Legal Title: Sisters of the Good Shepherd, Province of New York.

Legal Holdings or Titles: Good Shepherd Services, New York, NY; Good Shepherd Volunteers, Astoria, NY; Sisters of the Good Shepherd, Marlboro, MA; Collier Youth Services, Wickatunk, NJ.

Ministry in Counseling Centers; Social Service Agencies; Special Education Schools; Neighborhood Family Services; Adolescent Residential Programs; Human Services Workshops; Pastoral Ministry.

Programs sponsored: Good Shepherd Services; Collier Youth Services; Good Shepherd Volunteers.

Represented in the Archdioceses of Boston, Hartford and New York and in the Dioceses of Brooklyn and Trenton.

Province of Central South US (2014): Sisters of the Good Shepherd, 620 Roswell Rd., N.W., P.O. Box 340, Carrollton, OH 44615. Tel: 330-627-1641; Fax: 330-627-5789. Sr. Francisca Aguillón, R.G.S., Prov.

Professed Apostolic Sisters: 48.

Legal Title: Sisters of Our Lady of Charity of the Good Shepherd - Province Center.

Legal Holdings or Titles: Province Center and Convent Carrollton, OH; Convent, Erie, PA; Nativity Convent, Pittsburgh, PA; Good Shepherd Convent, Wheeling, WV; San Juan Convent, El Paso, TX; Mount St. Michael Convent, Dallas, TX; Convent Green Bay, WI.

Ministry in Domestic Abuse, Trafficked, Migrants, Immigration, Pastoral Ministry, Hispanic Ministry.

Represented in the Dioceses of Dallas, El Paso, Erie, Green Bay, Pittsburgh, San Diego, Steubenville and Wheeling-Charleston.

[1840] (G.N.S.H.)—GREY NUNS OF THE SACRED HEART (P)

Generalate, Congregational Offices: 14500 Bustleton Ave., Philadelphia, PA 19116-1188. Tel: 215-968-4236; Fax: 267-538-3442. Sr. Denise Roche, G.N.S.H., Pres.; Ms. Eileen Dickerson, Dir. Congregational Advancement Office.

Total in Community: 67.

Ministry in Intercommunity Finance; High Level Education; Hospice Chaplaincy; Pastoral Care; Social Services, Social Justice & Peace Activism; Retreat & Spiritual Direction; Addiction Consultant and Eco-Spirituality Advocacy.

Represented in the Archdiocese of Philadelphia and in the Diocese of Buffalo.

[1845] (M.G.SP.S.)—MISSIONARIES GUADALUPANAS OF THE HOLY SPIRIT (P)

Founded in Morelia, Michoacan, Mexico in 1930 by Rev. Felix de Jesus Rougier, M.Sp.S.

General Motherhouse: Hidalgo #7, Tlalpan 14000, Mexico, D.F., Mexico Mother Ana Maria Pacheco, Supr. Gen.

Provincial House: 5467 W. 8th St., Los Angeles, CA 90036-3811. Tel: 323-424-7208.

Total Sisters in U.S.: 43

Legal Title; Missionary Guadalupanas of the Holy Spirit, Inc. Ministry in Religious Education; Pastoral and Parish Ministries.

Represented in the Archdioceses of Atlanta and Los Angeles and in the Dioceses of Birmingham, Jackson, San Bernardino and Stockton. Also in the Dominican Republic.

U.S. Novitiate: 758 S. Dunsmuir Ave., Los Angeles, CA 90036.

[1850] (S.A.C.)—SISTERS OF THE GUARDIAN ANGEL (P)

Founded in Quillan, France in 1839.

General Motherhouse: Avda, del Valle, 42, Madrid 3, Spain Sr. Sagrario Escudero, S.A.C., Supr. Gen.

U.S. Foundation: 1245 S. Van Ness, Los Angeles, CA 90019. Tel: 213-732-7881.

Represented in the Archdiocese of Los Angeles.

[1855] (H.H.C.J.)—CONGREGATION OF THE HANDMAIDS OF THE HOLY CHILD JESUS (P)

Founded in Calabar, Nigeria in 1931 by Sister Mary Charles Magdalen Walker. Obtained Pontifical Status in 1971; first foundation in United States in 1992.

Generalate and Motherhouse: Handmaids of the Holy Child Jesus - The Generalate, Ifuho, P.O. Box 155, Ikot Ekpene, Nigeria Tel: 080-388-78670. Sr. Leonie Martha O'Karaga, H.H.C.J., Supr. Gen.

U.S.A. Mission: Ancilla Convent, 3614 Englewood Dr., Pearland, TX 77584. Tel: 281-692-0098; Fax: 281-692-0049; Email: usa@hhcj.org; Web: www.hhcj.org. Sr. Germaine Ocansey, H.H.C.J., U.S.A. Mission Supr.; Sr. Betty Kalu, H.H.C.J., Devel. Dir.

Universal Number of Professed Sisters: 802; Professed Sisters in U.S. & Canada: 60.

Ministry in the field of Education at all levels; Pastoral Work; Health Care services; Women Empowerment; Education; Special Education; Youth Ministry; Catechesis; Pastoral Ministry.

Represented in the Archdioceses of Galveston-Houston, Mobile, New York and Washington and in the Dioceses St. Petersburg.

[1857] (H.L.M.C.)—HANDMAIDS OF OUR LADY OF MOUNT CARMEL (CARMELITE SISTERS) (D)

Founded in 1959.

Motherhouse: Zimbabwe, Africa.

12 Cedarwood Way, Apt. B, Newport News, VA 23608. Sr. Judith Madeline Chapisa, Prioress.

Total Sisters: 100.

Ministry in Pastoral Work, Education, Nursing and Social Work.

Represented in the Diocese of Richmond.

[1860] (H.P.B.)—HANDMAIDS OF THE PRECIOUS BLOOD (P)

Founded in Jemez Springs, New Mexico in 1947.

Motherhouse and Novitiate: Cor Jesu Monastery, 596 Callaway Ridge Rd., New Market, TN 37820. Tel: 423-241-7065. Rev. Mother Sarah Michael, H.P.B., Mother Prioress.

Professed Sisters: 14.

Ministry as Contemplative, Life of Eucharistic Adoration (Perpetual) for the sanctification of priests and for the entire world.

[1870] (A.C.I.)—THE HANDMAIDS OF THE SACRED HEART OF JESUS (P)

Founded in Spain in 1877. First foundation in the United States in 1926.

General Motherhouse: Via XX Settembre, 65/b 00187 Rome, Italy. Sr. Rosario Fernández Villarán, Supr. Gen. Universal total in Congregation: 850.

Provincial Motherhouse: 616 Coopertown Rd., Haverford, PA 19041-1135. Tel: 610-642-5715; Fax: 610-642-6788; Web: www.acjusa.org. Sr. Belén Escauriaza, A.C.I., Prov.

Total in Community: 28.

Properties owned: St. Raphaela Center, Haverford, PA; Ancillae Assumpta Academy, Wyncote, PA; facilities in Georgia and Florida.

Sisters serve and staff: Elementary School; Retreat Center; Mission Center; Parish Ministry; CCD; Hispanic Pastoral Ministry; Social Workers; Pastoral Ministry; Mission work.

Represented in the Archdioceses of Atlanta, Miami, Philadelphia and St. Louis.

[1880] (A.R.)—HANDMAIDS OF REPARATION OF THE SACRED HEART OF JESUS (P)

Founded in Messina, Italy in 1918.

U.S. Foundation (1958): 6300 Capella Ave., Burke, VA 22015. Tel: 703-455-4180. Sr. Donatella Merulla, A.R., Contact Person.

Total number in U.S.: 6.

Ministry in Apostolic Work in Religious & Academic Education: Education All Levels; Religious Education; Parish and Diocesan Ministry; CCD Work; Orphanages; Missionary Work in Africa, Brazil and Poland.

Represented in the Dioceses of Arlington and Steubenville. Also in Africa, Brazil, Italy and Poland.

[1890] (H.H.S.)—SOCIETY OF HELPERS (P)

Founded in France in 1856. First foundation in the U.S. in 1892.

Generalate: 16 rue St. J. Baptiste de la Salle, Paris, France, 75006. Sr. Gudrun Bohle, Supr. Gen.

American Provincial Office (1921): 2226 W. Pratt Blvd., Chicago, IL 60645. Tel: 773-405-9884. Leadership Team: Sr. Alicia Gutierrez, S.H.; Tel: 773-209-7597; Email: gutier.ali23@gmail.com; Sr. Jean Kielty, S.H. Tel: 773-405-9884; Email: jeankielty@yahoo.com; Sr. Rayo Cuaya-Castillo, S.H. Tel: 773-301-7128; Email: rayo.javito@hotmail.com.

Total number in U.S. Province: 18.

Legal Title: Society of the Helpers of the Holy Souls; Helpers of the Holy Souls; Province of the Helpers of the Holy Souls in the United States.

Represented in the Archdioceses of Boston, Chicago and San Francisco and in the Dioceses of Joliet.

[1895] (C.S.J.)—HERMANAS CARMELITAS DE SAN JOSE (P)

Founded in El Salvador C.A. in 1916. First foundation in the United States in 2003.

Motherhouse: Final 14 Ave. Norte, Colonia San Antonio Las Palmeras Depto., De La Libertad, El Salvador.

Regional House: 141 W. 87th Pl., Los Angeles, CA 90003. Tel: 424-208-9264. Email: lupagoz@yahoo.com. Sr. Lucia Padilla, C.S.J., Regl. Supr. U.S. Community.

Total in Congregation: 201; U.S. Community: 4.

Ministry in Pastoral Care: Pastoral assistance in spiritual guidance and counseling; visitation of the sick and elderly; sacramental preparation; religious education for children, youth and/or adults; pastoral visits to the poor; faith formation.

[1900] (H.C.G.)—HERMANAS CATEQUISTAS GUADALUPANAS (P)

Founded in Saltillo, Coahuila, Mexico in 1923. First United States foundation in 1950.

Motherhouse and Novitiate: Saltillo, Coahuila, Mexico

U.S. Address: Hermanas Catequistas Guadalupanas Convent, 4110 S. Flores, San Antonio, TX 78214. Tel: 210-532-9344. Sr. Maria Martha Ruiz, H.C.G., Regl. Delegate.

Total number in the U.S.: 10.

Represented in the Archdioceses of San Antonio and in the Diocese of Fort Worth.

[1905] (H.F.I.C.)—HERMANAS FRANCISCANAS DE LA IMMACULADA CONCEPCION

General Motherhouse: 209 1st St., Brooklyn, NY 11215. Tel: 718-624-6720.

[1910] (H.J.)—HERMANAS JOSEFINAS (P)

General Motherhouse: Condor 336, Col. las Aguilas, Delg. Alvaro Obregon, Mexico, 01710. Mother Isabel Vargas Huante, H.J., Gen. & Supr.

U.S. Address: Santa Maria de Guadalupe Casa Delegacion, 2622 W. Summit Ave., San Antonio, TX 78228. Tel: 210-734-0039.

Sisters: 10.

Represented in the Archdioceses of Chicago, Los Angeles and San Antonio and in the Diocese of Joliet in Illinois.

[1920] (C.S.C.)—CONGREGATION OF THE SISTERS OF THE HOLY CROSS (P)

Founded at Le Mans, France in 1841. First foundation in the U.S. in 1843.

General Administration: Sisters of the Holy Cross Generalate, 301 Bertrand Hall-Saint Mary's, Notre Dame, IN 46556-5000. Tel: 574-284-5550; Fax: 574-284-5779. Communications Email: communications@cscsisters.org. Sr. M. Veronique Wiedower, C.S.C., Pres.; Sr. Catherine Osimo, C.S.C., Gen. Sec.

Professed Members: 286; Temporarily Professed: 36; Novices: 17; Candidates: 18.

Legal Title: Sisters of the Holy Cross, Inc.; The Academy of the Holy Cross, Inc., MD; The Corporation of Saint Mary's College, Notre Dame, IN; Holy Cross Ministries of Utah; Society of the Congregation of the Sisters of the Holy Cross, Bangladesh.

Areas and Coordinators:

Area of Africa - Ghana and Uganda Tel: 256-752-247637. Sr. Theresia W. Mbugua, C.S.C., Coord.

Area of Asia-Bangladesh and India. Tel: 88-02-9114712. Sr. Violet Rodrigues, C.S.C., Coord.

Area of North America - USA & Mexico, Notre Dame, IN, Tel: 574-284-5646. Sr. Joan Marie Steadman, C.S.C., Coord.

Area of South America - Brazil and Peru. Tel: 5511-2198-0600. Sr. Diane Cundiff, C.S.C., Coord.

Sisters serve and staff: Colleges; High Schools; Grade Schools; Adult Education Centers; Social Service Centers; Prayer Centers; Counseling Centers; Human Rights Centers; Women's Development Center; Hospitals and other Health Ministries, including Health Systems, Primary Health Care and Long Term Health Care; Parish Ministry; Diocesan Catechetical Services; Other Parish and Diocesan Ministries; Retirement Homes; Senior Citizen Residences; Pastoral Ministry with the Deaf; Correctional Institution.

Represented in the Archdioceses of Chicago, Indianapolis and Washington and in the Dioceses of Austin, Boise, Fort Wayne-South Bend, Joliet in Illinois, Lafayette in Indiana, Lexington, Oakland and Salt Lake City. Also in Bangladesh, Brazil, Ghana, India, Peru, Mexico and Uganda.

[1930] (C.S.C.)—SISTERS OF HOLY CROSS (P)

Founded in Le Mans, France in 1841. First foundation in Canada in 1847.

General Administration: 905 rue Basile-Moreau, St-Laurent, Montreal, Canada, H4L 4A1. Sr. Raymonde Maisonneuve, C.S.C., Congregational Leader.

Universal total in Congregation: 318.

North American Region/U.S. Sector Office: Sisters of Holy Cross, 365 Island Pond Rd., Manchester, NH 03109-4811. Tel: 603-622-9504; Fax: 603-622-9782. Sr. Diane Y. Dupere, C.S.C., Sector Leader. Email: dydupere@srsofholycross.com. Sr. Suzanne Levesque, C.S.C., Development. Email: cscdevoffice@srsofholycross.com.

Total number in Region: 68.

Ministry in the field of Early Childhood Education; ESL to assist refugees and immigrants; Parish Ministry; Spiritual Direction.

Properties owned: Holy Cross Early Childhood Center, Manchester, NH; St. George Manor, Manchester, NH; 136 Lynwood Ln., Manchester, NH 03109; 113 Wedgewood Ln., Manchester, NH 03109.

Represented in the Dioceses of Manchester, Norwich and St. Petersburg. Also in Burkina Faso, Mali, Chile, Haiti, Peru, Italy, Vietnam and Canada.

[1940] (C.H.F.)—CONGREGATION OF THE SISTERS OF THE HOLY FAITH (P)

Founded in Ireland in 1856. First foundation in U.S. in 1953. St. John of God School, 13817 Pioneer Blvd., Norwalk, California, 90650.

Motherhouse: Glasnevin, Dublin II, Ireland

U.S. Region: 12322 S. Paramount Blvd., Downey, CA 90242. Tel: 504-621-4530. Sr. Teresa Rooney, C.H.F., Regl. Leader.

Total in Community: 12.

Represented in the Archdioceses of Los Angeles, New Orleans and San Francisco.

[1950] (S.S.F.)—CONGREGATION OF THE SISTERS OF THE HOLY FAMILY (P)

Founded in New Orleans, Louisiana, in 1842.

Motherhouse: 6901 Chef Menteur Hwy., New Orleans, LA 70126-5215. Tel: 504-241-3088, Ext. 102. Sr. Alicia Costa, Ph.D., S.S.F., Congregational Leader.

Total in Community: 65.

Ministry in Secondary and Elementary Schools; Day Care Centers; Pastoral and Social Services; Nursing Home and Apartments for the Elderly, Disabled and Handicapped.

Represented in the Archdiocese of New Orleans and in the Dioceses of Alexandria, Baton Rouge and Lafayette (LA).

[1960] (S.H.F.)—SISTERS OF THE HOLY FAMILY (P)

Founded in San Francisco, California, in 1872.

General Motherhouse: P.O. Box 3248, Fremont, CA 94539. Tel: 510-624-4596; Fax: 510-933-7395. Email: congsecy@holyfamilysisters.org. Sr. Gladys Guenther, S.H.F., Congregational Pres.

Total in Community: 39.

Ministry in the following areas: Pastoral Care; Parish Administration and Ministries; Social Justice Ministry; Ministry to Immigrants.

Represented in the Dioceses of Oakland and Stockton.

[1970] (C.S.F.N.)—SISTERS OF THE HOLY FAMILY OF NAZARETH (P)

Founded in Italy in 1875. First foundation in the United States in 1885.

General Motherhouse: Rome, Italy. Sr. Angela Marie Mazzeo, C.S.F.N., Supr. Gen.

Holy Family Province (1885): 310 N. River Rd., Des Plaines, IL 60016-1211. Tel: 847-298-6760; Fax: 847803-1941. Email: info@nazarethesfn.org. Sr. Kathleen Maciej, C.S.F.N., Provincial Supr.; Sr. Rebecca Sullivan, C.S.F.N., Archivist.

Total number in United States: 187.

Ministry in Academic Education; Hospitals and Health Care; Social Work; Retreat Work; Religious Education; Child Care; Parish Ministry.

Represented in the Archdiocese of Chicago.

[1980] (O.S.F.)—CONGREGATION OF THE SERVANTS OF THE HOLY CHILD JESUS OF THE THIRD ORDER REGULAR OF SAINT FRANCIS (P)

Founded in Germany in 1855. First founded in the United States on April 9, 1929, at Staten Island, New York.

General Motherhouse: Kloster Oberzell, Wuerzburg, Germany Sister Katharina Ganz, Supr. Gen.

Regional House: Servants of the Holy Child Jesus Regional House Epiphany Convent, 99 Harrison Ave., North Plainfield, NJ 07060-3606. Tel: 908-370-3616; Fax: 908-756-3933. Sr. M. Antonia Cooper, Reg. Min. Total in American Region: 5.

Ministry in Social Work.

Represented in the Dioceses of Metuchen and Trenton.

[1990] (S.N.J.M.)—SISTERS OF THE HOLY NAMES OF JESUS AND MARY (P)

Founded by Blessed Marie Rose Durocher, in Longueuil, Quebec, Canada in 1843. First foundation in the U.S. in 1859.

Generalate: 80, rue Saint-Charles Est, Longueuil, Canada, J4H 1A9. Tel: 450-651-8104. Sr. Linda Haydock, Supr.

An international congregation of 550 religious women with missions in Lesotho, Nicaragua, Peru and Brazil. Congregational sponsored works include colleges; adult centers; secondary, elementary and preschools; continuing care retirement community and health clinics.

U.S.-Ontario Province: Provincial Administration, Box 398, Marylhurst, OR 97036. Tel: 503-675-7100; Fax: 503-697-3264; Email: info@snjmuson.org; Web: www.snjmusontario.org. Sr. Maureen Delaney, S.N.J.M., Prov.

Total in Province: 322.

Properties owned and/or sponsored: Academy of the Holy Names, Albany, NY; Academy of the Holy Names, Tampa, FL; Convent, Marylhurst, OR; St. Mary's Academy, Portland, OR; Mary's Woods at Marylhurst, Inc., Marylhurst, OR; Holy Names University, Oakland, CA; Holy Names High School, Oakland, CA; Ramona Convent Secondary School, Alhambra, CA; Villa Maria del Mar, Santa Cruz, CA; Next Step Learning Center, Oakland, CA; Holy Names Academy, Seattle, WA.

Sisters ministering in works sponsored by other institutions/agencies include Formal Education in Universities, Secondary, Elementary and Preschools; Adult Basic Education/Literacy; Administration in Diocesan Offices; Campus Ministry; Pastoral Ministry; Religious Education, Health Care and Social Services.

Represented in the Archdioceses of Los Angeles, Portland, Oregon, San Francisco, Seattle and Washington and in the Dioceses of Albany, Monterey, Oakland, St. Petersburg, Spokane, Venice and Yakima.

[2000] (C.S.R.)—SISTERS OF THE REDEEMER (P)

First foundation in the United States on March 19, 1924 in Baltimore, Maryland.

American Province of the Immaculate Conception: 1600 Huntingdon Pike, Meadowbrook, PA 19046. Tel: 215-914-4100; Fax: 215-914-4171. Sr. Ellen Marvel, C.S.R., Province Leader. Email: emarvel@holyredeemer.com.

Legal Holdings and Titles: Holy Redeemer Ministries; Holy Redeemer Health System; Holy Redeemer Hospital; Holy Redeemer St. Joseph Manor; Holy Redeemer Lafayette; Holy Redeemer Transitional Care Unit; Holy Redeemer Home Health and Hospice Services; Redeemer Village & Redeemer Village II; Drueding Center; HRH Management Corporation; Holy Redeemer Multi-Care, Inc.; Convents—Epiphany Community; St. Teresa of Avila Community Convent; Redeemer Community; Annunciation-Formation Community.

Represented in the Archdioceses of Newark and Philadelphia and in the Dioceses of Camden, Metuchen and Trenton.

[2010] (O.SS.R.)—ORDER OF THE MOST HOLY REDEEMER (P) (Redemptoristine Nuns)

Founded 1731 by St. Alphonsus de Liguori and Blessed Maria Celeste. (Contemplative). Rule approved 1750 by Pope Benedict XIV. First United States Monastery (1957) Esopus, New York.

Monastery of St. Alphonsus (1960): 200 Liguori Dr., Liguori, MO 63057. Tel: 636-464-1093; Fax: 636-464-1073. Email: rednuns@gmail.com. Sr. Janice Marie Klein, O.Ss.R., Prioress; Sr. Ann Marie Gool, O.Ss.R., Supr.

Total in Community: 5.

Properties owned and/or sponsored: Order of the Most Holy Redeemer, Monastery of the Most Holy Redeemer, Thailand.

Represented in the Archdioceses of New York and St. Louis.

Redemptoristine Nuns: 89 Hiddenbrooke Dr., Beacon, NY 12508-2230. Tel: 845-831-3132; Email: rednunsny@gmail.com; Web: www.rednunsny.org. Sr. Moira K. Quinn, O.SS.R., Prioress.

Total in Community: 5; Solemnly Professed Nuns: 5. Solemn Vows, Papal Enclosure.

[2040] (S.H.S.)—SISTERS OF THE HOLY SPIRIT (D)

Founded in the United States in 1913 at Donora, Pennsylvania.

5246 Clarwin Ave., Ross Township, Pittsburgh, PA 15229-2208. Tel: 412-931-1917; Fax: 412-931-3711; Email: SHS5246info@gmail.com; Web: www.sistersoftheholyspirit.com. Sr. Diane Smith, S.H.S., Supr.

Total in Community: 22.

Facilities owned and staffed: Martina Spiritual Renewal Center Inc.

Sisters serve: Elementary Schools; Religious Education; Health and Social Services; Retreat Services; Pastoral Ministry.

Represented in the Diocese of Pittsburgh.

[2050] (S.H.Sp.)—SISTERS OF THE HOLY SPIRIT AND MARY IMMACULATE (P)

Founded in America in 1893. Papal Approbation 1930; final Approbation, 1938.

General Motherhouse: Convent of the Holy Spirit and Mary Immaculate, 300 Yucca St., San Antonio, TX 78203. Tel: 210-533-5149. Sr. Geraldine Klein, S.H.Sp., Gen. Supr.

Professed Sisters: 65.

Legal Holdings: Holy Spirit Trust; Holy Spirit Motherhouse; Healy Murphy Center, Inc., San Antonio, TX.

Ministry in the following areas: Education; Health Care; Pastoral Ministry; Catechetical Ministry; Social Service; Retreats.

Represented in the Archdiocese of San Antonio and in the Dioceses of Brownsville, El Paso, Fort Worth, Jackson, Lafayette (LA) and Shreveport. Also in Zambia.

[2060] (O.SS.T.)—SISTERS OF THE MOST HOLY TRINITY (P)

Founded in Rome in 1198. First foundation in the United States in 1920.

General Motherhouse: Rome, Italy.

Provincial House: Immaculate Conception Province, 21281 Chardon Rd., Euclid, OH 44117. Tel: 216-481-8232; Fax: 216-481-6577. Sr. Phyllis Ann Lavalle, O.SS.T., Supr.

Total in Community: 15.

Properties owned and/or sponsored: Our Lady of Lourdes Shrine, Euclid, OH.

Represented in the Diocese of Cleveland.

[2070] (S.U.S.C.)—HOLY UNION SISTERS (P)

Founded in France in 1826. First foundation in the United States in 1886.

Generalate: Rome, Italy. Sr. Paula Coelho, S.U.S.C., Supr. Gen.

United States Province: 444 Centre St., P.O. Box 410, Milton, MA 02186-0006. Tel: 617-696-8765; Fax: 617-696-8571. Email: kathleen.corrigan@husmilton.org. Province Leadership Team: Sr. Kathleen Corrigan, S.U.S.C.; Sr. Joan Guertin, S.U.S.C.; Sr. Carol Regan, S.U.S.C.

Total in Community: 54.

Legal Title: Holy Union Sisters, Inc.

Ministry in the field of Religious and Academic Education; Social Services; Pastoral Care; Pastoral Ministry; Spiritual Renewal; Ministry Education; Family Ministry; Peace & Justice; Spanish Apostolate; Ministry to the Handicapped; Ministry to Immigrants and Refugees.

Represented in the Archdioceses of Baltimore and Boston and in the Dioceses of Brooklyn, Fall River, Lexington, Providence and Rockville Centre.

[2080] (G.H.M.S.)—HOME MISSION SISTERS OF AMERICA (D) (Glenmary Sisters)

Founded July 16, 1952.

Motherhouse: Glenmary Sisters - Glenmary Center, P.O. Box 22264, Owensboro, KY 42304-2264. Tel: 270-686-8401. Sr. Darlene Presley, Mother Supr.

Total in Community: 6.

Service to Home Missions.

Represented in the Dioceses of Lexington, Owensboro and Springfield Cape-Girardeau.

[2090] (H.V.M.)—SISTERS HOME VISITORS OF MARY (D)

Founded in Detroit, Michigan in 1949.

Motherhouse: 121 E. Boston Blvd., Detroit, MI 48202. Tel: 313-869-2160; Email: homevisitors@att.net.

Total in Community: 40.

Ministry in Urban Parishes; Schools and Preschools; Religious Education, RCIA.

Represented in the Archdiocese of Detroit. Also in Nigeria.

[2100] (C.H.M.)—CONGREGATION OF THE HUMILITY OF MARY (P)

Founded in France in 1854. First United States foundation in 1864.

Motherhouse: Humility of Mary Center, 820 West Central Park Ave., Davenport, IA 52804. Email: sisters@chmiowa.org. Sr. Mary Ann Vogel, C.H.M., Pres.

Total in Community: 63.

Legal Titles: Congregation of the Humility of Mary; Congregation of the Humility of Mary Charitable Trust.

Ministry in Schools and Colleges; Migrant Programs; Pastoral Ministry; Social Services; Inner City Programs; Health Services; Ministry to the Elderly; and Retreat Center.

Represented in the Archdiocese of Denver and in the Dioceses of Arlington, Davenport, Des Moines, Great Falls-Billings, Jackson, Rockford and Syracuse. Also in Mexico.

[2110] (H.M.)—SISTERS OF THE HUMILITY OF MARY, INC. (P)

Founded in France in 1854. First foundation in the United States in 1864 at Villa Maria, Lawrence County, Pennsylvania, 16155.

Motherhouse: Villa Maria Community Center, P.O. Box 914, Villa Maria, PA 16155-0914. Tel: 724-964-8861; Fax: 724-964-8082. Email: treardon@humilityofmary.org; scunningham@humilityofmary.org. Sr. Carol Anne Smith, H.M., Pastoral Leader & Major Supr.; Sr. Joanne Gardner, H.M., Community Archivist.

Total in Community: 107.

Ministry in the field of Academic and Religious Education; Hospitals and Nursing Home, Assisted Living; Parish and Pastoral Ministries; Legal Services; Social Services; Ministry to persons who are Native Americans, Migrants, Hispanics, Haitians and Rural Poor; Housing Ministry to Single Parents, Independent Elderly; Retreat Ministry; Spirituality and Counseling; Advocacy for Eco-justice.

Legal Holdings and Titles: Sisters of the Humility of Mary (Motherhouse), Villa Maria, PA; Sisters of the Humility of Mary Charitable Trust, Villa Maria, PA; Magnificat High School, Rocky River, OH; Villa Maria Education and Spirituality Center, Villa Maria, PA; Humility of Mary Housing, Inc., Akron, OH; HM Housing Development Corporation, Akron, OH; HM Life Opportunity Services, Akron, OH; Villa Maria Residential Services, Villa Maria, PA.

Represented in the Dioceses of Cleveland, Erie, Grand Island, Palm Beach, Pittsburgh, Wheeling-Charleston and Youngstown.

[2140]—SISTERS OF THE IMMACULATE CONCEPTION OF THE BLESSED VIRGIN MARY (LITHUANIAN) (P)

Founded in Marijampole, Lithuania in 1918. First foundation in the United States in 1936.

American Headquarters: Immaculate Conception Convent, 600 Liberty Hwy., Putnam, CT 06260-2503. Tel: 860-928-7955. Sr. Igne Marijosius, Supr.

Total in Community: 8.

Legal Titles & Holdings: Immaculate Conception Convent; Matulaitis Nursing Home, Putnam, CT.

Ministry in Nursing Homes; Retreat House; Catechetical Work in Parishes; Summer Camp for Children and Young Adults.

Represented in the Archdiocese of Chicago and in the Dioceses of Norwich.

[2145] (O.S.A.)—CONGREGATION OF AUGUSTINIAN SISTERS SERVANTS OF JESUS AND MARY (P)

Generalate: via Nomentana 514, Rome, Italy. Mother Tessie Bezzina, Gen.

Malta Province: 208 Fleur-de-Lys, B'Kara, Malta Mother Atanasia Buhagiar, Prov.

U.S. Foundation: St. John Convent, 531 E. Broadway, Brandenburg, KY 40108. Sr. Lydia Falzon, Supr.

Total in Community: 4.

Represented in the Archdiocese of Louisville.

[2150] (I.H.M.)—SISTERS, SERVANTS OF THE IMMACULATE HEART OF MARY (P)

Founded in the United States in 1845.

SSIHM Leadership Council: 610 W. Elm Ave., Monroe, MI 48162-7909. Tel: 734-240-9700; Fax: 734-240-9784. Sr. Mary Jane Herb, I.H.M., Pres.

Total in Congregation: 208.

Legal Titles: Marian High School for Young Women, Bloomfield Hills, MI; Visitation North Spirituality Center; IHM Senior Living Community, Inc., Monroe, Mich.

Ministry in Academic and Religious Education at all levels; Pastoral Ministry (parish, healthcare, campus and prison settings); Diocesan and Parish Administration; Peace and Justice; Social Service and Counseling; Spiritual Growth and Development; Overseas Ministries; Ministry in Health Care.

Represented in the Archdioceses of Boston, Chicago, Detroit, Milwaukee, Oklahoma City, Philadelphia,

San Juan and Washington and in the Dioceses of Cleveland, El Paso, Gaylord, Green Bay, Joliet, Lansing, Marquette, Oakland, Orlando, Raleigh, Richmond, Saginaw and Toledo. Also in Mexico and South Africa.

River House - IHM Spirituality Center: 805 W. Elm Ave., Monroe, MI 48162. Tel: 734-240-5494; Email: riverhouse@ihmsisters.org; Web: www.ihmsisters.org.

Sisters: 3.

Sponsorship of I.H.M. Congregation.

Visitation North Spirituality Center: 7227 Lahser Rd., Bloomfield Hills, MI 48301. Tel: 248-433-0950; Fax: 248-433-0952; Email: visitationnorth@ihmsisters.org; Web: www.visitationnorth.org.

Sisters: 2.

Sponsorship of I.H.M. Congregation.

[2160] (I.H.M.)—SISTERS, SERVANTS OF THE IMMACULATE HEART OF MARY (P)

Founded in 1845. Established in Scranton, Pennsylvania in 1871.

General Motherhouse: Immaculate Heart of Mary Center, 2300 Adams Ave., Scranton, PA 18509. Tel: 570-342-6850; Fax: 570-346-5439. Email: communications@sistersofihm.org; Web: www.sistersofihm.org. Sr. Ellen Maroney, I.H.M., Pres.

Total in Community: 291.

Properties owned and/or sponsored: IHM Center; Pascucci Family Our Lady of Peace Residence; Our Lady of Grace Center; Manhasset, NY. Ministry in the field of Academic Education; Health Care; Retreat Ministries; Directors of Religious Education; Pastoral Ministries; Social Services; Campus Ministry; Volunteer Services; Family Ministry; Ministry to Hispanics; Diocesan Offices.

Represented in the Archdioceses of Baltimore, Boston, Chicago, New York, Santa Fe, San Antonio, St. Louis and Washington and in the Dioceses of Albany, Brooklyn, Camden, Harrisburg, Paterson, Pittsburgh, Rockville Centre, St. Augustine, St. Petersburg, Scranton and Syracuse. Also in Mexico and Peru.

[2170] (I.H.M.)—SISTERS, SERVANTS OF THE IMMACULATE HEART OF MARY (P)

Founded in 1845. Established in West Chester, Pennsylvania in 1872.

General Motherhouse: Villa Maria House of Studies, 1 Our Lady Circle, Malvern, PA 19355. Tel: 610-647-2160; Fax: 610-889-0509. Email: ihmsisters1845@gmail.com. Sr. Mary Ellen Tennity, I.H.M., Gen. Supr.

Total in Congregation: 585.

Ministry in the field of Academic Education at all levels in the U.S. and Peru; Pastoral Ministry; Literacy Centers; Infirmary Work.

Represented in the Archdioceses of Miami and Philadelphia and in the Dioceses of Allentown, Arlington, Camden, Harrisburg, Manchester, Metuchen, Richmond, Savannah and Trenton.

[2180] (I.H.M.)—SISTERS OF THE IMMACULATE HEART OF MARY (P)

Founded in Spain in 1848. First foundation in the United States in 1871.

General Motherhouse: Girona, Spain

U.S. Province: 3820 N. Sabino Canyon Rd., Tucson, AZ 85750-6534. Tel: 520-419-3605. Sr. Alice M. Martinez, Supr.; Sr. Veronica Loya, Sec. & Community Archivist.

Total in Community: 12.

Ministry in the field of Academic and Religious Education.

Represented in the Diocese of Tucson.

[2182] (I.H.M.M.)—SISTERS OF THE IMMACULATE HEART OF MARY OF MIRINAE (P)

Founded in 1976 by Rev. Francis Haengman Tiyeng, Mirinae, Diocese of Suwon, Korea, under the motto, Through the Immaculate Heart of Mary to the Most Holy Trinity.

Motherhouse: Surichigol, Korea, South

U.S. Foundation: Immaculate Heart of Mary Pre School, 423 South Commonwealth Ave., Los Angeles, CA 90020. Sr. Cyrilla Kim, I.H.M.M., Sec.

Properties owned and/or sponsored: Sisters of the Immaculate Heart of Mary of Mirinae, Los Angeles, CA.

Ministry in retreat work, school, youth and care for the aged.

Represented in the Archdiocese of Los Angeles.

[2183] (I.H.M.)—SISTERS OF THE IMMACULATE HEART OF MARY MOTHER OF CHRIST, NIGERIA (P)

Founded in Nigeria, West Africa in 1937. Classified with the Pontifical Institute Right in 1973.

Motherhouse-Immaculate Heart Generalate: P.O. Box 1551, Odoakpu-Onitsha Anambra State, Nigeria Tel: 234-706-385-0098; Fax: 234-813-569-4827. Mother Mary Claude Oguh, Mother Gen.

Total in Congregation: 983.

U.S.A. Regional House: Immaculate Heart Convent, 1209A South Walnut Ave., Freeport, IL 61032. Tel: 815-297-8287. Email: guadaluperegion@gmail.com. Sr. Marilyn Umunnakwe, Regl. Supr.

Total number of Sisters in the U.S.: 44.

Legal Title: The Congregation of the Sisters of the Immaculate Heart of Mary Mother of Christ - Nigeria.

Ministry in Education; Hospital/Clinic, Pastoral/Social Services; Care of the Aged; Diocesan House Care.

Represented in the Archdioceses of Milwaukee, St. Paul-Minneapolis and Santa Fe and in the Dioceses of Belleville, Des Moines, Gallup, Oklahoma, Phoenix, Rockford and Syracuse.

[2185] (I.H.M.)—SISTERS OF THE IMMACULATE HEART OF MARY OF WICHITA (D)

Founded in Olot, Spain, in 1848. First foundation in United States in 1871. Wichita foundation in 1979. Canonically established as a religious institute of Diocesan right in 2007.

Motherhouse: 3550 N. 167th St. W., Colwich, KS 67030. Tel: 316-722-9316. Mother Mary Magdalene O'Halloran, I.H.M., Gen. Supr.

Total in Community: 30.

Apostolate: Contemplation of the Word and the spread of His Message of salvation through the various works and levels of education and retreat work.

Represented in the Diocese of Wichita.

[2187] (I.C.M.)—SISTERS OF INCARNATION-CONSECRATION-MISSION (P)

Founded in Vietnam in 1969. First foundation in the United States in 1975.

Motherhouse: 403 Tan Ha, Xa Loc Tien, Huyen Bao Loc, Tinh Lam Dong, Vietnam Tel: 011-84-02633-743-666; Email: tuhoiicm@yahoo.com.

U.S. Regional House: Incarnatio-Consecratio-Missio, Inc., 5185 Jetsail Dr., Orlando, FL 32812. Tel: 407-658-4124; Fax: 407-658-4124; Email: icmorlando@yahoo.com. Sr. Marie Nguyen, I.C.M., Contact Person.

Universal Membership: 149; Aspirants: 12.

Ministry in the areas of Education; Healthcare; Missionary Outreach; Parish Ministries, Social Services and Pastoral Care.

Represented in the Dioceses of Baton Rouge and Orlando. Also in Vietnam.

[2190] (C.V.I.)—CONGREGATION OF THE INCARNATE WORD AND BLESSED SACRAMENT (P)

Founded in France in 1625. First foundation in the United States in 1853.

Motherhouse and Novitiate: Incarnate Word Convent, 3400 Bradford Pl., Houston, TX 77025-1398. Tel: 713-668-0423. Sr. Lauren Beck, C.V.I., Gen. Supr.; Sr. Dympna Lyons, Archivist.

Total in Community: 23.

Ministry in the field of Academic Education; Administration; Pastoral Care; Nursing.

Represented in the Archdiocese of Galveston-Houston.

[2200] (I.W.B.S.)—CONGREGATION OF THE INCARNATE WORD AND BLESSED SACRAMENT (P)

Founded in France in 1625. First founded in the United States in 1853.

Motherhouse and Novitiate: Incarnate Word Convent, 1101 N.E. Water St., Victoria, TX 77901-9233. Tel: 361-575-2266; Fax: 361-575-2165. Email: skgoike@gmail.com. Sr. M. Kathleen Goike, I.W.B.S., Supr. Gen. & Community Archivist.

Perpetually Professed: 47; Postulants: 1.

Legal Titles: Sisters of the Incarnate Word and Blessed Sacrament, Victoria, Texas; Sisters of the Incarnate Word and Blessed Sacrament of Victoria, Texas Medical and Retirement Trust, Victoria, TX.

Ministry in the field of Education; Social Work; Hospitals; Pastoral Ministry.

Properties owned or sponsored: Nazareth Academy, Victoria, TX; Blessed Sacrament Academy, San Antonio, TX; Amor Meus Spirituality Center, Victoria, TX.

Represented in the Archdiocese of San Antonio and in the Diocese of Victoria.

[2205] (I.W.B.S.)—SISTERS OF THE INCARNATE WORD AND BLESSED SACRAMENT (P)

Founded in France in 1625. First founded in the United States in 1853.

Motherhouse and Novitiate: Incarnate Word Convent, 5201 Lipes Blvd., Corpus Christi, TX 78413. Tel: 361-882-5413; Fax: 361-880-4152. Sr. Annette Wagner, I.W.B.S., Supr. Gen.

Sisters: 37.

Legal Titles: Convent Academy of the Incarnate Word; Incarnate Word Academy Foundation; Fannie Bluntzer Nason Renewal Center, Inc., Corpus Christi, TX.

Sisters serve and staff: Private High Schools; Private Kindergartens; Montessori; Day Care; Private Middle Schools; Private Elementary Schools; Other ministries include Vocation Ministry; Social Service; Adult Faith Formation; General Administration; Retreat Ministry; Spiritual Direction.

Represented in the Dioceses of Brownsville and Corpus Christi.

[2210] (S.I.W.)—SISTERS OF THE INCARNATE WORD AND BLESSED SACRAMENT (P)

Founded in France in 1625. First foundation in the United States in 1853.

Motherhouse and Novitiate: 6618 Pearl Rd., Parma Heights, OH 44130-3808. Tel: 440-886-6440. Sr. Margaret Taylor, S.I.W., Congregational Leader.

Total in Community: 14.

Ministry includes Evangelization; Elementary and Religious Education; Spiritual Ministry; Pastoral Ministry in Nursing Homes.

Represented in the Diocese of Cleveland.

[2230] (C.I.J.)—CONGREGATION OF THE INFANT JESUS (D)

Founded in France in 1835. First foundation in the United States in 1905.

General Motherhouse: 984 North Village Ave., Rockville Centre, NY 11570. Tel: 516-823-3800; Tel: 516-823-3808; Fax: 516-594-0412. Email: hmkearney@aol.com. Sr. Helen Kearney, C.S.J., Canonical Trustee.

Total in Community: 20.

Corporate Title: Nursing Sisters of the Sick Poor Inc. Ministry in the fields of Nursing; Social Work; Physical Therapy; Pastoral Care; Chaplains; Retreat Work; Parish Ministry; and other works related to Health Services.

Represented in the Diocese of Rockville Centre.

[2250] (O.S.B.)—CONGREGATION OF BENEDICTINES OF JESUS CRUCIFIED (P)

Founded in France in 1930. First foundation in the United States in Devon, PA in 1955. Second foundation in Newport, RI in 1962. Both foundations merged in Branford, CT in 2001 at the Monastery of the Glorious Cross. Monastery building closed in 2019.

General Motherhouse: Brou-sur-Chantereine, France Sr. Anne Sophie Robitaillie, Prioress Gen.

U.S. Foundations: Community resides at St. Mary Home, 2021 Albany Ave.,West Hartford, CT 06117. Tel: 203-640-5959. Email: mzwenker_osb@hotmail.com. Sr. Marie-Zita Wenker, O.S.B., Prioress.

Total number in the U.S.: 6.

Represented in the Archdiocese of Hartford.

[2265] (S.V.)—SISTERS OF LIFE

Founded 1991.

Annunciation (Motherhouse): 38 Montebello Rd., Suffern, NY 10901. Tel: 845-357-3547; Fax: 845-357-5040. Email: sistersoflife@sistersoflife.org. Mother Agnes Mary Donovan, S.V., Supr. Gen.

Legal Title: Sisters of Life, Inc. Ministry: to advance a sense of the sacredness of human life through prayer and missions which include serving vulnerable, pregnant women; accompaniment of women suffering after abortion; campus ministry; the operation of a retreat center; staffing of the Respect Life Office of the Archdiocese of New York; and a wide spectrum of evangelization events nationally and internationally on the dignity of the human person.

Represented in the Archdioceses of Denver, New York, Philadelphia and Washington DC and in the Dioceses of Albany, Bridgeport and Phoenix. Also in Canada.

[2270] (L.C.M.)—LITTLE COMPANY OF MARY SISTERS - USA (P)

Founded in England in 1877. First foundation in the United States in 1893.

Generalate: Little Company of Mary Sisters CIO, 28 Trinity Crescent, Tooting Bec London, England, SW17 7AE.

Universal total in Congregation: 196; Final Professed Sisters: 182; Temporary Professed Sisters: 3; Novices: 3; Candidates: 2.

Region Office: Region of the Immaculate Conception, Little Company of Mary Sisters USA, 9350 S. California Ave., Evergreen Park, IL 60805. Tel: 708-229-5490. Sr. Carol Pacini, L.C.M., Region Leader.

Total in Community: 10.

Ministry in Hospitals and Health Care; Pastoral/Parish areas.

Properties owned: Little Company of Mary Hospital and Health Care Centers, Evergreen Park, IL; Memorial Hospital and Health Care Center, Jasper, IN; Little Company of Mary Health Services (Little Company of Mary Hospital, Torrance, CA)

Represented in the Archdioceses of Chicago and Los Angeles and in the Diocese of Evansville.

[2280] (P.F.M.)—LITTLE FRANCISCANS OF MARY (U.S.)

Founded in the United States in 1889.

General Motherhouse: Baie St. Paul (Charlevoix), Canada Sr. Francoise Duchesne, P.F.M., Supr. Gen.

American Region: 12 Jones St., Apt. 1, Worcester, MA 01604. Tel: 508-755-0878. Sr. Jacquelyn Alix, Treas.

Total number in Congregation including Canada and the United States: 160.

Represented in the Dioceses of Portland (In Maine) and Worcester.

[2300] (L.S.I.C.)—LITTLE SERVANT SISTERS OF THE IMMACULATE CONCEPTION (P)

(Congregatio Sororum Servularum Beatae Mariae Virginis Immaculatae Conceptae)

Founded by Blessed Edmund Bojanowski in Poland on May 3, 1850. First foundation in the United States on December 8, 1926.

General Motherhouse: Stara Wies 460, 36-200 Brzozow, skr. poczt. 66, woj. Podkarpackie, Poland Mother Beata Chwistek, L.S.I.C., Supr. Gen.

Total in Congregation: 1182.

Holy Trinity Province: Little Servants Sisters of the Immaculate Conception Provincialate-Novitiate, 1000 Cropwell Rd., Cherry Hill, NJ 08003. Tel: 856-424-1962; Fax: 856-424-5333; Email: s.dorotab@gmail.com; Web: www.lsic.com. Mother Dorota Baranowska, L.S.I.C., Supr. Prov.; Sr. Bozena Tyborowska, L.S.I.C., Vocation Dir.

Professed Sisters: 61.

Legal Titles: Congregation of the Little Servant Sisters of the Blessed Virgin Mary of the Immaculate Conception (Congregatio Sororum Servularum Beatae Mariae Virginis Immaculatae Conceptae), (Properties owned) Immaculate Conception Convent: Provincialate-Novitiate, Cherry Hill, NJ; Blessed Edmund Early Childhood Education Center, Cherry Hill, NJ; Marian Residence, Cherry Hill, NJ; St. John's Retreat House, Atlantic City, NJ; St. Joseph's Convent, Woodbridge, NJ; St. Joseph's Senior Home (Assisted Living and Nursing Center), Woodbridge, NJ.

Ministry: all levels of Religious Education, Pre-school and Academic Education; Parish Work; Social Work, Hospital Pastoral Care; Visiting Home Nursing Service; Senior Residential Homes; Assisted Living; Skilled Nursing Homes; Retreat House; Prayer Groups & Youth Ministry.

Represented in the Archdiocese of Newark and in the Dioceses of Camden, Columbus, Metuchen and Palm Beach. Also in the Philippines.

[2310] (L.S.A.)—LITTLE SISTERS OF THE ASSUMPTION (P)

Founded in France in 1865. First foundation in the United States in 1891.

General Motherhouse: 57 rue Violet, Paris, France, 75015. Sr. Nathalie Lafforgue, Supr. Gen.

United States Territory: Little Sisters of the Assumption, 475 E. 115th St., 1st Fl., New York, NY 10029. Tel: 212-289-4014; Web: www.littlesisters.org. Sr. Annette Allain, L.S.A., Territory Coord.

Total in Community: 6.

Ministry in Home Health; Community Development Supportive Family Services Located in Poverty Areas; Services are predominantly provided in the Home Setting and Center-Based.

Represented in the Archdioceses of Boston and New York and in the Diocese of Worcester.

[2330] (L.S.J.)—LITTLE SISTERS OF JESUS (P)

Founded in the Sahara in 1939. First foundation in the United States in 1952.

General Motherhouse: Rome, Italy. Sr. Dolores Francisca Gusi Castello, Prioress Gen.

Universal total in Congregation: 1100.

U.S. Regional House: 400 N. Streeper St., Baltimore, MD 21224-1230. Tel: 410-327-7863. Sr. Lynn Flear, L.S.J., Reg. Dir.

Total number in U.S.: 24.

Represented in the Archdioceses of Anchorage-Juneau, Baltimore and Washington and in the Diocese of Altoona-Johnstown.

[2331] (L.S.J.M.)—LITTLE SISTERS OF JESUS AND MARY (D)

Founded in the United States in 1974. Sr. Mary Elizabeth Gintling, Foundress.

Joseph House: P.O. Box 1755, Salisbury, MD 21802. Tel: 410-543-1645; Fax: 410-742-3390. Sr. Marilyn R. Bouchard, L.S.J.M., Supr. Gen.

Total in Community: 6.

Represented in the Diocese of Wilmington.

[2335] (L.S.O.S.F.)—LITTLE SISTERS OF ST. FRANCIS OF ASSISI

Founded in 1923.

Motherhouse: Nkokonjeru, Uganda. Generalate: Jinja, Uganda.

Provincial House: St. Francis Convent, 11300 Continental Road, Quinton, VA 23141.

Total Sisters in Order: 890

Ministry in Education, Healthcare, Social Work, Faith Formation, Dieticians, Fashion Designers.

Represented in the Archdioceses of Baltimore, Milwaukee and New York and in the Dioceses of Brooklyn, Richmond and Scranton. Also in Binghampton.

[2340] (L.S.P.)—LITTLE SISTERS OF THE POOR (P)

Founded in France in 1839. First foundation in the United States in 1868.

General Motherhouse: 3 La Tour St. Joseph, 35190, St. Pern, France Mother Maria del Monte Auxiliadora, Supr. Gen.

Province of Brooklyn (1868): Queen of Peace Residence, 110-30 221st St., Queens Village, NY 11429. Mother Alice Marie Jones, L.S.P., Prov.

Total number in Province: 90.

Ministry in Homes for the Aged.

Represented in the Archdioceses of Hartford, Philadelphia and New York and in the Dioceses of Brooklyn, Metuchen, Paterson and Providence.

Province of Baltimore: Little Sisters of the Poor, 601 Maiden Choice Ln., Catonsville, MD 21228-3698. Tel: 410-744-9367; Fax: 410-747-0601. Sr. Loraine Marie Maguire, L.S.P., Prov.

Total number in Province: 88.

Ministry in Homes for the Aged.

Represented in the Archdioceses of Baltimore, Cincinnati, Indianapolis, Mobile, New Orleans and Washington and in the Dioceses of Cleveland, Pittsburgh, Richmond, Toledo and Wilmington.

Province of Chicago: Little Sisters of the Poor, Chicago Province, Inc., 80 W. Northwest Hwy., Palatine, IL 60067-3582. Tel: 847-358-5700; Fax: 847-934-6852. Sr. Julie Horseman, L.S.P., Prov.

Total number in Province: 77.

Ministry in Homes for the Aged.

Represented in the Archdioceses of Chicago, Denver, Los Angeles, Louisville, St. Louis, St. Paul-Minneapolis and San Francisco and in the Dioceses of Gallup and Kansas City-St. Joseph.

[2345] (P.O.S.C.)—LITTLE WORKERS OF THE SACRED HEARTS (P)

Founded in Italy in 1892. First foundation in the U.S. in 1948.

General House: Via dei Pamphili 3, Rome, Italy, 00152. Motherhouse and Novitiate: Our Lady of Grace Convent, 635 Glenbrook Rd., Stamford, CT 06906-1409. Tel: 203-348-5531. Sr. Gesuina Gencarelli, P.O.S.C., U.S. Delegate & Supr.

Ministry in Day Care; Catechetics; Preschool.

Represented in the Archdioceses of Philadelphia and Washington and in the Diocese of Bridgeport.

[2350] (SLW)—SISTERS OF THE LIVING WORD (D)

Founded in the United States in 1975.

General Motherhouse: The Living Word Center, 950 Lee St., Ste. 200, Des Plaines, IL 60016. Tel: 847-577-5972; Fax: 847-577-5980; Web: www.slw.org. Congregational Leadership: Sr. Sharon Glumb, SLW; Sr. Carrie Miller, SLW; Sr. Kristine Vorenkamp, SLW.

Total in Community: 45.

Ministry in the field of Academic and Religious Education; Health Care; Parish Ministry and Social Services.

Represented in the Archdioceses of Chicago, New Orleans, St. Louis and St. Paul-Minneapolis and in the Diocese of Tampa.

[2360] (S.L.)—SISTERS OF LORETTO AT THE FOOT OF THE CROSS (P)

Founded in America in 1812.

General Motherhouse & Novitiate: Loretto Motherhouse and Novitiate, Nerinx, KY 40049. Tel: 270-865-5811.

Administrative Office: 515 Nerinx Rd., Nerinx, KY 40049. Tel: 270-431-0100; Fax: 270-865-2200. Sr. Barbara Nicholas, S.L., Pres.

Legal Title: Loretto Literary and Benevolent Institution.

Ministry in the field of Academic and Religious Education at all levels; Health Care-Aging; Community Administration; Pastoral Ministry; Social Justice-Social Service; Administration; Medicine and Nursing; Prayer Retreats; Clerical Offices; Consultants; Spirituality Center.

Represented in the Archdioceses of Denver, Indianapolis, Louisville, St. Louis, Santa Fe and in the Dioceses of El Paso, Kansas City-St. Joseph, Knoxville and Lexington.

[2370] (I.B.V.M.)—INSTITUTE OF THE BLESSED VIRGIN MARY (LORETTO SISTERS) (P)

Founded in St. Omer, Belgium, 1609. First foundation in Canada in 1847; in the United States in 1880.

Generalate: Casa Loreto, Via Massaua 3, Rome, Italy, 00162. Sr. Noelle Corscadden, I.B.V.M., Institute Leader.

Total in Congregation: 675.

Regional Office United States: P.O. Box 508, Wheaton, IL 60187. Tel: 630-653-4740; Fax: 630-653-4886. Development Office Email: development@ibvm.us. Web: www.ibvm.us. Leadership Team: Sr. Mary Carton, I.B.V.M.; Sr. Judy Illig, I.B.V.M.; Sr. Helen Timothy, I.B.V.M. Tel: 630-665-3814. Total in Community: 45.

Ministries: High School; Grade School; Mary Ward Center-English as a Second Language; Pastoral Ministry; Social Work; Spiritual Direction, Art and Spirituality, Regional Office; Loretto Development Office; Vocation Ministry.

Properties owned: Houses in Arizona and Illinois.

Represented in the Archdioceses of Chicago and Milwaukee and in the Dioceses of El Paso, Joliet and Phoenix.

[2375] (L.H.C.)—LOVERS OF THE HOLY CROSS (D)

Founded in 1670.

Motherhouse: Vietnam.

U.S. Community Office: 14116 Heritage Lane, Silver Spring, MD 20906. Archdiocese of Washington: Agnes Convent, 14116 Heritage Lane, Silver Spring, MD 20906. Diocese of Richmond: Paula Convent, 320 Whealton Road, Hampton, VA 23666. Sr. Therese Nu Tran, L.H.C., Supr. Gen. in Vietnam; Sr. Mary Thu Do, L.H.C., Local Supr. Email: lhchnhk@gmail.com; Tel: 832-758-7096.

Total Sisters: 476

Ministry in Education, Healthcare, Evangelization and Social Work.

Represented in the Archdiocese of Washington and in the Diocese of Richmond.

[2385] (L.H.C.N.T.)—LOVERS OF THE HOLY CROSS OF NHA TRANG (D)

Founded in Vietnam in 1950. First Foundation in the United States in 2003.

Motherhouse: 89 Van Tu Tay Cam Hoa Cam Ranh, Khanh Hoa, Nha Trang, Vietnam

Regional House: 12323 Alondra Blvd., Norwalk, CA 90650. Tel: 562-567-1502; 562-377-2844. Email: lovershollycrossnt@gmail.com; anhtram69@yahoo.com. Sr. Anna Anh Tram Tran, L.H.C.N.T., Rel. Supr.

Total in Congregation: 539; U.S. Community: 10.

Ministry in Pastoral Care: religious education for youth and/or adults, faith formation.

[2390] (L.H.C.)—LOVERS OF THE HOLY CROSS SISTERS (D)

Founded in 1670 in Vietnam by Bishop Pierre Lambert de la Motte. First foundation in the United States in 1976. Established as an autonomous institute of Consecrated Life of Diocesan Right in 1992.

General Motherhouse: Holy Cross Convent, 14700 South Van Ness Ave., Gardena, CA 90249. Tel: 714-426-0859. Sr. Grace Duc Le, L.H.C., Supr. Gen.

Sisters: 65; Novices: 9; Postulants: 3; Aspirants: 9; Oblates: 1.

Legal Title: Lovers of the Holy Cross Sisters, Inc.

Represented in the Archdiocese of Los Angeles and in the Dioceses of Orange and San Bernardino.

[2392] (L.H.C.)—LOVERS OF THE HOLY CROSS SISTERS (P) (Sisters, Lovers of the Holy Cross)

Founded in Vietnam in 1670 by Bishop Pierre Lambert de la Motte. First foundation in the United States in 1975.

U.S. Foundation: St. Theresa Convent, 43 Crown Ln., Westbury, NY 11590. Tel: 516-333-9464. Sr. Theresa Nguyen, L.H.C., Supr.

Legal Title: Sisters, Lovers of the Holy Cross, Inc.

Represented in the Diocese of Rockville Centre.

[2397] (L.H.C.]—QUINHON MISSIONARY SISTERS OF THE HOLY CROSS (D)

Founded in Vietnam in 1670 by Bishop Pierre Lambert de la Motte. First community established in the United States in 1986. U.S. Province established in 2011. The QuiNhon Missionary Sisters of the Holy Cross are residing in seven convents in California.

Motherhouse: Qui Nhon, Vietnam.

U.S. Province: QuiNhon Missionary Sisters of the Holy Cross, 1685 Humphrey Dr., Concord, CA 94519. Tel.: 925-674-9639. Email: menthangiaqn@gmail.com; Web: newhome.mtgqn.org/en/. Sr. Catherine Phuong Dang, L.H.C., Prov. Supr.

Professed Sisters: 30; Aspirant: 1.

Ministry in Religious Education; Catholic School Education; Pastoral Care; Nursing; Spiritual Direction; Parish work.

Represented in Archdiocese of San Francisco and the Dioceses of Oakland and San Jose.

[2400] (M.S.)—MARIAN SISTERS OF THE DIOCESE OF LINCOLN (D)

Marycrest Motherhouse: 6765 N. 112th, Waverly, NE 68462. Tel: 402-786-2750; Fax: 402-786-7256; Email: sr.annmarie-zierke@cdolinc.net. Mother Ann Marie Zierke, M.S., Major Supr.

Total in Community: 37.

Ministry in the field of Education; Special Education; Health Care; Catechetics; Social Work.

Represented in the Diocese of Lincoln.

[2410] (M.S.C.)—CONGREGATION OF THE MARIANITES OF HOLY CROSS (P)

Founded in France in 1841. First foundation in the United States in 1843.

Congregational Administration Headquarters: 21388 Smith Rd., Covington, LA 70435. Tel: 985-893-5201; Web: www.marianites.org. Sr. Ann Lacour, M.S.C., Congregational Leader.

Total Number in North America: 82.

Ministry in Diocesan Administration and Parishes; Social & Health Services; and the field of Education.

Legal Holdings or Titles: Prompt Succor Nursing Home, Opelousas, LA; C'est la Vie (Senior Citizen Independent Living Units), Opelousas, LA.

Represented in the Archdiocese of New Orleans and in the Dioceses of Baton Rouge, Houma-Thibodaux, Lafayette (LA) and Trenton. Also in Burkina-Faso, Canada, France and Ireland.

[2420] (S.M.S.M.)—MARIST MISSIONARY SISTERS (MISSIONARY SISTERS OF THE SOCIETY OF MARY) INC. (P)

Founded in France in 1845 for the mission in the South Pacific. First foundation in the United States in Boston, MA in 1922.

Motherhouse: Via Cassia, 1243, Rome, Italy, 00189.

North American Regional Office: 349 Grove St., Waltham, MA 02453. Tel: 781-893-0149; Fax: 781-899-6838; Email: admin@maristsmsm.org. Sr. Helen Muller, S.M.S.M., Regl. Leader, Region of the Americas.

Universal Total in Congregation: 397; Total in Region of Americas: 95.

Legal Title: Missionary Sisters of the Society of Mary

Ministries include: catechetical, medical, educational and social services; pastoral ministry; formation of laity for leadership and a great concern for the poorest and most neglected. Working by preference among people of different cultures and languages, to bring about greater understanding, dignity and mutual respect. Formation is international with the novitiate in Belmont, MA.

Represented in 25 countries around the world including the Archdiocese of Boston and in the Dioceses of Oakland and San Diego. Also in Jamaica and Peru.

[2440] (S.M.I.)—CATECHIST SISTERS OF MARY IMMACULATE HELP OF CHRISTIANS, INC. (P)

Catechist Sisters of Mary Immaculate, Help of Christians Founded in India in 1948 by the late Bishop Louis LaRavoire Morrow, Bishop of Krishnagar, India.

General Motherhouse: Krishnagar, Nadia Dist., West Bengal, India, 741 101. Sr. Dina Vellamaruthunkal, S.M.I., Supr. Gen.

Universal total in Congregation: 665.

U.S. Foundation (1981): Sisters of Mary Immaculate, 118 Park Rd., Leechburg, PA 15656. Tel: 724-845-2828; Email: lbgsmi@gmail.com. Sr. Jessy George, S.M.I., Delegation Supr.

Total in Community: 5.

Legal Holdings and Titles: Bishop Morrow Personal Care Home, Leechburg, PA

[2445] (S.M.I.)—SISTERS OF MARY IMMACULATE OF NYERI (P)

Founded in 1918 in Nyeri, Kenya. Established in U.S. in 1999.

Motherhouse: Nyeri, Kenya.

Generalate: Sisters of Mary Immaculate Generalate, P.O. Box 306, 10100, Nyeri, Kenya. U.S. Delegation: 400 State St., Elmer, NJ 08318. Sr. Esther Njoki Munyiri, S.M.I., Supr. Gen.; Sr. Anne Mugo, S.M.I., Delegation Supr.

Professed Sisters: 373; Novices: 25; U.S. Professed Sisters: 18

Ministry in Nursing and Pastoral Work.

Represented in the Dioceses of Camden and Brooklyn.

[2450] (S.M.P.)—SISTERS OF MARY OF THE PRESENTATION (P)

Founded in France. First foundation in the United States in 1903.

General Motherhouse: 27 Rue de la Barriere, B.P. 31, 22250 Broons, France.

U.S. Regional Convent & Novitiate at Maryvale: 3150 116A Ave. SE, Valley City, ND 58072-9620. Tel: 701-845-2864. Email: maryvaleSMP@gmail.com. Sr. Suzanne Stahl, Reg. Supr.

Total in Community: 15.

Ministry in the field of Retreat Centers; Parish Ministry; Hospitals, Nursing Homes and Home Health Agency.

Represented in the Diocese of Fargo.

[2460] (S.M.R.)—SOCIETY OF MARY REPARATRIX (P)

Founded in France in 1857. First foundation in the United States in 1908.

Generalate: Society Di Maria Riparatrice, Via dei Lucchesi 3, Rome, Italy, 00187. Sr. Aurora Torres Hernandez, Supr. Gen.

Total International Membership: 403.

U.S. Region: 10065 Northway Ave., Allen Park, MI 48101. Tel: 313-383-3312. Region Team Sr. Veronica Blake, S.M.R.; Sr. Ann Kasparek, S.M.R.

Total in Community: 11.

Represented in the Archdioceses of Detroit and New York and in the Diocese of Brooklyn.

[2470] (M.M.)—MARYKNOLL SISTERS OF ST. DOMINIC (P)

Founded in New York 1912.

Orientation Program: Maryknoll Sisters, Sr. Shu Chen Wu, M.M., Dir.

Center: Maryknoll Sisters Center, Maryknoll, NY 10545-0311. Tel: 914-941-7575. Sr. Jeong Mi Lee, Dir.; Sr. Teresa Hougnon, M.M., Community Pres.; Sr. Genie Castillo Natividad, M.M., Vice Pres.; Sr. Maria Leonor Montiel, M.M., General Sec.; Sr. Claris Zwareva, M.M., Team Member. Center Coordinators: Sr. Rebecca Macugay, M.M.; Sr. Carolyn White, M.M.; Sr. Mercy Mtaita, M.M.

Total in Congregation: 303

Legal Titles and Holdings: Maryknoll Sisters of St. Dominic, Inc.; Maryknoll Mission Institute.

Represented in the Archdioceses of Baltimore, Boston, Chicago, Cincinnati, Detroit, Galveston-Houston, Hartford, Los Angeles, New York, Portland in Oregon, San Antonio and Washington and in the Dioceses of Baker, Brownsville, Charlotte, Gallup, Harrisburg, Honolulu, Kansas City-St. Joseph, Madison, Oakland, Palm Beach, Phoenix, Providence and San Jose.

[2480] (M.M.M.)—MEDICAL MISSIONARIES OF MARY (P)

Founded in Nigeria in 1937. First United States Foundation in 1950.

Congregation Centre: Rosemount, Booterstown Ave., Blackrock. County Dublin, Ireland. Sr. Ursula Sharpe, M.M.M., Congregational Leader.

Medical Missionaries of Mary: 179 Highland Ave., Somerville, MA. Tel: 617-666-3223. Email: mdommm2014@gmail.com; Web: www.mmmworldwide.org. Sr. Therese McDonough, M.M.M., Area Councilor, Area of the Americas.

Total in Congregation: 310.

Represented in the Archdioceses of Boston, Chicago and in the Diocese of Richmond.

[2490] (M.M.S.)—MEDICAL MISSION SISTERS (P)

Generalate: London, England. Sr. Agnes Lanfermann, M.M.S.

Universal total in Congregation: 500.

North American Headquarters (1925): 8400 Pine Rd., Philadelphia, PA 19111. Tel: 215-742-6100; North America Coordinating Team: Sr. M. Sue Sopczynski, M.M.S., Sr. Helen Lembeck, M.M.S.; Sr. Suzanne Maschek, M.M.S.; Sr. Lucy Klien-Gebbinck, M.M.S.

Total number in North America: 65.

Legal Titles: Society of Catholic Medical Missionaries, Inc.; Society of Catholic Medical Missionaries Generalate, Inc.

Represented in the Archdioceses of Boston, Hartford, Philadelphia and in the Dioceses of Richmond and Tucson.

[2500] (M.S.J.)—MEDICAL SISTERS OF ST. JOSEPH (P)

Founded in Kerala, South India, 1946.

General Motherhouse: Dharmagiri, P.O. Kothamangalam, Kerala, India, 686691. Sr. Philomy, M.S.J., Supr. Gen.

U.S. Foundation (1985): Medical Sisters of Joseph, 3435 E. Funston, Wichita, KS 67218. Tel: 316-686-4746. Sr. Laly Josmy George, M.S.J., Supr.

Total in Congregation: 900.

Ministry as Health Care Apostolates.

Represented in the Diocese of Wichita.

[2510] (M.M.B.)—MERCEDARIAN MISSIONARIES OF BERRIZ (P)

Order originated in Berriz, Spain 1548. Transformed into a missionary institute in 1930 in Spain. First foundation in U.S. in 1946 in Kansas City, MO.

Total Number of Sisters in the Institute: 383.

Generalate: Mercedarie Missionarie di Berriz, Via Iberia 8, Rome, Italy, 00183. Tel: 39-068-41-3441. Sr. Lourdes Garostola, M.M.B., Gen. Coord.

U.S. Regional House: Mercedarian Missionaries of Berriz, 2115 Maturanna Dr., #101B, Liberty, MO 64068-7985. Tel: 816-781-8202; Fax: 816-781-8205; Email: mmbus@sbcglobal.net; Web: mmberriz.org. Sr. Sandra Thibodeaux, M.M.B., Reg. Coord.

Total in Region: 10; Total in Institute: 383.

Ministries in Health, Pastoral Care and Religious Education.

Property sponsored: Our Lady of Mercy Country Home. Liberty, MO.

Represented in the Diocese of Kansas City-St. Joseph. Also in Africa, Japan, Taiwan, Philippines, Guam, Federated States of Micronesia, Republic of Palau, Commonwealth of the Northern Marianas, Peru, Ecuador, Guatemala, Mexico, Democratic Republic of Congo, Zambia, Spain and Rome, Italy.

[2519] (R.S.M.)—RELIGIOUS SISTERS OF MERCY OF ALMA, MICHIGAN (P)

The Religious Sisters of Mercy of Alma was officially founded on September 1, 1973; Accepted for a foundation in Saginaw Diocese on January 25, 1974; Official pontifical status and approval of Constitutions on June 18, 1982. Final approval of Constitutions May 31, 1991.

Motherhouse and Novitiate: Religious Sisters of Mercy, 1965 Michigan Ave., Alma, MI 48801. Tel: 989-463-6035. Email: religious.sisters.of.mercy@gmail.com. Mother Mary McGreevy, R.S.M., Supr.

Total in Community: 112.

Represented in the Archdioceses of Denver, Philadelphia, Seattle, St. Louis and Washington and in the Dioceses of Knoxville, Lake Charles, Lansing, Phoenix, Saginaw, Toledo, Tulsa and Winona-Rochester. Also in Australia, Germany, Italy and Scotland.

[2549] (R.S.M.)—SISTERS OF MERCY (P)

Founded in Ireland in 1831. First foundation in the United States in 1956.

General Motherhouse: Congregation of the Sisters of Mercy, 13/14 Moyle Park, Clondalkin, Dublin 22, Ireland Tel: 01-467-3737. Sr. Margaret Casey, Congregational Leader.

Total in Congregation: 2200.

U.S. Provincial House: Sisters of Mercy, 1075 Bermuda Dr., Redlands, CA 92374. Tel: 909-798-4747; Fax: 909-798-5300. Sr. Rosaline O'Connor, R.S.M., Prov. Leader.

Professed Sisters in U.S. Province: 52.

Legal Title: Congregation of the Sisters of Mercy-San Bernardino.

Ministry in the field of Religious Education; Parishes; Social Services; Diocesan Offices.

Represented in the Archdioceses of Chicago, Miami and in the Dioceses of Memphis, Mobile, Monterey, Oakland, Orlando, Palm Beach, Providence, Sacramento, St. Augustine, San Diego, San Jose, Santa Rosa, San Bernardino and Venice.

U.S. Foundation: St. Joan of Arc, 500 S.W. 4th Ave., Boca Raton, FL 33432. Tel: 561-368-6655. Sr. Rosaline O'Connor, R.S.M., Prov. Leader.

Professed Sisters: 2.

Represented in the Diocese of Palm Beach.

[2575] (R.S.M.)—SISTERS OF MERCY OF THE AMERICAS (P)

Catherine McAuley founded the Sisters of Mercy in Dublin, Ireland, in 1831. Ten years later, she received confirmation of the Rule by Pope Gregory XVI. In 1843 the Sisters of Mercy established their first U.S.A. foundation in Pittsburgh, followed by various amalgamations.

In 1991, the members of the nine provinces of the Union and of 16 other Mercy congregations founded the Sisters of Mercy of the Americas consisting of 25 regional communities.

In 2009, the Sisters of Mercy of the Americas completed a restructuring of the 25 Regional Communities into six Communities within the Institute: Caribbean, Central America, South America Community; Mid-Atlantic Community; Northeast Community; New York, Pennsylvania, Pacific West Community; West Midwest Community and South Central Community.

In 2019 the six Communities were canonically suppressed, forming one Community (PJP) of the Sisters of Mercy of the Americas with one elected President and Leadership Team.

Institute Administrative Offices: 8403 Colesville Road, Suite 400, Silver Spring, MD 20910

Institute Leadership Team: Sister Patricia McDermott, R.S.M., Pres.; Sister Patricia Flynn, R.S.M., Vice Pres.; Sister Áine O'Connor, R.S.M.; Sister Judith Frikker, R.S.M.; Sister Anne Marie Miller, R.S.M.

Total in Congregation: 2,035

Legal Title: Sisters of Mercy of the Americas, Inc.

Legal Holdings: Mercy Volunteer Corp, Inc.; Conference for Mercy Higher Education, Inc.; Mercy Education System of the Americas, Inc.; Mercy Investment Services, Inc.; Mercy Ministry Corporation; Mercy Real Estate Holding Corporation; Sisters of Mercy Operating Trust; Sisters of Mercy Fund for Ministry Trust; Sisters of Mercy Fund for Infirmed, Disabled, or Elderly Sisters Trust; Mercy Real Estate Trust; Sisters of Mercy of the Americas CCASA Community, Inc.; Sisters of Mercy of the Americas-New York, Pennsylvania, Pacific West Community, Inc.; Sisters of Mercy of the Americas West Midwest Community, Inc.; Sisters of Mercy of the Americas South Central Community, Inc.; Sisters of Mercy of the Americas Northeast Community, Inc.; Sisters of Mercy of the Americas Mid-Atlantic Community, Inc.; Sisters of Mercy of the Americas South Central on Guam, Inc.; NyPPaW FIDES, Inc.; West Midwest FIDES, Inc.; South Central FIDES, Inc.

Sponsored and Co-sponsored Ministries:

Colleges & Universities: Carlow University, Pittsburgh, PA; College of Saint Mary, Omaha, NE (affiliated); Georgian Court University, Lakewood, NJ; Gwynedd Mercy University, Gwynedd Valley, PA; Maria College, Albany, NY; Mercy College of Health Sciences, Des Moines, IA (affiliated); Mercy College of Ohio, Toledo, OH (affiliated); Mercyhurst University, Erie, PA; Misericordia University, Dallas, PA; Mount Aloysius College, Cresson, PA; Mount Mercy University, Cedar Rapids, IA; St. Joseph's College of Maine, Standish, ME; Saint Xavier University, Chicago, IL; Salve Regina University, Newport, RI; Trocaire College, Buffalo, NY; University of Detroit Mercy, Detroit, MI (co-sponsored); University of Saint Joseph, West Hartford, CT.

Secondary Education: Academy of Our Lady of Mercy, Louisville, KY; Academy of Our Lady of Mercy Lauralton Hall, Milford, CT; Alpha Institute, Kingston, Jamaica; Assumption High School, Louisville, KY; Colegio Santa Ethnea, Bella Vista, Argentina; Convent of Mercy Academy (Alpha), Kingston, Jamaica; Cristo Rey Sacramento High School, Sacramento, CA (co-sponsored); Gwynedd Mercy Academy High School, Gwynedd Valley, PA; Mercy Career and Technical High School, Philadelphia, PA; Mercy High School, Baltimore, MD; Mercy High School, Burlingame, CA; Mercy High School, Farmington Hills, MI; Mercy High School, Omaha, NE; Mercy Junior College, Mindanao, Philippines; Mercyhurst Preparatory School, Erie, PA; Mercy McAuley High School, Cincinnati, OH; Merion Mercy Academy, Merion Station, PA; Mother McAuley Liberal Arts High School, Chicago, IL; Mount de Sales Academy, Macon, GA; Mount Mercy Academy, Buffalo, NY; Mount Saint Mary Academy, Little Rock, AR; Mount Saint Mary Academy, Watchung, NJ; Mount Saint Mary Catholic High School, Oklahoma City, OK (co-sponsored); Muffles College, Orange Walk Town, Belize; Notre Dame High School, Elmira, NY; Our Lady of Mercy Academy, Syosset, NY; Our Lady of Mercy School for Young Women, Rochester, NY; Saint Catharine Academy, Bronx, NY; Saint Catherine Academy, Belize City, Belize; Saint John Bosco Career Advancement Institute, Mandeville, Jamaica; Saint Mary Academy – Bay View, Riverside, RI; Saint Vincent's Academy, Savannah, GA; Walsingham Academy, Williamsburg, VA.

Elementary Education: Alpha Infant School, Kingston, Jamaica; Alpha Primary School, Kingston, Jamaica; Colegio Santa Ethnea, Bella Vista, Argentina; Gwynedd-Mercy Academy Elementary, Spring House, PA; Infant of Prague Nursery-K, Mangilao, Guam; Jessie Ripoll Primary School, Kingston, Jamaica; Mater Christi School, Burlington, VT; Mercy Heights Nursery & Kindergarten, Tamuning, Guam; Mercy Montessori, Cincinnati, OH; Mercymount Country Day School, Cumberland, RI; Mount St. Joseph Preparatory School, Mandeville, Jamaica; Saint Mary Academy – Bay View, Riverside, RI; Waldron Mercy Academy, Merion Station, PA; Walsingham Academy, Williamsburg, VA.

Hospitals & Health Care Services: Bon Secours Mercy Health, Cincinnati, OH (co-sponsored); Catholic Health Care Federation/Catholic Health Initiatives, Denver, CO (participating entity); Catholic Health Ministries/Trinity Health, Livonia, MI (participating entity); Elder Care Alliance, Alameda, CA (Facility and Program Sponsor); Elder Care Alliance, Oakland, CA (Facility and Program Sponsor); Marian Woods, Hartsdale, NY (co-sponsored); McAuley Hall, Watchung, NJ; Mercy Center, Dallas, PA; Mercy Circle, Chicago, IL; Mercy Community Hospital, Iligan City, Philippines; Mercy Crest, Barling, AR; Mercy Health Services (Mercy Medical Center & Stella Maris), Baltimore, MD; Mercy Hospital, Iowa City, IA; Mercy Medical Center; Cedar Rapids, IA; Mercy Retirement and Care Center, Oakland, CA; Mercy Urgent Care, Inc., Asheville, NC; Northern Light Health/Mercy Hospital, Portland, ME; Presence Health Ministries/Presence Health, Chicago, IL (participating entity); Scripps Mercy Hospital Chula Vista, Chula Vista, CA; Scripps Mercy Hospital, San Diego, CA; St. Joseph Mercy Hospital, Georgetown, Guyana; St. Joseph's/Candler Health System, Savannah, GA.

Social Services: ARISE Adelante, Alamo, TX (co-sponsored); Casa de la Mujer, Chimbote, Peru; Catherine McAuley Center, Cedar Rapids, IA; Catherine McAuley Center, Scranton, PA; Catherine's House, Belmont, NC; Centro Betania, Chulucanas, Peru; Circles of Mercy, Albany, NY; Holy Angels, Belmont, NC; House of Mercy, Belmont, NC; Marian House, Baltimore, MD (co-sponsored); McAuley Ministries, Providence, RI; McGlynn Center, Wilkes Barre, PA; Mercy Care for the Adirondacks, Lake Placid, NY; Mercy Center, Asbury Park, NJ; Mercy Center, Bronx, NY; Mercy Center for Women, Erie, PA; Mercy Connections, Burlington, VT; Mercy Consultation Center, Dallas, PA; Mercy First, Syosset, NY; Mercy Hilltop Center, Erie, PA; Mercy Home, Brooklyn, NY; Mercy Neighborhood Ministries, Cincinnati, OH; Mercy Services, Wilkes Barre, PA; Nande Roga Guaza, Clorinda Formosa, Argentina; Sisters Place (Mercy Outreach Center), Pittsburgh, PA (co-sponsored); Together in Peace, Georgetown, Guyana (co-sponsored).

Spirituality Centers & Retreat Houses: Cranaleith Spiritual Center, Philadelphia, PA; Mercy Center, Auburn, CA; Mercy Center, Burlingame, CA; Mercy Center, Madison, CT; Mercy Conference and Retreat Center, St. Louis, MO; Mercy Ecology, Cumberland, RI; Mercy Spirituality Center, Rochester, NY; Mount St. Mary House of Prayer, Watchung, NJ; Our Lady of the Pines Retreat Center, Fremont, OH; Well of Mercy, Hamptonville, NC.

Foundations: Mercy Foundation Sacramento, Rancho Cordova, CA; Mercy Foundation North, Redding, CA; The Mercy Foundation, Dallas, PA; Sisters of Mercy NC Foundation, Belmont, NC.

Housing: Gerard Place, Buffalo, NY (co-sponsored); Mercy Housing, Denver, CO (co-sponsored); Mercy Terrace Apartments, Erie, PA.

Other: Collaborative Center for Justice, Hartford, CT (co-sponsored); Mercy Action Marianas, Ltd., Perezville-Tamuning, Guam; Mercy Center of the Arts, Erie, PA; POWR Partnership for Woman Religious, Erie, PA (co-sponsored); The Sisters of Mercy of Jamaica, British West Indies; Regional Superior of Sisters of Mercy, Inc. (Philippines).

Represented in the Archdioceses of Agana, Atlanta, Baltimore, Boston, Chicago, Cincinnati, Denver, Detroit, Dubuque, Hartford, Indianapolis, Los Angeles, Louisville, Miami, Milwaukee, Mobile, New Orleans, New York, Newark, Oklahoma City, Omaha, Philadelphia, Portland in Oregon, San Francisco, San Jose, St Louis and Washington, DC and in the Dioceses of Albany, Allentown, Altoona-Johnstown, Biloxi, Birmingham, Boise, Bridgeport, Brooklyn, Brownsville, Buffalo, Burlington, Camden, Charlotte, Cleveland, Colorado Springs, Davenport, Des Moines, El Paso, Erie, Fall River, Fresno, Gaylord, Grand Rapids, Greensburg, Harrisburg, Jackson, Joliet, Kalamazoo, Lansing, Laredo, Lexington, Little Rock, Madison, Manchester, Memphis, Metuchen, Nashville, Norwich, Oakland, Ogdensburg, Orlando, Palm Beach, Paterson, Phoenix, Pittsburgh, Portland in Maine, Providence, Richmond, Rochester, Rockford, Rockville Centre, Sacramento, Saginaw, San Diego, Savannah, Scranton, Springfield-Cape Girardeau, Stockton, Syracuse, Toledo, Trenton, Tucson, Venice, Wheeling-Charleston, Winona-Rochester, Worcester and Youngstown. Also in Argentina, Belize, Chile, Guyana, Honduras, Jamaica, Panama, Peru and the Philippines.

[2590] (H.M.S.S.)—MERCEDARIAN SISTERS OF THE BLESSED SACRAMENT (P)
(Hermanas Mercedarias del Santísimo Sacramento)

Founded in Mexico City in 1910. First foundation in the United States in 1926.

Mercedarian Sisters of the Blessed Sacrament: 227 Keller St., San Antonio, TX 78204. Tel: 210-223-5013; Fax: 210-444-0779.

General Motherhouse: Fernandez Leal #130, Coyoacán, Mexico, 04330. Sr. Mary Rosario Vega-R., H.M.S.S., Regl. Supr.

Regional House: 1355 W. 70th St., Cleveland, OH 44102. Tel: 216-281-9304; Cell: 216-533-8607.

Professed Sisters in the U.S.: 27.

Represented in the Archdiocese of San Antonio and in the Dioceses of Baton Rouge, Cleveland, San Diego and Saint Augustine.

[2630] (S.C.S.C.)—SISTERS OF MERCY OF THE HOLY CROSS (P)

Founded in Switzerland in 1856. First foundation in the U.S. in 1912.

General Motherhouse: Ingenbohl, Switzerland Sr. Marie-Marthe Schoenenberger, S.C.S.C., Supr. Gen.

U.S. Office: Holy Cross Sisters, 1400 O'Day St., Merrill, WI 54452. Tel: 715-539-1460; Fax: 715-539-1456. Email: lsongy@holycrosssisters.org. Sr. Linda Songy, S.C.S.C., Coord.

Total in Community: 20.

Legal Title: Sisters of Mercy of the Holy Cross of Merrill, WI, Inc.

Ministry in the following areas: Schools; Hospitals; Social Ministries and Parishes; Retirement Homes; Adult Education; Prison Ministry.

Represented in the Diocese of Superior.

[2655] (R.S.M.)—DIOCESAN SISTERS OF MERCY OF PORTLAND (D)

Motherhouse: Diocesan Sisters of Mercy of Portland, 265 Cottage Rd., South Portland, ME 04106. Tel: 207-767-5804. Sr. Karen Hopkins, R.S.M.

[2675] (C.F.M.M.)—MINIM DAUGHTERS OF MARY IMMACULATE (P)

Founded in Leon, Guanajuato, Mexico 1886. Came to the United States in 1926.

U.S. Regional House: Minim Daughters of Mary Immaculate, 555 Patagonia Hwy., Nogales, AZ 85628. Tel: 520-287-3377; Fax: 520-287-2910. Sr. Rosa Maria Ruiz, C.F.M.M., Reg. Supr.

Total Sisters in U.S.: 17.

Properties owned and/or sponsored: Lourdes Catholic School, Nogales, AZ. Ministry in Academic and Religious Education and Health Care.

Represented in the Diocese of Tucson.

[2690] (M.C.D.P.)—MISSIONARY CATECHISTS OF DIVINE PROVIDENCE, SAN ANTONIO, TEXAS (P)

Autonomy with Pontifical status granted Dec. 12, 1989.

Administrative House: Administrative Offices, 515 SW 24th St., San Antonio, TX 78207. Tel: 210-432-0113; Fax: 210-432-1709. Email: mainoffice@mcdp.org. Sr. Sofia Berrones, M.C.D.P., Congregational Leader.

Total in Community: 24.

Represented in the Archdioceses of Galveston-Houston and San Antonio and in the Dioceses of Brownsville, Dallas, Fort Worth and San Jose.

[2700] (M.C.S.H.)—MISSIONARY CATECHISTS OF THE SACRED HEARTS OF JESUS AND MARY (P)

Founded in Mexico City, D.F. in 1918. U.S. foundation in 1943 in Victoria, Texas.

Central House: Mexico City, Mexico Sr. Felisa Nava, Gen. Supr.

Immaculate Heart of Mary Province: 203 E. Sabine St., Victoria, TX 77901. Tel: 361-570-3332; Fax: 361-570-3377. Sr. Midory Wu, M.C.S.H., Prov. Supr.

Total number in U.S. Province: 36.

Ministry in Catechetical family ministry in parishes and missions.

Represented in the Archdiocese of Santa Fe and in the Dioceses of Fort Worth, Lubbock, Metuchen and Victoria.

[2710] (M.C.)—MISSIONARIES OF CHARITY (P)

Founded in India, 1950.

General Motherhouse: 54A AJC Bose Rd., Kolkata, India, 700016. Sr. M. Joseph, M.C., Supr. Gen.

U.S. Foundation & Office (1971): Missionaries of Charity, 335 E. 145th St., Bronx, NY 10451. Tel: 718-292-0019. Sr. Maria Agnes, M.C., Regl. Supr.

Professed Sisters in Congregation: 5029.

Legal Title: Missionaries of Charity, Inc. Sisters serve and staff: Soup Kitchens; Emergency Shelters for Women; Homes for Unwed Mothers; Shelters for Unwed Mothers; Shelters for Men; Religious Education Programs; After-School and Bible Camp Programs for Children; Homes for AIDS Patients; Prison Ministry; Nursing Homes; Hospital and Shut-in Ministry; Family Counseling and Ministry; Foreign Missionary Work.

Represented in the Archdioceses of Atlanta, Baltimore, Boston, Chicago, Denver, Detroit, Galveston-Houston, Indianapolis, Los Angeles, Miami, New York, Newark, Philadelphia, San Francisco, St. Louis, St. Paul-Minneapolis and Washington and in the Dioceses of Baton Rouge, Bridgeport, Brooklyn, Charlotte, Dallas, Fall River, Gallup, Gary, Lafayette, Lexington, Little Rock, Memphis, Oakland, Peoria, Phoenix, Sacramento, San Diego, Spokane and Trenton. Also in Canada, Mexico, Central America and South America.

[2715] (MChR)—MISSIONARY SISTERS OF CHRIST THE KING FOR POLONIA (P)

Founded in Poland on Nov. 21, 1959 by Father Ignacy Posadzy, TChR. First foundation in the U.S. 1978.

General Motherhouse: Siostry Misjonarki Chrystusa Krola dla Polonii, ul. Siostr Misjonarek 10, Poznan, 50, Poland, 61-680. Sr. Ewa Kaczmarek, MChR, Supr. Gen.

Total in Congregation: 230.

Delegation Superior in the U.S.: Missionary Sisters of Christ the King for Polonia, 4910 North Menard Ave., Chicago, IL 60630. Tel: 773-481-1831; Fax: 773-545-4171. Sr. Katarzyna Zaremba, MChR, Supr.; Sr. Malgorzata Tomalka, MChR, Treas.; Sr. Anna Blauciak, MChR, Sec.

Total in Congregation: 230; Professed in U.S. & Canada: 50.

Legal Title: Missionary Sisters of Christ the King for Polonia.

Ministry among Polish immigrants and people of Polish heritage.

Represented in the Archdioceses of Chicago, Detroit and Newark and in the Dioceses of Joliet and Phoenix. Also in Canada.

[2717] (M.D.P.V.M.)—MISSIONARY DAUGHTERS OF THE MOST PURE VIRGIN MARY (P)

Founded in Mexico. First foundation in the United States in the Diocese of Corpus Christi 1916.

General Motherhouse: Heroe de Nacocariz, 721 Sur Aguascalientes, Ags, Mexico, 20240. Mother Guillermina Arroyo, M.D.P.V.M., Gen. Supr.

Missionary Daughters of the Most Pure Virgin Mary: 919 N. 9th St., Kingsville, TX 78363. Tel: 361-595-1087. Sr. Consuelo Ramirez, M.D.P.V.M., Supr.; Sr. Carmen Villalpando, M.D.P.V.M., Sec.; Sr. Maximina Cruz, M.D.P.V.M., Treas.

Total in Congregation: 400; Present in U.S.A.: 24.

Legal Title: Missionary Daughters of the Most Pure Virgin Mary.

Ministry in the field of Religious and Academic Education at the elementary level; Pastoral Ministry.

Represented in the Dioceses of Camden, Corpus Christi and Yakima.

[2720] (M.H.S.H.)—MISSION HELPERS OF THE SACRED HEART (P)

Founded in the United States in 1890.

Mission Helper Center: 1001 W. Joppa Rd., Baltimore, MD 21204. Tel: 410-823-8585; Fax: 410-825-6355. Sr. Elizabeth Langmead, M.H.S.H., Pres.

Total in Community: 43.

Legal Title: Institute of Mission Helpers of Baltimore City.

Represented in the Archdioceses of Baltimore, Boston, Cincinnati and in the Dioceses of Birmingham, Erie, Orlando, Pittsburgh, Rochester and Tucson. Also in Venezuela.

[2725] (M.S.E.)—MISSIONARY SISTERS OF THE EUCHARIST

Founded in Guatemala, C.A. in 1975. First foundation in the United States in 2001.

Motherhouse: San Andres Semetabaj, Solola, Guatemala Sr. Francisca Sisimit, M.S.E., Supr. Gen.

Total in Community: 54.

Visitation Convent, Magnificat Houses: 3301 San Jacinto St., Houston, TX 77004. Tel: 713-523-8831.

Mailing Address: P.O. Box 88147, Houston, TX 77288-0147. Sr. Gabina Coló, M.S.E., Local Supr. and Contact Person.

Ministry in parishes, missionary work, health care and social services.

Represented in the Archdiocese of Galveston-Houston.

[2730] (M.S.H.R.)—MISSIONARY SISTERS OF THE HOLY ROSARY (P)

Generalate (1924): 23 Cross Ave., Blackrock County, Dublin, Ireland Sr. Francesca Onyibor, Congregational Leader.

U.S. Regional Headquarters (1954): Missionary Sisters of the Holy Rosary, 741 Polo Rd., Bryn Mawr, PA 19010. Tel: 610-520-1976. Sr. Florence Enechukwu, Regl. Leader.

Total in Community: 334.

Represented in the Archdiocese of Philadelphia.

[2740] (M.S.SP.)—MISSION SISTERS OF THE HOLY SPIRIT (D)

Motherhouse and Novitiate: 915 N. River Rd., Saginaw, MI 48609. Tel: 989-781-0934. Sr. Mary Lou Owczarzak, Pres.

Total in Community: 3.

Legal Title: Society of the Mission Sisters of the Holy Spirit of the Diocese of Saginaw Holy Spirit Sisters Charitable Trust, Saginaw, MI.

Ministry in Special Religious Education for the disabled; Pastoral Ministry.

Represented in the Diocese of Saginaw.

[2750] (I.C.M.)—MISSIONARY SISTERS OF THE IMMACULATE HEART OF MARY (P)

Founded in India in 1897. First foundation in the United States in 1919.

Generalate: Via Filogaso 40, Rome, Italy, 00173. Sr. Lieve Stragier, I.C.M., Supr. Gen. Universal total in Congregation: 484.

American Province: 18110 Queen Palm Dr., P.O. Box 1017, Peñitas, TX 78576. Tel: 956-585-5488; 956-257-4308; Fax: 956-519-9123. Email: fatima.santiago@gmail.com. Sr. Fatima Mary Santiago, I.C.M., Mission Contact.

Total in Community: 11.

Missionaries Minister in Education; Catechetical; Pastoral and Social Ministry; Health Care; Ecology; Leprosaria; International Justice and the Promotion of Human Dignity.

Represented in the Archdiocese of New York and in the Diocese of Brownsville. Also in Belgium, Brazil, Burundi, Cameroon, Guatemala, Hong Kong, India, Italy, Philippines, Taiwan, Mongolia, Caribbean Islands, Congo and Senegal.

[2760] (S.M.I.C.)—MISSIONARY SISTERS OF THE IMMACULATE CONCEPTION OF THE MOTHER OF GOD (P)

Founded in Brazil in 1910. First foundation in the United States in 1922.

Generalate: 47 Garden Ave., Woodland Park, NJ 07424. Tel: 973-279-1484. Email: smicgen@optonline.net. Sr. Livramento Melo de Oliveira, S.M.I.C., Coord. Gen.

U.S. Province (1960): Provincialate of the Immaculate Conception, 779 Broadway, Paterson, NJ 07514. Tel: 973-279-3790.

Professed Sisters: 28.

Legal Titles: Missionary Sisters of the Immaculate Conception, Inc.; Province of the Immaculate Conception, Inc.

Sisters serve and staff: Religious Education; Pastoral Ministries; Health and Social Work.

Represented in the Archdioceses of Newark and in the Dioceses of Austin, Paterson, Portland (In Maine) and San Bernardino.

[2770] (M.J.M.J.)—MISSIONARY SISTERS OF JESUS, MARY AND JOSEPH (P)

Founded in Spain in 1944. First foundation in the United States in 1956. Mother Maria Dolores de la Cruz Domingo, Foundress.

Motherhouse: Plaza Inmaculada Concepcion 1, Madrid, Spain, 28019. Sr. Isabel Aguado, M.J.M.J., Supr. Gen.

Delegation Headquarters: Mount Thabor Convent, 12940 Leopard St., Corpus Christi, TX 78410. Tel: 361-241-1955; Fax: 361-241-2271. Sr. Irene Ybarra, M.J.M.J., Delegation Supr.; Sr. Gloria Rodriguez, M.J.M.J., Local Supr.

Sisters: 22.

Properties owned and/or sponsored: The Ark Assessment Center & Emergency Shelter for Youth.

Represented in the Archdiocese of San Antonio and in the Dioceses of Corpus Christi and El Paso. Also in Mexico.

[2780] (M.SS.S.)—MISSIONARY SISTERS OF THE MOST BLESSED SACRAMENT (P)

General Motherhouse: Calle Navarro Amandi, 11, Madrid, Spain, 28033. Mother Leonor Gutierreg, Mother Gen.

U.S. Foundation: Convent of Mary Immaculate, 1111 Wordin Ave., Bridgeport, CT 06605. Tel: 203-

334-5681; Email: januariab@gmail.com. Sr. Marian Macias, Mother General; Sr. Januaria Beleno, Local Supr.

[2790] (M.S.B.T.)—MISSIONARY SERVANTS OF THE MOST BLESSED TRINITY (P)

Founded in the United States in 1912.

Motherhouse-Generalate-Novitiate and Candidacy: 3501 Solly Ave., Philadelphia, PA 19136. Tel: 215-335-7550. Email: gensec@msbt.org. Sr. Barbara McIntyre, M.S.B.T., Gen. Custodian.

Total in Community: 92.

Properties owned and sponsored: Blessed Trinity Mother Missionary Cenacle, Philadelphia, PA; Blessed Trinity Shrine Retreat Cenacle, Holy Trinity, AL; Trinita Ecumenical Retreat Center, New Hartford, CT; Mother Boniface Spirituality Center, Philadelphia, PA.

Represented in the Archdioceses of Baltimore, Chicago, Hartford and Philadelphia and in the Dioceses of Birmingham, Camden, Fall River, San Bernardino and Savannah. Also in Puerto Rico and Mexico.

[2800] (M.S.C.)—MISSIONARY SISTERS OF THE MOST SACRED HEART OF JESUS (OF HILTRUP) (P)

Founded in Germany in 1899. First foundation in the United States in 1908.

Generalate: Via Martiri di Via Fani, 22, Sutri (Viterbo), Italy, 01015. Sr. Barbara Winkler, M.S.C., Gen. Supr.

American Province-Motherhouse (1908): Sacred Heart Villa, 51 Seminary Ave., Reading, PA 19605. Tel: 610-929-5751. Sr. Mary Anne Bigos, M.S.C., Coord.

Total number in U.S. Province: 44.

Legal Title: Missionary Sisters of the Most Sacred Heart of Jesus, Inc.

Ministry in Education; Health Care; Home Health Care; Parish Ministry; Pastoral Ministry to people on the move; Prison Ministry; Counseling; Social Ministry; Spiritual Ministry; Care of the Aged.

Properties owned or sponsored: MSC Province Center; Chevalier House, Sacred Heart Villa, Reading, PA.

Represented in the Archdioceses of Atlanta, Galveston-Houston and Philadelphia and in the Dioceses of Allentown, Harrisburg, Syracuse and Venice. Also in Mexico.

MSC Province Center: 2811 Moyers Ln., Reading, PA 19605. Tel: 610-929-5944. Email: USAMSC@mscreading.org. Sr. Dorothy Fabritze, M.S.C., Prov. Leader.

[2810] (M.S.M.G.)—MISSIONARY SISTERS OF MOTHER OF GOD (D) (Byzantine Ukrainian Rite-Philadelphia)

U.S. Province: 711 N. Franklin St., Philadelphia, PA 19132. Tel: 215-627-7808. Email: msmgnuns@gmail.com. Mother Maria Kelly, M.S.M.G., Gen. Supr.

Professed Sisters: 7.

Ministry in the field of Education.

Represented in the Ukrainian Archdiocese of Philadelphia.

[2820] (M.S.O.L.A.)—MISSIONARY SISTERS OF OUR LADY OF AFRICA (P) (Sisters of Africa)

Founded in Algiers, N. Africa in 1869. First foundation in the United States in 1929.

General Headquarters: Rome, Italy. Sr. Carmen Sammut, Supr. Gen.

Universal total in Congregation: 440.

American Headquarters: 47 West Spring St., Winooski, VT 05404. Tel: 802-655-2395 Ext. 2217. Sr. Felicia Nowak, Contact Person.

Total number in U.S.: 9.

Represented in the Diocese of Burlington.

[2830] (M.O.M.)—MISSIONARY SISTERS OF OUR LADY OF MERCY (D)

Founded in Piaui, Brazil in 1938. First foundation in the United States at Lackawanna, New York in 1955.

General Motherhouse: Salvador, Bahia, Brazil Mother Maria Ilsa Mascarenhas de Jesus, Supr. Gen.

U.S. Headquarters: Rainbow K, 388 Franklin St., Buffalo, NY 14202. Tel: 716-854-5198. Sr. Janice Benfield, M.O.M., Supr.

Total in Community: 3.

Represented in the Diocese of Buffalo.

[2840] (M.C.)—POOR CLARE MISSIONARY SISTERS (P)

Founded in Mexico by Blessed Maria Ines Teresa Arias of the Blessed Sacrament.

General Motherhouse: Via Cardinale Garampi 17, Pineta Sachetti, Rome, Italy. Mother Martha G. Hernandez, Gen. Supr.

U.S. Foundation: Regional House and Novitiate, 1019 N. Newhope, Santa Ana, CA 92703.

Total in Community: 42.

Ministry in Day Nurseries, Schools and Retreat House. Represented in the Archdiocese of Los Angeles and in the Dioceses of Orange in California and Springfield-Cape Girardeau.

[2850] (C.P.S.)—MISSIONARY SISTERS OF THE PRECIOUS BLOOD (P)

Founded in South Africa on Sept. 8, 1885. First founded in the United States at Princeton, New Jersey on August 15, 1925.

Generalate: Casa Generalizia, Suore Missionarie del Preziosissimo Sangue Mariannhill, Via San Giovanni Eudes 95, Rome, Italy, I-00163.

Universal total in Congregation: 715

North American Province: Precious Blood Convent, 1094 Welsh Rd., Reading, PA 19607-9363. Tel: 610-777-1624; Fax: 610-777-3359. Email: pbcpatreas@comcast.net. Sr. Helena Hyo Sun Kang, C.P.S., Prov.

Total number in Province: 53.

Represented in the Archdiocese of Philadelphia and in the Dioceses of Allentown and Lexington. Also in Canada.

[2860] (M.S.C.)—MISSIONARY SISTERS OF THE SACRED HEART OF JESUS (P) (Cabrini Sisters)

Founded in Italy in 1880, by Saint Frances Xavier Cabrini. First foundation in the United States in 1889.

Motherhouse: Viale Cortina D'Ampezzo 269, Rome, Italy, 00135. Sr. Maria Eliane Azevedo da Silva, M.S.C., Supr. Gen.

Provincial Office: 222 E. 19th St., 5B, New York, NY 10003. Sr. Diane Olmstead, M.S.C., Prov. Supr.

Professed Sisters: 200; Total in Congregation: 207.

Ministry in the field of Education; Hospitals; Immigration; Nursing Homes; Child Care; Retreat Centers; Shrines; Parishes.

Represented in the Archdioceses of Chicago, Denver, New Orleans, New York, Philadelphia and Seattle. Also in Argentina, Australia, Brazil, Central America, England, Ethiopia, Italy, Paraguay, Eswatini, Siberia, Spain, Switzerland and Uganda.

[2865] (M.S.C.GPE.)—MISSIONARIES OF THE SACRED HEART OF JESUS AND OUR LADY OF GUADALUPE (P)

National Address: 1212 E. Euclid Ave., Arlington Heights, IL 60004. Tel: 847-255-5616. Sr. Guadalupe Rosales, Local Supr.

Ministry in Schools, Nursing Homes, Seminaries and Foreign Missions.

Represented in the Archdioceses of Chicago, San Francisco and Washington and in the Diocese of Joliet.

[2880] (S.S.C.)—MISSIONARY SISTERS OF ST. COLUMBAN (P) (Columban Sisters)

Founded in Ireland in 1922. First foundation in the United States in 1930.

General Motherhouse: Wicklow, Ireland Sr. Ann Gray, S.S.C., Congregational Leader.

U.S. Region: St. Columban's on the Lake, 2546 Lake Road, Silver Creek, NY 14156. Tel: 716-934-4515; Fax: 716-934-3919. Email: sscarea@gmail.com. Sr. Corona Colleary, S.S.C., U.S. Area Leader; Sr. Susanna Choi, S.S.C., Congregational Leader.

Professed Sisters: 13.

Ministry in the fields of Evangelization, Pastoral Education, Health and Social ministry. Special programs for mission education and animation.

Represented in the Diocese of Buffalo. Also in Ireland, Myanmar, China, England, Scotland, Korea, Philippines and Pakistan

[2890] (M.S.S.A.)—MISSIONARY SERVANTS OF ST. ANTHONY (D)

Founded in the United States in 1929.

General Motherhouse: 100 Peter Baque Rd., San Antonio, TX 78209-1805. Tel: 210-824-4553. Sr. Mary Ann Domagalski, M.S.S.A., Supr.

Total in Community: 2.

Represented in the Archdiocese of San Antonio.

[2900] (M.S.C.S.)—MISSIONARY SISTERS OF ST. CHARLES BORROMEO (P) (Scalabrinians)

Founded in Italy in 1895. Began its mission in the United States in 1941 which developed to be the USA Province, Our Lady of Fatima Province USA.

Motherhouse: Via Monte del Gallo 68, Rome, Italy, 00165. Sr. Neusa de Fatima Mariano, M.S.C.S., Gen. Supr.

Total in Congregation: 520.

Our Lady of Fatima Province, USA & Bishop Scalabrini Community: 1406 N. 37th Ave., Melrose Park, IL 60160. Tel: 708-223-0977. Email: provincial.olf@scalabriniansisters.org; Sr. Luiza Dal Moro, M.S.C.S., Prov. Supr.; Sr. Vitalina Pietrobiasi, M.S.C.S., First Councilor & Admin.; Sr. Nyzelle Juliana Donde, M.S.C.S., Councilor & Apostolate; Sr. Alma Rosa Huerta Reyes, M.S.C.S., Councilor & Formation; Sr. Marizete Schiavon, M.S.C.S., Councilor & Prov. Sec.; Sr. Catherine Petalcurin, M.S.C.S., Prov. Treas.

Total in Community: 48.

Ministry in the fields of Education; Pastoral Care of the Sick; Catechesis; Social Service; Pastoral Care of Migrants and Refugees.

Represented in the Archdioceses of Chicago, New York and Washington. Also in Canada, Costa Rica, Dominican Republic, Honduras and Mexico.

[2910] (M.S.B.A.V.)—MONASTIC SISTERS OF BETHLEHEM AND OF THE ASSUMPTION OF THE VIRGIN (P)

Founded in 1951.

Motherhouse: France.

393 Our Lady of the Lourdes Camp Rd., Livingston Manor, NY 12758. Sr. Rafqa.

Total Sisters: 560.

Ministry in Monastic Life.

Represented in the Archdioceses of New York.

[2920] (M.D.)—MOTHERS OF THE HELPLESS (D)

Founded in Malaga, Spain in 1881. Founded in the United States in 1916.

General Motherhouse: Avda. San Jose de la Montana No. 15, Valencia, Spain, 46008. Mother Paloma Garcia, Supr. Gen.

U.S. Address: Mothers of the Helpless, 432 W. 20th St., New York, NY 10011. Mother Josefina Jimenez, Supr.

Professed Sisters in U.S.: 5.

Properties owned and sponsored: Sacred Heart Residence; San Jose Day Nursery, New York, NY.

Represented in the Archdiocese of New York.

[2930] (I.H.M.)—THE CALIFORNIA INSTITUTE OF THE SISTERS OF THE MOST HOLY AND IMMACULATE HEART OF THE BLESSED VIRGIN MARY (P)

Founded in Spain in 1848. First foundation in the United States in 1871.

Pontifical Commissary: 3424 Wilshire Blvd., 5th Fl., Los Angeles, CA 90010-2241. Tel: 213-637-7534; Email: eeobrien@la-archdiocese.org.

Professed Sisters: 3.

Represented in the Archdiocese of Los Angeles.

[2940] (M.H.S.)—SISTERS OF THE MOST HOLY SACRAMENT (P)

Founded in France in 1851. First foundation in the United States in 1872. Pontifical Approbation 1935.

Generalate: Sisters of the Most Holy Sacrament, 313 Corona Dr., Lafayette, LA 70503-4757. Tel: 337-981-8475. Sr. Ann Lacour, M.S.C., Major Supr.; Sr. Diane Dornan, M.H.S., Prov.

Total in Community: 11.

Legal Titles: St. Augustine Trust Fund, Lafayette, LA; Bethany Health Care Center, Lafayette, LA. Ministry in the field of Homes for the Aged.

Represented in the Diocese of Lafayette (LA).

[2950] (N.D.S.)—CONGREGATION OF NOTRE DAME DE SION (P)

Founded in France in 1843. First foundation in the United States in 1892.

Generalate: Rome, Italy. Sr. Oonah O'Shea, Supr. Gen. Universal total in Congregation: 250.

Notre Dame de Sion: 3823 Locust St., Kansas City, MO 64109. Tel: 816-753-3810.

Represented in the Dioceses of Brooklyn and Kansas City-St. Joseph.

[2955] (C.N.D.)—CONGREGATION OF NOTRE-DAME OF MONTREAL (P)

Founded in 1658.

Motherhouse: Montreal, Canada.

Holy Spirit Church, Jonesville, Saint Charles, VA 24282. Sr. Maryanne Foley, Supr.

Total Sisters: 560.

Ministry in Education and Community Development.

[2960] (N.D.)—NOTRE DAME SISTERS (P)

Founded in Czechoslovakia, Europe in 1853. First foundation in the United States in 1910.

General Motherhouse: Hradec Kralove, Czech Republic. Mother Metoda Piatnickova, N.D., Supr. Gen.

U.S. Provincial Motherhouse: Notre Dame Convent, 3501 State St., Omaha, NE 68112-1709. Tel: 402-455-2994; Fax: 402-455-3974. Email: info@notredamesisters.org. Sr. Rita Ostry, N.D., Prov.

Total in Community: 30.

Sisters serve and staff: all levels of education; Hispanic Ministry; Pastoral Care; Housing for low income elderly; Religious Education; Chaplaincy; Health Care; Adult Education; Service to abused and trafficked; Community Administration and Services.

Represented in the Archdioceses of Denver, Dubuque and Omaha and in the Dioceses of Grand Island and Pueblo.

[2970] (S.S.N.D.)—SCHOOL SISTERS OF NOTRE DAME (P)

Founded in Germany in 1833. First foundation in the United States in 1847.

General Motherhouse: Rome, Italy. Sr. Roxanne Schares, Supr. Gen.

Atlantic-Midwest Province: School Sisters of Notre Dame, 6401 N. Charles St., Baltimore, MD 21212-1099. Tel: 410-377-7774; Fax: 410-377-5363. Sr. Charmine Krohe, S.S.N.D., Prov. Leader.

Total in Community: 493.

Properties Owned and Legal Titles: School Sisters of Notre Dame in the City of Baltimore; Maria Health Care Center, Inc.; Atlantic-Midwest Province of the School Sisters of Notre Dame, Inc.; The Northeastern Province of the School Sisters of Notre Dame in the State of Connecticut; Lourdes Health Care Center, Inc.; School Sisters of Chicago Province, Inc.; Atlantic-Midwest Province Endowment Trust; SSND Service Corp.; SSND Care, Inc.; SSND Real Estate Holding Corp.; SSND Real Estate Trust; SSND Continuing Care Trust; SSND Charitable Annuity Trust.

Ministries: Teaching and Administering in the field of Academic Education at all levels; ESL and Tutoring for Women and Children; Nursing; Apostolate of the Aging; D.R.E.'s and Pastoral Associates.

Represented in the Archdioceses of Baltimore, Boston, Chicago, Hartford, Los Angeles, Newark, New York, Philadelphia and Washington and in the Dioceses of Albany, Bridgeport, Brooklyn, Charleston, El Paso, Jackson, Joliet, La Crosse, Lexington, Norwich, Oakland, Ogdensburg, Orlando, Palm Beach, Peoria, Pittsburgh, Providence, Rochester, Rockford, Rockville Centre, St. Petersburg, Venice, Wichita and Wilmington. Also in Canada, England, Rome and South Sudan.

Sponsored Corporate Ministries: Notre Dame of Maryland University; Notre Dame Preparatory School; Institute of Notre Dame, Baltimore, MD; Academy of the Holy Angels, Demarest, NJ; The Caroline Friess Center, Inc.' Academy of Our Lady, Chicago, Inc.; Caroline House, Inc.; School Sisters of Notre Dame Educational Center, Inc.; SisterHouse; Corazon A Corazon, NFP; Notre Dame Learning Center, Inc.

Co-Sponsored Ministries: Sisters Academy of Baltimore, Inc.; Mother Seton Academy, Inc.; Marian House, Incorporated.

Northeast Office (1957): School Sisters of Notre Dame, Atlantic-Midwest Province, 345 Belden Hill Rd., Wilton, CT 06897. Tel: 203-762-1220; Fax: 203-762-9434. Sr. Charmine Krohe, S.S.N.D., Prov. Leader.

Legal Holdings and Titles: The Northeastern Province of the School Sisters of Notre Dame in the State of Connecticut; Motherhouse and Lourdes Health Care Center, Wilton, CT; Academy of the Holy Angels, Demarest, NJ.

Ministries: Teaching and Administering in the field of Academic Education at all levels; ESL and Tutoring for Women and Children; Nursing; Apostolate of the Aging; D.R.E.'s and Pastoral Associates.

Central Pacific Province (2011): School Sisters of Notre Dame, 320 E. Ripa Ave., St. Louis, MO 63125. Tel: 314-544-0455; Fax: 314-544-6754. Sr. Debra M. Sciano, S.S.N.D., Prov. Leader.

Total in Central Pacific Province: 734.

Legal Title: School Sisters of Notre Dame Central Pacific Province, Inc.; The School Sisters of Notre Dame of Dallas Charitable Trust; School Sisters of Notre Dame at Mankato, Minnesota, Inc. - Charitable Trust; School Sisters of Notre Dame Cooperative Investment Fund; School Sisters of Notre Dame at Milwaukee, Wisconsin, Inc. Charitable Trust; The School Sisters of Notre Dame of St. Louis Caroline Trust.

Ministries to the Needy and Elderly; Women and Youth; all levels of Academic Education; D.R.E.'s; Pastoral Associates.

Sponsored/Co-Sponsored and Affiliated Ministries: East Side Learning Center, St. Paul, MN; Good Counsel Learning Center, Mankato, MN; Marian Middle School, St. Louis, MO; MORE, St. Paul, MN; Mount Mary University, Milwaukee, WI; Notre Dame School of Dallas, Dallas, TX; Notre Dame School of Milwaukee, Milwaukee, WI; Notre Dame High School Guam, Talofofo, GU; Notre Dame High School St. Louis, St. Louis, MO; Theresa Living Center, St. Paul, MN.

Represented in the Archdioceses of Baltimore, Denver, Detroit, Indianapolis, Los Angeles, Milwaukee, Mobile, New Orleans, San Antonio, Seattle, St. Louis, and St. Paul/Minneapolis and in the Dioceses of Amarillo, Belleville, Bismarck, Brooklyn, Brownsville, Dallas, Davenport, El Paso, Fargo, Fort Wayne-South Bend, Fort Worth, Fresno, Great Falls-Billings, Green Bay, Houma-Thibodaux, Jackson, Jefferson City, La Crosse, Lincoln, Madison, Manchester, Monterey, New Ulm, Orange, Owensboro, Peoria, Phoenix, San Diego, San Jose, Springfield in Cape Girardeau, Salt Lake City, Springfield in Illinois, St. Cloud, Superior, Tucson, and Winona-Rochester. Also in Guam, Italy, Japan, and Nepal.

Milwaukee Office: 10700 W. Research Dr., Ste. 145, Wauwatosa, WI 53226. Tel: 262-782-9850. Sr. Debra M. Sciano, S.S.N.D., Prov. Leader.

Total in Central Pacific Province: 734.

Legal Titles: School Sisters of Notre Dame of the Central Pacific Province; School Sisters of Notre Dame at Milwaukee, Wisconsin, Inc. Charitable Trust.

Mankato Office: School Sisters of Notre Dame, 170 Good Counsel Dr., Mankato, MN 56001-3138. Tel: 507-389-4200; Fax: 507-389-4125. Sr. Debra M. Sciano, Prov. Leader.

Total in Central Pacific Province: 734.

Legal Titles: School Sisters of Notre Dame at Mankato, Minnesota, Inc. - Charitable Trust; School Sisters of Notre Dame Cooperative Investment Fund.

Dallas Office: Notre Dame of Dallas - School Sisters of Notre Dame, 1421 W. Mockingbird Lane, Dallas, TX 75247. Tel: 214-330-9152; Fax: 214-330-9197. Sr. Debra M. Sciano, S.S.N.D., Prov. Leader.

Total in Central Pacific Province: 734.

[2980] (C.N.D.)—SISTERS OF THE CONGREGATION DE NOTRE DAME (P)

Founded in Canada in 1653. First Foundation in the United States in 1860. American Novitiate established at Bourbonnais, Illinois.

Blessed Sacrament Province: Sacred Heart University, 3135 Easton Turnpike, Fairfield, CT 06825.

Generalate and Motherhouse: 2330 Sherbrooke St., West, Montreal, Canada H3H 1G8. Sr. Ona Bessette, C.N.D., Congregational Leader.

U.S. Province (1946): Blessed Sacrament Province, Sacred Heart University, 3135 Easton Turnpike, Fairfield, CT 06825. Tel: 203-365-4303. Sr. Mary Anne Foley, C.N.D., Prov. Leader.

Total number in the U.S. Province: 87.

Represented in the Archdioceses of Chicago, Hartford, New York and Oklahoma City and in the Dioceses of Albany, Bridgeport, Brooklyn and Richmond.

[2990] (S.N.D.)—THE SISTERS OF NOTRE DAME OF THE UNITED STATES (P)

Founded in Germany in 1850. First foundation in the United States in 1874.

Generalate: Rome, Italy. Sr. Mary Ann Culpert, S.N.D., Supr. Gen.

Universal total in Congregation: 1,738.

Cleveland Province (1874): Notre Dame Educational Center - Provincial Center, Juniorate, & Novitiate, 13000 Auburn Rd., Chardon, OH 44024-9331. Tel: 440-286-7101. Sr. Margaret Mary Gorman, S.N.D., Prov. Supr.; Sr. M. Patricia Teckman, Prov. Sec.

Total in Community: 242.

Legal Titles: The Corporation of the Sisters of Notre Dame of Chardon, Ohio; The Sisters of Notre Dame Charitable Trust.

National and Diocesan Offices; Ministry in the field of Academic Education (preschool through college); Literacy, tutors; Special Education (K-8) for Children with Learning Disabilities; Youth, Young Adult Ministry; Parish Ministry (Pastoral Associates, Ministers, DREs); Health Care (Nurses, Chaplains, Hospice, Pastoral Care); Spiritual Direction, Speakers, Retreat work; Counseling; Respite Home for Children; Administration and Finance; Mission Effectiveness; Internet, Social Media Strategist; Donor Relations; Writers; Artists; Musicians; Peace and Justice Work; Outreach to the Homeless, Homebound, Marginalized, Human Trafficked, Incarcerated; Service to SND Community.

Properties owned and sponsored: Notre Dame Cathedral Latin School, Chardon, OH; Notre Dame Elementary School, Chardon, OH; Julie Billiart School, Lyndhurst, OH.

Represented in the Archdioceses of Detroit, Los Angeles, and Washington and in the Dioceses of Cleveland, Orlando, St. Petersburg, and Youngstown.

Covington Region (1924): Provincial Center and Novitiate of the Sisters of Notre Dame, 1601 Dixie Hwy., (St. Joseph Heights), Covington, KY 41011. Tel: 859-291-2040; Fax: 859-291-1774. Email: infoKY@sndusa.org.

Total in Community: 74.

Legal Title: Sisters of Notre Dame of Covington, KY, Inc. Ministry in the field of Education; Hospital and Health Care Services; Child Care.

Properties sponsored: Saint Claire Regional Medical Center, Morehead, KY; St. Charles Care Center, Inc., Covington, KY; Notre Dame Academy, Park Hills, KY; Notre Dame Urban Education Center, Inc., Covington, KY; Julie Learning Center, Park Hills, KY.

Represented in the Archdiocese of Cincinnati, Covington and Lexington.

Province of USA, Toledo Region: 1656 Henthorne Dr., Ste. 200, Maumee, OH 43537. Tel: 419-474-5485. Sr. Margaret Mary Gorman, S.N.D., Prov. Supr.

Total in Toledo Region Community: 144.

Ministry in the field of Academic Education; Foreign Mission Work; Religious Education, Pastoral Ministry, Vocational School, Health Care Ministry, Counseling Ministry, Community Service, Diocesan Offices, Spiritual Life, Hispanic and Migrant, Campus Ministries, Child Care, Care for Handicapped.

Properties owned and sponsored: Notre Dame Academy; Maria Early Learning Center; Lial Catholic School; Convent & Renewal Center, Whitehouse, OH; Holy Trinity Mission, Papua, New Guinea.

Represented in the Archdioceses of Detroit, Green Bay, Indianapolis and New Orleans and in the Dioceses of St. Augustine and Toledo.

Province of Los Angeles (1961): Sisters of Notre Dame, 1776 Hendrix Ave., Thousand Oaks, CA 91360. Tel: 805-496-3243; Fax: 805-379-3616. Email: bbienlein@sndca.org. Sr. Rita Marie Schroeder, S.N.D., Community Coord., Tel: 419-708-7075; Sr. Mary Judeen Julier, S.N.D., Community Coord., Tel: 562-301-7373.

Total number in Province: 47.

Legal Titles: Corporation of the Sisters of Notre Dame of Los Angeles; Notre Dame Academy Schools of Los Angeles; Notre Dame Center; La Reina High & Middle School, Thousand Oaks, CA; Providence House, Long Beach, CA; Notre Dame Learning Center Preschool, Thousand Oaks, CA.

Ministry in the field of Education, Parish and Social Ministry; Catechetics; Foreign Mission Work.

Represented in the Archdiocese of Los Angeles.

[3000] (S.N.D.DEN.)—SISTERS OF NOTRE DAME DE NAMUR (P)

Founded in France in 1804. First foundation in the United States in 1840.

Generalate: Suore di Nostra Signora di Namur,Via Raffaello Sardiello 20, Rome, Italy, 00165. Tel: 011-3906-6641-8704. Sr. Teresita Weind, S.N.D.deN., Gen. Mod.

U.S. Notre Dame Congregational Center: Congregational Mission Office, 30 Jeffreys Neck Rd., Ipswich, MA 01938. Tel: 978-356-2159; Fax: 978-356-2118. Sr. Lorraine Connell, S.N.D.deN., Treas.

Part of the Sisters of Notre Dame de Namur United States East-West Province: Sisters of Notre Dame de Namur, 351 Broadway, Everett, MA 02149-3425. Tel: 617-387-2500; Fax: 617-387-1303. Prov. Team: Sr. Mary M. Farren, S.N.D.deN.; Sr. Barbara Barry, S.N.D.deN.; Sr. Elaine Bain, S.N.D.deN; Sr. Eileen Burns, S.N.D.deN.; Sr. Patricia Chappell, S.N.D.deN.

Total in Community: 126.

Legal Title: Boston Province of the Sisters of Notre Dame de Namur, Inc.

Ministry in the field of Academic Education at all levels; Adult Education Programs; Parish Ministries; Religious Education Programs; and Social Services.

Properties owned and sponsored: Notre Dame Academy, Worcester, MA, Notre Dame Education Center, South Boston, MA; St. Patrick School and Education Center, Lowell, MA.

Represented in the Archdioceses of Boston, Hartford and Washington and in the Dioceses of Gallup, Manchester, Springfield in Massachusetts and Worcester.

Part of the Sisters of Notre Dame de Namur United States East-West Province: Sisters of Notre Dame de Namur, 30 Jeffrey's Neck Rd., Ipswich, MA 01938. Tel: 978-356-4381; Fax: 978-356-9759. Prov. Admin. Team: Sr. Catherine Waldron, S.N.D.deN.; Sr. Mary M. Farren, S.N.D.deN.; Sr. Barbara Barry, S.N.D.deN.; Sr. Elaine Bain, S.N.D.deN; Sr. Eileen Burns, S.N.D.deN.; Sr. Patricia Chappell, S.N.D.deN.

Total in Community: 79.

Legal Titles: Notre Dame Training School, Inc.; The Sisters of Notre Dame de Namur, Ipswich, MA.

Ministry in all fields of Education; Pastoral Ministry; Health, Social and Community Services; Retreat Work.

Properties owned and sponsored: Academy of Notre Dame, Tyngsboro, MA; Notre Dame Academy, Hingham, MA; Notre Dame Long Term Health Care Facility, Worcester, MA; Notre Dame Education Center, Lawrence, MA; Cuvilly Arts and Earth Center, Ipswich, MA; Notre Dame du Lac, Worcester, MA; St. Julie Billiart Residential Care Center, Ipswich, MA.

Represented in the Archdiocese of Boston and in the Dioceses of Baton Rouge, Manchester and Worcester.

Part of the Sisters of Notre Dame United States East-West Province: 468 Poquonock Ave., Windsor, CT 06095-2473. Tel: 860-688-1832. Prov. Admin. Team: Sr. Catherine Waldron, S.N.D.deN.; Sr. Mary M. Farren, S.N.D.deN.; Sr. Barbara Barry, S.N.D.deN.; Sr. Elaine Bain, S.N.D.deN; Sr. Eileen Burns, S.N.D.deN.; Sr. Patricia Chappell, S.N.D.deN.

Total in Community: 43.

Legal Title: The Connecticut Province of the Sisters of Notre Dame de Namur, Inc.

Sisters serve and staff: Colleges, High Schools, Grammar Schools; Sisters Engaged in Specialized Educational Programs: Pastoral Ministry and Religious Education, Social Health and Community Services, Diocesan Offices, Spiritual Direction and Adult Basic Education.

Represented in the Archdioceses of Boston, Hartford and Washington and in the Dioceses of Bridgeport, Norwich, Providence, Scranton, Springfield in Massachusetts and Worcester.

Part of the Sisters of Notre Dame United States East-West Province: Sisters of Notre Dame de Namur Administrative Offices, 305 Cable St., Baltimore, MD 21210-2511. Tel: 410-243-1993; Fax: 410-243-2279. Prov. Team: Sr. Catherine Waldron, S.N.D.deN.; Sr. Mary M. Farren, S.N.D.deN.; Sr. Barbara Barry, S.N.D.deN.; Sr. Elaine Bain, S.N.D.deN; Sr. Eileen Burns, S.N.D.deN.; Sr. Patricia Chappell, S.N.D.deN.

Total in Community: 34

Legal Title: Chesapeake Province of the Sisters of Notre Dame de Namur, Inc.

Represented in the Archdioceses of Baltimore, Miami, New York, Philadelphia and Washington and in the Dioceses of Arlington, Raleigh, and Wheeling-Charleston.

Part of the Sisters of Notre Dame United States East-West Province: 1520 Ralston Ave., Belmont, CA 94002. Tel: 650-593-2045. Provincial Team: Sr. Catherine Waldron, S.N.D.deN.; Sr. Mary M. Farren, S.N.D.deN.; Sr. Barbara Barry, S.N.D.deN.; Sr. Elaine Bain, S.N.D.deN; Sr. Eileen Burns, S.N.D.deN.; Sr. Patricia Chappell, S.N.D.deN.

Total in Community: 85.

Legal Title: Sisters of Notre Dame de Namur, California Province.

Ministries in the field of Academic Education at all levels; Adult Education Programs; Parish Ministries; Religious Education Programs; Social Services; Diocesan Administration; and Health.

Properties owned or sponsored: Notre Dame de Namur University, Belmont, CA; Moreland Notre Dame Elementary, Watsonville, CA; Notre Dame Elementary, Belmont, CA; Notre Dame High School, Belmont, CA; Notre Dame High School, San Jose, CA; Cristo Rey, Sacramento, CA. (Co-sponsored with Sisters of Mercy and Jesuits).

Represented in the Archdioceses of Cincinnati, Los Angeles, Portland in Oregon, San Francisco and Seattle and in the Dioceses of Burlington, Monterey, Oakland, Phoenix, Sacramento, San Jose and Stockton.

Ohio Province (1840): Sisters of Notre Dame de Namur Provincial House, 701 E. Columbia Ave., Cincinnati, OH 45215. Tel: 513-761-7636. Sr. Kathleen Harmon, S.N.D.deN.

Total in Community: 81.

Legal Titles: St. Mary's Educational Institute at Cincinnati; Sisters of Notre Dame de Namur - Ohio Province; Sisters of Notre Dame de Namur, Ohio Province, Charitable Trust.

Ministry in the field of Education at all levels; Pastoral Ministry; Administration and Services; Social Services; Communication; Health Care; Community Services.

Represented in the Archdioceses of Boston, Chicago, Cincinnati, Los Angeles, Louisville and Washington and in the Dioceses of Buffalo, Columbus, Covington, Phoenix and Youngstown. Also in Brazil and Kenya.

Part of Sisters of Notre Dame de Namur, Ohio Provincial House Baltimore Province (1934): Sisters of Notre Dame de Namur, Maryland Province Center, 701 E. Columbia Ave., Cincinnati, OH 45215. Tel: 513-761-7636.

Total in Community: 23.

Properties owned or sponsored: Maryvale Preparatory School, Brooklandville, MD; Notre Dame Academy, Villanova, PA; Trinity School, Ellicot City, MD; Sisters Academy of Baltimore, Inc.

Represented in the Archdiocese of Baltimore and in the Dioceses of Brooklyn and Rockville Centre.

Leadership Team: Sr. Sr. Kathleen Harmon, S.N.D.deN., Prov.; Sr. Donna Jurick, S.N.D.deN.; Sr. Patricia Loome, S.N.D.deN.

Base Communities Province (1989): Sisters of Notre Dame de Namur Base Communities Province Office:, 125 Michigan Ave., N.E., Washington, DC 20017-1004. Tel: 202-884-9750. Email: sndbcunit@aol.com. Communications Network: Sr. Maura Browne, SNDdeN; Sr. Loretta Fleming, SNDdeN; Sr. Mary Hayes, SNDdeN; Sr. Elizabeth Smoyer, SNDdeN.

Total in Province: 39.

Legal Title: Sisters of Notre Dame de Namur Base Communities, Inc.

Ministry in Formal Education; Social Services/ Community Development; Pastoral Ministry.

Represented in the Archdioceses of Baltimore, Boston, Cincinnati, Philadelphia and Washington and in the Dioceses of Albany, Charleston, Fort Wayne-South Bend, Orlando, Richmond, Rockville Centre, St. Petersburg, San Jose and Wilmington. Also in Brazil and Republic of Congo.

[3010] (O.S.B.S.)—OBLATE SISTERS OF THE BLESSED SACRAMENT (D)

Founded in 1935 by Rev. Sylvester Eisenman, O.S.B.

Motherhouse: St. Sylvester's Convent, 103 Church Dr., P.O. Box 204, Marty, SD 57361. Tel: 605-384-3305. Sr. Miriam Shindelar, O.S.B.S., Supr.

Total in Community: 4.

Represented in the Diocese of Sioux Falls.

[3020] (O.B.T.)—SISTERS OBLATES TO THE BLESSED TRINITY (D)

Founded in the Archdiocese of New York, United States, in 1987.

Generalate & Novitiate: St. Aloysius Gonzaga Novitiate, 306 Beekman Rd., P.O. Box 98, Hopewell Junction, NY 12533. Tel: 845-226-5671; Email: Jstab35097@aol.com. Sr. Julia Berdugo, O.B.T., Supr. Gen.

Total in Community: 25.

Represented in the Archdioceses of New York and San Juan and in the Diocese of Madison. Also in El Salvador.

[3040] (O.S.P.)—OBLATE SISTERS OF PROVIDENCE (P)

Founded in the United States in 1829.

General Motherhouse: Our Lady of Mount Providence Convent, 701 Gun Rd., Baltimore, MD 21227. Tel: 410-242-8500. Sr. Rita Michelle Proctor, O.S.P., Supr. Gen.; Sr. Mary Annette Beecham, O.S.P., Asst. Supr.; Sr. Mary Crescentia Proctor, O.S.P., Sec. Gen.; Sr. Mary Sharon Young, O.S.P., Treas.

Professed Sisters: 55; Serving in Baltimore: 43.

Legal Title: The Oblate Sisters of Providence of the City of Baltimore.

Sisters serve as Pastoral Ministry-Associates; in the field of Education; Reading Center; Day Care Centers; Teaching; Counseling; Hispanic & Migrant Ministry.

Represented in the Archdiocese of Baltimore and Miami and in the Diocese of Buffalo. Also in Costa Rica.

[3050] (O.S.H.J.)—OBLATE SISTERS OF THE SACRED HEART OF JESUS (P)

Founded in 1894. First foundation in the United States in 1949.

General Motherhouse: Rome, Italy.

American Headquarters: Villa Maria Teresa, 50 Warner Rd., Hubbard, OH 44425. Tel: 330-759-9329; Fax: 330-759-7290. Email: vmtoblate@aol.com. Sr. Joyce Candidi, O.S.H.J., Regl. Delegate.

Total in Community: 18; Total in Congregation: 167.

Represented in the Diocese of Youngstown.

[3060] (O.S.F.S.)—OBLATE SISTERS OF ST. FRANCIS DE SALES (P)

Founded in France in 1866. First foundation in the United States in 1951.

General Motherhouse: 4 rue des Terrasses, Troyes, France

American Headquarters: Villa Aviat Convent, 399 Childs Rd., Childs, MD 21916. Tel: 410-398-3699. Email: oblatesisters@mountaviat.org. Sr. Anne Elizabeth, O.S.F.S., Supr.

Total in Community: 12.

Ministry in the field of Academic and Religious Education.

Represented in the Archdiocese of Baltimore and Diocese of Wilmington.

[3080] (R.C.D.)—SISTERS OF OUR LADY OF CHRISTIAN DOCTRINE (D)

Founded in New York in 1910 for the work of religious education and social service.

Central Office: Marydell Convent, 110 Larchdale Ave., Nyack, NY 10960. Tel: 845-512-8669. Sr. Mary Murray, O.P., Pres.

Total in Community: 11.

Ministry in the field of Religious Education and Spirituality; Social Work, Nursing and Counseling.

Represented in the Archdiocese of New York.

[3090] (C.L.H.C.)—CONGREGATION OF OUR LADY, HELP OF THE CLERGY (D)

Maryvale Sisters

Founded in the United States in 1961.

Motherhouse: Maryvale Motherhouse, 2522 June Bug Rd., Vale, NC 28168. Tel: 704-276-2626. Mother Mary Louis, Supr.

Total in Community: 4.

Represented in the Diocese of Charlotte.

[3100] (R.S.R.)—CONGREGATION OF OUR LADY OF THE HOLY ROSARY (P)

Founded in Rimouski, P.Q., Canada in 1874. First foundation in the United States in 1899.

General Motherhouse: 300 Alle du Rosaire, Rimouski, Canada, G5L 3E3. Tel: 418-724-5940. Sr. Mary-Alma Dube, R.S.R., Supr. Gen.

Our Lady of the Holy Rosary Regional House: 25 Portland Ave., Old Orchard Beach, ME 04064-2211. Tel: 207-934-0592; Tel: 207-937-3214. Email: rsr@maine.rr.com. Sr. Jeannette Roy, R.S.R., Regl. Coord.

Total number in the Region: 9.

Ministry in the fields of Education; Diocesan Ministry; Pastoral Ministry; Retreat Ministry.

Represented in the Diocese of Portland (In Maine)

[3105] (S.O.L.T.)—SISTERS OF THE SOCIETY OF OUR LADY OF THE MOST HOLY TRINITY

Founded in 1958 in New Mexico by Fr. James H. Flanagan. The family of the Society of Our Lady of the Most Holy Trinity is composed of priests, brothers, sisters, and laity. The Sisters serve on Ecclesial

Teams with other SOLT members and live a Marian-Trinitarian spirituality.

Motherhouse & U.S. Regionalate: 1200 Lantana St., Corpus Christi, TX 78407. Tel: 361-654-0054; Fax: 361-289-0087; Email: generalsisterservant@solt.net. U.S. Regionalate: Tel: 361-387-8090; Email: info@solt.net. Sr. Megan Mary Thibodeau, S.O.L.T., Gen. Sister Servant.

Total number of Sisters in Community: 117.

Professed Sisters: 117; Novices: 4; Candidates: 11.

Represented in the Archdioceses of Santa Fe and Seattle and in the Dioceses of Corpus Christi, Fargo, Kansas City-St. Joseph, Phoenix, Pueblo and Sioux City.

[3110] (R.C.)—N AMERICAN PROVINCE OF THE CONGREGATION OF OUR LADY OF THE RETREAT IN THE CENACLE (P)

Founded in France in 1826. First foundation in the United States in 1892.

Generalate: Piazza Madonna del Cenacolo, 15, Rome, Italy, 00136.

North American Province (2000): Congregation of Our Lady of the Retreat in the Cenacle, 3800 W. Peterson Ave., Chicago, IL 60659-3116. Tel: 773-528-6300. Province Email: cenacleprovincialate@usa.net; Web: www.cenaclesisters.org. Sr. Pamela Falkowski, R.C., Prov. Email: pamelajeanrc@gmail.com.

Total in Community: 38.

Represented in the Archdioceses of Atlanta, Chicago and Galveston-Houston and in the Dioceses of Green Bay, Paterson and Rockville Centre.

[3120] (O.L.S.)—SISTERS OF OUR LADY OF SORROWS (P)

Founded in Italy in 1839. First foundation in the United States in 1947.

General Motherhouse: Viale Vaticano 90, Rome, Italy, 00165. Mother Carla Bertani, O.L.S., Supr. Gen.

American Headquarters: Sisters of Our Lady of Sorrows Convent, 9894 Norris Ferry Rd., Shreveport, LA 71106. Fax: 318-797-7003. Email: srsandraols@yahoo.com. Sr. Sandra Norsworthy, O.L.S., USA Delegate of Supr. Gen.

Total in Community: 19; Novices: 2. Universal total in Congregation: 280.

Ministry in the field of Education; Work with people with mental disability; Outreach to the poor; Pastoral Ministry; CCD & Adult Education; elementary, middle school and early childhood education; afterschool art & education program.

Represented in the Dioceses of Alexandria, Lafayette, Shreveport and Las Cruces.

[3130] (O.L.V.M.)—OUR LADY OF VICTORY MISSIONARY SISTERS (P)

Founded in the United States in 1922.

Motherhouse: Victory Noll, 1900 West Park Dr., Door 17, Huntington, IN 46750-8957. Tel: 260-200-1677; Fax: 260-356-1504; Email: victorynoll@olvm.org. Sr. Jenny Howard, S.P., Congregational Leader.

Total in Community: 29.

Legal Holding: Victory Noll Sisters Community Support Trust.

Represented in the Archdioceses of Chicago, Denver and Santa Fe and in the Dioceses of Charleston, Fort Wayne-South Bend and Lafayette in Indiana.

[3135] (S.B.S.)—SISTERS OF THE BLESSED SACRAMENT (P)

Founded in 1891.

Office: Four Neshaminy Interplex Drive, Suite 205, Trevose, PA 19053. Tel: 215-244-8174. Sr. Stephanie Henry, Pres.

Provincial House: 2260 Scottville Road, Powhatan, VA 23139.

Sisters: 4; Total Sisters in Order: 60

Ministry in Education, Healthcare, Ecosocial Justice, Chaplaincy and Missionaries.

Represented in the Archdioceses of Philadelphia and New Orleans and in the Dioceses of Cleveland, Nashville, Richmond and Savannah.

[3140] (C.S.A.C.)—SISTERS OF THE CATHOLIC APOSTOLATE (PALLOTTINE) (P)

Founded in Italy in 1835. First foundation in the United States in 1889.

General Motherhouse: Via Caio Canuleio 162, Rome, Italy, 00174. Mother Ivete Garlet, C.S.A.C., Supr. Gen. Universal total in Congregation: 480.

Provincial Motherhouse in America: Queen of Apostles Convent, 98 Harriman Heights Rd., Monroe, NY 10950. Sr. Ann Joachim Firneno, C.S.A.C., Prov. Moderator.

Total in Community: 32.

Ministry in the field of Academic and Religious Education at Elementary and Secondary Levels; Pastoral Services; Youth Ministry - PTAF.

Represented in the Archdioceses of Newark and New York.

Provincial: 98 Harriman Heights Rd., Monroe, NY 10950. Tel: 845-492-5080.

[3150] (S.A.C.)—PALLOTTINE MISSIONARY SISTERS - QUEEN OF APOSTLES PROVINCE (P) (Missionary Sisters of the Catholic Apostolate)

Founded in Rome, Italy. in 1838. First founded in the United States in 1912.

General Motherhouse: Rome, Italy. Sr. Izabela Swierad, S.A.C., Supr. Gen.

American Provincialate: St. Mary's Convent, 2810 North Staunton Rd., Huntington, WV 25702. Tel: 304-522-3790; Fax: 314-526-1538. Email: provincial@pallottinesac.org. Sr. Mary Grace Barile, S.A.C., Prov.; Sr. Phyllis Carpenter, S.A.C., Archivist/Historian.

Total in Congregation: 552; U.S. Province: 20.

Properties owned and/or sponsored: Pallottine Renewal Center, Florissant, MO; St. Mary's Convent, Huntington, WV; Convent, Buckhannon, WV; St. Vincent Pallotti Convent, High School Laurel, MD.

Sisters minister in the fields of Health Care; Education; Retreat and Renewal Ministry; Social Services; Parish and Pastoral Work.

Represented in the Archdioceses of St. Louis and Washington and in the Diocese of Wheeling-Charleston.

[3160] (P.V.M.I.)—PARISH VISITORS OF MARY IMMACULATE (P)

Founded in New York City in 1920 for family visitation and religious education. A contemplative-missionary community serving the Church by person-to-person evangelization.

Motherhouse and Novitiate: Marycrest, P.O. Box 658, Monroe, NY 10949-0658. Tel: 845-783-2251. Communications Email: marycrest@frontiernet.net.; Vocation Director Email: pvmi@frontiernet.net. Mother Maria Catherine Iannotti, Gen. Supr.; Sr. Mary Beata Im, Novice Dir.

Total in Community: 60.

Ministry in evangelization, catechetics, & spiritual counseling; liaison for social services.

Represented in the Archdioceses of New York and Philadelphia and in the Dioceses of Brooklyn, Phoenix Wilmington and Youngstown. Also in Nigeria and Philippines.

[3170] (C.P.)—CONGREGATION OF THE NUNS OF THE PASSION OF JESUS CHRIST (P) (Passionist Nuns)

Founded in Italy in 1771 by St. Paul of the Cross. First foundation in the United States in 1910.

2715 Churchview Ave., Pittsburgh, PA 15227. Tel: 412-881-1155; Email: passionistnuns@gmail.com. Mother Joyce Foga, C.P., Supr.

Perpetual Vows: 8.

The Religious of the Passion of Jesus Christ (Contemplative) (1926): St. Gabriel's Monastery, 631 Griffin Pond Rd., Clarks Summit, PA 18411. Tel: 570-586-2791; Fax: 570-586-8210. Sr. Teresita Kho, C.P., Supr. Professed Sisters: 7.

Sisters serve and staff: Retreats and other Programs for Women and Men of all Faiths; Clergy and Religious; Ecumenical Groups; Business and Civic Groups.

Legal Holding: St. Gabriel's Monastery and Retreat Center.

Passionist Nuns (Cloistered Contemplative) (1946): Passionist Nuns, 8564 Crisp Rd., Whitesville, KY 42378-9782. Tel: 270-233-4571. Mother John Mary Read, C.P., Supr.

Perpetually Professed Nuns: 9; Temporary Vows: 2.

Legal Title: Passionist Nuns of Covington, KY.

Passionist Nuns (Cloistered Contemplative) (1948): Passionist Monastery, 15700 Clayton Rd., Ellisville, MO 63011. Tel: 636-527-6867. Mother Mary Veronica, C.P., Supr.

Total in Community: 4.

[3180] (C.P.)—SISTERS OF THE CROSS AND PASSION (P) (Passionist Sisters)

Founded in 1852. First foundation in the United States in 1924.

Generalate: Drumalis Centre, 47 Glenarm Rd., Larne BT40 1DT Northern Ireland. Tel: +44(0)2828 267005; Email: cpclt@icloud.com. Sr. Eileen Fucito, C.P., Congregational Leader.

Diversified apostolic works according to the needs of the church; catechetical, pastoral and social work; education functions; retreats; missionary work in the United States and Africa, Argentina, Australia, Bosnia, Botswana, Chile, England, Europe, Ireland, Peru, Scotland and Vietnam.

Provincial House in United States: Holy Family Convent, One Wright Ln., North Kingstown, RI 02852. Tel: 401-667-4813; 401-480-7766. Email: passcom12@gmail.com. Sr. Bernadette Hughes, C.P. Province Leader.

Professed Sisters: 29.

Sisters minister in Retreat Centers; Elementary Education; Parish Ministry; Religious Education; Social Services.

Properties owned and operated: Our Lady of Calvary Retreat, Farmington, CT.

Represented in the Archdioceses of Hartford and in the Dioceses of Providence and Rockville Centre.

[3190] (A.P.)—NUNS OF THE PERPETUAL ADORATION OF THE BLESSED SACRAMENT (P)

Founded in Rome in 1807. First foundation in the United States in 1925.

El Paso: Expiatory Shrine of Christ the King and Monastery of Perpetual Adoration, 145 N. Cotton Ave., El Paso, TX 79901. Tel: 915-533-5323; Email: mary.guadalupe@att.net. Mother Maria Zoila Flores, A.P., Supr.

Sisters: 12.

Represented in the Archdioceses of Anchorage-Juneau and San Francisco and in the Dioceses of El Paso and Sioux Falls.

San Francisco: Monastery of Perpetual Adoration, 771 Ashbury St., San Francisco, CA 94117. Tel: 415-566-2743. Mother Rosalba Maria, A.P., Supr.

Sisters: 12.

Represented in the Archdiocese of San Francisco. Also in Africa, Chile, Italy, Mexico and Spain.

[3195] (A.P.G.)—SISTERS OF PERPETUAL ADORATION OF GUADALUPE, INC. (P)

U.S. Foundation: 2403 W. Travis, San Antonio, TX 78207. Tel: 210-227-5546. Mother Luz del Carmen Sanchez O., A.P.G., Gen. Counsel.

Total in Community: 10.

[3200] (SCH.P.)—SISTERS OF THE PIOUS SCHOOLS (P) (Escolapias)

Founded in Figueras, Spain in 1829.

Universal total in Congregation: 675.

General Motherhouse: Via Crescenzio 77, Rome, Italy, 00193. Mother M. Divina Garcia, Sch.P., Supr. Gen.

U.S. Headquarters (1954): 17601 Nordhoff St., Northridge, CA 91325. Tel: 818-885-6265; Fax: 818-718-6752. Sr. Guadalupe Gonzalez, Sch.P.

Total in Community: 8.

Ministry in Religious Education; Parish Schools.

Represented in the Archdiocese of Los Angeles.

[3210] (P.C.P.A.)—POOR CLARES OF PERPETUAL ADORATION (P)

Founded in France, 1854. First foundation in the United States at Cleveland, Ohio, 1921. Poor Clares of Perpetual Adoration, cloistered, contemplative, solemn vows. Object: Perpetual Adoration in spirit of Praise and Thanksgiving and Gospel living. Solemn Exposition day and night. Each monastery is autonomous.

Sancta Clara Monastery (1946): 4200 N. Market Ave., Canton, OH 44714. Tel: 330-492-1171; Web: www.poorclares.org. Mother Gertrude Espenilla, P.C.P.A., Abbess.

Total in Community: 20.

Saint Joseph Adoration Monastery (1956): Timber Drive, Mooresboro, NC 28114. Tel: 205-795-5739; Email: altarbread@olamnuns.com; Web: www.stjosephmonastery.com.

Legal Title: Poor Clares of Perpetual Adoration-Saint Joseph Adoration Monastery, Inc.

Adoration Monastery (1921): 4108 Euclid Ave., Cleveland, OH 44103. Tel: 216-361-0783. Email: angelspcpa@sbcglobal.net. Mother Mary James, P.C.P.A., Abbess.

Total in Community: 20.

Poor Clares of Perpetual Adoration (1954): Our Lady of the Most Blessed Sacrament Monastery, 3900 13th St., N.E., Washington, DC 20017-2699. Tel: 202-526-6808; Fax: 202-526-0678; Email: ourprayer4u@poorclareswdc.org; Web: www.poorclareswdc.org. Mother Mary Angela Perry, P.C.P.A., Abbess.

Total in Community: 5.

Our Lady of the Angels Monastery: Shrine of the Most Blessed Sacrament, 3222 County Rd. 548, Hanceville, AL 35077. Tel: 205-271-2917; Fax: 205-795-5701. Email: secretary@olamnuns.com; Web: www.olamnuns.com. Mother Mary Paschal, P.C.P.A., Apostolic Admin. Total in Community: 13.

Legal Title: Our Lady of the Angels Monastery in Hanceville, Alabama

Represented in the Diocese of Birmingham.

[3230] (P.H.J.C.)—POOR HANDMAIDS OF JESUS CHRIST (P)
(The Ancilla Domini Sisters, Inc.)

Founded in Germany in 1851. First foundation in the United States in 1868.

General Motherhouse: Dernbach, Westerwald, Germany Sr. Judith Diltz, P.H.J.C., Supr. Gen.

American Province-Provincialate: Convent Ancilla Domini, 9601 Union Rd., P.O. Box 1, Donaldson, IN 46513. Tel: 574-936-9936; Fax: 574-935-1785. Email: sbell@poorhandmaids.org. Sr. Shirley Bell, P.H.J.C., Prov. Provincial Councilors: Sr. Deborah Davis, P.H.J.C.; Sr. Marybeth Martin, P.H.J.C; Sr. Nkechi Iwuoha, P.H.J.C.; Amy Brown, Chief Accounting Officer; Amanda Maynard, Develop. Dir.

Professed Sisters: 55.

Ministry in the fields of Academic Education at all levels; Healthcare; Parish Ministries; Retreat Ministries; Child Care Ministry; Retirement Communities; Environmental Care and Homeless Ministries.

Properties owned or sponsored: Convent Ancilla Domini; Catherine Kasper Life Center, Inc.; Lindenwood Retreat & Conference Center; MoonTree Community, Donaldson, IN; Poor Handmaids of Jesus Christ Community Support Trust, Donaldson, IN; Poor Handmaids of Jesus Christ Foundation, Inc., Donaldson, IN; HealthVisions Midwest, Hammond, IN; Emmaus House, East Chicago, IN; Sojourner Truth House, Gary, IN; St. Catherine Convent, East Chicago, IN; Annunciation Convent, Hoffman Estates, IL; St. Joseph Community Health Foundation, Ft. Wayne, IN; Catherine Kasper Place, Ft. Wayne, IN; St. Joseph Medical Center of Ft. Wayne, Inc., Ft. Wayne, IN; Sarah House, South Bend, IN; St. Elizabeth Convent, Chicago, IL.

Represented in the Archdioceses of Chicago and Cincinnati and in the Dioceses of Fort Wayne-South Bend and Gary. Also in Brazil, Germany and Mexico.

[3240] (C.J.C.)—POOR SISTERS OF JESUS CRUCIFIED AND THE SORROWFUL MOTHER (D)

Founded in the United States in 1924.

General Motherhouse and Novitiate: Our Lady of Sorrows Convent, 261 Thatcher St., Brockton, MA 02302-3997. Sr. Mary Valliere, C.J.C., Gen. Supr.

Total in Community: 7.

Properties owned and/or sponsored: Our Lady of Sorrows Convent, Brockton, MA. Ministry in Nursing Homes; Education Center; Elementary Schools; Assisted Living facilities; and Pastoral Ministry.

Represented in the Archdiocese of Boston.

[3242] (C.S.N.)—THE CONGREGATION OF THE SISTERS OF NAZARETH (P)

Founded in England by Victoire Lermenier.

Motherhouse: 167-175 Hammersmith Rd., London, England, W6 8DB United Kingdom. Sr. Brenda McCall, C.S.N., Supr. Gen.

Regional Headquarters: Nazareth House, 6333 Rancho Mission Rd., San Diego, CA 92108-2001. Tel: 619-573-8538. Sr. Rose Hoye, C.S.N., Area Supr. Email: srrose.hoye@sistersofnazareth.com.

Professed Sisters: 15.

Legal Title: The Congregation of the Sisters of Nazareth Mother House U.S.A., Inc.

Represented in the Archdioceses of Los Angeles and San Francisco and in the Dioceses of Fresno and San Diego.

[3250] (P.S.S.J.)—POOR SISTERS OF ST. JOSEPH (P)

Founded in Buenos Aires, Argentina in 1880.

U.S. Motherhouse: St. Gabriel Convent, 4319 Sano St., Alexandria, VA 22312. Tel: 703-354-0395. Email: pssjalexandria@gmail.com. Mother Maria Gonzalez.

Casa Nazareth: 532 Spruce St., Reading, PA 19602. Tel: 610-378-1947. Total in Community: 9.

Saint Gabriel Preschool, 4319 Sano Street, Alexandria, VA 22312. Tel: 703-354-0395; Email: stgdaycare@gmail.com; Web: stgdaycare.org. Sr. Eneyda Martinez, P.S.S.J., Dir. Care for children ages 2-5 years.

General Motherhouse: Pte. Peron 734, 1663 Muñiz, Buenos Aires, Argentina Mother Raquel del Carmen Brambilla, Supr. Gen.

Represented in the Dioceses of Allentown and Arlington.

[3255] (P.C.M.)—PREACHERS OF CHRIST AND MARY (D)

Founded in 1995.

General Motherhouse: 8734 Whitney Ave., Elmherst, NY 11373. Mother Maria Amador, P.C.M., Supr.

Professed Sisters: 4.

Ministries in Evangelization through the Arts, the Media, Preaching in Retreats, Organization of Events, Religious Education Programs and Social Development.

Represented in the Diocese of Brooklyn.

[3260] (C.PP.S.)—SISTERS OF THE PRECIOUS BLOOD (DAYTON, OHIO) (P)

Founded in Switzerland in 1834. First foundation in the United States in 1844.

C.PP.S. Administration Offices: 4000 Denlinger Rd., Dayton, OH 45426. Tel: 937-837-3302; Fax: 937-715-4669. Sr. Edna Hess, C.PP.S., Pres.; Sr. Patty Kramer, C.PP.S., Vice Pres & Councilor; Sr. Margo Young, C.PP.S., M.D., Congregational Sec. & Councilor; Sr. Ann Clark, C.PP.S., Councilor; Sr. Maria Gipson, C.PP.S., Councilor; Sarah Aisenbrey, Archivist.

Total Membership: 82.

Ministry in Elementary Schools; Pastoral Ministry in Hospitals and Long-term Care Centers; Religious and Adult Education; Ethnic Minorities and Marginalized Peoples; Retreat and Music Ministry; Missionary and Volunteer Services.

Properties owned and sponsored: C.PP.S. Administration Offices, Dayton, OH; Salem Heights Convent, Dayton, OH.

Represented in the Archdioceses of Chicago, Cincinnati, Denver and in the Dioceses of Lansing, Saginaw, San Bernardino and San Diego. Also in Chile and Guatemala.

[3270] (C.PP.S.)—SISTERS OF THE MOST PRECIOUS BLOOD (O'FALLON, MO) (P)

Founded in Switzerland in 1845. First foundation in the United States in 1870.

General Administration: St. Mary's Institute of O'Fallon, 204 N. Main St., O'Fallon, MO 63366-2299. Tel: 636-240-6010; Fax: 636-272-5031. Sr. Janice Bader, C.PP.S., Supr. Gen. General Councilors: Sr. Marie Fennewald, C.PP.S., Councilor & Sec.; Sr. Susan Borgel, C.PP.S., Councilor & Treas.; Sr. Barbara Payne, Community Archivist.

Total in Community: 72.

Ministry in the field of Education; Care of the Elderly; Pastoral and Parish Ministry; Foreign Missions; Social Services; Prayer/Presence.

Properties owned: St. Mary's Institute of O'Fallon, O'Fallon, MO; Charitable Trust, Sisters of the Most Precious Blood of O'Fallon, MO.

Represented in the Archdiocese of St. Louis and in the Diocese of Wheeling-Charleston. Also in Bolivia and Peru.

[3310] (P.M.)—SISTERS OF THE PRESENTATION OF MARY (P)

Founded in France in 1796. First foundation in the United States in 1873.

General Administration: Presentazionne di Maria, Viale Pio XI, 29 - C.P. 104, Castelgandolfo, Italy, 00073. Mother Maria des Anjos Alves, p.m., Supr. Gen.

House of Formation: 186 Lowell Rd., Hudson, NH 03051-4908. Tel: 603-882-1347.

Provincial Administration: 209 Lawrence St., Methuen, MA 01844-3884. Tel: 978-687-1369. Sr. Helene Cote, P.M., Provincial Supr.

Total Number in Province: 108.

Properties owned and/or sponsored: Marie Joseph Spiritual Center, Biddeford, ME; Presentation of Mary Academy, Hudson, NH; St. Joseph Residence, Manchester, NH; Rivier University, Nashua, NH.

Represented in the Archdiocese of Boston and the Dioceses of Manchester and Portland in Maine.

[3320] (P.B.V.M.)—SISTERS OF THE PRESENTATION OF THE B.V.M. (P)

Founded in Ireland in 1775.

Represented in the United States in the following Archdioceses and Dioceses.

Dubuque (P)

Mt. Loretto Convent, Motherhouse and Novitiate: 2360 Carter Rd., Dubuque, IA 52001-2997. Tel: 563-588-2008; Fax: 563-588-4463. Email: carmen@dbqpbvms.org. Sr. Carmen Hernandez, P.B.V.M., Congregational Leader.

Total in Community: 80.

Legal Title: Sisters of the Presentation of the B.V.M., Dubuque, IA.

Ministry in the field of Religious and Academic Education; Hospital Chaplaincy; Elder Care; Parish Ministries; South American Bolivian Mission; Retreat & Spiritual Direction; Hispanic Ministry; Peace and Justice; Social Services; Internal Community Ministry.

Represented in the Archdioceses of Chicago, Dubuque, Louisville, New Orleans and St. Paul-Minneapolis and in the Dioceses of Davenport, Jackson, Pittsburgh, Sioux Falls and Winona-Rochester. Also in Bolivia.

New York (P)

Mt. St. Joseph Administration Center: Sisters of the Presentation of the Blessed Virgin Mary, 84 Presentation Way, New Windsor, NY 12553. Tel: 845-564-0513; Fax: 845-567-0219. Email: administration@sistersofthepresentation.org. Sr. Mary Catherine Redmond, P.B.V.M., Pres.

Total in Community: 83.

Ministry in the field of Academic Education at all levels; Pastoral Services; Health Care and Social Services.

Represented in the Archdioceses of New York and Washington and in the Dioceses of Brooklyn, Paterson and Worcester.

Our Lady of the Presentation Motherhouse: 419 Woodrow Rd., Staten Island, NY 10312. Tel: 718-356-2121. Sr. Lorraine Hale, Congregational Leader.

Professed Sisters: 11.

Ministry in Elementary Schools; University; Campus Ministry; Pastoral Counseling; Adult Education; Healing & Parish Ministry.

Represented in the Archdioceses of New York and Philadelphia.

San Francisco Presentation Congregational Offices: 281 Masonic Ave., San Francisco, CA 94118. Tel: 415-422-5001. Sr. Rosina Conrotto, P.B.V.M., Pres. Tel: 415-422-5012; Andrea Hetley, Archivist.

Total in Community: 50.

Legal Title: Sisters of the Presentation.

Ministry in the field of Religious and Academic Education at all levels; Parish Ministry; Social and Health Ministry; Retreat Work; Internal Ministry.

Represented in the Archdioceses of Los Angeles, San Francisco and Washington and in the Dioceses of Monterey, Oakland, San Jose and Sioux Falls.

Albany (P)

St. Colman's Presentation Convent, Motherhouse and Novitiate: Sisters of the Presentation of the Blessed Virgin Mary P.V.B.M., 11 Haswell Rd, Watervliet, NY 12189. Tel: 518-273-4911; Fax: 518-273-3312. Mother Mary Louise Kane, P.B.V.M., Supr.

Total in Community: 19.

Ministry in the field of Special Education; Child Caring Institution; Resident/Day School for Autistic & Day School for Emotionally Challenging Children, Students with Learning Disabilities.

Represented in the Diocese of Albany.

Sioux Falls (P)

Presentation Convent, Motherhouse and Novitiate: Sisters of the Presentation of the Blessed Virgin Mary, 1500 N. Second St., Aberdeen, SD 57401. Tel: 605-225-0420. Sr. Mary Thomas, P.B.V.M., Pres.; Kathleen Daly, Congregation Archivist.

Total in Community: 45.

Ministry in the field of Academic Education; Hospitals; Homes for the Aged; Parish Pastoral Ministry; Hispanic Ministry.

Represented in the Diocese of Sioux Falls.

Worcester (P)

Presentation Convent: 99 Church St., Leominster, MA 01453. Email: administration@sistersofthepresentation.org. Sr. Mary Catherine Redmond, P.B.V.M., Pres.

Total in Community: 83.

Sisters staff: Elementary School Education; Pastoral Ministry; Social Services; Nursing.

Represented in the Archdioceses of New York and Washington and in the Dioceses of Brooklyn, Paterson and Worcester.

[3330] (P.B.V.M.)—UNION OF SISTERS OF THE PRESENTATION OF THE BLESSED VIRGIN MARY (P)

The Congregation of the Presentation was founded in Cork, Ireland, 1775. By decree of the Sacred Congregation for Religious, the Union of Sisters of the Presentation was established in Ireland in 1976. First U.S.A. Province was established in 1989.

Generalate: Monasterevin Co., Kildare, W34 PV32 Ireland Tel: 045-525-335. Sr. Julie Watson, P.B.V.M., Supr. Gen.

Provincial Offices: 2715 Zurich, San Antonio, TX 78230. Email: sectypbvmus@gmail.com. Sr. Katherine Fennell, P.B.V.M., Prov.; Sr. Jocelyn Quijano, P.B.V.M., Asst. Prov.; Sr. Antonio Heaphy, P.B.V.M.; Sr. Mary Margaret Mooney, P.B.V.M., Treas.; Sr. Philippa Wall, P.B.V.M., Archivist.

Perpetual Sisters: 64

Sisters Serve in: Elementary and Religious Education; Parish Ministry; RCIA; Minstry to Immigrants; Retreat Ministry; Professor of Sacred Scriptures; Health and Hospital Services and Social Services.

Represented in the Archdioceses of Los Angeles and San Antonio and in the Dioceses of Fargo and New Ulm and Orange.

Sponsored Ministries: Presentation Prayer Center, Fargo, ND; Presentation Partners in Housing, Fargo, ND.

[3340] (S.P.)—SISTERS OF PROVIDENCE (D)

Established in Holyoke, MA as a mission of the Sisters of Charity of the House of Providence, Kingston, Ontario, Canada in 1873. Founded as an independent diocesan foundation in 1892 in the Diocese of Springfield, MA.

Administrative Office: 5 Gamelin St., Holyoke, MA 01040-4081. Tel: 413-536-7511; Fax: 413-536-7917; Email: sisters@sisofprov.org. Sr. Kathleen Popko, S.P., Congregation Pres.

Professed Sisters: 17.

Legal Holdings and Titles: Sisters of Providence, Inc: The Hillside at Providence, Inc.; Hillside Residence, Inc.; Sisters of Providence Ministry Corporation: Family Services - Providence Ministries for the Needy, Holyoke, MA; Retreat Center - Genesis Spiritual Life and Conference Center, Inc., Westfield, MA; Senior Services - Mary's Meadow at Providence Place, Inc., Holyoke, MA; Providence Place, Inc., Holyoke, MA.

Represented in the Diocese of Springfield in Massachusetts.

[3350] (S.P.)—SISTERS OF PROVIDENCE (P)

Founded in Montreal in 1843. First foundation in the United States in 1856.

General Administration: 12055 rue Grenet, Montreal, Canada, H4J 2J5. Sr. Alba Letelier, S.P., Congregational Leader.

Mother Joseph Province (2000): Sisters of Providence, 1801 Lind Ave., SW, #9016, Renton, WA 98057-9016. Tel: 425-525-3999; Fax: 425-525-3335; Web: www.sistersofprovidence.net. Sr. Barbara Schamber, S.P., Prov. Leader.

Total in Community: 331; Sisters in Province: 92.

Ministry for women and children; education, healthcare, parish, aid to poor people, care for the environment; socially responsible investing; repository for history of the Catholic Church in the Northwest; skilled nursing for our senior and disabled sisters from our own and other congregations.

Properties, entities and divisions owned or operated: Sisters of Providence-Mother Joseph Province; St. Joseph Residence, Seattle, WA; Providence Archives, Seattle, WA; Sisters of Providence Retirement Trust, Renton, WA.

Represented in the Archdioceses of Los Angeles, Portland in Oregon and Seattle and in the Dioceses of Spokane and Yakima. Also in El Salvador and the Philippines.

Novitiate House: 1016 N. Superior St., #4, Spokane, WA 99202-2096. Tel: 206-488-9989. Email: julie.macasieb@providence.org. Sr. Julie Macasieb, S.P., Novitiate Dir.

Vocation Office: 4800 37th Ave., S.W., Seattle, WA 98126-2724. Tel: 206-979-0577. Sr. Margarita Hernandez, S.P., Vocation Dir.

Our Lady of Province: 47 W. Spring St., Winooski, VT 05404. Tel: 802-655-2395; Fax: 802-655-3888. Sr. Carmen Proulx, S.P., Supr.

Total in Community: 10.

Emilie Gamelin Province (2005): Sisters of Providence, 47 W. Spring St., Winooski, VT 05404. Tel: 802-655-2395; Fax: 802-655-3888. Sr. Carmen Proulx, S.P., Supr.

Total in Community: 7.

[3360] (S.P.)—SISTERS OF PROVIDENCE OF SAINT MARY-OF-THE-WOODS, INDIANA (P)

Founded in France in 1806. First foundation in the United States in 1840.

General Administration: Sisters of Providence, 1 Sisters of Providence, Saint Mary-of-the-Woods, IN 47876-1007. Tel: 812-535-4193; Web: www.sistersofprovidence.org. Sr. Dawn Tomaszewski, S.P., Gen. Supr.; Sr. Janet Gilligan, S.P., Congregation Archivist; Vicki Layton, Gen. Sec.

Total number Professed Sisters: 196.

Legal Titles and Sponsored Institutions: Saint Mary-of-the-Woods College, Saint Mary-of-the-Woods, IN; Sisters of Providence Community Support Trust (1969-Foundation to provide support for the aged and infirm members of the Congregation) Indianapolis, IN; Providence Health Care, Inc., St. Mary-of-the-Woods, IN; Providence Cristo Rey High School, Indianapolis, IN.

Ministry in the fields of Education at all levels; Diocesan Offices; Parish and Pastoral Ministry; Health Care and Retirement Facilities; Congregation Administration; Social Services; Therapeutic/Rehabilitative/ Mental Health Services.

Represented in the Archdioceses of Boston, Chicago, Indianapolis, Louisville, Los Angeles and Washington and in the Dioceses of Charlotte, Cleveland, Evansville, Joliet, Lafayette (LA), Lafayette in Indiana, Lexington, San Diego and Tuscon. Also in Taiwan.

Area of Taiwan: Providence University, 200 Taiwan Blvd., Section 7, Shalu, Taichung 43301, Taiwan, Republic of China Tel: 011-886-4-2631-1182. Sr. Rose Chiu, S.P., Area Rep.

Total in Community: 7.

Ministry in the field of Education; Elderly Care

Represented in the Archdiocese of Taipei and in the Diocese of Taichung.

[3390] (R.A.)—RELIGIOUS OF THE ASSUMPTION (P)

Founded in France in 1839. Established in the United States in 1919.

Generalate: 17 rue de l'Assomption, Paris, France, 75016.

Universal total in Congregation: 1200.

Represented in 33 countries through Europe, Africa, Asia, North America, Central America and South America.

U.S. Province: Provincial House, 1001 South 47th St., Philadelphia, PA 19143. Tel: 215-386-5016. Sr. Anne Christopher Wright, R.A., Prov. Supr.

Business Office: 506 Crestview Rd., Lansdale, PA 19446. Tel: 215-368-4427; Tel: 215-362-6296.

Total number in Province: 21.

Ministry in Pastoral and Social Ministry; Education; Advocacy for Migrants; Spiritual Formation; Youth and Young Adult Ministry; Catechesis; Care for Creation; Peace and Justice.

Represented in the Archdiocese of Philadelphia and in the Dioceses of Las Cruces and Worcester.

[3400] (R.S.C.)—RELIGIOUS SISTERS OF CHARITY (P)

Founded in Dublin, Ireland in 1815. Sisters in entire Congregation 334.

Motherhouse: Caritas, 15 Gilford Rd., Sandymount, Dublin 4, Ireland. Sr. Patricia Lenihan, Supr. Gen.

U.S. Headquarters & Novitiate (1953): Regional Residence, 10668 St. James Dr., Culver City, CA 90230. Tel: 310-559-0176; Fax: 310-559-3530. Email: bridoshearsc@gmail.com. Sr. Brid O'Shea, R.S.C., Regl. Leader.

Total in U.S. Community: 14.

Represented in the Archdiocese of Los Angeles.

[3410] (R.C.E.)—RELIGIOUS OF CHRISTIAN EDUCATION (P)

Founded in France in 1817. First foundation in the United States in 1905.

General Motherhouse: France

Provincial Residence: 444 Centre St., Milton, MA 02186. Tel: 781-894-2008; Fax: 401-349-4970. Sr. Martha Brigham, R.C.E., Pres.

Total in Community: 6.

Legal Title: Religious of Christian Education, Inc.

Represented in the Archdiocese of Boston.

[3430] (M.P.F.)—RELIGIOUS TEACHERS FILIPPINI (P)

Founded in Italy in 1692. First foundation in the United States in 1910.

General Motherhouse: Villa Maria Regina, Via Stazione Ottavia, 72, Rome, Italy. Sr. Nicolina Bandiera, M.P.F., Supr. Gen.

St. Lucy Filippini Province: Villa Walsh, Morristown, NJ 07960-4928. Tel: 973-538-2886. Sr. Ascenza Tizzano, M.P.F., Prov. Supr.; Sr. Patricia Martin, M.P.F., Community Archivist.

Total in Community: 155.

Ministry in the field of Religious and Academic Education in elementary and secondary schools; Child Care Centers; Parish Ministry; Pastoral Care; Foreign Mission Work; House of Prayer; Retreat House.

Properties owned and sponsored: Villa Walsh, Morristown, NJ; Villa Victoria, Trenton, NJ; St. Joseph by The Sea, South Mantoloking, NJ; St. Joseph Convent, Bristol, CT; Villa Ferretti, Winchester Ctr, CT.

Represented in the Archdioceses of Hartford, Newark, Philadelphia and Santa Fe, and in the Dioceses of Brooklyn, Cleveland, Camden, Metuchen, Orlando, Paterson, Pittsburgh, Providence, Scranton and Trenton.

[3449] (C.V.I.)—RELIGIOUS OF THE INCARNATE WORD (P)

Founded in Lyon, France, in 1625. First foundation in the United States in 1853, in Mexico 1894.

General Motherhouse: Industria #1-Col. Toriello Guerra, Deleg., Tlalpan, Mexico, D.F. 14050. Sr. Margarita Dibildox, C.V.I., Gen. Supr.

U.S. Vice Provincial House: 153 Rainier Ct., Chula Vista, CA 91911. Tel: 619-869-7337. Sr. Camille Crabbe, C.V.I., Vice Prov.

Total in Congregation: 465.

Ministry in Parishes; Schools; Missions and Boarding for Students.

Represented in the Diocese of San Diego. Also in Africa, Argentina, El Salvador, France, Guatemala, Mexico, Spain and Uruguay.

[3450] (R.J.M.)—RELIGIOUS OF JESUS AND MARY (P)

Founded at Lyons, France, 1818. First foundation in the United States in 1877.

Motherhouse: Via Nomentana 325, Rome, Italy. Sr. Monica Joseph, R.J.M., Supr. Gen. Universal total in Congregation: 989.

United States Province: 821 Varnum St., N.E., Ste. 225, Washington, DC 20017. Tel: 202-526-3203; Email: amagner@rjmusa.org. Sr. Margaret Perron, R.J.M., Prov.

Total in Community: 57.

Legal Title: U.S. Province of the Religious of Jesus and Mary, Inc.

Ministry in the field of Academic and Religious Education; Pastoral Ministry; Social Services; Volunteer Program.

Represented in the Archdioceses of Boston, New York and Washington and in the Dioceses of Fall River, Providence and San Diego. Also in Haiti.

[3460] (R.M.I.)—RELIGIOUS OF MARY IMMACULATE (P)

Founded in Madrid, Spain in 1876.

Mother House: Madrid, Spain Generalate: Rome, Italy.

U.S. Foundation (1954): Villa Maria, 719 Augusta St., San Antonio, TX 78215. Tel: 210-226-0025; Fax: 210-226-3305. Sr. Maria de Jesus Lozano, R.M.I., Local Supr. Total in Community: 5.

Headquarters: Centro Maria, 3103 Arlington Ave., Bronx, NY 10463. Tel: 718-708-4661. Sr. Clara Echeverria, R.M.I., Local Supr.

Total in Community: 6.

Represented in the Archdioceses of New York, San Antonio and Washington.

[3465] (R.S.H.M.)—RELIGIOUS OF THE SACRED HEART OF MARY (P)

Founded in France in 1849. First foundation in the United States in 1877.

Generalate: Via Sorelle Marchisio 41, Rome, Italy, 00168. Sr. Margaret Fielding, R.S.H.M., Institute Leader.

Universal total in Congregation: 494.

Eastern American Area (1907): 50 Wilson Park Dr., Tarrytown, NY 10591. Tel: 914-631-8872. Sr. Rosamond Blanchet, R.S.H.M., Area Leader. Email: rozrshm@gmail.com.

Total in Community: 94.

Legal Title: Sisters of the Sacred Heart of Mary.

Ministries including Education; Pastoral Ministry; Retreat and Spiritual Direction; Social Work.

Represented in the Archdioceses of New York and in the Dioceses of Arlington, Rockville Centre and Venice. Also in Africa and Europe.

Western American Area (1959): Religious of the Sacred Heart of Mary R.S.H.M. Area Administration Center, 441 N. Garfield Ave., Montebello, CA 90640-2901. Tel: 323-887-8821; Fax: 323-887-8952. Email: rshmwap@earthlink.net. Sr. Kathleen Kelemen, R.S.H.M., Area Leader.

Total number in Province: 43.

Legal Titles or Holdings: Religious of the Sacred Heart of Mary, Western American Province, a California nonprofit corporation, Marymount School Corporation, a California nonprofit public benefit corporation.

Ministry in the field of Education; Diverse Pastoral Ministries; Prison Ministry; Justice and Peace Advocacy; Youth at Risk.

Represented in the Archdiocese of Los Angeles. Also in Mexico.

[3468] (S.M.M.I) SALESIAN MISSIONARIES OF MARY IMMACULATE (P)

Founded in France in 1872.

St. Louis: 798 Buckley Rd., St Louis, MO 63125. Sr. Jolly Joseph, Supr.

Chicago: 3954 N. Meade Ave., Chicago, IL 60634

Total in Community: 1400

Ministry in the fields of Healing; Education; Pastoral and Social Work.

Represented in the Archdioceses of Chicago and St. Louis.

[3469] (S.F.C.C.)—SISTERS FOR CHRISTIAN COMMUNITY

Founded in 1970.

Motherhouse: Vietnam.

International Communication Coordinator: Email: iccsfcc@yahoo.com

Vowed Members: 324; In Formation: 75.

Ministry in Education, Healthcare, Pastoral Services and Social Work.

[3470] (S.R.C.M.)—SISTERS OF REPARATION OF THE CONGREGATION OF MARY, INC. (D)

St. Zita's Villa, 50 Saddle River Rd., N., Monsey, NY 10952. Tel: 845-356-2011; Fax: 845-364-6520. Sr. Maureen Francis, S.R.C.M.

Total in Community: 2.

Represented in the Archdiocese of New York.

[3475] (S.R.)—SISTERS OF REPARATION OF THE SACRED WOUNDS OF JESUS (D)

Founded in 1954 in New York by Mother Mary Rose Therese, S.R. Established in the Diocese of San Diego in 1959. Motherhouse and Novitiate transferred to the Archdiocese of Portland in Oregon in 1973.

General Motherhouse and Novitiate: Sacred Wounds of Jesus Convent, 2120 S.E. 24th Ave., Portland, OR 97214. Tel: 503-236-4207; Fax: 503-236-3400; Email: repsrs@comcast.net; Email: MMAngels@comcast.net; Web: www.reparationsisters.org. Mother Mary of the Angels, S.R., Supr.

Sisters: 1; Donne Members: 164.

Legal Title: Sisters of Reparation of the Sacred Wounds of Jesus, Inc., Portland, OR.

Ministry in Health Care; Education; Pastoral Animation.

Represented in the Archdiocese of Portland in Oregon.

[3480] (C.R.)—SISTERS OF THE RESURRECTION (P)

Founded in Rome, Italy, in 1891. First foundation in the United States in 1900.

General Motherhouse: Via Marcantonio Colonna 52A, Rome, Italy. Sr. Dorota Zygmunt, C.R., Supr. Gen.

Universal total in Congregation: 350.

Western Province Provincial House and Novitiate: 7260 W. Peterson, Suite 216, Chicago, IL 60631. Tel: 773-792-6363. Email: Srdonna01@gmail.com. Sr. Donna Marie Wolowicki, C.R., Prov. Supr.

Total in Community: 21.

Represented in the Archdioceses of Chicago and Milwaukee.

Eastern Province Provincial House and Novitiate: Sisters of the Resurrection, 35 Boltwood Ave., Castleton On Hudson, NY 12033. Tel: 518-732-2226; Fax: 518-732-2898; Email: crsister@resurrectionsisters.org. Sr. Danielle Marie Baran, C.R., Prov. Supr.

Total in Community: 30.

Legal Title: Sisters of the Resurrection, New York, Inc.

Ministry in Nursing Homes; Elementary Schools; Christian Doctrine Centers; High School for Girls; Preschools; Pastoral Associates.

Represented in the Archdiocese of New York and in the Dioceses of Albany and Trenton.

[3490] (O.S.S.)—RELIGIOUS OF THE ORDER OF THE BLESSED SACRAMENT AND OF OUR LADY (P)

Founded in France in 1639. First foundation in the United States in 1912. The Sisters devote their lives to the perpetual adoration of Christ in the Eucharist.

Blessed Sacrament Monastery: 86 Dromore Rd., Scarsdale, NY 10583-1706. Tel: 914-722-1657. Sr. Mary Francis Blackmore, O.S.S., Prioress.

Professed Sisters: 5.

Monastery of Perpetual Adoration (1951): 2798 U.S. 31 N., P.O. Box 86, Conway, MI 49722. Tel: 231-347-0447. Sr. Mary Rosalie Smith, O.S.S., Prioress.

Professed Sisters: 1.

Represented in the Diocese of Gaylord.

[3499] (S.J.S.)—SISTER SERVANTS OF THE BLESSED SACRAMENT (P)

Founded in Mexico in 1904. First foundation in the United States in 1926.

General Motherhouse: Juan Bernardino 650, Guadalajara, Jalisco, Mexico, 45000. Sr. Maria de los Angeles Rodriguez De Anda, S.J.S., Supr. Gen.

U.S. Province: 3173 Winnetka Dr., Bonita, CA 91902. Tel: 619-267-0720; Email: provincial@usasjs.org. Sr. Adriana Rebeca Zuro, S.J.S., Prov. Supr.

Total in Community: 40.

Legal Title: Sister Servants of the Blessed Sacrament, Inc.

Ministry in the field of Education.

Represented in the Archdiocese of Los Angeles and in the Dioceses of Fresno, Sacramento and San Diego.

Province of the Immaculate Conception.

[3500] (S.S.S.)—SERVANTS OF THE BLESSED SACRAMENT (P)

Founded in France in 1859; First foundation in the United States in 1947.

General Motherhouse: 580 Dufferin, Sherbrooke, Canada, J1H 4N1.

U.S. Address: Blessed Sacrament Convent, 101 Silver St., Waterville, ME 04901. Tel: 207-872-7072; Fax: 207-873-2317. Sr. Mary Catherine Perko, S.S.S., Local Supr.

Total in Community: 10.

Represented in the Dioceses of Portland in Maine and Pueblo.

[3510] (S.S.C.K.)—CONGREGATION OF SISTER SERVANTS OF CHRIST THE KING (D)

Founded in the United States in 1936.

General Motherhouse: Loretto Convent, N.8114Co. W.W. Calvary St., Mount Calvary, WI 53057. Tel: 920-753-1053. Sr. Stephen Bloesl, Supr.

Professed Sisters: 4.

Represented in the Archdiocese of Milwaukee and in the Diocese of Fargo.

[3520] (S.S.C.M.)—SERVANTS OF THE HOLY HEART OF MARY (P)

Founded in Paris, France in 1860. First foundation in the United States in 1889.

Generalate: 2029 rue Holy Cross, Montreal, Canada, H4E 2A4. Sr. Kathleen Mulchay, S.S.C.M., Supr. Gen.

United States Region-Holy Family Province: Province Center, 2041 W., Ste. 113, Kankakee, IL 60901. Tel: 815-937-2380. Sr. Carol Karnitsky, S.S.C.M., Prov. Supr.

Total number in Region: 26.

Legal Title: Servants of the Holy Heart of Mary.

Ministry in Education; Pastoral Ministry; Ministry to the Aged; Spiritual Direction; Retreats and Home Missions.

Represented in the Dioceses of Joliet, Peoria and Rockford.

[3530] (S.SP.S.)—MISSIONARY SISTERS SERVANTS OF THE HOLY SPIRIT (P)

Founded in Holland in 1889. First foundation in the United States in 1901.

General Motherhouse: Convento dello Spirito Santo, Via Cassia 645, Rome, Italy, 00189. Sr. Maria Theresia Hörnemann, S.Sp.S., Congregational Leader.

Universal total in Congregation: 3,045.

American Motherhouse (1901): Convent of the Holy Spirit, 319 Waukegan Rd., Northfield, IL 60093; P.O. Box 6026, Techny, IL 60082-6026. Tel: 847-441-0126; Fax: 847-441-5587. Email: provinceleader@ssps-us.org. Sr. Dorota Maria Piechaczek, S.Sp.S., Prov.

Total in Community: 51.

Legal Titles: Arnold Janssen Foundation, Techny, IL; Helena Stollenwerk Foundation, Techny, IL; The Holy Spirit Life Learning Center, Chicago, IL. Ministry in Schools; Catechetical Work; Parish Ministry & Administration.

Represented in the Archdioceses of Chicago and New York and in the Dioceses of Memphis and Dubuque.

[3540] (S.SP.S.DEA.P.)—SISTER-SERVANTS OF THE HOLY SPIRIT OF PERPETUAL ADORATION (P)

Founded in Holland in 1896. First foundation in the United States in 1915. Second foundation in the United States in 1928.

Generalate: Convent of the Most Holy Trinity, Bad Driburg, Germany. Mother Maria Magdalena, S.Sp.S.deA.P., Supr. Gen.

U.S. House of Formation: Convent of Divine Love, 2212 Green St., Philadelphia, PA 19130-3197. Tel: 215-567-0123. Email: cdlvocations@gmail.com.

Blessed Sacrament Convent: 4105 Ocean Dr., Corpus Christi, TX 78411. Tel: 361-852-6212. Email: blessedsacramentconvent4105@gmail.com. Sr. Mary Angelica Nigos, S.Sp.S.A.P., Supr.; Sr. Stella Mary Marrero, S.Sp.S.A.P., Asst. Supr.; Sr. Mary Rebecca Juba, S.Sp.S.A.P., Councilor.

Professed Sisters: 7.

Adoration Convent of Christ the King Church: 1040 S. Cotner Blvd., Lincoln, NE 68510. Tel: 402-489-0765. Sr. Mary Christia, S.Sp.S.deA.P., Supr.

Professed Sisters: 7.

Represented in the Diocese of Lincoln.

[3550] (S.C.I.M.)—SERVANTS OF THE IMMACULATE HEART OF MARY (P)

Good Shepherd Sisters of Quebec

Founded in Canada in 1850. First foundation in the United States in 1882.

Generalate: 2550, rue Marie-Fitzbach, Canada Sr. Lise Gagne, S.C.I.M., Supr. Gen.

Universal total in Congregation: 248.

Provincial Headquarters: St. Joseph Province, 409 Pool St., Biddeford, ME 04005. Tel: 207-282-4976; Fax: 207-282-7376. Sr. Therese Gauvin, S.C.I.M., Prov.

Total in Community: 25.

Parish Ministry; Apostolate to the Elderly; Prison/Jail Ministry; Home and Advocacy for Women in Transition; Safe House for Trafficked Women; Ministry to immigrants.

Represented in the Diocese of Portland in Maine.

[3560] (S.J.)—SERVANTS OF JESUS (P)

Founded in Detroit, Michigan in 1974.

Headquarters: Servants of Jesus, 8080 Kinmore, Dearborn Heights, MI 48127. Tel: 313-562-6156. Sr. Corinne Weiss, S.J., Pres.

Total in Community: 13.

Ministries: Diocesan Offices; Parish Ministry; Religious Education; Catholic Schools; Legal Aid; Health Care.
Represented in the Archdiocese of Detroit and in the Dioceses of Grand Rapids, Gaylord and Saginaw.

[3570] (O.S.M.)—MANTELLATE SISTERS, SERVANTS OF MARY OF BLUE ISLAND (P)

Founded in Italy in 1861. First foundation in the United States in 1916.
Generalate and Novitiate: Rome, Italy.
Convent of Our Mother of Sorrows: 13811 S. Western Ave., Blue Island, IL 60406. Sr. Marianne Talian, O.S.M., Supr.
Legal Title: Mantellate Sisters Servants of Mary.
Represented in the Archdiocese of Chicago and in the Diocese of Joliet.

[3572] (O.S.M.)—MANTELLATE SISTERS SERVANTS OF MARY OF PLAINFIELD (P)

Founded October 6, 1861 in Treppio, Italy. First founded in the United States 1916.
Universal Number of Mantellate Sisters: 319.
Mantellate Sisters Servants of Mary of Plainfield (1977): 16949 S. Drauden Rd., Plainfield, IL 60586-9168. Tel: 815-436-5796. Sr. Marianne Talian, O.S.M., Supr.
Sisters: 6.
Ministry in the field of Academic Education; Parish Ministry; Retreats; Social Work; Nursing; Homes for the Aged; Foreign Missions.
Represented in the Archdiocese of Chicago and in the Diocese of Joliet.

[3580] (O.S.M.)—SERVANTS OF MARY (P)

Founded in Italy in the 13th Century. First foundation in the United States in 1893.
Congregational Motherhouse: 19 Avenue Gustave, Rodet, F93250 Villemomble, France. Sr. Chantal-Mari LeDiraison, O.S.M., Congregational Prioress
U.S./Jamaica Community (1893) Community Motherhouse: Community Motherhouse, Convent of Our Lady of Sorrows, 7400 Military Ave., Omaha, NE 68134-3351. Tel: 402-571-2547; Fax: 402-573-6055; Web: osms.org. Sr. Jackie Ryan, O.S.M., U.S./Jamaica Community Prioress.
Total in Community: 56.
Properties owned and/or sponsored: Marian High School, Omaha, NE.
Ministry in the field of Religious and Academic Education at all levels; Parishes; Social Service Agencies; Pastoral Care; Counseling; Campus Ministry; Consulting; Spiritual Direction; Retreat Work.
Represented in the Archdioceses of Detroit and Omaha and in the Dioceses of Des Moines and Ogdensburg. Also in Jamaica.

[3590] (O.S.M.)—SERVANTS OF MARY (SERVITE SISTERS) (D)

Founded in Italy in the 13th Century. First foundation in the United States in 1912.
General Motherhouse: Servants of Mary, 1000 College Ave. W., P.O. Box 389, Ladysmith, WI 54848-0389. Tel & Fax: 715-532-6153. Email: info@servitesisters.org. Web: www.servitesisters.org. Sr. Theresa H. Sandok, O.S.M., Pres.
Total in Community: 26.
Legal Titles: Mary Bradley Corporation; Pooled Investment Trust of the Servants of Mary, Inc.; Servants of Mary Continuing Care Charitable Trust.
Ministry in the fields of Education, Health Care, Pastoral Ministry and Social Services.
Represented in the Archdioceses of Chicago, Milwaukee and St. Paul-Minneapolis and in the Dioceses of Joliet, Phoenix and Superior.

[3595] (S.S.J.)—SERVANTS OF ST. JOSEPH (P)

Founded in Spain in 1874.
Motherhouse: Salamanca, Spain
General House: Rome, Italy. Mother Josefa Somoza, Supr. Gen.
U.S. Address (1957): 203 N. Spring St., Falls Church, VA 22046. Tel: 703-533-8441; Fax: 703-534-9549. Sr. Augustina Temprano.
Total in Community: 7.
Represented in the Diocese of Arlington.

[3600] (S.DEM.)—SISTERS SERVANTS OF MARY (P)

Founded in Madrid, Spain by St. Maria Soledad Torres, August 15, 1851. First foundation in the United States in 1914.
Total Membership 1,360 Sisters.
General Motherhouse: Via Antonio Musa 16, Rome, Italy, 00161. Mother Alfonsa Bellido, S.deM., Supr. Gen.
Provincial Motherhouse: 800 N. 18th St., Kansas City, KS 66102. Provincial Curia Email: supprovsdemusa@gmail.com; Sr. Alicia Hermosillo, S.deM., Prov. Supr.; Sr. Bernadette Proctor, S.deM., First Provincial Counselor; Sr. Lucero Garcia, S.deM., Local Supr. Email: superiorasdemkc@gmail.com; Sr. Claudia Zamora, S.deM., Community Archivist Email: secprovusakc@gmail.com; Sr. Germana Contreras, S.deM., Treas. Email: ecoprovsdemkc@gmail.com. Vocation Director Email: vocservantsmkc@yahoo.com.
Total number in Province: 198.
Represented in the Archdioceses of Kansas City in Kansas, Los Angeles, New Orleans and New York.

[3610] (S.S.M.I.)—SISTERS SERVANTS OF MARY IMMACULATE (P)

Founded in Zhuzhel, Ukraine on August 28, 1892. Approved by the Holy See, 1932. Arrived in the United States on August 15, 1935 at Stamford, Connecticut.
Generalate: Via Cassia Antica 104, Rome, Italy, 00191. Sr. Theresa Slota, S.S.M.I., Supr. Gen., Sr. Sofia Lebedowicz.
Sisters Servants of Mary Immaculate: Sisters Servants Ln., 9 Emmanuel Dr., P.O. Box 9, Sloatsburg, NY 10974-0009. Tel: 845-753-2840. Email: ssminy@aol.com. Sr. Kathleen Hutsko, S.S.M.I., Prov. Supr.
Total in Community: 23.
Properties owned and/or sponsored: Immaculate Conception Provincialate & Novitiate; St. Joseph's Home (for the aged); Saint Mary's Villa Spiritual, Cultural and Educational Center, Sloatsburg, NY.
Ministry in the field of Education; Parish and Pastoral ministry; Health Care; Administration; Retreat Ministry; Hospitality; Holy Dormition Pilgrimage; Catechetical; Seminary Library; Youth Ministry.
Represented in the Ukrainian and Byzantine Rite Catholic Dioceses of the United States.

[3615] (E.I.N.)—SERVANTS OF THE IMMACULATE CHILD MARY (ESCLAVASDE LA INMACULADA NINA) (P)

Founded in Mexico in 1901. First foundation in the United States in 1978.
Motherhouse: Dr. Espina #10, 28019 Madrid, Spain Maria Del Pilar Ordaz Mendez.
Provincial House: Matamoros #100, Tlalpan D.F., México, C.P. 14000. Sr. Maria del Carmen Salmerón Gutierrez.
U.S. Foundation: 5135 Dartmouth Ave., Los Angeles, CA 90032. Tel: 323-225-3279. Sr. Maria del Refugio Carlos, E.I.N.
House of Formation: 350 S. Boyle Ave., Los Angeles, CA 90033. Tel: 323-269-7786. Sr. Petra Lopez Cruz, E.I.N.; Sr. Maria R. Carlos; Sr. Maria Muniz Lopez; Sr. Maria Espindola; Sr. Maria Estela Navarro. In Casper, Wyoming: Sr. Josefina Guzman; Sr. Maria del Carmen Ruelas; Sr. Alejandra Austria.
Total number of Sisters in the U.S.: 8.
Ministry in the field of religious education, adult faith formation and pastoral care.
Represented in the Archdiocese of Los Angeles.

[3620] (S.S.M.I.)—SISTERS SERVANTS OF MARY IMMACULATE (P)

First founded in Poland in 1878.
General Motherhouse: Mariowka-Opoczynska, Poland Mother Miroslawa Grunt.
Total number of Sisters in the U.S.: 32; Universal total in Congregation: 740.
American Province (1935): 1220 Tugwell Dr., Catonsville, MD 21228. Tel: 410-747-1353. Sr. Danuta Zielinska, Prov. Supr.; Sr. Marianna Danko, Community Archivist.
Total in Community: 32.
Represented in the Archdioceses of Baltimore and Washington and in the Diocese of Cleveland.

[3625] S.S.V.M.—SERVANTS OF THE LORD AND VIRGIN OF MATARA, INC. (D)

Founded in Argentina in 1988.
General House: Rome, Italy.
Provincial House: 28 15th Street SE, Washington, DC 20003. Tel: 202-543-2064; Web: ssvmusa.org. Universal Total in Congregation: 1,603; Total in U.S.: 155.
Ministry in the areas of the formation of the consciences and faith of inner city children, youth and families throughout the U.S.; assisting in after-school care for children; pastoral care in homes for the elderly and hospitals; apostolate with university students; serving as directors of religious education and as catechists in parishes and schools.

[3630] (S.S.C.J.)—SERVANTS OF THE MOST SACRED HEART OF JESUS (P)

Founded in Poland in 1894.
General Motherhouse: 24 Garncarska St., Cracow, Poland. Mother Olga Podsadnia, Supr. Gen.
Sister Servants of the Most Sacred Heart of Jesus (1959): Sacred Heart Province, 866 Cambria St., Cresson, PA 16630-1713. Tel: 814-886-4223. Email: sscjusaprovince@gmail.com; Web: sacredheartsisters.org. Mother Klara Slonina, S.S.C.J., Prov. Supr.
Total Professed: 23.
Represented in the Dioceses of Altoona-Johnstown, Buffalo, Columbus and Grand Rapids. Also in Mandeville, Jamaica.

[3640] (S.M.G.)—POOR SERVANTS OF THE MOTHER OF GOD (P)

Founded in London, England in 1869. First foundation in the United States in 1947.
General Motherhouse: Maryfield, Roehampton, London, England, S.W. 15. Sr. Rosarii O'Connor, S.M.G., Supr. Gen.
American Foundation: Maryfield Nursing Home, 1315 Greensboro Rd., High Point, NC 27260. Tel: 336-821-4000. Sr. Julia Ann Cannane.
Total in Community: 5.
Ministry in Hospitals; Nursing Homes.
Represented in the Diocese of Charlotte.

[3658] (S.S.H.J.)—SISTERS OF THE SACRED HEART OF JESUS (P)

Founded in Ragusa, Italy in 1889. First foundation in the United States in 1951.
Generalate House: Instituto Sacro Cuore di Ragusa, Via Cassia 1714, Rome, Italy, 00123. Universal total in Congregation: 610.
Motherhouse: Instituto Sacro Cuore, Via Suor Maria Schinina 2, Ragusa, Italy, 97100.
American Headquarters: Sacred Heart Villa School & Convent, 5269 Lewiston Rd., Lewiston, NY 14092. Tel: 716-284-8273.
Legal Titles: Sacred Heart Villa School & Convent, Lewiston, NY; Saint Frances Cabrini Nursery and Convent, North Haven, CT.
Ministry in the field of Religious and Academic Education at all levels; Hospitals; Homes for the Aged; Orphanages; Parish Ministry; Youth Ministry; Foreign Missions; Social Services.
Represented in the Archdiocese of Hartford and in the Diocese of Buffalo.

[3660] (S.S.H.J.P.)—SERVANTS OF THE SACRED HEART OF JESUS AND OF THE POOR (P)

Founded in Leon, Gto., Mexico in 1885. First foundation in U.S. in 1907.
Motherhouse: Apartado 92, Puebla, Pue, Mexico, 72000. Tel: 01152-2222-42-18-69. Ma. Guadalupe Cortez, S.S.H.J.P., Gen. Supr.
U.S. Address: Sacred Heart Children's Home Convent, 3310 S. Zapata Hwy., Laredo, TX 78046. Tel: 956-723-3343. Email: regionyermousa@gmail.com. Mother Elia Lucía Hernández, S.S.H.J.P., Major Supr.; Mother Magdalena Sofía Juárez, S.S.H.J.P., Supr.; Sr. Maria Isidra Valdez, S.S.H.J.P., Admin.
Professed Sisters in U.S.: 38.
Ministry in academic and religious education at all levels; Children's Home.
Represented in the Dioceses of Laredo and El Paso.

[3670] (S.S.C.J.)—SISTERS OF THE SACRED HEART OF JESUS OF SAINT JACUT (P)

Founded in France in 1816. First foundation in the United States in 1903.
Generalate: Villa des Otages, No. 8 85 rue Haxo, Paris, France, 75020.
Motherhouse: St. Jacut les Pins, St. Jacut les Pins, France, 56220.
USA/Mexico Province (1916): Provincialate Offices, 11931 Radium St., San Antonio, TX 78216. Tel: 210-344-7203; Fax: 210-341-0721. Sr. Nell Marie Knezek, S.S.C.J., Prov.
Total in Community: 26.

Ministry in Education; Pastoral Work; Health Care; Mexico Missions.

Properties owned or sponsored: Holy Spirit, San Antonio, TX; Santa Maria Community, San Antonio, TX; St. Joseph's Community, San Antonio, TX; Beth Rachamim Community, San Antonio, TX; Casa Ste. Emilie, San Antonio, TX; Provincialate Office, San Antonio, TX; Firefly Residence, San Antonio, TX.

Represented in the Archdiocese San Antonio. Also in Mexico City.

[3680] (S.H.J.M.)—SISTERS OF THE SACRED HEARTS OF JESUS AND MARY (P)

Founded in France in 1866. First foundation in United States in 1953.

Motherhouse: Chigwell Convent, Essex, England

Regional House: 1607 Liberty St., El Cerrito, CA 94530. Tel: 510-234-2702; Web: sacredheartsjm.org.

Universal total in Congregation: 86; U.S. Community: 1.

Ministry in Nursing; Healthcare Management.

Represented in the Diocese of Oakland.

[3690] (SS.CC.)—CONGREGATION OF THE SACRED HEARTS AND OF PERPETUAL ADORATION (P)

Founded in France in 1800 as a Congregation of men and women. Members are consecrated to the Hearts of Jesus and Mary. Special Ministries are Perpetual Adoration, the education of youth, especially the poor, parish work and foreign missions. First Catholic missionaries to Hawaii in 1827: Sisters started Catholic Schools for girls in Hawaii 1859. First foundation in the continental United States in 1908.

Generalate: Via Aurelia 145, Scala C-Int 10-14, Rome, Italy, 00165. Sr. Patricia Villarroel, SS.CC., Supr. Gen.

Pacific Province: Sisters of the Sacred Hearts, 1120 Fifth Ave, Honolulu, HI 96816. Tel: 808-737-5822. Sr. Regina Mary Jenkins, SS.CC., Prov.

Total in Community: 20.

Legal Holdings and Titles: Sisters of the Sacred Hearts Corporation; Regina Pacis Convent; Sacred Hearts Academy Corporation; Saint Anthony Retreat Center Corporation; Malia O Ka Malu Community, Honolulu, HI.

East Coast Region: Sisters of the Sacred Hearts of Jesus and Mary and of Perpetual Adoration,35 Huttleston Ave., Fairhaven, MA 02719-3154. Tel: 508-994-9341. Sr. Claire M. Bouchard, SS.CC., Supr.

Total in Community: 3.

Represented in the Diocese of Fall River.

[3710] (C.S.A.)—CONGREGATION OF SISTERS OF SAINT AGNES (P)

Founded in the United States in 1858.

General Motherhouse: St. Agnes Convent, 320 County Rd. K, Fond du Lac, WI 54937-8158. Tel: 920-907-2300; Fax: 920-923-3194; Email: jquinn@csasisters.org. Sr. Sharon Pollnow, C.S.A., Gen. Supr.; Sr. Peg (Margaret) Spindler, C.S.A., Gen. Vicar. Councilors: Sr. Madeline Gianforte, C.S.A.; Sr. Lael Niblick, C.S.A.

Total in Congregation: 146.

Ministry in the field of Academic and Religious Education; Parish Ministry; Foreign Missions; Social Services; Healthcare; Spirituality.

Legal Holdings or Titles: Cold Springs Charitable Trust.

Properties owned or sponsored: Hazotte Ministries, Inc.; Marian University, Fond du Lac, WI.

Represented in the Archdioceses of Chicago, Milwaukee, and New York and in the Dioceses of Columbus, Fort Wayne-South Bend, Gallup, Madison, Raleigh, Tucson, Venice and Youngstown. Also in Nicaragua.

[3718] (S.S.A.)—SISTERS OF ST. ANN

Founded in Italy in 1834.

General Motherhouse: Via degli Aldobrandeschi, 100 00163 Rome, Italy. Sr. Francesca Sarcia, S.S.A., Supr. Gen.

Universal total in Congregation: 1,200.

U.S. Delegation (1952): Mount St. Ann, 1120 N. Center St., P.O. Box 328, Ebensburg, PA 15931. Tel: 814-472-9354; Fax: 814-472-9354. Sr. Marykutty Vellaplamuriyil, S.S.A., Delegate; Sr. Anna Maria Lorenzon, S.S.A., Community Archivist. Total in Community: 11.

Ministry in the field of Education; Retreat Ministry; Youth Ministry, Social Service, Foreign Mission; Pastoral Ministry.

Represented in the Dioceses of Altoona-Johnstown and Corpus Christi.

[3720] (S.S.A.)—SISTERS OF SAINT ANNE (P)

Founded in Vaudreuil, Province of Quebec, Canada, 1850. First foundation in the United States in 1866.

Legal Title: The Community of the Sisters of St. Anne.

General Motherhouse: 1754 Provost St., H8S 1P1, Lachine, Canada Sr. Rita Larivee, Congregational Leader.

Saint Marie Province (1887): 720 Boston Post Rd. E., Marlborough, MA 01752. Tel: 508-481-4934. Email: ssaprovsec@gmail.com. Provincial Leaders: Sr. Yvette Bellrose, S.S.A.; Sr. Therese Noury, S.S.A.

Total number in Province: 47; Total in Community: 268.

Properties owned and/or sponsored: 2 Residences, Marlborough, MA; 2 Residences, Worcester, MA; 1 Residence, Lachine, PQ, Canada.

Ministry in the field of Academic and Religious Education at all levels; Various Apostolates; Pastoral Ministry; Tutoring; Ministry to the Aged, Shut-ins and the Poor; Assisted-Living Nursing.

Represented in the Archdiocese of Boston and in the Dioceses of Worcester.

[3730] (O.S.B.M.)—SISTERS OF THE ORDER OF ST. BASIL THE GREAT (P) (International Byzantine Rite)

Founded in Cappadocia in the 4th Century by St. Basil the Great and his sister St. Macrina. First foundation in the United States in 1911.

Basilian Generalate: Via San Alessio 26, Rome, Italy, 00153. M. Marcela Runcan, O.S.B.M., Gen. Supr.

Philadelphia-Ukrainian Byzantine Rite: Provincial and Motherhouse, 710 Fox Chase Rd., Jenkintown, PA 19046. Tel: 215-663-9153; Fax: 215-380-1872. Email: province@stbasils.com. Sr. Joann Sosler, O.S.B.M., Prov. Supr.

Solemnly Professed Sisters: 26.

Sponsored Institutions: Manor College; Basilian Spirituality Center.

Ministry in Education at all levels; Pastoral & Social Ministry.

Represented in the Ukrainian Archdiocese of Philadelphia.

Pittsburgh Ruthenian Byzantine Rite-Motherhouse and Novitiate: Mount St. Macrina, 500 W. Main St., P.O. Box 878, Uniontown, PA 15401. Tel: 724-438-8644. Email: osbmolph@verizon.net. Sr. Susan Sisko, O.S.B.M., Prov.

Professed Sisters: 28.

Legal Titles: Declaration of the Sisters of the Order of St. Basil the Great Endowment Trust; Declaration of Trust of the Sisters of the Order of St. Basil the Great Community Support Program; Mount St. Macrina Cemetery, Inc., Uniontown, PA.

Sisters serve in Diocesan, Parish and Religious Education Ministry; Health Care; Pastoral Ministry.

Represented in the Byzantine Archdiocese of Pittsburgh.

[3735] (C.S.B.)—CONGREGATION OF ST. BRIGID (P)

Founded in Ireland in 1807.

U.S. Foundation (1953): St. Brigid's Convent, 5118 Loma Linda Dr., San Antonio, TX 78201. Tel: 210-733-0701. U.S. Team Coordinators: Sr. Teresa Carter, C.S.B.; Sr. Mary Teresa Cullen, C.S.B.; Sr. Margaret Doyle, C.S.B.

Total in Community: 9.

Properties owned and/or sponsored: Community House San Antonio.

Pastoral Ministry in Parishes, Detention Center and Adult Education.

Represented in the Archdiocese of San Antonio.

[3750] (S.S.CH.)—SISTERS OF ST. CHRETIENNE (P)

Founded in France in 1807. First foundation in the United States in 1903.

General Motherhouse: Metz (Moselle), France, 57000.

Regional Offices: 297 Arnold St., Wrentham, MA 02093-1798. Tel: 508-384-8066; Fax: 508-507-3634. Sr. Suzanne Beaudoin, S.S.Ch., Regl. Leader.

Total number in Region: 41.

Properties owned and/or sponsored: St. Chretienne Retirement Residence, Marlborough, MA; Our Lady Thrift Shop, Marlborough, MA; St. Chretienne Residence, Wrentham, MA.

Legal Titles: St. Chretienne Educational Institute, Inc., Marlborough, MA; St. Chretienne Educational Institute Trust Wrentham, MA.

Represented in the Archdiocese of Boston and in the Dioceses of Providence, Portland in Maine and St. Petersburg.

[3760] (O.S.C.P.C.C.)—ORDER OF ST. CLARE POOR CLARE COLETTINES

Founded in Assisi, Italy in 1212. First permanent foundation in the United States in 1878.

Assisi, Italy, is called the Motherhouse of the Order, but the Abbess of said Monastery has no jurisdiction over other Communities of Poor Clares. Some Monasteries, such as those at Omaha, Evansville, New Orleans, Memphis, Jamaica Plain, Travelers Rest, Greenville, Lowell and Spokane, are subject to a Father General and to the Provincial of the Franciscan Province in which the Monastery is located. Monasteries at Cleveland, Kokomo, Los Altos Hills, Barhamsville, Rockford, Roswell and Santa Barbara.

Franciscan Monastery of St. Clare: 22625 Edgewater Rd., Omaha, NE 68022. Tel: 402-558-4916 & 402-990-5970; Fax: 402-558-5046. Web: www.omahapoorclare.org. Email: srkathy@omahapoorclare.org. Sr. Kathleen R. Hawkins, O.S.C., Abbess.

Professed Sisters: 6; Novices: 1.

Cloistered.

Monastery of St. Clare: 70 Nelson Ave., Wappingers Falls, NY 12590-1121. Tel: 845-297-1685; Fax: 845-297-7657. Email: claresny@gmail.com; Web: www.poorclaresny.com.

Solemnly Professed Sisters: 7; Professed: 6; Novice: 1.

St. Clare's Monastery of the Blessed Sacrament O.S.C: 720 Henry Clay Ave., New Orleans, LA 70118. Tel: 504-895-2019. Sr. Elizabeth Mortell, O.S.C., Abbess. Total in Community: 8.

Cloistered.

Franciscan Monastery of St. Clare O.S.C: 6825 Nurrenbern Rd., Evansville, IN 47712-8518. Tel: 812-425-4396; Web: poorclare.org/evansville. Sr. Jane Marie DeLand, O.S.C., Abbess; Sr. Catherine Janeway, O.S.C., Vicaress.

Total in Community: 5.

Monastery of St. Clare (1932): 1310 Dellwood Ave., Memphis, TN 38127. Tel: 901-357-6662. Email: memphisclares@gmail.com. Sr. Mary Marguerite, O.S.C., Abbess.

Total in Community: 4.

Solemnly Professed Cloistered.

The Franciscan Monastery of St. Clare: 920 Centre St., Jamaica Plain, MA 02130. Tel: 617-524-1760; Fax: 617-983-5205. Email: poorclarenunsboston@gmail.com; Web: www.poorclarenunsboston.org. Sr. Clare Frances McAvoy, O.S.C., Abbess.

Total in Community: 12.

Monastery of St. Clare O.S.C: 150 White Pine Rd., Chesterfield, NJ 08515. Tel: 609-324-2638; Fax: 609324-2938. Sr. Miriam Varley, O.S.C., Abbess.

Total in Community: 13.

Franciscan Monastery of Saint Clare aka Monastery of St. Clare: 1271 Langhorne-Newtown Rd., Langhorne, PA 19047-1297. Tel: 215-968-5775; Fax: 215-968-6254. Email: stclare@poorclarepa.org. Sr. Patricia A. Coogan, O.S.C., Abbess.

Total in Community: 9.

Franciscan Monastery of St. Clare, Spokane, Washington: Poor Clare Nuns, 4419 N. Hawthorne St., Spokane, WA 99205. Tel: 509-327-4479. Sr. Marcia Kay LaCour, O.S.C., Abbess; Sr. Debbie Brown, O.S.C., Vocation Directress.

Professed Nuns: 5.

Solemn Vows, Papal Enclosure Franciscan Province of Santa Barbara. Mother Bentivoglio Federation of Poor Clares.

St. Clare's Monastery: 421 S. Fourth St., Sauk Rapids, MN 56379. Tel: 320-251-3556; Fax: 320-203-7052. Mother Mary Matthew, O.S.C., Abbess.

Total in Community: 16.

Monastery of Poor Clares (1877): Order of St. Clare, Poor Clare Colettine Nuns P.C.C., 3501 Rocky River Dr., Cleveland, OH 44111-2998. Tel: 216-941-2820. Mother Mary Dolores, P.C.C., Abbess.

Total in Community: 13.

Poor Clare Nuns (Colettines), observing the Primitive Rule of St. Clare. Strictly cloistered, Solemn Vows, Perpetual Exposition of the Most Blessed Sacrament.

Franciscan Monastery of St. Clare: Order of St. Clare, 1505 Miles Rd., Cincinnati, OH 45231-2427. Tel: 513-825-7177; Fax: 513-825-4071; Email: poorclareprayers@gmail.com; Web: www.poorclarescincinnati.org. Sr. Anna Marie Covely, O.S.C., Abbess.

Total in Community: 10.
Solemn vows; papal enclosure.

Corpus Christi Monastery (Solemn Vows, Papal Enclosure): Poor Clare Colettines P.C.C., 2111 S. Main St., Rockford, IL 61102. Tel: 815-963-7343. Email: vicarforclergy@rockforddiocese.org. Mother Maria Dominica, P.C.C., Abbess.
Total in Community: 26.
Cloistered.

Annunciation Monastery: Poor Clare Colettines P.C.C., 6200 E. Minooka Rd., Minooka, IL 60447-9458.

Monastery of Poor Clares-P.C.C. (1928): 215 E. Los Olivos St., Santa Barbara, CA 93105. Tel: 805-682-7670. Mother Aimee Marie of the Eucharist, Abbess.
Total in Community: 15.

Monastery of St. Clare: 445 River Rd., Andover, MA 01810-4213. Tel: 978-683-7599; Fax: 978-683-6085. Sr. Therese Marie Lacroix, O.S.C., Abbess.
Total in Community: 9.
Cloistered.

Poor Clares Immaculate Heart Monastery: 28210 Natoma Rd., Los Altos Hills, CA 94022-3220. Tel: 650-948-2947. Mother Maura, P.C.C., Abbess.
Total in Community: 23.

Monastery of St. Clare: 37 McCauley Rd., Travelers Rest, SC 29690. Tel: 864-834-8015; Fax: 864-834-5402. Email: info@poorclaresc.com; Vocation Email: vocation@poorclaresc.com. Sr. Nancy Shively, O.S.C., Abbess.
Total in Community: 15.
Contemplative Community.

Monastery of Poor Clares Colettine P.C.C: 5500 Holly Fork Rd., Barhamsville, VA 23011. Tel: 757-566-1684. Email: mtstfrancis@gmail.com. Mother Mary Joyce, P.C.C., Abbess.
Total in Community: 21.
Solemn Vows. Cloistered.

Maria Regina Mater Monastery P.C.C: Poor Clare Nuns, 1175 N., 300 W., Kokomo, IN 46901. Tel: 765-457-5743. Mother Miriam, Abbess.
Total in Community: 8.
Cloistered.

Christ the King Monastery of St. Clare O.S.C: 457 Glenbrook Dr., Atlantis, FL 33462. Tel: 561-498-3295. Sr. Leanna Chrostowski, O.S.C., Abbess.
Total in Community: 6.

Monastery of St. Clare of the Immaculate Conception O.S.C: Poor Clares, 200 Marycrest Dr., Saint Louis, MO 63129. Tel: 314-846-2618. Mother Mary Elizabeth Smith, O.S.C., Abbess.
Total in Community: 10.
Legal Title: Nuns of the Order of St. Clare of St. Louis.

San Damiano Monastery of St. Clare (Solemn Vows, Papal Enclosure): 6029 Estero Blvd., Fort Myers Beach, FL 33931-4325. Tel: 239-463-5599; Fax: 239463-4993. Email: saintclare@comcast.net. Sr. Mary Frances Fortin, O.S.C., Abbess.
Cloistered Sisters: 4.

Poor Clares of Montana: 3020 18th Ave., S., Great Falls, MT 59405-5167. Tel: 406-453-7891. Email: sisters@poorclaresmt.org Sr. Jane Sorenson, O.S.C., Abbess.
Sisters: 6.

Monastery of St. Clare: 4875 Shattuck Rd., Saginaw, MI 48603. Tel: 989-797-0593; Email: srsclare@protonmail.com. Sr. Dianne Doughty, O.S.C., Abbess.
Solemnly Professed: 2.

[3761]—POOR CLARES OF OUR LADY OF GUADALUPE

Poor Clare Monastery of Our Lady of Guadalupe: 809 E. 19th St., Roswell, NM 88201. Tel: 575-622-0868. Mother M. Angela Kelly, Abbess.
Total in Community: 25.
Legal Title: The Community of Poor Clares of New Mexico, Inc.
Cloistered.

[3765] (O.S.C.CAP.)—CAPUCHIN POOR CLARES (P)

Federation of Our Lady of the Angels in North America (1991): Monastery of the Blessed Sacrament, 4201 N.E. 18th St., Amarillo, TX 79107. Tel: 806-383-6771; Fax: 806-383-9877. Mother Theresa Cortes, O.S.C., Pres.

[3770] (O.S.C.)—SISTERS OF ST. CLARE (P)

St. Clare's Convent (Generalate): 63 Harold's Cross Rd., Dublin 6W, Ireland Fax: 011-353-1-496-6388. Sr. Anne Kelly, O.S.C., Abbess Gen.

Santa Clara: 1171 Via Santa Paulo, Vista, CA 92081. Tel: 760-295-0611. Sr. Madeline Fitzgerald, O.S.C., California-Pastoral Coord.; Sr. Therese Carolan, O.S.C., Regl. Supr.-Florida.
Total in Congregation: 100; Total in Guatemala & El Salvador: 24; Total in U.S.: 11; Total in England: 5; Total in Ireland: 60.
Ministry in the field of Academic and Religious Education at all Levels; Pastoral & Social Ministry; Retreats; Ministry to the sick, poor and imprisoned.
Represented in the Dioceses of Orange, St. Petersburg, San Bernardino, and San Diego. Also in El Salvador, England, Guatemala and Ireland.

[3780] (SS.C.M.)—SISTERS OF SAINTS CYRIL AND METHODIUS (P)

Founded in the United States in 1909.

General Motherhouse: Villa Sacred Heart, 1002 Railroad St., Danville, PA 17821-1873. Tel: 570-275-3581; Fax: 570-275-4037. Sr. Barbara Sable, SS.C.M., Gen. Supr.
Total in Community: 52.
Ministry in the field of Education; Parish Ministry and Religious Education; Retreat/Spiritual Direction; Hospital Chaplaincy; Deaf Apostolate; Homes for the Aged; Continuing Care Retirement Community.
Properties owned or sponsored: St. Cyril Preschool and Kindergarten; St. Cyril Academy Spiritual Center; Villa Sacred Heart; Maria Hall, Inc.; Maria Joseph Manor, Inc.; The Meadows at Maria Joseph Manor, Inc., Danville, PA; St. Francis Center, St. Helena Island, SC; Villa St. Cyril, Highland Park, IL.
Represented in the Archdioceses of Chicago and San Antonio and in the Dioceses of Charleston, Gary, Harrisburg and Scranton.

[3790] (S.S.D.)—INSTITUTE OF THE SISTERS OF ST. DOROTHY (P)

Founded in Italy in 1834. First foundation in the United States in 1911.

General Motherhouse: Via del Gianicolo 4-a, Rome, Italy, 00165. Sr. Sao Ribeiro, S.S.D., Gen. Coord.

Province of United States of America (1920): Mount Saint Joseph Vice-Provincialate, 13 Monkeywrench Ln., Bristol, RI 02809-2916. Tel: 401-253-5434. Sr. Sharon A. McCarthy, S.S.D., Vice Prov. Coord.
Universal total in Congregation: 876; Total number in the U.S.: 27.
Ministry in the field of Education; Spiritual Life Centers; Hospital Chaplaincies; Social work with immigrants.
Properties owned or sponsored: Villa Fatima, Taunton, MA; Mt. St. Joseph, Bristol, RI; Academy of St. Dorothy, Staten Island, NY.

[3810] (X.S.)—SOCIETY OF CATHOLIC MISSION SISTERS OF ST. FRANCIS XAVIER, INC. (D)
(Xavier Sisters)

Founded in the United States in 1946.

Convent: 37179 Moravian Dr., Clinton Township, MI 48036. Tel: 586-465-5082; Fax: 586-465-1990. Email: carmelctwp@sbcglobal.net. Sr. Mary Therese, O.C.D., Prioress.
Professed Nuns: 7; Sisters in temporary vows: 3; Postulants: 5.
Represented in the Archdiocese of Detroit.

[3820] (C.S.JB.)—SISTERS OF ST. JOHN THE BAPTIST (P)

Founded in Italy in 1878. First foundation in the United States in 1906.

General Motherhouse: Rome, Italy. Sr. Lina Pantano, Supr. Gen.

U.S. Provincial House: 3308 Campbell Dr., Bronx, NY 10465-1358. Tel: 718-518-7820. Sr. Claudette Marie Jaszczynski, C.S.JB., Prov. Supr.
Total in Community: 62.
Legal Titles and Holdings: Mt. St. John Convent, Purchase, NY.
Ministry in the field of Education; Health Care for Aged Women & Men; Pastoral Ministry.

[3830] (C.S.J. or S.S.J.)—SISTERS OF ST. JOSEPH

The Independent Motherhouses of the Sisters of St. Joseph are represented in the United States in the following Archdioceses and Dioceses:

[3830-01] BOSTON (D)

Motherhouse of the Congregation of the Sisters of St. Joseph of Boston-CSJ (1873): 637 Cambridge St., Brighton, MA 02135. Tel: 617-783-9090; Fax: 617-783-8246. Vocations Email: vocation.office@csjboston.org; Communications Email: communications.office@csjboston.org. Sr. Leila Hogan, C.S.J., Pres.; Katie McNally, Community Archivist.
Total in Community: 190.
Legal Holdings or Titles: Motherhouse of the Sisters of Saint Joseph of Boston, Brighton, MA; Bethany Health Care Center, Inc., Framingham, MA; Bethany Hill Place, Inc.; Framingham, MA; St. Joseph Hall, Framingham, MA; Walnut Park Montessori School, Newton, MA; Jackson School, Newton, MA; Fontbonne Academy, Milton, MA; St. Joseph Preparatory High School, Brighton, MA; Regis College, Weston, MA; Corporation for the Sponsored Ministries of the Sisters of St. Joseph of Boston, Brighton, MA; The Literacy Connection, Brighton, MA.; The Women's Table, Brighton, MA; Casserly House, Roslindale, MA; Jackson Walnut Park Educational Collaborative, Inc.

[3830-03] ORANGE (P)

Sisters of St. Joseph of Orange - Motherhouse: 440 S. Batavia St., Orange, CA 92868. Tel: 714-633-8121; Fax: 717-744-3165. Sr. Mary Beth Ingham, C.S.J., Gen. Supr.; Leo Catahan, Community Archivist.
Total in Community: 88.
Legal Holdings and Titles: Sisters of St. Joseph of Orange; Sisters of St. Joseph Healthcare Foundation, Orange, CA; St. Joseph College, Orange, CA; St. Joseph Health System; St. Joseph Health System Foundation, Irvine, CA.
Sponsoring the following ministries: St. Jude Medical Center, Fullerton, CA; St. Jude Memorial Foundation, Fullerton, CA; St. Joseph Hospital Orange; Yorba Linda, CA; Mission Hospital Regional Medical Center, Mission Viejo, CA; Santa Rosa Memorial Hospital, Santa Rosa, CA; St. Joseph Hospital of Eureka, Eureka, CA; Redwood Memorial Hospital, Fortuna, CA; Redwood Memorial Foundation, Fortuna, CA; Queen of the Valley Medical Center of Napa, Napa, CA; St. Mary of the Plains Hospital, Lubbock, TX; St. Mary Medical Center, Apple Valley, CA; St. Joseph Health Ministry.
Ministry in the field of Education; Health & Hospital Services; Pastoral and Social Services.
Represented in the Archdioceses of Los Angeles and San Francisco and in the Dioceses of Orange and San Diego.

[3830-05] ROCKVILLE CENTRE (D)

St. Joseph's Convent - Congregation of the Sisters of Saint Joseph of Brentwood, NY CSJ: Brent-wood, NY 11717. Tel: 631-273-1187. Sr. Tesa Fitzgerald, C.S.J., Pres.; Virginia Dowd, Community Archivist. Total in Community: 339.
Ministry in the field of Education; Health & Hospital Services; Social Services.
Represented in the Dioceses of Brooklyn and Rockville Centre. Also in Puerto Rico.

[3830-06] BUFFALO (P)

Generalate - Congregation of the Sisters of St. Joseph SSJ: Administration, 4975 Strickler Rd., Suite A, Clarence, NY 14031. Tel: 716-759-6454. Sr. Patrice Ryan, S.S.J., Pres.; Tel: 716-759-6454, Ext. 110; Email: pryan@buffalossj.org. Sr. Janet DiPasquale, S.S.J., Community Archivist. Email: jdipasquale@buffalossj.org.
Total in Community: 45.
Ministry in the field of Education at all levels; School for Deaf; Youth Ministry; Justice Ministry; Pastoral Ministry; Hospital Chaplaincy.
Properties owned or sponsored: Administrative Office; Sisters of St. Joseph Residence.

[3830-09] ERIE (D)

Sisters of St. Joseph SSJ: 5031 W. Ridge Rd., Erie, PA 16506-1249. Tel: 814-836-4100; Fax: 814-836-4278. Email: jennifer.woodard@ssjerie.org. Sr. Mary Drexler, S.S.J., Pres.
Total in Community: 77.
Legal Title: Sisters of St. Joseph of Northwestern Pennsylvania Inc.
Ministry in the field of Education at all levels; Social Ministries; Nursing Home; Health Care; Pastoral Work and other Diocesan Ministries.

Institutions sponsored: Saint Mary's Home of Erie; Sisters of St. Joseph Neighborhood Network, Inc.; St. Patrick's Haven; St. James Haven.

Represented in the Archdiocese of Louisville and in the Diocese of Cleveland.

[3830-12] OGDENSBURG (D)

Motherhouse of the Society of the Sisters of St. Joseph SSJ: 1425 Washington St., Watertown, NY 13601-4533. Tel: 315-782-3460; Web: www.ssjwatertown.org. Sr. Mary Eamon Lyng, S.S.J., Major Supr.; Sr. Norma Bryant, S.S.J., Community Archivist.

Total in Community: 40.

Ministry in the field of Education at all levels; Parish and Diocesan Administration.

Represented in the Diocese of Ogdensburg.

[3830-13] PITTSBURGH (P)

Sisters of St. Joseph CSJ - Motherhouse: Sisters of St. Joseph: 1020 State St., Baden, PA 15005. Tel: 724-869-2151; Fax: 724-869-3336. Leadership Team: Sr. Sharon Costello, Congregational Mod.; Sr. Mary Parks; Sr. Lyn Szymkiewicz; Sr. Jean Uzupis; Kathleen Washy, Community Archivist.

Total in Community: 110.

Properties owned and/or sponsored: Motherhouse and 12 residences.

Ministry in the field of Education; Health Care; Social Services; Spiritual Development; Congregational Services.

Represented in the Archdioceses of Boston, Hartford, New York, Philadelphia and Washington and in the Dioceses of Altoona-Johnstown, Cheyenne, Greensburg, Pittsburgh and Wheeling-Charleston.

[3830-14] ROCHESTER (P)

Sisters of St. Joseph SSJ - Motherhouse: 150 French Rd., Rochester, NY 14618-3822. Tel: 585-641-8100; Fax: 585-641-8524. Sr. Eileen Daly, S.S.J., Congregational Pres.; Kathleen Urbanic, Archivist. Email: kfleckenstein@ssjrochester.org.

Total in Community: 150.

Ministry in the field of Education PreK-6th grade; Health Care; Pastoral Ministry; Foster Care for Children; Parish and Diocesan Evangelization; College Campus Outreach; Social Service; Justice and Peace; Retreats & Spiritual Direction; Home Pastoral Care; Spirituality Programs; Domestic and Foreign Missions; Outreach and Volunteer Corps Programs.

Properties owned and/or sponsored: Nazareth Elementary; Motherhouse; Conference Center and 9 residences.

Represented in the Archdiocese of Mobile and in the Diocese of Rochester. Also in Brazil.

[3830-15] SALINA (P)

General Administration Office (1884): Sisters of St. Joseph of Concordia, 215 Court St., P.O. Box 279, Concordia, KS 66901. Tel: 785-243-2149. Email: csjcenter@csjkansas.org. Sr. Jean Rosemarynoski, C.S.J., Pres.

Motherhouse (1884): Sisters of St. Joseph of Concordia CSJ, 1300 Washington St., P.O. Box 279, Concordia, KS 66901. Tel: 785-243-2113.

Total Sisters in Community: 78.

Legal Titles: Nazareth Convent and Academy Corporation, Concordia, KS; Neighborhood Initiatives, Inc., Concordia, KS; Manna House of Prayer, Concordia, KS; Neighbor to Neighbor, Concordia, KS. Ministry in Care for Elderly; Homeless; Education; Parish and Diocesan Evangelization; Social Services; Justice and Peace Offices; Youth Formation; Healthcare; Consultants; Refugees; Continuous Prayer.

Represented in the Archdiocese of St. Paul-Minneapolis and in the Dioceses of Fargo, Grand Island, Las Cruces and Salina. Also in Brazil.

[3830-16] SPRINGFIELD (MA) (D)

Motherhouse: The Congregation of the Sisters of St. Joseph of Springfield (SSJ), 577 Carew St., Springfield, MA 01104. Tel: 413-536-0853; Fax: 413-533-3275. Joan Ryzewicz, S.S.J., Pres.; Sherry Enserro, Archivist.

Total in Community: 172.

Legal Holdings and Titles: The Friends of the Sisters of St. Joseph Springfield, Inc.

Ministry in the field of Religious & Academic Education; Parish Ministry; Cross-Cultural; Diocesan Administration; Chaplaincy; Health Care, Social Services; Restorative Justice; Creative Arts.

Represented in the Archdioceses of Baltimore and Boston and in the Dioceses of Burlington, Fall River, Portland (ME), Providence, Springfield (MA) and Worcester.

[3832] (C.S.J.)—CONGREGATION OF THE SISTERS OF ST. JOSEPH (P)

Legal Holdings: Congregation of the Sisters of St. Joseph Ministries, Inc. d/b/a CSJ Ministries: A.B.L.E. Families, Inc.; Caregiver Companion, Inc.; Christ in the Wilderness, Inc.; Congregation of St. Joseph Ministry Against the Death Penalty, Inc.; Holy Family Childcare & Development Center, Inc.; Nazareth Academy, Inc.; People Program, Inc.; River's Edge, A Place for Reflection and Action, Inc.; St. Joseph Academy, Inc. (Cleveland, OH); St. Joseph's Academy, Inc. (Baton Rouge, LA); SJA Foundation, Inc.*; St. Joseph Adoption Referral Services, Inc. d/b/a St. Joseph Adoption Ministry; St. Joseph Health Initiative, Inc.; St. Joseph Spirituality Center, Inc.; Sisters of St. Joseph Charitable Fund, Inc./d/b/a/: Sisters Health Foundation, Inc.; Sisters of St. Joseph Dear Neighbor. Ministries, Inc.; Sisters of St. Joseph Health and Wellness Foundation, Inc.; StepStone, Inc.*; Taller de Jose, Inc.; School and Tutors on Wheels, Inc.; The Well Spirituality Center, Inc. CSJ Initiatives, Inc: Dillon Complex for Independent Living, Inc.; Sheridan Village, Inc.

Legal Title: Congregation of the Sisters of St. Joseph, Inc. d/b/a Congregation of St. Joseph. 3430 Rocky River Dr., Cleveland, OH 44111-2297. Tel: 216-252-0440; Fax: 216-941-3430; Web: www.csjoseph.org.

Total in Community: 489.

Cleveland Center: 3440 Rocky River Dr., Cleveland, OH 44111-2997. Tel: 216-252-0440; Fax: 216-941-3430. Web: www.csjoseph.org. Kathleen Brazda, C.S.J., Pres.; Mary Zavoda, Coord Community Life. Email: mzavoda@csjoseph.org.

Sisters 64

Ministry in the field of Academic and Religious Education at all levels; Parish and Pastoral Ministry; Deaf Apostolate; Parish Team Member; Justice Work; Health Care; Social Services; Radio; Social Concerns; Retreat Work.

Represented in the Archdioceses of Chicago and Washington and in the Dioceses of Cleveland and Youngstown.

LaGrange Center: 1515 W. Ogden Ave., La Grange Park, IL 60526. Tel: 708-354-9200; Fax: 708-354-9573. Email: cmarsh@csjoseph.org; Web: www.csjoseph.org. Kathleen Brazda, C.S.J., Pres.; Chris March, C.S.J., Coord. of Community Life.

Sisters: 50

Ministry in the field of Education; School Administration; Nursing; Pastoral Care in Hospitals; Nursing Homes; Work with the Elderly; Parish Ministry; Archdiocesan Administration; Spiritual Direction and Retreats; Administrative Services; Immigration Services.

Represented in the Archdiocese of Chicago and the Dioceses of Joliet.

Nazareth Center: 2929 Nazareth Rd., Kalamazoo, MI 49048. Tel: 269-381-6290; Fax: 269-381-4909. Email: pwarbritton@csjoseph.org; Web: www.csjoseph.org. Kathleen Brazda, C.S.J., Pres.; Marjorie Bassett, C.S.J., Coordinator of Community Life. Email: mbassett@csjoseph.org.

Ministry in the field of Education; Social Services; Parish and Church-related Ministries; Healthcare; Spirituality; Transformations Spirituality Center.

Represented in the Archdioceses of Detroit and Santa Fe and in the Dioceses of Grand Rapids, Kalamazoo, Lafayette in Indiana, Lansing and Saginaw.

Wheeling Center: 137 Mount St. Joseph Rd., Wheeling, WV 26003. Tel: 304-232-8160; Fax: 304-232-1401. Email: pwarbritton@csjoseph.org; Web: www.csjoseph.org. Kathleen Brazda, C.S.J., Pres.; Rose Mathes, Coord of Community Life. Email: rmathes@csjoseph.org.

Sisters: 52.

Ministry in the following areas: Parish Ministry; Pastoral Services; Health Care; Social Services; Spiritual Formation; Direction and Retreat Ministries; Diocesan, Administration and Service.

Represented in the Diocese of Lafayette, IN and Wheeling-Charleston.

Wichita Center: 3700 E. Lincoln, Wichita, KS 67218. Tel: 316-686-7171; Fax: 316-689-4056. Legal Title: Sisters of St. Joseph of Wichita, Kansas.

Ministry in the fields of Religious and Academic Education; Pro-Life Ministry to Women; Hospital and Clinical Care; Pastoral Ministry; Senior Care; Social Services; Transitional Housing; Low Income Senior Housing; Retreat Ministry.

Represented in the Archdiocese of Kansas City in Kansas and in the Dioceses of Dodge City, Grand Island, Kansas City-St. Joseph, Salina and Wichita. Also in Japan.

[3840] (C.S.J.)—SISTERS OF ST. JOSEPH OF CARONDELET (P)

Founded in France in 1650. First foundation in the United States in 1836.

Congregational Offices: 10777 Sunset Office Dr., Ste. 10, Saint Louis, MO 63127-1019. Tel: 314-394-1985; Fax: 314-735-4476. Email: congctroffice@csjcarondelet.org. Congregational Leadership Team for Provinces & Vice Province: Sr. Sally Harper, C.S.J.; Sr. Patricia Johnson, C.S.J.; Sr. Mary McGlone, C.S.J.; Sr. Sean Peters, C.S.J.

Province of St. Louis (1836): St. Joseph's Provincial House, 6400 Minnesota Ave., St. Louis, MO 63111. Tel: 314-481-8800; Fax: 314-351-3111. Province Leadership Team: Sr. Margaret Schulz, C.S.J.; Sr. Amy Hereford, C.S.J.; Sr. Frances Maher, C.S.J.; Sr. Jeanne Janssen, C.S.J.; Sr. Maria Jeanne Tipton, C.S.J.

Total in Community: 216.

Legal Title: Sisters of St. Joseph of Carondelet, St. Louis Province.

Sponsored Institutions: Universities 2; Academies 2; Institute for the Deaf 1; Long Term Care Facility Co-Owner 1; Health System Co-sponsor 1.

Ministries in the field of Academic Education; Pastoral Ministries; Health Care; Child Care; Geriatric Care; Foreign Missions; Social Services; Community Services.

Represented in the Archdioceses of Chicago, Denver, Indianapolis, Kansas City in Kansas, Mobile, St. Louis and Seattle and in the Dioceses of Green Bay, Kansas City-St. Joseph, San Jose and Savannah.

Province of St. Paul (1851): St. Joseph's Administration Center, 1884 Randolph Ave., Saint Paul, MN 55105. Tel: 651-690-7000; Fax: 651-690-7039. Province Leadership Team: Sr. Catherine Mary Rosengren, C.S.J.; Sr. Katherine Rossini, C.S.J.; Sr. Jill Underdahl, C.S.J.; Michelle Hueg, Archivist.

Total in Community: 122.

Legal Holdings or Titles: Sisters of St. Joseph of Carondelet.

Ministry in the fields of Education; Health; Social Services; Spirituality.

Represented in the Archdiocese of St. Paul-Minneapolis and in the Diocese of Fargo.

Province of Albany (1858): St. Joseph's Provincial House, 385 Watervliet-Shaker Rd., Latham, NY 12110-4799. Tel: 518-783-3500; Fax: 518-783-5209; Web: https://csjcarondelet.org/. Province Leadership Team: Sr. Joan Mary Hartigan, C.S.J., Province Dir.; Sr. Margaret M. Edic, C.S.J., First Councilor & Province Treas.; Sr. Diane Zigo, C.S.J.; Sr. Rose Casaleno, C.S.J.; Sr. Mary Catherine Ryan, C.S.J.; Rev. Geoffrey D. Burke, Chap.

Total in Community: 197.

Novitiate:

Ministry in the fields of Academic and Special Education at all levels; Healthcare and Infirmary Services; Pastoral Ministries; Parish Ministry and Religious Education; Diocesan Offices; Youth Ministry; Counseling; Retreat and Spiritual Direction; Social and Community Services; Fine Arts.

Represented in the Archdioceses of Cincinnati, Philadelphia, St. Paul-Minneapolis and St. Louis and in the Dioceses of Albany, Baton Rouge, Rochester, Spokane and Syracuse.

Province of Los Angeles (1878): St. Mary's Provincialate and Carondelet Center, 11999 Chalon Rd., Los Angeles, CA 90049-1524. Tel: 310-889-2108; Fax: 310-472-5982. Email: lupe@csjla.org. Sr. Patricia Nelson, C.S.J., Prov. Dir.; Sr. Patricia Rose Shanahan, C.S.J., Archivist.

Professed Sisters: 239.

Legal Titles or Holdings: Sisters of St. Joseph in California; Sisters of St. Joseph in Arizona; Sisters of St. Joseph Ministerial Services.

Sisters serve in the fields of Education; Health Services; Social Services; Pastoral Ministry.

Represented in the Archdioceses of Los Angeles and San Francisco and in the Dioceses of Boise, Fresno, Honolulu, Monterey, Oakland, Orange, San Bernardino, San Diego, San Jose, Springfield-Cape Girardeau and Tucson. Also in Japan.

Legal Title: Sisters of St. Joseph of Carondelet-Hawaii Vice Province.
Ministries include: Elementary Schools; Services to the Elderly; Prayer & Spirituality; Religious Education Directors; Social Ministry; Adult Faith Formation; Social Justice.
Represented in the Archdiocese of Honolulu.

[3850] (C.S.J.)—SISTERS OF ST. JOSEPH OF CHAMBERY (P)

Founded in France in 1650. First foundation in United States in 1885.
Generalate: Via del Casaletto, 260, Rome, Italy, 00151. Sr. Dolores Lahr, C.S.J., Supr. Gen.
Provincial House: Convent of Mary Immaculate, 27 Park Rd., West Hartford, CT 06119. Tel: 860-233-5734; Fax: 860-232-4649. Sr. Sally Hodgdon, C.S.J., Prov. Supr.
Total in Community: 57.
Legal Title: The Sisters of St. Joseph Corporation. Ministry in the field of Academic and Religious Education at all levels; Social Services; Pastoral and Parish Ministries; Hospitals and Health Care; Retreat work and Spiritual Direction; Theologian; Finances.
Represented in the Archdiocese of Hartford and in the Dioceses of Bridgeport and Norwich. Also in Canada.

[3860] (S.J.C.)—SISTERS OF ST. JOSEPH OF CLUNY (P)

Founded in France in 1807.
Generalate: Paris, France Sr. Clare Stanley, S.J.C.
Provincialate: 7 Restmere Ter., Middletown, RI 02842. Tel: 401-846-4757. Sr. Genevieve Marie Vigil, S.J.C., Province of U.S.A. & Canada.
Professed Sisters in U.S. & Canada: 14.
Legal Title: Sisters of St. Joseph of Cluny, Inc. Ministry in Evangelization & Catechesis; Outreach; Parish Ministry.
Represented in the Archdiocese of Los Angeles and in the Dioceses of Norwich and Providence. Also in Canada.

[3870] (C.S.J.)—SISTERS OF ST. JOSEPH OF LYON, FRANCE (P)

Founded in France October 15, 1650. First foundation in United States in 1906 in Jackman, Maine.
General Motherhouse: Lyon, France Sr. Catherine Barange, Supr. Gen. Maine Sector: Sisters of St. Joseph, 80 Garland Rd., Winslow, ME 04901. Tel: 207-873-4512. Email: CSJsofLyon.Maine@gmail.com. Sr. Judith Donovan, C.S.J., Leader.
Total in Community: 14.
Ministries in Adult Faith Formation; Spirituality and Ecology; Pastoral Ministry.
Represented in the Diocese of Portland (In Maine).

[3890] (C.S.J.P.)—SISTERS OF ST. JOSEPH OF PEACE (P)

Founded in England 1884. First United States foundation 1885.
Shalom Center: Sisters of St. Joseph of Peace Generalate, Inc., 399 Hudson Ter., Englewood Cliffs, NJ 07632. Tel: 201-608-5401; Archives: 201-608-5408. Email: jlinley@csjp.org. Sr. Andrea Nenzel, C.S.J.P., Congregation Leader; Sr. Susan Francois, C.S.J.P., Asst. Congregation Leader; Sr. Margie Fort, C.S.J.P.; Sr. Sheena George, C.S.J.P.; Sr. Kathleen Pruitt, C.S.J.P.; Melody Maravillas, Congregation C.F.O.
Total in Community: 115; Total Number in the Eastern U.S.: 44.
Properties owned or sponsored: St. Joseph's Home for the Blind; St. Mary's Residence; St. Joseph's Home; The Nurturing Place; St. Joseph's School for the Blind; Waterspirit; The York Street Project; St. Michael Villa; The Kenmare School; Holy Name Medical Center; Peace Ministries, Inc.; Peace Care, Inc.; Margaret Anna Cusack Center, Inc. (dba Peace Care St. Joseph's) and St. Ann's Home for the Aged (dba Peace Care St. Ann's).
Ministry in the field of Education; Health & Social Services; Religious Education; Parish Ministry, Retreat Ministry, Social & Minority Ministry.
Represented in the Archdioceses of Newark, Portland in Oregon and Seattle and in the Dioceses of Camden and Paterson. Also in El Salvador, Haiti and the United Kingdom.
Western U.S. (1909): St. Mary's Residence and Novitiate, 1663 Killarney Way, P.O. Box 248, Bellevue, WA 98009-0248. Tel: 425-467-5499; Fax: 425-462-9760. Email: afleming@csjp-olp.org. Sr. Andrea Nenzel, C.S.J.P., Congregation Leader.
Total Number in Western U.S.: 42.
Corporate Titles: Sisters of St. Joseph of Peace; Sisters of St. Joseph of Peace Charitable Trust, Bellevue, WA.
Properties owned: St. Mary's Residence, Bellevue, WA; Prospect House, Seattle, WA; St. Therese Residence, Seattle, WA.

[3893] (S.S.J.)—SISTERS OF SAINT JOSEPH OF CHESTNUT HILL, PHILADELPHIA (P)

Founded in France in 1650. First foundation in Philadelphia in 1847.
Motherhouse (1847): Mount St. Joseph Convent, 9701 Germantown Ave., Philadelphia, PA 19118-2694. Tel: 215-248-7200; Fax: 215-248-7277; Email: kshelly@ssjphila.org; Web: www.ssjphila.org. Sr. Maureen G. Erdlen, S.S.J., Congregational Pres.; Sr. Margaret Mary Smith, S.S.J., Archivist.
Total in Congregation: 563.
Legal Holdings or Titles: Saint Joseph Villa; Saint Joseph Guild; Bethlehem Retirement Village, Flourtown, PA; Academy Village, McSherrystown, PA; Saint Joseph Housing Corporation; Cecilian, Philadelphia, PA; Mount Saint Joseph Academy, Flourtown, PA; Norwood-Fontbonne Academy, Philadelphia, PA; Chestnut Hill College, Philadelphia, PA; Cecilian Village, McSherrystown, PA; Saint Joseph Academy, McSherrystown, PA; The Convent of the Sisters of St. Joseph, Chestnut Hill, PA; Elizabeth House, Philadelphia, PA; Saint Joseph Village, McSherrystown, PA; Sisters of Saint Joseph Welcome Center, Philadelphia, PA; Sisters of Saint Joseph Neighborhood Center, Camden, NJ; Saint Joseph by-the-Sea, Sea Isle City, NJ.
Ministry in the field of Academic and Religious Education at all levels; Pastoral Ministry; Campus Ministry; Care of the Aged; Social Services; Prison Ministry; Health Care; Psychologists; Hospice Ministry; Hospital Chaplaincy; Spiritual Directors; Drug and Alcohol Counselors.
Represented in the Archdioceses of Baltimore, Los Angeles, Miami, Newark, Philadelphia and Washington and in the Dioceses of Allentown, Arlington, Camden, Charlotte, Fort Wayne-South Bend, Harrisburg, Metuchen, Paterson, Raleigh, St. Petersburg, Rockville Centre, Savannah, Trenton, Venice, Wheeling-Charleston and Wilmington.

[3900] (S.S.J.)—SISTERS OF ST. JOSEPH OF ST. AUGUSTINE, FLORIDA (D)

Founded in France in 1650. First foundation in the United States in 1866. Classified as an American Congregation in 1899.
Motherhouse (1847): St. Joseph Convent, 241 St. George St., P.O. Box 3506, St. Augustine, FL 32085. Tel: 904-824-1752; Email: srkathleencarr@ssjfl.org. Sr. Kathleen Carr, S.S.J., Gen. Supr.; Sr. Catherine Bitzer, S.S.J., Community Archivist.
Total in Community: 45.
Ministry in: Social Services; Hospital Pastoral Care; Care of Aged; Academic and Religious Education at all levels; Parish Ministry; Diocesan Office Administration; Retreat Ministry; Ministry to the Handicapped.
Represented in the Archdiocese of Miami and in the Diocese St. Augustine.

[3910] (S.J.S.M.)—SISTERS OF ST. JOSEPH OF ST. MARK (D)

Founded in France in 1845. First foundation in the United States in October, 1937.
Generalate: Colmar, France Sr. Sophie Moog, Gen. Supr. Universal total in Congregation: 249.
General Motherhouse (Cleveland) (1939): 21800 Chardon Rd., Euclid, OH 44117-2199. Mother M. Raphael Gregg, Supr. Gen.
Youngstown Diocese: Sisters of St. Joseph of St. Mark, Community Center, 2300 Reno Dr., Ste. 319, Louisville, OH 44641. Tel: 330-875-7967. Sr. Mary Ann De Plain, S.J.S.M., Supr.
Total number in U.S.: 10.
Represented in the Dioceses of Cleveland and Youngstown.

[3920] (S.J.W.)—SISTERS OF ST. JOSEPH THE WORKER (D)

General Motherhouse: St. William Convent, 1 St. Joseph Ln., Walton, KY 41094. Mother Mary Christina Murray, S. J.W., Supr. Gen.
Total in Community: 8.
Properties owned and operated: Taylor Manor Nursing Home, Versailles, KY; 16-acre property in Walton, KY: Motherhouse Formation House; St. Joseph Academy, Walton, KY.
Represented in the Dioceses of Covington and Lexington.

[3930] (SSJ-TOSF)—SISTERS OF ST. JOSEPH OF THE THIRD ORDER OF ST. FRANCIS (P)

Founded in the United States in 1901.
Corporate Office: 2801 Hoover Rd., Unit 1F, Stevens Point, WI 54481. Tel: 715-341-8457. Sr. Marjorie White, S.S.J.-T.O.S.F., Pres.; Sr. Judith Wood, S.S.J.-T.O.S.F., Vice Pres.; Sr. Michelle Wronkowski, S.S.J.-T.O.S.F., Vice Pres.; Sr. Barb Krakora, S.S.J.-T.O.S.F., Vice Pres.
Total number in the Congregation: 136.
Sponsors: Learning Center; 2 High Schools; Health Care System.
Ministries in the following areas: Academic Education at all levels; Pastoral Ministry; Health Care Services; Ministry in Puerto Rico; Social Services.
Represented in the Archdioceses of Chicago, Detroit, Hartford and Milwaukee and in the Dioceses of Arecibo, Cleveland, Fort Wayne-South Bend, Gary, Grand Island, Green Bay, Knoxville, La Crosse, Oakland and Superior. Also in Peru.

[3935] (S.S.L.)—THE CONGREGATION OF THE SISTERS OF ST. LOUIS, JUILLY MONAGHAN (P)

Founded in France in 1842. First foundation in the United States in 1949.
General Motherhouse: Louisville Monaghan, Ireland Sr. Patricia Ojo, S.S.L.
Regional House: Louisville Convent, 22300 Mulholland Dr., Woodland Hills, CA 91364. Tel: 818-883-1678; Email: sslca4@sistersofsaintlouis.com (Region); Email: admin@saintlouis.ie (Institute). Sr. Judith Dieterle, S.S.L.
Finally Professed Sisters: 33.
Legal Title: Sisters of St. Louis, Juilly-Monaghan, Inc. Ministry in the field of Education; Pastoral and Social Ministries.
Represented in the Archdioceses of Los Angeles and New York. Also in Brazil.

[3950] (S.S.M.N.)—SISTERS OF SAINT MARY OF NAMUR (P)

Founded in Namur, Belgium, in 1819. First foundation in the United States in 1863.
General Motherhouse: Namur, Belgium Sr. Maureen Quinn, Gen. Supr.
Universal total in Congregation: 379; Professed: 368; Novices: 11.
Eastern Province: Provincial House, 241 Lafayette Ave., Buffalo, NY 14213-1453. Tel: 716-884-8221; Fax: 716-884-6598. Email: ssmnprov@verizon.net. Sr. Caroline Smith, S.S.M.N., Prov. Supr.
Total in Community: 65.
Legal Holdings or Titles: 6 Residences.
Ministry in the field of Religious and Academic Education; Pastoral Ministry; Community Organization; Social Services; Diocesan and Health related services; Refugee Assistance.
Represented in the Dioceses of Buffalo, Charleston and Savannah. Also in Canada.
Western Province: Provincial House - Our Lady of Victory Center, 909 W. Shaw St., Fort Worth, TX 76110. Tel: 817-923-8393. Email: ssmnamur@sbcglobal.net. Sr. Patricia Ridgley, S.S.M.N., Prov.
Total in Community: 24.
Ministry in the field of Religious and Academic Education; Pastoral Ministry; Social Services; Health Care and Missions.
Properties owned or sponsored: Our Lady of Victory Center, Fort Worth, TX; Our Lady of Victory Catholic School, Fort Worth, TX; Sisters of St. Mary of Namur, Fort Worth, TX; Mercy Convent, Wichita Falls, TX.
Represented in the Dioceses of Dallas and Fort Worth.

[3960] (S.S.M.O.)—SISTERS OF ST. MARY OF OREGON

Founded in Oregon in 1886.
General Motherhouse: Sisters of St. Mary of Oregon, 4440 S.W. 148th Ave., Beaverton, OR 97078. Tel: 503-644-9181. Email: info@ssmo.org. Sr. Michael Francine Duncan, Supr. Gen.
Total in Congregation: 46.

Ministry in the field of Education; Nursing Homes; Parish Services; Social Services; and Counseling.
Properties owned or sponsored: Maryville Nursing Home; SSMO Campus Schools.
Represented in the Archdioceses of Portland in Oregon.

[3980] (S.P.C)—SISTERS OF SAINT PAUL DE CHARTRES (P)

Founded in France in 1696.
General House: 193 Via della Vignaccia, Rome, Italy, 1-00163. Sr. Maria Goretti Lee, S.P.C., Supr. Gen.
Universal total in Congregation: 4135.
U.S. Province: 1300 County Rd. 492, Marquette, MI 49855-9632. Tel: 906-226-3932. Sr. Mary Ann Laurin, S.P.C., District Supr.
Total in Community: 12.
Legal Holding: Bishop Noa Home for Senior Citizens, Escanaba, MI.
Ministry in the field of Academic and Religious Education; Hospital Chaplaincy; Pastoral Ministry.
Represented in the Archdiocese of Washington and in the Diocese of Marquette.

[3990] (S.S.P.C.)—MISSIONARY SISTERS OF ST. PETER CLAVER (P)

Founded in 1894. First Foundation in the United States, 1914.
General House: 16 via dell' Olmata, Rome, Italy, 00184. Sr. Selin Karikkattil, S.S.P.C., Supr. Gen.
Legal Title: The Sodality of St. Peter Claver for the African Missions-Missionary Sisters of St. Peter Claver.
American Headquarters: 225 Century Ave., S., Saint Paul, MN 55125-1155. Tel: 651-738-9704.
Total in Community: 17.
Represented in the Archdioceses of Chicago, St. Louis and St. Paul-Minneapolis.

[4010] (O.S.A.)—SISTERS OF ST. RITA (D)

General Motherhouse: Friedrich-Spee-Str. 32, 97072 Wurzburg, Germany Sr. Rita Maria Kaes, O.S.A., Gen.
Universal total in Congregation: 61.
U.S. Address: St. Rita's Convent, 4014 Green Bay Rd., Racine, WI 53404. Tel: 262-639-1766. Sr. Angelica Summer, O.S.A., Supr. Email: sr.angelica@sbcglobal.net.
Represented in the Archdiocese of Milwaukee.

[4020] (S.T.J.)—SOCIETY OF ST. TERESA OF JESUS (P) (Teresian Sisters)

Founded in Spain in 1876. First foundation in the United States in 1910. Total Membership 1,307.
Generalate: Via Valcannuta, 134, Rome, Italy, 00166.
Formation House: 18080 St. Joseph's Way, Covington, LA 70435-5623. Tel: 985-893-1470; Fax: 985-893-2476. Sr. Clarice Suchy, S.T.J., Vocation Dir.; Sr. Martha L. Gonzalez, Community Archivist.
Total in Community: 27.
Properties owned and/or sponsored: Provincialate, Covington, LA; Blessed Mercedes Prat Convent, New Orleans, LA.
Ministry in the field of Academic Education at all levels; Education in underdeveloped areas; Youth Ministry; Pastoral Ministry.
Represented in the Archdioceses of Miami, New Orleans and San Antonio.

[4030] (S.S.T.V.)—CONGREGATION OF SISTERS OF SAINT THOMAS OF VILLANOVA (P)

Founded in France in 1661. First foundation in the United States in 1948.
General Motherhouse: 52 Blvd. d'Argenson, Neuilly-sur Seine, France, 92200. Tel: 01 47 47 42 20; Fax: 01 47 47 38 00; Email: neuillystv@wanadoo.com; Web: www.congregation-stv.org.
Universal total in Congregation: 106.
Sisters of St. Thomas of Villanova Convent: 76 West Rocks Rd., Norwalk, CT 06851. Tel: 203-847-2885; Email: sstv_usa@sbcglobal.net; Web: www.saintthomasofvillanova.com. Sr. Marie Lucie Monast, S.S.T.V., Liaison.
Total in Community: 3.
Properties owned and/or sponsored: Notre Dame Convalescent Home dba Notre Dame Health & Rehabilitation Center.
Represented in the Diocese of Bridgeport.

[4035] (D.S.T.)—DAUGHTERS OF ST. THOMAS CONGREGATION

Founded in 1969.
Motherhouse: Daughters of St. Thomas Congregation, 2319 Clarence Ave., Berwyn, IL 60402. Tel: 708-898-8622; Email: dsttexas2010@gmail.com; Web: dstsisters.org. Sr. Nirmala Joseph, D.S.T., Mother Supr.
Sisters: 4

[4040] (S.U.)—SOCIETY OF ST. URSULA (P)

Founded in Dole, France, in 1606. First foundation in the United States in 1901.
General Motherhouse: St. Cyr-Loire, France. Sr. Rose McNamara, S.U., Supr. Gen.
Provincialate: 50 Linwood Rd., Rhinebeck, NY 12572. Tel: 845-876-2341. Sr. Elizabeth DiTolla, S.U., Regl. Supr.
Total in Community: 20.
Legal Title: Sisters of St. Ursula of the Blessed Virgin of New York.
Ministry in the field of Education; Parish Ministry; Spiritual Direction and Retreats.
Represented in the Archdiocese of New York and in the Diocese of Raleigh.

[4048] (F.C.J.)—SOCIETY OF THE SISTERS FAITHFUL COMPANIONS OF JESUS (P)

Founded in France in 1820. First founded in the United States in 1895.
FCJ Generalate: Gumley House F.C.J., Twickenham Rd., Isleworth, England, TW7 6DN.
Area Office: 300 Palmerston Ave., Toronto, Canada, M6J 2J4. Tel: 416-588-1791.
U.S. Business Office: 350 Mt. Pleasant Ave., Providence, RI 02908. Tel: 401-683-2222. Sr. Katherine Mary O'Flynn, F.C.J., Supr. Gen.; Sr. Bonita M. Moser, Prov. Leader; Sr. Marguerite Goddard, F.C.J., Novice Dir.
Sisters: 11.

[4050] (S.D.S.H.)—SISTERS OF THE SOCIETY DEVOTED TO THE SACRED HEART (D)

Founded in Hungary in 1940.
Motherhouse (1956): 9814 Sylvia Ave., Northridge, CA 91324. Tel: 818-772-9961; Fax: 818-772-2742; Web: www.sacredheartsisters.com. Sr. Mary Tomasella, S.D.S.H., Supr. Gen.
Novitiate House (1956): 10480 Winnetka Ave., Chatsworth, CA 91311. Tel: 818-831-9710; Fax: 818-831-0790; Web: www.sacredheartsisters.com.
Total in Community: 48.
Properties owned and/or sponsored: Sacred Heart Motherhouse, Northridge CA; Heart of Jesus Retreat Center, Santa Ana, CA; Sacred Heart Novitiate, Chatsworth, CA; Sacred Heart Retreat Camp, Big Bear, CA; Sacred Heart Convent, Los Angeles, CA.
Ministry in Parish Religious Education Centers; Catechist Formation Centers; Camp for year-round Retreatsmotherhouse and summer Family Retreat Camps; Catechesis; Youth Leadership Programs; Day Retreat Center for Children and Adults; "Sacred Heart Kids' Club" Video/DVD Catechesis; Ministries in Spanish and Chinese; Young Adult Prayer Ministry; Catechetical Programs on Military Bases; Catechetical Missions to Dioceses; Asian Pacific Mission in Taiwan; Mission in Hungary.
Represented in the Archdiocese of Los Angeles and the Dioceses of Orange and San Bernardino. Also in Taiwan and Hungary.

[4060] (S.H.C.J.)—SOCIETY OF THE HOLY CHILD JESUS (P)

Founded in England in 1846. First foundation in the United States in 1862.
Motherhouse: Via della Maglianella 379, Rome, Italy, 00166. Sr. Pauline Darby, S.H.C.J., Society Leader.
American Province: Provincial Offices, 1341 Montgomery Ave, Rosemont, PA 19010. Tel: 610-626-1400. Email: americanprovince@shcj.org. Sr. Carroll Juliano, S.H.C.J., Prov. Leader; Sr. Roseanne McDougall, S.H.C.J., Archivist.
Total number in Province: 92.
Ministry in a variety of Educational and Pastoral Work. Properties owned or sponsored: Connelly School of the Holy Child, Potomac, MD; Mayfield Junior School of the Holy Child Jesus; Mayfield Senior School of the Holy Child Jesus, Pasadena, CA; Oak Knoll School of the Holy Child, Summit, NJ; Old Westbury School of the Holy Child, Old Westbury, NY; Rosemont School of the Holy Child, Rosemont, PA; School of the Holy Child, Drexel Hill, PA; School of the Holy Child, Rye, NY; Providence Center, Philadelphia, PA; Cornelia Connelly Center for Education; Holy Child Middle School, New York, NY.
Represented in the Archdioceses of Chicago, Los Angeles, Milwaukee, Newark, New York, Philadelphia, Portland in Oregon and Washington DC and in the Dioceses of Camden, Rockford, San Bernardino and San Diego. Also in Chile.

[4070] (R.S.C.J.)—SOCIETY OF THE SACRED HEART (P)

Founded in France in 1800. First foundation in the United States in 1818.
Generalate: Via Tarquinio Viper, 16, Rome, Italy, 00152. Sr. Barbara Dawson, Supr. Gen.
United States-Canada Provincial House: 4120 Forest Park Ave., St. Louis, MO 63108. Tel: 314-652-1500; Fax: 314-534-6800; Email: provincialhouse@rscj.org. Sr. Sheila Hammond, R.S.C.J., Prov.; Sr. Carolyn Osiek, R.S.C.J., Prov. Archivist.
Total number in the Province: 281.
Ministry in the field of Religious and Academic Education at all levels; Adult Education; Parish, Pastoral, Social and Health Care Ministries.
Province Corporations: Society of the Sacred Heart, United States Province, Inc.; California Province of the Society of the Sacred Heart, Inc.; Society of the Sacred Heart, Chicago Province, Inc.; Religious of the Sacred Heart, Washington Province, Inc.; Religious of the Sacred Heart, New York Province, Inc.; Ladies of the Sacred Heart, MO; Religious of the Sacred Heart in Massachusetts, Inc.; Network of the Sacred Heart Schools, Inc., 700 N. Third St., St. Charles, MO 63301, Phone: 636-724-7003.
Represented in the Archdioceses of Boston, Chicago, Cincinnati, Detroit, Galveston-Houston, Louisville, Miami, Milwaukee, New Orleans, New York, Omaha, St. Louis, San Francisco, Seattle and Washington and in the Dioceses of Albany, Baton Rouge, Fall River, Fort Wayne-South Bend, Lafayette (LA), Oakland, Portland, San Bernardino, San Diego, San Jose, and Trenton.

[4080] (S.S.S.)—SISTERS OF SOCIAL SERVICE OF LOS ANGELES, INC. (P)

Founded in Hungary. Established in the United States at Los Angeles, California in 1926.
General Motherhouse: 4316 Lanai Rd., Encino, CA 91436. Tel: 818-285-3355; Fax: 818-285-3366. Sr. Maribeth Larkin, S.S.S., Gen. Dir.
Total in Community: 60.
Legal Titles: Sisters of Social Service of Los Angeles; Sisters of Social Service Support Trust Fund.
Social Service Work in Parishes and in Diocesan Agencies; Leadership Training of Youth and Adults; Summer Camps for Children and Families; Programs for the Elderly; Peace and Justice Work; Religious Education; Settlement Houses; Health Programs; Family Counseling Services; International houses in Mexico, Philippines and Taiwan.
Represented in the Archdioceses of Los Angeles, Portland in Oregon and San Francisco and in the Dioceses of Oakland, Sacramento and San Diego.

[4090] (S.S.S.)—SISTERS OF SOCIAL SERVICE OF BUFFALO, INC. (P)

Founded in Budapest, Hungary in 1923; Sr. Margaret Slachta, Foundress.
Generalate: H-1029, Bathori Laszlo u. 10, Budapest, Hungary
U.S. District Residence: 296 Summit Ave., Buffalo, NY 14214-1936. Tel: 716-834-0197; Fax: 716-834-6168; Email: agnes.patakisss@gmail.com. Sr. Agnes Pataki, S.S.S., Delegate; Sr. Magdolna Kovari, S.S.S., Gen. Mod.
Total number in the United States: 9.
Ministry in Pastoral Care, Spirituality and Education.
Represented in the Diocese of Buffalo.

[4100] (S.S.M.)—SISTERS OF THE SORROWFUL MOTHER (THIRD ORDER OF ST. FRANCIS) (P)

Founded in Italy in 1883. First foundation in the United States in 1889.
General Motherhouse: Casa Generalizia della Suore dell'Addolorata, Via Paolo III 7-9, Rome, Italy, I-00165. Sr. Catherine Marie Hanegan, S.S.M., Gen. Supr.

SSM St. Clare of Assisi Region Administration: 815 Westhaven Dr., Ste. 100, Oshkosh, WI 54904. Tel: 920-230-2040; Fax: 920-230-2041. Email: eanderson@ssm-uscaribbean.org. Sr. M. Lois Bush, S.S.M., Regl. Supr.

Total number in the U.S. Community: 69.

Legal Holding: Sisters of the Sorrowful Mother; St. Clare of Assisi Region

Ministry in the fields of Social Justice; Religious and Academic Education; Nursing Homes; Social Work; Hospitals and Hospital Administration; Parish Ministry; Pastoral Care.

Represented in the Archdiocese of Milwaukee and in the Dioceses of Green Bay, La Crosse, Paterson and Tulsa. Also in Trinidad, Grenada, St. Lucia, Dominican Republic, Austria, Germany, Brazil, Tanzania and Italy.

[4110] (O.S.U.)—URSULINE NUNS (P) (Roman Union)

Founded in Italy in 1535. First foundation in the United States New Orleans, Louisiana in 1727.

Generalate: Via Nomentana 236, Rome, Italy, 00162. Sr. Susan Flood, O.S.U., Prioress Gen.

Eastern Province of the U.S. (1900): Ursuline Provincialate, 1338 North Ave., New Rochelle, NY 10804. Tel: 914-712-0060; Fax: 914-712-3134.

Total number in the Province: 54.

Legal Titles: Ursuline Provincialate, Eastern Province of the United States, Inc.; Marian Residence Fund, New Rochelle, NY; OSU Charitable Trust, New Rochelle, NY.

Ministry in the field of Academic Education at all levels; varied Pastoral and Social Services.

Represented in the Archdiocese of New York and in the Dioceses of Bridgeport and Wilmington.

Central Province of the U.S.: Ursuline Provincialate, 353 S. Sappington Rd., Saint Louis, MO 63122. Tel: 314-821-6884; Fax: 314-821-6888. Sr. Elisa Ryan, O.S.U., Prov. Prioress.

Total in Community: 72.

Ministry in the field of Religious and Academic Education.

Represented in the Archdioceses of Boston, New Orleans, St. Louis, St. Paul-Minneapolis and San Antonio and in the Dioceses of Dallas, Portland in Maine and Springfield in Illinois.

Western Province U.S. (1932): Ursuline Provincialate, 9248 Lakewood Dr., Windsor, CA 95492. Tel: 707-484-7841. Mailing Address: 9248 Lakewood Drive, Windsor, CA 95492. Sr. Shirley Ann Garibaldi, O.S.U., Prov.

Total number in the Province: 13.

Ministry in the field of Elementary Education; Work with the Eskimos, American Indians, & Hispanics; Parish Ministry.

Represented in the Archdioceses of Anchorage-Juneau and San Francisco and in the Dioceses of Boise, Fairbanks, Great Falls-Billings and Santa Rosa.

[4120] (O.S.U.)—URSULINE NUNS (P)

Founded in Italy in 1535. First foundation in the United States in New Orleans, Louisiana in 1727.

Motherhouse (1845): Ursulines of Brown County, 20860 St. Rte. 251, Fayetteville, OH 45118-9705. Tel: 513875-2020; Fax: 513-875-2311; Web: www.ursulinesofbc.org. Sr. Patricia Homan, O.S.U., Congregational Min.

Total in Community: 17.

Legal Title: St. Ursula Literary Institute; Ursulines of Brown County; Ursuline Academy of Cincinnati, Chatfield College.

Ministry in the field of Academic Education at all levels; Adult Education; Catechetical Instruction; Administration; Retreats; Counseling; Organization Consultation; Senior Services; Campus and Parish Ministry; Social Services - Inner City and Rural; Social Justice; Spiritual Direction.

Represented in the Archdiocese of Cincinnati.

[4120-01] CINCINNATI (P)

Motherhouse: Ursulines of Cincinnati, St. Ursula Convent, 1339 E. McMillan St. (Walnut Hills), Cincinnati, OH 45206. Tel: 513-961-3410. Sr. Margaret Mary Efkeman, O.S.U.

Total in Community: 4.

Legal Title: Ursulines of Cincinnati.

Ministry in the field of Academic Education; Parish; Social Services; Communications; Adult Education; Social Justice.

Represented in the Archdiocese of Cincinnati.

[4120-03] LOUISVILLE (P)

Ursuline Sisters of the Immaculate Conception: 3115 Lexington Rd., Louisville, KY 40206. Tel: 502897-1811; Fax: 502-896-3913. Email: jzappa@ursulineslou.org. Sr. Jean Anne Zappa, O.S.U., Pres.

Total in Community: 43.

Legal Title: Ursuline Society and Academy of Education aka Ursuline Sisters.

Ministry in the field of Academic Education; Pastoral Ministry; Social Services; Spirituality; Special Education.

Represented in the Archdiocese of Louisville and in the Dioceses of Lexington. Also in Peru.

[4120-04] CLEVELAND (P)

Ursuline Sisters of Cleveland: 6085 Parkland Blvd., Suite 175, Cleveland, OH 44124. Fax: 440-683-1371. Sr. Ritamary Welsh, O.S.U., Pres.; Sr. Cynthia Glavac, O.S.U., Community Archivist.

Total in Community: 117.

Legal Titles: Ursuline Academy of Cleveland; Ursuline Sisters of Cleveland.

Ministry in the field of Academic Education at all levels; Parish Ministry; Seminary; Social Service Agency; Hospital and Health Care Ministry; Spiritual Direction and Retreat Ministry.

Properties sponsored: Ursuline College; Beaumont High School; Villa Angela/St. Joseph High School.

[4120-05] OWENSBORO (P)

Ursuline Sisters of Mount Saint Joseph: 8001 Cummings Rd., Maple Mount, KY 42356. Tel: 270-229-4103; Fax: 270-229-4127. Sr. Sharon Sullivan, O.S.U., Congregational Leader.

Total in Community: 82.

Legal Holdings and Titles: St. Joseph's Female Ursuline Academy, Inc.

Ministry in Colleges; Elementary Schools; Parishes; Retreats and Spiritual Direction; Pastoral Care; Health Care; Social Services; Social Justice.

Represented in the Archdioceses of Kansas City in Kansas, Indianapolis and Louisville and in the Dioceses of Belleville, Owensboro, Shreveport and Springfield in Illinois. Also in Chile.

[4120-06] TOLEDO (P)

Ursuline Convent of the Sacred Heart: 4045 Indian Rd., Toledo, OH 43606. Tel: 419-536-9587. Sr. Sandra Sherman, O.S.U., Pres. & Gen. Supr.

Total in Community: 25; Associates: 100.

Legal Title: Ursuline Convent of the Sacred Heart.

Ministry in the field of Religious and Academic Education; Pastoral Ministry; Retreat Work; Spiritual Direction; Volunteer Work.

Properties owned or sponsored: St. Ursula Academy, Toledo, OH.

[4120-07] YOUNGSTOWN (P)

Motherhouse: Ursuline Motherhouse and Educational Center, 4250 Shields Rd., Canfield, OH 44406. Tel: 330-792-7636. Sr. Mary McCormick, O.S.U., Gen. Supr.

Total in Community: 43.

Properties owned and/or sponsored: Ursuline Motherhouse; Ursuline Center; Ursuline Preschool & Kindergarten; Beatitude House.

Ministry in the field of Religious and Academic Education at all levels; Parish Ministry; Social Services; Hospital Services; Single Parenting; AIDS Ministry; Preschool; Kindergarten; Nursing Home Service.

Represented in the Dioceses of Cleveland and Youngstown.

[4130] (O.S.U.)—URSULINE SISTERS OF THE CONGREGATION OF TILDONK, BELGIUM (P) International Congregation

Founded in Italy in 1535 by St. Angela Merici (Ursulines). Congregation of Tildonk founded in Belgium in 1832. First foundation in the United States in Ozone Park, New York, in 1924.

Generalate: Brussels, Belgium Sr. Bimla Minj, O.S.U., Gen. Supr.

Ursuline Provincialate: 81-15 Utopia Pkwy., Jamaica, NY 11432. Tel: 718-591-0681. Email: jcallahan@tildonkursuline.org. Sr. Joanne Callahan, O.S.U., Prov. Supr.

Total in Community: 32.

Properties owned and/or sponsored: Ursuline Provincialate, Jamaica NY. Ministry in the field of Education in all its aspects; Retreat Work; Chaplaincies.

Represented in the Archdiocese of Hartford and in the Dioceses of Brooklyn and Rockville Centre.

[4140] V.D.M.F.—VERBUM DEI MISSIONARY FRATERNITY (P)

Founded in Mallorca, Spain in 1963.

Motherhouse: Rome, Italy. 3365-3373 19th St., San Francisco, CA 94110.

Sisters: 20.

Ministry in the fields of retreat work; campus ministry; formation ministry.

Represented in the Archdiocese of San Francisco.

[4155] (M.T.G.)—SISTERS ADORERS OF THE HOLY CROSS (P)

Founded in 1670 in Vietnam by Bishop Pierre Lambert de la Motte. First foundation in the U.S. 1979.

General Motherhouse: 7408 S.E. Alder, Portland, OR 97215. Tel: 503-254-3284. Sr. Mary Kim Chi Bui, M.T.G., Supr.

Sisters: 33.

Represented in the Archdiocese of Portland in Oregon and in the Dioceses of Arlington, Sacramento and Stockton.

[4170] (V.S.C.)—VINCENTIAN SISTERS OF CHARITY (D)

Founded in Bedford in 1928.

5900 Delhi Rd., Mount Saint Joseph, OH 45051. Email: pat.hayden@srcharitycinti.org.

[4180] (M.P.V.)—RELIGIOUS VENERINI SISTERS (P)

Founded in Italy in 1685. First foundation in the United States in 1909.

General Motherhouse: via Gioachino Belli 31, Rome, Italy. Mother Eliana Massimi, Supr. Gen.

Universal total in Congregation: 359.

Provincial House for the U.S.: 23 Edward St., Worcester, MA 01605. Sr. Carmen Capriole, M.P.V., Prov.

Total in Community: 16.

Legal Holdings: Venerini Academy, Worcester, MA.

Ministry in the field of Education; Health Care; Social Services; Parish and Diocesan Ministry; Foreign Missions.

Represented in the Archdiocese of Boston and in the Dioceses of Albany and Worcester.

[4190] (V.H.M.)—VISITATION NUNS (P)

Founded in France in 1610. First foundation in the United States in Georgetown, Washington, DC in 1799.

First Federation of North America: Tel: 419-536-1343; Fax: 419-536-6025. Email: vhm-toledo@toast.net; Web: https://visitationsistersfirstfederation.org. Sr. Sharon Elizabeth Gworek, V.H.M., Federation Pres. 1745 Parkside Blvd., Toledo, OH 43607-1599. Jane de Chantal Foundation. Monasteries listed in the order of foundation.

Monastery of the Visitation (1833): 2300 Springhill Ave., Mobile, AL 36607-3202. Tel: 251-473-2321; Fax: 251-476-9761; Web: www.VisitationMonasteryMobile.org. Mother Margaret Mary Rumpf, V.H.M., Supr.

Perpetual Vows: 12; Temporary Vows: 4; Novices: 2; Postulants: 4.

Monastery of the Visitation: 14 Beach Rd., P.O. Box 432, Tyringham, MA 01264. Tel: 413-243-3995; Fax: 413-243-3543; Email: vistyr3@aol.com; Web: www.vistyr.org. Mother Miriam Rose Niethus, Supr.

Total in Community: 15.

Legal Title: Visitation of Holy Mary.

Monastery of the Visitation: 12221 Bienvenue Rd., Rockville, VA 23146. Tel: 804-749-4885. Rev. Mother Maria Theresa Yang, V.H.M., Supr.

Professed Sisters: 8.

Legal Title: Visitation of Holy Mary.

Monastery of the Visitation: 5820 City Ave., Philadelphia, PA 19131-1295. Tel: 215-473-5888. Email: viznunphil@aol.com. Mother Antoinette Marie Walker, V.H.M., Supr.

Professed Sisters Cloistered: 5.

Legal Title: Sisters of the Visitation of Philadelphia.

Monastery of the Visitation (Contemplative): 1745 Parkside Blvd., Toledo, OH 43607-1599. Tel: 419-536-1343; Fax: 419-536-6025; Email: vhm-superior@

toast2.net; Web: www.toledovisitation.org. Mother Marie de Sales Kasper, V.H.M., Supr.
Professed Sisters: 14; In Formation: 5.
Legal Title: The Contemplative Order of the Visitation of Toledo, Ohio.

Monastery of the Visitation (Strictly Cloistered): 2055 Ridgedale Dr., Snellville, GA 30078. Tel: 770-972-1060. Sr. Teresa Maria Kulangara, V.H.M., Supr.
Professed Sisters: 5; Temporarily Professed: 2; Novices: 2; Aspirants: 3.
Legal Title: Order of the Visitation of the Holy Mary.

Second Federation of North America

Monastery of the Sisters of the Visitation of Georgetown: 1500 35th St., N.W., Washington, DC 20007. Tel: 202-337-0305; Fax: 202-558-7976. Email: berchmans@visi.org. Mother Mary Berchmans Hannan, Supr.; Sr. Mada-anne Gell, Community Archivist.
Total number in the School Community: 500; Total in Community: 10.
Legal Holdings and Titles: Sisters of the Visitation of Georgetown; Georgetown Visitation Preparatory School.

Monastery of the Visitation (1833): 3020 N. Ballas Rd., St. Louis, MO 63131. Tel: 314-625-9247. Sr. Karen Mohan, V.H.M., Administrator Supr.
Total in Community: 3.
Legal Holdings: Visitation Academy of St. Louis County; Monastery of the Visitation, St. Louis, MO.
Ministry in Education.

Monastery of the Visitation (1855): 8902 Ridge Blvd., Brooklyn, NY 11209-5716. Tel: 718-745-5151; Fax: 718-745-3680. Mother Susan Marie Kasprzak, V.H.M., Supr. Professed Sisters: 12.
Legal Title: Sisters of the Visitation of Brooklyn, NY.

Monastery of the Visitation: 2455 Visitation Dr., St. Paul, MN 55120. Tel: 651-683-1700. Email: info@vischool.org. Sr. Mary Denise Villaume, V.H.M., Supr.
Total in Community: 3.
Ministry in Prayer and Education.

[4200] (S.V.M.)—SISTERS OF THE VISITATION OF THE IMMACULATE HEART OF MARY (D)

Founded in France in 1610. First foundation in the United States in 1799.

Visitation Convent: 2360 Carter Rd., Dubuque, IA 52001-2997. Tel: 563-588-2008. Email: dbqsvm@dbqarch.org. Sr. Patricia Clark, S.V.M., Pres.
Total in Community: 3.
Ministry in prayer and community service.
Represented in the Archdiocese of Dubuque.

[4210] (S.D.V.)—VOCATIONIST SISTERS (P) (Sisters of the Divine Vocations)

Founded in Italy in 1921. First established in the United States in 1967.

General Motherhouse: Corso Duca D'Aosta, 22 Pianura, Naples, Italy, 80126. Sr. Chiara Stela Vitale, S.D.V., Supr. Gen.

U.S. Foundation: Perpetual Help Day Nursery, 170 Broad St., Newark, NJ 07104. Tel: 973-484-3535. Sr. Romilda Borges, S.D.V., Supr.
Total in Community: 5.
Ministry in Nursery Schools & Kindergartens; CCD Program and Parish Services.
Represented in the Archdiocese of Newark.

Sister Joanna Formation House: 88 Brooklake Rd., Florham Park, NJ 07932. Tel: 973-966-9762. Sr. Josephine Sabesaje, Supr.
Total in Community: 10.
Ministry in Nursery School; Formation House; Religious Education.
Represented in the Archdiocese of Newark and in the Dioceses of Metuchen and Paterson.

[4230] (X.M.M.)—XAVERIAN MISSIONARY SOCIETY OF MARY, INC. (P)

Founded in Italy in 1945. First established in the United States in 1954.

General Motherhouse: Missionarie di Maria - Saveriane, Via Omero 4, Parma, Italy 43123. Sr. Giordana Bertacchini, X.M.M., Supr. Gen.
Total Membership: 218.

U.S. Headquarters: Xaverian Missionary Society of Mary, 242 Salisbury St., Worcester, MA 01609. Tel: 508-757-0514; Email: xavsistersusa@yahoo.com.mx. Sr. Rebeca Sanchez Perez, X.M.M., Supr.
Ministry to Hispanics; Elderly; Families; CCD Programs and Mission Education.
Represented in the Diocese of Worcester.

AN ALPHABETICAL LIST OF DIOCESAN AND RELIGIOUS PRIESTS OF THE UNITED STATES

(Cardinals, Archbishops, Bishops, Archabbots and Abbots are listed in previous section)

ABBREVIATIONS

A.A.	Assumptionists
B.C.S.	Brothers of Christian Service
B.G.S.	Little Brothers of the Good Shepherd
B.S.O.	Basilian Salvatorian Fathers
C.F.A.	Alexian Brothers
C.F.C.	Congregation of Christian Brothers
C.F.M.M.	Brothers of Our Lady, Mother of Mercy
C.F.P.	Brothers of the Poor of St. Francis
C.F.R.	Franciscan Friars of the Renewal
C.F.X.	Brothers of St. Francis Xavier
C.I.C.M.	Missionhurst Congregation of the Immaculate Heart of Mary
C.J.	Josephite Fathers
C.J.M.	Congregation of Jesus and Mary
C.M.	Congregation of the Mission
C.M.C.	Congregation of Mother Coredemptrix
C.M.F.	Claretian Missionaries
C.M.I.	Carmelites of Mary Immaculate
C.M.L.M.	The Congregation of Maronite Lebanese Missionaries
C.M.M.	Congregation of Mananhill Missionaries, Marianhill Fathers and Brothers
C.M.Vd.	Mekhitarist Fathers
C.O.	Oratorians
C.P.	Congregation of the Passion
C.P.M.	Congregation of the Fathers of Mercy
C.P.P.S.	Society of the Precious Blood
C.R.	Congregation of the Resurrection
C.R.I.C.	Canons Regular of the Immaculate Conception
C.R.L.	Canons Regular of the Lateran
C.R.M.	Adorno Fathers
C.R.S.	Somascan Fathers
C.R.S.P.	Clerics Regular of St. Paul
C.S.	Missionaries of St. Charles Scalabrinians
C.S.B.	Basilian Fathers
C.S.C.	Priests of the Congregation of Holy Cross
C.S.J.	Congregation of St. Joseph
C.S.J.B.	Congregation of St. John the Baptist
C.S.P.	Paulist Fathers
C.S.P.X.	Brothers of Saint Pius X
C.S.S.	Stigmatine Fathers and Brothers
C.S.Sp.	Congregation of the Holy Spirit
C.SS.R.	Redemptorist Fathers
C.S.V.	Clerics of St. Viator
D.L.P.	Diocesan Labor Priests
Er.Cam.	Camaldolese Hermits of the Congregation of Monte Corona
F.C.	Brothers of Charity
F.D.P.	Sons of Divine Providence
F.F.I.	Franciscan Friars of the Immaculate
F.F.S C.	Franciscan Brothers of the Holy Cross
F.I.C.	Brothers of Christian Instruction
F.J.	Congregation of St. John
F.M.M.	Brothers of Mercy
F.M.M.	Missionary Fraternity of Mary
F.M.S.	The Marist Brothers
F.M.S.I.	Sons of Mary Missionary Society
F.P.M.	Presentation Brothers
F.S.C.	Brothers of the Christian Schools
F.S.C.B.	Priestly Fraternity of the Missionaries of St. Charles Borromeo, Inc
F.S.E.	Brothers of the Holy Eucharist
F.S.P.	Brothers of St. Patrick
F.S.R.	Brothers of the Congregation of Our Lady of the Holy Rosary
F.S.S.P.	Priestly Fraternity of St. Peter
G.H.M.	The Glenmary Home Missioners
H.J.D.	Los Hermanos de Juan Diego
H.M.C.	Hermits of Mount Carmel
I.C.	Institute of Charity
I.C.	Incarnational Consecration
I.H.M.	Brothers of the Immaculate Heart of Mary
I.M.C.	Consolata Missionaries
I.S.S.S.	Schoenstatt Institute of Secular Priests
L.B.S.F.	Little Brothers of Saint Francis
L.C.	Legionaries of Christ
M.Afr.	Missionaries of Africa
M.C.B.S.	Missionary Congregation of the Blessed Sacrament
M.C.C.J.	Comboni Missionaries of the Heart of Jesus (Verona)
M.Des.	Mercedarios Descalzos
M.E.P.	Paris Foreign Mission Society
M.G.	Guadalupe Missioners
M.H.M.	Mill Hill Missionaries
M.I.C.	Congregation of Marians of the Immaculate Conception
M.J.	Missionaries of St. Joseph (Mexico)
M.M.	Maryknoll
M.S.	The Missionaries of Our Lady of La Salette
M.S.A.	Missionaries of the Holy Apostles
M.S.C.	Missionaries of the Sacred Heart
M.S.F.	Congregation of the Missionaries of the Holy Family
M.S.P.	Missionaries of St. Paul
M.Sp.S.	Missionaries of the Holy Spirit
M.SS.CC.	Missionaries of the Sacred Hearts of Jesus and Mary
O.A.R.	Order of the Augustinian Recollects
O.Carm.	Carmelite Fathers and Brothers
O.Cart.	Order of Carthusians
O.C.D.	Discalced Carmelite Fathers
O.Cist.	Cistercian Fathers
O.C.S.O.	The Cistercian Order of the Strict Observance (Trappists)
O.de.M.	Order of Our Lady of Mercy
O.F.M.	Franciscan Friars
O.F.M.Cap.	The Capuchin Friars
O.F.M.Conv.	Conventual Franciscans
O.H.	Hospitaller Brothers of St. John of God
O.I.C.	Order of the Imitation of Christ
O.L.P.	Brothers of Our Lady of Providence
O.M.	Minim Fathers
O.Mar.	Congregation of Maronite Monks
O.M.I.	Oblates of Mary Immaculate
O.M.V.	Oblates of the Virgin Mary
O.P.	Order of Preachers (Dominicans)
O.Praem.	Canons Regular of Premontre
O.R.C.	Operarios del Reina de Cristo
O.S.A.	The Augustinians
O.S.B.	Benedictine Monks
O.S.B.Cam.	Camaldolese Hermits
O S.B.M.	Order of St. Basil the Great
O.S.C.	Canons Regular of the Order of the Holy Cross
O.S.Cam.	Camillian Fathers and Brothers
O.S.F.	Congregation of the Religious Brothers of the Third Order Regular of St. Francis
O.S.F.	Franciscan Brothers of Christ the King
O.S.F.	Franciscan Brothers of the Third Order Regular
O.S.F.	Franciscan Missionary Brothers of the Sacred Heart of Jesus
O.S.F.S.	Oblates of St. Francis de Sales
O.S.J.	Oblates of St. Joseph
O.S.M.	Servites
O.S.P.P.E.	Pauline Fathers
O.Ss.S.	Order of the Holy Trinity
P.I.M.E.	Pontifical Institute for Foreign Missions
R.C.J.	Rogationist Fathers
S.A.	Franciscan Friars of the Atonement
S.A.C.	Society of the Catholic Apostolate
S.C.	Brothers of the Sacred Heart
S.C.	Servants of Charity
S.Ch.	Society of Christ
Sch.P.	Piarist Fathers
S.C.J.	Congregation of the Priests of the Sacred Heart
S.D.B.	Salesians of Don Bosco
S.D.S.	Society of the Divine Savior
S.D.V.	Vocationist Fathers
S.F.	Sons of the Holy Family
S.F.M.	Scarboro Foreign Missions
S.J.	Jesuit Fathers and Brothers
S.M.	Society of Mary (Marianists)
S.M.	Marist Fathers
S.M.A.	Society of African Missions
S.M.M.	Montfort Missionaries
S.M.P.	Society of Our Mother of Peace
S.O.Cist.	Cistercian Monks of the Strict Observance
S.O.L.T.	Society of Our Lady of the Most Holy Trinity
s.P.	Servants of the Paraclete
S.P.S.	St. Patrick Missionary Society
S.S.	Society of the Priests of Saint Sulpice
S.S.C.	Society of St. Columban
SS.CC.	Congregation of the Sacred Hearts of Jesus and Mary
S.S.E.	Society of Saint Edmund
S.S.J.	St. Joseph's Society of the Sacred Heart
S.S.P.	Pauline Fathers and Brothers
S.S.S.	Congregation of the Blessed Sacrament
S.S.T.	Missionary Society of St. Thomas the Apostle
S.T.	Missionary Servants of the Most Holy Trinity
S.X.	Xaverian Missionary Fathers
S.V.D.	Society of the Divine Word
T.O.R.	Third Order Regular of Saint Francis
V.C.	Vincentian Congregation (India)
V.D.C.	Verbum Dei Community

Index Usage Guide – sample entry:

Abt, Rev. John, O.F.M. '90 (STL) [MON] Franciscan Friary of St. Anthony of Padua, St. Louis, MO

- Priests are sorted alphabetically by last name, first name, middle name.
- Religious order initials and ordination year, when provided, follow the Priest's name.
- Letters within parenthesis represent the diocese where the priest/assignment can be found.
- An arrow preceding the letters indicates a priest is on loan to the specified diocese, e.g., (>ALB).
- See the full list of diocesan abbreviations by using the table of contents on page A-3.
- Assignments consist of entity name and location or miscellaneous assignment (e.g., Retired, On Special Assignment, etc.). Multiple assignments are separated by a semi-colon.
- The three-letter 'index codes' enclosed in brackets correspond to Section Headers under which the priest/assignment can be found in the Institutions section. See list of headers/codes below:

ASSOCIATIONS	[ASN]
CAMPUS MINISTRY / NEWMAN CENTERS	[CAM]
CATHOLIC CHARITIES	[CCH]
CEMETERIES	[CEM]
COLLEGES & UNIVERSITIES	[COL]
CONVENTS, MONASTERIES, AND RESIDENCES FOR WOMEN	[CON]
ENDOWMENTS / FOUNDATIONS / TRUSTS	[EFT]
HOSPITALS / HEALTH SERVICES	[HOS]
MISCELLANEOUS	[MIS]
MONASTERIES AND RESIDENCES FOR PRIESTS AND BROTHERS	[MON]
NURSING / REHABILITATION / CONVALESCENCE / ELDERLY CARE	[NUR]
PRESCHOOLS / CHILDCARE CENTERS	[PRE]
RETREAT HOUSES / RENEWAL CENTERS	[RTR]
SEMINARIES	[SEM]
SHRINES	[SHR]
SPECIAL CARE FACILITIES	[SPF]

Aamodt, Rev. Aric, '17 (STP) St. Hubert, Chanhassen, MN
Aaron, Rev. Andrew D., '96 (BAL) St. Clement, Lansdowne, MD; St. Philip Neri, Linthicum Heights, MD
Aaron, Rev. Derek, '16 (LFT) Curia: Clergy and Religious Services St. John Vianney Parish, Fishers, IN
Aaron, Rev. Sean, (LFT) St. Louis de Montfort, Fishers, IN
Aaron, Rev. Shawn, *LC* '02 (ATL) [MON] Legionaries of Christ, Incorporated, Cumming, GA
Aarons, Very Rev. Anthony, '06 (ORL) Curia: Spiritual Life Basilica of the National Shrine of Mary Queen of the Universe, Orlando, FL
Ababio, Rev. George, '17 (ALN) Holy Guardian Angels, Reading, PA
Abadano, Rev. Rogelio L., '11 (RIC) St. Francis of Assisi, Amherst, VA; St. Mary Catholic Church, Lovingston, VA
Abadie, Rev. Travis, '15 (LAF) St. Catherine, Arnaudville, LA; St. John Francis Regis, Arnaudville, LA
Abadilla, Rev. Gregg, '16 (TR) St. Catharine-St. Margaret, Spring Lake, NJ
Abah, Rev. Joseph A., '82 (JC) St. Jude Thaddeus, Mokane, MO; St. Peter, Fulton, MO
Abainza, Rev. Alphonsus Zaldy, *SOLT* (PHX) Most Holy Trinity Roman Catholic Parish, Phoenix, AZ
Abalahin, Rev. Emiel, *O.Carm.* (NY) Parish of St. Simon Stock and St. Joseph, Bronx, NY
Aballe, Rev. Antonio Marrero, '01 (FAJ) San Francisco de Asis, Rio Grande, PR
Abalodo, Rev. Bakpenam Sebastien, *S.M.* '02 (CIN) [COL] The University of Dayton, Dayton, OH
Abalodo, Rev. Sebastien, *SM* (CIN) [MON] Marianist Community, Dayton, OH
Abalon, Rev. Jose Amante M., '01 (NEW) Our Lady of Most Holy Rosary/St. Michael, Elizabeth, NJ
Abalon, Rev. Jose Manuel, '00 (NEW) Saint Joseph Parish, East Orange, NJ
Abano, Rev. Edgardo D., '85 (MET) On Duty Outside Diocese.
Abano, Rev. Felix, '03 (GB) St. Anne Parish, Lena, WI
Abao, Rev. Marlee, *C.I.C.M.* '09 (R) Our Lady of the Rosary, Louisburg, NC
Abara, Rev. Lawrence N., '78 (LAF) Retired. Curia: (>MO) Offices and Directors
Abarca, Rev. Alfonso, *S.D.B.* (LA) St. John Chrysostom, Inglewood, CA
Abasilim, Rev. Maurice, '97 (MAN) Chap, Concord Hosp Christ the King Parish, Concord, NH
Abaskhron, Rev. Francis Fayez, (BRK) Resurrection Catholic Coptic Church, Brooklyn, NY; [CCH] Arabic Speaking Ministry, ,
Abasso, Rev. Rodney, (EST) Mart Mariam Chaldean Catholic Church, Northbrook, IL
Abaya, Rev. Pascual, '96 (HON) Curia: Consultative Bodies Cathedral Basilica of Our Lady of Peace, Honolulu, HI
Abba, Rev. Daniel, *C.S.Sp.* (PIT) [MON] Congregation of the Holy Spirit Province of the United States, Bethel Park, PA
Abba, Rev. William, '95 (PHX) Blessed Sacrament Roman Catholic Parish, Scottsdale, AZ
Abban, Rev. Mark, '03 (LR) Holy Child Church, Dumas, AR; St. Mark, Monticello, AR; St. Mary, McGehee, AR
Abbatiello, Rev. Robert J., *O.F.M.Cap.* (NY) Roman Catholic Church of the Sacred Heart, Yonkers, NY; Sacred Heart High School, Yonkers, NY; [MON] The Province of St. Mary of the Capuchin Order, White Plains, NY
Abbott, Rev. Gregory E., '07 (STP) Annunciation, Northfield, MN
Abbruzzese, Rev. Msgr. John A., (BO) On Duty Outside Diocese.
Abdella, Rev. Peter, *C.S.P.* '85 (LA) Retired. St. Paul the Apostle, Los Angeles, CA
Abdoo, Rev. Louis, *I.M.C.* '73 (SB) St. Francis de Sales, Riverside, CA
Abdulai, Rev. Sampson, '12 (NO) St. Thomas, Pointe-A-La-Hache, LA
Abegg, Rev. Victor P., *O.F.M.Conv.* '74 (OAK) [MON] Conventual Franciscans (Province of St. Joseph Cupertino) Provincial Center, Castro Valley, CA; [MON] Conventual Franciscans (Province of St. Joseph of Cupertino), Castro Valley, CA
Abeldaño, Rev. Mauricio, (MEM) Sacred Heart, Humboldt, TN; St. Matthew Mission, Milan, TN
Abele, Rev. Alan Carl, '73 (AJ) Retired.
Abella, Rev. Ray, '93 (STO) On Duty Outside Diocese. Hospital Chaplain, Northport, NY
Abella, Rev. Ray G., (MO) Curia: Offices and Directors
Abellan, Rev. Jose Antonio Murcia, '01 (CHI) Curia: Leadership Mary, Mother of Mercy, Chicago, IL
Abels, Rev. Kevin P., '03 (BRK) Our Lady of Angels, Brooklyn, NY
Abercrombie, Rev. Jamie M., *C.S.B.* '73 (GAL) Retired. [MON] The Basilian Fathers of Dillon House, Houston, TX
Aberion, Rev. Alvin B., '04 (GBG) Nativity of the Blessed Virgin Mary, Uniontown, PA; St. John the Evangelist, Uniontown, PA; St. Joseph, Uniontown, PA; St. Therese, the Little Flower of Jesus, Uniontown, PA
Abernethy, Rev. David S, '94 (PBR) SS. Peter and Paul, Duquesne, PA
Abert, Rev. Richard P., *S.J.* '76 (MIL) Our Lady of Guadalupe Congregation, Milwaukee, WI; St. Patricks Congregation, Milwaukee, WI; [MON] Arrupe House Jesuit Community, Milwaukee, WI
Abi Chedid, Rev. Elie, '85 (SAM) St. Jude, Orlando, FL
Abi-Akar, Rev. Dany, '10 (SAM) Saint John Paul II, Sleepy Hollow, NY
Abiamiri, Rev. Anthony, '97 (BAL) Our Lady of Perpetual Help, Ellicott City, MD; [MIS] Nigeria-Igbo Catholic Community, Baltimore, MD
Abiera, Rev. Fredric, *O.A.R.* (LA) St. Benedict, Montebello, CA
Abiero, Rev. Michael Charles, '15 (OWN) Curia: Advisory Boards, Commissions, Committees, and Councils Holy Guardian Angels, Irvington, KY; St. Rose, Cloverport, KY
Abinader, Rev. Marnan, *M.L.M.* (OLL) St. Therese of the Child Jesus Maronite Catholic Church, Tulsa, OK
Abiog, Rev. Merlito, (DAL) St. Francis of Assisi Catholic Parish - Whitesboro, Whitesboro, TX; St. Mary Catholic Parish, Sherman, TX; [CEM] St. Mary Parish-St. Mary Cemetery, Sherman, TX
Abisaad, Rev. Joseph, '16 (SAM) St. Theresa, Brockton, MA
Ablanida, Rev. Joachim E., *M.M.H.C.* '02 (LA) St. John of God, Norwalk, CA
Abler, Rev. Larry, *O.F.M.Cap.* '64 (MIL) [MON] St. Lawrence Friary, Mount Calvary, WI
Ables, Rev. Abner Marcelo, *C.S.* '12 (KC) Holy Rosary, Kansas City, MO
Abogado, Rev. Peter Magadya, *SSS* '13 (PBL) St. Francis Xavier, Pueblo, CO
Aboh, Rev. Bede C., '88 (KNX) Curia: Offices and Directors ETSU Catholic Center, Johnson City, TN; [CAM] ETSU-Catholic Center, Johnson City, TN
Aboyi, Rev. James, *V.C.* '04 (PHX) Curia: Leadership; Offices and Directors St. Benedict Roman Catholic Parish, Phoenix, AZ
Abraham, Rev. Anthony, '08 (STV) Our Lady of Mt. Carmel Parish, St. John, VI; [MIS] Catholic Charismatic Renewal, St. John, VI
Abraham, Rt. Rev. Msgr. Augustine Mangalath, '79 (MCE) Curia: Administration; Advisory Boards, Commissions, Committees, and Councils; Communications
Abraham, Rev. Johnson C., '88 (OAK) St. Agnes, Concord, CA
Abraham, Rev. Joseph, (KAL) St. Joseph, St. Joseph, MI
Abraham, Rev. Joseph, '90 (RNO) Curia: Leadership; Offices and Directors St. Rose of Lima, Reno, NV
Abraham, Rev. Mathew, (RVC) Our Lady of Peace, Lynbrook, NY
Abraham, Rev. Sunny, (PHX) Our Lady of Perpetual Help Roman Catholic Parish, Scottsdale, AZ
Abraham, Rev. Thaddeus, '90 (BRK) St. Matthew, Brooklyn, NY
Abraham, Rev. Tojan, *M.C.B.S.* (MEM) St. Mary Church, Savannah, TN
Abraham, Rev. Tomy, (CHI) St. Edna, Arlington Heights, IL
Abrahamczyk, Rev. Kazimierz, *SVD* '85 (SFR) All Souls, South San Francisco, CA
Abrahams, Rev. John J., '79 (BAL) Retired.
Abrahim, Rev. Jirjis, '67 (EST) Retired.
Abrego, Rev. Martin, '92 (SJ) On Leave.
Abreu, Rev. John E., '74 (PRO) Saint Thomas the Apostle Church Corporation of Warren, Warren, RI
Abrica Benitez, Friar Christian Emmanuel, *OFM Conv.* (SAT) [MON] San Damiano Friary, San Antonio, TX; [SEM] San Damiano Friary, Initial House of Formation, San Antonio, TX
Absalon, Rev. Burt H., '01 (RCK) St. Mary, Woodstock, IL; St. Patrick, Hartland, IL
Abts, Rev. John, *O.F.M.* '90 (STL) [MON] Franciscan Friary of St. Anthony of Padua, St. Louis, MO
Abu, Rev. Isaac, *O.M.V.* (BO) [MIS] St. Clement Archdiocesan Eucharistic Shrine, Boston, MA; [MIS] St. Francis Chapel, Boston, MA
Abugu, Rev. Benedict, '19 (ATL) Holy Cross Catholic Church, Atlanta, Inc., Atlanta, GA
Abuh, Rev. Emmanuel, (FTW) Queen of Peace, Mishawaka, IN
Abuh, Rev. Julius, '92 (KNX) St. Joseph the Worker, Madisonville, TN
Abulag, Rev. John, '20 (JOL) Sacred Heart, Joliet, IL; The Cathedral of St. Raymond, Joliet, IL
Abu-Lail, Rev. Samir, '94 (NTN) St. Joseph Mission, Seattle, WA
Abundiz, Rev. Jaime, *I.V.E.* '21 (DAL) City Hospo at White Rock, Dallas
Abúndiz, Rev. Jaime, *IVE* (FBK) Holy Mary of Guadalupe Catholic Church Healy, Healy, AK; Immaculate Conception Catholic Parish Fairbanks, Fairbanks, AK; Sacred Heart Cathedral Catholic Church Fairbanks, Fairbanks, AK; St. Theresa Catholic Church Nenana, Nenana, AK; [MON] St. Ignatius Residence, Fairbanks, AK
Abuya, Rev. Gregory, (FTW) Sacred Heart of Jesus (Lakeville), South Bend, IN; St. Jude Church, South Bend, IN
Abyad, Rev. Zyad, '22 (NTN) St. John of the Desert Melkite Catholic Church, Phoenix, AZ
Accardi, Rev. Joseph N., '90 (PH) St. Bernard, Philadelphia, PA
Accinni Reinhardt, Rev. Michael, '01 (PHX) Our Lady of the Lake Roman Catholic Parish, Lake Havasu City, AZ
Acebo, Rev. Jeff, (OAK) Retired. On Leave.
Acero, Rev. Romen A., '08 (R) St. Gabriel Catholic Parish of Greenville, Greenville, NC
Acervo, Rev. Lee E., '08 (DET) Curia: Administration; Consultative Bodies St. Edward on the Lake Parish Lakeport, Lakeport, MI
Acevedo, Rev. Alan, '21 (SR) Pastor of St. Eugene Cathedral of Santa Rosa, A Corporation Sole, Santa Rosa, CA
Acevedo, Rev. Dario, '13 (WOR) Curia: Offices and Directors St. Joseph's, Fitchburg, MA
Acevedo, Rev. Edward, '97 (MGZ) Parroquia San Jose, Custodio de la Sagrada Familia, Boqueron, PR
Acevedo, Rev. Jaime H., '99 (MIA) St. Mark, Southwest Ranches, FL
Acevedo, Rev. William, '08 (BO) St. Patrick, Lowell, MA
Acevedo, Rev. William, '08 (BO) Curia: Consultative Bodies
Acevedo Vizcaya, Rev. Natividad, (SJN) San Valentin, Carolina, PR
Acevedo-Fabian, Rev. Milton Rene, '00 (FRS) St. Augustine, Lamont, CA
Achacoso, Rev. Msgr. Jonas, '02 (BRK) Curia: Leadership Corpus Christi, Woodside, NY
Achadinha, Rev. James M., (BO) Holy Family, Gloucester, MA; Our Lady of Good Voyage, Gloucester, MA
Achbach, Rev. Kevin Lee, '03 (RC) Curia: Leadership St. Joseph, Spearfish, SD
Acheme, Rev. Augustine, *VC* '18 (PHX) St. Timothy Roman Catholic Parish, Mesa, AZ
Achi, Rev. Charles, '06 (NY) St. Martin de Porres, Poughkeepsie, NY
Achidi, Rev. Denning, '20 (BUF) Mary Immaculate, Pavilion, NY; St. Isidore, Perry, NY; St. Michael's R.C. Church Society, Warsaw, NY
Achu, Rev. Stanislaus, (SPR) St. Thomas the Apostle, West Springfield, MA
Acker, Rev. Karl H., '63 (MIL) Retired.
Ackeret, Rev. Dennis, '68 (MIL) Retired. Curia: Leadership
Ackerman, Rev. Donald K., '61 (EVN) Retired.
Ackerman, Rev. J. Thomas, '97 (BIR) Curia: Evangelization; Leadership St. Francis of Assisi Catholic Parish, Tuscaloosa, Tuscaloosa, AL
Ackerman, Rev. James, (CIN) [MON] Jesuit Community at St. Xavier High School, Cincinnati, OH
Ackerman, Rev. James C., *SJ* (CIN) St. Francis Xavier Church, Cincinnati, OH
Ackerman, Rev. Michael R., '14 (PIT) Curia: Consultative Bodies Resurrection, Pittsburgh, PA
Ackerman, Rev. Phillip, '78 (FAR) Holy Cross Church of West Fargo, West Fargo, ND
Ackerman, Rev. Raymond K., '91 (OKL) Curia: Consultative Bodies St. John the Baptist, Edmond, OK;

[CAM] University of Central Oklahoma, Edmond, OK
Ackerman, Rev. Thomas, (BIR) Curia: Leadership St. Robert, Reform, AL; [CAM] Campus Ministry Office - University of Alabama, Tuscaloosa, AL
Ackley, Rev. Randall Wasyl, '05 (HPM) Retired.
Acklin, Rev. Thomas, *O.S.B.* '80 (GBG) St. Bartholomew, Crabtree, PA; [MON] Saint Vincent Archabbey, Latrobe, PA
Acob, Rev. Augusto Tana, '80 (OAK) St. David of Wales, Richmond, CA
Acosta, Rev. Edgardo, '83 (MGZ) Church of San Isidro, Sabana Grande, PR
Acosta, Rev. Francisco, '70 (BWN) Our Lady of Guadalupe, Brownsville, TX
Acosta, Rev. Juan Gabriel, '13 (BGP) On Academic Leave. Graduate Studies
Acosta, Rev. Max Kenneth, '17 (COL) St. Mary, Delaware, OH
Acosta, Rev. Yovanny A., (SB) Saint John XXIII Catholic Community, Inc., Fontana, CA; [MIS] Columbia Worship Site, Redlands, CA
Acosta Pena, Very Rev. Jorge E., '02 (NEW) Immaculate Conception, Newark, NJ; Our Lady of Good Counsel, Newark, NJ
Acosta-Escobar, Rev. Bill John, '02 (R) Curia: Leadership St. Catherine of Siena, Wake Forest, NC
Acquaro, Rev. Philip Anthony, *C.S.B.* '70 (GAL) Retired. [MON] The Basilian Fathers of Dillon House, Houston, TX
Acquaye, Rev. Emmanuel, *O.F.M. Conv.* '06 (BAL) [HOS] MedStar Good Samaritan Hospital, Baltimore, MD
Acrea, Rev. John, '62 (DM) Retired.
Acri, Rev. John A., '65 (HBG) Retired.
Acton, Rev. Msgr. Sean A., '48 (LA) Retired.
Acuna Delgado, Rev. Jesus, '06 (TUC) On Administrative Leave.
Adagatla, Rev. Jojappa, *MSC* '11 (ALN) St. Thomas More, Allentown, PA
Adaikalam, Rev. Britto, (MAN) Gate of Heaven, Lancaster, NH
Adain, Rev. Dieuseul, '98 (NEW) Shrine of Divine Mercy St. Francis Xavier, Newark, NJ
Adaja, Rev. Paul O., '09 (CHI) SS. Peter and Lambert Parish, Skokie, IL
Adajar, Rev. Wayne, '98 (ORG) Holy Spirit, Fountain Valley, CA
Adam, Rev. Charles A., '86 (DAV) St. Thomas More Church of Coralville, Iowa, Coralville, IA; [EFT] St. Thomas More New Season Charitable Trust, Coralville, IA
Adam, Rev. Nicholas J., '76 (DAV) St. Mary's Church of Fairfield, Iowa, Fairfield, IA
Adam, Rev. Nick, '18 (JKS) Curia: Consultative Bodies; Offices and Directors St. Peter Cathedral, Jackson, MS; [CAM] Belhaven College Catholic Student Association, Jackson, MS; [CAM] Millsaps College Catholic Student Association, Jackson, MS; [CAM] University of Mississippi Medical Center - Catholic Student Association, Jackson, MS
Adam, Rev. Richard A., '88 (DAV) St. John Vianney Church of Bettendorf, Iowa, Bettendorf, IA
Adamcik, Rev. Bryan F.J., '96 (NEW) St. John the Evangelist, Leonia, NJ
Adamczak, Rev. Dawid, *S.D.S.* (NEW) St. Stanislaus Kostka, Garfield, NJ
Adamczyk, Rev. Kyle M., '18 (PH) St. Andrew, Newtown, PA
Adamczyk, Rev. Kyle M., (PH) On Special Assignment. Asst Master of Ceremonies, St Andrew Rectory, Newtown
Adamczyk, Rev. Lawrence, '03 (BAL) St. Clement, Lansdowne, MD; St. Philip Neri, Linthicum Heights, MD
Adamczyk, Rev. Witold, *O.F.M.Conv.* '01 (RCK) (>PEO) Sacred Heart, Rock Island, IL; (>PEO) St. Mary, Rock Island, IL; (>PEO) St. Pius X, Rock Island, IL
Adamczyk, Rev. Wojciech, *SCJ* '04 (MIL) [MON] St. Joseph's at Monastery Lake (Priests of the Sacred Heart), Franklin, WI
Adamczyk, Rev. Wojciech, (GAL) Our Lady of Guadalupe, Houston, TX
Adame, Rev. Alejandro, *C.S.V.* '00 (CHI) [MON] Viatorian Province Center-Clerics of St. Viator, Arlington Heights, IL
Adamiak, Rev. Aleksander, (STU) [MON] Holy Family Hermitage, Bloomingdale, OH
Adamich, Rev. Albert R., '48 (CHI) Retired. Most Holy Redeemer, Evergreen Park, IL
Adamo, Rev. Robert B., '98 (BRK) St. Ephrem, Brooklyn, NY
Adamo, Rev. Robert B., (BRK) [CON] Convent, Brooklyn, NY
Adamo, Rev. Robert B., '98 (BRK) Curia: Pastoral Services
Adamonis, Rev. Pio, *O.S.B.* (GBG) Assoc Chap, Excela Health - Westmoreland Hosp, Greensburg [MON] Saint Vincent Archabbey, Latrobe, PA
Adams, Rev. Alvin J., '67 (PIT) Retired.
Adams, Rev. J. Scott, '16 (PMB) Curia: Leadership St. Martin de Porres, Jensen Beach, FL
Adams, Rev. James, '09 (KAL) SS. John & Bernard, Benton Harbor, MI
Adams, Rev. James Francis, '04 (STP) St. Francis De Sales, St. Paul, MN
Adams, Rev. James P., '82 (ATL) Retired.
Adams, Rev. Jason P., '12 (SAV) Curia: Offices and Directors St. Matthew, Statesboro, GA
Adams, Rev. JK, *SJ* (SPK) [COL] Gonzaga University, Spokane, WA
Adams, Rev. Joel K., *S.J.* '95 (P) On Duty Outside Diocese.
Adams, Rev. John E., '69 (WDC) On Special Assignment. [MIS] Community of Christ, Washington, DC
Adams, Rev. John Michael, '85 (BIR) Cathedral of St. Paul Catholic Parish, Birmingham, Birmingham, AL
Adams, Rev. John W., '14 (BUF) Basilica of St. Mary of the Angels, Olean, NY; St. John, Olean, NY
Adams, Rev. Joseph M., *O.S.B.* '09 (MO) Curia: Offices and Directors
Adams, Rev. Joseph M., *O.S.B.* '09 (GBG) [MON] Saint Vincent Archabbey, Latrobe, PA
Adams, Rev. Larry, (PIT) Curia: Leadership St. Philip, Pittsburgh, PA
Adams, Rev. Msgr. Michael J., '59 (CHI) Retired. Christ the King, Chicago, IL
Adams, Rev. Michael J., '06 (TYL) Retired. Sacred Heart, Texarkana, TX
Adams, Rev. Nathan Daniel, '19 (PRM) (>HPM) Our Lady of Wisdom Italo-Greek, Las Vegas, AZ
Adams, Rev. Nathan Simeon, (PHX) Curia: (>HPM) Offices and Directors
Adams, Rev. Rob, (LEX) St. Francis of Assisi, Pikeville, KY; St. George, Jenkins, KY
Adams, Rev. Rodney T., '91 (OM) St. Mary Magdalene, Omaha, NE
Adams, Rev. Ryan J., '14 (DET) Most Holy Trinity Parish Detroit, Detroit, MI; Ste. Anne Basilica Parish de Detroit, Detroit, MI
Adams, Rev. Terry, *T.O.R.* '67 (ALT) [MON] St. Francis Friary at Mount Assisi, Loretto, PA
Adams, Rev. Ukeyima Emmanuel, (TUC) Saint Augustine Cathedral Roman Catholic Parish - Tucson, Tucson, AZ
Adams, Rev. William, '78 (VEN) Ascension Parish in Fort Myers Beach, Inc., Fort Myers Beach, FL
Adams, Rev. William, *C.Ss.R.* '63 (LA) Retired. [MON] Redemptorists of Whittier, Whittier, CA
Adamski, Rev. John S., '71 (ATL) Retired.
Adamski, Rev. Peter J., '20 (BGP) St. James R.C. Church Corporation, Stratford, CT
Adamson, Rev. Fredrick J., '95 (PHX) Curia: Leadership
Adamson, Rev. Joseph J., '90 (CAM) Retired. Mary, Mother of Mercy Parish, Glassboro, N.J., Glassboro, NJ
Adamus, Rev. Pawel, '15 (CHI) St. Gilbert, Grayslake, IL
Addam, Rev. Abraham Markos, *IMC* (OAK) St. Theresa of the Infant Jesus (The Little Flower), Oakland, CA
Addari, Rev. Enzo, *S.D.C.* '76 (LAN) [PRE] St. Louis Center for Exceptional Children & Adults, Chelsea, MI
Addey, Rev. Frank T., (RVC) Chap, Nassau Univ Med Ctr
Adebote, Rev. Michael, *SMA* '07 (PRT)
Adebote, Rev. Michael, *SMA* '07 (NEW) [MON] Society of African Missions, Provincialate, S.M.A. Fathers, Tenafly, NJ
Adegboyega, Rev. Johnrita, '00 (SAN) TDCJ-Parole, Big Spring, TX
Adejoh, Rev. Abraham O., '10 (BEL) Curia: (>MO) Offices and Directors
Adejoh, Rev. Patrick, '92 (JC) Harry S Truman Memorial Veteran's Hospital, Columbia
Adejoh, Rev. Patrick O., (MO) Curia: Offices and Directors
Adekola, Rev. Patrick, (NY) Parish of Saint Joseph/ Saint Boniface, Spring Valley, NY
Adelmann, Rev. Edward, *O.Carm.* '75 (JOL) [MON] Carmelite Provincial Office, Darien, IL
Adeoye, Rev. James, (PIT) St. Mary Magdalene, Pittsburgh, PA
Adetola, Rev. Augustine, (BAL) [MIS] Friends of Ijebu-Ode Diocese, Inc., Glen Burnie, MD
Adewole, Rev. Olusola, *OP* (HBG) St. Catherine of Siena, Quarryville, PA; [CAM] Bloomsburg University of Pennsylvania, Bloomsburg, PA
Adeyemi, Rev. Joachim, '04 (PHX) Our Lady of the Valley Roman Catholic Parish, Phoenix, AZ
Adhav, Rev. Satish Baburao, '06 (BLX) Curia: Advisory Boards, Commissions, Committees, and Councils St. John the Evangelist, Gulfport, MS
Adhunga, Rev. Joseph Okech, *A.J.* '92 (LA) Curia: (>MO) Offices and Directors St. Mary Magdalen, Los Angeles, CA
Adigwe, Rev. Simon, (NY) Chap, Bellevue Hosp, New York
Adike, Rev. Christian, (NU) Our Lady of the Lakes, Spicer, MN; St. Clara, Clara City, MN; St. Mary, Willmar, MN
Adiletta, Rev. David, *O.P.* '98 (NY) Memorial Sloan Kettering; NY Presbyterian [MIS] Dominican Mission Secretariat, , ; [MON] St. Catherine of Siena Priory, New York, NY
Adimakkeel, Rev. Joy J., '80 (AUS) Holy Family Catholic Church - Lexington, Texas, Lexington, TX; St. Joseph, Dime Box, TX
Adinuba, Rev. Christopher, (STL) St. Augustine Catholic Church, St. Louis, MO
Aditya, Rev. Dionisius, *O.Carm.* (WDC) [SEM] Whitefriars Hall, Washington, DC
Adkins, Rev. Howard R., '07 (BR) Retired. Congregation of St. Helena's Roman Catholic Church, Amite, Louisiana, Amite, LA
Adoboli, Rev. Francis, '91 (SUP) Our Lady of Perpetual Help, Danbury, WI; Sacred Hearts of Jesus and Mary, Webster, WI; St. John the Baptist, Webster, WI
Adoko-Enchill, Rev. Peter, '86 (SEA) St. Mary Star of the Sea, Port Townsend, WA
Adolf, Rev. Gregory P., '91 (TUC) Sacred Heart of Jesus Roman Catholic Parish - Tombstone, Tombstone, AZ; Saint Andrew the Apostle Roman Catholic Parish - Sierra Vista, Sierra Vista, AZ; Saint Patrick Roman Catholic Parish - Bisbee, Bisbee, AZ
Adongo, Rev. Crispine, '12 (EVN) St. Francis of Assisi, Dale, IN
Adonizio, Rev. Joseph J., '56 (SCR) Retired.
Adoppillil, Rev. Joseph Mathew, '96 (SYM) Sacred Heart Syro-Malabar Knanaya Catholic Church, Tampa, Brandon, FL
Adorjan, Rev. Ryan, (JOL) Sts. Peter and Paul, Naperville, IL
Adorno, Rev. Anibal, '92 (DAL) Retired.
Adrian, Rev. Stephen J., '68 (STP) Retired. St. Matthew, St. Paul, MN
Adrian, Rev. Steve, '68 (STP) Community of Saints Regional Catholic School, West St. Paul, MN
Adrie, Rev. Michael, *SMA* '92 (PEO) St. Mary's, Delavan, IL
Adu, Rev. Martin, '75 (MIA) Retired.
Adu Addai, Rev. Emmanuel, (COL) St. Michael, Worthington, OH
Aduaka, Rev. Anthony, '04 (LEX) On Duty Outside Diocese. VA Services, Martinsburg, WV
Aduaka, Rev. Anthony, '04 (MO) Curia: Offices and Directors
Adukus, Rev. Thaddeus Idanosi, '91 (SFD) Little Flower, Springfield, IL
Adu-Kwaning, Rev. Stephen, (MO) Curia: Offices and Directors
Adu-Kwaning, Rev. Msgr. Stephen, (HRT) Chap, VA CT Health Care System, West Haven
Adunchezor, Rev. Christopher, '90 (MO) Curia: Offices and Directors
Aduri, Rev. Thomas Reddy, '03 (KCK) Curia: Offices and Directors Mother Teresa of Calcutta, Topeka, KS
Aduseh Poku, Rev. John, '98 (MIA) St. Edward, Pembroke Pines, FL
Adusupalli, Rev. Bhaskar, (AMA) Holy Family, Nazareth, TX; [EFT] Holy Family Parish of Nazareth, Texas Endowment Foundation, Amarillo, TX
Adwan, Rev. Elias Khalil, (SAM) St. John Maron, Williamsville, NY
Adzaklui-Tume, Rev. Kofi, *FM* (GAL) St. Pius V, Pasadena, TX
Aelavanthara, Rev. Antony, '68 (ALX) Retired.
Aenekatt, Rev. Thomas Sunil, *V.C.* (SYM) [MIS] Vincentian House & Divine Prayer Center, Washington, NJ
Aerts, Rev. John F., '02 (FAR) Our Lady of Mt. Carmel Church of Balta, Balta, ND; St. Mary's Church of Knox, Knox, ND; St. Theresa, Little Flower Church of Rugby, Rugby, ND
Aetharyil, Rev. Pradeep Baby, *CMI* (STA) St. Matthew, Jacksonville, FL
Afagbegee, Rev. Edmund, *S.V.D.* (SB) Chap, St Bernardine Med Ctr, San Bernardino
Afangide, Rev. Anthony, *MSP* '86 (BEA) Sacred Heart -

St. Mary Parish, Port Arthur, TX
Affleck, Rev. David M., '12 (PRT) Retired. (>MAN) Corpus Christi Parish, Portsmouth, NH
Affum, Rev. John, (VIC) Sacred Heart, Hallettsville, TX; St. John the Baptist, Schulenburg, TX; St. Mary, Hallettsville, TX
Afina, Rev. Alphonsus, '10 (FBK) Curia: Leadership Church of the Holy Angels Catholic Church Unalakleet, Unalakleet, AK; St. Ann Catholic Church Teller, Nome, AK; St. Bernard Catholic Church Stebbins, Stebbins, AK; St. Francis Xavier Catholic Church Kotzebue, Kotzebue, AK; St. Joseph Catholic Church Nome, Nome, AK; St. Michael Catholic Church St. Michael, St. Michael, AK
Afonso, Rev. Samuel, (BO) [MON] Francis Xavier House, Brighton, MA
Afor, Rev. Maurice Sunde, '22 (BAL) Church of the Holy Spirit, Joppa, MD; St. Stephen, Kingsville, MD
Afu, Rev. Pio Gamig, '15 (SPP) Sacred Heart of Jesus, Pago Pago, AS
Afuecheta, Rev. Johnpaul O, '16 (SFE) St. Anne-Tucumcari, Tucumcari, NM
Afugwobi, Rev. Celestine, '99 (SB) St. Thomas the Apostle, Riverside, CA
Afunugo, Rev. Emmanuel, (GBG) [SEM] St. Vincent Seminary, Latrobe, PA
Afunugo, Rev. Emmanuel, *D.D.* '83 (AMA) On Duty Outside Diocese.
Agada, Rev. Jude Blaise, (TUC) Our Lady of Grace Roman Catholic Parish - Maricopa, Maricopa, AZ
Againglo, Rev. Rene, '09 (PH) Curia: Evangelization St. Cyprian, Philadelphia, PA
Agaloos, Rev. Reinerio, '89 (NEW) St. Leo, Elmwood Park, NJ
Agan, Rev. Msgr. Jose, '70 (NEW) Retired.
Agapito, Rev. John, *C.P.M.* '89 (OWN) [MON] Fathers of Mercy, Auburn, KY
Agba, Rev. Theodore T, '19 (SAV) St. Teresa of Avila, Grovetown, GA
Agbadugo, Rev. Robinson, (DAL) Sacred Heart Catholic Parish, Rowlett, TX
Agbasonu, Rev. Thaddeus, *SMMM* '12 (LA) St. James, Redondo Beach, CA
Agbata, Rev. Alex, (SP) [HOS] St. Joseph's Hospital, Inc., Tampa, FL
Agbata, Rev. Boniface, (MAN) Our Lady of the Miraculous Medal, Hampton, NH
Agbaw-Ebai, Rev. Maurice, (BO) St. Anne, Salem, MA
Agbedo, Rev. Jonathan, '96 (FTW) St. Mary of the Presentation, Geneva, IN
Agbeko, Rev. Patrick K., '10 (NY) St. Raymond, Bronx, NY
Agber, Rev. Philip, *C.S.Sp.* '01 (PH) [MON] Congregation of the Holy Spirit, Bensalem, PA
Agber, Rev. Philip, (MO) Curia: Offices and Directors
Agbir, Rev. Justin, '19 (TUC) Saints Peter and Paul Roman Catholic Parish - Tucson, Tucson, AZ
Agbley, Rev. Francis Kwasi, (LAF) St. Edmond, Lafayette, LA
Agbo, Rev. Chikere A, *SJ* '11 (OAK) [MON] Jesuit Fathers and Brothers, Berkeley, CA
Agbo, Rev. Robert, '17 (BUF) Blessed Sacrament, Andover, NY; Holy Family of Jesus, Mary & Joseph, Belmont, NY; Immaculate Conception, Wellsville, NY; SS. Brendan and Jude, Alfred, NY; St. Mary, Bolivar, NY
Agbodi, Rev. Patrick, *SMA* '00 (PRT) All Saints Parish, Brunswick, ME
Agbodza, Rev. Paul, '94 (BRK) St. Matthew, Brooklyn, NY
Agbowai, Rev. Jean-Lou Marrel Franck, '01 (DAL) Mary Immaculate Catholic Parish, Dallas, TX
Agila, Rev. Angel Vincente, '91 (GAL) Notre Dame, Houston, TX
Agirembabazi, Rev. Nestorio, *A.J.* '90 (NY) St. Angela Merici, Bronx, NY
Agliardo, Rev. Michael, (OAK) [ASN] US-China Catholic Association, Berkeley, CA (>SFR) [MON] Jesuit Community at St. Ignatius College Preparatory, San Francisco, CA
Agnew, Rev. Francis H., *C.M.* '60 (STL) Retired.
Agnew, Rev. John C., '90 (POD) Curia: Clergy and Religious Services
Agnew, Rev. John C., '90 (NY) [MIS] Prelature of the Holy Cross and Opus Dei, New York, NY
Agoda, Rev. Sylvester, '20 (NO) St. Rita, Harahan, LA
Agorsor, Rev. Aaron, (PHX) Our Lady of Mt. Carmel Roman Catholic Parish, Tempe, AZ
Agostinelli, Rev. Gianni, '86 (ORL) Saint Paul Catholic Church, Leesburg, FL; San Pedro de Jesus Maldonado Mission, Wildwood, FL; St. Patrick's, Mount Dora, FL
Agostino, Rev. Emil, *O.Carm.* '64 (JOL) Retired.
Agostino, Rev. Joseph V., *C.M.* '83 (PH) [MIS] Vincentian Family Office, Philadelphia, PA; [MON] Congregation of the Mission, Philadelphia, PA
Agostino, Rev. Steven J., '93 (Y) St. Brendan, Youngstown, OH
Agresti, Rev. Frank P., '03 (PAT) Curia: Administration Our Lady of Pompei, Paterson, NJ
Agu, Rev. Emmanuel O., '14 (NEW) Saint Michael the Archangel, Union, NJ
Agu, Rev. Hyginus Ndubueze, '95 (BGP) St. Vincent's Medical Center, Bpt., CT The Saint Andrew Roman Catholic Church Corporation, Bridgeport, CT
Aguason, Rev. Anthony O., '10 (CHK) San Jose, Tinian, MP
Aguason, Rev. Anthony O., (CHK) Curia: Advisory Boards, Commissions, Committees, and Councils; Consultative Bodies; Faith Formation
Aguayo, Rev. Jose Miguel, '19 (MRY) Sacred Heart/St. Benedict Catholic Community, Hollister, CA
Agudelo, Rev. Carlos A., '98 (BRK) St. Leo, Corona, NY
Agudelo, Rev. German Correa, '00 (FR) Curia: Offices and Directors Our Lady of Guadalupe Parish at St. James Church, New Bedford, MA
Agudelo, Rev. Henry, '11 (NOR) Curia: Offices and Directors Our Lady of Grace, New London, CT; St. Brendan the Navigator Parish, New London, CT
Agudelo, Rev. Oswaldo, (MIA) St. Mary's Cathedral, Miami, FL; [MIS] Catholic Hospice, Inc., Miami, FL
Agudelo Perdomo, Rev. Gabriel, '20 (BRK) On Leave. Our Lady of Sorrows, Corona, NY
Agudo, Rev. Moises, '97 (SFR) Curia: Advisory Boards, Commissions, Committees, and Councils; Leadership; Offices and Directors St. Charles Borromeo, San Francisco, CA; St. Peter, San Francisco, CA; [MIS] Immaculate Conception Chapel, San Francisco, CA
Agudo, Rev. Moises R., '97 (SFR) On Special Assignment. St. Anthony of Padua, San Francisco, CA
Agudo, Rev. Teodoro, *O.F.M.Cap.* '54 (NO) Retired.
Aguera, Rev. Jorge, *D.C.J.M.* '97 (DEN) St. Pius X Catholic Parish in Aurora, Aurora, CO
Aguggia, Rev. Msgr. Steven J., '93 (BRK) Curia: Consultative Bodies; Leadership; Organizations (affiliated, inter-Diocesan, miscellaneous/other); Pastoral Services St. Pancras, Glendale, NY; [MIS] National Italian Apostolate Conference, Glendale, NY; [MIS] Pro Sanctity Movement, Flushing, NY (>NY) [SEM] St. Joseph's Seminary, Yonkers, NY
Aughara, Rev. Fidelis, '88 (BUR) Chap, Univ of Vermont Med Ctr, Burlington
Aguilar, Rev. Arturo, *S.S.C.* '84 (OM) [MON] Missionary Society of St. Columban, St. Columbans, NE
Aguilar, Rev. Arturo, *SSC* (SB) St. Mary, Fontana, CA
Aguilar, Rev. Benjamin, *O.Carm.* '94 (CHI) [MON] Sant'Angelo Community at St. Cyril Priory, Chicago, IL
Aguilar, Rev. Benjamin, *O.Carm* '94 (LA) [MON] Our Lady of Mount Carmel Priory (Fathers of the Order of Mount Carmel, Corporation), Encino, CA
Aguilar, Rev. Francis V., '09 (LA) St. Mary Magdalen, Camarillo, CA
Aguilar, Rev. Genaro P, *CSC* '83 (FTW) [MON] Congregation of Holy Cross, United States Province of Priests and Brothers, Notre Dame, IN
Aguilar, Rev. Jesus Francisco Garcia, *C.O.R.C.* '86 (LA) Immaculate Conception, Los Angeles, CA
Aguilar, Rev. Rogelio Mur, *O.Carm.* '56 (MGZ) Curia: Leadership
Aguilar Alamilla, Friar Guillermo, *OFM Conv.* (AUS) Cristo Rey, Austin, TX
Aguilera, Rev. George, (LA) St. Anthony, Long Beach, CA
Aguilera, Rev. George, '83 (LA) Our Lady of Mt. Carmel Cambodian Catholic Center, Long Beach, CA
Aguilera, Rev. George, '83 (LA) Curia: Pastoral Services
Aguilera, Rev. Salvador, '84 (ELP) On Duty Outside Diocese. US Naval Acad, Annapolis, MD
Aguirre, Rev. Carlos, '13 (TR) Our Lady of the Angels Parish, Trenton, NJ
Aguirre, Rev. Eduardo, '08 (SB) Chap, Loma Linda Univ Med Ctr, Loma Linda
Aguirre, Rev. Francisco E., '13 (WDC) Curia: Consultative Bodies St. Catherine Laboure, Wheaton, MD
Aguirre, Rev. Ignacio, *O.S.B.* '53 (FAJ) [MON] San Antonio Abad Abbey of the Order of St. Benedict, Humacao, PR
Aguirre, Very Rev. Osmar R., '93 (YAK) Curia: Leadership; Offices and Directors St. Joseph's, Wenatchee, WA; [CCH] St. Joseph Parish Conference, St. Vincent de Paul, Wenatchee, WA
Aguirre Palacio, Rev. Juan Angel, '16 (NOR) Curia: Offices and Directors St. Mary Church of the Visitation, Clinton, CT
Aguirre-Garza, Rev. Jesus, *O.F.M.* '96 (STL) [MON] Franciscan Friary of St. Anthony of Padua, St. Louis, MO
Agustin, Rev. Honesto, '82 (RNO) St. Albert the Great, Reno, NV
Agustina, Rev. Leo, '08 (CHI) [MIS] Prelature of the Holy Cross and Opus Dei, Chicago, IL
Aguwa, Rev. Henry, (FRS) Chap, California Substance Abuse Treatment Facility & Stat St. Joseph, Avenal, CA
Aguwa, Rev. Jude, '78 (NY) St. Joseph, Somers, NY
Aguzie, Very Rev. Basil, *M.S.P.* '98 (AUS) Curia: Leadership Holy Cross, Austin, TX
Agwu, Rev. John Okeke, *S.M.M.M.* '04 (FRS) St. Patrick, Kerman, CA
Agwu, Rev. John Okeke, *SMMM* '04 (FRS) St. Paul, Tranquillity, CA
Agyapong, Rev. Dominic, '08 (MAR) Curia: Advisory Boards, Commissions, Committees, and Councils Immaculate Conception of the Blessed Virgin Mary, Wakefield, MI; St. Sebastian, Bessemer, MI
Agyapong, Rev. Nana Kofi, *SJ* '22 (OAK) [MON] Jesuit Fathers and Brothers, Berkeley, CA
Agyei, Rev. Philip, '12 (DUB) Basilica of St. Francis Xavier, Dyersville, Iowa, Dyersville, IA; S.S. Peter and Paul Church, Petersburg, Iowa, Dyersville, IA; St. Boniface Church of New Vienna, New Vienna, Iowa, New Vienna, IA; St. Joseph's Church, Earlville, Iowa, Earlville, IA; St. Paul Church, Worthington, Iowa, Worthington, IA
Agyemang, Rev. Msgr. Seth, '80 (NY) St. Joseph, Bronxville, NY
Agyemang, Rev. William, '13 (HRT) Saint Therese Parish Corporation, Granby, CT
Ahamefule, Rev. Anthony, '16 (P) Curia: Offices and Directors Holy Trinity Catholic Parish, Bandon, OR
Ahanatu, Rev. Leonard, '94 (TLS) Curia: Offices and Directors
Ahanotu, Rev. Leonard U., '94 (TLS) Holy Cross, Wagoner, OK; St. Vincent de Paul, Coweta, OK
Ahearn, Rev. Thomas A., *M.M.* '68 (NY) Retired.
Ahenkora, Rev. James, '07 (DM) St. Patrick, Council Bluffs, IA
Ahern, Rev. Adam L., '15 (IND) Curia: (>MO) Offices and Directors Sacred Heart Catholic Church, Jeffersonville, Inc., Jeffersonville, IN; St. Augustine Catholic Church, Jeffersonville, Inc., Jeffersonville, IN
Ahern, Rev. Dennis, *S.J.* '79 (DET) [MON] Colombiere Center, Clarkston, MI
Ahern, Rev. John J., '80 (BO) Curia: Consultative Bodies St. Gregory, Boston, MA
Ahern, Rev. John V., '67 (SY) Retired.
Ahern, Rev. Thomas W., '94 (BRK) Curia: Leadership; Pastoral Services Our Lady of Perpetual Help, South Ozone Park, NY
Aherne, Rev. James J., *M.S.* '73 (HRT) Our Lady of Sorrows Church Corporation of Parkville, Hartford, Hartford, CT; [MON] Our Lady of Sorrows Rectory, Hartford, CT
Aherne, Rev. John, *O.F.M.* (PAT) Our Lady of the Assumption, Pompton Lakes, NJ
Ahiaba, Rev. Martin, '21 (TYL) Our Lady of Victory, Paris, TX
Ahiaba, Rev. Paul A., *C.S.Sp* (SB) Our Lady of the Valley, Hemet, CA
Ahiarakwem, Rev. Gabriel A., '98 (BRK) Chap, Elmhurst Gen Hosp Our Lady of Fatima, Jackson Heights, NY
Ahlemeyer, Rev. Msgr. Richard J., '78 (BRK) Curia: Pastoral Services Saint Camillus-Saint Virgilius, Rockaway Park, NY
Ahlers, Rev. Garrett, (NU) Curia: Offices and Directors St. Joseph, Lamberton, MN; St. Raphael, Springfield, MN; St. Thomas (Oratory), Sanborn, MN
Ahles, Rev. Donald M., '71 (RCK) Retired.
Ahlin, Rev. Robert J., '71 (PIT) Retired. Blessed Trinity, Pittsburgh, PA
Ahlstrom, Rev. Michael P., '69 (CHI) Retired.
Ahmadu, Rev. Michael, (OM) St. Pius X, Omaha, NE
Ahn, Rev. Edward, *A.V.I.* (STL) [SEM] Kenrick School of Theology, ,
Ahn, Rev. Edward, '11 (KCK) St. Michael the Archangel, Overland Park, KS
Ahn, Rev. Simon Hyo Sung, '91 (RIC) St. Rose of Lima and the Korean Martyrs, Hampton, VA
Aho, Rev. Charles A., '70 (SY) Retired.
Ahyuwa, Rev. Lawrence David, (LA) Our Lady of the Assumption, Ventura, CA
Aiden, Rev. Yakubu, '13 (FBK) Church of the Nativity Catholic Church St. Marys, St. Marys, AK; St. Charles Spinola Catholic Church Pilot Station, Pilot Station, AK; St. Lawrence Catholic Church Mountain Village,

Mountain Village, AK
Aidoo, Rev. Augustine Kingsford, '04 (COV) Blessed Sacrament, Fort Mitchell, KY
Aiello, Rev. Anthony, '69 (DM) Retired.
Aiello, Rev. Ryan, (SEA) Eastside Catholic School, Sammamish, WA
Aigner, Rev. Edward M., '72 (WIL) Retired. Chap, Eastern Corr Inst St. Francis De Sales, Salisbury, MD
Aiken, Rev. Richard J., '70 (MIL) Retired.
Ailer, Rev. Gellert Jozsef, '06 (WDC) On Duty Outside Diocese. Szechenyi, Hungary
Aime, Rev. Moise, '80 (RVC) SS. Cyril and Methodius, Deer Park, NY
Aineto, Rev. Luis, *SDB* '61 (SP) [RTR] Mary Help of Christians Center, Tampa, FL
Ainikkal, Rev. Jose, *C.M.I.* '85 (CAM) The Parish of St. Maximilian Kolbe, Marmora, N.J., Marmora, NJ
Aisa, Rev. Francisco, *Sch.P.* '87 (PH) Devon Preparatory School (Piarist Fathers), Devon, PA; [MON] Piarist Fathers (Order of the Pious Schools), Devon, PA
Aita, Rev. Mark C., *S.J.* '83 (PH) [MIS] Jesuit Fathers, ,
Ajaero, Rev. Walter, '15 (ALX) On Leave.
Ajayi, Rev. Vincent, (BLX) St. Thomas the Apostle, Long Beach, MS
Ajemian, Rev. David J., '01 (BO) On Leave.
Ajewole, Rev. Michael, *M.S.P.* '96 (SAT) St. Luke-Loire, Pleasanton, TX
Ajic, Rev. Marvin, *C.S.* '05 (LA) Our Lady of Zapopan, North Hollywood, CA; [CON] Our Lady of the Holy Rosary Convent, Sun Valley, CA
Ajiki, Rev. Pius Titus, '84 (LAF) Our Mother of Mercy, Church Point, LA; Our Mother of Mercy, Rayne, LA
Ajpacaja Tzoc, Rev. Nicholas, '16 (IND) On Leave. St. Gabriel the Archangel Catholic Church, Indianapolis, Inc., Indianapolis, IN
Ajuka, Rev. Canon Nnaemeka Paschal, '03 (SAC) Chap, UC Davis Health Center, Davis
Ajuluchukwu, Rev. Nathaniel, (BRK) Our Lady of the Blessed Sacrament, Bayside, NY
Ajuruchi, Rev. George Bede, *SSJ* (LAF) St. Francis of Assisi, Breaux Bridge, LA
Akabueze, Rev. Evaristus, (BEL) SS. Peter and Paul, Waterloo, IL
Akajiofor, Rev. Pius, (MO) Curia: Offices and Directors
Akalawu, Rev. Ambrose, '71 (LAF) On Special Assignment. Chap, Our Lady of Lourdes
Akalue, Rev. Emmanuel, '94 (ORL) Curia: Evangelization St. Rose of Lima, Kissimmee, FL
Akanaefu, Rev. Martin Enyinna, '08 (LA) Maria Regina, Gardena, CA
Akano, Rev. Francis, (GLP) St. Mary, Bloomfield, NM; St. Rose of Lima, Blanco, NM
Akar, Rev. Dany Abi, '10 (NY) Immaculate Conception, Sleepy Hollow, NY
Akeriwe, Rev. Raymond A., *S.M.A.* (MO) Curia: Offices and Directors
Akers, Rev. Stephen, '15 (MRY) Curia: Advisory Boards, Commissions, Committees, and Councils Sacred Heart/St. Benedict Catholic Community, Hollister, CA
Aketch, Rev. Charles Osewe, *G.H.M.* (NSH) Holy Family, Lafayette, TN
Akiki, Rev. Wissam, '14 (OLL) Curia: Offices and Directors St. Joseph Maronite Catholic Church, Phoenix, AZ
Akindele, Rev. Nicholas O., '00 (DAV) Curia: Leadership Holy Family Church of Davenport, Iowa, Davenport, IA; St. Alphonsus Church of Davenport, Iowa, Davenport, IA
Akin-Otiko, Rev. Peter, '96 (STA) Curia: Leadership San Juan Del Rio, St. John, FL
Akinyemi, Rev. Julius B., '14 (AGN) Curia: Miscellaneous / Other Offices
Akiona, Very Rev. Lane K., *SS.CC.* '81 (HON) [MON] Sacred Hearts Center, Congregation of the Sacred Hearts of Jesus and Mary and of Perpetual Adoration, Kaneohe, HI
Akiona, Rev. Lane K., (FR) [MIS] Congregation of the Sacred Hearts - United States Province (Sacred Hearts Fathers; Sacred Hearts Missions), Fairhaven, MA
Akiona, Very Rev. Lane K., *SS.CC.* '81 (HON) Curia: Consultative Bodies; Offices and Directors St. Augustine by the Sea, Honolulu, HI
Akkala, Rev. Balaraju, '10 (LR) Blessed Stanley Rother Catholic Church, Decatur, AR; Immaculate Conception, Fort Smith, AR; Our Lady of the Ozarks Shrine, Winslow, AR
Akkalayil-Lucka, Rev. Binoy, *O.SS.T* (LAV) St. James the Apostle, Las Vegas, NV
Akkanath, Rev. Peter, *CMI* (MET) St. James the Less, Jamesburg, NJ
Akkin, Rev. Florentinus, '93 (CI) Curia: Leadership St. Anthony's, Chuuk, FM; Weito Parish, Chuuk, FM
Akoh, Rev. Valery, '16 (ATL) St. Matthew Catholic Church, Tyrone, Inc., Tyrone, GA
Akomeah, Rev. Joseph Peh, (NY) St. Augustine, Highland, NY
Akor, Rev. Joseph, (SEA) Sacred Heart, Bellevue, WA; St. Monica, Mercer Island, WA
Akordor, Rev. Edmund, '80 (NO) Sacred Heart of Jesus, Norco, LA
Akoury, Rev. Tony, '95 (SAM) Curia: Offices and Directors St. Joseph's Maronite Church, Sandy Springs, GA
Akpa, Rev. Onwuham, *O. Praem.* '04 (GB) [MON] St. Norbert Abbey, De Pere, WI
Akpabio, Rev. Felix, '78 (RVC) St. John the Evangelist, Center Moriches, NY
Akpaidem, Rev. Emmanuel, '01 (GAL) Sacred Heart, Crosby, TX
Akpan, Rev. Godwin, *S.S.J* (WDC) [SEM] St. Joseph's Seminary, Washington, DC
Akpan, Rev. Godwin, *SSJ* '10 (LA) Transfiguration, Los Angeles, CA
Akpan, Rev. James, (RVC) Curia: (>MO) Offices and Directors
Akpan, Rev. Linus Gabriel, '92 (BIR) Our Lady of Fatima, Birmingham, AL
Akpanobong, Rev. Patrick, '11 (SAN) Curia: Advisory Boards, Commissions, Committees, and Councils San Miguel Arcangel Church (Our Lady of San Juan), Midland, TX
Akpobolokemi, Rev. Emmanuel, '06 (TYL) St. Pius I, Hemphill, TX
Akpoghiran, Very Rev. Peter O., '92 (NO) Curia: Leadership; Offices and Directors
Akpoghiran, Rev. Peter O., '92 (NO) St. Mark Roman Catholic Church, Ama, Louisiana, Ama, LA
Aksamit, Rev. Stanley J., '77 (SPR) Our Lady of Peace, Turners Falls, MA
Aku, Rev. Edmund, '90 (MIA) [NUR] St. Anne's Nursing Center, St. Anne's Residence, Inc., Miami, FL
Akuh, Rev. Sunday, '05 (FTW) Holy Family, South Bend, IN; St. John the Baptist, South Bend, IN
Akujobi, Rev. Stephen, '98 (COS) Chap, Penrose-St Francis; St Francis Med Ctr [HOS] Penrose Hospital, Colorado Springs, CO
Akula, Rev. Prasad, (CHI) St. Juliana, Chicago, IL
Akumbilim, Rev. Raymond Asagdem, *SVD* (DUB) [SEM] Divine Word College, Epworth, IA
Akunaeziri, Rev. Joseph, (NY) Parish of Our Lady of Victory and Sacred Heart, Mount Vernon, NY
Akuti, Rev. Macdonald, (P) St. Mary by the Sea, Rockaway, OR
Akuti, Rev. Macdonald, *A.J.* (LA) St. Mary Magdalen, Los Angeles, CA
Akwa, Rev. Maurice M., (ARL) St. Lawrence, Alexandria, VA
Akwue, Rev. Francis, *C.S.Sp.* '71 (MIA) St. Henry, Pompano Beach, FL; [MIS] Congregation of the Holy Spirit Province of Nigeria South East, Inc., Miami Gardens, FL
Al Mimass, Rev. Fadi, '00 (NTN) St. Barbara the Great - Martyr Mission, Houston, TX
Alabre, Rev. Pierre Michel, (TR) Our Lady of Sorrows-St. Anthony Parish, Hamilton, NJ
Aladi, Rev. Uche, (DAL) St. Elizabeth of Hungary Catholic Parish, Dallas, TX
Alaeto, Rev. Justus, (P) Star of the Sea Catholic Church, Brookings, OR
Alagia, Rev. Vincent de P., *S.J.* '58 (PH) Retired. [MON] Jesuit Community at St. Joseph's University, Merion Station, PA
Alaka, Rev. Allan Oluoch, '13 (ELP) Curia: Advisory Boards, Commissions, Committees, and Councils Queen of Peace, El Paso, TX; St. Gertrude, ,
Alam, Rev. Alam, '81 (NTN) Retired.
Alam, Rev. Sarfraz, *O.S.A.* '19 (SD) Pastor of Saint Patrick Catholic Parish, San Diego, a corporation sole, San Diego, CA; [MON] Augustinian Community, San Diego, CA
Alamat, Rev. Ala, '03 (LA) St. Joseph, Pomona, CA
Alangram, Rev. Jesuraja, '06 (SAT) Our Lady of Guadalupe, Helotes, TX
Alanis, Rev. Francisco, '01 (SFE) San Clemente, Los Lunas, NM
Alapaty, Rev. Lourduraj, '89 (R) Saint Joseph Catholic Parish of Raleigh, Raleigh, NC
Alar, Very Rev. Christopher, *M.I.C.* '14 (SPR) [MON] Congregation of Marian Fathers of The Immaculate Conception of the Most Blessed Virgin Mary, Stockbridge, MA
Alarcon, Rev. Felix, '63 (RVC) Retired.
Alarcon, Rev. Servio, (FRS) St. Anne's Parish, Porterville, CA
Alaribe, Rev. Felix Okey, (LKC) [HOS] CHRISTUS Health Southwestern Louisiana, Lake Charles, LA
Alatorre, Rev. Jesus, (YAK) Blessed Sacrament, Grandview, WA
Alava, Rev. Andres, '63 (ELP) Retired.
Alava, Rev. Basilio S., *O.S.A.* (NY) Holy Rosary, New York, NY
Alba, Rev. Gerard, '14 (KCK) St. Pius X, Mission, KS
Alba Hernandez, Rev. Pabel, *O. de M.* (PCE) Colegio Mercedario San Judas Tadeo, Ponce, PR
Alba Hernandez, Rev. Pabel Amaury, *O. de M.* '18 (PCE) Parroquia San Judas Tadeo, Ponce, PR
Alba Hernandez, Rev. Pavel, *O.de.M.* (SJN) Colegio Nuestra Senora de La Merced, Hato Rey, PR
Alba-Infante, Rev. Saul, '02 (ORG) St. Joseph, Santa Ana, CA
Albanese, Rev. Charles, *O.C.S.O.* '05 (DEN) [MON] St. Benedict's Monastery, Snowmass, CO
Albano, Rev. Alwyn, (RIC) Military Chap
Albano, Rev. Alwyn M., '90 (MO) Curia: Offices and Directors
Albano, Rev. Peter J., *C.M.* '68 (BRK) [MON] Reverend John B. Murray, C.M. House, Jamaica, NY
Albarano, Rev. Richard, '68 (LA) Retired.
Albarracin, Rev. Luis, '67 (VEN) Retired.
Albee, Rev. Msgr. Paul M., '84 (LA) St. Maximilian Kolbe, Westlake Village, CA
Albenesius, Rev. Paul M., '97 (OM) Retired.
Alber, Rev. Michael J., '02 (GR) St. Patrick, Portland, MI; [EFT] The Father Flohe Foundation, Portland, MI
Alber, Rev. Thomas L., '85 (JC) St. Peters Church Parish, Jefferson City, MO
Albero, Rev. Steven J., *O. Praem.* '92 (PH) St. Norbert, Paoli, PA; [MON] Daylesford Abbey, Inc., Paoli, PA
Albers, Rt. Rev. James R., *O.S.B.* '00 (KCK) Curia: Advisory Boards, Commissions, Committees, and Councils [MON] St. Benedict's Abbey, Atchison, KS
Albers, Rev. Thomas, *C.PP.S.* '67 (CIN) Retired.
Albert, Rev. Alexander, '16 (LAF) Curia: Offices and Directors St. John the Evangelist, Jeanerette, LA (>BR) [MIS] International Institute of Culture and Gender Studies, Baton Rouge, LA
Albert, Rev. Andrew, *S.M.* '65 (BO) [MIS] Marist Fathers Residence, , ; [MON] Marist Fathers Lourdes Residence, Boston, MA
Albert, Rev. James R., '86 (PRT) Retired.
Albert, Rev. Patrick L., '92 (SCR) Curia: Leadership Nativity of Blessed Virgin Mary, Tunkhannock, PA
Albertine, Rev. Richard, *M.M.* '66 (NY) Retired. [MON] Maryknoll Fathers and Brothers (Catholic Foreign Mission Society of America, Inc.), Ossining, NY
Alberto, Rev. Jose Gerardo, *M.Sp.S.* (LA) Our Lady of Guadalupe Parish, Oxnard, CA
Alberto, Rev. Jose Gerardo, *M.Sp.S.* '00 (P) On Duty Outside Diocese. [EFT] Felix Rougier Religious Care Trust, Banks, OR
Alberts, Rev. Gregory, '22 (JOL) Visitation, Elmhurst, IL
Albertson, Rev. Eric J., '86 (ARL) Chap, CH (Co) Curia: (>MO) Offices and Directors
Albietz, Rev. Henry F., '74 (CIN) Retired.
Albin, Rev. Joseph Paul, *O.P.* '20 (DAL) Church of the Incarnation, Irving, TX; [COL] University of Dallas, Irving, TX; [MON] Dominican Priory of St. Albert the Great and Novitiate, Irving, TX
Albino, Rev. Msgr. Ramon E., '84 (MGZ) Curia: Leadership La Milagrosa, Aguadilla, PR; [COL] Corpus Christi College, Aquadilla, PR
Albino Guzman, Rev. Ramon Emilio, (MGZ) Curia: Leadership
Albosta, Rev. John T., '64 (SCR) Retired. [MON] Villa St. Joseph, Dunmore, PA
Al-Botany, Rev. Mazin Hanna, (SPA) St. Barbara Chaldean Catholic Church, Las Vegas, NV
Albrecht, Rev. James W., '58 (NY) [MIS] Prelature of the Holy Cross and Opus Dei, New York, NY
Albrecht, Rev. Louis Henry, '86 (BAK) Retired.
Albrecht, Rev. Tomasz, (NOR) On Leave.
Albright, Rev. Matthew, '07 (Y) On Leave.
Albright, Rev. R. Gerard, *S.J.* '58 (DET) [MON] Colombiere Center, Clarkston, MI
Albright, Rev. Robert E., '72 (BAL) Retired.
Albuquerque, Rev. Messius, (SFR) Curia: Offices and Directors
Alcantara, Rev. Patricio, (RIC) Holy Family, Pearisburg, VA; Holy Spirit Catholic Church, Christiansburg, VA
Alcantara, Rev. Radley, (CHI) St. Mary, Lake Forest, IL
Alcazar, Rev. Emanuel, '89 (ELP) La Purisima, Socorro, TX
Alchouefati, Rev. Kamil, '95 (SAM) Our Lady Star of the East, Pleasantville, NJ
Alciati, Rev. Paul J., '77 (SY) Retired. St. Patrick, Truxton, NY

Alco, Rev. James J., '90 (SCR) Retired.
Alcocer, Rev. Jose, '60 (ELP) Retired.
Alcombright, Rev. Matthew, '12 (SPR) On Leave.
Alcott, Rev. Stephen, *O.P.* '01 (COL) St. Patrick, Columbus, OH; [MIS] Shrine of Blessed Margaret of Castello, Columbus, OH
Alcuino, Rev. Miguel, '79 (ELP) Curia: Advisory Boards, Commissions, Committees, and Councils Santa Teresa de Jesus, Presidio, TX
Aldaba, Rev. Joachim, *O.Praem.* '17 (ORG) Archangel Institute (St. Michael's Preparatory School), Silverado, CA; [MON] Norbertine Fathers of Orange, Inc., Silverado, CA; [PRE] St. Michael's Summer Camp, Silverado, CA
Alderson, Rev. John, (PAT) Our Lady of the Assumption, Pompton Lakes, NJ
Alejandro, Rev. Armando, (BAL) St. Joseph, Sykesville, MD
Alejandro, Rev. Armando, (POC) St. Timothy Catholic Community, Sykesville, MD
Alejunas, Rev. Richard, *S.D.B* (CHI) St. James, Chicago, IL; St. John Bosco, Chicago, IL
Alejunas, Rev. Richard, *S.D.B.* '89 (NY) St. Michael, Staten Island, NY
Aleksa, Rev. Thomas M., '75 (E) Retired.
Alello, Very Rev. Michael J., '07 (BR) Curia: Administration Congregation Of St. Thomas More Roman Catholic Church, East Baton Rouge Parish, Baton Rouge, LA; [EFT] Pamphile and Mabyn Donaldson Trust for St. Thomas More, Baton Rouge, LA
Alemeo, Rev. Ryan, (ARL) St. John the Beloved, McLean, VA
Alenchery, Rev. Joseph, '87 (RVC) Assumption of the Blessed Virgin Mary, Centereach, NY
Alengadan, Rev. George, '82 (OAK) Retired.
Alesandro, Rev. Msgr. John A., '66 (RVC) Curia: Leadership St. Thomas, the Apostle, West Hempstead, NY
Alex, Rev. Dels, '08 (SYM) Holy Family Syro-Malabar Catholic Church (Phoenix), Phoenix, AZ
Alexander, Rev. Allen, *M.I.C.* '15 (NOR) [MIS] Congregation of Marian Fathers of the Immaculate Conception of the B.V.M., Thompson, CT; [MON] Marians of the Immaculate Conception of the B.V.M., Thompson, CT
Alexander, Rev. Andrew, *S.J.* (OM) [MON] Jesuit Community at Creighton University, Omaha, NE
Alexander, Rev. Fred, *S.O.L.T.* '98 (FAR) St. Ann's Church of Belcourt, Belcourt, ND
Alexander, Rev. Fred, *O.C.D.* '82 (MIL) [MON] Discalced Carmelite Friars of Holy Hill, Inc., Hubertus, WI
Alexander, Rev. Jon, *OP* '86 (CHI) Retired. [MON] St. Pius V Priory, Chicago, IL
Alexander, Rev. Joseph, '73 (LAF) On Administrative Leave.
Alexander, Rev. Matthew, '15 (CHI) On Duty Outside Diocese. St John Vianney College Seminary, St Paul, MN
Alexander, Rev. Matthew, (STP) [SEM] St. John Vianney Seminary, St. Paul, MN
Alexandre-Caldeira, Rev. Marcos V., (FR) Curia: Offices and Directors
Alexandre-Caldeira, Rev. Marcos Vinicius, (FR) St. Francis Xavier's, Hyannis, MA
Alexandrunas, Rev. Albert, *O.F.M.Cap.* '65 (PIT) [MON] St. Mary's Friary, Butler, PA
Alexius, Rev. Jay, '15 (LKC) Our Lady of the Lake, Lake Arthur, LA
Alexius, Rev. Vincent, (PT) St. Thomas the Apostle, Quincy, FL
Alexopoulos, Rev. Stefanos, '77 (WDC) [COL] Catholic University of America, The, Washington, DC
Alfano, Rev. Michael A., '87 (BO) St. Linus, Natick, MA; St. Patrick, Natick, MA
Alfaro, Rev. Msgr. Alfaro, '62 (SAT) Retired.
Alfaro, Rev. Gustavo A., '02 (NEW) St. Aloysius, Jersey City, NJ
Alfaro, Very Rev. Jose N., '03 (MIA) Curia: Clergy and Religious Services; Leadership St. John Neumann, Miami, FL
Alfaro, Rev. Msgr. Juan, '62 (SAT) Retired.
Alfonso, Rev. Bonilla, (ELP) Saint Therese of the Little Flower Parish, El Paso, TX
Alfonso, Rev. Yosbany, '21 (MIA) St. Andrew, Coral Springs, FL
Alford, Very Rev. Brian C., '11 (SFD) Curia: Leadership Cathedral of the Immaculate Conception, Springfield, IL
Alforque, Rev. Benjamin E., *MSC* (SB) Our Lady of Perpetual Help, Riverside, CA
Alforque, Rev. Elmer, '94 (GBG) St. John the Baptist, Scottdale, PA; St. Joseph, Everson, PA
Algarin, Rev. Carlos Ruben, (SJN) Santa Rosa de Lima, Bayamon, PR
Algarin, Rev. Rodney, (SJN) San Juan de Dios, Carolina, PR
Algarin Lopez, Rev. Carlos Ruben, *O.S.A.* '04 (SJN) Curia: Leadership
Algarin-Rosado, Rev. Rodney, '01 (SJN) Curia: Leadership San Felipe Apostol, Carolina, PR
Alger, Rev. Paul, *L.C.* '14 (ATL) St. Brendan Catholic Church, Cumming, Inc., Cumming, GA; [MON] Legionaries of Christ, Incorporated, Cumming, GA
Ali, Rev. Peter Yakubu, '82 (STP) Chap, Mercy Hosp, Coon Rapids; Mercy Hosp - Unity Campus
Aliba, Rev. Samuel, '13 (PHX) St. Rose Philippine Duchesne Roman Catholic Parish, Anthem, AZ
Alicea, Rev. Luis A, (CGS) Curia: Leadership Santisimo Sacramento, Caguas, PR; [MIS] Diocesan Tribunal of Caguas, Caguas, PR
Alicea, Rev. Luis Antonio, (BGP) Curia: Tribunal
Alimaji, Rev. Christian, *M.S.P.* (GAL) St. Philip Neri, Houston, TX
Alimnonu, Rev. Anthony, (BRK) St. Anselm, Brooklyn, NY
Alindogan, Rev. Peter J., '90 (TR) Curia: Canonical Services St. Veronica, Howell, NJ
Aliunzi, Rev. Robert, *A.J.* '12 (PHX) Curia: Leadership Our Lady of Mt. Carmel Roman Catholic Parish, Tempe, AZ; [MIS] EENU-USA, Inc. (E3 Africa), Queen Creek, AZ
Alkire, Rev. Thomas, *O.Carm.* '64 (JOL) Retired.
Alkire, Rev. Timothy M., '85 (LFT) Curia: Tribunal
Allam, Rev. Joji R., '95 (MAD) Saint Dennis Congregation, Madison, WI
Allan, Rev. Jason, (FWT) Immaculate Conception, Denton, TX
Allan, Rev. Jeffrey D., '14 (DET) Chap, Beaumont Hosp, Royal Oak
Allard, Rev. John E., *O.P.* '86 (PRO) [MON] St. Thomas Aquinas Priory at Providence College, Providence, RI
Allard, Rev. Marcel M., '65 (MAN) Retired.
Allbright, Rev. Brian V., '83 (P) St. Cyril, Wilsonville, OR
Allder, Rev. Dale Jonathan, '21 (LIN) Curia: Leadership St. Patrick, McCook, NE
Alle, Rev. Anthony, (OLL) Curia: Leadership
Allega, Rev. Ernest P., '76 (WOR) Retired.
Allen, Rev. Albert F., '12 (SFD) Annunciation, Shumway, IL
Allen, Rev. Charles, *SJ* (BO) [MON] Campion Health & Wellness, Inc., Weston, MA
Allen, Rev. David, '95 (DEN) Christ on the Mountain Catholic Parish in Lakewood, Lakewood, CO
Allen, Rev. David, '21 (MRY) St. Patrick, Arroyo Grande, CA
Allen, Rev. David E., '78 (BR) Retired.
Allen, Rev. David G., *S.J.* (PH) Retired. [MON] Jesuit Community at St. Joseph's University, Merion Station, PA
Allen, Rev. James F., *O.M.I.* '65 (BEL) [MON] Missionary Oblates of Mary Immaculate - St. Henry's Oblate Residence, Belleville, IL
Allen, Rev. John, '90 (CHL) St. Matthew, Charlotte, NC
Allen, Rev. Joseph, *O.P.* '67 (NY) Parish of St. Vincent Ferrer and St. Catherine of Siena, New York, NY; St. Catherine of Siena, New York, NY; [MON] St. Catherine of Siena Priory, New York, NY
Allen, Rev. Joshua, '11 (ATL) On Leave.
Allen, Rev. Kenneth, '04 (NO) Curia: Offices and Directors St. Jane de Chantal Roman Catholic Church, Abita Springs, Louisiana, Abita Springs, LA
Allen, Rev. Loren, '94 (SR) Retired.
Allen, Rev. Nicholas, '08 (NSH) Curia: Offices and Directors St. Stephen, Old Hickory, TN
Allen, Rev. Patrick, '13 (POC) Corpus Christi Catholic Community, Charleston, SC
Allen, Rev. Patrick, (CHR) St. Mary of the Annunciation, Charleston, SC
Allen, Rev. Peter, '71 (RVC) Retired.
Allen, Rev. Philip T., '59 (OG) Curia: Canonical Services Saint Joseph's Church, Minerva, Olmstedville, NY; St. Mary's and St. Paul's Parish, Indian Lake, NY
Allen, Very Rev. Richard J., '97 (E) Curia: (>MO) Offices and Directors Notre Dame, Hermitage, PA; St. Bartholomew, Sharpsville, PA
Allen, Rev. Richard L., '61 (GB) Retired.
Allen, Rev. Shawn W., '99 (BO) Curia: Advisory Boards, Commissions, Committees, and Councils St. Mary of the Annunciation, Melrose, MA
Allen, Rev. Terrance, *LC* '19 (ATL) Pinecrest Academy, Inc., Cumming, GA; [MON] Legionaries of Christ, Incorporated, Cumming, GA
Allender, Rev. Thomas G., *S.J.* '71 (SJ) [MON] Sacred Heart Jesuit Center, Los Gatos, CA
Allers, Rev. Rodney M., '08 (DUB) St. Mark's Church, Iowa Falls, Iowa, Iowa Falls, IA; St. Mary's Church, Eldora, Iowa, Eldora, IA
Alles, Rev. Anthony J., *M.M.J.M.J.* '14 (OLL) [MON] Oblates of Jesus, Mary & Joseph, Beaverton, OR; [MON] Sacred Heart Maronite Monastery, Beaverton, OR
Alles, Rev. Tyrell J., *O.S.B.* '93 (FTW) St. Louis, New Haven, IN
Allgaier, Rev. Sebastian, *O.S.B.* '99 (KC) St. Peter's, Stanberry, MO; [MON] Conception Abbey (Benedictine Monks), Conception, MO
Alliata, Rev. Peter R., '61 (WDC) Retired.
Allin, Rev. Benedict, *O.S.B.* '67 (STL) [MON] The Abbey of St. Mary and St. Louis, St. Louis, MO
Allison, Msgr. Bruce R., '61 (E) Retired.
Allison, Rev. Jeffrey, *C.S.C.* '96 (P) On Duty Outside Diocese.
Allison, Rev. Jeffrey L., *C.S.C.* '96 (FR) [COL] Holy Cross Fathers Religious, North Easton, MA; [COL] Stonehill College, North Easton, MA
Alloggia, Rev. Benoit, *O.S.B.* '09 (GBG) [MON] Saint Vincent Archabbey, Latrobe, PA
Alloy, Rev. Daniel, *FSSP* '20 (GAL) Regina Caeli, Houston, TX
Allt, Rev. John F., '73 (TUC) Retired. Chap, Assisting Priest, Christ the King Chapel, Tucson
Alluri, Rev. Joseph Raj, '05 (SUP) Immaculate Conception, Grantsburg, WI; St. Dominic, Frederic, WI
Almade, Rev. Frank D., '78 (PIT) St. Joseph the Worker, Pittsburgh, PA
Almagno, Rev. Romano S., *O.F.M.* '65 (NY) [MON] Padua Friary, New York, NY
Almeida, Rev. Joseph, '19 (BO) St. Patrick, Lowell, MA
Almendras, Rev. Joel P., '75 (MRY) Retired.
Almeter, Rev. Jacob N., '13 (SAV) Church of the Most Holy Trinity, Augusta, GA
Almeus, Rev. Enel, *C.S.Sp.* '03 (BRK) Chap, New York Presbyterian/Queens Mary's Nativity-Saint Ann Roman Catholic Church, Flushing, NY
Al-Mimass, Rev. Fadi, (NTN)
Almonor, Rev. Eugene, *O.M.I.* (PH) St. William, Philadelphia, PA
Almonor, Rev. Eugene R., *O.M.I.* (PH) Curia: Evangelization
Almonte, Rev. Yunior, '05 (NEW) St. Anthony of Padua, Union City, NJ
Almonte-Mendez, Rev. Yunior, '05 (NEW) Chap, Hoboken Univ Med Ctr
Alnas, Rev. Cipriano, '03 (HON) Sacred Hearts, Lanai City, HI
Alobaidi, Rev. Joseph, *O.P.* '80 (CIN) St. Gertrude, Cincinnati, OH; [MON] St. Gertrude Priory, Cincinnati, OH
Alonso, Rev. Armando, '90 (MIA) On Leave. Ministry in the prison system in Orange County, FL
Alonso, Rev. Guillermo, '22 (LA) St. Genevieve, Panorama City, CA
Alonso, Rev. Ignacio, *C.M.* (SJN) Sagrado Corazon de Jesus, San Juan, PR
Alonso, Rev. Jose, (GAL) St. Elizabeth Ann Seton, Houston, TX; St. Helen, Pearland, TX
Alonso Sanchez, Rev. Gabriel, (ARE) Curia: Leadership San Raphael, Quebradillas, PR
Alonzo, Rev. Baltazar Sanchez, '96 (BRK) St. Mary Gate of Heaven, Ozone Park, NY
Alookaran, Rev. Charles, '91 (BIR) Our Lady Queen of the Universe, Huntsville, AL
Alozie, Rev. Kelechi, '08 (SLC) Our Lady of Lourdes LLC 209, Magna, UT
Alphonse, Rev. Satheesh C., *S.D.C.* (LAN) Chap, Duane Waters Hosp Our Lady of Fatima Parish Michigan Center, Michigan Center, MI; [MIS] The Pious Union of St. Joseph, Grass Lake, MI
Alphonse, Rev. Thainese, '85 (LAF) St. Bernadette, Bayou Vista, LA
Alphonso, Rev. John, '68 (DAL) On Administrative Leave.
Alquiros, Rev. Jun Joseph, '21 (MET) Cathedral of St. Francis of Assisi, Metuchen, NJ
Al-Shaikh, Rev. Msgr. Emad Hanna, '00 (OLD) Our Mother of Perpetual Help Church, El Cajon, CA; Saint Joseph Mission, El Cajon, CA
Alt, Rev. Kenneth, (CIN) Holy Redeemer, New Bremen, OH; Most Precious Blood, Chickasaw, OH; Nativity of the Blessed Virgin Mary, Maria Stein, OH; St. Augustine, Minster, OH; St. John the Baptist, Maria Stein, OH; St. Rose, Maria Stein, OH; St. Sebastian, Celina, OH
Altamirano, Rev. Reynaldo Jose Escobar, (BO) St. Rose of Lima, Chelsea, MA

Altavilla, Rev. Philip A., '92 (SCR) On Administrative Leave.

Altavista, Rev. Salvatore D., *M.S.* '64 (HRT) [MIS] Missionaries of LaSalette, Hartford, CT

Al-Tawil, Rev. Muhanned, (EST) St. Paul Caldean Catholic Church, Grand Blanc, MI

Alteme, Rev. Celillon, (HRT) [HOS] Saint Francis Hospital and Medical Center (Catholic Health Ministries), Hartford, CT

Altenhofen, Rev. Joseph F., '10 (SEA) Our Lady of Hope, Everett, WA

Altermatt, Rev. Charles K., '08 (DET) St. Alfred Parish Taylor, Taylor, MI

Altermatt, Rev. Gregory M., '76 (HRT) Retired.

Altier, Rev. Robert J., '89 (STP) Holy Trinity, South St. Paul, MN

Altine, Rev. Richard L., '95 (KAL) St. Basil, South Haven, MI; St. Jude, Gobles, MI

Altman, Rev. David, (L) [MON] Abbey of Our Lady of Gethsemani, of the Order of Cistercians of the Strict Observance, Trappist, KY

Altman, Rev. James F., '08 (LC) On Administrative Leave.

Altman, Rev. Joseph W., '76 (CHI) Retired.

Altonji, Rev. Joshua, (BIR) Holy Spirit Catholic Parish, Huntsville, Huntsville, AL

Altrui, Rev. Ronald P., '81 (NY) On Leave.

Altuna, Rev. Javier, *S.J.* '66 (LA) Retired.

Alumam, Rev. Rudolph, '91 (ORG) Holy Family Catholic Church, Orange, CA

Aluthwatte, Rev. Joseph Benedict, (SAT) [NUR] Oblate Madonna Residence, San Antonio, TX

Alvarado, Rev. John Paul, '88 (MET) Sacred Heart, South Plainfield, NJ

Alvarado, Rev. Jorge, *C.C.* '15 (GAL) [MIS] Catholic Charismatic Center, Houston, TX

Alvarado, Rev. Roberto, '89 (ELP) Our Lady of the Light, El Paso, TX

Alvarado De Jesus, Rev. Jose Rafael, '94 (PCE) Nuestra Senora del Carmen, Villalba, PR

Alvarado de Jesus, Rev. Jose Rafael, '94 (PCE) Military Chap Colegio Nuestra Senora del Carmen, Villalba, PR; Cristo de la Salud, Villalba, PR; Espiritu Santo, Villalba, PR; Jesus Crucificado, Villalba, PR; La Milagrosa, Villalba, PR; La Providencia, Bo. Hatillo, PR; Ntra. Sra. del Carmen, Villalba, PR; Nuestra Senora del Carmen, Villalba, PR; Sagrado Corazon, Villalba, PR; San Antonio, Villalba, PR; San Francisco de Asis, Villalba, PR; San Juan Evangelista, Villalba, PR; San Pablo, Villalba, PR; San Pedro, Villalba, PR; Santa Cecilia, Villalba, PR; Santisima Trinidad, Villalba, PR; Santisimo Sacramento, Villalba, PR; Vigen Dolorosa, Villalba, PR

Alvarado Flores, Rev. Felix Emilio, (PCE) Retired.

Alvarez, Rev. Abel, *O.S.A.* '58 (NY) Holy Rosary, New York, NY

Alvarez, Very Rev. Carlos A., '01 (PBL) Curia: Leadership; Offices and Directors Sacred Heart, Alamosa, CO

Alvarez, Rev. Eduardo, *S.J.* '74 (MIA) Curia: Leadership Gesu, Miami, FL; [EFT] Father Tino Foundation, Inc., Miami, FL

Alvarez, Rev. Enrique, '03 (SAC) Curia: Offices and Directors Pastor of Holy Family Parish, Citrus Heights, a corporation sole, Citrus Heights, CA

Alvarez, Rev. Javier, *O.F.M.* '89 (LA) Assumption, Los Angeles, CA

Alvarez, Rev. Jay, (GAL) [MIS] Opus Dei, Houston, TX

Alvarez, Rev. John J., '81 (POD) Curia: Clergy and Religious Services

Alvarez, Rev. Jonathan, (CHK) Curia: Tribunal

Alvarez, Rev. Jonathan, '97 (AGN) Curia: Administration; Advisory Boards, Commissions, Committees, and Councils; Leadership; Tribunal Nino Perdido Y Sagrada Familia, Asan, GU

Alvarez, Rev. Jose, '03 (MIA) Epiphany, Miami, FL

Alvarez, Rev. Jose M., '12 (SEA) Holy Family, Seattle, WA

Alvarez, Rev. Luis E., '14 (ATL) St. Helena Catholic Church, Clayton, Inc., Clayton, GA

Alvarez, Rev. Manuel, '02 (MIA) Curia: Clergy and Religious Services Little Flower, Coral Gables, FL

Alvarez, Rev. Milton, *C.M.F.* '77 (LA) Retired. [MON] Dominguez Seminary Inc., Rancho Dominguez, CA

Alvarez, Rev. Porfirio, '69 (LA) Retired.

Alvarez, Rev. Ramiro, (DAL) St. Ann Catholic Parish - Coppell, Coppell, TX

Alvarez, Rev. Ramon, '82 (DAL) On Administrative Leave.

Alvarez, Rev. Yuvan A., '04 (NEW) Curia: Advisory Boards, Commissions, Committees, and Councils Our Lady of Fatima, North Bergen, NJ

Alvarez Infiesta, Rev. Ramon, '81 (SJN) [MIS] Opus Dei, Guaynabo, PR

Alvarez-Galindo, Rev. Miguel, (CHI) [MON] Missionaries of Saint Charles, Oak Park, IL

Alvarez-Lara, Rev. Fernando, *SJ* '09 (DEN) [MON] Regis Jesuit Community (The Jesuits at Regis University), Denver, CO

Alvarez-Posada, Rev. Fabio, '14 (ATL) St. Paul the Apostle Catholic Church, Cleveland, Inc., Cleveland, GA

Alvero, Rev. Ronnie, (MO) Curia: Offices and Directors

Alves, Rev. Adauto, (NEW) Our Lady of Fatima, Elizabeth, NJ

Alvial Moreno, Rev. Felipe Andres, *S.J.S.* '13 (MAD) On Duty Outside Diocese. Serves in Ecuador

Alvizures, Rev. Miguel, '08 (LEX) Mary, Queen of the Holy Rosary, Lexington, KY

Alzate, Rev. Alberto, '77 (LAV) Retired.

Alzate, Rev. German, '18 (ELP) San Pedro de Jesus Maldonado Mission, El Paso, TX

Alzate, Rev. German, '18 (ELP) Curia: Advisory Boards, Commissions, Committees, and Councils; Offices and Directors

Amabile, Rev. Patsy L., '73 (CAM) Retired.

Amadeo, Rev. Michael, '92 (DM) Curia: Leadership; Offices and Directors Our Lady's Immaculate Heart, Ankeny, IA; St. Mary/Holy Cross, Elkhart, IA

Amadeo, Rev. Michael A., '92 (DM) Curia: Leadership

Amadi, Rev. Alvan, '13 (GB) Divine Savior Catholic Elementary School, Inc., Kiel, WI; Holy Rosary, New Holstein, WI; SS. Peter & Paul Congregation, Kiel, WI

Amadi, Rev. Anselm, (GLP) St. Helena, Alpine, AZ; St. Peter, Springerville, AZ

Amadi, Rev. Anthony Obgonna, (B) Holy Trinity, Nezperce, ID; SS. Peter and Paul, Grangeville, ID

Amadi, Rev. Ernest E., '10 (CAM) Our Lady of Guadalupe Parish, Lindenwold, N.J., Lindenwold, NJ; The Catholic Community of Christ Our Light, Cherry Hill, N.J., Cherry Hill, NJ

Amadi, Rev. Kenneth, (FTW) St. Joseph, Mishawaka, IN

Amadi, Rev. Marcel, '03 (CHL) [CAM] NC Agricultural and Technical State University, Greensboro, NC; [CAM] Wake Forest University, Winston-Salem, NC

Amador, Rev. Roberto, '11 (PAT) Our Lady of Mercy, Whippany, NJ

Amaechi, Rev. Jerome, (SPC) Chap, Springfield Hosp Ministry

Amagba, Rev. Paschal, *C.M.F.* '97 (ATL) Corpus Christi Catholic Church, Stone Mountain, Inc., Stone Mountain, GA

Amah, Rev. Christian, '16 (NY) St. Benedict, Bronx, NY

Amah, Rev. Peter O., '05 (SPK) On Leave.

Amah, Rev. Pius, '90 (SAC) Chap, California Med Facility Pastor of St. Peter Parish, Dixon, a corporation sole, Dixon, CA

Amaladass, Rev. Ilayaraja, *H.G.N.* '09 (BUR) Our Lady of Fatima, Wilmington, VT; St. Joachim, Readsboro, VT

Amalanathan, Rev. Jayaseelan, (HBG) Sacred Heart of Jesus, Lewistown, PA

Amalfitano, Rev. Joseph A., '63 (PH) Retired.

Amaliri, Rev. Paul Obi, '00 (TLS) On Duty Outside Diocese. Military Chap, US Air Force Curia: (>MO) Offices and Directors

Amalorpavanathan, Rev. Rayapillai, *S.D.C.* '13 (LAN) [PRE] St. Louis Center for Exceptional Children & Adults, Chelsea, MI

Amalraj, Rev. Loyola, '81 (MIL) Retired.

Amalraj, Rev. Suresh, (P) Our Lady of the Lake, Lake Oswego, OR

Amalraj Selvanayagam, Rev. Arul, *O.Praem.* '90 (PH) St. Patrick, Malvern, PA

Amande, Rev. Lito D., (MO) Curia: Offices and Directors

Amandua, Rev. Caesar, *A.J.* '01 (CLV) Chap, SouthWest Gen Hosp

Amankwaa, Rev. Andrew, (SCR) Most Holy Trinity Parish, Susquehanna, PA

Amankwah, Rev. Alfred, '14 (RVC) Church of St. Mary, East Islip, NY

Amankwah, Rev. John, '79 (CIN) [COL] Mount St. Joseph University, Cincinnati, OH

Amann, Rev. John J., '66 (BRK) Retired.

Amann, Rev. Steven J., '74 (MIL) Retired.

Amann, Rev. William, '54 (ROC) Retired.

Amantia, Rev. Damian, *T.O.R.* '90 (SP) St. Mary Our Lady of Grace, St. Petersburg, FL

Amaobi, Rev. Sylvanus, '02 (TLS) St. Cecilia, Claremore, OK

Amar, Rev. Joseph P., '74 (SAM) Retired.

Amar, Rev. Zab, '74 (E) St. Basil the Great, Coalport, PA

Amaral, Rev. Angelo, '91 (TR) [MIS] Our Lady of the Rosary Chapel, Lawrenceville, NJ; [MON] Villa Vianney, Trenton, NJ

Amaral, Rev. Mark C., '04 (OAK) St. Edward, Newark, CA

Amaral, Rev. Stephen P., '78 (PRO) Retired.

Amarante, Rev. Alfonso V., *C.Ss.R.* '97 (STL) [MON] Alphonsian Foundation, Liguori, MO

Amarillas, Rev. Lucius, *O.S.B.* (SP) [MON] St. Leo Abbey, Saint Leo, FL

Amarlapudi, Rev. Lurdhu Vijaya, (LSC) Our Lady of Grace Parish, Artesia, Inc., Artesia, NM

Amaro, Rev. Martin, '19 (LR) Blessed Sacrament, Jonesboro, AR

Amasa, Rev. Sheldon, '90 (TR) Parish of Our Lady of Hope, West Long Branch, N.J., West Long Branch, NJ

Amasi, Rev. James, (FWT) Our Lady of Guadalupe, DeLeon, TX; Sacred Heart, Comanche, TX; St. Brendan, Stephenville, TX; St. Mary, Dublin, TX (>DET) [MON] Society of the Catholic Apostolate (Pallottine Fathers), Wyandotte, MI

Amasiorah, Rev. Innocent, '96 (CHL) St. Thomas Aquinas, Charlotte, NC; [CAM] University of North Carolina-Charlotte, Charlotte, NC

Amato, Rev. Anthony, '17 (ROC) St. Peter's Roman Catholic Parish, Ontario County, Clifton Springs, NY

Amato, Rev. Antonio, '61 (PRT) Retired.

Amato, Rev. Joseph, '59 (ALB) Retired.

Amato, Rev. Msgr. Nicholas P., '70 (BAL) Retired.

Amato, Rev. Salvatore J., '69 (BRK) Retired.

Amatrucola, Rev. Mark Paul, *C.O.* '20 (BRK) Assumption of the Blessed Virgin Mary, Brooklyn, NY; [MON] Oratory of Saint Philip Neri, Congregation Pontifical Rite, Brooklyn, NY

Amayun, Rev. Alejandro A., '92 (LA) Our Lady of the Valley, Canoga Park, CA; St. Francis of Assisi, Fillmore, CA

Amazeen, Rev. Ryan C., '20 (MAN) St. Rose of Lima, Littleton, NH

Ambadan, Rev. Raphael, (SYM) Curia: Administration

Ambalathingal, Rev. Robert, *O.C.D.* '96 (BRK) Chap, Long Island Jewish Hosp Our Lady of Lourdes, Queens Village, NY; [CCH] Indian Latin Rite Ministry, ,

Ambalathuruthel, Rev. Noble Dominic, *MSFS* '14 (ATL) [MON] The Missionaries of St. Francis de Sales - MSFS USA Vice Province, Loganville, GA

Amberger, Rev. Frank G., '96 (CIN) St. Angela Merici, Fayetteville, OH; St. George, Georgetown, OH; St. Mary, Georgetown, OH; St. Michael, Mt. Orab, OH; St. Michael, Ripley, OH

Ambert, Rev. Jorge, *S.J.* '66 (SJN) Curia: Offices and Directors San Ignacio de Loyola, San Juan, PR; [EFT] Renovacion Conyugal (Fundacion Fernando Martinez), San Juan, PR

Ambooken, Rev. Jose, '75 (NY) Our Lady of Mercy, Bronx, NY

Ambosta, Rev. Dawson, '75 (NY) St. Joseph, Bronxville, NY

Ambre, Rev. Efren C., '97 (GBG) St. Cecilia, Brownsville, PA; The Historic Church of St. Peter, Brownsville, PA

Ambrose, Very Rev. Alexander, *H.G.N.* '09 (FWT) Curia: Leadership Our Lady Queen of Peace, Wichita Falls, TX

Ambrose, Rev. Malcolm, '72 (LA) Retired.

Ambrosy, Rev. David J., '85 (DUB) SS. Peter and Paul Church, Springbrook, Iowa, Springbrook, IA; St. Catherine Church, St. Catherine, Iowa, Dubuque, IA; St. Donatus Church, St. Donatus, Iowa, St. Donatus, IA; St. Joseph's Church, Bellevue, Iowa, Bellevue, IA

Amburose, Rev. Alexander, *HGN* '12 (LUB) St. Michaels Church Anson, Anson, TX

Amburose, Rev. Stanley, '05 (FRS) St. Francis of Assisi, Bakersfield, CA

Ameche, Rev. William, *SJ* (P) [MON] Colombiere Jesuit Community, Portland, OR

Amede, Rev. Taroh, *S.J.* '21 (WDC) [MON] The Jesuit Community of St. Aloysius Gonzaga, Washington, DC

Amedeka, Rev. Patrick K., (DM) Holy Spirit Church of Creston, Creston, IA; St. Edward, Afton, IA

Amegble, Rev. Jean, *S.J.* (BO) [MON] Walter Ciszek House, Brighton, MA

Ameh, Rev. Mark Thomas, *M.S.P.* '06 (LAV) St. Joseph, Husband of Mary, Las Vegas, NV

Ameh, Rev. Samuel, (LSC) St. Thomas Aquinas Parish, Inc., Lovington, NM

Ameh, Rev. Victor, (MIA) (>NY) St. Bartholomew, Yonkers, NY

Amell, Rev. Gustavo, *S.T.* (JKS) (>PAT) [MON] Shrine of St. Joseph, Stirling, NJ

Ament, Rev. Richard J., '66 (DUB) Retired.

Americo Santos, Rev. Joel, (BO) Most Holy Redeemer, Boston, MA

Ames, Rev. Gregory, '86 (DEN) On Leave.
Ames, Rev. John J., '82 (PH) St. Colman, Ardmore, PA
Ames, Rev. Mark, *CFR* '18 (NY) [MON] St. Joseph's Friary, New York, NY
Amesse, Rev. Michael J., *O.M.I.* (BO) [MIS] St. Joseph the Worker Shrine, Lowell, MA
Amey, Rev. Msgr. Robert G., '69 (WDC) St. Mary, Rockville, MD; [MIS] Archdiocesan Council of Catholic Women, Rockville, MD
Amezcua, Rev. Pedro E., *C.O.R.C.* '86 (SB) Our Lady of Guadalupe, San Bernardino, CA
Amezcua Nuñez, Rev. Pedro E., *C.O.R.C.* '86 (SB) [MIS] Confraternity of Operarios Del Reino De Cristo, C.O.R.C., Corona, CA
Amezcua-Martin, Rev. Julio C., (DEN) On Duty Outside Diocese. Chap, Bishop Machebeuf High School Bishop Machebeuf High School, Denver, CO
Amico, Rev. Alexander D., '73 (E) Retired.
Amico, Rev. Charles R., '52 (BUF) Retired. [MON] Bishop Head Residence, Lackawanna, NY
Amidar, Rev. Venancio, '78 (ORG) Curia: Offices and Directors St. Justin Martyr, Anaheim, CA
Amine, Rev. Restom, *O.F.M.Cap.* '02 (DEN) [MON] St. Anthony of Padua Friary, Denver, CO
Amirtham, Rev. Xavier, *O. Praem.* '95 (GB) All Saints, Denmark, WI; Holy Trinity Mission, Denmark, WI; St. Mary, Glenmore Stark, WI; [MON] St. Norbert Abbey, De Pere, WI
Ammer, Rev. Michael, '21 (FTW) St. Jude, Fort Wayne, IN
Amo, Rev. Steven S., '92 (SPR) Sacred Heart, Feeding Hills, MA
Amo Gyau, Rev. Michael, (SCR) Christ the King Parish, Archbald, PA
Amoako-Opare, Rev. Ernest, '97 (SAL) Immaculate Heart of Mary Parish, Hill City, Inc., Hill City, KS; St. Joseph Parish, Damar, Inc., Damar, KS
Amobi, Rev. Bart, (NY) Chap, Terence Cardinal Cooke Health Care Ctr, Manhattan
Amodeo, Rev. Donald, '22 (SP) Church of the Nativity, Brandon, FL
Amodio, Rev. Francis, *O.Carm.* '83 (NY) Transfiguration, Tarrytown, NY; [MON] Carmelite Friars (North American Province of St. Elias), Middletown, NY
Amofa, Rev. Felix Rex, (RIC) Good Samaritan, Amelia, VA; St. Gabriel, Chesterfield, VA
Amojo, Rev. Christopher, *C.M.* '04 (LSC) St. Cecilia Parish, Inc., Jal, NM
Amora, Rev. Eduardo B., (MO) Curia: Offices and Directors
Amora, Rev. Silvano B., '77 (TR) Retired.
Amore, Rev. Mario V., '15 (DET) Curia: Administration; Consultative Bodies; Leadership St. Aloysius Parish Detroit, Detroit, MI; [MIS] St. Dominic Outreach Center, Detroit, MI
Amorose, Rev. Victor, '12 (SP) Curia: Faith Formation; Pastoral Services St. John Vianney, St. Pete Beach, FL
Amortegui, Rev. Gilberto, *A.I.C* '06 (MIA) St. Boniface, Pembroke Pines, FL
Amoruso, Rev. Roberto, *F.S.C.B.* '93 (WDC) [MIS] Priestly Fraternity of the Missionaries of St. Charles Borromeo, Inc., Bethesda, MD
Amos, Rev. George, (SAG) Our Lady of Perpetual Help Parish of Caseville, Caseville, MI; [MIS] St. Felix of Valois Church, Pinnebog, MI
Amoy, Rev. Roleto, (YAK) St. Peter Claver, Wapato, WA
Ampatt, Rev. Joseph, (SHP) Curia: Leadership
Ampatt, Rev. Joseph, '77 (SHP) Curia: Leadership
Ampong, Rev. Bernard Osei, '97 (ALB) Sacred Heart, Sidney, NY
Amponsah, Rev. Anthony A., (NY) Sacred Heart Church, Monroe, NY; St. John the Evangelist, Goshen, NY
Amrhein, Rev. Robert, *O.F.M.Conv.* '62 (SY) Assumption B.V.M., Syracuse, NY
Amsberry, Rev. John, '95 (P) Chap, San Diego Airport, San Diego
Amsberry, Rev. John, (SD) Pastor of Saint Charles Borromeo Catholic Parish, San Diego, a corporation sole, San Diego, CA; [MIS] Saint Charles Borromeo Catholic Parish in San Diego, CA Real Property Support Corporation, San Diego, CA
Amthor, Rev. Bryan C., '15 (KC) On Special Assignment. St. George, Odessa, MO; St. Jude the Apostle, Oak Grove, MO
Amundsen, Rev. Msgr. Robert L., '69 (DEN) Retired.
Amy, Rev. Msgr. Peter L., '64 (LA) Retired. St. Didacus, Sylmar, CA
Amyot, Rev. Andrew J., '64 (OG) Retired. The Parish of the Visitation and St. Raymond, Norfolk, NY
An Ninh, Rev. Vincent Nguyen, '71 (DET) Retired.
Anaeche, Rev. Collins I., '08 (HRT) St. Patrick's Church Corporation Collinsville, Connecticut, Collinsville, CT
Anaele, Rev. Ignatius I., '98 (CHI) St. Mary of Vernon, Indian Creek, IL
Anaeto, Rev. Dominic, '94 (HRT) Our Lady Queen of Angels Parish Corporation, Meriden, CT
Anagbogu, Rev. Michael A., (DET) St. John the Baptist Parish Monroe, Monroe, MI; St. Mary Parish Monroe, Monroe, MI
Anala, Rev. Anthony A., *S.V.D.* '07 (LAF) St. Paul the Apostle, Lafayette, LA
Anandan, Rev. Baskar, (GF) Immaculate Conception, Forsyth, MT; St. Margaret Mary, Colstrip, MT; [MIS] Fort Kipp, St. Anthony, , ; [MIS] Sacred Heart, Bainville, MT; [MIS] St. Thomas, Brockton, MT
Anandan, Rev. Rajendran, '91 (LC) Sacred Heart, Wauzeka, WI
Anandan, Very Rev. Rajendran, '91 (LC) Curia: Leadership St. Wenceslaus, Eastman, WI
Anandarayar, Rev. Perianayagasamy, *SdC* '13 (PRO) Church of the Sacred Heart, East Providence, RI
Anandarayar, Rev. Perianayagasamy, *SdC* '13 (PRO) Curia: Clergy and Religious Services
Anane, Rev. Francis Kwame, '98 (DUB) S.S. Peter and Paul Church, Gilbert, Iowa, Ames, IA; St. Mary Church, Williams, Iowa, Williams, IA; St. Thomas Aquinas Church, Webster City, Iowa, Webster City, IA; [EFT] St. Thomas Aquinas Foundation of Webster City, Iowa, Webster City, IA
Anania, Rev. Alexis D., *OFM* (Y) Retired.
Anarado, Rev. Ethel, '01 (RVC) St. Joseph, Babylon, NY
Anarcon, Rev. Angelito, '81 (TR) St. Catherine of Siena, Farmingdale, NJ
Anasiudu, Rev. John, '02 (SFE) San Miguel, Socorro, NM
Anastasia, Rev. Thomas J., '91 (SP) St. Michael the Archangel, Clearwater, FL
Anatolios, Rev. Khaled, '15 (NTN) On Special Assignment. Professor, Notre Dame University (>FTW) [COL] University of Notre Dame Du Lac, Notre Dame, IN
Anatuanya, Rev. Gregory, '01 (R) [CAM] Newman Catholic Student Center (Catholic Student Center UNC-W), Wilmington, NC
Anaya, Rev. Angel, '09 (MIL) St. Adalbert's Congregation, Milwaukee, WI
Anaya, Rev. Francisco, *Sch.P.* '01 (MIA) [MON] Piarist Fathers, Province of the USA & Puerto Rico, Miami, FL
Anaya, Rev. Oscar, '22 (FRS) Our Lady of Mt. Carmel, Fresno, CA; St. Alphonsus, Fresno, CA
Anaya Estrada, Rev. Jose-Angel, (MIL) Curia: (>MO) Offices and Directors
Anchanithadathil, Rev. Praneesh, (MCE) Curia: Advisory Boards, Commissions, Committees, and Councils
Ancharski, Rev. John J., '83 (TUC) Retired.
Ancheril, Rev. Jose, '86 (BEL) Retired.
Ancheta, Rev. Noel, (PHX) (>SLC) Saint Mary of the Assumption LLC 238, Park City, UT
Ancona, Rev. Msgr. Gaspar F., '63 (GR) Retired.
Anctil, Rev. Peter Claude, *O.S.B.* '67 (BUR) [MON] The Benedictine Foundation of the State of Vermont, Inc., Weston, VT
Andama, Rev. Geofrey, '13 (CHI) St. Michael, Orland Park, IL
Andarias, Rev. Arokiasamy, '00 (OKL) Sacred Heart, Mangum, OK
Andebo, Rev. Hillary, (GB) [HOS] Langlade Hospital - Hotel Dieu of St. Joseph of Antigo Wisconsin (Aspirus Langlade Hospital), Antigo, WI
Andel, Very Rev. David, '95 (SB) Curia: Advisory Boards, Commissions, Committees, and Councils; Offices and Directors
Andem, Rev. John, '03 (VEN) Ave Maria Parish, Inc., Ave Maria, FL
Anderl, Rev. Peter J., '01 (FAR) St. Boniface Church of Lidgerwood, Lidgerwood, ND; St. Martin's Church of Geneseo, Geneseo, ND; Sts. Peter & Paul Church of Cayuga, Cayuga, ND
Andersen, Rev. Eric, '09 (P) St. Stephen, Portland, OR
Anderson, Rev. Alexander R., '75 (STL) St. Rose of Lima Catholic Church, DeSoto, De Soto, MO
Anderson, Rev. Msgr. Andrew L., '74 (MIA) Retired.
Anderson, Rev. Arthur, *O.F.M.* (CHI) Curia: Tribunal [MON] St. Peter's Friary, Chicago, IL
Anderson, Rev. Arthur T., '58 (CAM) Retired.
Anderson, Rev. Barg G., '05 (SUP) Retired.
Anderson, Rev. Bruce T., (WIL) St. Joseph, Middletown, DE
Anderson, Rev. Daniel J., *O.F.M.* '76 (CIN) [MON] St. Francis Seraph Friary, Cincinnati, OH
Anderson, Rev. David, '97 (SEA) [COL] Seattle University, Seattle, WA; [MON] Arrupe Jesuit Community at Seattle University, Seattle, WA
Anderson, Rev. David, '83 (STN) (>CHY) [COL] Wyoming Catholic College, Lander, WY
Anderson, Rev. Edwin C., '08 (SUP) Curia: Offices and Directors Holy Trinity, Haugen, WI; Our Lady of Lourdes, Rice Lake, WI; St. John Evangelist, Birchwood, WI; St. Joseph, Rice Lake, WI
Anderson, Rev. Gabriel C., '89 (DUB) Immaculate Conception Church, Masonville, Iowa, Masonville, IA; St. John Church, Delhi, Iowa, Delhi, IA; St. Mary's Church, Manchester, Iowa, Manchester, IA; St. Patrick's Church, Ryan, Iowa, Ryan, IA
Anderson, Rt. Rev. Hugh R., *O.S.B.* '65 (JOL) Retired. [MON] St. Procopius Abbey, Lisle, IL
Anderson, Rev. Jake, '15 (STP) St. Lawrence, Minneapolis, MN; [CAM] Newman Center at St. Lawrence, Minneapolis, MN
Anderson, Rev. James, *M.S.A.* '77 (NOR) [MON] Society of the Missionaries of the Holy Apostles, Cromwell, CT
Anderson, Rev. Msgr. James B., '78 (GAL) Queen of Peace, La Marque, TX
Anderson, Rev. James W., *M.S.A.* (LA) Retired.
Anderson, Rev. John C., '93 (SUP) Curia: Offices and Directors Immaculate Conception, New Richmond, WI; St. Patrick, New Richmond, WI
Anderson, Rev. Msgr. John E., '66 (LSC) Retired. Curia: Evangelization; Tribunal
Anderson, Rev. Joseph W., '62 (PEO) Retired.
Anderson, Rev. Kenneth, '98 (CHI) St. John Newman, Evanston, IL
Anderson, Very Rev. Kenneth J., '87 (RCK) St. Peter Cathedral, Rockford, IL
Anderson, Rev. Kevin, '83 (SCL) Curia: Leadership; Offices and Directors The Church of Christ Our Light, Princeton, MN
Anderson, Rev. Lawrence, *O.F.M.* '10 (ALB) [CAM] Siena College, Loudonville, NY; [COL] Siena College, Loudonville, NY
Anderson, Rev. Louis, '07 (NY) On Leave.
Anderson, Rev. Louis L., '63 (GR) Retired.
Anderson, Rev. Luke, *O.Cist.* '54 (ALN) Retired.
Anderson, Rev. Michael F., '83 (STP) St. Joseph of the Lakes, Lino Lakes, MN; [CEM] St. Joseph Cemetery, Lino Lakes, MN
Anderson, Rev. Nathanael Peter, '20 (WDC) St. John the Baptist, Silver Spring, MD
Anderson, Rev. Patrick S., '10 (CLV) [SEM] Borromeo Seminary, Wickliffe, OH
Anderson, Rt. Rev. Philip, *O.S.B.* '84 (TLS) [EFT] Foundation for the Annunciation Monastery of Clear Creek, Hulbert, OK; [MON] Our Lady of the Annunciation of Clear Creek Abbey, Hulbert, OK
Anderson, Rev. R. Bentley, *S.J.* '96 (NY) [MON] Jesuit Community at Fordham University, New York, NY
Anderson, Rev. Ronald, '72 (DET) Retired.
Anderson, Rev. Shawn Matthew, *O.S.B.* '07 (GBG) [MON] Saint Vincent Archabbey, Latrobe, PA
Anderson, Rev. Steven D., '03 (LAN) Holy Redeemer Parish Flint, Burton, MI
Anderson, Rev. Terence, '84 (SFS) Curia: Leadership Saint Thomas More Parish of Brookings County, Brookings, SD
Anderson, Rev. Thomas, '07 (SFS) Curia: Leadership Sacred Heart Parish of Yankton County, Yankton, SD; Saint Benedict Parish of Yankton County, Yankton, SD
Anderson, Rev. Thomas S., *S.J.* '98 (MIL) Gesu Parish, Milwaukee, WI; [MON] Jesuit Community at Marquette University (Marquette Jesuit Associates, Inc.), Milwaukee, WI
Anderson, Rev. William A., '63 (WH) Retired.
Andert, Rev. Thomas, *O.S.B.* '75 (SCL) [MON] St. John's Abbey, of the Order of St. Benedict, Collegeville, MN; [NUR] John Paul Apartments, Cold Spring, MN
Andinam, Rev. Emmanuel O., '77 (CHR) Curia: Advisory Boards, Commissions, Committees, and Councils St. Gerard, Aiken, SC
Andoh, Rev. Godfrey, '02 (BLX) Curia: Advisory Boards, Commissions, Committees, and Councils; Leadership Cathedral of the Nativity of the Blessed Virgin Mary, Biloxi, MS
Andrade, Rev. Bernardino, '65 (OAK) Retired.
Andrade, Rev. J. Anthony, '92 (STP) St. Thomas Aquinas, St. Paul Park, MN; [CEM] St. Thomas Aquinas Cemetery, St. Paul Park, MN
Andrade, Rev. Michael, '16 (FRS) Curia: Advisory Boards, Commissions, Committees, and Councils Our Lady of Perpetual Help, Clovis, CA
Andrade, Rev. Victor Hugo, '19 (AMA) Our Lady of Guadalupe, Cactus, TX; St. Joseph's, Stratford, TX

Andrade-Limon, Rev. Juan Luis, '14 (CHI) Our Lady of the Snows, Chicago, IL
Andrae, Rev. Henry C., '78 (E) Retired.
Andraschko, Rev. Msgr. James, '59 (SFS) Retired.
Andre, Rev. Msgr. Ludwig, '57 (SJ) Retired.
Andreano, Rev. Msgr. Michael A., '00 (NEW) Cathedral Basilica of the Sacred Heart, Newark, NJ; Ss. Peter and Paul, Hoboken, NJ
Andreassi, Rev. Anthony, *C.O.* '07 (NY) Retired.
Andreassi, Rev. Anthony, *C.O.* '07 (BRK) Assumption of the Blessed Virgin Mary, Brooklyn, NY; [MON] Oratory of Saint Philip Neri, Congregation Pontifical Rite, Brooklyn, NY
Andree, Very Rev. Daniel, *C.Ss.R.* '80 (CHI) Curia: Offices and Directors; Tribunal [MON] The Redemptorist Fathers of Chicago, Chicago, IL
Andrejek, Rev. Michael J., '98 (PEO) Curia: Deaneries St. Joseph Catholic Church, Pekin, IL; [ASN] Catholic Cemetery Association of Pekin, IL, Pekin, IL
Andres, Rev. Edmundo, *CMF* '56 (LA) Retired.
Andres, Rev. James, *O.F.M.Cap.* '63 (DET) [MON] St. Bonaventure Monastery, Detroit, MI
Andres, Rev. Jon, (P) [HOS] Providence Health & Services-Oregon (Providence Portland Medical Center), Portland, OR
Andres, Rev. Napoleon, *M.S.* '85 (HON) Christ the King, Kahului, HI
Andres, Rev. Timothy P., *O.Carm.* '86 (JOL) Historic St. Joseph, Joliet, IL
Andrews, Rev. Christopher, *O.S.B.* '06 (TLS) [MON] Our Lady of the Annunciation of Clear Creek Abbey, Hulbert, OK
Andrews, Rev. Christopher, *O.S.B.* '06 (HPM) St. Philip the Apostle, Sacramento, CA
Andrews, Rev. Daniel R., '01 (OM) Curia: Leadership St. John Paul II Newman Center, Inc., Omaha, NE; [CAM] St. John Paul II Newman Center, Inc., Omaha, NE; [MIS] Marianna, Inc., Omaha, NE
Andrews, Rev. Edward, *O.S.A.* '59 (CHI) Retired. [MON] Austin Friary, Matteson, IL
Andrews, Rev. Eric P., *C.S.P.* '95 (NY) [MON] Paulist Fathers' Motherhouse, New York, NY
Andrews, Rev. Gregory J., '76 (SP) Retired.
Andrews, Rev. John S., '96 (OM) On Leave.
Andrews, Rev. Peter J., '88 (PRO) On Leave.
Andrews Neenan, Rev. Philip Patrick, *C.Ss.R.* '74 (PCE) San Antonio de Padua, Guayama, PR
Andrey, Rev. Roberto A., '83 (SFR) St. Patrick, San Francisco, CA
Andriamamitahina, Rev. Galson Angelot, *MSF* (SAT) Our Lady of Perpetual Help, New Braunfels, TX
Andrie, Rev. Donald, *C.S.P.* '94 (KNX) Curia: Offices and Directors Saint John XXIII University Parish/ Catholic Center, Knoxville, TN; [CAM] UT-Knoxville, Newman Foundation, Inc., Knoxville, TN; [MON] Paulist Fathers (Missionary Society of St. Paul the Apostle), Knoxville, TN
Andrie, Rev. Leonard, '13 (STP) St. Therese, Deephaven, MN; [NUR] St. Therese of Deephaven Senior Living (Deephaven Woods Senior Livin)g, Deephaven, MN
Andriitso, Rev. Roman, (PBR) SS. Peter and Paul, Patton, PA; St. John the Baptist, Northern Cambria, PA
Andrino, Rev. Guilherme A., *S.V.D.* '07 (TR) The Parish of Our Lady of Guadalupe, Lakewood, NJ
Andriot, Rev. Eric L., '16 (COV) St. Paul, Florence, KY
Andro, Rev. Sebastian T., '98 (BRK) Curia: Leadership St. Rosalia-Regina Pacis, Brooklyn, NY
Andrus, Rev. Albin A., '73 (PRT) Retired.
Andrus, Rev. Charles, *S.S.J.* '76 (NO) Blessed Sacrament-St. Joan of Arc, New Orleans, LA
Andrus, Rev. David, *S.J.* '79 (CI) [MON] Jesuit Community of Pohnpei, Kolonia, FM
Andrus, Rev. David L., *S.J.* '79 (CI) [MON] Jesuit Community of Micronesia, Chuuk, FM
Andrus, Rev. Rick, *SVD* (LAF) St. Anthony Catholic Church, Lafayette, LA
Andujar, Rev. J. Iriarte, *O.P.* '86 (PRO) [MON] St. Thomas Aquinas Priory at Providence College, Providence, RI
Aneke, Rev. Kris, *M.S.P.* (AUS) St. John Neumann, Westlake Hills, TX
Aneke, Rev. Paulinus, '01 (JC) St. Thomas More Newman Center, University of Missouri, Columbia, MO; [CAM] St. Thomas More Newman Center, Columbia, MO
Anel, Rev. Paul, (BRK) Curia: Consultative Bodies Saint Paul and Saint Agnes Roman Catholic Church, Brooklyn, NY
Anello, Rev. Robert, *M.S.A.* '07 (NOR) [MON] Society of the Missionaries of the Holy Apostles, Cromwell, CT
Anemelu, Rev. Charles I., (WH) St. Anthony, Charleston, WV
Anfone, Rev. Alwyn B., (SB) Sacred Heart, Palm Desert, CA
Ange, Rev. Sam, (LKC) Curia: Advisory Boards, Commissions, Committees, and Councils
Ange, Rev. Sam A. Trey, (LKC) Immaculate Conception, Jennings, LA
Angel, Rev. Ariel Oliver, '01 (BWN) Curia: Leadership Basilica of Our Lady of San Juan del Valle-National Shrine, San Juan, TX
Angel, Rev. Fredy A., '05 (SAV) Curia: Leadership Holy Trinity, Swainsboro, GA
Angel, Rev. Jose Rene, '93 (BWN) Resurrection, Alamo, TX
Angeles, Rev. Joey F., '00 (BR) The Congregation of St. Agnes Roman Catholic Church, Baton Rouge, LA
Angelicchio, Rev. Paul F., '77 (SY) St. John the Baptist, Rome, NY; Transfiguration, Rome, NY
Angelini, Friar Joseph, *OFM Conv.* (ALB) [MON] Franciscan Friars Conventual, Rensselaer, NY
Angelini, Rev. Joseph, '67 (MIA) Retired.
Angelino, Rev. David, (GAL) St. Theresa, Sugar Land, TX
Angell, Rev. Charles, *S.A.* '60 (NY) Retired.
Angell, Rev. Stephen J., '04 (SAV) On Leave.
Angel-Neri, Rev. Gilberto, '07 (NY) Our Lady of Lourdes, New York, NY
Angelo, Rev. Thomas M., '85 (NOR) On Leave.
Angeloni, Rev. Michael A., '75 (WIL) SS. Peter and Paul, Easton, MD
Angelov, Very Rev. Archpriest Kiril, '90 (STF) Curia: Leadership; Offices and Directors St. Michael, Yonkers, NY
Angelovic, Rev. Michael, '65 (SEA) Retired.
Angelucci, Rev. Patrick, *S.D.B.* '76 (NY) Parish of St. John Bosco, Port Chester, NY
Angert, Rev. James, *TOR* '71 (STU) [COL] Franciscan University of Steubenville, Steubenville, OH; [MON] Holy Spirit Friary, Steubenville, OH
Angi, Rev. Steve J., '85 (CIN) Guardian Angels, Cincinnati, OH; Immaculate Heart of Mary, Cincinnati, OH
Angi, Rev. Steve J., '85 (CIN) Curia: Administration; Leadership St. John Fisher, Cincinnati, OH
Angilella, Rev. Joseph T., *S.J.* '65 (SJ) [MON] Sacred Heart Jesuit Center, Los Gatos, CA
Anginoli, Rev. Msgr. Joseph T., '75 (PAT) Curia: Leadership St. Joseph's, Mendham, NJ
Angkel, Rev. Julio, '83 (CI) St. Francis Assisi, Chuuk, FM
Anglin, Rev. John, *O.F.M.* '71 (SP) Retired. [MON] St. Anthony Friary (St. Petersburg) Franciscan Friars-Holy Name Province, Inc., St. Petersburg, FL
Angrand, Rev. Medenel, '03 (OG) Catholic Community of Burke and Chateaugay, Chateaugay, NY; St. Mary's of the Fort, Fort Covington, NY, Fort Covington, NY; The Catholic Community of Constable, Westville and Trout River, Constable, NY
Angucho, Rev. Pedro, '19 (BRK) Divine Mercy Roman Catholic Church, Brooklyn, NY
Anguiano, Rev. James M., '82 (LA) Curia: Offices and Directors
Anguiano, Rev. Jesus, '09 (SAT) St. Joseph's, Dilley, TX
Anguiano-Rodriguez, Rev. Rafael, *O.F.M.Cap.* '16 (PIT) [MON] The Capuchin Franciscan Friars Province of Saint Augustine, Pittsburgh, PA
Angulo, Rev. Raul, '85 (MIA) Retired.
Angulo Viloria, Rev. Filadelfo Segundo, '06 (LA) Our Lady of Peace, North Hills, CA
Anhur, Rev. Siarhei, *S. Chr* (LAV) St. Joan of Arc, Las Vegas, NV
Anhur, Rev. Siarhei, *SCH* (CHI) St. Albert the Great, Burbank, IL
Ani, Rev. Edmund, (RVC) Holy Name of Mary, Valley Stream, NY
Ani, Rev. Godwin, *S.S.J.* '07 (NO) Our Lady of Grace Roman Catholic Church, Reserve, LA
Anicama, Rev. Cesar, '15 (JC) St. Vincent de Paul, Sedalia, MO
Aniekwe, Rev. Samuel, '96 (SAV) St. Mary, Americus, GA
Aniello, Rev. Frederick M., '79 (HRT) Saint Joseph Parish Corporation, Waterbury, CT; The Church of Our Lady of Mount Carmel, Waterbury, CT
Anil Kumar, Rev. Kakumanu, (SLC) Saint Kateri Tekakwitha Catholic Mission, Fort Duchesne, UT
Aniszczyk, Rev. Leon S., '73 (MET) Retired.
Anki-Reddy, Rev. Ananda, '10 (VEN) Curia: Leadership St. Andrew Parish in Cape Coral, Inc., Cape Coral, FL
Ankley, Rev. Christopher J., '09 (KAL) St. Jerome, Battle Creek, MI; St. Joseph, Battle Creek, MI
Anleu-Sandoval, Rev. Oswaldo, (RIC) Our Lady of Mount Carmel, Newport News, VA
Annese, Rev. Joseph P., '62 (LAV) Retired.
Annie, Rev. Msgr. Frederick P., '78 (WH) Retired. Curia: Offices and Directors
Annino, Rev. Sebastian V., '61 (CAM) Retired.
Annor-Ohene, Rev. James K., '02 (NY) St. Ann, Yonkers, NY
Anokwute, Rev. Victor, (SPC) Immaculate Conception, New Madrid, MO; Sacred Heart, Caruthersville, MO; St. Ann, Malden, MO; St. Teresa, Campbell, MO
Anokye, Rev. Eric, (RIC) Holy Family Parish, Tazewell, VA
Anonuevo, Rev. Arturo, *S.O.L.T.* '98 (PBL) St. Joseph, Capulin, CO
Anonuevo, Very Rev. Salvador, '86 (RIC) Curia: Administration; Deaneries Holy Cross, Lynchburg, VA
Anore, Rev. Joseph, '97 (AGN) Curia: Consultative Bodies St. Joseph, Inarajan, GU
Anover, Rev. Albert C, (L) St. Elizabeth Ann Seton, Louisville, KY
Anozie, Rev. Casmir, (LSC) Infant Jesus Parish, Inc., Hurley, NM; Santa Clara Parish, Inc., Santa Clara, NM
Anschutz, Rev. Larry L., '82 (SFD) Retired. Saint John Paul II, Mount Olive, IL
Anselment, Rev. Joseph E., '61 (ALB) Retired.
Ansems, Rev. Bruce, '05 (KCK) Curia: Tribunal Immaculate Conception, Louisburg, KS
Anson, Rev. Cesar R., '77 (TR) Parish of Mary, Mother of the Church, Bordentown N.J., Bordentown, NJ
Anstey, Rev. Kevin J., '14 (DAV) On Leave.
Anstoetter, Rev. Donald, (STL) [SEM] Kenrick School of Theology, ,
Antall, Rev. Msgr. Richard C., '80 (CLV) Curia: Advisory Boards, Commissions, Committees, and Councils Holy Name, Cleveland, OH
Antao, Rev. Msgr. John S., '60 (NEW) Retired.
Antao, Rev. Paul, *S.D.B.* '99 (BAK) Holy Redeemer Roman Catholic Parish, La Pine, OR
Antao, Rev. Paul, *S.D.B.* '99 (BAK) Curia: Leadership Holy Family, Fort Rock, OR; Holy Trinity, Sunriver, OR; Our Lady of the Snows, Gilchrist, OR
Antecini, Rev. Claudio, '96 (BRK) Visitation of the Blessed Virgin Mary, Brooklyn, NY; [MIS] Federation of Oases of Koinonia John the Baptist, Brooklyn, NY
Antekeier, Rev. Charles R., '62 (GR) Retired.
Antes, Rev. Esteban D., '93 (DAL) Holy Spirit Catholic Parish, Duncanville, TX
Anthappa, Rev. Anthony Swamy, *M.S.F.S.* (HBG) St. Peter, Columbia, PA
Anthony, Very Rev. Aloysius Royan, '95 (SUP) Curia: Leadership Holy Family, Bayfield, WI; Most Holy Rosary, Mellen, WI; Most Precious Blood, Glidden, WI; St. Ann, Cornucopia, WI; St. Anne, Sanborn, WI; St. Anthony, Highbridge, WI; St. Francis, Red Cliff, WI; St. George, Clam Lake, WI; St. Joseph, La Pointe, WI; St. Louis, Washburn, WI
Anthony, Rev. Angelo, *C.PP.S.* '89 (CIN) Emmanuel, Dayton, OH; Holy Trinity, Dayton, OH; St. Joseph, Dayton, OH; [EFT] Community Support Charitable Trust, Dayton, OH
Anthony, Rev. Fred Jeffrey, '09 (P) St. Helen Catholic Church, Sweet Home, OR
Anthony, Rev. Joseph, '80 (LAV) Retired.
Anthony, Rev. Julian, '66 (PBR) Retired.
Anthony, Rev. Patrick, '95 (NY) Chap, Staten Island Univ Hosp South, Staten Island Holy Rosary, Staten Island, NY; St. John Neumann, Staten Island, NY
Anthony, Rev. Robert Alex Sander, *MSC* '15 (ALN) Holy Family, Nazareth, PA
Antillon, Rev. William R., '79 (RCK) SS. Peter and Paul, Virgil, IL; St. Mary, Maple Park, IL
Antinarelli, Rev. Ronald A., *KCHS* '74 (ROC) Our Lady of Victory-St. Joseph, Rochester, NY
Antiporek, Rev. James, '81 (JOL) Retired.
Antoh, Rev. Michael, (DM) St. Boniface, Westphalia, IA
Anton, Rev. Ronald J., *S.J.* '83 (WDC) [MON] The Jesuit Community at Georgetown University, Washington, DC
Anton, Rev. William J., '02 (LUB) Curia: Leadership
Anton, Rev. William John, '02 (LUB) Curia: Leadership Our Lady of Guadalupe, Plainview, TX
Antonacci, Rev. Michael, *O.S.B.* '14 (GBG) [MON] Saint Vincent Archabbey, Latrobe, PA
Antone, Rev. William, *OMI* '80 (SAT) [MON] Missionary Oblates of Mary Immaculate of Texas, Southern Province (San Antonio USP Support Office), San Antonio, TX
Antonelle, Rev. John N., '06 (NOR) Curia: Leadership; Offices and Directors St. Mary, Portland, CT; [CAM] University of Connecticut, Storrs, CT
Antonelli, Rev. Robert, *C.S.C.* '65 (P) Retired. [MON] Priests of Holy Cross in Oregon, Inc., Portland, OR
Antonelli, Rev. Robert J., (SCR) On Special Assignment. St. Boniface, Williamsport, PA; St. Lawrence,

Williamsport, PA
Antoney, Rev. Benny, *O.S.B.* '01 (STO) St. Joseph Church of Modesto (Pastor of), Modesto, CA
Antoney, Rev. Jose Thundathil, *C.M.I.* '88 (SPC) Curia: Consultative Bodies Sacred Heart, Salem, MO
Antonicelli, Rev. Msgr. Charles V., '93 (WDC) Curia: Consultative Bodies; Deaneries; Tribunal Our Lady of Mercy, Potomac, MD
Antonik, Rev. Jan, '03 (VEN) St. Therese Parish in North Fort Myers, Inc., North Fort Myers, FL
Antonio, Rev. James, *S.J.* (SEA) [MON] Jesuit House, Seattle, Seattle, WA
Antonio, Rev. Pio, '91 (DUL) [MIS] Christ Child Society of Duluth, Inc., Proctor, MN
Antonisamy, Rev. Peter, *OMI* '04 (LAR) Sacred Heart (Parroquia Sagrado Corazon), Eagle Pass, TX
Antonucci, Rt. Rev. Richard J., *O. Praem.* '72 (PH) [MON] Daylesford Abbey, Inc., Paoli, PA; [SEM] Daylesford Abbey (Norbertine Fathers, Inc.), Paoli, PA
Antony, Rev. Anson, (OAK) St. Jarlath, Oakland, CA
Antony, Rev. Arockia, *H.G.N.* (MAN) St. Catherine of Siena, Woodsville, NH; St. Joseph, Woodsville, NH
Antony, Rev. Arulanandam Robert, *H.G.N.* (SEA) St. Stephen the Martyr, Renton, WA
Antony, Rev. Biju, *I.M.S.* '03 (BIS) St. Gertrude, Raleigh, ND; St. Lawrence, Flasher, ND; St. Theresa the Child Jesus, Carson, ND
Antony, Rev. John Britto, *C.S.C.* '11 (ORL) St. John the Evangelist, Viera, FL
Antony, Rev. John Francis, '91 (NY) Roman Catholic Church of Sacred Heart and Saint Francis of Assisi, Newburgh, NY
Antony, Rev. John K., '96 (LR) Curia: Leadership; Offices and Directors Immaculate Conception, Fort Smith, AR; Our Lady of the Ozarks Shrine, Winslow, AR; Trinity Catholic School, Fort Smith, AR; [CEM] Calvary, Fort Smith, AR
Antony, Rev. John K., '96 (LR) Curia: Leadership
Antony, Rev. John Berchmans, '90 (NEW) St. John the Baptist, Jersey City, NJ
Antony, Rev. Joy Retnazihamoni, '98 (ALX) Chaplain at CHRISTUS St. Francis Cabrini Hospital Our Lady of Prompt Succor, Alexandria, LA; [HOS] Christus Health Central Louisiana (Christus St. Frances Cabrini Hospital), Alexandria, LA
Antony, Rev. Leo, *S.D.V.* '10 (PAT) Curia: Leadership St. Gerard Majella, Paterson, NJ
Antony, Rev. Michael Jeeva, '99 (P) St. Mark, Eugene, OR; St. Peter, Eugene, OR
Antony, Rev. Prasad, *M.S.S.C.C.* (CHR) Holy Trinity, Orangeburg, SC; St. Andrew, Barnwell, SC; St. Mary Mission, Allendale, SC; St. Theresa Mission, Springfield, SC
Antony, Rev. Reehan Soosai, *S.A.C.* '08 (FWT) Assumption of the Blessed Virgin Mary, Decatur, TX
Antony, Rev. Royson Menolickal, *O.F.M.Cap.* '98 (SYM) Retired. St. Joseph Syro-Malabar Catholic Mission Hudson Valley, New York of St. Thomas Syro-Malabar Catholic Diocese of Chicago, Buchanan, NY
Antony, Rev. Stanislaus Michael, '04 (LC) Holy Rosary, Owen, WI; St. Bernard-St. Hedwig Parish, Thorp, WI
Antony, Rev. Theophane, *OCD* '97 (FRS) St. Francis of Assisi, Bakersfield, CA
Antony, Rev. Varghese, (SAT) St. John Bosco, Natalia, TX
Antony, Rev. Varghese, '91 (SAT) Curia: Administration St. Andrew, Lytle, TX
Antony, Rev. Wilson, '09 (SYM) St. Alphonsa Syro-Malabar Catholic Church Baltimore, Halethorpe, MD
Antonysamy, Rev. Pushpa, *I.S.P.* '03 (AUS) [MON] Schoenstatt Fathers, Austin, TX
Antoo Alappat, Rev. George, '94 (SYM) St. Alphonsa Syro-Malabar Catholic Church, Austin, Texas, Inc. of St. Thomas Syro-Malabar Catholic Diocese of Chicago, Manor, TX
Antoszewski, Rev. Pawel, '96 (LAR) Sacred Heart, Cotulla, TX
Antoszewski, Rev. Pawel, '96 (LAR) Curia: Offices and Directors
Antunes, Rev. Ezio, '02 (NEW) Holy Trinity - Epiphany, Newark, NJ
Antunez, Rev. Roy, *S.J.* '71 (LA) [MON] Jesuit Community, Los Angeles, CA (>SJ) [MON] Sacred Heart Jesuit Center, Los Gatos, CA
Antunez-Olea, Rev. Bardo Fabian, '03 (TUC) Our Lady Queen of All Saints Roman Catholic Parish - Tucson, Tucson, AZ
Antweiler, Rev. Donald J., '73 (JC) Retired.
Antwi, Rev. Emmanuel, '21 (SAV) St. Joseph, Macon, GA
Antwi-Boasiako, Rev. Dominic, '81 (VIC) Curia: Leadership Queen of Peace, Sweet Home, TX; St. John the Baptist, Sweet Home, TX
Anumata, Rev. Christopher C., (MO) Curia: Offices and Directors
Anumba, Rev. Damian, (CAM) [MON] Villa Pieta. Missionaries of the Sacred Hearts of Jesus & Mary, Linwood, NJ
Anumba, Rev. Damian, (LEX) Sacred Heart, Corbin, KY
Anung, Rev. Ronelo, '92 (NY) Parish of St. John Nepomucene, St. Frances Cabrini, and St. John the Martyr, New York, NY; St. Frances Cabrini, New York, NY
Anusiem, Rev. Boniface, (NEW) Epiphany, Cliffside Park, NJ
Anuszewski, Rev. Albert Michael, *O.SS.T.* '91 (BAL) St. Mark, Catonsville, MD; [MON] Holy Trinity Monastery, Sykesville, MD
Anuszewski, Rev. Damian, *O.SS.T.* '79 (BAL) [MON] Holy Trinity Monastery, Sykesville, MD
Anuta, Rev. Hyginus Chuks, '97 (SFE) Holy Ghost, Albuquerque, NM
Anweting, Rev. Livinus, (BAL) St. Francis Xavier, Baltimore, MD; [HOS] St. Agnes HealthCare, Ascension Health, Baltimore, MD; [HOS] University of Maryland St. Joseph Medical Center, Towson, MD
Anweting, Rev. Livinus, '04 (NY) Parish of Annunciation-Our Lady of Fatima, Crestwood, NY
Anyaeche, Rev. Jude, (MO) Curia: Offices and Directors
Anyama, Very Rev. Vincent C., '09 (DAL) On Duty Outside Diocese. [SEM] Holy Trinity Seminary, Irving, TX
Anyamele, Rev. Faustinus, '06 (DEN) Our Lady of the Mountains Catholic Parish in Estes Park, Estes Park, CO
Anyanike, Rev. Vitalis E., '02 (OM) Our Lady of Lourdes-St. Adalbert Parish, Omaha, NE; St. Andrew Kim Taegon Catholic Community, Omaha, NE
Anyanwu, Rev. Cajetan Amaechi, *CMF* (SAT) St. Mary's, Fredericksburg, TX
Anyanwu, Rev. Christian, '79 (SFR) Church of the Nativity, Menlo Park, CA
Anyanwu, Rev. Christopher, '95 (BEL) St. Anthony, Oakdale, IL; St. Barbara, Okawville, IL
Anyaoku, Rev. Charles, '03 (BEL) St. Edward, Fairfield, IL; St. Stephen, Flora, IL
Anzoategui Peiro, Rev. Francisco J., '88 (BO) Curia: Pastoral Services St. Stephen, Framingham, MA
Anzora, Very Rev. Juan, '08 (ATL) Curia: Leadership St. Andrew Catholic Church, Roswell, Inc., Roswell, GA
Apassa, Rev. Cyril, '71 (RNO) Retired.
Apel, Rev. John A., *S.J.* '69 (STL) [COL] Saint Louis University, St. Louis, MO
Aperocho, Rev. Romil, '91 (ORL) Divine Mercy Catholic Community, Merritt Island, FL
Apetorgbor, Rev. Nicholas, (HON) St. Catherine, Kapaa, HI
Apfelbeck, Rev. Kurt J., '99 (LC) On Special Assignment. Curia: Leadership; Offices and Directors [MIS] Holy Cross (Seminary) Diocesan Center, La Crosse, WI
Apoldite, Rev. Msgr. Dennis A., '78 (TR) Curia: Leadership Parish of the Sacred Heart, Trenton, N.J., Trenton, NJ
Apolinar, Rev. Moises R., '81 (LA) St. Patrick, Los Angeles, CA
Apollonio, Rev. Nicholas, (BRK) St. Gabriel, East Elmhurst, NY
Aponte Rivera, Rev. Eliud, '86 (PCE) Sagrado Corazon de Jesus, Ensenada, PR; San Antonio Abad, Guanica, PR
Apostol, Rev. Moises A., '78 (RCK) St. Elizabeth Ann Seton, Crystal Lake, IL
Appanapalle, Rev. Madhu, *H.G.N.* '12 (STO) St. Anthony Church of Manteca (Pastor of), Manteca, CA
Apparcel, Rev. Gregory, (WDC) [SEM] Paulist Washington Community, Washington, DC
Appel, Rev. Paul J., '03 (DAV) Curia: Leadership Jesus Christ, Prince of Peace Roman Catholic Church of Clinton, Iowa, Clinton, IA
Appel, Rev. William A., '14 (COV) On Duty Outside Diocese. Archdiocese of Military Services Curia: (>MO) Offices and Directors
Appiagyei, Rev. Joseph Maxwell, (RIC) Richmond International Airport St. John the Evangelist, Highland Springs, VA; St. Patrick, Richmond, VA; St. Peter, Richmond, VA
Appiah, Rev. Anthony, '92 (ARL) St. Anthony, Falls Church, VA
Appiah, Rev. Kwaku John, '98 (KNX) On Special Assignment. Serving outside diocese Curia: (>MO) Offices and Directors
Appiasi, Very Rev. Samuel, '83 (VIC) Curia: Leadership; Offices and Directors Holy Family, Wharton, TX
Appiasi, Very Rev. Samuel K, (VIC) St. Joseph, Boling, TX
Applegate, Rev. Michael, (GAL) St. John of the Cross, New Caney, TX
Appleyard, Rev. Msgr. George, (E) Retired.
Appleyard, Rev. George, '68 (SJP) Retired.
Appleyard, Rt. Rev. Archmandrite George, '68 (SJP) Retired. Curia: Offices and Directors
Appleyard, Rev. Joseph A., *S.J.* '66 (BO) [MON] Campion Health & Wellness, Inc., Weston, MA
Appreh, Rev. Francis G., '96 (NSH) St. Vincent de Paul, Nashville, TN
Aquino, Rev. Alexander, '74 (SD) Retired.
Aquino, Rev. Francisco, '90 (ORL) Curia: Evangelization Divine Mercy Catholic Community, Merritt Island, FL
Aquino, Rev. Javier, '06 (MGZ) Immaculate Heart of Mary, Las Marias, PR
Aquino, Rev. Joel, '09 (FRS) Santa Rosa, Lone Pine, CA
Aquino, Rev. Joseph G., *M.S.* '69 (ATL) St. Ann Catholic Church, Marietta, Inc., Marietta, GA
Aquino, Rev. Msgr. Oscar A., '62 (NY) St. Malachy's, New York, NY
Aquino, Rev. Paul Malinit, *S.V.D.* '16 (DUB) [SEM] Divine Word College, Epworth, IA
Aquino, Rev. Peter M., '69 (NEW) Retired. Our Lady of Mount Carmel, Nutley, NJ
Aracil, Rev. Javier, *S.D.B.* '63 (NEW) [MON] The Salesian Community, Orange, NJ
Aracil, Rev. Javier, *S.D.B.* (NY) [RTR] Don Bosco Retreat Center and Marian Shrine, Stony Point, NY; [RTR] Marian Shrine, Stony Point, NY
Arackal, Rev. Bony, '93 (SAC) Pastor of SS. Peter and Paul Parish, Rocklin, a corporation sole, Rocklin, CA
Arackal, Rev. Joseph J., *V.C.* '67 (SYM) [MON] Vincentian House, Bensenville, IL
Arakkamparambil, Rev. Job, *O.F.M. Cap.* (DEN) [MON] San Antonio Friary, Denver, CO
Arakkaparambil, Rev. Job, *OFM Cap.* '09 (SYM) St. Thomas Syro-Malabar Catholic Mission, Denver, CO, Inc. of St. Thomas Syro-Malabar Catholic Diocese of Chicago, Denver, CO
Arana, Rev. Francisco, '64 (SJN) [SPF] Centro Medico de P.R., San Juan, PR
Aranciba Bermudez, Rev. Carlos A., '12 (CHI) St. Bede the Venerable and St. Denis Parish, Chicago, IL
Arango, Rev. Andres, '95 (PHX) St. William Roman Catholic Parish, Cashion, AZ
Arango, Rev. Gilberto, '75 (STO) St. Anthony Church of Manteca (Pastor of), Manteca, CA
Arango-Medina, Rev. Miguel, '65 (SAT) Retired.
Aranha, Rev. George, '75 (SJ) Santa Teresa, San Jose, CA
Arano-Ponce, Rev. Gerardo, '03 (KCK) Queen of the Holy Rosary, Bucyrus, KS
Araque, Rev. Alvaro U., '72 (STO) Retired. St. George Church (Pastor of), Stockton, CA
Araque, Rev. Andres A., '15 (WOR) Blessed Sacrament, Worcester, MA
Arata, Rev. Miguel A., '95 (NEW) On Duty Outside Diocese. Rooma Katoliku Kirik Kogudus, Tartu
Arattukulam, Rev. Varghese, '08 (GAL) Christ the King, Houston, TX
Araujo, Rev. Arturo, *S.J.* '99 (SEA) [COL] Seattle University, Seattle, WA
Arauz, Rev. Erick E., (SFR) Sacred Heart, Olema, CA
Aravindathu, Rev. Thadeus, '83 (NY) St. Patrick, Armonk, NY
Arboleda, Rev. Jorge W., '93 (STO) St. Joachim Church of Newman (Pastor of), Newman, CA
Arboleda Ibarra, Rev. Dairo Hernando, *O.S.S.T.* '03 (SJN) Ascension del Senor, Bayamon, PR
Arbuckle, Rev. Matthew J., '11 (LFT) Holy Trinity, Bryant, IN; Immaculate Conception, Portland, IN; St. Joseph, Winchester, IN; St. Mary, Union City, IN
Arcan, Rev. Lenjenie, '08 (FRS) St. John's Cathedral, Fresno, CA
Arce, Rev. Carlos N., '91 (R) Curia: Leadership St. Bernadette, Fuquay-Varina, NC
Arce, Rev. Diego, (NEW) St. Andrew, Westwood, NJ
Arce, Rev. Neil A., '05 (BEA) On Duty Outside Diocese. On Leave
Arceneaux, Very Rev. Chester C., '92 (LAF) Curia: Leadership Cathedral of St. John the Evangelist, Lafayette, LA
Arceneaux, Rev. Jules, '90 (LAF) On Administrative Leave.
Arceneaux, Rev. Louis, *C.M.* '66 (NO) [MON] Congregation of the Mission Western Province (Vincentians) (DePaul Residence), New Orleans, LA
Arceo, Rev. Ruben, *S.J.* '02 (SD) Pastor of Saint Francis of Assisi Catholic Parish, Vista, a corporation sole, Vista, CA; [MIS] Saint Francis of Assisi Catholic Parish in Vista, CA Real Property Support Corporation, Vista,

CA
Archambault, Rev. Donald, '70 (DET) Retired.
Archer, Rev. Charles J., '21 (STL) St. Peter Catholic Church, Kirkwood, Kirkwood, MO
Archer, Rev. Jeffrey S., '14 (BO) St. Elizabeth of Hungary, Acton, MA; St. Isidore, Acton, MA
Archer, Rev. Scott, '90 (PEO) St. Andrew, Fairbury, IL
Archibong, Rev. Cosmas, '88 (HRT) Chap, VA CT Health Care System, West Haven
Archibong, Rev. Cosmas P., (MO) Curia: Offices and Directors
Archibong, Rev. Felix, '15 (SAN) St. Ann's, Sonora, TX
Archibong, Rev. Felix, '15 (SAN) Curia: Advisory Boards, Commissions, Committees, and Councils
Archibong, Rev. Joseph, '10 (LR) St. Anne, Berryville, AR; St. Elizabeth of Hungary, Eureka Springs, AR
Arciga, Rev. Ephraim P., *M.S.C.* (SB) St. Catherine of Alexandria, Riverside, CA
Arcila, Rev. Manuel, (CHI) Mary, Mother of Martyrs, Des Plaines, IL
Arcila, Rev. Sergio, '01 (STO) St. Stanislaus Church (Pastor of), Modesto, CA
Arciniegas, Rev. Juan, '92 (RCK) Sacred Heart, Aurora, IL
Arcoleo, Rev. Douglas R., '98 (RVC) Curia: Leadership St. Catherine of Sienna, Franklin Square, NY
Arcosa, Rev. Carl Tacuyan, '07 (OAK) Curia: Leadership; Offices and Directors St. Michael, Livermore, CA
Arcuri, Rev. Dominic, '18 (NO) St. Charles Borromeo, Destrehan, LA
Ardagh, Rev. Brian, '95 (CHI) St. Alphonsus and St. Patrick Parish, Lemont, IL
Ardianto, Rev. Hendrik, *S.C.J.* (JKS) Christ the King, Southaven, MS; Good Shepherd Catholic Church, Robinsonville, MS; Holy Spirit, Hernando, MS; Queen of Peace, Olive Branch, MS; St. Gregory the Great, Senatobia, MS; St. Joseph, Holly Springs, MS; [MON] St. Michael Community House, Nesbit, MS
Ardila, Rev. Carlos, '21 (WOR) Curia: Offices and Directors Saint John Paul II, Southbridge, MA
Ardis, Rev. John B, *CSP* '90 (SFR) Old St. Mary's Cathedral & Chinese Mission, San Francisco, CA
Ardouin, Rev. Msgr. Beaubrun, '93 (NEW) Curia: Offices and Directors St. Leo, Irvington, NJ
Arechabala, Rev. Daniel J., '15 (PH) Curia: Advisory Boards, Commissions, Committees, and Councils St. Agnes, West Chester, PA
Arechua, Rev. Ramon J., '96 (GAL) St. Raphael the Archangel, Houston, TX
Areepparampil, Rev. Daison, '99 (TR) St. James, Red Bank, NJ
Areiza, Rev. Juan F., '08 (ATL) St. Pius X Catholic Church, Conyers, Inc., Conyers, GA
Arejola, Rev. Rodolfo G., '68 (AGN) Retired.
Arel, Rev. Donald, *OMI* '64 (OAK) Retired. [MON] Missionary Oblates of Mary Immaculate Western, Oakland, CA
Arellano, Rev. Adondee, *M.S.* (HON) St. Joseph, Waipahu, HI
Arellano, Rev. Jesus, *C.M.* '73 (NY) Holy Agony, New York, NY; [MON] Vincentian Fathers (Padres Paules Community (Vincentians) Inc.), New York, NY
Arellano, Rev. Mario, '96 (LA) San Francisco, Los Angeles, CA
Arellano Devia, Rev. Ramon J., '03 (PCE) Nuestra Senora de la Medalla Milagrosa, Castaner, PR
Arenas, Rev. Carlos Urrego, '94 (RVC) Our Holy Redeemer, Freeport, NY
Arends, Rev. Todd, '02 (CR) Assumption, Barnesville, MN; St. Cecilia (Sabin), Sabin, MN
Arens, Rev. John F., '74 (BO) St. Bartholomew, Needham, MA; St. Sebastian's School, Inc., Needham, MA
Arens, Very Rev. Patrick O., '00 (WIN) Curia: Advisory Boards, Commissions, Committees, and Councils; Offices and Directors Basilica of St. Stanislaus, Winona, MN; St. John Nepomucene, Winona, MN
Arens, Rev. Tyler Lee, '22 (LAN) St. Mary Star of the Sea Parish Jackson, Jackson, MI
Arensberg, Rev. Patrick J., '12 (MOB) Corpus Christi Parish, Mobile, Mobile, AL
Ares, Rev. Francisco J., '83 (BRK) Chap, Wyckoff Heights Hosp St. Rita, Brooklyn, NY
Arevalo, Rev. Joseph V., '65 (RVC) [MON] St Pius X Residence for Retired Priests LLC, Ronkonkoma, NY
Arey, Rev. Michael, '19 (CR) St. Charles Catholic Church of Pennington, Pennington, MN; St. Philip's, Bemidji, MN; [CAM] Holy Spirit Newman Center, Bemidji, MN
Argano, Rev. Christopher, '09 (NY) Parish of Annunciation-Our Lady of Fatima, Crestwood, NY; St. Columba, Chester, NY; St. Mary, Washingtonville, NY; [SEM] Cathedral Prep Program, Yonkers, NY
Argentieri, Rev. Nicholas J., '08 (PIT) Children's Hosp, Allegheny Cty Our Lady of the Angels, Pittsburgh, PA; St. Maria Goretti Parish, Pittsburgh, PA
Argentino, Rev. Ralph J., '68 (SP) Retired.
Arguelles, Rev. I. Anthony, '74 (BLX) Retired. Curia: Leadership
Arias, Rev. Alfredo, (FRS) St. Isidore the Farmer, Orange Cove, CA
Arias, Rev. Ariel, '85 (RNO) Retired.
Arias, Rev. Guillermo, *S.J.* '72 (MIA) Belen Jesuit Preparatory School, Inc., Miami, FL
Arias, Rev. Hernan, '85 (PAT) On Sick Leave. Curia: Administration St. Margaret of Scotland, Morristown, NJ; [EFT] Catholic Foundation of the Diocese of Paterson, Inc., Clifton, NJ
Arias, Rev. Jesus J., '92 (MIA) Good Shepherd, Miami, FL
Arias, Rev. Jorge, *O.P.* (TR) St. Rose of Lima, Freehold, NJ
Arias, Rev. Jose Antonio, *O.A.R.* '60 (ORG) Our Lady of the Pillar, Santa Ana, CA
Arias Galvis, Rev. Rolando, '13 (BGP) Saint Mary Parish Corporation of Stamford, Stamford, CT
Arias Salazar, Rev. Jorge Eduardo, '03 (SFR) St. Matthew, San Mateo, CA
Aribe, Rev. Stephen, '55 (NEW) Chap, Trinitas Rgnl Med Ctr, Elizabeth St. Leo, Irvington, NJ; [HOS] Trinitas Regional Medical Center (Sisters of Charity of Saint Elizabeth and Elizabethtown Healthcare Foundation), Elizabeth, NJ
Arickappalil, Rev. Isaac, (MIA) St. Andrew, Coral Springs, FL
Arico, Rev. Carl J., '60 (NEW) Retired. St. Vincent de Paul, Bayonne, NJ
Ariko, Rev. John Stephen, *A.J.* (SAV) Holy Redeemer, McRae, GA; Immaculate Conception, Dublin, GA; St. Mark, Eastman, GA
Arikotla, Rev. Vidya S., '03 (GI) Curia: Offices and Directors Holy Spirit, North Platte, NE
Arimboor, Rev. Xavier, '91 (GF) St. Ann's Cathedral, Great Falls, MT; [MIS] Heisey Community Center at St. Ann's, Great Falls, MT
Arimond, Rev. James C.L., *S.J.* (DET) [MON] Colombiere Center, Clarkston, MI
Arinze, Very Rev. Paul Ugo, '99 (MAD) St. John Vianney Cure of Ars, Janesville, WI; St. Mary's Congregation, Janesville, WI
Aririguzo, Rev. Kentigern, *M.S.S.C.C.* (CHR) Our Lady of the Valley, Gloverville, SC; St. Mary of the Immaculate Conception, Edgefield, SC
Arisman, Rev. Steven M., '14 (SFD) St. Francis Solanus, Quincy, IL
Aristil, Rev. Edmond, *C.S.Sp.* '03 (CHI) St. John Neumann, Homewood, IL
Arisukwu, Rev. Vincent, (BAL) Christ the King Roman Catholic Congregation, Inc., Glen Burnie, MD; St. Bernadette, Severn, MD
Ariwaodo, Rev. Augustine, '13 (AUS) Holy Family, Copperas Cove, TX
Arizpe, Rev. Samuel, '87 (BWN) Hosp Ministry Basilica of Our Lady of San Juan del Valle-National Shrine, San Juan, TX
Arkins, Rev. Michael J, *SSS* '77 (CLV) St. Paschal Baylon, Highland Heights, OH
Arle, Rev. David, '84 (VEN) Retired.
Arledge, Rev. Joseph H., '97 (OKL) St. Patrick Church, Oklahoma City, OK
Arlia, Rev. William, *O.F.M.Cap.* '06 (WIL)
Arlotta, Rev. Jack, '92 (NY) St. Joseph, Florida, NY; St. Stephen, Warwick, NY
Armano, Rev. Patrick S., '03 (BO) Austin Preparatory School, Reading, MA
Armato, Rev. Robert J., '95 (BRK) St. Margaret, Middle Village, NY
Armbruster, Rev. Timothy, *C.PP.S.* '01 (DAV) St. Mary Church of Centerville, Iowa, Centerville, IA; St. Patrick Church of Melrose, Iowa, Melrose, IA; [EFT] St. Mary's Foundation of Centerville, Centerville, IA
Armbruster, Rev. Timothy, *C.PP.S.* '01 (KC) [MIS] St. Gaspar Society, Liberty, MO
Armenio, Rev. Peter V., '80 (CHI) [MIS] Prelature of the Holy Cross and Opus Dei, Chicago, IL
Armenio, Very Rev. Peter V., '80 (POD) Curia: Leadership
Armenta, Rev. Benito, (LA) St. Martha, Valinda, CA
Armentrout, Rev. Benjamin, (KC) On Special Assignment. Bishop LeBlond HS, St. Joseph Cathedral of St. Joseph, St. Joseph, MO; St. Mary Catholic Church, St. Joseph, MO
Armistead, Rev. Msgr. John M., '71 (STO) Retired.
Arms, Rev. Michael M., '68 (STP) Retired.
Armstrong, Rev. Anthony, *O.Carm.* (VEN) Our Lady of Mount Carmel Parish in Osprey, Inc., Osprey, FL
Armstrong, Rev. Christopher R., '80 (CIN) Curia: Administration [SEM] Mount St. Mary's Seminary of the West, Cincinnati, OH
Armstrong, Rev. John F., *S.J.* '78 (STL) [MON] Leo Brown Jesuit Community, St. Louis, MO; [MON] USA Central & Southern Province, Society of Jesus, St. Louis, MO
Armstrong, Rev. John F., *S.J.* '78 (NO) [MON] Jesuit Provincial Office (Catholic Society of Religious and Literary Education), New Orleans, LA
Armstrong, Rev. Regis, *O.F.M.Cap.* '67 (WDC) [COL] Catholic University of America, The, Washington, DC
Armstrong, Rev. Richard, '09 (SJP) On Leave. Curia: Offices and Directors
Armstrong, Rev. Rodney J, *SSJ* (GAL) Our Mother of Mercy, Houston, TX
Arnaiz, Rev. Domingo Pon-an, *MHM* '02 (NY) Our Lady of Mount Carmel, White Plains, NY; Parish of St. John the Evangelist and Our Lady of Mount Carmel, White Plains, NY; [MON] Mill Hill Fathers Residence, Hartsdale, NY
Arnao, Rev. Thomas V., '82 (RVC) Curia: Leadership
Arnaud, Rev. Michael, '75 (LAF) Retired.
Arnberg, Rev. Todd, '76 (SAG) Retired. On Duty Outside Diocese. Denver, CO
Arneaud, Rev. Allan, (RVC) The Roman Catholic Church of Saint Rose of Lima, Massapequa, NY
Arnett, Rev. Russell L., '11 (MIL) Congregation of the Resurrection, Allenton, WI; St. Lawrence Congregation, Hartford, WI; St. Peter's Congregation, Slinger, WI
Arnhols, Rev. Msgr. Richard J., '73 (NEW) St. John the Evangelist, Bergenfield, NJ
Arnister, Rev. Msgr. Edward J., '79 (TR) Curia: Canonical Services; Leadership St. Rose, Belmar, NJ
Arnold, Rev. Chad, '10 (WCH) Curia: Offices and Directors [EFT] Priests' Retirement and Education Fund of Wichita, Wichita, KS
Arnold, Rev. Erik J., '99 (BAL) St. John the Evangelist, Severna Park, MD
Arnold, Rev. John P., '98 (TUC) On Special Assignment. Curia: Advisory Boards, Commissions, Committees, and Councils; Consultative Bodies; Leadership; Offices and Directors; Organizations (affiliated, inter-Diocesan, miscellaneous/other); Tribunal Saint Mark Roman Catholic Parish - Tucson, Oro Valley, AZ
Arnold, Rev. Rex A., '04 (OKL) Christ the King, Oklahoma City, OK
Arnold, Rev. Seth, '22 (WCH) Church of the Magdalen, Wichita, KS
Arnold, Rev. Wayne H., '00 (MEM) St. Jude the Apostle Catholic Church, Selmer, TN; St. Mary Church, Bolivar, TN
Arnold, Rev. William, '18 (MIL) Congregation of the Holy Family, Reeseville, WI; St. Columbkille, Columbus, WI; St. John's Congregation, Clyman, WI; St. Katharine Drexel Parish, Beaver Dam, WI
Arnold, Rev. William L., '80 (COL) Holy Spirit, Columbus, OH; St. Philip the Apostle, Columbus, OH
Arnoldt, Rev. David L., '68 (SAV) Retired.
Arnoldt, Rev. David L., '68 (WIN) Retired.
Arnone, Rev. Alan, '80 (SJ) On Leave.
Arnone, Rev. Leo F., '93 (ALT) St. Aloysius, Cresson, PA; St. Francis Xavier, Cresson, PA
Arnoult, Rev. Paul, '02 (SFR) St. Cecilia, San Francisco, CA
Arnout, Rev. Eric A., '96 (ALN) Assumption B.V.M., Slatington, PA
Arnsparger, Rev. Roger K., '77 (CHL) Curia: Leadership Basilica of St. Lawrence, Asheville, NC; [MIS] Charlotte Catholic Women's Group, Charlotte, NC
Arnzen, Rev. Mark, '05 (SJ) Curia: Leadership; Offices and Directors St. Lawrence, the Martyr, Santa Clara, CA
Arocho, Rev. Marcelino, '88 (MGZ) San Sebastian Martir, San Sebastian, PR
Arockia Dass, Rev. Sengole, *O. Praem.* '09 (GB) St. John, Seymour, WI; St. Sebastian, Isaar, WI; [MON] St. Norbert Abbey, De Pere, WI
Arockiadoss, Rev. Antony, '03 (MET) Curia: Leadership
Arockiam, Rev. Arockiam, '02 (BR) Congregation Of St Paul The Apostle Roman Catholic Church, East Baton Rouge Parish, Baton Rouge, LA
Arockiam, Rev. Michael Arputham, '78 (NY) Chap, Richmond Univ Med Ctr, Staten Island
Arockiam, Rev. Michaelsami, '84 (BEL) Curia: Offices and Directors St. Mary, Belleville, IL
Arockiam, Rev. Panneer Selvam, '91 (JKS) All Saints, Belzoni, MS; St. Mary, Yazoo City, MS
Arockiam, Rev. SamyDurai, *O.S.M* '99 (LA) Divine Saviour, Los Angeles, CA; St. Ann, Los Angeles, CA
Arockiaraj, Rev. Chris, *P.S.S.* (WDC) [SEM] Theological

College of the Catholic University of America, Washington, DC
Arockiaraj, Rev. Inniah Christy, *P.S.S.* '95 (BAL) [MIS] St. Mary's Seminary & University, Baltimore, MD; [MON] Society of St. Sulpice, Province of the United States, Baltimore, MD
Arockiasamy, Rev. Arockiadoss, '13 (LEX) St. Joseph, Winchester, KY
Arockiasamy, Rev. Chinnappan, *MSFS* (SAT) St. Louis, Castroville, TX
Arockiasamy, Rev. Joseph, '85 (ALB) Curia: Leadership St. Joseph, Worcester, NY; St. Vincent de Paul, Cobleskill, NY
Arockiasamy, Rev. Leo, *H.G.N.* '07 (SPC) Curia: Deaneries Immaculate Heart of Mary, Mansfield, MO; Sacred Heart, Mountain Grove, MO
Arockiasamy, Rev. Prabhu, *HGN* (MOB) Our Lady of Lourdes Parish, Mobile, AL
Arogyasami, Rev. John J., *I.M.S.* '89 (BUF) St. Mark, Kendall, NY; St. Mary, Holley, NY
Arokiasamy, Rev. Hendry Jesu Rajan, *H.G.N.* (SEA)
Arokiasamy, Rev. Joseph Lawrence, *HGN* '16 (PBL) Our Lady of the Annunciation, Springfield, CO; St. Frances of Rome, Holly, CO; St. Francis De Sales-Our Lady of Guadalupe, Lamar, CO
Arokiasamy, Rev. Kulan-Daisamy, '71 (DET) St. Veronica Parish Eastpointe, Eastpointe, MI
Arokiasamy, Rev. Raj, (LUB) Our Lady of Guadalupe, Snyder, TX
Arokisamy, Rev. Arokiades, (LEX) St. Patrick, Mount Sterling, KY
Arokiyam, Rev. Antony, '99 (WIN) Queen of Peace, Lyle, MN; Sacred Heart, Adams, MN; St. John's, Adams, MN; St. Peter's, Rose Creek, MN
Arolaiadoss, Rev. Michael Irudayanathan Franklin, *S.D.C.* '13 (LAN) [PRE] St. Louis Center for Exceptional Children & Adults, Chelsea, MI
Arouje, Rev. Lonachan W., '70 (STO) St. Andrew Church of San Andreas (Pastor of), San Andreas, CA
Arputham, Rev. Arul Francis, (SAT) St. Anthony Mary Claret, San Antonio, TX
Arputharaj, Rev. Selvam, *HGN* (MOB) St. John the Baptist, Grand Bay, AL; [MON] Divine Mercy Province of Heralds of Good News, Inc., Mobile, AL
Arraiza, Friar Luis Gerardo, *OFM, Cap.* (FWT) Our Lady of Guadalupe, Fort Worth, TX
Arralde, Rev. Ambrose, *O.P.* (BAL) SS. Philip and James, Baltimore, MD
Arrambide, Rev. James C., *C.Ss.R.* '73 (BR) Congregation Of St. Gerard Majella Roman Catholic Church, Parish Of East Baton Rouge, Louisiana, Baton Rouge, LA; [MIS] Redemptorist Fathers of Baton Rouge, Inc., Baton Rouge, LA; [MON] St. Gerard Residence, Baton Rouge, LA
Arrando, Rev. Angelo S., '71 (BGP) Retired.
Arras, Rev. Cesar, *C.R.* '18 (PBL) St. Ignatius Parish, Ignacio, CO
Arrazola, Rev. Rodrigo A., '01 (HBG) Sacred Heart of Jesus, Cornwall, PA
Arredondo, Rev. Francisco, (NEW) [MON] Capuchin Friars - Province of the Sacred Stigmata of St. Francis, Union City, NJ
Arredondo, Friar Francisco, (WIL) [MON] Capuchin Franciscan Friars, St. Francis of Assisi Friary, Wilmington, DE
Arreola, Rev. Alberto, '02 (LA) Sacred Heart, Pomona, CA; Santa Rosa, San Fernando, CA
Arriaga, Rev. Joaquin S., '97 (FRS) On Academic Leave.
Arriagada, Very Rev. Pedro Pablo, '14 (POD) Curia: Clergy and Religious Services
Arribas, Rev. Santiago, *C.M.* '66 (SJN) Curia: Offices and Directors [MIS] Servicios Pastorales Paules, San Juan, PR
Arrieta Correa, Rev. Juan Carlos, '09 (CHI) St. Pio of Pietrelcino Parish, Chicago, IL
Arrieta Viloria, Rev. Isaac, (LA) St. Paul, Los Angeles, CA; St. Rose of Lima, Maywood, CA
Arriola, Rev. James, (MIA) Mother of Christ, Miami, FL
Arriola, Rev. Ricardo, '19 (GAL) St. Bartholomew the Apostle, Katy, TX
Arrizurieta, Rev. Candido, *C.M.* '54 (NY) [MON] Vincentian Fathers (Padres Paules Community (Vincentians) Inc.), New York, NY
Arrouk, Rev. Georges, (SAM) Saints Joachim and Anne Maronite Catholic Church, Inc., Allentown, PA
Arroyabe, Rev. Pastor, (CGS) Curia: Leadership El Salvador, Caguas, PR
Arroyave, Rev. Jesus Rodrigo, '96 (TYL) Our Lady of Guadalupe, Tyler, TX
Arroyave, Rev. Luis Fernando, '88 (TYL) Our Lady of Guadalupe, Diboll, TX
Arroyo, Rev. Msgr. Brigido U., '61 (AGN) Retired.
Arroyo, Rev. Edward, *S.J.* '75 (STL) [MIS] Office, St. Louis, MO
Arroyo, Rev. Jose, '18 (FTW) St. Paul of the Cross, Columbia City, IN
Arroyo, Rev. Mario J., '77 (GAL) St. Cyril of Alexandria, Houston, TX
Arruda, Rev. Henry S., '67 (FR) Retired. Curia: Advisory Boards, Commissions, Committees, and Councils
Arsenault, Rev. James M., '89 (RIC) St. Elizabeth, Richmond, VA; St. Michael, Glen Allen, VA
Arsenault, Rev. Joseph, *S.S.A.* '00 (KCK) Curia: Advisory Boards, Commissions, Committees, and Councils; Leadership; Tribunal Holy Family, Kansas City, KS; St. John the Baptist, Kansas City, KS; [CON] Servants of Mary, Ministers to the Sick, Kansas City, KS; [MIS] Society of St. Augustine - Public Association of the Faithful, Kansas City, KS
Arsenault, Rev. Joseph B., *M.M.* '59 (NY) Retired.
Arsenault, Rev. Joseph G., (BO) Retired.
Arseneau, Rev. Vernon, '72 (JOL) Retired.
Arseneault, Rev. David J., '81 (ALT) On Leave.
Arstikaitis, Rev. Audrius, '02 (LIT) Curia: Education
Arteaga, Rev. Pedro, *M.Sp.S.* '97 (P) [MON] Missionaries of the Holy Spirit, M.Sp.S., Milwaukie, OR; [SEM] Felix Rougier House of Studies, Mount Angel, OR
Arteaga, Rev. Peter, *M.Sp.S.* '97 (P) [SEM] Mount Angel Seminary, Saint Benedict, OR
Arteaga y Pinon, Rev. Eulalio, *FdCC* '09 (SFE) San Jose-Albuquerque, Albuquerque, NM
Arthasseril, Rev. Jerome S., '66 (NEW) Retired. Our Lady of the Lake, Verona, NJ
Arthur, Rev. Charles, (BLX) Our Lady of Fatima, Biloxi, MS
Arthur, Rev. James, '83 (MIL) Congregation of All Saints Catholic Church, Milwaukee, WI; Congregation of St. Martin de Porres Catholic Church, Milwaukee, WI
Artman, Rev. Brandon, (PH) On Special Assignment. Asst Master Ceremonies, Saint Anastasia Rec, Newtown Square
Artman, Rev. Brandon M., '18 (PH) St. Anastasia, Newtown Square, PA
Artmann, Rev. Robert J., '64 (MIL) Retired.
Arts, Rev. Paul-Louis, '64 (SC) Retired. Curia: Leadership
Arturi, Rev. Bradley K., '62 (POD) Curia: Clergy and Religious Services
Arturi, Rev. Bradley K., '62 (NY) [MIS] Personal Prelature, ,
Arturo-Gonzalez, Rev. Juan Andres, *C.O.* '97 (R) Holy Name of Jesus Cathedral, Raleigh, NC
Arty, Rev. Rodolphe, *C.S.C.* '94 (JOL) St. Patrick, Joliet, IL
Artymovych, Rev. Roman, '12 (STN) Curia: Offices and Directors SS. Volodymyr and Olha, Chicago, IL
Artysiewicz, Rev. Chester, *G.H.M* '73 (R) Holy Spirit Catholic Church, Windsor, NC; Holy Trinity, Williamston, NC
Artysiewicz, Rev. Chet, '73 (CIN) [MON] Headquarters of Glenmary Home Missioners (The Home Missioners of America), Fairfield, OH
Arulanandu, Rev. Alphonse, '93 (BUF) Our Lady of Charity, Buffalo, NY
Arulandu, Rev. Suvakin, '04 (NO) St. Louis King of France, Metairie, LA
Arulandu, Rev. Thaines, '82 (FAR) Immaculate Heart of Mary Church of Rock Lake, Rock Lake, ND; St. Joachim's Church of Rolla, Rolla, ND
Arulappa, Rev. Devaraj, '86 (TYL) On Duty Outside Diocese.
Arulappan, Rev. Albert, *H.G.N.* (SEA) St. Francis, Friday Harbor, WA
Arulappan, Rev. Francis, *H.G.N.* '01 (SEA) Chap, Clallam Bay Correction Ctr; Clearwater / Olympic Corr…
Arularasu, Rev. Mathias, (CC) [HOS] CHRISTUS Spohn Hospital Corpus Christi - Shoreline, Corpus Christi, TX
Aruldurai, Rev. Charles, *H.G.N.* (MAN) Saints Mary and Joseph, Salem, NH
Arulraj, Rev. Joseph, *MSFS* '14 (GAL) St. Thomas Aquinas, Sugar Land, TX
Arulraj, Rev. Karunaya Xavier, (BO) St. Anthony of Padua, Revere, MA
Arulsamy, Rev. Arputham, '90 (BRK) Our Lady of Angels, Brooklyn, NY
Arulsamy, Rev. Gnanavoli, *SVD* '15 (BEA) St. Pius X, Beaumont, TX
Arulsamy, Rev. Jeganathan, *HGN* '10 (LUB) St. Mary, Spur, TX; [MIS] St. Joseph, Crosbyton, TX
Arumugam, Rev. Antony Raj Kumar, *H.G.N.* (GF) Curia: Leadership St. Joseph, Plentywood, MT; St. Philip Bonitus, Scobey, MT; [MON] Mary Queen of Apostles Province HGN, Inc., Plentywood, MT
Arvizu, Rev. Hector, '18 (TYL) St. Francis of Assisi, Gilmer, TX
Arvlanandu, Rev. John Kennady, *MMI* '13 (NY) Holy Cross, Callicoon, NY
Arwady, Rev. James Fredrick, '10 (DET) St. Christopher Parish Marysville, Marysville, MI
Arwady, Rev. Raymond E., '09 (DET) St. Augustine Parish Richmond, Richmond, MI
Aryanto, Rev. Sonny, *C.I.C.M.* '16 (SAT) St. James the Apostle, San Antonio, TX
Arzate, Rev. Roman, '96 (LA) St. Cecilia, Los Angeles, CA
Asagba, Very Rev. Francis Kwame, '91 (BRK) Curia: Leadership St. Bonaventure-St. Benedict the Moor RC Church, Jamaica, NY
Asalemo, Rev. Asalemo, '08 (SPP) Christ the King, Pago Pago, AS
Asalemo, Rev. Asalemo, '08 (SPP) Curia: Offices and Directors
Asamoah-Bekoe, Rev. Emmanuel Kofi, '10 (LC) Holy Rosary, Durand, WI; Sacred Heart of Jesus, Mondovi, WI; St. Mary's Assumption, Durand, WI; [EFT] St. Mary Catholic School Endowment Trust, Durand, WI
Asante, Rev. Augustine N., '98 (VIC) St. Anthony's, Columbus, TX
Asante, Rev. Eric K., '12 (WOR) Sacred Heart of Jesus-St. Catherine of Sweden, Worcester, MA
Asare, Rev. Dominic, *SVD* (SD) Pastor of Our Lady of the Sacred Heart Catholic Parish, San Diego, a corporation sole, San Diego, CA; [MIS] Our Lady of the Sacred Heart Catholic Parish in San Diego, CA Real Property Support Corporation, San Diego, CA
Asare, Very Rev. John, '97 (RIC) Curia: Deaneries St. Mary, Blacksburg, VA
Ascan, Rev. Romeo, *A.M.* (NY) St. Pius X, Scarsdale, NY
Ascencio, Rev. Joseph A., '82 (COL) On Duty Outside Diocese. Chap, Federal Prison System, Florence, CO
Ascheman, Rev. Thomas J., *S.V.D.* '82 (DUB) [SEM] Divine Word College, Epworth, IA
Aschenbrener, Rev. Thomas G., '03 (CHI) St. Mary of Perpetual Help, All Saints and St. Anthony, Chicago, IL
Aschenbrenner, Rev. George, *S.J.* '65 (PH) Retired.
Ascik, Rev. Peter, '17 (CHL) Curia: Leadership
Ascik, Rev. Peter, '17 (CHL) St. Mary Help of Christians, Shelby, NC
Asebias, Rev. Anacleto, '80 (BRK) Ascension, Elmhurst, NY
Aseleku, Rev. Samuel, (RVC) Chap, St Charles Hosp, Port Jefferson, New York
Aseleku, Rev. Samuel Pius, (RVC) St. Gerard Majella, Port Jefferson Station, NY
Asencio, Rev. Ivan, '13 (DAL) On Administrative Leave.
Asenjo, Rev. Cristobal, *I.S.P.* '13 (AUS) [MON] Schoenstatt Fathers, Austin, TX
Asenjo, Rev. Jose Maria, '65 (GAL) Retired.
Asghedom, Rev. Tesfaldet, '85 (LA) Sacred Heart, Los Angeles, CA
Ashbaugh, Rev. William A., '93 (LAN) Curia: Offices and Directors St. Thomas the Apostle Parish Ann Arbor, Ann Arbor, MI
Ashbeck, Rev. David, (PHX) St Clare of Assisi Roman Catholic Parish Surprise, Surprise, AZ
Ashbeck, Rev. David K., '68 (GB) Retired.
Ashe, Rev. John F., '63 (NOR) Retired.
Ashe, Rev. Joseph C., '76 (NOR) Christ the King, Old Lyme, CT
Ashe, Rev. Kevin P., '63 (NEW) Retired.
Ashenbrenner, Rev. Robert D., *O.S.F.S.* '54 (WIL) Retired. [MON] Retirement and Assisted Care Facility, Childs, MD
Ashibuogwu, Rev. Michael, '00 (PHX) Holy Spirit Roman Catholic Parish, Tempe, AZ
Ashkar, Chorbishop Dominic, (WDC) Chap, National Insts of Health, Clinical Ctr, Bethesda, MD
Ashkar, Rev. Msgr. Dominic, (SAM) Retired.
Ashman, Rev. Robert, '86 (NY) Immaculate Conception, Irvington, NY
Ashmore, Rev. Nicholas, '19 (KCK) St. Catherine, Emporia, KS; St. Joseph, Olpe, KS
Ashmore, Rev. Ronald M., '76 (IND) Retired.
Asia, Rev. Thomas Frederick, '98 (LA) St. Martha, Valinda, CA
Asiegbulem, Rev. Chibueze, '22 (CIN) St. Albert the Great, Kettering, OH; St. Charles Borromeo, Kettering, OH
Asih, Rev. Paul, *M.S.P.* (BIR) St. Francis of Assisi Catholic Parish, Bessemer, Bessemer, AL
Asika, Rev. Raphael I., *M.S.P.* '92 (BR) St. Catherine of

Siena, Donaldsonville, LA
Asir, Rev. Antony, '82 (RVC) Curia: Offices and Directors St. Thomas More, Hauppauge, NY
Asirvatham, Rev. Joseph, *H.G.N.* '09 (SAL) St. Francis of Assisi Parish, St. Francis, Inc., St. Francis, KS; St. John Nepomucene Parish, Beardsley, Inc., Beardsley, KS; St. Joseph Parish, Bird City, Inc., Bird City, KS
Asirvatham, Rev. Selvam J., '93 (TR) St. Joseph, Toms River, NJ
Asma, Rev. Lawrence F., *C.M.* '83 (ALB) On Special Assignment. Chap to Daughters of Charity, Albany [MON] Vincentian Fathers Residence, Albany, NY
Asma, Rev. Lawrence F., *C.M.* '83 (STL) [MON] Congregation of the Mission, Perryville, MO
Asmar, Rev. Msgr. Maroun, '93 (SAM) Retired.
Asoh, Rev. Paul, (CHL) St. Mary, Sylva, NC
Asomah, Rev. Stephen, (SCR) Our Lady of the Snows, Clarks Summit, PA
Asomkase, Rev. Francis, *S.S.J.* (BAL) St. Peter Claver, Baltimore, MD; St. Pius V, Baltimore, MD
Asproni, Rev. Francesco S., '11 (AGN) Chap, Guam Mem Hosp & Guam Rgnl Med Ctr San Vicente Ferrer and San Roke, Barrigada, GU
Assalone, Rev. John T., '09 (LAV) Curia: Advisory Boards, Commissions, Committees, and Councils St. Francis of Assisi, Henderson, NV
Assamah, Rev. Raphael, (DM) St. Theresa of the Child Jesus, Des Moines, IA
Assamah, Rev. Raphael, (DM) Curia: Offices and Directors
Asselin, Rev. Jason, '06 (FAR) Curia: Leadership St. Boniface Church of Walhalla, Walhalla, ND; Sts. Nereus & Achilleus Church of Neche, Neche, ND
Assenga, Rev. Laurent, *A.L.C.P.* '86 (PMB) Our Lady Queen of the Apostles, Royal Palm Beach, FL
Assi, Rev. Nicholas, '72 (LA) Retired.
Assim, Rev. Dominic, '03 (DM) Assumption of the Blessed Virgin Mary, Granger, IA
Assisi, Rev. Francis, *O.I.C.* '72 (MCE) Curia: Advisory Boards, Commissions, Committees, and Councils
Assogba, Rev. Simon, *SMA* '12 (PRT) Parish of the Precious Blood, Caribou, ME (>NEW) [MON] Society of African Missions, Provincialate, S.M.A. Fathers, Tenafly, NJ
Ast, Rev. Nicholas K., *O.S.B.* '01 (OKL) [MON] St. Gregory's Abbey (Benedictine Fathers of Sacred Heart Mission, Inc.), Shawnee, OK
Astarita, Rev. Joseph J., '03 (NEW) Curia: Advisory Boards, Commissions, Committees, and Councils St. Joseph, East Rutherford, NJ
Astigarraga, Rev. Oscar, '18 (WDC) Curia: Consultative Bodies St. Bartholomew, Bethesda, MD
Astillero, Friar John, (NOR) [MON] Marian Friary of Our Lady of Guadalupe, Griswold, CT
Astrab, Rev. Anthony, (SP) Church of the Nativity, Brandon, FL
Astrab, Rev. Anthony, '19 (SP) Curia: Pastoral Services
Astudillo, Rev. Roland, '89 (LA) Our Lady of Lourdes, Tujunga, CA
Astudillo, Rev. Tony P., '73 (LA) St. Lorenzo Ruiz, Walnut, CA
Asucan, Rev. Julian I., '00 (BUR) St. Augustine, Montpelier, VT
Asue, Rev. Daniel, (MO) Curia: Offices and Directors
Asuncion, Rev. Alfred, '13 (DAL) Chap, Parkland Health & Hosp System, Dallas
Asuncion, Rev. Leonardo, '79 (OAK) St. Rose of Lima, Crockett, CA
Asuquo, Rev. Godwin Nsikan-Ubom, '03 (RCK) Curia: Offices and Directors St. Patrick Church, McHenry, IL
Ata, Friar Nader, *O.F.M.Conv.* (SY) Assumption B.V.M., Syracuse, NY; [MIS] Franciscorps, Inc., Syracuse, NY
Ata, Rev. Nader, *OFM, Conv.* '17 (BRK) Most Holy Trinity - Saint Mary, Brooklyn, NY
Atamian, Msgr. Andon, (OLN) St. Vartan's, Farmington Hills, MI
Atanasio, Rev. David, '14 (RVC) Curia: Offices and Directors St. John the Baptist Diocesan High School, West Islip, NY; St. Joseph, Babylon, NY
Atanga, Rev. Martin B., '91 (TUC) Curia: Consultative Bodies
Atanga, Rev. Martin B., '91 (TUC) On Special Assignment. Curia: Leadership The Roman Catholic Parish of Our Lady of Lourdes - Benson, Benson, AZ
Atangana, Rev. Edouard, '02 (BWN) St. Joseph the Worker, McAllen, TX
Atcher, Rev. Joseph, *O.Carm.* '76 (JOL) [MON] St. Simon Stock Priory, Darien, IL
Atem, Very Rev. Henry, '08 (ATL) Curia: Leadership St. Lawrence Catholic Church, Lawrenceville, Inc., Lawrenceville, GA
Aten, Rev. Robert L., '79 (STL) On Special Assignment. Heart of Mary Hermitage, Rocky Mountain [MON] Contemplative Heart of Mary Hermitage, Rocky Mount, MO
Atendido, Rev. Marlon, *SVD* (SR) Pastor of Our Lady Queen of Peace Catholic Church of Clearlake, A Corporation Sole, Clearlake, CA
Atherton, Rev. Jay, '11 (ALB) Curia: Leadership; Offices and Directors Sacred Heart, Cairo, NY; Sacred Heart-Immaculate Conception Church, Haines Falls, NY; St. John the Baptist, Greenville, NY; St. Mary, Coxsackie, NY; St. Patrick, Athens, NY; St. Patrick, Catskill, NY; St. Patrick, Ravena, NY; St. Theresa of Child Jesus, Windham, NY
Athipozhi, Rev. Shaji, (FRS) Shrine of Our Lady of Guadalupe, Co-Patroness of the Unborn, Bakersfield, CA
Athishu, Rev. Dominic, (WH) St. Edward the Confessor Mission, Terra Alta, WV; St. Sebastian, Kingwood, WV; St. Zita Mission, Masontown, WV
Atienza, Rev. Abdon, *O.S.A.* '61 (MGZ) St. Rose of Lima, San German, PR
Atienza, Rev. Brian C., '02 (SAC) Curia: Offices and Directors
Atienza, Rev. Brian C., '02 (SAC) On Special Assignment. Curia: Offices and Directors
Atinaja, Rev. Constantino T, (HON) Malia Puka O Kalani (Mary Gate of Heaven), Hilo, HI
Atisha, Rev. Perrin, (EST) Our Lady of Chaldeans Cathedral, Mother of God Chaldean Parish, Southfield, MI
Atkin, Rev. Tim, (ARL) Retired.
Atkins, Rev. J. Daniel, '87 (IND) Retired. Our Lady of Providence Junior - Senior High School, Inc., Clarksville, IN
Atkins, Rev. James Mary, *C.F.R.* '72 (NY) [MON] St. Crispin Friary, Bronx, NY
Ato, Rev. Lorenzo, '88 (NY) Sacred Heart of Jesus, New York, NY; St. Emeric, New York, NY
Atonio, Rev. Falaniko, (HON) Our Lady of Sorrows, Wahiawa, HI
Atonio, Rev. Pio, '91 (DUL) Immaculate Conception, Cromwell, MN; St. Louis, Floodwood, MN; St. Mary, Meadowlands, MN
Atoyebi, Rev. John B., '94 (CHI) SS. Peter and Lambert Parish, Skokie, IL
Atraga, Rev. Tamiru, '08 (ATL) Holy Spirit Catholic Church, Atlanta, Inc., Atlanta, GA
Attah, Rev. Clement, (PHX) Curia: Offices and Directors Our Lady of Joy Roman Catholic Parish, Carefree, AZ
Attah-Nsiah, Rev. Paul, '94 (DUB) Curia: Administration; Leadership [NUR] Stonehill Franciscan Services, Inc., Dubuque, IA
Attanasio, Rev. Scott, '95 (NEW) Queen of Peace, North Arlington, NJ
Attappattu, Rev. Binil Jose, *C.R.M.* '09 (CHR) Immaculate Conception, Goose Creek, SC; St. Francis Caracciolo Mission, Goose Creek, SC
Atto, Rev. Dennis D., '02 (RCK) On Administrative Leave.
Atuah, Rev. Charles, *MSP* '90 (DOD) Sacred Heart Catholic Church of Pratt, Kansas, Pratt, KS; St. John the Apostle Catholic Church of St. John, Kansas, St. John, KS; [EFT] The Sacred Heart Endowment, Inc., Pratt, KS
Atuegbu, Rev. Amobi, (HRT) [HOS] Saint Mary's Hospital, Waterbury, CT
Atukunda, Rev. Nazario, '98 (P) Curia: Offices and Directors; Tribunal St. John the Baptist, Milwaukie, OR
Atunzu, Rev. Kevin O., '79 (LR) Retired.
Atwell, Rev. Basil, *O.S.B.* '02 (BIS) Immaculate Conception, Max, ND; Sacred Heart, White Shield, ND; St. Nicholas, Garrison, ND; [MON] Assumption Abbey, Richardton, ND
Atwood, Rev. Ray E., '94 (DUB) Immaculate Conception Church, Fairbank, Iowa, Fairbank, IA; Sacred Heart Church, Oelwein, Iowa, Oelwein, IA
Atwood, Rev. Ronald E., '84 (OAK) Retired.
Au, Rev. Thomas, '79 (LIN) St. Vincent Ferrer, Osceola, NE
Au, Rev. Valentine Phu Ngoc, '15 (SFE) St. Thomas Apostle, Abiquiu, NM
Au, Rev. Vincent Thanh, *CRM* '00 (SPC) [MON] Congregation of the Mother of the Redeemer, Carthage, MO
Au, Rev. William A., '75 (BAL) Shrine of the Sacred Heart, Baltimore, MD
Aubert, Rev. Jerome, *O.S.B.* '22 (NO) [SEM] Saint Joseph Seminary College, Saint Benedict, LA
Aubespin, Rev. Borgia, *S.V.D.* '65 (LAF) (>BLX) [MON] St. Augustine's Residence, Bay St. Louis, MS
Aubin, Rev. Jean P., '01 (BO) St. Mary, Walpole, MA
Aubin, Rev. Pierre, *M.S.C.* '58 (OG) Retired. The Roman Catholic Community of Cape Vincent, Rosiere and Chaumont, Cape Vincent, NY; [MIS] Mission Project Service, Chaumont, NY; [MON] Missionaries of the Sacred Heart, Watertown, NY
Aubin, Rev. Msgr. Ronald B., '81 (SP) Curia: Leadership; Pastoral Services Our Lady of the Rosary, Land O' Lakes, FL
Auble, Rev. Theodore J., '75 (ROC) Retired.
Aubol, Rev. Canon Richard, '19 (SCL) St. Alexius, West Union, MN; St. Francis De Sales, Belgrade, MN
Aubrey, Rev. Robert J., '71 (DM) Retired.
Aubuchon, Rev. Christopher M., '14 (JC) St. Anthony, St. Anthony, MO; St. Lawrence, St. Elizabeth, MO
Aucoin, Rev. Msgr. Robert H., '70 (OG) Retired. Curia: Consultative Bodies; Offices and Directors St. Mary's Church, Ogdensburg, Ogdensburg, NY
Audet, Rev. Dennis J., '78 (MAN) St. Patrick, Milford, NH
Audet, Rev. Phil, '01 (LAV) On Duty Outside Diocese. Curia: (>MO) Offices and Directors
Audet, Rev. Philip, '01 (BLX) VA Medical Center Chaplain
Audette, Rev. Albert D., '93 (BGP) Retired.
Audino, Rev. John Paul, *FSSP* '21 (OM) Immaculate Conception, B.V.M., Omaha, NE
Audu, Rev. Stephen, (DM) [HOS] MercyOne - Des Moines, Des Moines, IA
Audziayuk, Rev. Aliaksandr, '09 (CHI) St. Thomas Apostle, Chicago, IL
Auer, Rev. Andrew A, '19 (STL) St. Clare of Assisi Catholic Church, Ellisville, MO
Auer, Rev. Benedict L., *O.S.B.* '80 (SEA) Retired. [COL] Saint Martin's University (Order of St. Benedict Master's Comprehensive University), Lacey, WA
Auer, Rev. John, '79 (COS) Retired.
Auer, Rev. Peter, '93 (MAD) St. Francis de Sales, Hazel Green, WI; St. Joseph, Hazel Green, WI
Auerbach, Rev. Shay W., *S.J.* '99 (RIC) Sacred Heart, Richmond, VA; [MIS] Sacred Heart Center, Inc., Richmond, VA
Auerback, Very Rev. Shay, *S.J.* (RIC) Curia: Deaneries
Aufdermauer, Rev. Joseph A., '68 (MIL) St. Elizabeth Ann Seton, New Berlin, WI
Aufiero, Rev. David, '13 (SPR) St. Marks, Conway, MA; [CEM] St. Stanislaus Cemetery, ,
Aufiero, Rev. David, (SPR) Holy Family Parish, South Deerfield, MA
Augenstein, Rev. Eric M., '04 (IND) Curia: Offices and Directors Nativity of Our Lord Jesus Christ Catholic Church, Indianapolis, Inc., Indianapolis, IN
Auger, Rev. Raymond D., '56 (PRT) Retired.
Auguscik, Rev. Jerzy, *O.F.M., Conv.* (ALT) St. Augustine, Dysart, PA; St. Monica, Chest Springs, PA
Auguste, Rev. Jean-Miguel, '93 (BRK) St. Pius X, Rosedale, NY
Augustin, Rev. Felix, *O.S.B.* '12 (SP) [MON] St. Leo Abbey, Saint Leo, FL
Augustin, Rev. Franz, '13 (DUB) St. Mary Church (Roseville), Marble Rock, Iowa, Marble Rock, IA; St. Mary Church, Greene, Iowa, Greene, IA; The Holy Name Church, Rockford, Iowa, Rockford, IA
Augustine, Rev. Gabriel Selvanathan, *M.F.* '06 (OAK) Our Lady of Guadalupe, Fremont, CA; [MON] Missionaries of Faith-India Inc., Fremont, CA
Augustine, Very Rev. Joseph Mandokkara, '05 (WH) Curia: Leadership; Offices and Directors Our Lady of Peace, Wheeling, WV
Augustine, Rev. Kenneth J., '77 (MIL) St. Luke Congregation, Brookfield, WI
Augustine, Rev. Libin, *C.M.I.* (CHR) Christ Our King, Mount Pleasant, SC
Augustine, Rev. Liju, (BRK) St. John's Preparatory School, Astoria, NY
Augustine, Rev. Liju, *C.M.I.* '03 (BRK) Immaculate Conception, Astoria, NY
Augustine, Rev. Mark, '13 (CHI) On Special Assignment. Student, Advanced Studies
Augustine, Rev. Regimon, *MSFS* (NSH) St. John the Evangelist, Lewisburg, TN
Augustine, Rev. Russell, '89 (BGP) St. Mark Roman Catholic Church, Stratford, CT
Augustine, Rev. Shiju, *C.M.I.* (BEA) St. Anne, Beaumont, TX
Augustine, Rev. Titus, '99 (NSH) St. Ignatius of Antioch, Antioch, TN
Augustinowitz, Rev. Michael E., '75 (BUR) Our Lady of the Snows, Woodstock, VT; [CAM] Goddard College (Plainfield), Montpelier, VT
Augustyn, Rev. Boguslaw Adam, *C.Ss.R.* '93 (MO) Curia: Offices and Directors
Augustyn, Rev. James M., '63 (BUF) Retired. [MON] Bishop Head Residence, Lackawanna, NY

Augustyn, Rev. Richard H., '76 (BUF) Curia: Offices and Directors
Augustyniak, Rev. Pawel, (SFD) Assumption B.V.M., Assumption, IL; Immaculate Conception, Shelbyville, IL; St. Frances de Sales, Moweaqua, IL
Auletta, Rev. Andrew J., '22 (PH) St. Joseph, Downingtown, PA
Aune, Rev. Mark, '20 (BIS) St. Anthony, Linton, ND; St. Katherine, Braddock, ND; St. Paul, Hazelton, ND
Aung, Rev. Mahka "Philip", (SB) St. Paul the Apostle, Chino Hills, CA
Aung, Rev. Philip Naw, *M.S.* (SB) [MON] The Pacific Region Missionaries of Our Lady of La Salette, MS, Moreno Valley, CA
Aurelien, Rev. Yvon-Hector, '16 (BRK) Holy Family - Saint Laurence, Brooklyn, NY
Aurilia, Rev. John, *O.F.M.Cap.* '66 (NY) [MON] Immaculate Conception Friary (Capuchin Friars of the Province of the Stigmata of St. Francis), New York, NY
Aurillo, Rev. Arnold, '96 (TUC) Our Mother of Sorrows Roman Catholic Parish - Tucson, Tucson, AZ
Auro, Rev. Fadi, (STL) [SEM] Kenrick School of Theology, ,
Ausperk, Rev. Michael D., '89 (CLV) On Administrative Leave.
Austgen, Rev. Robert J., *C.S.C.* '58 (FTW) [MIS] Holy Cross House, Notre Dame, IN
Austin, Rev. Brian, *FSSP* '09 (ATL) St. Francis de Sales Catholic Church, Mableton, Inc., Mableton, GA
Austin, Rev. Charles Gerard, *O.P.* '59 (MIA) [MON] Dominican Fathers of Miami, Inc., Miami, FL
Austin, Rev. David M., '03 (RCK) St. Mary, McHenry, IL
Austin, Rev. Jonathan, '97 (DAL) On Administrative Leave.
Austin, Rev. Leo, '08 (POD) Curia: Clergy and Religious Services
Austin, Rev. Luke P., '10 (BUR) Curia: Leadership Assumption of the Blessed Virgin Mary, Middlebury, VT; [CAM] Middlebury College, Middlebury, VT
Austin, Rev. Michael P., '00 (BLX) Curia: Advisory Boards, Commissions, Committees, and Councils; Faith Formation; Miscellaneous / Other Offices; Spiritual Life Holy Family Parish, Pass Christian, MS
Austin, Rev. Michael Paul, (BLX) Curia: Advisory Boards, Commissions, Committees, and Councils
Austin, Rev. Stephen E., '84 (TLS) St. Francis De Sales, Idabel, OK
Austriaco, Rev. Nicanor P.G., *O.P.* '04 (PRO) [MON] St. Thomas Aquinas Priory at Providence College, Providence, RI
Auta, Rev. Samuel, '12 (PBL) Immaculate Heart of Mary, Pagosa Springs, CO; Pope John Paul II (Immaculate Heart of Mary), Pagosa Springs, CO; [MIS] Archuleta Housing Corporation, Pagosa Springs, CO
Auth, Rev. Clifford H., '99 (SY) Curia: Leadership St. Augustine, Baldwinsville, NY; St. Mary of the Assumption, Baldwinsville, NY
Auth, Rev. James E., '61 (TOL) Retired.
Auther, Rev. John, *S.J.* '90 (SJ) [RTR] Jesuit Retreat Center of Los Altos, Los Altos, CA
Auva'a, Rev. Eneliko, '91 (SPP) St. Peter Chanel Parish Fagasa, Pago Pago, AS
Auve, Rev. Msgr. Perron J., '62 (YAK) Retired. Holy Spirit, Kennewick, WA
Available, Rev. Not, (E) [CAM] University of Pittsburgh - Bradford Campus, Bradford, PA
Avant, Rev. Frank, '15 (STN) Retired. St. Sophia Ukrainian Catholic Church, The Colony, TX
Avarez, Rev. Tegin, '13 (PHX) St. Maria Goretti Roman Catholic Parish, Scottsdale, AZ
Avella, Very Rev. Alberto, '80 (GLP) Our Lady of Sorrows, Ceboyeta, NM
Avella, Rev. Steven M., '79 (MIL) On Special Assignment. Faculty, Milwaukee
Avendano, Rev. Alvaro D., '92 (ATL) Retired.
Avendano, Rev. Eliseo, (SR) Curia: Leadership
Avendano, Rev. Eliseo, '08 (SR) Curia: Leadership Pastor of St. Mary Immaculate Catholic Church of Lakeport, a Corporation Sole, Lakeport, CA
Avendano, Rev. Henry, (HRT) Chap Hartford Police Dept Maria, Reina de la Paz Parish Corporation, Hartford, CT; [MIS] Trinity College Chapel, Hartford, CT
Avendano, Rev. Hilario, '97 (BAL) St. John the Evangelist, Columbia, MD
Aveni, Rev. Paul J., '98 (BO) Saint Matthew the Evangelist Parish, Billerica, MA; St. Andrew, Billerica, MA; St. Mary, Billerica, MA; St. Theresa of Lisieux, Billerica, MA
Avenido, Rev. Albert H., '95 (LA) [MIS] Filipino Pastoral Ministry, Monterey Park, CA
Avenido, Rev. Serafin P., '77 (SAN) Holy Trinity Parish, Big Spring, TX
Avestruz, Rev. Lester S., '72 (LA) Chap, Hospital Chaplain, Cedars-Sinai Med Ctr, Los Angeles
Avicolli, Rev. Maurice C., *O.Praem.* '68 (PH) Retired. [MON] Daylesford Abbey, Inc., Paoli, PA
Avila, Rev. Daniel, '87 (FRS) On Special Assignment. Curia: Advisory Boards, Commissions, Committees, and Councils; Leadership Shrine of Our Lady of Miracles, Gustine, CA
Avila, Rev. Israel, '91 (FRS) St. Frances Cabrini, Huron, CA; St. Peter Prince of Apostles, Lemoore, CA
Avila, Rev. Jader, '18 (PAT) On Leave.
Avila, Rev. Maximilian, *OFM Conv.* '18 (BUF) [MON] St. Francis of Assisi Friary, Hamburg, NY
Avila, Rev. Misael, '98 (STO) St. Frances of Rome Church (Pastor of), Riverbank, CA
Avila, Rev. Ricardo, *S.J.* '19 (WDC) [MON] The Jesuit Community of St. Aloysius Gonzaga, Washington, DC
Avila, Rev. Msgr. Stephen J., '81 (FR) Curia: Leadership; Offices and Directors St. Joseph, Guardian of the Holy Family, East Falmouth, MA
Avila Piña, Rev. Federico, *Sch. P.* '17 (PCE) San Joaquin y Santa Ana, Adjuntas, PR
Avila Vivero, Rev. Mario, '11 (MIA) St. Bernadette, Hollywood, FL
Avila-Ibarra, Rev. Juan Pablo, '08 (CHI) Transfiguration, Wauconda, IL
Aviles, Rev. Juan Alberto, '03 (MIA) St. Francis de Sales, Miami Beach, FL
Aviles Mercado, Rev. Javier Montalvo, *C.P.* '18 (NY) [MON] The Congregation of the Passion - St. Paul of the Cross Province, Jamaica, NY
Aviles Rosa, Rev. Edgardo Javier, '21 (ARE) St. Joseph, Lares, PR
Avilla, Rev. Melvin Ilagan, *C.R.M.* '08 (CHK) San Jude Parish, Saipan, MP
Avis, Rev. William, (PIT) Most Precious Blood of Jesus, Pittsburgh, PA
Avittappally, Rev. Baiju Augustine, *M.S.* '01 (R) St. Stephen the First Martyr, Sanford, NC
Avula, Rev. Maria Susai J., '80 (TYL) St. Luke, Wills Point, TX
Avvakumov, Rev. Yury, (FTW) [COL] University of Notre Dame Du Lac, Notre Dame, IN
Awad, Rev. Msgr. Assad, '57 (SAM) Retired.
Awada, Rev. Bechara, '03 (OLL) St. Sharbel Maronite Catholic Church, Peoria, IL
Awange, Rev. Richard T., *C.S.Sp.* '99 (TUC) Saint Margaret Mary Alacoque Roman Catholic Parish - Tucson, Tucson, AZ
Award, Rev. Richard, *C.P.* '81 (NY) [MON] The Congregation of the Passion - St. Paul of the Cross Province, Jamaica, NY
Awe, Rev. Emmanuel, *S.S.J.* '13 (LAF) (>BLX) St. Peter the Apostle, Pascagoula, MS
Awe, Rev. Emmanuel, *S.S.J.* '13 (LA) St. Brigid, Los Angeles, CA
Awiliba, Rev. Christopher, '21 (SAV) St. Joseph, Augusta, GA
Awo Doku, Rev. Seth N., '90 (RVC) St. Frances de Chantal, Wantagh, NY
Awobi, Rev. Godfrey, *A.J.* (NY) Holy Agony, New York, NY; Parish of St. Cecilia and Holy Agony, New York, NY
Awotwe-Mensah, Rev. Andrew, '04 (DUB) Sacred Heart Church (Oxford Junction, Iowa), Oxford Junction, IA; Saint Isidore Church, Springville, Iowa, Springville, IA; St. John's Church, Mt. Vernon, Iowa, Mount Vernon, IA
Awotwi, Rev. Charles K., '11 (SAL) On Duty Outside Diocese. Military Archdiocese
Awuah Gyamfi, Rev. Eric, '04 (DOD) Holy Spirit, Coldwater, KS; St. Joseph Catholic Church of Ashland, Kansas, Ashland, KS
Axalan, Rev. Romeo J., '97 (MO) Curia: Offices and Directors
Axalan, Rev. Romeo Jose, (WDC) Chap, VA Med Ctr, Washington
Axe, Rev. Thomas R., '60 (CIN) Retired.
Axline, Rev. R. Christopher, '13 (PHX) Curia: Offices and Directors St. Mary Magdalene Roman Catholic Parish, Gilbert, AZ
Axtmann, Rev. David, '06 (SFS) Retired.
Axtmann, Rev. Mark, '01 (SFS) Saint Joseph Parish of McPherson County, Eureka, SD
Axtmann, Rev. Mark A., '01 (SFS) Saint Anthony Parish of Walworth County, Selby, SD; Saint Joseph Parish of Walworth County, Mobridge, SD
Ayala, Rev. Andrés, *IVE* (BAL) Our Lady of Mount Carmel, Thurmont, MD; St. Anthony Shrine, Emmitsburg, MD; St. Joseph, Emmitsburg, MD
Ayala, Rev. H. Alejandro, '06 (CHL) St. William, Murphy, NC
Ayala, Rev. Ismael (Mel) N., '10 (WDC) [SHR] Basilica of the National Shrine of the Immaculate Conception, Washington, DC
Ayala, Rev. Juan, '10 (RCK) St. Mary, Woodstock, IL; St. Patrick, Hartland, IL
Ayala, Rev. Juan, *O.M.I.* '07 (LA) St. Ferdinand, San Fernando, CA
Ayala, Rev. Lino Garcia, *CS* (BO) St. Anthony of Padua, Somerville, MA
Ayala, Rev. Patrick, '21 (LA) Santa Clara, Oxnard, CA
Ayala, Rev. Ramon, (NSH) Our Lady of Guadalupe, Antioch, TN
Ayala, Rev. Robert M., '06 (MIA) Nativity, Hollywood, FL
Ayala, Rev. Saul, '71 (SB) Retired.
Ayala Rosales, Rev. Fernando E., (BO) St. John the Evangelist, Chelmsford, MA; St. Margaret of Scotland, Lowell, MA; St. Mary, Chelmsford, MA
Ayala-Santiago, Rev. Andres, '10 (PBL) Queen of All Saints, Crested Butte, CO; St. Peter, Gunnison, CO
Ayathupadam, Rev. Joseph, '61 (CHL) Retired.
Ayem, Rev. Alfred, *SVD* (LAF) Immaculate Heart of Mary, Lafayette, LA
Ayers, Rev. Andrew, '19 (GR) St. Catherine, Ravenna, MI; St. Francis Xavier, Conklin, MI; St. Joseph Wright, Conklin, MI
Ayers, Rev. Dan, '99 (COS) [HOS] Penrose Hospital, Colorado Springs, CO
Ayers, Very Rev. Eric J., '11 (RIC) Curia: Deaneries
Ayers, Rev. Eric James, '11 (RIC) Blessed Sacrament, Norfolk, VA
Ayima, Rev. Joseph, (PHX) St. Mary Roman Catholic Parish Chandler, Chandler, AZ
Ayirwanda, Rev. Edouard, *C.M.* '18 (CHI) [MON] DePaul Vincentian Residence, Chicago, IL
Ayisu, Rev. Stephen, *S.V.D.* '02 (OAK) St. Bernard, Oakland, CA
Aylward, Rev. James W., '64 (SFR) Retired.
Aylward, Rev. Richard, *M.M.* '53 (NY) Retired. [MON] Maryknoll Fathers and Brothers (Catholic Foreign Mission Society of America, Inc.), Ossining, NY
Ayo, Rev. Nicholas R., *C.S.C.* '59 (FTW) [COL] University of Notre Dame Du Lac, Notre Dame, IN; [MON] Holy Cross Community, Corby Hall, University of Notre Dame, Notre Dame, IN
Ayodi, Friar Benedict, *OFM Cap* (NY) Our Lady of Sorrows, New York, NY; [MIS] Franciscans International, Inc., New York, NY
Ayoob, Rev. John, '65 (PIT) Retired.
Ayoub, Rev. Lucian, (SPA) Our Lady of Perpetual Help Chaldean Catholic Church, Orangevale, CA
Aytona, Rev. Joseph R, *CPM* '10 (GB) [SHR] The National Shrine of Our Lady of Good Help, Inc., New Franken, WI
Ayubi, Rev. Omar, '18 (MIA) St. Katharine Drexel, Weston, FL
Ayuso, Rev. Miguel Eli, '76 (OKL) St. Joseph Old Cathedral, Oklahoma City, OK
Ayuyu, Rev. Isaac M., '86 (CHK) Curia: Advisory Boards, Commissions, Committees, and Councils
Ayyaneth, Rev. Thomas, '07 (MCE) Curia: Administration; Advisory Boards, Commissions, Committees, and Councils; Communications; Tribunal St. Vincent de Paul Malankara Catholic Cathedral, Elmont, NY
Az Cuc, Rev. Basilio, '16 (OWN) St. Thomas More, Paducah, KY
Aza, Rev. Robinson, (PMB) St. Joan of Arc, Boca Raton, FL
Azagbor, Rev. Dominic, *O.P.* (HBG) St. Rose of Lima, York, PA
Azah, Rev. Francis Perry, (NEW) Chap (Adjunct), Hackensack Univ Med Ctr
Azah, Rev. Francis Perry, '97 (NEW) St. Elizabeth, Wyckoff, NJ
Azanwi, Rev. Rigo, *OFM Cap.* (HBG) St. Joseph, York, PA
Azar, Rt. Rev. John, '88 (NTN) Retired. Curia: Consultative Bodies
Azar, Rev. Nicholas G., '09 (ATL) On Duty Outside Diocese. St Vincent de Paul Regional Seminary
Azar, Rev. Nicholas George, (PMB) [SEM] St. Vincent de Paul Regional Seminary, Boynton Beach, FL
Azar, Rev. Msgr. Peter, (OLL) Curia: Offices and Directors
Azar, Rev. Msgr. Peter Fahed, '80 (SAM) Curia: Offices and Directors [SEM] Our Lady of Lebanon Maronite Seminary, Washington, DC
Azaro, Rev. Stanley, (PRO) Retired. St. Joseph's Church Providence Rhode Island, Providence, RI
Azike, Rev. Gerald, '04 (MEM) Curia: Advisory Boards,

Commissions, Committees, and Councils St. James, Memphis, TN
Azizo, Chorbishop Toma B., '54 (OLD) Retired.
Aznar, Rev. Manuel, *CM* (SJN) Jesus Maestro, San Juan, PR
Aznar, Rev. Manuel, *CM* (SJN) Colegio San Vicente de Paul, San Juan, PR
Azorji, Rev. Eugene, '80 (DAL) [SEM] Holy Trinity Seminary, Irving, TX
Azpericueta, Rev. Lucas, '69 (FRS) Retired.
Azudiugwu, Rev. Emmanuel, (SB) Chap, Temecula Valley Hosp
Azudiugwu, Rev. Emmanuel C., (SB) St. Catherine of Alexandria, Temecula, CA
Azzarto, Rev. Anthony, (NY) [MON] Murray-Weigel Hall (A Jesuit Community at Murray-Weigel Hall and Kohlmann Hall), Bronx, NY
Azzarto, Rev. Anthony J., *S.J.* '69 (NEW) [MIS] Jesuit Community, Jersey City, NJ
Baab, Rev. John, (RIC) On Administrative Leave.
Baafi, Rev. Edward Baah, '06 (MAR) Precious Blood Church, Stephenson, MI
Baalbaki, Rev. Seraphim Pio, *C.F.R.* '22 (NY) [MON] Our Lady of the Angels Friary, Bronx, NY; [SEM] St. Joseph's Seminary, Yonkers, NY
Babcock, Rt. Rev. Archmandrite James, '81 (NTN) Retired. Virgin Mary Mission, Temecula, CA
Babeu, Rev. Gill C., '87 (BGP) Retired.
Babic, Rev. Ivica, (DET) Retired.
Babich, Rev. Ronald J., '77 (DET) Retired.
Babick, Rev. Bryan P., '07 (CHR) On Administrative Leave.
Babicz, Rev. Edmund A., '84 (MAN) Retired.
Babiczuk, Rev. Fred, '86 (FR) St. Anthony's, Taunton, MA; St. Jude the Apostle Parish, Taunton, MA
Babiczuk, Rev. Freddie, (FR) St. Mary's, Taunton, MA
Babin, Rev. Victor J., '75 (MIA) Nativity, Hollywood, FL
Babiuch, Rev. Thomas, '02 (ALB) Roman Catholic Community of Hudson Falls/Kingsbury, Hudson Falls, NY; St. Joseph, Fort Edward, NY
Babota, Rev. Ilie, '14 (STF) On Duty Outside Diocese. Prison Ministry, Diocese of Syracuse, NY Curia: (>MO) Offices and Directors
Babowitch, Rev. John F., '96 (PH) On Special Assignment. Dean, Deanery 11, Our Lady of Calvary Rectory, Philadelphia Curia: Advisory Boards, Commissions, Committees, and Councils Our Lady of Calvary, Philadelphia, PA
Babu, Rev. Bobin, '14 (RNO) St. Rose of Lima, Reno, NV; [CAM] Our Lady of Wisdom Catholic Parish Corporation, Reno, NV
Babu, Rev. Thomas, (RNO) Curia: Leadership; Offices and Directors
Babu, Rev. Thomas P, (RNO) St. Teresa of Avila Parish Corporation, Carson City, NV
Babychan, Rev. Arackathara, (SAT) Curia: Administration
Babychan, Rev. Arackathara Mathai, *M.S.F.S.* (SAT) St. John the Evangelist, Hondo, TX
Baca, Rev. Alfred S., '89 (ORG) Curia: Leadership St. Anne Church, Seal Beach, CA
Baca, Rev. Jamie, *C.S.P.* '06 (LA) Curia: Offices and Directors St. Paul the Apostle, Los Angeles, CA
Bacalso, Rev. Romeo, *S.V.D.* '05 (WH) Holy Spirit, Monongah, WV; St. Anthony, Fairmont, WV
Bacatan, Rev. Francisco Sebastian, *A.M.* '94 (NY) St. Pius X, Scarsdale, NY
Bacchi, Rev. James, (JOL) Retired.
Bacchi, Rev. Lee, '76 (JOL) Retired. [NUR] St. John Vianney Villa, Naperville, IL
Bacchi, Rev. Robert A., '77 (CHI) Retired.
Bacevice, Rev. Joseph A., '77 (CLV) Curia: Tribunal St. Casimir, Cleveland, OH
Bacevicius, Rev. John J., *O.F.M.* '62 (PRT) [MON] Society of Franciscan Fathers of Greene, Maine, Kennebunk, ME
Bach, Rev. Gregory J., '99 (COV) St. Benedict, Covington, KY
Bach, Rev. James N., '96 (NO) Retired.
Bachman, Rev. Martin E., '09 (CIN) Our Lady of the Visitation, Cincinnati, OH
Bachman, Rev. Michael J., '84 (BGP) Retired. [MON] The Catherine Dennis Keefe Queen of the Clergy Retired Priests' Residence, Stamford, CT
Bachmann, Rev. Mark, *O.S.B.* '91 (TLS) [MON] Our Lady of the Annunciation of Clear Creek Abbey, Hulbert, OK
Bachmeier, Rev. Brian, '97 (FAR) Sacred Heart Church of Sanborn, Sanborn, ND; St. Agatha's Church of Hope, Hope, ND; St. Bernard's Church of Oriska, Oriska, ND
Bachmeier, Rev. Mark, '89 (P) Holy Cross Catholic Church, Portland, OR
Bachmeier, Rev. Mark V., '89 (P) Curia: Offices and Directors
Bachner, Very Rev. Daniel, '05 (JOL) Curia: Leadership St. Raphael, Naperville, IL
Bachner, Rev. James M., '96 (PIT) St. Teresa of Kolkata, Pittsburgh, PA
Bacik, Rev. James J., '62 (TOL) Retired.
Bacik, Rev. Leonard M., '72 (CLV) Retired.
Bacik, Rev. Robert Crowley, '15 (LAN) Curia: Leadership St. Gerard Parish Lansing, Lansing, MI
Backer, Rev. Dennis J., '07 (STP) St. Luke, Clearwater, MN; [CEM] St. Luke Cemetery, Clearwater, MN
Backes, Rev. John J., '73 (NY) St. Stanislaus Kostka, Pleasant Valley, NY
Backmann, Rev. Albert P., '00 (STP) Retired.
Backous, Rev. Timothy, *O.S.B.* '86 (SCL) [MON] St. John's Abbey, of the Order of St. Benedict, Collegeville, MN
Backowski, Rev. Joseph, '12 (SCL) St. Lawrence's, Foley, MN; St. Marcus, Clear Lake, MN
Bacleon, Rev. Misael, '83 (NY) St. Ann, Bronx, NY
Bacovin, Rev. Msgr. Ronald J., '66 (TR) Retired. [MON] Villa Vianney, Trenton, NJ
Badawi, Chorbishop Alfred, '91 (OLL) Curia: Offices and Directors St. Sharbel Maronite Catholic Church, Clinton Township, MI
Baddick, Rev. Msgr. Thomas D., '81 (ALN) Notre Dame of Bethlehem, Bethlehem, PA
Badding, Rev. Joseph P., '69 (BUF) Retired.
Badeaux, Rev. James, '99 (PSC) Curia: Advisory Boards, Commissions, Committees, and Councils; Leadership St. Mary's, Hillsborough, NJ; St. Nicholas, Dunellen, NJ
Badeaux, Very Rev. Kevin, '84 (BEA) Curia: Administration; Leadership Our Lady of the Assumption, Beaumont, TX
Badenes, Rev. Jose Ignacio, *S.J.* '93 (LA) [MON] Jesuit Community, Los Angeles, CA
Bader, Very Rev. Edward, '82 (NY) Curia: Leadership St. Aloysius, Livingston Manor, NY; St. Peter, Liberty, NY
Bader, Rev. Paul A., '61 (CIN) Retired.
Bader, Rev. Raed, '10 (JOL) St. Isaac Jogues, Hinsdale, IL
Badgley, Rev. T. Augustine, (NY) Holy Rosary, Greenwood Lake, NY
Badiani, Rev. Tommaso, *FSCB* '21 (WDC) [MIS] Priestly Fraternity of the Missionaries of St. Charles Borromeo, Inc., Bethesda, MD
Badillo, Rev. Robert P., *M.Id* '95 (NY) Our Lady of Solace, Bronx, NY; St. Dominic, Bronx, NY; [EFT] Foundation of Christ the Redeemer, Bronx, NY; [MON] Idente Missionaries - Santa Maria Residence, Bronx, NY
Bado, Rev. Walter, *S.J.* (CIN) [MON] Cincinnati Jesuit Community, Cincinnati, OH
Bado, Rev. Walter, *S.J.* '59 (LEX) [MON] Jesuit Fathers & Brothers, Lexington, KY
Badway, Very Rev. Gavin J., '00 (PMB) Curia: Leadership Cathedral of St. Ignatius Loyola, Palm Beach Gardens, FL
Bae, Rev. Christopher W., '16 (BO) St. Columbkille, Brighton, MA
Bae, Rev. Emmanuel, (RVC) Chap, St Francis Hosp
Baenziger, Rev. Edward J., *C.S.B.* '76 (GAL) [MON] Keon House, Houston, TX
Baer, Rev. Chrysostom Anthony, *O.Praem* '04 (ORG) [MON] Norbertine Fathers of Orange, Inc., Silverado, CA; [SEM] St. Michael's Norbertine Postulancy, Novitiate and Juniorate, Silverado, CA
Baer, Rev. Mitchell, '21 (STL) Ste. Genevieve Catholic Church, Ste. Genevieve, Ste. Genevieve, MO
Baer, Rev. Timothy K., '13 (WDC) Curia: Consultative Bodies St. Nicholas, Laurel, MD
Baetzold, Rev. David, (E) Holy Rosary, Erie, PA; St. John the Baptist, Erie, PA
Baez, Rev. Alejandro, (SEA) Bellarmine Preparatory School, Tacoma, WA
Baez, Rev. O. Alejandro, *S.J.* '18 (SFR) St. Agnes, San Francisco, CA; [MON] Loyola House Jesuit Community, San Francisco, CA
Baez, Rev. Ramon A., '05 (ARL) Holy Family, Dale City, VA
Baeza Gama, Rev. Jose Manuel, *M.C.C.J.* '96 (LA) Our Lady of Peace, North Hills, CA
Baffour Asamoah, Rev. Eric, (RIC) Church of the Holy Spirit, Jonesville, VA; Sacred Heart, Big Stone Gap, VA; St. Anthony, Norton, VA; St. Joseph, Clintwood, VA
Baffour-Akoto, Rev. Patrick, (RIC) Immaculate Heart of Mary, Blackstone, VA
Baffuor-Awuah, Rev. Paul, (HRT) Saint Isaac Jogues Ghanaian Catholic Parish Corporation, East Hartford, CT
Bagan, Rev. Vincent, *O.P.* (PRO) [MON] St. Thomas Aquinas Priory at Providence College, Providence, RI
Bagattini, Rev. Paolo, *C.S.S.* (SPR) Our Lady of Mt. Carmel, Springfield, MA
Baggio, Rev. Gianantonio, *C.S.* '92 (LA) St. Peter, Los Angeles, CA
Baghdassarian, Msgr. Parsegh Manuel, (OLN) Curia: Leadership St. Gregory Armenian Catholic Cathedral, Glendale, CA
Bagley, Rev. Ronald, *CJM* '77 (SD) Pastor of Saint Patrick Catholic Parish , Carlsbad, a corporation sole, Carlsbad, CA
Bagnato, Rev. James D., *O.Praem.* '79 (WIL) [MON] Immaculate Conception Priory of the Canons Regular of Premontre, Middletown, DE
Baguio, Rev. Daniel S., '91 (GAL) St. Jude Thaddeus, Highlands, TX
Baguna, Rev. Victor, (GBG) St. Patrick, East Brady, PA
Bagyo, Rev. Samuel, '15 (SFD) On Special Assignment.
Bahash, Rev. James, '99 (SD) Pastor of Saint John the Evangelist Catholic Parish, Encinitas, a corporation sole, Encinitas, CA; [MIS] Saint John the Evangelist Catholic Parish Encinitas in Encinitas, CA Real Property Support Corporation, Encinitas, CA
Bahhuth, Msgr. Albert M., '96 (LA) Holy Family, South Pasadena, CA
Bahl, Rev. Greg E., '06 (DUB) Curia: Advisory Boards, Commissions, Committees, and Councils; Leadership; Offices and Directors
Bahrke, Rev. Scott, '22 (MEM) Church of the Incarnation, Collierville, TN
Bai, Rev. Jerome, *SVD* '15 (SFR) All Souls, South San Francisco, CA
Bai, Rev. Lianjiang Peter, '07 (BRK) St. Agatha's, Brooklyn, NY
Baidoo, Rev. Joseph, '85 (RVC) Curia: Leadership Queen of the Most Holy Rosary, Roosevelt, NY; St. Boniface, Elmont, NY
Baier, Rev. Scott, '15 (P) St. Paul Catholic Church, St. Paul, OR
Baier, Rev. William J., '82 (STL) Retired.
Baikauskas, Rev. Patrick H., *O.P.* '08 (STL) [MON] St. Dominic Priory, St. Louis, MO; [SEM] Aquinas Institute of Theology, St. Louis, MO
Bailey, Rev. Casey, (P) [MON] The Cistercian (Trappist) Abbey of Our Lady of Guadalupe (Order of Cistercians of the Strict Observance), Carlton, OR
Bailey, Rev. David P., '21 (TYL) Holy Family, Lindale, TX
Bailey, Rev. Fred K., '83 (ORG) Santa Clara de Asis, Yorba Linda, CA
Bailey, Rev. James L. "Larry", '86 (SEA) Retired.
Bailey, Rev. Robert L., '93 (PRO) Retired.
Bailey, Rev. Scott, (DEN) Risen Christ Catholic Parish in Denver, Denver, CO
Bailey, Rev. Thomas, *O.S.B.* '04 (RCK) [MON] Marmion Abbey, Aurora, IL
Baillargeon, Rev. Daniel J., '07 (PRT) Corpus Christi Parish, Winslow, ME; [CAM] Colby College, Waterville, ME; [CAM] Thomas College, Waterville, ME
Bailon Martinez, Rev. Cirilo, (CHR) Church of the Infant Jesus, Marion, SC; St. Louis, Dillon, SC
Baily, Rev. Harold, '69 (PIT) Retired.
Bain, Rev. Andre M., '04 (BRK) On Leave.
Bain, Rev. Daniel, '64 (RIC) Retired.
Bain, Rev. John, '70 (RNO) Retired.
Baird, Rev. James, '93 (DEN) St. Mark Catholic Parish in Westminster, Westminster, CO
Baird, Rev. Msgr. Lawrence J., '69 (ORG) Retired.
Baird, Rev. Msgr. Lawrence J., '69 (ORG) Curia: Offices and Directors
Bajkowski, Rev. Dennis W., '71 (CAM) Retired.
Bak, Rev. Charles, *M.S.A.* '09 (NOR) [MON] Society of the Missionaries of the Holy Apostles, Cromwell, CT; [SEM] Holy Apostles College and Seminary, Cromwell, CT
Baker, Rev. Msgr. Andrew R., '91 (BAL) [COL] Mount Saint Mary's University, Emmitsburg, MD; [SEM] Mount St. Mary's Seminary, Emmitsburg, MD
Baker, Rev. Msgr. Andrew R., '91 (ALN) On Duty Outside Diocese. Rector, Vice Pres, Emmitsburg, MD
Baker, Rev. Anthony, *O.S.B.* '12 (BIS) [CON] Annunciation Monastery, Bismarck, ND; [MON] Assumption Abbey, Richardton, ND
Baker, Rev. Bartley, '93 (NEW) St. Francis of Assisi, Ridgefield Park, NJ
Baker, Rev. Brad, '00 (JOL) Sts. Peter and Paul, Naperville, IL
Baker, Rev. Brian H., '14 (ATL) St. Monica Catholic Church, Duluth, Inc., Duluth, GA
Baker, Rev. David D, '07 (BUF) Curia: Offices and Directors

Baker, Rev. Dennis, *S.J.* (CI) Xavier High School, Chuuk, FM
Baker, Very Rev. Donald C., '95 (NY) Parish of St. Monica, St. Elizabeth of Hungary, and St. Stephen of Hungary, New York, NY; St. Elizabeth of Hungary, New York, NY; St. Stephen of Hungary, New York, NY
Baker, Rev. Donald P., '80 (CHL) Retired.
Baker, Rev. Dwight H., '09 (BUR) Curia: Offices and Directors St. Catherine of Siena Parish Charitable Trust, Shelburne, VT
Baker, Rev. George E., '81 (NY) St. Mary, Obernburg, NY
Baker, Rev. Jack H., '93 (DET) On Leave.
Baker, Rev. Jay, '92 (HT) Curia: Administration; Clergy and Religious Services
Baker, Rev. Jay L., '92 (HT) Curia: Leadership; Tribunal Cathedral of St. Francis De Sales, Houma, LA; [MIS] The Diocese of Houma-Thibodaux Historical Research Center, Thibodaux, LA
Baker, Rev. Jeffrey, '16 (LA) St. Gregory the Great Church, Whittier, CA
Baker, Very Rev. John C., '82 (MIA) Curia: Leadership St. Mary Star of the Sea Basilica, Key West, FL
Baker, Rev. John Sims, '94 (NSH) Curia: Leadership
Baker, Rev. Joseph, '15 (PEO) St. Ambrose, Milan, IL; St. Patrick Church, Taylor Ridge, IL
Baker, Rev. Joseph, '16 (MAD) Curia: Consultative Bodies Blessed Trinity Parish, Lodi, WI
Baker, Rev. Justin J., '99 (BUR) Christ the King-St. Anthony, Burlington, VT
Baker, Rev. Kenneth, (SJ) [MON] Sacred Heart Jesuit Center, Los Gatos, CA
Baker, Rev. Kenneth R., '62 (CIN) Retired.
Baker, Rev. Michael Allen, *M.I.C.* '19 (SPR) (>MIL) St. Peter's Congregation, Kenosha, WI
Baker, Rev. Nicholas J., '63 (LIN) Retired. St. Joseph's, Alma, NE
Baker, Rev. Paul, (STP) Church of the Epiphany, Coon Rapids, MN
Baker, Rev. Richard, '90 (NY) St. Francis of Assisi, West Nyack, NY
Baker, Rev. Richard M., *M.M.* '71 (NY) Retired. [MON] Maryknoll Fathers and Brothers (Catholic Foreign Mission Society of America, Inc.), Ossining, NY
Baker, Rev. Simon, *O.S.B.* '15 (KCK) On Leave. [MON] St. Benedict's Abbey, Atchison, KS
Baker, Rev. Stephen J., *O.S.A.* '90 (PH) [COL] Villanova University, Villanova, PA; [MON] Saxony Hall, Rosemont, PA; [MON] St. Thomas Monastery, Villanova, PA
Baker, Rev. Thomas E., '89 (LA) St. Rita, Sierra Madre, CA
Baker, Rev. W. Pierre, '78 (MAN) Retired.
Baker, Rev. Msgr. William T., '82 (ALN) All Saints Parish, McAdoo, PA
Bakey, Rev. Christopher T., '98 (CAM) Curia: Clergy and Religious Services
Bakey, Rev. Christopher T., '98 (CAM) Holy Trinity Parish, Margate, N.J., Margate City, NJ
Bakh, Rev. Msgr. Antoine, '88 (OLL) Curia: Offices and Directors St. John Maron Maronite Catholic Church, Orange, CA
Bakkar, Rev. Gabriel Mary, *C.F.R.* '07 (NY) [MON] St. Joseph's Friary, New York, NY
Bakke, Rev. Msgr. Lawrence M., '75 (MAD) Curia: Offices and Directors Our Lady, Queen of Peace, Madison, WI; [MIS] Apostolate to the Handicapped, Inc., Madison, WI
Bakkelund, Rev. Jonathan P., '11 (RCK) Curia: Leadership; Offices and Directors St. Peter, Geneva, IL
Bakker, Rev. Neil Edward, '16 (STP) St. John the Baptist, Jordan, MN; [CEM] St. John the Baptist Cemetery, Jordan, MN
Bakle, Rev. John, *S.M.* '67 (CIN) Retired.
Bakowski, Rev. Dominik, '16 (PAT) On Duty Outside Diocese. Curia: (>MO) Offices and Directors
Baky, Rev. Isidore, '72 (MIA) Retired.
Bakyil, Rev. Alphonsus, *S.O.L.T.* '85 (PHX) St. Frances Cabrini Roman Catholic Parish, Camp Verde, AZ
Bakyil, Rev. William K., *S.O.L.T.* '06 (CC) Christ the King, Corpus Christi, TX; [MON] Society of Our Lady of the Most Holy Trinity, Corpus Christi, TX
Bakyor, Rev. Francis, '82 (KCK) Immaculate Conception, Louisburg, KS
Bala, Rev. Pawel, '11 (PAT) Sacred Heart, Rockaway, NJ
Balagapo, Rev. Victorio R., '66 (SFR) Retired. Visitacion, Church of the, San Francisco, CA
Balagtas, Rev. Rodel G., '91 (LA) Incarnation, Glendale, CA
Balajadia, Rev. James, (CHK) Santa Remedios Parish, Saipan, MP
Balajadia, Rev. James, (CHK) Kristo Rai Parish, Saipan, MP
Balamaze, Rev. Charles, '17 (LA) St. Lawrence Martyr, Redondo Beach, CA
Balang, Rev. Joevensie, '95 (PHX) All Saints Roman Catholic Parish, Mesa, AZ
Balarote, Rev. Venancio R., '01 (RIC) St. Nicholas, Virginia Beach, VA
Balasamy, Rev. Karmalraj, '12 (FAR) Holy Cross Church of West Fargo, West Fargo, ND
Balash, Very Rev. Michael D., '87 (Y) Curia: Leadership; Pastoral Services Our Lady of Mount Carmel Parish, Niles, OH; St. William, Warren, OH
Balash, Very Rev. Michael D., (Y) Curia: Clergy and Religious Services
Balasko, Rev. George J., '67 (Y) Retired.
Balaswamy, Rev. Gali, (BIR) Holy Family, Lanett, AL
Balavendra, Rev. Gerald Kumar, *CMF* '05 (LA) San Gabriel Mission, San Gabriel, CA
Balcerski, Rev. Duane, *C.S.C.* '71 (PHX) [MON] Holy Cross Congregation/Casa Santa Cruz, Phoenix, AZ
Balchunas, Rev. Henry A., '65 (HRT) Retired.
Baldaresa, Rev. Erick, (BRK) Our Lady of Light Roman Catholic Church, St. Albans, NY
Baldelovar, Rev. Jayferson, *O.A.R.* '17 (CHK) San Francisco de Borja Parish, Rota, MP
Baldelovar, Rev. Jayferson, *O.A.R.* (CHK) San Isidro Parish, Rota, MP
Balderas, Rev. Jose Luis, '68 (LAR) Retired. St. John Neumann, Laredo, TX
Balderas, Rev. Sergio A., '06 (BLX) Curia: Advisory Boards, Commissions, Committees, and Councils St. Elizabeth Ann Seton, Ocean Springs, MS
Baldonado, Rev. Msgr. Bonifacio, '85 (STO) St. Frances of Rome Church (Pastor of), Riverbank, CA
Baldonieri, Rev. Thomas F., '90 (CHI) All Saints Parish, Niles, IL
Baldovin, Rev. John, *S.J.* '75 (BO) [MON] Edmund Campion House, Brighton, MA
Baldwin, Rev. Kevin, *L.C.* '98 (ATL) [MIS] Legionaries of Christ, Atlanta, GA
Baldwin, Rev. Paul C., '97 (DUB) Sacred Heart Church (Monticello, Iowa), Monticello, IA; St. Luke's Church, Hopkinton, Iowa, Hopkinton, IA
Baldyga, Rev. William, (HRT) Church Corporation of the Sacred Heart of Jesus of New Britain, New Britain, CT
Baldyga, Rev. William L., '69 (HRT) Retired.
Balen, Rev. Adlso Luis, *C.S.* (LA) [NUR] Villa Scalabrini (Missionary Fathers of St. Charles), Sun Valley, CA
Balen, Rev. Moacir, (PMB) Our Lady Queen of Peace, Delray Beach, FL
Bales, Rev. Francis, *O.S.B.* '87 (TLS) [MON] Our Lady of the Annunciation of Clear Creek Abbey, Hulbert, OK
Bales, Rev. Robert, '57 (MIL) Retired.
Balestino, Rev. Francis P., '60 (ALT) Retired.
Baliar-Singh, Rev. Ajit, *SS.CC.* '14 (BWN) Sacred Heart, Edinburg, TX
Balinda, Rev. Thadeus, '92 (FTW) St. Patrick, Fort Wayne, IN
Balisnomo, Rev. Ian Chris, *F.L.P.* '11 (GAL) [MIS] The Catholic Chaplain Corps, Houston, TX
Balistreri, Rev. Anthony, '92 (SJP) Retired. Curia: Offices and Directors
Balius, Rev. Sameem, (EST) St. Joseph Chaldean Parish, Troy, MI
Balius, Rev. Sameem, '08 (EST) Curia: Offices and Directors
Balizan, Rev. Daniel M., '89 (SFE) On Leave.
Ball, Rev. Raymond A., '87 (MAN) Curia: Faith Formation Immaculate Heart of Mary, Concord, NH
Ball, Rev. Richard D., '77 (SC) Retired.
Ball, Rev. Wayne L., '89 (RIC) St. Augustine, North Chesterfield, VA
Ballacillo, Rev. R. Joy, '21 (TR) St. Gregory the Great, Hamilton Square, NJ
Ballacillo, Rev. Roy, (TR) St. Mary of the Lakes, Medford, NJ
Ballard, Rev. Christopher J., '10 (SY) Curia: Offices and Directors Holy Family, Vernon, NY; St. Agatha, Canastota, NY; St. Helena, Sherrill, NY; St. John, North Bay, NY; St. Joseph, Oneida, NY; St. Patrick, Oneida, NY
Ballard, Rev. Kevin, *S.J.* (SEA) Sacred Heart, Tacoma, WA (>SJ) [MON] Sacred Heart Jesuit Center, Los Gatos, CA
Ballard, Rev. Kevin, *S.J.* '85 (SJ) Chap, Santa Clara Valley Med Ctr
Ballard, Rev. Mark E., '02 (BO) On Leave.
Ballard, Rev. Richard, (CHR) Our Lady of the Rosary, Greenville, SC
Ballecer, Rev. Robert R, *S.J.* '07 (SJ) [MON] USA West Province, Society of Jesus, Los Gatos, CA
Ballesteros, Rev. Enrique, '89 (OAK) St. Louis Bertrand, Oakland, CA
Ballesteros, Rev. Jesus, '10 (RNO) Curia: Offices and Directors Holy Family, Yerington, NV; Our Lady of Perpetual Help, Hawthorne, NV
Ballesteros, Rev. Jose, (PHX) Christ the King Roman Catholic Parish, Mesa, AZ
Ballesteros, Rev. Juan Ignacio, '04 (POD) Curia: Clergy and Religious Services
Ballesteros, Rev. Juan Ignacio, (SJN) [MIS] Opus Dei, Guaynabo, PR
Ballien, Rev. Paul K., '99 (DET) Saint John Neumann Parish Canton, Canton, MI
Ballman, Rev. Luke R., '01 (ATL) On Duty Outside Diocese. USCCB, Washington, DC
Ballman, Very Rev. Robert, '14 (MEM) Curia: Leadership
Ballman, Very Rev. Robert Dale, '14 (MEM) St. Alphonsus Church, Covington, TN
Ballou, Rev. Jeffrey A., '01 (SPR) Curia: (>MO) Offices and Directors St. Catherine of Siena, Springfield, MA
Balluff, Very Rev. John, '88 (JOL) Curia: Leadership St. Anthony, Joliet, IL; [EFT] Diocese of Joliet Priests' Pension Plan, Crest Hill, IL; [EFT] Diocese of Joliet Retired Priests' Other Benefits Plan, Crest Hill, IL
Balluff, Rev. Thomas J., '06 (STP) Church of Saint John the Evangelist of Little Canada, Little Canada, MN; [CEM] Saint John's Church of Little Canada Cemetery, Little Canada, MN
Balogh, Rev. Laszlo, (PAT) St. Stephen's, Passaic, NJ
Baloza, Rev. Sylvere, *C.I.C.M.* (CHR) St. Ann, Florence, SC; St. Anthony, Florence, SC
Balta, Rev. Msgr. Raymond A., '69 (PBR) St. Mary's, Johnstown, PA
Baltes, Rev. Gabriel, *O.S.B.* '91 (JOL) St. Joan of Arc, Lisle, IL; [MON] St. Procopius Abbey, Lisle, IL
Baltes, Rev. Timothy, '76 (SCL) Retired. Curia: Offices and Directors
Balthazar, Rev. Rodolphe, (LR) St. Vincent de Paul, Rogers, AR
Baltrus, Rev. Michael, '08 (NSH) St. Philip, Franklin, TN
Baltz, Rev. Albert G., '70 (BUR) Retired.
Baltz, Rev. David Paul, *MCCJ* '60 (CIN) Retired. [MON] Comboni Missionaries (Verona Fathers)-Comboni Mission Center, Cincinnati, OH
Baltz, Rev. Joseph, '20 (SFE) St. Francis Xavier-Clayton, Clayton, NM
Balwinski, Rev. Gerald E., '69 (SAG) Retired. Saint Mark Parish of Au Gres, Au Gres, MI
Bambenek, Rev. Joseph J., '10 (STP) Curia: Evangelization
Bambrick, Rev. John P., '91 (TR) Curia: Leadership St. Aloysius, Jackson, NJ
Bame, Rev. Jeffrey, '15 (GAL) Co-Cathedral of the Sacred Heart, Houston, TX
Bamman, Rev. John, *O.F.M.Conv.* '09 (TOL) Our Lady of Consolation, Carey, OH; [SHR] Basilica and National Shrine of Our Lady of Consolation, Carey, OH
Bamman, Rev. John, *O.F.M.Conv.* '09 (IND) St. Anthony of Padua Catholic Church, Clarksville, Inc., Clarksville, IN
Banal, Rev. Jose Vaughn A., '96 (LA) On Administrative Leave.
Bananal, Rev. Jay T., '12 (SD) Curia: Advisory Boards, Commissions, Committees, and Councils Pastor of Saint Pius X Catholic Parish, Chula Vista, a corporation sole, Chula Vista, CA
Banares, Rev. Bernard, (BR) Congregation Of St. George Roman Catholic Church, Baton Rouge, Louisiana, Baton Rouge, LA
Banasula, Rev. Zaverio, '13 (RIC) Good Shepherd, Lebanon, VA; St. Therese, St. Paul, VA; [CAM] Catholic Campus Ministry, University of Virginia at Wise, Norton, VA
Banazak, Rev. Gregory, '85 (DET) [SEM] SS. Cyril and Methodius Seminary, Orchard Lake, MI
Banchs Plaza, Rev. Luis Roberto, *S.E.M.V.* '02 (ARE) Our Lady of Guadalupe, Hatillo, PR
Bancroft, Rev. Hartley, '16 (NY) Parish of St. Joseph and Immaculate Conception, Millbrook, NY
Bancroft, Rev. Martin, '01 (RVC) Chap, Consolation Nursing Home
Bandanadam, Rev. Arogyriah, *MF* '04 (SR) Pastor of St. Anthony of Padua Catholic Church of Willits, a Corporation Sole, Willits, CA
Bandari, Rev. Jayaraju, *HGN* '12 (IND) Saint Luke Catholic Church, Indianapolis, Inc., Indianapolis, IN
Banden, Rev. Joseph W., '69 (STL) Retired. St. Sabina Catholic Church, Florissant, MO

Bandsuch, Rev. Mark, *S.J.* '00 (LA) [MON] Jesuit Community, Los Angeles, CA
Bandura, Rev. Tyler J., '13 (GBG) Curia: Advisory Boards, Commissions, Committees, and Councils; Leadership; Offices and Directors St. James, New Alexandria, PA
Bandurski, Rev. Pawel, *SChr* (PHX) Our Lady of Czestochowa Roman Catholic Parish, Phoenix, AZ
Banecker, Rev. Eric, '18 (PH) St. Francis de Sales, Philadelphia, PA
Banet, Rev. Stephen J., (IND) Retired.
Bang, Rev. Aloysio Kyeongseok, (SEA) St. Andrew Kim Personal Parish, Seattle, WA
Bang, Rev. S., (NSH) Curia: Offices and Directors
Bani, Rev. Cary, (BR) Curia: Administration; Clergy and Religious Services
Bani, Rev. J. Cary, '07 (BR) Curia: Administration Congregation of St. Joseph Roman Catholic Cathedral of Baton Rouge, Baton Rouge, LA; [EFT] St. Joseph Cathedral Cemetery Fund, Baton Rouge, LA; [EFT] St. Joseph Cathedral Trust & Bettie Womack Dedicated Cathedral Trust Funds, Baton Rouge, LA
Banick, Rev. Msgr. Thomas V., '63 (SCR) Retired.
Banico, Rev. Emmanuel, (MO) Curia: Offices and Directors
Baniulis, Rev. Algis, *S.J.* '74 (CHI) [MON] Lithuanian American Jesuits (Jesuit Fathers of Della Strada Inc.), Chicago, IL
Banjare, Rev. Stephen, *SS.CC.* '08 (FR) St. Joseph's, Fairhaven, MA; [MIS] Congregation of the Sacred Hearts - United States Province (Sacred Hearts Fathers; Sacred Hearts Missions), Fairhaven, MA
Banka, Rev. Yesobu, '05 (STO) Curia: Leadership St. Patrick Church of Sonora (Pastor of), Sonora, CA
Bankemper, Rev. Stephen M., '03 (COV) Curia: Advisory Boards, Commissions, Committees, and Councils St. Catherine of Siena, Fort Thomas, KY
Banker, Rev. Richard A., '88 (STP) St. Edward, Bloomington, MN
Banks, Rev. Charles, *O.M.I.* '66 (SAT) [NUR] Oblate Madonna Residence, San Antonio, TX
Banks, Rev. Gary M., *S.T.* '76 (WDC) [MON] Father Judge Missionary Cenacle, Adelphi, MD; [MON] Holy Spirit Missionary Cenacle, Riverdale, MD
Banks, Rev. Michael, *OFM Cap.* (NY) [MON] St. Clare Friary (Capuchin Franciscan Friars, Province of St. Mary), Yonkers, NY
Banks, Rev. Peter M, *OFM Cap* '73 (LA) Retired. Old Mission Santa Ines, Solvang, CA
Bankston, Rev. James, (PHX) Curia: (>HPM) Offices and Directors
Bankston, Rev. James Patrick, '04 (HPM) Holy Angels, San Diego, CA
Bannan, Rev. Peter F., '67 (NY) Retired.
Banowsky, Rev. William, '19 (OKL) Curia: Tribunal Bishop McGuinness Catholic High School, Oklahoma City, OK; St. Charles Borromeo, Oklahoma City, OK
Banyk, Rev. Vasyl, '11 (PBR) Holy Trinity, Sykesville, PA; Nativity of the Mother of God, Du Bois, PA
Banzin, Rev. Robert S., '64 (CHI) Retired. St. John Brebeuf, Niles, IL
Baok, Rev. Dominikus, *S.V.D.* '06 (WH) Immaculate Conception, Montgomery, WV; St. Anthony's Shrine, Boomer, WV
Baptista, Rev. Diego, '69 (SR) On Duty Outside Diocese. Chaplain, Mule Creek State Prison, Ione
Baptista, Rev. Diogo, '69 (SAC) Retired.
Baptista, Rev. Jose L., *S.F.X.* '85 (CHI)
Baptiste, Rev. Charles J., '96 (PIT) On Sick Leave.
Baptiste, Rev. Eden Jean, '83 (RVC) St. Boniface, Elmont, NY
Baquero, Rev. Andres, '13 (PAT) Our Lady of Mt. Carmel, Passaic, NJ
Baraan, Rev. Geoffrey, '97 (OAK) Curia: Leadership St. Joseph, Pinole, CA
Barajas, Rev. Abel, (SD) Pastor of Church of the Resurrection Catholic Parish, Escondido, a corporation sole, Escondido, CA
Barajas, Rev. Abel E., '96 (MIA) On Leave.
Barajas, Rev. Juan Martin, (LA) On Duty Outside Diocese.
Barakeh, Rev. Imad N., *B.S.O.* '05 (MO) Curia: Offices and Directors
Barakeh, Rev. Imad N., (RIC) Military Chap
Baraki, Rev. Tesfamariam, '75 (WDC) Chap, Hospital & Nursing Home Ministry, Howard Univ Hosp St. Gabriel, Washington, DC
Baran, Rev. Blaise R., '82 (LAV) La Virgen de Guadalupe, Mesquite, NV
Baran, Rev. Blaise R., '82 (MET) On Duty Outside Diocese. Diocese of Las Vegas, NV
Baraniak, Rev. James T., *O. Praem.* '93 (GB) Curia: Advisory Boards, Commissions, Committees, and Councils Our Lady of Lourdes, De Pere, WI; [MON] St. Norbert Abbey, De Pere, WI
Baranowski, Rev. Arthur R., '68 (DET) Retired. [MIS] National Alliance of Parishes Restructuring into Communities (NAPRC), Macomb, MI
Baranski, Rev. Andrew E., '92 (SY) Curia: Leadership Basilica of the Sacred Heart, Syracuse, NY
Baransky, Rev. Francis J., '79 (ALN) Retired.
Baratelli, Rev. David J., '82 (NEW) Retired.
Baratelli, Rev. David J., '82 (PSC) Curia: Advisory Boards, Commissions, Committees, and Councils St. George, Newark, NJ
Barattero, Rev. Alberto, *I.V.E.* (NY) [MON] Institute of the Incarnate Word, Inc., New York, NY
Barattero, Rev. Alberto, (WDC) [EFT] IVE Real Estate Trust, Mount Rainier, MD; [MON] Institute of the Incarnate Word, Chillum, MD
Barattero, Rev. Alberto, *IVE* '97 (BAL) Our Lady of Mount Carmel, Thurmont, MD; St. Anthony Shrine, Emmitsburg, MD; St. Joseph, Emmitsburg, MD; [MON] St. Vincent's House, Chillum, MD
Baraza, Rev. Patrick, '82 (SPK) St. Ann Parish-Spokane, Spokane, WA; [SEM] Bishop White Seminary, Spokane, WA
Barba, Rev. Alfredo, '09 (FWT) On Leave.
Barbaric, Rev. Zegko, *O.F.M.* (NY) SS. Cyril and Methodius - St. Raphael, New York, NY
Barbarossa, Rev. Michael, '21 (SEA) Immaculate Heart of Mary, Kelso, WA; St. Mary, Castle Rock, WA; St. Rose de Viterbo, Longview, WA
Barbato, Rev. Robert A., *O.F.M.Cap.* '87 (LA) Old Mission Santa Ines, Solvang, CA (>SFR) [SEM] Capuchin Franciscan Order San Buenaventura Friary, San Francisco, CA
Barbee, Rev. William, '20 (HBG) Immaculate Conception of the Blessed Virgin Mary, Berwick, PA; St. Joseph's, Berwick, PA; St. Theresa of the Infant Jesus, New Cumberland, PA
Barbella, Rev. John J., '87 (MET) Curia: Consultative Bodies; Education; Evangelization St. Philip & St. James, Phillipsburg, NJ
Barber, Rev. Hal L., '67 (SFS) Retired.
Barber, Rev. Michael D., *S.J.* '79 (STL) [COL] Saint Louis University, St. Louis, MO; [MON] Sacred Heart Jesuit Community, St. Louis, MO
Barberi de Carvalho, Rev. Rafael, '13 (WDC) On Special Assignment. [SEM] Redemptoris Mater Archdiocesan Missionary Seminary, Hyattsville, MD
Barbian, Rev. Leonard M., '65 (MIL) Retired.
Barbieri, Rev. Giuseppe, '88 (SAN) St. Elizabeth Ann Seton, Odessa, TX
Barbieri, Rev. Joseph, '88 (SAN) Curia: Advisory Boards, Commissions, Committees, and Councils; Canonical Services
Barbiero, Rev. Adriano, (CHI) Our Lady of Mount Carmel, Melrose Park, IL
Barbieto, Rev. Paciano A., '86 (NEW) Our Lady of Mount Carmel, Nutley, NJ
Barbin, Rev. Josemaria, (NOR) [MON] Marian Friary of Our Lady of Guadalupe, Griswold, CT
Barbin, Rev. JoseMaria M., *F.I.* '17 (SY) [RTR] Mount St. Francis Hermitage, Inc., Endicott, NY
Barbone, Rev. Joseph F., '72 (NEW) St. James, Springfield, NJ
Barbour, Rev. Hugh C., *O.Praem.* '90 (ORG) [MON] Norbertine Fathers of Orange, Inc., Silverado, CA
Barboutz, Rev. Paul, '09 (PAT) Curia: Administration Our Lady of the Lake, Mount Arlington, NJ
Barcellona, Rev. Thomas J., '95 (CAM) Curia: Advisory Boards, Commissions, Committees, and Councils; Leadership; Tribunal The Church of Our Lady of the Angels, Cape May Court House, N.J., Cape May Court House, NJ
Barcellona, Rev. Thomas T., (CAM) Chap, Cape Rgnl Med Ctr, Cape May Court House
Barcelos, Rev. Roberto, *OCD* (SB) [RTR] El Carmelo Retreat House, Redlands, CA
Barch, Rev. Howard C., '93 (RCK) On Special Assignment. Prison & Jail Ministry Holy Trinity, Scales Mound, IL; St. Mary, Galena, IL; St. Michael, Galena, IL
Barclay, Rev. Robert F., '75 (BRK) Retired.
Barczak, Rev. Rene, (SP) Retired. [MON] St. Anthony Friary (St. Petersburg) Franciscan Friars-Holy Name Province, Inc., St. Petersburg, FL
Barder, Rev. Luke Christopher, *O.P.* '14 (DEN) St. Dominic Parish, Denver, CO; St. Mary Magdalene Catholic Parish in Denver, Denver, CO; [MON] Dominican Friars, St. Dominic Priory, Denver, Inc., Denver, CO
Bareno, Rev. Javier, (PAT) St. Therese, Succasunna, NJ
Barfi, Rev. Peter Calixtus, (RIC) Church of the Holy Angels, Portsmouth, VA; Church of the Resurrection, Portsmouth, VA; St. Mary, Chesapeake, VA; St. Paul, Portsmouth, VA
Barfield, Rev. Richard G., '22 (VIC) Our Lady of the Gulf, Port Lavaca, TX
Baricuatro, Rev. J. Michael B., '10 (SAC) Curia: Leadership Pastor of St. Rose of Lima Parish, Roseville, a corporation sole, Roseville, CA
Barile, Rev. Ralph E., '82 (BRK) Retired.
Barimah-Apau, Rev. Msgr. Michael, '82 (RVC) St. Thomas, the Apostle, West Hempstead, NY
Baris, Rev. Bernard B., *M.S.* '69 (FR) [MON] La Salette Missionary Association (Missionaries of La Salette (MA), Inc.), Attleboro, MA; [MON] La Salette Shrine & Retreat Center, Attleboro, MA
Barita, Rev. Joseph, *A.L.C.P./O.S.S.* '87 (P) Our Lady of Victory, Seaside, OR
Bariviera, Rev. Jefferson, *C.S.* (WDC) Our Lady of Fatima Parish, Riverdale, MD; St. Bernard, Riverdale Park, MD
Barkemeyer, Rev. John F., '90 (CHI) Chap, Wilmette Curia: (>MO) Offices and Directors
Barker, Rev. Brian, (BEL) St. Joseph, Marion, IL; St. Paul, Johnston City, IL
Barker, Rev. Jack, '92 (SB) Retired.
Barker, Rev. Msgr. James, '80 (BAL) St. Ignatius, Forest Hill, MD
Barker, Rev. Joseph F., '53 (ALB) Retired.
Barker, Rev. Richard E., '92 (GAL) St. Philip the Apostle, Huffman, TX
Barker, Rev. Ronald A., '75 (BO) St. Joseph, Wakefield, MA
Barkett, Very Rev. James S., '91 (ARL) St. Mary of Sorrows, Fairfax, VA
Barkey, Rev. Patrick C., '90 (PIT) Triumph of the Holy Cross, Jefferson Hills, PA
Barkhausen, Rev. Christopher S., '14 (PAT) Curia: Administration; Leadership St. Francis de Sales, Vernon, NJ
Barkin, Rev. Martin F., '77 (PIT) St. Joseph the Worker, Pittsburgh, PA
Barko, Rev. Robert Joseph, *OFM* '16 (STL) [MON] Franciscan Friary of St. Anthony of Padua, St. Louis, MO
Barlett, Rev. Joshua, '15 (KC) On Special Assignment. Missouri Western State Univ St. Rose of Lima, Savannah, MO; [CAM] Newman Catholic Center, Northwest Missouri State University, Maryville, MO
Barley, Very Rev. Tom, '91 (SAN) Curia: Advisory Boards, Commissions, Committees, and Councils; Canonical Services; Leadership St. Thomas, Miles, TX
Barmann, Rev. Karl, *OSB* '65 (SPC) St. Joseph, Springfield, MO
Barmasse, Rev. Gerardo R., *C.S.C.* '76 (PHX) St. Philip the Deacon Mission, A Quasi-Parish, Phoenix, AZ; [MON] Holy Cross Congregation/Casa Santa Cruz, Phoenix, AZ
Barna, Rev. Dariusz P., *O.F.M.Cap.* (MO) Curia: Offices and Directors
Barnabass, Rev. Robert, (NY) Parish of Sts. Peter and Paul and St. Ursula, Mount Vernon, NY
Barnad, Rev. Maria Julian, *SdC.* (PRO) Church of Our Lady of Loreto, East Providence, East Providence, RI
Barnekow, Rev. Kevin, '11 (MIL) On Leave.
Barnell, Rev. Robert, (L) Immaculate Conception, LaGrange, KY
Barnes, Rev. Austin Leonard, '20 (STP) Church of St. Michael, Stillwater, MN; St. Mary, Stillwater, MN
Barnes, Rev. Charles, *S.J.* (MO) Curia: Offices and Directors
Barnes, Rev. Charles, *S.J.* (SEA) [MON] Jesuit House, Seattle, Seattle, WA
Barnes, Rev. Charles, *S.J.* (SEA) Chap, Veterans Administration Med Ctr
Barnes, Rev. Christopher M., '10 (E) St. Ann, Marienville, PA; St. Titus, Titusville, PA; [CAM] University of Pittsburgh - Titusville Campus, Titusville, PA
Barnes, Rev. David, (BO) [SEM] Saint John's Seminary, Brighton, MA
Barnes, Rev. David J., '97 (BO) Curia: Pastoral Services
Barnes, Rev. James H., '69 (LA) Retired.
Barnes, Rev. Nicholas R., '13 (ARL) St. Theresa, Ashburn, VA
Barnes, Rev. Patrick Thomas, '10 (STP) St. Henry, Monticello, MN; [CEM] St. Nicholas Cemetery, Elko New Market, MN
Barnes, Rev. Thomas C., '87 (COV) Retired. Holy Cross, Covington, KY
Barnett, Rev. Bruce, (CHR) Sacred Heart, Gaffney, SC; St. Augustine, Union, SC
Barnett, Very Rev. Daniel J., '00 (SPK) Curia: Offices and Directors St. Catherine of Alexandria, Oakesdale, WA; [SEM] Bishop White Seminary, Spokane, WA

Barnett, Rev. James, *O.P.* (CHI) Retired.
Barnett, Rev. Msgr. Stephen, '70 (SFS) Retired.
Barnhill, Rev. Robert K., '85 (LIN) Curia: Leadership; Offices and Directors St. Wenceslaus, Wilber, NE
Barnum, Rev. Martin, '74 (CHI) Retired.
Barnum, Rev. Martin, (TUC) Retired.
Barnum, Rev. Matthew J., '07 (GR) St. Ann - St. Ignatius, Baldwin, MI; St. Bernard, Irons, MI
Barnwell, Rev. Gerald P., '77 (FR) Retired.
Baroma, Rev. R. Roy C., '97 (SEA) Holy Family, Auburn, WA
Baron, Rev. James, '11 (COS) Curia: Offices and Directors
Baron, Rev. John B., '73 (NEW) Retired.
Baron, Rev. Mark, *M.I.C.* '04 (JOL) Our Lady of Peace, Darien, IL
Barona, Rev. Msgr. Jaime, '98 (ATL) Retired.
Barone, Rev. Jason K., '12 (CHL) Curia: Leadership Our Lady of the Mountains, Highlands, NC; St. Jude, Sapphire, NC
Barone, Rev. Matthew, '20 (SPR) St. Mary's, Lee, MA
Barone, Rev. Michael, (SAM) Curia: Offices and Directors
Barone, Rev. Michael J., '75 (TYL) Retired.
Baronti, Rev. David, '76 (SPK) Retired.
Baroody, Rev. David, '22 (NTN) Holy Transfiguration, McLean, VA
Barose, Rev. Febin, (L) [MON] Sacred Heart Retreat, Louisville, KY
Barota, Rev. Michael, '04 (SPA) St. Mary Assyrian-Chaldean Parish (Assyrian Chaldean Catholic Church California Corporation), Campbell, CA; St. Paul Assyrian-Chaldean Catholic Parish, North Hollywood, CA
Barozzi, Rev. Italo, '65 (BRK) Retired. St. Mel, Flushing, NY
Barr, Rev. Benjamin, (PIT) Westminster Coll, New Wilmington Holy Spirit, New Castle, PA
Barr, Rev. Brian P., '93 (RVC) St. Mary of the Isle, Long Beach, NY
Barr, Rev. Brian P., '93 (RVC) Curia: Leadership; Offices and Directors Our Lady of the Miraculous Medal, Point Lookout, NY
Barr, Rev. Msgr. Eric R., '84 (RCK) Retired.
Barr, Rev. Frederick L., '76 (BO) Retired.
Barr, Rev. Joseph F., '78 (BAL) [EFT] The Immaculate Conception Elementary School Endowment Trust, Towson, MD
Barr, Rev. Msgr. Liam M., '74 (LIN) Retired.
Barr, Rev. Mark D., '08 (BO) On Leave.
Barr, Rev. Timothy J., '06 (RCK) St. Joseph, Freeport, IL; St. Mary, Freeport, IL
Barra, Rev. Nonito Jesus, '93 (GB) St. Margaret Mary, Neenah, WI
Barragan, Rev. Lalo, '02 (YAK) Our Lady of the Desert, Mattawa, WA
Barragan Mendoza, Rev. Juan Pablo, *T.O.R.* (AUS) St. Anthony Marie De Claret, Kyle, TX
Barrameda, Rev. Arnel B., '86 (GAL) Curia: Offices and Directors St. Anthony de Padua, Danbury, TX
Barrand, Rev. James, '89 (IND) [HOS] Franciscan Health, Indianapolis, IN
Barrand, Rev. James, (PHX) Curia: (>HPM) Offices and Directors
Barranger, Rev. Richard L, *OP* (CHI) St. Vincent Ferrer, River Forest, IL
Barras, Rev. Gregory, '84 (BLX) Retired.
Barras, Rev. Michael J., '73 (LKC) Retired. St. John Bosco, Westlake, LA
Barras, Rev. Robert S., '80 (GAL) St. Bernadette Soubirous, Houston, TX
Barratt, Very Rev. Anthony M., '85 (ALB) On Special Assignment. Dir, Office of Prayer & Worship, Pastoral Ctr, Albany Curia: Leadership; Offices and Directors Parish of the Holy Trinity, Hudson, NY
Barraza, Rev. Jeider S., '16 (PAT) St. Andrew the Apostle, Clifton, NJ
Barre, Rev. Michael L., *P.S.S.* '70 (BAL) Retired. [MIS] St. Mary's Seminary & University, Baltimore, MD; [MON] Society of St. Sulpice, Province of the United States, Baltimore, MD
Barrera, Rev. Abraham, *Rev* '16 (MRY) St. Patrick, Watsonville, CA
Barrera, Rev. Albino F., *O.P.* '93 (PRO) [MON] St. Thomas Aquinas Priory at Providence College, Providence, RI
Barrera, Rev. Constantino, '06 (BEA) St. Catherine of Siena, Port Arthur, TX
Barrera, Rev. Filiberto, '98 (OAK) The Catholic Community of Pleasanton, Pleasanton, CA
Barrera, Rev. Gabriel, (PAT) SS. Cyril and Methodius, Clifton, NJ
Barrera, Rev. Msgr. Gustavo, '79 (BWN) Curia: Advisory Boards, Commissions, Committees, and Councils; Leadership Our Lady of Sorrows, McAllen, TX
Barrera, Rev. Jose Alberto, '92 (SLC) Saint Therese of the Child Jesus LLC 246, Midvale, UT
Barrera, Rev. Julio, '13 (OWN) Holy Redeemer, Beaver Dam, KY; Holy Trinity, Morgantown, KY
Barrera, Rev. Luis, '95 (ORL) Holy Cross, Orlando, FL
Barrera-Cruz, Rev. Jose Fidel, (SLC) Curia: Offices and Directors
Barret, Rev. Jichael J., (NY) [MIS] Prelature of the Holy Cross and Opus Dei, New York, NY
Barret, Rev. Kevin, (PCE) On Duty Outside Diocese. Diocese of Cheyenne
Barreto Medina, Very Rev. Javier, '15 (MIA) Curia: Leadership Little Flower, Hollywood, FL
Barrett, Friar Daniel, *OFM* (NO) St. Mary of the Angels, New Orleans, LA
Barrett, Rev. David A., '97 (STP) Retired.
Barrett, Rev. David S., '64 (GB) Retired.
Barrett, Rev. Edward J., '75 (CHI) Retired.
Barrett, Rev. James L., '82 (CHI) Retired. Our Lady of Perpetual Help, Glenview, IL
Barrett, Rev. John J., '78 (RVC) St. Patrick's, Southold, NY
Barrett, Rev. Joseph, '05 (FAR) St. James Basilica of Jamestown, Jamestown, ND; St. Margaret Church of Buchanan, Buchanan, ND; St. Mathias Church of Windsor, Windsor, ND
Barrett, Rev. Michael, '85 (NY) Curia: (>POD) Clergy and Religious Services St. Agnes, New York, NY
Barrett, Rev. Michael, '76 (MIL) Retired.
Barrett, Rev. Miles J., '82 (SC) Retired. On Duty Outside Diocese. Cdr, North Cape May, NJ
Barrett, Rev. Thomas, *C.Ss.R.* '67 (BAL) [SPF] St. John Neuman Residence, Timonium, MD
Barrett, Rev. Thomas E., '93 (PMB) Curia: Leadership Holy Cross, Vero Beach, FL; John Carroll High School, Inc., Fort Pierce, FL
Barrett, Rev. Thomas G., '88 (ORL) St. Brendan, Ormond Beach, FL
Barrett, Rev. Thomas M., '71 (BEL) Retired.
Barrett, Rev. Msgr. Walter C., '75 (RIC) Retired.
Barricks, Rev. Robert L., '94 (P) Sacred Heart, Portland, OR
Barrie, Rev. Giles, *CFR* (NY) [MON] St. Crispin Friary, Bronx, NY
Barrios, Rev. Gustavo, (MIA) St. Gregory, Plantation, FL
Barrios, Rev. Julio, '13 (PAT) On Academic Leave.
Barrios, Rev. Manuel Rafael, '22 (SJ) St. John Vianney, San Jose, CA
Barrios Delgado, Rev. Jose Luis, *OFM* (OAK) St. Elizabeth, Oakland, CA; [MON] Franciscan Friars of California (Province of St. Barbara), Oakland, CA
Barron, Rev. Clemente, (LA) [MON] Passionist Residence, Sierra Madre, CA
Barron, Rev. Dale F., *M.M.* '65 (NY) Retired. [MON] Maryknoll Fathers and Brothers (Catholic Foreign Mission Society of America, Inc.), Ossining, NY
Barron, Rev. Daniel, '96 (DEN) [SEM] Saint John Vianney Theological Seminary, Denver, CO
Barron, Rev. Gerald, *O.F.M., Cap* (SFR) Our Lady of Angels, Burlingame, CA
Barron, Rev. John, *S.J.* (PH) [MON] Jesuit Community at St. Joseph's University, Merion Station, PA
Barron, Rev. Joseph, *PES* '21 (STP) Curia: Leadership St. Mark, St. Paul, MN
Barron, Rev. Stanley C., '74 (PAT) Curia: Administration; Leadership St. Elizabeth Ann Seton, Flanders, NJ
Barron, Rev. William R., '07 (E) Immaculate Conception Parish, Osceola Mills, PA; St. Agnes, Morrisdale, PA
Barrons, Rev. Brian, *M.M.* '84 (NY) [MON] Maryknoll Fathers and Brothers (Catholic Foreign Mission Society of America, Inc.), Ossining, NY
Barros, Rev. Joao Baptista, *C.S.Sp.* '99 (PRO) Immaculate Heart of Mary, Pawtucket, RI
Barros, Rev. Joao Baptista, (PRO) Saint Anthony's Church Corporation, Pawtucket, Pawtucket, RI
Barrosa, Rev. Michael A., '91 (GAL) St. Cecilia, Houston, TX
Barrow, Rev. John A., '80 (PMB) Curia: Leadership St. Andrew, Stuart, FL
Barrow, Rev. Joseph A., '96 (NEW) Retired.
Barrow, Rev. Joshua A., '15 (PRO) Church of Saint Teresa of the Child Jesus, Pawtucket, Rhode Island, Pawtucket, RI
Barry, Rev. Msgr. Edward M., '73 (NY) Retired. On Leave.
Barry, Rev. James, *C.P.* '69 (BRK) [MON] Immaculate Conception Monastery, Jamaica, NY
Barry, Rev. James, *C.P.* '69 (NY) [MON] The Congregation of the Passion - St. Paul of the Cross Province, Jamaica, NY
Barry, Rev. James D., '61 (NU) Retired.
Barry, Rev. James J., '69 (BO) Retired. Immaculate Conception, Malden, MA
Barry, Rev. Msgr. John F., '61 (LA) American Martyrs, Manhattan Beach, CA
Barry, Rev. Maurice J., '67 (HRT) Retired.
Barry, Rev. Michael, *SS.CC.* '64 (SB) On Special Assignment. Mary's Mercy Ctr [MIS] Mary's Mercy Center, Inc., San Bernardino, CA; [MON] Congregation of the Sacred Hearts of Jesus and Mary, SS.CC., Hemet, CA
Barry, Rev. Michael T., '06 (RCK) Retired.
Barry, Rev. Michael W., *SS.CC.* '64 (LA) [MON] Congregation of the Sacred Hearts of Jesus and Mary, La Verne, CA
Barry, Rev. Peter J., *M.M.* '65 (NY) Retired. [MON] Maryknoll Fathers and Brothers (Catholic Foreign Mission Society of America, Inc.), Ossining, NY
Barry, Rev. Robert, *O.P.* '73 (DEN) St. Dominic Parish, Denver, CO; [MON] Dominican Friars, St. Dominic Priory, Denver, Inc., Denver, CO
Barry, Rev. Thomas, '16 (TR) Curia: (>MO) Offices and Directors
Barry, Msgr. Thomas J., (HRT) Retired. Curia: Tribunal
Barry, Rev. Zachary, '14 (FTW) St. Patrick, Ligonier, IN
Barsness, Rev. Michael, '14 (STP) Church of St. Henry, Le Sueur, MN; Church of the Nativity, Cleveland, MN; Immaculate Conception of Marysburg, Madison Lake, MN; St. Mary, Le Center, MN
Barstad, Rev. Joel, (PHX) Curia: (>HPM) Offices and Directors
Barstad, Rev. Joel, '18 (HPM) On Special Assignment. Holy Protection of the Mother of God, Denver, CO
Barta, Rev. Ardel H., '63 (DUB) Retired.
Barta, Rev. Msgr. James O., '55 (DUB) Retired. Curia: Administration
Bartczyszyn, Rev. Steven, *C.R.* '86 (CHI) St. Hyacinth Basilica, Chicago, IL; [MON] Provincial Office of the Congregation of the Resurrection, Chicago, IL
Bartek, Rev. Valerian, '82 (LIN) Sacred Heart, Lincoln, NE
Bartel, Rev. Franklin L., '70 (PHX) Retired. St. Thomas More Roman Catholic Parish, Glendale, AZ
Bartel, Rev. Martin, *O.S.B.* (BAL) [MIS] The Benedictine Society of Baltimore, Inc., Baltimore, MD
Bartel, Rt. Rev. Martin R., *O.S.B.* '85 (GBG) [COL] Saint Vincent College Corporation, Latrobe, PA; [EFT] Benedictine Society of St. Vincent Archabbey, O.S.B., Charitable Trust, Latrobe, PA; [MON] Saint Vincent Archabbey, Latrobe, PA
Bartelme, Rev. James P., '92 (SUP) Retired. On Administrative Leave.
Barth, Rev. Michael D., '94 (COV) Curia: Tribunal St. Joseph, Warsaw, KY
Barth, Rev. Michael K., *S.T.* '79 (WDC) [MON] Missionary Servants of the Most Holy Trinity, Silver Spring, MD
Barthel, Very Rev. Charles W., '82 (STL) Curia: Leadership Mary, Mother of the Church Catholic Church, St. Louis, MO
Bartholomew, Rev. Gregory, *FSSP* '12 (RC) Immaculate Conception Church of Rapid City, Rapid City, SD
Bartholomew, Rev. Michael J., '09 (RVC) Curia: Leadership Immaculate Conception, Westhampton Beach, NY
Bartko, Rev. Louis, *O.F.M.* '90 (CIN) Retired.
Bartkus, Rev. Msgr. Algimantas A., '65 (ALN) Retired.
Bartlett, Rev. Brendan W., '13 (ARL) On Leave.
Bartniski, Rev. William D., '67 (GAL) Retired.
Bartolay, Rev. Rolando, '08 (OAK) Curia: Leadership St. Anne, Union City, CA
Bartolo, Rev. Salvador, *O.Carm.* '52 (JOL) Retired.
Bartoloma, Rev. James L., '03 (CAM) Curia: Advisory Boards, Commissions, Committees, and Councils; Clergy and Religious Services; Tribunal Church of the Holy Family, Washington Township, Sewell, NJ; Korean Catholic Mission (St. Yun Yi II Korean Mission), , ; [EFT] The Sharkey Family Charitable Trust, Camden, NJ
Bartolome, Rev. Cyrus, '07 (BGP) Curia: Consultative Bodies; Leadership Church of Assumption, Westport, Connecticut, Westport, CT
Bartolotta, Rev. Victor W., '90 (ROC) Retired.
Bartos, Rev. Andrzej A., '83 (CHI) SS. Bruno and Richard Parish, Chicago, IL
Bartos, Rev. Francis J., '54 (PH) Retired.
Bartos, Rev. Kris, '85 (MIA) San Pablo, Marathon, FL
Bartosz, Rev. Andrzej, '91 (CHI)
Bartoszek, Rev. Richard, '89 (DET) Chap, Beaumont

Hosp, Grosse Pointe

Bartoul, Rev. William, '77 (SAM) Retired.

Bartoul, Rev. William, (RVC) Chap, Veteran's Administration Hosp

Bartow, Rev. Matthew, (BIR) [MON] Franciscan Missionaries of the Eternal Word, A Public Clerical Association of the Christian Faithful, Irondale, AL

Bartsch, Rev. Ken, *OFM, Conv.* (L) VA Medical Center

Bartsch, Rev. Ken, *O.F.M.Conv.* '75 (IND) [RTR] Mount Saint Francis Friary and Retreat Center, Mount St. Francis, IN

Bartulica, Rev. Matthew, '10 (KC) On Special Assignment. Abbey of Our Lady of Ephesus, Gower Seven Dolors, Hurlingen, MO

Bartunek, Rev. John, '03 (ATL) [MON] Legionaries of Christ, Incorporated, Cumming, GA

Bartylla, Rev. Msgr. James R., '01 (MAD) Curia: Advisory Boards, Commissions, Committees, and Councils; Consultative Bodies; Leadership; Offices and Directors [MIS] Holy Name Catholic Center, Inc., Madison, WI; [MIS] Holy Name Seminary, Inc. (St. Joseph Fund), Madison, WI; [MON] Holy Name Heights, Madison, WI

Barusefski, Very Rev. Ronald, '89 (PSC) On Special Assignment. Curia: Advisory Boards, Commissions, Committees, and Councils (>PBR) [SEM] Byzantine Catholic Seminary of SS. Cyril and Methodius, Pittsburgh, PA

Barusefski, Very Rev. Ronald, '89 (PSC) Curia: Leadership

Barut, Rev. Edmundo N., '92 (HON) Curia: Consultative Bodies; Offices and Directors Our Lady of Perpetual Help, Ewa Beach, HI

Barutwanayo, Rev. Felix, (BO) [MON] Miguel Pro House, Brighton, MA

Barwikowski, Rev. Pawel, '16 (CHI) St. James, Arlington Heights, IL

Barytskyy, Rev. Bohdan, '97 (SJP) Curia: Offices and Directors Epiphany of Our Lord, St. Petersburg, FL

Barzare, Rev. Matthew, '14 (LAF) St. Anne, Abbeville, LA

Basa, Rev. Frank, (CLV) Retired. St. Bernard Parish, Akron, OH

Basanez, Rev. Hector, '10 (SJ) Curia: Leadership; Offices and Directors Christ the King (Parroquia Cristo Rey), San Jose, CA

Basarab, Very Rev. John G., '79 (PSC) Curia: Advisory Boards, Commissions, Committees, and Councils; Leadership Epiphany of Our Lord, Annandale, VA

Basbas, Rev. Larry, '20 (CHI) Our Lady of Perpetual Help, Glenview, IL

Baseford, Rev. Paul, '57 (SB) Retired.

Basekela, Rev. Balufu, (STP) Retired.

Bashista, Rev. Brian, '99 (ARL) St. Elizabeth Ann Seton, Lake Ridge, VA

Basil, Rev. Joseph Stanly, *H.G.N.* '15 (SAL) Sacred Heart Cathedral Parish, Salina, Inc., Salina, KS; St. Joseph Parish, Brookville, Inc., Brookville, KS

Basile, Rev. Giovanni Pietro, (BO) [MON] The Jesuit Community at Boston College, Chestnut Hill, MA

Basilious, Rev. Reynolds, *O.C.D.* '97 (BRK) On Duty Outside Diocese. India Incarnation, Queens Village, NY

Basler, Rev. Robert, *O.S.A.* '13 (JOL) St. Walter, Roselle, IL

Basquel, Rev. Thomas, *C.S.Sp.* '76 (BRK) [MIS] St. Virgilius Church, Broad Channel, NY; [MIS] World Compassion Link, Long Island City, NY

Basquel, Rev. Thomas, *C.S.Sp* (SFR) St. Dunstan, Millbrae, CA

Bass, Rev. Frank B., '03 (BR) St. Isidore the Farmer (Congregation Of Saint Isidore Roman Catholic Church, Baker, Louisiana), Baton Rouge, LA

Bass, Rev. Wade, (DAL) [CAM] Catholic Campus Ministry at Southern Methodist University, Dallas, TX

Bassano, Rev. Michael, *M.M.* '75 (SY) On Duty Outside Diocese. Mary Knoll (Incardinated)

Bassey, Rev. Emmanuel, (DM) St. Patrick, Corning, IA; St. Patrick, Lenox, IA

Bassey, Rev. Peter, '18 (BUF) Curia: Consultative Bodies Basilica of St. Mary of the Angels, Olean, NY; St. John, Olean, NY

Bassil, Rev. Pierre, '98 (OLL) Curia: Communications; Offices and Directors Our Lady of Lebanon Maronite Catholic Church, Flint, MI

Basso, Rev. Anthony, (STA) St. Francis Xavier, Live Oak, FL

Basso, Rev. Anthony, '93 (LSC) On Duty Outside Diocese. on loan, Orange Park, FL

Basso, Rev. Francesco, '17 (DEN) St. Francis de Sales Catholic Parish in Denver, Denver, CO

Bastia, Rev. Msgr. Raymond B., '75 (PRO) Curia: Advisory Boards, Commissions, Committees, and Councils; Finance; Leadership SS. Peter and Paul's Church, Providence, RI

Bastian, Rev. James R., '95 (BUF) Retired. Curia: (>MO) Offices and Directors

Bastianelli, Rev. Daniel, *S.S.J.* '64 (BAL) Retired.

Bastidas, Rev. Alexis, '82 (NY) St. Teresa, New York, NY

Bastidas, Rev. Jorge, '20 (RVC) St. John of God, Central Islip, NY

Bastien, Rev. Emmanuel, '09 (MIA) Retired.

Basulto, Rev. Marco Antonio, '00 (TUC) Saint Bernard Roman Catholic Church - Pirtleville, Pirtleville, AZ

Basulto-Pitol, Rev. Marco, '00 (TUC) Immaculate Conception Roman Catholic Parish - Douglas, Douglas, AZ

Basulto-Pitol, Rev. Marco Antonio, '00 (TUC) Saint Luke Roman Catholic Church - Douglas, Douglas, AZ

Baswekundola, Rev. Nsongolo, *C.P.* '91 (R) On Special Assignment.

Basznianin, Rev. Richard, '84 (TR) St. Pius X, Forked River, NJ

Bataille, Rt. Rev. Vincent, *O.S.B.* (IND) [MIS] Swiss-American Benedictine Congregation, Inc., St. Meinrad, IN

Bataille, Rt. Rev. Vincent, *O.S.B.* '65 (RCK) Retired. [MON] Marmion Abbey, Aurora, IL

Batcha, Rev. James J., '85 (PRM) Curia: Leadership Saint George, Bay City, MI; St. Michael, Flushing, MI

Batchelder, Rev. George, '05 (MRY) Retired.

Batcheldor, Rev. C. Joseph, '57 (L) Retired. Basilica of St. Joseph Proto-Cathedral, Bardstown, KY

Bateman, Very Rev. John B., '96 (HBG) Curia: Offices and Directors; (>MO) Offices and Directors St. Patrick Parish York Charitable Trust, York, PA

Bateman, Very Rev. John R., '96 (HBG) Curia: Offices and Directors

Bates, Rev. James, (BGP) The Saint Bridget Roman Catholic Church Corporation, Stamford, CT; The Saint Maurice Roman Catholic Church Corporation, Stamford, CT

Bath, Rev. Winston L., '72 (ALB) Retired. Curia: Offices and Directors Parish of the Holy Trinity, Hudson, NY

Bathineni, Rev. Mohan, '01 (KCK) Cure of Ars, Leawood, KS

Bathini, Rev. Balaswamy, (OKL) St. Joseph's, Blackwell, OK; St. Joseph's, Tonkawa, OK

Bathke, Rev. Joseph, *C.PP.S.* '78 (KC) Curia: Leadership (>CIN) [MON] Society of the Precious Blood, United States Province, Inc., Dayton, OH

Bathke, Rev. Joseph C., *C.PP.S.* (LC) Retired.

Bathouche, Rev. Ezzat, '08 (NTN) St. Jude, Miami, FL

Bathula, Rev. Kishore, (SAT) Sacred Heart of Mary, Rocksprings, TX

Batista, Rev. Jiobani, '93 (VEN) Curia: Leadership; Organizations (affiliated, inter-Diocesan, miscellaneous/other) Our Lady Queen of Heaven Parish in LaBelle, Inc., LaBelle, FL (>SAT) [MIS] Asociacion Nacional de Sacerdotes Hispanos, EEUU (Inc.), San Antonio, TX

Batres, Rev. Miguel, *O.Praem.* '17 (ORG) [MON] Norbertine Fathers of Orange, Inc., Silverado, CA

Batsis, Rev. Thomas, *O.Carm.* '70 (LA) Retired.

Batt, Rev. Anthony, (STU) Retired. (>CIN) [MON] St. Charles, Celina, OH

Batta, Rev. Nicolas, (SB) St. Anthony, Riverside, CA

Batterberry, Rev. Michael J., '70 (SEA) Retired.

Battey, Rev. Stephen M., (PRO) Saint John Paul II Parish, Pawtucket, Rhode Island, Pawtucket, RI

Battey, Rev. Stephen M., (PRO) Curia: Evangelization

Battiato, Rev. Patrick, (COS) Retired.

Battiato, Rev. Ronald A., '61 (OM) Retired.

Battisti, Rev. Lewis A., '62 (CAM) Retired.

Batts, Rev. Peter, *O.P.* '81 (PRO) [MON] St. Thomas Aquinas Priory at Providence College, Providence, RI

Battu, Rev. Kishore, *SAC* '08 (DET) St. Michael Parish Monroe, Monroe, MI

Battula, Rev. Babu, '96 (LR) Holy Rosary, Stuttgart, AR; Holy Trinity Church, England, AR

Batule, Rev. Msgr. Robert J., '85 (RVC) On Duty Outside Diocese. Dunwoodie St. Dominic's, Oyster Bay, NY

Batungbacal, Rev. Eugene T., *C.Ss.R.* '10 (GR) St. Alphonsus, Grand Rapids, MI; [MIS] The Society of the Redemptorists of the City of Grand Rapids, Grand Rapids, MI

Batykefer, Rev. John J., '90 (PIT) Saint Luke the Evangelist, Sewickley, PA

Bau, Rev. Chau Xuan, *C.Ss.R.* '62 (LA) [MON] Vietnamese Redemptorist Mission, Baldwin Park, CA

Bauer, Rev. Charles A., '78 (MEM) Retired.

Bauer, Rev. Donald J., '01 (LC) St. Aloysius, Hillsboro, WI; St. Jerome, Wonewoc, WI

Bauer, Rev. Elmer, *C.M.* '93 (PH) [SEM] DePaul Novitiate, Philadelphia, PA; [SEM] St. Vincent's Seminary, Philadelphia, PA

Bauer, Rev. Elmer, *C.M.* '88 (PH) [MON] Congregation of the Mission, Philadelphia, PA

Bauer, Rev. John, *C.Ss.R.* (BAL) [SPF] St. John Neuman Residence, Timonium, MD

Bauer, Rev. John James, '08 (STP) Immaculate Heart of Mary, Minnetonka, MN; Notre Dame Academy, Minnetonka, MN

Bauer, Very Rev. John M., '79 (STP) Curia: Leadership Our Lady of Lourdes, Minneapolis, MN

Bauer, Rev. Mark F., '86 (GR) SS. Peter and Paul, Grand Rapids, MI

Bauer, Rev. Richard W., *M.M.* '85 (NY) [MON] Maryknoll Fathers and Brothers (Catholic Foreign Mission Society of America, Inc.), Ossining, NY

Bauer, Rev. Robert A., '87 (DET) St. Mary, Our Lady Queen of Families Parish Warren, Center Line, MI

Bauer, Rev. Stephan, *O.S.C.* '92 (PHX) [MON] Crosier Community of Phoenix (Canons Regular of the Order of the Holy Cross) (Conventual Priory of the Holy Cross), Phoenix, AZ

Bauer, Rev. Steven, '04 (CHI) St. Alphonsus, Chicago, IL

Bauerle, Rev. Bernhard, *O.Carm.* '64 (JOL) [MIS] National Shrine Museum of St. Therese of Lisieux, Darien, IL; [MON] St. Simon Stock Priory, Darien, IL

Baugh, Rev. David G., '57 (CLV) Retired. Our Lady of Mount Carmel, Wickliffe, OH

Baugh, Rev. Matthew, *S.J.* '19 (STL) [MON] Bellarmine House of Studies, St. Louis, MO

Bauhoff, Rev. Msgr. Richard C., '73 (RVC) Curia: Leadership; Offices and Directors Holy Name of Jesus, Woodbury, NY

Bauknecht, Rev. Peter, (DAL) Mater Dei Personal Parish, Irving, TX

Bauler, Rev. Msgr. Gary Patrick, '67 (LA) Retired.

Baum, Very Rev. Matthew B., '09 (ALT) Chap, Sac Min, State Corr Inst, Huntingdon St. John Gualbert Cathedral, Johnstown, PA; St. Patrick, Johnstown, PA; St. Peter in Chains, Somerset, PA

Baum, Rev. Terrence, *SJ* '81 (CIN) [MON] Jesuit Community at St. Xavier High School, Cincinnati, OH

Bauman, Rev. Dale A., '82 (FTW) St. Catherine of Alexandria, Columbia City, IN; St. Joseph, Roanoke, IN

Bauman, Rev. John, '69 (NEW) Retired.

Bauman, Rev. Kevin M., '08 (FTW) St. Joseph, Fort Wayne, IN

Bauman, Rev. Rodger, '82 (STP) Retired. [CEM] Guardian Angels Cemetery, Oakdale, MN

Baumann, Rev. Charles, *S.J.* '80 (MIL) [MON] St. Camillus Jesuit Community (Society of Jesus, USA Midwest Province), Wauwatosa, WI

Baumann, Rev. John A., *S.J.* '69 (OAK) [MIS] Faith in Action, Oakland, CA; [MON] Jesuit Fathers and Brothers, Oakland, CA

Baumann, Rev. Lawrence L., '64 (PHX) Retired.

Baumann, Rev. Richard, *S.J.* (LAN) [MON] USA Midwest Province of the Society of Jesus - Jesuit Residence, Ann Arbor, MI

Baumann, Rev. Stephen A., '92 (ORL) Retired.

Baumann, Rev. Msgr. Theodore J., '67 (BEL) Retired.

Baumberger, Rev. Richard, '89 (SFS) Saint John The Evangelist Parish of Kingsbury County, Arlington, SD; Saint Mary Parish of Hamlin County, Bryant, SD; Saint Thomas Aquinas Parish of Kingsbury, De Smet, SD

Baumert, Rev. Frank J., '78 (OM) St. Joan of Arc, Omaha, NE; St. Thomas More, Omaha, NE

Baumgardner, Rev. John J., '17 (MIL) [SEM] Saint Francis de Sales Seminary, St. Francis, WI

Baumgardner, Rev. Nicholas, '19 (MIL) Curia: Leadership St. Joseph's Congregation, Grafton, WI

Baumgartner, Rev. Msgr. David, '90 (CR) Cathedral of the Immaculate Conception, Crookston, MN; Sacred Heart, Frazee, MN; St. Peter's (Gentilly), Crookston, MN

Baunach, Rev. David, '16 (SPC) Curia: Administration; Consultative Bodies; Offices and Directors St. Cecilia, Kennett, MO; St. Eustachius, Portageville, MO

Baus, Rev. Antonio, *C.PP.S.* (COL) St. James the Less, Columbus, OH

Bausch, Rev. Michael, '79 (ROC) Retired.

Bausch, Rev. William J., '55 (TR) Retired.

Bautista, Rev. Ariel, '21 (MET) Immaculate Conception, Annandale, NJ

Bautista, Rev. Arthur, (CHI) Holy Child Jesus, Chicago, IL

Bautista, Very Rev. Efrain, '10 (SD) Curia: Advisory Boards, Commissions, Committees, and Councils Pastor of Corpus Christi Catholic Parish, Bonita, a corporation sole, Bonita, CA

Bautista, Rev. Gasper, '75 (FRS) Our Lady of Mt. Carmel, Fresno, CA; St. Alphonsus, Fresno, CA

Bautista, Rev. Jose, '91 (ORL) Curia: Canonical Services St. Isaac Jogues, Orlando, FL
Bautista, Rev. Jose A., '99 (LA) Our Lady of Perpetual Help, Los Nietos, CA
Bautista, Rev. Renato J., '07 (NEW) [COL] Seton Hall University, South Orange, NJ; [SEM] Immaculate Conception Seminary School of Theology, South Orange, NJ
Bautista, Rev. Tony, '05 (NY) St. Patrick, Staten Island, NY; [SEM] Society of St. Paul, Staten Island, NY
Bautista Camargo, Rev. Juan C., (CHI) St. Agnes of Bohemia, Chicago, IL
Bautista Peraza, Rev. Pedro, '04 (SPK) Sacred Heart, Brewster, WA
Bava, Rev. David, '73 (WDC) Holy Redeemer, Washington, DC
Baver, Rev. John J., '91 (PIT) All Saints, Butler, PA
Baver, Rev. Msgr. William F., '81 (ALN) Curia: Leadership; Organizations (affiliated, inter-Diocesan, miscellaneous/other) Our Lady Help of Christians, Allentown, PA; SS. Simon and Jude, Bethlehem, PA; [CEM] Diocesan Cemetery Perpetual Care Trust, Allentown, PA; [CEM] Diocesan Cemetery Perpetual Care Trust, Bethlehem, PA; [EFT] Diocesan Cemetery Perpetual Care Charitable Trust, Allentown, PA
Bavinger, Rev. Bruce, *S.J.* '78 (R) St. Raphael the Archangel, Raleigh, NC; [MON] Jesuit Community, Raleigh, NC
Bavugayabo, Rev. Jean Damascene, (BO) [MON] Edmund Campion House, Brighton, MA
Bawyn, Very Rev. Anthony E., '82 (SEA) On Special Assignment. Judicial Vicar, Seattle Curia: Leadership; Offices and Directors; Tribunal
Bawyn, Very Rev. Anthony E., '82 (SEA) Curia: Offices and Directors St. Madeleine Sophie, Bellevue, WA
Baxa, Rev. Henry, '90 (SAL) Retired. St. Edward Parish, Belleville, Inc., Belleville, KS; St. George Parish, Munden, Inc., Munden, KS; St. Isidore Parish, Cuba, Inc., Cuba, KS
Baxter, Rev. Gregory P., '88 (OM) St. Patrick Catholic Church of Gretna, Gretna, NE; [EFT] St. Patrick's Church of Gretna Cemetery Endowment Trust Fund, Gretna, NE
Baxter, Rev. Gregory P., '88 (OM) Curia: Leadership
Baxter, Very Rev. M. Shane, '03 (BEA) Curia: Leadership
Baxter, Rev. Nicholas, *O.F.M.* '62 (SFE) Retired. [MON] The Province of Our Lady of Guadalupe of the Order of Friars Minor, Inc., Albuquerque, NM
Baxter, Rev. Shane, '03 (BEA) St. Anthony Cathedral Basilica, Beaumont, TX
Baxter, Rev. Thomas Benedict, *O.S.B.* '62 (SFE) [MON] Monastery of Christ in the Desert, Abiquiu, NM
Baxter, Rev. Thomas F., '76 (MAD) Retired.
Bay, Rev. Joseph N., '94 (COL) Columbus Vietnamese Catholic Community, Columbus, OH; Sts. Augustine and Gabriel, Columbus, OH
Bay, Rev. Richard, '04 (PAT) Curia: Leadership St. Simon the Apostle, Green Pond, NJ
Baybay, Rev. Felicito S., '74 (ORL) Retired.
Bayer, Rev. Ernest, '01 (DEN) Immaculate Heart of Mary Catholic Parish in Northglenn, Northglenn, CO
Bayer, Rev. John, *O.Cist.* '13 (DAL) [MON] Our Lady of Dallas Cistercian Abbey, Irving, TX
Bayer, Rev. Lawrence J., '58 (CLV) Retired. St. Bridget of Kildare, Parma, OH
Bayer, Rev. Peter T., '71 (ROC) Retired.
Bayhi, Rev. M. Jeffery, '79 (BR) Congregation Of St. John The Baptist Roman Catholic Church Of Zachary, Zachary, LA; [MIS] Closer Walk Catholic Communications, Baton Rouge, LA
Bayiha, Rev. Mathias, (DEN) St. Anne Catholic Parish in Grand Lake, Grand Lake, CO; St. Ignatius Catholic Parish in Walden, Walden, CO; St. Peter Catholic Parish in Kremmling, Kremmling, CO
Bayim, Rev. Cyril Obi, '79 (RVC) St. Patrick's, Bay Shore, NY
Bayler, Rev. Frederick C., '09 (FBK) Retired.
Bayles, Rev. Aaron, (POC) Military Chap
Bayless, Rev. Aaron, (MO) Curia: Offices and Directors
Baylon, Rev. R.V., *S.J.* (GAL) Strake Jesuit College Preparatory Inc., Houston, TX
Baynham, Rev. Michael, (DAL) St. Rita Catholic Parish, Dallas, TX
Bayta, Rev. Joker R., '96 (RIC) St. Peter the Apostle, Ebony, VA; St. Richard, Emporia, VA
Bayuk, Rev. Richard, *C.PP.S.* '75 (KC) Retired. [MON] Society of the Precious Blood, Liberty, MO; [SEM] Gaspar Mission House, Kansas City, MO
Baz, Rev. Msgr. Louis, '81 (OLL) Retired.
Bazan, Rev. Msgr. Joaquin, '62 (WDC) Retired.
Bazan, Rev. Michael J., '84 (ARL) St. Clare of Assisi, Clifton, VA
Bazar, Rev. Ty J., '02 (VIC) Immaculate Conception, Goliad, TX
Bazemo, Rev. Barthelemy, *M.Afr.* '05 (WDC) [MON] Society of Missionaries of Africa, Washington, DC
Bazikila, Rev. Ghislain C., '08 (SFR) Curia: Offices and Directors
Bazimenyera, Rev. John, '80 (PEO) Retired. St. Monica Church, East Peoria, IL; St. Patrick's, Washington, IL
Bazouzi, Rev. Fadi, (OLL) St. Joseph Maronite Catholic Mission, Riverside, CA
Bazzel, Very Rev. Kevin M., '01 (BIR) Curia: Leadership
Bazzi, Rev. Michael J., '64 (SPA) St. Peter Chaldean Cathedral, El Cajon, CA
Bazzoli, Rev. Robert L., *O.S.F.S.* '88 (PH) (>WIL) [MON] Wilmington-Philadelphia Province of the Oblates of St. Francis de Sales, Wilmington, DE
Beach, Rev. Msgr. Francis W., '76 (PH) St. Katharine of Siena, Wayne, PA
Beach, Rev. R. Paul, '01 (L) Curia: Leadership St. Martin of Tours, Louisville, KY
Beagles, Rev. David, '20 (SFD) Robinson Correctional Center Our Lady of Lourdes, Oblong, IL; St. Elizabeth, Robinson, IL
Beahen, Rev. Sean-Patrick, '18 (POC) On Special Assignment. St John Evangelist, Calgary, AB
Beal, Rev. Brian, (COL) Holy Redeemer, Portsmouth, OH; St. Mary, Portsmouth, OH; St. Peter, Wheelersburg, OH
Beal, Rev. John P., '74 (WDC) [COL] Catholic University of America, The, Washington, DC
Beal, Rev. John P., '74 (E) On Duty Outside Diocese. The Catholic University of America, Washington D.C.
Beal, Rev. Wesley, '20 (LUB) Holy Spirit, Lubbock, TX
Beale, Rev. Kenneth R., '92 (NEW) Chap, Tampa, FL
Bean, Rev. E. Gray, '03 (BIR) St. Theresa Catholic Parish, Leeds, Leeds, AL
Beard, Rev. Mark B., '09 (BR) Congregation of St. Helena's Roman Catholic Church, Amite, Louisiana, Amite, LA
Beardslee, Rev. Samuel, (LIN) Curia: Leadership Pius X Catholic High School, Lincoln, NE; St. Teresa Catholic Church, Lincoln, NE
Bearer, Rev. Jacob, (CLV) St. Edward, Parkman, OH; St. Lucy, Middlefield, OH
Bearis, Rev. Marvin, *O.F.M. Cap.* (BO) [MON] St. Francis of Assisi Friary, Jamaica Plain, MA
Bearss, Rev. James M., '97 (GLD) Holy Childhood of Jesus of Harbor Springs, Harbor Springs, MI; Holy Cross of Cross Village, Cross Village, MI; Saint Ignatius of Good Hart, Good Hart, MI; Saint Nicholas of Larks Lake, Pellston, MI
Beaton, Rev. Kevin J., *S.F.O.* '87 (SAM) Retired.
Beatty, Very Rev. Steven L., '07 (BEL) Curia: Leadership St. Bernard, Albers, IL; St. Damian, Damiansville, IL; St. George, New Baden, IL; [EFT] Catholic Community Foundation for the Diocese of Belleville, Belleville, IL; [EFT] Ministry Formation Fund, NFP, Belleville, IL; [EFT] Property & Liability Insurance Fund, NFP, Belleville, IL; [EFT] The Catholic Diocese of Belleville Parish & Agency Resource Fund, Belleville, IL; [MIS] Catholic Diocese of Belleville General Fund, Belleville, IL; [MIS] Diocese of Belleville The Catholic Service and Ministry Appeal, Belleville, IL
Beaubien, Rev. David W., '93 (WDC) Curia: Deaneries St. Aloysius, Leonardtown, MD
Beauchamp, Rev. E. William, *C.S.C.* '82 (FTW) [MON] Congregation of Holy Cross, Southern Province, Inc., Notre Dame, IN; [MON] Congregation of Holy Cross, United States Province of Priests and Brothers, Notre Dame, IN; [MON] Congregation of Holy Cross-Eastern Province, Inc., Notre Dame, IN; [MON] Priests of Holy Cross, Indiana Province, Inc., Notre Dame, IN
Beauchamp, Rev. William, *C.S.C.* '82 (FTW) [MON] Holy Cross Community, Corby Hall, University of Notre Dame, Notre Dame, IN
Beauclair, Rev. Stephen, *O.S.B.* '67 (SCL) [MON] St. John's Abbey, of the Order of St. Benedict, Collegeville, MN; [NUR] St. Benedict's Senior Community, St. Cloud, MN
Beaudin, Rev. William L., *O.F.M.* '81 (HRT) St. Patrick and St. Anthony Roman Catholic Church Corporation, Hartford, CT; [MON] St. Patrick-St. Anthony Friary (Franciscan Friars), Hartford, CT
Beaudin, Rev. William R., '82 (BUR) Curia: Leadership; Offices and Directors Christ Our Savior Parish, Manchester Center, VT
Beaudry, Rev. David, (GB) Roncalli Catholic Schools, Inc., Manitowoc, WI; St. Thomas the Apostle, Newton, WI
Beaudry, Very Rev. David B., '82 (GB) Curia: Advisory Boards, Commissions, Committees, and Councils
Beaugrand, Rev. Hugues, *I.B.P.* (MAN) St. Stanislaus Parish, Winchester, NH
Beaulaurier, Very Rev. Brooks F., '08 (YAK) Curia: Offices and Directors St. John, Naches, WA; St. Juan Diego, Cowiche, WA
Beaulieu, Rev. Msgr. Kerry, '74 (ORG) Retired. St. Justin Martyr, Anaheim, CA
Beaulieu, Rev. Msgr. Peter R., '83 (WOR) On Special Assignment. Dir, Mission Integration & Pastoral Care, St Vincent Hosp. [MIS] Catholic Restoration Apostolate, Worcester, MA
Beaumier, Rev. Casey C., *S.J.* '05 (BO) [MON] The Jesuit Community at Boston College, Chestnut Hill, MA
Beaumont, Rev. Gregory J., '96 (FRS) St. Malachy, Tehachapi, CA
Beaumont, Rev. Msgr. Joachim, (NY) Retired. St. Margaret Mary, Bronx, NY
Beaumont, Rev. Msgr. Joachim B., '59 (NY) Parish of St. Brendan and St. Ann, Bronx, NY
Beaupre, Rev. R. Bradley, *C.S.C.* '68 (ORL) Retired. [MON] Congregation of Holy Cross, United States Province, Cocoa Beach, FL
Beauregard, Rev. Andrew M., *F.P.O.* '08 (BO) [MON] Franciscans of Primitive Observance, Lawrence, MA
Beauregard, Rev. David, *O.M.V.* '80 (SFD) St. Mary's, Alton, IL
Beausoleil, Rev. Charles, *O.M.I.* '56 (BO) [NUR] Immaculate Heart of Mary Residence, Tewksbury, MA
Beausoleil, Rev. Kent, *S.J.* '05 (OM) [MON] Jesuit Community at Creighton University, Omaha, NE
Beauvais, Rev. David E., '62 (RCK) Retired.
Beaven, Rev. Robert W., '68 (CHI) Retired. St. Benedict, Chicago, IL
Beaver, Rev. Nelson G., '76 (TOL) Resurrection, Lexington, OH
Bebak, Rev. Brian D., '86 (WCH) Holy Family, Marion, KS
Becerra, Rev. Chris, (CC) St. Joseph, Alice, TX; St. Peter Mission, Ben Bolt, TX
Becerra, Very Rev. Christopher E., '13 (CC) Curia: Leadership
Becerra, Rev. Manuel, '15 (P) St. Vincent de Paul, Salem, OR
Becerra, Rev. Rafael, *C.S.* '95 (GAL) St. Jerome, Houston, TX
Becerra, Rev. Robert L., '89 (NEW) On Duty Outside Diocese. Newark
Becerra Mendez, Rev. Gustavo Adolfo, (DEN) St. John the Evangelist Catholic Parish in Loveland, Loveland, CO
Becerra Reyes, Rev. Roberto Carolos, (CIN) St. Bernard, Cincinnati, OH
Bechard, Rev. Gerard V., '80 (DET) Retired.
Becher, Rev. Albert B., '84 (DAL) On Administrative Leave.
Bechill, Rev. David, '11 (DET) Curia: Administration; Consultative Bodies Christ the Good Shepherd Parish Lincoln Park, Lincoln Park, MI
Bechtel, Rev. David W., '08 (SCR) Curia: Leadership St. Joseph the Worker, Williamsport, PA
Bechter, Rev. Paul, '16 (DAL) Curia: Offices and Directors [COL] University of Dallas, Irving, TX
Bechtold, Rev. Mitchell, '14 (SCL) Christ the King, Browerville, MN; St. Joseph, Clarissa, MN
Beck, Rev. Edward L., *C.P.* '85 (NY) [MON] St. Vincent Strambi Residence (The Passionists), Pelham Manor, NY; [MON] The Congregation of the Passion - St. Paul of the Cross Province, Jamaica, NY
Beck, Rev. Henry, *O.F.M.* '80 (ALN) [MON] St. Francis Friary (Franciscan Province of St. John the Baptist), Easton, PA; [RTR] St. Francis Retreat House, Inc., Easton, PA
Beck, Rev. Joseph C., '84 (PIT) Chap, Health South Hosp of Pittsburgh; McKeesport UPMC; Kan… Mary, Mother of God, White Oak, PA
Beck, Rev. Lawrence J., '88 (SAC) Pastor of Holy Trinity Parish, El Dorado Hills, a corporation sole, El Dorado Hills, CA
Beck, Rev. R. Patrick, '76 (BEA) Retired.
Beck, Rev. Richard W., '74 (SCR) Curia: Leadership Blessed Virgin Mary, Queen of Peace, Hawley, PA
Beck, Rev. Robert R., '66 (DUB) Retired.
Becker, Rev. Aaron, '17 (LC) St. Paul, Mosinee, WI; [EFT] St. Paul Parish Endowment Trust, Mosinee, WI
Becker, Rev. Brian, (CHL) St. Margaret Mary, Swannanoa, NC
Becker, Rev. Charles P., '86 (CHI) On Duty Outside Diocese. Wauconda
Becker, Rev. David R., '66 (ALT) Retired.
Becker, Rev. Edward, '05 (ORG) Curia: Offices and Directors Our Lady of Guadalupe, La Habra, CA
Becker, Rev. Jayson, '18 (KC) Church of the Santa Fe, Buckner, MO; Immaculate Conception, Lexington, MO
Becker, Rev. Jayson, '18 (KC) On Special Assignment. Jeanne Jugan Ctr

Becker, Rev. John J., '72 (GB) Retired.
Becker, Rev. Msgr. Michael A., '75 (ALT) Curia: Offices and Directors St. John the Evangelist, Altoona, PA; St. Rose of Lima, Altoona, PA; [CAM] Office of Campus Ministry, Altoona, PA
Becker, Rev. Michael C., '99 (STP) Sts. Joachim and Anne, Shakopee, MN
Becker, Rev. Nickolas, *O.S.B.* '02 (SCL) [MON] St. John's Abbey, of the Order of St. Benedict, Collegeville, MN
Becker, Rev. Paul D., '73 (BIS) Retired.
Becker, Rev. Thomas, '80 (SCL) Retired.
Becker, Rev. Msgr. Vincent J., '62 (BUF) Retired.
Becker, Rev. William M., '88 (WIN) Holy Trinity, Owatonna, MN; Sacred Heart, Hayfield, MN; St. Columbanus, Blooming Prairie, MN
Beckermann, Rev. Julius, *OSB* (SCL) St. Anthony Catholic Church, Albany, MN; St. Benedict's, Avon, MN
Beckley, Rev. John, *S.M.* '73 (WDC) Retired. [MON] Marist Center (The Marist Finance Center of the Atlanta Province of the Society of Mary, Marist Fathers and Brothers), Washington, DC
Beckley, Rev. John P., *S.M.* '73 (WH) Retired.
Beckman, Rev. David M., '92 (DUB) St. John's Church, Independence, Iowa, Independence, IA; St. Patrick Church, Winthrop, Iowa, Winthrop, IA
Beckman, Rev. Gary L., '95 (DAV) St. Bernadette Church of West Branch, Iowa, West Branch, IA; St. Wenceslaus Church of Iowa City, Iowa, Iowa City, IA
Beckman, Rev. Mark, '90 (NSH) St. Henry, Nashville, TN
Beckman, Rev. Martin A., '58 (STP) Retired.
Beckmann, Rev. Msgr. Donald M., '70 (RVC) Retired. St. Ignatius Martyr, Long Beach, NY
Becnel, Rev. Msgr. Terry B., '64 (NO) Retired.
Beczek, Rev. Mariusz, *O.S.J.* '98 (SCR) Annunciation, Hazleton, Hazleton, PA
Bedard, Rev. Ernest, *O.F.M., Cap.* '12 (NOR) St. Pius X, Middletown, CT
Bedel, Rev. Jason Edward, '08 (CIN) Mary Help of Christians, Fairborn, OH; Sacred Heart, New Carlisle, OH; St. Augustine, Jamestown, OH; St. Brigid, Xenia, OH; St. Paul, Yellow Springs, OH
Bedenikovic, Rev. Stephen, *O.F.M.* '85 (CHI) Sacred Heart, Chicago, IL
Bediako, Rev. Richard, (VIC) Our Lady of Guadalupe, Cuero, TX; SS. Peter & Paul, Meyersville, TX; St. Michael, Cuero, TX
Bedient, Rev. Anthony, '19 (LIN) Curia: Leadership Church of the Holy Spirit, Plattsmouth, NE
Bedillion, Rev. James R., '75 (PIT) Retired. Manorcare Health Svcs, Allegheny
Bednar, Rev. Gerald J., '83 (CLV) Retired. St. John of the Cross, Euclid, OH
Bednarik, Rev. John, *O.F.M. Cap.* '68 (PIT) [MON] St. Augustine Friary, Pittsburgh, PA
Bednarowicz, Rev. Andrzej, '01 (BUR) Our Lady of Perpetual Help, Bradford, VT
Bednarski, Rev. Piotr D., *O.S.P.P.E.* '09 (NY) St. Stanislaus Bishop and Martyr, New York, NY
Bednarz, Rev. Jan, '72 (SLC) Retired.
Bedore, Rev. Donald E., '11 (DOD) Curia: Offices and Directors St. Joseph Catholic Church of Scott City, Kansas, Scott City, KS; St. Theresa Catholic Church of Dighton, Kansas, Dighton, KS
Bedoya, Rev. Carlos, '90 (ORL) St. Mary of the Lakes, Eustis, FL
Bedoya, Rev. Hector, '91 (ORG) St. Mary's, Fullerton, CA
Bedoya, Rev. Jorge, '13 (TR) The Church of Jesus, the Good Shepherd, Beverly, NJ
Bedoya, Rev. Julio, *ICC* (STA) Christ the King, Jacksonville, FL; [SHR] Mission Nombre de Dios and Shrine of Our Lady of La Leche, St. Augustine, FL
Bedoya, Rev. Ruben, '91 (LAV) On Administrative Leave.
Bedrossian, Rev. Armenag, '99 (OLN) Our Lady Queen of Martyrs, Los Angeles, CA
Bedzinski, Rev. Robert, *S.Ch.* '02 (BO) [SHR] Saint John Paul II Shrine of Divine Mercy, Salem, MA
Beebe, Rev. Msgr. Charles J., '70 (PEO) Retired.
Beegan, Rev. James, *M.S.F.* '00 (SAT) [NUR] Missionary Servants of St. Anthony (Padua Place), San Antonio, TX
Beekman, Rev. Carl E., '00 (RCK) St. Anthony of Padua, Rockford, IL
Beeman, Very Rev. W. Daniel, '07 (RIC) Curia: Deaneries Our Lady of Mount Carmel, Newport News, VA
Beeri, Rev. Clement, (HON) St. Anthony of Padua, Kailua, HI
Beerman, Rev. Andrew J., '96 (WIN) Curia: Advisory Boards, Commissions, Committees, and Councils Holy Family, Fairmont, MN; SS. Peter and Paul's, Blue Earth, MN; St. John Vianney, Fairmont, MN; St. Mary's, Winnebago, MN
Beeson, Rev. Msgr. Lawrence A., '60 (DM) Retired.
Beeson, Rev. Terry P., '05 (STP) St. Joseph, Hastings, MN; St. Pius V, Cannon Falls, MN; [CEM] St. Joseph Cemetery, Hastings, MN; [CEM] St. Pius V Cemetery, Cannon Falls, MN
Beever, Rev. Carlton J., '74 (IND) Retired.
Beezam, Rev. Kishore Raju, *SAC* '04 (DET) St. Augustine Parish Richmond, Richmond, MI
Befort, Rev. Daryl, '95 (WCH) St. Joseph, Andale, KS
Befort, Rev. Earl, *O.F.M.Cap.* '69 (SAL) St. Catherine Parish, Catharine, Inc., Catharine, KS; [MON] St. Fidelis Friary, Victoria, KS
Begany, Rev. David Patrick, *S.S.J.* '14 (GAL) Holy Family, McNair, TX
Begay, Rev. Joseph N., *S.S.J.* (BAL) Retired.
Begg, Rev. Christopher T., '77 (WDC) On Special Assignment. Catholic Univ of America St. Joseph's on Capitol Hill, Washington, DC; [COL] Catholic University of America, The, Washington, DC
Beggiani, Rev. Seely, '61 (SAM) Retired.
Beggiani, Chorbishop Seely, '61 (SAM) Curia: Offices and Directors
Beggin, Rev. Thomas M., '79 (GF) Retired.
Begley, Rev. James J., '82 (RIC) St. Paul, Richmond, VA
Begley, Rev. John J., *S.J.* '62 (SCR) [COL] The University of Scranton, Scranton, PA
Begly, Very Rev. Mark S., '84 (ALT) Curia: Deaneries; Offices and Directors Our Mother of Sorrows, Johnstown, PA; St. Michael the Archangel, Johnstown, PA
Begolly, Rev. Msgr. Michael J., '81 (GBG) Curia: Advisory Boards, Commissions, Committees, and Councils Mother of Sorrows, Murrysville, PA
Behan, Rev. Harry P., '73 (NU) Retired.
Behan, Rev. Msgr. Philip A., '70 (SB) Retired. St. Vincent Ferrer, Sun City, CA
Beharry, Rev. Marlon Ricardo, *O. Carm* '21 (NY) [MON] St. Albert's Priory, Middletown, NY; [RTR] National Shrine of Our Lady of Mount Carmel, Middletown, NY
Behay, Rev. Vasyl S., '11 (STF) Curia: (>MO) Offices and Directors; Offices and Directors St. Michael, Yonkers, NY
Behling, Rev. Patrick, '16 (MIL) St. Mary's Congregation, Elm Grove, WI; St. Monica's Congregation, Whitefish Bay, WI
Behm, Very Rev. Patrick M., '12 (SC) Curia: Leadership St. John Paul II Catholic Parish, Carroll, IA
Behna, Rev. Max, '18 (JOL) St. Margaret Mary, Naperville, IL
Behnke, Rev. John J., *C.S.P.* '76 (NY) [MON] Paulist Fathers' Motherhouse, New York, NY
Behrend, Rev. Thomas J., '00 (CLV) St. Rita, Solon, OH
Beidelman, Very Rev. Patrick J., (IND) Curia: Offices and Directors Saint Mary of the Immaculate Conception Catholic Church, Indianapolis, Inc., Indianapolis, IN; SS. Peter and Paul Cathedral, Indianapolis, Inc., Indianapolis, IN
Beighlie, Rev. James T., *C.M.* '79 (STL) Our Lady, Queen of Peace Catholic Church, House Springs, MO; St. Vincent De Paul Catholic Church, St. Louis, St. Louis, MO; [MON] Congregation of the Mission, Perryville, MO
Beirne, Rev. Gerald E., '62 (PRO) Retired.
Beirne, Rev. M. Christen, '69 (NEW) Retired. St. Rose of Lima, Short Hills, NJ
Beirne, Rev. Robert M., '63 (PRO) Retired. [MON] St. John Vianney Residence, Providence, RI
Beischel, Rev. Thomas, *C.PP.S.* '58 (CIN) Retired.
Beisel, Rev. Msgr. James D., '80 (PH) Curia: Evangelization St. Robert Bellarmine, Warrington, PA
Beiter, Rev. Eugene J., '64 (LAN) Retired.
Beiter, Rev. Isaiah, *OP* '20 (NY) St. Joseph, New York, NY
Bejan, Rev. Ciprian, '00 (BGP) Curia: Consultative Bodies Saint Lawrence Corporation, Shelton, CT
Bejan, Rev. Flavian, (BGP) The St. Theresa's Roman Catholic Church Corporation, Trumbull, CT
Bejarano, Rev. Cesar, (RVC) Queen of the Most Holy Rosary, Roosevelt, NY
Bejgrowicz, Rev. Joseph J., '70 (NEW) St. Raphael, Livingston, NJ; St. Theresa, Kenilworth, NJ
Bejgrowicz, Rev. Joseph S., (NEW) Retired.
Bejo, Rev. Lauro, *SOLT* (PHX) Most Holy Trinity Roman Catholic Parish, Phoenix, AZ
Bekala, Rev. Mariadas, '04 (MAD) St. Mary, Palmyra, WI; St. Mary Help of Christians, Sullivan, WI
Belanger, Rev. Daniel R., *C.S.V.* '07 (CHI) [MON] Viatorian Province Center-Clerics of St. Viator, Arlington Heights, IL
Belanger, Rev. Daniel R., *C.S.V.* '07 (JOL) St. George, Bourbonnais, IL
Belanger, Rev. Francis, (NY) Parish of St. Vincent Ferrer and St. Catherine of Siena, New York, NY
Belanger, Rev. Msgr. Gerald R., '75 (MAN) St. Charles Borromeo, Meredith, NH
Belanger, Rev. Thomas G., '06 (CHI) Curia: Leadership St. Josephine Bakhita Parish, Chicago, IL
Belanich, Rev. Giordano, '75 (NEW) Retired. Chap, Hudson Cty Juvenile Corr Ctr, Secaucus Curia: Offices and Directors
Belardi, Rev. Todd, '04 (MIL) Curia: Leadership St. Anthony's Congregation, Kenosha, WI; St. Joseph Catholic Academy, Inc., Kenosha, WI
Belauskas, Rev. August J., '68 (CHI) Retired. [SEM] University of Saint Mary of the Lake/Mundelein Seminary, Mundelein, IL
Belczak, Rev. Edward, '72 (DET) Retired.
Belczak, Rev. Thomas A., '80 (DET) St. Kenneth Parish Plymouth, Plymouth, MI
Belden, Rev. Corey T., '02 (STP) Ave Maria Academy, Maple Grove, MN; St. Anne, Hamel, MN; [CEM] St. Anne Cemetery, Hamel, MN
Belford, Rev. Msgr. William J., '74 (NY) Curia: Leadership St. Teresa, Staten Island, NY
Belgarde, Rev. George H., *S.J.* (NY) [MON] Murray-Weigel Hall (A Jesuit Community at Murray-Weigel Hall and Kohlmann Hall), Bronx, NY
Belger, Rev. Jeffry, '03 (DAV) [CAM] Newman Catholic Student Center, Iowa City, IA
Belgica, Rev. Erwin, '94 (SP) Our Lady of Grace, Beverly Hills, FL
Belhumeur, Rev. Paul N., *M.S.* '61 (HRT) [MIS] Missionaries of LaSalette, Hartford, CT
Beligotti, Rev. Richard J., '68 (ROC) Retired.
Beligotti, Rev. Robert L., '68 (ROC) Retired.
Belina, Rev. Scott A., '13 (OG) On Leave.
Belinsky, Rev. Michael, *CSC* (P) Holy Redeemer, Portland, OR
Belisch, Rev. Carl L., *C.S.B.* '65 (GAL) Retired. [MON] The Basilian Fathers of Dillon House, Houston, TX
Belisle, Rev. Ronald H., '62 (SEA) Retired.
Belitz, Rev. Ronald C., '79 (GB) St. John Nepomucene (St. John Congregation), Little Chute, WI
Belizaire, Rev. Hilaire, '00 (BRK) Sacred Heart, Cambria Heights, NY
Belizario, Rev. Nelson, *O.Carm.* '68 (NY) St. Joseph, Bronx, NY
Belizario, Rev. Nelson, (NEW) St. Cecilia, Englewood, NJ
Belken, Rev. Daniel, '20 (SPC) Curia: Offices and Directors Cathedral of St. Mary of the Annunciation, Cape Girardeau, MO; Notre Dame Regional High School, Cape Girardeau, MO
Bell, Rev. Msgr. Carl F., '66 (LA) Retired.
Bell, Rev. Edward H., '77 (PH) Curia: Advisory Boards, Commissions, Committees, and Councils Nativity of the Blessed Virgin Mary, Media, PA
Bell, Rev. Gerald L., '73 (L) Retired. Curia: Leadership; Offices and Directors
Bell, Rev. Msgr. John P., *J.C.L.* '75 (DAL) Curia: Administration Our Lady of Angels Catholic Parish, Allen, TX
Bell, Rev. Joseph, '74 (SPK) Curia: Leadership
Bell, Rev. Joseph W., '74 (SPK) Retired.
Bell, Rev. Kyle, '18 (SP) [CAM] Catholic Student Center, University of South Florida, Temple Terrace, FL; [MIS] DOSP USF Housing, Inc., Tampa, FL
Bell, Rev. Kyle, '18 (SP) Curia: Pastoral Services
Bell, Rev. Marc, *O.Carm.* '15 (JOL) [MON] Carmelite Provincial Office, Darien, IL
Bell, Rev. Steven, *CSP* (OAK) (>NY) [MON] Paulist Fathers - Generalate, New York, NY
Bellafiore, Rev. I. Michael, *S.J.* '03 (BO) [SEM] Pope Saint John XXIII National Seminary, Weston, MA
Bellafiore, Rev. Samuel, (ALB) Immaculate Heart of Mary, Watervliet, NY
Bellamkonda, Rev. Joseph, '11 (MAD) St. John the Baptist, Waunakee, WI; St. Mary of the Lake, Waunakee, WI
Belland, Rev. David, '87 (SCL) On Special Assignment.
Bellantonio, Rev. Albert, '69 (BRK) Retired.
Bellen, Rev. Louie, (MRY) St. Mary of the Nativity, Salinas, CA
Bellenoit, Rev. George C., '72 (FR) Retired. Curia: Offices and Directors
Belleque, Very Rev. Thomas, '85 (SEA) Curia: Leadership St. Anthony, Renton, WA
Bellew, Rev. Francis, '66 (NY) Retired.
Belli, Rev. Bryan W., '02 (ARL) On Leave.
Bellino, Rev. Samuel P., *S.J.* '88 (SJ) [MON] Jesuit

Community at Santa Clara University, Inc., Santa Clara, CA

Bellittiere, Rev. David A., '89 (BUF) Fourteen Holy Helpers, West Seneca, NY

Belliveau, Rev. Gary J., '85 (MAN) Corpus Christi Parish, Portsmouth, NH

Belliveau, Rev. Paul D., *M.M.* '69 (NY) Retired. [MON] Maryknoll Fathers and Brothers (Catholic Foreign Mission Society of America, Inc.), Ossining, NY

Bello, Rev. Iden Jose, '05 (LAR) San Agustin Cathedral, Laredo, TX

Bello, Rev. Jorge Luis, '03 (MIA) Retired.

Bello, Rev. Jose Wilson, '98 (NEW) Parish of the Transfiguration, Newark, NJ

Bello, Rev. Manuel Aznar, *C.M* (SJN) Chap, Hospital Pavia-Santurce, Santurce

Bello-Ayala, Rev. Carlos Wilson, '09 (DEN) Holy Trinity Catholic Parish in Westminster, Westminster, CO

Bello-Carrillo, Rev. Juan Carlos, *T.O.R.* '08 (SAT) St. Benedict, San Antonio, TX

Bello-Carrillo, Rev. Juan Carlos, *T.O.R.* '00 (SAT) Holy Name, San Antonio, TX

Bellonce, Rev. Fritzner, '06 (MIA) Holy Family, North Miami, FL

Bellopede, Rev. Louis P., '91 (PH) Curia: Advisory Boards, Commissions, Committees, and Councils St. Agnes, West Chester, PA

Bellow, Rev. Msgr. Richard, '70 (CHL) Retired.

Belmonte, Rev. John, *S.J.* (VEN) Institute for Catholic Studies and Formation, Inc., Arcadia, FL

Belmonte, Rev. John, *S.J.* (VEN) Curia: Leadership

Belmonte-Luna, Rev. Luis Gerardo, *O.C.D.* '07 (OKL) Our Lady of Mount Carmel and St. Therese Little Flower, Oklahoma City, OK; [MON] Monastery of Our Lady of Mount Carmel and Little Flower, Oklahoma City, OK

Belmontes, Rev. Jesus, '04 (DAL) Cathedral Santuario de Guadalupe, Dallas, TX

Belocura, Rev. Roy, (CHI) Saint Julie Billiart, Tinley Park, IL

Belogi, Very Rev. James, '81 (ALB) Curia: Leadership Our Lady Queen of Peace, Schenectady, NY; St. Gabriel the Archangel, Schenectady, NY; St. Madeleine Sophie, Schenectady, NY; [MIS] Christ Child Society of Albany, Schenectady, NY

Belongia, Very Rev. Brian S., '05 (GB) Curia: Administration; Leadership St. Francis Xavier Cathedral, Green Bay, WI; St. John the Evangelist, Green Bay, WI

Belschner, Rev. Wayne L., '95 (BO) St. Mary, Dedham, MA

Belsole, Rev. Kurt J., *O.S.B.* '78 (GBG) [MON] Saint Vincent Archabbey, Latrobe, PA

Belt, Rev. David D., '90 (OM) Curia: Leadership; Offices and Directors St. Stephen the Martyr, Omaha, NE

Beltowski, Rev. Andrzej, (CHI) Retired.

Beltran, Rev. Jacque, (MO) Curia: Offices and Directors

Beltran, Rev. Jacque B., '87 (CHI) On Special Assignment. Formation Faculty, University of St. Mary of the Lake

Beltran, Rev. Jo Andre B., '01 (CHI) St. Pio of Pietrelcino Parish, Chicago, IL

Beltran, Rev. Jorge Paredes, (ARE) Curia: Leadership

Beltran, Rev. Jose J., '11 (SAC) Pastor of St. Rose Parish, Sacramento, a corporation sole, Sacramento, CA

Beltran, Rev. Rene Mena, '05 (CHI) Cristo Rey Parish, Chicago, IL

Beltran Arias, Rev. Yorman A., '10 (CHI) SS. Genevieve and Stanislaus Bishop and Martyr, Chicago, IL

Beltzner, Rev. Lucian, *O.Carm.* '63 (NY) [MON] St. Albert's Priory, Middletown, NY

Bempong, Rev. Philip Yaw, (DM) St. John, Greenfield, IA; St. Patrick, Massena, IA

Benander, Rev. Alan V., *O.Praem.* '13 (ORG) [MON] Norbertine Fathers of Orange, Inc., Silverado, CA

Benas, Rev. Randy, '85 (SJ) On Leave.

Benavente, Rev. Msgr. James L.G., '94 (AGN) Curia: Miscellaneous / Other Offices

Benavente, Rev. Msgr. James Leon Guerrero, '94 (AGN) Dulce Nombre de Maria Cathedral - Basilica, Agana, GU

Benavides, Rev. Xavier, (SJ) Curia: Leadership

Benavides Mesones, Rev. Gonzalo, *S.J.* '16 (CHI) [COL] Jesuit Community at Loyola University Chicago, Chicago, IL

Benden, Rev. Stephen Joseph, *C.Ss.R.* '89 (STL) St. Alphonsus Liguori Catholic Church, St. Louis, MO; [MON] Redemptorist Fathers, St. Louis, MO

Bender, Rev. Arthur C., *S.J.* '78 (NY) Regis High School, New York, NY; [MON] St. Ignatius Loyola Residence, New York, NY

Bender, Rev. Donald H., '15 (HBG) Saint Patrick, Carlisle, PA

Bender, Rev. John, *LC* (HRT) [MON] Legionaries of Christ, Cheshire, CT; [SEM] Novitiate of the Legion of Christ, Cheshire, CT

Bendik, Rev. Msgr. John J., '67 (SCR) Retired. [MON] Villa St. Joseph, Dunmore, PA

Bendzella, Rev. Sylvester J., '59 (ALT) Retired.

Bene, Very Rev. Philip J., '94 (STL) Curia: Leadership; (>JC) Tribunal St. Joseph Catholic Church, Clayton, Clayton, MO

Benecki, Rev. Stanley, '84 (COL) Retired.

Benedetto, Rev. James F., '70 (NEW) Retired. [MON] The Rev. Msgr. James F. Kelley Residence for Retired Priests, Caldwell, NJ

Benedetto, Rev. William F., '07 (NEW) Madonna, Fort Lee, NJ; Our Lady of Lourdes, Mountainside, NJ

Benedi-an, Rev. Edgar, *O.S.M.* (P) [MON] The Grotto, The National Sanctuary of Our Sorrowful Mother, Portland, OR

Benedict, Rt. Rev. Francis, *O.S.B.* '76 (LA) [MON] St. Andrew's Abbey (Benedictine Monks), Valyermo, CA

Benedict, Rev. Joseph, '97 (SJ) On Special Assignment. Curia: Leadership; Offices and Directors Sacred Heart, Saratoga, CA

Benedict, Rev. Joseph M., '97 (SJ) Curia: Leadership

Benedict, Rev. Rejimon K., (RVC) Blessed Sacrament, Valley Stream, NY

Beneleit, Rev. Edward L., '74 (Y) Retired. Holy Family Parish, Navarre, OH; St. Joseph, Canton, OH

Benestad, Rev. Msgr. Thomas J., '70 (ALN) Retired.

Benetti, Rev. Michele, *FSCB* '14 (BO) Sacred Heart, Boston, MA

Bengert, Rev. Tony, '65 (ELP) On Leave.

Bengford, Rev. Ronald J., '94 (PRO) St. Matthew's Church Corporation, Cranston, RI

Bengry, Rev. Robert-Charles, '18 (POC) On Special Assignment.

Benicewicz, Rev. Joseph, *OFM Conv.* '88 (HRT) Saint Paul Parish Corporation, Kensington, CT; [MIS] St. Paul Friary (St. Paul Parish Corporation), Kensington, CT

Beninati, Rev. Francis H., *M.M.* '55 (NY) Retired. [MON] Maryknoll Fathers and Brothers (Catholic Foreign Mission Society of America, Inc.), Ossining, NY

Benioff, Rev. Edward C., '07 (LA) Good Shepherd, Beverly Hills, CA

Benitez, Rev. Carlos A., '04 (WDC) On Duty Outside Diocese. Philadelphia, PA

Benitez, Rev. Carlos A., '04 (PH) [SEM] Redemptoris Mater Archdiocesan Missionary Seminary, Yeadon, PA

Benitez, Rev. Juan, '17 (ROC) On Leave.

Benitez-Camacho, Rev. Gustavo, '96 (TUC) On Leave.

Benjamin, Rev. Joseph, *S.S.J.* '10 (BLX) Curia: Advisory Boards, Commissions, Committees, and Councils (>BR) The Congregation Of St. Augustine Roman Catholic Church, New Roads, LA

Benjamin, Rev. Matthew, '10 (KC) On Duty Outside Diocese. Archdiocese for Military Svcs Curia: (>MO) Offices and Directors

Benjamin, Rev. Robert, '00 (SR) Retired.

Benjamine, Rev. Anthony, '94 (CHR) St. Ann, Santee, SC; St. Mary Mission, Summerton, SC; St. Mary, Our Lady of Hope, Manning, SC

Benko, Rev. Robert, *OFM Conv.* (PMB) Curia: Leadership St. Mark, Boynton Beach, FL

Benn, Rev. Walter J., '77 (PH) St. Lawrence, Riegelsville, PA

Bennerfield, Rev. Herbert, '99 (LAF) Curia: Miscellaneous / Other Offices St. Joseph, Patterson, LA

Bennett, Rev. Ambrose, *O.S.B.* '04 (STL) [MON] The Abbey of St. Mary and St. Louis, St. Louis, MO

Bennett, Rev. Christopher, (SJ) (>OAK) [MIS] Italian Catholic Federation, Oakland, CA

Bennett, Rev. Christopher, '90 (SJ) Curia: Leadership; Offices and Directors St. Christopher, San Jose, CA; [MIS] Catholic Professional and Business Club, San Jose, CA

Bennett, Rev. Msgr. Donald T., '67 (RVC) Retired.

Bennett, Rev. Eric M., '12 (BO) Our Lady of the Visitation Parish, Milton, MA

Bennett, Rev. Joshua Tobias, '11 (LFT) Sacred Heart of Jesus, Remington, IN; SS. Peter and Paul, Goodland, IN; St. Augustine, Rensselaer, IN

Bennett, Rev. Michael X., '71 (HBG) Retired.

Bennett, Rev. Nicholas, '19 (STA) San Juan Del Rio, St. John, FL

Bennett, Rev. Norman S., *C.Ss.R.* '71 (BRK) Our Lady of Perpetual Help Basilica, Brooklyn, NY

Bennett, Rev. Richard S., *C.Ss.R.* '96 (PH) St. Peter the Apostle, Philadelphia, PA

Bennett, Rev. Thomas, '91 (PHX) Curia: Leadership Queen of Peace Roman Catholic Parish, Mesa, AZ

Bennis, Rev. Terrence W., '04 (GRY) All Saints, San Pierre, IN; Ss. Cyril and Methodius, North Judson, IN

Beno, Rev. Patrick C, (GB) St. Agnes, Green Bay, WI

Benoit, Rev. Adrian J., '65 (SPR) Retired.

Benoit, Rev. Charles, *O.S.B.* '01 (NO) On Special Assignment. Vicar, Pastoral Planning Curia: Leadership St. Benedict Roman Catholic Church, Covington, Louisiana, Covington, LA; [MON] St. Joseph Abbey, St. Benedict, LA

Benoit, Rev. Louis, '79 (RIC) Retired.

Benoit, Rev. Vincent, *O.P.* '84 (P) Retired. St. Thomas More Catholic Church, Eugene, OR; [CAM] University of Oregon (Eugene), Eugene, OR

Benonis, Rev. Richard R., '58 (PH) Retired.

Bensman, Rev. Gerald E., *S.T.L.* '64 (CIN) Retired.

Benson, Rev. Joseph A., '84 (NO) Retired.

Benson, Rev. Richard B., *C.M.* '78 (CHI) [MON] Vincentian Community, Congregation of the Mission, Western Province, Chicago, IL

Bentil, Rev. Augustine Kofi, '94 (LC) St. Joseph, Wittenberg, WI; St. Ladislaus, Hatley, WI; [EFT] St. Ladislaus Parish Bevent Endowment Trust, Hatley, WI

Bentil, Very Rev. Gabriel, '84 (VIC) Curia: Leadership; Offices and Directors Holy Family of Joseph, Mary & Jesus, Victoria, TX

Bentley, Rev. John, (SAT) [MIS] Brothers of the Beloved Disciple, San Antonio, TX

Bentley, Rev. Marc, '19 (LEX) Prince of Peace, West Liberty, KY; Ss. John & Elizabeth, Grayson, KY

Benton, Rev. James F., '73 (LIN) Retired.

Bentz, Rev. John, *S.J.* '04 (NY) [MON] Cardinal Spellman Hall, Jesuit Community, Bronx, NY (>LA) [MON] Colombiere House (Jesuit Fathers), Los Angeles, CA

Bentz, Rev. John C, *SJ* '04 (LA) Blessed Sacrament, Los Angeles, CA

Bentz, Rev. Mark A., '13 (P) St. Alice, Springfield, OR

Benusa, Rev. Jeffrey M., '03 (HEL) Saint James Parish: Series 542, LLC, Plains, MT; Saint William Parish: Series 549, LLC, Thompson Falls, MT

Benwell, Rev. Msgr. William, '80 (MET) Mount St. Mary Academy, Watchung, NJ; St. Mary-Stony Hill, Watchung, NJ

Benwell, Rev. Msgr. William, '80 (MET) Curia: Consultative Bodies; Leadership; Tribunal

Benz, Rev. Msgr. David H., '75 (PH) Retired.

Benz, Rev. Gary, '99 (BIS) Sacred Heart of Jesus, Glen Ullin, ND; St. Joseph, Glen Ullin, ND

Benz, Rev. James J., '74 (STL) St. Cletus, St. Charles, MO

Benz, Rev. Michael J., '13 (STL) St. Agnes Catholic Church, Bloomsdale, MO; St. Lawrence Catholic Church, Bloomsdale, MO

Benz, Rev. Thomas G., *S.J.* '00 (BRK) [MON] Carroll Street Jesuit Community, Brooklyn, NY

Benzmiller, Rev. James T., '99 (LC) Retired.

Benzoni, Rev. Martin, *O.Praem.* '81 (ORG) [MON] Norbertine Fathers of Orange, Inc., Silverado, CA

Beof, Rev. Marlon, *O.A.R.* '97 (LA) [MON] Order of Augustinian Recollects (O.A.R.), St. Augustine Priory, Oxnard, CA

Beong, Rev. Zakarias, *SMM* (RVC) [MON] Montfort Missionaries, Bay Shore, NY

Beran, Rev. Mark T., '02 (OM) St. Augustine Catholic Church, Winnebago, NE; St. Joseph, Walthill, NE

Berard, Rev. Jonathan A., '16 (WDC) Holy Redeemer, College Park, MD

Berardi, Rev. Thomas F., '76 (ALB) Retired. Curia: Leadership; Offices and Directors

Berbary, Rev. Richard J., '04 (NEW) Retired. St. Mary, Nutley, NJ

Berbena, Rev. Christopher, '80 (OAK) Retired. St. John Vianney, Walnut Creek, CA

Berberian, Rev. David V., '74 (ALB) Curia: Offices and Directors

Berberian, Rev. David V., '74 (ALB) Curia: Leadership St. Mary's Church, Waterford, NY

Berberich, Rev. Thomas E., '59 (HRT) Retired.

Bercasio, Rev. Rafael, '93 (PHX) El Cristo Rey Roman Catholic Parish, Grand Canyon, AZ

Berchmans, Rev. Britto, '81 (CHI) Retired.

Berchmanz, Rev. Anthony, '67 (NEW) Chap, San Diego, CA

Berchmanz, Rev. Antony N., (MO) Curia: Offices and Directors

Bercier, Rev. Barry, *A.A.* (BO) [MON] Augustinians of the Assumption, Inc., Boston, MA

Berdugo-Sanjuan, Rev. Hernan, (SJN) San Esteban, Protomartir, Toa Alta, PR

Berean, Rev. Christopher H., '87 (NY) Parish of St. Mary of the Snow/St. Joseph/St. John the Evangelist, Saugerties, NY

Bereda, Rev. Stanislaw J., '65 (GLD) Retired.

Berendt, Rev. George, *PIME* '74 (DET) [MON] PIME Missionaries, Detroit, MI
Berens, Rev. Cyprian, *O.F.M.* '51 (CIN) Retired.
Beres, Rev. Kevin J., '00 (ARL) St. Peter, Washington, VA
Beretta, Rev. J. Christian, *O.S.F.S.* '97 (WIL) Salesianum School, Wilmington, DE
Beretta, Rev. Patrick, '82 (HEL) Curia: Leadership Butte Catholic Community North: Series 211, LLC, Butte, MT
Bereza, Rev. Stepan, '93 (STF) St. Josaphat, New Britain, CT
Berg, Rev. Blaise R., '98 (SAC) On Duty Outside Diocese. St. Patrick Seminary & University, Menlo Park Curia: Leadership (>SFR) [SEM] St. Patrick's Seminary and University (The Roman Catholic Seminary of San Francisco), Menlo Park, CA
Berg, Rev. Brandon, (COS) [MIS] Catholic Center at the Citadel, Colorado Springs, CO
Berg, Rev. Daniel J., '00 (BIS) Curia: Leadership St. John the Baptist, Beach, ND; St. Mary's Golva, Golva, ND; [SPF] Home On The Range, Sentinel Butte, ND
Berg, Rev. John Marcus, *FSSP* '97 (OM) Immaculate Conception, B.V.M., Omaha, NE
Berg, Rev. Ralph, *C.M.F.* (PHX) Sacred Heart Roman Catholic Parish Prescott, Prescott, AZ
Berg, Rev. Richard, *C.S.C.* '63 (P) Retired. [MON] Priests of Holy Cross in Oregon, Inc., Portland, OR
Berg, Rev. Thomas V., '00 (NY) [SEM] St. Joseph's Seminary, Yonkers, NY
Bergamo, Rev. Msgr. John A., (SCR) Retired. St. Matthew, East Stroudsburg, PA
Bergbower, Very Rev. Daniel J., '88 (SFD) Curia: Deaneries
Bergbower, Rev. Daniel J., '88 (SFD) St. Agnes, Springfield, IL
Bergen, Rev. William J., *S.J.* '65 (NY) St. Ignatius Loyola, New York, NY; [MON] St. Ignatius Loyola Residence, New York, NY
Berger, Rev. John G., '67 (NU) Retired.
Berger, Rev. John W., '77 (HON) Retired.
Berger, Rev. Lawrence B., '66 (LC) Retired.
Berger, Rev. Peter J., '05 (MIL) St. Mary's Congregation, Elm Grove, WI
Berger, Rev. Robert F., '62 (HBG) Retired.
Bergeron, Rev. Msgr. Albert G., '62 (HT) Retired.
Bergeron, Rev. C. Paul, '81 (LAF) Retired.
Bergeron, Rev. Michael, '96 (HT) Retired. Curia: Administration
Berggreen, Rev. Msgr. Robert H., '64 (BR) Retired.
Berghouse, Rev. Jordan, '19 (MIL) St. James Congregation, Mukwonago, WI; St. Theresa's Congregation, Eagle, WI
Berghout, Rev. Paul A., '96 (ARL) Curia: Tribunal Queen of Apostles, Alexandria, VA
Bergida, Rev. Joseph D., '12 (ARL) Curia: Tribunal
Bergin, Rev. James, *S.V.D.* '69 (DUB) Curia: Leadership [SEM] Divine Word College, Epworth, IA
Bergin, Rev. Karl, '04 (ORL) Epiphany, Port Orange, FL; [CAM] Catholic Campus Ministry at Embry-Riddle Aeronautical University, Daytona Beach, FL
Bergin, Rev. Paschal, '57 (CC) Retired.
Bergin, Rev. Patrick A., *M.M.* '59 (NY) Retired.
Bergin, Rev. Msgr. Thomas, '61 (NY) Retired.
Bergkamp, Rev. Andrew, (WCH) St. Joseph, Wichita, KS
Bergkamp, Rev. Roger, *O.M.I.* (CC) [RTR] Oblate La Parra Center, Sarita, TX
Bergman, Rev. Eric, '07 (POC) St. Thomas More Catholic Church, Scranton, PA
Bergquist, Rev. Patrick, '90 (FBK) On Leave.
Bergquist, Rev. Patrick D., *O.Praem.* (WIL) Sacred Heart, Chestertown, MD
Bergs, Rev. David, '76 (LSC) Retired.
Bergsbaken, Very Rev. Dennis L., '78 (GB) Retired.
Bergschneider, Very Rev. Matthew M., '05 (RCK) On Special Assignment. Curia: Leadership; Tribunal St. Mary, Durand, IL
Bergstadt, Rev. John P., '68 (GB) Retired.
Berhorst, Rev. Brad T., '19 (JC) Curia: Administration; Tribunal St. Peters Church Parish, Jefferson City, MO
Berinti, Rev. Benjamin, *C.PP.S.* '85 (CIN) [MON] Society of the Precious Blood, United States Province, Inc., Dayton, OH
Berinti, Very Rev. Benjamin A., *C.PP.S.* '85 (ORL) Curia: Advisory Boards, Commissions, Committees, and Councils; Leadership Immaculate Conception, Melbourne Beach, FL; St. Joseph, Palm Bay, FL
Berjuega, Rev. Noly, *C.R.M.* '11 (CHR) Immaculate Conception, Goose Creek, SC; St. Francis Caracciolo Mission, Goose Creek, SC
Berkhout, Rev. Frans J., '87 (ALN) Sacred Heart of Jesus, Bethlehem, PA
Berkmans, Rev. Albert, *HGN* '09 (PBL) Holy Name of Mary, Del Norte, CO; St. Francis Jerome, Center, CO; St. Joseph, Monte Vista, CO
Berkmans, Rev. Joselin Pens, *M.M.I.* '10 (NY) St. Thomas Aquinas, Forestburgh, NY
Berko, Rev. Abraham A., '88 (NY) Holy Name of Jesus, Valhalla, NY
Bermudez, Rev. Alberto, '86 (NO) Chap, Chateau de Notre Dame Assisted Living, New Orleans
Bermudez, Rev. Duvan, '96 (PMB) Curia: Education; Offices and Directors; Organizations (affiliated, inter-Diocesan, miscellaneous/other) St. John Fisher, West Palm Beach, FL
Bermudez, Rev. Duverney, '10 (NEW) Immaculate Conception, Elizabeth, NJ; [COL] Seton Hall University, South Orange, NJ; [SEM] College Seminary of the Immaculate Conception (Saint Andrew's Hall), South Orange, NJ
Bermudez, Rev. Jaime, '03 (POD) Curia: Clergy and Religious Services
Bermudez, Rev. Jaime, (SJN) [MIS] Opus Dei, Guaynabo, PR
Bermudez, Rev. Jose A., '80 (SPR) Chap, Hampden Cty Women's Corr Ctr; Franklin Cty Jail &...
Bernabe, Rev. Christopher Denzell, '14 (SFE) St. Anthony of Padua-Fort Sumner, Fort Sumner, NM; St. Rose of Lima, Santa Rosa, NM
Bernabe, Rev. Humberto, '92 (LA) St. Albert the Great, Rancho Dominguez, CA
Bernal Rodriguez, Rev. Miguel, (BGP) St. Catherine of Siena and St. Agnes Parish Corporation, Riverside, CT
Bernales, Rev. Joal, (PHX) St. Anne Roman Catholic Parish, Gilbert, AZ
Bernaola, Rev. Javier, (POD) Curia: Clergy and Religious Services
Bernaola, Rev. Javier, '85 (MGZ) [MIS] Opus Dei (Prelature of the Holy Cross and Opus Dei), Mayaguez, PR
Bernaola Hortigüela, Rev. Javier, (PCE) [MIS] Prelatura de la Santa Cruz y Opus Dei, Ponce, PR
Bernard, Rev. Bernard, (SAT) Retired.
Bernard, Rev. Donald, '19 (LAF) St. Edward, New Iberia, LA
Bernard, Rev. Donald, (SAT) Retired. [NUR] Oblate Madonna Residence, San Antonio, TX
Bernard, Rev. George C., *C.S.C.* '49 (P) Retired. (>FTW) [MIS] Holy Cross House, Notre Dame, IN
Bernard, Rev. Harold, '03 (BRK) St. Finbar, Brooklyn, NY
Bernard, Rev. James Andrew, '21 (STP) Our Lady of Guadalupe, St. Paul, MN
Bernard, Rev. Kiran Kumar, (GF) Sacred Heart, Cascade, MT
Bernardi, Rev. Peter J., *S.J.* '87 (CHI) [COL] Jesuit Community at Loyola University Chicago, Chicago, IL
Bernardino, Rev. Eduardo, '91 (SD) Pastor of Church of the Resurrection Catholic Parish, Escondido, a corporation sole, Escondido, CA; [MIS] Church of the Resurrection Catholic Parish in Escondido, CA Real Property Support Corporation, Escondido, CA
Bernardo, Rev. Joel, *C.M.* '95 (PH) [MON] Congregation of the Mission, Philadelphia, PA
Bernardo, Rev. Joel, *C.M.* '95 (STL) [MIS] Vincentian Solidarity Office, St. Louis, MO
Bernardo, Rev. Joseph J., '03 (LIN) Cathedral of the Risen Christ, Lincoln, NE; Pius X Catholic High School, Lincoln, NE; St. Joseph, Lincoln, NE
Bernas, Rev. Anthony N., '03 (MO) Curia: Offices and Directors
Bernas, Rev. Casimir, '59 (L) [MON] Abbey of Our Lady of Gethsemani, of the Order of Cistercians of the Strict Observance, Trappist, KY
Bernas, Rev. Eugene, '66 (NEW) Retired.
Bernauer, Rev. James W., *S.J.* '75 (BO) [MON] The Jesuit Community at Boston College, Chestnut Hill, MA
Bernavas, Rev. Edison, *I.C.* (SP) St. Francis of Assisi, Seffner, FL
Berndt, Rev. Michael, '20 (SFD) St. Anthony of Padua, Effingham, IL
Bernelli, Rev. Msgr. Matthew, '64 (BGP) Retired. The Saint Andrew Roman Catholic Church Corporation, Bridgeport, CT
Berner, Rev. Albert J., '68 (NEW) Retired.
Berner, Rev. Michael, '86 (DM) Our Lady of Grace, Griswold, IA; St. Timothy, Cumberland, IA
Berngeh, Rev. Roland, '85 (PRT) Parish of the Transfiguration, Bar Harbor, ME
Bernhard, Rev. Mark, (JOL) Notre Dame, Clarendon Hills, IL
Bernier, Rev. Paul, '00 (FR) St. George's, Westport, MA; St. John the Baptist, Westport, MA
Bernier, Rev. Paul, *S.S.S.* '62 (CLV) Retired.
Bernier, Rev. Philip, *O.F.M. Cap.* '01 (CLV) St. Peter, Cleveland, OH; [MON] St. Paul Friary, Cleveland, OH
Berning, Rev. James, *S.D.B.* '93 (NEW) [MON] The Salesian Community, Orange, NJ
Berning, Rev. James C., '91 (WIN) Curia: Advisory Boards, Commissions, Committees, and Councils St. Francis of Assisi, Rochester, MN
Bernotas, Rev. Robert J, (LFT) [EFT] St. Joseph School Foundation, Inc., ,
Bernotas, Rev. Robert J., '83 (LFT) Retired.
Berns, Rev. Eric R., '96 (LC) St. John the Baptist, Norwalk, WI; St. Patrick, Sparta, WI; [EFT] Endowment Trust of the Friends and Parishioners of St. Patrick Parish, Sparta, WI
Berny, Rev. Paul W., '72 (ATL) Retired. St. Thomas Aquinas Catholic Church, Alpharetta, Inc., Alpharetta, GA
Beroch, Rev. Tomas, '10 (SAV) St. Joseph's, Bainbridge, GA
Berran, Rev. Donald M., '60 (BRK) Retired. Our Lady of Perpetual Help, South Ozone Park, NY
Berrelleza, Rev. Erick, (BO) [MON] The Jesuit Community at Boston College, Chestnut Hill, MA
Berret, Rev. Anthony J., *S.J.* '71 (PH) Retired. [MIS] Jesuit Fathers, , ; [MON] Jesuit Community at St. Joseph's University, Merion Station, PA
Berrette, Rev. Hugues, '91 (BRK) Our Lady of Miracles, Brooklyn, NY
Berrio, Rev. Augusto, *S.J.* '63 (LA) [MON] Colombiere House (Jesuit Fathers), Los Angeles, CA
Berrio Guitierrez, Rev. Ignacio de Jesus, (BO) St. Mary of the Assumption, Lawrence, MA
Berrios, Rev. Angel Berrios, '65 (PCE) Retired.
Berrios, Rev. Giovanni Perez, (SJN) Santa Teresa de Jesus Jornet, San Juan, PR
Berrios, Rev. Matthew J, *CSP* '17 (NY) [MON] Paulist Fathers - Generalate, New York, NY
Berrum, Rev. Aristeo, '20 (DAL) Mary Immaculate Catholic Parish, Dallas, TX
Berry, Rev. Dennis, *S.T.* '86 (PAT) [MON] Trinity House at the Shrine of St. Joseph, Stirling, NJ
Berry, Very Rev. Michael, *OCD* '06 (MIL) St. Florian's Congregation, West Milwaukee, WI; [MON] Washington Province of Discalced Carmelite Friars, Inc., Milwaukee, WI
Bersabal, Rev. Rey B., '91 (SAC) Curia: Offices and Directors Pastor of St. Francis of Assisi Parish, Sacramento, a corporation sole, Sacramento, CA
Berschied, Rev. Paul L., '86 (COV) Retired.
Bertelli, Rev. Mark, '06 (SB) St. Anthony, San Jacinto, CA
Bertha, Rev. Joseph, '80 (PSC) Curia: Advisory Boards, Commissions, Committees, and Councils St. John the Baptist, Bayonne, NJ; St. Mary's, Jersey City, NJ
Berthelette, Rev. Ernest H., '74 (PRO) On Duty Outside Diocese. Diocese of St John's-Basseterre, Antigua & Barbuda, West...
Bertin, Rev. Gerard L., '89 (MAN) Retired.
Bertino, Rev. Dominic V., '75 (GRY) Retired.
Bertke, Rev. Jason M., '16 (COV) St. Henry District High School, Erlanger, KY; St. Paul, Florence, KY
Bertogli, Rev. John, '77 (DM) Retired. Curia: Offices and Directors
Bertolacci, Rev. Caesar, *MC* '96 (DET) [MON] Miles Christi, South Lyon, MI
Bertolotti, Rev. David P., '91 (BRK) St. Mary Star of the Sea and St. Gertrude, Far Rockaway, NY
Bertonazzi, Rev. Steven J., (CAM) R.C. Church of the Incarnation, Township of Mantua, New Jersey, Mantua, NJ
Bertone, Rev. Thomas C., *C.S.C.* '81 (FTW) [SEM] Moreau Seminary, Notre Dame, IN
Bertoniere, Rev. Gabriel, *O.C.S.O.* '58 (WOR) [MON] St. Joseph's Abbey (Cistercian Abbey of Spencer, Inc., Cistercian Order of the Strict Observance (Trappists)), Spencer, MA
Bertram, Rev. Michael, *O.F.M.Cap* '88 (MIL) St. Benedict the Moor, Milwaukee, WI; [MIS] Capuchin Community Services, Milwaukee, WI
Bertram, Rev. Michael, *O.F.M.Cap.* '88 (MIL) Curia: Leadership St. Francis of Assisi, Milwaukee, WI
Bertrand, Rev. Armand J., '89 (SC) Retired.
Bertrand, Rev. Conley, '59 (LAF) Retired.
Bertrand, Rev. Conley, '59 (LAF) [MIS] Come Lord Jesus! Inc., Lafayette, LA
Bertrand, Rev. Emmanuel, *O.P.* (L) Retired. St. Louis Bertrand, Louisville, KY
Bertrand, Rev. Joshua, '20 (SP) On Duty Outside Diocese. St. John Vianney, St. Pete Beach, FL
Bertrand, Rev. Vincent E., '87 (SPC) Curia: Offices and Directors
Bertrand Lemoine, Rev. Louis, *O.P.* (Y) [COL] Walsh University, North Canton, OH

Beseau, Rev. Steven, '95 (KCK) On Duty Outside Diocese. Rector, Pontifical College Josephinum
Beseau, Rev. Steven P., (COL) [SEM] Pontifical College Josephinum, Columbus, OH
Besel, Rev. Patrick E., '06 (BAL) Our Lady, Queen of Peace, Middle River, MD
Bessellieu, Rev. Mel, '97 (FWT) Curia: Leadership St. Francis of Assisi, Grapevine, TX
Bessert, Rev. James W., '80 (SAG) Retired. Curia: Offices and Directors Saint Catherine of Siena Parish of Bay City, Bay City, MI
Best, Rev. Craig, '18 (CIN) St. Francis de Sales, Lebanon, OH; St. Philip the Apostle, Morrow, OH
Betancourt, Rev. Cesar, '09 (TYL) Most Holy Trinity, Trinity, TX
Betancourt, Rev. Johan D., '15 (NEW) The Parish of Blessed Miriam Teresa Demjanovich Church, Bayonne, NJ
Betancourt, Rev. Jorge R., *O.Carm.* '03 (ARE) [MIS] Chapel Buen Pastor, Ciales, PR; [MIS] Chapel Divino Nino Jesus, Ciales, PR; [MIS] Chapel Inmaculado Corazon de Maria, Ciales, PR; [MIS] Chapel Maternidad Divina de Maria, Ciales, PR; [MIS] Chapel Sagrado Corazon, Ciales, PR; [MIS] Chapel San Antonio, Ciales, PR; [MIS] Chapel San Elias, Ciales, PR; [MIS] Chapel San Ignacio, Ciales, PR; [MIS] Chapel San Jose, Ciales, PR; [MIS] Chapel Santa Clara, Ciales, PR
Betancourt, Rev. Jose Luis, '17 (CGS) Santos Angeles Cutodios, Yabucoa, PR
Betancourt Ramirez, Rev. Jorge R., *O.Carm.* '03 (ARE) Holy Rosary, Ciales, PR
Betancourt Suriel, Rev. Cesar Yohel, (MIA) St. John Neumann, Miami, FL
Betancur, Rev. Nelson, '75 (PAT) Retired. [MIS] Nazareth Village, Chester, NJ
Betasso, Rev. Emmanuel, *O.C.D.* '05 (WDC) [SEM] Discalced Carmelite Friars, Inc., Washington, DC
Bethel, Rev. Francis, *O.S.B.* '83 (TLS) [MON] Our Lady of the Annunciation of Clear Creek Abbey, Hulbert, OK
Bethge, Rev. Christopher J., '15 (BRK) Curia: Leadership; Organizations (affiliated, inter-Diocesan, miscellaneous/other)
Betley, Rev. Michael E., '80 (GB) St. John-Sacred Heart, Sherwood, WI; St. Mary, Stockbridge, WI; St. Mary Congregation, Hilbert, WI
Betoni, Rev. John P., *O.S.A.* '62 (PH) [MON] St. Thomas Monastery, Villanova, PA
Betschart, Rev. Msgr. Joseph, '99 (P) Curia: Offices and Directors
Betschart, Rev. Msgr. Joseph V., '99 (P) [SEM] Mount Angel Seminary, Saint Benedict, OR
Betters, Rev. John D., '03 (CLV) Chap, Richmond UHHS Med Ctr SS. Robert & William, Euclid, OH; St. John of the Cross, Euclid, OH
Betti, Rev. Frederick G., *S.J.* '90 (BUF) St. Michael, Buffalo, NY
Betti, Rev. Mark J., '96 (R) St. Brendan the Navigator, Shallotte, NC
Bettin, Rev. John, (DET) Curia: Administration; Consultative Bodies St. Daniel Parish Clarkston, Clarkston, MI
Bettinger, Rev. Eugene Joseph, *O.Carm.* '76 (NEW) Retired. Assumption, Emerson, NJ; Carmelite Chapel of St. Therese, Teaneck, NJ
Bettinger, Rev. Mark T., '93 (PBL) Holy Family, Pueblo, CO
Betts, Rev. John C., '68 (P) Retired.
Betz, Rev. James, '71 (CAM) Retired. St. Brendan the Navigator Parish, Avalon, N.J., Avalon, NJ
Betz, Rev. Kenneth, '65 (EVN) St. James, Haubstadt, IN
Betz, Rev. Robert, '73 (MIL) Retired. St. James Congregation, Franklin, WI
Betz, Rev. Thomas, (PH) Curia: Evangelization St. John the Evangelist, Philadelphia, PA
Betzen, Rev. James G., *C.PP.S.* '81 (DAV) Church of St. Mary of the Visitation, Ottumwa, IA
Betzen, Rev. John D., (WCH) Curia: Leadership St. Joseph, Humboldt, KS; St. Patrick, Chanute, KS
Beuther, Rev. Richard J., '96 (BRK) St. Bartholomew, Elmhurst, NY
Bevacqua, Rev. James M., '03 (LA) Curia: Pastoral Services St. Bede the Venerable, La Canada Flintridge, CA
Bevak, Very Rev. Jon-Paul, *C.O.* '12 (CIN) Old St. Mary, Cincinnati, OH; Sacred Heart, Cincinnati, OH; [MIS] Society of Saint Philip Neri, Inc. (The Cincinnati Oratory), Cincinnati, OH
Bevan, Rev. James J., '75 (LAV) Retired.
Bevans, Rev. Stephen B., *S.V.D.* '71 (CHI) [SEM] Catholic Theological Union, Chicago, IL; [SEM] Divine Word Theologate, Chicago, IL
Beveridge, Rev. John P., '72 (SFD) Retired. SS. Peter and Paul, Collinsville, IL
Beverung, Rev. Michael, '21 (LKC) Our Lady of Prompt Succor, Sulphur, LA
Bevins, Rev. Msgr. John J., '58 (HRT) Retired. Corporation of the Church of the Immaculate Conception, Waterbury, Connecticut, Waterbury, CT
Beya-Tshingimba, Rev. Zacharie, '75 (LC) St. Joseph, Prescott, WI
Beyuo, Rev. Christopher, (CHR) St. Michael, Murrells Inlet, SC
Bezner, Rev. Kevin, '19 (SJP) Curia: Offices and Directors St. Nicholas Mission, Nashville, TN; St. Thomas the Apostle Mission, Knoxville, TN
Bezruchka, Rev. Michael S., '16 (HPM) Curia: Leadership; Offices and Directors Saint Anne, San Luis Obispo, CA
Bezzegato, Rev. Richard, *C.S.* '72 (DAL) St. Luke Catholic Parish, Irving, TX
Bhastati, Rev. Sudhakar, '09 (EVN) St. Peter, Montgomery, IN
Biagi, Rev. Vincent L., *S.J.* '78 (NY) Xavier High School, New York, NY (>RVC) St. Anthony, Oceanside, NY
Bialas, Rev. Aleksander, '12 (PAT) Our Lady Queen of Peace, Hewitt, NJ
Bialek, Rev. Mark S., '06 (BAL) St. John, Westminster, MD; St. Joseph, Taneytown, MD
Bialkowski, Rev. Jacek J., '96 (SCR) St. Peter's, Wellsboro, PA; St. Thomas the Apostle, Elkland, PA
Bialorucki, Rev. Michael, '20 (TOL) St. Paul, Norwalk, OH
Biancalana, Rev. Angelo, *M.C.C.J.* '52 (CHI) Retired.
Bianco, Rev. Louis A., '05 (BAL) Cathedral of Mary Our Queen, Baltimore, MD
Biber, Rev. Joseph, '85 (RIC) Retired.
Bickel, Rev. Timothy C., '92 (MIL) St. Gabriel Congregation, Hubertus, WI
Bicsko, Rev. Stephen Charles, *C.M.* '70 (PH) Retired. [MON] Congregation of the Mission, Philadelphia, PA
Bicz, Rev. Marian, '88 (RVC) St. Hyacinth, Glen Head, NY
Bidwell, Rev. Michael L., '89 (CIN) Retired.
Biedrzycki, Rev. Matthew, '16 (PH) Cathedral Basilica of Saints Peter and Paul and the Shrine of Saint Katharine Drexel, Philadelphia, PA
Bieganowski, Rev. Ronald, *S.J.* '72 (MIL) [MON] Jesuit Community at Marquette University (Marquette Jesuit Associates, Inc.), Milwaukee, WI
Biegler, Rev. Patrick, *M.S.A.* '05 (NOR) [MON] Society of the Missionaries of the Holy Apostles, Cromwell, CT
Bielak, Rev. Andrew, '95 (NY) Chap, Henry J Carter Specialty Hosp, New York Our Lady of Peace, New York, NY
Bielasiewicz, Rev. Slawomir, '08 (STA) Curia: Clergy and Religious Services St. Francis of Assisi Catholic Church, Yulee, FL
Bielecki, Rev. Paul, *OFM Cap.* (NY) Our Lady of Sorrows, New York, NY
Bielewicz, Rev. Harry R., '86 (PIT) Curia: Consultative Bodies St. Isidore the Farmer, Imperial, PA
Bien, Rev. Dan, '85 (AGN) Santa Barbara, Dededo, GU
Bien, Rev. Danilo (Dan) C., '85 (AGN) Curia: Miscellaneous / Other Offices; Organizations (affiliated, inter-Diocesan, miscellaneous/other)
Bienvenu, Rev. Paul G., '92 (LAF) Our Lady of Perpetual Help, Maurice, LA; St. Alphonsus, Maurice, LA
Bier, Rev. Louis C., '76 (PH) [CAM] University of the Sciences in Philadelphia, Philadelphia, PA
Bierbaum, Rev. Gregory W., '15 (COS) Curia: Leadership St. Mark Catholic Church, Highlands Ranch, CO
Biernat, Rev. Leon J., '92 (BUF) Curia: Consultative Bodies; Offices and Directors St. Gregory the Great, Williamsville, NY
Biernat, Rev. Ryszard S., '09 (BUF) On Administrative Leave.
Biernat, Rev. Wayne C., '04 (SPR) St. Michael's, East Longmeadow, MA
Biersack, Rev. Thomas E., '81 (MIL) Retired.
Bierschenk, Rev. Stephen W., (DAL) St. Jude Chapel, Dallas, TX
Biewend, Rev. Michael, '80 (P) St. Mary Magdalene, Portland, OR
Bigam, Rev. Brandon J., (LEX) St. Martha, Prestonsburg, KY
Bigelow, Rev. William R., '67 (BUF) Retired.
Bigg, Rev. Dort A., '15 (ARL) St. Elizabeth Ann Seton, Lake Ridge, VA
Bignall, Rev. Douglas, '93 (DET) St. Hubert Parish Harrison Township, Harrison Township, MI
Bigney, Rev. Anthony, *O.Cist.* '13 (DAL) [MON] Our Lady of Dallas Cistercian Abbey, Irving, TX
Bihr, Rev. Msgr. Louis J., '68 (PAT) Retired.
Bihuniak, Rev. Michael J., '90 (MET) On Sick Leave.
Bik, Rev. Michael, *O.S.B.* '93 (SCL) [MON] St. John's Abbey, of the Order of St. Benedict, Collegeville, MN
Bilavendiran, Rev. Xavier, '16 (GAL) St. Katharine Drexel, Hempstead, TX
Bilinsky, Rev. Msgr. William, '65 (NO) Retired.
Bilinsky, Rev. Msgr. Canon William M., '65 (STN) Retired.
Bill, Rev. Msgr. Ronald C., '57 (SY) Retired. Immaculate Conception, Fayetteville, NY
Billett, Rev. Robert, *C.M.F.* '57 (LA) [MON] Dominguez Seminary Inc., Rancho Dominguez, CA
Billian, Rev. Msgr. Michael R., '84 (TOL) [EFT] U.T. Newman Foundation for Student Education and Development, Toledo, OH
Billian, Rev. Msgr. Michael Richard, '84 (TOL) St. Joseph, Sylvania, OH
Billiard, Rev. Donald, *OFM* (COS) Divine Redeemer, Colorado Springs, CO
Billing, Rev. Msgr. Jerome D., '71 (STL) Curia: Leadership; Offices and Directors [MIS] San Luis Apartments, Inc., St. Louis, MO
Billinger, Rev. James J., '83 (WCH) Curia: Leadership Holy Savior, Wichita, KS
Billman, Rev. George, '72 (FAR) Retired.
Billote, Rev. Dindo, '09 (JOL) St. Mary Church, Mokena, IL
Billotte, Rev. Philip J., '66 (ROC) Retired.
Billotti, Rev. Joseph E., *S.J.* '63 (NY) [MON] Murray-Weigel Hall (A Jesuit Community at Murray-Weigel Hall and Kohlmann Hall), Bronx, NY
Billy, Rev. Dennis J., *C.Ss.R.* (BAL) [SEM] St. Mary's Seminary and University, Baltimore, MD
Bilodeau, Rev. Leopold J., '73 (BUR) Retired.
Bilot, Rev. James D., '92 (DET) St. Paul Parish Grosse Pointe Farms, Grosse Pointe Farms, MI
Bilotte, Rev. Philip, (E) Retired.
Bilski, Rev. Artur, (LA) [MIS] Koinonia John the Baptist California, Palmdale, CA
Biltz, Rev. Maximilian K., (WCH) St. Mary, Newton, KS
Bily, Rev. Msgr. John C., '58 (VIC) Retired.
Bily, Rev. Lambert S., '63 (SAT) Retired.
Bily, Rev. Msgr. Lambert S., '63 (SAT) Retired. [NUR] Casa De Padres, San Antonio, TX
Bilyk, Rev. Ivan, '90 (STF) Protection of B.V.M., Willimantic, CT
Bilyk, Rev. Stepan, '01 (PHU) St. John the Baptist, Whippany, NJ
Bim-Merle, Rev. Gregory A., (GRY) Curia: Leadership St. James the Less, Highland, IN
Bindas, Rev. Stanislav, *C.M.* '01 (CHI) [MON] DePaul Vincentian Residence, Chicago, IL
Binder, Rev. Mark J., '71 (SPC) Retired. Curia: Advisory Boards, Commissions, Committees, and Councils Immaculate Conception, New Madrid, MO; Sacred Heart, Caruthersville, MO
Binet, Rev. Scott Francis, (CHR) Curia: Advisory Boards, Commissions, Committees, and Councils
Bingham, Rev. John Marie, *O.P.* '10 (OAK) [MON] Order of Preachers (Province of the Most Holy Name of Jesus - Western Dominican Province), Oakland, CA
Biniek, Rev. Joseph P., '78 (ARL) Retired.
Binsfeld, Rev. Douglas, '98 (SFS) Christ the King Parish of Day County, Webster, SD; Immaculate Conception Parish of Day County, Waubay, SD
Bioh, Rev. Sylvester, '07 (ROC) St. Luke the Evangelist Roman Catholic Church Society of Livingston County, Geneseo, NY
Biondi, Rev. Alberto, '16 (WDC) St. Catherine Laboure, Wheaton, MD; St. Michael, Silver Spring, MD
Biondi, Rev. Lawrence, *S.J.* '70 (CHI) [MON] Clark Street Jesuit Residence Community, Chicago, IL
Biosca, Rev. Emilio, *O.F.M.Cap.* '94 (WDC) Curia: Consultative Bodies Shrine of the Sacred Heart, Washington, DC (>PIT) [MON] The Capuchin Franciscan Friars Province of Saint Augustine, Pittsburgh, PA
Bircumshaw, Rev. Msgr. Colin F., '75 (SLC) Curia: Leadership; Offices and Directors
Bird, Rev. Stephen J., '76 (OKL) Curia: Consultative Bodies; Deaneries; Spiritual Life Church of the Epiphany of the Lord, Oklahoma City, OK
Bird, Rev. Steven, '00 (PEO) On Sick Leave.
Birdsall, Rev. Anthony J., '60 (GB) Retired.
Birdsall, Rev. Hugh G., *S.D.S.* '62 (MIL) [MIS] Salvatorians - Jordan Hall, Milwaukee, WI
Birdsall, Rev. Paul, '18 (HT) Annunziata, Houma, LA
Biren, Rev. Timothy E., '99 (WIN) Curia: Advisory Boards, Commissions, Committees, and Councils; Offices and Directors Holy Redeemer, Eyota, MN; St. Charles Borromeo, St. Charles, MN

Biriruka, Very Rev. Ernest, '81 (MIA) Curia: Leadership Saint John XXIII Church, Miramar, FL
Birk, Rev. John W., '70 (L) Retired.
Birkel, Rev. John B., '96 (LIN) Curia: Leadership St. Michael's, Fairbury, NE
Birket, Rev. Dwight J., '72 (WCH) Retired.
Birkle, Rev. Msgr. Walter A., '58 (NY) Retired.
Birkmaier, Rev. James, '68 (GF) Retired.
Birmingham, Rev. Robert F., '93 (HRT) Retired.
Birney, Rev. Timothy P., '98 (DET) SS. Andrew and Benedict Parish Detroit, Detroit, MI; St. Frances Cabrini Allen Park, Allen Park, MI; St. Mary Magdalen Parish Melvindale, Melvindale, MI
Birollo, Rev. Isaia, *C.S.* (MIA) Curia: Pastoral Services St. Vincent, Margate, FL
Biron, Rev. Robert G., '74 (MAN) Retired. Our Lady of the Miraculous Medal, Hampton, NH
Birungyi, Rev. George, '75 (RCK) Provena St. Joseph Hospital, Elgin
Biryomumeisho, Rev. Alex, '19 (CIN) Immaculate Heart of Mary, Cincinnati, OH; St. John Fisher, Cincinnati, OH
Bisbee, Rev. Bernie, *SJ* (OM) Retired.
Bisbee, Rev. Burnell B., *S.J.* '75 (MIL) [MON] St. Camillus Jesuit Community (Society of Jesus, USA Midwest Province), Wauwatosa, WI
Bischoff, Rev. Albert J., *S.J.* '56 (CIN) Retired. [CAM] Xavier University Dorothy Day Center for Faith & Justice, Cincinnati, OH; [MON] Cincinnati Jesuit Community, Cincinnati, OH
Bischoff, Rev. Tyler A., '15 (GLD) Curia: Advisory Boards, Commissions, Committees, and Councils; Leadership All Saints of Alpena, Alpena, MI; Saint Rose of of Lima of Herron, Herron, MI
Bishop, Rev. E. Louis, *S.J.* '64 (SJ) [MON] Sacred Heart Jesuit Center, Los Gatos, CA
Bishop, Rev. Jerome R., '13 (CIN) Our Lady of Good Hope, Miamisburg, OH; St. Henry, Dayton, OH; St. Mary of the Assumption, Springboro, OH
Bishop, Rev. Marc J., '01 (BO) Curia: Consultative Bodies Saint Agnes, Arlington, MA; St. Camillus, Arlington, MA
Bishop, Rev. Msgr. Patrick A., '74 (ATL) Retired.
Bishop, Rev. Robert, *C.M.F.* '71 (LA) [MON] Dominguez Seminary Inc., Rancho Dominguez, CA
Bishop, Rev. Thomas, '75 (CHI) St. Theresa, Palatine, IL
Bishop, Rev. Thomas G., '70 (Y) Retired. Holy Family Parish, Navarre, OH
Bisig, Rev. Josef, *F.S.S.P.* '77 (LIN) [SEM] Our Lady of Guadalupe Seminary, Inc., Denton, NE
Bisoffi, Rev. Joseph, *M.I.* '72 (MIL) Retired. [MON] St. Camillus Communities, Inc., Wauwatosa, WI
Bissex, Rev. Michael, (RVC) St. Patrick's, Huntington, NY
Bisson, Rev. Andrew R., *O.F.M.* '93 (PRT) [MON] Society of Franciscan Fathers of Greene, Maine, Kennebunk, ME
Bissonette, Rev. James B., '88 (DUL) Curia: Leadership; (>SUP) Leadership; Offices and Directors St. Raphael, Duluth, MN; St. Rose, Proctor, MN
Biszek, Rev. Msgr. Robert J., '65 (ALN) Retired. Curia: Leadership St. Paul, Allentown, PA
Bittel, Rev. Patrick M., '82 (OWN) St. Martin, Owensboro, KY
Bitterman, Rev. Francis M., '12 (CHI) St. Josaphat, Chicago, IL
Bittmenn, Rev. David J., '94 (SLC) Curia: Offices and Directors Saint Christopher LLC 219, Kanab, UT; St. George LLC 223, St. George, UT
Bittner, Rev. Gregory T., '85 (BIR) Curia: Leadership
Bitz, Rev. Al, '69 (BIS) Retired. [NUR] Emmaus Place, Bismarck, ND
Bitz, Rev. Longinus (Al) M., '69 (FAR) Retired.
Bixenman, Rev. Msgr. Joseph E., '72 (AMA) Retired.
Bizzotto, Rev. Giovanni, *C.S.* '72 (LA) [MON] Scalabrini House of Discernment, Sun Valley, CA
Bjorum, Rev. James L., '76 (DET) Our Lady of Hope Parish St. Clair Shores, St. Clair Shores, MI
Blacet, Rev. Msgr. William J, '46 (KC) Retired.
Blach, Rev. Leo M., '53 (DEN) Retired.
Black, Rev. Francis A., '80 (BRK) St. Matthew, Brooklyn, NY; [CCH] West Indian Ministry, ,
Black, Rev. James P., '88 (COL) St. Joan of Arc, Powell, OH
Black, Rev. Michael A., '15 (COV) St. Patrick, Maysville, KY; St. Patrick High School, Maysville, KY
Black, Rev. Michael G, '00 (RCK) On Administrative Leave.
Black, Rev. Oliver, '20 (NTN) Holy Cross, Placentia, CA
Blackburn, Rev. Michael, *O.F.M.* '86 (SPK) St. Francis of Assisi, Spokane, WA
Blackwell, Rev. Edward A., '76 (HBG) On Duty Outside Diocese. Punta Gorda, FL
Blackwell, Rev. Nicholas Dustin, *O.Carm.* '17 (NY) (>WDC) [SEM] Whitefriars Hall, Washington, DC
Blad, Rev. Karl Lino, (NY) Chap, VA Hudson Valley Healthcare, Castle Point
Blaettler, Rev. James R., *S.J.* '80 (SJ) [MON] Jesuit Community, Santa Clara, CA; [MON] Jesuit Community at Santa Clara University, Inc., Santa Clara, CA
Blaha, Rev. Nicholas, '11 (KCK) Blessed Sacrament Church, Kansas City, KS; Christ the King, Kansas City, KS
Blahnik, Rev. Jason J., '09 (GB) St. Francis of Assisi, Manitowoc, WI; [CAM] Newman Center of Oshkosh, Inc., Oshkosh, WI
Blaine, Rev. Philip, *O.F.M.Conv.* '63 (NY) [MON] St. Francis Friary, Staten Island, NY
Blair, Rev. Samuel, (RVC) Chap, Good Shepherd Hospice (Nassau)
Blais, Rev. George P., '90 (ORG) St. Nicholas, Laguna Woods, CA
Blais, Rev. Robert L., '63 (PRO) Retired.
Blake, Rev. Andrew P., '63 (RVC) Retired. [MON] St Pius X Residence for Retired Priests LLC, Ronkonkoma, NY
Blake, Rev. David D., *O.F.M.* '95 (BUF) [MON] St. Bonaventure Friary, St. Bonaventure, NY
Blake, Rev. Gary W., '08 (PEO) Curia: Deaneries St. Joseph's, Peru, IL; St. Mary, Peru, IL; St. Valentine, Peru, IL
Blake, Rev. Jerry W., '00 (DUB) St. Francis Church, Belmond, Iowa, Belmond, IA; St. John Church, Clarion, Iowa, Clarion, IA; The Sacred Heart Church, (Eagle Grove, Iowa), Eagle Grove, IA
Blake, Rev. John Vincent, *O.P.* '51 (CHI) [MON] St. Pius V Priory, Chicago, IL
Blake, Rev. Peter M., '84 (STL) Immaculate Conception Catholic Church, Maplewood, Maplewood, MO; St. Luke the Evangelist Catholic Church, St. Louis, MO
Blake, Rev. Richard, *S.J.* '69 (BO) [MON] The Jesuit Community at Boston College, Chestnut Hill, MA
Blake, Rev. Robert, '77 (SR) Retired.
Blakely, Rev. Paige, '64 (ORL) Retired.
Blaker, Rev. John R., '96 (OAK) Retired. Chap, Kaiser-Permanente Med Ctr; Walnut Creek Campus of... [NUR] Bishop Begin Villa, Oakland, CA
Blanc, Rev. Armand, *O.F.M.Cap.* '08 (WDC) Shrine of the Sacred Heart, Washington, DC
Blanchard, Rev. Donald V., '69 (BR) Retired.
Blanchett, Rev. Edward H., '04 (TR) Curia: Leadership; Miscellaneous / Other Offices Visitation, Brick, NJ
Blanchette, Rev. Melvin C., *P.S.S.* '67 (BAL) Retired. [MON] Society of St. Sulpice, Province of the United States, Baltimore, MD
Blanchfield, Rev. David W., '82 (BGP) Retired. Curia: Consultative Bodies Saint Jerome's Roman Catholic Church Corporation, Norwalk, CT
Blanco, Rev. Adalberto, '77 (LA) Retired.
Blanco, Rev. Gildardo, (LA) Our Lady of the Holy Rosary, Sun Valley, CA
Blanco, Rev. Gonzalo, *O.S.B.* '92 (BIS) [MON] Assumption Abbey, Richardton, ND
Blanco, Rev. Leandro, *M.I.* '04 (MIL) [MIS] St. Camillus Health System, Inc., Wauwatosa, WI; [MIS] St. Camillus Ministries, Inc., Wauwatosa, WI; [MON] St. Camillus Communities, Inc., Wauwatosa, WI; [NUR] St. Camillus, Wauwatosa, WI; [NUR] St. Camillus Health Center, Inc., Wauwatosa, WI
Blanco, Rev. Lustein, '98 (OWN) St. Michael, Sebre, KY
Blanco, Rev. Miguel Angel, '02 (MIA) St. Kevin, Miami, FL
Blanco, Rev. Vincent, '90 (AJ) St. Anthony, Anchorage, AK
Blanco, Rev. Yamid, '12 (MIL) St. Louis' Congregation, Caledonia, WI; St. Paul The Apostle Congregation, Racine, WI
Blanco-Rivera, Rev. Juan Antonio, '19 (CGS) Nuestra Senora del Carmen, Cidra, PR
Bland, Rev. Thomas A., '74 (SAC) Retired. Pastor of St. John the Evangelist Parish, Carmichael, a corporation sole, Carmichael, CA
Blanda, Very Rev. William C., '91 (LAF) Curia: Leadership St. Peter, New Iberia, LA
Blandon Rojas, Rev. Leandro Antonio, (SJN) Maria Madre de Mi Senor, Guaynabo, PR
Blanes, Rev. Mario Elias, (ARE) Holy Family, Corozal, PR
Blaney, Rev. Dennis J., '58 (GRY) Retired. Chap, Sharing Meadows, Rolling Prairie
Blaney, Rev. Robert James, '07 (BO) Most Precious Blood, Dover, MA
Blaney, Rev. Robert M., '92 (BO) Curia: Clergy and Religious Services; Consultative Bodies St. Denis, Westwood, MA; St. Margaret Mary, Westwood, MA; St. Theresa of Lisieux, Sherborn, MA
Blangiardi, Rev. B. Jeffrey, *S.J.* '86 (SD) Chap, Veterans Administration Hosp, La Jolla
Blangiardi, Rev. B. Jeffrey, *S.J.* (MO) Curia: Offices and Directors
Blank, Rev. Matthew J., '07 (SAC) Pastor of St. John Parish, Quincy, a corporation sole, Quincy, CA
Blank, Rev. Nicholas, '19 (ARL) St. John the Evangelist, Warrenton, VA
Blank, Rev. William A., (NO) Retired.
Blankinship, Rev. Msgr. Calvin L., '96 (B) Retired.
Blantz, Rev. James R., *C.S.C.* '59 (PHX) St. Helen Roman Catholic Parish, Glendale, AZ; [MON] Holy Cross Congregation/Casa Santa Cruz, Phoenix, AZ
Blantz, Rev. Thomas E., *C.S.C.* '60 (FTW) [COL] University of Notre Dame Du Lac, Notre Dame, IN; [MIS] Holy Cross House, Notre Dame, IN
Blas, Rev. M. Wilson, (SAT) Chap, Veterans' Administration Hosp, Kerrville
Blas, Rev. Mario W., (MO) Curia: Offices and Directors
Blaser, Rev. John R., '64 (TOL) Retired.
Blasi, Rev. Leo, '17 (SAL) Sacred Heart Parish, Plainville, Inc., Plainville, KS; St. Thomas Parish, Stockton, Inc., Stockton, KS
Blasick, Rev. George, *C.Ss.R.* '01 (TYL) St. Catherine of Siena Church, Atlanta, TX
Blasko, Rev. Joseph A., '99 (GLD) Retired.
Blasko, Rev. Zvonko, '82 (CLV) St. Paul, Cleveland, OH; [MIS] Joseph House of Cleveland, Inc., Cleveland, OH
Blastic, Friar Michael, *OFM* (SD) Pastor of Immaculate Conception Catholic Parish, San Diego, a corporation sole, San Diego, CA
Blaszcak, Rev. Gerald R., *S.J.* '79 (BGP) [MON] The Fairfield Jesuit Community-Fairfield University, Fairfield, CT
Blaszczak, Rev. Gerald R., *S.J.* '79 (BGP) Curia: Consultative Bodies
Blaszkowski, Rev. Andy, '08 (STA) Annunciation School, Middleburg, FL; St. Luke, Middleburg, FL; [PRE] St. Luke Early Learning Center, Middleburg, FL
Blaszkowski, Rev. Remek, '05 (STA) San Jose, Jacksonville, FL
Blatchford, Rev. Colin, '14 (KNX) On Special Assignment. Serving outside diocese
Blatchford, Rev. Colin, (BGP) St. Pius X Corporation, Fairfield, CT; [MIS] Courage International, Inc., Trumbull, CT
Blatt, Rev. Adam, '15 (ATL) Prince of Peace Catholic Church, Flowery Branch, Inc., Flowery Branch, GA
Blau, Rev. Thomas, *O.P.* '99 (COL) St. Patrick, Columbus, OH
Blawie, Rev. Brendan, '21 (BGP) On Academic Leave. Pontifical North American Studies, Rome, Italy
Blaxton, Rev. Stephen, (SAG) Holy Family Parish of Sandusky, Sandusky, MI
Blazejewski, Rev. Richard W., '74 (BUF) Retired.
Blazek, Rev. David J., '97 (DET) St. Rita Parish Holly, Holly, MI
Blazek, Rev. James F., '79 (CHI) Holy Cross, Deerfield, IL
Blazek, Rev. John, *C.S.C.* '67 (CLV) Gilmour Academy, Gates Mills, OH
Blazek, Rev. William, *SJ* '12 (CHI) St. Ignatius Jesuit Community, Chicago, IL
Blazovich, Rev. Victor M., '00 (SPK) Curia: Leadership Sacred Heart, Spokane, WA; [SEM] Bishop White Seminary, Spokane, WA
Bleeser, Rev. Peter, '67 (NY) [MIS] Deutschsprachige Katholische Gemeinde New York-German Speaking Catholic Congregation New York, White Plains, NY
Bleich, Rev. Msgr. Russell M., '60 (DUB) Retired.
Bleichner, Rev. Howard P., *P.S.S.* '67 (BAL) Retired. [MON] Society of St. Sulpice, Province of the United States, Baltimore, MD
Bleiler, Rev. William James, '66 (CAM) Retired.
Blenkle, Rev. Joseph A., '90 (NY) Church of St. Mary, Mother of the Church, Fishkill, NY
Blessing, Rev. Gerald J., '05 (STL) St. Paul Catholic Church, St. Paul, St. Paul, MO
Blessing, Rev. Howard, '76 (LAF) Retired.
Blessing, Rev. Loren, '81 (FRS) Retired.
Blevins, Rev. Payden, (AUS) Curia: Leadership Holy Trinity Catholic Church - Llano, Texas, Llano, TX; St. Joseph, Mason, TX; [EFT] Diocese of Austin Pension Plan and Trust, Austin, TX
Blewett, Rev. John Patrick, *S.J.S.* '09 (MAD) St. Mary, Platteville, WI
Blichar, Rev. Radko, (PBR) St. Andrew the Apostle, Gibsonia, PA; St. John the Baptist, Lyndora, PA
Blicharski, Rev. Lukasz, (MET) Sacred Heart, South Amboy, NJ

Blicharski, Rev. Michael, *O.Cist.* '95 (CHI) Our Lady, Mother of the Church Polish Mission, Willow Springs, IL; [MON] Cistercian Fathers, Our Lady Mother of the Church Polish Mission, Willow Springs, IL
Blicharz, Rev. Dariusz Piotr, '91 (BRK) Curia: Leadership St. Matthias, Ridgewood, NY
Blick, Rev. Ned J., '92 (WCH) St. Margaret Mary, Wichita, KS
Blick, Rev. W. Scott, (POC) Retired.
Blickhan, Rev. Donald, '74 (SFD) Retired.
Blind, Rev. Thomas F., '81 (NEW) Retired. St. Aloysius, Caldwell, NJ
Bline, Rev. G. David, '98 (CLV) [SEM] Saint Mary Seminary and Graduate School of Theology, Wickliffe, OH
Bliss, Rev. Msgr. Michael C., '91 (PEO) St. Michael, Bement, IL; St. Philomena, Monticello, IL
Bliszcz, Rev. Michael, '87 (SJP) Retired. Curia: Offices and Directors
Blocher, Rev. James Francis, *C.S.B.* '75 (GAL) Retired.
Block, Rev. Michael, (LFT) Our Lady of Grace, Noblesville, IN
Block, Very Rev. Nathanael Z., '14 (GLP) Curia: Leadership Our Lady of the Snow, Snowflake, AZ
Blondell, Rev. Robert H., '66 (DET) Retired.
Blonski, Rev. Joachim, (GLP) San Rafael, Concho, AZ
Blonski, Rev. Joachim, '92 (GLP) St. John the Baptist, St. Johns, AZ
Blonski, Rev. Joachim, '92 (GLP) Curia: Leadership
Blood, Rev. Francis J., *O.S.F.S.* '72 (WIL) [MON] Retirement and Assisted Care Facility, Childs, MD
Blood, Rev. Robert, '19 (RCK) On Special Assignment. Curia: Clergy and Religious Services St. Edward Central Catholic High School, Elgin, IL
Bloom, Rev. Phillip A., '71 (SEA) St. Mary of the Valley, Monroe, WA
Bloshchynskyy, Rev. Ihor, '03 (PHU) Curia: Leadership Annunciation of the B.V.M., Melrose Park, PA
Blostic, Rev. Leonard J., *T.O.R.* '63 (ALT) Retired. [MON] St. Bernardine Monastery, Hollidaysburg, PA
Blotsky, Rev. Hugo L., *O.S.B.* '88 (BIS) [MON] Assumption Abbey, Richardton, ND
Blottman, Rev. William P., '65 (FR) Retired.
Blount, Rev. Anthony, *S.O.L.T.* (DET) Holy Redeemer Parish Detroit, Detroit, MI; St. Cunegunda Parish Detroit, Detroit, MI; St. Gabriel Parish Detroit, Detroit, MI
Blount, Rev. James E., (ATL) Society of Our Lady of the Most Holy Trinity, Covington, GA
Blout, Rev. Daniel L., '86 (GBG) Curia: Advisory Boards, Commissions, Committees, and Councils; Miscellaneous / Other Offices Our Lady of Grace, Greensburg, PA; St. Benedict, Greensburg, PA
Blowers, Rev. Leslie F., *M.M.* '63 (NY) Retired. [MON] Maryknoll Fathers and Brothers (Catholic Foreign Mission Society of America, Inc.), Ossining, NY
Blubaugh, Rev. Homer D., '69 (COL) Retired.
Bluejacket, Very Rev. David, '88 (DEN) Curia: Deaneries Our Lady of Loreto Catholic Parish in Foxfield, Foxfield, CO
Bluett, Rev. Anthony, '69 (ORL) Retired.
Bluett, Rev. James K., '67 (PT) Retired.
Bluett, Rev. John J., '63 (ORL) Retired.
Blum, Rev. John, '96 (SP) St. Timothy, Lutz, FL; [PRE] St. Timothy Catholic Early Childhood Learning Center, Lutz, FL
Blum, Rev. Stephen J., '76 (TOL) Retired. St. John the Evangelist, Delphos, OH
Blum, Rev. William G., *C.S.C.* '65 (FTW) [MON] Congregation of Holy Cross, United States Province of Priests and Brothers, Notre Dame, IN
Blume, Rev. David, '04 (STP) Curia: Offices and Directors
Blumenfeld, Rev. Donald E., '79 (NEW) Retired. [COL] Seton Hall University, South Orange, NJ
Blumeyer, Rev. James A., *S.J.* '63 (STL) [MIS] Office, St. Louis, MO
Boachie-Yiadom, Rev. Godfred, '95 (SAV) St. Augustine, Thomasville, GA
Boackle, Rev. Paul H., '89 (SAM) Retired.
Boafo, Rev. Joseph Kwadwo O., *CSSp* (BO) St. John the Baptist, Quincy, MA; St. Joseph, Quincy, MA
Boak, Rev. Dominikus, *S.V.D.* '06 (WDC) [MON] Society of the Divine Word/Divine Word House, Washington, DC
Boansi, Rev. Raphael, '05 (NY) St. Raymond, Bronx, NY
Boateng, Rev. Francis, (RIC) St. Mary the Mother of God, Wytheville, VA
Boateng, Rev. Francis K., '91 (RIC) Saint Edward, Pulaski, VA
Boateng-Mensah, Rev. Semanhyia, '73 (PH) Chap, Veterans Administration Med Ctr, Coatesville
Boazman, Rev. Zachary, '19 (OKL) Curia: Clergy and Religious Services; Spiritual Life Church of the Epiphany of the Lord, Oklahoma City, OK
Bobal, Rev. Msgr. Joseph K., '63 (E) Retired.
Bobba, Rev. Rajeev, (TUC) Saints Peter and Paul Roman Catholic Parish - Tucson, Tucson, AZ
Bobbin, Rev. Kevin J., '05 (ALN) Nativity B.V.M. High School, Inc., Pottsville, PA; St. John the Baptist, Pottsville, PA
Bober, Rev. Charles S., '72 (PIT) Holy Sepulcher, Butler, PA; St. Kilian, Cranberry Township, PA; [MIS] Priests' Benefit Plan of the Diocese of Pittsburgh, Pittsburgh, PA
Bober, Rev. Kamil, '17 (BRK) On Leave. Released from Diocesan Assignment
Boberek, Rev. Aurelius, *O.S.B.* '57 (IND) [MON] St. Meinrad Archabbey, St. Meinrad, IN
Bobesiuk, Rev. Roman, (STN) St. Nicholas Ukrainian Catholic Cathedral, Chicago, IL
Bobesiuk, Rev. Roman, (STN) Curia: Offices and Directors
Bobick, Rev. Cody W., (RVC) St. Anne, Garden City, NY
Bobier, Rev. Anselmo, (HON) Our Lady of Lourdes, Honokaa, HI
Bobis, Rev. Antonio D., '79 (HON) Retired. St. Philomena, Honolulu, HI
Boboh, Rev. Hyginus, *SSJ* (BLX) St. Therese, Gulfport, MS
Bocala, Rev. Henry, '00 (POD) Curia: Clergy and Religious Services
Bocanegra, Rev. Jose, '13 (PAT) On Leave.
Boccabella, Rev. James D., '09 (WDC) Our Lady of Grace, Silver Spring, MD
Boccacci, Rev. Lucio, (IND) [PRE] Camp River Ridge, Oldenburg, IN
Boccaccio, Rev. Michael A., '71 (BGP) Curia: Tribunal St. Philip Roman Catholic Church Corporation, Norwalk, CT
Boccafola, Rev. Msgr. Kenneth, '63 (RVC) Retired. [MON] St Pius X Residence for Retired Priests LLC, Ronkonkoma, NY
Bochanski, Rev. Philip G., '99 (BGP) [MIS] Courage International, Inc., Trumbull, CT
Bochanski, Rev. Philip G., *C.O.* '99 (PH) On Duty Outside Diocese. Assoc Dir, St Catherine of Siena Church, Trumbull, CT
Bochenek, Rev. Joseph G., '71 (BAL) Retired.
Bochicchio, Rev. Msgr. Paul L., '71 (NEW) Retired. Curia: Organizations (affiliated, inter-Diocesan, miscellaneous/other) St. Francis of Assisi, Hoboken, NJ
Bochnak, Rev. Zenon A., '85 (MET) On Duty Outside Diocese. Archdiocese for the Military Services, USA
Bocian, Rev. Msgr. Ronald C., '72 (ALN) Curia: Organizations (affiliated, inter-Diocesan, miscellaneous/ other) Divine Mercy, Shenandoah, PA
Bocianowski, Rev. Thaddeus Nicholas, '71 (BUF) St. Padre Pio, Oakfield, NY
Bock, Rev. David R., *O.C.S.O.* '76 (DUB) [MON] New Melleray Abbey, Order of Cistercians of the Strict Observance (Corporation of New Melleray), Peosta, IA
Bock, Rev. Jeremy, '17 (DUL) Our Lady of the Snows, Bigfork, MN; St. Catherine, Squaw Lake, MN; St. Michael, Northome, MN
Bock, Rev. Lawrence R., '62 (HRT) Retired. Curia: Advisory Boards, Commissions, Committees, and Councils Annunciation Parish Corporation, Newington, CT
Bockman, Rev. Garrett, (DAL) All Saints Catholic Parish, Dallas, TX
Bockrath, Rev. Nathan, '13 (TOL) Curia: Advisory Boards, Commissions, Committees, and Councils; Deaneries Mother of Sorrows, Put-In-Bay, OH; St. Ann, Fremont, OH; St. Joseph, Fremont, OH; St. Michael, Put-In-Bay, OH
Bockskopf, Rev. Richard J., '70 (STL) Ascension Catholic Church, Chesterfield, Chesterfield, MO
Boczek, Rev. Zenon, *S.D.S.* '96 (NEW) Saint John Paul II Church, Bayonne, NJ; [MON] The Salvatorian Fathers, Verona, NJ
Bodah, Rev. Henry J., '78 (PRO) Chap, South Cty Hosp St. Joseph's Church Providence Rhode Island, Providence, RI
Bodde, Rev. Frederick A., '53 (DET) Retired.
Boddicker, Rev. Jacob, *SJ* '17 (CIN) St. Francis Xavier Church, Cincinnati, OH; [MON] Jesuit Community at St. Xavier High School, Cincinnati, OH
Boddie, Rev. Msgr. James R., '78 (STA) Curia: Evangelization Christ the King, Jacksonville, FL
Bodin, Rev. Daniel J., '05 (STP) St. Peter, Forest Lake, MN; [CEM] Calvary Cemetery, Forest Lake, MN
Bodo, Rev. Murray L., *O.F.M.* '64 (CIN) [MIS] Franciscans Network, Cincinnati, OH; [MON] Pleasant Street Friary, Cincinnati, OH
Bodziak, Rev. Charles F., '67 (ALT) On Leave.
Bodzioch, Very Rev. Michael, '11 (DEN) Curia: Deaneries Sacred Heart in Peetz, Peetz, CO; St. Anthony Catholic Parish in Sterling, Sterling, CO; St. Catherine in Iliff, Iliff, CO
Boeckman, Rev. Scott A., '03 (OKL) St. James the Greater, Oklahoma City, OK
Boedy, Rev. Thomas G., *S.J.* '70 (MIL) [MON] Arrupe House Jesuit Community, Milwaukee, WI
Boegel, Friar Peter, *O.F.M.* (TUC) San Solano Missions Roman Catholic Parish - Topawa, Topawa, AZ; [MON] San Francisco Solano Friary, Topawa, AZ
Boeglin, Very Rev. John L., '78 (EVN) Retired. Curia: Leadership; Offices and Directors
Boehling, Very Rev. Michael G., '06 (RIC) Curia: Administration
Boehm, Rev. Dustin M., '11 (IND) St. Bridget Catholic Church, Liberty, Inc., Liberty, IN; St. Gabriel Catholic Church, Connersville, Inc., Connersville, IN
Boehm, Rev. Msgr. James A., '58 (STU) Retired.
Boehm, Rev. Michael P., '94 (STL) Curia: Leadership
Boehm, Rev. Michael P., (STL) Curia: Leadership
Boehm, Rev. Michael Patrick, (STL) St. Francis Borgia Catholic Church, Washington, MO
Boehme, Rev. Arnold, *O.C.D.* '68 (MIL) [MON] Washington Province of Discalced Carmelite Friars, Inc., Milwaukee, WI
Boehme, Rev. Ferdinand J., '97 (LIN) Curia: Leadership St. Joseph's, Superior, NE
Boehme, Rev. Walter E., *S.J.* '70 (MIL) [MON] St. Camillus Jesuit Community (Society of Jesus, USA Midwest Province), Wauwatosa, WI
Boekelman, Rev. Timothy J., '77 (SC) Retired.
Boelscher, Rev. Eric M., '15 (COV) St. Joseph, Crescent Springs, KY
Boenzi, Rev. Joseph, *S.D.B.* '79 (OAK) [MON] Salesians of Don Bosco, Berkeley, CA; [SEM] Dominican School of Philosophy and Theology, Berkeley, CA
Boersma, Rev. Karel, (RVC) Chap, St Francis Hosp
Boes, Rev. Clair L., '65 (SC) Retired. St. Francis of Assisi, Rockwell City, IA
Boes, Rev. Steven, '85 (OM) Immaculate Conception B.V.M., Boys Town, NE
Boettcher, Rev. John, '91 (SR) Retired.
Boettner, Very Rev. David, '94 (KNX) Curia: Leadership Cathedral of the Most Sacred Heart of Jesus, Knoxville, TN; [EFT] St. Mary's Legacy Foundation of East Tennessee, Inc., Knoxville, TN
Boever, Rev. Richard, *C.Ss.R.* '73 (NO) St. Alphonsus, New Orleans, LA; [SHR] National Shrine of Blessed Francis Xavier Seelos, New Orleans, LA
Bogacki, Very Rev. Phillip A., '08 (MIL) Curia: Leadership Christ King Congregation, Wauwatosa, WI; St. Bernard's Congregation, Wauwatosa, WI
Bogacz, Rev. John A., '09 (TR) Our Lady of Good Counsel, Moorestown, NJ
Bogdan, Rev. Msgr. Leonard A., '60 (KAL) Retired.
Bogert, Rev. James, '67 (RVC) Retired.
Boghossian, Rev. G. Scott, '02 (PSC) Curia: Advisory Boards, Commissions, Committees, and Councils; Leadership St. Mary's, Freeland, PA
Bognanno, Rev. Msgr. Frank E., (DM) Retired.
Bogniak, Rev. Msgr. Casimir A., '57 (E) Retired. St. James, Erie, PA
Boguslawski, Very Rev. Steven C., '87 (HRT) Curia: Administration; Advisory Boards, Commissions, Committees, and Councils; Clergy and Religious Services; Offices and Directors; Tribunal [SEM] St. Thomas Seminary, Bloomfield, CT
Boh, Rev. Aloysius N, '01 (WH) St. Bernadette Catholic Church, Hedgesville, WV
Bohan, Rev. Philip, *O.F.M.Cap.* '67 (NY) Retired.
Boharic, Rev. Thomas, '12 (CHI) Mother of the Americas Parish, Chicago, IL
Bohlin, Rev. Msgr. Thomas G., '97 (NY) [MIS] Personal Prelature, New York, NY; [MIS] Prelature of the Holy Cross and Opus Dei, New York, NY
Bohlin, Rev. Msgr. Thomas G., '97 (POD) Curia: Clergy and Religious Services
Bohn, Rev. John, '97 (JKS) On Leave.
Bohnert, Rev. Edward A., '85 (SFR) Retired.
Bohorquez, Rev. Carlos M., '99 (SFD) On Leave.
Bohorquez, Rev. Jesus Alberto, '01 (MIA) On Leave.
Bohr, Rev. Aaron, *SJ* '22 (CHI) St. Ignatius Jesuit Community, Chicago, IL
Bohr, Rev. Msgr. David A., '71 (SCR) Curia: Offices and Directors [MON] Villa St. Joseph, Dunmore, PA
Bohr, Rev. Gail G., *S.J.* '73 (CHI) [COL] Jesuit Community at Loyola University Chicago, Chicago, IL
Bohren, Rev. Gregory J., '09 (LC) St. Agnes, Weston, WI; St. Florian, Hatley, WI
Boiko, Rev. John, '87 (AUS) St. Mary's Church of the

Assumption, West, TX
Boisvert, Rev. Keith W., '79 (BAL) St. Katharine Drexel, Frederick, MD
Boisvert, Rev. Robert G., '58 (MAN) Retired.
Boivin, Rev. John P., '76 (CHI) Retired.
Bojczuk, Rev. Thaddeus J., '73 (CHI) Retired.
Boji, Rev. Manuel Y., '68 (EST) Curia: Offices and Directors
Bok, Rev. James M., *O.F.M.* '74 (CIN) [MON] St. Francis Seraph Friary, Cincinnati, OH
Bok, Rev. John, *O.F.M.* '62 (CIN) Retired. [MIS] Franciscan Missionary Union, Cincinnati, OH; [MON] St. Clement Friary, Cincinnati, OH; [MON] St. Francis Seraph Friary, Cincinnati, OH
Bokinskie, Rev. Richard A., '79 (SAG) Saint Thomas Aquinas Parish of Saginaw, Saginaw, MI
Bokota, Rev. Marek, (NEW) St. Philip the Apostle, Saddle Brook, NJ
Boks, Rev. Lawrence E., '66 (GLD) Retired.
Boksay, Rev. Peter, (PRM) Curia: Leadership St. Emilian, Brunswick, OH
Boland, Rev. Eamonn, '69 (DUL) Retired.
Boland, Rev. James, '14 (WOR) St. Patrick, Rutland, MA
Boland, Rev. Jeremiah M., '81 (CHI) Our Lady of Perpetual Help, Glenview, IL
Boland, Rev. John, '75 (GLP) Retired.
Boland, Rev. Joseph, (GLP) On Leave.
Boland, Rev. Msgr. Michael M., '86 (CHI)
Boland, Rev. Stephen Joseph, *MSC* '86 (ALN) [MON] Sacred Heart Villa, Missionaries of the Sacred Heart, Center Valley, PA
Bolanos, Rev. Victor M., '16 (BRK) Presentation of the Blessed Virgin Mary, Jamaica, NY
Bolatete, Rev. Ramon, '85 (ORL) St. Faustina Catholic Church, Clermont, FL
Bolcic, Rev. Dragan, *OFM* (CHI) Sacred Heart, Chicago, IL (>MIL) Sacred Heart Congregation, Milwaukee, WI
Bolda, Rev. Eugemoisz, *SChr* (SFR) Nativity, San Francisco, CA
Bolderson, Rev. John D., '81 (KC) Retired. St. Cyril's Catholic Church - Sugar Creek, Sugar Creek, MO
Bolding, Rev. Robert, '09 (PHX) St. Mary's Roman Catholic High School, Phoenix, AZ; St. Thomas the Apostle Roman Catholic Parish, Phoenix, AZ
Bolduc, Rev. John, *S.M.* '70 (WDC) [MON] Marist Center (The Marist Finance Center of the Atlanta Province of the Society of Mary, Marist Fathers and Brothers), Washington, DC
Bolduc, Rev. John P., *S.M.* '70 (BO) Curia: Consultative Bodies
Bolek, Rev. Eric, '15 (PEO) St. Mary of Lourdes, Germantown Hills, IL
Boley, Rev. Robert, *O.Carm.* '75 (JOL) [MON] Carmelite Provincial Office, Darien, IL
Bolger, Rev. Jesse L., '07 (BAL) St. Joseph, Baltimore, MD; [MIS] Catholic Evidence League of Baltimore, Baltimore, MD
Bolger, Rev. Michael J., '92 (RCK) On Special Assignment. Aquin Central Catholic High School, Freeport, IL; St. Wendelin, Shannon, IL
Bolger, Rev. Msgr. Richard T., '66 (PH) Retired.
Bolger, Rev. Msgr. William, '53 (SD) Retired.
Bolieau, Rev. Henry G., '72 (NOR) On Leave.
Bolin, Rev. Kenneth M., '13 (POC) Military Chap St. Thomas Becket Catholic Church, Fort Worth, TX
Boll, Rev. John E., '70 (SAC) Retired.
Boll, Rev. John Joseph Blase, *O.P.* '82 (ATL) [CAM] Emory University, Agnes Scott College, Atlanta, GA; [MON] Augustine House, Dominicans Friars of Atlanta (The Monastery on the Hill), Atlanta, GA
Boller, Rev. Kenneth, *SJ* (NY) [MON] Xavier Jesuit Community, New York, NY
Boller, Rev. Kenneth, *SJ* (NY) St. Francis Xavier, New York, NY; [MIS] Xavier Mission, Inc., New York, NY
Bolling, Rev. Francis Joseph, '04 (MOB) Retired.
Bolling, Rev. Joseph M., '91 (MOB) St. Matthew Parish, Mobile, Mobile, AL
Bollman, Rev. Richard W., *S.J.* '69 (CIN) [MON] Cincinnati Jesuit Community, Cincinnati, OH
Bolls, Rev. Donald McChesney, '15 (PBR) Church of the Resurrection, Monroeville, PA; Holy Trinity, Wall, PA
Bologo, Rev. Christopher, (SJ) St. Simon, Los Altos, CA
Bolser, Rev. Charles G., *C.S.V.* '73 (CHI) St. Viator High School, Arlington Heights, IL; [MON] Viatorian Province Center-Clerics of St. Viator, Arlington Heights, IL
Bolster, Rev. M. Thomas, '82 (GR) Retired.
Bolster, Rev. Rhodes Winslow, (NSH) Curia: Leadership; Offices and Directors [MIS] FrassatiUSA Inc. (University Catholic), Nashville, TN
Bolte, Rev. Richard G., '83 (COV) St. Timothy, Union, KY
Bolte, Rev. Thomas L., '80 (CIN) St. John the Evangelist, New Paris, OH; St. Mary, Camden, OH; St. Mary Church, Oxford, OH; Visitation of the Blessed Virgin Mary, Eaton, OH
Bolton, Rev. Bill, *S.D.B.* '87 (LA) St. Jerome, Los Angeles, CA
Bolton, Rev. Norman B., '83 (SPR) Retired. Saint Elizabeth Parish, Ludlow, MA; [CAM] Western New England University, Springfield, MA
Boly, Rev. Craig, *S.J.* '74 (P) Jesuit High School (The Society of Jesus), Portland, OR; [MON] Colombiere Jesuit Community, Portland, OR
Boman, Rev. Timothy, (NY) Parish of St. Margaret of Cortona and St. Gabriel, Bronx, NY
Bomba, Rev. Paul M., '77 (WOR) St. Joseph's, Auburn, MA
Bombardier, Rev. Paul A., '82 (SPR) On Duty Outside Diocese. Canada
Bomberger, Rev. Raymond P., *S.S.J.* (BAL) [MON] St. Joseph Society of the Sacred Heart House of Central Administration, Baltimore, MD
Bommarito, Rev. Msgr. Vincent, (STL) St. Joan of Arc Catholic Church, St. Louis, MO
Bommarito, Rev. Msgr. Vincent R., '77 (STL) St. Ambrose Catholic Church, St. Louis, MO
Bona, Rev. Richard, (CLV) St. Elizabeth of Hungary, Cleveland, OH; St. Emeric, Cleveland, OH
Bona, Rev. Richard, (PRM) Curia: Advisory Boards, Commissions, Committees, and Councils; Leadership
Bona, Rev. Richard, '03 (CLV) Curia: Tribunal
Bonacci, Rev. Paul, '91 (ROC) St. Pius Tenth, Rochester, NY
Bonacci, Rev. Thomas, *C.P.* '72 (NY) [MON] The Congregation of the Passion - St. Paul of the Cross Province, Jamaica, NY
Bonafed, Rev. Joseph E., '92 (GBG) On Leave.
Bonagiri, Rev. Joseph Thambi, '04 (GI) Our Lady of Guadalupe, Scottsbluff, NE
Bonagiri, Rev. ViJay, (COS) Sacred Heart, Cheyenne Wells, CO
Bonar, Rev. Clyde A., '84 (ORL) Retired.
Bonarrigo, Rev. David, *T.O.R.* '78 (ALT) [MON] St. Francis Friary at Mount Assisi, Loretto, PA
Bonavitacola, Rev. John, '88 (PHX) Curia: Leadership; Offices and Directors Our Lady of Lourdes Roman Catholic Parish, Sun City West, AZ
Bond, Rev. Christopher A., (CHL) St. Lucien, Spruce Pine, NC
Bond, Rev. Ernest W., '88 (COS) Retired.
Bond, Rev. Samuel, '20 (LKC) Immaculate Conception Cathedral, Lake Charles, LA
Bond, Rev. Samuel E., '20 (LKC) Curia: Advisory Boards, Commissions, Committees, and Councils
Bond, Rev. William D., '99 (OM) Assumption of the Blessed Virgin Mary-Our Lady of Guadalupe Church of Omaha, Omaha, NE; St. Mary, Omaha, NE; Sts. Peter and Paul Church of Omaha, Omaha, NE
Bondi, Rev. Steven, '86 (JOL) St. John Vianney, Lockport, IL
Bondy, Rev. Alberto P., '86 (DET) Retired. St. Lawrence Parish Utica, Utica, MI; St. Lucy (Croatian) Parish Troy, Troy, MI
Bonela, Rev. Anthony, *MSFS* '97 (ATL) [MON] The Missionaries of St. Francis de Sales - MSFS USA Vice Province, Loganville, GA
Bonela, Rev. Anthony, *M.S.F.S.* '97 (STA) St. Monica, Palatka, FL
Bonello, Rev. Pablo, *I.V.E.* '84 (WDC) St. James, Mount Rainier, MD; [MON] Institute of the Incarnate Word, Chillum, MD
Bonete, Rev. Jay J., (SEA) St. Theresa, Federal Way, WA
Boney, Rev. Vincent, *C.P.* '57 (NY) Retired. [MON] The Congregation of the Passion - St. Paul of the Cross Province, Jamaica, NY
Bonfiglio, Rev. Gregory R., *S.J.* '94 (SFR) St. Ignatius, San Francisco, CA; [MON] Loyola House Jesuit Community, San Francisco, CA
Bongard, Rev. Joseph W., '86 (PH) Immaculate Heart of Mary, Philadelphia, PA; Roman Catholic High School for Boys, Philadelphia, PA
Boni, Rev. Frederick G., '10 (MOB) St. Catherine of Siena, Mobile, AL
Bonian, Rev. Stephen J., *S.J.* '82 (BO) [MON] Campion Health & Wellness, Inc., Weston, MA
Bonifacio, Rev. Edwin, (NY) Incarnation, New York, NY
Bonifazi, Rev. Jason, '13 (AUS) On Administrative Leave.
Bonilla, Rev. Msgr. Humberto Lopez, '86 (MGZ) Curia: Leadership Cathedral of Our Lady of Purification, Mayaguez, PR
Bonilla, Rev. Juan Manuel, '12 (DEN) On Duty Outside Diocese. Holy Trinity Catholic Parish in Westminster, Westminster, CO
Bonilla, Rev. Nelson Angel, *F.M.M.* (SB) Immaculate Conception, Colton, CA
Bonilla Sanchez, Rev. Fernando, *M.S.P.* (SB) St. Charles Borromeo, Bloomington, CA; St. John the Evangelist, Riverside, CA
Bonilla-Moreno, Rev. Fredy, '15 (P) On Leave.
Bonk, Rev. Carl A., *S.J.* '82 (DET) [MON] Colombiere Center, Clarkston, MI
Bonk, Rev. Matthew, (LAN) St. John Vianney Parish Flint, Flint, MI
Bonk, Rev. Paul, '16 (SFD) St. Gertrude, Grantfork, IL; St. Nicholas, Pocahontas, IL
Bonk, Rev. Paul J., (SFD) Immaculate Conception, Pierron, IL
Bonke, Rev. James R., (IND) Retired.
Bonner, Rev. Charles E., '65 (PH) Retired. St. Cecilia, Philadelphia, PA
Bonner, Rev. Patrick, '00 (NY) Parish of St. Patrick and St. Mary, Newburgh, NY
Bonner, Rev. Sean P., '15 (DET) Curia: Administration; Consultative Bodies St. Mary Parish Wayne, Wayne, MI; St. Richard Parish Westland, Westland, MI
Bonneville, Rev. Lionel E., '63 (SPR) Retired. Chap, Veterans Administration Hosp, Northampton
Bonnici, Rev. John S., '91 (NY) Curia: Leadership SS. John and Paul, Larchmont, NY; St. Augustine, Larchmont, NY; St. Columba, Chester, NY
Bonnot, Rev. Bernard R., '67 (Y) Retired.
Bonsignore, Rev. Dennis, '81 (ROC) Chaplain, Monroe Cmty Hosp, Roch; Strong Health Sys, Roch St. Anne, Rochester, NY
Bonsor, Rev. Jack, '74 (SJ) Retired.
Bonsu, Rev. Anthony, (RVC) St. Catherine of Sienna, Franklin Square, NY
Bonzagni, Rev. Msgr. John J., '80 (SPR) Curia: Leadership; Tribunal St. Ann, Lenox, MA; St. Patrick's, West Stockbridge, MA; St. Vincent de Paul, Lenox Dale, MA
Book, Very Rev. Matthew, '10 (DEN) Curia: Deaneries Light of the World Roman Catholic Parish in Littleton, Littleton, CO; [ASN] Companions of Christ, Denver, CO
Booms, Rev. Andrew D., '07 (SAG) Curia: Leadership Saint Brigid of Kildare Parish of Midland, Midland, MI; Saint Mary University Parish of Mt. Pleasant, Mount Pleasant, MI
Boone, Rev. Scott F., '01 (DUB) Saint Joseph's Church, Farley, Iowa, Farley, IA; St. Clement Church, Bankston, Iowa, Epworth, IA; St. John Church, Placid, Epworth, Iowa, Epworth, IA; St. John the Baptist Church of Peosta, Iowa, Peosta, IA; St. Patrick Church, Epworth, Iowa, Epworth, IA
Boosel, Rev. Brian D., *O.S.B.* '03 (GBG) [MON] Saint Vincent Archabbey, Latrobe, PA
Booth, Rev. Adam David Patrick, *CSC* (FR) [COL] Holy Cross Fathers Religious, North Easton, MA
Booth, Rev. Edward, '74 (STA) Retired.
Booth, Rev. Jim W., '07 (BIR) Blessed Sacrament Catholic Parish, Birmingham, Birmingham, AL; [EFT] Blessed Sacrament Catholic Church Endowment Fund, Birmingham, AL
Booth, Rev. Michael, (MO) Curia: Offices and Directors
Booth, Rev. Steven, '20 (FR) St. Joan of Arc, Orleans, MA
Bopda, Rev. Armand, *CJ* (LA) St. Louis de Montfort, Santa Maria, CA
Boquet, Rev. Gregory M., *O.S.B.* '88 (NO) [MON] St. Joseph Abbey, St. Benedict, LA; [SEM] Saint Joseph Seminary College, Saint Benedict, LA
Boquet, Rev. Shenan, (MIA) [MIS] Vida Humana Internacional (Hispanic Division of Human Life International), Miami, FL
Boquet, Rev. Shenan J., '93 (HT) On Duty Outside Diocese.
Boquet, Rev. Shenan J., '93 (ARL) [MIS] Human Life International, Front Royal, VA
Bora, Rev. Vittorio, *O.F.M. Cap.* (DEN) [MON] St. Anthony of Padua Friary, Denver, CO
Boras, Rev. Drazan, *OFM* (CHI) Blessed Alojzije Stepinac Croatian Mission, Chicago, IL
Boras, Rev. Kurt D., '86 (CHI) Curia: Offices and Directors
Borbor, Rev. Hanz Christian, (GB) St. Anthony, Neopit, WI; St. Michael, Keshena, WI
Borchard, Rev. Craig, '16 (FTW) St. Vincent de Paul, Elkhart, IN
Borchardt, Rev. Edgar, '96 (SPK) Retired.
Borda Rojas, Rev. Oscar, (CHR) St. James the Younger, Conway, SC
Bordelon, Very Rev. Kevin P., '05 (LAF) Curia:

Leadership; Tribunal
Bordonaro, Rev. Joseph C., '89 (PH) St. Joseph, Warrington, PA
Bordonaro, Rev. Richard D., '76 (BUF) Retired.
Borek, Rev. Derek J., '99 (BO) St. John the Baptist, Peabody, MA; St. Thomas the Apostle, Peabody, MA
Borel, Rev. Albert W., '81 (LKC) Retired. Curia: Leadership
Borello, Rev. Steven, '11 (JOL) Curia: Leadership
Boren, Rev. Edward, *O.F.M.* (IND) Sacred Heart of Jesus Catholic Church, Indianapolis, Inc., Indianapolis, IN
Borer, Rev. Robert D., '76 (STU) Retired.
Boretto, Rev. Krzysztof, '87 (SY) Chap, Our Lady of Lourdes Mem Hosp, Binghamton
Borgelt, Rev. Daniel E., '93 (TOL) Curia: Advisory Boards, Commissions, Committees, and Councils; Deaneries St. Mary, Edgerton, OH; St. Michael, Hicksville, OH
Borgen, Rev. Alfonso, *O.F.M.Conv.* '98 (LA) St. Alphonsus, Los Angeles, CA
Borgen, Rev. Alfonso, *O.F.M.Conv.* '98 (OAK) St. Edward, Newark, CA
Borger, Rev. Msgr. Marvin G., '91 (TOL) St. Joan of Arc, Toledo, OH
Borges, Rev. Charles, *S.J.* '81 (BAL) [COL] Jesuit Community of Loyola University, Inc., Baltimore, MD; [MON] Jesuit Community of Loyola University Maryland, Inc., Baltimore, MD
Borges, Rev. Mario L., '82 (OAK) Transfiguration, Castro Valley, CA
Borges, Rev. Miguel Garcia, *S.D.B.* (SJN) Chap, Doctors Cmty Hosp, Santurce
Borges, Rev. Miguel Rivera, (SJN) Chap, Doctors Cmty Hosp, Santurce
Borges, Rev. Robert B., '04 (FRS) Curia: Advisory Boards, Commissions, Committees, and Councils; Leadership St. Patrick's Parish and Our Lady of Mercy Church, Merced, CA
Borgman, Rev. E. Scott, '10 (ORG) Curia: Leadership (>P) [SEM] Mount Angel Seminary, Saint Benedict, OR
Borgmeyer, Rev. Msgr. Dean G., '81 (WH) Curia: Leadership; Offices and Directors St. Joseph Parish, Huntington, WV
Borgos, Rev. Carlos J., (BRK) Holy Child Jesus, Richmond Hill, NY; SS. Peter and Paul, Brooklyn, NY
Boric, Rev. James E., '14 (BAL) [EFT] Basilica of the Assumption Historic Trust, Inc., Baltimore, MD
Borino, Rev. David J., '86 (HRT) Retired.
Borja, Rev. Charlito A., '03 (CHK) Curia: Advisory Boards, Commissions, Committees, and Councils; Consultative Bodies; Faith Formation; Leadership Santa Soledad Mission Parish, Saipan, MP
Borja, Rev. Ricardo, (HRT) Saint John XXIII Parish Corporation, West Haven, CT
Bork, Rev. Vincent D., '95 (ARL) Holy Trinity, Gainesville, VA
Borkenhagen, Rev. Jason W., '01 (WCH) Immaculate Conception (St. Mary, Aleppo), Garden Plain, KS
Borkowski, Rev. Frank, (NY) St. Stanislaus Mission, Pine Island, NY
Borkowski, Rev. Mark, '96 (DET) Our Lady of the Scapular (Our Lady of Mount Carmel and St. Stanislaus Kostka), Wyandotte, MI
Borkowski, Rev. Raymond, *OFM Conv.* '61 (HRT) Retired. Saint Paul Parish Corporation, Kensington, CT; [MIS] St. Paul Friary (St. Paul Parish Corporation), Kensington, CT
Borkowski, Rev. Thomas, '81 (KC) Retired. (>JOL) [RTR] Mayslake Ministries, Inc., Oakbrook Terrace, IL
Borkowski, Rev. Tomasz J., '01 (WOR) St. Patrick, Whitinsville, MA
Borkowski, Rev. Walter M. (Waldystaw), '85 (SAC) Retired.
Borlakunta, Rev. Naveen, (CAM) Our Lady of Peace Parish, Monroe Township, N.J., Williamstown, NJ
Borlakunta, Rev. Naveen, (CAM) Chap, Jefferson Washington Township Hosp; Inspira Med Ctr
Borlang, Rev. Stephen M., '86 (SAC) Retired.
Borlik, Rev. Daniel P., *C.M.* (CHI) [MON] DePaul Vincentian Residence, Chicago, IL
Bormann, Rev. Paul, '85 (SC) St. Mary's, Hawarden, IA; St. Patrick, Akron, IA
Bornhauser, Rev. Emmanuel, '98 (NEW) On Duty Outside Diocese. Montpellier
Borno, Rev. Saint Charles, '04 (BRK) Blessed Sacrament, Jackson Heights, NY; [CCH] Haitian Ministry, ,
Borntrager, Rev. Conrad M., *O.S.M.* '60 (CHI) [MIS] Monastery of Our Lady of Sorrows, ,
Boroch, Rev. Andrzej, (PHX) St. Theresa Roman Catholic Parish, Phoenix, AZ
Boroch, Rev. Andrzej, '95 (SAG) On Duty Outside Diocese. Milwaukee, WI
Boroff, Rev. David Gregory, '13 (COS) Holy Trinity, Colorado Springs, CO
Boroughs, Rev. Philip L., *S.J.* '78 (WOR) [COL] College of the Holy Cross, Inc., Worcester, MA; [MON] Jesuits of the Holy Cross, Inc., Worcester, MA
Boroughs, Rev. Philip L., *S.J.* (SEA) St. Leo the Great, Tacoma, WA
Boroviy, Rev. Ruslan, '14 (PHU) Curia: Administration
Borovyi, Rev. Ruslan, '14 (PHU) St. Nicholas Ukrainian Catholic Church, Philadelphia, PA
Borowiak, Rev. David J., '71 (BUF) Retired. [MON] Msgr. Conniff Residence, Depew, NY
Borowiak, Rev. Kenneth A., '87 (LIN) Curia: Leadership St. Michael, Lincoln, NE
Borowiejski, Rev. Rafal, '20 (RVC) Our Lady of Victory, Floral Park, NY
Borowski, Rev. Paul, *C.Ss.R.* (BAL) [MON] The Redemptorists, Baltimore, MD
Borowski, Rev. Paul J., *C.Ss.R.* '87 (BRK) [MON] Redemptorist Fathers of New York, Inc.-Baltimore Province, Brooklyn, NY
Borre, Rev. Robert J., '60 (MAD) Retired.
Borrero Rivera, Rev. Victor R., (ARE) On Duty Outside Diocese. Spain
Borrow, Rev. Anthony, *S.J.* (SJN) San Ignacio de Loyola, San Juan, PR
Borrow, Rev. Anthony R., *S.J.* '10 (FWT) [EFT] Montserrat Foundation, Inc., ,
Borruel, Rev. Alberto J., '06 (AUS) Our Lady of Guadalupe, Taylor, TX
Bors, Rev. James, '22 (BAL) Our Lady of the Chesapeake, Pasadena, MD; St. Jane Frances de Chantal, Pasadena, MD
Borski, Rev. Msgr. Chester L., '67 (GAL) Curia: Offices and Directors [SEM] St. Mary's Seminary, Houston, TX
Borski, Rev. Jerome, *O.S.B.* '92 (PAT) [MON] St. Mary's Abbey, Morristown, NJ
Borstelmann, Rev. James E., '67 (NY) Retired.
Bortz, Very Rev. Thomas P., '04 (ALN) Curia: Leadership St. Francis de Sales, Robesonia, PA; St. Ignatius Loyola, West Lawn, PA
Borzych, Rev. Alexander J., '80 (GI) Retired.
Bosch, Rev. Stan, *ST* '86 (LA) St. Raphael, Los Angeles, CA
Bosch, Rev. William J., *S.J.* '60 (SY) [MON] Jesuits at LeMoyne, Inc., Syracuse, NY
Boschert, Rev. Hubert G., *S.J.* '68 (MIL) Retired. [MON] St. Camillus Jesuit Community (Society of Jesus, USA Midwest Province), Wauwatosa, WI
Boschetto, Rev. Dan, *S.X.* '70 (PAT) [MON] Xaverian Missionary Fathers, Wayne, NJ
Bosco, Rev. John, (HT) Thanh Gia, Morgan City, LA
Bosco, Rev. Mark, *S.J.* '99 (WDC) [MON] The Jesuit Community at Georgetown University, Washington, DC
Boscoe, Rev. John L., *C.S.B.* '72 (GAL) [MON] The Basilian Fathers of Dillon House, Houston, TX
Boscutti, Rev. Darrio L., '86 (CHI) St. Edna, Arlington Heights, IL
Bosken, Rev. Robert E., *S.J.* '56 (STL) Retired.
Boslett, Rev. Donald E., '59 (ALT) Retired.
Bosnich, Very Rev. David A., '95 (PBR) Curia: Leadership St. Michael, Sheffield, PA
Bosomafi, Rev. Stephen K, (SCR) St. Thomas More, Lake Ariel, PA
Bosques, Rev. Eric J, '18 (MGZ) St. John the Baptist, Maricao, PR
Bosse, Rev. Austin Lee, '21 (PEO) Marquette Academy of Ottawa, Inc., Ottawa, IL; SS. Peter and Paul's, Tonica, IL; St. Michael the Archangel Parish, Streator, IL
Bosse, Rev. Dennis, *O.F.M.* (TUC) Saint Pius X Roman Catholic Parish - Tucson, Tucson, AZ
Bossi, Rev. Paul R., '69 (BUF) Retired. [MON] O'Hara Residence, Tonawanda, NY
Bosso, Rev. Msgr. Stephen C., '78 (PT) Retired. Curia: Leadership
Bostwick, Rev. John, '69 (RIC) Retired.
Bot, Rev. Daniel, (SP) St. Ignatius of Antioch, Tarpon Springs, FL
Bot, Rev. Joshua, '22 (NU) Cathedral of the Holy Trinity, New Ulm, MN; St. George, New Ulm, MN; St. John the Baptist, New Ulm, MN; St. Mary, New Ulm, MN
Boteju, Rev. Bernard, '85 (TYL) Retired.
Boteler, Rev. William M., *M.M.* '68 (SJ) Retired. [MON] Maryknoll, Los Altos, CA
Botsko, Rev. Jerome G., '82 (PBR) [CON] Monastery and Novitiate of the Sisters of St. Basil the Great, Uniontown, PA
Botsko, Rev. Jerome G., '82 (PBR) St. Stephen, Leisenring, PA
Bottehagen, Rev. Paul, *OFM* '82 (MRY) [MON] Franciscan Friars, San Juan Bautista, CA
Bottino, Rev. Msgr. Dominic J., '78 (CAM) Chap, Jefferson Univ Hosps; Jefferson Health at Stratford Curia: Leadership; Tribunal St. Mary's R.C. Church, Delaware Township, N.J., Cherry Hill, NJ
Botz, Rev. Roger, *O.S.B.* '60 (SCL) [MON] St. John's Abbey, of the Order of St. Benedict, Collegeville, MN
Botzet, Rev. Mark, '19 (SCL) Our Lady of the Angels, Sauk Centre, MN; SS. Peter and Paul, Sauk Centre, MN; St. Donatus, Sauk Centre, MN; St. Paul's, Sauk Centre, MN
Bou, Rev. Pedro L., *S.V.D.* '74 (TR) The Parish of Our Lady of Guadalupe, Lakewood, NJ
Bouchard, Rev. Charles E., *O.P.* '79 (STL) [MON] Dominican Community of St. Louis, St. Louis, MO
Bouchard, Rev. Denis, *F.S.S.P.* '00 (Y) Retired.
Bouchard, Rev. Lucien, *O.M.I.* '55 (BO) Retired. [NUR] Immaculate Heart of Mary Residence, Tewksbury, MA
Bouchard, Rev. Marcel H., '72 (FR) Retired.
Bouchard, Rev. Msgr. Paul L., '72 (MAN) Curia: Consultative Bodies; Tribunal Our Lady of Mercy, Merrimack, NH
Boucher, Rev. Alexander Robert, '20 (PRT) St. John Paul II Parish, Scarborough, ME
Boucher, Rev. Kevin, '91 (FAR) St. Anthony Church of Selz, Selz, ND; St. Cecilia's Church of Harvey, Harvey, ND
Boucher, Rev. Roger R., '73 (WOR) Retired.
Boucheron, Rev. Antoine M., (GB) St. Patrick, Green Bay, WI; [MIS] Oratory of St. Patrick, Green Bay, WI
Bouck, Rev. Dominic, '18 (BIS) [COL] University of Mary, Bismarck, ND
Bouck, Rev. William Gabriel, '22 (MEM) St. Paul the Apostle, Memphis, TN
Boudoin, Rev. Burt, '82 (SD) Pastor of Saint Charles Catholic Parish, San Diego, a corporation sole, San Diego, CA
Boudreau, Rev. George, (MIA) [COL] Barry University, Miami, FL; [MON] Dominican Fathers of Miami, Inc., Miami, FL
Boudreau, Rev. Thomas C., '95 (BO) St. Joseph, Holbrook, MA; St. Michael, Avon, MA
Boudreaux, Rev. John S., '73 (MOB) Retired.
Boudreaux, Rev. Ronald J., *S.J.* '05 (STL) [MON] Leo Brown Jesuit Community, St. Louis, MO; [MON] USA Central & Southern Province, Society of Jesus, St. Louis, MO
Bouffier, Rev. Robert, *S.M.* (MIA) Chaminade-Madonna College Preparatory, Hollywood, FL
Boufford, Rev. Thomas F., '81 (GR) St. Michael the Archangel, Remus, MI
Boughton, Rev. John Anthony, *C.F.R.* (NY) [MON] St. Crispin Friary, Bronx, NY
Boughton, Rev. Michael G., *S.J.* '79 (BO) [MON] Saint Peter Faber Jesuit Community, Brighton, MA
Bouhall, Rev. William G., '94 (CLV) [SEM] Borromeo Seminary, Wickliffe, OH
Boulet, Rev. Marshall, '71 (LKC) Retired.
Boulette, Rev. James J., '22 (WOR) St. Ann, North Oxford, MA; St. Roch, Oxford, MA
Boulin, Rev. Jean Wesner, '04 (PMB) Sacred Heart, Lake Worth, FL; St. Peter, Jupiter, FL
BouMerhi, Rev. Jibran, '88 (OLL) Curia: Offices and Directors Saint Jude Maronite Catholic Church, Murray, UT
Boumerhi, Rev. Joubran, '88 (SLC) Saint Jude LLC, Murray, UT
Bourcy, Rev. Robert Scott, '82 (ROC) Church of the Transfiguration, Pittsford, NY; St. Catherine of Siena, Mendon, NY
Bourdon, Rev. Norman W., '73 (PRO) Saint Joan's Church, Cumberland, Rhode Island, Cumberland, RI
Bourek, Rev. David F., '79 (LIN) St. Patrick's, Lincoln, NE
Bourg, Rev. Rodney P., '78 (NO) Curia: Leadership Most Holy Trinity Roman Catholic Church, Louisiana, Covington, LA
Bourgault, Rev. Ronald L., '63 (BO) Retired.
Bourgeois, Rev. Msgr. Bernard W., '95 (BUR) Curia: Leadership Christ the King, Rutland, VT; St. Patrick, Wallingford, VT
Bourgeois, Rev. Donald E., '85 (SY) Retired.
Bourgeois, Rev. Roger, *s.s.s.* (CLV) Retired.
Bourgeois, Rev. Canon Ross, (PIT) Most Precious Blood of Jesus, Pittsburgh, PA
Bourke, Rev. Charles E., '70 (BO) Retired. Saint Agnes, Arlington, MA
Bourke, Rev. Martin, '74 (SEA) The Proto-Cathedral of St. James the Greater, Vancouver, WA; [MIS] Skagit Valley Catholic Churches, Mount Vernon, WA

Bourke, Rev. Ulick, *SMA* '68 (BO) Retired. [MON] Society of African Missions, Dedham, MA
Bourque, Rev. Msgr. Charles J., '62 (BO) Retired.
Bourque, Rev. John Joseph, *CJC* '20 (LAF) [MIS] Community of Jesus Crucified, St. Martinville, LA; [MIS] Community of Jesus Crucified - Priest Brother and Sister Servants, St. Martinville, LA
Bourque, Rev. Thomas G., *T.O.R.* '82 (ARL) St. Joseph, Herndon, VA
Bouterie, Rev. Thomas, '80 (HT) On Duty Outside Diocese.
Boutin, Rev. Christopher G., '16 (MOB) Curia: Leadership St. John the Evangelist Parish, Ozark, Ozark, AL; St. Martin of Tours, Troy, AL; [CAM] Mother Teresa Catholic Newman Ministry at Troy University, Troy, AL
Bouton, Rev. Thomas F., '83 (BO) St. Ambrose, Boston, MA
Boutros, Very Rev. Peter, '00 (NTN) Curia: Consultative Bodies St. John of the Desert Melkite Catholic Church, Phoenix, AZ
Bouzi, Rev. Quilin, *O.M.I.* '07 (BO) St. William, Tewksbury, MA
Bova, Rev. Michael, *SMA* '19 (NEW) [MON] Society of African Missions, Provincialate, S.M.A. Fathers, Tenafly, NJ
Bova Conti, Rev. Michael J., '71 (BO) Retired.
Bove, Rev. Ralph A., '78 (SY) St. Bartholomew the Apostle, Norwich, NY; St. Paul, Norwich, NY
Bovino, Rev. Michael, (NOR) St. Patrick Cathedral, Norwich, CT
Bowden, Rev. Andrew, '22 (JKS) St. Richard of Chichester, Jackson, MS
Bowe, Rev. Matthew L., '22 (LC) Queen of the Apostles Parish, Tomah, WI
Bowen, Rev. Brent, (LFT) [CAM] St. Thomas Aquinas Parish and Foundation for Catholic Students Attending Purdue University, West Lafayette, IN
Bowen, Rev. Brent, *O.P.* '19 (LFT) [MIS] Dominicans, Community of St. Thomas Aquinas, Inc., West Lafayette, IN
Bowen, Rev. Brent, (LFT) St. Thomas Aquinas, West Lafayette, IN
Bowen, Rev. Daniel, *O. de M.* '15 (CLV) (>COL) Holy Family, Columbus, OH
Bowen, Rev. Gerard J., '77 (BAL) St. John the Evangelist, Columbia, MD
Bower, Rev. Alan, '89 (STA) Corpus Christi, St. Augustine, FL
Bower, Rev. Alan E., '89 (STA) Retired.
Bower, Rev. Lawrence C., '88 (BAK) Retired.
Bower, Rev. Michael, (LFT) St. Bernard, Crawfordsville, IN
Bowers, Rev. Robert J., '87 (BO) On Leave.
Bowers, Rev. Ronald J., '64 (STP) Retired.
Bowers, Rev. Ronald J., '64 (SFE) Retired. Curia: Offices and Directors
Bowes, Rev. James, *S.J.* (NY) [MON] Murray-Weigel Hall (A Jesuit Community at Murray-Weigel Hall and Kohlmann Hall), Bronx, NY
Bowker, Very Rev. Jeffrey A., '95 (R) Curia: Leadership; Offices and Directors Church of St. Therese, Wilson, NC
Bowlds, Rev. Kent, '93 (JKS) Curia: Consultative Bodies; Leadership Our Lady of Victories, Cleveland, MS; [CAM] Delta State University Newman Center, Cleveland, MS
Bowler, Rev. James M., (BO) [MON] Campion Center, Inc., Weston, MA
Bowlin, Rev. John-Mary Sayf, '12 (TYL) St. Jude, Gun Barrel City, TX
Bowling, Rev. William M., '97 (L) Curia: Leadership Holy Name, Louisville, KY; St. Martin de Porres, Louisville, KY
Bowman, Rev. Eric A., '04 (CIN) St. Boniface, Piqua, OH; St. Mary, Piqua, OH; St. Patrick, Troy, OH; St. Teresa of the Infant Jesus, Covington, OH; Transfiguration, West Milton, OH
Bowman, Rev. James C., '65 (RVC) Retired.
Bowman, Rev. John, '65 (SEA) Retired.
Bowman, Rev. Ronald P., '82 (ALN) [CON] St. Joseph Villa, Reading, PA
Bowora, Rev. Sheunesu, '16 (PHX) Curia: Offices and Directors St. Daniel the Prophet Roman Catholic Parish, Scottsdale, AZ
Bowski, Rev. Eugene, '77 (GLP) Retired.
Boxie, Rev. Robert P., '16 (WDC) Howard Univ Curia: Clergy and Religious Services; Consultative Bodies [CAM] Howard University Newman Center, Washington, DC
Boyack, Rev. Kenneth, (OAK) Holy Spirit Parish/ Newman Hall, Berkeley, CA
Boyalla, Rev. Balaji, *S.A.C.* '99 (FWT) St. Michael, Bedford, TX
Boyalla, Very Rev. Balaji, *S.A.C.* '99 (FWT) Curia: Leadership
Boyapati, Rev. Joji Reddy, '02 (SUP) Cathedral of Christ the King, Superior, WI; Holy Assumption, Superior, WI; St. Anthony, Superior, WI; St. Anthony Catholic Church, Lake Nebagamon, WI; St. William, Foxboro, WI
Boyce, Rt. Rev. Edmund, (KC) [MON] Conception Abbey (Benedictine Monks), Conception, MO
Boyce, Rt. Rev. Edmund J., *O.S.B.* '74 (MIL) [MON] St. Benedict's Abbey (Benedictine Monks of Wisconsin, Inc.), Benet Lake, WI
Boyd, Rev. Andrew M., '18 (E) Chap, SCI Mercer Immaculate Heart of Mary, Mercer, PA
Boyd, Rev. Benjamin, '14 (OM) St. James, Omaha, NE
Boyd, Rev. C. Morris, '78 (CHL) Retired.
Boyd, Rev. Douglas A., '79 (PIT) Retired. Magee-Women's Hosp, Allegheny Cty Our Lady of the Angels, Pittsburgh, PA; St. Maria Goretti Parish, Pittsburgh, PA
Boyd, Rev. Ian, '63 (NEW) [COL] Seton Hall University, South Orange, NJ
Boyd, Rev. James, '63 (SD) Retired. Chap, Port of San Diego, San Diego Curia: Miscellaneous / Other Offices
Boyd, Rev. James A., '63 (BRK) Retired.
Boyd, Rev. Robert, '10 (PAT) Our Lady of Fatima Chapel (Tridentine), Pequannock, NJ
Boyd, Rev. Robert J., '02 (BGP) On Duty Outside Diocese. The Priestly Fraternity of St. Peter, Pequannock, NJ
Boyer, Rev. Mark G., '76 (SPC) Retired.
Boyer, Rev. Millard G., '75 (LAF) On Special Assignment. Chap, Lafayette Gen Med Ctr, Lafayette
Boyer, Rev. Thomas J., '68 (OKL) Retired.
Boyer, Rev. Wayne M., '87 (JC) Retired.
Boyeye, Rev. Corneille, *M.S.C.* '02 (OG) St. Lawrence Psychiatric Center, Ogdensburg [MON] Missionaries of the Sacred Heart, Watertown, NY
Boyhan, Rev. J. Patrick, *M.S.A.* '77 (NOR) [MON] Society of the Missionaries of the Holy Apostles, Cromwell, CT
Boykow, Rev. Joseph, (PAT) On Leave.
Boylan, Rev. Martin M., '80 (SCR) On Administrative Leave.
Boyle, Rev. Christopher J., '19 (BO) Gate of Heaven, Boston, MA; St. Brigid of Kildare, Boston, MA
Boyle, Rev. Daniel J., '78 (SPR) Retired.
Boyle, Rev. David, (STL) [HOS] SSM Health De Paul Hospital - St. Louis, Bridgeton, MO
Boyle, Rev. Gregory, *S.J.* '84 (LA) Dolores Mission, Los Angeles, CA
Boyle, Rev. James E., '66 (ROC) Retired.
Boyle, Rev. John B., '76 (SCR) St. Vincent de Paul, Milford, PA
Boyle, Rev. John J., '97 (P) Curia: Offices and Directors; Tribunal Our Lady of Perpetual Help (St. Philip Benizi), Cottage Grove, OR
Boyle, Rev. Michael, '95 (CHR) Retired.
Boyle, Rev. Patrick, *O.F.M.* '80 (NY) [MON] Franciscan Province of the Immaculate Conception, New York, NY
Boyle, Rev. Patrick M., *S.J.* '56 (CHI) Retired. [SEM] University of Saint Mary of the Lake/Mundelein Seminary, Mundelein, IL
Boyle, Rev. Richard P., *S.J.* '75 (TUC) [MON] Jesuit Community of the Vatican Observatory, Tucson, AZ
Boyle, Rev. Ryan, (MO) Curia: Offices and Directors
Boyle, Rev. Ryan C., '15 (SP) On Duty Outside Diocese. Archdiocese for the Military Services, U.S.A.
Boyle, Rev. Silvan, *O.Carm.* '48 (PHX) Retired. [MON] Carmelite Community, Phoenix, AZ
Boyle, Rev. Stephen M., *O.Praem.* '90 (ORG) [MON] Norbertine Fathers of Orange, Inc., Silverado, CA
Boyle, Rev. Valentine, *O.Carm.* '46 (JOL) Retired.
Bozada, Rev. Mark S., '81 (STL) St. James Catholic Church, Catawissa, Catawissa, MO; St. Mary of Perpetual Help Catholic Church, Moselle, Villa Ridge, MO
Bozant, Rev. Ian, (BAL) The National Shrine of St. Alphonsus Liguori, Baltimore, MD
Bozant, Rev. Ian M., '14 (NO) On Duty Outside Diocese. National Shrine of St Alphonsus Liguori, Baltimore, MD
Bozek, Rev. Jozef A., '99 (CLV) St. Sebastian, Akron, OH
Bozek, Rev. Robert, '78 (WDC) Retired. On Leave.
Boznar, Rev. Joseph P., '70 (CLV) Retired. [MIS] St. Vitus Development Corporation, Cleveland, OH
Bozovsky, Rev. Matthew, '13 (CHI) Our Lady of Ransom, Niles, IL
Bozung, Rev. James M., '61 (GR) Retired.
Bozza, Rev. Nicholas, (PAT) Curia: Administration St. Lawrence the Martyr, Chester, NJ
Bozzelli, Rev. Msgr. Richard J., '94 (BAL) Curia: Miscellaneous / Other Offices St. Bernardine, Baltimore, MD
Braaten, Rev. Msgr. James B., '89 (BIS) Curia: Leadership; Offices and Directors Ascension, Bismarck, ND
Braathen, Rev. Scott, *SOLT* '03 (CC) [MON] Society of Our Lady of the Most Holy Trinity, Corpus Christi, TX
Braband, Rev. James, *S.V.D.* '80 (CHI) [MON] Divine Word Residence, Techny, IL
Brabazon, Rev. Kenneth C., '11 (PH) Curia: Advisory Boards, Commissions, Committees, and Councils St. Isidore, Quakertown, PA
Bracamontes, Rev. Juan Francisco, '90 (SAC) Pastor of Our Lady of Guadalupe Parish, Sacramento, a corporation sole, Sacramento, CA
Bracke, Rev. James A., *C.S.C.* '80 (FTW) [COL] University of Notre Dame Du Lac, Notre Dame, IN; [HOS] University Health Services, Notre Dame, IN; [MON] Congregation of Holy Cross, United States Province of Priests and Brothers, Notre Dame, IN; [MON] Holy Cross Community, Corby Hall, University of Notre Dame, Notre Dame, IN
Bracken, Rev. Jerome, *C.P.* '68 (BRK) [MON] Immaculate Conception Monastery, Jamaica, NY
Bracken, Rev. Jerome, *C.P.* '68 (NY) [MON] The Congregation of the Passion - St. Paul of the Cross Province, Jamaica, NY
Bracken, Rev. Msgr. John J., '67 (BRK) Retired.
Bracken, Rev. Joseph, *S.J.* '62 (MIL) [MON] St. Camillus Jesuit Community (Society of Jesus, USA Midwest Province), Wauwatosa, WI
Bracken, Rev. W. Jerome, *C.P.* '68 (NEW) [COL] Seton Hall University, South Orange, NJ
Brackin, Rev. James D., *S.C.J.* '75 (MIL) Retired. [MON] Sacred Heart at Monastery Lake, Franklin, WI
Braden, Rev. Michael, *S.J.* '79 (LA) [MON] Jesuit Community, Los Angeles, CA (>SJ) [MON] Sacred Heart Jesuit Center, Los Gatos, CA
Bradford, Rev. Richard S., '98 (BO) Retired. Congregation of Saint Athanasius, Boston, MA
Bradler, Rev. Robert C., '62 (ROC) Retired.
Bradley, Rev. Adam, (GB) Curia: Advisory Boards, Commissions, Committees, and Councils; Clergy and Religious Services
Bradley, Rev. Alfred E., *C.Ss.R.* '88 (PH) Holy Name of Jesus, Philadelphia, PA
Bradley, Very Rev. Bruce, '78 (DAL) St. Elizabeth Ann Seton Catholic Parish, Plano, TX; [CEM] St. Elizabeth Ann Seton Parish Columbarium, Plano, TX
Bradley, Rev. Charles, (PAT) Retired.
Bradley, Rev. Ed, '75 (OWN) Curia: Advisory Boards, Commissions, Committees, and Councils
Bradley, Rev. Msgr. Edward G., '66 (NEW) Retired. Curia: Advisory Boards, Commissions, Committees, and Councils
Bradley, Rev. Hugh J., '89 (CAM) Curia: Parish Services St. Teresa of Calcutta Parish, Collingswood, NJ
Bradley, Rev. J. Richard, '81 (TLS) Retired.
Bradley, Rev. J. Edward, '75 (OWN) Retired.
Bradley, Rev. James P., '73 (BRK) Retired.
Bradley, Rev. James P., *S.J.* '67 (LAF) [MON] St. Charles College, Grand Coteau, LA
Bradley, Rev. John J., '67 (ALB) Retired. Curia: Offices and Directors
Bradley, Rev. Michael, '91 (TUC) On Administrative Leave.
Bradley, Rev. Michael, '78 (CHI) Retired. St. Gertrude, Chicago, IL
Bradley, Rev. Richard, (TLS) Retired.
Bradley, Rev. Stephen, (SHP) [HOS] CHRISTUS Health Northern Louisiana, Shreveport, LA
Bradshaw, Rev. Alexander H., '85 (ROC) Retired. Church of St. John of Rochester of Perinton, New York, Fairport, NY
Bradshaw, Rev. Benjamin, '06 (MEM) St. Michael Church, Memphis, TN
Bradshaw, Rev. Terry L., '80 (L) Curia: Leadership Basilica of St. Joseph Proto-Cathedral, Bardstown, KY
Bradtke, Rev. Marcin, '16 (PAT) St. Joseph's, Lincoln Park, NJ
Brady, Rev. Daniel J., '61 (CHI) Retired. Our Lady of the Wayside, Arlington Heights, IL; St. Cecilia, Mt. Prospect, IL
Brady, Rev. Daniel O., '84 (RIC) St. Michael, Glen Allen, VA
Brady, Rev. Dermot, *S.S.J.* (BAL) Retired.
Brady, Rev. Edmund P., '59 (BRK) Retired. Our Lady of Mount Carmel, Long Island City, NY
Brady, Rev. Edward E., '90 (PH) St. Dominic, Philadelphia, PA
Brady, Rev. Edward J., *S.J.* '59 (BAL) On Special

Assignment. Chap, Holy Redeemer Health Sys (Huntingdon Valley), St Domi…
Brady, Rev. James, '06 (LAF) St. Pius X, Lafayette, LA
Brady, Rev. Msgr. James J., '72 (TR) Retired.
Brady, Rev. James Paul, *S.M.M.* '92 (RVC) [EFT] Missionaries of the Company of Mary General House Charitable Trust, Bay Shore, NY; [MON] Montfort Missionaries, Bay Shore, NY
Brady, Rev. John, '55 (SFS) Retired.
Brady, Rev. Jude, *O.S.B.* '80 (GBG) [MON] Saint Vincent Archabbey, Latrobe, PA; [SEM] St. Vincent Seminary, Latrobe, PA
Brady, Rev. Justin, '05 (B) Curia: Leadership Queen of Heaven Chapel, Nampa, ID; St. Joseph's Chapel, Melba, ID; St. Paul's, Nampa, ID
Brady, Rev. Michael, '01 (STO) St. Joseph Church of Modesto (Pastor of), Modesto, CA
Brady, Rev. Patrick J., '93 (PH) On Special Assignment. Vice Rec, St Charles Borromeo Seminary Overbrook, Wynnewood Curia: Clergy and Religious Services [SEM] Theological Seminary of St. Charles Borromeo, Wynnewood, PA
Brady, Rev. Patrick J., '64 (CAM) Retired.
Brady, Rev. Reginald, '93 (DET) On Leave.
Brady, Rev. Ryan, '21 (CHI) Our Lady of the Ridge and St. Linus Parish, Oak Lawn, IL
Brady, Rev. Timothy J., (WIL) St. Michael the Archangel, Georgetown, DE
Brady, Rev. Vincent M., '95 (PSC) Curia: Advisory Boards, Commissions, Committees, and Councils Holy Dormition, Ormond Beach, FL
Brady, Rev. William J., '80 (SFR) St. Emydius, San Francisco, CA
Braganza, Rev. Simon F., '92 (CHI) Queen of All Saints Basilica, Chicago, IL
Bragotti, Rev. Joseph, *M.C.C.J.* '62 (CIN) [MON] Comboni Missionaries (Verona Fathers)-Comboni Mission Center, Cincinnati, OH
Brahill, Rt. Rev. John, *O.S.B.* '82 (RCK) [MON] Marmion Abbey, Aurora, IL
Brahill, Rt. Rev. John, *O.S.B.* '82 (RCK) Marmion Academy, Aurora, IL
Brailsford, Rev. William M., '04 (WDC) Resurrection Parish, Burtonsville, MD
Braley, Rev. James E., '76 (BO) Retired.
Brambilla, Rev. Charles A., '70 (STP) Retired.
Bramble, Rev. Donald, *O.P.* '76 (LA) St. Dominic, Los Angeles, CA
Bramlage, Rev. Gregory D., '96 (IND) On Special Assignment. Diocese of Colorado Springs, CO for Missionary Ministry
Bramlage, Rev. James A., '64 (CIN) Retired.
Bramwell, Rev. Bevil, *O.M.I.* '85 (WDC) [MON] Oblate Community, Washington, DC
Branch, Rev. Msgr. Edward B., '74 (ATL) Retired.
Brancich, Rev. John, *F.S.S.P.* (MAN) St. Stanislaus Parish, Nashua, NH
Brancolini, Rev. Luca, *F.S.C.B.* '99 (BO) Sacred Heart, Boston, MA
Brand, Rev. Samuel R., '14 (WCH) Sacred Heart, Arkansas City, KS
Branden, Very Rev. Brad Vanden, *O.Praem.* (GB) Curia: Advisory Boards, Commissions, Committees, and Councils
Brandenburg, Rev. Daniel, *LC* '07 (ATL) [MIS] Catholic World Mission (GA), Inc., Roswell, GA; [MON] Legionaries of Christ, Incorporated, Cumming, GA
Brandenburg, Rev. Daniel, *LC* (NY) [CCH] Catholic World Mission, Inc., Rye, NY
Brandenhoff, Rev. Peter B., '70 (WIN) Retired.
Brandi, Rev. John, '19 (PAT) On Duty Outside Diocese. serving in Archdiocese of Newark, NJ
Brandimarti, Rev. Paul Joseph, '19 (COL) St. Luke, Danville, OH; St. Vincent de Paul, Mt. Vernon, OH
Brandl, Rev. Mark J., '09 (MIL) Congregation of the Holy Name, Sheboygan, WI; St. Clement's Congregation, Sheboygan, WI; St. Dominic Congregation, Sheboygan, WI; [MIS] The Sheboygan County Catholic Fund, Inc., Sheboygan, WI
Brandow, Rev. Stephen J., '96 (ALX) Chap, Central Louisiana State Hosp, Pineville; Vet Admin… Curia: Miscellaneous / Other Offices
Brandstrup, Rev. Christian, '79 (STA) On Leave.
Brandt, Rev. Daniel J., '99 (CHI) Curia: Offices and Directors
Brandt, Rev. Joseph D., '83 (PH) St. Luke the Evangelist, Glenside, PA; [CAM] Arcadia University, Glenside, PA
Brandt, Rev. Paul C., '84 (PH) Saint Teresa of Calcutta, Schwenksville, PA
Brandt, Rev. Timothy, '09 (GB) On Leave.
Brankatelli, Rev. Joseph R., '08 (CLV) Curia: (>MO) Offices and Directors
Brankatelli, Rev. Joseph R., (CLV) St. Clare, Lyndhurst, OH
Brankin, Rev. Anthony J., '75 (CHI) Retired.
Brankin, Rev. Msgr. Patrick M., '79 (CHI) On Duty Outside Diocese. St Theresa, Collinsville, OK
Brankin, Rev. Msgr. Patrick M., '79 (TLS) On Special Assignment. Deliverance Ministry, Chancery Office
Brannen, Rev. Brett A., '91 (SAV) [EFT] Foundation for Priestly Vocations, Inc., Savannah, GA
Brannen, Rev. Brett A., '91 (COL) [SEM] Pontifical College Josephinum, Columbus, OH
Brannigan, Rev. John, *S.S.C.* '67 (OM) [MON] Missionary Society of St. Columban, St. Columbans, NE
Bransfield, Rev. Christopher, '98 (SJ) St. Justin, Santa Clara, CA
Bransfield, Rev. Msgr. J. Brian, '94 (PH) On Duty Outside Diocese. USCCB Secretariat of Evangelization and Catechesis, Washi… Curia: Advisory Boards, Commissions, Committees, and Councils St. Joseph, Aston, PA
Bransfield, Rev. Sean P., '02 (PH) On Special Assignment. Chancellor Curia: Advisory Boards, Commissions, Committees, and Councils; Leadership Immaculate Heart of Mary, Philadelphia, PA
Branson, Rev. Dale A., '97 (TUC) Saint Michael the Archangel Roman Catholic Parish - San Tan Valley, Florence, AZ
Branson, Rev. Keith, *C.PP.S.* '00 (KC) [MON] Society of the Precious Blood, Liberty, MO
Brant, Rev. David A., '65 (SEA) Retired.
Braquet, Rev. David J., '94 (ALX) St. Rita, Alexandria, LA
Braschoss, Rev. Carl, *O. Praem.* '10 (PH) [MON] Daylesford Abbey, Inc., Paoli, PA
Brashears, Very Rev. Christopher T., '14 (OKL) Curia: Consultative Bodies; Deaneries; Tribunal St. Peter's, Guymon, OK; [CAM] Oklahoma Panhandle State University, Goodwell, OK
Brasher, Rev. C. John, '75 (SFE) Retired.
Brassard, Rev. Ronald E., '74 (PRO) Retired.
Brasseur, Rev. Zachary, '22 (SP) Our Lady of Lourdes, Dunedin, FL
Bratkowski, Rev. Allen J., '89 (MIL) Retired.
Braud, Rev. Colin V., '13 (NO) Curia: Leadership The Visitation of Our Lady Roman Catholic Church, Marrero, Louisiana, Marrero, LA
Brauer, Rev. Mark S., '92 (DET) St. Hugo of the Hills Parish Bloomfield Hills, Bloomfield Hills, MI
Brault, Rev. Bernard, (RVC) Retired. [MON] Montfort Missionaries, Bay Shore, NY
Brault, Rev. Laurence V., '77 (WOR) St. Gabriel the Archangel, Upton, MA
Brault, Rev. Y. David, '77 (WDC) St. John the Baptist, Silver Spring, MD
Braun, Rev. Beau, '17 (DUL) Holy Cross, Orr, MN; St. Martin, Tower, MN; St. Mary, Cook, MN
Braun, Rev. Douglas A., '15 (GR) Sacred Heart, Muskegon Heights, MI; St. Thomas the Apostle, Muskegon, MI
Braun, Rev. Douglas A., '15 (GR) Curia: Leadership
Braun, Rev. Drew, '12 (DUL) On Leave.
Braun, Rev. Garrett, '21 (EVN) St. Francis Xavier, Vincennes, IN; St. Philip Neri, Bicknell, IN
Braun, Rev. Gary G., '77 (STL) On Special Assignment. Catholic Student Ctr, Washington Univ, St Louis [CAM] Catholic Student Center at Washington University, St. Louis, MO
Braun, Rev. H. Gerard, '85 (FAR) Curia: Leadership St. Anthony of Padua's Church of Fargo, Fargo, ND; [ASN] Calvary Cemetery Association, Grand Forks, ND
Braun, Rev. Justin, '12 (TYL) Curia: Advisory Boards, Commissions, Committees, and Councils; Miscellaneous / Other Offices Sacred Heart, Texarkana, TX
Braun, Rev. Msgr. Michael R., '67 (FRS) Retired.
Braun, Rev. Stephen, *FSSP* '18 (SAC) Pastor of St. Stephen the First Martyr Parish, Sacramento, a corporation sole, Sacramento, CA
Brauninger, Rev. Jason E, *S.J.* '16 (DEN) [MON] Regis Jesuit Community (The Jesuits at Regis University), Denver, CO
Braunreuther, Rev. Robert, (BO) [MON] Campion Health & Wellness, Inc., Weston, MA
Brausch, Rev. Anthony R., '02 (CIN) [SEM] Mount St. Mary's Seminary of the West, Cincinnati, OH; [SEM] The Athenaeum of Ohio, Cincinnati, OH
Braverman, Rev. John M., *S.J.* '09 (PH) [MIS] Jesuit Fathers, ,
Bravo, Rev. Flavio I., *S.J.* '05 (SJN) Colegio San Ignacio de Loyola, San Juan, PR; [MON] Compania de Jesus en Puerto Rico, Inc, San Juan, PR
Bravo, Rev. Joseph, '77 (SFR) Retired.
Bravo, Rev. Manuel Leon, '12 (LA) St. Madeleine, Pomona, CA
Bravo, Rev. Miguel Angel, (PH) St. Barnabas, Philadelphia, PA
Brawanski, Rev. Robert, (DAL) St. Francis of Assisi Catholic Parish - Frisco, Frisco, TX
Brawner, Rev. Frank, '05 (LEX) Our Lady of the Mountains, Stanton, KY; St. Joseph, Winchester, KY; [CEM] St. Thomas, Mt. Sterling, KY
Bray, Rev. Benjamin, (SEA) Holy Trinity, Bremerton, WA; Sacred Heart, La Conner, WA
Bray, Rev. Kevin, '67 (FRS) Retired.
Bray, Rev. Kevin, '67 (LA) Retired.
Brazaskas, Rev. Robert, '66 (TUC) Retired. [MIS] Retorno (Marriage Retorno), Marana, AZ
Bream, Rev. James I., '64 (SFS) Retired.
Breault, Rev. Charles, *O.M.I.* '59 (BO) [CEM] St. Joseph Cemetery, Inc., Chelmsford, MA; [MON] Missionary Oblates of Mary Immaculate Northern Province, Lowell, MA
Breaux, Rev. John, '04 (LAF) Curia: Advisory Boards, Commissions, Committees, and Councils Our Lady of the Lake, Delcambre, LA; Saint Martin de Porres, Delcambre, LA
Breaux, Rev. Louis Allen, '81 (LAF) Retired.
Breck, Rev. Steven H., '00 (CLV) St. Mary Magdalene, Willowick, OH
Breczinski, Rev. Paul, '98 (BAL) Our Lady of the Fields, Millersville, MD
Bredestege, Rev. Mark, '19 (CIN) Holy Trinity, West Union, OH; St. Benignus, Greenfield, OH; St. Mary Catholic Church, Hillsboro, OH; St. Mary Queen of Heaven, Peebles, OH
Breed, Rev. Glenn, (MO) Curia: Offices and Directors
Breen, Rev. Bernard J., '72 (L) Retired.
Breen, Rev. Damian B., '98 (MET) Corpus Christi, South River, NJ
Breen, Rev. Francis J., *M.M.* '70 (NY) Retired. [MON] Maryknoll Fathers and Brothers (Catholic Foreign Mission Society of America, Inc.), Ossining, NY; [MON] Maryknoll Fathers and Brothers Charitable Trust, Maryknoll, NY
Breen, Rev. James E., '80 (BGP) Retired. [MON] The Catherine Dennis Keefe Queen of the Clergy Retired Priests' Residence, Stamford, CT
Breen, Rev. Joseph Anthony, *O.P.* '63 (L) St. Louis Bertrand, Louisville, KY
Breen, Rev. Kenneth, *OdeM* '85 (BUF) St. Brigid, Bergen, NY
Breidenbach, Rev. John, '87 (EVN) On Leave.
Breier, Rev. Msgr. Henry J., '94 (STL) Cathedral Basilica of Saint Louis Catholic Church, St. Louis, MO
Breig, Rev. Gary R., '78 (STL) Retired.
Breighner, Rev. Joseph F., '71 (BAL) Retired. Cathedral of Mary Our Queen, Baltimore, MD
Breitbach, Rev. Richard C., '61 (MIL) Retired.
Brembah, Rev. Philip, '98 (FWT) St. Vincent de Paul, Arlington, TX
Bremer, Rev. Albert, '02 (OWN) Curia: Advisory Boards, Commissions, Committees, and Councils Sacred Heart, Russellville, KY; St. Francis of Assisi Catholic Church, Guthrie, KY
Bremer, Rev. Michael, '18 (ATL) [MIS] Catholic Student Center at The University of Georgia, Athens, GA
Brenberger, Rev. Thomas, *C.PP.S.* '66 (CIN) [MON] St. Charles, Celina, OH
Brender, Rev. John, *L.C.* '15 (CHI) [MON] Legion of Christ, Hickory Hills, IL
Breneville, Rev. Garcia, (BO) Our Lady of Mount Carmel Parish, Boston, MA
Brenkle, Rev. Msgr. John J., '58 (SR) Retired. Curia: Leadership
Brenkus, Rev. Pavol, '01 (ATL) Holy Trinity Catholic Church, Peachtree City, Inc., Peachtree City, GA
Brenna, Rev. William D., '09 (SUP) Retired. (>LC) Nativity of the Blessed Virgin Mary, River Falls, WI
Brennan, Rev. Chris, (P) Chap, Columbia River Corr Inst, Portland
Brennan, Rev. Christopher, *CSC* (FTW) [COL] University of Notre Dame Du Lac, Notre Dame, IN; [MON] Holy Cross Community, Corby Hall, University of Notre Dame, Notre Dame, IN
Brennan, Rev. George P., '68 (STL) Retired.
Brennan, Rev. James, *C.Ss.R.* '64 (BAL) [SPF] St. John Neuman Residence, Timonium, MD
Brennan, Rev. John D., '70 (PIT) Retired. Chap, West Penn Allegheny Health Sys-Alle-Kiski Med Ctr, Al… Guardian Angels, Natrona Heights, PA
Brennan, Rev. John J., '78 (SPR) St. Christopher's, Brimfield, MA; St. Patrick's, Monson, MA
Brennan, Rev. John P., *S.M.A.* '64 (LA) [SEM] St. John's Seminary, Camarillo, CA
Brennan, Rev. John P., *SMA* '68 (NEW) [MON] Society of African Missions, Provincialate, S.M.A. Fathers,

Tenafly, NJ
Brennan, Rev. John W., *O.S.F.S.* '65 (WIL) Retired. [MON] Retirement and Assisted Care Facility, Childs, MD
Brennan, Rev. Joseph (Dennis), *O.S.B.* '74 (LA) [MON] St. Andrew's Abbey (Benedictine Monks), Valyermo, CA
Brennan, Rev. Joseph T., *O.S.F.S.* '98 (ARL) St. John Neumann, Reston, VA
Brennan, Rev. Msgr. Keith R., '84 (STA) Curia: Leadership Our Lady Star of the Sea, Ponte Vedra Beach, FL
Brennan, Rev. Msgr. Mark E., '76 (WDC) On Duty Outside Diocese. Auxiliary Bishop - Baltimore
Brennan, Rev. Matthew, '62 (BIR) Retired.
Brennan, Rev. Michael, *O. Praem.* '17 (GB) St. Norbert College Parish, De Pere, WI; [MON] St. Norbert Abbey, De Pere, WI
Brennan, Rev. Msgr. Michael J., '71 (BRK) Retired.
Brennan, Rev. Pat, *C.P.* (DET) [RTR] St. Paul of the Cross Passionist Retreat and Conference Center, Detroit, MI
Brennan, Rev. Patrick, *C.P.* '73 (DET) [MON] St. Paul of the Cross Community, Congregation of the Passion, Detroit, MI
Brennan, Rev. Msgr. Patrick, '77 (P) Retired. Curia: Offices and Directors; Tribunal
Brennan, Rev. Pierce A., *S.J.* '76 (NY) [MON] Murray-Weigel Hall (A Jesuit Community at Murray-Weigel Hall and Kohlmann Hall), Bronx, NY
Brennan, Rev. Robert J., *C.S.C.* '68 (FTW) [MIS] Holy Cross House, Notre Dame, IN
Brennan, Rev. Msgr. Seamus F., '72 (MET) Curia: Consultative Bodies St. Matthias, Somerset, NJ
Brennan, Rev. Terrence, '99 (SFE) Retired.
Brennan, Rev. Thomas J., *S.J.* '96 (PH) [MIS] Jesuit Fathers, , ; [MON] Arrupe Jesuit Community, Merion Station, PA
Brennan, Rev. Thomas J., '74 (PH) Retired.
Brennan, Rev. Msgr. William P., '63 (CAM) Retired. Curia: Leadership
Brennell, Rev. Msgr. John J., '78 (STL) Curia: Leadership Seven Holy Founders Catholic Church, St. Louis, MO
Brenner, Rev. Raymond, '69 (EVN) Retired.
Brenninkmeijer, Rev. Paul A., *O.S.B.* '67 (CHR) Retired.
Brenon, Rev. Terence V., '91 (SAN) St. Patrick's, Brady, TX
Brensinger, Rev. Richard C., '92 (ALN) Curia: Organizations (affiliated, inter-Diocesan, miscellaneous/other) St. Francis of Assisi, Allentown, PA
Brent, Rev. James, *O.P.* '10 (WDC) [COL] Catholic University of America, The, Washington, DC; [SEM] Dominican House of Studies, Washington, DC
Brentwood, Rev. Scottston F., *OdeM* (BUF) [MON] Our Lady of Mercy Friary, Le Roy, NY
Breski, Rev. Martin, *O.F.M.Conv.* '69 (BAL) (>ATL) St. Philip Benizi Catholic Church, Jonesboro, Inc., Jonesboro, GA
Breslin, Rev. J. Michael, '65 (RIC) St. Charles Borromeo, Cape Charles, VA
Breslin, Rev. John, *S.M.M.* '56 (RVC) Retired. [MON] Montfort Missionaries, Bay Shore, NY
Breslin, Rev. Matthew, '21 (NY) St. Joseph, Somers, NY
Breslin, Rev. Paul J, *O.F.M.* '88 (PAT) St. Bonaventure, Paterson, NJ
Breslin, Rev. Peter W., *S.J.* '91 (CHI) [COL] Jesuit Community at Loyola University Chicago, Chicago, IL
Breslin, Rev. William E., '74 (DEN) Retired.
Bresnahan, Rev. Edward J., '10 (ARL) Church of the Nativity, Burke, VA
Bresowar, Rev. Vincent E., '11 (BIR) Curia: Leadership Good Shepherd Catholic Parish, Russellville, Russellville, AL
Brethour, Rev. Gary G., '89 (LIN) St. James, Trenton, NE
Breton, Rev. Richard D., '08 (NOR) Guardian Angels Parish, Colchester, CT; [SEM] Holy Apostles College and Seminary, Cromwell, CT
Bretone, Rev. Richard, '88 (BRK) Retired.
Bretone, Rev. Richard, '91 (BRK) [CAM] Campus Ministers and Ministry Centers (Newman Apostolate, Inc.), Brooklyn, NY
Bretone, Rev. Richard, '89 (NY) Parish of St. Anthony of Padua and St. Thomas Aquinas, Yulan, NY; [SPF] Kolping Society of New York Residence (Catholic Kolping Society New York, Inc.), New York, NY
Bretone, Rev. Richard J., '89 (BRK) Retired. [MIS] Eternal Flame of Hope Ministries, Inc., Jackson Heights, NY
Brett, Rev. Stephen, (NSH) Retired. Curia: Leadership
Bretzke, Rev. James, *S.J.* (CLV) [COL] John Carroll Jesuit Community, University Heights, OH
Breu, Rev. David L., '73 (NU) Retired.
Breunig, Rev. Rudy, *S.T.* '65 (WDC) [MON] Father Judge Missionary Cenacle, Adelphi, MD
Brevil, Rev. Reynold, '19 (MIA) St. Mary's Cathedral, Miami, FL
Brewczynski, Rev. Jacek M., '96 (DET) On Leave.
Brewer, Rev. Dexter S., '89 (NSH) Curia: Leadership; Offices and Directors Christ the King, Nashville, TN
Brewer, Rev. Timothy M., '79 (WOR) Curia: Leadership; Offices and Directors St. Mary, Jefferson, MA
Brewer, Rev. Vincent, '13 (MAD) St. Bernard, Watertown, WI; St. Henry, Watertown, WI
Brewer, Rev. Vincent Bryan, (MO) Curia: Offices and Directors
Brey, Rev. Christopher J., '97 (SFD) On Leave.
Breza, Rev. Paul J., '63 (WIN) Retired.
Brezovec, Rev. John F., '66 (ALT) Retired.
Brice, Rev. Donald, '58 (WDC) Retired. [NUR] Cardinal O'Boyle Residence for Priests, Washington, DC
Brice, Rev. Jean Robert, (WOR) St. John's, Worcester, MA
Brice, Rev. Joseph, (PRO) St. Michael's Providence, Rhode Island, Providence, RI
Brice, Rev. Steven J., '82 (LC) Holy Spirit Parish, Stevens Point, WI; [EFT] Newman Campus Ministry Endowment Trust, Stevens Point, WI; [EFT] St. Stanislaus Kostka Congregation, Stevens Point Endowment Trust, Stevens Point, WI
Bricker, Rev. Brian G., *O.P.* '89 (CHI) St. Pius V, Chicago, IL; [MON] St. Pius V Priory, Chicago, IL
Brickler, Rev. Richard, '61 (ROC) Retired. Curia: Tribunal
Brickner, Rev. Charles W., '75 (RIC) Retired.
Brickner, Rev. Ronald J., '92 (TOL) St. Mary, Vermilion, OH; St. Mary, Wakeman, OH; [EFT] St. Mary's Church Education Endowment Foundation, Vermilion, OH
Bridges, Rev. Clarence S., '88 (ALT) Retired.
Bridges, Rev. Msgr. James P., '62 (SAN) Retired.
Bridgman, Rev. Mark M., '96 (OM) St. Augustine Catholic Church, Winnebago, NE; St. Joseph, Walthill, NE
Bridling, Rev. David I., '95 (Y) St. Mary, Orwell, OH
Bried, Rev. William, *O.F.M.* (SP) Retired. [MON] St. Anthony Friary (St. Petersburg) Franciscan Friars-Holy Name Province, Inc., St. Petersburg, FL
Bried, Rev. William K., *O.F.M.* '79 (PHX) Our Lady of the Angels Conventual Church, Scottsdale, AZ; [RTR] Franciscan Renewal Center, Inc. (Casa de Paz Y Bien), Scottsdale, AZ
Brienz, Rev. Edward R., '96 (Y) Curia: Leadership Our Lady of Perpetual Help, McDonald, OH
Brierley, Rev. Andrew, '08 (PMB) St. Luke, Palm Springs, FL
Bries, Rev. Marvin J., '73 (DUB) Immaculate Conception Church, North Buena Vista, Iowa, North Buena Vista, IA; St. Joseph Church, Garnavillo, Iowa, Garnavillo, IA; St. Mary Church, Guttenberg, Iowa, Guttenberg, IA
Briese, Very Rev. Dominic, *O.P.* '96 (SLC) Curia: Offices and Directors Saint Martin de Porres LLC 236, Taylorsville, UT
Briese, Rev. Llane, (PMB) [SEM] St. Vincent de Paul Regional Seminary, Boynton Beach, FL
Briese, Rev. Llane B., '10 (ATL) On Duty Outside Diocese. St Vincent de Paul Rgnl Seminary, FL
Briese, Rev. Michael W., '09 (WDC) On Leave. Holy Name, Washington, DC
Brietske, Rev. Msgr. Richard C., '62 (TR) Retired.
Briffa, Rev. Salvino P., '71 (DET) Retired.
Brigandi, Rev. Stephen J., '97 (RVC) Curia: Leadership Sacred Heart, North Merrick, NY
Briganti, Rev. Philip, '73 (PAT) On Leave.
Briggs, Very Rev. Philip, '20 (ARL) St. Philip, Falls Church, VA
Brighenti, Rev. Kenneth D., '88 (MET) (>COL) [SEM] Pontifical College Josephinum, Columbus, OH
Brignac, Rev. H. L., '83 (NO) Retired.
Brilhante, Rev. Jason, '12 (FR) St. John of God, Somerset, MA
Brillantes, Rev. Edgar B., '80 (HON) Our Lady of the Mount, Honolulu, HI
Brillantes, Rev. Michael, '83 (SFR) St. Bruno, San Bruno, CA
Brincat, Rev. George, '57 (LA) Retired.
Brindamour, Rev. Maurice L., '74 (PRO) Retired. St. Joseph's Church Providence Rhode Island, Providence, RI
Bringas, Rev. Daniel, '76 (FRS) Retired.
Bringas, Rev. Salvador, '87 (SAC) Pastor of St. Dominic Parish, Colfax, a corporation sole, Colfax, CA
Bringuela, Rev. Francisco, '02 (P) St. Patrick Church, Independence, OR; [CAM] Western Oregon University (Monmouth), Monmouth, OR
Brinker, Rev. Brian J., '88 (RVC) [MON] St Pius X Residence for Retired Priests LLC, Ronkonkoma, NY
Brinkman, Rev. Andrew R., '13 (STP) Holy Childhood, St. Paul, MN; Maternity of the Blessed Virgin, St. Paul, MN
Brinkman, Rev. Msgr. Barry E., '91 (SAL) Curia: Tribunal [CON] Sisters of St. Joseph of Concordia, Concordia, KS; [MIS] Nazareth Convent & Academy Corporation, Concordia, KS
Brinkman, Rev. James J., '81 (SUP) Retired.
Brinkman, Rev. John T., '71 (NY) Retired. [MON] Maryknoll Fathers and Brothers (Catholic Foreign Mission Society of America, Inc.), Ossining, NY
Brinkman, Rev. Terence P., '73 (GAL) Curia: Leadership St. John the Evangelist, Baytown, TX
Brinkmann, Rev. Charles J., '56 (HBG) Retired. [MON] St. Clement's Mission House, Ephrata, PA
Brinsmade, Rev. John F., '81 (HRT) Saint Raphael Parish Corporation, Milford, CT
Briones, Rev. Jesus, *SVD* '76 (CHI) [MON] Divine Word Residence, Techny, IL
Briones, Rev. Jose Maria, '93 (TLS) St. Thomas More, Tulsa, OK
Briones, Rev. Osvaldo, *S.J.S.* '09 (MAD) Divine Mercy Parish, Sauk City, WI; Holy Cross Parish (St. Barnabas Parish), Mazomanie, WI; St. Norbert, Sauk City, WI
Brioni, Rev. Luigi, *S.X.* '61 (PAT) [MON] Xaverian Missionary Fathers, Wayne, NJ
Brioschi, Rev. Marco, *PIME* (DET) [MON] PIME Missionaries, Detroit, MI
Briscoe, Rev. Patrick Mary, *O.P.* '16 (PRO) [MON] St. Pius V Priory (Dominican Fathers), Providence, RI
Briscoe, Rev. Patrick Mary, *O.P.* '16 (WDC) [SEM] Dominican House of Studies, Washington, DC
Briseno, Rev. Miguel, *O.F.M.Conv.* '90 (ELP) Curia: Advisory Boards, Commissions, Committees, and Councils; Leadership Our Lady of Mt. Carmel, El Paso, TX; [MIS] Franciscans, Secular Order of Franciscans, El Paso, TX
Briseno, Rev. Msgr. Pedro, '81 (BWN) St. Cecilia, Los Fresnos, TX
Briseño, Friar Miguel, *OFM, Conv.* (ELP) [MIS] Apostolado de la Cruz (Apostolate of the Cross), El Paso, TX
Brislin, Rev. Thomas, *C.P.* '68 (NY) [MON] The Congregation of the Passion - St. Paul of the Cross Province, Jamaica, NY
Brislin, Rev. Thomas P., *C.P.* '68 (BRK) [MON] Immaculate Conception Monastery, Jamaica, NY
Brisotti, Rev. William F., '68 (RVC) Retired. Our Lady of the Miraculous Medal, Wyandanch, NY
Brissette, Rev. Reginald R., '63 (PRT) Retired. St. Anthony of Padua Parish, Westbrook, ME
Brisson, Rev. Robert A., '85 (NY) Curia: (>POD) Clergy and Religious Services St. Agnes, New York, NY; [MIS] Prelature of the Holy Cross and Opus Dei, New York, NY
Bristol, Rev. Mark C., '16 (BRK) Chap, Lt, CHC, USN, APO Pacific American Martyrs, Oakland Gardens, NY
Bristol, Rev. Mark C., (MO) Curia: Offices and Directors
Britanico, Rev. Rafael, (MO) Curia: Offices and Directors
Brito, Rev. Cristiano Aparecido, *O.S.B.* '91 (RIC) St. Gregory the Great, Virginia Beach, VA
Brito, Rev. Cristiano E., *O.S.B.* '91 (GBG) [MON] Saint Vincent Archabbey, Latrobe, PA
Brito, Rev. Larry R., '00 (SFE) Curia: Offices and Directors St. Anne Catholic Church, Santa Fe, NM
Brittain, Rev. Gerald W., '62 (MIL) Retired.
Britto, Rev. Msgr. Federico A., '82 (PH) On Special Assignment. Dean, Deanery 9, St Cyprian Rectory, Philadelphia Curia: Advisory Boards, Commissions, Committees, and Councils; Deaneries St. Cyprian, Philadelphia, PA; St. Ignatius of Loyola, Philadelphia, PA
Britto, Rev. Irudayaraj John, *C.M.F.* '67 (PHX) Sacred Heart Roman Catholic Parish Prescott, Prescott, AZ
Britto Fernandez, Rev. Roger, (BAL) On Administrative Leave. Extern Priest - no longer with for Archdiocese of Batlimore
Britton, Rev. Blake, '18 (ORL) St. Joseph's, Lakeland, FL
Brizio, Rev. Michael, *I.M.C.* (TR) Monmouth Cty Jail St. Rose of Lima, Freehold, NJ
Brobbey, Rev. John, (DM) St. Francis of Assisi, West Des Moines, IA
Brobst, Rev. James, *O.M.I.* '90 (WDC) [MON] Missionary Oblates of Mary Immaculate, Washington, DC; [MON] Oblate Community, Washington, DC
Brobst, Rev. James P., *O.M.I.* '90 (CHI) [EFT] Oblates for International Pastoral (Oblate International Pastoral

Investment Trust), Chicago, IL
Brobst, Rev. Richard A., '65 (Y) Retired.
Brocato, Rev. John K., '03 (ALX) Curia: Leadership St. Joseph, Colfax, LA; [CCH] Catholic Charities and Special Ministries, Alexandria, LA
Brocato, Rev. Robert S., '95 (SJ) Retired.
Broccolo, Rev. Gerard T., '65 (CHI) Retired.
Brock, Rev. Herald Joseph, *C.F.R.* '94 (PAT) [MIS] Saint Michael's Friary (Franciscan Friars of the Renewal), Paterson, NJ (>NY) [MIS] Franciscan Mission Outreach, Inc., Bronx, NY
Brock, Rev. Steven, '92 (POD) Curia: Clergy and Religious Services
Brock, Rev. William, '91 (DEN) Retired.
Brockett, Rev. Norman L., '87 (HRT) The Church of the Holy Infant, Orange, CT
Brockhaus, Rev. Msgr. Edward, '64 (SD) Retired. Curia: Advisory Boards, Commissions, Committees, and Councils
Brockland, Rev. John A., '91 (STL) Sts. Joachim and Ann Catholic Church, St. Charles, St. Charles, MO
Brockland, Very Rev. John A., '91 (STL) Curia: Leadership
Brockland, Rev. Robert J., *C.M.* '74 (STL) [MON] Congregation of the Mission, Perryville, MO
Brockman, Rev. Blaise N., '77 (LA) Holy Angels, Arcadia, CA
Brockman, Rev. Msgr. David D., '90 (R) Holy Name of Jesus Cathedral, Raleigh, NC
Brockmeier, Rev. James, '16 (IND) Curia: Offices and Directors St. Mary Catholic Church, Rushville, Inc., Rushville, IN
Brockmyre, Rev. Philip C., '02 (SY) Retired.
Brockson, Rev. Scott D., '96 (PH) Assumption B.V.M., West Grove, PA
Broderick, Rev. Michael, '87 (WOR) Our Lady of the Lake, Leominster, MA
Broderick, Rev. Richard J., '70 (ALB) Retired.
Broderick, Rev. Sean A., *C.S.Sp.* '65 (MET) Retired. Mary, Mother of God, Hillsborough, NJ
Brodersen, Rev. Steven W., '85 (SC) Retired.
Brodeski, Rev. Aaron R, '98 (RCK) On Administrative Leave.
Brodnick, Rev. Edward J., '76 (COV) Bishop Brossart High School, Alexandria, KY; St. Mary of the Assumption, Alexandria, KY
Brodnick, Rev. Joseph, '69 (CLV) On Administrative Leave.
Brodsky, Rev. Edward, *FSSP* '16 (MAN) St. Stanislaus Parish, Nashua, NH
Brody, Rev. Matthew D., '17 (PH) On Special Assignment. Asst Master Ceremonies, Our Lady Mount Carmel, Doylestown St. Richard, Philadelphia, PA
Brogan, Rev. Jared J., '11 (PAT) On Academic Leave. Curia: Leadership
Brogan, Rev. Leo, '67 (PHX) Retired.
Brogan, Rev. William, '68 (NY) Retired. St. Raymond, Bronx, NY
Brohammer, Rev. Ronald, '60 (MIA) Retired.
Broheimer, Rev. John P., '03 (OM) St. Peter, Omaha, NE; [MIS] Legion of Mary, Omaha, NE
Brohl, Rev. John Eudes, (STU) [MON] Order of the Holy Cross, Inc., Carrollton, OH
Brohl, Rev. John Eudes, (STU) [MON] Opus Angelorum, Inc., Carrollton, OH
Brokaw, Rev. Lee, '17 (PEO) Curia: Clergy and Religious Services Corpus Christi, Galesburg, IL; Immaculate Heart of Mary, Galesburg, IL; Sacred Heart, Abingdon, IL; St. Patrick's, Galesburg, IL
Brokke, Rev. David, *SOLT* '20 (FAR) St. Ann's Church of Belcourt, Belcourt, ND; St. Michael the Archangel Dunseith, Dunseith, ND
Brokman, Rev. James P., '97 (DUB) On Special Assignment. Chap, Mercy Med Ctr, Cedar Rapids Sacred Heart Church, Walker, Iowa, Walker, IA; St. Mary Church, Vinton, Iowa, Vinton, IA; St. Mary's Church, Urbana, Iowa, Urbana, IA; [HOS] Mercy Medical Center-Cedar Rapids, Cedar Rapids, IA
Brom, Rev. Joseph, *S.J.C.* '22 (CHI) St. John Cantius, Chicago, IL
Brommer, Very Rev. Joshua R., '06 (HBG) Curia: Leadership
Brommer, Rev. Joshua R., '06 (HBG) Cathedral Parish of St. Patrick, Harrisburg, PA
Bromwich, Rev. James S., '03 (L) On Duty Outside Diocese. Fort Wayne, IN
Broniak, Rev. Leonard R., *C.Ss.R.* '79 (GAL) Curia: Offices and Directors Holy Ghost, Houston, TX
Bronkiewicz, Rev. Msgr. Laurence R., '73 (BGP) Retired. [MON] The Catherine Dennis Keefe Queen of the Clergy Retired Priests' Residence, Stamford, CT
Bronovskyy, Rev. Elias, *OSBM* '10 (STF) St. George, New York, NY
Bronovskyy, Rev. Ilya, *O.S.B.M.* (STF) Curia: Offices and Directors
Bronsema, Rev. Gregg, '15 (P) St. Aloysius, Estacada, OR; St. Michael the Archangel, Sandy, OR
Brookbank, Rev. Scott, *O.F.M.* (TR) St. Francis of Assisi, Long Beach Township, NJ
Brooks, Rev. Anthony, (LAN) St. Isidore Parish Laingsburg, Laingsburg, MI
Brooks, Rev. Armond, '97 (FAR) [CON] Franciscan Sisters of Dillingen, Hankinson, ND
Brooks, Very Rev. Bryan, '93 (TLS) Curia: Leadership; Offices and Directors Church of Saint Benedict, Broken Arrow, OK
Brooks, Rev. David, (BAL) Retired. [MIS] Colombiere Jesuit Community, Baltimore, MD
Brooks, Rev. Jason, *L.C.* (DET) [MIS] Clarkston Pastoral Center, Inc., Bloomfield Hills, MI; [RTR] Queen of the Family Retreat Center, Bloomfield Hills, MI
Brooks, Rev. Nathan W., '19 (SY) Curia: Leadership Holy Family, Vernon, NY; St. Agatha, Canastota, NY; St. Helena, Sherrill, NY; St. John, North Bay, NY; St. Joseph, Oneida, NY; St. Patrick, Oneida, NY
Brooks, Rev. Robert C., '61 (ARL) Retired.
Brooks, Rev. Robert E., '95 (SAC) Retired.
Brooks, Rev. Thomas M., '78 (E) St. Gregory Thaumaturgus, North East, PA
Brooks, Rev. Msgr. William C., '76 (AUS) Retired.
Broom, Rev. Edward, *O.M.V.* '86 (LA) St. Peter Chanel, Hawaiian Gardens, CA
Broome, Rev. William, *M.S.A.* '05 (NOR) [MON] Society of the Missionaries of the Holy Apostles, Cromwell, CT
Brophy, Rev. John L., '69 (MIL) Retired.
Brophy, Rev. Justin, *O.P.* '12 (PRO) [MON] St. Thomas Aquinas Priory at Providence College, Providence, RI
Brophy, Rev. Lawrence, *O.Cist.* '12 (DAL) [MON] Our Lady of Dallas Cistercian Abbey, Irving, TX
Brosamer, Rev. Patrick, '13 (AJ) Our Lady of Perpetual Help, Soldotna, AK; Our Lady of the Angels, Kenai, AK
Brosk, Rev. Steven J., '90 (NEW) On Duty Outside Diocese. Sugarloaf, PA
Brosmer, Rev. John, '05 (EVN) St. Joseph, Jasper, IN
Brosnan, Rev. Thomas F., '81 (BRK) Retired. St. Rosalia-Regina Pacis, Brooklyn, NY
Brossart, Rev. Scott, *S.O.L.T.* (KC) [MON] Society of Our Lady of the Most Holy Trinity, Kansas City, MO
Brost, Rev. Corey D., *C.S.V.* '06 (CHI) [MON] Viatorian Province Center-Clerics of St. Viator, Arlington Heights, IL; [SPF] Viator House of Hospitality, Des Plaines, IL
Brost, Rev. Frederick, '56 (SUP) Retired.
Broudou, Rev. Joseph G., '96 (OM) On Duty Outside Diocese. St Mary Cathedral, Grand Island, NE (>GI) Cathedral of the Nativity of the Blessed Virgin Mary, Grand Island, NE
Brougher, Rev. Douglas C., '62 (NO) Dir, Pastoral Care & Chap, Touro Infirmary, New Orleans Good Shepherd Roman Catholic Church, New Orleans, Louisiana, New Orleans, LA
Brouillard, Rev. John, '56 (P) Retired.
Brouillette, Rev. Andre, (BO) [MON] Isaac Jogues House, Brighton, MA
Brouillette, Rev. Daniel E., '09 (NO) Annunciation Catholic Church, Bogalusa, LA; St. Peter, Covington, LA
Brouillette, Rev. Thomas S., '96 (LIN) St. Cecilia's Middle School/High School, Hastings, NE; [EFT] Hastings Catholic Schools Foundation, Hastings, NE
Broussard, Rev. A. Rex, '66 (LAF) Retired.
Broussard, Rev. David, (LAF) On Administrative Leave.
Broussard, Rev. Henry J., '72 (LAF) Retired.
Broussard, Rev. John, *CPM* '14 (OWN) [MON] Fathers of Mercy, Auburn, KY
Broussard, Very Rev. Ken, '03 (LAF) Curia: Leadership; Tribunal [CON] The Carmelite Monastery of Lafayette, Louisiana, Inc., Lafayette, LA
Broussard, Rev. Patrick, '14 (LAF) Our Lady of Wisdom, University of Louisiana, Lafayette, LA; [CAM] Our Lady of Wisdom Catholic Student Center, Lafayette, LA
Broussard, Rev. Paul, '98 (LAF) St. Leo IV, Rayne, LA
Broussard, Rev. Richard Dale, '00 (LAF) Retired.
Broussard, Rev. Msgr. Ronald, '88 (LAF) Our Lady of the Assumption, Carencro, LA; Saint Martin de Porres, Scott, LA
Broussard, Rev. Ted, '98 (LAF) St. Bridget, Lawtell, LA
Broussard, Rev. Theodore, '98 (LAF) Curia: Miscellaneous / Other Offices Sacred Heart, Opelousas, LA; [MIS] Cursillo Center, Opelousas, LA
Brouwers, Rev. Msgr. Hans A.L., '78 (PH) On Special Assignment. Dean, Deanery 2, St Katharine of Siena Rectory, Wayne St. Katharine of Siena, Wayne, PA
Brown, Rev. Avram E., '04 (SAC) Pastor of St. Isidore Parish, Yuba City, a corporation sole, Yuba City, CA
Brown, Rev. Benedict J., '73 (L) St. Ambrose, Cecilia, KY; St. Ignatius, White Mills, KY
Brown, Rev. Charles, '58 (SFE) Retired.
Brown, Rev. Charles, *S.C.J.* '84 (MIL) [MON] St. Francis Residence, Franklin, WI
Brown, Rev. Charles D., '93 (GR) Holy Name of Jesus, Wyoming, MI; San Juan Diego Academy, Wyoming, MI
Brown, Rev. Charles L., '73 (BRK) On Leave. Resigned
Brown, Rev. Msgr. Charles L., '67 (WIL) Retired. Curia: Advisory Boards, Commissions, Committees, and Councils
Brown, Rev. David, *OSM* '48 (CHI) Retired.
Brown, Rev. David, '07 (P) Curia: Offices and Directors St. Paul Catholic Church, Eugene, OR
Brown, Rev. David A., *S.J.* '02 (TUC) [MON] Jesuit Community of the Vatican Observatory, Tucson, AZ
Brown, Rev. David A., *S.J.* '02 (NO) [MON] Jesuit Provincial Office (Catholic Society of Religious and Literary Education), New Orleans, LA
Brown, Rev. David G., *O.S.B.* '75 (CHL) [MON] Belmont Abbey (Southern Benedictine Society of North Carolina, Inc.), Belmont, NC
Brown, Rev. Douglas T., '06 (CLV) Cleveland Police Department; Cleveland Fire Department Curia: Advisory Boards, Commissions, Committees, and Councils Mary Queen of Peace, Cleveland, OH
Brown, Rev. Edward J., *M.S.* '81 (FR) [MON] La Salette Shrine & Retreat Center, Attleboro, MA; [RTR] La Salette Retreat and Conference Center, Attleboro, MA
Brown, Rev. Erin, '07 (TR) Parish of St. Teresa of Calcutta, Bradley Beach, N.J., Bradley Beach, NJ; [CAM] Bede House, College of New Jersey, Trenton, NJ
Brown, Rev. Eugene M., '60 (NU) Retired.
Brown, Rev. Francis Xavier, *O.S.B.* '84 (TLS) [MON] Our Lady of the Annunciation of Clear Creek Abbey, Hulbert, OK
Brown, Rev. Frank, '20 (COL) St. Brendan, Hilliard, OH
Brown, Rev. George, *O.M.I.* '64 (BO) [MON] Missionary Oblates of Mary Immaculate Northern Province, Lowell, MA
Brown, Rev. Gerald L., *P.S.S.* '64 (BAL) Retired. [CCH] Associated Catholic Charities Inc., Baltimore, MD; [MON] Society of St. Sulpice, Province of the United States, Baltimore, MD
Brown, Rev. Gregory, (SP) [HOS] St. Joseph's Hospital, Inc., Tampa, FL
Brown, Rev. Gregory J., *O.F.M.Cap.* '04 (PIT) (>WDC) [SEM] St. Francis Friary-Capuchin College, Washington, DC
Brown, Rev. Harold C., *C.PP.S.* '59 (TOL) [MON] Mary Lay Center, Bellevue, OH; [RTR] Sorrowful Mother Shrine, Bellevue, OH
Brown, Rev. James E., '72 (TOL) St. Joseph, Marblehead, OH
Brown, Rev. James T., '97 (NEW) Ascension, New Milford, NJ; Sacred Heart, Bloomfield, NJ
Brown, Rev. James V., *O.A.R.* '46 (LA) [MON] Order of Augustinian Recollects (O.A.R.), St. Augustine Priory, Oxnard, CA
Brown, Rev. Jerry W., '01 (OAK) Retired.
Brown, Rev. John, *S.J.* '11 (NO) Jesuit High School, New Orleans, LA; [MIS] 124 Airline Drive, Inc., New Orleans, LA; [MON] Loyola Jesuit Community, New Orleans, LA
Brown, Rev. Joseph, *C.PP.S.* '61 (CIN) Retired. [MON] St. Charles, Celina, OH
Brown, Rev. Joshua S., '10 (GI) St. Mary's, Wood River, NE
Brown, Rt. Rev. Justin, *O.S.B.* '90 (NO) [MON] St. Joseph Abbey, St. Benedict, LA; [SEM] Saint Joseph Seminary College, Saint Benedict, LA
Brown, Rev. Keenan Wynn, '02 (LAF) St. Augustine, Basile, LA
Brown, Rev. Kenneth A., '77 (STL) Curia: Leadership
Brown, Rev. Lawrence, *O.S.B.* '84 (BUR) [CON] Monastery of the Immaculate Heart of Mary, Westfield, VT
Brown, Rev. Lawrence, *O.S.B.* '84 (TLS) [MON] Our Lady of the Annunciation of Clear Creek Abbey, Hulbert, OK
Brown, Rev. Michael K., '16 (BUF) St. Christopher, Tonawanda, NY
Brown, Rev. Michael O., '74 (TOL) Retired.
Brown, Rev. Michael R., '89 (ROC) Chaplain, Groveland Corr Fac, Sonyea; Auburn Corr Fac Holy Family, Auburn, NY; Sacred Heart, Auburn, NY; St. Alphonsus, Auburn, NY
Brown, Rev. Mitchell Athanasius, '17 (GLP) Curia:

Leadership Cathedral of the Sacred Heart, Gallup, NM; Sacred Heart Catholic School, Gallup, NM
Brown, Rev. Ned J., '98 (CIN) Holy Family, Versailles, OH; Immaculate Conception, Bradford, OH; St. Denis, Versailles, OH; St. Louis, North Star, OH; St. Mary, Greenville, OH; St. Nicholas, Osgood, OH; St. Remy, Russia, OH
Brown, Rev. Nicholas, *S.C.J.* (MIL) Retired. [MON] Sacred Heart at Monastery Lake, Franklin, WI
Brown, Rev. Nicholas, '15 (HON) Immaculate Conception Church, Ewa, HI
Brown, Rev. Nicholas J., '13 (L) Most Blessed Sacrament, Louisville, KY; SS. Simon and Jude, Louisville, KY
Brown, Rev. Phillip J., *S.S.* '89 (BIS) On Duty Outside Diocese. Pres & Rector, St Mary's Seminary & Univ, Baltimore, MD
Brown, Rev. Phillip J., *P.S.S.* '89 (BAL) [MON] Society of St. Sulpice, Province of the United States, Baltimore, MD; [SEM] St. Mary's Seminary and University, Baltimore, MD
Brown, Rev. Robert W., '66 (ORL) Retired.
Brown, Very Rev. Samuel Moses, '13 (SR) Curia: Leadership; Offices and Directors Pastor of St. Rose of Lima Catholic Church of Santa Rosa, A Corporation Sole, Santa Rosa, CA
Brown, Rev. Seth A., '14 (SFD) Chap, Vandalia Corr Ctr Mother of Dolors, Vandalia, IL; St. Joseph, Ramsey, IL; [MIS] Our Sorrowful Mothers Ministry, Vandalia, IL
Brown, Rev. Shaun S., '94 (NTN) St. Jacob Melkite Catholic Church, Inc., San Diego, CA
Brown, Rev. Stephan, *S.V.D.* '93 (CHI) [MON] Divine Word Residence, Techny, IL
Brown, Rev. Steven P., '77 (SJ) Retired.
Brown, Rev. Thomas E., '78 (E) St. Raphael, Eldred, PA
Brown, Rev. Thomas J., '99 (GR) Curia: Leadership SS. Peter and Paul, Ionia, MI; St. Edward, Lake Odessa, MI
Brown, Rev. Timothy, '88 (ROC) Peace of Christ Roman Catholic Parish of Rochester, NY, Rochester, NY
Brown, Rev. Timothy B., *S.J.* '86 (BAL) [COL] Jesuit Community of Loyola University, Inc., Baltimore, MD; [MON] Jesuit Community of Loyola University Maryland, Inc., Baltimore, MD
Brown, Rev. Victor, *O.P.* '63 (NO) Retired.
Brown, Rev. Warren, *O.M.I.* '82 (WDC) [MON] Missionary Oblates of Mary Immaculate, Washington, DC
Brown, Rev. Warren, *O.M.I.* '82 (SAT) [MON] De Mazenod House, San Antonio, TX
Brown, Rev. Wilbur J., '04 (LAF) Retired.
Brown, Rev. William E., '88 (SFR) St. Anselm, Ross, CA
Brown, Rev. William M., *O.M.V.* '94 (BO) Curia: Consultative Bodies [EFT] Lanteri Charitable Trust, Boston, MA; [MON] Oblate Residence (St. Joseph House), Milton, MA
Brown, Rev. William P., '80 (PT) Retired. Our Lady Queen of Peace, Fountain, FL; Our Lady Queen of Peace Mission, Fountain, FL
Browne, Rev. Msgr. J. Patrick, '67 (SJ) Retired. Curia: Offices and Directors
Browne, Rev. Jeremiah, (NEW) Curia: Organizations (affiliated, inter-Diocesan, miscellaneous/other) [MIS] RENEW International, Plainfield, NJ
Browne, Rev. Robert M., '61 (BO) Retired.
Browne, Very Rev. Ronald T., '91 (DET) Curia: Tribunal
Browne, Rev. William, '98 (CHI) St. Gerald, Oak Lawn, IL
Browne, Rev. William E., '04 (CLV) Retired.
Brownell, Rev. Patrick, '94 (KNX) On Leave.
Brownell, Rev. Patrick P., '94 (KNX) Curia: (>MO) Offices and Directors
Brownell, Rev. Robert A., '69 (RIC) Retired.
Brownfield, Rev. David L., '90 (DAV) Church of All Saints of Keokuk, Iowa, Keokuk, IA
Brownholtz, Rev. Andrew C., '01 (PH) Curia: Advisory Boards, Commissions, Committees, and Councils St. Ignatius of Antioch, Yardley, PA
Browning, Rev. Ryan B., '13 (RCK) On Special Assignment. Curia: Offices and Directors St. Thomas More, Elgin, IL; [COL] Saint Anthony College of Nursing, Rockford, IL
Brownsey, Rev. Msgr. Brian, '96 (PEO) Curia: Clergy and Religious Services St. Mark's, Peoria, IL; [CAM] Newman Foundation at Bradley University & Illinois Central College, Peoria, IL
Brozonowicz, Rev. Grzegorz P., '96 (NOR) Curia: Leadership; Offices and Directors Saint Pio Parish, Old Saybrook, CT
Brubaker, Rev. Msgr. George J., '80 (WIL) Chap, Governor Bacon Health Ctr Curia: Tribunal Our Lady of Fatima, New Castle, DE; St. Paul, Delaware City, DE
Brubaker, Rev. Msgr. George J., '80 (WIL) Curia: Miscellaneous / Other Offices
Brubaker, Rev. W. Scott, '82 (PHX) St. Bridget Roman Catholic Parish, Mesa, AZ
Bruce, Rev. Dillon, '22 (RIC) On Academic Leave. Pontifical University of Saint Thomas Aquinas, Rome.
Bruce, Rev. Joseph J., *S.J.* '81 (BO) Boston College High School, Boston, MA
Bruce, Rev. Rusty Paul, '20 (HT) Community of St. Anthony, Gheens, LA; St. Hilary of Poitiers, Raceland, LA
Bruce, Rev. Terry, '67 (KC) Retired. Curia: Leadership
Bruch, Rev. James A., '65 (SC) Retired. St. Thomas, Manson, IA
Bruch, Rev. Lynn A., '86 (SC) Chap, North Central Corr Fac St. Francis of Assisi, Rockwell City, IA; St. Mary's, Lake City, IA; St. Thomas, Manson, IA
Bruck, Rev. Donald, '68 (DM) Retired.
Brucker, Rev. G. Fredrick, '76 (GR) Retired.
Brucker, Rev. George W., '56 (ALB) Retired.
Brucksch, Rev. Msgr. James L., '69 (GLD) Retired.
Brucz, Rev. James M., *C.S.P.* '74 (PMB) [MON] Paulist Fathers Residence, Vero Beach, FL
Bruecken, Rev. Albert, *O.S.B.* '77 (KC) Curia: Leadership St. Gregory Barbarigo, Maryville, MO; [MON] Conception Abbey (Benedictine Monks), Conception, MO
Bruener, Rev. David P., '12 (LC) St. Joseph, Friendship, WI
Bruggeman, Rev. Sidney B., '09 (GI) Chaplain, US Veterans' Hospital Curia: Offices and Directors St. Libory's, St. Libory, NE
Brugger, Rev. Msgr. Robert L., '68 (E) Retired.
Brum, Rev. Msgr. Louis L., '74 (BWN) Retired.
Brumleve, Rev. Matthew, '88 (KC) Curia: Leadership St. Patrick, Kansas City, MO
Brummel, Rev. Mark J., *C.M.F.* '60 (CHI) [MIS] St. Jude League, Chicago, IL; [MON] Provincial Residence, Oak Park, IL; [SPF] Villa Guadalupe Senior Services Corporation, Chicago, IL
Brune, Rev. Meinrad, *O.S.B.* '61 (IND) [MON] St. Meinrad Archabbey, St. Meinrad, IN
Brune, Rev. Philip, '14 (VIC) Curia: Leadership St. Robert Bellarmine, El Campo, TX
Brunelle, Rev. J. Ernest, *M.M.* '59 (NY) Retired.
Brunet, Rev. Msgr. Frederic, '60 (HT) Retired.
Brunet, Rev. Jules A., '55 (BR) Retired.
Brunet, Rev. Paul J., '11 (SEA) St. Frances Cabrini, Lakewood, WA
Brunette, Rev. Larry H., '99 (SFD) Retired.
Brungardt, Rev. Michael G., '18 (WCH) Holy Name of Jesus, Bushton, KS; St. Paul, Lyons, KS
Bruni, Rev. John E., '76 (CAM) Retired.
Brunick, Rev. Charles, *C.S.P.* (GR) Retired. (>NY) [MON] Paulist Fathers' Motherhouse, New York, NY
Bruning, Rev. David R., '78 (TOL) Our Lady of Lourdes, Toledo, OH
Bruning, Rev. William, '93 (KCK) Queen of the Holy Rosary, Overland Park, KS
Brunn, Rev. Nate, '18 (CR) St. Joseph's, Moorhead, MN; [CAM] St. Thomas Aquinas Newman Center, Moorhead, MN
Brunn, Rev. Nathan, '18 (CR) Curia: Offices and Directors
Brunner, Rt. Rev. Michael, *O.S.B.* (PRO) [MON] Abbey of St. Gregory the Great (Order of St. Benedict in Portsmouth, Rhode Island, Benedictines of the English Congregation), Portsmouth, RI
Brunner, Rev. Stephen, '19 (MAD) Curia: Organizations (affiliated, inter-Diocesan, miscellaneous/other) Christ the King, McFarland, WI
Brunner, Rev. William, *S.S.C.* '62 (OM) Retired. [MON] Missionary Society of St. Columban, St. Columbans, NE
Brunner, Rev. William, *S.S.C.* (PRO) [MON] St. Columban's Retirement House (St. Columban's Foreign Mission Society), Bristol, RI
Brunner, Rev. William J., '11 (GB) Holy Trinity, Kiel, WI; St. Anna's Congregation, New Holstein, WI; St. Gregory, St. Nazianz, WI
Brunnert, Rev. Jude, *M.S.* '64 (LKC) Retired. Our Lady of Prompt Succor, Sulphur, LA
Bruno, Rev. Anthony J., '68 (HRT) Retired.
Bruno, Rev. John, *RCJ* (LA) [MON] Congregation of Rogationists, Inc., Van Nuys, CA
Bruno, Rev. John, *R.C.J.* '74 (FRS) St. Mary, Sanger, CA
Bruno, Rev. Michael, '10 (NY) [SEM] St. Joseph's Seminary, Yonkers, NY
Bruno, Rev. Michael J. S., '10 (BRK) On Duty Outside Diocese. 201 Seminary Ave., Yonkers, 10704 Curia: Leadership St. Edmund, Brooklyn, NY
Bruno, Rev. Robert, *O.F.M.* (CIN) [MON] St. Francis Seraph Friary, Cincinnati, OH
Bruno, Rev. Robert, (RIC) Military Chap
Bruno, Rev. Schned, '09 (BRK) St. Brendan, Brooklyn, NY
Bruno, Rev. Steven V., '05 (NO) Curia: Miscellaneous / Other Offices St. Rita, Harahan, LA
Brunovsky, Rev. Michael, *O.S.B.* '93 (CLV) Benedictine High School, Cleveland, OH; [MON] Benedictine Order of Cleveland (St. Andrew Abbey), Cleveland, OH
Brunovsky, Rev. Steven K., '92 (CLV) St. Hilary, Fairlawn, OH
Bruns, Rev. Corey D., '21 (OWN) St. Joseph, Bowling Green, KY
Brunton, Rev. Daniel B., '60 (SPR) Retired. [MIS] Apostolate of the Suffering, Inc., Palmer, MA
Brusatti, Rev. Louis, *C.M.* '75 (AUS) Retired.
Bruse, Rev. James C., '84 (ARL) Our Lady of the Blue Ridge, Madison, VA
Brutus, Rev. Ferry, '80 (MIA) San Pedro, Tavernier, FL
Bruun, Rev. Nate, (CR) Curia: Offices and Directors
Bryan, Rev. Kevin J., '76 (L) Curia: Leadership
Bryant, Rev. F. Michael, '69 (WDC) DC Detention Center Holy Comforter - St. Cyprian, Washington, DC
Bryant, Rev. Michael M, '78 (SCR) Curia: Leadership Nativity of Our Lord Parish, Duryea, PA
Bryce, Rev. Edward M., '60 (PIT) Retired.
Bryda, Rev. Ronald J., '66 (CLV) Retired.
Bryerton, Rev. Robert R., '74 (TUC) Retired.
Brylinski, Rev. Bruce C., '83 (CIN) [MON] Headquarters of Glenmary Home Missioners (The Home Missioners of America), Fairfield, OH
Bryon, Rev. Thomas C., '63 (STL) Retired.
Brzek, Rev. Jon, (PIT) St. Catherine Laboure, Pittsburgh, PA
Brzezicki, Rev. Zbigniew Canon, '88 (STF) Curia: Offices and Directors Annunciation of the B.V.M., Fresh Meadows, NY
Brzezinski, Rev. Jerome A., '69 (DET) Retired.
Brzezowski, Very Rev. Michael, '00 (YAK) Curia: Leadership Holy Spirit, Kennewick, WA
Brzezowski, Very Rev. Michael E., '00 (YAK) Curia: Leadership; Offices and Directors
Brzoska, Rev. David, '00 (CHL) On Duty Outside Diocese.
Brzoska, Rev. Jerzy, *S.I.* '92 (CHI) [MIS] Jan Beyzym Society, Inc., Chicago, IL; [MON] Sacred Heart Mission House (The Polish Messenger of The Sacred Heart, Inc.), Chicago, IL
Brzozowski, Rev. Simon, (SAT) [NUR] Missionary Servants of St. Anthony (Padua Place), San Antonio, TX
Bubel, Rev. Robert J., '08 (NY) On Sick Leave. Saint Peter the Apostle, Kingston, NY
Bubnevych, Rev. Artur, (PHX) Curia: (>HPM) Offices and Directors
Bubnevych, Rev. Artur, '14 (HPM) Curia: Offices and Directors Our Lady of Perpetual Help, Albuquerque, NM
Buby, Rev. Bertrand A., *S.M.* '64 (CIN) Retired. [COL] The University of Dayton, Dayton, OH; [MON] Marianist Community, Dayton, OH
Bucalo, Rev. Peter, '15 (L) St. Stephen, Martyr, Louisville, KY
Bucaro, Rev. Michael, '80 (SB) Retired.
Buccarello, Rev. Luigi, *O.SS.T.* (BAL) [MON] Holy Trinity Monastery, Sykesville, MD
Bucchino, Rev. John, *O.F.M.* '73 (MAN) Blessed Sacrament, Manchester, NH
Bucci, Rev. Richard A., '73 (PRO) Church of the Sacred Heart, Natick RI, West Warwick, RI
Bucciantini, Rev. Charles, '72 (JKS) Retired.
Bucciarelli, Rev. Michael R., '75 (TUC) Retired.
Buccicone, Rev. Ananias, *O.S.B.* '93 (ALT) Queen of Peace, Patton, PA
Buccicone, Rev. Ananias G., *O.S.B.* '93 (GBG) [MON] Saint Vincent Archabbey, Latrobe, PA
Buccilli, Rev. Gustavo, '89 (NEW) [MON] Society of African Missions, Provincialate, S.M.A. Fathers, Tenafly, NJ
Buccilli, Rev. Gustavo, (BO) Immaculate Conception, Everett, MA
Buchanan, Rev. Andrew, (JOL) St. Mary, West Chicago, IL
Buchanan, Rev. Caleb A., '97 (BRK) On Leave.
Buchanan, Rev. Paul, '14 (CHL) Queen of the Apostles, Belmont, NC
Buchanan, Rev. Robert E., '68 (SB) Retired.
Buchheit, Rev. Edward, *C.P.* '63 (NY) Retired.
Buchholz, Rev. Samuel James, '01 (R) Annunciation, Havelock, NC
Buchignani, Rev. Msgr. Peter P., '65 (MEM) Retired.

Buchlein, Rev. Neil R., '98 (WH) St. Barbara, Chapmanville, WV; St. Mary Queen of Heaven, Madison, WV
Buchleitner, Rev. Donald N., '70 (PIT) Retired.
Buchmeier, Rev. Robert P., '91 (WDC) Holy Cross, Garrett Park, MD
Buchmiller, Rev. Ronald J., '69 (SD) Retired.
Buck, Rev. Frank, '85 (ORL) Retired.
Buck, Rev. Jason E., '14 (PH) Curia: Advisory Boards, Commissions, Committees, and Councils [SEM] Theological Seminary of St. Charles Borromeo, Wynnewood, PA
Buckalew, Rev. Jack, '74 (SEA) Retired.
Bucki, Rev. John P., *S.J.* '79 (SY) [CAM] LeMoyne College Campus Ministry, Syracuse, NY
Buckler, Rev. Brendan, (CHL) St. Elizabeth, Boone, NC
Buckler, Rev. Brendan J., '11 (R) On Duty Outside Diocese. Diocese of Charlotte
Buckles, Rev. David, (NEW) St. Vincent de Paul, Bayonne, NJ
Buckles, Rev. David J., '88 (LFT) [HOS] Franciscan Health Lafayette East, Lafayette, IN
Buckles, Rev. Luke D., *O.P.* (NO) [SEM] Notre Dame Seminary Graduate School of Theology, New Orleans, LA
Buckles, Rev. Luke D., *O.P.* '78 (OAK) [MON] Order of Preachers (Province of the Most Holy Name of Jesus - Western Dominican Province), Oakland, CA
Buckley, Rev. Brendan, *OFM, Cap.* '81 (BRK) St. Michael - Saint Malachy, Brooklyn, NY
Buckley, Friar Brendan Patrick, *OFM Cap.* '81 (BRK) [MON] St. Michael Friary, Brooklyn, NY
Buckley, Rev. Charles J., *O.S.B.* '70 (OKL) [MON] St. Gregory's Abbey (Benedictine Fathers of Sacred Heart Mission, Inc.), Shawnee, OK
Buckley, Rev. Cornelius M., *S.J.* '62 (SJ) [MON] Sacred Heart Jesuit Center, Los Gatos, CA
Buckley, Rev. Dominic, '13 (ORL) On Duty Outside Diocese.
Buckley, Rev. Dominic James, (PMB) [SEM] St. Vincent de Paul Regional Seminary, Boynton Beach, FL
Buckley, Rev. Frank C., *S.J.* '08 (LA) [MON] Colombiere House (Jesuit Fathers), Los Angeles, CA
Buckley, Rev. James, (DAL) Mater Dei Personal Parish, Irving, TX
Buckley, Rev. James, '82 (GLP) On Leave.
Buckley, Rev. James F., '59 (FR) Retired.
Buckley, Rev. James M., '90 (OM) St. Cecilia Cathedral, Omaha, NE
Buckley, Rev. John, *S.S.C.* '68 (PRO) [MON] St. Columban's Retirement House (St. Columban's Foreign Mission Society), Bristol, RI
Buckley, Rev. John, *S.S.C.* '68 (OM) Retired. [MON] Missionary Society of St. Columban, St. Columbans, NE
Buckley, Rev. Patrick F., '04 (NY) St. Charles, Staten Island, NY; St. Sylvia, Tivoli, NY
Buckley, Rev. Thomas J., *S.J.* '74 (WDC) [MON] The Jesuit Community at Georgetown University, Washington, DC
Buckley, Rev. Thomas R., '76 (ALN) St. Joseph, Coopersburg, PA
Buckley, Rev. Thomas W., '55 (BO) Retired.
Buckley, Rev. Timothy J., '92 (PH) St. Cyril of Jerusalem, Jamison, PA
Buckman, Rev. Frank, '63 (ORG) Retired.
Buckman, Rev. Thomas J, '00 (OWN) Christ the King, Scottsville, KY
Buckman, Rev. Thomas J., '00 (OWN) Curia: Advisory Boards, Commissions, Committees, and Councils
Buckman, Rev. Tom, (OWN) St. Mary, Franklin, KY
Buckman, Rev. Tom, '00 (OWN) Curia: Advisory Boards, Commissions, Committees, and Councils
Buckner, Rev. Christopher M., '80 (ARL) Retired.
Buckner, Rev. Mark A., '02 (OWN) St. Anthony, Utica, KY
Bucko, Rev. Michal, (PRM) St. Michael, Merrillville, IN
Bucko, Rev. Raymond A., *S.J.* '83 (NY) [MON] Murray-Weigel Hall (A Jesuit Community at Murray-Weigel Hall and Kohlmann Hall), Bronx, NY
Bucon, Rev. Raymond H., '79 (DET) Retired.
Bucsek, Rev. Basil, '68 (STN) Retired.
Buczek, Rev. Piotr S., '13 (HRT) Saint Bridget of Sweden Parish Corporation, Cheshire, CT
Buda, Rev. Jacek, *OP* '95 (SLC) Saint Catherine of Siena Catholic Newman Center LLC 218, Salt Lake City, UT
Budash, Rev. Vladyslav, '10 (PSC) Byzantine Catholic Church of the Resurrection, Smithtown, NY
Budde, Rev. Msgr. John G., '77 (DET) Retired.
Budde, Rev. Todd, '01 (MIL) St. Gregory the Great Congregation, Milwaukee, WI
Budhi, Rev. Adrianus, *M.S.C.* '89 (SB) Chap, Riverside Cmty Hosp
Budka, Rev. Dennis G., '84 (MIL) Retired.
Budke, Rev. John, *L.C.* '01 (HRT) [SEM] Novitiate of the Legion of Christ, Cheshire, CT
Budke, Rev. Jon, *L.C.* '01 (HRT) [MON] Legionaries of Christ, Cheshire, CT
Budnar, Rev. Randy J., '88 (MAD) St. Ann, Stoughton, WI
Budwick, Rev. Msgr. John J., '64 (NY) Retired. St. Francis of Assisi, Mt. Kisco, NY
Budzikowski, Rev. Kenneth A., '80 (CHI) Curia: Leadership St. Cajetan, Chicago, IL; St. John Fisher, Chicago, IL
Budzinski, Rev. Andrew, '10 (FTW) Curia: Leadership St. John the Baptist, Fort Wayne, IN
Bueche, Rev. William C., *C.Ss.R.* '78 (GAL) Holy Ghost, Houston, TX
Buechele, Rev. Andrew C., *Sch.P.* '69 (WDC) [SEM] Queen of Pious Schools, Inc., Washington, DC
Buehler, Rev. John A., '74 (SY) Retired. Curia: Leadership
Buehler, Rev. Raymond, '13 (STL) Assumption Catholic Church, Mattese, St. Louis, MO; Church of the Good Shepherd Catholic Church, Hillsboro, Hillsboro, MO
Buelt, Rev. Msgr. Edward, '82 (DEN) Notre Dame Catholic Parish in Denver, Denver, CO
Buena, Rev. Joey R., '06 (MRY) St. Elizabeth Ann Seton, Los Osos, CA
Buena, Rev. Julio Ciraco Barrameda, '90 (RIC) Church of the Sacred Heart, South Prince George, VA; St. James Church, Hopewell, VA; St. John, Petersburg, VA
Buenaflor, Rev. Evelio, '85 (HT) Sacred Heart, Montegut, LA; St. Charles Borromeo, Montegut, LA; St. Lawrence, Schriever, LA
Buencamino, Rev. Joey, (SAV) St. James, Savannah, GA
Buenger, Rev. Bryan, (PHX) Blessed Sacrament Roman Catholic Parish, Scottsdale, AZ
Buening, Rev. Matthew T., '03 (BAL) Blessed Sacrament Church, Baltimore, MD; St. Matthew, Baltimore, MD
Bueno, Rev. Alberto, *T.O.R.* (SP) St. Patrick, Tampa, FL
Bueno, Rev. Raymond, *O.C.D.* '12 (OM) Curia: Leadership
Bueno, Rev. Raymond, *O.C.D.* '12 (P) [MON] Discalced Carmelite Friars (O.C.D.), Mount Angel, OR
Bueno Martinez, Rev. Benjamin, *FM* '11 (GAL) St. Pius V, Pasadena, TX
Buentello, Rev. Michael Anthony, *CSB* '95 (DET) Retired.
Buersmeyer, Rev. David A., '80 (DET) St. Regis Parish Bloomfield Hills, Bloomfield Hills, MI
Buerster, Rev. Msgr. James A., '79 (BEL) St. Boniface, Germantown, IL; St. Cecilia, Bartelso, IL
Buettner, Rev. Brian E., '13 (OKL) Curia: Clergy and Religious Services; Consultative Bodies St. Joseph Old Cathedral, Oklahoma City, OK; St. Thomas More University Parish, Norman, OK
Bueza, Rev. Ritche S., '03 (SJ) On Special Assignment. Curia: Offices and Directors Holy Spirit, San Jose, CA
Buffardi, Rev. Joseph G., '76 (PAT) St. Christopher, Parsippany, NJ
Buffer, Rev. Thomas J., '91 (COL) Sacred Hearts, Cardington, OH; St. Mary, Marion, OH
Bufford, Rev. Brian J., '15 (ATL) St. Gerard Majella Catholic Church, Fort Oglethorpe, Inc., Fort Oglethorpe, GA
Buffum, Rev. David M, '19 (PH) SS. Peter and Paul, West Chester, PA
Bufogle, Rev. Arthur, '04 (WH) St. John Neumann, Marlinton, WV; St. Mark the Evangelist Mission, Bartow, WV; [MIS] St. Bernard, Snowshoe, WV
Bugarin, Rev. Fred, '75 (AJ) Retired.
Bugarin, Rev. Msgr. G. Michael, '91 (DET) Curia: Offices and Directors St. Joan of Arc Parish St. Clair Shores, St. Clair Shores, MI
Bugas, Rev. Joel O., '09 (SFE) San Ignacio, Albuquerque, NM
Bugay, Rev. Stephen R., '84 (GBG) SS. Simon and Jude, Blairsville, PA
Bugayong, Rev. Demetrio L., '70 (LA) Retired.
Buggert, Rev. Donald W., *O.Carm.* '66 (JOL) [MON] St. Elias Carmelites, Joliet, IL
Bugler, Rev. Msgr. Henry J., '75 (NO) Retired. Mary, Queen of Peace Roman Catholic Church, Mandeville, Louisiana, Mandeville, LA
Bugner, Rev. Joseph, *S.V.D.* '63 (CHI) Retired. [MON] Divine Word Residence, Techny, IL
Bugno, Rev. Krzysztof, *S.D.S.* '85 (ORL) Curia: Evangelization St. Teresa, Titusville, FL
Buhake, Rev. Longin, (MO) Curia: Offices and Directors
Buhake, Rev. Longin, (PT) Chap, Tyndall Air Force Base [MIS] Christ the King Chapel, Freeport, FL
Buhl, Rev. Wilbert L., '60 (GB) Retired.
Buhler, Rev. Richard, *S.J.* (NO) [MON] Loyola Jesuit Community, New Orleans, LA
Buhler, Rev. Richard, *S.J.* '70 (BR) [RTR] Manresa House of Retreats, Convent, LA
Buhler, Rev. Richard, *S.J.* '70 (STL) [COL] Saint Louis University, St. Louis, MO
Buhman, Rev. Jay M., '04 (LIN) Curia: Leadership All Saints, Holdrege, NE
Buhrman, Very Rev. Donald A., '86 (GI) Curia: Leadership; Offices and Directors; Tribunal St. Leo, Grand Island, NE
Bui, Rev. Anthony, '11 (SB) St. Adelaide, Highland, CA
Bui, Rev. Christian, (GAL) St. Edward, Spring, TX
Bui, Rev. Dong, '92 (JOL) Our Lady of Lourdes, Gibson City, IL; St. Mary, Paxton, IL
Bui, Rev. Duc, (HT) Our Lady of the Rosary, Larose, LA
Bui, Rev. Dung Quang, '02 (STA) Our Lady of Consolation, Callahan, FL
Bui, Rev. Francis Quyet, *S.D.D.* '90 (DAL) St. Joseph Vietnamese Parish, Grand Prairie, TX; [MIS] Domus Dei Clerical Society of Apostolic Life, Kaufman, TX
Bui, Rev. Francis Ty, '75 (LA) Retired.
Bui, Rev. Joseph, '00 (PHX) Curia: Offices and Directors St. Louis the King Roman Catholic Parish, Glendale, AZ
Bui, Rev. Joseph T.P., '97 (GAL) Christ, The Incarnate Word, Houston, TX
Bui, Rev. Khue Si, '01 (BEA) St. Joseph, Beaumont, TX
Bui, Rev. Linh N., '14 (OKL) Cristo Rey Oklahoma City Catholic High School, Oklahoma City, OK; St. Francis of Assisi, Oklahoma City, OK
Bui, Friar Marion, *OCD* (DAL) Mount Carmel Center, Dallas, TX; [MON] Mt. Carmel Center (Discalced Carmelite Fathers of Dallas, Inc.), Dallas, TX
Bui, Rev. Martin Philip Nhan Thai, *O.P.* '08 (GAL) [MON] Vietnamese Dominican Vicariate of St. Vincent Liem, Houston, TX
Bui, Rev. Martin Phuoc, '11 (ORG) St. Joseph, Placentia, CA; St. Nicholas, Laguna Woods, CA
Bui, Rev. Msgr. Peter Dai, '03 (PHX) Curia: Leadership; Offices and Directors
Bui, Rev. Peter Tam, '01 (WOR) Our Lady of Vilna, Worcester, MA
Bui, Rev. Tam M., '01 (WOR) Curia: Offices and Directors
Bui, Rev. Thaddeus, *O.H.* (LA) [NUR] St. John of God Retirement and Care Center, Los Angeles, CA
Bui, Rev. Thaddeus, *O.H. sac* (SB)
Bui, Rev. Tho, *S.D.B.* '07 (SFR) SS. Peter and Paul, San Francisco, CA; [EFT] Father Raphael Piperni Charitable Trust, San Francisco, CA; [EFT] Philip Rinaldi Charitable Trust, San Francisco, CA; [MON] Salesian Provincial Residence, San Francisco, CA
Builes, Rev. Oscar Londono, '90 (GR) SS. Peter and Paul, Ionia, MI
Buitrago, Rev. Alejandro, (DAL) On Administrative Leave.
Buitrago, Rev. Tarsicio, '64 (ARL) Retired.
Buitron, Rev. Luis Segundo, '00 (CR) Assumption - Church of Florian, Strandquist, MN; St. Rose of Lima, Argyle, MN; St. Stephen's, Stephen, MN
Bujalance, Rev. Javier, '13 (WDC) [MIS] Tenley Study Center, Washington, DC
Bujalance, Rev. Javier, '13 (OAK) [MIS] Opus Dei, Berkeley, CA
Bujalance, Rev. Javier, '13 (POD) Curia: Clergy and Religious Services
Bujdos, Rev. Peter, (NY) Parish of St. Paul and St. Ann, Congers, NY
Bukaty, Rev. Msgr. Lawrence J., '76 (ALN) Retired.
Bukauskas, Rev. Raimundas, *O.F.M.* '04 (PRT) [MON] Society of Franciscan Fathers of Greene, Maine, Kennebunk, ME
Bukenya, Rev. Sebastian, '06 (SD) Pastor of Saint Brigid Catholic Parish, San Diego, a corporation sole, San Diego, CA
Bula, Rev. Sebastine Tor Orya, *V.C.* '04 (SFR) St. Cecilia, San Francisco, CA
Bulfer, Rev. Stephen, (FRS) Retired.
Bulger, Rev. John, '64 (SEA) Retired.
Bulinda, Rev. Ernest Livasia, '88 (RIC) St. Ann, South Chesterfield, VA; St. John, Petersburg, VA
Bulinski, Rev. Marcin J., '07 (CHI) Curia: (>MO) Offices and Directors
Bullene, Rev. Richard S., *C.S.C.* '83 (FTW) [COL] University of Notre Dame Du Lac, Notre Dame, IN; [MON] Holy Cross Community, Corby Hall, University of Notre Dame, Notre Dame, IN
Buller, Very Rev. Ruben J., '08 (LKC) Curia: Advisory Boards, Commissions, Committees, and Councils; Leadership Immaculate Conception Cathedral, Lake

Charles, LA; [MIS] Society of Roman Catholic Church of the Dioceses of Lake Charles, Lake Charles, LA

Bullman, Rev. Rudolph, '00 (HEL) Retired.

Bullock, Very Rev. Scott E., '91 (DUB) On Special Assignment. Dean of the Waterloo Deanery Cedar Valley Catholic Schools, Waterloo, Iowa, Waterloo, IA; St. Edward's Church, Waterloo, Iowa, Waterloo, IA; [CEM] Catholic Cemeteries of Waterloo, Waterloo, Iowa, Waterloo, IA

Bullos, Rev. Neil, *O.A.R.* (CHK) Curia: Advisory Boards, Commissions, Committees, and Councils; Faith Formation

Bulso, Rev. Andrew, '15 (NSH) Curia: Leadership; Offices and Directors St. Edward, Nashville, TN

Bulter, Rev. Francis, *S.S.J.* '85 (BAL) Retired.

Bulus, Rev. Vincent Hassan, (RVC) St. Raymond's, East Rockaway, NY

Bumbar, Rev. Canon Philip, '68 (SJP) Ss. Peter and Paul, Aliquippa, PA

Bumbar, Rev. Philip, '68 (SJP) Retired. Curia: Offices and Directors

Bumbarger, Rev. Bruce, '92 (BIR) Our Lady of Lourdes, Birmingham, AL

Bump, Friar Dominic J, *O.P.* '13 (PH) St. Patrick, Philadelphia, PA

Bundz, Rev. Michael, '81 (STF) Curia: Offices and Directors St. Volodymyr the Great, Utica, NY

Bunger, Rev. Kevin J., '83 (SY) Church of the Annunciation, Clark Mills, NY; St. John the Evangelist, New Hartford, NY

Bungo, Rev. Samuel, '77 (E) St. Charles Church, New Bethlehem, PA

Bunik, Rev. Wasyl, '93 (PHU) St. John the Baptist, Northampton, PA; St. Vladimir's, Palmerton, PA

Bunnell, Rev. Adam, *O.F.M.Conv.* '73 (L) St. Paul, Louisville, KY

Bunnell, Rev. Thomas J/, *S.J.* '74 (P) (>SJ) [MON] Sacred Heart Jesuit Center, Los Gatos, CA

Bunny, Rev. Msgr. J. Michael, '65 (LA) Retired.

Buntel, Rev. Richard A., '71 (BO) On Leave.

Bunyan, Rev. Gregory, '96 (AMA) St. Ann's, Bovina, TX; St. Teresa of Jesus, Friona, TX

Buonanno, Rev. Msgr. Vito A., '81 (BRK) On Duty Outside Diocese. Basilica of the Natnl Shrine of the Imm. Conc., DC (>WDC) [SHR] Basilica of the National Shrine of the Immaculate Conception, Washington, DC

Buongirno, Rev. Robert F., '02 (NOR) Divine Mercy Parish, Uncasville, CT

Buono, Rev. Carmen, '07 (PAT) Retired. Morris Catholic High School, Denville, NJ; Sacred Heart Church and Our Lady Queen of the Most Holy Rosary, Dover, NJ

Buonocore, Rev. Maximillian, *O.S.B.* '17 (NEW) [MON] Benedictine Abbey of Newark, Newark, NJ

Buonopane, Rev. Gerald J., '06 (NEW) Curia: Advisory Boards, Commissions, Committees, and Councils [COL] Seton Hall University, South Orange, NJ

Buote, Rev. Martin L., '60 (FR) Retired.

Bur, Rev. George W., *S.J.* '72 (PH) [MON] Arrupe Jesuit Community, Merion Station, PA

Buranosky, Rev. Dennis M., '72 (PIT) Retired. Holy Sepulcher, Butler, PA; St. Kilian, Cranberry Township, PA

Burba, Rev. Edward A., '75 (CLV) St. Anthony of Padua, Akron, OH

Burbeck, Very Rev. Michael J., '14 (R) Curia: Leadership St. Michael the Archangel Catholic Church, Cary, NC

Burch, Rev. Edward, '03 (R) Retired.

Burch, Rev. Thaddeus J., *S.J.* '61 (MIL) [MON] St. Camillus Jesuit Community (Society of Jesus, USA Midwest Province), Wauwatosa, WI

Burchell, Rev. Jason C., '13 (ARL) On Duty Outside Diocese. Curia: (>MO) Offices and Directors

Burchill, Rev. John P., *O.P.* '65 (PRO) [MON] St. Pius V Priory (Dominican Fathers), Providence, RI

Burdick, Rev. Msgr. Thomas J., '84 (SB) St. Mother Teresa of Calcutta Catholic Community, Inc., Winchester, CA

Burdikoff, Friar Igor, (ALB) Chap, Stratton Veterans' Administration Med Ctr

Burdzy, Rev. Krystian S., '03 (MET) Good Shepherd Parish, Hopelawn, NJ

Burek, Rev. Frank J., '71 (CHI) Retired.

Burgaleta, Rev. Claudio, *S.J.* '92 (NEW) [COL] St. Peter University Jesuit Community, Jersey City, NJ; [MIS] Jesuit Community, Jersey City, NJ; [MON] Jesuits of Saint Peter College, Inc., Jersey City, NJ

Burgard, Rev. David G., '94 (DET) St. John the Baptist Parish Monroe, Monroe, MI; St. Mary Parish Monroe, Monroe, MI

Burge, Rev. Robert, '71 (CLV) Retired.

Burgener, Rev. Eric, (FTW) On Administrative Leave.

Burger, Rev. Francis, '69 (KCK) Retired. [MIS] Catholic Care Campus, Inc. (Santa Marta), Olathe, KS

Burger, Rev. John, *S.S.C.* '73 (PH) [NUR] Camilla Hall Nursing Home, Immaculata, PA

Burger, Rev. John, *S.S.C.* '73 (OM) [MON] Missionary Society of St. Columban, St. Columbans, NE

Burger, Rev. John E., *S.S.C.* '73 (PRO) [MON] St. Columban's Retirement House (St. Columban's Foreign Mission Society), Bristol, RI

Burger, Rev. Mark J., '80 (CIN) Corpus Christi, Cincinnati, OH; St. John Neumann, Cincinnati, OH; St. John the Baptist, Cincinnati, OH

Burger, Rev. Philip G., (HBG) Curia: Offices and Directors Immaculate Heart of Mary, Abbottstown, PA

Burger, Rev. Msgr. Raymond, '60 (KCK) Retired.

Burgess, Rev. Yancey Q., '10 (WCH) Mary Queen of Angels, Fort Scott, KS

Burian, Rev. Msgr. Ed, '65 (SFS) Retired.

Burish, Very Rev. Jesse D., '09 (LC) Curia: Leadership Holy Ghost, Chippewa Falls, WI; Notre Dame, Chippewa Falls, WI; St. Bridget, Chippewa Falls, WI; [EFT] Notre Dame Children's Endowment Trust, Chippewa Falls, WI; [EFT] Notre Dame Parish Endowment Trust, Chippewa Falls, WI; [EFT] The Education/Sustaining Endowment Trust (Holy Ghost Parish Trust), Chippewa Falls, WI

Buritica, Rev. Diego A., '16 (WOR) Curia: Offices and Directors; Spiritual Life St. Luke the Evangelist, Westborough, MA

Burkard, Rev. Msgr. Paul J.E., '69 (BUF) Retired. Our Lady of Victory National Shrine and Basilica, Lackawanna, NY

Burkart, Rev. James, '93 (GAL) Curia: Leadership Christ the Good Shepherd, Spring, TX

Burkauskas, Rev. Peter M., '79 (PH) Retired.

Burke, Rev. Adrian, *O.S.B.* (IND) [MON] St. Meinrad Archabbey, St. Meinrad, IN

Burke, Rev. Alfred J., '69 (NEW) Retired.

Burke, Rev. Alfred M., *O.S.A.* '57 (CHI) [MON] St. Rita Monastery, Chicago, IL

Burke, Rev. Christopher R., '86 (PBR) St. Mary's, New Salem, PA; St. Nicholas, Brownsville, PA

Burke, Rev. Donal, *O.F.M.Cap.* '75 (SFR) (>OAK) [MON] Capuchin Franciscan Friars, Berkeley, CA

Burke, Rev. Edward P., '73 (PH) Retired.

Burke, Rev. Geoffrey D., '79 (ALB) Our Lady of the Assumption, Latham, NY; [CON] Sisters of St. Joseph of Carondelet (Albany Province), Latham, NY

Burke, Very Rev. Herbert T., '92 (CHL) Immaculate Conception, Forest City, NC

Burke, Rev. Msgr. James A., '56 (NEW) Retired. Church of the Nativity, Midland Park, NJ

Burke, Rev. James C., '64 (ROC) Retired.

Burke, Rev. James G., '77 (BO) Sacred Heart, Lexington, MA; St. Brigid, Lexington, MA

Burke, Rev. Msgr. James M., '64 (PMB) Retired. St. Lucie, Port St. Lucie, FL

Burke, Rev. John R., '72 (L) Retired. St. William, Louisville, KY

Burke, Rev. Joseph F., *S.J.* '78 (BO) [MON] Campion Health & Wellness, Inc., Weston, MA

Burke, Rev. Kevin F., *SJ* '86 (DEN) [COL] Regis University, Denver, CO; [MON] Regis Jesuit Community (The Jesuits at Regis University), Denver, CO

Burke, Rev. Mark, (NY) [MON] Jesuit Community at Fordham University, New York, NY

Burke, Rev. Paul A., '96 (ATL) Curia: Offices and Directors; (>MO) Offices and Directors [SPF] Our Lady of Perpetual Help Home, Atlanta, GA

Burke, Rev. Richard, *C.P.* '76 (NY) [MON] The Congregation of the Passion - St. Paul of the Cross Province, Jamaica, NY

Burke, Rev. Richard, *C.P.* '76 (SCR) St. Ann's Basilica Parish, Scranton, PA; [EFT] St. Ann's Foundation, Scranton, PA; [MON] Saint Ann's Passionist Monastery of Scranton PA, Scranton, PA

Burke, Rev. Thomas J., *O.SS.T.* '78 (BAL) Resurrection of Our Lord, Laurel, MD; [MON] Holy Trinity Monastery, Sykesville, MD

Burke, Rev. Thomas J., '01 (PIT) St. Benedict the Moor Parish, Pittsburgh, PA; St. Mary Magdalene, Pittsburgh, PA

Burke, Rev. William A., '65 (CHI) Retired. St. Cajetan, Chicago, IL

Burke, Rev. William F., '75 (MEM) Retired.

Burke, Rev. Msgr. William F., '59 (BAL) St. Francis of Assisi, Baltimore, MD

Burkemper, Rev. Andrew V., '14 (STL) St. Bridget of Kidare Catholic Church, Pacific, MO

Burkemper, Rev. Robert W., '81 (STL) St. Elizabeth Ann Seton Catholic Church, St. Charles, MO

Burkert, Rev. William C., '71 (MIL) Retired. Our Lady of Lourdes Congregation, Milwaukee, WI

Burkey, Rev. Blaine, *O.F.M.Cap.* '61 (DEN) [MON] Capuchin Province of Mid-America, Inc. (Capuchin Province of St. Conrad), Denver, CO

Burkhalter, Rev. Ross C., '94 (OM) Curia: Leadership

Burkhalter, Rev. Ross C., '94 (OM) Sacred Heart Parish of Boyd County, Butte, NE; St. Boniface, Stuart, NE; St. Joseph, Atkinson, NE; St. Patrick, O'Neill, NE

Burkhard, Rev. John, *O.F.M.Conv.* '67 (WDC) [SEM] St. Bonaventure Friary, Silver Spring, MD

Burkhardt, Rev. Alan T., '86 (LC) Curia: Offices and Directors Holy Name of Jesus, Wausau, WI; Mary, Mother of Good Help Parish, Wausau, WI

Burkle, Rev. Raymond A., '90 (DUB) Curia: Leadership Sacred Heart Church (Osage, Iowa), Osage, IA; Visitation Church, Stacyville, Iowa, Stacyville, IA; [CEM] St. Patrick's Cemetery Association, McIntire, Mitchell County, Iowa, Osage, IA

Burkley, Rev. John T., '70 (CLV) Retired. Chap, Geauga Cty Jail, Chardon

Burks, Rev. William P., '86 (L) St. Lawrence, Louisville, KY

Burla, Rev. Frank J., '63 (NEW) Retired.

Burmester, Rev. William Wyatt, '17 (LR) Curia: Leadership

Burmester, Rev. William Wyatt, '17 (LR) Curia: Leadership; Offices and Directors Sacred Heart Church, Foreman, AR; St. Edward, Texarkana, AR; St. Elizabeth Ann Seton Church, Ashdown, AR

Burnell, Rev. Robert J., '70 (CHI) Retired. St. Paul VI, Riverside, IL

Burnett, Rev. Msgr. James E., '74 (DAV) Retired.

Burnett, Rev. Timothy J., *O.S.B.* '80 (NO) [MON] St. Joseph Abbey, St. Benedict, LA

Burnett, Rev. Travis J., '11 (MOB) Sacred Heart, Grove Hill, AL; St. John the Evangelist, Butler, AL

Burnette, Rev. John C., '85 (SFD) Retired. Saints James and Patrick Parish, Decatur, IL

Burney, Rev. Keith T., '16 (WDC) Curia: Consultative Bodies

Burnham, Rev. Martin J., '02 (BAL) [MIS] St. Mary's Seminary & University, Baltimore, MD; [MON] Society of St. Sulpice, Province of the United States, Baltimore, MD

Burnham, Rev. Martin Joseph, (SAT) [SEM] The Seminary of the Assumption of the Blessed Virgin Mary-St. John of San Antonio, TX (Assumption-St. John's Seminary), San Antonio, TX

Burnia, Rev. Scott A., '88 (SD) Pastor of Saint Louise de Marillac Catholic Parish, El Cajon, a corporation sole, El Cajon, CA

Burnie, Rev. James, *C.S.Sp.* '84 (LR) St. Mary, Hattieville, AR

Burns, Rev. Andrew, (SP) Christ the King, Tampa, FL

Burns, Rev. Andrew, (PAT) On Duty Outside Diocese. Diocese of Saint Petersburg, FL

Burns, Rev. Claude T., '02 (EVN) Curia: Offices and Directors St. John the Baptist, Newburgh, IN

Burns, Rev. Devin T., '15 (WCH) Christ the King, Wichita, KS

Burns, Rev. Douglas C., *O.S.F.S.* '99 (ALN) [COL] DeSales University, Center Valley, PA; [MON] Oblates of St. Francis de Sales, Center Valley, PA

Burns, Rev. Edward M., '04 (CIN) St. Gabriel, Cincinnati, OH; St. John the Evangelist, West Chester, OH; St. Michael, Cincinnati, OH

Burns, Rev. Garett, '18 (WCH) St. Margaret Mary, Wichita, KS

Burns, Very Rev. Gerald, '09 (SEA) Curia: Leadership St. Andrew, Sumner, WA; [MIS] Pierce County Deanery, Sumner, WA

Burns, Rev. Gerald H., '69 (BR) Retired.

Burns, Rev. Hugh, *O.P.* '69 (BRK) Saint Teresa of Avila-Saint Anthony of Padua, South Ozone Park, NY

Burns, Rev. James P., '93 (STP) On Duty Outside Diocese. Pres, St Mary's Univ of Minnesota

Burns, Rev. James P., *I.V.D.* '93 (WIN) [COL] Saint Mary's University of Minnesota, Winona, MN

Burns, Rev. James P., *I.V.D.* '93 (BO) [COL] Woods College of Advancing Studies, ,

Burns, Rev. John, '10 (MIL) On Special Assignment. Voc Promoter, Voc Ofc, St Francis de Sales Sem, St Francis Curia: Leadership

Burns, Rev. John M., *O.Carm.* '82 (STP) [CON] Carmel of Our Lady of Divine Providence, Lake Elmo, MN; [MON] Carmelite Hermitage of the Blessed Virgin Mary, Lake Elmo, MN

Burns, Rev. Laurence J., '64 (SC) Retired.

Burns, Rev. Malcolm J., '85 (RVC) Corpus Christi, Mineola, NY

Burns, Rev. Michael, *S.D.S.* '05 (MIL) [MON] Salvatorian Provincial Offices (Society of the Divine Savior), Milwaukee, WI

Burns, Rev. Michael E., *S.D.S.* '05 (IND) [HOS] Franciscan Health, Indianapolis, IN
Burns, Rev. Michael J., '73 (TR) Retired. [MON] Villa Vianney, Trenton, NJ
Burns, Rev. Norbert C., *S.M.* '53 (CIN) Retired.
Burns, Rev. Patrick J., *S.J.* '63 (MIL) [MON] St. Camillus Jesuit Community (Society of Jesus, USA Midwest Province), Wauwatosa, WI
Burns, Rev. Patrick J., '13 (MIL) Curia: Leadership Congregation of St. Francis Borgia, Cedarburg, WI
Burns, Rev. Paul D., *C.S.S.* '62 (BO) Retired.
Burns, Rev. Peter, *S.J.* '53 (SJ) [MON] Sacred Heart Jesuit Center, Los Gatos, CA
Burns, Rev. Thomas, *S.C.J.* '65 (SP) Retired.
Burns, Rev. Thomas J., '54 (SFR) Retired.
Burns, Rev. Thomas J., *M.M.* '69 (NY) Retired.
Burns, Rev. Vincent P., '67 (PH) On Duty Outside Diocese. Glenmary Home Missioners, Cincinnati, OH
Burns, Rev. Zachary, *TOR* '20 (FWT) Good Shepherd, Colleyville, TX
Burr, Rev. Jeremiah R., *M.M.* '67 (NY) Retired. [MON] Maryknoll Fathers and Brothers (Catholic Foreign Mission Society of America, Inc.), Ossining, NY
Burr, Rev. Stephen, '02 (DET) On Special Assignment. Sacred Heart Major Seminary, Detroit [SEM] Sacred Heart Major Seminary, Inc., Detroit, MI
Burrascano, Rev. Anthony, *O.S.A.* '79 (CAM) St. Augustine Preparatory School, Richland, NJ
Burrell, Rev. David B., *C.S.C.* '59 (FTW) [MIS] Holy Cross House, Notre Dame, IN
Burrill, Rev. Msgr. Jeffrey D., '98 (LC) St. Teresa of Kolkata Parish, West Salem, WI
Burrows, Rev. Michael, *O.S.B.* '80 (RCK) Marmion Academy, Aurora, IL; [MON] Marmion Abbey, Aurora, IL
Burshek, Rev. James J., *S.J.* '75 (STL) [COL] Saint Louis University, St. Louis, MO; [MON] Saint Jean de Brebeuf Jesuit Community, St. Louis, MO
Burt, Rev. Michael E., '09 (GR) Our Lady of the Lake, Holland, MI
Burton, Rev. Charles, '80 (KNX) Curia: Leadership St. Jude, Chattanooga, TN
Burton, Rev. Jeffrey D., '18 (GRY) St. John Bosco, Hammond, IN; St. Joseph, Hammond, IN
Burton, Rev. William, *O.F.M.* '89 (CHI) [MON] St. Peter's Friary, Chicago, IL
Burton, Rev. William L., *O.F.M.* (BAL) [SEM] St. Mary's Seminary and University, Baltimore, MD
Burusu, Rev. Valery, '92 (SFD) St. Aloysius, Paris, IL; St. Mary, Paris, IL
Bury, Rev. Antoni, '91 (CHI) St. Marcelline, Schaumburg, IL
Bury, Rev. Harold J., '55 (STP) Retired.
Buryadnyk, Rev. Mykola, '02 (STN) Chap Curia: Offices and Directors St. Joseph, Chicago, IL
Buryska, Rev. James F., '65 (WIN) Retired.
Burzynski, Rev. Michael H., '89 (BUF) Retired.
Bus, Rev. Anthony, *C.R.* '84 (CHI) St. Stanislaus Kostka, Chicago, IL
Busch, Rev. Douglas, '19 (NO) Our Lady of the Lake Roman Catholic Church, Mandeville, LA
Busch, Very Rev. Joseph G., '80 (ALB) Curia: Leadership Our Lady of Hope, Whitehall, NY; Our Lady of the Annunciation, Queensbury, NY; Sacred Heart, Lake George, NY; St. Ann's Roman Catholic Church, Fort Ann, NY; St. Mary's Roman Catholic Church Roman Catholic Community of Granville, Granville, NY
Busch, Rev. Matthew, '14 (PT) Immaculate Conception, Perry, FL
Buse, Rev. Harold J., '77 (OM) Retired. Curia: Leadership; Offices and Directors St. Robert Bellarmine, Omaha, NE
Bush, Rev. Msgr. Robert, '69 (SAN) St. Anthony, Odessa, TX; St. Joseph, Odessa, TX
Bush, Rev. Thomas B., '99 (LIN) Mother of Sorrows, Grant, NE; St. Mary's, Wallace, NE
Bush, Rev. William C., '62 (LEX) Retired.
Busher, Rev. Robert J., '76 (DAV) Retired.
Bushmaker, Rev. Godfrey E., *O.Praem.* '00 (ORG) St. John the Baptist, Costa Mesa, CA; [MON] Norbertine Fathers of Orange, Inc., Silverado, CA
Bushu, Rev. Edwin, '11 (AGN) Retired. Chap, Guam Mem Hosp & Guam Rgnl Med Ctr St. Anthony and St. Victor, Tamuning, GU
Bushy, Rev. Timothy F., '83 (CR) On Duty Outside Diocese.
Busse, Rev. Brendan P., *S.J.* '17 (LA) Dolores Mission, Los Angeles, CA
Bussen, Rev. Msgr. Robert J., '71 (SLC) Retired.
Bustamante, Rev. Carlos, '99 (ATL) Our Lady of the Americas Catholic Mission, Lilburn, GA
Bustamante, Rev. John Christopher, '03 (DET) Curia: Administration; Consultative Bodies Assumption of the Blessed Virgin Mary (Grotto) Parish Detroit, Detroit, MI
Bustamante, Rev. Robert, '17 (SFE) Immaculate Conception-Albuquerque, Albuquerque, NM
Bustillos, Rev. Guillermo, (DEN) On Duty Outside Diocese.
Busto, Rev. George, *C.O.* '05 (NOR) St. Therese of Lisieux Parish, Putnam, CT
Bustos, Rev. Martin Alonso, *M.N.M.* (ELP) San Lorenzo, Clint, TX
Bustos-Lopez, Very Rev. Javier, '01 (MIL) Curia: Leadership Our Lady, Queen of Peace Congregation, Milwaukee, WI
Butch, Rev. Brian T., '93 (TR) Co-Cathedral of St. Robert Bellarmine, Freehold, NJ
Butera, Rev. Christopher, (ALN) Kolbe Academy, Inc., Bath, PA
Butera, Rev. Christopher S., '07 (ALN) Curia: (>MO) Offices and Directors; Organizations (affiliated, inter-Diocesan, miscellaneous/other) Sacred Heart of Jesus, Bath, PA
Butera, Rev. George J., '68 (BO) Retired.
Buting, Rev. Stephen, '19 (MIL) Curia: Leadership Lumen Christi Congregation, Mequon, WI; St. Monica's Congregation, Whitefish Bay, WI
Butkowski, Rev. Charles, (CLV) St. Adalbert, Berea, OH
Butler, Rev. Allan L. W., '67 (BO) Retired.
Butler, Rev. Benjamin, '15 (NSH) St. Martha, Ashland City, TN
Butler, Rev. James P., '86 (BO) Retired.
Butler, Rev. John, (CIN) Retired. [MON] St. Charles, Celina, OH
Butler, Rev. John, '14 (TR) St. Michael, West End, NJ
Butler, Rev. John, *S.J.* '00 (BO) [MON] The Jesuit Community at Boston College, Chestnut Hill, MA
Butler, Rev. John J., '60 (HON) Retired.
Butler, Rev. Kevin M., '07 (RCK) St. John the Baptist, Somonauk, IL
Butler, Rev. Leo J., '98 (NEW) Immaculate Conception, Norwood, NJ
Butler, Rev. Michael A., '85 (R) On Leave.
Butler, Rev. Msgr. Michael T., '89 (STL) Curia: (>MO) Offices and Directors St. Clement of Rome Catholic Church, St. Louis, MO
Butler, Rev. Patrick J., '82 (ALB) St. Edward the Confessor, Clifton Park, NY
Butler, Rev. Paul F., '87 (RVC) St. Margaret of Scotland, Selden, NY
Butler, Rev. Rene J., *M.S.* '73 (HRT) [MIS] Missionaries of LaSalette, Hartford, CT
Butler, Rev. Rene J., *M.S.* '73 (FR) [MON] La Salette Missionary Association (Missionaries of La Salette (MA), Inc.), Attleboro, MA
Butler, Rev. Robert, *MS* '69 (ATL) Retired. St. Oliver Plunkett Catholic Church, Snellville, Inc., Snellville, GA
Butler, Rev. Robert J., '62 (BO) Retired.
Butler, Rev. Ted, '16 (SFE) San Jose-Los Ojos, Los Ojos, NM; Santo Nino-Tierra Amarilla, Tierra Amarilla, NM; St. Patrick-Chama, Chama, NM
Butler, Rev. Thomas, *O.Carm.* '50 (TUC) Retired. Salpointe Catholic High School, Tucson, AZ
Butler, Rev. Timothy, (RIC) Military Chap
Butler, Rev. Timothy A., '88 (BO) On Leave.
Butor, Rev. Walter, *O.M.I.* (BEL) [MON] Missionary Oblates of Mary Immaculate - St. Henry's Oblate Residence, Belleville, IL
Butrus, Rev. Nimatullah Muneam, '11 (OLD) Our Lady of Peace Syriac Catholic Church Incorporated, Jacksonville, FL
Butta, Rev. C. Gregory, '91 (WDC) Chap, Hospital & Nursing Home Ministry, St John XXIII Curia: Consultative Bodies
Butta, Rev. C. Gregory, '91 (WDC) Curia: Clergy and Religious Services [NUR] Cardinal O'Boyle Residence for Priests, Washington, DC
Butters, Rev. Craig M., '83 (ORG) Santa Margarita Catholic High School, Rancho Santa Margarita, CA
Buttner, Rev. Michael J., '78 (CHL) Retired.
Buttner, Rev. Michael T., '75 (BAL) Retired.
Buttrick, Rev. Dean T., '63 (SUP) Retired. Curia: Offices and Directors
Butts, Rev. James, *S.D.V.* (PAT) St. Gerard Majella, Paterson, NJ
Butz, Rev. Joseph, *C.Ss.R.* '70 (LA) Retired.
Butz, Rev. Joseph, *C.Ss.R.* '70 (MIL) [RTR] Our Mother of Perpetual Help Retreat Center (The Redemptorist Retreat Center), Oconomowoc, WI
Butz, Rev. Robert J., '00 (MAD) St. Christopher Parish, Verona, WI
Buu, Rev. Francis X., '74 (NY) Retired.
Buvala, Rev. Andrew, *OFM* (GB) Retired.
Buxkemper, Rev. Msgr. Roland, '65 (LUB) Retired.
Buxman, Rev. Msgr. Donald, '70 (P) Retired.
Buya, Rev. Gideon K., '14 (MIL) St. Charles Borromeo Congregation, Milwaukee, WI; St. Roman Congregation, Milwaukee, WI
Buyeera, Rev. Cyril, (NO) Ascension of Our Lord Roman Catholic Church, LaPlace, Louisiana, La Place, LA
Buzbuzian, Rev. Harry, '09 (MIL) Retired.
Buzzelli, Rev. Aaron N., *O.S.B.* '77 (GBG) [MON] Saint Vincent Archabbey, Latrobe, PA
Byabato, Rev. Deus-Dedit B., '93 (PEO) [HOS] OSF HealthCare St. Mary Medical Center, Galesburg, IL
Byambaasa, Rev. Rogers, *A.J.* '91 (PEO) [HOS] OSF HealthCare St. Joseph Medical Center, Bloomington, IL
Byarugaba, Rev. Dismas, *A.J.* '03 (CLV) St. John the Baptist, Akron, OH; Visitation of Mary, Akron, OH
Byaruhanga, Rev. Frederick, '89 (LA) Chap, Veterans Administration Greater Los An…
Byaruhanga, Rev. Frederick K., (MO) Curia: Offices and Directors
Byeck, Rev. Mitch, '81 (BUF) Epiphany of Our Lord, North Collins, NY
Byekwaso, Very Rev. Celestine, '82 (GB) Curia: Advisory Boards, Commissions, Committees, and Councils Holy Family, Marinette, WI
Byer, Rev. James M., '81 (CHL) Prince of Peace, Robbinsville, NC
Byerley, Rev. E. Joseph, '93 (CAM) Curia: Leadership
Byerley, Rev. E. Joseph, '93 (CAM) Holy Angels Parish, Woodbury, N.J., Woodbury, NJ
Byerley, Rev. Timothy E., '85 (CAM) St. Peter's Catholic Church, Merchantville, N.J., Merchantville, NJ; [MIS] Collegium Center for Faith and Culture, Haddon Heights, NJ
Byers, Rev. Dohrman W., '74 (CIN) Retired.
Byers, Rev. George D., *C.P.M.* '81 (CHL) Holy Redeemer, Andrews, NC
Byers, Rev. John, '95 (LAN) [ASN] Catholic Lay Association of the Holy Spirit Oratory, Lansing, MI
Byomuhangi, Rev. Bruno, (PEO) Holy Family, Peoria, IL
Byomuhangi, Rev. Deusdedit, '96 (PEO) [HOS] OSF HealthCare Sacred Heart Medical Center (Presence Central and Suburban Hospitals Network d/b/a Presence United Samaritans Medical Center), Danville, IL
Byrd, Rev. Charles A., '01 (ATL) Mary Our Queen Catholic Church, Peachtree Corners, Inc., Peachtree Corners, GA
Byrd, Rev. Freddie, '88 (OWN) John Paul II Catholic School, Morganfield, KY; St. Ann, Morganfield, KY
Byrd, Rev. Howard W., *S.S.J.* '75 (NO) [MIS] The Josephite Faculty House of St. Augustine High School,
Byrd, Rev. Jerry L., '12 (IND) St. Ann Catholic Church, Jennings County, Inc., North Vernon, IN; St. Joseph Catholic Church, Jennings County, Inc., North Vernon, IN; St. Mary Catholic Church, North Vernon, Inc., North Vernon, IN
Byrne, Rev. Msgr. Albert J., '79 (ALN) Retired. St. John the Baptist, Whitehall, PA
Byrne, Rev. Bernard, *M.M.* (NY) Retired.
Byrne, Rev. Edward G., '64 (NY) Retired.
Byrne, Rev. Frederick, *O.S.B.* '82 (GBG) [MON] Saint Vincent Archabbey, Latrobe, PA
Byrne, Rev. George, '69 (SD) Retired.
Byrne, Rev. Harry M., *OP* '78 (STL) [MON] Dominican Community of St. Louis, St. Louis, MO; [SEM] Aquinas Institute of Theology, St. Louis, MO
Byrne, Rev. Hugh A., '62 (BRK) Retired. [MON] Bishop Mugavero Residence, Douglaston, NY
Byrne, Rev. J. Peter, *F.S.S.P.* '03 (FWT) (>RIC) St. Joseph, North Chesterfield, VA
Byrne, Rev. Keith, '04 (LA) On Leave.
Byrne, Rev. Matthew J., '14 (CLV) St. John Bosco, Parma Heights, OH
Byrne, Rev. Peter, *SJ* (B) Sacred Heart, DeSmet, ID
Byrne, Rev. Peter J., *S.J.* '75 (SPK) [MON] Regis Community, Spokane, WA
Byrne, Rev. Robert H., '75 (SAG) Retired. Curia: Offices and Directors
Byrne, Rev. Thomas, '13 (CHI) [SEM] University of Saint Mary of the Lake/Mundelein Seminary, Mundelein, IL
Byrne, Rev. William D., '94 (WDC) On Duty Outside Diocese. Bishop of Springfield, MA
Byrnes, Rev. James J., '80 (STL) Cure' of Ars Catholic Church, St. Louis, MO
Byrnes, Rev. John D, '94 (ALT) [MIS] Diocese of Altoona-Johnstown, Altoona, PA

Byrnes, Very Rev. John D., '94 (ALT) Basilica of St. Michael the Archangel, Loretto, PA
Byrnes, Very Rev. John D., '94 (ALT) Curia: Leadership; Offices and Directors
Byrnes, Rev. Robert R., '67 (GBG) Retired. [NUR] Neumann House, Greensburg, PA
Byrnes, Rev. Thomas J., '99 (NY) St. Anthony of Padua, West Harrison, NY
Byrolly, Rev. Bruce, '58 (WIL) Retired.
Byron, Rev. William, '62 (YAK) Holy Trinity, Goldendale, WA
Byron, Rev. William J., *S.J.* '61 (PH) [MIS] Jesuit Fathers, , ; [MON] Jesuit Community at St. Joseph's University, Merion Station, PA
Bytomski, Rev. Kris, (SAT) Sacred Heart, Floresville, TX
Cabala, Rev. Thomas S., '79 (CHI) Our Lady at St. Germaine, Oak Lawn, IL
Caballejo, Rev. Yuen Servanez, '06 (ATL) Chap, United States Regular Army, Germany Curia: (>MO) Offices and Directors
Caballero, Rev. Francisco, '53 (TOL) Retired.
Caballero, Rev. Rodolfo, '93 (SAT) Holy Trinity, San Antonio, TX
Caban Vazquez, Rev. Carlos J., *SDB* '05 (ORL) St. John Vianney, Orlando, FL
Cabanas, Rev. R. Jaime, '55 (BWN) Retired.
Cabardo, Rev. Donato, '99 (NEW) St. Paul of the Cross, Jersey City, NJ
Cabasagan, Rev. Arbel S., '07 (SAC) Pastor of St. Teresa of Avila Parish, Auburn, a corporation sole, Auburn, CA
Cabasino, Rev. Philip, *C.Ss.R.* '47 (BAL) Retired. [SPF] St. John Neuman Residence, Timonium, MD
Cabello Miguelez, Rev. Tomas, *C.M.F.* (SJN) Casa Mision Claret, Bayamon, PR
Cabello Miguelez, Rev. Tomas, *CMF* (SJN) San Jose, Bayamon, PR
Cabezas, Rev. Richard E., '99 (NEW) Retired. Holy Trinity, Fort Lee, NJ
Caboboy, Rev. Juan, '76 (ORG) Holy Family, Seal Beach, CA
Cabra, Rev. Miguel Arturo, '98 (R) St. Elizabeth Ann Seton, Fayetteville, NC
Cabral, Rev. Clifford J., '79 (PRO) Retired.
Cabral, Rev. Fernando A., '86 (PRO) Church of Our Lady of Fatima, Valley Falls, Cumberland, RI
Cabral, Very Rev. Jeffrey, '02 (FR) Curia: Tribunal Santo Christo, Fall River, MA
Cabras, Rev. Fred, *O.F.M. Cap.* (DET) [CCH] Capuchin Services, Detroit, MI; [MON] St. Mary's Friary, Detroit, MI
Cabrera, Rev. Alberto, *C.P.* '65 (BRK) [MON] Immaculate Conception Monastery, Jamaica, NY
Cabrera, Rev. Alberto, '99 (MRY) San Juan Bautista, San Juan Bautista, CA
Cabrera, Rev. Alberto, *C.P.* '65 (NY) Retired. [MON] The Congregation of the Passion - St. Paul of the Cross Province, Jamaica, NY
Cabrera, Rev. Carlos J., '13 (MIA) St. Kieran, Miami, FL; [HOS] Mercy Hospital, Inc., Miami, FL
Cabrera, Rev. Diego, *S.S.C.* '95 (OM) [MON] Missionary Society of St. Columban, St. Columbans, NE
Cabrera, Rev. E. Julian, '08 (CC) [HOS] CHRISTUS Spohn Hospital Corpus Christi - Shoreline, Corpus Christi, TX
Cabrera, Rev. Emilio, (CHY) St. Joseph's, Cheyenne, WY
Cabrera, Rev. Emilio, '00 (CHY) St. Christopher, Eden, WY
Cabrera, Friar Jorge, *OCD* '09 (SAT) Basilica of the National Shrine of the Little Flower, Our Lady of Mt. Carmel and St. Therese Parish, San Antonio, TX; [MON] Discalced Carmelite Fathers of San Antonio, San Antonio, TX
Cabrera, Rev. Jose, '07 (SAG) Curia: Leadership
Cabrera, Rev. Jose Maria, (SAG) All Saints Parish of Bay City, Bay City, MI
Cabrera, Rev. Mario F., '81 (LA) Santa Rosa, San Fernando, CA
Cabrera, Rev. Rolando, '93 (MIA) Immaculate Conception, Hialeah, FL
Cabrera Duran, Rev. Cayetano, (TUC) Most Holy Nativity of Our Lord Jesus Christ Roman Catholic Parish - Rio Rico, Rio Rico, AZ
Cabrera-Carranza, Rev. Claudio, '02 (MRY) Our Lady of Solitude, Soledad, CA
Cabrerizo, Rev. Juan L., *Sch.P.* '77 (SJN) Colegio Calasanz, San Juan, PR; Santisimo Salvador, San Juan, PR
Cabrisos, Rev. Cromwell, '78 (ORL) Retired.
Cabrita, Rev. Paul M., *SM* '86 (WH) Retired.
Cabroas, Rev. Arn, (OAK) Good Shepherd, Pittsburg, CA
Cabuenas, Rev. Cyrain, (BUR) St. Francis of Assisi, Windsor, VT
Cabueñas, Rev. Cyrain G., (BUR) St. Anthony, White River Junction, VT
Caccavale, Rev. Charles, '91 (NY) [SEM] St. Joseph's Seminary, Yonkers, NY
Caccavale, Rev. Charles, '81 (BRK) On Duty Outside Diocese. St. Joseph Seminary, 201 Seminary Ave., Yonkers, 10704
Caccavale, Rev. Charles, '91 (RVC) Curia: Leadership
Cacciapuoti, Rev. Msgr. Antonio, '90 (LA) Cathedral of Our Lady of the Angels, Los Angeles, CA
Caceres, Rev. Msgr. Alonso, '59 (ORG) Retired.
Caceres, Rev. Jacob A., '08 (SAC) St. Joseph, Princeton, CA; [MIS] Our Lady of Sorrows, Grimes, CA
Caceres, Rev. Jacobo A., '08 (SAC) Pastor of Our Lady of Lourdes Parish, Colusa, a corporation sole, Colusa, CA
Caceres, Rev. Leonardo M., '03 (NEW) On Duty Outside Diocese. Notre Dame Le Rouet, Marseille
Caceres, Rev. Luis Alberto, '08 (AUS) St. Margaret Mary, Cedar Park, TX
Caceres, Rev. Marco A., '67 (MET) Retired. [MON] Maria Regina Residence, Somerset, NJ
Cachat, Rev. Leo P., *S.J.* '66 (DET) [RTR] Manresa Jesuit Retreat House, Bloomfield Hills, MI
Cacherco, Rev. Dionisio C., *O.A.R.* (LA) St. Benedict, Montebello, CA
Cadavid, Rev. Diego, '02 (CHI) SS. Genevieve and Stanislaus Bishop and Martyr, Chicago, IL; St. Donatus, Blue Island, IL
Cadavid, Rev. Jose Augusto, '97 (ORL) Blessed Sacrament, Clermont, FL
Cadavid-Rivera, Rev. Gonzalo, '09 (BAL) Curia: Tribunal
Caddy, Rev. James L., '64 (CLV) Retired.
Cadena, Rev. Jose G., (LAR) Curia: Leadership; Offices and Directors Christ the King, Laredo, TX
Cadena, Rev. Lorenzo Gamboa, '11 (CHI) Our Lady of Mercy, Chicago, IL
Cadigan, Rev. Timothy J., *S.J.* '91 (SCR) [COL] The University of Scranton, Scranton, PA
Cadin, Rev. Eric F., '12 (BO) Curia: Clergy and Religious Services; Consultative Bodies; Pastoral Services St. Mary, Dedham, MA
Cadorette, Rev. Curtis R., *M.M.* '77 (NY) Retired. [MON] Maryknoll Fathers and Brothers (Catholic Foreign Mission Society of America, Inc.), Ossining, NY
Cadran, Rev. Raymond G., *M.S.* '78 (ATL) St. Ann Catholic Church, Marietta, Inc., Marietta, GA
Cadrecha, Rev. Robert, '04 (SP) St. Jerome, Largo, FL
Cadri, Rev. Diego, '95 (KCK) Chaplain, Veterans Health Administration, Topeka
Cadri, Rev. Diego, (MO) Curia: Offices and Directors
Cady, Rev. Frank G., '81 (TUC) Retired. Saint Odilia Roman Catholic Community - Tucson, Oro Valley, AZ
Caesar, Rev. Floyd, '75 (ALN) Retired.
Cafarelli, Rev. Francis T., *C.S.C.* '65 (FTW) [MIS] Holy Cross House, Notre Dame, IN
Caffrey, Rev. Gerald, *C.M.F.* '80 (PHX) Chap, United States Veterans Hosp (Prescott), Prescott Sacred Heart Roman Catholic Parish Prescott, Prescott, AZ
Cafiero, Rev. Johnpaul, *OFM* (CLV) [MON] St. Anthony of Padua Friary, Brooklyn, OH
Cafiero, Friar Johnpaul, *O.F.M.* '95 (CHI) Hales Franciscan High School, Inc., Chicago, IL; [MON] Holy Evangelists Friary, Chicago, IL
Caggianelli, Rev. Gregg, '02 (VEN) On Duty Outside Diocese. Curia: (>MO) Offices and Directors (>PMB) [SEM] St. Vincent de Paul Regional Seminary, Boynton Beach, FL
Caggiano, Rev. Kyrin, *O.Carm.* '62 (JOL) Retired.
Cahalan, Rev. Patrick J., *S.J.* '65 (LA) [COL] Loyola Marymount University, Los Angeles, CA
Cahalane, Rev. Msgr. Thomas, '63 (TUC) Retired. Our Mother of Sorrows Roman Catholic Parish - Tucson, Tucson, AZ
Cahill, Rev. Colm, (NO) Curia: Leadership; Offices and Directors Our Lady of the Rosary, New Orleans, LA
Cahill, Rev. Daniel, '73 (TR) Retired. [MON] Villa Vianney, Trenton, NJ
Cahill, Rev. Dennis H., '77 (DUB) Retired.
Cahill, Rev. J. Patrick, '07 (CHL) Curia: Leadership St. Eugene, Asheville, NC
Cahill, Rev. J. Donald, (SAT) [NUR] Marianist Residence: Skilled Nursing, San Antonio, TX
Cahill, Rev. James, '61 (CHL) Retired.
Cahill, Rev. Joseph W., '76 (PRT) Retired.
Cahoon, Rev. John E., '89 (GAL) Curia: Leadership
Cahoon, Rev. John E., '89 (GAL) St. Angela Merici, Missouri City, TX
Cai My Loc, Rev. Bonaventure, *C.M.C.* (DEN) Queen of Vietnamese Martyrs Catholic Parish in Wheat Ridge, Wheat Ridge, CO
Caiazzo, Rev. Gregory G., '76 (RIC) Retired.
Caime, Rev. James, *S.J.* (KC) Curia: Leadership
Caime, Rev. James N., *S.J.* '02 (KC) St. Francis Xavier, Kansas City, MO; [MON] St. Peter Claver Jesuit Community, Kansas City, MO
Cain, Rev. Dennis R., '79 (DUB) Retired.
Cain, Rev. Frederick L., '70 (PIT) [CON] Sisters of St. Francis of the Providence of God, Pittsburgh, PA
Cain, Rev. Fredrick, (PIT) Retired.
Cain, Rev. Henry J., *S.J.* '63 (BO) [MON] Campion Health & Wellness, Inc., Weston, MA
Cain, Very Rev. Martin, '13 (MRY) Old Mission Church (Mission San Luis Obispo de Tolosa), San Luis Obispo, CA
Cain, Rev. William P., *S.J.* '76 (BRK) [MON] Carroll Street Jesuit Community, Brooklyn, NY
Cairnes, Rev. Michael, '13 (PMB) Cathedral of St. Ignatius Loyola, Palm Beach Gardens, FL
Cairns, Rev. John L., '63 (ALB) Retired.
Cairone, Rev. A. Robert, '64 (CAM) Retired.
Cajigal, Rev. Orville, *R.C.J.* (CHI) [MON] Rogationists of the Heart of Jesus - St. Matthew Province, Blue Island, IL
Calabrese, Rev. Charles L., '72 (STU) On Duty Outside Diocese. Fort Worth, TX
Calabrese, Rev. Mario Aquinas, *O.P.* (RIC) St. Thomas Aquinas, Charlottesville, VA
Calabrese, Rev. Peter M., *C.R.S.P.* '00 (BUF) Holy Family, Sanborn, NY; [SEM] St. Anthony M. Zaccaria Seminary, Youngstown, NY; [SHR] Basilica of the National Shrine of Our Lady of Fatima, Inc., Youngstown, NY
Calabria, Rev. Michael D., *O.F.M.* '03 (BUF) [MON] St. Bonaventure Friary, St. Bonaventure, NY
Calabro, Rev. John E., '73 (PH) Retired. St. Monica, Philadelphia, PA
Calais, Rev. Floyd J., '50 (LAF) Retired.
Calapan, Rev. Richard, (BUR) St. Mary, Cambridge, VT
Calapan, Rev. Richard, (BUR) St. Thomas, Underhill Center, VT
Caldarella, Rev. James J., '71 (WOR) Retired.
Calder, Rev. Kenneth J., '60 (BRK) Retired. Our Lady of Angels, Brooklyn, NY
Calderon, Rev. Christopher A., *S.J.* '17 (SAC) [MON] Sacramento Jesuit Community, Carmichael, CA
Calderon, Rev. Cruz, '08 (DAL) St. Cecilia Catholic Parish, Dallas, TX
Calderon, Rev. Jairo A., (CHR) St. Mary of the Angels, Anderson, SC
Calderon, Rev. Jonathan Santiago Vanegas, '16 (WDC) St. Martin of Tours, Gaithersburg, MD
Calderon Espinoza, Rev. Angel Renato, '93 (MIA) St. Timothy, Miami, FL
Calderone, Rev. Joseph D., *O.S.A.* '73 (PH) [COL] Villanova University, Villanova, PA; [MON] St. John Stone Friary, Villanova, PA; [MON] St. Thomas of Villanova Friary, Villanova, PA
Calderoni, Rev. Alessandro, '21 (TLS) Church of Saint Benedict, Broken Arrow, OK
Caldognetto, Rev. Dominic, *S.X.* '66 (MIL) [SEM] Xaverian Missionary Fathers College Seminary, Franklin, WI
Caldwell, Rev. Msgr. Francis J., (RVC) Cure of Ars Roman Catholic Church, Merrick, NY
Caldwell, Rev. Msgr. Frank J., *C.S.W.* '81 (RVC) Curia: Leadership
Caldwell, Rev. Fred, '95 (DAL) Retired.
Caldwell, Rev. Gregory, '21 (BUR) St. Michael, Brattleboro, VT
Caldwell, Rev. Jim, (TLS) On Special Assignment. Jim E Hamilton Corr Ctr, Hodgen
Caldwell, Rev. John A., '70 (L) Retired.
Caldwell, Rev. Teresio, *O.S.B.* '14 (P) [MON] Mt. Angel Abbey, Saint Benedict, OR; [SEM] Mount Angel Seminary, Saint Benedict, OR
Caldwell, Rev. Thomas A., *S.J.* '56 (MIL) [MON] St. Camillus Jesuit Community (Society of Jesus, USA Midwest Province), Wauwatosa, WI
Caldwell, Rev. Msgr. William, '68 (KC) Retired.
Calero, Rev. Luis F., *S.J.* '83 (SJ) [MON] Jesuit Community at Santa Clara University, Inc., Santa Clara, CA
Calero, Rev. Nomar J, '91 (MGZ) San Sebastian Martir, San Sebastian, PR
Calgaro, Friar John, *OFM Conv.* (AUS) Cristo Rey, Austin, TX
Calhoun, Rt. Rev. Michael, *O.S.B.* '02 (PEO) [SEM] St. Bede Abbey (Benedictine Society of St. Bede,

Benedictine Fathers and Brothers), Peru, IL
Calhoun, Rev. Ronald G., '72 (BO) Retired.
Calia, Rev. Jeffrey, *C.O.* '10 (MET) Holy Trinity, Bridgewater, NJ; [MON] The Raritan Congregation of the Oratory of St. Philip Neri, Raritan, NJ
Caliba, Rev. Jude C., (MO) Curia: Offices and Directors
Caliente, Rev. Ervin Pio M., '15 (RCK) On Duty Outside Diocese. St. Michael's Abbey of Norbertine Fathers, Silverado, CA
Caligiuri, Rev. Msgr. Angelo M., '58 (BUF) Retired. Curia: Consultative Bodies [MON] O'Hara Residence, Tonawanda, NY
Calik, Very Rev. Piotr, '13 (SPR) Curia: Leadership
Calik, Very Rev. Piotr S., (SPR) Immaculate Conception, Indian Orchard, MA
Calis, Rev. Joseph A., '99 (WDC) Curia: Deaneries St. John the Evangelist, Silver Spring, MD
Calise, Rev. Msgr. Joseph P., '80 (BRK) Parish of Transfiguration – Saint Stanislaus Kostka, Maspeth, NY
Calisin, Rev. Carlo, '14 (TR) Curia: Leadership St. Paul, Princeton, NJ
Calkins, Rev. Msgr. Arthur B, (LKC) Retired. Our Lady of Prompt Succor, Sulphur, LA
Calkins, Rev. Msgr. Arthur B., '70 (NO) Retired.
Calkins, Rev. Ronald L., '78 (NO) Curia: Leadership
Callaghan, Rev. Msgr. Aloysius R., '71 (ALN) Retired.
Callaghan, Rev. Msgr. Aloysius R., '71 (STP) [SEM] St. John Vianney Seminary, St. Paul, MN
Callaghan, Rev. John, (CAM) Curia: Advisory Boards, Commissions, Committees, and Councils
Callaghan, Rev. Michael, *C.M.* '76 (PH) [MON] Congregation of the Mission, Philadelphia, PA; [NUR] Camilla Hall Nursing Home, Immaculata, PA
Callaghan, Rev. Michael J., *C.O.* '90 (BRK) Assumption of the Blessed Virgin Mary, Brooklyn, NY; [MON] Oratory of Saint Philip Neri, Congregation Pontifical Rite, Brooklyn, NY
Callaghan, Rev. Nicholas E., '04 (NY) Curia: Leadership
Callaghan, Rev. Vincent, *O.F.M.* '75 (GB) Retired. [MON] Blessed Giles Friary, Manitowoc, WI
Callahan, Rev. Daniel, (NY) [MIS] New Hope Manor, Inc., Barryville, NY
Callahan, Rev. Daniel, *S.A.* '87 (NY) [MON] Franciscan Friars of the Atonement, Minister General Office, Garrison, NY
Callahan, Rev. David P., '87 (BO) Saints Louis and Zelie Martin Parish, Somerville, MA; St. Ann, Somerville, MA; St. Catherine of Genoa, Somerville, MA; St. Joseph, Somerville, MA
Callahan, Rev. James A., '73 (PH) Christ the King, Philadelphia, PA
Callahan, Rev. James B., '98 (WOR) St. Francis of Assisi Parish, South Barre, MA
Callahan, Rev. James F., '75 (WIN) St. Mary's, Worthington, MN
Callahan, Rev. Msgr. James P., '74 (STL) St. Joseph Catholic Church, Cottleville, St. Charles, MO
Callahan, Rev. Joseph H., '86 (CLV) Our Lady of Lourdes, Cleveland, OH; [CCH] Our Lady of Lourdes, Cleveland, OH
Callahan, Rev. Msgr. Kevin G., '84 (STL) St. Paul Catholic Church, Fenton, Fenton, MO
Callahan, Rev. Richard B., *M.M.* '64 (NY) [MON] M.M.A.F. Charitable Trust, Maryknoll, NY
Callahan, Very Rev. Msgr. Steven F., '87 (SD) Curia: Leadership Pastor of Saint Brigid Catholic Parish, San Diego, a corporation sole, San Diego, CA; [MIS] Saint Brigid Catholic Parish in San Diego, CA Real Property Support Corporation, San Diego, CA
Callahan, Rev. Zachary, '58 (RVC) Retired. Cure of Ars Roman Catholic Church, Merrick, NY
Callan, Rev. Dennis, *S.V.D.* '87 (CHI) [EFT] Divine Word Missionaries, Inc., Techny, IL; [EFT] Divine Word Techny Community Corporation, Techny, IL; [MON] Divine Word Residence, Techny, IL; [RTR] Techny Towers Retreat and Conference Center, Techny, IL
Callan, Rev. John, *Sch.P.* (WDC) [MON] Piarist Fathers, Province of the U.S.A. and Puerto Rico, Washington, DC; [SEM] Queen of Pious Schools, Inc., Washington, DC
Callanan, Rev. Michael G., *M.M.* '60 (LA) Retired. [MON] Maryknoll Fathers and Brothers, Los Angeles, CA
Callanan, Rev. Michael G., *M.M.* '60 (NY) Retired. [MON] Maryknoll Fathers and Brothers (Catholic Foreign Mission Society of America, Inc.), Ossining, NY
Calle, Rev. Juan de la, '54 (PMB) Retired.
Calledo, Rev. James, '94 (RVC) St. Mark, Shoreham, NY
Callery, Rev. William, (BIS) Retired. [NUR] Emmaus Place, Bismarck, ND
Callery, Rev. William V., '01 (FAR) Retired.
Callipare, Very Rev. Joseph P., '85 (PT) Retired. Curia: Leadership; Offices and Directors
Callis, Rev. Elbert, '76 (MEM) Retired.
Calloway, Very Rev. Donald, *M.I.C.* '03 (SPR) [MON] Congregation of Marian Fathers of The Immaculate Conception of the Most Blessed Virgin Mary, Stockbridge, MA
Caloca-Rivas, Rev. Rigoberto, *O.F.M.* '82 (OAK) [MIS] Multicultural Institute, Berkeley, CA; [MON] Franciscan Friars of California (Province of St. Barbara), Oakland, CA
Cal-Ortiz, Rev. Rodolfo L., '93 (GAL) [MIS] The Catholic Chaplain Corps, Houston, TX
Calovini, Rev. Msgr. Gerald E., '73 (STU) Curia: Offices and Directors Holy Family, Steubenville, OH
Calvario, Very Rev. Fredy, '10 (MRY) Curia: Administration; Deaneries St. Mary of the Nativity, Salinas, CA
Calvert, Rev. Roland, (TOL) [MON] Oblates of St. Francis de Sales, Toledo, OH
Calvillo, Rev. Ernesto, '10 (TLS) Curia: Leadership
Calvillo, Rev. Jose, (TLS) St. Therese Church and Diocesan Eucharistic Shrine of Saint Therese, Collinsville, OK
Caly, Rev. Roman, *M.M.* '91 (ROC) St. Stanislaus, Rochester, NY
Camacho, Rev. Gabriel, '21 (NEW) St. John the Apostle, Linden, NJ
Camacho, Rt. Rev. Isaac, *O.S.B.* '01 (SP) [MON] St. Leo Abbey, Saint Leo, FL; [RTR] Saint Leo Abbey Retreat Center, St. Leo, FL
Camacho, Rev. Jesus, '06 (SAT) Immaculate Heart of Mary, Pearsall, TX
Camacho, Rev. Jesus, '75 (B) St. Mary's, Boise, ID
Camacho, Rev. Juan Manuel, '12 (MIL) Congregation of St. Richard, Racine, WI; St. Edward's Congregation, Racine, WI; St. Patrick's Congregation, Racine, WI; [MIS] Community of St. Paul, Inc., Racine, WI
Camacho, Rev. Lemmuel, '15 (PAT) Curia: Leadership St. Mary's, Wharton, NJ
Camacho, Rev. Luis, '13 (AGN) On Duty Outside Diocese.
Camacho, Rev. Robert J., '79 (RCK) Retired. St. Laurence, Elgin, IL
Camacho-Monserrate, Rev. Enrique Manuel, '07 (SJN) Curia: Offices and Directors Stella Maris, Condado, San Juan, PR; [MIS] Caritas de Puerto Rico, Inc., San Juan, PR
Camacho-Torres, Rev. Jose Orlando, *C.S.Sp.* '92 (SJN) Curia: Offices and Directors [SPF] Santuario del Espiritu Santo-Congregacion del Espiritu Santo, Dorado, PR
Camacho-Torres, Rev. José O., (CGS) San Pedro Apostol, Caguas, PR
Camaioni, Rev. Matthew J., '07 (RCK) Immaculate Conception, Fulton, IL; St. Patrick, Albany, IL
Camara, Rev. Michael M., '89 (FR) Retired.
Camarda, Rev. Ronald A., '90 (STA) St. John the Baptist, Jacksonville, FL
Camargo, Rev. Carlos E., '06 (B) Retired.
Camargo, Rev. Milton, '15 (PAT) Saint Brendan and Saint George, Clifton, NJ
Camarillo, Rev. Joel Arciga, '98 (CAM) Divine Mercy, Vineland, N.J., Vineland, NJ
Cambe, Rev. Don Einars, '08 (CHI) Holy Name Cathedral, Chicago, IL
Cambi, Very Rev. Michael, '07 (ALB) Curia: Leadership St. Mary, Cooperstown, NY
Cambra, Rev. Daniel, *M.I.C.* '86 (NOR) [MIS] Congregation of Marian Fathers of the Immaculate Conception of the B.V.M., Thompson, CT; [MON] Marians of the Immaculate Conception of the B.V.M., Thompson, CT
Cambra, Rev. Raymond, '77 (FR) Our Lady Queen of Martyrs, Seekonk, MA
Cambre, Rev. Christopher, '17 (LAF) Immaculate Conception, Charenton, LA
Cambre, Rev. Christopher B., '17 (LAF) Sacred Heart, Baldwin, LA
Cameli, Rev. Louis J., '69 (CHI) Holy Name Cathedral, Chicago, IL
Camello, Rev. Ignatius, *O.S.B.* '20 (GBG) [MON] Saint Vincent Archabbey, Latrobe, PA
Camera, Rev. Bede, *O.S.B.* (MAN) Retired. [MON] St. Anselm Abbey, Manchester, NH
Cameron, Rev. Lachlan, '08 (RVC) [MIS] Sacred Heart Institute, Huntington, NY
Cameron, Rev. Lachlan, '08 (RVC) Curia: Leadership; Offices and Directors
Camilleri, Rev. Anthony, '07 (DET) Our Lady of Good Counsel Parish Plymouth, Plymouth, MI
Camilleri, Rev. Joseph M., '74 (BR) Retired.
Camilli, Rev. E. Michael, *M.S.C.* '60 (ALN) Curia: Leadership Holy Guardian Angels, Reading, PA; [ASN] Mission Vehicle Association, Inc., Center Valley, PA
Caminiti, Rev. Antonino, '08 (AGN) Curia: Miscellaneous / Other Offices San Juan Bautista, Ordot, GU
Camire, Rev. Bernard J., *S.S.S.* '66 (NY) St. Jean Baptiste, New York, NY
Camiring, Rev. Paul John T., (WDC) St. Augustine, Washington, DC
Camiring, Rev. Paul John, (HON) St. Elizabeth, Aiea, HI
Cammayo, Rev. Rubenus, '80 (NY) St. Anthony of Padua, West Harrison, NY
Camou, Rev. Fernando, '15 (PHX) Curia: Offices and Directors SS. Simon and Jude Roman Catholic Cathedral, Phoenix, AZ
Camp, Rev. Msgr. Steven, '89 (RVC) Chap, St Patrick, Huntington; Nassau Cty Firemen's Assn Curia: Leadership; Offices and Directors St. Patrick's, Huntington, NY
Campagna, Rev. Robert M., *O.F.M.* '77 (NY) [MON] Franciscan Province of the Immaculate Conception, New York, NY
Campagna, Rev. Robert M., *O.F.M.* '77 (NY) [MIS] St. Dymphna Devotion (Province of the Immaculate Conception), Mount Vernon, NY; [MON] Franciscan Mission Associates (Province of the Immaculate Conception), Mount Vernon, NY
Campana, Rev. Thomas J., '80 (CHI) St. Monica and St. Rosalie Parish, Chicago, IL
Campbell, Rev. Bernard J., *C.S.P.* '68 (NY) [MON] Paulist Fathers' Motherhouse, New York, NY
Campbell, Rev. Brian, '09 (PMB) St. John of the Cross, Vero Beach, FL
Campbell, Rev. Donald, *C.S.P.* '62 (NY) Retired. [MON] Paulist Fathers' Motherhouse, New York, NY
Campbell, Rev. Douglas L., '76 (WCH) Retired.
Campbell, Rev. Dwight, '91 (PEO) On Duty Outside Diocese. Our Lady of Mount Carmel Parish, Kenosha, WI
Campbell, Rev. Dwight P., '91 (MIL) Our Lady of Mount Carmel, Kenosha, WI; St. Therese Congregation, Kenosha, WI
Campbell, Rev. Howard W., '88 (PIT) Our Lady of the Valley, Beaver, PA
Campbell, Rev. Msgr. J. Michael, '71 (STU) Curia: Deaneries
Campbell, Rev. Jack, '18 (PT) Curia: Leadership Little Flower, Pensacola, FL
Campbell, Rev. James C., '06 (E) St. Patrick, Franklin, PA
Campbell, Rev. Msgr. James F., '64 (BUF) Retired. [MON] Bishop Head Residence, Lackawanna, NY
Campbell, Rev. Msgr. John G., '55 (ORG) Retired.
Campbell, Rev. Msgr. John Michael, '71 (STU) Basilica of St. Mary of the Assumption, Marietta, OH; St. Henry, Lower Salem, OH; [CAM] Marietta College, Marietta, OH
Campbell, Rev. Msgr. John S., '66 (ALN) Retired. Queenship of Mary Parish, Northampton, PA
Campbell, Rev. Joseph, (LAN) Lansing Catholic High School, Lansing, MI
Campbell, Rev. Joseph C., '06 (E) On Duty Outside Diocese. Army Chaplain Curia: (>MO) Offices and Directors
Campbell, Rev. Msgr. Mark A., '71 (SD) Curia: Tribunal
Campbell, Rev. Norbert J., '60 (PIT) Retired. [MON] St. John Vianney Manor, Pittsburgh, PA
Campbell, Rev. Paul F., '65 (WOR) Retired.
Campbell, Rev. Robert, *O.Praem* '08 (SFE) Chap, Westside Hosps; Presbyterian Hosp
Campbell, Rev. Robert E., *O.Praem.* '08 (SFE) [MON] Santa Maria de la Vid Abbey, Albuquerque, NM
Campbell, Rev. Ruben, *C.C.* '17 (GAL) Queen of Peace, Houston, TX
Campbell, Rev. Shane, (BIS) St. Bernard, Belfield, ND
Campbell, Rev. Shane, '08 (BIS) Curia: Offices and Directors St. Mary, South Heart, ND; St. Mary (Medora), Medora, ND
Campbell, Rev. Theodore C., '72 (STP) Retired.
Campbell, Rev. Wayne, '86 (OAK) Retired.
Campbell, Rev. William D., '58 (SCR) Retired.
Campbell, Rev. William F., *S.J.* '98 (WOR) [MON] Jesuits of the Holy Cross, Inc., Worcester, MA
Campbell, Rev. William G., '63 (FR) Retired.
Campeaux, Rev. Corey, '10 (LAF) St. Peter the Apostle, Gueydan, LA
Campion, Rev. Joseph, (LAF) St. Edmond, Lafayette, LA
Campion, Rev. Owen F., '66 (NSH) Retired.

Campo, Rev. David A., '21 (BO)
Campo, Rev. Frank, (BO) St. Mary, Franklin, MA
Campo, Rev. Lance, '93 (NO) St. Theresa of Avila, New Orleans, LA; [RTR] Center of Jesus the Lord, New Orleans, LA
Campos, Rev. Daniel, '04 (TLS) St. Thomas More, Tulsa, OK
Campos, Rev. Felipe, *CSC* (AUS) St. Ignatius Martyr, Austin, TX
Campos, Rev. Jose Antonio, '90 (SAC) Pastor of Holy Spirit Parish, Fairfield, a corporation sole, Fairfield, CA; Pastor of St. Joseph Parish, Lincoln, a corporation sole, Lincoln, CA
Campos, Rev. Miguel, '98 (FRS) Our Lady of Guadalupe, Delano, CA
Campos, Rev. Miguel, (SD) Pastor of Saint Rose of Lima Catholic Parish, Chula Vista, a corporation sole, Chula Vista, CA
Campos, Rev. Pedro, '02 (CHI) Our Lady of Mercy, Chicago, IL
Campos, Rev. Randy Raul, '08 (LA) St. Matthew, Long Beach, CA
Campos-Covarrubias, Rev. Jorge, '15 (SAT) Our Lady of Grace, San Antonio, TX; St. Anthony School, San Antonio, TX; St. Peter Prince of the Apostles, San Antonio, TX
Campos-Garcia, Rev. Jose, '12 (P) St. Joseph, Roseburg, OR
Campos-Garcia, Rev. Jose Manuel, '12 (P) St. Francis Xavier, Sutherlin, OR
Campuzano, Rev. Guillermo, *CM* '93 (CHI) [COL] De Paul University, Chicago, IL; [MON] DePaul Vincentian Residence, Chicago, IL
Camurati, Friar Leo, *OP* (NY) Church of the Holy Innocents, Pleasantville, NY
Camuso, Rev. Robert, '92 (SEA) Retired.
Canaan, Rev. Timothy G., '93 (OG) Retired.
Canales, Rev. Rene L., '06 (CAM) Curia: Advisory Boards, Commissions, Committees, and Councils; Parish Services Our Lady of Guadalupe Parish, Lindenwold, N.J., Lindenwold, NJ
Canary, Rev. Msgr. John, (CHI) Retired. [RTR] Joseph and Mary Retreat House, Mundelein, IL
Canary, Rev. Msgr. John F., '69 (CHI) Curia: Finance
Canas, Rev. Eugene, *OMI* (SAT) Retired. [NUR] Oblate Madonna Residence, San Antonio, TX
Canas, Rev. Eugene, *O.M.I.* '64 (GAL) Curia: Offices and Directors
Canavan, Rev. Gerald D., '69 (PH) Retired. Sacred Heart, Havertown, PA
Canavan, Rev. Mark P., '71 (CHI) Retired.
Canavan, Rev. Msgr. Martin, (STF) Curia: Leadership
Canavan, Very Rev. Archpriest Martin A., '68 (SJP) Retired. Curia: Offices and Directors
Canavera, Rev. Lawrence J., '67 (GB) Retired.
Cancino, Rev. Francisco J., '10 (SEA) St. Joseph, Lynden, WA
Cancino, Rev. Victor, *S.J.* (HEL) Saint Ignatius Mission Parish: Series 645, LLC, St. Ignatius, MT
Cancro, Rev. Francis, '81 (MIA) Curia: Canonical Services
Cancro, Rev. Francis T., '81 (CHL) Retired.
Candalisa, Rev. Frank, '02 (NO) Retired.
Candanosa, Rev. Agustin Garcia, (CHI) Our Lady of Unity Parish, Chicago, IL
Candela, Rev. Rafael, '59 (SJN) Retired.
Candelaria, Rev. Dino, '04 (SFE) Retired.
Candreva, Rev. Msgr. Thomas D., '63 (RVC) Retired.
Canela, Rev. Jorge, '09 (GI) Curia: Leadership Cathedral of the Nativity of the Blessed Virgin Mary, Grand Island, NE
Canela, Rev. Victor M., *S.T.* '14 (SAV) St. Joseph's, Bainbridge, GA
Canfield, Rev. Francis E., *S.J.* '67 (DET) [MON] Colombiere Center, Clarkston, MI
Caniglia, Rev. Ross P, '19 (SC) Holy Trinity Parish of Webster County, Fort Dodge, IA
Canino, Rev. Louis, *O.F.M.* '69 (CHL) [MIS] Franciscan Center, Greensboro, NC; [MON] Franciscan Friary, Stoneville, NC
Canizares, Rev. Dwight M., '81 (GAL) St. Michael, Lake Jackson, TX
Canna, Rev. Jeremy A.J., '14 (BRK) Blessed Trinity Roman Catholic Church, Rockaway Point, NY
Cannaday, Rev. Mark, '12 (POC) Retired.
Cannariato, Rev. Paul A., '83 (NEW) Curia: Advisory Boards, Commissions, Committees, and Councils; Offices and Directors Assumption, Emerson, NJ; St. Mary, Closter, NJ
Canning, Rev. Wilfred S., *C.S.B.* '55 (GAL) Retired. [MON] The Basilian Fathers of Dillon House, Houston, TX
Cannoles, Rev. Gordon, *C.Ss.R.* '69 (HBG) [MON] St. Clement's Mission House, Ephrata, PA
Cannon, Rev. Col. Robert R., '78 (VEN) On Duty Outside Diocese. Chaplin, Chancellor, Archdiocese of the Military
Cannon, Very Rev. John, '04 (SFE) Curia: Offices and Directors Cristo Rey Parish, Santa Fe, NM; The Cathedral Basilica of St. Francis of Assisi, Santa Fe, NM
Cannon, Rev. Kenneth V., *S.X.* '97 (BO) St. Albert the Great, Weymouth, MA; St. Francis Xavier, Weymouth, MA
Cannon, Rev. Matthew E., (HBG) Holy Name of Jesus, Harrisburg, PA
Cannon, Rev. Michael J., '81 (VEN) St. Michael the Archangel Parish in Sarasota, Inc., Sarasota, FL
Cannon, Rev. Richard E., '86 (BO) St. John the Evangelist, Hopkinton, MA
Cannon, Very Rev. Robert R., '78 (MO) Curia: Offices and Directors
Canny, Rev. Michael T., '77 (SAC) Retired.
Canny, Rev. Stephen, '61 (SR) Retired.
Cano, Rev. Andres, '09 (KNX) Holy Trinity Catholic Church, Jefferson City, TN
Cano, Rev. Hugo, '12 (WOR) Curia: Offices and Directors
Cano, Rev. Juan, '15 (LA) On Administrative Leave.
Cano, Rev. Nicolas, *O.S.B.* '97 (BIS) [MON] Assumption Abbey, Richardton, ND
Canorro, Rev. John, '01 (SY) Curia: Offices and Directors Christ the Good Shepherd, Oswego, NY; Church of the Holy Trinity, Fulton, NY; Our Lady of Perpetual Help, Minetto, NY; Our Lady of the Rosary, Hannibal, NY
Canova, Rev. James C., '01 (RCK) St. Rita, Rockford, IL
Canoy, Rev. Charles, '05 (LAN) St. John the Evangelist Parish Jackson, Jackson, MI
Canterna, Rev. Charles, '76 (BAL) Retired. St. Vincent de Paul, Baltimore, MD
Cantley, Rev. Msgr. Michael J., '55 (BRK) Retired. [MON] Bishop Mugavero Residence, Douglaston, NY
Cantones, Rev. Joel P., '81 (NO) St. Hubert, Garyville, LA
Cantrell, Rev. William, '13 (POC) Military Chap St. John the Baptist, Bridgeport, PA
Cantu, Rev. Jose Helio, *L.C.* '07 (NY) Parish of St. Peter and St. Denis, Yonkers, NY; [MON] Legionaries of Christ, Rye, NY
Cantwell, Rev. Edward F., '54 (ALB) Retired.
Cantwell, Rev. John, '69 (SAC) Retired. Curia: Organizations (affiliated, inter-Diocesan, miscellaneous/other) Pastor of St. Patrick Parish, Placerville, a corporation sole, Placerville, CA
Cantwell, Rev. Stephen, '82 (BRK) St. John the Baptist, Brooklyn, NY
Cantwell, Rev. Stephen F., *C.M.* '82 (PH) [MON] Congregation of the Mission, Philadelphia, PA
Canuel, Rev. Paul E., '66 (FR) Retired.
Canzio, Rev. Celestino, *O.F.M.* '73 (NY) [MON] Franciscan Province of the Immaculate Conception, New York, NY
Cao, Rev. (Joseph) Thanh Xuan, *CRM* '87 (SPC) [MON] Congregation of the Mother of the Redeemer, Carthage, MO
Cao, Rev. Bill T., '01 (ORG) St. Anthony Claret, Anaheim, CA
Cao, Rev. Binh The, *S.D.D.* '01 (NO) [MIS] Domus Dei Clerical Society of Apostolic Life, U.S.A., Inc., New Orleans, LA
Cao, Rev. Chuong, *C.Ss.R.* '01 (GAL) Holy Ghost, Houston, TX
Cao, Rev. John Mary Vu, *C.M.C.* '01 (SB) On Special Assignment.
Cao, Rev. Joseph, '01 (DEN) Cure d'Ars Catholic Parish in Denver, Denver, CO
Cao, Rev. Nghia, *C.Ss.R.* '05 (STL) [MON] St. Clement Health Care Center, Liguori, MO
Cao, Rev. Paul D., '01 (CHI) Curia: Leadership St. Mother Theodore Guerin, Elmwood Park, IL
Cao, Rev. Victor, *C.S.J.B.* '06 (BRK) St. John Vianney, Flushing, NY; [MON] Congregation of St. John the Baptist of China, Elmhurst, NY
Cao, Rev. Vincent Minh, *C.Ss.R.* '68 (STL) [MON] St. Clement Health Care Center, Liguori, MO
Cao, Rev. Vu, *CRM* '01 (SAC) Vietnamese Martyrs Parish, Sacramento, CA
Cao Vinh Phuc, Rev. Pierre, (PH) Visitation B.V.M., Philadelphia, PA
Capadano, Rev. Mathew, '14 (OM) St. Mary, Laurel, NE
Capadano, Rev. Matthew, '14 (OM) St. Mary, Wayne, NE; [CAM] Wayne State College Newman Center, Wayne, NE
Capalbo, Rev. Kenneth, *O.F.M.* (CHI) [MON] St. Peter's Friary, Chicago, IL
Caparas, Rev. Allain B., '06 (CAM) Mary, Mother of Mercy Parish, Glassboro, N.J., Glassboro, NJ
Capdepon, Rev. Federico, '83 (MIA) Retired. Curia: Leadership Corpus Christi, Miami, FL
Capeding, Rev. Lito J., '86 (MOB) Curia: Organizations (affiliated, inter-Diocesan, miscellaneous/other) Shrine of the Holy Cross Parish, Daphne, Daphne, AL; St. John Mission Parish, Bromley, Bromley, AL
Capella, Rev. Joseph P., *S.A.C.* '90 (CAM) The Catholic Community of Christ Our Light, Cherry Hill, N.J., Cherry Hill, NJ
Capella, Rev. Joseph P., '90 (CAM) Curia: Tribunal
Capewell, Rev. Timothy J., '83 (TR) Curia: Leadership Church of St. David the King, Princeton Jct., NJ
Capik, Rev. Msgr. William J., '54 (MET) Retired.
Capitani, Rev. Sylvan P., (HBG) Retired.
Capizzi, Rev. Marc F., '06 (PH) St. Andrew, Newtown, PA
Caplis, Rev. Roger J., '58 (CHI) Retired. St. Juliana, Chicago, IL; St. Pio of Pietrelcino Parish, Chicago, IL
Capo, Rev. Rafael, '96 (MIA) Curia: Pastoral Services [COL] St. Thomas University, Inc., Miami Gardens, FL; [MIS] Federacion de Institutos Pastorales, Inc., Miami, FL
Capone, Rev. Albert L., '80 (BO) Immaculate Conception, Malden, MA
Capone, Rev. Robert, (SD) [COL] University of San Diego, San Diego, CA
Capone, Rev. Robert, '00 (ORG) On Duty Outside Diocese.
Capongpongan, Rev. Julius U., (GBG) Geibel Catholic Junior-Senior High School, Connellsville, PA; Immaculate Conception, Connellsville, PA; St. Aloysius, Dunbar, PA; St. John the Evangelist, Connellsville, PA; St. Rita, Connellsville, PA
Caponi, Rev. Francis J., *O.S.A.* '89 (PH) [COL] Villanova University, Villanova, PA; [MON] St. Thomas Monastery, Villanova, PA
Caporiccio, Rev. Louis, *CPM* '97 (OWN) [MON] Fathers of Mercy, Auburn, KY
Capoverdi, Rev. Giacomo D., '97 (PRO) Church of the Immaculate Conception of Westerly, Rhode Island, Westerly, RI
Cappella, Rev. Romeo, '20 (MAR) St. Joseph, Sault Sainte Marie, MI; [CAM] Lake Superior State University, Newman Center, Sault Sainte Marie, MI
Cappelloni, Rev. David, '86 (SCR) [MIS] St. Anthony of Padua, Dunmore, Dunmore, PA
Cappelloni, Rev. David P., '86 (SCR) Curia: Leadership SS. Anthony & Rocco Parish, Dunmore, PA
Cappeloni, Rev. David, (SCR) Curia: Offices and Directors
Cappeloni, Rev. Thomas A., (SCR) Retired.
Capperella, Rev. Thomas S., '01 (CAM) Retired.
Cappleman, Rev. Garry, *O.P.* (P) St. Thomas More Catholic Church, Eugene, OR; [CAM] University of Oregon (Eugene), Eugene, OR
Capra, Rev. Paolo, '12 (DAL) Chap, Choice Moore Transfer Facility, Bonham Santa Clara of Assisi Catholic Parish, Dallas, TX
Caprio, Rev. Robert J., *O.F.M.* '63 (BO) [MON] St. Christopher Friary, Boston, MA
Capuano, Very Rev. Brian W., '11 (RIC) Curia: Administration
Capuano, Rev. Vincent, *S.J.* (MIA) Belen Jesuit Preparatory School, Inc., Miami, FL
Capucci, Rev. Giovanni, '03 (DEN) Curia: Tribunal [SEM] Redemptoris Mater House of Formation, Denver, CO
Capuci, Rev. John M., '90 (BO) St. Charles Borromeo, Woburn, MA; St. Malachy, Burlington, MA
Caputo, Rev. Louis, *SDV* '67 (PAT) [RTR] Sanctuary of Mary-Our Lady of the Holy Spirit (Vocationist Fathers), Branchville, NJ
Caputo, Rev. Louis, *S.D.V.* '67 (NEW) St. Nicholas, Palisades Park, NJ
Caputo, Rev. Ralph J., '75 (BRK) Retired. Our Lady Help of Christians, Brooklyn, NY
Caputo, Rev. Salvatore, '76 (OM) Retired.
Caputo, Rev. Salvatore S., *S.S.C.* '76 (PRO) Retired. [MON] St. Columban's Retirement House (St. Columban's Foreign Mission Society), Bristol, RI
Caraballo, Rev. Antonio, '81 (ARE) Retired.
Caraballo, Rev. Gerardo E, '09 (MGZ) Church de El Buen Pastor, Mayaguez, PR
Carabello, Rev. Francis J., '68 (NO) Retired.
Carabez, Rev. Miguel Angel, (ORG) St. Joachim, Costa Mesa, CA
Carandang, Rev. Alexander, *O.S.J.* '07 (STA) Sacred Heart, Jacksonville, FL
Carasala, Rev. Arul, '94 (KCK) Curia: Leadership SS.

Peter and Paul, Seneca, KS
Carasala, Rev. Lazar, '89 (KCK) Corpus Christi, Atchison, KS; St. Joseph, Nortonville, KS; St. Mary's Immaculate Conception, Valley Falls, KS
Caraway, Rev. Joseph, '20 (LKC) Curia: Advisory Boards, Commissions, Committees, and Councils St. Henry, Lake Charles, LA
Caraway, Rev. Michael Eugene, '19 (LKC) Curia: Advisory Boards, Commissions, Committees, and Councils; Leadership
Caraway, Rev. Michael J, '19 (LKC) [CAM] Vianney House of Discernment, Lake Charles, LA
Carazo, Very Rev. Jacob, *O.F.M. Conv.* '04 (MRY) (>WDC) [SEM] St. Bonaventure Friary, Silver Spring, MD
Carbajal, Rev. Francisco, '17 (SFE) St. Helen, Portales, NM; [CAM] University Catholic Center - St. Thomas More Chapel, Portales, NM
Carballo, Very Rev. Rafael, '06 (ATL) Curia: Leadership St. Mary Catholic Church, Rome, Inc., Rome, GA
Carbine, Rev. Msgr. Francis A., '62 (PH) Retired.
Carbonaro, Rev. Dennis J., '81 (PH) [SEM] Theological Seminary of St. Charles Borromeo, Wynnewood, PA
Carbone, Rev. Anthony J., '93 (GBG) Curia: Leadership; Miscellaneous / Other Offices; Offices and Directors Holy Trinity, Ligonier, PA
Carbonneau, Rev. Rob, *C.P.* '78 (NY) [MON] The Congregation of the Passion - St. Paul of the Cross Province, Jamaica, NY
Carbonneau, Rev. Robert, *C.P.* '78 (SCR) [MON] Saint Ann's Passionist Monastery of Scranton PA, Scranton, PA
Carcar, Rev. Geraldo, (CHI) [MIS] Instituto De Liderazgo Pastoral (Hispanic Programs for Lay Ministry and Permanent Diaconate), ,
Carcar, Rev. Gerardo Raul, *I.Sch.* '88 (MIL) Congregation of the Holy Assumption, West Allis, WI; St. Augustine Congregation, West Allis, WI; St. Rita's Congregation, West Allis, WI
Carcerano, Rev. Michael J., '76 (LA) Retired.
Cardelli, Rev. Msgr. Daniel E., '57 (OAK) Retired.
Cardenas, Rev. Arturo, '13 (BWN) On Duty Outside Diocese. Diocese of Oakland (in California)
Cardenas, Rev. Eugenio, *M.Sp.S.* '82 (LA) Our Lady of Guadalupe Parish, Oxnard, CA; [SEM] St. John's Seminary, Camarillo, CA
Cardenas, Rev. Juan, *O.S.A.* (PH) Annunciation B.V.M., Philadelphia, PA; [MON] Augustinian Community (O.S.A.), Philadelphia, PA
Cardenas, Rev. Juan Raul, '00 (PMB) St. Mary, Pahokee, FL
Cardenas, Rev. Marco J., *C.M.F.* '91 (CHI) [MON] Claretian Missionaries U.S.A.-Canada Province, Inc., Chicago, IL
Cardenas, Rev. Neiser, '12 (TR) St. Joseph, Toms River, NJ
Cardenas Bonilla, Rev. Jose C., '99 (PRO) On Duty Outside Diocese. Diocese of Charlotte
Cardenas-Bonilla, Rev. Jose Camilo, (CHL) Holy Trinity, Taylorsville, NC
Cardente, Very Rev. Edward S., '74 (PRO) Curia: Leadership Saint Anthony's Church Corporation, North Providence, North Providence, RI; St. Edward (The Church of St. Joseph Geneva Rhode Island), Providence, RI; The Church of the Presentation of the Blessed Virgin Mary, North Providence, RI
Cardilicchia, Rev. Vincenzo, '14 (BRK) All Saints – Our Lady of the Rosary of Pompeii, Brooklyn, NY
Cardinale, Rev. Kenneth, '98 (WOR) Saint John Paul II, Southbridge, MA
Cardo, Rev. Daniel, *S.C.V.* '06 (DEN) Holy Name Catholic Parish in Englewood, Englewood, CO
Cardona, Rev. Carlos Garcia, '92 (LKC) St. Joseph, Vinton, LA
Cardona, Rev. Edwin, '18 (ORL) Holy Cross, Orlando, FL
Cardona, Rev. Edwuin, (NSH) St. William of Montevergine, Shelbyville, TN
Cardona, Rev. Jorge D., '93 (CGS) Curia: Leadership San Juan Apostol y Evangelista, Caguas, PR
Cardona, Rev. Julian, '14 (KNX) St. Thomas the Apostle, Lenoir City, TN
Cardona, Rev. Luis Ferneidy, *AIC* (GRY) St. Margaret Mary, Hammond, IN
Cardona Diaz, Rev. Jose Juan, (SJN) San Juan de La Cruz, San Juan, PR
Cardone, Rev. Anthony, '11 (RVC) St. Thomas, the Apostle, West Hempstead, NY
Cardone, Rev. Anthony F., '11 (WIL) On Duty Outside Diocese. East Meadow, NY
Cardone, Rev. Joseph P., '87 (TOL) On Duty Outside Diocese.
Cardone, Rev. Thomas A., *S.M.* '85 (RVC) Kellenberg Memorial High School, Uniondale, NY; [MON] Provincial Residence and Novitiate, Mineola, NY
Cardosa, Rev. Carlos, (BAL) Chap, Roxbury Corr Inst, Hagerstown
Cardosi, Rev. James J., '15 (PH) St. Denis, Havertown, PA
Cardoso, Rev. Timothy N., '83 (FRS) St. Mary Queen of Apostles Catholic Church, Fresno, CA
Cardoza, Rev. Manuel, '09 (SB) Our Lady of Hope Catholic Community, Inc., San Bernardino, CA
Cardozo, Rev. Orlando, *O.P.* '06 (MIA) St. Dominic, Miami, FL; [MON] Dominican Fathers of Miami, Inc., Miami, FL
Cardozo Vargas, Rev. Homero, (COS) St. Francis of Assisi, Castle Rock, CO
Cardy, Rev. William, *O.F.M.* '72 (STL) [HOS] Mercy Hospital South, St. Louis, MO
Carew, Rev. Lawrence F., '66 (BGP) Retired.
Carey, Rev. David C., '04 (HRT) Retired. Holy Disciples Parish Corporation, Watertown, CT
Carey, Rev. Gerald P., '98 (PH) Curia: Advisory Boards, Commissions, Committees, and Councils Our Lady of the Assumption, Strafford, PA
Carey, Rev. James H., '66 (SY) Immaculate Conception, Pompey, NY; St. Joseph, Lafayette, NY; St. Leo, Tully, NY
Carey, Rev. Joseph H., *C.S.C.* '69 (FTW) [COL] University of Notre Dame Du Lac, Notre Dame, IN; [MON] Holy Cross Community, Corby Hall, University of Notre Dame, Notre Dame, IN
Carey, Rev. Louis Michael, *O.S.B.* '18 (CLV) Assumption, Broadview Heights, OH
Carey, Rev. Michael, *O.P.* '77 (OAK) (>LA) St. Dominic, Los Angeles, CA
Carey, Rev. Michael, *O.P.* '77 (LA) [CON] Monastery of the Angels (Contemplative) (Nuns of the Order of Preachers), Los Angeles, CA
Carey, Rev. Raymond, '70 (P) On Special Assignment. Salem
Carey, Rev. Shawn P., '09 (BO) Curia: Pastoral Services St. Jude, Waltham, MA
Carey, Rev. Stephen A., '98 (NEW) Curia: Advisory Boards, Commissions, Committees, and Councils St. Mary, Dumont, NJ
Carey, Rev. William F., '67 (BGP) Retired.
Carey, Rev. William G., '81 (BGP) Retired. [MON] The Catherine Dennis Keefe Queen of the Clergy Retired Priests' Residence, Stamford, CT
Carfagna, Rev. Msgr. Frank A., '67 (Y) Retired. St. Joseph, Canton, OH
Cargo, Very Rev. Jason, '07 (DAL) St. Mark the Evangelist Catholic Parish, Plano, TX; [CEM] St. Mark the Evangelist Parish - Columbarium, Plano, TX
Cargo, Rev. Thomas, '78 (JOL) Retired.
Caridi, Rev. Michael A., '94 (PIT) St. Paul of the Cross, Pittsburgh, PA
Cariglio, Rev. Msgr. Michael J., '70 (Y) Curia: Offices and Directors Basilica of Our Lady of Mount Carmel - St. Anthony of Padua Parish, Youngstown, OH
Carillo, Rev. John, '16 (OAK) Curia: Leadership Assumption of the Blessed Virgin Mary, San Leandro, CA
Carina, Rev. Chester H., '85 (MET) Curia: Evangelization; Tribunal Most Holy Redeemer, Matawan, NJ
Carini, Rev. Msgr. James P., '65 (NOR) Retired.
Carl, Rev. Gregory P., '12 (OM) Sacred Heart Church of Norfolk, Norfolk, NE; St. Patrick's, Battle Creek, NE
Carl, Rev. Scott M., '00 (STP) St. Odilia, Shoreview, MN; [SEM] The Saint Paul Seminary, St. Paul, MN
Carles, Rev. Alexander J., '88 (MET) Mary, Mother of God, Hillsborough, NJ
Carleton, Rev. Robert J., *M.M.* '64 (SJ) Retired. (>NY) [MON] Maryknoll Fathers and Brothers (Catholic Foreign Mission Society of America, Inc.), Ossining, NY
Carley, Rev. Patrick F., '69 (SLC) Retired.
Carlin, Rev. Bernard, *C.Ss.R.* '78 (STL) Retired. [MON] St. Clement Health Care Center, Liguori, MO
Carlin, Rev. Jacob K., (WCH) Curia: Offices and Directors
Carlin, Rev. John T., '76 (CLV) St. Charles Borromeo, Parma, OH
Carlin, Rev. Leagon, '22 (OG) Saint Augustine's Church, Peru, NY, Peru, NY; St. James Church, Cadyville, NY, Cadyville, NY; The Roman Catholic Community of St. Alexander and St. Joseph, Morrisonville, NY
Carlin, Rev. Warren, *O.Carm.* '58 (JOL) Retired.
Carlino, Rev. Richard A., '79 (ALB) Curia: Leadership St. Anthony, Schenectady, NY; St. John the Evangelist, Schenectady, NY
Carlo, Rev. Cyprian, '73 (LA) Retired. St. Cyril, Encino, CA
Carlo, Very Rev. Raymond J., '87 (CHR) Curia: Advisory Boards, Commissions, Committees, and Councils; Deaneries St. John the Beloved, Summerville, SC
Carloose, Rev. Anto Vijayan, *SAC* '06 (FWT) Assumption of the Blessed Virgin Mary, Decatur, TX; St. John the Baptizer, Bridgeport, TX; St. Mary, Jacksboro, TX
Carlos, Rev. Joseph P., *O.F.M.* '75 (SFD) St. Francis of Assisi, Teutopolis, IL; [MON] St. Francis Assisi Friary, Teutopolis, IL
Carlos, Rev. Joshua A., '16 (BWN) Holy Family, Brownsville, TX
Carlson, Rev. Alex Bernard, '10 (STP) St. John the Baptist, Excelsior, MN; [CEM] Resurrection Cemetery, Excelsior, MN
Carlson, Rev. Curtis, *O.F.M.Cap.* '95 (SAL) Our Lady Help of Christians Parish, Antonino, Inc., Antonino, KS; St. Anthony Parish, Schoenchen, Inc., Schoenchen, KS; [MON] St. Fidelis Friary, Victoria, KS
Carlson, Rev. Msgr. George F., '66 (BO) Retired.
Carlson, Rev. Gregory I., *S.J.* '74 (OM) [MON] Jesuit Community at Creighton University, Omaha, NE
Carlson, Rev. James R., '73 (SAG) Retired.
Carlson, Rev. Michael, (CHL) St. Mark, Huntersville, NC
Carlson, Rev. Paul, '10 (PEO) Curia: Clergy and Religious Services Holy Family, Oglesby, IL
Carlson, Rev. Richard D., '69 (NEW) Retired.
Carlson, Rev. Msgr. Steven V., '96 (R) Retired.
Carlton, Rev. Maurice T., '68 (MET) Our Lady of Lourdes, Whitehouse Station, NJ
Carlton, Rev. Thomas, (MET) Retired.
Carlucci, Rev. Antonio, *R.C.J.* '78 (LA) St. Jane Frances de Chantal, North Hollywood, CA; [MON] Congregation of Rogationists, Inc., Van Nuys, CA
Carman, Rev. Bernie, *S.A.C.* (BAL) St. Leo the Great, Baltimore, MD
Carmel, Rev. Alex, '09 (MAD) St. Gabriel the Archangel Parish (Saint Gabriel Congregation, Jefferson County WI, Inc.), Lake Mills, WI
Carmichael, Rev. Eugene, *S.J.* '73 (DET) [MON] Colombiere Center, Clarkston, MI
Carmichael, Rev. John F., '97 (BO) St. Ann by the Sea, Marshfield, MA
Carmody, Rev. James F., '70 (WOR) Retired.
Carmody, Rev. Michael J., '83 (GAL) Retired.
Carmody, Rev. Stephen F., *O.P.* '81 (COL) St. Matthew the Apostle Catholic Church & School, Gahanna, OH
Carmola, Rev. Michael J., '64 (SY) Retired.
Carmona, Rev. Fernando, (MIA) St. Patrick, Miami Beach, FL
Carmona, Rev. Henry, '78 (B) Curia: Leadership Holy Spirit Catholic Community, Pocatello, ID
Carnazzo, Rev. Hezekias, (ARL) [MIS] Institute of Catholic Culture, McLean, VA
Carnazzo, Rev. Hezekias, '16 (NTN) St. George Melkite Church Inc., Sacramento, CA
Carnazzo, Rev. Sebastian A., '16 (NTN) St. Elias, San Jose, CA
Carnecer, Rev. Ryan, *C.I.C.M.* '10 (SAT) Curia: Administration Divine Providence, San Antonio, TX
Carneiro, Rev. Denis, '68 (CHI) St. Mary, Buffalo Grove, IL
Carnes, Rev. Matthew E., *S.J.* '03 (WDC) [COL] Georgetown University, Washington, DC; [MON] The Jesuit Community at Georgetown University, Washington, DC
Carnevale, Rev. Michael, *O.F.M.* '61 (NY) St. Francis of Assisi, New York, NY
Carney, Rev. Brian, (BRK) Our Lady of the Blessed Sacrament, Bayside, NY
Carney, Rev. Bryan J., '07 (BRK) Chap, Flushing Hosp and Med Ctr
Carney, Rev. Edward, '63 (PEO) Retired.
Carney, Rev. John F., '91 (SFE) Retired.
Carney, Rev. John J., '63 (BAL) Retired.
Carney, Rev. Lawrence D., '07 (WCH) On Duty Outside Diocese.
Carney, Rev. Patrick, '55 (NY) Retired.
Caro, Rev. Eddie, *O.F.M.* (SJN) Post-Noviciado San Jose Obrero, Sabana Seca, PR
Caro, Rev. Robert V., *S.J.* '70 (LA) [COL] Loyola Marymount University, Los Angeles, CA
Carola, Rev. Joseph A., *S.J.* '93 (NO) [MON] Jesuit Provincial Office (Catholic Society of Religious and Literary Education), New Orleans, LA
Carolan, Rev. Craig, (SAG) Annunciation of the Lord Parish of Port Austin, Port Austin, MI
Carolan, Rev. Craig G., '91 (BWN) On Duty Outside Diocese. Diocese of Saginaw (in Michigan)
Carolan, Rev. Emmet, (SAT) Retired. [NUR] Casa De

Padres, San Antonio, TX
Carolan, Rev. Robert, '21 (NY) Parish of Annunciation-Our Lady of Fatima, Crestwood, NY
Caron, Rev. David G., *O.P.* '89 (NO) (>MIA) [MON] Dominican Fathers of Miami, Inc., Miami, FL
Caron, Rev. Gerard J., '94 (PRO) St. John's Church Society, Rhode Island, Slatersville, RI
Caron, Rev. Msgr. Marc B., '89 (PRT) On Special Assignment. Scarborough;Portland Curia: Consultative Bodies; Leadership; Offices and Directors St. John Paul II Parish, Scarborough, ME; [CCH] Catholic Charities Maine, Portland, ME
Caronan, Rev. John, (OLL) Curia: Leadership
Caronan, Rev. John, *O.Praem.* '94 (ORG) Curia: Leadership [MON] Norbertine Fathers of Orange, Inc., Silverado, CA
Caronan, Rev. John E., *O.Praem.* '94 (ORG) Curia: Leadership
Carongay, Rev. Jovito B., '92 (BRK) St. Nicholas of Tolentine, Jamaica, NY
Carosella, Rev. Jerome A., '63 (VEN) Curia: Advisory Boards, Commissions, Committees, and Councils Our Lady of Mercy Parish in Boca Grande, Inc., Boca Grande, FL
Carotenuto, Rev. Anthony M., '68 (TR) Retired.
Carpe, Rev. Gleen, '14 (ELP) Christ the Savior, El Paso, TX
Carpenter, Rev. Brian, '09 (ROC) On Duty Outside Diocese. St. Matthew Cathedral, South Bend, IN
Carpenter, Rev. Brian, '09 (FTW) Cathedral of Saint Matthew, South Bend, IN
Carpenter, Rev. Edward C., '95 (ELP) Curia: Advisory Boards, Commissions, Committees, and Councils St. Luke, El Paso, TX
Carpenter, Rev. Sean G., '09 (SCR) Resurrection, Muncy, PA
Carpentier, Rev. Scott J., '13 (PRO) St. Brendan, Riverside, RI
Carpine, Rev. Eric, *O.F.M.* '75 (SP) Retired. [MON] St. Anthony Friary (St. Petersburg) Franciscan Friars-Holy Name Province, Inc., St. Petersburg, FL
Carpio, Rev. Ernie, *CMI* (BEA) St. Henry, Bridge City, TX
Carpio, Rev. Ernie, (BEA) Curia: Administration
Carr, Rev. Alton, *C.Ss.R.* '60 (SAT) Retired. [MON] The Redemptorists/San Antonio, San Antonio, TX
Carr, Rev. Andrew, *C.Ss.R.* '55 (BAL) Retired. [SPF] St. John Neuman Residence, Timonium, MD
Carr, Rev. Damian, *O.C.S.O.* '87 (WOR) [MON] St. Joseph's Abbey (Cistercian Abbey of Spencer, Inc., Cistercian Order of the Strict Observance (Trappists)), Spencer, MA (>DEN) [MON] St. Benedict's Monastery, Snowmass, CO
Carr, Rev. Daniel, '18 (GBG) Curia: Advisory Boards, Commissions, Committees, and Councils; Offices and Directors St. Pius X, Mount Pleasant, PA; Visitation of the Blessed Virgin Mary, Mount Pleasant, PA
Carr, Rev. David J., '12 (L) St. Martin of Tours, Louisville, KY
Carr, Rev. Dom Elias, *Can.Reg.* '99 (RVC) All Saints Regional Catholic School, Glen Cove, NY; St. Patrick's, Glen Cove, NY
Carr, Rev. Ephrem, *O.S.B.* '67 (IND) [MON] St. Meinrad Archabbey, St. Meinrad, IN
Carr, Rev. Eugene R., '63 (SCR) Retired. [MON] Villa St. Joseph, Dunmore, PA
Carr, Rev. Gary M., '82 (SPC) Retired.
Carr, Rev. James, (NY) Loyola School, New York, NY; [MON] St. Ignatius Loyola Residence, New York, NY
Carr, Rev. James V., '69 (RIC) Retired.
Carr, Rev. Joseph A., '06 (PIT) Chap, Maplewood Personal Care Saint Luke the Evangelist, Sewickley, PA
Carr, Rev. Mark A., *S.J.* '05 (MIL) (>GB) [RTR] Jesuit Retreat House, Oshkosh, WI
Carr, Rev. Michael, '68 (CHY) Retired.
Carr, Rev. Patrick, '16 (NO) Curia: Offices and Directors St. Rita Catholic Church, New Orleans, LA
Carr, Rev. Richard T., '01 (ARL) Holy Trinity, Gainesville, VA
Carr, Rev. Robert J., (BO) St. Anthony of Padua, Boston, MA
Carr, Rev. Msgr. William H., '69 (RIC) Retired.
Carrano, Rev. David A., '10 (MAD) Good Shepherd Parish, Madison, WI
Carranza, Rev. Fernando, '95 (DAL) [SEM] The Redemptoris Mater House of Formation (Redemptoris Mater Seminary), Dallas, TX
Carranza, Rev. Fernando, '95 (NEW) On Duty Outside Diocese. Redemptoris Mater Seminary, Dallas, TX
Carranza, Rev. Rizalino J., '80 (LA) Curia: Pastoral Services St. Peter Claver, Simi Valley, CA
Carrara, Rev. Christopher C., '94 (OG) Curia: Consultative Bodies; Offices and Directors Our Lady of Grace Parish, Morristown, NY
Carraro, Rev. Francesco, '95 (NEW) St. Mary, Plainfield, NJ
Carrasco, Rev. Juan, '22 (LA) St. Mariana de Paredes, Pico Rivera, CA
Carrasco, Rev. Marco, '14 (TUC) Saint Helen of the Cross Roman Catholic Church - Eloy, Eloy, AZ
Carrasco, Rev. Mauricio, '12 (LR) Curia: Leadership; Offices and Directors Assumption B.V.M., Atkins, AR; St. Augustine, Dardanelle, AR
Carrasco, Rev. Maurico, '12 (LR) Saint Andrew Church, Danville, AR
Carre, Rev. Joseph P. Edwidge, '83 (NSH) St. Lawrence, Joelton, TN
Carreiro, Rev. Walter A., '95 (BO) Parish of the Transfiguration, Wilmington, MA
Carrella, Rev. Eugene J., '84 (NY) St. Rita, Staten Island, NY
Carreño Carreño, Rev. Edwin, '99 (GR) Shrine of St. Francis Xavier and Our Lady of Guadalupe, Grand Rapids, MI
Carreon, Rev. Regidor, '75 (PHX) St. Joseph Roman Catholic Parish, Phoenix, AZ
Carrero, Rev. Luis E. Serrano, '02 (CHR) St. Anthony, Ridgeland, SC; St. Gregory the Great, Bluffton, SC; St. Mary Mission, Hampton, SC
Carrico, Rev. Adam, '15 (L) Ascension of Our Lord, Louisville, KY
Carrier, Rev. Michael J., *K.H.S.* '95 (WIL) Curia: Education Church of the Holy Child, Wilmington, DE
Carrigg, Rev. George A., '57 (BO) Retired.
Carrillo, Rev. Agustin, *CMF* '04 (FRS) St. Anthony Claret, Fresno, CA
Carrillo, Rev. Arthur, *C.P.* '70 (CHI) [MON] Passionist Community of St. Vincent Strambi, Chicago, IL
Carrillo, Rev. Augustine, (CHY) Curia: Consultative Bodies St. Mary Magdalen, Evanston, WY
Carrillo, Rev. Ivan, (JOL) St. Dominic, Bolingbrook, IL
Carrillo, Rev. Ivan, (GRY) Curia: Leadership
Carrillo, Rev. Ronald, *S.F.* '74 (WDC) [SEM] Holy Family Seminary, Silver Spring, MD
Carrington, Rev. Richard J., '76 (NEW) Our Lady of Lourdes, Mountainside, NJ
Carrion, Rev. Patrick M., '82 (BAL) Curia: Administration St. Ignatius of Loyola, Ijamsville, MD; [CEM] New Cathedral Cemetery, Baltimore, MD
Carriveau, Rev. Kenneth L., '03 (AGN) Retired.
Carro, Rev. Curtis V., '15 (SP) Curia: Administration; Pastoral Services St. Raphael, St. Petersburg, FL
Carrola, Rev. Rudy, (SAT) Sacred Heart, Comfort, TX
Carrola, Rev. Rudy T., (SAT) Curia: Administration St. Anthony, Harper, TX
Carroll, Rev. Msgr. Aidan M., '63 (LA) Retired. St. Martha, Valinda, CA
Carroll, Rev. Edward E., '50 (MIL) Retired.
Carroll, Rev. Francis, *S.S.C.* '62 (OM) Retired. [MON] Missionary Society of St. Columban, St. Columbans, NE
Carroll, Rev. Francis P., *S.S.C.* '62 (PRO) Retired. [MON] St. Columban's Retirement House (St. Columban's Foreign Mission Society), Bristol, RI
Carroll, Rev. James, *O.F.M.* '79 (PSC) St. Mary's, Brockton, PA; St. Mary's, Mahanoy City, PA
Carroll, Rev. Msgr. John J., '66 (PAT) Retired. Curia: Leadership Our Lady of the Magnificat, Kinnelon, NJ
Carroll, Rev. John R., (BO) Retired.
Carroll, Rev. Keith M., '09 (HBG) Curia: Offices and Directors
Carroll, Rev. Matthew Paul, *OP* '13 (NY) [MON] St. Vincent Ferrer Priory, New York, NY
Carroll, Rev. Michael A., '72 (SAC) Retired.
Carroll, Rev. Msgr. Michael J., '61 (PH) Retired.
Carroll, Rev. Michael J., *CM* '77 (BUF) [ASN] Our Lady of Angels Association, Lewiston, NY
Carroll, Rev. Norman P., '93 (WIL) Curia: Administration; Miscellaneous / Other Offices St. Elizabeth Ann Seton, Bear, DE
Carroll, Rev. Owen, (OAK) Retired. [NUR] Mercy Retirement and Care Center, Oakland, CA
Carroll, Rev. Patrick, *CSSp* (STA) Retired.
Carroll, Rev. Robert, *O.Carm.* '71 (JOL) Our Lady of Mount Carmel, Darien, IL
Carroll, Rev. Msgr. Robert B., '63 (PAT) Retired.
Carroll, Rev. Msgr. Robert J., '75 (PH) St. Dorothy, Drexel Hill, PA
Carroll, Very Rev. Sean, *S.J.* '00 (P) [MON] Colombiere Jesuit Community, Portland, OR; [MON] Society of Jesus, Oregon Province, Portland, OR
Carroll, Rev. Sean, *S.J.* '00 (SJ) [EFT] USA West Province, Society of Jesus Irrevocable Aged-Infirm Fund Charitable Trust, Los Gatos, CA; [EFT] USA West Province, Society of Jesus Irrevocable Apostolic Fund Charitable Trust, Los Gatos, CA; [EFT] USA West Province, Society of Jesus Irrevocable Formation Fund Charitable Trust, Los Gatos, CA; [EFT] USA West Province, Society of Jesus Irrevocable Foundations Fund Charitable Trust, Los Gatos, CA; [MON] USA West Province, Society of Jesus, Los Gatos, CA
Carroll, Rev. Thomas, (PHX) St. Francis Xavier Roman Catholic Parish, Phoenix, AZ
Carroll, Rev. Thomas R., *Sch.P.* '70 (LEX) The Piarist School, Hagar Hill, KY; [MON] Piarist Fathers, Martin, KY
Carroll, Rev. William R., '70 (BO) Retired.
Carrozza, Rev. Andrew P., '90 (NY) St. Denis, Hopewell Junction, NY
Carrozzo, Rev. Anthony, *O.F.M.* '66 (SP) Retired. [MON] St. Anthony Friary (St. Petersburg) Franciscan Friars-Holy Name Province, Inc., St. Petersburg, FL
Carruthers, Rev. Msgr. Michael, '91 (SP) Curia: Administration Cathedral of St. Jude the Apostle, St. Petersburg, FL
Carson, Rev. Daniel B., '12 (WDC) St. Peter, Washington, DC
Carson, Rev. Maxwell, (DM) St. Patrick, Council Bluffs, IA
Carson, Rev. Michael, '98 (SJ) On Special Assignment. Assoc Dir for Native American Affairs, USCCB, Washington, DC
Carson, Rev. Msgr. Stanley B., '79 (ALT) Cathedral of the Blessed Sacrament, Altoona, PA; Our Lady of Fatima, Altoona, PA
Cartagena, Rev. Antonio, '85 (CGS) Curia: Leadership Parroquia Nuestra Senora del Perpetuo Socorro, Caguas, PR
Cartagena, Rev. Leo, '85 (KAL) St. Anthony, Buchanan, MI
Cartagenas, Rev. Tito Jesus, '10 (SJ) Curia: Leadership Church of the Transfiguration, San Jose, CA
Cartaya, Rev. Pedro, *S.J.* '67 (MIA) Belen Jesuit Preparatory School, Inc., Miami, FL
Carter, Rev. Augustine, *O.Carm.* '67 (JOL) Retired.
Carter, Rev. Daniel E., '79 (SFR) All Hallows Chapel, San Francisco, CA
Carter, Rev. David E., '16 (E) Our Lady Queen of the Americas, Conneaut Lake, PA
Carter, Rev. H. Todd, '11 (TR) Holy Innocents, Neptune, NJ
Carter, Very Rev. J. David, '05 (KNX) Curia: Leadership; Offices and Directors Basilica of Sts. Peter and Paul, Chattanooga, TN; [CEM] Mount Olivet Cemetery, Chattanooga, TN
Carter, Rev. Msgr. James A., '66 (CHR) Retired.
Carter, Rev. James C., *S.J.* '58 (NO) Retired.
Carter, Rev. Kevin E., '86 (NEW) Curia: Organizations (affiliated, inter-Diocesan, miscellaneous/other) St. Margaret of Cortona, Little Ferry, NJ
Carter, Rev. Mark, *O.F.M.Cap.* '92 (PIT) (>BAL) [MON] Our Lady of the Mountains Friary, Cumberland, MD
Carter, Rev. Mark, *O.F.M. Cap.* (BAL) Our Lady of the Mountains, Roman Catholic Congregation, Inc., Cumberland, MD
Carter, Rev. Martin, *S.A.* '75 (NY) Retired. [MON] Franciscan Friars of the Atonement, Garrison, NY; [MON] Franciscan Friars of the Atonement, Minister General Office, Garrison, NY
Carter, Rev. Noah C., '16 (CHL) Holy Cross, Kernersville, NC
Carter, Rev. Partrick, *O.S.B.* '15 (TLS) [MON] Our Lady of the Annunciation of Clear Creek Abbey, Hulbert, OK
Carton, Rev. A. Richard, '93 (PAT) St. Vincent de Paul, Stirling, NJ
Cartwright, Rev. Chris, *SJ* (SEA) Curia: Leadership St. Joseph, Seattle, WA
Cartwright, Rev. Steven G., '15 (PRT) Parish of the Holy Eucharist, Falmouth, ME
Carucci, Rev. David P., '95 (MOB) Our Lady of the Gulf Parish, Gulf Shores, Gulf Shores, AL
Carusi, Rev. Angelo N., '98 (PRO) Saint Rocco Church of Johnston, Johnston, RI
Caruso, Rev. Carmine, '21 (NY) Church of St. Mary, Mother of the Church, Fishkill, NY
Caruso, Rev. Daniel M., '94 (SY) Our Lady of Pompei/ St. Peter, Syracuse, NY; St. John the Baptist/Holy Trinity, Syracuse, NY
Caruso, Rev. Michael P., *S.J.* '82 (CHI) (>STL) [MON] Saint Jean de Brebeuf Jesuit Community, St. Louis, MO
Caruso, Rev. Philip J., '78 (NY) St. John the Evangelist, Mahopac, NY
Caruso, Rev. Robert J., '80 (PHX) Curia: Offices and Directors All Saints Roman Catholic Parish, Mesa, AZ
Carvajal, Rev. Msgr. Felipe N., '68 (PAT) Retired.
Carvajal, Rev. Jorge A., '94 (MIA) Mother of Christ, Miami, FL

Carvajal, Rev. Jose, '21 (WOR) St. Mary's, Shrewsbury, MA
Carvajal, Rev. Raul H., '65 (MRY) Retired.
Carvajal Casal, Rev. David, '19 (TLS) St. Pius X, Tulsa, OK
Carvajal y Basto, Rev. Tomas, (COL) Church of the Holy Trinity, Bolivar, OH
Carvajal-Salazar, Rev. Gabriel, '10 (CHL) Our Lady of the Highways, Thomasville, NC
Carvalho, Rev. Antonio, '93 (COL) Holy Name of Jesus, Columbus, OH; Santa Cruz Parish, Columbus, OH
Carvalho, Rev. Gordian, '85 (HON) Retired.
Carvalho, Rev. Joaquim, *O.S.B.* '82 (KCK) [MON] St. Benedict's Abbey, Atchison, KS
Carver, Rev. Dennis J., '94 (BLX) Retired. Curia: Advisory Boards, Commissions, Committees, and Councils
Carvill, Very Rev. Michael, *F.S.C.B.* '90 (DEN) Curia: Deaneries Nativity of Our Lord Catholic Parish in Broomfield, Broomfield, CO; [MON] Priestly Fraternity of St. Charles Borromeo (F.S.C.B.), Broomfield, CO
Carville, Rev. John, '63 (BR) Retired.
Cary, Rev. Robert, *CSP* '84 (LA) St. Paul the Apostle, Los Angeles, CA
Cary, Rev. Robert M., *C.S.P.* '84 (NY) Retired.
Carzon, Rev. Thomas, *O.M.V.* '96 (BO) (>VEN) San Pedro Parish in North Port, Inc., North Port, FL
Casado, Rev. Cristian, '22 (DAL) St. Gabriel the Archangel Catholic Parish, McKinney, TX
Casado Carmona, Rev. Cristian, '22 (TYL) Curia: Tribunal
Casagram, Rev. Michael, *O.C.S.O.* '82 (L) [MON] Abbey of Our Lady of Gethsemani, of the Order of Cistercians of the Strict Observance, Trappist, KY
Casale, Rev. Msgr. Franklyn M., '67 (NEW) Retired.
Casaleggio, Rev. Dave, (LAV) Retired.
Casari, Rev. Michael T., '95 (WIL) Retired.
Casavantes, Rev. Carlos, *FSSP* '86 (CIN) Holy Family, Dayton, OH
Cascione, Rev. James, *C.Ss.R.* '83 (BRK) Our Lady of Perpetual Help Basilica, Brooklyn, NY
Cascione, Rev. James R., *C.Ss.R.* '83 (NY) Parish of Most Holy Redeemer and Nativity, New York, NY
Casciotti, Rev. James A, *S.J.* (NY) [MON] St. Ignatius Loyola Residence, New York, NY
Case, Rev. Frank, *S.J.* '69 (SJ) [MON] Sacred Heart Jesuit Center, Los Gatos, CA
Case, Rev. Nicholas, (SFR) Junipero Serra High School (Boys), San Mateo, CA
Case, Rev. Nicholas, (SFR) St. Catherine of Siena, Burlingame, CA
Case, Rev. Richard, *S.J.* '75 (SJ) [MON] Sacred Heart Jesuit Center, Los Gatos, CA
Casellas Rivera, Rev. Ramón Jaime, *O.F.M. Cap.* '85 (PCE) Santa Teresita del Nino Jesus, Ponce, PR
Caseres, Rev. Blas, *C.Ss.R.* (CHR) Our Lady of the Hills, Columbia, SC
Caserta, Rev. Msgr. Thomas G., '80 (BRK) Curia: Organizations (affiliated, inter-Diocesan, miscellaneous/other) St. Bernadette, Brooklyn, NY
Casey, Very Rev. Christopher J., '07 (BO) Curia: Leadership Our Lady of Good Counsel, Methuen, MA
Casey, Rev. David J., *S.J.* '69 (NY) [MON] Murray-Weigel Hall (A Jesuit Community at Murray-Weigel Hall and Kohlmann Hall), Bronx, NY
Casey, Rev. Diarmuid, *C.S.Sp.* '69 (BRK)
Casey, Rev. Diarmuid C., *C.S.Sp.* '69 (SFR) St. Dunstan, Millbrae, CA
Casey, Rev. Edward, (SCR) Good Shepherd, Blooming Grove, PA
Casey, Rev. Edward J., '79 (PH) Immaculate Heart of Mary, Philadelphia, PA
Casey, Rev. Edward J., (SCR) St. Ann's, Shohola, PA; St. John Neumann, Hawley, PA
Casey, Rev. James R., '00 (PH) Epiphany of Our Lord, Philadelphia, PA
Casey, Rev. John, *S.A.C.* (DET) Retired.
Casey, Rev. Msgr. John F., '54 (BRK) Retired.
Casey, Rev. John J., *M.M.* '56 (NY) Retired.
Casey, Rev. John P., *M.M.* '56 (NY) Retired.
Casey, Rev. Kevin P., *S.J.* '72 (SD) Retired.
Casey, Rev. Michael T., '13 (HRT) Curia: Offices and Directors Divine Providence Parish Corporation (St. Joseph Church St. Peter Church), New Britain, CT; Holy Apostles Parish Corporation, New Britain, CT; Saint Katharine Drexel Parish Corporation, New Britain, CT; St. Francis of Assisi Church Corporation of New Britain, New Britain, CT; [CAM] Central Connecticut State University Newman House, New Britain, CT
Casey, Rev. Patrick, *S.J.* (LAN) St. Mary Student Parish Ann Arbor, Ann Arbor, MI; [CAM] St. Mary Student Parish, Ann Arbor, MI; [MON] USA Midwest Province of the Society of Jesus - Jesuit Residence, Ann Arbor, MI
Casey, Rev. Patrick, (WDC) [MON] Oblate Community, Washington, DC
Casey, Rev. Patrick L., '65 (NU) Retired.
Casey, Rev. Patrick P., '97 (DET) On Leave.
Casey, Rev. Patrick T., *O.M.I.* '80 (AJ) Co-Cathedral of the Nativity of the Blessed Virgin Mary, Juneau, AK
Casey, Rev. Peter J., '68 (BO) Retired.
Casey, Rev. Richard L., '65 (BO) Retired.
Casey, Very Rev. Robert E., '87 (BO) Curia: Leadership Gate of Heaven, Boston, MA; St. Brigid of Kildare, Boston, MA
Casey, Rev. Robert G., '94 (CHI) Curia: Offices and Directors
Casey, Rev. Ryan P, *C.S.P.* '18 (LA) (>OAK) Holy Spirit Parish/Newman Hall, Berkeley, CA
Casey, Rev. Thomas J., *O.S.A.* '69 (PH) [MON] St. Thomas Monastery, Villanova, PA
Casey, Rev. William, *C.P.M.* '91 (OWN) [MON] Fathers of Mercy, Auburn, KY
Cash, Rev. Richard, '89 (OWN) On Special Assignment. Chap, Carmel Home and Owensboro Health Rgnl Hosp
Cashen, Rev. Michael E., '91 (TLS) On Special Assignment. Northeast Oklahoma Correction Ctr, Vinita Holy Ghost, Vinita, OK
Cashman, Rev. Christopher T, '89 (BRK) St. Mary Star of the Sea, Brooklyn, NY
Cashman, Rev. John, *C.P.* '67 (NY) Retired. [MON] The Congregation of the Passion - St. Paul of the Cross Province, Jamaica, NY
Casillas, Rev. Rafael, '72 (LA) St. Joseph, Los Angeles, CA
Casillas, Rev. Richard D., *S.V.D.* (SB) St. Catherine of Siena, Rialto, CA
Casimir, Rev. Benjamin, '03 (VEN) Curia: Leadership St. Peter the Apostle Parish in Naples, Inc., Naples, FL
Cassani, Rev. John A., '13 (BO) On Leave.
Cassar, Rev. Edward A., '69 (BRK) Retired. Our Lady of Grace, Brooklyn, NY; St. Joseph, Astoria, NY
Cassar, Rev. Michael, '20 (LAN) St. Thomas Aquinas Parish East Lansing, East Lansing, MI
Cassato, Rev. Msgr. David L., '72 (BRK) Retired. Curia: Leadership; Pastoral Services Our Lady of Mount Carmel - Annunciation of the Blessed Virgin Mary, Brooklyn, NY; [CCH] Italian Ministry, ,
Casserly, Rev. Eugene D., '69 (PT) Retired. Curia: Leadership
Cassiano-Amaya, Rev. Erick, *F.M.M.* '07 (MIL) St. Anthonys Congregation, Milwaukee, WI; St. Hyacinth's Congregation, Milwaukee, WI
Cassidy, Rev. Daniel J., '78 (CHI) Divine Mercy, Winnetka, IL
Cassidy, Rev. James, '78 (STP) St. Joan of Arc, Minneapolis, MN
Cassidy, Rev. James, *O.S.A.* (PH) [MON] St. Thomas Monastery, Villanova, PA
Cassidy, Rev. James M., '61 (CLV) Retired.
Cassidy, Rev. Msgr. John, '79 (PT) Retired.
Cassidy, Rev. Matthew J., *S.J.* '99 (NEW) [MIS] Jesuit Community, Jersey City, NJ
Cassidy, Rev. Matthew J., *S.J.* '99 (CI) [MON] Jesuit Community of Micronesia, Chuuk, FM
Cassidy, Rev. Richard, '67 (DET) On Special Assignment. Sacred Heart Major Seminary, Detroit [MON] St. Paul of the Cross Community, Congregation of the Passion, Detroit, MI
Cassidy, Rev. Theodore K., *S.M.* '68 (CIN) Retired. [COL] The University of Dayton, Dayton, OH; [MON] Marianist Community, Dayton, OH
Cassidy, Rev. Thomas, *S.C.J.* '71 (MIL) Retired. [MON] Sacred Heart at Monastery Lake, Franklin, WI
Cassin, Rev. Msgr. Andrew J., '54 (WDC) Retired.
Castagnola, Rev. Mario, *PES* '10 (STP) Church of the Risen Savior, Burnsville, MN
Castaldi, Rev. Joseph, '63 (NOR) Retired.
Castanas, Rev. Edilberto S., '11 (OAK) Holy Spirit, Fremont, CA
Castaneda, Rev. Brian, '99 (LA) St. Brendan, Los Angeles, CA
Castaneda, Very Rev. Heibar, '94 (MRY) Curia: Deaneries Immaculate Conception, Tres Pinos, CA; Sacred Heart/St. Benedict Catholic Community, Hollister, CA
Castaneda, Rev. Jose, '17 (LA) St. Emydius, Lynwood, CA
Castaneda, Friar Luis Joaquin, *OCD* '03 (SAT) Basilica of the National Shrine of the Little Flower, Our Lady of Mt. Carmel and St. Therese Parish, San Antonio, TX; [MON] Discalced Carmelite Fathers of San Antonio, San Antonio, TX
Castaneda, Rev. Mario, (PMB) [MIS] Magnificat Palm Beach Chapter, Inc., West Palm Beach, FL
Castaneda, Rev. Oscar F., '87 (MIA) Retired. [MIS] Opus Caritatis Corp., Hialeah, FL
Castaneda, Rev. Severiano, '71 (LA) Retired.
Castañeda, Rev. Mario, '95 (PMB) St. Rita, Wellington, FL
Castañeda, Rev. Martin, (DAL) St. Mary Catholic Parish, Sherman, TX
Castano, Rev. Archmandrite Hector, (BRK) Our Lady of Angels, Brooklyn, NY
Castano, Rev. Jorge, '18 (PAT) Cathedral of St. John the Baptist, Paterson, NJ
Castano Fernandez, Rev. Rafael, '88 (ATL) Sacred Heart of Jesus Catholic Church, Hartwell, Inc., Hartwell, GA
Casteel, Rev. Michael J., '84 (SPC) Retired.
Castelblanco, Rev. Johnathan, *SJ* '14 (NY) [MON] Jesuit Community at Fordham University, New York, NY
Castellani, Rev. Paul J., '96 (PH) St. Philomena, Lansdowne, PA
Castellano, Rev. Rogie, *C.P.* '05 (BRK) Immaculate Conception, Jamaica, NY; [MON] Immaculate Conception Monastery, Jamaica, NY
Castellino, Rev. Albert J., *C.Ss.R.* '62 (STL) Retired. [MON] St. Clement Health Care Center, Liguori, MO
Castello, Rev. Anthony B, *SFX* (CHI) All Saints Parish, Niles, IL
Castelow, Rev. Ralph T., '89 (WIL) Retired.
Caster, Rev. Gary C., '92 (PEO) St. Columba, Ottawa, IL; St. Francis of Assisi, Ottawa, IL; St. Patrick's, Ottawa, IL
Castiblanco, Rev. Michael, '19 (NOR) Corpus Christi Catholic Parish, Willimantic, CT
Castiblanco, Rev. Michael, '19 (NOR) Curia: Leadership; Offices and Directors
Castilla, Rev. Carlos, '12 (TR) St. Mark, Sea Girt, NJ
Castillo, Rev. Arturo, '13 (BWN) San Martin de Porres, Alton, TX
Castillo, Rev. Eduardo, '01 (POD) Curia: Clergy and Religious Services
Castillo, Rev. Eduardo J., '01 (MIL) [MIS] Prelature of the Holy Cross and Opus Dei Layton Study Center, Brookfield, WI
Castillo, Rev. Federico, *Sch.P.* '15 (LA) Our Lady Help of Christians (Maria Auxiliadora), Los Angeles, CA; [MON] Piarist Fathers, Los Angeles, CA
Castillo, Rev. Francisco, '67 (BWN) Our Lady of St. John of the Fields, Mission, TX
Castillo, Rev. Gustavo, '01 (LA) [SEM] St. John's Seminary, Camarillo, CA
Castillo, Rev. Jeremias, (BRK) Curia: Leadership
Castillo, Rev. Lucio, *OMI* '15 (SAT) [MON] Missionary Oblates of Mary Immaculate of Texas, Southern Province (San Antonio USP Support Office), San Antonio, TX
Castillo, Rev. Pedro, '85 (AUS) St. Joseph, Rockdale, TX
Castillo, Rev. Rene R., '89 (RIC) Holy Family, Virginia Beach, VA
Castillo, Rev. Ricardo, '03 (CHI) St. Gall, Chicago, IL
Castillo, Very Rev. Rolo B., '92 (RIC) On Special Assignment. Christ the King, Abington & St. John the Evangelist, Marion Christ the King, Abingdon, VA; St. John the Evangelist Church, Marion, VA
Castillo, Rev. Ruben Dario, '95 (PAT) Our Lady of Victories, Paterson, NJ
Castillo, Rev. Santos, (JOL) Mary, Queen of Heaven, Elmhurst, IL
Castillo, Rev. Santos Perez, *O.F.M.* (SJN) San Jose Obrero, Toa Baja, PR
Castillo Liranzo, Rev. Jeremias E, '08 (BRK) Transfiguration, Brooklyn, NY
Castle, Rev. Nathan, *O.P.* (TUC) [CAM] University of Arizona Newman Center, Tucson, AZ
Castle, Rev. Robert, (TUC) Saint Thomas More Roman Catholic Newman Parish - Tucson, Tucson, AZ
Castles, Rev. Patrick J., '69 (TR) Retired.
Castoldi, Rev. Heitor, *C.S.* '05 (ORL) Curia: Evangelization Resurrection Catholic Church, Winter Garden, FL
Castor, Rev. Timothy William, '01 (RC) St. Francis of Assisi, Sturgis, SD; St. Mary Star of the Sea, Newell, SD
Castori, Rev. Michael T., *S.J.* '98 (OAK) Curia: Offices and Directors All Saints, Hayward, CA
Castrejon, Very Rev. Javier, '03 (R) Curia: Leadership Sacred Heart, Pinehurst, NC
Castrillon, Rev. Carlos, '14 (HRT) Our Lady, Queen of the Apostles Parish Corporation, Derby, CT
Castro, Rev. Alex, *A.A.* '11 (WOR) St. Anne and St. Patrick, Fiskdale, MA (>BO) [MON] Augustinians of the Assumption, Inc., Boston, MA
Castro, Rev. Angel, '08 (LA) St. Helen, South Gate, CA
Castro, Rev. Angel Alfredo, *MSP* '13 (SAN) Curia: Advisory Boards, Commissions, Committees, and

Councils Holy Redeemer, Odessa, TX
Castro, Rev. Antonio A., '84 (GAL) St. Mary, La Porte, TX
Castro, Rev. Dominic Joseph, '98 (MRY) On Special Assignment. Chap, Seaside Curia: (>MO) Offices and Directors
Castro, Rev. Elixavier, (SP) Curia: Faith Formation St. Lawrence, Tampa, FL
Castro, Rev. Geronimo, *M.S.* '99 (HON) St. Joseph, Waipahu, HI
Castro, Rev. John G., *O.M.I.* '62 (SAT) [MON] Oblate Benson Residence, San Antonio, TX
Castro, Rev. Jorge E., '12 (HRT) Saint Junipero Serra Parish Corporation, South Windsor, CT
Castro, Rev. Mario A., '00 (BWN) Basilica of Our Lady of San Juan del Valle-National Shrine, San Juan, TX
Castro, Rev. Oscar M., '93 (GAL) St. Mark the Evangelist, Houston, TX
Castro, Rev. Patrick, *O.F.M.Cap.* '88 (AGN) Curia: Consultative Bodies; Miscellaneous / Other Offices St. Jude Thaddeus, Sinajana, GU; [MIS] Secular Franciscans, Agana Heights, GU; [MON] St. Fidelis Friary, Agana Heights, GU
Castro, Rev. Robert, '85 (SR) Retired.
Castro, Rev. Warli de Araujo, '14 (DEN) Holy Cross Catholic Parish in Thornton, Thornton, CO
Castro Martinez, Friar Cristian Ubaldo, *OFM Conv.* (SAT) [SEM] San Damiano Friary, Initial House of Formation, San Antonio, TX
Castro Martinez, Friar Cristian Ublado, *OFM Conv.* (SAT) [MON] San Damiano Friary, San Antonio, TX
Castronovo, Rev. Edmund A., '76 (SY) Our Lady of Good Counsel, Verona, NY
Caswell, Rev. Joshua, *S.J.C.* '14 (CHI) St. John Cantius, Chicago, IL; [MIS] Canons Regular of Saint John Cantius, Chicago, IL
Caswell, Rev. Nathan, *S.J.C.* '14 (CHI) St. Peter, Volo, IL; [MIS] Canons Regular of Saint John Cantius, Chicago, IL
Caswell, Rev. Thomas C., '66 (SPK) Retired.
Catada, Rev. Apolonio C, '05 (SAC) Pastor of St. Joseph Parish, Elk Grove, a corporation sole, Elk Grove, CA
Catagnus, Rev. James N., '70 (PH) Retired. St. Ambrose, Philadelphia, PA; St. Paul, East Norriton, PA
Catalano, Rev. James, *O.S.J.* '63 (FRS) St. Joachim, Madera, CA
Catanach, Rev. Richard, '88 (LSC) Curia: Consultative Bodies; Evangelization; Leadership; Tribunal Holy Cross Parish, Inc., Las Cruces, NM; [MIS] The Priests' Retirement Plan of the Catholic Diocese of Las Cruces, Inc., Las Cruces, NM
Catania, Rev. Jason, '12 (POC) Saint Luke, Fort Washington, MD
Catanise, Rev. Joseph R., '82 (ROC) St. Leo, Hilton, NY
Cataudo, Rev. Anthony I., *O.P.* '60 (CAM) Retired.
Catella, Rev. Anthony, '10 (ALX) On Leave.
Catena, Rev. Paul G., '07 (ALB) Curia: Leadership; Offices and Directors Annunciation, Ilion, NY; Our Lady Queen of Apostles, Frankfort, NY
Caton, Rev. Scott, '11 (ROC) On Leave.
Catron, Rev. A. Cory, '16 (CHL) St. Francis of Assisi, Jefferson, NC
Cattany, Rev. Ronald, '13 (DEN) Guardian Angels Catholic Parish in Mead, Mead, CO
Catuiran, Rev. Joeffrey B., (AGN) Curia: Tribunal
Catungal, Rev. Mario T., *O.C.D.* '04 (MO) Curia: Offices and Directors
Catura, Rev. Mariano, '96 (ORL) St. Anthony Catholic Church, Lakeland, FL
Caughey, Rev. Daniel, (SY) On Academic Leave. St. Malachy, Sherburne, NY; St. Margaret, Homer, NY; St. Theresa of the Infant Jesus, New Berlin, NY
Caul, Rev. Robert F., '61 (PRO) Retired.
Cauley, Rev. Thomas F., '81 (PMB) Retired. Holy Family, Port St. Lucie, FL
Caulfield, Rev. Sean, '49 (B) Retired.
Causton, Rev. Paul, (STP) [HOS] United Hospital, Hastings Regina Campus, Hastings, MN
Cauterucci, Rev. Francis J., '90 (PH) Our Lady of Mt. Carmel, Philadelphia, PA
Cavagnaro, Rev. John A., '75 (CAM) Retired.
Cavagnaro, Rev. Mark, '70 (CAM) Retired.
Cavagnuolo, Rev. Salvatore F., '67 (HRT) Retired.
Cavalier, Rev. Robert C., '72 (NO) Retired. Curia: Miscellaneous / Other Offices
Cavalier, Rev. Wayne A., *O.P.* (NO) [MIS] Congar Institute for Ministry Development, New Orleans, LA
Cavalier, Rev. Wayne A., *O.P.* '93 (SAT) [COL] Oblate School of Theology, San Antonio, TX; [CON] Dominican Community of San Juan Macias (San Juan Macias Community), San Antonio, TX
Cavallari, Rev. Nicholas, '15 (CHI) St. Paul of the Cross, Park Ridge, IL
Cavalluzzi, Rev. Kevin P., '93 (BRK) Saint John the Evangelist-Saint Rocco Roman Catholic Church, Brooklyn, NY; St. Saviour, Brooklyn, NY; [CAM] Campus Ministers and Ministry Centers (Newman Apostolate, Inc.), Brooklyn, NY
Cavanagh, Rev. Msgr. Brian M., '58 (LA) Retired. Sacred Heart, Covina, CA
Cavanagh, Rev. David J., '85 (POD) Curia: Clergy and Religious Services
Cavanagh, Rev. David J., '85 (BO) [MIS] Prelature of the Holy Cross and Opus Dei, Cambridge, MA
Cavanagh, Rev. James, '80 (LA) On Sick Leave.
Cavanaugh, Rev. Brian, *T.O.R.* '82 (STU) [COL] Franciscan University of Steubenville, Steubenville, OH; [MON] Holy Spirit Friary, Steubenville, OH
Cavanaugh, Rev. James K., '51 (Y) Retired.
Cavanaugh, Rev. John, '90 (FAR) Our Lady of Perpetual Help Church of Reynolds, Reynolds, ND; St. Jude's Church of Thompson, Thompson, ND
Cavanaugh, Rev. Kevin P., '86 (HRT) Retired. Curia: (>MO) Offices and Directors
Cavara, Rev. Kenneth, '21 (PH) St. Monica, Philadelphia, PA
Cavara, Rev. Mark J., '16 (PH) Archbishop John Carroll High School, Radnor, PA; St. Patrick, Malvern, PA
Cavazos-Gonzales, Rev. Gilberto, *O.F.M.* '85 (CHI) [MON] Holy Spirit Friary, Order of Friars Minor, Chicago, IL
Caveglia, Rev. Patrick, *O.S.B.* '94 (KC) [SEM] Conception Seminary College, Conception, MO
Cavender, Rev. Joshua, (HBG) St. Pius X, Selinsgrove, PA; [CAM] Franklin and Marshall College, Lancaster, Lancaster, PA; [CAM] Millersville University, Millersville, PA
Cavera, Rev. Thomas J., '16 (GR) Curia: Offices and Directors St. Patrick, Ada, MI
Caverte, Rev. Rolando A., '62 (SFR) Retired. Church of the Epiphany, San Francisco, CA
Caviedes, Rev. Victor, '99 (VEN) St. Jude Parish in Sarasota, Inc., Sarasota, FL
Cavitt, Rev. Arthur J., '02 (STL) St. Nicholas Catholic Church, St. Louis, MO; [MIS] St. Charles Lwanga Center, St. Louis, MO
Cavoto, Rev. Joseph F., *OFM* '80 (NY) [SPF] St. Francis Counseling Center, Inc., New York, NY
Cavoto, Rev. Joseph Francis, *OFM* '80 (PAT) [MON] Holy Name Friary, Inc., Ringwood, NJ
Cawley, Rev. Martin, *O.C.S.O.* '61 (P) [MON] The Cistercian (Trappist) Abbey of Our Lady of Guadalupe (Order of Cistercians of the Strict Observance), Carlton, OR
Cawley, Rev. Patrick, '70 (GR) Retired.
Cawley, Rev. William M., '73 (GF) Retired.
Cayer, Rev. John, (PT) Curia: Leadership Our Lady of the Assumption Mission, Pensacola Beach, FL; St. Ann, Gulf Breeze, FL; [NUR] Casa Calderon, Inc., Tallahassee, FL
Cayer, Very Rev. John B., '96 (PT) Chap, Federal Corr Inst Curia: Leadership
Cayetano, Rev. Alvin, *S.O.L.T.* '95 (PHX) St. Joseph Roman Catholic Mission, A Quasi-Parish, Mayer, AZ
Caylor, Rev. Dennis J., '75 (CIN) Retired. Curia: Administration
Cazares, Rev. Everardo, (AUS) Sacred Heart Catholic Church - Latium, Texas, Latium, TX; St. Mary of the Immaculate Conception, Brenham, TX
Cazares, Rev. Felix A., '03 (BWN) Sacred Heart Church, Mercedes, TX; San Martin de Porres, Weslaco, TX
Ceballos-Gonzalez, Rev. Gerardo, '16 (ATL) On Special Assignment. Curia: Leadership; Offices and Directors
Cebula, Rev. Joseph, '75 (ALB) St. Mary's Church, Waterford, NY
Cebula, Rev. Thomas, '68 (Y) Sacred Heart of Mary, Louisville, OH; St. Louis, Louisville, OH
Cebula, Rev. Thomas W., '68 (Y) Retired.
Cebulka, Rev. Peter, *C.O.* '93 (MET) [MON] The Raritan Congregation of the Oratory of St. Philip Neri, Raritan, NJ
Cebulka, Rev. Peter R., *C.O.* '93 (MET) [MON] Clairvaux House, Raritan, NJ; [SHR] Shrine Chapel of the Blessed Sacrament, Raritan, NJ
Cecero, Rev. John J., *S.J.* '89 (NY) [COL] Fordham University, Bronx, NY; [EFT] Aged and Infirm Trust, New York, NY; [EFT] Apostolic Works Trust, New York, NY; [EFT] Formation Trust, New York, NY; [EFT] Foundation Trust, New York, NY; [EFT] Religious Property Trust, New York, NY; [MIS] Centro Altagracia de Fe y Justicia, Inc. (Altagracia Center of Faith and Justice, Inc.), New York, NY; [MON] Jesuit Community at Fordham University, New York, NY
Cecil, Rev. Anthony Leo, *STB* '19 (L) St. Raphael the Archangel, Louisville, KY
Cecil, Rev. Bruce, *C.S.C* '92 (OAK) Moreau Catholic High School, Hayward, CA; [MON] Priests of the Congregation of Holy Cross, Berkeley, CA
Cecil, Rev. Zachary, '19 (CIN) St. Teresa of Avila, Cincinnati, OH; St. William, Cincinnati, OH
Cedeno, Rev. Jose Miguel, (SJN) Curia: Leadership
Cedeño Velez, Rev. Jose Miguel, (SJN) Nuestra Senora del Carmen, San Juan, PR
Cedolia, Rev. Robert J., (PIT) On Administrative Leave.
Ceja, Rev. Miguel R., '90 (SB) Saint Kateri Tekakwitha Catholic Community, Inc., Beaumont, CA
Ceja, Rev. Vianney, '17 (ORG) Curia: Leadership Archangel Institute (St. Michael's Preparatory School), Silverado, CA; [MON] Norbertine Fathers of Orange, Inc., Silverado, CA; [SEM] St. Michael's Norbertine Postulancy, Novitiate and Juniorate, Silverado, CA
Celano, Rev. Freddy, '87 (TYL) On Special Assignment. Studies Our Lady of Sorrows, Jacksonville, TX
Celano, Rev. Msgr. Joseph G., '87 (MET) Curia: Administration; Consultative Bodies Church of the Immaculate Conception, Somerville, NJ
Celentano, Rev. Christopher, '08 (SY) St. Rose of Lima, North Syracuse, NY
Celeste, Rev. Charles R., '80 (ALB) On Leave.
Celestial, Rev. Ramonito, '12 (TUC) Our Lady of Guadalupe, Bowie, AZ; Our Lady of Perpetual Help, San Simon, AZ
Celestine, Rev. Patrick, '20 (SJN) Ntra. Sra. de la Caridad del Cobre, San Juan, PR
Celestino dos Santos, Rev. Ivanildo, '02 (BGP) The Roman Catholic Church of St. Charles, Bridgeport, CT
Celiano, Rev. Alfred V., '53 (NEW) Retired. [COL] Seton Hall University, South Orange, NJ
Celichowski, Rev. John, *OFM Cap.* (LA) [SEM] San Lorenzo Seminary - Novitiate, Santa Ynez, CA
Celino, Rev. Anthony C., '97 (ELP) Curia: Advisory Boards, Commissions, Committees, and Councils; Leadership; Tribunal St. Raphael, El Paso, TX
Cella, Rev. John, *O.F.M.* '78 (MIL) [MIS] Franciscan Pilgrimage Programs, Inc., Franklin, WI; [MON] Francis and Clare Friary, Franklin, WI
Cellars, Rev. Michael, '20 (CHR) St. Theresa the Little Flower, Summerville, SC
Cellini, Rev. Msgr. Ronald R., '79 (CHR) Curia: Advisory Boards, Commissions, Committees, and Councils; Deaneries; Offices and Directors St. Anthony Mission, Hardeeville, SC; St. Gregory the Great, Bluffton, SC
Celso, Rev. B. Thomas, '64 (ROC) Retired.
Celuch, Very Rev. Martin, '03 (Y) Curia: Leadership; Offices and Directors Holy Family, Poland, OH; Our Lady of the Holy Rosary, Lowellville, OH; [MIS] Conference of Slovak Clergy, Youngstown, OH; [MIS] Midwest Canon Law Society, Youngstown, OH
Cely, Rev. Alfonso, *O.P.* '00 (ORL) St. Ann, Haines City, FL
Cely, Rev. Hernan, '13 (PAT) Curia: Leadership St. Anthony of Padua, Passaic, NJ
Cely, Rev. Manuel, *O.S.B.* '05 (BIS) [MON] Assumption Abbey, Richardton, ND
Celzo, Rev. Msgr. Juan R., '78 (MOB) Our Lady Queen of Mercy Parish, Montgomery, Montgomery, AL; St. John the Baptist Parish, Montgomery, Montgomery, AL
Cembor, Rev. Thomas M., '79 (NEW) Chap, Mountainside Hosp, Montclair
Cencula, Rev. Leonard T., '63 (STU) Retired.
Centeno, Rev. Yader F., '96 (MIA) St. John Bosco, Miami, FL
Centina, Rev. Gilbert Luis R., *O.S.A.* (NY) Holy Rosary, New York, NY
Centner, Rev. David Joseph, *O.C.D.* (MIL) [MON] Discalced Carmelite Friars of Holy Hill, Inc., Hubertus, WI
Centner, Rev. David Joseph, *O.C.D.* (BO) [MON] Carmelite Monastery, Boston, MA
Cepeda, Rev. Jose R, *OSA* '12 (MGZ) St. Francis of Assisi, Aguada, PR
Cepeda Contreras, Rev. Marco Antonio, *M.N.M* '90 (ARE) Our Lady of Asumption, Camuy, PR
Cepil, Rev. Krzysztof, (CHI) St. James, Chicago, IL; St. John Bosco, Chicago, IL
Cerank, Rev. Gerald A., '72 (OG) Retired.
Ceranowski, Rev. Albert B., '64 (TOL) Retired.
Ceranowski, Rev. Gerald L., '67 (TOL) Retired.
Cerbone, Rev. James, *S.D.B.* '80 (NEW) [MON] Don Bosco Prep Salesian Residence, Ramsey, NJ
Cerda, Rev. Jesus Ramirez, *C.S.* (CHI) St. Charles Borromeo, Melrose Park, IL
Cerezo, Rev. Alberto F., '60 (YAK) Retired.
Ceriello, Rev. Joseph A., '78 (BRK) Queen of All Saints, Brooklyn, NY
Cerio, Rev. Frank, '86 (ORL) Our Lady of the Lakes,

Deltona, FL
Cerkas, Rev. John W., '70 (GB) Retired.
Cermak, Rev. Michael Gilmary, *M.M.A.* '95 (SAM) [MON] Maronite Monks of Adoration - Most Holy Trinity Monastery, Petersham, MA
Cerna, Rev. Jose, '19 (JOL) Immaculate Conception, Elmhurst, IL
Cerniglia, Rev. George, *SM* '69 (STL) [MON] Marianist Province of the United States (Society of Mary), St. Louis, MO
Cerniglia, Rev. George James, *SM* '69 (STL) Our Lady of the Pillar Catholic Church, St. Louis, MO; [MON] Chaminade Community, Creve Coeur, MO
Ceron Valdez, Rev. Manuel de Jesus, '07 (SLC) Chap, Central Utah Corr Fac Saint Elizabeth LLC 220, Central Valley, UT
Cerpich, Rev. Richard J., '61 (MIL) Retired.
Cerratos, Rev. Ramon, *S.X.* '99 (PAT) [MON] Xaverian Missionary Fathers, Wayne, NJ
Cerrone, Rev. Michael J., '81 (SAV) Retired.
Cervantes, Rev. Cirilo, *M.C.* '99 (SAC) Curia: Offices and Directors Pastor of Our Lady of Mercy Parish, Redding, a corporation sole, Redding, CA
Cervantes, Rev. Fidel, '55 (ELP) Retired.
Cervantes, Rev. Miguel, (AGN) On Duty Outside Diocese.
Cervero, Rev. Joseph, '89 (BGP) The Saint Margaret Mary Roman Catholic Church Corporation, Shelton, CT
Cervine, Rev. Keith, '09 (MET) Immaculate Conception, Annandale, NJ
Cervinski, Rev. Paul, '61 (BIS) Retired. [NUR] Emmaus Place, Bismarck, ND
Cerwonka, Rev. Clarence J., '61 (SY) Retired.
Cesa, Rev. Dean, '98 (CHL) St. Joan of Arc, Candler, NC
Cesanek, Rev. Damian, *O.F.M.* '69 (CIN) Retired. [MON] St. Clement Friary, Cincinnati, OH
Cesarek, Rev. Adam, '15 (PEO) St. Mary's, Pontiac, IL
Cesarone, Rev. Jeffrey T., *O.Praem.* (WIL) [MON] Immaculate Conception Priory of the Canons Regular of Premontre, Middletown, DE
Cespedes, Rev. Carlos J., '75 (MIA) [SHR] National Shrine of Our Lady of Charity, Miami, FL
Cespedes, Rev. Jorge A., '11 (MEM) On Leave.
Cesta, Rev. James M., '74 (SY) St. Mary of Mt. Carmel/ Blessed Sacrament, Utica, NY
Cestare, Rev. Gerald, '95 (RVC) Good Shepherd, Holbrook, NY
Chaanine, Rev. George, '96 (LAV) On Administrative Leave.
Chabaan, Rev. Zaid, '21 (DET) Our Lady of Good Counsel Parish Plymouth, Plymouth, MI
Chaback, Rev. Msgr. Michael J., '70 (ALN) Retired. Curia: Leadership
Chabak, Rev. Msgr. Robert M., '72 (NEW) Retired.
Chabala, Rev. Brian J., '77 (DET) Retired.
Chabot, Rev. Peter L., *M.M.* '65 (NY) Retired. [MON] Maryknoll Fathers and Brothers (Catholic Foreign Mission Society of America, Inc.), Ossining, NY
Chabot, Rev. Roger P., '65 (PRT) Retired.
Chachlowski, Rev. Marek, '82 (NEW) St. Thomas More, Fairfield, NJ
Chackaleckel, Rev. Davis, *M.S.F.S.* '80 (NSH) St. Stephen, Old Hickory, TN
Chacko, Rev. Abraham Kalarickal, (SYM) Christ the King Syro-Malabar Knanaya Catholic Church DFW, Farmers Branch, TX
Chacko, Rev. Benny Alikandayil, '98 (EVN) Curia: Leadership Annunciation of the Lord, Evansville, IN
Chacko, Rev. Chanlis, '04 (PH) Our Lady of Mt. Carmel, Philadelphia, PA
Chacko, Rev. Doney, *R.C.J.* '15 (WH) St. James, McMechen, WV; St. John, Benwood, WV
Chacko, Rev. Jose B., '87 (BIR) Curia: Leadership St. James Catholic Parish, Gadsden, Gadsden, AL; [CAM] Gadsden State Campus Ministry - St. James Church, Gadsden, AL; [EFT] St. James Educational Foundation, Gadsden, AL
Chacko, Rev. Joseph, *I.M.S.* (HT) St. Andrew, Amelia, LA
Chacko, Rev. Joseph, '94 (MO) Curia: Offices and Directors
Chacko, Rev. Joseph M. C., '95 (MOB) St. Agatha Parish, Bay Minette, Bay Minette, AL; St. Robert Bellarmine, Atmore, AL
Chacko, Rev. Joseph T., '84 (NY) Holy Family, New York, NY
Chacko, Rev. Joy T., '92 (TR) Sacred Heart, Bay Head, NJ; St. Gabriel, Marlboro, NJ; The Church of St. Pio of Pietrelcina, Lavallette, N.J., Lavallette, NJ
Chacko, Rev. Mathai Pallurathil, (SYM) St. Antony Syro Malabar Catholic Mission, Milwaukee, WI
Chacko, Rev. Mathew, *C.M.I.* '84 (SAL) Immaculate Conception of the Blessed Virgin Mary Parish, Leoville, Inc., Leoville, KS; Sacred Heart Parish, Oberlin, Inc., Oberlin, KS; Sacred Heart Parish, Selden, Inc., Selden, KS
Chacko, Rev. Philip, '85 (FAR) Retired.
Chacko, Rev. Reji, (MIL) [MON] St. Camillus Communities, Inc., Wauwatosa, WI
Chacko, Rev. Sebastian V., '76 (HON) Retired.
Chacko, Rev. Thomas Pulikkeel, *SAC* '98 (MIL) [MON] Pallotti House, Milwaukee, WI
Chacko, Rev. Tojo, *H.G.N.* '09 (OG) St. Bernard's and St. Edmund's Parish, Ellenburg Center, NY
Chacon, Very Rev. Frank, '89 (GLP) Curia: Leadership St. Mary's, Farmington, NM
Chacon, Very Rev. Jaime H., '04 (YAK) Curia: Leadership; Offices and Directors Holy Rosary, Moxee, WA
Chacon, Rev. Jorge, '74 (NEW) Retired.
Chacon, Rev. William, '91 (BRK) St. Rita, Brooklyn, NY
Chacon Gonzalez, Rev. Oscar, *O.SS.T.* (ARE) Curia: Leadership
Chacon Gonzalez, Rev. Oscar A., *O.SS.T.* (PCE) Curia: Leadership
Chacon Gonzalez, Rev. Oscar Alexander, *O.SS.T.* (PCE) Santisima Trinidad, Ponce, PR
Chacon-Mora, Rev. Tomas Felipe, '03 (SJN) Inmaculada Concepcion, Carolina, PR; Ntra. Sra. Reina de la Paz, Carolina, PR
Chadwick, Very Rev. Brian D., '01 (GRY) Curia: Leadership; Offices and Directors Our Lady of Grace, Highland, IN
Chadwick, Rev. John J., '95 (NEW) Curia: Advisory Boards, Commissions, Committees, and Councils; Leadership; Offices and Directors; Organizations (affiliated, inter-Diocesan, miscellaneous/other) [COL] Seton Hall University, South Orange, NJ
Chadwick, Rev. John J., '95 (NEW) Curia: Advisory Boards, Commissions, Committees, and Councils
Chadwick, Rev. Keith Edward, '21 (KCK) Holy Trinity, Lenexa, KS
Chadwick, Rev. Lawrence A., '75 (RVC) St. John Nepomucene, Bohemia, NY
Chaffman, Rev. Msgr. Charles, '84 (LA) On Duty Outside Diocese.
Chaffman, Rev. Msgr. Charles J., '84 (LAV) Curia: Tribunal
Chagala, Rev. Arturo, '13 (DEN) On Duty Outside Diocese. Parochial Admin, St Michael Parish, Philadelphia, PA St. Anthony of Padua Catholic Parish in Denver, Denver, CO
Chahin, Rev. Krikor Gregory, '98 (SAT) Curia: Leadership
Chajkowski, Rev. Daniel, '15 (PAT) Chap, Morristown Mem Hosp
Chaker, Rev. Victor, '03 (NOR) Retired. Curia: Offices and Directors
Chakian, Rev. Joy, '78 (DET) Chap, Ascension Crittenton Hosp, Rochester; Beaumont Hosp... Our Mother of Perpetual Help Parish Oak Park, Oak Park, MI
Chakkappan, Rev. Poulose K., *M.F.* (OAK) [MON] Missionaries of Faith-India Inc., Fremont, CA
Chakkunny, Rev. Peter Akkanath, *C.M.I.* '98 (MET) Chap, Univ Med Ctr of Princeton at Plainsboro, Plainsboro
Chalackal, Rev. A. David, *C.M.I.* '88 (MET) Our Lady of Fatima, Piscataway, NJ; [HOS] Saint Peter's University Hospital, New Brunswick, NJ
Chalaco Vega, Rev. Jorge Luis, '06 (LA) Our Lady of the Rosary of Talpa, Los Angeles, CA
Chalbhagam, Rev. George, *C.M.I.* '86 (SAL) St. Columba Parish, Elmo, Inc., Elmo, KS; St. John the Evangelist Parish, Herington, Inc., Herington, KS; St. Phillip Parish, Hope, Inc., Hope, KS
Chalissery, Rev. Joy, '90 (BIR) Curia: Leadership Most Merciful Jesus Catholic Church, Madison, AL
Chalissery, Rev. Paul, '99 (SYM) Curia: Administration; Offices and Directors
Chalkey, Rev. Andrew, *OMI* '56 (BEL) Retired.
Challinor, Rev. Michael F., '91 (NY) Holy Name of Jesus, New Rochelle, NY; Sacred Heart of Jesus, Port Chester, NY
Challman, Rev. Stephen G., '96 (NY) On Sick Leave. St. Rita, Staten Island, NY
Chalmers, Rev. H. Edward, '79 (WOR) Curia: Leadership
Chalmers, Rev. H. Edward, (WOR) Prince of Peace, Princeton, MA
Chalmers, Rev. Jon, '12 (BIR) John Carroll Catholic High School, Birmingham, AL; Prince of Peace Catholic Parish, Birmingham, Birmingham, AL
Chalupa, Rev. Fred, '73 (AUS) Retired.
Chamberlain, Rev. James, '86 (AUS) St. Matthew, Rogers, TX; St. Monica, Cameron, TX
Chamberlain, Rev. Msgr. Robert J., '64 (DM) Retired.
Chamberlain, Rev. Thomas G., '70 (AUS) Retired.
Chamberland, Rev. Gary S., *C.S.C.* '98 (FTW) [COL] University of Notre Dame Du Lac, Notre Dame, IN; [MON] Holy Cross Community, Corby Hall, University of Notre Dame, Notre Dame, IN
Chamberland, Rev. Ross, *O.F.M.* '15 (BUF) [CAM] St. Bonaventure University, St. Bonaventure, NY; [MON] St. Bonaventure Friary, St. Bonaventure, NY
Chamberlin, Rev. Msgr. Mark, '68 (CC) Retired. Curia: Leadership
Chambers, Rev. Francis, *O.S.A.* '78 (PH) [COL] Villanova University, Villanova, PA; [MON] St. Thomas Monastery, Villanova, PA
Chambers, Rev. James, *O.M.I.* '06 (BO) [MON] Andre Garin Residence, Lowell, MA
Chambers, Rev. James, *O.M.I.* (CC) [CON] Oblate La Parra Center, Sarita, TX; [RTR] Oblate La Parra Center, Sarita, TX
Chambers, Rev. James, (MAN) [MON] Shrine of Our Lady of Grace, Colebrook, NH
Chambers, Rev. James, *O.M.I.* '06 (SAT) [MON] Missionary Oblates of Mary Immaculate of Texas, Southern Province (San Antonio USP Support Office), San Antonio, TX
Chambers, Rev. James, *O.M.I.* '06 (WDC) [MON] Missionary Oblates of Mary Immaculate, Washington, DC; [MON] Oblate Community, Washington, DC (>CHI) [EFT] Oblates for International Pastoral (Oblate International Pastoral Investment Trust), Chicago, IL
Chamblain, Rev. Joseph, *O.S.M.* '84 (CHI) Assumption of the Blessed Virgin Mary, Chicago, IL; [MON] Assumption Priory, Chicago, IL; [MON] Order of Friar Servants of Mary (Servites) United States of America Province, Inc., Chicago, IL
Chami, Rev. Christian Joseph, '22 (VEN) On Duty Outside Diocese.
Chamorro, Rev. Hans, '21 (MIA) St. Coleman, Pompano Beach, FL
Champagne, Rev. Michael, *C.J.C.* '94 (LAF) [MIS] Community of Jesus Crucified, St. Martinville, LA; [MIS] Community of Jesus Crucified - Priest Brother and Sister Servants, St. Martinville, LA; [RTR] Our Lady of Sorrows Retreat Center, St. Martinville, LA
Champagne, Rev. Michael, *C.J.C.* (NO) [SEM] Notre Dame Seminary Graduate School of Theology, New Orleans, LA
Champigny, Rev. Richard, *O.Carm.* '65 (PMB) St. Jude, Boca Raton, FL
Champlin, Rev. Eunice, (SY) Chap, St Joseph's Hosp Health Ctr, Syracuse
Champlin, Rev. William E., '93 (WOR) Curia: Social Services St. Leo, Leominster, MA
Champoux, Rev. Msgr. Thomas C., '67 (YAK) Curia: Leadership; Offices and Directors Christ the King, Richland, WA; St. Frances Xavier Cabrini, Benton City, WA; [CCH] Christ the King Parish Conference, Richland, WA
Chamwaza, Rev. Kasweka Joseph, '11 (BAL) [MIS] St. Mary's Seminary & University, Baltimore, MD; [MON] Society of St. Sulpice, Province of the United States, Baltimore, MD
Chan, Rev. Joseph, (LR) St. Leo, Hartford, AR
Chanama, Rev. Oliver, '80 (NY) Holy Innocents, New York, NY
Chanama, Rev. Oliver, (NY) Chap, Eric M Taylor Ctr, East Elmhurst
Chanan, Rev. Anthony S., '90 (BRK) St. Ephrem, Brooklyn, NY
Chanas, Rev. Stefan, '96 (NY) Parish of St. John Nepomucene, St. Frances Cabrini, and St. John the Martyr, New York, NY; St. Frances Cabrini, New York, NY; St. John the Martyr, New York, NY
Chanassery, Rev. Johnson, *O.C.D.* '99 (BRK) St. Joan of Arc, Jackson Heights, NY
Chan-A-Sue, Rev. Andrew, '00 (MIA) St. Bartholomew, Miramar, FL
Chancler, Rev. Joseph, *T.O.R.* '83 (ALT) [MON] St. Francis Friary at Mount Assisi, Loretto, PA
Chandler, Rev. Anthony L., '89 (L) Curia: Leadership (>FWT) [CCH] Catholic Charities, Diocese of Fort Worth, Inc., Fort Worth, TX
Chandy, Rev. Jose Panamattathil, (FTW) St. Vincent de Paul, Fort Wayne, IN
Chandy, Rev. Regimon, '91 (SAC) Pastor of Holy Spirit Parish, Fairfield, a corporation sole, Fairfield, CA
Chandy, Rev. Regimon Thandassery, '91 (SYM) St. John Paul II Syro-Malabar Knanaya Catholic Mission, Sacramento, Fairfield, CA
Chaney, Rev. Robert E., '88 (SAV) Curia: Leadership;

Offices and Directors Resurrection of Our Lord, Savannah, GA
Chang, Rev. Augustine, '11 (LA) St. Gregory Nazianzen, Los Angeles, CA
Chang, Rev. Cornelius P., *O.S.B.* '62 (GBG) [MON] Saint Vincent Archabbey, Latrobe, PA
Chang, Rev. John O., '00 (TR) St. Veronica, Howell, NJ
Chang, Rev. Joseph, *O.S.B.* '57 (JOL) Retired. [MON] St. Procopius Abbey, Lisle, IL
Chapa, Rev. Emilio Landeros, '08 (TUC) Saint Francis of Assisi Roman Catholic Parish - Yuma, Yuma, AZ; [MIS] Rachel's Vineyard Retreat Ministries Tucson and Southern Arizona, Inc., Hereford, AZ
Chapa, Rev. Eric G., '16 (CC) St. Martin, Kingsville, TX; [MIS] St. Thomas Aquinas Newman Center and Chapel (Texas A&M University Kingsville), Kingsville, TX
Chaparin, Rev. Taras, '13 (STF) Curia: Leadership Holy Protection of the Mother of God, Mt. Kisco, NY
Chaparin, Rev. Taras, (STF) Curia: Leadership
Chaparin, Rev. Taras, (STF) Curia: Offices and Directors
Chapdelaine, Rev. Gerard E., *S.J.* '66 (SEA) Bellarmine Preparatory School, Tacoma, WA
Chapel, Rev. Joseph, (NEW) Curia: Advisory Boards, Commissions, Committees, and Councils Our Lady of Mercy, Park Ridge, NJ
Chapel, Rev. Msgr. Joseph, (NEW) St. Andrew, Westwood, NJ
Chapin, Rev. Daniel L., '72 (OG) Retired. The Roman Catholic Church of St. Augustine in North Bangor, NY, North Bangor, NY
Chapin, Friar Jacinto Mary, (SY) [MON] Mount St. Francis Hermitage, Inc., Endicott, NY; [RTR] Mount St. Francis Hermitage, Inc., Endicott, NY
Chaplin, Rev. John G., '68 (E) Retired.
Chapman, Rev. Bonaventure, *O.P.* '17 (WDC) [SEM] Dominican House of Studies, Washington, DC
Chapman, Rev. Bonaventure, *O.P.* '17 (PRO) [MON] St. Thomas Aquinas Priory at Providence College, Providence, RI
Chapman, Rev. Lawrence J., '77 (MIL) Retired.
Chapman, Rev. Michael L., '69 (OKL) Retired.
Chapman, Rev. Robert J., '67 (PH) Retired. St. John Neumann, Bryn Mawr, PA
Chappell, Rev. James T., '67 (DUB) Retired.
Charboneau, Rev. Marion, *O.S.B.* '06 (KCK) [COL] Benedictine College, Atchison, KS; [MON] St. Benedict's Abbey, Atchison, KS
Charbonneau, Rev. Roger, (VEN) Curia: Leadership
Charbonneau, Rev. Roger L., '71 (BUR) Retired. Curia: Leadership
Charbonnet, Rev. Clayton J., '03 (NO) St. Angela Merici Roman Catholic Church, Metairie, Louisiana, Metairie, LA
Charchaflian, Rev. Michael Marie, '22 (SAM) Our Lady of Lebanon, Miami, FL
Charelus, Rev. Sudzer, (BO) [MON] Alberto Hurtado House, Boston, MA
Charito, Rev. Suan, (SFR) Good Shepherd, Pacifica, CA
Charland, Rev. George A., '60 (WOR) Retired.
Charland, Rev. Paul A., '71 (PRO) Retired.
Charles, Rev. Hayden, '20 (WCH) St. Patrick, Wichita, KS
Charles, Rev. Patrick, '06 (MIA) St. Clement, Fort Lauderdale, FL
Charles, Rev. Pierre Listo, (MIA) St. Bartholomew, Miramar, FL
Charles, Rev. Robes C., '99 (MIA) Sacred Heart, Homestead, FL
Charlton, Rev. Robert, *SS.CC.* '88 (BWN) Curia: Advisory Boards, Commissions, Committees, and Councils; Leadership Queen of Peace, Harlingen, TX (>FR) [MIS] Congregation of the Sacred Hearts - United States Province (Sacred Hearts Fathers; Sacred Hearts Missions), Fairhaven, MA
Charman, Rev. Eugene J., '71 (HRT) Retired.
Charnley, Rev. George, '76 (DET) Retired.
Charron, Rev. Jason, '08 (PIT) Chap, Jefferson Rgnl Med Ctr, Allegheny Cty; Baldwin Health... Curia: (>SJP) Offices and Directors (>SJP) Holy Trinity Ukrainian Catholic Church, Carnegie, PA; (>SJP) Our Lady of Perpetual Help, Wheeling, WV
Charters, Rev. Thomas, *G.H.M.* '75 (KNX) St. Michael the Archangel Catholic Church, Erwin, TN
Charuc Mox, Rev. Jaime E., *F.M.M.* '04 (MIL) St. Anthonys Congregation, Milwaukee, WI; St. Hyacinth's Congregation, Milwaukee, WI
Chase, Rev. Geoffrey P., *O.S.B.* '59 (PRO) Retired. [MON] Abbey of St. Gregory the Great (Order of St. Benedict in Portsmouth, Rhode Island, Benedictines of the English Congregation), Portsmouth, RI
Chase, Rev. Kenneth M., '84 (DET) Sacred Heart Parish Dearborn, Dearborn, MI
Chase, Very Rev. Lee P., '93 (ROC) Curia: Deaneries St. Lawrence, Rochester, NY
Chase, Rev. P. Geoffrey, *O.S.B.* '59 (PRO) Retired.
Chase, Rev. Raymond C., '78 (BAL) St. Vincent de Paul, Baltimore, MD; [NUR] The Neighborhoods at St. Elizabeth (St. Elizabeth Rehabilitation and Nursing Center), Baltimore, MD
Chatagnier, Rev. Cody, '16 (HT) St. Ann, Bourg, LA
Chatagnier, Rev. Cody, '16 (HT) Curia: Administration
Chateau, Rev. Ishmael Ixon, '06 (BO) Immaculate Conception, Stoughton, MA; St. James, Stoughton, MA
Chateau, Rev. Paul, '66 (DET) Our Mother of Perpetual Help Parish Oak Park, Oak Park, MI
Chathely, Rev. A. Biju, *C.M.I.* '05 (L) St. Bernadette Parish, Prospect, KY
Chau, Rev. Pedro Bismarck, '08 (NEW) Curia: Advisory Boards, Commissions, Committees, and Councils
Chau, Rev. Pedro Bismarck, '08 (NEW) Curia: Advisory Boards, Commissions, Committees, and Councils [CAM] The Newman Catholic Center at University Heights (Rutgers-Newark/NJIT/Essex), Newark, NJ
Chau, Rev. Peter, (NSH) Retired.
Chauvin, Rev. Gregory, '07 (LAF) St. Jules, Lafayette, LA
Chavajay, Rev. Juan, (JKS) Sacred Heart, Canton, MS
Chavajay, Rev. Juan, '97 (MGZ) Our Lady of the Purification, Lajas, PR
Chavarria, Rev. Horacio, '66 (BWN) Retired.
Chavarria, Rev. Jerome L., *C.Ss.R.* (CHL) St. James, Concord, NC
Chavarria, Rev. John, '11 (CC) Saint Michael the Archangel, Banquete, TX; St. Frances of Rome, Agua Dulce, TX
Chavenia, Rev. Nestor, '94 (TR) St. Mary, Barnegat, NJ
Chavez, Rev. Alberto, *S.D.B.* '07 (LA) St. Mary, Los Angeles, CA
Chavez, Rev. Alex, '12 (FRS) Good Shepherd Catholic Parish, Visalia, CA
Chavez, Rev. Arturo, '91 (SB) Retired. St. Vincent Ferrer, Sun City, CA
Chavez, Rev. Carlos, '84 (SFE) On Duty Outside Diocese. Cross International Ministry
Chavez, Rev. Eduardo, (YAK) St. Joseph's, Wenatchee, WA
Chavez, Rev. Frank, '76 (SAN) St. Anthony, Odessa, TX; St. Joseph, Odessa, TX
Chavez, Rev. Jose, '96 (MRY) Our Lady of Solitude, Soledad, CA
Chavez, Rev. Jose, *C.Ss.R.* '84 (SAT) [MON] North American Redemptorist Theology Residence, San Antonio, TX
Chavez, Rev. Jose M., '98 (GI) Curia: Offices and Directors St. Ann's, Lexington, NE
Chavez, Rev. Manuel, '96 (SR) Pastor of St. Helena Catholic Church of St. Helena, A Corporation Sole, St. Helena, CA
Chavez, Rev. Rafael L., '93 (OAK) Queen of All Saints, Concord, CA
Chavez, Rev. Ricardo, '16 (BWN) Christ the King, Brownsville, TX
Chavez, Rev. Ricardo A., '63 (OAK) Retired.
Chavez, Rev. Vincent P., '91 (SFE) On Leave.
Chavez Garnica, Rev. Jesus, '19 (DAL) On Administrative Leave.
Chavez Godoy, Rev. Alberto Jose, '21 (MIA) Our Lady of Lourdes, Miami, FL
Chavira, Rev. Manuel, *S.J.* (SFR) [MON] Loyola House Jesuit Community, San Francisco, CA
Cheah, Rev. Joseph, *O.S.M.* '92 (HRT) St. Ann's Church of Avon, Avon, CT
Cheah, Rev. Joseph M, *OSM* (CHI) [MON] Order of Friar Servants of Mary (Servites) United States of America Province, Inc., Chicago, IL
Cheba, Rev. Simon, *P.S.S.* '02 (BAL) [MON] Society of St. Sulpice, Province of the United States, Baltimore, MD
Cheble, Rt. Rev. Michel, '02 (NTN) Curia: Administration; Consultative Bodies Our Lady of Redemption, Warren, MI
Chebli, Rev. Samir, (SAM) Our Lady of Victory, Pittsburgh, PA
Check, Rev. Paul N., '97 (BGP) On Duty Outside Diocese. Exec. Dir. Shrine of Our Lady of Guadalupe, LaCrosse, WI (>LC) [MIS] Holy Cross (Seminary) Diocesan Center, La Crosse, WI; (>LC) [SHR] Shrine of Our Lady of Guadalupe, La Crosse, WI
Checkai, Rev. Ronald Leo, *O.P.* '14 (PRO) [MON] St. Thomas Aquinas Priory at Providence College, Providence, RI
Cheerakathil, Rev. Rijo, (SYM) St. Joseph Syro-Malabar Catholic Church (Tampa), Seffner, FL
Cheesman, Rev. Robert, *C.Ss.R.* '57 (BAL) Retired.
Chekri, Rev. Roger, (OLL) [MON] Maronite Order of the Blessed Virgin Mary, Ann Arbor, MI
Chelakunnel, Rev. Jobimon Joseph, *MCBS* '09 (SYM) St. Mary's Syro-Malabar Catholic Church, Pearland, TX
Chelena, Rev. Thomas, '68 (PRM) On Leave.
Chelich, Rev. James A., '76 (GR) St. Thomas the Apostle Parish, Grand Rapids, MI
Chembakassery, Rev. Vincent Lazar, (MO) Curia: Offices and Directors
Chemino, Rev. Stephen Scott, '93 (ALX) Curia: Miscellaneous / Other Offices St. Anthony of Padua, Bunkie, LA
Chen, Rev. Cesar, '19 (NEW) Sacred Heart, Lyndhurst, NJ
Chen, Rev. John S., (BO) St. Eulalia, Winchester, MA
Chen, Rev. Joseph Tongchun, *O.P.* '11 (WDC) [SEM] Dominican House of Studies, Washington, DC
Chen, Rev. Paul Feng, '07 (OAK) Queen of All Saints, Concord, CA
Chen, Rev. Reuben, '12 (DAL) On Administrative Leave.
Chen, Rev. Tommy, '08 (VIC) Curia: Leadership; Offices and Directors Our Lady of the Gulf, Port Lavaca, TX
Chen, Rev. Vincent P., '57 (MET) Retired. [MON] Maria Regina Residence, Somerset, NJ
Chenault, Rev. Richard A., '08 (BIR) Our Lady of the Valley Catholic Parish, Fort Payne, Fort Payne, AL
Chendumalli, Rev. Anthony, '16 (KCK) Annunciation, Frankfort, KS; St. Columbkille, Blaine, KS; St. Monica - St. Elizabeth, Blue Rapids, KS
Cheney, Rev. Craig I., '03 (MAN) Chap, Coos Cty House of Corrections North American Martyrs Parish, Colebrook, NH
Cheney, Rev. James, '95 (FAR) St. Paul's Newman Church of Fargo, Fargo, ND; [CAM] St. Paul's Newman Church of Fargo, Fargo, ND
Cheney, Rev. James W., '95 (FAR) Curia: (>MO) Offices and Directors [MIS] Newman Living, Fargo, ND
Chenier, Rev. Michael D., '09 (MAR) Curia: Offices and Directors Immaculate Conception of the Blessed Virgin Mary, Iron Mountain, MI
Chenot, Rev. Paul, *C.P.* '72 (BRK) Retired. [MON] Immaculate Conception Monastery, Jamaica, NY
Chenot, Rev. Paul, *C.P.* '72 (NY) [MON] The Congregation of the Passion - St. Paul of the Cross Province, Jamaica, NY
Cheon, Rev. Joachim, '01 (FRS) St. Mary, Buttonwillow, CA; St. Mary, Taft, CA
Cheong, Rev. Lucas Gyu Whan, *MG* '86 (LA) [MON] Guadalupe Missioners Procure, Los Angeles, CA
Cheong, Rev. Seonghoon, (CLV) St. Andrew Kim Pastoral Center, Cleveland, OH
Chepaitis, Rev. Peter, *O.F.M.* '72 (ALB) On Special Assignment. Bethany Ministries, Middleburgh [RTR] Bethany Ministries, Middleburgh, NY
Chepelskyy, Rev. Vasyl, '10 (PSC) Curia: Advisory Boards, Commissions, Committees, and Councils; Leadership SS. Peter and Paul, Beaver Meadows, PA; St. Mary's, Beaver Meadows, PA; St. Mary's, Nesquehoning, PA
Cheplic, Rev. Msgr. Peter A., '72 (NEW) Retired. [MON] St. John Vianney Residence for Retired Priests, Rutherford, NJ
Chepponis, Rev. James J., '85 (PIT) Curia: Leadership Resurrection, Pittsburgh, PA
Cherian, Rev. Jose, '01 (MAR) St. Agnes, Iron River, MI; St. Cecilia, Caspian, MI
Cherian, Rev. Reginon, (NY) Parish of St. Christopher and St. Patrick, Buchanan, NY
Cheriankunnel, Rev. Shibu, (OWN) St. Stephen Cathedral, Owensboro, KY
Chermeil, Rev. Tony, '91 (VEN) Curia: Leadership St. Francis of Assisi Parish in Grove City, Inc., Englewood, FL
Chern, Rev. James N., '99 (NEW) Curia: Offices and Directors [CAM] Newman Catholic Center at Montclair State University, Upper Montclair, NJ
Cherolikal, Rev. John, '74 (LUB) Retired.
Cherrez, Rev. Omoldo, '97 (LA) St. Alphonsus, Los Angeles, CA
Cherrez, Rev. Ornoldo, '97 (HON) St. Theresa, Kihei, HI
Cherry, Rev. Athanasius C., *O.S.B.* '68 (GBG) [MON] Saint Vincent Archabbey, Latrobe, PA (>PBR) St. Mary's, Bradenville, PA
Cherubini, Rev. Perry A., '85 (CAM) Curia: Leadership; Tribunal Holy Spirit High School, Absecon, N.J., Absecon, NJ; St. Joseph's Catholic Church, Sea Isle City, N.J., Sea Isle City, NJ
Cherunilath, Rev. Johnus S., *V.C.* (SYM) [MON] Vincentian House, Bensenville, IL

Cheruparambil, Rev. Francis, *V.C.* '81 (TR) Holy Family, Union Beach, NJ
Cheruparambil, Rev. Saji Matthew, *O.S.B.Silv.* '03 (STL) Sacred Heart Catholic Church, Crystal City, Crystal City, MO
Chervenak, Rev. Gregory, *O.F.M.Cap.* '79 (BAL) Our Lady of the Mountains, Roman Catholic Congregation, Inc., Cumberland, MD; [MON] Our Lady of the Mountains Friary, Cumberland, MD
Chesley, Rev. Michael, (DET) Chap, Wayne Cty Jail, Detroit; Monroe Cty Jail; St Clair…
Chesney, Rev. Michael E., *S.J.* '91 (LAF) [MON] St. Charles College, Grand Coteau, LA
Chester, Rev. Paschal, *S.V.D.* (PT) Curia: Offices and Directors
Chethalil, Rev. Bins Jose, (PH) Curia: Evangelization
Chethalil, Rev. Bins Jose, (PH) Assumption B.V.M., Feasterville, PA
Chethalil, Rev. Bins Jose, '05 (SYM) Christ the King Knanaya Catholic Church of New Jersey, Carteret, NJ
Chettaniyil, Rev. Roy, '04 (NY) Immaculate Conception, Irvington, NY
Chettiyath, Rev. Shoby M., '06 (SPC) Curia: Administration; Advisory Boards, Commissions, Committees, and Councils; Consultative Bodies; Leadership; Offices and Directors St. Francis of Assisi, Nixa, MO
Chettoor, Rev. Jose, (SCL) Holy Cross, Pierz, MN; St. John Nepomuk, Lastrup, MN
Chevalier, Rev. Martin, (MO) Curia: Offices and Directors
Chevalier, Rev. Martin G., '83 (DM) Retired.
Chevalier, Rev. Thomas H., '80 (ALB) St. Peter, Saratoga Springs, NY
Cheverria Jimenez, Rev. Jose Orlando, '97 (CHR) San Sebastian Mission, Greenville, SC; St. Mary, Greenville, SC
Chew, Rev. Randolph G., '71 (PRO) Retired.
Chi, Rev. SangWoo, (PH) St. Christopher, Philadelphia, PA
Chia, Rev. James, (CLV) St. Rocco, Cleveland, OH; [MON] Mercedarians (Fathers of Our Lady of Mercy, Inc. / Order of the B.V.M. of Mercy / Mercedarian Friars USA), Cleveland, OH
Chiagorom, Rev. Michael, '94 (SFE) San Felipe de Neri, Albuquerque, NM
Chiang, Rev. Msgr. Joseph, '59 (NEW) Retired. [MON] St. John Vianney Residence for Retired Priests, Rutherford, NJ
Chiantella, Rev. David M., '82 (R) Saint Mary, Mother of the Church Catholic Parish of Garner, Garner, NC
Chiapa-Villarreal, Rev. Hector, '06 (DEN) St. Therese Catholic Parish in Aurora, Aurora, CO
Chiaramonte, Rev. Anthony, '65 (ALB) Retired. Curia: Offices and Directors
Chiaravalle, Rev. Dominic M., '65 (PH) Retired.
Chiawa, Rev. Francis, '96 (MEM) St. Augustine, Memphis, TN
Chica, Rev. Esterminio, '07 (NEW) Curia: Advisory Boards, Commissions, Committees, and Councils Christ, the King, Jersey City, NJ
Chica, Rev. Esterminio, '06 (NEW) Curia: Advisory Boards, Commissions, Committees, and Councils
Chicas, Rev. Hector, *O. P.* '96 (ELP) St. Patrick, Canutillo, TX
Chicas, Rev. Jose Anibal, '13 (DEN) On Leave. St. Augustine Catholic Parish in Brighton, Brighton, CO
Chicas, Rev. Santos Rafael Ramirez, '15 (RIC) Our Lady of Lourdes, Richmond, VA
Chichester, Rev. Jeff, '18 (ROC) Church of St. John of Rochester of Perinton, New York, Fairport, NY
Chichester, Rev. Zachariah, (ALB) Our Lady of Hope, Whitehall, NY; St. Ann's Roman Catholic Church, Fort Ann, NY; St. Mary's Roman Catholic Church Roman Catholic Community of Granville, Granville, NY
Chichetto, Rev. James W., *C.S.C.* '68 (FR) [COL] Holy Cross Fathers Religious, North Easton, MA; [COL] Stonehill College, North Easton, MA
Chick, Rev. Jesse Chi, *C.F.I.C.* (COL) Chap, Hospital Ministry St. Elizabeth, Columbus, OH
Chicoine, Rev. Trevor, '17 (DM) Curia: Offices and Directors SS. Peter and Paul, Atlantic, IA; St. Mary, Anita, IA
Chidiac, Rev. Msgr. Bakhos, (OLL) Our Lady of Lebanon Maronite Catholic Church, Wheeling, WV
Chidozie, Rev. Marcus, '93 (DAL) St. Joseph Catholic Parish - Commerce, Commerce, TX
Chieffo, Rev. Msgr. Ralph J., '75 (PH) St. Mary Magdalen, Media, PA
Chiffriller, Rev. Edward, *S.S.J.* '74 (BR) St. Francis Xavier Catholic Church, Baton Rouge, LA
Chigbo, Rev. Chijioke A., (MO) Curia: Offices and Directors
Chikankheni, Rev. Dominic, (SEA) Holy Disciples, Puyallup, WA
Chikawe, Rev. Hugh, '71 (SP) Curia: Administration [CEM] Miserere Guild, Inc. (Calvary Catholic Cemetery), Clearwater, FL
Chikere, Rev. Angelbert, '20 (SJ) On Special Assignment. Dir., Office of Life, Justice & Peace Curia: Offices and Directors St. Lawrence, the Martyr, Santa Clara, CA
Chikerizi Ihuoma, Rev. Robert, (SB) Sacred Heart, Rancho Cucamonga, CA
Chikezie, Rev. Emmanuel, '89 (BEA) [HOS] CHRISTUS Southeast Texas Health System - St. Elizabeth, Beaumont, TX
Chikweto, Rev. Timothy C., *P.S.S.* '02 (BAL) [MON] Society of St. Sulpice, Province of the United States, Baltimore, MD
Chilczuk, Rev. Marcin L., '14 (BRK) On Leave.
Child, Rev. John F., '59 (DET) Retired.
Childress, Rev. Richard, '18 (NSH) St. John Vianney, Gallatin, TN
Childs, Rev. Guy A., '00 (ALB) St. Michael the Archangel, South Glens Falls, NY
Chilen, Rev. Msgr. Michael D., '69 (CC) Retired.
Chiles, Rev. Richard, *O. Praem.* '88 (GB) Retired. [MON] St. Norbert Abbey, De Pere, WI
Chillikulam, Rev. Thomas, *S.J.* (CHI) [MIS] President's Office, Chicago, IL
Chillog, Rev. Thomas A., '84 (STU) Curia: Deaneries; Offices and Directors St. Frances Cabrini, Colerain, OH; St. Mary's, St. Clairsville, OH; [CAM] Ohio University - Eastern, St. Clairsville, OH
Chilou, Rev. Raphael Jacques, *C.F.R.* '93 (NEW) [MON] Franciscan Friars of the Renewal (Most Blessed Sacrament Friary), Newark, NJ
Chilson, Very Rev. Elbert, '78 (DEN) St. Stephen Catholic Parish in Glenwood Springs, Glenwood Springs, CO
Chilson, Rev. Richard, *C.S.P.* '72 (SFR) Retired. Old St. Mary's Cathedral & Chinese Mission, San Francisco, CA
Chimera, Rev. Angelo M., '69 (BUF) Retired. All Saints, Buffalo, NY
Chimese, Rev. Abraham, *OMI* (SAT) [SEM] Blessed Mario Borzaga Formation Community, San Antonio, TX
Chimezie, Rev. Ngozichukwu, (RVC) Corpus Christi, Mineola, NY
Chimiak, Rev. Msgr. Karl A., '80 (WDC) Retired. St. Joseph, Beltsville, MD (>CHR) Our Lady Star of the Sea, North Myrtle Beach, SC
Chincha, Rev. Eddie, *SDB* '19 (SP) Cristo Rey Tampa Salesian High School, Tampa, FL
Chincha, Rev. Eduardo, *SDB* '19 (SP) [RTR] Mary Help of Christians Center, Tampa, FL
Chinchar, Rev. Gerald, (SAT) [NUR] Marianist Residence: Skilled Nursing, San Antonio, TX
Chinchilla, Rev. Ricardo Antonio, *CJM* '93 (SD) Pastor of Saint James Catholic Parish, Solana Beach, a corporation sole, Solana Beach, CA; [MIS] Saint James Catholic Parish in Solana Beach, CA Real Property Support Corporation, Solana Beach, CA
Chinedu, Rev. Emmanuel, (B) Holy Apostles, Meridian, ID
Chineke, Rev. Peter O., '20 (SFD) St. Thomas the Apostle, Decatur, IL
Ching, Rev. Brian C., *C.S.C.* '13 (FTW) Curia: Offices and Directors [COL] University of Notre Dame Du Lac, Notre Dame, IN; [EFT] Father Edward Sorin Trust, Notre Dame, IN; [MON] Holy Cross Community, Corby Hall, University of Notre Dame, Notre Dame, IN
Ching, Rev. Philip, '09 (DET) Holy Family Parish Memphis, Memphis, MI; St. Augustine Parish Richmond, Richmond, MI; St. Mary Mystical Rose Parish Armada, Armada, MI
Chinnabathini, Rev. Antony, (B) St. Ann's, Bonners Ferry, ID
Chinnabathini, Rev. Rayappa, (SPC) Chap, South Central Corr Ctr St. Mark, Houston, MO
Chinnaiyan, Rev. Anthony Kanagaraj, *HGN* '05 (PRT) Our Lady of the Eucharist Parish, Lincoln, ME
Chinnapan, Rev. Robert K., *M.F.* (GB) St. Edward, Appleton, WI; St. Nicholas, Freedom, WI (>OAK) [MON] Missionaries of Faith-India Inc., Fremont, CA
Chinnappan, Rev. Alwin, '21 (BO) Saint Agnes, Arlington, MA; St. Camillus, Arlington, MA
Chinnappan, Rev. Benjamin, (CHI) [MIS] Dalit Solidarity, Des Plaines, IL
Chinnappan, Rev. Benjamin, '88 (MO) Curia: Offices and Directors
Chinnappan, Rev. John Buckthese, (CAM) The Parish of Saint Monica, Atlantic City, NJ
Chinnappan, Rev. Peter, '85 (DAL) Holy Family Catholic Parish, Van Alstyne, TX; St. Michael Catholic Parish - McKinney, McKinney, TX
Chinnappan, Rev. Philip, (GF) Curia: Offices and Directors St. John the Evangelist, Baker, MT
Chinnappan, Rev. Raymond, *OFM Cap* (DET) [MIS] Solanus Casey Center, Detroit, MI; [MON] St. Bonaventure Monastery, Detroit, MI
Chinnici, Friar Joseph, *OFM* (SD) Pastor of Immaculate Conception Catholic Parish, San Diego, a corporation sole, San Diego, CA
Chinthamalla, Rev. Francis, (FWT) Santa Rosa, Knox City, TX; St. Joseph, Munday, TX
Chiodo, Rev. Msgr. Frank, '76 (DM) Retired.
Chiola, Rev. Richard L., '72 (SFD) Retired.
Chipiro, Rev. Welcome, '08 (FBK) Curia: Leadership Holy Rosary Catholic Church Tok, Tok, AK; Our Lady of Sorrows Catholic Church Delta Junction, Delta Junction, AK; St. Nicholas Catholic Church North Pole, North Pole, AK; [MIS] St. Mary's of the Lake, Fairbanks, AK
Chirappurathu, Rev. Joseph, '88 (SYM) St. Jude Syro-Malabar Knanaya Catholic Parish of South Florida, Fort Lauderdale, FL
Chirayath, Rev. Chummar, *OSJ* '78 (MRY) St. Vincent De Paul, Davenport, CA; [MON] Oblates of St. Joseph Provincial House and Shrine, Santa Cruz, CA; [SHR] Shrine of St. Joseph Guardian of the Redeemer, Santa Cruz, CA
Chirayath, Rev. Joseph, '75 (TLS) Retired.
Chirayath, Rev. Sijo, *CMI* '11 (SAC) Chap, St. Patrick-St. Vincent High School, Vallejo
Chiriaco, Rev. William, (PH) Bishop Shanahan High School, Downingtown, PA
Chiriaco, Rev. William J., '86 (PH) Curia: Advisory Boards, Commissions, Committees, and Councils St. Agnes, West Chester, PA
Chirichella, Rev. Vincent G., '07 (BRK) St. Joseph, Astoria, NY
Chirichiello, Rev. Richard, *O.S.B.* '95 (GBG) Assoc Chap, Excela Health - Westmoreland Hosp, Greensburg [MON] Saint Vincent Archabbey, Latrobe, PA
Chirino Gonzalez, Rev. Wilmer, '20 (PH) St. Thomas Aquinas, Philadelphia, PA
Chirovsky, Mitred Archpriest Andriy, '80 (STN) Curia: Offices and Directors [MIS] Metropolitan Andrey Sheptytsky Institute of Eastern Christian Studies, Flagstaff, AZ
Chirovsky, Rev. Ivan, '90 (PBR) [SEM] Byzantine Catholic Seminary of SS. Cyril and Methodius, Pittsburgh, PA
Chirovsky, Rev. Ivan, '90 (SJP) Curia: Offices and Directors
Chirovsky, Rev. John, '90 (SJP) Curia: Offices and Directors
Chishimba, Rev. Adrian, '10 (AUS) On Sick Leave.
Chisholm, Rev. Gregory, *S.S.J.* (BAL) [MON] Jesuit Community of Loyola University Maryland, Inc., Baltimore, MD
Chisholm, Rev. Gregory, *S.J.* '93 (NY) All Saints, New York, NY
Chisholm, Rev. Thomas, *O.S.B.* '89 (JOL) Retired. [MON] St. Procopius Abbey, Lisle, IL
Chittattukara, Rev. Shiju, *S.D.V.* (SYM) St. Thomas Syro-Malabar Catholic Mission, Brooklyn, New York, Inc., Brooklyn, NY
Chittattukara, Rev. Shiju, *SDV* '07 (PAT) [MON] Father Justin Vocationary (Vocationist Fathers), Florham Park, NJ; [RTR] Sanctuary of Mary-Our Lady of the Holy Spirit (Vocationist Fathers), Branchville, NJ; [RTR] Vocationist Fathers Retreat Center, Florham Park, NJ
Chitteth, Rev. Biju, (AUS) On Special Assignment. St. Paul Chong Hasang, Harker Heights, TX
Chitteth, Rev. Mathai Chacko, *CFIC* (STP) St. Bonaventure, Bloomington, MN; [MON] Congregation of the Sons of the Immaculate Conception, Bloomington, MN
Chittilapilly, Rev. Benny, *SDV* '11 (BUR) Mater Dei, Newport, VT
Chittilappilly, Rev. Benny, *S.D.V.* (PAT) St. Gerard Majella, Paterson, NJ
Chiu, Rev. Bit-Shing Abraham, '90 (SAC) Pastor of St. John the Evangelist Parish, Carmichael, a corporation sole, Carmichael, CA
Chizmar, Rev. Msgr. John G., '75 (ALN) Curia: Leadership St. Peter the Fisherman, Lake Harmony, PA; [MIS] Retirement Plan for the Ordained Diocesan Priests of the Diocese of Allentown, Allentown, PA
Chlebo, Rev. John C., '80 (CLV) Curia: Clergy and Religious Services St. Christopher, Rocky River, OH
Chleborad, Rev. Gerald, '60 (CHY) Retired.
Chlopecki, Rev. Robert J., '74 (BEL) Retired.
Chmiel, Rev. Bronislaw, '69 (CHI) Retired.

Chmiel, Rev. Gerald J., '70 (TOL) Retired.
Chmielewski, Rev. Philip J., *S.J.* '81 (LA) [MON] Jesuit Community, Los Angeles, CA
Chmil, Rev. John J., '95 (SCR) St. Ann, Williamsport, PA
Chmura, Rev. Gary, '78 (CLV) Chap, Northcoast Behavioral Healthcare Sys North Campus; So… Our Lady of Peace, Cleveland, OH
Chmura, Rev. Gary D., '78 (CLV) Cleveland Psychiatric Institute; Cuyahoga County Juvenile St. Adalbert, Cleveland, OH
Chmura, Rev. Julian, '64 (DET) Retired.
Chmurski, Rev. Marek, '95 (FR) St. Margaret, Buzzards Bay, MA
Cho, Rev. Hong-Ray Peter, '11 (NEW) Curia: Organizations (affiliated, inter-Diocesan, miscellaneous/ other) [COL] Seton Hall University, South Orange, NJ; [SEM] College Seminary of the Immaculate Conception (Saint Andrew's Hall), South Orange, NJ
Cho, Rev. James, (NEW) Parish of St. Joseph, Demarest, NJ
Cho, Rev. Min (Joseph) Hyun, '99 (NEW) Curia: Organizations (affiliated, inter-Diocesan, miscellaneous/ other)
Cho, Rev. Minhyun, '99 (NEW) Curia: (>MO) Offices and Directors; Offices and Directors St. Michael, Palisades Park, NJ
Cho, Rev. Ray P., (NEW) On Duty Outside Diocese. Casa Santa Maria, Rome
Chocarro, Rev. Antonio, (CGS) Retired.
Chochol, Rev. Ronald C., '64 (STL) Retired.
Chodakowski, Rev. Ireneusz, *M.I.C.* '78 (MIL) St. Peter's Congregation, Kenosha, WI
Chodkowski, Rev. Grzegorz, '03 (WOR) St. Joseph Basilica, Webster, MA
Chodzynski, Rev. Jacek, *O.C.D.* '88 (GRY) [MON] Discalced Carmelite Fathers Monastery, Munster, IN
Choi, Rev. DaeJe, *S.J.* '03 (LA) St. Agnes, Los Angeles, CA
Choi, Rev. Hakseng, '13 (R) St. Andrew Kim, Fayetteville, NC
Choi, Rev. Joseph, '17 (LA) St. John Vianney, Hacienda Heights, CA
Choi, Rev. Jungjin Leo, '11 (BIR) St. Luke Hwang, Birmingham, AL
Choi, Rev. Martino I., '15 (WDC) St. Patrick, Rockville, MD
Chojda, Rev. Artur, *O.C.D.* '03 (STA) [MON] Discalced Carmelite Fathers of Florida, Bunnell, FL
Chojnacki, Rev. Anthony, (MIL) [MON] Queen of Peace Friary (Franciscan Friars of the Assumption B.V.M. Province), Burlington, WI
Cholewa, Rev. Gregory, *OMI* '76 (BEL) [MON] Missionary Oblates of Mary Immaculate - St. Henry's Oblate Residence, Belleville, IL
Chompoochan, Rev. Weersak (Lee), '06 (OAK) Christ the King, Pleasant Hill, CA
Chong, Rev. Vicente, (BO) [MON] Isaac Jogues House, Brighton, MA
Chontos, Rev. Joseph, '82 (KCK) Chaplain, KS Juvenile Correctional Complex, Topeka
Choorackal, Rev. Vijumon, '02 (GI) Curia: Offices and Directors Church of the Resurrection, Grand Island, NE
Choorackunnel, Rev. John V., *C.M.I.* '64 (TLS) On Special Assignment. Chap, Saint Francis Hosp, Tulsa [HOS] Saint Francis Hospital, Tulsa, OK
Choquet, Rev. Alexei H., '83 (CHL) On Duty Outside Diocese.
Choquette, Rev. David, '98 (NOR) Curia: Leadership
Choquette, Rev. David P., '98 (NOR) Curia: Leadership; Offices and Directors St. Therese of Lisieux Parish, Putnam, CT
Choragwicki, Rev. Stanislaw, (RVC) St. Frances de Chantal, Wantagh, NY
Chorey, Rev. Robert W, (RNO) Our Lady of the Snows, Reno, NV
Chorey, Rev. Robert W., '02 (RNO) Curia: Leadership; Offices and Directors
Chornopyskii, Rev. Andrii, (PHU) Saints Joachim and Anna Ukrainian Catholic Church, Front Royal, VA; Ukrainian Catholic National Shrine of the Holy Family, Washington, DC
Chorpenning, Rev. Joseph, *O.S.F.S.* (WIL) Salesianum School, Wilmington, DE
Chorpenning, Rev. Joseph F., *O.S.F.S.* '79 (PH) [MON] Villa de Sales Oblate Residence, Wyndmoor, PA
Chortos, Rev. Donald, '66 (PIT) Retired. St. James, Washington, PA; St. Katharine Drexel Parish, Bentleyville, PA
Chortos, Rev. George F., '64 (PIT) Retired. St. James, Washington, PA
Choutapalli, Very Rev. Joseph, '90 (SAN) Curia: Advisory Boards, Commissions, Committees, and Councils St. Ambrose, Wall, TX
Chovanec, Rev. Paul R., '72 (GAL) St. Justin Martyr, Houston, TX
Chowaran, Rev. Tomy, '99 (BAK) Curia: Offices and Directors Immaculate Conception (St. Mary's Catholic Church), Hood River, OR
Chowning, Rev. Daniel, *O.C.D.* '88 (MIL) [MON] Discalced Carmelite Friars of Holy Hill, Inc., Hubertus, WI
Chowning, Rev. Michael, *O.F.M.* '63 (IND) Holy Family Catholic Church, Oldenburg, Inc., Oldenburg, IN
Chowrappa, Rev. Anthony, (SFD) All Saints, White Hall, IL; St. John the Evangelist, Carrollton, IL; St. Michael, Greenfield, IL
Choy, Rev. Byung, (PHX) St. Columba Kim Roman Catholic Mission, Chandler, AZ
Chripko, Rev. Vladimir, *C.O.* '95 (NY) Parish of St. Paul and St. Ann, Congers, NY; St. Ann, Congers, NY; [CON] Dominican Convent of Our Lady of the Rosary, Sparkill, NY; [MIS] New York Oratory of St. Philip Neri, Inc., Sparkill, NY
Chrisman, Rev. Michael, '11 (PBL) Curia: Leadership; Offices and Directors Shrine of St. Therese, Pueblo, CO
Christensen, Rev. Brian Patrick, '99 (RC) Curia: Leadership; Offices and Directors Cathedral of Our Lady of Perpetual Help, Rapid City, SD; St. Michael's, Hermosa, SD
Christensen, Rev. Christian, *I.S.P.* '71 (AUS) Retired. [MON] Schoenstatt Fathers, Austin, TX
Christensen, Rev. Christopher P., '14 (ARL) St. Rita, Alexandria, VA
Christensen, Rev. Joseph, *F.M.I.* '97 (FAR) [CCH] Saint Gianna and Pietro Molla Maternity Home, Minto, ND; [MIS] Third Order Franciscans of Mary Immaculate, Minto, ND
Christensen, Rev. Michael R., '79 (LIN) Curia: Leadership St. Anthony, Steinauer, NE
Christiaens, Rev. Matthew, '22 (HEL) Resurrection Parish: Series 158, LLC, Bozeman, MT
Christian, Rev. Jason M., '13 (CHL) St. John the Baptist, Tryon, NC
Christian, Rev. John, (RIC) St. Bridget, Richmond, VA
Christian, Rev. Lawrence J., '83 (SAT) On Leave.
Christiansen, Rev. Cal R., '08 (SEA) Curia: Leadership St. Pius X, Mountlake Terrace, WA
Christiansen, Rev. Drew, *S.J.* '72 (WDC) [COL] Georgetown University, Washington, DC
Christianson, Rev. John, '15 (CR) Curia: Offices and Directors Sacred Heart (Wilton), Wilton, MN; St. Mary's Mission Church, Red Lake, MN
Christianson, Rev. Raphael, *O.P.* '17 (WDC) [SEM] Dominican House of Studies, Washington, DC
Christofferson, Rev. Kevin, '97 (HEL) Curia: Offices and Directors Immaculate Conception Parish: Series 543, LLC, Polson, MT; Sacred Heart Parish: Series 544, LLC, Ronan, MT; Santo Tomas, Helena, MT
Christopher, Rev. Brian J., *S.J.* '09 (STL) [MON] USA Central & Southern Province, Society of Jesus, St. Louis, MO
Christopher, Rev. Patrick J., '91 (STL) Sacred Heart Catholic Church, Valley Park, Valley Park, MO; St. Joseph Catholic Church, Apple Creek, Apple Creek, MO; St. Maurus Catholic Church, Biehle, MO
Christy, Very Rev. Timothy A., '92 (MET) Cathedral of St. Francis of Assisi, Metuchen, NJ
Christy, Very Rev. Timothy A., '92 (MET) Curia: Consultative Bodies; Evangelization
Christy, Rev. William H., *C.S.Sp.* '92 (PIT) [COL] Duquesne University of the Holy Spirit, Pittsburgh, PA; [MON] Congregation of the Holy Spirit Province of the United States, Bethel Park, PA
Chriszt, Rev. Dennis, *C.PP.S.* '82 (CIN) [MON] Society of the Precious Blood, United States Province, Inc., Dayton, OH
Chrusciel, Rev. Bogumil, '68 (NEW) Retired. St. Stanislaus, Newark, NJ
Chryst, Rev. Robert D., '68 (SY) Retired.
Chrzan, Rev. John P., '03 (CHI) St. Gilbert, Grayslake, IL
Chrzastek, Rev. Brian, *O.P.* '92 (WDC) [SEM] Dominican House of Studies, Washington, DC
Chu, Rev. Ly, (DM) Church of St. Peter Vietnamese Catholic Community, Des Moines, IA
Chu, Rev. Peter Minh Quang, *S.J.* '68 (SJ) [MON] Sacred Heart Jesuit Center, Los Gatos, CA
Chu, Rev. Peter Ngoc Thanh, '55 (GAL) Retired.
Chu, Rev. Quang Vinh, '91 (ORG) St. Mary's by the Sea, Huntington Beach, CA
Chua, Rev. Freddie T., '98 (LA) Annunciation, Arcadia, CA
Chudy, Rev. Carl, *sx* '86 (BO) [MIS] Our Lady of Fatima Shrine, Holliston, MA; [MON] Xaverian Missionaries, Holliston, MA
Chukwu, Rev. Evaristus, *MSP* (GAL) St. Peter the Apostle, Houston, TX
Chukwu, Rev. Kenneth, (SEA) [HOS] Providence Regional Medical Center Everett, Everett, WA
Chukwu, Rev. Michael, '11 (NO) [SEM] Saint Joseph Seminary College, Saint Benedict, LA
Chukwuani, Rev. Charles, (NY) Chap, Dir, Bon Secours Cmty Hosp, Port Jervis; St Anthony…
Chukwudiebere, Rev. Maxwell U., (BO) St. Catherine of Siena, Norwood, MA
Chukwukere, Rev. Maurice Ejikeme, '08 (SPC) St. Mary, West Plains, MO
Chukwuleta, Rev. Daniel, '91 (FTW) St. Francis Xavier, Pierceton, IN
Chukwuma, Rev. Bartholomew, '09 (NO) Chap, East Jefferson Gen Hosp, Metairie Blessed Trinity, New Orleans, LA
Chukwuma, Rev. Felix, '05 (BEL) Holy Cross, Newton, IL; St. Joseph, Olney, IL; St. Lawrence, Lawrenceville, IL
Chukwuma, Rev. Francis, '96 (FTW) Curia: Offices and Directors Most Precious Blood, Fort Wayne, IN
Chukwumalume, Rev. Sylvester, (RVC) Chap, Northwell, Southside Hosp
Chumo, Rev. Augustine, '98 (ROC) Immaculate Conception, Ithaca, NY
Chun, Rev. Cheeyoon, '21 (ORG) Curia: Offices and Directors Holy Family Catholic Church, Orange, CA
Chun, Rev. Francis, '63 (P) Retired.
Chun, Rev. Glen, *S.J.* '08 (CHI) [COL] Jesuit Community at Loyola University Chicago, Chicago, IL; [MIS] Holy Family Church, Inc., Chicago, IL; [MIS] Jesuit International Missions, Inc., Chicago, IL; [MIS] Society of Jesus Worldwide, Chicago, IL; [MIS] The Jesuit Partnership, Chicago, IL; [MIS] USA Midwest Province of the Society of Jesus, Inc., Chicago, IL; [MON] Chicago Province of the Society of Jesus, Chicago, IL; [MON] Wisconsin Province of the Society of Jesus, Chicago, IL
Chun, Rev. Steve, '19 (NEW) Madonna, Fort Lee, NJ
Chung, Rev. Andrew, '14 (LA) St. Pancratius, Lakewood, CA
Chung, Rev. Anthony, '71 (SFR) Retired.
Chung, Rev. Brian, '00 (LA) Mother of Sorrows, Los Angeles, CA
Chung, Rev. Francis, '93 (AUS) St. Andrew Kim Taegon Korean Catholic Church, Austin, TX
Chung, Rev. John Mary, '11 (SFR) (>LA) [COL] Thomas Aquinas College, Santa Paula, CA
Chung, Rev. John Y., (SFR) On Academic Leave.
Chung, Rev. Maurice Haechul, (BAL) Holy Korean Martyrs, Baltimore, MD
Chuong Doan, Rev. Joseph Huy, '64 (SPC) Retired. [MON] Congregation of the Mother of the Redeemer, Carthage, MO
Chuong Nguyen, Rev. Paul, *S.D.B.* (LA) [RTR] St. Joseph's Salesian Youth Renewal Center, Rosemead, CA
Church, Rev. Wenceslaus, '59 (CHI) [MON] St. Peter's Friary, Chicago, IL
Churchill, Rev. Michael, '22 (WIN) Pax Christi, Rochester, MN
Churran, Rev. Jason, (PIT) Chap, Southwestern Nursing and Rehab Ctr, Allegheny Cty
Chuwa, Rev. Leonard, *A.J.* (STA) On Special Assignment. St Vincents/Ascension Health, Jacksonville St. Paul's, Jacksonville, FL
Chwalek, Rev. Kazimierz, *M.I.C.* '87 (SPR) [MON] Congregation of Marian Fathers of The Immaculate Conception of the Most Blessed Virgin Mary, Stockbridge, MA
Chwalek, Rev. Kazimierz, *M.I.C.* '87 (LIT) Curia: Clergy and Religious Services
Chycinski, Rev. Gregory A., '71 (MIL) Retired.
Chylinski, Rev. Keith J., '07 (PH) Curia: Clergy and Religious Services [SEM] Theological Seminary of St. Charles Borromeo, Wynnewood, PA
Chylko, Rev. Gerard, *C.Ss.R.* '79 (PH) St. Peter the Apostle, Philadelphia, PA
Ciaccio, Rev. Accursio, *F.S.C.B.* '08 (DEN) Nativity of Our Lord Catholic Parish in Broomfield, Broomfield, CO; [MON] Priestly Fraternity of St. Charles Borromeo (F.S.C.B.), Broomfield, CO
Ciampaglio, Rev. Msgr. Joseph M., (PAT) Retired.
Ciancimino, Rev. David S., *S.J.* '88 (BUF) Canisius High School, Buffalo, NY; [MON] The Canisius Jesuit Community, Inc., Buffalo, NY
Ciappi-Azcorra, Rev. Angel L., '98 (SJN) Cristo Redentor, San Juan, PR
Ciaramitaro, Rev. James, *O.F.M. Conv.* '88 (MIL) St. Josaphat Congregation, Milwaukee, WI
Ciaramitaro, Rev. Msgr. Victor P., '72 (MEM) Retired.

Curia: Advisory Boards, Commissions, Committees, and Councils Our Lady of Perpetual Help, Germantown, TN
Ciaston, Rev. Krzysztof D., '07 (CHI) St. Paul the Apostle, Gurnee, IL
Ciavaglia, Rev. Julio M., *C.R.S.P.* '66 (BUF) [SEM] St. Anthony M. Zaccaria Seminary, Youngstown, NY; [SHR] Basilica of the National Shrine of Our Lady of Fatima, Inc., Youngstown, NY
Ciba, Rev. Thomas J., '74 (NEW) Retired. Our Lady of Czestochowa, Jersey City, NJ
Cibelli, Rev. Ernest W., '09 (BAL) St. Mary, Hagerstown, MD
Ciccarino, Rev. Christopher M., '96 (NEW) Curia: Organizations (affiliated, inter-Diocesan, miscellaneous/ other) [COL] Seton Hall University, South Orange, NJ; [SEM] Immaculate Conception Seminary School of Theology, South Orange, NJ
Ciccolini, Rev. Samuel R., '69 (CLV) Retired. Immaculate Conception, Akron, OH
Ciccone, Rev. Joseph Anthony, *CSP* '89 (NY) [MON] Paulist Fathers' Motherhouse, New York, NY
Ciccone, Rev. Mark, *S.J.* '85 (LA) [HOS] Providence Saint Joseph Medical Center, Burbank, CA; [MON] Colombiere House (Jesuit Fathers), Los Angeles, CA
Ciccone, Rev. Michael, *O.P.* (BAL) SS. Philip and James, Baltimore, MD; St. Thomas Aquinas, Baltimore, MD
Ciccone, Rev. Nicholas C., '84 (BO) On Leave.
Cicerale, Rev. Msgr. Charles W., '75 (MET) Retired.
Cicero, Rev. Christopher, '10 (Y) Blessed Sacrament, Warren, OH; St. Elizabeth Ann Seton Parish, Warren, OH
Cicero, Rev. Frankie, (PHX) Queen of Peace Roman Catholic Parish, Mesa, AZ
Cichon, Rev. Michael W, '85 (NY) St. Christopher and St. Margaret Mary, Staten Island, NY
Cichon, Rev. Michael W., '85 (NY) Parish of Sts. Peter and Paul and Assumption, Staten Island, NY; St. Paul, Staten Island, NY
Cichoski, Rev. Adam J., (CAM) Curia: Advisory Boards, Commissions, Committees, and Councils; Leadership; Tribunal The Parish of the Cathedral of the Immaculate Conception, Camden, N.J., Camden, NJ
Cicinato, Rev. Michael Jerome, '76 (MRY) Retired.
Cid, Rev. Roberto M., '07 (MIA) Curia: Pastoral Services St. Patrick, Miami Beach, FL; [MIS] Stella Maris Seamen Center, Inc., Miami, FL
Ciechanowski, Rev. Konrad, *O.Cist.* '07 (CHI) [MON] Cistercian Fathers, Our Lady Mother of the Church Polish Mission, Willow Springs, IL
Cieniewicz, Rev. Donald W., '83 (ALN) Cathedral of St. Catharine of Siena, Allentown, PA
Cienik, Rev. Kenneth, *S.A.* '77 (NY) [MON] Franciscan Friars of the Atonement, Minister General Office, Garrison, NY
Cieri, Rev. Domenic L., '81 (BAL) Retired.
Ciesla, Rev. Marek, *S.Chr.* '82 (DEN) St. Joseph Catholic Parish in Akron, Akron, CO; St. Mary Catholic Parish in Brush, Brush, CO
Ciesla, Rev. Walter M., '81 (GRY) St. Stanislaus Kostka, Michigan City, IN
Cieslak, Rev. William, (GB) Retired. [MON] St. Fidelis Friary, Appleton, WI
Cieslewicz, Very Rev. Vincent P., '94 (E) Chap, Federal Correction Inst-McKean, Bradford St. Elizabeth, Smethport, PA
Cieslik, Rev. R. Dale, '82 (L) Curia: Leadership St. Francis Xavier, Mount Washington, KY
Cieslik, Rev. Shaun, '16 (JOL) St. Mary of Gostyn, Downers Grove, IL
Cieslikowski, Rev. Thomas J., '88 (HRT) Saint Nicholas Parish Corporation, Seymour, CT
Ciferni, Rev. Andrew D., *O.Praem.* '68 (PH) [MON] Daylesford Abbey, Inc., Paoli, PA
Cifuentes, Rev. Carlos, '16 (ATL) On Leave.
Cigainero, Rev. Robert Kenneth, '14 (LR) (>TYL) St. Michael, Mount Pleasant, TX
Cigan, Rev. John J., '74 (PSC) Curia: Advisory Boards, Commissions, Committees, and Councils Holy Ghost, Jessup, PA; St. John the Baptist, Forest City, PA
Cihak, Rev. Msgr. John, '98 (P) Christ the King, Milwaukie, OR
Cihak, Msgr. John, '92 (P) Curia: Offices and Directors
Cilia, Rev. Msgr. Francis V., '79 (SJ) Curia: Leadership; Offices and Directors St. Clare, Santa Clara, CA
Cilia, Rev. Joseph O., *O. Carm.* '68 (SAC) Pastor of Our Lady of Mount Carmel Parish, Fairfield, a Corporation Sole, Fairfield, CA
Cilibraise, Rev. Michael, '08 (GR) Holy Family, Caledonia, MI
Cilinski, Very Rev. Robert C., '79 (ARL) Curia: Leadership; Offices and Directors Church of the Nativity, Burke, VA
Cima, Rev. Thomas E., '67 (CHI) Curia: Leadership
Cimbala, Rev. Edward G., '88 (PSC) Curia: Advisory Boards, Commissions, Committees, and Councils; Leadership Greek Rite Catholic Church of Exaltation of Holy Cross (and) Exaltation of the Holy Cross Byzantine Catholic Church, New York, NY; St. Mary's, New York, NY
Cimerman, Rev. Krizolog, *O.F.M.* '73 (NY) St. Cyril, New York, NY (>CHI) [MON] The Slovene Franciscan Fathers, Order of Friars Minor, Commissariat of the Holy Cross, Lemont, IL
Cimino, Rev. Michael, '86 (SFE) Our Lady of the Assumption-Albuquerque, Albuquerque, NM
Cimpl, Rev. Charles L., '78 (SFS) Retired. Curia: Leadership [EFT] Holy Spirit School Permanent Trust, Sioux Falls, SD; [MIS] Diocese of Sioux Falls Outreach Ministry Property Corporation, Sioux Falls, SD
Cincinnati, Rev. Msgr. Anthony, '87 (WH) St. Francis de Sales Catholic Church, Morgantown, WV
Cinco, Rev. Msgr. Francisco, (SD) Pastor of Saint Michael Catholic Parish, San Diego, a corporation sole, San Diego, CA; [MIS] Saint Michael Catholic Parish San Diego in San Diego, CA Real Property Support Corporation, San Diego, CA
Cingle, Rev. Martin A., '73 (ALT) On Leave.
Cini, Rev. Msgr. J. Thomas, '68 (WIL) Retired.
Cink, Rev. James J., '85 (MOB) Curia: Leadership Blessed Francis Xavier Seelos Parish, Malbis, Spanish Fort, AL
Cinnante, Rev. Justin, *O. Carm.* (NY) Transfiguration, Tarrytown, NY
Cinquegrani, Rev. David, *C.P.* '96 (HRT) [MON] Holy Family Monastery/Retreat, West Hartford, CT; [RTR] Holy Family Passionist Retreat Center (Passionist Fathers of CT, Inc.), West Hartford, CT
Cinquegrani, Rev. David, *C.P.* '96 (NY) [MON] The Congregation of the Passion - St. Paul of the Cross Province, Jamaica, NY
Cinquegrani, Rev. R. Bruce, '79 (MEM) St. Anne's, Memphis, TN
Cinson, Rev. Victor, '74 (STU) St. Francis Xavier, Malvern, OH; St. Gabriel the Archangel, Minerva, OH
Cintron, Rev. Angel L., '91 (CGS) Curia: Leadership Santo Cristo de la Salud, Comerio, PR
Cintron, Rev. Frederick, '87 (BRK) On Duty Outside Diocese. 39-38 29th Street, Long Island City, NY 11101 St. Patrick, Long Island City, NY
Cintron, Rev. Frederick, (NY) Chap, Otis Bantum Corr Ctr, East Elmhurst
Cintron Gonzalez, Rev. Kevin, '11 (CGS) San Juan Bautista, Las Piedras, PR
Cintron Orengo, Rev. Segismundo, '89 (PCE) Curia: Leadership; Offices and Directors Sagrado Corazon de Jesus, Penuelas, PR
Cioch, Rev. Gregory, '00 (DEN) Holy Name Catholic Parish in Steamboat Springs, Steamboat Springs, CO
Cioffi, Rev. Alfred, '85 (MIA) St. Monica, Miami Gardens, FL; [COL] St. Thomas University, Inc., Miami Gardens, FL
Cioffi, Rev. Ronald J., '69 (TR) Retired.
Ciomek, Rev. Christopher, '98 (CHI) Curia: Leadership St. Peter Damian, Bartlett, IL
Cioppa, Rev. John, *M.M.* '59 (NY) Retired. [MON] Maryknoll Fathers and Brothers (Catholic Foreign Mission Society of America, Inc.), Ossining, NY
Cioppi, Rev. Martin T., '81 (PH) On Special Assignment. Dean, Deanery 6, Mother of Divine Providence Rec, King of P… Curia: Advisory Boards, Commissions, Committees, and Councils Mother of Divine Providence, King of Prussia, PA
Ciordia, Rev. Jose Antonio, '61 (NEW) St. Augustine, Union City, NJ
Ciordia, Rev. Pedro M., '61 (LA) Retired.
Ciorra, Rev. Anthony J., '73 (NY) [MIS] Voluntas Dei USA, New York, NY
Cipolla, Rev. Richard G., '84 (BGP) Retired.
Cipolle, Rev. Anthony, '17 (PRT) On Administrative Leave.
Cipot, Rev. Edwin H., '00 (NY) Holy Child, Staten Island, NY
Cippel, Rev. Msgr. John A., '60 (SP) Retired.
Cipriani, Rev. Peter A., '04 (BGP) Curia: Clergy and Religious Services; Consultative Bodies The Church of Our Lady of the Assumption, Fairfield, CT
Cirata, Rev. David J., '06 (TOL) Curia: Pastoral Services St. Michael the Archangel, Toledo, OH
Cirba, Rev. Richard J., '89 (SCR) Curia: Leadership Exaltation of the Holy Cross, Hanover Township, PA; St. Robert Bellarmine Parish, Wilkes-Barre, PA
Circe, Very Rev. Scott M., '05 (ORL) Curia: Advisory Boards, Commissions, Committees, and Councils; Deaneries Holy Name of Jesus, Indialantic, FL
Cirera, Rev. Arsenio G., '89 (SFR) St. Bartholomew, San Mateo, CA
Ciriaco, Rev. Dominic, *P.S.S.* '99 (BAL) Retired. [MIS] St. Mary's Seminary & University, Baltimore, MD; [MON] Society of St. Sulpice, Province of the United States, Baltimore, MD
Ciriaco, Rev. Dominic G., '99 (NEW) On Duty Outside Diocese. Theological College, Washington, DC
Ciriaco, Rev. Dominic G., '99 (WDC) [SEM] Theological College of the Catholic University of America, Washington, DC
Cirignani, Rev. Anthony, *O.F.M.* '83 (GB) Retired.
Cirino, Rev. Andre, *O.F.M.* '67 (NY) [MON] St. Bernardine of Siena Friary (Franciscan Friars, Province of Immaculate Conception), Mount Vernon, NY
Ciro, Rev. Rafael, '13 (PAT) St. Stephen's, Paterson, NJ
Cirujeda, Rev. Pablo, '03 (MIL) On Duty Outside Diocese. Delg Alvaro Obregon, Ciudad de Mexico
Ciryak, Rev. Michael A., '98 (FR) Transfiguration of the Lord, North Attleborough, MA
Ciscar, Rev. Tomas, *O.Carm.* '78 (MGZ) St. Anthony Abbot, Anasco, PR
Ciscar Nadal, Rev. Tomás, *O. Carm.* (ARE) Nuestra Senora del Carmen, Morovis, PR
Cisco, Rev. Bede, *O.S.B.* '78 (IND) [MON] St. Meinrad Archabbey, St. Meinrad, IN
Cisetti, Rev. Joseph, '91 (KC) St. Therese Parish, Kansas City, MO
Cisewski, Rev. Msgr. John, '71 (NO) Retired.
Ciski, Rev. Michael, *T.O.R.* '00 (FWT) St. Maria Goretti, Arlington, TX
Cisneros, Rev. Adrian Ruben, '19 (STO) Curia: Leadership St. Stanislaus Church (Pastor of), Modesto, CA; [EFT] Father John C. Silva Education Foundation, Modesto, CA
Cisneros, Rev. Gerardo, (YAK) St. Pius X, Quincy, WA
Cisneros, Rev. Gerardo, (P) [EFT] Felix Rougier Religious Care Trust, Banks, OR
Cisneros, Rev. Pablo Cesar, *O.F.M.* (LAR) Our Lady of Guadalupe, Hebbronville, TX
Cisneros, Rev. Ramon, '99 (ORG) St. Barbara Catholic Church, Santa Ana, CA
Cisneros, Rev. Richard Mederich Marcelino, '98 (NY) St. Peter and St. Paul, Bronx, NY
Cisneros-Luna, Rev. Antonio, '95 (GAL) St. Charles Borromeo, Houston, TX
Ciszkowski, Rev. Slawomir, '00 (NY) Roman Catholic Church of St. Catherine Laboure and St. Colman, Lake Katrine, NY
Citero, Rev. Samuel, *O.Carm.* '84 (NEW) St. Therese of Lisieux, Cresskill, NJ
Citino, Rev. Msgr. Angelo R., '77 (PH) SS. Peter and Paul, West Chester, PA
Citro, Rev. Anthony M., '94 (GLD) Curia: Advisory Boards, Commissions, Committees, and Councils; Leadership Immaculate Conception of Traverse City, Traverse City, MI
Ciuba, Rev. Msgr. Edward J., '59 (NEW) Retired. Church of the Presentation, Upper Saddle River, NJ
Ciucci, Rev. Daniel, (DEN) Most Precious Blood Catholic Parish in Denver, Denver, CO
Ciupek, Rev. James D., '97 (BUF) Curia: Consultative Bodies Nativity of Our Lord, Orchard Park, NY
Ciurpita, Rev. John, '89 (PHU) [CON] Provincial Motherhouse of the Sisters of St. Basil the Great, Fox Chase Manor, PA
Civeles Villanueva, Rev. Manuel, *SchP* '19 (SJN) Santisimo Salvador, San Juan, PR
Civille, Rev. John R., '66 (CIN) Holy Family, Middletown, OH; Holy Name, Trenton, OH; Our Lady of Sorrows, Monroe, OH
Cizewski, Rev. Albert, '71 (SFS) Saint John de Britto Parish of Marshall County, Britton, SD
Cizik, Rev. Ladis, '87 (PIT) Chap, Providence Care Ctr St. Monica, Beaver Falls, PA
Cizmar, Rev. Jan, '09 (PRM) On Leave. Left the Catholic Church for the Orthodox Church in 2021
Clair, Rev. John J., '82 (CHI) [SPF] Misericordia Home (Misericordia Foundation), Chicago, IL
Clancy, Rev. Msgr. Douglas P., '71 (HRT) Retired. Curia: Clergy and Religious Services
Clancy, Rev. Richard F., '91 (BO) St. Mary Magdalen, Tyngsborough, MA; St. Rita, Lowell, MA
Clancy, Rev. Richard F., (BO) Ste. Marguerite d'Youville, Dracut, MA
Clancy, Rev. Robert E., '74 (CLV) Retired.
Clancy, Rev. Timothy R., *S.J.* '89 (SPK) Our Lady of the Lake, Nine Mile Falls, WA; [COL] Gonzaga University, Spokane, WA
Clanton, Rev. Bruce, *S.D.S.* '78 (MIL) [MON] Salvatorian Provincial Offices (Society of the Divine Savior), Milwaukee, WI
Clapham, Rev. Bruce R., '95 (CHY) Curia: (>MO) Offices and Directors

Clara Giron, Rev. Dario, *M.N.M.* '03 (DAL) St. James Catholic Church, Dallas, TX
Claravall, Rev. Justin, *S.J.* '20 (LA) Dolores Mission, Los Angeles, CA
Clarin, Rev. Rolando, '93 (LA) Immaculate Heart of Mary, Los Angeles, CA
Clark, Rev. Alexander, '21 (CLV) St. John Vianney, Mentor, OH
Clark, Rev. Anthony, '79 (LSC) Retired.
Clark, Rev. Augustine, *O.S.B.* '97 (ORL) Retired.
Clark, Rev. Bede, *O.S.B.* (SD) [MON] Prince of Peace Abbey, Oceanside, CA
Clark, Rev. Dana, '01 (SAL) St. Mary Parish, Ellis, Inc., Ellis, KS
Clark, Rev. Douglas K., '76 (SAV) St. Matthew, Statesboro, GA
Clark, Rev. Douglas K., '76 (SAV) Curia: Leadership; Offices and Directors
Clark, Rev. Eric A, '14 (LIN) St. Peter, Lincoln, NE
Clark, Rev. Gary, '15 (OWN) St. Francis de Sales, Paducah, KY; [CEM] Mt. Carmel Cemetery, Inc., Paducah, KY
Clark, Rev. J. Michael, '95 (OWN) Curia: Leadership Blessed Mother, Owensboro, KY
Clark, Rev. James B., '95 (BO) On Leave.
Clark, Very Rev. James M., '11 (MEM) Curia: Advisory Boards, Commissions, Committees, and Councils; Leadership; Offices and Directors St. Francis of Assisi, Cordova, TN
Clark, Rev. James W., '84 (GBG) Retired. [NUR] Neumann House, Greensburg, PA
Clark, Rev. Joseph J., '96 (ARL) Retired.
Clark, Rev. Joseph L., '76 (RIC) Retired.
Clark, Rev. Lucian, *C.P.* '65 (NY) Retired. [MON] The Congregation of the Passion - St. Paul of the Cross Province, Jamaica, NY
Clark, Rev. Lucian, *C.P.* (PMB) [MON] Our Lady of Florida Spiritual Center, North Palm Beach, FL
Clark, Rev. Luke, *O.P.* (WDC) St. Dominic Church & Priory, Washington, DC
Clark, Rev. Malachi, '20 (SY) Church of the Holy Family, Syracuse, NY
Clark, Rev. Matthew R., *O.S.B.* '87 (NO) [MON] St. Joseph Abbey, St. Benedict, LA; [SEM] Saint Joseph Seminary College, Saint Benedict, LA
Clark, Rev. Michael, (OWN) Curia: Advisory Boards, Commissions, Committees, and Councils
Clark, Rev. Patrick S., '61 (SEA) Retired.
Clark, Rev. Paul, '16 (NO) Our Lady of the Holy Rosary, Hahnville, LA
Clark, Rev. Paul J., '17 (JC) Curia: Advisory Boards, Commissions, Committees, and Councils; Faith Formation; Offices and Directors Helias Catholic High School, Jefferson City, MO
Clark, Very Rev. Paul M., '03 (HBG) Curia: Leadership; Offices and Directors St. Matthew, Apostle and Evangelist, Dauphin, PA
Clark, Rev. Peter A., *S.J.* '92 (PH) [MIS] Jesuit Fathers, , ; [MON] Jesuit Community at St. Joseph's University, Merion Station, PA
Clark, Rev. Peter J., '02 (LAN) Retired.
Clark, Rev. Ray, (OWN) [NUR] Carmelite Sisters of the Divine Heart of Jesus, Owensboro, KY
Clark, Rev. Ray, '91 (OWN) On Special Assignment. Chap, Prison Ministry Curia: Advisory Boards, Commissions, Committees, and Councils; Organizations (affiliated, inter-Diocesan, miscellaneous/other) [COL] Brescia University, Owensboro, KY
Clark, Rev. Robert J., '99 (CHI) Retired.
Clark, Rev. Ronald Lee, '17 (LA) St. Dorothy, Glendora, CA
Clark, Rev. Thomas F., *S.J.* '81 (BR) Congregation of Immaculate Conception Roman Catholic Church Scotlandville LA, Baton Rouge, LA; [CAM] Martin Luther King, Jr. Catholic Student Center, Baton Rouge, LA
Clark, Rev. Thomas R., '62 (L) Retired.
Clark, Rev. Timothy, *O.C.S.O.* '80 (P) [MON] The Cistercian (Trappist) Abbey of Our Lady of Guadalupe (Order of Cistercians of the Strict Observance), Carlton, OR
Clark, Rev. Timothy, '80 (SEA) Our Lady of the Lake, Seattle, WA
Clark, Rt. Rev. Victor J., *O.S.B.* '54 (BIR) Retired. [MON] St. Bernard Abbey, Cullman, AL
Clark, Rev. Willaim, *OMI* '55 (BEL) Retired.
Clark, Rev. William A., *S.J.* '93 (WOR) [MON] Jesuits of the Holy Cross, Inc., Worcester, MA
Clarke, Rev. Andrew, '82 (SJP) Retired. Curia: Offices and Directors
Clarke, Rev. Brian J.T., '07 (SCR) Curia: Offices and Directors Christ the King Parish, Archbald, PA
Clarke, Rev. Brian J.W., (SCR) Most Holy Trinity Parish, Cresco, PA
Clarke, Rev. Brian J.W., '02 (SCR) Curia: Leadership
Clarke, Rev. James, '81 (LA) St. Anthony, San Gabriel, CA
Clarke, Rev. Msgr. James A., '70 (Y) Retired. St. Paul, North Canton, OH
Clarke, Rev. Msgr. John A., '59 (CAM) Retired.
Clarke, Rev. Kevin T., *S.J.* '73 (P) [HOS] Providence Health & Services-Oregon (Providence Portland Medical Center), Portland, OR; [MON] Colombiere Jesuit Community, Portland, OR
Clarke, Rev. Mark, *C.M.F.* '03 (SAT) Immaculate Heart of Mary, San Antonio, TX
Clarke, Rev. Paul, *O.P.* (WDC) St. Dominic Church & Priory, Washington, DC
Clarke, Rev. Peter J., '04 (PAT) Morris Catholic High School, Denville, NJ; Our Lady of Good Counsel, Pompton Plains, NJ
Clarke, Rev. Ransford, '11 (NY) St. Joseph of the Holy Family, New York, NY; St. Margaret of Antioch, Pearl River, NY
Clarke, Rev. Steven E., '90 (NY) St. Francis of Assisi, Mt. Kisco, NY
Clarke, Rev. Steven P., '98 (RCK) St. Joseph, Harvard, IL
Claro, Rev. Carlos Luis, *C.S.V.* '98 (CHI) [MON] Viatorian Province Center-Clerics of St. Viator, Arlington Heights, IL
Claro, Rev. Mario R., '67 (WH) Retired.
Clary, Rev. Brian M., '97 (BO) Curia: Clergy and Religious Services Sacred Heart, Boston, MA
Clary, Rev. Drew, *C.S.C.* (FTW) St. Adalbert, South Bend, IN; St. Casimir, South Bend, IN
Class, Rev. Michael, *S.J.* (GLD) Saint Wenceslaus of Gills Pier, Suttons Bay, MI
Claudio, Rev. Miguel, '06 (CGS) Curia: Leadership Nuestra Senora de Fatima, Cidra, PR
Claver, Rev. James, '14 (DEN) On Duty Outside Diocese. Chap, The Augustine Inst, Greenwood Village
Claver, Rev. Peter, '93 (NY) Chap, Westchester Med Ctr, Valhalla
Clavero, Rev. Jose M., *Sch.P.* '64 (NY) St. Ann's School Annunciation, New York, NY; [MON] Calasanzian Fathers (Piarists), New York, NY
Clavin, Rev. M. Oliver, '70 (SPC) Retired.
Clavin, Rev. Nicholas P., '73 (SD) Pastor of Saint Gregory the Great Catholic Parish, San Diego, a corporation sole, San Diego, CA
Clawson, Rev. Michael, '22 (IND) St. Malachy Catholic Church, Brownsburg, Inc., Brownsburg, IN
Clay, Rev. Catesby, '07 (LEX) St. Leo, Versailles, KY
Clay, Rev. Chris, '07 (LEX) Curia: Offices and Directors
Clay, Rev. David, *S.S.C.* '62 (OM) Retired. [MON] Missionary Society of St. Columban, St. Columbans, NE
Clay, Rev. Msgr. Michael G., '80 (WDC) [COL] Catholic University of America, The, Washington, DC
Clay, Rev. Msgr. Michael G., '80 (R) Curia: Leadership Saint Francis of Assisi Catholic Parish of Raleigh, Raleigh, NC
Clayton, Rev. Barry R., '11 (KCK) Our Lady of Lourdes, La Cygne, KS; Sacred Heart Shrine to St. Philippine Duchesne, Mound City, KS; St. Philip Neri, Osawatomie, KS
Clayton, Rev. Daniel, '68 (DAL) Retired.
Cleary, Rev. Christopher, *C.P.* '86 (NY) [MON] The Congregation of the Passion - St. Paul of the Cross Province, Jamaica, NY
Cleary, Rev. Christopher, *C.P.* '86 (BRK) [MON] Immaculate Conception Monastery, Jamaica, NY
Cleary, Rev. Dennis W., *M.M.* '77 (NY) Retired.
Cleary, Rev. Hugh, *C.S.C.* '73 (BUR) Sacred Heart St. Francis de Sales Parish Charitable Trust, Bennington, VT; St. John the Baptist, North Bennington, VT
Cleary, Rev. Paul, '74 (SAT) Retired. [NUR] Casa De Padres, San Antonio, TX
Cleary, Rev. Philip C., '79 (CHI) On Special Assignment.
Cleary, Rev. Richard, *O.S.B.* '55 (KC) [MON] Conception Abbey (Benedictine Monks), Conception, MO
Cleary, Rev. William, '04 (NY) [SEM] St. Joseph's Seminary, Yonkers, NY
Cleary, Rev. William, (PIT) [COL] Duquesne University of the Holy Spirit, Pittsburgh, PA
Cleary, Rev. William M., *C.Ss.R.* '62 (SEA) Retired. Sacred Heart of Jesus, Seattle, WA; [MON] The Redemptorist Society of Washington, Seattle, WA
Cleaton, Rev. C. Thomas, '75 (CLV) St. Mary of the Immaculate Conception, Avon, OH
Cleator, Rev. Gerard B., *O.P.* '65 (CHI) [MON] St. Pius V Priory, Chicago, IL
Cleatus, Rev. Biju Chitteth, (MO) Curia: Offices and Directors
Cleetus, Rev. Jackson, (HT) The Congregation of St. Joseph's Roman Catholic Cathedral, Thibodaux, LA
Cleetus, Rev. Jackson, (SP) [HOS] St. Anthony's Hospital, Inc., St. Petersburg, FL
Clegg, Rev. Thomas E., '90 (IND) Curia: Offices and Directors St. John Paul II Catholic Church, Sellersburg, Inc., Sellersburg, IN
Clegg, Rev. Timothy W., '71 (LFT) Retired.
Clem, Rev. Kenneth, '19 (KCK) Sacred Heart, Ottawa, KS
Clem, Rev. Peter J., (ARL) Basilica of St. Mary, Alexandria, VA
Clemence, Rev. Steven, '14 (BO) Immaculate Conception, Marlborough, MA
Clemence, Rev. William, '13 (DEN) [SEM] Redemptoris Mater House of Formation, Denver, CO
Clemens, Rev. Bailey, '98 (BAK) Curia: Leadership
Clemens, Rev. John W., '72 (CHI) Retired. [MIS] The Aquin Guild, Chicago, IL
Clemens, Rev. Neal C., '01 (OAK) Queen of All Saints, Concord, CA
Clement, Rev. D. Blaine, '08 (LAF) Annunciation of the B.V.M., Eunice, LA; Our Lady of Mount Carmel, Chataignier, LA
Clement, Rev. Frederick, *M.SS.CC.* '94 (CAM) [MON] Villa Pieta. Missionaries of the Sacred Hearts of Jesus & Mary, Linwood, NJ
Clement, Rev. Philip, '08 (PRT) Our Lady of the Lakes, Oquossoc, ME
Clement, Rev. Philip, '08 (SP) On Duty Outside Diocese. Diocese of Portland, Maine
Clement, Rev. Richard H., '85 (ALN) St. Columbkill, Boyertown, PA
Clement, Rev. Thomas, '95 (SFS) Curia: Offices and Directors Saint Ann Parish of Charles Mix County, Geddes, SD; Saint Peter the Apostle Parish of Charles Mix County, Platte, SD
Clemente, Rev. Dominic, '16 (CHI) St. Edward, Chicago, IL
Clemente, Rev. Joseph J., '81 (SY) St. Marianne Cope Parish, Solvay, NY
Clemente, Rev. Steven, '12 (VEN) Curia: Advisory Boards, Commissions, Committees, and Councils St. William Parish in Naples, Inc., Naples, FL
Clemente, Rev. Vincent L., '76 (VEN) St. James Catholic Parish in Lake Placid, Inc., Lake Placid, FL
Clements, Rev. Robert, '90 (PHX) All Saints Roman Catholic Newman Center, Tempe, AZ; [CAM] All Saints Catholic Newman Center Tempe, Tempe, AZ
Clements, Rev. Thomas P., '55 (CHL) Retired.
Clemo, Rev. Ronald C., *S.J.* '67 (SFR) [MON] Jesuit Community at St. Ignatius College Preparatory, San Francisco, CA
Clemons, Rev. Delma, '66 (OWN) Retired.
Clennon, Rev. Raymond, *O. Carm.* '67 (JOL) [MON] St. Simon Stock Priory, Darien, IL
Clerkin, Rev. Msgr. Robert J., '80 (RVC) St. Peter of Alcantara, Port Washington, NY
Clerkin, Rev. Thomas J., *C.S.P.* '85 (LA) Retired. St. Paul the Apostle, Los Angeles, CA
Clerveau, Rev. Germain, *S.J.* '18 (SFR) [MON] Loyola House Jesuit Community, San Francisco, CA
Cleto, Rev. Jorge Luis, *O.S.A.* '08 (NY) St. Ann, Ossining, NY
Cletus, Rev. Ranjan, '84 (AUS) SS. Cyril and Methodius Catholic Church - Marak, Texas, Buckholts, TX; St. Joseph, Burlington, TX
Cleveland, Rev. Gregory, *O.M.V.* (DEN) Holy Ghost Catholic Parish in Denver, Denver, CO
Cleves, Rev. Simeon, *O.F.M.* '55 (CIN) Retired.
Cleves, Rev. Msgr. William F., '78 (COV) Curia: Offices and Directors Holy Spirit, Newport, KY
Click, Rev. Patrick R., '71 (LFT) Retired.
Clifford, Rev. Donald P., '61 (BO) Retired.
Clifford, Rev. Edward R., '14 (PRT) Curia: Consultative Bodies Saint Teresa of Calcutta Parish, Norway, ME; St. Joseph, Bridgton, ME
Clifford, Rev. James, *O.S.A.* '72 (P) Retired. [HOS] Providence Health & Services-Oregon (Providence Medford Medical Center), Medford, OR; [MON] Augustinian Community, San Diego, CA
Clifford, Rev. Joseph G., '89 (VEN) On Duty Outside Diocese. Diocese of Lansing
Clifford, Rev. Paul T., (BO) St. Clare, Braintree, MA; St. Francis of Assisi, Braintree, MA
Clifford, Rev. Peter C., '76 (ROC) Church of St. John of Rochester of Perinton, New York, Fairport, NY
Clifford, Rev. Richard J., *S.J.* '66 (BO) [MON] Noel Chabanel House, Brighton, MA
Clifford, Rev. Thomas F., *S.J.* '81 (WDC) St. Ignatius, Port Tobacco, MD; [MON] The Jesuit Community at Georgetown University, Washington, DC
Clift, Rev. Benton M., '18 (COV) St. William,

Williamstown, KY
Clifton, Rev. James F., *S.J.* '88 (OM) [MON] Jesuit Community at Creighton University, Omaha, NE
Clifton, Rev. Joshua, (P) St. Birgitta, Portland, OR; St. Mary of Immaculate Conception, Vernonia, OR
Clifton, Rev. Joshua, '12 (MRY) On Special Assignment. St Birgitta Church, Portland, OR
Climaco, Rev. Julian, *S.J.* (SJ) [MON] Jesuit Community at Santa Clara University, Inc., Santa Clara, CA
Climaco, Rev. Julian, '15 (SEA) [MON] Jesuit House, Seattle, Seattle, WA
Climaco, Rev. Julian, *S.J.* '15 (LA) [MON] Jesuit Community, Los Angeles, CA
Clinch, Rev. Craig J., '11 (LIN) Chap, Nebraska Penal Complex, Lincoln Curia: Offices and Directors St. Cecilia's, Hastings, NE
Cline, Rev. Brian James, '10 (Y) St. Joan of Arc, Canton, OH; St. Joseph, Canton, OH
Cline, Rev. Martin E., '05 (OG) Curia: Consultative Bodies; Offices and Directors Saint Bernard's Church, Saranac Lake, Saranac Lake, NY
Clinton, Rev. Donald E., '90 (MAN) Chap, Rockingham Cty House of Corrections Our Lady of Fatima, New London, NH
Clinton, Rev. Kevin I., '74 (STP) Retired.
Cloherty, Rev. Francis J., '62 (BO) Retired. Sacred Heart, Lynn, MA; Saint Mary of the Sacred Heart Parish, Lynn, MA
Cloherty, Rev. John J., '60 (SFR) Retired.
Cloherty, Rev. Thomas, (DAL) Retired.
Cloney, Rev. Michael W., '68 (SR) Retired.
Cloos, Rev. Robert J., '14 (DAV) Assumption and St. Patrick Church of Charlotte, Iowa, Charlotte, IA; Immaculate Conception Church of Petersville, Iowa, Petersville, IA; Our Lady of the Holy Rosary Catholic Church of Lost Nation, Iowa, Lost Nation, IA; Ss. Mary and Joseph Church of Sugar Creek, Iowa, Preston, IA; St. Patrick Church of Delmar, Iowa, Delmar, IA
Clore, Rev. Victor, '65 (DET) Retired. [MIS] Dominican Center for Religious Development, Farmington Hills, MI
Close, Rev. Corey C., '12 (DAV) On Special Assignment. Washington, D.C.
Close, Rev. Frederick J., '01 (WDC) Curia: Consultative Bodies; Pastoral Services St. Anthony of Padua, Washington, DC
Close, Rev. John, '82 (ALB) Immaculate Conception, New Lebanon, NY; St. Mary, Nassau, NY
Clote, Rev. John, (PHX) Holy Spirit Roman Catholic Parish, Tempe, AZ
Clough, Rev. Wulfstan F., *O.S.B.* '96 (GBG) [MON] Saint Vincent Archabbey, Latrobe, PA
Cloutier, Rev. Roland C., '66 (NOR) Curia: Leadership
Cloutier, Rev. Roland C., '66 (NOR) Retired. Curia: Offices and Directors
Cloutier, Rev. Ronald F., '72 (GAL) Retired.
Cloutier, Rev. Timothy D., '83 (STP) Retired.
Clovis, Rev. Stephen, '89 (P) [SEM] Mount Angel Seminary, Saint Benedict, OR
Clutario, Rev. Reynaldo, '93 (PHX) Corpus Christi Roman Catholic Parish, Phoenix, AZ
Clyne, Rev. Andrew, '18 (WDC) Holy Redeemer, College Park, MD
Co, Rev. Anthony, '05 (PEO) St. Mary's, Champaign, IL; St. Patrick, Urbana, IL
Coady, Rev. Frank, '76 (SAL) Curia: Advisory Boards, Commissions, Committees, and Councils; Consultative Bodies; Faith Formation; Spiritual Life St. Thomas More Parish, Manhattan, Inc., Manhattan, KS
Coakley, Rev. Patrick, *M.S.C.* '86 (AUS) St. Catherine of Siena, Austin, TX
Coan, Rev. Gregory S., '03 (WDC) Holy Ghost, Newburg, MD
Coan, Rev. Gregory S., '03 (WDC) Chap, Hosp & Nursing Home Min, Adventist HealthCare Washing…
Coaquira, Rev. Rodolpho, *MCCJ* '92 (CIN) St. Boniface, Cincinnati, OH
Coaquira Hilaje, Rev. Rodolfo, *M.CCJ.* (CIN) Holy Family, Cincinnati, OH; St. Joseph, Cincinnati, OH; St. Leo the Great, Cincinnati, OH; St. Therese Little Flower, Cincinnati, OH
Coates, Rev. Roderick, *S.S.J.* (NO) St. Augustine High School, New Orleans, LA
Cobb, Rev. Jerry, *S.J.* '81 (SEA) [COL] Seattle University, Seattle, WA; [MON] Arrupe Jesuit Community at Seattle University, Seattle, WA
Cobb, Rev. Richard E., *S.J.* '62 (SJ) Bellarmine College Preparatory, San Jose, CA; [MON] Sacred Heart Jesuit Center, Los Gatos, CA
Cobel, Rev. Lawrence F., '73 (BUF) Retired. [MON] Msgr. Conniff Residence, Depew, NY
Cobenas, Rev. Pedro A., '92 (LA) On Administrative Leave.
Coble, Rev. Scott W, *S.J.* (LA) [SEM] Ignatius House, The Novitiate of the U.S. West Province, Society of Jesus, Culver City, CA
Cobona, Rev. Kusitino, '84 (LAN) St. James Parish Mason, Mason, MI
Cobos, Rev. J. Abelardo, '03 (GAL) Curia: Leadership Our Lady of Mt. Carmel, Houston, TX
Cocco, Rev. William T., '04 (WIL) St. Edmond, Rehoboth Beach, DE
Cochrac, Rev. Joshua, '20 (CLV) St. Charles Borromeo, Parma, OH
Cochran, Rev. Paul, *S.J.* '94 (HEL) Saint Francis Xavier Parish: Series 640, LLC, Missoula, MT
Cochran, Rev. Paul W., '88 (LFT) Curia: Miscellaneous / Other Offices St. Joseph, Lebanon, IN; St. Mary, Frankfort, IN
Cochran, Rev. Ronald, '01 (SD) Retired. [MIS] The Church of Saint Luke Catholic Parish in El Cajon, CA Real Property Support Corporation, El Cajon, CA
Coci, Rev. Anthony J., (TOL) Curia: Advisory Boards, Commissions, Committees, and Councils St. Joseph, Tiffin, OH; St. Pius X, Tiffin, OH; [EFT] Tiffin Calvert Foundation, Tiffin, OH
Cockayne, Rev. John E., '85 (HRT) Retired.
Cockson, Rev. David A., '14 (L) Retired.
Cocucci, Rev. Joseph M.P.R., *K.H.S.* '96 (WIL) St. John Neumann Roman Catholic Church, Berlin, MD
Coda, Rev. Joseph F., '63 (NEW) Retired. [MON] St. John Vianney Residence for Retired Priests, Rutherford, NJ
Codd, Rev. Matthew P., '12 (CHL) St. Thomas Aquinas, Charlotte, NC
Coddaire, Rev. Louis, '78 (SR) Retired.
Code, Rev. Sean K., '93 (ALT) Retired. Chap, Main Campus, Johnstown
Codega, Rev. John C., '99 (PRO) Saint Lucy's Church Corp., Middletown, RI
Codoner-Contell, Rev. Andres, '08 (NEW) St. Augustine, Newark, NJ; St. Columba, Newark, NJ
Codori, Rev. Joseph, (PIT) Archangel Gabriel, McKees Rocks, PA
Cody, Rev. Henry P., '58 (HRT) Retired.
Cody, Rev. John, *C.Ss.R.* '81 (STL) Retired. [MON] St. Clement Health Care Center, Liguori, MO
Cody, Rev. Msgr. John K., '73 (COL) Retired. Curia: Offices and Directors
Cody, Rev. Kevin W., (MAN) On Duty Outside Diocese.
Cody, Rev. Thomas, '68 (STA) Retired.
Coelho, Rev. Adilso, *C.O.* '01 (CHR) Divine Saviour, York, SC; [MON] Oratory of St. Philip Neri, Congregation of the Oratory of Pontifical Rite, Rock Hill, SC
Coelho, Rev. Brian Alick, '07 (WDC) St. Mary Star of the Sea, Indian Head, MD
Coelho, Rev. Gabriel P., '78 (CC) Our Lady of Mount Carmel, Corpus Christi, TX; Our Lady of the Rosary, Corpus Christi, TX
Coelho, Very Rev. Oscar W., '08 (SFE) Curia: Offices and Directors Santuario San Martin de Porres, Albuquerque, NM
Coelho, Very Rev. Oscar W., '08 (SFE) Curia: Offices and Directors
Coellho-Harguindeguyg, Rev. Msgr. John, '67 (FRS) Retired.
Coen, Rev. Msgr. Charles P., '68 (NY) Retired.
Coens, Rev. Frank, *OFM* (BEL) [MON] St. Benedict the Black Friary, East Saint Louis, IL
Coens, Friar Frank, *OFM* '73 (STL) [MIS] The Franciscan Connection, St. Louis, MO
Coerver, Very Rev. Richard V., '76 (STL) Curia: Leadership St. John, The Beloved Disciple Catholic Church, Imperial, MO
Coffaro, Rev. Nicholas F., '08 (SAG) Prince of Peace Parish of Linwood, Linwood, MI; [MIS] St. Anne Church, ,
Coffas, Very Rev. William G., '04 (ROC) Curia: Clergy and Religious Services; Consultative Bodies; Deaneries Holy Cross, Rochester, NY; Our Mother of Sorrows, Rochester, NY
Coffey, Rev. Michael J., '91 (CAM) Retired. Holy Eucharist Parish, Cherry Hill, N.J., Cherry Hill, NJ
Coffey, Rev. Stephen G., *O.S.B. Cam.* '07 (MRY) [MON] Monastery of the Risen Christ, San Luis Obispo, CA
Coffi Gonzalez, Rev. Alexis, (PAT) Our Lady of Mercy, Whippany, NJ
Coffiey, Rev. Christopher R., '13 (WIL) St. Benedict, Ridgely, MD
Cogan, Rev. James, '04 (VEN) Incarnation Parish in Sarasota, Inc., Sarasota, FL
Cogan, Rev. Patrick, *S.A.* '77 (NY) [MON] Franciscan Friars of the Atonement, Minister General Office, Garrison, NY
Coggeshall, Rev. Canon Benjamin L, *ICRSP* '14 (STL) Oratory of St. Francis de Sales, St. Louis, MO; [MIS] Friends of St. Francis de Sales Oratory, Inc., St. Louis, MO
Coghlan, Rev. John P., '74 (MOB) St. Cecilia Parish, Mt. Vernon, Mount Vernon, AL; St. Theresa Parish, West Mount Vernon, West Mount Vernon, AL; St. Thomas Aquinas Parish, Citronelle, Citronelle, AL
Cogollodo, Rev. Ignacio, *SDV* '20 (MET) St. James, Woodbridge, NJ
Cogut, Rev. Daniel A., '15 (RIC) Our Lady of Perpetual Help, Salem, VA; St. Gerard, Roanoke, VA; [CAM] Catholic Campus Ministry, Roanoke College, Salem, VA
Cohan, Rev. Dennis J., '74 (NEW) Retired.
Cohea, Rev. Victor H., '80 (NO) Chap, Lafon Nursing Facility of the Holy Family, New Orleans St. Raymond-St. Leo the Great, New Orleans, LA
Coindreau, Rev. James M., *L.C.* '67 (MO) Curia: Offices and Directors
Coine, Rev. Robert E., '76 (WIL) St. Michael the Archangel, Georgetown, DE
Coiro, Rev. Mark J., '94 (BO) St. Mary, Holliston, MA
Cokonougher, Rev. Brian K., '99 (DET) St. Andrew Parish Rochester, Rochester, MI
Cokus, Rev. Msgr. Joseph J., '58 (LA) Retired.
Colacino, Rev. John A., *C.PP.S.* '80 (ROC) [MON] Missionaries of the Precious Blood, Rochester, NY
Colagreco, Rev. Michael A., '77 (PH) St. Anastasia, Newtown Square, PA
Colaj, Rev. Rene Otzoy, *O.S.B.* '82 (RCK) [MON] Marmion Abbey, Aurora, IL
Colamaria, Rev. Francis A., '01 (BRK) St. Helen, Howard Beach, NY
Colankin, Rev. Dimitrij, '76 (AUS) Retired.
Colaresi, Rev. Robert E., *O.Carm.* '67 (JOL) [MON] St. Simon Stock Priory, Darien, IL; [RTR] Carmelite Spiritual Center, Darien, IL
Colarusso, Rev. Darin V., '06 (BO) Curia: (>MO) Offices and Directors St. Lucy, Methuen, MA; St. Monica, Methuen, MA
Colas, Rev. Wilbert, (ELP) St. Pius X, El Paso, TX
Colasito, Rev. Francisco "Bing", '99 (PHX) Curia: Leadership; Offices and Directors Good Shepherd Mission, A Quasi-Parish, New River, AZ; St. Philip Benizi Roman Catholic Mission, A Quasi-Parish, Black Canyon City, AZ; St. Rose Philippine Duchesne Roman Catholic Parish, Anthem, AZ
Colaste, Rev. Sherwin S., '06 (SAC) On Leave.
Colasurdo, Rev. Peter, '77 (STA) Retired.
Colavito, Rev. Christopher, '16 (TR) Curia: Pastoral Services
Colbert, Rev. Richard K., *S.M.* '64 (WDC) Retired. [MON] Marist Center (The Marist Finance Center of the Atlanta Province of the Society of Mary, Marist Fathers and Brothers), Washington, DC
Colchin, Rev. Stephen E., '84 (FTW) Retired.
Cole, Rev. Basil Burr, *O.P.* '66 (WDC) [SEM] Dominican House of Studies, Washington, DC
Cole, Friar Casey, (SAV) Curia: Offices and Directors Holy Spirit, Macon, GA
Cole, Rev. Casey Allen, *OFM* '19 (SAV) St. Peter Claver, Macon, GA
Cole, Rev. G. Barry, '82 (POD) Curia: Clergy and Religious Services
Cole, Rev. G. Max, '14 (CLV) Holy Angels, Chagrin Falls, OH
Cole, Rev. James J., '71 (BGP) Retired.
Cole, Rev. Matthew, *SMA* '96 (PEO) Sacred Heart Roman Catholic Congregation of Moline Illinois, Moline, IL (>NEW) [MON] Society of African Missions, Provincialate, S.M.A. Fathers, Tenafly, NJ
Cole, Rev. Msgr. Raymond L., '72 (MET) Retired.
Cole, Very Rev. Robert F., '71 (MAN) Curia: Consultative Bodies St. Katharine Drexel, Alton, NH
Cole, Rev. Robert J., '72 (CLV) Retired. St. Mary, Berea, OH
Cole, Rev. Robert J., '06 (RIC) Curia: Advisory Boards, Commissions, Committees, and Councils St. John the Apostle Church, Virginia Beach, VA
Cole, Rev. Vincent P., *M.M.* '71 (NY) Retired. [MON] Maryknoll Fathers and Brothers (Catholic Foreign Mission Society of America, Inc.), Ossining, NY
Colello, Rev. Michael A., '01 (PRO) On Leave.
Coleman, Rev. C. Michael, '67 (KC) Retired.
Coleman, Rev. Casey A., '15 (CHL) Our Lady of Grace, Greensboro, NC
Coleman, Rev. Donald, (SD) Retired. Pastor of The Church of Saint Luke Catholic Parish, El Cajon, a corporation sole, El Cajon, CA
Coleman, Rev. Ed, '86 (P) St. Michael Catholic Church, Oakridge, OR

Coleman, Rev. Gerald D., *P.S.S.* '68 (BAL) Retired. [MON] Society of St. Sulpice, Province of the United States, Baltimore, MD
Coleman, Rev. Gerald D., *P.S.S.* '68 (SFR) Retired.
Coleman, Rev. Gerald J., '78 (TLS) On Special Assignment. Chap, Ascension St John Med Ctr, Tulsa
Coleman, Rev. James, '76 (COL) Our Lady of the Miraculous Medal, Columbus, OH
Coleman, Rev. James, '73 (P) Retired.
Coleman, Rev. Msgr. James G., '62 (HRT) Retired. Curia: Advisory Boards, Commissions, Committees, and Councils
Coleman, Rev. Msgr. James G., '62 (TUC) Retired.
Coleman, Rev. James Montini, '99 (MOB) Retired.
Coleman, Rev. Msgr. John, '50 (SJ) Retired.
Coleman, Rev. John A., *S.J.* '67 (SJ) [MON] Sacred Heart Jesuit Center, Los Gatos, CA
Coleman, Rev. John K., '71 (SFR) Retired.
Coleman, Rev. Msgr. John R., '50 (SFR) Retired. St. Francis of Assisi, East Palo Alto, CA
Coleman, Rev. Michael A., '81 (JC) Curia: Faith Formation Fr. Augustine Tolton Regional Catholic High School, Columbia, MO; Holy Spirit, Centralia, MO
Coleman, Rev. Paul, '03 (OAK) Curia: Leadership St. Monica, Moraga, CA
Coleman, Rev. Msgr. Robert F., '78 (NEW) Retired. Curia: Organizations (affiliated, inter-Diocesan, miscellaneous/other) [COL] Seton Hall University, South Orange, NJ
Coleman, Rev. Robert J., '87 (JOL) Retired.
Coleman, Rev. Robert P., '78 (CHI) Retired.
Coless, Rev. Gabriel M., *O.S.B.* '57 (PAT) Retired. [MON] St. Mary's Abbey, Morristown, NJ
Coletta, Rev. Ralph V., '61 (CLV) Retired.
Colgan, Rev. Thomas, *S.J.* '75 (SPK) [COL] Gonzaga University, Spokane, WA
Colgan, Rev. Tobias, *O.S.B.* '82 (IND) [MON] St. Meinrad Archabbey, St. Meinrad, IN; [SEM] Saint Meinrad School of Theology, St. Meinrad, IN
Colhour, Rev. David, *C.P.* '94 (CHI) [MON] Passionist Community of St. Vincent Strambi, Chicago, IL; [MON] Passionist Provincial Office (The Congregation of the Passion, Holy Cross Province), Park Ridge, IL
Colina, Rev. Jose C., '89 (SP) On Duty Outside Diocese.
Coll, Rev. Eduardo, '88 (VEN) Curia: Leadership St. Andrew Parish in Cape Coral, Inc., Cape Coral, FL
Coll, Rev. Msgr. Robert J., '59 (ALN) Retired. Assumption B.V.M., Bethlehem, PA
Collard, Rev. Bruce W., '80 (MAN) Retired.
Collazo Santiago, Rev. Carlos A., '15 (PCE) Curia: Leadership Santa Maria Reina, Ponce, PR
Colle, Rev. Matthew, (GB) St. Francis of Assisi, Manitowoc, WI
Colleoni, Rev. Xavier, *M.C.C.J.* '52 (LA) Holy Cross, Los Angeles, CA
Collette, Rev. Msgr. Richard, '52 (WOR) Retired.
Colletti, Rev. Arnold F., '62 (BO) Retired.
Colletti, Rev. Peter, '84 (CLV) St. Eugene, Cuyahoga Falls, OH
Colletti, Rev. Msgr. Richard M., '78 (WIN) Curia: Miscellaneous / Other Offices Our Lady of Good Counsel, Wilmont, MN; St. Adrian, Adrian, MN; St. Anthony's, Lismore, MN
Collier, Rev. Joseph, '58 (SD) Retired.
Colligan, Rev. James P., *M.M.* '55 (NY) Retired.
Colling, Rev. Paul J., '87 (GI) Curia: Leadership; Offices and Directors Prince of Peace, Kearney, NE
Collins, Rev. Austin I., *C.S.C.* '82 (FTW) [COL] University of Notre Dame Du Lac, Notre Dame, IN; [MON] Holy Cross Community, Corby Hall, University of Notre Dame, Notre Dame, IN
Collins, Rev. Carl, (HT) Curia: Organizations (affiliated, inter-Diocesan, miscellaneous/other) St. Charles Borromeo, Thibodaux, LA
Collins, Rev. Charles E., '72 (BO) Retired.
Collins, Rev. Charlie I., '82 (WIN) Retired.
Collins, Rev. Christopher, (STP) [COL] University of St. Thomas, St. Paul, MN
Collins, Rev. Christopher S., *S.J.* '06 (STL) [COL] Saint Louis University, St. Louis, MO
Collins, Rev. Chuck R., '05 (PT) Chap, Saufley Field Fed Prison Camp St. Anne's, Pensacola, FL
Collins, Rev. Daniel J., '58 (CHI) Retired. St. Mary of the Lake and Our Lady of Lourdes Parish, Chicago, IL
Collins, Rev. David J., *S.J.* '98 (WDC) [COL] Georgetown University, Washington, DC; [MON] The Jesuit Community at Georgetown University, Washington, DC
Collins, Rev. Dustin A., (MO) Curia: Offices and Directors
Collins, Rev. Dustin Alan, '12 (KNX) Curia: Leadership; Offices and Directors St. Mary's Catholic Church, Johnson City, TN
Collins, Rev. George E., (BO) [MON] Campion Center, Inc., Weston, MA; [RTR] Campion Center Conference & Renewal, Weston, MA
Collins, Rev. James B., '04 (NY) Chap, NY Army Nat Guard, St. Robert, MO Curia: (>MO) Offices and Directors
Collins, Rev. James M., '95 (CHL) St. Joseph, Newton, NC
Collins, Rev. James R., '81 (PRO) Retired.
Collins, Rev. John, '98 (LA) Ss. Felicitas and Perpetua, San Marino, CA
Collins, Rev. John, *C.Ss.R.* '87 (TR) [RTR] San Alfonso Retreat House, Long Branch, NJ
Collins, Rev. John E., *C.S.P.* '70 (NY) [MON] Paulist Fathers' Motherhouse, New York, NY
Collins, Rev. John P., '72 (PH) Retired. [SEM] Theological Seminary of St. Charles Borromeo, Wynnewood, PA
Collins, Rev. Kevin A., *O.M.I.* '82 (BWN) St. Eugene de Mazenod, Brownsville, TX
Collins, Rev. Lawrence, '77 (CHI)
Collins, Rev. Leonard J., *C.S.C.* '69 (FTW) St. Augustine, South Bend, IN; [MON] Congregation of Holy Cross, United States Province of Priests and Brothers, Notre Dame, IN
Collins, Rev. Matthew Carl, '21 (HRT) Most Holy Trinity Parish Corporation, Wallingford, CT
Collins, Rev. Neil J., '58 (NEW) Retired. [MON] St. John Vianney Residence for Retired Priests, Rutherford, NJ
Collins, Rev. Patrick, '64 (PEO) Retired.
Collins, Rev. Raymond, (BAL) (>PH) [MIS] Perpetual Help Center, Philadelphia, PA; (>PH) [MIS] Redemptorist Office for Mission Advancement, Philadelphia, PA
Collins, Rev. Raymond F., '59 (PRO) Retired.
Collins, Rev. Richard, '04 (FWT) Curia: Miscellaneous / Other Offices All Saints, Fort Worth, TX
Collins, Rev. Robert C., *S.J.* '67 (NY) [MON] America; Residence and Publication Office of the America Press, New York, NY
Collins, Rev. Shannon M., *M.S.J.B.* '00 (COV) Our Lady of Lourdes Parish, Park Hills, KY
Collins, Rev. Stephen L., '83 (E) St. Bonaventure, Grampian, PA; St. Timothy, Curwensville, PA
Collins, Rev. Thomas E., '92 (NY) Archbishop Stepinac High School, White Plains, NY; Our Lady of Sorrows, White Plains, NY
Collins, Rev. Thomas R., '72 (RIC) Retired.
Collins, Rev. Thomas S., '92 (PT) Holy Spirit, Pensacola, FL
Collins, Rev. Msgr. William A., '61 (BAL) Retired.
Collins, Rev. William B., '74 (PAT) Retired.
Colliou, Rev. Alain, (WDC) Our Lady Help of Christians, Waldorf, MD
Collison, Rev. Craig A., '78 (SC) Curia: Offices and Directors Church of the Resurrection, Pocahontas, IA; Our Lady of Good Counsel, Fonda, IA
Collogan, Rev. Robert, '82 (JOL) On Leave.
Colloton, Rev. Paul, *O.S.F.S.* (WIL) [MON] Oblates of St. Francis De Sales, Childs, MD
Collum, Rev. Patrick, '92 (NO) Holy Spirit Roman Catholic Church, New Orleans, Louisiana, New Orleans, LA
Colmenares, Rev. Wilson, (STA) Blessed Trinity, Jacksonville, FL; St. John the Evangelist, Chiefland, FL
Colocho, Rev. Walter, '06 (FRS) St. Thomas the Apostle, Arvin, CA
Colom, Rev. Marti, '00 (MIL) On Duty Outside Diocese. Parroquia la Resurreccion, Bogota [MIS] Community of St. Paul, Inc., Racine, WI
Colombo, Rev. Felipe, '22 (DEN) St. Michael the Archangel Catholic Parish in Aurora, Aurora, CO
Colombo, Rev. Ronald A., '72 (GB) Retired.
Colombo, Rev. Stefano, *FSCB* '99 (STP) Convent of the Visitation School, Mendota Heights, MN
Colon, Rev. Alberto Diaz, '85 (ARE) Curia: Leadership
Colon, Rev. Angel, '95 (CGS) Curia: Leadership San Isidro Labrador, Maunabo, PR
Colon, Rev. Jackson, '90 (CHI) Chap, John H Stroger, Jr Hosp of Cook Cty, Chicago
Colon, Rev. Jose, (FAJ) Curia: Leadership Maria Reina de la Paz, Humacao, PR
Colon, Rev. Jose, (SY) Chap, Mgr, St Joseph's Hosp Health Ctr, Syracuse
Colon, Rev. Juan J., '95 (CGS) Chap, Hosp Interamericano de Medicina Avanzada (HIMA); Hosp... Curia: Offices and Directors Catedral Dulce Nombre de Jesus, Caguas, PR
Colón, Rt. Rev. Economos Fray Roberto, *O.F.M.Cap.* '19 (SJN) [MON] The Custody of Saint John the Baptist, Puerto Rico, of the Order Friars Minor Capuchin, San Juan, PR
Colon Claudio, Rev. Josue Efrain, '18 (ARE) Curia: Offices and Directors
Colon Claudio, Rev. Josue Efraín, (ARE) [MIS] Chapel San Jose Obrero, Arecibo, PR
Colon Claudio, Rev. Josue Efraín, (ARE) Curia: Offices and Directors
Colon Claudio, Rev. Josue Efrain, (ARE) Church of San Martin de Porres, Arecibo, PR
Colon Ferrer, Rev. Hector L., *C.Ss.R.* '76 (PCE) San Antonio de Padua, Guayama, PR
Colon Gutierrez, Rev. Fernando Rafael, '19 (SJN) Maria Madre de La Iglesia, San Juan, PR
Colon Gutierrez, Rev. Fernando Rafael, (SJN) Asuncion de La Virgen, San Juan, PR
Colon Ortiz, Friar Roberto, *O.F.M.Cap.* '19 (SJN) San Antonio de Padua, San Juan, PR; [MON] Fraternidad San Antonio, San Juan, PR
Colon Rivera, Rev. Luis A., *S.E.M.V.* (ARE) Curia: Leadership; Offices and Directors
Colon Rivera, Rev. Luis A., *S.E.M.V.* '81 (ARE) Curia: Leadership Our Lady of Guadalupe, Hatillo, PR
Colon Rivera, Rev. Rene A., *S.E.M.V.* '84 (ARE) Our Lady of Guadalupe, Hatillo, PR
Colon Rivera, Rev. Rene A., *S.E.M.V.* '84 (ARE) [MIS] Chapel Inmaculada Concepcion, Hatillo, PR; [MIS] Chapel San Jose, Hatillo, PR; [MIS] Chapel Santa Rosa de Lima, Hatillo, PR
Colon-Gutierrez, Rev. Fernando Rafael, '19 (SJN) Curia: Offices and Directors
Colopelnic, Rev. Vasile, '04 (STF) SS. Peter and Paul, Auburn, NY
Colopelnic, Rev. Vasile, '04 (STF) Curia: Leadership; Offices and Directors
Colopy, Rev. James L., '86 (COL) Retired. The Basilica of St. Mary of the Assumption, Lancaster, OH
Colorado Prieto, Rev. Harold, (AGN) San Dimas and Our Lady of the Rosary, Malesso, GU; San Dionisio, Humåtak, GU
Colozzi, Rev. Charles J., '02 (CAM) Saint Gabriel the Archangel Parish, Carneys Point, N.J., Carney's Point, NJ
Colpitts, Rev. Albert B., '73 (PRT) Retired.
Colton, Rev. Gary P., '68 (HON) Retired.
Colucci, Rev. Thomas, '16 (NY) Church of St. Mary, Mother of the Church, Fishkill, NY; Most Precious Blood, Walden, NY
Colunga, Rev. Miguel, '21 (LAN) St. Patrick Parish Brighton, Brighton, MI
Colvin, Rev. Andrew, '02 (BAK) Chap, CHC, USN Curia: (>MO) Offices and Directors
Colwell, Very Rev. Michael P., '94 (AMA) Curia: Family Life; Leadership; Offices and Directors
Coly, Rev. Remy, *MSC* '03 (ALN) Our Lady of Mt. Carmel, Bangor, PA
Coman, Rev. Christopher M., '08 (SAG) Saint Christopher Parish of Caro and Mayville, Caro, MI
Comandini, Rev. Glenn J., '86 (MET) Curia: Evangelization
Combs, Rev. Gordon, *O.F.M.Cap.* '64 (HON) Retired.
Combs, Rev. Gordon, *O.F.M.Cap.* (NY) Retired. [MON] St. Clare Friary (Capuchin Franciscan Friars, Province of St. Mary), Yonkers, NY
Combs, Rev. Ronald, '03 (CIN) On Special Assignment. Cincinnati Curia: Pastoral Services
Combs, Rev. Timothy, *O.P.* (STP) [MON] St. Albert the Great Priory, Minneapolis, MN
Combs, Rev. William H., '04 (SAT) St. Mary Magdalen, San Antonio, TX; [MIS] Brothers of the Beloved Disciple, San Antonio, TX
Comeau, Rev. Ronald R., '71 (LFT) On Duty Outside Diocese. Aurora, ON
Comeaux, Rev. Nathan A., '11 (LAF) St. Peter, New Iberia, LA
Comer, Rev. Michael E., '80 (COV) Mother of God, Covington, KY; Newport Central Catholic High School, Newport, KY
Comerford, Rev. Christopher J., '96 (SFD) Chap, Decatur Corr Ctr Saints James and Patrick Parish, Decatur, IL; [ASN] Calvary Cemetery Association, Decatur, IL
Comerford, Rev. John J., *O.Carm.* '77 (JOL) [MON] Titus Brandsma Priory (Society of Mount Carmel), Darien, IL
Comerford, Rev. Patrick, '69 (LA) Retired.
Comiskey, Rev. John, *S.S.C.* '68 (OM) [MON] Missionary Society of St. Columban, St. Columbans, NE
Commins, Rev. Canon Jean-Baptiste, *I.C.R.S.S.* (DET) St. Joseph Shrine Parish Detroit (St. Joseph Roman Catholic Church), Detroit, MI
Commyn, Rev. James E., '86 (DET) St Lucy Parish, St. Clair Shores, St. Clair Shores, MI

Compaired Cortes, Rev. Fernando, '63 (MIA) Retired.

Comparan, Rev. Jose Luis, '03 (AUS) Holy Cross, Bertram, TX; Our Mother of Sorrows, Burnet, TX

Complo, Rev. Daniel C., '54 (DET) Retired.

Compton, Rev. Matthew Ross, '04 (CHI) Two Holy Martyrs Parish, Chicago, IL

Comstock, Rev. Douglas G., '67 (OG) Retired. Roman Catholic Community of Alexandria, Alexandria Bay, NY

Comtois, Rev. Norman, *O.M.I.* '73 (BO) [MON] Missionary Oblates of Mary Immaculate Northern Province, Lowell, MA

Conahan, Rev. Msgr. John J., '62 (PH) Retired.

Conard, Rev. James A., *M.M.* '56 (SJ) Retired.

Conard, Rev. James A., *M.M.* '56 (NY) Retired.

Conaty, Rev. Charles, '88 (CAM) Retired.

Concepcion, Rev. Mervin P., '03 (SAC) Pastor of St. Joseph Parish, Rio Vista, a corporation sole, Rio Vista, CA

Concepcion, Rev. Norlito, (HON) St. Pius X, Honolulu, HI

Concepcion, Rev. Vincent A. Yee, '02 (GBG) Seven Dolors, Yukon, PA

Concepcion, Rev. Vincent A. Yee, (GBG) Chap, Uniontown Hosp

Concepcion, Rev. Vincent A. Yee, '02 (GBG) Curia: Advisory Boards, Commissions, Committees, and Councils St. Edward, Herminie, PA

Concha, Rev. Alfonso J., '76 (PH) St. William, Philadelphia, PA

Concha, Rev. Augusto M., '72 (PH) Retired. St. William, Philadelphia, PA

Concordia, Rev. Stephen P., *O.S.B.* '95 (GBG) [MON] Saint Vincent Archabbey, Latrobe, PA

Conde, Rev. Francis Enrico, '74 (PAT) [HOS] St. Joseph's University Medical Center, Paterson, NJ

Conde, Rev. Norberto, '89 (GAL) Retired.

Conde, Rev. Thomas P., '87 (CHI) St. Christina, Chicago, IL

Conde Ocampo, Rev. Ramon, *O.de.M.* (SJN) Retired. Ntra. Sra. de Fatima, San Juan, PR

Condon, Rev. Daniel J., '81 (ROC) Curia: Clergy and Religious Services; Consultative Bodies; Leadership St. Thomas More, Rochester, NY

Condon, Rev. Denis, '78 (CHI) Retired.

Condon, Rev. Liam, '63 (ALB) Retired.

Condon, Rev. Msgr. Mark, (NEW) Curia: Offices and Directors

Condon, Rev. Sean, '57 (ORG) Retired. Our Lady of Mount Carmel, Newport Beach, CA

Condon, Rev. Msgr. T. Mark, '89 (PAT) Curia: Administration; Leadership Our Lady of the Holy Angels, Little Falls, NJ; Pope John XXIII Middle School, Inc., Sparta, NJ; [EFT] Catholic Foundation of the Diocese of Paterson, Inc., Clifton, NJ; [EFT] Diocese of Paterson Mission Fund, Inc., Clifton, NJ; [MIS] DePaul Catholic Diocesan High School, Inc., Wayne, NJ; [MIS] Paterson Diocese Central Investment & Lending Agency, Inc., Clifton, NJ; [MIS] Pope John XXIII Regional High School, Inc., Sparta, NJ; [MIS] St. Joseph's Fund, Clifton, NJ; [MIS] The Catholic Academy of Sussex County, Inc., Sparta, NJ

Condori, Rev. Delfin, *I.V.E.* '08 (DAL) St. Elizabeth Catholic Parish - Bonham, Bonham, TX

Conduah, Rev. Emmanuel, '04 (BRK) Chap, NY Presbyterian Brooklyn Methodist; NYU Langone Hosp Holy Name, Brooklyn, NY

Cone, Rev. Timothy, (SFS) Curia: Offices and Directors Holy Cross Parish of Edmunds County, Ipswich, SD; Our Lady of Perpetual Help Parish of McPherson County, Leola, SD

Cone, Rev. Timothy, '19 (SFS) Saint Thomas Apostle Parish of Edmunds County, Roscoe, SD

Cone Lombarte, Rev. Christian, (CIN) St. Ignatius of Loyola, Cincinnati, OH

Conedera, Rev. Sam, '17 (PHX) (>STL) [MON] Jesuit Community Corporation at Saint Louis University - Jesuit Hall, St. Louis, MO

Conesa, Rev. Msgr. Diego, '57 (STA) Retired.

Confer, Rev. Bernard, *O.P.* '73 (Y) St. Dominic, Youngstown, OH

Conforti, Rev. Sam, '21 (JOL) St. Mary Church, Mokena, IL

Congdon, Rev. John, '00 (FRS) Retired.

Congdon, Rev. Robert J., '87 (BO) On Leave.

Conger, Rev. Matthew, '21 (OG) Curia: Offices and Directors Saint Anthony's Church, Watertown, NY; The Church of the Holy Family, Watertown, NY; The Society of St. Patrick's Church, Watertown, NY

Congote, Rev. Jairo E., (OM) Divine Mercy, Schuyler, NE

Coning, Rev. Jeffrey J., '97 (COL) Immaculate Conception, Dennison, OH; Sacred Heart, New Philadelphia, OH

Conka, Rev. Frantisek, *C.O.* '98 (NY) [MIS] New York Oratory of St. Philip Neri, Inc., Sparkill, NY

Conklin, Rev. Ronald, *L.C.* (GRY) Sacred Heart Apostolic School, Inc., Rolling Prairie, IN

Conklin, Rev. Ross E., '14 (BAL) St. Joseph, Baltimore, MD; [EFT] St. Luke Parish Education Endowment Trust, Baltimore, MD

Conlan, Rev. Walter J., *S.J.* '76 (BO) [MON] Campion Health & Wellness, Inc., Weston, MA

Conley, Rev. Brian J., *S.J.* '01 (BO) Boston College High School, Boston, MA

Conley, Rev. Brian J., *SJ* '01 (PRT) Our Lady of Hope Parish, Portland, ME; [MON] St. Ignatius Residence (The Jesuits of Maine), Portland, ME

Conley, Rev. Charles, '74 (MIL) Retired.

Conley, Rev. John, *C.P.* '76 (SAC) [MON] Christ the King Passionist Retreat Center, Inc. (The Passionists (Chicago, IL)), Citrus Heights, CA

Conley, Rev. John E., *C.S.C.* '79 (FTW) Sacred Heart, Notre Dame, IN; [MON] Holy Cross Community, Corby Hall, University of Notre Dame, Notre Dame, IN

Conley, Rev. John J., *S.J.* '83 (BAL) [COL] Jesuit Community of Loyola University, Inc., Baltimore, MD; [MON] Jesuit Community of Loyola University Maryland, Inc., Baltimore, MD

Conley, Rev. Matthew J., '16 (BO) St. Mary of the Nativity, Scituate, MA

Conley, Rev. Msgr. Peter V., '63 (BO) Retired. Curia: Consultative Bodies [SEM] Pope Saint John XXIII National Seminary, Weston, MA

Conley, Rev. Rory T., '89 (WDC) On Special Assignment. Curia: Consultative Bodies St. Mary, Bryantown, MD

Conlin, Rev. Daniel C., '90 (STP) On Leave.

Conlon, Rev. Columbanus, '59 (ORG) Retired.

Conlon, Rev. James P., '02 (LAN) St. Francis of Assisi Parish Ann Arbor, Ann Arbor, MI

Conlon, Rev. Richard W., '90 (BRK) Resurrection Ascension - Our Lady of the Angelus Roman Catholic Church, Rego Park, NY

Connaghan, Rev. Daniel H., '90 (HRT) Retired.

Connall, Very Rev. Darrin, '92 (SPK) Curia: Leadership Cathedral of Our Lady of Lourdes, Spokane, WA

Connaughton, Rev. John, '13 (BGP) Curia: Clergy and Religious Services; Consultative Bodies St. Cecilia-St. Gabriel Parish Corporation, Stamford, CT

Connealy, Rev. Daniel, '16 (PHX) Curia: Offices and Directors St. Joan of Arc Roman Catholic Parish, Phoenix, AZ

Connealy, Rev. Gerald A., '87 (OM) Curia: Offices and Directors St. Mary, Laurel, NE; St. Mary, Wayne, NE

Connel, Rev. Loren, *OFM* (ALN) [RTR] St. Francis Retreat House, Inc., Easton, PA

Connell, Rev. Dennis P., *M.S.A.* '12 (NOR) [MON] Society of the Missionaries of the Holy Apostles, Cromwell, CT

Connell, Rev. James E., '87 (MIL) Retired. Curia: Leadership

Connell, Rev. John Andrew, '81 (PAT) Retired. [MIS] Nazareth Village, Chester, NJ

Connell, Rev. John M, '85 (LR) Curia: Leadership; Offices and Directors

Connell, Rev. John M., '85 (LR) Curia: Offices and Directors St. Raphael, Springdale, AR

Connell, Rev. Kevin, *S.J.* (SPK) [COL] Gonzaga University, Spokane, WA

Connell, Rev. Mark J., '86 (NY) [MIS] Newburgh San Miguel Program, Newburgh, NY

Connell, Rev. Martin T, *SJ* '94 (OAK) [MON] Jesuit Fathers and Brothers, Berkeley, CA

Connell, Rev. Patrick J., '92 (DET) Our Lady of La Salette Parish Berkley, Berkley, MI

Connell, Rev. William, '75 (MAD) Retired.

Connell, Rev. Msgr. William J., '76 (Y) Retired. Curia: Offices and Directors

Connelly, Rev. Msgr. Christopher D., '93 (SPR) Curia: Tribunal Cathedral of St. Michael the Archangel, Springfield, MA

Connelly, Rev. James, (RIC) Chap, McGuire VA Med Ctr

Connelly, Rev. James T., *C.S.C.* '64 (FTW) [MON] Congregation of Holy Cross, United States Province of Priests and Brothers, Notre Dame, IN

Connelly, Rev. Joseph, '19 (STP) Guardian Angels, Oakdale, MN

Connelly, Rev. Laurence, (AUS) Retired.

Connelly, Rev. Peter, *O.S.B.* '87 (WOR) [MON] Benedictine Monks, St. Benedict Abbey, Still River, MA

Connely Quintero, Rev. Marco A., (ARE) On Duty Outside Diocese. Spain

Conner, Rev. Jacob Scott, '10 (LKC) On Leave. Non-Active

Conner, Rev. James, *O.C.S.O.* '57 (L) [MON] Abbey of Our Lady of Gethsemani, of the Order of Cistercians of the Strict Observance, Trappist, KY

Conner, Rev. Paul, (OAK) [MON] Order of Preachers (Province of the Most Holy Name of Jesus - Western Dominican Province), Oakland, CA

Conner, Rev. Paul M., *O.P.* '67 (PRO) [MON] St. Thomas Aquinas Priory at Providence College, Providence, RI

Conner, Rev. Steven, '94 (NEW) St. Matthew, Ridgefield, NJ

Conners, Rev. Quinn, *O.Carm.* '71 (NY) [MON] Brandsma Priory (Carmelite Friars (North American Prov. of St. Elias and Most Pure Heart of Mary Province)), Middletown, NY

Connerton, Rev. Msgr. Barry R.L., '70 (PRO) Retired.

Connery, Rev. J. Thomas, '63 (ALB) Retired.

Connery, Rev. Sean P., *O.S.F.S.* '71 (WIL) Salesianum School, Wilmington, DE

Connery, Rev. Thomas, '83 (ORL) St. Theresa, Belleview, FL

Connole, Rev. Marlin J., '68 (SEA) Retired.

Connolly, Rev. Andrew P., '56 (RVC) Retired.

Connolly, Rev. Brian T., '17 (PH) Curia: Advisory Boards, Commissions, Committees, and Councils St. Helena, Blue Bell, PA

Connolly, Msgr. Clement J., '64 (LA) Retired. Holy Family, South Pasadena, CA

Connolly, Rev. Edward B., '66 (ALN) Retired.

Connolly, Rev. James M.T., '78 (RIC) Military Chap

Connolly, Rev. James M.T., '78 (ALN) On Duty Outside Diocese. Hampton, VA Curia: (>MO) Offices and Directors

Connolly, Rev. Jerry, '67 (GF) Retired.

Connolly, Rev. John J., '94 (BO) St. John Chrysostom, Boston, MA; St. Theresa of Avila, Boston, MA

Connolly, Rev. K. Scott, '95 (SEA) Curia: Leadership St. Edward, Seattle, WA; St. George, Seattle, WA; St. Paul, Seattle, WA; St. Peter, Seattle, WA; [MIS] St. Mary, Seattle, WA

Connolly, Rev. Kevin, '85 (WIN) St. Bernard's, Stewartville, MN; St. Bridget's, Rochester, MN

Connolly, Rev. Leo L., '81 (COL) Curia: Consultative Bodies Seton Parish, Pickerington, OH

Connolly, Rev. Michael, '78 (NY) [MON] St. Clare Friary (Capuchin Franciscan Friars, Province of St. Mary), Yonkers, NY

Connolly, Rev. Michael, '18 (NY) St. Martin de Porres, Poughkeepsie, NY; St. Mary, Wappingers Falls, NY

Connolly, Rev. Michael C., *O.S.F.S.* '74 (WIL) Curia: Tribunal Salesianum School, Wilmington, DE

Connolly, Rev. Michael J., *S.J.* '68 (SPK) [COL] Gonzaga University, Spokane, WA

Connolly, Rev. Patrick, *S.J.* '66 (LA) [MON] Jesuit Community, Los Angeles, CA

Connolly, Rev. Patrick, *S.J.* '66 (SJ) [MON] Sacred Heart Jesuit Center, Los Gatos, CA

Connolly, Rev. Paul E., '83 (DAV) St. Alphonsus Church of Mt. Pleasant, Iowa, Mount Pleasant, IA

Connolly, Rev. Peter, *C.Ss.R.* '07 (TUC) Retired. [MON] Redemptorist Society of Arizona Desert House of Prayer Residence, Tucson, AZ; [RTR] Redemptorist Society of Arizona Redemptorist Renewal Center, Tucson, AZ

Connolly, Rev. Sean, '15 (NY) Parish of Immaculate Conception and Assumption, Tuckahoe, NY; Parish of Most Holy Redeemer and Nativity, New York, NY; St. Brigid, New York, NY

Connolly, Rev. Thomas, *S.J.* '63 (SJ) [MON] Sacred Heart Jesuit Center, Los Gatos, CA

Connolly, Rev. Thomas, '00 (SPK) St. Mary Presentation, Deer Park, WA

Connolly, Rev. Thomas, '00 (SPK) St. Joseph, Colbert, WA

Connolly, Rev. Thomas, (SPK) Curia: Leadership

Connor, Rev. Brian P., '89 (LIN) St. Mary's, David City, NE

Connor, Rev. Charles P., '90 (SCR) Retired. Curia: Offices and Directors

Connor, Rev. J. Patrick, '61 (NSH) Retired.

Connor, Rev. James, '78 (HEL) Saint Francis of Assisi Parish: Series 631, LLC, Hamilton, MT

Connor, Rev. John, *C.S.C.* (FTW) [MIS] Holy Cross House, Notre Dame, IN

Connor, Rev. John J., *C.P.* '84 (SCR) Retired.

Connor, Rev. Patrick L., '83 (ROC) Saints Isidore and Maria Torribia, Addison, NY

Connor, Rev. Robert A., '64 (POD) Curia: Clergy and Religious Services

Connor, Rev. Sean M., '01 (BO) Curia: Consultative Bodies Sacred Heart, Weymouth, MA; St. Thomas

More, Braintree, MA
Connor, Rev. Vincent, '71 (SB) Retired.
Connor, Rev. William Joseph, '66 (LA) Retired.
Connors, Rev. Cletus, *O.S.B.* '68 (SCL) [MON] St. John's Abbey, of the Order of St. Benedict, Collegeville, MN
Connors, Rev. Cletus, *OSB* '72 (SCL) Church of Saint Boniface, Cold Spring, MN; SS. Peter and Paul, Richmond, MN; St. James, Cold Spring, MN
Connors, Rev. Francis E., '73 (BUR) Retired.
Connors, Rev. John E., '01 (SPR) St. Cecilia's, Wilbraham, MA
Connors, Rev. Michael E., *C.S.C.* '84 (FTW) [COL] University of Notre Dame Du Lac, Notre Dame, IN; [MON] Holy Cross Community, Corby Hall, University of Notre Dame, Notre Dame, IN
Connors, Rev. Richard P., '79 (PH) Retired.
Connors, Very Rev. Robert L., '71 (BO) Retired. Curia: Advisory Boards, Commissions, Committees, and Councils; Clergy and Religious Services; Consultative Bodies; Leadership
Connors, Rev. Ryan, '12 (BO) [SEM] Saint John's Seminary, Brighton, MA
Connors, Rev. Ryan W., '12 (PRO) On Duty Outside Diocese. St John Seminary, Brighton, MA
Connors, Rev. Msgr. Terrence L., '75 (MAD) Retired.
Conoboy, Rev. Shawn, '06 (Y) Curia: Leadership Our Lady of Perpetual Help, Aurora, OH; St. Ambrose, Garrettsville, OH; St. Joseph, Mantua, OH
Conoscenti, Rev. Frederick M., '65 (BUF) Retired.
Conover, Rev. James, (TR) St. Rose of Lima, Freehold, NJ
Conroy, Rev. Donald B., '64 (GBG) (>WDC) [MIS] National Institute for the Family, Washington, DC
Conroy, Rev. Francis M., '64 (BO) Retired.
Conroy, Rev. Francis X., '72 (BEA) Retired.
Conroy, Rev. James R., *S.J.* '78 (BAL) [MIS] Ignatian Volunteer Corps, Baltimore, MD (>WDC) [MON] The Jesuit Community at Georgetown University, Washington, DC
Conroy, Rev. Sean, '21 (DEN) Our Lady of Lourdes Catholic Parish in Denver, Denver, CO; St. Louis-King of France Catholic Parish in Englewood, Englewood, CO
Conry, Rev. Austin, '65 (MOB) Retired.
Consani, Rev. Robert E., '63 (KAL) Retired. St. Monica, Kalamazoo, MI
Conselva, Rev. Edwin, *MS* '15 (HON) St. Theresa, Kekaha, HI
Consemino, Rev. Angelo R., '84 (LUB) Sacred Heart, Littlefield, TX; Sacred Heart, Plainview, TX
Conserva, Rev. Stephen, *OMI* '74 (BO) [MIS] St. Joseph the Worker Shrine, Lowell, MA
Considine, Rev. James F., '02 (MET) Curia: Consultative Bodies St. Frances Cabrini, Piscataway, NJ
Considine, Rev. Matthew, *SMM* '77 (RVC) Sts. Peter & Paul, Manorville, NY; [MON] Montfort Missionaries, Bay Shore, NY; [PRE] Montfort Missionaries Charitable Trust, Bay Shore, NY
Considine, Rev. Matthew J., *S.M.M.* '77 (BRK) [MON] Montfort Missionaries Provincialate (Missionaries of the Company of Mary; Montfort Missionaries; Montfort Publications; Montfort Spiritual Association), Ozone Park, NY
Considine, Rev. William, *S.M.M.* '73 (HRT) [MON] Montfort Missionaries, Litchfield, CT
Consiglio, Rev. Cyprian, *O.S.B.Cam.* '98 (MRY) [MON] New Camaldoli Hermitage (Camaldolese Hermits of America), Big Sur, CA
Constant, Rev. Van, '93 (HT) Curia: (>MO) Offices and Directors [MIS] The Chapel of the Blessed Sacrament, Gibson, LA
Constantin, Rev. Rodrigue, '03 (OLL) St. Rafka Maronite Catholic Church, Livonia, MI
Constantine, Rev. Albert, '13 (OLL) Curia: Leadership; Offices and Directors
Constantine, Rev. Cyprian G., *O.S.B.* '77 (GBG) [MON] Saint Vincent Archabbey, Latrobe, PA; [SEM] St. Vincent Seminary, Latrobe, PA
Contadino, Rev. J. Eugene, *S.M.* '70 (CIN) Retired.
Contadino, Rev. J. Eugene, *SM* (CIN) [MON] Marianist Community, Dayton, OH
Contarin, Rev. Robert, '19 (BUF) Our Lady of Victory National Shrine and Basilica, Lackawanna, NY
Conte, Rev. James W., '48 (NY) Retired.
Contons, Rev. Msgr. Albert J., '48 (BO) Retired.
Contreras, Rev. David, '93 (AMA) Curia: Advisory Boards, Commissions, Committees, and Councils Church of the Holy Spirit, Tulia, TX
Contreras, Rev. Elizandro, *O.S.A.* (PH) Annunciation B.V.M., Philadelphia, PA; [MON] Augustinian Community (O.S.A.), Philadelphia, PA
Contreras, Rev. Fredy, *C.S.V.* (CHI) [MON] Viatorian Province Center-Clerics of St. Viator, Arlington Heights, IL
Contreras, Rev. Rodolfo, '10 (MRY) St. Rose of Lima Church, Paso Robles, CA
Contreras, Rev. Victor Manuel, (FWT) St. Matthew, Arlington, TX
Contreras, Rev. Wilfredo, '03 (MIA) San Isidro, Pompano Beach, FL
Contreras Tribaldo, Rev. Carlos Alberto, (SJN) Exaltacion de la Santa Cruz, Trujillo Alto, PR; Santa Cruz, Trujillo Alto, PR
Contu, Rev. Joseph, (GLP) On Leave.
Converse, Rev. Brian J., '91 (NOR) Curia: Leadership; (>MO) Offices and Directors; Offices and Directors Our Lady of Lourdes, Gales Ferry, CT; Sacred Heart, Groton, CT; St. Mary Mother of the Redeemer, Groton, CT
Converset, Rev. John M., *M.C.C.J.* '71 (CIN) [MON] Comboni Missionaries (Verona Fathers)-Comboni Mission Center, Cincinnati, OH
Converset, Rev. John Michael, *M.C.C.J.* '71 (NEW) [MON] Comboni Missionaries of the Heart of Jesus (Verona Fathers), Newark, NJ
Convertino, Rev. David I., *O.F.M.* (PAT) [MIS] St. Anthony's Guild, Paterson, NJ
Convery, Rev. Paul C., *C.O.* '84 (PH) St. Francis Xavier, Philadelphia, PA; [MON] The Philadelphia Congregation of The Oratory of St. Philip Neri, Philadelphia, PA
Convocar, Very Rev. Romeo Duetao, '96 (AGN) Curia: Leadership
Convocar, Rev. Romeo (Romy) D., (AGN) Curia: Consultative Bodies; Organizations (affiliated, inter-Diocesan, miscellaneous/other); Tribunal Blessed Diego Luis de San Vitores Church, Tumon, GU
Conway, Rev. Dennis C., '17 (DUB) Immaculate Conception Church, Cedar Rapids, Iowa, Cedar Rapids, IA; St. Wenceslaus Church, Cedar Rapids, Iowa, Cedar Rapids, IA
Conway, Rev. James, '65 (SAT) Retired. [NUR] Missionary Servants of St. Anthony (Padua Place), San Antonio, TX
Conway, Rev. John E., *M.M.* '73 (SJ) Retired.
Conway, Rev. John E., *M.M.* '73 (NY) Retired.
Conway, Rev. John T., '00 (ATL) St. Anthony Catholic Church, Blue Ridge, Inc., Blue Ridge, GA
Conway, Rev. Msgr. John T., '77 (PH) Mary, Mother of the Redeemer, North Wales, PA
Conway, Rev. Msgr. Michael, '60 (PAT) Retired.
Conway, Rev. Michael, *O.SS.T.* '73 (BAL) Retired. [MON] Holy Trinity Monastery, Sykesville, MD
Conway, Rev. Michael, *S.D.B.* (NY) [MON] Salesian Provincial House, New Rochelle, NY
Conway, Rev. Michael P., '14 (PIT) Curia: Consultative Bodies Christ the Divine Shepherd, Monroeville, PA
Conway, Rev. Richard C., '63 (BO) Retired. St. Ambrose, Boston, MA
Conway, Rev. Richard T., '83 (BO) St. Robert Bellarmine, Andover, MA
Conway, Rev. Robert, *C.PP.S.* '53 (CIN) Retired.
Conway, Rev. Robert R., '04 (CHL) Retired.
Conway, Rev. Thomas, '86 (JKS) Curia: Consultative Bodies
Conway, Rev. Thomas, *O.F.M.* '05 (BO) Curia: Consultative Bodies [MIS] St. Anthony Shrine, Boston, MA
Conway, Rev. Thomas S., '86 (BLX) Curia: Advisory Boards, Commissions, Committees, and Councils
Conway, Rev. Thomas S., '86 (BLX) Curia: Tribunal St. Fabian Catholic Parish, Hattiesburg, MS
Conway, Rev. William, '77 (JOL) Retired.
Conwill, Rev. Giles, '73 (SD) Retired.
Conyers, Rev. James C., '14 (WH) Curia: Offices and Directors St. Catherine of Siena, Ronceverte, WV; St. Charles Borromeo, White Sulphur Springs, WV
Conyers, Rev. Richard J., *CSC* (FTW) Retired. [MIS] Holy Cross House, Notre Dame, IN
Coogan, Rev. Msgr. Thomas M., '97 (RVC) Curia: Offices and Directors St. Dominic's, Oyster Bay, NY
Cook, Rev. Adrian L., '72 (MOB) Retired.
Cook, Rev. Brian J., '85 (CHL) Retired.
Cook, Rev. Christian, (CHL) Curia: Consultative Bodies
Cook, Rev. Damien J., '99 (OM) St. Philip Neri-Blessed Sacrament Parish of Omaha, Omaha, NE
Cook, Rev. Daniel A., '90 (ALX) On Leave.
Cook, Rev. Msgr. Douglas J., '94 (ORG) Curia: Leadership Our Lady of Mount Carmel, Newport Beach, CA
Cook, Rev. Edward J., '67 (MIL) Congregation of the Great Spirit, Milwaukee, WI
Cook, Rev. John Joseph Mary, *F.I.* '02 (SY) [MON] Mount St. Francis Hermitage, Inc., Endicott, NY; [RTR] Mount St. Francis Hermitage, Inc., Endicott, NY
Cook, Rev. Kevin, (STL) [HOS] SSM Health De Paul Hospital - St. Louis, Bridgeton, MO
Cook, Rev. Kevin A., '01 (FR) Curia: Offices and Directors
Cook, Rev. Kevin A., '01 (FR) Our Lady of Mt. Carmel, Seekonk, MA
Cook, Rev. Michael J., '73 (WIL) Retired.
Cook, Rev. Msgr. Paul G., '59 (BAL) Retired.
Cook, Rev. Philip C., *O.S.A.* '97 (TLS) Cascia Hall Preparatory School, Tulsa, OK
Cook, Rev. Raymond, *O.M.I.* '12 (WDC) [MON] Missionary Oblates of Mary Immaculate, Washington, DC
Cook, Rev. Raymond, *O.M.I.* '12 (GAL) [CAM] Catholic Student Center and St. Mary Chapel, Houston, TX (>CHI) [EFT] Oblates for International Pastoral (Oblate International Pastoral Investment Trust), Chicago, IL
Cook, Rev. Robert, *O.F.M.Conv.* '10 (CHI) Mary, Mother of God, Chicago, IL; [MIS] Saint Bonaventure Friary, ,
Cook, Rev. Robert J., '65 (LC) Retired. [MIS] Holy Cross (Seminary) Diocesan Center, La Crosse, WI
Cook, Rev. Robert P., '03 (B) Curia: Leadership [MIS] Sacred Heart, Clark Fork, ID
Cook, Rev. Robert P., '03 (B) Curia: Leadership St. Joseph's, Sandpoint, ID
Cook, Rev. Robert W., '00 (CHY) Retired.
Cook, Rev. Msgr. Thomas E., '97 (WIN) On Duty Outside Diocese. Dicastery for the Clergy, Vatican City
Cook, Rev. Thomas S., '88 (LA) St. Mary of the Assumption, Santa Maria, CA
Cook, Rev. Timothy R., '83 (STL) Mary, Queen of Peace Catholic Church, Webster Groves, MO; Sts. Teresa and Bridget Catholic Church, St. Louis, MO
Cook, Rev. W. Christian, '17 (CHL) Immaculate Conception, Hendersonville, NC
Cook, Rev. William, (SAV) St. Anne, Columbus, GA
Cook, Rev. William G., '88 (NEW) Retired.
Cooke, Rev. Christopher R., '06 (PH) [SEM] Theological Seminary of St. Charles Borromeo, Wynnewood, PA
Cooke, Rev. Jared, (AUS) Our Lady of Wisdom University Parish (Our Lady of Wisdom Catholic Church - San Marcos, Texas), San Marcos, TX
Cookson, Rev. Edward L., *M.M.* '65 (NY) [MON] Maryknoll Fathers and Brothers (Catholic Foreign Mission Society of America, Inc.), Ossining, NY
Cool, Rev. Brian, '93 (ROC) [CAM] Catholic Newman Community at the University of Rochester, Rochester, NY; [CAM] Eastman School of Music Catholic Students Organization, Rochester, NY; [CAM] Newman (Catholic Campus) Parish, RIT/NTID, Rochester, NY
Cooley, Rev. Stephen, *O.Carm.* '67 (JOL) Retired.
Coolidge, Rev. Martin P, '21 (DUB) St. Bridget Church (Postville, Iowa), Postville, IA; St. Mary's Church, McGregor, Iowa, McGregor, IA; St. Patrick's Church, Monona, Iowa, Monona, IA
Coolong, Rev. Raymond, *S.M.* '71 (SP) Our Lady of Perpetual Help, Tampa, FL
Coon, Rev. David N., '93 (SPC) Curia: Offices and Directors Sacred Heart, Dexter, MO
Coon, Rev. J.C., '01 (BEA) Immaculate Conception-St. Peter, Groves, TX
Coonan, Very Rev. Matthew M., '11 (FTW) Curia: Leadership; Offices and Directors St. Henry, Fort Wayne, IN; St. Therese, Fort Wayne, IN
Coonan, Rev. Robert J., '65 (SPR) Retired.
Coonan, Rev. Terrence M., '11 (FTW) Curia: Offices and Directors St. Elizabeth Ann Seton, Fort Wayne, IN
Cooney, Rev. Albert, *SMA* '55 (NEW) Retired. [MON] Society of African Missions, Provincialate, S.M.A. Fathers, Tenafly, NJ
Cooney, Rev. Art, (DET) [MON] St. Bonaventure Monastery, Detroit, MI
Cooney, Rev. David C., *S.D.S.* '67 (MIL) Retired. [MON] Salvatorian Provincial Offices (Society of the Divine Savior), Milwaukee, WI
Cooney, Rev. Frank, *M.S.* '69 (ORL) Good Shepherd, Orlando, FL
Cooney, Rev. John M., '62 (HRT) Retired.
Cooney, Rev. Patrick, *O.S.B.* '91 (IND) [MON] St. Meinrad Archabbey, St. Meinrad, IN
Cooney, Rev. Patrick, *O.S.B.* (OWN) Curia: Leadership
Cooney, Rev. Msgr. Roger P., '70 (COV) Retired. Curia: Advisory Boards, Commissions, Committees, and Councils
Cooney, Rev. Sean K., '59 (ORL) Retired.
Cooney, Rev. Stephen A., '76 (LIN) St. Mary, Lincoln, NE
Cooney, Rev. Theophane, *C.P.* '52 (BRK) Retired. [MON] Immaculate Conception Monastery, Jamaica, NY

Cooney, Rev. Theophane, *C.P.* '52 (BRK) Retired. [MON] Immaculate Conception Monastery, Jamaica, NY
Cooney, Rev. Xavier, *SVD* (CHI) Retired.
Cooper, Rev. David E., '70 (MIL) Retired.
Cooper, Rev. Jeffrey, *C.S.C.* (COS) [MON] Holy Cross Novitiate (Congregation of Holy Cross, United States Province), Cascade, CO
Cooper, Rev. John A., '80 (LIN) Retired.
Cooper, Rev. Joseph M., '95 (MAN) On Administrative Leave.
Cooper, Rt. Rev. Mark A., *O.S.B.* '76 (MAN) [COL] Saint Anselm College, Manchester, NH; [MON] St. Anselm Abbey, Manchester, NH; [SEM] St. Anselm Abbey Seminary, Manchester, NH
Cooper, Rev. Nicholas, (GLD) Holy Family of East Tawas, East Tawas, MI
Cooper, Rev. Patrick E., '91 (CHR) Retired. St. Elizabeth Ann Seton, Simpsonville, SC
Cooper, Rev. Robert T., '07 (NO) Divine Mercy Roman Catholic Church, Kenner, Louisiana, Kenner, LA
Cooper, Rev. Warren L., '71 (NO) On Special Assignment. Min to Infirm St. Luke the Evangelist Roman Catholic Church, Slidell, Louisiana, Slidell, LA
Cooray, Rev. Joe, *OMI* '88 (FRS) Sacred Heart, Fresno, CA
Copeland, Rev. Leonard, *O.C.D.* '67 (BO) [MON] Carmelite Monastery, Boston, MA
Copeland, Rev. Robert F., '99 (LAN) St. John the Evangelist Parish Fenton, Fenton, MI
Copelin, Rev. Boniface T., *O.S.B.* '08 (OKL) [MON] St. Gregory's Abbey (Benedictine Fathers of Sacred Heart Mission, Inc.), Shawnee, OK
Copenhagen, Rev. Michael, '15 (NTN) St. Nicholas, Rochester, NY
Copp, Rev. Rodney J., '73 (BO) Retired.
Copping, Rev. Gary P., '13 (NO) St. Anthony, Gretna, LA; St. Joseph Church and Shrine on the Westbank, Gretna, LA
Coppinger, Rev. Edmund, '59 (WIL) Retired.
Coppinger, Rev. John W., *S.A.* '72 (NY) Retired. [MON] St. Christopher's Inn Friary, Garrison, NY
Coppola, Rev. Anthony, '02 (SP) Curia: Pastoral Services Most Holy Redeemer, Tampa, FL
Copsey, Rev. Robert A., '78 (SAC) Retired.
Coquilla, Rev. German J., *C.R.M.* (CHR) St. Anne and St. Jude, Sumter, SC
Coquillo, Rev. German, *C.R.M.* (NEW) Chap, Hackensack Univ Med Ctr
Corazon Lopez, Rev. Jose Gabriel, '19 (SJN) Nuestra Senora del Carmen, Catano, PR
Corbally, Rev. Christopher, *S.J.* '76 (TUC) [MON] Jesuit Community of the Vatican Observatory, Tucson, AZ
Corbelli, Rev. Vincent, *M.M.* '60 (ROC) Retired.
Corbelli, Rev. Vincent F., *M.M.* '60 (NY) Retired. [MON] Maryknoll Fathers and Brothers (Catholic Foreign Mission Society of America, Inc.), Ossining, NY
Corbett, Rev. John, *O.P.* '80 (CIN) St. Gertrude, Cincinnati, OH; [MON] St. Gertrude Priory, Cincinnati, OH
Corbett, Rev. John F., '95 (NEW) Curia: Offices and Directors
Corbett, Rev. Msgr. W. Joseph, '95 (ATL) St. Jude the Apostle Catholic Church, Sandy Springs, Inc., Sandy Springs, GA
Corbin, Rev. Raymond G., '04 (BUF) St. Stephen, Grand Island, NY
Corbino, Rev. Thomas, '72 (JOL) Retired.
Corbley, Rev. Timothy L., *I.V. Dei* '93 (COS) Chap, Penrose-St Francis; St Francis Med Ctr
Corbo, Rev. Alfred P., '56 (CHI) Retired. St. Gertrude, Franklin Park, IL
Corces, Rev. Pedro M., '88 (MIA) Our Lady of Divine Providence, Miami, FL
Corcoran, Rev. Brian, '72 (SD) Retired.
Corcoran, Rev. C. Timothy, '12 (SP) Curia: Leadership
Corcoran, Rev. Kevin, '88 (SY) Curia: Leadership St. Patrick, Chittenango, NY; [CAM] Cazenovia College Newman Center, Cazenovia, NY
Corcoran, Rev. Kevin, (PAT) Curia: Leadership
Corcoran, Rev. Kevin J., (SY) St. James, Cazenovia, NY
Corcoran, Rev. Michael P., *S.J.* '88 (BUF) [MON] The Canisius Jesuit Community, Inc., Buffalo, NY
Corcoran, Rev. T. Kevin, '99 (PAT) Curia: Leadership [EFT] Catholic Foundation of the Diocese of Paterson, Inc., Clifton, NJ; [EFT] Diocese of Paterson Mission Fund, Inc., Clifton, NJ
Corcoran, Rev. T. Kevin, '99 (PAT) Corpus Christi, Chatham, NJ
Corcoran, Rev. William, (SCR) Retired.
Corcoran, Rev. William T., '81 (CHI) Curia: Leadership St. Elizabeth Seton, Orland Hills, IL
Cordaro, Rev. Salvatore, *O.F.M.Cap.* '12 (NY) St. Joseph, New Paltz, NY; [MON] St. Joseph Friary (Capuchin Franciscans, Province of St. Mary), New Paltz, NY
Cordeiro, Rev. Luis, '98 (STO) St. Anthony Church of Hughson (Pastor of), Hughson, CA
Cordell, Rev. Hyacinth, *O.P.* '11 (WDC) St. Dominic Church & Priory, Washington, DC
Cordell, Friar Hyacinth M, *O.P.* '11 (PH) St. Patrick, Philadelphia, PA
Cordeno, Rev. Peter, '85 (ORL) Holy Name of Jesus, Indialantic, FL
Cordero, Friar Carlos, *O.S.A.* '99 (SJN) Santa Rita de Casia, Bayamon, PR
Cordero, Rev. Enrique, (MGZ) Our Lady of Monserrate, Moca, PR
Cordero, Rev. Msgr. Faustino, '71 (BRK) Retired.
Cordero, Rev. John, *M.M.H.C.* '94 (LA) Holy Family, Artesia, CA
Cordero, Rev. Martin G., '99 (LSC) Curia: Consultative Bodies; Leadership; Spiritual Life Our Lady of Purification Parish, Inc., Dona Ana, NM
Cordero, Rev. Mert, '74 (NEW) Chap, Valley Hosp, Ridgewood Our Lady of Mount Carmel, Ridgewood, NJ
Cordery, Rev. Robert J., '80 (BO) Retired.
Cordes, Rev. Christopher L., '95 (JC) Curia: Administration; Advisory Boards, Commissions, Committees, and Councils Our Lady of Lourdes, Columbia, MO
Cordes, Rev. John, '03 (KCK) Our Lady of Unity, Kansas City, KS
Cordier, Rev. Michael L., '02 (CIN) St. Simon the Apostle, Cincinnati, OH
Cordoba, Rev. Luis Guillermo, '00 (ATL) Our Lady of the Americas Catholic Mission, Lilburn, GA
Cordonnier, Rev. Andrew P., '14 (CIN) St. Angela Merici, Fayetteville, OH; St. Michael, Mt. Orab, OH
Core, Rev. Jeffrey, '11 (SPK) Curia: Leadership Holy Family, Clarkston, WA
Corel, Very Rev. Joseph S., '00 (JC) Curia: Administration; Deaneries St. Vincent de Paul, Sedalia, MO
Coric, Rev. Christopher, *O.F.M.Conv.* '71 (BUF) Chap, Veterans Hosp Our Lady of Bistrica, Lackawanna, NY
Coric, Rev. Zvonimir, '03 (LA) St. Anthony, Los Angeles, CA
Coriden, Rev. James A., '57 (GRY) Retired.
Corkery, Rev. Daniel, '55 (ALX) Retired. St. Martin of Tours, Hessmer, LA
Corley, Rev. Theodosius, *O.F.M.Cap.* '74 (NY) Retired. [MON] St. Clare Friary (Capuchin Franciscan Friars, Province of St. Mary), Yonkers, NY
Cormack, Rev. James B., *C.M.* '76 (STL) St. Catherine Laboure Catholic Church, St. Louis, MO; [MON] Congregation of the Mission Vincentian Fathers Lazarist Residence, St. Louis, MO
Cormack, Rev. John, (GLP) St. Catherine, Cibicue, AZ; St. Francis, Whiteriver, AZ
Cormack, Rev. Michael J., '54 (SAC) Retired. Pastor of St. Rose of Lima Parish, Roseville, a corporation sole, Roseville, CA
Cormie, Rev. Justin, '19 (GAL) Our Lady of Fatima, Galena Park, TX
Cormier, Rev. Gregory P., '83 (LAF) St. Joseph, Cecilia, LA; St. Rose of Lima, Cecilia, LA
Cormier, Very Rev. Matthew, '14 (LKC) Curia: Advisory Boards, Commissions, Committees, and Councils; Leadership St. Henry, Lake Charles, LA
Cormier, Rev. Michael, '00 (SP) Incarnation Catholic Church, Tampa, FL
Cormier, Rev. Roger C., '61 (BO) Retired.
Cormier, Rev. William N., '71 (WOR) Retired.
Cornea, Rev. Sergiu, '96 (ROM) Curia: Offices and Directors Ss. Peter and Paul Church, Chicago, IL
Corneille, Rev. Cecil C., '95 (STV) On Duty Outside Diocese. Curia: (>MO) Offices and Directors
Cornejo, Very Rev. Martin, '01 (LSC) Curia: Leadership Immaculate Conception Parish, Alamogordo, Inc., Alamogordo, NM
Cornejo-Castillero, Rev. Justino, '05 (NEW) [SEM] Redemptoris Mater Archdiocesan Missionary Seminary, Kearny, NJ
Corneli, Rev. Luis R., *P.S.S.* '91 (BAL) [MIS] St. Mary's Seminary & University, Baltimore, MD; [MON] Society of St. Sulpice, Province of the United States, Baltimore, MD
Cornelia, Rev. Jose D., *D.S.* '99 (PHX) Immaculate Conception Roman Catholic Parish, Cottonwood, AZ
Cornelio, Rev. Noel Emmanuel, '03 (DET) Sacred Heart Parish Imlay City, Imlay City, MI; St. Cornelius Parish Dryden, Dryden, MI; St. Nicholas Parish Capac, Capac, MI
Cornelius, Rev. John, '13 (POC) Retired.
Cornelius, Rev. Leonard, *O.F.M.* '69 (PIT) [MON] Holy Family Friary, Pittsburgh, PA
Cornell, Rev. Richard P., (BO) St. Cecilia, Ashland, MA
Cornett, Rev. David, '85 (STU) Curia: Deaneries Assumption, Barnesville, OH; St. Mary's, Barnesville, OH
Corona, Rev. Andrew J., '93 (GRY) Retired.
Corona, Rev. Dominic, '10 (SP) St. James the Apostle, Port Richey, FL
Corona, Rev. Enrique, '07 (PAT) St. Agnes, Paterson, NJ; St. Michael the Archangel, Paterson, NJ
Corona, Rev. John, '71 (RNO) Retired.
Corona, Rev. Miguel, '05 (MRY) Chap, Salinas Valley State Prison St. Theodore, Gonzales, CA
Corona, Rev. Rufino, *TOR* '20 (STU) [COL] Franciscan University of Steubenville, Steubenville, OH; [MON] Holy Spirit Friary, Steubenville, OH
Corona Bernal, Rev. Santiago (James), '19 (JOL) St. Matthew, Glendale Heights, IL
Coronado, Rev. Daniel, (KCK) Our Lady of Guadalupe, Topeka, KS
Coronado, Rev. Victorino B., '95 (CAM) St. Andrew the Apostle R.C. Church, Gibbsboro, N.J., Gibbsboro, NJ
Corpora, Rev. Joseph V., *C.S.C.* '84 (FTW) [COL] University of Notre Dame Du Lac, Notre Dame, IN; [MON] Holy Cross Community, Corby Hall, University of Notre Dame, Notre Dame, IN
Corradi, Rev. Frank, '85 (LC) Retired.
Corradin, Rev. Albert, *C.S.* '54 (LA) Retired.
Corrado, Rev. Dennis M., *C.O.* '70 (BRK) Retired. Assumption of the Blessed Virgin Mary, Brooklyn, NY; [MON] Oratory of Saint Philip Neri, Congregation Pontifical Rite, Brooklyn, NY
Corral, Rev. Arturo N., '98 (LA) Our Lady Queen of Angels, Los Angeles, CA
Corral, Rev. Jose M., '79 (SFR) Our Lady of the Pillar, Half Moon Bay, CA; [MIS] Catholic Charismatic Renewal (CCR), San Francisco, CA
Corral, Rev. Miguel, '18 (LAV) Curia: Advisory Boards, Commissions, Committees, and Councils; Faith Formation St. Anne, Las Vegas, NV
Corral, Rev. Miguel, (LAV) Curia: Advisory Boards, Commissions, Committees, and Councils; Clergy and Religious Services
Corrales, Rev. Alirio, '78 (LAR) Santa Margarita de Escocia, Laredo, TX; [MIS] National Nocturnal Adoration Society (Congregation of the Blessed Sacrament), Laredo, TX
Corrales-Diaz, Rev. Roger A., '02 (CHI) St. Mary, Star of the Sea, Chicago, IL
Correa, Rev. Fabio Correa, '97 (OAK) St. Leander, San Leandro, CA
Correa, Rev. Gino, *O.F.M.* (WDC) [SEM] Holy Name College, Silver Spring, MD
Correa, Rev. Luis Norberto, (FAJ) Curia: Leadership Santisimo Redentor, Fajardo, PR
Correa-Llano, Rev. Javier, *I.V.E.* (NY) St. Jerome's, Bronx, NY
Correa-Torres, Rev. Elias, *O.S.B.* '14 (CHL) [MON] Belmont Abbey (Southern Benedictine Society of North Carolina, Inc.), Belmont, NC
Corredor, Rev. Gustavo, '91 (CHR) Curia: Offices and Directors Corpus Christi, Lexington, SC; Minor Basilica of St. Peter, Columbia, SC
Correia, Rev. Edward E., '68 (FR) Retired.
Correio, Rev. Bruce, '85 (LA) San Roque, Santa Barbàra, CA
Correz, Rev. Steven, '00 (ORG) Curia: Offices and Directors St. Mary's, Fullerton, CA
Corriente, Rev. Andrew, *OFM Cap* '22 (GBG) St. Bernard of Clairvaux, Indiana, PA; St. Thomas More University Parish, Indiana, PA
Corriere, Rev. Basil, *E.C.* '87 (STU) [MON] Holy Family Hermitage, Bloomingdale, OH
Corrigan, Rev. Allen F., '82 (CLV) Mother of Sorrows, Peninsula, OH; St. Victor, Richfield, OH
Corrigan, Rev. David J., *S.J.* '65 (STL) [COL] Saint Louis University, St. Louis, MO
Corrigan, Rev. George, (ARL) St. Francis of Assisi, Triangle, VA
Corrigan, Rev. Msgr. Hugh J., '63 (NY) Retired.
Corrigan, Rev. Michael T., '75 (GAL) Retired.
Corriseau, Rev. Ernest J., *M.S.* '64 (FR) Retired.

Corriveau, Rev. Ernest, (FR) [MON] La Salette Shrine & Retreat Center, Attleboro, MA
Corriveau, Rev. Roger R., *A.A.* '74 (WOR) [MON] Augustinians of the Assumption at Assumption University, Worcester, MA
Cortado, Rev. Dick Anthony, '07 (GBG) Nativity of the Blessed Virgin Mary, Uniontown, PA; St. John the Evangelist, Uniontown, PA; St. Joseph, Uniontown, PA; St. Therese, the Little Flower of Jesus, Uniontown, PA
Cortens, Rev. Cameron, (P) Holy Redeemer, Portland, OR
Cortes, Rev. Ariel, '96 (TYL) St. Michael, Mount Pleasant, TX
Cortes, Rev. Jesse, '63 (LAV) Retired.
Cortes, Rev. Jose Maria, *F.S.C.B.* '95 (WDC) (>STP) St. Peter, North St. Paul, MN
Cortes, Rev. Mario, '98 (PHX) Our Lady of Perpetual Help Roman Catholic Parish, Glendale, AZ
Cortes, Rev. Oscar, '94 (RCK) St. Rita of Cascia, Aurora, IL
Cortes, Rev. Roberto J., '02 (WDC) Curia: Pastoral Services St. Mark, Hyattsville, MD
Cortes, Rev. Victor G., '96 (POD) Curia: Clergy and Religious Services
Cortese, Rev. Matthew, *S.J.* '22 (FTW) [MIS] Jesuit Community, South Bend, IN
Cortez, Rev. Alejandro, *MG* '05 (LA) St. Martha, Huntington Park, CA
Cortez, Rev. Fernando J., '77 (OAK) Retired.
Cortez, Rev. Filiberto, '20 (LA) Our Lady of Lourdes, Northridge, CA
Cortez, Rev. Marcelino, (OAK) All Saints, Hayward, CA
Cortez, Rev. Octavio, (SB) St. Patrick, Moreno Valley, CA
Cortez, Rev. Octavio, *I.V.E.* '12 (FR) [MIS] The Institute of the Incarnate Word, Inc., New Bedford, MA
Cortez, Rev. Ramiro, (SAT) Retired. [NUR] Oblate Madonna Residence, San Antonio, TX
Cortezano, Rev. Teodoro, (GBG) St. Agnes, North Huntingdon, PA
Cortinovis, Rev. Charles A., '09 (WDC) Curia: Pastoral Services
Cortinovis, Rev. Charles A., '15 (WDC) On Special Assignment. Curia: Leadership
Coruna, Rev. Roberto, '77 (MET) Church of the Annunciation, Bloomsbury, NJ
Corzo, Rev. Wilson O., '98 (FTW) Our Lady of Hungary, South Bend, IN
Cos, Rev. Rafael, '82 (MIA) Curia: Pastoral Services St. Ann Mission, Naranja, FL
Cosby, Rev. Msgr. R. Roy, '54 (ARL) Retired.
Coschignano, Rev. Joseph C., '69 (RVC) Retired.
Cosgrave, Rev. Raymond, *L.C.* '78 (HRT) [MON] Legionaries of Christ, Cheshire, CT; [SEM] Novitiate of the Legion of Christ, Cheshire, CT
Cosgrove, Rev. Francis J., '65 (JKS) Retired.
Cosgrove, Rev. Joseph J., '92 (BAL) Retired.
Cosgrove, Rev. William, '55 (ROC) Retired.
Cosgrove, Rev. William B., '74 (NY) Chap, Rockland Cty Jail, New City Curia: Leadership St. Augustine, New City, NY; [MIS] Catholic Charismatic Renewal Office, Scarsdale, NY; [MIS] Charismatic Renewal Office, Scarsdale, NY
Cosgrove, Rev. William P., '99 (BIS) Retired.
Cosmas, Rev. Brendan, (PMB) St. Ann, West Palm Beach, FL
Coss, Rev. John, *F.M.S.I.* '56 (BO) [SEM] Sylva Maria, Framingham, MA
Cossavella, Rev. Anthony J., '81 (PH) Retired. On Leave.
Cossio Sepulveda, Rev. Cristian, '20 (ATL) St. Lawrence Catholic Church, Lawrenceville, Inc., Lawrenceville, GA
Costa, Rev. Anthony J., '90 (PH) St. Jude, Chalfont, PA
Costa, Rev. David A., '85 (FR) St. Louis de France, Swansea, MA; St. Patrick's, Somerset, MA; St. Thomas More, Somerset, MA; [CEM] St. Mary, Attleboro Falls, MA; [CEM] St. Patrick, Somerset, MA
Costa, Rev. Gabriel B., '79 (NEW) Curia: Leadership [COL] Seton Hall University, South Orange, NJ
Costa, Rev. Gene, (CLV) Lutheran Medical Center St. Rocco, Cleveland, OH; [MON] Mercedarians (Fathers of Our Lady of Mercy, Inc. / Order of the B.V.M. of Mercy / Mercedarian Friars USA), Cleveland, OH
Costa, Rev. Lucas Torrell deAlmeida, *O.S.B.* '67 (GBG) [MON] Saint Vincent Archabbey, Latrobe, PA
Costa, Rev. Raimundo, *I.S.P.* (MIA) [SHR] Schoenstatt Movement of Florida, Inc., Miami, FL
Costa, Rev. Raimundo, *I.S.P.* '07 (AUS) [MON] Schoenstatt Fathers, Austin, TX
Costa, Rev. Rizal, (HON) St. Raphael, Koloa, HI
Costa, Rev. Msgr. Thomas C., '78 (RVC) Curia: Leadership; Offices and Directors [MON] St Pius X Residence for Retired Priests LLC, Ronkonkoma, NY
Costa, Rev. Thomas E., '05 (FR) St. Dominic's, Swansea, MA
Costa, Rev. Thomas Edward, (FR) Saint Francis of Assisi, Swansea, MA
Costales, Rev. Frederick A., *M.S.* '02 (SB) St. Vincent Ferrer, Sun City, CA; [MON] The Pacific Region Missionaries of Our Lady of La Salette, MS, Moreno Valley, CA
Costantino, Rev. Anthony, (PHX) St. John the Baptist, Laveen, AZ
Costantino, Rev. Joseph S., *S.J.* '87 (NEW) [MON] Jesuits of Saint Peter College, Inc., Jersey City, NJ
Costanza, Rev. Jared J., '99 (PRO) Christ the King Church Corporation, Kingston, Kingston, RI
Costanzo, Rev. John J., '64 (PBL) Retired.
Costello, Rev. Andrew, *C.Ss.R* '65 (TR) [RTR] San Alfonso Retreat House, Long Branch, NJ
Costello, Rev. Coleman J., '67 (BRK) Retired. [MON] Bishop Mugavero Residence, Douglaston, NY
Costello, Friar Cyprian, (FR) [MON] Marian Friary of Our Lady, Queen of the Seraphic Order, New Bedford, MA
Costello, Rev. Daniel F., '98 (CHI) St. Mary of the Annunciation, Mundelein, IL
Costello, Rev. David M., '95 (BO) Curia: Clergy and Religious Services St. Stephen, Boston, MA; [MON] The Society of St. James the Apostle, Inc., Boston, MA
Costello, Rev. Edward, *O.F.M.Conv.* '61 (NY) [MON] St. Francis Friary, Staten Island, NY
Costello, Rev. John, '96 (VEN) Curia: Leadership
Costello, Rev. John F., '96 (VEN) Retired. Curia: Advisory Boards, Commissions, Committees, and Councils; Leadership
Costello, Rev. John F., *S.J.* '83 (CHI) [COL] Jesuit Community at Loyola University Chicago, Chicago, IL
Costello, Rev. John J., '89 (BRK) Curia: Leadership St. Luke, Whitestone, NY
Costello, Rev. John M., *S.J.* '84 (NY) [MON] Murray-Weigel Hall (A Jesuit Community at Murray-Weigel Hall and Kohlmann Hall), Bronx, NY
Costello, Rev. Mark Joseph, *O.F.M.Cap.* '91 (GF) St. Francis Xavier, St. Xavier, MT; [MON] St. Katharine Friary, Crow Agency, MT
Costello, Rev. Mark Joseph, *O.F.M. Cap.* (DET) [MON] St. Bonaventure Monastery, Detroit, MI
Costello, Rev. Steven, *L.C.* '11 (R) St. Michael the Archangel Catholic Church, Cary, NC
Costello, Rev. Ted, '85 (SP) St. Michael the Archangel, Clearwater, FL
Costello, Rev. Theodore, '85 (SP) Curia: Organizations (affiliated, inter-Diocesan, miscellaneous/other)
Costello, Rev. Timon, *O.F.M.Cap.* '58 (GB) Retired.
Costello, Rev. Vincent F., '76 (CHI) Retired.
Costigan, Rev. Christopher M., '08 (RVC) Chap, St Martin Tours, Bethpage; Nassau Cty Firemen's Assn Curia: Leadership; Offices and Directors St. Martin of Tours, Bethpage, NY
Costigan, Rev. James P., *C.P.M.* '02 (OWN) [MON] Fathers of Mercy, Auburn, KY
Costigan, Rev. Msgr. P. James, '68 (SAV) Retired.
Costik, Rev. Michael, '13 (ROC) St. Benedict Roman Catholic Parish Ontario County, NY, Canandaigua, NY
Cota, Rev. Valentin, (ELP) Christ the King, Pecos, TX
Cota, Rev. Valentin A., *M.N.M.* (ELP) Santa Rosa de Lima, Pecos, TX
Cota, Rev. Valentin A., *M.N.M.* (ELP) St. Catherine, Pecos, TX
Cote, Rev. David P., '68 (PRT) Retired.
Cote, Rev. Duaine, '62 (FAR) Retired. [MIS] Cursillo Movement of the Fargo Diocese, Fargo, ND
Cote, Rev. Mark, '04 (JOL) St. Paul the Apostle, Joliet, IL
Cote, Rev. Norman C., '58 (OG) Retired. Holy Cross Parish, Plattsburgh, NY
Cote, Rev. Roland P., '71 (MAN) Retired. [CON] Holy Cross Health Center, Inc., Manchester, NH; [CON] St. George Manor / Holy Cross Health Center, Manchester, NH
Cotone, Rev. Michael, *O.S.C.* '74 (PHX) [MON] Conventual Priory of the Holy Cross (Crosier Fathers and Brothers Province, Inc.), Phoenix, AZ
Cotta, Rev. Robbie, '21 (ATL) Immaculate Heart of the Blessed Virgin Mary Catholic Church, Atlanta, Inc., Atlanta, GA
Cotter, Rev. David, '79 (WOR) St. Columba, Paxton, MA; [CAM] Anna Maria College, Paxton, MA
Cotter, Rev. George C., *M.M.* '60 (NY) Retired.
Cotter, Rev. John F., '80 (SAG) Mary of the Immaculate Conception Parish of St. Charles, St. Charles, MI; Saint Michael Parish of Maple Grove, New Lothrop, MI
Cotter, Rev. Stephen D., '12 (BAL) Curia: (>MO) Offices and Directors
Cotter, Rev. Vincent, '83 (OAK) Retired. St. Benedict, Oakland, CA
Cotto Soto, Rev. Juan Carlos, *C.M.V.* '03 (ARE) Nuestra Senora de Fatima, Sabana Hoyos, PR
Cotton, Rev. Charles E., '73 (COL) Retired.
Cottrill, Very Rev. Paul Nicholas, '13 (R) Curia: Leadership Holy Family, Elizabeth City, NC
Coucelo, Rev. Andres, '68 (MIA) Retired.
Coughlin, Rev. Msgr. Daniel P., '60 (CHI) Retired.
Coughlin, Rev. James K., *S.J.* (STL) (>NY) [MON] Jesuit Community at Fordham University, New York, NY
Coughlin, Rev. John, *O.F.M.* (PAT) Our Lady of the Assumption, Pompton Lakes, NJ
Coughlin, Rev. John J., *O.F.M.* '83 (NY) Parish of Holy Name of Jesus and St. Gregory the Great, New York, NY
Coughlin, Rev. Kenneth F., '90 (LAN) SS. Charles and Helena Parish Clio, Clio, MI; St. Francis Xavier Parish Otisville, Otisville, MI
Coughlin, Rev. Paul E., '66 (PRT) Retired.
Coughlin, Rev. Paul F., '91 (BO) St. Raphael, Medford, MA
Coughlin, Rev. Thomas, '77 (HON) On Duty Outside Diocese. Archdiocese of San Antonio
Coughlin, Rev. Thomas, *O.M.I.* '70 (WDC) [MON] Missionary Oblates of Mary Immaculate, Washington, DC; [MON] Oblate Community, Washington, DC
Coughlin, Rev. Thomas, (NEW) Curia: Offices and Directors
Coughlin, Rev. William D., '66 (BO) Retired. Immaculate Conception, Malden, MA
Couhig, Rev. Michael D., *C.S.C.* '80 (PHX) St. Paul Roman Catholic Parish, Phoenix, AZ; [MON] Holy Cross Congregation/Casa Santa Cruz, Phoenix, AZ
Coulter, Rev. Gary L., '99 (LIN) Curia: Leadership
Coulter, Rev. Gary L., '99 (LIN) Curia: Leadership [RTR] Our Lady of Good Counsel Retreat House, Waverly, NE
Coulter, Rev. Zachary, (Y) St. Joseph, Mogadore, OH; St. Peter of the Fields, Rootstown, OH
Counce, Very Rev. Paul D., '79 (BR) Curia: Canonical Services; Leadership
Courier, Rev. Rick L., '85 (MAR) St. Anthony of Padua, Wells, MI; St. Thomas the Apostle, Escanaba, MI
Cournoyer, Rev. Alfred C., '85 (SPR) Retired.
Courtemanche, Rev. Normand L., '65 (PRO) Retired.
Courtney, Rev. Scott M., '00 (LIN) Chap, Nebraska Penal Complex, Lincoln
Courtney, Friar Thomas, *O.F.M.* (WDC) [MON] Franciscan Monastery USA Inc., Washington, DC
Courtney, Rev. William Liam, '99 (PBL) Retired.
Courtright, Rev. Lawrence P., '61 (TLS) Retired.
Courtright, Rev. Raymond P., '92 (FAR) St. Michael's Church of Grand Forks, Grand Forks, ND
Courville, Rev. Carl James, '74 (GAL) Curia: Offices and Directors St. Helen, Pearland, TX
Courville, Rev. Msgr. J. Douglas, '76 (LAF) St. Stephen, Berwick, LA (>NO) [SEM] Saint Joseph Seminary College, Saint Benedict, LA
Courville, Rev. Randy, '19 (LAF) St. Helena, Franklin, LA; St. Nicholas, New Iberia, LA
Courville, Rev. Robert, '63 (LAF) Retired.
Coury, Rev. Charles, *C.Ss.R.* '76 (NY) Parish of Most Holy Redeemer and Nativity, New York, NY
Coury, Rev. Paul, *C.Ss.R.* '72 (LA) [MON] Redemptorists of Whittier, Whittier, CA
Coury, Rev. Paul, *C.Ss.R.* '72 (TUC) Retired.
Coury, Rev. Philip J., *C.M.* '71 (STL) [MON] Congregation of the Mission, Perryville, MO
Cousens, Rev. Dennis L., '77 (L) Retired.
Cousins, Rev. John, *OFM, Cap.* '76 (KCK) St. John the Evangelist Catholic Church, Lawrence, KS; [MON] St. Conrad Friary, Lawrence, KS
Coutinho, Rev. Absalom, (PAT) Retired.
Couto, Rev. Nelson, '79 (NY) Holy Name of Mary, Croton-on-Hudson, NY
Couture, Rev. Jeffrey W., '10 (BGP) Curia: Clergy and Religious Services Saint Matthew's Roman Catholic Church Corporation, Norwalk, CT
Couturier, Rev. David, *O.F.M.Cap.* '79 (BUF) [MON] St. Bonaventure Friary, St. Bonaventure, NY
Couturier, Rev. Dominic T, '20 (GR) Our Lady of Consolation, Rockford, MI
Couturier, Rev. George M., '81 (HRT) Saint Josephine Bakhita Parish Corporation, Rocky Hill, CT
Couvillon, Rev. Louis, (MET) (>PRO) [MON] Brothers of the Sacred Heart Residence, Pascoag, RI
Covarrubias, Rev. Raul R., '83 (B) Retired.
Covarrubias-Pina, Rev. Salomon, '91 (YAK) St. Joseph, White Salmon, WA

Coveney, Rev. James B., '64 (ALT) Retired. On Leave.

Cover, Rev. Phillip B., '70 (LFT) Retired.

Coveyou, Rev. Michael, '18 (R) St. Ann, Fayetteville, NC

Covington, Rev. Charles, '85 (AUS) St. Theresa, Austin, TX

Covos, Rev. Ruben, '06 (SAN) Captain Rev. Ruben Covos, Kessler AFB, Biloxi, MS Curia: (>MO) Offices and Directors

Covos, Rev. Ruben, '06 (BLX) Chap, Keesler Airforce Base

Cowan, Rev. George R., '65 (BRK) Retired. [MON] Bishop Mugavero Residence, Douglaston, NY

Cowan, Rev. Matthew John, '14 (GLD) On Duty Outside Diocese. Diocese of Salina (>SAL) St. Francis of Assisi Parish, Norton, Inc., Norton, KS; (>SAL) St. Joseph Parish, New Almelo, Inc., New Almelo, KS

Cowart, Rev. Conrad, '96 (STA) Retired.

Cowles, Rev. James, '90 (RIC) Church of the Redeemer, Mechanicsville, VA

Cowles, Rev. Kristopher, '11 (SFS) Our Lady of Guadalupe Parish of Minnehaha County, Sioux Falls, SD

Cox, Rev. Alonzo Q., '10 (BRK) Curia: Pastoral Services Saint Martin de Porres, Brooklyn, NY; [CCH] African American Ministry, ,

Cox, Rev. Bernard, '91 (IND) Retired.

Cox, Rev. Christopher A., '14 (CLV) St. Anselm, Chesterland, OH

Cox, Rev. Msgr. Craig A., '78 (LA) Curia: Pastoral Services Our Lady of Perpetual Help, Santa Clarita, CA

Cox, Rev. Msgr. David D., '81 (JC) St. Margaret of Antioch, Osage Bend, MO; St. Stanislaus, Wardsville, MO

Cox, Rev. Msgr. Gregory A., '76 (LA) Curia: Offices and Directors St. Anastasia, Los Angeles, CA; [CCH] Catholic Charities Community Development Corporation, Inc., Los Angeles, CA; [CCH] Catholic Charities of Los Angeles, Inc., Los Angeles, CA; [MIS] Opus Caritatis, Inc., Los Angeles, CA

Cox, Rev. James M., '98 (PH) St. Mary, Schwenksville, PA

Cox, Rev. John, *O.M.I.* '87 (CR) St. Ann, Waubun, MN; St. Anne, Naytahwaush, MN; St. Frances Cabrini (Big Elbow Lake), Waubun, MN

Cox, Rev. Joseph, *O.S.B.* '91 (IND) [MON] St. Meinrad Archabbey, St. Meinrad, IN

Cox, Rev. Michael, (FRS) Divine Mercy Catholic Church, Clovis, CA

Cox, Rev. Paul C., '54 (ALB) Retired. Curia: Offices and Directors St. Cecilia, Warrensburg, NY

Coy, Rev. Richard D., '00 (MEM) Retired. Chap, Memphis VA Med Ctr [MIS] Society of St. Vincent DePaul, Memphis, TN

Coyle, Rev. Msgr. Arthur M., '77 (BO) Retired.

Coyle, Rev. Msgr. Edward J., '80 (ALN) Curia: Organizations (affiliated, inter-Diocesan, miscellaneous/other) St. Ann, Emmaus, PA

Coyle, Rev. Kevin J., (HBG) Curia: Offices and Directors Bishop McDevitt High School of Harrisburg, Harrisburg, PA; St. Paul the Apostle, Annville, PA; [CAM] Lebanon Valley College, Annville, PA

Coyle, Rev. Patrick P., *SS.CC.* '61 (LA) Retired. [MON] Congregation of the Sacred Hearts of Jesus and Mary, La Verne, CA

Coyle, Rev. Thomas J., '70 (MAD) St. Francis of Assisi, Jefferson, WI

Coyne, Rev. Emmett A., '66 (MAN) Retired.

Coyne, Rev. Msgr. George R., '59 (STU) Retired.

Coyne, Rev. Gregory, '89 (STL) [MIS] Prelature of the Holy Cross and Opus Dei, Kirkwood, MO

Coyne, Rev. Gregory J., '89 (POD) Curia: Clergy and Religious Services

Coyne, Rev. Liam, '98 (ATL) St. James Catholic Church, McDonough, Inc., McDonough, GA

Coyne, Rev. Msgr. Michael J., '55 (CAM) Retired.

Coyne, Rev. Robert, *M.M.* '83 (NY) Retired.

Coyne, Rev. Robert F., *M.M.* '83 (SJ) Retired.

Coyne, Rev. Ronald D., '73 (BO) Blessed Mother of the Morning Star Parish, Revere, MA

Coyte, Rev. Thomas, '74 (DEN) Retired.

Cozzi, Rev. Phillip M., '06 (ARL) St. Mary of the Immaculate Conception, Fredericksburg, VA

Cozzubbo, Rev. Gregory P., *CM* '84 (BUF) [MON] Vincentian Community at Niagara University (Congregation of the Mission of St. Vincent de Paul), Niagara University, NY

Craddock, Rev. Joseph F., '04 (PRO) Holy Family Parish, Pawtucket, Pawtucket, RI

Crafts, Rev. George, '65 (PRO) [MIS] Prelature of the Holy Cross and Opus Dei, Providence, RI

Crafts, Rev. George A., '65 (POD) Curia: Clergy and Religious Services

Crager, Rev. Richard, *SDB* '78 (SP) [RTR] Mary Help of Christians Center, Tampa, FL

Crahen, Rev. Daniel, *O.M.I.* '71 (SAT) Retired. [NUR] Oblate Madonna Residence, San Antonio, TX

Craig, Rev. Anthony John, '11 (DUL) Holy Family, Duluth, MN; St. Lawrence, Duluth, MN

Craig, Rev. Arthur, *O.M.I.* '55 (WDC) [MON] Oblate Community, Washington, DC

Craig, Rev. Bruce, *S.D.B.* '74 (SP) [RTR] Mary Help of Christians Center, Tampa, FL

Craig, Rev. Christopher A., '93 (IND) Most Sorrowful Mother of God Catholic Church, Vevay, Inc., Vevay, IN; Prince of Peace Catholic Church, Madison, Inc., Madison, IN; [CAM] Hanover College, Madison, IN

Craig, Rev. Dale, *SOLT* '97 (SFE) St. Gertrude the Great, Mora, NM

Craig, Rev. Dale, *S.O.L.T.* '97 (PHX) Most Holy Trinity Roman Catholic Parish, Phoenix, AZ

Craig, Rev. Donal, (SB) Chap, Desert Rgnl Med Ctr, Palm Springs

Craig, Rev. Donald R., '74 (CHI) Retired.

Craig, Rev. Jeffrey, '20 (PIT) Regina Coeli, Pittsburgh, PA

Craig, Rev. John, *S.J.* (DEN) [MON] Regis High Jesuit Community, Centennial, CO

Craig, Rev. Patrick H., '05 (KAL) St. Joseph, Watervliet, MI

Craig, Rev. Paul, *O.F.M.Cap.* '66 (MIL) [MON] St. Lawrence Friary, Mount Calvary, WI

Craig, Rev. Robert, *O.F.M. Cap.* '67 (PIT) Chap, Univ Drive; HJ Heinz III (Aspinwall); VA Pittsburgh… [MON] St. Augustine Friary, Pittsburgh, PA

Craig, Rev. Rod L., '77 (FRS) On Special Assignment. [RTR] St. Anthony's Retreat Center, Three Rivers, CA

Craig, Rev. Roderick L., '77 (FRS) [RTR] Santa Teresita Youth Center, Three Rivers, CA

Cramblitt, Rev. Msgr. Richard E., '72 (BAL) Retired.

Cramer, Rev. David W., '91 (SCR) St. Eulalia, Roaring Brook Twp., PA

Cramer, Rev. Harry N., '84 (WH) Retired.

Cramer, Rev. William N., '77 (PAT) Retired.

Crane, Rev. Gregory, '19 (BIS) Bishop Ryan Catholic School, Minot, ND; St. Leo, Minot, ND; St. Mary, Foxholm, ND; St. Philomena, Glenburn, ND

Crane, Rev. Mark W., '05 (TR) Retired.

Crane, Rev. Matthew, (SCL) Curia: Leadership

Crane, Rev. Matthew, '11 (SCL) Curia: Leadership

Crane, Rev. Msgr. Thomas E., '57 (BUF) Retired. [MON] O'Hara Residence, Tonawanda, NY

Cranor, Rev. Bernard, *O.S.B.* '62 (SFE) [MON] Monastery of Christ in the Desert, Abiquiu, NM

Crasta, Rev. Rudolf, '89 (LUB) Our Lady of Grace, Lubbock, TX

Cravalho, Rev. Allan, (OWN) [MON] Fathers of Mercy, Auburn, KY

Crawford, Rev. Msgr. C. Slade, '65 (PT) Retired.

Crawford, Rev. Douglas Y., '07 (NY) Parish of St. Matthew and Our Lady of Perpetual Help, Hastings-on-Hudson, NY

Crawford, Rev. John G., '63 (CLV) Retired. St. Francis de Sales, Parma, OH

Crawford, Rev. Robert F., *M.M.* '61 (NY) Retired. [MON] Maryknoll Fathers and Brothers (Catholic Foreign Mission Society of America, Inc.), Ossining, NY

Crawley, Rev. Richard, *O.F.M. Cap.* (ROC) [MON] St. Fidelis Friary, Interlaken, NY

Cray, Rev. David G., *S.S.E.* '72 (BUR) [COL] St. Michael's College, Colchester, VT; [MON] Society of St. Edmund, Colchester, VT

Creagan, Rev. Michael, '97 (STP) Chap, Army National Guard Curia: (>MO) Offices and Directors St. Joseph, West St. Paul, MN

Creagan, Very Rev. Robert, '88 (KAL) Curia: Consultative Bodies; Deaneries; Leadership St. Augustine Cathedral, Kalamazoo, MI

Creagh, Rev. Kevin G., *C.M.* '96 (BUF) (>BRK) [MON] Reverend John B. Murray, C.M. House, Jamaica, NY

Creagh, Rev. Richard C., '76 (CHI) Retired.

Creamer, Rev. Ryan, '12 (RVC) Most Holy Trinity, East Hampton, NY

Creane, Rev. Anthony, '56 (SPR) Retired.

Creary, Rev. Msgr. J. Edwin, '73 (MEM) Retired.

Creed, Rev. Peter M., '67 (RIC) Retired. Military Chap

Creed, Rev. William E., *S.J.* '71 (CHI) [COL] Jesuit Community at Loyola University Chicago, Chicago, IL

Creeden, Rev. Brendan D., *O.S.B.* '78 (CHI) [MON] Monastery of the Holy Cross, Chicago, IL

Creedon, Rev. Joseph D., '68 (PRO) Retired.

Creegan, Rev. Kevin G., '01 (PEO) St. Mary, Tiskilwa, IL; St. Mary's, DePue, IL

Cregan, Rev. David A., *O.S.A.* '99 (PH) [COL] Villanova University, Villanova, PA; [MON] Fray de Leon Community, Villanova, PA

Cregan, Rev. Msgr. John C., '87 (ARL) Retired.

Cregan, Rev. Mark T., (BRK) Christ the King, Springfield Gardens, NY

Crehan, Rev. Lawrence F., '74 (PH) Queen of Peace, Ardsley, PA

Crehan, Rev. Matthias, *O.F.M.* '75 (CIN) [MON] St. Francis Seraph Friary, Cincinnati, OH

Creighton, Rev. Bernard R., *O.F.M.* '67 (PAT) [MON] St. Anthony Friary (Order of Friars Minor), Butler, NJ

Creighton, Rev. James J., *S.J.* '70 (DET) [MON] Colombiere Center, Clarkston, MI

Crelencia, Rev. Eric, *OAR* (NY) Sacred Heart, Suffern, NY

Cremaldi, Rev. Angelo, '60 (LAF) Retired.

Cremers, Rev. Bill, (OM) St. Patrick, Fremont, NE

Cremers, Rev. William, (OM) St. Rose of Lima, Hooper, NE

Cremonie, Rev. Louis D., '72 (HRT) Retired.

Crenwelge, Rev. Brian J., '16 (WH) Curia: Offices and Directors St. John University, Morgantown, WV

Crepeau, Rev. John, '72 (DET) On Leave.

Creson, Rev. Mike, (KNX) Retired.

Crespin, Rev. George E., '62 (OAK) Retired. [NUR] Bishop Begin Villa, Oakland, CA; [NUR] Bishop Begin Villa, Retirement Facility for Priests in the Oakland Diocese, ,

Crespo, Rev. Alexander, (MGZ) Cathedral of Our Lady of Purification, Mayaguez, PR

Cretella, Rev. Joseph J., (HRT) Retired.

Creus, Rev. John Therese, (DEN) Notre Dame Catholic Parish in Denver, Denver, CO

Crevcoure, Rev. Stuart, '01 (TLS) Church of St. Mary, Tulsa, OK; [CAM] Northeastern State University Catholic Student Organization, Tahlequah, OK

Crewe, Rev. Ronald O., '63 (MIL) Retired.

Crews, Rev. Clyde F., '73 (L) Retired. [COL] Bellarmine University, Louisville, KY

Cribben, Rev. Andrew G., *O. Praem.* '94 (GB) St. Willebrord, Green Bay, WI; [MON] St. Norbert Abbey, De Pere, WI

Cribben, Rev. Msgr. Philip J., '62 (PH) Retired.

Cricchio, Rev. Santo, *O.F.M.Conv.* '91 (MO) Curia: Offices and Directors

Cricchio, Friar Santo, *OFM Conv.* '91 (ATL) St. Philip Benizi Catholic Church, Jonesboro, Inc., Jonesboro, GA

Crilly, Rt. Rev. Marc, *O.S.B.* '93 (WOR) [MON] Benedictine Monks, St. Benedict Abbey, Still River, MA; [RTR] Benedictine Monks, St. Benedict Abbey, Still River, MA

Crimmins, Rev. Msgr. Michael, (NY) Retired. St. Gregory, New York, NY

Crincoli, Rev. Vito, *L.C.* '09 (WDC) [MON] Legionaries of Christ, Potomac, MD

Crino, Rev. Patrick M., '88 (TUC) Curia: Consultative Bodies; Organizations (affiliated, inter-Diocesan, miscellaneous/other); Pastoral Services Saint Thomas the Apostle Roman Catholic Parish - Tucson, Tucson, AZ

Criqui, Rev. J. Kenneth, '63 (KC) St. Mary's, Carrollton, MO

Crisanto, Rev. Avelino S., *O.deM.* '81 (LA) St. Aloysius Gonzaga, Los Angeles, CA

Criscione, Rev. Daniele, *PIME* '13 (DET) [MON] PIME Missionaries, Detroit, MI

Criscitelli, Rev. Anthony, *T.O.R.* '80 (ALT) [MON] St. Bernardine Monastery, Hollidaysburg, PA

Criscuolo, Rev. Msgr. Salvatore A., '78 (WDC) Retired. DC Police Curia: Consultative Bodies St. Patrick, Washington, DC

Crisman, Rev. James H., '01 (DEN) St. Francis of Assisi Catholic Parish in Longmont, Longmont, CO

Crisostomo, Rev. Armando S., '93 (NEW) Chap, Overlook Hosp, Summit; Hackensack Univ Med Ctr Holy Trinity, Hackensack, NJ

Crisostomo, Rev. Michael, '96 (AGN) Curia: Administration; Advisory Boards, Commissions, Committees, and Councils; Communications; Consultative Bodies; Leadership; Organizations (affiliated, inter-Diocesan, miscellaneous/other); Social Services Saint Anthony Catholic School, Tamuning, GU; St. Anthony and St. Victor, Tamuning, GU; [MIS] Federal Grant (St. Anthony Church -STOP Violence Against Women), Tamuning, GU

Crisp, Rev. Michael L., '97 (SUP) Retired.

Crisp, Rev. Robert R., '75 (DAL) On Administrative Leave.

Crispin, Rev. John Paul, *F.M.H.* '14 (SHP) Our Lady of Fatima, Monroe, LA

Crispin, Rev. John Paul, *F.M.H.* '14 (SHP) [CAM] Catholic Campus Ministry at the University of Louisiana at Monroe, Monroe, LA

Cristancho, Rev. Lisandro, '98 (RCK) St. Mary, Elgin, IL; St. Patrick, St. Charles, IL
Criste, Rev. Ambrose, *O.Praem.* '08 (ORG) [MON] Norbertine Fathers of Orange, Inc., Silverado, CA; [SEM] St. Michael's Norbertine Postulancy, Novitiate and Juniorate, Silverado, CA (>SFD) [MIS] The Evermode Institute, Springfield, IL
Cristler, Rev. Richard F., '00 (TLS) On Special Assignment. Jack C Mongomery Veterans Med Ctr, Muskogee, Eddie Warrio... Saint Joseph Church, Muskogee, OK; [EFT] St. Joseph School Endowment Trust, Muskogee, OK
Cristobal, Rev. Adrian, '89 (AGN) On Duty Outside Diocese.
Critch, Rev. Gerard F., '89 (VEN) St. Peter the Apostle Parish in Naples, Inc., Naples, FL
Crivello, Rev. Peter A., '93 (MRY) St. Angela Merici Church, Pacific Grove, CA
Cro, Rev. Robert J., *P.S.S.* '12 (TR) (>WDC) [SEM] Theological College of the Catholic University of America, Washington, DC
Cro, Rev. Robert J., *P.S.S.* '12 (BAL) [MIS] St. Mary's Seminary & University, Baltimore, MD; [MON] Society of St. Sulpice, Province of the United States, Baltimore, MD
Croak, Rev. Msgr. David P., '66 (DEN) Retired.
Croak, Rev. Thomas, *C.M.* '65 (STL) Retired. [MON] Congregation of the Mission, Perryville, MO
Crochet, Rev. Barry F., '93 (LAF) Our Lady of Victory, Loreauville, LA; St. Joseph, Loreauville, LA
Crofut, Rev. Msgr. Robert J., '72 (BGP) [MON] The Catherine Dennis Keefe Queen of the Clergy Retired Priests' Residence, Stamford, CT
Croghan, Rev. James, *S.J.* (BO) Curia: Consultative Bodies
Croghan, Rev. John Francis, '21 (DEN) Holy Family in Meeker, Meeker, CO; St. Ignatius of Antioch in Rangely, Rangely, CO; St. Michael Catholic Parish in Craig, Craig, CO
Croghan, Rev. John P., '75 (SY) Retired. [CAM] Hamilton College Newman Center, Clinton, NY
Croglio, Rev. James C., '80 (BUF) Curia: Consultative Bodies St. Joseph's Collegiate Institute, Buffalo, NY; [MIS] Diocesan Counseling Center for Clergy & Religious, Cheektowaga, NY
Crohan, Rev. Robert F., *M.M.* '62 (NY) Retired.
Croisetiere, Rev. David N., '77 (SD) Curia: Tribunal Pastor of Our Lady of Refuge Catholic Parish, San Diego, a corporation sole, San Diego, CA
Crombie, Rev. Francis H., '68 (SPR) Retired.
Cromly, Rev. Nathan, *C.S.J.* (DEN) All Souls Catholic Parish in Englewood, Englewood, CO; [MIS] Saint John Institute, Englewood, CO
Cron, Rev. Steven D., '78 (GR) Retired.
Cronauer, Rev. Patrick T., *O.S.B.* '84 (GBG) [MON] Saint Vincent Archabbey, Latrobe, PA; [SEM] St. Vincent Seminary, Latrobe, PA
Crone, Rev. Patrick H., '71 (CIN) Retired. St. Veronica, Cincinnati, OH
Crone, Rev. Terence, '02 (ATL) St. Mary Magdalene Catholic Church, Newnan, Inc., Newnan, GA
Cronin, Rev. Brian, *C.S.Sp.* (PIT) [COL] Duquesne University of the Holy Spirit, Pittsburgh, PA
Cronin, Rev. Edward J., '80 (CHI) St. Stephen, King of Hungary Mission, Chicago, IL
Cronin, Rev. John, (ALB) Curia: Leadership; Offices and Directors Holy Trinity, Cohoes, NY; St. Michael, Cohoes, NY
Cronin, Rev. Joseph R., '98 (HRT) Curia: Advisory Boards, Commissions, Committees, and Councils Saint Luke Parish Corporation, Southington, CT
Cronin, Rev. Kevin M., *O.F.M.* '74 (PAT) [MON] St. Anthony Friary (Order of Friars Minor), Butler, NJ
Cronin, Very Rev. Michael J., '95 (WIN) Curia: Advisory Boards, Commissions, Committees, and Councils; Miscellaneous / Other Offices; Tribunal St. Mary's, Winona, MN; St. Paul's, Minnesota City, MN
Cronin, Rev. Michael J., '73 (CHI) Retired.
Cronin, Rev. Michael J., '15 (SC) Curia: Offices and Directors Sacred Heart, Manning, IA; St. Ann's, Vail, IA; St. Rose of Lima, Denison, IA
Cronin, Rev. Peadar, *SS.CC.* '72 (LA) [MON] Congregation of the Sacred Hearts of Jesus and Mary, La Verne, CA
Cronin, Rev. Richard F., *O.S.B.* '66 (PAT) Retired. [MON] St. Mary's Abbey, Morristown, NJ
Cronin, Rev. Msgr. Sylvester J., '88 (MET) St. James, Basking Ridge, NJ
Cronin, Rev. Thomas, '69 (KC) Retired.
Cronin, Rev. Msgr. Timothy P., '85 (STL) St. Clement of Rome Catholic Church, St. Louis, MO; St. Mary Magdalen Catholic Church, Brentwood, Brentwood, MO
Cronk, Rev. James F., '69 (DET) Retired.
Cronkleton, Rev. Thomas, '86 (CHY) [CEM] Olivet Cemetery, Cheyenne, WY
Cronkleton, Rev. Thomas E., '86 (CHY) Curia: Advisory Boards, Commissions, Committees, and Councils; Consultative Bodies; Leadership St. Mary's Cathedral, Cheyenne, WY; [EFT] St. Mary's School Foundation, Cheyenne, WY
Crook, Rev. David G., '81 (BEL) Retired.
Crookston, Rev. James F., '71 (ALT) Retired. St. Clement, Johnstown, PA
Crookston, Rev. Michael J., '80 (GBG) Curia: Advisory Boards, Commissions, Committees, and Councils; Leadership; Offices and Directors SS. Cyril and Methodius, Fairchance, PA; St. Hubert, Point Marion, PA; St. Sebastian, Belle Vernon, PA; The Epiphany of Our Lord, Monessen, PA
Crosby, Rev. Daniel, *OFM Cap.* (DET) [MON] St. Bonaventure Monastery, Detroit, MI
Crosby, Rev. Michael, *O.F.M.* '64 (GB) Retired. [MON] Blessed Giles Friary, Manitowoc, WI
Crosby, Rev. Theodore A., '00 (OG) Saint Joseph's Church, West Chazy, NY, West Chazy, NY; The Sacred Heart Church of Chazy, NY, Chazy, NY
Crosby, Rev. Vincent R., *O.S.B.* '72 (GBG) [MON] Saint Vincent Archabbey, Latrobe, PA
Cross, Rev. Michael L., '62 (MRY) Retired.
Cross, Very Rev. William D., '85 (STU) Curia: Deaneries; Offices and Directors St. Adalbert, Dillonvale, OH; St. Casimir Church, Adena, OH; St. Joseph, Tiltonsville, OH
Cross, Rev. William H., '74 (CIN) Retired.
Crossen, Rev. Jason K., '00 (DAV) Our Lady of Lourdes Church of Bettendorf, Iowa, Bettendorf, IA
Crossin, Rev. John W., (ARL) St. John Neumann, Reston, VA
Crossin, Rev. John W., *O.S.F.S.* '76 (WDC) [SEM] Deshairs Community-Oblates of St. Francis de Sales Residence, Washington, DC; [SEM] Oblates of St. Francis de Sales, Washington, DC
Crossmyer, Rev. Robert, *C.P.* (L) [MON] Sacred Heart Retreat, Louisville, KY
Croteau, Rev. Roger H., '67 (MAN) Retired.
Crotty, Rev. Kevin (Columban), *SS.CC.* '58 (FR) Retired. [MIS] Damien Residence Retirement Home, , ; [MIS] National Center of the Enthronement, Fairhaven, MA
Crotty, Rev. Travis, '20 (SC) Curia: Offices and Directors Cathedral of the Epiphany, Sioux City, IA; Gehlen Catholic School, Le Mars, IA
Crow, Rev. Alexander M, '21 (MOB) Corpus Christi Parish, Mobile, Mobile, AL
Crowe, Rev. Brent, (P) Our Lady of the Mountain, Ashland, OR
Crowe, Rev. George W., '65 (PH) Retired.
Crowe, Rev. Peter D., (ALT) Curia: Offices and Directors St. Andrew, Johnstown, PA; [MIS] Office of Vocations, Altoona, PA
Crowe, Rev. William R., '08 (LA) St. Bernardine of Siena, Woodland Hills, CA
Crowley, Rev. Cale J., *P.S.S.* '69 (BAL) Retired.
Crowley, Rev. Daniel J., '68 (BO) Retired.
Crowley, Rev. Dennis J., '89 (PAT) Retired. Assumption of the Blessed Virgin Mary, Morristown, NJ
Crowley, Rev. Edmund G., '70 (MAN) Retired. St. Patrick, Nashua, NH; [CEM] Holy Rosary Cemetery, Hooksett, NH
Crowley, Rev. James M., '87 (CHR) Retired. Our Lady Star of the Sea, North Myrtle Beach, SC
Crowley, Rev. Joseph P., '06 (HRT) Curia: Advisory Boards, Commissions, Committees, and Councils Saint Maximillian Kolbe Parish Corporation, Thomaston, CT
Crowley, Rev. Patrick J., *SS.CC.* '63 (SB) [MON] Congregation of the Sacred Hearts of Jesus and Mary, SS.CC., Hemet, CA
Crowley, Rev. Patrick J., *SS.CC.* '63 (LA) [MON] Congregation of the Sacred Hearts of Jesus and Mary, La Verne, CA
Crowley, Rev. Richard P., '64 (BO) Retired.
Crowley, Rev. Zachary, '20 (BAL) Sacred Heart, Glyndon, MD
Crozier, Rev. John, '20 (RVC) Church of St. Mary, East Islip, NY
Crozzoletto, Rev. Provvido, *M.C.C.J.* '70 (NEW) [MON] Comboni Missionaries of the Heart of Jesus (Verona Fathers), Newark, NJ
Cruickshank, Rev. Mike, *C.S.P.* '20 (GR) On Special Assignment. Curia: Education Cathedral of St. Andrew, Grand Rapids, MI; [MIS] Catholic Information Center, Grand Rapids, MI
Crummy, Rev. Michael E., '86 (MET) Chap, Parker at McCarrick, Somerset Our Lady of Lourdes, Milltown, NJ
Crump, Rev. Michael Edward, *S.O.L.T.* '09 (CC) [MON] Society of Our Lady of the Most Holy Trinity, Corpus Christi, TX
Crutchfield, Rev. John, '14 (HEL) Madison County Catholic Community: Series 236, LLC, Sheridan, MT; Saint Catherine Parish: Series 208, LLC, Boulder, MT; Saint Teresa of Avila Parish: Series 254, LLC, Whitehall, MT
Cruz, Rev. Alexander, (NEW) Divine Mercy Parish, Rahway, NJ
Cruz, Rev. Alexander T., '91 (NEW) Curia: Advisory Boards, Commissions, Committees, and Councils
Cruz, Rev. Anthony, *HGN* '14 (FAR) Nativity Church of Fargo, Fargo, ND
Cruz, Rev. Bernardo, '10 (DET) St. Francis D'Assisi - St. Hedwig Parish, Detroit, MI
Cruz, Rev. Camilo E, '10 (NEW) St. Patrick Pro-Cathedral, Newark, NJ
Cruz, Rev. Camilo E., '10 (NEW) St. John, Newark, NJ
Cruz, Rev. Daniel, (PHX) St. Mary Roman Catholic Parish Chandler, Chandler, AZ
Cruz, Rev. Msgr. David, '89 (LUB) Curia: Leadership St. John the Baptist Catholic Church, Lubbock, TX
Cruz, Rev. Dennys W, '00 (MGZ) San Sebastian Martir, San Sebastian, PR
Cruz, Rev. Domingo, (HT) Retired. Our Lady of the Rosary, Larose, LA
Cruz, Rev. Eric, '03 (NY) Curia: Offices and Directors St. Luke, Bronx, NY
Cruz, Rev. Gilbert, '81 (LA) Epiphany, South El Monte, CA; St. Marcellinus, Commerce, CA
Cruz, Rev. Gilbert J., '81 (SJN) Retired.
Cruz, Rev. Gustavo, '74 (LAV) Retired.
Cruz, Rev. Hector, *S.M.* (SP) Our Lady of Perpetual Help, Tampa, FL
Cruz, Friar Humberto Flores, *O.A.R.* (ELP) Guardian Angel, El Paso, TX
Cruz, Rev. James A., '05 (NY) St. Raymond, Bronx, NY
Cruz, Rev. Jamilcar, (MO) Curia: Offices and Directors
Cruz, Rev. Luciano, '86 (PAT) Retired.
Cruz, Rev. Luis, *Sch.P.* '15 (WDC) [MON] Piarist Fathers, Province of the U.S.A. and Puerto Rico, Washington, DC
Cruz, Rev. Miguel, '15 (MGZ) San Jose Obrero, San Antonio, PR
Cruz, Rev. Noel, *M.S.* '92 (SB) St. Joseph the Worker, Loma Linda, CA; [MON] The Pacific Region Missionaries of Our Lady of La Salette, MS, Moreno Valley, CA
Cruz, Rev. Msgr. Remberto, '49 (SJN) Retired.
Cruz, Rev. Renato, '81 (LUB) [MIS] Our Lady of Guadalupe, Matador, TX; [MIS] St. Elizabeth, Paducah, TX
Cruz, Rev. Robert Joel, '96 (HT) Curia: Miscellaneous / Other Offices
Cruz, Rev. Robin Pena, '03 (SLC) Saint Thomas Aquinas LLC 247, Hyde Park, UT
Cruz, Rev. Vincente DeLa, (HT) The Congregation of St. Joseph's Roman Catholic Cathedral, Thibodaux, LA
Cruz Alverez, Rev. Jose, '15 (NY) Sacred Heart, Bronx, NY
Cruz Baerga, Rev. Luis Alberto, *Sch. P.* '15 (PCE) Colegio Ponceno, Ponce, PR
Cruz Collazo, Rev. Jose A., *O.F.M.Cap.* '83 (SJN) [MON] The Custody of Saint John the Baptist, Puerto Rico, of the Order Friars Minor Capuchin, San Juan, PR
Cruz Córdova, Rev. Ernest Jr., '19 (ARE) Nuestra Senora del Carmen, Arecibo, PR
Cruz Cruz, Rev. Ferdinand, '05 (PCE) Curia: Leadership San Antonio de Padua, Coamo, PR
Cruz Cuevas, Rev. Dennys, *C.P.* '00 (SJN) [COL] Universidad Central de Bayamon, Inc., Bayamon, PR
Cruz Garcia, Rev. Edwin A., '95 (SJN) La Resurreccion del Senor, Bayamon, PR; Santo Domingo de Guzman, Bayamon, PR
Cruz Gonzalez, Rev. Gil, '48 (SJN) Retired.
Cruz Rodriguez, Rev. Jose Gabriel, '98 (CHR) Blessed Trinity, Greer, SC
Cruz Rosa, Rev. Fausto, *C.M.F.* (SJN) Casa Mision Claret, Bayamon, PR
Cruz Santiago, Friar Hector Luis, *O.Carm.* '19 (SJN) Santa Teresita del Nino Jesus, San Juan, PR
Cruz Velosa, Rev. Francisco, '69 (CHR) Retired.
Cruz-Collazo, Rev. Jose A, *ofm Cap.* '83 (MGZ) Santuario Protomártires de la Inmaculada Concepción, Aguada, PR
Cruz-Santiago, Rev. Hector Luis, *O.Carm.* '19 (SJN) Curia: Offices and Directors
Cruz-Zapata, Rev. Jose, (MEM) Curia: Advisory Boards, Commissions, Committees, and Councils
Cryan, Rev. Jack, (NEW) Curia: Offices and Directors

Cryan, Rev. James F., *O.S.F.S.* '65 (TOL) Retired. [MON] Oblates of St. Francis de Sales, Toledo, OH
Cryan, Rev. John J., '81 (NEW) Retired. Curia: Offices and Directors St. Aloysius, Caldwell, NJ
Cryans, Rev. Andrew W., '75 (MAN) St. Thomas More, Durham, NH; [CAM] St. Thomas More Catholic Student Center at the University of New Hampshire, Durham, NH
Crynes, Msgr. J. Peter, (SCR) On Administrative Leave.
Csete, Rev. Ivan L., '81 (NY) Retired. Immaculate Conception, Port Jervis, NY
Csizmar, Rev. Richard A., '68 (BUF) Holy Family, Albion, NY
Cu Hong, Rev. Phuc (Joseph), *CM* (BRK) [MON] Reverend John B. Murray, C.M. House, Jamaica, NY
Cuadrado, Rev. Hector, *C.M.F.* '91 (SJN) Casa Mision Claret, Bayamon, PR; San Jose, Bayamon, PR
Cuadrado Calvo, Rev. Angel, *O.de.M.* '86 (PCE) Parroquia San Judas Tadeo, Ponce, PR
Cuadros, Rev. Jesus, '66 (BRK) Retired. Holy Family-Saint Thomas Aquinas, Brooklyn, NY
Cuahutemoc Ramirez, Rev. Jose Maria, '01 (LA) St. Philip Neri, Lynwood, CA
Cuario, Rev. Dindo C., '91 (PHX) St. Paul Roman Catholic Parish, Phoenix, AZ
Cuarto, Rev. Jonathan, '05 (SJ) Sacred Heart of Jesus, San Jose, CA
Cuarto, Rev. Samuel Aceves, *M.I* '96 (LA) Our Lady of the Valley, Canoga Park, CA
Cuasito, Rev. Rolando, *M.S.C.* (MI) Curia: Leadership Queen of Peace, Ebeye, MH
Cuba, Rev. Barry, '13 (AUS) St. Theresa, Austin, TX
Cubas, Rev. Franklin, '89 (LA) St. Matthias, Huntington Park, CA
Cubera, Rev. Ryan J., '13 (CLV) St. Mary of the Falls, Olmsted Falls, OH
Cudden, Rev. Jerome, *O.P.* '07 (SFR) St. Raymond, Menlo Park, CA
Cuddihy, Rev. Msgr. William, '56 (SD) Retired.
Cuddy, Rev. Cajetan, *O.P.* '14 (WDC) [SEM] Dominican House of Studies, Washington, DC
Cuddy, Rev. Msgr. William F., '79 (BO) Curia: (>MO) Offices and Directors St. Michael, Bedford, MA
Cuellar, Rev. Henry, '18 (AUS) St. Joseph, Manor, TX
Cuellar, Rev. Manuel, '19 (PAT) Our Lady of Mercy, Whippany, NJ
Cuenin, Rev. Walter H., '70 (BO) Retired. [CAM] Brandeis University Catholic Chaplaincy, Waltham, MA
Cuevas, Rev. Alberto, '98 (LA) Our Lady of Guadalupe, Santa Barbara, CA
Cuevas, Rev. Diego O., '03 (MAD) On Duty Outside Diocese. VA Chaplain in Puerto Rico Curia: (>MO) Offices and Directors
Cuevas, Rev. Randy M., '82 (BR) Curia: Administration The Congregation of St. Aloysius Roman Catholic Church, Baton Rouge, LA; [EFT] St. Aloysius School Endowment Fund, Baton Rouge, LA
Cuevas, Rev. Trinidad Jose, '12 (NEW) St. Anthony of Padua, Union City, NJ
Cuevas, Rev. Wilson, '81 (ELP) Curia: Advisory Boards, Commissions, Committees, and Councils Our Lady of the Light, El Paso, TX; Santo Nino De Atocha, El Paso, TX
Cuevas-Contreras, Rev. Hernan, '11 (CHI) Curia: Leadership Christ Our Hope Parish, Highland Park, IL
Cuff, Rev. John P., *M.M.* '69 (CHI) Retired. St. Mother Teresa of Calcutta, Chicago, IL; [MON] Maryknoll Fathers & Brothers (Catholic Foreign Mission Society of America, Inc.), Chicago, IL
Cuizon, Rev. Manuel P., (SFD) St. Joseph, Springfield, IL
Culaba, Rev. Rey V., *C.S.S.R.* '72 (SFR) Our Lady of Mercy, Daly City, CA
Culbertson, Rev. Terry Ruth, (SY) Chap, Dir, Upstate Univ Hosp, Syracuse
Culhane, Rev. Alberic, *O.S.B.* '57 (SCL) [MON] St. John's Abbey, of the Order of St. Benedict, Collegeville, MN
Culic, Rev. Dennis, (NEW) St. Mary, West Orange, NJ
Culkin, Rev. Michael, '78 (WDC) On Duty Outside Diocese. Lancaster, PA
Culkin, Rev. Michael J., (HBG) Chap, Lancaster Gen Hosp
Cullen, Rev. Anthony F., '78 (SPR) Retired.
Cullen, Rev. Christopher, *S.J.* '94 (NY) [MON] Jesuit Community at Fordham University, New York, NY; [SEM] St. Joseph's Seminary, Yonkers, NY
Cullen, Rev. Christopher M., *S.J.* '94 (NY) [MON] Cardinal Spellman Hall, Jesuit Community, Bronx, NY
Cullen, Rev. Donald, '71 (KCK) Retired.
Cullen, Rev. Harold F., '68 (TR) Retired.
Cullen, Rev. Msgr. J. Peter, '67 (BGP) Retired. [MON] The Catherine Dennis Keefe Queen of the Clergy Retired Priests' Residence, Stamford, CT
Cullen, Rev. John J., '99 (BUF) Curia: Consultative Bodies St. Mary, Canaseraga, NY
Cullen, Rev. Kevin L., *S.J.* '86 (STL) (>COS) [RTR] Sacred Heart Jesuit Retreat House, Sedalia, CO
Cullen, Rev. Kevin L., *S.J.* '86 (STL) [COL] Saint Louis University, St. Louis, MO
Cullen, Rev. Patrick, (BIR) Retired.
Cullen, Rev. Patrick P., '68 (BIR) Curia: Catholic Charities St. Francis Xavier Catholic Parish, Birmingham, Birmingham, AL
Cullen, Rev. William, '83 (JOL) Retired.
Cullen, Rev. William, '83 (JKS) Retired. (>JOL) [NUR] St. John Vianney Villa, Naperville, IL
Culler, Rev. Eric J., '08 (TOL) Curia: Advisory Boards, Commissions, Committees, and Councils; Leadership
Culley, Rev. Brian, *CMF* '84 (LA) [MON] Dominguez Seminary Inc., Rancho Dominguez, CA
Culligan, Rev. Kevin, *OCD* '63 (MIL) [MON] Discalced Carmelite Friars of Holy Hill, Inc., Hubertus, WI
Culligan, Rev. Michael A., '59 (SR) Retired.
Cullinane, Rev. Brian, *O.F.M.* '71 (BO) Retired. [MIS] St. Anthony Shrine, Boston, MA
Cullings, Rev. David Ronald, '67 (P) Retired.
Cullota, Rev. Joachim, *OP* '64 (CHI) Retired.
Culnane, Rev. William R., '60 (SCR) Retired. [MON] Villa St. Joseph, Dunmore, PA
Culotta, Rev. Joachim, *OP* '64 (CHI) Retired. [MON] St. Pius V Priory, Chicago, IL
Culotta, Rev. Joseph G., '83 (BIR) Curia: Leadership St. Francis Xavier Catholic Parish, Birmingham, Birmingham, AL; [EFT] St. Francis Xavier Catholic School Education Foundation, Birmingham, AL
Culotta, Rev. Msgr. Salvador J., '53 (BEA) Retired.
Culver, Rev. Maurice Milton, (STA) St. Catherine of Siena, Orange Park, FL
Cumberland, Rev. Matthew T., '92 (LA) Our Lady of the Assumption, Claremont, CA
Cumin, Rev. Paolo, *F.S.C.B.* '02 (BO) Sacred Heart, Boston, MA
Cummings, Rev. Brian J., *S.S.E.* '96 (BUR) Curia: Offices and Directors [COL] St. Michael's College, Colchester, VT; [SHR] St. Anne's Shrine, Isle La Motte, VT
Cummings, Rev. Msgr. Carl F., '75 (BAL) [EFT] St. Jane Frances Educational Endowment Trust, Pasadena, MD
Cummings, Rev. Charles J., '68 (SCR) Retired.
Cummings, Rev. Evan, *CSP* '19 (COL) (>NY) [MON] Paulist Fathers' Motherhouse, New York, NY
Cummings, Rev. Gabriel, '84 (SAV) St. Frances Xavier Cabrini, Savannah, GA
Cummings, Rev. Keith D., '12 (ARL) St. Mary of Sorrows, Fairfax, VA
Cummings, Rev. Maurice, *O.Carm.* '71 (NY) [MON] St. Albert's Priory, Middletown, NY
Cummings, Rev. Msgr. McLean A., '98 (BAL) On Special Assignment. Mount St Mary's Univ [SEM] Mount St. Mary's Seminary, Emmitsburg, MD
Cummings, Rev. Timothy P., '08 (SP) Curia: Organizations (affiliated, inter-Diocesan, miscellaneous/ other) Prince of Peace, Sun City Center, FL
Cummings-Espada, Rev. Msgr. Jose Emilio, '72 (SJN) Curia: Leadership Academia Perpetuo Socorro, San Juan, PR; Ntra. Sra. del Perpetuo Socorro, Santurce, PR
Cummins, Rev. Anthony, (SAT) [NUR] Casa De Padres, San Antonio, TX
Cummins, Rev. Anthony O., '65 (SAT) Retired. Curia: Administration
Cummins, Rev. Anthony O., '65 (SAT) Curia: Administration
Cummins, Rev. Charles T., '68 (SLC) Saint Joseph LLC 230, Ogden, UT; [CAM] Weber State University, Newman Center, Ogden, UT
Cummins, Rev. Joseph V., *C.M.* '72 (BRK) [MON] Our Lady of Good Counsel, Brooklyn, NY
Cummins, Rev. Michael E., '95 (KNX) Curia: Leadership; Offices and Directors St. Dominic, Kingsport, TN
Cummins, Rev. Michael J., *C.M.* '77 (BRK) [MON] DePaul Residence, Queens Village, NY; [MON] Reverend John B. Murray, C.M. House, Jamaica, NY
Cundall, Rev. Brian, (LR) Christ the King, Fort Smith, AR
Cuneo, Rev. Msgr. J. James, '67 (BGP) Retired. Curia: Offices and Directors
Cung, Rev. Pius Kei, '02 (KAL) St. Jerome, Battle Creek, MI; St. Joseph, Battle Creek, MI
Cunnane, Rev. Jarlath, '77 (LA) St. Cornelius, Long Beach, CA
Cunniff, Rev. Charles, *CSP* (BO) [MIS] Chapel of the Holy Spirit, Boston, MA; [MIS] Paulist Center, Boston, MA; [MON] Missionary Society of St. Paul the Apostle in Massachusetts, Boston, MA
Cunningham, Rev. Douglas D., '87 (SY) Retired. On Special Assignment. Curia: (>MO) Offices and Directors
Cunningham, Rev. James B., '87 (BUF) Retired.
Cunningham, Rev. James K., '95 (BRK) St. Francis de Sales, Belle Harbor, NY
Cunningham, Rev. John D., *S.J.* '05 (NY) [MON] Jesuit Community at Fordham University, New York, NY
Cunningham, Rev. John F., '74 (PHX) Retired.
Cunningham, Rev. John H., '65 (ALX) Retired.
Cunningham, Rev. John P., '79 (BAL) Retired.
Cunningham, Rev. Joseph L., '63 (BRK) Retired.
Cunningham, Rev. Msgr. Joseph L., '63 (BRK) Retired. Our Lady Queen of Martyrs, Forest Hills, NY
Cunningham, Rev. Michael, '86 (OAK) Retired.
Cunningham, Rev. Michael, (DAL) Mater Dei Personal Parish, Irving, TX
Cunningham, Rev. Michael, *C.Ss.R.* '18 (BRK) Our Lady of Perpetual Help Basilica, Brooklyn, NY
Cunningham, Rev. Nicholas J., '79 (TOL) Sacred Heart of Jesus, New Bavaria, OH; St. Mary, Holgate, OH
Cunningham, Rev. Patrick M., '13 (BIS) St. Bonaventure, Underwood, ND; St. Catherine, Turtle Lake, ND; St. Edwin's Church, Washburn, ND
Cunningham, Rev. Sam, *S.V.D.* (DUB) [SEM] Divine Word College, Epworth, IA
Cunningham, Rev. Vianney, *TOR* (ALT) [MON] St. Bernardine Monastery, Hollidaysburg, PA
Cupple, Rev. Gerard J., '85 (DET) St. Gabriel Parish Ida, Ida, MI
Curalli, Rev. Joseph M., *C.Ss.R.* '78 (STL) [MIS] Redemptorist Fathers, Liguori, MO; [MON] St. Clement Health Care Center, Liguori, MO
Curci, Rev. Msgr. Richard G., '72 (GBG) Curia: Advisory Boards, Commissions, Committees, and Councils [MIS] Christ Our Shepherd Center, Greensburg, PA; [NUR] Neumann House, Greensburg, PA
Curesky, Friar Mark L., *O.F.M.Conv.* '75 (NOR) Curia: Leadership; Offices and Directors St. John, Cromwell, CT
Curiel, Rev. James A., *OCD* (DAL) Mount Carmel Center, Dallas, TX; St. Mary of Carmel Catholic Parish, Dallas, TX; [MON] Mt. Carmel Center (Discalced Carmelite Fathers of Dallas, Inc.), Dallas, TX
Curley, Rt. Rev. Augustine J., *O.S.B.* '88 (NEW) St. Mary of the Immaculate Conception, Newark, NJ; [MON] Benedictine Abbey of Newark, Newark, NJ
Curley, Rev. Msgr. Joseph K., '62 (RVC) Retired. [MON] St Pius X Residence for Retired Priests LLC, Ronkonkoma, NY
Curley, Rev. P. J., (JKS) Retired.
Curley, Rev. Patrick K., '08 (NY) Retired.
Curran, Rev. Anthony, '72 (ALB) Retired.
Curran, Rev. Anthony T., '67 (ATL) Retired.
Curran, Rev. Brendan A., *O.P.* '01 (CHI) [MON] Dominican Community of St. Martin de Porres, Oak Park, IL
Curran, Rev. Charles, '58 (ROC) Retired.
Curran, Rev. David, *C.I.C.M.* '71 (ARL) Retired.
Curran, Rev. Francis T., '69 (GI) Retired.
Curran, Rev. James, *CMF* '83 (LA) Retired. [MON] Dominguez Seminary Inc., Rancho Dominguez, CA
Curran, Rev. Msgr. James J., '63 (CAM) Retired.
Curran, Rev. James P., '00 (RIC) Basilica of St. Mary of the Immaculate Conception, Norfolk, VA
Curran, Rev. John, *L.C.* '96 (R) Catholic Student Center, North Carolina State University, Raleigh, NC; [CAM] NC State University Catholic Campus Ministry, Raleigh, NC
Curran, Rev. Joseph L., '76 (BO) Sacred Heart, Cambridge, MA
Curran, Rev. Oliver, '76 (RNO) Retired.
Curran, Rev. Richard G., '76 (BO) Retired. St. Ann, Somerville, MA; St. Catherine of Genoa, Somerville, MA; St. Joseph, Somerville, MA
Curran, Rev. Thomas B., *S.J.* '84 (KC) (>DEN) [MON] Regis Jesuit Community (The Jesuits at Regis University), Denver, CO
Curran, Rev. Thomas M., '70 (BO) On Leave.
Curran, Rev. Vincent J., '98 (HRT) Saint Mary Parish Corporation, New Haven, CT
Curran, Rev. William J, *MAfr* (SP) Retired. [MON] Missionaries of Africa, St. Petersburg, FL
Current, Rev. Maurice H., '80 (LIN) Curia: Leadership; Offices and Directors St. Mary's, Orleans, NE
Currie, Rev. John A., '97 (BO) Curia: Consultative Bodies Holy Family, Boston, MA; St. Patrick, Boston, MA; St. Peter, Boston, MA
Currin, Rev. John M., '98 (DET) On Leave.
Curry, Rev. Andrew, '08 (FTW) Immaculate Conception,

Laotto, IN; St. John Bosco, Churubusco, IN

Curry, Rev. Msgr. Joseph M., '86 (MET) Curia: Clergy and Religious Services Mary, Mother of God, Hillsborough, NJ

Curry, Rev. Robert S., *S.J.* '64 (PH) Retired.

Curry, Rev. Stephen, *O.S.A.* '96 (CAM) St. Augustine Preparatory School, Richland, NJ

Curry, Rev. Stephen M., *O.S.A.* (CHI) [MON] St. Rita Monastery, Chicago, IL

Curry, Rev. Terrence, (BRK) Saint John the Evangelist-Saint Rocco Roman Catholic Church, Brooklyn, NY

Curry, Rev. Terrence W., *S.J.* '77 (BO) [MON] Campion Center, Inc., Weston, MA

Curry, Rev. Thomas, *OSB* (E) Sacred Heart, St. Marys, PA

Curry, Rev. Thomas P., *O.S.B.* '03 (GBG) [MON] Saint Vincent Archabbey, Latrobe, PA

Curso, Rev. Manuel, '72 (SFR) Retired.

Curtin, Rev. James, '69 (JOL) Retired. [NUR] St. John Vianney Villa, Naperville, IL

Curtin, Rev. Martin, *O.F.M.Cap.* (RVC) St. Joseph the Worker, East Patchogue, NY

Curtin, Rev. Martin, *O.F.M., Cap.* '90 (NOR) St. Pius X, Middletown, CT

Curtin, Rev. Vincent C., *S.J.* (BAL) [MIS] Colombiere Jesuit Community, Baltimore, MD

Curtis, Rev. Bonaventure J., *O.S.B.* '10 (GBG) [MON] Saint Vincent Archabbey, Latrobe, PA

Curtis, Rev. John, (LEX) Retired. Holy Cross, Jackson, KY

Curtis, Rev. John C., '84 (LEX) Retired. Curia: Offices and Directors

Curtis, Rev. Joseph C., '69 (CHI) St. Paul the Apostle, Gurnee, IL

Curtis, Rev. Joshua C., *F.S.S.P.* '14 (SAC) Curia: Offices and Directors Pastor of St. Stephen the First Martyr Parish, Sacramento, a corporation sole, Sacramento, CA

Curtiss, Rev. Donald J., '71 (ROC) Retired. Curia: Tribunal

Curto, Rev. Antonio, *C.P.* '77 (GAL) [MON] Congregation of the Passion, Holy Name Passionist Community and Retreat Center, Houston, TX

Cusack, Rev. Anthony M., '15 (BO) St. Mary of the Nativity, Scituate, MA

Cusack, Rev. Msgr. John J., '71 (PAT) Retired.

Cusack, Rev. Msgr. John J., '71 (TUC) [MIS] Rachel's Vineyard Retreat Ministries Tucson and Southern Arizona, Inc., Hereford, AZ

Cusack, Rev. Thomas, *S.S.C.* '62 (OM) Retired. [MON] Missionary Society of St. Columban, St. Columbans, NE

Cusatis, Rev. Girard J., '63 (PH) Retired.

Cush, Rev. John P., '98 (BRK) On Duty Outside Diocese. St. Joseph Seminary, 201 Seminary Ave., Yonkers, 10704 Curia: Leadership; Pastoral Services Immaculate Heart of Mary, Brooklyn, NY (>NY) [SEM] St. Joseph's Seminary, Yonkers, NY

Cushing, Rev. Matthew A., '09 (COV) Curia: Advisory Boards, Commissions, Committees, and Councils All Saints, Walton, KY

Cushing, Rev. Walter F., '56 (ROC) Retired.

Cusicanqui, Rev. Wilfredo, (SCR) Holy Rosary, Hazleton, PA

Cusicanqui, Rev. Wilfredo Milan, (SCR) Holy Name of Jesus Parish, West Hazleton, PA

Cusick, Rev. John C., '70 (CHI) Retired.

Cusick, Rev. Kevin M., '92 (WDC) St. Francis de Sales, Benedict, MD

Cusick, Rev. Mark A., '13 (WDC) St. Francis Xavier, Washington, DC

Cusick, Rev. Thomas H., '64 (DET) Retired.

Cusick, Rev. Timothy, '00 (STA) On Duty Outside Diocese. St. Vincent de Paul Regional Seminary, Boynton Beach

Cusick, Rev. Timothy, (PMB) [SEM] St. Vincent de Paul Regional Seminary, Boynton Beach, FL

Custer, Rev. Edward O., *M.M.* '72 (NY) Retired. [MON] Maryknoll Fathers and Brothers (Catholic Foreign Mission Society of America, Inc.), Ossining, NY

Custer, Very Rev. John S., '83 (PSC) Curia: Advisory Boards, Commissions, Committees, and Councils; Leadership Holy Wisdom, Flanders, NJ; St. Michael Cathedral, Passaic, NJ

Custodio, Rev. Rinaldo B., '62 (STP) Retired.

Cutrara, Rev. Vincent, *C.S.* '57 (LA) Retired.

Cutrone, Rev. Dominick F., '55 (BRK) Retired. Our Lady of Grace, Brooklyn, NY

Cwiekowski, Rev. Bruce, '79 (P) Retired.

Cwiekowski, Rev. Frederick J., *P.S.S.* '62 (BAL) Retired. [MON] Society of St. Sulpice, Province of the United States, Baltimore, MD

Cwierz, Rev. Marcin, *OSPPE* (PH) [MON] The Order of Saint Paul, First Hermit - The Pauline Fathers, Doylestown, PA; [RTR] National Shrine of Our Lady of Czestochowa, Doylestown, PA

Cwik, Rev. Joseph, (WDC) Our Lady of Mercy, Potomac, MD

Cwik, Rev. Tom, *S.J.* '00 (STL) St. Francis Xavier Catholic Church, St. Louis, MO

Cwik, Rev. Tom, *S.J.* '00 (COS) [RTR] Sacred Heart Jesuit Retreat House, Sedalia, CO

Cybulski, Rev. David, '09 (DET) Curia: Administration; Consultative Bodies St. Isaac Jogues Parish St. Clair Shores, St. Clair Shores, MI

Cymer, Rev. Daniel, '12 (SPR) On Duty Outside Diocese. St Colman Parish, Pompano Beach, Florida St. Charles, Pittsfield, MA

Cymerman, Rev. Alexander, *OFM Conv* '65 (BUF) Retired. [MON] St. Maximilian Kolbe Friary, Hamburg, NY

Cyr, Rev. Joel R., '71 (PRT) Retired.

Cyr, Rev. John, '02 (PEO) St. Dominic's, Wyoming, IL; St. John the Baptist, Bradford, IL

Cyr, Rev. L. Philip, '69 (PRT) Retired.

Cyr, Rev. William F., '71 (SPR) Retired.

Cyriac, Rev. John, *MSFS* (SAT) St. John the Evangelist, Hondo, TX

Cyriac, Rev. John, *MSFS* (SAT) Holy Cross, D'Hanis, TX

Cyscon, Rev. Peter J., '73 (CHI) Retired.

Cyscon, Rev. Philip E., '84 (CHI) [HOS] Franciscan Health Olympia Fields (Franciscan Alliance, Inc.), Olympia Fields, IL

Czabala, Rev. Teodor, '98 (STF) Sacred Heart Ukrainian Catholic Church, Johnson City, NY; St. Nicholas, Elmira Heights, NY (>PHU) Ascension of Our Lord, Sayre, PA

Czachor, Rev. Richard E., '77 (SCR) Curia: Leadership; Offices and Directors Our Lady of Victory, Tannersville, PA

Czahur, Rev. John P., '77 (TR) Curia: Leadership Sacred Heart, Mount Holly, NJ

Czaicki, Rev. Franciszek, *O.C.D.* '97 (GRY) [MON] Discalced Carmelite Fathers Monastery, Munster, IN

Czaja, Rev. Blaise, *C.P.* '64 (SAC) (>GAL) [MON] Congregation of the Passion, Holy Name Passionist Community and Retreat Center, Houston, TX

Czajkowski, Rev. Andrew A., '74 (LAN) Curia: Leadership St. John the Evangelist Parish Davison, Davison, MI

Czajkowski, Rev. Richard J., *M.M.* '61 (NY) Retired.

Czapinski, Rev. Richard J., '58 (PIT) Retired.

Czapla, Rev. Bruce C., *O.F.M.* '89 (HRT) St. Josephs Roman Catholic Church Corporation, Winsted, Connecticut, Winsted, CT

Czapla, Rev. Donald J., '03 (DUB) St. Cecilia Church, Ames, Iowa, Ames, IA

Czarcinski, Rev. Edward A., '88 (MET) Our Lady of Lourdes, Milltown, NJ

Czarkowski, Rev. Joseph R., '74 (E) Chap., SCI Houtzdale Christ the King, Houtzdale, PA

Czarnecki, Rev. Andrew, '98 (DET) St. Louise de Marillac Parish Warren, Warren, MI

Czarnecki, Rev. Msgr. Anthony S., '66 (WOR) Retired. Curia: Leadership

Czarnecki, Rev. Eryk, '01 (CHI) St. Gertrude, Franklin Park, IL

Czarnecki, Rev. Stanislaw, *S.J.* '97 (CHI) [MON] Canisius House Jesuit Community, Evanston, IL

Czarnota, Rev. Paul, '03 (DET) Curia: Tribunal

Czaster, Rev. Herman, *O.F.M.Conv.* '65 (BRK) St. Adalbert, Elmhurst, NY

Czeck, Rev. Thomas, *OFM, Conv.* '98 (MRY) St. Paul the Apostle, Pismo Beach, CA

Czelusniak, Rev. Donald, '78 (ALB) Retired. Church of the Holy Spirit, Gloversville, NY

Czerniak, Rev. Ryszard, *S.Chr.* (BAL) Holy Rosary, Baltimore, MD

Czerniakowski, Rev. Boguslaw, *O.F.M.Conv.* (PAT) St. John Kanty, Clifton, NJ

Czerwonka, Rev. Paul G., '03 (LC) On Sick Leave.

Czok, Rev. Robert W., '66 (BRK) Retired.

Czop, Rev. Cyprian, *O.M.I.* (STP) Holy Cross, Minneapolis, MN; St. Casimir, St. Paul, MN; St. Patrick, St. Paul, MN

Czyz, Rev. Marcin Pawel, *SDS* '09 (SAT) St. Helena, San Antonio, TX; [MON] Salvatorian Fathers Community of Texas, Falls City, TX

Czyzewski, Rev. Michal, *OSPPE* (NY) St. Stanislaus Bishop and Martyr, New York, NY

Czyzynski, Rev. John, *S.C.J.* '63 (MIL) [MON] Sacred Heart at Monastery Lake, Franklin, WI

Da Silva, Rev. Marcelo, *IVE* (FR) Our Lady of the Immaculate Conception, New Bedford, MA; St. Anthony of Padua's, New Bedford, MA

Da Costa, Rev. Darrell, '97 (BRK) Our Lady of Fatima, Jackson Heights, NY

da Cunha, Rev. Domingos M., '71 (PRO) Retired. St. Joseph's Church Providence Rhode Island, Providence, RI

da Luz, Rev. Alessandro, '15 (RVC) St. Agnes Cathedral, Rockville Centre, NY

Da Roza, Rev. George, *S.S.C.* '85 (OAK) St. Anne, Walnut Creek, CA

da Silva, Rev. Antonio, *S.D.V.* (FR) St. Patrick's, Wareham, MA

da Silva, Rev. Antonio F., '88 (NEW) Curia: Advisory Boards, Commissions, Committees, and Councils Our Lady of Fatima, Newark, NJ

Da Silva, Rev. Arlindo Paul, '98 (MET) Curia: Consultative Bodies

Da Silva, Rev. Jose Carlos, '92 (BRK) St. Rita, Long Island City, NY; [CCH] Brazilian Ministry, ,

da Silva, Rev. Marcio Antonio Bueno, '04 (BGP) Immaculate Heart of Mary, Roman Catholic Church Corporation, Danbury, CT

da Silva, Rev. Ricardo, *SJ* '21 (NY) [MON] Xavier Jesuit Community, New York, NY

da Silva, Rev. Roberto, *S.D.V.* (NEW) St. Nicholas, Palisades Park, NJ

Da Silva Oliviera, Rev. Edivaldo, '02 (MIA) Curia: Pastoral Services Archbishop Edward A. McCarthy High School, Inc., Southwest Ranches, FL; Saint David, Davie, FL

Dabanka, Rev. Stephen, (DOD) Holy Trinity Catholic Church of Timken, Kansas, Timken, KS; St. Joseph Catholic Church of Liebenthal, Kansas, Liebenthal, KS; St. Michael Catholic Church of LaCrosse, Kansas, LaCrosse, KS

Dabash, Rev. G. Adrian, *O.P.* '71 (PRO) [MON] St. Thomas Aquinas Priory at Providence College, Providence, RI

D'Abele, Rev. Peter, *S.M.M.* '75 (RVC) [MON] Shrine of Our Lady of the Island, Manorville, NY

Dabney, Rev. Philip, *C.Ss.R.* '78 (BRK) [MON] Redemptorist Fathers of New York, Inc.-Baltimore Province, Brooklyn, NY

Dabria, Rev. Jerry J., '55 (NO) Retired.

Dabrowski, Rev. Klemens, *S.Ch.* (SEA) SS. Peter & Paul, Tacoma, WA

Dabu, Rev. Raynier Q., *C.R.S.* '13 (CHR) Divine Redeemer, Hanahan, SC

Daccache, Rev. Joe, (OLL) Saint Sharbel Maronite Catholic Mission of Milwaukee Inc., Union Grove, WI

Dacechen, Rev. Mario, *O.S.B.M.* '88 (STF) Holy Cross, Long Island City, NY

D'Achille, Rev. Arnold V., '59 (DET) Retired.

D'Aco, Rev. Joseph, '99 (FAR) Retired.

Dacoco, Rev. Rommel Rodriguez, (GB) St. Louis, Dyckesville, WI

DaCorte, Rev. Allan, *O.F.M.* '77 (CLV) [MON] St. Anthony of Padua Friary, Brooklyn, OH

Dada, Rev. Augustine, (NY) Our Lady of Mt. Carmel, Elmsford, NY

Dada, Rev. Jacek A., '92 (CHI) Queen of Peace Parish, Chicago, IL

D'Addezio, Rev. Msgr. Louis A., '61 (PH) Retired.

Daddona, Very Rev. Nicholas A., (PSC) Curia: Advisory Boards, Commissions, Committees, and Councils; Leadership St. Andrew the Apostle, Westbury, NY

Dadey, Rev. Neil R., '81 (ALT) Retired.

Dadiri, Rev. Joseph Aline, (LA) Our Lady of Perpetual Help, Downey, CA; St. Christopher, West Covina, CA

Daduya, Rev. Noel Abao, *CMI* '00 (BRK) St. Nicholas of Tolentine, Jamaica, NY

Daffron, Rev. Justin, *S.J.* '05 (NO) On Special Assignment. Academy of the Sacred Heart [COL] Loyola University New Orleans, New Orleans, LA; [MON] Loyola Jesuit Community, New Orleans, LA

Daganta, Rev. Felizardo J., (LA) Mary Star of the Sea, Oxnard, CA

Dagelen, Rev. Anthony L., *S.J.* '65 (MIL) [MON] St. Camillus Jesuit Community (Society of Jesus, USA Midwest Province), Wauwatosa, WI

Daghir, Rev. Benjamin Joseph, '22 (E) Assumption of Blessed Virgin Mary, Sykesville, PA; DuBois Area Catholic School System, Du Bois, PA; St. Bernard, Falls Creek, PA; St. Catherine of Siena, Du Bois, PA; St. Mary, Reynoldsville, PA

Dagit, Rev. Rick D., '86 (DUB) St. Gabriel Church, Zearing, Iowa, Zearing, IA; St. Joseph's Church, State Center, Iowa, State Center, IA; St. Mary Church, Colo, Iowa, Colo, IA; St. Patrick Church, Nevada, Iowa, Nevada, IA

Dagle, Rev. Harold F., '59 (ALN) Retired. Immaculate Conception, Allentown, PA; Immaculate Conception, Douglassville, PA

Dagle, Rev. Thomas W., '02 (WH) Retired.

Dagnoli, Rev. Albert, *SS.CC.* '68 (FR) Retired.
D'Agostino, Rev. Vincent, '16 (NEW) Curia: Offices and Directors St. Theresa, Kenilworth, NJ
Daguplo, Rev. Gene P., '84 (TR) St. Raphael-Holy Angels Parish, Hamilton, NJ
Daheim, Rev. Joseph, (AUS) Curia: Leadership St. Anthony Marie De Claret, Kyle, TX
Dahlberg, Rev. Daniel J., '67 (SUP) Retired.
Dahlinger, Rev. James H., *S.J.* '91 (SY) [MON] Jesuits at LeMoyne, Inc., Syracuse, NY
Dahm, Rev. Charles W., *O.P.* '64 (CHI) Curia: Parish Services St. Pius V, Chicago, IL; [MON] St. Pius V Priory, Chicago, IL
Daiber, Rev. Msgr. Sean J., '67 (CAM) On Duty Outside Diocese. Brazilian Missions
Daigle, Rev. Christopher, '78 (TLS) Retired.
Daigle, Rev. David A., '03 (BGP) Curia: (>MO) Offices and Directors
Daigle, Rev. Gregory J., '93 (BR) The Congregation Of Saint John The Evangelist Roman Catholic Church Of The Parish Of Iberville, State Of Louisiana, Plaquemine, LA
Daigle, Rev. Jerry J., '14 (SHP) Curia: Leadership St. Paschal, West Monroe, LA
Daigle, Rev. Karl J., '97 (SHP) Curia: Leadership St. Jude, Benton, LA
Daigle, Rev. Robert E., '63 (HPM) Retired.
Daigle, Rev. Steven, '89 (DUL) Retired.
Daiif, Rev. Joseph, '10 (SAM) Saint Sharbel Maronite Catholic Church, Newtown Square, PA
Dail, Rev. Nathan, '18 (B) [CAM] Boise State University, St. Paul's Catholic Center, Boise, ID; [MIS] St. Paul's Student Center, Boise, ID
Dail, Rev. Nathan, (B) Curia: Offices and Directors
Dailey, Rev. Gary, '85 (SPR) [CAM] Center for Religious Life, Springfield, MA; [CAM] University of Massachusetts, Amherst, MA
Dailey, Rev. Gary M., '85 (SPR) Curia: Offices and Directors St. Brigid's, Amherst, MA
Dailey, Rev. Joseph E., '77 (DET) Retired.
Dailey, Rev. Stash, (COL) Curia: Consultative Bodies
Dailey, Rev. Thomas F., *O.S.F.S.* (PH) [SEM] Theological Seminary of St. Charles Borromeo, Wynnewood, PA
Dailey, Rev. William R., *C.S.C.* '01 (FTW) [COL] University of Notre Dame Du Lac, Notre Dame, IN; [MON] Holy Cross Community, Corby Hall, University of Notre Dame, Notre Dame, IN
Daily, Rev. Cole, (LFT) Holy Spirit Church, Fishers, IN; St. John Vianney Parish, Fishers, IN
Daily, Rev. Vincent E., '90 (BO) [SEM] Pope Saint John XXIII National Seminary, Weston, MA
Daise, Rev. Richard, '10 (SAL) Curia: Administration; Advisory Boards, Commissions, Committees, and Councils; Consultative Bodies St. Joseph Parish, Hays, Inc., Hays, KS
Daisy, Rev. George R., '97 (LAN) Curia: Offices and Directors Immaculate Heart of Mary Parish Lansing, Lansing, MI
Dakes, Rev. John T., '87 (WDC) Jesus the Divine Word Parish, Huntingtown, MD
Dakin, Rev. Kenneth M., '88 (SAT) Retired.
D'Albro, Rev. Thomas G., '71 (BRK) Retired.
Dale, Rev. John Douglas, '88 (ORG) Retired.
Daleo, Rev. Joseph P., '71 (BEA) [CEM] St. Mary Cemetery, Orange, TX; [EFT] St. Mary School Foundation, Inc., Orange, TX
Dalessandro, Rev. Dennis G., '83 (HBG) Our Lady of Mercy, Catawissa, PA
Daley, Rev. Brian, *S.J.* '70 (WDC) (>NY) [MON] Murray-Weigel Hall (A Jesuit Community at Murray-Weigel Hall and Kohlmann Hall), Bronx, NY
Daley, Rev. Daniel P., '70 (GLP) Retired. Sacred Heart, Quemado, NM; St. Mary of the Angels, Pinetop, AZ
Daley, Rev. Francis E., '66 (BO) Retired.
Daley, Rev. Frederick D., '74 (SY) Curia: Leadership All Saints, Syracuse, NY
Daley, Rev. James D., '54 (ALB) Retired.
Daley, Rev. Raymond, *O.P.* (PRO) [MON] St. Thomas Aquinas Priory at Providence College, Providence, RI
Dalimata, Rev. Joseph, *FSSP* '21 (ELP) Immaculate Conception, El Paso, TX
Dalin, Rev. Jonathan J., '09 (PH) Saint Martha, Philadelphia, PA
Dall, Rev. Lincoln, '08 (JKS) Chap, Rankin Cty Prison; Mississippi State Hosp Curia: Consultative Bodies; Leadership Holy Savior, Clinton, MS; St. John, Charleston, MS; [CAM] Mississippi College Catholic Student Association, Clinton, MS
Dall'Agnese, Rev. Sergio, *C.S.* (WDC) Holy Rosary, Washington, DC
Dall'Agnese, Rev. Sergio, *C.S.* '79 (NY) [MIS] Scalabrini International Migration Network, New York, NY
Dallas, Rev. Benjamin, '02 (SAV) Holy Family, Columbus, GA
D'Almeda, Rev. Jeevan, *O.C.D.* (DEN) St. Frances Cabrini Catholic Parish in Littleton, Littleton, CO
D'Almeida, Rev. Edward P., '09 (LR) Holy Redeemer, El Dorado, AR; St. Luke Church, Warren, AR
Dalpiaz, Rev. Gino, *C.S.* '51 (CHI) [MON] Scalabrini House of Theology, Chicago, IL
Dalrymple, Rev. Matthew C., '14 (ATL) St. Luke the Evangelist Catholic Church, Dahlonega, Inc., Dahlonega, GA; [CAM] University of North Georgia (Dahlonega), Dahlonega, GA
Dalseth, Rev. Gerald, '64 (SCL) Retired.
Dalton, Rev. George R., '84 (PIT) Holy Family, Pittsburgh, PA
Dalton, Rev. James, '68 (SEA) Retired.
Dalton, Rev. James E., *O.S.F.S.* '72 (PH) SS. John Neumann and Maria Goretti Catholic High School, Philadelphia, PA
Dalton, Rev. Michel, *O.F.M.Cap.* '78 (HON) Curia: Consultative Bodies Holy Trinity, Honolulu, HI
Dalton, Rev. Robert, '62 (CIN) Retired. [MON] Headquarters of Glenmary Home Missioners (The Home Missioners of America), Fairfield, OH
Dalupang, Rev. Arturo O., '95 (CHR) Retired.
Daly, Rev. Anthony C., *S.J.* '72 (STL) [COL] Saint Louis University, St. Louis, MO
Daly, Rev. Christopher H., '60 (NY) Retired. [MON] John Cardinal O'Connor Residence, Bronx, NY
Daly, Rev. David, *LC* '01 (ATL) [MON] Legionaries of Christ, Incorporated, Cumming, GA
Daly, Rev. Msgr. Desmond, '66 (SP) Retired.
Daly, Rev. Francis J., *S.J.* '72 (DET) [RTR] Manresa Jesuit Retreat House, Bloomfield Hills, MI
Daly, Rev. Francis J., (BO) Our Lady of Sorrows, Sharon, MA
Daly, Rev. J. Daniel, '92 (NO) [EFT] Jesuit Seminary and Mission Fund, New Orleans, LA; [MON] Jesuit Provincial Office (Catholic Society of Religious and Literary Education), New Orleans, LA
Daly, Rev. J. Daniel, *S.J.* '92 (STL) [COL] Saint Louis University, St. Louis, MO; [EFT] US Central and Southern Province, Society of Jesus Aged/Infirm Fund, St. Louis, MO; [EFT] US Central and Southern Province, Society of Jesus Formation Fund, St. Louis, MO; [MON] Sacred Heart Jesuit Community, St. Louis, MO; [MON] USA Central & Southern Province, Society of Jesus, St. Louis, MO
Daly, Rev. Jerome R., '87 (ARL) Retired.
Daly, Rev. Kevin, *O.F.M.* (PAT) St. Anthony, Butler, NJ
Daly, Rev. Leo, *S.J.* '61 (NY) [MON] Murray-Weigel Hall (A Jesuit Community at Murray-Weigel Hall and Kohlmann Hall), Bronx, NY
Daly, Rev. Manus P., '65 (JC) Retired.
Daly, Rev. Michael Peter, '16 (STP) On Leave.
Daly, Rev. Peter J., '86 (WDC) Retired.
Daly, Rev. Robert J., *S.J.* '63 (BO) [MON] Campion Health & Wellness, Inc., Weston, MA
Daly, Rev. Shawn T., '95 (HRT) Curia: Advisory Boards, Commissions, Committees, and Councils; Clergy and Religious Services Saint Damien of Molokai Parish Corporation, Windsor, CT
Daly, Rev. Timothy P., '96 (ORL) Retired.
Daly, Rev. Vincent M., '71 (BRK) Retired. Holy Trinity, Whitestone, NY
Daman, Rev. Timoteus, *SMM* (RVC) [MON] Montfort Missionaries, Bay Shore, NY
D'Amato, Rev. Frank, '18 (PMB) St. Jude, Tequesta, FL
Damboise, Rev. Aaron L., '08 (PRT) Parish of the Holy Savior, Mexico, ME; St. Joseph's, Rockwood, ME
D'Ambrosia, Rev. Peter J., '85 (PRO) Saint Clare's Church Corporation, Misquamicut, Westerly, RI; Saint Vincent's Church Corporation, Bradford, Bradford, RI
Damian, Rev. Lawrence, (OKL) St. Benedict, Shawnee, OK
Damian, Rev. Lawrence P., '71 (BUF) Retired.
Damian, Rev. Peter, '05 (GR) St. Paul the Apostle, Grand Rapids, MI
Damian, Rev. Peter, *OCSO* '19 (ATL) [MON] The Monastery of the Holy Spirit, Conyers, GA
D'Amico, Rev. Carmen A., '82 (PIT) St. Oscar Romero, Canonsburg, PA
D'Amico, Rev. Francesco M., '19 (PH) St. Aloysius, Pottstown, PA
D'Amico, Rev. Francisco, (PH) Curia: Deaneries
D'Amico, Rev. Frank A., '87 (STL) St. Elizabeth Ann Seton Catholic Church, St. Charles, MO
D'Amico, Rev. Joseph A., '95 (NEW) Chap, Hudson Cty Corr Ctr, South Kearny; Offc Prison Minis... Curia: Advisory Boards, Commissions, Committees, and Councils St. Anastasia, Teaneck, NJ
D'Amico, Rev. Joseph A., '95 (NEW) Curia: Advisory Boards, Commissions, Committees, and Councils
Damien, Rev. Paul, '97 (SAM) St. Michael the Archangel, Fayetteville, NC
Dammay, Rev. Dante U., '77 (STO) Sacred Heart Church of Turlock (Pastor of), Turlock, CA
Damoah, Rev. Francis, *S.V.D.* (LAF) Our Lady of the Rosary, Jeanerette, LA; St. Peter the Apostle, Franklin, LA
Damron, Rev. Robert, '83 (LEX) Mother of Good Counsel, Hazard, KY
Danaher, Rev. Msgr. Mortimer, '53 (STA) Retired.
Danaher, Rev. Philip M., '83 (JOL) Retired.
Danaher, Rev. Timothy, *O.P.* '18 (MAN) [CAM] The Catholic Student Center at Dartmouth, Aquinas House, Aquinas at Dartmouth, Inc., Hanover, NH
Danavelil, Rev. George, (SYM) Curia: Administration
Danavelil, Rev. George, (SYM) Curia: Leadership; Offices and Directors St. Raphel Syro-Malabar Mission Cleveland, OH, Cleveland, OH
Danber, Rev. Bernard, *O.S.A.* '86 (CHI) [MON] St. Rita Monastery, Chicago, IL
Danczyk, Rev. Mark J., '92 (MIL) St. Benedict's Congregation, Fontana, WI
Danda, Rev. Sean R., '06 (IND) Curia: Offices and Directors St. Malachy Catholic Church, Brownsburg, Inc., Brownsburg, IN
Dandeneau, Rev. Stephen J., '11 (PRO) Saint Joseph's Roman Catholic Church of Pascoag, Pascoag, RI; St. Eugene's Church Corporation, Chepachet, Chepachet, RI
Dandou, Rev. Pepin, '97 (SAC) Pastor of St. Joseph Parish, Vacaville, a corporation sole, Vacaville, CA
D'Andrea, Rev. Steven D., '97 (NEW) Most Sacred Heart of Jesus, Wallington, NJ
Dandu, Rev. Asirvadam, (JOL) St. Isidore, Bloomingdale, IL
Dandurand, Rev. Douglas E., '82 (STP) Retired.
Dandurand, Very Rev. Michael G., '97 (TOL) Curia: Advisory Boards, Commissions, Committees, and Councils; (>MO) Offices and Directors Holy Trinity, Swanton, OH
Dandurand, Rev. Michael M., (TOL) Curia: Deaneries
Dane, Rev. James E., '83 (MOB) St. Columba Parish, Dothan, Dothan, AL
Dane, Rev. John, '91 (LEX) Retired.
Danek, Rev. Timothy, (LIN) St. Joseph's, Auburn, NE
Danella, Rev. Francis W., *O.S.F.S.* '73 (WIL) [MON] Wilmington-Philadelphia Province of the Oblates of St. Francis de Sales, Wilmington, DE
Dang, Rev. Anthony, (PHX) [CAM] Holy Trinity Newman Center, A Quasi-Parish, Flagstaff, AZ
Dang, Rev. Bernie Tan, *C.R.M.* (STA) Christ the King, Jacksonville, FL
Dang, Rev. Brandon, '16 (ORG) Curia: Leadership St. Elizabeth Ann Seton, Irvine, CA
Dang, Rev. Hai Duc, '99 (GAL) Curia: Offices and Directors St. Philip of Jesus, Houston, TX
Dang, Rev. Hoang, '95 (LA) St. Catherine Laboure, Torrance, CA
Dang, Rev. Johnny, '15 (SB) Our Lady of Perpetual Help, Riverside, CA
Dang, Rev. Joseph, (BLX) [MON] St. Augustine's Residence, Bay St. Louis, MS
Dang, Rev. Joseph Q.A., *O.P.* (ARL) Holy Martyrs of Vietnam Catholic Church, Arlington, VA
Dang, Rev. Peter A., '12 (BR) Chap, Baton Rouge Gen Med Ctr, Baton Rouge The Congregation Of Sacred Heart Roman Catholic Church, Baton Rouge, LA
Dang, Rev. Peter Ha Dinh, (SPR) Curia: Offices and Directors St. Paul the Apostle, Springfield, MA
Dang, Rev. Quy Ngoc, *S.V.D.* '09 (WH) Holy Family, Richwood, WV; St. Anne, Webster Springs, WV
Dang, Rev. Vincent H., '95 (SCR) St. Leo, Ashley, PA
Dang, Rev. Vincent Tinh Thanh, '08 (SJ) St. Frances Cabrini, San Jose, CA
Dang Cao, Rev. Khiet, *CS* '21 (BO) St. Anthony of Padua, Everett, MA
Dang Ha, Rev. Dominic Thuy, '84 (SLC) Retired.
D'Angelo, Rev. Donald S., '68 (SFR) Retired.
D'Angelo, Rev. Joseph, '68 (RVC) Retired. Chap Curia: Offices and Directors
D'Angelo, Rev. Paul R., '09 (VEN) Our Lady Queen of Martyrs Parish in Sarasota, Inc., Sarasota, FL
Dango, Rev. Enno H, *CP* '10 (DET) [MON] St. Paul of the Cross Community, Congregation of the Passion, Detroit, MI; [RTR] St. Paul of the Cross Passionist Retreat and Conference Center, Detroit, MI
Daniel, Rev. Ambrose Ladu, (DM) St. Ambrose Cathedral, Des Moines, IA
Daniel, Rev. Ambrose Ladu, (DM) Curia: Offices and Directors
Daniel, Rev. Avery, '22 (ATL) St. Catherine Laboure Catholic Church, Jefferson, Inc., Jefferson, GA; St.

Joseph Catholic Church, Athens, Inc., Athens, GA
Daniel, Rev. John C., '92 (SFE) Curia: Offices and Directors Immaculate Heart of Mary, Los Alamos, NM
Daniel, Rev. Timothy G., '14 (WDC) Ascension, Bowie, MD
Danielewicz, Rev. Noel, *O.F.M.Conv.* (HRT) [MIS] Enfield Convent (Felician Sisters), Enfield, CT
Daniels, Rev. Desmond, (GAL) [MIS] The Catholic Chaplain Corps, Houston, TX
Daniels, Rev. Jerry, '01 (KNX) St. Catherine Laboure, Copperhill, TN; [RTR] Christ Prince of Peace Retreat Center, Benton, TN
Daniels, Rev. Lawrence, *O.C.D.* '65 (MIL) [MON] Washington Province of Discalced Carmelite Friars, Inc., Milwaukee, WI
Daniels, Very Rev. Leo Francis, *C.O.* '65 (BWN) Oratory Academy of St. Philip Neri, Pharr, TX; Oratory Athenaeum for University Preparation, Pharr, TX; St. Jude Thaddeus, Pharr, TX; [MON] Pharr Oratory of St. Philip Neri of Pontifical Right, Pharr, TX
Danielsen, Rev. Francis Thomas, *C.Ss.R.* '64 (KC) Retired. Our Lady of Perpetual Help, Kansas City, MO
Danielsen, Rev. Thomas, *C.Ss.R.* '64 (KC) [MON] Redemptorists Fathers of Kansas City, Missouri, Kansas City, MO
Danielski, Rev. Francis, *O.Praem.* '11 (PH) [MON] Daylesford Abbey, Inc., Paoli, PA
Danielson, Rev. Charles R., '92 (BUR) Curia: Leadership
Danielson, Rev. Tage A., *O.F.M.Cap.* (GBG) (>WDC) Shrine of the Sacred Heart, Washington, DC
Danik, Rev. Daniel, (NEW) Curia: Organizations (affiliated, inter-Diocesan, miscellaneous/other)
d'Anjou, Rev. John R., *S.J.* '72 (PRT) Our Lady of Hope Parish, Portland, ME
D'Anjou, Very Rev. Lawrence C., '00 (OAK) Curia: Leadership; Offices and Directors St. Bonaventure, Concord, CA
Dankasa, Rev. Jacob, '04 (DAL) Holy Family of Nazareth Catholic Parish, Irving, TX
Dankoski, Rev. Francis, '09 (STU) On Leave.
Danneker, Rev. David L., '82 (HBG) On Leave. [CAM] Catholic Campus Ministry, Harrisburg, PA
Danneker, Rev. Edward A.J., '64 (ATL) Retired.
Danner, Rev. Brian J., '95 (SC) On Leave.
Danner, Rev. James L., '74 (MEM) Retired.
Dansak, Rev. Thomas E., '73 (PIT) Retired.
Dansak, Rev. Thomas J., '73 (PIT) Retired.
Dansereau, Rev. Kevin J., '15 (ARL) Curia: Tribunal Cathedral of St. Thomas More, Arlington, VA
Danso, Rev. Samuel, '10 (DM) St. Brendan, Leon, IA; St. Francis, Corydon, IA
Danstrom, Rev. Connor Coyle, '14 (CHI) [CAM] University of Illinois at Chicago - St. John Paul II Newman Center, Chicago, IL
Dant, Rev. J. Nicholas, (IND) Retired. Curia: Offices and Directors
Dante, Rev. Neal F., '64 (CAM) Retired.
Dantinne, Rev. Gary J., '68 (GB) Retired.
D'Antonio, Rev. John A., '73 (SP) Retired.
D'Antonio, Rev. Ronald M., '76 (BRK) Saint Athanasius - Saint Dominic, Brooklyn, NY
Danyluk, Rev. Richard, *SS.CC.* (SB) [MON] Congregation of the Sacred Hearts of Jesus and Mary, SS.CC., Hemet, CA
Danyluk, Rev. Richard J., *SS.CC.* (FR) [MIS] Congregation of the Sacred Hearts - United States Province (Sacred Hearts Fathers; Sacred Hearts Missions), Fairhaven, MA
Danyluk, Rev. Richard J., *SS.CC.* '75 (LA) [MON] Congregation of the Sacred Hearts of Jesus and Mary, La Verne, CA
Danzi, Rev. Rocco C., *S.J.* (NEW) [COL] Saint Peter University, Jersey City, NJ
Danzi, Rev. Rocco C., *S.J.* '00 (NEW) St. Aedan, Jersey City, NJ; [MON] Jesuits of Saint Peter College, Inc., Jersey City, NJ
Dao, Rev. (John Bosco M.) Bang Thanh, *CRM* '19 (SPC) [MON] Congregation of the Mother of the Redeemer, Carthage, MO
Dao, Rev. Anthony C., '82 (SB) St. Catherine of Alexandria, Temecula, CA
Dao, Rev. Joseph Vu, *S.V.D.* '88 (BLX) [MON] St. Augustine's Residence, Bay St. Louis, MS
Dao, Rev. Khahn T., (BO) St. Mary Magdalen, Tyngsborough, MA; St. Rita, Lowell, MA; Ste. Marguerite d'Youville, Dracut, MA
Dao, Rev. Ngo Van, *C.Ss.R.* '86 (LA) [MON] Vietnamese Redemptorist Mission, Baldwin Park, CA
Dao, Rev. Simon, *C.R.M.* (VEN) St. John XXIII Catholic Parish in Fort Myers, Inc., Fort Myers, FL
Dao, Rev. Thanh X., '03 (SEA) Vietnamese Martyrs Personal Parish, Tukwila, WA
Daoust, Rev. Joseph, *SJ* '69 (RC) [MON] Holy Rosary Mission Jesuit Community, Pine Ridge, SD
Daprile, Rev. James M., '76 (Y) Retired.
D'Aquila, Rev. Ulysses L., '04 (SFR) Retired. St. James, San Francisco, CA
Darbouze, Rev. Joseph, '55 (NY) St. Raymond, Bronx, NY
Darbouze, Rev. Joseph, '58 (NY) Retired.
Darbouze, Rev. Msgr. Rollin, '69 (BRK) Retired.
Darcy, Rev. Brendan, *SMA* '67 (BO) Curia: Consultative Bodies [MON] Society of African Missions, Dedham, MA
Darcy, Rev. David M., '94 (SPR) Curia: Offices and Directors St. Francis of Assisi, Belchertown, MA
Darcy, Rev. James F., '66 (BO) Retired.
Darcy, Very Rev. Michael J., *C.O.* '02 (PIT) [MON] Congregation of the Oratory of St. Philip Neri, Pittsburgh, PA
Darcy, Rev. Michael P., *K.H.S.* '00 (WIL) Corpus Christi, Wilmington, DE; St. Matthew, Wilmington, DE
D'Arcy, Rev. Patric, (NY) Our Lady of Refuge, Bronx, NY
Dardis, Very Rev. Stephen, '12 (NO) Curia: Leadership Holy Family Roman Catholic Church, Luling, Louisiana, Luling, LA
Dare, Rev. Glenn, '74 (SAC) Retired.
Dargis, Rev. Andre, (PHX) Retired. St. Patrick Roman Catholic Parish, Scottsdale, AZ
Dargis, Rev. Andre E., '67 (WOR) Retired.
Darilek, Rev. Dennis, '73 (SAT) Retired.
Darin, Rev. Msgr. David M., '91 (BEL) Curia: Offices and Directors St. Mary, Trenton, IL
Darlak, Rev. Mateusz, '18 (PAT) St. Cecilia's, Rockaway, NJ
Darling, Rev. George E., '84 (GR) Blessed Sacrament, Grand Rapids, MI; St. Alphonsus, Grand Rapids, MI
Darmanin, Rev. Daniel, '19 (NO) St. Margaret Mary Roman Catholic Church, Slidell, Louisiana, Slidell, LA
Darnell, Rev. Lawrence T., *O.M.V.* '82 (LA) St. Peter Chanel, Hawaiian Gardens, CA
Daro, Rev. Douglas, '18 (LIN) Curia: Leadership; Offices and Directors St. Cecilia's, Hastings, NE
Darow, Rev. Robert G., '63 (CHI) Retired. St. Pio of Pietrelcino Parish, Chicago, IL
DaRoza, Rev. George, *S.S.C.* '85 (OM) [MON] Missionary Society of St. Columban, St. Columbans, NE
D'Arpino, Rev. John A., '11 (BO) On Leave.
Darragh, Rev. John, '69 (HEL) Retired.
Darsi, Rev. Don Bosco, '06 (NO) [SEM] Saint Joseph Seminary College, Saint Benedict, LA
D'Arthenay, Rev. Marcelino D., '76 (BO) Cathedral of the Holy Cross, Boston, MA
D'Arthenay, Rev. Marcelino D., '76 (BO) Curia: Tribunal
Das, Rev. Arokodias, '13 (LEX) Curia: Leadership
Dasari, Rev. Pavikiran, (NY) Chap, Nyack Hosp
Dasari, Rev. Ravi K., *C.O.* (NY) Nyack Hosp
Dash, Rev. George J., *O.F.M.Cap.* '92 (NY) Chap, Fishkill Corr Fac, Beacon
Dashner, Rev. Daniel L., (NO) Most Holy Trinity Roman Catholic Church, Louisiana, Covington, LA
DaSilva, Rev. Arlindo Paul, '98 (MET) Our Lady of Fatima, Piscataway, NJ
DaSilva, Rev. Edivar Ribeiro, (FR) Curia: Offices and Directors Good Shepherd, Oak Bluffs, MA
Dass, Rev. Joseph, '90 (LA) Retired.
Dass David, Rev. Arokia, '09 (SLC) Good Shepherd LLC 204, Price, UT; Notre Dame de Lourdes LLC 207, Price, UT
Daszewski, Rev. Alexander, (RVC) Chap, Good Shepherd Hospice (Nassau)
Dattilo, Rev. Anthony A., '90 (STL) St. Joachim Catholic Church, Old Mines, Cadet, MO; St. Joseph Catholic Church, Tiff, Cadet, MO
Dattilo, Rev. Anthony M., '84 (CIN) St. Antoninus, Cincinnati, OH; St. Catharine of Siena, Cincinnati, OH
Datzman, Rev. Harold L., *O.S.B.* '65 (PEO) Retired. [SEM] St. Bede Abbey (Benedictine Society of St. Bede, Benedictine Fathers and Brothers), Peru, IL
Dau, Rev. Paul, '10 (ORL) Our Lady of Hope, Port Orange, FL
d'Auby, Rev. Phillip, *S.M.* '61 (SFR) Retired. [MON] Marist Center of the West, San Francisco, CA
Daugherty, Rev. Patrick, *C.P.* '02 (NY) [MON] The Congregation of the Passion - St. Paul of the Cross Province, Jamaica, NY
Daugherty, Rev. Patrick, '02 (ATL) St. Paul of the Cross Catholic Church, Atlanta, Inc., Atlanta, GA
Daugherty, Rev. Msgr. Scott, '83 (FRS) St. Anne's Parish, Porterville, CA
Dauphinais, Rev. Louis Marie, *M.M.A.* '70 (SAM) [MON] Maronite Monks of Adoration - Most Holy Trinity Monastery, Petersham, MA
Dauphine, Rev. Marc Rene, '09 (MRY) On Leave.
Dauses, Rev. Jeffrey S., '90 (BAL) Immaculate Heart of Mary, Baltimore, MD; St. Thomas More, Baltimore, MD; [EFT] The Immaculate Heart of Mary School Endowment Trust, Baltimore, MD
Davalos, Rev. Juan Pablo, '07 (BWN) Sacred Heart, Hidalgo, TX
Davantes, Rev. Carlo B., (MO) Curia: Offices and Directors
Davanzo, Rev. Joseph V., '97 (RVC) Curia: Organizations (affiliated, inter-Diocesan, miscellaneous/other) Our Lady of Grace, West Babylon, NY
Dave, Rev. Kyle V., '01 (NO) Our Lady of Perpetual Help, Belle Chasse, LA
Davenport, Rev. Thomas, *O.P.* (PRO) [MON] St. Thomas Aquinas Priory at Providence College, Providence, RI
D'Aversa, Rev. Robert, *T.O.R.* '73 (ALT) [MON] St. Bernardine Monastery, Hollidaysburg, PA
Davey, Rev. Edward M., '53 (PAT) Retired. [MIS] Nazareth Village, Chester, NJ
Davey, Rev. Philip D., *O.S.B.* '75 (PEO) [SEM] St. Bede Abbey (Benedictine Society of St. Bede, Benedictine Fathers and Brothers), Peru, IL
Davich, Rev. Msgr. George, '62 (SLC) Retired.
David, Rev. Angelo, '11 (SJ) St. Julie Billiart, San Jose, CA
David, Very Rev. Arokia Dass, '09 (SLC) Curia: Offices and Directors
David, Rev. Arulanandu, (SEA) St. Philip, Woodland, WA
David, Rev. Craig, (SY) Chap, Veterans Administration Hosp, Syracuse
David, Rev. Craig, '96 (ATL) On Duty Outside Diocese. VA East Syracuse, NY Curia: (>MO) Offices and Directors
David, Rev. Fontaine, *O.Carm.* '79 (TUC) Retired.
David, Very Rev. George, '71 (ROM) Curia: Offices and Directors St. Basil, Trenton, NJ; St. Mary, Roebling, NJ
David, Very Rev. Jamin S., '08 (BR) Curia: Administration; Canonical Services; Leadership St. Margaret Queen of Scotland (Congregation Of St. Margaret Roman Catholic Church), Hammond, LA; [MIS] Baton Rouge Chancery Office, Baton Rouge, LA
David, Rev. Joseph, '09 (OKL) Prince of Peace, Altus, OK
Davids, Rev. Peter, '14 (POC) Retired.
Davids, Rev. Peter, (AUS) Retired.
Davidson, Rev. Al M., '12 (BR) Curia: Administration Congregation Of St. Joseph The Worker Roman Catholic Church Of Assumption, Louisiana, Pierre Part, LA; The Congregation Of Our Lady Of Prompt Succor Roman Catholic Church, Of The Parish Of Iberville, State Of Louisiana, White Castle, LA
Davidson, Rev. James, '18 (SJP) Annunciation of the Mother of God, Ramey, PA; Immaculate Conception, Altoona, PA; St. John the Baptist, Johnstown, PA
Davidson, Rev. James, '18 (SJP) Curia: Offices and Directors
Davidson, Rev. John, '64 (EVN) Retired.
Davidson, Rev. Michael F., *S.J.* '09 (BO) [MON] The Jesuit Community at Boston College, Chestnut Hill, MA
Davied, Rev. Matthew, (WCH) (>SAL) St. Isidore Catholic Student Center Parish, Manhattan, Inc., Manhattan, KS; (>SAL) [CAM] St. Isidore Catholic Student Center Parish, Manhattan, Inc., Manhattan, KS
Davies, Rev. Julian A., *O.F.M.* '60 (ALB) [COL] Siena College, Loudonville, NY
Davignon, Rev. Philip A., '62 (FR) Retired.
Davila, Rev. Rafael R., *M.M.* '58 (GAL) [SEM] St. Mary's Seminary, Houston, TX (>NY) [MON] Maryknoll Fathers and Brothers (Catholic Foreign Mission Society of America, Inc.), Ossining, NY
Davila, Rev. Rito, '05 (AUS) St. Albert the Great, Austin, TX
Davila, Rev. Vincent, *O.P.* (STP) (>STL) [MON] St. Dominic Priory, St. Louis, MO
Davila Lopez, Rev. Reinaldo I., '90 (ARE) St. Joseph, Camuy, PR
Davin, Rev. Neil, *C.P.* '52 (BRK) Retired.
Davin, Rev. Neil, *C.P.* '52 (NY) Retired.
Davis, Rev. Anthony, '15 (COL) St. Matthias, Columbus, OH
Davis, Rev. Anthony K. A., '85 (SEA) Sacred Heart of Jesus, Enumclaw, WA; St. Barbara, Black Diamond, WA
Davis, Rev. Anthony Maxwell, '21 (DEN) St. Stephen Catholic Parish in Glenwood Springs, Glenwood

Springs, CO
Davis, Rev. Binoy P., '15 (CHL) St. Matthew, Charlotte, NC
Davis, Rev. Christopher, *O.S.B.* '58 (PRO) Retired. [MON] Abbey of St. Gregory the Great (Order of St. Benedict in Portsmouth, Rhode Island, Benedictines of the English Congregation), Portsmouth, RI
Davis, Rev. Christopher J., '98 (CHL) On Leave.
Davis, Rev. Clement T., '70 (IND) Retired. Holy Trinity Catholic Church, Edinburgh, Inc., Edinburgh, IN; St. Bartholomew Catholic Church, Columbus, IN, Columbus, IN
Davis, Rev. Daniel, *O.P.* '94 (MAD) [CON] Sinsinawa Dominican Congregation of the Most Holy Rosary., Sinsinawa, WI
Davis, Rev. Dwayne D., '13 (BRK) Our Lady Help of Christians, Brooklyn, NY; St. Thomas Aquinas, Brooklyn, NY
Davis, Rev. Edward V., *M.M.* '61 (NY) Retired. [MON] Maryknoll Fathers and Brothers (Catholic Foreign Mission Society of America, Inc.), Ossining, NY
Davis, Rev. F. Hampton, '90 (LAF) St. Anthony of Padua, Eunice, LA
Davis, Rev. Frassati, *O.P.* '21 (WDC) [SEM] Dominican House of Studies, Washington, DC
Davis, Rev. Gary G., '75 (L) Retired.
Davis, Rev. Hampton, (LAF) St. Edmund Catholic School, Eunice, LA; St. Mathilda, Eunice, LA
Davis, Very Rev. Henry J., *S.S.J.* '93 (NO) Curia: Leadership Corpus Christi-Epiphany, New Orleans, LA
Davis, Rev. Jacob W., '99 (YAK) Resurrection, Zillah, WA
Davis, Rev. Jeremy, *S.O.L.T.* (DET) Holy Redeemer Parish Detroit, Detroit, MI; St. Cunegunda Parish Detroit, Detroit, MI; St. Gabriel Parish Detroit, Detroit, MI
Davis, Rev. John P., '63 (PRT) Retired.
Davis, Rev. Jonathan, (KC) On Special Assignment. Bishop LeBlond HS Bishop LeBlond High School, St. Joseph, MO; St. Patrick Catholic Church, St. Joseph, St. Joseph, MO
Davis, Rev. Joseph P., '72 (PAT) Retired. [MIS] Nazareth Village, Chester, NJ
Davis, Rev. Karl, *O.M.I.* '05 (WDC) [MON] Oblate Community, Washington, DC
Davis, Rev. Kenneth, *O.F.M.Conv.* '86 (IND) [RTR] Mount Saint Francis Friary and Retreat Center, Mount St. Francis, IN
Davis, Rev. Kenneth G., *O.F.M.* (NO) [SEM] Saint Joseph Seminary College, Saint Benedict, LA
Davis, Rev. Kirk, *O. S. A.* '10 (LA) St. Thomas Aquinas, Ojai, CA
Davis, Rev. Mark E., '96 (TOL) Curia: Advisory Boards, Commissions, Committees, and Councils; Deaneries St. Aloysius, Bowling Green, OH
Davis, Rev. Michael J., '87 (PH) Assumption B.V.M., Feasterville, PA
Davis, Rev. Michael W., '90 (MIA) Curia: Leadership St. Gregory, Plantation, FL
Davis, Rev. Nathan, (POC) St. Alban's Catholic Church, Henrietta, NY
Davis, Rev. Nathan, '20 (ROC) Kateri Tekakwitha Roman Catholic Parish, Rochester, NY
Davis, Rev. Noel, '62 (LAR) St. Frances Cabrini, Laredo, TX
Davis, Rev. Ralph E., '17 (DUB) Holy Name Church, West Union, Iowa, West Union, IA; Immaculate Conception Church, Sumner, Iowa, Sumner, IA; St. Francis Church, Fayette, Iowa, Fayette, IA; St. Peter Church, Clermont, Iowa, Clermont, IA
Davis, Rev. Richard L., *T.O.R.* '80 (ALT) [MON] St. Francis Friary at Mount Assisi, Loretto, PA
Davis, Rev. Thomas, '19 (NTN) St. Ann, Danbury, CT
Davis, Very Rev. Thomas R., '83 (R) Curia: Offices and Directors Basilica Shrine of Saint Mary, Wilmington, NC
Davis, Rev. Thomas X., *O.C.S.O.* '58 (SAC) [SEM] Abbey of New Clairvaux, Trappist Seminary, Vina, CA
Davis, Rev. Msgr. Wilbur, '64 (ORG) Retired. Our Lady Queen of Angels, Newport Beach, CA
Davis, Rev. William, (VEN) St. Ann Catholic Parish in Naples, Inc. a Florida non-profit corporation, Naples, FL
Davis, Rev. William, *O.M.I.* '57 (SAT) Retired. [NUR] Oblate Madonna Residence, San Antonio, TX
Davis, Rev. William Thomas Porter, *OSA* '10 (SD) Pastor of Saint Patrick Catholic Parish, San Diego, a corporation sole, San Diego, CA
Davison, Rev. Andreas R., '07 (BO) Curia: Tribunal Our Lady of the Visitation Parish, Milton, MA
Davison, Rev. Ben, '92 (SD) Pastor of Saint Kieran Catholic Parish, El Cajon, a corporation sole, El Cajon, CA
Davison, Rev. Donald J., *C.PP.S.* (FTW) St. Patrick, Walkerton, IN
Davison, Rev. Timothy L., (STU) St. John the Baptist, Woodsfield, OH; St. Sylvester, Woodsfield, OH
Davitti, Rev. Michael, *S.X.* '70 (PAT) [MON] Xaverian Missionary Fathers, Wayne, NJ
Davoren, Rev. Stephen, '96 (LA) St. Mel, Woodland Hills, CA
Davy, Rev. Andrew Peter, *M.I.C.* '09 (SPR) [MON] Congregation of Marian Fathers of The Immaculate Conception of the Most Blessed Virgin Mary, Stockbridge, MA
Davy, Rev. Andy, *M.I.C.* '09 (JOL) St. Mary, Plano, IL
Davy, Rev. Kavungal, *C.M.I.* '89 (SAC) Curia: Offices and Directors Pastor of St. Mary Parish, Sacramento, a corporation sole, Sacramento, CA
Daw, Rev. Timothy M., '91 (CLV) St. Christopher, Rocky River, OH
Dawley, Rev. Robert, (RVC) Chap, Good Shepherd Hospice (Nassau)
Dawson, Rev. Andrew, (DET) St. Joan of Arc Parish St. Clair Shores, St. Clair Shores, MI
Dawson, Rev. Brendan H., '19 (PIT) St. Jude, Pittsburgh, PA
Dawson, Rev. David L., '21 (BR) On Special Assignment. Notre Dame Seminary Congregation Of Immaculate Heart Of Mary Roman Catholic Church Of Maringouin, Maringouin, LA; Congregation Of St. Frances Xavier Cabrini Roman Catholic Church Of Livonia, Louisiana, Livonia, LA; The Congregation Of St. Joseph Roman Catholic Church, Of The Parish Of Iberville, State Of Louisiana, Grosse Tete, LA
Dawson, Rev. M. David, '14 (HRT) Saint Martin of Tours Parish Corporation, Canaan, CT
Dawson, Rev. Richard, '81 (PT) Curia: Offices and Directors Blessed Trinity, Bonifay, FL; St. Margaret, De Funiak Springs, FL
Dawson, Rev. W. Penn, *S.J.* '18 (NO) [COL] Loyola University New Orleans, New Orleans, LA; [MON] Loyola Jesuit Community, New Orleans, LA
Dawson, Rev. Wayne, '98 (MRY) St. Joseph, Capitola, CA
Day, Rev. Dennis C., '76 (B) Curia: Leadership
Day, Rev. James R., *O.SS.T.* '72 (BAL) [MON] Holy Trinity Monastery, Sykesville, MD
Day, Rev. James R., *O.SS.T.* '72 (WDC) DeMatha Catholic High School, Hyattsville, MD
Day, Rev. James Richard, '96 (NO) Chap, Ochsner Med Ctr, West Bank, Gretna; W Jefferson Gener…
Day, Very Rev. Jeffrey, '99 (DET) Curia: Consultative Bodies; Leadership
Day, Rev. Jerome J., *O.S.B.* '95 (MAN) [MON] St. Anselm Abbey, Manchester, NH
Day, Rev. John Patrick, (L) On Special Assignment. St. Andrew, Sparta, TN [MON] Sacred Heart Retreat, Louisville, KY
Day, Rev. Martin, *O.F.M.Conv.* '91 (IND) Curia: Offices and Directors [MON] Provincial Headquarters, Our Lady of Consolation Province, Conventual Franciscans (Province of Our Lady of Consolation), Mount St. Francis, IN; [RTR] Province of Our Lady of Consolation, Inc., Mount St. Francis, IN
Day, Rev. Wilfred E., (IND) St. John the Baptist Catholic Church, Starlight, Inc., Floyds Knobs, IN; St. Mary of the Annunciation Catholic Church, Navilleton, Inc., Floyds Knobs, IN
Day, Rev. William F., '86 (GLP) Retired.
Daya, Rev. John, *O.F.M. Cap.* (BAL) Our Lady of the Mountains, Roman Catholic Congregation, Inc., Cumberland, MD
Daya, Rev. John, *O.F.M.Cap.* '78 (PH) Holy Redeemer, Philadelphia, PA (>BAL) [MON] Our Lady of the Mountains Friary, Cumberland, MD
Dayto, Rev. Paolo, '13 (P) St. Jude, Eugene, OR
Dayton, Rev. Christopher James, '18 (TR) St. Rose, Belmar, NJ
Daz, Rev. Msgr. Rudolph A., '54 (SLC) Retired.
Daza, Rev. Diego, '98 (POD) Curia: Clergy and Religious Services
Daza, Rev. Diego, '98 (WDC) The Heights School, Potomac, MD; [MIS] Tenley Study Center, Washington, DC
Daza, Very Rev. Wilmer de Jesus, '99 (DAL) Divine Mercy of Our Lord Catholic Parish, Mesquite, TX
Daza-Jaller, Rev. Daniel, (PMB) St. Paul of the Cross, North Palm Beach, FL
Daza-Jaller, Rev. Daniel, '18 (PMB) Curia: Leadership
D'Costa, Rev. Maxy, '96 (P) Chap, Washington Cty Jail, Oregon City Curia: Offices and Directors St. John the Apostle, Oregon City, OR
D'Cruz, Rev. Michael, *O.F.M.* '57 (NY) [MON] Franciscan Province of the Immaculate Conception, New York, NY
D'Cunha, Rev. Theodore, *S.A.C.* '90 (DET) Retired.
de Anda, Rev. James R., '05 (OM) Curia: Leadership St. Mary, Bellevue, NE
de Angel, Rev. Miguel A., '05 (CGS) Curia: Leadership Church of St. Joseph, Aibonito, PR; [RTR] Casa Manresa, Aibonito, PR
De Brasi, Rev. Richard Thaddeus, '17 (NEW) Saint Paul the Apostle, Jersey City, NJ
de Cardenas, Rev. Msgr. Javier Garcia, '85 (NY) [MIS] Prelature of the Holy Cross and Opus Dei, New York, NY
De Carlo Mena, Rev. Francisco, '50 (SJN) Retired.
De Celles, Rev. John C., '96 (ARL) St. Raymond of Penafort, Springfield, VA
de Cendra, Rev. Jamie, *D.C.J.M.* '08 (DEN) St. Mary Catholic School, Littleton, CO; [MON] Disciples of the Hearts of Jesus and Mary, Littleton, CO
De Class, Rev. Edmundus Yosef Soni, *S.V.D.* '05 (DUB) [SEM] Divine Word College, Epworth, IA
de Cristobal, Rev. Fernando, '65 (GRY) Retired.
De Fillipps, Rev. James, '12 (MET) St. Magdalen de Pazzi, Flemington, NJ
de Gaal, Rev. Emery, '00 (CHI) [SEM] University of Saint Mary of the Lake/Mundelein Seminary, Mundelein, IL
De Grocco, Rev. Msgr. Joseph, '88 (RVC) Curia: Leadership
de Guzman, Rev. Antonio, (SFR) St. Pius, Redwood City, CA
De Guzman, Rev. Antonio, (ELP) Most Holy Trinity, El Paso, TX
De Guzman, Rev. Dennis, '91 (OM) Curia: (>MO) Offices and Directors
De Guzman, Rev. John Michael, '22 (R) St. Michael the Archangel Catholic Church, Cary, NC
De Heredia, Rev. Agnel, '80 (SFR) Curia: Offices and Directors St. John the Evangelist, San Francisco, CA
De Herrera Sandoval, Rev. Christopher, *O.S.* '97 (PCE) On Duty Outside Diocese. [MIS] Oblates of Wisdom, Ponce, PR
de Herrera Sandoval, Rev. Christopher C., *O.S.* '97 (PCE) On Duty Outside Diocese. Curia: Leadership
De Jesus, Rev. Alejandro, (MO) Curia: Offices and Directors [MIS] National Conference of Veterans Affairs Catholic Chaplains, Inc., San Francisco, CA
De Jesus, Rev. Dwight, '85 (ALX) Curia: Miscellaneous / Other Offices St. Francis de Sales, Echo, LA; St. Joseph, Cheneyville, LA
De Jesus, Rev. Jose Daniel, *CMF* (CGS) Inmaculado Corazon de Maria, Caguas, PR; [MON] Misioneros Hijos del Inmaculado Corazon de Maria (Claretianos), Caguas, PR
De Jesus, Rev. Julio Enrique, '15 (MIA) St. Benedict, Hialeah, FL
de Jesus, Rev. Orlando, (CGS) Curia: Leadership
de Jesus Garcia, Rev. Jose, '09 (DEN) St. James Catholic Parish in Denver, Denver, CO
de Jesus Gomez, Rev. Orlando, '86 (CGS) Santisima Trinidad, Caguas, PR; [MIS] Diocesan Tribunal of Caguas, Caguas, PR
de Jong, Rev. Jan, *S.C.J.* '64 (MIL) Retired. [MON] Sacred Heart at Monastery Lake, Franklin, WI
de la Cruz, Rev. Jenaro, *OCD* (DAL) St. Mary of Carmel Catholic Parish, Dallas, TX; [EFT] St. Mary of Carmel Building Trust, Dallas, TX; [MON] Mt. Carmel Center (Discalced Carmelite Fathers of Dallas, Inc.), Dallas, TX
De La Cruz, Rev. Martin, '01 (BWN) Our Lady of Perpetual Help, McAllen, TX
De la Cruz, Rev. Pablo Roberto, *O. Carm.* (ARE) Nuestra Senora del Carmen, Morovis, PR
De la Cruz, Rev. Perlito G., '03 (SAC) St. Anthony Parish, Winters, a corporation sole, Winters, CA
De La Cruz, Rev. Ronnie, *D.S.* '05 (GAL) [MIS] The Catholic Chaplain Corps, Houston, TX
De La Cruz, Rev. Vicente, (HT) Curia: Administration; Clergy and Religious Services; Leadership; Tribunal
de la Cruz, Rev. Vincente N., (HT) Curia: Administration
de la Cruz Quen, Rev. Luis A., *MSP* (SB) St. Charles Borromeo, Bloomington, CA; St. John the Evangelist, Riverside, CA
de la Cruz Turcios, Rev. Juan, (GRY) [MON] Our Lady of Lourdes Friary, Cedar Lake, IN
de la Pena, Rev. Cosme R., (CAM) Church of Saint Elizabeth Ann Seton, Absecon, N.J., Absecon, NJ
De la Pena, Rev. Ericson, (BRK) St. Adalbert, Elmhurst, NY
de la Pena, Rev. Jose Manuel, '00 (NEW) St. Anthony of Padua, Union City, NJ
De La Pena, Rev. Ordanico, '98 (NEW) St. Nicholas, Jersey City, NJ
de la Puebla, Rev. Tomas, *C.M.* '49 (MGZ) Retired.

De La Rama, Rev. Eugenio P., '14 (NEW) Curia: Leadership; Offices and Directors; Organizations (affiliated, inter-Diocesan, miscellaneous/other)

De La Rosa, Rev. Caleb J., '22 (BWN) Mary, Mother of the Church, Brownsville, TX

De La Rosa, Rev. Carlos Tomas, '22 (CC) St. Pius X, Corpus Christi, TX

De La Rosa, Rev. Esteban Antonio, (SJN) [SPF] Asylum For The Aged and Infirm, Puerta De Tierra, PR

de la Rosa, Rev. Frank, '78 (SJN) [HOS] Hospital de la Universidad de Puerto Rico, Dr. Federico Trilla, Carolina, PR

de la Rosa, Rev. Jose, (SAT) Retired.

de la Rosa, Rev. Pedro Edgardo N, (OG) Holy Angels Church, Altona, N.Y., Altona, NY; St. Ann, Mooers Forks, NY

De la Rosa, Rev. Rolando S., '95 (SFR) Curia: Leadership Mater Dolorosa, South San Francisco, CA

de la Rosa Peguero, Rev. Frank, '78 (SJN) San Francisco de Asis, Carolina, PR

De la Rosa-Martinez, Rev. Esteban, *C.Ss.R.* (SJN) San Agustin, San Juan, PR

De La Texera Rojas, Rev. Diego, '18 (ARE) St. Paul Apostle, Morovis, PR

De La Texera Rojas, Rev. Diego Francisco, (ARE) [MIS] Chapel Divino Nino Jesus de Praga, Morovis, PR; [MIS] Chapel Nuestra Senora de La Providencia, Morovis, PR; [MIS] Chapel Senor de los Milagros, Morovis, PR

de la Torre, Rev. Carlos V., '81 (GAL) Curia: Offices and Directors St. Alphonsus, Houston, TX

de la Torre, Rev. Jorge, '97 (FRS) On Duty Outside Diocese. Archdiocese of Dhaka, Bangladesh

de la Torre, Rev. Miguel, *LC* (HRT) [MON] Legionaries of Christ, Cheshire, CT

de la Torre, Rev. Miguel Angel, *LC* (HRT) [SEM] Novitiate of the Legion of Christ, Cheshire, CT

De la Torre Carrillo, Rev. Sergio, '10 (CHI) Our Lady, the Mystical Rose Parish, Cicero, IL

De la Vega, Rev. Agustin, *L.C.* '85 (LA) [MON] Legionaries of Christ, Pasadena, CA (>MAD) Oaklawn Academy, Edgerton, WI; (>MAD) [MIS] Oaklawn Incorporated, Edgerton, WI

de Laire, Rev. Georges F., '97 (MAN) Curia: Clergy and Religious Services; Consultative Bodies; Leadership; Tribunal St. Pius X, Manchester, NH

De Leo, Rev. Jared Salvatore, (STA) St. Anastasia, St. Augustine, FL

de Leon, Rev. Christopher, '15 (BAL) On Administrative Leave.

De Leon, Rev. Eddie, *CMF* '91 (CHI) [MON] Claret House (Formation Residence), Chicago, IL

De Leon, Rev. Jose Angel, '14 (LAR) Curia: Offices and Directors

De Leon, Rev. Juancho D., '94 (NEW) St. Aloysius, Jersey City, NJ

De Leon, Very Rev. Matthew, (SAT) Curia: Administration; Leadership St. Patrick Catholic Church, Sabinal, TX

De Leon, Rev. Michael, '95 (LAR) Divine Mercy, Laredo, TX

De Leon, Rev. Michael August, *A.M.* '03 (CAM) Saint Simon Stock Parish, Berlin, N.J., Berlin, NJ

De León, Rev. Marco, '01 (PMB) St. Rita, Wellington, FL

De Loera, Rev. Cristobal, '14 (OKL) St. Peter's, Woodward, OK

de Loera, Rev. Marco A., '11 (WCH) Curia: Leadership

De Los Reyes, Rev. Francisco, *S.S.S.* '91 (HON) Curia: Consultative Bodies Mary, Star of the Sea, Honolulu, HI

de los Reyes, Rev. Joel, (AGN) Curia: Miscellaneous / Other Offices San Vicente Ferrer and San Roke, Barrigada, GU

de los Reyes, Rev. Joel, '75 (AGN) Curia: Miscellaneous / Other Offices

de los Santos, Rev. Antonio, (GB) Curia: Advisory Boards, Commissions, Committees, and Councils Annunciation of the Blessed Virgin Mary, Green Bay, WI

de los Santos, Rev. Antonio, (GB) St. Joseph, Green Bay, WI; St. Jude, Green Bay, WI

De Los Santos, Rev. Edgardo S., '17 (MIA) St. John the Baptist Catholic Church, Fort Lauderdale, FL

de los Santos, Rev. Msgr. Jorge, '91 (DEN) Our Lady Mother of the Church Catholic Parish in Commerce City, Commerce City, CO

De Martinis, Rev. O. Robert, '86 (ALB) St. Joseph-St. Michael-Our Lady of Mount Carmel, Amsterdam, NY; St. Stanislaus, Amsterdam, NY; The Parish of St. Joseph/St. Michael/Our Lady of Mount Carmel, Amsterdam, NY

De Medeiros Cabral, Rev. Pedro, *OFM* '08 (FRS) St. Ann, Riverdale, CA

de Mesa, Rev. Rodel, '12 (P) Holy Family, Portland, OR

De Nard, Rev. Silvio, *SdC* '79 (PRO) Church of the Sacred Heart, East Providence, RI

de Nazaret Malanga, Rev. Messias, (FR) [MON] La Salette Shrine & Retreat Center, Attleboro, MA

De Oca, Rev. Jose Monte, '96 (NEW) Our Lady of the Visitation, Paramus, NJ

de Oliveira, Rev. Pedro, *O.F.M. Conv.* '00 (SPR) Our Lady of Fatima, Ludlow, MA

de Oliveira Joaquim, Rev. Alvaro, *O.S.J.* '70 (SCR) [SEM] St. Joseph's Oblate Seminary, Pittston, PA

de Orbegozo, Rev. Joseph, '18 (LR) Cathedral of St. Andrew, Little Rock, AR

De Pascale, Rev. Daniel F., '61 (ALB) Retired.

de Paula, Rev. Cleber, '22 (WOR) Curia: Offices and Directors Holy Family Parish, Worcester, MA

De Paulis, Rev. Alexander, '14 (SD) Curia: Advisory Boards, Commissions, Committees, and Councils Pastor of Saint Vincent de Paul Catholic Parish, San Diego, a corporation sole, San Diego, CA; [MIS] Saint Vincent de Paul Catholic Parish in San Diego, CA Real Property Support Corporation, San Diego, CA

De Prinzio, Rev. Kevin, *O.S.A.* '04 (PH) [MON] Bellesini Friary, Ardmore, PA

de Ribera, Rev. Ignacio, *D.C.J.M.* (ARL) Our Lady of Angels, Woodbridge, VA

de Ribera Martin, Rev. Ignacio, *D.C.J.M.* '08 (WDC) [COL] Catholic University of America, The, Washington, DC

de Rosa, Very Rev. Francis M., '97 (ARL) St. Elizabeth of Hungary, Colonial Beach, VA

De Salvo, Rev. William Michael, '88 (JOL) Visitation, Elmhurst, IL

De Santiago-Carreon, Rev. Rito, '11 (MEM) Church of the Ascension, Memphis, TN

De Silva, Rev. Andrew, '19 (NEW) St. Agnes, Clark, NJ; St. Peter the Apostle, River Edge, NJ

De Silva, Rev. Andrew, (MO) Curia: Offices and Directors

de Silva, Rev. Terrence, '16 (LEX) St. Stephen, Cumberland, KY

De Souza, Rev. Anderson Luis, (BEA) St. Joseph, Livingston, TX; St. Martin de Porres Mission, Corrigan, TX

De Souza, Rev. Owen, '70 (LA) Retired.

De Tomasi, Rev. Gerardo, *M.C.C.J.* '63 (LA) [MIS] Comboni Mission Center, Covina, CA

de Verteuil, Rev. Jack, '89 (FBK) Retired.

De Villa, Rev. Camilo, '92 (PHX) Good Shepherd of the Desert Mission, Congress, AZ; St. Francis of Assisi Roman Catholic Parish, Scottsdale, AZ

De Vita, Rev. James C., '57 (RVC) Retired.

Deaconson, Rev. James N., '85 (AUS) Retired.

DeAguilar, Rev. Arturo, '97 (CHL) On Leave.

Dean, Rev. Harry, '96 (AUS) [RTR] Cedarbrake Catholic Retreat Center, Temple, TX

Dean, Rev. James N., '91 (MOB) Our Lady of Guadalupe Parish, Wetumpka, Wetumpka, AL

Dean, Rev. Mark, *O.M.I.* '83 (BEL) [RTR] King's House Retreat and Renewal Center, Belleville, IL (>SAT) [MON] Missionary Oblates of Mary Immaculate of Texas, Southern Province (San Antonio USP Support Office), San Antonio, TX

Dean, Rev. Mark, *OMI* (WDC) [MON] Missionary Oblates of Mary Immaculate, Washington, DC

Dean, Rev. William E., '76 (PH) On Special Assignment. Chap, Camilla Hall, Camilla Hall, Immaculata

Deane, Rev. Msgr. Joseph, '59 (AUS) Retired.

DeAngelis, Rev. Mark J., '88 (BO) St. Bridget, Framingham, MA

DeAngelis, Rev. Sante, *O.F.M.* '62 (MIL) Retired. [MON] Francis and Clare Friary, Franklin, WI

DeAngelo, Rev. Jude, *O.F.M.Conv.* (WDC) [COL] Catholic University of America, The, Washington, DC

DeAngelo, Rev. Jude, *OFM Conv* '84 (SY) Assumption B.V.M., Syracuse, NY

DeAntoniis, Rev. Paul J., *O. Praem.* '63 (PH) Retired. [MON] Daylesford Abbey, Inc., Paoli, PA

Deardorff, Rev. Joseph F., *C.PP.S.* '82 (CIN) [MON] Society of the Precious Blood, United States Province, Inc., Dayton, OH

Dearhammer, Rev. John W., '91 (CHI) Mision San Juan Diego, Arlington Heights, IL

DeArila, Rev. Rafael, (SFR) Retired.

DeArmond, Rev. Augustine, *O.P.* '13 (NO) St. Anthony of Padua, New Orleans, LA; [MON] Dominican Friars, Southern Dominican Province of St. Martin de Porres, New Orleans, LA

Deary, Rev. John F., *O.S.A.* '66 (PH) Our Mother of Good Counsel, Bryn Mawr, PA; [MON] Augustinians Friars (O.S.A.), Bryn Mawr, PA

Deas, Rev. Msgr. George T., '51 (BRK) Retired. [MON] Bishop Mugavero Residence, Douglaston, NY

DeAscanis, Rev. Michael, '04 (BAL) St. Francis of Assisi, Fulton, MD; St. Louis, Clarksville, MD

Dease, Rev. Dennis J., '78 (STP) Retired.

Dease, Rev. Dennis J., '69 (STP) [COL] University of St. Thomas, St. Paul, MN

Deasio, Rev. August, '75 (ROC) Retired.

Deasio, Rev. August J., '75 (STU) Retired.

Deasy, Rev. Kenneth H., '87 (LA) Retired.

Deatrick, Rev. John D., '66 (L) Retired.

Deaver, Rev. Stephen F., '59 (GI) Retired.

DeBellis, Rev. John A., '85 (NY) Holy Spirit, Cortlandt Manor, NY

Debes, Friar Donald, *O.F.M.Cap.* '70 (SAL) Retired. [MON] St. Fidelis Friary, Victoria, KS

DeBlanc, Rev. Msgr. Jefferson J., '77 (LAF) Our Lady of Fatima, Lafayette, LA

DeBlanc, Rev. Michael, '14 (LAF) St. Anthony of Padua, Krotz Springs, LA

DeBlasio, Rev. Ernie, '88 (MEM) St. Ann, Bartlett, TN

DeBlock, Rev. Matthew M., '08 (RCK) Sacred Heart, Marengo, IL

Debo, Rev. William D., '95 (JC) Curia: Advisory Boards, Commissions, Committees, and Councils Holy Family, Freeburg, MO; Sacred Heart, Rich Fountain, MO

DeBoe, Rev. Stanley, *O.S.S.T.* (TR) The Church of the Incarnation-St. James, Trenton, NJ

DeBona, Rev. Guerric, *O.S.B.* '86 (IND) [MON] St. Meinrad Archabbey, St. Meinrad, IN

DeBritto, Rev. A. John, *M.S.S.C.C.* (CHR) Holy Trinity, Orangeburg, SC; St. Andrew, Barnwell, SC; St. Mary Mission, Allendale, SC; St. Theresa Mission, Springfield, SC

DeBruycker, Rev. James R., '82 (STP) Church of Gichitwaa Kateri, Minneapolis, MN; St. Joan of Arc, Minneapolis, MN; [CEM] St. Joan of Arc Memorial Garden, Minneapolis, MN

Debski, Rev. Joseph E., '64 (MIL) Retired.

Dec, Rev. Ignatius, *M.M.A.* '84 (SAM) [MON] Maronite Monks of Adoration - Most Holy Trinity Monastery, Petersham, MA

Decal, Rev. Wilfredo, '77 (HT) Retired.

DeCandia, Rev. Anthony, '07 (R) On Leave.

DeCarlo, Rev. Christian Michael, '18 (LFT) St. Francis of Assisi, Muncie, IN; St. Lawrence, Muncie, IN; St. Mary, Muncie, IN

DeCarlo, Rev. Thomas M., '69 (DM) Retired.

DeCelles, Rev. Mark J., '21 (SCR) Curia: Leadership Our Lady of Fatima Parish, Wilkes-Barre, PA; St. Nicholas, Wilkes-Barre, PA

DeCesare, Rev. Robert, (GRY) Sacred Heart Apostolic School, Inc., Rolling Prairie, IN

Dechant, Rev. Leo, *C.S.J.* '80 (LA) St. Junipero Serra, Lancaster, CA

Dechant, Rev. Leo Ambrose, *CSJ* '80 (CLV) St. Bartholomew, Middleburg Heights, OH; [RTR] St. Leonard Youth Retreat Center (Fathers of St. Joseph, Inc.), Avon, OH

Dechant, Rev. Paul Gerald, *o.s.f.s.* (VEN) St. Cecilia Parish in Fort Myers, Inc., Fort Myers, FL

Dechenne, Rev. Jason, (PHU) Curia: (>MO) Offices and Directors

Decipeda, Rev. Vicente Raymond, *M.M.H.C.* '91 (LA) Curia: Pastoral Services St. John of God, Norwalk, CA

Deck, Rev. Alan Figueroa, *S.J.* '76 (SJ) [MON] USA West Province, Society of Jesus, Los Gatos, CA

Deck, Rev. Allan Figueroa, *S.J.* '76 (LA) [MON] Jesuit Community, Los Angeles, CA

Decker, Rev. Christopher J., '07 (BR) Curia: Administration The Congregation Of Saint Mary False River Roman Catholic Church Of The Parish Of Pte. Coupee, State Of Louisiana, New Roads, LA

Decker, Rev. Douglas A., '78 (OG) Curia: Canonical Services Catholic Community of St. Peter and St. Mary and St. Hedwig, Lowville, NY

Decker, Rev. Raymond G., '58 (SFR) Retired.

Decker, Rev. Robert L., '83 (OG) Curia: Offices and Directors St. Cecilia's Church, Adams, NY, Adams, NY

Decker, Rev. W. Jonathan, *M.M.J.M.J.* '76 (OLL) [MON] Sacred Heart Maronite Monastery, Beaverton, OR

Decker, Rev. W. Jonathan, *M.M.J.M.J.* '76 (OLL) Retired. [MON] Oblates of Jesus, Mary & Joseph, Beaverton, OR

DeClippel, Rev. Ludo, *C.J.* '68 (LA) [MON] St. Joseph Seminary (Josephite Fathers' Novitiate), Santa Maria, CA

DeClippel, Rev. Ludovic, (LA) [EFT] American Region of the Josephite Fathers Charitable Trust, Santa Maria, CA

DeCola, Rev. Vincent P., *S.J.* '88 (NY) [MON] America; Residence and Publication Office of the America Press, New York, NY

DeCosta, Rev. Joseph F., '90 (NOR) Curia: Offices and

Directors St. Lawrence, Killingworth, CT; St. Peter, Higganum, CT
DeCoste, Rev. Wade, '03 (ALX) Curia: Miscellaneous / Other Offices Our Lady of Lourdes, Winnfield, LA; St. Anthony of Padua, Natchitoches, LA
DeCrane, Rev. Timothy, '19 (IND) Our Lady of the Greenwood Catholic Church, Inc., Greenwood, IN; St. Rose of Lima Catholic Church, Franklin, Inc., Franklin, IN
DeCrans, Rev. Joseph J., (CR) Retired.
DeCrans, Rev. William, '08 (CR) Curia: Offices and Directors St. Charles Catholic Church of Pennington, Pennington, MN; St. Philip's, Bemidji, MN
Dede, Rev. Paul M., '64 (IND) Retired.
Dederick, Rev. Joseph S., *O.F.M.Cap.* '09 (SFR) [MIS] San Buenaventura Center for Ministry and Studies, San Francisco, CA; [MIS] St. Conrad Center for Ministry and Studies, Berkeley, CA; [MON] Capuchin Provincial House, Burlingame, CA
Dederick, Rev. Joseph Seraphin, (OAK) St. Jarlath, Oakland, CA
DeDomenico, Rev. Dominic, *O.P.* '66 (OAK) [MON] Order of Preachers (Province of the Most Holy Name of Jesus - Western Dominican Province), Oakland, CA
Dee, Rev. Msgr. Dacian, '56 (SP) Retired.
Dee De, Rev. Peter, '08 (FTW) Cathedral of the Immaculate Conception, Fort Wayne, IN
Dee Du, Rev. Richard, *MF* (AUS) St. Francis of Assisi, Franklin, TX; St. Mary, Bremond, TX
Deegan, Rev. John E., *O.S.A.* '61 (PH) [MON] Provincial Offices of the Order of St. Augustine, Province of St. Thomas of Villanova, Villanova, PA; [MON] St. John Stone Friary, Villanova, PA
Deehan, Rev. Robert J., '83 (BO) Curia: Clergy and Religious Services; Leadership Holy Family, Duxbury, MA
Deehr, Rev. Anselm, *S.T.* '90 (WDC) [MON] Father Judge Missionary Cenacle, Adelphi, MD
Deeke, Rev. Von C., '03 (BEL) Curia: Leadership; Offices and Directors St. Agatha, New Athens, IL; St. Joseph, Freeburg, IL
Deeley, Rev. Kevin J., '74 (BO) Curia: Consultative Bodies St. Michael, North Andover, MA
Deely, Rev. Thomas, *C.Ss.R.* '65 (PH) St. Peter the Apostle, Philadelphia, PA
Deely, Rev. Thomas (Martin), *C.Ss.R.* '65 (NY) [RTR] Redemptorist Community at Esopus (Redemptorist Fathers and Brothers), Ulster Park, NY
Deely, Rev. Timothy X., '19 (PIT) Curia: Consultative Bodies Regina Coeli, Pittsburgh, PA
Deering, Rev. Charles, (BIR) Annunciation of the Lord Catholic Parish, Decatur (St. Ann Catholic Church), Decatur, AL
Deering, Rev. Msgr. Michael J., '02 (BIR) Curia: Leadership Holy Spirit, Tuscaloosa, AL; [EFT] Holy Spirit School of Tuscaloosa Endowment Foundation, Tuscaloosa, AL; [EFT] The Harrison Family Endowment Trust for the Benefit of Holy Spirit School, Tuscaloosa, AL
Dees, Rev. Elliott Richard, '11 (CHI) St. Juliana, Chicago, IL
Defayette, Rev. Jeffrey M., '88 (WDC) Resurrection Parish, Burtonsville, MD
DeFazio, Rev. Peter F., '14 (BO) On Leave. St. Peter, Boston, MA
DeFelice, Rev. Jonathan, *O.S.B.* '74 (MAN) [MON] St. Anselm Abbey, Manchester, NH
DeFelice, Rev. Jonathan P., *O.S.B.* (BO) St. John the Baptist, Quincy, MA
Deffenbaugh, Rev. Joseph T., '79 (Y) Retired.
Deffenbaugh, Rev. Terry A., *O.S.A.* '75 (CHI) [MON] Austin Friary, Matteson, IL
Deffenbaugh, Rev. Terry A., *O.S.A.* '75 (JOL) [COL] University of St. Francis, Joliet, IL
Define, Rev. William, *F.S.S.P.* '02 (TLS) On Special Assignment. Hillcrest Hosp Most Precious Blood Parish, Tulsa, OK
DeFolco, Rev. Jay, '85 (SEA) Chap, Snohomish Cty Jail & Juvenile Detention
DeFolco, Rev. Joseph, '85 (SEA) Holy Cross Parish, Lake Stevens, WA; St. Hubert, Langley, WA
DeForest, Rev. Matthew J., '09 (ARL) On Leave.
DeFrange, Rev. Jonathan, *OSB* (PRO) [MON] Brothers of the Sacred Heart Residence, Pascoag, RI
DeFrange, Rev. Jonathan M., *O.S.B.* '78 (NO) [MON] St. Joseph Abbey, St. Benedict, LA
DeFronzo, Rev. Anthony P., '81 (PSC) Retired.
DeFusco, Rev. Andrew T., '14 (BAL) St. Andrew by the Bay, Annapolis, MD; [EFT] St. Andrew by the Bay Endowment Trust, Annapolis, MD
DeFusco, Rev. Matthew, '19 (BAL) St. John the Evangelist, Frederick, MD; St. Joseph-on-Carrollton Manor, Frederick, MD
DeGaetano, Rev. Louis J., '79 (BRK) Retired. Mary's Nativity-Saint Ann Roman Catholic Church, Flushing, NY
DeGance, Rev. Matthew, (PMB) St. Helen, Vero Beach, FL
DeGaris, Rev. Herbert T., '91 (NY) Immaculate Conception, Stony Point, NY
Degasperi, Rev. Paolo, '21 (FTW) St. John the Baptist, Fort Wayne, IN
Degele, Rev. Jacob, '21 (BIS) Our Lady of Grace, Minot, ND
Degenhardt, Rev. Gervase, *O.F.M. Cap.* '58 (PIT) [CON] Sisters of St. Francis of the Neumann Communities, Western Pennsylvania Region, Warrendale, PA; [MON] St. Augustine Friary, Pittsburgh, PA
DeGeorge, Rev. Salvatore, *O.M.I.* (GAL) Retired. Immaculate Conception, Houston, TX
DeGerolami, Rev. Michael, '74 (SAT) Retired.
Degeyter, Rev. Edward, '70 (LAF) Retired.
DeGiacomo, Rev. Albert J., '08 (LEX) Cathedral of Christ the King, Lexington, KY
DeGrand, Rev. Robert L., '80 (SFD) On Leave.
DeGrandis, Rev. Robert, *S.S.J.* '59 (BAL) Retired.
DeGrassa, Rev. James R., '10 (PH) Resurrection of Our Lord, Philadelphia, PA
DeGrocco, Rev. Msgr. Joseph, '88 (RVC) Our Lady of Perpetual Help, Lindenhurst, NY
DeGrood, Rev. Donald E., '97 (STP) [CEM] St. John the Baptist Catholic Cemetery, Savage, MN
DeGroot, Rev. Francis J., '93 (MAR) Curia: Offices and Directors St. Anne, Escanaba, MI
DeGroot, Rev. Ignatius, *OFM* (OAK) [MON] Franciscan Friars of California (Province of St. Barbara), Oakland, CA
DeGroot, Rev. Kenneth, *O. Praem.* '61 (GB) [MON] St. Norbert Abbey, De Pere, WI
DeHondt, Rev. Ronald, '73 (DET) St. Margaret of Scotland Parish St. Clair Shores, St. Clair Shores, MI
Deiak, Rev. Sergij, (PSC) Patronage of the Mother of God, Arbutus, MD
Deiak, Rev. Sergij, (PSC) Curia: Leadership St. Gregory of Nyssa, Beltsville, MD
Deibel, Rev. David, '83 (MRY) On Special Assignment. Indian River, MI
Deichert, Rev. Joseph, '84 (BIS) On Duty Outside Diocese. Bismarck
Deichert, Rev. Joseph, (MO) Curia: Offices and Directors
Deimeke, Rev. L. Edward, '75 (ALB) Retired. St. Mary, Albany, NY
Deiters, Rev. James E., '91 (BEL) Curia: Leadership St. Clare of Assisi Parish, O'Fallon, IL
Deiters, Rev. James R., '91 (BEL) Curia: Offices and Directors
Deitz, Rev. Andrew J, '14 (RCK) On Administrative Leave.
DeJesus, Rev. Alejandro, *O.S.B.* '84 (MO) Curia: Offices and Directors
DeJulio, Rev. David, '90 (SP) St. Frances Xavier Cabrini, Spring Hill, FL
DeJulio, Rev. Robert J., '72 (NY) Retired. St. Catharine, Pelham, NY
Deka, Rev. Robbie, '07 (GLD) Curia: (>MO) Offices and Directors
Dekaa, Rev. Thomas, (HRT) [HOS] Saint Francis Hospital and Medical Center (Catholic Health Ministries), Hartford, CT
Dekat, Rev. Earl, '66 (KCK) Retired.
Deken, Rev. John C., '72 (STL) Assumption Catholic Church, New Haven, New Haven, MO; St. Paul Catholic Church, Berger, New Haven, MO
DeKeyser, Rev. Andrew R., '10 (LFT) St. Ann, Kewanna, IN; St. Anne, Monterey, IN; St. Francis Solano, Francesville, IN; St. Joseph, Rochester, IN; St. Joseph, Star City, IN; St. Peter, Winamac, IN
Del Angel, Rev. Jesus, '00 (FRS) On Special Assignment. Curia: Leadership Our Lady of Victory, Fresno, CA
Del Brocco, Rev. Salvatore Enzo, *C.P.* (BRK) [MIS] St. Paul's Benevolent, Educational and Missionary Institute, Inc. (Congregation of the Passion - St. Paul of the Cross Province), Jamaica, NY
Del Brocco, Rev. Salvatore Enzo, *C.P.* '96 (NY) [MON] St. Vincent Strambi Residence (The Passionists), Pelham Manor, NY; [MON] The Congregation of the Passion - St. Paul of the Cross Province, Jamaica, NY
Del Carmen, Rev. Leonardo, '91 (STO) San Joaquin Co Hosp Curia: Leadership St. George Church (Pastor of), Stockton, CA
Del Carmen-Espinoza, Rev. Sergio, *C.Ss.R.* (CGS) Church of Tres Santos Reyes, Aguas Buenas, PR
del Castillo, Very Rev. Javier, '05 (POD) Curia: Leadership
Del Duca, Rev. John A., '68 (CAM) Retired.
Del Olmo, Rev. Jose, '92 (VEN) Jesus the Worker Parish in Fort Myers, Inc. (Jesus Obrero), Fort Myers, FL
del Olmo, Rev. Jose, '92 (VEN) Curia: Organizations (affiliated, inter-Diocesan, miscellaneous/other)
Del Prete, Rev. Msgr. Frank G., '77 (NEW) Curia: Offices and Directors St. Gabriel the Archangel, Saddle River, NJ
Del Priore, Rev. John, *S.J.S.* '08 (MAD) [CAM] St. Augustine Newman Center, Platteville, WI
Del Priore, Rev. Kenneth, '83 (SD) Retired.
Del Rio, Rev. Manuel, '20 (SD) Pastor of Good Shepherd Catholic Parish, San Diego, a corporation sole, San Diego, CA
del Rivero, Rev. Eduardo, (FAJ) Maria Reina de la Paz, Humacao, PR
Del Rosario, Rev. Anulfo, *C.M.* '92 (SJN) Colegio Sagrado Corazon de Jesus, San Juan, PR
del Rosario, Rev. Mark, *SSS* '80 (PBL) St. Mary Help of Christians, Pueblo, CO
del Rosario Sosa, Rev. Anulfo, *CM* (SJN) Sagrado Corazon de Jesus, San Juan, PR
del Toro, Rev. Alejandro, '07 (RCK) On Administrative Leave.
del Torro, Rev. Juan Pablo Marrufo, *S.J.* '15 (PHX) [MON] Society of Jesus, Phoenix, AZ
Del Valle, Rev. Tomas, '79 (SJN) On Duty Outside Diocese.
Dela Cruz, Rev. Leandro B., '10 (TR) Curia: Pastoral Services St. Ann, Lawrenceville, NJ
Dela Cruz, Rev. Ronnie, (GAL) St. Anthony of Padua, The Woodlands, TX
DeLacy, Rev. Stephen P., '04 (PH) On Special Assignment. Dir, Voc Ofc Diocesan Priesthood St. Bridget, Philadelphia, PA; [CAM] Newman Apostolate for Archdiocese of Philadelphia, Philadelphia, PA
deLadurantaye, Rev. Paul F., '88 (ARL) On Duty Outside Diocese. Vatican City State
Delahanty, Rev. Patrick D., '69 (L) Retired.
Delahunty, Rev. Richard A., '65 (ORG) Retired.
Delaney, Rev. Brian, '75 (LA) Retired.
Delaney, Rev. Msgr. Dennis M., '76 (STL) Curia: Offices and Directors St. John the Apostle and Evangelist Catholic Church, St. Louis, MO; [CEM] Calvary Cemetery, St. Louis, MO
Delaney, Rev. John, '81 (FTW) Curia: Offices and Directors Sacred Heart of Jesus (Lakeville), South Bend, IN; St. Jude Church, South Bend, IN
Delaney, Rev. Msgr. John W., '64 (MIA) Retired.
Delaney, Rev. John W., (BO) Curia: Leadership Sacred Hearts, Haverhill, MA
Delaney, Rev. Larry, '90 (CR) Curia: Offices and Directors St. Joseph, Fertile, MN; St. Lawrence, Mentor, MN
Delaney, Rev. Msgr. Michael J., '85 (SCR) On Administrative Leave.
Delaney, Rev. Thomas, '57 (JKS) Retired.
Delaney, Rev. William, *C.PP.S.* '63 (KC) (>CIN) [MON] Society of the Precious Blood, United States Province, Inc., Dayton, OH
Delaney, Rev. William, (OAK) [NUR] Mercy Retirement and Care Center, Oakland, CA
Delaney, Rev. William K., *S.J.* '85 (LA) [MIS] SCRC (Southern California Renewal Communities), Burbank, CA; [MON] Colombiere House (Jesuit Fathers), Los Angeles, CA
Delange, Rev. Maurice, '71 (COV) Retired.
Delargy, Rev. Torlach, '66 (POD) Curia: Clergy and Religious Services
DeLaRiva, Rev. John, *O.F.M.Cap.* '99 (SFR) St. Francis of Assisi, National Shrine, San Francisco, CA; [SEM] Capuchin Franciscan Order San Buenaventura Friary, San Francisco, CA
DeLaTorre, Rev. Jorge, (FRS) On Duty Outside Diocese.
DeLay, Rev. Dominic, *O.P.* '93 (SFR) St. Raymond, Menlo Park, CA
DeLay, Rev. Dominic, *OP* (SJ) Catholic Community at Stanford, Stanford, CA
Delay, Rev. Donald R., '83 (BO) Retired.
Delcambre, Rev. Michael L., '05 (LAF) Sacred Heart of Jesus, Broussard, LA
DelConte, Rev. Eugene, *O.S.A.* '55 (PH) [MIS] National Shrine of Saint Rita of Cascia, Philadelphia, PA
DelDuca, Rev. John A., '68 (CAM) Retired. Our Lady of Hope Parish, Blackwood, N.J., Blackwood, NJ
Delendick, Rev. Msgr. John E., '77 (BRK) St. Jude Shrine Church, Brooklyn, NY
DeLeon, Very Rev. Esteban, (RIC) Curia: Deaneries Star of the Sea, Virginia Beach, VA
DeLeon, Rev. Jose Raul, '08 (WDC) St. Bernardine of Siena, Suitland, MD
DeLerno, Rev. Christian W., '11 (NO) St. Mary Magdalen, Metairie, LA

DeLerno, Rev. Kevin T., '09 (NO) SS. Peter and Paul Roman Catholic Church, Pearl River, Louisiana, Pearl River, LA
Delfin, Rev. Emmanuel, '19 (LA) St. Anthony, Oxnard, CA
DelFra, Rev. Louis A., *C.S.C.* '04 (FTW) [COL] University of Notre Dame Du Lac, Notre Dame, IN; [MON] Holy Cross Community, Corby Hall, University of Notre Dame, Notre Dame, IN
Delgado, Rev. Alvaro H., '02 (STO) Curia: Leadership St. Edward Church (Pastor of), Stockton, CA
Delgado, Rev. Lenin, *C.Ss.R.* '91 (MO) Curia: Offices and Directors
Delgado, Rev. Lenin, *C.Ss.R.* '91 (NY) Chap, VA Hudson Valley Healthcare, Castle Point
Delgado, Rev. Leslie N., '55 (LA) Our Lady of Guadalupe Sanctuary, Los Angeles, CA
Delgado, Rev. Octavio, (PHX) St. Augustine Roman Catholic Parish, Phoenix, AZ
Delgado, Rev. Ruben, '90 (BWN) Our Lady of the Assumption, Harlingen, TX
Delgado-Diaz, Rev. Rafael, *O.P.* (SJN) San Bartolome, Trujillo Alto, PR
DelGiudice, Rev. Carl, (CHL) Retired.
Delia, Rev. Stephen A., '22 (PAT) St. Mary's, Denville, NJ
D'Elia, Rev. Ralph F., (SP) St. Petersburg Catholic High School, Inc., St. Petersburg, FL
Delich, Rev. David, *O.P.* '63 (CHI) [MON] St. Pius V Priory, Chicago, IL
DeLillio, Rev. Richard, *O.S.F.S.* (WIL) Salesianum School, Wilmington, DE
DeLillio, Rev. Richard, *O.S.F.S.* '66 (WDC) [SEM] Deshairs Community-Oblates of St. Francis de Sales Residence, Washington, DC
Delisandru, Rev. Andriy, (STN) On Special Assignment. St. Joseph, Chicago, IL
Delisle, Rev. Eric T., '03 (MAN) Chap, Maple Leaf Nursing Home; Elliott Hosp; Hillsborough… Curia: Tribunal St. Hedwig, Manchester, NH; St. Joseph Cathedral, Manchester, NH
Delka, Rev. Joseph D., '15 (SLC) Curia: Offices and Directors Saint Andrew Catholic Church LLC 233, Riverton, UT
Dellaert, Rev. Brian M., '05 (DUB) St. Joseph the Worker Church of Dubuque, Dubuque, Iowa, Dubuque, IA
DellaGiovanna, Rev. Mariano, '07 (PH) Blessed Virgin Mary, Darby, PA; [SEM] Redemptoris Mater Archdiocesan Missionary Seminary, Yeadon, PA
Dellagiovanna, Rev. Mariano N., '07 (NEW) On Duty Outside Diocese. St Barnabas Rectory, Philadelphia, PA
DellaPenna, Rev. Michael, *O.F.M.* (BO) St. Leonard of Port Maurice, Boston, MA
Dellaporte, Rev. Dominick, '85 (NEW) On Duty Outside Diocese. Brooklyn, NY
Dellasega, Rev. Andrew, '19 (WCH) St. Thomas Aquinas, Wichita, KS
Dellinger, Rev. Jonathan, '05 (DEN) Sacred Heart of Mary Catholic Parish in Boulder, Boulder, CO; St. Martin de Porres Catholic Parish in Boulder, Boulder, CO
Dello Russo, Very Rev. Albert A., '10 (PMB) Curia: Leadership; Offices and Directors
Dello Russo, Rev. John F., *O.S.A.* '87 (BO) St. Augustine, Andover, MA
Dellota, Rev. Ryan Salvador, (OAK) St. Michael, Livermore, CA
Delmonte, Rev. Albert L., '64 (ROC) Retired.
Delmore, Rev. Eugene P., *S.J.* '69 (SEA) Bellarmine Preparatory School, Tacoma, WA
DeLoera, Rev. Marco A, '11 (WCH) Our Lady of Perpetual Help, Wichita, KS
DeLong, Rev. James Allen, *S.M.* '77 (HON) [MON] Marianist Hall Community, , (>SJ) [MON] The Marianist Center, Cupertino, CA
DeLong, Rev. Robert, *MSF* '11 (SAT) Our Lady of Guadalupe, Seguin, TX
Delonnay, Rev. Lawrence, '75 (DET) Retired.
DeLorenzo, Rev. John R., '76 (SY) St. Patrick, Jordan, NY
DeLorme, Rev. R. Daniel, '57 (SY) Retired.
delos Reyes, Rev. Joselito, '91 (CLV) Curia: Parish Services Cathedral of St. John the Evangelist, Cleveland, OH; [EFT] St. John Cathedral Endowment Trust, Cleveland, OH
delos Reyes, Rev. Roel, (HON) St. Mary, Hana, HI
DeLoza, Rev. Jose, '87 (YAK) Retired.
DeLuca, Rev. David, *M.S.C.* '66 (OG) Retired. [MON] Missionaries of the Sacred Heart, Watertown, NY
DeLuca, Rev. Paul F., '81 (CIN) Retired.
DeLuca, Rev. Stephen J., '65 (BGP) Retired.
DeLucia, Rev. Gerald M., '78 (Y) Retired.
DeLucia, Rev. Vincent, *O.P.* '94 (Y) St. Dominic, Youngstown, OH
Delva, Rev. Jean, '07 (BRK) Our Lady of Miracles, Brooklyn, NY
DelValle, Rev. Tomas, (NY) St. Columba, New York, NY
Delvard, Rev. Quesnel, '03 (PMB) Curia: Leadership St. Ann, West Palm Beach, FL
Delys, Rev. Gastin, *ofm Cap.* '13 (ARE) (>MGZ) Santuario Protomártires de la Inmaculada Concepción, Aguada, PR
Delzingaro, Rev. Richard M., *C.R.S.P.* '96 (BUF) [SEM] St. Anthony M. Zaccaria Seminary, Youngstown, NY; [SHR] Basilica of the National Shrine of Our Lady of Fatima, Inc., Youngstown, NY
DeMaio, Rev. Dominic, *OP* (OAK) [MON] Order of Preachers (Province of the Most Holy Name of Jesus - Western Dominican Province), Oakland, CA
DeMaio, Rev. Joseph, *O.Carm.* '65 (ROC) [MON] Whitefriars Priory, Rochester, NY
Deman, Rev. Shane A., '08 (SC) On Duty Outside Diocese. Vice-Rector: Kenrick-Glennon Seminary, St. Louis, MO
DeMan, Rev. Thomas, *O.P.* (TUC) Saint Thomas More Roman Catholic Newman Parish - Tucson, Tucson, AZ; [CAM] University of Arizona Newman Center, Tucson, AZ
Demarais, Rev. Garvin J., '81 (OG) Retired. Curia: Canonical Services
DeMarco, Rev. David G., *S.J.* '05 (CHI) [COL] Jesuit Community at Loyola University Chicago, Chicago, IL
DeMartinis, Rev. Michael J, (E) St. Patrick, Erie, PA
DeMartino, Rev. Robert J., '92 (ARL) St. William of York, Stafford, VA
DeMattia, Rev. John A., '68 (PAT) Retired.
deMayo, Rev. Martin P., '03 (BGP) The Church of the Sacred Heart Corporation, Stamford, Stamford, CT
Dembowski, Rev. Aleksander, '20 (B) Cathedral of St. John the Evangelist, Boise, ID
Demek, Rev. Martin H., '75 (BAL) Corpus Christi, Baltimore, MD
Demers, Rev. Francis, *O.M.I.* '55 (BO) [NUR] Immaculate Heart of Mary Residence, Tewksbury, MA
Demers, Rev. Francis, *O.M.I.* (AGN) Curia: Tribunal
Demers, Rev. Richard D., '83 (OG) Retired.
Demesmin, Rev. Dimitri, (CAM) St. Padre Pio Parish, Vineland, N.J., Vineland, NJ
DeMeulemeester, Rev. Patrick, '95 (PEO) Curia: Clergy and Religious Services Sacred Heart of Jesus, Granville, IL; St. Patrick's, Hennepin, IL
DeMeulenaere, Rev. Martin, *O.S.B.* '73 (KC) [MON] Conception Abbey (Benedictine Monks), Conception, MO
Demkiv, Rev. Ivan, '92 (PHU) Curia: Offices and Directors St. Mary's, Bristol, PA
Demko, Rev. James J., '82 (PSC) Retired.
Demkovich, Very Rev. Michael T., *O.P.* '81 (SFE) Curia: Leadership Immaculate Conception-Tome, Tome, NM
Demma, Rev. Jonathan, (FWT) Sacred Heart, Wichita Falls, TX
Demma, Rev. Jonathan Michael, '18 (FWT) Curia: Advisory Boards, Commissions, Committees, and Councils
D'Emma, Rev. Gregory J., '70 (HBG) Retired. Saint Patrick, Carlisle, PA
D'Emma, Rev. Gregory J., '70 (NEW) Retired.
Demmer, Rev. Donald L., '75 (DET) Christ Our Light Parish Troy, Troy, MI
Demnyan, Rev. Jack, '16 (PIT) Our Lady of Mount Carmel, Pittsburgh, PA
Demo, Rev. John M., '88 (OG) Curia: Consultative Bodies Saint Anthony's Church, Watertown, NY; The Church of the Holy Family, Watertown, NY; The Society of St. Patrick's Church, Watertown, NY
DeMoreno, Rev. Raphael Paul, '87 (SFD) St. James, Riverton, IL
Dempsey, Rev. Albert Connor, *O.P.* '22 (COL) St. Patrick, Columbus, OH
Dempsey, Rev. Msgr. James, '56 (BEA) Retired.
Dempsey, Rev. Nicholas, '71 (SD) Retired.
Dempsey, Rev. Msgr. Patrick E., '97 (WDC) Retired.
Dempsey, Rev. Msgr. Robert J., '80 (CHI) St. Patrick, Lake Forest, IL
Dempsey, Rev. Sean T., *S.J.* '08 (LA) [MON] Jesuit Community, Los Angeles, CA
Dempsey, Rev. Terrence E., *S.J.* '85 (STL) [COL] Saint Louis University, St. Louis, MO
Dempsey, Rev. Msgr. Thomas J., '61 (RCK) Retired.
Dempsey, Rev. Msgr. Thomas J., '62 (STL) Retired.
Demse, Rev. Thomas P., '76 (MIL) Retired.
Demski, Rev. Ronald G., '69 (TYL) Retired.
Demuth, Rev. Paul E., '68 (GB) Retired.
Denault, Rev. Paul, *O.Carm.* '80 (NY) Our Lady of Mt. Carmel, Middletown, NY
Denburger, Rt. Rev. John, *O.C.S.O.* '63 (ROC) Retired. [MON] Abbey of the Genesee, Inc., Piffard, NY
Denchira, Rev. Simon Atta, '04 (ROC) St. Louis, Pittsford, NY
Dene, Rev. Charles J., '58 (ALN) Retired.
Dengler, Rev. Pier Giorgio, *O.P.* (L) St. Louis Bertrand, Louisville, KY
Denig, Rev. Philip P., '85 (DEN) Curia: (>MO) Offices and Directors
DeNigris, Rev. Emanuele, '05 (WDC) On Special Assignment. Redemptoris Mater Seminary
DeNigris, Rev. Emanuele, '05 (MIA) Curia: Leadership St. Cecilia, Hialeah, FL; [SEM] The Redemptoris Mater Seminary Archdiocese of Miami, Inc., Hialeah, FL
Denina, Rev. Melvin, (LA) Holy Family, Artesia, CA
DeNinno, Rev. Dale E., '78 (PIT) Retired. Christ the King, Pittsburgh, PA
DeNinno, Rev. Louis L., '76 (PIT) Retired. Curia: Tribunal Christ Our Savior, Pittsburgh, PA
Denison, Rev. Frederick J., '73 (IND) Retired. St. Joseph Catholic Church, Marengo, Inc., Marengo, IN
Denk, Rev. Michael J., '07 (CLV) St. Matthias, Parma, OH
Denn, Rev. James J., *C.S.C.* '61 (FTW) [MIS] Holy Cross House, Notre Dame, IN
Dennehy, Rev. John D., '81 (NEW) [COL] Seton Hall University, South Orange, NJ
Dennemann, Rev. Thomas J., '73 (CIN) Retired.
Dennerlein, Rev. John L., '74 (JOL) Retired.
Denning, Rev. John F., *C.S.C.* '87 (FR) [COL] Holy Cross Fathers Religious, North Easton, MA; [COL] Stonehill College, North Easton, MA
Dennis, Rev. Jack, *S.J.* (BAL) [COL] Jesuit Community of Loyola University, Inc., Baltimore, MD; [MON] Jesuit Community of Loyola University Maryland, Inc., Baltimore, MD
Dennis, Rev. Jack, *S.J.* (BAL) (>SCR) [COL] The University of Scranton, Scranton, PA
Dennis, Rev. Jamie, (OWN) Blessed Mother, Owensboro, KY
Dennis, Rev. John J., *O.S.F.S.* '45 (WIL) Retired.
Dennis, Rev. Patrick, '78 (B) Retired.
Dennis, Rev. Peter K., *SS.CC.* '62 (LA) Retired. [MON] Congregation of the Sacred Hearts of Jesus and Mary, La Verne, CA
Dennis, Rev. Thomas J., '92 (SFD) On Leave.
Dennis, Rev. Tyler, '09 (RC) Our Lady of the Sacred Heart, Martin, SD
Dennis, Rev. Tyler, '09 (RC) Our Lady of Victory, Kadoka, SD; St. Patrick's, Wall, SD
Denniston, Rev. John, '79 (RVC) On Duty Outside Diocese. Notre Dame, New Hyde Park, NY
Denny, Rev. Charles J., '69 (TOL) Retired.
Denny, Rev. Thomas, (BO) [MON] Campion Center, Inc., Weston, MA
Deno, Rev. Msgr. Lawrence M., '59 (OG) Retired.
Densmore, Rev. Anthony M., '04 (DAL) St. Anthony Catholic Parish - Wylie, Wylie, TX; [CEM] St. Paul Cemetery, Wylie, TX
Denson, Rev. Johnathan, *OSB* (BIR) [MON] St. Bernard Abbey, Cullman, AL
Dente, Rev. Thomas A., '93 (NEW) Curia: Offices and Directors Notre Dame, North Caldwell, NJ; St. Joseph, Maplewood, NJ
Denzer, Rev. Joseph W., '68 (BRK) Retired. [MON] Bishop Mugavero Residence, Douglaston, NY
DeOliveira, Rev. Edinardo, (BO) St. Anthony of Padua, Cambridge, MA; St. Francis of Assisi, Cambridge, MA
DePalma, Rev. John P., (SEA) St. Vincent De Paul, Federal Way, WA
DePalma, Rev. Michael, '03 (SFE) St. Thomas Aquinas University Parish, Albuquerque, NM; [CAM] St. Thomas Aquinas University Parish, Albuquerque, NM
DePasquale, Rev. Leonard D., *I.M.C.* '71 (SB) St. Bernardine Church, San Bernardino, CA
Depatie, Rev. Donald L., '78 (PRO) Retired.
Depcik, Rev. Michael, *O.S.F.S.* (DET) Curia: Offices and Directors [SPF] St. John's Deaf Center, Eastpointe, MI
DePew, Rev. Daniel R., '85 (GR) St. John Cantius, Free Soil, MI; St. Mary-St. Jerome Parish, Custer, MI
DePeyster, Rev. Aaron Earl, '04 (SR) Pastor of Resurrection Catholic Church of Santa Rosa, A Corporation Sole, Santa Rosa, CA
Depinet, Rev. Robert L., *M.M.* '61 (NY) Retired.
DePinto, Rev. Basil, '58 (OAK) Retired. Corpus Christi, Piedmont, CA
Depman, Rev. Msgr. Francis J., '81 (PH) St. Rocco, Avondale, PA
Deponai, Rev. Joseph J., '83 (NY) St. Anthony, Nanuet, NY
DePrinzio, Rev. Kevin M., *O.S.A.* '04 (PH) [COL]

Villanova University, Villanova, PA
DeProspero, Rev. Nicholas, '70 (PSC) St. John's Greek Catholic Church Pottstown PA, Pottstown, PA
Deptula, Rev. Matthew, '15 (PEO) St. Mary's, Downs, IL; St. Patrick Church of Merna, Bloomington, IL
Deptula, Rev. Msgr. Stanley L., '96 (PEO) Saint Matthew Roman Catholic Congregation of Champaign, Champaign, IL; St. Boniface, Seymour, IL; [EFT] Archbishop Fulton J. Sheen Foundation, Peoria, IL
DePuydt, Rev. Francesco, (P) St. Henry, Gresham, OR
DeRammelaere, Rev. Bruce A., '06 (DAV) St. Paul the Apostle Church of Davenport, Iowa, Davenport, IA; [EFT] St. Paul the Apostle Foundation, Davenport, IA
Derasmo, Rev. John, '81 (RVC) St. James, Seaford, NY
Derasmo, Rev. John M., '81 (RVC) Curia: Offices and Directors
Derda, Rev. Christopher, '06 (KAL) St. Mary's Visitation, Byron Center, MI; St. Stanislaus, Dorr, MI
Derilus, Rev. Beauplan, *CMF* '09 (CHI) [MON] Claret House (Formation Residence), Chicago, IL
Derise, Rev. Mark, '97 (LAF) Curia: Miscellaneous / Other Offices Sts. Peter and Paul, Scott, LA
DeRiso, Rev. John M., *C.S.C.* '02 (FTW) [COL] University of Notre Dame Du Lac, Notre Dame, IN; [MON] Holy Cross Community, Corby Hall, University of Notre Dame, Notre Dame, IN
Derivan, Rev. Msgr. Thomas B., '72 (NY) St. Theresa of the Infant Jesus, Bronx, NY
Derivera, Rev. Raj R., '16 (SAC) Curia: Leadership Pastor of Sacred Heart Parish, Anderson, a corporation sole, Anderson, CA
Dermond, Rev. Msgr. John K., '68 (TR) Retired. Curia: Canonical Services [MON] Villa Vianney, Trenton, NJ
Dernek, Rev. Richard J., '70 (WIN) Retired.
DeRosa, Rev. Vincent John, (WDC) St. Mary, Mother of God, Washington, DC
DeRose, Rev. Martin, '88 (ALB) Retired.
DeRosia, Rev. Volney, (MAN) (>STU) [MIS] Fraternity of Priests, Inc., Steubenville, OH
DeRosia, Rev. Volney J., '03 (MAN) Curia: Clergy and Religious Services St. Patrick, Pelham, NH
Derosier, Rev. Edmond M., '73 (BO) St. Anthony of Padua, Shirley, MA; St. Mary, Ayer, MA
DeRouchey, Rev. Gary K., '02 (SFS) Saint Lawrence Parish of Grant County, Milbank, SD
DeRouen, Rev. Andrew M, '20 (LKC) St. Margaret, Lake Charles, LA
DeRouen, Rev. Msgr. Keith J., '83 (LAF) Our Lady Queen of Angels, Opelousas, LA
Derpich, Rev. Nikola P., *L.C.* '06 (R) On Special Assignment.
Derrane, Rev. Mark G., '95 (BO) Our Lady of the Assumption, Marshfield, MA
Derry, Rev. Daniel, '63 (SJ) Retired.
Dery, Rev. Cornelius, '05 (RVC) Chap, Mercy Med Ctr St. Christopher's Parish, Baldwin, NY
Des Rosiers, Rev. Denis A., '69 (OAK) Retired.
Desam, Rev. Balaraju, '03 (LR) St. Joseph, Conway, AR
DeSanctis, Rev. Peter, (RVC) Our Lady of the Isle, Shelter Island Heights, NY
DeSandre, Rev. John G., '64 (TR) Retired.
DeSantis, Rev. Msgr. Joseph A., '75 (ALN) Curia: Leadership Holy Rosary, Reading, PA; Sacred Heart, West Reading, PA
Desaulniers, Rev. Richard P., '70 (PRO) Retired.
DeSaye, Rev. Michael, '18 (TR) On Duty Outside Diocese.
Deschamps, Rev. Wilfred H., '90 (MAN) Sacred Heart of Jesus, Greenville, NH; St. Patrick, Jaffrey, NH
DeSciose, Rev. Michael, '75 (DEN) Retired.
DeSciose, Rev. Michael C., '75 (PBL) Retired.
Descoteaux, Rev. Lee, (RVC) Our Lady of Good Counsel, Inwood, NY
Descoteaux, Rev. Lee R., '07 (RVC) Curia: Leadership
Deshaies, Rev. Richard A., *S.J.* '92 (BO) [MON] Loyola House, Boston, MA
Deshautelle, Rev. Blake Paul, '07 (ALX) Our Lady of Prompt Succor, Mansura, LA; St. Paul the Apostle, Mansura, LA
Deshotels, Rev. James Michael, *S.J.* '93 (PRM) St. Louis Mission, St. Louis, MO
DeSiano, Rev. Francis P., *C.S.P.* '72 (WDC) [MIS] Paulist Evangelization Ministries, Washington, DC; [SEM] Paulist Washington Community, Washington, DC
Desiderio, Rev. Frank, (ALB) [RTR] St. Mary's of the Lake, Lake George, NY
Desiderio, Rev. Frank, *C.S.P.* '82 (NY) [EFT] Paulist Religious Property Trust, New York, NY; [MON] Paulist Fathers - Generalate, New York, NY; [MON] Paulist Fathers' Motherhouse, New York, NY
deSilva, Rev. Terrence, '16 (LEX) Church of the Resurrection, Lynch, KY; Holy Trinity, Harlan, KY
Desimone, Rev. Joseph C., '15 (ALX) Immaculate Conception, Dupont, LA
Desimone, Rev. Nicholas, '10 (WOR) Curia: Leadership; Offices and Directors St. Mary's, Uxbridge, MA
Desir, Rev. Jean Hugues, '04 (ORL) St. John the Baptist, Dunnellon, FL
Desjardins, Rev. George A., '59 (MAN) Retired.
Deskevich, Very Rev. Andrew J., '97 (PBR) Curia: Leadership; Offices and Directors Saint Nicholas Chapel, Beaver, PA; St. John the Baptist Cathedral, Munhall, PA
Desmarais, Rev. Paul E., '79 (PRO) Saint Mary's Church Corporation, Carolina, RI, Carolina, RI
Desmond, Rev. Hubert E., '58 (BO) Retired.
Desmond, Rev. Joseph L., '74 (MET) Retired.
Desmond, Rev. Joseph L., '74 (MET) Most Holy Redeemer, Matawan, NJ
Desmond, Rev. Msgr. Michael J., '71 (NEW) Retired.
DeSocio, Rev. John, '78 (ROC) Retired.
Desormeaux, Rev. Roland, *C.S.* '82 (PMB) Our Lady of Perpetual Help Mission, Delray Beach, FL
DesOrmeaux, Rev. Scott, '91 (LKC) Retired. On Sick Leave. Medical Retired Non-Active
DeSousa, Rev. John C., '11 (NEW) Holy Cross, Harrison, NJ
DeSouza, Rev. Eucinei, *F.D.P.* (BO) St. Joseph-St. Lazarus, Boston, MA
Desrosiers, Rev. Philip J., '66 (BO) Retired.
DesRosiers, Rev. Ronald, '63 (STP) Retired. (>WDC) [MON] Marist Center (The Marist Finance Center of the Atlanta Province of the Society of Mary, Marist Fathers and Brothers), Washington, DC
DesRuisseaux, Rev. Msgr. Charles E., '60 (MAN) Retired.
Desruisseaux, Rev. Gerard Frantz, '78 (BGP) Retired. [MON] The Catherine Dennis Keefe Queen of the Clergy Retired Priests' Residence, Stamford, CT
Desruisseaux, Rev. Pierre, *C.Ss.R.* (BO) Our Lady of Perpetual Help, Boston, MA
Desso, Rev. Leo C., '79 (AJ) Retired.
Dessureault, Rev. Marc, *O.M.I.* '91 (CHI) [EFT] Oblates for International Pastoral (Oblate International Pastoral Investment Trust), Chicago, IL
DeStefano, Rev. Salvatore, '08 (NY) St. Clare of Assisi, Bronx, NY; St. Francis Xavier, Bronx, NY
Deston, Rev. David C., (FR) Annunciation of the Lord, Taunton, MA; St. Nicholas of Myra Parish, North Dighton, MA
Destura, Rev. Mark Robin, (FRS) St. Katherine, , (>LA) [MON] Congregation of Rogationists, Inc., Van Nuys, CA
DeSutter, Rev. Mark, '82 (PEO) Sacred Heart Roman Catholic Congregation of Moline Illinois, Moline, IL
DeSutter, Rev. Mark, '82 (PEO) [MIS] Lee Parish Center, Moline, IL
DeTemple, Rev. Michael, *OP* (SFD) [CON] Dominican Sisters of Springfield, Il, Springfield, IL
Deters, Rev. Gregory J., '87 (DET) St. Alphonsus - St. Clement Parish Dearborn, Dearborn, MI
Detisch, Rev. John J., '88 (E) St. Tobias, Brockway, PA
Detisch, Rev. Scott P., '87 (E) St. John the Evangelist, Girard, PA
DeToma, Rev. Brandon, '18 (L) Curia: Leadership St. Michael, Fairfield, KY
Detscher, Rev. Msgr. Alan F., '71 (BGP) Retired. [MON] The Catherine Dennis Keefe Queen of the Clergy Retired Priests' Residence, Stamford, CT
Dettenwanger, Rev. Dennis, '64 (CIN) Retired.
Dettmer, Rev. David J., '80 (BRK) St. Anastasia, Douglaston, NY
Detwiler, Rev. Joseph, '21 (STL) Queen of All Saints Catholic Church, Oakville, MO
Deutsch, Very Rev. Msgr. Daniel J., '94 (RCK) On Special Assignment. Curia: Clergy and Religious Services; Leadership St. Patrick, St. Charles, IL
Deutsch, Rev. George E., '57 (TR) Retired.
Deutsch, Rev. Marvin, *M.M.* '57 (SJ) Retired.
Deutsch, Rev. Marvin F., *M.M.* '57 (NY) Retired. [MON] Maryknoll Fathers and Brothers (Catholic Foreign Mission Society of America, Inc.), Ossining, NY
Deutsch, Rev. Paul, *S.J.* '90 (LAF) [MON] St. Charles College, Grand Coteau, LA; [RTR] Jesuit Spirituality Center (St. Charles College), Grand Coteau, LA
Deutsch, Rev. Timothy, '94 (SD) Pastor of Saint Elizabeth of Hungary Catholic Parish, Julian, a corporation sole, Julian, CA; Pastor of Santa Ysabel Indian Mission Catholic Parish, Santa Ysabel, a corporation sole, Santa Ysabel, CA
Deutsch, Rev. Timothy, '94 (DUL) On Duty Outside Diocese. Alpine, CA
Devanapalle, Rev. George, '95 (BUF) SS. Joachim & Anne, Attica, NY
Devaney, Rev. John M., *O.P.* '15 (NY) Chap, Memorial Sloan Kettering Cancer Ctr, New York; Hosp...
Devaraj, Rev. Chinnappan M., *O.F.M.* '94 (DM) St. Boniface, Waukee, IA
Devaraj, Rev. Fredrick, *C.Ss.R.* '97 (STL) St. Alban Roe Catholic Church, Wildwood, MO
Devaraj, Rev. Peter, *S.A.C.* '81 (RVC) Queen of the Most Holy Rosary, Bridgehampton, NY; St. Andrew's, Sag Harbor, NY
Devasahayam, Rev. Thomas, *D.S.* '07 (GAL) St. James the Apostle, Spring, TX; [MON] Disciples of Hope (Texas), Houston, TX
Devasia, Rev. Sovi, (HT) Chap, Thibodaux Rgnl Med Ctr
Devassy, Rev. Biju T., '06 (WH) St. Luke the Evangelist, Morgantown, WV
Devassy, Rev. Joy K., *O.F.M.* '98 (MIL) [MIS] General Secretariat of the Franciscan Missions, Inc., Burlington, WI
Devassy, Rev. Shaju, (RVC) St. Barnabas the Apostle, Bellmore, NY
Devasya, Very Rev. Sebastian Embrayil, (WH) Curia: Leadership; Offices and Directors Sacred Heart, Bluefield, WV; Sacred Heart, Princeton, WV
Deveau, Rev. Daniel R., '75 (MAN) St. Marguerite d'Youville Parish, Groveton, NH; [CEM] Sacred Heart Cemetery, North Stratford, NH; [CEM] St. Francis Xavier Cemetery, Groveton, NH
DeVeer, Rev. Richard S., '65 (BO) Retired.
DeVelis, Rev. Mark-Joseph, *O.C.D.* '99 (MIL) [MON] Discalced Carmelite Friars of Holy Hill, Inc., Hubertus, WI; [MON] Washington Province of Discalced Carmelite Friars, Inc., Milwaukee, WI
DeVelis, Rev. Mark-Joseph, *O.C.D.* '99 (BO) [MON] Carmelite Monastery, Boston, MA
Dever, Rev. James T., *O.S.F.S.* '73 (CAM) The Church of Our Lady Star of the Sea, Cape May, Cape May, NJ
Dever, Msgr. William, '65 (MIA) St. Paul the Apostle, Lighthouse Point, FL
DeVera, Rev. Percival P., '91 (ORL) Church of Our Saviour, Cocoa Beach, FL
Devereaux, Rev. Martin C., '54 (PMB) Retired.
Devereux, Rev. Peter C., *L.C.* '00 (R) Saint Joseph Catholic Parish of Raleigh, Raleigh, NC
Devett, Rev. Aaron, '75 (SUP) Retired.
DeVilder, Rev. Daniel, (STL) [HOS] SSM Health De Paul Hospital - St. Louis, Bridgeton, MO
DeVille, Rev. George T., '57 (PIT) Retired. St. Oscar Romero, Canonsburg, PA
DeVille, Rev. William H., '62 (COL) Retired.
Devillers, Rev. Arnaud, (Y) (>SFD) St. Rose of Lima Parish, Quincy, IL; (>SFD) [MIS] Priestly Fraternity of St. Peter, Quincy, IL
Devin, Rev. John, *C.Ss.R.* '58 (BO) Our Lady of Perpetual Help, Boston, MA
Devina, Rev. Edgar, '97 (NY) St. Christopher and St. Margaret Mary, Staten Island, NY
Devine, Rev. Finbarr Columba, '70 (LA) Retired.
Devine, Rev. James T., '60 (BRK) Retired. [MON] Bishop Mugavero Residence, Douglaston, NY
Devine, Rev. Joseph T., '80 (HRT) Saint Gianna (Beretta Molla) Parish Corporation, West Hartford, CT
Devine, Rev. Msgr. Michael F., '57 (SP) Retired. St. Brendan, Clearwater, FL
Devine, Rev. Patrick A., '69 (HBG) Retired.
Devine, Rev. Richard J., *C.M.* '55 (BRK) [MON] DePaul Residence, Queens Village, NY
Devine, Rev. Terry, '85 (OWN) Immaculate Conception, Hawesville, KY; St. Columba, Lewisport, KY
Devine, Rev. Thomas, *O.A.R* (ORG) Our Lady of the Pillar, Santa Ana, CA
Devine, Rev. Thomas J., *O.A.R.* '68 (NEW) Holy Family, Union City, NJ; St. Augustine, Union City, NJ
Devine, Rev. William D., '73 (BO) Curia: Leadership St. Thomas Aquinas, Bridgewater, MA
Devino, Rev. Terrence, *S.J.* '87 (BO) [COL] Emmanuel College, Boston, MA
Devis, Rev. Sanjai, *V.C.* '97 (CAM) Our Lady of Peace Parish, Monroe Township, N.J., Williamstown, NJ
DeVito, Rev. Michael C., '76 (HRT) Retired.
Devlin, Rev. David J., *O.S.F.S.* '77 (CAM) The Church of Our Lady Star of the Sea, Cape May, Cape May, NJ
Devlin, Rev. Francis X., *O.S.A.* '73 (CAM) St. Augustine Preparatory School, Richland, NJ
Devlin, Rev. James E., '72 (BRK) Retired. Good Shepherd, Brooklyn, NY
Devlin, Rev. Joseph P., '91 (PH) St. Matthew, Conshohocken, PA
Devlin, Rev. Mark, '79 (TR) Retired.
DeVolder, Rev. Philip, '80 (FTW) Retired. [MIS] Saint Anne at Victory Noll (Saint Anne Home of the Diocese of Fort Wayne-South Bend, Inc.), Huntington, IN
DeVolder, Rev. Philip, '80 (FTW) Retired.

Devorak, Rev. James, '72 (NU) Retired.
Devorak, Rev. James William, '72 (STP) [CEM] Immaculate Conception Cemetery, Watertown, MN
Devore, Rev. Daniel B., '79 (BGP) Retired.
Devot, Rev. Paul D., *S.J.* '72 (SFR) St. Ignatius, San Francisco, CA; [MON] Loyola House Jesuit Community, San Francisco, CA
DeVous, Rev. Phillip W., '04 (COV) St. Charles Borromeo, Flemingsburg, KY; St. Rose of Lima, May's Lick, KY
DeVries, Rev. Thomas D., '89 (MIL) Retired. Holy Trinity Congregation, Newburg, WI
Devron, Rev. Christopher, *S.J.* '01 (NY) Fordham Preparatory School, Bronx, NY; Regis High School, New York, NY; [MON] St. Ignatius Loyola Residence, New York, NY
Devron, Rev. Christopher J., *S.J.* '01 (NY) [MON] Cardinal Spellman Hall, Jesuit Community, Bronx, NY
Dewaele, Rev. Joseph, *C.I.C.M.* '49 (ARL) Retired.
Dewan, Rev. Wilfed F., *C.S.P.* '53 (NY) Retired.
Dewan, Rev. Wilfred F., *C.S.P.* '53 (BRK) Retired.
Dewan, Rev. Wilfrid, (NY) Retired.
Dewan, Rev. William G., '86 (JOL) Sacred Heart, Joliet, IL; The Cathedral of St. Raymond, Joliet, IL
Dewane, Rev. Msgr. John B., '62 (GB) Retired.
deWater, Rev. Joseph M., '67 (NO) Retired.
DeWitt, Rev. David D., '84 (PIT) Holy Family, Pittsburgh, PA
Dewitt, Rev. Sean Regan, '16 (AUS) On Duty Outside Diocese. Apostolic Signatura, 00164 Rome
DeWitt, Rev. Stephen Nathaniel, *OFM* '12 (PH) [MON] Order of Friars Minor of the Province of the Most Holy Name, Philadelphia, PA; [SPF] St. Francis Inn, Philadelphia, PA
Dey, Rev. Charles, (STL) [HOS] SSM Health St. Joseph Hospital - St. Charles, St. Charles, MO
Deye, Rev. Walter C., *S.J.* '75 (CIN) [MIS] St. Xavier Church Property Corporation, Cincinnati, OH; [MON] Cincinnati Jesuit Community, Cincinnati, OH
DeYoung, Rev. Craig, (AUS) St. Louis, Austin, TX
DeYoung, Rev. Thomas J., '83 (GR) Retired.
Deziel, Rev. William, '97 (STP) Annunciation, Minneapolis, MN; [CEM] Guardian Angels Cemetery, Chaska, MN; [CEM] St. Nicholas Cemetery, Carver, MN
Dhabliwala, Very Rev. Neil, '08 (ATL) Curia: Leadership St. Catherine of Siena Catholic Church, Kennesaw, Inc., Kennesaw, GA
Dhanwar, Rev. Walter, *I.M.S.* '91 (AUS) St. Joseph, Elk, TX; St. Joseph, West, TX; St. Martin, West, TX
Dharelli, Rev. Thomas, *HGN* (SPC) Immaculate Heart of Mary, Mansfield, MO; Sacred Heart, Mountain Grove, MO
Dharmaraj, Rev. Anthony, *M.S.F.S.* '92 (ALX) Curia: Miscellaneous / Other Offices St. Rita, Alexandria, LA
Dhason, Rev. Ignas Maria, *MMI* (NY) Immaculate Conception, Woodbourne, NY
Dhein, Very Rev. William A., '02 (LC) Curia: Leadership; Offices and Directors [MIS] Holy Cross (Seminary) Diocesan Center, La Crosse, WI
Di Benedetto, Rev. Dennis M., '17 (FTW) St. Robert Bellarmine, North Manchester, IN
Di Gennaro, Rev. Paolo, *FSCB* '10 (STP) Hill-Murray School, Maplewood, MN
Di Giovanni, Rev. Alfonso, '96 (NEW) On Duty Outside Diocese. SS Peter and Paul, Tallinn
Di Giovanni, Rev. Msgr. Stephen M., '77 (BGP) Retired. St. John's Catholic Church, Stamford, Connecticut, Stamford, CT
Di Lella, Rev. Mario, *O.F.M.* '53 (SP) Retired. [MON] St. Anthony Friary (St. Petersburg) Franciscan Friars-Holy Name Province, Inc., St. Petersburg, FL
Di Marzio, Rev. Vito, *R.C.J.* '75 (LA) [MON] Congregation of Rogationists, Inc., Van Nuys, CA
Di Marzio, Rev. Vito, *RCJ* (FRS) Retired. St. Anthony of Padua, Reedley, CA
Di Raimondo, Rev. Domenico, (ORG) [RTR] House of Prayer for Priests, Orange, CA
Di Raimondo Romo, Rev. Dominico, *M.Ss.P.* On Special Assignment. Dir, Orange
Di Russo, Rev. Anthony, '63 (MAN) Retired.
Di Spigno, Rev. Francis, *O.F.M.* '96 (TR) St. Francis of Assisi, Long Beach Township, NJ
Di Tomo, Rev. Christopher P., '11 (RCK) St. Mary, Huntley, IL
Di Ulio, Rev. Albert J., *S.J.* '74 (CHI) [MON] Clark Street Jesuit Residence Community, Chicago, IL
Diala, Rev. Innocent, '91 (BUF) Curia: Consultative Bodies St. Josephs Roman Catholic Church Society Inc., Gowanda, NY; St. Mary, Cattaraugus, NY
Diamond, Rev. Msgr. David E., '83 (PH) St. Cornelius, Chadds Ford, PA
Dias, Rev. D. Francis, '71 (NY) Retired.
Dias, Rev. Dedigamuqage, (NY) Retired.
Dias, Rev. Francis Xavier, (GB) St. John, Gillett, WI; St. Michael, Suring, WI
Dias, Rev. Paulo, (DET) Saint John Neumann Parish Canton, Canton, MI
Dias, Rev. Prakash, *SAC* '13 (FWT) Jesus of Nazareth, Albany, TX; Sacred Heart of Jesus, Breckenridge, TX
Dias da Costa, Rev. Josias, *O.S.B.* '86 (KCK) [MON] St. Benedict's Abbey, Atchison, KS
Diatta, Rev. Jean Baptiste, (BO) [MON] The Jesuit Community at Boston College, Chestnut Hill, MA
Diaz, Rev. Alejandro, '11 (WDC) Our Lady Queen of the Americas (Parroquia Nuestra Senora Reina de las Americas), Washington, DC; St. Ambrose, Cheverly, MD
Diaz, Rev. Alexander, '06 (ARL) Queen of Apostles, Alexandria, VA
Diaz, Rev. Alvaro, '73 (CAM) Retired. St. Gianna Beretta Molla Parish, Northfield, N.J., Northfield, NJ
Diaz, Rev. Alvaro, '45 (SJN) Retired.
Diaz, Rev. Claudio, '00 (CHI) Our Lady of Unity Parish, Chicago, IL
Diaz, Rev. Dairo E., '01 (HRT) On Duty Outside Diocese. Moody Air Force Base, Georgia. Curia: (>MO) Offices and Directors
Diaz, Rev. Dairo E., (MO) Curia: Offices and Directors
Diaz, Rev. David, '79 (CGS) Santos Angeles Cutodios, Yabucoa, PR
Diaz, Rev. Edgardo, (GLP) Our Lady of Blessed Sacrament, Ft. Defiance, AZ; St. Michael, St. Michaels, AZ
Diaz, Rev. Erno, '69 (NY) Retired. [MIS] Chapel San Lorenzo Ruiz (Philippine Pastoral Center), New York, NY
Diaz, Rev. Fernando, (NEW) St. John the Baptist, Fairview, NJ
Diaz, Rev. Francisco, '87 (FRS) Chap, Kern Valley State Prison, Delano
Diaz, Rev. Francisco Gerardo, '77 (MIA) Retired.
Diaz, Rev. German Perez, '97 (KAL) Sacred Heart of Jesus, Bangor, MI
Diaz, Rev. Gilbert M., '94 (KNX) Holy Family, Seymour, TN
Diaz, Rev. Gonzalo, '52 (POD) Curia: Clergy and Religious Services
Diaz, Rev. Gonzalo, '63 (MGZ) On Special Assignment. Vicar General, Mayaguez
Diaz, Rev. Gonzalo, '52 (SJN) [MIS] Opus Dei, Guaynabo, PR
Diaz, Rev. Msgr. Gonzalo, '63 (MGZ) Curia: Leadership
Diaz, Rev. Msgr. Heberto M., '89 (BWN) Curia: Advisory Boards, Commissions, Committees, and Councils; Leadership Mary, Mother of the Church, Brownsville, TX; [CCH] Catholic Charities of the Rio Grande Valley San Juan Main Office, San Juan, TX; [EFT] Catholic Foundation of the Rio Grande Valley, Brownsville, TX
Diaz, Rev. Hector, '82 (SJN) Curia: (>MO) Offices and Directors [SPF] Centro Medico de P.R., San Juan, PR
Diaz, Rev. Hermes, '15 (NEW) St. Vincent de Paul, Bayonne, NJ
Diaz, Rev. Hernando, '71 (SLC) Retired.
Diaz, Rev. Javier A., '98 (TR) Curia: Canonical Services The Church of Christ the King, Long Branch, N.J., Long Branch, NJ
Diaz, Rev. Jose, '18 (BRK) Curia: Leadership St. Bartholomew, Elmhurst, NY; St. Leo, Corona, NY
Diaz, Rev. Jose Matias, (WDC) On Special Assignment.
Diaz, Rev. Jose Matías, (WDC) [SEM] Redemptoris Mater Archdiocesan Missionary Seminary, Hyattsville, MD
Diaz, Rev. Jose Glenn, '87 (SP) St. Thomas the Apostle, Homosassa, FL
Diaz, Rev. Joseph A., '94 (HON) Curia: Offices and Directors
Diaz, Rev. Luis F., '15 (NEW) St. Joseph, Bogota, NJ
Diaz, Rev. Luther Alvaro, '19 (LA) Our Lady of Perpetual Help, Santa Clarita, CA
Diaz, Rev. Manuel, (MET) Our Lady of Fatima, Perth Amboy, NJ
Diaz, Very Rev. Martin L., '78 (SLC) Curia: Offices and Directors Cathedral of the Madeleine LLC 202, Salt Lake City, UT
Diaz, Rev. Michael, '73 (SD) Retired.
Diaz, Rev. Raul, '97 (FRS) On Sick Leave.
Diaz, Rev. Thomas K., '81 (SR) Pastor of St. Elizabeth Catholic Church of Rohnert Park, A Corporation Sole, Rohnert Park, CA
Diaz Aponte, Rev. Melvin, '02 (PCE) Inmaculada Concepcion, Guayanilla, PR
Diaz De Leon, Rev. Juan Ramon, '72 (SR) Retired.
Diaz Gaytan, Rev. Eleazar, (MRY) St. Francis Xavier, Seaside, CA
Diaz Guerra, Rev. Salvador, (MIA) St. John Bosco, Miami, FL
Diaz Llamas, Rev. Salvador, *MNM* '04 (KCK) St. Mary-St. Anthony, Kansas City, KS
Diaz Marrero, Rev. Angel, '85 (ARE) Curia: Leadership [MIS] Chapel San Jose, Vega Baja, PR; [MIS] Chapel San Pedro Apostol, Vega Baja, PR
Diaz Marrero, Rev. Angel R., '85 (ARE) Ntra. Sra. de la Providencia, Vega Baja, PR
Diaz y Diaz, Rev. Javier, *S.J.* '16 (OAK) [MON] Jesuit Fathers and Brothers, Berkeley, CA
Diaz-Perez, Rev. Angel Antonio, *O.P.* (NO) Annunciation Catholic Church School, Bogalusa, LA
DiBacco, Rev. John V., '67 (WH) Retired.
DiBardino, Rev. Anthony R., '76 (CAM) Retired.
Dibble, Rev. Michael, '60 (NY) Retired.
Dibeashi, Rev. Ignatius, '89 (SD) Pastor of Immaculate Heart of Mary Catholic Parish, Ramona, a corporation sole, Ramona, CA
DiBiccaro, Rev. Dominic M., '04 (HBG) St. Ignatius Loyola, Orrtanna, PA
Dibongue, Msgr. Emile Martin, '05 (DEN) Sts. Peter & Paul Catholic Parish in Wheat Ridge, Wheat Ridge, CO
DiBuo, Very Rev. Roger F., '89 (WIL) Curia: Advisory Boards, Commissions, Committees, and Councils; Deaneries; Miscellaneous / Other Offices St. Elizabeth, Wilmington, DE
Dice, Rev. Armand, (AJ) Our Lady of the Lake Church, Big Lake, AK
DiCicco, Rev. Mario, *O.F.M.* (CHI) [MON] St. Peter's Friary, Chicago, IL
Dick, Rev. Gregory M., *O.Praem.* '96 (ORG) [MON] Norbertine Fathers of Orange, Inc., Silverado, CA
Dick, Rev. John, '96 (DAL) Epiphany Catholic Parish, Italy, TX; St. John Nepomucene Catholic Parish, Ennis, TX
Dickey, Rev. Bryon A., '09 (SEA) Retired.
Dickie, Rev. Clement, *O.P.* (NY) St. Joseph, New York, NY
Dickinson, Rev. Andrew, '06 (SFS) Curia: Leadership Sacred Heart Parish of Brown County, Aberdeen, SD; Sacred Heart Parish of Westport, Westport, SD; Saint Mary Parish of Brown County, Aberdeen, SD; [CAM] Saint Thomas Aquinas Newman Center, Aberdeen, SD
Dickinson, Rev. John D., '11 (PRT) Curia: Consultative Bodies; Offices and Directors St. John Paul II Parish, Scarborough, ME; [CAM] Southern Maine Community College, South Portland, ME
Dickinson, Rev. William R., '89 (CLV) On Leave.
Dickman, Rev. Richard C., '93 (LC) Retired.
Dicks, Rev. Thomas, '87 (NY) Parish of St. Mary and St. James, Marlboro, NY
Dickson, Rev. Jonathan J., (ALT) Chap, Mount Nittany Med Ctr, State College
Dicristina, Rev. Frank T., '86 (SB) Retired.
Didone, Rev. Matthew, *C.S.* '67 (NY) [MIS] American Committee on Italian Migration, Inc., New York, NY
Dieckhaus, Rev. Anthony W., (PH) Retired.
Dieckhaus, Rev. Joseph C., '74 (PH) Curia: Leadership SS. Philip and James, Exton, PA
Dieckmann, Rev. Msgr. Michael E., '74 (STL) Curia: Leadership Holy Infant Catholic Church, Ballwin, MO
Diederichs, Rev. Carl, (GB) SS. Peter & Paul Congregation, Kiel, WI
Diederichs, Rev. Carl E., '02 (MIL) Retired.
Diedrick, Rev. Charles T., '78 (CLV) St. Agnes, Elyria, OH; St. Mary, Elyria, OH
Diegel, Rev. Msgr. Ronald L., '75 (TYL) Retired.
Diego, Rev. Menniti, (LA) Mary Star of the Sea, San Pedro, CA
Diego, Rev. Saleh, (CHR) St. Gregory the Great, Bluffton, SC
Diehm, Rev. Noah J., '11 (DUB) Curia: Leadership Bosco Catholic School System, Gilbertville, Iowa, Gilbertville, IA; Immaculate Conception Church, Gilbertville, Iowa, Gilbertville, IA; St. Joseph's Church, Raymond, Iowa, Raymond, IA
Dieker, Rev. James P., '93 (DOD) Curia: Offices and Directors St. Anthony Catholic Church of Fowler, Kansas, Fowler, KS; St. John the Baptist Catholic Church of Meade, Kansas, Meade, KS; St. Patrick Catholic Church of Plains, Kansas, Plains, KS
Diekhans, Rev. Joseph, '65 (GF) Retired.
Diem, Rev. Joseph, '85 (BO) On Leave.
Diemer, Rev. Michael, *M.J.* '96 (TOL) St. Francis Xavier, Willard, OH
Diemer, Rev. Michael J., '96 (TOL) St. Bernard, New Washington, OH
Diemke, Rev. L. Edward, (ALB) Retired.
Dien, Rev. Raymond M. Nguyen, *C.M.C.* '88 (SPC) [SHR] Shrine of Immaculate Heart of Mary, Carthage, MO
Dien Nguyen, Rev. Raymond M., *CRM* '88 (SPC) [MON]

Congregation of the Mother of the Redeemer, Carthage, MO
Diener, Rev. Joshua, '16 (LA) Our Lady Queen of Angels, Lompoc, CA; St. Anthony, Oxnard, CA
Dieringer, Rev. James J., '58 (P) Retired.
Diermeier, Rev. Msgr. Joseph G., '78 (LC) Curia: Leadership; Offices and Directors Nativity of the Blessed Virgin Mary, Marathon, WI; [EFT] Nativity of the Blessed Virgin Mary, Marathon Endowment Trust, Marathon, WI
Diesbourg, Rev. Raymond, *M.S.C.* (OG) Curia: Consultative Bodies The Roman Catholic Community of Cape Vincent, Rosiere and Chaumont, Cape Vincent, NY; [MON] Missionaries of the Sacred Heart, Watertown, NY
Diesen, Rev. Edwin, (MIA) St. James, Miami, FL
Dietrich, Rev. Douglas D., '96 (LIN) Curia: Leadership; Offices and Directors St. Mary's, Davey, NE
Dietrich, Rev. John James, '93 (HRT) Curia: Advisory Boards, Commissions, Committees, and Councils The Saint Gregory Roman Catholic Church Corporation of Bristol, Connecticut, Bristol, CT; The St. Matthew's Church Corporation of Forestville, Connecticut, Forestville, CT
Dietsch, Rev. William, '71 (EVN) Retired.
Dietz, Rt. Rev. Elias, *O.C.S.O.* '03 (L) [MON] Abbey of Our Lady of Gethsemani, of the Order of Cistercians of the Strict Observance, Trappist, KY
Dietzenbach, Rev. Alan J., '12 (DUB) St. Francis Catholic School, Marshalltown, Iowa, Marshalltown, IA; St. Francis of Assisi Parish, Marshalltown, Iowa, Marshalltown, IA
Dietzenbach, Rev. Msgr. John A., '80 (BAL) Resurrection, Ellicott City, MD; St. Paul, Ellicott City, MD; [EFT] The St. Paul's Parish Endowment Trust, Ellicott City, MD
Dietzler, Rev. William J., '69 (MIL) Retired.
Diez, Rev. Alvaro, '68 (YAK) Retired.
Diez, Rev. Msgr. Antonio, '59 (SP) Retired.
Diez, Rev. Oscar, '68 (DAL) On Administrative Leave.
DiFazio, Rev. Silverio, '10 (STA) Retired.
Diffley, Rev. James, '63 (BRK) [MON] Bishop Mugavero Residence, Douglaston, NY
DiFolco, Rev. Thomas P., '83 (CIN) Retired.
DiGeronimo, Rev. Michael A., '76 (WOR) Curia: Leadership; Offices and Directors St. Mark, Sutton, MA
DiGiralamo, Rev. Gerald, *S.A.* '81 (NY) Retired.
DiGirolamo, Rev. Msgr. Paul A., '83 (PH) On Special Assignment. Judicial Vicar, Met Tribunal, Old St Mary's, Philadelphia Curia: Leadership Old St. Mary's, Philadelphia, PA
DiGiulio, Rev. Richard S., '69 (BUF) Retired. Curia: Offices and Directors [MON] Msgr. Conniff Residence, Depew, NY
Digmann, Rev. Kyle M., '14 (DUB) St. Thomas Aquinas Church, Ames, Iowa, Ames, IA; [CAM] St. Thomas Aquinas Church, Ames, Iowa, Ames, IA
Dignan, Rev. Eamon, '59 (WDC) Retired. St. John Francis Regis, Hollywood, MD
DiGregorio, Rev. Joseph L., '66 (PH) Retired.
DiGregorio, Rev. Michael F., *O.S.A.* '73 (PH) [MON] St. Thomas Monastery, Villanova, PA
DiGuglielmo, Rev. Anthony J., '03 (PH) St. Gabriel of the Sorrowful Mother, Avondale, PA
Digwou, Rev. Modeste, '02 (STV) Cathedral of SS. Peter and Paul, Charlotte Amalie, VI
DiIanni, Rev. Albert, *S.M.* '60 (BO) Retired. (>WDC) [MON] Marist Center (The Marist Finance Center of the Atlanta Province of the Society of Mary, Marist Fathers and Brothers), Washington, DC
DiIorio, Rev. Michael C., '77 (PH) St. Michael the Archangel, Levittown, PA
Dike, Rev. Anthony O., (GLP) Curia: Leadership Sacred Heart, Quemado, NM; Santo Nino, Reserve, NM
Dike, Rev. Casmir, *M.S.P.* (SAT) Chap, Santa Rosa Hosp System, San Antonio
Dike, Rev. Ernest, '05 (JC) Immaculate Conception, Montgomery City, MO; St. Patrick, Jonesburg, MO
Dikete, Rev. Fidele O., '02 (SAT) St. John Berchmans, San Antonio, TX
DiLella, Rev. Msgr. Christopher C., (PAT) Curia: Administration
DiLeo, Rev. Anthony, '64 (SB) Retired.
Dilettuso, Rev. Joseph, '72 (BLX) Retired.
Dilg, Rev. Donald W., *C.S.C.* (FTW) [MIS] Holy Cross House, Notre Dame, IN
Dilger, Rev. Donald, '59 (EVN) Retired.
Dill, Very Rev. Anthony R., '12 (HBG) Curia: Leadership; Offices and Directors Holy Spirit Parish Charitable Trust, Palmyra, PA; [EFT] Roman Catholic Diocese of Harrisburg Charitable Trust, Harrisburg, PA
Dill, Rev. Edwin, *S.T.* '59 (WDC) [MON] Father Judge Missionary Cenacle, Adelphi, MD
Dillabough, Rev. Msgr. Daniel J., '74 (SD) Curia: Tribunal [COL] University of San Diego, San Diego, CA
Dillard, Rev. Daniel, (OWN) Owensboro Catholic High School, Owensboro, KY
Dillard, Rev. Daniel C., '09 (OWN) Curia: Advisory Boards, Commissions, Committees, and Councils SS. Joseph and Paul, Owensboro, KY
Dillard, Rev. Steven, *S.J.* '86 (P) [MON] Colombiere Jesuit Community, Portland, OR
Dillard, Rev. William, '98 (P) [SEM] Mount Angel Seminary, Saint Benedict, OR
Dillenburg, Rev. Msgr. James E., '65 (GB) Retired.
Dillinger, Rev. Joseph A., '96 (SC) St. Joseph's, Wall Lake, IA
Dillingham, Rev. Charles C., '73 (WIL) Curia: Advisory Boards, Commissions, Committees, and Councils St. Mary of the Assumption, Hockessin, DE
Dillon, Rev. David, *O.Carm.* '65 (JOL) Retired.
Dillon, Rev. Dennis T., *S.J.* (DET) [MON] Colombiere Center, Clarkston, MI
Dillon, Rev. Msgr. Edward J., '67 (ATL) Curia: Advisory Boards, Commissions, Committees, and Councils; Offices and Directors Holy Spirit Catholic Church, Atlanta, Inc., Atlanta, GA; [COL] Holy Spirit College, Inc. (Pontifex University), Atlanta, GA
Dillon, Rev. Edward J., '60 (ROC) Retired.
Dillon, Rev. J. Thomas, '11 (PT) St. John Paul II Catholic High School, Tallahassee, FL
Dillon, Rev. Jeffry T., '81 (BRK) Retired. Curia: Organizations (affiliated, inter-Diocesan, miscellaneous/ other) St. Kevin, Flushing, NY
Dillon, Rev. Jerome V., (OM) Retired.
Dillon, Rev. John J., '98 (WDC) Curia: Deaneries St. Francis of Assisi, Derwood, MD
Dillon, Rev. Jonathan, '14 (RC) Curia: Leadership Immaculate Conception, Bonesteel, SD; Sacred Heart, Burke, SD; St. Anthony's, Fairfax, SD; St. Joseph, Gregory, SD
Dillon, Rev. Kevin J., '03 (RVC) Church of Our Lady of Hope, Carle Place, NY; St. Boniface Martyr, Sea Cliff, NY
Dillon, Rev. Kevin M., '00 (HRT) St. George's Church, Guilford, CT
Dillon, Rev. Michael J., '61 (SAC) Retired. Pastor of SS. Peter and Paul Parish, Rocklin, a corporation sole, Rocklin, CA
Dillon, Rev. Richard J., '61 (NY) Retired.
Dillon, Rev. Robert W., '97 (NY) St. John Neumann, Staten Island, NY; St. Patrick, Staten Island, NY
Dillon, Rev. Tristan P. A., '22 (SLC) St. George LLC 223, St. George, UT
Dilone, Rev. Mark, (NEW) [MON] Benedictine Abbey of Newark, Newark, NJ
DiLorenzo, Rev. Thomas A., '79 (BO) Retired. St. John the Baptist, Quincy, MA
DiLuzio, Rev. James M., *C.S.P.* '93 (NY) [MON] Paulist Fathers' Motherhouse, New York, NY
Dilworth, Rev. Kevin, *S.J.* '84 (PHX) St. Francis Xavier Roman Catholic Parish, Phoenix, AZ; [MON] Society of Jesus, Phoenix, AZ
Dim, Rev. Leonard, '12 (PMB) St. Matthew, Lake Worth, FL
DiMarco, Rev. Anthony J., '06 (NOR) Curia: Leadership Our Lady of Grace, New London, CT; St. Brendan the Navigator Parish, New London, CT
DiMaria, Rev. Peter J., '93 (PH) Sacred Heart, Swedesburg, PA
DiMaria, Rev. Sean E., '05 (BUF) Curia: Leadership Saint John Paul II, Lake View, NY
DiMascola, Rev. Charles J., '81 (SPR) Retired.
DiMassimo, Rev. Steven T., '21 (R) St. Thomas More, Chapel Hill, NC
DiMattei, Rev. Robert A., '91 (BAL) St. Athanasius, Baltimore, MD; St. Rose of Lima, Baltimore, MD
DiMauro, Rev. Joseph A., (PH) St. Thomas the Apostle, Glen Mills, PA
DiMauro, Rev. Msgr. Joseph V., '67 (CAM) Retired.
Dimic, Rev. Milan, '85 (BGP) The Saint Andrew Roman Catholic Church Corporation, Bridgeport, CT
Dimler, Rev. Richard G., *S.J.* '63 (PH) Retired.
D'Imperio, Rev. Robert J., '07 (CAM) Saint Gabriel the Archangel Parish, Carneys Point, N.J., Carney's Point, NJ
Din, Rev. Rudin, (DOD) St. Helen Catholic Church of Hugoton, Kansas, Hugoton, KS; St. Joan of Arc Catholic Church of Elkhart, Kansas, Elkhart, KS
Dinan, Rev. Dennis M., '92 (NY) St. Francis Xavier, Narrowsburg, NY
DiNardo, Rev. Daniel A., '66 (CAM) Retired.
DiNardo, Very Rev. Lawrence A., '74 (PIT) Retired. Curia: Consultative Bodies; Leadership Christ Our Savior, Pittsburgh, PA
Dinelli, Rev. William J., '61 (SAC) Retired.
Dinga, Rev. Eric J., '15 (GBG) Curia: Advisory Boards, Commissions, Committees, and Councils; Leadership; Miscellaneous / Other Offices; Offices and Directors Christ, Prince of Peace Parish, Ford City, PA; St. Lawrence, Ford City, PA
Dinga, Rev. William, '75 (RIC) Retired.
Dinguis, Rev. Jorge, '06 (TYL) Sacred Heart of Jesus, Rusk, TX; Venerable Antonio Margil-Alto, Alto, TX
Dingwall, Rev. William, *O.C.S.O.* '06 (WOR) [MON] St. Joseph's Abbey (Cistercian Abbey of Spencer, Inc., Cistercian Order of the Strict Observance (Trappists)), Spencer, MA
Dinh, Rev. Andrew, (AUS) St. Mary, College Station, TX
Dinh, Rev. Chien X., *S.V.D.* (SP) St. Joseph Vietnamese Parish, Tampa, FL
Dinh, Rev. Dominic Hai, *C.Ss.R.* '95 (DAL) [MON] St. John Neumann Formation House, Dallas, TX
Dinh, Rev. Hai D., '08 (DAV) St. Joseph Church of Hills, Iowa, Hills, IA; St. Mary Church of Lone Tree, Iowa, Lone Tree, IA; St. Mary Church of Nichols, Iowa, Nichols, IA
Dinh, Very Rev. Hao, '93 (SJ) On Special Assignment. Curia: Leadership; Offices and Directors Church of the Ascension, Saratoga, CA; [MIS] Roman Catholic Seminary Corporation of San Jose, San Jose, CA; [MIS] The Roman Catholic Welfare Corporation of San Jose, San Jose, CA
Dinh, Rev. Hoan Q., '07 (ROC) St. Luke the Evangelist Roman Catholic Church Society of Livingston County, Geneseo, NY
Dinh, Rev. Huong, '21 (OAK) St. Anthony-Mary Help of Christians, Oakland, CA
Dinh, Rev. Huy Quang, *C.S.Sp.* '00 (GAL) St. Benedict the Abbot, Houston, TX
Dinh, Rev. Joseph Long, '00 (CHL) Christ the King, High Point, NC
Dinh, Rev. Joseph Tu, (GAL) St. Ambrose, Houston, TX
Dinh, Rev. Ky Ngoc, *S.V.D.* '08 (DUB) [SEM] Divine Word College, Epworth, IA
Dinh, Rev. Peter, (DEN) Sacred Heart Catholic Parish in Roggen, Roggen, CO
Dinh, Rev. Peter Vien T., *CRM* '14 (SPC) [MON] Congregation of the Mother of the Redeemer, Carthage, MO
Dinh, Rev. Quang Duc, *S.V.D.* '92 (CHI) [EFT] Divine Word Techny Community Corporation, Techny, IL; [MON] Divine Word Residence, Techny, IL; [MON] Society of the Divine Word, Provincial Headquarters-Chicago Prov., Techny, IL
Dinh, Rev. Tien, *O.F.M.Cap.* (GF) [MON] St. Katharine Friary, Crow Agency, MT
Dinh, Rev. Tran, (VIC) St. Mary's, Victoria, TX
Dinh, Rev. Tran Thuc, '61 (OAK) Retired.
Dinh, Rev. Tri M., *S.J.* '00 (LA) Dolores Mission, Los Angeles, CA; [MIS] Christus Ministries, Culver City, CA; [MON] Jesuit Community, Los Angeles, CA
Dinh, Rev. Victor T., '03 (FRS) Our Lady of La Vang, Fresno, CA; St. Genevieve, Fresno, CA
Dinh-Van-Thiep, Rev. Philip, '83 (GB) Annunciation of the Blessed Virgin Mary, Green Bay, WI; St. Joseph, Green Bay, WI; St. Jude, Green Bay, WI
Dinkel, Rev. Brian, *I.V.E.* '13 (SJ) Curia: Leadership Our Lady of Peace, Santa Clara, CA; [EFT] IVE West Coast Trust, Santa Clara, CA; [MON] The Institute of the Incarnate Word (IVE), Santa Clara, CA; [SHR] Shrine of Our Lady of Peace, Santa Clara, CA
Dinkel, Rev. Harvey, *O.F.M.Cap.* '61 (SAL) [MON] St. Fidelis Friary, Victoria, KS; [RTR] Capuchin Center for Spiritual Life, Victoria, KS
DiNoia, Rev. Joseph Augustine, *O.P.* '70 (WDC) On Duty Outside Diocese. Sub-Sec, Congregation of the Doctrine of the Faith, Rome
Dinovo, Rev. Anthony A., '01 (COL) St. Michael, Worthington, OH
Dinsdale, Rev. Samuel, '03 (SLC) Curia: Offices and Directors Saint Vincent de Paul LLC 250, Salt Lake City, UT
Dio, Rev. Jacob, *M.S.F.S.* '02 (NSH) Curia: Leadership Immaculate Conception, Clarksville, TN
Dioka, Rev. Jude, '80 (RVC) St. Mary's, Manhasset, NY
Diokno, Rev. Msgr. Rolando V., '70 (GAL) Retired.
Diolata, Rev. Victor, (HON) Mary, Star of the Sea, Honolulu, HI
Dion, Rev. Gerard, '92 (MAN) Retired.
Dion, Very Rev. Michael, '16 (SEA) Curia: Leadership St. Michael, Snohomish, WA
Dion, Rev. Richard H., '99 (MAN) St. Anthony of Padua, Manchester, NH

Dionisio, Rev. Romeo, '84 (PHX) Curia: Leadership; Offices and Directors Church of the Resurrection Roman Catholic Parish, Tempe, AZ
Dionne, Rev. Francis, '81 (SP) Retired.
Dionne, Very Rev. J. Joseph, *C.Ss.R.* '04 (R) Curia: Leadership Immaculate Conception, Clinton, NC
DiOrio, Rev. John R., '99 (PH) Stella Maris, Philadelphia, PA
Diorio, Rev. Ralph A., '57 (WOR) Retired.
DiPerri, Rev. James M., '88 (BO) Curia: Advisory Boards, Commissions, Committees, and Councils Our Lady, Comforter of the Afflicted, Waltham, MA
Diphe, Rev. Juan M., '76 (HEL) Chap, US Air Force
DiPietro, Rev. Leroy A., '70 (PIT) Retired. Curia: Clergy and Religious Services
Direen, Rev. John, '01 (OAK) Chap, Highland Hosp; Kaiser-Permanente Med Ctr Curia: Offices and Directors St. Leo the Great, Oakland, CA
Dirichukwu, Rev. Emanuel, (NSH) St. Andrew, Sparta, TN; St. Gregory, Smithville, TN
Dirkx, Rev. Dennis A., '72 (MIL) Retired.
DiRocco, Rev. Cassian, '13 (STP) Chap, Regions Hosp, St Paul
DiRocco, Rev. Michael Anthony (Cassian), '13 (STP) St. Joseph, Hastings, MN
Dirscherl, Rev. Denis, (DET) [MON] Colombiere Center, Clarkston, MI
DiSalvatore, Rev. Remo, *O.F.M.Cap.* '97 (NEW) St. Ann, Hoboken, NJ; [MON] Capuchin Friars - Province of the Sacred Stigmata of St. Francis, Union City, NJ
Dischler, Rev. Raymond J., '73 (MAD) Retired.
DiSciacca, Rev. Joseph V., '73 (HRT) Retired.
Disco, Rev. Bernard, *O.S.B.* '06 (MAN) [MON] St. Anselm Abbey, Manchester, NH
Diskin, Rev. Michael L., '77 (PHX) Retired. Curia: Offices and Directors
DiSpigno, Rev. Gennaro J., '81 (RVC) Good Shepherd, Holbrook, NY
Distefano, Rev. Simeon C., *O.F.M.* '63 (NY) [MON] Padua Friary, New York, NY
Distor, Rev. Leo, *S.S.C.* '96 (CHI) [MON] Columban Fathers Theologate, Chicago, IL
Ditchuk, Rev. Sviatoslav, '19 (SJP) St. Josaphat Cathedral, Parma, OH
Ditchuk, Rev. Sviatoslav, '19 (SJP) Curia: Offices and Directors
Ditillo, Rev. James J., *S.J.* '74 (PH) [MON] Jesuit Community at St. Joseph's University, Merion Station, PA
DiTomasso, Rev. Peter, *M.SS.CC.* (HBG) Immaculate Conception of the Blessed Virgin Mary, Fairfield, PA; St. Rita, Blue Ridge Summit, PA; [MIS] Missionaries of the Sacred Hearts of Jesus & Mary House of Studies, Fairfield, PA
Ditta, Rev. Angelo J., '86 (RVC) Retired.
Dittmeier, Rev. Charles R., '70 (L) On Duty Outside Diocese. Louisville
Dittmer, Rev. Antonio, '97 (PEO) Curia: Consultative Bodies; Deaneries St. Mary's, Moline, IL
Ditto, Rev. Anthony W., '90 (GBG) Mother of Sorrows, Murrysville, PA
Ditton, Rev. Edmund Augustine, *O.P.* (L) St. Rose, Springfield, KY
Ditullio, Rev. Brian, '06 (PAT) St. John Vianney, Stockholm, NJ; St. Thomas, the Apostle, Oak Ridge, NJ
Diurczak, Rev. Eugene, '68 (NEW) Retired. [MON] The Rev. Msgr. James F. Kelley Residence for Retired Priests, Caldwell, NJ
Divine, Rev. Finbarr, '70 (LA) Retired.
Divine, Rev. Nicholas, *C.P.* '21 (GAL) [MON] Congregation of the Passion, Holy Name Passionist Community and Retreat Center, Houston, TX; [RTR] Holy Name Retreat Center, Houston, TX
Divis, Rev. Daniel O., '79 (CLV) St. Mary, Lorain, OH
Divis, Rev. M. James, '76 (LIN) Curia: Leadership; Offices and Directors [SEM] St. Gregory the Great Seminary, Seward, NE
Dixey, Rev. Edward, *O.S.A.* '57 (PH) [MON] St. Thomas Monastery, Villanova, PA
Dixon, Rev. David C., '57 (PIT) Retired. [MON] St. John Vianney Manor, Pittsburgh, PA
Dixon, Rev. Francis F., *O.Carm.* '76 (NY) [CAM] Iona College, New Rochelle, NY; [MON] St. Albert's Priory, Middletown, NY
Dixon, Rev. Isadore, (WDC) St. Jerome, Hyattsville, MD
Dixon, Rev. James M., *S.J.* '73 (MIL) [MON] St. Camillus Jesuit Community (Society of Jesus, USA Midwest Province), Wauwatosa, WI
Dixon, Rev. Msgr. James R., '70 (NO) Retired.
Dizon, Rev. Jonathan, '15 (KCK) St. Dominic, Holton, KS; St. Francis Xavier, Mayetta, KS; [SHR] Our Lady of the Snows Oratory, Mayetta, KS
Djonovic, Rev. Marko, '13 (DET) Curia: Administration; Consultative Bodies St. Moses the Black Parish Detroit, Detroit, MI
Dlabal, Rev. Norbert, '72 (SAL) Retired. Curia: Organizations (affiliated, inter-Diocesan, miscellaneous/ other)
Dlugos, Rev. Raymond F., *O.S.A.* '83 (BO) Curia: Pastoral Services [CAM] Merrimack College Campus Ministry Center, North Andover, MA; [COL] Merrimack College, North Andover, MA
D'Mello, Rev. John, '73 (PMB) St. Patrick, Palm Beach Gardens, FL
Dmoch, Rev. Paul, '76 (NY) Retired.
Dmytryszyn, Rev. Glen J., (HRT) Curia: Offices and Directors; Spiritual Life The Church of the Assumption, Woodbridge, Woodbridge, CT; [CAM] Southern Connecticut State University Catholic Center, New Haven, CT
Do, Rev. (Francis Xavier M.) Tung Cao, *CRM* '98 (SPC) [MON] Congregation of the Mother of the Redeemer, Carthage, MO
Do, Rev. Andrew Mary Sang Linh, *C.M.C.* '83 (SB) Retired.
Do, Rev. Ba, *CRM* '14 (SAC) Vietnamese Martyrs Parish, Sacramento, CA
Do, Rev. Msgr. Dominic Dinh, '72 (SJ) Retired.
Do, Rev. Long, '10 (MIA) St. Ambrose, Deerfield Beach, FL
Do, Rev. Minh Q., '14 (SD) Pastor of Our Lady of Perpetual Help Catholic Parish Lakeside in Lakeside California, A Corporation Sole, Lakeside, CA
Do, Rev. Nho Duy, '66 (LR) Retired. [MON] St. John Manor, Little Rock, AR
Do, Rev. Peter, *O.P.* '09 (P) Holy Rosary Parish Dominican, Portland, OR; [MON] Holy Rosary Priory, Portland, OR
Do, Rev. Peter Quan, '02 (L) Curia: Leadership St. John Paul II, Louisville, KY
Do, Rev. Thanh (Philip M.), *CRM* '09 (SPC) [MON] Congregation of the Mother of the Redeemer, Carthage, MO
Do, Rev. Timothy Truong, '10 (SB) St. Joseph, Upland, CA
Do, Rev. Toan, (L) St. John the Apostle, Brandenburg, KY
Do, Rev. Tuyen, (LR) St. Anthony, Weiner, AR; St. John Newman University Parish, Jonesboro, AR; [CAM] Arkansas State University, St. John Newman University Parish, Jonesboro, AR; [EFT] Arkansas State Univ. St. John Newman Univ. Parish Trust Fund Agreement, Jonesboro, AR
Do, Rev. Vien Van, '90 (PEO) Retired.
Do, Rev. Vincentius T., '07 (BRK) Curia: Consultative Bodies St. Michael, Flushing, NY; [CCH] Chinese Ministry-Brooklyn, ,
Do Ba Cong, Rev. James, '61 (SPC) Retired.
Doan, Rev. Basil Toan Quang, *CRM* '99 (CIN) [MIS] Catholic Vietnamese Community of Dayton, Dayton, OH
Doan, Rev. Nam, (ORG) St. Norbert, Orange, CA
Doan, Rev. Peter Khoi Anh, *S.D.D.* (SEA) Our Lady of Lourdes, Seattle, WA
Doan Nguyen, Rev. Joseph Tan, *O.F.M.* '86 (STL) [MON] Franciscan Friary of St. Anthony of Padua, St. Louis, MO
Dobbs, Rev. Jeffrey L., '08 (WIN) [SEM] Immaculate Heart of Mary Seminary, Winona, MN
Dober, Rev. Edward J., '76 (LA) Retired.
Dober, Rev. Martin, (CLV) Curia: Advisory Boards, Commissions, Committees, and Councils St. John Vianney, Mentor, OH
Dobes, Rev. Msgr. George E., '68 (CHI) On Duty Outside Diocese. Arlington, VA
Dobes, Rev. George E., '68 (WDC) Curia: Tribunal
Dobosz, Rev. Jerzy George, '95 (TYL) On Leave.
Dobrowski, Rev. Peter P., '71 (PHX) Retired. Curia: Leadership San Francisco de Asis Roman Catholic Parish, Flagstaff, AZ
Dobrozsi, Rev. Ambrose, '19 (CIN) Holy Cross, Dayton, OH; Mary Help of Christians, Fairborn, OH; Our Lady of the Rosary, Dayton, OH; Sacred Heart, New Carlisle, OH
Dobrzenski, Rev. Francis G., '77 (MAR) Retired.
Dobrzynski, Rev. Martin J., '84 (GRY) Curia: Offices and Directors St. Michael, Schererville, IN
Dobson, Rev. Christopher, (ALT) [MON] St. Francis Friary at Mount Assisi, Loretto, PA
Dobson, Rev. Gregory J., '83 (BUF) Retired. St. Thomas Aquinas, Buffalo, NY
Dockendorf, Rev. Ronald, '82 (SCL) St. John the Baptist, Swanville, MN; St. Joseph's, Grey Eagle, MN
Doctor, Rev. John, *O.F.M.* '76 (SFD) [COL] Quincy University Corporation, Quincy, IL; [MON] Holy Cross Friary (Quincy University Friary), Quincy, IL
Doda, Rev. Eugene J., '77 (MIL) Retired.
Dodd, Rev. David, *T.O.R.* '19 (ARL) St. Joseph, Herndon, VA
Dodds, Rev. Michael J., *O.P.* '77 (OAK) [MON] Order of Preachers (Province of the Most Holy Name of Jesus - Western Dominican Province), Oakland, CA; [SEM] Dominican School of Philosophy and Theology, Berkeley, CA
Dodge, Rev. Billy J., '15 (LC) Blessed Sacrament Parish, La Crosse, WI; Roncalli Newman Parish, La Crosse, WI; [CAM] Roncalli Newman Parish, La Crosse, WI; [EFT] Blessed Sacrament Parish Endowment Trust, La Crosse, WI; [EFT] Roncalli Newman Parish Student Endowment Trust, La Crosse, WI
Dodge, Rev. Edwin J., *O.S.A.* '57 (CHI) [MON] St. Rita Monastery, Chicago, IL
Dodge, Rev. Thomas E., '05 (FAR) Sacred Heart Church of Carrington, Carrington, ND; St. Elizabeth's Church of Sykeston, Sykeston, ND
Dodo, Rev. Wilfred Y., (NY) Chap, Richmond Univ Med Ctr, Staten Island Holy Child, Staten Island, NY
Dodson, Rev. James C., '11 (BUR) Curia: Offices and Directors Nativity of the Blessed Virgin Mary-St. Louis, Swanton, VT
Doering, Rev. Christopher, '98 (CHI)
Doering, Rev. Christopher E., '98 (CHI) Curia: (>MO) Offices and Directors
Doerr, Rev. Brian M., '98 (LFT) St. Elizabeth Seton, Carmel, IN
Doerr, Rev. Richard J., '93 (LFT) Our Lady of Mount Carmel, Carmel, IN
Doerre, Rev. Edmund J, '63 (LC) Retired.
Doffing, Rev. Gordon, (PHX) All Saints Roman Catholic Parish, Mesa, AZ
Doffing, Rev. Gordon M., '60 (STP) Retired.
Dogali, Rev. Michael F., '92 (BGP) The St. Joseph's Church of Shelton, Shelton, CT
Dogaru, Rev. Alin Nadir, '00 (ROM)
Dogo, Rev. Timothy, '96 (PHX) St. Anne Roman Catholic Parish, Gilbert, AZ
Doheny, Rev. Thomas R., '58 (MAD) Retired.
Doher, Rev. Jason, (LIN) St. Peter, Lincoln, NE
Doherty, Rev. Cathal, *S.J.* '09 (SFR) (>MIL) [MON] Jesuit Community at Marquette University (Marquette Jesuit Associates, Inc.), Milwaukee, WI
Doherty, Rev. Cathal, (MO) Curia: Offices and Directors
Doherty, Rev. Daniel G., *O.P.* '57 (NY) Church of the Holy Innocents, Pleasantville, NY
Doherty, Rev. Daniel J., *P.S.S.* '94 (BAL) [MON] Society of St. Sulpice, Province of the United States, Baltimore, MD
Doherty, Rev. Daniel J., *S.S.* '94 (SCR) On Duty Outside Diocese. Baltimore, MD
Doherty, Rev. Donald J., *M.M.* '62 (NY) Retired.
Doherty, Rev. Edward, *O.S.A.* (PH) [MON] St. Thomas Monastery, Villanova, PA
Doherty, Rev. James J., *C.S.C* '78 (FR) [COL] Holy Cross Fathers Religious, North Easton, MA; [RTR] Holy Cross Retreat House, North Easton, MA
Doherty, Rev. James M., '72 (GLD) Retired.
Doherty, Rev. John R., '64 (NEW) Retired.
Doherty, Rev. Mark D., '14 (SFR) On Special Assignment. Rector, St Patrick's Seminary & Univ [SEM] St. Patrick's Seminary and University (The Roman Catholic Seminary of San Francisco), Menlo Park, CA
Doherty, Rev. Michael, *O.F.M.* '76 (LA) [RTR] Serra Retreat, Malibu, CA
Doherty, Rev. Patrick J., '59 (MAD) Retired.
Doherty, Rev. Paul J., '95 (WOR) On Administrative Leave.
Doherty, Rev. Robert J., '70 (BO) Retired.
Doherty, Rev. Terrance M., *S.M.A.* '70 (NEW) Retired.
Dohman, Rev. William, '73 (STN) Retired.
Dohner, Rev. Stephen J., '76 (CLV) Holy Martyrs, Medina, OH
Dohogne, Rev. David J., '92 (SPC) Curia: Consultative Bodies; Offices and Directors St. Henry, Charleston, MO
Doiron, Rev. David E., '69 (WOR) Retired.
Doke, Very Rev. Jason T., '13 (JC) Curia: Administration; Organizations (affiliated, inter-Diocesan, miscellaneous/other) St. Martin, St. Martins, MO
Doktorczyk, Very Rev. Msgr. Stephen S., '05 (ORG) Curia: Leadership St. Martin de Porres, Yorba Linda, CA
Doktorczyk, Very Rev. Msgr. Stephen S., '05 (ORG) Curia: Leadership
Dolak, Rev. Mark J., (MET) On Leave.

Dolan, Rev. Gerald M., *O.F.M.* '56 (SP) Retired. [MON] St. Anthony Friary (St. Petersburg) Franciscan Friars-Holy Name Province, Inc., St. Petersburg, FL
Dolan, Rev. Guthrie, '11 (DM) On Special Assignment. Clinical Chaplaincy Formation
Dolan, Rev. James W., '75 (PIT) Retired. Chap, Kane Rgnl Ctr - Ross; Manorcare Health Services North...
Dolan, Rev. John J., (CAM) The Church of Our Lady Star of the Sea, Cape May, Cape May, NJ
Dolan, Rev. John R., *M.S.* '79 (FR) Our Lady of the Cape, Brewster, MA
Dolan, Rev. Joseph M., '92 (WOR) St. Bernard Parish at St. Camillus de Lellis, Fitchburg, MA
Dolan, Rev. Mark A., '76 (STL) Our Lady of the Presentation Catholic Church, Overland, MO
Dolan, Rev. Michael F., '97 (WDC) Retired.
Dolan, Rev. Michael J., '96 (HRT) Curia: Clergy and Religious Services; Parish Services Northwest Catholic High School, West Hartford, CT
Dolan, Rev. Msgr. Neal T., '64 (SD) Retired.
Dolan, Rev. Nicholas, (TR) St. Anthony Church, Red Bank, NJ
Dolan, Rev. Patrick, '95 (DEN) Holy Family Catholic Parish in Denver, Denver, CO
Dolan, Rev. Patrick G., '71 (JC) Retired. St. Bonaventure, Marceline, MO; St. Mary, Milan, MO
Dolan, Rev. Patrick J., '78 (L) Retired. Curia: Leadership Holy Redeemer, Greensburg, KY; Holy Spirit, Jamestown, KY
Dolan, Rev. Paul, '84 (RVC) Retired.
Dolan, Rev. Peter C., '54 (PMB) Retired. St. Lucie, Port St. Lucie, FL
Dolan, Rev. Robert G., *S.J.* '76 (LA) (>SJ) [MON] Sacred Heart Jesuit Center, Los Gatos, CA
Dolan, Rev. Timothy E., '83 (STP) Retired. Curia: Leadership
Dolan, Rev. William S., *S.J.* '82 (SY) [CAM] LeMoyne College Campus Ministry, Syracuse, NY; [MON] Jesuits at LeMoyne, Inc., Syracuse, NY
Dolce, Rev. Linus, *O.S.B.* '10 (STL) St. Barnabas Catholic Church, O'Fallon, MO; [MON] The Abbey of St. Mary and St. Louis, St. Louis, MO
Dolce, Rev. Thomas J., '09 (GAL) St. Martha, Porter, TX
Dolcic, Rev. Maurus, *T.O.R.* '99 (WDC) St. Blaise, Washington, DC
Dole, Rev. Jeffrey A., '14 (DUB) On Special Assignment. Graduate Studies in Rome Curia: Leadership
Dolejsi, Rev. Bryan, '06 (SEA) On Special Assignment. Dir Vocations, Seattle Curia: Leadership Holy Family, Kirkland, WA
Dolinic, Rev. Louis S., '66 (BUF) Retired. On Administrative Leave.
Dolinski, Rev. Pawel, *S.D.S.* '97 (NEW) [MON] The Salvatorian Fathers, Verona, NJ
Doll, Rev. Donald A., *S.J.* '68 (OM) [MON] Jesuit Community at Creighton University, Omaha, NE
Dollard, Rev. Mark E., '91 (MAN) Holy Trinity Parish, Plymouth, NH; [CEM] Old St. Rose of Lima Cemetery, Bethlehem, NH
Dollins, Very Rev. R. Michael, '07 (DEN) Curia: Leadership
Dollins, Very Rev. Randy Michael, '07 (DEN) St. Thomas More Catholic Parish in Centennial, Centennial, CO
Domanski, Rev. David, *OFM Cap.* '22 (WDC) (>CLV) [MON] St. Paul Friary, Cleveland, OH
Domanski, Rev. David, *OFM Cap* '22 (CLV) Cuyahoga County Jail - Clevelnad St. Agnes - Our Lady of Fatima, Cleveland, OH
Domaszewicz, Rev. Chester, '78 (VEN) Retired.
Dombroski, Rev. Dean W., '64 (GB) Retired.
Dombrowski, Rev. Francis, *O.F.M.Cap.* '59 (MIL) [MIS] Capuchin Community Services, Milwaukee, WI
Dombrowski, Rev. John, (GB) [MON] Blessed Giles Friary, Manitowoc, WI
Dombrowski, Rev. Ronald J., '72 (SAG) Retired.
Dome, Rev. Thomas J., *C.R.I.C.* '98 (LA) [MON] Canons Regular of the Immaculate Conception, Santa Paula, CA
Dome, Rev. Canon Thomas J., *C.R.I.C.* '98 (LA) Our Lady of Guadalupe, Santa Paula, CA
Domek, Rev. Kazimierz, '73 (SP) Blessed Sacrament, Tampa, FL
Domenech, Rev. Julio, (LA) Mary Immaculate, Pacoima, CA; St. Louis of France, La Puente, CA
Domfe, Rev. Joseph, *SMA* '02 (PEO) St. Paul's, Macomb, IL; St. Rose, Rushville, IL; [CAM] St. Francis of Assisi Newman Center, Macomb, IL
Domfeh-Boateng, Rev. Joseph, '95 (NY) St. Patrick, Bedford, NY
Domhoff, Rev. Ronald J., '72 (L) Retired.
Domin, Rev. Msgr. Edward R., '88 (ALN) St. Benedict's, Mohnton, PA
Domingo, Rev. Alberto, *C.M.F.* '79 (LA) Retired. [MON] Dominguez Seminary Inc., Rancho Dominguez, CA
Domingue, Rev. Kenneth J., '91 (LAF) Curia: Miscellaneous / Other Offices St. John Berchmans, Cankton, LA
Dominguez, Rev. Jesus, '02 (RCK) St. Patrick, Rochelle, IL
Dominguez, Rev. Juan Rumin, (MIA) St. Joseph, Miami Beach, FL
Dominguez, Very Rev. Julio C., '03 (CHL) Curia: Leadership [MIS] Diocesan Hispanic Ministry, Charlotte, NC
Dominguez, Rev. Ramon, '00 (FR) On Duty Outside Diocese. McLean, VA
Dominguez, Rev. Vincent, '02 (SFE) St. Charles Borromeo, Albuquerque, NM
Dominguez, Rev. Zachary, *LC* '13 (TYL) Cathedral of the Immaculate Conception, Tyler, TX
Dominic, Rev. Jaimon, '04 (CHY) St. Laurence O'Toole, Laramie, WY
Dominic, Rev. Joseph, *S.A.C.* '80 (MIL) Saint Mary's Congregation, Mayville, WI; St. Andrews Congregation, Lomira, WI; St. Theresa's Congregation, Theresa, WI; [MON] Pallotti House, Milwaukee, WI
Dominic, Rev. Rohan, *C.M.F.* '92 (NEW) St. Joseph, Jersey City, NJ
Dominic, Rev. Sunny, '94 (SC) Holy Name, Rock Rapids, IA; St. Mary, Larchwood, IA
Dominik, Rev. Kevin J., '88 (PIT) St. Andrew the Apostle, Donora, PA
Dominik, Rev. Stanley J., '58 (GRY) Retired.
Dominique, Rev. Todd M., '94 (TOL) Curia: Advisory Boards, Commissions, Committees, and Councils St. Caspar, Wauseon, OH; St. Wendelin, Fostoria, OH
Domme, Rev. Edward C., '79 (SFE) Our Lady of the Assumption-Albuquerque, Albuquerque, NM
Dommer, Rev. Ian, *O.S.B.* '79 (SCL) [MON] St. John's Abbey, of the Order of St. Benedict, Collegeville, MN
Dompke, Rev. Ramon, *C.Ss.R.* '64 (CHI) Retired. St. Michael in Old Town, Chicago, IL; [MON] The Redemptorist Fathers of Chicago, Chicago, IL
Domurat, Rev. Thomas S., '79 (BO) Most Holy Redeemer, Boston, MA
Donahue, Rev. Aidan, (HRT) Precious Blood Parish Corporation, Milford, CT
Donahue, Rev. Aidan N., '86 (HRT) Curia: Parish Services
Donahue, Rev. Msgr. Brian G., '83 (FAR) St. Anthony's Church of Fairmount, Fairmount, ND; St. Philip's Church of Hankinson, Hankinson, ND
Donahue, Rev. Cecil J., *O.S.B.* '54 (MAN) Retired. [MON] St. Anselm Abbey, Manchester, NH
Donahue, Rev. Charles, *C.S.P.* '05 (KNX) Immaculate Conception, Knoxville, TN; [CEM] Calvary Cemetery, Knoxville, TN; [MON] Paulist Fathers (Missionary Society of St. Paul the Apostle), Knoxville, TN
Donahue, Rev. Charles, *C.S.P.* '05 (KNX) Curia: Leadership; Offices and Directors [MON] Paulist Fathers (Missionary Society of St. Paul the Apostle), Knoxville, TN
Donahue, Rev. Denis M., '90 (ARL) St. Philip, Falls Church, VA
Donahue, Rev. Eugene L., *S.J.* '70 (GB) [RTR] Jesuit Retreat House, Oshkosh, WI
Donahue, Rev. John F., '06 (PIT) Saint Luke the Evangelist, Sewickley, PA
Donahue, Rev. John G., '60 (STP) Retired.
Donahue, Rev. John R., *S.J.* '64 (BAL) Retired. [MIS] Colombiere Jesuit Community, Baltimore, MD
Donahue, Rev. L. Scott, '82 (CHI) [PRE] Mission of Our Lady of Mercy-Mercy Home for Boys and Girls, Chicago, IL
Donahue, Rev. Matthew, '21 (KNX) On Special Assignment.
Donahue, Rev. Scott, '82 (CHI) Curia: Social Services
Donahue, Rev. Stephen D., '86 (IND) St. Michael Catholic Church, Cannelton, Inc., Tell City, IN; St. Pius V Catholic Church, Troy, Inc., Tell City, IN
Donahue, Rev. Timothy C., '00 (SAV) On Leave.
Donahue, Rev. William P., '86 (SR) Curia: Leadership
Donahue, Rev. William P., '86 (SR) Curia: Leadership St. Vincent de Paul High School, Petaluma, CA
Donahue, Rev. Williams, '86 (SR) Pastor of St. Vincent de Paul Catholic Church of Petaluma, A Corporation Sole, Petaluma, CA
Donahugh, Rev. Donald E., '62 (RCK) Retired.
Donajkowski, Rev. Charles G., '91 (GLD) Curia: Leadership Sacred Heart of Oscoda, Oscoda, MI
Donald, Rev. Michael L., '72 (STL) St. Joseph Catholic Church, Clayton, Clayton, MO; St. Monica Catholic Church, Creve Coeur, MO
Donaldson, Rev. Raymond, *SJ* '05 (PH) The Gesu School, Philadelphia, PA; [MON] Arrupe Jesuit Community, Merion Station, PA
Donaldson, Rev. Thomas, *C.Ss.R.* '77 (STL) St. Alphonsus Liguori Catholic Church, St. Louis, MO; [MON] Redemptorist Fathers, St. Louis, MO
Donat, Rev. Robert J., '66 (SB) Retired.
Donatelli, Rev. Gene, *S.J.* '82 (DET) Retired. [MON] Colombiere Center, Clarkston, MI
Donato, Rev. Carlos, (MEM) St. Francis of Assisi, Cordova, TN
Donato, Rev. John, *C.S.C.* '91 (P) [MON] Priests of Holy Cross in Oregon, Inc., Portland, OR
Donato Da Silva, Rev. Carlos, '17 (MEM) Curia: Offices and Directors
Dondanville, Rev. Joseph, '95 (PEO) Holy Family, Lincoln, IL; St. Patrick, Elkhart, IL
Donelan, Rev. Jeb S., '11 (ARL) San Francisco de Asis, Banica, Arlington, VA; San Jose, Pedro Santana, Arlington, VA
Doner, Rev. Roy, '81 (SAC) Retired.
Dong, Rev. Quang Minh, '91 (OAK) Curia: Leadership Immaculate Heart of Mary, Brentwood, CA
Dong Ping, Rev. Li F., (CHI) St. Mother Teresa of Calcutta, Chicago, IL
Dongo, Rev. Bruno, *A.J.* '01 (ALN) [MIS] Apostles of Jesus, Northampton, PA
Donia, Rev. John E., '07 (PH) Bishop Shanahan High School, Downingtown, PA; St. Joseph, Downingtown, PA
Donini, Rev. Leone, '95 (NEW) On Duty Outside Diocese. c/o Seminaire Redemptoris Mater, La Seyne sur mer
Donio, Rev. Frank, *S.A.C.* '94 (NEW) [MIS] Pallottine Intra-Community Operating Corporation, Fairview, NJ
Donio, Rev. Frank S., *S.A.C.* (WDC) [MIS] Catholic Apostolate Center, Inc., West Hyattsville, MD
Donio, Rev. Frank S., *S.A.C.* '94 (WDC) [SEM] Pallottine Seminary at Green Hill, West Hyattsville, MD
Donio, Rev. Thomas S., '95 (CAM) Chap, New Jersey State Psychiatric Hosp, Hammonton
Donis, Rev. Agustin Alonso Sigaran, '16 (R) Saint Mary, Mother of the Church Catholic Parish of Garner, Garner, NC
Donish, Rev. Peter M., '70 (PSC) Retired.
Donlan, Rev. Paul A., '62 (POD) Curia: Clergy and Religious Services
Donlan, Rev. Paul A., '62 (LA) [MIS] Tilden Study Center, Los Angeles, CA
Donlan, Rev. Phillip, *CP* '22 (SAC) [MON] Christ the King Passionist Retreat Center, Inc. (The Passionists (Chicago, IL)), Citrus Heights, CA
Donley, Rev. Christopher D., '11 (PIT) Point Park Univ, Pittsburgh Divine Mercy, Pittsburgh, PA
Donlon, Rev. James I., '75 (ALB) Retired. Curia: Leadership; Offices and Directors
Donnarumma, Rev. Francesco, '05 (NEW) Holy Family, Nutley, NJ
Donnay, Rev. David, *O.S.C.* '01 (SCL) [EFT] Crosier International Trust for Religious Life and Service, Onamia, MN
Donnelly, Rev. J. Patrick, *S.J.* '65 (MIL) [MON] St. Camillus Jesuit Community (Society of Jesus, USA Midwest Province), Wauwatosa, WI
Donnelly, Rev. Msgr. Joseph T., '71 (HRT) Retired.
Donnelly, Rev. Msgr. Lawrence Edward, '49 (LA) Retired.
Donnelly, Rev. Michael, *S.S.C.* '63 (OM) Retired. [MON] Missionary Society of St. Columban, St. Columbans, NE
Donnelly, Rev. Michael J., *S.S.C.* '63 (PRO) Retired. [MON] St. Columban's Retirement House (St. Columban's Foreign Mission Society), Bristol, RI
Donnelly, Rev. Robert, '91 (ALB) Retired.
Donnelly, Rev. Sean J., '82 (CLV) Immaculate Conception, Madison, OH
Donnelly, Rev. Thomas F., *M.M.* '57 (NY) Retired.
Donnelly, Rev. William, '64 (ROC) Retired.
Donnelly, Rev. William, *M.M.* '65 (NY) Retired. [MON] Maryknoll Fathers and Brothers (Catholic Foreign Mission Society of America, Inc.), Ossining, NY
Donnelly, Rev. William J., *MM* (ELP) Retired.
Donnelly, Rev. William J., *M.M.* '65 (CHI) Retired.
Dono, Rev. Abram E., *S.T.* '64 (TUC) (>PAT) [MON] Shrine of St. Joseph, Stirling, NJ
D'Onofrio, Rev. Joseph J., '05 (BO) St. Lucy, Methuen, MA; St. Monica, Methuen, MA
Donoghue, Rev. Denis G., *S.J.* '05 (BGP) [MON] The Fairfield Jesuit Community-Fairfield University, Fairfield, CT
Donoghue, Rev. Patrick, '82 (P) St. Anthony, Portland, OR
Donohoe, Rev. Patrick K., '82 (CC) St. John of the

Cross, Orange Grove, TX
Donohoe, Rev. Richard E., '84 (BIR) Our Lady Queen of the Universe, Birmingham, AL
Donohoe, Rev. Stephen S., '92 (BO) Curia: Consultative Bodies St. Catherine of Siena, Norwood, MA
Donohoe, Rev. Thomas P., '52 (BO) Retired.
Donohoo, Rev. Daniel B., (IND) Retired.
Donohue, Rev. John J., '73 (NEW) Retired.
Donohue, Rev. Msgr. Michael T., '75 (NOR) Retired.
Donohue, Rev. Patrick W., '75 (NEW) Retired. St. Mary, Dumont, NJ
Donohue, Rev. Paul, *M.C.C.J.* '75 (NEW) St. Lucy, Newark, NJ; [MON] Comboni Missionaries of the Heart of Jesus (Verona Fathers), Newark, NJ
Donohue, Rev. Peter M., *O.S.A.* '79 (PH) [COL] Villanova University, Villanova, PA; [MON] Fray de Leon Community, Villanova, PA
Donohue, Rev. Raymond A., '85 (BUF) Retired.
Donovan, Rev. Bernard Thomas, '05 (SFD) Curia: (>MO) Offices and Directors St. Anthony of Padua, Quincy, IL
Donovan, Rev. Charles, *C.Ss.R.* (CHL) St. James, Concord, NC
Donovan, Rev. Dennis, *S.D.B.* '83 (NY) [RTR] Don Bosco Retreat Center and Marian Shrine, Stony Point, NY; [RTR] Marian Shrine, Stony Point, NY
Donovan, Rev. Dennis, *S.D.B.* (NEW) [MIS] Salesians of Don Bosco, South Orange, NJ
Donovan, Rev. Edward M., '04 (NEW) Queen of Peace, North Arlington, NJ
Donovan, Rev. J. Michael, '65 (SY) Retired.
Donovan, Rev. James, *S.J.* '13 (RVC) St. Anthony, Oceanside, NY
Donovan, Rev. James J., '87 (CHI) St. Barnabas, Chicago, IL
Donovan, Rev. John P., '86 (SY) Curia: Canonical Services; Leadership Sacred Heart, Cicero, NY
Donovan, Rev. Joseph J., *M.M.* '79 (NY) Retired. [MON] Maryknoll Fathers and Brothers (Catholic Foreign Mission Society of America, Inc.), Ossining, NY
Donovan, Rev. Kevin G., '88 (HRT) The Church of St. Dunstan of Glastonbury Corporation, Glastonbury, CT
Donovan, Rev. Michael, *O.de.M.* '00 (BUF) (>COL) Holy Family, Columbus, OH
Donovan, Very Rev. Richard, *O.F.M.* (ALB) Curia: Leadership St. Anthony of Padua, Troy, NY
Donovan, Rev. Richard R., '58 (RVC) Retired. Our Lady of Lourdes, Malverne, NY
Donovan, Rev. Sean T., '12 (TLS) SS. Peter and Paul, Tulsa, OK
Donovan, Rev. Tim, (ORG) Santa Margarita Catholic High School, Rancho Santa Margarita, CA
Donovan, Rev. William G., '94 (PH) St. John Baptist Vianney, Gladwyne, PA
Donton, Rev. Joseph P., '91 (PEO) Holy Cross, Champaign, IL
Doody, Rev. Michael J., *S.J.* '78 (BGP) [MON] The Fairfield Jesuit Community-Fairfield University, Fairfield, CT
Doody, Rev. Msgr. Peter J., '71 (PAT) Retired.
Dool, Rev. Franz C., '11 (CLV) On Leave.
Dooley, Rev. Kevin F., '01 (MAD) Retired.
Dooley, Rev. Matthew R., '09 (NEW) Church of the Little Flower, Berkeley Heights, NJ; Oratory Preparatory School, Summit, NJ; St. Joseph, Maplewood, NJ
Dooley, Rev. Michael D., *S.J.* '85 (STL) [MON] Leo Brown Jesuit Community, St. Louis, MO; [MON] USA Central & Southern Province, Society of Jesus, St. Louis, MO
Dooley, Rev. Msgr. Peter C., '76 (RVC) Retired. St. Philip Neri, Northport, NY
Dooley, Rev. Sean, '15 (COL) Our Lady of Peace, Columbus, OH
Dooley, Rev. Thomas V., '91 (DM) Curia: Offices and Directors St. Joseph, Winterset, IA; St. Patrick Catholic Church, Irish Settlement, Cumming, IA
Dooling, Rev. Patrick, '82 (MRY) Retired. Cathedral of San Carlos Borromeo, Monterey, CA
Dooner, Rev. William B., '70 (PH) Retired. Curia: Advisory Boards, Commissions, Committees, and Councils St. Philip Neri, Lafayette Hill, PA
Dooner, Rev. William B., '70 (PH) Retired. Our Lady of Grace, Penndel, PA
Dora, Rev. Msgr. Peter A., '72 (ATL) Retired.
Dorado, Rev. Jaime, '93 (PMB) St. Anastasia, Fort Pierce, FL
Doran, Rev. Msgr. Austin C., '71 (LA) Retired.
Doran, Rev. Brian D., '78 (LA) Retired.
Doran, Rev. Msgr. Edward P., '81 (BRK) Retired. Curia: Leadership; Pastoral Services Parish of Transfiguration – Saint Stanislaus Kostka, Maspeth, NY
Doran, Rev. James, *O.M.V.* (BO) [MIS] St. Francis Chapel, Boston, MA; [MON] Oblate Residence (St. Joseph House), Milton, MA
Doran, Rev. James, '88 (SAM) St. Joseph, Waterville, ME
Doran, Rev. James, *O.S.B.* '00 (WOR) [MON] Benedictine Monks, St. Benedict Abbey, Still River, MA; [RTR] Benedictine Monks, St. Benedict Abbey, Still River, MA
Doran, Rev. Msgr. John E., '72 (NEW) Retired.
Doran, Rev. Msgr. John E., '66 (WOR) Retired. Curia: Finance
Doran, Rev. Joseph A., '10 (GAL) Sts. Peter & Paul, Bellville, TX
Dorantes, Rev. Manuel, '10 (CHI) Curia: Leadership St. Mary of the Lake and Our Lady of Lourdes Parish, Chicago, IL
Dorau, Rev. Daniel R., '17 (DAV) St. Boniface Church of Farmington, Iowa, Farmington, IA; St. James Church of St. Paul, Iowa, St. Paul, IA; St. John Church of Houghton, Iowa, Houghton, IA; St. Mary Church of West Point, Iowa, West Point, IA
Dorcey, Rev. Joseph, *C.Ss.R.* '79 (CHI) [MON] The Redemptorist Fathers of Chicago, Chicago, IL; [MON] The Redemptorists/Denver Province, Chicago, IL
Dorcey, Rev. Theodore, *C.Ss.R.* '12 (CHI) [MON] The Redemptorists/Denver Province, Chicago, IL
Dore, Rev. M.J. Bernard, '82 (PRO) St. Paul's Church Corporation, Foster, Foster, RI
Dore, Rev. Robert, '89 (JKS) St. Michael, Vicksburg, MS
Dorelus, Rev. Patrick, '18 (BRK) On Academic Leave.
Dorham, Rev. Elias, '20 (NTN) Holy Transfiguration, McLean, VA
Dorhauer, Rev. C. Robert, '63 (STL) Retired.
Doris, Rev. John A., '75 (SCR) Curia: Leadership Our Lady of Mount Carmel Parish, Dunmore, PA
Dorival, Rev. Samson, (SPC) Sacred Heart, Poplar Bluff, MO; St. Benedict, Doniphan, MO
Dormer, Rev. David J., '77 (SCR) Retired.
Dormevil, Rev. Guy, (BGP) Curia: Consultative Bodies; Leadership Notre Dame du Perpetuel Secours Corporation, Stamford, CT
Dormido, Rev. Arecio P., '83 (NY) Chap, Downstate Corr Fac, Fishkill
Dorn, Rev. Louis E., '72 (JC) Retired. Sacred Heart, Vandalia, MO
Dorn, Rev. Michael, *OFM Cap.* '21 (CHI) (>GF) Our Lady of Loretto, Lodge Grass, MT; (>GF) St. Dennis, Crow Agency, MT
Dorn, Rev. Thomas E., '03 (CIN) St. Mary, Bethel, OH; St. Peter, New Richmond, OH; St. Thomas More, Cincinnati, OH
Dornak, Rev. Melvin, '92 (AUS) Holy Rosary, Caldwell, TX; St. Mary, Caldwell, TX
Dornbos, Rev. William, '68 (HEL) Retired. Holy Spirit Parish: Series 219, LLC, Butte, MT
Dorner, Rev. Dennis, '13 (ATL) Immaculate Conception Catholic Church, Atlanta, Inc., Atlanta, GA
Dorner, Rev. Joseph, '95 (GB) Curia: Advisory Boards, Commissions, Committees, and Councils St. Bernadette, Appleton, WI
Dorner, Rev. William E., '07 (PIT) Curia: Tribunal
Dorney, Rev. Msgr. Dennis C., '67 (TLS) Retired. Church of St. Mary, Tulsa, OK
Dorniak, Rev. Joseph, (PMB) St. Mark, Boynton Beach, FL
Dornquast, Rev. Steven (Chuck), '15 (SP) Curia: Leadership; Pastoral Services
Dorosh, Rev. Emilian, '11 (STF) St. George High School, New York, NY (>STN) St. Josaphat, Warren, MI
Dorr, Rev. James F., *C.M.* '58 (BRK) (>PH) [MON] Congregation of the Mission, Philadelphia, PA
Dorr, Rev. Jeffrey R, *S.J.* '21 (DET) Gesu Parish Detroit, Detroit, MI; [MON] Jesuit Community at the University of Detroit Mercy, Detroit, MI
Dorrego, Rev. Paolo, *P.E.S.* '17 (SAC) Pastor of St. Anthony Parish, Walnut Grove, a corporation sole, Walnut Grove, CA; Pastor of St. Therese Parish, Isleton, a corporation sole, Isleton, CA
Dorrmann, Rev. William J., '55 (CIN) Retired. St. John the Baptist, Harrison, OH
Dorsa, Rev. Anthony, *FSSP* (SCR) St. Michael's, Scranton, PA
Dorsch, Rev. Henry L., '68 (SPR) Retired.
Dorsch, Rev. Larry W., '75 (WH) Retired.
Dorsey, Rev. Christopher, '15 (ORL) On Duty Outside Diocese.
Dorsey, Rev. Christopher, (MO) Curia: Offices and Directors
Dorsey, Rev. Daniel, '78 (CIN) [MON] Headquarters of Glenmary Home Missioners (The Home Missioners of America), Fairfield, OH
Dorsey, Rev. Garrett D., '59 (PIT) Retired.
Dorton, Rev. John, '70 (DM) Retired. Curia: Offices and Directors
Dorula, Rev. Douglas E., (GBG) On Administrative Leave.
Dorula, Rev. Douglas E., '02 (GBG) On Administrative Leave. SS. Cyril and Methodius, Fairchance, PA; St. Hubert, Point Marion, PA; [NUR] Neumann House, Greensburg, PA
Dorvil, Rev. Pierre A, *S.M.M.* '84 (SP) Immaculate Conception Haitian Catholic Mission, ,
Dorwart, Rev. William, *C.S.C.* (FTW) [MON] Congregation of Holy Cross, United States Province of Priests and Brothers, Notre Dame, IN
Dory, Rev. Michael, '76 (GB) Chap, Lt Cmdr, Surprise, AZ
dos Reis, Rev. Jose Q., '64 (PRO) [MON] St. John Vianney Residence, Providence, RI
dos Santos, Rev. Antonio, *C.S.S.* '90 (BO) St. Joseph Parish, Kingston, MA; St. Mary, Plymouth, MA
Dos Santos, Rev. Joseph E.S., '10 (NEW) Curia: Offices and Directors Our Lady of Fatima, Newark, NJ
Dos Santos, Rev. Joseph Emmanuel Simon, (STA) Queen of Peace Catholic Community, Gainesville, FL
Dos Santos, Rev. Kenneth, *M.I.C.* '10 (SPR) [MON] Congregation of Marian Fathers of The Immaculate Conception of the Most Blessed Virgin Mary, Stockbridge, MA
Dos Santos, Rev. Stephen, *C.PP.S.* '06 (CIN) [MON] Society of the Precious Blood, United States Province, Inc., Dayton, OH
Dos Santos, Rev. Tarcisio, *S.D.B.* '89 (NY) Parish of St. John Bosco, Port Chester, NY
Dosch, Rev. Jordan, (BIS) Curia: Offices and Directors
Dosch, Rev. Michael Mary, *O.P.* '05 (CIN) St. Gertrude, Cincinnati, OH; [MON] St. Gertrude Priory, Cincinnati, OH; [SEM] Dominican Novitiate, Cincinnati, OH
Dosdos, Rev. Siegfred, (HON) St. Benedict, Captain Cook, HI
Doseck, Rev. David A., '17 (CIN) St. John the Evangelist, New Paris, OH; St. Mary, Camden, OH; St. Mary Church, Oxford, OH; Visitation of the Blessed Virgin Mary, Eaton, OH
Dosen, Rev. Anthony, *CM* '82 (STL) [MON] Congregation of the Mission Vincentian Fathers Lazarist Residence, St. Louis, MO
Doss, Rev. Alex Anthony Maria, *H.G.N.* '08 (PRT) [RTR] Christian Life Center, Frenchville, ME
Doss, Rev. Arockia, (BLX) St. Mary, Gautier, MS
Dosyak, Rev. Mykhaylo, '95 (STF) St. John-the-Baptist, Fall River, MA; St. Michael, Woonsocket, RI
Dotson, Rev. Msgr. Paul T., '68 (LA) St. Lawrence Martyr, Redondo Beach, CA
Dotson, Rev. William F., '12 (STL) St. Charles Borromeo Catholic Church, St. Charles, MO
Doty, Rev. Craig A., '97 (LIN) Curia: Leadership St. Mary's, Denton, NE
Dou, Rev. Paul Ming, *SOLT* '94 (CC) [MON] Society of Our Lady of the Most Holy Trinity, Corpus Christi, TX
Dougherty, Rev. C. Peter, '61 (LAN) Retired.
Dougherty, Rev. Charles, *C.P.* '68 (NY) Retired. [MON] The Congregation of the Passion - St. Paul of the Cross Province, Jamaica, NY
Dougherty, Rev. Charles T., *C.P.* '68 (SFE) Retired.
Dougherty, Rev. Edward C.A., *S.J.* (PH) Retired.
Dougherty, Rev. Edward M., *M.M.* '79 (NY) Cathedral of St. Patrick, New York, NY; [MON] Maryknoll Fathers and Brothers (Catholic Foreign Mission Society of America, Inc.), Ossining, NY
Dougherty, Rev. Hugh J., '69 (PH) Retired.
Dougherty, Rev. James, '67 (JOL) Retired.
Dougherty, Rev. James R., '68 (BEL) Retired.
Dougherty, Rev. John, (AUS) St. Ignatius Martyr, Austin, TX
Dougherty, Rev. Joseph V., '05 (E) St. Eulalia, Coudersport, PA; St. Gabriel the Archangel, Port Allegany, PA
Dougherty, Rev. Matthew, *O. Praem.* '15 (GB) [MON] St. Norbert Abbey, De Pere, WI
Dougherty, Rev. Msgr. Paul V., '80 (PH) On Special Assignment. Chap, Apostolate Deaf Persons, St Margaret Rectory, Narberth Curia: Advisory Boards, Commissions, Committees, and Councils; Evangelization St. Margaret, Narberth, PA
Dougherty, Rev. Terrence, *O.C.D.* '63 (BO) [MON] Carmelite Monastery, Boston, MA
Dougherty, Rev. Terrence, *O.C.D.* (WOR) Our Lady of the Angels, Worcester, MA
Doughty, Rev. Rees W., '94 (NY) St. Joseph, New Windsor, NY; St. Marianne Cope, Cornwall-on-Hudson, NY
Douglas, Rev. Gordon W., '68 (SEA) Retired.
Douglas, Rev. Norman K., '74 (CLV) St. Vincent de Paul

Parish, Akron, OH
Doussan, Rev. Msgr. Douglas A., '60 (NO) Retired.
Doustou, Rev. Kyle L., '14 (PRT) Curia: Consultative Bodies; Offices and Directors Parish of the Resurrection of the Lord, Old Town, ME; [CAM] University of Maine, Orono, ME
Dovari, Rev. Joseph, (WIL) St. Ann, Bethany Beach, DE
Dover, Rev. Edward R., '85 (LA) Beatitudes of Our Lord, La Mirada, CA
Dovzhuk, Rev. Mykola, '89 (STN) Protection of the Mother of God, Houston, TX
Dow, Rev. Robert, *FSSP* '14 (ATL) St. Francis de Sales Catholic Church, Mableton, Inc., Mableton, GA
Dowalgo, Rev. Mitch, *C.S.B.* '82 (GAL) [MON] Keon House, Houston, TX
Dowd, Rev. Barry G., '82 (BUR) Retired.
Dowd, Rev. Brian P., '91 (BRK) St. Patrick, Brooklyn, NY; [CCH] Irish Ministry, ,
Dowd, Rev. Robert A., *C.S.C.* '94 (FTW) [COL] University of Notre Dame Du Lac, Notre Dame, IN; [MON] Holy Cross Community, Corby Hall, University of Notre Dame, Notre Dame, IN
Dowd, Rev. William J., '67 (NEW) Retired.
Dowdel, Rev. Lawrence J., '91 (LA) St. Louis of France, La Puente, CA; St. Mary Magdalen, Camarillo, CA
Dowds, Rev. James, *C.Ss.R.* '85 (FRS) Chap, China Lake Naval Air Weapons Station
Dowdy, Rev. James H., '69 (BAL) Retired.
Dower, Rev. Daniel P., '84 (TYL) St. Mary, Longview, TX; [EFT] Longview Catholic School Endowment Fund, Longview, TX
Dowling, Rev. Edward T., *S.J.* '69 (NY) [MON] Murray-Weigel Hall (A Jesuit Community at Murray-Weigel Hall and Kohlmann Hall), Bronx, NY
Dowling, Rev. Finbarr, *O.S.B.* '68 (STL) [MON] The Abbey of St. Mary and St. Louis, St. Louis, MO
Dowling, Rev. John J., *O.S.A.* '68 (CHI) St. Turibius, Chicago, IL
Dowling, Rev. John R., '83 (KNX) St. Augustine, Signal Mountain, TN
Dowling, Rev. Kevin, '80 (NSH) Retired.
Dowling, Rev. Lawrence R., '91 (CHI) Curia: Leadership St. Agatha and St. Martin De Porres Parish, Chicago, IL; [EFT] Foundation for Adult Catechetical Teaching Aids, Mundelein, IL
Dowling, Rev. Patrick, '82 (JC) Retired.
Dowling, Rev. Ray, '61 (AUS) Retired.
Dowling, Rev. Timothy, '93 (PAT) Curia: Leadership Good Shepherd, Andover, NJ
Downer, Rev. Jason G, *S.J.* '20 (SY) [MON] Jesuits at LeMoyne, Inc., Syracuse, NY
Downer, Rev. Jason G., *S.J.* (CHK) Curia: Advisory Boards, Commissions, Committees, and Councils
Downes, Rev. Msgr. Stephen N., '66 (LA) Retired. Our Lady of Mount Carmel, Santa Barbara, CA
Downey, Rev. Christopher J., '09 (AUS) St. Joseph, Killeen, TX; [EFT] Diocese of Austin Pension Plan and Trust, Austin, TX
Downey, Rev. David C., '03 (PMB) St. Therese de Lisieux, Wellington, FL
Downey, Rev. James, (DM) St. Luke the Evangelist Catholic Church, Ankeny, IA
Downey, Rev. Michael D., '72 (SAC) Retired. Pastor of Holy Spirit Parish, Fairfield, a corporation sole, Fairfield, CA
Downing, Rev. Aaron, '21 (RCK) Curia: Offices and Directors St. Bridget, Loves Park, IL
Downing, Rev. Andrew, (NEW) [COL] Saint Peter University, Jersey City, NJ; [MON] Jesuits of Saint Peter College, Inc., Jersey City, NJ
Downing, Rev. Luke, (WCH) Church of Blessed Sacrament, Wichita, KS; St. Francis of Assisi, Wichita, KS
Downing, Rev. Sean Richard, *SM* '08 (STL) [MON] Maryland Avenue Marianist Community, St. Louis, MO
Downs, Rev. Bruce, '94 (PHX) All Saints Roman Catholic Newman Center, Tempe, AZ; [CAM] All Saints Catholic Newman Center Tempe, Tempe, AZ
Downs, Rev. Gregory Todd, '91 (LAF) Retired.
Downs, Rev. James, *M.S.A.* '02 (NOR) [MON] Society of the Missionaries of the Holy Apostles, Cromwell, CT
Downs, Rev. James A., (E) Retired.
Downs, Rev. John L., '55 (OG) Retired. The Parish of the Visitation and St. Raymond, Norfolk, NY
Downs, Rev. L. James, '66 (WDC) Retired.
Dowsey, Rev. Gary, '82 (SP) Curia: Pastoral Services
Dowsey, Rev. Gary, '80 (SP) Curia: Pastoral Services St. Peter the Apostle Catholic Church in Trinity, Inc., Trinity, FL
Doyen, Rev. Mitchell S., '91 (STL) St. John the Baptist Catholic Church, St. Louis, St. Louis, MO
Doyle, Rev. Bradley A., '15 (BR) Congregation Of Our Lady Of Mt. Carmel Roman Catholic Church, St. Francisville, LA
Doyle, Rev. Brendan P., '63 (JC) Retired.
Doyle, Rev. Dennis J., '65 (STL) Retired. Christ, Prince of Peace Catholic Church, Manchester, MO
Doyle, Rev. Dennis M., '92 (STL) Curia: Leadership St. Vincent Catholic Church, Dutzow, Marthasville, MO
Doyle, Rev. Eugene, '76 (SCL) Retired.
Doyle, Rev. Francis J., *O.S.A.* '70 (PH) [MON] St. Thomas Monastery, Villanova, PA
Doyle, Rev. Francis W., '10 (JC) Curia: Faith Formation St. Joseph, Slater, MO; St. Peter Catholic Church Marshall, Marshall, MO
Doyle, Rev. Msgr. James Michael, '57 (SFS) Retired.
Doyle, Rev. Msgr. Jerald A., '69 (BGP) Retired.
Doyle, Rev. John, (GRY) Sacred Heart Apostolic School, Inc., Rolling Prairie, IN
Doyle, Rev. John J., '58 (JOL) Retired.
Doyle, Rev. John J., '70 (CHI) Retired.
Doyle, Rev. Joseph C., '72 (NEW) St. Anne, Fair Lawn, NJ
Doyle, Rev. Kenneth, '66 (ALB) Curia: Offices and Directors
Doyle, Rev. Kennth, '66 (ALB) Retired.
Doyle, Rev. Kevin, '08 (SFS) Saint Charles Borromeo Parish of Sanborn County, Artesian, SD; Saint Joseph Parish of Jerauld County (St. Joseph's Catholic Church of Wessington Springs), Wessington Springs, SD; Saint Wilfrid Parish of Sanborn County (St. Wilfrid Church, Woonsocket, SD), Woonsocket, SD
Doyle, Rev. Lawrence Michael, *O.S.M.* '65 (CHI) [MON] Assumption Priory, Chicago, IL
Doyle, Rev. Luke, '21 (KCK) St. Michael the Archangel, Overland Park, KS
Doyle, Rev. Michael, *O.S.M.* '65 (CHI) Assumption of the Blessed Virgin Mary, Chicago, IL
Doyle, Rev. Msgr. Michael J., '59 (CAM) The Church of Sacred Heart, Camden, NJ
Doyle, Rev. Michael J., '59 (CAM) Retired.
Doyle, Rev. Michael J., '85 (BO) Curia: Consultative Bodies St. Mary of the Annunciation, Danvers, MA
Doyle, Rev. Michael M., '89 (NU) St. Leo, St. Leo, MN; St. Peter, Canby, MN
Doyle, Rev. Oliver, '78 (GF) [COL] University of Providence, Great Falls, MT
Doyle, Rev. Paul F., *C.S.C.* '77 (FTW) [MIS] Holy Cross House, Notre Dame, IN
Doyle, Rev. Msgr. Seamus, '56 (MIA) Retired.
Doyle, Rev. Thomas, '08 (RCK) St. John the Baptist, Savanna, IL
Doyle, Rev. Thomas, '84 (BRK) Curia: Organizations (affiliated, inter-Diocesan, miscellaneous/other) Good Shepherd, Brooklyn, NY
Doyle, Rev. Thomas D., '82 (BUF) Retired. Curia: Consultative Bodies
Doyle, Rev. Thomas J., '08 (RCK) SS. John and Catherine, Mount Carroll, IL
Doyle, Rev. Thomas R., '62 (DAV) Retired. [MON] St. Vincent Center, Davenport, IA
Doyle, Rev. Thomas V., '82 (BRK) [MIS] Confraternity of the Precious Blood, Brooklyn, NY
Dozier, Rev. Daniel, (PHX) Curia: (>HPM) Offices and Directors
Dozier, Rev. Daniel, (HPM) St. George Byzantine Catholic Church, Olympia, WA
Drabik, Rev. Richard, *M.I.C.* '60 (SPR) [MON] Congregation of Marian Fathers of The Immaculate Conception of the Most Blessed Virgin Mary, Stockbridge, MA
Dragga, Rev. Thomas M., '83 (CLV) Chap, Cuyahoga Hills Juvenile Corr Fac Curia: Advisory Boards, Commissions, Committees, and Councils; Clergy and Religious Services Resurrection of Our Lord, Solon, OH
Drago, Friar Calogero, *OFM Conv.* '75 (AUS) Cristo Rey, Austin, TX
Drake, Rev. Timothy A., '71 (RIC) Retired. St. Bernard, Gate City, VA
Drance, Rev. George W., *S.J.* '95 (NY) [MON] Jesuit Community at Fordham University, New York, NY
Draper, Rev. Andrew, (ALT) [MON] St. Francis Friary at Mount Assisi, Loretto, PA
Draper, Rev. Timothy J., '12 (RCK) St. Anne, Dixon, IL
Draugialis, Rev. Josef, '63 (LA) Our Lady of Perpetual Help, Los Nietos, CA
Drea, Rev. Michael E., '04 (BO) On Duty Outside Diocese.
Drees, Rev. John M., '13 (STP) St. Joseph's, Taylors Falls, MN; The Church of Saint Francis Xavier, Shafer, MN; [CEM] St. Francis Xavier Cemetery, Taylors Falls, MN
Dreese, Rev. Msgr. John J., '59 (COL) Retired.
Dreger, Rev. Msgr. Francis X., '51 (PH) Retired.
Dreher, Rev. John D., '64 (PRO) Retired. [MON] St. John Vianney Residence, Providence, RI
Dreiling, Rev. Msgr. Raymond C., '75 (FRS) Shrine of St. Therese, Fresno, CA
Dreisbach, Rev. Charles V., '59 (BAK) Retired.
Drennan, Rev. Jimmy, (SAT) St. Catherine, San Antonio, TX
Drennan, Rev. Jimmy David, '96 (SAT) St. Margaret Mary, San Antonio, TX
Drennan, Rev. Theodore P., (SB) St. Thomas the Apostle, Riverside, CA
Drennen, Rev. Christopher J., *O.S.A.* '83 (PH) Malvern Preparatory School for Boys, Malvern, PA; [MON] Augustinian Friars (O.S.A.), Malvern, PA
Drenzek, Rev. Peter C., '69 (MIL) Retired. Good Shepherd Congregation, Menomonee Falls, WI
Dresden, Rev. Shawn, '14 (LAV) Christ the King, Las Vegas, NV
Dressler, Rev. Paul, *OFM Cap.* '99 (PIT) [MON] St. Augustine Friary, Pittsburgh, PA
Dressman, Rev. Richard E., '72 (CIN) Retired.
Dreves, Rev. Mark, (SAT) Curia: Administration Holy Spirit, San Antonio, TX
Dreves, Rev. Mark, '95 (LEX) On Duty Outside Diocese. Our Lady of Perpetual Help, Selma, TX
Drevitch, Rev. Michael, (SCR) On Administrative Leave.
Drew, Rev. Andrew, *O.F.M.Cap.* '61 (NY) Retired.
Drew, Rev. James F., '74 (RVC) St. Joseph's, Hewlett, NY
Drew, Rev. Kevin, '12 (KC) Immaculate Conception, Richmond, MO; St. Ann, Excelsior Springs, MO
Drewniak, Rev. Stanley, '78 (JOL) Sacred Heart, Kinsman, IL; St. Lawrence, South Wilmington, IL
Drewniak, Rev. Stanley, (JOL) St. Mary, Reddick, IL
Dreyer, Rev. Nathaniel, *I.V.E.* '15 (WDC) St. James, Mount Rainier, MD
Driesch, Rev. David, *O.Praem.* (WIL) [MON] Immaculate Conception Priory of the Canons Regular of Premontre, Middletown, DE
Driesch, Rev. David, *O.Praem.* '82 (PH) [COL] Cabrini University (Missionary Sisters of the Sacred Heart of Jesus), Radnor, PA; [MON] Daylesford Abbey, Inc., Paoli, PA
Drilling, Rev. Peter J., '67 (BUF) Retired. Curia: Offices and Directors [MON] Bishop Head Residence, Lackawanna, NY
Driscoll, Rev. Msgr. Eugene J., '70 (LUB) Retired.
Driscoll, Rt. Rev. Jeremy, *O.S.B.* '81 (P) [MON] Mt. Angel Abbey, Saint Benedict, OR; [SEM] Mount Angel Seminary, Saint Benedict, OR
Driscoll, Rev. Joseph J., '79 (BO) Retired.
Driscoll, Rev. Michael, '77 (HEL) On Duty Outside Diocese. Notre Dame Univ, South Bend, IN
Driscoll, Rev. Michael, *O. Carm.* (PMB) Curia: Leadership
Driscoll, Rev. Michael, '67 (PMB) St. Jude, Boca Raton, FL
Driscoll, Rev. Michael J., '92 (PEO) St. Mary, Utica, IL; [HOS] OSF HealthCare Saint Elizabeth Medical Center, Ottawa, IL
Driscoll, Rev. Patrick J., '08 (SFR) St. Veronica, South San Francisco, CA
Driscoll, Rev. Patrick R., '04 (MOB) St. Dominic Parish, Mobile, Mobile, AL
Driscoll, Rev. Paul G., '64 (RVC) Retired.
Driscoll, Rev. Richard, *S.D.S.* '65 (MIL) Retired. [MIS] Salvatorians - Jordan Hall, Milwaukee, WI
Driscoll, Rev. Samuel, *O.F.M. Cap.* '59 (PIT) [MON] St. Augustine Friary, Pittsburgh, PA
Driscoll, Rev. William D., '55 (NEW) Retired.
Drobach, Rev. William, *S.A.* '88 (NY) [MON] St. Christopher's Inn, Garrison, NY; [MON] St. Christopher's Inn Friary, Garrison, NY
Drobin, Rev. Paul J., '66 (SY) Retired.
Drobinski, Rev. Joseph J., '75 (WIL) Retired.
Droessler, Rev. Chad M., '10 (MAD) Curia: Organizations (affiliated, inter-Diocesan, miscellaneous/ other) Immaculate Heart of Mary, Monona, WI
Droessler, Rev. Jeffrey A., '09 (ORG) St. John Neumann, Irvine, CA
Droessler, Rev. Wayne J., '69 (DUB) Retired.
Drofych, Rev. Mykola, '08 (STF) St. John the Baptist, Kenmore, NY
Drogon, Rev. Greg, (PAT) Retired.
Droll, Very Rev. Adam, '15 (SAN) Holy Family, Abilene, TX
Droll, Rev. Msgr. Larry J., '73 (SAN) Curia: Advisory Boards, Commissions, Committees, and Councils; Canonical Services; Offices and Directors St. Ann's, Midland, TX
Droll, Rev. Nicholas L., '13 (COL) On Special Assignment. Canonical Studies in Washington, D.C.

Drolshagen, Rev. Jerry, *S.O.L.T.* '04 (CC) [MON] Society of Our Lady of the Most Holy Trinity, Corpus Christi, TX
Drongowski, Rev. Stanley, '79 (GR) [COL] Aquinas College, Grand Rapids, MI
Droski, Rev. Norman P., '64 (GR) Retired.
Droste, Rev. Christopher Lee, '13 (EVN) On Special Assignment. Curia: Offices and Directors Mater Dei High School, Evansville, IN; St. Boniface, Evansville, IN
Drouin, Very Rev. Marc B., '90 (MAN) Chap, Belknap Cty House of Corrections St. Andre Bessette, Laconia, NH; St. Joseph, Belmont, NH
Drouncheck, Rev. Anthony M., '89 (ALN) Retired.
Drozd, Rev. Henry J., '62 (LAR) Retired.
Drozdovsky, Rev. Canon Michael, '92 (SJP) Curia: Offices and Directors
Drozdovsky, Rev. Mykhaylo, '92 (SJP) Pokrova Ukrainian Catholic Parish, Parma, OH
Drozdzik, Rev. Roch T., '96 (R) St. Mary, Goldsboro, NC
Droze, Rev. Msgr. D. Anthony, '85 (CHR) Curia: Advisory Boards, Commissions, Committees, and Councils; Offices and Directors Cathedral of St. John the Baptist, Charleston, SC; St. Mary of the Annunciation, Charleston, SC
Drucker, Rev. James N., '78 (PSC) Retired. On Leave.
Druding, Rev. Vincent J., '09 (NY) Holy Cross, Bronx, NY
Drummer, Rev. Desmond, '14 (ATL) Chap, Hartsfield Jackson International Airport, Atlanta Most Blessed Sacrament Catholic Church, Atlanta, Inc., South Fulton, GA
Drummond, Rev. Alexander R., '94 (ARL) St. Michael, Annandale, VA
Drummy, Rev. John A., '71 (SUP) Retired.
Drury, Rev. Dennis G., '82 (GB) St. Isidore the Farmer, Tisch Mills, WI; St. Therese de Lisieux, Denmark, WI
Drury, Rev. Michael, '84 (HEL) Retired.
Drury, Rev. Michael J., '74 (PAT) Retired.
Drury, Rev. Robert, '79 (OWN) Curia: Advisory Boards, Commissions, Committees, and Councils Sacred Heart, Hickman, KY; St. Edward, Fulton, KY; St. Jude, Clinton, KY
Drybka, Friar Krzysztof, (RVC) St. Isidore, Riverhead, NY
Drzaic, Rev. Francis, *S.V.D.* '62 (CHI) [MON] Divine Word Residence, Techny, IL
D'Sa, Rev. Bernard, '94 (SR) Curia: Leadership Pastor of Sacred Heart Catholic Church of Eureka, A Corporation Sole, Eureka, CA; Pastor of St. Bernard Catholic Church of Eureka, A Corporation Sole, Eureka, CA
D'Silva, Rev. Joseph R., '67 (R) Retired.
D'Silva, Rev. Mark, (BGP) Sacred Heart Church of East Port Chester, Connecticut, Greenwich, CT
D'Silva, Rev. Percival L., '64 (WDC) Retired. Blessed Sacrament, Shrine of the Most, Washington, DC
Dsouza, Rev. Sylvester, (LUB) [MIS] San Jose de Calasanz, Lockney, TX
Dsouza, Rev. Thomas, *SAC* '88 (FWT) Our Lady of Lourdes, Mineral Wells, TX; St. Francis of Assisi, Graford, TX
D'Souza, Rev. Amit, *S.J.* (OM) [MON] Jesuit Community at Creighton University, Omaha, NE
D'Souza, Rev. Bruno, *C.P.* '04 (LA) [MON] Passionist Residence, Sierra Madre, CA; [RTR] Mater Dolorosa Passionist Retreat Center, Inc., Sierra Madre, CA
D'Souza, Rev. Claude J., '65 (RVC) Retired. [MON] St Pius X Residence for Retired Priests LLC, Ronkonkoma, NY
D'Souza, Very Rev. Darryl J., '93 (CC) Curia: Leadership Holy Family Church, Corpus Christi, TX
D'Souza, Rev. Denis, '79 (CHY) Immaculate Conception, Green River, WY
D'Souza, Rt. Rev. Gerard, *O.C.S.O.* '01 (ROC) [MON] Abbey of the Genesee, Inc., Piffard, NY
D'Souza, Rev. Gilbert P., '73 (BGP) Retired. [MON] The Catherine Dennis Keefe Queen of the Clergy Retired Priests' Residence, Stamford, CT
D'Souza, Rev. Jerome, '00 (SUP) Curia: Leadership Our Lady of the Lake Catholic Community, Ashland, WI; SS. Peter and Paul, Moquah, WI; St. Florian, Mason, WI; St. Mary, Odanah, WI; St. Peter, Moquah, WI
D'Souza, Rev. Maurice, *C.S.C.* (MO) Curia: Offices and Directors
D'Souza, Rev. Nobert, (RVC) St. Joseph's, Hewlett, NY
D'Souza, Rev. Norbert, *O.F.M.Cap* (RVC) Chap, Mercy Med Ctr
D'Souza, Rev. Peter, '79 (LUB) Retired.
D'Souza, Rev. Robert, '73 (FTW) Retired.
D'Souza, Rev. Sudhir, '05 (BGP) St. Philip Roman Catholic Church Corporation, Norwalk, CT
D'Souza, Rev. Thomas, (BAK) St. Katherine's, Enterprise, OR
D'Souza, Rev. Tony A., '14 (WDC) St. Martin of Tours, Gaithersburg, MD
D'Souza, Rev. William, '76 (GF) Retired.
Duaime, Rev. Jeffrey T., *C.S.Sp.* '86 (PIT) Curia: Consultative Bodies [COL] Duquesne University of the Holy Spirit, Pittsburgh, PA; [EFT] Spiritan Support Trust, Bethel Park, PA
Duarte, Rev. J. Scott, '78 (RIC) St. Elizabeth Ann Seton, Quinton, VA
Duarte, Rev. Luis, '20 (NO) Divine Mercy Roman Catholic Church, Kenner, Louisiana, Kenner, LA
Duarte, Rev. Miguel, '89 (AUS) St. Mary, Pin Oak, TX
Duarte Miranda, Friar Darwing, *T.C.* (SJN) [SPF] Casa de Ninos Manuel Fernandez Juncos, San Juan, PR
Dube, Rev. Emile H., '12 (PRT) Curia: Leadership Parish of the Transfiguration, Bar Harbor, ME; St. Joseph, Ellsworth, ME; Stella Maris Parish, Bucksport, ME; [CAM] Maine Maritime Academy, Castine, ME
Dube, Rev. Gregory P., '07 (PRT) On Special Assignment. Curia: Consultative Bodies; Offices and Directors
Dube, Rev. Marcel, *O.Carm.* '54 (JOL) Retired.
Dube, Rev. Marcel, *O.Carm.* '54 (VEN) [MON] Carmel at Mission Valley, Nokomis, FL
Dubell, Rev. Msgr. James H., '65 (TR) Retired.
Dubert, Rev. James W., '98 (DUB) Retired.
Dubi, Rev. Leonard A., '68 (CHI) Retired. Jesus, Shepherd of Souls, Câlumet City, IL
Dubitsky, Rev. Roman, '65 (PHU) Retired.
Dublinski, Rev. Steven L., '85 (SPK) Curia: Leadership Sacred Heart, Pullman, WA
Dubois, Rev. Msgr. Andrew, '95 (PRT) Curia: Consultative Bodies; Leadership Saint Paul the Apostle Parish, Bangor, ME
Dubois, Rev. Msgr. Charles J., '64 (LKC) Retired.
DuBois, Rev. David J., '80 (GAL) Sacred Heart, Pattison, TX
DuBois, Rev. Francis J., '70 (ALB) Retired.
Dubois, Rev. Msgr. Patrick, '04 (VEN) Curia: Leadership Epiphany Cathedral Catholic Parish in Venice, Inc., Venice, FL; [NUR] St. Mark's Housing of Venice, Inc. (Villa San Marco), Venice, FL
Dubois, Rev. Samuel, '16 (HBG) St. Elizabeth Ann Seton, Mechanicsburg, PA
Dubon, Rev. Oscar H., '14 (GAL) Church Of The Resurrection, Houston, TX
Dubovici, Rt. Rev. Mitred Archpriest Mihai, '94 (STF) St. John the Baptist, Syracuse, NY
Dubroc, Rev. Blake, '18 (LAF) Curia: Offices and Directors
Dubrouillet, Rev. James N., '97 (CHR) Holy Cross, Pickens, SC; St. Luke Mission, Easley, SC
Duc, Rev. Dominic Tran Minh, '90 (PH) St. Thomas Aquinas, Philadelphia, PA
Duc Minh, Rev. Msgr. Joseph N., '61 (LA) Retired.
Duch, Rev. Robert G., '64 (PIT) Retired.
Duchaine, Rev. Msgr. R. Mark, '78 (SC) Retired. Curia: Leadership
DuCharme, Rev. Paul, '55 (GB) Retired.
Duchnowicz, Rev. Arthur F., '01 (GLD) Saint Casimir of Posen, Posen, MI; Saint Dominic of Metz, Posen, MI
Duchschere, Rev. Paul C., '90 (FAR) Curia: Leadership St. Catherine's Church of Valley City, Valley City, ND; [CAM] Valley City State University Newman Center, Valley City, ND
Duck, Rev. Robert, *STL* '18 (TLS) St. Michael, Henryetta, OK; St. Stephen's, Holdenville, OK
Ducote, Rev. David, '16 (NO) On Special Assignment. St. Charles Catholic HS, LaPlace Curia: Miscellaneous / Other Offices St. Joan of Arc, La Place, LA
Ducote, Rev. Derek, '17 (ALX) Immaculate Conception, Natchitoches, LA
Ducre, Rev. Kennon Y., '83 (ELP) St. Thomas Aquinas, El Paso, TX
Duda, Rev. Lukasz, (ARL) St. Rita, Alexandria, VA
Duda, Rev. Rafal, (SAT) Notre Dame, Kerrville, TX
Duda, Rev. Rafal P., '11 (OAK) St. Joseph, Pinole, CA
Duda, Rev. Robert, '84 (JOL) Christ the Servant Parish, Woodridge, IL
Dudak, Rev. Msgr. George A., '56 (PAT) Retired. [MIS] Nazareth Village, Chester, NJ
Dudash, Rev. Derrick F., '74 (GRY) Retired.
Dudek, Rev. Christopher, *O.F.M.Conv.* (BAL) Archbishop Curley High School, Baltimore, MD
Dudek, Rev. John, '21 (DET) Divine Child Parish Dearborn, Dearborn, MI
Dudek, Rev. Ladislaus J., '66 (ALN) Retired.
Dudek, Rev. Stanislaus, *O.F.M. Conv.* '87 (HRT) Church Corporation of the Sacred Heart of Jesus of New Britain, New Britain, CT
Dudek, Rev. Stephen S., '84 (GR) Retired. Curia: Leadership; Offices and Directors [MIS] The Society For The Propagation Of The Faith, Grand Rapids, MI
Dudkevych, Rev. Andriy, '95 (PHU) St. Nicholas, Passaic, NJ
Dudo, Rev. Nicholas, '08 (CAM) Curia: Advisory Boards, Commissions, Committees, and Councils; Clergy and Religious Services; Leadership; Tribunal Holy Angels Parish, Woodbury, N.J., Woodbury, NJ
Dudziak, Rev. Marcin, '15 (MOB) Chaplain to all area hospitals in the Mobile area
Dudziak, Rev. Msgr. Paul, '69 (WDC) St. Stephen Martyr, Washington, DC
Dudzik, Rev. Dariusz K., *J.C.L.* '95 (NOR) Curia: Leadership St. John Paul II, East Hampton, CT
Dudzik, Rev. Jozef W., '00 (BUF) Our Lady Help of Christians, Cheektowaga, NY; Resurrection, Cheektowaga, NY; St. Josaphat, Cheektowaga, NY
Dudzinski, Very Rev. Andrew J., '96 (LFT) Curia: Leadership; Miscellaneous / Other Offices St. Boniface, Lafayette, IN; St. Lawrence, Lafayette, IN
Dudzinski, Rev. Brian A., '97 (LFT) St. Maria Goretti, Westfield, IN
Dudzinski, Rev. Paul L., '86 (ARL) St. Theresa, Ashburn, VA
Dudzinski, Very Rev. Theodore C., '97 (LFT) Curia: Advisory Boards, Commissions, Committees, and Councils; Leadership; Miscellaneous / Other Offices; Pastoral Services; Tribunal Blessed Sacrament, West Lafayette, IN; [MIS] Hamilton County Catholic High School Corporation (St. Theodore Guerin High School; Guerin Catholic High School), Noblesville, IN
Duell, Rev. James S., '82 (CIN) St. Boniface, Piqua, OH; St. Patrick, Troy, OH; St. Teresa of the Infant Jesus, Covington, OH; Transfiguration, West Milton, OH
Duenas, Rev. Manuel, '07 (NEW) Curia: Offices and Directors [SEM] Redemptoris Mater Archdiocesan Missionary Seminary, Kearny, NJ
Duenas, Rev. Roniel, (GBG) St. Elizabeth Ann Seton, North Huntingdon, PA
Duenas, Rev. Roniel Bantugan, (GBG) Immaculate Conception, Irwin, PA
Duerr, Rt. Rev. Gregory, *O.S.B.* '64 (P) Retired. [MON] Mt. Angel Abbey, Saint Benedict, OR
Duesman, Rev. Msgr. Jerry, (DAL) Retired.
Duesman, Rev. Msgr. Leon, '65 (DAL) Retired.
Duesterhaus, Rev. Michael R., (ARL) St. John the Baptist, Front Royal, VA
Duet, Rev. Wayne J., '75 (LAF) Retired. St. Thomas, Savoy, LA
Duff, Rev. Daniel J., '07 (LFT) St. Joseph, Lebanon, IN; St. Mary, Frankfort, IN
Duff, Rev. John J., '77 (NY) Retired. Holy Family, New Rochelle, NY
Duffeck, Rev. David A., '06 (GB) On Sick Leave.
Duffell, Rev. John P., '69 (NY) Retired.
Duffert, Rev. William D., '21 (STP) The Nativity of Our Lord, St. Paul, MN
Duffner, Rev. Paul A., *O.P.* '40 (P) Retired.
Dufford, Rev. Robert J., *S.J.* '73 (OM) [MON] Jesuit Community at Creighton University, Omaha, NE
Duffy, Rev. Christopher, *S.J.* (BAL) [COL] Jesuit Community of Loyola University, Inc., Baltimore, MD; [MON] Jesuit Community of Loyola University Maryland, Inc., Baltimore, MD
Duffy, Rev. Christopher J., *S.J.* '06 (WDC) [COL] Georgetown University, Washington, DC
Duffy, Rev. Darrell G., '05 (BUF) SS. Peter and Paul, Hamburg, NY
Duffy, Rev. Msgr. Francis J., '70 (PAT) Retired.
Duffy, Rev. George, '63 (MIA) Retired.
Duffy, Rev. Hugh, '66 (PMB) Retired.
Duffy, Rev. Hugh E., *O.S.F.S.* '60 (WIL) Retired.
Duffy, Rev. James D., *S.M.* '79 (ATL) Our Lady of the Assumption Catholic Church, Brookhaven, Inc., Brookhaven, GA
Duffy, Rev. James F., *S.J.* '06 (WDC) [COL] Georgetown University, Washington, DC (>SCR) [COL] The University of Scranton, Scranton, PA
Duffy, Rev. John F., *C.S.P.* '75 (NY) [MON] Paulist Fathers' Motherhouse, New York, NY
Duffy, Rev. Joseph P., *S.J.* '57 (BO) [MON] Campion Center, Inc., Weston, MA
Duffy, Rev. Michael, *O.F.M.* (PH) [MON] Order of Friars Minor of the Province of the Most Holy Name, Philadelphia, PA
Duffy, Rev. Michael A., *O.F.M.* '71 (PH) [SPF] St. Francis Inn, Philadelphia, PA
Duffy, Rev. Michael F., '12 (RVC) Curia: Leadership; Offices and Directors Our Lady of Lourdes, Malverne, NY
Duffy, Rev. Michael M., '76 (RIC) Curia: Administration Immaculate Conception, Buckner, VA; St. Jude, Mineral, VA

Duffy, Rev. Patrick P., '74 (CIN) Retired.
Duffy, Rev. Paul J., *M.M.* '79 (NY) Retired. [MON] Maryknoll Fathers and Brothers (Catholic Foreign Mission Society of America, Inc.), Ossining, NY
Duffy, Rev. Richard, *OFM* (GB) Retired.
Dufner, Rev. Dan, '96 (YAK) Our Lady of Fatima, Moses Lake, WA
Dufner, Very Rev. Daniel G., '96 (YAK) Curia: Offices and Directors
Dufner, Rev. Thomas W., '83 (STP) Curia: Consultative Bodies Church of the Epiphany, Coon Rapids, MN; [CEM] Epiphany Cemetery, Coon Rapids, MN
Dufour, Rev. David W., '94 (NO) St. Jerome Roman Catholic Church, Kenner, Louisiana, Kenner, LA
Dufour, Rev. Phillip J, '18 (PRO) St. Philip's Church Greenville Rhode Island, Greenville, RI
Dufrene, Rev. Stephen Marie, *C.F.R.* (NY) (>NEW) [MON] Franciscan Friars of the Renewal (Most Blessed Sacrament Friary), Newark, NJ
Dufresne, Rev. David A., '14 (ARL) St. Charles Borromeo, Arlington, VA
Dufresne, Rev. Jeffrey, (IND) Our Lady of the Most Holy Rosary Catholic Church, Indianapolis, Inc., Indianapolis, IN; St. Philip Neri Catholic Church, Indianapolis, Inc., Indianapolis, IN
Dufresne, Rev. Vincent J., '83 (BR) Curia: Canonical Services Congregation Of St. Joseph's Roman Catholic Church, Paulina, LA; Most Sacred Heart of Jesus (Congregation Of Sacred Heart Roman Catholic Church Of Gramercy), Gramercy, LA; St. Michael the Archangel (Congregation Of St. Michael Roman Catholic Church), Convent, LA
Dugal, Rev. James, *C.PP.S.* '56 (CIN) Retired. [MON] St. Charles, Celina, OH
Dugan, Rev. Dennis, *SOLT* (PHX) Most Holy Trinity Roman Catholic Parish, Phoenix, AZ
Dugan, Rev. James Lee, *S.J.* '73 (BUF) St. Michael, Buffalo, NY
Dugan, Rev. James M., '89 (ALT) Chap, State Corr Inst, Huntingdon Our Lady of Lourdes, Altoona, PA
Dugan, Rev. Kyle, '17 (WCH) St. Joseph, Conway Springs, KS
Dugan, Rev. T. Michael, '88 (DAL) On Administrative Leave.
Dugan, Rev. Thomas P., *C.S.B.* '60 (ROC) Retired. [MON] Basilian Fathers, Rochester, NY; [MON] Basilian Residence, Rochester, NY
Dugandzic, Rev. Peter, '95 (RVC) St. Joseph's, Kings Park, NY
Dugas, Rev. Scott, '77 (HT) Retired. On Duty Outside Diocese.
Dugas, Rev. Willard, '77 (LAF) Retired.
Duggan, Rev. Albert, *O.P.* (NY) [EFT] St. Thomas Aquinas Foundation of the Dominican Fathers of the United States (STAF), New York, NY; [MON] St. Vincent Ferrer Priory, New York, NY
Duggan, Rev. Kevin F.X., '98 (SEA) Our Lady of Guadalupe, Seattle, WA
Duggan, Rev. Kevin J., *S.M.* '86 (ATL) Our Lady of the Assumption Catholic Church, Brookhaven, Inc., Brookhaven, GA
Duggan, Rev. Michael A., *M.M.* '59 (NY) [MON] Maryknoll Fathers and Brothers (Catholic Foreign Mission Society of America, Inc.), Ossining, NY
Duggan, Rev. Oliver, '71 (SEA) Assumption, Seattle, WA
Duggan, Rev. Paul O'Donnell, '70 (PAT) Retired.
Duggan, Rev. Robert D., '69 (WDC) Retired.
Duggan, Rev. Sean, *O.S.B.* '88 (BUF) St. Dominic, Westfield, NY
Duggan, Rev. Sean B., *O.S.B.* '88 (NO) [MON] St. Joseph Abbey, St. Benedict, LA
Duggan, Rev. Thomas S., '13 (R) Curia: Leadership St. Ann, Clayton, NC
Duggempudi, Rev. Joseph Reddy, '12 (OKL) Sacred Heart, Konawa, OK
Duggins, Rev. Dominic R., '74 (CIN) Retired. [MIS] Glenmary Home Missioners Charity, Inc., Fairfield, OH; [MON] Headquarters of Glenmary Home Missioners (The Home Missioners of America), Fairfield, OH
Duhe, Rev. Thomas P., '49 (BR) Retired.
Duhon, Rev. Edward, (LAF) Our Lady Queen of Peace, Lafayette, LA
Duke, Rev. Jerome J., '68 (CLV) Retired.
Duker, Rev. Msgr. Russell A., *S.E.O.D.* '70 (PBR) Retired.
Dulek, Rev. Lawrence V., '73 (MIL) Retired.
Duling, Rev. Daniel J., '11 (WCH) St. Louis, Murdock, KS; St. Rose, Cheney, KS
Dulli, Rev. Brian D., '08 (MAD) St. Patrick, Cottage Grove, WI
Dulock, Rev. Vincent J., *C.S.B.* '69 (GAL) [MON] Basilian Fathers Missions, Sugar Land, TX
Duma, Rev. Msgr. Gregory, '64 (ROM) Retired.
Dumag, Rev. Peter, '92 (HON) On Duty Outside Diocese. Military Archdiocese, US Air Force Curia: (>MO) Offices and Directors
Dumain, Rev. Canon Pierre, *ICRSP* '15 (STL) Oratory of St. Francis de Sales, St. Louis, MO; [MIS] Friends of St. Francis de Sales Oratory, Inc., St. Louis, MO
Dumais, Rev. George J., *S.J.* '71 (SJ) Retired. [MON] Sacred Heart Jesuit Center, Los Gatos, CA
Dumais, Rev. Paul H., '04 (PRT) Curia: Leadership St. Joseph's, Farmington, ME; St. Rose of Lima, Jay, ME; [CAM] University of Maine at Farmington, Farmington, ME
Dumais, Rev. Steve, (SP) Mary Help of Christians, Tampa, FL; [RTR] Mary Help of Christians Center, Tampa, FL
Dumais, Rev. Steven, *S.D.B.* '78 (NEW) [MON] The Salesian Community, Orange, NJ
Duman, Rev. Charles J., '52 (SFS) Retired.
Dumas, Rev. Emile E., *M.M.* '67 (NY) Retired. [MON] Maryknoll Fathers and Brothers (Catholic Foreign Mission Society of America, Inc.), Ossining, NY
Dumas, Rev. John, '10 (DET) Our Lady on the River Parish Marine City, Marine City, MI
Dumas, Rev. Terrence J., '88 (LAN) Retired.
Dumenko, Rev. Alexander, '01 (PHU) Curia: Leadership Annunciation of the Blessed Virgin Mary, Manassas, VA; Holy Trinity, Silver Spring, MD
Dumlao, Rev. Jonathan Yu, *I.V.E.* '14 (SJ) Our Lady of Peace, Santa Clara, CA; [MON] The Institute of the Incarnate Word (IVE), Santa Clara, CA
Dumnych, Rev. Andrii, (PSC) St. Michael, Pittston, PA; St. Nicholas, Pittston, PA
Dumont, Rev. Msgr. C. Peter, '71 (MAN) Retired. Curia: Clergy and Religious Services; Consultative Bodies
Dumont, Rev. Msgr. C. Peter, '71 (MAN) St. Joseph Cathedral, Manchester, NH
Dumont, Rev. Gerald, '80 (BRK) St. Francis of Assisi-St. Blaise, Brooklyn, NY
Dumphrey, Rev. Joseph C., *O.S.F.S.* '64 (BUF) St. John the Baptist Roman Catholic Congregation, Lockport, NY
Dumphy, Rev. Charles, '55 (WOR) Retired.
Dumych, Rev. Myroslav, (STN) St. John the Baptist, Detroit, MI
Duncan, Rev. Andrew, '93 (CHY) Chap, Wyoming Women's Ctr (Correctional Facility) St. Stephen's, St. Stephens, WY
Duncan, Rev. Msgr. John C., '60 (LFT) Retired.
Duncan, Rev. Jonathan, '14 (POC) On Duty Outside Diocese.
Duncan, Rev. Jonathan C., (CHR) St. Joseph's Catholic School, Greenville, SC; St. Mary, Greenville, SC; [CAM] Furman University Campus Ministry, Greenville, SC
Duncan, Rev. Msgr. Joseph P., '89 (PH) Curia: Deaneries St. Albert the Great, Huntingdon Valley, PA
Duncan, Rev. Joshua J., '16 (JC) St. Joseph, Fayette, MO; St. Mary, Glasgow, MO
Duncan, Rev. Nicholas, '22 (SHP) St. Joseph, Shreveport, LA
Duncan, Very Rev. Msgr. William H., '90 (GR) Curia: Leadership St. Sebastian, Byron Center, MI
Dunch, Rev. Matthew, *S.J.* '17 (CHI) [COL] Jesuit Community at Loyola University Chicago, Chicago, IL
Dunccklee, Rev. Lawrence, '80 (RVC) St. John the Evangelist, Riverhead, NY
Dunccklee, Rev. Lawrence T., '80 (RVC) Curia: Leadership
Dun-Dery, Rev. William, '06 (KCK) St. Patrick's, Kansas City, KS
Dundon, Rev. Luke R., '11 (ARL) On Duty Outside Diocese. CH (LT), APO Pacific Curia: (>MO) Offices and Directors
Dunfee, Rev. Dirk, *S.J.* '97 (DEN) St. Ignatius Loyola Catholic Parish in Denver, Denver, CO; [MON] Society of Jesus - St. Ignatius Loyola Jesuit Community, Denver, CO
Dunfee, Very Rev. James M., '84 (STU) Curia: Deaneries; Leadership; Offices and Directors St. Agnes, Mingo Junction, OH
Dung, Rev. Nguyen Quoc, *C.Ss.R.* '05 (LA) [MON] Vietnamese Redemptorist Mission, Baldwin Park, CA
Dunham, Rev. Larry, *O.F.M.* '74 (CIN) [MON] St. Francis Seraph Friary, Cincinnati, OH
Dunkelberger, Rev. Benjamin, (HBG) Our Lady of the Visitation, Shippensburg, PA; St. John the Baptist, New Freedom, PA; [CAM] York College, York, PA
Dunkle, Rev. Brian, *S.J.* '09 (BO) [MON] Francis Xavier House, Brighton, MA
Dunkley, Rev. George, '70 (WOR) Retired.
Dunkley, Rev. George, '70 (SD) Retired.
Dunlap, Rev. Christopher J., '06 (STL) Christ, Prince of Peace Catholic Church, Manchester, MO
Dunlap, Rev. William M., '74 (TR) Retired. St. Catharine-St. Margaret, Spring Lake, NJ
Dunleavy, Rev. Thomas, *M.M.* '75 (NY) Retired. [MON] Maryknoll Fathers and Brothers (Catholic Foreign Mission Society of America, Inc.), Ossining, NY
Dunleavy, Rev. Msgr. Thomas J., '75 (PH) SS. Simon and Jude, West Chester, PA; St. Thomas More, Pottstown, PA
Dunmire, Rev. Mark R., '20 (GBG) [NUR] Neumann House, Greensburg, PA
Dunmyer, Rev. Raymond A., '76 (BIR) Prince of Peace Catholic Parish, Birmingham, Birmingham, AL
Dunn, Rev. Bob, '85 (CC) St. Gertrude, Kingsville, TX
Dunn, Rev. Charles, '16 (SPC) Curia: Administration St. Canera, Neosho, MO
Dunn, Rev. Christopher J., (ARL) St. Francis of Assisi, Triangle, VA
Dunn, Rev. Edmond J., '72 (DAV) Retired.
Dunn, Rev. Harold, *M.S.A.* '78 (NOR) [MON] Society of the Missionaries of the Holy Apostles, Cromwell, CT
Dunn, Rev. Harold F., *M.S.A* '78 (WH) Retired.
Dunn, Rev. Laurence J., '68 (CHI) Retired. St. Norbert and Our Lady of the Brook Parish, Northbrook, IL
Dunn, Rev. Mathew, (BR) Congregation of Christ the King Roman Catholic Church of the Diocese of Baton Rouge, Baton Rouge, LA; [CAM] Christ the King Parish and Catholic Center (Congregation of Christ the King Roman Catholic Church of the Diocese of Baton Rouge), Baton Rouge, LA
Dunn, Rev. Michael G., '03 (TR) St. Isaac Jogues, Marlton, NJ; St. John Neumann, Mount Laurel, NJ
Dunn, Rev. Michael L., '94 (BGP) Curia: Clergy and Religious Services; Consultative Bodies Saint Gregory the Great Roman Catholic Church Corporation, Danbury, CT
Dunn, Rev. Richard B., '80 (SY) St. Mary's of the Lake, Skaneateles, NY
Dunn, Rev. Stephen, '71 (SD) Retired.
Dunn, Rev. Stephen, *C.P.* '64 (NY) [MON] The Congregation of the Passion - St. Paul of the Cross Province, Jamaica, NY
Dunn, Rev. Thomas, '15 (JOL) Sacred Heart, Lombard, IL
Dunn, Rev. Msgr. William A., '65 (COL) Retired.
Dunne, Rev. Dermot, '00 (SP) St. Stephen, Riverview, FL
Dunne, Rev. Gerald, *O.S.F.S.* '77 (WIL) Immaculate Conception, Elkton, MD
Dunne, Rev. Gerard, *S.S.C.* '67 (OM) Retired. [MON] Missionary Society of St. Columban, St. Columbans, NE
Dunne, Rev. Jacob A, '21 (DUB) Epiphany Parish, Mason City, Iowa, Mason City, IA; Sacred Heart Church, Manly, Iowa, Manly, IA
Dunne, Rev. Mark, '02 (TYL) Curia: Deaneries Sacred Heart, Mount Vernon, TX
Dunne, Rev. Martin, (PMB) Holy Redeemer, Palm City, FL
Dunne, Rev. Patrick J., '70 (NY) Retired.
Dunne, Rev. Thomas, *S.D.B.* '72 (NY) [MON] Salesian Cooperators of St. John Bosco, New Rochelle, NY
Dunne, Rev. Victor, *S.P.S.* '80 (NY) Retired.
Dunning, Rev. James Patrick, '63 (ORG) Retired.
Dunphy, Rev. James, *M.S.* '57 (HRT) [MIS] Missionaries of LaSalette, Hartford, CT
Duns, Rev. Ryan Gerard, *S.J.* '15 (MIL) [MON] Jesuit Community at Marquette University (Marquette Jesuit Associates, Inc.), Milwaukee, WI
Dunson, Rev. Donald, '82 (CLV) St. Angela Merici, Fairview Park, OH
Dunton, Rev. Thomas J., *C.S.J.* '10 (PEO) [MON] Congregation of St. John, Princeville, IL
Duong, Rev. Cu Minh, '87 (MOB) Curia: Organizations (affiliated, inter-Diocesan, miscellaneous/other) St. Monica Parish, Mobile, Mobile, AL
Duong, Rev. James Duc H., '01 (CHL) St. Benedict, Greensboro, NC
Duong, Rev. Minh Quang, (IND) St. Joseph Catholic Church, Indianapolis, Inc., Indianapolis, IN
Duong, Rev. Paul, '74 (SJ) Retired.
Duong, Rev. Quy, *C.Ss.R.* '17 (STP) St. Alphonsus, Brooklyn Center, MN; [MON] Redemptorist Fathers of Hennepin County, Brooklyn Center, MN
Duong, Rev. Tien H., '01 (CHL) St. Francis of Assisi, Franklin, NC
Duong, Rev. Tri Minh, *C.M.* '05 (BRK) [MON] Reverend John B. Murray, C.M. House, Jamaica, NY
Duong, Rev. Vincent, *S.J.* (SEA) [CAM] Seattle University Campus Ministry, Seattle, WA
Duplantis, Rev. Daniel, (HT) Cathedral of St. Francis De Sales, Houma, LA
Duplantis, Rev. Daniel, (MO) Curia: Offices and

Directors
Duplissey, Rev. Josh, (LSC) Retired.
Dupont, Rev. Quentin, *S.J.* '14 (SEA) [MON] Arrupe Jesuit Community at Seattle University, Seattle, WA
Dupont, Rev. Quentin, *S.J.* '14 (WDC) [MON] The Jesuit Community at Georgetown University, Washington, DC
Dupre, Rev. Daniel, '22 (SFE) Shrine of Our Lady of Guadalupe-Santa Fe, Santa Fe, NM; [SHR] Shrine of Our Lady of Guadalupe, Santa Fe, NM
Dupre, Rev. Matthew C., (BR) Ascension of Our Lord Jesus Christ (The Congregation Of Ascension Roman Catholic Church, Of The Parish Of Ascension, State Of Louisiana), Donaldsonville, LA; The Congregation Of Saint Francis Of Assisi Roman Catholic Church, Donaldsonville, LA; [EFT] Ascension Catholic Interparochial School Endowment Fund, ,
Dupre, Very Rev. Matthew C., '98 (BR) Curia: Administration
Duprey, Rev. Msgr. Dennis J., '70 (OG) Retired. Curia: Canonical Services; Consultative Bodies Saint Augustine's Church, Peru, NY, Peru, NY
Duprey, Rev. Manuel, '17 (SJN) Nuestra Senora de Lourdes, San Juan, PR
Duquaine, Rev. Stephen J., '14 (LFT) Curia: Tribunal St. Joan of Arc, Kokomo, IN; St. Patrick, Kokomo, IN
Duquette, Rev. Don Bosco, *O.F.M.Cap.* '64 (NOR) Retired.
Duquette, Rev. Don Bosco, *OFM Cap* (NY) Retired. [MON] St. Clare Friary (Capuchin Franciscan Friars, Province of St. Mary), Yonkers, NY
Dura, Rev. Eduardo, '77 (SFR) St. Augustine, South San Francisco, CA
Durairaj, Rev. Timothy, *O.F.M.Cap.* '14 (WDC) [SEM] St. Francis Friary-Capuchin College, Washington, DC
Duraisamy, Rev. JohnBosco, '87 (CHR) St. Ann, Florence, SC; St. Anthony, Florence, SC
Duran, Rev. Franklin, '12 (JOL) On Leave.
Duran, Rev. John Paul, *LC* '11 (ATL) Holy Spirit Preparatory School, Inc., Atlanta, GA; [MIS] Legionaries of Christ, Atlanta, GA
Duran, Rev. Jorge, '75 (SAT) On Leave.
Duran, Rev. Marek J., '04 (CHI) [SEM] University of Saint Mary of the Lake/Mundelein Seminary, Mundelein, IL
Duran, Very Rev. Miguel Duarte, '89 (AUS) Curia: Leadership St. Margaret, Giddings, TX; St. Mary, Giddings, TX
Duran, Rev. Roberto C, *S.J.* '18 (SJ) [MON] USA West Province, Society of Jesus, Los Gatos, CA
Duran, Rev. Said, '95 (TYL) On Duty Outside Diocese. Colombia
Durand, Rev. Donald, '58 (P) Retired.
Durango, Rev. Pedro, (AGN) On Duty Outside Diocese.
Durango Agudelo, Rev. Pedro Luis, '15 (MIA) St. Cecilia, Hialeah, FL; [SEM] The Redemptoris Mater Seminary Archdiocese of Miami, Inc., Hialeah, FL
Durant, Rev. Thomas P., '76 (SY) St. Paul, Whitesboro, NY
Durante, Rev. Charles, '94 (RNO) Curia: Leadership; Offices and Directors St. Mary's in the Mountains, Virginia City, NV; St. Thomas Aquinas Cathedral, Reno, NV
Durante, Rev. Chuck, (RNO) Curia: Leadership
Durazo, Rev. Marco Antonio, '08 (LA) [SEM] St. John's Seminary, Camarillo, CA
Durbin, Rev. John G., '79 (R) Curia: Leadership St. Andrew the Apostle, Apex, NC
Durchholz, Rev. Jack J., '95 (EVN) Curia: Leadership
Durchholz, Rev. Jack J., '95 (EVN) Curia: Leadership St. Clement, Boonville, IN
Durette, Rev. Mathias D., *O.S.B.* '93 (MAN) [MON] St. Anselm Abbey, Manchester, NH
Durham, Rev. DePorres, *O.P.* '90 (STL) [MON] St. Dominic Priory, St. Louis, MO
Durham, Rev. Neil, *S.D.S.* '82 (MIL) Retired. [MON] Salvatorian Provincial Offices (Society of the Divine Savior), Milwaukee, WI
Duri Raj, Rev. Mount Joseph, *S.J.* '91 (ELP) St. John the Apostle and Evangelist, Monahans, TX
Durian, Rev. Ariel F, *C.S.* (SLC) Saint Peter LLC 242, American Fork, UT
Durig, Rev. D. Kent, '93 (WH) Retired.
Durkee, Rev. David R., '80 (CLV) Queen of Heaven, Uniontown, OH
Durkee, Rev. Stephen J., '17 (GR) On Special Assignment. St. Pius X Parish, Grandville Curia: Clergy and Religious Services St. Pius X, Grandville, MI
Durkin, Rev. Daniel, '73 (FTW) Retired.
Durkin, Rev. Edward J., *S.J.* '75 (BUF) The NativityMiguel Middle School of Buffalo, Buffalo, NY; [MON] The Canisius Jesuit Community, Inc., Buffalo, NY
Durkin, Rev. James J., '68 (CAM) Retired.
Durkin, Rev. John F., '99 (ATL) St. Monica Catholic Church, Duluth, Inc., Duluth, GA
Durkin, Rev. Riley Riley, '20 (FAR) St. Mary's Cathedral of Fargo, Fargo, ND
Durosier, Rev. Wilner, '06 (VEN) Curia: Leadership St. Michael Parish in Wauchula, Inc., Wauchula, FL
Duru, Rev. Hippolytus, '97 (NY) Chap, Jacobi Med Ctr, Bronx; North Central Bronx Hosp. St. Francis Xavier, Bronx, NY
Duru, Rev. Innocent, *C.M.F.* (RVC) Chap, Nassau Univ Med Ctr
Duru, Rev. Onyekachi Innocent, (RVC) St. Bernard, Levittown, NY
Dury, Rev. Daniel J., '10 (COL) St. John Neumann, Sunbury, OH
Duschl, Rev. Frederick J., '65 (TOL) Retired.
Dusecina, Rev. Regis, '73 (PBR) St. Mary's, Hannastown, PA
Dusecina, Rev. Regis J., '73 (PBR) St. Nicholas of Myra, Greensburg, PA
Dusheck, Rev. Leo, *S.V.D.* '61 (TR) Retired.
Dussouy, Rev. Charles W., '14 (NO) Our Lady of Perpetual Help, Kenner, LA
Duston, Rev. Thomas L., '92 (MAN) Curia: (>MO) Offices and Directors St. Mary, Rochester, NH; St. Peter, Farmington, NH; [CEM] St. Mary's Cemetery, Rochester, NH
Dustou, Rev. Kyle L., (PRT) Curia: Consultative Bodies
Dusza, Rev. Donald W., '83 (ALT) On Leave.
Dutan, Rev. Joseph F., '18 (BRK) St. Brigid, Brooklyn, NY
Dutkiewicz, Rev. Lukasz, '07 (BRK) St. Frances de Chantal, Brooklyn, NY
Dutko, Rev. Andrew, (PAT) On Leave. Curia: Leadership
Dutra, Rev. David, '07 (STO) Curia: Leadership St. Bernard Church (Pastor of), Tracy, CA
DuVall, Rev. Scott, '09 (RCK) On Administrative Leave.
Duvall, Rev. Shayne R., '15 (L) Holy Trinity, Louisville, KY
Duvelius, Rev. Dennis M., '96 (IND) Curia: Offices and Directors St. John the Apostle Catholic Church, Bloomington, Inc., Bloomington, IN; St. Jude Catholic Church, Spencer, Inc., Spencer, IN
DuWell, Very Rev. Ralph, '00 (ORL) Curia: Advisory Boards, Commissions, Committees, and Councils; Deaneries St. Timothy, Lady Lake, FL
Duyshart, Rev. Edwin C., '84 (LA) St. Ignatius of Loyola, Los Angeles, CA
Dvorak, Rev. Franklin A., '70 (OM) Retired. On Administrative Leave.
Dvorak, Rev. Gerald, '79 (STP) Retired.
Dvorak, Rev. Grant, '22 (BIS) Dickinson Catholic Schools (Trinity Catholic Schools), Dickinson, ND; Queen of Peace Church, Dickinson, ND; Trinity High School, Dickinson, ND
Dvorak, Rev. James M., '20 (VIC) Sacred Heart, Hallettsville, TX; St. John the Baptist, Schulenburg, TX; St. Mary, Hallettsville, TX
Dvorscak, Rev. James, '76 (JOL) St. Dennis, Lockport, IL
Dwayer, Rev. Wlliam, '22 (COS) St. Mark Catholic Church, Highlands Ranch, CO
Dwomoh, Rev. Charles O., '86 (VIC) St. John the Baptist, Hungerford, TX
Dworak, Rev. Walter W., '72 (PIT) Retired.
Dwyer, Rev. Arthur J., *M.M.* '49 (NY) Retired.
Dwyer, Rev. Curtiss, '05 (DEN) Chap, Lt CMDR, USN Curia: (>MO) Offices and Directors
Dwyer, Rev. Curtiss, (MO) Curia: Offices and Directors
Dwyer, Rev. Daniel J., '12 (PH) On Sick Leave.
Dwyer, Rev. Daniel P., *O.F.M.* '88 (ALB) [COL] Siena College, Loudonville, NY
Dwyer, Rev. David P., *C.S.P.* '00 (NY) [MON] Paulist Fathers - Generalate, New York, NY; [MON] Paulist Fathers' Motherhouse, New York, NY
Dwyer, Rev. Msgr. Donald M., '79 (NY) Curia: Leadership Resurrection, Rye, NY
Dwyer, Rev. Edwin G., '11 (SAG) Curia: Offices and Directors Saint Paul the Apostle Parish of Ithaca, Ithaca, MI
Dwyer, Rev. James, *S.S.C.* '58 (PRO) Retired. [MON] St. Columban's Retirement House (St. Columban's Foreign Mission Society), Bristol, RI
Dwyer, Rev. James, *S.S.C.* '58 (OM) Retired. [MON] Missionary Society of St. Columban, St. Columbans, NE
Dwyer, Rt. Rev. Jean Thomas, (SAT) [CON] Daughters of Charity Residence, San Antonio, TX
Dwyer, Rev. John A., '74 (WOR) Retired.
Dwyer, Rev. Thomas P., *O.S.A.* '58 (PH) [MON] St. Thomas Monastery, Villanova, PA
Dwyer, Rev. Timothy, *S.M.* '68 (SAT) [MON] Marianist Residence, San Antonio, TX
Dyachim, Rev. Joshua, (SP) [HOS] St. Joseph's Hospital, Inc., Tampa, FL
Dyachok, Rev. Petro, '89 (STN) Immaculate Conception Catholic Church, San Francisco, CA; St. Volodymyr Ukrainian Catholic Mission, Santa Clara, CA
Dye, Rev. David M., '92 (ATL) Retired.
Dye, Rev. Robert M., '91 (TLS) On Special Assignment. David L Moss Corr Fac Saint Joseph Church, Muskogee, OK
Dyer, Rev. Francis X., *O.P.* '69 (CHI) Retired. [MON] St. Pius V Priory, Chicago, IL
Dyer, Rev. Hugh Vincent, *O.P.* (BAL) (>WDC) [SEM] Dominican House of Studies, Washington, DC
Dyer, Rev. James W., '97 (STL) Retired.
Dyer, Rev. Joseph, '74 (JKS) Retired. Curia: Consultative Bodies Christ the King, Jackson, MS
Dyer, Rev. Kevin B., *S.J.* '10 (NO) Jesuit High School, New Orleans, LA (>DEN) [MON] Regis Jesuit Community (The Jesuits at Regis University), Denver, CO
Dyer, Rev. Richard E., '11 (ARL) St. Veronica, Chantilly, VA
Dyer, Rev. Thomas P., '69 (Y) Retired.
Dyer, Rev. Msgr. Timothy J., '74 (LA) St. Patrick, Los Angeles, CA; St. Stephen of Hungary, Los Angeles, CA
Dygert, Rev. C. Joseph, '11 (COS) Curia: Tribunal
Dygert, Rev. Joseph, (COS) Divine Redeemer, Colorado Springs, CO
Dygula, Rev. Rafal, '96 (LA) Our Lady of the Bright Mount, Los Angeles, CA
Dykalski, Rev. Michal, (PAT) Holy Rosary, Passaic, NJ
Dykes, Rev. Reuben, '15 (BR) Congregation Of Mater Dolorosa Roman Catholic Church, Independence, Louisiana, Independence, LA
Dymek, Rev. Janusz, '01 (BRK) Our Lady of Czestochowa-St. Casimir, Brooklyn, NY
Dymek, Rev. Mariusz, *O.S.P.P.E.* '02 (BUF) Corpus Christi, Buffalo, NY; St. Stanislaus, Buffalo, NY
Dymowski, Rev. Tom, *O.SS.T.* '85 (BAL) Curia: Leadership St. Mark, Catonsville, MD; [MON] Holy Trinity Monastery, Sykesville, MD
Dyrwal, Rev. Justin, *O.S.B.* '98 (CLV) Assumption, Broadview Heights, OH
Dysinger, Rev. Luke, *O.S.B.* '86 (LA) [MON] St. Andrew's Abbey (Benedictine Monks), Valyermo, CA; [SEM] St. John's Seminary, Camarillo, CA
Dzekoe, Rev. Richmond, '03 (DUB) St. John XXIII Parish, Cedar Rapids, Iowa, Cedar Rapids, IA; Xavier High School, Cedar Rapids, Iowa, Cedar Rapids, IA
Dzengeleski, Rev. Martin G., (BO) Holy Trinity, Quincy, MA
Dziak, Rev. Theodore A., (BO) [MON] Campion Center, Inc., Weston, MA
Dziedziak, Rev. Robert T., '05 (VEN) Curia: Leadership
Dziedziak, Rev. Robert T., '05 (VEN) Curia: Advisory Boards, Commissions, Committees, and Councils; Leadership St. Mary Star of the Sea Parish in Longboat Key, Inc., Longboat Key, FL
Dziedzic, Rev. Gerald H., '74 (HRT) Retired. Curia: Deaneries
Dziedzic, Rev. Grzegorz, '04 (BRK) [CAM] Campus Ministers and Ministry Centers (Newman Apostolate, Inc.), Brooklyn, NY
Dzieglewicz, Rev. John T., *S.J.* '83 (NY) [MON] Jesuit Community at Fordham University, New York, NY
Dziekan, Rev. Wayne H., '94 (GLD) Curia: Offices and Directors; Organizations (affiliated, inter-Diocesan, miscellaneous/other)
Dzielak, Rev. Msgr. Thomas L., '63 (RCK) Retired. Curia: Offices and Directors SS. Peter and Paul, Virgil, IL; St. Mary, Maple Park, IL
Dzien, Rev. Joseph Duc, '83 (NO) St. John the Baptist, Paradis, LA
Dzien, Rev. Mark, '95 (STA) St. Madeleine Sophie Parish and Santa Fe Shrine of Our Lady of La Leche, High Springs, FL
Dzieszko, Rev. Thaddeus, '88 (CHI) St. Faustina Kowalska, Chicago, IL
Dzikowicz, Rt. Rev. Justin E., *O.S.B.* '73 (PAT) [MON] St. Paul's Abbey (Order of St. Benedict, Congregation of St. Ottilien), Newton, NJ
Dzikowski, Rev. Piotr, *S.Ch.* '87 (P) St. Stanislaus, Portland, OR
Dziordz, Rev. Walter, *M.I.C.* '84 (SPR) [MON] Congregation of Marian Fathers of The Immaculate Conception of the Most Blessed Virgin Mary, Stockbridge, MA
Dziorek, Rev. Anthony, *C.R.* '75 (CHI) St. Hyacinth Basilica, Chicago, IL
Eads, Rev. Kyle, '19 (ALB) St. Theresa of Child Jesus, Windham, NY

Eagan, Rev. William Joseph, *S.J.* '75 (BO) [MON] Campion Health & Wellness, Inc., Weston, MA
Eale, Rev. Francois, (RVC) St. Francis of Assisi, Greenlawn, NY
Earl, Rev. John P, '94 (RCK) On Administrative Leave.
Earl, Rev. Patrick, *SJ* '74 (WDC) Holy Trinity, Washington, DC; [MON] The Jesuit Community at Georgetown University, Washington, DC
Earley, Friar Jerome, *O.C.D.* '95 (LR) [SEM] Discalced Carmelite Friars of St. Therese, Little Rock, Little Rock, AR
Earleywine, Rev. Kevin R., '17 (DUB) St. Mary's Church of Ackley, Ackley, Iowa, Ackley, IA; St. Patricks Church, Hampton, Iowa, Hampton, IA
Earls, Rev. John Patrick, *O.S.B.* '65 (SCL) [MON] St. John's Abbey, of the Order of St. Benedict, Collegeville, MN
Early, Rev. Francis J., '85 (WDC) Retired.
Earner, Rev. Msgr. Thomas, '62 (SP) Retired.
Earthedath, Rev. Sebastian, *M.S.T.* '86 (SP) Our Lady Queen of Peace, New Port Richey, FL
Earthman, Rev. Michael G, '07 (GAL) [SEM] St. Mary's Seminary, Houston, TX
East, Rev. Msgr. Raymond G., '81 (WDC) St. Teresa of Avila, Washington, DC
Easterling, Rev. William T., '82 (LA) Curia: Pastoral Services Sacred Heart, Covina, CA
Eastman, Rev. Patrick W., '84 (TLS) Retired.
Easton, Rev. Colin, '17 (RCK) On Sick Leave.
Easton, Rev. Msgr. Frederick, '66 (IND) Curia: Offices and Directors
Eaton, Rev. John, *O.F.M.* '78 (BEL) [MON] St. Benedict the Black Friary, East Saint Louis, IL
Ebach, Rev. Aloys, *C.PP.S.* '74 (KC) Saint Francis Xavier Catholic Church, St. Joseph, MO; [MON] Society of the Precious Blood, Liberty, MO
Ebbesmier, Rev. John, '78 (PHX) Curia: Offices and Directors
Ebel, Rev. Stephen P., '70 (DAV) Retired.
Eberhart, Rev. Lewis, '04 (LAN) Chap, Univ of Michigan Hosps/Pastoral Dept
Eberle, Rt. Rev. Peter, *O.S.B.* '68 (P) Retired. [MON] Mt. Angel Abbey, Saint Benedict, OR
Ebert, Rev. Douglas A., '09 (STP) Retired. Curia: Consultative Bodies
Ebert, Very Rev. James A., '09 (ALB) On Special Assignment. Vicar for Clergy, in Residence at Sacred Heart Rectory Curia: Leadership; Offices and Directors Notre Dame-Visitation, Schuylerville, NY; St. Clement, Saratoga Springs, NY
Ebey, Rev. Carl F., *C.S.C.* '72 (FTW) [MON] Holy Cross Community, Corby Hall, University of Notre Dame, Notre Dame, IN
Eblen, Rev. James, '64 (SEA) Retired.
Ebner, Rev. Patrick, '04 (AUS) St. John Vianney, Round Rock, TX
Eboh, Rev. Geoffrey, (SB) Chap, Riverside Univ Health Sys Rgnl Med Ctr, Moreno Valley
Ebong, Rev. Thomas, (CIN) Immaculate Heart of Mary, Cincinnati, OH
Ebright, Rev. James A., '05 (CHL) St. Michael, Gastonia, NC
Ebron, Rev. Jose Erlito, '93 (NEW) St. Raphael, Livingston, NJ
Ebulueme, Rev. Theophilus, '95 (NSH) Holy Name Catholic Church, Nashville, TN
Eburn, Rev. Brian, '66 (STA) Retired.
Eburuche, Rev. Eugene, *S.M.M.M.* '65 (SB) Chap, California Inst for Men, Chino
Ebuziem, Rev. Cajetan, (CHI) [HOS] Saint Anthony Hospital (Saint Anthony Health Ministries), Chicago, IL
Echavarria, Rev. Carlos Andres, '10 (HRT) On Administrative Leave.
Echavarria, Rev. Juan David, '11 (WOR) Curia: Leadership St. Mary of the Hills, Boylston, MA
Echeandia, Rev. Jesus, *C.P.* '59 (NY) [MON] The Congregation of the Passion - St. Paul of the Cross Province, Jamaica, NY
Echekwu, Rev. Kyrian C., '92 (BRK) Ascension, Elmhurst, NY
Echert, Rev. John P., '87 (STP) Curia: (>MO) Offices and Directors Holy Trinity, South St. Paul, MN
Echevarria, Rev. Julio A, '12 (MGZ) San Sebastian Martir, San Sebastian, PR
Echevarria Lopez, Rev. Wilfredo, *O.SS.T* '86 (ARE) St. Anthony, Isabela, PR
Echeverria Murillo, Rev. Pedro Faustino, '84 (PCE) Nuestra Senora del Carmen, Villalba, PR
Echeverry, Rev. Angelus, *O.S.B.* '17 (LA) [MON] St. Andrew's Abbey (Benedictine Monks), Valyermo, CA
Eck, Rev. Ivan C., '51 (WCH) Retired.
Eck, Rev. Timothy Mark, '21 (MET) On Special Assignment. Curia: Consultative Bodies; Evangelization St. Bartholomew, East Brunswick, NJ
Eckart, Rev. Frank K., '69 (TOL) Retired.
Eckberg, Rev. Joseph A., '00 (WCH) St. Mary, Derby, KS
Ecker, Rev. Msgr. John A., '58 (YAK) Curia: Leadership; Offices and Directors St. Paul Cathedral, Yakima, WA
Ecker, Rev. Msgr. Robert J., '51 (BRK) Retired.
Eckert, Rev. Msgr. John C., '72 (PH) Holy Trinity, Morrisville, PA
Eckert, Rev. John J., '10 (CHL) Sacred Heart, Salisbury, NC
Eckert, Rev. Sidney J., '66 (DET) Retired.
Eckert, Rev. Thomas, *CSC* '03 (FTW) [COL] University of Notre Dame Du Lac, Notre Dame, IN; [MIS] Holy Cross Foreign Mission Society, Inc. (Holy Cross Mission Center), Notre Dame, IN; [MON] Holy Cross Community, Corby Hall, University of Notre Dame, Notre Dame, IN
Eckert, Rev. Thomas J., *C.S.C.* '02 (PHX) [EFT] St. John Vianney School Development Fund, Goodyear, AZ
Eckinger, Rev. Ambrose, *O.P.* (COL)
Eckley, Rev. Michael P., '91 (OM) St. Wenceslaus, Omaha, NE
Eckrich, Rev. Brian, (SFS) Saint Joseph the Workman Parish of Minnehaha County, Colton, SD; Saint Rose of Lima Parish of Minnehaha County, Garretson, SD
Eckrich, Rev. Christopher M., (LIN) Curia: Offices and Directors
Eckrich, Rev. Christopher M., (LIN) Cathedral of the Risen Christ, Lincoln, NE
Eckroth, Rev. Leonard A., '58 (BIS) Retired. [NUR] Emmaus Place, Bismarck, ND
Eckstein, Rev. Francis J., '58 (IND) Retired.
Eco, Rev. Roy V., '80 (ORL) Blessed Sacrament, Clermont, FL
Edailakatt, Rev. Daniel, (MCE) St. Mary's Malankara Catholic Church, North Hollywood, CA
Edamattam, Rev. Thomas, (RVC) Retired.
Edassery, Rev. Davies, *S.A.C.* '88 (MIL) [MON] Pallotti House, Milwaukee, WI
Edathil, Rev. Michael P, '13 (WDC) Church of the Holy Spirit, Forestville, MD
Edathil, Rev. Michael Philipose, '13 (MCE) Curia: Advisory Boards, Commissions, Committees, and Councils; Offices and Directors St. Mary's Malankara Catholic Church, Forestville, MD
Edayadiyil, Rev. Jose, *VC* '73 (SYM) [MON] Vincentian House, Bensenville, IL
Eddy, Rev. Corbin, '68 (MAR) Retired.
Eddy, Rev. Joseph, *O.de.M.* '08 (SP) (>COL) Holy Family, Columbus, OH
Edeh, Rev. Charles, (WDC) St. Jerome, Hyattsville, MD
Edel, Rev. Ralph, '16 (BRK) Holy Family, Flushing, NY; St. Francis Preparatory School, Fresh Meadows, NY
Edelen, Rev. Luke A., *O.S.B.* '80 (NEW) Curia: Organizations (affiliated, inter-Diocesan, miscellaneous/ other) [MON] Benedictine Abbey of Newark, Newark, NJ
Edelen, Rev. Luke A., *O.S.B.* '80 (OLD) Curia: Leadership St. Ignatius of Antioch Syriac Catholic Mission, Worcester, MA
Edelen, Rev. Thomas, '01 (TYL) Retired.
Eden, Rev. Timothy, *SM* (CIN) [MON] Marianist Community, Novitiate, Dayton, OH
Edens, Rev. William, *C.S.P.* '81 (GR) Cathedral of St. Andrew, Grand Rapids, MI
Edet, Rev. Xavier, *S.S.J.* (BAL) Curia: (>MO) Offices and Directors St. Ann, Baltimore, MD; St. Francis Xavier, Baltimore, MD; St. Wenceslaus, Baltimore, MD
Edet, Rev. Xavier, *S.S.J.* (WDC) [MIS] African Conference of Catholic Clergy & Religious in the United States, Inc., Washington, DC
Edgar, Rev. Zachary T, (SFD) St. Rose of Lima Parish, Quincy, IL
Edgar, Rev. Zachary T., '12 (SFD) Chap, Illinois Veterans' Home, Quincy
Edgerly, Rev. Leo J., '84 (OAK) Curia: Offices and Directors Corpus Christi, Piedmont, CA
Ediza, Rev. Manuel, '79 (SD) Pastor of Saint Michael Catholic Parish, San Diego, a corporation sole, San Diego, CA; [MIS] Saint Michael Catholic Parish San Diego in San Diego, CA Real Property Support Corporation, San Diego, CA
Edlefsen, Rev. Frederick H., '01 (ARL) Our Lady of Lourdes, Arlington, VA
Edmunds, Rev. John S., *S.T.* '76 (CHI) St. James, Chicago, IL
Edney, Rev. Mark, '97 (SD) [MIS] The San Diego Catholic Account for Parishes and Schools, Incorporated, San Diego, CA
Edney, Rev. Ron Mark, '97 (SD) Pastor of Our Lady of the Valley Catholic Parish in El Centro, a corporation sole, El Centro, CA
Edogwo, Rev. Linus V., '86 (NEW) St. Mary of the Immaculate Conception, Newark, NJ
Edoka, Rev. Martins, (TUC) Chap, MCAS Chapel, Yuma
Edquist, Rev. Nate, '17 (GRY) Holy Family, La Porte, IN
Edquist, Rev. Nathaniel, (GRY) Curia: Offices and Directors
Eduarte, Rev. Edmund P., '93 (GAL) Curia: Leadership Blessed Sacrament, Houston, TX
Eduvala, Rev. Andre, *O.F.M.Cap.* '04 (AGN) Curia: Advisory Boards, Commissions, Committees, and Councils Our Lady of the Blessed Sacrament, Agana Heights, GU; [MON] St. Fidelis Friary, Agana Heights, GU
Edwards, Rev. (Bill) Guy F., (OG) [RTR] Our Lady of the Adirondacks Inc. House of Prayer, Ellenburg Center, NY
Edwards, Rev. Cassian, (PIT) St. Joseph the Worker, Pittsburgh, PA
Edwards, Rev. Cassian, *OSB* '21 (GBG) [MON] Saint Vincent Archabbey, Latrobe, PA
Edwards, Rev. Charles A., '86 (SFD) St. Jude, Rochester, IL
Edwards, Rev. Cyril D., '84 (SCR) Curia: Leadership Holy Cross High School, Dunmore, PA; Mary, Mother of God Parish, Scranton, PA
Edwards, Rev. Dale, '83 (FWT) Retired.
Edwards, Rev. David A., '02 (BEA) St. James, Port Arthur, TX
Edwards, Rev. Kelly L., (OKL) Curia: Consultative Bodies St. Eugene's, Weatherford, OK; [CAM] Southwestern Oklahoma State University, Weatherford, OK
Edwards, Rev. Michael W., '79 (PMB) Retired. Curia: Leadership
Edwards, Rev. Philip, *O.S.B.* '67 (LA) [MON] St. Andrew's Abbey (Benedictine Monks), Valyermo, CA; [RTR] St. Andrew's Abbey Retreat Center, Valyermo, CA
Edwards, Rev. Robert R., '81 (Y) Retired. Curia: Miscellaneous / Other Offices
Edwin, Rev. Jacob, *OCD* (PMB) St. Anastasia, Fort Pierce, FL
Effiong, Rev. Noel, *MSP* '89 (GAL) St. Gregory the Great, Houston, TX
Eftink, Rev. Glenn A., '93 (SPC) Curia: Advisory Boards, Commissions, Committees, and Councils; Organizations (affiliated, inter-Diocesan, miscellaneous/ other) St. Joseph, Advance, MO
Egan, Rev. Brennan, *O.F.M.* (NY) [MON] Franciscan Province of the Immaculate Conception, New York, NY
Egan, Rev. David J., '20 (PIT) Divine Grace, Cranberry Township, PA
Egan, Rev. Gerard P., '65 (CHI) Retired.
Egan, Rev. Harvey D., *S.J.* '69 (BO) [MON] The Jesuit Community at Boston College, Chestnut Hill, MA
Egan, Rev. Patrick, *O.S.B.* '08 (BIR) Sacred Heart of Jesus Catholic Parish, Cullman, Cullman, AL; [EFT] Friends of Sacred Heart School Endowment Foundation, Cullman, AL; [EFT] Natalie Collier Memorial Scholarship Fund, Cullman, AL; [MON] St. Bernard Abbey, Cullman, AL
Egan, Rev. Patrick, '66 (LAN) Retired.
Egan, Rev. Philip, '82 (KC) Holy Family, Kansas City, MO
Egan, Rev. Robert M., *C.S.V.* '78 (CHI) [MON] Viatorian Province Center-Clerics of St. Viator, Arlington Heights, IL
Egan, Rev. Thomas F., '75 (WOR) Retired.
Egan, Rev. Thomas R., *M.M.* '64 (CHI) Retired. (>NY) [MON] Maryknoll Fathers and Brothers (Catholic Foreign Mission Society of America, Inc.), Ossining, NY
Egbe, Rev. Dozie Romanus, '95 (PIT) Chap, UPMC Univ of Pittsburgh Med Ctr, Allegheny Cty
Egbeji, Rev. Jude, '89 (NY) Chap, Westchester Cty Jail, Valhalla; Calvary Hosp, Bronx
Egbi, Rev. Msgr. Cletus, (HT) St. Lucy, Houma, LA; St. Luke, Thibodaux, LA
Egging, Rev. Martin L., '93 (GI) Curia: Offices and Directors Blessed Sacrament, Grand Island, NE
Eggleston, Rev. Earl, '96 (SD) Pastor of Saint Anne Catholic Parish, San Diego, a corporation sole, San Diego, CA
Egiguren, Rev. Antonio, *OFM* '80 (FRS) St. Patrick's Parish and Our Lady of Mercy Church, Merced, CA
Egitto, Rev. Philip J., '88 (ORL) Our Lady of Lourdes, Daytona Beach, FL

Ego, Rev. Anthony M., '85 (PEO) Mary, Our Lady of Peace, Orion, IL; St. Maria Goretti, Coal Valley, IL
Eguino, Rev. Michael, (NY) Parish of St. Anselm and St. Roch, Bronx, NY
Ehalt, Rev. William L., '99 (IND) St. Catherine of Siena Parish, Decatur County, Inc., Greensburg, IN
Ehli, Rev. Joshua, '09 (BIS) Curia: Leadership Cathedral of the Holy Spirit, Bismarck, ND
Ehmke, Rev. Matthew, '70 (STP) Retired.
Ehrich, Rev. John D., '00 (PHX) St. Thomas More Roman Catholic Parish, Glendale, AZ
Ehrman, Rev. Dale, *O.S.C.* (LFT) Curia: Leadership
Ehrman, Rev. Dale W., '90 (LFT) Holy Spirit Church, Fishers, IN; St. John Vianney Parish, Fishers, IN
Ehrman, Rev. Terrence P., *C.S.C.* '00 (FTW) [COL] University of Notre Dame Du Lac, Notre Dame, IN; [MON] Holy Cross Community, Corby Hall, University of Notre Dame, Notre Dame, IN
Eichenberger, Rev. Thomas P., '76 (MIL) Retired.
Eichhorst, Rev. Franklin, *O.F.M.Cap.* '50 (MIL) Retired.
Eichhorst, Rev. Franklin, (GB) Retired. [MON] St. Fidelis Friary, Appleton, WI
Eichman, Rev. James, *FSSP* (KCK) On Special Assignment. Asst Chap, Community of St. John-Mary Vianney, Maple Hill
Eichman, Rev. Nicholas, *FSSP* '21 (B) St. Joan of Arc, Post Falls, ID
Eichor, Rev. Barnabas, *O.F.M.Cap.* '11 (KCK) St. Aloysius, Meriden, KS; St. Theresa, Perry, KS; [MON] St. Conrad Friary, Lawrence, KS
Eickhoff, Rev. Jeffrey R., '95 (LIN) St. Wenceslaus, Wahoo, NE
Eickhoff, Rev. Matthew F., '89 (LIN) Curia: Leadership; Offices and Directors
Eickhoff, Rev. Matthew F., '89 (LIN) St. Joseph's, Benkelman, NE
Eickhoff, Rev. Stephen, '10 (JOL) St. Anne, Oswego, IL
Eid, Rev. Elie, '07 (NTN) St. Michael, Plymouth, MI
Eid, Rev. Ronald W., '21 (OLL) Our Lady of the Cedars of Mt. Lebanon Maronite Catholic Church, Fairlawn, OH
Eifler, Rev. John G., '61 (L) Retired.
Eikhuemelo, Rev. Bernardine, '96 (STA) Church of the Crucifixion, Jacksonville, FL; Holy Rosary, Jacksonville, FL; St. Pius V, Jacksonville, FL
Eilen, Rev. Allan Paul, '09 (STP) St. Patrick, Oak Grove, MN; The Way of the Shepherd, Blaine, MN; [CEM] St. Patrick of Cedar Creek Cemetery, Oak Grove, MN
Eilerman, Rev. Craig R., '87 (COL) The Basilica of St. Mary of the Assumption, Lancaster, OH; [EFT] St. Mary of the Assumption Foundation, Lancaster, OH
Eilers, Rev. Brian, '04 (AUS) St. Joseph, Bryan, TX
Eilert, Rev. Msgr. Edward J., '64 (NEW) Retired. [MON] St. John Vianney Residence for Retired Priests, Rutherford, NJ
Eiroa, Rev. Andres, (POD) Curia: Clergy and Religious Services
Eiroa, Rev. Andres, '88 (SJN) [MIS] Opus Dei, Guaynabo, PR
Eirvin, Rev. Jeffrey, '12 (P) St. Therese of the Child Jesus, Portland, OR
Eis, Rev. Charles R., '66 (SPK) Retired.
Eisele, Rev. James F., '88 (LAN) St. Michael Parish Grand Ledge, Grand Ledge, MI
Eisele, Rev. Paul F., '68 (SC) Retired.
Eisweirth, Rev. Thomas C., '74 (Y) Retired. Blessed Sacrament, Warren, OH
Ejaidu, Rev. Cyril Ngbede, '95 (AUS) St. John the Baptist, Waco, TX
Ejike, Rev. John, '78 (FAR) St. Timothy's Church of Manvel, Manvel, ND
Ejimadu, Rev. Festus N., '93 (DET) Ss. John and Paul Parish Washington Township, Washington, MI
Ejiofo, Rev. Lawrence, (MO) Curia: Offices and Directors
Ejiogu, Rev. Cornelius K., '13 (WDC) Curia: Consultative Bodies St. Luke, Washington, DC
Ejsymont, Rev. Cezary, (FBK) Sacred Heart Cathedral Catholic Church Fairbanks, Fairbanks, AK; [MON] St. Ignatius Residence, Fairbanks, AK
Ekaitis, Very Rev. Timothy M., '07 (MAR) Curia: Offices and Directors St. Louis the King (Harvey), Marquette, MI
Ekanem, Rev. Anthony, *M.S.P.* (NY) Immaculate Conception, Yonkers, NY
Ekanem, Rev. Peter, (BUF) Blessed Sacrament, Tonawanda, NY; St. Paul, Kenmore, NY
Ekdahl, Rev. Kenneth W., '91 (TR) Retired.
Eke, Rev. Anselm, *MSP* '92 (DOD) Curia: Offices and Directors St. Ann Catholic Church of Olmitz, Kansas, Olmitz, KS; St. John the Evangelist Catholic Church of Hoisington, Kansas, Hoisington, KS
Eke, Rev. Casimir, *C.S.Sp.* '74 (CHI)
Eke, Rev. Martin, (GAL) St. Francis of Assisi, Houston, TX
Eke, Rev. Peter, (GLD) Our Lady of the Lake of Prudenville, Prudenville, MI
Eke, Rev. Peter O., '97 (GLD) Curia: Offices and Directors Saint Hubert of Higgins Lake, Higgins Lake, MI; Saint James the Greater of Houghton Lake, Houghton Lake, MI
Eke, Rev. Rafael E., '01 (SAT) Chap, US Army
Eke, Rev. Raphael, (MO) Curia: Offices and Directors
Eke, Rev. Raphael E., '01 (SAT) Chap, Brooke Army Med Ctr, Fort Sam Houston
Ekebe, Rev. Divine, (GLP) Sacred Heart, Quemado, NM
Ekechukwu, Rev. Alexander, *C.S.Sp.* '73 (MIA) Holy Redeemer, Miami, FL
Ekeh, Rev. Paul, '97 (PBL) Sacred Heart, Fruita, CO
Ekekwe, Rev. Kenneth D., '00 (CHI) St. Mother Theodore Guerin, Elmwood Park, IL
Ekenedo, Rev. Marcelinus, (FRS) St. Paul, Tranquillity, CA
Ekeno, Rev. Augustine E., *S.J.* '17 (WDC) [MON] The Jesuit Community of St. Aloysius Gonzaga, Washington, DC
Ekeocha, Very Rev. James M., '07 (AUS) Curia: Leadership St. Jerome, Waco, TX
Ekeocha, Rev. John O., '93 (WDC) [HOS] Medstar Georgetown University Hospital, Washington, DC
Ekete, Rev. Damian, '95 (NY) Holy Spirit, Bronx, NY
Ekezie, Rev. Franklin Ifeanyichukwu, '21 (MIA) St. Coleman, Pompano Beach, FL
Ekiert, Rev. Ireneusz, '00 (MIA) Epiphany, Miami, FL
Ekisa, Rev. Deogratias O., '98 (NO) [SEM] Notre Dame Seminary Graduate School of Theology, New Orleans, LA
Ekka, Rev. Alexius, '81 (JC) Our Lady of the Snows, Mary's Home, MO; Sacred Heart, Eldon, MO
Ekka, Rev. Louis T., '89 (LAN) St. Mary Queen of Angels Parish Swartz Creek, Swartz Creek, MI
Ekosse, Rev. Raymond, (CHL) St. Thomas Aquinas, Charlotte, NC
Ekpenyong, Rev. Andrew E., (OM) St. Mary Magdalene, Omaha, NE
Ekwebelam, Rev. Chrisantus, (SB) Chap, Kaiser Permanente Hosp, Fontana
Ekwelum, Rev. Emeka Emmanuel, *M.S.S.C.C.* (CHR) Our Lady of the Valley, Gloverville, SC; St. Mary of the Immaculate Conception, Edgefield, SC
Ekwere, Rev. Ofonmbuk (Oscar), (WIL) SS. Peter and Paul, Easton, MD; St. Dennis, Galena, MD
El Basha, Rev. Assaad, *M.L.M.* '92 (OLL) Our Lady of Lebanon Maronite Catholic Church, Lewisville, TX; [MON] The Congregation of Maronite Lebanese Missionaries, Houston, TX
El Hachem, Rev. Boutros, (SAM) St. Louis Gonzaga, Utica, NY
El Hachem, Rev. Boutros, (SAM) Curia: Offices and Directors
El Haddad, Rev. Ibrahim, *B.S.O.* (NTN) [MON] Monastery of St. Basil the Great, Methuen, MA
El Helou, Rev. Jean-Maroun, '02 (OLL) St. Elias Maronite Catholic Church, Birmingham, AL
El Khoury, Rev. Pierre, *M.L.M.* '98 (OLL) Our Lady of Lebanon Maronite Catholic Church, Lombard, IL; [MON] The Congregation of Maronite Lebanese Missionaries, Houston, TX
El Tabchi, Rev. Fadi (Andrawos), '17 (SAM) St. Maron, Philadelphia, PA
Elam, Rev. Raymond, *O.S.A.* '70 (SD) Retired. [MON] Augustinian Community, San Diego, CA
Elambasseril, Rev. George, '92 (SYM) St. Thomas Syro-Malabar Catholic Church (Bronx), Bronx, NY; St. Thomas Syro-Malabar Catholic Mission Westchester, New York of St. Thomas Syro-Malabar Catholic Diocese of Chicago, Bronx, NY
Elamparo, Rev. Edgar, '18 (SJ) St. John the Baptist, Milpitas, CA
Elamturuthil, Rev. Babu Joseph, '87 (WH) St. Augustine, Grafton, WV; St. Elizabeth Parish, Philippi, WV
Elanjileth, Rev. J. Matthew, '45 (PIT) Retired.
Elanjimattathil, Rev. Michael, *C.M.I.* '96 (SAL) St. Mary Help of Christians Parish, Gorham, Inc., Gorham, KS; St. Mary, Queen of Angels Parish, Russell, Inc., Russell, KS
Elavungal, Rev. Roy Isac, *SDB* '01 (BAK) St. Alphonsus, Dufur, OR; St. Mary, Wasco, OR
Elbert, Rev. Colby J., (SPC) Curia: Consultative Bodies Notre Dame Regional High School, Cape Girardeau, MO; St. Francis Xavier, Sikeston, MO
Elbert, Rev. Kevin P., '10 (CLV) Curia: Advisory Boards, Commissions, Committees, and Councils St. Luke, Lakewood, OH
Elder, Rev. Gregory, '06 (SB) Curia: Advisory Boards, Commissions, Committees, and Councils Christ of the Desert, Palm Desert, CA; Sacred Heart, Palm Desert, CA
Elder, Rev. Joseph Mary, *O.F.M.Cap.* '12 (DEN) [MON] St. Francis of Assisi Friary, Denver, CO
Elder, Rev. Ryan W., '13 (R) Holy Family, Hillsborough, NC
Elder, Rev. William S., '81 (NY) [SEM] St. Joseph's Seminary, Yonkers, NY
Eldridge, Rev. Darren J., '07 (LAF) St. Catherine, Leonville, LA; St. Leo the Great, Leonville, LA
Eldridge, Rev. Francis, *S.A.* '77 (NY) [MIS] Atonement Friars, New York, NY; [MON] Franciscan Friars of the Atonement, Garrison, NY; [MON] Franciscan Friars of the Atonement, Minister General Office, Garrison, NY
Eldridge, Rev. Frank, (BGP) St. Peter's Corporate Society, Danbury, CT
Elewaut, Rev. Thomas J., '86 (LA) Mission Basilica San Buenaventura, Ventura, CA
Elford, Rev. Ricardo, *C.Ss.R.* '64 (TUC) [MON] Redemptorist Society of Arizona Desert House of Prayer Residence, Tucson, AZ; [RTR] Redemptorist Society of Arizona Redemptorist Renewal Center, Tucson, AZ
Elhajj, Rev. Simon, (SAM) [EFT] Saint Sharbel Maronite Catholic Church Endowment Trust, Somerset, NJ
El-hajj, Rev. Simon, '10 (SAM) Saint Sharbel Maronite Catholic Church, Somerset, NJ
Eli, Rev. Jude, *O.P.* '76 (LA) St. Dominic, Los Angeles, CA
Elia, Chorbishop Faouzi, '77 (OLL) Curia: Facilities; Offices and Directors St. Sharbel Maronite Catholic Church, Peoria, IL
Elia, Rev. Victor, *C.M.* '57 (NY) [MON] Vincentian Fathers (Padres Paules Community (Vincentians) Inc.), New York, NY
Elias, Rt. Rev. Alistar, *C.Ss.R.* (BAL) St. Mary, Annapolis, MD
Elias, Rev. Mazen Michael, '21 (STA) Holy Faith, Gainesville, FL
Elie, Rev. Matthew J., '05 (BEL) Blessed Sacrament, Belleville, IL; Our Lady Queen of Peace, Belleville, IL
Elis, Rev. Patrick H., '69 (BUF) Retired.
Elis, Rev. Tomas Alfonso, '70 (LA) Retired.
Elizardo, Rev. Pedro T., '01 (CC) Curia: Administration; Leadership Corpus Christi Cathedral, Corpus Christi, TX; Sacred Heart, Corpus Christi, TX; [MIS] The Cathedral Concert Series, Corpus Christi, TX
Elizarraras, Rev. Edson, '16 (TUC) Saint Christopher Roman Catholic Parish - Marana, Marana, AZ
Elizondo, Rev. Ernesto, '00 (AUS) Retired.
El-Khalli, Rev. Msgr. Georges Y., '81 (SAM) Curia: Offices and Directors
El-Khalli, Rev. Msgr. Georges Y., '81 (SAM) Our Lady of the Cedars of Lebanon Maronite Catholic Church, Jamaica Plain, MA
Elkhourey, Rev. Armando, (SAM) [SEM] Our Lady of Lebanon Maronite Seminary, Washington, DC
Elkhoury, Rev. Armando, '04 (OLL) On Special Assignment. Our Lady of Lebanon Seminary, Washington, DC Curia: Offices and Directors
Elkin, Rev. Msgr. Frederic F., '77 (SY) Retired.
Elko, Rev. Joseph M., '70 (HRT) Saint Martin de Porres Church Corporation, New Haven, CT
Ellerman, Rev. Thomas E., *S.M.* '67 (ATL) Retired. Marist School, Atlanta, GA
Ellias, Rev. John J., '64 (ALT) Retired.
Ellickal Joseph, Rev. Saji, (VEN) Our Lady of Lourdes Parish in Venice, Inc., Venice, FL
Elliott, Rev. Cuthbert, *O.S.B.* '15 (STL) St. Louis Priory School, Creve Coeur, MO; [MON] The Abbey of St. Mary and St. Louis, St. Louis, MO
Elliott, Rev. George T., '15 (TYL) Curia: Advisory Boards, Commissions, Committees, and Councils Sacred Heart, Nacogdoches, TX; [CAM] St. Mary's Catholic Campus Ministry, Nacogdoches, TX
Elliott, Rev. Joseph W., '71 (OG) Retired.
Elliott, Rev. Ronald J., '02 (KC) Retired.
Elliott, Rev. Thomas, *C.S.C.* (FTW) [MIS] Holy Cross House, Notre Dame, IN
Elliott, Rev. Timothy P., '82 (STL) St. Gianna Catholic Church, Wentzville, MO
Elliott, Rev. Trumie Culpepper, '88 (L) Retired.
Elliott, Rev. W. Gregg, '00 (TLS) Retired.
Elliott, Rev. Msgr. William, '60 (SD) Retired.
Elliott, Rev. Zachary, *O.F.M.* '08 (SP) Sacred Heart, Tampa, FL
Ellis, Rev. Jeffrey R., '16 (NOR) Curia: Tribunal
Ellis, Rev. Joah, '83 (STP) Our Lady of Peace, Minneapolis, MN
Ellis, Rev. Kail C., *O.S.A.* '67 (PH) [COL] Villanova University, Villanova, PA; [MON] St. John Stone

Friary, Villanova, PA
Ellis, Rev. Matthew, '98 (DET) St. Isidore Parish Macomb Township, Macomb, MI
Ellison, Rev. Joseph T., (SB) St. Mel, Norco, CA
Ellorin, Rev. Raymund, '91 (HON) St. George, Waimanalo, HI
Elmer, Rev. John, *O.F.M.Conv.* '73 (IND) [RTR] Mount Saint Francis Friary and Retreat Center, Mount St. Francis, IN
Elmer, Rev. Msgr. Timothy S., '73 (SY) On Special Assignment. Curia: Leadership Blessed Sacrament, Syracuse, NY; [EFT] Grimes Foundation, Syracuse, NY; [MIS] The Syracuse Diocesan Investment Fund, Inc., Syracuse, NY
Elmhorst, Rev. Clayton R., '14 (LC) On Sick Leave.
Elsasser, Rev. Thomas G., '88 (CLV) St. Mary of the Assumption, Mentor, OH
Elsbernd, Rev. James H., '90 (CIN) Bethesda North Hosp St. Joseph, Hamilton, OH
Elser, Rev. Stephen, '18 (LR) Curia: Leadership; Offices and Directors St. John the Baptist, Engelberg, AR; St. Joseph the Worker Church, Corning, AR; St. Paul the Apostle, Pocahontas, AR
Elser, Rev. William, '86 (LR) Curia: Offices and Directors Sacred Heart of Jesus, Hot Springs, AR
Elshoff, Rev. Matthew, *O.F.M.Cap.* '82 (LA) St. Lawrence of Brindisi, Los Angeles, CA
Elskamp, Rev. Frederick J., '62 (JC) Retired.
Elston, Rev. Joseph G., '85 (SCR) On Special Assignment. Curia: Leadership; Offices and Directors St. John the Evangelist, Pittston, PA; St. Joseph Marello Parish, Pittston, PA
Elue, Rev. Callistus, (ALT) SS. Gregory & Barnabas, Johnstown, PA
Eluka, Rev. Akajiaku, (MO) Curia: Offices and Directors
Eluka, Rev. Akajiaku Pius, (RVC) Chap, Stony Brook Univ Hosp
Elukkunel, Rev. Binoj Jose, (SAT) St. Peter Prince of the Apostles, San Antonio, TX
Elukkunnel, Rev. Binoj Jose, *H.G.N.* '07 (SAT) Our Lady of Grace, San Antonio, TX; Our Lady of Sorrows, San Antonio, TX
Eluo, Rev. Jean-B Kikwaya, *S.J.* '98 (TUC) [MON] Jesuit Community of the Vatican Observatory, Tucson, AZ
Eluvathingal, Rev. Jose, *S.A.C.* '85 (MIL) [MON] Pallotti House, Milwaukee, WI
Ely, Rev. Peter B., *S.J.* '69 (SEA) [COL] Seattle University, Seattle, WA; [MON] Arrupe Jesuit Community at Seattle University, Seattle, WA
Elyse, Rev. Esteker, *S.M.M.* '94 (MIA) [NUR] Villa Maria West Skilled Nursing Facility, Hialeah, FL
Elzner, Rev. Taylor J, '20 (AMA) St. Laurence Church, Amarillo, TX
Emanuel, Rev. John, '92 (TUC) Retired.
Emanuel, Rev. Sergiy, '12 (BRK) Guardian Angel, Brooklyn, NY; [CCH] Russian Speaking/Ukrainian Ministry, ,
Emanuel, Rev. Steven, '93 (OM) St. Francis, Humphrey, NE
Embach, Rev. Kevin, *S.J.* '18 (OM) [MON] Jesuit Community at Creighton University, Omaha, NE
Emechete, Rev. Innocent, '72 (SB) Chap, Federal Corrections Inst, Victorville
Emeh, Rev. Marcel, *S.D.S.* '18 (SAC) Pastor of Holy Trinity Parish, El Dorado Hills, a corporation sole, El Dorado Hills, CA
Emeh, Rev. Martins, '02 (GAL) St. Monica, Houston, TX
Emeh, Rev. Martins C., '02 (RCK) On Duty Outside Diocese. Archdiocese of Galveston-Houston
Emeh, Rev. Wilfred E., '04 (PH) St. Agnes, West Chester, PA
Emeli, Rev. Edwin O., '88 (TUC) Curia: (>MO) Offices and Directors
Emerick, Rev. Stephen J., '58 (CIN) Retired.
Emerson, Rev. George F., '56 (BO) Retired.
Emerson, Rev. Scott J., '15 (MAD) Curia: Offices and Directors St. Maria Goretti Congregation, Madison, WI
Emery, Rev. Jonathan, '14 (SP) St. Matthew, Largo, FL
Emery, Rev. Msgr. Robert E., '87 (NEW) St. Aloysius, Caldwell, NJ
Emile Dormil, Rev. Athas S., *C.M.* (PCE) San Vicente de Paul, Ponce, PR
Emmanuel, Rev. Binu, *C.S.T.* '14 (WH) St. Patrick, Mannington, WV; St. Peter, Farmington, WV; [CAM] Fairmont State University Newman Center, Fairmont, WV
Emmanuel, Rev. Joseph A., '81 (NY) Our Lady of Mount Carmel, Tuxedo, NY; Parish of St. Joan of Arc-Our Lady of Mount Carmel, Sloatsburg, NY
Emmanuel, Rev. Sagayaraj, *M.S.C.* (SB) Our Lady of Mount Carmel, Rancho Cucamonga, CA
Emmanuelli, Rev. Andres, '17 (SAC) On Leave.
Emmanuelli, Rev. Andres M., (OAK) Our Lady of Lourdes, Oakland, CA
Emmick, Rev. Brian S., '12 (EVN) Curia: Leadership Precious Blood, Jasper, IN
Emminger, Rev. Christopher, '20 (BUF) Assumption, Buffalo, NY; Holy Spirit, Buffalo, NY; St. Mark, Buffalo, NY
Emmons, Rev. Rayford E., '74 (PH) Holy Cross, Philadelphia, PA
Empereur, Rev. James L., *S.J.* '65 (SAT) (>MIL) [MON] St. Camillus Jesuit Community (Society of Jesus, USA Midwest Province), Wauwatosa, WI
Emrisek, Rev. Gene, *O.F.M.Cap.* '68 (COS) [MIS] Catholic Center at the Citadel, Colorado Springs, CO; [MON] Solanus Casey Friary, Colorado Springs, CO
Emumwen, Rev. Victor O., (NY) St. Aloysius, New York, NY
Emunemu, Rev. Jude O., '08 (NO) The Visitation of Our Lady Roman Catholic Church, Marrero, Louisiana, Marrero, LA
Emusa, Rev. Peter, '97 (LAF) St. Jules, Franklin, LA
Emwalu, Rev. Romple, (HON) St. Michael, Waialua, HI
Encinares, Rev. Msgr. Cesar E., '77 (SB) Retired.
Encinas, Rev. Carlos Alberto, (VEN) St. Agnes Parish in Naples, Inc., Naples, FL
Encisco, Rev. Frank, *C.S.V.* (CHI) [MON] Viatorian Province Center-Clerics of St. Viator, Arlington Heights, IL
Enderle, Rev. Gilbert, *C.Ss.R.* '62 (NO) St. Alphonsus, New Orleans, LA; [SHR] National Shrine of Blessed Francis Xavier Seelos, New Orleans, LA
Enderlin, Rev. R. E., '69 (PEO) Retired.
Enderlin, Rev. Ronald, '69 (PEO) Retired.
Endiape, Rev. Dario Z, (RCK) St. Mary, Huntley, IL
Endorf, Rev. Boniface, (NY) St. Joseph, New York, NY
Endres, Rev. David J., '09 (CIN) Curia: Administration; Offices and Directors St. Mary, Bethel, OH; St. Peter, New Richmond, OH; [SEM] Mount St. Mary's Seminary of the West, Cincinnati, OH; [SEM] The Athenaeum of Ohio, Cincinnati, OH
Endres, Rev. James F., '82 (PH) Retired. St. Robert Bellarmine, Warrington, PA
Endres, Rev. William, '69 (ROC) Retired. St. Jerome, East Rochester, NY
Endress, Rev. James, '60 (EVN) Retired.
Ene, Rev. Herbert, '97 (MEM) St. Mary Church, Camden, TN
Ene, Rev. Martin, (NY) Chap, NY Univ Med Ctr, New York; Hosp for Joint Disease
Eneh, Rev. Barry C., (MO) Curia: Offices and Directors
Eneji, Rev. Richard, *C.S.Sp.* '05 (BUR) Chap, Univ of Vermont Med Ctr, Burlington
Enelichi, Rev. Alphonsus, *M.S.P.* '90 (GF) Curia: Leadership Our Lady of Lourdes, Great Falls, MT
Enemali, Rev. Aloysius, (BRK) Curia: Leadership
Enemali, Rev. Mark, *CssP* '06 (FTW) Immaculate Conception, Auburn, IN
Engbarth, Rev. David R., '76 (RCK) Retired.
Engebretson, Rev. Aaron, *S.J.* '15 (SAC) Jesuit High School, Carmichael, CA; [MON] Sacramento Jesuit Community, Carmichael, CA
Engelbrecht, Rev. S. Stephen, '00 (PEO) Sacred Heart, Annawan, IL; St. Anthony's, Atkinson, IL
Engelhart, Rev. Henry R., '63 (BEL) Retired.
Engh, Rev. Michael, *S.J.* '81 (LA) [MON] Jesuit Community, Los Angeles, CA
England, Rev. Barry C., '68 (FTW) Retired.
Engler, Rev. Clarence A., *M.M.* '59 (NY) Retired.
Engler, Rev. John Chapin, '07 (WH) Christ the King, Dunbar, WV; Holy Trinity, Nitro, WV; [MIS] Daily Living Ministries, Inc., Wheeling, WV
Englert, Rev. Michael, *OFM Conv.* '89 (HRT) Saint Paul Parish Corporation, Kensington, CT; [MIS] St. Paul Friary (St. Paul Parish Corporation), Kensington, CT
English, Rev. Joseph, *O.F.M.Cap.* '90 (AGN) Curia: Miscellaneous / Other Offices Santa Teresita Catholic Church, Mangilao, GU; [MON] St. Fidelis Friary, Agana Heights, GU
English, Rev. Michael, '18 (SAT) St. Thomas More, San Antonio, TX
English, Rev. Paul F, *CSB* '85 (GAL) [CAM] University of St. Thomas Campus Ministry, Houston, TX; [MON] Keon House, Houston, TX
English, Rev. Robert K., (OM) Retired.
English, Rev. Sean P., '14 (PH) St. Stanislaus, Lansdale, PA
English, Rev. Msgr. William J., '69 (WDC) Retired. Curia: Consultative Bodies
Engurait, Rev. Simon Peter, '13 (HT) Curia: Administration; Faith Formation; Leadership
Engurait, Rev. Simon Peter, *V.G.* (HT) St. Bridget, Schriever, LA
Enke, Rev. Msgr. Paul P., '72 (COL) St. Edward the Confessor, Granville, OH
Enlow, Rev. Msgr. Leo, '75 (SFD) Curia: Deaneries
Enlow, Rev. Msgr. Leo J., '75 (SFD) St. Peter, Quincy, IL; [ASN] Catholic Cemetery Association, Quincy, IL
Enman, Rev. Frederick, *S.J.* '88 (BO) [MON] The Jesuit Community at Boston College, Chestnut Hill, MA
Enneking, Rev. Marvin, '91 (SCL) Curia: Leadership St. Andrew's, Greenwald, MN; St. John's, Melrose, MN; St. Mary's, Melrose, MN; St. Michael's, Melrose, MN
Enneking, Rev. Thomas, *O.S.C.* '84 (CHI) [MON] Crosier Community of Chicago, Chicago, IL
Enneking, Rev. Thomas A., *O.S.C.* '84 (PHX) [MON] Conventual Priory of the Holy Cross (Crosier Fathers and Brothers Province, Inc.), Phoenix, AZ; [MON] Crosier Community of Phoenix (Canons Regular of the Order of the Holy Cross) (Conventual Priory of the Holy Cross), Phoenix, AZ; [MON] Crosier Village of Phoenix, Phoenix, AZ
Ennis, Rev. Timothy, *O.Carm.* '02 (NY) [MON] Brandsma Priory (Carmelite Friars (North American Prov. of St. Elias and Most Pure Heart of Mary Province)), Middletown, NY
Ennis, Rev. Msgr. William, '64 (ORL) Retired.
Enoh, Rev. Emmanuel, '10 (OWN) Curia: (>MO) Offices and Directors
Enoh, Rev. Uwem, '10 (OWN) On Duty Outside Diocese. Air Force Chaplain, Atlus, OK
Enright, Rev. James C., '69 (BUF) Retired.
Enright, Rev. Michael P., '84 (CHI) St. Paul, Chicago, IL
Enrique, Rev. Marcos, (BO) St. Ambrose, Boston, MA; St. Mark, Boston, MA
Enriquez, Rev. Alexander, '85 (TR) Church of St. Monica, Jackson, NJ
Enriquez, Rev. Bonfilio, *SJS* '08 (MET) Our Lady of Mt. Carmel, New Brunswick, NJ; [MON] Society of Jesus Christ the Priest, Stewartsville, NJ
Ensey, Rev. Eric S., '95 (SCR) On Leave.
Ensman, Rev. Raymond E., '66 (TOL) Retired.
Enudu, Rev. Simon M., '13 (SPC) Sacred Heart, Conway, MO; St. William, Buffalo, MO
Enyan-Boadu, Rev. Peter, '84 (ROC) Retired. St. John the Evangelist, Rochester, NY
Enyiaka, Rev. Canice, '01 (WDC) St. Matthias Apostle, Lanham, MD
Enyinmful, Rev. Anthony, '99 (NY) Holy Family, Staten Island, NY
Enzeani, Rev. Fidelis, (NY) St. Ann, Congers, NY
Enzler, Rev. Msgr. John, '73 (WDC) [CCH] Catholic Charities of the Archdiocese of Washington, Inc., Washington, DC
Enzler, Rev. Msgr. John J., '73 (WDC) On Special Assignment. Curia: Consultative Bodies St. Bartholomew, Bethesda, MD
Enzweiler, Rev. Msgr. Donald A., '87 (COV) On Leave.
Enzweiler, Rev. Raymond N., '06 (COV) Curia: Advisory Boards, Commissions, Committees, and Councils St. Thomas, Fort Thomas, KY; [COL] Thomas More University, Crestview Hills, KY
Epah, Rev. Mugagga, '10 (BIR) St. Francis of Assisi Catholic Parish, Tuscaloosa, Tuscaloosa, AL
Eppenbrock, Rev. Donald J., '60 (SAG) Retired. Ave Maria Parish of Lexington, Lexington, MI
Epperson, Rev. Frank, '01 (SR) Curia: Leadership; Offices and Directors Pastor of St. Eugene Cathedral of Santa Rosa, A Corporation Sole, Santa Rosa, CA
Epping, Rev. Robert, *C.S.C.* '70 (FTW) [MON] Holy Cross Community, Corby Hall, University of Notre Dame, Notre Dame, IN
Epping, Rev. Ross M., '16 (DAV) St. Peter Church of Buffalo, Iowa, Buffalo, IA; [COL] St. Ambrose University, Davenport, IA
Eppler, Rev. Jeff, '03 (FAR) Sacred Heart Church of Oakwood, Grafton, ND; St. John the Evangelist's Church of Grafton, Grafton, ND
Epstein, Rev. Jacob, '21 (DM) Corpus Christi, Council Bluffs, IA
Eraly, Rev. Mathew, '75 (NEW) Chap, Veterans Administration Hosp, East Orange St. Philomena, Livingston, NJ
Eraly, Rev. Mathew, '75 (MO) Curia: Offices and Directors
Eranimus Fernandez, Rev. Cyprian, (IND) St. Gabriel the Archangel Catholic Church, Indianapolis, Inc., Indianapolis, IN
Erazo, Rev. Henry, (DAL) St. Ann Catholic Parish - Kaufman, Kaufman, TX
Erbland, Rev. Philip N., *M.M.* '66 (NY) Retired. [MON] Maryknoll Fathers and Brothers (Catholic Foreign Mission Society of America, Inc.), Ossining, NY

Erdle, Rev. Thomas M., '55 (ROC) Retired.
Erdlen, Rev. Harry J., *O.S.A.* '57 (PH) [MON] St. Thomas Monastery, Villanova, PA
Erdman, Rev. Jonathan, '17 (POC) Our Lady and Saint John Catholic Church, Louisville, KY
Ericksen, Rev. Matthew, '09 (SAV) [HOS] St. Joseph's Hospital, Inc., Savannah, GA
Erickson, Rev. David, '97 (CHY) St. Patrick's, Diamondville, WY
Erickson, Rev. John Paul, '06 (STP) Transfiguration, Oakdale, MN
Erickson, Rev. Joshua, '18 (STU) Curia: Deaneries Blessed Sacrament, Wintersville, OH; Our Lady of Lourdes, Wintersville, OH
Erickson, Friar Matthew, *O.P.* '90 (RIC) St. Thomas Aquinas, Charlottesville, VA
Erickson, Rev. Paul, (LAN) St. Mary Magdalen Parish Brighton, Brighton, MI
Erickson, Very Rev. Philip Lee, '95 (L) Curia: Leadership Our Mother of Sorrows, Louisville, KY; St. Elizabeth of Hungary, Louisville, KY; St. Therese, Louisville, KY
Erickson, Rev. Robert, (SPK) [MON] Regis Community, Spokane, WA
Erikson, Rev. Richard M., '85 (BO) On Duty Outside Diocese.
Erlander, Rev. Michael, '68 (STP) Retired.
Erlenbush, Rev. Ryan, '09 (GF) Curia: Leadership; Offices and Directors Corpus Christi, Great Falls, MT; [EFT] St. Joseph's Education Trust, Great Falls, MT
Ermatinger, Rev. Cliff O., '97 (MIL) On Special Assignment. Waukesha
Ermatinger, Rev. Roderick, '05 (HEL) Curia: Leadership Saint Anne Parish: Series 333, LLC, Heart Butte, MT; Saint Teresa of the Little Flower Parish: Series 310, LLC, Browning, MT
Ermer, Rev. James, '78 (FAR) St. Leo's Church of Casselton, Casselton, ND; St. Thomas Church of Buffalo, Buffalo, ND
Ermis, Rev. Norman, '83 (SAT) St. Peter the Apostle, Boerne, TX
Ernest, Rev. Bryan D., '82 (GI) Curia: Leadership; Offices and Directors St. Luke's, Ogallala, NE
Ernest, Rev. Matthew S., '04 (NY) Curia: Leadership; Offices and Directors [SEM] St. Joseph's Seminary, Yonkers, NY
Ernst, Rev. Anthony, '98 (EVN) Curia: Leadership St. Francis Xavier, Vincennes, IN; St. Philip Neri, Bicknell, IN; [CEM] Calvary, Vincennes, IN; [MIS] Old Cathedral Library & Museum, Inc., Vincennes, IN
Ernst, Rev. Anthony R., '98 (EVN) On Special Assignment. Curia: Offices and Directors
Ernst, Rev. Msgr. Norbert A., '72 (STL) St. Margaret Mary Alacoque Catholic Church, St. Louis, MO
Ernst, Rev. Stephen T., *S.T.* '86 (WDC) [MON] Father Judge Missionary Cenacle, Adelphi, MD
Ernst, Rev. William W., '64 (IND) Retired.
Erondu, Rev. Isaac Emeka, '93 (BWN) Curia: Leadership St. Paul, Mission, TX
Erpelding, Rev. Edward, '66 (FTW) Retired.
Erpelding, Rev. Michael J., '89 (SC) Curia: Leadership St. John, Onawa, IA; St. Joseph's, Salix, IA
Erps, Rev. James D., *S.J.* (BO) St. Ignatius Loyola, Chestnut Hill, MA; [MON] The Jesuit Community at Boston College, Chestnut Hill, MA
Errecalde Conte, Rev. Javier, *O. de M.* (PCE) Retired. Parroquia San Judas Tadeo, Ponce, PR
Ertle, Rev. Thomas J., *O.P.* '56 (PRO) [MON] St. Thomas Aquinas Priory at Providence College, Providence, RI
Eruaga, Rev. Donald, *M.S.P.* (CHI) SS. Martha, Mary, and Lazarus Parish, Chicago, IL
Eruo, Rev. Basil, (MO) Curia: Offices and Directors
Ervin, Rev. Dalton, '20 (VIC) The Cathedral of Our Lady of Victory, Victoria, TX
Erwin, Rev. Michael J., '98 (MIL) St. Jude Congregation, Wauwatosa, WI
Ery, Rev. Chandra, '13 (SUP) Assumption of the Blessed Virgin Mary, Rice Lake, WI; St. Boniface, Chetek, WI; St. Joseph, Barron, WI; St. Peter, Cameron, WI
Ery, Rev. Sunder, '00 (SFD) Sacred Heart, Sigel, IL; St. Mary Help of Christians, Effingham, IL; St. Mary of the Assumption, Neoga, IL; St. Michael the Archangel, Sigel, IL
Ery, Rev. Suresh Babu, '05 (STO) St. Joseph Church of Modesto (Pastor of), Modesto, CA
Esack, Rev. Susaikannua, *SAC* '98 (DET) St. Patrick Parish White Lake, White Lake, MI
Esarey, Rev. Brian G., '04 (IND) Holy Cross Catholic Church, St. Croix, Inc., St. Croix, IN; St. Augustine Catholic Church, Leopold, Inc., Leopold, IN
Escalante, Rev. Agustin, '88 (SFR) (>LAR) St. Peter the Apostle, Laredo, TX
Escalante, Rev. Agustin, '88 (LAR) Curia: Leadership
Escalante, Rev. Jose Manuel, '11 (WH) Curia: Offices and Directors St. Agnes, Charleston, WV; [CAM] St. John Paul II Catholic Campus Ministry Center, Charleston, WV
Escalante, Rev. Peter, '78 (SD) Curia: Advisory Boards, Commissions, Committees, and Councils
Escalante, Rev. Ronald S., '95 (ARL) On Leave.
Escalona, Rev. Warren, (MIA) St. Henry, Pompano Beach, FL
Escamez, Rev. Juan, (MIA) Little Flower, Coral Gables, FL
Escamez, Rev. Juan, (MO) Curia: Offices and Directors
Escanilla, Rev. Elias F., '84 (HON) Sacred Heart, Hawi, HI
Escano, Rev. Mariano, '09 (P) Curia: Offices and Directors Our Lady of Perpetual Help (St. Mary), Albany, OR; [CAM] Southern Oregon University (Ashland), Ashland, OR
Escarcega, Rev. Rafael, (PHX) SS. Simon and Jude Roman Catholic Cathedral, Phoenix, AZ
Esch, Rev. Aaron J., '09 (MIL) On Duty Outside Diocese. Rome - Dicastery for Bishops
Eschbach, Rev. Victor J., '72 (PH) Retired.
Esclanda, Rev. Derek, '99 (POD) Curia: Clergy and Religious Services
Esclanda, Rev. Roderick, (CHI) St. Mary of the Angels, Chicago, IL
Escobar, Rev. Joseph A., '88 (PRO) Church of Our Lady of the Rosary, Providence, RI
Escobar, Rev. Ricardo, (STL) St. Joseph Catholic Church, Manchester, Manchester, MO
Escobedo, Rev. Juan M., *M.S.P.* (SB) St. Joseph, Fontana, CA
Escribano, Rev. Pedro, '88 (MAD) Divine Mercy Parish, Sauk City, WI; St. Norbert, Sauk City, WI
Escudero, Rev. Diogo, *O.F.M.Cap.* '20 (WDC) Shrine of the Sacred Heart, Washington, DC
Escudero, Rev. Juan, '15 (WOR) St. Rose of Lima, Northboro, MA
Escurel, Rev. Armando P., '79 (SD) Curia: Advisory Boards, Commissions, Committees, and Councils Pastor of Our Lady of Mt. Carmel Catholic Parish, San Ysidro, a corporation sole, San Ysidro, CA; [MIS] Our Lady of Mount Carmel Catholic Parish San Ysidro in San Ysidro, CA Real Property Support Corporation, San Ysidro, CA
Esenther, Rev. Keith J., *S.J.* (DET) [MON] Colombiere Center, Clarkston, MI
Esker, Rev. Karl, *C.Ss.R.* '76 (BRK) Our Lady of Perpetual Help Basilica, Brooklyn, NY
Eskind, Rev. Msgr. Jace F., '87 (LKC) Curia: Leadership St. Martin de Porres, Lake Charles, LA
Esmero-Carcueva, Rev. Rodolfo, '92 (FRS) St. Joseph, Mariposa, CA
Esmilla, Rev. Efren V., '93 (PH) On Special Assignment. Deanery 12, Chaplain, Filipino Apostolate Curia: Evangelization St. James, Elkins Park, PA; St. Martin of Tours, Philadelphia, PA
Espades, Rev. Miguel, '09 (MEM) On Leave.
Esparza, Rev. Carlos, (AUS) (>STL) [MON] Jesuit Community Corporation at Saint Louis University - Jesuit Hall, St. Louis, MO
Esparza, Rev. Carlos D., *S.J.* '15 (DAL) [MON] St. Aloysius Gonzaga Jesuit Community, Dallas, TX
Esparza, Rev. Erik L., '08 (SB) Curia: Advisory Boards, Commissions, Committees, and Councils; Leadership The Holy Name of Jesus Catholic Community, Inc., Redlands, CA
Esparza, Rev. Jose Luis, *F.N.* '99 (DAL) Good Shepherd Catholic Parish, Garland, TX
Esparza-Perez, Rev. Hugo, *C.P.* '11 (NY) [MON] The Congregation of the Passion - St. Paul of the Cross Province, Jamaica, NY
Espelage, Rev. Arthur, *O.F.M.* '71 (CIN) [MON] St. Francis Seraph Friary, Cincinnati, OH
Espelage, Rev. Arthur J., *O.F.M.* (TUC) Curia: Tribunal
Espenilla, Rev. Silverio, '89 (SD) Pastor of Saint Rita Catholic Parish, San Diego, a corporation sole, San Diego, CA
Esper, Rev. Jerome C., *C.S.C.* (FTW) [MIS] Holy Cross House, Notre Dame, IN
Esper, Rev. John C., '83 (DET) St. Vincent Ferrer Parish Madison Heights, Madison Heights, MI
Esper, Rev. Joseph M., '82 (DET) Immaculate Conception Parish Ira Township, Ira Township, MI
Espiga, Rev. Francis, '08 (LA) Our Lady of Loretto, Los Angeles, CA; St. Columban, Los Angeles, CA; St. Lucy, Long Beach, CA
Espinal, Rev. Jason N., '14 (BRK) SS. Peter and Paul, Brooklyn, NY
Espiniella Garcia, Rev. Jaime, (BO) [MON] Alberto Hurtado House, Boston, MA
Espino, Rev. Alexander A, (SB) Corpus Christi, Corona, CA
Espino, Rev. Jose, '83 (MIA) [MIS] Centro de Artes y Oficios De La Salle, Inc., Homestead, FL; [SHR] National Shrine of Our Lady of Charity, Miami, FL
Espino, Rev. Juan, *D.C.J.M.* '13 (ARL) Our Lady of Angels, Woodbridge, VA
Espinosa, Rev. Boris, '78 (CGS) Catedral Dulce Nombre de Jesus, Caguas, PR
Espinosa, Rev. Eduardo, *O.F.M.* '10 (LSC) St. John Parish, Inc., Roswell, NM
Espinosa, Rev. Gabriel D., '07 (VIC) Our Lady of Guadalupe, Bay City, TX
Espinosa, Rev. Gerson, (MRY) Curia: Offices and Directors
Espinosa, Rev. Tonatiuh, *O.A.R.* (NEW) St. Augustine, Union City, NJ
Espinoza, Rev. Adalberto, '10 (DET) Our Lady of Guadalupe Parish Detroit, Detroit, MI
Espinoza, Very Rev. Carlos A., '85 (LSC) Curia: Clergy and Religious Services; Leadership San Jose Parish, La Mesa, Inc., La Mesa, NM; San Luis Rey, Chamberino, NM; San Miguel Parish, Inc., San Miguel, NM
Espinoza, Rev. Carlos A., '85 (LSC) San Pedro (Del Cerro), Vado, NM
Espinoza, Rev. Galo, *O.A.R.* '92 (LA) St. Benedict, Montebello, CA
Espinoza, Rev. Luis, '16 (LA) Curia: Pastoral Services St. Agnes, Los Angeles, CA
Espinoza, Rev. Martin, '11 (MET) On Leave.
Espinoza, Rev. Nerio A., '05 (OKL) St. Catherine of Siena, Pauls Valley, OK
Espinoza, Rev. Pedro, '02 (MRY) Curia: Tribunal St. Joseph, Cayucos, CA
Espona Jimenez, Rev. Juan, '82 (PCE) Retired.
Esposito, Rev. Alberto, (STA) Queen of Peace Catholic Community, Gainesville, FL
Esposito, Rev. Alberto, '01 (STA) Curia: Evangelization; Leadership
Esposito, Rev. Giuseppe, '19 (ALN) Curia: Leadership St. Charles Borromeo, Ashland, PA; St. Joseph the Worker Parish, Frackville, PA
Esposito, Rev. Lawrence J., '76 (WOR) Retired.
Esposito, Rev. Mario, *O.Carm.* '77 (ALB) [MIS] Postulation Office, ,
Esposito, Rev. Mario, *O.Carm.* '77 (NY) [MON] Carmelite Friars (North American Province of St. Elias), Middletown, NY
Esposito, Rev. Ralph J., '67 (LR) Retired.
Esposito, Rev. Samuel J., '78 (PIT) Curia: Consultative Bodies
Esposito, Rev. Thomas, *O.Cist.* '11 (DAL) [MON] Our Lady of Dallas Cistercian Abbey, Irving, TX
Esposito-Garcia, Rev. Juan, '08 (WDC) On Duty Outside Diocese. Rome, Italy
Esqueda, Rev. Jesse, *OMI* '14 (SAT) [MON] Missionary Oblates of Mary Immaculate of Texas, Southern Province (San Antonio USP Support Office), San Antonio, TX
Esquen, Rev. Rafael, (TR) On Special Assignment. Military The Church of Jesus, the Good Shepherd, Beverly, NJ
Esquen, Rev. Rafael E., (MO) Curia: Offices and Directors
Esquiliano, Very Rev. J. David, '13 (SC) Curia: Leadership; Offices and Directors Cathedral of the Epiphany, Sioux City, IA
Esquivel, Rev. Carlos, *O.S.J.* '83 (FRS) St. Joachim, Madera, CA
Esquivel, Rev. Msgr. John, '68 (FRS) Retired.
Esquivel, Rev. Oscar Esquivel, *M.S.C.* '00 (LA) San Miguel, Los Angeles, CA
Esquivel, Rev. Reynaldo, (MRY) San Carlos Borromeo Basilica, Carmel, CA
Ess, Rev. Thomas, *O.F.M.* '66 (CHI) [MON] St. Peter's Friary, Chicago, IL
Esse, Rev. Julien, *SMA* '13 (NEW) [MON] Society of African Missions, Provincialate, S.M.A. Fathers, Tenafly, NJ
Esseff, Rev. Msgr. John A., '53 (SCR) Retired. [MON] Villa St. Joseph, Dunmore, PA
Essel, Rev. John, '89 (MAR) Ste. Anne de Michilimackinac, Mackinac Island, MI
Esselman, Rev. Thomas E., *C.M.* '80 (STL) [MON] Congregation of the Mission Vincentian Fathers Lazarist Residence, St. Louis, MO
Esser, Rev. James, *O.F.M.* (GB) [MON] Assumption of B.V.M. Friary, Pulaski, WI
Essex, Rev. Msgr. Donald S., '73 (WDC) Retired.
Esshaki, Rev. Simon, '15 (SPA) Curia: Leadership; Offices and Directors St. Michael Chaldean Catholic Church, El Cajon, CA; [SEM] Seminary of Mar Abba

the Great, El Cajon, CA
Essien, Rev. Anthony, '01 (CLV) [MON] St. Paul Friary, Cleveland, OH
Essiet, Rev. Emmanuel J., (MIA) Curia: Canonical Services
Essig, Rev. Edward J., '94 (ALN) Curia: Organizations (affiliated, inter-Diocesan, miscellaneous/other) St. John Baptist de la Salle, Shillington, PA
Essig, Rev. Herbert, '74 (JOL) St. Francis of Assisi, Bolingbrook, IL
Essling, Rev. Harold W, *CSC* (FTW) [MIS] Holy Cross House, Notre Dame, IN
Essling, Rev. Harold W., *C.S.C.* '78 (AUS) Retired.
Essman, Rev. Ronald, '80 (DET) Retired. St. Therese of Lisieux Parish Shelby Township, Shelby Twp., MI
Esson, Rev. Joseph, '94 (TUC) Saint Ann's Roman Catholic Parish and Its Missions - Tubac, Tubac, AZ
Esswein, Rev. Michael, (STL) Holy Cross Academy - St. Louis, St. Louis, MO
Esswein, Rev. Michael J., '98 (STL) Annunciation Catholic Church, Webster Groves, MO
Estabrook, Rev. Kevin E., '09 (CLV) St. Ignatius of Antioch, Cleveland, OH
Estacio, Rev. Jeffrey, '11 (LEX) St. Lawrence, Lawrenceburg, KY
Estadilla, Rev. Lino, *O.M.V.* (VEN) (>LA) St. Peter Chanel, Hawaiian Gardens, CA
Estaniel, Rev. Jose, *MSP* '85 (SAC) Pastor of St. Catherine of Siena Parish, Vallejo, a corporation sole, Vallejo, CA; [MON] Missionary Society of the Philippines, Vallejo, CA
Estaris, Rev. Michael J., '10 (SAC) Curia: Offices and Directors Pastor of St. Monica Parish, Willows, a corporation sole, Willows, CA
Esteban, Rev. Juan Pablo, (NEW) Immaculate Conception, Elizabeth, NJ
Esteban, Rev. Pedro Antonio, '85 (LA) St. Aloysius Gonzaga, Los Angeles, CA
Estefan, Rev. Levon Joulian, (OLN) St. Gregory Armenian Catholic Cathedral, Glendale, CA
Estefont, Rev. Pierre-Soul, '13 (PMB) St. Philip Benizi, Belle Glade, FL
Estepa, Rev. Isaias, '94 (CC) Our Lady of Guadalupe Mission, Edroy, TX; Sacred Heart, Odem, TX
Estiverne, Rev. Saint Martin, (BRK) Holy Cross, Brooklyn, NY
Estok, Rev. Edward T., '85 (CLV) Curia: Advisory Boards, Commissions, Committees, and Councils St. Albert the Great, North Royalton, OH
Estorque, Rev. Roger O., '85 (GAL) St. Dominic, Houston, TX
Estrada, Rev. Agustin, (MIA) St. Gregory, Plantation, FL
Estrada, Rev. Agustin, (SAT) St. Dominic, San Antonio, TX
Estrada, Rev. Eder, *F.M.* '13 (PH) St. Joseph, Coatesville, PA
Estrada, Rev. Enrique J., '93 (MIA) Our Lady of Divine Providence, Miami, FL
Estrada, Rev. Hector Diaz, '82 (SJN) [HOS] VA Medical Center, San Juan, PR
Estrada, Rev. Ignacio M, '03 (MO) Curia: Offices and Directors
Estrada, Rev. Canon Joel, *ICRSS* '14 (HRT) Saint Patrick Parish Corporation, Waterbury, CT
Estrada, Rev. Luis Rivera, (LA) St. Rose of Lima, Simi Valley, CA
Estrada, Rev. Martin, '19 (EVN) Holy Rosary, Evansville, IN
Estrada, Rev. Rafael A., '05 (SAV) Good Shepherd, Hazlehurst, GA
Estrada, Rev. Reinaldo, '20 (CGS) Curia: Leadership; Offices and Directors Parroquia Nuestra Senora de la Providencia, Caguas, PR
Estrada, Rev. Sabino, '72 (BRK) Retired.
Estrella, Rev. Alexander A., '16 (SAC) Curia: Leadership; Offices and Directors Pastor of Immaculate Conception Parish, Downieville, a corporation sole, Downieville, CA; Pastor of St. Canice Parish, Nevada City, a corporation sole, Nevada City, CA; Pastor of St. Patrick Parish, Grass Valley, a corporation sole, Grass Valley, CA
Esty, Rev. Gregory L., '75 (STP) St. Genevieve, Centerville, MN; [CEM] St. Genevieve Cemetery, Centerville, MN
Etenduk, Rev. Jerome, (PIT) St. Raphael the Archangel, Carnegie, PA
Etheredge, Very Rev. F. William, '83 (RCK) On Special Assignment. Curia: Leadership St. Mary, Sycamore, IL
Etienne, Rev. Bernard T., '93 (EVN) On Special Assignment. Curia: Leadership Holy Rosary, Evansville, IN
Etienne, Rev. Zachary J., '04 (EVN) Curia: Leadership All Saints, Evansville, IN; Good Shepherd, Evansville, IN
Etim, Rev. Idongesit A., '09 (WIL) St. Francis De Sales, Salisbury, MD
Etim, Rev. Sampson, (BAL) [HOS] University of Maryland St. Joseph Medical Center, Towson, MD
Etim, Rev. Sampson U., *M.S.P.* (MO) Curia: Offices and Directors
Etonu, Rev. Simeon A., '15 (JC) St. Aloysius, Baring, MO; St. John, Memphis, MO; St. Joseph, Edina, MO; [CAM] Catholic Newman Center, Truman State University, Kirksville, MO
Ettel, Rev. Dale, '82 (SCL) [MON] Crosier Priory, Onamia, MN
Ettensohn, Rev. John Mark, *OMI* (OAK) Sacred Heart, Oakland, CA
Ettinger, Rev. John, '14 (Y) Our Lady of Hope, Andover, OH; St. Joseph Calasanctius, Jefferson, OH
Ettner, Rev. Wilhelm J., '93 (ARL) On Leave.
Etuale, Rev. Kolio, '03 (SPP) Curia: Offices and Directors St. Joseph the Worker Futiga, Pago Pago, AS; St. Paul, Pago Pago, AS; St. Theresa, Leone, AS
Etuale, Rev. Msgr. Viane, '90 (SPP) Curia: Leadership; Offices and Directors Church of the Immaculate Conception, Pago Pago, AS; Our Lady of Fatima, Pago Pago, AS
Etuge, Friar Akolla, *O.F.M. Cap* '19 (PH) St. John the Evangelist, Philadelphia, PA
Etzel, Rev. Peter J, *S.J.* '94 (STP) St. Thomas More, St. Paul, MN; [MON] Markoe House Jesuit Community, Minneapolis, MN
Eugene, Rev. Rodney, (BAL) [HOS] Mercy Health Services Inc., Baltimore, MD
Eugenio, Rev. Peter Ronald, (SFR) Our Lady of Angels, Burlingame, CA
Euk, Rev. Vincent, (TR) Retired.
Eurico, Rev. Francisco, '94 (HRT) The Church of Our Lady of Fatima Corporation, Waterbury, CT
Eusterman, Rev. Daniel, (DEN) On Academic Leave. Pontifical Univ of Santa Croce, Rome
Euvrard, Rev. Scott A., '94 (BO) Curia: Clergy and Religious Services St. Anthony of Padua, Cohasset, MA; St. Mary of the Assumption, Hull, MA
Evancho, Very Rev. Robert, '79 (PSC) Curia: Leadership St. Therese, St. Petersburg, FL; [EFT] Maria Theresa Foundation, Inc., New York, NY
Evangelista, Rev. Damien, *O.S.B.* (SD) [MON] Prince of Peace Abbey, Oceanside, CA
Evangelista, Rev. Reynald, '01 (SD) Pastor of Saint Mary, Star of the Sea Catholic Parish, Oceanside, a corporation sole, Oceanside, CA
Evangelista, Rev. Romeo, '02 (MRY) Resurrection, Aptos, CA
Evangelista, Rev. Victor, (RVC) St. Anne's, Brentwood, NY
Evanick, Rev. Michael, '60 (PRM) Retired.
Evanish, Rev. Robin, '83 (PIT) Chap, St Clair Mem Hosp; Asbury Hts, Allegheny Cty; Concord... St. Raphael the Archangel, Carnegie, PA
Evanko, Rev. Joseph J., '91 (SCR) Curia: Leadership Our Lady Help of Christians, Wapwallopen, PA; St. Jude, Mountain Top, PA
Evanofski, Rev. Bernard P., '86 (VEN) Retired.
Evans, Rev. Bryce, '17 (STP) St. Mary, St. Paul, MN
Evans, Rev. George P., '77 (BO) Curia: Leadership Holy Name, Boston, MA
Evans, Rev. James L., '94 (AUS) Retired.
Evans, Rev. John L., '80 (WIN) Curia: Advisory Boards, Commissions, Committees, and Councils St. Peter's, Hokah, MN; The Church of the Crucifixion, La Crescent, MN
Evans, Rev. John R., '09 (RCK) St. Patrick, Dixon, IL
Evans, Rev. John S., '04 (SLC) Curia: Offices and Directors
Evans, Rev. John S., '04 (SLC) Curia: Offices and Directors Saint Thomas More Catholic Church LLC 248, Cottonwood Heights, UT
Evans, Rev. Joshua R., '15 (WCH) Sacred Heart, Frontenac, KS
Evans, Rev. Ken, '86 (NEW) Retired.
Evans, Rev. Larry, '01 (NEW) St. Francis of Assisi, Ridgefield Park, NJ
Evans, Rev. Michael J., '92 (LA) St. Bernardine of Siena, Woodland Hills, CA
Evans, Rev. Richard A., '82 (CLV) Holy Family, Parma, OH
Evans, Rev. Robert T., '03 (STL) Holy Spirit Catholic Church, Maryland Heights, MO
Evans, Rev. William, '19 (GB) St. Joseph, Wautoma, WI
Evans-Campos, Rev. Blake, '10 (WDC) Nativity, Washington, DC; St. Andrew Apostle, Silver Spring, MD
Evanstock, Rev. Philip, *C.S.Sp.* '60 (PHX) Notre Dame Preparatory Roman Catholic High School, Scottsdale, AZ
Evard, Rev. Patrick, *OFM* (OAK) [NUR] Mercy Retirement and Care Center, Oakland, CA
Evernden, Rev. Michael, *C.S.P.* '74 (SFR) Old St. Mary's Cathedral & Chinese Mission, San Francisco, CA
Evers, Very Rev. Glenn M., *V.C.* '13 (WIL) Curia: Administration; Advisory Boards, Commissions, Committees, and Councils; Leadership; Miscellaneous / Other Offices; Offices and Directors St. Joseph's R.C. Church of Wilmington, Inc., Wilmington, DE
Evers, Rev. Leonard M., '68 (GB) Retired.
Evers, Rev. Linus, *C.PP.S.* '71 (CIN) Retired. [MON] St. Charles, Celina, OH
Evers, Rev. Paul H., '80 (HON) Retired.
Eversole, Rev. Paul M., '95 (ARL) St. Matthew, Spotsylvania, VA
Everton, Rev. Joseph, *MS* '21 (ATL) St. Oliver Plunkett Catholic Church, Snellville, Inc., Snellville, GA
Everts, Rev. Chad, '04 (CHI) On Special Assignment. Vocations Dir. at Oaklawn Academy (>MAD) Oaklawn Academy, Edgerton, WI
Everts, Rev. Donald E., '95 (GB) Holy Cross, Kaukauna, WI; St. Katharine Drexel, Kaukauna, WI
Evinger, Rev. Joseph A., '13 (BIS) St. Joseph, Killdeer, ND; St. Joseph, Twin Buttes, ND; St. Paul, Halliday, ND
Ewen, Rt. Rev. Sharbel, *O.S.B.* '88 (SD) [MON] Prince of Peace Abbey, Oceanside, CA
Ewenteang, Rev. Tatieru, *M.S.C.* (MI) Curia: Leadership
Ewers, Rev. Paul, '65 (LA) [MIS] Comboni Mission Center, Covina, CA
Ewers, Rev. Paul J., *MCCJ* '65 (CIN) Retired. [MON] Comboni Missionaries (Verona Fathers)-Comboni Mission Center, Cincinnati, OH
Ewing, Rev. Kevin B., (BAL) [CAM] Towson University, Towson, MD
Ewing, Rev. Matt J., *O.Carm.* '54 (LA) Retired. [MON] Our Lady of Mount Carmel Priory (Fathers of the Order of Mount Carmel, Corporation), Encino, CA
Ewing, Rev. Matthias, *O.Carm.* '54 (JOL) Retired.
Ewulu, Rev. Donald C., (CLV) Chap, Parma Cmty Hosp
Exaltacion, Rev. Chryostom, *S.J.* (BO) [MON] Alberto Hurtado House, Boston, MA
Exner, Rev. David, '16 (SD) Pastor of Queen of Angels Catholic Parish, Alpine, a corporation sole, Alpine, CA; [MIS] Queen of Angels Catholic Parish in Alpine, CA Real Property Support Corporation, Alpine, CA
Extejt, Rev. John I., *O.S.F.S.* '85 (WDC) Retired. [SEM] Oblates of St. Francis de Sales, Washington, DC
Extejt, Rev. Thomas J., '73 (TOL) Curia: Advisory Boards, Commissions, Committees, and Councils; Deaneries St. Anthony of Padua, Columbus Grove, OH
Exume, Rev. Gilbert, '08 (ATL) St. Matthew Catholic Church, Winder, Inc., Winder, GA
Eyerman, Rev. Matthew, '95 (CHI) Blessed Maria Gabriella Parish, Chicago, IL
Eyinla, Rev. Patrick O., '92 (CHR) Curia: Advisory Boards, Commissions, Committees, and Councils St. Joseph, Charleston, SC; [NUR] Carter-May Home Assisted Living & St. Joseph Residence for Retired Priests, Charleston, SC
Eyman, Rev. Bryan R., '85 (PRM) Curia: Advisory Boards, Commissions, Committees, and Councils; Leadership St. Mary Magdalene, Fairview Park, OH
Eyyazo, Rev. Julius M., (NEW) Saint Joseph Parish, East Orange, NJ
Ezaki, Rev. Bernard J., '88 (ALN) Curia: Organizations (affiliated, inter-Diocesan, miscellaneous/other) Bethlehem Catholic High School, Inc., Bethlehem, PA; Notre Dame of Bethlehem, Bethlehem, PA
Ezama, Rev. Ruffino, *M.C.C.J.* '94 (CIN) [MON] Comboni Missionaries (Verona Fathers)-Comboni Mission Center, Cincinnati, OH
Eze, Rev. Msgr. Anthony, (SB) [SEM] Saint Junipero Serra House of Formation, Grand Terrace, CA
Eze, Rev. Cyprian, '88 (LAF) On Special Assignment. Hospital Ministry - Lafayette General Southwest, Lafayette Cathedral of St. John the Evangelist, Lafayette, LA
Eze, Rev. John, '97 (FTW) Queen of Peace, Mishawaka, IN
Ezeador, Rev. Martin Chukwunenye, (SJ) St. Clare, Santa Clara, CA
Ezeador, Rev. Martin Chukwunenye, (SJ) Chap, Regional Med Ctr
Ezealla, Rev. Athanasius O., (SB) St. Louis, Cathedral City, CA
Ezeani, Rev. Damian, (CLV) Mercy Regional Medical Center St. Richard, North Olmsted, OH
Ezeani, Rev. Fidelis, '99 (RVC) Our Lady of Perpetual Help, Lindenhurst, NY

Ezeanokwasa, Rev. Jude O., '89 (MIA) Curia: Canonical Services
Ezeanya, Rev. Albert, '05 (SAN) Sts. Joachim and Ann, Clyde, TX
Ezeanya, Rev. Albert, '05 (SAN) Curia: Advisory Boards, Commissions, Committees, and Councils Sacred Heart, Abilene, TX
Ezeanya, Rev. Gregory, '89 (PBL) Parkview Hospital, Pueblo St. Aloysius, Rye, CO
Ezeaputa, Rev. Anthony Obinna, '20 (SFE) Nuestra Senora De Guadalupe - Pena Blanca, Pena Blanca, NM
Ezeatu, Rev. Mike, (RVC) St. James, Setauket, NY
Ezeh, Rev. Christian, '95 (STO) On Special Assignment. St. Joseph Hospital Stockton St. Mary of the Assumption Church (Pastor of), Stockton, CA
Ezeh, Rev. Gabriel, *S.M.M.M.* (SB) St. Joseph, Barstow, CA; St. Philip Neri (Lenwood), Barstow, CA
Ezeh, Rev. Gabriel I., '94 (BWN) On Leave.
Ezeh, Rev. Kevin, (OAK) Most Holy Rosary, Antioch, CA
Ezeh, Rev. Raphael, *M.S.P.* (NY) St. Bartholomew, Yonkers, NY
Ezeigbo, Rev. Pius, '99 (SAT) St. Ann's, Stockdale, TX
Ezeihuaku, Rev. Martin, *M.S.P.* '02 (GF) Curia: Offices and Directors Immaculate Conception, Wolf Point, MT
Ezeiloaku, Rev. Cornelius, '03 (NU) St. Anne, Wabasso, MN; St. Catherine, Redwood Falls, MN
Ezeiruaku, Rev. Vitus Arinze, '96 (RVC) Chap, Stony Brook Univ Hosp
Ezenneh, Rev. Emmanuel, (LSC) Curia: Tribunal Immaculate Heart of Mary Cathedral Parish, Inc., Las Cruces, NM
Ezenwa, Rev. Hippolytus, *SMMM* (B) Our Lady of Good Counsel, Mountain Home, ID
Ezenwachi, Rev. Ferdinand, (BAL) St. Margaret, Bel Air, MD
Ezenwata, Rev. Aloysius, *M.S.P.* (SP) [HOS] St. Joseph's Hospital, Inc., Tampa, FL
Ezenwelem, Rev. Bartholomew, '10 (LSC) St. Francis Newman Center Parish, Inc., Silver City, NM
Ezeoke, Rev. Benedict, '96 (CHI) [HOS] Saint Anthony Hospital (Saint Anthony Health Ministries), Chicago, IL
Ezeokeke, Rev. Edwin, (NY) Parish of Our Lady of Victory and St. Andrew, New York, NY; Parish of Saint Peter and Our Lady of the Rosary, New York, NY
Ezeonyeka, Rev. Aloysius, '02 (LA) Sacred Heart, Ventura, CA
Ezeora, Rev. Franklin, (RVC) Chap, Pilgrim Psychiatric Ctr
Ezeorah, Rev. Franklin, '07 (BRK) Saint Martin de Porres, Brooklyn, NY
Ezeuchenne, Rev. Eliseus, '95 (MIA) All Saints, Sunrise, FL
Ezeugwu, Rev. Gilbert U., (BO) St. Charles Borromeo, Woburn, MA
Ezeugwu, Rev. Romanus Obiora, *M.S.P.* '00 (SAV) St. Benedict the Moor, Savannah, GA
Eziefule, Rev. Innocent, '13 (SAN) St. Francis of Assisi, Abilene, TX
Ezop, Rev. Dwight M., '97 (LAN) St. Mary Parish Charlotte, Charlotte, MI; [MIS] FAITH Magazine, ,
Ezulike, Rev. Ephraim, (LSC) Curia: Tribunal Assumption Parish Inc., Roswell, NM
Ezuma, Rev. Jude E., '11 (GAL) Curia: Offices and Directors Holy Family, Galveston, TX; St. Mary's Cathedral Basilica, Galveston, TX
Ezung, Rev. Mhonchan, '16 (MET) Church of the Immaculate Conception, Somerville, NJ
Ezurike, Rev. Paschal, '95 (P) St. Philip Benizi, Oregon City, OR
Faber, Rev. Christopher, '15 (OLL) Saint Sharbel Maronite Catholic Church, Portland, OR
Fabian, Rev. Jack V., '68 (DET) Retired.
Fabian, Rev. John, '68 (MAR) [MIS] Companions of Christ the Lamb, Paradise, MI
Fabien, Rev. Rony, (RVC) St. Martha, Uniondale, NY
Fabing, Rev. Robert J., *S.J.* '74 (SJ) [MIS] Jesuit Institute for Family Life, Los Altos, CA; [RTR] Jesuit Retreat Center of Los Altos, Los Altos, CA
Fabish, Rev. Rapael A., *O.P.* '53 (CHI) [MON] St. Pius V Priory, Chicago, IL
Fabiszewski, Rev. Brian C., '14 (SP) Most Holy Name of Jesus, Gulfport, FL
Fabre, Rev. Christopher, '15 (P) [HOS] Providence Health & Services-Oregon (Providence Medford Medical Center), Medford, OR; [HOS] Providence Health & Services-Oregon (Providence Newberg Medical Center), Newberg, OR; [HOS] Providence Health & Services-Oregon (Providence St. Vincent Medical Center), Portland, OR
Fabre, Rev. Richard, '73 (LAF) Retired.
Facci, Rev. John, *S.A.C.* '71 (ALB) Retired.
Fackler, Rev. Neil E., '98 (CHI) Mary, Mother of Divine Grace, Westchester, IL
Factora, Rev. Julius Paul, *O.P.* (AGN) Curia: Tribunal
Facura, Rev. Joseph C., '68 (RIC) Retired.
Fadallan, Rev. Elbert A., '80 (LUB) Curia: (>MO) Offices and Directors
Fadini, Rev. Emanuele, (DEN) Nativity of Our Lord Catholic Parish in Broomfield, Broomfield, CO
Fadok, Very Rev. Christopher, *O.P.* (OAK) [EFT] Dominican Community Support Charitable Trust, Oakland, CA; [MON] Order of Preachers (Province of the Most Holy Name of Jesus - Western Dominican Province), Oakland, CA (>NY) [EFT] St. Thomas Aquinas Foundation of the Dominican Fathers of the United States (STAF), New York, NY
Fadok, Very Rev. Christopher Paul, *O.P.* (OAK) [MON] Order of Preachers (Province of the Most Holy Name of Jesus - Western Dominican Province), Oakland, CA; [SEM] Dominican School of Philosophy and Theology, Berkeley, CA
Fador, Rev. Francis R., '96 (HRT) Retired.
Fadrowski, Rev. Msgr. William J., '87 (NEW) Retired.
Faes, Rev. Julio Cesar, '14 (STV) Curia: Leadership; Offices and Directors Cathedral of SS. Peter and Paul, Charlotte Amalie, VI; [MIS] Hispanic Ministry, St. Thomas, VI
Faesser, Rev. Arthur A., '76 (GI) Retired.
Fagan, Rev. Christopher B., '09 (LA) St. Augustine, Culver City, CA
Fagan, Rev. George V., '69 (COS) Curia: Leadership; Tribunal
Fagan, Rev. John, (BRK) Our Lady of the Presentation-Our Lady of Mercy Roman Catholic Church, Brooklyn, NY (>NY) [MON] Xavier Jesuit Community, New York, NY
Fagan, Rev. Michael, '16 (POD) Curia: Clergy and Religious Services
Fagan, Rev. Paul R., *C.P.* '86 (NY) [MIS] Passionist Communications, Inc., Rye Brook, NY; [MON] St. Vincent Strambi Residence (The Passionists), Pelham Manor, NY; [MON] The Congregation of the Passion - St. Paul of the Cross Province, Jamaica, NY
Fagone, Rev. Benedict, *O.F.M.Conv.* '67 (SPR) Retired.
Fagone, Rev. Benedict, *O.F.M. Conv.* '67 (FR) Retired.
Fahey, Rev. Msgr. Charles J., '58 (SY) Retired.
Fahey, Rev. Edward J., '89 (WIL) Retired. St. Helena, Wilmington, DE
Fahey, Rev. Fiacre, (MRY) St. Joseph, Nipomo, CA
Fahey, Rev. Timothy, '16 (CIN) [CAM] Catholic Campus Ministry, Fairborn, OH
Fahey-Guerra, Rev. John, *C.Ss.R.* '96 (DEN) (>BR) Congregation Of St. Gerard Majella Roman Catholic Church, Parish Of East Baton Rouge, Louisiana, Baton Rouge, LA; (>BR) [MIS] Redemptorist Fathers of Baton Rouge, Inc., Baton Rouge, LA; (>BR) [MON] St. Gerard Residence, Baton Rouge, LA
Fahrbach, Rev. Paul A., '84 (TOL) Holy Trinity, Bucyrus, OH; St. Joseph, Galion, OH
Faiella, Rev. William W., *C.S.C.* '79 (PHX) [MON] Holy Cross Congregation/Casa Santa Cruz, Phoenix, AZ
Faimega, Rev. Peter, (STL) St. Joseph Catholic Church, Imperial, Imperial, MO
Fain, Rev. John M., '03 (LAN) St. Therese Parish Lansing, Lansing, MI
Faiola, Rev. Thomas, *O.F.M.Cap.* '85 (NY) Good Shepherd, New York, NY
Fairbanks, Rev. Msgr. Gregory J., '90 (PH) [SEM] Theological Seminary of St. Charles Borromeo, Wynnewood, PA
Fairbanks, Rev. Patrick Alexis, *S.J.* '00 (CHI) St. Ignatius Jesuit Community, Chicago, IL
Fairman, Rev. Derek, '06 (ALT) St. John the Evangelist, Everett, PA; St. Stephen, McConnellsburg, PA
Fairman, Rev. Timothy J., '88 (CHI) Curia: Leadership St. Theresa, Palatine, IL
Fait, Rev. Thomas G., '74 (MIL) Retired.
Faix, Rev. Michael, (PIT) Corpus Christi, Bridgeville, PA
Fajardo, Rev. Ramil E., '04 (CHI) Holy Name Cathedral, Chicago, IL; [SHR] National Shrine of St. Frances Xavier Cabrini, Inc., Chicago, IL
Faker, Rev. Dennis A., '08 (LFT) Cathedral of St. Mary of the Immaculate Conception, Lafayette, IN; St. Ann, Lafayette, IN
Falabella, Rev. Robert, *C.H.S.* '61 (CHR) St. Mary Magdalene, Simpsonville, SC
Falana, Rev. Arkadiusz, '06 (CHI) Incarnation and St. Terrence Parish, Crestwood, IL
Falardeau, Rev. Ernest, *S.S.S.* (CLV) Retired.
Falardeau, Rev. Ernest R., *S.S.S.* '56 (NY) St. Jean Baptiste, New York, NY
Falce, Rev. Joshua, '21 (B) All Saints Catholic Parish, Lewiston, ID
Falce, Rev. Michael, '19 (BRK) St. Patrick, Brooklyn, NY
Falco, Rev. Frank M., *O.S.M.* '67 (CHI) [MIS] Monastery of Our Lady of Sorrows, ,
Falco, Rev. Ronald, '81 (WOR) Curia: Leadership; Offices and Directors St. Bernadette, Northboro, MA
Falcone, Rev. Mark D., *O. Praem* '66 (GB) [MON] St. Norbert Abbey, De Pere, WI
Faletoi, Rev. Konelio, '92 (HON) Curia: Consultative Bodies; Offices and Directors St. Michael the Archangel, Kailua-Kona, HI
Falgowski, Rev. Michal A, '13 (PAT) St. Virgilius, Morris Plains, NJ
Falgowski, Rev. Michal A., (MO) Curia: Offices and Directors
Faliskie, Rev. Edmund, *C.Ss.R.* (TR) [RTR] San Alfonso Retreat House, Long Branch, NJ
Falk, Rev. Gerald R., '59 (GB) Retired. St. Thomas More, Appleton, WI
Falkenhan, Rev. Pierre M., '80 (PIT) St. John XXIII, McMurray, PA
Falkenthal, Rev. Thomas W., '75 (CHI) Retired. On Duty Outside Diocese. Chap, Aventura, FL
Falla, Rev. Gustavo A., '96 (BGP) Saint Mary Parish Corporation of Stamford, Stamford, CT
Faller, Rev. Cameron M., '15 (SFR) On Special Assignment. Curia: Leadership St. Stephen, San Francisco, CA; Visitacion, Church of the, San Francisco, CA
Faller, Rev. Kyle J., (SFR) St. Raphael, San Rafael, CA
Faller, Rev. Rodel, '08 (BEA) Curia: Offices and Directors [CAM] Lamar University-Catholic Student Center, Beaumont, TX
Falletta, Rev. Joseph, '72 (ALB) Retired.
Fallgren, Rev. Matthew, '01 (RC) Cathedral of Our Lady of Perpetual Help, Rapid City, SD; St. Michael's, Hermosa, SD
Fallon, Rev. Brian S., '12 (STL) Curia: Offices and Directors St. Mary Magdalen Catholic Church, St. Louis, St. Louis, MO
Fallon, Rev. Daniel R., '76 (CHI) Retired.
Fallon, Rev. James P., *S.S.J.* '68 (LAF) Immaculate Conception, Lebeau, LA
Fallon, Rev. John, '69 (BIR) Retired. Prince of Peace Catholic Parish, Birmingham, Birmingham, AL
Fallon, Rev. John C., '71 (ATL) Retired.
Fallon, Rev. Joseph, '96 (NY) St. Gregory Barbarigo, Garnerville, NY
Fallon, Rev. Marc F., *C.S.C.* '91 (FR) [COL] Holy Cross Fathers Religious, North Easton, MA
Fallone, Rev. Thomas H., '02 (PAT) St. Thomas More, Morristown, NJ
Fallouh, Rev. Paul (Adham), '14 (NTN) St. Philip, San Bernardino, CA; Virgin Mary Mission, Temecula, CA
Falsey, Friar Edward, *OFM Conv.* (ALB) [MON] Franciscan Friars Conventual, Rensselaer, NY
Falsey, Rev. James E., '72 (SAG) Retired. On Duty Outside Diocese. North Pole, AK
Falsey, Rev. Jim, '72 (FBK) Retired. Our Lady of Guadalupe Catholic Church Russian Mission, , ; St. Michael Catholic Church McGrath, McGrath, AK
Fama, Rev. Lawrence J., '92 (NEW) Church of St. Thomas the Apostle, Bloomfield, NJ
Famave, Rev. Tony Terwase, '21 (SJ) Holy Family (Roman Catholic Bishop of San Jose, a Corporation Sole), San Jose, CA
Fambrini, Rev. Robert A, *S.J.* '79 (PHX) St. Francis Xavier Roman Catholic Parish, Phoenix, AZ; [MON] Society of Jesus, Phoenix, AZ
Familiar, Rev. Rex, (SPK) St. Patrick, Pasco, WA
Famiyeh, Rev. Emmanuel, '90 (LC) Holy Family, Willard, WI; St. Anthony of Padua, Loyal, WI; St. Mary Help of Christians, Greenwood, WI; [EFT] Holy Family Parish, Willard Endowment Trust, Willard, WI
Fanale, Rev. James, *C.S.V.* '69 (JOL) Retired.
Fane, Rev. Kevin R., *O.P.* '69 (CHI) [MON] St. Pius V Priory, Chicago, IL
Fanelli, Rev. Charles V., '71 (CHI) Retired. [MIS] Italian Catholic Federation, Chicago, IL
Fangman, Rev. Thomas M., '92 (OM) St. Patrick (Elkhorn), Elkhorn, NE; [EFT] Saint Patrick's Parish Foundation, Elkhorn, NE
Fangmeyer, Rev. LeRoy J., '89 (WDC) Curia: Deaneries Mother Seton Parish, Germantown, MD
Fanning, Rev. John, (NY) Retired.
Fanning, Rev. Patrick, (HON) St. Damien, Kaunakakai, HI; St. Francis, Kalaupapa, HI
Fanning, Rev. Patrick, *SS.CC.* (LA) [MON] Congregation of the Sacred Hearts of Jesus and Mary, La Verne, CA
Fano, Rev. Frank J., (NEW) Our Lady of Mount Carmel, Ridgewood, NJ
Fanomezantsoa Rarivoson, Rev. Amedee, (BO) [MON]

Miguel Pro House, Brighton, MA
Fanta, Rev. Thomas G., '88 (CLV) St. Dominic, Shaker Heights, OH; [EFT] St. Dominic Endowment Fund, Shaker Heights, OH
Faour, Rev. George, '91 (NEW) St. John, Orange, NJ
Farabaugh, Rev. Luke, (PT) Co-Cathedral of St. Thomas More, Tallahassee, FL
Farah, Rev. Robert, (SAM) Saint Sharbel Maronite Catholic Church, Raleigh, NC
Farana, Rev. Mario P., '71 (SFR) St. James, San Francisco, CA; St. Paul, San Francisco, CA
Farao, Rev. John, *OFM Conv.* '88 (MRY) Chap, California Men's Colony West and East St. Paul the Apostle, Pismo Beach, CA
Farbolin, Rev. Alberic R., *O.C.S.O.* '02 (DUB) [MON] New Melleray Abbey, Order of Cistercians of the Strict Observance (Corporation of New Melleray), Peosta, IA
Fares, Rev. Lawrence T., '50 (DET) Retired.
Faretra, Rev. Albert M., '86 (BO) St. Blaise, Bellingham, MA
Farfaglia, Rev. James, (CC) St. Francis de Paula, San Diego, TX
Farfaglia, Rev. Salvatore James, '87 (CC) Our Lady of Guadalupe, Corpus Christi, TX
Farge, Rev. William J., *S.J.* '78 (NO) [MON] Loyola Jesuit Community, New Orleans, LA
Farhat, Rev. Vincent, '10 (SAM) Curia: Offices and Directors Our Lady of Purgatory, New Bedford, MA
Faria, Rev. Carl M.D., '88 (MRY) Retired.
Farias, Rev. Joseph, *S.D.B.* '64 (LA) St. Mary, Los Angeles, CA
Farias, Rev. Joseph G., '75 (PAT) Retired.
Farias-Saucedo, Rev. Jorge, '12 (TUC) Curia: Pastoral Services St. James Roman Catholic Parish - Coolidge, Coolidge, AZ
Farinto, Rev. Solomon, '07 (DUB) [HOS] MercyOne Waterloo Medical Center, Waterloo, IA
Faris, Chorbishop John, (OLL) Curia: Communications
Faris, Chorbishop John D., '76 (SAM) Curia: Leadership; Offices and Directors Saint Anthony Maronite Catholic Church, Glen Allen, VA; [MIS] Saint Anthony Maronite Scholarship Endowed Trust Agreement, Glen Allen, VA; [MIS] Saint Maron Publications, Glen Allen, VA
Farke, Rev. Rodney, '72 (SFS) Retired. Curia: Leadership; Offices and Directors
Farland, Rev. Msgr. George A., '68 (SPR) Curia: Offices and Directors; Tribunal Sacred Heart, Springfield, MA
Farleo, Rev. Brenann Joseph, *O.F.M.Conv.* (TR) St. Peter's, Point Pleasant Beach, NJ
Farleo, Rev. Brennan-Joseph, *O.F.M.Conv.* '86 (NY) [MON] St. Francis Friary, Staten Island, NY
Farley, Rev. Bernard C., '68 (PH) Retired.
Farley, Rev. James V., '65 (PRO) Retired.
Farley, Rev. John, '93 (PBL) Sangre de Cristo, San Luis, CO
Farley, Rev. Msgr. John, '62 (NY) Retired.
Farley, Rev. Leo O., '54 (NEW) Retired. [MON] The Rev. Msgr. James F. Kelley Residence for Retired Priests, Caldwell, NJ
Farley, Rev. Leslie A., '93 (LR) Church of Our Lady of the Assumption, Booneville, AR; St. Jude Thaddeus Church, Waldron, AR; [CON] St. Scholastica Monastery-Motherhouse, Fort Smith, AR
Farley, Rev. Louis, '11 (KC) On Special Assignment. St Joseph's Med Ctr & St Mary's Med Ctr Christ the King, Kansas City, MO
Farmer, Rev. Cyril, '03 (PRM) St. John the Baptist, Minneapolis, MN
Farmer, Rev. J. Kevin, '92 (BAL) Catholic Community of St. Francis Xavier, Hunt Valley, MD; Our Lady of Grace, Parkton, MD
Farmer, Rev. Msgr. James P., '79 (BAL) Church of the Immaculate Conception, Towson, MD; [MIS] St. Thomas More Society of Maryland Inc., Baltimore, MD
Farmer, Rev. Msgr. Michael L., '95 (MOB) Curia: Leadership St. Michael, Auburn, AL
Farnan, Rev. Donald P., '87 (KC) On Special Assignment. Rockhurst Univ, Kansas City St. James, Kansas City, MO; St. Therese Little Flower, Kansas City, MO
Farnan, Rev. James B., '00 (PIT) St. Matthias, Waynesburg, PA
Farrar, Rev. Brandon, '06 (KCK) St. John Paul II Catholic Church, Olathe, KS
Farrell, Rev. Bernard P., '65 (BLX) Retired.
Farrell, Rev. David, '18 (L) St. Dominic, Springfield, KY
Farrell, Rev. David E., *CSC* (FTW) Retired. [MIS] Holy Cross House, Notre Dame, IN
Farrell, Rev. Emmett L., '65 (SC) Retired.
Farrell, Rev. George A., '96 (MET) On Leave. [MON] Maria Regina Residence, Somerset, NJ
Farrell, Rev. Gerald, *M.M.* '57 (NY) Retired.
Farrell, Rev. James M., (IND) Retired.
Farrell, Rev. John E., '62 (BO) Retired.
Farrell, Rev. Joseph J., '74 (TR) Retired.
Farrell, Rev. Joseph L., '95 (PH) Our Lady of Consolation, Philadelphia, PA
Farrell, Rev. Joseph W., '15 (ARL) [CAM] George Mason University, Catholic Campus Ministry, Fairfax, VA
Farrell, Rev. Kevin R., '65 (JOL) Retired.
Farrell, Rev. Kurt P., '98 (WIN) Curia: Advisory Boards, Commissions, Committees, and Councils St. James, Albert Lea, MN; St. Theodore, Albert Lea, MN; [EFT] St. Theodore Catholic School Endowment, Albert Lea, MN
Farrell, Rev. Martin, *O.P.* '78 (NY) Chap, Hospital for Special Surgery, New York
Farrell, Rev. Michael A., '70 (ORL) Retired.
Farrell, Rev. Michael J., '11 (BO) On Leave.
Farrell, Rev. Msgr. Patrick, '60 (JKS) Retired.
Farrell, Very Rev. Philip N., '93 (PIT) Curia: Consultative Bodies; Leadership
Farrell, Rev. Richard T., '84 (ROC) Chap, Elmira Corr Fac, Ctr and Camp Monterey; Southport Cor… The Parish of the Most Holy Name of Jesus, Chemung County, NY, Elmira, NY
Farrell, Rev. Robert, *S.J.* '64 (BO) [MON] Campion Health & Wellness, Inc., Weston, MA
Farrell, Rev. Robert J., '80 (CIN) St. Francis de Sales, Lebanon, OH; St. Philip the Apostle, Morrow, OH
Farrell, Rev. Ronald J., '00 (CHR) Holy Family, Hilton Head Island, SC
Farrell, Rev. Seamus J., '67 (OAK) St. Bede, Hayward, CA
Farrell, Rev. Thomas J., '92 (GB) Stella Maris, Egg Harbor, WI
Farrell, Rev. Thomas P., '82 (LEX) St. Mark, Richmond, KY; [CAM] Catholic Campus Ministry of St. Mark (St. Stephen the Martyr Newman Center), Richmond, KY
Farrell, Rev. Timothy W., '89 (GLP) Curia: Leadership Sacred Heart, Farmington, NM
Farrell, Rev. Tom, '82 (LEX) Curia: Leadership
Farrelly, Rev. Paul, *O.S.B.* '10 (SD) [MON] Prince of Peace Abbey, Oceanside, CA
Farren, Rev. John Aquinas, *O.P.* '64 (NY) Retired. St. Catherine of Siena, New York, NY; [MIS] Dominican Shrine of St. Jude, Inc., New York, NY
Farris, Rev. William, *O.F.M.* '77 (CIN) [MON] St. Francis Seraph Friary, Cincinnati, OH; [SHR] St. Anthony Shrine, Cincinnati, OH
Farrugia, Rev. David, *O.P.* '60 (SAC) Retired. St. Dominic, Benicia, CA
Farrugia, Rev. Pierre John, *O.F.M.* '05 (NY) [MIS] Franciscan Mission Associates, Mount Vernon, NY
Farrugia, Rev. William C., '63 (BRK) Retired. St. Joseph, Astoria, NY
Farsaci, Rev. Francis A., *O.S.A.* '64 (PH) [MON] St. Thomas Monastery, Villanova, PA
Farwell, Rev. Richard, (CHL) Retired.
Farynets, Rev. Mykhaylo, '09 (PBR) Curia: Leadership Infant Jesus of Prague, Boardman, OH; St. Nicholas, Youngstown, OH
Fasano, Rev. Eric R., '02 (RVC) Curia: Leadership; Offices and Directors; Organizations (affiliated, inter-Diocesan, miscellaneous/other) Campus Parish of Long Island, Rockville Centre, NY
Fasano, Rev. Jerome W., '77 (ARL) Retired.
Fasching, Rev. Jeffery A., '97 (WCH) On Leave.
Fasciglione, Rev. Massimo S., '74 (CAM) Retired.
Fase, Rev. Matthew, *C.S.C.* (FTW) Curia: Leadership St. Joseph, South Bend, IN
Fasnacht, Rev. Jonathan Joseph, '15 (WIN) Curia: Advisory Boards, Commissions, Committees, and Councils Good Shepherd, Jackson, MN; St. Joseph, Lakefield, MN; St. Luke's, Sherburn, MN
Fasnacht, Rev. Matthew J., '07 (WIN) St. Mary's of the Lake, Lake City, MN; St. Patrick of West Albany, Millville, MN
Faso, Rev. Charles, *O.F.M.* '67 (CHI) [MON] St. Gratian Friary, Franciscan Friars, Countryside, IL
Fassero, Rev. Jonathan, *O.S.B.* '78 (IND) [MON] St. Meinrad Archabbey, St. Meinrad, IN
Fassett, Rev. Edward S., *S.J.* '88 (SJ) [ASN] Jesuit Seminary Association, Los Gatos, CA; [MON] Jesuit Community at Santa Clara University, Inc., Santa Clara, CA; [MON] USA West Province, Society of Jesus, Los Gatos, CA
Fassett, Rev. Edward S., *S.J.* (P) [MON] Society of Jesus, Oregon Province, Portland, OR
Fater, Rev. Msgr. Douglas, '70 (SAT) Retired.
Fath, Rev. Robert, '07 (FBK) Curia: Leadership; Offices and Directors [MIS] Bl. Pier Giorgio Frassati House of Discernment, Fairbanks, AK
Fatooh, Rev. Msgr. Charles G., '85 (MRY) Retired. St. Joseph, Cayucos, CA
Faucett, Rev. Matthew, '19 (GB) On Special Assignment. Military duty Curia: (>MO) Offices and Directors
Faulhaber, Rev. Gregory M., '79 (BUF) Curia: Consultative Bodies Queen of Heaven, West Seneca, NY
Faulk, Rev. Joel Christopher, '16 (LAF) Assumption B.V.M., Franklin, LA; St. Joseph, Centerville, LA
Faulk, Rev. Peter, (SHP) Curia: Leadership
Faulk, Very Rev. Peter A., '06 (ALX) Curia: Miscellaneous / Other Offices St. Margaret, Boyce, LA
Faulkner, Rev. Joseph J., '05 (LIN) St. Joseph's, Beatrice, NE
Faulstich, Rev. Paul J., *S.J.* '68 (CHI) [COL] Jesuit Community at Loyola University Chicago, Chicago, IL
Fauser, Very Rev. Steven W., '03 (HBG) Curia: Offices and Directors Our Lady of Lourdes, New Holland, PA
Faust, Rev. Louis J., '74 (WDC) Retired. Mother Seton Parish, Germantown, MD
Faustino, Rev. Archie Filoteo, '93 (ORL) Holy Redeemer, Kissimmee, FL
Fausz, Rev. Kevin P., *C.M.* '91 (SAT) Curia: Administration Holy Redeemer, San Antonio, TX; Our Lady of Perpetual Help, San Antonio, TX; St. Michael, San Antonio, TX
Favazza, Rev. Robert D., '09 (MEM) Church of the Resurrection, Memphis, TN
Favole-Mihm, Rev. Joseph, *F.S.S.P.* (BAL) The National Shrine of St. Alphonsus Liguori, Baltimore, MD
Fawls, Rev. Daniel J., '97 (BUF) Curia: Consultative Bodies St. Aloysius, Springville, NY; St. John the Baptist, West Valley, NY
Fay, Rev. David E., '64 (CIN) Retired.
Fay, Rev. Gregory J., '76 (STA) Retired.
Fay, Rev. William J., '64 (PIT) Retired.
Fay, Rev. Msgr. William P., '73 (BO) Curia: Advisory Boards, Commissions, Committees, and Councils
Fay, Rev. Msgr. William P., '74 (BO) Curia: Consultative Bodies [SEM] Pope Saint John XXIII National Seminary, Weston, MA
Fayez, Rev. Francis, (BRK) Holy Family-Saint Thomas Aquinas, Brooklyn, NY
Faylona, Rev. Joey, '03 (SAN) St. Mary's, San Angelo, TX
Fazio, Rev. Kevin C., '12 (PIT) All Saints, Butler, PA
Fazio, Rev. Msgr. Mariano, '91 (POD) Curia: Leadership
Fazio, Rev. Paul, *O.F.M. Conv* '74 (OAK) Our Lady of Grace, Castro Valley, CA
Fazolini, Rev. Leandro, *S.F.* (BAL) Sacred Heart, Glyndon, MD; St. John, Westminster, MD; St. Joseph, Taneytown, MD
Feain, Rev. Andre M., *FI* '04 (FR) [MON] Marian Friary of Our Lady, Queen of the Seraphic Order, New Bedford, MA
Feather, Rev. Ronald Joseph, '11 (AUS) Retired.
Fecht, Rev. Geoffrey, *O.S.B.* '88 (SCL) [MON] St. John's Abbey, of the Order of St. Benedict, Collegeville, MN
Fecko, Rev. Leonard J., '89 (CIN) Retired.
Fedak, Rev. Dennis Z., '98 (PH) Corpus Christi, Lansdale, PA
Fedak, Rev. Paul C., '98 (FR) Good Shepherd, Oak Bluffs, MA
Fedchyk, Rev. Roman, '12 (STN) St. Michael the Archangel Ukrainian Greek Catholic Church, Grand Rapids, MI
Feddon, Rev. Dustin, (PT) Chap, Wakulla Corr Inst Blessed Sacrament, Tallahassee, FL; Sacred Heart of Jesus, Carrabelle, FL; [MIS] Joseph House LLC, Pensacola, FL
Fedek, Rev. Robert M., '05 (CHI) Curia: Offices and Directors
Fedele, Rev. Giuseppe, '05 (NEW) On Duty Outside Diocese. c/o St James Roman Catholic Church, Denver, CO
Federico, Rev. Anthony, '19 (HRT) Curia: Advisory Boards, Commissions, Committees, and Councils; Offices and Directors
Federico, Rev. Anthony J., '19 (HRT) Saint Mary Parish Corporation, New Haven, CT
Federico, Rev. Matthew, (SAG) Holy Trinity Parish of Pinconning, Pinconning, MI; [EFT] St. Michael Catholic School Foundation Endowment Fund, Pinconning, MI
Feders, Rev. Joseph, *O.S.B.* '99 (SCL) [MON] St. John's Abbey, of the Order of St. Benedict, Collegeville, MN
Federspiel, Rev. Nicholas, '04 (RCK) On Special Assignment. Prison Ministry & Poor Clares Monastery, Rockford, IL
Fedewa, Rev. Eric, '10 (DET) St. Basil Parish Eastpointe, Eastpointe, MI
Fedewa, Rev. Matthew, '58 (LAN) Retired.

Fedigan, Rev. James, (BRK) Our Lady of Fatima, Jackson Heights, NY

Fedor, Rev. Gregory F., '83 (Y) Immaculate Heart of Mary, Austintown, OH; St. Joseph, Austintown, OH

Fedor, Rev. Mark Q., '72 (CLV) Retired.

Fedoryshyn, Rev. Christopher, '14 (SPR) St. Mark's, Pittsfield, MA; [CAM] Berkshire Community College, Pittsfield, MA

Fedrigoni, Rev. Paolo, *I.M.C.* '82 (MET) [MON] Consolata Society for Foreign Missions, North Brunswick, NJ

Fee, Rev. James, *O.M.I.* (BEL) Holy Rosary, Fairmont City, IL; St. Stephen, Caseyville, IL; [MON] Shrine of Our Lady of the Snows, Belleville, IL

Feehily, Rev. John W., '73 (OKL) Retired.

Feela, Rev. Paul F., '78 (STP) Retired.

Feely, Rev. Msgr. James B., '58 (GB) Retired.

Feely, Rev. Thomas H., *S.J.* '75 (NY) [MON] Xavier Jesuit Community, New York, NY

Feeney, Rev. Joseph J., *S.J.* '65 (PH) [MIS] Jesuit Fathers, , ; [MON] Jesuit Community at St. Joseph's University, Merion Station, PA

Feeney, Rev. Kevin J., '77 (CHI) Retired. [CAM] Northwestern University, Sheil Center, Evanston, IL

Feeney, Rev. Msgr. Thomas P., '79 (CC) Curia: Administration; Leadership

Feeney, Rev. William P., '72 (PIT) Retired. [NUR] Little Sisters of the Poor Home for the Aged, Pittsburgh, PA

Fegan, Rev. Peter, *O.P.* (WDC) (>COL) St. Patrick, Columbus, OH

Fehn, Rev. Jerome W., '78 (STP) Retired.

Fehrenbacher, Rev. Canon Jonathon, *I.C.R.S.S.* '16 (TUC) Curia: Miscellaneous / Other Offices Holy Family Roman Catholic Parish - Tucson, Tucson, AZ; [MIS] The Oratory of St. Gianna, Tucson, AZ

Feicht, Rev. Donald L., '70 (Y) Retired.

Feierfeil, Rev. Gerald F., '67 (SC) Retired.

Feigh, Rev. Jason R., '11 (E) St. Francis Xavier, Mc Kean, PA

Feild, Rev. Msgr. Martin E., '59 (BAL) Retired. St. Joseph, Taneytown, MD

Feiss, Rev. Hugh, *O.S.B.* '66 (B) [MON] Monastery of the Ascension, Jerome, ID

Feist, Rev. Matthew S., '16 (CIN) Holy Family, Versailles, OH; Immaculate Conception, Bradford, OH; St. Denis, Versailles, OH; St. Louis, North Star, OH; St. Mary, Greenville, OH; St. Nicholas, Osgood, OH; St. Remy, Russia, OH

Feketie, Rev. Michael J., '57 (NEW) Retired. St. Mary, Plainfield, NJ

Felago, Rev. John F., *M.M.* '68 (NY) Retired. [MON] Maryknoll Fathers and Brothers (Catholic Foreign Mission Society of America, Inc.), Ossining, NY

Feldcamp, Rev. Msgr. William J., '65 (SCR) Retired. [MON] Villa St. Joseph, Dunmore, PA

Feldmeier, Rev. Russell J., *M.M.* '80 (CHI) [MON] Maryknoll Fathers & Brothers (Catholic Foreign Mission Society of America, Inc.), Chicago, IL

Feldtz, Rev. Michael J, '18 (CLV) St. Thomas More, Brooklyn, OH

Felice, Rev. John M., *O.F.M.* '68 (NY) Retired.

Felice-Pace, Rev. Albert, *O.P.* '60 (LAV) Retired. [MON] Dominican Rectory, Fra Angelico House, Las Vegas, NV

Felices Sanchez, Rev. Msgr. Fernando B., '82 (SJN) Curia: Leadership

Felices Sanchez, Rev. Msgr. Fernando Benicio, (SJN) Gruta de Lourdes, Trujillo Alto, PR

Felices-Sanchez, Rev. Msgr. Fernando B., '82 (SJN) Curia: Offices and Directors

Feliciano, Rev. Abraham, *S.D.B.* '06 (NY) [MON] Salesian Office of Youth & Young Adult Ministry, New Rochelle, NY

Felicichia, Rev. Stephen, '20 (FTW) St. Elizabeth Ann Seton, Fort Wayne, IN

Felicien, Rev. Jean, '14 (TR) Curia: Canonical Services; Leadership St. George, Titusville, NJ; St. James, Pennington, NJ

Felicitas, Rev. Godofredo, '84 (BRK) St. Robert Bellarmine, Bayside, NY

Felipe, Rev. Marvin Paul, *S.D.B.* '92 (SFR) Chap, San Francisco State Univ, Newman Ctr [CAM] Newman Center, San Francisco State University, San Francisco, CA

Felix, Rev. Bernard H., '92 (DOD) Curia: Offices and Directors Sacred Heart of Jesus Catholic Church of Larned, Kansas, Larned, KS; St. Bernard Catholic Church of Belpre, Kansas, Belpre, KS; [EFT] Sacred Heart Endowment Fund, Inc., Larned, KS

Felix, Rev. Christopher M., '14 (LA) Resurrection, Los Angeles, CA

Felix, Rev. Paul G., '90 (GAL) Curia: Leadership The Church of the Annunciation, Houston, TX

Felix, Rev. William P., '81 (LC) Curia: Leadership; Offices and Directors All Saints, Stanley, WI; [EFT] St. Rose of Lima Catholic Church Endowment Trust, Stanley, WI; [MIS] Institute of St. Joseph, Boyd, WI

Felix-Rosas, Rev. Rogelio, '05 (SLC) Curia: Offices and Directors Saint Thomas Aquinas LLC 247, Hyde Park, UT

Feliz, Rev. Normando, '75 (VEN) Retired.

Feliz Sena, Rev. Neftali, (SCR) Church of the Most Precious Blood, Hazleton, PA

Felkner, Rev. Christian, *O.S.B.* '14 (TLS) [MON] Our Lady of the Annunciation of Clear Creek Abbey, Hulbert, OK

Fell, Rev. Msgr. John N., '88 (MET) Curia: Clergy and Religious Services; Consultative Bodies; Leadership

Fellenz, Rev. Ralph, *O.F.M.Cap.* '68 (GB) Retired. [MON] St. Fidelis Friary, Appleton, WI

Fellrath, Rev. Frank W., '89 (MET) On Leave.

Felt, Rev. Richard R., '69 (PHX) Retired.

Felter, Rev. Francis J., *M.M.* '69 (NY) Retired. [MON] Maryknoll Fathers and Brothers (Catholic Foreign Mission Society of America, Inc.), Ossining, NY

Feltes, Rev. Victor C., '09 (LC) St. John the Baptist, Bloomer, WI; St. Paul, Bloomer, WI; [EFT] St. Paul Catholic Parish of Bloomer Wisconsin Endowment Trust, Bloomer, WI

Feltman, Rev. Philip S., '66 (TOL) Retired.

Feltman, Rev. Thomas, '01 (FAR) Blessed Sacrament Church of West Fargo, West Fargo, ND

Feltz, Rev. John G., '73 (BUR) Curia: Leadership St. Ann, Milton, VT

Feltz, Rev. Joseph M., '02 (IND) Our Lady Of Perpetual Help Catholic Church, New Albany, Inc., New Albany, IN

Felux, Rev. Jonathan W., '09 (SAT) On Leave.

Fenili, Rev. J. Robert, *C.Ss.R.* '62 (CHI) Retired. St. Michael in Old Town, Chicago, IL; [MON] The Redemptorist Fathers of Chicago, Chicago, IL

Fenili, Rev. Joseph, *C.Ss.R.* (CHI) Retired.

Fenlon, Rev. Thomas B., '61 (NY) Retired. Chap, Vernon C Bain Ctr, Bronx Parish of St. Charles Borromeo and All Saints, New York, NY

Fennell, Rev. Patrick A., *O.S.B.* '89 (PEO) [SEM] St. Bede Abbey (Benedictine Society of St. Bede, Benedictine Fathers and Brothers), Peru, IL

Fennessy, Rev. James, '02 (ROC) St. Francis & St. Clare Roman Catholic Parish, Seneca County, NY, Waterloo, NY; [CAM] New York Chiropractic College, Waterloo, NY; [EFT] Patrician Fund Trust, Waterloo, NY

Fennessy, Rev. Msgr. James J., '68 (ATL) Retired.

Fennessy, Rev. Peter J., *S.J.* '70 (DET) [RTR] Manresa Jesuit Retreat House, Bloomfield Hills, MI

Fenstermaker, Rev. James E., *C.S.C.* '84 (FTW) Holy Cross, South Bend, IN

Fenton, Rev. Joseph, *S.M.* '72 (WDC) [MON] Marist Center (The Marist Finance Center of the Atlanta Province of the Society of Mary, Marist Fathers and Brothers), Washington, DC

Fenton, Rev. Joseph, *S.M.* '72 (LA) Curia: Offices and Directors

Fenton, Rev. Patrick, '08 (TYL) Retired. Mary, Queen of Heaven Church, Malakoff, TX

Fenzl, Rev. Roderick R., *O. Praem.* '55 (GB) [MON] St. Norbert Abbey, De Pere, WI

Ferch, Rev. Matthew, '22 (MIL) Congregation of St. Francis Borgia, Cedarburg, WI

Ferdzefer, Very Rev. Cyprian Tatah, (STV) Church of St. Patrick, Frederiksted, VI

Ference, Rev. Damian J., '03 (CLV) Curia: Advisory Boards, Commissions, Committees, and Councils; Leadership; Parish Services [SEM] Borromeo Seminary, Wickliffe, OH

Ferguson, Rev. Anthony, '20 (RIC) St. Bede, Williamsburg, VA

Ferguson, Rev. James, (SHP) Curia: Leadership

Ferguson, Rev. James A., '85 (ALX) Curia: Miscellaneous / Other Offices St. Francis Xavier Cathedral, Alexandria, LA

Ferguson, Rev. James J., *C.S.C.* '64 (FTW) [MIS] Holy Cross House, Notre Dame, IN

Ferguson, Rev. Justin R., '06 (SAV) On Leave.

Ferguson, Rev. Paul A., '02 (EVN) Curia: Leadership Our Lady of Hope, Washington, IN

Ferguson, Rev. Peter A., '90 (GAL) Retired.

Ferguson, Rev. Robert, *F.S.S.P.* '02 (LIN) [SEM] Our Lady of Guadalupe Seminary, Inc., Denton, NE

Ferguson, Rev. Thomas P., '94 (ARL) Curia: Tribunal Good Shepherd, Alexandria, VA

Ferguson, Very Rev. Timothy, (WIN) Curia: Tribunal

Ferguson, Very Rev. Timothy T., '15 (MAR) Curia: Advisory Boards, Commissions, Committees, and Councils; Offices and Directors; Organizations (affiliated, inter-Diocesan, miscellaneous/other) St. Joseph & St. Patrick, Escanaba, MI

Ferguson, Rev. Timothy T., (OAK) Curia: Offices and Directors

Ferguson, Rev. William J., '06 (COL) St. Andrew, Columbus, OH

Ferland, Rev. Thomas J., '87 (PRO) Curia: Advisory Boards, Commissions, Committees, and Councils Saint James Church of Manville, Rhode Island, Manville, RI; St. Ambrose Church, Albion, Rhode Island, Albion, RI

Ferme, Rev. Joseph A., '22 (BO) On Duty Outside Diocese. St. Margaret of Scotland, Lowell, MA

Fernan, Rev. Matthew F., '89 (NY) St. Eugene, Yonkers, NY

Fernandes, Rev. Cosme S., '95 (NY) St. Martin of Tours, Bronx, NY

Fernandes, Rev. Cyril, '88 (FTW) St. Hedwig, South Bend, IN; St. Patrick, South Bend, IN

Fernandes, Rev. David A., '97 (PH) St. Thomas Aquinas, Croydon, PA

Fernandes, Rev. John, '77 (OAK) Retired.

Fernandes, Rev. Louis Mariano, *SCJ* '04 (JKS) Christ the King, Southaven, MS; Good Shepherd Catholic Church, Robinsonville, MS; Holy Spirit, Hernando, MS; Queen of Peace, Olive Branch, MS; St. Gregory the Great, Senatobia, MS; St. Joseph, Holly Springs, MS; [MON] St. Michael Community House, Nesbit, MS

Fernandes, Rev. Lourdino, '69 (FTW) Retired.

Fernandes, Rev. Patrick O., '83 (BUF) Retired.

Fernandes, Rev. Roque A.D., '69 (LA) Retired. St. Frances of Rome, Azusa, CA

Fernandes, Rev. Socorro, *S.A.C.* '99 (DET) Our Lady of Loretto Parish Redford, Redford, MI; St. Valentine Parish Redford, Redford, MI; [MON] Society of the Catholic Apostolate-Indian Province of the State of Michigan, Redford, MI

Fernandes, Rev. Stephen, *O.F.M.Cap.* (HBG) Curia: Offices and Directors St. Joseph, York, PA

Fernandez, Rev. Altaire, (LA) Curia: Pastoral Services

Fernandez, Rev. Archie, (TLS) St. Bernard of Clairvaux, Tulsa, OK

Fernandez, Rev. Eduardo C., *S.J.* '92 (OAK) [MON] Jesuit Fathers and Brothers, Berkeley, CA; [SEM] Jesuit School of Theology of Santa Clara University (Berkeley, California Campus), Berkeley, CA

Fernandez, Rev. Emmanuel, '79 (LAF) St. John, Erath, LA

Fernandez, Rev. Felipe, (MGZ) St. Francis of Assisi, Aguada, PR

Fernandez, Rev. Gerardo, (SD) Pastor of Mission San Antonio de Pala Catholic Parish, Pala, a corporation sole, Pala, CA; [CEM] Pala Indian Missions, Pala, CA; [MIS] Mission San Antonio de Pala Catholic Parish in Pala, CA Real Property Support Corporation, Pala, CA

Fernandez, Rev. Jeff, '14 (SJ) On Special Assignment. Curia: Offices and Directors Queen of Apostles, San Jose, CA

Fernandez, Rev. Jorge Ivan, *mxy* '88 (NY) Church of Our Saviour, Bronx, NY; [MON] Yarumal Mission Society, Inc., Bronx, NY

Fernandez, Rev. L. Wilfredo, '16 (L) St. Joseph, Louisville, KY

Fernandez, Rev. Luis J., '71 (NO) Retired.

Fernandez, Rev. Msgr. Manuel, '62 (ORL) Retired.

Fernandez, Rev. Marcellus, '68 (B) Retired.

Fernandez, Rev. Matthew, *M.M.H.C.* '94 (LA) Holy Family, Artesia, CA

Fernandez, Rev. Sydney, '79 (HON) Retired.

Fernandez, Rev. Vince, '18 (TLS) Church of St. Mary, Tulsa, OK

Fernandez, Rev. Wilfredo Luder, '16 (L) Curia: Leadership

Fernandez Ceja, Rev. Miguel A., '11 (BWN) Sacred Heart, Roma, TX

Fernandez Minguez, Rev. Serapio, '50 (ARE) Retired.

Fernandez Triana, Rev. Julio, '03 (MIA) St. John the Apostle, Hialeah, FL

Fernandez-Bangueses, Rev. Jose, '70 (TR) Retired.

Fernandez-Boscan, Rev. Mauricio, '15 (MIL) On Leave.

Fernandez-Torres, Rev. Ismael, *O.P.* (SJN) San Pio X, Trujillo Alto, PR

Fernando, Rev. Antony, '85 (CR) Curia: Offices and Directors Our Lady of the Pines, Nevis, MN; St. Theodore of Tarsus (Laporte), Laporte, MN

Fernando, Rev. Augustine, '64 (RVC) Retired. St. Kilian, Farmingdale, NY

Fernando, Rev. Bernard, '65 (NEW) Retired.

Fernando, Rev. Camillus, '80 (BAK) St. Patrick, Vale, OR

Fernando, Rev. Cresus, '82 (NY) St. Anthony, Nanuet, NY

Fernando, Rev. Damian, '70 (LA) Retired.

Fernando, Rev. Gamini E., '71 (NY) Retired. Holy Trinity, Poughkeepsie, NY

Fernando, Rev. Jude, *T.O.R.* (LKC) Our Lady of Perpetual Help, Jennings, LA
Fernando, Rev. Jude Gregory, *S.S.S.* '07 (NY) St. Jean Baptiste, New York, NY
Fernando, Rev. Peter Damian, '70 (LA) Retired. Mission Basilica San Buenaventura, Ventura, CA
Fernando, Rev. Polycarp, '78 (FTW) St. Vincent de Paul, Fort Wayne, IN
Fernando, Rev. Roger, (B) Sacred Heart, Boise, ID
Fernando, Rev. Simon, '60 (RVC) Retired.
Fernando, Rev. Susil, '87 (LKC) Our Lady of Seven Dolors, Welsh, LA
Fernando, Rev. Susil, '87 (LKC) Curia: Leadership
Fernando, Rev. Msgr. Venantius M., '61 (NEW) Retired. St. Theresa, Kenilworth, NJ
Ferone, Rev. John M., *S.J.* (DET) [MON] Colombiere Center, Clarkston, MI
Ferrandiz, Rev. Danilo D., '95 (AGN) San Miguel, Talo'fo'fo', GU
Ferrante, Rev. Frank, *C.M.F.* '70 (LA) [MON] Dominguez Seminary Inc., Rancho Dominguez, CA
Ferrara, Rev. Charles F., '90 (STL) St. David Catholic Church, Arnold, MO
Ferrara, Rev. John, *O.M.V.* '82 (BO) [MON] Oblate Residence (St. Joseph House), Milton, MA
Ferrara, Rev. Joseph R., '77 (CAM) Retired.
Ferrarese, Rev. Msgr. Fernando A., '77 (BRK) Curia: Consultative Bodies Immaculate Conception, Astoria, NY
Ferrari, Rev. Msgr. Steven A., '80 (BRK) St. Teresa, Woodside, NY
Ferrario, Rev. Ettore, *F.S.C.B.* (STP) St. Peter, North St. Paul, MN; [CEM] St. Mary's Cemetery, North St. Paul, MN
Ferraro, Rev. Msgr. Joseph, '67 (OAK) Retired.
Ferraro, Rev. Joseph A., '90 (NEW) Holy Family, Nutley, NJ
Ferraro, Rev. Michael M., '68 (BO) Retired.
Ferraro, Rev. Ronald A., '60 (HRT) Retired.
Ferraro, Rev. Vincent J., '70 (BUF) Retired.
Ferras, Rev. Jesus, '04 (AUS) [MON] Schoenstatt Fathers, Austin, TX
Ferras, Rev. Jesus, *I.S.P.* (MIA) St. Kieran, Miami, FL
Ferrecchia, Rev. Leonard, *C.S.S.* (WOR) Retired.
Ferreira, Rev. Alfonse, *O.F.M.* '72 (BO) Curia: Social Services [MON] Franciscan Community (Province of Immaculate Conception), Lynn, MA
Ferreira, Rev. James, '10 (NY) Our Lady Help of Christians, Staten Island, NY
Ferrence, Rev. John J., *O.S.A.* '52 (PH) [MON] St. Thomas Monastery, Villanova, PA
Ferrer, Rev. Antonio, '98 (NY) St. Anthony, Nanuet, NY
Ferrer, Rev. Charles M., '64 (CHI) [MIS] Midtown Residence, Chicago, IL
Ferrer, Rev. Charles R., '64 (POD) Curia: Clergy and Religious Services
Ferrer, Very Rev. Christopher, '01 (AUS) Curia: Leadership; Tribunal St. Peter the Apostle, Austin, TX
Ferrer, Rev. Gonzalo, *TOR* '81 (AUS) Retired.
Ferrer, Rev. Melchor, *S.D.B.* '74 (NY) Chap, New York Presbyterian-Columbia Med Ctr, New York St. Rose of Lima, New York, NY
Ferrera, Rev. Fernando, *C.M.F.* '92 (CHI) [MON] Claretian Missionaries U.S.A.-Canada Province, Inc., Chicago, IL
Ferretti, Rev. Samuel J., '74 (SCR) SS. Peter and Paul, Scranton, PA; St. Lucy's, Scranton, PA
Ferrick, Very Rev. Michael P., '99 (E) St. Peter Cathedral, Erie, PA
Ferrick, Rev. Raymond J., '77 (PRO) Retired.
Ferrie, Rev. Francis, '65 (NO) Retired. Mater Dolorosa, New Orleans, LA
Ferris, Rev. Aaron R., '19 (GR) On Duty Outside Diocese. Serving as Chaplain Officer in the U.S. Air Force Curia: (>MO) Offices and Directors
Ferris, Rev. Brennan H., '22 (WIL) Holy Cross, Dover, DE; Immaculate Conception, Marydel, MD
Ferris, Very Rev. Luke A., '11 (GB) Curia: Advisory Boards, Commissions, Committees, and Councils; Clergy and Religious Services
Ferris, Rev. Robert M., '01 (CHL) Retired.
Ferris, Rev. Timothy F., '03 (TOL) Our Lady of Lourdes, Genoa, OH; St. Boniface, Oak Harbor, OH
Ferroni, Rev. Jose, (MO) Curia: Offices and Directors
Ferroni, Rev. Jose Luis, (TUC) Chap, US Veterans Hosp, Tucson
Ferroni, Rev. Jose Luis, (SB) [RTR] El Carmelo Retreat House, Redlands, CA
Ferruzzi, Rev. William, *S.D.B.* '76 (NY) [RTR] Don Bosco Retreat Center and Marian Shrine, Stony Point, NY; [RTR] Marian Shrine, Stony Point, NY
Ferry, Rev. James, '84 (FR) Retired.
Ferry, Rev. James P., '06 (NEW) Curia: Advisory Boards, Commissions, Committees, and Councils Our Lady of Lourdes, West Orange, NJ
Ferry, Rev. Msgr. John T., '84 (NY) St. Patrick, Bedford, NY
Ferus, Rev. James P., *SJ* '20 (NY) Regis High School, New York, NY; [MON] St. Ignatius Loyola Residence, New York, NY
Fery, Rev. Yohanes, '16 (CHI) [MON] DePaul Vincentian Residence, Chicago, IL
Fesniak, Rev. Mark, '03 (PHU) Curia: Leadership
Fesniak, Rev. Mark, '03 (PHU) Curia: Leadership
Fesniak, Rev. Mark Michael, '03 (PHU) Nativity of B.V.M., Middleport, PA; St. Nicholas, Minersville, PA
Fessenden, Rev. Joseph, (NSH) On Leave.
Fessio, Rev. Joseph D., *S.J.* '72 (SFR) [MON] Jesuit Community at St. Ignatius College Preparatory, San Francisco, CA
Fest, Rev. Donald M., *S.S.J.* '76 (ARL) St. Joseph's, Alexandria, VA
Fetcko, Rev. Jordan C., '15 (GRY) Queen of All Saints, Michigan City, IN
Fetscher, Msgr. James F., '68 (MIA) St. Sebastian, Fort Lauderdale, FL
Fetters, Rev. Donald G., *C.S.C.* '76 (FTW) [SEM] Moreau Seminary, Notre Dame, IN
Fetz, Rev. Thomas A., *O.F.C.V.* (CHI) Mary, Mother of God, Chicago, IL
Feusahrens, Rev. Frederick J., '72 (RIC) Retired.
Fewel, Rev. John Matthew, '14 (STV) On Duty Outside Diocese.
Fey, Rev. Thomas J., '70 (ALX) Retired. On Duty Outside Diocese. Curia: (>MO) Offices and Directors
Fiala, Rev. Vit, *O.F.M.* '98 (Y) [MON] Mt. Alverna Friary, Youngstown, OH
Fialkowski, Rev. Edward R., '78 (CHI) St. Luke and St. Bernardine Parish, River Forest, IL
Fialkowski, Rev. Thomas M., '66 (E) Retired.
Ficara, Rev. Jonathan J., '14 (NOR) Curia: Offices and Directors [CAM] Connecticut College, New London, CT
Ficek, Rev. Ryszard, '98 (RVC) St. Ignatius Martyr, Long Beach, NY
Fichter, Rev. Stephen J., '00 (NEW) Curia: Organizations (affiliated, inter-Diocesan, miscellaneous/other) St. Elizabeth, Wyckoff, NJ
Fichtinger, Rev. Richard J., *S.J.*, '17 (STP) St. Thomas More, St. Paul, MN; [SEM] Jesuit Novitiate of St. Alberto Hurtado, St. Paul, MN
Fickel, Rev. Patrick, '16 (GR) St. Mary-St. Paul Parish, Big Rapids, MI
Fickel, Rev. William, *S.S.S.* '81 (SP) St. Vincent De Paul, Holiday, FL
Fickes, Rev. Daniel R., '91 (CLV) Holy Spirit, Avon Lake, OH
Ficorilli, Rev. Chad R., *O.S.B.* '79 (GBG) [MON] Saint Vincent Archabbey, Latrobe, PA
Fictum, Rev. Robert A., '78 (MIL) Retired.
Fidalgo, Rev. Federico, '63 (CC) Retired.
Fider, Rev. William P., '66 (DUL) Retired.
Fiebelkorn, Rev. Daniel F., '97 (BUF) Our Lady of Mt. Carmel, Silver Creek, NY
Fiedurek, Rev. Jan, *S.Chr.* '89 (SJ) St. Brother Albert Chmielowski Polish Catholic Pastoral Mission, San Jose, CA
Fiedurek, Rev. Jan, *T.Chr* (WDC) Our Lady Queen of Poland and Saint Maximilian Kolbe, Silver Spring, MD
Field, Rev. Eugene J., '94 (NEW) Curia: Offices and Directors Our Lady of the Visitation, Paramus, NJ
Field, Rev. Michael J., '82 (CAM) Catholic Community of the Holy Spirit, Mullica Hill, N.J., Mullica Hill, NJ
Fields, Rev. Robert H., '82 (JC) St. Michael the Archangel, Kahoka, MO; The Shrine of St. Patrick, St. Patrick, MO
Fields, Rev. Stephen M., *S.J.* '86 (WDC) [COL] Georgetown University, Washington, DC; [MON] The Jesuit Community at Georgetown University, Washington, DC
Fier, Rev. Brian, '89 (STP) Church of St. Patrick, Inver Grove Heights, MN; [CEM] St. Patrick Cemetery, Inver Grove Heights, MN
Fifagrowicz, Rev. Joseph G., '62 (BUF) Retired. [MON] Bishop Head Residence, Lackawanna, NY
Figel, Rev. Terence J, *OMI* '64 (BEL) Retired. [MON] Shrine of Our Lady of the Snows, Belleville, IL; [NUR] Apartment Community of Our Lady of the Snows (Benedictine Living Community | At The Shrine), Belleville, IL
Figliola, Rev. Nicholas J., '64 (RVC) Retired.
Figliozzi, Rev. Msgr. Richard M., '79 (RVC) Curia: Offices and Directors St. Vincent de Paul, Elmont, NY
Figueredo, Rev. Sergio, *S.J.* '60 (MIA) Gesu, Miami, FL
Figueroa, Rev. Honecimo, '99 (BWN) On Leave.
Figueroa, Rev. John, '19 (NY) St. Augustine, Ossining, NY
Figueroa, Rev. Jose R., (CGS) Curia: Offices and Directors San Jose, Gurabo, PR
Figueroa, Rev. Jose Ramón, (CGS) Curia: Leadership
Figueroa, Rev. Juan Antonio, (FAJ) Curia: Offices and Directors Nuestra Senora del Carmen, Punta Santiago, PR
Figueroa, Rev. Ruben, '70 (TYL) Retired.
Figueroa, Rev. Tomas Galarza, '86 (MGZ) St. Charles Borromeo, Aguadilla, PR
Figueroa Farias, Rev. Miguel Angel, (P) St. Anne, Gresham, OR
Figueroa Moran, Rev. Juan Francisco, *OFM* (ELP) St. Francis of Assisi, El Paso, TX; [SEM] St. Anthony's School of Theology, El Paso, TX
Figueroa-Esquer, Rev. Francisco, '01 (OAK) Retired. Curia: Leadership; Offices and Directors St. Joseph, Pinole, CA
Figura, Rev. Msgr. Juanito, '81 (ORL) Curia: Advisory Boards, Commissions, Committees, and Councils Saints Peter and Paul, Winter Park, FL
Figurelli, Rev. Nicholas G., '82 (NEW) [COL] Seton Hall University, South Orange, NJ
Fikiri Kamunto, Rev. Deogratias, *SJ* '19 (OAK) (>MIL) [MON] Jesuit Community at Marquette University (Marquette Jesuit Associates, Inc.), Milwaukee, WI
Filacchione, Rev. Msgr. Marc J., '80 (NY) Chap, New York Fire Department Curia: Offices and Directors St. Michael, New York, NY; [ASN] Missionary Childhood Association, New York, NY; [MIS] Pontifical Mission Society Propagation of the Faith, New York, NY
Filardi, Rev. Msgr. Edward J., '94 (WDC) St. Paul, Damascus, MD
Filary, Rev. Richard M., '82 (SAG) Curia: Offices and Directors Our Lady of Czestochowa Parish of Bay City, Bay City, MI; [CON] Convent, Bay City, MI
Filima, Rev. Richard, *SPS* '08 (NY) [MIS] St. Patrick's International Inc., New York, NY
Filipkowski, Rev. Peter, '86 (PAT) Retired.
Filippelli, Rev. John, *S.S.J.* '57 (BAL) Retired.
Filippini, Rev. Renato, *S.X.* '97 (PAT) [MON] Xaverian Missionary Fathers, Wayne, NJ
Filippucci, Rev. Andrea, (STV) Church of St. Joseph, Frederiksted, VI
Fillion, Rev. Stephen, '79 (SAG) Retired. All Saints Parish of Bay City, Bay City, MI
Filmer, Rev. Eric R., '04 (SAV) St. Patrick, Kathleen, GA
Fils Aime, Rev. Franckel, (VEN) Curia: Leadership
Fils-Aime, Rev. Franckel, (VEN) St. Peter the Apostle Parish in Naples, Inc., Naples, FL
Filut, Rev. David C., '68 (MIL) Retired.
Fimian, Rev. Kevin, (MO) Curia: Offices and Directors
Fimian, Rev. Kevin J., '06 (ARL) On Duty Outside Diocese. Virginia Beach
Finamore, Rev. Robert A., '70 (WDC) Retired.
Finbarr, Rev. Emmanual T, (GLD) Holy Family of Klacking Creek, West Branch, MI; Saint Joseph of West Branch, West Branch, MI
Finch, Rev. Henry, '19 (AUS) [CAM] St. Peter Catholic Student Center at Baylor University, Waco, TX
Finch, Rev. Raymond J., *M.M.* '76 (NY) [MON] Maryknoll Fathers and Brothers (Catholic Foreign Mission Society of America, Inc.), Ossining, NY
Fincher, Rev. Jon, '20 (TLS) On Special Assignment. North American College, Rome Curia: Offices and Directors
Fincher, Rev. Jon Paul, '20 (TLS) Christ the King, Tulsa, OK
Finder, Rev. James, '91 (JC) Retired.
Finegan, Rev. Lawrence J., '70 (SFR) Retired.
Finelli, Rev. Jay A., '92 (PRO) Church of the Holy Ghost, North Tiverton, Tiverton, RI
Finelli, Rev. Victor, '89 (LEX) Curia: Leadership
Finelli, Rev. Msgr. Victor F., '89 (ALN) Curia: Leadership St. Joseph the Worker, Orefield, PA
Fineo, Rev. Richard, '02 (FAR) St. Benedict, Belcourt, ND; St. Benedict's Church of Belcourt, Belcourt, ND; St. John's Church of St. John, St. John, ND
Finerty, Rev. D. Bryan, '59 (PRO) Retired.
Fink, Rev. Daniel G., *O.F.M.Conv.* '84 (PMB) (>BUF) [MON] St. Maximilian Kolbe Friary, Hamburg, NY
Fink, Rev. Frederick T., '61 (NU) Retired.
Fink, Rev. John L., '69 (IND) Retired.
Fink, Rev. Joseph, '83 (STP) Retired.
Fink, Rev. Peter, *SJ* '69 (ATL) Retired.
Finlan, Rev. Robert T., '94 (ALN) Curia: Leadership; Organizations (affiliated, inter-Diocesan, miscellaneous/ other) St. John XXIII, Tamaqua, PA; St. Richard, Barnesville, PA
Finley, Rev. James F., '63 (BRK) Retired.
Finley, Rev. Thomas, '75 (LAF) Retired. St. Jules,

Lafayette, LA
Finley, Rev. William, '81 (ORL) Retired.
Finn, Rev. Daniel, (WDC) [MIS] Irish Apostolate USA, Inc., Upper Marlboro, MD
Finn, Rev. Daniel J., '72 (BO) Retired.
Finn, Rev. David, '03 (RCK) Boylan Central Catholic High School, Rockford, IL
Finn, Rev. John A., *O.S.F.S.* '62 (WIL) Retired.
Finn, Rev. Joseph P., '98 (LIN) St. Mary, Lincoln, NE
Finn, Rev. Michael E., '77 (SCR) Retired.
Finn, Rev. Patrick, '18 (PRT) Prince of Peace Parish, Lewiston, ME; [CAM] Bates College, Lewiston, ME
Finn, Rev. Seamus P., *O.M.I.* '76 (WDC) [MON] Missionary Oblates of Mary Immaculate, Washington, DC; [MON] Oblate Community, Washington, DC
Finn, Rev. Seamus P., *O.M.I.* '71 (CHI) [EFT] Oblates for International Pastoral (Oblate International Pastoral Investment Trust), Chicago, IL
Finnegan, Rev. Gerald F., *S.J.* '67 (BO) St. Ignatius Loyola, Chestnut Hill, MA; [MON] The Jesuit Community at Boston College, Chestnut Hill, MA
Finnegan, Rev. Kevin, '96 (STP) Our Lady of Grace, Edina, MN; St. John Paul II Catholic Preparatory School, Minneapolis, MN
Finnegan, Rev. Robert K., *O.Praem.* '52 (GB) [MON] St. Norbert Abbey, De Pere, WI
Finnegan, Rev. William J., '57 (CHI) Retired. Our Lady of the Woods, Orland Park, IL
Finnell, Rev. John H., '78 (WH) Retired.
Finnell, Rev. Terrell M., '92 (KC) Good Shepherd Catholic Church, Smithville, MO
Finnerty, Rev. Daniel, '15 (Y) Assumption B.V.M., Geneva, OH
Finnerty, Rev. James J., '55 (NEW) Retired.
Finnerty, Rev. Vincent Henry, *CM* (CHR) Curia: Offices and Directors St. William, Ward, SC
Finnestad, Rev. Jerald L.C., '80 (FAR) Retired.
Finney, Rev. Donald T., '94 (PMB) St. Peter, Jupiter, FL
Finnigan, Rev. Francis, *C.P.* '68 (NY) [MON] The Congregation of the Passion - St. Paul of the Cross Province, Jamaica, NY
Finnigan, Rev. Francis, *C.P.* '68 (PMB) [MON] Our Lady of Florida Spiritual Center, North Palm Beach, FL
Finno, Rev. James, '72 (CHI) Retired.
Fino, Rev. Joseph Michael, *C.F.R.* '21 (NY) [MON] St. Leopold's Friary, Yonkers, NY
Fioramonti, Rev. Jonathan R., (ARL) St. Leo the Great, Fairfax, VA
Fiore, Rev. Arthur B., '75 (WIL) Retired.
Fiore, Rev. Benjamin, *S.J.* '74 (BUF) St. Michael, Buffalo, NY
Fiore, Rev. Joseph A., '70 (BUF) Immaculate Heart of Mary, Darien Center, NY
Fiorelli, Rev. Lewis S., *O.S.F.S.* '70 (WIL) (>ARL) Our Lady of Good Counsel, Vienna, VA
Fiorenza, Rev. Antonio, *R.C.J.* '78 (LA) St. Elizabeth, Van Nuys, CA; [MON] Congregation of Rogationists, Inc., Van Nuys, CA
Fiorillo, Rev. Patrick J., '16 (BO) St. Paul, Cambridge, MA; [CAM] Harvard Catholic Center, Cambridge, MA
Fiorino, Rev. Dominic J., '61 (NEW) Retired. [MON] The Rev. Msgr. James F. Kelley Residence for Retired Priests, Caldwell, NJ
Firestone, Rev. Thomas, '78 (LAN) Christ the King Parish Flint, Flint, MI; St. John Vianney Parish Flint, Flint, MI; [MIS] Alma Redemptoris Mater, Fenton, MI
Firko, Very Rev. Frank A., '77 (PBR) Curia: Leadership Holy Ghost, McKees Rocks, PA; Holy Ghost, Pittsburgh, PA
Firmin, Very Rev. Daniel F., '04 (SAV) Curia: Leadership; Offices and Directors St. James, Savannah, GA
Firpo, Rev. John A., '77 (ROC) St. Charles Borromeo, Rochester, NY
Fischer, Rev. Adrian, *O.F.M.* '75 (SHP) Little Flower of Jesus, Monroe, LA
Fischer, Rev. Andrew, (PIT) Guardian Angels, Natrona Heights, PA
Fischer, Rev. Barry, *C.PP.S.* (IND) [COL] Marian University (Sisters of the Third Order Regular of St. Francis), Indianapolis, IN
Fischer, Rev. Barry J., *C.PP.S.* '73 (CIN) [MON] Society of the Precious Blood, United States Province, Inc., Dayton, OH
Fischer, Rev. Benedict, *O.S.B.* '07 (BIS) [MON] Assumption Abbey, Richardton, ND
Fischer, Rev. Brian J., '79 (CHI) Retired.
Fischer, Rev. Brian K., '21 (STP) On Special Assignment. Holy Trinity Hermitage St Paul, MN
Fischer, Very Rev. Brian R., '03 (STL) St. Patrick Catholic Church, Wentzville, MO
Fischer, Rev. Charles, '90 (FAR) St. Mary's Cathedral of Fargo, Fargo, ND
Fischer, Rev. Charles H., '71 (KAL) Retired.
Fischer, Rev. Msgr. Don L., '67 (DAL) Retired.
Fischer, Rev. G. William, *O.S.F.S.* '69 (E) [NUR] Saint Mary's at Asbury Ridge, Erie, PA
Fischer, Rev. John, '86 (SFS) Holy Name of Jesus Parish of Codington County, Watertown, SD
Fischer, Rev. John M., '63 (E) Retired.
Fischer, Rev. John P., '76 (CIN) Retired.
Fischer, Rev. Jonathan, *O.S.B.* '61 (SCL) [MON] St. John's Abbey, of the Order of St. Benedict, Collegeville, MN
Fischer, Rev. Kenneth J., '71 (CHI) Retired. Holy Cross, Deerfield, IL
Fischer, Rev. Mark, *FSSP* '95 (LEX) Curia: Offices and Directors
Fischer, Rev. Norman, '00 (LEX) Curia: Leadership St. Peter Claver, Lexington, KY
Fischer, Rev. Richard Owen, '76 (BAK) Curia: Leadership; Offices and Directors St. Kateri Tekakwitha, Warm Springs, OR
Fischer, Rev. Ryan M., '15 (HBG) Curia: Offices and Directors
Fischler, Rev. James, *C.I.C.M.* '76 (SAT) St. Louis, Castroville, TX
Fischler, Rev. James P., *C.I.C.M.* '76 (SAT) Curia: Administration
Fisette, Rev. Carl B., '06 (PRO) Curia: Clergy and Religious Services The Prout School, Wakefield, RI; [CAM] University of Rhode Island Catholic Center, Kingston, RI
Fish, Rev. Alfred H., '77 (OG) St. Ann's Church, St. Regis Falls, NY, St. Regis Falls, NY; The Church of the Holy Cross of Hopkinton, NY, Hopkinton, NY
Fish, Rev. Justin, '05 (DUL) Resurrection, Eveleth, MN; St. Joseph, Gilbert, MN
Fish, Rev. Matthew J., '15 (WDC) Curia: Consultative Bodies St. Mary, Charlotte Hall, MD
Fishel, Rev. Gregory, *S.D.B.* '89 (CHI) St. John Bosco, Chicago, IL
Fisher, Rev. A. J., '56 (BAK) Retired.
Fisher, Rev. Albert, '81 (BIR) Retired.
Fisher, Very Rev. Andrew J., '98 (ARL) St. Ambrose, Annandale, VA
Fisher, Rev. Clarence L., '61 (HON) Retired.
Fisher, Rev. David, '84 (OLL) On Special Assignment. Disability Leave- Philadelphia, PA
Fisher, Rev. David A., '84 (PH) St. Cyprian, Philadelphia, PA
Fisher, Rev. David E., '86 (LAN) Retired.
Fisher, Rev. Edward K., '92 (MEM) Retired.
Fisher, Rev. Harold, *O.M.I.* '00 (BEL) Holy Rosary, Fairmont City, IL; St. Stephen, Caseyville, IL; [MON] Shrine of Our Lady of the Snows, Belleville, IL
Fisher, Rev. John J., *OSFS* '88 (PH) Our Mother of Consolation, Philadelphia, PA
Fisher, Rev. Leo, *C.F.R.* '05 (SFE) [MON] Community of the Franciscans of the Renewal San Juan Diego Friary, Albuquerque, NM
Fisher, Rev. Martin J., '86 (ALB) Roman Catholic Community of All Saints on the Hudson, Mechanicville, NY; Sacred Heart, Stamford, NY
Fisher, Rev. Raymond A., '71 (TOL) Retired.
Fisher, Rev. Robert, '65 (CHI) Retired. [MON] Divine Word Residence, Techny, IL
Fisher, Rev. Robert D., '80 (DEN) Retired.
Fisher, Rev. Terry, '85 (FTW) Cathedral of Saint Matthew, South Bend, IN
Fisher, Rev. William, '93 (KCK) Retired.
Fishwick, Rev. Joseph, '75 (MIA) Retired.
Fiske, Rev. Jack Jason, *C.Ss.R.* '80 (BAL) [SPF] St. John Neuman Residence, Timonium, MD
Fister, Rev. Daniel, '09 (LEX) Annunciation of the Blessed Virgin Mary, Paris, KY; Shrine of Our Lady of Guadalupe, Carlisle, KY; [MIS] Our Lady of Guadalupe Shrine, Carlisle, KY
Fister, Rev. Stephen J., '82 (P) Retired. [RTR] St. Rita's Retreat Center, Central Point, OR
Fitch, Rev. John, '02 (VEN) St. Charles Borromeo Parish in Port Charlotte, Inc., Port Charlotte, FL; [NUR] St. Charles Housing I, Inc. (Villa San Carlos), Port Charlotte, FL; [NUR] St. Charles Housing II, Inc. (Villa San Carlos II), Port Charlotte, FL
Fitterer, Rev. L. Paul, *S.J.* '63 (SJ) [MON] Sacred Heart Jesuit Center, Los Gatos, CA
Fittin, Very Rev. Edward Seton, *O.S.B.* '93 (PAT) [MON] St. Mary's Abbey, Morristown, NJ
Fitz, Rev. James, *S.M.* '74 (CIN) [COL] The University of Dayton, Dayton, OH
Fitz, Rev. James F., *S.M.* '74 (CIN) [MON] Marianist Community, Dayton, OH
Fitzgerald, Rev. Allan, *O.S.A.* '67 (PH) [COL] Villanova University, Villanova, PA; [MON] Bellesini Friary, Ardmore, PA
Fitzgerald, Rev. Brendan, '20 (BAL) Basilica of the National Shrine of the Assumption of the Blessed Virgin Mary, Baltimore, MD
Fitzgerald, Very Rev. Brendan A., '00 (NY) St. Barnabas, Bronx, NY
Fitzgerald, Rev. David, *s.P.* '78 (STL) [RTR] Vianney Renewal Center, Dittmer, MO
Fitzgerald, Rev. David, *S.A.* '65 (NY) Retired. [MIS] Atonement Friars, New York, NY; [MON] Franciscan Friars of the Atonement, Garrison, NY; [MON] Franciscan Friars of the Atonement, Minister General Office, Garrison, NY
Fitzgerald, Rev. Edmund H., '57 (PRO) Retired.
Fitzgerald, Rev. Msgr. Edmund J., '68 (FR) Retired.
Fitzgerald, Very Rev. Edward W., '95 (CHR) Curia: Advisory Boards, Commissions, Committees, and Councils; Deaneries; Tribunal St. Michael, Murrells Inlet, SC
Fitzgerald, Rev. Msgr. J. Terrence, '62 (SLC) Retired. Curia: Leadership; Offices and Directors
Fitzgerald, Rev. John E., '63 (STO) Retired. All Saints Church (Pastor of), Twain Harte, CA
Fitzgerald, Rev. Msgr. John Gerard, '62 (LA) Retired.
Fitzgerald, Rev. John J., '58 (RVC) Retired. St. James, Setauket, NY
FitzGerald, Rev. Msgr. John L., '67 (BAL) Retired. [MIS] Stella Maris Seafarers' Center, Baltimore, MD
Fitzgerald, Rev. John P., '74 (PIT) Retired.
Fitzgerald, Rev. Joseph H., '07 (RVC) Curia: Leadership St. William the Abbot, Seaford, NY
FitzGerald, Rev. Kevin, *S.J.* '84 (OM) [MON] Jesuit Community at Creighton University, Omaha, NE
FitzGerald, Rev. Kevin T., *S.J.* '88 (WDC) [COL] Georgetown University, Washington, DC
Fitzgerald, Rev. Paul J., *S.J.* '92 (SFR) [COL] University of San Francisco, San Francisco, CA; [MON] Loyola House Jesuit Community, San Francisco, CA
Fitzgerald, Rev. R. Martin, '89 (R) On Duty Outside Diocese. Diocese of Orlando
Fitzgerald, Rev. Richard W., '87 (BO) Curia: Clergy and Religious Services; Leadership St. Columbkille, Brighton, MA; [SEM] Saint John's Seminary, Brighton, MA
Fitzgerald, Rev. Thomas J., '75 (PAT) St. Clare, Clifton, NJ
Fitzgerald, Rev. Thomas P., '66 (STP) Retired.
Fitzgerald, Rev. Timothy, *C.P.* '56 (PIT) Retired.
Fitzgerald, Rev. Timothy, (DM) Retired.
Fitzgerald, Rev. Timothy, *C.P.* '56 (NY) Retired.
Fitzgerald, Rev. William, *O.Praem.* '79 (ORG) [MON] Norbertine Fathers of Orange, Inc., Silverado, CA
Fitzgerald, Rev. William, (PHX) Our Lady of Perpetual Help Roman Catholic Parish, Scottsdale, AZ
Fitzgerald, Rev. William J., '58 (OM) Retired.
Fitzgerald, Rev. William M., *O.Praem.* '79 (ORG) [MON] Norbertine Fathers of Orange, Inc., Silverado, CA
Fitzgibbons, Rev. Peter L., '84 (CHL) Chap, US Army Our Lady of the Annunciation, Albemarle, NC
Fitzmaurice, Msgr. V. Paul, (GBG) [NUR] St. Anne Home, Greensburg, PA
Fitzpatrick, Rev. Charles P., '16 (RCK) St. Thomas the Apostle, Crystal Lake, IL
Fitzpatrick, Rev. Daniel J., *S.J.* '66 (NY) [ASN] Brooklyn Prep Alumni Association, New York, NY; [MON] Murray-Weigel Hall (A Jesuit Community at Murray-Weigel Hall and Kohlmann Hall), Bronx, NY
Fitzpatrick, Rev. Edward, *O.S.F.S.* (WIL) Salesianum School, Wilmington, DE
Fitzpatrick, Rev. Edward J., '70 (DAV) Retired.
Fitzpatrick, Rev. Edward T., *O.S.F.S.* '74 (PH) [MON] Villa de Sales Oblate Residence, Wyndmoor, PA
Fitzpatrick, Rev. James M., (GLD) Retired.
Fitzpatrick, Rev. James M., '71 (SAG) Retired. On Duty Outside Diocese. Alpena
Fitzpatrick, Rev. James M., '84 (FR) Curia: Leadership St. Ann, Raynham, MA
Fitzpatrick, Rev. John, (MO) Curia: Offices and Directors
Fitzpatrick, Rev. Joseph, (BO) [MON] Campion Health & Wellness, Inc., Weston, MA
Fitzpatrick, Rev. Michael, *S.J.* '77 (SPK) [MIS] Kateri Northwest Ministry Institute, Spokane, WA
Fitzpatrick, Rev. Michael, (ORG) St. John Neumann, Irvine, CA
Fitzpatrick, Rev. Michael J., '83 (PH) On Special Assignment. Dean, Deanery 3, St Peter Rectory, West Brandywine St. Peter, West Brandywine, PA
Fitzpatrick, Rev. Michael J., '03 (FR) St. Francis Xavier's, Hyannis, MA
Fitzpatrick, Rev. Michael J., *S.J.* '77 (BAK) St. Andrew Catholic Mission of Pendleton, Inc., Pendleton, OR
Fitzpatrick, Rev. Michael R., '71 (OM) Retired.

Fitzpatrick, Rev. Paul, *SM* (CIN) Retired. [COL] The University of Dayton, Dayton, OH; [MON] Marianist Community, Dayton, OH
Fitzpatrick, Rev. Paul K., '98 (LA) Curia: Advisory Boards, Commissions, Committees, and Councils St. Martin of Tours, Los Angeles, CA
Fitzpatrick, Rev. Robert J., '73 (STP) Retired.
Fitzpatrick, Rev. Thomas, '04 (SFS) Saint Katharine Drexel Parish of Minnehaha County, Sioux Falls, SD
Fitzpatrick, Rev. Thomas J., *S.J.* '68 (BGP) [MON] The Fairfield Jesuit Community-Fairfield University, Fairfield, CT
Fitzpatrick, Rev. Thomas P., '61 (SY) Retired.
Fitzpatrick, Rev. Vincent, '92 (FAR) Retired.
Fitz-Patrick, Rev. David M., '79 (WDC) Retired.
Fitzsimmons, Rev. Donald J., *C.S.V.* '60 (CHI) [MON] Viatorian Province Center-Clerics of St. Viator, Arlington Heights, IL
Fitzsimmons, Rev. George E., '14 (BO) On Duty Outside Diocese.
Fitzsimmons, Rev. Gerald J., *S.M.M.* '75 (RVC) [MON] Montfort Missionaries, Bay Shore, NY
Fitzsimmons, Rev. J. Thomas, '62 (CIN) Retired. St. Stephen, Cincinnati, OH
Fitzsimmons, Rev. Msgr. Thomas B., '62 (CAM) Retired.
Fitzsimons, Rev. Patrick, '01 (LEX) On Duty Outside Diocese. VA Administration Services Nashville, TN Curia: (>MO) Offices and Directors
Fiuk, Rev. Stanislaw, '90 (SAT) St. James, Seguin, TX
Fix, Rev. Donald P., '80 (PIT) Retired.
Fixsen, Rev. Patrick, '07 (PEO) On Leave.
Flach, Rev. James A., '86 (SFD) Retired. Our Lady of Lourdes, Oblong, IL; St. Elizabeth, Robinson, IL
Flach, Rev. Msgr. Thomas D., '71 (BEL) Retired. Curia: Leadership
Flack, Rev. Robert Stanley, *SJ* '74 (DET) [RTR] Manresa Jesuit Retreat House, Bloomfield Hills, MI
Fladung, Rev. Charles J., '92 (DAV) St. Mary Church of Solon, Iowa, Solon, IA
Flagg, Rev. Wayne, '88 (VIC) Curia: Leadership
Flagg, Rev. Wayne N., '88 (VIC) Curia: Leadership St. Michael, Weimar, TX
Flagstadt, Rev. Christian, '22 (MAR) Sacred Heart, Champion, MI; St. Augustine, Republic, MI; St. John the Evangelist, Ishpeming, MI; St. Joseph, Ishpeming, MI
Flaherty, Rev. Charles, *S.S.C.* '50 (OM) Retired.
Flaherty, Rev. Frederick R., *M.S.* '57 (HRT) [MIS] Missionaries of LaSalette, Hartford, CT
Flaherty, Rev. Msgr. James, '80 (PT) Retired.
Flaherty, Rev. John R., '90 (DUB) All Saints Church, Cedar Rapids, Iowa, Cedar Rapids, IA; Regis Middle School, Cedar Rapids, Iowa, Cedar Rapids, IA
Flaherty, Rev. Malachy, *O.F.M.Cap.* (RVC) Chap, Long Island Developmental Ctr
Flaherty, Rev. Michael T., '73 (CIN) Retired.
Flaherty, Rev. Richard C., *O.F.M.* '82 (BO) Retired. [MIS] St. Anthony Shrine, Boston, MA
Flaherty, Rev. William J., '52 (CHI) Retired. SS. Faith, Hope and Charity, Winnetka, IL
Flajole, Rev. John Paul, *O.F.M.* '64 (CIN) Retired. [MON] St. Clement Friary, Cincinnati, OH
Flammia, Rev. Paul G., '96 (BO) Visitation Parish, Manchester by the Sea, MA
Flanagan, Rev. Austin E., (SCR) On Administrative Leave.
Flanagan, Rev. Brian, '98 (PMB) Retired. St. Patrick, Palm Beach Gardens, FL
Flanagan, Rev. Damian, '91 (MIA) St. Mary Magdalen, Sunny Isles Beach, FL
Flanagan, Rev. David J., '87 (MAD) St. Patrick, Benton, WI; St. Rose of Lima, Cuba City, WI
Flanagan, Rev. John B., '97 (PH) St. Madeline, Ridley Park, PA
Flanagan, Rev. Michael D., '10 (LEX) Curia: Leadership St. Michael Catholic Church, Paintsville, KY
Flanagan, Rev. Msgr. Michael T., '65 (JC) Retired. Our Lady of Lourdes, Columbia, MO
Flanagan, Rev. Msgr. P. Kevin, '59 (PAT) Retired. St. Philip the Apostle, Clifton, NJ
Flanagan, Rev. Patrick S., *C.M.* '92 (BRK) [MON] Reverend John B. Murray, C.M. House, Jamaica, NY
Flanagan, Rev. Thomas J., '74 (SC) Retired. [MIS] Opus Spiritus Sancti, Spirit Lake, IA
Flanigan, Rev. Msgr. Thomas P., '69 (PH) Retired. St. Joseph, Aston, PA
Flannagan, Rev. Bruce G., '78 (BO) St. Richard of Chichester, Danvers, MA
Flannery, Rev. Michael, '97 (ALB) Sacred Heart of Jesus, Albany, NY
Flannery, Rev. Msgr. Michael, (BLX) Curia: Tribunal
Flannery, Rev. Msgr. Michael, '64 (JKS) Retired. Curia: Canonical Services; Leadership
Flannery, Rev. Robert B., '73 (BEL) Curia: Offices and Directors St. Francis Xavier, Carbondale, IL
Flatley, Rev. Brian M., '66 (BO) Retired. Holy Name, Boston, MA
Flatley, Rev. Matthew J., '12 (JC) Immaculate Conception, Jefferson City, MO
Flattery, Rev. James, '20 (DAV) Divine Mercy Parish of Burlington-West Burlington, West Burlington, IA; St. Mary Church of Dodgeville, Iowa, Sperry, IA
Flavin, Rev. James A., '87 (BO) On Leave.
Flax, Rev. Myron, *O.F.M.Cap.* '64 (SAL) Retired.
Fleck, Very Rev. David G., '75 (EVN) On Leave. Curia: Leadership
Fleck, Rev. John W., '59 (TOL) Retired.
Fleck, Rev. Kenneth J., '76 (CHI) Retired.
Fleck, Rev. Luke, '18 (LIN) Curia: Leadership St. Michael, Lincoln, NE
Fleckenstein, Rev. John D., '02 (KAL) Curia: Consultative Bodies St. Joseph, St. Joseph, MI; St. Joseph, Watervliet, MI
Flecky, Rev. Michael, *S.J.* '77 (OM) [MON] Jesuit Community at Creighton University, Omaha, NE
Fleischhacker, Rev. John J., *O.S.C.* '61 (SCL) [MON] Crosier Priory, Onamia, MN
Fleischman, Rev. Richard J., '68 (MIL) Retired.
Fleming, Rev. Austin H., '73 (BO) Good Shepherd Parish, Wayland, MA; St. Joseph, Belmont, MA
Fleming, Rev. David, '90 (DM) Curia: Leadership St. Pius X, Urbandale, IA
Fleming, Rev. George, '94 (ALB) Corpus Christi, Round Lake, NY; Roman Catholic Community of All Saints on the Hudson, Mechanicville, NY; [MIS] Worship Site, Stottville, NY
Fleming, Rev. James J, *SJ* '95 (BO) (>ATL) [MON] Atlanta Jesuit Community, Inc., Decatur, GA
Fleming, Rev. James J., *SJ* '75 (ATL) [RTR] Ignatius House Jesuit Retreat Center, Sandy Springs, GA
Fleming, Rev. John M., '61 (CAM) Retired.
Fleming, Rev. John W., '96 (MAN) Curia: Tribunal Parish of the Transfiguration, Manchester, NH
Fleming, Rev. Joseph, '13 (HEL) Chap, Montana State Prison; Warm Springs State Hosp Immaculate Conception Parish: Series 223, LLC, Deer Lodge, MT
Fleming, Rev. Joseph, (GF) [MIS] Retrouvaille of Montana, Great Falls, MT
Fleming, Very Rev. Joseph W., '74 (ALT) St. Catherine of Siena, Mount Union, PA
Fleming, Very Rev. Joseph W., '74 (ALT) Curia: Deaneries St. Mary, Orbisonia, PA
Fleming, Rev. Nicholas, '20 (BEL) Holy Childhood of Jesus, Mascoutah, IL; St. Liborius, St. Libory, IL
Fleming, Rev. Nicholas T., '15 (PRO) SS. John and James Parish, West Warwick, RI; St. Mary's Church, Crompton Rhode Island, West Warwick, RI
Fleming, Rev. Raymond H., '82 (ROC) Emmanuel Church of the Deaf of the Diocese of Rochester, Rochester, NY; Immaculate Conception/St. Bridget, Rochester, NY; St. Monica, Rochester, NY
Fleming, Rev. Rodger P., '07 (STL) St. James Catholic Church, Potosi, Potosi, MO
Fleming, Rev. Sean Paul, '12 (BUF) St. Joseph Cathedral, Buffalo, NY
Fleming, Rev. Sean Paul, (WDC) St. Anthony of Padua, Washington, DC
Fleming, Rev. Msgr. Terrance L., '73 (LA) Curia: Offices and Directors; Pastoral Services St. Brendan, Los Angeles, CA
Fleming, Rev. Thomas J., '85 (SAG) Saint Hubert Parish of Bad Axe, Bad Axe, MI
Flemming, Rev. James K., '86 (VEN) Retired.
Flens, Rev. Daniel, '89 (VEN) St. Andrew Parish in Cape Coral, Inc., Cape Coral, FL
Fletcher, Rev. John Michael, (MO) Curia: Offices and Directors
Fletcher, Rev. Luke Mary, *C.F.R.* '03 (NY) [MON] St. Leopold's Friary, Yonkers, NY
Fletcher, Rev. Peregrine, *O.Praem.* '20 (ORG) [MON] Norbertine Fathers of Orange, Inc., Silverado, CA; [SEM] St. Michael's Norbertine Postulancy, Novitiate and Juniorate, Silverado, CA
Fleurimond, Rev. Louis Jacques, *OFM Cap.* (NY) Immaculate Conception, Bronx, NY
Fleury, Rev. Joseph M., *S.M.* '84 (WDC) [MON] Marist Center (The Marist Finance Center of the Atlanta Province of the Society of Mary, Marist Fathers and Brothers), Washington, DC
Fleury, Rev. Joseph M., *S.M.* '84 (MO) Curia: Offices and Directors
Flick, Rev. Michael, (B) St. Joan of Arc, Post Falls, ID
Flickenger, Rev. Don D, '64 (FRS) Retired.
Flint, Rev. James, *O.S.B.* '83 (JOL) [MON] St. Procopius Abbey, Lisle, IL
Fliss, Rev. James W., '75 (BUF) St. Anthony's, Farnham, NY
Fliss, Rev. Paul J., '92 (MIL) Immaculate Conception Congregation, Sheboygan, WI; St. Peter Claver Congregation, Sheboygan, WI; Sts. Cyril and Methodius' Congregation, Sheboygan, WI; [MIS] The Sheboygan County Catholic Fund, Inc., Sheboygan, WI
Floch, Rev. W. Roy, '77 (SPK) Retired.
Floeder, Rev. John P., '07 (STP) Curia: Consultative Bodies
Floeder, Rev. Louis Sebastian, '19 (STP) Annunciation, Northfield, MN; St. Dominic, Northfield, MN
Floersh, Rev. Christopher, '17 (KNX) Curia: Offices and Directors St. John Neumann, Farragut, TN
Flonder, Rev. Hans, *O.F.M.Conv.* '12 (CHI) [MON] Marytown, Our Lady of Fatima Friary, Libertyville, IL
Flood, Rev. Charles J., *O.SS.T.* '90 (TR) On Duty Outside Diocese. Outside of the Diocese
Flood, Rev. Eric, *F.S.S.P.* '00 (KCK) On Special Assignment. Chaplain, Community of St. John-Mary Vianney, Maple Hill St. John Vianney School, Maple Hill, KS
Flood, Rev. Francis, *O.S.B.* '93 (NEW) [MON] Benedictine Abbey of Newark, Newark, NJ
Flood, Rev. Msgr. J. Michael, '68 (PH) Retired. On Special Assignment. Admin, Regina Coeli Residence for Priests, Warminster [SPF] Regina Coeli Residence for Priests, Warminster, PA
Flood, Rev. Paul A., '90 (ATL) St. Benedict Catholic Church, Johns Creek, Inc., Johns Creek, GA
Flood, Rev. Msgr. Peter J., '69 (TR) Retired.
Flood, Rev. Reed, '22 (DM) Dowling Catholic High School (Dowling College Inc.), West Des Moines, IA
Flor, Rev. Carlos F., (BO) Curia: Consultative Bodies
Flor, Rev. Carlos F., '97 (NEW) (>BO) Our Lady of Lourdes, Boston, MA; (>BO) St. Mary of the Angels, Boston, MA; (>BO) St. Thomas Aquinas, Boston, MA
Flora, Rev. Giandomenico M., '06 (NEW) On Duty Outside Diocese. St Raphael Parish, Bridgeport, CT [MIS] Our Lady of Mt. Carmel Oratory, Montclair, NJ
Florczyk, Rev. Franciszek, '81 (CHI) SS. Constance and Robert Bellarmine Parish, Chicago, IL
Florczyk, Rev. Walter, '62 (SY) Retired.
Florea, Rev. Eugene, '07 (PHX) [RTR] Merciful Heart Hermitage: A House of Prayer for Priests, Black Canyon City, AZ
Florek, Rev. Richard T., *O.F.M.Conv.* '72 (PMB) St. Mark, Boynton Beach, FL
Florek, Rev. Thomas W., *S.J.* '86 (CHI) [MON] Canisius House Jesuit Community, Evanston, IL
Flores, Rev. Alejandro F., '09 (BWN) St. Anthony, Harlingen, TX
Flores, Rev. Amadito, (CAM) Christ the Good Shepherd Parish, Vineland, N.J., Vineland, NJ
Flores, Rev. Amadito, (PAT) On Duty Outside Diocese. Lindenwold, NJ
Flores, Rev. Arthur, *O.M.I.* '92 (WDC) [MON] Missionary Oblates of Mary Immaculate, Washington, DC; [MON] Oblate Community, Washington, DC
Flores, Rev. Arthur, *O.M.I.* '92 (SAT) [MON] Missionary Oblates of Mary Immaculate of Texas, Southern Province (San Antonio USP Support Office), San Antonio, TX; [MON] Oblate Benson Residence, San Antonio, TX
Flores, Very Rev. Benjamin, '93 (ELP) Curia: Advisory Boards, Commissions, Committees, and Councils; Leadership; Offices and Directors St. Frances Xavier Cabrini Parish, El Paso, TX
Flores, Rev. Carlos Alberto, *O.S.A.* '05 (SD) Pastor of Saint Patrick Catholic Parish, San Diego, a corporation sole, San Diego, CA; [MIS] Saint Patrick Catholic Parish San Diego in San Diego, CA Real Property Support Corporation, San Diego, CA; [MON] Augustinian Community, San Diego, CA
Flores, Rev. Cristobal Martin, *M.Id* (NY) Santa Maria, Bronx, NY
Flores, Rev. Danilo Ramiro, (AGN) Curia: Tribunal
Flores, Rev. Darwin A., '07 (RCK) St. Therese of Jesus, Aurora, IL
Flores, Rev. Eduardo, '19 (JOL) St. Andrew the Apostle, Romeoville, IL
Flores, Friar Emilio, *O.F.M.* '96 (ELP) [SEM] St. Anthony's School of Theology, El Paso, TX
Flores, Rev. Eric, '14 (SAC) Curia: Leadership; Offices and Directors Pastor of Divine Mercy Parish, Sacramento, a corporation sole, Sacramento, CA
Flores, Rev. Francisco, *RCJ* '07 (FRS) St. Mary, Sanger, CA
Flores, Rev. Francisco Q., (B) St. John Paul II Parish, Idaho Falls, ID; [CAM] North Idaho College, Coeur d'Alene, ID
Flores, Rev. Gabriel, '85 (SFR) Retired. St. Francis of Assisi, East Palo Alto, CA
Flores, Rev. Harry, *SMM* (RVC) [MON] Montfort

Missionaries, Bay Shore, NY
Flores, Rev. Javier E., *R.C.J.* (LA) [MON] Congregation of Rogationists, Inc., Van Nuys, CA
Flores, Rev. Jesus, '85 (ROC) Curia: Pastoral Services
Flores, Rev. Joel R., '16 (BWN) San Pedro Quasi Parish, Brownsville, TX; [CAM] Ministry with Young People, San Juan, TX
Flores, Rev. Jose Siesquen, '88 (SPR) All Souls, Springfield, MA; Blessed Sacrament, Springfield, MA
Flores, Rev. Juan, '98 (YAK) Christ the King, Richland, WA
Flores, Rev. Juan Manuel, (YAK) St. Frances Xavier Cabrini, Benton City, WA
Flores, Rev. Juan Manuel, '03 (FRS) Sacred Heart, Bakersfield, CA
Flores, Rev. Lee A., '85 (GAL) Our Lady of Guadalupe, Rosenberg, TX
Flores, Rev. Luis, (MIA) SS. Peter and Paul, Miami, FL
Flores, Rev. Luis, *SDB* '86 (LAR) San Luis Rey, Laredo, TX
Flores, Rev. Manuel J., '18 (PH) St. Patrick, Norristown, PA
Flores, Rev. Micah, '22 (DEN) Most Precious Blood Catholic Parish in Denver, Denver, CO
Flores, Rev. Miguel, '94 (FRS) On Administrative Leave.
Flores, Rev. Miguel, (AUS) St. Louis, Waco, TX; St. Philip Catholic Church - China Spring, Texas, China Spring, TX
Flores, Rev. Miguel, '16 (CHI) St. Nicholas of Tolentine, Chicago, IL
Flores, Rev. Octavio Trejo, *SDS* '18 (SAC) Divine Savior, Orangevale, CA
Flores, Rev. Ramiro, (OAK) Most Holy Rosary, Antioch, CA
Flores, Rev. Ramiro, '95 (OAK) Curia: Offices and Directors
Flores, Rev. Raymond, *OSA* (JOL) St. Jude, New Lenox, IL
Flores, Rev. Richard, (MO) Curia: Offices and Directors
Flores, Rev. Roberto Cristobal, *S.V.D.* '96 (SB) Our Lady of Guadalupe, Ontario, CA
Flores Chirino, Rev. Javier, '08 (BRK) Our Lady of Solace, Brooklyn, NY
Flores Duarte, Rev. Ramon, *S.T.* (SB) Our Lady of Soledad, Coachella, CA
Flores Gonzalez, Rev. Hector I., '17 (ARE) Curia: Leadership St. Joseph, Camuy, PR; [MIS] Chapel Espiritu Santo, Camuy, PR; [MIS] Chapel Inmaculada Concepcion, Camuy, PR; [MIS] Chapel La Milagrosa, Camuy, PR; [MIS] Chapel Nuestra Senora de la Monserrate, Camuy, PR; [MIS] Chapel Nuestra Senora del Rosario, Camuy, PR; [MIS] Chapel Sagrado Corazon, Camuy, PR
Flores-Alva, Rev. Luis M., '06 (BAK) Curia: Offices and Directors Our Lady of Guadalupe, Boardman, OR
Flores-Cota, Rev. Antonio, (DEN) [MON] The Theatine Fathers, Denver, CO
Flores-Nina, Rev. Constancio Alipio, *C.Ss.R.* (BAL) Sacred Heart of Jesus-Sagrado Corazon de Jesus, Baltimore, MD
Flores-Perez, Rev. Miguel, (MO) Curia: Offices and Directors
Florez, Rev. Andrew, '93 (NY) Sacred Heart, Mount Vernon, NY
Florez, Rev. Carlos A., '11 (TR) St. Barnabas, Bayville, NJ
Florez, Rev. Diego, *A.I.C.* (GRY) Our Lady of Guadalupe, East Chicago, IN; St. Patrick Roman Catholic Church, East Chicago, IN
Florez, Rev. Jhon Jaime, (GAL) Our Lady of St. John, Houston, TX
Florez, Rev. Parmenio, (VIC) Our Lady of Sorrows, Victoria, TX
Florez Albarracin, Rev. Hernan, '05 (DEN) St. Theresa Catholic Parish in Frederick, Frederick, CO
Flórez Carmona, Rev. Jhonnatan, '15 (MRY) Our Lady of Mt. Carmel, Carmel Valley, CA
Florez-Ardila, Rev. Carlos A., '03 (MIL) St. Mark's Congregation, Kenosha, WI
Floridi, Rev. Nicholas A., '00 (PHX) Church of St. Joachim & St. Anne Roman Catholic Parish, Sun City, AZ
Florido, Rev. Robert, '79 (LA) Chap, Veterans Admin Long Beach Healthcare System
Florio, Rev. Philip A., *S.J.* '01 (NY) [CAM] Fordham University at Rosehill, Bronx, NY; [MON] St. Ignatius Loyola Residence, New York, NY
Flott, Rev. Phil, (OM) Retired. Holy Ghost, Omaha, NE
Flott, Rev. Phil L, '02 (GI) Retired.
Flowers, Rev. Thomas A., '77 (WIL) Retired. Curia: Miscellaneous / Other Offices
Flowers, Rev. Thomas J, *S.J.* '18 (SJ) (>STL) [MON] Bellarmine House of Studies, St. Louis, MO
Floyd, Rev. Ronnie, '06 (GR) Sacred Heart of Jesus, Grand Rapids, MI
Floyd, Rev. Ronnie P., '08 (FR) On Duty Outside Diocese. Grand Rapids MI
Fluet, Rev. Gregoire, (NY) [CAM] Mt. St. Mary College, Newburg, NY
Fluet, Rev. Gregoire, (NY) [COL] Mt. St. Mary College, Newburgh, NY
Fluet, Rev. Gregoire J., '82 (NOR) On Duty Outside Diocese. Curia: Leadership
Fluetsch, Rev. John P., '91 (FRS) St. Columba, Chowchilla, CA
Flum, Rev. Martin E., '01 (WDC) Sacred Heart, La Plata, MD; St. Michael's, Brandywine, MD
Flynn, Rev. Brian L., '03 (BO) Sacred Heart, Lynn, MA; Saint Mary of the Sacred Heart Parish, Lynn, MA; St. Mary, Lynn, MA
Flynn, Rev. Charles P., '69 (DUL) Retired.
Flynn, Rev. Dennis, *SVD* '61 (CHI) Retired. [MON] Divine Word Residence, Techny, IL
Flynn, Rev. Francis J., '69 (OG) Retired. Saint Augustine's Church, Peru, NY, Peru, NY
Flynn, Rev. James, '06 (FWT) Curia: Leadership St. Elizabeth Ann Seton, Keller, TX
Flynn, Rev. James B., '64 (WOR) St. Matthew, Southborough, MA
Flynn, Rev. James E., '55 (L) Retired.
Flynn, Rev. James F., '67 (CHI) Retired.
Flynn, Rev. James R., *O.S.A.* '72 (PH) [MON] St. Thomas Monastery, Villanova, PA
Flynn, Rev. Msgr. John, '52 (TYL) Retired. On Leave.
Flynn, Rev. John Joseph, *O.F.M.Cap.* (NY) [CAM] College of New Rochelle, New Rochelle, NY
Flynn, Rev. Joseph, *O.F.M.Cap.* '66 (NY) [MON] The Province of St. Mary of the Capuchin Order, White Plains, NY
Flynn, Rev. Lawrence W., *M.M.* '87 (NY) Retired.
Flynn, Rev. Martin, '12 (MAR) St. Barbara, Vulcan, MI; St. Mary, Norway, MI
Flynn, Rev. Michael, '91 (BGP) Retired. The Church of Our Lady of the Assumption, Fairfield, CT
Flynn, Rev. Michael, '94 (PT) Retired.
Flynn, Rev. Michael E., '77 (CHI) Retired.
Flynn, Rev. Msgr. Sean P., '75 (TR) St. Mark, Sea Girt, NJ
Flynn, Rev. Stephen A., '08 (CLV) St. Francis of Assisi, Gates Mills, OH
Flynn, Rev. Thomas, '61 (HEL) On Duty Outside Diocese.
Flynn, Rev. Msgr. Thomas M., '58 (CAM) Retired.
Flynn, Rev. William J., '64 (NOR) Retired.
Foelker, Rev. James, *OMI* (SAT) Retired. [NUR] Oblate Madonna Residence, San Antonio, TX
Foertsch, Rev. Robert, '22 (FAR) Sts. Anne & Joachim Church of Fargo, Fargo, ND
Fogal, Rev. Joseph B., '75 (WIN) Retired.
Fogarty, Rev. Gerald P., *S.J.* '70 (WDC) (>NY) [MON] Murray-Weigel Hall (A Jesuit Community at Murray-Weigel Hall and Kohlmann Hall), Bronx, NY
Fogarty, Rev. John, (PIT) [COL] Duquesne University of the Holy Spirit, Pittsburgh, PA
Fogarty, Rev. Msgr. Paul, '67 (ATL) Retired.
Fogle, Rev. Bruce, '83 (OWN) St. John the Evangelist, Paducah, KY
Fogle, Rev. Randall, '15 (POC) St. Michael and All Angels Catholic Church, Denison, TX
Fogliasso, Rev. John P., '11 (WCH) Chap, Sedgwick Cty Juvenile Detention Facility St. Jude, Wichita, KS
Fohlin, Rev. Paul, *O.C.D.* '72 (BO) [MON] Carmelite Monastery, Boston, MA
Fohn, Rev. Kurt M., '01 (CHL) Retired.
Folan, Rev. Peter, *S.J.* '13 (WDC) [MON] The Jesuit Community at Georgetown University, Washington, DC
Folbrecht, Rev. Robert, '75 (LA) Retired.
Folchetti, Rev. John T., '74 (TR) St. Leo the Great, Lincroft, NJ
Foley, Rev. Augustine E., *O.S.B.* '88 (NO) [MON] St. Joseph Abbey, St. Benedict, LA; [SEM] Saint Joseph Seminary College, Saint Benedict, LA
Foley, Rev. Brendan Daniel, '21 (SY) Curia: Leadership Holy Cross, DeWitt, NY; St. Anthony of Padua, Syracuse, NY
Foley, Rev. David M., '72 (MEM) Retired.
Foley, Rev. Edward, *O.F.M.Cap.* (CHI) [MON] St. Clare Friary, Chicago, IL; [SEM] Catholic Theological Union, Chicago, IL
Foley, Rev. Francis P., '84 (PH) Military Chap Curia: Advisory Boards, Commissions, Committees, and Councils St. Gabriel, Philadelphia, PA
Foley, Rev. George, '58 (FWT) Retired.
Foley, Rev. Gerald J., '59 (GB) Retired.
Foley, Rev. Jerome P., '84 (SFR) Curia: Leadership St. Peter, Pacifica, CA
Foley, Rev. John J., *C.S.P.* '67 (BRK) [EFT] Paulist Mission Trust, Jamaica Estates, NY
Foley, Rev. John J., *C.S.P.* '67 (NY) Retired. [MON] Paulist Fathers' Motherhouse, New York, NY
Foley, Rev. John P., *S.J.* '67 (CHI) (>DET) [MON] Colombiere Center, Clarkston, MI
Foley, Rev. Joseph F., *S.M.A.* '67 (NEW) Retired.
Foley, Rev. Joseph P., *C.M.* '68 (BRK) [MON] DePaul Residence, Queens Village, NY; [MON] Reverend John B. Murray, C.M. House, Jamaica, NY
Foley, Rev. Marc, *O.C.D.* '81 (WDC) [SEM] Discalced Carmelite Friars, Inc., Washington, DC
Foley, Rev. Matthew, *O.F.M.* (BUF) Curia: Consultative Bodies St. Francis High School, Hamburg, NY; [MON] St. Francis of Assisi Friary, Hamburg, NY
Foley, Rev. Matthew E., '89 (CHI) St. Gall, Chicago, IL
Foley, Very Rev. Michael, '70 (PT) Curia: Leadership; Offices and Directors Good Shepherd, Tallahassee, FL
Foley, Rev. Michael G., '86 (CHI) Our Lady of the Woods, Orland Park, IL
Foley, Rev. Patrick, '72 (PT) Retired.
Foley, Rev. Peter J., '67 (PH) Retired.
Foley, Rev. Scott, '19 (DAV) St. Mary Church of Grinnell, Iowa, Grinnell, IA
Foley, Rev. Thomas F., *C.S.P.* '77 (SFR) Old St. Mary's Cathedral & Chinese Mission, San Francisco, CA
Foley, Rev. Thomas S., '86 (BO) Curia: (>MO) Offices and Directors
Foley, Rev. Timothy M., '65 (STL) Retired.
Foley, Rev. William E., '79 (WDC) [MIS] The Washington Cursillo Movement, Washington, DC
Foley, Rev. William P., '74 (BAL) Curia: Clergy and Religious Services Basilica of the National Shrine of the Assumption of the Blessed Virgin Mary, Baltimore, MD; St. Mark, Fallston, MD
Folino, Rev. Frank, *O.F.M.* (SFD) St. Isidore the Farmer Church, Dieterich, IL; [MON] St. Francis Assisi Friary, Teutopolis, IL
Follmann, Rev. Roland F., *O.S.A.* '60 (TLS) Cascia Hall Preparatory School, Tulsa, OK
Folmar, Rev. Michael J., (ARL) St. Michael, Annandale, VA
Folorunso, Rev. Stephen, (BIS) St. Martin of Tours, Center, ND; St. Mary, Queen of Peace, Almont, ND; St. Pius V, New Salem, ND
Folsey, Rev. William David, *O.P.* '60 (PRO) [MON] St. Thomas Aquinas Priory at Providence College, Providence, RI
Folsom, Rev. Paul, '65 (SCL) Retired.
Foltyn, Rev. Andrzej, '08 (MIA) St. Agnes, Key Biscayne, FL
Foltyn, Rev. Paul A., '18 (GAL) St. Augustine, Houston, TX
Foltz, Rev. Msgr. Michael H., '89 (CR) Holy Trinity Catholic (Tabor), Angus, MN; Sacred Heart, East Grand Forks, MN; St. Francis of Assisi, Fisher, MN
Folwaczny, Rev. Dan Ignatius, '14 (CHI) Our Lady of the Blessed Sacrament, Elk Grove Village, IL
Folzenlogen, Rev. John N., *S.J.* '65 (STL) Retired.
Folzenlogen, Rev. Joseph D., *S.J.* '71 (CIN) [MIS] Claver Jesuit Ministry, Cincinnati, OH (>DET) [MON] Colombiere Center, Clarkston, MI
Fomukong, Rev. Frankline, '04 (BIR) St. Charles Borromeo, Jacksonville, AL; [CAM] Jacksonville State University, Jacksonville, AL
Fones, Very Rev. Michael, *OP* (OAK) [EFT] Dominican Community Support Charitable Trust, Oakland, CA; [MON] Order of Preachers (Province of the Most Holy Name of Jesus - Western Dominican Province), Oakland, CA
Fongemie, Rev. John, *F.S.S.P.* (Y) Queen of the Holy Rosary, Vienna, OH
Fons, Rev. David Michael, '15 (LAN) Curia: Offices and Directors St. Mary Parish Williamston, Williamston, MI
Fonseca, Rev. Msgr. Harvey, '92 (FRS) Shrine of Saint Jude Thaddeus, Livingston, CA
Fonseca, Rev. Luis, '09 (SAV) St. Peter the Apostle Church, Savannah, GA
Fonseca, Rev. Oscar D., '07 (NEW) Chap, Sheppard AFB, TX Curia: (>MO) Offices and Directors
Fonseca, Rev. Peter J., '15 (STL) Curia: Offices and Directors St. Theodore Catholic Church, Wentzville, MO
Fonseca, Rev. Rolando, '94 (ELP) San Juan Diego Parish, El Paso, TX
Fonseka, Rev. Matthew, '69 (NEW) Retired.
Fonseka, Rev. Peduru, '18 (IND) [MON] St. Meinrad Archabbey, St. Meinrad, IN
Fontana, Rev. Alphonso R., '97 (HRT) Curia: Advisory Boards, Commissions, Committees, and Councils St.

Ann's Church of Avon, Avon, CT
Fontana, Rev. Glenn J., '92 (PEO) Retired. On Sick Leave.
Fontana, Rev. John, (CHI) [MIS] National Shrine of St. Peregrine, O.S.M., ,
Fontana, Rev. John M., *O.S.M.* '78 (CHI) [MON] Assumption Priory, Chicago, IL
Fontanella, Rev. Paul C., '02 (SCR) On Administrative Leave.
Fontanini, Rev. Christopher, '97 (DM) Retired. Curia: Leadership St. Joseph Catholic Church, Des Moines, IA
Fontenot, Rev. Anthony M., '01 (LKC) Curia: Advisory Boards, Commissions, Committees, and Councils; Leadership St. Raphael, Iowa, LA
Fonti, Rev. Joseph G., '92 (BRK) Curia: Leadership St. Mel, Flushing, NY
Foote, Rev. Job J., *O.S.B.* '89 (GBG) Ascension, Jeannette, PA; Sacred Heart, Jeannette, PA; [MON] Saint Vincent Archabbey, Latrobe, PA
Fopa Lonfo, Rev. Yacob, '19 (STV) Curia: Offices and Directors
Foppiano, Rev. Michael, '07 (BAL) Curia: Clergy and Religious Services St. Mark, Fallston, MD
Foradori, Very Rev. V. David, '86 (E) Curia: Leadership Beloved Disciple, Grove City, PA; [CAM] Grove City College, Grove City, PA
Forbes, Rev. Eric, *O.F.M.Cap.* '90 (AGN) Curia: Miscellaneous / Other Offices [MON] St. Fidelis Friary, Agana Heights, GU
Forbes, Very Rev. John J., '91 (R) Curia: Leadership Sacred Heart, Pinehurst, NC
Forbes, Rev. Richard L., '67 (CAM) Retired.
Forbidussi, Rev. John E., '94 (PIT) Our Lady of Perpetual Help, Glenshaw, PA
Forcelle, Rev. Joseph, '80 (SFS) Saint Leo The Great Parish of Bon Homme County, Tyndall, SD; Saint Vincent de Paul Parish of Bon Homme County, Springfield, SD; Saint Wenceslaus Parish of Bon Homme County, Tabor, SD
Forcier, Rev. Richard-Jacob, *O.F.M.Conv.* '86 (BAL) [MIS] Shrine of St. Anthony, Ellicott City, MD
Forcier, Rev. Robert H., '03 (PRO) Saint Augustine's Church, Providence, Rhode Island, Providence, RI
Ford, Rev. Christopher, '19 (BGP) On Special Assignment. Pursue Ph.D @Fordham
Ford, Rev. Christopher M., '87 (HRT) Curia: Administration; Advisory Boards, Commissions, Committees, and Councils; Tribunal The St. Peter Claver Church Corporation of West Hartford, West Hartford, CT
Ford, Rev. Msgr. J. Joseph, '67 (PRT) Retired.
Ford, Rev. Lawrence D., *O.F.M.* '96 (NY) St. Gregory, New York, NY
Ford, Rev. Michael F., *S.J.* '75 (WOR) [MON] Jesuits of the Holy Cross, Inc., Worcester, MA
Ford, Rev. Michail, *O.P.* '10 (CHI) [MON] St. Pius V Priory, Chicago, IL; [SHR] Dominican Shrine of St. Jude Thaddeus, ,
Ford, Rev. Nathan, *S.J.C.* '21 (CHI) St. John Cantius, Chicago, IL; [MIS] Canons Regular of Saint John Cantius, Chicago, IL
Ford, Rev. Ryan T., '11 (MAR) Curia: Advisory Boards, Commissions, and Committees, and Councils; Offices and Directors; Organizations (affiliated, inter-Diocesan, miscellaneous/other) Sacred Heart, Champion, MI; St. Augustine, Republic, MI; St. John the Evangelist, Ishpeming, MI; St. Joseph, Ishpeming, MI
Forester, Rev. Raymond L., '66 (WIL) Retired.
Forge, Very Rev. Michael D., '97 (DAL) Curia: Administration Prince of Peace Catholic Parish, Plano, TX
Forget, Rev. Timothy W., '02 (OM) St. John, Valley, NE
Forintos, Rev. Bradley, '91 (DET) Holy Trinity Parish Port Huron, Port Huron, MI
Foriska, Rev. John M., '70 (GBG) Retired. Holy Family, Latrobe, PA; [NUR] Neumann House, Greensburg, PA
Forkuoh, Rev. John, '00 (DOD) Curia: Offices and Directors St. Anthony Catholic Church of Hanston, Kansas, Hanston, KS; St. John the Baptist Catholic Church of Spearville, Kansas, Spearville, KS; St. Lawrence Catholic Church of Jetmore, Kansas, Jetmore, KS
Forlano, Rev. Albert, (STF) On Duty Outside Diocese. Diocese of Bridgeport, CT
Forlano, Rev. Albert, (BGP) Retired. Chap, Saint Vincent's Med Ctr, Danbury
Forlano, Rev. Philip M., '03 (PH) St. Charles Borromeo, Bensalem, PA
Forler, Rev. Christopher, '08 (EVN) Reitz Memorial High School, Evansville, IN; St. Bernard, Fort Branch, IN; St. John the Evangelist, Evansville, IN
Forliti, Rev. John E., '62 (STP) Retired.
Forman, Rev. Bruce H., '74 (STL) Sts. Peter and Paul Catholic Church, St. Louis, MO
Forman, Rev. Patrick J., '89 (BUR) Curia: Leadership; Offices and Directors St. Monica, Barre, VT; St. Monica - St. Michael School, Barre, VT
Formolo, Rev. Frank, *L.C.* '03 (ATL) [MIS] Horizons Institute, Inc. (CT), a Connecticut Non-Stock Corporation, Roswell, GA; [MIS] Horizons Institute, Inc. (MA), a Massachusetts Non-Profit Corporation, Roswell, GA; [MIS] Human Resources ITA, Inc., Roswell, GA; [MIS] LC RC Family Centers, Inc., Roswell, GA; [MIS] LCNA Atlanta, Incorporated, Roswell, GA; [MIS] Legion of Christ, Atlanta, Inc., Roswell, GA; [MIS] Lux et Vita, Inc., Roswell, GA; [MIS] Mission Network USA, Inc., Roswell, GA; [MIS] RC Education (GA), Inc., Roswell, GA; [MIS] Sierra Madre, Inc., Roswell, GA; [MIS] Sviluppo Risorse Umane, Inc., Roswell, GA; [MIS] Vocation Action Circle, Inc., Cumming, GA; [MON] Legionaries of Christ, Incorporated, Cumming, GA; [MON] Norcross Pastoral Center, Inc., Roswell, GA
Formolo, Rev. Frank, (LA) [MIS] Hombre Nuevo, El Monte, CA; [MON] Ramona Blvd., Inc., Pasadena, CA
Formolo, Rev. Frank, (PRO) [MIS] Hombre Nuevo (RI), Inc., North Smithfield, RI; [MIS] LC Pastoral Services, Inc., Greenville, RI; [MIS] Ocean Pastoral Center, Inc., North Smithfield, RI; [MIS] Regnum Christi, Greenville, RI
Formolo, Rev. Frank, (DET) [MIS] Clarkston Pastoral Center, Inc., Bloomfield Hills, MI; [MIS] Opdyke, Inc., Bloomfield Hills, MI
Formolo, Rev. Frank, (ARL) [MIS] Alpha Omega Clinic and Consultation Services, Fairfax, VA
Formolo, Rev. Frank, *L.C.* '03 (HRT) [COL] Legion of Christ College, Inc., Cheshire, CT
Formolo, Rev. Frank, *L.C.* (MAN) [MIS] L.C. Center Harbor, Inc., Center Harbor, NH
Formolo, Rev. Frank, (WDC) [MIS] Potomac Pastoral Center Inc., Potomac, MD; [RTR] Alpha Omega, Inc. (Our Lady of Bethesda), Bethesda, MD
Formolo, Rev. Frank, (NY) [EFT] Legion of Christ and Consecrated Regnum Christi Members Assistance Foundation, Rye, NY; [MIS] Alpha Omega Family Center, Inc., Rye, NY; [MIS] Arke, Inc., Rye, NY; [MIS] Catholic Net, Inc., Rye, NY; [MIS] Consolidated Catholic Administrative Services, Inc., Rye, NY; [MIS] Helping Hands Medical Missions, Inc., Rye, NY; [MIS] Legion of Christ North America, Inc., Rye, NY; [MIS] Legion of Christ, Incorporated, Rye, NY; [MIS] Logos, Inc., Rye, NY; [MIS] Nueva Primavera Inc., Rye, NY; [MIS] Regina Apostolorum, Inc., Rye, NY; [MIS] Rossotto, Inc., Rye, NY; [MIS] The Legion of Christ, Incorporated, Rye, NY
Forner, Rev. Clayton A., '20 (STP) Divine Mercy Catholic Church, Faribault, MN
Forner, Rev. Craig W., '75 (SFR) Retired.
Forni, Rev. John V., '77 (ROC) Retired.
Fornkwa, Rev. Hyacinth, '08 (PRT) St. Anthony, Jackman, ME
Fornkwa, Rev. Hyacinth Ndifon, '08 (PRT) Holy Family, Greenville, ME
Forno, Rev. Adam, (ALB) Retired.
Fornwalt, Rev. Athanasius, *FHS* '17 (DET) St. Mary of Redford Parish Detroit, Detroit, MI
Fornwalt, Rev. Richard, (PHX) St. John the Baptist, Laveen, AZ
Foro, Rev. Emmanuel, *S.J.* (OM) [MON] Jesuit Community at Creighton University, Omaha, NE
Forrai, Rev. Tamas G., *S.J.* (ATH) Curia: Organizations (affiliated, inter-Diocesan, miscellaneous/other)
Forrey, Very Rev. William C., (HBG) Curia: Leadership; Offices and Directors Holy Infant, Manchester, PA; [EFT] Roman Catholic Diocese of Harrisburg Charitable Trust, Harrisburg, PA; [EFT] Roman Catholic Diocese of Harrisburg Real Estate Trust, Harrisburg, PA
Forsen, Rev. Msgr. James, '79 (LA) Retired. Visitation, Los Angeles, CA
Forsman, Rev. David, '01 (DUL) Immaculate Heart Church, Crosslake, MN; St. Emily, Emily, MN
Forson, Rev. Cletus, '92 (BRK) Sacred Hearts of Jesus and Mary and St. Stephen, Brooklyn, NY
Forster, Rev. Francis P., *O.S.B.* '64 (CHL) [MON] Belmont Abbey (Southern Benedictine Society of North Carolina, Inc.), Belmont, NC
Forsyth, Rev. Kevin J., '86 (HRT) Retired.
Forsythe, Rev. Andrew, (NSH) Sacred Heart, Lawrenceburg, TN
Forte, Rev. Anthony, '91 (RIC) St. Benedict, Chesapeake, VA
Forte, Rev. Anthony R., '91 (NEW) On Duty Outside Diocese. Chesapeake, VA
Forte, Rev. John Paul, *O.P.* '93 (TUC) [CAM] University of Arizona Newman Center, Tucson, AZ
Forte, Rev. John Paul, *O.P.* '93 (TUC) Saint Thomas More Roman Catholic Newman Parish - Tucson, Tucson, AZ
Fortener, Rev. Kenneth R., '69 (L) Retired.
Fortier, Rev. Joel, '69 (JOL) Retired.
Fortier, Rev. Joseph, *S.J.* '90 (SPK) St. Michael's Mission, Inchelium, WA; St. Rose of Lima, Keller, WA; [MON] Regis Community, Spokane, WA
Fortin, Rev. John R., *O.S.B* '76 (MAN) Retired. [MON] St. Anselm Abbey, Manchester, NH
Fortin, Rev. LeeAllen, '22 (FTW) St. Mary of the Assumption, Decatur, IN
Fortin, Rev. Philip, '00 (PT) Chap, Washington Corr Inst; Florida Corr Insts Curia: Leadership St. Anne, Marianna, FL; St. Joseph the Worker, Chipley, FL
Fortin, Rev. Richard A., '62 (WOR) Retired.
Fortman, Rev. Anthony, *C.PP.S.* '01 (TOL) St. John the Baptist, Glandorf, OH (>CIN) Precious Blood, Dayton, OH; (>CIN) St. Rita, Dayton, OH
Fortman, Rev. Anthony, *C.PP.S.* '01 (CIN) St. Paul, Englewood, OH
Fortner, Rev. Mark, *S.C.J.* '68 (MIL) Retired. [MON] Sacred Heart at Monastery Lake, Franklin, WI
Fortuna, Rev. Joseph, '80 (CLV) Chap, Euclid Hosp, Cleveland
Fortuna, Rev. Joseph J., '80 (CLV) Euclid Hospital Our Lady of the Lake Parish, Euclid, OH; St. Jerome, Cleveland, OH
Fortuna, Rev. Stanley, *C.F.R.* '90 (NY) [MIS] Francesco Productions Inc., Bronx, NY; [MON] Our Lady of the Angels Friary, Bronx, NY
Fortunato, Rev. Anthony, (SP) [MON] St. Peter Nolasco Residence, St. Petersburg, FL
Fortunato, Rev. Vincent, *O.F.M. Cap.* '80 (NEW) St. Ann, Hoboken, NJ
Fortunio, Rev. Carlo, '85 (NEW) Holy Redeemer, West New York, NJ
Foschiatto, Rev. Edi, *S.X.* '81 (PAT) [MON] Xaverian Missionary Fathers, Wayne, NJ
Foshage, Rev. Nathanael, *O.S.B.* '68 (OM) [MON] Mount Michael Benedictine Abbey, Elkhorn, NE
Foshage, Rev. Nathanael, *O.S.B.* '68 (PBL) St. Daniel the Prophet, Ouray, CO
Foshage, Rev. Ronald B., *M.S.* '75 (HRT) [MON] Missionaries of La Salette Province of Mary, Mother of the Americas (The Missionaries of La Salette Corporation., MLS Religious Trust), Hartford, CT
Foshage, Very Rev. Ronald B., *M.S.* '75 (BEA) Curia: Leadership Our Lady of the Pines, Woodville, TX; St. Michael, Jasper, TX; St. Raymond Mission, Brookland, TX
Foshee, Rev. Aaron J., '15 (OKL) St. Joseph, Ada, OK; [CAM] East Central State University, Ada, OK
Fosnot, Rev. James, '94 (RIC) Retired.
Fossa, Rev. Leandro, *CS* (CHI) Our Lady of Mount Carmel, Melrose Park, IL
Fossoh, Rev. Divine, '14 (PRT) Saint Brendan the Navigator Parish, Camden, ME
Foster, Rev. Clyde, '75 (CLV) St. Vincent de Paul, Cleveland, OH
Foster, Rev. Clyde K., '75 (CLV) St. Patrick, Cleveland, OH
Foster, Rev. Dominic, *TOR* (STU) [COL] Franciscan University of Steubenville, Steubenville, OH; [MON] Holy Spirit Friary, Steubenville, OH
Foster, Rev. James A., '72 (ALX) Retired. On Leave.
Foster, Rev. James J., '80 (STL) Holy Family Catholic Church, Port Hudson, New Haven, MO
Foster, Rev. James K., *C.S.C.* '95 (FTW) [COL] University of Notre Dame Du Lac, Notre Dame, IN; [EFT] Saint Andre Bessette Continuing Care Trust, Notre Dame, IN; [MON] Holy Cross Community, Corby Hall, University of Notre Dame, Notre Dame, IN
Foster, Very Rev. John J.M., '91 (STO) Curia: Canonical Services; Leadership Cathedral of the Annunciation (Pastor of), Stockton, CA
Foster, Rev. John Mary, *M.D.M.* '87 (SAT) On Special Assignment. New Braunfels
Foster, Rev. Jonathan, *OFM* (GB) Retired.
Foster, Rev. Joseph R., '91 (BO) On Leave.
Foster, Rev. Msgr. Michael S., '80 (BO) Curia: Tribunal
Foster, Rev. Thomas J., '82 (DUL) Curia: (>MO) Offices and Directors [HOS] St. Mary's Medical Center, Duluth, MN; [HOS] St. Mary's Medical Center (Essentia Health-St. Mary's Medical Center), Duluth, MN
Foster, Rev. Thomas J., '82 (DUL) Chap, St Mary's Med Ctr
Fostner, Rev. Jay J., *O. Praem.* '88 (GB) [MON] St. Norbert Abbey, De Pere, WI (>CHI) [MON] Premonstratensian Fathers and Brothers (Norbertines), Chicago, IL
Fosu, Rev. Daniel, '11 (MAR) St. Louis the King

(Harvey), Marquette, MI
Fosu, Rev. Msgr. Dominic K., '94 (COV) Curia: Advisory Boards, Commissions, Committees, and Councils; Leadership Immaculate Heart of Mary, Burlington, KY
Fosu, Rev. Peter H., '86 (MAR) Immaculate Conception, Watersmeet, MI
Fournier, Rev. William, (PHX) St. Elizabeth Seton Roman Catholic Parish, Sun City, AZ
Fournier, Rev. William, '73 (DUL) Retired.
Foutts, Rev. Patrick D., *O.Praem.* '93 (ORG) [MON] Norbertine Fathers of Orange, Inc., Silverado, CA
Fowler, Very Rev. Joseph, '02 (PT) Basilica of St. Michael the Archangel, Pensacola, FL
Fowler, Rev. Joseph M., '61 (L) Retired.
Fowler, Rev. Michael, *OFM* (CHI) St. Peter's, Chicago, IL
Fowler, Rev. Michael G., '15 (ROC) St. Agnes, Avon, NY; St. Paul of the Cross, Honeoye Falls, NY; St. Rose, Lima, NY
Fowler, Very Rev. T. Joseph, '02 (PT) Curia: Leadership; Offices and Directors
Fowlkes, Rev. Eric L., '89 (NSH) Curia: Leadership Cathedral of the Incarnation, Nashville, TN
Fowoyo, Rev. Louis, '85 (FTW) St. Gaspar del Bufalo, Rome City, IN
Fox, Rev. Brian P., *S.S.J.* '91 (GAL) Retired.
Fox, Rev. Charles D., '06 (DET) [SEM] Sacred Heart Major Seminary, Inc., Detroit, MI
Fox, Rev. Charles D., '06 (DET) On Special Assignment. Sacred Heart Major Seminary, Detroit St. Therese of Lisieux Parish Shelby Township, Shelby Twp., MI
Fox, Rev. Daniel, *O.F.M.Cap.* (SAG) Our Lady of Grace Parish of Sanford, Sanford, MI
Fox, Rev. Daniel J., *O.F.M.Cap.* '75 (DET) [MON] St. Bonaventure Monastery, Detroit, MI
Fox, Rev. James E., '74 (DEN) Good Shepherd Catholic Parish in Denver, Denver, CO
Fox, Rev. James R., '90 (DEN) Christ the King Catholic Parish in Evergreen, Evergreen, CO
Fox, Rev. Joseph, *O.P.* '74 (LA) Curia: Offices and Directors St. Victor, West Hollywood, CA
Fox, Rev. Kevin, '19 (CLV) St. Charles Borromeo, Parma, OH
Fox, Rev. Martin E., '03 (CIN) Our Lady of Good Hope, Miamisburg, OH; St. Henry, Dayton, OH; St. Mary of the Assumption, Springboro, OH
Fox, Rev. Melvin E., '63 (GR) Retired.
Fox, Rev. Richard D., '85 (SFS) Curia: Leadership Immaculate Conception Parish of Codington County, Watertown, SD; [EFT] Immaculate Conception School Foundation, Inc., Watertown, SD
Fox, Rev. Richard E., '92 (SCR) Curia: Leadership St. Patrick, Scranton, PA
Fox, Rev. Robert L., '01 (CHY) Retired.
Fox, Rev. Sean P., '53 (SEA) Retired.
Fox, Rev. Tom, *OFM* '62 (IND) Retired. Sacred Heart of Jesus Catholic Church, Indianapolis, Inc., Indianapolis, IN
Fox, Rev. William, (KC) St. Joseph's Catholic Church, Trenton, MO; [MIS] Cursillo, Kansas City, MO
Foxen, Rev. David K., *M.S.C.* '97 (SB) Our Lady of Guadalupe, Palm Springs, CA; Our Lady of Solitude, Palm Springs, CA
Foynes, Rev. Msgr. Aiden, '61 (SP) Retired. St. Cecelia, Clearwater, FL
Frackowiak, Rev. Adrian, (MAN) St. Gabriel, Franklin, NH
Frade, Rev. Paulo, '97 (NEW) On Duty Outside Diocese.
Fragomeni, Rev. Richard, '75 (CHI) Our Lady of Pompeii, Chicago, IL; [SEM] Catholic Theological Union, Chicago, IL; [SHR] Shrine of Our Lady of Pompeii, ,
Fragomeni, Rev. Richard N., '75 (ALB) On Duty Outside Diocese. Chicago, IL
Fragoso, Rev. Michael, '13 (MET) Parish of the Visitation, New Brunswick, NJ
Fragoso-Carranza, Rev. Manuel, '05 (TUC) Immaculate Conception & Guadalupe Missions Roman Catholic Parish & Guadalupe Mission - Yuma, Yuma, AZ
Fragoso-Carranza, Rev. Manuel, '05 (TUC) Curia: Consultative Bodies; Leadership Our Lady of Guadalupe, Yuma, AZ
Frain, Rev. Brian B., *S.J.* (BAL) St. Ignatius Church, Baltimore, MD
Fraini, Rev. Frederick D., '08 (WOR) North American Martyrs, Auburn, MA
Fraley, Rev. Mason, (DEN) On Leave.
Frambes, Rev. John, *O.F.M.* '79 (TR) St. Francis of Assisi, Long Beach Township, NJ
Framboise, Rev. Ronald, *O.M.I.* '14 (SAT) [SEM] Blessed Mario Borzaga Formation Community, San Antonio, TX
Franca, Rev. Hugo, '04 (OAK) St. Leander, San Leandro, CA
Franceschini, Rev. Mark, *O.S.M.* '59 (DEN) Our Lady of Mount Carmel Catholic Parish in Denver, Denver, CO
Francesco, Rev. Richard G., '87 (NEW) On Duty Outside Diocese. Diocese of Helena, St Mary Catholic Cmty, Helena, MT
Francese, Rev. Francesco, '12 (PRO) Chap, Rhode Island Hosp, Providence Curia: Offices and Directors Corporation of the Church of the Holy Ghost, Rhode Island, Providence, RI
Franchomme, Rev. Emilio, '04 (DEN) [SEM] Redemptoris Mater House of Formation, Denver, CO
Franchuk, Rev. Ben, '21 (BIS) St. Charles, Bowman, ND; St. Mary, Marmarth, ND; St. Mel, Rhame, ND
Francik, Rev. Gerard C., '87 (BAL) Sacred Heart, Glyndon, MD
Francis, Rev. Bernard C., '69 (NO) Retired.
Francis, Rev. Bijoy, *O.Praem.* '05 (MO) Curia: Offices and Directors
Francis, Rev. Bijoy, '05 (SFE) Veteran's Hosp St. Francis Xavier-Albuquerque, Albuquerque, NM
Francis, Rev. Emmanuel, '96 (LA) St. Louise de Marillac, Covina, CA
Francis, Rev. Msgr. Eugene, '52 (GAL) Retired.
Francis, Rev. Jaya Kumar, *MSC* '98 (ALN) St. Jane Frances de Chantal, Easton, PA
Francis, Rev. John, '90 (BRK) St. Fidelis, College Point, NY
Francis, Rev. John, *S.J.* (ORG) Curia: Leadership
Francis, Rev. Jose, *TOR* '96 (FWT) Sacred Heart, Wichita Falls, TX
Francis, Rev. Joseph A., '78 (NY) Parish of St. Monica, St. Elizabeth of Hungary, and St. Stephen of Hungary, New York, NY; St. Joseph Parish, Yonkers, NY
Francis, Rev. Mark R., *C.S.V.* '82 (CHI) [MON] Viatorian Province Center-Clerics of St. Viator, Arlington Heights, IL; [SEM] Catholic Theological Union, Chicago, IL
Francis, Rev. Mathew, '91 (KCK) St. Bede, Kelly, KS; St. Patrick, Corning, KS; St. Vincent de Paul, Onaga, KS
Francis, Rev. R. Peter, *O.F.M.* '80 (MO) Curia: Offices and Directors
Francis, Rev. Sean M., '04 (PIT) St. Faustina, Slippery Rock, PA
Francis, Rev. Thomas C., *O.M.* '15 (LA) All Saints, Los Angeles, CA; [MON] Minim Fathers, Los Angeles, CA
Francisco, Rev. Rolyn B., '88 (PHX) Christ the King Roman Catholic Parish, Mesa, AZ
Franciscus, Rev. Thomas J., *C.SS.R.* (RNO) Retired.
Franck, Rev. James, *C.PP.S.* (CIN) [MON] St. Charles, Celina, OH
Franck, Rev. John, *A.A.* (WOR) St. Anne and St. Patrick, Fiskdale, MA
Franco, Rev. Anthony, '16 (SAN) Curia: Advisory Boards, Commissions, Committees, and Councils Our Lady of Guadalupe, Eldorado, TX
Franco, Rev. David, (RIC) St. Joseph, North Chesterfield, VA
Franco, Rev. Efren, *M.S.P.* '22 (LA) St. Mary, Palmdale, CA
Franco, Rev. Federico M., *O.S.M.* '89 (ELP) Our Lady of Sorrows, El Paso, TX; Saint John Paul II, El Paso, TX
Franco, Rev. Msgr. Hilary, '55 (NY) Retired.
Franco, Rev. Joseph E., '04 (NY) Our Lady of Angels, Bronx, NY
Franco, Rev. Juan, '08 (OAK) St. Clement, Hayward, CA
Franco, Rev. Robert J., '82 (CLV) Curia: Advisory Boards, Commissions, Committees, and Councils St. Julie Billiart, North Ridgeville, OH; St. Peter, North Ridgeville, OH
Franco, Rev. Rodolfo, '99 (BWN) Curia: Advisory Boards, Commissions, Committees, and Councils St. Francis Xavier, La Feria, TX
Franco, Rev. Ronald A., *C.S.P.* (NY) [MON] Paulist Fathers' Motherhouse, New York, NY
Franco Luna, Rev. Marco Antonio, '19 (CHI) San Jose Luis Sanchez del Rio, Chicago, IL
Franco-Gomez, Rev. Emanuel, *O.Carm.* (TUC) [MON] Carmelite Priory, Tucson, AZ
Francois, Very Rev. Ducasse, '98 (PMB) Curia: Leadership St. Juliana, West Palm Beach, FL
Francois, Rev. Jean-Augustin, '90 (BRK) St. Jerome, Brooklyn, NY
Francois, Rev. Kerly, '14 (STV) Holy Family Parish, St. Thomas, VI
Francois, Rev. Kerly, '14 (STV) [MIS] Miscellaneous Organizations, Charlotte Amalie, VI
Francois, Rev. Marc-Arthur, '94 (NEW) St. Patrick and Assumption/All Saints Church, Jersey City, NJ
Francois, Rev. Yves, '05 (PMB) Sacred Heart, Okeechobee, FL
Franey, Rev. John A., '63 (PH) Retired.
Frangie, Rev. Butros (Peter), '21 (SAM) On Special Assignment. Brooklyn, NY Saint Anthony Maronite Catholic Church, Glen Allen, VA
Frank, Rev. Chrysostom, '85 (DEN) Retired. On Duty Outside Diocese.
Frank, Rev. David, '19 (NO) St. Rita, Harahan, LA
Frank, Rev. Gerald W., '70 (BWN) Retired.
Frank, Rev. Paul G., '04 (LIN) Sacred Heart, Red Cloud, NE
Frank, Rev. Richard W., '72 (JC) Retired.
Frank, Rev. Msgr. Thomas, '70 (AUS) Retired.
Frank, Rev. Thomas Robert, *SSJ* '78 (GAL) Our Lady Star of the Sea, Houston, TX; St. Peter Claver, Houston, TX
Franken, Rev. William F., '88 (BAL) St. Joan of Arc, Aberdeen, MD
Frankenberger, Rev. William Joseph, *C.S.B.* '73 (GAL) Retired. [MON] The Basilian Fathers of Dillon House, Houston, TX
Franklin, Rev. Claude W., '97 (SAM) Curia: Offices and Directors St. Joseph Maronite Catholic Church, Olean, NY
Franklin, Rev. Colin P., '12 (JC) Our Lady Help of Christians, Frankenstein, MO; St. George, Linn, MO
Franklin, Rev. David W., '85 (BGP) St. Aloysius Church Corporation of Connecticut, New Canaan, CT
Franklin, Rev. Mark E., '02 (SHP) St. Joseph, Mansfield, LA
Franklin, Rev. Osvaldo, (NY) Our Lady of Fatima Portuguese Roman Catholic Church, Yonkers, NY
Frankman, Rev. Gregory L., '81 (SFS) Saint John the Baptist Parish of Roberts County, Rosholt, SD; Saint Kateri Tekakwitha Parish of Roberts County, Sisseton, SD; Saint Peter Parish of Roberts County, Sisseton, SD
Frankovich, Rev. Francis A., *C.C.* '68 (GAL) Retired.
Frankovich, Rev. Lawrence, *O.F.M.* '66 (MIL) Retired.
Franks, Rev. T. Becket, *O.S.B.* '86 (JOL) [MON] St. Procopius Abbey, Lisle, IL
Franks, Rev. Thomas, *O.F.M.Cap.* '08 (NY) Parish of Holy Cross and St. John the Baptist, New York, NY; St. John the Baptist, New York, NY
Franquiz, Rev. Francisco, (MEM) St. Michael Church, Memphis, TN
Fransco, Rev. Peter J., '58 (SC) Retired.
Fransiscus, Rev. Thomas, *C.Ss.R.* '65 (TUC) Retired. [MON] Redemptorist Society of Arizona Desert House of Prayer Residence, Tucson, AZ; [RTR] Redemptorist Society of Arizona Redemptorist Renewal Center, Tucson, AZ
Fransiscus, Rev. Thomas Joseph, (TUC) Curia: Tribunal
Franz, Rev. S. Michael, '69 (CLV) Retired.
Franzman, Rev. Thomas R., '70 (CHI) Retired.
Frappier, Rev. Msgr. George L., '56 (PRO) Retired.
Frascadore, Rev. Henry C., '59 (HRT) Retired.
Fraser, Rev. Bernard, '00 (DET) On Leave.
Fraser, Rev. Christopher J., '01 (PHX) Curia: Leadership
Fraser, Rev. Donald C., '74 (B) Retired.
Fraser, Rev. Gerald C., '72 (BO) Retired.
Fraser, Rev. James, (PBR) St. Mary Holy Protection, Morgantown, WV
Fraser, Rev. James, (PSC) On Special Assignment.
Fraser, Rev. John, '96 (NY) St. Malachy's, New York, NY
Fraszczak, Rev. Zbigniew, *S.V.D.* '93 (ORG) [CCH] Pope John Paul II Polish Center, Yorba Linda, CA
Fratic, Rev. Joseph P., '64 (BO) On Leave.
Fratt, Rev. Gregory Perkins, '98 (HT) The Congregation of the Sacred Heart Roman Catholic Church, Cut Off, LA (Sacred Heart Church), Cut-Off, LA
Fratus, Rev. Nicholas J., '22 (E) St. George, Erie, PA
Frawley, Rev. Gerard, *S.A.C.* '68 (DET) Retired.
Frawley, Rev. Patrick J., '78 (BRK) Retired. Our Lady of Fatima, Jackson Heights, NY
Frayna, Rev. Ramon, '86 (AUS) St. Mary, Hearne, TX
Frazer, Very Rev. Christopher R., '07 (SAC) On Special Assignment. Curia: Leadership; Offices and Directors; Organizations (affiliated, inter-Diocesan, miscellaneous/ other)
Frazer, Rev. Edward J., *P.S.S.* '61 (BAL) Retired.
Frazer, Rev. Edward J., *S.S.* '61 (GF) Retired.
Frazer, Rev. Edward J., *S.S.* '61 (AUS) Retired.
Frazer, Rev. J. Francis, '75 (PIT) Retired. St. Matthias, Waynesburg, PA
Frazer, Rev. Joseph, '84 (AUS) Retired.
Frazier, Rev. Lawrence K., '71 (BAL) Retired. St. Joseph-on-Carrollton Manor, Frederick, MD
Frechette, Rev. Paul, *S.M.* '76 (WDC) [MON] Marist Center (The Marist Finance Center of the Atlanta Province of the Society of Mary, Marist Fathers and Brothers), Washington, DC

Frechette, Archimandrite Paul G., '78 (NTN) St. George's Syrian Congregation, Milwaukee, WI
Frechette, Rev. Richard, *C.P.* '79 (NY) [MON] The Congregation of the Passion - St. Paul of the Cross Province, Jamaica, NY
Frechette, Rev. Thomas A., '86 (FR) St. John the Evangelist, Pocasset, MA
Frecker, Rev. Msgr. A. Anthony, '72 (COL) Retired.
Frederici, Very Rev. David C., '01 (FR) Curia: Advisory Boards, Commissions, Committees, and Councils; Leadership; Offices and Directors; Tribunal St. Mary's, South Dartmouth, MA
Frederick, Rev. Allan R., '13 (COV) Cristo Rey, Florence, KY
Frederick, Rev. Curt J., '75 (MIL) Retired. Curia: Leadership
Frederick, Rev. Isaiah, (SCL) [MON] St. John's Abbey, of the Order of St. Benedict, Collegeville, MN
Frederick, Rev. Msgr. Lawrence A., '66 (LR) Catholic High School of Little Rock, AR, Little Rock, AR; Mount St. Mary Academy, Little Rock, AR
Frederick, Rev. Robert, '00 (ATL) [CAM] Berry College, Rome, GA
Fredericks, Rev. James L., '77 (SFR) Retired.
Fredericks, Rev. Michael J., '87 (SB) St. Paul the Apostle, Chino Hills, CA
Frederico, Rev. Charles A., *S.J.* '06 (BUF) [MON] The Canisius Jesuit Community, Inc., Buffalo, NY
Freeh, Rev. Vincent T., *M.S.C.* (ALN) [MON] Sacred Heart Villa, Missionaries of the Sacred Heart, Center Valley, PA
Freehill, Rev. Jeremy, '13 (PEO) St. Ann, Peoria, IL
Freeman, Rt. Rev. Brendan J., *O.C.S.O.* '69 (DUB) Retired. [MON] New Melleray Abbey, Order of Cistercians of the Strict Observance (Corporation of New Melleray), Peosta, IA
Freeman, Rev. James, '65 (DM) Retired.
Freeman, Rev. Justin, *O.de.M.* '10 (CLV) (>PH) Our Lady of Lourdes, Philadelphia, PA; (>PH) [MON] Monastery of Our Lady of Mercy (Fathers of Our Lady of Mercy, Inc. / Order of the B.V.M. of Mercy (Mercedarian Friars)), Philadelphia, PA
Freeman, Rev. Roland P., '67 (DEN) Retired. [MIS] Special Religious Education-Pastoral Care of Developmentally Disabled Persons, Denver, CO
Freer, Rev. Douglas A, '07 (TR) [MON] Villa Vianney, Trenton, NJ
Frei, Rev. William C., '20 (CHR) Cardinal Newman School, Columbia, SC; St. Joseph, Columbia, SC
Freiburger, Rev. Jason, '07 (FTW) Curia: Offices and Directors St. Monica, Mishawaka, IN
Freihofer, Rev. Michael, '06 (DEN) On Special Assignment. On sabbatical
Freitag, Friar Joseph, *OFM Conv.* (ALB) [MON] Franciscan Friars Conventual, Rensselaer, NY
Freitas, Rev. Patrick, '65 (HON) Retired.
Freitez, Rev. Pedro, '83 (MIA) San Isidro, Pompano Beach, FL
Frels, Rev. Jonathon, '16 (TYL) Retired. Curia: Advisory Boards, Commissions, Committees, and Councils Sacred Heart, Palestine, TX
French, Rev. Michael O, *CPM* '22 (GB) [SHR] The National Shrine of Our Lady of Good Help, Inc., New Franken, WI
French, Rev. Raymond D., *C.S.Sp.* '91 (PIT) [COL] Duquesne University of the Holy Spirit, Pittsburgh, PA
French, Rev. Thomas, *S.M.* '97 (STL) Our Lady of the Pillar Catholic Church, St. Louis, MO
Frenier, Rev. Steven, *OFM Conv* (SY) Retired. Assumption B.V.M., Syracuse, NY
Frerichs, Rev. Glenn K., '00 (WIN) Curia: Advisory Boards, Commissions, Committees, and Councils; Tribunal St. Mary, Chatfield, MN
Frerking, Rev. Thomas, *O.S.B.* '86 (STL) [MON] The Abbey of St. Mary and St. Louis, St. Louis, MO
Freson, Rev. Kenan, *O.F.M.* '67 (CIN) [EFT] Community Support Charitable Trust for the Province of St. John the Baptist of the Order of Friars Minor, Cincinnati, OH; [SHR] St. Anthony Shrine, Cincinnati, OH
Freund, Rev. John B., *C.M.* '69 (PH) [MON] Congregation of the Mission, Philadelphia, PA
Freund, Rev. Jospeh, *C.Ss.R.* '66 (BAL) Retired.
Frey, Rev. Msgr. John T., '70 (CAM) Retired.
Frey, Rev. Reed, *C.O.* (PIT) [CAM] Carnegie-Mellon University, Pittsburgh, PA; [CAM] Chatham College, Pittsburgh, PA; [CAM] University of Pittsburgh, Pittsburgh, PA; [MON] Congregation of the Oratory of St. Philip Neri, Pittsburgh, PA
Freyer, Rev. Timothy, '89 (ORG) Curia: Offices and Directors
Frez, Rev. Joseph S., '10 (SLC) On Duty Outside Diocese. Diocese of Broken Bay, Australia
Frias, Rev. Martin, '03 (PBL) On Leave. Par.Vic. St. Rose of Lima, Denver, CO
Frias Santana, Rev. Reynaldo, *O.F.M. Cap.* '17 (PH) [MON] Padre Pio Friary, Province of St. Augustine, Philadelphia, PA
Frias-Guardado, Rev. Martin, (DEN) St. Rose of Lima Catholic Parish in Denver, Denver, CO
Friberg, Rev. Daniel, '62 (STP) Retired.
Fricke, Rev. Colin, '20 (DET) St. Paul Parish Grosse Pointe Farms, Grosse Pointe Farms, MI
Fride, Rev. Edward O., '86 (LAN) Curia: Leadership Christ the King Parish Ann Arbor, Ann Arbor, MI
Friebel, Rev. Richard, *C.PP.S.* '78 (CIN) [MON] Society of the Precious Blood, United States Province, Inc., Dayton, OH
Friebel, Rev. Richard, *C.PP.S.* '78 (TOL) SS. Peter and Paul, Ottawa, OH; St. John the Baptist, Continental, OH; St. John the Baptist, Glandorf, OH; St. Michael, Kalida, OH
Friebohle, Rev. Charles, '16 (DUL) St. Anthony, Ely, MN; St. Pius X, Babbitt, MN
Fried, Rev. Francis L., '68 (STP) Retired.
Friedel, Rev. John (J.) F., '86 (SPC) Curia: Advisory Boards, Commissions, Committees, and Councils; Consultative Bodies; Offices and Directors Our Lady of the Lake, Branson, MO; Our Lady of the Ozarks, Forsyth, MO; [CAM] Catholic Campus Ministry, Branson, MO
Friedel, Rev. Michael, (SFD) Our Lady of Lourdes, Decatur, IL; [CAM] Millikin University Newman Catholic Community, Decatur, IL
Friedell, Rev. Ronald G., '66 (DUB) Retired.
Friedl, Rev. Erwin J., '71 (CHI) Retired. Sacred Heart and St. Eulalia, Melrose Park, IL
Friedl, Rev. Thomas, '92 (CR) Curia: Offices and Directors
Friedley, Rev. Craig W.M., '07 (PHX) Our Lady of Guadalupe Roman Catholic Parish, Queen Creek, AZ
Friedman, Rev. Daniel L., '72 (BEL) St. Francis of Assisi, Aviston, IL
Friedman, Rev. Gregory, *O.F.M.* '76 (SFE) [EFT] Anselm Weber Fund, Albuquerque, NM; [EFT] Roger Huser Fund, Albuquerque, NM; [MON] The Province of Our Lady of Guadalupe of the Order of Friars Minor, Inc., Albuquerque, NM
Friedrich, Rev. Jim, '89 (SFS) Assumption of the Blessed Virgin Mary Parish of Charles Mix County, Dante, SD; Saint Paul Parish of Charles Mix County, Marty, SD
Friedrich, Rev. Jim Duane, '89 (SFS) Saint John the Baptist Parish of Charles Mix County, Wagner, SD
Friedrichs, Rev. Richard M., '70 (PRO) Retired.
Friedrichsen, Rev. Timothy A., '84 (SC) Sacred Heart, Sioux City, IA
Friel, Rev. David M., '11 (PH) On Academic Leave. Catholic Univ of America; Washington, DC Curia: Advisory Boards, Commissions, Committees, and Councils; Clergy and Religious Services [SEM] Theological Seminary of St. Charles Borromeo, Wynnewood, PA
Friel, Rev. Edward M., '89 (CAM) Mary, Queen of All Saints, Pennsauken, N.J., Pennsauken, NJ
Friel, Rev. John F., '70 (TUC) Retired. Saint John Neumann Roman Catholic Church - Yuma, Yuma, AZ
Friend, Rev. Joseph S., '20 (LR) Curia: Offices and Directors Sacred Heart, Morrilton, AR; St. Joseph, Center Ridge, AR
Friend, Rev. Msgr. Scott, '87 (LR) Curia: Leadership; Offices and Directors [EFT] Blessed Sacrament Educational Endowment Fund, ,
Friend, Rev. Msgr. Scott, (LR) Blessed Sacrament, Jonesboro, AR
Frigo, Rev. William, *O.F.M.Cap.* (GF) Retired.
Frimpong, Rev. Ernest, (NY) Parish of Our Lady of Perpetual Help and St. Catharine, Pelham Manor, NY
Frimpong, Rev. Nicholas, (RVC) St. Anne, Garden City, NY
Frink, Rev. John A., '87 (ALN) [CAM] Muhlenberg College (Allentown), Allentown, PA
Frinsko, Rev. Donald S., *T.O.R.* '79 (STU) [COL] Franciscan University of Steubenville, Steubenville, OH; [MON] Holy Spirit Friary, Steubenville, OH
Frisch, Rev. Kenneth J., '78 (MAD) Retired.
Frisch, Rev. Michael F., *O. Praem.* '97 (GB) [MON] St. Norbert Abbey, De Pere, WI
Frisch, Rev. Ralph, (WDC) [MON] Father Judge Missionary Cenacle, Adelphi, MD
Friske, Rev. Joseph P., '62 (SAG) Retired. On Duty Outside Diocese. Munich
Frison, Rev. Theodore, '72 (P) Retired.
Frisoni, Very Rev. Matthew H., '05 (ALB) On Special Assignment. Judicial Vicar, Diocesan Tribunal, Pastoral Ctr, Albany Curia: Leadership; Offices and Directors Church of St. Adalbert, Schenectady, NY; Our Lady of Mt. Carmel, Schenectady, NY; St. Paul the Apostle, Schenectady, NY
Fritsch, Rev. Albert, *S.J.* (CIN) [MON] Cincinnati Jesuit Community, Cincinnati, OH
Fritsch, Rev. Albert, *S.J.* '67 (LEX) St. Elizabeth of Hungary, Ravenna, KY
Fritsch, Rev. Michael C., (IND) Queen of Peace Catholic Church, Danville, Inc., Danville, IN
Fritz, Rev. Msgr. John, *F.S.S.P.* '00 (FTW) St. Stanislaus Bishop and Martyr, South Bend, IN
Fritz, Rev. Peter, *OFM* (GB) Retired.
Fritz, Rev. Richard A., '75 (KAL) Retired.
Fritz, Rev. Robert J., '75 (CAM) Retired. The Parish of Saint John Neumann, North Cape May, N.J., North Cape May, NJ
Fritzen, Rev. James C., '69 (SY) Retired. Chap, St Camillus Health & Rehab Ctr, Syracuse
Frizzell, Rev. Lawrence E., '62 (NEW) Curia: Organizations (affiliated, inter-Diocesan, miscellaneous/ other) [COL] Seton Hall University, South Orange, NJ
Froehle, Rev. Nicholas, (STP) Church of St. Michael, Farmington, MN
Froehlich, Rev. James P., *O.F.M.Cap.* '82 (WDC) Shrine of the Sacred Heart, Washington, DC; [SEM] Theological College of the Catholic University of America, Washington, DC
Froehlich, Rev. Msgr. Mark J., '69 (STU) Retired.
Froeschl, Rev. Robert J., '20 (LIN) Curia: Leadership
Froeschl, Rev. Robert J., (LIN) St. John the Apostle, Lincoln, NE
Frohlich, Rev. Attila, '01 (MIA) Blessed Trinity, Virginia Gardens, FL
Frohlich, Rev. Tyler, '22 (HEL) Christ the King Parish: Series 638, LLC, Missoula, MT
Froidurot, Rev. Michel, '78 (SD) Pastor of Saint Gabriel Catholic Parish, Poway, a corporation sole, Poway, CA; [MIS] Saint Gabriel Catholic Parish in Poway, CA Real Property Support Corporation, Poway, CA
Fromholzer, Rev. Francis J., '58 (ALN) Retired.
Fronckowiak, Rev. Dennis F., '77 (BUF) St. Timothy, Tonawanda, NY
Fronek, Rev. Randy J., '05 (RCK) Our Lady of Perpetual Help, Sublette, IL; St. Mary, West Brooklyn, IL; St. Patrick, Amboy, IL
Fronske, Friar Edward, *O.F.M.* '67 (TUC) Retired.
Fronske, Rev. Edward, *O.F.M.* (TUC) Retired.
Frontiero, Rev. Msgr. Anthony R., '91 (MAN) On Duty Outside Diocese. St. Matthew, Windham, NH
Frost, Rev. John M., '87 (DM) St. Mary of Nazareth, Des Moines, IA; [EFT] Shelby County Catholic Education Foundation, Harlan, IA
Frost, Rev. Krzysztof, *S.A.C.* (VEN) St. Martha Parish in Sarasota, Inc., Sarasota, FL
Frost, Rev. Msgr. Stephen A., '77 (FRS) Christ the King, Bakersfield, CA
Frost, Rev. Stephen W., (ORG) Retired.
Frost, Rev. Thomas, *OFM* (OAK) [NUR] Mercy Retirement and Care Center, Oakland, CA
Frozena, Rev. Kenneth R., '60 (GB) Retired.
Fruth, Rev. Paul, '74 (DUL) Retired.
Fry, Rev. Wallace Blake, '07 (ELP) Retired.
Fryar, Rev. James, *F.S.S.P.* '04 (LA) St. Vitus, San Fernando, CA
Fryar, Very Rev. Msgr. Thomas S., '78 (DEN) Retired.
Fryer, Rev. Marcus C, *SJ* '17 (DEN) [MON] Regis Jesuit Community (The Jesuits at Regis University), Denver, CO
Fryer, Rev. Msgr. Patrick L., '73 (WH) Retired.
Fryml, Rev. Andrew Jaroslav, '17 (CHR) Curia: Advisory Boards, Commissions, Committees, and Councils Bishop England High School, Charleston, SC; Christ Our King, Mount Pleasant, SC; [CAM] Catholic Campus Ministry at the College of Charleston and Medical University of South Carolina, Charleston, SC
Fuccile, Rev. Dominic G., '66 (NEW) Retired.
Fucheck, Rev. Robert, '66 (ORL) Retired.
Fuchs, Rev. Eric W., '04 (NEW) Curia: Advisory Boards, Commissions, Committees, and Councils St. Lawrence, Weehawken, NJ
Fuchs, Rev. John D., *S.J.* '75 (SEA) Bellarmine Preparatory School, Tacoma, WA
Fuchs, Rev. Kristopher L., '15 (VIC) Curia: Leadership; Offices and Directors St. Mary's, Victoria, TX
Fucinaro, Rev. Msgr. Thomas J., '89 (LIN) On Duty Outside Diocese. Rome Cathedral of the Risen Christ, Lincoln, NE
Fuentes, Rev. Alberto, *OAR* (ORG) Our Lady of Guadalupe, Santa Ana, CA; [MON] Augustinian Recollects, Santa Ana, CA
Fuentes, Rev. Enrique, '95 (SD) Pastor of Our Lady of Light Catholic Parish, Descanso, a corporation sole, Descanso, CA; [MIS] Our Lady of Light Catholic Parish in Descanso, CA Real Property Support Corporation,

Descanso, CA
Fuentes, Rev. Pablo, '95 (STA) St. John the Evangelist, Interlachen, FL
Fuentes, Rev. Roselio, '17 (TYL) Our Lady of Grace, Hallsville, TX
Fuentes, Rev. Theo, *C.M.F.* '51 (LA) [CON] Convent, San Gabriel, CA
Fuentes Rodriguez, Rev. Jose, '45 (SJN) Retired.
Fuertes, Rev. Agustin, '02 (DAL) Epiphany Catholic Parish, Italy, TX; St. John Nepomucene Catholic Parish, Ennis, TX
Fuhrman, Rev. Msgr. Robert J., '81 (NEW) Curia: Offices and Directors; Organizations (affiliated, inter-Diocesan, miscellaneous/other) St. Philomena, Livingston, NJ
Fukes, Rev. Gary, (MO) Curia: Offices and Directors
Fukes, Rev. Gary M., '88 (SY) On Special Assignment. Seffner, FL Curia: (>MO) Offices and Directors
Fuks, Rev. Marcin, (NEW) Immaculate Heart of Mary, Mahwah, NJ
Fuks, Rev. Mariusz K., '08 (SAV) Our Lady Star of the Sea, St. Marys, GA
Fuld, Rev. Charles, '86 (SD) Retired.
Fulgenzi, Rev. Mario A., *O.S.B.* '68 (GBG) [MON] Saint Vincent Archabbey, Latrobe, PA
Fullam, Rev. Msgr. T. Dominick, '94 (BLX) Curia: Advisory Boards, Commissions, Committees, and Councils; Leadership; Miscellaneous / Other Offices; Tribunal St. Michael, Biloxi, MS; [MIS] Catholic Foundation of the Diocese of Biloxi, Inc., Biloxi, MS
Fullam, Rev. Msgr. Vincent F., '65 (BRK) Retired. Immaculate Conception, Astoria, NY
Fuller, Rev. Jon D., *S.J.* '90 (BO) Boston College High School, Boston, MA
Fuller, Rev. Michael J. K., '97 (CHI) [EFT] Civitas Dei Foundation, Mundelein, IL
Fuller, Rev. Michael J.K., '97 (RCK) On Duty Outside Diocese. USCCB, Washington, DC
Fuller, Rev. Neil D., *S.V.D.* '69 (SB) St. Frances Xavier Cabrini, Crestline, CA
Fuller, Rev. Timothy M., '93 (OKL) Curia: Deaneries; (>MO) Offices and Directors St. Mark the Evangelist, Norman, OK
Fullerton, Rev. Daniel, '91 (SCR) On Duty Outside Diocese. Navy Chaplain
Fullmer, Rev. Hugh, '72 (JOL) Retired.
Fullum, Rev. John J., '67 (BRK) Retired. Sacred Heart of Jesus Church, Glendale, NY
Fulton, Rev. Msgr. David I., '67 (MET) Retired.
Fulton, Rev. David L., '02 (OM) St. Michael, Central City, NE; St. Peter, Clarks, NE; St. Peter, Fullerton, NE
Fulton, Rev. Eugene J., '67 (PSC) Retired. On Duty Outside Diocese. Larchmont, NY (>NY) [RTR] Trinity Retreat, Larchmont, NY
Fulton, Rev. Eugene J., '67 (NY) [MIS] Spiritual Development Office, Larchmont, NY
Fulton, Rev. Justin R., '15 (LIN) Chap, Dir, Nebraska Penal Complex, Lincoln Curia: Leadership; Offices and Directors Bishop Bonacum Chancery, Lincoln, NE; [CCH] Catholic Social Services, Lincoln, NE; [EFT] Lincoln Diocesan Investment Trust and Loan, Lincoln, NE; [MIS] Diocesan Housing Ministries, Inc., Lincoln, NE; [MIS] John XXIII Diocesan Center, Lincoln, NE; [NUR] Bonacum House, Lincoln, NE
Fulton, Rev. Michael R., '20 (COL) Christ the King, Columbus, OH; St. Thomas the Apostle, Columbus, OH
Fulton, Rev. Patrick W., *C.S.B.* '97 (DET) Detroit Catholic Central High School, Novi, MI
Fulton, Rev. Robert P., '04 (LA) St. Louise de Marillac, Covina, CA
Funa, Rev. Harold, (CHK) Curia: Advisory Boards, Commissions, Committees, and Councils
Funk, Rev. C. Alan, '91 (LFT) Retired.
Funk, Rev. David J., *O.F.M.Cap.* '68 (GB) [MON] St. Fidelis Friary, Appleton, WI
Funk, Rev. Msgr. David R., '74 (COL) Retired.
Funk, Rev. Peter, *O.S.B.* '04 (CHI) [MON] Monastery of the Holy Cross, Chicago, IL
Funk, Rev. Peter C., '64 (PH) Retired.
Funk, Rev. Virgil C., '63 (RIC) Retired.
Funke, Rev. Gerald, '80 (B) Curia: Leadership
Funke, Rev. Gerald J., '80 (B) St. Agnes, Weiser, ID; St. Jude Station, Council, ID
Funke, Rev. Msgr. Richard P., '60 (DUB) Retired. Curia: Administration
Funtila, Rev. Aloysius, '83 (CHI) St. Pio of Pietrelcino Parish, Chicago, IL
Furca, Rev. Marian, *C.Ss.R.* '87 (CHI) Our Lady of Czestochowa and Charity Parish, Cicero, IL
Furdzik, Rev. Pawel, *O.C.D.* '95 (GRY) [MON] Discalced Carmelite Fathers Monastery, Munster, IN
Furey, Rev. John, *C.Ss.R.* '60 (BO) Our Lady of Perpetual Help, Boston, MA
Furey, Rev. Matthew J., '99 (NY) St. Martin de Porres, Poughkeepsie, NY
Furey, Rev. Thomas J., '73 (PH) Retired.
Furfaro, Rev. Virgil, '73 (SFE) Retired.
Furgiuele, Rev. Matthew A., '13 (GLD) Curia: Offices and Directors Saint Joseph of East Jordan, East Jordan, MI
Furlan, Rev. Michael J., '75 (CHI) Retired.
Furlong, Rev. Aidan M., *A.A.* '53 (WOR) Retired. [MON] Assumptionists (Augustinians of the Assumption), Worcester, MA
Furlong, Rev. Richard V., '72 (BUF) Retired.
Furlong, Rev. Ryan A., '20 (Y) Curia: Pastoral Services St. Thomas the Apostle Parish, Vienna, OH
Furlow, Rev. Timothy, '15 (P) St. Patrick Catholic Church, Portland, Oregon, Portland, OR
Furman, Rev. Frank W., '18 (SPR) Our Lady of the Valley, Sheffield, MA
Furman, Rev. Henry P., '02 (BUR) Curia: Leadership St. Michael, Brattleboro, VT
Furnaguera, Rev. Joseph Anthony, '18 (NEW) On Duty Outside Diocese. Casa Santa Maria, Roma
Furnari, Rev. Casper J., '68 (BRK) Retired. Holy Family, Flushing, NY
Furnari, Rev. Salvatore C., *S.A.C.* '05 (BAL) St. Jude Shrine, Baltimore, MD
Furrell, Rev. Reynold, '98 (ORG) Sts. Simon & Jude, Huntington Beach, CA
Furrevig, Rev. Edward G., '67 (NEW) Retired.
Furtado, Rev. Alwyn, *C.S.Sp.* '64 (SFR) St. Dunstan, Millbrae, CA
Fusare, Rev. Francis, *CPM* '96 (OWN) [MON] Fathers of Mercy, Auburn, KY
Fusco, Rev. Albin, *O.F.M.* (NY) [MON] Franciscan Province of the Immaculate Conception, New York, NY
Fusco, Rev. Thomas M., '85 (RVC) Curia: Leadership Our Lady of Victory, Floral Park, NY
Futter, Rev. Volker, *O.S.B.* '69 (OM) [MON] Benedictine Mission House - Christ the King Priory, Schuyler, NE
Fwamba, Rev. Evans, *C.P.* '05 (RVC) Chap, Northwell North Shore Univ Hosp, Manhasset
Fwamba, Rev. Evans, *C.P.* '05 (NY) [MON] The Congregation of the Passion - St. Paul of the Cross Province, Jamaica, NY
Fwamba, Rev. Evans Barasa, *C.P.* '05 (BRK) [MON] Immaculate Conception Monastery, Jamaica, NY
Fye, Rev. Michael, '14 (NSH) St. Ann, Nashville, TN
Fynn, Rev. Isaac A., '79 (TUC) Chap, St Joseph's Hosp, Tucson
Gaa, Rev. David, *O.F.M.* '98 (OAK) [EFT] Province of Saint Barbara Fraternal Care Trust, Oakland, CA; [MIS] Franciscan Charities, Inc., Oakland, CA; [MON] Franciscan Friars of California (Province of St. Barbara), Oakland, CA
Gaa, Rev. David, *OFM* (SFR) St. Boniface, San Francisco, CA
Gaalaas, Rev. Msgr. Patrick J., '72 (TLS) Retired. On Special Assignment. Hillcrest Hosp South (>KC) [SEM] Conception Seminary College, Conception, MO
Gabage, Very Rev. John B., '07 (WIL) Curia: Advisory Boards, Commissions, Committees, and Councils; Deaneries St. Christopher, Chester, MD
Gabel, Rev. Martin M., '68 (JOL) Retired. [NUR] St. John Vianney Villa, Naperville, IL
Gabet, Rev. George, *F.S.S.P.* (CIN) Holy Family, Dayton, OH
Gabin, Rev. John D., '75 (PH) On Special Assignment. Chap, St Joseph Rectory, Collingdale St. Joseph, Collingdale, PA
Gable, Rev. Justin C., *O.P.* '14 (OAK) [SEM] Dominican School of Philosophy and Theology, Berkeley, CA
Gable, Rev. Justin Charles, *O.P.* '14 (SFR) [MON] St. Dominic Priory, San Francisco, CA
Gabler, Rev. Michael, *O.S.B.* (ALT) St. Benedict, Carrolltown, PA
Gabler, Rev. Michael J., *O.S.B.* '08 (GBG) [MON] Saint Vincent Archabbey, Latrobe, PA
Gabor, Rev. Pavel, *S.J.* '04 (TUC) [MON] Jesuit Community of the Vatican Observatory, Tucson, AZ
Gaboury, Rev. Victor, *S.S.C.* '57 (OM) Retired. [MON] Missionary Society of St. Columban, St. Columbans, NE
Gaboury, Rev. Victor, *S.S.C.* '57 (PRO) Retired. [MON] St. Columban's Retirement House (St. Columban's Foreign Mission Society), Bristol, RI
Gabriel, Rev. Abelardo, *SVD* (LAF) Notre Dame de Perpetuel Secours, St. Martinville, LA
Gabriel, Rev. Alexander, '83 (JC) Holy Family, Hannibal, MO; St. Joseph, Palmyra, MO
Gabriel, Rev. John, (HON) St. John Apostle and Evangelist, Mililani Town, HI
Gabriel, Rev. John, *M.S.* '91 (ATL) (>HRT) [MIS] Missionaries of LaSalette, Hartford, CT
Gabriel, Rev. John B., (MO) Curia: Offices and Directors
Gabriel, Rev. John D., '87 (NEW) Church of St. Paul, Ramsey, NJ
Gabriel, Rev. Michael A., '84 (CHI) St. Gertrude, Chicago, IL
Gabriel, Rev. Paul, *O.F.M.Conv.* '05 (PMB) St. Lucie, Port St. Lucie, FL
Gabriel, Rev. William C., *O.S.A.* (PH) Malvern Preparatory School for Boys, Malvern, PA; [MON] Augustinian Friars (O.S.A.), Malvern, PA
Gabrielli, Rev. Ted, *S.J.* '96 (LA) Dolores Mission, Los Angeles, CA
Gabrielli, Rev. Theodore, *S.J.* '96 (SJ) [MIS] California Jesuit Missionaries, Los Gatos, CA; [MON] USA West Province, Society of Jesus, Los Gatos, CA
Gabriel-Masonet, Rev. Guillermo, '11 (TYL) Curia: Advisory Boards, Commissions, Committees, and Councils St. Elizabeth Ann Seton, Madisonville, TX
Gabutera, Rev. Rolando, (SD) Pastor of Saint Columba Catholic Parish, San Diego, a corporation sole, San Diego, CA; [MIS] Saint Columba Catholic Parish in San Diego, CA Real Property Support Corporation, San Diego, CA
Gabuzda, Rev. Richard J., '81 (OM) On Special Assignment.
Gabuzda, Rev. Richard J., '81 (OM) [MIS] The Community of IPF Priests, Inc., Omaha, NE
Gacad, Rev. Manuel, *M.J.* '78 (LA) Precious Blood, Los Angeles, CA; St. Kevin, Los Angeles, CA; [MON] Missionaries of Jesus, Inc., Los Angeles, CA
Gadaj, Rev. Bartlomiej, (STA) Resurrection, Jacksonville, FL
Gadaj, Rev. Bartlomiej L., (MO) Curia: Offices and Directors
Gadalia, Rev. Nathaniel Maria, *pfgm* '21 (HT) Holy Family, Dulac, LA; St. Eloi, Theriot, LA
Gadberry, Rev. Stephen, '16 (LR) Curia: Leadership
Gaddy, Rev. Msgr. James, '65 (LKC) Retired. Curia: Leadership
Gaddy, Rev. Msgr. James M., (LKC) St. Mary of the Lake, Lake Charles, LA
Gaddy, Rev. Kenneth, *C.Ss.R.* (BAL) Sacred Heart of Jesus-Sagrado Corazon de Jesus, Baltimore, MD
Gade, Rev. Hrudaya Raj, '96 (TLS) Sacred Heart, Fairfax, OK
Gade, Rev. Sagar Kumar, '13 (SAC) Pastor of St. Rose of Lima Parish, Roseville, a corporation sole, Roseville, CA
Gadenz, Rev. Pablo T., '96 (NEW) Curia: Organizations (affiliated, inter-Diocesan, miscellaneous/other) [COL] Seton Hall University, South Orange, NJ
Gadenz, Rev. Pablo T., '96 (TR) On Duty Outside Diocese. Mount St. Mary Seminary, Emmitsburg, MD Curia: Leadership
Gadoury, Rev. Mark Gabriel, '22 (PRO) Saint Luke's Church Corporation, Barrington, Barrington, RI
Gadziala, Very Rev. Timothy A., '94 (ATL) Curia: Leadership; Miscellaneous / Other Offices St. Peter Catholic Church, LaGrange, Inc., LaGrange, GA
Gaesser, Rev. Ronald E., '61 (ROC) Retired.
Gaeta, Rev. Bernard N., '73 (Y) Retired.
Gaeta, Rev. David R., '80 (SLC) Retired.
Gaeta, Rev. Msgr. Francis X., '63 (RVC) Retired. [MON] St Pius X Residence for Retired Priests LLC, Ronkonkoma, NY
Gaetano, Rev. Msgr. Lewis F., '73 (Y) Christ the Servant Parish, Canton, OH
Gaetner, Rev. Stephen A., *O.Praem.* '16 (SFE) [MON] Santa Maria de la Vid Abbey, Albuquerque, NM
Gaffey, Rev. Eugene F., '69 (PRT) Retired.
Gaffey, Rev. Msgr. James P., '60 (SR) Retired. Curia: Leadership
Gaffney, Rev. Andrew, '22 (KCK) Prince of Peace, Olathe, KS; Saint Thomas Aquinas High School, Inc., Overland Park, KS
Gaffney, Rev. David F., '00 (PRO) St. Bernard's Roman Catholic Church of Wickford, Rhode Island, Wickford, RI
Gaffney, Rev. J. Michael, '73 (OG) Retired.
Gaffney, Rev. John, *S.O.L.T.* '09 (CC) [MON] Society of Our Lady of the Most Holy Trinity, Corpus Christi, TX
Gaffney, Rev. William, *C.Ss.R.* '60 (BRK) Retired.
Gaffny, Rev. David J., '57 (NSH) Retired. On Duty Outside Diocese. Columbus Ohio
Gaffrey, Rev. Christopher, *O.F.M.* (MAN) St. Thomas Aquinas, Derry, NH
Gagan, Rev. Charles, *S.J.* (SFR) [EFT] The Megan Furth Memorial Fund, San Francisco, CA
Gagan, Rev. Charles R., *S.J.* '68 (SFR) Mission Dolores

Academy, San Francisco, CA; [MON] Jesuit Community at St. Ignatius College Preparatory, San Francisco, CA
Gagan, Rev. Phillip R., '79 (STA) Retired.
Gage, Rev. George D., '79 (ROM) Retired.
Gage, Rev. Philip S., *S.M.* '69 (WDC) Retired. [MON] Marist Center (The Marist Finance Center of the Atlanta Province of the Society of Mary, Marist Fathers and Brothers), Washington, DC
Gaglia, Rev. Fred R., '63 (SB) Retired.
Gaglione, Rev. John R., '76 (BUF) Retired.
Gaglione, Rev. Joseph B., *C.S.Sp.* '64 (SB) Retired. [MON] Congregation of the Holy Spirit, Hemet, CA
Gagne, Rev. Marc R., '85 (MAN) Curia: Consultative Bodies St. Anne, Hampstead, NH
Gagne, Rev. Roger C., '75 (PRO) Curia: Advisory Boards, Commissions, Committees, and Councils St. Peter's Church, Warwick, Rhode Island, Warwick, RI
Gagne, Rev. Ronald, '66 (DUL) Retired.
Gagne, Rev. Ronald G., *M.S.* '71 (FR) [MON] La Salette Shrine & Retreat Center, Attleboro, MA
Gagnepain, Rev. John F., *C.M.* '62 (STL) [MON] Congregation of the Mission, Perryville, MO
Gagnier, Rev. John F., '78 (ROC) St. Elizabeth Ann Seton, Hamlin, NY
Gagnon, Rev. David, '21 (MAN) St. Joseph, Epping, NH
Gagnon, Rev. Joseph A., '61 (DET) Retired.
Gagnon, Rev. Raymond E., '72 (MAN) Retired.
Gagnon, Rev. Ronald P., '56 (TUC) Retired.
Gago, Rev. Jose Maria, (SAT) Retired. [NUR] Oblate Madonna Residence, San Antonio, TX
Gahagan, Rev. Msgr. William H., '70 (KNX) Retired.
Gahan, Rev. Dermot, '95 (FTW) [COL] University of Saint Francis, Fort Wayne, IN
Gahan, Rev. James L., '68 (STL) Retired. Sts. Joachim and Ann Catholic Church, St. Charles, St. Charles, MO
Gahan, Rev. Timothy, (CHR) Retired.
Gahan, Rev. Timothy M., '07 (CHR) Retired.
Gahng, Rev. Chahm, '15 (MAD) St. Michael the Archangel, Mount Horeb, WI
Gaiardo, Rev. Martin J., '70 (SCR) Retired. Mary, Mother of God Parish, Scranton, PA
Gaines, Rev. David, '14 (SPK) Sacred Heart, Tekoa, WA
Gaines, Rev. Timothy, (DEN) St. Elizabeth in Buffalo Creek, ,
Gaitan, Rev. Raymond, *OAR* (SAT) Retired. [CEM] Resurrection Cemetery, San Antonio, TX
Gajardo, Rev. Leonardo, '06 (GRY) Curia: Offices and Directors St. Maria Goretti, Dyer, IN
Gajda, Rev. Piotr J., '55 (CC) Green Beret Chap, Oklahoma City, OK Curia: (>MO) Offices and Directors
Gajdos, Rev. Msgr. T. George, '70 (MIL) Retired. Curia: Leadership St. James Congregation, Franklin, WI
Gajdzinski, Rev. Norman A., '63 (CLV) Retired.
Gajettan, Rev. Ronald, *HGN* (SEA) St. Mary Magdalen, Everett, WA
Gajewski, Rev. Mariusz, '14 (PAT) On Duty Outside Diocese. Catholic Univ, Lublin, Poland
Gajewski, Rev. Robert, (PAT) [RTR] Hermits of Bethlehem in the Heart of Jesus, Chester, NJ
Gajewski, Rev. Robert S., '07 (NEW) St. Anthony of Padua, Newark, NJ
Galadza, Archpriest Peter, '81 (STN) [MIS] Metropolitan Andrey Sheptytsky Institute of Eastern Christian Studies, Flagstaff, AZ
Galang, Rev. Danilo Corpuz, *M.S.* (HON) Holy Cross, Kalaheo, HI
Galang, Rev. Jose P.A., '78 (SJ) Curia: Offices and Directors
Galang, Rev. Restituto O., *MSP* (SB) St. Margaret Mary, Chino, CA
Galant, Rev. Andrzej, *S.Ch.* '81 (SEA) St. Margaret of Scotland, Seattle, WA
Galarneault, Rev. Thomas, '07 (DUL) St. Columban, Littlefork, MN; St. Thomas Aquinas, International Falls, MN
Galarza, Rev. Edison, *O.C.C.S.S.* '99 (STP) Sacred Heart, St. Paul, MN
Galarza, Rev. Raul Ivan, (SJN) San Francisco Javier, San Juan, PR
Galarza Roldan, Rev. Raul Ivan, '20 (SJN) Maria Llena de Gracia, Trujillo Alto, PR
Galarza-Roldan, Rev. Raul Ivan, (SJN) Curia: Leadership; Offices and Directors
Galasso, Rev. Michael S., '71 (HRT) Retired.
Galati, Rev. Anthony, '21 (P) St. Charles, Portland, OR
Galaviz, Rev. Gerardo, '07 (LA) Curia: Offices and Directors St. Alphonsus, Los Angeles, CA; St. John Chrysostom, Inglewood, CA
Galaz, Rev. Jesse Cayetano, '81 (LA) Retired.
Galazka, Rev. Symeon, *OSB oliv.* '09 (SFE) [MON] Our Lady of Guadalupe Abbey, Pecos, NM
Galazyn, Rev. Szymon A, '16 (BRK) Holy Family - Saint Laurence, Brooklyn, NY
Galbraith, Rev. Michael D., '15 (AJ) Curia: Offices and Directors St. Paul the Apostle, Juneau, AK
Galea, Rev. Michael A., '80 (BR) Congregation Of Our Lady Of Pompeii Roman Catholic Church, Tickfaw, LA, Tickfaw, LA
Galeana, Rev. David, '12 (SR) Curia: Leadership Pastor of St. Peter Catholic Church of Cloverdale, A Corporation Sole, Cloverdale, CA
Galens, Very Rev. Jeffrey R., '90 (ROC) Curia: Deaneries Blessed Trinity, Owego, NY; St. Patrick, Owego, NY
Galens, Rev. Jeffrey R., '90 (NY) Retired. On Leave.
Galeon, Rev. Jhay B., '13 (SAC) Pastor of Holy Cross Parish, West Sacramento, a corporation sole, West Sacramento, CA
Galeone, Rev. Victor, (BAL) Retired.
Galetto, Rev. Paul W., *O.S.A.* '82 (PH) St. Paul, Philadelphia, PA; [MON] Augustinian Community (O.S.A.), Philadelphia, PA
Gali, Rev. Naresh, (SEA) Queen of Angels, Port Angeles, WA; St. Anne Parish, Forks, WA; St. Joseph, Sequim, WA
Gali, Rev. Pradeep, *HGN* '14 (LKC) St. Joan of Arc, Oberlin, LA; St. Joseph, Welsh, LA
Galic, Rev. Msgr. Bernard J., '70 (FTW) Retired.
Galic, Rev. Josip N., *O.F.M.* '66 (CHI) [MON] St. Anthony's Friary, ,
Galicia-Ramirez, Rev. Cain, (MEM) St. Brigid, Memphis, TN
Galido, Rev. Msgr. Ariel A., *M.S.C.* '04 (MI) Cathedral of the Assumption, Majuro, MH; Outer Island Missions, Majuro, MH; [MIS] Catholic Pastoral Center: Ajeltake, Majuro, MH
Galido, Rev. Msgr. Ariel Alaan, *M.S.C.* '04 (MI)
Galier, Very Rev. Victor A., '98 (ATL) St. Anthony of Padua Catholic Church, Atlanta, Inc., Atlanta, GA
Galindo Carreon, Rev. Antonio, *OFM* (OAK) St. Elizabeth, Oakland, CA; [MON] Franciscan Friars of California (Province of St. Barbara), Oakland, CA
Galiyas, Rev. Zachary A., '15 (PIT) St. Isidore the Farmer, Imperial, PA
Gall, Rev. Jacob M., '62 (FTW) Retired.
Gallagher, Rev. Anthony, (TOL) Retired.
Gallagher, Rev. Cathal, '74 (SFS) Retired.
Gallagher, Rev. Charles M., '10 (WDC) Curia: Consultative Bodies Immaculate Conception, Washington, DC; Our Lady of the Wayside, Chaptico, MD
Gallagher, Rev. Charles R., *S.J.* '10 (BO) [MON] The Jesuit Community at Boston College, Chestnut Hill, MA
Gallagher, Rev. Cyrus, *O.F.M.Cap.* '65 (COS) [MON] Our Lady of the Angels Friary, Colorado Springs, CO
Gallagher, Rev. Daniel, '65 (JKS) Retired.
Gallagher, Rev. Dennis, *A.A.* (BO) [MON] Augustinians of the Assumption, Inc., Boston, MA; [MON] Priests of the Assumption, Inc., Brighton, MA
Gallagher, Rev. Edward, *C.M.* '78 (STL) [MON] Congregation of the Mission, Perryville, MO
Gallagher, Rev. Edward, *S.A.* '71 (NY) Retired.
Gallagher, Rev. Gregory R, *O.M.I.* '92 (CR) Most Holy Redeemer, Ogema, MN; St. Benedict (White Earth), White Earth, MN; St. Theodore of Ponsford, Ponsford, MN
Gallagher, Rev. James E., '87 (RIC) Holy Cross, Lynchburg, VA; Our Lady of Peace, Appomattox, VA; St. Victoria, Hurt, VA
Gallagher, Rev. James R., '65 (CHI) Retired. [HOS] OSF Little Company of Mary Medical Center (The Little Company of Mary Hospital and Health Care Centers), Evergreen Park, IL
Gallagher, Rev. Jim, *C.S.C.* '07 (P) [CAM] University of Portland, Portland, OR (>FTW) [SEM] Moreau Seminary, Notre Dame, IN
Gallagher, Rev. John, *OFM Cap.* '78 (NY) Retired. Roman Catholic Church of the Sacred Heart, Yonkers, NY
Gallagher, Rev. Msgr. John Gerald, '57 (CAM) Retired.
Gallagher, Rev. John M., '71 (GB) Retired.
Gallagher, Rev. John P., '80 (DAV) Retired. Curia: Leadership [MON] St. Vincent Center, Davenport, IA
Gallagher, Rev. John P., '68 (PIT) Divine Grace, Cranberry Township, PA
Gallagher, Rev. John R., '93 (WH) Curia: Leadership; Offices and Directors St. Michael, Vienna, WV
Gallagher, Rev. Kevin J., '02 (PH) St. Denis, Havertown, PA
Gallagher, Rev. Kevin P., '83 (ALN) St. Teresa of Calcutta Parish, Mahanoy City, PA
Gallagher, Rev. Martin, '17 (BUF) Blessed Sacrament, Tonawanda, NY; St. Paul, Kenmore, NY
Gallagher, Rev. Michael, *S.J.* (ELP) Sacred Heart, El Paso, TX
Gallagher, Rev. Msgr. Michael J., '66 (SD) Retired.
Gallagher, Rev. Michael J., '69 (WIL) Retired.
Gallagher, Rev. Msgr. Patrick J., '70 (MOB) Retired.
Gallagher, Rev. Patrick M., '10 (MEM) Curia: Leadership Holy Rosary, Memphis, TN
Gallagher, Friar Paul, *OFM* '92 (STL) [MIS] The Franciscan Connection, St. Louis, MO
Gallagher, Rev. Paul, *OFM* (BEL) [MON] St. Benedict the Black Friary, East Saint Louis, IL
Gallagher, Rev. Peter, (CAM) Holy Angels Parish, Woodbury, N.J., Woodbury, NJ
Gallagher, Rev. Richard, '72 (TR) Retired. [MON] Villa Vianney, Trenton, NJ
Gallagher, Rev. Richard, '36 (SEA) Retired.
Gallagher, Rev. Richard, '60 (SEA) Retired. Catholic Chap, Regional Justice Ctr
Gallagher, Rev. Simeon, *O.F.M. Cap.* (DEN) [MON] St. Francis of Assisi Friary, Denver, CO
Gallagher, Rev. Simon P., *O.S.B.* '73 (PAT) Retired. [MON] St. Mary's Abbey, Morristown, NJ
Gallagher, Rev. Steven P., '11 (AJ) St. Paul the Apostle, Juneau, AK
Gallagher, Rev. Thomas, (SJ) [MON] Sacred Heart Jesuit Center, Los Gatos, CA
Gallagher, Rev. Thomas, *OFM* '82 (NY) St. Francis of Assisi, New York, NY
Gallagher, Rev. Msgr. Thomas G., '68 (RVC) Retired.
Gallagher, Rev. Thomas P., *O.S.F.S.* '67 (PH) Resurrection of Our Lord, Philadelphia, PA; [MON] Villa de Sales Oblate Residence, Wyndmoor, PA
Gallagher, Rev. Thomas R., '12 (WH) St. Joseph's, Martinsburg, WV
Gallagher, Rev. Timothy, '09 (ATL) St. Bernadette Catholic Church, Cedartown, Inc., Cedartown, GA
Gallagher, Rev. William G., '53 (RVC) Retired.
Gallant, Rev. Jon-Paul, '78 (FR) Curia: Offices and Directors St. Theresa of the Child Jesus, Attleboro, MA
Gallardo, Rev. Carlos, (COS) Curia: Leadership
Gallas, Rev. John A., '05 (STP) Curia: Consultative Bodies St. Agnes, St. Paul, MN
Galle, Rev. Maciej D., '08 (CHI) Curia: Leadership St. Priscilla, Chicago, IL
Gallego Cifuentes, Rev. Patricio Antonio, (ARE) Perpetual Help, Hatillo, PR; [MIS] Chapel Nuestra Senora de la Milagrosa, Hatillo, PR
Gallegos, Rev. Andres D, *OFM* '15 (SFE) Holy Family-Albuquerque, Albuquerque, NM
Gallegos, Rev. David D, *OSM* (ORG) St. Philip Benizi, Fullerton, CA
Gallegos, Rev. Stephen, *C.M.* '88 (STO) Sacred Heart Church of Patterson (Pastor of), Patterson, CA
Gallegos, Rev. Valentine, '09 (SAT) On Leave.
Gallenstein, Rev. Joseph A., '90 (COV) St. Mary of the Assumption, Alexandria, KY
Gallerini, Rev. Philip G., '62 (SPR) Retired.
Galles, Very Rev. Andrew J., '17 (SC) Curia: Leadership; Offices and Directors Cathedral of the Epiphany, Sioux City, IA
Galley, Rev. Charles "Gino", '19 (SB) St. Andrew Newman Center, Riverside, CA; [CAM] St. Andrew Newman Center, Riverside, CA
Galligan, Rev. Charles H., '87 (PRO) St. Joseph's Church, Ashton, Rhode Island, Cumberland, RI
Gallina, Rev. Leo J., '65 (E) Retired.
Gallinger, Very Rev. Carl, '89 (CHY) Curia: Advisory Boards, Commissions, Committees, and Councils; Consultative Bodies [CCH] Catholic Charities of Wyoming, Inc., Cheyenne, WY; [EFT] Holy Trinity Youth Education Trust, Cheyenne, WY
Gallinger, Very Rev. Carl J., '89 (CHY) Curia: Consultative Bodies; Leadership Church of the Holy Trinity, Cheyenne, WY; St. Joseph, Albin, WY; St. Peter, Carpenter, WY
Gallivan, Rev. Msgr. David M., '66 (BUF) Retired. St. Anthony, Lackawanna, NY
Gallo, Rev. Gerardo D., '85 (NEW) Blessed Sacrament, Elizabeth, NJ
Gallo, Rev. Manuel, (NY) [RTR] Don Bosco Retreat Center and Marian Shrine, Stony Point, NY; [RTR] Marian Shrine, Stony Point, NY
Gallo, Rev. Regis, *O.F.M.* (NY) [MON] Franciscan Province of the Immaculate Conception, New York, NY
Gallo, Rev. Vincent, '60 (BRK) Retired.
Galluzzo, Rev. James, '90 (P) Retired.
Galonek, Rev. David B., '96 (WOR) Retired. Curia: Leadership; Offices and Directors
Galos, Rev. Artemio, '85 (DET) St. Michael Parish Sterling Heights, Sterling Heights, MI
Galuppi, Rev. Michael, '07 (SY) Our Lady of Hope, Syracuse, NY; St. Michael & St. Peter, Syracuse, NY

Galuschik, Very Rev. Steven, '14 (PSC) Curia: Leadership All Saints Byzantine Catholic, North Fort Myers, FL
Galvan, Rev. Alfred, '65 (LSC) Retired.
Galvan, Rev. Michael, (OAK) On Leave.
Galvan Gonzalez, Rev. Omar, '21 (LR) St. Joseph, Tontitown, AR; St. Raphael, Springdale, AR
Galvan Vargas, Rev. Manuel, (MIA) Sacred Heart, Homestead, FL
Galvez, Rev. Arnulfo Jara, '03 (CHR) Blessed Sacrament, Charleston, SC
Galvez, Rev. Elias, *O.F.M.* (TUC) Retired.
Galvez, Rev. Manuel, (MRY) Our Lady of the Assumption, Royal Oaks, CA
Galvez, Rev. Miguel, *S.J.S.* '01 (MAD) Divine Mercy Parish, Sauk City, WI; Holy Cross Parish (St. Barnabas Parish), Mazomanie, WI
Galvez, Rev. Salvador, '87 (NO) Retired.
Galvez Badillo, Rev. Josep Emmanuel, *I.V.E.* '20 (PHX) Immaculate Heart of Mary Roman Catholic Parish, Phoenix, AZ; St. Anthony Roman Catholic Parish, Phoenix, AZ
Galvin, Rev. Edward, *SMA* '62 (NEW) Retired. [MON] Society of African Missions, Provincialate, S.M.A. Fathers, Tenafly, NJ
Galvin, Rev. Garrett, *O.F.M.* '00 (SD) Pastor of Immaculate Conception Catholic Parish, San Diego, a corporation sole, San Diego, CA; [COL] Franciscan School of Theology, San Diego, CA; [MIS] Immaculate Conception Catholic Parish in San Diego, CA Real Property Support Corporation, San Diego, CA
Galvin, Rev. Gregory P., '94 (NOR) Our Lady Queen of Peace Parish, Coventry, CT
Galvin, Rev. James Gerard, '94 (SAT) Retired.
Galvin, Rev. John David, *S.M.* '63 (BO) Retired. (>WDC) [MON] Marist Center (The Marist Finance Center of the Atlanta Province of the Society of Mary, Marist Fathers and Brothers), Washington, DC
Galvin, Rev. John P., '68 (BO) Retired. On Duty Outside Diocese. (>WDC) [COL] Catholic University of America, The, Washington, DC
Galvin, Rev. Shaun, (DEN) Immaculate Conception Catholic Parish in Lafayette, Lafayette, CO
Galvin, Rev. Thomas J., '82 (PIT) Chap, West Penn Allegheny Health Sys-Canonsburg Hosp St. Oscar Romero, Canonsburg, PA; [MIS] Cursillo Movement-Diocese of Pittsburgh, Pittsburgh, PA
Galvis, Rev. Mauricio, (HRT) Saint Paul VI Parish Corporation, Hamden, CT
Galvizo, Rev. Aaron, (ORG) St. Irenaeus, Cypress, CA
Galvo, Rev. Jeudiel, '94 (SPP) Cathedral of the Holy Family, Pago Pago, AS
Galvo, Rev. Jeudiel, '94 (SPP) Curia: Offices and Directors
Gama, Rev. Christopher, *O.F.M.Cap.* '13 (DEN) [MON] St. Anthony of Padua Friary, Denver, CO
Gamache, Rev. Barry J., '81 (PRO) Saint Mary's Church, Bristol, Rhode Island, Bristol, RI
Gamalo, Rev. Augusto L., '16 (TR) St. Benedict, Holmdel, NJ
Gamas, Rev. Giovanni B., '07 (SAC) Pastor of St. John Vianney Parish, Rancho Cordova, a Corporation Sole, Rancho Cordova, CA
Gambaro, Rev. Giampiero, *O.F.M.Cap.* '90 (NY) [EFT] St. Francis of Assisi Foundation, White Plains, NY
Gamel, Rev. Robert, '90 (FRS) On Administrative Leave.
Gameros, Rev. Ignacio L., '81 (TUC) Retired.
Gamez, Rev. Alfonso, '19 (CHL) Our Lady of Mercy, Winston-Salem, NC
Gamez, Rev. Juan Fernando, '92 (CC) Nuestra Senora de San Juan de Los Lagos, Madre de la Iglesia, Corpus Christi, TX
Gamez, Rev. Steven A., '08 (SAT) Curia: Administration SS. Peter and Paul, New Braunfels, TX
Gami, Rev. Eric, (BIR) Our Lady of Sorrows Catholic Parish, Birmingham, Birmingham, AL
Gamino, Rev. Alex, '10 (SB) Our Lady of Perpetual Help, Indio, CA
Gamino, Rev. Juan Victor, *M.N.M.* '94 (ELP) San Elceario, San Elizario, TX
Gamm, Rev. David B., '72 (COV) Retired. St. Joseph, Warsaw, KY
Gammad, Rev. Engelberto, '84 (SJ) St. Joseph, Mountain View, CA
Gamrot, Rev. Jaroslaw S., '91 (WDC) Holy Face, Great Mills, MD
Gancarz, Rev. Eugeniusz, '71 (SP) Retired. Resurrection, Riverview, FL
Gancarz, Rev. John E., '19 (HRT) Curia: Leadership; Offices and Directors
Gancayco, Rev. Richard K., '92 (WDC) St. Mary's Catholic Church, Landover Hills, MD
Gancayo, Rev. Richard K., (WDC) On Sick Leave.
Ganci, Rev. William Philip, '09 (PT) St. John the Evangelist, Pensacola, FL
Gang, Rev. Dennis, *TOR* '76 (STU) [COL] Franciscan University of Steubenville, Steubenville, OH; [MON] Holy Spirit Friary, Steubenville, OH
Ganiel, Rev. Joseph F., '83 (CAM) Holy Child Parish, Runnemede, N.J., Runnemede, NJ
Ganir, Rev. Philip A., *S.J.* '13 (WDC) [MON] The Jesuit Community at Georgetown University, Washington, DC
Ganley, Rev. Thomas P., '85 (MET) On Leave.
Gann, Rev. Sean J., '94 (RVC) Chap Curia: Offices and Directors St. Patrick's, Bay Shore, NY
Gannon, Rev. Bernard J., '71 (CAM) Retired.
Gannon, Rev. Brian P., '97 (BGP) The St. Theresa's Roman Catholic Church Corporation, Trumbull, CT
Gannon, Rev. George, '02 (BAL) Church of the Holy Spirit, Joppa, MD; St. Stephen, Kingsville, MD
Gannon, Rev. James, *O.F.M.* '87 (MIL) [MON] Francis and Clare Friary, Franklin, WI
Gannon, Rev. James Gerard, *OFM* '87 (GB) Assumption of the Blessed Virgin Mary Congregation, Pulaski, WI; St. Casimir Congregation, Krakow, WI; St. Stanislaus Congregation, Hofa Park, WI; [MON] Assumption of B.V.M. Friary, Pulaski, WI
Gannon, Rev. Josephjude C., '03 (BRK) Curia: Organizations (affiliated, inter-Diocesan, miscellaneous/ other) St. Gerard Majella, Hollis, NY
Gannon, Rev. Patrick, '76 (NO) Retired.
Ganser, Rev. Joseph S., '13 (ALN) Sacred Heart, Palmerton, PA
Ganshert, Rev. Msgr. Daniel, '74 (MAD) Retired.
Ganta, Rev. Suresh, *HGN* (IND) St. Anthony of Padua Catholic Church, Morris, Inc., Morris, IN; St. Louis Catholic Church, Batesville, Inc., Batesville, IN
Gantley, Very Rev. Mark J., '91 (HON) Curia: Consultative Bodies; Tribunal
Ganuza, Rev. Felix, *Sch.P.* '76 (NY) St. Ann's School Annunciation, New York, NY; [MON] Calasanzian Fathers (Piarists), New York, NY
Gapayao, Rev. Jay, *S.O.L.T.* '06 (PBL) St. Joseph, Capulin, CO
Gapinski, Rev. Timothy, '14 (SCL) St. Joseph's, Waite Park, MN; St. Michael, St. Cloud, MN
Gappa, Rev. Herbert T., *M.M.* '68 (NY) Retired. [MON] Maryknoll Fathers and Brothers (Catholic Foreign Mission Society of America, Inc.), Ossining, NY
Garand, Rev. J. Douglas, '01 (TOL) St. Augustine, Napoleon, OH
Garanzini, Rev. Michael, *S.J.* (WDC) [ASN] Association of Jesuit Colleges and Universities, Washington, DC; [MON] The Jesuit Community at Georgetown University, Washington, DC
Garapati, Rev. Tulasi Babu, *O.F.M. Cap.* '14 (NEW) St. Francis of Assisi, Hackensack, NJ
Garatea, Rev. Juan M., '59 (B) Retired.
Garaventa, Rev. Louis T., *S.J.* '76 (NY) Xavier High School, New York, NY; [MON] Xavier Jesuit Community, New York, NY
Garbacz, Rev. Marcin Stanislaw, '04 (RC) On Administrative Leave. Without Faculties
Garbarino, Rev. Joseph J., '83 (PAT) St. Ann, Parsippany, NJ
Garbo, Rev. Francis M.P., '90 (SFR) Curia: Advisory Boards, Commissions, Committees, and Councils Mission Dolores Basilica, San Francisco, CA
Garboso, Rev. Joemar, '13 (MET) On Leave.
Garceau, Rev. Hildebrand J., *O.Praem.* '84 (ORG) Archangel Institute (St. Michael's Preparatory School), Silverado, CA; [MON] Norbertine Fathers of Orange, Inc., Silverado, CA
Garces, Rev. Luis Eduardo, (BRK) St. Elizabeth, Ozone Park, NY
Garcia, Rev. Albert, *SS.CC.* '69 (HON) [MON] St. Patrick's Monastery, Honolulu, HI
Garcia, Rev. Alberto, (MIA) Belen Jesuit Preparatory School, Inc., Miami, FL; [EFT] Father Tino Foundation, Inc., Miami, FL; [MON] Belen Jesuit Fathers, Inc., Miami, FL; [MON] Villa Javier, Miami, FL
Garcia, Rev. Alejandro, '21 (BWN) Immaculate Conception, Rio Grande City, TX; St. Paul the Apostle, Rio Grande City, TX
Garcia, Rev. Alonzo M, (TUC) Saint Rita in the Desert Roman Catholic Parish - Vail, Vail, AZ
Garcia, Rev. Andres Arambula, '93 (PH) St. Patrick, Kennett Square, PA; St. Rocco, Avondale, PA
Garcia, Rev. Andrew, *S.J.* '04 (SJ) Most Holy Trinity, San Jose, CA
Garcia, Rev. Andrey, '08 (SJ) Curia: Offices and Directors St. Lucy, Campbell, CA
Garcia, Rev. Brian, '16 (SAT) St. Anthony Parish, San Antonio, TX
Garcia, Very Rev. Brian, '16 (SAT) Curia: Administration
Garcia, Rev. Bryan Anthony, '15 (MIA) Curia: Leadership [SEM] St. John Vianney College Seminary, Inc., Miami, FL
Garcia, Rev. Camilo, '08 (B) Curia: Leadership St. Catherine's, Hagerman, ID; St. Nicholas, Rupert, ID
Garcia, Rev. Camilo, '00 (STO) St. Mary of the Assumption Church (Pastor of), Stockton, CA
Garcia, Rev. Cesar, (ELP) Most Holy Trinity, El Paso, TX; St. Mark, El Paso, TX
Garcia, Rev. Daniel, '20 (LA) Our Lady of Perpetual Help, Downey, CA
Garcia, Rev. David, '75 (SAT) Retired. Curia: Administration
Garcia, Friar David Ulises, *O.Carm.* (JOL) Our Lady of Mount Carmel, Joliet, IL
Garcia, Rev. Dennis M., '00 (SFE) Curia: Offices and Directors Immaculate Conception-Las Vegas, Las Vegas, NM; [CAM] Highlands University Newman Center, Las Vegas, NM
Garcia, Rev. Derlis R., '17 (BWN) Curia: Offices and Directors Prince of Peace, Lyford, TX
Garcia, Rev. Edgar R., *O.M.I.* '85 (BWN) Immaculate Conception Cathedral, Brownsville, TX
Garcia, Rev. Eliberto, (ARL) Cathedral of St. Thomas More, Arlington, VA
Garcia, Rev. Eric I, '17 (MGZ) Church de El Buen Pastor, Mayaguez, PR
Garcia, Rev. Erlin, *I.C.C.* (STA) [SHR] Mission Nombre de Dios and Shrine of Our Lady of La Leche, St. Augustine, FL
Garcia, Rev. Esau, '87 (ORL) Curia: Consultative Bodies Holy Cross, Orlando, FL
Garcia, Rev. Francisco D., '18 (SAT) [NUR] Missionary Servants of St. Anthony (Padua Place), San Antonio, TX
Garcia, Rev. Francisco Gius, '95 (RVC) SS. Cyril and Methodius, Deer Park, NY
Garcia, Rev. Frank, (SAT) Our Lady of Perpetual Help, Selma, TX
Garcia, Rev. Gabriel, *O.F.M.* '99 (AMA) Curia: Advisory Boards, Commissions, Committees, and Councils; Consultative Bodies; Offices and Directors SS. Peter and Paul, Dumas, TX
Garcia, Rev. Gildardo, '85 (MO) Curia: Offices and Directors
Garcia, Rev. Guillermo C., '75 (LA) Retired.
Garcia, Rev. Higinio, '99 (SD) Pastor of Saint Pius X Catholic Parish, Jamul, a corporation sole, Jamul, CA
Garcia, Rev. Isidore, *O.M.I.* '64 (SAT) [NUR] Oblate Madonna Residence, San Antonio, TX
Garcia, Rev. Ismael, (CHI) St. Norbert and Our Lady of the Brook Parish, Northbrook, IL
Garcia, Rev. Jaime A., '08 (PRO) Saint Charles Borromeo Roman Catholic Church, Providence, Rhode Island, Providence, RI
Garcia, Rev. James L., '70 (SFR) Retired.
Garcia, Rev. Jesus, '98 (LA) Our Lady Queen of Angels, Los Angeles, CA
Garcia, Rev. Jesus (Jesse), '14 (GAL) St. Anthony of Padua, The Woodlands, TX
Garcia, Rev. Jet, '97 (DAL) Holy Family Catholic Parish, Van Alstyne, TX; St. Michael Catholic Parish - McKinney, McKinney, TX
Garcia, Rev. Jhakson, '05 (RCK) Church of Holy Apostles, McHenry, IL
Garcia, Rev. Jhon Mario, (KNX) Cathedral of the Most Sacred Heart of Jesus, Knoxville, TN
Garcia, Very Rev. Jorge A., '08 (SB) Curia: Offices and Directors [SEM] Saint Junipero Serra House of Formation, Grand Terrace, CA
Garcia, Rev. Jorge E., (B) Curia: Leadership Immaculate Conception, Buhl, ID
Garcia, Rev. Jose, '64 (GAL) Curia: Leadership
Garcia, Rev. Jose L., (ARE) Retired.
Garcia, Rev. Jose Luis, '00 (BWN) On Leave.
Garcia, Rev. Juan Antonio, *F.M.M.* '95 (FRS) St. Mary, Cutler, CA
Garcia, Rev. Msgr. Juan F., '67 (SPR) Retired.
Garcia, Rev. Lino, *C.S.* (WDC) Our Lady of Fatima Parish, Riverdale, MD; St. Bernard, Riverdale Park, MD
Garcia, Rev. Luis F., '11 (GR) St. Francis de Sales, Holland, MI
Garcia, Rev. Luis G., '97 (MIA) Retired.
Garcia, Rev. Msgr. Luis Javier, '76 (BWN) Immaculate Heart of Mary, Harlingen, TX
Garcia, Rev. Luis Mario, '13 (NEW) St. Joseph the Carpenter (Sisters of St. Joseph, Chestnut Hill), Roselle, NJ
Garcia, Rev. Marcelino, *S.J.* '70 (MIA) [RTR] Ignatian Spirituality Center, Inc. - Manresa Retreat House,

Miami, FL
Garcia, Rev. Marcial I., '95 (VEN) St. Joseph the Worker Parish in Moore Haven, Inc., Moore Haven, FL
Garcia, Rev. Martin, (PHX) Mater Misericordiae Catholic Church, Phoenix, AZ
Garcia, Rev. Martin, (FAJ) Nuestra Senora del Carmen, Culebra, PR
Garcia, Rev. Michael, '15 (SFE) San Francisco de Asis, Ranchos De Taos, NM
Garcia, Rev. Michael A., '15 (MIA) Curia: Clergy and Religious Services; Leadership St. Coleman, Pompano Beach, FL
Garcia, Rev. Michael Augustine, *OP* '81 (CHI) Retired. [MON] St. Pius V Priory, Chicago, IL
Garcia, Rev. Millan, '62 (SFE) Retired.
Garcia, Rev. Msgr. Otto L., '73 (BRK) St. Teresa, Woodside, NY
Garcia, Rev. P. Miguel, *C.Ss.R.* (CGS) Academia San Alfonso, Aguas Buenas, PR
Garcia, Rev. Paolo, '16 (LA) Curia: Offices and Directors
Garcia, Rev. Pedro, '65 (GR) Retired.
Garcia, Rev. Msgr. Pedro F., '64 (MIA) Retired.
Garcia, Friar Philip, *OP* (OAK) [RTR] San Damiano Retreat, Danville, CA
Garcia, Rev. Philip, *OFM* (OAK) [MON] Franciscan Friars of California (Province of St. Barbara), Oakland, CA
Garcia, Rev. Porfirio, '08 (GAL) Immaculate Conception, Houston, TX
Garcia, Rev. Rafael, *S.J.* '93 (ELP) Curia: Advisory Boards, Commissions, Committees, and Councils Sacred Heart, El Paso, TX
Garcia, Rev. Ramon Israel, '15 (HRT) On Administrative Leave.
Garcia, Rev. Raymundo, '74 (TYL) Our Lady of Victory, Paris, TX; St. Joseph, Clarksville, TX
Garcia, Rev. Ricardo, '15 (NY) Our Lady of Angels, Bronx, NY; St. Frances de Chantal, Bronx, NY
Garcia, Rev. Rizalino P., *C.M.* '99 (NY) Holy Rosary, Staten Island, NY; Sacred Heart, Staten Island, NY; St. Joseph-St. Thomas St. John Neumann Parish, Staten Island, NY
Garcia, Rev. Rodolfo, (DAL) St. Francis of Assisi Catholic Parish - Frisco, Frisco, TX
Garcia, Rev. Ruben, '97 (SAT) Cathedral of San Fernando, San Antonio, TX
Garcia, Rev. Salomon, '09 (ATL) St. Joseph Catholic Church, Dalton, Inc., Dalton, GA
Garcia, Rev. Sebastian, (STA) Sacred Heart, Fleming Island, FL
Garcia, Rev. Sergio E., '94 (LA) On Administrative Leave.
Garcia, Rev. Victor, (MIA) Nativity, Hollywood, FL
Garcia, Rev. Yojaneider, '14 (PAT) St. Vincent Martyr, Madison, NJ; [MIS] St. Paul Inside The Walls: The Catholic Center for Evangelization at Bayley-Ellard, Madison, NJ
Garcia Arias, Rev. Msgr. Justiniano, '98 (SJN) [MIS] Opus Dei, Guaynabo, PR
Garcia Arias, Rev. Msgr. Justiniano, '98 (POD) Curia: Leadership
Garcia Blay, Rev. Msgr. Roberto, '86 (PCE) Corazon de Jesus, Ponce, PR
Garcia de Cardenas, Rev. Msgr. Javier, '85 (POD) Curia: Clergy and Religious Services
Garcia Fernandez, Rev. Francisco, (MIA) Our Lady of Lourdes, Miami, FL
Garcia Gil, Rev. Misabet, '18 (CHI) St. Agnes of Bohemia, Chicago, IL
Garcia Morales, Rev. Hector Manuel, *O.Carm* '94 (ARE) Nuestra Senora del Carmen, Morovis, PR
Garcia Ortiz, Rev. Alejandro A, *IVE* (CHI) St. Francis of Assisi, Chicago, IL
Garcia Oviedo, Rev. Jose, (SB) Sacred Heart, Jurupa Valley, CA
Garcia Rodriguez, Rev. Jesus, '94 (SJN) Buen Pastor, Guaynabo, PR
Garcia Vargas, Rev. Guillermo, *C.S.* '88 (LA) Retired.
Garcia-Almodovar, Rev. Angel L., '03 (ALN) St. Margaret, Reading, PA
Garcia-Avila, Rev. Martin, '09 (SAT) Christ the King, San Antonio, TX
Garcia-Chavez, Rev. Luis, (COS) Curia: (>MO) Offices and Directors
Garcia-Concepcion, Rev. Eric Ivan, (MGZ) Curia: Leadership
Garcia-Elizalde, Rev. Enrique, (DM) On Administrative Leave.
Garcia-Ferrer, Rev. Eduardo, '93 (CHI) St. Ansgar, Hanover Park, IL
Garcia-Flores, Rev. Hector, *C.Ss.R.* (CGS) Nuestra Senora de la Mercedes, San Lorenzo, PR
Garcia-Gonzalez, Rev. Francisco Javier, '80 (R) St. Andrew, Red Springs, NC
Garcia-Hernandez, Rev. Alfredo, (BRK) Holy Innocents, Brooklyn, NY
Garcia-Icedo, Rev. Mario, '78 (PHX) St. William Roman Catholic Parish, Cashion, AZ
Garcia-Jimenez, Rev. Gerardo, (DEN) Sacred Heart in Silt, Silt, CO
Garcia-Lora, Rev. Toribio Nicolas, *C.M.F.* (SJN) Casa Mision Claret, Bayamon, PR
Garcia-Maldonado, Rev. Jose Maria, '09 (CHI) San Jose Luis Sanchez del Rio, Chicago, IL
Garcia-Molina, Rev. Rafael, '15 (SJN) Curia: Leadership Sagrada Familia, San Juan, PR; Santos Pedro y Pablo los Apostoles, San Juan, PR
Garcia-Perez, Rev. Msgr. Manuel, '75 (SJN) Cristo Rey, San Juan, PR
Garcia-Ramirez, Rev. Pedro, (AUS) St. John the Evangelist, Marble Falls, TX
Garcias, Rev. Anthony, '16 (LA) Holy Family, Glendale, CA
Garcia-Tunon, Rev. Guillermo, *S.J.* '00 (MIA) Belen Jesuit Preparatory School, Inc., Miami, FL; [MIS] Compania de Jesus, Provincia de las Antillas, LLC, ,
Garcia-Vazquez, Rev. Jaime, '12 (BAL) St. Augustine, Williamsport, MD; St. James Boonsboro, Boonsboro, MD; St. Joseph, Hagerstown, MD
Garcia-Velazquez, Rev. Edgardo, '17 (SAC) Pastor of Holy Cross Parish, Tulelake, a corporation sole, Tulelake, CA
Garcon, Rev. Barthelemy, *S.M.M.* '86 (ORL) St. Andrew, Orlando, FL
Gardin, Rev. Msgr. Vernon E., '71 (STL) Curia: Leadership Immacolata Catholic Church, Richmond Heights, MO
Gardiner, Rev. Christopher B., '68 (MAR) Retired.
Gardiner, Rev. James, *S.A.* '69 (WDC) [MON] Franciscan Monastery USA Inc., Washington, DC
Gardiner, Rev. James, *S.A.* '69 (NY) [MON] Franciscan Friars of the Atonement, Minister General Office, Garrison, NY
Gardiner, Rev. James K., '69 (GLD) Retired.
Gardiner, Rev. Richard E., '67 (WDC) Retired.
Gardner, Rev. Clement, '67 (ALT) Retired.
Gardner, Rev. Daniel, '78 (KCK) St. Ann, Hiawatha, KS; St. Leo, Horton, KS
Gardner, Rev. Jerome J., '79 (CIN) Church of the Resurrection - Bond Hill, Cincinnati, OH; Holy Trinity Church, Cincinnati, OH; Nativity of Our Lord, Cincinnati, OH; St. John the Evangelist, Cincinnati, OH; St. Saviour, Cincinnati, OH
Gardner, Rev. John Paul, '05 (BIS) Cathedral of the Holy Spirit, Bismarck, ND
Gardner, Rev. Thomas, '15 (COL) Sacred Heart, Coshocton, OH; St. Francis de Sales, Newcomerstown, OH; St. Peter, Millersburg, OH; [HOS] Trinity Hospital Twin City, an Affiliate of Catholic Health, Dennison, OH
Gardner, Rev. Thomas J., '10 (PH) On Special Assignment. Newman Chap, W Chester Univ, St Maximilian Kolbe, W Chester St. Patrick, Malvern, PA
Gardner, Rev. Thomas J., '10 (PH) [CAM] West Chester University, West Chester, PA
Gardner, Rev. William M., '92 (PEO) On Duty Outside Diocese.
Gareau, Rev. Timothy W., '88 (CLV) St. Raphael, Bay Village, OH
Gargani, Rev. Francis, *C.Ss.R.* '71 (BRK) [MON] Redemptorist Fathers of New York, Inc.-Baltimore Province, Brooklyn, NY
Gargiulo, Rev. Giuliano, (BAL) Our Lady of Fatima, Baltimore, MD
Gargol, Rev. Sebastian, '12 (JOL) St. Patrick, Manhattan, IL; St. Rose, Wilmington, IL
Garibaldi, Rev. Anthony, *O.F.M.* '76 (SD) [MON] Old Mission San Luis Rey, Oceanside, CA
Garibay, Rev. Zoilo, *O.F.M.Cap.* '13 (MIL) [MON] St. Lawrence Friary, Mount Calvary, WI; [SEM] St. Lawrence Seminary High School, Mount Calvary, WI
Gariboldi, Rev. Ronald J., '61 (BO) Retired.
Gariepy, Rev. Thomas P., *C.S.C.* '74 (FR) [COL] Holy Cross Fathers Religious, North Easton, MA; [COL] Stonehill College, North Easton, MA
Garinger, Rev. Grant S., *S.J.* '97 (MIL) [MON] Jesuit Community at Marquette University (Marquette Jesuit Associates, Inc.), Milwaukee, WI
Garisto, Rev. James, '77 (NY) On Leave.
Garkowski, Rev. John, '66 (BRK) Retired. Our Lady of Perpetual Help, South Ozone Park, NY
Garland, Rev. Brett, '18 (COL) St. Mary, Delaware, OH
Garneau, Rev. James F., '84 (R) On Leave.
Garner, Rev. Andrew, '01 (OWN) On Duty Outside Diocese. Holy Family Church, Ashland
Garner, Rev. Andy, (LEX) Holy Family, Ashland, KY; [CEM] Calvary, Ashland, KY
Garner, Rt. Rev. Joel P., *O.Praem.* '65 (SFE) [MON] Santa Maria de la Vid Abbey, Albuquerque, NM
Garner, Rev. Kirby D., '77 (AUS) Retired.
Garner, Rev. Steven M., '09 (DUB) Holy Spirit Church, Dubuque, Iowa, Dubuque, IA; [CEM] Mount Calvary Cemetery Association, Dubuque, IA
Garnica, Rev. Francisco Honorato, *CSJ* (CLV) Sagrada Familia, Cleveland, OH
Garnier, Rev. David, '09 (GAL) Our Lady of Sorrows, Houston, TX
Garon, Rev. Robert E. J., '05 (LA) St. Didacus, Sylmar, CA; [MIS] Magnificat, A Ministry to Catholic Women West San Fernando Valley Chapter, Santa Susana Knolls, CA
Garone, Rev. Thomas, *O.F.M.* '73 (NY) [RTR] Mt. Alvernia Retreat House, Wappingers Falls, NY
Garramone, Rev. Dominic M., *O.S.B.* '92 (PEO) St. Bede Academy (Benedictine Fathers and Brothers), Peru, IL; [SEM] St. Bede Abbey (Benedictine Society of St. Bede, Benedictine Fathers and Brothers), Peru, IL
Garrett, Rev. Benton, (PT) Chap, Naval Air Station Pensacola
Garrett, Rev. Benton Lee, '06 (WDC) Military Chap Curia: (>MO) Offices and Directors
Garrett, Rev. John C., '04 (TR) The Church of the Resurrection, Delran Township, N.J., Delran, NJ
Garrett, Rev. Mark, (DAL) Cathedral Santuario de Guadalupe, Dallas, TX
Garrett, Rev. Patrick Stuart, '09 (GAL) Curia: Offices and Directors Sts. Simon and Jude, The Woodlands, TX
Garrett, Rev. Scott, '03 (AJ) Curia: Tribunal Holy Rosary, Dillingham, AK
Garrett, Rev. Scott, '03 (FBK) Curia: Leadership
Garrido, Rev. Alejandro, '92 (CHI) St. Anthony of Padua, Cicero, IL
Garrido, Rev. Jose Rafael, (BO) [MON] Noel Chabanel House, Brighton, MA
Garrigan, Rev. Gerard, *O.S.B.* '89 (STL) [MON] The Abbey of St. Mary and St. Louis, St. Louis, MO
Garris, Rev. Eric S., (CLV) Curia: Advisory Boards, Commissions, Committees, and Councils; Clergy and Religious Services Cathedral of St. John the Evangelist, Cleveland, OH
Garrison, Rev. G. Matthew, '04 (LR) Sacred Heart of Mary, Barling, AR; SS. Sabina and Mary Church, Fort Smith, AR
Garrison, Rev. Gary M., '04 (LR) Curia: (>MO) Offices and Directors
Garrity, Rev. Msgr. G. Patrick, '76 (KNX) Retired. St. Albert the Great Church, Knoxville, TN
Garrity, Rev. James, (TLS) [MON] Our Lady of the Annunciation of Clear Creek Abbey, Hulbert, OK
Garrity, Rev. Msgr. Paul V., '73 (BO) Retired.
Garrity, Rev. Robert M., '81 (RCK) On Duty Outside Diocese. Ave Maria Univ, Naples, FL
Garrote, Rev. Sancho, '76 (NY) Chap, Jacobi Med Ctr, Bronx; North Central Bronx Hosp, Bronx Parish of St. Brendan and St. Ann, Bronx, NY
Garrott, Rev. Bill, *O.P.* (WDC) St. Dominic Church & Priory, Washington, DC
Garrou, Rev. Dennis, '11 (DEN) Retired.
Garrow, Rev. Robert, '16 (FTW) Curia: Offices and Directors St. Stanislaus Kostka, New Carlisle, IN; [MIS] The Fort Wayne-South Bend Diocesan Division: World Apostolate of Fatima, The Blue Army, Fort Wayne, IN
Garry, Rev. Michael, (DUL) Our Lady of the Lakes, Pequot Lakes, MN
Garry, Rev. Michael, '13 (DUL) Curia: Leadership All Saints, Brainerd, MN; St. Francis, Brainerd, MN; St. Thomas, Brainerd, MN
Garry, Rev. Ron, '83 (RC) Curia: Leadership St. John, Fort Pierre, SD; [ASN] Priest Retirement and Aid Association/Pension Plan Board, Rapid City, SD
Gartland, Rev. Daniel B., '82 (LFT) Our Lady of Mount Carmel, Carmel, IN
Gartland, Rev. James, *SJ* '93 (LAN) St. Mary Student Parish Ann Arbor, Ann Arbor, MI; [CAM] St. Mary Student Parish, Ann Arbor, MI; [MON] USA Midwest Province of the Society of Jesus - Jesuit Residence, Ann Arbor, MI
Gartland, Rev. Msgr. R. Vincent, '81 (TR) Retired. [MON] Villa Vianney, Trenton, NJ
Garvey, Rev. James W., '76 (PIT) Retired.
Garvey, Rev. Michael, '71 (Y) Retired.
Garvin, Rev. Msgr. Joseph P., '73 (PH) St. Christopher, Philadelphia, PA
Garvin, Very Rev. Keith, '14 (SHP) Curia: Leadership St. Joseph, Zwolle, LA
Gary, Rev. Paul, '84 (CHL) St. Luke, Mint Hill, NC

Garza, Rev. Amador, '85 (BWN) Holy Spirit, Progreso, TX
Garza, Rev. Baldemar, '18 (PHX) St. Margaret Mary Roman Catholic Parish, Bullhead City, AZ
Garza, Rev. Baldemar, '18 (BO) On Duty Outside Diocese.
Garza, Rev. Charlie, (AUS) St. Albert the Great, Austin, TX
Garza, Rev. David, '07 (SFS) Annunciation Parish of Grant County, Revillo, SD; Saint Charles Borromeo Parish of Grant County, Big Stone City, SD
Garza, Rev. Jesus Guadalupe, '15 (BWN) Our Lady Star of the Sea, Port Isabel, TX
Garza, Rev. Jose, '14 (BWN) St. Joseph the Worker, Edinburg, TX
Garza, Rev. Juan G., '02 (WCH) Our Lady of Perpetual Help, Wichita, KS
Garza, Msgr. Roberto, '96 (MIA) Curia: Catholic Charities; Clergy and Religious Services; Leadership; Pastoral Services St. Joachim, Miami, FL; [EFT] Schott Memorial Center Foundation, Inc., Cooper City, FL; [MIS] Pax Catholic Communications, Inc., Miami, FL
Garza, Rev. Steve, (BAK) St. Peter, The Dalles, OR
Garza, Rev. Steve, '19 (BAK) Curia: Offices and Directors
Garzon, Very Rev. Fabio, '86 (KAL) Curia: Catholic Charities; Clergy and Religious Services; Consultative Bodies; Deaneries San Felipe de Jesus, Fennville, MI; St. Basil, South Haven, MI; St. Peter, Douglas, MI
Garzon Pastrana, Rev. Jose, (PHX) Blessed Sacrament Roman Catholic Parish, Tolleson, AZ
Garzon-Pastrana, Rev. Jose Carlos, '12 (NEW) St. Columba, Newark, NJ
Gaskin, Rev. Grantley DaCosta, '06 (WDC) Military Chap Curia: (>MO) Offices and Directors
Gaspar, Rev. Antony J., '98 (LA) St. Barnabas, Long Beach, CA
Gaspar, Rev. John Antonydas, '01 (CHR) Curia: Advisory Boards, Commissions, Committees, and Councils Holy Spirit, Johns Island, SC
Gaspar, Rev. Jonathan M., (BO) Curia: Clergy and Religious Services
Gaspar, Rev. Jonathan M., '04 (BO) Curia: Consultative Bodies St. Mary of the Assumption, Brookline, MA
Gaspar, Rev. Joseph A., (NY) Regina Coeli, Hyde Park, NY
Gaspar, Rev. Joseph C, (RVC) Our Lady of the Snow, Blue Point, NY
Gaspar, Rev. Juan, *O.M.I.* '13 (BEL) [MON] Shrine of Our Lady of the Snows, Belleville, IL
Gaspar, Rev. Kennedy, '10 (GB) Curia: Advisory Boards, Commissions, Committees, and Councils Holy Family, Elcho, WI; St. Joseph, Crandon, WI; St. Mary, Pickerel, WI
Gaspar, Rev. Roach, *O.F.M.Cap.* '15 (MIL) (>CHI) [MON] St. Clare Friary, Chicago, IL
Gasparik, Rev. Francis, *O.F.M.Cap.* '86 (NY) Parish of Holy Cross and St. John the Baptist, New York, NY
Gasparin, Rev. Giampietro, *C.S.J.* '79 (LA) Paraclete High School, Lancaster, CA; St. Junipero Serra, Lancaster, CA
Gasparini, Rev. Louis, *M.C.C.J.* '66 (CIN) [MIS] The Comboni Missionaries Auxiliary, Inc., Cincinnati, OH; [MON] Comboni Missionaries (Verona Fathers)-Comboni Mission Center, Cincinnati, OH
Gaspeny, Rev. Peter J., '83 (SAG) Curia: Offices and Directors Holy Spirit Parish of Saginaw, Saginaw, MI
Gass, Rev. Michael W., '77 (DEN) Retired.
Gaston, Rev. Msgr. James T., (GBG) Retired.
Gaston, Rev. Msgr. James T., '70 (GBG) Curia: Advisory Boards, Commissions, Committees, and Councils; Leadership [NUR] Neumann House, Greensburg, PA
Gately, Rev. R. Troy, '89 (GAL) St. John Vianney, Houston, TX
Gates, Rev. Joseph, '13 (VEN) Curia: Leadership; Miscellaneous / Other Offices St. Frances Xavier Cabrini Parish in Parrish, Inc., Parrish, FL
Gathenya, Rev. John, '86 (ROC) Holy Family Catholic Community, Wayland, NY
Gathungu, Rev. John, '90 (B) St. Charles, Salmon, ID; St. John Paul II Parish, Idaho Falls, ID
Gatitu, Rev. Timothy Kinyua, *I.M.C.* '12 (MET) [MON] Consolata Society for Foreign Missions, North Brunswick, NJ
Gatla, Rev. Pratap, (PHX) Our Lady of Perpetual Help Roman Catholic Parish, Glendale, AZ
Gatlin, Rev. Bernard J., '68 (LA) Retired.
Gatlin, Rev. Jeffrey D., '00 (L) St. Brigid, Vine Grove, KY; St. John the Baptist, Elizabethtown, KY
Gatman, Rev. Ronald, *O.S.B.* '79 (GBG) [MON] Saint Vincent Archabbey, Latrobe, PA
Gatman, Rev. Ronald P., *O.S.B.* '79 (SAV) Benedictine Military School, Savannah, GA; [MON] The Benedictine Priory, Savannah, GA
Gatschet, Very Rev. Fred, '93 (SAL) Curia: Administration; Consultative Bodies Sacred Heart Cathedral Parish, Salina, Inc., Salina, KS; St. Joseph Parish, Brookville, Inc., Brookville, KS
Gatti, Rev. Daniel J., *S.J.* '72 (NY) [MON] America; Residence and Publication Office of the America Press, New York, NY; [MON] Kolhmann Hall Jesuit Community, Bronx, NY
Gatti Florian, Rev. Fabio, *C.M.V.* '97 (ARE) Nuestra Senora de Fatima, Sabana Hoyos, PR
Gatto, Rev. Reynold J., *S.J.* '68 (SJ) [MON] Sacred Heart Jesuit Center, Los Gatos, CA
Gatus, Rev. Josh David, *O.P.* '22 (OAK) (>P) St. Thomas More Catholic Church, Eugene, OR; (>P) [CAM] Lane Community College (St. Thomas More Catholic Church, Eugene, Newman Center), Eugene, OR
Gatzak, Rev. John P., '75 (HRT) Curia: Communications [MIS] ORTV, Inc., Prospect, CT
Gau, Rev. David H., *S.J.* '62 (MIL) [MON] St. Camillus Jesuit Community (Society of Jesus, USA Midwest Province), Wauwatosa, WI
Gauchat, Rev. Eric, *O.F.M.Cap.* '92 (BAL) Divine Mercy Parish, Frostburg, MD; [MON] Our Lady of the Mountains Friary, Cumberland, MD
Gauci, Rev. John, *C.Ss.R.* '59 (BAL) Retired. [SPF] St. John Neuman Residence, Timonium, MD
Gaudet, Rev. Alex, '15 (HT) Curia: Administration
Gaudet, Rev. Alex Gerard, '15 (HT) Christ the Redeemer, Thibodaux, LA
Gaudet, Rev. Joseph A., '57 (BO) Retired.
Gaudio, Rev. Robert, '74 (ROC) On Leave.
Gaudreau, Rev. Bernard E., '75 (BUR) Retired.
Gaudreau, Rev. James E., '69 (BO) On Leave.
Gaudreau, Rev. Walter L., *S.M.* '64 (WDC) Retired. [MON] Marist Center (The Marist Finance Center of the Atlanta Province of the Society of Mary, Marist Fathers and Brothers), Washington, DC
Gaudreau, Rev. Walter L., *S.M.* '64 (BO) [EFT] Senior Religious Trust Fund of Marist Fathers of Boston, Boston, MA
Gaudreault, Rev. Lucien, *S.V.D.* '88 (CHI) Retired. [MON] Divine Word Residence, Techny, IL
Gaughan, Rev. Joseph, '94 (FTW) On Administrative Leave.
Gaughan, Rev. Msgr. Patrick E., '68 (STU) Retired.
Gaughan, Rev. Thomas E., *CSC* (P) [MON] Priests of Holy Cross in Oregon, Inc., Portland, OR
Gaughan, Rev. Tom, *CSC* (P) St. Andre Bessette Church, Portland, OR
Gaul, Rev. Thomas J., '73 (R) Retired.
Gaunay, Rev. Placid, *O.S.B.* '18 (BUR) [MON] The Benedictine Foundation of the State of Vermont, Inc., Weston, VT
Gaunt, Rev. James Joseph, *C.S.B.* '64 (GAL) Retired. [MON] The Basilian Fathers of Dillon House, Houston, TX
Gaunt, Rev. Thomas P., *S.J.* '81 (WDC) [MIS] CARA, Center for Applied Research in the Apostolate, Washington, DC; [MON] The Jesuit Community at Georgetown University, Washington, DC
Gauthier, Rev. Ernest, '62 (KC) Retired.
Gauthier, Rev. John C., '65 (PHX) Retired.
Gautreau, Rev. Henry W., '79 (BR) Retired.
Gauvin, Rev. Maurice O., '86 (FR) Espirito Santo, Fall River, MA; St. Anthony of Padua, Fall River, MA
Gavaler, Rev. Campion P., *O.S.B.* '59 (GBG) [MON] Saint Vincent Archabbey, Latrobe, PA
Gavancho, Rev. Juan C., '07 (CHI) SS. Paul, Agnes, and Kieran Parish, Chicago Heights, IL
Gavin, Rev. Emmett, *O.Carm.* '87 (NEW) Our Lady of Mount Carmel, Tenafly, NJ
Gavin, Rev. Emmett J., *O.Carm.* (PAT) Curia: Leadership
Gavin, Rev. John F., *S.J.* '11 (WOR) [MON] Jesuits of the Holy Cross, Inc., Worcester, MA
Gavin, Rev. Kenneth J., *S.J.* '75 (BRK) [MON] Carroll Street Jesuit Community, Brooklyn, NY
Gavin, Rev. Patrick Arthur, *O.Carm* '97 (SAC) Pastor of Our Lady of Mount Carmel Parish, Fairfield, a Corporation Sole, Fairfield, CA
Gavin, Rev. Thomas M., *S.J.* '75 (NY) [RTR] Mount Manresa Jesuit Retreat House (Society of Jesus), Staten Island, NY
Gavin, Rev. Thomas Michael, *S.J.* '75 (WDC) [MON] The Jesuit Community of St. Aloysius Gonzaga, Washington, DC
Gaviola, Rev. Raul R., '95 (NEW) St. Henry, Bayonne, NJ
Gaviria, Rev. Jesus Antonio, '06 (PAT) St. Jude, Budd Lake, NJ
Gaviria, Rev. Juan Carlos, '13 (MET) Curia: Family Life St. James the Less, Jamesburg, NJ
Gavit, Rev. Steven M., '97 (SAG) Curia: Leadership; Offices and Directors Saint Dominic Parish of Saginaw, Saginaw, MI
Gavitt, Rev. J. Duane, '84 (SCR) St. Rita, Gouldsboro, PA
Gavitt, Rev. J. Duane, (SCR) Holy Redeemer High School, Wilkes-Barre, PA; St. Elizabeth, Bear Creek, PA
Gavotto, Rev. Robert W., *O.S.A.* '64 (SD) Retired. [MON] Augustinian Community, San Diego, CA
Gawed, Rev. Amlesom Gaim, *O.F.M. Cap.* (COS) [MIS] Catholic Center at the Citadel, Colorado Springs, CO; [MON] Solanus Casey Friary, Colorado Springs, CO
Gawienowski, Rev. John, '00 (SPR) Our Lady of the Hills, Haydenville, MA
Gawlik, Rev. Przemyslaw, '16 (PAT) Chap, Morristown Mem Hosp St. Thomas of Aquin, Ogdensburg, NJ
Gawlowski, Rev. Michael R., '02 (DET) St. John the Evangelist Parish Allenton, Allenton, MI
Gawlowski, Rev. Paul, *O.F.M. Conv* '99 (LA) Our Lady of Guadalupe, Hermosa Beach, CA
Gawlowski, Rev. Paul T., *O.F.M.Conv.* '99 (OAK) [MON] Conventual Franciscans (Province of St. Joseph Cupertino) Provincial Center, Castro Valley, CA
Gawronski, Rev. Gerald, '01 (LAN) St. Thomas the Apostle Parish Ann Arbor, Ann Arbor, MI
Gawronski, Rev. Marc A., '91 (DET) Sacred Heart Parish Grosse Ile, Grosse Ile, MI; St. Cyprian Parish Riverview, Riverview, MI; St. Joseph Parish Trenton, Trenton, MI; St. Timothy Parish Trenton, Trenton, MI
Gawrylewski, Rev. Patrick, *O.F.M.* (GRY) Holy Name, Cedar Lake, IN; [MON] Our Lady of Lourdes Friary, Cedar Lake, IN
Gay, Rev. James A., '59 (BGP) Retired.
Gayam, Rev. Francis, '78 (SR) Pastor of Christ the King Catholic Church of McKinleyville, A Corporation Sole, McKinleyville, CA; Pastor of St. Kateri Tekakwitha Catholic Mission of Hoopa, A Corporation Sole, Hoopa, CA; Pastor of St. Mary Catholic Church of Arcata, A Corporation Sole, Arcata, CA; [CAM] Cal Poly Humboldt Newman Center, Arcata, CA
Gayarre, Rev. Eugenio, '61 (ARE) Retired.
Gaydosik, Rev. David L., '87 (STU) Curia: Deaneries Our Lady of Mercy, Lowell, OH; St. John the Baptist, Marietta, OH
Gaynes, Rev. Blair, '12 (STA) Curia: Evangelization Basilica of the Immaculate Conception, Jacksonville, FL; [CAM] Flagler College Catholic Fellowship, St. Augustine, FL
Gaynor, Rev. Santiago (Jim), (COL) St. James the Less, Columbus, OH
Gaytan, Rev. Jose Alfredo, *S.O.L.T.* '82 (LAR) Retired.
Gaytan, Rev. Rene, '15 (BWN) Our Lady of Good Counsel, Brownsville, TX
Gaytan Ramirez, Rev. Rodolfo, '02 (CHI) St. Anne, Barrington, IL
Gayton, Rev. John J., '86 (WIL) Holy Rosary, Claymont, DE
Gaza, Rev. J. Patrick, '68 (GRY) Retired.
Gaza, Rev. Kerwin, (PAT)
Gazdowicz, Very Rev. Krzysztof, '04 (SP) Curia: Pastoral Services Sacred Heart, Dade City, FL
Gazzingan, Rev. Mark, '07 (SJ) St. Victor, San Jose, CA
Gazzingan, Rev. Michael, '03 (SJ) St. Nicholas and St. William Catholic Parish, Los Altos, CA
Gbedey, Rev. Mebounou, (MIA) Our Lady of Guadalupe, Doral, FL
Gbur, Rev. Andrzej, *O.C.D.* '98 (GRY) [MON] Discalced Carmelite Fathers Monastery, Munster, IN
Geaney, Rev. James, *O.Carm.* '59 (JOL) Retired.
Geaney, Rev. John, *CSP* (BO) Retired. [MON] Missionary Society of St. Paul the Apostle in Massachusetts, Boston, MA
Geaney, Rev. John, *CSP* (BRK) [EFT] The Paulist Foundation, Inc., Jamaica Estates, NY
Geany, Rev. Nash P., (NY) Chap, Stewart Field
Gearhart, Rev. Lawrence, (CIN) St. Teresa of the Child Jesus, Springfield, OH
Gearheard, Rev. William, '94 (ALX) Rapides Rgnl Med Ctr, Alexandria St. Francis Xavier Cathedral, Alexandria, LA
Gearing, Rev. Barry T., '00 (CLV) St. John Neumann, Strongsville, OH
Geary, Rev. Brian, '22 (JOL) Holy Family, Shorewood, IL
Geary, Rev. Brian A., '98 (RCK) St. James, Belvidere, IL
Gebbia, Rev. Gregory, (ALB) [COL] Siena College, Loudonville, NY
Gebelein, Rev. Gary M., '74 (STL) Retired.
Gebhard, Rev. Robert L., '87 (BUF) Blessed Trinity,

Buffalo, NY
Gebhardt, Rev. Paul L., '91 (CIN) Holy Family, Middletown, OH; Holy Name, Trenton, OH; Our Lady of Sorrows, Monroe, OH
Gebremichael, Rev. Abayneh, '96 (BO) Curia: Pastoral Services
Gebremichael, Rev. Abayneh Franswa, *Rev* '96 (WDC) [MIS] Kidane-Mehret Ge'ez Rite Ethiopian Catholic Church, Washington, DC
Geders, Rev. Joseph C., *C.M.* '84 (STL) Christ the Savior Catholic Church, Perryville, MO; Our Lady of Victory Catholic Church, Perryville, MO; St. Rose of Lima Catholic Church, Silver Lake, Perryville, MO; St. Vincent De Paul Catholic Church, Perryville, Perryville, MO; [MON] Congregation of the Mission, Perryville, MO
Geditz, Rev. Roger, '69 (SFS) Retired.
Gedney, Rev. A.J., '22 (COV) Holy Cross, Covington, KY
Gee, Rev. Daniel N., '95 (ARL) St. John the Baptist, Front Royal, VA
Geer, Rev. Stephen, '06 (P) Retired.
Geerling, Rev. Steven, '17 (GR) On Leave.
Geers, Friar Fran, *OFM* '60 (CIN) Retired.
Geers, Rev. Frank, *O.F.M.* '58 (CIN) Retired.
Geers, Rev. Frank, *OFM* '60 (CIN) Retired.
Geers, Rev. Harold, *O.F.M.* '60 (CIN) [MON] St. Francis Seraph Friary, Cincinnati, OH
Geffrard, Rev. Yves, '01 (PMB) Curia: Offices and Directors Notre Dame Mission, Fort Pierce, FL
Geger, Rev. Bart, (BO) [MON] Walter Ciszek House, Brighton, MA
Gegotek, Rev. Tadeusz, (MO) Curia: Offices and Directors
Gegotek, Rev. Tadeusz Jozef, '91 (BEL) Retired.
Gehling, Rev. Kenneth B., '62 (DUB) Retired.
Gehring, Rev. Robert P., '66 (GRY) Retired.
Gehringer, Rev. Andrew N., '00 (ALN) Curia: Leadership Holy Infancy, Bethlehem, PA; Incarnation of Our Lord Parish, Bethlehem, PA
Geib, Rev. Harry F., *S.J.* '92 (WDC) [MON] The Jesuit Community of St. Aloysius Gonzaga, Washington, DC
Geiger, Rev. Christopher M., '16 (CIN) [SEM] Mount St. Mary's Seminary of the West, Cincinnati, OH
Geiger, Rt. Rev. Damon, '71 (NTN) Retired. Curia: Consultative Bodies
Geiger, Rev. James, *C.Ss.R.* (HBG) Retired.
Geiger, Rev. Michael A., '02 (TOL) Most Blessed Sacrament, Toledo, OH
Geinzer, Rev. Eugene M., *S.J.* (PH) [MON] Arrupe Jesuit Community, Merion Station, PA
Geinzer, Rev. John A., '67 (PIT) Retired.
Geinzer, Rev. Patrick, *C.P.* '95 (PIT) [RTR] St. Paul of the Cross Retreat Center, Pittsburgh, PA
Geinzer, Rev. Patrick, *C.P.* (BRK) [MON] Immaculate Conception Monastery, Jamaica, NY
Geinzer, Rev. Patrick, *C.P.* '95 (NY) [MON] The Congregation of the Passion - St. Paul of the Cross Province, Jamaica, NY
Geis, Rev. John F., '64 (IND) Retired.
Geiser, Rev. Allen A., '90 (GB) Retired.
Geleney, Rev. Joseph, '01 (AUS) St. Mary of the Assumption, Waco, TX
Gelfant, Rev. Michael L., '05 (BRK) Blessed Trinity Roman Catholic Church, Rockaway Point, NY
Gelfenbien, Rev. Gary Paul, '71 (ALB) Retired.
Gelido, Rev. Manuel T., '79 (WH) St. Joseph's, Martinsburg, WV
Geller, Rev. Charles H., '73 (BEL) Retired.
Gelmetti, Rev. Jean-Michael, *C.S.Sp.* (PIT) [COL] Duquesne University of the Holy Spirit, Pittsburgh, PA
Gelson, Rev. James N., *S.J.* '60 (BAL) [MIS] Colombiere Jesuit Community, Baltimore, MD
Gembala, Rev. Joseph J., '87 (DET) Curia: Administration; Consultative Bodies St. Malachy Parish Sterling Heights, Sterling Heights, MI
Gemme, Rev. Stephen M., '02 (WOR) On Special Assignment. St Vincent Hosp, Worcester
Gemza, Rev. Richard J., '95 (BGP) Christ the King Roman Catholic Church Corporation, Trumbull, CT
Genabia, Rev. Joel S., '03 (SAC) Curia: Leadership; Offices and Directors Pastor of Holy Spirit Parish, Fairfield, a corporation sole, Fairfield, CA
Genao, Rev. Rumando Peralta, *C.R.L.* (NY) St. Teresa of Avila, Sleepy Hollow, NY
Gendreau, Rev. Claude R., '93 (PRT) On Special Assignment. St Res Peter Rectory, Portland Curia: Consultative Bodies; Offices and Directors [MIS] St. Bartholomew Church, Cape Elizabeth, ME
Gendron, Rev. Michael E., '95 (MAN) Curia: Consultative Bodies; Tribunal Holy Rosary, Hooksett, NH; St. John the Baptist, Suncook, NH; St. Peter, Auburn, NH
Genereux, Rev. Wayne C., '97 (SP) Blessed Trinity, St. Petersburg, FL
Generose, Rev. Anthony J., (SAM) Curia: Leadership
Generose, Rev. Anthony J., '99 (SCR) Curia: Leadership Church of the Most Precious Blood, Hazleton, PA; Queen of Heaven, Hazleton, Hazelton, PA
Geng, Rev. Dennis, *O.C.D.* '89 (MIL) [MON] Washington Province of Discalced Carmelite Friars, Inc., Milwaukee, WI
Gengaro, Rev. Nicholas S., '81 (NEW) [COL] Seton Hall University, South Orange, NJ
Genito, Rev. Joseph A., *O.S.A.* '75 (PH) St. Thomas of Villanova Parish, Rosemont, PA
Genito, Rev. Walter, '19 (NY) St. Columba, Hopewell Junction, NY
Genovesi, Rev. James, '71 (LC) On Special Assignment. Our Lady of the Bl. Sacrament Hermitage, Custer
Genovesi, Rev. Vincent J., *S.J.* '69 (PH) Retired. [MIS] Jesuit Fathers, , ; [MON] Jesuit Community at St. Joseph's University, Merion Station, PA
Gensler, Rev. Gael, *O.S.F.* (CHI) St. Francis of Assisi, Orland Park, IL
Gente, Rev. Msgr. Gilbert C., '93 (GBG) St. Mary, Freeport, PA
Gentile, Rev. Carl J., '60 (PIT) Retired.
Gentile, Rev. Robert A., '03 (SPR) Blessed Sacrament, Holyoke, MA
Gentile, Rev. Thomas E., '73 (L) Retired. Mary Queen of Peace Parish, Louisville, KY
Gentili, Rev. Msgr. Joseph P., '87 (PH) Our Lady of Guadalupe, Doylestown, PA
Gentleman, Rev. Gerard J., '97 (RVC) Holy Trinity Diocesan High School, Hicksville, NY; The Roman Catholic Church of Saint Rose of Lima, Massapequa, NY
Gentry, Rev. Michael C., '13 (COL) Holy Cross, Columbus, OH
Gentry-Akin, Rev. David, '14 (STO) On Duty Outside Diocese. Venerable English College, Rome Italy
Genuardi, Rev. Gasper A., '68 (PH) Retired.
Geoghegan, Rev. James, *O.C.D.* '60 (SJ) [MON] Carmelite Monastery, Novitiate, San Jose, CA
George, Rev. Baby, (FWT) St. Mark, Argyle, TX
George, Rev. Benny, *C.M.I.* '88 (LA) (>BEL) St. Barbara, Scheller, IL; (>BEL) St. Mary the Immaculate Conception, Mount Vernon, IL
George, Rev. Msgr. David, (SPR) Holy Cross, Springfield, MA
George, Rev. Msgr. David M., '76 (SAM) Retired.
George, Rev. Figi Philip, *CMI* (STA) Queen of Peace Catholic Community, Gainesville, FL
George, Rev. Francis M., '87 (LAN) St. John the Baptist Parish Howell, Howell, MI
George, Rev. Gary, (SAM) Mary Mother of the Light Maronite Catholic Church, Tequesta, FL
George, Rev. George C., '86 (SYM) St. Thomas Syro-Malabar Catholic Church of San Antonio, San Antonio, TX
George, Rev. Jacob, (MO) Curia: Offices and Directors
George, Rev. Jacob C., '95 (WDC) St. Elizabeth, Rockville, MD
George, Rev. Jacob C., (PRT) Chap, Togus VA Med Ctr
George, Rev. Jerish, *MOC* '91 (LKC) Our Lady Star of the Sea, Cameron, LA; Sacred of Heart of Jesus Catholic Church, Cameron, LA; St. Eugene, Grand Chenier, LA
George, Rev. Jilson, *CMI* '00 (BO) [MIS] St. Theresa Carmelite Chapel, Peabody, MA
George, Rev. Jofin, '09 (JKS) St. Jude, Pearl, MS
George, Rev. Johnykutty, '97 (SYM) St. Joseph Syro-Malabar Catholic Church, Missouri City, TX
George, Rev. Jolly, '05 (BIS) St. Peter - Catholic Indian Mission, Fort Yates, ND; [MIS] Oratory of Sacred Heart, Solen, Solen, ND; [MIS] Oratory of St. James, Porcupine, Porcupine, ND; [MIS] Oratory of St. Philomena, Selfridge, Selfridge, ND
George, Rev. Lloyd D., *S.J.* '73 (BAL) Retired. [COL] Jesuit Community of Loyola University, Inc., Baltimore, MD; [MIS] Colombiere Jesuit Community, Baltimore, MD; [MON] Jesuit Community of Loyola University Maryland, Inc., Baltimore, MD
George, Rev. Madhu, '98 (TUC) Our Lady of the Blessed Sacrament Roman Catholic Church - Miami, Miami, AZ
George, Rev. Mani, *M.C.* (LEX) St. Gregory, Barbourville, KY; St. William, London, KY; [CAM] St. Gregory Church-Union College, Barbourville, KY
George, Rev. Mark, *S.J.* '98 (DET) [MON] Jesuit Community at the University of Detroit Mercy, Detroit, MI
George, Rev. Philip, '99 (RNO) Curia: Leadership; Offices and Directors Immaculate Conception, Sparks, NV
George, Very Rev. Rejimon, *C.M.I.* '03 (BEA) Curia: Leadership St. Elizabeth, Port Neches, TX; St. Therese the Little Flower of Jesus, Port Arthur, TX
George, Rev. Richard E., '95 (PMB) Curia: Leadership St. Anastasia, Fort Pierce, FL
George, Rev. Robert J., '95 (ALN) Marian High School, Inc., Tamaqua, PA; St. Joseph, Summit Hill, PA
George, Rev. Robert J., '76 (PIT) Retired.
George, Rev. Santhosh, *O.SS.T.* '07 (BAL) St. Mark, Catonsville, MD; [MON] Holy Trinity Monastery, Sykesville, MD
George, Rev. Sebastian K., *C.M.I.* '80 (STA) St. Joseph, Jacksonville, FL
George, Rev. Sijo Muthanattu, '09 (BRK) Most Precious Blood – Ss. Simon and Jude, Brooklyn, NY
George, Rev. Sojan, *H.G.N.* '00 (FWT) St. Francis of Assisi, Grapevine, TX
George, Rev. Tijo, *M.C.B.S.* '08 (WH) Our Lady of Fatima, Huntington, WV; St. Stephen, Ona, WV
George, Rev. Varghese, *MST* (SYM) Holy Trinity Syro-Malabar Catholic Church, Delaware, Inc. of St. Thomas Syro-Malabar Catholic Diocese of Chicago, Hammonton, NJ; St. Jude Syro-Malabar Catholic Church, South Jersey of St. Thomas Syro-Malabar Catholic Diocese of Chicago, Inc., Hammonton, NJ
George, Rev. Vensus, *S.A.C.* (BAL) St. Jude Shrine, Baltimore, MD
George, Rev. Vinod Madathiparambil, '98 (SYM) Curia: Administration St John Paul 2 Syro Malabar Catholic Church Inc., Loganville, GA; St. Alphonsa Syro-Malabar Catholic Church, Atlanta, Loganville, GA
George, Rev. Vipin, *MSFS* (GAL) Holy Rosary, Rosenberg, TX; St. Wenceslaus Mission, Beasley, TX
George, Rev. William, *SJ* '73 (WDC) [MON] The Jesuit Community at Georgetown University, Washington, DC
George, Rev. William L, *S.J.* '73 (WDC) [EFT] Gregorian University Foundation, Washington, DC
George-Obilonu, Rev. Kingsley, '98 (TLS) St. Joseph's, Krebs, OK
Georgia, Rev. Msgr. John J., '75 (HRT) Curia: Advisory Boards, Commissions, Committees, and Councils The Church of the Resurrection, Wallingford, CT
Gepiga, Rev. Rufino J.O., '99 (SFR) St. Matthew, San Mateo, CA
Gera, Rev. Francis, '64 (PSC) Retired.
Geraci, Rev. Anthony J., '75 (CIN) Retired.
Geraci, Rev. Kenneth, *C.P.M.* '12 (OWN) [MON] Fathers of Mercy, Auburn, KY
Geraghty, Rev. Msgr. Martin T., '64 (BRK) Retired. St. Robert Bellarmine, Bayside, NY
Gerald, Rev. John J., '82 (SC) St. Joseph's, Jefferson, IA
Gerber, Rev. Anthony J., '11 (STL) Sacred Heart Catholic Church, Florissant, Florissant, MO
Gerber, Very Rev. Brian C., '08 (MAR) Curia: Advisory Boards, Commissions, Committees, and Councils Our Lady of Peace, Ironwood, MI
Gerber, Rev. Martin, '76 (ORL) Retired.
Gerber, Rev. Nicholas, '15 (AMA) Blessed Sacrament, Amarillo, TX
Gerber, Rev. Canon Nicholas J., '08 (AMA) Curia: Advisory Boards, Commissions, Committees, and Councils; Consultative Bodies; Offices and Directors
Gerena Lopez, Rev. Roberto C., '19 (ARE) On Duty Outside Diocese. Nuestra Senora del Mar, Manati, PR
Gerg, Rev. Joseph U., *O.S.B.* '65 (GBG) [MON] Saint Vincent Archabbey, Latrobe, PA
Gergel, Rev. Stephen J., '62 (ALT) Retired. On Leave.
Gergel, Rev. Stephen J., '62 (SAV) Retired.
Gergen, Rev. Michael, *SDB* '79 (LA) St. Dominic Savio, Bellflower, CA
Gerhart, Rev. Gregory Don, '16 (AUS) Curia: Leadership
Geris, Rev. Thierry, '09 (SJ) Retired.
Gerl, Rev. Robert, '79 (LAN) Retired.
Gerlach, Rev. Grant, '14 (RC) Sacred Heart, Philip, SD; St. Anthony of Padua, Hot Springs, SD; St. William, Midland, SD
Gerlach, Rev. Matthew J., '96 (TLS) On Special Assignment. Ascension St John, Broken Arrow Curia: Offices and Directors St. Anne, Broken Arrow, OK
Gerlach, Rev. Michael J., '82 (PH) SS. Simon and Jude, West Chester, PA
Gerlach, Rev. William P., '04 (FAR) Nativity Church of Fargo, Fargo, ND
Gerlich, Rev. Robert, '80 (BO) [MON] The Jesuit Community at Boston College, Chestnut Hill, MA
Gerlich, Rev. Robert S., *S.J.* '80 (NO) Retired.
Germain, Rev. Levelt, '02 (NY) Parish of Saint Joseph/ Saint Boniface, Spring Valley, NY
German, Rev. Michael J., '68 (NEW) Retired. [MON] St. John Vianney Residence for Retired Priests, Rutherford, NJ

Gernetzke, Rev. Christopher, '15 (MAD) St. Martin of Tours, Cross Plains, WI; St. Peter Catholic Church, Middleton, WI

Gerona, Rev. Rene F., *S.V.D.* '13 (WH) Curia: Offices and Directors St. John the Evangelist, Summersville, WV

Geronimo, Rev. Generoso, '92 (SJ) St. Martin of Tours, San Jose, CA

Geronimo, Rev. Jerald, '22 (SFR) Cathedral of St. Mary (Assumption), San Francisco, CA

Gerosa, Rev. Julian, *C.R.S.* '78 (GAL) Christ the King, Houston, TX

Gerovac, Rev. Ivan, *S.J.* '72 (LA) Retired. Mary Star of the Sea, San Pedro, CA

Gerres, Rev. Daniel W., '66 (WIL) Retired.

Gerritts, Very Rev. John R., '91 (SUP) Curia: Leadership; Offices and Directors Assumption of the Blessed Virgin Mary, Osceola, WI; Assumption of the Blessed Virgin Mary, Rice Lake, WI; Immaculate Conception, Grantsburg, WI; Sacred Heart of Jesus Church, Almena, WI; St. Ann, Turtle Lake, WI; St. Anne, Somerset, WI; St. Anthony Abbot, Cumberland, WI; St. Boniface, Chetek, WI; St. Dominic, Frederic, WI; St. Joseph, Barron, WI; St. Joseph, Osceola, WI; St. Patrick, Hudson, WI; St. Peter, Cameron, WI

Gersbach, Rev. Karl A., *O.S.A.* '61 (CHI) [MON] St. John Stone Friary, Chicago, IL

Gerth, Rev. Kenneth, *M.C.C.J.* '65 (CIN) [MON] Comboni Missionaries (Verona Fathers)-Comboni Mission Center, Cincinnati, OH

Gerth, Rev. Kenneth, *M.C.C.J.* '64 (SP) [HOS] St. Joseph's Hospital, Inc., Tampa, FL

Gerut, Rev. William, *S.J.* '67 (MIL) [MON] St. Camillus Jesuit Community (Society of Jesus, USA Midwest Province), Wauwatosa, WI

Gervacio, Rev. Adrian R., '67 (HON) Retired. Our Lady of the Mount, Honolulu, HI

Gervasio, Rev. Msgr. Thomas N., '82 (TR) Curia: Leadership Our Lady of Sorrows-St. Anthony Parish, Hamilton, NJ

Gese, Rev. David, '78 (SEA) Retired. [MIS] Catholic Pastoral Care - Hospital Tacoma Ministry, Tacoma, WA

Gessler, Rev. James, *SMA* '63 (NEW) Retired. [MON] Society of African Missions, Provincialate, S.M.A. Fathers, Tenafly, NJ

Getigan, Rev. Bernard, '85 (SAN) St. Mary's Church, Odessa, TX

Getigan, Rev. Bernardito, '85 (SAN) Curia: Advisory Boards, Commissions, Committees, and Councils

Getsy, Rev. John, *O.F.M.Cap.* '66 (PIT) [MON] St. Augustine Friary, Pittsburgh, PA

Gettinger, Rev. Msgr. Robert J., '64 (STL) St. Augustine Catholic Church, St. Louis, MO

Geurtz, Rev. Gary, '81 (FWT) Retired.

Gevera, Rev. Peter, (MO) Curia: Offices and Directors

Geyman, Rev. Donald R., '96 (GLD) Curia: Leadership Saint Francis of Assisi of Traverse City, Traverse City, MI

Ghani, Rev. Adnan, *O.S.A.* '19 (SD) [MON] Augustinian Community, San Diego, CA

Ghanoum, Rt. Rev. Exarch Gabriel, *B.S.O.* '93 (NTN) St. Nicholas, Delray Beach, FL

Ghattamaneni, Rev. Jayaraju, *SJ* '16 (OAK) [MON] Jesuit Fathers and Brothers, Berkeley, CA

Ghattas, Rev. Rafael Boshra, '21 (CHR) Curia: Advisory Boards, Commissions, Committees, and Councils John Paul II Catholic School, Ridgeland, SC; St. Gregory the Great, Bluffton, SC

Ghazarian, Rev. Tavit, (OLN)

Ghebray, Rev. Araia Ghiday, '81 (WDC) Chap, St Elizabeths Hosp (Government Operated), Washington Holy Comforter - St. Cyprian, Washington, DC; Kidane-Mehret Ge'ez Rite Catholic Church, Washington, DC

Gherardi, Rev. Marc, *O.S.F.S.* '08 (WIL) [MON] Wilmington-Philadelphia Province of the Oblates of St. Francis de Sales, Wilmington, DE

Ghezzi, Rev. Richard G., '86 (SCR) Retired. Our Lady of Hope Parish, Wilkes-Barre, PA

Ghiloni, Rev. Mark V., '83 (COL) Retired. Church of the Blessed Sacrament, Newark, OH

Ghiorso, Rev. David A., '81 (SFR) St. Charles, San Carlos, CA; St. Matthias, Redwood City, CA

Ghyselinck, Rev. Mark, *C.S.C.* '88 (P) [MON] Priests of Holy Cross in Oregon, Inc., Portland, OR

Giacabazi, Rev. Vincent, *S.J.* '15 (KC) Rockhurst High School, Kansas City, MO; [MON] St. Peter Claver Jesuit Community, Kansas City, MO

Giacona, Rev. Anthony, '17 (NY) Immaculate Conception, Port Jervis, NY; St. John the Evangelist, Goshen, NY

Gialogo, Rev. Msgr. Agustin, '73 (STO) St. Michael Church of Stockton (Pastor of), Stockton, CA

Giamello, Rev. Anthony, '05 (WIL) Chap, Delaware Air National Guard, New Castle Curia: (>MO) Offices and Directors St. John the Apostle, Milford, DE

Giampietro, Rev. Anthony E., *C.S.B.* '93 (WDC) St. Anselm's Abbey School, Inc, Washington, DC; [MIS] Fellowship of Catholic Scholars, Washington, DC

Giandurco, Rev. Msgr. Joseph R., '87 (NY) Curia: Leadership St. Patrick, Yorktown Heights, NY; [MIS] The Cardinal Cooke Guild, Yorktown Heights, NY

Giannamore, Rev. Msgr. Anthony J., '56 (STU) Retired.

Gianni, Rev. Vincent J., '70 (BO) Retired.

Giannini, Very Rev. Stephen W., '93 (IND) Curia: Leadership SS. Francis and Clare of Assisi Catholic Church, Greenwood, Inc., Greenwood, IN; St. Martin of Tours Catholic Church, Martinsville, Inc., Martinsville, IN; [MIS] Indianapolis South Deanery, Indianapolis, IN

Giannitelli, Rev. Michael C., '91 (NOR) St. Philip the Apostle, Ashford, CT

Giannone, Rev. Ronald, *O.F.M.Cap.* '90 (WIL) [MIS] Sacred Heart Oratory, Inc., Wilmington, DE; [MON] St. Felix Friary, Wilmington, DE; [SPF] Ministry of Caring, Wilmington, DE

Giannoni, Friar Gregory, *O.F.M.* (WDC) [MON] Franciscan Monastery USA Inc., Washington, DC

Gianola, Rev. William, '62 (CHY) Retired.

Giap, Rev. Damien V., *O.Praem.* '07 (ORG) St. John the Baptist, Costa Mesa, CA; [MON] Norbertine Fathers of Orange, Inc., Silverado, CA

Giardina, Rev. Robert J., '76 (PRO) SS. Peter and Paul's Church, Phoenixville, Rhode Island, West Warwick, RI

Giardini, Rev. Alessandro, '19 (PH) Saint Teresa of Calcutta, Schwenksville, PA

Gibbens, Rev. Randy, (GAL) Jesuit Cristo Rey High School of Houston, Inc. (Cristo Rey Jesuit College Preparatory School of Houston, Inc.), Houston, TX

Gibbons, Rev. Donald Patrick, '91 (SFD) St. Cecilia, Glen Carbon, IL

Gibbons, Rev. Ian R., *S.J.* '06 (STL) St. Louis University High School, George H. Backer Memorial, St. Louis, MO; [MON] Saint Jean de Brebeuf Jesuit Community, St. Louis, MO

Gibbons, Rev. James, *OMI* '61 (SAT) Retired. [NUR] Oblate Madonna Residence, San Antonio, TX

Gibbons, Friar John, *O.F.M.* '01 (TUC) San Solano Missions Roman Catholic Parish - Topawa, Topawa, AZ; [MON] San Francisco Solano Friary, Topawa, AZ

Gibbons, Rev. Msgr. John, '60 (TR) Retired.

Gibbons, Rev. John M., '10 (ALT) Chap, Sacr Min, State Corr Inst - Rockview Our Lady of…

Gibbons, Rev. John M., '89 (ALN) Immaculate Conception, Allentown, PA; Sacred Heart of Jesus, Allentown, PA

Gibbons, Rev. Joseph Marie of Jesus, *M.Carm.* '10 (CHY) On Special Assignment. In Res, Monks of the Most Blessed Virgin Mary of Mt Carme... [MON] Monks of the Most Blessed Virgin Mary of Mt. Carmel (Carmelite Monks), Meeteetse, WY

Gibbons, Rev. Msgr. Robert C., '81 (SP) Curia: Leadership; Pastoral Services St. Paul, St. Petersburg, FL; [MIS] Partners with Haiti, Inc., St. Petersburg, FL

Gibbons, Rev. Thomas C., *C.S.P.* '12 (LA) St. Paul the Apostle, Los Angeles, CA

Gibbons, Rev. Tom, (LA) [MIS] Paulist Productions, Los Angeles, CA

Gibbs, Rev. Alexander R., '15 (PH) On Duty Outside Diocese. St. Albert the Great, Huntingdon Valley, PA

Gibbs, Very Rev. Phillip G., '94 (DUB) On Special Assignment. Dean of the Dubuque Deanery Church of the Resurrection, Dubuque, Iowa, Dubuque, IA; [EFT] Declaration of Trust of the Paul & Janet Auterman Charitable Educational Trust, Dubuque, IA

Gibino, Very Rev. Joseph R., '81 (BRK) Curia: Consultative Bodies; Pastoral Services Holy Trinity, Whitestone, NY; [MIS] Office of Faith Formation, Brooklyn, NY (>NY) [SEM] St. Joseph's Seminary, Yonkers, NY

Gibowski, Rev. Boguslaw T., '69 (PRO) Retired.

Gibson, Rev. Ajani K., '21 (NO) St. Peter Claver, New Orleans, LA

Gibson, Rev. Brendan, *S.J.C.* '05 (CHI) St. Peter, Volo, IL; [MIS] Canons Regular of Saint John Cantius, Chicago, IL (>SFD) St. Katharine Drexel, Springfield, IL

Gibson, Rev. Bruno, *OP* '60 (SFR) [MON] St. Dominic Priory, San Francisco, CA

Gibson, Rev. Chris, (L) [MON] Sacred Heart Retreat, Louisville, KY

Gibson, Rev. James M., *C.R.* '79 (SB) Our Lady of the Desert, Apple Valley, CA; St. Paul, Lucerne Valley, CA; [MON] Congregation of the Resurrection, CR, Needles, CA

Gibson, Rev. John, *S.D.B.* '70 (OAK) [MON] Salesians of Don Bosco, Berkeley, CA

Gibson, Rev. John S., '14 (MIL) St. Jerome's Congregation, Oconomowoc, WI

Gibson, Rev. Stephen, '81 (GRY) All Saints, Hammond, IN

Gibson, Rev. Stephen, (GRY) St. Casimir, Hammond, IN

Gicheru, Rev. Leonard, '14 (KC) On Special Assignment. VA Med Ctr St. Monica, Kansas City, MO

Gicheru, Rev. Leonard M., (MO) Curia: Offices and Directors

Gick, Rev. Francois, *S.J.* '80 (NY) [MON] Murray-Weigel Hall (A Jesuit Community at Murray-Weigel Hall and Kohlmann Hall), Bronx, NY

Gideon, Rev. Peter M., '76 (COL) St. Joseph, Sugar Grove, OH; St. Mark, Lancaster, OH

Gideon, Rev. Stephen G., '97 (NSH) Retired. On Duty Outside Diocese. Teaching Curia: Offices and Directors

Giel, Very Rev. John, '78 (ORL) Curia: Advisory Boards, Commissions, Committees, and Councils; Canonical Services; Leadership St. Stephen, Winter Springs, FL

Gielow, Rev. Richard, *C.M.* '70 (STL) [MON] Congregation of the Mission Vincentian Fathers Lazarist Residence, St. Louis, MO

Gielow, Rev. Robert, *C.M.* '71 (STL) [MON] Congregation of the Mission Vincentian Fathers Lazarist Residence, St. Louis, MO

Gier, Rev. Msgr. Gregory A., '67 (TLS) Retired. Holy Family Cathedral, Tulsa, OK

Giera, Rev. Craig, '10 (DET) Curia: Consultative Bodies; Offices and Directors

Gierasimczyk, Rev. Wojciech, '12 (DEN) St. Mary Catholic Parish in Greeley, Greeley, CO

Giese, Rev. Samuel C., '85 (WDC) St. Jane Frances de Chantal, Bethesda, MD

Giesige, Rev. Randy P., '98 (TOL) Curia: Advisory Boards, Commissions, Committees, and Councils; Deaneries St. Mary, Defiance, OH

Giesing, Rev. Msgr. Anthony, '55 (SD) Retired.

Gieske, Rev. Elias, '13 (DUL) Our Lady of Fatima, Garrison, MN; St. Joseph's Church, Crosby, Crosby, MN

Giesler, Rev. Michael E., '79 (POD) Curia: Clergy and Religious Services

Giesler, Rev. Michael E., '79 (STL) [MIS] Prelature of the Holy Cross and Opus Dei, Kirkwood, MO

Gifford, Rev. Daniel, '13 (PEO) St. Malachy's, Geneseo, IL

Gifford, Rev. Joseph Leo, '18 (STP) The Church of St. Peter Claver of Saint Paul, Minnesota, St. Paul, MN

Gigantiello, Rev. Msgr. Jamie J., '95 (BRK) Curia: Consultative Bodies; Leadership Our Lady of Mount Carmel - Annunciation of the Blessed Virgin Mary, Brooklyn, NY; [EFT] Catholic Foundation for Brooklyn & Queens, Brooklyn, NY

Gigliotti, Rev. James, *T.O.R.* '80 (FWT) St. Andrew, Fort Worth, TX

Gignac, Rev. J. Thomas, '16 (BO) St. Bartholomew, Needham, MA

Gignac, Rev. Thomas, (BO) Curia: Consultative Bodies

Gikenyi, Rev. Mark O., '11 (P) Nativity B.V.M., Rainier, OR

Gil, Rev. Fernando, '88 (ORL) Curia: Tribunal

Gil, Rev. Paul R., '66 (SB) Retired.

Gilbaugh, Rev. Eric C., '05 (HEL) Holy Family Parish: Series 150, LLC, Three Forks, MT; Saint John Vianney Parish: Series 165, LLC, Belgrade, MT

Gilbeau, Rev. Jeremy Aquinas, *O.P.* '02 (WDC) [SEM] Dominican House of Studies, Washington, DC

Gilbert, Rev. Dan, '20 (GI) St. Leo's, Gordon, NE

Gilbert, Rev. Dennis M., '71 (MRY) Retired.

Gilbert, Rev. Msgr. Donald J., '68 (MAN) Retired.

Gilbert, Rev. Edward, (PHX) St. Mary Magdalene Roman Catholic Parish, Gilbert, AZ

Gilbert, Rev. Francis, '18 (NOR) Divine Mercy Parish, Uncasville, CT

Gilbert, Rev. John Mary, '03 (LC) [MIS] Institute of St. Joseph, Boyd, WI

Gilbert, Rev. Michael, (PHX) St. Catherine of Siena Roman Catholic Parish, Phoenix, AZ

Gilbert, Very Rev. Patrick N., '01 (MAN) Chap, Carroll Cty House of Correction St. Anthony, Sanbornville, NH; St. Joseph, Center Ossipee, NH; [CEM] Mount Calvary Cemetery, Sanbornville, NH

Gilbert, Rev. Robert J., '98 (CHI) Our Lady of Kibeho Parish, Chicago, IL; Sacred Heart Mission of Holy Name of Mary, Chicago, IL

Gilbert, Rev. Thomas R., '05 (BRK) On Leave. Excardinated

Gilbert, Rev. Thomas-Mary, *O.C.D.* (MIL) [MON] Discalced Carmelite Friars of Holy Hill, Inc., Hubertus,

WI
Gilbertson, Rev. Lee C., '63 (SPR) Retired.
Gilbertson, Rev. Samuel Robert, '22 (STP) On Duty Outside Diocese. Pontifical North American Coll, Rome
Gilborges, Rev. Anthony, *O.S.F.S.* '89 (VEN) Our Lady of Light Parish in Fort Myers, Inc., Fort Myers, FL
Gilbreath, Rev. Patrick J., '19 (MOB) Holy Spirit Parish, Montgomery, Montgomery, AL
Gilday, Rev. Robert J., (IND) Curia: Offices and Directors St. Therese of the Infant Jesus Catholic Church, Indianapolis, Inc., Indianapolis, IN
Gilde, Rev. Lothar, (LIN) St. Patrick, Imperial, NE
Gilde, Rev. Lothar M., '06 (LIN) Curia: Offices and Directors
Gildea, Rev. Arthur, *C.Ss.R.* (HBG) Retired.
Gildea, Rev. Msgr. John J., '66 (BRK) Retired. Our Lady of the Snows, Floral Park, NY
Gile, Rev. Joseph M., '88 (WCH) [COL] Newman University, Wichita, KS; [CON] Wichita Center, Congregation of the Sisters of St. Joseph, Wichita, KS
Gilg, Rev. Msgr. James E., '66 (OM) Retired. Immaculate Conception B.V.M., Boys Town, NE
Gilger, Rev. Patrick, (NY) (>CHI) [COL] Jesuit Community at Loyola University Chicago, Chicago, IL
Giljum, Rev. Stephen P., '03 (STL) St. Elizabeth, Mother of John the Baptist Catholic Church, St. Louis, MO
Gill, Rev. David H., *S.J.* '67 (BO) [MON] Campion Health & Wellness, Inc., Weston, MA
Gill, Rev. Gerald Dennis, '83 (PH) On Special Assignment. Dir, Ofc for Worship Curia: Advisory Boards, Commissions, Committees, and Councils; Leadership Cathedral Basilica of Saints Peter and Paul and the Shrine of Saint Katharine Drexel, Philadelphia, PA; St. Agnes-St. John Nepomucene, Philadelphia, PA; St. Andrew, Philadelphia, PA; [MIS] Concerts at the Cathedral, Philadelphia, PA
Gill, Rev. Ilyas, *O.F.M.* '93 (BRK) Immaculate Heart of Mary, Brooklyn, NY; [CCH] Pakistani Ministry, ,
Gill, Rev. Joseph, '13 (BGP) The St. Jude Roman Catholic Church Corporation, Monroe, CT
Gill, Rev. Kenneth, '14 (ORL) Basilica of Saint Paul, Daytona Beach, FL
Gill, Rev. Kenneth J., '14 (WDC) Shrine of St. Jude, Rockville, MD; St. Ignatius Loyola, Port Tobacco, MD
Gill, Rev. Matthew, (FR) Holy Family, East Taunton, MA
Gill, Rev. Matthew, '18 (FR) Curia: Offices and Directors
Gill, Rev. Michael J., '66 (NOR) Retired.
Gill, Rev. Richard, '91 (NY) Sacred Heart, Patterson, NY; St. Lawrence O'Toole, Brewster, NY
Gill, Rev. Msgr. William J., '55 (RVC) Retired. [MON] St Pius X Residence for Retired Priests LLC, Ronkonkoma, NY
Gillelan, Rev. Robert M., '89 (HBG) Assumption of the Blessed Virgin Mary, Lebanon, PA
Gillen, Rev. Gabriel, *O.P.* '00 (WDC) [SHR] Rosary Shrine of St. Jude, Washington, DC
Gillen, Rev. George D., '71 (NEW) Curia: Advisory Boards, Commissions, Committees, and Councils
Gillen, Rev. Niles, *O.Carm.* '56 (JOL) Retired.
Gillen, Rev. Peter D., '78 (BRK) St. Brendan, Brooklyn, NY
Giller, Rev. Roderic, *O.S.B.* '62 (KCK) Kansas State Prison, Lansing [MON] St. Benedict's Abbey, Atchison, KS
Gilles, Rev. Msgr. Richard W., '94 (LC) St. Joseph the Workman Cathedral, La Crosse, WI; [EFT] Cathedral of St. Joseph the Workman Endowment Trust, La Crosse, WI
Gillespie, Rev. C. Kevin, *S.J.* '86 (WDC) Holy Trinity, Washington, DC; [MON] The Jesuit Community at Georgetown University, Washington, DC
Gillespie, Rev. Hugh, *S.M.M.* '06 (RVC) [MON] Shrine of Our Lady of the Island, Manorville, NY
Gillespie, Rev. Jerome F., '82 (BO) Retired. St. Mary - St. Catherine of Siena, Boston, MA
Gillespie, Rev. John D., '72 (STA) San Sebastian, St. Augustine, FL
Gillespie, Rev. John L., '95 (R) Retired.
Gillespie, Rev. Joseph, (PRO) Curia: Clergy and Religious Services
Gillespie, Rev. Joseph P., *O.P.* '70 (STP) Risen Christ Catholic School, Minneapolis, MN; [MON] St. Albert the Great Priory, Minneapolis, MN
Gillespie, Rev. Martin Joseph, '00 (BLX) St. Mary, Biloxi, MS
Gillespie, Rev. Philip S., '10 (CHR) St. Joseph, Anderson, SC; [MIS] Family Honor, Inc., Columbia, SC
Gillespie, Rev. Thomas, *O.S.B.* '64 (SCL) [MON] St. John's Abbey, of the Order of St. Benedict, Collegeville, MN
Gillespie, Rev. Thomas E., '72 (MAD) Retired.
Gillespie, Rev. Thomas L., '10 (PIT) St. Oscar Romero, Canonsburg, PA
Gillespie, Rev. Thomas M., (BO) Retired.
Gillette, Rev. James, *C.P.* '71 (NY) Retired. [MON] The Congregation of the Passion - St. Paul of the Cross Province, Jamaica, NY
Gilley, Rev. Charles F., *I.V.Dei.* '96 (BRK) St. Patrick, Long Island City, NY
Gillgannon, Rev. Michael, '58 (KC) Retired.
Gillick, Rev. Lawrence D., *S.J.* '72 (OM) [MON] Jesuit Community at Creighton University, Omaha, NE
Gilligan, Rev. Adrian, *O.S.A.* '68 (PH) [MON] St. Thomas Monastery, Villanova, PA
Gilligan, Rev. Michael J., '69 (CHI) [MIS] American Catholic Press, South Holland, IL; [MIS] San Rocco Oratory, Chicago Heights, IL
Gillin, Rev. Thomas P., '74 (PH) Our Lady of Fatima, Secane, PA
Gillio, Rev. Flavio, *M.S.* '01 (FR) [MON] La Salette Shrine & Retreat Center, Attleboro, MA
Gillis, Rev. David C., '79 (ALN) Retired.
Gillis, Rev. Kevin, *L.C.* '20 (ATL) [MON] Legionaries of Christ, Incorporated, Cumming, GA
Gillmeyer, Rev. Patrick S., *O.S.B.* '03 (RCK) Curia: Leadership Annunciation of the Blessed Virgin Mary, Aurora, IL; [MON] Marmion Abbey, Aurora, IL
Gillmore, Rev. Vincent M., '19 (IND) St. Lawrence Catholic Church, Lawrence, Inc., Indianapolis, IN
Gillon, Rev. James Aloysius, *S.J.* '74 (BO) [MON] Campion Health & Wellness, Inc., Weston, MA
Gills, Rev. Thomas, '86 (BAL) St. Peter the Apostle, Oakland, MD
Gillum, Rev. William, *O.F.M.Cap.* '76 (WDC) [SEM] St. Francis Friary-Capuchin College, Washington, DC
Gilmartin, Rev. Msgr. John, (RVC) St. John Nepomucene, Bohemia, NY
Gilmore, Rev. Alan, *O.C.S.O.* '70 (L) [MON] Abbey of Our Lady of Gethsemani, of the Order of Cistercians of the Strict Observance, Trappist, KY
Gilmour, Rev. James, *C.Ss.R.* '72 (BRK) Our Lady of Perpetual Help Basilica, Brooklyn, NY
Gilmour, Rev. Robert, *CSC* (FTW) Retired. [MIS] Holy Cross House, Notre Dame, IN
Gilson, Rev. Michael, (SJ) [MON] USA West Province, Society of Jesus, Los Gatos, CA
Gilson, Rev. Michael C., *S.J.* '02 (P) [MON] Colombiere Jesuit Community, Portland, OR; [MON] Society of Jesus, Oregon Province, Portland, OR
Gilstrap, Rev. Austin, (NSH) Our Lady of the Lake, Hendersonville, TN
Gilstrap, Rev. Austin, '15 (NSH) Curia: Offices and Directors
Gimeno, Rev. Msgr. Fabian G., '60 (ORL) Retired.
Giner, Rev. Richard, *O.SS.T.* (BAL) [MON] Holy Trinity Monastery, Sykesville, MD
Ging, Rev. Regis, *M.M.* '66 (NY) Retired. [MON] Maryknoll Fathers and Brothers (Catholic Foreign Mission Society of America, Inc.), Ossining, NY
Ginnetti, Rev. Nicholas, '19 (STU) Curia: Deaneries Holy Name Cathedral, Steubenville, OH; Triumph of the Cross, Steubenville, OH
Gins, Rev. Paul M., *O.S.M.* '75 (CHI) [MON] Order of Friar Servants of Mary (Servites) United States of America Province, Inc., Chicago, IL
Ginter, Rev. Andrew W., '16 (SFR) St. Mary Star of the Sea, Sausalito, CA
Ginther, Very Rev. Richard, '83 (IND) Curia: Leadership; Offices and Directors
Ginther, Rev. Richard M., (IND) Our Lady of Lourdes Catholic Church, Indianapolis, Inc., Indianapolis, IN
Gintoli, Rev. Msgr. Blase M., '69 (BGP) Retired.
Ginty, Rev. Msgr. Thomas M., '85 (HRT) Mary, Mother of the Church Parish Corporation, Waterbury, CT; Saint Basil the Great Parish Corporation, Wolcott, CT
Gioeli, Rev. Leonard, '05 (VEN) Retired.
Giombetti, Rev. Jason R., (BO) Curia: Consultative Bodies
Gion, Rev. Chad, '02 (BIS) Curia: Offices and Directors Oratory of St. Elizabeth, Cannon Ball, Cannon Ball, ND; St. Peter - Catholic Indian Mission, Fort Yates, ND; [MIS] Oratory of Sacred Heart, Solen, Solen, ND; [MIS] Oratory of St. James, Porcupine, Porcupine, ND; [MIS] Oratory of St. Philomena, Selfridge, Selfridge, ND
Gion, Rev. Chad O., '02 (BIS) Curia: (>MO) Offices and Directors
Giordano, Rev. John C., '67 (MET) Retired.
Giordano, Rev. Joseph, *C.I.C.M.* '72 (ARL) Retired.
Giordano, Rev. Pasquale T., *S.J.* '72 (NY) [MON] Murray-Weigel Hall (A Jesuit Community at Murray-Weigel Hall and Kohlmann Hall), Bronx, NY
Giorno, Rev. Stephen, (SR) (>SAV) Our Lady of Lourdes, Columbus, GA
Giorno, Rev. Stephen, *S.T.* '86 (WDC) [MON] Holy Spirit Missionary Cenacle, Riverdale, MD
Giovanoni, Rev. Peter M., '01 (WDC) St. Michael, Ridge, MD
Gipson, Rev. Msgr. Laurence A., (POC) Retired.
Gipson, Rev. Msgr. Robert W., '62 (LA) Retired.
Giragori Chinnappan, Rev. Thomas Aquinas, *HGN* (BUR) Mary Queen of All Saints Parish, Hardwick, VT
Giraldo, Rev. Antonio, (KNX) St. Francis of Assisi, Townsend, TN
Giraud, Rev. Gael, *S.J.* (WDC) [MON] The Jesuit Community at Georgetown University, Washington, DC
Giroir, Rev. Msgr. Frank J., '81 (NO) On Special Assignment. St. Scholastica Academy Curia: Leadership St. Anselm, Madisonville, LA
Giron, Rev. Olvin, (KC) Holy Cross, Kansas City, MO
Girone, Rev. Joseph D., '83 (NEW) Curia: Advisory Boards, Commissions, Committees, and Councils; Organizations (affiliated, inter-Diocesan, miscellaneous/other) Saint Rocco/Saint Brigid, Union City, NJ
Girotti, Very Rev. John, '02 (GB) Curia: Advisory Boards, Commissions, Committees, and Councils [CON] Monastery of the Holy Name of Jesus, Ltd., Denmark, WI
Girotti, Very Rev. John W., '02 (GB) Curia: Administration; Advisory Boards, Commissions, Committees, and Councils; Leadership
Giroux, Rev. Garry B., '76 (OG) Curia: Canonical Services Church of St. John the Baptist Madrid, Madrid, NY; St. Mary's, Waddington, Waddington, NY
Giroux, Rev. Joseph W., '00 (OG) Curia: Canonical Services; Offices and Directors Saint Patrick's Church, Colton, NY, Colton, NY; The Roman Catholic Church of Saint Mary in Potsdam, NY, Potsdam, NY
Giroux, Rev. Peter F., *F.P.O.* '98 (BO) On Special Assignment. [MON] Franciscans of Primitive Observance, Lawrence, MA
Giroux, Rev. William P., '80 (BUR) Retired.
Girres, Very Rev. Msgr. Edward M., '79 (SC) Retired. [MIS] Shrine of the Grotto of the Redemption, West Bend, IA
Gismondi, Rev. Carl, *F.S.S.P.* '02 (PH) St. Mary Roman Catholic Church, Conshohocken, PA
Gitau, Rev. Paul, '94 (ROC) Curia: Evangelization St. Paul, Webster, NY
Githinji, Rev. Charles, '13 (DAL) St. Patrick Catholic Parish - Dallas, Dallas, TX
Gitter, Rev. Paul, '93 (STP) [SEM] St. John Vianney Seminary, St. Paul, MN
Gittins, Rev. Anthony, *C.S.Sp.* '67 (CHI) [SEM] Catholic Theological Union, Chicago, IL
Giuffre, Very Rev. Carmelo, '07 (MIL) Nativity of the Lord Congregation, Cudahy, WI; St. Paul's Congregation, Milwaukee, WI; St. Veronica's Congregation, Milwaukee, WI; [CEM] Holy Sepulcher, Cudahy, WI
Giuffre, Rev. Frank A., '97 (PH) [SEM] Theological Seminary of St. Charles Borromeo, Wynnewood, PA
Giuliani, Rev. John P., *C.O.* '80 (CHR) All Saints Parish, Lake Wylie, SC; [MON] Oratory of St. Philip Neri, Congregation of the Oratory of Pontifical Rite, Rock Hill, SC
Giuliano, Rev. Carmen, *S.A.* '61 (NY) Retired.
Giuliano, Rev. Steven B., '80 (WIL) Our Lady of Lourdes Church, Inc., Seaford, DE
Giulietti, Rev. Stephen, (WDC) Little Flower, Bethesda, MD
Giulietti, Rev. Stephen M., '13 (BRK) On Leave. St. Helen, Howard Beach, NY
Gizler, Rev. John B., '02 (PIT) On Sick Leave. [MIS] Ascension Worship Site, PIttsburgh, PA
Gjengdahl, Rev. Nels H., '07 (STP) Holy Family Catholic High School, Victoria, MN; SS. Peter and Paul, Loretto, MN; St. Thomas the Apostle, Corcoran, MN
Gjergji, Rev. Nue, '73 (DET) Our Lady of Albanians Parish Southfield, Southfield, MI
Gjonaj, Rev. Damien, *O.S.B.* '00 (DET) [MON] St. Benedict Monastery, Oxford, MI; [SEM] St. Benedict Monastery, House of Formation, Oxford, MI
Glab, Rev. Joseph, *C.R.* '75 (CHI) St. Matthew, Schaumburg, IL
Glab, Rev. Stephen, *C.R.* '82 (RCK) Resurrection, Woodstock, IL
Glabik, Rev. Peter S., '07 (PAT) Curia: Leadership St. Clare, Clifton, NJ
Glabinski, Rev. Janusz, '86 (LAR) Curia: Leadership St. Joseph, Laredo, TX
Glabinski, Rev. Jozef, (SAT) St. Rose of Lima, Charlotte, TX
Glabinski, Rev. Jozef Michal, (SAT) St. Joseph, Tilden, TX

Glade, Rev. Albert G., *O.P.* '72 (CHI) (>STL) [MON] St. Dominic Priory, St. Louis, MO
Gladysz, Rev. Martin, '02 (KNX) Curia: Leadership Cathedral of the Most Sacred Heart of Jesus, Knoxville, TN
Glanzmann, Rev. Edward J., *O.S.B.* '79 (CHI) [MON] Monastery of the Holy Cross, Chicago, IL; [RTR] Monastery of the Holy Cross/Ascension Guest House, Chicago, IL
Glaser, Rev. Kenneth J., '00 (DUB) Curia: Advisory Boards, Commissions, Committees, and Councils St. Ludmila's Church, Cedar Rapids, Iowa, Cedar Rapids, IA; [CEM] St. John's Cemetery Association, Cedar Rapids, Iowa, Cedar Rapids, IA
Glaser, Rev. Lawrence A., *O.C.S.O.* '58 (SAC) Retired.
Glasgow, Rev. Brendan, '19 (WDC) St. Peter, Washington, DC
Glasgow, Rev. Dennis T., *S.J.* '84 (DET) [MON] Colombiere Center, Clarkston, MI
Glasgow, Rev. James, '20 (WDC) St. Mary, Rockville, MD
Glasgow, Rev. Mark W., '62 (PIT) Chap, Pastoral Care, VA Pittsburgh Health Care System
Glasgow, Very Rev. Robert K., '85 (MAN) Curia: Consultative Bodies St. John Neumann, Merrimack, NH
Glasgow, Rev. Msgr. T. Gaspard, '69 (NO) Retired.
Glass, Rev. James M., *O.S.B.* '04 (RIC) Chap, Old Dominion Univ Holy Trinity, Norfolk, VA
Glass, Rev. Robert H., *C.S.B.* '74 (GAL) [MON] The Basilian Fathers of Dillon House, Houston, TX
Glassmire, Rev. David R., '94 (BUF) Curia: Offices and Directors Ascension Roman Catholic Church Society of Batavia, New York, Batavia, NY
Glastetter, Rev. Donald A., '65 (STL) Retired.
Glavin, Rev. Patrick, *OFM Cap* (NY) Retired. [MON] St. Clare Friary (Capuchin Franciscan Friars, Province of St. Mary), Yonkers, NY
Glazier, Rev. Kirk Matthew, '21 (WCH) Church of the Holy Cross, Hutchinson, KS
Gleason, Rev. Jack, '95 (TLS) Curia: Leadership St. Bernard of Clairvaux, Tulsa, OK
Gleason, Rev. Joseph F., '87 (PH) On Special Assignment. Chap, Lankenau and Bryn Mawr Hosps
Gleeson, Rev. Edward D., '69 (CHI) Retired.
Gleeson, Friar Martin J., *O.P.* '98 (GAL) Holy Rosary, Houston, TX
Gleixner, Rev. Joseph, *M.S.C.* '65 (ALN) [MON] Sacred Heart Villa, Missionaries of the Sacred Heart, Center Valley, PA
Glenn, Rev. Nathaniel, '20 (PHX) Curia: Offices and Directors Xavier College Preparatory Roman Catholic High School, Phoenix, AZ
Glenn, Rev. Ryan, (SCR) Curia: Leadership Notre Dame Jr./Sr. High School, East Stroudsburg, PA
Glenn, Rev. Ryan P., (SCR) St. Matthew, East Stroudsburg, PA
Glennon, Rev. Bertin, *S.T.* (MOB) St. Joseph Parish Holy Trinity, Fort Mitchell, AL; St. Patrick Parish, Phenix City, Phenix City, AL; [MON] St. Joseph Cenacle, Fort Mitchell, AL
Glennon, Rev. Thomas, *S.S.C.* '79 (OM) Retired. [MON] Missionary Society of St. Columban, St. Columbans, NE
Glinkowski, Rev. Raphael K., *O.S.P.P.E.* '62 (GBG) [MON] Pauline Fathers Monastery, Kittanning, PA
Glisson, Rev. Nicholas, '79 (OAK) St. Mary Magdalen, Berkeley, CA
Glockner, Rev. David, '66 (CIN) Retired. [MON] Headquarters of Glenmary Home Missioners (The Home Missioners of America), Fairfield, OH
Glodd, Rev. Taj Van Courtlan, '14 (LAF) St. Joseph, Opelousas, LA
Glogowski, Rev. John F., '71 (SFR) Retired.
Glorie, Rev. Msgr. John W., '60 (MIA) Retired.
Gloss, Rev. John C., '03 (MET) St. John Vianney, Colonia, NJ; [MON] Maria Regina Residence, Somerset, NJ
Glosser, Rev. Msgr. William F., '84 (ALN) Chap, Schuylkill Manor Curia: Leadership Holy Cross Parish, New Philadelphia, PA; St. Clare of Assisi Parish, Saint Clair, PA
Gloudeman, Rev. Francis M., *O.Praem.* '91 (ORG) [MON] Norbertine Fathers of Orange, Inc., Silverado, CA
Gloudeman, Rev. Robert J., '64 (MIL) Retired.
Glover, Rev. Donald F., *M.M.* '70 (NY) Retired. [MON] Maryknoll Fathers and Brothers (Catholic Foreign Mission Society of America, Inc.), Ossining, NY
Glover, Rev. Jason A., '01 (E) Holy Trinity, Erie, PA
Glover, Rev. Jason A., *S.T.L.* '02 (E) St. Stanislaus, Erie, PA
Glover, Rev. Mark, '08 (SPR) On Leave.
Glover, Rev. S. Matthew, '04 (PRO) On Leave.
Glovik, Rev. Msgr. Karl L., '61 (DUB) Retired.
Glueckert, Rev. Leopold, (CHI) [MON] Sant'Angelo Community at St. Cyril Priory, Chicago, IL
Glynn, Rev. Joseph, *C.S.Sp.* '76 (SFR) St. Dunstan, Millbrae, CA
Glynn, Rev. Joseph, *C.S.Sp.* '76 (BRK)
Glynn, Rev. Martin G., '78 (PAT) St. Mary's, Denville, NJ
Glynn, Rev. Robert, *SJ* (SJ) Catholic Community at Stanford, Stanford, CA; [RTR] Jesuit Retreat Center of Los Altos, Los Altos, CA
Glynn, Rev. Seamus A., '58 (ORG) Retired.
Gnall, Rev. Julian, '55 (SD) Retired.
Gnanapragasam, Rev. Charles, '01 (RVC) Church of St. Mary, East Islip, NY
Gnanaraj, Rev. Michael, '76 (BWN) St. Theresa of the Infant Jesus, Edcouch, TX
Gnanaraj, Very Rev. Sengole Thomas, '07 (IND) Chap, Richmond State Hosp Curia: Leadership St. Elizabeth Ann Seton Catholic Church, Richmond, Inc., Richmond, IN; [CAM] Earlham College, Richmond, IN; [MIS] Connersville Deanery, Indianapolis, IN
Gnarackatt, Rev. Joseph, '67 (TR) Retired. St. Dominic, Brick, NJ
Gniewyk, Rev. Eugene, '90 (NEW) Retired.
Gnirk, Rev. Lloyd A., '78 (OM) Roncalli Catholic High School of Omaha, Omaha, NE
Gnoinski, Rev. Piotr, '05 (CHI) St. Ferdinand, Chicago, IL
Gobbo, Rev. Paolo, '94 (SJ) St. Christopher, San Jose, CA
Gober, Very Rev. Christopher M., '00 (CHL) Curia: Leadership St. Leo the Great, Winston-Salem, NC
Gobitas, Rev. Msgr. Gerald E., '75 (ALN) St. John the Baptist, Whitehall, PA
Godecker, Rev. Jeffrey H., '69 (IND) Retired. St. Andrew the Apostle Catholic Church, Indianapolis, Inc., Indianapolis, IN
Godefroid, Rev. Edward J., '21 (STL) St. Charles Borromeo Catholic Church, St. Charles, MO
Godenciuc, Rev. Iura, '94 (STF) Saint Michael the Archangel Ukrainian Catholic Church, New Haven, CT
Godenciuc, Rev. Vasile, '81 (STF) Holy Trinity, Staten Island, NY
Godfrey, Rev. Donal, *S.J.* '92 (SFR) [MON] Loyola House Jesuit Community, San Francisco, CA
Godfrey, Rev. Joseph J., *S.J.* '69 (PH) [MIS] Jesuit Fathers, , ; [MON] Jesuit Community at St. Joseph's University, Merion Station, PA
Godfrey, Rev. Joseph J., *S.J.* '60 (PH) Retired.
Godfrey, Rev. Timothy, *S.J.* '85 (SFR) [MON] Loyola House Jesuit Community, San Francisco, CA
Godic, Rev. Frank G., '73 (CLV) Immaculate Conception, Cleveland, OH; [MIS] Joseph House of Cleveland, Inc., Cleveland, OH
Godinez, Rev. Eulices, (SB) The Holy Name of Jesus Catholic Community, Inc., Redlands, CA
Godinez, Rev. Eulices, '08 (LEX) On Duty Outside Diocese. St. Margaret Mary Church, Chino, CA
Godinez, Rev. Felix Antonio Castro, (NEW) Chap (Adjunct), Bergen Rgnl Med Ctr, Paramus
Godinez, Rev. Francisco H., '10 (B) Curia: Leadership Corpus Christi Catholic Church, Fruitland, ID
Godinez, Rev. Rodolfo, '91 (STA) San Jose, Jacksonville, FL
Godito, Rev. Rene, *sP* (STL) [MON] Servants of the Paraclete, Dittmer, MO
Godleski, Rev. David A., *S.J.* '98 (CHI) [COL] Jesuit Community at Loyola University Chicago, Chicago, IL
Godleski, Rev. David A., *S.J.* '98 (WDC) [MON] Leonard Neale House, Washington, DC
Godley, Rev. Patrick, '53 (SEA) Retired.
Goebel, Rev. Nathan, '14 (DEN) St. Joan of Arc Catholic Parish in Arvada, Arvada, CO
Goebel, Rev. Robert W., '74 (CIN) Retired.
Goeckner, Very Rev. Jeffrey H., '95 (SFD) Curia: Deaneries Father McGivney Catholic High School, Glen Carbon, IL; St. Boniface, Edwardsville, IL
Goehring, Rev. Msgr. Raymond, '64 (LAN) Retired.
Goehring, Rev. Msgr. Raymond J., '64 (LAN) Curia: Offices and Directors
Goeke, Rev. James, *S.J.* (DEN) [MON] Regis High Jesuit Community, Centennial, CO
Goellen, Rev. Richard M., '63 (FAR) Retired.
Goerend, Rev. James, '19 (DUB) Holy Family Church, New Hampton, Iowa, New Hampton, IA; Immaculate Conception Church, North Washington, Iowa, North Washington, IA; St. Boniface Church (Ionia, Iowa), Ionia, IA; St. John School of Religion, New Hampton, Iowa, New Hampton, IA
Goergen, Rev. David J., *M.Afr.* '69 (WDC) [MON] Society of Missionaries of Africa, Washington, DC
Goergen, Rev. Donald, *OP* '75 (CHI) St. Pius V, Chicago, IL; [MON] Dominicans (Provincial Office), Chicago, IL
Goering, Rev. Msgr. Joseph P., '00 (FAR) Curia: Leadership; Offices and Directors St. Mary's Cathedral of Fargo, Fargo, ND
Goerner, Rev. James E., '93 (PH) Our Lady of Perpetual Help, Morton, PA
Goertz, Rev. Howard, '77 (AUS) St. John the Evangelist, Luling, TX
Goertz, Rev. Jonathan, '10 (RIC) Our Lady of Lourdes, Richmond, VA
Goertz, Rev. Msgr. Victor, '52 (AUS) Retired.
Goethals, Rev. Gregory M., *S.J.* '88 (LA) Loyola High School of Los Angeles, Los Angeles, CA
Goetz, Rev. Gerald E., *S.J.* '73 (MIL) [MON] St. Camillus Jesuit Community (Society of Jesus, USA Midwest Province), Wauwatosa, WI
Goetz, Rev. J. Raymond, '81 (OWN) [COL] Brescia University, Owensboro, KY
Goetz, Rev. Martin G., '92 (DAV) Divine Mercy Parish of Burlington-West Burlington, West Burlington, IA; St. Mary Church of Dodgeville, Iowa, Sperry, IA
Gofigan, Rev. Paul A.M., '04 (AGN) Curia: Advisory Boards, Commissions, Committees, and Councils; Consultative Bodies; Family Life Our Lady of Lourdes, Yigo, GU
Goggin, Rev. John T., '64 (NU) On Duty Outside Diocese.
Goggins, Rev. James K., '94 (DEN) Sts. Peter & Paul Catholic Parish in Wheat Ridge, Wheat Ridge, CO
Gogolin, Rev. Seth, '12 (DUL) Curia: Leadership St. Benedict, Duluth, MN; St. John, Duluth, MN
Gohm, Rev. Robert S., '75 (SAG) Retired. Saint John Vianney Parish of Saginaw, Saginaw, MI
Gohring, Rev. William, '84 (ORL) Retired.
Goins, Rev. James A., '92 (OKL) Curia: Evangelization St. Eugene's, Oklahoma City, OK
Gojuk, Rev. Peter P., *O.M.V.* '81 (BO) [MON] Oblate Residence (St. Joseph House), Milton, MA
Golab, Rev. Tomasz, '18 (BLX) Our Lady of Victories, Pascagoula, MS; St. Peter, Bassfield, MS
Golamari, Rev. Louis R., '97 (CHI) (>GB) St. Jude the Apostle, Oshkosh, WI
Golas, Rev. John S., '81 (HRT) Curia: Advisory Boards, Commissions, Committees, and Councils; Clergy and Religious Services Saint Jeanne Jugan Parish Corporation, Enfield, CT
Golba, Rev. Gregorz, '97 (PAT) Curia: Administration St. Francis of Assisi, Haskell, NJ
Gold, Rev. William, '65 (SD) Retired.
Goldasich, Rev. Mark, '81 (KCK) Curia: Offices and Directors Sacred Heart, Tonganoxie, KS
Goldberg, Rev. James M., '76 (GBG) Retired.
Goldberg, Rev. James M., (GBG) [NUR] Neumann House, Greensburg, PA
Golden, Very Rev. Msgr. Patrick D., '96 (RIC) Curia: Deaneries Our Lady of Nazareth, Roanoke, VA
Goldin, Rev. William Brewer, '14 (ORG) St. Vincent de Paul, Huntington Beach, CA
Golding, Rev. Edward, '88 (ALB) St. John the Baptist, Walton, NY; St. Peter, Delhi, NY
Goldrick, Rev. Timothy J., '72 (FR) Retired.
Goldsmith, Very Rev. Joseph F., '12 (RIC) Curia: Deaneries Church of the Sacred Heart, South Prince George, VA; St. James Church, Hopewell, VA; St. John, Petersburg, VA; [CEM] Sacred Heart Cemetery Corporation, South Prince George, VA
Golemba, Rev. Msgr. Roman, '75 (STF) Retired.
Golias, Rev. Msgr. Andrew J., '70 (PH) Retired.
Golias, Rev. Msgr. Andrew J., '70 (PH) Retired. [SEM] Theological Seminary of St. Charles Borromeo, Wynnewood, PA
Golini, Rt. Rev. Ronald, '68 (NTN) Retired.
Golino, Rev. Arthur A., '80 (NY) Cathedral of St. Patrick, New York, NY
Gollob, Rev. Timothy, '58 (DAL) Retired.
Golna, Rev. Justin M., '20 (WH) On Duty Outside Diocese. Casa Santa Maria, Rome Curia: Leadership St. John the Evangelist, Wellsburg, WV
Golombek, Rev. Msgr. Robert K., '65 (BUF) Retired.
Goloran, Rev. Mauricio O., '84 (LA) St. Catherine of Siena, Reseda, CA
Golyzniak, Rev. Gregory, '98 (COS) Curia: Leadership St. Peter, Monument, CO
Goman, Rev. Ralph J., '64 (STP) Retired.
Gomes, Rev. Christopher, (BO) Our Lady of Fatima, Peabody, MA
Gomes, Rev. Herman, *SS.CC.* '78 (HON) Our Lady of Good Counsel, Pearl City, HI; [MON] St. Patrick's Monastery, Honolulu, HI
Gomes, Rev. John Stanley, '95 (NEW) Curia: Advisory Boards, Commissions, Committees, and Councils; Offices and Directors [MON] St. John Vianney

Residence for Retired Priests, Rutherford, NJ
Gomes, Rev. Martin T., *SS.CC.* '69 (FR) [MIS] Damien Residence Retirement Home, ,
Gomes, Rev. Robert M., '66 (CAM) Retired.
Gomes, Rev. Ronald A., '87 (BO) Retired.
Gomes, Rev. Msgr. William J., '69 (RVC) Retired. (>CHR) St. Mary Help of Christians, Aiken, SC
Gomez, Rev. Anthony J., '98 (LA) St. Philip the Apostle, Pasadena, CA
Gomez, Rev. Arnulfo, *S.S.P.* '92 (LA) [MON] The Society of St. Paul, Los Angeles, CA
Gomez, Rev. Augustin A. Anda, (BO) St. Theresa of Lisieux, North Reading, MA
Gomez, Rev. Aurelio Yanez, '74 (NEW) Curia: Organizations (affiliated, inter-Diocesan, miscellaneous/other)
Gomez, Rev. Aurelio Yanez, '74 (NEW) St. Catherine of Siena, Hillside, NJ
Gomez, Rev. Cesar, '98 (AMA) Immaculate Conception, Perryton, TX
Gomez, Rev. Edmund, '93 (SB) Our Lady of Guadalupe, Chino, CA
Gomez, Rev. Edmundo, '69 (NY) Retired. St. Theresa of the Infant Jesus, Bronx, NY
Gomez, Rev. Eduardo, '07 (BWN) Mother Cabrini Parish, Pharr, TX
Gomez, Rev. Edwin A., '05 (WOR) Chap, Travis AFB, CA Curia: (>MO) Offices and Directors
Gomez, Rev. Egren, '18 (LA) Holy Cross, Santa Barbara, CA
Gomez, Rev. Emilio, '16 (BR) Curia: Pastoral Services
Gomez, Rev. Eugenio Francisco, '13 (SJN) Nuestra Senora de la Altagracia, San Juan, PR
Gomez, Rev. Francisco, *ST* '83 (SB) Our Lady of Soledad, Coachella, CA
Gomez, Rev. Msgr. Henry, '58 (LA) Retired.
Gomez, Rev. Homero Sanchez, *O.S.F.* '13 (CHI) St. Rita of Cascia, Chicago, IL
Gomez, Rev. Humberto, '88 (SAC) Chap, Folsom State Prison, Represa Curia: Offices and Directors
Gomez, Rev. Jhon, (BGP) Curia: Consultative Bodies St. Peter's R.C. Church of Bridgeport, Bridgeport, CT
Gomez, Very Rev. John J., '09 (TYL) Curia: Advisory Boards, Commissions, Committees, and Councils; Leadership; Tribunal [CCH] Catholic Charities - Diocese of Tyler, Tyler, TX
Gomez, Rev. Jorge A., '04 (BWN) Curia: Advisory Boards, Commissions, Committees, and Councils Basilica of Our Lady of San Juan del Valle-National Shrine, San Juan, TX; [MIS] The Basilica of Our Lady of San Juan del Valle-National Shrine, San Juan, TX; [NUR] St. John Vianney Retirement Home, San Juan, TX
Gomez, Rev. Jose, '95 (AMA) Curia: Offices and Directors Our Lady of Guadalupe, Amarillo, TX
Gomez, Rev. Juan Luis, (L) St. James, Elizabethtown, KY
Gomez, Rev. Msgr. Leo, '63 (SFE) Retired.
Gomez, Rev. Msgr. Leo, '63 (GLP) Retired.
Gomez, Rev. Matthew, '18 (MIA) Curia: Clergy and Religious Services; Leadership St. Mary's Cathedral, Miami, FL
Gomez, Rev. Miguel, '81 (MIA) Retired.
Gomez, Rev. Octavio, '03 (MIA) St. Maximilian Kolbe, Pembroke Pines, FL
Gomez, Rev. Orlando Perez, *O.S.B.* '01 (RCK) [MON] Marmion Abbey, Aurora, IL
Gomez, Rev. Orlando R., '97 (SAC) Pastor of Immaculate Conception Parish, Corning, a corporation sole, Corning, CA
Gomez, Rev. Otoniel J., '90 (PRO) Holy Spirit Parish Central Falls, Central Falls, RI
Gomez, Rev. Ramon, '85 (OAK) Curia: Leadership All Saints, Hayward, CA
Gomez, Rev. Raul, (KAL) Holy Angels, Sturgis, MI
Gomez, Rev. Roberto, '15 (CGS) Church of St. Anthony of Padua, Barranquitas, PR
Gomez, Rev. Roberto, '09 (SJ) Curia: Leadership; Offices and Directors St. Martin, Sunnyvale, CA
Gomez, Rev. Romulo Cesar, '84 (RVC) Church of Saint Brigid, Inc., Westbury, NY
Gomez Alfaro, Rev. Marlon Nicolas, '11 (FRS) Our Lady of Guadalupe, Delano, CA
Gomez Barajas, Rev. Pedro, *MXY/IMEY* (CHR) St. Gregory the Great, Bluffton, SC
Gomez Franyutty, Rev. Juan Alberto, '18 (MIA) St. Brendan, Miami, FL
Gomez Limon, Rev. David, '97 (DEN) On Duty Outside Diocese.
Gomez Lopez, Rev. Luis Gabriel, *SF* '07 (SFE) Holy Cross, Santa Cruz, NM
Gomez Rueda, Friar Silvestre, *O.P.* '97 (PCE) San Blas de Illescas, Coamo, PR
Gomez Sotres, Rev. Lorenzo, *L.C.* '73 (LA) [MON] Legionaries of Christ, Pasadena, CA
Gomez-Amaya, Rev. Hernando, '02 (SAC) Curia: Organizations (affiliated, inter-Diocesan, miscellaneous/other) Pastor of St. Patrick Parish, Placerville, a corporation sole, Placerville, CA
Gomez-Baca, Rev. Walter S., '80 (SJN) Curia: Leadership Preescolar San Juan Evangelista, Guaynabo, PR; San Juan Evangelista, Guaynabo, PR
Gomez-Baca, Rev. Walter Salomon, '80 (SJN) Curia: Leadership; (>MO) Offices and Directors
Gómez-Cuadrado, Rev. Roberto, (CGS) Curia: Offices and Directors
Gomez-Medina, Rev. Oscar, '02 (SAC) Pastor of St. Charles Borromeo Parish, Sacramento, a corporation sole, Sacramento, CA
Gomez-Rivera, Rev. Carlos, '03 (PHX) St. Augustine Roman Catholic Parish, Phoenix, AZ
Gomez-Rivera, Rev. Eduardo, '11 (NY) St. Anthony of Padua, Bronx, NY
Gomez-Ruiz, Rev. Miller, '20 (ATL) Transfiguration Catholic Church, Marietta, Inc., Marietta, GA
Gómez-Ruiz, Very Rev. Raúl, *S.D.S.* '87 (MIL) [MON] Salvatorian Provincial Offices (Society of the Divine Savior), Milwaukee, WI; [SEM] Sacred Heart Seminary and School of Theology, Franklin, WI
Gomeztorres, Rev. Fredi, '02 (PEO) [HOS] OSF HealthCare Saint Francis Medical Center, East Peoria, IL
Gomez-Zapien, Rev. Gerardo, (SD) Pastor of Saint Jude Shrine of the West Catholic Parish, San Diego, a corporation sole, San Diego, CA
Gomide, Rev. Tomaz, '71 (RVC) Retired.
Gomolski, Rev. Joseph T., '81 (WIL) Retired.
Gomori, Rev. Marcus, '11 (HPM) Curia: Leadership St. Gabriel the Archangel, Las Vegas, NV
Gonchar, Rev. John Joseph, *O.F.M.* '56 (PIT) [MON] Holy Family Friary, Pittsburgh, PA
Gonchar, Rev. John Joseph, *OFM* (CIN) [MON] St. John the Baptist Friary, Cincinnati, OH
Gondek, Rev. Albert J., *O.S.F.S* '66 (WIL) Retired.
Gonderinger, Rev. Gerald E., '74 (OM) Retired.
Goni, Rev. Joaquin, *O.A.R.* '40 (LA) [MON] Order of Augustinian Recollects (O.A.R.), St. Augustine Priory, Oxnard, CA
Gonnella, Rev. Robert, '17 (RCK) On Special Assignment. Curia: Clergy and Religious Services; Education Christ the Teacher, University Parish of Northern Illinois University, DeKalb, IL; [CAM] Newman Foundation for Catholic Students of Northern Illinois University, DeKalb, IL; [RTR] Newman Center of Northern Illinois University Educational Program and Development Fund, Inc., DeKalb, IL
Gonsalves, Rev. Lino, '86 (NY) Parish of Our Lady of Victory and St. Andrew, New York, NY
Gonsalves, Rev. Valerian, '02 (TLS) St. Elizabeth, Grove, OK
Gonser, Rev. Richard A., '62 (CLV) Retired. St. Jude, Elyria, OH
Gonyeau, Rev. Patrick, (DET) Corpus Christi Parish Detroit, Detroit, MI
Gonyo, Rev. Lance, '93 (ROC) Kateri Tekakwitha Roman Catholic Parish, Rochester, NY
Gonzales, Rev. Adam Gregory, *O.C.D.* '05 (SB) [MON] Discalced Carmelites, OCD, Redlands, CA; [RTR] El Carmelo Retreat House, Redlands, CA
Gonzales, Rev. Anthony, (NY) St. Rita, Staten Island, NY
Gonzales, Rev. Dennis, '13 (PMB) St. Vincent Ferrer, Delray Beach, FL
Gonzales, Rev. Edward, '21 (SAT) Holy Trinity, San Antonio, TX
Gonzales, Rev. George, '71 (SB) Retired.
Gonzales, Rev. Hily Buyco, *c.s.* '96 (SD) Pastor of Our Lady of Guadalupe Catholic Parish, Chula Vista, a corporation sole, Chula Vista, CA; [MIS] Our Lady of Guadalupe Catholic Parish Chula Vista in Chula Vista, CA Real Property Support Corporation, Chula Vista, CA
Gonzales, Rev. John, '18 (TUC) Curia: Pastoral Services
Gonzales, Rev. John Juarez, '18 (TUC) Our Mother of Sorrows Roman Catholic Parish - Tucson, Tucson, AZ
Gonzales, Very Rev. Jose, (VEN) Curia: Leadership
Gonzales, Very Rev. Julio, *S.F.* '00 (SFE) Curia: Offices and Directors San Antonio, , ; San Jose, , ; San Miguel, , ; [SHR] Santuario de Chimayo, Chimayo, NM
Gonzales, Rev. Msgr. Loreto, '78 (LA) Retired. St. Bernadette, Los Angeles, CA
Gonzales, Rev. Randy V., *C.I.C.M.* '04 (R) Transfiguration of Jesus, Wallace, NC
Gonzales, Very Rev. Richard, '98 (CC) Curia: Leadership St. Joseph, Beeville, TX
Gonzales, Very Rev. Richard, '98 (CC) Curia: Leadership
Gonzales, Rev. Robert A., '78 (TUC) Saint John the Evangelist Roman Catholic Parish - Tucson, Tucson, AZ
Gonzales, Rev. Ronald, *S.J.* (SJN) San Ignacio de Loyola, San Juan, PR
Gonzalez, Rev. Abdias Gonzalez, *C.O.R.C.* '11 (LA) Immaculate Conception, Los Angeles, CA
Gonzalez, Rev. Alberto I, '18 (MGZ) La Milagrosa, Aguadilla, PR
Gonzalez, Rev. Alvaro Pio, '03 (PT) Curia: Leadership; Offices and Directors Saint Sylvester, Gulf Breeze, FL
Gonzalez, Rev. Andres, (BO) [MON] Miguel Pro House, Brighton, MA
Gonzalez, Rev. Andrew J., '19 (CLV) Holy Family, Stow, OH
Gonzalez, Rev. Andy, '22 (NO) Our Lady of Prompt Succor, Chalmette, LA
Gonzalez, Rev. Angel, '52 (FRS) Retired.
Gonzalez, Rev. Anthony E., '92 (LA) Retired.
Gonzalez, Rev. Aquilino, *OSA* '72 (PH) [MON] St. Thomas Monastery, Villanova, PA
Gonzalez, Rev. Avelino A., '06 (WDC) St. Gabriel, Washington, DC
Gonzalez, Rev. Christopher L, '21 (MGZ) San Sebastian Martir, San Sebastian, PR
Gonzalez, Rev. Daniel, '92 (TYL) Retired.
Gonzalez, Rev. David, *O.Praem.* '14 (ORG) Archangel Institute (St. Michael's Preparatory School), Silverado, CA; [MON] Norbertine Fathers of Orange, Inc., Silverado, CA
Gonzalez, Rev. Dulibber, '18 (PAT) St. Therese, Succasunna, NJ
Gonzalez, Very Rev. Elkin, '08 (TLS) Christ the King, Tulsa, OK; [EFT] Priest Retirement Trust of the Roman Catholic Diocese of Tulsa, Broken Arrow, OK; [EFT] Saint Francis of Assisi Tuition Assistance Trust, Broken Arrow, OK
Gonzalez, Rev. Elvis Antonio, '13 (MIA) Curia: Clergy and Religious Services; Pastoral Services St. Michael the Archangel, Miami, FL
Gonzalez, Rev. Emelio R., '88 (SEA) Retired.
Gonzalez, Rev. Esteban, *C.S.J.* (LAR) St. Patrick, Laredo, TX
Gonzalez, Rev. Felipe, '16 (SP) Curia: Pastoral Services Our Lady of the Rosary, Land O' Lakes, FL
Gonzalez, Rev. Felipe de Jesus, '12 (BO) On Special Assignment.
Gonzalez, Rev. Felix, (VEN) St. James Catholic Parish in Lake Placid, Inc., Lake Placid, FL
Gonzalez, Rev. Felix, '81 (NY) Our Lady of Grace, Bronx, NY
Gonzalez, Rev. Fernando, '95 (BWN) Curia: Advisory Boards, Commissions, Committees, and Councils; Offices and Directors St. Luke, Brownsville, TX
Gonzalez, Rev. Flavio V., '97 (CHI) Little Flower Parish, Waukegan, IL
Gonzalez, Rev. Francisco Alanis, (FWT) Holy Name of Jesus, Fort Worth, TX
Gonzalez, Rev. Freddy D., '92 (LA) St. Rose of Lima, Maywood, CA
Gonzalez, Rev. George A., '67 (SAV) Retired.
Gonzalez, Rev. George A., '87 (BWN) Prison & Jail Ministry, San Juan Immaculate Heart of Mary, Harlingen, TX
Gonzalez, Rev. George G., '67 (SAT) Chap, Major, Columbus, GA
Gonzalez, Rev. Guillermo J., (ARL) All Saints, Manassas, VA
Gonzalez, Rev. Israel, '11 (DAL) Good Shepherd Catholic Parish, Garland, TX
Gonzalez, Very Rev. J. Eduardo, '98 (DAL) Curia: Administration St. Philip the Apostle Catholic Parish, Dallas, TX
Gonzalez, Rev. John Alex, '02 (R) Saint Francis of Assisi Catholic Parish of Raleigh, Raleigh, NC
Gonzalez, Rev. John-Paul, '06 (LA) St. Victor, West Hollywood, CA
Gonzalez, Rev. Jorge L., *S.D.B.* '89 (SJN) San Juan Bosco, San Juan, PR
Gonzalez, Rev. Jose, '05 (MIL) Congregation of St. John's Cathedral, Milwaukee, WI; [SEM] Sacred Heart Seminary and School of Theology, Franklin, WI
Gonzalez, Rev. Jose, '69 (SR) Pastor of Resurrection Catholic Church of Santa Rosa, A Corporation Sole, Santa Rosa, CA
Gonzalez, Very Rev. Jose Antonio, '91 (VEN) Curia: Advisory Boards, Commissions, Committees, and Councils; Leadership St. Catherine Parish in Sebring, Inc., Sebring, FL; [RTR] Campo San Jose, Lake Placid, FL
Gonzalez, Rev. Jose de Dios, '16 (LUB) Curia: Leadership St. James, Seminole, TX

Gonzalez, Rev. Jose de Jesus, '08 (B) St. Bernard's, Blackfoot, ID
Gonzalez, Rev. Jose Luis, '98 (P) Curia: Offices and Directors St. Anne, Gresham, OR
Gonzalez, Rev. Jose Duvan, '96 (ATL) St. Catherine of Siena Catholic Church, Kennesaw, Inc., Kennesaw, GA
Gonzalez, Rev. Juan, *C.PP.S.* '76 (CIN) Retired. [MON] St. Charles, Celina, OH
Gonzalez, Rev. Juan, *S.M.* '82 (SFR) Curia: Leadership Notre Dame des Victoires, San Francisco, CA (>WDC) [MON] Marist Center (The Marist Finance Center of the Atlanta Province of the Society of Mary, Marist Fathers and Brothers), Washington, DC
Gonzalez, Rev. Juan Francisco, '94 (LA) Our Lady Queen of Angels, Los Angeles, CA
Gonzalez, Rev. Juan Jose, *M.Sp.S.* '00 (P) [MON] Missionaries of the Holy Spirit, M.Sp.S., Hillsboro, OR
Gonzalez, Rev. Juan Pedro, '19 (TYL) Cathedral of the Immaculate Conception, Tyler, TX
Gonzalez, Rev. Juan R, '03 (MGZ) St. Michael, Cabo Rojo, PR
Gonzalez, Rev. Juan Jose, *MSpS* '00 (P) St. Matthew Catholic Church, Hillsboro, OR
Gonzalez, Rev. Julio, (LA) Our Lady of the Rosary, Paramount, CA
Gonzalez, Very Rev. Julio, *S.F.* '00 (SFE) Curia: Offices and Directors Holy Family-Chimayo, Chimayo, NM
Gonzalez, Rev. Lauro Regulo, *M.N.M.* '94 (SAT) St. Agnes, San Antonio, TX
Gonzalez, Rev. Lorenzo, '01 (VEN) St. Columbkille Parish in Fort Myers, Inc., Fort Myers, FL
Gonzalez, Rev. Luis O., '00 (NEW) On Duty Outside Diocese. Our Lady of Divine Providence RC Mission, Providenciales
Gonzalez, Rev. Luis P., '94 (NEW) On Duty Outside Diocese. Calle Constructora Naval 7, Cadiz, MD
Gonzalez, Rev. Marco Antonio, '06 (AMA) Curia: Organizations (affiliated, inter-Diocesan, miscellaneous/ other)
Gonzalez, Rev. Marcos J., '94 (LA) St. Andrew, Pasadena, CA
Gonzalez, Rev. Martin, '17 (LA) Immaculate Conception, Monrovia, CA
Gonzalez, Very Rev. Miguel, '06 (YAK) Curia: Offices and Directors Our Lady of the Assumption Parish, Peshastin, WA
Gonzalez, Very Rev. Miguel A., '98 (ORL) Curia: Advisory Boards, Commissions, Committees, and Councils; Clergy and Religious Services; Leadership; Organizations (affiliated, inter-Diocesan, miscellaneous/ other) St. James Cathedral, Orlando, FL
Gonzalez, Rev. Octavio, '01 (NEW) Holy Trinity, Hackensack, NJ
Gonzalez, Rev. Orestes, '86 (NY) [MIS] Personal Prelature, New Rochelle, NY
Gonzalez, Rev. Pablo, '07 (NY) Parish of St. Rita of Cascia and St. Pius V, Bronx, NY; St. Pius V, Bronx, NY
Gonzalez, Rev. Msgr. Ricardo, '57 (NEW) Retired. St. John, Orange, NJ
Gonzalez, Rev. Robinson, *SDV* '10 (ORL) St. Francis of Assisi, Apopka, FL
Gonzalez, Rev. Rogelio, '11 (SB) Our Lady of the Assumption, San Bernardino, CA
Gonzalez, Rev. Rudolph Francis, '87 (NY) St. Margaret Mary, Bronx, NY
Gonzalez, Rev. Salvador, *O.M.I.* '04 (BEL) [RTR] King's House Retreat and Renewal Center, Belleville, IL
Gonzalez, Very Rev. Salvador, '01 (FRS) Curia: Advisory Boards, Commissions, Committees, and Councils; Leadership St. John's Cathedral, Fresno, CA
Gonzalez, Rev. Steven, '21 (NY) Our Lady of Angels, Bronx, NY
Gonzalez, Rev. Vidal, (PAT) Curia: Administration Saint Kateri Tekakwitha, Sparta, NJ
Gonzalez, Rev. Yoelvis Aloysius, '14 (MEM) Blessed Sacrament, Memphis, TN; St. Therese the Little Flower, Memphis, TN; [MIS] Serra Club of Memphis, Memphis, TN
Gonzalez Ayala, Rev. Rafael De Jesus, (SJN) Cristo Rey, Carolina, PR
Gonzalez Betancourt, Rev. Adonis, (MIA) St. Thomas the Apostle Church, Miami, FL
Gonzalez Cedeno, Rev. William Enrique, *S.J.S.* '16 (MAD) On Duty Outside Diocese. Serves in Ecuador
Gonzalez Chao, Rev. Luis, '58 (SJN) Retired.
Gonzalez Delgadillo, Rev. Ricardo, *SVD* '16 (OAK) (>LA) Our Lady of Lourdes, Los Angeles, CA
Gonzalez Gonzalez, Rev. Ernesto, (SJN) Catedral de San Juan Bautista, San Juan, PR
Gonzalez Gonzalez, Rev. Tomas, (SJN) Curia: Leadership
González González, Rev. Juan Rolando, (ARE) Our Lady of Lourdes, Vega Baja, PR
Gonzalez Herrera, Rev. Robinson, *S.V.D.* (NEW) St. Michael, Newark, NJ
Gonzalez Nieto, Rev. Nelson, (VIC) St. Anthony's, Columbus, TX
Gonzalez Padro, Rev. Rafael, *O.P.* '11 (PCE) Nuestra Senora del Rosario, Yauco, PR
Gonzalez Padro, Friar Rafael, *O.P.* (SJN) [COL] Universidad Central de Bayamon, Inc., Bayamon, PR
Gonzalez Padro, Friar Rafael, *O.P.* (SJN) Nuestra Senora del Perpetuo Socorro, Bayamon, PR; Santo Domingo de Guzman, Bayamon, PR
Gonzalez Santiago, Rev. Carlos, *S.F.M.* (SJN) Nuestra Senora del Pilar, San Juan, PR
Gonzalez y Perez, Rev. Belen, '13 (POC) On Duty Outside Diocese. Curia: (>MO) Offices and Directors
Gonzalez Zapata, Rev. Jesus Mario, (SJN) Ntra. Sra. del Carmen, Carolina, PR
Gonzalez-Cabrera, Rev. Javier, '08 (SB) St. Adelaide, Highland, CA
Gonzalez-Gonzalez, Rev. Ernesto, (SJN) Curia: Leadership; Offices and Directors
Gonzalez-Gonzalez, Rev. Tomas, '01 (SJN) Curia: Leadership; Offices and Directors Santa Luisa de Marillac, San Juan, PR
Gonzalez-Hernandez, Rev. Marco Antonio, '07 (R) St. Elizabeth of Hungary, Farmville, NC
Gonzalez-Torres, Rev. Marcos A., '06 (MAN) St. Aloysius of Gonzaga, Nashua, NH
Gonzalo, Rev. Andrew, (WDC) Our Lady of Victory, Washington, DC
Gonzalo, Rev. Andrew B., '94 (WDC) St. Benedict the Moor, Washington, DC; St. Vincent De Paul, Washington, DC
Goo, Rev. Youngsaeng, '09 (SFR) St. Michael Korean Catholic Church, San Francisco, CA
Good, Rev. Daniel, (FAR) Curia: Leadership
Good, Rev. Daniel F., '10 (MOB) Curia: Offices and Directors St. Michael Parish, Heron Bay, Coden, AL; St. Philip Neri Parish, Belle Fontaine, Theodore, AL
Good, Rev. Karl, *CMOP* '99 (KCK) Kansas City Hospice, MO
Good, Rev. Mark S., '12 (CHR) Curia: Advisory Boards, Commissions, Committees, and Councils St. Benedict, Mount Pleasant, SC
Goodavish, Rev. Michael John, '87 (STP) Corpus Christi, Roseville, MN
Goode, Rev. Francis, *O.P.* '87 (LA) St. Dominic, Los Angeles, CA
Goode, Rev. Msgr. Joseph J., '73 (PAT) Retired. Curia: Leadership
Goode, Rev. Lawrence C., '64 (SFR) St. Francis of Assisi, East Palo Alto, CA; [MIS] Legion of Mary, East Palo Alto, CA
Goode, Rev. Michael, *C.PP.S.* '79 (KC) [MIS] St. Gaspar Society, Liberty, MO; [MON] Precious Blood Center, Liberty, MO; [MON] Society of the Precious Blood, Liberty, MO; [SEM] Society of the Precious Blood Provincial Offices, Liberty, MO
Goodfellow, Rev. Scott D, '14 (CLV) St. Mary, Chardon, OH
Goodfellow, Rev. Scott D., '14 (CLV) St. Patrick, Thompson, OH
Goodin, Rev. Richard, (L) Curia: Leadership Holy Cross, Loretto, KY; St. Francis of Assisi Church, Loretto, KY
Goodly, Rev. Timothy, '93 (LKC) Immaculate Conception of the B.V.M., Sulphur, LA
Goodman, Rev. Chase, (VIC) Nativity of the Blessed Virgin Mary, Schulenburg, TX; St. John the Baptist, Schulenburg, TX; St. Rose of Lima, Schulenburg, TX
Goodman, Rev. Leo M., '91 (HBG) Curia: Offices and Directors St. Margaret Mary Alacoque Parish and School Charitable Trust, Harrisburg, PA
Goodreau, Rev. Michael J., '20 (SPR) Immaculate Heart of Mary, Granby, MA
Goodrow, Rev. David C., '00 (BO) On Leave.
Goodrum, Rev. Gerald, '05 (GAL) St. Juan Diego, Pasadena, TX
Goodson, Rev. Todd Michael, (IND) Curia: Offices and Directors Holy Trinity Catholic Church, Edinburgh, Inc., Edinburgh, IN; Our Lady of the Greenwood Catholic Church, Inc., Greenwood, IN; St. Rose of Lima Catholic Church, Franklin, Inc., Franklin, IN; [CAM] Franklin College, Franklin, IN
Goodwin, Rev. Christopher P., '04 (LIN) Curia: Leadership
Goodwin, Rev. James, '97 (FAR) Curia: Leadership St. Maurice Church of Kindred, Kindred, ND
Goodwin, Rev. Michael J., '20 (GR) St. Anthony, Saranac, MI; St. Mary Great Mother of God Catholic Church, Lowell, MI; St. Paul the Apostle, Grand Rapids, MI
Goodwin, Rev. Raymond M., '69 (WOR) Retired.
Goodyear, Rev. Michael, (COS) St. Benedict Catholic Church, Falcon, CO; St. Michael's, Calhan, CO
Goodyear, Rev. Robert, *S.T.* '75 (JKS) Holy Rosary, Philadelphia, MS
Gooley, Rev. Laurence L., *S.J.* '65 (SJ) Retired. [MON] Sacred Heart Jesuit Center, Los Gatos, CA
Goolsby, Rev. Gregory D., '93 (ATL) Retired.
Gootee, Rev. Jason E., '99 (ALX) St. Mary, Winnsboro, LA; St. William, Olla, LA
Gopaul, Rev. Antonious Peter, '97 (BRK) St. Vincent Ferrer, Brooklyn, NY
Gora, Rev. Tomasz, (WOR) Our Lady of Czestochowa, Worcester, MA
Goraieb, Rev. Charles, '91 (PHX) Our Lady of Mt. Carmel Roman Catholic Parish, Tempe, AZ
Gorazd, Rev. Mariusz, (RVC) St. Ladislaus, Hempstead, NY
Gorczyca, Rev. Andrzej, *M.I.C.* '74 (SPR) [MON] Congregation of Marian Fathers of The Immaculate Conception of the Most Blessed Virgin Mary, Stockbridge, MA
Gorczyca, Rev. Grzegorz P., '05 (CHI) St. John the Evangelist, Streamwood, IL
Gordon, Rev. Dennis M., *F.S.S.P.* '08 (B) Chap St. Joan of Arc, Post Falls, ID; [CON] Monastery of Jesus, Mary and Joseph, Post Falls, ID
Gordon, Rev. Gerard, '88 (RVC) Chap Curia: Offices and Directors St. Martin of Tours, Amityville, NY
Gordon, Rev. Gerard A., '88 (RVC) Curia: Leadership
Gordon, Rev. Jacob A., '06 (TOL) St. Gaspar del Bufalo, Bellevue, OH
Gordon, Rev. James, *I.C.* '69 (SP) Blessed Sacrament, Seminole, FL
Gordon, Rev. James Edward, (RIC) St. Ann, Ashland, VA
Gordon, Rev. James J., *F.S.S.P.* '04 (COS) Curia: Leadership Immaculate Conception Parish, Security, CO
Gordon, Rev. John, '88 (PAT) [ASN] The Association of the Marian Apostolate of Mercy, Inc., Wayne, NJ
Gordon, Rev. Msgr. John B., '85 (MET) St. Joseph, Carteret, NJ
Gordon, Rev. John F., '88 (NEW) Curia: Offices and Directors; Organizations (affiliated, inter-Diocesan, miscellaneous/other)
Gordon, Rev. John F., '88 (NEW) Curia: Offices and Directors
Gordon, Rev. John J., *O.M.I.* '01 (SAT) St. Mary, San Antonio, TX
Gordon, Rev. Joseph A., '71 (SFR) Retired.
Gordon, Rev. L. William, '65 (OG) Retired. Curia: Canonical Services The Roman Catholic Community of St. Alexander and St. Joseph, Morrisonville, NY
Gore, Rt. Rev. Aidan, *O.S.B. Oliv.* '11 (SFE) [MON] Our Lady of Guadalupe Abbey, Pecos, NM; [RTR] Our Lady of Guadalupe Olivetan Benedictine Abbey, Pecos, NM
Gore, Rev. William R., *O.S.F.S.* '69 (WIL) [MON] Wilmington-Philadelphia Province of the Oblates of St. Francis de Sales, Wilmington, DE
Gorena, Rev. Pedro, *O.SS.T.* '68 (SJN) [SPF] Hogar Santisima Trinidad, Toa Alta, PR
Gorenski, Rev. Kyle, (ALB) Notre Dame-Visitation, Schuylerville, NY; St. Clement, Saratoga Springs, NY
Gorges, Rev. Bernard X, '95 (WCH) St. Joseph, Mount Hope, KS
Gorges, Rev. Bernard X., '95 (WCH) Curia: Leadership St. Peter the Apostle, Wichita, KS
Gorgies, Rev. Fadi, '18 (EST) St. Joseph Chaldean Parish, Troy, MI
Gori, Rev. Peter G., *O.S.A.* (BO) St. Augustine, Andover, MA
Goris, Rev. Carlos M., (BRK) St. Michael, Brooklyn, NY
Gorka, Rev. Tadeusz, '88 (PH) Sacred Heart, Royersford, PA
Gorman, Rev. Anthony, *O.S.B.* '90 (SCL) [MON] St. John's Abbey, of the Order of St. Benedict, Collegeville, MN
Gorman, Rev. Edward M., *O.P.* '92 (MO) Curia: Offices and Directors
Gorman, Rev. James P., '73 (PH) Retired. Saint John Paul II Parish, Philadelphia, PA
Gorman, Rev. Msgr. Michael J., '80 (LC) Curia: Leadership; Miscellaneous / Other Offices; Offices and Directors St. Charles Borromeo, Chippewa Falls, WI; St. Peter, Chippewa Falls, WI; [EFT] St. Charles Future Fund Trust, Chippewa Falls, WI; [EFT] St. Peter Parish Endowment Trust, Chippewa Falls, WI
Gorman, Rev. Patrick, '20 (CHI) St. Alphonsus, Chicago, IL
Gorman, Rev. Robert G., '80 (MET) Curia: Evangelization St. John Vianney, Colonia, NJ

Gorman, Rev. Thomas J., '59 (TOL) Retired.
Gormley, Rev. Brendan, '07 (NY) St. Clare, Staten Island, NY
Gormley, Rev. Daniel, '22 (TLS) St. Anne, Broken Arrow, OK
Gormley, Rev. George, *S.V.D.* '07 (BLX) [MON] Southern Province of St. Augustine - Provincial Offices, Bay St. Louis, MS; [MON] St. Augustine's Residence, Bay St. Louis, MS
Gormley, Rev. Gerard, '85 (SR) Curia: Leadership Pastor of St. James Catholic Church of Petaluma, A Corporation Sole, Petaluma, CA
Gormley, Rev. Kevin W., '64 (JC) Retired.
Gormley, Rev. Raymond P., '92 (CAM) Curia: Tribunal R.C. Church of the Incarnation, Township of Mantua, New Jersey, Mantua, NJ
Gormley, Rev. Raymond P., (CAM) Curia: Advisory Boards, Commissions, Committees, and Councils; Leadership
Gorny, Rev. Ed, '68 (CIN) Retired. [MON] Headquarters of Glenmary Home Missioners (The Home Missioners of America), Fairfield, OH
Gorny, Rev. Tomasz J., '10 (SPR) On Leave.
Gorospe, Rev. Paterno, '66 (NEW) Retired.
Gorsic, Very Rev. Gregor, '97 (JOL) Curia: Leadership St. Matthew, Glendale Heights, IL
Gorski, Rev. John F., *M.M.* '63 (NY) Retired. [MON] Maryknoll Fathers and Brothers (Catholic Foreign Mission Society of America, Inc.), Ossining, NY
Gorski, Rev. Lawrence E., '75 (CHI) Retired.
Gorski, Rev. Robert E., '80 (MAN) St. Jude, Londonderry, NH
Gorski, Rev. Terrence, *O.F.M.* '75 (BWN) Holy Family, Edinburg, TX
Gortland, Rev. Msgr. R. Vincent, '81 (TR) Retired.
Gorton, Rev. Timothy J., '82 (PRO) Retired.
Gorzo, Rev. Vasile, '03 (ROM) On Administrative Leave.
Gosciniak, Rev. Dariusz, '92 (HRT) The Church of the Holy Cross, New Britain, New Britain, CT
Gosele, Rev. Andreas, (PH) [MON] Arrupe Jesuit Community, Merion Station, PA
Gosma, Rev. Robert D., '59 (MIL) Retired.
Gosselin, Rev. Andre L., *S.M.* '64 (WDC) Retired. [MON] Marist Center (The Marist Finance Center of the Atlanta Province of the Society of Mary, Marist Fathers and Brothers), Washington, DC
Gosselin, Rev. Andre L., *S.M.* '64 (BO) Retired.
Gosselin, Rev. Fernand L., *M.M.* '70 (NY) Retired. [MON] Maryknoll Fathers and Brothers (Catholic Foreign Mission Society of America, Inc.), Ossining, NY
Gosselin, Rev. Msgr. Homer P., '69 (SPR) Saint Elizabeth Parish, Ludlow, MA
Gosselin, Rev. Joseph, (MAN) [MON] Shrine of Our Lady of La Salette (La Salette of Enfield, Inc.), Enfield, NH; [RTR] Shrine of Our Lady of La Salette (La Salette of Enfield, Inc), Enfield, NH
Gosselin, Rev. Larry, *O.F.M.* '81 (LA) Old Mission Santa Barbara, Santa Barbara, CA; [MON] Franciscan Friary, Order of Friars Minor (Old Mission), Santa Barbara, CA
Gosselin, Rt. Rev. Lawrence, '76 (NTN) Retired.
Gossen, Rev. Christopher, '19 (PHX) St. Thomas Aquinas Roman Catholic Parish, Avondale, AZ
Gossett, Rev. Matthew W.J., '16 (STU) Holy Name Cathedral, Steubenville, OH; Triumph of the Cross, Steubenville, OH
Gossett, Rev. Michael, '11 (STU) Blessed Sacrament, Wintersville, OH; Our Lady of Lourdes, Wintersville, OH
Gossman, Rev. John A., '71 (DUB) Retired.
Goth, Rev. Dennis J., '84 (LFT) Curia: Leadership St. John the Baptist, Tipton, IN; St. Joseph, Elwood, IN
Gothie, Rev. George J., '67 (PAT) Retired. [MIS] Nazareth Village, Chester, NJ
Gothman, Rev. Augie, '93 (CR) Curia: Offices and Directors St. Andrew, Hawley, MN
Gothman, Rev. August, '93 (CR) St. Elizabeth, Dilworth, MN
Gott, Rev. Camillus, *OFM Conv.* '60 (STP) (>LSC) [RTR] Holy Cross Retreat and Friary (Franciscan Fathers), Mesilla Park, NM
Gottschalk, Friar David, *O.F.M.Cap.* '69 (COS) [MON] Our Lady of the Angels Friary, Colorado Springs, CO
Gotwalt, Rev. Joseph F., '65 (HBG) Retired. St. Vincent de Paul, Hanover, PA
Goudreau, Rev. Paul, '60 (SP) Retired.
Gouger, Rev. John, *C.Ss.R.* '65 (STL) Retired. [MON] St. Clement Health Care Center, Liguori, MO
Gough, Rev. Justin, (BAL) Cathedral of Mary Our Queen, Baltimore, MD
Gouin, Rev. Msgr. Joseph O., '65 (MAR) American Martyrs, Kingsford, MI
Gould, Rev. Clayton, '81 (LR) Retired. [MON] St. John Manor, Little Rock, AR
Gould, Rev. James R., '81 (ARL) Curia: Consultative Bodies St. Francis de Sales, Purcellville, VA
Gould, Rev. Lawrence, *SAC* '76 (DET) Retired. [MON] Society of the Catholic Apostolate (Pallottine Fathers), Wyandotte, MI
Gould, Rev. Michael, *M.M.* '54 (SJ) Retired. [MON] Maryknoll, Los Altos, CA
Gould, Rev. Michael, *M.M.* '54 (NY) Retired.
Gould, Rev. Shawn D., *P.S.S.* (BAL) [MON] Society of St. Sulpice, Province of the United States, Baltimore, MD
Gouldrick, Rev. John William, *C.M.* '69 (PH) [MON] Congregation of the Mission, Philadelphia, PA
Goulet, Rev. Daniel R., '07 (BAL) Battalion Chap, Capt, US Army Curia: (>MO) Offices and Directors
Goulet, Rev. Xavier, *O.F.M.Conv.* (TOL) [SHR] Basilica and National Shrine of Our Lady of Consolation, Carey, OH
Gournas, Rev. John Victor, '10 (R) Curia: Leadership Infant of Prague, Church of the Holy Spirit, Jacksonville, NC
Gousse, Rev. Paul M., '99 (MAN) On Special Assignment. Senior Priest Ste. Marie, Manchester, NH
Gouthro, Rev. Arthur, *S.A.* '69 (NY) Retired. [MON] Franciscan Friars of the Atonement, Minister General Office, Garrison, NY
Governale, Rev. Russell, *O.F.M.Conv.* '88 (BRK) Most Holy Trinity - Saint Mary, Brooklyn, NY
Govin, Rev. Lazarus J., '17 (MIA) St. Matthew, Hallandale Beach, FL
Govind, Rev. Anthony, '10 (EVN) Christ the King, Ferdinand, IN
Govindu, Rev. Bala, (SPC) St. Lawrence, Benton, MO
Govindu, Rev. Bala Anthony, '15 (SAN) Curia: Advisory Boards, Commissions, Committees, and Councils
Govindu, Rev. Bala Anthony, '15 (SAN) St. Charles Borromeo Catholic Church, Eden, TX
Govindu, Rev. Bala Swamy, (SPC) St. Denis, Benton, MO
Govindu, Rev. Balaswamy, '77 (SR) Curia: Leadership; Offices and Directors Pastor of St. Philip Catholic Church of Occidental, a Corporation Sole, Occidental, CA
Govindu, Rev. Joseph, (FRS) Sacred Heart, Planada, CA
Gow, Rev. John, '08 (RCK) St. Flannen, Harmon, IL; St. Mary, Walton, IL; St. Patrick, Amboy, IL
Gowen, Rev. Daniel, '89 (TR) Retired. Our Lady of Sorrows-St. Anthony Parish, Hamilton, NJ
Gower, Rev. Peter J., '84 (PRO) Church of Our Lady of Grace, Johnston, RI
Goyette, Rev. Giles R., *M.M.A.* '82 (SAM) [MON] Maronite Monks of Adoration - Most Holy Trinity Monastery, Petersham, MA
Goyette, Rev. Michael J., '04 (CAM) Church of Our Lady of the Lakes, Collings Lakes, N.J., Collings Lakes, NJ
Goyo, Very Rev. Jimwell, '89 (DAL) Curia: Administration Blessed Sacrament Catholic Parish, Dallas, TX
Graap, Rev. Augustine, *O.Carm.* '66 (NY) Chap, Otisville Corr Fac [MON] St. Albert's Priory, Middletown, NY
Grabert, Rev. Colman, *O.S.B.* '65 (IND) [MON] St. Meinrad Archabbey, St. Meinrad, IN
Grabish, Rev. Msgr. John J., '72 (ALN) Curia: Leadership St. Joseph, Reading, PA; St. Paul, Reading, PA
Grabner, Rev. Donald, *O.S.B.* '54 (KC) Retired. [MON] Conception Abbey (Benedictine Monks), Conception, MO
Grabner, Rev. Robert J., '00 (STP) Retired.
Grabowski, Rev. Dennis, '76 (Y) Retired.
Grabowski, Rev. Eugene M., '89 (R) Retired.
Grabowski, Rev. Walter P., '81 (BUF) Curia: Consultative Bodies St. Gabriel, Elma, NY
Grabowsky, Rev. Msgr. Myron, '67 (PHU) St. Michael's, Shenandoah, PA; St. Nicholas, Saint Clair, PA
Grabrian, Rev. Dennis, '70 (COS) Retired.
Grace, Rev. Edward D., '67 (CHI) Retired. Queen of All Saints Basilica, Chicago, IL; SS. Peter and Lambert Parish, Skokie, IL
Grace, Rev. James N., '59 (CHI) Retired.
Grace, Rev. John, *O.S.A.* '62 (SD) Retired. [MON] Augustinian Community, San Diego, CA
Grace, Rev. John, (RIC) Immaculate Conception, Hampton, VA
Grace, Rev. John M., '88 (MAN) Parish of the Resurrection, Nashua, NH
Grace, Rev. Patrick, '79 (RVC) SS. Cyril and Methodius, Deer Park, NY
Grace, Rev. Peter, *C.P.* '72 (NY) [MON] The Congregation of the Passion - St. Paul of the Cross Province, Jamaica, NY
Grace, Rev. Peter A., *C.P.* '72 (R) Curia: Leadership St. Ann, Clayton, NC
Gracey, Rev. John, '93 (FRS) Our Lady of Perpetual Help, Bishop, CA
Grachanin, Rev. Terrence M., '13 (CLV) St. Noel, Willoughby Hills, OH
Gracz, Rev. Msgr. Henry C., '65 (ATL) Curia: Leadership Immaculate Conception Catholic Church, Atlanta, Inc., Atlanta, GA
Grady, Rev. Bernard C., '68 (DUB) Retired.
Grady, Rev. Brian D., '00 (RCK) On Special Assignment. Curia: Clergy and Religious Services St. Rita, Rockford, IL
Grady, Rev. Francis, *S.S.C.* '63 (PRO) Retired. [MON] St. Columban's Retirement House (St. Columban's Foreign Mission Society), Bristol, RI
Grady, Rev. Joseph, '16 (DEN) On Duty Outside Diocese. Chap, Holy Family High School
Grady, Rev. Matthew, '12 (VEN) On Leave.
Grady, Rev. Michael, '19 (COV) Covington Latin School, Covington, KY; St. Therese of the Infant Jesus, Southgate, KY; [MIS] Shrine of the Little Flower, Southgate, KY
Grady, Rev. Michael, '94 (MIA) St. Anthony, Fort Lauderdale, FL
Graebe, Rev. Henry, '22 (PH) St. Eleanor, Collegeville, PA
Graeve, Rev. Stephen L., '15 (LIN) St. Joseph's, Nebraska City, NE
Graf, Rev. Gary M., '84 (CHI) Lord of Mercy Parish, Harvey, IL; SS. Paul, Agnes, and Kieran Parish, Chicago Heights, IL
Graf, Rev. James W., '72 (L) Retired.
Graf, Rev. Paul M., '82 (LFT) Retired.
Graf, Rev. William E., '60 (ROC) Retired.
Graff, Rev. Joseph P., '76 (GLD) Retired.
Graff, Rev. Timothy G., '85 (NEW) Curia: Advisory Boards, Commissions, Committees, and Councils; Offices and Directors; Organizations (affiliated, inter-Diocesan, miscellaneous/other) St. Joseph, Bogota, NJ
Graffis, Rev. Joseph T., '71 (L) Retired.
Grafsgaard, Rev. Thomas, '13 (BIS) Curia: Leadership St. Joseph, Beulah, ND; St. Martin, Hazen, ND
Grafsky, Rev. George J., '71 (STP) Retired.
Graham, Rev. Daniel M., '70 (BO) Retired.
Graham, Very Rev. David, '91 (MEM) St. John's Church, Brownsville, TN; St. Mary's Church, Jackson, TN
Graham, Rev. George Nelson, '92 (LC) St. Anthony de Padua, Athens, WI; St. Thomas, Athens, WI; [EFT] Saint Anthony Parish Endowment Trust, Athens, WI
Graham, Rev. Msgr. James J., '73 (PH) Curia: Leadership St. Rose of Lima, North Wales, PA
Graham, Rev. James K., '93 (NTN) Retired.
Graham, Rev. Jerry, *S.J.* '00 (SEA) Bellarmine Preparatory School, Tacoma, WA
Graham, Rev. Jerry D., *S.J.* '00 (P) [MON] Colombiere Jesuit Community, Portland, OR
Graham, Rev. John J., '90 (BO) St. Joseph Parish, Kingston, MA; St. Mary, Plymouth, MA
Graham, Rev. Msgr. John K., '74 (NY) Curia: Leadership St. Frances de Chantal, Bronx, NY
Graham, Rev. Matthew J., '15 (BR) Curia: Administration Congregation Of The Immaculate Conception Roman Catholic Church, Denham Springs, Louisiana, Denham Springs, LA
Graham, Rev. Michael J., *S.J.* '88 (CIN) [MON] Cincinnati Jesuit Community, Cincinnati, OH
Graham, Rev. Richard, '21 (PT) Curia: Leadership St. Dominic, Panama City, FL
Graham, Rev. William C., '76 (DUL) On Leave. St. Michael, Duluth, MN
Grajeda, Rev. Juan Angel, (TLS) Curia: Leadership; Offices and Directors St. Francis Xavier Church and Diocesan Marian Shrine & Expiatory Temple of Our Lady of Guadalupe, Tulsa, OK
Grajeda, Very Rev. Miguel Angel, '97 (MRY) On Special Assignment. Vicar Gen & Vicar for Priests, St Patrick's Church, Monterey Curia: Administration; Advisory Boards, Commissions, Committees, and Councils Santa Rosa, Cambria, CA
Grajek, Rev. Lawrence, '57 (SB) Retired.
Grala, Rev. Paul, *SOLT* '95 (SFE) St. Gertrude the Great, Mora, NM
Gramann, Rev. Robert B., (ATL) St. Dominic, Atlanta, GA
Gramata, Rev. Raymond C., '70 (E) Retired. St. Francis of Assisi, Bradford, PA
Grambow, Rev. Arnold J., '69 (MAR) Retired.
Gramc, Rev. Thomas, (PIT) Our Lady of the Angels,

Pittsburgh, PA; St. Maria Goretti Parish, Pittsburgh, PA
Gramlich, Rev. Anthony, *M.I.C.* '02 (SPR) [MON] Congregation of Marian Fathers of The Immaculate Conception of the Most Blessed Virgin Mary, Stockbridge, MA
Grams, Rev. Msgr. Douglas L., '87 (NU) On Special Assignment. Curia: Leadership; Offices and Directors Cathedral of the Holy Trinity, New Ulm, MN; New Ulm Area Catholic Schools, New Ulm, MN; St. George, New Ulm, MN; St. Gregory the Great, Lafayette, MN; St. John the Baptist, New Ulm, MN; St. Mary, New Ulm, MN
Gramza, Rev. Ronald, '73 (MIL) Retired.
Granado, Rev. Jason, '08 (AGN) On Duty Outside Diocese.
Granado, Rev. Jason, '08 (CHK) Curia: Advisory Boards, Commissions, Committees, and Councils; Consultative Bodies; Faith Formation; Pastoral Services San Jose Parish, Saipan, MP
Granados, Rev. Jorge, (YAK) Queen of All Saints, Moses Lake, WA; St. Michael the Archangel, Royal City, WA
Granados, Rev. Julio R., '22 (WOR) Curia: Offices and Directors St. John the Guardian of Our Lady, Clinton, MA
Granados, Rev. Oscar, (MGZ) El Salvador, Hormigueros, PR
Granados del Valle, Rev. Oscar, *SFM* (SJN) Nuestra Senora del Pilar, San Juan, PR
Granados Penagos, Rev. Carlos Eduardo, '88 (ARE) La Candelaria, Manati, PR
Granados-Benavides, Rev. Jairo Enrique, (SJN) Maria Madre de Mi Senor, Guaynabo, PR; Nuestra Senora de la Paz, Guaynabo, PR
Granados-Garcia, Rev. Enrique, '09 (MEM) Church of the Resurrection, Memphis, TN
Granato, Rev. John, '06 (HRT) Our Lady of Hope Parish Corporation, New Hartford, CT
Granato, Rev. Msgr. Joseph J., '55 (NEW) Retired. St. Lucy, Newark, NJ
Graner, Rev. Thomas, '94 (FAR) Curia: Offices and Directors Holy Family Church of McClusky, McClusky, ND; St. Francis Xavier Church of Anamoose, Anamoose, ND; St. Margaret Mary Church of Drake, Drake, ND
Graney, Rev. Paul W., '16 (DET) St. Lawrence Parish Utica, Utica, MI
Graney, Rev. William F., '71 (WIL) Retired.
Granger, Rev. Sean S., '07 (MIL) Congregation of St. Elizabeth, Kenosha, WI; St. James Congregation, Kenosha, WI
Granito, Rev. Mark E., '98 (SFE) Holy Child, Tijeras, NM; San Lorenzo, ,
Grankauskas, Rev. Paul, (ARL) St. Bridget of Ireland Parish, Berryville, VA
Grankowski, Rev. Zbigniew, '83 (DET) St. Barbara Parish Dearborn, Dearborn, MI
Granstrand, Rev. Charles P., '66 (NEW) Retired.
Grant, Rev. Benedict W., *F.P.O.* '08 (BO) On Leave.
Grant, Rev. Douglas, (PRO) Saint Mark Church of Jamestown, Jamestown, RI
Grant, Rev. Francis A., (SB) St. Anthony, San Jacinto, CA
Grant, Rev. James A., '66 (PH) Retired.
Grant, Rev. Jeffery A., '82 (SFD) Blessed Sacrament, Springfield, IL
Grant, Rev. John L., '12 (TLS) Curia: Offices and Directors St. Catherine, Tulsa, OK
Grant, Rev. Robert, '84 (DM) On Duty Outside Diocese. Teacher, St. Ambrose University, Davenport
Grant, Rev. Robert J., '93 (HRT) Retired.
Grant, Rev. Robert L., '84 (DAV) St. Andrew Church of Blue Grass, Iowa, Blue Grass, IA; St. Mary Church of Wilton, Iowa, Wilton, IA; [COL] St. Ambrose University, Davenport, IA
Granyak, Rev. Esteban Nelson, '12 (NEW) On Duty Outside Diocese. Saint Charles Borromeo Rectory, Philadelphia, PA
Granzotto, Rev. Peter, *S.D.B.* '57 (NY) Parish of St. John Bosco, Port Chester, NY
Grappoli, Rev. Frank B., *S.X.* '63 (PAT) [MON] Xaverian Missionary Fathers, Wayne, NJ
Grasher, Rev. Albert, '86 (SPK) Retired.
Grassel, Rev. Martin, *O.S.B.* '04 (P) [EFT] The Abbey Foundation of Oregon, St. Benedict, OR; [MON] Mt. Angel Abbey, Saint Benedict, OR; [SEM] Mount Angel Seminary, Saint Benedict, OR
Grasselli, Rev. Msgr. Renato, '94 (NEW) Curia: Advisory Boards, Commissions, Committees, and Councils [SEM] Redemptoris Mater Archdiocesan Missionary Seminary, Kearny, NJ; [SHR] Eucharistic Shrine of the Adorable Face of Jesus, Kearny, NJ
Grassi, Rev. Dominic J., '73 (CHI) Retired.
Grassi, Very Rev. Timothy J., '00 (WH) Curia: Leadership St. James, Charles Town, WV; [RTR] Priest Field Pastoral Center, Kearneysville, WV
Grasso, Rev. Anthony R., *C.S.C.* '78 (SCR) (>ORL) [MON] Congregation of Holy Cross, United States Province, Cocoa Beach, FL
Grasso, Rev. Joseph, *C.PP.S.* '91 (ALB) Chap, Stratton Veterans' Administration Med Ctr
Grasso, Rev. Joseph, '92 (ALB) On Special Assignment. Chap Stratton Veterans Administration Medical Center, Albany
Grasso, Rev. Joseph A., *C.PP.S.* '91 (MO) Curia: Offices and Directors
Gratkowski, Rev. Eugene W., '67 (CHI) Retired.
Grattarola, Rev. Robert A., '62 (WOR) St. Joseph's, Charlton, MA
Gratton, Rev. Scott, (MO) Curia: Offices and Directors
Gratton, Rev. Scott A., '15 (BUR) Our Lady of the Angels, Randolph, VT; Our Lady of the Valley Parish, Bethel, VT; St. John the Evangelist, Northfield, VT; [CAM] Norwich Newman Apostolate, Northfield, VT
Grau, Rev. James, (DET) St. John Vianney Parish Shelby Township, Shelby Twp., MI
Grave de Peralta, Rev. Miguel, '96 (ATL) Holy Family Catholic Church, Marietta, Inc., Marietta, GA
Graves, Rev. Edwin, '92 (LR) Retired. [MON] St. John Manor, Little Rock, AR
Grawe, Rev. Michael, *O.F.M.* '70 (GB) Retired. [MON] Blessed Giles Friary, Manitowoc, WI
Gray, Very Rev. Christopher P., '13 (SLC) Curia: Offices and Directors Saint Mary of the Assumption LLC 238, Park City, UT
Gray, Rev. Daniel J., '76 (PRO) Saint Anthony's Church of Portsmouth, Portsmouth, RI
Gray, Rev. James C., '88 (STL) St. Jude Catholic Church, Overland, MO
Gray, Rev. Msgr. Jason A., '97 (PEO) Curia: Tribunal St. Thomas, Peoria Heights, IL
Gray, Rev. John W., '58 (PRO) Retired.
Gray, Rev. Joseph B., '09 (KAL) Retired. St. John the Evangelist, Albion, MI
Gray, Rev. Josh, '17 (SAN) Curia: Advisory Boards, Commissions, Committees, and Councils St. Margaret, San Angelo, TX; St. Therese, Carlsbad, TX
Gray, Rev. Kevin J., '84 (HRT) Retired.
Gray, Rev. Peter W., *P.S.S.* '79 (BAL) [MON] Society of St. Sulpice, Province of the United States, Baltimore, MD
Gray, Rev. Richard, '03 (BAL) Our Lady of Perpetual Help, Edgewater, MD; Our Lady of Sorrows, West River, MD
Gray, Rev. Ryan, '16 (STU) On Leave.
Gray, Rev. S. Matthew, (MO) Curia: Offices and Directors
Gray, Rev. Samuel M., (CHR) On Duty Outside Diocese. Vocations Director for Archdiocese for the Military Services Curia: (>MO) Offices and Directors
Gray, Rev. Tim, *S.C.J.* '78 (GAL) Retired.
Gray, Rev. Zackary, '22 (ORL) St. Joseph's, Lakeland, FL
Graziadio, Rev. Msgr. Domenick T., '66 (RVC) Retired.
Graziano, Rev. Gerard J., '61 (NEW) Retired. St. Matthew, Ridgefield, NJ
Graziano, Rev. J. Damien, '67 (JOL) Retired.
Graziano, Rev. Peter N., '63 (FR) Retired.
Grazulis, Rev. Antanas, *S.J.* '78 (CHI) [MON] Baltic Jesuits Advancement Project, Lemont, IL
Grbavac, Rev. Charbel R., *O.Praem.* '06 (ORG) [MON] Norbertine Fathers of Orange, Inc., Silverado, CA
Greaves, Rev. Gerald F., '74 (NEW) Retired. Sacred Heart, Bloomfield, NJ; St. Raphael, Livingston, NJ
Greb, Rev. John, '06 (PHX) St. Timothy Roman Catholic Parish, Mesa, AZ
Greb, Rev. Michael P., *O.F.M.Cap.* '89 (PIT) Chap, Dir Pastoral Care, McGuire Mem Home, New Brighton [MON] St. Fidelis Friary, Beaver, PA
Grecco, Rev. Robert J., '93 (PIT) St. Raphael the Archangel, Carnegie, PA
Grecia, Rev. Rholly, (HT) Chap, Terrebonne Gen Med Ctr
Grecia, Rev. Rholondo T., '98 (HT) The Congregation of St. Joseph's Roman Catholic Cathedral, Thibodaux, LA
Greco, Rev. Michael, *OFM Cap* (NY) [MON] Capuchin Friars of North America (NAPCC/North America Pacific Capuchin Conference), White Plains, NY; [MON] The Province of St. Mary of the Capuchin Order, White Plains, NY
Greco, Rev. Michael, '15 (FWT) Curia: Miscellaneous / Other Offices
Greco, Rev. Raymond, (PHX) St. Elizabeth Seton Roman Catholic Parish, Sun City, AZ
Greeley, Rev. John Carlos, *MSP* '08 (LA) St. Camillus de Lellis, Los Angeles, CA
Greeley, Rev. Msgr. Joseph F., '74 (LA) Retired.
Green, Rev. Benjamin F., '12 (WCH) On Duty Outside Diocese. Missionary Service -Diocese of Dodge City (>DOD) St. Joseph Catholic Church of Offerle, Kansas, Offerle, KS; (>DOD) St. Nicholas Catholic Church of Kinsley, Kansas, Kinsley, KS
Green, Rev. Chad, (SEA) Mary, Queen of Peace, Sammamish, WA
Green, Rev. Daniel H., '13 (NO) St. Maria Goretti, New Orleans, LA
Green, Rev. David, (PIT) Chap, Ladies of the Grand Army Republic, Allegheny Cty St. John XXIII, McMurray, PA
Green, Rev. Fred J., *S.J.* (SJ) [MON] USA West Province, Society of Jesus, Los Gatos, CA
Green, Rev. John, '10 (DEN) St. Mary Assumption in Central City, Central City, CO; St. Paul Catholic Parish in Idaho Springs, Idaho Springs, CO
Green, Rev. Michael R., *O.S.B.* '70 (DET) [MON] St. Benedict Monastery, Oxford, MI
Green, Rev. Romuald, *O.F.M.* '55 (WDC) [MON] Franciscan Monastery USA Inc., Washington, DC
Green, Rev. Ronald L., '61 (MRY) Sacred Heart, Salinas, CA
Green, Rev. Thomas P., *S.J.* '61 (NY) St. Aloysius, New York, NY
Green, Rev. William, (PHX) St. Elizabeth Seton Roman Catholic Parish, Sun City, AZ
Green, Rev. William H., '63 (SUP) Retired.
Greene, Rev. John C., '85 (GLD) Retired.
Greene, Rev. John L., '76 (SFR) Chap, San Francisco Fire Department
Greene, Rev. Michael, *C.P.* '82 (BRK) [MON] Immaculate Conception Monastery, Jamaica, NY
Greene, Rev. Michael, *C.P.* '82 (NY) [MON] The Congregation of the Passion - St. Paul of the Cross Province, Jamaica, NY
Greene, Rev. Michael M., '79 (BRK) On Leave.
Greene, Rev. Padraig, '76 (OAK) Retired.
Greene, Rev. Msgr. Richard, '65 (LAF) Retired.
Greene, Rev. Thomas P., *S.J.* '07 (NO) [MON] Jesuit Provincial Office (Catholic Society of Religious and Literary Education), New Orleans, LA
Greene, Rev. Thomas P., *S.J.* '07 (STL) [MON] Sacred Heart Jesuit Community, St. Louis, MO; [MON] USA Central & Southern Province, Society of Jesus, St. Louis, MO
Greenfield, Rev. David J., '08 (MAD) Retired.
Greenfield, Rev. James J., *O.S.F.S.* '90 (ALN) [COL] DeSales University, Center Valley, PA; [MON] Oblates of St. Francis de Sales, Center Valley, PA
Greenhalgh, Rev. Donald C., '84 (ARL) Retired.
Greenleaf, Rev. Daniel P., '95 (PRT) Prince of Peace Parish, Lewiston, ME
Greenough, Rev. Patrick, *O.F.M.Conv.* '87 (PEO) St. Ann Parish, Toluca, IL; St. John the Baptist, Lostant, IL; St. Mary's, Wenona, IL; St. Patrick's, Minonk, IL
Greenway, Rev. George G., '87 (SAV) Retired.
Greenwell, Rev. Charles C., '82 (SAN) Retired.
Greenwell, Rev. Michael A., *O.Carm.* '79 (SFR) Chap, St Mary's Med Ctr Curia: Advisory Boards, Commissions, Committees, and Councils St. Teresa, San Francisco, CA
Greenwell, Rev. Zachary L., '14 (MOB) St. John, Enterprise, AL; St. Mary Mission Parish, Geneva, Geneva, AL
Greer, Very Rev. Bradley W., '09 (STU) Curia: Deaneries; Leadership; Offices and Directors St. Peter's, Steubenville, OH
Greer, Rev. G. Michael, '81 (COV) St. John, Covington, KY; [MIS] Shrine of St. Ann, Covington, KY
Greer, Rev. Gabriel, '16 (WCH) Curia: Leadership; Offices and Directors
Greer, Very Rev. Michael J., '75 (MIA) Curia: Leadership Assumption Church, Lauderdale-by-the-Sea, FL
Gregerson, Rev. Royce, '15 (FTW) Curia: Offices and Directors St. John the Evangelist, Goshen, IN
Gregg, Rev. Stephen, *O.Cist.* '12 (DAL) [MON] Our Lady of Dallas Cistercian Abbey, Irving, TX
Gregoire, Rev. Jocelyn, *C.S.Sp.* '86 (PIT) [COL] Duquesne University of the Holy Spirit, Pittsburgh, PA
Gregor, Rev. Robert M., *C.P.M.* '00 (L) On Special Assignment. Holy Angels Academy, Inc., Louisville, KY
Gregorek, Rev. Joseph C., '65 (E) Retired. [COL] Gannon University, Erie, PA
Gregorek, Rev. Stan M., '66 (PIT) Retired. St. Thomas the Apostle, Homestead, PA
Gregorich, Rev. Carl, '18 (MEM) Immaculate Conception, Union City, TN
Gregorio, Rev. Robert J., '68 (CAM) Retired.

Gregory, Rev. James T., '99 (HRT) Prince of Peace Parish Corporation, Woodbury, CT
Gregory, Rev. Kenneth W., '73 (ALB) Retired.
Gregory, Rev. Peter A., '73 (SPR) Retired.
Gregory, Rev. Msgr. Robert S., '69 (KC) Retired.
Greig, Rev. Msgr. Harry D., '76 (LKC) Retired. Curia: Leadership
Grein, Rev. Blane, *O.F.M.* '62 (CIN) [MON] St. Francis Seraph Friary, Cincinnati, OH
Grein, Rev. Blane, *O.F.M.* '62 (GLP) Our Lady of Blessed Sacrament, Ft. Defiance, AZ
Greiner, Rev. Jacob M., '13 (DAV) Curia: Offices and Directors Our Lady of Victory Church of Davenport, Iowa, Davenport, IA
Greiner, Rev. James A., '63 (OKL) Retired.
Greiner, Very Rev. Robert, (BAK) St. Catherine, Fossil, OR
Greiner, Rev. Robert, '93 (BAK) Curia: Leadership; Offices and Directors St. Francis, Arlington, OR; St. John, Condon, OR
Greiner, Rev. Roch, *CFR* '17 (SFE) [MON] Community of the Franciscans of the Renewal San Juan Diego Friary, Albuquerque, NM
Greisen, Rev. Thomas A., '82 (OM) St. Columbkille, Papillion, NE
Greiten, Rev. Gregory J., '92 (MIL) Northwest Catholic School, Milwaukee, WI; Our Lady of Good Hope Congregation, Milwaukee, WI; St. Bernadette Congregation, Milwaukee, WI; St. Catherine, Milwaukee, WI
Grelak, Rev. Andrew T., '71 (BO) Retired. St. Stanislaus, Chelsea, MA; St. Stephen, Framingham, MA
Grelinger, Rev. Adam E., (WCH) [COL] Newman University, Wichita, KS
Grell, Rev. Loras, '96 (LIN) St. Joseph's, Giltner, NE
Grell, Rev. Loras K., '96 (LIN) St. Mary's, Aurora, NE; St. Mary's, Wymore, NE
Gremillion, Rev. Rick, '98 (ALX) Immaculate Heart of Mary, Ball, LA
Gremmels, Rev. John, '91 (FWT) On Leave.
Grenier, Rev. David, *OFM* '15 (WDC) [MON] Commissariat of the Holy Land, Franciscan Monastery - Mount St. Sepulchre, Washington, DC; [MON] Franciscan Monastery USA Inc., Washington, DC
Grenon, Rev. Paul R., '78 (PRO) Saint Joseph's Church Corporation, North Scituate, North Scituate, RI
Greschel, Rev. Mark, '01 (CHI) Military Chap
Greskiewicz, Rev. Joseph A., '69 (SCR) Retired. [MON] Villa St. Joseph, Dunmore, PA
Gresko, Rev. Gregory, *O.S.B.* '05 (RIC) [MON] Mary Mother of the Church Abbey, Richmond, VA
Greskowiak, Rev. David F., '09 (GB) St. Lawrence, Navarino, WI; St. Mary, Black Creek, WI
Gretchko, Rev. A. Edward, '72 (PBR) St. Michael the Archangel, Pleasant City, OH
Gretz, Rev. James R., '94 (PIT) St. Matthew, Pittsburgh, PA
Grevatch, Rev. William N., '64 (LC) Retired.
Greving, Rev. Daniel M., '97 (SC) Curia: Offices and Directors Spalding Catholic Schools, Inc., Alton, IA; St. Anthony's, Hospers, IA; St. Joseph, Granville, IA; St. Mary's, Alton, IA
Grewe, Rev. Michael W., '79 (OM) Curia: Leadership; Offices and Directors St. Cecilia Cathedral, Omaha, NE; [CEM] Calvary, Omaha, NE; [CEM] Catholic Cemeteries of the Archdiocese of Omaha, Omaha, NE; [CEM] Holy Sepulchre, Omaha, NE; [CEM] Resurrection, Omaha, NE; [CEM] St. Mary, Omaha, NE; [CEM] St. Mary Magdalene, Omaha, NE
Grey, Rev. Michael T., *C.S.Sp.* '79 (GAL) [MON] US Foundation for the Congregation of the Holy Ghost and the Immaculate Heart of Mary, Inc., Houston, TX
Gribble, Rev. Richard E., *C.S.C.* '89 (FR) [COL] Stonehill College, North Easton, MA
Gribbon, Rev. Michael C., '81 (BRK) Curia: Pastoral Services Resurrection, Brooklyn, NY
Gribik, Rev. John, '89 (SJP) Curia: Offices and Directors Patronage of the Mother of God, Ford City, PA; St. Michael, West Leechburg, PA
Gribowich, Rev. John, '15 (BRK) On Duty Outside Diocese. Piffard, NY St. Augustine, Brooklyn, NY; St. Charles Borromeo, Brooklyn, NY
Grice, Rev. Edward M., '80 (NO) Retired.
Gricius, Rev. Aurelijus, *O.F.M.* '96 (PRT) [MON] Society of Franciscan Fathers of Greene, Maine, Kennebunk, ME
Gricoski, Rev. Thomas, *O.S.B.* '10 (IND) [MON] St. Meinrad Archabbey, St. Meinrad, IN
Grieco, Rev. Frank M., '01 (RVC) Holy Spirit, New Hyde Park, NY
Grieco, Rev. John, '11 (POD) Curia: Clergy and Religious Services
Grieco, Rev. Michael S., '83 (LA) Holy Redeemer, Montrose, CA; St. Frances of Rome, Azusa, CA; St. James the Less, La Crescenta, CA
Grieman, Rev. Gerald G., '79 (STP) Retired.
Griener, Rev. George E., *S.J.* '73 (OAK) [MON] Jesuit Fathers and Brothers, Berkeley, CA; [SEM] Jesuit School of Theology of Santa Clara University (Berkeley, California Campus), Berkeley, CA
Gries, Rev. Eugene, *O.Praem.* '68 (SFE) Retired. [MON] Santa Maria de la Vid Abbey, Albuquerque, NM
Gries, Rev. Jason B., '04 (EVN) Curia: Leadership Holy Redeemer, Evansville, IN
Gries, Very Rev. Jeremy M., '09 (IND) Curia: Leadership Holy Family Catholic Church, New Albany, Inc., New Albany, IN; [MIS] New Albany Deanery, New Albany, IN
Griesbach, Rev. Msgr. John, '76 (FRS) On Special Assignment. Curia: Leadership; Spiritual Life [RTR] Santa Teresita Youth Center, Three Rivers, CA; [RTR] St. Anthony's Retreat Center, Three Rivers, CA
Griesbach, Rev. Seamus P., '07 (PRT) Curia: Consultative Bodies Cathedral of the Immaculate Conception, Portland, ME; Sacred Heart/St. Dominic, Portland, ME; St. Christopher's, Peaks Island, ME; St. Louis, Portland, ME; St. Peter's, Portland, ME
Griesedieck, Rev. Msgr. Edmund, '65 (STL) Retired. [MIS] St. Louis Catholic Charismatic Renewal, Crestwood, MO
Griesedieck, Rev. Msgr. Edmund O., '65 (STL) Retired. [RTR] Vision of Peace Ministries, Pevely, MO; [SEM] Kenrick School of Theology, ,
Griesemer, Rev. Edward, *S.C.J.* '57 (MIL) Retired. [MIS] Milwaukee Archdiocesan Holy Name Union, New Berlin, WI; [MON] Sacred Heart at Monastery Lake, Franklin, WI
Griesgraber, Rev. Paul Gerard, '06 (LA) Chap, Los Angeles Cty Men's Central Jail
Griffey, Rev. Brendan, '74 (JC) Retired.
Griffin, Rev. Carter H., '04 (WDC) On Special Assignment. Curia: Clergy and Religious Services [SEM] Saint John Paul II Seminary, Washington, DC
Griffin, Rev. Daniel, (RVC) Kellenberg Memorial High School, Uniondale, NY
Griffin, Rev. David G., '66 (BUF) Retired. [MON] Bishop Head Residence, Lackawanna, NY
Griffin, Rev. David R., *O.S.B.* '76 (ALT) [CAM] Penn State Catholic Community, University Park, PA; [CAM] Penn State University, University Park, University Park, PA
Griffin, Rev. David R., *O.S.B.* '76 (GBG) [MON] Saint Vincent Archabbey, Latrobe, PA
Griffin, Rev. James C., '82 (RIC) Retired.
Griffin, Rev. John, '72 (SR) Retired.
Griffin, Rev. John, '77 (MRY) Retired.
Griffin, Rev. Joseph M., '82 (SAG) Retired.
Griffin, Rev. Michael, '90 (SFS) Saint Anthony Parish of Walworth County, Selby, SD; Saint Joseph Parish of McPherson County, Eureka, SD; Saint Joseph Parish of Walworth County, Mobridge, SD; Saint Michael Parish of Campbell County, Herreid, SD
Griffin, Rev. Patrick J., *C.M.* '79 (BRK) [MON] Reverend John B. Murray, C.M. House, Jamaica, NY
Griffin, Rev. Thomas, '16 (NOR) St. Catherine of Siena, Preston, CT; St. Mary, Jewett City, CT; St. Thomas the Apostle, Voluntown, CT
Griffin-Smolenski, Rev. Thomas, *S.J.* '00 (PHX) (>SJ) [MON] Sacred Heart Jesuit Center, Los Gatos, CA
Griffith, Very Rev. Daniel F., '02 (STP) The Basilica of St. Mary Co-Cathedral, Minneapolis, MN
Griffith, Rev. Darragh, '97 (ATL) St. Brigid Catholic Church, Johns Creek, Inc., Johns Creek, GA
Griffith, Rev. Sidney H., *S.T.* '65 (WDC) [MON] Holy Spirit Missionary Cenacle, Riverdale, MD
Griffith, Rev. Thomas, *SVD* '69 (CHI) Retired. [MON] Divine Word Residence, Techny, IL
Griffith, Rev. Zachary, '20 (KNX) Our Lady of Perpetual Help, Chattanooga, TN
Griffiths, Rev. Charles L., '05 (TR) On Leave.
Griffiths, Rev. John, (WIN) Curia: Tribunal
Griffiths, Rev. John M., '76 (CHI) Curia: Tribunal St. Elizabeth of the Trinity, Chicago, IL
Grigassy, Rev. Daniel P., *O.F.M.* '77 (PAT) St. Bonaventure, Paterson, NJ
Griggs, Rev. Gabriel J., *CSC* '22 (FTW) [COL] University of Notre Dame Du Lac, Notre Dame, IN; [MON] Holy Cross Community, Corby Hall, University of Notre Dame, Notre Dame, IN
Grile, Rev. Harry, *C.Ss.R.* '68 (SEA) Sacred Heart of Jesus, Seattle, WA; [MON] The Redemptorist Society of Washington, Seattle, WA
Grile, Rev. Patrick, *C.Ss.R.* '71 (TUC) [MON] Redemptorist Society of Arizona Desert House of Prayer Residence, Tucson, AZ; [RTR] Redemptorist Society of Arizona Redemptorist Renewal Center, Tucson, AZ
Grimaldi, Rev. Joseph, (DET) Sacred Heart Parish Auburn Hills, Auburn Hills, MI
Grimaldi, Rev. Joseph A., (HON) Retired.
Grimaldi, Rev. Msgr. Joseph R., '83 (BRK) Curia: Consultative Bodies; Leadership St. Bernard of Clairvaux, Brooklyn, NY
Grimalia, Rev. Msgr. Vincent J., '68 (SCR) Retired. On Special Assignment. Curia: Offices and Directors
Grimard, Rev. Rocky, *O.M.I.* '91 (WDC) [MON] Missionary Oblates of Mary Immaculate, Washington, DC; [MON] Oblate Community, Washington, DC
Grimditch, Rev. Kevin C., '14 (PHX) Curia: Leadership; Offices and Directors
Grimes, Rev. John C., '00 (MET) Curia: Evangelization; Leadership St. Ambrose, Old Bridge, NJ
Grimes, Rev. John J., '71 (BO) Retired. St. Timothy, Norwood, MA
Grimes, Rev. Price D., '88 (OKL) Retired. On Sick Leave.
Grimes, Rev. Robert R., *S.J.* '84 (NY) [MON] Murray-Weigel Hall (A Jesuit Community at Murray-Weigel Hall and Kohlmann Hall), Bronx, NY
Grimes, Rev. Timothy, '19 (BR) The Congregation Of Sacred Heart Roman Catholic Church, Baton Rouge, LA
Grimm, Rev. Robert, *S.J.* '76 (SEA) [COL] Seattle University, Seattle, WA; [MON] Arrupe Jesuit Community at Seattle University, Seattle, WA
Grimm, Rev. William J., *M.M.* '77 (SJ) [MON] Maryknoll, Los Altos, CA
Grimme, Rev. D. Timothy, '77 (ALT) Asst Chap, UMPC Altoona, Altoona St. Therese of the Child Jesus, Altoona, PA
Grinko, Rev. Frank X., *O.F.M. Cap.* '81 (COS) [MIS] Catholic Center at the Citadel, Colorado Springs, CO; [MON] Solanus Casey Friary, Colorado Springs, CO
Grinnell, Rev. Horace H., '74 (ARL) Retired.
Grinsell, Rev. John, *S.D.B.* '71 (NY) Parish of St. John Bosco, Port Chester, NY
Grippe, Rev. Louis A., '69 (SCR) Retired.
Grippo, Very Rev. Robert F., '72 (NY) Curia: Leadership Annunciation-Our Lady of Fatima, Tuckahoe, NY; Parish of Annunciation-Our Lady of Fatima, Crestwood, NY
Gripshover, Rev. Ronald J., '96 (ARL) St. Lawrence, Alexandria, VA
Grisafi, Rev. Jason, '13 (RVC) St. Joseph, Babylon, NY
Grismer, Rev. Sean, '16 (RCK) On Special Assignment. Curia: Clergy and Religious Services Aurora Central Catholic High School, Aurora, IL
Grisolano, Rev. Michael, '12 (CHI) St. Elizabeth of the Trinity, Chicago, IL
Grispino, Rev. Francis, *S.M.* '56 (BO) [MIS] Marist Fathers Residence, , ; [MON] Marist Fathers Lourdes Residence, Boston, MA
Grissom, Rev. Joel, *S.M.* (WH) [NUR] Good Shepherd Nursing Home LC, Wheeling, WV
Grissom, Rev. Joel R., *S.M.* '03 (SFR) (>WDC) [MON] Marist Center (The Marist Finance Center of the Atlanta Province of the Society of Mary, Marist Fathers and Brothers), Washington, DC
Griswold, Rev. Edward J., '73 (TR) Retired. St. Barnabas, Bayville, NJ
Grizzelle-Reid, Rev. Paul, *S.C.J.* '72 (SP) Retired. [MON] Priests of the Sacred Heart, Pinellas Park, FL
Groark, Rev. Michael J, *OFM Cap.* (CHI) [MON] St. Clare Friary, Chicago, IL
Groarke, Rev. Francis P., '73 (PH) Retired.
Grobe, Rev. Lewis, *O.S.B.* '15 (SCL) [MON] St. John's Abbey, of the Order of St. Benedict, Collegeville, MN
Grochowski, Rev. Bernard J., '63 (WOR) Retired.
Grode, Rev. Patrick M., '18 (SFS) Saint Paul Parish of Brookings County, White, SD; [CAM] Pope Pius XII Newman Center, Brookings, SD
Grodecki, Rev. Christopher, (FTW) [MIS] Jesuit Community, South Bend, IN
Grodecki, Rev. Henry W, *C.M.* '75 (AJ) Cathedral of Our Lady of Guadalupe, Anchorage, AK
Grodi, Rev. Peter D., '20 (TOL) St. Michael the Archangel, Findlay, OH; [CAM] University of Findlay Newman Campus Ministry, Findlay, OH
Grodnicki, Rev. Robert S., '88 (TR) Curia: Leadership St. Luke, Toms River, NJ
Groeger, Rev. Mark, '21 (ALT) Prince of Peace, Northern Cambria, PA
Groeschel, Rev. Benedict Joseph, *C.F.R.* '59 (NY)
Grogan, Rev. James Clyde, '68 (BEL) Retired.
Grogan, Rev. James J., '15 (TR) Our Lady of Good Counsel, Moorestown, NJ
Grogan, Rev. Todd O., '90 (CIN) On Leave.
Grogan, Rev. William E., '83 (PH) Holy Cross, Philadelphia, PA

Grogan, Rev. William P., '76 (CHI) Curia: Offices and Directors St. Gertrude, Chicago, IL; [MIS] The Catholic Education Institute, Chicago, IL
Groh, Very Rev. Christopher, '79 (JOL) Curia: Leadership St. Bernard, Joliet, IL; St. Mary Magdalene, Joliet, IL
Grohe, Rev. Eugene, *C.Ss.R.* '50 (TR) [RTR] San Alfonso Retreat House, Long Branch, NJ
Grohe, Rev. Eugene J., *C.Ss.R.* '50 (NY) [RTR] Redemptorist Community at Esopus (Redemptorist Fathers and Brothers), Ulster Park, NY
Groher, Rev. Robert C., '66 (GB) Retired.
Gromadzki, Rev. Michael J., '01 (MET) St. Mary of Ostrabrama, South River, NJ
Gromadzki, Rev. Stanley G., '89 (MET) Sacred Heart, South Amboy, NJ
Gron, Rev. Ryszard, '88 (CHI) St. William, Chicago, IL
Groncki, Rev. Msgr. Richard F., '66 (NEW) Retired. Curia: Offices and Directors Annunciation, Paramus, NJ
Grondin, Rev. Charles R., '03 (PRO) The Church of the Blessed Sacrament in Providence, Rhode Island, Providence, RI
Gronert, Rev. Stephen F., '86 (WCH) Retired.
Gronifillo, Rev. Alejandro, (TR) Retired. [MON] Villa Vianney, Trenton, NJ
Gronotte, Rev. Andrew, '16 (ATL) [MIS] Legionaries of Christ, Atlanta, GA
Gronotte, Rev. Christopher, *L.C.* (GRY) Sacred Heart Apostolic School, Inc., Rolling Prairie, IN
Groody, Rev. Daniel G., *C.S.C.* '93 (FTW) [COL] University of Notre Dame Du Lac, Notre Dame, IN; [MON] Holy Cross Community, Corby Hall, University of Notre Dame, Notre Dame, IN
Grooms, Rev. Kenneth, '19 (RVC) St. Aidan's Church, Williston Park, NY
Gros, Rev. Edwin L., *S.J.* '80 (NO) Holy Name of Jesus, New Orleans, LA; [MON] Loyola Jesuit Community, New Orleans, LA
Gros, Rev. Paul A., '09 (BR) Curia: Administration; Clergy and Religious Services St. Margaret Queen of Scotland (Congregation Of St. Margaret Roman Catholic Church), Hammond, LA
Grosch, Rev. Michael J., '11 (STL) St. Gerard Majella Catholic Church, Kirkwood, MO; St. Michael Catholic Church, Shrewsbury, MO
Grosch, Rev. Robert, '74 (GF) Retired. Curia: Leadership
Grosch, Rev. Robert, '74 (HEL) Curia: Leadership
Grosch, Rev. Robert D., '74 (GF) Retired. Curia: Leadership; Offices and Directors
Groshek, Rev. Msgr. Richard, '62 (LAN) Retired.
Gross, Rev. Brian P., '10 (BIS) Curia: Leadership Epiphany, Watford City, ND; Our Lady of Consolation, Alexander, ND
Gross, Rev. Donald L., '59 (LFT) Retired.
Gross, Rev. G. Robert, '07 (DUB) Curia: Leadership Marquette High School, Bellevue, Iowa, Bellevue, IA; SS. Peter and Paul Church, Springbrook, Iowa, Springbrook, IA; St. Catherine Church, St. Catherine, Iowa, Dubuque, IA; St. Donatus Church, St. Donatus, Iowa, St. Donatus, IA; St. Joseph's Church, Bellevue, Iowa, Bellevue, IA
Gross, Rev. Gary, '83 (LIN) St. James, Mead, NE
Gross, Rev. Gary L., '83 (LIN) Curia: Leadership
Gross, Rev. Gerard, *O.C.S.O.* '78 (ATL) [MON] The Monastery of the Holy Spirit, Conyers, GA
Gross, Rev. James, '99 (FAR) St. Mary Church of Grand Forks, Grand Forks, ND
Gross, Rev. Ken, (DM) Retired. Curia: Offices and Directors
Gross, Rev. Lee W., '87 (ARL) On Duty Outside Diocese. Mount St Mary's Seminary, Emmitsburg, MD
Gross, Rev. Lee W., '87 (BAL) [SEM] Mount St. Mary's Seminary, Emmitsburg, MD
Gross, Friar Matthew, *O.F.M.Cap.* '61 (COS) [MON] Our Lady of the Angels Friary, Colorado Springs, CO
Gross, Rev. Nile C., '09 (NO) Curia: Offices and Directors St. Nicholas of Myra Byzantine Catholic Mission, New Orleans, LA; [SEM] Notre Dame Seminary Graduate School of Theology, New Orleans, LA (>PBR) St. Nicholas of Myra Byzantine Catholic Mission, New Orleans, LA
Gross, Rev. Ralph C., '70 (MIL) Retired. Curia: Leadership
Gross, Rev. Richard C., '62 (NU) Retired.
Gross, Rev. Robert M., '14 (PH) Visitation B.V.M., Norristown, PA
Gross, Rev. Thomas L., '75 (HON) Retired.
Grossenburg, Rev. Tony, '99 (RC) Blessed Sacrament, Rapid City, SD
Grossi, Rev. Anthony J., *O.S.B.* '99 (GBG) Clelian Heights School for Exceptional Children (Clelian Heights, Inc., Apostles of the Sacred Heart of Jesus), Greensburg, PA; [CON] Apostles of the Sacred Heart of Jesus, Greensburg, PA; [MON] Saint Vincent Archabbey, Latrobe, PA
Grosskopf, Rev. Albert, (SJ) [MON] Sacred Heart Jesuit Center, Los Gatos, CA
Grosskopf, Rev. Albert A., *S.J.* '83 (ORG)
Grossman, Rev. Jered, '20 (FAR) St. Michael's Church of Grand Forks, Grand Forks, ND
Grosso, Rev. James D., '79 (BGP) Saint Leo Roman Catholic Church Corporation, Stamford, CT
Grote, Rev. Alan W., '82 (GBG) Chap, Armstrong Cty Hosp, Kittanning Curia: Miscellaneous / Other Offices Christ, Prince of Peace Parish, Ford City, PA; St. Lawrence, Ford City, PA
Groth, Rev. Michael, '20 (JOL) St. Joseph, Downers Grove, IL; [MIS] Companions of Christ of the Diocese of Joliet, Crest Hill, IL
Grous, Rev. Msgr. Albin J., '87 (PH) St. Andrew, Drexel Hill, PA
Grove, Rev. Kevin G., *C.S.C.* '10 (FTW) [COL] University of Notre Dame Du Lac, Notre Dame, IN; [MON] Holy Cross Community, Corby Hall, University of Notre Dame, Notre Dame, IN
Grove, Rev. Stanley, *M.S.A.* '00 (NOR) [MON] Society of the Missionaries of the Holy Apostles, Cromwell, CT
Grovenburg, Rev. Gregg, *S.J.* '88 (NO) [COL] Loyola University New Orleans, New Orleans, LA; [MON] Loyola Jesuit Community, New Orleans, LA
Grover, Rev. Daniel G., '15 (OKL) St. Matthew's, Elk City, OK
Grover, Rev. David A., '83 (CAM) Curia: Advisory Boards, Commissions, Committees, and Councils Church of St. Rose, Haddon Heights, N.J., Haddon Heights, NJ
Grover, Rev. Peter W., *O.M.V.* '90 (BO) [MIS] St. Clement Archdiocesan Eucharistic Shrine, Boston, MA; [SEM] Our Lady of Grace Seminary, Boston, MA
Grozio, Rev. Stephen M., *C.M.* '78 (PH) [MON] Congregation of the Mission, Philadelphia, PA; [SEM] St. Vincent's Seminary, Philadelphia, PA
Grubb, Rev. Hyacinth, *O.P.* '20 (NY) Archcare [MIS] Dominican Friars Health Care Ministry of New York, Inc., New York, NY; [MON] St. Vincent Ferrer Priory, New York, NY
Grubba, Rev. Dale W., '66 (MAD) St. James, Neshkoro, WI; St. John the Baptist, Princeton, WI
Gruben, Rev. John, *O.A.R.* '74 (NY) Sacred Heart, Suffern, NY; [SEM] Tagaste Monastery, Suffern, NY
Gruber, Rev. Eric J., '91 (ALN) St. John Fisher, Catasauqua, PA
Gruber, Rev. Francis, *O.Cist.* '21 (DAL) [MON] Our Lady of Dallas Cistercian Abbey, Irving, TX
Gruber, Rev. Frederick, (PIT) Christ the Divine Shepherd, Monroeville, PA
Gruber, Rev. Frederick W., '12 (PIT) Chap, Golden Living Ctr Monroeville and Oakmont; Allegheny
Gruber, Rev. Peter, (PIT) [CAM] Chatham College, Pittsburgh, PA; [CAM] University of Pittsburgh, Pittsburgh, PA
Gruber, Rev. Peter, *C.O.* (PIT) [CAM] Carnegie-Mellon University, Pittsburgh, PA
Gruber, Rev. Peter J., *C.O.* (PIT) [MON] Congregation of the Oratory of St. Philip Neri, Pittsburgh, PA
Gruden, Rev. William J., '79 (SAG) Retired.
Grudowski, Rev. Msgr. Robert J., '61 (PH) Retired.
Gruenbauer, Rev. Hans H., '76 (CIN) Retired.
Grullon Capellan, Rev. Carlos M., (PCE) Curia: Leadership
Grullon Capellan, Rev. Carlos Manuel, '08 (PCE) Curia: Leadership Nuestra Senora de la Monserrate, Salinas, PR
Grumsey, Rev. Dennis, *O.F.M.Conv.* '86 (BAL) St. Casimir, Baltimore, MD
Grundhaus, Rev. Msgr. Roger, (CR) Retired.
Grundman, Rev. David, '97 (SCL) St. Edward's, Bowlus, MN; St. Francis of Assisi, Freeport, MN; St. Mary, Upsala, MN
Grundowski, Rev. Francis M., '71 (ALN) Retired.
Grunow, Rev. Stephen E., '97 (CHI) On Duty Outside Diocese. Word on Fire Catholic Ministries, Santa Barbara, CA
Grupczynski, Rev. Gerald, *S.Chr.* '88 (LAV) Curia: Advisory Boards, Commissions, Committees, and Councils Our Lady of Las Vegas, Las Vegas, NV
Gruszka, Rev. Artur, '04 (LA) St. Pius X, Santa Fe Springs, CA
Grytner, Rev. Eugene, *S.D.S.* '79 (ORL) St. Thomas Aquinas, Bartow, FL
Grzelak, Rev. Thaddeus A., '65 (BRK) Retired.
Grzesik, Rev. Michael, '15 (CHI) Our Lady of the Lakes, Ingleside, IL
Grzeskiewicz, Rev. Piotr, *C.Ss.R.* '08 (MET) Christ the Redeemer Parish, Manville, NJ
Grzybowski, Rev. Jakub, '15 (PAT) St. Joseph, West Milford, NJ
Grzymski, Rev. Donald, *O.F.M.Conv.* '80 (BAL) Archbishop Curley High School, Baltimore, MD; [EFT] Archbishop Curley High School Endowment Trust, Baltimore, MD; [MIS] The Maryland State Council, Knights of Columbus, Bowie, MD
Gschwend, Rev. James P., *S.J.* '65 (CHI) [RTR] Bellarmine Jesuit Retreat House, Inc., Barrington, IL
Guadagnoli, Rev. Michael, '97 (DAL) Curia: Administration St. Monica Catholic Parish, Dallas, TX
Guadalquiver, Rev. Msgr. Leonardo C., '92 (MOB) Curia: Offices and Directors St. Edmund-by-the-Sea Parish, Dauphin Island, Dauphin Island, AL; St. Rose of Lima Parish, Mon Luis Island, Coden, AL
Guadalupe, Rev. Gerard Leoval C., '90 (RIC) St. Andrew the Apostle, Chincoteague Island, VA
Guaipo, Rev. Jose Gregorio, '88 (SJN) Santa Rosa de Lima, Guaynabo, PR
Guajardo, Rev. Hilario, '89 (AUS) SS. Cyril and Methodius, Granger, TX
Gualano, Rev. Kevin M., '04 (ALN) St. Francis of Assisi, Allentown, PA
Guanchez, Rev. Omar, '09 (SCL) St. Mary of Mt. Carmel, Long Prairie, MN
Guanella, Rev. Alan M., '13 (LC) Our Lady, Queen of Heaven, Wisconsin Rapids, WI; [EFT] Our Lady Queen of Heaven Parish Endowment Trust, Wisconsin Rapids, WI
Guanga, Rev. Esteban Sanchez, '13 (NY) Church of the Assumption, Peekskill, NY
Guanipa, Rev. Luis M., '00 (RCK) St. Monica, Carpentersville, IL
Guarascio, Rev. James, (JOL) Our Lady of Mercy, Aurora, IL
Guardado Delgado, Rev. Jaime Antonio, (MIA) Good Shepherd, Miami, FL
Guardado Marin, Rev. Cesar, '21 (LA) St. Emydius, Lynwood, CA
Guardiano, Rev. Peter, (GBG) Immaculate Conception, Connellsville, PA; St. Aloysius, Dunbar, PA; St. John the Evangelist, Connellsville, PA; St. Rita, Connellsville, PA
Guardiola, Rev. Louis, *C.P.M.* '01 (OWN) [MON] Fathers of Mercy, Auburn, KY
Guarino, Rev. Domenico, *M.C.C.J* '89 (LA) Holy Cross, Los Angeles, CA
Guarino, Rev. Mario, '81 (BO) St. Christine, Marshfield, MA
Guarino, Rev. R. Michael, '68 (BO) Retired.
Guarino, Rev. Randy, (SEA) Queen of Angels, Port Angeles, WA; St. Anne Parish, Forks, WA; St. Joseph, Sequim, WA
Guarino, Rev. Msgr. Thomas G., '77 (NEW) Curia: Organizations (affiliated, inter-Diocesan, miscellaneous/ other) [COL] Seton Hall University, South Orange, NJ
Guarnieri, Rev. Leo J., '77 (RIC) Retired.
Guarnieri, Rev. Richard M., '71 (NY) Retired.
Guarnizo, Rev. Jhon, '03 (STA) Curia: Social Services Blessed Trinity, Jacksonville, FL
Guastello, Rev. Michael, '17 (KCK) St. Benedict, Bendena, KS; St. Charles, Troy, KS; St. Joseph, Wathena, KS
Guativa, Rev. Javier, '11 (MIL) On Duty Outside Diocese. La Sagrada Familia, Dominican Republic [MIS] Community of St. Paul, Inc., Racine, WI
Guay, Rev. Robert, '73 (PIT) Retired. Holy Sepulcher, Butler, PA; St. Kilian, Cranberry Township, PA
Gubbels, Rev. Wayne, '71 (DM) Retired.
Gubbins, Rev. John, '70 (MIA) Retired.
Gubbiotti, Rev. Jeffrey A., '04 (HRT) Holy Rosary Church Corporation of Ansonia, Connecticut, Ansonia, CT; The Church of the Assumption of the B.V., Ansonia, CT
Gubernat, Rev. Michael E., '77 (NEW) Our Lady of Victories, Jersey City, NJ
Guberovic, Rev. Zeljko J., '06 (GLD) Divine Mercy of Manistee, Manistee, MI
Guberovic, Rev. Zeljko J., '06 (NEW) On Duty Outside Diocese. Diocese of Gaylord, Gaylord, MI
Guckin, Rev. Matthew W., '99 (PH) Our Lady of Mount Carmel, Doylestown, PA
Gucor, Rev. Fredhelito E., '12 (SAC) Pastor of St. Joseph

Parish, Lincoln, a corporation sole, Lincoln, CA
Gude, Rev. Udayameena V., *O.F.M.Cap.* (WIL) [MON] St. Felix Friary, Wilmington, DE; [SPF] Emmanuel Dining Room, West, Wilmington, DE
Gudewicz, Rev. John L., '70 (PIT) Retired.
Gudimalla, Rev. Raju, *H.G.N*'11 (STO) Curia: Leadership St. Joachim Church of Lockeford (Pastor of), Lockeford, CA
Gudime, Rev. Devasahayam, '90 (KC) Blessed Sacrament, Bethany, MO
Gudime, Rev. Jesudas, (CHI) St. Mary of the Woods, Chicago, IL
Gudipalli, Rev. Ravi Rayappa, (LR) St. Mary of the Springs, Hot Springs, AR
Gudipalli, Rev. Thomas, '03 (GI) St. John the Evangelist, Stapleton, NE
Guenter, Rev. Frank, '66 (GAL) Retired.
Guenther, Rev. Brandon, '19 (LC) Holy Ghost, Chippewa Falls, WI; Notre Dame, Chippewa Falls, WI; St. Bridget, Chippewa Falls, WI
Guenther, Very Rev. Daniel C., '82 (SC) Curia: Leadership St. Mary's, Humboldt, IA
Guenther, Rev. Msgr. Donald E., '62 (NEW) Retired. St. Bartholomew, Scotch Plains, NJ
Guentner, Rev. Hugh M., *O.S.M.* '91 (DEN) Our Lady of Mount Carmel Catholic Parish in Denver, Denver, CO
Guerin, Rev. Louis T., '87 (PMB) Retired.
Guerin-Boutaud, Rev. Bernard Marie, *C.S.J.* (NEW) Our Lady of Mt. Carmel, Orange, NJ
Guerra, Rev. Enrique, '07 (ORL) St. Isaac Jogues, Orlando, FL
Guerra, Rev. Henry, (FAJ) Concathedral Dulce Nombre de Jesus, Humacao, PR
Guerra, Rev. Jose Sobarzo, '04 (RNO) St. Paul, Winnemucca, NV
Guerra, Rev. Ricardo V., *O.M.I.* '78 (SAT) Retired. [NUR] Oblate Madonna Residence, San Antonio, TX
Guerra, Rev. Robert F., '00 (VIC) Parish of the Nativity, Eagle Lake, TX
Guerra-Mayaudon, Rev. Gerardo, *O.P.* '69 (AUS) [MON] Dominican Friars of Austin, Austin, TX
Guerreiro, Rev. Clyde, *SS.CC.* (HON) St. Patrick, Honolulu, HI; St. Patrick School, Honolulu, HI
Guerrera, Rev. Richard P., *SJ* '73 (BO) [MON] Campion Health & Wellness, Inc., Weston, MA
Guerrera, Rev. Vittorio, '12 (HRT) The Church of Our Lady of Loreto of Waterbury Corporation, Waterbury, CT; The Corporation of the Church of the Blessed Sacrament in Waterbury, Waterbury, CT
Guerrero, Rev. Alfred, (HON) Curia: Consultative Bodies; Offices and Directors
Guerrero, Rev. Alfred Omar B., (HON) Newman Center-Holy Spirit Parish, Honolulu, HI
Guerrero, Rev. Felixberto Leon, *O.F.M.Cap.* (AGN) Curia: Miscellaneous / Other Offices
Guerrero, Rev. Felixberto Leon, *O.F.M.Cap.* '86 (AGN) Curia: Tribunal [MON] St. Fidelis Friary, Agana Heights, GU
Guerrero, Rev. Jose Abraham, '98 (TUC) Saint Monica Roman Catholic Parish - Tucson, Tucson, AZ
Guerrero, Rev. Jose Ma., (ARE) Retired.
Guerrero, Rev. Joseph Ricardo, *M.J.* '85 (LA) [MON] Missionaries of Jesus, Inc., Los Angeles, CA
Guerrero, Rev. Juan Carlos Ruiz, *O.F.M* (CHI) [MON] St. Peter's Friary, Chicago, IL
Guerrero, Rev. Lawrence M., '83 (STO) Retired. St. Bernadette Church (Pastor of), Stockton, CA
Guerrero, Rev. Servando, '14 (SAT) St. Leonard's, San Antonio, TX
Guerrero, Rev. Toribio C., '96 (LAR) Curia: Leadership San Francisco Javier, Laredo, TX
Guerrero, Rev. Toribio C., (LAR) Curia: Offices and Directors
Guerrero Rodriguez, Rev. Jesus, '15 (KNX) St. Mary's Catholic Church, Johnson City, TN
Guerrero-Oeta, Rev. Abel, '00 (ATL) St. Patrick Catholic Church, Norcross, Inc., Norcross, GA
Guerrini, Rev. Brian, *SS.CC.* '08 (LA) [MON] Congregation of the Sacred Hearts of Jesus and Mary, La Verne, CA
Guesnier, Rev. Rene, *O.S.B.* '61 (KC) [MON] Conception Abbey (Benedictine Monks), Conception, MO
Guessetto, Rev. Robert Joseph, *O.S.A.* '79 (PH) St. Rita of Cascia, Philadelphia, PA; [MON] Augustinian Community (O.S.A.), Philadelphia, PA
Guest, Rev. Richard M., '94 (ARL) St. Luke, McLean, VA
Guest, Rev. Vincent G., '12 (CAM) Curia: Advisory Boards, Commissions, Committees, and Councils; Pastoral Services; Tribunal The Church of Sacred Heart, Camden, NJ
Guevara, Rev. Alfonso M., '77 (BWN) Curia: Advisory Boards, Commissions, Committees, and Councils; Leadership St. John the Baptist, San Juan, TX; [NUR] San Juan Nursing Home, Inc., San Juan, TX
Guevara, Rev. Jose Maria, '68 (LAR) Curia: Leadership St. Jude, Laredo, TX
Guevara, Rev. Manuel, '10 (PAT) On Leave. Curia: Leadership
Guevin, Rev. Benedict M., *O.S.B.* '85 (MAN) [MON] St. Anselm Abbey, Manchester, NH
Guffey, Rev. David, *C.S.C.* '91 (LA) St. Monica, Santa Monica, CA
Guffey, Rev. David, *C.S.C.* '91 (FR) [MIS] Holy Cross Family Ministries, North Easton, MA
Guglielmi, Rev. Msgr. Donald A., '84 (BGP) On Duty Outside Diocese. Curia: Canonical Services (>NY) [SEM] St. Joseph's Seminary, Yonkers, NY
Guglielmo, Rev. Alan F., '68 (NEW) Retired. [MON] St. John Vianney Residence for Retired Priests, Rutherford, NJ
Gugliotta, Rev. Kevin, (NEW) [CAM] Ramapo College, Mahwah, NJ
Guiao, Rev. Raymond P., *S.J.* '86 (CLV) St. Ignatius High School, Cleveland, OH; [MIS] St. Ignatius High School Scholarship Granting Organization, Cleveland, OH
Guichard, Rev. Benoit, *F.S.S.P.* '04 (LIN) [SEM] Our Lady of Guadalupe Seminary, Inc., Denton, NE
Guida, Rev. Amedeo G., '85 (SY) Sacred Heart, Cicero, NY; St. Joseph and St. Patrick, Utica, NY
Guidi, Rev. Matthew, '12 (SPR) Our Lady of the Lake, Southwick, MA
Guidini, Rev. Jairo Francisco, *C.S.* '93 (NY) Our Lady of Pompeii, New York, NY; [MIS] Scalabrini International Migration Network, New York, NY
Guido, Rev. Joseph J., *O.P.* '81 (PRO) [MON] St. Thomas Aquinas Priory at Providence College, Providence, RI
Guido, Rev. Juan J., '14 (LR) Curia: Leadership; Offices and Directors Christ the King, Little Rock, AR; St. Francis of Assisi Church, Roland, AR
Guido, Rev. Luis, '07 (SB) St. Louis, Cathedral City, CA
Guido, Rev. Paul, *O.F.M.* '66 (ALB) (>NY) [RTR] Mt. Alvernia Retreat House, Wappingers Falls, NY
Guido, Rev. Thomas J., '87 (PT) Church of the Resurrection, Miramar Beach, FL
Guidon, Rev. Patrick, *OMI* (SAT) [NUR] Oblate Madonna Residence, San Antonio, TX
Guidry, Rev. Michael, '91 (LAF) On Administrative Leave.
Guidry, Rev. Mitchell, '97 (LAF) Our Lady Queen of All Saints, Ville Platte, LA
Guijarro, Rev. Msgr. Mario, (SJN) Curia: Offices and Directors Colegio San Pedro Martir, Guaynabo, PR
Guijarro de Corzo, Rev. Msgr. Mario A., '78 (SJN) San Pedro Martir de Verona, Guaynabo, PR
Guilbeau, Very Rev. Aubrey V., '82 (LKC) Curia: Advisory Boards, Commissions, Committees, and Councils; Leadership St. Theodore, Lake Charles, LA; [MIS] Society of Roman Catholic Church of the Dioceses of Lake Charles, Lake Charles, LA
Guilbert, Rev. Norman J., '97 (BGP) The Church of the Sacred Heart of Jesus, Danbury, Danbury, CT
Guilfoil, Rev. Brendan, '13 (CHI) SS. Constance and Robert Bellarmine Parish, Chicago, IL
Guillen, Rev. Alfredo, *O.Carm.* '12 (JOL) [MON] Carmelite Provincial Office, Darien, IL
Guillen, Rev. Fernando E., '90 (NEW) St. Francis of Assisi, Ridgefield Park, NJ
Guillen, Rev. Jorge, *S.D.B.* '69 (LA) St. Anne, Santa Monica, CA
Guillen, Rev. Oswaldo, *S.D.B.* '02 (CHI) St. Cecilia, Mt. Prospect, IL
Guillen, Rev. Randy, (ORG) St. Angela Merici, Brea, CA
Guillen, Rev. Robert, '70 (WDC) Retired.
Guillen, Rev. Tomas, (SB) Saint Oscar Romero Catholic Community, Inc., Eastvale, CA
Guillen-Vega, Rev. Henry, '11 (P) On Leave.
Guillory, Rev. Brad D., '09 (LAF) On Special Assignment. Archdiocese of the Military Services
Guillory, Rev. Brad D., (MO) Curia: Offices and Directors
Guillory, Rev. Joshua P., '07 (LAF) St. Patrick, Lafayette, LA
Guillory, Rev. Joshua P., '07 (LAF) Curia: Tribunal
Guilloux, Rev. Edouard B., '19 (ARL) St. John the Apostle, Leesburg, VA
Guilmain, Rev. Roland, *A.A.* '53 (BO) Retired. [MON] Augustinians of the Assumption, Inc., Boston, MA
Guimon, Rev. Michael M., *O.S.M.* '70 (CHI) [MON] Assumption Priory, Chicago, IL
Guinan, Rev. Frank, '66 (PMB) Retired.
Guinto, Rev. Danilo, '18 (LA) St. Paschal Baylon, Thousand Oaks, CA
Guiral Cadavid, Rev. Willmar, *O.S.S.T.* '02 (SJN) [COL] Universidad Central de Bayamon, Inc., Bayamon, PR
Guiral Cadavid, Rev. Willmar A., *O.SS.T* '02 (ARE) St. Anthony, Isabela, PR; [MIS] Chapel Nuestra Senora de la Providencia, Isabela, PR
Guiriba, Rev. Aniceto, (P) St. James, Molalla, OR
Guiriba, Rev. Aniceto, '13 (P) Curia: Offices and Directors
Guise, Rev. Cyril, *O.C.D.* '59 (MIL) [MON] Discalced Carmelite Friars of Holy Hill, Inc., Hubertus, WI
Guiteau, Rev. Pierre Toussaint, *CFR* '18 (NY) [MON] Our Lady of the Angels Friary, Bronx, NY
Guitron, Rev. Steven, '94 (LA) St. Joseph, Pomona, CA
Gula, Rev. Richard, *P.S.S.* (E) On Duty Outside Diocese.
Gula, Rev. Richard M., *P.S.S.* '73 (BAL) [MON] Society of St. Sulpice, Province of the United States, Baltimore, MD
Gulash, Rev. George M., '92 (ALT) Resurrection Roman Catholic Church, Johnstown, PA; St. Clare of Assisi, Johnstown, PA; [CAM] University of Pittsburgh at Johnstown, Johnstown, PA
Guld, Rev. Jerome, '14 (TR) The Parish of St. Katharine Drexel, Burlington, N.J., Burlington, NJ
Gulfam, Rev. Nasir, (RVC) Our Lady of Mercy, Hicksville, NY
Gulfam, Rev. Nasir, (RVC) Curia: Leadership
Gulino, Rev. Stephen S., '97 (NOR) Curia: Offices and Directors
Guljas, Rev. Andrew R., *C.S.C.* '68 (FTW) [MIS] Holy Cross House, Notre Dame, IN
Gullo, Rev. Joseph A., '86 (BUF) Retired. St. Mary, Arcade, NY
Gully, Rev. Msgr. Bernard L., '62 (SAN) Retired.
Gumalay, Rev. Rowell, *MOP* '13 (SR) Pastor of St. Francis Solano Catholic Church of Sonoma, A Corporation Sole, Sonoma, CA
Gummess, Rev. Matthew, *OCarm.* (FTW) [SEM] Moreau Seminary, Notre Dame, IN
Gumula, Rev. Stanislaus, *O.C.S.O.* '04 (CHR) Retired. On Duty Outside Diocese. Ecuador [MON] Mepkin Abbey, Moncks Corner, SC
Gunderson, Rev. Gerald T., '76 (CHI) Retired.
Gundiga, Rev. V. Sagar, '19 (WOR) St. Gabriel the Archangel, Upton, MA
Gunn, Rev. Msgr. James L., '77 (MAD) Curia: Offices and Directors St. John the Baptist, Waunakee, WI; St. Mary of the Lake, Waunakee, WI
Gunning, Rev. Eugene L., '55 (SCR) Retired.
Gunningham, Rev. John, '07 (SB) On Special Assignment.
Gunwall, Rev. Kurtis, '08 (FAR) Curia: Offices and Directors
Gunwall, Rev. Kurtis L., '08 (FAR) St. Alphonsus Church of Langdon, Langdon, ND; St. Edward Church of Nekoma, Nekoma, ND; St. Michael's Church of Wales, Wales, ND
Guppenberger, Rev. August, '61 (CIN) Retired.
Gural, Rev. William S., *SS.CC.* '21 (BWN) Sacred Heart, Edinburg, TX
Gurath, Rev. Guy G., '64 (MIL) Retired.
Gurdak, Rev. Joseph, *OFM Cap* (NY) Retired. [MON] St. Clare Friary (Capuchin Franciscan Friars, Province of St. Mary), Yonkers, NY
Gurka, Rev. Gerald J., '80 (SCR) All Saints Parish, Plymouth, PA; St. John the Baptist, Larksville, PA
Gurnee, Rev. William H., '00 (WDC) Curia: Clergy and Religious Services; Tribunal St. Joseph's on Capitol Hill, Washington, DC
Gurnick, Rev. Michael K., '98 (CLV) St. Malachi, Cleveland, OH; St. Patrick, Cleveland, OH
Gurrola, Rev. Roberto, *I.V.E.* (PH) St. Veronica, Philadelphia, PA
Gurtler, Rev. Gary M., *S.J.* '79 (BO) [MON] Campion Center, Inc., Weston, MA
Gurtner, Very Rev. Mark A., '96 (FTW) Curia: Leadership; Offices and Directors Our Lady of Good Hope, Fort Wayne, IN; [CCH] Catholic Charities of the Diocese of Ft. Wayne-South Bend, Inc., Fort Wayne, IN; [MIS] Scholarship Granting Organization of Northeast Indiana, Inc., Fort Wayne, IN
Gurtner, Very Rev. Mark A., '96 (FTW) Curia: Leadership; Offices and Directors
Gusiora, Rev. Alphonsus, '83 (PCE) Retired. On Leave.
Gusmer, Rev. Msgr. Charles W., '66 (NEW) Retired. Curia: Offices and Directors St. Catherine of Siena, Cedar Grove, NJ
Gustafson, Rev. Christopher M., '95 (CHI) St. Norbert and Our Lady of the Brook Parish, Northbrook, IL
Gustafson, Rev. Daniel, *S.J.* (BO) [MON] The Jesuit Community at Boston College, Chestnut Hill, MA
Gustafson, Rev. Roger G., '14 (SFR) Chap, St Thomas

More Society St. Hilary, Tiburon, CA
Guste, Rev. Placid, *S.M.P.* '61 (SPC) [MON] The Society of Our Mother of Peace, Sons of Our Mother of Peace - Queen of Heaven Solitude, High Ridge, MO
Guste, Rev. Placid, *S.M.P.* '61 (STL) [MON] Society of Our Mother of Peace, High Ridge, MO
Gutay, Rev. Jose Femilou, *O.F.M.* (GLP) Our Lady of Blessed Sacrament, Ft. Defiance, AZ
Gutgsell, Rev. Michael F., '74 (OM) On Administrative Leave.
Gutgsell, Rev. Stephen J., '84 (OM) St. John the Baptist, Fort Calhoun, NE
Guthneck, Rev. Peter E., '71 (GF) Retired.
Guthridge, Rev. Timothy, *C.PP.S.* '97 (LA) St. Agnes, Los Angeles, CA
Guthrie, Rev. Douglas J., '77 (GAL) St. Luke the Evangelist, Houston, TX
Guthrie, Rev. Raymond, '84 (MIL) Congregation of St. Francis de Sales, Lake Geneva, WI
Guthrie, Rev. Raymond P., '84 (PEO) On Duty Outside Diocese. Holy Family Church, Whitefish Bay, WI
Gutierrez, Rev. Alfonso, '85 (SAV) Immaculate Conception, Moultrie, GA
Gutierrez, Rev. Alvin P., '61 (PIT) Retired.
Gutierrez, Rev. Andres E., '12 (BWN) Curia: Leadership Holy Spirit, McAllen, TX
Gutierrez, Rev. Andrew, '19 (NO) On Special Assignment. Studies, University of St. Mary of the Lake, Mundelein, IL St. Catherine of Siena, Metairie, LA
Gutierrez, Rev. Armando J., '12 (SFR) On Duty Outside Diocese. Studies, Rome [SEM] St. Patrick's Seminary and University (The Roman Catholic Seminary of San Francisco), Menlo Park, CA
Gutierrez, Rev. Celestino, '64 (VEN) St. Jude Parish in Sarasota, Inc., Sarasota, FL
Gutierrez, Rev. Dionisio, *O.A.R.* '63 (NEW) Holy Family, Union City, NJ
Gutierrez, Rev. Eduar, (HRT) [CAM] Central Connecticut State University Newman House, New Britain, CT
Gutierrez, Rev. Eduardo, (RNO) St. Teresa of Avila Parish Corporation, Carson City, NV
Gutierrez, Rev. Francisco, '01 (YAK) Sacred Heart, Prosser, WA
Gutierrez, Rev. Fulgencio, '00 (BRK) St. Michael, Brooklyn, NY
Gutierrez, Rev. Gilberto, '73 (PAT) Retired.
Gutierrez, Rev. Ismael, '04 (OAK) St. Francis of Assisi, Concord, CA
Gutierrez, Rev. Javier, *S.F.* '91 (SFE) Holy Cross, Santa Cruz, NM
Gutierrez, Rev. Msgr. Jeronimo, '81 (SJ) Retired.
Gutierrez, Rev. Jose, '73 (STP) Retired.
Gutierrez, Rev. Jose Luis, (GAL) St. John Fisher, Richmond, TX
Gutierrez, Rev. Juan, '22 (LA) St. John the Baptist, Baldwin Park, CA
Gutierrez, Rev. Juan Rogelio, '07 (BWN) Sacred Heart, McAllen, TX
Gutierrez, Rev. Luis, '98 (JOL) St. Joseph, Addison, IL
Gutierrez, Rev. Miguel Angel, *M.S.C.* '99 (LA) Sagrado Corazon y Santa Maria de Guadalupe, Cudahy, CA
Gutierrez, Rev. Nahum, *M.G.* '05 (LA) St. Anthony, San Gabriel, CA
Gutierrez, Rev. Oscar, '96 (PHX) Curia: Leadership; Offices and Directors Holy Family Roman Catholic Parish, Phoenix, AZ
Gutierrez, Rev. Richard, '19 (CC) Immaculate Conception, Skidmore, TX
Gutierrez, Rev. Rogelio, '09 (YAK) St Joseph Parish Sunnyside, Sunnyside, WA
Gutierrez, Rev. Toribio, *C.M.* '08 (LA) St. Bernard, Bellflower, CA
Gutierrez, Rev. Victor, '15 (SAC) Pastor of Sacred Heart Parish, Maxwell, a corporation sole, Williams, CA
Gutierrez del Toro, Rev. Manuel, (SD) Pastor of Saint Mary Catholic Parish, Escondido, a corporation sole, Escondido, CA
Gutierrez-Franco, Rev. Vicente, *M.Sp.S.* '73 (LA) Our Lady of Guadalupe Parish, Oxnard, CA
Gutmann, Rev. David, '83 (P) St. Wenceslaus, Scappoose, OR
Gutmann, Rev. Don, '91 (P) Curia: Offices and Directors
Gutmann, Rev. Donald, '91 (P) St. Clare, Portland, OR
Gutowski, Rev. Matthew J., '88 (OM) Curia: Leadership; Offices and Directors SS. Cyril and Methodius, Clarkson, NE; St. Wenceslaus, Dodge, NE
Gutting, Rev. James G., '75 (E) St. Bernard, Bradford, PA; St. Francis of Assisi, Bradford, PA
Guyol, Rev. John, *S.J.* '22 (LA) [MON] Jesuit Community, Los Angeles, CA
Guzaldo, Rev. John, '06 (AUS) St. Luke, Temple, TX
Guzik, Rev. Michael, (SY) [MON] Jesuits at LeMoyne, Inc., Syracuse, NY
Guzman, Rev. Agustin, *C.O.* '11 (CHR) Curia: Advisory Boards, Commissions, Committees, and Councils St. Joseph, Chester, SC; St. Mary, Rock Hill, SC; [CAM] Winthrop University, Rock Hill, SC; [MON] Oratory of St. Philip Neri, Congregation of the Oratory of Pontifical Rite, Rock Hill, SC
Guzman, Rev. Alexander, '17 (NO) On Special Assignment. Northshore Hispanic Community St. Jane de Chantal Roman Catholic Church, Abita Springs, Louisiana, Abita Springs, LA
Guzman, Rev. Alfredo, *S.J.* (SJN) San Ignacio de Loyola, San Juan, PR
Guzman, Rev. Antonio, (SB) Our Lady of Perpetual Help, Riverside, CA
Guzman, Rev. Armando, '86 (SEA) Retired.
Guzman, Rev. Baudilio, *S.J.* '91 (SJN) [MON] Compania de Jesus en Puerto Rico, Inc, San Juan, PR
Guzman, Rev. Baudilio, *S.J.* (SJN) Colegio San Ignacio de Loyola, San Juan, PR; San Ignacio de Loyola, San Juan, PR
Guzman, Rev. Baudilio, *S.J.* (SJN) Curia: Offices and Directors
Guzman, Rev. David, *O.C.D.* '10 (LA) St. Therese, Alhambra, CA
Guzman, Rev. Gilbert, '18 (LA) Sacred Heart, Altadena, CA
Guzman, Rev. Juan Jose, *O.A.R.* '08 (LA) Santa Clara High School, Oxnard, CA
Guzman, Rev. Julian, *S.D.S.* '68 (WDC) [SEM] Salvatorian Community, Silver Spring, MD
Guzman, Rev. Mark A., '08 (SEA) St. Nicholas, Gig Harbor, WA
Guzman, Rev. Paul, '14 (CHI) Curia: (>MO) Offices and Directors
Guzman, Rev. Paul, '12 (CHI) Most Holy Redeemer, Evergreen Park, IL
Guzman, Rev. Rito, *M.Sp.S.* (P) St. Matthew Catholic Church, Hillsboro, OR; [MON] Missionaries of the Holy Spirit, M.Sp.S., Hillsboro, OR
Guzman, Rev. Salvador, '00 (DAL) St. Pius X Catholic Parish, Dallas, TX
Guzman Quintana, Rev. Pedro J., '10 (PCE) Nuestra Senora del Rosario, Juana Diaz, PR; San Ramon Nonato, Juana Diaz, PR
Guzman-Alfaro, Rev. Alfonso, *O.F.M.* '71 (SJN) Curia: Leadership San Jose Obrero, Toa Baja, PR; [COL] Universidad Central de Bayamon, Inc., Bayamon, PR
Guzman-Alvarez, Rev. Walter F., '02 (HBG) St. Mark the Evangelist, Greencastle, PA
Guzman-Diaz, Rev. Cesar Jaime, (AUS) Santa Teresa, Bryan, TX
Guzmán-Dominguez, Rev. Josemaría, *O.P.* (BAL) SS. Philip and James, Baltimore, MD
Gveric, Rev. Drago, *O.F.M.* '78 (SJ) St. Mary of the Assumption, San Jose, CA
Gwinner, Rev. David E., '84 (COL) Retired. St. Paul the Apostle, Westerville, OH
Gworek, Rev. Matthew G., '16 (HRT) Curia: Advisory Boards, Commissions, Committees, and Councils; Communications St. Patricks Church Society of Farmington, Connecticut, Farmington, CT; The Star of the Sea Church Corporation of Unionville, Connecticut, Unionville, CT
Gwozdz, Rev. John P., '86 (HRT) Saint Edmund Campion Parish Corporation, East Hartford, CT
Gwozdz, Rev. Thomas, *SDB* '75 (SP) Retired. [RTR] Mary Help of Christians Center, Tampa, FL
Gwudz, Rev. John S., '72 (NOR) Retired.
Gyamerah, Rev. Anthony, (NY) St. Eugene, Yonkers, NY
Gyamfi, Rev. Martin Adu, (RVC) Our Lady of Grace, West Babylon, NY
Gyan, Rev. Eric V., '86 (BR) St. Theresa of Avila (Congregation Of St. Theresa Roman Catholic Church, Gonzales, Louisiana), Gonzales, LA
Gyanobeng, Rev. Simon, (NY) St. Ann, Congers, NY
Gyasi, Rev. George, (SP) [HOS] St. Joseph's Hospital, Inc., Tampa, FL
Gyau, Rev. Francis, '21 (LSC) San Albino Parish, Inc., Mesilla, NM
Gyhra, Rev. Richard A., '99 (LIN) On Duty Outside Diocese. Secretariat of State
Gyure, Rev. William L., '91 (NEW) Retired.
Gyves, Rev. Peter W., '08 (BO) [MON] Loyola House, Boston, MA
Ha, Rev. Abraham, '02 (ALN) St. Ann, Emmaus, PA
Ha, Rev. Alex H., '93 (ORG) [CCH] St. Thomas Korean Catholic Center, Anaheim, CA
Ha, Rev. Dominic Vinh Van, '93 (CHI) St. Edward, Chicago, IL
Ha, Rev. Hieu Minh, '00 (ATL) Chap, Prison Apostolate
Ha, Rev. Kanh, '20 (BRK) St. Michael, Flushing, NY
Ha, Rev. Louis Pham, *C.R.M.* '94 (STP) [MIS] Queen Anne Communities, Minneapolis, MN
Ha, Rev. Thomas, '10 (LAV) Our Lady of La Vang, Las Vegas, NV
Haag, Rev. Michael B., '05 (SFD) SS. Peter and Paul, Collinsville, IL
Haag, Rev. Ralph L., *C.S.C.* '04 (FTW) [COL] University of Notre Dame Du Lac, Notre Dame, IN; [MON] Holy Cross Community, Corby Hall, University of Notre Dame, Notre Dame, IN
Haag, Rev. Theodore, *O.F.M.* '79 (CLV) Transfiguration, Lakewood, OH; [MON] St. Anthony of Padua Friary, Brooklyn, OH
Haake, Rev. Adam, '12 (KC) On Special Assignment. Univ of Missouri - Kansas City Coronation of Our Lady, Grandview, MO; Our Lady of Lourdes, Raytown, MO
Haake, Rev. Chris G., '97 (PEO) St. Patrick's, Dwight, IL; St. Paul's, Odell, IL
Haake, Rev. Gregory P., *C.S.C.* '07 (FTW) [COL] University of Notre Dame Du Lac, Notre Dame, IN; [MON] Holy Cross Community, Corby Hall, University of Notre Dame, Notre Dame, IN
Haaland, Rev. Byron, *S.C.J.* '77 (MIL) [MON] Sacred Heart Novitiate, Franksville, WI
Haan, Rev. Thomas J., '13 (LFT) Curia: Miscellaneous / Other Offices St. Louis de Montfort, Fishers, IN
Haarer, Rev. Eric, '01 (PBL)
Haas, Rev. Joseph H., '59 (MIL) Retired.
Haas, Friar Julian, (COS) Retired. [MON] Our Lady of the Angels Friary, Colorado Springs, CO
Haase, Rev. Albert, *O.F.M.* '83 (CHI) [MON] Holy Spirit Friary, Order of Friars Minor, Chicago, IL
Haase, Rev. Howard G., '83 (MIL) Congregation of Holy Angels, West Bend, WI; Holy Trinity Congregation, Newburg, WI
Habash, Rev. Andrwos, '05 (OLD) Our Lady of Deliverance Parish, Bayonne, NJ
Habash, Rev. Rabee, (OLD) Christ the King Church, Troy, MI
Habash, Rev. Msgr. Safaa, '99 (OLD) St. Isaac of Nineveh Syriac Catholic Church, Lansing, MI
Habchi, Rev. Nabil, *O.M.M.* '02 (OLL) [MON] Maronite Order of the Blessed Virgin Mary, Ann Arbor, MI
Haberkorn, Rev. Timothy A., '92 (KCK) Sacred Heart-St. Joseph, Topeka, KS
Habib, Rev. ElBadaoui, (OLL) [MON] The Congregation of Maronite Lebanese Missionaries, Houston, TX
Habib, Rev. El-Badaoui, (OLL) St. Rafka Maronite Catholic Church, Lakewood, CO
Habiger, Rev. Matthew, *O.S.B.* '68 (KCK) [MON] St. Benedict's Abbey, Atchison, KS
Habila, Rev. Joseph Shemgwan, (RVC) St. Matthew, Dix Hills, NY
Habing, Rev. Paul A., '80 (SFD) St. Elizabeth, Marine, IL
Habison, Rev. Gerhart, '76 (LA) Retired.
Hablewitz, Rev. James A., '67 (GB) Retired.
Haby, Rev. Gerald, (SAT) [MON] Marianist Residence, San Antonio, TX
Haby, Rev. Gerald, (SAT) Retired.
Haby, Rev. Gerald, *S.M.* '69 (SAT) Retired.
Hachey, Rev. Paul, *S.M.* '84 (WDC) [MON] Marist Center (The Marist Finance Center of the Atlanta Province of the Society of Mary, Marist Fathers and Brothers), Washington, DC
Hack, Rev. Michael, '70 (LEX) Curia: Leadership
Hackenmueller, Rev. Jerome B., '69 (STP) Retired.
Hacker, Rev. Louis, *O.S.B.* '85 (IND) [MON] St. Meinrad Archabbey, St. Meinrad, IN
Hackett, Rev. James F., '68 (L) Retired.
Hackman, Rev. Marvin R., '71 (CIN) Retired.
Hadarag, Rev. Constantin, (ROM) St. John the Baptist, Detroit, MI
Haddad, Rev. Cyrus M., '14 (COL) St. Colman, Washington Court House, OH
Haddad, Rev. George, '20 (NTN) St. Elias Melkite Church, Inc., Brooklyn, OH
Haddad, Rev. Hermiz, '10 (EST) Curia: Offices and Directors St. Ephrem's Chaldean Catholic Church, Chicago, IL
Haddad, Rev. Muntaser, '09 (OLD) Saint Toma Church, Farmington Hills, MI
Haddix, Rev. Ralph-Elias, *O.C.D.* '98 (MIL) [MON] Washington Province of Discalced Carmelite Friars, Inc., Milwaukee, WI
Hadel, Rev. Richard E., *S.J.* '65 (STL) [RTR] Retreat House, ,
Haden, Rev. Kyle, *O.F.M.* '97 (BUF) [CAM] St. Bonaventure University, St. Bonaventure, NY; [MON] St. Bonaventure Friary, St. Bonaventure, NY
Hadley, Rev. Christopher, *S.J.* '09 (OAK) [MON] Jesuit

Fathers and Brothers, Berkeley, CA; [SEM] Jesuit School of Theology of Santa Clara University (Berkeley, California Campus), Berkeley, CA
Hadley, Very Rev. Kurt, '19 (YAK) Curia: Offices and Directors Holy Redeemer, Yakima, WA; St. Mary's, White Swan, WA
Hadyka, Rev. Richard J., '67 (CAM) Retired.
Haefeli, Rev. Joaquin C., '51 (LA) Retired.
Haefling, Rev. Maurice C., *O.S.B.* '94 (KCK) [MON] St. Benedict's Abbey, Atchison, KS
Haefner, Rev. Douglas J., '83 (MET) Retired. On Leave.
Haemmerle, Rev. Gerald R., '67 (CIN) Retired.
Haesaert, Rev. William F., *C.S.V.* '80 (LAV) Retired. [MON] Clerics of St. Viator Retirement Home, Las Vegas, NV
Haesaert, Rev. William F., *C.S.V.* '80 (CHI) [MON] Viatorian Province Center-Clerics of St. Viator, Arlington Heights, IL
Hafeman, Rev. Harry G., '76 (GB) Retired.
Hafemann, Rev. George, '99 (NY) St. John the Evangelist, Goshen, NY
Haffey, Rev. Thomas P., '69 (HEL) Retired. Curia: Leadership
Haft, Rev. Ronald C., '07 (CIN) St. Bartholomew, Cincinnati, OH; St. Clare, Cincinnati, OH; St. Vivian, Cincinnati, OH
Hagan, Rev. Byron S., '15 (STP) Regions Hosp, St Paul St. Mary, St. Paul, MN
Hagan, Rev. Msgr. Charles H., '70 (PH) Retired.
Hagan, Rev. Harry, *O.S.B.* '86 (IND) [MON] St. Meinrad Archabbey, St. Meinrad, IN
Hagan, Rev. James, '69 (SFR) On Duty Outside Diocese. Mexico
Hagan, Rev. Joseph, *O.P.* '19 (NY) (>WDC) [SEM] Dominican House of Studies, Washington, DC
Hagan, Rev. Robert P., *O.S.A.* '03 (PH) [MON] Provincial Offices of the Order of St. Augustine, Province of St. Thomas of Villanova, Villanova, PA; [MON] Saxony Hall, Rosemont, PA; [MON] St. Augustine Friary, Villanova, PA; [MON] St. Thomas Monastery, Villanova, PA
Hagan, Rev. Vincent J., '66 (RVC) Retired.
Hagan, Rev. William Ian-Vincent, '18 (LA) St. Julie Billiart, Newbury Park, CA
Haganey, Rev. Colin, '19 (KCK) St. Francis Xavier, Burlington, KS; St. Joseph, Waverly, KS; St. Patrick, Williamsburg, KS; St. Teresa, Westphalia, KS
Hage, Rev. Jason, '14 (SY) Curia: Offices and Directors St. Bernard, Waterville, NY; St. Joseph, Oriskany Falls, NY; St. Mary, Hamilton, NY; [CAM] Newman Association at SUNY Morrisville, Morrisville, NY
Hagearty, Rev. Charles B., '59 (HRT) Retired.
Hagelin, Very Rev. Bradley R., '11 (SEA) St. Luke, Shoreline, WA
Hagemann, Rev. John, *O.S.B.* '75 (OM) Mount Michael Benedictine School, Elkhorn, NE; [EFT] Mount Michael Foundation, Elkhorn, NE; [MON] Mount Michael Benedictine Abbey, Elkhorn, NE
Hage-Moussa, Rev. Ramsine, *M.L.M.* (OLL) [MON] The Congregation of Maronite Lebanese Missionaries, Houston, TX
Hage-Moussa, Rev. Ramsine, '00 (OLL) Curia: Leadership St. Jude Maronite Catholic Church, West Covina, CA
Hagen, Rev. Gerald A., '91 (SUP) Holy Family, Woodruff, WI
Hagen, Rev. Nicholas, '21 (STP) St. Raphael, Crystal, MN
Hagen, Very Rev. Rob, *OSA* (PH) (>CHI) [MON] Federation of Augustinians of North America, Chicago, IL
Hager, Rev. Louis L, *O.Praem.* '22 (ORG) Archangel Institute (St. Michael's Preparatory School), Silverado, CA; [MON] Norbertine Fathers of Orange, Inc., Silverado, CA; [PRE] St. Michael's Summer Camp, Silverado, CA
Hagerman, Rev. James W., '86 (MET) St. Bernadette, Parlin, NJ
Haggar, Rt. Rev. Joseph S., '66 (NTN) Retired. Curia: Administration; Consultative Bodies St. Basil the Great, Lincoln, RI
Haggerty, Rev. Donald, '89 (NY) Cathedral of St. Patrick, New York, NY
Haggerty, Rev. Shaun T, '09 (SFS) Saint John Paul II Parish of Lincoln County, Harrisburg, SD
Haggerty, Rev. Theodore, *O.S.B.* '20 (RCK) [MON] Marmion Abbey, Aurora, IL
Haggerty, Rev. Thomas J., '79 (RVC) SS. Philip and James, St. James, NY
Haggerty, Rev. Thomas M., '64 (BRK) Retired. Curia: Pastoral Services
Haggins, Rev. Martin, (OAK) [MON] Capuchin Franciscan Friars, Berkeley, CA; [NUR] Mercy Retirement and Care Center, Oakland, CA
Hagman, Rev. Ed, (MIL) [MON] St. Lawrence Friary, Mount Calvary, WI
Hagos, Rev. Arman, *C.R.M.* (CHK) San Antonio Parish, Saipan, MP
Hagstrom, Very Rev. Thomas, '93 (SFD) Curia: Deaneries Sacred Heart, Livingston, IL; Saint John Paul II, Mount Olive, IL; St. Michael the Archangel, Staunton, IL
Hahn, Rev. Gerald T., '79 (NEW) St. Anthony, Northvale, NJ
Hahn, Rev. Jeremiah, (STU) Christ the King University Parish, Athens, OH; Holy Cross, Glouster, OH; Sacred Heart, Pomeroy, OH; St. Paul Church, Athens, OH; [CAM] Christ the King University Parish - Ohio University, Athens, OH
Hahn, Rev. Michael Leonard, *O.S.B.* '14 (SCL) [MON] St. John's Abbey, of the Order of St. Benedict, Collegeville, MN
Hahn, Very Rev. Peter I., '02 (HBG) Curia: Offices and Directors St. Leo the Great, Lancaster, PA
Hahn, Rev. Raymond W., '74 (E) Retired.
Hahn, Rev. Scott R., '03 (WDC) St. Jerome, Hyattsville, MD
Hahn, Rev. William P., '04 (COL) Curia: Consultative Bodies; Leadership; Offices and Directors
Hahr, Rev. Karl A., '04 (BUR) St. Luke, Fairfax, VT
Hai, Rev. Dinh Minh, *C.Ss.R.* '95 (LA) [MON] Vietnamese Redemptorist Mission, Baldwin Park, CA
Hai, Rev. Nguyen Tat, *C.Ss.R.* '95 (LA) [MON] Vietnamese Redemptorist Mission, Baldwin Park, CA
Haig, Rev. Frank, *S.J.* (PH) Retired. [MON] Jesuit Community at St. Joseph's University, Merion Station, PA
Haight, Rev. Roger D., *S.J.* '67 (NY) [MON] America; Residence and Publication Office of the America Press, New York, NY
Haile, Rev. Hagos Tesfagabir, '07 (ARL) Holy Spirit, Annandale, VA
Hailu, Rev. Atakelt, *S.J.* (CLV) [COL] John Carroll Jesuit Community, University Heights, OH
Haines, Rev. Kevin J., '87 (LFT) St. Maria Goretti, Westfield, IN
Hainsey, Rev. Jordan M., '20 (COV) Curia: Administration; Leadership
Haissig, Rev. Andrew W., '15 (ARL) St. Agnes, Arlington, VA
Hajj, Rev. George, '13 (OLL) St. Anthony of Padua Maronite Catholic Church, Cincinnati, OH
Hajj, Rev. George, '13 (OLL) Curia: Offices and Directors
Hajovsky, Rev. Bryan B., *O.F.M.Conv.* '14 (BUF) [MON] St. Francis of Assisi Friary, Hamburg, NY
Hake, Rev. Msgr. James E., '60 (SAL) Curia: Consultative Bodies; Tribunal
Hake, Rev. Patrick, '18 (FTW) St. Peter, Fort Wayne, IN
Hakeem, Rev. Samuel P., *OP* '17 (CHI) [MON] Dominicans (Provincial Office), Chicago, IL
Hakenwerth, Rev. Quentin, *S.M.* '60 (STL) [MON] Marianist Province of the United States (Society of Mary), St. Louis, MO
Halaiko, Rev. David J., '67 (CLV) Retired. St. Vincent de Paul Parish, Akron, OH
Halbur, Rev. Kenneth, '09 (DM) St. Luke the Evangelist Catholic Church, Ankeny, IA
Haldane, Rev. Richard S., '92 (B) Retired.
Haldas, Rev. Piotr, *SDS* (NEW) St. Stanislaus Kostka, Garfield, NJ
Hale, Rev. W. Robert, '22 (CIN) Holy Cross, Dayton, OH; Our Lady of the Rosary, Dayton, OH; St. Christopher, Vandalia, OH; St. John the Baptist, Tipp City, OH; St. Peter, Huber Heights, OH
Halepeska, Rev. Orrin, '12 (GAL) Curia: Offices and Directors Holy Rosary, Rosenberg, TX; St. Wenceslaus Mission, Beasley, TX
Haley, Rev. James A., *C.S.P.* '68 (KNX) Retired. [MON] Paulist Fathers (Missionary Society of St. Paul the Apostle), Knoxville, TN
Haley, Rev. James A., *C.S.P.* '68 (NY) Retired. [MON] Paulist Fathers - Generalate, New York, NY
Haley, Rev. Thomas J., '78 (STL) Blessed Teresa of Calcutta Catholic Church, Ferguson, MO; Sacred Heart Catholic Church, Valley Park, Valley Park, MO
Halfacre, Rev. Msgr. Philip D., '91 (PEO) Curia: Clergy and Religious Services; Consultative Bodies; Leadership; Offices and Directors; Social Services SS. Peter and Paul's, Tonica, IL; St. Michael the Archangel Parish, Streator, IL
Halka, Rev. Frantisek A., '98 (ALT) Chap, Fayetteville, NC Curia: (>MO) Offices and Directors
Hall, Rev. Charles D., '79 (GR) St. Francis de Sales, Norton Shores, MI; St. Michael the Archangel, Muskegon, MI
Hall, Rev. Daniel R., *C.S.V.* '88 (CHI) [MON] Viatorian Province Center-Clerics of St. Viator, Arlington Heights, IL
Hall, Rev. Emmett, '16 (DAL) Curia: Offices and Directors St. Elizabeth of Hungary Catholic Parish, Dallas, TX
Hall, Rev. James W., '70 (ELP) Retired. Curia: Advisory Boards, Commissions, Committees, and Councils; Tribunal
Hall, Rev. John M., '80 (IND) St. Anne Catholic Church, New Castle, Inc., New Castle, IN; St. Elizabeth of Hungary Catholic Church, Cambridge City, Inc., Cambridge City, IN
Hall, Rev. Michael, *O.S.B.* '65 (WDC) [MON] St. Anselm's Abbey, Washington, DC
Hall, Rev. Michael J., '10 (TR) Curia: Leadership; Offices and Directors St. Gregory the Great, Hamilton Square, NJ
Hall, Rev. Nathan, (LIN) North American Martyrs, Lincoln, NE
Hall, Rev. Richard, *O.M.I.* '93 (SAT) [MON] Oblate Benson Residence, San Antonio, TX; [SHR] Oblate Lourdes Grotto Shrine of the Southwest, Tepeyac de San Antonio, San Antonio, TX
Hall, Rev. Robert C., '79 (ALT) Church of the Transfiguration, Conemaugh, PA
Hall, Rev. Rodney L., '91 (SAC) Retired.
Hall, Rev. Roger L., *O.F.M.* '03 (HRT) St. Josephs Roman Catholic Church Corporation, Winsted, Connecticut, Winsted, CT
Hall, Rev. Thomas P., *C.S.P.* '77 (NY) Retired. [MON] Paulist Fathers - Generalate, New York, NY
Hall, Rev. Thomas P., *C.S.P.* '77 (MRY) Retired.
Hall, Rev. Timothy J., '06 (WIN) Curia: Advisory Boards, Commissions, Committees, and Councils; Miscellaneous / Other Offices St. James, St. James, MN; St. Mary, Madelia, MN
Hallada, Rev. Christopher James, '17 (SFE) Our Lady of Guadalupe-Albuquerque, Albuquerque, NM
Halladay, Rev. Paul A., '00 (MOB) On Duty Outside Diocese. Chaplain for Archdiocese for Military Services, USA Curia: (>MO) Offices and Directors
Halladay, Rev. Phillip A., '14 (NSH) Curia: Leadership St. Luke, Smyrna, TN
Hallahan, Rev. Kenneth P., '75 (CAM) Retired.
Hallee, Rev. Roger, *O.M.I.* '63 (WDC) [MON] Oblate Community, Washington, DC
Hallegado, Rev. Salvador Den, '03 (CHI) St. Odilo, Berwyn, IL
Halleron, Rev. James E., '97 (TOL) Sacred Heart, Montpelier, OH; St. Patrick, Bryan, OH
Halley, Rev. Msgr. James L., '04 (LA) St. Luke the Evangelist, Temple City, CA
Halligan, Rev. Damian, *S.J.* '67 (NY) [MON] Murray-Weigel Hall (A Jesuit Community at Murray-Weigel Hall and Kohlmann Hall), Bronx, NY
Hallinan, Rev. Edward J., '83 (PH) Curia: Advisory Boards, Commissions, Committees, and Councils St. John Chrysostom, Wallingford, PA
Hallinan, Rev. Mark, *S.J.* (NY) St. Ignatius Loyola, New York, NY; [MON] St. Ignatius Loyola Residence, New York, NY
Hallissey, Rev. LaSalle, *O.P.* '79 (OAK) [MON] Order of Preachers (Province of the Most Holy Name of Jesus - Western Dominican Province), Oakland, CA
Hallock, Rev. Addison, *M.S.A.* '74 (NOR) [MON] Society of the Missionaries of the Holy Apostles, Cromwell, CT
Halloran, Rev. Msgr. John C., '62 (PRO) Retired.
Halm, Rev. David, *C.S.C.* '15 (PHX) Saint John Vianney Roman Catholic Parish, Goodyear, AZ
Halovatch, Rev. Paul J., '70 (HRT) Retired.
Halphen, Rev. Jude, '94 (LAF) Curia: Offices and Directors St. Peter, Washington, LA
Halsema, Rev. Douglas G., '00 (PT) Curia: Leadership St. Mary Church, Fort Walton Beach, FL
Halstead, Rev. James R, *OSA* '76 (CHI) [MON] The Augustinians-Provincialate, Chicago, IL
Halter, Rev. Robert, *C.Ss.R.* '70 (BR) (>STL) [MON] St. Clement Health Care Center, Liguori, MO
Halvey, Rev. William, *S.V.D.* '76 (CHI) Retired. [MON] Divine Word Residence, Techny, IL
Halvorson, Rev. Richard, '04 (KCK) On Duty Outside Diocese. University of St Mary of the Lake, Mundelein, IL
Ham, Rev. Msgr. Jerome, '68 (PEO) Retired.
Hamak, Rev. William, '92 (SFS) Saint James Parish of Brule County, Chamberlain, SD; Saint Margaret Parish of Brule County, Kimball, SD
Haman, Rev. Gregory, '12 (FAR) Assumption Church of Dickey, Dickey, ND; Holy Rosary Church of La Moure, La Moure, ND; St. Raphael's Church of Verona,

Verona, ND
Hamaty, Rev. Anthony Edward, (STA) Holy Family, Williston, FL
Hambrough, Rev. Msgr. Patrick K., '85 (STL) Queen of All Saints Catholic Church, Oakville, MO
Hambur, Rev. Leonardus, *O.S.M.* (P) [MON] The Grotto, The National Sanctuary of Our Sorrowful Mother, Portland, OR
Hamel, Rev. James A., '92 (NEW) Chap, Col Curia: (>MO) Offices and Directors
Hamel, Rev. Philip N., '85 (FR) Our Lady of Lourdes, Wellfleet, MA; St. Peter the Apostle, Provincetown, MA; [CEM] Our Lady of Lourdes, Wellfleet, MA; [CEM] St. Peter, Provincetown, MA
Hamill, Rev. Gregory J., '94 (PH) On Duty Outside Diocese. Abbey of the Genesee, Piffard, NY
Hamill, Rev. John, *O.C.S.O.* (ROC) [MON] Abbey of the Genesee, Inc., Piffard, NY
Hamill, Rev. William A., *O.S.A.* '68 (TLS) Cascia Hall Preparatory School, Tulsa, OK
Hamilton, Rev. John W., '70 (BUR) Retired.
Hamilton, Rev. Justin, '17 (KCK) Immaculate Conception, St. Marys, KS; St. Stanislaus, Rossville, KS
Hamilton, Rev. Kenneth, *S.V.D.* '82 (CHI) [MON] Divine Word Residence, Techny, IL
Hamilton, Rev. Mark M., '94 (L) Curia: Leadership; Offices and Directors Holy Name of Mary, Lebanon, KY; St. Augustine, Lebanon, KY
Hamilton, Rev. Stephen V., '99 (OKL) Curia: Clergy and Religious Services St. Monica, Edmond, OK
Hamilton, Rev. Terence J., '73 (CIN) St. Antoninus, Cincinnati, OH; St. Martin of Tours, Cincinnati, OH
Hamilton, Rev. Thomas M., '88 (SFR) Grand Chap, Young Ladies' Inst Curia: Advisory Boards, Commissions, Committees, and Councils; Leadership St. Gabriel, San Francisco, CA
Hamilton, Rev. William, (SPR) Curia: Advisory Boards, Commissions, Committees, and Councils; Offices and Directors Most Holy Redeemer, Hadley, MA
Hamlet, Rev. Mark, '10 (AUS) Sacred Heart, Austin, TX; [EFT] Diocese of Austin Pension Plan and Trust, Austin, TX
Hamlett, Very Rev. Christopher M., '82 (E) St. Peter, Conneautville, PA; St. Philip the Apostle, Linesville, PA
Hamm, Rev. David A., *S.T.* '75 (MOB) Our Lady of Guadalupe Parish, Clio, AL; St. Joseph Parish Holy Trinity, Fort Mitchell, AL; St. Patrick Parish, Phenix City, Phenix City, AL; [MON] St. Joseph Cenacle, Fort Mitchell, AL
Hamm, Rev. John, '13 (WOR) Retired.
Hamm, Rev. M. Dennis, *S.J.* '70 (MIL) [MON] St. Camillus Jesuit Community (Society of Jesus, USA Midwest Province), Wauwatosa, WI
Hamm, Rev. Robert E., *S.J.* '68 (BAL) (>PH) [MON] Jesuit Community at St. Joseph's University, Merion Station, PA
Hamm, Very Rev. Thomas F., '00 (STU) Curia: Deaneries
Hamm, Very Rev. Thomas F., '00 (STU) Curia: Deaneries St. Louis, Gallipolis, OH; [MIS] RCIA, Gallipolis, OH
Hammeke, Rev. Andy, '18 (SAL) Curia: Consultative Bodies; Miscellaneous / Other Offices Thomas More Prep-Marian High Inc., Hays, KS; [CAM] Comeau Catholic Campus Center, Hays, Inc., Hays, KS; [MIS] Vocatio of Salina, Salina, KS
Hammelman, Rev. William, *O.S.B.* '71 (P) Retired. [MON] Mt. Angel Abbey, Saint Benedict, OR
Hammer, Rev. James, *O.F.M.Cap.* '65 (NOR) Retired.
Hammer, Rev. Michael J., '69 (MIL) Retired.
Hammer, Rev. William D., '80 (L) Curia: Leadership St. Margaret Mary, Louisville, KY; St. William, Louisville, KY
Hammerschmidt, Rev. Gale, '12 (SAL) St. Isidore Catholic Student Center Parish, Manhattan, Inc., Manhattan, KS; [CAM] St. Isidore Catholic Student Center Parish, Manhattan, Inc., Manhattan, KS
Hammerschmitt, Rev. Clemens, '73 (PMB) Curia: Organizations (affiliated, inter-Diocesan, miscellaneous/ other) St. Matthew, Lake Worth, FL; [MIS] Diocesan Council of Catholic Women, Port St. Lucie, FL
Hammes, Rev. Gregory, '07 (KCK) Prince of Peace, Olathe, KS
Hammett, Rev. Peter E., *O.S.B.* '72 (NO) [MON] St. Joseph Abbey, St. Benedict, LA
Hammond, Rev. Charles, '76 (SAG) Retired. On Duty Outside Diocese. Denver, CO
Hammond, Rev. David I., '10 (ALB) Curia: (>MO) Offices and Directors
Hammond, Rev. David J., (ALB) Chap, Lt, CHC, USN, Kailua, HI
Hammond, Rev. Jeremy, '20 (WDC) St. Jane Frances de Chantal, Bethesda, MD
Hammond, Rev. John, '14 (NSH) St. Patrick, Nashville, TN
Hammond, Rev. John, *O.S.B.* '50 (BUR) [MON] The Benedictine Foundation of the State of Vermont, Inc., Weston, VT
Hammond, Rev. John, '14 (NSH) Curia: Leadership
Hammond, Rev. Joseph, *C.H.S.* '89 (KNX) St. John Neumann, Farragut, TN
Hammond, Rev. Louis K., '92 (DAV) Chap, Univ of Iowa Hosps and Clinics
Hammond, Rev. Mark J., '89 (COL) St. Luke, Danville, OH; St. Vincent de Paul, Mt. Vernon, OH
Hammond, Rev. Martin, '73 (BAL) Retired.
Hamness, Rev. Adam A., '13 (CR) Curia: Leadership; Offices and Directors Assumption, Callaway, MN
Hamon, Rev. Victor, '93 (TYL) On Leave.
Hampe, Rev. Msgr. Raymond A., '54 (STL) Retired. Chap, SSM Health St Joseph Health Ctr - St Charles St. Robert Bellarmine Catholic Church, St. Charles, MO
Hampsch, Rev. John, *C.M.F.* '52 (LA) Retired.
Han, Rev. Sang Man, '83 (LA) Ventura Korean Catholic Church, Oxnard, CA
Hancock, Rev. Msgr. George, '47 (OWN) Retired.
Hand, Rev. Dennis M., '75 (GRY) Retired.
Hand, Rev. John D., '98 (PH) St. Gabriel, Norwood, PA
Hand, Rev. Kenneth J., '72 (BRK) Retired.
Handal, Rev. Ephrem, '03 (NTN) Holy Transfiguration, McLean, VA
Handapangoda, Rev. Godwin, '85 (SAC) On Duty Outside Diocese.
Handges, Rev. Msgr. William E., '64 (ALN) Retired.
Handwerker, Rev. Msgr. Valentine, (MEM) St. Patrick's, Memphis, TN
Handy, Rev. Edward, *O.F.M.Conv.* (PAT) St. John Kanty, Clifton, NJ
Hanel, Rev. Charles T., '83 (MIL) Queen of Apostles Congregation, Pewaukee, WI
Haney, Friar Michael Martin, *O.F.M.* '74 (NO) St. Mary of the Angels, New Orleans, LA
Hangholt, Rev. Anthony R., '12 (PH) Curia: Advisory Boards, Commissions, Committees, and Councils St. Philip Neri, Pennsburg, PA
Hanh, Rev. Joseph Phan Trong, '70 (KC) Retired.
Hanic, Rev. John D., '83 (CHL) St. John Baptist de LaSalle, North Wilkesboro, NC
Hanic, Rev. Johnathan, '02 (CHL) On Leave.
Hanifan, Rev. Mark, '07 (RNO) Curia: Offices and Directors St. Gall, Gardnerville, NV
Hanifin, Rev. Michael P., '87 (ORG) St. Joachim, Costa Mesa, CA
Hanincik, Rev. Frank A., '08 (PSC) SS. Cyril and Methodius, Fort Pierce, FL
Hankee, Rev. Robert Jason, '02 (IND) Curia: Offices and Directors Christ The King Catholic Church, Indianapolis, Inc., Indianapolis, IN
Hankiewicz, Rev. Msgr. Edward A., '79 (GR) St. Isidore, Grand Rapids, MI
Hankins, Rev. Brendan, *O.Praem.* '11 (ORG) St. John the Baptist, Costa Mesa, CA
Hankins, Rev. Brendan R., *O.Praem.* '11 (ORG) [MON] Norbertine Fathers of Orange, Inc., Silverado, CA
Hankomoone, Rev. Cornelius, *P.S.S.* '96 (BAL) [MON] Society of St. Sulpice, Province of the United States, Baltimore, MD
Hanks, Rev. Sebastian, (PH) [MON] The Order of Saint Paul, First Hermit - The Pauline Fathers, Doylestown, PA
Hankus, Rev. David J., '84 (JOL) Retired.
Hanley, Rev. Charles, *O.F.M. Cap.* '80 (NEW) St. Ann, Hoboken, NJ
Hanley, Rev. Christopher, '08 (WIL) St. John the Baptist-Holy Angels, Newark, DE
Hanley, Rev. Craig, '15 (HEL) Curia: Leadership Butte Catholic Community Central: Series 214, LLC, Butte, MT; Holy Spirit Parish: Series 219, LLC, Butte, MT; Saint Ann Parish: Series 213, LLC, Butte, MT
Hanley, Rev. Daniel F., '05 (ARL) On Duty Outside Diocese. USCCB, Washington, DC
Hanley, Rev. Jeffrey David, '17 (KAL) Curia: Offices and Directors; Tribunal St. Joseph, Kalamazoo, MI
Hanley, Rev. John A., *O.S.F.S.* '86 (R) Holy Redeemer by the Sea, Kitty Hawk, NC
Hanley, Rev. John F., *O.M.I.* '70 (BO) [MON] Missionary Oblates of Mary Immaculate Northern Province, Lowell, MA; [MON] Oblate World/ Missionary Association of Mary Immaculate, Tewksbury, MA; [NUR] Immaculate Heart of Mary Residence, Tewksbury, MA
Hanley, Rev. John P., '94 (PAT) Retired. Curia: Leadership
Hanley, Rev. Thomas E., '65 (WIL) Retired.
Hanley, Rev. William, '69 (ORL) Retired.
Hanlon, Rev. Francis, *O.S.F.S.* '76 (VEN) St. Cecilia Parish in Fort Myers, Inc., Fort Myers, FL
Hanlon, Rev. Kevin J., *M.M.* '89 (NY) [MON] Maryknoll Fathers and Brothers (Catholic Foreign Mission Society of America, Inc.), Ossining, NY
Hanly, Rev. Michael A., '67 (NEW) Retired. Curia: Advisory Boards, Commissions, Committees, and Councils St. Bartholomew, Scotch Plains, NJ
Hann, Rev. Michael, *C.I.C.M.* '73 (ARL) Retired. [MON] Missionhurst, C.I.C.M.-Central House and Provincialate (American I.H.M. Province, Inc., Immaculate Heart Missions, Inc., Missionhurst, Inc.), Arlington, VA
Hanna, Rev. Ayad, '99 (EST) Curia: Leadership; Offices and Directors Mart Mariam Chaldean Catholic Church, Northbrook, IL
Hanna, Rev. Dominique, '07 (SAM) Curia: Leadership; Offices and Directors Cathedral of Our Lady of Lebanon, Brooklyn, NY
Hanna, Rev. Edward, *M.L.M.* (OLL) Curia: Offices and Directors Our Lady of the Cedars Maronite Catholic Church, Houston, TX; [MIS] Maronite Youth Organization, St. Louis, MO; [MON] The Congregation of Maronite Lebanese Missionaries, Houston, TX
Hanna, Rev. Etienne, (OLL) Our Lady of Mt. Lebanon-St. Peter Maronite Catholic Cathedral, Los Angeles, CA; [MON] The Congregation of Maronite Lebanese Missionaries, Houston, TX
Hanna, Rev. George, *S.D.B.* '66 (NO) St. John Bosco Roman Catholic Church, Harvey, Louisiana, Harvey, LA; St. Rosalie, Harvey, LA
Hanna, Rev. Victor, (NTN) Our Lady of Mercy Melkite Mission, Allentown, PA
Hannafey, Rev. Francis T, *S.J.* '93 (PH) Old St. Joseph's, Philadelphia, PA
Hannafin, Rev. Steven J., '01 (RVC) St. Francis de Sales, Patchogue, NY
Hannah, Rev. Raymond, *S.V.D.* '60 (CHI) Retired. [MON] Divine Word Residence, Techny, IL
Hannappel, Rev. Joseph A., '84 (GI) Curia: Offices and Directors St. James, Kearney, NE
Hanneke, Rev. Msgr. Richard E., '76 (STL) Our Lady of Lourdes Catholic Church, University City, University City, MO
Hanneman, Rev. Dennis A., '72 (OM) Retired. Curia: Offices and Directors Immaculate Conception B.V.M., Boys Town, NE
Hannes, Rev. David A., '83 (PRM) Retired.
Hannigan, Rev. John T., '76 (CHI) Retired. Curia: (>MO) Offices and Directors
Hannon, Rev. Msgr. James W., '88 (BAL) On Sick Leave.
Hannon, Rev. Joseph, *S.D.B.* '73 (SP) Cristo Rey Tampa Salesian High School, Tampa, FL; [RTR] Mary Help of Christians Center, Tampa, FL
Hannon, Rev. Ken, *O.M.I.* '72 (SAT) [COL] Oblate School of Theology, San Antonio, TX; [MON] De Mazenod House, San Antonio, TX
Hannon, Rev. Patrick, *C.S.C.* '89 (P) [MON] Priests of Holy Cross in Oregon, Inc., Portland, OR
Hannon, Rev. Robert J., '79 (Y) Retired.
Hannosh, Rev. Royal, '15 (SPA) Mar Auraha Chaldean Catholic Parish (The Chaldean Catholic Church of Arizona Corporation), Scottsdale, AZ
Hanovsky, Rev. Canon Andrew, '88 (SJP) Curia: Leadership; Offices and Directors Ss. Peter and Paul, Cleveland, OH
Hanrahan, Rev. William, (AJ) Sacred Heart, Seward, AK
Hanrahan, Rev. William P., '69 (NEW) Chap, Seward, AK
Hans, Rev. Jeremy J., '15 (OM) St. Andrew, Bloomfield, NE; St. Ludger, Creighton, NE; St. Paul, Plainview, NE; St. Wenceslaus, Verdigre, NE
Hansen, Rev. Msgr. Fredrick, *P.S.S.* (BAL) [SEM] St. Mary's Seminary and University, Baltimore, MD
Hansen, Rev. Msgr. Fredrik, '07 (BAL) [MON] Society of St. Sulpice, Province of the United States, Baltimore, MD
Hansen, Rev. John, *SMP* (SPC) [MON] The Society of Our Mother of Peace, Sons of Our Mother of Peace - Queen of Heaven Solitude, High Ridge, MO
Hansen, Rev. John Richard, *SMP* '81 (STL) [MON] Society of Our Mother of Peace, High Ridge, MO
Hansen, Rev. Lawrence H., '68 (NU) Retired.
Hansen, Rev. Nathan, (NU) Cathedral of the Holy Trinity, New Ulm, MN; St. George, New Ulm, MN; St. John the Baptist, New Ulm, MN; St. Mary, New Ulm, MN
Hansen, Rev. Stephen, '06 (KC) Cathedral of St. Joseph, St. Joseph, MO; St. Mary Catholic Church, St. Joseph, MO
Hanser, Rev. F. Patrick, *C.M.* '70 (DAL) [MON]

Congregation of the Mission, Western Province, Dallas, TX
Hanson, Rev. Msgr. Donald, '72 (RVC) St. Louis de Montfort, Sound Beach, NY
Hanson, Rev. Msgr. James E., '61 (STL) Retired.
Hanson, Rev. John Henry, *O.Praem.* '06 (ORG) [MON] Norbertine Fathers of Orange, Inc., Silverado, CA; [SEM] St. Michael's Norbertine Postulancy, Novitiate and Juniorate, Silverado, CA
Hanson, Rev. Richard N., '75 (CHL) Retired.
Hanson, Rev. Msgr. William A., '72 (RVC) Mary Immaculate, Bellport, NY
Hanus, Rev. Thomas J., '66 (AUS) Retired.
Hanwell, Rev. John J., *S.J.* '91 (NY) [MON] America; Residence and Publication Office of the America Press, New York, NY
Hao, Rev. William T., '09 (ATL) Holy Name of Jesus Chinese Catholic Mission, Norcross, GA; St. Brigid Catholic Church, Johns Creek, Inc., Johns Creek, GA
Harahan, Rev. Msgr. Robert E., '74 (NEW) St. Rose of Lima, Short Hills, NJ
Haran, Rev. F. Ignatius, '59 (SAC) Retired. Pastor of St. John the Baptist Parish, Folsom, a corporation sole, Folsom, CA
Harb, Rev. Alex, (BR) The Congregation of St. Agnes Roman Catholic Church, Baton Rouge, LA
Harbaugh, Rev. James Michael, *S.J.* '76 (OAK) [MON] Jesuit Fathers and Brothers, Oakland, CA
Harbaugh, Rev. Jim, *S.J.* (SEA) Bellarmine Preparatory School, Tacoma, WA
Harbaugh, Rev. Paul E., '74 (BEL) On Leave.
Harbaugh, Rev. Russell D., '04 (MEM) Retired.
Harbour, Rev. Gerald G., '73 (PRO) Retired.
Harbour, Rev. Linn S., '86 (MOB) Retired. Curia: (>MO) Offices and Directors
Harburg, Rev. Nathan E., '11 (SAG) Curia: Leadership Good Shepherd Parish of Ubly, Ubly, MI
Harcarik, Rev. Bernard M., '63 (PIT) Retired.
Harder, Rev. Kenneth, (TLS) St. Anthony's, Okmulgee, OK
Harder, Very Rev. Kenneth J., '96 (TLS) Curia: (>STO) Leadership; Leadership
Hardesty, Rev. Matthew T., '11 (L) Immaculate Conception, New Haven, KY; St. Catherine, New Haven, KY; St. Vincent de Paul, New Hope, KY; [MIS] World Apostolate of Fatima (Blue Army), Springfield, KY
Hardiman, Rev. Msgr. Michael J., '78 (BRK) Queen of Peace, Flushing, NY
Hardin, Rev. John, *O.F.M.* '82 (OAK) [EFT] Province of Saint Barbara Fraternal Care Trust, Oakland, CA
Harding, Rev. Ignatius, *O.F.M.* (TUC) [MON] San Xavier Mission Friary, Tucson, AZ
Harding, Rev. Nicholas J., *O.M.I.* '99 (BWN) Immaculate Conception Cathedral, Brownsville, TX
Harding, Rev. Nick, *OMI* '99 (WDC) [MON] Oblate Community, Washington, DC
Harding, Rev. Pius X, *O.S.B.* '93 (P) [MON] Mt. Angel Abbey, Saint Benedict, OR; [RTR] Mount Angel Abbey Guest House & Retreat Center, St. Benedict, OR (>HEL) Saint Joseph Parish: Series 537, LLC, Libby, MT
Hardy, Rev. J. Patrick, '06 (SUP) Retired.
Hardy, Rev. L. Richard, '06 (PAT) Retired.
Hare, Rev. Joshua, (SP) St. Paul, St. Petersburg, FL
Hare, Rev. Robert, '70 (CIN) Retired. [MON] Headquarters of Glenmary Home Missioners (The Home Missioners of America), Fairfield, OH
Haremza, Rev. Shawn J., '00 (WIN) Resurrection, Rochester, MN; SS. Peter and Paul, Mazeppa, MN
Haren, Rev. Thomas A., '73 (CLV) Retired. St. Benedict Catholic School, Garfield Heights, OH
Hargaden, Very Rev. Kevin J., '99 (ATL) St. Francis of Assisi Catholic Church, Cartersville, Inc., Cartersville, GA
Harger, Rev. Bruce E., '01 (NEW) Epiphany, Cliffside Park, NJ
Hargesheimer, Rev. Msgr. Thomas J., '68 (WIN) Retired.
Harhager, Rev. John H., *S.M.* '79 (WDC) [MON] Marist Center (The Marist Finance Center of the Atlanta Province of the Society of Mary, Marist Fathers and Brothers), Washington, DC
Harkins, Rev. Simon James, *FSSP* '10 (FWT) St. Benedict Parish, Fort Worth, TX
Harkrader, Rev. Edward O., '69 (PEO) Retired.
Harlow, Rev. Lance W., '93 (BUR) Curia: Offices and Directors Corpus Christi Parish, St. Johnsbury, VT
Harlow, Rev. Sean R., *O.Carm.* '69 (NY) Our Lady of Mt. Carmel, Middletown, NY
Harman, Rev. Paul, *S.J.* (BO) [MON] Miguel Pro House, Brighton, MA
Harman, Rev. Paul F., *S.J.* '68 (WOR) [MON] Jesuits of the Holy Cross, Inc., Worcester, MA
Harman, Rev. Peter C., '99 (SFD) Curia: Leadership St. Anthony of Padua, Effingham, IL
Harmening, Rev. Adrian W., *O.S.B.* '55 (RIC) [MON] Mary Mother of the Church Abbey, Richmond, VA
Harmon, Rev. Kevin T., '22 (MIL) Congregation of the Immaculate Conception, West Bend, WI; St. Frances Cabrini Congregation, West Bend, WI
Harnan, Rev. James A., *M.S.C.* '64 (SAT) [MON] Missionaries of the Sacred Heart, San Antonio, TX
Harness, Rev. H. Robert, '82 (DAV) Retired.
Harnett, Rev. Edward F., '58 (CHI) Retired.
Harney, Rev. Thomas C., '62 (GF) Retired.
Harnish, Rev. Basil, *O.Praem.* '20 (ORG) Archangel Institute (St. Michael's Preparatory School), Silverado, CA; [MON] Norbertine Fathers of Orange, Inc., Silverado, CA
Haro, Rev. Jorge, *M.Sp.S* (SAT) St. Luke, San Antonio, TX
Haro, Rev. Jose, (KAL) Curia: Offices and Directors
Haro Gomez, Rev. Jose de Jesus, '16 (KAL) St. Mary, Kalamazoo, MI
Harold, Rev. Msgr. Thomas J., '91 (RVC) Curia: Leadership St. Anne, Garden City, NY
Haroldson, Rev. Delwyn, *C.R.* '12 (SB) Our Lady of the Desert, Apple Valley, CA; St. Paul, Lucerne Valley, CA; [MON] Congregation of the Resurrection, CR, Needles, CA
Haros-Mendez, Rev. Jesus, '19 (TUC) On Leave.
Harper, Rev. James, (MO) Curia: Offices and Directors
Harper, Rev. John H., '87 (GB) Retired.
Harpole, Rev. Ryan, '11 (OWN) St. Joseph, Bowling Green, KY; [MIS] Diocesan Shrine of Mary Mother of the Church and Model of all Christians, Bowling Green, KY
Harr, Rev. Gerald J., '62 (GI) Retired.
Harren, Rev. Robert, '66 (SCL) Retired. Curia: Leadership
Harren, Rev. Robert C., '66 (SCL) Retired. Curia: Leadership; Offices and Directors
Harrer, Rev. Ronald, *O.M.I.* (BEL) Retired. [MON] Shrine of Our Lady of the Snows, Belleville, IL; [NUR] Apartment Community of Our Lady of the Snows (Benedictine Living Community | At The Shrine), Belleville, IL
Harrigan, Rev. Maurice D., '96 (LA) Mary Star of the Sea, San Pedro, CA
Harriman, Rev. Msgr. Michael D., (SFR) Retired.
Harrington, Rev. Ashley J., *O.Carm.* '67 (NEW) Retired. Sacred Heart, Haworth, NJ; St. Cecilia, Englewood, NJ
Harrington, Rev. Brian, '13 (LAF) Our Lady of the Sacred Heart, Church Point, LA
Harrington, Rev. Brian J., '67 (FR) Retired.
Harrington, Rev. Donald J., *C.M.* '73 (BRK) [MON] Reverend John B. Murray, C.M. House, Jamaica, NY
Harrington, Rev. Ignatius, '82 (NTN) Holy Resurrection, Columbus, OH
Harrington, Rev. Jay M., *OP* '85 (STL) [MON] St. Dominic Priory, St. Louis, MO; [SEM] Aquinas Institute of Theology, St. Louis, MO
Harrington, Rev. Jeremy, '59 (DET) Church of the Transfiguration Parish Southfield, Southfield, MI
Harrington, Rev. Jeremy, *O.F.M.* '59 (CIN) [EFT] Community Support Charitable Trust for the Province of St. John the Baptist of the Order of Friars Minor, Cincinnati, OH
Harrington, Rev. John P., '66 (BRK) Retired. Our Lady of Mount Carmel, Long Island City, NY
Harrington, Rev. Msgr. Kieran E., '01 (BRK) On Duty Outside Diocese. MISSIO, 70 West 36th Street, 8th Floor, New York, NY 10018
Harrington, Rev. Michael C., '00 (BO) Curia: Clergy and Religious Services; Consultative Bodies; Pastoral Services St. Anthony of Padua, Cambridge, MA; St. Francis of Assisi, Cambridge, MA; St. Mary of the Annunciation, Cambridge, MA
Harrington, Rev. Msgr. Russell J., '79 (LAF) Assumption of the Blessed Virgin Mary, Church Point, LA
Harris, Rev. Alfred J., '94 (WDC) Retired.
Harris, Rev. Anton F, *S.J.* (LA) [SEM] Ignatius House, The Novitiate of the U.S. West Province, Society of Jesus, Culver City, CA
Harris, Rev. Arlen, *O.F.M.Cap.* '08 (NY) Allen Pavilion-Columbia Presbyterian, New York Our Lady of Sorrows, New York, NY
Harris, Rev. David, (MAN) St. Christopher, Nashua, NH
Harris, Rev. David G., '06 (GAL) Our Lady of Lourdes, Hitchcock, TX
Harris, Rev. David W., '08 (L) St. Albert the Great, Louisville, KY
Harris, Rev. Ebin Christopher, *MSFS* '07 (GAL) Prince of Peace, Houston, TX
Harris, Rev. Edwin, *S.J.* '75 (SAC) Jesuit High School, Carmichael, CA; [MON] Sacramento Jesuit Community, Carmichael, CA
Harris, Rev. Gerald P., '79 (SUP) Curia: Leadership Our Lady of the Lakes, Balsam Lake, WI; St. Joseph, Amery, WI
Harris, Rev. Glenn, '92 (PEO) St. John the Baptist, Rapids City, IL
Harris, Rev. Msgr. Jack D., '74 (LR) Curia: Leadership Sacred Heart, Morrilton, AR; St. Elizabeth, Oppelo, AR; St. Joseph, Center Ridge, AR; [CAM] University of Central Arkansas & Hendrix College Catholic Campus Ministry, Conway, AR; [EFT] Sacred Heart Catholic School Endowment Fund, Morrilton, AR
Harris, Rev. Msgr. James E., '85 (LAR) Curia: Leadership St. Frances Cabrini, Laredo, TX
Harris, Rev. James Jason, (L) St. Gabriel the Archangel, Louisville, KY
Harris, Rev. Julian P., '91 (PMB) St. Thomas More, Boynton Beach, FL
Harris, Rev. Mark, '21 (VEN) St. John the Evangelist Parish in Naples, Inc., Naples, FL
Harris, Rev. Michael B., '89 (SCR) On Administrative Leave.
Harris, Friar Peter Damian, *OP* (GAL) Holy Rosary, Houston, TX
Harris, Rev. Raymond L., '94 (BAL) Curia: Tribunal Holy Family, Randallstown, MD
Harris, Rev. Msgr. Richard D., '93 (CHR) Curia: Advisory Boards, Commissions, Committees, and Councils; Offices and Directors St. Joseph, Columbia, SC
Harris, Rev. Robert, '96 (DM) All Saints, Des Moines, IA
Harris, Rev. Msgr. Robert M., '59 (BRK) Retired.
Harris, Rev. Scott, (PHX) St. Helen Roman Catholic Parish, Glendale, AZ
Harris, Rev. Scott T., *M.M.* '78 (NY) Retired. [MON] Maryknoll Fathers and Brothers (Catholic Foreign Mission Society of America, Inc.), Ossining, NY
Harris, Friar Timothy, *T.O.R.* '06 (VEN) (>ALT) St. John Vianney, Mundy's Corner, PA
Harris, Rev. Tyler, (MO) Curia: Offices and Directors
Harris, Rev. Tyler, '20 (MRY) St. Joseph, Spreckels, CA
Harris, Rev. Msgr. Wallace A., '72 (NY) Retired.
Harris, Rev. Whitney G., '80 (LKC) Retired.
Harrison, Rev. Brian W., *O.S.* '85 (STL) [MIS] Oblates of Wisdom Study Center, St. Louis, MO
Harrison, Rev. Brian W., *O.S.* (LC) [MIS] Society of the Oblates of Wisdom, Eastman, WI
Harrison, Rev. Brian W., *O.S.* '85 (PCE) Retired. On Duty Outside Diocese. Saint Louis, MO
Harrison, Rev. Corey, (LIN) Curia: Leadership Sacred Heart, Roseland, NE
Harrison, Rev. Corey R., '15 (LIN) Curia: Leadership Sacred Heart, Lawrence, NE
Harrison, Rt. Rev. Cyprian, *O.C.S.O.* '57 (SPC) [MON] Assumption Abbey (O.Cist), Ava, MO; [SEM] Assumption Novitiate (Trappists), Ava, MO
Harrison, Rev. Cyprian, *O.C.S.O.* '57 (DUB) [MON] New Melleray Abbey, Order of Cistercians of the Strict Observance (Corporation of New Melleray), Peosta, IA
Harrison, Rev. George E., '68 (FR) Corpus Christi, East Sandwich, MA
Harrison, Rev. James, '55 (ATL) Retired.
Harrison, Rev. Jeffrey D., *S.J.* '87 (STL) [MON] St. Matthew Jesuit Community, St. Louis, MO
Harrison, Rev. John, *C.Ss.R.* '69 (BAL) Sacred Heart of Mary, Baltimore, MD; St. Rita, Baltimore, MD; [EFT] The Sacred Heart of Mary Cemetery Continuing Care Trust, Baltimore, MD; [SPF] St. John Neuman Residence, Timonium, MD
Harrison, Rev. Joseph, (NY) St. Clare, Staten Island, NY
Harrison, Rev. Patrick C., '91 (OM) St. Anthony, Columbus, NE; St. Bonaventure, Columbus, NE
Harrison, Rev. Timothy A., '91 (BO) Holy Redeemer, Merrimac, MA; Immaculate Conception, Newburyport, MA
Harrison, Rev. William S., '72 (PH) Presentation of Blessed Virgin Mary, Cheltenham, PA; St. Joseph, Cheltenham, PA
Harrold, Rev. John J., '92 (GBG) St. Ambrose, Avonmore, PA; St. Matthew, Avonmore, PA; St. Sylvester, Slickville, PA
Harry, Rev. William J., *O.Carm.* (TUC) Retired. Salpointe Catholic High School, Tucson, AZ
Harsha, Rev. Ignatius, *O.Praem.* '22 (LA) Mary Star of the Sea, San Pedro, CA
Harsha, Rev. Ignatius B, *O.Praem.* '22 (ORG) [MON] Norbertine Fathers of Orange, Inc., Silverado, CA
Harshaw, Rev. Albert E., '73 (CAM) Retired.
Hart, Rev. Andrew P., (LR) Curia: Leadership
Hart, Rev. Charles, *O.F.M.* '79 (SFD) (>CLV) [MON]

St. Anthony of Padua Friary, Brooklyn, OH

Hart, Rev. Daniel, '17 (ALX) St. Mary, Jena, LA

Hart, Rev. Msgr. E. James, (FWT) [EFT] Catholic Diocese of Fort Worth Advancement Foundation, Fort Worth, TX

Hart, Rev. Msgr. E. James, '96 (FWT) Curia: Advisory Boards, Commissions, Committees, and Councils; Leadership; Miscellaneous / Other Offices

Hart, Rev. James, '65 (KC) Retired.

Hart, Rev. Msgr. John E., '81 (PAT) Curia: Administration; Leadership Assumption of the Blessed Virgin Mary, Morristown, NJ

Hart, Rev. Joseph A., '73 (ROC) Our Lady Queen of Peace, Rochester, NY; St. Thomas More, Rochester, NY; [MIS] Providence Housing Development Corporation, Rochester, NY

Hart, Rev. Msgr. Kevin T., '74 (WDC) Curia: Tribunal St. Andrew Apostle, Silver Spring, MD

Hart, Rev. Richard M., '01 (SAV) Retired.

Hart, Rev. Robert H., '00 (STP) Retired. Curia: Leadership [CEM] Annunciation of Hazelwood Cemetery, Northfield, MN; [CEM] Calvary Cemetery, Northfield, MN

Hart, Rev. Stephen, '17 (LR) Curia: Leadership; Offices and Directors Holy Cross, Crossett, AR; Holy Spirit Church, Hamburg, AR; Our Lady of the Lake, Lake Village, AR

Hart, Rev. Thomas J., '74 (SC) Retired. Curia: Offices and Directors

Hart, Rev. Thomas Joseph, '07 (LR) St. Francis of Assisi, Fairfield Bay, AR

Hart, Rev. Thomas M., *O.S.B.* '88 (GBG) [MON] Saint Vincent Archabbey, Latrobe, PA

Harte, Rev. Paul D., '76 (CAM) The Church of Our Lady of Sorrows, Linwood, N.J., Linwood, NJ

Hartenbach, Rev. William, (STL) [MON] Congregation of the Mission, Perryville, MO

Harter, Rev. Michael G., *S.J.* '74 (STL) [MON] Sacred Heart Jesuit Community, St. Louis, MO

Harter, Rev. Scott M., '14 (GI) Curia: Offices and Directors Our Lady of Perpetual Help, Ord, NE

Hartford, Rev. Kevin F., '04 (WOR) St. Denis, Ashburnham, MA

Hartge, Rev. Michael R., '15 (COL) On Administrative Leave. Curia: Consultative Bodies

Hartgen, Rev. William E., *P.S.S.* '76 (BAL) Retired. [MON] Society of St. Sulpice, Province of the United States, Baltimore, MD

Harth, Rev. John M., '87 (SPC) Retired. Curia: Advisory Boards, Commissions, Committees, and Councils; (>MO) Offices and Directors

Hartigan, Rev. Dennis, *S.D.B.* '80 (NEW) [MON] The Salesian Community, Orange, NJ

Hartigan, Rev. Dennis, *SDB* '71 (SP) [RTR] Mary Help of Christians Center, Tampa, FL

Hartin, Rev. Patrick, '71 (SPK) Retired. Our Lady of Fatima, Spokane, WA; [SEM] Bishop White Seminary, Spokane, WA

Hartle, Rev. Levi, (PIT) Blessed Trinity, Pittsburgh, PA

Hartle, Rev. Thomas R., *O.F.M.* '71 (PAT) [MON] St. Anthony Friary (Order of Friars Minor), Butler, NJ

Hartley, Rev. Matthew, '06 (DEN) St. Thomas More Catholic Parish in Centennial, Centennial, CO

Hartley, Rev. Michael, '16 (PT) Curia: Leadership St. Rita, Santa Rosa Beach, FL

Hartley, Rev. Steven A., '07 (SFE) Retired.

Hartman, Rev. Glenn R., '76 (CAM) Chap, Elmwood Hills Healthcare Ctr, Blackwood; Virtua Heal [MIS] Mater Ecclesiae Mission, Berlin, NJ

Hartman, Rev. Thomas, (SFS) Curia: Leadership Saint Michael Parish of Minnehaha County, Sioux Falls, SD

Hartmann, Rev. Joseph A., '78 (DEN) St. Joseph Catholic Parish in Ft. Collins, Fort Collins, CO

Hartmann, Rev. Paul B.R., '94 (MIL) On Duty Outside Diocese. Assoc Secy Gen, USCCB

Hartmann, Rev. Richard A., '73 (DET) Retired.

Hartnett, Rev. Daniel F., *S.J.* (CHI) [COL] Jesuit Community at Loyola University Chicago, Chicago, IL

Hartnett, Rev. James, '72 (ORG) Retired. Holy Family, Seal Beach, CA

Hartnett, Rev. Patrick, '11 (TYL) On Leave.

Hartnett, Rev. Msgr. Robert L., '79 (BAL) Our Lady of Mount Carmel, Essex, MD

Hartrich, Rev. Kurt, *O.F.M.* '66 (CHI) [MIS] S.F.V., Inc., Chicago, IL; [MON] St. Peter's Friary, Chicago, IL

Hartshorn, Rev. Christopher, '94 (DM) Curia: Offices and Directors Sacred Heart, West Des Moines, IA

Hartwell, Rev. James W., '02 (BUF) Curia: Leadership Blessed Sacrament, Andover, NY; Holy Family of Jesus, Mary & Joseph, Belmont, NY; Immaculate Conception, Wellsville, NY; Immaculate Conception School of Allegany County, Wellsville, NY; SS. Brendan and Jude, Alfred, NY; St. Mary, Bolivar, NY; [CAM] Alfred University and Alfred State College Campus Ministry, Alfred, NY

Harvey, Rev. David W., '68 (LAN) Retired.

Harvey, Rev. Frederick R., '00 (BIS) Christ the King, Mandan, ND

Harvey, Rev. James P., '96 (KNX) Curia: Leadership Holy Trinity Catholic Church, Jefferson City, TN

Harvey, Rev. Jeffrey, *CM* '93 (LA) [MON] Congregation of the Mission Western Province (DePaul Center Residence), Montebello, CA; [SEM] St. John's Seminary, Camarillo, CA

Harvey, Rev. John A., '66 (PIT) Retired.

Harvey, Rev. John D., *O.F.M.Cap.* '72 (PIT) [MON] St. Fidelis Friary, Beaver, PA

Harvey, Rev. Michael L., *O.F.M.* (P) [HOS] Providence Health & Services-Oregon (Providence Portland Medical Center), Portland, OR

Harvey, Rev. Peter J., *O.S.F.S.* '60 (WIL) Retired.

Harvey, Rev. Warren, '88 (LR) Curia: Offices and Directors [HOS] St. Vincent Infirmary Medical Center, Little Rock, AR; [MON] St. John Manor, Little Rock, AR

Harvey, Rev. Wilfred, *O.M.I.* '63 (BO) [MON] Missionary Oblates of Mary Immaculate Northern Province, Lowell, MA

Haschka, Rev. David, *S.J.* '75 (STP) Curia: Consultative Bodies [MON] Markoe House Jesuit Community, Minneapolis, MN

Haschke, Rev. Jonathan, (LIN) Lourdes Elementary, Nebraska City, NE

Haschke, Rev. Jonathan J., '09 (LIN) Curia: Offices and Directors Lourdes Central Catholic Schools, Nebraska City, NE; St. Mary Catholic Church of Nebraska City, Nebraska City, NE; [EFT] Lourdes Central High School Endowment Fund, Nebraska City, NE

Hasenkamp, Rev. Robert, '63 (KCK) Retired.

Hasenoehrl, Rev. Chase R., '10 (B) Curia: Leadership St. Augustine's, Moscow, ID; St. Mary Station, Potlatch, ID; [CAM] St. Augustine's Catholic Center, Moscow, ID

Hasieber, Rev. Joseph S., '73 (ALX) Retired.

Haskamp, Rev. Gregory, '93 (KC) St. Elizabeth, Kansas City, MO

Haskin, Rev. Jay C., '67 (BUR) Retired.

Hasler, Rev. Clifford, *MS* '71 (STL) [MON] Missionaries of LaSalette, Province of Mary, Mother of the Americas, St. Louis, MO

Hasse, Rev. Benjamin J., '09 (MAR) Curia: Offices and Directors St. Albert the Great University Parish, Houghton, MI; St. Anne, Chassell, MI; [CAM] St. Albert the Great University Parish (Catholic Campus Ministry at Michigan Tech), Houghton, MI

Hassel, Rev. Christopher, (SAV) St. Teresa of Avila, Grovetown, GA

Hassel, Rev. Christopher, '18 (SAV) Curia: Leadership; Offices and Directors

Hassett, Rev. James F., '75 (BUF) Retired. [MON] O'Hara Residence, Tonawanda, NY

Hassler, Rev. Luke, '19 (EVN) Curia: Leadership Annunciation of the Blessed Virgin Mary, Jasper, IN

Hast, Rev. James, *OFM Cap.* (DET) [MON] St. Bonaventure Monastery, Detroit, MI

Hastings, Rev. Joel, '99 (DUL) Curia: Offices and Directors SS. Mary & Joseph, Sawyer, MN; St. Francis, Carlton, MN

Hastings, Rev. Joseph P., '20 (MEM) Curia: Advisory Boards, Commissions, Committees, and Councils St. Francis of Assisi, Cordova, TN

Hastings, Rev. Nathan Robert, '19 (STP) Holy Spirit, St. Paul, MN

Hastings, Rev. Scott A., '08 (OM) Curia: Leadership; Offices and Directors St. Joseph, Springfield, NE

Hatch, Very Rev. Lorenzo, '13 (SAN) Cathedral of the Sacred Heart, San Angelo, TX

Hatcher, Rev. John, (HON) Retired. St. Theresa, Kihei, HI

Hater, Rev. Robert J., '59 (CIN) Retired. St. Clare, Cincinnati, OH

Hatfield, Rev. James H., '10 (COL) Church of the Holy Trinity, Bolivar, OH; St. Joseph, Dover, OH

Hathaway, Rev. Christopher, *F.S.S.P.* (VEN) Christ the King Parish in Sarasota, Inc., Sarasota, FL

Hathaway, Rev. Edward C., '91 (ARL) Basilica of St. Mary, Alexandria, VA

Hathaway, Rev. Keith, '15 (FWT) St. Rita, Fort Worth, TX

Hattar, Rev. Fares, '89 (NY) Immaculate Conception, Yonkers, NY

Hatton, Very Rev. Ronald J., '95 (PSC) Curia: Advisory Boards, Commissions, Committees, and Councils; Leadership Holy Trinity Greek Catholic Church, New Britain, CT; Saint Nicholas Byzantine Catholic Church, Danbury, CT; Saints Peter and Paul's Byzantine Catholic Church, Peekskill, NY; St. Nicholas Greek Catholic Church, Meriden, CT

Hattrup, Rev. Theobald, *O.F.M.* '56 (CIN) Retired.

Hauber, Rev. Douglas, (JOL) SS. Mary and Joseph, Chebanse, IL

Hauber, Very Rev. Douglas L., '89 (JOL) Curia: Leadership Assumption of the Blessed Virgin Mary, Ashkum, IL; St. Peter's, Clifton, IL

Hauck, Very Rev. Stephen, (FWT) Curia: Advisory Boards, Commissions, Committees, and Councils; Leadership St. Martin De Porres Parish, Prosper, TX; [EFT] Catholic Diocese of Fort Worth Advancement Foundation, Fort Worth, TX

Hauf, Rev. Edward, *O.M.I.* '66 (SAT) St. Mary, San Antonio, TX

Haug, Rev. Joel, '19 (KCK) Bishop Ward High School, Kansas City, KS; St. Joseph, Shawnee, KS

Haugan, Rev. Daniel C., '03 (STP) Curia: Advisory Boards, Commissions, Committees, and Councils Church of Lumen Christi, St. Paul, MN; St. Stanislaus, St. Paul, MN

Haugen, Rev. John S., '84 (DUB) Sacred Heart Church (Volga City, Iowa), Volga, IA; St. Joseph's Church, Elkader, Iowa, Elkader, IA; St. Mark's Church, Edgewood, Iowa, Edgewood, IA; St. Mary Church, Strawberry Point, Iowa, Strawberry Point, IA; St. Patrick's Church, Colesburg, Iowa, Colesburg, IA

Hauser, Rev. Albert J., '81 (OG) Curia: Consultative Bodies; Miscellaneous / Other Offices Catholic Community of Moriah, Port Henry, NY; Church of the Sacred Heart of Jesus, Crown Point, NY

Hauser, Rev. John G., '71 (BRK) Retired.

Hauser, Rev. Nathanael, *O.S.B.* '83 (SCL) [MON] St. John's Abbey, of the Order of St. Benedict, Collegeville, MN

Hausfeld, Rev. Bruce, *O.F.M.* '61 (CIN) Retired.

Hausfeld, Rev. Bruce, (SFE) (>CIN) [MON] St. Clement Friary, Cincinnati, OH

Hausfeld, Rev. Bryant, (SFE) (>CIN) [MON] St. Clement Friary, Cincinnati, OH

Hausfeld, Rev. Bryant, *O.F.M.* '65 (CIN) Retired.

Hausladen, Rev. Robert T., '01 (IND) Curia: Offices and Directors St. Joseph Catholic Church, Indianapolis, Inc., Indianapolis, IN; St. Susanna Catholic Church, Plainfield, Inc., Plainfield, IN

Hausmann, Rev. Leo, '92 (RC) Curia: Leadership St. Ambrose, Deadwood, SD; St. Patrick's, Lead, SD

Haut, Rev. Msgr. Vincent J., '68 (STA) Retired.

Hautz, Rev. Roland, '53 (CIN) Retired.

Hauver, Rev. James H., '97 (NY) Retired. St. Columba, New York, NY

Hauwert, Rev. Gerardus, *IVE* (FBK) Immaculate Conception Catholic Parish Fairbanks, Fairbanks, AK; [MON] St. Ignatius Residence, Fairbanks, AK

Havel, Rev. Elias, *M.M.A.* '95 (SAM) [MON] Maronite Monks of Adoration - Most Holy Trinity Monastery, Petersham, MA

Havel, Very Rev. Gregory G., '90 (WIN) Curia: Advisory Boards, Commissions, Committees, and Councils; Deaneries Our Lady of Mount Carmel, Easton, MN; St. Casimir's, Wells, MN; St. John the Baptist, Minnesota Lake, MN

Haverland, Rev. Nathan, '13 (KCK) Most Pure Heart of Mary, Topeka, KS

Haverstock, Rev. Paul, '16 (STP) The Parish of Saint Gabriel the Archangel of Hopkins, Minnesota, Hopkins, MN

Havey, Rev. Lee, *C.P.* '06 (SCR) [MON] Saint Ann's Passionist Monastery of Scranton PA, Scranton, PA

Havey, Rev. Lee, *C.P.* '04 (NY) [MON] The Congregation of the Passion - St. Paul of the Cross Province, Jamaica, NY

Havill, Rev. Gregory J., *O.S.B.* '15 (PRO) [MON] Abbey of St. Gregory the Great (Order of St. Benedict in Portsmouth, Rhode Island, Benedictines of the English Congregation), Portsmouth, RI

Havrilka, Rev. Joseph, *KCHS* '05 (SFD) St. Clare, Altamont, IL

Havrilka, Rev. T. Joseph, '05 (SFD) St. Anne, Edgewood, IL; St. Mary, St. Elmo, IL

Havyarimana, Rev. Jean Claude, *SJ* '12 (OAK) [MON] Jesuit Fathers and Brothers, Berkeley, CA

Hawes, Rev. Msgr. Cletus J., '52 (DUB) Retired.

Hawes, Rev. Donald J., '53 (DUB) Retired.

Hawes, Very Rev. Roger, '01 (VIC) Curia: Leadership; Offices and Directors Holy Cross, Yorktown, TX

Hawk, Rev. Vincent J., '02 (CLV) Avon Hospital Curia: Advisory Boards, Commissions, Committees, and Councils Holy Trinity, Avon, OH

Hawken, Rev. Michael, '94 (KCK) Church of the Nativity, Leawood, KS

Hawker, Rev. James, '63 (CHL) Retired.

Hawkes-Teeples, Rev. Steven, *S.J.* '93 (PRM) St. Louis

Mission, St. Louis, MO
Hawkins, Rev. Allan R.G., '94 (FWT) Retired.
Hawkins, Rev. C. Matthew, (PIT) St. Benedict the Moor Parish, Pittsburgh, PA; St. Mary Magdalene, Pittsburgh, PA
Hawkins, Rev. Charles, '78 (PMB) Retired.
Hawkins, Rev. Edward, (PMB) Retired.
Hawkins, Rev. John, *O.S.C.* '66 (SCL) [MON] Crosier Priory, Onamia, MN
Hawkins, Rev. Matthew, '18 (ORL) Saint Paul Catholic Church, Leesburg, FL
Hawkins, Rev. Thomas J. D., '70 (KC) St. Mary's, Higginsville, MO
Hawley, Rev. Benjamin, *SJ* '00 (WDC) Holy Trinity, Washington, DC; [MON] The Jesuit Community at Georgetown University, Washington, DC
Hawley, Rev. Benjamin B., *S.J.* '00 (LAN) [MIS] Charismatic Renewal Diocesan Service Committee, Lansing, MI
Hawley, Rev. Gerard L., '92 (SCR) On Administrative Leave.
Hawthorne, Rev. Patrick J., '82 (WOR) Our Lady of the Rosary, Worcester, MA
Hawver, Rev. Carl, *O.F.M.* '74 (CIN) Retired.
Hawxhurst, Rev. Tom, '12 (GAL) St. Patrick, Houston, TX
Hay, Rev. Msgr. Theodore H., *S.T.L.* '55 (MOB) Retired.
Hay, Rev. W. Michael, '92 (CIN) St. Gabriel, Cincinnati, OH; St. John the Evangelist, West Chester, OH; St. Michael, Cincinnati, OH
Hayatsu, Rev. Richard K., '65 (SEA) St. Francis of Assisi, Burien, WA
Haycock, Rev. Anthony J., '72 (SEA) Retired. [CCH] Catholic Seafarer's Ministry, Seattle, WA
Hayden, Rev. James P., '91 (GLD) Retired. Curia: Advisory Boards, Commissions, Committees, and Councils; Leadership; Offices and Directors Immaculate Conception of Traverse City, Traverse City, MI; Saint Anthony of Padua of Mancelona, Mancelona, MI; Saint Luke the Evangelist of Bellaire, Bellaire, MI; [EFT] Northern Michigan Catholic Foundation, Inc., Gaylord, MI
Hayden, Rev. Joseph F., '63 (L) Retired.
Hayden, Rev. Joseph J., *S.J.* '70 (BAL) [MIS] Colombiere Jesuit Community, Baltimore, MD
Hayden, Rev. Michael T., '85 (SUP) Retired.
Hayden, Rev. Patrick T., '90 (STL) On Duty Outside Diocese. La Paz, Bolivia
Hayden, Rev. Terence, '77 (NO) Retired.
Haydinger, Rev. Christian J., '76 (RIC) Retired.
Haydock, Rev. Kenneth, '80 (SEA) Retired.
Haydu, Rev. Mark, *L.C.* '07 (NY) [MON] Legionaries of Christ, Rye, NY
Hayduk, Rev. Archpriest Michael, '77 (PRM) Retired.
Hayek, Rev. Herbert C, *OP* '71 (CHI) St. Katharine Drexel, Chicago, IL; [MON] Dominican Community of St. Martin de Porres, Oak Park, IL
Hayek, Rev. Msgr. Sami, '59 (SAM) Retired.
Hayer, Rt. Rev. Mitred Archpriest James, '89 (PSC) Curia: Advisory Boards, Commissions, Committees, and Councils; Leadership St. Thomas the Apostle, Rahway, NJ
Hayes, Rev. Brian, '92 (SD) Pastor of Saint Catherine Laboure Catholic Parish, San Diego, a corporation sole, San Diego, CA; [MIS] Saint Catherine Laboure Catholic Parish in San Diego, CA Real Property Support Corporation, San Diego, CA
Hayes, Rev. Christopher H., '13 (ARL) Church of the Nativity, Burke, VA
Hayes, Rev. Dennis J., '86 (NO) Chap, Univ of New Orleans, New Orleans Curia: Leadership
Hayes, Rev. Dennis J., '76 (SY) Retired.
Hayes, Rev. Edward A., *M.M.* '59 (NY) Retired.
Hayes, Rt. Rev. Eugene J., *O.Praem.* '77 (ORG) [EFT] St. Michael's Abbey Foundation, Silverado, CA; [MON] Norbertine Fathers of Orange, Inc., Silverado, CA; [SEM] St. Michael's Norbertine Postulancy, Novitiate and Juniorate, Silverado, CA
Hayes, Rev. James, *S.S.S.* '77 (NY) The Mount Sinai Hosp, New York St. Jean Baptiste, New York, NY
Hayes, Rev. James A., *S.S.J.* '55 (BAL) Retired.
Hayes, Rev. James M., *S.J.* '85 (WOR) [MON] Jesuits of the Holy Cross, Inc., Worcester, MA
Hayes, Rev. Jerome T., *S.J.* '07 (WDC) [MON] The Jesuit Community at Georgetown University, Washington, DC
Hayes, Rev. John, (NU) Church of the Holy Family, Silver Lake, MN; Holy Trinity, Winsted, MN; St. Pius X, Glencoe, MN
Hayes, Rev. John H., '87 (ROC) The Parish of Saint Martin de Porres, Livingston County, NY, Caledonia, NY
Hayes, Rev. John J., '60 (CLV) Retired. Immaculate Conception, Cleveland, OH
Hayes, Rev. Lawrence, *O.F.M.* '89 (NY) Parish of Holy Name of Jesus and St. Gregory the Great, New York, NY; [MON] Franciscan Friars, Holy Name Province (The Order of Friars Minor of the Province of the Most Holy Name), New York, NY
Hayes, Rev. Leo J., '61 (BEL) Retired.
Hayes, Rev. Madison, '21 (AJ) Curia: (>MO) Offices and Directors Our Lady of the Lake Church, Big Lake, AK; Sacred Heart, Wasilla, AK
Hayes, Rev. Maurice, *O.F.M.Conv.* '69 (L) Retired.
Hayes, Rev. Robert, '71 (MRY) Curia: Tribunal
Hayes, Rev. Robert E., '71 (SJ) Retired. On Special Assignment. Curia: Offices and Directors
Hayes, Rev. Robert E., '71 (RNO) Curia: Leadership
Hayes, Rev. Samuel, '83 (CHY) Retired.
Hayes, Rev. Stephen-Dominic, *O.P.* '88 (COL) St. Patrick, Columbus, OH
Hayes, Rev. Terrence M., '72 (STP) Our Lady of Victory, Minneapolis, MN
Hayes, Rev. Thomas, *O.M.I.* '64 (BEL) [MON] Missionary Oblates of Mary Immaculate - St. Henry's Oblate Residence, Belleville, IL
Hayes, Rev. Thomas J., '73 (ALB) Retired. St. Vincent de Paul, Albany, NY
Hayes, Rev. Timothy M., '85 (COL) St. Mary, Chillicothe, OH; St. Mary, Queen of the Missions, Waverly, OH; St. Peter, Chillicothe, OH
Hayman, Rev. Douglas, '13 (POC) Retired.
Hayman, Rev. Robert W., '66 (PRO) Retired. SS. Peter and Paul's Church, Providence, RI
Haynes, Rev. Scott, *S.J.C.* '07 (CHI) St. Bede the Venerable and St. Denis Parish, Chicago, IL; St. Thomas More Mission, Chicago, IL; [MIS] Canons Regular of Saint John Cantius, Chicago, IL; [MIS] Musica Pacis, Cicero, IL
Haynes, Rev. Thaddeus, *C.R.I.C.* '15 (LA) [MON] Canons Regular of the Immaculate Conception, Santa Paula, CA
Haynes, Rev. Thaddeus, *C.R.I.C.* '15 (LA) St. Sebastian, Santa Paula, CA
Hays, Rev. John S., '93 (SP) St. Anne, Ridge Manor, FL
Hays, Rev. Kevin W., '77 (CHI) Retired.
Hays, Rev. Timothy, '96 (SPK) Curia: Leadership Assumption of the Blessed Virgin Mary, Spokane, WA
Hayter, Rev. Timothy, '17 (SAN) St. Mary Star of the Sea, Ballinger, TX
Haywiaser, Rev. Isaac, *OSB* (ALT) St. Michael, West Salisbury, PA
Haywiser, Rev. Isaac (Paul), *O.S.B.* '15 (GBG) [MON] Saint Vincent Archabbey, Latrobe, PA
Hazard, Rev. Msgr. Michael, '72 (KAL) Curia: Consultative Bodies; Leadership St. Ambrose, Parchment, MI
Hazebrouck, Rev. Maurice L., '45 (PRO) Retired.
Hazel, Rev. Robert L., '66 (STP) Retired.
Hazuka, Rev. Jeremy L., '97 (LIN) Curia: Leadership St. Michael's, Hastings, NE
Hazzard, Rev. William M., '63 (WIL) Retired.
Headley, Rev. William R., (FTW) [COL] University of Notre Dame Du Lac, Notre Dame, IN
Heagerty, Rev. Msgr. John J., '54 (SY) Retired.
Heagle, Rev. John L., '65 (LC) Retired.
Healey, Very Rev. Bede, *OSB Cam* '19 (OAK) [MON] Incarnation Monastery, Camaldolese Benedictines, Berkeley, CA
Healey, Very Rev. Bernard A., '95 (PRO) Curia: Leadership; Offices and Directors Our Lady of Mercy, Greenwich, Rhode Island, East Greenwich, RI
Healey, Rev. Charles J., *S.J.* '65 (BO) [MON] Campion Center, Inc., Weston, MA
Healey, Rev. Edward J., '87 (FR) Christ the King, Mashpee, MA
Healey, Rev. Edward J., '87 (FR) Curia: Offices and Directors
Healey, Rev. John E., '70 (MAN) Retired. St. Patrick, Nashua, NH
Healey, Rev. Joseph G., *M.M.* '66 (NY) [MON] Maryknoll Fathers and Brothers (Catholic Foreign Mission Society of America, Inc.), Ossining, NY
Healey, Rev. Kenneth, *S.M.* '70 (BO) Holy Trinity, Lowell, MA; Immaculate Conception, Lowell, MA; St. Anthony of Padua, Lowell, MA
Healey, Rev. Robert, '20 (TLS) St. Francis Xavier Catholic Church, Stillwater, OK
Healy, Rev. Cornelius J., '66 (SFR) Retired. St. Isabella, San Rafael, CA
Healy, Rev. Daniel, '01 (ROC) [MIS] Anawim Community Center, Corning, NY
Healy, Rev. Daniel H., '01 (MET) [MIS] The Anawim Community, Oxford, NJ
Healy, Rev. Msgr. Gerard M., '61 (MAD) Retired.
Healy, Rev. Jack, *O.Carm.* '70 (ROC) [MON] Whitefriars Priory, Rochester, NY
Healy, Rev. James E., '72 (KC) Retired.
Healy, Rev. John J., '12 (BO) St. Mary, Walpole, MA
Healy, Rev. John J., '66 (SAC) Retired.
Healy, Rev. Kieran, (P) [RTR] St. Benedict Lodge Dominican Retreat & Conference Center, McKenzie Bridge, OR
Healy, Rev. Michael J., '71 (SFR) Chap, San Francisco Police Department St. Stephen, San Francisco, CA; St. Vincent de Paul, San Francisco, CA
Healy, Rev. Patrick S., *S.S.J.* '76 (BR) Retired.
Healy, Rev. Ryan, '19 (FR) St. Francis Xavier's, Acushnet, MA
Healy, Rev. Stephen M., '85 (BO) On Leave.
Healy, Rev. Terence P., '62 (ALB) Retired. St. Anthony-St. Joseph, Herkimer, NY; St. John the Baptist, Newport, NY
Healy, Rev. Thomas, '67 (SAV) Retired. Curia: Leadership
Healy, Rev. Msgr. Thomas J., '66 (BRK) Retired.
Healy, Rev. William, '66 (PHX) Retired.
Heanue, Rev. Christopher R., '15 (BRK) Co-Cathedral of Saint Joseph – Saint Teresa of Avila, Brooklyn, NY; [CCH] Catholic Kolping Society of Brooklyn (Katholischer Gesellen Verein), Glendale, NY
Hearn, Rev. Philip A., '66 (SY) Retired. Curia: Leadership Immaculate Conception, Fayetteville, NY
Hearne, Rev. William S., '11 (CHR) St. Francis of Assisi, Walhalla, SC; St. Paul the Apostle, Seneca, SC
Heasley, Rev. Peter Andrew, '13 (NY) Curia: Leadership Corpus Christi, New York, NY; Notre Dame, New York, NY; [SEM] St. Joseph's Seminary, Yonkers, NY
Heaslip, Rev. Andrew J., '09 (LIN) Curia: Offices and Directors
Heath, Rev. Christopher Raymond, '88 (ORG) Curia: Leadership; Offices and Directors
Heathershaw, Rev. Thomas, '19 (DUB) St. Michael's Church, Nashua, Iowa, Nashua, IA; The Immaculate Conception Church, Charles City, Iowa, Charles City, IA
Hebda, Rev. Martin J., '67 (CHI) Retired.
Hebda, Rev. Michael J., '96 (SAC) Retired.
Hebden, Rev. W. Scott, '99 (CHI) St. Raymond de Penafort, Mt. Prospect, IL
Heberlein, Rev. Kenneth, '71 (GAL) Retired.
Hebert, Rev. Daniel J., '79 (AJ) Holy Cross, Anchorage, AK
Hebert, Rev. David B., '11 (LAF) St. Elizabeth Seton, Lafayette, LA
Hebert, Rev. Gerard A., '81 (FR) Curia: Tribunal St. Bernard's, Assonet, MA
Hebert, Rev. Msgr. J. Gaston, '60 (LR) Retired.
Hebert, Rev. Jeffrey, '18 (LR) Curia: Offices and Directors [MIS] Diocese of Little Rock House of Formation, Little Rock, AR; [MIS] Monsignor James E. O'Connell Diocesan Seminarian Fund, Inc., Little Rock, AR
Hebert, Rev. Joseph Elmo, *M.Afr.* '63 (SP) Retired. [MON] Missionaries of Africa, St. Petersburg, FL
Hebert, Rev. Mark, '20 (GAL) Curia: Leadership
Hebert, Rev. Matthew, (LAF) Our Lady of Prompt Succor, New Iberia, LA; Our Lady of the Holy Rosary, Kaplan, LA
Hebert, Rev. Ronald, '65 (SD) Retired.
Hebert, Rev. T. J., '49 (LAF) Retired.
Hebl, Rev. Msgr. John H., '61 (MAD) Retired.
Heck, Rev. Thomas, '76 (VEN) Retired.
Heckel, Rev. Guerric Frederick A., *O.C.S.O.* '66 (CHR) [MON] Mepkin Abbey, Moncks Corner, SC
Hecker, Rev. Curtis D.L., '15 (WCH) Kapaun Mt. Carmel Catholic High School, Wichita, KS
Hecker, Rev. Msgr. Lawrence A., '58 (NO) Retired.
Hecktor, Rev. Brian E., '08 (STL) St. Mark Catholic Church, Affton, St. Louis, MO
Hedagbui, Rev. Prosper, '09 (LA) St. Monica, Santa Monica, CA
Hedderman, Rev. James P., '95 (BIR) Corpus Christi, Oneonta, AL
Hederman, Rev. James J., *S.J.* '99 (NY) Xavier High School, New York, NY; [MON] Xavier Jesuit Community, New York, NY
Hedges, Rev. John P., '87 (DET) St. Stephen Parish New Boston, New Boston, MI
Hedman, Rev. Paul James, '20 (STP) St. Peter, Forest Lake, MN
Hedrick, Rev. John H., '70 (MAD) Retired.
Hedrick, Rev. Msgr. Kenneth J., '73 (NO) Retired. Transfiguration of the Lord, New Orleans, LA
Hedrick, Rev. Timothy D., '14 (NO) Curia: Offices and Directors St. Catherine of Siena, Metairie, LA; [SEM] Notre Dame Seminary Graduate School of Theology,

New Orleans, LA
Hedstrom, Rev. Andrew Daniel, '21 (LA) Holy Family, South Pasadena, CA
Hedz, Rev. Bohdan, '10 (STF) Curia: Offices and Directors St. John the Baptist, Riverhead, NY
Heenan, Rev. Grayson D., (DET) Curia: Consultative Bodies St. Andrew Parish Rochester, Rochester, MI
Heet, Rev. Donald J., *O.S.F.S.* '76 (ARL) St. John Neumann, Reston, VA
Heffernan, Rev. Henry, *S.J.* (PH) Retired.
Heffernan, Rev. Henry G., *S.J.* '62 (WDC) Chap, St Elizabeths Hosp (Government Operated), Washington
Heffernan, Rev. Joseph, (LIN) [MIS] St. Francis of Assisi Church, Lincoln, NE
Heffernan, Rev. Raymond, '57 (SEA) Retired.
Heffner, Rev. Carroll, '61 (NO) Retired.
Hefner, Rev. Msgr. Helmut A., '69 (LA) Retired.
Hegarty, Rev. Frederick J., *M.M.* '53 (NY) Retired.
Hegemann, Rev. Matthew, *O.Cist.* '22 (DAL) [MON] Our Lady of Dallas Cistercian Abbey, Irving, TX
Hegnauer, Rev. Edward Anthony, '09 (WDC) Immaculate Heart of Mary, Lexington Park, MD; St. Philip the Apostle, Camp Springs, MD
Heher, Rev. Msgr. Michael, '78 (ORG) Curia: Leadership St. Anne Church, Seal Beach, CA
Hehir, Rev. J. Bryan, '66 (BO) Curia: Social Services
Hehir, Rev. J. Bryan, (BO) St. John the Evangelist, Wellesley, MA
Hehman, Rev. Lawrence W., '65 (LEX) Retired.
Heiar, Rev. Msgr. Donald J., '00 (MAD) St. Albert the Great, Sun Prairie, WI
Heiar, Rev. James, '70 (CHI) Retired. [MON] Divine Word Residence, Techny, IL
Heidecke, Rev. Albert J., '93 (JOL) St. Joseph, Downers Grove, IL
Heidenreich, Rev. Robert J., '69 (CHI) Retired.
Heidt, Rev. Ed, *C.S.B.* '76 (LSC) [MON] The Basilian Fathers of Las Cruces, Las Cruces, NM
Heier, Rev. Thomas, *C.M.M.* '58 (DET) [MON] Mariannhill Mission Society, Dearborn Heights, MI
Heier, Rev. Vergil, *C.M.M.* '63 (DET) [MON] Mariannhill Mission Society, Dearborn Heights, MI
Heikkala, Rev. Gregory R., '91 (MAR) St. Michael, Marquette, MI
Heil, Rev. John P., *S.S.D.* '74 (WDC) [COL] Catholic University of America, The, Washington, DC
Heil, Rev. John P., *S.S.D.* '74 (STL) On Duty Outside Diocese. Washington, DC
Heille, Rev. Gregory J., *OP* '75 (STL) [MON] Dominican Community of St. Louis, St. Louis, MO; [SEM] Aquinas Institute of Theology, St. Louis, MO
Heilman, Rev. Richard M., '88 (MAD) St. Mary of Pine Bluff, Cross Plains, WI
Heim, Rev. Edward L., '71 (STL) Retired.
Heim, Rev. John P., *S.J.* (DET) [MON] Colombiere Center, Clarkston, MI
Heim, Rev. Joseph A., *M.M.* '61 (NY) Retired. [MON] Maryknoll Fathers and Brothers (Catholic Foreign Mission Society of America, Inc.), Ossining, NY
Heim, Rev. Joseph A., *M.M.* (PH) Retired.
Heiman, Rev. Andrew E., '05 (WCH) Curia: Leadership Sacred Heart Parish, Halstead, KS
Heimer, Rev. Michael G., '71 (GRY) Curia: Leadership St. Anthony of Padua, Walkerton, IN; St. John Kanty, Walkerton, IN
Heimsoth, Rev. Larry, '97 (AUS) Retired.
Hein, Rev. Francis, *O.S.B.* '13 (STL) St. Anselm Catholic Church, St. Louis, MO; [MON] The Abbey of St. Mary and St. Louis, St. Louis, MO
Hein, Rev. Kenneth C., *O.S.B.* '69 (B) Retired. [MON] Monastery of the Ascension, Jerome, ID
Heina, Rev. Steven, '82 (SAL) St. John the Baptist Parish, Clyde, Inc., Clyde, KS; St. Mary Parish, Clifton, Inc., Clifton, KS
Heine, Rev. Michael, *OFM Conv.* '90 (BAL) [MON] Franciscan Friars - Our Lady of the Angels Province, Inc., Ellicott City, MD; [MON] Order of Friars Minor Conventual, Ellicott City, MD
Heinen, Rev. Miles J., *C.M.* '82 (STL) [MON] Congregation of the Mission Vincentian Fathers Lazarist Residence, St. Louis, MO
Heinen, Rev. Virgil O., '60 (SUP) Retired.
Heiney, Rev. Lawrence W., '75 (CHL) Retired.
Heinlein, Rev. Gregory, (RVC) Retired. [MON] St Pius X Residence for Retired Priests LLC, Ronkonkoma, NY
Heinlein, Rev. Msgr. John, (RVC) Retired. [MON] St Pius X Residence for Retired Priests LLC, Ronkonkoma, NY
Heinlein, Rev. Msgr. John T., '61 (RVC) Retired.
Heinrich, Rev. Matthew, '15 (CHI) Immaculate Conception, Chicago, IL
Heintz, Rev. Andrew J., '05 (ARL) St. Paul, Hague, VA
Heintz, Rev. Daniel, '54 (SY) Retired.
Heintz, Rev. Msgr. Michael, '93 (BAL) [SEM] Mount St. Mary's Seminary, Emmitsburg, MD
Heintz, Rev. Msgr. Michael W., '93 (FTW) On Special Assignment. Granger Curia: Offices and Directors
Heintzelman, Rev. Edward F., '84 (CAM) Curia: Advisory Boards, Commissions, Committees, and Councils; Leadership St. Vincent de Paul Parish, Mays Landing, N.J., Mays Landing, NJ
Heintzelman, Rev. Gerard T., '59 (HBG) Retired. [NUR] Maria Hall, Inc., Danville, PA
Heinz, Rev. David C., '77 (PEO) Retired.
Heinz, Rev. John, *O.F.M.Conv.* '93 (OAK) [MON] Conventual Franciscans (Province of St. Joseph Cupertino) Provincial Center, Castro Valley, CA; [MON] Conventual Franciscans (Province of St. Joseph of Cupertino), Castro Valley, CA
Heinz, Rev. Msgr. Martin G., '94 (RCK) St. Joseph, Richmond, IL
Heinz, Rev. Robert P., '80 (CHI) Retired.
Heinz, Rev. Walter E., '62 (STU) Retired.
Heinze, Rev. Arthur G., '69 (MIL) Retired.
Heinze, Rev. Markus, *O.F.M.* (NY) [MIS] Franciscans International, Inc., New York, NY
Heise, Rev. Bert, *O.F.M.* '57 (CIN) Retired. [MON] St. Francis Seraph Friary, Cincinnati, OH
Heiser, Very Rev. James, '05 (CHY) Curia: Consultative Bodies St. John the Baptist, Buffalo, WY
Heiser, Rev. John Paul (Ryan), *O.S.B.* '14 (GBG) [MON] Saint Vincent Archabbey, Latrobe, PA
Heiser, Rev. John Paul, *OSB* (SAV) [MON] The Benedictine Priory, Savannah, GA
Heiser, Rev. John Paul Ryan, (MO) Curia: Offices and Directors
Heiskell, Rev. Peter, *SM* (RVC) Chaminade High School (Boys), Mineola, NY
Heisler, Rev. John F., '99 (ARL) St. Francis de Sales, Purcellville, VA
Heisler, Rev. John Paul, '21 (ARL) St. James, Falls Church, VA
Heithoff, Rev. James H., '77 (GI) Retired.
Heiting, Rev. Msgr. R. Paul, '87 (WIN) Curia: Tribunal Immaculate Heart of Mary, Currie, MN; St. Anthony's, Westbrook, MN; St. Gabriel's, Fulda, MN
Heitz, Rev. Warren, *O.S.B.* '66 (IND) [MON] St. Meinrad Archabbey, St. Meinrad, IN
Hejdak, Rev. Andrew, '84 (CC) Immaculate Conception, Gregory, TX
Hejna, Rev. Lewis E., '81 (SPC) Cathedral of St. Agnes, Springfield, MO
Helbing, Rev. Brendan, *O.S.B.* '65 (TLS) On Special Assignment. Chap, Ascension St John Med Ctr, Tulsa
Helbing, Rev. Brendan J., *O.S.B.* '65 (OKL) Retired. [MON] St. Gregory's Abbey (Benedictine Fathers of Sacred Heart Mission, Inc.), Shawnee, OK
Held, Rev. Brad, *S.J.* (RC) Holy Rosary/Red Cloud Indian School Inc., Pine Ridge, SD; [MIS] Our Lady of Sorrows, Kyle, SD; [MIS] Saint Ignatius Loyola, Wanblee, SD
Held, Rev. Brad A., *S.J.* '17 (RC) St. Agnes, Manderson, SD; [MON] Holy Rosary Mission Jesuit Community, Pine Ridge, SD
Held, Rev. Thomas R., '12 (SAG) Saint Joseph the Worker Parish of Beal City, Mount Pleasant, MI
Helfrich, Rev. P. Frederick, '71 (ROC) Retired.
Helfrich, Rev. Paul D., *B.H.* '00 (BO) On Special Assignment. Curia: Pastoral Services [MON] Brotherhood of Hope, Boston, MA
Helfrich, Rev. Peter, '76 (ROC) Retired.
Helfrich, Rev. Peter G., '76 (OG) Retired.
Helfrich, Rev. Thomas J., *O.S.F.S.* '78 (LAN) St. Rita Parish Clarklake, Clarklake, MI
Heller, Rev. Msgr. Christopher J., '79 (RVC) Curia: Offices and Directors St. Louis de Montfort, Sound Beach, NY
Hellman, Rev. Stephen C., '12 (MOB) Annunciation, Monroeville, AL; St. Joseph Mission Parish, Camden, Camden, AL
Hellmann, Rev. Wayne, *O.F.M.Conv.* '67 (IND) [RTR] Mount Saint Francis Friary and Retreat Center, Mount St. Francis, IN
Hellstrom, Rev. Christopher, '88 (DEN) On Duty Outside Diocese.
Hellwig, Rev. Carl, '06 (PMB) Ascension, Boca Raton, FL
Hellwig, Rev. Lee, '86 (HRT) Saint Paul VI Parish Corporation, Hamden, CT; [MON] Basilica of the Immaculate Conception Rectory, Waterbury, CT
Helmick, Rev. Msgr. William M., '62 (BO) Retired.
Helmin, Rev. Virgil, '75 (SCL) Curia: Leadership
Helmin, Rev. Virgil, '75 (CR) Curia: Leadership
Helmin, Rev. Virgil A., '75 (SCL) Retired. Curia: Leadership
Helms, Rev. Michael L., '90 (DOD) Retired.
Helms, Rev. Walter B., '69 (DAV) Retired.
Helmueller, Rev. John J., '01 (SFS) Curia: Offices and Directors Saint Mark Parish of Charles Mix County, Lake Andes, SD; Saint Paul the Apostle Parish of Douglas County, Armour, SD
Helwig, Rev. Paul C., '74 (HBG) Retired.
Heman, Rev. Richard J., '67 (STL) Retired.
Hemann, Very Rev. David A., '85 (SC) Holy Cross Catholic Parish, Sioux City, IA
Hembrom, Rev. Benjamin, *TOR* '08 (FWT) St. Thomas the Apostle, Fort Worth, TX; [MON] Third Order Regular of St. Francis, Province of St. Thomas, Carrollton, TX
Hemelt, Very Rev. Jonathan P., '13 (NO) Curia: Leadership; Offices and Directors Our Lady of the Rosary, New Orleans, LA
Hemm, Rev. Thomas, *C.PP.S.* '78 (CIN) [MON] St. Charles, Celina, OH
Hemmelgarn, Rev. Larry J., *C.PP.S.* '84 (CIN) [MON] Society of the Precious Blood, United States Province, Inc., Dayton, OH
Hemmer, Rev. Joseph, *O.F.M.* '54 (FBK) St. Peter-in-Chains Catholic Church, Ruby, AK; St. Teresa Catholic Church, Kaltag, AK
Hemmerling, Rev. Henry L., '66 (MET) Retired. [MON] Maria Regina Residence, Somerset, NJ
Hemrick, Rev. Eugene, '63 (JOL) (>WDC) St. Joseph's on Capitol Hill, Washington, DC
Hemrick, Rev. Eugene F., '63 (JOL) Retired.
Hemsing, Rev. John D., '88 (MIL) Curia: Leadership St. James Congregation, Menomonee Falls, WI
Henao, Rev. Nelson, *Sch.P.* (PH) [MON] Piarist Fathers (Order of the Pious Schools), Devon, PA
Henao Rincon, Rev. Nelson, *Sch. P.* (PCE) Academia San Joaquin, Adjuntas, PR
Henao Rincón, Rev. Nelson, *Sch. P.* '10 (PCE) San Joaquin y Santa Ana, Adjuntas, PR
Henao-Lopez, Rev. John, '14 (TYL) Christ the King, Kilgore, TX
Henault, Rev. James, *M.S.* '93 (ORL) Good Shepherd, Orlando, FL
Henchey, Rev. Joseph, *C.S.S.* (CHI) [SEM] University of Saint Mary of the Lake/Mundelein Seminary, Mundelein, IL
Hendel, Rev. Lawrence, '77 (SJ) Retired.
Henden, Rev. Brian, (JOL) [MON] Titus Brandsma Priory (Society of Mount Carmel), Darien, IL
Hendershott, Rev. Michael, '15 (KNX) Holy Ghost, Knoxville, TN
Henderson, Rev. Agustin, '22 (SFE) Our Lady of Sorrows Church-Las Vegas, Las Vegas, NM
Henderson, Rev. Donald, '70 (PEO) Retired.
Henderson, Rev. John, '84 (P) Curia: Offices and Directors St. Anthony, Tigard, OR
Henderson, Rev. John A., '87 (JC) St. William, Perry, MO
Henderson, Rev. Robert J., '65 (COV) Retired. [HOS] St. Elizabeth, Covington (St. Elizabeth Medical Center, Inc.), Covington, KY; [HOS] St. Elizabeth, Edgewood (Saint Elizabeth Medical Center, Inc.), Edgewood, KY; [HOS] St. Elizabeth, Florence (Saint Elizabeth Medical Center, Inc.), Florence, KY; [HOS] St. Elizabeth, Fort Thomas (Saint Elizabeth Medical Center, Inc.), Fort Thomas, KY; [HOS] St. Elizabeth, Grant County (Saint Elizabeth Medical Center, Inc.), Williamstown, KY
Henderson, Rev. Timothy J., '04 (STL) Church of the Holy Martyrs of Japan Catholic Church, Sullivan, MO
Hendrianto, Rev. Stephanus, *S.J.* '19 (SJ) [MON] USA West Province, Society of Jesus, Los Gatos, CA
Hendrianto, Rev. Stephanus, *S.J.* '19 (SFR) Curia: Offices and Directors
Hendrick, Rev. Christianus, *S.C.J.* '98 (RC) St. Mary's, Lower Brule, SD; [MON] SCJ Community House, Lower Brule, SD
Hendrick, Rev. Christianus, *S.C.J.* '98 (SFS) Immaculate Conception Parish of Hyde County, Stephan, SD; Saint Catherine Parish of Hughes County, Big Bend, SD; Saint Joseph Parish of Buffalo County, Fort Thompson, SD
Hendrick, Rev. Msgr. Frank J., '54 (ARL) Retired.
Hendricks, Rev. Edward S., '77 (BAL) Divine Mercy Parish, Frostburg, MD; [EFT] St. Joseph Midland Cemetery Continuing Care Trust, Frostburg, MD; [EFT] St. Joseph Midland Parish Endowment Trust, Midland, MD; [EFT] St. Peter's, Westernport, School Endowment Trust, Frostburg, MD
Hendricks, Rev. Msgr. Joseph M., '72 (COL) St. Brigid of Kildare, Dublin, OH; [MIS] Diocesan Charities Membership Corporation, Columbus, OH; [MIS] Diocesan Retirement Community Corp., Columbus, OH; [MIS] The Villas at St. Therese Plain City Independent Living, Plain City, OH; [MIS] Villas at St.

Therese Plain City Assisted Living, Plain City, OH; [NUR] Seton Development, Inc., Dover, OH
Hendrickson, Rev. D. Scott, *S.J.* '08 (CHI) [COL] Jesuit Community at Loyola University Chicago, Chicago, IL; [MIS] President's Office, Chicago, IL
Hendrickson, Rev. Daniel S., *S.J.* '06 (OM) [COL] Creighton University, Omaha, NE; [MON] Jesuit Community at Creighton University, Omaha, NE
Hendrickson, Rev. Michael D., '01 (SJ) Curia: Leadership St. Mary, Gilroy, CA
Hendrickson, Rev. Michael D., '01 (SJ) Curia: Leadership
Hendry, Rev. Gerald, '85 (SP) St. Justin Martyr, Seminole, FL
Hendry, Rev. Msgr. Owen J., '60 (NEW) Retired.
Hendry, Rev. Simon J., *S.J.* '77 (DET) [MON] Jesuit Community at the University of Detroit Mercy, Detroit, MI
Heneghan, Rev. James A., '83 (CHI) Curia: Leadership Our Lady of the Rosary Parish, Chicago, IL
Henehan, Rev. Patrick, '98 (PEO) Curia: Consultative Bodies; Offices and Directors St. Jude, Peoria, IL
Henehan, Rev. Thomas P., *M.M.* '65 (CHI) Retired.
Henery, Rev. Ronald Eugene, *O.P* '78 (NY) [MON] St. Vincent Ferrer Priory, New York, NY
Heney, Rev. David, '78 (LA) St. Bruno, Whittier, CA
Hengle, Rev. John R., '68 (CLV) Retired.
Henke, Rev. Donald E., '93 (STL) [SEM] Kenrick School of Theology, ,
Henke, Rev. Msgr. James, '66 (SAT) Retired.
Henkes, Rev. Donald, (SAG) Retired.
Henkle, Friar Charles, (LSC) [RTR] Holy Cross Retreat and Friary (Franciscan Fathers), Mesilla Park, NM
Henley, Rev. Earl, *M.S.C.* '69 (SB) St. Joseph Mission, San Jacinto, CA
Henley, Rev. Earl Joseph, *M.S.C.* '69 (SB) [MIS] Our Lady of the Snows Chapel, Anza, CA; [MIS] Sacred Hearts of Mary and Jesus Chapel, Thermal, CA; [MIS] St. Mary Chapel, Banning, CA; [MIS] St. Michael Chapel, Temecula, CA; [MIS] St. Rose of Lima Chapel, Anza, CA
Henn, Rev. William, *O.F.M. Cap.* '78 (PIT) [MON] St. Augustine Friary, Pittsburgh, PA
Hennecke, Rev. William W., '07 (SPC) Curia: Advisory Boards, Commissions, Committees, and Councils Our Lady of the Cove, Kimberling City, MO
Hennelly, Rev. Michael F., '91 (PH) On Special Assignment. Asst Vicar for Clergy, St Bridget Rectory, Philadelphia Curia: Advisory Boards, Commissions, Committees, and Councils; Clergy and Religious Services St. Bridget, Philadelphia, PA
Hennen, Rev. David R., '05 (STP) Curia: Consultative Bodies St. Elizabeth Ann Seton, Hastings, MN; [CEM] St. Elizabeth Ann Seton Cemetery, Hastings, MN
Hennen, Rev. Joseph, '67 (HON) Retired.
Hennen, Rev. Thomas J., '04 (DAV) Curia: Leadership Sacred Heart Cathedral of Davenport, Iowa, Davenport, IA; St. Andrew Church of Blue Grass, Iowa, Blue Grass, IA; [EFT] Sacred Heart Cathedral Foundation, Inc., Davenport, IA; [MIS] Roman Catholic Ministries of Iowa City, Iowa, Davenport, IA; [MIS] Vietnamese Catholic Community of Our Lady of Mong Trieu, Davenport, IA
Hennes, Rev. Jeffrey W., '12 (LC) St. Joseph, Stevens Point, WI; St. Stephen, Stevens Point, WI; [EFT] St. Joseph Parish, Stevens Point Endowment Trust, Stevens Point, WI; [EFT] St. Stephen Parish Endowment Trust, Stevens Point, WI
Hennessey, Rev. Britton, '17 (COV) St. Francis Xavier, Falmouth, KY
Hennessey, Rev. Daniel F., '02 (BO) St. Agnes, Middleton, MA; St. Rose of Lima, Topsfield, MA
Hennessey, Rev. John E., '67 (CHI) Retired. St. Joseph, Libertyville, IL
Hennessey, Rev. Joseph M., '88 (BO) On Special Assignment. Good Shepherd Parish, Wayland, MA
Hennessey, Rev. Lawrence R., '71 (CHI) Retired. [SEM] University of Saint Mary of the Lake/Mundelein Seminary, Mundelein, IL
Hennessy, Rev. Msgr. Brian P., '99 (PH) St. Alphonsus, Maple Glen, PA
Hennessy, Msgr. Douglas, '63 (PEO) Retired.
Hennessy, Rev. James W., '61 (WIN) Retired.
Hennessy, Rev. John A., *S.J.* '69 (MIL) [MON] St. Camillus Jesuit Community (Society of Jesus, USA Midwest Province), Wauwatosa, WI
Hennessy, Rev. Joseph I., '63 (PHX) Retired.
Hennigen, Rev. Michael C., '13 (COV) Covington Catholic High School, Park Hills, KY; Holy Cross, Covington, KY
Henning, Rev. Michael L., '74 (STL) Holy Name of Jesus Catholic Church, St. Louis, MO
Henning, Rev. Phillip D., '93 (SAT) On Sick Leave.
Henning, Rev. Msgr. Richard G., '92 (RVC) Curia: Leadership; Offices and Directors [SEM] Diocesan Seminary of the Immaculate Conception, Huntington, NY
Henninger, Rev. George, '85 (VIC) Retired.
Henninger, Rev. Mark G., *S.J.* '78 (CHI) [COL] Jesuit Community at Loyola University Chicago, Chicago, IL; [MIS] President's Office, Chicago, IL
Hennings, Rev. Clifford, *OFM* (DET) Holy Family Parish Novi, Novi, MI
Hennington, Rev. Bruce M., '68 (MAD) Retired.
Henrich, Rev. Steven, *OSC* '74 (SCL) Retired. [MON] Crosier Priory, Onamia, MN
Henricks, Rev. Maron, *M.M.A.* '18 (SAM) [MON] Maronite Monks of Adoration - Most Holy Trinity Monastery, Petersham, MA
Henricksen, Rev. Msgr. Francis C., '55 (DAV) Retired.
Henriksen, Rev. Steven D., '13 (L) St. Michael, Louisville, KY
Henriksen, Rev. Steven D., '13 (L) Curia: Leadership
Henriot, Rev. Peter, (SEA) Bellarmine Preparatory School, Tacoma, WA
Henriquez, Rev. Genaro, '99 (BWN) Our Lady of the Holy Rosary, Mission, TX
Henriquez, Rev. Jose A., '15 (BRK) St. Finbar, Brooklyn, NY
Henriquez de Paz, Rev. Moises, (SB) San Salvador, Colton, CA
Henritzy, Rev. Elias Curtis, *OP* '92 (COL) [HOS] Mohun Health Care Center, Columbus, OH
Henry, Rev. Chad, (GAL) Holy Family, Galveston, TX; St. Mary's Cathedral Basilica, Galveston, TX
Henry, Rev. Donald H., '71 (VEN) Retired.
Henry, Rev. Earl J., *O.S.B.* '64 (GBG) [MON] Saint Vincent Archabbey, Latrobe, PA
Henry, Rev. James, '71 (MRY) Retired.
Henry, Rev. James, *S.V.D.* '59 (CHI) Retired.
Henry, Rev. Jeffrey F., '11 (SAC) Chap, Travis Air Force Base, Travis AFB Curia: (>MO) Offices and Directors
Henry, Rev. Joseph P., '58 (PRO) Retired.
Henry, Rev. Lawrence J., *C.S.C.* '61 (FTW) [MON] Congregation of Holy Cross, United States Province of Priests and Brothers, Notre Dame, IN
Henry, Rev. Matthew J., '10 (PHX) On Leave.
Henry, Rev. Patrick J., '92 (SAC) Retired.
Henry, Rev. Paul J., '70 (BAL) Retired.
Henry, Rev. Paul J., '68 (ORL) Retired.
Henry, Rev. Perry F., *C.M.* '83 (LA) [MON] Congregation of the Mission Western Province (DePaul Center Residence), Montebello, CA
Henry, Rev. Robert P., '79 (NY) Most Holy Trinity, Mamaroneck, NY; Our Lady of Perpetual Help, Ardsley, NY
Henry, Rev. Sixmund Nyabenda, '01 (PEO) St. Joseph's, Marseilles, IL
Henry, Rev. Terence, *T.O.R.* (ALT) [MON] St. Francis Friary at Mount Assisi, Loretto, PA
Henry, Rev. William F., '84 (JKS) Curia: Offices and Directors
Hensell, Rev. Eugene, *O.S.B.* '69 (IND) [MON] St. Meinrad Archabbey, St. Meinrad, IN
Henson, Rev. Jerome, '77 (ORG) Retired.
Henson, Rev. Joel, '93 (LA) Curia: Offices and Directors St. Columban, Los Angeles, CA
Henson, Rev. Paul, *O.Carm.* '02 (TUC) Salpointe Catholic High School, Tucson, AZ; [MON] Carmelite Priory, Tucson, AZ
Henson, Rev. Paul Anthony, *O. Carm.* '02 (TUC) Saint Cyril of Alexandria Roman Catholic Parish - Tucson, Tucson, AZ
Hensy, Rev. Patrick E., *C.S.P.* '78 (LA) Retired.
Hentz, Rev. Otto H., *S.J.* '68 (WDC) [MON] The Jesuit Community at Georgetown University, Washington, DC
Henyk, Rev. Canon Christopher, '08 (Y) Little Flower Catholic Church, Canton, OH
Hepburn, Rev. Timothy, '93 (ATL) St. Michael Catholic Church, Gainesville, Inc., Gainesville, GA
Hephner, Rev. John J., '59 (GB) Retired.
Hepner, Rev. Timothy, '12 (PEO) Immaculate Conception, Monmouth, IL; [CAM] St. Augustine Newman Club, Monmouth, IL
Heppe, Rev. Patrick E., '77 (MIL) Curia: Leadership St. John Neumann, Catholic Community of Waukesha, Waukesha, WI; St. Joseph, Catholic Community of Waukesha, Waukesha, WI; St. Mary, Catholic Community of Waukesha, Waukesha, WI; St. William, Catholic Community of Waukesha, Waukesha, WI
Heppler, Rev. Jeremy, *O.S.B.* '10 (KCK) Curia: Leadership St. Benedict, Atchison, KS; [MON] St. Benedict's Abbey, Atchison, KS
Heramb, Rev. James, '68 (JOL) Retired.
Herard, Rev. Raymond G., '21 (PT) Curia: Offices and Directors Nativity of Our Lord, Pensacola, FL
Herba, Rev. Stanislaw, '64 (SLC) Retired.
Herbein, Rev. Msgr. John J., '74 (E) Retired.
Herber, Rev. Stanley J., (IND) Retired.
Herberger, Rev. Roy T., '68 (BUF) Retired. [CAM] State University of New York at Buffalo (North Campus) Newman Center, Amherst, NY
Herbert, Rev. Eugene, '81 (LA) Retired. Annunciation, Arcadia, CA
Herbert, Rev. G. Paul, '86 (WDC) St. Ignatius, Fort Washington, MD
Herbert, Rev. Msgr. J. Gaston, '60 (LR) Retired.
Herbst, Rev. Robert, *O.F.M. Conv.* (SLC) Curia: Offices and Directors
Herbst, Very Rev. Robert M., *O.F.M.Conv.* '91 (LAV) Curia: Advisory Boards, Commissions, Committees, and Councils; Leadership; Tribunal
Herbster, Rev. Msgr. Kenneth J., '63 (NEW) Retired. [MON] The Rev. Msgr. James F. Kelley Residence for Retired Priests, Caldwell, NJ
Herbut, Rev. Marek, '13 (JOL) Immaculate Conception, Gilman, IL; St. Peter, Gilman, IL
Hercek, Rev. Joseph R., '72 (MRY) Retired.
Hercules, Rev. Jeivi Miguel, '12 (NEW) Queen of Peace, North Arlington, NJ
Herda, Rev. Jerome G., '90 (MIL) St. Mathias Congregation, Milwaukee, WI
Heredia, Rev. Javier, '14 (CHR) St. Catherine of Siena, Lancaster, SC; St. Michael Mission, Great Falls, SC
Heredia, Rev. Juan Victor, '91 (BWN) St. Anthony, Raymondville, TX
Heredia Hernandez, Friar Juan Manuel, *OFM* (ELP) Our Lady of Guadalupe, El Paso, TX
Hereley, Rev. Peter J., *O.P.* '63 (CHI) St. Vincent Ferrer, River Forest, IL; [MON] St. Pius V Priory, Chicago, IL
Herff, Rev. Jerome, *C.M.* '67 (LA) (>STL) [MON] Congregation of the Mission, Perryville, MO
Herge, Rev. Thomas, (COL) Holy Trinity, Jackson, OH; SS. Peter and Paul, Wellston, OH; St. Sylvester, Zaleski, OH
Hergenroeder, Rev. Charles, *C.Ss.R.* '73 (BO) Our Lady of Perpetual Help, Boston, MA
Hergenroeder, Rev. Charles, (NY) Immaculate Conception, Bronx, NY
Hergenroeder, Rev. Charles, '73 (BRK) Retired. Our Lady of Perpetual Help Basilica, Brooklyn, NY
Heria, Rev. Fernando, '96 (MIA) Retired.
Heric, Rev. Paul, '14 (SPK) St. Boniface, Uniontown, WA; St. Gall, Colton, WA; [CAM] Catholic Newman Center at Eastern Washington University, Cheney, WA; [CAM] St. Thomas More Catholic Student Center - Washington State University, Pullman, WA
Heric, Very Rev. William, '81 (SEA) Curia: Leadership St. Bridget, Seattle, WA
Herlihy, Rev. Msgr. Daniel J., '67 (MET) Retired.
Herlihy, Rev. Neil J., '05 (ATL) St. Brigid Catholic Church, Johns Creek, Inc., Johns Creek, GA
Herman, Rev. Robert D., '60 (WIN) Retired.
Herman, Rev. William J., '00 (DET) St. Ronald Parish Clinton Township, Clinton Township, MI
Hermann, Rev. Msgr. Carlton P., '52 (SFS) Retired.
Hermawan, Rev. Markus Rudy, *CM* (PH) St. Thomas Aquinas, Philadelphia, PA
Hermawar, Rev. Markus Rudy, (PH) Curia: Evangelization
Hermes, Rev. Alphonsus B., *O.Praem.* '01 (ORG) [MON] Norbertine Fathers of Orange, Inc., Silverado, CA
Hermes, Rev. Msgr. Daniel J., '69 (RCK) Retired.
Hermes, Rev. Joseph, *M.M.* '62 (SJ) Retired. [MON] Maryknoll, Los Altos, CA
Hermes, Rev. Michael, '91 (KCK) Curia: Leadership St. Paul, Olathe, KS
Hermes, Rev. Richard C., *S.J.* '98 (SP) Jesuit High School of Tampa, Inc., Tampa, FL
Hermes, Rev. Thomas W., '82 (KC) Mary Immaculate, Gallatin, MO; Sacred Heart, Hamilton, MO
Hermoso, Rev. Msgr. Seth F., '67 (GAL) Retired.
Hernandez, Rev. Alex, '20 (KNX) All Saints Catholic Church, Knoxville, TN
Hernandez, Rev. Alfred, '82 (LA) St. Catherine Laboure, Torrance, CA
Hernandez, Rev. Alfred Ricardo, '66 (SAT) Col Catholic Chap, Converse
Hernandez, Rev. Alfredo, '92 (PMB) [EFT] St. Vincent de Paul Regional Seminary Endowment Trust, Boynton Beach, FL; [SEM] St. Vincent de Paul Regional Seminary, Boynton Beach, FL
Hernandez, Rev. Andrew, '97 (RCK) St. Thomas the Apostle, Crystal Lake, IL
Hernandez, Rev. Angelo J., '93 (PH) St. John Bosco, Hatboro, PA
Hernandez, Rev. Anselmo, *L.C.* '01 (MO) Curia: Offices

and Directors
Hernandez, Rev. Msgr. Anthony, '95 (BRK) Curia: Leadership Transfiguration, Brooklyn, NY; [SPF] Casa Betsaida-Home for people with AIDS, Brooklyn, NY
Hernandez, Rev. Anthony, '00 (HPM) St. Basil the Great, Los Gatos, CA
Hernandez, Rev. Antonio, *C.Ss.R.* '67 (CGS) Nuestra Senora de la Mercedes, San Lorenzo, PR
Hernandez, Rev. Antonio, '00 (DAL) Our Lady of the Lake Catholic Parish, Rockwall, TX
Hernandez, Rev. Antonio X., '91 (SAT) St. Joseph, Devine, TX
Hernandez, Rev. Ariel, '03 (CAM) Our Lady of the Blessed Sacrament, Newfield, N.J., Newfield, NJ
Hernandez, Rev. Benito A., *C.R.* '03 (DEN) Our Lady of Guadalupe Catholic Parish in Denver, Denver, CO
Hernandez, Rev. Daniel, *O.S.C.* '22 (SCL) (>PHX) [MON] Crosier Community of Phoenix (Canons Regular of the Order of the Holy Cross) (Conventual Priory of the Holy Cross), Phoenix, AZ
Hernandez, Rev. Enrico, '96 (SJ) On Leave.
Hernandez, Rev. Esteban, '87 (BWN) San Martin de Porres, Weslaco, TX
Hernandez, Rev. Fernando A., '90 (NY) Parish of St. Patrick and St. Mary, Newburgh, NY; Roman Catholic Church of Sacred Heart and Saint Francis of Assisi, Newburgh, NY; St. Mary, Newburgh, NY
Hernandez, Rev. Fidel, *O.A.R.* '98 (LA) [MON] Order of Augustinian Recollects (O.A.R.), St. Augustine Priory, Oxnard, CA
Hernandez, Rev. Fidel, *O.A.R.* '97 (NY) Retired. [SEM] Tagaste Monastery, Suffern, NY
Hernandez, Friar Flavio Alberto, *O.F.M.* '70 (ELP) [SEM] Roger Bacon College, El Paso, TX
Hernandez, Rev. Francisco, '95 (SP) Most Holy Redeemer, Tampa, FL
Hernandez, Rev. Francisco, '16 (ELP) Curia: Advisory Boards, Commissions, Committees, and Councils; Tribunal Our Lady of Fatima, Van Horn, TX
Hernandez, Rev. Francisco J., '94 (MIA) St. Raymond, Miami, FL
Hernandez, Rev. Francisco Javier, (LAR) St. Patrick, Laredo, TX
Hernandez, Rev. Gerardo, *C.Ss.R.* (CGS) Church of Tres Santos Reyes, Aguas Buenas, PR
Hernandez, Rev. Gerardo, *C.Ss.R.* (CGS) [RTR] Casa Cristo Redentor, Aguas Buenas, PR
Hernandez, Rev. Gerardo (Gerry) N., '85 (AGN) Curia: Miscellaneous / Other Offices San Isidro, Inarajan, GU
Hernandez, Rev. Msgr. Gonzalo Diaz, '63 (MGZ) Curia: Leadership Shrine of the Order of Our Lady of Monserrate, Hormigueros, PR
Hernandez, Rev. Guillermo, '13 (SAC) On Special Assignment. Director of Vocations Curia: Offices and Directors
Hernandez, Rev. Israel A., '21 (SP) St. Stephen, Riverview, FL
Hernandez, Very Rev. J. Enrique, '12 (MIL) Holy Family Congregation, Whitefish Bay, WI; St. Robert's Congregation, Shorewood, WI
Hernandez, Rev. Jaime, (ORG) St. Anthony Claret, Anaheim, CA
Hernandez, Rev. Jaime, '05 (BRK) St. Michael, Flushing, NY
Hernandez, Rev. Jaime B., '03 (WDC) Church of St. John the Evangelist, Clinton, MD
Hernandez, Rev. Jesus, '18 (SAC) On Academic Leave.
Hernandez, Rev. Jimmy, '83 (ARE) Retired.
Hernandez, Rev. Joe Luis, '20 (BWN) Our Lady of Sorrows, McAllen, TX
Hernandez, Rev. Jorge, *O.F.M.* '98 (P) Holy Name, Coquille, OR; Holy Redeemer, North Bend, OR
Hernandez, Rev. Jose A., '60 (SFE) Retired.
Hernandez, Rev. Jose Luis, '99 (SPK) Chap
Hernandez, Rev. Msgr. Joseph F., '81 (LA) Holy Cross, Moorpark, CA
Hernandez, Rev. Juan Antonio, '09 (TLS) Curia: Offices and Directors SS. Peter and Paul, Tulsa, OK
Hernandez, Rev. Juan Jose, *L.C.* '12 (R) [CAM] Duke Catholic Center, Durham, NC
Hernandez, Rev. Lazaro, *MSP* '22 (SAN) St. Joseph, San Angelo, TX
Hernandez, Rev. Luis Alberto, '15 (PAT) St. Christopher, Parsippany, NJ
Hernandez, Rev. Luis Miguel, *FSCB* '05 (BO) Sacred Heart, Boston, MA
Hernandez, Rev. Manuel, '96 (CC) Retired.
Hernandez, Rev. Manuel Santiago, '85 (PCE) Curia: Leadership
Hernandez, Rev. Miguel A., '02 (ORG) Curia: Leadership St. Joseph, Placentia, CA
Hernandez, Rev. Nils, '04 (DUB) Queen of Peace Church, Waterloo, Iowa, Waterloo, IA
Hernandez, Rev. Osvaldo, '18 (NY) Parish of St. Peter and St. Mary of the Assumption, Haverstraw, NY
Hernandez, Rev. Pablo A., '06 (L) St. Bartholomew, Louisville, KY
Hernandez, Rev. Pedro, '20 (BWN) San Martin de Porres, Weslaco, TX
Hernandez, Rev. Ramon, '73 (SP) Retired.
Hernandez, Rev. Ricardo F., '97 (RCK) Rockford Memorial Hosp, Rockford St. Bernadette, Rockford, IL
Hernandez, Rev. Victor, '06 (TYL) Curia: Advisory Boards, Commissions, Committees, and Councils St. Celestine, Grand Saline, TX; St. James, Sulphur Springs, TX
Hernández, Rev. Rafael, (CGS) Curia: Offices and Directors
Hernandez Arriaga, Rev. Bradford, '08 (AUS) Nuestra Senora De Dolores, Austin, TX
Hernandez Fana, Rev. Elmon M., '97 (ARE) Curia: Offices and Directors The Blessed Trinity, Vega Baja, PR
Hernandez Figueroa, Rev. Eric, *M.N.M* '10 (ARE) Our Lady of the Miraculous Medal, Camuy, PR
Hernandez Figueroa, Rev. Eric, *M.N.M* '10 (ARE) Curia: Leadership [MIS] Chapel Cristo Rey, Camuy, PR; [MIS] Chapel Nuestra Senora del Carmen, Camuy, PR; [MIS] Chapel Sagrado Corazon, Camuy, PR; [MIS] Chapel Sagrado Corazon de Jesus, Isabela, PR; [MIS] Chapel Santiago Apostol, Isabela, PR
Hernandez Montoya, Rev. Enrique, *OFM Conv* (AUS) St. Helen, Georgetown, TX
Hernandez Morales, Rev. Ricardo, '98 (SJN) Curia: Offices and Directors
Hernandez Quintanilla, Rev. Marco, *O.F.M.* '00 (ORG) St. Edward the Confessor, Dana Point, CA
Hernandez Velazquez, Rev. Victor Manuel, '12 (PCE) Curia: Leadership Nuestra Senora de Lourdes, Juana Diaz, PR
Hernandez Velez, Rev. Daniel Enrique, '03 (MGZ) Curia: Offices and Directors San German de Auxerre, San German, PR
Hernandez-Alonso, Rev. Juan P., '89 (MIA) Mother of Our Redeemer, Hialeah, FL
Hernandez-Angulo, Rev. Jose Carmen, *C.S.* '88 (GAL) St. Leo the Great, Houston, TX
Hernandez-Ayala, Very Rev. Jose Luis, '06 (ATL) Curia: Leadership St. Mark Catholic Church, Clarkesville, Inc., Clarkesville, GA
Hernandez-Dominguez, Rev. Juan Adrian, '20 (DEN) Church of the Ascension Catholic Parish in Denver, Denver, CO
Hernandez-Gomez, Rev. Francisco J., '01 (SAC) Pastor of St. John the Baptist Parish, Chico, a corporation sole, Chico, CA
Hernandez-Hernandez, Rev. Oscar Manuel, '05 (SLC) Saint Joseph LLC 230, Ogden, UT
Hernandez-Melchor, Rev. Ivan, '09 (FRS) St. Rita, Tulare, CA
Hernández-Ortiz, Rev. Rafael, (CGS) Divino Nino, Caguas, PR
Hernandez-Ralat, Rev. Edwin, *P.B.R.O.* '01 (SJN) Sagrada Familia, Bayamon, PR
Hernando, Rev. Henry L., '67 (LA) Retired.
Hernando, Rev. Msgr. Jose Luis, '62 (MIA) Retired.
Hernando, Rev. Victor, '82 (FRS) Our Lady of the Snows, Oakhurst, CA
Hernando, Rev. Victor P., '82 (FRS) Our Lady of the Sierra, Oakhurst, CA
Herold, Rev. Anthony J., '79 (DAV) Sacred Heart Church of Newton, Iowa, Newton, IA
Heron, Rev. J. Thomas, '78 (PH) Retired.
Heron, Rev. J. Thomas, '78 (PH) Retired. Holy Saviour, Norristown, PA
Herondi, Rev. Fernandes de Araujo, *S.X.* '76 (PAT) [MON] Xaverian Missionary Fathers, Wayne, NJ
Herpin, Rev. Msgr. Michael, '66 (LAF) On Administrative Leave.
Herpin, Rev. Wayne, *S.J.* '74 (BIR) St. Cecilia Catholic Church, Jasper, AL
Herrera, Rev. David, '89 (SAN) Our Lady of Guadalupe, Midland, TX
Herrera, Rev. Msgr. Emigdio, '77 (LA) Retired.
Herrera, Very Rev. Enrique, '96 (MRY) Curia: Deaneries Holy Trinity, Greenfield, CA
Herrera, Rev. Felix J., (BRK) On Leave.
Herrera, Rev. Felix W., '14 (BRK) On Leave.
Herrera, Rev. Francisco, '67 (ELP) Retired.
Herrera, Rev. James, '13 (P) Sacred Heart-St. Louis, Gervais, OR
Herrera, Rev. John D., '19 (OKL) Curia: Clergy and Religious Services St. Francis Xavier, Enid, OK
Herrera, Rev. Jorge, '03 (RNO) St. Francis of Assisi, Incline Village, NV; St. Therese of the Little Flower Catholic Church, Reno, NV
Herrera, Rev. Jose, '89 (STV) On Duty Outside Diocese.
Herrera, Rev. Jose F., '88 (BRK) St. Fortunata, Brooklyn, NY
Herrera, Rev. Jose Geronimo, '89 (SFE) San Isidro, Santa Fe, NM
Herrera, Rev. Jose M., '09 (YAK) Curia: Offices and Directors St. Rose of Lima, Ephrata, WA
Herrera, Rev. Juan G., '11 (WOR) St. Edward the Confessor, Westminster, MA
Herrera, Rev. Pedro E., *C.S.V.* '80 (CHI) [MON] Viatorian Province Center-Clerics of St. Viator, Arlington Heights, IL
Herrera, Rev. Roberto, '08 (ATL) St. John Paul II Catholic Mission, Gainesville, GA
Herrera, Rev. Rocendo, *S.T.* (SB) Sanctuary of Our Lady of Guadalupe, Mecca, CA
Herrera, Rev. Rocendo, *S.T.* (FAJ) Curia: Leadership Espiritu Santo y San Patricio, Loiza, PR; Santiago Apostol, El Mayor, Loiza, PR
Herrera, Rev. Ruben, '06 (RCK) On Special Assignment. Curia: Offices and Directors St. Peter, Aurora, IL
Herrera, Rev. Scott, '04 (SD) Pastor of Saint Mary Catholic Parish, Escondido, a corporation sole, Escondido, CA
Herrera Guzman, Rev. Elmer, '20 (DAL) Holy Cross Catholic Parish, Dallas, TX
Herrera-Ciro, Rev. Albeiro, '08 (PBL) St. Michael, Delta, CO
Herrera-DosReis, Rev. Armando, '22 (RIC) On Special Assignment. Parochial Vicar, Blessed Sacrament, Harrisonburg. Blessed Sacrament, Harrisonburg, VA
Herrero, Rev. Msgr. Nicolas, '59 (FRS) Retired.
Herrero, Rev. Raul, (PHX) St. Augustine Roman Catholic Parish, Phoenix, AZ
Herres, Msgr. Joseph, '72 (LA) Retired. Holy Trinity, Los Angeles, CA
Herring, Rt. Rev. James B., *O.Praem.* '02 (WIL) [MON] Immaculate Conception Priory of the Canons Regular of Premontre, Middletown, DE; [MON] Norbertine Fathers of Delaware, Inc., Middletown, DE
Herring, Rt. Rev. James B., *O.Praem.* '02 (WIL) Curia: Tribunal
Herrmann, Rev. Francis R., *S.J.* '74 (BO) [MON] The Jesuit Community at Boston College, Chestnut Hill, MA
Herrmann, Rev. Simon, *OSB* '21 (IND) [MON] St. Meinrad Archabbey, St. Meinrad, IN
Herron, Rev. Msgr. Denis M., '73 (BRK) Retired. Resurrection Ascension - Our Lady of the Angelus Roman Catholic Church, Rego Park, NY
Herron, Rev. Jack B., '74 (FAR) Retired.
Hersey, Rev. Bryan L., (SEA) Christ Our Hope Parish, Seattle, WA
Hersey, Rev. Bryan L., '98 (SEA) Chap, First Hill Hosp Ministry [MIS] St. Patrick, Seattle, WA
Hertel, Rev. Joseph, *O.F.M.* '66 (SP) Retired. [MON] St. Anthony Friary (St. Petersburg) Franciscan Friars-Holy Name Province, Inc., St. Petersburg, FL
Hertges, Rev. Donald A., '07 (DUB) St. Benedict Church, Decorah, Iowa, Decorah, IA
Hertzfeld, Rev. Adam L., '02 (TOL) Curia: Advisory Boards, Commissions, Committees, and Councils St. Michael the Archangel, Findlay, OH; St. Richard, Swanton, OH
Herzing, Rev. Joseph, '99 (SCL) Curia: Leadership; Offices and Directors Christ Church, St. Cloud, MN; Holy Spirit, St. Cloud, MN; St. Anthony of Padua, St. Cloud, MN; [CAM] Newman Center, Inc., St. Cloud, MN
Herzog, Rev. Edmund M, '17 (WCH) Bishop Carroll Catholic High School, Wichita, KS; St. Francis of Assisi, Wichita, KS
Herzog, Rev. John M., '56 (DUB) Retired.
Herzog, Rev. Lawrence A., '80 (STL) Little Flower Catholic Church, Richmond Heights, MO
Herzog, Rev. Mark J., '79 (TOL) Retired. Our Lady of Mt. Carmel, Martin, OH; St. Ignatius, Oregon, OH
Hesketh, Rev. John E., *O.S.B.* '94 (PAT) [MON] St. Mary's Abbey, Morristown, NJ
Hesko, Rev. Daniel, '84 (TR) Curia: Leadership St. Catherine, Middletown, NJ
Heslin, Rev. Sean, '67 (ORL) Retired.
Hess, Rev. Aaron, '21 (CIN) Holy Angels, Sidney, OH; Sacred Heart of Jesus, Anna, OH
Hess, Rev. Andrew, '19 (CIN) St. Aloysius, Carthagena, OH; St. Bernard, Burkettsville, OH; St. Francis, Cranberry, OH; St. Henry, St. Henry, OH; St. Wendelin, Wendelin, OH
Hess, Rev. Brian J., '14 (CHY) Curia: Consultative Bodies; Faith Formation Church of Corpus Christi, Newcastle, WY
Hess, Very Rev. Christopher Martin, (RIC) Curia:

Deaneries St. Anne, Bristol, VA; St. Bernard, Gate City, VA
Hess, Rev. Daniel K., '11 (CIN) [SEM] Mount St. Mary's Seminary of the West, Cincinnati, OH
Hess, Rev. James, *O.Carm.* (ALB) [CON] St. Teresa's Motherhouse, Germantown, NY
Hess, Rev. Msgr. Michael, '71 (DM) Retired.
Hess, Rev. Stephen M., *SJ* (SPK) [COL] Gonzaga University, Spokane, WA (>KC) [MON] St. Peter Claver Jesuit Community, Kansas City, MO
Hesse, Rev. Anthony R., '01 (NU) Our Lady of Victory, Lucan, MN; St. Anne, Wabasso, MN; St. Catherine, Redwood Falls, MN; St. Mary, Wabasso, MN; St. Mathias, Wabasso, MN
Hesse, Very Rev. Paul A., '91 (CC) Curia: Leadership St. Pius X, Corpus Christi, TX
Hessel, Rev. Gerald J., '67 (MIL) Retired.
Hesseling, Rev. Jason E., '00 (MAD) On Duty Outside Diocese. Military Chaplain (United States Army) Curia: (>MO) Offices and Directors
Hessian, Rev. Roger J., '61 (STP) Retired.
Hession, Rev. Anthony, '99 (FAR) St. Ann's Church of Belcourt, Belcourt, ND
Hetland, Rev. John G., '11 (CHI) Prince of Peace, Lake Villa, IL
Hetzel, Rev. Connor, '22 (Y) St. Michael the Archangel, Canton, OH
Heuberger, Rev. Joseph, '70 (P) Retired.
Heuberger, Rev. Mark L., '80 (VEN) Ss. Peter and Paul the Apostles Parish in Bradenton, Inc., Bradenton, FL
Heusel, Rev. Daniel, '00 (STU) Curia: Offices and Directors St. John, Bellaire, OH; St. Mary's, Shadyside, OH
Heuser, Rev. James, *S.D.B.* '84 (NEW) Don Bosco Preparatory High School (Salesians of St. John Bosco), Ramsey, NJ; [MIS] Don Bosco Preparatory High School, Inc., Ramsey, NJ; [MON] Don Bosco Prep Salesian Residence, Ramsey, NJ (>NY) Salesian High School, New Rochelle, NY
Hever, Rev. Msgr. Thomas F., '62 (PHX) Retired. Our Lady of Perpetual Help Roman Catholic Parish, Scottsdale, AZ
Hevern, Rev. Vincent W., *S.J.* '76 (SY) [MON] Jesuits at LeMoyne, Inc., Syracuse, NY
Hevia, Rev. Todd O., '67 (PT) Retired.
Hewe, Rev. Manuel, '97 (HON) Curia: Consultative Bodies
Hewe, Rev. Manuel A., '97 (HON) Curia: Consultative Bodies; Offices and Directors Co-Cathedral of St. Theresa of the Child Jesus, Honolulu, HI
Hewes, Rev. James, '74 (ROC) Retired.
Hewes, Rev. Robert S., '78 (RVC) St. Matthew, Dix Hills, NY
Hewes, Rev. Russell L., '01 (OKL) Holy Angels, Oklahoma City, OK; Sacred Heart, Oklahoma City, OK
Hewitt, Rev. Anthony, '99 (VEN) Curia: Leadership St. Francis Xavier Parish in Fort Myers, Inc., Fort Myers, FL; [NUR] Villa Francisco, Fort Myers, FL
Hewitt, Rev. Matthew A., '04 (SC) On Administrative Leave.
Hewson, Very Rev. Shane, (TLS) Curia: Leadership
Heyd, Rev. James F., '89 (CHI) On Special Assignment. Priests for Life, Maryville, Chicago
Heyer, Very Rev. Bryan, '04 (VIC) Curia: Leadership; Offices and Directors SS. Cyril and Methodius, Shiner, TX
Heying, Rev. John, '00 (RC) Christ the King, Presho, SD; Sacred Heart, White River, SD; St. Martin, Murdo, SD
Heynen, Rev. Matthew, *OP* '22 (AJ) Holy Family Old Cathedral, Anchorage, AK
Heyrosa, Rev. Alfredo, '83 (SD) Pastor of Saint Jude Shrine of the West Catholic Parish, San Diego, a corporation sole, San Diego, CA
Hezel, Rev. Francis X., *S.J.* '69 (AGN) Curia: Consultative Bodies Santa Barbara, Dededo, GU; [MON] Society of Jesus Micronesia, Tamuning, GU
Hezel, Rev. Kenneth, *S.J.* '66 (BUF) St. Michael, Buffalo, NY
Hiaeshutter, Rev. Ryan, (DAL) Christ the King Catholic Parish, Dallas, TX
Hibner, Rev. Cyprian, *O.Carm.* '61 (TUC) Retired.
Hiciano, Rev. Antonio, *C.M.* (SJN) Sagrado Corazon de Jesus, San Juan, PR
Hickel, Rev. Robert, *OMI* (SAT) [NUR] Oblate Madonna Residence, San Antonio, TX
Hickey, Rev. Christopher J., '94 (BO) Our Lady of the Angels Parish, Hanover, MA
Hickey, Rev. Gregory J., '79 (PH) Retired.
Hickey, Rev. James F., '68 (BO) Holy Family Parish, Rockland, MA
Hickey, Rev. Kevin T., (BO) St. Mary, Foxborough, MA
Hickey, Rev. Thomas E., '70 (CHI) Retired. Our Lady of Perpetual Help, Glenview, IL
Hickey, Rev. Timothy J., *C.S.Sp.* '99 (ARL) Our Lady, Queen of Peace, Arlington, VA
Hickey, Rev. Timothy S., '13 (DOD) St. Anthony of Padua Catholic Church of Leoti, Kansas, Leoti, KS; St. Joseph the Worker Catholic Church of Tribune, Kansas, Tribune, KS; St. Mary Catholic Church of Marienthal, Kansas, Marienthal, KS
Hickey, Rev. Timothy W., '13 (HRT) On Duty Outside Diocese. Incardinated into Dodge City, Kansas
Hickie, Rev. Noel, (P) Retired.
Hickie, Rev. Noel, (BAK) Retired.
Hickin, Rev. Michael, '97 (FAR) St. Anthony's Church of Mooreton, Mooreton, ND; Sts. Peter & Paul Church of Mantador, Mantador, ND
Hickl, Rev. Robert, *OMI* '79 (LAR) Sacred Heart (Parroquia Sagrado Corazon), Eagle Pass, TX
Hickman, Rev. J. Stephen, '82 (RIC) Retired.
Hicks, Rev. Alfred J., (BO) [MON] Campion Center, Inc., Weston, MA
Hicks, Rev. Boniface, *O.S.B.* '04 (GBG) [MON] Saint Vincent Archabbey, Latrobe, PA; [SEM] St. Vincent Seminary, Latrobe, PA
Hicks, Rev. Msgr. Francis J., '00 (LA) St. Basil's Roman Catholic Church, Los Angeles, CA
Hicks, Rev. Steven, '82 (SAN) Retired.
Hidalgo, Rev. Gregorio, '16 (LA) St. Philomena, Carson, CA
Hidalgo, Rev. Sergio, '21 (LA) Santa Rosa, San Fernando, CA
Hien, Rev. Joachim L., '74 (SPK) Retired. Curia: Leadership [SEM] Bishop White Seminary, Spokane, WA
Hien Duc Tran, Rev. John M., *CRM* '16 (SPC) [MON] Congregation of the Mother of the Redeemer, Carthage, MO
Hiep Nguyen, Rev. Brandon Mother, *S.V.D.* (TR) The Church of Mother of Mercy, Asbury Park, N.J., Asbury Park, NJ
Hiers, Rev. Jeremy, *OSA* (PH) [MON] Augustinian Community (O.S.A.), Philadelphia, PA
Higdon, Rev. Francis B., *M.M.* '67 (NY) Retired.
Higdon, Rev. Ryan C., '12 (AUS) Curia: Leadership St. Louis, Waco, TX; St. Philip Catholic Church - China Spring, Texas, China Spring, TX
Higginbotham, Rev. Keith, '18 (LR) St. Vincent de Paul, Rogers, AR
Higginbotham, Rev. Matthew P., '94 (LAF) Holy Trinity, Washington, LA; Immaculate Conception, Washington, LA
Higginbotham, Rev. Robert P., '75 (BLX) Retired.
Higgins, Rev. Brian J., '99 (ATL) Christ the Redeemer Catholic Church, Dawsonville, Inc., Dawsonville, GA
Higgins, Rev. Charles J., '75 (BO) Curia: Clergy and Religious Services
Higgins, Rev. Charles J., '75 (BO) Mary Immaculate of Lourdes, Newton, MA; St. John Chrysostom, Boston, MA; St. Theresa of Avila, Boston, MA; [EFT] Massachusetts Catholic Self-Insurance Group, Inc., Braintree, MA
Higgins, Very Rev. Damien, (STN) [MON] Holy Transfiguration Monastery, Redwood Valley, CA
Higgins, Very Rev. Edward J., '76 (PSC) Curia: Advisory Boards, Commissions, Committees, and Councils; Leadership SS. Peter and Paul, Bethlehem, PA; SS. Peter and Paul, Palmerton, PA; SS. Peter and Paul, Phillipsburg, NJ; St. Michael, Allentown, PA
Higgins, Rev. Francis C., '68 (SAV) Retired.
Higgins, Rev. Francis E., '64 (SC) Retired.
Higgins, Rev. Jerome, *O.F.M.Cap.* '54 (MIL) Retired. [MON] St. Lawrence Friary, Mount Calvary, WI
Higgins, Rev. John, '81 (LA) Retired. St. Raymond, Downey, CA
Higgins, Rev. John F., *M.S.* '72 (HRT) Our Lady of Sorrows Church Corporation of Parkville, Hartford, Hartford, CT; [MON] Our Lady of Sorrows Rectory, Hartford, CT
Higgins, Rev. John J., '96 (NY) Holy Cross, Bronx, NY
Higgins, Rev. Leonard H., '82 (TLS) On Special Assignment. Jane Phillips Med Ctr, Bartlesville Our Lady of Guadalupe, Dewey, OK
Higgins, Rev. Michael, *TOR* '85 (FWT) Good Shepherd, Colleyville, TX
Higgins, Rev. Michael, *C.P.* '70 (LA) [MON] Passionist Residence, Sierra Madre, CA; [RTR] Mater Dolorosa Passionist Retreat Center, Inc., Sierra Madre, CA
Higgins, Rev. Patrick G., '10 (CC) Our Lady of the Assumption, Ingleside, TX
Higgins, Rev. Raymond, (DM) St. Cecilia, Panora, IA; St. Mary, Guthrie Center, IA; St. Patrick, Bayard, IA
Higgins, Rev. Robert F., '05 (CHR) St. Patrick, Charleston, SC
Higgins, Rev. Thomas M., '85 (PH) Curia: Advisory Boards, Commissions, Committees, and Councils; Deaneries Holy Innocents, Philadelphia, PA
Higgs, Very Rev. Donald X., '88 (WH) Curia: Leadership Basilica of the Co-Cathedral of the Sacred Heart, Charleston, WV
Highberger, Rev. Donald, *S.J.* '81 (STL) [COL] Saint Louis University, St. Louis, MO
Highberger, Rev. Msgr. George E., '61 (PHX) St. Charles Borromeo Roman Catholic Parish, Peoria, AZ
Hightower, Rev. Craig, *S.J.* (HEL) Curia: Leadership Saint Francis Xavier Parish: Series 640, LLC, Missoula, MT; Saint Ignatius Mission Parish: Series 645, LLC, St. Ignatius, MT
Higley, Rev. Msgr. Gregory L., '81 (JC) Curia: Tribunal Sacred Heart, Columbia, MO
Higuera, Very Rev. Francisco, '01 (YAK) Immaculate Conception, Roslyn, WA
Higuera, Rev. Francisco, '01 (YAK) St. John the Baptist, Cle Elum, WA
Higuera, Very Rev. Francisco P., '01 (YAK) Curia: Offices and Directors
Hilage, Rev. Rudolfo Coaquira, *M.C.C.J.* '92 (CIN) [MON] Comboni Missionaries (Verona Fathers)-Comboni Mission Center, Cincinnati, OH
Hilaire, Rev. Wesler, '14 (PMB) St. Peter, Jupiter, FL
Hiland, Rev. Gerard P., '85 (CIN) Our Lady of the Visitation, Cincinnati, OH
Hilbert, Rev. Michael P., *S.J.* '83 (NY) St. Ignatius Loyola, New York, NY; [MON] St. Ignatius Loyola Residence, New York, NY
Hilderbrand, Rev. H. Michael, (IND) Retired.
Hilderbrand, Rev. Ryan P., '09 (EVN) Curia: Offices and Directors St. Matthew, Mount Vernon, IN; St. Philip, Mount Vernon, IN
Hile, Rev. Caleb D., '20 (LIN) Curia: Leadership
Hile, Rev. Caleb D., '20 (LIN) Cathedral of the Risen Christ, Lincoln, NE
Hilferty, Rev. John G., '78 (ALN) [HOS] Sacred Heart Hospital, Allentown, PA
Hilgartner, Rev. Msgr. Richard B., '95 (BAL) St. Joseph, Cockeysville, MD; [EFT] St. Joseph, Texas Endowment Trust, Cockeysville, MD
Hilgeman, Rev. James L., *M.M.* '65 (NY) Retired. [MON] Maryknoll Fathers and Brothers (Catholic Foreign Mission Society of America, Inc.), Ossining, NY
Hilgenbrinck, Rev. Chase, '14 (PEO) Curia: Offices and Directors
Hilgendorf, Rev. Patrick J., '97 (DAV) St. Mary Magdalen Church of Bloomfield, Iowa, Bloomfield, IA; St. Patrick Church of Ottumwa, Iowa, Ottumwa, IA
Hilgendorf, Rev. Stephen, '21 (POC) St. Barnabas Church of the Personal Ordinariate of the Chair of St. Peter, Omaha, NE
Hilgendorf, Rev. Stephen, (OM) Christ the King, Omaha, NE
Hilgert, Rev. John, *C.P.* '75 (SAC) [MON] Christ the King Passionist Retreat Center, Inc. (The Passionists (Chicago, IL)), Citrus Heights, CA
Hilinski, Rev. Joseph, '74 (CLV) St. Barbara, Cleveland, OH
Hilinski, Rev. Joseph T., '76 (CLV) Curia: Advisory Boards, Commissions, Committees, and Councils
Hilinski, Rev. Joseph T., '74 (CLV) Curia: Parish Services
Hill, Rev. Allan J., '83 (HRT) Retired.
Hill, Rev. Chad, '22 (SEA) Christ the King, Seattle, WA
Hill, Rev. Msgr. Charles E., '64 (LA) Retired. Visitation, Los Angeles, CA
Hill, Very Rev. Eric J., '00 (ATL) Curia: Leadership Transfiguration Catholic Church, Marietta, Inc., Marietta, GA
Hill, Rev. Frederick, '67 (RVC) St. Patrick, Smithtown, NY
Hill, Rev. George H., '68 (NY) [CAM] Manhattan College, Bronx, NY
Hill, Rev. Mackenzie, '21 (STA) Cathedral - Basilica of St. Augustine, St. Augustine, FL
Hill, Rev. Michael, *O.F.M.* '77 (STL) [MON] Franciscan Friary of St. Anthony of Padua, St. Louis, MO
Hill, Rev. Patrick J., '68 (LA) Retired.
Hill, Rev. Peter, *C.Ss.R.* '08 (SAT) [MON] North American Redemptorist Theology Residence, San Antonio, TX
Hill, Rev. Msgr. Philip W., '70 (NY) Retired. Military Chap
Hill, Rev. Scott, *O.M.I.* '79 (OAK) Sacred Heart, Oakland, CA
Hill, Rev. Scott J., '15 (VIC) On Administrative Leave.
Hill, Rev. W. Paul, '64 (WDC) Retired.
Hill, Very Rev. William, '06 (CHY) Curia: Consultative

Bodies Holy Spirit Catholic Community, Rock Springs, WY; [EFT] Rock Springs Catholic School Foundation, Rock Springs, WY
Hill, Very Rev. William, '06 (CHY) Curia: Consultative Bodies
Hillenbrand, Rev. Thomas Andrew, *O.S.B.* '65 (OM) [MON] Benedictine Mission House - Christ the King Priory, Schuyler, NE
Hilley, Rev. Stephen J., '79 (MIA) St. Justin Martyr, Key Largo, FL
Hillier, Rev. John G., '88 (MET) Curia: Evangelization; Family Life St. Elizabeth - St. Brigid, Peapack, NJ
Hillyard, Rev. Matthew J., *OSFS* '91 (ARL) Our Lady of Good Counsel, Vienna, VA
Hils, Rev. Damian J., '95 (COV) Blessed Sacrament, Fort Mitchell, KY
Hilton, Rev. Adrian J., *C.O.* '15 (CIN) Old St. Mary, Cincinnati, OH; Sacred Heart, Cincinnati, OH; [MIS] Society of Saint Philip Neri, Inc. (The Cincinnati Oratory), Cincinnati, OH
Hilton, Rev. Adrian J., (BIR) On Special Assignment. Cincinnati
Hilton, Rev. Francis G., *S.J.* '92 (MET) Curia: Consultative Bodies St. Joseph, Hillsborough, NJ
Hilton, Very Rev. John L., '82 (DEN) Curia: Deaneries St. Vincent De Paul Catholic Parish in Denver, Denver, CO
Hilzendeger, Rev. Greg, '21 (BIS) St. Boniface, Grenora, ND; St. John the Baptist, Trenton, ND; St. Joseph, Williston, ND
Himes, Rev. Kenneth, *O.F.M.* '76 (BO) [MON] The Jesuit Community at Boston College, Chestnut Hill, MA (>ALB) [COL] Siena College, Loudonville, NY
Himes, Rev. Matthew T, '19 (BAL) Curia: Clergy and Religious Services Cathedral of Mary Our Queen, Baltimore, MD
Himes, Rev. Robert P., '58 (YAK) Retired.
Hincapie Ramirez, Rev. Lisimaco, '95 (ARE) Holy Family, Corozal, PR
Hincapie Ramirez, Rev. Lisimaco, '95 (ARE) Curia: Leadership [MIS] Chapel Nuestra Senora del Carmen, Corozal, PR; [MIS] Chapel Nuestra Senora del Perpetuo Socorro, Corozal, PR; [MIS] Chapel San Jose, Corozal, PR; [MIS] Chapel San Vicente de Paul, Corozal, PR; [MIS] Chapel Santa Teresita del Nino Jesus, Corozal, PR
Hincks, Rev. Matthew, *O.R.C.* '98 (STU) [MON] Opus Angelorum, Inc., Carrollton, OH; [MON] Order of the Holy Cross, Inc., Carrollton, OH
Hindelang, Rev. Joseph C., *S.M.* '78 (WDC) [MON] Marist Center (The Marist Finance Center of the Atlanta Province of the Society of Mary, Marist Fathers and Brothers), Washington, DC; [SEM] Marist College, Provincialate of the Marist Society in the USA, Washington, DC
Hindelang, Rev. Joseph C., *S.M.* '78 (DET) Notre Dame Preparatory School and Marist Academy, Pontiac, MI
Hindelang, Rev. Joseph C., *S.M.* (ATL) [MON] Marist Provincial Office, Society of Mary - Atlanta Province, Atlanta, GA
Hinders, Rev. Joseph, *C.PP.S.* '63 (CIN) Retired. [MON] St. Charles, Celina, OH
Hindman, Rev. John, '75 (SB) Retired.
Hinds, Rev. Nathaniel, (COS) Curia: Leadership Ave Maria, Parker, CO
Hindsley, Rev. Leonard P., '84 (FR) Retired.
Hines, Rev. George C., '04 (BO) Blessed Sacrament, Walpole, MA; St. Linus, Natick, MA; St. Patrick, Natick, MA
Hines, Rev. Hugh, *O.F.M.* '60 (BO) Retired. [MIS] St. Anthony Shrine, Boston, MA
Hinkle, Rev. James, (MO) Curia: Offices and Directors
Hinkle, Rev. James C., '14 (ARL) On Duty Outside Diocese.
Hinkley, Rev. Richard R., '14 (GAL) Curia: Offices and Directors [SEM] St. Mary's Seminary, Houston, TX
Hinnen, Rev. James W., '71 (MAD) Retired.
Hinni, Rev. Thomas R., *C.M.* '63 (STL) [MON] Congregation of the Mission, Perryville, MO
Hinojal, Rev. Ricardo, *O.A.R.* '62 (LSC) St. Anthony Parish, Anthony, Inc., Anthony, NM
Hinojos, Rev. Jaime, '02 (DET) St. Juan Diego Parish Detroit, Detroit, MI
Hinojosa, Rev. Damian, '87 (NO) [SEM] Saint Joseph Seminary College, Saint Benedict, LA
Hinojosa, Rev. P. Nolasco, '96 (LAR) Curia: Offices and Directors Holy Family, Laredo, TX; Immaculate Heart of Mary, Encinal, TX
Hinojosa, Rev. Rafael, '09 (OAK) St. Anthony, Oakley, CA
Hinojosa Avalos, Rev. Rafael, (OAK) Curia: Leadership
Hinsvark, Rev. John, '66 (FBK) Retired.
Hinterschied, Rev. Michael J., '12 (COL) Chap, London Corr Inst
Hinton, Rev. Frederick M., '70 (BUF) Retired.
Hipp, Rev. Branson S., '15 (ATL) [CAM] Georgia Tech Catholic Center, Atlanta, GA
Hippee, Rev. Msgr. Michael E., '73 (MAD) Retired.
Hipskind, Rev. J. Timothy, *S.J.* '00 (DET) [MON] Jesuit Community at the University of Detroit Mercy, Detroit, MI
Hipwell, Rev. Patrick J., '77 (STP) Curia: Consultative Bodies The Nativity of Our Lord, St. Paul, MN
Hiramatsu, Rev. Joseph, *S.A.* '82 (NY) [MON] Franciscan Friars of the Atonement, Minister General Office, Garrison, NY
Hirsch, Rev. Msgr. Joseph W., '86 (LC) On Duty Outside Diocese. Casa Hogar Juan Pablo II; Lurin, Peru, South America
Hirt, Rev. Alan, '15 (CIN) [MON] St. Francis Seraph Friary, Cincinnati, OH
Hirt, Rev. Alan, *OFM* '77 (CIN) St. Francis Seraph, Cincinnati, OH
Hirt, Friar Alan C, *OFM* '77 (CIN) [MON] Pleasant Street Friary, Cincinnati, OH
Hirtz, Rev. Daniel J., '73 (SPC) St. Catherine of Siena, Piedmont, MO
Hirtz, Rev. Patrick, '12 (MEM) Holy Angels Catholic Church, Dyersburg, TN
Hirudayasamy, Rev. Adam F., *SMA* '02 (MIL) St. Joseph Congregation, Wauwatosa, WI (>NEW) [MON] Society of African Missions, Provincialate, S.M.A. Fathers, Tenafly, NJ
Hislop, Rev. Edward, '73 (HEL) Curia: Leadership Blessed Trinity Parish: Series 661, LLC, Missoula, MT
Hissey, Rev. Leo Pierre, '66 (PHX) St. Steven Roman Catholic Parish, Sun Lakes, AZ
Hissrich, Rev. John E., '86 (PIT) Chap, Ridgepoint, Allegheny Cty Our Lady of Hope, Bethel Park, PA
Hitchens, Very Rev. Robert J., '94 (PHU) Curia: Leadership; Offices and Directors Saints Joachim and Anna Ukrainian Catholic Church, Front Royal, VA; Ukrainian Catholic National Shrine of the Holy Family, Washington, DC; [SEM] St. Josaphat Seminary, Washington, DC
Hite, Rev. Gregory R., '81 (TOL) Curia: Advisory Boards, Commissions, Committees, and Councils; Deaneries
Hite, Rev. Jordan, *T.O.R.* '70 (HBG) Curia: Offices and Directors St. Catherine Laboure, Harrisburg, PA
Hite, Rev. Jordan F., *T.O.R.* '70 (MO) Curia: Offices and Directors
Hite, Rev. Richard, *M.S.A.* '70 (NOR) [MON] Society of the Missionaries of the Holy Apostles, Cromwell, CT
Hitpas, Rev. Joseph, *O.M.I.* (BEL) [MON] Missionary Oblates of Mary Immaculate - St. Henry's Oblate Residence, Belleville, IL
Hitpas, Rev. Msgr. William J., '67 (BEL) St. Nicholas, O'Fallon, IL
Hivale, Rev. Kailas, *M.S.F.S.* (GAL) Sts. Simon and Jude, The Woodlands, TX
Hjelstrom, Rev. Timothy, '07 (DEN) St. Louis Catholic Parish in Louisville, Louisville, CO
Hlabse, Rev. Andrij, (FTW) [MIS] Jesuit Community, South Bend, IN
Hladik, Rev. Dusan, '83 (CHI) Czech Mission of Saints Cyril and Methodius, Brookfield, IL
Hlavaty, Very Rev. Kirby, '99 (VIC) Curia: Leadership; Offices and Directors The Cathedral of Our Lady of Victory, Victoria, TX
Hlond, Rev. Waclaw, *C.M.* '55 (HRT) Retired. The St. Joseph Church Corporation of Ansonia, Ansonia, CT
Hlubik, Rev. Joseph G., '93 (TR) Sacred Heart, Bay Head, NJ; The Church of St. Pio of Pietrelcina, Lavallette, N.J., Lavallette, NJ
Hnatkivskyy, Rev. Vasyl, '89 (STN) On Leave.
Ho, Rev. Antonius, *C.S.J.B.* '95 (BRK) [CCH] Chinese Ministry-Queens, ,
Ho, Rev. David Liang, *O.S.B.* '09 (GBG) [MON] Saint Vincent Archabbey, Latrobe, PA
Ho, Rev. Derek, '14 (CHI) Mary, Seat of Wisdom, Park Ridge, IL
Ho, Rev. Hai, *O.F.M.Cap.* '12 (OAK) St. Jarlath, Oakland, CA; [CAM] St. Mary's College Mission and Ministry Center, Moraga, CA
Ho, Rev. Joseph, *C.Ss.R.* (GAL) Sacred Heart Catholic Church, Richmond, TX
Ho, Very Rev. Joseph Khanh, '90 (BEA) Curia: Administration; Leadership Holy Trinity, Mont Belvieu, TX
Ho, Rev. M. Justin Cong Huu, *O.Cist.* '06 (SB) [MON] The Cistercian Congregation of the Holy Family, St. Joseph Monastery, Lucerne Valley, CA
Ho, Rev. Nicholas, '79 (SAC) Retired.
Ho, Rev. Phi Phu, *C.S.J.B.* '95 (NY) [MIS] Chinese Catholic Information Center, New York, NY
Ho, Rev. Thuc Si, '04 (SJ) St. Simon, Los Altos, CA
Ho, Rev. Viet Peter, '00 (ORG) Curia: Leadership St. Polycarp, Stanton, CA
Hoag, Rev. Michael R., *S.J.* '71 (NY) [MON] Jogues Retreat Center, Cornwall, NY
Hoag, Rev. Timothy S., '95 (RC) Curia: Leadership Blessed Sacrament, Rapid City, SD
Hoagland, Rev. Victor, *C.P.* '59 (BRK) [MON] Immaculate Conception Monastery, Jamaica, NY
Hoagland, Rev. Victor, *C.P.* '59 (NY) [MON] The Congregation of the Passion - St. Paul of the Cross Province, Jamaica, NY
Hoan, Rev. Michael Mai Khai, '72 (ORG) Retired.
Hoang, Rev. Benjamin Diep, '12 (ORG) St. Columban, Garden Grove, CA
Hoang, Rev. Dat, *OFM* '18 (SFD) St. Francis of Assisi, Teutopolis, IL; St. Rose of Lima, Montrose, IL; [MON] St. Francis Assisi Friary, Teutopolis, IL
Hoang, Rev. Dat, '03 (GAL) Curia: Offices and Directors St. Faustina Catholic Church, Fulshear, TX
Hoang, Rev. Doan T., *S.J.* '97 (LA) St. Francis Xavier Chapel, Los Angeles, CA
Hoang, Rev. Dominic Hung, '90 (OKL) Retired.
Hoang, Rev. Ignatius Trieu, *CRM* '16 (STP) Church of St. Anne - St. Joseph Hien, Minneapolis, MN
Hoang, Rev. John Baptist, *O.P.* (L) Curia: Offices and Directors
Hoang, Rev. John Minh Toan, '68 (GAL) Retired.
Hoang, Rev. John N., (VEN) Our Lady Queen of Martyrs Parish in Sarasota, Inc., Sarasota, FL
Hoang, Rev. John Nghia, *C.M.C.* '08 (VEN) Curia: Leadership
Hoang, Rev. John The, '19 (SJ) Holy Spirit, San Jose, CA
Hoang, Rev. John Baptist, *O.P.* (L) St. Louis Bertrand, Louisville, KY
Hoang, Rev. Joseph, '99 (P) St. Anthony, Waldport, OR
Hoang, Rev. Joseph, '04 (ORG) Curia: (>MO) Offices and Directors
Hoang, Rev. Joseph Duc Quang, '04 (ORG) Military Chap
Hoang, Rev. Joseph Vien, *S.D.B.* '83 (NY) Parish of St. John Bosco, Port Chester, NY
Hoang, Friar Joseph Martin, (OAK) [MON] Conventual Franciscans (Province of St. Joseph of Cupertino), Castro Valley, CA
Hoang, Rev. Khanh, '94 (HON) Curia: Consultative Bodies St. Jude, Kapolei, HI
Hoang, Rev. Linh, *O.F.M.* '09 (ALB) [COL] Siena College, Loudonville, NY
Hoang, Rev. Louis Trung Dinh, '95 (DOD) St. Mary Catholic Church of Garden City, Kansas, Garden City, KS
Hoang, Rev. Peter Nhat, (P) St. Anthony, Tigard, OR
Hoang, Rev. Petrus Binh, '96 (P) On Leave.
Hoang, Rev. Phuong V., '89 (SEA) St. Gabriel, Port Orchard, WA
Hoang, Rev. Randy, '21 (P) On Academic Leave. Student at Pontifical North American College, Rome, Italy
Hoang, Rev. Simon Thoi, *S.V.D.* '07 (DUB) [SEM] Divine Word College, Epworth, IA
Hoang, Rev. Son Thanh, *O.P.* (GAL) Our Lady of Lourdes, Houston, TX
Hoang, Rev. Tat Thang, *C.Ss.R.* '06 (CHI) (>BR) [MON] St. Gerard Residence, Baton Rouge, LA
Hoang, Rev. Tat Thang, *C.Ss R* '06 (BR) Congregation Of St. Gerard Majella Roman Catholic Church, Parish Of East Baton Rouge, Louisiana, Baton Rouge, LA; [MIS] Redemptorist Fathers of Baton Rouge, Inc., Baton Rouge, LA
Hoang, Rev. Thang, *S.V.D.* '04 (DUB) [SEM] Divine Word College, Epworth, IA
Hoang, Rev. The, '18 (WIN) Curia: Advisory Boards, Commissions, Committees, and Councils Sacred Heart, Waseca, MN
Hoang, Rev. Thi Van, '13 (OAK) Curia: Leadership Good Shepherd, Pittsburg, CA
Hoang, Rev. Thuan V., '97 (SFR) On Special Assignment. Tribunal, Office of Tyribunal (Part-time) Curia: Offices and Directors Visitacion, Church of the, San Francisco, CA
Hoang, Rev. Tuan, *S.V.D.* '18 (DUB) [SEM] Divine Word College, Epworth, IA
Hoar, Rev. Thomas, *S.S.E.* (MO) Curia: Offices and Directors
Hoar, Rev. Thomas F.X., *S.S.E.* '78 (NOR) Chap, US Submarine Base-New London, Groton [MON] St. Edmund's of Connecticut, Inc., Mystic, CT; [RTR] St. Edmund's Retreat, Inc., Mystic, CT
Hoare, Rev. Richard, '69 (BRK) Retired. Blessed Sacrament, Jackson Heights, NY
Hoat, Rev. Rochus Vu Dinh, '60 (SPC) Retired.
Hoban, Rev. Msgr. Thomas E., '60 (ALN) Retired. St.

Ann, Emmaus, PA
Hobbs, Rev. Charles R., '14 (LR) St. Michael, Van Buren, AR
Hober, Rev. Raymond, *S.V.D.* '60 (PIT) [MON] Society of The Divine Word, Pittsburgh, PA
Hober, Rev. Raymond, *S.V.D.* '59 (CHI) Retired. [MON] Divine Word Residence, Techny, IL
Hobson, Rev. J. Mark, '86 (CLV) On Leave.
Hobson, Rev. Michael A., (BO) Holy Apostles Parish, Halifax, MA
Hoc, Rev. Mark, (OAK) St. Raymond, Dublin, CA
Hoc Nguyen, Rev. (Thomas M.), *CRM* '17 (SPC) [MON] Congregation of the Mother of the Redeemer, Carthage, MO
Hochhalter, Rev. Kregg W., '12 (BIS) Saint Anne, Bismarck, ND
Hochreiter, Rev. Robert S., '68 (SCR) Retired. Chap, Col, USAF, Newport News, VA
Hock, Rev. Harry, *S.J.* '64 (PH) Retired.
Hock, Rev. Neal J., '11 (GI) Curia: Offices and Directors [CAM] St. Teresa of Calcutta Newman Center, Kearney, NE
Hockman, Rev. Richard C., *C.S.C.* (FTW) [MIS] Holy Cross House, Notre Dame, IN
Hodari, Rev. Raphael, (L) [MON] Abbey of Our Lady of Gethsemani, of the Order of Cistercians of the Strict Observance, Trappist, KY
Hodge, Rev. Msgr. William A., '74 (CAM) St. Mary's Church, Gloucester, Gloucester, NJ
Hodges, Rev. Anthony Leo, '86 (ORL) St. Andrew, Orlando, FL
Hodges, Rev. Michael G., '12 (GR) Curia: Leadership St. Mary, Marne, MI; St. Michael, Coopersville, MI
Hodges, Rev. Robert S., *O.Praem.* '74 (ORG) [MON] Norbertine Fathers of Orange, Inc., Silverado, CA
Hodges, Rev. Ronald E., '06 (DAV) Immaculate Conception Church of Colfax, Iowa, Colfax, IA
Hodgson, Rev. William M., '79 (SPC) Curia: Deaneries; Organizations (affiliated, inter-Diocesan, miscellaneous/ other) Holy Family, Shell Knob, MO; St. Edward, Cassville, MO
Hoeberechts, Rev. Dwight, *OMI* '97 (STP) St. Casimir, St. Paul, MN; St. Patrick, St. Paul, MN
Hoefer, Rev. Reginald, (NY) Parish of St. Vincent Ferrer and St. Catherine of Siena, New York, NY; [MON] St. Vincent Ferrer Priory, New York, NY
Hoeffner, Rev. Robert J., '73 (ORL) Retired.
Hoefler, Rev. Msgr. David J., '02 (SFD) On Special Assignment. Curia: Leadership [HOS] St. Mary's Hospital, Decatur, IL; [MIS] Catholic Care Center, Inc., Springfield, IL; [MIS] Diocesan Care Management, Inc., Springfield, IL; [MIS] Priests' Purgatorial Society, Springfield, IL; [MIS] St. Martin De Porres Center, Inc., Springfield, IL
Hoeft, Rev. Patrick, (SCL) Holy Family, Little Falls, MN; Our Lady of Lourdes, Little Falls, MN; St. Elizabeth, Elizabeth, MN; St. Leonard's, Pelican Rapids, MN; St. Mary, Little Falls, MN
Hoegerl, Rev. Carl, *C.Ss.R.* '50 (BAL) Retired. [SPF] St. John Neuman Residence, Timonium, MD
Hoehn, Rev. Daniel, '04 (JOL) St. Michael, Wheaton, IL; [EFT] Diocese of Joliet Priests' Pension Plan, Crest Hill, IL; [EFT] Diocese of Joliet Retired Priests' Other Benefits Plan, Crest Hill, IL
Hoelke, Rev. Augustine, *O.Cist.* '10 (DAL) [MON] Our Lady of Dallas Cistercian Abbey, Irving, TX
Hoelscher, Rev. Matthew, '14 (PEO) St. John's Catholic Chapel, Champaign, IL; [CAM] Newman Foundation at the University of IL (St. John's Catholic Newman Center), Champaign, IL
Hoelsken, Rev. Mark A., *S.J.* '91 (FBK) (>SJ) [MON] USA West Province, Society of Jesus, Los Gatos, CA
Hoerning, Rev. Richard P., '73 (RVC) Retired. Immaculate Conception, Westhampton Beach, NY; St. Agnes, Greenport, NY
Hoerter, Rev. James, '06 (RC) Assumption of the Blessed Virgin Mary, Kenel, SD; St. Bernard, McLaughlin, SD; [MIS] Standing Rock Reservation, McLaughlin, SD
Hoeser, Rev. Jerome G., '63 (LC) St. Henry, Eau Galle, WI
Hoesing, Rev. Kenneth F., '97 (LIN) St. Mary's, Dawson, NE
Hoesing, Rev. Paul, '02 (STL) Curia: Leadership; Offices and Directors [SEM] Kenrick School of Theology, ,
Hoesing, Rev. Paul C., '02 (OM) On Duty Outside Diocese. Kenrick-Glennon Seminary, St Louis, MO
Hofer, Rev. Adam, (MO) Curia: Offices and Directors
Hofer, Rev. Adam, '14 (RC) Curia: Offices and Directors Sacred Heart, Morristown, SD; St. Bonaventure's, McIntosh, SD; St. Mary's, Lemmon, SD; St. Michael, Watauga, SD
Hofer, Rev. Kenneth Andrew, *O.P.* '02 (WDC) St. Dominic Church & Priory, Washington, DC
Hoffa, Rev. Allen J., '09 (ALN) Holy Guardian Angels, Reading, PA
Hoffenkamp, Rev. Robert A., '89 (JOL) Retired.
Hoffer, Rev. Steven R., '05 (LAV) Curia: Social Services Holy Family, Las Vegas, NV
Hoffman, Rev. Andrew K., (WCH) On Duty Outside Diocese. Curia: Leadership St. Paul Parish, Wichita, KS; [CAM] St. Paul Catholic Student Center, Wichita, KS
Hoffman, Rev. Andrew W., '74 (SC) Retired.
Hoffman, Rev. Daniel R., '09 (E) Curia: Offices and Directors St. Bibiana, Galeton, PA; St. Eulalia, Coudersport, PA; St. Gabriel the Archangel, Port Allegany, PA
Hoffman, Rev. David J., '96 (GB) SS. Edward and Isidore, Flintville, WI
Hoffman, Rev. Dennis H., '70 (DUL) Retired.
Hoffman, Rev. Dennis L., '90 (DAV) Sacred Heart Church of Melcher, Iowa, Melcher, IA; St. Anthony Church of Knoxville, Iowa, Knoxville, IA; [MIS] St. Joseph's Church of Bauer, Iowa, Knoxville, IA
Hoffman, Rev. Edward, *O.C.S.O.* '72 (DEN) [MON] St. Benedict's Monastery, Snowmass, CO
Hoffman, Rev. Edward J., '21 (CIN) St. Joseph, Hamilton, OH; St. Julie Billiart, Hamilton, OH; St. Peter in Chains, Hamilton, OH
Hoffman, Rev. Francis J, '92 (POD) Curia: Clergy and Religious Services
Hoffman, Rev. Francis J., '92 (GB) (>CHI) [MIS] Relevant Radio, Inc., Lincolnshire, IL
Hoffman, Rev. Frank J., '92 (CHI) [MIS] Prelature of the Holy Cross and Opus Dei, Chicago, IL
Hoffman, Rev. Henry J., '03 (BGP) St. Stephen's Roman Catholic Church Corporation, Trumbull, CT
Hoffman, Rev. James, *O.F.M.* '67 (GB) Retired.
Hoffman, Rev. James A., *O.F.M.* '67 (CHI) [MON] St. Peter's Friary, Chicago, IL
Hoffman, Rev. James A., '67 (SUP) Retired.
Hoffman, Rev. John R., '75 (CHI) Retired.
Hoffman, Rev. Joseph M., '79 (BRK) Curia: Pastoral Services St. Barbara, Brooklyn, NY
Hoffman, Rev. Mark A., '90 (E) Our Lady of the Lake, Edinboro, PA; [CAM] Penn West, Edinboro, PA
Hoffman, Rev. Michael, *S.D.S.* '82 (MIL) [MIS] Salvatorians - Jordan Hall, Milwaukee, WI
Hoffman, Rev. Michael J., '05 (GRY) Retired.
Hoffman, Rev. Paul E., '10 (LC) Retired.
Hoffman, Rev. Philip, '64 (GB) Retired. On Sick Leave.
Hoffman, Rev. Pio Maria, *C.F.R.* '07 (NY) [MON] Our Lady of the Angels Friary, Bronx, NY
Hoffman, Rev. Raniero, *O.S.B.Cam.* '76 (MRY) [MON] New Camaldoli Hermitage (Camaldolese Hermits of America), Big Sur, CA
Hoffman, Rev. Robert, '56 (PEO) Retired.
Hoffman, Rev. Robert, '19 (STA) Epiphany, Lake City, FL
Hoffman, Rev. Robert, '19 (STA) Curia: Clergy and Religious Services
Hoffman, Rev. Robert E., *M.M.* '60 (SJ) Retired.
Hoffman, Rev. Steven B., '07 (STP) St. Peter, Mendota, MN; [CEM] St. Peter Cemetery, Mendota, MN
Hoffman, Rev. Thomas, '80 (CHI) Retired.
Hoffman, Rev. William A., '80 (GB) Curia: Advisory Boards, Commissions, Committees, and Councils
Hoffman, Rev. Msgr. William G., '61 (ATL) Retired.
Hoffmann, Rev. Charles, '63 (GB) Retired.
Hoffmann, Rev. Christopher, '87 (ORL) Our Lady of the Lakes, Deltona, FL
Hoffmann, Rev. Edward, '21 (CIN) Queen of Peace, Hamilton, OH; St. Aloysius, Hamilton, OH
Hoffmann, Rev. Francis T., '90 (BGP) Curia: Consultative Bodies; Leadership Church of Assumption, Westport, Connecticut, Westport, CT
Hoffmann, Rev. Henry, *C.O.* '21 (CIN) Old St. Mary, Cincinnati, OH; Sacred Heart, Cincinnati, OH; [MIS] Society of Saint Philip Neri, Inc. (The Cincinnati Oratory), Cincinnati, OH
Hoffmann, Rev. Lawrence, '71 (DM) Retired.
Hoffmann, Rev. Lawrence R., '71 (DM) Retired. Curia: Offices and Directors
Hoffmann, Rev. Robert E., *M.M.* '60 (SJ) Retired. [MON] Maryknoll, Los Altos, CA
Hoffmann, Rev. Robert E., *M.M.* '60 (NY) Retired.
Hofmann, Rev. Msgr. Thomas X., '77 (CHR) St. Anthony, Walterboro, SC; St. James the Greater, Walterboro, SC
Hofschulte, Rev. Charles L., *C.J.* '71 (LA) [EFT] American Region of the Josephite Fathers Charitable Trust, Santa Maria, CA; [MON] St. Joseph Seminary (Josephite Fathers' Novitiate), Santa Maria, CA
Hofstede, Rev. John Michael, '75 (STP) Retired. St. Cecilia, St. Paul, MN
Hogan, Rev. David J., '14 (STL) Immaculate Conception Catholic Church, Dardenne, Dardenne Prairie, MO; Incarnate Word Catholic Church, Chesterfield, MO
Hogan, Rev. James J., '61 (HEL) Retired.
Hogan, Rev. John F., '88 (SY) St. John the Evangelist, Camden, NY
Hogan, Rev. John J., *O.M.I.* '65 (BO) [NUR] Immaculate Heart of Mary Residence, Tewksbury, MA
Hogan, Rev. John Paul, *O.F.M.* (SP) Retired. [MON] St. Anthony Friary (St. Petersburg) Franciscan Friars-Holy Name Province, Inc., St. Petersburg, FL
Hogan, Rev. Joseph T., '88 (PEO) Our Lady of the Lake, Mahomet, IL
Hogan, Rev. Phil D., *O.F.M.* '62 (CHI) [MON] Holy Spirit Friary, Order of Friars Minor, Chicago, IL
Hogan, Rev. Richard, '86 (DET) On Leave.
Hogan, Rev. Robert E., *B.B.D.* '83 (SAT) St. Henry, San Antonio, TX; St. Mary Magdalen, San Antonio, TX; [MIS] Brothers of the Beloved Disciple, San Antonio, TX
Hogan, Rev. Sean M., *C.S.Sp.* '67 (PIT) [COL] Duquesne University of the Holy Spirit, Pittsburgh, PA
Hogan, Msgr. Terence, '80 (MIA) Retired.
Hogan, Rev. Msgr. Timothy D., '82 (DET) St. Fabian Parish Farmington Hills, Farmington Hills, MI
Hogan, Rev. Timothy J., '82 (SC) Sacred Heart, Spencer, IA; St. Joseph's, Hartley, IA
Hogan, Rev. Verne F., '57 (COV) Retired.
Hogan, Rev. William A., '66 (GF) Retired.
Hohenstein, Rev. Robert J., '68 (ALB) Retired. Curia: Leadership Roman Catholic Community of All Saints on the Hudson, Mechanicville, NY
Hohenwarter, Rev. Norman C., '96 (HBG) [NUR] St. Anne's Retirement Community, Columbia, PA
Hohman, Rev. Steve, '10 (OWN) St. Elizabeth of Hungary, Clarkson, KY; St. Paul, Leitchfield, KY
Hohosha, Very Rev. Archpriest Ihor, '07 (SJP) Curia: Leadership; Offices and Directors St. George, Pittsburgh, PA; St. John the Baptist, McKees Rocks, PA
Hoi, Rev. Joseph, '84 (JC) Retired.
Hoiland, Rev. Christopher, '16 (SEA) St. Augustine, Oak Harbor, WA
Hoisington, Rev. Thomas M., '95 (WCH) St. Martin of Tours, Caldwell, KS
Hokamp, Rev. Ethan, '19 (LC) McDonell Central Catholic High School, , ; Notre Dame Middle School, , ; St. Charles Borromeo, Chippewa Falls, WI; St. Peter, Chippewa Falls, WI
Hoke, Rev. John D., '76 (HBG) St. Joseph, Milton, PA
Holahan, Rev. Thomas J., *C.S.P.* '77 (NY) [MON] Paulist Fathers' Motherhouse, New York, NY
Holahan, Rev. Thomas J., *C.S.P.* '77 (NY) Chap, Mount Sinai West, New York
Holbrook, Rev. James A., '10 (STL) St. Joseph Catholic Church, Bonne Terre, Bonne Terre, MO; St. Joseph Catholic Church, Manchester, Manchester, MO
Holbrook, Rev. William M., '70 (LFT) Retired.
Holbrook, Rev. William M., '70 (CHI) Retired. St. Monica and St. Rosalie Parish, Chicago, IL
Holbus, Rev. Brian T., '81 (MIL) Retired.
Holcomb, Rev. Joseph T., '80 (BRK) [SEM] Cathedral Seminary House of Formation, Douglaston, NY
Holden, Rev. Charles E., '13 (P) On Leave.
Holden, Rev. James T., '62 (MOB) Retired.
Holden, Rev. Robert A., '62 (TOL) Retired.
Holder, Rev. Thomas, '95 (KC) Our Lady of the Presentation, Lees Summit, MO; St. John Francis Regis, Kansas City, MO
Holdren, Rev. Benjamin P., '07 (LIN) St. Peter's, Bellwood, NE
Holeda, Very Rev. Timothy Michael, '11 (PT) Chap, Federal Corr Inst Curia: Leadership; Offices and Directors Co-Cathedral of St. Thomas More, Tallahassee, FL
Holgren, Rev. Dan, '21 (SD) Pastor of Corpus Christi Catholic Parish, Bonita, a corporation sole, Bonita, CA
Holguin, Rev. Cruz Manuel, '12 (FWT) On Leave.
Holian, Rev. John P., '63 (NEW) Retired.
Holicky, Rev. Gregory, '72 (GRY) [HOS] Franciscan Health Dyer, Dyer, IN
Holicky, Rev. Gregory P., '71 (GRY) Retired.
Holiday, Rev. William P., '12 (POC) Incarnation Catholic Church, Orlando, FL
Holl, Rev. Kermit, *O.S.C.* '90 (SCL) [EFT] Crosier Continuing Care and Support Trust, Onamia, MN; [MON] Crosier Priory, Onamia, MN
Holladay, Rev. Matthew, *MIC* '19 (WDC) [SEM] Marian Fathers Scholasticate and Novitiate, Washington, DC
Holland, Rev. Daniel F., '65 (ROC) Retired.
Holland, Rev. Edward T., '97 (CLV) Chap, Grafton Reintegration Ctr, Grafton St. Elizabeth Ann Seton,

Columbia Station, OH
Holland, Rev. James P., '98 (PIT) Our Lady of the Lakes (The Catholic Communities of St. Victor & Transfiguration Parishes), Bairdford, PA
Holland, Rev. Jeremiah, *SS.CC.* '67 (LA) [MON] Congregation of the Sacred Hearts of Jesus and Mary, La Verne, CA
Holland, Rev. Jeremiah, *SS.CC.* '67 (SB) [MON] Congregation of the Sacred Hearts of Jesus and Mary, SS.CC., Hemet, CA
Holland, Rev. Kevin, (E) St. Boniface, Kersey, PA
Holland, Rev. Matthew, (SEA) Bellarmine Preparatory School, Tacoma, WA; Sacred Heart, Tacoma, WA
Holland, Rev. Paul D, *SJ* (PH) Old St. Joseph's, Philadelphia, PA
Holland, Rev. Stanley, *TOR* '96 (STU) (>FWT) St. Maria Goretti, Arlington, TX
Hollas, Rev. Eric, *O.S.B.* '75 (SCL) [MON] St. John's Abbey, of the Order of St. Benedict, Collegeville, MN
Holleman, Rev. John L., '81 (MOB) Retired.
Hollenbach, Rev. David, *S.J.* '71 (WDC) [COL] Georgetown University, Washington, DC; [MON] The Jesuit Community at Georgetown University, Washington, DC
Holler, Rev. Martin J., '66 (STU) Retired.
Holleran, Rev. Msgr. J. Warren, '52 (SFR) Retired.
Holleran, Rev. Leo, *M.S.* '78 (HRT) [MIS] Missionaries of LaSalette, Hartford, CT
Holleran, Rev. Michael K., '79 (NY) Corpus Christi, New York, NY; Notre Dame, New York, NY
Holley, Rev. George, '15 (TUC) [EFT] Parish Pooled Investment Trust, Tucson, AZ
Holley, Rev. George, '15 (TUC) Saint John Neumann Roman Catholic Church - Yuma, Yuma, AZ; [MIS] St. John Neumann Roman Catholic Church Regional Columbarium - Yuma, Yuma, AZ
Hollfelder, Rev. Eugene F., '68 (MAD) Retired.
Hollick, Rev. Ian F., '21 (SB) St. Martha, Murrieta, CA
Holliday, Rev. John, (BRK) [MON] Reverend John B. Murray, C.M. House, Jamaica, NY
Hollis, Rev. Mark L., '72 (CLV) Retired. St. Patrick, Cleveland, OH
Holloway, Rev. David L., '82 (KC) Curia: Offices and Directors
Holloway, Rev. Gerald, '98 (BIR) Holy Infant of Prague Catholic Parish, Trussville, Trussville, AL
Holloway, Rev. James, '70 (SAV) Retired.
Holloway, Rev. James P., '70 (WDC) Retired.
Holloway, Rev. Jim, (SAV) Retired. St. William, St. Simons Island, GA
Hollowell, Very Rev. Anthony P., '16 (IND) Curia: Leadership St. Mark's Catholic Church, Perry County, Inc., Tell City, IN; St. Paul Catholic Church, Tell City, Inc., Tell City, IN; [MIS] Tell City Deanery, Indianapolis, IN
Hollowell, Rev. John J., '09 (IND) Catholic Chap, Putnamville Correctional Fac Annunciation Catholic Church, Brazil, Inc., Brazil, IN; St. Paul the Apostle Catholic Church, Putnam County, Inc., Greencastle, IN; [CAM] DePauw University, Greencastle, IN
Holly, Rev. Dennis, '64 (CIN) Retired. [MON] Headquarters of Glenmary Home Missioners (The Home Missioners of America), Fairfield, OH
Holmberg, Rev. Michael, '73 (FWT) Retired.
Holmer, Rev. James J., '76 (TOL) Retired.
Holmer, Rev. Scott S., '13 (WDC) Curia: Clergy and Religious Services St. Edward, Bowie, MD
Holmes, Rev. Albert, '93 (SCL) Retired.
Holmes, Rt. Rev. Caedmon W., *O.S.B.* '97 (PRO) Retired. [MON] Abbey of St. Gregory the Great (Order of St. Benedict in Portsmouth, Rhode Island, Benedictines of the English Congregation), Portsmouth, RI
Holmes, Rev. Msgr. Kevin D., '84 (MAD) Cathedral Parish of St. Raphael, Madison, WI
Holmes, Rev. Paul A., '81 (NEW) [COL] Seton Hall University, South Orange, NJ
Holmes, Rev. Stephen, '00 (ARL) Sacred Heart, Manassas, VA
Holmes, Rev. Thomas F., '91 (ALB) Church of St. Mary at Clinton Heights, Rensselaer, NY; Parish of St. John the Evangelist and St. Joseph's, Rensselaer, NY; St. Henry, Averill Park, NY; St. Mary, Nassau, NY
Holmquist, Rev. Michael, (COS) Curia: Offices and Directors Our Lady of the Visitation, Kiowa, CO
Holoubek, Rev. Roger, '69 (MIA) Retired.
Holoubek, Rev. William, (LIN) St. Mary's, Ashland, NE
Holquin, Rev. Msgr. Arthur, '74 (ORG) Retired. Mission Basilica - San Juan Capistrano, San Juan Capistrano, CA
Holquin, Rev. Msgr. Arthur A., '74 (ORG) Retired.
Holroyd, Rev. Patrick, '74 (ARL) St. Mark, Vienna, VA
Holt, Rev. William Alexander, *OP* '76 (NY) [MON] St. Vincent Ferrer Priory, New York, NY
Holterhoff, Rev. Edward G., '70 (PAT) Retired.
Holtgrewe, Rev. Donald E., *O.F.M.* '63 (CIN) Retired.
Holtman, Rev. Msgr. Elmer, '64 (AUS) Retired.
Holtman, Rev. William Jeffry, *O.F.S.* '85 (SFD) Ss. Peter and Paul, Alton, IL; [CEM] Calvary Cemetery, Edwardsville, IL
Holtmann, Rev. Christopher F., '00 (STL) St. George Catholic Church, St. Louis, MO; St. John Paul II Catholic Church, St. Louis, MO
Holtschneider, Rev. Dennis H., *CM* '89 (WDC) [ASN] Association of Catholic Colleges and Universities, Washington, DC
Holtschneider, Rev. Dennis H., *C.M.* '89 (CHI) [COL] De Paul University, Chicago, IL
Holtschneider, Rev. Dennis H., *C.M.* '89 (PH) [MON] Congregation of the Mission, Philadelphia, PA
Holtz, Rev. Albert T., *O.S.B.* '69 (NEW) [MON] Benedictine Abbey of Newark, Newark, NJ
Holtz, Rev. Robert, '03 (TR) Parish of St. Isidore the Farmer, New Egypt, N.J., Wrightstown, NJ
Holtzinger, Rev. William, '00 (P) Curia: Offices and Directors Holy Trinity, Beaverton, OR
Holtzman, Rev. Jerome, '57 (SFS) Retired.
Holup, Rev. James, '59 (JOL) Retired.
Holway, Rev. Craig T., '10 (STL) Mary, Queen of Peace Catholic Church, Webster Groves, MO
Holy, Rev. Richard C., '08 (GRY) Curia: Leadership; Offices and Directors St. Edward, Lowell, IN
Holz, Rev. Robert, (RVC) Curia: Offices and Directors
Holz, Rev. Robert A., '08 (RVC) Curia: Leadership; Offices and Directors St. Raphael, East Meadow, NY
Holzhauser, Rev. J. Joseph, '82 (SFS) Saints Peter and Paul Parish of Hughes County, Pierre, SD
Holzhuter, Rev. Jared J., '17 (MAD) St. Olaf, De Forest, WI
Holzhuter, Rev. Jared J., '17 (MAD) Curia: Offices and Directors St. Joseph, Sun Prairie, WI
Holzmann, Rev. Michael F., '88 (RVC) Curia: Leadership Church of the Holy Cross, Nesconset, NY
Homes, Rev. Dennis, '72 (BAK) Retired.
Homes, Rev. Ronald G., '93 (LIN) St. Anthony, Bruno, NE
Homic, Rev. Russell, '11 (KAL) St. Monica, Kalamazoo, MI
Homick, Rev. Joseph, '91 (SFR) [MIS] The Contemplatives of Saint Joseph, South San Francisco, CA
Homick, Rev. Joseph, '91 (STN) On Leave.
Honan, Rev. Eugene D., '67 (SPR) Retired.
Hong, Rev. Sung Gye, '14 (NEW) Church of St. Paul, Ramsey, NJ; Our Lady of the Blessed Sacrament, Roseland, NJ
Hong Van Le, Rev. Anthony, (OAK) Curia: Leadership St. Joseph (Old Mission San Jose), Fremont, CA
Honhart, Rev. Mark A., '80 (SCR) On Administrative Leave.
Honiotes, Rev. John, (JOL) St. Michael, Wheaton, IL
Honkomp, Rev. Clinton, *O.P.* '88 (SFD) Christ the King, Springfield, IL
Honorio, Rev. Gregorio S., '95 (HON) Curia: Consultative Bodies; Offices and Directors
Hont, Rev. Leon, *O.S.B.* '80 (GBG) [MON] Saint Vincent Archabbey, Latrobe, PA
Hood, Rev. Carl J., '86 (MEM) Curia: Advisory Boards, Commissions, Committees, and Councils St. Francis of Assisi, Cordova, TN
Hood, Rev. Matthew, '17 (DET) Curia: Consultative Bodies; Offices and Directors [CAM] Detroit Catholic Campus Ministry, Detroit, MI; [CAM] Gabriel Richard Student Center, Dearborn, MI
Hoog, Rev. Eric, *C.Ss.R.* '73 (BAL) St. Mary, Annapolis, MD
Hoog, Rev. Eric R., *C.Ss.R.* '73 (MO) Curia: Offices and Directors
Hoogerwerf, Rev. Canon James, '19 (CHI) [MON] Institute of Christ the King Sovereign Priest, Chicago, IL
Hook, Rev. Stephen E., '03 (BAL) Our Lady of the Chesapeake, Pasadena, MD; St. Jane Frances de Chantal, Pasadena, MD
Hoolahan, Rev. Michael, *C.P.* '61 (LA) [RTR] Mater Dolorosa Passionist Retreat Center, Inc., Sierra Madre, CA
Hooper, Rev. Derek J., '21 (JC) Church of the Risen Savior, Rhineland, MO; Immaculate Conception, Owensville, MO; St. Alexander, Belle, MO; St. George Catholic Church, Hermann, MO
Hooper, Rev. Jeffery G., '88 (L) Curia: Offices and Directors
Hoorman, Rev. Albert F.H., '67 (PHX) Retired.
Hoover, Rev. Andrew J., '16 (CLV) Curia: Advisory Boards, Commissions, Committees, and Councils St. Ambrose, Brunswick, OH
Hoover, Rev. Conrad, '89 (CHL) Retired.
Hoover, Rt. Rev. Gary, *O.S.B.* '83 (CLV) Benedictine High School, Cleveland, OH; [MON] Benedictine Order of Cleveland (St. Andrew Abbey), Cleveland, OH
Hoover, Rev. John P., '79 (CHL) Retired.
Hoover, Rev. Matthew N., '95 (COL) Immaculate Conception, Columbus, OH
Hopcus, Rev. Daniel R., '64 (ORG) Retired.
Hope, Rev. Donald E., '76 (SLC) Retired.
Hopefl, Very Rev. Gregory J., '76 (SUP) Retired. Curia: Offices and Directors
Hopka, Rev. Jack W., '79 (DAL) St. Mark the Evangelist Catholic Parish, Plano, TX
Hopkins, Rev. Edward, *LC* '91 (ATL) [MIS] Legionaries of Christ, Atlanta, GA
Hopkins, Rev. John, (LA) [MON] Legionaries of Christ, Pasadena, CA
Hopkins, Rev. Msgr. John P., '78 (WIL) Curia: Advisory Boards, Commissions, Committees, and Councils St. Joseph on the Brandywine, Wilmington, DE
Hopkins, Rev. Peter, *L.C.* (WDC) [MON] Legionaries of Christ, Potomac, MD
Hopmeir, Rev. Ronald J., '91 (STL) St. Stephen Protomartyr Catholic Church, St. Louis, MO; Sts. Mary and Joseph Catholic Church, St. Louis, MO
Hopp, Rev. Raymond, '65 (BAK) Retired.
Hoppe, Rev. Sean, *O.S.B.* '82 (IND) [MON] St. Meinrad Archabbey, St. Meinrad, IN
Hoppe, Rev. Msgr. William M., '78 (BRK) Curia: Leadership
Hoppe, Rev. Msgr. William M., '78 (BRK) Curia: Leadership St. Joan of Arc, Jackson Heights, NY
Hopper, Rev. Jeffrey G., '06 (L) St. Christopher, Radcliff, KY; St. Martin of Tours, Vine Grove, KY
Hopper, Rev. Jeffrey G., '06 (L) Curia: (>MO) Offices and Directors [MIS] Sacred Heart Apostolate, Radcliff, KY
Hopper, Rev. Thomas W., '04 (GAL) St. Anne, Tomball, TX
Hopping, Rev. John Paul, '85 (STL) St. Charles Borromeo Catholic Church, St. Charles, MO; [MIS] Archdiocesan Stewardship Education Committee, St. Louis, MO
Hoppough, Rev. Gregory J., *C.S.S.* '74 (WOR) Sacred Heart of Jesus, Milford, MA
Hopps, Rev. Marc, (SAG) Saint Mary University Parish of Mt. Pleasant, Mount Pleasant, MI
Hora, Rev. Robert J., '83 (BUF) Retired.
Horak, Rev. Msgr. Donald E., '63 (STU) Retired. Curia: Deaneries
Horak, Rev. Mark F., *S.J.* '94 (WDC) [MON] The Jesuit Community of St. Aloysius Gonzaga, Washington, DC
Horan, Rev. Brendan, *S.J.* '93 (NY) [MON] Jesuit Community at Fordham University, New York, NY
Horan, Rev. George E., '72 (LA) Retired. Sacred Heart, Los Angeles, CA
Horan, Rev. Gerald M., *O.S.M.* '82 (ORG) St. Philip Benizi, Fullerton, CA
Horan, Rev. James, *SDB* '82 (SP) [RTR] Mary Help of Christians Center, Tampa, FL
Horan, Rev. John, (JOL) On Special Assignment. Bishop McNamara HS St. John Paul II Parish, Kankakee, IL
Horan, Rev. John F., *O.Carm.* '84 (PMB) Curia: Leadership St. Jude, Boca Raton, FL
Horan, Rev. Mike, '80 (SAT) St. Dominic, San Antonio, TX
Horan, Rev. Thomas, *OMI* (BEL) Retired.
Horan, Rev. Timothy E., '79 (ROC) Curia: Consultative Bodies Holy Trinity, Webster, NY
Horan, Rev. Tom, *OMI* (SAT) Retired. [NUR] Oblate Madonna Residence, San Antonio, TX
Horath, Rev. James R., '73 (SUP) Retired.
Horejsi, Rev. Jeffrey P., '91 (NU) Curia: Leadership Church of Our Lady, Grove City, MN; St. John, Darwin, MN; St. Philip, Litchfield, MN
Horgan, Rev. Daniel B., '98 (PMB) St. Lucy, Highland Beach, FL
Horgan, Rev. John E., '72 (WOR) Retired.
Horgas, Very Rev. Robert, '91 (E) St. Francis, Clearfield, PA; [CAM] Lock Haven University - Clearfield Campus, Clearfield, PA
Horihan, Rev. Robert S., '01 (WIN) [SEM] Immaculate Heart of Mary Seminary, Winona, MN
Horihan, Very Rev. Robert S., (WIN) Curia: Advisory Boards, Commissions, Committees, and Councils
Horkan, Rev. Edward R., '03 (ARL) Curia: Leadership St. Raymond of Penafort, Springfield, VA
Horn, Rev. Ben, '22 (LEX) Mary, Queen of the Holy Rosary, Lexington, KY
Horn, Rev. Francis J., *O.S.A.* '75 (PH) [MON] St. Thomas Monastery, Villanova, PA
Horn, Rev. John, *S.J.* '85 (PMB) [SEM] St. Vincent de

Paul Regional Seminary, Boynton Beach, FL

Horn, Rev. Joseph, (DET) Curia: Administration; Consultative Bodies National Shrine of the Little Flower Basilica, Royal Oak, MI

Horn, Rev. Joseph K., *O.Praem.* '81 (ORG) [MON] Norbertine Fathers of Orange, Inc., Silverado, CA

Horn, Rev. Mark E., '15 (RC) St. Rose of Lima, Hill City, SD

Hornacek, Rev. Joseph F., '66 (MIL) Retired. Curia: Leadership

Hornat, Rev. Stephen William, *S.S.E.* '76 (MOB) Immaculate Conception Parish, Orrville, Orrville, AL; Our Lady Queen of Peace Parish, Selma, Selma, AL; [CAM] Marion Military Institute Campus Ministry, Selma, AL; [MON] Fathers of St. Edmund Southern Missions, Inc., Selma, AL

Hornicak, Rev. John Joseph, '03 (JOL) Holy Ghost, Wood Dale, IL; [EFT] Diocese of Joliet Priests' Pension Plan, Crest Hill, IL; [EFT] Diocese of Joliet Retired Priests' Other Benefits Plan, Crest Hill, IL

Horning, Rev. Edward, '04 (SD) Pastor of Our Lady of the Valley Catholic Parish in El Centro, a corporation sole, El Centro, CA

Horning, Rev. Jay, '18 (FTW) Curia: (>MO) Offices and Directors St. Bernard, Wabash, IN

Horning, Rev. Roy, '01 (LAN) Holy Rosary Parish Flint, Flint, MI

Horning, Rev. Roy Theodore, '01 (LAN) St. Mary Parish Mt. Morris, Mount Morris, MI

Horobets, Rev. Oleksiy, (STF) St. George, New York, NY

Horowski, Rev. Janusz, '95 (CHI) [EFT] Divine Word Techny Community Corporation, Techny, IL; [MON] Divine Word Residence, Techny, IL

Horrigan, Rev. Kevin P., '70 (BO) Retired.

Horrigan, Rev. Sean P., '98 (GAL) Curia: Leadership Christ the Redeemer, Houston, TX

Horton, Rev. Geoffrey, '08 (PEO) Central Catholic High School, Bloomington, IL; St. Patrick Church, Wapella, IL; [MIS] Central Catholic High School of Bloomington, Inc., Bloomington, IL

Horton, Rev. John C., '66 (PEO) Retired.

Horvath, Rev. Gerlac A., *O.Praem.* '46 (ORG) Retired.

Horvath, Rev. Pius L., *O.S.B.* '53 (SFR) Retired.

Hosak, Rev. Peter J., '83 (PSC) On Leave. Curia: Advisory Boards, Commissions, Committees, and Councils

Hose, Rev. Samuel, '91 (AUS) Retired.

Hosey, Rev. P. Keith, '56 (LFT) Retired.

Hosler, Rev. Gregory, '01 (PSC) St. John the Baptist, Lansford, PA; St. Michael, McAdoo, PA

Hospodar, Rev. Robert, (ALB) Curia: Leadership

Hospodar, Rev. Msgr. Robert, '78 (NY) Curia: Leadership

Hospodar, Rev. Robert J., '78 (PSC) SS. Peter and Paul, New York, NY

Host, Rev. Richard, '74 (GR) Retired.

Hostetler, Rev. Seth, '22 (CHY) St. Mary's Cathedral, Cheyenne, WY

Hostetter, Rev. Larry, '87 (OWN) On Special Assignment. Pres, Owensboro [COL] Brescia University, Owensboro, KY

Hostettler, Rev. Paul A., '50 (KNX) Retired.

Hostios, Rev. Jaime E., '07 (CAM) St. Joseph Catholic Church, East Camden, N.J. (Pro-Cathedral), Camden, NJ

Hotop, Rev. Louis R., *S.J.* '21 (BWN) San Felipe de Jesus, Brownsville, TX

Hotovy, Rev. Dennis W., '57 (LIN) Retired.

Hottinger, Rev. David, *PES* '21 (STP) St. Mark, St. Paul, MN

Hottinger, Rev. Paul, '75 (JOL) Retired.

Hottle, Rev. Maximilian, *O.F.M.* '61 (TUC) Retired.

Hotze, Rev. John V., '93 (DOD) Curia: Leadership

Hotze, Rev. John V., '93 (WCH) Curia: Leadership St. Michael the Archangel, Mulvane, KS; [NUR] Villa Maria, Inc., Mulvane, KS

Houbeck, Rev. James, (DET) St. Anastasia Parish Troy, Troy, MI

Houck, Rev. Gregory, '92 (CHI) (>JOL) [MON] Carmelite Provincial Office, Darien, IL

Houck, Rev. Gregory, *O.Carm* '92 (JOL) Our Lady of Mount Carmel, Darien, IL

Houck, Rev. Joshua, *FSSP* (Y) Queen of the Holy Rosary, Vienna, OH

Houde, Rev. Daniel, *O.SS.T.* '87 (MIA) Our Lady of the Holy Rosary - St. Richard Church, Palmetto Bay, FL

Houde, Rev. Daniel, *O.SS.T.* '87 (BAL) [MON] Holy Trinity Monastery, Sykesville, MD

Houde, Rev. Paul C., '96 (BUR) Retired.

Hough, Rev. Charles A., '12 (POC) Retired.

Hough, Rev. Charles A., '12 (POC) The Cathedral of Our Lady of Walsingham, Houston, TX

Houle, Rev. Msgr. Michael, '79 (STA) Curia: Leadership St. Paul's, Jacksonville Beach, FL

Houle, Rev. Roger A., '77 (PRO) Retired. [MON] St. John Vianney Residence, Providence, RI

Houle, Rev. Thomas, *OFM Cap* (NY) Retired. [MON] St. Clare Friary (Capuchin Franciscan Friars, Province of St. Mary), Yonkers, NY

Houlihan, Rev. John J., '64 (GF) Retired.

Houlihan, Rev. Michael K., '79 (LIN) Curia: Leadership St. Catherine's, Indianola, NE

Houlihan, Rev. Ralph D., *S.J.* '65 (STL) [MON] Saint Jean de Brebeuf Jesuit Community, St. Louis, MO

Houlis, Rev. Paul C., '11 (NEW) Church of St. Paul, Ramsey, NJ

Hourican, Rev. John J., '05 (MEM) St. William, Millington, TN

House, Very Rev. Christopher A., '02 (SFD) Curia: Leadership Christ the King, Springfield, IL

Householder, Rev. Paul C., '73 (PIT) Retired.

Houseknecht, Rev. Eric, '95 (PHX) St. Steven Roman Catholic Parish, Sun Lakes, AZ

Houseknecht, Rev. Eric, '95 (CHL) On Duty Outside Diocese. Diocese of Phoenix

Houser, Rev. Michael, (STL) On Duty Outside Diocese. Ireland

Houser, Rev. Samuel E, (HBG) Retired.

Housey, Rev. Walter L., *C.M.* '56 (LA) Retired.

Houston, Rev. James A., '68 (WOR) Retired.

Houston, Rev. Michael, *C.Ss.R.* (BAL) St. Mary, Annapolis, MD

Hovanec, Rev. Craig M., '03 (CLV) Nativity of the Blessed Virgin Mary, Lorain, OH; St. Peter, Lorain, OH

Hoveling, Rev. Michael, *O.S.B.* '18 (BUR) [MON] The Benedictine Foundation of the State of Vermont, Inc., Weston, VT

Hovley, Rev. Vincent E., *S.J.* '69 (COS) [MON] Sacred Heart Jesuit Community, Sedalia, CO

Howard, Rev. Anthony, *O.F.M.Conv.* '84 (OAK) St. Paul, San Pablo, CA

Howard, Rev. Arthur, '06 (KAL) Our Lady Queen of Peace, Bridgman, MI

Howard, Rev. C. Donald, *S.A.* '72 (WDC) Retired. [SEM] Atonement Seminary-Franciscan Friars of the Atonement, Washington, DC

Howard, Rev. David G., '06 (CIN) Our Lady of Good Hope, Miamisburg, OH; St. Henry, Dayton, OH; St. Mary of the Assumption, Springboro, OH

Howard, Rev. Evan Arthur, *O.F.M.* '55 (OAK) Retired. [NUR] Mercy Retirement and Care Center, Oakland, CA

Howard, Rev. John W., *S.J.* '68 (BO) [MON] Campion Center, Inc., Weston, MA

Howard, Rev. Joseph R., '02 (HBG) On Sick Leave.

Howard, Rev. Kenneth J., *S.S.J.* (GAL) Retired.

Howard, Rev. Randy, '01 (OWN) Curia: Advisory Boards, Commissions, Committees, and Councils Holy Spirit, Bowling Green, KY

Howard, Rev. Msgr. Robert E., '62 (LA) Retired.

Howarth, Rev. Joseph E., '80 (PH) Immaculate Conception, Jenkintown, PA

Howe, Rev. Edward, *C.R.* '10 (JOL) St. Scholastica, Woodridge, IL

Howe, Rev. J. Norbert, '56 (TOL) Retired.

Howe, Rev. Robert J., '94 (SAG) Blessed Sacrament Parish of Midland, Midland, MI

Howe, Rev. Spencer J., '13 (STP) Holy Cross, Minneapolis, MN

Howe, Rev. Stephen, (NY) [MON] Legionaries of Christ, Rye, NY

Howe, Rev. Timothy, *S.J.* '98 (SJN) Colegio San Ignacio de Loyola, San Juan, PR; San Ignacio de Loyola, San Juan, PR

Howell, Rev. Charles W., '98 (LEX) St. Elizabeth Ann Seton, Lexington, KY

Howell, Rev. David F., '78 (LAN) Retired. St. Mark the Evangelist Parish Grand Blanc, Grand Blanc, MI

Howell, Rev. Jonathan, '18 (BIR) Curia: Leadership St. Francis Xavier Catholic Parish, Birmingham, Birmingham, AL

Howell, Rev. Msgr. Michael, '74 (CC) Retired. Curia: Leadership

Howell, Rev. Patrick J., *S.J.* '72 (SEA) [COL] Seattle University, Seattle, WA; [MON] Arrupe Jesuit Community at Seattle University, Seattle, WA

Howell, Rev. Stephen H., '74 (SFR) Curia: Advisory Boards, Commissions, Committees, and Councils; Leadership

Howells, Rev. Mary David, *O.C.S.O.* '10 (TLS) [MON] Our Lady of the Annunciation of Clear Creek Abbey, Hulbert, OK

Hower, Rev. William J., '64 (MAD) Retired.

Howes, Rev. Marc C., '04 (LAV) Curia: Advisory Boards, Commissions, Committees, and Councils St. John Neumann, North Las Vegas, NV

Howley, Rev. Vincent, (NY) On Sick Leave.

Howren, Very Rev. John T., '96 (ATL) Curia: Leadership Sacred Heart of Jesus Catholic Church, Atlanta, Inc., Atlanta, GA; [CAM] Georgia Gwinnett College, Lawrenceville, GA

Hoye, Rev. Msgr. Daniel F., '72 (FR) Retired. Curia: Tribunal

Hoye, Rev. Justin E., '06 (KC) Curia: Leadership; Offices and Directors St. Catherine of Siena, Kansas City, MO; St. Thomas More, Kansas City, MO

Hoye, Rev. Ronald, *C.M.* '91 (STL) [MIS] Catholic Home Study, St. Louis, MO; [MON] Congregation of the Mission Vincentian Fathers Lazarist Residence, St. Louis, MO

Hoyer, Rev. Michael, '80 (MIA) Retired. [HOS] Holy Cross Hospital, Inc., Fort Lauderdale, FL

Hoying, Rev. David, (CIN) [MON] St. Charles, Celina, OH

Hoying, Rev. Ethan, '22 (CIN) Holy Trinity, Coldwater, OH; Mary Help of Christians, Fort Recovery, OH; St. Anthony, Fort Recovery, OH; St. Mary, Coldwater, OH; St. Paul, Fort Recovery, OH

Hoying, Rev. John, *C.PP.S.* '62 (CIN) Retired. [MON] St. Charles, Celina, OH

Hoying, Rev. Mark, *C.PP.S.* (CIN) Holy Redeemer, New Bremen, OH; St. Augustine, Minster, OH

Hoying, Rev. Mark, *C.PP.S.* '85 (TOL) St. John the Baptist, Continental, OH; St. Michael, Kalida, OH (>CIN) Most Precious Blood, Chickasaw, OH; (>CIN) Nativity of the Blessed Virgin Mary, Maria Stein, OH; (>CIN) St. John the Baptist, Maria Stein, OH; (>CIN) St. Rose, Maria Stein, OH; (>CIN) St. Sebastian, Celina, OH

Hoying, Rev. Vincent, *C.PP.S.* '58 (CIN) Retired.

Hoyles, Rev. Monte J., '06 (TOL) Holy Angels, Sandusky, OH; SS. Adalbert & Hedwig, Toledo, OH; SS. Peter and Paul, Sandusky, OH; St. Mary's, Sandusky, OH; [CEM] Catholic Cemeteries of Sandusky, Sandusky, OH

Hoyng, Rev. William, *C.PP.S.* '61 (CIN) Retired. [MON] St. Charles, Celina, OH

Hoyt, Friar Luke, *OP* (NY) Church of the Holy Innocents, Pleasantville, NY

Hoyt, Very Rev. Stephen M., '92 (CHL) St. Francis of Assisi, Lenoir, NC

Hoyumpa, Rev. Santiago M., '09 (GLD) Saint Mary of Mio, Mio, MI

Hradil, Rev. Yevhenii, (PSC) St. John the Baptist Church, Hazleton, PA; St. Mary's, Hazleton, PA

Hrebenko, Rev. Pawel M., '04 (BGP) Curia: Consultative Bodies The Church of the Holy Name of Jesus, Stamford, CT

Hreha, Rev. James D., '87 (WIL) Chap, Delaware Home & Hosp for the Chronically Ill St. Dennis, Galena, MD; St. Polycarp, Smyrna, DE

Hrezo, Very Rev. Paul, '00 (STU) Curia: Deaneries Christ Our Light Parish, Cambridge, OH

Hrezo, Very Rev. Paul E., '00 (STU) Curia: Deaneries [MIS] SS. Peter and Paul, Lore City, OH

Hritsko, Rev. William A., '98 (COL) Our Lady of Mt. Carmel, Buckeye Lake, OH; St. Leonard, Heath, OH

Hrubiak, Rev. Archpriest Dennis M., '70 (PRM) Retired.

Hrubiak, Rt. Rev. Mitred Archpriest Dennis M., '70 (PRM) Retired.

Hruby, Rev. Paul, '82 (LA) Retired.

Hruska, Very Rev. Timothy W., '96 (MAR) Curia: Advisory Boards, Commissions, Committees, and Councils St. Francis Xavier, Brimley, MI; St. Joseph, Rudyard, MI

Hrynkiw, Rev. Wasyl, '91 (STF) Saint Vladimir Ukrainian Catholic Church, Hempstead, NY

Hrytsyuk, Very Rev. Archpriest Volodymyr, '06 (SJP) Curia: Leadership; Offices and Directors St. Josaphat Cathedral, Parma, OH

Hsieh, Rev. Jacob, *O.Praem.* '15 (ORG) [MON] Norbertine Fathers of Orange, Inc., Silverado, CA

Hsieh, Rev. Jacob, *O. Praem* (LA) SS. Peter and Paul, Wilmington, CA

Hsu, Rev. Aloysius Ming-te, *SJ* '18 (OAK) [MON] Jesuit Fathers and Brothers, Berkeley, CA

Hsu, Rev. Luke (Chien-Pang), *OSB* '21 (GBG) [MON] Saint Vincent Archabbey, Latrobe, PA

Htun, Rev. Francis Than, '02 (SFR) Chap, San Francisco Gen Hosp Curia: Offices and Directors

Htwe, Rev. James Tin Mg, '98 (LA) St. John Vianney, Hacienda Heights, CA

Hua, Rev. Lam M., *M.M.* '14 (NY) [MON] Maryknoll Fathers and Brothers (Catholic Foreign Mission Society of America, Inc.), Ossining, NY

Hualpa, Rev. Matias, (MIA) Blessed Trinity, Virginia Gardens, FL

Huan, Rev. Joseph Van Tran, '73 (RIC) Retired.
Huard, Rev. Etienne, *O.S.B.* (KC) [MON] Conception Abbey (Benedictine Monks), Conception, MO; [SEM] Conception Seminary College, Conception, MO
Huard, Rev. Leo, *O.Carm.* '65 (JOL) Retired.
Hubba, Rev. Msgr. David C., '74 (NEW) St. Joseph, New Milford, NJ
Hubbard, Rev. J. Randall, '90 (L) Curia: Leadership Epiphany Catholic Church, Louisville, KY
Hubbard, Rev. Joseph, '20 (BO) St. Michael, North Andover, MA
Hubbert, Rev. Joseph G., *C.M.* '77 (BUF) [MON] Vincentian Community at Niagara University (Congregation of the Mission of St. Vincent de Paul), Niagara University, NY
Hubbs, Rev. Martin, *O.Carm.* '12 (SAN) [MON] Hermits of the Blessed Virgin Mary of Mount Carmel, Christoval, TX
Hubbs, Rev. Timothy L., '84 (CAM) Retired. On Duty Outside Diocese. Chap (Major), Arlington, VA
Huber, Rev. Aaron, '22 (CHL) St. Mark, Huntersville, NC
Huber, Rev. Henry P., '02 (DUB) Our Lady of Seven Dolors Church, Festina, Iowa, Fort Atkinson, IA; St. Aloysius Church (Calmar, Iowa), Calmar, IA; St. Francis Church, Ossian, Iowa, Ossian, IA; St. Teresa of Calcutta Faith Formation, Calmar, Iowa, Calmar, IA; St. Teresa of Calcutta School, Calmar, Iowa, Ossian, IA; St. Wenceslaus Church, Spillville, Iowa, Spillville, IA
Huber, Rev. J. William, '59 (PBL) Retired.
Huber, Rev. Justin A., '10 (WDC) Curia: Tribunal Our Lady of the Presentation, Poolesville, MD
Huber, Rev. Kevin R., '91 (GRY) Curia: Leadership St. Mary, Crown Point, IN
Huber, Rev. Msgr. Mark D., '94 (LIN) Curia: Leadership; Offices and Directors Sacred Heart, Beaver Crossing, NE
Huber, Rev. Matthew P., '87 (HEL) Retired.
Huber, Rev. Vincent, '11 (KCK) On Duty Outside Diocese. Christ the King, Sarasota, FL
Huber, Rev. Vincent, *F.S.S.P.* (VEN) Christ the King Parish in Sarasota, Inc., Sarasota, FL
Huber, Rev. Vincent J., '64 (STU) Retired. Curia: Offices and Directors
Huberfeld, Rev. Canon Aaron, *ICRSS* '10 (LC) [MIS] St. Mary's Roman Catholic Oratory, Wausau, WI
Hubertus, Rev. Msgr. Albert, '50 (SAT) Retired.
Hubertus, Rev. Msgr. Albert H., '50 (SAT) Retired. [NUR] Missionary Servants of St. Anthony (Padua Place), San Antonio, TX
Huberty, Rev. Ronald V., '90 (NU) Curia: Leadership; Offices and Directors SS. Peter & Paul, Ivanhoe, MN; St. Dionysius, Tyler, MN; St. Genevieve, Lake Benton, MN; St. John Cantius, Ivanhoe, MN; St. Leo, St. Leo, MN; St. Peter, Canby, MN
Hubmann, Rev. William, *C.PP.S.* '79 (KC) (>CIN) [MON] Society of the Precious Blood, United States Province, Inc., Dayton, OH
Huck, Rev. Charles Joseph, '06 (CR) Holy Rosary, Detroit Lakes, MN
Huck, Rev. Chuck, '06 (CR) Curia: Offices and Directors Holy Rosary School, ,
Hudak, Rev. Mark J., *O.F.M.* '93 (CIN) Roger Bacon High School, Cincinnati, OH; [MON] Brother Juniper Friary, Cincinnati, OH
Hudak, Rev. Ralph, '77 (CLV) Immaculate Heart of Mary, Cleveland, OH
Hudak, Rev. Richard E., '68 (CLV) Retired.
Hudak, Rev. Thomas R., '73 (SCR) Retired.
Hudert, Rev. John P., *M.M.* '62 (NY) Retired.
Hudgin, Rev. Christopher, *O.S.F.S.* '81 (TOL) Little Flower of Jesus, Toledo, OH
Hudgins, Rev. James C., '98 (ARL) St. Theresa, Ashburn, VA
Hudock, Rev. Msgr. Paul A., '98 (WH) On Leave.
Hudson, Rev. Joseph, *O.S.B.* (TLS) [MON] Our Lady of the Annunciation of Clear Creek Abbey, Hulbert, OK
Hudson, Rev. Paul, '10 (AUS) Sacred Heart, Elgin, TX
Hudzan, Rev. Volodymyr, '93 (STN) St. Michael, Mishawaka, IN
Hudziak, Rev. Jerome M., '64 (MIL) Retired.
Huebner, Rev. Christian, (WDC) St. Raphael, Rockville, MD
Huebner, Rev. Terrance J., '74 (MIL) Retired.
Huehlefeld, Very Rev. Matthew H., '96 (VIC) Curia: Leadership; Offices and Directors St. Joseph, Yoakum, TX
Huehlefeld, Very Rev. Matthew H., '96 (VIC) Curia: Leadership
Huemmer, Rev. David G., '10 (LFT) Curia: Pastoral Services
Huerta, Rev. Enrique, '86 (LA) St. Francis of Assisi, Los Angeles, CA
Huertas, Rev. Alvaro, '81 (MIA) Santa Barbara, Hialeah, FL
Huertas Colon, Rev. Ivan Luis, (SJN) Santo Cristo de la Agonia, Carolina, PR
Huesca, Rev. Omar A., '81 (MIA) Retired.
Huesing, Rev. Paul, (PMB) [MON] Paulist Fathers Residence, Vero Beach, FL
Huete, Rev. Francis W., *S.J.* '82 (NO) [MON] Jesuit Provincial Office (Catholic Society of Religious and Literary Education), New Orleans, LA
Huete, Rev. Francis William, *S.J.* '82 (STL) [MON] Leo Brown Jesuit Community, St. Louis, MO; [MON] USA Central & Southern Province, Society of Jesus, St. Louis, MO
Huff, Rev. Thomas M., '90 (LC) St. Mary, Gays Mills, WI; St. Patrick, Eastman, WI; St. Philip, Soldiers Grove, WI
Huffman, Rev. David L., '72 (STU) St. Ambrose, Little Hocking, OH
Huffman, Very Rev. Timothy J., '93 (STU) Curia: Deaneries St. Peter's, Steubenville, OH
Hug, Rev. James, *S.J.* (LAN) [CON] Motherhouse of the Sisters of St. Dominic, Congregation of the Most Holy Rosary, Adrian, MI
Huggins, Rev. Scott, '01 (JOL) St. Elizabeth Seton, Naperville, IL
Hughes, Rev. Anthony, '93 (LAV) Retired.
Hughes, Rev. Brian C., '81 (SC) St. Joseph's, Milford, IA; St. Mary's, Spirit Lake, IA
Hughes, Rev. Christopher, '98 (SFS) Holy Rosary Parish of Codington County, Kranzburg, SD; Saint Francis de Sales Parish of Hamlin County, Estelline, SD; Saint Mary Parish of Deuel County, Clear Lake, SD
Hughes, Rev. Msgr. Dennis E., '75 (SP) Retired.
Hughes, Rev. Derek, '86 (MRY) Curia: Offices and Directors Holy Eucharist, Corralitos, CA
Hughes, Rev. James A., '80 (BRK) Immaculate Conception, Astoria, NY
Hughes, Rev. John, '94 (BEA) St. Charles Borromeo, Nederland, TX
Hughes, Rev. Kenneth J., *S.J.* '66 (BO) [MON] Alberto Hurtado House, Boston, MA
Hughes, Rev. Mark F., '82 (WDC) Curia: Consultative Bodies Holy Redeemer, Kensington, MD
Hughes, Rev. Michael, *O.S.A.* '75 (PH) St. Thomas of Villanova Parish, Rosemont, PA
Hughes, Rev. Paul F., *O.M.I.* '73 (BWN) St. Eugene de Mazenod, Brownsville, TX
Hughes, Rev. Peter, '15 (STP) Immaculate Conception, Watertown, MN; St. Boniface, St. Bonifacius, MN; [CEM] St. Boniface Cemetery, St. Bonifacius, MN; [CEM] St. Mary of Czestochowa Cemetery, Delano, MN
Hughes, Rev. Raymond E., '02 (TR) Retired. [MON] Villa Vianney, Trenton, NJ
Hughes, Rev. Robert, *S.M.* '59 (SJ) [MON] The Marianist Center, Cupertino, CA
Hughes, Rev. Robert E., '90 (CAM) Curia: Advisory Boards, Commissions, Committees, and Councils; Clergy and Religious Services; Leadership; Pastoral Services; Tribunal
Hughes, Rev. Robert W., '68 (MAD) Retired.
Hughson, Rev. D. Thomas, *S.J.* '71 (MIL) [MON] Arrupe House Jesuit Community, Milwaukee, WI
Hughson, Rev. Robert S., '79 (BUF) Catholic Academy of Niagara Falls, Niagara Falls, NY; St. Vincent de Paul (St.Leo/Prince of Peace), Niagara Falls, NY
Hugo, Rev. Josh, (BRK) Our Lady Help of Christians, Brooklyn, NY
Hugo, Rev. William, (DET) [MON] St. Bonaventure Monastery, Detroit, MI
Huguley, Rev. Vernon F., '93 (BIR) Curia: Leadership St. Peter the Apostle Catholic Parish, Birmingham, Birmingham, AL; [EFT] St. Peter Child Development Center Fund, Birmingham, AL
Huhn, Rev. Thomas, *M.S.* '69 (HRT) [MIS] Missionaries of LaSalette, Hartford, CT
Huhtanan, Rev. Andrew, *O.M.V.* '83 (DEN) Holy Ghost Catholic Parish in Denver, Denver, CO
Hullinger, Rev. Ty S., '04 (BAL) Most Precious Blood, Baltimore, MD; St. Anthony of Padua, Baltimore, MD; St. Dominic, Baltimore, MD
Hulot, Rev. Vincent, *O.S.B.* '97 (TLS) [MON] Our Lady of the Annunciation of Clear Creek Abbey, Hulbert, OK
Hulshof, Rev. David F., '82 (SPC) On Special Assignment. Director of Apostolic Formation, PNAC in Rome
Hultquist, Rev. Thomas H., '76 (WOR) Immaculate Conception, Lancaster, MA
Humbrecht, Rev. Msgr. T. Allen, '72 (KNX) Curia: Leadership; Offices and Directors Holy Spirit Catholic Church, Soddy Daisy, TN; [MIS] Diocesan Council of Catholic Women, Knoxville, TN
Hume, Rev. Kenneth, '63 (P) Retired.
Humerickhouse, Rev. Matthew, '20 (Y) St. Luke, Boardman, OH
Hummel, Rev. Donald K., '78 (NEW) Retired. Annunciation, Paramus, NJ; Paramus Catholic High School, Paramus, NJ
Hummel, Rev. Matthew, (POC) St. John the Baptist, Bridgeport, PA
Hummer, Rev. Lawrence L., '73 (COL) Retired.
Hummerickhouse, Rev. Matthew, '20 (Y) St. Charles Borromeo, Boardman, OH
Humphrey, Rev. Brian, '19 (LA) On Academic Leave.
Humphrey, Rev. Delos A., *M.M.* '54 (NY) Retired. [MON] Maryknoll Fathers and Brothers (Catholic Foreign Mission Society of America, Inc.), Ossining, NY
Humphries, Rev. Ryan P., '05 (ALX) St. Edward, Tallulah, LA
Hund, Rev. Francis, '82 (KCK) Prince of Peace, Olathe, KS
Hund, Rev. Joseph, *O.F.M.* '89 (NO) St. Mary of the Angels, New Orleans, LA
Hund, Rev. William, *C.S.C.* '60 (P) Retired.
Hund, Rev. William, *C.S.C.* (FTW) [MIS] Holy Cross House, Notre Dame, IN
Hundt, Rev. Msgr. George F., '81 (PAT) Curia: Administration; Leadership St. Vincent Martyr, Madison, NJ
Hundt, Rev. Msgr. Robert P., '61 (LC) Retired. Curia: Offices and Directors [MIS] Holy Cross (Seminary) Diocesan Center, La Crosse, WI
Hunegar, Rev. Msgr. Richard, '73 (P) [CAM] Willamette University (Salem), Salem, OR
Huneger, Rev. Msgr. Richard, '73 (P) Chap, Santiam Corr Inst, Salem; Oregon State Penitentiary Curia: Offices and Directors St. Joseph, Salem, OR
Hung, Rev. Bernard T., '95 (AUS) St. Paul Catholic Church, Smithville, TX; Sts. Peter and Paul, Flatonia, TX
Hung, Rev. Le Trong, *C.Ss.R.* '08 (LA) [MON] Vietnamese Redemptorist Mission, Baldwin Park, CA
Hung, Rev. Peter, '67 (CHI) Retired.
Hung, Rev. Pham Quoc, *C.Ss.R.* '94 (LA) [MIS] The Redemptorist Vietnamese Mission Corporation, Baldwin Park, CA; [MON] Vietnamese Redemptorist Mission, Baldwin Park, CA
Hung Long Tran, Rev. Francis M., *CRM* '99 (SPC) [MON] Congregation of the Mother of the Redeemer, Carthage, MO; [SHR] Office of the Immaculate Heart of Mary Shrine, Carthage, MO
Hunke, Rev. Norman F., (OM) Retired.
Hunkler, Rev. Jerome, '83 (FAR) Retired.
Hunko, Rev. Gerard A., '91 (GLD) Saint Helen of St. Helen, Saint Helen, MI; Saint Mary of Grayling, Grayling, MI; Saint Michael of Roscommon, Roscommon, MI
Hunstiger, Rev. Thomas, '65 (STP) Retired.
Hunt, Rev. Daniel P., '12 (CIN) All Saints, Cincinnati, OH; St. Vincent Ferrer, Cincinnati, OH
Hunt, Rev. Dennis, '81 (LIN) St. George, Morse Bluff, NE
Hunt, Rev. Henry Clay, '09 (SAT) On Leave.
Hunt, Rev. James M., '83 (GI) Curia: Offices and Directors St. Joseph's, Broken Bow, NE
Hunt, Rev. John W., '68 (PRO) Retired.
Hunt, Rev. Kevin, *O.C.S.O.* '79 (WOR) [MON] St. Joseph's Abbey (Cistercian Abbey of Spencer, Inc., Cistercian Order of the Strict Observance (Trappists)), Spencer, MA
Hunt, Rev. Msgr. Luke, '67 (PT) Curia: Leadership; Offices and Directors Our Lady of the Assumption Mission, Pensacola Beach, FL; St. Ann, Gulf Breeze, FL
Hunt, Rev. Mark, '01 (NSH) St. Mary Villa Chapel, Nashville, TN; [CON] Sisters of Mercy of Nashville, TN, Inc., Nashville, TN
Hunt, Rev. Mark J., '85 (PH) On Special Assignment. Prof, Holy Family Univ - Newtown Campus, St John Bosco [COL] Holy Family University, Philadelphia, PA
Hunt, Rev. Richard D., *S.J.* '71 (NY) [MON] Kolhmann Hall Jesuit Community, Bronx, NY
Hunter, Rev. Alan, '77 (SFD) Retired. [HOS] HSHS Holy Family Hospital, Inc., Greenville, IL
Hunter, Rev. Douglas, '16 (IND) St. Roch Catholic Church, Indianapolis, Inc., Indianapolis, IN
Hunter, Rev. Eric, '72 (SP) Retired.
Hunter, Rev. John J., '86 (ALB) Retired.
Huon, Rev. Phan Phat, *C.Ss.R.* '53 (LA) [MON] Vietnamese Redemptorist Mission, Baldwin Park, CA
Hurbanczuk, Rev. Adam, '91 (HRT) The Church of S.S. Cyril & Methodius of Hartford, Connecticut, Hartford,

CT
Hurd, Rev. Robert E., *S.J.* '91 (CIN) [MON] Cincinnati Jesuit Community, Cincinnati, OH
Hurd, Rev. Stephen F., *S.J.* '80 (DET) [MON] Jesuit Community at the University of Detroit Mercy, Detroit, MI
Hurd, Rev. Timothy C., '92 (SHP) Curia: Leadership
Hurkes, Rev. Charles, *O.M.I.* (BO) [NUR] Immaculate Heart of Mary Residence, Tewksbury, MA
Hurlbert, Rev. James F., '90 (CHI) Nativity of Our Lord and St. Gabriel Parish, Chicago, IL
Hurley, Rev. Brian K., '02 (DET) Curia: Consultative Bodies Immaculate Conception Parish Lapeer, Lapeer, MI
Hurley, Rev. Briggs, (STA) St. Joseph, Jacksonville, FL
Hurley, Rev. Msgr. Edward, '70 (DM) Retired. Curia: Leadership; Offices and Directors
Hurley, Rev. Gerard, '76 (JKS) Curia: Consultative Bodies St. Paul, Flowood, MS
Hurley, Rev. John, '82 (WDC) Retired. St. Matthew Cathedral, Washington, DC
Hurley, Rev. John, '13 (SPR) Curia: Offices and Directors St. John the Evangelist, Agawam, MA
Hurley, Rev. John E., *C.S.P.* '77 (SFR) Old St. Mary's Cathedral & Chinese Mission, San Francisco, CA
Hurley, Rev. John W., '74 (CHI) Retired. St. Alphonsus Liguori, Prospect Heights, IL
Hurley, Rev. Kevin H., '13 (LFT) Holy Family, Gas City, IN; St. John the Evangelist, Hartford City, IN; St. Mary, Dunkirk, IN
Hurley, Rev. Michael J., *O.P.* '07 (SFR) Curia: Leadership St. Dominic's Catholic Church, San Francisco, CA; [MON] St. Dominic Priory, San Francisco, CA
Hurley, Rev. Paul K., '95 (BO) On Special Assignment. Curia: Consultative Bodies St. Mary, Winchester, MA
Hurley, Rev. Sean Patrick, *F.P.O.* '11 (BO) [MON] Franciscans of Primitive Observance, Lawrence, MA
Hurley, Rev. Msgr. Steven P., '03 (WIL) Curia: Administration; Advisory Boards, Commissions, Committees, and Councils; Leadership; Offices and Directors; Organizations (affiliated, inter-Diocesan, miscellaneous/other) St. Thomas the Apostle, Wilmington, DE; [MIS] Catholic Ministry to the Elderly, Inc., Wilmington, DE; [MIS] Catholic Press of Wilmington, Inc., Wilmington, DE; [MIS] Catholic Youth Organization, Inc., Wilmington, DE; [MIS] Diocese of Wilmington Schools, Inc., Wilmington, DE
Hurlimann, Rev. Jakob, '22 (AUS) St. Mary Cathedral, Austin, TX
Hurst, Rev. Paul F., '77 (CIN) Retired.
Hurst, Rev. Thomas R., *S.S.* '73 (ALB) On Duty Outside Diocese. St Mary's Seminary & Univ, Baltimore, MD
Hurst, Rev. Thomas R., *P.S.S.* '73 (BAL) Retired. [MON] Society of St. Sulpice, Province of the United States, Baltimore, MD
Hurtado, Rev. Mauricio, '10 (SAC) Pastor of St. Dominic Parish, Orland, A corporation sole, Orland, CA
Hurtado, Rev. Tomas, '04 (ORL) St. Augustine, Casselberry, FL
Hurtado-Badillo, Rev. Domingo, '93 (CHI) On Special Assignment.
Hurtado-Olazo, Rev. Marco, '02 (NEW) St. Catherine of Siena, Hillside, NJ; St. Rose of Lima, Newark, NJ
Hurtuk, Rev. Joseph, *S.M.* '74 (STP) St. Louis King of France, St. Paul, MN
Huse, Rev. Ralph G., *S.J.* '75 (STL) [MON] White House Retreat Jesuit Community, St. Louis, MO; [RTR] White House Retreat, St. Louis, MO
Huse, Rev. Robert, *O.A.R.* '56 (LA) [MON] Order of Augustinian Recollects (O.A.R.), St. Augustine Priory, Oxnard, CA
Huser, Rev. Jeremy S., '11 (WCH) Chap, Correctional Facility St. Bridget's, Scammon, KS; St. Joseph, Baxter Springs, KS; St. Patrick, Galena, KS; St. Rose, Columbus, KS
Huske, Rev. Leonard G., '56 (CHI) Retired.
Hussey, Rev. Edmund M., '58 (CIN) Retired.
Hussey, Rev. Michael, *O.M.I.* '60 (BEL) [MON] Missionary Oblates of Mary Immaculate - St. Henry's Oblate Residence, Belleville, IL
Hussey, Rev. Robert, *S.J.* '00 (ATL) Curia: Leadership St. Thomas More Catholic Church, Decatur, Inc., Decatur, GA; [MON] Atlanta Jesuit Community, Inc., Decatur, GA
Hussey, Rev. Robert M., *S.J.* '00 (BAL) [COL] Jesuit Community of Loyola University, Inc., Baltimore, MD; [MON] Jesuit Community of Loyola University Maryland, Inc., Baltimore, MD
Hust, Rev. David, '18 (GAL) St. Anthony of Padua, The Woodlands, TX
Husted, Rev. Richard, *O.F.M.* (PAT) [MON] St. Anthony Friary (Order of Friars Minor), Butler, NJ
Hutcherson, Rev. Bartholomew J., *O.P.* '97 (OAK) [MON] Order of Preachers (Province of the Most Holy Name of Jesus - Western Dominican Province), Oakland, CA
Hutchins, Rev. H. James, '67 (PH) Retired.
Hutchins, Rev. Michael, *S.V.D.* '75 (CHI) [MON] Divine Word Residence, Techny, IL
Hutchinson, Very Rev. Ronald, '94 (GR) Curia: Leadership Basilica of St. Adalbert, Grand Rapids, MI; St. Mary, Grand Rapids, MI; [EFT] Basilica of St. Adalbert Education Foundation, Grand Rapids, MI
Hutmacher, Rev. Robert, *O.F.M.* '79 (CHI) [MON] St. Peter's Friary, Chicago, IL
Hutsko, Rev. Basil, '79 (PRM) Retired. On Leave.
Hutsko, Rev. Joseph, '79 (HPM) Retired.
Hutsko, Rev. Archpriest Michael, '84 (PHU) Curia: Offices and Directors Assumption of B.V.M., Centralia, PA; Patronage of the Mother of God, Marion Heights, PA; SS. Peter and Paul, Mount Carmel, PA
Hutta, Rev. John A, '18 (ALN) Curia: Leadership
Hutter, Rev. John S., '92 (PH) St. Mary of the Assumption, Phoenixville, PA
Hutton, Rev. Leon, '80 (LA) Curia: Pastoral Services Our Lady of the Assumption, Ventura, CA
Huvane, Rev. James H., *M.M.* '70 (NY) Retired. [MON] Maryknoll Fathers and Brothers (Catholic Foreign Mission Society of America, Inc.), Ossining, NY
Huy Quyen, Rev. Nguyen, '73 (JOL) Retired. Queenship of Mary, Glen Ellyn, IL
Huynh, Rev. Benjamin Joseph, '13 (KAL) St. Catherine of Siena, Portage, MI
Huynh, Rev. Peter Loi, '02 (SJ) Our Lady of La Vang Parish, San Jose, CA
Huynh, Rev. Viet, '93 (PT) Corpus Christi, Destin, FL
Hvozdovic, Rev. Andrew S., '87 (SCR) Curia: Offices and Directors Gate of Heaven, Dallas, PA; Our Lady of Victory, Harveys Lake, PA
Hwang, Rev. James, *O.F.M.* (CHI) [MON] St. Peter's Friary, Chicago, IL
Hwang, Rev. Pil-koo, '17 (BRK) St. Robert Bellarmine, Bayside, NY
Hwang, Rev. Stephen, *E.C.* '95 (STU) [MON] Holy Family Hermitage, Bloomingdale, OH
Hyatt, Rev. Donald F., *C.S.B.* '68 (LSC) [MON] The Basilian Fathers of Las Cruces, Las Cruces, NM
Hyatt, Rev. John R., *S.J.* '77 (NEW) St. Aedan, Jersey City, NJ; [COL] St. Peter University Jesuit Community, Jersey City, NJ; [MIS] St. Aedan: St. Peter University Church, Jersey City, NJ; [MON] Jesuits of Saint Peter College, Inc., Jersey City, NJ
Hyatt, Rt. Rev. Archmandrite Martin A., *B.S.O.* '84 (NTN)
Hyclak, Rev. Walter J., '69 (CLV) Retired.
Hyde, Rev. Gregory, *SJ* (CLV) Gesu, University Heights, OH
Hyde, Rev. Gregory, *S.J.* (CLV) [COL] John Carroll Jesuit Community, University Heights, OH
Hyde, Rev. Mark, *S.D.B.* '81 (NO) St. John Bosco Roman Catholic Church, Harvey, Louisiana, Harvey, LA; St. Rosalie, Harvey, LA
Hyde, Very Rev. Patrick F., *O.P.* '16 (IND) Curia: Leadership St. Paul Catholic Center, Bloomington, Inc., Bloomington, IN; [CAM] St. Paul Catholic Center, Parish and Newman Center at Indiana University, Bloomington, IN; [MIS] Bloomington Springs Deanery, Indianapolis, IN
Hyde, Rev. Robert P., '88 (SY) Curia: Leadership St. Joseph, Camillus, NY
Hyeyeon, Rev. Kim (John), '04 (CHK) Korean Catholic Church of Saipan, Saipan, MP
Hying, Rev. Donald J., (STL) [MIS] Society of St. Vincent de Paul, National Council of the United States, Maryland Heights, MO
Hykavy, Rev. Roman, *OSBM* '94 (STN) St. Josaphat, Warren, MI
Hyland, Rev. James M., '81 (CHI) Most Holy Redeemer, Evergreen Park, IL
Hyland, Rev. Msgr. John M., '68 (DAV) Retired. [MON] St. Vincent Center, Davenport, IA
Hyman, Very Rev. Daniel W., '12 (KAL) Curia: Consultative Bodies; Deaneries St. Charles Borromeo, Coldwater, MI; St. Mary Assumption, Bronson, MI
Hyman, Rev. David, *O.F.M.* '60 (CHL) [MIS] Franciscan Center, Greensboro, NC; [MON] Franciscan Friary, Stoneville, NC; [RTR] St. Francis Springs Prayer Center, Stoneville, NC
Hyman, Rev. Robert A., (GLP) St. Anthony, McNary, AZ
Hyman, Rev. Robert A., '61 (TUC) Retired.
Hymel, Rev. Ray A., '87 (NO) St. Gertrude, Des Allemands, LA
Hynes, Rev. Aidan, '81 (PMB) St. Christopher, Hobe Sound, FL
Hynes, Rev. Msgr. Christopher J., '92 (NEW) Curia: Offices and Directors [COL] Seton Hall University, South Orange, NJ
Hynes, Rev. John M., '65 (WIL) St. Catherine of Siena, Wilmington, DE
Hynes, Rev. Msgr. Richard P., '72 (CHI) Retired.
Hypolite, Rev. Douglas J., *S.J.* '80 (GAL) Strake Jesuit College Preparatory Inc., Houston, TX
Iaconis, Rev. Anthony, '97 (RVC) Curia: Leadership Church of St. Mary, East Islip, NY; St. Peter the Apostle, Islip Terrace, NY
Iacovacci, Rev. Msgr. Nicholas J., '51 (PRO) Retired.
Ianelli, Rev. Robert A., '12 (PH) St. Katharine Drexel, Chester, PA
Iannacone, Rev. Timothy, '17 (BGP) On Leave. St. Edward the Confessor, New Fairfield, CT
Iannizzotto, Rev. Christopher, (PMB) St. Jude, Boca Raton, FL
Iannizzotto, Rev. Christopher J., *O.Carm.* '08 (NY) St. Joseph, Bronx, NY
Iannone, Rev. Raphael, *O.F.M.Cap.* '64 (NY) St. Francis de Sales, Phoenicia, NY; [MON] St. Joseph Friary (Capuchin Franciscans, Province of St. Mary), New Paltz, NY
Iannotti, Rev. Pascal A., '61 (ALB) Retired.
Ianucci, Rev. Thomas, '94 (RIC) Curia: (>MO) Offices and Directors
Ianucci, Rev. Thomas, '94 (RIC) Military Chap
Iaquinta, Rev. Patsy J., '70 (WH) Retired.
Iaquinto, Rev. Richard, *O.S.B.* '68 (BUR) [MON] The Benedictine Foundation of the State of Vermont, Inc., Weston, VT
Iasiello, Rev. Louis, (ALB) [COL] Siena College, Loudonville, NY
Ibach, Very Rev. Michael J., '73 (YAK) Curia: Leadership; Offices and Directors Holy Family, Yakima, WA
Ibañez, Rev. Juan Diego, '99 (POD) Curia: Clergy and Religious Services
Ibarra, Rev. Alexis, (LA) St. John Chrysostom, Inglewood, CA
Ibarra, Rev. Arnold, '00 (SAT) St Lawrence the Martyr Catholic Church, San Antonio, TX
Ibarra, Rev. Brando, '99 (PAT) Curia: Administration; Leadership St. Mary's, Paterson, NJ
Ibarra, Rev. Javier, *I.V.E.* (WIN) SS. Peter and Paul Catholic Church, Mankato, MN; [SEM] IVE Formation Program, Inc., Mankato, MN
Ibarra, Rev. Javier, *I.V.E.* '06 (WDC) St. James, Mount Rainier, MD
Ibarra, Rev. Juan Jose, *O.F.M* (LAR) Our Lady of Guadalupe, Hebbronville, TX
Ibarra, Rev. Manuel, '98 (LSC) On Sick Leave.
Ibarra, Rev. Martin, *O.F.M.* '08 (OAK) [MON] Franciscan Friars of California (Province of St. Barbara), Oakland, CA (>TUC) San Xavier Mission Roman Catholic Parish - Tucson, Tucson, AZ
Ibarra, Rev. Martin D., '07 (CHI) SS. Viator and Wenceslaus Parish, Chicago, IL
Ibay, Rev. Yul, '98 (CC) Sacred Heart, Sinton, TX
Ibe, Rev. Nicholas, (NY) Chap, Calvary Hosp, Bronx
Ibe, Rev. Reginald, (SB) Holy Family Parish, Hesperia, CA
Ibe, Rev. Sanctus K., '00 (MAD) Holy Angels Congregation, Sauk County WI, Inc., La Valle, WI
Ibebuike, Rev. Faustinus, '06 (GLP) Our Lady of Sorrows, Ceboyeta, NM; St. Jude, Tuba City, AZ
Ibegbulem, Rev. Andrew, *OSA* (SFR) Our Lady of Lourdes, San Francisco, CA; St. Paul of the Shipwreck, San Francisco, CA
Ibegbunam, Rev. Anthony, (SB) St. Joan of Arc, Blythe, CA
Ibeh, Rev. Eliseus, *M.S.P.* '89 (GAL) St. Nicholas, Houston, TX
Ibeh, Rev. Hyacinth, (SB) St. Joan of Arc, Victorville, CA
Ibeh, Rev. Ikechukwu Titus, (SB) Chap, Chuckawalla Valley State Prison, Blythe
Ibeh, Rev. James Uzoma, *C.S.Sp.* '96 (LR) St. Andrew, Marianna, AR; St. Francis of Assisi, Forrest City, AR; St. John the Baptist, Brinkley, AR; St. Mary, Helena, AR; St. Mary of the Lake Church, Horseshoe Lake, AR
Ibeh, Rev. Livinus "Martin", '18 (STA) Chaplain, Flagler Hospital Our Lady of Good Counsel, St. Augustine, FL
Ibeh, Rev. Luke, '00 (NY) St. Augustine Our Lady of Victory, Bronx, NY
Ibeh, Rev. Valentine, (SR) [HOS] Providence Queen of the Family Medical Center (Providence Queen of the Valley Medical Center), Napa, CA
Ibemere, Rev. Julian, '98 (OWN) St. Michael the Archangel, Oak Grove, KY
Ibeneme, Rev. Desmond, (TLS) SS. Peter and Paul,

Cushing, OK; St. John, Pawnee, OK
Ibiapina, Rev. Thiago, '22 (WOR) Curia: Offices and Directors Annunciation Parish, Gardner, MA
Ibiwoye, Rev. Joseph, *MSP* (BEA) Our Mother of Mercy, Beaumont, TX
Ibok, Rev. Dominic, (SPC) Chap, Southeast Corr Ctr, Charleston Sacred Heart, Caruthersville, MO
Ibok, Rev. Dominic, (MO) Curia: Offices and Directors
Ibok, Rev. Matthew, '96 (STA) Cathedral - Basilica of St. Augustine, St. Augustine, FL; Corpus Christi, St. Augustine, FL
Ichidi, Rev. Emmanuel M., *P.S.S.* '11 (BAL) [MIS] St. Mary's Seminary & University, Baltimore, MD; [MON] Society of St. Sulpice, Province of the United States, Baltimore, MD
Idagbo, Rev. Osang, *C.M.* '05 (BEL) Holy Family, Cahokia, IL; Sacred Heart of Jesus, Dupo, IL
Idler, Rev. Peter M., '97 (CAM) Chap, Part Time, Federal Corr Inst, Fairton
Idler, Rev. Peter M., '97 (CAM) The Parish of All Saints, Millville, N.J., Millville, NJ
Idoko, Rev. Stephen, (SFR) St. Vincent de Paul, San Francisco, CA
Idomele, Rev. Joseph O., '95 (MO) Curia: Offices and Directors
Idra, Rev. Augustine L., *A.J.* '97 (ALN) [MIS] Apostles of Jesus, Northampton, PA
Idzik, Rev. George, '73 (NEW) Retired.
Ifamilik, Rev. Robert, '15 (CI) St. Paul, Kolonia, Pohnpei, FM; [MON] Vicariate Residence, Kolonia, Pohnpei, FM
Ifele, Rev. Andrew, '89 (SFE) St. Anthony-Questa, Questa, NM
Ifionu, Rev. Bartholomew, *SMMM* '04 (FRS) St. Patrick, Kerman, CA; St. Paul, Tranquillity, CA
Ifkovits, Rev. Edward, (BO) [MON] Campion Health & Wellness, Inc., Weston, MA
Igboerika, Rev. Maurice C, (SFR) Our Lady of the Pillar, Half Moon Bay, CA
Igbogidi, Rev. Raymond, '98 (NO) St. Christopher the Martyr, Metairie, LA
Ighacho, Rev. John, '90 (OWN) St. Joseph, Central City, KY
Iglesias, Rev. Antonio Romero, *MM.SS.CC.* (SJN) San Juan Bautista de la Salle, Bayamon, PR
Iglesias, Rev. Clement, '58 (BEA) Retired.
Ignacio, Rev. Alejandro, '74 (FRS) Retired.
Ignacio, Rev. Rodelio Santos, '08 (SLC) Blessed Sacrament LLC 201, Sandy, UT
Ignacio, Rev. Simon, (MO) Curia: Offices and Directors
Ignasik, Rev. Slawomir, '00 (JOL) On Special Assignment. Missionary in Kenya
Ignaszak, Rev. Michael A., '84 (MIL) St. John Paul II Congregation, Milwaukee, WI
Ignatius, Rev. John, *SCJ* '13 (DEN) On Duty Outside Diocese. [MON] Servants of Christ Jesus, Denver, CO
Igoe, Rev. Martin S., '62 (BGP) Retired. [MON] The Catherine Dennis Keefe Queen of the Clergy Retired Priests' Residence, Stamford, CT
Igrobay, Rev. Manuel D., '89 (SFR) Our Lady of Perpetual Help, Daly City, CA; St. Luke, Foster City, CA; St. Timothy, San Mateo, CA
Igwegbe, Rev. Azubuike, '05 (RVC) Chap, Northwell at Glen Cove
Igwegbe, Rev. Azubuike Anthony Clifford, (RVC) St. Boniface Martyr, Sea Cliff, NY
Igwenagu, Rev. Callistus, (GF) St. Joseph, Hardin, MT
Igwenwanne, Rev. Fidelis, '90 (PHX) Chap, Mercy Gilbert Med Ctr, Gilbert; Chandler Rgnl Med Ctr
Igwenwanne, Rev. Fidelis, (MO) Curia: Offices and Directors
Igweonu, Rev. Romanus, '92 (BUR) All Saints Parish Charitable Trust, Richford, VT; St. Anthony, Sheldon Springs, VT; St. John the Baptist, Enosburg Falls, VT
Igwilo, Rev. Collins, (RC) St. John the Baptist, Custer, SD; [MIS] St. James the Apostle, Edgemont, SD
Igwilo, Rev. Peter, '92 (WIL) Chap, Veteran's Hosp, Elsmere
Igwilo, Rev. Peter C., (MO) Curia: Offices and Directors
Iheaka, Rev. Emmanuel K., '90 (PH) Chap, Veterans Administration Med Ctr, Coatesville St. Peter, West Brandywine, PA
Iheaka, Rev. Emmanuel K., '90 (MO) Curia: Offices and Directors
Iheanacho, Rev. Kenneth, '90 (TLS) Sacred Heart, Skiatook, OK
Ihedioha, Rev. Hilary A., '85 (SAN) Our Lady of Perpetual Help, Ozona, TX
Ihediohamma, Rev. Paschal C., '06 (JC) Immaculate Conception, Brookfield, MO; St. Bonaventure, Marceline, MO; St. Raphael, Indian Grove, MO
Ihejirika, Rev. Kingsley, (SPR) Saint Elizabeth Ann Seton, Northampton, MA
Iheme, Rev. Iuvenis, *CM* '09 (BEL) Our Lady of Lourdes, Sparta, IL; St. Pius V, Walsh, IL
Iheme, Rev. Iuvenis N., *C.M.* '09 (BEL) St. Boniface, Evansville, IL
Ihemedu, Rev. Emmanuel I., '06 (HRT) Saint John Paul the Great Parish Corporation, Torrington, CT
Ihenacho, Rev. David, (BRK) Most Precious Blood – Ss. Simon and Jude, Brooklyn, NY
Ihim, Rev. Remigius, (B) St. Thomas the Apostle, Coeur d'Alene, ID
Ihm, Rev. Gregory S., '10 (MAD) Curia: Leadership; Offices and Directors St. Charles Borromeo, Cassville, WI; St. John, Patch Grove, WI; St. Mary, Bloomington, WI; St. Mary Help of Christians, Glen Haven, WI
Ihnatowicz, Rev. Janusz, '62 (GAL) [MON] Keon House, Houston, TX
Ihuoma, Rev. Stanley, *S.S.J.* '10 (NO) St. Raymond-St. Leo the Great, New Orleans, LA
IIoh, Rev. Theodore, (RVC) St. Raymond's, East Rockaway, NY
Ike, Rev. Anthony, (MO) Curia: Offices and Directors
Ike, Rev. Anthony, (OM) Holy Cross, Omaha, NE
Ike, Rev. Hilary, (MO) Curia: Offices and Directors
Ike, Rev. Hilary C., '04 (COL) Curia: Offices and Directors St. Mary, Groveport, OH; [MIS] The Nigerian Catholic Community in Columbus, Ohio, Inc., Columbus, OH
Ike, Very Rev. Roberto M., '94 (JC) Curia: Deaneries St. Andrew, Holts Summit, MO
Ike, Rev. Romanus, (SB) Chap, Loma Linda Univ Med Ctr, Loma Linda
Ikeatuegwu, Rev. James Nebolisa, (SAT) St. Mary Magdalen, Brackettville, TX
Ikemeh, Rev. JohnBosco, *O.P.* '96 (CHR) Chap, Medical Univ of South Carolina, Charleston
Ikeocha, Rev. Ikechukwu, '00 (LA) On Administrative Leave.
Ikponko, Rev. John, '94 (TUC) Saint Odilia Roman Catholic Community - Tucson, Oro Valley, AZ
Ikponko, Rev. John, (TUC) Sacred Heart Roman Catholic Parish - Parker, Parker, AZ
Ikuelogbon, Rev. Moses, '19 (BUF) Our Lady of Peace, Salamanca, NY
Ilango, Rev. Xavier, '88 (CR) Curia: Offices and Directors SS. Peter and Paul, Warren, MN; St. Joseph, Oslo, MN; St. Mary (Euclid), Euclid, MN
Ilano, Rev. Francis, '06 (LA) St. Philomena, Carson, CA
Ilano, Rev. Jovencio, '96 (RIC) Retired.
Ileka, Rev. Sylvester, '00 (RVC) Curia: (>MO) Offices and Directors St. Martin of Tours, Bethpage, NY
Ilg, Rev. Edmond P, (NEW) Our Lady of Victories, Harrington Park, NJ
Ilg, Rev. Philip, (WDC) Mother Seton Parish, Germantown, MD
Ilg, Rev. Phillip, '16 (WDC) St. Mary, Laurel, MD
Ilgen, Rev. Timothy W., '03 (SEA) Our Lady of Good Help, Hoquiam, WA; Sacred Heart of Jesus, Lacey, WA; St. Jerome, Ocean Shores, WA; St. Joseph, Elma, WA; St. Mary, Aberdeen, WA
Ilijic, Rev. Sasa, (BRK) Most Precious Blood, Long Island City, NY
Illes, Rev. Joseph Joseph, '19 (MET) Church of the Immaculate Conception, Somerville, NJ
Illikattil, Rev. Mathew K., '71 (KAL) Retired.
Illikkal, Rev. George, *C.M.I.* '05 (L) St. Mary Magdalen of Pazzi, Payneville, KY; St. Theresa, Payneville, KY
Illiotes, Rev. Alien, (FAJ) Nuestra Senora del Rosario, Naguabo, PR
Illo, Rev. Joseph, '91 (STO) On Duty Outside Diocese. Star of the Sea Catholic Church
Illo, Rev. Joseph, '91 (SFR) Star of the Sea, San Francisco, CA
Ilnicki, Rev. Roman Theodosious, *O.B.S.M* '88 (STN) Curia: Offices and Directors Nativity of B.V.M., Palos Park, IL
Ilnicki, Rev. Theodosius (Roman), *O.S.B.M.* '88 (RVC) [MON] St. Josaphat's Monastery, Novitiate and Retreat House, Glen Cove, NY
Iloha, Rev. Christopher, (LA) St. Pancratius, Lakewood, CA
Ilokaba, Rev. Damian, '86 (DAV) VA Med Ctr, Iowa City Ss. Joseph and Cabrini Catholic Church, East Pleasant Plain, IA
Ilokaba, Rev. Damian O., '86 (MO) Curia: Offices and Directors
Imamshah, Rev. Harold, '90 (ALX) On Leave.
Imbao, Rev. Eric, *C.I.C.M.* '16 (R) St. Catherine of Siena, Tarboro, NC
Imbarrato, Rev. Stephen, '05 (SFE) Retired.
Imbya, Rev. Timothy, *V.C.* '16 (TUC) Immaculate Conception & Guadalupe Missions Roman Catholic Parish & Guadalupe Mission - Yuma, Yuma, AZ
Imholte, Rev. Otto, *S.S.C.* '63 (OM) Retired.
Iminga, Rev. Wilfredo, *M.S.* (SB) Our Lady of Lourdes, Montclair, CA; [MON] The Pacific Region Missionaries of Our Lady of La Salette, MS, Moreno Valley, CA
Immel, Rev. Eric, *S.J.* (BO) (>OM) [MON] Jesuit Community at Creighton University, Omaha, NE
Imming, Rev. Donald, '60 (SFS) Retired.
Imo, Rev. Cletus, '91 (SB) Saint John XXIII Catholic Community, Inc., Fontana, CA
Imoru, Rev. Godwin B, '04 (MOB) St. James Major, Prichard, AL
Imperial, Rev. Michael Montalban, '08 (RIC) St. Peter the Apostle Catholic Church, Onley, VA
Inai, Rev. Ghislain, *SMA* '04 (PEO) Corpus Christi, Galesburg, IL; Immaculate Heart of Mary, Galesburg, IL; Sacred Heart, Abingdon, IL; St. Patrick's, Galesburg, IL (>NEW) [MON] Society of African Missions, Provincialate, S.M.A. Fathers, Tenafly, NJ
Inameti, Rev. Samuel M, '19 (STL) St. Margaret Mary Alacoque Catholic Church, St. Louis, MO
Incardona, Rev. Victor, *M.I.C.* (SPR) [MON] Congregation of Marian Fathers of The Immaculate Conception of the Most Blessed Virgin Mary, Stockbridge, MA
Ince, Rev. Michael W., '64 (STP) Retired. [CEM] Calvary Cemetery, Waterville, MN
Indrias, Rev. Pervais, '87 (MET) Sacred Heart, South Plainfield, NJ
Inekwere, Rev. Bede, '95 (DM) [NUR] Bishop Drumm Retirement Center, Johnston, IA
Infanger, Rev. Andrew, '18 (MIL) Curia: Leadership Holy Family Congregation, Whitefish Bay, WI; St. Robert's Congregation, Shorewood, WI; [CAM] Catholic Campus Ministry Newman Center - U.W. Milwaukee, Milwaukee, WI
Infanger, Rev. Frank, '02 (JOL) On Leave.
Infanger, Rev. Peter, '20 (JOL) St. Thomas the Apostle, Naperville, IL
Infante, Rev. Cesar A., '15 (NEW) St. John the Evangelist, Bergenfield, NJ; St. Joseph of the Palisades, West New York, NJ
Infante, Rev. Donato, '15 (WOR) Curia: Offices and Directors
Infante, Rev. Joseph, '92 (RNO) Chap, Renown Med Ctr, Reno; VA Sierra Nevada Hosp, Reno St. Robert Bellarmine, Fernley, NV
Infante, Rev. Richard A., '92 (PIT) St. Paul of the Cross, Pittsburgh, PA
Infanti, Rev. Anthony, (CAM) Christ the Good Shepherd Parish, Vineland, N.J., Vineland, NJ
Ingalls, Rev. Victor P., '12 (MOB) Curia: Offices and Directors Cathedral-Basilica of the Immaculate Conception Parish, Mobile, Mobile, AL
Ingels, Rev. Kyle, '05 (COS) Curia: Offices and Directors
Ingemie, Rev. Dominic, '67 (ALB) Retired. Curia: Offices and Directors Transfiguration Parish, Schaghticoke, NY
Ingham, Rev. G. Nicholas, *O.P.* '81 (PRO) [MON] St. Thomas Aquinas Priory at Providence College, Providence, RI
Ingham, Rev. Msgr. Jeffrey A., '75 (R) Curia: Leadership St. Luke the Evangelist, Raleigh, NC
Ingham, Rev. Nicholas, *O.P.* '81 (Y) St. Dominic, Youngstown, OH
Ingold, Rev. Michael L., '91 (GB) St. Francis Xavier, De Pere, WI; St. Mary, De Pere, WI
Ingram, Rev. Brian, '90 (RVC) St. Lawrence the Martyr, Sayville, NY
Ingram, Rev. Stephen, (DAL) St. Joseph Catholic Parish - Richardson, Richardson, TX
Ingram, Rev. Walter Y. (Mike), '02 (SAV) St. Teresa of Avila, Grovetown, GA
Injoalu, Rev. Stephen, '15 (PBL) Our Lady of the Assumption, Westcliffe, CO; St. Benedict, Florence, CO
Inke, Rev. Alexander, *A.J.* '02 (MO) Curia: Offices and Directors
Inman, Rev. Robert D., '03 (YAK) Retired.
Innaiah, Rev. Arul Raj, '02 (GI) St. John the Baptist, Crawford, NE
Innocenti, Rev. Mark, '99 (SCL) Curia: Leadership The Church of St. Andrew, Elk River, MN
Insco, Rev. Caleb, *FSSP* '16 (SEA) North American Martyrs Personal Parish, Edmonds, WA
Inserra, Rev. John J., '03 (BGP) The Cathedral Parish, Bridgeport, CT
Inskip, Rev. Jonathan, *M.I.C.* '15 (SPR) [MON] Congregation of Marian Fathers of The Immaculate Conception of the Most Blessed Virgin Mary, Stockbridge, MA
Intal, Rev. Arlan, *M.S.* '05 (HON) St. Anthony, Honolulu, HI
Intes, Rev. Jesryll, (MO) Curia: Offices and Directors

Intovigne, Rev. Raymond D., '64 (NOR) Curia: Offices and Directors
Intranuovo, Rev. Ralph, *S.C.J.* '83 (SP) Retired. [MON] Priests of the Sacred Heart, Pinellas Park, FL
Introini, Rev. Msgr. Elso C., (PAT) Retired.
Introvigne, Rev. Raymond, '64 (NOR) Retired. Sacred Heart, Taftville, CT
Invernizzi, Rev. Matteo, *FSCB* (DEN) Nativity of Our Lord Catholic Parish in Broomfield, Broomfield, CO
Inwang, Rev. Augustine Etemma, *M.S.P.* '90 (BAL) Transfiguration Catholic Community, Baltimore, MD; [HOS] Mercy Health Services Inc., Baltimore, MD
Iodice, Rev. Ciro, *O.F.M.* '72 (NY) [MON] Franciscan Province of the Immaculate Conception, New York, NY
Iorchir, Rev. Manasseh, *VC* '10 (PHX) St. Benedict Roman Catholic Parish, Phoenix, AZ
Iori, Rev. Claudio, *C.S.J.* '80 (LA) St. Elizabeth, Lake Hughes, CA
Iorio, Rev. Peter J., '93 (KNX) Curia: Leadership; Offices and Directors Our Lady of Fatima, Alcoa, TN
Iorlam, Rev. Clement, (SD) Curia: Advisory Boards, Commissions, Committees, and Councils
Iorliam, Rev. Clement, (SD) Chap, Scripps Mercy Hosp; UCSD Med Ctr
Iott, Friar Martin, *O.P.* '70 (GAL) Holy Rosary, Houston, TX
Iovino, Rev. Paul, '61 (PAT) Retired.
Ipolito, Rev. Pascal D., '70 (BUF) Retired. On Administrative Leave.
Ireland, Rev. Dave R., '83 (CLV) Curia: Advisory Boards, Commissions, Committees, and Councils Sacred Heart of Jesus Parish, South Euclid, OH
Iriarte, Rev. Edgardo, '95 (PHX) St. Mary Roman Catholic Parish Chandler, Chandler, AZ
Iriarte, Rev. Santiago, '12 (FRS) St. Ann, Ridgecrest, CA
Irish, Rev. Robert L., '92 (LAN) Curia: Leadership
Irizarry, Rev. Alan, (MO) Curia: Offices and Directors
Irizarry, Rev. Alan M., '83 (ARE) On Duty Outside Diocese. Fayetteville, NC Curia: (>MO) Offices and Directors
Irizarry Roman, Rev. Elvin A., '97 (ARE) San Pedro y San Pablo, Utuado, PR
Irizarry Santana, Rev. Jose F, *ofm Cap.* '01 (ARE) San Miguel Arcangel, Utuado, PR; [MIS] Fondita Santa Marta, Utuado, PR
Irizarry Santana, Rev. Jose F., '01 (ARE) [MIS] Chapel Nuestra Senora del Perpetuo Socorro, Utuado, PR; [MIS] Chapel San Fidel, Utuado, PR; [MIS] Chapel San Jose, Utuado, PR; [MIS] Chapel San Martin de Porres, Utuado, PR
Irizarry-Santana, Rev. Jose Fernando, *O.F.M.Cap.* '01 (ARE) (>SJN) [MON] The Custody of Saint John the Baptist, Puerto Rico, of the Order Friars Minor Capuchin, San Juan, PR
Iromenu, Rev. Anthony, '95 (FRS) Sacred Heart, Dos Palos, CA
Ironuma, Rev. Donatus, (SPR) Chap, Mercy Med Ctr
Ironuma, Rev. Donatus, '94 (SPR) Mary Mother of Hope Parish, Springfield, MA; [HOS] Trinity Health - Mercy Medical Center (Catholic Health Ministries - Trinity Health, Livonia, MI), Springfield, MA
Iroot, Rev. Francis, *A.J.* '01 (ALN) St. Joseph the Worker, Orefield, PA
Irudayanathan, Rev. Valanarasu, (STA) St. Paul's, Jacksonville Beach, FL
Irudayaraj, Rev. Amalanathan, '91 (P) St. Francis, Sherwood, OR
Irudayaraj, Rev. Amirtham, (P) St. James, McMinnville, OR
Irudayasamy, Rev. Albert, (WOR) St. Anne, Southborough, MA
Iruthayasamy, Rev. Augustin, *IVDei* (MOB) Our Lady of Sorrow Mission Parish, Fairford, Fairford, AL; St. Peter the Apostle, Chastang, AL
Iruthayasamy, Rev. Paul Vincent Ravi, *HGN* '01 (MOB) St. Thomas by the Sea, Orange Beach, AL
Irving, Rev. Alfred, Retired.
Irving, Rev. Alfred E., '71 (PRT) Retired.
Irving, Rev. G. Peter, '83 (LA) Holy Innocents, Long Beach, CA
Irwin, Rev. Craig, '22 (TOL) [MIS] Gesu Parish, Toledo, OH; [MIS] St. Pius X, Toledo, OH
Irwin, Rev. Joseph M., '05 (OKL) Curia: Clergy and Religious Services; Consultative Bodies St. Joseph's, Norman, OK
Irwin, Rev. Msgr. Kevin W., '71 (NY) Retired. (>WDC) [COL] Catholic University of America, The, Washington, DC
Irwin, Rev. Michael, (FWT) Retired.
Irwin, Rev. Michael Dennis, '01 (MOB) St. Joseph Parish, Prattville, Prattville, AL
Irwin, Rev. Msgr. Patrick, '69 (SP) Retired.
Irwin, Rev. Robert, '78 (FAR) Retired.
Isaac, Rev. Emmanuel, *O.S.A.* '22 (LA) St. Thomas Aquinas, Ojai, CA
Isaac, Rev. Guency, '05 (ALN) St. Jane Frances de Chantal, Easton, PA
Isaac, Rev. Jose, (RNO) Curia: Offices and Directors
Isaac, Rev. Justin, *H.G.N.* '02 (MOB) Curia: Leadership Our Mother of Mercy Parish, Mobile, Prichard, AL; St. Francis Xavier Parish, Mobile, Mobile, AL
Isaac, Rev. Mathieu, (HRT) Saint Justin - Saint Michael Parish Corporation, Hartford, CT
Isaac, Rev. Stephan A., '16 (ALN) Curia: Leadership Allentown Central Catholic High School, Inc., Allentown, PA; Cathedral of St. Catharine of Siena, Allentown, PA
Isaac, Rev. Tariq, '93 (PH) Curia: Evangelization St. William, Philadelphia, PA
Isaacson, Rev. James, *S.J.C.* '04 (CHI) [MIS] Canons Regular of Saint John Cantius, Chicago, IL
Isaacson, Rev. James E., *S.J.C.* '04 (SFD) Curia: Leadership St. Katharine Drexel, Springfield, IL
Isenbarger, Rev. Brian, '22 (FTW) St. Vincent de Paul, Fort Wayne, IN
Isenberg, Rev. Michael C., '13 (ARL) Curia: Offices and Directors; Tribunal St. Philip, Falls Church, VA
Ishaq, Rev. Dominic, '87 (PH) On Special Assignment. Ofc Met Tribunal, Our Lady of Peace Rec, Milmont Park Maternity B.V.M., Philadelphia, PA
Ishida, Rev. Michael L., '06 (SPK) Holy Ghost, Valley, WA; Mary Queen of Heaven, Sprague, WA
Isidor, Rev. Rahab, '06 (SPC) Sacred Heart, Verona, MO; St. Lawrence, Monett, MO
Isinta, Rev. Christopher D., '04 (NEW) Retired.
Isley, Rev. Stephen, *O.S.A.* (TLS) Cascia Hall Preparatory School, Tulsa, OK
Isopo, Rev. Dominic P., '80 (ALB) Curia: Offices and Directors St. Joseph, Schenectady, NY; St. Luke, Schenectady, NY
Israel, Rev. Jude, *O.S.B.* '10 (NO) [MON] St. Joseph Abbey, St. Benedict, LA; [SEM] Saint Joseph Seminary College, Saint Benedict, LA
Israel, Rev. Maria Joseph, *S.J.* '06 (SJ) [MON] Jesuit Community at Santa Clara University, Inc., Santa Clara, CA
Issa, Rev. Alaa, (SAM) St. Ann, Watervliet, NY
Issac, Rev. Jose, '75 (RNO) Holy Cross Catholic Community, Sparks, NV
Issac, Rev. Matthew Kurry, *O.S.F.S.* '03 (STO) On Special Assignment. St. Mary's High School, Stockton/ O'Connor Woods Retirement
Issing, Rev. Daniel J., *C.S.C.* '90 (SCR) [COL] King's College, Wilkes-Barre, PA
Iszezuck, Rev. Cyril, *O.S.B.M.* '89 (STF) St. George, New York, NY
Itamid, Rev. Julius, '09 (DM) St. Columbanus, Underwood, IA; St. Patrick, Neola, IA
Ita-Sam, Rev. Joseph, *C.M.* '18 (PH) St. Vincent de Paul, Philadelphia, PA
Itua, Rev. Mark O., '06 (BUF) St. John Vianney, Orchard Park, NY
Iturbe, Rev. Rene, *S.M.* '74 (SFR) [MON] Marist Center of the West, San Francisco, CA
Ityo, Rev. Simon, '08 (TUC) Our Lady of Fatima Roman Catholic Parish - Tucson, Tucson, AZ
Itzaina, Rev. John, *SDB* (OAK) Salesian College Preparatory (Salesians of St. John Bosco), Richmond, CA
Iurochkin, Rev. Valentin, '19 (KNX) Basilica of Sts. Peter and Paul, Chattanooga, TN
Iurochkin, Rev. Valentin, '19 (KNX) Curia: Offices and Directors
Ivanov, Rev. Mykola, '05 (PHU) Curia: Leadership Presentation of Our Lord, Lansdale, PA; St. Anne's, Warrington, PA
Ivany, Rev. Mark R., '08 (WDC) Curia: Clergy and Religious Services [SEM] Saint John Paul II Seminary, Washington, DC
Ivers, Rev. Msgr. Leslie, '79 (NY) Our Lady of the Rosary, New York, NY
Iverson, Rev. Paul, '15 (DAL) On Administrative Leave.
Ivey, Rev. David, (MO) Curia: Offices and Directors
Ivory, Rev. Msgr. Thomas, '64 (NEW) Retired.
Iwan, Rev. Janusz, '76 (DET) Our Lady Queen of Apostles Parish Hamtramck, Hamtramck, MI; St. Hyacinth Parish Detroit, Detroit, MI
Iwanczuk, Rev. Lukasz, '15 (PAT) SS. Cyril and Methodius, Boonton, NJ
Iwaniec, Rev. Wieslaw, '86 (SAT) Immaculate Conception of the Blessed Virgin Mary, Panna Maria, TX; Nativity of the Blessed Virgin Mary, Falls City, TX
Iwanowski, Rev. Thomas B., '75 (NEW) Curia: Advisory Boards, Commissions, Committees, and Councils; Offices and Directors
Iwasiw, Very Rev. Nestor, '93 (PHU) Curia: Leadership; Offices and Directors SS. Peter and Paul, Simpson, PA; St. Cyril's Church, Olyphant, PA
Iwuagwu, Rev. Christian, '96 (BEL) St. Mary, Eldorado, IL; St. Mary, Harrisburg, IL; St. Paul, Vienna, IL
Iwuagwu, Rev. Franklin, '21 (SFE) Sacred Heart-Clovis, Clovis, NM
Iwuala, Rev. Ishmael O., (MO) Curia: Offices and Directors
Iwuala, Rev. Peter O., '09 (NEW) Chap, Clara Maass Med Ctr, Belleville
Iwuji, Rev. Gordian, *MSP* (SAV) Sacred Heart, Vidalia, GA
Iwuji, Rev. Luke, '97 (DET) Chap, Beaumont Hosp [HOS] Trinity Health Livonia, Livonia, MI
Iwuji, Rev. Magnus Tochi, (RIC) Immaculate Heart of Mary, Blackstone, VA; Sacred Heart, Meherrin, VA; St. Theresa, Farmville, VA
Iwuji, Rev. Matthew, '74 (AUS) Retired. Curia: Tribunal
Iwuji, Rev. Paulinus, (SFR) Chap, Veterans' Hosp, Ft Miley St. Monica - St. Thomas the Apostle Parish, San Francisco, CA
Iwuji, Rev. Paulinus, (MO) Curia: Offices and Directors
Iwuji, Rev. Raymond, (STL) Holy Name of Jesus Catholic Church, St. Louis, MO
Iwuji, Rev. Tochi, (RIC) Curia: Administration [CAM] Catholic Campus Ministry, Hampden-Sydney & Longwood Univ., Farmville, VA
Iwunze, Rev. Christogonus, *S.D.V.* '04 (NEW) St. Nicholas, Palisades Park, NJ
Iwunze, Rev. Christogonus, *SDV* (BRK) St. Clement Pope, South Ozone Park, NY
Iwuoha, Rev. Anastasius, '94 (SLC) Saint Patrick LLC 241, Salt Lake City, UT
Iyogwoya, Rev. Moses, (AUS) St. Mary, Mexia, TX
Iyorember, Rev. Callistus, (TUC) Saint Thomas the Apostle Roman Catholic Parish - Tucson, Tucson, AZ
Izac, Rev. C. Andre, (WDC) Retired.
Izaguirre, Rev. Cesar, '20 (PH) Queen of the Universe, Levittown, PA
Izbicki, Rev. Adam, (STA) Most Holy Redeemer, Jacksonville, FL
Izquierdo, Very Rev. Cesar, '18 (YAK) St Joseph Parish, Kennewick, WA
Izquierdo, Very Rev. Cesar, '18 (YAK) Curia: Offices and Directors
Izuka, Rev. Emmanuel, '97 (SFE) Our Lady of Guadalupe-Peralta, Peralta, NM
Izyk, Rev. Andrew, '74 (CHI) Retired.
Izzo, Rev. Brian A., '98 (PH) St. Rose of Lima, Eddystone, PA
Izzo, Rev. John, *SJ* (SPK) [MON] Regis Community, Spokane, WA
Jabbour, Rev. Toni Gerges, *OMM* '00 (SAM) St. Rafka Maronite Mission, Greer, SC
Jablonski, Rev. Edward J., '96 (PH) Retired.
Jablonski, Rev. Michael, (OG) Saint Joseph's Church, Dannemora, Dannemora, NY; The Church of the Assumption, Redford, Redford, NY
Jablonski, Rev. Scott M., '14 (MAD) Curia: Offices and Directors St. Francis Xavier, Cross Plains, WI
Jabo, Rev. Scott W., '90 (E) [SEM] St. Mark Seminary, Erie, PA
Jabo, Rev. Scott W., '90 (E) Curia: Clergy and Religious Services St. James, Erie, PA
Jacinto, Rev. Marty Borbon, '01 (NEW) Our Lady of Mercy, Jersey City, NJ; Our Lady of Sorrows, Jersey City, NJ
Jack, Rev. Duane C., '67 (PEO) Retired.
Jack, Rev. J. Robert, '92 (CIN) On Special Assignment. Cincinnati
Jacklin, Rev. Richard, '84 (JOL) On Leave.
Jackson, Rev. Colon, (CHI) Our Lady of Mount Carmel, Melrose Park, IL
Jackson, Rev. James M., '75 (WIL) Retired.
Jackson, Rev. James R., *M.M.* '58 (SJ) Retired. [MON] Maryknoll, Los Altos, CA
Jackson, Rev. Joseph M., '74 (CHI) Retired.
Jackson, Rev. Lawrence J., '60 (DET) Retired.
Jackson, Rev. Pio, *O.F.M.* (STL) [RTR] Il Ritiro-The Little Retreat (Il Ritiro Franciscan Retreat Center), Dittmer, MO
Jackson, Rev. Pio, *O.F.M.* '91 (STL) [MON] Franciscan Friars Province of the Sacred Heart, Dittmer, MO
Jackson, Rev. Robert H., '84 (CLV) Prince of Peace, Norton, OH
Jackson, Rev. Thomas M., *O.P.* '92 (CHI) [MON] St. Pius V Priory, Chicago, IL
Jacob, Rev. Abraham M., (CHI) Our Lady of the Rosary Parish, Chicago, IL
Jacob, Rev. Abraham Mutholathu, '80 (SYM) Sacred Heart Knanaya Catholic Parish, Chicago, Maywood,

IL; St. Paul Knanaya Catholic Mission, Minnesota, Minneapolis, MN

Jacob, Rev. Anthony J., *O.S.B.* '65 (JOL) Retired. [MON] St. Procopius Abbey, Lisle, IL

Jacob, Rev. Jaison, *CMI* (BEA) St. Anthony Cathedral Basilica, Beaumont, TX

Jacob, Rev. Jaison, *C.M.I.* (BEA) Chap, Convalescent Home Ministry

Jacob, Rev. Jerome J., '92 (CHI) Curia: Leadership St. Mary of the Annunciation, Mundelein, IL

Jacob, Rev. Jose R., (BEL) St. Elizabeth Ann Seton, Kinmundy, IL; St. Theresa of Avila, Salem, IL

Jacob, Rev. Joseph, *CMI* (STA) St. Paul's, Jacksonville Beach, FL

Jacob, Rev. Joy, *SDB* '95 (HRT) The St. Michael's Church Corporation, Beacon Falls, Connecticut, Beacon Falls, CT

Jacob, Rev. Matthew, '07 (MIL) Lumen Christi Congregation, Mequon, WI

Jacob, Rev. Roy, (JOL) St. John Paul II Parish, Kankakee, IL

Jacob, Rev. Roy, '03 (BRK) Our Lady of Grace, Brooklyn, NY

Jacob, Rev. Sujan, *MCBS* (MIL) [MON] Missionary Congregation of the Blessed Sacrament, Inc., Zion Province, Cudahy, WI

Jacobi, Rev. Joseph A., '91 (OKL) Curia: Consultative Bodies Holy Spirit Catholic Church, Mustang, OK

Jacobo, Rev. Mario, '16 (LR) St. Boniface, Fort Smith, AR

Jacobs, Rev. Charles E., '86 (HRT) Lithuanian Roman Catholic Church of the Most Holy Trinity, Hartford, CT

Jacobs, Rev. Leonard, '88 (RCK) St. John Neumann, St. Charles, IL

Jacobs, Rev. Richard, *O.S.A.* '76 (PH) [COL] Villanova University, Villanova, PA

Jacobs, Rev. William, '03 (KAL) St. Catherine of Siena, Portage, MI

Jacobson, Very Rev. Cliff, '96 (CHY) Curia: Consultative Bodies St. Patrick's Catholic Church of Casper, Casper, WY

Jacobson, Very Rev. Clifford, '96 (CHY) Curia: Clergy and Religious Services; Consultative Bodies

Jacobson, Rev. Gary, '65 (P) Retired.

Jacobus, Rev. Michael J., '08 (MAR) Holy Family, Ontonagon, MI; Sacred Heart, Ewen, MI; St. Jude, White Pine, MI; St. Mary, Rockland, MI

Jacquel, Rev. John B., '83 (E) St. Bernard, Bradford, PA; St. Francis of Assisi, Bradford, PA

Jacquemin, Rev. George, '72 (CIN) St. Bartholomew, Cincinnati, OH; St. Clare, Cincinnati, OH; St. Vivian, Cincinnati, OH

Jacquemin, Rev. Louis, '21 (CIN) St. Aloysius, Carthagena, OH; St. Bernard, Burkettsville, OH; St. Francis, Cranberry, OH; St. Henry, St. Henry, OH; St. Wendelin, Wendelin, OH

Jacques, Rev. Alfred, '60 (PRT) Retired.

Jacques, Rev. Eugene F., '80 (NO) Curia: Leadership Holy Name of Mary (Algiers), New Orleans, LA

Jacques, Rev. Roger N., '78 (BO) Retired.

Jaddou, Rev. John, '18 (EST) Curia: Leadership St. George Chaldean Catholic Church, Shelby Twp., MI

Jadotte, Rev. Jean, (MIA) St. Pius X, Fort Lauderdale, FL

Jaeger, Very Rev. James P., '86 (ROC) Chap, Veteran's Hosp, Canandaigua Curia: Deaneries; (>MO) Offices and Directors St. John Vianney Roman Catholic Parish, Steuben County, NY, Bath, NY

Jaeger, Rev. Louis M., '73 (DUB) Retired.

Jaeger, Rev. Msgr. Robert E., '90 (COS) Curia: Advisory Boards, Commissions, Committees, and Councils; Consultative Bodies; Leadership; Offices and Directors Saint Paul, Colorado Springs, CO

Jaffe, Rev. Joel D., '03 (ARL) Christ the Redeemer, Sterling, VA

Jagela, Rev. Walter M., '94 (WH) All Saints, Bridgeport, WV

Jager, Rev. Robert, (PRM) Curia: Leadership

Jager, Rev. Robert, '02 (PRM) St. John Chrysostom, Columbus, OH

Jager, Rev. Robert, (PRM) Curia: Advisory Boards, Commissions, Committees, and Councils; Leadership

Jagodensky, Rev. Joe, *S.D.S.* '80 (MIL) [MON] Salvatorian Provincial Offices (Society of the Divine Savior), Milwaukee, WI

Jagodzinski, Rev. Msgr. John J., '62 (PH) Retired. St. Pius X, Broomall, PA

Jagudilla, Rev. Julian, *O.F.M.* '08 (NY) St. Francis of Assisi, New York, NY

Jaimes, Rev. Noe, *cs* '22 (ORL) Resurrection Catholic Church, Winter Garden, FL

Jaje, Rev. Damian, *S.D.S.* (SAT) Blessed Sacrament, Poth, TX; [MON] Salvatorian Fathers Community of Texas, Falls City, TX

Jakel, Rev. Pat G., '85 (SFD) St. Paul, Highland, IL; [HOS] HSHS St. Joseph's Hospital, Highland, IL

Jakopac, Rev. George I, (ALT) Our Lady of Victory, State College, PA

Jaks, Rev. Jacob, (PT) Cathedral of the Sacred Heart, Pensacola, FL; St. Anthony of Padua, Pensacola, FL

Jakub, Rev. Joseph A., '06 (TR) On Leave.

Jakubco, Rev. Bernard, *M.S.C.* '64 (PT) Retired. Blessed Sacrament, Tallahassee, FL

Jakubik, Rev. Richard, '93 (CHI) St. Mary of the Woods, Chicago, IL

Jakubowicz, Rev. Gregory P., *O.F.M.* '04 (BUF) Curia: Leadership St. Joseph-University, Buffalo, NY; [CAM] State University of New York at Buffalo (Main St. South Campus), Buffalo, NY

Jakubowski, Rev. Scott D., *C.M.* '21 (LA) St. Vincent De Paul, Los Angeles, CA

Jakupco, Rev. Matthew, (LFT) St. Ambrose, Anderson, IN

Jakupco, Rev. Matthew, (LFT) St. Mary, Alexandria, IN; St. Mary, Anderson, IN

Jalbert, Rev. Edward, *C.J.* '87 (LA) St. Joseph High School, Santa Maria, CA; [MON] St. Joseph Seminary (Josephite Fathers' Novitiate), Santa Maria, CA

Jalbert, Very Rev. Jason Y., '03 (MAN) Curia: Clergy and Religious Services; Consultative Bodies; Leadership St. Joseph Cathedral, Manchester, NH; St. Patrick, Hampton, NH; [CEM] Cathedral Cemetery, Manchester, NH

Jalbert, Rev. Robert A., *M.M.* '79 (SJ) [MON] Maryknoll, Los Altos, CA

Jalkh, Rev. Mikhael Chady, '21 (OLL) St. Sharbel Maronite Catholic Mission, El Paso, TX

Jallas, Rev. Robert J., '84 (SFD) St. Mary, Edwardsville, IL

James, Rev. David J., '91 (SY) On Special Assignment.

James, Rev. Msgr. David L., '96 (ALN) Curia: Leadership St. Peter, Coplay, PA

James, Rev. Dylan, '98 (COL) [SEM] Pontifical College Josephinum, Columbus, OH

James, Rev. Jibin, *O.F.M.Cap.* '14 (MIL) St. Francis of Assisi, Milwaukee, WI

James, Rev. Msgr. Joseph W., '57 (LUB) Retired. [RTR] Our Lady of Mercy Retreat Center, Slaton, TX

James, Rev. Joy, *O.S.H.* '01 (GAL) Holy Family, Missouri City, TX; [MON] The Society of the Oblates of Sacred Heart, Missouri City, TX

James, Rev. Mariya, *S.A.C.* '14 (FWT) Holy Angels, Clifton, TX

James, Rev. Richard W., '12 (ALN) Most Blessed Sacrament, Bally, PA

James, Rev. Saji, *M.S.T.* '98 (SP) Our Lady Queen of Peace, New Port Richey, FL

James, Rev. Thomas, *S.V.D.* '69 (LAF) Holy Ghost, Opelousas, LA

James, Rev. V. Warwick, '80 (SJ) Retired.

Jameson, Rev. David, '22 (GR) Holy Spirit, Grand Rapids, MI

Jameson, Rev. Msgr. W. Ronald, '68 (WDC) St. Matthew Cathedral, Washington, DC

Jamesson, Rev. Matthew, '14 (CHI) St. Theresa, Palatine, IL

Jamhoury, Rev. Charbel, *O.L.M.* '01 (BR) Congregation Of Our Lady Of Mercy Roman Catholic Church, Baton Rouge, LA

Jamieson, Rev. Andrew, '88 (TR) Holy Eucharist, Tabernacle, NJ

Jamison, Very Rev. Dale, *O.F.M.* '74 (GLP) Curia: Leadership; Offices and Directors St. Mary Church, Tohatchi, NM

Jamka, Rev. Tomasz, (COS) Our Lady of Victory, Limon, CO

Jamka, Rev. Tomasz, (COS) Chap, Diocesan Prison Curia: Leadership Holy Apostles, Colorado Springs, CO

Jamnicky, Rev. John, (CHI) Retired.

Jamnicky, Rev. John, (AUS) Retired.

Jampangi, Rev. Ravi, (LAF) Holy Cross, Lafayette, LA

Jamrog, Rev. Brett, (OM) Sacred Heart Church of Norfolk, Norfolk, NE; St. Patrick's, Battle Creek, NE

Jamros, Rev. Daniel P., *S.J.* '76 (BUF) [MON] The Canisius Jesuit Community, Inc., Buffalo, NY

Janas, Rev. Camillus, *O.F.M.* '60 (CHI) [MON] Holy Name Friary, Chicago, IL

Janas, Rev. Camillus, *O.F.M.* (JKS) St. Francis of Assisi, Greenwood, MS

Janas, Rev. Piotr, *SCH* (CHI) Holy Trinity Mission, Chicago, IL

Janasik, Very Rev. Daniel R., '09 (MIL) St. Leonard Congregation, Muskego, WI

Jancarz, Rev. Janusz Jay, '83 (VEN) Our Lady of Lourdes Parish in Venice, Inc., Venice, FL

Janczak, Rev. Krzysztof, '05 (CHI) St. Thomas of Villanova, Palatine, IL

Janczyk, Rev. Jacob Bertrand, *O.P.* (MAN) St. Denis, Hanover, NH

Jandaczek, Rev. Peter, '99 (OKL) Assumption, Duncan, OK

Jandeh, Rev. Samuel, *V.C.* '09 (TUC) Curia: Consultative Bodies; Leadership Saint Andrew the Apostle Roman Catholic Parish - Sierra Vista, Sierra Vista, AZ

Jandernoa, Rev. Ronald L., '94 (MET) St. Jude, Columbia, NJ

Jandonero, Rev. Ernesto M., '19 (SFR) St. Gabriel, San Francisco, CA

Janelli, Rev. Msgr. Anthony, '64 (FRS) Retired.

Janes, Rev. David, '75 (P) Retired.

Janes, Rev. David A., '83 (SFS) Retired.

Janezic, Rev. Larry, *O.F.M.* (JOL) St. John the Baptist, Joliet, IL

Janicki, Rev. Carl F., '94 (PH) St. Genevieve, Flourtown, PA

Janicki, Rev. Krzysztof, (JOL) Divine Mercy Parish, Lombard, IL

Janiga, Rev. Bruce G., '83 (NEW) St. Philip the Apostle, Saddle Brook, NJ

Janik, Rev. Anthony F., *O.F.M.* '70 (GRY) [HOS] Franciscan Health Crown Point, Crown Point, IN; [MON] Our Lady of Lourdes Friary, Cedar Lake, IN

Janik, Rev. Msgr. Leszek T., '92 (NOR) Curia: Leadership; Offices and Directors; Tribunal

Janik, Rev. Msgr. Leszek T., '92 (NOR) Curia: Offices and Directors Sacred Heart, Norwichtown, CT; St. Joseph, Norwich, CT

Janise, Rev. Johnathan J., '11 (LAF) Immaculate Heart of Mary, Crowley, LA

Janish, Rev. Msgr. James V, '69 (SAT) Retired. [NUR] Casa De Padres, San Antonio, TX

Janiszeski, Rev. Joseph, (ALT) [MON] St. Francis Friary at Mount Assisi, Loretto, PA

Jank, Rev. Tadeusz, '96 (NEW) Guardian Angel, Allendale, NJ

Jankaitis, Rev. Ronald V., '79 (ALN) Retired.

Janko, Rev. John Joseph, *SDB* '78 (BO) [MON] The Salesian Community, Boston, MA

Janko, Rev. Joshua, '06 (LFT) Chap, Air Force Acad, Colorado Curia: (>MO) Offices and Directors

Jankowiak, Rev. Patrick M., '92 (SAG) Blessed Trinity Parish of Frankenmuth, Frankenmuth, MI

Jankowski, Rev. Daniel C., '73 (CHI) Retired.

Jankowski, Rev. James Michael, '99 (LAV) Curia: Advisory Boards, Commissions, Committees, and Councils; Deaneries St. Elizabeth Ann Seton, Las Vegas, NV

Jankowski, Rev. Peter G., '96 (JOL) St. Patrick, Momence, IL

Jankowski, Rev. Peter G., (JOL) St. Anne, St. Anne, IL

Jankowski, Rev. Richard, '92 (SP) St. Mark the Evangelist, Tampa, FL

Jankowski, Rev. Stanislaw, *C.R.* '94 (CHI) St. Hyacinth Basilica, Chicago, IL

Jankowski, Very Rev. Valentine M., *O.F.M.Conv.* '61 (LSC) Curia: Clergy and Religious Services; Leadership Shrine and Parish of Our Lady of Guadalupe, Inc., Las Cruces, NM; [RTR] Holy Cross Retreat and Friary (Franciscan Fathers), Mesilla Park, NM

Janoch, Rev. Edward J., '00 (CLV) St. Gabriel, Concord Twp., OH; St. Rita, Solon, OH

Janocha, Rev. Carl William, '91 (OKL) Retired.

Janoski, Rev. Steven A., '88 (SFD) St. Ambrose, Godfrey, IL

Janovec, Rev. James J., '64 (GI) Retired.

Janowiak, Rev. Paul A., *S.J.* '84 (OAK) [MON] Jesuit Fathers and Brothers, Berkeley, CA; [SEM] Jesuit School of Theology of Santa Clara University (Berkeley, California Campus), Berkeley, CA

Janowicz, Rev. Richard, '80 (STN) Curia: Leadership; Offices and Directors Nativity of the Mother of God Byzantine Catholic Church, Springfield, OR

Janowski, Rev. Lawrence, *O.F.M.* '73 (CHI) [MON] Holy Name Friary, Chicago, IL

Janowski, Rev. Marek, *S.J.* '06 (CHI) [MIS] Jan Beyzym Society, Inc., Chicago, IL; [MON] Sacred Heart Mission House (The Polish Messenger of The Sacred Heart, Inc.), Chicago, IL

Janowski, Rev. Michael S., '03 (GLD) Curia: Leadership Saint Ann of Cadillac, Cadillac, MI; Saint Edward of Harrietta, Harrietta, MI; Saint Stephen of Lake City, Lake City, MI; Saint Theresa of Manton, Manton, MI

Janowski, Rev. Rock J., '64 (LA) Retired.

Janowski, Rev. Stan, *O.F.M.* '66 (MIL) [MON] Queen of Peace Friary (Franciscan Friars of the Assumption B.V.M. Province), Burlington, WI

Janowski, Rev. Wesley, '93 (LC) Our Lady of the Lake, Mauston, WI; St. Francis of Assisi, Necedah, WI
Jansen, Rev. Anthony, (SAT) [NUR] Marianist Residence: Skilled Nursing, San Antonio, TX
Jansen, Rev. Raymond L., '99 (LIN) Curia: Leadership Assumption, Dwight, NE; St. Wenceslaus, Bee, NE
Janson, Rev. Christian, (SAT) [NUR] Marianist Residence: Skilled Nursing, San Antonio, TX
Janton, Rev. Anthony W., '77 (PH) Our Lady Help of Christians, Abington, PA
Jantz, Rev. Brad, '17 (BIR) [CAM] University of Montevallo Catholic Campus Ministry, Montevallo, AL; [EFT] St. Thomas Education Foundation, Montevallo, AL
Jantz, Rev. Bradley, '17 (BIR) Curia: Leadership Church of the Resurrection, Clanton, AL; St. Thomas the Apostle Catholic Parish, Montevallo, Montevallo, AL
Janus, Rev. Mark-David, *C.S.P.* '79 (NEW) [MIS] Paulist Press, Mahwah, NJ; [MON] Paulist Fathers - Paulist Press, Mahwah, NJ
Janus, Rev. Mark-David, *C.S.P.* '79 (NY) [MON] Paulist Fathers' Motherhouse, New York, NY
Janvier, Rev. Paul, '00 (TR) The Church of Mother of Mercy, Asbury Park, N.J., Asbury Park, NJ
Janysek, Rev. Scott, '14 (SAT) Curia: Administration Our Lady of Guadalupe, Helotes, TX
Jao, Rev. Radmar, *S.J.* '11 (SJ) [MON] USA West Province, Society of Jesus, Los Gatos, CA
Jaramillo, Rev. Cesar, '17 (PAT) Curia: Administration Cathedral of St. John the Baptist, Paterson, NJ
Jaramillo, Rev. Cesar, (BO) Curia: Tribunal
Jaramillo, Rev. Cesar, (PAT) Curia: Leadership
Jaramillo, Rev. Domingo, '07 (RCK) SS. Peter & Paul, Cary, IL
Jaramillo, Rev. Ernesto, '11 (LA) St. Philip Neri, Lynwood, CA
Jaramillo, Rev. Jose Miguel, *S.J.* '13 (MIL) [MON] Jesuit Community at Marquette University (Marquette Jesuit Associates, Inc.), Milwaukee, WI
Jaramillo, Rev. Leonardo, '92 (PAT) St. Paul, Clifton, NJ
Jaramillo, Rev. Misael, (PAT) SS. Cyril and Methodius, Clifton, NJ
Jaramillo, Rev. Oscar, '90 (B) Curia: Leadership Sacred Heart, Emmett, ID; St. Jude's, Garden Valley, ID
Jaramillo, Rev. Peter, *S.S.A.* '81 (KCK) All Saints, Kansas City, KS; St. Mary-St. Anthony, Kansas City, KS; [MIS] Society of St. Augustine - Public Association of the Faithful, Kansas City, KS; [MIS] The Cursillo Movement of the Archdiocese of Kansas City in Kansas, Shawnee, KS
Jaranilla, Rev. Roberto F., '96 (LA) Nativity, El Monte, CA
Jarapa, Rev. Edilberto H., '97 (RCK) St. Thomas More, Elgin, IL
Jarboe, Rev. Msgr. J. Bruce, '86 (BAL) St. Ann, Hagerstown, MD
Jarmillo, Rev. Oscar, (B) [MIS] St. Jude, Garden Valley, ID
Jarmoluk, Rev. Msgr. Joseph F., '84 (RCK) St. Peter, Spring Grove, IL
Jaron, Rev. Glenn Giovanni, *M.S.P.* '91 (SAC) Pastor of St. Catherine of Siena Parish, Vallejo, a corporation sole, Vallejo, CA; [MON] Missionary Society of the Philippines, Vallejo, CA
Jaroszeski, Rev. Paul A., '76 (STP) St. Katharine Drexel, Ramsey, MN
Jarrell, Rev. Stephen T., '73 (IND) Retired.
Jarret, Rev. Peter A., *C.S.C.* '92 (FTW) [MON] Congregation of Holy Cross, United States Province of Priests and Brothers, Notre Dame, IN
Jarvis, Rev. Christopher A., '16 (GLD) Christ the King of Acme, Williamsburg, MI
Jarvis, Rev. Paul, '04 (STP) St. Bridget, Minneapolis, MN
Jarzabek, Rev. Mariusz, *M.I.C.* '90 (SPR) [MON] Congregation of Marian Fathers of The Immaculate Conception of the Most Blessed Virgin Mary, Stockbridge, MA
Jarzombek, Rev. Dennis, '79 (SAT) Curia: Administration
Jarzombek, Rev. Gregory, *O.S.B.* '12 (PEO) [SEM] St. Bede Abbey (Benedictine Society of St. Bede, Benedictine Fathers and Brothers), Peru, IL
Jas, Rev. Rofinus, *S.V.D.* (BLX) Our Mother of Mercy, Pass Christian, MS
Jasany, Rev. Robert J., '79 (CLV) St. John Nepomucene, Cleveland, OH
Jasilek, Rev. Bartlomiej, (BEA) St. Joseph, Livingston, TX; St. Martin de Porres Mission, Corrigan, TX
Jasinski, Rev. Andrew, '98 (FAR) St. Benedict's Church of Wild Rice, Horace, ND; [ASN] Catholic Chaplains Association, Fargo, ND
Jasinski, Rev. Andrew, '98 (FAR) Curia: Offices and Directors
Jaskierny, Rev. Joseph F., '11 (RCK) Curia: Tribunal St. Peter Cathedral, Rockford, IL
Jaskot, Rev. Msgr. Robert J., '98 (BAL) Holy Family Catholic Community, Middletown, MD; St. Francis of Assisi, Brunswick, MD
Jaskowiak, Rev. Wojciech B., '03 (NEW) Our Lady of Victories, Harrington Park, NJ
Jasniewicz, Rev. Mateusz, '15 (PAT) Curia: Leadership Immaculate Heart of Mary, Wayne, NJ
Jasper, Rev. Frank, *O.F.M.* '73 (CIN) [MIS] Franciscan Central Purchasing, Cincinnati, OH; [MON] St. Clement Friary, Cincinnati, OH
Jasper, Rev. Richard, (WIL) Curia: Administration St. Ann, Wilmington, DE
Jaspers, Rev. Andrew, (MO) Curia: Offices and Directors
Jaspers, Rev. Andrew M., '13 (STP) Chap, Hennepin Cty Med Ctr, Minneapolis
Jaspers, Rev. David Leo, '09 (P) Ascension, Portland, OR
Jaspers, Rev. J. Dennis, '66 (CIN) Retired.
Jastrab, Rev. David J., '75 (PIT) Retired. Divine Redeemer, Sewickley, PA
Jastrzebski, Rev. Cezariusz W., '14 (BRK) Our Lady of Czestochowa-St. Casimir, Brooklyn, NY
Jaszczuk, Rev. Radoslaw, *CSSR* (CHI) St. Mary Frances of the Five Wounds, Cicero, IL
Jaszek, Rev. Stanislaw, '88 (FBK) Curia: Leadership Sacred Heart Catholic Church Emmonak, Emmonak, AK; St. Ignatius Catholic Church Alakanuk, Alakanuk, AK; St. Joseph Catholic Church Kotlik, Kotlik, AK
Jauregui, Very Rev. Luke, '05 (SD) Curia: Advisory Boards, Commissions, Committees, and Councils Pastor of Saint Stephen Catholic Parish, Valley Center, a corporation sole, Valley Center, CA
Jauregui, Rev. Rene, '18 (SAC) Pastor of St. James Parish, Davis, a corporation sole, Davis, CA
Jauregui, Rev. Rene, '18 (SAC) Curia: Leadership; Offices and Directors
Java, Rev. Miguel B., '73 (LA) Retired. St. Basil's Roman Catholic Church, Los Angeles, CA
Javid, Rev. Akram, (NY) Chap, The Mount Sinai Hosp, New York
Javier, Rev. Nelson, *TOR* '96 (ALT) Holy Rosary, Altoona, PA; St. Mark, Altoona, PA
Javinez, Rev. Cerilo, (PAT) St. Mary's, Wharton, NJ
Jawa, Rev. Stanley, *S.V.D.* '07 (LAF) Holy Family, Lawtell, LA; St. Ann, Lawtell, LA
Jawidzik, Rev. Edward M., '81 (TR) Retired.
Jaworowski, Rev. Grzegorz, '93 (HRT) The St. Anthony's Church Corporation of Prospect, Prospect, CT
Jaworski, Rev. Richard, (GAL) [MON] The Companions of The Cross, Houston, TX
Jaworski, Rev. Rick, *C.C.* (DET) [MON] Companions of the Cross, Detroit, MI
Jayababu, Rev. Nuthulapati, *CPPS* '06 (GRY) Sacred Heart, Whiting, IN
Jayamanne, Rev. Dharshana, '94 (PH) Saint Elizabeth, Chester Springs, PA
Jayaraj, Rev. Arulappan, *HGN* (PT) St. Joseph, Pensacola, FL
Jayasuria, Rev. Wimal, (FTW) Curia: Offices and Directors
Jayasuriya, Rev. Wimal, '97 (FTW) St. Mary's Catholic Church, Fort Wayne, IN
Jayr, Rev. Canon Benoit, *I.C.R.S.S.* '92 (MIL) The St. Stanislaus Congregation, Milwaukee, WI
Jazdzewski, Rev. Brian J., '99 (LC) On Leave.
Jazmin, Very Rev. Romeo D., '85 (RIC) On Special Assignment. Mary Star of the Sea, Fort Monroe, St. Joseph, Hampton St. Joseph, Hampton, VA; St. Mary Star of the Sea, Fort Monroe, VA; St. Vincent de Paul, Newport News, VA
Jazon, Rev. Yvans, '07 (CAM) St. Teresa of Calcutta Parish, Collingswood, NJ
Jazo-Tarin, Friar Jose Eduardo, *TOR* (AUS) St. Francis on the Brazos, Waco, TX
Jean, Rev. Agapit H., '95 (MAN) Parish of the Assumption, Dover, NH
Jean, Rev. Anthonio, '99 (VEN) St. Katharine Drexel Parish in Cape Coral, Inc., Cape Coral, FL
Jean, Rev. Carl, '12 (ATL) Sts. Peter and Paul Catholic Church, Decatur, Inc., Decatur, GA
Jean, Rev. Edroud, '21 (ELP) St. Luke, El Paso, TX; St. Raphael, El Paso, TX
Jean, Rev. Franky, '93 (MIA) St. Stephen, Miramar, FL
Jean, Rev. Lesly, '83 (MIA) On Special Assignment. Chap, Jackson Mem Hosp
Jean, Rev. Thony Roody, '99 (ATL) On Leave.
Jean Paul, Rev. Souvenir, *S.M.* '97 (BRK) Chap, Kings Cty Hosp Ctr
Jean-Francois, Very Rev. Nixon, (BRK) SS. Joachim and Anne, Queens Village, NY
Jean-Louis, Rev. Joseph, '03 (MIA) Christ the King, Miami, FL
Jean-Mary, Rev. Reginald, '01 (MIA) Curia: Clergy and Religious Services; Leadership; Pastoral Services Notre Dame d'Haiti, Miami, FL; [MIS] Pierre Toussaint Leadership and Learning Center, Inc., Miami, FL
Jean-Paul, Rev. Souvenir, *S.M.* '97 (WDC) [MON] Marist Center (The Marist Finance Center of the Atlanta Province of the Society of Mary, Marist Fathers and Brothers), Washington, DC
Jean-Pierre, Rev. Jaccius, (NY) Parish of Saint Joseph/ Saint Boniface, Spring Valley, NY
Jean-Pierre, Rev. Nobert, '07 (PMB) St. Philip Benizi, Belle Glade, FL
Jeanty, Msgr. Chanel, '04 (MIA) Curia: Canonical Services St. James, Miami, FL
Jeanty, Rev. Succes, (BO) Sacred Heart, Boston, MA
Jecewicz, Rev. Jerome T., '75 (BRK) Retired. St. Kevin, Flushing, NY
Jednaki, Rev. P. Grzegorz, '08 (NOR) Curia: Offices and Directors
Jednaki, Rev. P. Grzegorz, '08 (NOR) Saint Andre Bessette Parish (St. John the Apostle Church), Plainfield, CT
Jedrychowski, Rev. Janusz, '95 (STF) St. Nicholas, Hudson, NY
Jedrzejewski, Rev. Richard, '74 (BUF) Retired.
Jeffers, Rev. Douglas, (AUS) Curia: Leadership; Tribunal St. Mary Cathedral, Austin, TX
Jeffers, Rev. Robert A., '54 (NY) Retired. Our Lady of the Rosary, New York, NY
Jeffrey, Rev. George A., '65 (SCR) Retired. Curia: Leadership [MON] Villa St. Joseph, Dunmore, PA
Jeganathan, Rev. Arockia dhass, *HGN* '10 (LUB) St. Ann, Stamford, TX; St. Michaels Church Anson, Anson, TX
Jekielek, Rev. Steven A., '11 (BUF) St. John the Baptist Roman Catholic Congregation, Lockport, NY
Jemigbola, Rev. Hyacinth, (RVC) St. Edward Confessor, Syosset, NY
Jemy Puthuseril, Rev. Joseph, '05 (SYM) St. Mary's Syro-Malabar Knanaya Catholic Church of Detroit, Berkley, MI
Jendrek, Rev. Michael J., '87 (BAL) Holy Family, Davidsonville, MD
Jenga, Rev. Fred, *CSC* '74 (FR) [COL] Holy Cross Fathers Religious, North Easton, MA
Jenkins, Rev. Aaron M., '08 (IND) Father Thomas Scecina Memorial High School, Inc., Indianapolis, IN; St. Michael Catholic Church, Greenfield, Inc., Greenfield, IN; St. Thomas the Apostle, Fortville, Inc., Fortville, IN
Jenkins, Rev. Alan, *S.V.D.* '73 (SB) [RTR] Divine Word Province/ Retreat Center, Riverside, CA
Jenkins, Rev. J. Wayne, '72 (L) Retired.
Jenkins, Rev. J. Wayne, (L) Retired.
Jenkins, Rev. John I., *C.S.C.* '83 (FTW) [COL] University of Notre Dame Du Lac, Notre Dame, IN; [MON] Holy Cross Community, Corby Hall, University of Notre Dame, Notre Dame, IN
Jenkins, Rev. Jon, (POC) Our Lady of the Atonement Catholic Church, San Antonio, TX
Jenkins, Rev. Joseph A., '86 (WDC) Holy Family, Mitchellville, MD
Jenkins, Rev. Kenneth F., '80 (SB) Retired.
Jenkins, Rev. Msgr. Ron, '89 (AUS) On Duty Outside Diocese. The Catholic Univ of America, Washington, DC
Jenkins, Rev. Msgr. Ronny E., '89 (WDC) [COL] Catholic University of America, The, Washington, DC
Jenkins, Rev. Walter, *C.S.C.* (PAT) [MIS] Pope John XXIII Regional High School, Inc., Sparta, NJ; [MIS] The Catholic Academy of Sussex County, Inc., Sparta, NJ
Jenkins, Rev. Wayne, *S.C.J.* '77 (MIL) [MON] Sacred Heart at Monastery Lake, Franklin, WI
Jenkins, Rev. Wayne, '72 (L) Retired.
Jenne, Rev. Walter H., '70 (CLV) Retired. Curia: Parish Services
Jennett, Rev. Msgr. Michael J., '74 (LA) Retired.
Jenniges, Rev. Bradley, *O.S.B.* '14 (SCL) Church of Saint Joseph of Saint Joseph, St. Joseph, MN; St. John the Baptist, St. Joseph, MN; [EFT] Holy Cross Trust, Collegeville, MN; [MON] St. John's Abbey, of the Order of St. Benedict, Collegeville, MN
Jennings, Rev. Paul F., '74 (WIL) St. Luke-St. Andrew, Ocean City, MD
Jennings, Rev. Thomas J., '69 (WIN) Retired.
Jennings, Rev. Tommie, '88 (SD) Pastor of Christ the King Catholic Parish, San Diego, a corporation sole,

San Diego, CA; [MIS] Christ the King Catholic Parish in San Diego, CA Real Property Support Corporation, San Diego, CA
Jennrich, Rev. Michael, (JOL) [COL] University of St. Francis, Joliet, IL; [MON] St. John the Baptist Friary, Joliet, IL
Jensen, Rev. Joseph, *O.S.B.* '54 (WDC) [MON] St. Anselm's Abbey, Washington, DC
Jenson, Rev. Glen T., '95 (STP) SS. Peter and Paul, Loretto, MN; St. Thomas the Apostle, Corcoran, MN; [CEM] Old St. Thomas Cemetery, Corcoran, MN; [CEM] St. Jean de Chantel Cemetery, Corcoran, MN; [CEM] St. Patrick's Cemetery, Corcoran, MN; [CEM] St. Thomas the Apostle Cemetery, Corcoran, MN; [CEM] Sts. Peter and Paul Cemetery, Loretto, MN
Jenuwine, Rev. David, '09 (SAG) Saints Francis and Clare Parish of Birch Run, Birch Run, MI
Jeon, Rev. Dong-Hyuk, '01 (CIN) [MIS] St. Andrew Kim Korean Catholic Community, Cincinnati, OH
Jeon, Rev. Leo Yongguk, (SEA) St. Andrew Kim Personal Parish, Seattle, WA
JeongHun Kim, Rev. Raphael, (DEN) St. Lawrence Korean Catholic Parish in Aurora, Aurora, CO
Jeorge, Rev. Anthoni, *M.I.* '04 (MIL) [MON] St. Camillus Communities, Inc., Wauwatosa, WI
Jerabek, Rev. Bryan W., '08 (BIR) Curia: Leadership Cathedral of St. Paul Catholic Parish, Birmingham, Birmingham, AL; [CAM] St. Stephen the Martyr Catholic University Chapel, Birmingham, AL; [EFT] Cathedral of St. Paul Columbarium Fund, Birmingham, AL
Jerek, Rev. John, '88 (Y) Curia: Leadership Our Lady of Sorrows Parish, Youngstown, OH; St. Christine, Youngstown, OH
Jeremiah, Rev. Ian, '08 (BGP) St. Ann Roman Catholic Church Corporation, Bridgeport, CT
Jerez Rivera, Rev. Froylan, (AUS) Santa Barbara Catholic Church - Austin, Texas, Austin, TX
Jerome, Rev. Louis R., '88 (NY) Assumption/St. Paul, Staten Island, NY; Our Lady of Good Counsel, Staten Island, NY
Jeronimo, Rev. Arturo, (BAK) Our Lady of Angels, Hermiston, OR
Jerse, Rev. William M., '80 (CLV) Retired.
Jervis, Rev. Msgr. Paul W., '73 (BRK) St. Francis of Assisi-St. Blaise, Brooklyn, NY
Jesudhason, Rev. Christopher, *S.A.C.* '01 (TOL) Holy Angels, Sandusky, OH; SS. Peter and Paul, Sandusky, OH; St. Mary's, Sandusky, OH
Jesuraj, Rev. Maria Salethu, *HGN* '03 (LEX) St. Julian, Middlesboro, KY
Jeyamani, Rev. Paul, (P) All Saints, Portland, OR
Jeyaraj, Rev. Gilbert, (OAK) [MON] Salesians of Don Bosco, Berkeley, CA
Jiang, Rev. Joseph Xiu Hui, '10 (STL) On Duty Outside Diocese. Casa Santa Maria, Rome Cathedral Basilica of Saint Louis Catholic Church, St. Louis, MO
Jiang, Rev. Joseph (You Guo), *SJ* '08 (BO) [MON] The Jesuit Community at Boston College, Chestnut Hill, MA
Jicha, Rev. John J., '95 (BAL) St. Augustine, Williamsport, MD; St. James Boonsboro, Boonsboro, MD; St. Joseph, Hagerstown, MD
Jimenez, Rev. Alvaro, '84 (ORL) Basilica of Saint Paul, Daytona Beach, FL
Jimenez, Rev. Benjamin P., *S.J.* '01 (CLV) St. Augustine, Cleveland, OH
Jimenez, Rev. Candelario, '21 (OAK) St. Isidore, Danville, CA
Jimenez, Rev. David J., (YAK) Curia: Leadership
Jimenez, Rev. Diego A., '11 (HRT) Curia: Advisory Boards, Commissions, Committees, and Councils; Spiritual Life All Saints Parish Corporation, Waterbury, CT; St. Francis Xavier's Church Corporation of Waterbury, Connecticut, Waterbury, CT; [CCH] Spanish-Speaking Center, Waterbury, CT
Jimenez, Rev. Eduardo, '82 (MIA) On Leave. personal request for employment
Jimenez, Rev. Eloy, '82 (FTW) St. Vincent de Paul, Elkhart, IN
Jimenez, Rev. Emilio, '99 (CC) St. Mary, Star of the Sea, Aransas Pass, TX
Jimenez, Rev. Emilio B., '99 (CC) Curia: Leadership
Jimenez, Rev. Fernando M., '09 (FTW) Curia: Offices and Directors St. Michael, Plymouth, IN
Jimenez, Rev. Gerardo Garcia, '99 (DEN) St. Mary Catholic Parish in Rifle, Rifle, CO
Jimenez, Rev. Jose Carmelo, '99 (OWN) St. Michael, Sebre, KY
Jimenez, Rev. Jose Miguel, '15 (PAT) [HOS] St. Joseph's University Medical Center, Paterson, NJ
Jimenez, Rev. Juan Bosco, *S.D.B.* '90 (LA) St. Frances Xavier Cabrini, Los Angeles, CA
Jimenez, Rev. Victor, *L.C.* '19 (HRT) [MON] Legionaries of Christ, Cheshire, CT; [SEM] Novitiate of the Legion of Christ, Cheshire, CT
Jimenez Alvarez, Rev. David J., '95 (YAK) Curia: Leadership St. Anne's, Chelan, WA; St. Francis de Sales, Chelan, WA
Jimenez Barros, Rev. Pedro, (MO) Curia: Offices and Directors
Jimenez Mocobono, Rev. Javier Fernando, (BO) [MON] Isaac Jogues House, Brighton, MA
Jimenez Nieto, Rev. Miguel, *C.O.R.C.* '94 (LA) Immaculate Conception, Los Angeles, CA
Jimenez Ortiz, Rev. Adrian N., '87 (ARE) Curia: Leadership; Offices and Directors [MIS] Chapel Ermita del Carmen, Arecibo, PR; [MIS] Chapel Sagrada Familia, Arecibo, PR; [MIS] Chapel San Juan Apostol, Arecibo, PR; [MIS] Chapel Santa Maria Reina, Arecibo, PR
Jimenez Ortiz, Rev. Adrian N., '87 (ARE) Curia: Leadership; Offices and Directors Cathedral of San Felipe Apostol, Arecibo, PR
Jimenez Soto, Rev. Julio, '13 (CHI) Chap, Hillside
Jimenez-Londono, Rev. Fredy A., '93 (PRO) On Leave.
Jimenez-Morales, Rev. Ignacio, (BLX) Immaculate Conception, Laurel, MS; St. Bernadette, Waynesboro, MS
Jiminez, Rev. Vinicio, (CHI) Blessed Maria Gabriella Parish, Chicago, IL
Jin, Rev. Francis, *OSB* '22 (GBG) [MON] Saint Vincent Archabbey, Latrobe, PA
Jin, Rev. Ho Seok, (LA) St. Paul, Los Angeles, CA
Jin, Rev. Joseph Lei, '01 (PH) St. John the Evangelist, Philadelphia, PA
Jindra, Rev. Frank E., '84 (OM) Curia: Leadership; Offices and Directors Assumption of the Blessed Virgin Mary-Our Lady of Guadalupe Church of Omaha, Omaha, NE; St. Joan of Arc, Omaha, NE; St. Mary, Omaha, NE; St. Thomas More, Omaha, NE; Sts. Peter and Paul Church of Omaha, Omaha, NE
Jingbe, Rev. Simon, (FBK) Curia: Leadership St. Raphael Catholic Church Fairbanks, Fairbanks, AK
Jirak, Rev. John F., '02 (WCH) Curia: Leadership; Offices and Directors Church of the Magdalen, Wichita, KS
Jirovsky, Rev. Lee T., '06 (LIN) Bishop Neumann Jr.-Sr. High School, Wahoo, NE; St. Wenceslaus, Wahoo, NE
Jirovsky, Rev. Lee Thomas, '06 (LIN) [EFT] Bishop Neumann High School Endowment Fund, Wahoo, NE
Job, Rev. John R., '11 (NEW) Curia: Advisory Boards, Commissions, Committees, and Councils Most Blessed Sacrament, Franklin Lakes, NJ
Jocco, Rev. Joseph, *O.S.F.S.* '84 (WIL) Retired.
Jocson, Rev. Edgardo P., '01 (NEW) Curia: Offices and Directors St. Elizabeth of Hungary, Linden, NJ
Jocson, Rev. Salvador, '57 (SFR) Retired.
Joda, Rev. Robert J., *S.J.* '45 (MIL) [MON] St. Camillus Jesuit Community (Society of Jesus, USA Midwest Province), Wauwatosa, WI
Joerger, Rev. Robert H., *C.P.* '77 (NY) [MON] St. Vincent Strambi Residence (The Passionists), Pelham Manor, NY; [MON] The Congregation of the Passion - St. Paul of the Cross Province, Jamaica, NY
Johanneck, Rev. Aaron T., '12 (NU) On Special Assignment. Curia: Advisory Boards, Commissions, Committees, and Councils; Offices and Directors
Johannes, Rev. David G., '12 (MAD) On Administrative Leave.
Johannssen, Rev. John-Mary, (NEW) (>NY) [MON] St. Leopold's Friary, Yonkers, NY
Johansen, Rev. Eric, '15 (NSH) On Leave. No assignment
Johansen, Rev. Robert J., '01 (KAL) St. Augustine Cathedral, Kalamazoo, MI
John, Rev. Boby, *CSC* '08 (FR) [COL] Holy Cross Fathers Religious, North Easton, MA
John, Rev. Cyriac, '93 (R) St. Mary Catholic Parish of Laurinburg, Laurinburg, NC
John, Rev. Jacob, '02 (PH) St. Hilary of Poitiers, Rydal, PA
John, Rev. Joshy, (HRT) Corporation of the Church of the Immaculate Conception, Waterbury, Connecticut, Waterbury, CT
John, Very Rev. Lawrence, '00 (AMA) Curia: Administration; Offices and Directors
John, Rev. Manoj, *Sch.P.* '13 (PHX) St. Germaine Roman Catholic Parish, Prescott Valley, AZ; St. Michael Roman Catholic Parish, Gila Bend, AZ
John, Rev. Sam, '10 (HRT) Saint Thomas & Saint Timothy Parish Corporation, West Hartford, CT
John, Rev. Sam, (MCE) Boston Syro-Malankara Mission, Waltham, MA
John, Rev. Sam, (MCE) Curia: Advisory Boards, Commissions, Committees, and Councils
John, Rev. Shanoy, '12 (SYM) St. Alphonsa Syro-Malabar Catholic Church, Richmond, VA of St. Thomas Syro-Malabar Catholic Diocese of Chicago, North Chesterfield, VA
John, Rev. Siby, *C.P.* '98 (SCR) [MON] Saint Ann's Passionist Monastery of Scranton PA, Scranton, PA
John Bosco, Rev. Lee, (SP) [RTR] Mary Help of Christians Center, Tampa, FL
John Bosco, Rev. Lee, (SP) Mary Help of Christians, Tampa, FL
John Puthiydath, Rev. Noble, (PHX) St. Germaine Roman Catholic Parish, Prescott Valley, AZ
Johns, Rev. Michael, (LR) Immaculate Heart of Mary, Magnolia, AR; St. Louis, Camden, AR
Johns, Rev. Thomas W., '78 (CLV) St. John Vianney, Mentor, OH
Johnson, Rev. Adam, '12 (KC) On Special Assignment. Curia: Offices and Directors Our Lady of Good Counsel, Kansas City, MO
Johnson, Rev. Andrew, '91 (FR) Corpus Christi, East Sandwich, MA
Johnson, Rev. Arthur D., *O.S.A.* (BO) St. Augustine, Andover, MA
Johnson, Rev. Ben, (GB) Curia: Faith Formation St. Francis Xavier, De Pere, WI; St. Mary, De Pere, WI
Johnson, Rev. Bernard, *O.Praem.* '81 (ORG) [MON] Norbertine Fathers of Orange, Inc., Silverado, CA
Johnson, Rev. Brian, *C.Ss.R.* '86 (TUC) [MON] Redemptorist Society of Arizona Desert House of Prayer Residence, Tucson, AZ; [RTR] Redemptorist Society of Arizona Redemptorist Renewal Center, Tucson, AZ
Johnson, Rev. Brian, '97 (OWN) St. Anthony of Padua, Grand Rivers, KY; St. Pius Tenth, Calvert City, KY
Johnson, Rev. Chad, '21 (Y) Curia: Clergy and Religious Services; Pastoral Services University Parish Newman Center, Kent, OH
Johnson, Rev. Charles, '21 (BUF) St. Amelia's Roman Catholic Church Society of the Town of Tonawanda, N.Y., Tonawanda, NY
Johnson, Friar Charles K., *OP* (GAL) Holy Rosary, Houston, TX
Johnson, Rev. Charles K., *O.P.* '06 (BR) Congregation Of Holy Ghost Roman Catholic Church, Hammond, Louisiana, Hammond, LA
Johnson, Rev. Charles W., '94 (AUS) On Special Assignment. Curia: (>MO) Offices and Directors
Johnson, Rev. Christopher, *O.C.D.* '93 (BGP) Staff Chap, Greenwich Hosp St. Catherine of Siena and St. Agnes Parish Corporation, Riverside, CT
Johnson, Rev. Christopher, *OP* '20 (CHI) Fenwick High School, Oak Park, IL
Johnson, Rev. Christopher, *SJ* '14 (IND) Brebeuf Jesuit Preparatory School, Inc. (Society of Jesus Community), Indianapolis, IN
Johnson, Rev. Cyril, (TR) St. Michael, West End, NJ
Johnson, Rev. Dave, '89 (OWN) Sacred Heart, Morganfield, KY; St. Peter, Waverly, KY
Johnson, Rev. Edward D., '55 (PRO) Retired.
Johnson, Very Rev. Eric M., '02 (IND) Curia: Leadership; Offices and Directors SS. Peter and Paul Cathedral, Indianapolis, Inc., Indianapolis, IN; St. Agnes Catholic Church, Nashville, Inc., Nashville, IN
Johnson, Friar Gary, *OFM Conv.* (SAT) [MON] San Damiano Friary, San Antonio, TX; [SEM] San Damiano Friary, Initial House of Formation, San Antonio, TX (>BAL) [MON] Order of Friars Minor Conventual, Ellicott City, MD
Johnson, Rev. Gerald, '04 (SFE) Retired.
Johnson, Rev. Msgr. H. Thomas, '78 (DET) On Leave.
Johnson, Rev. Howard, *S.S.J.* '60 (BAL) Retired.
Johnson, Rev. Howard J., '54 (MIL) Retired.
Johnson, Rev. James, *O.F.M. Cap.* '68 (LA) (>OAK) [MON] Capuchin Franciscan Friars, Berkeley, CA
Johnson, Rev. James B., '80 (SP) St. Scholastica, Lecanto, FL
Johnson, Rev. James B., '80 (SP) Curia: Faith Formation; Leadership; Pastoral Services
Johnson, Rev. James O., '00 (SEA) Holy Innocents, Duvall, WA; St. Jude, Redmond, WA
Johnson, Rev. Jared, (BIS) St. Mary, Bismarck, ND
Johnson, Rev. Jared M., '13 (BIS) Curia: Leadership; Offices and Directors
Johnson, Rev. Jeff G., '92 (MAR) On Special Assignment. Chap, Marquette Cty-Prison, Nursing Homes, Hosp
Johnson, Rev. Jeffrey C., *S.J.* '11 (GAL) Curia: Offices and Directors Strake Jesuit College Preparatory Inc., Houston, TX
Johnson, Rev. Jerome A., '86 (MET) St. Thomas the Apostle, Old Bridge, NJ
Johnson, Rev. Joachim, *O.C.S.O.* '02 (L) [MON] Abbey of Our Lady of Gethsemani, of the Order of Cistercians

of the Strict Observance, Trappist, KY
Johnson, Rev. Msgr. John G., '74 (COL) Retired. Curia: Offices and Directors [SEM] Pontifical College Josephinum, Columbus, OH
Johnson, Rev. John J., '66 (STL) Retired. St. Justin Martyr Catholic Church, Sunset Hills, MO
Johnson, Very Rev. John R., '07 (SAV) Curia: Leadership; Offices and Directors St. Joseph, Macon, GA
Johnson, Rev. John R., (LFT) St. Elizabeth Seton, Carmel, IN
Johnson, Rev. John R., '72 (SAG) Retired.
Johnson, Rev. Joseph R., '98 (STP) Holy Family, St. Louis Park, MN
Johnson, Rev. Joshua D., '14 (BR) Curia: Administration; Clergy and Religious Services; Organizations (affiliated, inter-Diocesan, miscellaneous/ other) The Congregation Of Sacred Heart Roman Catholic Church, Baton Rouge, LA; [EFT] Sacred Heart School Endowment Fund, Baton Rouge, LA
Johnson, Rev. Lawrence M., '83 (BAL) On Special Assignment. Stella Maris, Pastoral Care [NUR] Stella Maris, Timonium, MD
Johnson, Rev. Lawrence P., '76 (DUL) On Duty Outside Diocese. San Diego, CA
Johnson, Rev. Lawrence R., '75 (STP) Retired.
Johnson, Rev. Lyle, '76 (LIN) Curia: Leadership St. John the Apostle, Lincoln, NE
Johnson, Rev. Marcus, '02 (LKC) On Leave. Non-Active
Johnson, Rev. Michael, *O.F.M.* '02 (HRT) St. Patrick and St. Anthony Roman Catholic Church Corporation, Hartford, CT; [MON] St. Patrick-St. Anthony Friary (Franciscan Friars), Hartford, CT
Johnson, Rev. Michael, '20 (MAD) Congregation of St. Isidore, Hollandale, WI
Johnson, Rev. Michael, (BUF) Nativity of Our Lord, Orchard Park, NY
Johnson, Very Rev. Michael C., '09 (STP) Curia: Leadership; Tribunal
Johnson, Rev. Patrick D., *C.S.P.* '74 (CHI) Old St. Mary, Chicago, IL
Johnson, Rev. Peter, '91 (CHY) Retired.
Johnson, Rev. Philip G., '17 (R) On Duty Outside Diocese.
Johnson, Rev. Phillip M., '10 (CAM) Retired.
Johnson, Rev. Raney, (SHP) St. Mary of the Pines, Shreveport, LA
Johnson, Rev. Raney Christopher, '20 (SHP) Loyola College Prep, Shreveport, LA; St. Clement, Vivian, LA; St. Pius X, Shreveport, LA
Johnson, Rev. Rijo, *S.D.V.* '08 (BUR) Curia: Leadership Mater Dei, Newport, VT
Johnson, Rev. Robert, (LIN) St. Joseph, Lincoln, NE
Johnson, Rev. Robert, '18 (SFD) Mother of Perpetual Help, Maryville, IL
Johnson, Rev. Robert, '21 (ALX) St. Frances Xavier Cabrini, Alexandria, LA
Johnson, Rev. Robert, '09 (PT) Curia: Offices and Directors Christ Our Redeemer, Niceville, FL
Johnson, Rev. Robert Joseph, *SVD* '92 (DET) Our Lady of the Woods Parish Woodhaven, Woodhaven, MI
Johnson, Rev. Msgr. Robert K., '90 (WOR) Holy Family Parish, Worcester, MA; St. Stephen's, Worcester, MA
Johnson, Rev. Robert W., '20 (LIN) Curia: Leadership
Johnson, Rev. Shane, *L.C.* '09 (NY) St. Anthony of Padua, Bronx, NY
Johnson, Rev. Terrance, '94 (CHI) On Duty Outside Diocese. Sisters of Providence of St. Mary, Terre Haute, IN
Johnson, Rev. Terrence, (IND) [CON] Sisters of Providence General Administration, St. Mary of the Woods, IN
Johnson, Rev. Timothy A., '93 (SC) Sacred Heart, Boone, IA; St. Malachy's, Madrid, IA
Johnson, Rev. Timothy D., '01 (FAR) Retired.
Johnson, Rev. Timothy K., '71 (OAK) Retired.
Johnson, Rev. Tyler Y., (SEA) Immaculate Conception, Arlington, WA
Johnson, Rev. Walter E., *M.M.* '53 (NY) Retired.
Johnson, Rev. William B., '83 (OAK) Retired.
Johnson, Rev. William T., *S.J.* '91 (MIL) [MON] Arrupe House Jesuit Community, Milwaukee, WI
Johnson Vellachira, Rev. Varghese, (MIL) [MIS] St. Camillus Health System, Inc., Wauwatosa, WI; [MIS] St. Camillus Ministries, Inc., Wauwatosa, WI; [MON] St. Camillus Communities, Inc., Wauwatosa, WI; [NUR] St. Camillus, Wauwatosa, WI; [NUR] St. Camillus Health Center, Inc., Wauwatosa, WI
Johnston, Rev. Christian R., '05 (KAL) St. Anthony, Buchanan, MI; St. Mary of the Immaculate Conception Church, Niles, MI
Johnston, Rev. Jason, (BLX) Curia: Advisory Boards, Commissions, Committees, and Councils
Johnston, Rev. Jason, '16 (JKS) Curia: Canonical Services; Consultative Bodies St. Joseph, Starkville, MS
Johnston, Rev. Jeffrey, (RVC) Retired.
Johnston, Rev. Kenneth J., '68 (CAM) Retired.
Johnston, Rev. Matthew D., '14 (NO) Curia: Offices and Directors St. Benilde Roman Catholic Church, Metairie, Louisiana, Metairie, LA
Johnston, Rev. Michael, '96 (P) St. Philip, Dallas, OR
Johnston, Rev. Michael O., '70 (NSH) Retired.
Johnston, Rev. Robert F., '71 (SAT) Retired.
Johny, Rev. Reju Pynadath, (BIR) St. Aloysius Catholic Parish, Bessemer, Bessemer, AL
Joly, Rev. Michael, '94 (RIC) St. Joan of Arc, Yorktown, VA
Joly, Rev. Philip, '01 (VEN) On Duty Outside Diocese. Chaplain, St. Mary Medical Center
Joncas, Rev. Jan Michael, '69 (STP) Retired.
Jonczyk, Rev. Dariusz J., '97 (PRO) Saint Stanislaus Kostka Church of Woonsocket, Woonsocket, RI; St. Joseph's Church of Central Falls, Central Falls, RI
Jones, Rev. Andrew B, '18 (MOB) The City of St. Jude Parish, Montgomery, Montgomery, AL
Jones, Rev. Anthony, '89 (OWN) St. Romuald, Hardinsburg, KY
Jones, Rev. Brandon H., (CHL) St. Ann Catholic Church, Charlotte, NC
Jones, Rev. C. Gregory, *C.S.V.* '96 (CHI) [MON] Viatorian Province Center-Clerics of St. Viator, Arlington Heights, IL
Jones, Rev. Casey, '12 (VEN) Curia: Leadership St. Elizabeth Seton Parish in Naples, Inc., Naples, FL
Jones, Rev. Clarence, '94 (SEA) Sacred Heart of Jesus, Enumclaw, WA
Jones, Rev. Colin Daniel, '18 (STP) [SEM] St. John Vianney Seminary, St. Paul, MN
Jones, Rev. David A., '89 (CHI) Curia: Leadership St. Benedict the African, Chicago, IL
Jones, Rev. David J., *M.M.* '62 (ALB) Retired.
Jones, Rev. Douglas, *S.J.* (NY) [MON] Cardinal Spellman Hall, Jesuit Community, Bronx, NY
Jones, Rev. Glennon, (MO) Curia: Offices and Directors
Jones, Very Rev. Glennon F., '08 (SFE) Curia: Finance; Leadership; Offices and Directors; Pastoral Services Our Lady of the Assumption-Jemez Springs, Jemez Springs, NM
Jones, Rev. Gregory David, *O.S.B.* '13 (DET) [MON] St. Benedict Monastery, Oxford, MI; [SEM] St. Benedict Monastery, House of Formation, Oxford, MI
Jones, Rev. Herb, (SAT) (>IND) Sacred Heart of Jesus Catholic Church, Indianapolis, Inc., Indianapolis, IN
Jones, Rev. Herbert, *O.Carm.* (BO) Retired.
Jones, Rev. Joseph, *C.P.* '65 (NY) Retired.
Jones, Rev. Joseph F., *C.Ss.R.* '73 (ROC) [RTR] Notre Dame Retreat House, Canandaigua, NY
Jones, Rev. Joseph F., *C.Ss.R.* '73 (BRK) [MON] Immaculate Conception Monastery, Jamaica, NY
Jones, Rev. Joseph R., *C.P.* '65 (NY) Retired. [MON] The Congregation of the Passion - St. Paul of the Cross Province, Jamaica, NY
Jones, Rev. Kenneth, '69 (NEW) Retired.
Jones, Rev. Mark R., '92 (MIL) Good Shepherd Congregation, Eden, WI; St. Matthew's Congregation, Campbellsport, WI
Jones, Rev. Martin J.W., '94 (NOR) St. Lawrence, Killingworth, CT; St. Peter, Higganum, CT
Jones, Rev. Matthew F., '15 (ROC) On Leave.
Jones, Rev. Michael K., '92 (BGP) Curia: Clergy and Religious Services; Consultative Bodies St. Marys Rom. C. Church Greenwich Connecticut, Greenwich, CT
Jones, Rev. Michael P., *OFM* (SP) Sacred Heart, Tampa, FL
Jones, Rev. Michael T., '85 (WDC) St. Pius X, Bowie, MD
Jones, Rev. Paul W., '96 (JC) Retired.
Jones, Rev. Msgr. Raymond N., '59 (DEN) Retired.
Jones, Rev. Richard S., '88 (PIT) Chap, Mercy Health Sys of Pittsburgh-Pittsburgh Mercy Hosp.
Jones, Rev. Rick L., '90 (SPC) Curia: Consultative Bodies; Offices and Directors St. Vincent de Paul, Cape Girardeau, MO
Jones, Rev. Robert, *S.M.* (CIN) [CAM] University of Dayton Campus Ministry, Dayton, OH; [SEM] Marianist Community, Dayton, OH
Jones, Very Rev. Robert W., '92 (RCK) On Special Assignment. Curia: Leadership St. Thomas the Apostle, Crystal Lake, IL
Jones, Rev. Ronald A., '73 (RCK) Retired.
Jones, Very Rev. Scott, (STL) Curia: Leadership Sacred Heart Catholic Church, Valley Park, Valley Park, MO; [SEM] Kenrick School of Theology, ,
Jones, Rev. Stephen P., '22 (CIN) Holy Family, Versailles, OH; Immaculate Conception, Bradford, OH; St. Denis, Versailles, OH; St. Louis, North Star, OH; St. Mary, Greenville, OH; St. Nicholas, Osgood, OH; St. Remy, Russia, OH
Jones, Rev. Stephen W., '12 (JC) Curia: Offices and Directors
Jones, Rev. Steven Robert, '12 (SFS) Saint Mary, Help of Christians Parish of McCook County, Salem, SD; Saint Patrick Parish of McCook County, Montrose, SD; Saint Teresa of Calcutta of Union County, Dakota Dunes, SD
Jones, Rev. Thomas, '21 (FWT) St. Jude, Mansfield, TX
Jones, Rev. Thomas J., *CSC* (FTW) [MIS] Holy Cross House, Notre Dame, IN
Jones, Rev. Thomas P., *O.F.M.* '59 (SP) Retired. [MON] St. Anthony Friary (St. Petersburg) Franciscan Friars-Holy Name Province, Inc., St. Petersburg, FL
Jones, Rev. Tony, '89 (OWN) Curia: Advisory Boards, Commissions, Committees, and Councils
Jones, Rev. William R., '67 (SY) Retired. The Cathedral of the Immaculate Conception, Syracuse, NY
Jones, Rev. Zachary R., '22 (SC) On Duty Outside Diocese. Graduate studies at North American College, Rome
Jong, Rev. Lyndon A., (MO) Curia: Offices and Directors
Jong-A-Kiem, Rev. Walter, (OM) St. Joseph, Platte Center, NE; St. Stanislaus, Duncan, NE
Jonientz, Rev. Bernard, '63 (SEA) Retired.
Joo, Rev. Jae, (NEW) St. Elizabeth, Wyckoff, NJ
Joppa, Rev. Mark J., '07 (STP) Curia: Leadership Church of St. Rita, Cottage Grove, MN; [CEM] St. Michael Cemetery, Bayport, MN
Jordan, Rev. Brian, *O.S.F.* '83 (BRK) [CAM] Campus Ministers and Ministry Centers (Newman Apostolate, Inc.), Brooklyn, NY
Jordan, Rev. Daniel J., '99 (BUR) Curia: Leadership All Saints Parish Charitable Trust, Richford, VT; St. Anthony, Sheldon Springs, VT; St. John the Baptist, Enosburg Falls, VT
Jordan, Rev. Msgr. Harry J., '61 (CAM) Retired.
Jordan, Rev. Jeyanthan, '07 (BLX) St. Charles Borromeo, Picayune, MS
Jordan, Rev. John M., '83 (PIT) Retired. [MON] St. John Vianney Manor, Pittsburgh, PA
Jordan, Rev. Msgr. John W., '69 (SCR) Retired.
Jordan, Rev. Matthew, (CLV) St. Michael, Independence, OH
Jordan, Rev. Milton E., '72 (WDC) Retired.
Jordan, Rev. Salvador, *S.J.* (PH) Retired.
Jordan, Rev. Shawn William, '05 (BGP) St. Marguerite Bourgeoys, Brookfield, CT
Jorgensen, Rev. Alan P., '05 (KAL) St. John Bosco, Mattawan, MI; St. Jude, Gobles, MI; St. Mary, Paw Paw, MI
Jorgensen, Rev. Cody, *O.P.* '19 (SLC) Saint Catherine of Siena Catholic Newman Center LLC 218, Salt Lake City, UT; [CAM] University of Utah, Newman Center, Salt Lake City, UT
Jorgensen, Rev. Cody, *O.P.* '19 (SLC) Curia: Offices and Directors
Jose, Rev. Benny, *M.SS.CC.* '12 (HBG) St. Joseph the Worker, Gettysburg, PA
Jose, Rev. Jaime, '03 (HON) Sacred Heart, Waianae, HI
Jose, Rev. Raju, *M.S.T.* '96 (MAR) St. Joseph, Lake Linden, MI
Jose, Rev. Raneesh, (BO) [MON] Noel Chabanel House, Brighton, MA
Jose, Rev. Shaji, (LKC) Immaculate Heart of Mary, Lake Charles, LA
Jose, Rev. Shinoj, '10 (SC) Sacred Heart, Manning, IA; St. Ann's, Vail, IA; St. Rose of Lima, Denison, IA
Jose Chethalil, Rev. Bins, '05 (SYM) St. John Neumann Syro-Malabar Knanaya Catholic Mission of Greater Philadelphia, Feasterville, PA
Jose Volques, Rev. Luis Amaury, *CRL* (SJN) San Francisco de Asis, Trujillo Alto, PR
Josemandapathe, Rev. Tojy, (GRY) [MON] Our Lady of Lourdes Friary, Cedar Lake, IN
Joseph, Rev. Alexander, '13 (SAM) Our Lady of Mercy, Worcester, MA
Joseph, Rev. Antony, (LC) Sacred Heart of Jesus-St. Patrick, Eau Claire, WI; [EFT] St. Patrick of Eau Claire Endowment Trust, Eau Claire, WI; [EFT] The Sacred Heart Parish Endowment Trust, Eau Claire, WI
Joseph, Rev. Antony A., '75 (CHI)
Joseph, Rev. Augustine, '90 (OAK) St. Augustine, Oakland, CA
Joseph, Rev. Basil, *O.F.M. Cap.* (BO) [MON] San Lorenzo Friary, Boston, MA
Joseph, Rev. Benoy, (SYM) St. Mary's Syro-Malabar Catholic Church (Orlando), Sanford, FL
Joseph, Rev. Bijoy, *CFT* '02 (NOR) St. Luke, Ellington, CT
Joseph, Rev. Binu, (VEN) Sacred Heart Parish in

Bradenton, Inc., Bradenton, FL
Joseph, Rev. Charles Heston, '94 (NY) Parish of St. Mary-St. Joseph and Our Lady of Mount Carmel, Poughkeepsie, NY
Joseph, Rev. Charles Heston, (CHY) St. Anthony, Cody, WY
Joseph, Rev. Chellan, '80 (NY) Our Lady of Mount Carmel, White Plains, NY; Parish of St. John the Evangelist and Our Lady of Mount Carmel, White Plains, NY
Joseph, Rev. Cidouane, *OFM* '11 (BO) [MIS] St. Anthony Shrine, Boston, MA
Joseph, Rev. Denny, *R.C.J.* '09 (LA) [MON] Congregation of Rogationists, Inc., Van Nuys, CA
Joseph, Rev. Denny E., *R.C.J.* '09 (FRS) St. Anthony of Padua, Reedley, CA
Joseph, Rev. Eugene, '21 (COL) St. Joan of Arc, Powell, OH; St. Joseph Cathedral, Columbus, OH
Joseph, Rev. Francis, *OCD* '79 (ORL) Prince of Peace, Ormond Beach, FL
Joseph, Rev. George, '94 (NEW) St. Paul of the Cross, Jersey City, NJ
Joseph, Rev. George, '99 (AUS) Retired.
Joseph, Rev. Gregoire, *C.M.* '15 (PCE) Nuestra Senora de la Medalla Milagrosa, Ponce, PR
Joseph, Rev. Jacob P., *C.M.I.* '83 (CHR) Good Shepherd, McCormick, SC; Sacred Heart, Abbeville, SC
Joseph, Rev. James, *S.D.B.* '91 (SYM) Holy Family Syro-Malabar Catholic Mission, Seattle, Washington of St. Thomas Syro-Malabar Diocese of Chicago, Kirland, WA
Joseph, Rev. Jenesh, *HGN* (LKC) St. John Bosco, Westlake, LA
Joseph, Rev. Jimmy, *V.C.* '97 (SCL) Sacred Heart, Flensburg, MN; St. James, Randall, MN; St. Stanislaus, Little Falls, MN
Joseph, Rev. Joby, '21 (SYM) Curia: Offices and Directors Mar Thoma Sleeha Cathedral (Chicago), Bellwood, IL
Joseph, Rev. Jojan, *C.S.T.* '08 (WH) SS. Peter and Paul, Oak Hill, WV
Joseph, Rev. Jom, *HGN* '11 (LKC) St. Charles Borromeo, Fenton, LA
Joseph, Rev. Jomon, *MSFS* (SAT) Prince of Peace, San Antonio, TX
Joseph, Rev. Joseph K., '83 (GI) Immaculate Conception, Elm Creek, NE
Joseph, Rev. Joseph Panakkal, *S.A.C.* '14 (TOL) Our Lady of Hope, Attica, OH
Joseph, Rev. Joy, *T.O.R.* '95 (FWT) Curia: Miscellaneous / Other Offices Holy Cross, The Colony, TX; [MON] Third Order Regular of St. Francis, Province of St. Thomas, Carrollton, TX
Joseph, Rev. Jubish, '07 (MAR) Church of the Resurrection, Hancock, MI
Joseph, Rev. Justin, '12 (JKS) St. Joseph, Meridian, MS; St. Patrick, Meridian, MS
Joseph, Rev. Mamachan, *C.M.I.* '86 (SAN) Chaplain for San Angelo Hospitals
Joseph, Rev. Marialal, *CMI* (STA) St. Augustine Church and Catholic Student Center, Gainesville, FL
Joseph, Rev. Mathew Vettath, *SDV* '08 (ORL) St. Francis of Assisi, Apopka, FL
Joseph, Rev. Msgr. Milam, '64 (DAL) Retired. Our Lady of Perpetual Help Catholic Parish, Dallas, TX
Joseph, Rev. Norbert, *CSJ* '17 (LA) St. Junipero Serra, Lancaster, CA
Joseph, Rev. Pham M., *C.M.* (DAL) St. Peter Vietnamese Catholic Parish, Dallas, TX
Joseph, Rev. Pierre-Louis, '86 (MIA) [MIS] Catholic Hospice, Inc., Miami, FL
Joseph, Rev. Reji, *OSFS* '04 (VEN) St. Ann Catholic Parish in Naples, Inc. a Florida non-profit corporation, Naples, FL
Joseph, Rev. Reji, (SAC) Pastor of St. Mary Parish, Vacaville, a Corporation Sole, Vacaville, CA
Joseph, Rev. Roy M, *S.J.* '16 (DAL) [MON] St. Aloysius Gonzaga Jesuit Community, Dallas, TX
Joseph, Rev. Saju, '94 (SJ) St. Martin of Tours, San Jose, CA
Joseph, Rev. Satish Antony, '94 (CIN) Holy Angels, Dayton, OH; Our Lady of the Immaculate Conception, Dayton, OH; St. Anthony of Padua, Dayton, OH; St. Helen, Dayton, OH; St. Mary, Dayton, OH
Joseph, Rev. Saw, '93 (STP) Church of St. Bernard, St. Paul, MN
Joseph, Rev. Sinu Puthenpurackal, '00 (DAL) St. Elizabeth Ann Seton Catholic Parish, Plano, TX
Joseph, Rev. Sujan, (NY) Our Lady, Queen of Peace, Staten Island, NY
Joseph, Rev. Sunny, (ARL) St. Timothy, Chantilly, VA
Joseph, Rev. Thankachan, (BAK) St. Patrick's, Heppner, OR; St. William, Ione, OR
Joseph, Rev. Msgr. Theophilus, '74 (BRK) Retired. St. Ephrem, Brooklyn, NY
Joseph, Rev. Thomas, '11 (BRK) St. Nicholas of Tolentine, Jamaica, NY
Joseph, Rev. Thomas, *O.S.H.* '94 (GAL) St. Edward, Spring, TX; [MON] The Society of the Oblates of Sacred Heart, Missouri City, TX
Joseph, Rev. Thomas, (NY) Chap, White Plains Hosp, White Plains; NY Presbyterian
Joseph, Rev. Thomas J., '05 (STP) On Leave.
Joseph, Rev. Tomy Mamparampil, '98 (RNO) St. John Bosco, Battle Mountain, NV
Joseph, Rev. Vincent Ezhanikatt, '84 (WH) Catholic Church of the Ascension, Hurricane, WV
Joseph, Rev. Vincent Rathappillil, *VC* '85 (FTW) St. Michael the Archangel, Waterloo, IN
Joseph, Rev. William, '62 (PT) Retired.
Joseph HGN, Rev. Jojy, *HGN* '08 (OWN) St. Mark Church, Eddyville, KY; St. Paul, Princeton, KY
Joseph Williams, Rev. Jeyaraj, (LA) Mary Immaculate, Pacoima, CA
Joslyn, Rev. James W., '73 (CHI) Retired.
Josoma, Rev. Stephen S., (BO) St. Susanna, Dedham, MA
Jost, Rev. Aloys, *O.F.M.* '80 (SHP) Curia: Offices and Directors Our Lady of Perpetual Help, Farmerville, LA
Jost, Rev. Edward F., '96 (BUF) St. Mary of the Lake, Hamburg, NY
Josten, Rev. Paul, '87 (SFS) Saint Ann Parish of Hand County, Miller, SD; Saint Mary Parish of Hyde County, Highmore, SD
Joutras, Rev. Samuel L., *O.S.A.* (CHI) St. Rita of Cascia, Chicago, IL
Jovanovic, Rev. Msgr. Robert P., '61 (STL) Retired.
Jovicic, Rev. Goran, (SFR) [SEM] St. Patrick's Seminary and University (The Roman Catholic Seminary of San Francisco), Menlo Park, CA
Jowdy, Rev. Msgr. Albert W., '84 (ATL) Immaculate Heart of the Blessed Virgin Mary Catholic Church, Atlanta, Inc., Atlanta, GA
Joy, Rev. Joemon, (PHX) St. Vincent de Paul Roman Catholic Parish, Phoenix, AZ
Joy, Rev. Laurence, '60 (LA) Retired.
Joy, Very Rev. William P., '72 (BO) Curia: Advisory Boards, Commissions, Committees, and Councils; Clergy and Religious Services; Consultative Bodies; Leadership
Joyce, Rev. Daniel R.J., *S.J.* '01 (PH) [COL] Saint Joseph's University, Philadelphia, PA; [MIS] Jesuit Fathers, , ; [MON] Arrupe Jesuit Community, Merion Station, PA
Joyce, Rev. Msgr. David, (SPR) Holy Cross, Springfield, MA
Joyce, Rev. David J., '68 (SPR) Retired.
Joyce, Rev. Gerald P., '61 (CHI) Retired.
Joyce, Rev. James F., *S.J.* '75 (NY) [MON] Murray-Weigel Hall (A Jesuit Community at Murray-Weigel Hall and Kohlmann Hall), Bronx, NY
Joyce, Rev. James K., '72 (SPR) Retired.
Joyce, Rev. Kevin J., '01 (OM) Holy Cross, Bancroft, NE; St. Joseph, Lyons, NE; St. Patrick, Tekamah, NE; [MIS] His Global Love, Inc., Tekamah, NE
Joyce, Rev. Kevin P., '80 (SJ) Retired. (>SFR) [SEM] St. Patrick's Seminary and University (The Roman Catholic Seminary of San Francisco), Menlo Park, CA
Joyce, Rev. Michael, *O. Carm.* '22 (NEW) St. Therese of Lisieux, Cresskill, NJ
Joyce, Rev. Michael, *O.F.M.* '67 (PAT) Retired. [MON] St. Anthony Friary (Order of Friars Minor), Butler, NJ
Joyce, Rev. Michael, *O.F.M.Cap.* '85 (CLV) [SEM] Borromeo Seminary, Wickliffe, OH
Joyce, Rev. Michael P., *C.M.* '76 (SPC) Curia: Offices and Directors
Joyce, Rev. Michael P., *C.M.* '76 (STL) Curia: Leadership [MON] Congregation of the Mission Vincentian Fathers Lazarist Residence, St. Louis, MO
Joyce, Rev. Peter, '83 (WOR) Curia: Offices and Directors St. Mary of the Assumption, Milford, MA
Joyce, Rev. Msgr. Peter M., '92 (CAM) Curia: Leadership The Parish of St. Maximilian Kolbe, Marmora, N.J., Marmora, NJ
Joyce, Rev. Msgr. Peter M., '92 (CAM) Curia: Tribunal
Joyce, Rev. Timothy J., '59 (BO) [MON] Glastonbury Abbey, Hingham, MA
Jozefiak, Rev. Greg, '92 (PEO) Holy Family, Peoria, IL
Jozefiak, Rev. Matthew, *C.PP.S.* (CIN) Holy Redeemer, New Bremen, OH; Most Precious Blood, Chickasaw, OH; Nativity of the Blessed Virgin Mary, Maria Stein, OH; St. Augustine, Minster, OH; St. John the Baptist, Maria Stein, OH; St. Rose, Maria Stein, OH; St. Sebastian, Celina, OH; [EFT] Community Support Charitable Trust, Dayton, OH
Jozefiak, Rev. Matthew, *C.PP.S.* '87 (TOL) SS. Peter and Paul, Ottawa, OH
Jozwiak, Rev. Lawrence W., '87 (GAL) Curia: Leadership; Offices and Directors St. Maximilian Kolbe, Houston, TX
Jozwiak, Rev. Richard, '59 (SAG) Retired. Saint John Vianney Parish of Saginaw, Saginaw, MI
Jozwiak, Rev. Ronald J., '79 (DET) Prince of Peace Parish West Bloomfield, West Bloomfield, MI
Juan, Rev. Dennis R., '98 (ATL) Sacred Heart Catholic Church, Griffin, Inc., Griffin, GA
Juan, Rev. Vincent R., '03 (SAC) Pastor of Assumption of the Blessed Virgin Mary Parish, Truckee, a corporation sole, Truckee, CA
Juarbe-Perez, Friar Gabriel, *O.F.M.Cap.* (SJN) [MON] Fraternidad Santa Maria de Los Angeles, Rio Piedras, PR
Juarez, Rev. Lucio, '91 (LA) On Administrative Leave.
Juarez, Rev. Mario, '09 (ORG) St. Anne, Santa Ana, CA
Juarez, Rev. Ricardo, *CJM* '14 (SD) Pastor of Our Lady of Angels Catholic Parish, San Diego, a corporation sole, San Diego, CA
Juarez, Rev. Rudolph T., '80 (DAV) Curia: Leadership St. Anthony Church of Davenport, Iowa, Davenport, IA
Juchniewicz, Rev. Leon, '80 (SAC) Retired. Pastor of Good Shepherd Parish, Elk Grove, a corporation sole, Elk Grove, CA
Jucutan, Rev. Michael Vincent, '13 (AGN) Santa Barbara, Dededo, GU
Judd, Rev. Augustine, *O.P.* (SPR) Curia: Clergy and Religious Services
Judd, Rev. Stephen, *M.M.* '78 (SJ) Retired. [MON] Maryknoll, Los Altos, CA
Judd, Rev. Stephen P., *M.M.* '78 (NY) Retired.
Judge, Rev. James G., '72 (BUF) Retired.
Judge, Rev. Philip G., *S.J.* '93 (NY) [MON] America; Residence and Publication Office of the America Press, New York, NY
Judge, Rev. Philip G., *S.J.* '93 (ROC) McQuaid Jesuit High School, Rochester, NY
Judge, Rev. Russell R., '78 (JC) Retired.
Judge, Rev. Timothy M., '79 (PH) Retired. On Special Assignment. Chap, Holy Redeemer Health Sys, St David Rec, Willow Grove
Judie, Rev. John T., '87 (L) Retired.
Judkins, Rev. Brett, '16 (BEL) On Academic Leave.
Judy, Rev. Albert G., *O.P.* '62 (CHI) [MON] St. Pius V Priory, Chicago, IL
Judy, Rev. Myron, *O.Carm.* '63 (JOL) [MON] Carmelite Provincial Office, Darien, IL
Juelfs, Rev. Daniel, '73 (RC) Curia: Leadership
Juelfs, Rev. Daniel, '73 (RC) Retired. Curia: Leadership [MON] Casa Maria Residence for Retired Priests, Piedmont, SD
Juettner, Rev. Mark R., '79 (STP) Retired. [CEM] St. George Cemetery, Long Lake, MN
Jugenheimer, Rev. James R., '87 (GB) SS. Peter and Paul, Hortonville, WI; St. Pius X, Appleton, WI
Juguilon, Rev. Alex, *O.S.C.* (PHX) [COL] Benedictine University, Mesa, AZ; [MON] Crosier Community of Phoenix (Canons Regular of the Order of the Holy Cross) (Conventual Priory of the Holy Cross), Phoenix, AZ
Juhasz, Rev. Imre, '03 (MET) Curia: Family Life Holy Family Parish, New Brunswick, NJ
Juhl, Rev. Dennis D., '73 (DUB) Retired.
Jujjuvarapu, Rev. Kumar, '06 (SAN) St. Isidore, Coyanosa, TX
Jujjuvarapu, Rev. Kumar, '06 (SAN) Our Lady of Lourdes, Imperial, TX
Jujjuvarapu, Rev. Kumar, '06 (SAN) Good Shepherd, Crane, TX; Sacred Heart, McCamey, TX
Jujuvarapu, Rev. Bose, *H.G.N.* '11 (FWT) Sacred Heart, Seymour, TX; St. Mary, Megargel, TX
Juknialis, Rev. Joseph J., '69 (MIL) Retired. St. Mary's Congregation, Milwaukee, WI
Julce, Rev. Evans, (BRK) [CON] The Sisters Adorers of the Precious Blood, Brooklyn, NY
Juleen, Rev. Stuart, '77 (SAT) Retired.
Jules, Rev. Youry, (MIA) Notre Dame d'Haiti, Miami, FL
Julia, Rev. Peter, '19 (P) Curia: (>MO) Offices and Directors; Offices and Directors
Julian, Rev. Mario, *O.F.M.* (NY) St. Anthony of Padua, New York, NY; [RTR] Mt. Alvernia Retreat House, Wappingers Falls, NY
Julien, Rev. Jean Ridly, '96 (BGP) On Duty Outside Diocese. Columbia Univ Med Ctr, New York 10032
Julien, Rev. Roland M., '65 (STA) Retired.
Julio, Rev. Javier, '18 (WOR) Curia: Offices and Directors St. Louis, Webster, MA

Jumao-As, Rev. Vito, '02 (BRK) St. Fidelis, College Point, NY
Junak, Rev. Jacek, *CR* '95 (RCK) St. John the Baptist, Johnsburg, IL
Juncer, Rev. Bartholomew J., '08 (CHI) St. Odilo, Berwyn, IL
Jung, Rev. Chung Yeol, '16 (NEW) Our Lady of Mercy, Jersey City, NJ
Jung, Rev. Dennet, *OFM* '63 (DET) [MON] Dun Scotus Friary, Berkley, MI
Jung, Rev. Dominic K., *C.PP.S.* '95 (BO) Saint Antoine Daveluy, Newton, MA
Jung, Rev. Jaehoon, (SJ) Holy Korean Martyrs, San Jose, CA
Jung, Rev. Jay, *C.M.* (GLP) Our Lady of Guadalupe, Kayenta, AZ
Jung, Rev. Jerome L., '93 (POD) Curia: Clergy and Religious Services
Jung, Rev. John J, *C.M.* '53 (STL) [MON] Congregation of the Mission, Perryville, MO
Jung, Rev. Joseph B., '56 (PH) Retired.
Junge, Rev. Aaron R., '16 (DUB) Immaculate Conception Church, Cedar Rapids, Iowa, Cedar Rapids, IA; St. Wenceslaus Church, Cedar Rapids, Iowa, Cedar Rapids, IA
Jungmann, Rev. William, '03 (DEN) Retired.
Junianto, Rev. Hery, *S.X.* '14 (MIL) [SEM] Xaverian Missionary Fathers College Seminary, Franklin, WI
Juniet, Rev. Paul, *O.F.M.* '66 (SFE) Retired. [MON] The Province of Our Lady of Guadalupe of the Order of Friars Minor, Inc., Albuquerque, NM
Junker, Very Rev. Nicholas G., '08 (BEL) Curia: Leadership; Offices and Directors St. Barbara, Scheller, IL; St. Mary the Immaculate Conception, Mount Vernon, IL
Juracek, Rev. Joseph, *O.F.M.* (PAT) Curia: Leadership St. Anthony, Butler, NJ
Jurcak, Rev. Lawrence, '81 (CLV) Curia: Advisory Boards, Commissions, Committees, and Councils St. Mary, Hudson, OH
Jurek, Rev. Msgr. Daniel J., '73 (BEL) Retired. Curia: Leadership
Jurek, Rev. Norbert K., '11 (MOB) [CAM] Sacred Heart of Jesus Catholic Student Center at University of South Alabama, Mobile, AL
Jurgelonis, Rev. Joseph J., '73 (WOR) Retired.
Jurgensmeyer, Rev. Nicholaus L, '18 (WCH) Sacred Heart, Eureka, KS; St. John, Hamilton, KS; St. Teresa of Avila, Madison, KS
Juric, Rev. Jakov, (GLP) On Leave.
Jurisich, Friar Melvin A., *O.F.M.* '70 (LA) [RTR] Serra Retreat, Malibu, CA
Jurisich, Rev. Melvin A., *O.F.M.* '70 (OAK) [EFT] Province of Saint Barbara Fraternal Care Trust, Oakland, CA; [MON] Franciscan Friars of California (Province of St. Barbara), Oakland, CA; [RTR] San Damiano Retreat, Danville, CA
Jurkiewicz, Rev. Andrzej, '83 (ORL) St. Ann's, Debary, FL
Jurkovich, Rev. Robb M., '04 (MAR) [HOS] OSF HealthCare St. Francis Hospital & Medical Group, Escanaba, MI
Jurkowski, Rev. Joseph V., '58 (CAM) Retired.
Jurkus, Rev. Alan F., '70 (MIL) Retired.
Jurzyk, Rev. Marek, '91 (JOL) Corpus Christi, Carol Stream, IL
Jussen, Rev. Paul, *M.S.* (LKC) [CAM] Catholic Student Center, Lake Charles, LA
Jussen, Rev. Paul, *M.S.* (LKC) Curia: Leadership Our Lady of Good Counsel, Lake Charles, LA
Justice, Rev. Joseph Charles, '75 (ORG) Retired.
Juszczak, Rev. John Wladyslaw, *C.Ss.R.* '88 (MIA) Annunciation, West Park, FL
Juszczec, Rev. Andrzej, (CHI) SS. Bruno and Richard Parish, Chicago, IL
Jutte, Rev. Edgar, *C.PP.S.* '62 (CIN) Retired. [MON] St. Charles, Celina, OH
Juya, Rev. Jose, (CHL) St. Michael, Gastonia, NC; [MIS] Diocesan Hispanic Ministry, Charlotte, NC
Juza, Rev. Philip J., '95 (SUP) St. Catherine, Sarona, WI; St. Francis De Sales, Spooner, WI; St. Joseph, Shell Lake, WI
Kaanan, Rev. A. Solomon, '19 (SAV) St. Mary on the Hill, Augusta, GA
Kabagambe, Rev. Evarist, (TR) Church of St. Elizabeth Ann Seton, Whiting, NJ
Kabali, Rev. Joseph, '96 (MET) Curia: Tribunal St. Matthew the Apostle, Edison, NJ
Kabalisa, Rev. Francois, *O.S.B.* '16 (LA) [MON] St. Andrew's Abbey (Benedictine Monks), Valyermo, CA
Kabango, Rev. Jean-Marie, *O.F.M.* '99 (WDC) St. Camillus, Silver Spring, MD
Kabat, Rev. Robert J., '79 (GB) St. Matthew, Green Bay, WI
Kaberia, Rev. Silvio, '83 (RIC) Blessed Sacrament, Harrisonburg, VA
Kabipi, Rev. Narcis L., '98 (SFR) St. John of God, San Francisco, CA; [CAM] Catholic Student Association of UCSF, San Francisco, CA
Kabiru, Rev. Francis, '07 (DUL) Holy Angels, Moose Lake, MN; St. Isidore, Sturgeon Lake, MN; St. Mary, Willow River, MN
Kabran, Rev. Frederic, (FAJ) Santa Maria Madre de Dios, Canovanas, PR
Kabuk, Rev. Elias V., '09 (LAV) Holy Child, Caliente, NV; Sacred Heart, Ely, NV
Kaburu, Rev. Julius, '10 (SAC) Pastor of Good Shepherd Parish, Elk Grove, a corporation sole, Elk Grove, CA
Kacalo, Rev. Robert C., '06 (MIL) St. Stephens Congregation, Oak Creek, WI
Kacerguis, Rev. Edward, '82 (ALB) Curia: Offices and Directors [MIS] Chapel + Cultural Center, ,
Kachappilly, Rev. Joseph, (SPA) Assyrian Chaldean Catholic Church California Corporation, Campbell, CA
Kachel, Rev. Msgr. Steven J., '95 (LC) Curia: Leadership St. Patrick, Onalaska, WI; [EFT] Aquinas Catholic Schools Foundation, La Crosse, WI; [EFT] Father John Rossiter and Friends Endowment Trust of St. Patrick Parish, Onalaska, WI
Kachuba, Rt. Rev. Mitred Archpriest John S., '74 (PRM) Retired.
Kachuba, Rev. Archpriest John S., '74 (PRM) Retired.
Kachuba, Rev. Samuel S., '08 (BGP) Curia: Clergy and Religious Services; Consultative Bodies St. Pius X Corporation, Fairfield, CT
Kachurka, Rev. Edward M., '89 (BRK) Curia: Organizations (affiliated, inter-Diocesan, miscellaneous/ other) Mary's Nativity-Saint Ann Roman Catholic Church, Flushing, NY; St. Gregory the Great, Bellerose, NY
Kacprzak, Rev. Stanley, '85 (ROC) Our Lady of the Valley, Hornell, NY
Kaczkowski, Rev. Conrad J., *S.M.* '68 (SAT) Retired. [COL] St. Mary's University of San Antonio, Texas, San Antonio, TX; [MON] Marianist Residence, San Antonio, TX
Kaczmarczyk, Rev. Pawel, '03 (DET) On Leave.
Kaczmarek, Rev. James A., (MO) Curia: Offices and Directors
Kaczmarek, Rev. Msgr. James A., '69 (MAR) Retired. Chap, Veterans Administration Ctr
Kaczmarek, Rev. Peter, '69 (RVC) St. Francis of Assisi, Greenlawn, NY
Kaczmarek, Rev. Thaddeus J., '71 (GBG) Retired. [NUR] Neumann House, Greensburg, PA
Kaczmarzyk, Rev. Witold, (DEN) Our Lady of Lourdes Catholic Parish in Denver, Denver, CO; St. Louis-King of France Catholic Parish in Englewood, Englewood, CO
Kaczorowski, Rev. Msgr. James T., '73 (CHI) Queen of Apostles Parish, Chicago, IL
Kaczowka, Rev. Julian, *S.Chr.* (WIL) St. Hedwig, Wilmington, DE
Kaczynski, Rev. Krzysztof, '93 (MET) Our Lady of Victories, Baptistown, NJ; St. Edward the Confessor, Milford, NJ
Kadambukatt, Rev. Ambrose, (PMB) Holy Name of Jesus, West Palm Beach, FL
Kadaprayil, Rev. Joseph, *S.D.B.* '78 (GI) St. Patrick, North Platte, NE
Kadar, Rev. Vasyl, (PBR) SS. Peter and Paul, Punxsutawney, PA; St. Jude Thaddeus, Ernest, PA
Kadavil, Rev. Antony, '67 (MOB) Retired. [NUR] Little Sisters of the Poor, Home For the Aged, Inc., Mobile, AL
Kaddo, Rev. Msgr. Joseph, (SAM) Retired.
Kaddu, Rev. Fred, *S.S.J.* '20 (NO) All Saints, New Orleans, LA
Kadera, Rev. Thomas R., '87 (CHY) Retired.
Kaderabek, Rev. Matthew A., *L.C.* '03 (ATL) Pinecrest Academy, Inc., Cumming, GA; [MON] Legionaries of Christ, Incorporated, Cumming, GA
Kadlec, Rev. Jared, '97 (FAR) St. Mark's Church of Bottineau, Bottineau, ND
Kadlec, Rev. Jared, '97 (FAR) St. Andrew's Church of Westhope, Westhope, ND
Kadlec, Rev. Jared, '97 (FAR) Curia: Leadership
Kado, Rev. Paul, '06 (FRS) St. Anthony, Atwater, CA
Kado, Rev. Paul, (FRS) Immaculate Conception, Atwater, CA
Kadrmas, Rev. Christopher J., '00 (BIS) Curia: Leadership; Offices and Directors St. Henry, Regent, ND; St. John the Baptist, New Leipzig, ND; St. Vincent de Paul, Mott, ND
Kadukappillil, Very Rev. Thomas, '91 (SYM) Curia: Administration; Leadership Mar Thoma Sleeha Cathedral (Chicago), Bellwood, IL
Kadukunnel, Rev. Jose, *C.M.I.* '86 (JOL) Ascension of Our Lord, Oakbrook Terrace, IL
Kaduthodiyil, Rev. Abraham, '81 (GI) St. Nicholas, Valentine, NE
Kady, Rev. Scott, (BAL) Resurrection, Ellicott City, MD; St. Paul, Ellicott City, MD
Kadylo, Rev. Vasyl, '03 (STF) St. Josaphat, Rochester, NY
Kaech, Very Rev. Paul A., '06 (SEA) Curia: Leadership St. Edward, Shelton, WA
Kaeding, Rev. Robert F., '73 (TR) Retired.
Kaele, Rev. Raymond, (ORL) Immaculate Conception, Melbourne Beach, FL
Kaelin, Rev. Dennis J., '76 (NEW) Retired.
Kafara, Rev. Andrew, '85 (SAT) Retired. Our Lady of Perpetual Help, ,
Kafumu, Rev. Peter, *OFM Cap.* '18 (MIL) [MON] St. Lawrence Friary, Mount Calvary, WI; [SEM] St. Lawrence Seminary High School, Mount Calvary, WI
Kagere, Rev. Guy, (MO) Curia: Offices and Directors
Kaggwa, Very Rev. Gerald S., '90 (RIC) Curia: Deaneries Church of Francis de Sales, Mathews, VA; Church of the Visitation, Topping, VA
Kaggwa, Rev. Jude, (BO) St. Mary, Waltham, MA
Kagoo, Rev. Edwin, (AUS) St. John the Evangelist, San Marcos, TX
Kagumisa, Rev. Thomas R., '10 (PHX) Curia: Leadership Church of the Resurrection Roman Catholic Parish, Tempe, AZ
Kahan, Rev. Paul, *S.V.D.* '99 (BEA) Immaculate Conception, Liberty, TX; [CEM] Immaculate Conception Cemetery, Liberty, TX
Kahle, Rev. Jason J., '09 (TOL) St. Thomas More University Parish, Bowling Green, OH
Kahlich, Rev. Daniel P., '66 (VIC) Retired.
Kahmann, Rev. Kevin James, '10 (COV) Mary, Queen of Heaven, Erlanger, KY; St. Henry District High School, Erlanger, KY
Kahumburu, Rev. Joseph, '83 (NY) Most Holy Trinity, Mamaroneck, NY
Kail, Chorbishop Michael J., '74 (OLL) Retired.
Kaim, Very Rev. Phillip A., '03 (RCK) On Special Assignment. Curia: Leadership; Offices and Directors Holy Family, Rockford, IL
Kaiman, Rev. Tokabwebwe, *M.S.C.* '19 (MI) Holy Rosary, Likiep, MH
Kaimann, Rev. Gerald J., '70 (JC) Retired. St. Joseph, Palmyra, MO
Kaimukirwa, Rev. Adrian, '11 (DAV) [MON] St. Vincent Center, Davenport, IA
Kain, Rev. Carson, '19 (LIN) St. John's, Prague, NE
Kairouz, Rev. Antoine, '13 (SAM) Saint Teresa of Calcutta Maronite Mission, Baden, PA
Kairouz, Rev. Elie G., '01 (SAM) Curia: Leadership St. John Maron, Williamsville, NY
Kairouz, Rev. Elie G., '01 (BUF) Curia: Leadership
Kais, Rev. Paul D., '02 (POD) Curia: Clergy and Religious Services (>VIC) [MIS] Opus Dei, Schulenburg, TX
Kais, Rev. Paul D., '02 (GAL) [MIS] Opus Dei, Houston, TX
Kaiser, Rev. Gary Edward, '06 (EVN) Holy Cross, Fort Branch, IN; St. Joseph, Princeton, IN
Kaiser, Rev. Lawrence H., '64 (DET) Retired.
Kaithackal, Rev. Sebastian D., *C.M.I.* '81 (MET) Chap, John F Kennedy Med Ctr Our Lady of Peace, Edison, NJ
Kajko, Rev. Sebastian, (NY) (>NEW) [MON] Franciscan Friars of the Renewal (Most Blessed Sacrament Friary), Newark, NJ
Kakala, Rev. Kapiolani, '04 (SFR) Curia: Offices and Directors St. Timothy, San Mateo, CA
Kakareka, Rev. Joseph R., '72 (SCR) Retired.
Kakaty, Rt. Rev. Edward, '72 (NTN) Retired.
Kakkuzhiyil, Rev. John, '86 (GI) On Administrative Leave.
Kako, Rev. Fawaz, '10 (EST) Curia: Leadership; Offices and Directors St. George Chaldean Catholic Church, Shelby Twp., MI
Kakumanu, Rev. Anil Kumar, '12 (SLC) Our Lady of Lourdes LLC 211, Salt Lake City, UT; St. Francis of Assisi LLC 221, Orem, UT
Kala, Rev. Paul, '10 (SFD) On Duty Outside Diocese. Missionary Society of St Theresa
Kala, Rev. Sleeva R., *O.S.F.S.* (WIL) St. Anthony of Padua, Wilmington, DE
Kalaj, Rev. Frederik, '01 (DET) St. Paul (Albanian) Parish Rochester Hills, Rochester Hills, MI
Kalam, Rev. Thomas, *C.M.I.* '69 (NSH) Curia: Leadership Our Lady of the Lake, Hendersonville, TN
Kalamaja, Rev. Theodore M., *S.J.* '67 (MIL) [MON] St.

Camillus Jesuit Community (Society of Jesus, USA Midwest Province), Wauwatosa, WI
Kalamuzi, Rev. Ivan, '05 (COV) St. Anthony, Taylor Mill, KY
Kalange, Rev. Timothy, *O.S.B.* '20 (P) [MON] Mt. Angel Abbey, Saint Benedict, OR
Kalapurackal, Rev. Francis Joseph, '97 (IND) St. Andrew the Apostle Catholic Church, Indianapolis, Inc., Indianapolis, IN; St. Pius X Catholic Church, Indianapolis, Inc., Indianapolis, IN
Kalapurackal, Rev. Thomas K., '88 (WH) Our Lady of the Hills, Elkview, WV; St. Anthony, Charleston, WV
Kalarickal, Rev. Joseph, *M.S.T.* '90 (SP) Our Lady Queen of Peace, New Port Richey, FL
Kalarickal, Rev. Luke, *MSFS* '88 (TYL) Prince of Peace Catholic Church, Whitehouse, TX
Kalas, Rev. Ronald N., '59 (CHI) Retired. Curia: Leadership; Offices and Directors Mary, Seat of Wisdom, Park Ridge, IL
Kalata, Rev. Dominik P., '65 (ALN) Retired.
Kalayil, Rev. Roy, (CC) Holy Cross, Corpus Christi, TX; Our Lady Star of the Sea, Corpus Christi, TX
Kalcic, Rev. Dismas B., *O.S.B.* '65 (JOL) Retired. [MON] St. Procopius Abbey, Lisle, IL
Kalck, Rev. Michael V., '74 (CHI) Retired.
Kaldawi, Rev. Wadih, (OLL) St. John Maron Maronite Catholic Church, Orange, CA
Kalema, Rev. Joseph Kato, (NEW) Curia: Advisory Boards, Commissions, Committees, and Councils
Kalema, Rev. Josephat Kato, '85 (NEW) Parish of the Transfiguration, Newark, NJ
Kalema, Rev. Mark, '88 (CHI) All Souls Parish, Lansing, IL
Kalema, Rev. Raymond, '19 (SPK) Our Lady of Perpetual Help, St. John, WA; St. Joseph, LaCrosse, WA; St. Patrick, Colfax, WA
Kalenzi, Rev. Paul, *S.J.* '16 (CHI) St. Ignatius Jesuit Community, Chicago, IL
Kalert, Rev. David A., *OMI* (BEL) [MON] Missionary Oblates of Mary Immaculate - St. Henry's Oblate Residence, Belleville, IL
Kaley, Rev. Richard, *OFM Conv.* (SAT) [MON] San Damiano Friary, San Antonio, TX; [SEM] San Damiano Friary, Initial House of Formation, San Antonio, TX
Kalil, Rev. Gordon, '94 (SR) Retired.
Kalin, Rev. William A., '59 (LIN) Retired.
Kalina, Rev. Isaac, *O.S.B.* '89 (LA) [MON] St. Andrew's Abbey (Benedictine Monks), Valyermo, CA
Kalinowski, Rev. Dariusz, '99 (FR) Curia: Tribunal Santo Christo, Fall River, MA
Kalinowski, Rev. Joseph, '79 (E) St. John, Tidioute, PA
Kalinowski, Rev. Loren M., '75 (SAG) Curia: Leadership Sacred Heart Parish of Mt. Pleasant, Mount Pleasant, MI
Kalinowski, Rev. Ryszard, *S.V.D.* '74 (LAF) On Special Assignment. Rel Chap, Lafayette area Hosps Immaculate Heart of Mary, Lafayette, LA
Kalist, Rev. Pancrose, '88 (NY) Parish of Guardian Angel and St. Columba, New York, NY
Kalista, Rev. Timothy D., '03 (CLV) On Administrative Leave.
Kalita, Rev. Thomas M., '74 (WDC) Curia: Consultative Bodies St. Peter, Olney, MD
Kalivela, Rev. Prabhakar, '97 (OKL) Christ the King, Oklahoma City, OK
Kaliyadan, Rev. William, *M.S.* '94 (FR) Immaculate Conception, Brewster, MA
Kaliyadan, Rev. William, *M.S.* '94 (HRT) [MON] Missionaries of La Salette Province of Mary, Mother of the Americas (The Missionaries of La Salette Corporation., MLS Religious Trust), Hartford, CT
Kall, Rev. Anthony, *O.F.M.Conv.* '71 (ALB) [MIS] Assisi in Albany, Inc., Albany, NY; [MON] Immaculate Conception Friary - Order of Friars Minor Conventual, Rensselaer, NY
Kall, Friar Anthony, *O.F.M.Conv.* '71 (TR) Retired. St. Junipero Serra, Seaside Park, Seaside Park, NJ
Kallabat, Rev. Stephen, '66 (EST) Retired.
Kallabat, Rev. Stephen H., '66 (EST) Retired. Curia: Offices and Directors Mar Addai Chaldean Parish, Oak Park, MI
Kalladanthiyil, Rev. Geomon, (NY) Parish of Our Lady of the Assumption - St. Mary Star of the Sea, Bronx, NY
Kallaher, Rev. Timothy S., '72 (CIN) Retired.
Kallal, Rev. Paul, *O.M.V.* (SFD) St. Mary's, Alton, IL
Kallal, Rev. Scott, '11 (KCK) On Leave.
Kallarackal, Rev. Lijo Stephen, *O.S.B.Silv.* '03 (STL) St. Martin de Porres Catholic Church, Hazelwood, MO
Kallas, Rev. Mhanna Joseph, *M.L.M* (OLL) St. George Maronite Catholic Church, San Antonio, TX; [MON] The Congregation of Maronite Lebanese Missionaries, Houston, TX
Kallattil, Rev. John, *V.C.* '79 (NY) St. Teresa, Staten Island, NY
Kalliyathuparambil, Rev. James, (PHX) St. Charles Borromeo Roman Catholic Parish, Peoria, AZ
Kallock, Rev. Michael, (WDC) [SEM] Paulist Washington Community, Washington, DC
Kallock, Rev. Michael J., *C.S.P.* '73 (NY) Retired. Chap, Mount Sinai West, New York
Kallookalam, Rev. Joseph, *C.M.I.* '71 (SHP) St. Paul, Minden, LA
Kallukalam, Rev. Jose, '72 (STA) St. Michael's, Fernandina Beach, FL
Kalombo, Rev. Jean Rene, '13 (OWN) SS. Joseph and Paul, Owensboro, KY
Kalonga, Very Rev. Simon, '84 (DEN) Curia: Deaneries Holy Family Catholic Parish in Ft. Collins, Fort Collins, CO; St. Joseph Catholic Parish in Ft. Collins, Fort Collins, CO
Kalousieh, Rev. George, '81 (OLN) Sacred Heart, Little Falls, NJ; St. Ann's Armenian Catholic Church, Little Falls, NJ
Kalscheuer, Rev. Roger H., (OM) Retired.
Kalscheur, Rev. Gregory, *S.J.* '01 (BO) [COL] Graduate School of the Morrissey College of Arts and Sciences, , ; [MON] The Jesuit Community at Boston College, Chestnut Hill, MA
Kaltreider, Rev. Carl E., '79 (CHL) Our Lady of the Angels, Marion, NC
Kalu, Rev. Bernard, '06 (LA) St. John Fisher, Rancho Palos Verdes, CA
Kalu, Rev. Matthew, '91 (LFT) St. Boniface, Lafayette, IN; St. Lawrence, Lafayette, IN
Kalu, Rev. Samuel J., '95 (LFT) Curia: Miscellaneous / Other Offices; Tribunal Blessed Sacrament, West Lafayette, IN; [NUR] St. Anthony Health Care Inc.,, Lafayette, IN
Kalubi, Rev. Edouard, *O.de.M.* '05 (CHI) [MIS] Hales Services, Inc., ,
Kalumba, Rev. Michel Mbusa, *AA* '16 (WOR) [MON] Augustinians of the Assumption at Assumption University, Worcester, MA
Kaluza, Rev. Michael C., '07 (STP) Our Lady of the Prairie, Belle Plaine, MN; [CEM] St. Martin Cemetery, Rogers, MN; [CEM] St. Walburga Cemetery, Rogers, MN
Kalva, Rev. Showri Rayalu, '95 (SLC) Saint James the Greater LLC 227, Vernal, UT
Kamalu, Rev. Chika, (FRS) Chap, Fresno Heart & Surg Hosp; Kaiser Permanente Med Ctr Curia: Pastoral Services
Kamanzi, Rev. Speratus, '93 (ALN) St. John the Baptist, Allentown, PA
Kamas, Rev. John A., *S.S.S.* '75 (NY) St. Jean Baptiste, New York, NY
Kamau, Rev. Francis, *F.M.H.* '00 (SHP) St. John the Baptist, Many, LA
Kambala, Rev. Nirmalraj Mariadass, *C.P.P.S.* '08 (LR) Our Lady of Good Hope, Hope, AR
Kambale Sambya, Rev. Zawadi Jean-Marie, *osc* '12 (SCL) [MON] Crosier Priory, Onamia, MN
Kambale Sambya, Rev. Zawadi Jean-Marie, *OSC* '12 (SCL) [SHR] National Shrine of St. Odilia, Onamia, MN
Kambale Tsongo, Rev. Pacifique, *AA* '21 (WOR) [MON] Augustinians of the Assumption at Assumption University, Worcester, MA
Kamber, Rev. Kenneth L., '53 (L) Retired.
Kamina, Rev. Akizou Gerard, *S.V.D.* (DUB) [SEM] Divine Word College, Epworth, IA
Kaminski, Rev. Dariusz K., '91 (PAT) Curia: Administration; Leadership St. Joseph's, Passaic, NJ
Kaminski, Rev. Edward J., *C.S.C.* '75 (PHX) St. Raphael Roman Catholic Parish, Glendale, AZ
Kaminski, Rev. Frank, (PH) [MON] Arrupe Jesuit Community, Merion Station, PA
Kaminski, Rev. Gabriel, *SDS* (ORL) St. Teresa, Titusville, FL
Kaminski, Rev. Louis T., '77 (SCR) Corpus Christi, Glen Lyon, PA; St. Martha, Stillwater, PA; St. Mary, Our Lady of Perpetual Help, Mocanaqua, PA
Kaminski, Rev. Mark P., '01 (SY) St. Anthony and St. Agnes Church, Utica, NY; St. Mark, Utica, NY
Kaminsky, Rev. Joseph T., '61 (HRT) Retired.
Kammen, Rev. Paul A., '07 (STP) St. Joseph, Rosemount, MN; [CEM] St. Joseph Cemetery, Rosemount, MN
Kammer, Rev. Alfred C, *SJ* '76 (BR) Congregation of Immaculate Conception Roman Catholic Church Scotlandville LA, Baton Rouge, LA
Kammer, Rev. Alfred C., *S.J.* '76 (NO) Retired.
Kammerer, Rev. James, '97 (SAT) On Leave.
Kammerer, Rev. Joseph, '98 (LA) American Martyrs, Manhattan Beach, CA
Kampschneider, Rev. Daniel J., '79 (OM) St. Vincent de Paul, Omaha, NE
Kamwendo, Rev. John, '13 (IND) St. Michael the Archangel Catholic Church, Indianapolis, Inc., Indianapolis, IN
Kanattu, Rev. Devassya P., *C.M.I.* (L) Holy Cross Catholic Church, Burkesville, KY
Kandathikudy, Rev. Jose, (SYM) Retired.
Kandathikudy, Rev. Joseph, (CHI) [MIS] St. Mary's Malankara Catholic Church, ,
Kandora, Rev. Rafal Dominik, *OSPPE* '10 (ORL) St. Mark the Evangelist, Summerfield, FL
Kandt, Rev. Gregory R., '90 (RIC) St. Therese, the Little Flower, Gloucester, VA
Kandyuk, Rev. Valeriy, '90 (STN) Transfiguration of Our Lord, Denver, CO
Kane, Rev. Adam, '14 (KNX) St. Patrick, Morristown, TN
Kane, Rev. Brian P., '00 (LIN) On Duty Outside Diocese. St Charles Borromeo Seminary, Philadelphia Curia: (>MO) Offices and Directors [SEM] St. Gregory the Great Seminary, Seward, NE
Kane, Very Rev. Edward R. P., '79 (BRK) Holy Family - Saint Laurence, Brooklyn, NY
Kane, Rev. George J., '51 (CHI) Retired. Church of the Holy Spirit, Schaumburg, IL
Kane, Rev. James, '71 (ALB) Curia: Offices and Directors
Kane, Rev. James J., '71 (ALB) Retired. St. Clare, Colonie, NY
Kane, Rev. John A., '16 (R) St. Anthony of Padua, Southern Pines, NC
Kane, Rev. John E., *C.M.* '70 (PH) [MON] Congregation of the Mission, Philadelphia, PA
Kane, Rev. Joseph, '67 (EVN) Retired.
Kane, Rev. Matthew, (COS) Holy Apostles, Colorado Springs, CO
Kane, Rev. Michael, '80 (PSC) Our Lady of the Sign, Coconut Creek, FL
Kane, Rev. Patrick M., '16 (HRT) Saint Pio of Pietrelcina Parish Corporation, East Haven, CT
Kane, Rev. Philip M., '88 (JC) Sacred Heart, Vandalia, MO; St. Joseph, Martinsburg, MO
Kane, Rev. Thomas A., '52 (WDC) [NUR] Cardinal O'Boyle Residence for Priests, Washington, DC
Kane, Rev. Thomas Anthony, *C.S.P.* '75 (NY) Retired. [MON] Paulist Fathers' Motherhouse, New York, NY
Kane, Rev. Msgr. Thomas S., '67 (RVC) Retired.
Kane, Rev. Timothy J., '82 (DET) On Leave.
Kanfush, Rev. Philip, *OSB* (GBG) [COL] Saint Vincent College Corporation, Latrobe, PA
Kanfush, Rev. Philip M., *O.S.B.* '00 (GBG) [MON] Saint Vincent Archabbey, Latrobe, PA
Kang, Rev. James Kueh, (CHL) Holy Family, Winston-Salem, NC
Kanga, Rev. Florent, *SAC* (SFD) St. Mary, Farmersville, IL; St. Maurice, Morrisonville, IL; St. Raymond, Raymond, IL
Kania, Rev. Marcin, (PAT) St. Virgilius, Morris Plains, NJ
Kania, Rev. Marcin D., '10 (TR) St. Mary Cathedral, Trenton, NJ
Kanimea, Rev. Joseph, *M.S.C.* '01 (OG) Our Lady of the Sacred Heart, Watertown, NY; St. Mary's Roman Catholic Church of Evans Mills, NY, Evans Mills, NY; St. Paul's Church, Black River, NY; [MON] Missionaries of the Sacred Heart, Watertown, NY
Kaniparampil, Rev. James, *C.M.I.* '98 (STA) Sacred Heart, Jacksonville, FL
Kanippillil, Rev. Stephen, *M.C.B.S.* '07 (SYM) St. Thomas the Apostle Syro-Malabar Catholic Church (Boston), Framingham, MA
Kaniseli, Rev. Soane T., '87 (SAC) Retired.
Kanjira, Rev. Enoch, (BAL) [MON] Society of St. Sulpice, Province of the United States, Baltimore, MD
Kanjirakattu, Rev. Binesh Joseph, (SCR) Ascension Parish, Forest City, PA
Kanjiramparayil, Rev. Shaju K., *O.S.F.S.* '00 (ALN) [COL] DeSales University, Center Valley, PA; [MON] Oblates of St. Francis de Sales, Center Valley, PA (>PH) St. Agnes, Sellersville, PA
Kanjirathumkal, Rev. Albert Francis, (FWT) St. Jerome, Bowie, TX; St. Joseph, Nocona, TX; St. Mary, Henrietta, TX; St. William, Montague, TX
Kankolongo, Rev. Remy, (ARL) [MON] Missionhurst, C.I.C.M.-Central House and Provincialate (American I.H.M. Province, Inc., Immaculate Heart Missions, Inc., Missionhurst, Inc.), Arlington, VA
Kankolongo, Rev. Remy Konkolongo, *C.I.C.M.* '22 (R) Maria, Reina De Las Americas, Mount Olive, NC
Kanmury, Rev. Niranjan, '01 (SD) Pastor of San Rafael Catholic Parish, San Diego, a corporation sole, San

Diego, CA
Kanna, Rev. Jayanna, '93 (SUP) Good Shepherd Catholic Church, Rib Lake, WI; Our Lady of Perpetual Help, Medford, WI; Our Lady of the Holy Rosary, Medford, WI; Sacred Heart of Jesus, Stetsonville, WI
Kannai, Rev. Niby, (SYM) St. Mary Syro-Malabar Catholic Mission Columbus, OH, Columbus, KY
Kannai, Rev. Niby, '05 (COV) St. Edward, Cynthiana, KY
Kannampalackal, Rev. Abraham, (COS) Chap, Penrose-St Francis; St Francis Med Ctr
Kannamparabil, Rev. Justin Vakko, *O.C.D.* '98 (ORL) Prince of Peace, Ormond Beach, FL
Kannampilly, Rev. Paul, (OAK) St. Philip Neri-St. Albert the Great, Alameda, CA
Kannampuzha, Rev. Jose J., '92 (TYL) St. Jude, Henderson, TX
Kannampuzha, Rev. Thomas, (FRS) (>LA) [MON] Congregation of Rogationists, Inc., Van Nuys, CA
Kanonik, Rev. Stephen F., '82 (CHI) Curia: Parish Services St. Benedict, Chicago, IL
Kanowitz, Rev. Chris, (RNO) Curia: Offices and Directors
Kanowitz, Rev. Christopher, '17 (RNO) Our Lady of the Snows, Reno, NV
Kanshamba, Rev. George, '98 (NY) St. Anthony of Padua, West Harrison, NY
Kantor, Very Rev. Robert, '98 (VEN) Curia: Advisory Boards, Commissions, Committees, and Councils; Leadership; Organizations (affiliated, inter-Diocesan, miscellaneous/other) St. Agnes Parish in Naples, Inc., Naples, FL
Kanyike, Rev. Simon Jude, '05 (JC) Our Lady of Lourdes, Columbia, MO
Kao, Rev. Paulus, '59 (LSC) Retired.
Kapita, Rev. Jacob, *S.J.* '20 (STL) [MON] Jesuit Community Corporation at Saint Louis University - Jesuit Hall, St. Louis, MO
Kapitan, Rev. John J., *O.F.M.* '95 (PBR) St. John the Baptist, Mingo Junction, OH; St. Joseph, Toronto, OH
Kaplan, Rev. Jan F., '67 (CHI) Retired. St. Ladislaus, Chicago, IL
Kapolka, Rev. Michael, '21 (CIN) Holy Trinity, Coldwater, OH; Mary Help of Christians, Fort Recovery, OH; St. Anthony, Fort Recovery, OH; St. Joseph, Fort Recovery, OH; St. Mary, Coldwater, OH; St. Paul, Fort Recovery, OH; St. Peter Catholic Church, Fort Recovery, OH
Kappalumakkel, Rev. Mathew, (HRT) Saint Jeanne Jugan Parish Corporation, Enfield, CT
Kappe, Rev. John H., '71 (GAL) Retired.
Kapperman, Rev. Michael Thomas, '20 (SFS) Sacred Heart Parish of Brown County, Aberdeen, SD; Saint Mary Parish of Brown County, Aberdeen, SD
Kappes, Rev. Christiaan, '02 (PBR) [SEM] Byzantine Catholic Seminary of SS. Cyril and Methodius, Pittsburgh, PA
Kappes, Rev. Christiaan W., '02 (IND) On Special Assignment. Saints Cyril and Methodius Seminary, Pittsburg, PA
Kappilumakkal, Rev. Joseph, *C.M.I.* '86 (JOL) St. Thomas the Apostle, Naperville, IL
Kappler, Rev. Stephan, '94 (OAK) On Leave.
Kapumet Tambwe, Rev. Jean Pierre, *C.S.Sp.* (NY) St. Mark the Evangelist, New York, NY
Karakkat, Rev. Cleetus P., '00 (SAC) Pastor of St. John the Baptist Parish, Folsom, a corporation sole, Folsom, CA
Karalus, Rev. Peter J., '97 (BUF) Curia: Consultative Bodies; Leadership Blessed Sacrament, Buffalo, NY; [MIS] St. Joseph Investment Fund, Inc., Buffalo, NY
Karam, Rev. Hanna, '01 (SAM) St. John the Baptist, New Castle, PA
Karanauskas, Rev. Tomas, '98 (LA) St. Casimir, Los Angeles, CA
Karani, Rev. Stephen, '93 (ROC) Holy Family, Auburn, NY; Sacred Heart, Auburn, NY; St. Alphonsus, Auburn, NY
Karasek, Very Rev. Edward, '87 (AUS) Curia: Leadership St. Mary, Lockhart, TX; [EFT] Clerical Endowment Fund, Lockhart, TX; [EFT] Diocese of Austin Pension Plan and Trust, Austin, TX
Karcher, Rev. Jerome T., '83 (ORG) St. Vincent de Paul, Huntington Beach, CA
Karcsinski, Rev. Joseph J., '79 (BGP) The Church of the Blessed Sacrament of Bridgeport, Bridgeport, CT
Kardouh, Rev. Ephrem, *BSO* '13 (NTN) St. Basil the Great, Lincoln, RI
Kardzis, Rev. Krzysztof, '84 (TOL) Sacred Heart, Fremont, OH
Karekatt, Rev. Raphael, *MSFS* (SR) Pastor of St. John the Baptist Catholic Church of Healdsburg, A Corporation Sole, Healdsburg, CA
Karenga, Rev. Paul G., '02 (MIA) St. Mark, Southwest Ranches, FL; [MIS] Magnificat Broward County, Florida Chapter, Inc., Lauderdale Lakes, FL
Karg, Rev. Msgr. Andrew H., '64 (E) Retired.
Kargul, Rev. A. Waine, '67 (HRT) Retired.
Kari, Rev. Arnold, '77 (RC) Retired.
Kariakatt, Rev. Paul, (LUB) Retired.
Karickal, Rev. Rojin, '09 (BGP) Saint Jerome's Roman Catholic Church Corporation, Norwalk, CT
Karikunnel, Rev. Joseph, *C.S.T.* '83 (PHX) Holy Cross Roman Catholic Parish, Mesa, AZ
Karimalikkal, Rev. Benny, (BIR) Our Lady of the Shoals, Tuscumbia, AL
Kariuki, Rev. Alphonsus, '86 (MET) Curia: Family Life St. John the Evangelist, Dunellen, NJ
Kariuki, Rev. Isaac, '15 (PBL) St. Anthony of Padua, Aguilar, CO; St. Mary, Walsenburg, CO
Karle, Rev. Robert, (LAN) St. Mary Student Parish Ann Arbor, Ann Arbor, MI; [CAM] St. Mary Student Parish, Ann Arbor, MI; [MON] USA Midwest Province of the Society of Jesus - Jesuit Residence, Ann Arbor, MI
Karle, Rev. William J., '72 (SCR) Retired.
Karlen, Rev. Donald H., '64 (SY) Retired.
Karls, Rev. Victor, *C.Ss.R.* '70 (STL) [MON] St. Clement Health Care Center, Liguori, MO
Karmanocky, Rev. Bernard, *O.F.M.* '73 (ALT) St. Therese of the Child Jesus, Johnstown, PA (>CHI) [MON] The Slovene Franciscan Fathers, Order of Friars Minor, Commissariat of the Holy Cross, Lemont, IL
Karnik, Rev. George W., '58 (DUB) Retired.
Karnik, Rev. Scott, '17 (FAR) Holy Trinity Church of Fingal, Fingal, ND; Our Lady of the Scapular Church of Sheldon, Sheldon, ND; St. Patrick's Church of Enderlin, Enderlin, ND
Karnish, Rev. Robert, '66 (GI) Retired.
Karobo, Rev. Venatius T., *A.J.* '93 (ALN) Notre Dame of Bethlehem, Bethlehem, PA; [SPF] Holy Family Manor of Catholic Senior Housing and Health Care Services, Inc., Bethlehem, PA
Karoor, Rev. Isaac M., '69 (BAL) Retired.
Karpinski, Rev. Maciej, (PH) [MON] The Order of Saint Paul, First Hermit - The Pauline Fathers, Doylestown, PA
Karpyn, Rev. Gregory R., '87 (ALN) Retired.
Karris, Rev. Robert, *O.F.M.* '65 (CHI) [MON] St. Peter's Friary, Chicago, IL
Kartje, Rev. John F., '02 (CHI) Curia: Offices and Directors [SEM] University of Saint Mary of the Lake/ Mundelein Seminary, Mundelein, IL
Karuhn, Rev. Robert J., '65 (GB) Retired.
Karwacki, Rev. Bartholomew A., *O.F.M.Conv.* (BAL) St. Casimir, Baltimore, MD
Karwacki, Very Rev. Francis J., '83 (HBG) Curia: Offices and Directors Our Lady of Mount Carmel, Mount Carmel, PA
Karwot, Rev. Marcin, *SVD* (CHI) St. Joseph the Worker, Wheeling, IL
Karwowski, Rev. Edmund K., '87 (HRT) Retired.
Kasanziki, Rev. Pascal, '94 (HEL) Saint Anthony Parish: Series 639, LLC, Missoula, MT
Kaschenbach, Rev. Msgr. Arthur J., '51 (SCR) Retired.
Kasel, Rev. Randal J., '05 (STP) Curia: Consultative Bodies; Leadership St. Michael, Pine Island, MN; St. Paul, Zumbrota, MN; [CEM] St. Mary Cemetery, Goodhue, MN; [CEM] St. Michael Cemetery, Pine Island, MN; [CEM] St. Paul Cemetery, Zumbrota, MN
Kasela, Rev. Adam J., '01 (SAV) St. Stephen, First Martyr, Hinesville, GA
Kasele, Rev. Raphael Mbotela, *F.M.H.* '10 (NO) St. Maria Goretti, New Orleans, LA
Kaserow, Rev. John M., *M.M.* '69 (NY) Retired. [MON] Maryknoll Fathers and Brothers (Catholic Foreign Mission Society of America, Inc.), Ossining, NY
Kaseta, Rev. Peter, *O.F.M.Cap.* '67 (PRT) Parish of the Holy Eucharist, Falmouth, ME
Kashangaki, Rev. David, *C.S.C.* '99 (FTW) St. Hedwig, South Bend, IN; St. Patrick, South Bend, IN; [MON] Congregation of Holy Cross, United States Province of Priests and Brothers, Notre Dame, IN
Kashif, Rev. Javed, *O.F.M.Cap.* (HBG) Chap, Geisinger Med Ctr, Danville Saint Patrick, Carlisle, PA
Kasi, Rev. Selvaraj, *HGN* '13 (PRT) Cathedral of the Immaculate Conception, Portland, ME; Sacred Heart/ St. Dominic, Portland, ME; St. Christopher's, Peaks Island, ME; St. Louis, Portland, ME; St. Peter's, Portland, ME
Kasinski, Rev. James J., '66 (BUF) Retired.
Kasipogu, Rev. Bala, '03 (MAD) St. Jude, Beloit, WI; St. Thomas Congregation, Beloit, WI
Kasiyan, Rev. Andriy, '02 (STF) Our Lady of Perpetual Help, Lackawanna, NY; St. Basil, Lancaster, NY
Kasiyan, Rev. Dmytro, '21 (SJP) Curia: Offices and Directors Presentation of the Most Holy Mother of God (St. Mary's), North Port, FL
Kasiyan, Rev. Ihor, '92 (SJP) Curia: Leadership; Offices and Directors St. Andrew, Parma, OH
Kaska, Rev. E. William, '69 (DAV) Retired.
Kasongo, Rev. Eric, (RVC) Chap, Stony Brook Univ Hosp
Kasparek, Rev. John A., '69 (PMB) Retired.
Kasper, Rev. John, *O.S.F.S.* '79 (OAK) (>TOL) [MON] Oblates of St. Francis de Sales, Toledo, OH
Kasperczuk, Rev. Marek, (CHI) (>COL) [SEM] Pontifical College Josephinum, Columbus, OH
Kasperczuk, Very Rev. Marek, '99 (CHI) On Duty Outside Diocese. Pontifical College Josephinum, Columbus, OH
Kasperek, Rev. Milan, '06 (HPM) (>PRM) [MIS] St. Barbara Prayer Community, Fairborn, OH
Kasprick, Rev. Roger, *O.S.B.* '59 (SCL) [MON] St. John's Abbey, of the Order of St. Benedict, Collegeville, MN
Kasprzak, Rev. John F., '75 (BUF) Retired. Queen of Angels, Lackawanna, NY
Kasprzak, Rev. Przemyslaw, (BO) St. Patrick, Brockton, MA
Kaspustis, Rev. Thomas R., (CHI) Retired.
Kassa, Rev. Augustin, *SMA* (PH) Our Lady of the Assumption, Strafford, PA
Kassa, Rev. Bryan, (SPA) (>EST) Our Lady of Chaldeans Cathedral, Mother of God Chaldean Parish, Southfield, MI
Kassa, Rev. Bryan, '16 (EST) Curia: Leadership
Kassab, Rev. Patrick, (OLL) Curia: Offices and Directors St. Raymond - St. Elizabeth Maronite Catholic Church, Crestwood, MO; St. Raymond Maronite Catholic Cathedral, St. Louis, MO
Kassis, Very Rev. Daniel F., '81 (GLP) Curia: Leadership St. Rita, Show Low, AZ
Kasteel, Rev. Msgr. Ben, '64 (LUB) Retired.
Kastenholz, Rev. John P., *O. Praem.* '65 (GB) [MON] St. Norbert Abbey, De Pere, WI
Kastenholz, Very Rev. Nicholas E., '02 (STL) Curia: Leadership Assumption Catholic Church, O'Fallon, O'Fallon, MO
Kastl, Very Rev. Gary, '07 (TLS) Curia: Leadership; Offices and Directors Holy Family Cathedral, Tulsa, OK; [MIS] Veritas Tax School Scholarships, Inc., Broken Arrow, OK
Kastl, Very Rev. Gary D., '07 (TLS) Curia: Offices and Directors
Kasule, Rev. Dennis, '08 (CHI) [SEM] University of Saint Mary of the Lake/Mundelein Seminary, Mundelein, IL
Kasule, Rev. Gerald, (MO) Curia: Offices and Directors
Kasun, Rev. Paul L., *O.S.B.* '94 (OM) [MON] Benedictine Mission House - Christ the King Priory, Schuyler, NE
Kasza, Rev. Msgr. John C., '93 (DET) Curia: Offices and Directors Austin Catholic High School, Chesterfield, MI; St. Therese of Lisieux Parish Shelby Township, Shelby Twp., MI
Kaszczak, Rev. Archpriest Ivan, '85 (STF) Curia: Leadership; Offices and Directors Holy Trinity Ukrainian Catholic Church, Kerhonkson, NY; St. John the Baptist, Hunter, NY
Kasznel, Rev. Richard C., '65 (STL) Retired. Immaculate Conception Catholic Church, St. Mary, St. Mary, MO
Katafiasz, Rev. Robert, (BAL) Christ the King Roman Catholic Congregation, Inc., Glen Burnie, MD; St. Bernadette, Severn, MD
Katamba, Rev. John C., '84 (GB) Sacred Heart, Appleton, WI
Katambe, Rev. Narcis, (PEO) Holy Family, Lincoln, IL; St. Patrick, Elkhart, IL
Katanga, Rev. Wenceslaus, '03 (FAR) Curia: Leadership St. Andrew's Church of Zeeland, Zeeland, ND; St. David's Church of Ashley, Ashley, ND; St. Patrick Church of Wishek, Wishek, ND
Kathawa, Rev. Anthony, (MO) Curia: Offices and Directors
Kathol, Rev. Quentin, *O.S.B.* '63 (KC) [MON] Conception Abbey (Benedictine Monks), Conception, MO
Katompa, Rev. Zephyrin Kabengele, '98 (NEW) St. Peter Claver, Montclair, NJ
Katongole, Rev. Emmanuel, (FTW) [COL] University of Notre Dame Du Lac, Notre Dame, IN
Katongole, Rev. Herman, '02 (RIC) St. Joseph's, Woodlawn, VA
Katrinak, Rev. Frantisek, (Y) Saint Mary Saint Joseph Parish, Warren, OH
Katsouros, Rev. Stephen N, *S.J.* (NY) [MON] St. Ignatius Loyola Residence, New York, NY
Katta, Rev. Vijaya Babu "Sleeva", '10 (R) Holy Trinity, Williamston, NC
Kattakkara, Rev. Joseph, *C.M.I.* '89 (BEA) Chap,

Convalescent Home Ministry St. Anthony Cathedral Basilica, Beaumont, TX
Kattiakaran, Rev. Ligory Johnson, '91 (SYM) St. Thomas Syro-Malabar Catholic Church of San Francisco (Indian), Milpitas, CA
Kattikanayil, Rev. Tomy, *M.S.F.S.* (DET) St. Mary Parish Milford, Milford, MI
Kattookkaran, Rev. Elson, *M.S.* (MAN) St. Joseph Cathedral, Manchester, NH
Katz, Rev. Jerome A., '71 (SY) Retired.
Katzenberger, Rev. Scott, *C.Ss.R.* (CHI) [MON] The Redemptorists/Denver Province, Chicago, IL
Katziner, Rev. Stephen F., '74 (PH) St. Ephrem, Bensalem, PA
Kau, Rev. Garrett B., '13 (MAD) St. John the Evangelist, Spring Green, WI; St. Luke, Plain, WI
Kauchak, Rev. Justin, *O.P.* '66 (NO) St. Anthony of Padua, New Orleans, LA
Kaucheck, Rev. Kenneth R., '76 (DET) Retired.
Kauffman, Rev. Dennis, *C.S.B.* '79 (DET) Detroit Catholic Central High School, Novi, MI
Kauffman, Rev. John G., '75 (DEN) Retired.
Kaufman, Rev. Donald, *L.C.* (NY) Parish of St. Peter and St. Denis, Yonkers, NY; St. Denis, Yonkers, NY; [MON] Legionaries of Christ, Rye, NY
Kaufman, Rev. Harry J., '02 (BO) Retired.
Kaufman, Rev. Kent R., '93 (TOL) Curia: Clergy and Religious Services St. Charles Borromeo, Lima, OH
Kaufman, Rev. Msgr. William C., '74 (PH) On Special Assignment. Dean, Deanery 1, St Pius X Rectory, Broomall Curia: Advisory Boards, Commissions, Committees, and Councils St. Pius X, Broomall, PA
Kaul, Rev. John L., '75 (DET) Retired.
Kaump, Very Rev. Joey, '05 (MEM) Curia: Advisory Boards, Commissions, Committees, and Councils; Leadership St. Brigid, Memphis, TN
Kaup, Rev. Ryan A., '15 (LIN) Curia: Leadership; Offices and Directors St. Benedict's, Nebraska City, NE
Kauta, Rev. Felix, *A.J.* '94 (PHX) St. James Roman Catholic Parish, Glendale, AZ
Kauth, Rev. Matthew K., '00 (CHL) [SEM] St. Joseph College Seminary, Inc., Mount Holly, NC
Kautzky, Rev. Zachary, '10 (DM) On Duty Outside Diocese. USAF Chaplain, Shreveport, LA
Kautzky, Rev. Zachary, (MO) Curia: Offices and Directors
Kautzman, Rev. Jerome G., '59 (BIS) Retired. [NUR] Emmaus Place, Bismarck, ND
Kavanagh, Rev. Aelred, *O.S.B.* '94 (NO) [MON] St. Joseph Abbey, St. Benedict, LA
Kavanagh, Rev. James F., '64 (LA) St. James, Redondo Beach, CA
Kavanagh, Rev. Kevin J., '83 (COL) Our Lady of Lourdes, Marysville, OH
Kavanaugh, Rev. John J., '57 (WIL) Retired.
Kavanaugh, Rev. Michael J., '85 (SAV) Curia: Offices and Directors St. Peter the Apostle Church, Savannah, GA
Kavcak, Rev. John P., *M.S.C.* '73 (SB) St. Theresa, Palm Springs, CA
Kavishe, Rev. Apolinary, *A.J.* '98 (PRT) Chap, Eastern Maine Med Ctr, Bangor Saint Paul the Apostle Parish, Bangor, ME
Kavookjian, Rev. Msgr. Perry, '87 (FRS) Curia: Leadership Garces Memorial High School, Bakersfield, CA; St. Elizabeth Ann Seton, Bakersfield, CA
Kavumkal, Rev. Sebastian, *M.S.T.* '79 (MAR) Holy Family, Gladstone, MI
Kavungal, Rev. Davy, *C.M.I.* '96 (NSH) [RTR] Carmel Center of Spirituality, Liberty, TN
Kavusa, Rev. Hubert, *O.S.C.* (PHX) [MON] Crosier Community of Phoenix (Canons Regular of the Order of the Holy Cross) (Conventual Priory of the Holy Cross), Phoenix, AZ
Kawalec, Rev. Pawel, '96 (VEN) St. Catherine Parish in Sebring, Inc., Sebring, FL
Kawalec, Rev. Zachary M., '02 (CLV) Nativity of the Lord Jesus, Akron, OH
Kawecki, Rev. Andrew M., '80 (GBG) On Leave.
Kawka, Rev. Frederick J., '64 (SAG) Retired. Saint Vincent de Paul Parish of Shepherd, Shepherd, MI
Kay, Rev. Colin Adrian, '05 (NEW) Bergen Catholic High School, Oradell, NJ; St. Anne, Fair Lawn, NJ
Kayajan, Rev. Daniel R., (SP) Resurrection, Riverview, FL
Kayammakal, Rev. Thomas, '80 (SFE) Our Lady of the Annunciation, Albuquerque, NM
Kayatta, Rev. Francis P., '80 (PRO) Curia: Advisory Boards, Commissions, Committees, and Councils St. Mary, Star of the Sea Church Corporation, Point Judith, Narragansett, RI
Kayaye, Rev. Francis, (HT) Holy Cross, Morgan City, LA
Kaye, Rev. Joseph, '98 (CHI) All Souls Parish, Lansing, IL
Kayimbw Mbay, Rev. Bernard, *C.I.C.M.* '13 (R) Maria, Reina De Las Americas, Mount Olive, NC; St. Mary of the Angels, Mount Olive, NC
Kayitare, Rev. Olivier, *S.J.* '15 (SFR) [MON] Loyola House Jesuit Community, San Francisco, CA
Kayiwa, Rev. Julius, '92 (PHX) Our Lady of the Desert Mission, A Quasi-Parish, Dolan Springs, AZ
Kaylor, Rev. Lee, '81 (SFR) Retired.
Kaylor, Rev. Robert W., '70 (Y) Retired.
Kayondo, Rev. Leonard, '93 (FR) Curia: Offices and Directors Cathedral of St. Mary of the Assumption, Fall River, MA
Kayongo, Rev. Nicholas, (SEA) Sacred Heart, Battle Ground, WA
Kayrouz, Rev. Msgr. Victor, '64 (OLL) Retired.
Kaywell, Rev. Jerome P., '91 (VEN) Sacred Heart Parish in Punta Gorda, Inc.; Punta Gorda, FL
Kaza, Rev. Msgr. Charles A., '72 (E) Retired.
Kazadi, Rev. Andre, (ARL) [MON] Missionhurst, C.I.C.M.-Central House and Provincialate (American I.H.M. Province, Inc., Immaculate Heart Missions, Inc., Missionhurst, Inc.), Arlington, VA
Kazarnowicz, Rev. Anthony S., '75 (WOR) Chap, US Army, Fort Bragg, NC St. Joseph Basilica, Webster, MA
Kazibwe, Rev. John C., '03 (RIC) Curia: Administration Church of the Epiphany, North Chesterfield, VA
Kazzahchiyang, Rev. Didam David, (NEW) Saint Joseph Parish, East Orange, NJ
Kcira, Rev. Anton P., '67 (DET) Retired.
Kealey, Rev. Edward J., '89 (RVC) Retired.
Kealy, Rev. Sean, *C.S.Sp.* '65 (PIT) Retired. [COL] Duquesne University of the Holy Spirit, Pittsburgh, PA
Kean, Rev. Brian, '10 (CHI) Holy Guardian Angels, Brookfield, IL
Kean, Rev. Brian M., '08 (PH) Curia: Clergy and Religious Services St. Matthias, Bala Cynwyd, PA
Kean, Rev. James F., '97 (DET) St. John Fisher Chapel University Parish Auburn Hills, Auburn Hills, MI; St. Joseph Parish Lake Orion, Lake Orion, MI
Keane, Rev. Aquinas, *O.C.S.O.* '73 (WOR) [MON] St. Joseph's Abbey (Cistercian Abbey of Spencer, Inc., Cistercian Order of the Strict Observance (Trappists)), Spencer, MA
Keane, Rev. Msgr. Dennis P., '71 (NY) Curia: Offices and Directors Holy Family, New Rochelle, NY
Keane, Rev. John, *S.A.* '62 (NY) Retired. [MON] Franciscan Friars of the Atonement, Minister General Office, Garrison, NY
Keane, Rev. Michael F., '90 (NY) Curia: Leadership St. Anastasia, Harriman, NY; [CON] Queen of Apostles Convent, Monroe, NY
Keane, Rev. Patrick A., '03 (R) Our Lady of Lourdes, Raleigh, NC
Keane, Rev. Robert Lawrence, *S.J.* (PH) [MON] Jesuit Community at St. Joseph's University, Merion Station, PA
Kearney, Rev. Christopher, *O.F.M.Cap.* '68 (SFR) [SEM] Capuchin Franciscan Order San Buenaventura Friary, San Francisco, CA
Kearney, Rev. Daniel S., '87 (NY) Ascension, New York, NY
Kearney, Rev. Joseph A., '67 (SCR) Retired. Geisinger Wyoming Valley Hosp, Wilkes-Barre St. Andrew Parish, Wilkes-Barre, PA
Kearney, Rev. Michael, '16 (JOL) On Duty Outside Diocese. St John Vianney College Seminary, St Paul, MN Our Lady of Mercy, Aurora, IL
Kearney, Rev. Michael J., '82 (BO) On Leave.
Kearney, Very Rev. Timothy E., '96 (BO) Curia: Leadership Sacred Heart, Watertown, MA; St. Patrick, Watertown, MA
Kearns, Rev. Daniel P., *C.M.* '69 (STL) [MON] Congregation of the Mission Vincentian Fathers Lazarist Residence, St. Louis, MO
Kearns, Rev. Edward A., '63 (MET) Retired.
Kearns, Rev. Edward T., '77 (PH) St. Dominic, Philadelphia, PA
Kearns, Rev. Owens, *L.C.* '83 (DAL) [MON] Legionaries of Christ, Irving, TX
Keas, Rev. Jason, '13 (COS) Divine Redeemer, Colorado Springs, CO
Keating, Rev. Earl, *C.P.* '58 (NY) Retired.
Keating, Rev. Earl, *C.P.* (BRK) [MON] Immaculate Conception Monastery, Jamaica, NY
Keating, Rev. Earl, *C.P.* '58 (NY) Retired. [MON] The Congregation of the Passion - St. Paul of the Cross Province, Jamaica, NY
Keating, Rev. Edward J., '94 (HBG) Mary, Mother of the Church, Mount Joy, PA
Keating, Friar James R., *O.S.A.* '84 (PH) St. Augustine, Philadelphia, PA
Keating, Rev. John R., *S.J.* '61 (NY) [MON] Murray-Weigel Hall (A Jesuit Community at Murray-Weigel Hall and Kohlmann Hall), Bronx, NY
Keating, Rev. Joseph, '16 (FWT) Sacred Heart, Muenster, TX
Keating, Rev. Michael, (OM) St. Michael, South Sioux City, NE
Keating, Rev. Michael J., '02 (STP) Retired.
Keating, Very Rev. Patrick J., '05 (BRK) Curia: Consultative Bodies; Leadership; Organizations (affiliated, inter-Diocesan, miscellaneous/other); Pastoral Services [CCH] Catholic Charities Neighborhood Services, Inc., Brooklyn, NY; [CCH] Catholic Charities, Diocese of Brooklyn, Brooklyn, NY; [CCH] Catholic Migration Services, Inc., Brooklyn, NY
Keating, Rev. Ryan E, '21 (BUF) St. Mary, Swormville, NY
Keating, Rt. Rev. Thomas, *O.C.S.O.* (NY) [SPF] Contemplative Outreach, Ltd., Yonkers, NY
Keating, Rev. Timothy, *C.Ss.R.* '66 (BAL) [SPF] St. John Neuman Residence, Timonium, MD
Keating, Rev. Timothy G., *S.M.* '85 (WDC) [SEM] Marist College, Provincialate of the Marist Society in the USA, Washington, DC
Keating, Rev. Timothy G., *S.M.* '85 (ATL) [MON] Marist Provincial Office, Society of Mary - Atlanta Province, Atlanta, GA
Keck, Rev. Edward, '73 (COL) Retired.
Kedati, Rev. Andreas, (LR) St. Justin, Star City, AR; St. Peter, Pine Bluff, AR
Kedjierski, Rev. Walter F., '02 (RVC) On Duty Outside Diocese. [SEM] Diocesan Seminary of the Immaculate Conception, Huntington, NY
Kee, Rev. Msgr. James S, (SHP) Curia: Leadership
Kee, Rev. Msgr. James S., '95 (MOB) Curia: Leadership; Offices and Directors St. Vincent de Paul Parish, Mobile, Mobile, AL
Keebler, Rev. William, '91 (PEO) St. Joseph's, Chenoa, IL
Keech, Rev. William J., *O.S.F.S.* '57 (WIL) Salesianum School, Wilmington, DE
Keefe, Rev. Charles R., '76 (MIL) Retired.
Keefe, Very Rev. Daniel G., '83 (HRT) Curia: Advisory Boards, Commissions, Committees, and Councils Saint John Bosco Parish Corporation, Branford, CT
Keefe, Rev. Daniel T., '54 (OG) Retired.
Keefe, Rev. John J., '68 (LIN) Retired.
Keefe, Rev. John P., *C.S.C.* (FTW) [MON] Congregation of Holy Cross, United States Province of Priests and Brothers, Notre Dame, IN
Keefe, Rev. Joseph, (POD) Curia: Clergy and Religious Services
Keegan, Rev. David, '16 (STA) Holy Family, Jacksonville, FL
Keegan, Rev. John, *SJ* (BO) [MON] Campion Health & Wellness, Inc., Weston, MA
Keegan, Rev. John E., *M.M.* '60 (NY) Retired. [MON] Maryknoll Fathers and Brothers (Catholic Foreign Mission Society of America, Inc.), Ossining, NY
Keegan, Rev. Martin P., *M.M.* '65 (NY) Retired.
Keegan, Rev. Terence, *O.P.* '68 (PRO) [MON] St. Thomas Aquinas Priory at Providence College, Providence, RI
Keehan, Rev. Terence M., '86 (CHI) Holy Family, Inverness, IL
Keehner, Rev. John, '93 (Y) Curia: Offices and Directors St. Paul, North Canton, OH
Keehner, Rev. John E., '93 (Y) Holy Spirit, Uniontown, OH
Keeler, Rev. Roger H., '84 (SAT) [COL] Oblate School of Theology, San Antonio, TX
Keeley, Rev. Isaac, *O.C.S.O.* '92 (WOR) [MON] St. Joseph's Abbey (Cistercian Abbey of Spencer, Inc., Cistercian Order of the Strict Observance (Trappists)), Spencer, MA
Keen, Rev. Carlos F., '05 (PH) St. Agatha-St. James, Philadelphia, PA
Keena, Rev. James, *C.Ss.R.* '57 (CHI) Retired. St. Michael in Old Town, Chicago, IL; [MON] The Redemptorist Fathers of Chicago, Chicago, IL
Keenan, Rev. Christopher B., *O.F.M.* '71 (NY) FDNY Chaplain & PT Chaplain at Mt. St Vincent College
Keenan, Rev. Francis X., *C.P.* '61 (CHI) [MON] Passionist Community of St. Vincent Strambi, Chicago, IL
Keenan, Rev. James, *S.J.* '82 (BO) [MON] The Jesuit Community at Boston College, Chestnut Hill, MA
Keenan, Rev. James F., *S.J.* '69 (NY) [MON] Xavier Jesuit Community, New York, NY.
Keenan, Very Rev. James R., '99 (RCK) On Special Assignment. Curia: Leadership St. Mary, Sterling, IL;

[MIS] St. Mary's Conference, Sterling, IL
Keenan, Rev. Joseph, (WDC) [MON] Father Judge Missionary Cenacle, Adelphi, MD
Keenan, Rev. Joseph F., '84 (PIT) Retired.
Keenan, Rev. Patrick, '69 (NY) Retired.
Keenan, Rev. Msgr. Patrick J., '69 (NY) St. Columbanus, Cortlandt Manor, NY
Keenan, Rev. Paul, *O.F.M.* '13 (NEW) Assumption of Our Blessed Lady, Wood Ridge, NJ
Keene, Rev. James H., *S.J.* '73 (SJ) [MON] Sacred Heart Jesuit Center, Los Gatos, CA
Keene, Very Rev. Mark A., '84 (COV) Curia: Advisory Boards, Commissions, Committees, and Councils; Clergy and Religious Services; Leadership Covington Catholic High School, Park Hills, KY; St. Agnes, Fort Wright, KY
Keener, Rev. Robert J., '95 (CHI) Chap, USN Curia: (>MO) Offices and Directors
Keeney, Rev. Charles P., '78 (BRK) Retired.
Keeney, Rev. Msgr. Timothy E., '96 (RIC) Incarnation Catholic Church, Charlottesville, VA
Keenoy, Rev. John A., '87 (STL) St. Mary Catholic Church, Hawk Point, Hawk Point, MO
Keese, Rev. John H., '74 (LA) St. Elizabeth Ann Seton, Rowland Heights, CA
Keferl, Rev. Francis J., '73 (CIN) Retired.
Keffer, Rev. Robert, *O.S.B.* (GBG) Assoc Chap, Excela Health - Westmoreland Hosp, Greensburg [MON] Saint Vincent Archabbey, Latrobe, PA
Keffer, Rev. Robert F., '68 (WDC) Retired.
Keffler, Rev. Leopold, *O.F.M.Conv.* '63 (IND) [MIS] Mount Saint Francis Sanctuary, Inc., Indianapolis, IN; [RTR] Mount Saint Francis Friary and Retreat Center, Mount St. Francis, IN
Kegley, Rev. Jeffrey J., '96 (TR) Curia: Miscellaneous / Other Offices St. Mary, Middletown, NJ
Kehoe, Rev. James P., '70 (CHI) Retired.
Kehoe, Rev. Joseph F., '66 (SY) Retired. On Leave.
Kehoe, Rev. Mark, '99 (MET) St. Lawrence, Laurence Harbor, NJ
Kehres, Rev. Franklin P., '68 (TOL) Retired.
Keigher, Rev. Bernard J., '74 (TR) Retired.
Keijbou, Rev. Msgr. Zouhair Toma, '68 (EST) Holy Cross Chaldean Catholic Church, Farmington Hills, MI
Keikati, Rev. Youssef, '85 (SAM) Our Lady of Lebanon, Easton, PA
Keiser, Rev. Jerome F., '71 (STP) Retired.
Keiser, Rev. Raymond W., '70 (BIR) Retired.
Keiter, Rev. Adam J., '08 (WCH) Cathedral of the Immaculate Conception, Wichita, KS
Keiter, Rev. James E., '01 (OM) All Saints Church of Northeast Nebraska, Fordyce, NE; Holy Family Parish of Cedar County, Fordyce, NE; St. Rose of Lima, Crofton, NE; [EFT] Cemetery Endowment for St. Boniface Church, Fordyce, NE; [MIS] Christ Child Society of Omaha, Omaha, NE
Kejbou, Rev. Msgr. Zouhair T., '68 (EST) Curia: Offices and Directors
Kelash, Rev. David J., *V.F.* '94 (PHX) Curia: Leadership; Offices and Directors St. John Vianney Roman Catholic Parish, Sedona, AZ
Kelber, Rev. Vincent, *OP* (SFR) St. Dominic's Catholic Church, San Francisco, CA
Kelber, Rev. Vincent, *O.P.* '07 (P) (>SFR) [MON] St. Dominic Priory, San Francisco, CA
Keleher, Rev. Msgr. J. Patrick, '68 (BUF) [CAM] State University of New York at Buffalo (North Campus) Newman Center, Amherst, NY
Keliher, Rev. Nobert, *O.P.* (Y) Curia: Pastoral Services
Keliher, Rev. Norbert, (Y) St. Dominic, Youngstown, OH; [CAM] St. John Henry Newman Center at Youngstown State University aka YSU Newman Center, Youngstown, OH
Kelleher, Rev. James R., *S.O.L.T.* '96 (CC) [MON] Society of Our Lady of the Most Holy Trinity, Corpus Christi, TX
Kelleher, Rev. John, (FR) St. Pius X, South Yarmouth, MA
Kelleher, Rev. John P., *O.S.B.* '89 (FR) [MIS] Our Lady of the Highway, South Yarmouth, MA
Kelleher, Rev. Mark A., '96 (WIL) St. Joseph, Middletown, DE
Keller, Rev. Ben, (LFT) St. Thomas Aquinas, West Lafayette, IN; [CAM] St. Thomas Aquinas Parish and Foundation for Catholic Students Attending Purdue University, West Lafayette, IN
Keller, Rev. Brady, '20 (SCL) St. Augustine, St. Cloud, MN; St. John Cantius, St. Cloud, MN; St. Mary's Cathedral of St. Cloud, St. Cloud, MN
Keller, Rev. Gerald J., '65 (CLV) Retired. Curia: Advisory Boards, Commissions, Committees, and Councils
Keller, Rev. Herbert B., *S.J.* '81 (SCR) [COL] The University of Scranton, Scranton, PA
Keller, Rev. John, (SD) [EFT] The St. Augustine Foundation, San Diego, CA
Keller, Rev. John T., '74 (GAL) Retired.
Keller, Rev. Matthew A., '02 (GLP) San Mateo, San Mateo, NM; San Rafael, San Rafael, NM; St. John the Evangelist, Houck, AZ; St. Teresa of Avila, Grants, NM; St. Vivian, Milan, NM
Keller, Rev. Paul, *CMF* '96 (FRS) St. Paul Catholic Newman Center, Fresno, CA
Keller, Rev. Paul, *C.M.F.* '96 (CHI) [MON] Claretian Missionaries U.S.A.-Canada Province, Inc., Chicago, IL
Keller, Rev. Paul Jerome, *O.P.* '93 (CIN) (>COL) St. Patrick, Columbus, OH
Keller, Rev. Paul Jerome, *OP* '93 (COL) Curia: Offices and Directors
Keller, Rev. Robert, '16 (FAR) Holy Spirit Church of Fargo, Fargo, ND
Keller, Rev. Robert, '83 (GR) [COL] Aquinas College, Grand Rapids, MI
Keller, Rev. Robert L., '67 (CIN) Resurrection of Our Lord, Cincinnati, OH
Keller, Rev. Seth M., '20 (COL) Sacred Hearts, Cardington, OH; St. Mary, Marion, OH
Keller, Rev. Thomas, '84 (B) Retired.
Keller, Rev. Thomas G., '97 (STL) Assumption Catholic Church, Mattese, St. Louis, MO
Keller, Rev. Thomas W., '58 (LR) Retired. [MON] St. John Manor, Little Rock, AR
Kelley, Rev. Aloysius P., *S.J.* (BAL) Retired. [MIS] Colombiere Jesuit Community, Baltimore, MD
Kelley, Very Rev. Daniel P., '95 (FWT) Curia: Leadership St. Jude, Mansfield, TX
Kelley, Rev. Msgr. David F., '88 (WIL) Curia: Advisory Boards, Commissions, Committees, and Councils Holy Family, Newark, DE; Parish of the Resurrection, Wilmington, DE
Kelley, Rev. David J, *OSA* (ALB) St. Augustine, Lansingburgh, NY
Kelley, Rev. David J., *O.S.A.* '73 (ALB) St. Mary of the Assumption, Waterford, NY
Kelley, Rev. Edward J., '68 (PRO) Retired.
Kelley, Rev. Msgr. Edward J., '66 (MAN) Retired.
Kelley, Rev. Msgr. Francis H., '68 (BO) Retired. Curia: Clergy and Religious Services
Kelley, Rev. John, '91 (AUS) St. Ann, Rosebud, Rosebud, TX; St. Michael, Burlington, TX
Kelley, Rev. Joseph J., '87 (PH) On Special Assignment. Dean, Deanery 8, St Monica Rectory, Philadelphia Curia: Deaneries St. Monica, Philadelphia, PA
Kelley, Rev. Michael A., '00 (PRO) Saint Agatha's Church Corporation, Woonsocket, Woonsocket, RI; The Church of the Precious Blood Corporation, Woonsocket, RI, Woonsocket, RI
Kelley, Rev. Michael J., '75 (WDC) St. Martin of Tours, Washington, DC
Kelley, Rev. Msgr. Richard J., '72 (MAN) Retired. St. Patrick, Pelham, NH
Kelley, Rev. Stephen P., '13 (HBG) Holy Trinity, Columbia, PA
Kelley, Very Rev. Thomas L., '88 (MAD) Sacred Hearts of Jesus and Mary, Sun Prairie, WI
Kelley, Rev. William H., *C.S.C.* '70 (FR) [COL] Holy Cross Fathers Religious, North Easton, MA
Kelley, Rev. William J., *S.J.* '85 (WDC) Holy Trinity, Washington, DC; [MON] The Jesuit Community at Georgetown University, Washington, DC
Kellogg, Rev. Michael, '02 (SCL) Curia: Leadership The Church of Mary of the Visitation of Becker/Big Lake, Big Lake, MN
Kelly, Rev. Aaron, '22 (ROC) On Duty Outside Diocese. Studying Vatican
Kelly, Rev. Albert P., '72 (MOB) Retired.
Kelly, Rev. Andrew E., '70 (DAV) Retired.
Kelly, Rev. Augustine G., *O.S.B* '88 (MAN) [MON] St. Anselm Abbey, Manchester, NH
Kelly, Rev. Brendan R.J., '05 (LIN) Curia: Offices and Directors St. Stephen's, Exeter, NE
Kelly, Rev. Brian, (ALB) St. Ambrose, Latham, NY
Kelly, Rev. Brian F., '77 (SCR) Retired. Chap, Cap, USN, Carlsbad, CA
Kelly, Rev. Charles F., '64 (MET) Retired.
Kelly, Rev. Charles M., '11 (NEW) Assumption, Emerson, NJ
Kelly, Rev. Charles P., '99 (SAC) Pastor of Sacred Heart Parish, Red Bluff, a corporation sole, Red Bluff, CA
Kelly, Rev. Daniel A., '87 (PAT) Retired. Immaculate Heart of Mary, Wayne, NJ
Kelly, Rev. Daniel J., '56 (LC) Retired.
Kelly, Rev. Daniel L., '72 (RIC) St. Joseph, Clifton Forge, VA
Kelly, Rev. David, (NO) [SEM] Notre Dame Seminary Graduate School of Theology, New Orleans, LA
Kelly, Rev. David, *O.F.M.* '10 (GRY) [HOS] Franciscan Health Crown Point, Crown Point, IN; [MON] Our Lady of Lourdes Friary, Cedar Lake, IN
Kelly, Rev. David, *O.S.B.* (GBG) Curia: Leadership
Kelly, Rev. David A., *C.PP.S.* '82 (CHI) [MIS] Precious Blood Ministry of Reconciliation, Chicago, IL
Kelly, Rev. E. Francis, '67 (SCR) Retired.
Kelly, Rev. Edward C., '90 (PH) Holy Cross, Springfield, PA
Kelly, Rev. Edward J., '68 (PH) Retired.
Kelly, Rev. Edward M., '68 (MIA) St. Elizabeth Ann Seton, Coral Springs, FL
Kelly, Rev. Eugene L., *O.S.F.S.* '65 (WIL) Retired.
Kelly, Rev. Msgr. Francis D., '63 (WOR) Retired.
Kelly, Rev. Francis J., *F.P.O.* '98 (BO) On Special Assignment.
Kelly, Rev. Gerald E., *M.M.* '67 (GAL)
Kelly, Rev. Gerard P., *C.M.* '82 (CHI) [MON] Vincentian Community, Congregation of the Mission, Western Province, Chicago, IL
Kelly, Rev. Msgr. James A., '81 (POD) (>OAK) [MIS] Opus Dei, Berkeley, CA
Kelly, Rev. Msgr. James A., '82 (SFR) [MIS] Prelature of the Holy Cross and Opus Dei, San Francisco, CA
Kelly, Rev. Msgr. James A., '82 (POD) Curia: Clergy and Religious Services
Kelly, Rev. Msgr. James G., '62 (BUF) Retired. [MON] O'Hara Residence, Tonawanda, NY
Kelly, Rev. James J., '50 (PH) Retired.
Kelly, Rev. James J., *S.J.* '03 (BAL) [COL] Jesuit Community of Loyola University, Inc., Baltimore, MD; [MON] Jesuit Community of Loyola University Maryland, Inc., Baltimore, MD
Kelly, Rev. James J., '83 (LA) Sacred Heart, Covina, CA
Kelly, Rev. Msgr. James J., '60 (BRK) Retired. St. Brigid, Brooklyn, NY
Kelly, Rev. James P., *O.F.M.* '65 (HRT) St. Patrick and St. Anthony Roman Catholic Church Corporation, Hartford, CT
Kelly, Rev. James T., '92 (BO) St. John the Evangelist, Swampscott, MA; St. Thomas Aquinas, Nahant, MA
Kelly, Rev. John, *S.A.C.* '72 (DET) [MIS] Pallottine Missionary Center (Irish Province), Wyandotte, MI
Kelly, Rev. John, (NY) Retired.
Kelly, Rev. John, *O.S.F.S.* (MO) Curia: Offices and Directors
Kelly, Rev. John D., '86 (ARL) Blessed Sacrament, Alexandria, VA
Kelly, Rev. John E., '73 (BO) St. Joseph, Holbrook, MA; St. Michael, Avon, MA
Kelly, Rev. John E., '87 (BUF) On Sick Leave.
Kelly, Rev. John F., '84 (PT) Curia: Offices and Directors Saint Sylvester, Gulf Breeze, FL
Kelly, Rev. John J., '87 (PH) Retired. Assumption B.V.M., Feasterville, PA
Kelly, Rev. John J., '64 (BLX) Retired.
Kelly, Rev. John J., *O.S.F.S.* '71 (R) Retired.
Kelly, Rev. John R., '68 (R) Retired.
Kelly, Rev. Jonathan J., '11 (STP) [SEM] St. John Vianney Seminary, St. Paul, MN
Kelly, Rev. Jordan, *OP* (Y) St. Rose of Lima Parish, Girard, OH
Kelly, Rev. Jordan, *O.S.P.* '03 (WDC) Archbishop Carroll High School, Washington, DC
Kelly, Rev. Joseph, '15 (SPC) Curia: Consultative Bodies; Organizations (affiliated, inter-Diocesan, miscellaneous/other) Guardian Angel, Oran, MO; St. Ambrose, Chaffee, MO
Kelly, Rev. Msgr. Joseph P., '66 (SCR) Retired. [MON] Villa St. Joseph, Dunmore, PA
Kelly, Rev. Justin J., *S.J.* '66 (DET) [MON] Jesuit Community at the University of Detroit Mercy, Detroit, MI
Kelly, Rev. Kenneth W., '79 (KCK) Retired.
Kelly, Rev. Kevin, *C.O.* '06 (MET) [MON] The Raritan Congregation of the Oratory of St. Philip Neri, Raritan, NJ
Kelly, Rev. Kevin Patrick, *C.O.* '06 (MET) St. Joseph, Raritan, NJ
Kelly, Rev. Michael, '59 (STA) Retired.
Kelly, Rev. Michael, '73 (STO) On Leave.
Kelly, Rev. Michael, *SS.CC.* '63 (FR) Retired. [MIS] Damien Residence Retirement Home, ,
Kelly, Rev. Michael, (YAK) St. Joseph Parish, Yakima, WA
Kelly, Rev. Msgr. Michael E., '66 (NEW) Curia: Offices and Directors Seton Hall Preparatory School, West Orange, NJ
Kelly, Rev. Michael J., '82 (PH) On Duty Outside Diocese. Dir of Spiritual Form, Pontifical Coll Josephinum

Kelly, Rev. Michael J.R., '10 (ARL) St. John the Apostle, Leesburg, VA

Kelly, Rev. Neil A., '91 (NY) St. Joseph-St. Thomas St. John Neumann Parish, Staten Island, NY

Kelly, Rev. Patrick, *S.J.* '99 (SEA) [COL] Seattle University, Seattle, WA; [MON] Arrupe Jesuit Community at Seattle University, Seattle, WA

Kelly, Rev. Patrick M., *S.J.* '99 (DET) [MON] Jesuit Community at the University of Detroit Mercy, Detroit, MI

Kelly, Rev. Paul, '83 (SC) St. Patrick's, Estherville, IA

Kelly, Rev. Paul J., '74 (OG) Retired.

Kelly, Rev. Philip J., '93 (NY) St. Francis de Sales, New York, NY

Kelly, Rev. Randy J., '94 (SAG) Retired.

Kelly, Rev. Richard J., '88 (NEW) Sacred Heart, Rochelle Park, NJ; [COL] Lodi Campus, Lodi, NJ

Kelly, Rev. Robert, *O.P.* '89 (DEN) St. Dominic Parish, Denver, CO; [MON] Dominican Friars, St. Dominic Priory, Denver, Inc., Denver, CO

Kelly, Rev. Robert, *S.V.D.* '86 (CHI) Our Lady of Africa Parish, Chicago, IL

Kelly, Rev. Robert D., '00 (PRM) Retired.

Kelly, Rev. Robert J., '74 (ALT) On Leave.

Kelly, Rev. Robert L., '77 (SY) Curia: Offices and Directors St. Joseph, Lee Center, NY; St. Paul, Rome, NY

Kelly, Rev. Stephen M., *S.J.* '90 (OAK) [MON] Jesuit Fathers and Brothers, Oakland, CA

Kelly, Rev. Thomas J., '68 (ALB) Retired.

Kelly, Rev. Thomas M., '90 (BIR) Our Lady of the Valley, Birmingham, AL; [EFT] Our Lady of the Valley Educational Foundation, Birmingham, AL

Kelly, Rev. Thomas N., '10 (VEN) On Duty Outside Diocese. Chaplain, Military Curia: (>MO) Offices and Directors

Kelly, Rev. Thomas P., '70 (BO) Retired.

Kelly, Rev. Msgr. Thomas R., '67 (NY) Retired.

Kelly, Rt. Rev. Timothy, *O.C.S.O.* '65 (L) Retired. [MON] Abbey of Our Lady of Gethsemani, of the Order of Cistercians of the Strict Observance, Trappist, KY

Kelly, Rev. Timothy J., '99 (TYL) Curia: Pastoral Services

Kelly, Rev. Tom, '77 (MRY) Retired.

Kelly, Msgr. Vincent T., '56 (MIA) Retired.

Kelly, Rev. William A., '59 (STA) Retired. Curia: Clergy and Religious Services

Kelly, Rev. William J., '05 (CAM) Curia: Leadership St. Brendan the Navigator Parish, Avalon, N.J., Avalon, NJ

Kelly, Rev. William T., '88 (BO) Curia: Pastoral Services St. Paul, Cambridge, MA

Kelly, Rev. William T., (BO) [CAM] Harvard Catholic Center, Cambridge, MA

Kelm, Rev. Robert J., '15 (SAG) Holy Apostles Parish of Ruth, Ruth, MI; Saint Isidore Parish of Parisville, Ruth, MI

Kelpsas, Rev. A., *M.I.C.* '53 (JOL) Retired.

Kelpsas, Rev. Jaunius, '94 (CHI) Nativity of the Blessed Virgin Mary, Chicago, IL; Our Lady of Siluva Lithuanian Mission, Mundelein, IL

Kelpsas, Rev. Jaunius, '94 (LIT) Curia: Organizations (affiliated, inter-Diocesan, miscellaneous/other)

Kelsch, Rev. V. Ross, '17 (COV) St. Thomas, Fort Thomas, KY

Kelso, Rev. Francis E., '61 (MAN) Retired.

Kelso, Rev. Ronald, *S.S.C.* '73 (OM) Retired. [MON] Missionary Society of St. Columban, St. Columbans, NE

Kelso, Rev. Ronald, *SSC* (SD) Retired.

Kelt, Rev. Andriy, '16 (SJP) Curia: Offices and Directors Immaculate Conception (St. Mary's Ukrainian Catholic Church), Northern Cambria, PA; Protection Blessed Virgin Mary, Revloc, PA

Kelty, Rev. Edward J., *O.S.* '89 (PCE) Retired. On Duty Outside Diocese. Roma

Kemayou, Rev. Louis, '92 (STV) Curia: Offices and Directors St. Ann's Roman Catholic Congregation, Inc, Kingshill, VI; [MIS] Lumen 2000/Caribbean Region, Kingshill, VI

Kemayou, Rev. Louis, '92 (STV) [MIS] Miscellaneous Organizations, Charlotte Amalie, VI

Kemayou, Rev. Louis K, '92 (STV) Retired.

Kemberling, Rev. Andrew, '88 (DEN) Immaculate Heart of Mary Catholic Parish in Northglenn, Northglenn, CO

Kemboi, Rev. Albert, '14 (KAL) St. Ambrose, Parchment, MI

Kemme, Rev. Allen M., '91 (SFD) Little Flower, Springfield, IL

Kemo, Rev. Msgr. Kurt, (COV) Retired. Curia: Tribunal

Kemo, Rev. Msgr. Kurt H., '83 (STU) On Leave.

Kemp, Very Rev. Christopher J., '11 (SUP) Curia: Leadership Nativity of Our Lord, Rhinelander, WI; St. John, Pelican Lake, WI; St. John the Baptist, Gleason, WI

Kemp, Rev. Raymond B., '67 (WDC) Retired. On Special Assignment.

Kemper, Rev. Jeffrey M., '79 (CIN) St. Andrew, Milford, OH; St. Elizabeth Ann Seton, Milford, OH; St. Veronica, Cincinnati, OH

Kempf, Rev. Darrel C., '12 (GR) Curia: Leadership St. Joseph, Pewamo, MI

Kempf, Rev. Joseph G., '80 (STL) Most Sacred Heart Catholic Church, Eureka, Eureka, MO

Kempf, Rev. William, '84 (STL) St. Justin Martyr Catholic Church, Sunset Hills, MO

Kempinger, Rev. Stephen J., *C.S.C.* '01 (FTW) [COL] University of Notre Dame Du Lac, Notre Dame, IN; [MON] Holy Cross Community, Corby Hall, University of Notre Dame, Notre Dame, IN

Kempski, Rev. Leonard J., '66 (WIL) Retired. Holy Rosary, Claymont, DE

Kendzierski, Rev. Luiz, (LA) Our Lady of the Holy Rosary, Sun Valley, CA

Kenefick, Rev. Paul F., '56 (HRT) Retired.

Kenehan, Rev. David A., *OSFS* '74 (TOL) Retired. [MON] Provincial Offices, ,

Kenfack, Rev. Robert, '98 (STV) Curia: Leadership [MIS] Miscellaneous Organizations, Charlotte Amalie, VI

Kenkel, Rev. Leonard A., '60 (DM) Retired.

Kenna, Rev. Joseph J., '67 (YAK) Retired.

Kenna, Rev. Joseph R., '99 (ARL) Our Lady of Lourdes, Arlington, VA

Kennady, Rev. Joseph, (CR) St. Ann's (Blackduck), Blackduck, MN; St. John (Nebish), Nebish, MN; St. Patrick, Kelliher, MN

Kennealy, Rev. John H., '04 (WDC) St. Andrew Apostle, Silver Spring, MD; St. Matthias Apostle, Lanham, MD

Kennealy, Rev. Thomas P., *S.J.* '62 (CIN) Retired. [MON] Cincinnati Jesuit Community, Cincinnati, OH

Kennedy, Rev. Bernard, *O.F.M.* '88 (CHI) [MON] Holy Name Friary, Chicago, IL

Kennedy, Rev. Charles, '66 (TR) Retired.

Kennedy, Rev. Charles J., '66 (PH) Retired. St. Ignatius of Antioch, Yardley, PA

Kennedy, Rev. David, '97 (OWN) Holy Cross, Earlington, KY; Immaculate Conception, Earlington, KY; Resurrection, Dawson Springs, KY

Kennedy, Rev. Edward J., '68 (PH) Retired. On Special Assignment. Rector (Pro-Tem), Villa St Joseph Curia: Clergy and Religious Services Blessed Virgin Mary, Darby, PA

Kennedy, Rev. Edward M., '16 (CAM) St. Clare of Assisi Parish, Gibbstown, N.J., Gibbstown, NJ

Kennedy, Rev. Francis M., '64 (SPR) Retired.

Kennedy, Rev. Gary L., '68 (PBL) Retired.

Kennedy, Rev. Msgr. James M., '54 (SY) Retired.

Kennedy, Rev. John D., '93 (SHP) Retired.

Kennedy, Rev. Joseph P., '73 (WDC) Retired.

Kennedy, Rev. Kevin, '99 (SFR) Cathedral of St. Mary (Assumption), San Francisco, CA; Our Lady of Fatima Byzantine Catholic Church, San Francisco, CA

Kennedy, Rev. Kevin, '00 (SFR) Curia: Advisory Boards, Commissions, Committees, and Councils

Kennedy, Rev. Leo R., *M.M* '59 (NY) Retired.

Kennedy, Rev. Malcolm M., '61 (POD) Curia: Clergy and Religious Services

Kennedy, Rev. Malcolm M., '61 (NY) [MIS] Personal Prelature, New Rochelle, NY

Kennedy, Rev. Michael, (TR) Curia: Social Services Visitation, Brick, NJ

Kennedy, Rev. Michael E., *S.J.* '77 (LA) St. Albert the Great, Rancho Dominguez, CA

Kennedy, Rev. Patrick A., '77 (STP) Retired. Cretin-Derham Hall, St. Paul, MN

Kennedy, Rev. Msgr. Paul M., '77 (PH) St. David, Willow Grove, PA

Kennedy, Rev. Richard, *MSC* '67 (RCK) [MIS] The J. Chevalier Charitable Trust, Aurora, IL; [MON] Missionaries of the Sacred Heart Community, Aurora, IL

Kennedy, Rev. Robert E., *S.J.* '65 (NY) [MON] Murray-Weigel Hall (A Jesuit Community at Murray-Weigel Hall and Kohlmann Hall), Bronx, NY

Kennedy, Rev. Robert J., '74 (ROC) Retired.

Kennedy, Rev. Robert R., '66 (BO) Retired.

Kennedy, Rev. Russell F., '75 (NOR) Curia: Offices and Directors St. Francis of Assisi, Middletown, CT

Kennedy, Rev. Thomas, '15 (POC) Church of St. Mary the Virgin, Arlington, TX

Kennedy, Rev. Thomas, '21 (ALX) Our Lady of Prompt Succor, Alexandria, LA

Kennedy, Rev. Victor P., '77 (NEW) Immaculate Conception, Secaucus, NJ

Kennedy, Rev. William M., '87 (BO) Sacred Heart, Waltham, MA

Kennehan, Rev. John P., '62 (OG) Retired.

Kennell, Rev. Thomas, '16 (PT) Curia: Leadership St. John the Evangelist, Panama City, FL

Kennelly, Rev. Daniel, '77 (BGP) Retired.

Kennett, Rev. Timothy Cole, (LIN) St. Joseph's, Colon, NE

Kenney, Rev. Msgr. Albert A., '94 (PRO) Curia: Advisory Boards, Commissions, Committees, and Councils; Leadership Holy Apostles Church, Cranston, Rhode Island, Cranston, RI

Kenney, Rev. Brian A., '02 (L) Our Lady of Mercy, Hodgenville, KY; St. Ann, Howardstown, KY

Kenney, Rev. C. Douglas, '99 (BAL) Retired.

Kenney, Rev. C. Douglas, '99 (BAL) Retired.

Kenney, Rev. Msgr. Jeremiah F., '72 (BAL) Retired.

Kenney, Rev. Joachim, *O.P.* '17 (CIN) St. Gertrude, Cincinnati, OH; [MON] St. Gertrude Priory, Cincinnati, OH

Kenney, Rev. Keith Edwin, '14 (PHX) St. Anne Roman Catholic Parish, Gilbert, AZ

Kenney, Rev. Kevin T., '94 (STP) DeLaSalle High School, Minneapolis, MN; SS. Cyril and Methodius, Minneapolis, MN; St. Olaf, Minneapolis, MN

Kenney, Rev. Mark, *S.M.* '79 (ATL) Marist School, Atlanta, GA

Kenney, Rev. Paul C., *S.J.* '72 (BO) [MON] Campion Center, Inc., Weston, MA

Kenney, Rev. Sean W., *OFS* '91 (MET) Our Lady of the Mount, Warren, NJ

Kenney, Rev. Timothy, *S.M.* '82 (STL) [MON] Marianist Province of the United States (Society of Mary), St. Louis, MO

Kenney, Rev. William J., '56 (STP) Retired.

Kennington, Rev. John, (BAL) Retired.

Kenny, Rev. Gregory D., *C.M.F.* '59 (ATL) Corpus Christi Catholic Church, Stone Mountain, Inc., Stone Mountain, GA

Kenny, Rev. John F., *O.S.F.S.* '69 (WIL) Retired.

Kenny, Rev. Stephen K., '91 (MEM) St. Paul the Apostle, Memphis, TN

Kenny, Rev. Thomas Todd, *S.J.* '09 (CI) [MON] Jesuit Community of Micronesia, Chuuk, FM

Kenny, Rev. Msgr. Walter F., '54 (NY) Retired.

Kenny, Rev. William J.M., '71 (LAV) Curia: Advisory Boards, Commissions, Committees, and Councils; Deaneries Holy Spirit Catholic Church, Las Vegas, NV

Kent, Rev. Daniel, '63 (MIA) Retired.

Kent, Friar James, *OFM Conv* '91 (STP) [MON] St. Joseph Cupertino Friary, Prior Lake, MN; [RTR] Franciscan Retreats and Spirituality Center, Prior Lake, MN

Kenyon, Rev. Lee, '12 (POC) On Duty Outside Diocese.

Kenyon, Rev. Stephen, '19 (P) St. Mary, Eugene, OR

Keohane, Rev. Daniel G., '78 (BRK) Retired. [MON] Bishop Mugavero Residence, Douglaston, NY

Keohane, Rev. Donal, '68 (LA) Retired.

Keohane, Rev. Donal, '68 (SAV) Retired.

Keolker, Rev. Ricardo, '63 (YAK) St Joseph Parish, Kennewick, WA

Keolker, Rev. Richard F., '63 (YAK) Retired.

Keough, Rev. Joseph F., '96 (HRT) Sacred Heart Parish Corporation, Suffield, CT

Keown, Rev. William, (BAL) Our Lady of Victory, Baltimore, MD; [CAM] University of Maryland, Baltimore County (UMBC), Ellicott City, MD

Keown, Rev. William, (BAL) Curia: Clergy and Religious Services

Keppens, Rev. Gustaaf M., *S.J.* (BAL) Retired.

Keppens, Rev. Gustaaf M., *S.J.* '61 (WDC) Retired.

Keppler, Rev. Msgr. John F., '60 (BRK) Retired. [MON] Bishop Mugavero Residence, Douglaston, NY

Kerbawy, Rev. Kevin, '76 (SAG) Retired. Corpus Christi Parish of Bay City, Bay City, MI

Kerber, Rev. Joseph P., '88 (SFD) Retired.

Kerber, Rev. Justin, *C.P.* '72 (NY) [MON] The Congregation of the Passion - St. Paul of the Cross Province, Jamaica, NY

Kerber, Rev. Justin, *C.P.* '72 (PIT) Curia: Consultative Bodies [MON] St. Paul of the Cross Monastery, Pittsburgh, PA

Kerestes, Rev. Michael, '89 (PSC) Curia: Advisory Boards, Commissions, Committees, and Councils; Leadership St. Mary's, Wilkes-Barre, PA

Kerin, Rev. Michael, (SAV) Holy Family, Blakely, GA

Kerkemeyer, Rev. Carl, '02 (TLS) On Special Assignment. Mack Alford Corr Ctr, Stringtown St. William, Durant, OK

Kerketta, Rev. Noas, '94 (HT) Cathedral of St. Francis De Sales, Houma, LA

Kerketta, Rev. Sylverius, *SM* (CIN) [MON] Marianist Community, Huntsville, OH

Kern, Rev. Jason L., '12 (WIN) Curia: Advisory Boards, Commissions, Committees, and Councils; Offices and Directors [SEM] Immaculate Heart of Mary Seminary, Winona, MN
Kern, Rev. John Paul, *O.P.* (L) (>NY) [EFT] The Dominican Foundation of Dominican Friars, Province of St. Joseph, Inc., New York, NY; (>NY) [MIS] Dominican Friars' Guilds, New York, NY; (>NY) [MON] St. Vincent Ferrer Priory, New York, NY
Kern, Rev. John Paul, *O.P.* (WDC) St. Dominic Church & Priory, Washington, DC
Kern, Rev. Martin F., '94 (ALN) Curia: Organizations (affiliated, inter-Diocesan, miscellaneous/other) Our Lady of Perpetual Help, Bethlehem, PA
Kernan, Rev. William A., '93 (SD) Pastor of Saint Margaret Catholic Parish, Oceanside, a corporation sole, Oceanside, CA
Kerner, Rev. Terrence D., '72 (DET) St. Kateri Tekakwitha Parish Dearborn, Dearborn, MI
Kerns, Rev. Bryan, *O.S.A.* (BO) [COL] Merrimack College, North Andover, MA
Kerns, Rev. John W., '85 (P) Chap, Coffee Creek Corr Fac, Wilsonville Curia: Offices and Directors Our Lady of the Lake, Lake Oswego, OR
Kerper, Rev. Michael, '85 (MAN) Curia: Tribunal St. Patrick, Nashua, NH
Kerr, Rev. Robert, '95 (KC) Retired.
Kerr, Rev. Seamus, '60 (YAK) Retired. Holy Apostles, East Wenatchee, WA
Kerrigan, Rev. Msgr. Joseph J., '90 (MET) St. Joseph, Bound Brook, NJ
Kerrigan, Rev. Michael, '87 (NY) Parish of St. John and Visitation, Bronx, NY; Visitation, Bronx, NY
Kerrigan, Rev. Michael F., '64 (DEN) Retired.
Kersch, Rev. Terence, *C.S.B.* '01 (GAL) [MON] Basilian Fathers Missions, Sugar Land, TX
Kerschen, Rev. Leon J., '62 (WCH) Retired.
Kerschen, Rev. Michael L., '18 (WCH) Church of the Magdalen, Wichita, KS
Kerst, Rev. Patrick, '90 (SPK) Curia: Leadership; Offices and Directors St. Thomas More, Spokane, WA
Kersten, Rev. Jay J., '98 (LAN) On Duty Outside Diocese. Curia: (>MO) Offices and Directors
Kersten, Rev. Kevin, *S.J.* (MIL) [MON] St. Camillus Jesuit Community (Society of Jesus, USA Midwest Province), Wauwatosa, WI
Kerstiens, Rev. Christopher, *OFM* (GLP) San Esteban, Acoma Catholic Indian Mission, Pueblo of Acoma, NM; St. Joseph, Laguna, NM
Kersys, Rev. Gediminas, '08 (CHI) Nativity of the Blessed Virgin Mary, Chicago, IL
Kersys, Rev. Gediminas, (GRY) St. Ann, Beverly Shores, IN
Kertys, Rev. Martin, '95 (NY) Parish of St. John Nepomucene, St. Frances Cabrini, and St. John the Martyr, New York, NY; St. Frances Cabrini, New York, NY; [MIS] New York Oratory of St. Philip Neri, Inc., Sparkill, NY
Kertz, Rev. Msgr. Raymond N., '67 (MAD) Retired.
Kerul-Kmec, Rev. Miron, '21 (PBR) St. John Chrysostom, Pittsburgh, PA; St. John the Baptist, Pittsburgh, PA
Kerul-Kmec, Rev. Miron, '90 (PRM) Curia: Advisory Boards, Commissions, Committees, and Councils; Leadership St. Nicholas, Barberton, OH
Kerze, Rev. William F., '69 (LA) Retired. Our Lady of Malibu, Malibu, CA
Kesicki, Rev. Michael T., (E) [CAM] Gannon University, Erie, PA; [COL] Gannon University, Erie, PA
Kesicki, Rev. Timothy, *S.J.* '94 (WDC) [MON] Leonard Neale House, Washington, DC; [MON] The Jesuit Community of St. Aloysius Gonzaga, Washington, DC
Kessel, Rev. Gerald, (GB) [MON] St. Fidelis Friary, Appleton, WI
Kessler, Rev. Thomas, '84 (CHL) St. Philip the Apostle, Statesville, NC
Kessler, Rev. Thomas, '75 (EVN) Retired.
Kessler, Rev. William F., '99 (SFD) St. Alphonsus, Brighton, IL; St. John the Evangelist, Medora, IL
Kessler, Rev. William Thomas, '74 (COL) Retired. St. Catharine, Columbus, OH; [SEM] Pontifical College Josephinum, Columbus, OH
Kestermeier, Rev. Charles T., *S.J.* '75 (OM) [MON] Jesuit Community at Creighton University, Omaha, NE
Ketcham, Rev. Robert W., '08 (RVC) Christ the King, Commack, NY
Kettelberger, Rev. John A., *C.M.* '78 (PH) [MON] Congregation of the Mission, Philadelphia, PA
Kettenring, Rev. Michael J., '01 (NO) Retired.
Ketter, Very Rev. Daniel P., '08 (ATL) Curia: Leadership; Offices and Directors Holy Family Catholic Church, Marietta, Inc., Marietta, GA
Ketterer, Rev. Bryan, '14 (TLS) On Special Assignment. Chap, St Philip Neri Newman Ctr, Tulsa, OK Sacred Heart, Wilburton, OK
Ketterlin, Rev. Kendall, '19 (KC) St. Ann's, Independence, MO; St. Joseph the Worker, Independence, MO; St. Mary's, Independence, MO
Keucher, Very Rev. Michael T., '15 (IND) Curia: Leadership; Offices and Directors St. Joseph Catholic Church, Shelbyville, Inc., Shelbyville, IN; St. Vincent De Paul Catholic Church, Shelby County, Inc., Shelbyville, IN; [MIS] Batesville Deanery, Indianapolis, IN
Keusenkothen, Rev. Aquinas, *O.SB.* (KC) [MON] Conception Abbey (Benedictine Monks), Conception, MO
Keusenkothen, Rev. Stephen, (KC) [SEM] Conception Seminary College, Conception, MO
Keveny, Rev. M. Valentine, (WDC) St. Mary, Rockville, MD
Keville, Rev. Joseph F, '96 (BO) St. Patrick, Stoneham, MA
Key, Rev. Paul R., '07 (TYL) St. Boniface, Chandler, TX
Key, Rev. William W., '75 (MIL) Retired.
Keyes, Rev. David E., '20 (MET) St. Ambrose, Old Bridge, NJ
Keyes, Rev. Jeffrey, (SR) Curia: Offices and Directors Pastor of St. Eugene Cathedral of Santa Rosa, A Corporation Sole, Santa Rosa, CA; [CAM] Newman Center at Sonoma State University, Penngrove, CA
Keyes, Rev. Patrick, *C.Ss.R.* '89 (LA) St. Mary of the Assumption, Whittier, CA; [MON] Redemptorists of Whittier, Whittier, CA
Keyes, Rev. Samuel, '21 (POC) St. Augustine of Canterbury, Escondido, TX
Keyes, Rev. Thomas E., '73 (BO) Our Lady of Hope, Ipswich, MA
Keymont, Rev. Walter F., '80 (BO) On Special Assignment.
Kezmarsky, Rev. Kenneth E., '86 (PIT) St. Joseph the Worker, Pittsburgh, PA
Khachan, Rev. Charles H., *M.L.M.* '99 (OLL) Curia: Offices and Directors St. George Maronite Catholic Church, San Antonio, TX; [MON] The Congregation of Maronite Lebanese Missionaries, Houston, TX
Khallouf, Rev. Raymond, '13 (SAM) St. Maron Maronite, Jacksonville, FL
Kharuk, Rev. Wasyl, '92 (PHU) St. Michael the Archangel, Jenkintown, PA
Khdmyn, Rev. Eugene (Andriy), *O.S.B.M.* '10 (RVC) [MON] St. Josaphat's Monastery, Novitiate and Retreat House, Glen Cove, NY
Khembo, Rev. James, (CR) Holy Trinity Catholic (Tabor), Angus, MN; Sacred Heart, East Grand Forks, MN
Khin, Rev. Theodore, '99 (WCH) St. Ambrose, Erie, KS; St. Francis, St. Paul, KS
Khoi, Rev. Jim N., (FWT) Immaculate Conception of Mary, Wichita Falls, TX
Khomyn, Rev. Andriy, (MO) Curia: Offices and Directors
Khomytskyy, Rev. Ihor, (STN) St. Nicholas Ukrainian Catholic Cathedral, Chicago, IL
Khong, Rev. Michael Tuan, (ORG) Curia: Leadership; Offices and Directors
Khoueiry, Rev. Joseph, '00 (SAM) Our Lady of Lebanon, Waterbury, CT
Khoury, Rev. Ghattas, '90 (OLL) Our Lady of the Rosary Mission, Carmichael, CA; St. Sharbel Maronite Catholic Mission, Stockton, CA
Khoury, Rev. Jean Paul, (OLL) Saint Ignatius of Antioch Maronite Catholic Church, Dayton, OH
Khue, Rev. Thomas, '91 (OAK) Our Lady, Queen of the World, Bay Point, CA
Kiamo-oh, Rev. Peter, '22 (BAL) St. Ignatius, Forest Hill, MD
Kibaki, Rev. Robert, *A.J.* (SD) Pastor of Saint John the Evangelist Catholic Parish, Encinitas, a corporation sole, Encinitas, CA
Kibambe Kya Bela Mema, Rev. Crispin, (DEN) St. Mary Catholic Parish in Greeley, Greeley, CO
Kibby, Rev. Patrick J., '84 (NSH) Retired. Curia: Leadership St. Henry, Nashville, TN
Kibler, Rev. Joshua, *C.O.* '09 (PIT) [MON] Congregation of the Oratory of St. Philip Neri, Pittsburgh, PA
Kick, Rev. Caleb, *F.S.S.P.* '17 (PH) St. Mary Roman Catholic Church, Conshohocken, PA
Kickham, Rev. Robert T., (BO) Curia: Advisory Boards, Commissions, Committees, and Councils Cathedral of the Holy Cross, Boston, MA
Kidaagen, Very Rev. Baiju, *V.C.* '01 (COV) Curia: Advisory Boards, Commissions, Committees, and Councils; Leadership St. Pius X, Edgewood, KY; Villa Madonna Academy High School/Junior High, Villa Hills, KY
Kidaha, Rev. Silvanus S, (CHI) St. Andrew, Chicago, IL
Kidd, Rev. David D., '16 (TOL) Curia: Advisory Boards, Commissions, Committees, and Councils St. Joseph, Toledo, OH
Kidd, Rev. Richard Meno, '13 (AGN) Curia: Advisory Boards, Commissions, Committees, and Councils; Consultative Bodies; Faith Formation; Leadership; Pastoral Services Our Lady of Guadalupe, Santa Rita, GU
Kidder, Rev. Msgr. James C., '67 (SAC) Retired. Curia: Leadership; Offices and Directors
Kiddy, Rev. Curtis, *C.P.* '92 (NY) [MON] The Congregation of the Passion - St. Paul of the Cross Province, Jamaica, NY
Kiddy, Rev. Curtis, *C.P.* '92 (PIT) [MON] St. Paul of the Cross Monastery, Pittsburgh, PA
Kidney, Rev. Msgr. Liam J., '68 (LA) Curia: Pastoral Services Corpus Christi, Pacific Palisades, CA
Kiefer, Rev. John D., '70 (LFT) Retired.
Kiefer, Rev. Thomas P., '81 (SPC) Curia: Advisory Boards, Commissions, Committees, and Councils; Consultative Bodies; Leadership; Offices and Directors St. Elizabeth Ann Seton, Springfield, MO
Kiefer, Rev. William J., '58 (SB) Retired.
Kieffer, Rev. Charles G., '80 (PHX) Curia: Leadership
Kieffer, Rev. John L., *S.J.* '68 (LEX) (>DET) [MON] Colombiere Center, Clarkston, MI
Kieffer, Rev. Joseph, '04 (SAL) Curia: Consultative Bodies Sacred Heart Parish, Greenleaf, Inc., Greenleaf, KS; St. Augustine Parish, Washington, Inc., Washington, KS; St. John the Baptist Parish, Hanover, KS
Kieffer, Very Rev. Peter J., '17 (LC) Curia: Leadership Immaculate Conception Parish, Alma Center, WI; St. Joseph, Fairchild, WI
Kieffer, Rev. Robert, '69 (SCL) Retired.
Kiehl, Rev. Matthew Allen, '15 (RIC) Holy Spirit, Virginia Beach, VA
Kieler, Rev. Michael, '21 (STA) On Academic Leave. Catholic Univ of America, Washington, DC
Kielkowski, Rev. Andrzej, *S.D.S.* '81 (NEW) [MON] The Salvatorian Fathers, Verona, NJ
Kielkowski, Rev. Andrzej, *S.D.S.* '81 (MO) Curia: Offices and Directors
Kielkowski, Rev. Andrzej, *S.D.S.* '81 (MET) Chap, US Veterans Med Ctr
Kieltyka, Rev. Robert, '58 (NO) Retired.
Kiely, Rev. Brian R., '78 (BO) [SEM] Pope Saint John XXIII National Seminary, Weston, MA
Kiely, Rev. Cornelius, '67 (BAK) Retired.
Kiely, Rev. Thomas, (SD) Pastor of Sacred Heart Catholic Parish, San Diego, a corporation sole, San Diego, CA; [MIS] Sacred Heart Catholic Parish San Diego in San Diego, CA Real Property Support Corporation, San Diego, CA
Kiely, Rev. Thomas P., '88 (NY) St. John, Woodstock, NY
Kiely, Rev. Thomas R., '03 (CAM) On Duty Outside Diocese.
Kienzle, Rev. Jerome C., '72 (MIL) Retired.
Kiepura, Rev. Kenneth, '69 (CHI) Retired.
Kieran, Rev. John C., '67 (ATL) Retired.
Kiernan, Rev. Michael F., '73 (SAC) Retired. Pastor of Our Lady of the Assumption Parish, Carmichael, a corporation sole, Carmichael, CA
Kiernan, Rev. Steven W., '15 (PH) Holy Cross, Springfield, PA
Kiesel, Rev. James P., '95 (BAL) St. Joseph, Odenton, Odenton, MD
Kiesel, Rev. Leo C., '63 (EVN) Retired.
Kiesling, Rev. John F., *S.A.* '68 (NY) [MON] St. Christopher's Inn Friary, Garrison, NY
Kieton, Rev. Dennis J., '85 (PRO) Retired. SS. John and Paul Parish Corporation, Coventry, Coventry, RI
Kieu, Rev. Kien, (SB) Sacred Heart, Anza, CA
Kiff, Rev. Herbert J., '95 (NO) Mater Dolorosa, New Orleans, LA
Kifolo, Rev. Patrick, *O.S.F.S.* (WIL) Salesianum School, Wilmington, DE
Kifolo, Rev. Patrick J., *O.S.F.S.* '07 (ARL) Our Lady of Good Counsel, Vienna, VA
Kiggins, Rev. Roy, '64 (ROC) Retired.
Kightlinger, Rev. Jon, '02 (BAL) On Special Assignment.
Kigozi, Rev. Denis S., '91 (COL) Church of the Resurrection, New Albany, OH
Kihm, Rev. Frederick C., '93 (STU) Sacred Heart, Hopedale, OH; St. Matthias Mission, Freeport, OH; St. Teresa, Cadiz, OH
Kik, Rev. Jacques, (OLL) St. Maron Maronite Catholic Church, Youngstown, OH
Kikoba, Rev. Athanasius, '04 (SJ) St. Francis of Assisi, San Jose, CA
Kilanowski, Rev. Humbert, *O.P.* (PRO) [MON] St.

Thomas Aquinas Priory at Providence College, Providence, RI
Kilburn, Rev. Clayton, *C.M.* '79 (STL) [MON] Congregation of the Mission Vincentian Fathers Lazarist Residence, St. Louis, MO
Kilcawley, Rev. Sean P., '05 (LIN) Curia: Leadership; Offices and Directors St. Leo's, Palmyra, NE
Kilcomons, Rev. Richard, '06 (PAT) St. Therese, Succasunna, NJ
Kilcourse, Rev. George A., '76 (L) Retired.
Kilcoyne, Rev. Patrick, '75 (SJ) Retired.
Kilcoyne, Rev. Terence T., '76 (WOR) Curia: Leadership Holy Trinity, Harvard, MA
Kileen, Rev. William, (CHI) Retired.
Kileo, Rev. Albert Noepachio, *A.L.C.P.* '92 (SLC) Saint Anthony of Padua Catholic Church LLC 216, Helper, UT
Kiley, Rev. J. Cletus, '74 (CHI) Retired.
Kiley, Rev. John A., '66 (PRO) Retired. Curia: Clergy and Religious Services
Kiley, Rev. John G., '70 (BO) Retired. Our Lady of Hope, Ipswich, MA
Kilgallon, Rev. John J., '69 (PH) Retired.
Kilian, Rev. Waldemar A., '87 (CHI) Military Chap., Gurnee
Kilidjian, Rev. Vincent, *M.S.A.* '68 (NOR) [MON] Society of the Missionaries of the Holy Apostles, Cromwell, CT
Kilisara, Rev. Thomas, '85 (NO) Sacred Heart, Lacombe, LA
Kilkelly, Rev. Timothy O., *M.M.* '90 (NY) [MON] Maryknoll Fathers and Brothers (Catholic Foreign Mission Society of America, Inc.), Ossining, NY
Kill, Rev. Donald H, *S.S.C.* '72 (OM) Retired. [MON] Missionary Society of St. Columban, St. Columbans, NE
Kill, Rev. Robert J., '71 (TOL) Retired. St. Isidore, Defiance, OH; St. Michael, Defiance, OH
Killeen, Rev. Andrew, (LAF) Sacred Heart of Jesus, Ville Platte, LA; St. Joseph, Ville Platte, LA
Killeen, Rev. John C., '59 (CAM) Retired.
Killeen, Rev. Msgr. Michael F., '59 (LA) Retired. St. Elizabeth Ann Seton, Rowland Heights, CA
Killeen, Rev. Thomas, *O.M.I.* (BEL) [MON] Missionary Oblates of Mary Immaculate - St. Henry's Oblate Residence, Belleville, IL
Killian, Rev. Anthony J., '08 (ARL) Our Lady of Hope, Potomac Falls, VA
Killilea, Rev. Patrick J., *SS.CC.* '69 (HON) St. Francis, Kalaupapa, HI
Killips, Rev. Aaron, '07 (SAV) On Leave.
Kilmas, Rev. Johanis, *M.S.C.* '18 (MI) Curia: Leadership Sacred Heart of Jesus, Jaluit, MH
Kilmurray, Rev. Fintan J., '77 (BLX) Our Lady of Perpetual Help, Lumberton, MS
Kilpatrick, Rev. Andrew W., '96 (SCR) On Administrative Leave.
Kilpatrick, Rev. John J., '61 (SCR) Retired. Curia: Offices and Directors Our Lady of the Abingtons, Dalton, PA; [MON] Villa St. Joseph, Dunmore, PA
Kilpatrick, Rev. Kyle, '17 (GR) Muskegon Catholic Central, Muskegon, MI; Muskegon Catholic Central Elementary School, Muskegon, MI; St. Mary of the Immaculate Conception, Muskegon, MI
Kilroy, Rev. Paul E., '70 (BO) Retired. Curia: Pastoral Services St. Camillus, Arlington, MA; [CAM] Regis College Office of Campus Ministry, Weston, MA
Kilty, Rev. Cornelius F., *O.S.F.S.* '69 (WIL) [MON] Retirement and Assisted Care Facility, Childs, MD
Kilumbu, Rev. Claudes, '94 (MO) Curia: Offices and Directors
Kilzer, Rev. James, *O.S.B.* '98 (BIS) [MON] Assumption Abbey, Richardton, ND
Kim, Rev. Adrian, '02 (FRS) St. Lucy, Fowler, CA
Kim, Rev. Alapaki, '82 (HON) Curia: Consultative Bodies St. Rita, Nanakuli, HI
Kim, Rev. Alfonso, *M.M.* '97 (NY) [EFT] Maryknoll Missionary Education Trust, Maryknoll, NY; [MON] Maryknoll Fathers and Brothers (Catholic Foreign Mission Society of America, Inc.), Ossining, NY
Kim, Rev. Andrew M., '98 (BRK) St. Paul Chong Ha-Sang Roman Catholic Chapel, Flushing, NY
Kim, Rev. Bede, '07 (MET) St. John Vianney, Colonia, NJ
Kim, Rev. Byeong Hoon, *O.F.M. Conv.* '17 (LA) St. Francis Korean Center, Torrance, CA
Kim, Rev. Carlos C., '93 (BO) On Leave.
Kim, Rev. Chan Mi, '06 (PH) Holy Angels, Philadelphia, PA; Holy Mary Korean Catholic Church, Newtown Square, PA
Kim, Rev. Daeseon (Paul), *M.S.C.* (SB) St. Andrew Kim Korean Community, Riverside, CA
Kim, Rev. David, *S.D.D.* (NO) [MIS] Domus Dei Clerical Society of Apostolic Life, U.S.A., Inc., New Orleans, LA
Kim, Rev. Didaco Yung Soo, '01 (NEW) Curia: Organizations (affiliated, inter-Diocesan, miscellaneous/ other)
Kim, Rev. Dominicus, '17 (STP) St. Andrew Kim, St. Paul, MN
Kim, Rev. Dongyoung Augustine, '13 (COS) St. Andrew Kim Parish, Colorado Springs, CO
Kim, Rev. Dukwoo Antonio, '06 (COL) St. Andrew Kim Taegon Korean Catholic Community, Columbus, OH
Kim, Rev. Francis, '12 (CAM) Church of St. Rose, Haddon Heights, N.J., Haddon Heights, NJ; Korean Catholic Mission (St. Yun Yi II Korean Mission), ,
Kim, Rev. Francis Beth, '21 (LA) St. Mel, Woodland Hills, CA
Kim, Rev. Francis K., *O.F.M.* '96 (NY) [MIS] Franciscan Missionary Charities, Inc., New York, NY
Kim, Rev. Francis K., *O.F.M.* '96 (PAT) [MON] St. Anthony Friary (Order of Friars Minor), Butler, NJ
Kim, Rev. Hae In, (LA) St. Gregory Nazianzen, Los Angeles, CA
Kim, Rev. Hyun-jhik, (BO) [MON] Miguel Pro House, Brighton, MA
Kim, Rev. InShik, '08 (SAV) St. Joseph, Augusta, GA
Kim, Rev. Jeong Gon, '01 (SFR) Curia: Offices and Directors
Kim, Rev. Jihoon, '21 (LA) St. Kateri Tekakwitha, Santa Clarita, CA
Kim, Rev. Jinmo, '08 (STA) St. Francis Choe Korean Catholic Mission, Jacksonville, FL
Kim, Rev. Jinyeol, *OFM* (NY) St. Francis of Assisi, New York, NY
Kim, Rev. Jiwan, '93 (LA) St. Matthew Korean Catholic Center, Tujunga, CA
Kim, Rev. John Hyun Guk, (OAK) Curia: Offices and Directors
Kim, Rev. JooHyeon, (JOL) St. Andrew Kim, Itasca, IL
Kim, Rev. Joseph, (BO) St. Joseph, Needham, MA
Kim, Rev. Joseph, *O.F.M.Conv.* '11 (LA) Our Lady of Guadalupe, Hermosa Beach, CA; Our Savior Parish & U.S.C. Caruso Catholic Center, Los Angeles, CA
Kim, Rev. Joseph, '10 (SJ) Curia: Leadership; Offices and Directors St. John Vianney, San Jose, CA
Kim, Rev. Joseph (Sae Eul), '84 (AUS) Retired.
Kim, Rev. Joseph L., (MO) Curia: Offices and Directors
Kim, Rev. Joseph S., '90 (LAN) St. Andrew Dung Lac Parish Lansing, Lansing, MI
Kim, Rev. Joseph Soon-Jin, '92 (PH) Holy Angels, Philadelphia, PA
Kim, Rev. Jungsoo, '03 (NEW) Madonna, Fort Lee, NJ
Kim, Rev. Jungtack (John), '10 (AUS) St. Mary of the Assumption, Taylor, TX
Kim, Rev. Mary Joseph, *O.Cart.* '92 (BUR) [MON] Carthusian Foundation in America, Inc., Charterhouse of the Transfiguration, Arlington, VT
Kim, Rev. Michael Hak Hyeon, *KMS* '10 (AJ) St. Joseph, Cordova, AK
Kim, Rev. Nam, *P.P.S.* '90 (STO) St. Gertrude Church (Pastor of), Stockton, CA
Kim, Rev. Nam J., *P.S.S.* '90 (BAL) [MON] Society of St. Sulpice, Province of the United States, Baltimore, MD
Kim, Rev. Nam Joseph, '90 (ELP) On Duty Outside Diocese. Society of St Sulpice
Kim, Rev. Nam Gil Andrew, (DAL) St. Andrew Kim Catholic Parish, Irving, TX
Kim, Rev. Paul Y., '13 (BRK) St. Raphael, Long Island City, NY
Kim, Rev. Robert C., '09 (TLS) St. Catherine, Tulsa, OK
Kim, Rev. Samuel, *O.S.B.* '95 (PAT) [MON] St. Paul's Abbey (Order of St. Benedict, Congregation of St. Ottilien), Newton, NJ
Kim, Rev. Sangkyun, (NEW) St. Andrew Kim, Maplewood, NJ
Kim, Rev. Silvester, '06 (BAL) On Administrative Leave.
Kim, Rev. Simon Cheng ban, (ORG) On Sick Leave.
Kim, Rev. Steve, '11 (SJ) Saint John XXIII College Prep, Campbell, CA
Kim, Rev. Steve, '11 (SJ) Curia: Offices and Directors St. Leo the Great, San Jose, CA
Kim, Rev. Sung Ho, (RVC) St. Raphael, East Meadow, NY
Kim, Rev. Sunghyun, (ATL) Korean Martyrs Catholic Church, Doraville, Inc., Doraville, GA
Kim, Rev. Tae Jin, (ARL) St. Paul Chung, Fairfax, VA
Kim, Rev. Tu-Jin Paul, *C.P.* '00 (CHI) [MON] Passionist Community of St. Vincent Strambi, Chicago, IL
Kim, Rev. Woo-jung Stephen, (BO) [MON] Francis Xavier House, Brighton, MA
Kim, Rev. Yoonsok, (TUC) Our Lady Star of the Sea Roman Catholic Parish - Tucson, Tucson, AZ
Kim, Rev. Yoonsok (Paul), (TUC) Curia: Miscellaneous / Other Offices
Kim, Rev. YoungKun, (HON) [MIS] Korean Catholic Community, Honolulu, HI
Kim, Rev. Young-Kwan, (SEA) St. Paul Chong Hasang Personal Parish, Fife, WA
Kim Ban, Rev. Albert M. P., *CRM* '03 (SPC) [MON] Congregation of the Mother of the Redeemer, Carthage, MO
Kimani, Rev. John, '18 (SFE) Curia: Offices and Directors San Antonio de Padua, Penasco, NM; St. Anthony-Dixon, Dixon, NM
Kimani, Rev. Peter Patrick, '14 (MIL) St. Catherine's Congregation, Milwaukee, WI; St. Sebastian's Congregation, Milwaukee, WI
Kimario, Rev. Lucas, (LAV) St. Francis de Sales, Las Vegas, NV
Kimaryo, Rev. Alfred, *I.C.* (SP) St. Francis of Assisi, Seffner, FL
Kimaryo, Rev. Simon, *AJ* '90 (ALN) [MIS] Apostles of Jesus, Northampton, PA
Kimbro, Rev. Clay, '17 (WCH) Holy Name, Winfield, KS; St. Anne, Wichita, KS
Kime, Rev. David W., (GRY) Curia: Leadership Queen of All Saints, Michigan City, IN
Kime, Rev. David W., '97 (GRY) St. Mary of the Immaculate Conception, Michigan City, IN
Kimel, Rev. Alvin, '06 (NEW) On Duty Outside Diocese. Roanoke, VA
Kimes, Rev. John Paul, '00 (OLL) On Special Assignment. Notre Dame Univ, IN Curia: Leadership
Kimes, Rev. John Paul, '00 (SAM) Curia: Leadership
Kimes, Rev. John Paul, (OLL) Curia: Offices and Directors (>FTW) [COL] University of Notre Dame Du Lac, Notre Dame, IN
Kimm, Rev. Gregory C., '87 (SJ) St. Mary of the Immaculate Conception, Los Gatos, CA
Kimminau, Rev. Bernard, '94 (LIN) Curia: Leadership St. Patrick, McCook, NE
Kimminau, Rev. Irenaeus, *O.F.M.* '49 (SFD) Retired. [MON] Holy Cross Friary (Quincy University Friary), Quincy, IL
Kimmons, Rev. Steve, *S.J.* (BR) [RTR] Manresa House of Retreats, Convent, LA
Kimmons, Rev. Steven E., *S.J.* '94 (LAF) Curia: Miscellaneous / Other Offices (>NO) [MON] Loyola Jesuit Community, New Orleans, LA
Kimtis, Rev. Kevin J., '11 (TR) On Duty Outside Diocese. India Vatican Diplomatic Corps
Kinane, Rev. William P., '57 (SAC) Retired.
Kincl, Rev. Robert L., '67 (AUS) Retired.
Kinda, Rev. Joseph, (NY) St. Joseph of the Holy Family, New York, NY
Kindel, Rev. Joseph, '08 (CIN) On Special Assignment. Dayton St. Peter, Huber Heights, OH
Kinderman, Rev. Dennis, *C.PP.S.* '67 (CHI) [MIS] Precious Blood Ministry of Reconciliation, Chicago, IL
Kindon, Rev. W. Frederick, '74 (PH) St. Martin of Tours, New Hope, PA
Kindong, Rev. Dieudonne Nsom Nsom, *S.T.* '16 (WDC) [MON] Missionary Servants of the Most Holy Trinity, Silver Spring, MD
Kinerk, Rev. Edward, *S.J.* '72 (COS) [MON] Sacred Heart Jesuit Community, Sedalia, CO; [RTR] Sacred Heart Jesuit Retreat House, Sedalia, CO
King, Rev. Andrew, '96 (NY) Cathedral of St. Patrick, New York, NY
King, Rev. Brian, '00 (PMB) Curia: Leadership; Offices and Directors
King, Rev. Brian Madison, '97 (LKC) Curia: Leadership [HOS] CHRISTUS Health Southwestern Louisiana, Lake Charles, LA
King, Rev. Bruce, *I.C.* '85 (SP) St. Theresa, Spring Hill, FL
King, Rev. Chad, '10 (PHX) St. Gabriel Roman Catholic Parish, Cave Creek, AZ
King, Rev. Donald E., '74 (Y) Retired. Central Catholic High School, Canton, OH; St. Joan of Arc, Canton, OH; St. Thomas Aquinas High School & Middle School, Louisville, OH; [EFT] St. Thomas Aquinas High School Endowment Fund, Louisville, OH
King, Rev. Garrett, '21 (KC) St. Andrew the Apostle, Gladstone, MO
King, Rev. Howard J., '63 (E) Retired.
King, Rev. James B., *CSC* (P) (>FTW) [COL] University of Notre Dame Du Lac, Notre Dame, IN; (>FTW) [MON] Holy Cross Community, Corby Hall, University of Notre Dame, Notre Dame, IN
King, Rev. Msgr. James E., '71 (PBL) Holy Rosary, Pueblo, CO; Our Lady of the Meadows, Pueblo, CO
King, Rev. James H., '11 (CAM) Richard Stockton University, Pomona, NJ; [MIS] St. John of God, North Cape May, , ; [MIS] St. Raymond, Villas, Villas, NJ
King, Rev. James J., *S.J.* '63 (MIL) [MON] St. Camillus

Jesuit Community (Society of Jesus, USA Midwest Province), Wauwatosa, WI

King, Rev. James W., '91 (BRK) St. Patrick, Brooklyn, NY; [SEM] Cathedral Seminary House of Formation, Douglaston, NY

King, Rev. Jeffrey W., '87 (GLP) Curia: Offices and Directors St. Mary's, Farmington, NM

King, Rev. Jeremy, *O.S.B.* (EVN) [CON] Sisters of St. Benedict of Ferdinand, IN, Inc., Monastery Immaculate Conception, Ferdinand, IN

King, Rev. Jeremy, *O.S.B.* '76 (IND) [MON] St. Meinrad Archabbey, St. Meinrad, IN

King, Rev. Lawrence J., '89 (GR) Retired. Curia: Leadership

King, Rev. Martin L., '96 (P) Curia: Offices and Directors St. Thomas More, Portland, OR

King, Rev. Matthew, '19 (STA) Assumption, Jacksonville, FL

King, Rev. Michael J., '77 (WDC) Curia: Consultative Bodies; Deaneries Jesus the Good Shepherd, Owings, MD

King, Rev. Nicholas, '66 (ORL) Retired.

King, Rev. Norman, '88 (RNO) Retired.

King, Rev. Paul Stephen, '10 (SFS) Saint Lambert Parish of Minnehaha County, Sioux Falls, SD

King, Rev. Stephen, *OFM Conv* (HBG) Mother Cabrini, Shamokin, PA

King, Rev. Stuart, '12 (HT) On Duty Outside Diocese.

King, Rev. Stuart, (MO) Curia: Offices and Directors

King, Rev. Thomas, *C.S.C.* (FTW) [MIS] Holy Cross House, Notre Dame, IN

King, Rev. Thomas M., '73 (CIN) Guardian Angels, Cincinnati, OH; Immaculate Heart of Mary, Cincinnati, OH

King, Rev. Msgr. William J., '83 (HBG) Curia: Offices and Directors [CAM] Messiah College, Mechanicsburg, PA

King, Rev. Msgr. William J., (BAL) [SEM] Mount St. Mary's Seminary, Emmitsburg, MD

King, Rev. William J., (SAM) Curia: Leadership

Kingery, Rev. Patrick J., '93 (ATL) Retired.

Kingori, Rev. James, *I.M.C.* '88 (MET) [MON] Consolata Society for Foreign Missions, North Brunswick, NJ

Kingsbury, Rev. John, *C.Ss.R* '80 (BAL) Sacred Heart of Jesus-Sagrado Corazon de Jesus, Baltimore, MD

Kingsley, Rev. Daniel O., '15 (BRK) St. Clare, Rosedale, NY

Kingsley, Rev. Richard M., '83 (TUC) Retired. Corpus Christi Roman Catholic Parish - Tucson, Tucson, AZ

Kingsley, Rev. S. **Thomas**, '03 (CHR) Curia: Advisory Boards, Commissions, Committees, and Councils; Offices and Directors Church of the Nativity, Charleston, SC

Kiniry, Rev. Msgr. Lawrence R., '65 (GBG) Retired. [NUR] Neumann House, Greensburg, PA

Kinkel, Rev. Msgr. Robert J., '70 (DEN) Retired.

Kinn, Rev. James W., '57 (CHI) Retired. Santa Maria Del Popolo, Mundelein, IL

Kinnally, Rev. Msgr. Robert M., '05 (BGP) Curia: Clergy and Religious Services; Community Services; Consultative Bodies; Leadership St. Aloysius Church Corporation of Connecticut, New Canaan, CT

Kinnaman, Rev. Leroy G., '73 (LFT) Retired.

Kinnane, Rev. Msgr. James F., (HRT) Retired. Curia: Tribunal Annunciation Parish Corporation, Newington, CT

Kinnane, Rev. James R., (HRT) Retired.

Kinney, Rev. Donald, *OCD* '88 (SR) [MON] Carmelite House of Prayer, Oakville, CA; [RTR] Carmelite House of Prayer, Oakville, CA

Kinney, Rev. Eugene M, (LAV) St. Joseph, Husband of Mary, Las Vegas, NV

Kinney, Rev. George R., '63 (STP) Retired.

Kinney, Rev. James J., '98 (SUP) Retired. (>LEX) St. Patrick, Mount Sterling, KY

Kinney, Rev. John M., '76 (LFT) Chap, San Antonio, TX Curia: (>MO) Offices and Directors

Kinney, Rev. Matthew, '06 (AUS) On Leave.

Kinsella, Rev. Charles R., '65 (BO) Retired.

Kintiba, Rev. Georges, *S.V.D.* '96 (WDC) [MON] Society of the Divine Word/Divine Word House, Washington, DC

Kinyua, Rev. James Mwangi, (RVC) Chap, NYU Winthrop Univ Hosp; St Francis Hosp

Kinzamba, Rev. Jeremie, *SJ* '20 (OAK) [MON] Jesuit Fathers and Brothers, Berkeley, CA

Kinzler, Rev. Dale H., '74 (FAR) Curia: Offices and Directors Sacred Heart Church of Aneta, Aneta, ND; St. George Church of Cooperstown, Cooperstown, ND; St. Lawrence Church of Jessie, Jessie, ND; St. Olaf Church of Finley, Finley, ND; [MIS] Marriage Encounter, Cooperstown, ND

Kinzler, Rev. Herman, *O.Carm.* '08 (NEW) St. Cecilia, Englewood, NJ; St. John the Baptist, Fairview, NJ

Kiocha, Rev. Process Milton, *A.J.* '01 (COL) St. Mary, Chillicothe, OH; St. Mary, Queen of the Missions, Waverly, OH; St. Peter, Chillicothe, OH

Kipchirchir, Rev. Ignatius, '03 (SD) Pastor of Our Lady of Mt. Carmel Catholic Parish, San Diego, a corporation sole, San Diego, CA

Kipfer, Rev. David M., '88 (PEO) St. Mary's, Metamora, IL

Kipper, Rev. Nicholas A., '06 (LIN) Curia: Leadership; Offices and Directors St. Teresa Catholic Church, Lincoln, NE; [CON] Adoration Convent and Church of Christ the King (Sister Servants of the Holy Spirit of Perpetual Adoration), Lincoln, NE

Kirangu, Rev. Zack, (NSH) St. Patrick's, McEwen, TN

Kiratu, Rev. Bernard, '10 (ORL) Blessed Trinity, Ocala, FL

Kirby, Rev. Daniel J., '94 (DM) St. John the Apostle Church, Norwalk, IA

Kirby, Rev. Donald J., *S.J.* '72 (SY) Curia: Leadership [COL] Le Moyne College, Syracuse, NY; [MON] Jesuits at LeMoyne, Inc., Syracuse, NY

Kirby, Rev. Gerald S., (NOR) All Saints, Somersville, CT

Kirby, Rev. Jeffrey F., '07 (CHR) Our Lady of Grace, Lancaster, SC

Kirby, Rev. Joh P., *SVD* (SB) [RTR] Divine Word Province/ Retreat Center, Riverside, CA

Kirby, Rev. Shane L., '04 (SCR) On Duty Outside Diocese. Serving in Rome at the Vatican

Kirby, Rev. Thomas M., '57 (PIT) Retired.

Kirch, Rev. Jeffrey, *C.PP.S.* '04 (CIN) [MON] Society of the Precious Blood, United States Province, Inc., Dayton, OH (>KC) [MIS] St. Gaspar Society, Liberty, MO

Kirchgessner, Rev. Christopher A., *O.S.B.* '80 (CHL) [MON] Belmont Abbey (Southern Benedictine Society of North Carolina, Inc.), Belmont, NC

Kirchhoefer, Rev. Thomas A., '98 (STL) Military Chap Curia: (>MO) Offices and Directors

Kirchner, Rev. Allen, '20 (SPC) Springfield Catholic High School, Springfield, MO

Kirialdeniyage, Rev. Ajith, *OMI* (NY) St. Peter, Poughkeepsie, NY

Kirigia, Rev. Lazarus, '07 (DM) Curia: Leadership St. Mary, Red Oak, IA; St. Patrick, Imogene, IA

Kirila, Rev. Michael, '87 (ROM) Retired.

Kirincic, Rev. Vedran, '08 (BRK) Most Precious Blood, Long Island City, NY; [CCH] Croatian Ministry, ,

Kirk, Rev. Msgr. Albert E., '68 (MEM) Retired.

Kirk, Rev. Daniel E., '12 (TR) Curia: Leadership St. Charles Borromeo, Cinnaminson, NJ

Kirk, Rev. David, (RIC) Military Chap

Kirk, Rev. David R., '83 (TOL) Chap, US Army Curia: (>MO) Offices and Directors

Kirk, Very Rev. James T., '86 (WIL) Curia: Deaneries St. Mary Magdalen, Wilmington, DE

Kirk, Rev. John L., '70 (NSH) Retired.

Kirk, Rev. Matthew J., '22 (MIL) Congregation of the Holy Assumption, West Allis, WI; St. Rita's Congregation, West Allis, WI

Kirk, Rev. Msgr. Raymond, '59 (SD) Retired.

Kirk, Rev. Raymond, (SB) St. Vincent Ferrer, Sun City, CA

Kirk, Rev. Robert, (POC) Christ the King Catholic Church, Towson, MD; Mount Calvary Church, Baltimore, MD

Kirk, Rev. William S., '72 (PH) Retired. Our Lady of Calvary, Philadelphia, PA

Kirkconnell, Rev. Joseph D., '14 (DET) On Academic Leave. Catholic Univ of America, Washington (>WDC) St. Anthony of Padua, Washington, DC

Kirke, Rev. Eugene K., '62 (BO) Retired.

Kirkendoll, Rev. Thomas, '87 (CIN) Retired. [MON] Headquarters of Glenmary Home Missioners (The Home Missioners of America), Fairfield, OH

Kirkham, Rev. Richard, '11 (FWT) On Leave.

Kirkman, Rev. Kenneth R., '16 (SY) Curia: Leadership St. Ambrose, Endicott, NY; St. Anthony of Padua, Endicott, NY; St. Joseph, Endicott, NY

Kirkpatrick, Rev. James W., '08 (BUF) Immaculate Conception, Ransomville, NY; St. John de La Salle, Niagara Falls, NY; St. Jude the Apostle Roman Catholic Parish of North Tonawanda, New York, North Tonawanda, NY

Kirlin, Rev. Bernard G., '71 (MIA) Retired.

Kirouac, Rev. Richard, (STN) On Leave.

Kirsch, Rev. Gerard D., *O.S.B.* '70 (SEA) [COL] Saint Martin's University (Order of St. Benedict Master's Comprehensive University), Lacey, WA

Kirsch, Rev. Gregory G., '88 (STL) On Duty Outside Diocese. Irvine, CA

Kirsch, Rev. Myron M., *O.S.B.* '73 (GBG) [MON] Saint Vincent Archabbey, Latrobe, PA

Kirschman, Rev. Andrew, (LAF) [SEM] Jesuit Novitiate of St. Stanislaus Kostka at St. Charles College, Grand Coteau, LA

Kirwen, Rev. Michael C., *M.M.* '63 (NY) Retired. [MON] Maryknoll Fathers and Brothers (Catholic Foreign Mission Society of America, Inc.), Ossining, NY

Kirwin, Rev. Arthur, *O.P.* '84 (ATL) [MON] Augustine House, Dominicans Friars of Atlanta (The Monastery on the Hill), Atlanta, GA (>STL) [MON] St. Dominic Priory, St. Louis, MO

Kirwin, Rev. George, *O.M.I.* '58 (WDC) [MON] Oblate Community, Washington, DC

Kirwin, Rev. John D., '66 (ALB) Retired. Curia: Offices and Directors

Kirwin, Rev. Michael J., '76 (SCR) St. John Vianney, Scott Twp., PA

Kirwin, Rev. Peter, *O.F.M.* '81 (PHX) Our Lady of the Angels Conventual Church, Scottsdale, AZ; [RTR] Franciscan Renewal Center, Inc. (Casa de Paz Y Bien), Scottsdale, AZ

Kisaka, Rev. Odemary Bahati, *AJ* '00 (ALN) [MIS] Apostles of Jesus, Northampton, PA (>CLV) Visitation of Mary, Akron, OH

Kiselica, Rev. John J., '84 (DET) St. Paul of Tarsus Parish Clinton Township, Clinton Township, MI

Kiser, Rev. Karl J, *S.J.* '97 (CHI) [MIS] USA Midwest Province of the Society of Jesus, Inc., Chicago, IL; [MON] Chicago Province of the Society of Jesus, Chicago, IL

Kish, Rev. Carl, '62 (Y) St. Robert Bellarmine Parish, Cortland, OH

Kish, Rev. Jerome, '98 (JOL) Holy Cross, Joliet, IL; St. Mary Nativity, Joliet, IL

Kish, Rev. Leslie P., '97 (B) Retired.

Kish, Rev. Michael A., '65 (MIA) Retired.

Kisonia, Rev. Kasereka Moise, *OSC* '16 (SCL) [MON] Crosier Priory, Onamia, MN

Kiss, Friar Barnabas G., *O.F.M.* '78 (DET) Holy Cross (Hungarian) Parish Detroit, Detroit, MI

Kiss, Rev. Barnabas G., *O.F.M.* '78 (ATH) Curia: Leadership; Organizations (affiliated, inter-Diocesan, miscellaneous/other)

Kissane, Rev. Maurice J., '64 (CHI) Retired.

Kissane, Rev. Michael, *O.Carm.* '86 (NY) Parish of St. Simon Stock and St. Joseph, Bronx, NY

Kissel, Rev. Anthony, '73 (EVN) Retired.

Kissel, Rev. Francis J., *S.M.* '71 (ATL) Marist School, Atlanta, GA

Kissel, Rev. Ignatius M., *O.S.M.* '65 (P) Retired. [MON] The Grotto, The National Sanctuary of Our Sorrowful Mother, Portland, OR

Kissell, Very Rev. Terrence, '78 (DEN) St. Michael the Archangel Catholic Parish in Aurora, Aurora, CO

Kissner, Rev. Mark, *OCD* (SR) [MON] Carmelite House of Prayer, Oakville, CA; [RTR] Carmelite House of Prayer, Oakville, CA

Kistner, Rev. Hilarion, *O.F.M.* '55 (CIN) Retired.

Kiszelewski, Very Rev. Mark M., '13 (SEA) Curia: Leadership St. Cecilia, Bainbridge Island, WA

Kiszka, Rev. Kamil, '18 (PAT) Our Lady of the Lake, Sparta, NJ

Kita, Rev. John M., '98 (SCR) On Administrative Leave.

Kitchin, Rev. George R., '70 (BLX) Retired.

Kithinji, Rev. Lawrence M., '03 (SAC) Pastor of St. Anne Parish, Sacramento, a corporation sole, Sacramento, CA

Kitsmiller, Rev. Robert J., '04 (COL) Curia: Offices and Directors St. Joseph Cathedral, Columbus, OH

Kituli, Rev. Christopher, '10 (CHI) St. Patricia, Hickory Hills, IL

Kitzhaber, Rev. Keith J., '08 (LC) Corpus Christi, Marshfield, WI; Sacred Heart of Jesus, Marshfield, WI

Kitzke, Rev. Timothy L., '89 (MIL) Our Lady of Divine Providence Congregation, Milwaukee, WI; SS. Peter and Paul, Milwaukee, WI; St. Mary's Congregation, Milwaukee, WI; Three Holy Women Congregation, Milwaukee, WI; [MIS] SPRED Partners, Inc., Milwaukee, WI

Kiwan, Rev. Naji, '98 (SAM) St. Anthony, Danbury, CT

Kiyimba, Rev. Pontian, *A.J.* '05 (KNX) St. Mary, Oak Ridge, TN

Kizewski, Rev. Justin J., '08 (LC) On Duty Outside Diocese. Faculty: St. Francis de Sales Seminary, Milwaukee (>MIL) [SEM] Saint Francis de Sales Seminary, St. Francis, WI

Kizhakedan, Rev. John, *C.M.I.* '74 (BEL) Our Lady of Good Counsel, Renault, IL; Seven Dolors of the B.V.M., Valmeyer, IL; St. Patrick, Waterloo, IL

Kizhakkeparambil, Rev. Peter, (LEX) St. Peter, Lexington, KY

Kizhavana, Rev. Joseph, (PHX) St. Thomas the Apostle Roman Catholic Parish, Phoenix, AZ
Kizito, Rev. John Fisher, '02 (FAR) St. Philip's Church of Napoleon, Napoleon, ND
Kizza, Rev. Patrick, '19 (CHI) Our Lady of Perpetual Help, Glenview, IL
Kizza, Rev. Tonny, '22 (MIL) St. Eugene Congregation, Fox Point, WI; St. Monica's Congregation, Whitefish Bay, WI
Kladar, Rev. John, '19 (RCK) On Special Assignment. Curia: Clergy and Religious Services; Leadership Holy Cross, Batavia, IL
Klag, Rev. Michael A., '03 (WCH) On Duty Outside Diocese. St. Joseph, Arma, KS; St. Michael, Girard, KS
Klak, Rev. Jan Piotr, '79 (SAT) St. Anthony Mary Claret, San Antonio, TX
Klamut, Rev. Charles, '99 (PEO) St. Anthony, Bartonville, IL
Klanichka, Very Rev. Volodymyr, '01 (PHU) Curia: Leadership St. Basil the Great, Chesapeake City, MD; St. Nicholas, Wilmington, DE
Klanichka, Rev. Volodymyr, (WIL) Chap, Wilmington Hosp; Christiana Care Health Srvcs, Inc.
Klasek, Rev. Stephen A., '83 (NSH) St. Mark, Manchester, TN; St. Paul the Apostle Catholic Church, Tullahoma, TN
Klasinski, Rev. Stanley J., '77 (CLV) St. Clare, Lyndhurst, OH
Klassen, Rt. Rev. John, *O.S.B.* '77 (SCL) [MON] St. John's Abbey, of the Order of St. Benedict, Collegeville, MN
Klassen, Rev. Roger, *O.S.B.* '66 (SCL) [MON] St. John's Abbey, of the Order of St. Benedict, Collegeville, MN
Klauck, Rev. Michael, '94 (BIR) On Special Assignment.
Klaus, Rev. John Mark, *T.O.R.* '99 (FWT) Good Shepherd, Colleyville, TX
Klaver, Rev. Wilhelmus J, *M.H.M* '95 (NY) Parish of St. Charles Borromeo and All Saints, New York, NY; [MON] Mill Hill Fathers Residence, Hartsdale, NY
Kleas, Rev. Msgr. Milam, '51 (GAL) Retired.
Kleba, Rev. Gerald J., '67 (STL) Retired.
Klecha, Rev. Joseph A., *M.M.* '69 (SJ) Retired.
Klecker, Rev. David, (SAV) Curia: (>MO) Offices and Directors Benedictine Military School, Savannah, GA; [MON] The Benedictine Priory, Savannah, GA
Kleckner, Rev. Brandon M., '12 (E) St. Michael, Greenville, PA; [CAM] Thiel College, Greenville, PA
Klee, Rev. Joseph C., '01 (COL) Chap, Marion Corr Inst; Ross Corr Inst, Chillicothe
Kleespie, Rev. Nickolas, *O.S.B.* '15 (SCL) [MON] St. John's Abbey, of the Order of St. Benedict, Collegeville, MN
Klein, Rev. Anthony, '19 (SFS) Cathedral of Saint Joseph Parish, Sioux Falls, SD
Klein, Rev. David F., *S.J.* '71 (SJ) Retired. [MON] Sacred Heart Jesuit Center, Los Gatos, CA
Klein, Rev. David J., '90 (CAM) Curia: Tribunal St. Mary's Church, Gloucester, Gloucester, NJ
Klein, Rev. David O., *C.S.B.* '70 (LSC) [MON] The Basilian Fathers of Las Cruces, Las Cruces, NM
Klein, Rev. Dennis, *O.P.* (OAK) [MON] Order of Preachers (Province of the Most Holy Name of Jesus - Western Dominican Province), Oakland, CA; [SEM] Dominican School of Philosophy and Theology, Berkeley, CA
Klein, Rev. Dennis D., '66 (BRK) Retired.
Klein, Rev. Donald L., '65 (DUB) Retired.
Klein, Rev. Douglas M., '96 (SC) All Saints Roman Catholic Church, Le Mars, IA
Klein, Rev. Eugene M., '74 (WIN) On Leave.
Klein, Rev. George W., '59 (CHI) Retired.
Klein, Rev. Gregory, *O.Carm.* '75 (VEN) [MON] Carmel at Mission Valley, Nokomis, FL
Klein, Rev. James J., '03 (COS) St. Anthony of Padua, Hugo, CO; St. Mary, ,
Klein, Rev. James T., '78 (CLV) Retired.
Klein, Rev. John, *LC* '17 (ATL) [MIS] Legionaries of Christ, Atlanta, GA
Klein, Rev. John, '02 (JOL) St. Ann Parish, Channahon, IL
Klein, Rev. John J., '70 (PAT) Retired. [MIS] Nazareth Village, Chester, NJ
Klein, Rev. John Paul, *O.M.V.* (DEN) Holy Ghost Catholic Parish in Denver, Denver, CO
Klein, Rev. Louis S., '81 (BUF) Curia: Consultative Bodies Queen of Martyrs, Cheektowaga, NY
Klein, Rev. Martin L., '91 (RVC) Retired.
Klein, Rev. Pascal, (DOD) Holy Family School, Great Bend, KS; Sacred Heart School, ,
Klein, Rev. Pascal L., '87 (DOD) Sacred Heart Catholic Church of Ness City, Kansas, Ness City, KS; St. Aloysius Catholic Church of Ransom, Kansas, Ransom, KS
Klein, Rev. Peter J., '74 (WIN) Retired.
Klein, Rev. Pius, *O.S.B.* '74 (IND) [MON] St. Meinrad Archabbey, St. Meinrad, IN
Klein, Rev. Terrance W., '84 (DOD) Curia: Offices and Directors Holy Family Catholic Church of Odin, Kansas, Odin, KS; Immaculate Conception Catholic Church of Claflin, Kansas, Claflin, KS; St. Joseph Catholic Church of Ellinwood, Kansas, Ellinwood, KS; [EFT] St. Joseph School Education Endowment Fund, Ellinwood, KS
Klein, Rev. Tony, (SFS) O'Gorman Junior High, Sioux Falls, SD
Kleine, Rev. Andrew, '19 (KC) St. Thomas More, Kansas City, MO
Kleine, Rev. Andrew, '19 (KC) On Special Assignment. Curia: Offices and Directors
Kleiner, Rev. James, '67 (DEN) Retired.
Kleinfehn, Rev. Walter J., '60 (DUB) Retired.
Kleinmann, Rev. Dennis W., '93 (ARL) St. Veronica, Chantilly, VA
Kleinschmidt, Rev. John, '02 (GB) Most Precious Blood Parish, New London, WI; St. Patrick, New London, WI
Kleinschmidt, Rev. John, '02 (FAR) On Duty Outside Diocese. Wisconsin
Kleinwachter, Rev. John, '77 (CR) Curia: Offices and Directors Sacred Heart, Roseau, MN; St. Mary's (Badger), Badger, MN; St. Philip (Falun), Roseau, MN
Kleissler, Rev. Msgr. Thomas A., '57 (NEW) Retired. On Special Assignment. Pastor Emeritus, Caldwell [MIS] RENEW International, Plainfield, NJ
Klekas, Rev. Patrick, '18 (RNO) St. Albert the Great, Reno, NV
Klem, Rev. Daniel N., '83 (RIC) Church of the Holy Angels, Portsmouth, VA; Church of the Resurrection, Portsmouth, VA; St. Mary, Chesapeake, VA; St. Paul, Portsmouth, VA
Klem, Rev. Robert James, *C.S.B.* '56 (GAL) Retired. [MON] The Basilian Fathers of Dillon House, Houston, TX
Klemash, Rev. Dennis, *O.F.M. Cap.* (PIT) [MON] St. Augustine Friary, Pittsburgh, PA
Klemme, Rev. Robert W., '91 (LFT) Retired.
Klemmer, Rev. Marvin J., '66 (BIS) Retired. Curia: Leadership [NUR] Emmaus Place, Bismarck, ND
Klepac, Rev. Msgr. Kenneth J., '58 (MOB) Retired. [NUR] Little Sisters of the Poor, Home For the Aged, Inc., Mobile, AL
Klepac, Rev. Richard, (CC) St. Anthony, Robstown, TX
Klepacki, Rev. Michael S., '78 (CHL) Retired. On Leave.
Kleponis, Rev. Jerome A., '22 (HBG) Saint Katharine Drexel, Mechanicsburg, PA
Klettner, Rev. Frederick J., '65 (DET) Retired.
Kletzel, Rev. Thomas P., '83 (PH) St. Malachy, Philadelphia, PA
Klevence, Rev. John P., *K.H.S.* '85 (WIL) St. Ann, Bethany Beach, DE
Klich, Rev. Grzegorz, (VEN) Ascension Parish in Fort Myers Beach, Inc., Fort Myers Beach, FL
Klimczyk, Rev. Leon, *S.J.* '76 (MIL) [MON] St. Camillus Jesuit Community (Society of Jesus, USA Midwest Province), Wauwatosa, WI
Klimek, Rev. Daniel, *TOR* '20 (STU) [COL] Franciscan University of Steubenville, Steubenville, OH; [MON] Holy Spirit Friary, Steubenville, OH
Klimko, Rev. Anthony J., '15 (GBG) Curia: Advisory Boards, Commissions, Committees, and Councils Nativity of the Blessed Virgin Mary, Uniontown, PA; St. John the Evangelist, Uniontown, PA; St. Joseph, Uniontown, PA; St. Therese, the Little Flower of Jesus, Uniontown, PA
Kline, Rev. Donald J., '95 (PHX) Curia: Leadership St. Bernadette Roman Catholic Parish, Scottsdale, AZ
Kline, Rev. Edmond G., '04 (WCH) Holy Trinity, Little River, KS
Kline, Rev. Edmond G., '04 (TLS) [HOS] Saint Francis Hospital, Tulsa, OK
Kline, Rev. Robert J., '04 (RVC) Retired.
Kline, Rev. Tyler G., '19 (BAL) Curia: Leadership Basilica of the National Shrine of the Assumption of the Blessed Virgin Mary, Baltimore, MD
Klingeisen, Rev. Richard H., '72 (GB) Immaculate Conception, Cato, WI; St. Michael, Whitelaw, WI
Klingele, Rev. Brian, '02 (KCK) On Leave.
Klinger, Rev. Charles, '83 (COL) Retired.
Klinger, Rev. Msgr. Nevin J., '82 (ALN) Assumption B.V.M., Bethlehem, PA
Klinger, Rev. Msgr. Nevin J., (SAM) Curia: Leadership
Klingler, Rev. Donald P., '61 (KAL) Retired.
Klink, Rev. Kenneth J., '66 (MAD) Retired.
Klink, Rev. Peter J., *S.J.* '81 (RC) [MON] Holy Rosary Mission Jesuit Community, Pine Ridge, SD
Klinzing, Rev. Msgr. Thomas J., '71 (PMB) Retired.
Klismet, Rev. Kurt J., *O.SS.T.* '02 (BAL) [EFT] Cardinal Denhoff Trust, Sykesville, MD; [MON] Holy Trinity Monastery, Sykesville, MD
Klizek, Rev. Duane R., '82 (BUF) Holy Family of Jesus, Mary and Joseph, Niagara Falls, NY
Kloak, Rev. David G., '78 (CHI) Military Chap
Klobuka, Rev. John, (CIN) (>SJ) [MON] The Marianist Center, Cupertino, CA
Klocek, Rev. Andrzej Wojciech, '89 (BRK) St. Elizabeth, Ozone Park, NY
Klockeman, Rev. John A., '00 (STP) St. Bartholomew, Wayzata, MN
Klonowski, Rev. Kevin J., '16 (CLV) St. Joseph, Strongsville, OH
Klores, Rev. Stanley P., '82 (NO) Retired.
Klores, Rev. Stanley P., '82 (NO) Retired.
Klos, Rev. Joseph, '80 (BUF) Retired.
Klos, Rev. Michael E., '00 (LC) Nativity of the Blessed Virgin Mary, Norwalk, WI; Sacred Heart of Jesus, Cashton, WI; St. Augustine of Hippo, Norwalk, WI; [EFT] Holy Family Endowment Trust Fund, Cashton, WI; [EFT] Sacred Heart of Jesus Education Endowment Trust, Cashton, WI
Kloss, Rev. Anthony, *O.S.B.* '91 (WOR) [MON] Benedictine Monks, St. Benedict Abbey, Still River, MA
Kloster, Rev. Everson L., *SX* '22 (MIL) [SEM] Xaverian Missionary Fathers College Seminary, Franklin, WI
Klosterkamp, Rev. Thomas, *OMI* (SAT) [COL] Oblate School of Theology, San Antonio, TX; [MON] De Mazenod House, San Antonio, TX
Klosterman, Rev. Timothy Clement, '08 (LA) On Administrative Leave.
Kloton, Rev. Michael J., (SCR) Church of the Good Shepherd, Drums, PA
Kloton, Rev. Michael J., '87 (SCR) Curia: (>MO) Offices and Directors Our Lady of the Immaculate Conception, Freeland, PA; St. Patrick, White Haven, PA
Klotter, Rev. Frederick W., '96 (L) Curia: Leadership Holy Spirit, Louisville, KY
Kluba, Rev. Zbigniew, '73 (PAT) Retired.
Kluckman, Rev. Anthony, *S.C.J.* '73 (MIL) Retired. [MON] Sacred Heart at Monastery Lake, Franklin, WI
Kluckman, Rev. Anthony, *S.C.J.* (SFS) St. Joseph Indian School, Chamberlain, SD
Klucsarits, Rev. Linus, *O.S.B.* '17 (BIR) [MON] St. Bernard Abbey, Cullman, AL
Kluge, Rev. Daniel, (RIC) St. Benedict, Chesapeake, VA
Kluge, Rev. Daniel, '15 (COV) On Duty Outside Diocese. Priestly Fraternity of St. Peter
Kluge, Rev. Stephen E., *O.F.M.* (SP) Sacred Heart, Tampa, FL
Kluk, Rev. David, *LC* '91 (MAD) Oaklawn Academy, Edgerton, WI
Klump, Rev. Gregory S., '98 (STL) Our Lady Catholic Church, Festus, MO; Sts. Philip and James Catholic Church, Ste. Genevieve, MO
Klunk, Rev. David, '09 (ORG) St. Hedwig, Los Alamitos, CA
Klunk, Rev. Timothy, '79 (BAL) Retired.
Klusman, Rev. Christopher L., '11 (MIL) Curia: Leadership
Klybus, Rev. Edward George, '01 (NEW) Church of the Nativity, Midland Park, NJ
Kmetz, Rev. Andy, *IVE* '19 (DAL) St. Bernard of Clairvaux Catholic Parish, Dallas, TX
Kmiecik, Rev. Piotr A., '14 (BLX) Holy Spirit Catholic Church, Vancleave, MS
Knab, Rev. George, *O.M.I.* '67 (BEL) [MON] Missionary Oblates of Mary Immaculate - St. Henry's Oblate Residence, Belleville, IL
Knapik, Rev. Andrew, (CLV) Chap, Hillcrest Hosp, Cleveland
Knapik, Rev. Andrew G., '57 (ALT) Retired.
Knapik, Rev. Andrzej, '78 (CLV) St. Francis of Assisi, Gates Mills, OH
Knapp, Rev. Charles, '63 (TUC) Retired.
Knapp, Rev. Gerard J., *C.Ss.R.* '75 (BRK) [MON] Redemptorist Fathers of New York, Inc.-Baltimore Province, Brooklyn, NY
Knapp, Rev. John M., '86 (NY) Parish of Our Lady of the Assumption - St. Mary Star of the Sea, Bronx, NY; St. Mary Star of the Sea, Bronx, NY
Knapp, Rev. Msgr. Kenneth, '63 (EVN) Retired.
Knapp, Msgr. Kenneth R., '63 (EVN) Retired. Curia: Leadership
Knappik, Rev. Richard, *C.S.s.R.* '58 (HBG) Retired. [MON] St. Clement's Mission House, Ephrata, PA
Knecht, Rev. Marcus E., '16 (OM) St. Gerald, Ralston, NE
Kneeland, Rev. David L., '06 (MAN) St. Lawrence, Goffstown, NH
Kneemiller, Rev. William C., '99 (DAV) Retired. [MIS] Holy Land Military Rosary, Inc., Davenport, IA;

[MON] St. Vincent Center, Davenport, IA
Kneifl, Rev. Rodney V., '85 (OM) [MIS] Servants of the Heart of the Father, Platte Center, NE
Knepper, Rev. Msgr. Daniel J., '70 (DUB) Retired. Curia: Leadership
Knerr, Rev. Joseph, '80 (ORG) Curia: Leadership St. Bonaventure, Huntington Beach, CA
Knickerbocker, Rev. Knick, '09 (SAN) Retired.
Knight, Rev. Christopher, '20 (STA) Our Lady Star of the Sea, Ponte Vedra Beach, FL
Knight, Rev. Dennis, '77 (LEX) Retired.
Knight, Rev. Msgr. Jeffrey N., '88 (STL) Immaculate Conception Catholic Church, Arnold, Arnold, MO; St. Joseph Catholic Church, Zell, Ste. Genevieve, MO
Knight, Rev. John (Jack) Philp, '18 (ATL) St. John Vianney Catholic Church, Lithia Springs, Inc., Lithia Springs, GA
Knight, Rev. Robert D., '83 (STL) St. Francis of Assisi Catholic Church, Luebbering, MO; St. Stephen Catholic Church, Richwoods, MO
Knight, Rev. Trinity, '14 (COV) St. Agnes, Fort Wright, KY
Knight, Rev. Vernon, '14 (SAV) St. Mary on the Hill, Augusta, GA
Knipe, Very Rev. Michael J., '88 (TLS) Curia: Leadership Resurrection, Tulsa, OK
Knippel, Rev. Kenneth P., '76 (MIL) Retired.
Knippenberg, Rev. Patrick S., '12 (VIC) Our Lady of Lourdes, Victoria, TX
Knippenberg, Very Rev. Robert E., '00 (VIC) Curia: Leadership; Offices and Directors SS. Peter and Paul, New Ulm, TX; St. Roch, Alleyton, TX
Knipper, Rev. Daniel J., '67 (DUB) Retired. Curia: Organizations (affiliated, inter-Diocesan, miscellaneous/ other)
Knittel, Rev. Kilian J., '60 (CHI) Retired. Christ Our Light Parish, Chicago, IL
Knoblach, Rev. Thomas, '87 (SCL) Curia: Offices and Directors Annunciation, Sauk Rapids, MN; Church of Sacred Heart, Sauk Rapids, MN
Knoebel, Rev. Thomas L., '69 (MIL) Retired.
Knoll, Rev. Lester, *O.F.M. Cap.* '64 (PIT) [MON] St. Augustine Friary, Pittsburgh, PA
Knoll, Rev. Urban H., '69 (STL) Retired.
Knop, Rev. Andrew, *OMI* (DUL) St. Joseph, Gnesen, MN
Knop, Rev. Andy, (DUL) St. Michael, Duluth, MN
Knopik, Rev. Andrew J., '83 (BEL) Our Lady of Perpetual Help, Nashville, IL; St. Ann, Nashville, IL
Knopik, Rev. John Paul, '11 (SCL) Ave Maria, Wheaton, MN; St. Mary's, Chokio, MN
Knopp, Rev. John, '78 (ELP) On Leave.
Knotek, Rev. Michael P., '96 (CHI) Curia: Leadership; Offices and Directors Our Lady of the Holy Family, Chicago, IL
Knott, Rev. J. Ronald, '70 (L) Retired.
Knox, Rev. Sean Vincent, '01 (PT) Andrews AFB, Maryland Blessed Sacrament, Tallahassee, FL
Knox, Rev. Msgr. Stephen J., '89 (RCK) On Special Assignment. Curia: Clergy and Religious Services; Leadership St. Bridget, Loves Park, IL
Knudsen, Rev. Ronald W., '72 (SEA) Retired. Holy Cross, Tacoma, WA
Ko, Rev. Bong Ho Peter, (GAL) St. Andrew Kim, Houston, TX
Ko, Rev. Michael, *K.M.S.* '08 (AJ) Sacred Heart, Haines, AK
Ko, Rev. Taehoon, (SJ) Holy Korean Martyrs, San Jose, CA
Koba, Rev. Bartlomiej, (RVC) St. Hyacinth, Glen Head, NY
Kobak, Rev. David, *OFM* '03 (GB) Assumption of the Blessed Virgin Mary Congregation, Pulaski, WI; St. Stanislaus Congregation, Hofa Park, WI
Kobbeman, Rev. Msgr. Gerald P., '66 (RCK) Retired.
Kobe, Rev. Robert S., '79 (ELP) Retired. Curia: Tribunal
Kobos, Rev. Martin, *OFM Conv.* '76 (HBG) Mother Cabrini, Shamokin, PA (>HRT) Saint Paul Parish Corporation, Kensington, CT
Kobus, Rev. Boguslaw, '92 (PAT) Immaculate Conception, Franklin, NJ
Kobuszewski, Rev. Thomas P., '64 (SY) Transfiguration, Syracuse, NY
Koch, Rev. Albert, *SM* (CIN) [MON] Siena Woods Marianist Community, Dayton, OH
Koch, Rev. David J., '69 (GB) Retired.
Koch, Rev. Garry, '13 (TR) Curia: Offices and Directors St. Benedict, Holmdel, NJ
Koch, Rev. Jason, '03 (KC) Immaculate Conception, Montrose, MO; St. Patrick's, Butler, MO
Koch, Rev. Kevin A., '85 (CHY) St. Paul's, Pine Bluffs, WY
Koch, Rev. Mariusz, *C.F.R.* '69 (NEW) [SEM] Immaculate Conception Seminary School of Theology, South Orange, NJ
Kochan, Rev. Frederick A., '55 (WIL) Retired.
Kocher, Rev. Donald, '63 (JOL) Retired.
Kocherla, Rev. Sundar Raj, '72 (JOL) Retired.
Kochery, Rev. Msgr. Peter, '70 (MCE) St. Thomas Malankara Catholic Church, Elizabeth, NJ
Kochery, Rev. Msgr. Peter, '70 (TR) Retired. St. Thomas More, Manalapan, NJ
Kochery, Rt. Rev. Msgr. Peter, '70 (MCE) Curia: Advisory Boards, Commissions, Committees, and Councils
Kochivar, Rev. Erin, '16 (COS) St. Francis of Assisi, Colorado Springs, CO
Kochlin, Rev. Lester, *OFM* (GB) Retired. [MON] Blessed Giles Friary, Manitowoc, WI
Kochu, Rev. Paul, '74 (SP) St. Luke the Evangelist, Palm Harbor, FL; [PRE] St. Luke Early Childhood Center, Palm Harbor, FL
Kochumoodapuvail, Rev. Mathew Abraham, '99 (PT) St. Joseph, Port St. Joe, FL
Kochuparambil, Rev. George J., '91 (ALN) Most Blessed Trinity Parish, Tremont, PA
Kochuparambil, Very Rev. Jose M, '12 (LUB) Curia: Leadership
Kochuparampil, Rev. Jose M., '87 (ATL) St. Mary Mother of God Catholic Church, Jackson, Inc., Jackson, GA
Kochupurackal, Rev. Abraham George, *C.M.I.* (STP) Ascension Catholic Church, Norwood, MN; St. Bernard, Cologne, MN; [CEM] Ascension Cemetery, Norwood, MN; [CEM] St. Bernard Cemetery, Cologne, MN; [CEM] St. Patrick's Cemetery, Norwood, MN
Kociemba, Rev. Benjamin, '12 (SCL) Curia: Offices and Directors Holy Family, Little Falls, MN; Our Lady of Lourdes, Little Falls, MN; St. Mary, Little Falls, MN
Kociolek, Rev. Charles J., *C.S.C.* '79 (SCR) [COL] King's College, Wilkes-Barre, PA
Kocurek, Rev. Antonin, '90 (BRK) Our Lady Queen of Martyrs, Forest Hills, NY; [CCH] Czech/Slovak Ministry, ,
Koczera, Rev. Joseph A., *S.J.* '15 (WDC) [MON] Leonard Neale House, Washington, DC
Kodakarakaran, Rev. Paul, '75 (TLS) (>SYM) Holy Family Syro-Malabar Catholic Church Oklahoma, Oklahoma City, OK
Kodavatikanti, Rev. Chandra, (LR) St. John the Evangelist, Huntsville, AR
Koday, Rev. Mishael J., '08 (BWN) Hosp Ministry Our Lady of Sorrows, McAllen, TX
Kodet, Rev. John, *FSSP* '15 (LA) St. Vitus, San Fernando, CA
Kodigandla, Rev. Sudeep, '22 (KCK) Church of the Nativity, Leawood, KS
Kodiganti, Rev. Maria Joseph, '11 (SUP) Our Lady Queen of Peace, Manitowish Waters, WI; St. Anthony of Padua, Lac du Flambeau, WI; St. Isaac Jogues and Companions, Mercer, WI
Kodjo, Rev. Msgr. Paul, '91 (BRK) St. Elizabeth, Ozone Park, NY
Koehl, Rev. Daniel, '21 (FTW) St. Charles Borromeo, Fort Wayne, IN
Koehl, Very Rev. Keith, '97 (AUS) Curia: Leadership St. Thomas More, Austin, TX; [EFT] Diocese of Austin Pension Plan and Trust, Austin, TX
Koehler, Rev. Jon C., '74 (BR) Retired.
Koehler, Rev. Kenneth, '72 (DEN) Retired.
Koehler, Rev. Steven C., '82 (DET) St. Rene Goupil Parish Sterling Heights, Sterling Heights, MI
Koehn, Rev. Christopher Scott, '18 (R) Curia: Leadership St. Mary Magdalene, Apex, NC
Koehr, Rev. Sean T, '19 (ARL) St. Mary of the Immaculate Conception, Fredericksburg, VA
Koelle, Rev. John, *O.F.M. Cap.* (NY) St. Joseph, New Paltz, NY
Koen, Rev. Stephen A., '58 (BO) Retired.
Koenemann, Rev. Cassian, *O.S.B.* '13 (STL) St. Louis Priory School, Creve Coeur, MO; [MON] The Abbey of St. Mary and St. Louis, St. Louis, MO
Koenig, Rev. Paul, *OCD* '93 (SJ) [MON] Carmelite Monastery, Novitiate, San Jose, CA
Koenig, Rev. Paul J., *OFM Cap* '93 (MIL) Our Lady of the Holyland, Mount Calvary, WI; [MON] St. Lawrence Friary, Mount Calvary, WI
Koenig, Rev. Msgr. William E., '83 (RVC) Curia: Leadership; Offices and Directors St. Agnes Cathedral, Rockville Centre, NY
Koenigsfeld, Rev. Msgr. James F., '68 (PBL) Retired. Curia: Offices and Directors
Koenigsknecht, Rev. Gary K., '14 (LAN) St. Joseph Parish Howell, Howell, MI
Koenigsknecht, Rev. Todd W., '14 (LAN) Curia: Leadership Sacred Heart Parish Hudson, Hudson, MI; St. Mary on the Lake Parish Manitou Beach, Manitou Beach, MI
Koenigsknecht, Rev. William J., '68 (LAN) Retired.
Koeninger, Rev. Francis F., '79 (STL) Our Lady, Help of Christians Catholic Church, Ste. Genevieve, MO
Koesel, Rev. Douglas H., '78 (CLV) Blessed Trinity Parish, Cleveland, OH
Koester, Rev. Timothy J., '83 (BUF) Most Precious Blood, Angola, NY
Koeth, Rev. Stephen, *CSC* (FTW) [COL] University of Notre Dame Du Lac, Notre Dame, IN; [MON] Holy Cross Community, Corby Hall, University of Notre Dame, Notre Dame, IN
Koeth, Rev. Stephen M., *C.S.C.* '09 (NY) Holy Trinity, New York, NY
Koether, Very Rev. Jacob A., '15 (VIC) Curia: Leadership; Offices and Directors Our Lady of Sorrows, Victoria, TX
Koetter, Rev. David A., *OFM* '94 (SAV) Most Blessed Sacrament, Savannah, GA
Koeune, Rev. August, '84 (CHY) Curia: Clergy and Religious Services; Consultative Bodies Church of St. Ann, Saratoga, WY; St. Mary's Cathedral, Cheyenne, WY
Koeune, Rev. George, '95 (CHI) Our Lady of the Lakes, Ingleside, IL
Koffi, Rev. Augustin N'guessan Kouacou, *SJ* '22 (OAK) [MON] Jesuit Fathers and Brothers, Berkeley, CA
Koffi, Rev. Komi Sedomo (Antonio), '11 (WDC) [MON] Society of Missionaries of Africa, Washington, DC
Kofi-Amo, Rev. Peter Oscar, '16 (VIC) St. Patrick's, Bloomington, TX
Kofski, Rev. James W., *M.M.* '91 (NY) [MON] Maryknoll Fathers and Brothers (Catholic Foreign Mission Society of America, Inc.), Ossining, NY
Kogut, Rev. Daniel J., '11 (LAN) Curia: Leadership St. Mary Parish Pinckney, Pinckney, MI
Koh, Rev. Soonhyun Macario, *O.F.M.Conv.* '18 (LA) St. Francis Korean Center, Torrance, CA
Koharchik, Rev. Edward, '05 (AUS) St. Mary, Our Lady of the Lake Catholic Church - Lago Vista, Texas, Lago Vista, TX
Kohler, Rev. Girard J., *C.S.Sp.* '63 (PIT) Retired.
Kohler, Rev. Lawrence A., *M.S.* '61 (LKC) Retired. Our Lady of LaSalette, Sulphur, LA
Kohler, Rev. William E., '67 (MIL) Retired.
Kohlerman, Rev. Charles W., *C.S.C.* '63 (FTW) [MON] Congregation of Holy Cross, United States Province of Priests and Brothers, Notre Dame, IN
Kohli, Rev. Charles F., '61 (RVC) Retired.
Kohls, Rev. Msgr. Eugene C., '57 (STA) Retired.
Kohn, Rev. Jarred, '18 (CIN) Holy Angels, Sidney, OH; Sacred Heart of Jesus, Anna, OH; St. Michael, Fort Loramie, OH
Kohner, Rev. David W., '90 (STP) St. Bridget of Sweden, Lindstrom, MN
Kohrman, Rev. Glenn, '92 (FTW) Curia: Offices and Directors Holy Family, South Bend, IN; St. John the Baptist, South Bend, IN; [MIS] The Fort Wayne-South Bend Diocesan Division: World Apostolate of Fatima, The Blue Army, Fort Wayne, IN
Kohut, Rev. David, *O.F.M.* '79 (CIN) [MON] St. Clare Friary, Cincinnati, OH
Koka, Rev. Benjamin, *A.J.* (CLV) St. Colman, Cleveland, OH; St. Stephen, Cleveland, OH
Kokeram, Rev. Sudash Joseph, '99 (NEW) Chap, Fayetteville, NC Curia: (>MO) Offices and Directors
Kokorian, Rt. Rev. Patrick, *M.M.A.* '13 (SAM) [MON] Maronite Monks of Adoration - Most Holy Trinity Monastery, Petersham, MA
Kokorzycki, Rev. Marian, (TR) St. Dominic, Brick, NJ
Kokose, Rev. Pius Eusebius, *C.S.Sp.* '98 (CHI) Immaculate Conception and St. Michael, Chicago, IL
Kokoszka, Rev. Michael, '18 (LA) St. Vitus, San Fernando, CA
Kokoszka, Rev. Michael, '18 (SPR) On Duty Outside Diocese. Priestly Fraternity of St Peter
Kola, Rev. Prakash, *MSFS* '04 (DOD) Prince of Peace Catholic Church of Great Bend, Kansas, Great Bend, KS
Kolakowski, Very Rev. Robert B., '02 (MET) Curia: Consultative Bodies; Evangelization; Tribunal St. John the Evangelist, Lambertville, NJ
Kolanti, Rev. Raju, *MSFS* (SR) Pastor of St. John the Baptist Catholic Church of Napa, A Corporation Sole, Napa, CA
Kolawole, Rev. Jacob, (JOL) St. Michael, Wheaton, IL
Kolb, Rev. James M., *C.S.P.* '76 (NY) Retired. [MON] Paulist Fathers - Generalate, New York, NY
Kolberg, Rev. Lawrence Floyd, '68 (ORG) Retired.
Kolencherry, Rev. John, *O.F.M.Cap.* '97 (KCK) St. John the Evangelist Catholic Church, Lawrence, KS; [MON]

St. Conrad Friary, Lawrence, KS
Kolenkiewicz, Rev. Louis J., '93 (PH) On Sick Leave.
Kolenski, Rev. Robert D., '62 (LAN) Retired.
Kolesar, Rev. Msgr. John C., '64 (STU) Retired. Curia: Deaneries St. Adalbert, Dillonvale, OH; St. Casimir Church, Adena, OH
Kolf, Rev. Gerald, '95 (POD) Curia: Clergy and Religious Services
Kolibas, Rev. Kenneth R., '94 (MET) Our Lady of Peace, North Brunswick, NJ
Kolinski, Rev. Dennis, *S.J.C.* '04 (CHI) St. John Cantius, Chicago, IL; [MIS] Canons Regular of Saint John Cantius, Chicago, IL
Kolisnyk, Rev. Ihor, (PHU) St. John the Baptist, Newark, NJ
Kollannoor, Rev. Andrews, *MS* '85 (ATL) St. Ann Catholic Church, Marietta, Inc., Marietta, GA
Kollar, Rev. Rene M., *O.S.B.* '74 (GBG) [MON] Saint Vincent Archabbey, Latrobe, PA
Kollasch, Rev. Merle F., '64 (SC) Retired.
Kollath, Very Rev. Robert, '97 (GB) Curia: Advisory Boards, Commissions, Committees, and Councils St. Gabriel the Archangel, Neenah, WI
Koller, Rev. Michael, '04 (KCK) Holy Trinity, Lenexa, KS
Kollithanath, Rev. Philip, '84 (CHL) St. Joseph, Asheboro, NC
Kollman, Rev. Paul V., *C.S.C.* '91 (FTW) [COL] University of Notre Dame Du Lac, Notre Dame, IN; [MON] Holy Cross Community, Corby Hall, University of Notre Dame, Notre Dame, IN
Kolmaga, Rev. Jan, *O.S.P.P.E.* '82 (PH) [MON] The Order of Saint Paul, First Hermit - The Pauline Fathers, Doylestown, PA
Kolo, Rev. Vincent F., '95 (PIT) Our Lady of the Lakes (The Catholic Communities of St. Victor & Transfiguration Parishes), Bairdford, PA; Sts. Martha and Mary, Allison Park, PA
Kolodiejchuk, Rev. Brian, (SD) [MIS] The Mother Teresa of Calcutta Center, San Diego, CA
Kolodziej, Rev. John, *O.S.F.S.* '99 (WIL) [MIS] Brisson Fund, Wilmington, DE; [MIS] Oblate Development Fund, Wilmington, DE; [MIS] OSFS Real Estate Holding Corporation, Wilmington, DE; [MIS] OSFS Real Estate Trust, Wilmington, DE; [MIS] OSFS Service Corporation, Wilmington, DE; [MON] OSFS Wilmington-Philadelphia Province, Inc., Wilmington, DE; [MON] Wilmington-Philadelphia Province of the Oblates of St. Francis de Sales, Wilmington, DE
Kolodziej, Rev. Ryszard W., '96 (R) St. Egbert, Morehead City, NC
Kolodziejczyk, Rev. Sebastian J., '99 (LC) St. Matthew, Wausau, WI
Kolodziejski, Rev. Karl, *O.F.M.Conv.* '78 (ALT) Chap, Sacr Min, State Corr Inst, Laurel Highlands, Somerset St. Anne, Davidsville, PA
Kolp, Rev. Msgr. James, '50 (Y) Retired.
Kolson, Rev. Lawrence F., '74 (BAL) Retired.
Koltz, Rev. Dennis, *PIME* '90 (DET) [MON] PIME Missionaries, Detroit, MI
Komar, Rev. Adrian, (SLC) Christ the King LLC 203, Cedar City, UT
Komar, Rev. Adrian, '06 (SLC) Curia: Offices and Directors
Komatz, Rev. David M., *O. Praem.* '75 (GB) [MON] St. Norbert Abbey, De Pere, WI
Kombo, Rev. Honore M., '90 (LC) On Special Assignment. Chaplain: Mayo Clinic Health System, La Crosse
Kommathoti, Rev. Bala, '02 (TUC) Blessed Sacrament Roman Catholic Parish - Mammoth, Mammoth, AZ; Saint Bartholomew Roman Catholic Parish - San Manuel, San Manuel, AZ
Kommers, Rev. Thomas M., '80 (STP) Retired. Christ the King, Minneapolis, MN; [CEM] Calvary Cemetery, Red Wing, MN
Komo, Rev. George, '09 (DM) St. Elizabeth Seton, Carlisle, IA
Komoroski, Rev. Christopher, '20 (CIN) Annunciation of the Blessed Virgin Mary, Cincinnati, OH; St. Monica-St. George Parish Newman Center, Cincinnati, OH; [CAM] University of Cincinnati Newman Center, Cincinnati, OH
Komperda, Rev. Pawel, '06 (CHI) Incarnation and St. Terrence Parish, Crestwood, IL
Koncik, Rev. Adam M., *C.Ss.R.* '82 (NY) Parish of Most Holy Redeemer and Nativity, New York, NY
Koncik, Rev. Adam Michael, *C.Ss.R.* (CHR) Corpus Christi, Lexington, SC; [CCH] Office of Prison Ministry, Columbia, SC
Kondamudi, Rev. Hrudaya, (AMA) Sacred Heart Catholic Church, White Deer, TX; St. Theresa, Panhandle, TX
Kondik, Rev. Curtis L., '00 (CLV) Our Lady Help of Christians Parish, Litchfield, OH; St. Francis Xavier, Medina, OH
Kondziolka, Rev. Ronald L., '76 (CHI) On Special Assignment. St James Hosp, Olympia Fields St. Veronica, Flossmoor, IL
Konen, Rev. Lyle E., *C.Ss.R.* '61 (SEA) Retired. Sacred Heart of Jesus, Seattle, WA; [MON] The Redemptorist Society of Washington, Seattle, WA
Konerman, Rev. Gregory J., '93 (CIN) Retired.
Konicki, Rev. William C., '78 (WOR) Sacred Heart of Jesus, Hopedale, MA
Konieczka, Rev. Edward J., '63 (SAG) Retired.
Konieczny, Rev. Stanley J., '06 (BEL) Curia: Leadership St. John the Baptist, Smithton, IL; St. Michael, Waterloo, IL
Konikattil, Very Rev. Joseph M., (WH) Curia: Leadership; Offices and Directors St. Peter the Fisherman, Fairmont, WV
Konja, Rev. Pierre, (EST) St. Thomas Chaldean Catholic Parish, West Bloomfield, MI
Konja, Rev. Pierre, '11 (EST) Curia: Leadership; Offices and Directors
Konka, Rev. Rayappa, '89 (GI) St. Agnes, Scottsbluff, NE
Konkler, Rev. Paul Jerome, *O.C.S.O.* '68 (SAC) [SEM] Abbey of New Clairvaux, Trappist Seminary, Vina, CA
Kono, Rev. Mario, '91 (VEN) Sacred Heart Parish in Punta Gorda, Inc., Punta Gorda, FL
Konold, Rev. Lon, *O.M.I.* '77 (STP) [RTR] Christ the King Retreat Center, Buffalo, MN
Konopa, Very Rev. Brian D., '98 (LC) Curia: Offices and Directors Mary, Mother of the Church, La Crosse, WI; [EFT] Mary, Mother of the Church Parish Endowment Trust, La Crosse, WI
Konopacky, Rev. Joseph R., '82 (LC) On Leave.
Konopelski, Rev. Louis, *S.D.B.* '02 (NEW) Don Bosco Preparatory High School (Salesians of St. John Bosco), Ramsey, NJ; [MON] Don Bosco Prep Salesian Residence, Ramsey, NJ
Konopik, Rev. Michael J., '07 (SFR) Star of the Sea, San Francisco, CA
Konopka, Rev. Edward M., '60 (NOR) Retired.
Konopka, Rev. Thomas, '90 (ALB) Chap, Sacramental Min, Capital District Psychiatric Ctr
Konopka, Rev. Thomas E., '90 (ALB) On Special Assignment. Dir, Consultation Center, Albany Curia: Offices and Directors Immaculate Conception, Glenville, NY; Our Lady of Grace, Ballston Lake, NY; St. Joseph Church, Scotia, NY
Konowalek, Rev. Zenon, '89 (CC) Retired.
Konrade, Rev. Jarett, '05 (SAL) Curia: Consultative Bodies Sacred Heart Parish, Esbon, Inc., Esbon, KS; Saints Peter and Paul Parish, Cawker City, Inc., Cawker City, KS; St. John the Baptist Parish, Beloit, Inc., Beloit, KS; St. Theresa Parish, Mankato, Inc., Mankato, KS
Konyeaso, Rev. Emmanuel, (SPC) Ste. Marie Du Lac, Ironton, MO
Konz, Rev. Gregory N.P., *S.J.* (BGP) [MON] The Fairfield Jesuit Community-Fairfield University, Fairfield, CT
Konzman, Rev. Brian G., (BGP) [MON] The Fairfield Jesuit Community-Fairfield University, Fairfield, CT
Koo, Rev. Msgr. Matthew, '88 (SJ) Retired.
Koo, Rev. Sukhun, (MIA) Curia: Pastoral Services St. Paul Chung Ha Sang Korean Mission, West Park, FL
Kookoothe, Rev. Neil P., '95 (CLV) St. Clarence, North Olmsted, OH
Koomson, Rev. Augustine, '99 (SFD) Christ the King, Greenup, IL; St. Charles Borromeo, Casey, IL; St. Mary, Marshall, IL
Koons, Rev. Msgr. Thomas P., '97 (ALN) Curia: Leadership Assumption of the Blessed Virgin Mary, Northampton, PA
Koop, Rev. Evan Steven, '12 (STP) The Church of Saint Stephen-Holy Rosary, Minneapolis, MN; [SEM] The Saint Paul Seminary, St. Paul, MN
Koopman, Rev. Dennis, *OFM* '70 (SFD) [MON] St. Francis Assisi Friary, Teutopolis, IL
Koopman, Rev. Dennis, *OFM* '70 (SFD) St. Francis of Assisi, Teutopolis, IL
Koopman, Rev. Dennis, *O.F.M.* '70 (CHI) [MON] St. Gratian Friary, Franciscan Friars, Countryside, IL
Koopman, Rev. Joseph M., '01 (CLV) [SEM] Saint Mary Seminary and Graduate School of Theology, Wickliffe, OH
Koopmann, Rev. Robert, *O.S.B.* '81 (SCL) [MON] St. John's Abbey, of the Order of St. Benedict, Collegeville, MN
Kooran, Rev. George, (DET) [MIS] Solanus Casey Center, Detroit, MI; [MON] St. Bonaventure Monastery, Detroit, MI
Kooro, Rev. Fredrick Mwangi, '02 (SY) [MIS] Catholic Diocese of Nakuru Mission Office, Inc., Canastota, NY
Koos, Rev. Msgr. Gerald J., '66 (E) Retired.
Koottappillil, Rev. George, *S.V.D.* '81 (DUB) [SEM] Divine Word College, Epworth, IA
Kopacek, Very Rev. Jerry F., '88 (DUB) On Special Assignment. Dean of the New Hampton Deanery Immaculate Conception Church, Riceville, Iowa, Riceville, IA; Our Lady of Lourdes Church, Lourdes, Iowa, Elma, IA; Saint Bernard's Church, Alta Vista, Iowa, Alta Vista, IA; St. Peter's Church, New Haven, Iowa, Osage, IA; The Immaculate Conception Church, Elma, Iowa, Elma, IA
Kopacz, Rev. K. S., '95 (FAR) St. Stephen's Church of Larimore, Larimore, ND
Kopacz, Rev. Msgr. Matthew S., '63 (BUF) Retired.
Kopacz, Rev. Stephen A., '72 (NEW) Retired. St. Catherine of Siena, Cedar Grove, NJ
Kopaczynski, Rev. Germain, *O.F.M.Conv.* '74 (PMB) St. Mark, Boynton Beach, FL
Kopala, Rev. Lukasz, '15 (BUF) Sacred Heart of Jesus Roman Catholic Church Society of Bowmansville NY, Bowmansville, NY
Kopczynski, Rev. Sean P., *M.S.J.B.* '00 (COV) Our Lady of Lourdes Parish, Park Hills, KY
Kopec, Rev. Christopher A., '93 (WIL) Military Chap
Kopec, Rev. Edward, (MO) Curia: Offices and Directors
Kopec, Rev. Edward S., '92 (PEO) On Duty Outside Diocese. Zablocki VA Med Ctr, Milwaukee, WI
Kopec, Rev. Jerome E., '79 (BUF) Curia: Consultative Bodies; Leadership Infant of Prague, Cheektowaga, NY
Kopec, Rev. Rajmund, '92 (NEW) Chap, Major, Clarksville, TN Curia: (>MO) Offices and Directors
Kopel, Rev. Jerome, '77 (SFS) Retired.
Koper, Rev. Msgr. Francis B., '71 (SAG) Our Lady of Hope Parish of Clare, Clare, MI
Koper, Rev. Msgr. Francis B., '71 (WIL) Retired.
Koper, Rev. Ryszard, '85 (BRK) Nativity of the Blessed Virgin Mary-Saint Stanislaus Bishop and Martyr Roman Catholic Church, Ozone Park, NY
Koperski, Rev. Matthew J., '04 (GI) Curia: Leadership; Offices and Directors Holy Rosary, Alliance, NE
Kopfensteiner, Rev. Thomas R., '81 (STL) On Duty Outside Diocese. Englewood, CO
Kopil, Rev. Michael J., '08 (GRY) St. Elizabeth Seton, Valparaiso, IN
Kopinski, Rev. Msgr. Richard P., '64 (RVC) Retired.
Koplinka, Rev. Steven, '79 (PRM) Saint Nicholas, Munster, IN
Kopp, Rev. Msgr. Richard M., '69 (SY) Retired. Curia: Offices and Directors
Kopp, Rev. Scott, (Y) Christ the Servant Parish, Canton, OH
Koppes, Rev. Albert P., *O.Carm.* '59 (JOL) Retired.
Koppes, Rev. Albert P., *O.Carm.* '59 (LA) Retired. [COL] Loyola Marymount University, Los Angeles, CA
Kopson, Rev. John D., '14 (DET) St. Anne Parish Warren, Warren, MI
Korba, Rev. Msgr. Frank, '66 (PRM) Retired.
Korban, Rev. Janusz, '97 (RC) St. Joseph, Faith, SD
Korbelak, Rev. John J., '74 (NEW) Retired.
Korchinski, Rev. Leonard, '60 (STN) Retired.
Korcsmar, Rev. John S., *C.S.C.* '74 (FTW) [MON] Congregation of Holy Cross, United States Province of Priests and Brothers, Notre Dame, IN
Korcz, Rev. Krzysztof, '94 (WOR) St. Andrew Bobola, Dudley, MA
Kordek, Rev. Frank, *OFM* '72 (GB) [MON] Blessed Giles Friary, Manitowoc, WI
Korenek, Very Rev. Gregory E., '93 (VIC) Curia: Leadership; Offices and Directors Assumption of the B.V.M., Ganado, TX
Koressel, Rev. James E., '69 (EVN) Retired. Curia: Leadership
Korf, Rev. Joseph, '74 (SCL) Retired. Curia: Leadership
Korir, Rev. Anthony, *SMA* '06 (NEW) [MON] Society of African Missions, Provincialate, S.M.A. Fathers, Tenafly, NJ (>PRT) Parish of the Precious Blood, Caribou, ME
Kornath, Very Rev. Edwin M., '84 (MIL) St. John Vianney Congregation, Brookfield, WI
Kornmeyer, Rev. Thomas E., '90 (OG) St. Anthony of Padua Parish of Inlet and Raquette Lake, Inlet, NY; St. Bartholomew's Church of Old Forge, Old Forge, NY
Kornu, Rev. Godwin Kwame, *MCCJ* '99 (CHI) [MON] Comboni Missionaries, La Grange Park, IL
Kornyckyi, Rev. Vasyl, (STF) On Duty Outside Diocese. Ireland
Koro, Rev. Nicholas Erias, *A.J.* '07 (PHX) St. Andrew the Apostle Roman Catholic Parish, Chandler, AZ
Koroba, Rev. Bura Aloysius, *S.S.J.* '13 (MOB) Most Pure Heart of Mary Parish, Mobile, Mobile, AL; St. Joseph Parish, Maysville, Mobile, AL
Korogi, Rev. Dale J., '83 (STP) Ascension, Minneapolis,

MN
Korostil, Rev. Iaroslav, '12 (PSC) Nativity of Our Lord, East Brunswick, NJ
Korte, Rev. Owen W., '81 (OM) Curia: Leadership; Offices and Directors Cedar Catholic High School, Hartington, NE; Holy Trinity, Hartington, NE; St. Michael, Coleridge, NE
Korte, Rev. William, '83 (JC) St. Cornelius, Crocker, MO; St. Theresa, Dixon, MO
Kortendick, Rev. Steve, (MO) Curia: Offices and Directors
Kortendick, Rev. Steven J., '85 (MAD) Chap, Univ of Wisconsin Hosps and Clinics, Madison St. Thomas Aquinas, Madison, WI
Korth, Rev. David M., (OM) Curia: Leadership
Korth, Rev. David M., '92 (OM) Curia: Leadership; Offices and Directors CUES School System, Omaha, NE; Sacred Heart, Omaha, NE
Kos, Rev. Sebastian K., '10 (HRT) St. Stanislaus' Church of New Haven Connecticut, New Haven, CT
Kos, Rev. Stanislaw, '96 (RCK) Retired.
Kosak, Rev. Michael, '70 (STV) Retired.
Kosak, Rev. Msgr. Michael F., '70 (STV) Retired.
Kosaka, Rev. Paulo R., *O.F.M.Cap.* '84 (HON) Our Lady of Mt. Carmel, Kaneohe, HI
Kosanke, Rev. Msgr. Charles G., '85 (DET) Curia: Administration Ste. Anne Basilica Parish de Detroit, Detroit, MI; [EFT] Ste. Anne Restoration Fund, Detroit, MI; [MIS] Cabrini Clinic, Detroit, MI; [MIS] Gabriel Richard Historical Society, Detroit, MI
Kosanke, Rev. Msgr. Charles G., '85 (DET) Curia: Consultative Bodies Most Holy Trinity Parish Detroit, Detroit, MI
Kosch, Rev. Leo, '93 (LIN) Curia: Leadership
Kosch, Rev. Leo D., '93 (LIN) Curia: Offices and Directors St. Joseph's, Beatrice, NE
Kosco, Rev. William "Billy" J., '00 (PHX) Saint Henry Roman Catholic Parish, Buckeye, AZ
Kose, Rev. Robert E., *OFM, Cap* '92 (LA) Old Mission Santa Ines, Solvang, CA
Kosem, Rev. Frank P., '70 (CLV) Retired. St. Jude, Elyria, OH
Koshko, Rev. Dennis, '75 (HON) Retired.
Koshyk, Rev. Ihor, '05 (STN) Nativity of B.V.M., Los Angeles, CA
Kosikumah, Rev. Emmanuel, '91 (DOD) Holy Rosary Catholic Church of Medicine Lodge, Kansas, Medicine Lodge, KS; St. Boniface Catholic Church of Sharon, Kansas, Sharon, KS; St. John the Apostle Catholic Church of Kiowa, Kansas, Kiowa, KS
Kosinski, Rev. Stephen D., '81 (GRY) Retired.
Kosisko, Rev. Richard J., '85 (GBG) Curia: Leadership Holy Family, Latrobe, PA; St. John the Evangelist, Latrobe, PA
Kosk, Rev. Piotr, '20 (SFD) Taylorville Correctional Center Holy Trinity, Stonington, IL; St. Mary, Taylorville, IL; St. Rita, Kincaid, IL
Kosler, Rev. Msgr. Timothy, '71 (VIC) Retired. Curia: Leadership
Kosmicki, Rev. Raymond M., '68 (GI) Retired.
Kosmoski, Rev. David B., '83 (MET) St. Andrew, Avenel, NJ
Kosmowski, Rev. Gary J., '90 (MAN) Our Lady of the Miraculous Medal, Hampton, NH; St. Theresa, Rye Beach, NH
Kosowicz, Rev. Wojciech, (LAR) Retired. Nuestra Senora del Rosario, Laredo, TX
Kosse, Rev. Msgr. Gerald C., '76 (WIN) Curia: Advisory Boards, Commissions, Committees, and Councils; Deaneries; Organizations (affiliated, inter-Diocesan, miscellaneous/other) St. Catherine's, Luverne, MN; St. Leo, Pipestone, MN
Kostelc, Rev. Daniel, '21 (CHY) St. Anthony's, Guernsey, WY; St. Leo's, Lusk, WY; St. Rose, Torrington, WY
Kostelnik, Rev. Msgr. Kevin J., '82 (LA) St. Joseph, Long Beach, CA
Koster, Rev. Kenneth J., '76 (SFS) Curia: Leadership
Koster, Rev. Ryan, '15 (KC) St. Columban, Chillicothe, MO
Kostiha, Rev. Darrell, (AUS) Church of the Visitation, Lott, TX
Kostiuk, Rev. Stepan, '06 (STN) SS. Volodymyr and Olha, Chicago, IL
Kostka, Rev. Leonard, *C.PP.S.* '40 (CIN) Retired.
Kostka, Rev. Paul, '13 (DEN) Chap, LT, CHC, USNR, US Naval Acad, Annapolis, MD
Kostka, Rev. Paul, (MO) Curia: Offices and Directors
Kostyk, Rev. Marian, '90 (STF) St. Nicholas, Amsterdam, NY
Kostyk, Rev. Nicholas, (STN) St. Michael Ukrainian Greco-Catholic Church, Tucson, AZ
Kostyk, Very Rev. Yaroslav, (STF) St. Volodymyr, Campbell Hall, NY
Kostyk, Very Rev. Yaroslav, '90 (STF) St. Andrew's, Campbell Hall, NY
Kostyk, Rev. Yaroslaw, '90 (STF) Curia: Offices and Directors
Kostyuk, Rev. Volodymyr, '98 (PHU) On Special Assignment. St. Nicholas, Great Meadows, NJ; St. Paul, Ramsey, NJ
Koszalka, Rev. Tomasz, (NEW) St. Theresa of the Child Jesus, Linden, NJ
Koszarek, Rev. Msgr. Paul P., '54 (GB) Retired.
Koszarek, Rev. Robert J., '74 (SUP) Retired.
Koszyk, Rev. Dariusz, '04 (RVC) Our Lady of the Assumption, Copiague, NY
Koszyk, Rev. Severyn J., *S.A.C.* '59 (BUF) Retired. [MON] Society of the Catholic Apostolate, North Tonawanda, NY; [SHR] Shrine of the Infant Jesus, North Tonawanda, NY
Kotara, Rev. James M., '76 (SAT) Curia: Administration St. Peter the Fisherman, Von Ormy, TX
Kotara, Rev. James M., (SAT) St. Mary's, Somerset, TX
Kotch, Rev. James, '16 (MAD) Divine Mercy Parish, Sauk City, WI; St. Norbert, Sauk City, WI
Kotecki, Rev. Ronald E., '72 (MIL) Retired.
Koterski, Rev. Joseph W., *S.J.* '92 (NY) [MON] Cardinal Spellman Hall, Jesuit Community, Bronx, NY
Kote-Witah, Rev. Anthony, (DET) [MON] St. Bonaventure Monastery, Detroit, MI
Kothalamuthu, Rev. Michael Raj, *H.G.N.* '15 (SAL) St. Joseph Parish, Hays, Inc., Hays, KS
Kotlarczyk, Rev. Mark E., '88 (SB) St. Mary of the Valley, Yucca Valley, CA
Kotlarz, Rev. Robert J., '68 (DET) Retired.
Kotlinski, Rev. Bede, *O.S.B.* '85 (CLV) Benedictine High School, Cleveland, OH; [MON] Benedictine Order of Cleveland (St. Andrew Abbey), Cleveland, OH
Kotlinski, Rev. Eugeniusz, *C.M.* '88 (BRK) SS. Cyril and Methodius, Brooklyn, NY
Kotrba, Rev. Patrick S., '13 (WCH) Curia: Leadership St. Cecilia, Haysville, KS
Kottana, Rev. Kishore, '09 (TOL) St. Mary of the Snows, Mansfield, OH; St. Rose, Perrysburg, OH
Kottas, Rev. Charles, '70 (DM) St. Peter, Council Bluffs, IA; [CEM] St. Joseph Catholic Cemetery Association, Council Bluffs, IA; [EFT] St. Albert Educational Foundation, Council Bluffs, IA
Kottayil, Rev. Joseph, '79 (MIA) Saint David, Davie, FL
Kouam, Rev. Gervais Kamwa, (BRK) [MON] Reverend John B. Murray, C.M. House, Jamaica, NY
Koury, Very Rev. James, '92 (NTN) Curia: Administration; Consultative Bodies; Pastoral Services
Koury, Rev. Joseph, (LEX) Retired.
Koury, Rev. Joseph J., '77 (ALB) Curia: Leadership
Koutnik, Rev. Jerome P., '99 (RCK) St. Mary, Huntley, IL
Kouts, Rev. Michael, '91 (SJP) Curia: Offices and Directors St. Andrew, Brooksville, FL
Kovacevich, Rev. Steve, (OG) Retired.
Kovach, Very Rev. Andriy, '11 (PSC) Curia: Leadership Holy Ghost, Philadelphia, PA
Kovacik, Rev. Jozef, '98 (ALT) Church of the Good Shepherd, Port Matilda, PA
Kovacik, Rev. Mark S., '07 (DEN) Sacred Heart of Jesus Catholic Parish in Boulder, Boulder, CO
Kovacina, Rev. Peter T., '12 (CLV) St. Francis of Assisi, Gates Mills, OH
Koval, Rev. Yaroslav, '10 (SJP) Nativity of the Mother of God, New Alexandria, PA; St. John the Baptist, Pittsburgh, PA; St. Vladimir, Arnold, PA
Koval, Rev. Yaroslav, '10 (SJP) Curia: Offices and Directors
Kovalchuk, Rev. Serhiy, (STN) St. Nicholas Ukrainian Catholic Cathedral, Chicago, IL
Kovalchuk, Very Rev. Serhiy, (STN) Curia: Leadership; Offices and Directors
Kovalcin, Rev. John, (STL) Retired.
Kovalenko, Rev. Andrey, '06 (PRM) On Leave.
Kovalyshin, Rev. Severyn, '00 (SJP) On Academic Leave. Curia: (>MO) Offices and Directors; Offices and Directors
Kovanis, Rev. Joel, '94 (SP) Corpus Christi, Temple Terrace, FL
Kovar, Rev. Matthew, '21 (LIN) Curia: Leadership Blessed Sacrament, Lincoln, NE
Kovash, Rev. Russell P., '09 (BIS) Curia: Offices and Directors St. Boniface, Grenora, ND; St. John the Baptist, Trenton, ND; St. Joseph, Williston, ND
Kovatch, Rev. Thomas G., '07 (IND) St. Charles Borromeo Catholic Church, Bloomington, Inc., Bloomington, IN
Kowalczyk, Rev. Adolph M., '88 (BUF) Curia: Consultative Bodies Our Lady of the Sacred Heart, Orchard Park, NY
Kowalczyk, Rev. Andrzej, *C.S.M.A.* '93 (DET) Curia: Consultative Bodies St. Clare of Montefalco Parish Grosse Pointe Park, Grosse Pointe Park, MI; [MON] Congregation of St. Michael the Archangel - Michaelite Fathers, Grosse Pointe Park, MI
Kowalczyk, Rev. Joseph W., *M.M.* '61 (NY) Retired.
Kowalczyk, Rev. Kyle Patrick, '16 (STP) The Church of Saint Maximilian Kolbe, Delano, MN; [CEM] Calvary Cemetery, Delano, MN; [CEM] St. Joseph Cemetery, Delano, MN; [CEM] St. Peter Cemetery, Delano, MN
Kowalczyk, Rev. Miroslaw, *F.D.P.* '88 (BO) St. Joseph-St. Lazarus, Boston, MA; [NUR] Don Orione Nursing Home, East Boston, MA
Kowalczyk, Rev. Thomas M., '67 (SAG) Retired. Saint Mark Parish of Au Gres, Au Gres, MI
Kowalik, Rev. Jacek, '79 (VEN) Retired.
Kowalske, Rev. Kevin J., '95 (MIL) On Leave. [EFT] St. Michael's Priest Fund Trust, St. Francis, WI
Kowalski, Rev. Eric, '93 (CHL) St. Francis of Assisi, Mocksville, NC
Kowalski, Rev. George, '56 (DET) Retired.
Kowalski, Rev. Janusz A., '98 (LC) St. Lawrence, Wisconsin Rapids, WI; St. Philip, Rudolph, WI; [EFT] St. Lawrence Parish, Wisconsin Rapids Endowment Trust, Wisconsin Rapids, WI
Kowalski, Rev. Matthew, *O.S.B.* '87 (CHI) St. Raphael the Archangel, Old Mill Creek, IL
Kowalsky, Rev. Myron, *OFM Cap.* (MIL) St. Francis of Assisi, Milwaukee, WI
Kowatch, Rev. Thomas, '85 (CLV) SS. Robert & William, Euclid, OH
Koyickal, Rev. Joseph, (SFD) SS. Mary & Joseph, Carlinville, IL; SS. Simon and Jude, Gillespie, IL; St. Joseph, Benld, IL
Koyickal, Rev. Joseph, *S.A.C.* '80 (MIL) [EFT] Pallottine Fathers and Brothers, Inc., Disability Trust, Milwaukee, WI; [EFT] Pallottine Fathers and Brothers, Inc., Educational and Apostolic Ministry Trust, Milwaukee, WI; [MON] Pallotti House, Milwaukee, WI (>SFD) [CAM] Blackburn College Newman Club, Carlinville, IL
Koys, Rev. Thomas R., '85 (CHI) SS. Cyril and Methodius, Lemont, IL
Kozacheson, Rev. Roman, *O.F.M.Cap* (ALT) St. John the Baptist, New Baltimore, PA
Kozak, Rev. David J., '83 (ALN) Curia: Leadership Holy Ghost, Bethlehem, PA; St. Ursula, Fountain Hill, PA
Kozak, Rev. Richard J., '67 (CHI) Retired.
Kozak, Rev. Timothy J., '04 (STU) Curia: Deaneries St. Bernard, Beverly, OH; St. James, McConnelsville, OH
Kozar, Rev. Msgr. John E., '71 (PIT) Retired.
Kozar, Rev. Joseph F., *S.M.* '77 (CIN) [COL] The University of Dayton, Dayton, OH; [MON] Marianist Community, Dayton, OH
Kozar, Rev. Petro, '89 (STN) Assumption of B.V.M., Omaha, NE; St. George's, Lincoln, NE; St. Joseph's, St. Joseph, MO
Kozel, Rev. Msgr. Robert F., '61 (ALN) Retired.
Kozen, Rev. Bert S., '63 (SCR) Curia: Leadership
Kozen, Rev. Bert S., '82 (SCR) Immaculate Conception of the Blessed Virgin Mary, Jersey Shore, PA; Saint John Neumann Regional Academy High School Campus, Williamsport, PA; St. Luke, Williamsport, PA
Kozhaya Akoury, Rev. Tanios, '82 Curia: (>SAM) Leadership
Koziczuk, Rev. Andrzej A., '79 (SAC) Retired.
Koziel, Rev. Piotr A., '97 (CC) Our Lady of Mount Carmel, Portland, TX
Koziol, Rev. John, *O.F.M.Conv.* '88 (ATL) (>SPR) St. Stanislaus Basilica, Chicopee, MA
Koziol, Rev. Ryszard, (CC) St. Theresa, Corpus Christi, TX
Koziola, Rev. Marcin, '05 (VEN) On Leave.
Koziolkiewicz, Rev. Piotr, '07 (NEW) St. Mary, Rutherford, NJ
Koziolkiewicz, Rev. Piotr, (MO) Curia: Offices and Directors
Kozlowski, Rev. John Chrysostom, *O.P.* '10 (WDC) (>NY) [MON] St. Vincent Ferrer Priory, New York, NY
Kozlowski, Rev. Lukasz, (MO) Curia: Offices and Directors
Kozlowski, Rev. Theodore, '58 (GR) Our Lady of Sorrows, Grand Rapids, MI
Kozminski, Rev. Andrzej, *SAC* '88 (COL) Sacred Heart, Columbus, OH; St. John the Baptist, Columbus, OH
Kozub, Rev. Tomasz, '93 (CC) St. Anthony, Violet, TX
Kozyra, Rev. Oscar, *O.de.M.* '73 (SP) [MON] St. Peter Nolasco Residence, St. Petersburg, FL
Kracke, Rev. Cole T., '11 (STP) On Leave. [CEM] St. John the Baptist Cemetery, Hampton, MN; [CEM] St. Mary Cemetery, Hampton, MN; [CEM] St. Mathias

Cemetery, Hampton, MN
Kraeger, Rev. David, *T.O.R.* '68 (ALT) [MON] St. Francis Friary at Mount Assisi, Loretto, PA
Kraemer, Rev. Edwin, '55 (SCL) Retired.
Kraemer, Rev. Matthew M, '12 (FAR) Sts. Peter & Paul Church of Karlsruhe, Karlsruhe, ND
Kraemer, Rev. Matthew M., '12 (FAR) St. Cecilia's Church of Velva, Velva, ND
Krafft, Rev. Joseph M., '02 (NO) Curia: Miscellaneous / Other Offices [SEM] Notre Dame Seminary Graduate School of Theology, New Orleans, LA
Kraft, Rev. Bill L., '86 (STO) Holy Cross Church (Pastor of), Linden, CA
Kraft, Rev. Philip G., '62 (SFD) Retired.
Krahenbuhl, Rev. Gary L., '84 (MAD) St. Mary Help of Christians, Briggsville, WI; St. Mary of the Immaculate Conception, Portage, WI
Krahman, Rev. Philip G., '72 (STL) On Special Assignment. Archbishop's Liaison Sr Priests of the Archdiocese, St Louis Curia: Leadership
Kraig, Rev. Robert J., '72 (CLV) Retired.
Krajewski, Rev. Joseph A., '73 (MET) Retired.
Krajnak, Rev. Jozef, '91 (NEW) Chap, Robert Wood Johnson Univ Hosp, Rahway Divine Mercy Parish, Rahway, NJ; Holy Family, Linden, NJ
Kraker, Rev. Joseph H., '64 (CLV) Retired.
Krakowski, Rev. Damian, '12 (MEM) On Leave.
Kraljic, Rev. John R., '69 (NY) Retired. Cardinal Spellman High School, Bronx, NY
Krall, Rev. Christopher J, *S.J.* (OM) [MON] Jesuit Community at Creighton University, Omaha, NE
Krall, Rev. Kenneth R., *S.J.* '71 (SPK) [COL] Gonzaga University, Spokane, WA
Kramberg, Rev. Donald F., '74 (OG) Retired. On Duty Outside Diocese.
Kramer, Rev. Alex, '22 (DM) On Special Assignment.
Kramer, Rev. Daniel J., *C.M.* '47 (PH) [MON] Congregation of the Mission, Philadelphia, PA
Kramer, Rev. Gary J., '93 (PH) St. John Bosco, Hatboro, PA
Kramer, Rev. George, '62 (JC) Retired.
Kramer, Rev. James F., '68 (CLV) Retired.
Kramer, Rev. Mark, *S.J.* '05 (LAF) St. Charles Borromeo, Grand Coteau, LA; [MON] St. Charles College, Grand Coteau, LA
Kramer, Rev. Mark, *S.J.* '05 (STL) [SEM] Kenrick School of Theology, ,
Kramer, Rev. Richard D., '12 (POC) Retired. Curia: Leadership
Kramer, Rev. Richard R., '66 (RCK) Retired.
Kramer, Rev. Scott, *C.PP.S.* '90 (TOL) Curia: Advisory Boards, Commissions, Committees, and Councils [MON] Mary Lay Center, Bellevue, OH; [RTR] Sorrowful Mother Shrine, Bellevue, OH
Kramer, Rev. Stephen Alphonsus, *S.J.* '19 (NO) Immaculate Conception, New Orleans, LA; [MON] Loyola Jesuit Community, New Orleans, LA
Kramer, Rev. Thomas J., '77 (DET) Resurrection Parish Canton, Canton, MI
Kramis, Rev. Joseph, '57 (SEA) Retired.
Kramper, Rev. James V., '73 (OM) Retired.
Kranc, Rev. Maciej, '15 (PAT) Curia: Leadership St. Rose of Lima, East Hanover, NJ
Krantz, Rev. Robert V., '78 (SFS) Saint Martin Parish of Hanson County, Emery, SD; Saint Mary of Mercy Parish of Hanson County, Alexandria, SD; Saint Stephen Parish of McCook County, Bridgewater, SD
Krapfl, Rev. Gary F., '72 (DUB) Retired.
Krasevac, Rev. Edward, *O.P.* '77 (OAK) [SEM] Dominican School of Philosophy and Theology, Berkeley, CA
Krasic, Rev. Ljubo, *O.F.M.* (CHI) [MON] St. Anthony's Friary, ,
Kraszewski, Rev. Thomas P., '97 (Y) St. Anthony/All Saints Parish, Canton, OH; St. Mary/St. Benedict Parish, Canton, OH
Kratz, Rev. Alex, *OFM* '99 (DET) [MIS] Terra Sancta Pilgrimages, Pontiac, MI
Kraus, Rev. Leonard E., *S.J.* '72 (BR) [RTR] Manresa House of Retreats, Convent, LA
Kraus, Rev. Leonard E., *S.J.* '72 (STL) [RTR] Retreat House, ,
Kraus, Rev. Stephen, '75 (ROC) Retired.
Kraus, Rev. William, *O.F.M. Cap.* (DEN) [MON] Capuchin Province of Mid-America, Inc. (Capuchin Province of St. Conrad), Denver, CO
Kraus, Rev. William, *O.F.M. Cap.* (COS) [MIS] Catholic Center at the Citadel, Colorado Springs, CO; [MON] Our Lady of the Angels Friary, Colorado Springs, CO
Krause, Rev. Edward, *C.S.C.* '40 (STL) [MIS] Central Bureau of the C.C.V.A., St. Louis, MO
Krause, Rev. Edward C., *C.S.C.* '66 (FTW) [MIS] Holy Cross House, Notre Dame, IN
Krauth, Rev. Lothar, '73 (GF) Retired.
Krautsack, Rev. Blaise R., *O.Praem.* '74 (PH) [MON] Daylesford Abbey, Inc., Paoli, PA
Krautter, Rev. Francis Therese, *CSJ* (DEN) All Souls Catholic Parish in Englewood, Englewood, CO
Kravatz, Rev. Daniel E., '14 (ALN) Curia: Leadership Notre Dame High School, Inc., Easton, PA; Our Lady of Mt. Carmel, Bangor, PA; [CAM] Lafayette College (Easton), Hellertown, PA
Kravchuk, Rev. Mykhaylo, '07 (PSC) Saints Peter and Paul Byzantine Catholic Church, Somerset, NJ; St. Joseph, New Brunswick, NJ
Krawczenko, Rev. Arthur, '03 (SY) Church of Sacred Heart and St. Mary, New York Mills, NY
Krawczenko, Rev. Arthur, '07 (SY) [HOS] St. Elizabeth Medical Center, Utica, NY
Krawczyk, Rev. Brad A., '12 (MIL) On Special Assignment. Saint Francis de Sales Seminary, St Francis [MIS] St. Thomas More Lawyers Society of Wisconsin, Milwaukee, WI; [SEM] Saint Francis de Sales Seminary, St. Francis, WI
Kraynak, Rev. Nicholas, '59 (PSC) Retired.
Kraynak, Rev. William B., '81 (Y) Curia: Leadership Immaculate Conception, Ravenna, OH
Krebs, Rev. Bruce D., '78 (BIS) Retired.
Krebs, Rev. Doug S., '16 (BIS) On Duty Outside Diocese. Rome; Schuster, Frank, Rome Curia: Leadership
Krebs, Rev. Msgr. Henry L., '60 (E) Retired. St. Francis, Clearfield, PA
Kreckel, Rev. Robert G., '54 (ROC) Retired. St. Joseph, Penfield, NY
Kredel, Rev. Thomas E., '72 (PIT) Retired.
Kreder, Rev. Mark, '03 (TR) St. Justin, Toms River, NJ
Kreder, Rev. Michael J., '85 (NEW) St. Mary, Rutherford, NJ
Kreidler, Rev. Alex, '15 (KC) On Special Assignment. St Michael the Archangel HS Curia: Offices and Directors St. Gabriel Archangel, Kansas City, MO
Kreidler, Rev. Rodney A., '05 (CLV) Chap, Samaritan Hosp, Ashland St. Edward, Ashland, OH
Kreidler, Rev. Thomas W., '77 (CIN) Retired.
Kreilein, Rev. Ronald, '07 (EVN) St. Bernard, Rockport, IN; St. Martin, Chrisney, IN
Kreilein, Rev. Ronald L., '07 (EVN) Curia: Leadership
Kreimer, Rev. Richard, '79 (CIN) Retired.
Kreis, Rev. Marek, *OSPPE* (BUF) Corpus Christi, Buffalo, NY; St. Stanislaus, Buffalo, NY
Kreis, Rev. Mark, *OSPPE* (GBG) [MON] Pauline Fathers Monastery, Kittanning, PA
Kreis, Rev. Mark, *O.S.P.P.E.* '87 (NY) St. Casimir, Yonkers, NY
Kreiser, Rev. Thomas L., '94 (NY) On Leave.
Kreitinger, Rev. Todd, '00 (BIS) Curia: Leadership St. Leo, Minot, ND; St. Mary, Foxholm, ND; St. Philomena, Glenburn, ND
Krekelberg, Rev. Msgr. Richard G., '73 (LA) Retired.
Krekelberg, Rev. William F., '70 (ORG) Retired. Curia: Offices and Directors
Kremen, Rev. Timothy, *OSM* (CHI) Assumption of the Blessed Virgin Mary, Chicago, IL; [MIS] Monastery of Our Lady of Sorrows, ,
Kreml, Rev. Curt, *O.F.M.Conv.* '76 (PMB) St. Lucie, Port St. Lucie, FL
Kremmell, Rev. William T., '66 (BO) Retired. Curia: Organizations (affiliated, inter-Diocesan, miscellaneous/ other)
Krempa, Rev. Stanley J., '70 (ARL) Retired.
Krempel, Rev. Matthew, '74 (PHX) St. Margaret Roman Catholic Parish, Tempe, AZ
Krengiel, Rev. Corey, '14 (PEO) St. Mary of the Woods, Princeville, IL
Krenik, Rev. Michael J., '84 (STP) Our Lady of Mount Carmel, Minneapolis, MN; St. Frances Cabrini, Minneapolis, MN
Krenik, Rev. Thomas, '77 (STP) Retired.
Krenzke, Rev. John W., '57 (COS) Retired.
Kresak, Rev. Stephen, (PIT) Blessed Trinity, Pittsburgh, PA
Kresinski, Rev. Daniel J., '70 (E) Retired.
Kress, Rev. Dennis, '99 (KNX) St. Anthony of Padua Catholic Church, Mountain City, TN; St. Elizabeth, Elizabethton, TN
Kress, Rev. Joseph-Anthony, (RIC) Chap, Univ of Virginia St. Thomas Aquinas, Charlottesville, VA; [CAM] Catholic Campus Ministry, University of Virginia, Charlottesville, VA
Kretowicz, Rev. Antoni, '87 (RCK) St. Mary, Aurora, IL
Krettek, Rev. Daniel F., '78 (DM) Retired. Curia: Offices and Directors
Krettek, Rev. Thomas, *S.J.* (CHI) [COL] Jesuit Community at Loyola University Chicago, Chicago, IL
Krettek, Rev. Tom, (CHI) [RTR] Bellarmine Jesuit Retreat House, Inc., Barrington, IL
Kretz, Rev. James C., '91 (PEO) Retired.
Kreul, Rev. Ronald, *OP* '78 (STP) St. Joseph the Worker, Maple Grove, MN
Kreutzer, Rev. Dan, '97 (OWN) Retired.
Kricek, Rev. Henry C., '80 (CHI) SS. Peter and Lambert Parish, Skokie, IL
Krieg, Rev. Charles F., *C.M.* '63 (PH) [MON] Congregation of the Mission, Philadelphia, PA
Krieg, Rev. Msgr. Gerard C., '53 (ROC) Retired.
Krieg, Rev. Thomas J., '92 (LC) St. James the Greater, Eau Claire, WI; [EFT] Friends of St. James the Greater Catholic School at Eau Claire Tuition Endowment Trust, Eau Claire, WI; [EFT] The St. James the Greater Catholic Church Endowment Trust, Eau Claire, WI
Kriegel, Rev. Msgr. Henry A., '70 (E) Retired.
Kriegshauser, Rev. Laurence, *O.S.B.* '69 (STL) [MON] The Abbey of St. Mary and St. Louis, St. Louis, MO
Krile, Rev. Stephen L., '83 (COL) St. John, Logan, OH
Krill, Rev. Jude Michael, *O.F.M.Conv.* '83 (ATL) Holy Cross Catholic Church, Atlanta, Inc., Atlanta, GA
Krill, Rev. Philip D., '81 (STL) St. Andrew Catholic Church, St. Louis, MO; St. Ann Catholic Church, Clover Bottom, Washington, MO; St. Gertrude Catholic Church, Washington, MO; St. Richard Catholic Church, St. Louis, MO
Krings, Rev. Doug, (GF) Holy Spirit, Great Falls, MT
Krip, Rev. Andriy, '15 (STF) Holy Ghost, South Deerfield, MA; SS. Peter and Paul, Ludlow, MA
Krische, Rev. James J., '91 (BRK) Curia: (>MO) Offices and Directors St. Mary Gate of Heaven, Ozone Park, NY
Krische, Rev. Msgr. Vincent E., '64 (KCK) Retired.
Kriski, Rev. Frank, *C.Ss.R.* '63 (KC) Retired. (>STL) [MON] St. Clement Health Care Center, Liguori, MO
Krisman, Rev. Ronald, '73 (ORL) Retired.
Kriss, Rev. Aaron J., '91 (PIT) Holy Spirit, New Castle, PA
Kristancic, Rev. Dennis J., '83 (CLV) Retired.
Kristofak, Rev. Terence, *C.P.* '69 (NY) [MON] The Congregation of the Passion - St. Paul of the Cross Province, Jamaica, NY
Kristofak, Rev. Terence J., *C.P.* '69 (HRT) Retired. [MON] Holy Family Monastery/Retreat, West Hartford, CT
Krittenbrink, Rev. Carson, '14 (OKL) Curia: Consultative Bodies; Deaneries St. Mary's Catholic Church, Ponca City, OK; [CAM] Northern Oklahoma College, Tonkawa, OK; [NUR] St. Mary's Housing Foundation, Ponca City, OK
Krivak, Rev. John A., '82 (ALN) Curia: Leadership St. Theresa of the Child Jesus, Hellertown, PA
Kriz, Rev. Dennis, *O.S.M.* '99 (CHI) [MIS] Servite Secular Order, Inc., Chicago, IL
Kriz, Rev. Dennis, *O.S.M.* '99 (ORG) Servite High School, A California Corporation, Anaheim, CA; St. Philip Benizi, Fullerton, CA
Krizner, Rev. William R., '79 (CLV) St. Colette, Brunswick, OH
Krlis, Rev. William F., '68 (BRK) Retired. Curia: Pastoral Services Most Precious Blood, Long Island City, NY
Kroeger, Rev. James H., *M.M.* '75 (NY) [MON] Maryknoll Fathers and Brothers (Catholic Foreign Mission Society of America, Inc.), Ossining, NY
Kroeger, Rev. John, '72 (CIN) Retired.
Kroes, Rev. Ralph S., *M.M.* '58 (NY) Retired. [MON] Maryknoll Fathers and Brothers (Catholic Foreign Mission Society of America, Inc.), Ossining, NY
Kroger, Rev. Daniel, *O.F.M.* '73 (CIN) [MIS] Franciscan Media, LLC, Cincinnati, OH; [SHR] St. Anthony Shrine, Cincinnati, OH
Krogman, Rev. David, '81 (SFS) Retired. [HOS] Avera McKennan, Sioux Falls, SD
Krol, Rev. Jan, *C.S.M.A.* (SJN) Jesus Mediador, San Juan, PR
Krol, Rev. Marek, '95 (COS) Chap, Diocesan Prison Our Lady of the Woods Catholic Parish, Woodland Park, CO
Krol, Rev. Miroslaw K., '99 (NEW) On Duty Outside Diocese. Orchard Lake Schools, Orchard Lake, MI
Krolczyk, Rev. David B., '72 (CHI) Retired.
Kroll, Rev. Alexander, (OKL) St. John the Baptist, Edmond, OK; [CAM] University of Central Oklahoma, Edmond, OK
Kroll, Rev. Anthony, '61 (SCL) Retired.
Kroll, Rev. Robert J., *S.J.* '99 (MIL) [MON] Jesuit Community at Marquette University (Marquette Jesuit Associates, Inc.), Milwaukee, WI; [SEM] Saint Francis de Sales Seminary, St. Francis, WI
Kromholtz, Rev. Bryan, *O.P.* '00 (OAK) [MON] Order of Preachers (Province of the Most Holy Name of Jesus - Western Dominican Province), Oakland, CA; [SEM] Dominican School of Philosophy and Theology,

Berkeley, CA
Krondon, Friar Joseph, *O.F.M.Conv.* (SY) Assumption B.V.M., Syracuse, NY
Kropac, Rev. Robert J., '82 (CLV) St. Wendelin Parish, Cleveland, OH
Kropf, Rev. Richard, '58 (GLD) [MIS] Stella Maris Hermitage, Johannesburg, MI
Kropf, Rev. Richard, '58 (LAN) On Duty Outside Diocese. Johannesburg
Kropiwnicki, Rev. Henry, '58 (FR) Retired.
Kropp, Rev. Steven R., *O.F.M.Cap.* '04 (DET) [MIS] Solanus Casey Center, Detroit, MI; [MON] St. Bonaventure Monastery, Detroit, MI
Krosfield, Rev. George, '70 (ALX) Retired.
Krosnicki, Rev. Thomas A, *SVD* '66 (CHI) Retired. [MON] Divine Word Residence, Techny, IL
Krotec, Rev. Ivan, '70 (STN) SS. Volodymyr and Olha, Chicago, IL
Krotkiewicz, Rev. Luke, '83 (DET) Chap, Henry Ford Macomb Hosp, Clinton Twp; Karmanos Cancer
Krouse, Rev. Dennis, '68 (SD) Retired.
Krouse, Rev. Jack, *SJ* (P) [MON] Colombiere Jesuit Community, Portland, OR
Krueger, Rev. Robert, (CHI) St. Pius X and St. Leonard Parish, Berwyn, IL
Krueger, Rev. Ryan E., '12 (GB) Corpus Christi, Sturgeon Bay, WI; St. Mary (Holy Name of Mary), Maplewood, WI
Krug, Rev. Clement, *C.Ss.R.* '65 (BRK) Our Lady of Perpetual Help Basilica, Brooklyn, NY
Krug, Rev. Clement M., *C.Ss.R.* '65 (NEW) Curia: Offices and Directors St. James, Newark, NJ
Krug, Rev. Jerome, '19 (OKL) Curia: Consultative Bodies St. Eugene's, Oklahoma City, OK
Krugel, Rev. Stephen A., '88 (HRT) Retired.
Kruger, Rev. Brent, '97 (SD) Pastor of Saint Thomas More Catholic Parish, Oceanside, a corporation sole, Oceanside, CA; [MIS] Saint Thomas More Catholic Parish in Oceanside, CA Real Property Support Corporation, Oceanside, CA
Krul, Rev. Valentine C., '77 (SY) On Leave.
Krulak, Rev. Michael, '84 (PSC) On Leave.
Krull, Rev. Michael G., '86 (MET) Our Lady of Peace, North Brunswick, NJ
Krumm, Rev. John E., '76 (CIN) Retired.
Krupa, Rev. Stephen T., *S.J.* '88 (CHI) [MON] Clark Street Jesuit Residence Community, Chicago, IL
Krupa, Rev. Thomas, '71 (ALB) Curia: Offices and Directors Sacred Heart, Castleton On Hudson, NY
Krupa, Rev. Thomas J., '71 (ALB) Curia: Leadership
Krupka, Rev. Canon Michael, '77 (SJP) Retired. Curia: Offices and Directors
Krupka, Rev. Canon Michael, '77 (SJP) Retired.
Krupnik, Rev. Marion I., '54 (HRT) Retired.
Krupp, Rev. Joseph, (LAN) St. Mark the Evangelist Parish Grand Blanc, Grand Blanc, MI
Krupp, Rev. Joseph J., '98 (LAN) Holy Family Parish Grand Blanc, Grand Blanc, MI
Kruse, Rev. Anthony J., '11 (DUB) Blessed Sacrament Church, Waterloo, Iowa, Waterloo, IA
Kruse, Rev. David, '15 (SPK) St. Augustine, Spokane, WA
Kruse, Rev. David B., '94 (BAL) Chap, Maj, US Air Force
Kruse, Rev. Msgr. James E., '96 (PEO) St. Louis, Princeton, IL
Kruse, Rev. Phillip F., '81 (DUB) Retired.
Krutcik, Rev. Stanley F., '80 (WOR) St. Christopher, Worcester, MA
Krylowicz, Rev. Mark J., '91 (CHI) St. Anthony of Padua, Chicago, IL
Krymski, Rev. Christopher M., *O.S.M.* '83 (CHI) Our Lady of Sorrows, Basilica of, Chicago, IL; [MIS] Monastery of Our Lady of Sorrows, , ; [MIS] National Shrine of St. Peregrine, O.S.M., ,
Krysa, Rev. Czeslaw M., '80 (BUF) St. Bernard, Buffalo, NY; St. Casimir Church, Buffalo, NY
Krystosek, Rev. Glenn A., '07 (SCL) Curia: Leadership St. Agnes, Roscoe, MN; St. Louis, Paynesville, MN; St. Margaret's, Lake Henry, MN
Kryszkiewicz, Rev. Pawel, '93 (CAM) Holy Trinity Parish, Margate, N.J., Margate City, NJ
Kryvikulsky, Rev. Oleh, (STN) Curia: Offices and Directors
Kryvokulsky, Rev. Oleh, '98 (STN) SS. Volodymyr and Olha, Chicago, IL
Krzanowski, Rev. Lukasz, *MS* (MIL) [MON] La Salette Missionaries, Twin Lakes, WI
Krzeszowski, Rev. Dawid, (MO) Curia: Offices and Directors
Krzyston, Rev. Stanley, '85 (TR) St. Vincent de Paul, Trenton, NJ
Krzywda, Rev. Jerzy, '89 (LAR) Curia: Leadership; Offices and Directors Our Lady of Guadalupe, Carrizo Springs, TX
Krzywicki, Rev. Lance P., '83 (PT) On Duty Outside Diocese. Chap, Nadliwe
Kselman, Rev. John S., *P.S.S.* '67 (BAL) Retired. [MON] Society of St. Sulpice, Province of the United States, Baltimore, MD
Kselman, Rev. John S., *P.S.S.* '67 (SFR) Curia: Leadership
Ksiazek, Rev. Karol J., '10 (BGP) St. Rose's Church Newtown, Newtown, CT
Ksiazkiewicz, Rev. Tymoteusz, '19 (DAL) [CAM] Catholic Center on Campbell, Richardson, TX; [CAM] University Catholic Center at UT Dallas, Richardson, TX
Ku, Rev. Tonguk, '01 (ATL) Korean Martyrs Catholic Church, Doraville, Inc., Doraville, GA
Kub, Rev. Francis Q., '65 (CHI) Curia: Offices and Directors St. Gall, Chicago, IL
Kuba, Rev. William M., '62 (E) Retired. St. Eusebius, East Brady, PA
Kubacki, Rev. Msgr. William J., '78 (TOL) Curia: Advisory Boards, Commissions, Committees, and Councils; Leadership Our Lady Queen of the Most Holy Rosary Cathedral, Toledo, OH
Kubajak, Rev. James, '77 (PRM) Retired.
Kubat, Rev. Christopher K., '99 (LIN) Curia: Offices and Directors St. Andrew's, Tecumseh, NE (>OM) [MIS] Marianna, Inc., Omaha, NE
Kubeck, Rev. John C., '65 (POD) Curia: Clergy and Religious Services
Kubeck, Rev. John C., '65 (MIL) [MIS] Prelature of the Holy Cross and Opus Dei Layton Study Center, Brookfield, WI
Kubiak, Rev. Joseph, *O.F.M.Cap.* '74 (MET) St. Helena, Edison, NJ
Kubiak, Rev. Lukasz, '16 (BRK) On Leave.
Kubicki, Rev. James, (RC) (>MIL) [MON] Jesuit Community at Marquette University (Marquette Jesuit Associates, Inc.), Milwaukee, WI
Kubina, Rev. Eugene, *T.O.R.* '53 (ALT) Retired. [MON] St. Bernardine Monastery, Hollidaysburg, PA
Kubinski, Rev. Scott, '84 (ROC) The Parish of the Most Holy Name of Jesus, Chemung County, NY, Elmira, NY
Kubinski, Rev. Scott M., '84 (ROC) [CAM] Elmira College, Elmira, NY
Kubisa, Rev. Jan, '82 (GAL) Curia: Offices and Directors St. Pius V, Pasadena, TX
Kubishyn, Rev. Ivan, '79 (SJP) Curia: Offices and Directors
Kubista, Rev. Paul Basil, '10 (STP) St. Mary of Czestochowa, Delano, MN
Kubrak, Rev. Wladyslaw Z., '06 (BRK) St. Pancras, Glendale, NY
Kuca, Rev. Stanislaw, '91 (CHI) Curia: Leadership St. Luke and St. Bernardine Parish, River Forest, IL
Kucer, Very Rev. Peter, *M.S.A.* '03 (NOR) [MON] Society of the Missionaries of the Holy Apostles, Cromwell, CT; [SEM] Holy Apostles College and Seminary, Cromwell, CT
Kucera, Rev. David G., '98 (DUB) Holy Family Church, Reinbeck, Iowa, Reinbeck, IA
Kucera, Rev. Edward C., '73 (GAL) St. Mary, Plantersville, TX
Kucera, Rev. Jeremy G., '04 (NU) Curia: Leadership Church of the Sacred Heart, Murdock, MN; Church of the Visitation (Oratory), Danvers, MN; St. Bridget, DeGraff, MN; St. Francis, Benson, MN; St. John, Appleton, MN; St. Malachy, Clontarf, MN
Kucera, Rev. John, (B) Curia: Leadership Mary Immaculate, St. Anthony, ID
Kuchar, Rev. Michael W., '80 (LAN) Retired.
Kucharczyk, Rev. Dennis H., '85 (SAG) Retired.
Kucharski, Rev. Steven M., '77 (MAN) Retired.
Kuchinski, Rev. John, '16 (HBG) Immaculate Conception of the Blessed Virgin Mary, York, PA
Kuchinsky, Rev. William J., '97 (WH) On Leave. Curia: Offices and Directors
Kuczborski, Rev. Joseph, '82 (PMB) Retired.
Kuczera, Rev. Frank, (SFD) [SEM] Immaculate Heart of Mary Novitiate, Godfrey, IL
Kuczora, Rev. Matthew C., *C.S.C.* '12 (FTW) [COL] University of Notre Dame Du Lac, Notre Dame, IN; [SEM] Moreau Seminary, Notre Dame, IN
Kuczynski, Rev. Edward P., '77 (PH) St. Philip Neri, Philadelphia, PA
Kuczynski, Rev. James H., *M.S.* '73 (GAL) Mary Queen Catholic Church, Friendswood, TX
Kuczynski, Rev. Kazimierz, '76 (NEW) St. Ann, Jersey City, NJ
Kuczynski, Rev. Krzysztof, '13 (BGP) Saint Lawrence Corporation, Shelton, CT
Kuder, Rev. Stephen R., *S.J.* '73 (SPK) [COL] Gonzaga University, Spokane, WA
Kueber, Rev. Michael, '00 (STP) [CEM] Assumption Cemetery, Richfield, MN
Kueber, Rev. Michael I., '00 (P) Curia: Offices and Directors
Kuehnemund, Rev. Thomas, '93 (DET) Curia: Administration; Consultative Bodies Our Lady of Mount Carmel Parish Emmett, Emmett, MI; Sacred Heart Parish Yale, Yale, MI
Kuffel, Rev. Thomas P., '89 (LIN) On Duty Outside Diocese. Diocese of Fairbanks
Kuffner, Rev. Patrick J., '02 (MET) On Leave.
Kuforiji, Rev. George, '15 (P) St. Francis of Assisi, Portland, OR
Kuhar, Rev. Jonathan, '20 (SCR) Curia: Leadership; Offices and Directors Saint John Neumann Parish, Scranton, PA; Saint Paul of the Cross, Scranton, Scranton, PA
Kuharski, Rev. Joseph H., '14 (STP) [SEM] St. John Vianney Seminary, St. Paul, MN
Kuhlman, Rev. Joseph, '15 (STA) Curia: Evangelization St. Patrick, Jacksonville, FL
Kuhlmann, Rev. Steve, (LFT) St. Thomas Aquinas, West Lafayette, IN; [CAM] St. Thomas Aquinas Parish and Foundation for Catholic Students Attending Purdue University, West Lafayette, IN
Kuhlmann, Rev. Steven F., *O.P.* '92 (CHI) (>LFT) [MIS] Dominicans, Community of St. Thomas Aquinas, Inc., West Lafayette, IN
Kuhn, Rev. Aaron, (SFD) Holy Family, Mount Sterling, IL; St. Thomas, Camp Point, IL; [ASN] Catholic Cemetery Association, Mt. Sterlin, IL
Kuhn, Rev. Aaron J., '07 (SCL) Sacred Heart, Staples, MN; St. Ann's, Wadena, MN; St. Frederick, Verndale, MN; St. Hubert, Sebeka, MN; St. John the Baptist, Bluffton, MN; St. Joseph, Bertha, MN; St. Michael, Motley, MN; The Church of the Assumption of Our Lady of Menahga, Menahga, MN
Kuhn, Rev. Christopher A., *C.S.C.* (FTW) [MON] Congregation of Holy Cross, United States Province of Priests and Brothers, Notre Dame, IN
Kuhn, Rev. Christopher J., '97 (RCK) Curia: Offices and Directors St. Mary, Elgin, IL
Kuhn, Rev. Dennis R., '82 (CHL) On Leave.
Kuhn, Rev. James G., '71 (MAD) Retired.
Kuhn, Rev. Matthew, '10 (SCL) Immaculate Conception, Osakis, MN; St. Nicholas, Carlos, MN; The Church of St. Mary, Alexandria, MN
Kuhn, Rev. Melvin T., '14 (SFS) Our Lady of Good Counsel Parish of Brookings County, Elkton, SD; Saint Peter Parish of Moody County, Colman, SD; Saints Simon and Jude Parish of Moody County, Flandreau, SD; [PRE] Preschool, Jefferson, SD
Kuhn, Rev. Nathaniel W., '14 (LC) Curia: Offices and Directors [MIS] Holy Cross (Seminary) Diocesan Center, La Crosse, WI; [SEM] Holy Cross Seminary House of Formation, La Crosse, WI
Kuhn, Rev. Paul, '17 (FAR) St. John's Church of Wahpeton, Wahpeton, ND
Kuhn, Rev. Richard W., '53 (DUB) Retired.
Kuhneman, Very Rev. Timothy M., '06 (RIC) Curia: Administration
Kuhns, Rev. James, '61 (SPK) Retired.
Kuhr, Rev. Bryan J., '17 (ATL) St. Catherine Laboure Catholic Church, Jefferson, Inc., Jefferson, GA; St. Joseph Catholic Church, Athens, Inc., Athens, GA
Kuhr, Rev. William, '67 (GB) Retired.
Kujawa, Rev. Andrzej, *S.D.S.* '08 (NEW) Saint John Paul II Church, Bayonne, NJ; St. Stanislaus Kostka, Garfield, NJ
Kujawa, Rev. Bryan, '15 (CR) St. Anne (Goodridge), Goodridge, MN; St. Clement (Grygla), Grygla, MN; St. Francis Xavier's (Oklee), Oklee, MN
Kujawinski, Rev. Matthew J., '03 (E) Curia: Offices and Directors Our Lady of Mercy, Harborcreek, PA
Kukana, Rev. Raphael Munday, '07 (BRK) St. Catherine of Genoa, Brooklyn, NY
Kukatla, Rev. Jones, '82 (WIL) St. John the Apostle, Milford, DE; St. Jude the Apostle, Lewes, DE
Kukielka, Rev. Zbigniew, '11 (NEW) [SEM] Redemptoris Mater Archdiocesan Missionary Seminary, Kearny, NJ
Kukielka, Rev. Zbigniew, (BGP) Curia: Clergy and Religious Services [SEM] Redemptorist Mater Diocesan Missionary Seminary Diocese of Bridgeport Inc., Stamford, CT
Kuklich, Rev. Stepan, '95 (STF) On Duty Outside Diocese. Diocese of Buffalo, NY
Kukulka, Rev. Janusz, '85 (HRT) Saint Teresa of Calcutta Parish Corporation, Manchester, CT
Kulacz, Rev. Sean, '09 (BGP) Retired. Holy Family and St. Emery Parish Corporation, Fairfield, CT
Kulah, Rev. Henry N., '84 (CHR) Our Lady of Good

Counsel, Folly Beach, SC
Kulak, Rev. Joseph F., '66 (RCK) Retired.
Kulandai, Rev. Gnanasekar, *H.G.N.* '09 (SAL) Curia: Consultative Bodies St. Francis Xavier Parish, Junction City, Inc., Junction City, KS
Kulandaijesu, Rev. Lourthuantony, *H.G.N.* '10 (SAL) St. Joseph Parish, Dorrance, Inc., Dorrance, KS; St. Mary Parish, Holyrood, Inc., Holyrood, KS; St. Wenceslaus Parish, Wilson, Inc., Wilson, KS
Kulandaisamy, Rev. David, '90 (PHX) St. Gabriel Roman Catholic Parish, Cave Creek, AZ
Kulas, Rev. William J., '74 (WIN) Retired. Curia: (>LC) Offices and Directors
Kulas, Rev. William J., '74 (WIN) Retired.
Kulathanapatikal, Rev. Suneesh Mathew, *H.G.N.* '08 (OWN) Precious Blood, Owensboro, KY
Kulathinal, Rev. Jose J., *C.M.I.* '92 (STA) Curia: Leadership Holy Faith, Gainesville, FL
Kulathumkal, Rev. Babu, *H.G.N.* '96 (OWN) St. Pius Tenth Parish, Owensboro, KY
Kulbicki, Rev. Timothy, *O.F.M. Conv.* '86 (R) Newman Catholic Student Center, University of North Carolina, Chapel Hill, NC; [CAM] Newman Catholic Student Center, Chapel Hill, NC
Kulczyk, Rev. Aaron F., '19 (BUF) Blessed Mother Teresa of Calcutta (dba Saint Mother Teresa of Calcutta), Depew, NY; Our Lady of Pompeii, Lancaster, NY
Kulczynski, Rev. Jason V., '89 (PH) Holy Martyrs, Oreland, PA
Kulick, Rev. Michael, '12 (SJP) St. John the Baptist Mission, Charlotte, NC
Kulick, Rev. Michael, '09 (SJP) Curia: Offices and Directors
Kulig, Rev. Msgr. Anthony J., '61 (NEW) Retired. [COL] Seton Hall University, South Orange, NJ
Kulig, Rev. Krzysztof A., (CHI) St. Thomas Becket, Mt. Prospect, IL
Kuligowski, Rev. Peter, '97 (ALX) On Leave. St. Anthony of Padua, Natchitoches, LA
Kuligowski, Rev. Peter J., '97 (ALT) On Duty Outside Diocese. St Joseph, LA
Kull, Rev. John J., *O.F.M.* (HRT) Retired. St. Patrick and St. Anthony Roman Catholic Church Corporation, Hartford, CT
Kull, Rev. Martin R., '76 (BRK) Retired. St. Josaphat, Bayside, NY
Kuller, Rev. Thomas, *S.J.* (PH) [MON] Jesuit Community at St. Joseph's University, Merion Station, PA
Kullmann, Rev. Charles, *C.S.P.* '78 (AUS) St. Austin, Austin, TX
Kulma, Rev. Ryszard, '02 (GAL) St. Edith Stein, Katy, TX
Kulway, Rev. James J., '16 (CLV) St. Barnabas, Northfield, OH
Kulwiec, Rev. Richard, *O.M.I.* '81 (LAR) St. Joseph, Eagle Pass, TX
Kumai, Rev. Felix K., '86 (MO) Curia: Offices and Directors
Kumakech, Rev. Patrick, *AJ* (CLV) Akron City Hospital
Kumanda, Rev. Pascal Ngboloma, *C.I.C.M.* '13 (ARL) [MON] Missionhurst, C.I.C.M.-Central House and Provincialate (American I.H.M. Province, Inc., Immaculate Heart Missions, Inc., Missionhurst, Inc.), Arlington, VA
Kumar, Rev. Mathias, *OSFS* (ARL) Our Lady of Good Counsel, Vienna, VA
Kumar, Rev. Micheal, *SS.CC* '13 (LA) Holy Name of Mary, San Dimas, CA
Kumar, Rev. Pradeep, *H.G.N.* (WH) Our Lady of Fatima, Huntington, WV; St. Stephen, Ona, WV
Kumar, Rev. Raj, *S.J.* '06 (CHI) [COL] Jesuit Community at Loyola University Chicago, Chicago, IL
Kumar Embeti, Rev. Jaya, (SEA) Our Lady of Good Help, Hoquiam, WA; St. Jerome, Ocean Shores, WA; St. Joseph, Elma, WA; St. Mary, Aberdeen, WA
Kumarthusseril, Rev. Joy, *M.F.* '88 (OAK) Curia: Leadership Our Lady of Guadalupe, Fremont, CA; [MON] Missionaries of Faith-India Inc., Fremont, CA
Kumbakeel, Rev. Kuriakose, (PH) Curia: Evangelization
Kumbakeel, Rev. Kuriakose, (SYM) St. Thomas Syro-Malabar Catholic Church (Philadelphia), Philadelphia, PA
Kumbakeel, Rev. Kuriakose, '86 (SYM) Curia: Administration
Kumbakkeel, Rev. James, *O.S.B.* '86 (FTW) St. Charles Borromeo, Fort Wayne, IN
Kumbalaprampil, Rev. Xavier, '66 (SAV) Retired.
Kumblolickal, Rev. Jose, *MSFS* '92 (GAL) St. Ignatius of Loyola, Spring, TX
Kumblumkal, Rev. Jose, *CMI* (SPC) St. Francis De Sales, Lebanon, MO
Kummer, Rev. William J., '75 (FTW) Curia: Leadership; Offices and Directors St. Joseph, Fort Wayne, IN
Kummerer, Rev. Timothy M., '83 (TOL) All Saints, New Riegel, OH; SS. Patrick & Andrew, Bascom, OH
Kump, Rev. Thomas, (GLP) On Leave.
Kumplam, Rev. Chacko, (HRT) Saint Francis Xavier Parish Corporation, New Milford, CT
Kumse, Rev. John M., '79 (CLV) St. Mary, Cleveland, OH
Kumulmac, Rev. Moises, '12 (P) Sacred Heart of Jesus, Medford, OR
Kuna, Rev. Matthew J., '22 (ALN) Berks Catholic High School, Inc., Reading, PA; St. Catharine of Siena, Reading, PA
Kuna, Rev. Vincent A., *C.S.C.* '09 (LA) St. Monica, Santa Monica, CA
Kunat, Rev. Bartosz T., '11 (BLX) Chap, Industrial and Training School Cathedral of the Nativity of the Blessed Virgin Mary, Biloxi, MS
Kunath, Rev. A. Conor, '19 (COV) Curia: Offices and Directors; Spiritual Life
Kunco, Rev. Edward J., '69 (PIT) Retired.
Kunderevych, Rev. Orest, '98 (PHU) Nativity of B.V.M., New Brunswick, NJ; St. Michael's, Hillsborough, NJ
Kundoni, Rev. Job, '08 (PHX) St. Jerome Roman Catholic Parish, Phoenix, AZ
Kunes, Rev. James, *S.M.* '60 (CIN) Retired.
Kunigonis, Rev. Mark S., '00 (PH) St. John Cantius, Philadelphia, PA
Kunisch, Rev. Robert, *C.PP.S.* '56 (CIN) Retired.
Kunisch, Rev. William, '02 (HON) St. Anthony of Padua, Kailua, HI
Kunisch, Rev. William J., '02 (HON) Curia: Consultative Bodies; Offices and Directors
Kunitz, Rev. Michael David, '21 (PBR) Holy Spirit, Pittsburgh, PA; St. Pius X, Pittsburgh, PA
Kunjukutty, Rev. Biju Chennala, *M.S.F.S.* '02 (LC) St. Joseph, La Crosse, WI; St. Peter, Rockland, WI
Kunkel, Rev. George C., '77 (CIN) Retired.
Kunkel, Rev. James E., '73 (PIT) Retired.
Kunkel, Rev. Ronald T., '00 (CHI) [SEM] University of Saint Mary of the Lake/Mundelein Seminary, Mundelein, IL
Kunkel, Rev. Steven A., '01 (PHX) Curia: Leadership; Offices and Directors St. Thomas the Apostle Roman Catholic Parish, Phoenix, AZ
Kunnakkattuthara, Msgr. Zacharias S., '75 (TYL) Curia: Advisory Boards, Commissions, Committees, and Councils; Deaneries Immaculate Conception, Jefferson, TX; St. Joseph, Marshall, TX
Kunnalakattu, Rev. Peter, *BCC* (STA) Chaplain, Malcom Randall VA Med Ctr, Gainesville
Kunnalakattu, Rev. Peter Raphael, (MO) Curia: Offices and Directors
Kunnath, Rev. Matthew, '60 (NEW) Retired.
Kunnath, Rev. Sebastian, '73 (NEW) Retired. [MON] St. John Vianney Residence for Retired Priests, Rutherford, NJ
Kunnath, Rev. Thomas, '85 (TR) Retired.
Kunnel, Rev. George, *M.S.F.S.* '76 (TUC) Saint Joseph Roman Catholic Parish - Hayden, Hayden, AZ
Kunnel, Rev. George, *MSFS* '76 (TUC) Infant Jesus of Prague Roman Catholic Parish - Kearny, Kearny, AZ
Kunnel, Rev. Thomas, *C.O.* '83 (NY) St. John Henry Newman, Tappan, NY; [MIS] New York Oratory of St. Philip Neri, Inc., Sparkill, NY
Kunnelaya, Rev. Joseph T., '84 (BAK) Curia: Leadership St. Joseph, Prineville, OR
Kunninu, Rev. Sibi, *M.S.* (GAL) Mary Queen Catholic Church, Friendswood, TX
Kunninu Chacko, Rev. Sibi, *M.S.* '02 (LKC) St. Theresa, Sulphur, LA
Kunnumpuram, Rev. Paul, *M.S.F.S.* '76 (ALX) Christ the King, Simmesport, LA
Kunst, Rev. Richard, '98 (DUL) St. James, Duluth, MN
Kuntz, Rev. Kenneth E., '77 (DAV) Retired.
Kunz, Rev. Msgr. David C., '80 (LC) Queen of the Apostles Parish, Tomah, WI; [EFT] The St. Mary's Catholic Church Educational Endowment Trust, Tomah, WI
Kunz, Rev. Eric J., '08 (STL) St. Clare Catholic Church, St. Clair, St. Clair, MO
Kunz, Rev. James H., '73 (WIN) Retired.
Kunz, Rev. John M., '76 (WIN) St. John the Baptist, Mankato, MN
Kunz, Very Rev. Thomas W., '04 (PIT) Curia: Consultative Bodies; Leadership; Tribunal
Kunz, Very Rev. Thomas W., '04 (PIT) Curia: Consultative Bodies; Leadership
Kunze, Rev. Robert W., '74 (NEW) Retired.
Kunzman, Rev. Richard T., '63 (CAM) Retired.
Kupar, Rev. Vasyl, (PRM) St. Joseph, Brecksville, OH
Kuperski, Rev. Marcin, '04 (NEW) Most Sacred Heart of Jesus, Wallington, NJ; Notre Dame, North Caldwell, NJ
Kupka, Rev. Marek S., '01 (PRO) Church of Our Lady of Lourdes, Providence, RI; Saint Adalbert's Church, Providence, RI
Kupke, Rev. Msgr. Raymond J., '73 (PAT) Curia: Leadership St. Anthony's, Hawthorne, NJ
Kuppe, Rev. Paul, *O.F.M.Cap.* '70 (PIT) Our Lady of the Valley, Beaver, PA; [MON] St. Fidelis Friary, Beaver, PA
Kurber, Rev. Robert, '60 (ORL) Retired.
Kurc, Rev. Slawomir, '95 (CHI) St. John Brebeuf, Niles, IL
Kurgan, Rev. John J., '04 (SY) Curia: Leadership; Offices and Directors Holy Cross, DeWitt, NY; St. Anthony of Padua, Syracuse, NY; [EFT] Grimes Foundation, Syracuse, NY; [EFT] The Robert L. McDevitt, K.S.G., K.C.H.S. and Catherine H. McDevitt, L.C.H.S. Foundation, Inc., Syracuse, NY; [EFT] The Saint Thomas Aquinas Fund Inc., Syracuse, NY; [MIS] The Robert L. McDevitt, K.S.G., K.C.H.S. and Catherine H. McDevitt, L.C.H.S. Fund of St. James Church of Lestershire, N.Y., Johnson City, NY; [MIS] The Syracuse Diocesan Investment Fund, Inc., Syracuse, NY
Kuriakose, Rev. John, '99 (MCE) Curia: Advisory Boards, Commissions, Committees, and Councils; Offices and Directors
Kuriakose, Rev. Jossey, '02 (P) St. Paul, Silverton, OR
Kuriakose, Rev. Siju, '04 (LA) Chap, Hospital Chaplain, St Francis Med Ctr, Lynwood
Kuriakose, Rev. Thomas, '83 (HT) Curia: Administration St. Lawrence the Martyr, Thibodaux, LA
Kurian, Rev. Binoy, *T.O.R.* (FWT) Curia: Miscellaneous / Other Offices St. Patrick Cathedral, Fort Worth, TX
Kurian, Rev. Msgr. Cyriac, *C.M.I.* (NSH) St. Rose of Lima, Murfreesboro, TN
Kurian, Rev. George, *CMI* '00 (BRK) St. Anthony-St. Alphonsus, Brooklyn, NY; [MON] Carmelites of Mary Immaculate, Inc., Brooklyn, NY
Kurian, Rev. Roy, (LAV) St. John Neumann, North Las Vegas, NV
Kurian, Rev. Shijomon, (NEW) St. Joseph Church, Lodi, NJ
Kuriapilly, Rev. Johnson, '90 (BR) [HOS] Our Lady of the Lake Hospital, Inc. (Our Lady of the Lake Regional Medical Center; DBA Our Lady of the Lake Children's Hospital; DBA Our Lady of the Lake Ascension), Baton Rouge, LA
Kuriappilly, Rev. Jose Joseph, (SCR) SS. Peter and Paul, Towanda, PA
Kurimay, Rev. Michael D., *S.J.* '73 (MIL) [MON] St. Camillus Jesuit Community (Society of Jesus, USA Midwest Province), Wauwatosa, WI
Kurimsky, Rev. Francis M., '86 (PIT) Robert Morris Univ, Moon Twp Most Sacred Heart of Jesus, Moon Township, PA
Kurnath, Rev. Joseph G.M., '91 (HRT) Retired.
Kuroly, Rev. James, (BRK) [MIS] Office of Faith Formation, Brooklyn, NY
Kuroly, Rev. James A., '07 (BRK) [SEM] Cathedral Preparatory School and Seminary, Elmhurst, NY
Kurovsky, Rev. Andrew, (SCR) Sacred Heart of Jesus, Peckville, PA
Kurovsky, Rev. Andrew, '85 (SCR) Curia: Offices and Directors
Kurpel, Rev. Yaroslav, '93 (PHU) Christ the King Ukrainian Catholic Church, Philadelphia, PA
Kurpios, Rev. Szymon, *Sch.P.* '02 (NY) St. James the Apostle, Carmel, NY; [MON] Calasanzian Fathers (Piarists), New York, NY
Kurps, Rev. Jack, *S.C.J.* '77 (JKS) [MIS] Sacred Heart Southern Missions, Inc., Walls, MS; [MON] St. Michael Community House, Nesbit, MS
Kurtz, Rev. James, *O.F.M.Cap.* '87 (PIT) St. Clare of Assisi, Chicora, PA; St. Francis of Assisi, Cabot, PA; St. John the Evangelist, Fenelton, PA; St. Mary of the Assumption, Butler, PA; [MON] St. Mary's Friary, Butler, PA
Kurtz, Rev. Jeffrey A., '90 (MAR) Retired.
Kurucz, Rev. Frank A., '98 (CHI) St. Michael, Orland Park, IL
Kurumbel, Rev. Joseph, *O.S.B.* '76 (LUB) Retired. St. Mary Magdalen, Floydada, TX
Kurutz, Rev. Joseph V., '59 (PIT) Retired.
Kuruvila, Rev. Prince, '92 (CC) Retired.
Kuruvilla, Rev. Baby, (HT) St. Joseph, Chauvin, LA
Kurwicki, Rev. Msgr. Robert A., '85 (JC) Curia: Administration; Advisory Boards, Commissions, Committees, and Councils; Organizations (affiliated, inter-Diocesan, miscellaneous/other) St. Michael, Russellville, MO

Kury, Rev. Canon Ignatius, '06 (SJP) On Leave. Curia: Offices and Directors
Kurz, Rev. Andrew J., '12 (GB) Holy Rosary, Kewaunee, WI; St. Mary, Algoma, WI
Kurz, Rev. William S., *S.J.* '70 (MIL) [MON] St. Camillus Jesuit Community (Society of Jesus, USA Midwest Province), Wauwatosa, WI
Kurzaj, Rev. Msgr. Franciszek, '76 (SAT) St. Stanislaus, Bandera, TX
Kurzak, Rev. John F., '75 (SC) Retired. On Duty Outside Diocese. Palm Springs, CA
Kurzawa, Rev. Ronald, '64 (DET) Retired.
Kurzyna, Rev. Andrew E., '74 (NY) Retired. Parish of Our Saviour and St. Stephen/Our Lady of the Scapular, New York, NY
Kurzyna, Rev. Zenon, '13 (VEN) On Leave.
Kurzynski, Very Rev. James R., '03 (LC) Curia: Leadership St. Olaf, Eau Claire, WI; [EFT] St. Olaf Parish Endowment Trust, Eau Claire, WI
Kus, Rev. Robert J., '98 (R) Retired.
Kusa, Rev. Daniel K., (CHI) St. Priscilla, Chicago, IL
Kuse, Rev. Msgr. Michael R., '67 (SFD) Retired.
Kushamba, Rev. Tafadzwa, '19 (MAD) St. Clare of Assisi Parish, Monroe, WI
Kushnir, Rev. Volodymyr, '09 (STN) St. Josaphat, Munster, IN
Kushnir, Rev. Volodymyr, '09 (STN) Chap Curia: Offices and Directors
Kusi, Rev. Benjamin Asibvo, '03 (CIN) St. Stephen, Cincinnati, OH
Kusi, Rev. Gordon P., '95 (BRK) Christ the King, Springfield Gardens, NY; St. Mary Magdalene, Springfield Gardens, NY
Kusibab, Rev. Justin, *O.F.M.Conv.* '87 (CHI) (>BUF) [MON] St. Maximilian Kolbe Friary, Hamburg, NY
Kusibab, Rev. Miroslaw, (NEW) St. Genevieve, Elizabeth, NJ
Kusmirek, Rev. Mark, '77 (TYL) Curia: Deaneries St. Charles Borromeo Catholic Church, Frankston, TX
Kuss, Rev. Allen R., '84 (STP) Curia: Leadership St. Patrick, Edina, MN
Kusugh, Rev. Richard T., '04 (TUC) Saint Francis de Sales Roman Catholic Parish - Tucson, Tucson, AZ
Kusy, Rev. Jerzy, '86 (CLV) St. Cyprian, Perry, OH
Kutch, Rev. Joseph P., '88 (SCR) Curia: Leadership St. Michael (St Johns - St. Michaels Church), Canton, PA
Kutiuk, Rev. Casimir, '57 (GB) Retired.
Kutlesa, Rev. Zvonimir, *O.F.M.* '66 (CHI) [MON] St. Anthony's Friary, ,
Kutner, Rev. Msgr. Raymond W., '64 (BRK) Retired.
Kutsch, Rev. Eugene C., '51 (DUB) Retired.
Kuttner, Rev. David, '09 (SPK) St. Rose of Lima, Cheney, WA
Kutubebi, Rev. Frederick K.A., '97 (SR) Pastor of Holy Family Catholic Church of American Canyon, A Corporation Sole, American Canyon, CA; [HOS] Providence Queen of the Family Medical Center (Providence Queen of the Valley Medical Center), Napa, CA
Kutys, Rev. Msgr. Daniel J., '80 (PH) On Special Assignment. Curia: Advisory Boards, Commissions, Committees, and Councils; Leadership St. Dorothy, Drexel Hill, PA; [MIS] Catholic Charities Appeal of the Archdiocese of Philadelphia, Philadelphia, PA; [MIS] Heritage of Faith - Vision of Hope, Philadelphia, PA
Kutz, Rev. Lawrence A., '65 (POD) Curia: Clergy and Religious Services
Kutzner, Rev. Roger, '90 (JOL) St. Boniface, Monee, IL; St. Paul the Apostle, Peotone, IL
Kuubeta, Rev. Jonas, (VIC) Holy Family of Joseph, Mary & Jesus, Victoria, TX
Kuukole, Rev. Beyuo, '05 (KCK) Providence & St John Hosp, Kansas City Christ the King, Kansas City, KS
Kuupuo, Rev. Severo, '91 (SJ) St. Catherine of Alexandria, Morgan Hill, CA
Kuwornu, Rev. Frank, (OAK) Holy Spirit, Fremont, CA
Kuykendall, Rev. Henry, '86 (EVN) Retired. Curia: Offices and Directors
Kuzara, Rev. Yuri (George) J., *C.PP.S.* '78 (TOL) [MON] Mary Lay Center, Bellevue, OH
Kuzhichalil, Rev. Joseph, *C.M.I.* (BIR) St. Joseph Catholic Church, Florence, AL; [CAM] University of North Alabama, Florence, AL; [EFT] St. Joseph School Foundation, Florence, Florence, AL
Kuzhikottayil, Rev. John, *SDB* (HRT) Saint Francis of Assisi Parish Corporation, Naugatuck, CT
Kuzhimannil, Rev. Paul, *C.Ss.R.* (TOL) St. Gerard, Lima, OH
Kuzhupil, Rev. Joseph, *M.S.F.S.* '85 (KNX) Notre Dame, Greeneville, TN; [MIS] Diocesan Council of Catholic Women, Knoxville, TN
Kuzma, Rev. John Paul, *OFM Cap.* '15 (CLV) [SEM] Borromeo Seminary, Wickliffe, OH
Kuzma, Mitred Archpriest Mykhailo, '81 (STN) Chap Immaculate Conception Ukrainian Catholic Church, Palatine, IL
Kuzmich, Rev. Msgr. John M., '65 (FTW) Retired.
Kuźmicki, Rev. Ireneusz, (DEN) Our Lady of Loreto Catholic Parish in Foxfield, Foxfield, CO
Kuzminskyi, Rev. Roman, '08 (SJP) Curia: Offices and Directors Protection of the Mother of God, Apopka, FL
Kvedas, Rev. Leonard J., '61 (HRT) Retired.
Kwaleyela, Rev. Peter M., *P.S.S.* '10 (BAL) [MIS] St. Mary's Seminary & University, Baltimore, MD; [MON] Society of St. Sulpice, Province of the United States, Baltimore, MD
Kwame, Rev. Joel Yao, '14 (ARL) St. James, Falls Church, VA
Kwan, Rev. Robin, *S.J.C.* '13 (CHI) St. Peter, Volo, IL; [MIS] Canons Regular of Saint John Cantius, Chicago, IL
Kwan, Rev. Roger, (NY) Parish of Transfiguration and St. James/St. Joseph, New York, NY
Kwatera, Rev. Michael, *O.S.B.* '77 (SCL) [MON] St. John's Abbey, of the Order of St. Benedict, Collegeville, MN
Kweder, Rev. Joseph J., '85 (ALN) St. Rocco, Martins Creek, PA
Kwiatkowski, Rev. Dawid A., '11 (SAV) St. Anne, Richmond Hill, GA
Kwiatkowski, Rev. Joseph, '06 (NEW) St. Rose of Lima, Newark, NJ
Kwiatkowski, Rev. Michael, '78 (SPK) Retired. [SEM] Bishop White Seminary, Spokane, WA
Kwiatkowski, Rev. Richard P., '72 (NEW) Retired. St. John the Evangelist, Leonia, NJ
Kwiatkowski, Very Rev. Robert M., '83 (HRT) Curia: Advisory Boards, Commissions, Committees, and Councils The Roman Catholic Parish of Middlebury and Southbury Church Corporation, Southbury, CT
Kwiatkowski, Rev. Sylvester, '89 (SAC) Pastor of St. Maria Goretti Parish, Elk Grove, a corporation sole, Elk Grove, CA
Kwiecien, Rev. John S., '76 (BUF) Retired. [MON] Bishop Head Residence, Lackawanna, NY
Kwiecien, Rev. Michael E., *O.Carm.* '80 (SFR) Chap, Kaiser Hosp San Francisco St. Teresa, San Francisco, CA
Kwiecien, Rev. Wojciech, '79 (CHI) Curia: Leadership Blessed Martyrs of Chimbote Parish, Argo, IL
Kwofie, Rev. Emmanuel, '97 (BWN) Our Lady of Guadalupe, Raymondville, TX
Kwoka, Rev. Edward, '78 (TR) Retired.
Kwon, Rev. Jinwon, '08 (KCK) On Special Assignment. Chaplain, Korean Catholic Community, Lenexa
Kwon, Rev. Sun Joong, (BRK) [CCH] Korean Ministry, ,
Ky, Rev. Joseph T., *P.S.S.* '59 (BAL) Retired.
Ky, Rev. Joseph T., *S.S.* '59 (HON) Retired.
Kyabuta, Rev. Jean Baptiste, '88 (NSH) Curia: Leadership
Kyabuta, Rev. Jean Baptiste, (NSH) St. Joseph, Madison, TN
Kyallo, Rev. Thomas, '85 (SR) Pastor of St. Apollinaris Catholic Church of Napa, A Corporation Sole, Napa, CA
Kyara, Rev. Bernard, *A.J.* (CLV) Visitation of Mary, Akron, OH
Kyara, Rev. Bernard P., *A.J.* (CLV) Chap, Akron Gen Hosp
Kyara, Rev. Gasper, *ALCP* (HEL) Saint Michael the Archangel Parish: Series 321, LLC, Conrad, MT; Saint William Parish: Series 326, LLC, Dutton, MT
Kyeah, Rev. Barnabas, '95 (VIC) St. Joseph Catholic Church, Inez, TX
Kyebasuuta, Rev. John, '98 (LA) Curia: Pastoral Services St. Thomas Aquinas, Monterey Park, CA
Kyerematen, Rev. Enoch, (WOR) Curia: Offices and Directors St. Anne, Shrewsbury, MA
Kyfes, Rev. Robert J., '77 (CHI) Retired.
Kynam, Rev. Victor, '07 (GR) Curia: Offices and Directors Our Lady of LaVang, Wyoming, MI
Kyrpczak, Rev. James A., '96 (MET) St. Joseph, High Bridge, NJ
Kysely, Rev. Andrew T., '07 (MIL) St. Joseph's Congregation, Big Bend, WI
Kythe, Rev. Jay, *O.S.B.* '17 (KCK) [MON] St. Benedict's Abbey, Atchison, KS
La Buda, Rev. David E., *M.M.* '71 (NY) Retired. [MON] Maryknoll Fathers and Brothers (Catholic Foreign Mission Society of America, Inc.), Ossining, NY
La Chance, Rev. Matthew, (TLS) On Special Assignment. Ascension St John, Owasso
La Plante, Rev. David W., (OM) Retired.
La Rocca, Rev. Christopher, *OCD* (SR) [MON] Carmelite House of Prayer, Oakville, CA; [RTR] Carmelite House of Prayer, Oakville, CA
La Russa, Rev. Thomas George, *SDV* '19 (BUR) Mater Dei, Newport, VT
Laba, Rev. Gerald, *C.P.* '73 (PIT) [MON] St. Paul of the Cross Monastery, Pittsburgh, PA; [RTR] St. Paul of the Cross Retreat Center, Pittsburgh, PA
Laba, Rev. Gerald, *C.P.* '73 (NY) [MON] The Congregation of the Passion - St. Paul of the Cross Province, Jamaica, NY
Labacevic, Rev. Ihar, '06 (PRM) On Duty Outside Diocese. Air Force Chaplain Curia: (>MO) Offices and Directors
LaBaff, Rev. Arthur J., '66 (OG) Retired. Curia: Consultative Bodies Roman Catholic Community of Alexandria, Alexandria Bay, NY; St. Mary's of Clayton, Clayton, NY
Labaire, Rev. Steven M., '87 (WOR) Our Lady of Good Counsel, West Boylston, MA
Labak, Rev. Joseph L., '77 (CLV) Sacred Heart of Jesus, Wadsworth, OH
LaBarbera, Rev. Robert, '70 (OAK) Retired. [NUR] Mercy Retirement and Care Center, Oakland, CA
Labarda, Rev. Nathaniel C., '93 (HRT) The Saint Gregory Roman Catholic Church Corporation of Bristol, Connecticut, Bristol, CT
LaBarge, Rev. Christopher W., '85 (WIL) St. Francis De Sales, Salisbury, MD
Labat, Rev. Dennis C., '74 (NU) Curia: Offices and Directors Holy Redeemer, Marshall, MN; St. Mary, Cottonwood, MN; St. Mary, Tracy, MN; St. Michael, Milroy, MN
Labat, Rev. Sean, (RIC) Military Chap
LaBat, Rev. Sean J., '99 (SJP) On Duty Outside Diocese. Richmond, VA Curia: (>MO) Offices and Directors; Offices and Directors
Labatorio, Rev. Andrew, *C.I.C.M.* '03 (PH) Our Lady of Hope, Philadelphia, PA
LaBauve, Rev. J. Joel, '70 (BR) Retired.
LaBauve, Rev. Joel, (BR) Curia: Administration
Labbe, Rev. Clifton, *S.V.D.* '69 (LAF) St. Joseph, Maurice, LA
Labbe, Rev. Donavan J., '97 (LAF) St. Peter, Morrow, LA
Labbe, Rev. Wilfred P., '99 (PRT) Curia: Consultative Bodies; Leadership Saint Therese of Lisieux Parish, Sanford, ME; St. Matthew, Limerick, ME
LaBelle, Rev. Jeffrey T., *S.J.* '88 (MIL) [MON] Jesuit Community at Marquette University (Marquette Jesuit Associates, Inc.), Milwaukee, WI
LaBelle, Rev. Joseph, *O.M.I.* '92 (SAT) [COL] Oblate School of Theology, San Antonio, TX; [MON] De Mazenod House, San Antonio, TX
Labenz, Rev. Andrew, '17 (WCH) Our Lady of Lourdes, Pittsburg, KS
Labinski, Rev. Jacek W., '83 (TR) Curia: Leadership St. Hedwig, Trenton, NJ
LaBo, Very Rev. Timothy P., '86 (ORL) Curia: Advisory Boards, Commissions, Committees, and Councils; Deaneries Church of the Resurrection, Lakeland, FL; St. Anthony Catholic Church, Lakeland, FL; St. Joseph's, Lakeland, FL; St. Joseph's, Winter Haven, FL; [CAM] Florida Southern College Newman Center, Lakeland, FL
Laboe, Rev. Timothy A., '99 (DET) On Special Assignment. Sacred Heart Major Seminary, Detroit [SEM] Sacred Heart Major Seminary, Inc., Detroit, MI
Laborde, Rev. Lucas, *S.S.J.* '05 (P) Curia: Offices and Directors St. Mary, Corvallis, OR; [MON] Saint John Society, Corvallis, OR
Laborde, Rev. Lucas, (WDC) On Duty Outside Diocese.
Labosky, Rev. James M., '79 (R) Retired.
Laboy, Rev. Lorenzo, '13 (NY) Immaculate Conception, New York, NY; St. Elizabeth, New York, NY
Labrador, Rev. Rene, (BAK) St. Francis of Assisi Catholic Church of Bend, Inc., Bend, OR
LaBranche, Rev. Raymond, '94 (NEW) On Duty Outside Diocese. Redemptoris Mater Seminary, Quebec
Labre, Rev. Michael M., '07 (NO) St. James Major, New Orleans, LA
LaBrecque, Rev. Frederick, '67 (CHR) Retired.
LaBree, Rev. Paul, '03 (PRT) On Sick Leave.
Labrie, Rev. Jean-Paul, '82 (PRT) Curia: Consultative Bodies; Leadership St. John Vianney Parish, Fort Kent, ME; [CAM] University of Maine at Fort Kent, Fort Kent, ME; [RTR] Christian Life Center, Frenchville, ME
Labrie, Rev. Ray J., '03 (MAN) Immaculate Conception, Nashua, NH
Labrie, Rev. Robert G., '64 (BO) Retired.
LaBurt, Rev. Brian R., '86 (SAV) St. John the Evangelist, Valdosta, GA
Labus, Rev. Gregory T., '06 (BWN) Curia: Advisory

Boards, Commissions, Committees, and Councils; Offices and Directors St. Joseph, Edinburg, TX
LaCanne, Rev. Stephen J., '76 (STP) Retired.
LaCasse, Rev. Andre-Joseph, *O.P.* (COL) Holy Trinity, Somerset, OH; St. Joseph, Somerset, OH
Lacasse, Rev. Eugene, *O.C.S.O.* '54 (WOR) [MON] St. Joseph's Abbey (Cistercian Abbey of Spencer, Inc., Cistercian Order of the Strict Observance (Trappists)), Spencer, MA
LaCasse, Rev. James, *S.J.* '74 (FRS) Retired.
Lacasse, Rev. Robert, *O.M.I.* '59 (BO) [NUR] Immaculate Heart of Mary Residence, Tewksbury, MA
Lacerna, Rev. Rodolfo, '68 (ELP) Retired.
Lacey, Rev. Grant, '15 (SFS) Curia: Leadership [COL] Mount Marty University, Yankton, SD
Lacey, Rev. Joseph P., *S.J.* '71 (BAL) Retired. (>PH) [MON] Jesuit Community at St. Joseph's University, Merion Station, PA
Lacey, Rev. Michael, '78 (OAK) Retired. St. Leander, San Leandro, CA
Lacey, Rev. Robert Edward, '05 (SFS) Curia: (>MO) Offices and Directors Sacred Heart Parish of Yankton County, Yankton, SD; Saint Benedict Parish of Yankton County, Yankton, SD
Lach, Rev. Piotr, *MIC* '98 (JOL) Our Lady of Peace, Darien, IL
LaChance, Rev. Matthew G., '03 (TLS) St. Henry, Owasso, OK
LaChance, Rev. Roger, (B) Curia: Offices and Directors
LaChance, Rev. Roger, '67 (B) Retired.
LaChapelle, Rev. Hector, *M.S.* '68 (R) Retired. St. Stephen the First Martyr, Sanford, NC
Lache-Avila, Rev. Jose Rodolfo, '81 (CHR) St. John of the Cross, Batesburg-Leesville, SC
Lachica, Rev. Jose Nestor P., '02 (MO) Curia: Offices and Directors
Lachowitzer, Very Rev. Charles V., '90 (STP) Curia: Consultative Bodies; Leadership
Lachowitzer, Very Rev. Charles Vincent, '90 (STP) St. Gerard Majella, Brooklyn Park, MN
Lack, Rev. Chris, '90 (CIN) St. Dominic, Cincinnati, OH
Lackenmier, Rev. James R., *CSC* (FTW) [MON] Congregation of Holy Cross, United States Province of Priests and Brothers, Notre Dame, IN
Lackie, Rev. Daniel, *O.F.M.* '96 (LA) Old Mission Santa Barbara, Santa Barbara, CA
Lackland, Rev. Anthony F., '06 (DAL) Christ the King Catholic Parish, Dallas, TX
LaCombe, Rev. C. Terrence, '87 (GB) Retired.
Lacovic, Rev. Lawrence L., '69 (ALT) Retired. SS. Cyril and Methodius, Windber, PA; St. Anthony of Padua, Windber, PA
LaCroix, Rev. Charles, '05 (FAR) St. Brigid of Ireland Church of Cavalier, Cavalier, ND; St. Patrick's Church of Crystal, Crystal, ND
LaCroix, Rev. Robert A., '98 (DET) Holy Family Parish Novi, Novi, MI
Lacroix, Rev. Stephen A., *C.S.C.* '08 (FTW) Christ the King, South Bend, IN; [COL] University of Notre Dame Du Lac, Notre Dame, IN
LaCruz, Rev. Cecilio, *Sch.P.* '59 (SJN) Colegio Calasanz, San Juan, PR
LaCuesta, Rev. Don A., '06 (DET) Our Lady of Mount Carmel Parish Temperance, Temperance, MI
Lacy, Rev. Aidan, '93 (PMB) St. Patrick, Palm Beach Gardens, FL
Laczko, Rev. Msgr. T. Ansgar, '60 (WDC) Retired.
Ladd, Rev. John O., '79 (GLD) Retired.
Ladda, Rev. Paul, '93 (BUF) St. John Gualbert, Cheektowaga, NY
Ladkau, Rev. William D., '84 (CHR) Retired.
Ladzinski, Rev. Msgr. Casimir H., '62 (TR) Retired. [MON] Villa Vianney, Trenton, NJ
Laferrera, Rev. Msgr. John J., '73 (NEW) Retired.
Laferrera, Rev. Robert G., '88 (NEW) Retired. Our Lady of the Blessed Sacrament, Roseland, NJ
Lafey, Rev. Harold, (PHX) St. Agnes Roman Catholic Parish, Phoenix, AZ
Lafey, Rev. Kevin, *O.Carm.* '72 (PHX) [MON] St. Therese Priory, Phoenix, AZ
Laffey, Rev. Matthew T., *O.S.B.* '00 (ALT) [CAM] Penn State Catholic Community, University Park, PA; [CAM] Penn State University, University Park, University Park, PA
Laffey, Rev. Matthew T., *O.S.B.* '00 (GBG) [MON] Saint Vincent Archabbey, Latrobe, PA
Laflamme, Rev. Steven, '09 (DUL) Holy Spirit, Two Harbors, MN
Laflamme, Rev. Steven, '09 (DUL) Curia: Leadership; Offices and Directors St. Mary, Silver Bay, MN
LaFleur, Rev. Luke, '18 (ALX) Curia: Miscellaneous / Other Offices St. Juliana, Alexandria, LA
LaFleur, Rev. Paul J., '85 (LAF) St. Joseph, Evangeline, LA
Lafontaine, Rev. James, *S.J.* '87 (RC) St. Bridget, Rosebud, SD; St. Charles Borromeo, St. Francis, SD; [MON] Kino Jesuit Community, Mission, SD
Lafontaine, Rev. James, *S.J.* '87 (RC) St. Agnes, Parmelee, SD; St. Francis Mission, St. Francis, SD
Laforet, Very Rev. Albert, '02 (AUS) Curia: Leadership St. Thomas Aquinas Catholic Parish, College Station, TX; [EFT] Diocese of Austin Pension Plan and Trust, Austin, TX
LaFramboise, Rev. Andrew S., '14 (SAG) Curia: Leadership Saint Elizabeth of Hungary Parish of Reese, Reese, MI; Saint Frances Xavier Cabrini Parish of Vassar, Vassar, MI
Laframboise, Rev. Ross, '03 (FAR) Curia: Offices and Directors Holy Spirit Church of Fargo, Fargo, ND
LaFreniere, Very Rev. Thomas R., '09 (PMB) Curia: Leadership St. Paul of the Cross, North Palm Beach, FL
Lagarde, Rev. Benedicto, *M.J.* '97 (BWN) Saint Anne, Penitas, TX
Lagattuta, Rev. Enzie, '78 (SJ) Retired.
Lagco, Rev. Policarp, (RIC) On Leave.
Lager, Rev. Brian, '12 (SAL) Curia: Advisory Boards, Commissions, Committees, and Councils; Consultative Bodies Sacred Heart Parish, Colby, Inc., Colby, KS
Lager, Rev. John, *O.F.M. Cap.* (DEN) [MON] St. Francis of Assisi Friary, Denver, CO
Lagges, Rev. Patrick, (CHI) Retired.
Lagges, Rev. Patrick R., '77 (TUC) Curia: Tribunal
Lagges, Rev. Msgr. Patrick R., '77 (CHI) Curia: Tribunal
Laghezza, Rev. Pasquale, *SS.CC.* '60 (LA) Retired. [MON] Congregation of the Sacred Hearts of Jesus and Mary, La Verne, CA
Laghezza, Rev. Pasquale V., *SS.CC.* '60 (NY) Chap, New York City Veterans Administration Hosp, New York
Lagiovane, Rev. John M., '92 (NY) St. Joseph, Somers, NY
Lago, Rev. Danilo, *S.X.* '77 (PAT) [MON] Xaverian Missionary Fathers, Wayne, NJ
Lago, Rev. William J. P., '99 (TR) St. Denis, Manasquan, NJ
Lagodinski, Rev. Dale, '72 (FAR) Curia: Leadership St. John's Church of Wahpeton, Wahpeton, ND
Lagos, Rev. Jose Maria, *O.S.B.* '12 (TLS) [MON] Our Lady of the Annunciation of Clear Creek Abbey, Hulbert, OK
LaGuerre, Rev. Jean Gerard, '95 (BRK) Chap, The Mount Sinai Hosp of Queens Our Lady of Mount Carmel, Long Island City, NY; St. Joseph, Astoria, NY
Lagunilla, Rev. Ariel R., '06 (SAN) St. Boniface, Rowena, TX; St. Joseph's, Rowena, TX; St. Thomas, Miles, TX
Laguros, Rev. Mario, '96 (SR) Pastor of Assumption of Our Lady Catholic Church of Ferndale, A Corporation Sole, Ferndale, CA; Pastor of Our Lady of the Redwoods Catholic Church of Garberville, A Corporation Sole, Garberville, CA
Lahens, Rev. Albert, '95 (MIA) St. Edward, Pembroke Pines, FL
LaHood, Rev. Thomas G., '00 (WDC) Curia: Consultative Bodies; Deaneries Saint Mary of the Assumption, Upper Marlboro, MD
Lahoud, Rev. Msgr. Joseph F., '59 (SAM) Retired.
Lai, Rev. Joseph Toan, *C.Ss.R.* '17 (GAL) Sacred Heart Catholic Church, Richmond, TX
Lai, Rev. M. Robert Canh X, *O. Cist.* (SB) [MON] The Cistercian Congregation of the Holy Family, St. Joseph Monastery, Lucerne Valley, CA
Laible, Rev. Jeffrey G., '88 (PEO) On Duty Outside Diocese. Vicar General in the Archdiocese of the Military, USA
Laible, Rev. Msgr. Jeffrey G., (MO) Curia: Leadership; Offices and Directors
Laicha, Rev. Michael, '89 (HBG) St. Cecilia, Lebanon, PA
Laiju, Rev. Augustine K.M., '20 (GLP) San Rafael, San Rafael, NM; St. Teresa of Avila, Grants, NM
Laing, Rev. Vincent Thu, '87 (SAL) St. Frances Cabrini Parish, Hoxie, Inc., Hoxie, KS; St. Martin Parish, Seguin, Inc., Seguin, KS
Laini, Rev. Valerian, '69 (CHI) Retired.
Laird, Rev. Kenneth W., '75 (BR) Retired.
Laird, Rev. Martin, *O.S.A.* '90 (PH) [COL] Villanova University, Villanova, PA; [MON] St. Thomas Monastery, Villanova, PA
Laird, Rev. Martin L., '08 (ALX) Curia: Miscellaneous / Other Offices Mater Dolorosa, Plaucheville, LA
Laird, Rev. Martin S., *O.S.A.* '90 (PH) [MON] Saxony Hall, Rosemont, PA
Laird, Rev. Matthew F., '22 (FR) St. Joseph, Guardian of the Holy Family, East Falmouth, MA
Laird, Rev. William F., '75 (ROC) Curia: Tribunal St. Mary, Our Lady of the Hills, Honeoye, NY; St. Matthew Catholic Church Society, Livonia, NY
Laizer, Rev. Raphael L., '08 (SFR) St. Patrick, San Francisco, CA
Lajack, Rev. Jerome M., '66 (CLV) Retired.
Lajato, Rev. Anthony, *O.F.M.Conv.* '10 (CHI) [MIS] Saint Bonaventure Friary, ,
Lajiness, Rev. Msgr. Todd J., '95 (DET) On Special Assignment. Sacred Heart Major Seminary, Detroit Our Lady of Good Counsel Parish Plymouth, Plymouth, MI
LaJoie, Rev. Joseph, '13 (DEN) St. John XXIII Catholic Parish in Ft. Collins, Fort Collins, CO
Lajoie, Rev. Roland, *SM* '74 (STP) Retired.
Lakkisetti, Rev. Praveen, '17 (SAT) St. Mary, Stockdale, TX
Lakkisetti, Rev. Praveen, '17 (SAT) St. Pius X, San Antonio, TX
Lakra, Rev. Arun, (SCR) Ascension Parish, Forest City, PA; St. Katharine Drexel Parish, Pleasant Mount, PA
Lakra, Rev. Prabhu, '02 (LAN) Good Shepherd Parish Montrose, Montrose, MI; St. Robert Bellarmine Parish Flushing, Flushing, MI
Lakra, Rev. Thomas, '97 (BGP) On Duty Outside Diocese. Returned to Diocese in Varanasi, India
Lakra, Rev. Virchand, *I.M.S.* (AUS) St. Paul Chong Hasang, Harker Heights, TX
Lal, Rev. Joseph, '95 (LA) Ascension, Los Angeles, CA
LaLiberte, Rev. Nathan, '11 (STP) Nativity of the Blessed Virgin Mary, Bloomington, MN
Laliberte, Rev. Msgr. Robert, '73 (FAR) Retired.
Lally, Rev. Brendan G., *S.J.* '77 (PH) [MIS] Jesuit Fathers, , ; [MON] Jesuit Community at St. Joseph's University, Merion Station, PA
Lally, Rev. Joachim, *C.S.P.* '65 (NY) Retired.
Lally, Rev. Joachim, *C.S.P.* '65 (GR) Retired. Cathedral of St. Andrew, Grand Rapids, MI
Lally, Rev. Joachim, *C.S.P.* '65 (NY) Retired.
Lally, Rev. Martin, '78 (DEN) Retired.
LaLonde, Rev. Jason, *S.J.* '18 (FTW) [MIS] Jesuit Community, South Bend, IN
Lalor, Rev. Thomas, '66 (JKS) Retired.
Lalte, Rev. Stephen Van Lal Than, '20 (OWN) Holy Name of Jesus, Henderson, KY
Lam, Rev. Ba "Phillip" S., *C.R.M.* (SB) St. Mary Magdalene, Corona, CA
Lam, Rev. Hoang Chi, '06 (DET) Our Lady of Grace (Vietnamese) Parish Warren, Warren, MI
Lam, Rev. John, *S.D.B.* '71 (LA) St. Bridget, Los Angeles, CA; [MON] Dominic Savio Salesian Residence, Los Angeles, CA
Lam, Rev. Julio, '15 (CHI) Queen of All Nations, Hillside, IL
Lam, Rev. Peter Vu, '04 (SD) Pastor of Holy Family Catholic Parish, San Diego, a corporation sole, San Diego, CA
Lam, Rev. Tom, '08 (GAL) Epiphany of the Lord, Katy, TX
Lamanna, Rev. Michael J., *S.J.* '21 (SP) (>WDC) [MON] The Jesuit Community of St. Aloysius Gonzaga, Washington, DC
Lamanna, Rev. Thomas, *SJ* (SPK) [COL] Gonzaga University, Spokane, WA
Lamanna, Rev. Tom, *S.J.* (SPK) St. Aloysius, Spokane, WA
Lamansky, Rev. John D., '18 (DAV) Jesus Christ, Prince of Peace Roman Catholic Church of Clinton, Iowa, Clinton, IA
LaMar, Rev. Joseph P., *M.M.* '83 (NY) Retired. [MON] Maryknoll Fathers and Brothers (Catholic Foreign Mission Society of America, Inc.), Ossining, NY
LaMarca, Rev. Michael, '16 (BUF) Curia: Consultative Bodies Mary Immaculate, Pavilion, NY; St. Isidore, Perry, NY; St. Michael's R.C. Church Society, Warsaw, NY
LaMartina, Rev. Liborio J., *S.J.* '67 (BAL) [MIS] Colombiere Jesuit Community, Baltimore, MD
Lamas, Rev. Rodolfo, '80 (SJN) Divino Nino Jesus, Guaynabo, PR
Lamb, Rev. Gary, '83 (MEM) St. Anne's, Memphis, TN; St. Mary Church, Memphis, TN
Lamb, Rev. Patrick H., '83 (ALN) Queenship of Mary Parish, Northampton, PA
Lamb, Rev. Thomas J., '71 (NY) [MIS] Personal Prelature, ,
Lamb, Rev. Wes, '81 (SAV) Retired.
Lamba, Rev. Robain, '20 (SJ) St. Nicholas and St. William Catholic Parish, Los Altos, CA
Lambert, Rev. Curtis, '74 (CHI) Retired.
Lambert, Rev. James J., '80 (PT) Retired.
Lambert, Rev. John C., '84 (SCR) SS. Peter and Paul,

Plains, PA
Lambert, Rev. Matthew, *O.S.B.* '16 (GBG) [MON] Saint Vincent Archabbey, Latrobe, PA
Lambert, Rev. Peter, '72 (MIA) Retired.
Lambert, Rev. Peter S., '79 (DUL) Retired.
Lambert, Rev. Richard D., '80 (CR) St. Bernards, Thief River Falls, MN
Lambert, Very Rev. Richard I., '75 (PBR) Curia: Leadership Assumption of the Blessed Virgin, Youngstown, OH
Lambert, Rev. Timothy J., '90 (BRK) St. Columba, Brooklyn, NY
Lambrecht, Rev. Matthias, *OCD* '18 (SJ) [MON] Carmelite Monastery, Novitiate, San Jose, CA
Lambro, Rev. Edward J., (PAT) Retired. Curia: Leadership
Lamendola, Rev. Salvatore R., '90 (GBG) St. Joseph, Derry, PA; St. Martin, Derry, PA
Lamica, Rev. Alan J., '78 (OG) Bare Hill Correctional Facility, Malone Curia: Canonical Services; Consultative Bodies The Roman Catholic Church of St. Augustine in North Bangor, NY, North Bangor, NY
Lamirez, Rev. Roberto A., '95 (NEW) St. Thomas More, Fairfield, NJ
Lammers, Rev. Msgr. Donald W., '66 (JC) Retired.
Lammert, Rev. Edward, *O.F.M.* '58 (CIN) Retired.
LaMoine, Rev. Gary, '81 (CR) Retired.
LaMorte, Rev. Msgr. Joseph P., '81 (NY) Curia: Leadership; Offices and Directors
LaMorte, Rev. Richard, '66 (NY) [CAM] Marist College, Poughkeepsie, NY
Lamothe, Rev. Msgr. Daniel O., '62 (MAN) Retired.
Lamothe, Rev. Donat R., *A.A.* '62 (WOR) Retired. [MON] Assumptionists (Augustinians of the Assumption), Worcester, MA
Lamoureux, Rev. Matthew, *M.I.C.* '05 (JOL) St. Mary, Plano, IL; St. Patrick, Yorkville, IL
Lamoureux, Rev. Richard E., *A.A* '71 (WOR) [COL] Assumption University, Worcester, MA; [MON] Augustinians of the Assumption at Assumption University, Worcester, MA
Lamp, Rev. Edward, '82 (SP) Retired. Curia: Organizations (affiliated, inter-Diocesan, miscellaneous/ other)
Lampe, Rev. Michael, (STL) Immaculate Conception Catholic Church, Dardenne, Dardenne Prairie, MO
Lampe, Rev. Stephen J., '82 (MIL) Retired. Congregation of Our Lady of the Lakes, Random Lake, WI; Divine Savior Congregation, Fredonia, WI
Lampert, Rev. Vincent P., '91 (IND) St. Michael the Archangel Catholic Church, Brookville, Inc., Brookville, IN; St. Peter Catholic Church, Franklin County, Inc., Brookville, IN
Lamping, Rev. Thomas E., '84 (CHI) Retired.
Lampitt, Rev. Robert, '08 (PEO) St. John's Catholic Chapel, Champaign, IL; [CAM] Newman Foundation at the University of IL (St. John's Catholic Newman Center), Champaign, IL
Lampitt, Rev. Robert, (SFD) [CAM] Newman Connection, Inc., Teutopolis, IL
Lampron, Rev. Alfred J., '75 (PAT) St. Bernard's, Wharton, NJ
Lampron, Rev. Maurice W., '63 (MAN) Retired.
Lamy, Rev. Michael, '21 (NO) St. Ann Roman Catholic Church and Shrine, Metairie, Louisiana, Metairie, LA
Lana, Rev. Charles, '19 (PAT) Holy Family, Florham Park, NJ
Lanahan, Rev. Daniel J., *O.F.M.* '62 (PAT) Retired. [MON] St. Anthony Friary (Order of Friars Minor), Butler, NJ
Lancaster, Rev. Robert, '99 (SFE) Estancia Valley Catholic Parish, Moriarty, NM
Landa, Rev. Florencio, *C.P.* '63 (SJN) Nuestra Senora de la Piedad School, Carolina, PR
Landa, Rev. Salvador, '94 (ORG) St. Boniface, Anaheim, CA
Landauer, Rev. Joe, (WDC) [MIS] Prelature of the Holy Cross and Opus Dei, Washington, DC
Landauer, Rev. Joseph P., '78 (POD) Curia: Clergy and Religious Services
Landauer, Rev. Joseph P., (PIT) [MIS] Prelature of the Holy Cross and Opus Dei, Pittsburgh, PA
Landback, Rev. Robert N., '12 (HRT) Saint Kateri Tekakwitha Parish Corporation, Kent, CT
Landenwitch, Rev. Shawn R., '09 (CIN) Immaculate Conception, North Lewisburg, OH; Sacred Heart (St. Paris), St. Paris, OH; St. Mary, Urbana, OH; St. Mary of the Woods, Russells Point, OH; St. Michael Church, Mechanicsburg, OH; St. Patrick, Bellefontaine, OH
Landeza, Rev. Jayson J., '91 (OAK) Curia: Offices and Directors Divine Mercy Parish, Oakland, CA; St. Benedict, Oakland, CA
Landfried, Rev. Christopher, '21 (CHI) Santa Maria Del Popolo, Mundelein, IL; St. Elizabeth of the Trinity, Chicago, IL
Landgraff, Rev. Thomas A., *O.S.F.S.* '64 (TOL) Retired.
Landi, Rev. Lodovico Joseph, '90 (SFR) Retired. St. Cecilia, San Francisco, CA
Landicho, Rev. Rey D, (BAL) St. John, Westminster, MD; St. Joseph, Taneytown, MD
Landis, Rev. Gabriel, *O.S.B.* '04 (KCK) [MON] St. Benedict's Abbey, Atchison, KS
Landman, Rev. Max, '17 (VIC) On Administrative Leave.
Landman, Rev. Max A., *SJ* '16 (VIC) On Administrative Leave. (>CHI) [COL] Jesuit Community at Loyola University Chicago, Chicago, IL
Landrau Roman, Rev. Jose Antonio, (SJN) San Jorge, San Juan, PR
Landrigan, Rev. Benjamin, '21 (FTW) St. Vincent de Paul, Elkhart, IN
Landry, Rev. Bart, *C.S.P.* '07 (SAC) On Special Assignment. Curia: Offices and Directors
Landry, Rev. Bartholomew K., *C.S.P.* '07 (SFR) Old St. Mary's Cathedral & Chinese Mission, San Francisco, CA
Landry, Rev. Charles R., '83 (BR) The Congregation Of Saint Gabriel Roman Catholic Church, St. Gabriel, LA
Landry, Rev. Francis, *C.P.* '76 (NY) [MON] The Congregation of the Passion - St. Paul of the Cross Province, Jamaica, NY
Landry, Rev. Francis, *C.P.* '76 (SCR) [MON] Saint Ann's Passionist Monastery of Scranton PA, Scranton, PA
Landry, Rev. Michael Keith, '08 (LAF) Sacred Heart of Jesus, New Iberia, LA
Landry, Rev. Oneil Anthony, '47 (LAF) Retired.
Landry, Very Rev. Philip G., '88 (NO) Curia: Offices and Directors Cathedral - Basilica of St. Louis King of France, New Orleans, LA; [MIS] Catholic Cultural Heritage Center St. Mary Chapel, New Orleans, LA; [SHR] Shrine of St. Lazarus of Jerusalem, New Orleans, LA
Landry, Rev. Roger J., '99 (FR) On Duty Outside Diocese. Permanent Observer Mission of the Holy See to the UN
Landry, Rev. Thomas, '83 (WOR) Blessed Sacrament, Worcester, MA
Landwerlen, Rev. Paul E., '54 (IND) Retired.
Lane, Rev. Andrew F., '22 (PH) St. Timothy, Philadelphia, PA
Lane, Rev. Brian, '89 (RC) Curia: Leadership Holy Cross, Timber Lake, SD
Lane, Rev. Msgr. Frank P., '67 (COL) Retired.
Lane, Rev. George, *S.J.* '67 (DET) [MON] Colombiere Center, Clarkston, MI
Lane, Rev. James, (PHX) Retired.
Lane, Very Rev. John Thomas Joseph, *S.S.S.* '92 (CLV) St. Paschal Baylon, Highland Heights, OH; [MON] Congregation of the Blessed Sacrament Provincial House, Highland Heights, OH
Lane, Rev. Mark J., *C.O.* '83 (BRK) Assumption of the Blessed Virgin Mary, Brooklyn, NY; St. Boniface, Brooklyn, NY; [MON] Oratory of Saint Philip Neri, Congregation Pontifical Rite, Brooklyn, NY
Lane, Rev. Msgr. Mark Richard, '74 (RIC) Retired.
Lane, Rev. Michael, '74 (JOL) St. Jude, Joliet, IL
Lane, Rev. Timothy R., *C.J.* '95 (LA) [MON] St. Joseph Seminary (Josephite Fathers' Novitiate), Santa Maria, CA
Lanese, Rev. John, '73 (ALB) Retired.
Lang, Rev. Brian E., '98 (SY) St. Ann, Manlius, NY
Lang, Rev. Charles F., '75 (CIN) Retired.
Lang, Rev. Frederick, *C.PP.S.* '54 (CIN) Retired.
Lang, Rev. Hugh J., '56 (PIT) Retired.
Lang, Rev. Msgr. James P., '75 (SY) On Special Assignment. Curia: Leadership; Offices and Directors Church of the Annunciation, Clark Mills, NY; Epiphany Parish, Liverpool, NY; Immaculate Heart of Mary, Liverpool, NY; St. John the Evangelist, New Hartford, NY; St. Mary, Clinton, NY
Lang, Rev. James Paul, '75 (Y) Retired.
Lang, Rev. Joseph, '05 (DET) National Shrine of the Little Flower Basilica, Royal Oak, MI
Lang, Rev. Lawton, '16 (VEN) Curia: Leadership; Organizations (affiliated, inter-Diocesan, miscellaneous/ other) St. Thomas More Parish in Sarasota, Inc., Sarasota, FL
Lang, Rev. Michael P., '92 (TR) St. Joseph, Millstone Township, NJ
Langager, Rev. Matthew, '16 (SCL) SS. Peter and Paul, Gilman, MN; St. Elizabeth of Hungary, Foley, MN; St. Joseph's, Foley, MN
Langan, Rev. Jeffrey, '15 (POD) Curia: Clergy and Religious Services
Langan, Rev. Jeffrey J., '15 (NY) [MIS] Prelature of the Holy Cross and Opus Dei, New York, NY
Langan, Rev. John, *S.D.B.* '20 (NO) On Special Assignment. Archbishop Shaw High School (Salesians of St. John Bosco), Marrero, LA
Langan, Rev. John P., *S.J.* '72 (WDC) [COL] Georgetown University, Washington, DC
Langan, Rev. Patrick, (HRT) [MON] Legionaries of Christ, Cheshire, CT; [SEM] Novitiate of the Legion of Christ, Cheshire, CT
Langan, Rev. William J.P., '77 (SCR) St. John the Evangelist, Honesdale, PA
Langbiir, Rev. Lazarus, *CSSp* (PIT) [RTR] The Spiritan Center, Bethel Park, PA
Lange, Rev. Donald F., '70 (MAD) Retired.
Lange, Rev. Jeremiah, *O.S.B.* '13 (GBG) Assoc Chap, Excela Health - Latrobe Area Hosp, Latrobe
Lange, Rev. Jeremiah, *OSB* (ALT) Bishop Carroll Catholic High School, Ebensburg, PA; St. Nicholas, Nicktown, PA
Lange, Rev. Jeremiah (George), *O.S.B.* '13 (GBG) [MON] Saint Vincent Archabbey, Latrobe, PA
Lange, Rev. John J., *M.M.* '58 (NY) Retired. [MON] Maryknoll Fathers and Brothers (Catholic Foreign Mission Society of America, Inc.), Ossining, NY
Lange, Rev. Joshua L., '09 (COV) St. Henry, Elsmere, KY
Lange, Rev. Ronald, *S.V.D.* '71 (CHI) [MON] Divine Word Residence, Techny, IL
Lange, Rev. Steven J., '02 (RCK) [HOS] Saint Anthony Medical Center (OSF Saint Anthony Medical Center), Rockford, IL
Lange, Rev. Theodore, '09 (P) Shepherd of the Valley, Central Point, OR
Lange, Rev. Timothy John, '14 (DUL) Sacred Heart, Hackensack, MN; St. Agnes, Walker, MN
Lange, Rev. William T, '92 (PH) On Sick Leave. St. Maximilian Kolbe, West Chester, PA
Langenbrunner, Rev. Norman, '70 (CIN) Retired.
Langenbrunner, Rev. Steven, '17 (DUL) Curia: Leadership Holy Rosary, Grand Portage, MN; St. John, Grand Marais, MN
Langenderfer, Rev. Carl, *O.F.M.* '71 (IND) Holy Family Catholic Church, Oldenburg, Inc., Oldenburg, IN
Langenderfer, Rev. Max, *O.F.M.* '73 (CIN) Retired. [MON] St. Francis Seraph Friary, Cincinnati, OH
Langenkamp, Rev. Peter, '17 (CIN) On Special Assignment. Roma
Langevin, Rev. Dominic, *O.P.* '05 (WDC) [SEM] Dominican House of Studies, Washington, DC
Langevin, Very Rev. Paul Joseph, *O.F.M. Conv.* (CHI) [MIS] Franciscan Friars Retirement Corporation, Chicago, IL; [MON] Conventual Franciscans of St. Bonaventure Province, Chicago, IL
Langevin, Rev. Peter J., '16 (NOR) Curia: Leadership; Offices and Directors St. Patrick Cathedral, Norwich, CT; [EFT] The Donor Advised Funds of the Diocese of Norwich, Inc., Norwich, CT
Langford, Rev. Terry L., '96 (L) St. Aloysius, Shepherdsville, KY; St. Benedict, Lebanon Junction, KY
Langhans, Rev. Victor, (P) Retired.
Langhans, Rev. Victor E., '84 (HEL) Retired.
Langhorst, Rev. Randall, '92 (LIN) St. Elizabeth Ann Seton, North Platte, NE; St. Joseph's, Tobias, NE
Langley, Rev. Barry James, *OFM* '94 (NY) St. Francis of Assisi, New York, NY
Langley, Rev. Terence, *S.C.J.* '79 (MIL) Retired. [MON] St. Joseph's at Monastery Lake (Priests of the Sacred Heart), Franklin, WI
Langlois, Rev. Charles, '96 (LAF) Retired. [NUR] Consolata Home, New Iberia, LA
Langlois, Rev. Frederick M., '91 (HRT) Retired.
Langlois, Rev. John, *O.P.* '91 (CIN) St. Gertrude, Cincinnati, OH; [MON] St. Gertrude Priory, Cincinnati, OH
Langlois, Rev. William A., '74 (GR) Retired.
Langone, Rev. Robert, *S.A.* '89 (NY) [MON] Franciscan Friars of the Atonement, Minister General Office, Garrison, NY
Langsdorf, Rev. Karl, '72 (JOL) St. Francis Xavier, Joliet, IL
Langston, Rev. Micheas, *O.S.B.* '65 (IND) [MON] St. Meinrad Archabbey, St. Meinrad, IN
Langton, Rev. Bernard F., *O.P.* '69 (PRO) [MON] St. Thomas Aquinas Priory at Providence College, Providence, RI
Laniauskas, Rev. Lukas, *SJ* '15 (CLV) Gesu, University Heights, OH; [COL] John Carroll Jesuit Community, University Heights, OH
Lanik, Rev. Robert H., '11 (TYL) Curia: Advisory Boards, Commissions, Committees, and Councils; Leadership Cathedral of the Immaculate Conception, Tyler, TX; [MIS] Catholic Parish and Mission Assistance Program, Tyler, TX

Lankenau, Rev. Tom, *S.J.* (HEL) St. Philip Benizi, Darby, MT

Lankford, Rev. Christopher, '16 (JOL) St. John the Baptist, Winfield, IL

Lankford, Rev. Michael G., '92 (TR) On Duty Outside Diocese. Veterans Administration Curia: (>MO) Offices and Directors

Lannan, Rev. Paul A., '66 (LA) Retired. St. Paul the Apostle, Los Angeles, CA

Lannen, Rev. Daniel T., *O.S.F.S.* '11 (ALN) [COL] DeSales University, Center Valley, PA; [MON] Oblates of St. Francis de Sales, Center Valley, PA

Lanning, Rev. Michael J., '78 (CLV) St. Angela Merici, Fairview Park, OH

Lannon, Rev. Timothy, *S.J.* (CHI) [MON] Detroit Province of the Society of Jesus - Provincial Office, Chicago, IL

Lannon, Rev. Timothy, *S.J.* (CIN) [MIS] St. Xavier Church Property Corporation, Cincinnati, OH

Lannon, Rev. Timothy R., *S.J.* '86 (CHI) [ASN] Jesuit Seminary Association, Chicago, IL; [MIS] Ignatius Productions, Inc., Chicago, IL; [MIS] Jesuit International Missions, Inc., Chicago, IL; [MIS] Society of Jesus Worldwide, Chicago, IL; [MIS] The Jesuit Partnership, Chicago, IL; [MIS] USA Midwest Province of the Society of Jesus, Inc., Chicago, IL

Lanoue, Rev. Marc L., '09 (BAL) On Leave. St. John the Evangelist, Columbia, MD

Lanser, Rev. Wilbert, (GB) Retired. [MON] St. Fidelis Friary, Appleton, WI

Lanshima, Rev. Peter, (SAV) St. James, Savannah, GA

Lanterman, Rev. Robert, '12 (Y) On Leave.

Lantry, Rev. Stephen C., *S.J.* '81 (SEA) Bellarmine Preparatory School, Tacoma, WA

Lantsberger, Rev. John, '76 (SFS) Saint Mary Parish of Minnehaha County School, Dell Rapids, SD

Lantz, Rev. Msgr. David S., '78 (SFD) Christ the King, Springfield, IL

Lantz, Rev. Gary, *S.C.J.* '80 (MIL) Retired. [MON] Sacred Heart at Monastery Lake, Franklin, WI

Lanuevo, Rev. Victor, '75 (HON) Retired.

Lanza, Rev. Daniel A., *M.M.* '59 (NY) Retired.

Lanza, Rev. Steven M., '81 (CHI) Divine Mercy, Winnetka, IL

Lanza, Rev. Thomas, '20 (MET) St. Peter the Apostle, New Brunswick, NJ; [CAM] Catholic Center at Rutgers University, New Brunswick, NJ

Lanzaderas, Rev. Francisco, '82 (NY) Blessed Sacrament, Staten Island, NY

Lanzrath, Rev. John, '88 (WCH) Curia: Offices and Directors St. Joseph, Wichita, KS

Lanzrath, Rev. John P., '88 (WCH) Chap, El Dorado Corr Fac St. John the Evangelist, El Dorado, KS

Lap, Rev. Gilbert D., '03 (RVC) St. Frances Cabrini, Coram, NY

LaPacz, Rev. Patrick, *O. Praem.* '18 (GB) [MON] St. Norbert Abbey, De Pere, WI

LaPalme, Rev. Paul M., '97 (ALX) Congregation of Mary, Mother of Jesus Roman Catholic Church, Woodworth, Louisiana, Woodworth, LA

LaPastina, Rev. Cyprian P., '97 (BGP) St. John's Catholic Church, Stamford, Connecticut, Stamford, CT

Lape, Rev. Crespo, *M.J.* '89 (LA) Precious Blood, Los Angeles, CA; St. Kevin, Los Angeles, CA

Lape, Rev. Lydell T., '90 (OM) St. Mary, Bellevue, NE

Lape, Rev. Steven W., '99 (ROC) The Parish of the Holy Family, Monroe County, NY, Rochester, NY

Lapensky, Rev. John G., '77 (STP) Most Holy Trinity, Veseli, MN; [CEM] Most Holy Trinity Cemetery, Veseli, MN; [CEM] St. John's Cemetery, Veseli, MN

Lapera, Rev. John M., '84 (SCR) Curia: Offices and Directors St. Gregory, Clarks Green, PA

Laperle, Rev. Theodore R., '54 (WOR) Retired.

Lapeyre, Rev. Louis Charles, '13 (DET) Our Lady on the River Parish Marine City, Marine City, MI

Lapeyrouse, Rev. Brett, '19 (HT) Curia: Administration

LaPlante, Rev. Bob J., '95 (CR) St. Francis Xavier's, Lake Park, MN; St. Mary of the Lakes, Detroit Lakes, MN

LaPlante, Rev. Roland M., '62 (HRT) Retired.

LaPlante, Rev. Roland M., '56 (HRT) Retired.

Lapointe, Rev. J. Donald R., (SPR) Retired. Curia: Tribunal [MIS] Mary's House of Prayer, Chicopee, MA

LaPointe, Rev. Laurence A.M., '70 (NOR) Curia: Leadership; Offices and Directors Corpus Christi Catholic Parish, Willimantic, CT; [CAM] Campus Ministry, Willimantic, CT; [MIS] Sagrado Corazon de Jesus, Inc. of Windham, Windham, CT

Lapomarda, Rev. Vincent A., *S.J.* '64 (WOR) [MON] Jesuits of the Holy Cross, Inc., Worcester, MA

Lapommeray, Rev. Rodney, '12 (BRK) Curia: Organizations (affiliated, inter-Diocesan, miscellaneous/ other) St. Agatha's, Brooklyn, NY

LaPore, Rev. Arthur, '76 (JOL) Retired.

LaPorte, Rev. Gerard B., *C.Ss.R.* '65 (NO) Retired. (>STL) [MON] St. Clement Health Care Center, Liguori, MO

Laporte, Rev. Paul J., '65 (PRO) Retired.

Lapp, Rev. Christopher R., '13 (FTW) Curia: Offices and Directors St. Joseph, Mishawaka, IN

Lappe, Rev. Derek J., '00 (SEA) Our Lady, Star of the Sea, Bremerton, WA

Lappe, Rev. Joseph L., *M.I.C.* '18 (MIL) Congregation of the Holy Rosary of Pompeii, Kenosha, WI

Lara, Rev. Bernardo, '15 (SD) Pastor of Sacred Heart Catholic Parish, Brawley, a corporation sole, Brawley, CA; Pastor of Saint Joseph Catholic Parish, Westmorland, a corporation sole, Westmorland, CA; Pastor of Saint Margaret Mary Catholic Parish, Brawley, a corporation sole, Brawley, CA; [MIS] Sacred Heart Catholic Parish Brawley in Brawley, CA Real Property Support Corporation, Brawley, CA

Lara, Rev. Isaac, '14 (CHI) St. Catherine Laboure, Glenview, IL

Lara, Rev. Josue, '94 (RCK) St. Nicholas, Aurora, IL

Lara, Rev. Rafael, (LA) Guardian Angel, Pacoima, CA

Laracy, Rev. Joseph R., '13 (NEW) On Duty Outside Diocese. Casa Santa Maria, Roma [COL] Seton Hall University, South Orange, NJ

Lara-Hernandez, Rev. Fernando E., '11 (LC) St. John the Baptist, Norwalk, WI; St. Patrick, Sparta, WI

Laramie, Rev. Joseph W., *S.J.* '11 (MIL) [MIS] Apostleship of Prayer, Pope's Worldwide Prayer Network, Milwaukee, WI; [MON] Jesuit Community at Marquette University (Marquette Jesuit Associates, Inc.), Milwaukee, WI

L'Arche, Rev. Jeffrey, '75 (ALB) Chap, Teresian House St. Mary, Amsterdam, NY; St. Stephen, Hagaman, NY; [NUR] Teresian House, Albany, NY

L'Arche, Rev. Jeffrey M., *M.S.* '75 (HRT) [MIS] Missionaries of LaSalette, Hartford, CT

Largaespada, Very Rev. Luis Roger, '09 (MIA) Curia: Clergy and Religious Services; Leadership St. Hugh, Miami, FL

Large, Rev. John, '15 (TR) St. Theresa, Little Egg Harbor Twp, NJ

Large, Rev. John J., '75 (PH) St. Anselm, Philadelphia, PA

Larger, Rev. Raymond E., '77 (CIN) The Cathedral Basilica of St. Peter in Chains, Cincinnati, OH

Largoza, Rev. Rogelio A. S., (RIC) On Special Assignment. Saint Mary of the Presentation, Suffolk St. Mary of the Presentation, Suffolk, VA

Larion, Rev. Steven, '06 (SD) Pastor of Our Mother of Confidence Catholic Parish, San Diego, a corporation sole, San Diego, CA; [MIS] Our Mother of Confidence Catholic Parish in San Diego, CA Real Property Support Corporation, San Diego, CA

Larios Martinez, Rev. Sergio Alfonso, *O.SS.T.* '16 (PCE) La Resurreccion, Ponce, PR

Lariviere, Rev. Robert D., '78 (PRT) Immaculate Heart of Mary Parish, Auburn, ME

Larkin, Rev. Msgr. Alexander C., '67 (SJ) Retired.

Larkin, Rev. Andrew, (SAV) Curia: Leadership

Larkin, Rev. Andrew, '18 (SAV) Curia: Offices and Directors Cathedral Basilica of St. John the Baptist, Savannah, GA

Larkin, Rev. Brian, (DEN) Our Lady of Lourdes Catholic Parish in Denver, Denver, CO; St. Louis-King of France Catholic Parish in Englewood, Englewood, CO

Larkin, Rev. Dan, (CIN) [CAM] Xavier University Dorothy Day Center for Faith & Justice, Cincinnati, OH

Larkin, Rev. Msgr. Kevin John, '59 (LA) Retired.

Larkin, Rev. Michael J., '59 (STA) Retired.

Larkin, Rev. Nicholas, (DEN) Assumption of the Blessed Virgin Mary Catholic Parish in Denver, Denver, CO

Larlick, Rev. Matthew R., '15 (HBG) Sacred Heart of Jesus, Lewisburg, PA

LaRocca, Rev. Frank, *S.J.* '98 (CHI) (>SY) [MON] Jesuits at LeMoyne, Inc., Syracuse, NY

LaRocca, Rev. Jack, '75 (SJ) Retired.

LaRocca, Rev. John J., *S.J.* '75 (CIN) Retired. [MON] Cincinnati Jesuit Community, Cincinnati, OH

Laroche, Rev. Brendon M., '15 (ALN) Curia: Leadership St. Thomas More, Allentown, PA

Laroche, Rev. Leonidas B., '61 (BUR) Retired.

Laroche, Rev. Victor, *O.P.* '02 (NO) St. Anthony of Padua, New Orleans, LA

Larochelle, Rev. John L., '21 (WOR) Divine Mercy Parish, Blackstone, MA

Larochelle, Rev. Maurice R., '87 (MAN) Ste. Marie, Manchester, NH

LaRocque, Rev. Msgr. Richard P., '63 (NOR) Retired.

LaRosa, Rev. John J., '81 (PH) Retired.

LaRose, Rev. Joseph, *S.M.M.* (BO) Christ the King, Brockton, MA; Our Lady of Lourdes, Brockton, MA; St. Edith Stein, Brockton, MA

Larrea, Rev. Hector, '94 (NEW) St. Columba, Newark, NJ

Larrea, Rev. Luis Eduardo, *M.F.E.* '77 (TYL) St. Peter Claver, Tyler, TX

Larrivee, Rev. Leo J., *S.S.* '77 (SEA) On Duty Outside Diocese.

Larrivee, Rev. Leo J., *P.S.S.* '77 (BAL) Our Lady of the Angels Catholic Community, Catonsville, MD; [MON] Society of St. Sulpice, Province of the United States, Baltimore, MD

Larroque, Rev. Msgr. H. Alexandre, '55 (LAF) Retired.

Larry, Rev. Anthony J., *O.S.F.S.* '67 (WIL) Retired.

Larsen, Rev. Kevin J., '93 (ARL) St. John the Apostle, Leesburg, VA

Larson, Rev. Dustin, '18 (MAR) [CAM] Catholic Campus Ministry-Northern Michigan University, Marquette, MI

Larson, Rev. Jan, '68 (SEA) Retired.

Larson, Rev. John L., *MIC* '06 (MIL) Congregation of the Holy Rosary of Pompeii, Kenosha, WI

Larson, Rev. Lawrence A., '77 (BGP) St. Thomas Church Fairfield Connecticut, Fairfield, CT

LaRue, Rev. Caleb J., '14 (LIN) On Academic Leave. Catholic Univ of America, Washington DC Curia: Leadership St. Thomas Aquinas, Lincoln, NE; [MIS] Chancery, Lincoln, NE

Las, Rev. A. Stefan, '88 (PAT) Curia: Leadership

Las, Rev. A. Stefan, '88 (PAT) Holy Rosary, Passaic, NJ

Las, Rev. Wlodzimierz R., *S.D.S.* '86 (NEW) St. Joseph, Hackensack, NJ

LaSalle, Rev. Donald Gregory, *S.M.M.* '83 (HRT) [MIS] Lourdes Shrine Guild, Inc., Litchfield, CT; [MON] Montfort Missionaries, Litchfield, CT

Lascelle, Rev. Roger L., '77 (DEN) Retired. (>MAN) St. Anthony of Padua, Manchester, NH

Lascelles, Rev. William A., '73 (PBR) Retired.

Lasch, Rev. Msgr. Kenneth E., '62 (PAT) Retired.

Laschuk, Rev. Alexander Michael, '10 (STN) [MIS] Metropolitan Andrey Sheptytsky Institute of Eastern Christian Studies, Flagstaff, AZ

LaSelva, Rev. Giacomo, *O.F.M.* '10 (NY) [MON] Franciscan Province of the Immaculate Conception, New York, NY

Lasheras, Rev. Antonio, *O.A.R.* '62 (ELP) Our Lady of the Light, El Paso, TX; Santo Nino De Atocha, El Paso, TX

Lasheras Gonzalez, Rev. Jesus Antonio, (LSC) St. Anthony Parish, Anthony, Inc., Anthony, NM

Laska, Rev. William M., '88 (E) Immaculate Conception, Brookville, PA

Laske, Rev. Kenneth S., '58 (CHI) Retired.

Laski, Rev. Adam J., '15 (SUP) Curia: Leadership; Offices and Directors Holy Trinity, Haugen, WI; Our Lady of Lourdes, Rice Lake, WI; St. John Evangelist, Birchwood, WI; St. Joseph, Rice Lake, WI

Laskiewicz, Rev. Aaron R., '18 (MIL) St. Mary Congregation, Hales Corners, WI

Laskowski, Rev. Keith R., '02 (ALN) Our Lady of Mercy Parish, Easton, PA; St. Anthony of Padua, Easton, PA

Lasky, Friar Michael, *OFM, Conv.* (HBG) Our Lady of Hope, Coal Township, PA

Laslavich, Rev. Luke, *O.Praem.* '94 (ORG) [MON] Norbertine Fathers of Orange, Inc., Silverado, CA

Laslo, Rev. Cristian, '09 (ROM) St. Mary, Dearborn, MI

Lasota, Rev. Stanislaw, *C.R.* '79 (CHI) St. Hyacinth Basilica, Chicago, IL

Lasrado, Rev. Francis, '80 (RVC) Infant Jesus, Port Jefferson, NY

Lasrado, Rev. Max, '92 (RCK) Blessed Sacrament Catholic Church, North Aurora, IL

Lastimosa, Rev. Philip Neri, *O.Cist.* '10 (DAL) [MON] Our Lady of Dallas Cistercian Abbey, Irving, TX

Lastra, Rev. Darwin J., '15 (PAT) Our Lady of Good Counsel, Pompton Plains, NJ

Lasuba, Rev. John Lugala, '93 (WIN) Christ the King, Byron, MN; Holy Family, Kasson, MN; St. John Baptist de La Salle, Dodge Center, MN

Lasutaz, Rev. Joel, *SSS* '97 (PBL) St. Peter the Apostle, Rocky Ford, CO

Latcovich, Rev. Mark, '81 (CLV) Curia: Advisory Boards, Commissions, Committees, and Councils [MIS] Center for Pastoral Leadership Services, Inc., Wickliffe, OH; [SEM] Borromeo Seminary, Wickliffe, OH; [SEM] Saint Mary Seminary and Graduate School of Theology, Wickliffe, OH

Lathem, Rev. Msgr. E. Christopher, '65 (CHR) Retired.

Lathrop, Rev. Robert A., '01 (DAV) Holy Trinity Church of Keota/Harper, Iowa, Keota, IA; Ss. Joseph and Cabrini Catholic Church, East Pleasant Plain, IA; St.

Mary Church of Sigourney, Iowa, Sigourney, IA
Latkowski, Rev. Waldemar, *CSSR* (CHI) Curia: Leadership Our Lady of Czestochowa and Charity Parish, Cicero, IL
Latosynski, Rev. Roger, '84 (PT) St. Patrick, Apalachicola, FL
Latronico, Rev. Philip F. A., '86 (NEW) Curia: Organizations (affiliated, inter-Diocesan, miscellaneous/ other) [MIS] The Community of God's Love, Rutherford, NJ
Latsko, Rev. Andrew, '92 (CHL) Retired.
Lattner, Rev. Stephen, *O.S.B.* '07 (CIN) Holy Name, Trenton, OH; Our Lady of Sorrows, Monroe, OH
Latus, Rev. Charles J., '68 (ROC) Retired.
Latzko, Rev. Frank J., '84 (CHI) St. Teresa of Avila, Chicago, IL
Lau, Rev. Ignatius, '58 (ORG) Retired. Immaculate Heart of Mary, Santa Ana, CA
Lau, Rev. John-Raymond, (OAK) Sacred Heart, Oakland, CA
Lau, Rev. Michael, '61 (P) Retired.
Laubenthal, Rev. Allan R., '61 (CLV) Retired.
Laude, Rev. Segundino R., (GBG) Mt. St. Peter, New Kensington, PA; St. Joseph, New Kensington, PA; St. Margaret Mary, Lower Burrell, PA; St. Mary of Czestochowa, New Kensington, PA
Lauder, Rev. Robert E., '60 (BRK) Retired.
Laudick, Rev. John R., '64 (TOL) Retired.
Laudwein, Rev. James R, *S.J.* '62 (SJ) [MON] Sacred Heart Jesuit Center, Los Gatos, CA
Lauenstein, Rev. Gary, *C.Ss.R.* '71 (NY) Immaculate Conception, Bronx, NY
Lauer, Rev. Douglas J., '94 (COV) On Sick Leave.
Laughery, Rev. Kevin Michael, '83 (SFD) Curia: Leadership St. James, St. Jacob, IL; St. Jerome, Troy, IL
Laughlin, Rev. James J., '91 (BO) Curia: Consultative Bodies St. Ann, Wayland, MA; St. John the Evangelist, Wellesley, MA; St. Paul, Wellesley, MA; St. Zepherin, Wayland, MA
Laughlin, Rev. Msgr. Martin T., '52 (CHR) Retired.
Laughlin, Rev. Msgr. Martin T., '52 (DUB) Retired.
Launderville, Rev. Dale, *O.S.B.* '79 (SCL) [MON] St. John's Abbey, of the Order of St. Benedict, Collegeville, MN; [SEM] St. John's School of Theology and Seminary, Collegeville, MN
Laupe Dorvil, Rev. Socrate, *C.M.* '08 (PCE) Nuestra Senora de la Medalla Milagrosa, Ponce, PR
Laurance, Rev. John D., *S.J.* '70 (MIL) [MON] Jesuit Community at Marquette University (Marquette Jesuit Associates, Inc.), Milwaukee, WI
Laurent, Rev. Sterling, (MIA) St. Kieran, Miami, FL; [HOS] Mercy Hospital, Inc., Miami, FL
Laurenzo, Rev. James, '69 (DM) Retired.
Lauri, Rev. John F., '73 (NY) Parish of Sts. Peter and Paul and St. Ursula, Mount Vernon, NY; St. Ursula, Mount Vernon, NY
Lauricella, Rev. Andrew R., '12 (BUF) St. Brendan on the Lake, Newfane, NY; St. John the Baptist Roman Catholic Congregation, Lockport, NY
Laurick, Rev. Richard, *C.S.C.* (FTW) [MIS] Holy Cross House, Notre Dame, IN
Lause, Rev. James, *O.F.M.* '98 (STL) St. Anthony of Padua Catholic Church, St. Louis, MO; [MON] Franciscan Friary of St. Anthony of Padua, St. Louis, MO
Lause, Rev. Richard L., *C.M.* '77 (STL) [MON] Congregation of the Mission, Perryville, MO
Lautz, Rev. Boniface, *O.S.B.* '60 (B) [MON] Monastery of the Ascension, Jerome, ID
Lauzon, Rev. Kris C., '91 (OG) Catholic Community of Holy Name and St. Matthew's, Au Sable Forks, NY; The Roman Catholic Community of Keeseville, Keeseville, NY
Lavagetto, Rev. Xavier, *O.P.* '96 (SJ) Catholic Community at Stanford, Stanford, CA
Lavagetto, Rev. Xavier M., *O.P.* '96 (SFR) St. Raymond, Menlo Park, CA
Lavallee, Rev. Michael N., '05 (WOR) St. Peter, Northbridge, MA
Lavalley, Rev. Msgr. Richard G., '64 (BUR) St. Francis Xavier, Winooski, VT
Lavan, Rev. Michael G., '06 (RCK) Curia: Leadership Holy Angels, Aurora, IL
Lavaroni, Rev. Rino, '67 (NEW) Retired.
Lavastida, Very Rev. Jose I., '87 (NO) Curia: Leadership; (>MO) Offices and Directors Blessed Francis Xavier Seelos, New Orleans, LA
Lavelle, Rev. Edward R., '63 (HBG) Retired. Curia: Offices and Directors
Lavelle, Rev. John-Michael, '00 (Y) Curia: Leadership St. Michael, Canfield, OH
Lavely, Rev. Charles J., *C.S.C.* '65 (FTW) [MIS] Holy Cross House, Notre Dame, IN
LaVerde, Rev. Calogero N., '68 (CAM) Retired.
Laverde, Rev. Luis F., '89 (BRK) Blessed Sacrament - Saint Sylvester, Brooklyn, NY
LaVerghetta, Rev. Msgr. Richard D., '86 (TR) St. Joan of Arc, Marlton, NJ
LaVergne, Rev. Korey, '18 (LAF) St. Edward, Church Point, LA
Laverone, Rev. Ken, *O.F.M.* '79 (LA) [MIS] The Cause of Blessed Junipero Serra, Santa Barbara, CA
Laverone, Rev. Kenneth J., *O.F.M.* '79 (MRY) On Special Assignment. Judicial Vicar, Diocesan Tribunal, Monterey Curia: Tribunal
Laverty, Rev. Seamus, '68 (SEA) Retired.
Lavery, Rev. Bruce Dean, '67 (ORG) Retired.
Laviano, Rev. Vincent, *O.F.M.* '74 (SP) [MON] St. Anthony Friary (St. Petersburg) Franciscan Friars-Holy Name Province, Inc., St. Petersburg, FL
Lavich, Rev. David, *O.C.S.O.* '73 (WOR) [MON] St. Joseph's Abbey (Cistercian Abbey of Spencer, Inc., Cistercian Order of the Strict Observance (Trappists)), Spencer, MA
Lavilla, Rev. Rafael, '05 (STA) Curia: Evangelization St. John the Baptist, Jacksonville, FL
Lavin, Rev. John J., '64 (PRO) Retired.
Lavin, Rev. Peter, *A.M.* (ORG) Curia: Leadership
Lavin, Rev. Thomas, *O.F.M.* (WDC) Our Lady of Good Counsel High School, Olney, MD
Lavoie, Rev. Merle L., '68 (SPR) Retired.
Lawinger, Rev. Michael J., '21 (MIL) Christ King Congregation, Wauwatosa, WI; St. Bernard's Congregation, Wauwatosa, WI
Lawir, Rev. Anthony, '98 (PRT) Good Shepherd Parish, Saco, ME
Lawler, Rev. Bruce A., '80 (SC) Curia: Offices and Directors All Saints Roman Catholic Church, Le Mars, IA; Gehlen Catholic School, Le Mars, IA
Lawler, Rev. David J., '62 (IND) Retired.
Lawler, Rev. Msgr. Joseph A., '61 (BEL) Retired.
Lawler, Rev. Scott J., '16 (GLD) Saint Monica of Afton, Afton, MI; Saint Paul of Onaway, Onaway, MI
Lawler, Rev. Thomas, *SJ* '99 (STP) [RTR] Jesuit Retreat House, Lake Elmo, MN
Lawler, Rev. Thomas A., *S.J.* (CHI) [MIS] The Jesuit Partnership, Chicago, IL
Lawless, Rev. Thomas, '07 (ALB) All Saints Catholic Church, Albany, NY
Lawlor, Rev. Brendan, '55 (SP) Retired.
Lawlor, Rev. Frank, '14 (SPR) On Leave.
Lawlor, Rev. J. Michael, '73 (BO) St. Paul, Hamilton, MA
Lawlor, Rev. James F., '63 (ROC) Retired. Our Lady of Lourdes, Rochester, NY; St. Anne, Rochester, NY
Lawlor, Rev. Mark S., '95 (CHL) St. Therese, Mooresville, NC
Lawongkerd, Rev. Peter, (OAK) Holy Spirit, Fremont, CA
Lawrence, Rev. Andrew F., '00 (DUB) On Duty Outside Diocese. Chap, COL, Springfield, VA Curia: (>MO) Offices and Directors
Lawrence, Rev. Basil, *O.S.B.* '14 (P) [MON] Mt. Angel Abbey, Saint Benedict, OR
Lawrence, Rev. Bradley, (MO) Curia: Offices and Directors
Lawrence, Rev. Brijil, *S.A.C.* (FWT) Curia: Miscellaneous / Other Offices
Lawrence, Rev. Candance, (SY) Chap, St Camillus Health & Rehab Ctr, Syracuse
Lawrence, Rev. David, *S.J.* '74 (OAK) Retired. St. Bonaventure, Concord, CA
Lawrence, Rev. David, '97 (JOL) St. Mary, West Chicago, IL
Lawrence, Rev. James A., '70 (BUR) Retired.
Lawrence, Rev. John M., '76 (SAC) Retired.
Lawrence, Rev. Msgr. Kevin C., '87 (PH) Curia: Deaneries St. John the Baptist, Philadelphia, PA; [CAM] Roxborough Memorial School of Nursing, Philadelphia, PA
Lawrence, Rev. Martin E, '03 (SFS) Saint Magdalen Parish of Lincoln County, Lennox, SD
Lawrence, Rev. Martin E., '03 (SFS) Curia: Leadership Saint Dominic Parish of Lincoln County, Canton, SD
Lawrence, Rev. Peter, *P.V.* '16 (LAN) Most Holy Trinity Parish Fowler, Fowler, MI; St. Mary Parish Westphalia, Westphalia, MI
Lawrence, Rt. Rev. Philip, *O.S.B.* '77 (SFE) [MON] Monastery of Christ in the Desert, Abiquiu, NM
Lawrence, Rev. Msgr. Robert E., '66 (HBG) Retired. St. Columba, Bloomsburg, PA
Lawrence, Rev. Thomas Bagley, '21 (RIC) St. Joseph, Hampton, VA; St. Mary Star of the Sea, Fort Monroe, VA; St. Vincent de Paul, Newport News, VA
Lawrence, Rev. William, *F.S.S.P.* '06 (LIN) [SEM] Our Lady of Guadalupe Seminary, Inc., Denton, NE (>SCR) [MON] Priestly Fraternity of St. Peter (F.S.S.P.), North American District Headquarters, S. Abington Twp., PA
Lawryniuk, Rev. Lawrence, *O.S.B.M.* '64 (STF) St. Mary Protectress, Bronx, NY
Laws, Rev. Joshua, '15 (BAL) Catholic Community of South Baltimore Roman Catholic Congregation, Inc., Baltimore, MD
Lawson, Rev. Meinrad J., *O.S.B.* '67 (GBG) [MON] Saint Vincent Archabbey, Latrobe, PA
Lawson, Rev. Stephen, *O.S.B.* '17 (MAN) [MON] St. Anselm Abbey, Manchester, NH
Lawson, Rev. Theodore, *C.Ss.R.* '89 (MIL) [RTR] Our Mother of Perpetual Help Retreat Center (The Redemptorist Retreat Center), Oconomowoc, WI
Lawson, Rev. Walter G., '03 (BRK) On Leave. Released from Diocesan Assignment
Lawton, Rev. Robert B., *S.J.* '81 (BAL) [MIS] Colombiere Jesuit Community, Baltimore, MD
Laygo, Rev. Kristian, *S.D.B.* (MRY) [MON] Saint Francis Salesian Community, ,
Laylan, Rev. Kyle N., '18 (LC) Holy Family, Arcadia, WI; Most Sacred Heart, Dodge, WI; [EFT] Arcadia Catholic School to Holy Family School, Arcadia, WI
Layosa, Rev. Doroteo B., '14 (NEW) Paramus Catholic High School, Paramus, NJ
Layous, Rev. Ziad, '19 (NTN) St. Joseph, Lawrence, MA
Layton, Rev. Richard, *O.C.S.O.* '82 (P) [MON] The Cistercian (Trappist) Abbey of Our Lady of Guadalupe (Order of Cistercians of the Strict Observance), Carlton, OR
Layton, Rev. Thomas Michael, '09 (P) Retired.
Laz, Rev. Medard P., '69 (CHI) Retired. [MIS] Joyful Again, La Grange Park, IL
Laz, Rev. Medard P., '69 (CHI) Retired. Holy Family, Inverness, IL
Lazar, Rev. Arul, (KAL) Holy Family, Decatur, MI; Holy Maternity of Mary, Dowagiac, MI; Sacred Heart of Mary, Dowagiac, MI
Lazar, Rev. John E., '80 (BRK) On Leave.
Lazar, Rev. Justin, '04 (RNO) Curia: Offices and Directors St. Therese of the Little Flower Catholic Church, Reno, NV
Lazar, Rev. Thadayoose, *HGN* '06 (LSC) St. Rita Parish, Inc., Carrizozo, NM
Lazarra, Rev. Alexis, '10 (HT) Curia: Administration St. Gregory Barbarigo, Houma, LA
Lazer, Rev. Francis, '09 (LSC) Curia: Leadership St. Anthony Parish, Artesia, Inc., Artesia, NM
Lazerna, Rev. Alberic, (PT) St. Louis, Tallahassee, FL
Lazo, Rev. Alonso, *S.M.M.* (RVC) [MON] Montfort Missionaries, Bay Shore, NY
Lazzarato, Rev. Mauro, *C.S.* '86 (CHI) [MON] Scalabrini House of Theology, Chicago, IL
Lazzeroni, Very Rev. Gary F., '07 (SEA) Curia: Leadership St. Joseph, Vancouver, WA
Lazzeroni, Very Rev. Gary F., '07 (SEA) Curia: Leadership
Le, Rev. Anthony V., (BO) St. James, Haverhill, MA; St. John the Baptist, Haverhill, MA
Le, Rev. Ben, '98 (LA) St. Christopher, West Covina, CA
Le, Rev. Canon David, '21 (CHI) [SHR] Shrine of Christ the King Sovereign Priest, Chicago, IL
Le, Rev. Canon David, '21 (CHI) [MON] Institute of Christ the King Sovereign Priest, Chicago, IL
Le, Rev. Duy T., (ORG) San Francisco Solano Catholic Church, Rancho Santa Margarita, CA
Le, Rev. Francis, *O.P.* '04 (SEA) Blessed Sacrament, Seattle, WA
Le, Rev. James Vinh, '87 (KAL) St. Augustine Cathedral, Kalamazoo, MI
Le, Rev. John Paul, *O.S.B.* '15 (P) [MON] Mt. Angel Abbey, Saint Benedict, OR
Le, Rev. John Vianney, *O.S.B.* '17 (P) [MON] Mt. Angel Abbey, Saint Benedict, OR
Le, Rev. Johnson, '18 (SAT) St. Ann, La Vernia, TX
Le, Rev. Joseph, '16 (JKS) St. Francis of Assisi, Aberdeen, MS; St. Helen, Amory, MS
Le, Rev. Joseph, (DAL) [MON] St. John Neumann Formation House, Dallas, TX
Le, Rev. Joseph, *C.Ss.R.* '14 (LAV) St. Elizabeth Ann Seton, Las Vegas, NV
Le, Rev. Joseph N., (CHI) St. Alphonsus Liguori, Prospect Heights, IL
Le, Rev. Joseph Quoc Quang, *OP* (OAK) [MON] Order of Preachers (Province of the Most Holy Name of Jesus - Western Dominican Province), Oakland, CA
Le, Rev. Joseph Thu, '03 (GAL) St. Christopher, Houston, TX
Le, Rev. Joseph Tuan Anh, '14 (OAK) St. Francis of

Assisi, Concord, CA
Le, Rev. Justin, '09 (SJ) Curia: Leadership St. Maria Goretti, San Jose, CA
Le, Rev. Khoa, '15 (DAV) SS. Mary and Mathias Church of Muscatine, Iowa, Muscatine, IA
Le, Rev. Khoa T., '06 (RVC) St. Hugh of Lincoln, Huntington Station, NY
Le, Rev. Khoa T., (RVC) St. Peter of Alcantara, Port Washington, NY
Le, Rev. Khoi, (GAL) Most Holy Trinity Catholic Church, Angleton, TX
Le, Rev. Lam T., '04 (GR) Curia: Clergy and Religious Services Mary, Queen of Apostles, Sand Lake, MI; Saint John Paul II, Cedar Springs, MI
Le, Rev. Nicolas Thanh Quang, *OCist.* (SAC) [MON] Our Lady of Sacramento Monastery, Walnut Grove, CA
Le, Rev. Peter Tai Thanh, '98 (HT) St. Joseph, Galliano, LA
Le, Rev. Simon M. Diem Phuc, *CRM* '03 (SPC) [MON] Congregation of the Mother of the Redeemer, Carthage, MO
Le, Rev. Son Peter, *S.V.D.* '13 (DUB) [SEM] Divine Word College, Epworth, IA
Le, Rev. Tan Van, '73 (CHL) Retired.
Le, Rev. Thai, '08 (LA) St. Thomas More, Alhambra, CA
Le, Rev. Tuan, *S.J.* '99 (CHI) [COL] Jesuit Community at Loyola University Chicago, Chicago, IL; [MIS] President's Office, Chicago, IL
Le Bouteiller des Haries, Rev. Philippe, *O.S.B.* '95 (TLS) [MON] Our Lady of the Annunciation of Clear Creek Abbey, Hulbert, OK
Le Fevre, Rev. Francis J., '71 (BAL) On Leave.
Le Jacq, Rev. Peter M., *M.M.* '87 (NY) [MON] Maryknoll Fathers and Brothers (Catholic Foreign Mission Society of America, Inc.), Ossining, NY
Le Thanh, Rev. Huan, *C.Ss.R.* (PH) St. Peter the Apostle, Philadelphia, PA
Lea, Rev. Joseph P., '04 (PH) On Duty Outside Diocese. Curia: (>MO) Offices and Directors
Leach, Rev. Gregory, '80 (DM) Retired. Curia: Offices and Directors
Leach, Rev. Msgr. Phillip, '85 (R) Retired.
Leach, Rev. Thomas F., '73 (BRK) Mary Queen of Heaven, Brooklyn, NY
Leach, Rev. Msgr. William J., '58 (STL) Retired. St. Margaret Mary Alacoque Catholic Church, St. Louis, MO
Leahy, Rev. Edwin D., *O.S.B.* '72 (NEW) Saint Benedict Preparatory School, Newark, NJ; [MON] Benedictine Abbey of Newark, Newark, NJ
Leahy, Rev. Liam, '72 (TUC) Retired.
Leahy, Rev. William, '66 (SAV) Retired.
Leahy, Rev. William P., *S.J.* '78 (BO) [COL] Boston College, Chestnut Hill, MA; [MON] The Jesuit Community at Boston College, Chestnut Hill, MA; [SEM] The Ecclesiastical Faculty at Boston College, Newton, MA
Leake, Rev. Jerome L., '68 (RCK) Retired. Our Lady of Good Counsel, Aurora, IL
Leake, Rev. Stephen, *S.D.B.* '00 (NO) Christ the King, Terrytown, LA; Immaculate Conception, Marrero, LA; St. Joachim Roman Catholic Church, Marrero, Louisiana, Marrero, LA
Leal, Rev. Moises, (P) Chap, Federal Corr Inst, Sheridan St. Luke, Woodburn, OR
Leal de Sa, Rev. Nilson, *C.B.* '01 (DEN) St. Catherine of Siena Catholic Parish in Denver, Denver, CO; [ASN] The Catholic Community of the Beatitudes, Denver, CO
Lealofi, Rev. Msgr. Etuale, '69 (SPP) Retired. Curia: Leadership; Offices and Directors Cathedral of the Holy Family, Pago Pago, AS
Leary, Rev. Daniel P., '97 (WDC) On Duty Outside Diocese. Valle de Chalco, Mexico
Leary, Rev. James P., *O.F.M.Cap* '70 (MIL) [MON] St. Lawrence Friary, Mount Calvary, WI
Lease, Rev. James E., '06 (HBG) Curia: Offices and Directors St. Catherine Laboure, Harrisburg, PA
Lease, Rev. James E., '06 (HBG) Curia: Offices and Directors
Leaver, Rev. Kevin P., (BO) On Leave. Sacred Hearts, Malden, MA; St. John the Baptist, Peabody, MA; St. Thomas the Apostle, Peabody, MA
Leavins, Rev. Brice, *O.F.M.* '69 (PAT) Retired. [MON] St. Anthony Friary (Order of Friars Minor), Butler, NJ
Leavitt, Rev. Robert F., *P.S.S.* '68 (BAL) Retired. [MIS] St. Mary's Seminary & University, Baltimore, MD; [MON] Society of St. Sulpice, Province of the United States, Baltimore, MD
Leavitt, Rev. Robert F., *S.S.* '68 (HRT) On Duty Outside Diocese. St Mary Seminary, Baltimore, MD
Leavy, Rt. Rev. Matthew K., *O.S.B.* '75 (MAN) Retired. [MON] St. Anselm Abbey, Manchester, NH
Leavy, Rt. Rev. Matthew Kenneth, *O.S.B.* (SFR) [MON] Woodside Priory, Portola Valley, CA
Lebanowski, Rev. Jerry, *MS* '59 (STL) Retired. [MON] Missionaries of LaSalette, Province of Mary, Mother of the Americas, St. Louis, MO
Lebdowicz, Rev. Jan Krzystof, '80 (NEW) St. Bernard of Clairvaux and St. Stanislaus Kostka, Plainfield, NJ
Lebel, Rev. Maurice T., '67 (PRT) Retired.
LeBlanc, Rev. Alvin J., '82 (HRT) Curia: Advisory Boards, Commissions, Committees, and Councils Saint Thomas & Saint Timothy Parish Corporation, West Hartford, CT
LeBlanc, Rev. Charles L., '79 (NOR) On Leave.
LeBlanc, Rev. Clyde, *S.J.* '75 (LAF) St. Charles Borromeo, Grand Coteau, LA; [MON] St. Charles College, Grand Coteau, LA
LeBlanc, Rev. Daniel, *O.M.I.* (NY) Ascension, New York, NY
LeBlanc, Rev. Daniel, *O.M.I.* '78 (WDC) [MON] Oblate Community, Washington, DC
LeBlanc, Rev. Gregory, '94 (DOD) Retired.
LeBlanc, Rev. Msgr. James L., '96 (CHR) Curia: Advisory Boards, Commissions, Committees, and Councils St. Theresa, Winnsboro, SC; Transfiguration, Blythewood, SC
LeBlanc, Rev. Leo A., '74 (MAN) Retired.
LeBlanc, Rev. Leo-Paul J., '79 (WOR) Retired. St. Cecilia, Leominster, MA
LeBlanc, Rev. Paul J., (NY) St. Joan of Arc, Bronx, NY
LeBlanc, Rev. Robert A., '21 (BO) St. Mary of the Assumption, Brookline, MA
Leblanc, Rev. Stephen R., '16 (BO) Curia: Tribunal Mary Immaculate of Lourdes, Newton, MA
LeBlanc, Rev. Steven C., '77 (LAF) Curia: Leadership St. Basil, Duson, LA
LeBleu, Rev. V. Wayne, '95 (LKC) St. Joseph's, DeRidder, LA
LeBoeuf, Rev. Gerard, '93 (DET) St. Irenaeus Parish Rochester Hills, Rochester Hills, MI
Lebrun, Rev. Raymond A., *O.M.I.* '68 (WDC) [MON] Oblate Community, Washington, DC; [SHR] Basilica of the National Shrine of the Immaculate Conception, Washington, DC
Lebsock, Rev. Christopher, '15 (HEL) Curia: Leadership Saints Cyril and Methodius Parish: Series 427, LLC, East Helena, MT
LeCaptain, Rev. Douglas E., '93 (GB) Curia: Advisory Boards, Commissions, Committees, and Councils St. Francis of Assisi, Manitowoc, WI
Lech, Rev. Hank, '88 (PT) Curia: Offices and Directors
Lech, Rev. Henry A, '88 (PT) Nativity of Our Lord, Pensacola, FL
Lech, Rev. Lukasz, '15 (BRK) On Duty Outside Diocese. Diocese of Fukuoka, Japan
Lech, Rev. Waclaw L., *O.C.D.* '74 (GRY) [MON] Discalced Carmelite Fathers Monastery, Munster, IN
Lechnar, Rev. William J., '97 (GBG) Holy Family, Seward, PA
Lechner, Rev. Msgr. Roger A., '66 (SD) Retired.
Lechtenberg, Rev. Msgr. Edward W., '51 (DUB) Retired.
Lechukwu, Rev. Joachim, '02 (SB) Our Lady of the Snows, Wrightwood, CA; Saint Junipero Serra, Phelan, CA
Lecias, Rev. J. Michael O., '10 (WH) St. Vincent de Paul, Berkeley Springs, WV
Leckie, Rev. Michael J., '90 (PRO) Retired.
LeClaire, Rev. H. Fred, *C.M.F.* '87 (PHX) St. Catherine Laboure Roman Catholic Parish, Chino Valley, AZ
LeCompte, Rev. Glenn, (HT) St. Charles Borromeo, Thibodaux, LA
LeCompte, Rev. Glenn, '86 (HT) Curia: Faith Formation
Lecomte, Rev. Gerard, *CJM* '78 (SD) [MON] The Eudists - Congregation of Jesus and Mary, Vista, CA
Ledesma, Rev. Jose Salvador, '99 (STO) Curia: Leadership; Offices and Directors Our Lady of Guadalupe Church (Pastor of), Lathrop, CA
Ledesma, Rev. Michael, '21 (TYL) St. John the Evangelist, Emory, TX
Ledezma, Rev. Jesus, '16 (NY) Our Lady of Guadalupe at St. Bernard's, New York, NY; St. Rose of Lima, New York, NY
Ledford, Very Rev. John S., '75 (WH) Curia: Leadership; Offices and Directors St. James, McMechen, WV; St. John, Benwood, WV; St. Jude, Glen Dale, WV
Ledoux, Rev. Albert H., '87 (ALT) St. Demetrius, Gallitzin, PA
LeDoux, Rev. Louis Vernon, '52 (LAF) Retired.
Ledoux, Rev. Mark, '99 (LAF) St. Peter, Carencro, LA
Ledoux, Very Rev. William J., '93 (PRO) Curia: Advisory Boards, Commissions, Committees, and Councils; Clergy and Religious Services; Leadership Holy Apostles Church, Cranston, Rhode Island, Cranston, RI
Leduc, Rev. Roger, (FRS) Retired.
LeDuc, Rev. Roger D., '60 (FR) Retired.
Ledwon, Rev. Jacob C., '72 (BUF) St. Joseph-University, Buffalo, NY; [CAM] State University of New York at Buffalo (Main St. South Campus), Buffalo, NY
Lee, Rev. Andrew H., (NY) St John Nam, Bronx, NY
Lee, Rev. Anthony S., '97 (LA) St. Agatha, Los Angeles, CA
Lee, Rev. Cha Yong (Paul), (TR) Immaculate Conception, Eatontown, NJ
Lee, Rev. Chang Hyon, *S.J.* '17 (LA) St. Agnes, Los Angeles, CA
Lee, Rev. Chang-Jun, (FWT) Korean Martyrs, Hurst, TX
Lee, Rev. Changwoo, *O.F.M.Conv.* '04 (LA) St. Francis Korean Center, Torrance, CA
Lee, Rev. Chongman John the Baptist, '05 (SAT) Korean Martyrs Catholic Church, Boerne, TX
Lee, Rev. Msgr. David M., '68 (BUF) Retired.
Lee, Rev. Dongsik, '02 (MOB) St. Andrew Kim Taegon Parish, Montgomery, Montgomery, AL
Lee, Rev. Dongwook, '01 (R) St. Ha-Sang Paul Jung, Apex, NC
Lee, Rev. Duy Ahn, (SPR) St. Mary's, Westfield, MA
Lee, Rev. Eugene, '04 (ORG) St. Thomas More, Irvine, CA; [CCH] Korean Martyrs Catholic Center, Westminster, CA
Lee, Rev. Gabriel, '17 (SJ) St. Mary of the Immaculate Conception, Los Gatos, CA
Lee, Rev. Gabriel, '97 (BRK) St. Robert Bellarmine, Bayside, NY
Lee, Rev. HyoSuk, (CHL) St. Peter Yu, Greensboro, NC
Lee, Rev. Jaehwa John, '07 (PH) On Duty Outside Diocese.
Lee, Rev. Jaehwa John, '07 (PH) On Duty Outside Diocese. Diocese of Cheju, GwangYang Catholic Church, Jeju-do
Lee, Rev. Jaeung Damian, (ALB) On Special Assignment. Chap, Holy Family Korean Apostolate, Albany Curia: Offices and Directors [MIS] Korean Apostolate of the Roman Catholic Diocese of Albany, Albany, NY
Lee, Rev. James E., '75 (SEA) St. Michael, Olympia, WA
Lee, Rev. Jeffrey E., '92 (TR) Curia: Leadership St. Mary's, Colts Neck, NJ
Lee, Rev. John Michael, *C.P.* '72 (NY) [MON] The Congregation of the Passion - St. Paul of the Cross Province, Jamaica, NY
Lee, Rev. John Michael, *C.P.* (SCR) [MON] Saint Ann's Passionist Monastery of Scranton PA, Scranton, PA
Lee, Rev. Joseph, *F.S.S.P.* '06 (LIN) [SEM] Our Lady of Guadalupe Seminary, Inc., Denton, NE
Lee, Rev. Joseph, (MO) U.S. Army Fort Drum
Lee, Rev. Archmandrite Joseph (Richard), '72 (PHU) [MON] Monastery of the Holy Cross, Washington, DC
Lee, Rev. Joseph C., '91 (DAL) St. Francis of Assisi Catholic Parish - Frisco, Frisco, TX
Lee, Rev. Joshua, '22 (RC) St. Joseph, Spearfish, SD
Lee, Rev. Joshua Peter, '89 (LA) Retired.
Lee, Rev. Jun Hee, '13 (BRK) On Academic Leave. St. Patrick, Brooklyn, NY
Lee, Rev. Keun-Soo, '95 (BR) Congregation Of St. Anne's Roman Catholic Church Of Sorrento, Sorrento, LA; St. Anthony of Padua (The Congregation Of St. Anthony Roman Catholic Church Of Darrow, Louisiana), Darrow, LA
Lee, Rev. Kwang H., (BO) Our Lady of Grace, Pepperell, MA; St. John the Evangelist, Townsend, MA
Lee, Rev. Matthew K., '09 (CIN) St. Boniface, Piqua, OH; St. Patrick, Troy, OH; St. Teresa of the Infant Jesus, Covington, OH; Transfiguration, West Milton, OH
Lee, Rev. Michael, *S.J.* '96 (LA) Dolores Mission, Los Angeles, CA
Lee, Rev. Michael, '14 (PRM) St. Luke, Byzantine Catholic Parish, Sugar Creek, MO
Lee, Rev. Michael, '11 (PAT) St. Michael's, Netcong, NJ
Lee, Rev. Mike, *SJ* (SD) Pastor of Our Lady of Guadalupe Catholic Parish, San Diego, a corporation sole, San Diego, CA
Lee, Rev. Myoungsang, '99 (RIC) St. Kim Taegon, Richmond, VA
Lee, Rev. Namwoong, (MET) Curia: Family Life Our Lady of Mercy, South Bound Brook, NJ
Lee, Rev. Patrick J, *S.J.* '78 (SFR) [MON] Loyola House Jesuit Community, San Francisco, CA
Lee, Rev. Patrick J., '81 (CHI) Our Lady of Mount

Carmel, Chicago, IL
Lee, Rev. Paul D., '83 (WDC) Shrine of St. Jude, Rockville, MD
Lee, Rev. Paul Kyung, '06 (NEW) Curia: Organizations (affiliated, inter-Diocesan, miscellaneous/other) St. Andrew Kim, Maplewood, NJ
Lee, Rev. Peter John, '18 (MAD) St. John, South Wayne, WI; St. Joseph, Gratiot, WI; St. Matthew, Shullsburg, WI
Lee, Rev. Raphael, '08 (NEW) Curia: Leadership; Offices and Directors Church of Korean Martyrs, Saddle Brook, NJ
Lee, Rev. Roy A., '86 (MIL) On Duty Outside Diocese. Decatur, GA
Lee, Rev. Roy Arthur, '86 (ATL) On Duty Outside Diocese. St Leo Univ, St Leo, FL
Lee, Rev. Ryan, '16 (PHX) Saint Henry Roman Catholic Parish, Buckeye, AZ
Lee, Rev. Sang Yil, '92 (AUS) Retired.
Lee, Rev. Sang Sun, (HRT) Sacred Heart of Jesus Korean Catholic Parish Corporation, Wethersfield, CT
Lee, Rev. Se Ho, (SEA) St. Paul Chong Hasang Personal Parish, Fife, WA
Lee, Rev. Sebastian, *SF* '97 (SFE) Holy Family-Chimayo, Chimayo, NM
Lee, Rev. Taeseop, (ARL) St. Paul Chung, Fairfax, VA
Lee, Rev. Tuan, '06 (DAL) St. Elizabeth Ann Seton Catholic Parish, Plano, TX
Lee, Rev. Yong Hyuk, '01 (GAL) St. Joseph, Baytown, TX
Leeser, Rev. James R., '14 (MAD) St. William, Janesville, WI
Leete, Rev. Timothy, '18 (KC) [NUR] Jeanne Jugan Center (Little Sisters of the Poor), Raytown, MO
LeFaivre, Rev. Rick, '18 (P) On Leave.
Lefebure, Rev. Leo D., '78 (CHI) On Duty Outside Diocese. (>WDC) Our Lady of Victory, Washington, DC
LeFevre, Rev. Msgr. Michael C., '82 (DET) Curia: Tribunal St. Owen Parish Bloomfield Hills, Bloomfield Hills, MI
Leffler, Rev. Richard J., '78 (MAD) SS. Andrew and Thomas, Potosi, WI
Leffler, Rev. Taylor, (OM) St. Wenceslaus, Omaha, NE
LeFleur, Rev. R. Keith, '76 (SAG) Retired.
Lefor, Rev. Jason, '99 (FAR) St. John Nepomucene's Church of Pisek, Pisek, ND; St. Joseph's Church of Lankin, Lankin, ND; Sts. Peter & Paul Church of Bechyne, Lankin, ND
LeFort, Very Rev. David R., '98 (ALB) On Special Assignment. Vicar Gen, Pastoral Ctr, Albany Curia: Leadership; Offices and Directors
LeFort, Very Rev. David R., '98 (ALB) Curia: Leadership [EFT] Diocesan Investment and Loan Trust, Albany, NY
LeGallic, Rev. Philippe-Joseph, *C.S.J.* (NEW) Our Lady of Mt. Carmel, Orange, NJ
Legarreta, Rev. Felipe DeJesus, '93 (JOL) On Leave.
Legaspi, Rev. Alex L., '76 (SFR) Holy Angels, Colma, CA
Legaspi, Rev. Alwin P., '96 (MOB) St. Joseph, Lillian, AL
Legaspi, Very Rev. Dennis L., '93 (SB) Saint Kateri Tekakwitha Catholic Community, Inc., Beaumont, CA
Legaspi, Rev. Josemarie, '89 (NY) (>PH) St. John the Baptist, Ottsville, PA
Leger, Rev. Arthur F., *S.J.* '02 (CI) [MON] Jesuit Community of Palau, Manresa Jesuit House, Koror, PW
Leger, Rev. Austin, '62 (LAF) Retired.
Leger, Rev. G. Robert, '71 (SJ) Retired.
Leger, Rev. Jeffrey P., '97 (L) Guardian Angels, Louisville, KY
Leger, Rev. Robert, (SJ) Curia: Offices and Directors
Leger, Very Rev. Steven L., '86 (BEA) Curia: Administration; Leadership St. Jude Thaddeus, Beaumont, TX
Legge, Rev. David Dominic, *O.P.* '07 (WDC) [SEM] Dominican House of Studies, Washington, DC
Leggieri, Rev. Joseph, (PH) [CAM] Thomas Jefferson University, Philadelphia, PA
Lego, Rev. William E., *O.S.A.* '83 (CHI) St. Turibius, Chicago, IL
Lehane, Rev. Brian, (TOL) St. John's Jesuit High School and Academy, Toledo, OH; [MON] St. John's Jesuit High School Jesuit Community, Holland, OH
Leheny, Rev. Msgr. Bernard, '66 (LA) Retired.
Lehigh, Rev. Todd, '18 (COL) Church of the Atonement, Crooksville, OH; St. Bernard, Corning, OH; St. Patrick, Junction City, OH; St. Rose of Lima, New Lexington, OH
Lehman, Rev. Joseph J., *T.O.R.* '96 (ALT) [MON] St. Bonaventure Hall, Loretto, PA
Lehner, Rev. John, *O.S.F.S.* '70 (TOL) St. Pius X, Toledo, OH
Lehnert, Rev. Brian, (ALB) Curia: Leadership Parish of Mater Christi, Albany, NY
Lehnertz, Rev. Benjamin, '13 (ORL) St. Joseph, Orlando, FL; St. Maximilian Kolbe, Orlando, FL
Lehning, Rev. Thomas J., '70 (ARL) Curia: Tribunal
Lehocky, Rev. Msgr. Leigh A., '68 (CHR) Retired.
Lehr, Rev. James W., *M.M.* '53 (NY) Retired.
Lehrberger, Rev. James, *O.Cist.* '76 (DAL) [MON] Our Lady of Dallas Cistercian Abbey, Irving, TX
Leibham, Very Rev. David, '87 (AUS) Curia: Leadership Church of the Resurrection, Emmaus, Lakeway, TX
Leibrecht, Rev. Robert G., '58 (STL) Retired.
Leidich, Rev. Kevin, *S.J.* '82 (SJ) [RTR] Jesuit Retreat Center of Los Altos, Los Altos, CA
Leier, Rev. Darrick, (DEN) St. Mary Catholic Parish in Aspen, Aspen, CO
Leif, Rev. Gregory P., '78 (WIN) Retired.
Leigh, Rev. David J., *S.J.* '68 (SEA) [COL] Seattle University, Seattle, WA; [MON] Arrupe Jesuit Community at Seattle University, Seattle, WA
Leigh, Rev. David J., *S.J.* '68 (SJ) [MON] Sacred Heart Jesuit Center, Los Gatos, CA
Leighton, Rev. Msgr. Donald E., '62 (PH) Retired.
Leiker, Rev. Michael, '19 (SAL) Seven Dolors of the Blessed Virgin Mary Parish, Manhattan, KS
Leiker, Rev. Perry D., '76 (LA) St. Bernard, Los Angeles, CA
Lein, Rev. Lambert, *S.V.D.* '00 (LAF) Holy Ghost, Opelousas, LA
Leiphon, Rev. Donald A., '68 (FAR) Retired. [CON] Sisters of Mary of the Presentation, Valley City, ND
Leise, Rev. Gerald, '74 (OM) Sacred Heart, Emerson, NE; St. John, Pender, NE
Leising, Rev. Msgr. Frederick D., '71 (BUF) Retired. Curia: Consultative Bodies [MON] Msgr. Conniff Residence, Depew, NY
Leising, Rev. John J., '69 (BUF) Retired.
Leising, Rev. Robert, *O.M.I.* (CC) [RTR] Oblate La Parra Center, Sarita, TX
Leisy, Rt. Rev. Christian, *O.S.B.* '88 (SFE) [MON] Monastery of Christ in the Desert, Abiquiu, NM
Leitem, Rev. Leon, *O.F.M. Cap.* '57 (PIT) [MON] St. Augustine Friary, Pittsburgh, PA
Leitner, Rev. Msgr. John E., '55 (KC) Retired.
Leitner, Rev. Thomas Aquinas, *O.S.B.* '92 (OM) Curia: Offices and Directors [MON] Benedictine Mission House - Christ the King Priory, Schuyler, NE; [RTR] Saint Benedict Center, Schuyler, NE
Leiva-Merikakis, Rev. Simeon, *O.C.S.O.* '13 (WOR) [MON] St. Joseph's Abbey (Cistercian Abbey of Spencer, Inc., Cistercian Order of the Strict Observance (Trappists)), Spencer, MA
Lek, Rev. Basil, (GLD) Divine Mercy of Manistee, Manistee, MI
Leke, Rev. Charles, '82 (SP) St. Patrick, Largo, FL
Leland, Rev. Thomas H., '99 (WCH) On Leave.
Leliaert, Rev. Richard M., '67 (DET) Retired.
Leloczky, Rev. Julius, *O.Cist.* '61 (DAL) [MON] Our Lady of Dallas Cistercian Abbey, Irving, TX
Lemaine, Rev. Calonge, '89 (STA) Curia: Evangelization Prince of Peace, Jacksonville, FL
Lemaire, Rev. Seth, (LAF) St. Joseph, Centerville, LA
Lemaster, Rev. Scott G., '85 (DAV) St. Bridget Church of Victor, Iowa, Victor, IA; St. Patrick Church of Brooklyn, Iowa, Brooklyn, IA
Lemautu, Rev. Faitau, '11 (SPP) Co-Cathedral of St. Joseph the Worker, Pago Pago, AS
Lemautu, Rev. Faitau, '11 (SPP) Curia: Offices and Directors
Lemay, Rev. Donald H., '89 (RIC) St. Edward the Confessor, North Chesterfield, VA
Lemay, Rev. Jean M., '75 (MAN) Retired.
Lemchi, Rev. Fidelis, (SPR) Chap, Baystate Med Ctr, Springfield Our Lady of the Sacred Heart, Springfield, MA
Lemkuhl, Rev. David A., '79 (CIN) Church of the Resurrection - Bond Hill, Cincinnati, OH; Holy Trinity Church, Cincinnati, OH; Nativity of Our Lord, Cincinnati, OH; St. John the Evangelist, Cincinnati, OH; St. Saviour, Cincinnati, OH
Lemme, Rev. Christopher, *T.O.R.* (ALT) Holy Family, Colver, PA
Lemmert, Rev. Ronald D., '79 (NY) On Leave.
Lemmert, Rev. Ronald J., '79 (NY) Chap, Phelps Mem Hosp, Sleepy Hollow
Lemoi, Rev. Paul R., '75 (PRO) Church of Our Lady of Good Counsel, Warwick RI, West Warwick, RI
Lemoine, Rev. Louis Bertrand, (Y) St. Dominic, Youngstown, OH
Lemon, Rev. Msgr. Clement P., '64 (WIL) Retired.
Lemoncelli, Rev. Hank, *OMI* '79 (STP) [RTR] Christ the King Retreat Center, Buffalo, MN
Lemor, Rev. Kiskama, *C.S.Sp.* '00 (MO) Curia: Offices and Directors
Lemos, Rev. Blas S., '04 (BRK) St. John the Baptist, Brooklyn, NY
Lemos, Rev. Thomas F., *C.S.C.* '74 (PHX) Saint John Vianney Roman Catholic Parish, Goodyear, AZ
Lemus, Rev. Angel Randolfo, '21 (KC) Our Lady of the Presentation, Lees Summit, MO
Lemus, Rev. Raul, '02 (SR) Curia: Leadership; Offices and Directors Pastor of St. Joseph Catholic Church of Cotati, A Corporation Sole, Cotati, CA
Lenaghan, Rev. James, *O.P.* '95 (HRT) [CAM] Quinnipiac Catholic Chaplaincy, Hamden, CT
Lenchak, Rev. Timothy, *S.V.D.* '75 (CHI) [MON] Divine Word Novitiate, Techny, IL; [MON] Divine Word Residence, Techny, IL
Lendvai, Rev. John B., '94 (PIT) Guardian Angels, Natrona Heights, PA
Lenehan, Rev. Claude T., *O.F.M.* '55 (PAT) Retired. [MON] St. Anthony Friary (Order of Friars Minor), Butler, NJ
Lengwin, Rev. Msgr. Ronald P., '66 (PIT) Retired. Curia: Consultative Bodies; Leadership
Lenhart, Rev. Erik, (NY) [PRE] Capuchin Youth and Family Ministries, Garrison, NY
Lenihan, Rev. Michael, '71 (CC) Retired. (>SAT) [NUR] Missionary Servants of St. Anthony (Padua Place), San Antonio, TX
Lenius, Rev. Kevin, '21 (SAN) St. Stephen's, Midland, TX
Lenk, Rev. Dominic, *O.S.B.* '98 (STL) St. Louis Priory School, Creve Coeur, MO; [MON] The Abbey of St. Mary and St. Louis, St. Louis, MO
Lenneman, Rev. Marc J., '06 (HEL) Curia: Leadership; Offices and Directors [COL] Carroll College, Helena, MT
Lennie, Rev. Francis H., '21 (PAT) St. Anthony's, Hawthorne, NJ
Lennon, Rev. Raymond, *S.V.D.* '64 (CHI) Retired. [MON] Divine Word Residence, Techny, IL
Lennon, Rev. Raymond T., *S.V.D.* '64 (TR) Retired.
Lennon, Rev. Robert, *C.Ss.R.* '57 (BO) Our Lady of Perpetual Help, Boston, MA
Lennon, Rev. Robert, *C.Ss.R.* '57 (BO) Curia: Organizations (affiliated, inter-Diocesan, miscellaneous/other)
Lenoci, Rev. Dominick J., '95 (NEW) St. Joseph, West Orange, NJ
Lenox, Rev. Peter F., '00 (BGP) Curia: Consultative Bodies; Leadership [SHR] Shrine of Saint Margaret, Bridgeport, CT
Lentini, Very Rev. James S., '03 (WIL) Curia: Administration; Deaneries Holy Cross, Dover, DE; Immaculate Conception, Marydel, MD
Lentz, Rev. Lawrence D., *C.S.V.* '81 (CHI) [MON] Viatorian Province Center-Clerics of St. Viator, Arlington Heights, IL
Lenz, Rev. Brian, *P.V.* '16 (LAN) Lumen Christi Catholic School, Jackson, MI
Lenz, Rev. Clark, (CHY) Our Lady of Fatima, Casper, WY
Lenz, Rev. Daniel, *O.S.B.* '85 (OM) Mount Michael Benedictine School, Elkhorn, NE; [MON] Mount Michael Benedictine Abbey, Elkhorn, NE
Lenz, Rev. David, *O.F.M.Conv.* '86 (IND) [RTR] Mount Saint Francis Friary and Retreat Center, Mount St. Francis, IN
Lenz, Rev. Frank, '69 (MAR) Retired.
Lenz, Rev. Frank, '94 (VIC) Retired.
Lenz, Rev. Michael George, *OFM* '76 (DET) [MON] Dun Scotus Friary, Berkley, MI
Leo, Rev. Dominic, *OSB* (RIC) St. Gregory the Great, Virginia Beach, VA
Leon, Rev. Armando, '22 (PMB) St. Helen, Vero Beach, FL
Leon, Rev. Bartholomew, '85 (SAM) St. Rafka Maronite Mission, Greer, SC
Leon, Rev. Dave, '05 (SD) St. Mary Magdalene, Jacumba, CA; [MIS] Saint Adelaide of Burgundy Catholic Parish in Campo, CA Real Property Support Corporation, Campo, CA
Leon, Rev. Fr Dave, '05 (SD) Pastor of Saint Adelaide of Burgundy Catholic Parish, Campo, a corporation sole, Campo, CA
Leon, Rev. Francisco, *O.S.A.* '78 (LAR) Holy Redeemer, Laredo, TX
Leon, Rev. Gregorio, '88 (LAV) St. Anne, Las Vegas, NV
Leon, Rev. Jose M., '81 (OAK) Retired.
Leon, Rev. Victor, *O.S.J.* '00 (SCR) Annunciation, Hazleton, Hazleton, PA
Leon Aguirre, Rev. Luis Enrique, *SS.CC.* (SJN) Sagrados

Corazones, Guaynabo, PR
Leon Guerrero, Rev. Felixberto, *OFM Cap.* '86 (AGN) San Francisco de Asis, Yona, GU
Leon-Angulo, Rev. Marcos, '03 (R) Curia: Offices and Directors St. Bernadette, Butner, NC
Leonard, Rev. Albert P., '89 (SCR) On Administrative Leave.
Leonard, Rev. Daniel, '94 (DEN) [SEM] Saint John Vianney Theological Seminary, Denver, CO
Leonard, Very Rev. Edwin, '12 (DAL) Curia: Administration St. Ann Catholic Parish - Coppell, Coppell, TX
Leonard, Rev. John J., *O.F.M.* '96 (HRT) St. Patrick and St. Anthony Roman Catholic Church Corporation, Hartford, CT; [MON] St. Patrick-St. Anthony Friary (Franciscan Friars), Hartford, CT
Leonard, Rev. Peter, *O.S.F.S.* '86 (CHL) Immaculate Heart of Mary, High Point, NC
Leonard, Rev. Raymond Joseph, (CHR) Curia: Advisory Boards, Commissions, Committees, and Councils Church of the Resurrection, Loris, SC; Our Lady Star of the Sea, North Myrtle Beach, SC
Leonard, Rev. William T., '69 (BO) Retired.
Leondhas, Rev. Edward, '09 (SLC) Saint Helen LLC 224, Roosevelt, UT
Leone, Rev. James M., '60 (BRK) Retired.
Leone, Rev. Msgr. Kenneth J., '67 (DEN) Retired.
Leone, Rev. William B., '74 (ROC) Chap, Veteran's Hosp, Canandaigua St. Jerome, East Rochester, NY; [MIS] Rochester Comitium, Penfield, NY
Leong, Rev. Francis J., *M.M.* '87 (NY) Retired. [MON] Maryknoll Fathers and Brothers (Catholic Foreign Mission Society of America, Inc.), Ossining, NY
Leonhardt, Rev. Douglas J., *S.J.* '69 (MIL) [MON] Jesuit Community at Marquette University (Marquette Jesuit Associates, Inc.), Milwaukee, WI
Leonhardt, Rev. Louis J., '56 (DAV) Retired.
Leon-Valencia, Rev. Rafael A., '04 (R) Curia: Leadership St. James, Henderson, NC
Leopold, Rev. David C., '82 (BGP) Retired. The St. Theresa's Roman Catholic Church Corporation, Trumbull, CT
Leopold, Rev. Martin J., '01 (SAT) Mary, Mother of the Church Catholic Parish, San Antonio, TX
Leopold, Rev. Martin J., '01 (SAT) Curia: Leadership [MIS] The Archdiocese of San Antonio Capital Campaign Inc., San Antonio, TX
LePage, Rev. Joseph Francis, *F.H.S.* '03 (PHX) On Leave. St. John the Baptist, Laveen, AZ
Lepak, Rev. Brannon, '21 (OKL) Sacred Heart, Oklahoma City, OK
Lepak, Rev. Przemyslaw, '06 (PRO) Saint Christopher's Church of Tiverton, Tiverton, RI; St. Theresa's Parish Corporation, Tiverton, Tiverton, RI
Lepak, Rev. Roy C., '62 (STP) Retired.
Lepcha, Rev. Joachim, '96 (LA) Immaculate Conception, Monrovia, CA
Lepez, Rev. Isidro, (SEA) Bellarmine Preparatory School, Tacoma, WA
Lepez, Rev. Isidro, (PHX) St. Francis Xavier Roman Catholic Parish, Phoenix, AZ
Lepez, Rev. Isidro, *S.J.* (SEA) Chap, Northwest Detention Ctr
Lepine, Rev. Steven M., '06 (MAN) On Leave. Holy Rosary, Hooksett, NH
Lequin, Rev. Thomas, '77 (PRT) Retired.
Lerma, Rev. Carlos H., '12 (RIC) St. Francis of Assisi, Rocky Mount, VA; St. Joseph, Martinsville, VA
Lerner, Rev. Ryan M., '14 (HRT) Saint Mary Parish Corporation, New Haven, CT; St. Stanislaus' Church of New Haven Connecticut, New Haven, CT; [CAM] Saint Thomas More Catholic Chapel and Center at Yale University, New Haven, CT
Lery, Rev. Bruce J., *S.M.* '87 (SFR) [MON] Marist Center of the West, San Francisco, CA
Lesak, Rev. William P., '75 (NEW) Chap, New Bern, NC
Lescher, Rev. Raymond C., '63 (JOL) Retired.
Leser, Rev. Msgr. William J., '63 (LA) Retired.
Lesher, Rev. Gregory, '15 (DEN) Chap, CHC, USN, CLB6 H&S Co RMT, Camp Lejeune, NC
Lesher, Rev. Gregory L., (MO) Curia: Offices and Directors
LeSieur, Rev. Msgr. David, '76 (LR) St. Vincent de Paul, Rogers, AR
Lesiriam, Rev. Seraphine, (CIN) Emmanuel, Dayton, OH; St. Joseph, Dayton, OH
Lesko, Rev. Andrew Paul, '20 (STV) Cathedral of SS. Peter and Paul, Charlotte Amalie, VI; [MIS] Miscellaneous Organizations, Charlotte Amalie, VI
Leskovar, Rev. Richard J., '68 (ALB) Retired. Curia: Offices and Directors
Leslie, Rev. Patrick J., '69 (SAC) Retired.
Lesly Andre, Rev. Freddo, '06 (ARE) Our Lady of Carmen-Playa, Vega Baja, PR
Lesly Andre, Rev. Fredo, (ARE) [MIS] Chapel Divino Nino Jesus, Vega Baja, PR; [MIS] Chapel San Judas Tadeo, Vega Baja, PR
Lesniak, Rev. David, '91 (DET) St. Maria Goretti Parish Dearborn Heights, Dearborn Heights, MI
Lesniak, Rev. Richard D., '66 (MAD) Retired.
Lesniewski, Rev. Stephen F., '93 (CHI) On Duty Outside Diocese. Santiago De Compostela, Lake Forest, CA
Lessa Natalino, Rev. Adriano, *C.Ss.R.* '07 (WOR) Our Lady of Good Counsel, West Boylston, MA
Lessard, Rev. Eugene R., '59 (PRO) Retired. Saint Joseph's Church Corporation, North Scituate, North Scituate, RI
Lessard, Rev. Gerard, *O.P.* '84 (WDC) St. Dominic Church & Priory, Washington, DC
Lessard-Thibodeau, Very Rev. John G., '92 (SPR) Curia: Leadership; Offices and Directors; Tribunal
Lesser, Rev. F. Richard, '15 (ALB) St. Matthew, Voorheesville, NY; St. Thomas the Apostle (St. Thomas' Church of Delmar, N.Y.), Delmar, NY
Lesser, Rev. Richard, (ALB) Curia: Leadership Christ the King, Albany, NY
Lesupati, Rev. Paul, '22 (SFD) Cathedral of the Immaculate Conception, Springfield, IL
Leszczynski, Rev. Jacek, *OFMConv.* '98 (SPR) Our Lady of the Cross, Holyoke, MA; St. Anthony of Padua, Chicopee, MA
Leszko, Rev. Adrian, '21 (B) St. Mark's, Boise, ID
Letak, Rev. Tobias, '16 (OM) Curia: Offices and Directors St. Margaret Mary, Omaha, NE
Leto, Rev. Nelo A., '54 (DM) Retired.
Letona, Rev. Robert M., '09 (LC) Curia: Leadership St. James the Less, La Crosse, WI; [EFT] St. James Parish Endowment Trust, La Crosse, WI
Letourneau, Rev. Larry, '00 (SAL) Retired.
Letran, Rev. Benjamin, (MO) Curia: Offices and Directors
Letteer, Rev. Michael C., '96 (HBG) Immaculate Conception of the Blessed Virgin Mary, New Oxford, PA; Sacred Heart of Jesus, Spring Grove, PA
Lettre, Rev. Raymond, '88 (SP) Retired.
Leu, Rev. Beni, *S.V.D.* '99 (SB) Queen of Angels, Riverside, CA
Leuthardt, Rev. Henry, '10 (RVC) Cure of Ars Roman Catholic Church, Merrick, NY; St. Rosalie's, Hampton Bays, NY
Leva, Rev. Stephen F., '88 (PH) On Special Assignment. Dean, Deanery 4, St Joseph Rectory, Downingtown Curia: Deaneries St. Joseph, Downingtown, PA
LeVasseur, Rev. Giles, '84 (WH) Retired.
LeVecke, Rev. John R., '84 (ORG) On Administrative Leave.
Leveille, Rev. Andre E., *C.S.C.* '78 (FTW) [MIS] Holy Cross House, Notre Dame, IN
Levels, Rev. Karen, (SY) Chap, Our Lady of Lourdes Mem Hosp, Binghamton
Levens, Rev. Robert, (BO) [MON] Campion Center, Inc., Weston, MA
Levesque, Rev. Gerald A., '64 (PRT) Retired.
Levesque, Rev. Sylvio J., '55 (PRT) Retired.
Levine, Rev. Joseph, '10 (BAK) Curia: Offices and Directors Holy Family Catholic Church of Burns, Inc., Burns, OR
Leviste, Rev. Vic Karljohn Rouie Reyes, '22 (PAT) St. Joseph's, Mendham, NJ
Levitt, Rev. Donald L., '79 (PEO) Christ the King, Moline, IL
Levko, Rev. John J., *S.J.* '78 (SCR) [COL] The University of Scranton, Scranton, PA
Levra, Rev. Ronald W., '07 (SUP) Retired.
Levreault, Very Rev. Raymond G., '05 (SAV) Curia: Leadership St. Teresa, Albany, GA
Levri, Rev. Fid, '67 (CIN) Retired. [MON] Headquarters of Glenmary Home Missioners (The Home Missioners of America), Fairfield, OH
Levri, Rev. Fideles, *G.H.M.* '67 (OWN) Curia: Advisory Boards, Commissions, Committees, and Councils
Lewandowski, Rev. Andrew, *O.F.M.* '76 (STL) St. Anthony of Padua Catholic Church, St. Louis, MO; [MON] Franciscan Friary of St. Anthony of Padua, St. Louis, MO
Lewandowski, Rev. Andrew, *C.R.* '89 (JOL) St. Mark, Wheaton, IL
Lewandowski, Rev. Dennis, (JOL) [COL] Lewis University, Romeoville, IL
Lewandowski, Rev. Glen, *O.S.C.* '74 (SCL) Curia: Leadership [MON] Crosier Priory, Onamia, MN
Lewandowski, Rev. John, '96 (FAR) Retired.
Lewandowski, Rev. Leonard A., '77 (PH) Retired.
Lewandowski, Rev. Raymond H., '85 (DET) St. Roch Parish Flat Rock, Flat Rock, MI
Lewandowski, Rev. Richard P., '74 (WOR) Retired.
Lewandowski, Rev. Thomas J., '00 (PIT) Wash. & Jeff. Coll, California Univ of PA, Waynesburg Coll St. Hilary, Washington, PA; St. James, Washington, PA; St. Katharine Drexel Parish, Bentleyville, PA
Lewerenz, Rev. Spencer, '18 (LA) St. Anthony, San Gabriel, CA
Lewinski, Rev. Cassian, (OAK) Retired. [MON] Order of Preachers (Province of the Most Holy Name of Jesus - Western Dominican Province), Oakland, CA
Lewis, Rev. Brian S., '13 (WIL) Curia: Miscellaneous / Other Offices St. Jude the Apostle, Lewes, DE
Lewis, Rev. Clyde A., '64 (OG) Curia: Consultative Bodies Saint Patrick's Church, Rouses Point, Rouses Point, NY; The Church of Saint Mary of Champlain, Champlain, NY
Lewis, Rev. David, '90 (CI) [MON] St. John Vianney Formation House, Chuuk, FM
Lewis, Rev. David C., '04 (BO) Curia: Consultative Bodies St. Adelaide, Peabody, MA; St. Ann, Peabody, MA
Lewis, Rev. Dennis J., '75 (MIL) Retired.
Lewis, Rev. Dwight P., '11 (SEA) Chap, CHI Franciscan/ Multicare Health St. Charles Borromeo, Tacoma, WA
Lewis, Rev. Eric, '69 (LA) Retired.
Lewis, Rev. Msgr. Gerald L., '61 (R) Retired. Curia: Leadership; Offices and Directors
Lewis, Rev. Jeffrey, '11 (SPK) Curia: Leadership St. Mary, Spokane Valley, WA; [SEM] Bishop White Seminary, Spokane, WA
Lewis, Rev. John Paul, '16 (OKL) Curia: Clergy and Religious Services Blessed Sacrament, Lawton, OK
Lewis, Rev. Lawrence J., *M.M.* '75 (NY) [MON] Maryknoll Fathers and Brothers (Catholic Foreign Mission Society of America, Inc.), Ossining, NY
Lewis, Rev. Leo T., '60 (STL) Retired.
Lewis, Rev. Mark, *S.J.* '91 (NO) [MON] Jesuit Provincial Office (Catholic Society of Religious and Literary Education), New Orleans, LA
Lewis, Rev. Mark W., '12 (POC) Our Lady of the Atonement Catholic Church, San Antonio, TX
Lewis, Rev. Patrick S., '12 (WDC) Curia: Consultative Bodies Little Flower, Bethesda, MD
Lewis, Rev. Ryan P., '99 (OM) Curia: Offices and Directors St. Elizabeth Ann, Omaha, NE
Lewis, Rev. Scott M., *S.J.* (SJ) [MON] USA West Province, Society of Jesus, Los Gatos, CA
Lewis, Rev. Steven, '21 (ROC) Blessed Trinity, Owego, NY; St. Patrick, Owego, NY
Lewis, Rev. Walter G., '79 (RIC) St. John Neumann, Powhatan, VA
Lewkiewicz, Rev. Richard, '68 (BRK) Retired.
Ley, Friar Philip, *O.F.M.Conv.* '84 (SAT) [MON] San Damiano Friary, San Antonio, TX
Ley, Friar Phillip, *O.F.M.Conv.* '57 (SAT) [SEM] San Damiano Friary, Initial House of Formation, San Antonio, TX
Ley, Rev. Richard J., '71 (ARL) Retired.
Leyba, Rev. John Paul, '02 (DEN) St. Frances Cabrini Catholic Parish in Littleton, Littleton, CO
Leyble, Rev. Eric, '12 (HT) Curia: Leadership; Tribunal St. Genevieve, Thibodaux, LA
Leykam, Rev. Msgr. John J., '72 (STL) Curia: Leadership Church of the Annunziata Catholic Church, Ladue, MO
Leykam, Rev. Lambert, *OFM* (GB) Retired.
Leyrita, Rev. Norbert, '63 (GR) Retired.
Leyton-Rodriguez, Rev. Sandro, '13 (NY) Parish of St. Margaret of Cortona and St. Gabriel, Bronx, NY
L'Heureux, Rev. William D., '91 (OM) Curia: Leadership; Offices and Directors SS. Peter and Paul, Genoa, NE; St. Edward, St. Edward, NE; St. Lawrence, Silver Creek, NE; St. Rose of Lima, Genoa, NE
Lhoposo, Rev. Jean-Pierre Swamunu, '04 (CHL) Divine Redeemer (Divino Redentor), Boonville, NC
Li, Rev. Dong Min (Paul), '07 (HON) Curia: Consultative Bodies St. Philomena, Honolulu, HI
Li, Rev. Mingwei, '19 (PIT) Most Sacred Heart of Jesus, Moon Township, PA
Liaugminas, Rev. Andrew, *S.T.D.* (CHI) On Duty Outside Diocese. Cong. for the Doctrine of the Faith, Vatican City
Libby, Rev. Donald L., '05 (GLD) Holy Rosary of Cedar, Cedar, MI
Libby, Very Rev. Richard A., '99 (CC) Curia: Administration; Leadership Saint Helena of the True Cross of Jesus, Corpus Christi, TX
Libens, Rev. John F., *S.J.* '70 (DET) [MON] Colombiere Center, Clarkston, MI
Libera, Rev. F. Nelson, *J.C.D.* '00 (PHX) Curia: Leadership
Libera, Rev. Thomas A., '69 (CHI) Retired. St. Pio of Pietrelcino Parish, Chicago, IL
Liberatore, Rev. David D., '60 (CLV) Retired.

Liberman-Ormaza, Rev. Antonio, '85 (DAL) St. Edward Catholic Parish, Dallas, TX
Libiszewski, Rev. Dominik, *OSPPE* (ORL) St. Mark the Evangelist, Summerfield, FL
Libone, Very Rev. John, '80 (DAL) Curia: Administration St. Thomas Aquinas Catholic Parish, Dallas, TX
Libra, Rev. Matthew (Matt), '12 (P) Chap, Donald E Long Juvenile Detention Ctr, Portland Curia: Offices and Directors St. Rose of Lima, Portland, OR
Librizzi, Rev. Mark, '12 (ORL) St. Mary Catholic Church, Rockledge, FL
Licari, Rev. John J., '02 (PT) Chap, Saufley Field Fed Prison Camp Curia: Leadership St. John the Evangelist, Pensacola, FL
Licari, Rt. Rev. Jonathan, *O.S.B.* (PAT) [MON] St. Mary's Abbey, Morristown, NJ
Licari, Rt. Rev. Jonathan, *O.S.B.* '76 (SCL) Curia: Leadership [MON] St. John's Abbey, of the Order of St. Benedict, Collegeville, MN
Licciardi, Rev. Fred, *C.PP.S.* '82 (CIN) [MON] Society of the Precious Blood, United States Province, Inc., Dayton, OH
Licciardi, Rev. Giuseppe, '67 (DET) Retired.
Lichtenthal, Rev. Msgr. James J., '63 (BUF) Retired.
Lichter, Rev. Mark, '92 (SFS) Saint Boniface Parish of Turner County, Idylwilde, SD; Saint George Parish of Bon Homme County, Scotland, SD; St. John the Baptist Parish of Yankton County, Lesterville, SD
Lickteig, Rev. Anthony, '54 (KCK) Retired. Cure of Ars, Leawood, KS
Lickteig, Very Rev. Anthony E., '10 (WDC) On Special Assignment. Curia: Clergy and Religious Services; Consultative Bodies; Leadership Holy Angels, Avenue, MD; Sacred Heart, Bushwood, MD
Lickteig, Rev. Gabriel, (KC) [CAM] Newman Center Catholic Campus Ministry for University of Central Missouri, Warrensburg, MO
Lickteig, Rev. Gabriel, '15 (KC) On Special Assignment. Northwest Missouri State Univ Curia: Leadership Sacred Heart, Warrensburg, MO
Lickteig, Rev. Paul A., (CIN) St. Francis Xavier Church, Cincinnati, OH
Lickteig, Rev. Paul A., *SJ* (CIN) [MIS] St. Xavier Church Property Corporation, Cincinnati, OH; [MON] Cincinnati Jesuit Community, Cincinnati, OH
Licznerski, Rev. Henry, *C.R.* '92 (SB) St. Ann, Needles, CA; [MON] Congregation of the Resurrection, CR, Needles, CA
Liddy, Rev. Msgr. Richard M., '63 (NEW) [COL] Seton Hall University, South Orange, NJ
Liderbach, Rev. Daniel P., *S.J.* '73 (DET) [MON] Colombiere Center, Clarkston, MI
Lieb, Rev. Benedict Mary, *F.H.S.* '13 (PHX) On Leave.
Liebert, Rev. Aaron, *FSSP* '18 (SD) Pastor of Saint Anne Catholic Parish, San Diego, a corporation sole, San Diego, CA
Lieberth, Rev. Joseph, '68 (CLV) On Administrative Leave.
Liebhardt, Rev. Kevin M., '74 (CLV) St. Justin Martyr, Eastlake, OH
Liebl, Rt. Rev. Michael, *O.S.B.* '77 (OM) Mount Michael Benedictine School, Elkhorn, NE; [EFT] Mount Michael Foundation, Elkhorn, NE; [MON] Mount Michael Benedictine Abbey, Elkhorn, NE
Liebler, Rev. Thomas R., '81 (SFD) Our Lady Queen of Peace, Bethalto, IL
Liebner, Rev. James, (SFR) St. Paul, San Francisco, CA; St. Philip the Apostle, San Francisco, CA
Liebsch, Rev. Douglas, '16 (SCL) Curia: Offices and Directors The Cathedral High School, St. Cloud, MN
Liebscher, Rev. Arthur F., *S.J.* '84 (SJ) [MON] Jesuit Community at Santa Clara University, Inc., Santa Clara, CA
Liekhus, Rev. James C., '05 (STP) Curia: Leadership Blessed Trinity Catholic School of Richfield, Minnesota, Richfield, MN; St. Peter, Richfield, MN; St. Richard, Richfield, MN; The Church of the Assumption/La Iglesia de La Asuncion, Richfield, MN; [CEM] St. Margaret's Cemetery, Hopkins, MN
Lien, Rev. Lambert, *S.V.D.* '00 (NO) St. Katharine Drexel, New Orleans, LA
Lienert, Rev. Msgr. Charles, '68 (P) Retired.
Lienhard, Rev. Joseph T., *S.J.* '71 (NY) [MON] Jesuit Community at Fordham University, New York, NY
Lies, Rev. C. Jarrod, '01 (WCH) St. Francis of Assisi, Wichita, KS
Lies, Rev. David J., '98 (WCH) Curia: Leadership; Offices and Directors
Lies, Rev. James M., *C.S.C.* '97 (FTW) [COL] University of Notre Dame Du Lac, Notre Dame, IN; [MON] Holy Cross Community, Corby Hall, University of Notre Dame, Notre Dame, IN
Lies, Rev. William M., *C.S.C.* '94 (FTW) [MON] Congregation of Holy Cross, United States Province of Priests and Brothers, Notre Dame, IN
Lieser, Rev. Gregory, '63 (SCL) Retired. Curia: Leadership
Lieser, Rev. Vincent, '67 (SCL) Retired.
Liewer, Rev. David F., '74 (OM) Retired. Curia: Offices and Directors
Ligato, Rev. Anthony, '95 (ALB) On Special Assignment. Vicar, Vocations, Pastoral Ctr, Albany
Ligato, Very Rev. Anthony F., '95 (ALB) Curia: Leadership; Offices and Directors Cathedral of the Immaculate Conception, Albany, NY; St. Francis of Assisi Parish, Albany, NY
Ligenza, Rev. Rafal, '11 (VEN) St. Joseph Parish in Bradenton, Inc., Bradenton, FL
Ligeti, Friar Angelus, *O.F.M.* '79 (DET) Holy Cross (Hungarian) Parish Detroit, MI
Ligeza, Rev. Jan A., '03 (STA) On Academic Leave. Post Graduate Studies St. Edward, Starke, FL
Liggio, Rev. Jasper, '14 (VIC) Curia: Leadership Nativity of the Blessed Virgin Mary, Schulenburg, TX; St. John the Baptist, Schulenburg, TX; St. Rose of Lima, Schulenburg, TX
Lightner, Rev. Michael, (GB) St. John the Baptist, Menasha, WI; St. Mary, Menasha, WI
Lightner, Rev. Michael F., '05 (MIL) On Duty Outside Diocese. Niagara, Diocese of Green Bay
Ligonde, Rev. Jean-Marie Fritz, '89 (VEN) Curia: Advisory Boards, Commissions, Committees, and Councils; Leadership St. Columbkille Parish in Fort Myers, Inc., Fort Myers, FL
Ligory, Rev. Joseph, '80 (NY) St. Theresa of the Infant Jesus, Bronx, NY
Ligot, Rev. Andres, '92 (SJ) Curia: Offices and Directors
Ligot, Rev. Andres C., '92 (SJ) On Special Assignment. St. Elizabeth, Milpitas, CA
Liguori, Rev. Christopher, '03 (STA) St. Patrick, Jacksonville, FL
Liias, Rev. Jurgen, '13 (POC) Retired.
Lijana, Rev. John, (LEX) Good Shepherd, Frankfort, KY
Lijewski, Rev. Thomas F., '70 (MIL) Retired.
Lijewski, Rev. Timothy M., '93 (CHR) Retired.
Lijo, Rev. Kochuparambil, '09 (SYM) St. Mary's Syro-Malabar Knanaya Catholic Parish (Morton Grove), Morton Grove, IL
Likoudis, Rev. Michael, (DAL) St. Mark the Evangelist Catholic Parish, Plano, TX
Liliedahl, Rev. Michael, (SFR) St. Stephen, San Francisco, CA
Lill, Rev. Kenneth J., '91 (TOL) Retired.
Lillard, Rev. Rhone, *F.S.S.P.* '10 (LIN) [SEM] Our Lady of Guadalupe Seminary, Inc., Denton, NE
Lillpopp, Rev. Michael, '05 (SPR) [CAM] Springfield College Campus Ministry, Springfield, MA
Lillpopp, Rev. Michael C., '05 (SPR) St. John the Evangelist, Agawam, MA
Lilly, Rev. Robert A., *M.M.* '62 (NY) Retired.
Lilly, Rev. Thomas C., '03 (AJ) St. Benedict, Anchorage, AK
Lim, Rev. Felix, (SFR) St. Anthony of Padua, Novato, CA
Lim, Rev. Jiha, '16 (RVC) St. Mary's, Manhasset, NY
Lim, Rev. Jong Un, (CHL) St. John Lee (Korean), Charlotte, NC
Lim, Rev. Marc, '07 (OM) Mary Our Queen, Omaha, NE
Lim, Rev. Roque G., '06 (BAL) On Special Assignment. Chap, Harford Cty Parishes St. Ignatius, Forest Hill, MD
Lima, Rev. Joao Bosco, '92 (NEW) On Duty Outside Diocese. Aracaju, SE
Lima, Rev. John H., '63 (OAK) Retired.
Lima, Rev. Ranjan Kumar, (CHI) [MON] DePaul Vincentian Residence, Chicago, IL
Lima, Rev. Vivian B., '85 (LA) Retired. St. Madeleine, Pomona, CA
Limanni, Rev. Joseph, (GAL) Curia: Offices and Directors
Limmer, Rev. George A., '64 (BAL) Retired.
Limongi, Rev. Carlos, '18 (NY) Church of the Assumption, Peekskill, NY; Saint Joseph and Saint Mary Immaculate, Staten Island, NY
Limpiado, Rev. Edwin, '04 (MRY) St. William's, Atascadero, CA
Lin, Rev. Peter Yunping, '97 (MIA) Curia: Pastoral Services
Lin, Rev. Sheng Jiao, *C.M.* '08 (BRK) St. Rosalia-Regina Pacis, Brooklyn, NY
Linardi, Rev. Alessandro, '18 (BRK) St. Joseph, Astoria, NY
Linares, Rev. Jose R., '86 (HRT) Saint Augustine Parish Corporation, Hartford, CT
Lincon, Rev. Joseph B., '89 (BGP) Retired.
Lind, Rev. Msgr. Joseph G., '65 (BO) Retired.
Lindblad, Rev. Karl-Albert, '87 (NY) Chap, USN, Suffolk, VA Curia: (>MO) Offices and Directors
Lindemann, Rev. Msgr. Gene E., '83 (BIS) Curia: Leadership; Offices and Directors Sacred Heart, Wilton, ND; St. Hildegard, Menoken, ND; [EFT] The Parish Expansion Fund of the Diocese of Bismarck, Bismarck, ND
Linden, Rev. John A., '07 (LAN) St. Andrew Parish Saline, Saline, MI
Linden, Rev. Michael D., *S.J.* (CHK) Curia: Advisory Boards, Commissions, Committees, and Councils; Consultative Bodies; Leadership
Linden, Rev. Phillip J., *S.S.J.* '69 (NO) Retired.
Linden, Rev. Phillip J., *S.S.J.* '69 (PBR) Retired.
Lindenfelser, Rev. Timothy M., '94 (STA) Curia: Advisory Boards, Commissions, Committees, and Councils; Leadership St. Anastasia, St. Augustine, FL
Lindle, Rev. Jacob, '22 (CIN) Immaculate Conception, North Lewisburg, OH; Sacred Heart (St. Paris), St. Paris, OH; St. Mary, Urbana, OH; St. Mary of the Woods, Russells Point, OH; St. Michael Church, Mechanicsburg, OH; St. Patrick, Bellefontaine, OH
Lindner, Rev. Jerold W., *S.J.* '76 (SJ) [MON] Sacred Heart Jesuit Center, Los Gatos, CA
Lindner, Rev. Thomas F., '95 (LC) Church of the Resurrection, Wausau, WI; St. Anne, Wausau, WI; St. Michael, Wausau, WI; [EFT] Church of the Resurrection Parish Church Building Endowment Trust, Wausau, WI; [EFT] Newman Catholic Schools Endowment Trust, Wausau, WI; [EFT] St. Michael Parish Endowment Trust, Wausau, WI
Lindsay, Rev. John, *O.S.F.S.* (BUF) Retired.
Lindsay, Rev. Michael P., '87 (LSC) On Duty Outside Diocese. Military base, Louisiana Curia: (>MO) Offices and Directors
Lindsay, Rev. Stewart M., *O.S.F.S.* '74 (BUF) Holy Family of Jesus, Mary and Joseph, Niagara Falls, NY
Lindsey, Very Rev. John, '10 (JOL) Curia: Leadership St. Joseph, Manhattan, IL
Lindsey, Rev. Robert H., *C.Ss.R.* '09 (SAT) St. Gerard Majella, San Antonio, TX; [MON] The Redemptorists/San Antonio, San Antonio, TX
Linebach, Rev. Martin A., '87 (L) Curia: Leadership; Offices and Directors Cathedral of the Assumption, Louisville, KY; [EFT] Catholic Foundation of Louisville, Inc., Louisville, KY
Linehan, Rev. Stephen J., '75 (BO) [SEM] Pope Saint John XXIII National Seminary, Weston, MA
Ling, Rev. Martin Ma Na, '22 (OWN) Holy Spirit, Bowling Green, KY
Lingan, Rev. Joseph E., *S.J.* '79 (WDC) [COL] Georgetown University, Washington, DC; [MON] The Jesuit Community of St. Aloysius Gonzaga, Washington, DC
Lingaur, Rev. Michael Anthony, '21 (GLD) All Saints of Alpena, Alpena, MI; Saint Rose of Lima of Herron, Herron, MI
Lingle, Rev. Brent C., '07 (SC) Curia: Leadership; Offices and Directors St. Mary's, Storm Lake, IA; [EFT] St. Mary's Foundation of Storm Lake, Iowa, Storm Lake, IA
Lingo, Rev. Benjamin Mac, (OAK) St. Anthony, Oakley, CA
Link, Rev. David, '91 (OAK) Retired. Curia: Offices and Directors [NUR] Bishop Begin Villa, Oakland, CA; [NUR] Bishop Begin Villa, Retirement Facility for Priests in the Oakland Diocese, ,
Link, Rev. David T., '08 (GRY) Retired.
Link, Rev. Fred, *O.F.M.* '70 (CIN) Retired. [MON] St. Clement Friary, Cincinnati, OH
Link, Rev. Frederick G., '69 (CAM) Retired.
Link, Rev. Joshua J, '19 (DUB) Sacred Heart Church (Rockwell, Iowa), Rockwell, IA; St. Patrick Church, Clear Lake, Iowa, Clear Lake, IA
Link, Rev. Matthew B., *C.PP.S.* '05 (SFR) Most Holy Redeemer, San Francisco, CA
Linkchorst, Rev. William J., '73 (ALN) Retired.
Linkenheld, Rev. James E., '21 (RCK) On Duty Outside Diocese. Pontifical North American College, Rome
Linn, Rev. Andrew J.T., '16 (MIL) Curia: Leadership St. Anthony's Congregation, Menomonee Falls, WI; St. Mary's Congregation, Menomonee Falls, WI
Linn, Rev. Matthew L., *S.J.* '73 (STP) [MON] Markoe House Jesuit Community, Minneapolis, MN
Linnan, Rev. Roger J., '62 (SC) Retired. Curia: Leadership
Linnane, Rev. Brian F., *S.J.* '86 (BAL) Retired. [MON] Jesuit Community of Loyola University Maryland, Inc., Baltimore, MD (>NY) [MON] Xavier Jesuit Community, New York, NY

Lino-Salinas, Rev. Andres T., *CORC* (SB) St. Edward, Corona, CA; [MIS] Confraternity of Operarios Del Reino De Cristo, C.O.R.C., Corona, CA
Linsky, Rev. Canon Gary S., '95 (CHR) Curia: Advisory Boards, Commissions, Committees, and Councils; Deaneries Minor Basilica of St. Peter, Columbia, SC
Linsler, Rev. Christopher E., '78 (ROC) St. Mary Our Mother, Horseheads, NY
Linster, Rev. Msgr. Joseph B., '69 (RCK) Retired.
Linton, Rev. Edward, *O.S.B.* '91 (IND) [MON] St. Meinrad Archabbey, St. Meinrad, IN
Lintz, Rev. Charles, *S.S.C.* '70 (PRO) [MON] St. Columban's Retirement House (St. Columban's Foreign Mission Society), Bristol, RI
Lintz, Rev. Charles, *S.S.C.* '70 (OM) [MON] Missionary Society of St. Columban, St. Columbans, NE
Lintz, Rev. Christoph, '94 (NEW) On Duty Outside Diocese. Holy Family Parish, Muenchen
Lintzenich, Rev. Stephen, '74 (EVN) Retired.
Lintzenich, Rev. Stephen P., '74 (EVN) Retired. Curia: Leadership
Linzmaier, Rev. Eric G., '00 (LC) Holy Cross, Cornell, WI; Sacred Heart of Jesus, Jim Falls, WI; St. Anthony, Cadott, WI
Lioi, Very Rev. Frank E., '67 (ROC) Curia: Deaneries Our Lady of the Snow, Auburn, NY; Saints Mary and Martha Roman Catholic Parish Cayuga County, NY, Auburn, NY; St. Mary, Auburn, NY
Lionelli, Rev. Anthony J., '72 (NEW) Retired.
Lipalata, Rev. Benny, *O.M.I.* (CR) Most Holy Redeemer, Ogema, MN; St. Ann, Waubun, MN; St. Benedict (White Earth), White Earth, MN; St. Theodore of Ponsford, Ponsford, MN
Lipareli, Rev. Michael A., '80 (NY) Curia: (>MO) Offices and Directors
Lipiec, Rev. Bartholomew W., '83 (BUF) FBI St. Martha, Depew, NY
Lipinski, Rev. Edward J., '71 (CAM) Retired.
Lipinski, Rev. Paul M., '73 (RCK) Retired.
Lipnicki, Rev. Thomas P., '78 (NEW) Curia: Organizations (affiliated, inter-Diocesan, miscellaneous/ other) Our Lady of Perpetual Help, Oakland, NJ
Lippert, Rev. Donald F., *O.F.M.Cap* '85 (WDC) [MIS] Spanish Catholic Center, Washington, DC
Lippert, Rev. Paul R., '61 (MIL) Retired.
Lippstock, Rev. Paul E., '78 (DUB) [HOS] MercyOne - North Iowa, Mason City, IA
Lipscomb, Rev. John B., '09 (SP) Curia: Leadership; Pastoral Services [RTR] Bethany Center, Inc., Lutz, FL
Lipscomb, Rev. William W., '97 (GLD) Retired.
Lipski, Rev. Janusz, '67 (RVC) Our Lady of Poland, Southampton, NY
Liptak, Rev. Edward, *S.D.B.* '59 (SFR) Corpus Christi, San Francisco, CA
LiPuma, Rev. Msgr. David G., '87 (BUF) Curia: Consultative Bodies Our Lady of Victory National Shrine and Basilica, Lackawanna, NY; St. Anthony, Lackawanna, NY; [MIS] Our Lady of Victory Institutions, Inc., Lackawanna, NY; [SPF] Baker Victory Services (OLV Human Services), Lackawanna, NY
Lirette, Rev. Joey, '18 (HT) The Congregation of the Sacred Heart Roman Catholic Church, Cut Off, LA (Sacred Heart Church), Cut-Off, LA
Lis, Rev. John S., '73 (SPR) Retired.
Lis, Rev. Mariusz, (CHI) Holy Trinity Mission, Chicago, IL
Lisabet, Rev. Dailon, '19 (PAT) St. Margaret of Scotland, Morristown, NJ
Lisabet, Rev. Dailon, '19 (PAT) Curia: Leadership
Lisante, Rev. Msgr. James P., '81 (RVC) Our Lady of Lourdes, Massapequa Park, NY
Liscinsky, Rev. Steven, *L.C.* (GRY) Sacred Heart Apostolic School, Inc., Rolling Prairie, IN
Lisik, Rev. Paul A., '81 (GBG) Curia: Advisory Boards, Commissions, Committees, and Councils; Leadership; Offices and Directors Immaculate Conception, Connellsville, PA; St. Aloysius, Dunbar, PA; St. John the Evangelist, Connellsville, PA; St. Pius X, Mount Pleasant, PA; St. Rita, Connellsville, PA; Visitation of the Blessed Virgin Mary, Mount Pleasant, PA
Lisovski, Rev. Valdemaras, (BRK) On Special Assignment. Annunciation of the BVM, Brooklyn, NY Our Lady of the Miraculous Medal, Ridgewood, NY
Lisowski, Rev. Lawrence M., '84 (CHI) Curia: Leadership Immaculate Conception and St. Joseph, Chicago, IL
Lisowski, Rev. Robert J., *CSC* (FTW) [COL] University of Notre Dame Du Lac, Notre Dame, IN; [MON] Holy Cross Community, Corby Hall, University of Notre Dame, Notre Dame, IN
Lisowski, Rev. Thomas, '86 (SPR) St. Patrick, Northfield, MA
List, Rev. John E., '85 (LEX) Curia: Leadership
List, Rev. John E., '85 (LEX) Curia: Leadership St. Sylvester, Waynesburg, KY; St. William, Lancaster, KY
Liston, Rev. Msgr. Daniel P., '85 (SPR) Curia: Tribunal St. Patrick's, Springfield, MA
Liszewski, Rev. Peter B., '78 (NOR) Curia: Offices and Directors St. Edward, Stafford Springs, CT
Litak, Rev. Matthew, '16 (CHI) St. Clement, Chicago, IL
Litavec, Rev. Edward S., '60 (PIT) Retired.
Litcheck, Rev. Michael P., '71 (SCR) Retired.
Literal, Rev. Peter, (BAL) St. John the Evangelist-Long Green Valley, Hydes, MD
Litt, Rev. Andrew, (LIN) Curia: Leadership Sacred Heart, Shelby, NE
Littelmann, Rev. Edward J., '69 (TOL) Retired.
Little, Rev. Ambrose, *O.P.* '13 (WDC) [SEM] Dominican House of Studies, Washington, DC
Little, Rev. Ambrose, *O.P.* '13 (PRO) [MON] St. Thomas Aquinas Priory at Providence College, Providence, RI
Little, Rev. Msgr. Anthony B., '82 (ALT) On Leave.
Little, Rev. Benjamin, '12 (STP) Curia: Leadership St. John the Baptist, Savage, MN; [CEM] St. Michael Cemetery, Farmington, MN
Little, Rev. John J.L., '88 (ALN) Retired.
Littlefield, Rev. Joseph, '22 (FAR) St. Joseph Church, Devils Lake, ND
Litwack, Rev. Joshua E., '00 (TLS) St. Pius X, Tulsa, OK
Litwin, Rev. Msgr. Paul A., '79 (BUF) Christ the King, Snyder, NY
Litzner, Very Rev. Corey J., '04 (MAR) Curia: Advisory Boards, Commissions, Committees, and Councils; Organizations (affiliated, inter-Diocesan, miscellaneous/ other) Sacred Heart, L'Anse, MI; St. Ann, Baraga, MI; The Most Holy Name of Jesus-Saint Kateri Tekakwitha, Baraga, MI
Liu, Very Rev. Daniel, '08 (AUS) St. Mary Cathedral, Austin, TX
Liu, Rev. Gregory, *O.P.* '20 (SAC) St. Dominic, Benicia, CA
Liu, Rev. Peter T., '60 (RVC) Retired. [MON] St Pius X Residence for Retired Priests LLC, Ronkonkoma, NY
Liuzzi, Very Rev. Kenneth, '75 (DEN) Retired.
Liuzzi, Rev. Peter, *O.Carm.* '65 (JOL) Retired.
Liuzzi, Rev. Peter J., *O.Carm.* '65 (LA) Retired.
Lively, Rev. Gregory, '01 (HEL) Saint Rose of Lima Parish: Series 224, LLC, Dillon, MT
Livigni, Rev. Salvatore, '61 (BAL) Retired.
Livingston, Rev. James, '91 (DET) Our Lady of Sorrows Parish Farmington, Farmington, MI
Livingston, Rev. James T., '90 (STP) Church of Saint Paul, Ham Lake, MN
Livingston, Rev. Joshua M., '20 (MAN) Our Lady of the Mountains, North Conway, NH
Livingston, Rev. Mark, (DET) National Shrine of the Little Flower Basilica, Royal Oak, MI
Livingstone, Rev. James W., '03 (SFR) Retired.
Livojevich, Rev. Ronald, '70 (KCK) Retired.
Liwanag, Friar Bernard, (OAK) Holy Spirit, Fremont, CA
Liwarski, Rev. Krzysztof P., '16 (PAT) St. Vincent Martyr, Madison, NJ
Lizalde, Rev. Jesus, '93 (GAL) St. Charles Borromeo, Houston, TX
Lizama, Rev. Sergio, *S.A.C.* '06 (MIL) [MON] Pallotti House, Milwaukee, WI
Lizcano, Rev. Otoniel, '99 (BGP) Pope John Paul II Healthcare
Lizewski, Rev. John M., '99 (WOR) St. Aloysius-St. Jude, Leicester, MA
Lizinczyk, Rev. Tadeusz, '98 (PH) [MON] The Order of Saint Paul, First Hermit - The Pauline Fathers, Doylestown, PA; [RTR] National Shrine of Our Lady of Czestochowa, Doylestown, PA
Lizor, Rev. Msgr. Joseph S., '58 (BAL) Retired.
Llamas, Rev. Rodolfo D., '93 (SAC) Pastor of St. Joseph Parish, Sacramento, a corporation sole, Sacramento, CA
Llambias, Rev. Martin, (POD) Curia: Clergy and Religious Services
Llanera, Rev. Alex A., *S.J.* '18 (SJ) [MON] USA West Province, Society of Jesus, Los Gatos, CA
Llanos, Rev. Philip, '78 (FRS) Retired.
Llanos, Rev. Phillip S., '78 (LA) Retired.
Llenas-Urenas, Rev. Victor Manuel, (SJN) Ntra. Sra. de Fatima, Carolina, PR
Lleo, Rev. Pedro, '76 (MIA) Retired.
Llorente, Rev. Ignacio, *S.S.J.* '09 (P) Church of St. Michael the Archangel, Portland, OR; [MON] Saint John Society, Corvallis, OR
Lloyd, Rev. C. Todd, '11 (BR) Congregation Of The Most Blessed Sacrament Parish, Baton Rouge, LA
Lloyd, Rev. James B., *C.S.P.* '48 (NY) Retired. [MIS] Courage International, Incorporated, New York, NY; [MON] Paulist Fathers' Motherhouse, New York, NY
Lloyd, Rev. Patrick, *S.C.J.* '69 (SP) Retired. [MON] Priests of the Sacred Heart, Pinellas Park, FL
Lloyd, Rev. Philip P., '78 (GAL) St. Theresa, Houston, TX
Lloyd, Rev. Robert J., *M.M.* '62 (NY) Retired. [MON] Maryknoll Fathers and Brothers (Catholic Foreign Mission Society of America, Inc.), Ossining, NY
Llywelyn, Rev. Dorian, *S.J.* '90 (LA) [MIS] The Institute for Advanced Catholic Studies, Los Angeles, CA
Loaiza, Rev. Carlos, '03 (TLS) Curia: Offices and Directors St. James, Bartlesville, OK; St. John's, Bartlesville, OK
Loaiza, Rev. Jorge H., '98 (RCK) St. Peter, South Beloit, IL
Lobacz, Very Rev. James E., '79 (MIL) On Special Assignment. Vicar for Sr Clergy; Master of Ceremonies/ Logistics Coord f... Curia: Leadership
Lobaton, Rev. Jose R., *O.F.M.* '73 (PHX) St. Anthony of Padua Roman Catholic Parish, Wickenburg, AZ
Lobert, Rev. Richard C., '75 (BAL) On Leave.
LoBianco, Rev. Msgr. Francis R., '54 (NEW) Retired.
LoBianco, Rev. Richard J., '79 (CHI) Holy Cross, Deerfield, IL
LoBiondo, Rev. Gasper F., *S.J.* '68 (WDC) Gonzaga College High School, Washington, DC (>PH) [MON] Jesuit Community at St. Joseph's University, Merion Station, PA
Lobo, Rev. Joseph, (RVC) SS. Philip and James, St. James, NY
Lobo, Rev. Maicaal, '94 (FTW) St. Rose of Lima, Monroeville, IN
Lobo, Rev. Manuel Morales, *CRS* '02 (CHR) St. Thomas the Apostle, North Charleston, SC
Lobo, Rev. Prashanth, *M.SS.CC.* (LEX) Holy Spirit Church - the Newman Center, Lexington, KY; Our Lady of Perpetual Help, Williamsburg, KY; St. Boniface, Williamsburg, KY
Lobo, Rev. Raul Venust, '62 (NO) Retired.
Lobo, Rev. Stanley M., '65 (NEW) Retired. St. Michael, Palisades Park, NJ
Loch, Rev. Killian (Richard), *O.S.B.* '79 (GBG) [MON] Saint Vincent Archabbey, Latrobe, PA
Lock, Rev. Bertram, *SS.CC.* '89 (HON) St. Patrick, Honolulu, HI
Lockard, Rev. Msgr. David A., '75 (ALT) St. Michael's, St. Michael, PA
Locke, Rev. James E., '61 (PH) Retired.
Lockey, Rev. Paul E., '87 (GAL) [SEM] St. Mary's Seminary, Houston, TX
Lockwood, Rev. Gregory J., '88 (KC) Christ the King, Kansas City, MO
Lockwood, Rev. Keeton, (FTW) St. Michael, Plymouth, IN
LoCoco, Rev. John C., '18 (MIL) On Special Assignment. Vocations Director, St Francis de Sales Seminary Curia: Leadership
Loda, Rev. Mauro, *S.X.* '99 (PAT) [MON] Xaverian Missionary Fathers, Wayne, NJ
Lodge, Rev. John G., '73 (CHI) Retired. [SEM] University of Saint Mary of the Lake/Mundelein Seminary, Mundelein, IL
Lodge, Rev. Simon, '00 (SAC) Pastor of Sacred Heart Parish, Sacramento, a corporation sole, Sacramento, CA
Lodi, Rev. George C., '74 (NY) Parish of St. Margaret of Cortona and St. Gabriel, Bronx, NY
Lody, Rev. John, '62 (Y) Retired.
Lody, Rev. Joseph Delano, '03 (BIR) Church of the Resurrection, Clanton, AL
Loeb, Rev. Karl E., '95 (BUF) St. Vincent de Paul Roman Catholic Church, Springbrook, NY
Loebl, Rev. Jeffrey R., *S.J.* '82 (MIL) [MON] St. Camillus Jesuit Community (Society of Jesus, USA Midwest Province), Wauwatosa, WI
Loecke, Rev. Douglas J., '89 (DUB) St. Matthew's Church, Cedar Rapids, Iowa, Cedar Rapids, IA; [CEM] Mt. Cavalry Cemetery Association, Cedar Rapids, Iowa, Cedar Rapids, IA
Loecker, Rev. Craig J., '92 (OM) St. Leo, Omaha, NE
Loeffler, Rev. David, '16 (PHX) Curia: Offices and Directors Bourgade Catholic High School, Phoenix, AZ; [CAM] Holy Spirit Roman Catholic Newman Center Phoenix, Phoenix, AZ
Loehr, Rev. Jared, *LC* '19 (DAL) [MON] Legionaries of Christ, Irving, TX
Loeper, Rev. David J., '83 (ALN) Chap, York Terrace Nursing Home Curia: Leadership St. Mary, Hamburg, PA
Loera, Rev. Abel, '03 (LA) On Duty Outside Diocese.

Loera, Rev. Abel, '03 (LA) On Duty Outside Diocese.
Loester, Rev. Christopher Brenden, '22 (CHR) St. Francis By the Sea, Hilton Head Island, SC
Loew, Rev. James H., *O.S.B.* '97 (GBG) Curia: Advisory Boards, Commissions, Committees, and Councils Christ the King, Leechburg, PA; St. Gertrude, Vandergrift, PA; [MON] Saint Vincent Archabbey, Latrobe, PA
Lofgren, Rev. Eric D., '93 (SAC) Curia: Leadership Pastor of St. Joseph Parish, Redding, a corporation sole, Redding, CA
Loftin, Rev. Don, '94 (AUS) Retired.
Lofton, Rev. Msgr. Edward D., '82 (CHR) Retired. Curia: Offices and Directors
Lofton, Rev. James J., '61 (ALN) Retired.
Loftus, Rev. David C., '94 (LA) Our Lady of Lourdes, Northridge, CA
Loftus, Rev. Joseph, *F.S.S.P.* (SEA) St. Joseph, Tacoma, WA
Loftus, Rev. Msgr. Padraic, '62 (LA) Retired.
Loftus, Rev. Robert A., '91 (WOR) St. Joseph-St. Pius X Parish, Leicester, MA
Loftus, Rev. Steven P., '02 (PEO) Curia: Deaneries Holy Family, Danville, IL; St. Anthony Church, Hoopeston, IL
Logan, Rev. Aidan (Arthur H.), *O.C.S.O.* '85 (WOR) [MON] St. Joseph's Abbey (Cistercian Abbey of Spencer, Inc., Cistercian Order of the Strict Observance (Trappists)), Spencer, MA
Logan, Rev. James J., '59 (LC) Retired.
Logan, Rev. Nilsen, (CAM) Church of Saint Elizabeth Ann Seton, Absecon, N.J., Absecon, NJ
Loggiodice, Rev. Omar, '09 (ATL) On Sick Leave. St. Vincent De Paul Catholic Church, Dallas, Inc., Dallas, GA
Logiste, Rev. Eduardo, *O.P.* '10 (MIA) St. Dominic, Miami, FL; [MON] Dominican Fathers of Miami, Inc., Miami, FL
Logsdon, Rev. Peter F., '14 (LFT) Holy Trinity, Bryant, IN; Immaculate Conception, Portland, IN; St. Joseph, Winchester, IN; St. Mary, Union City, IN
Logue, Rev. Joseph, *S.V.D.* '83 (CHI) Retired. [MON] Divine Word Residence, Techny, IL
Logue, Rev. Mark J., '73 (BAL) Retired.
Logue, Rev. Stephen, (HBG) Lancaster Catholic High School, Lancaster, PA
Logue, Rev. Thomas, '22 (JOL) St. Raphael, Naperville, IL
Lohan, Rev. Louis, '71 (BLX) Retired.
Lohan, Rev. William P., (BO) On Leave.
Lohse, Rev. Msgr. Edward M., '89 (E) Curia: Leadership; Offices and Directors St. Julia, Erie, PA
Loiacono, Rev. James, *O.M.I.* '79 (BUF) Holy Cross, Buffalo, NY
Lojek, Rev. Robert J., '03 (CHI) SS. Constance and Robert Bellarmine Parish, Chicago, IL
Lokidiryo, Rev. Benson Lotiang'a, '20 (CIN) St. Andrew, Milford, OH; St. Elizabeth Ann Seton, Milford, OH; St. Veronica, Cincinnati, OH
Lokpo, Rev. Jean Philippe, *MCCJ* '10 (CHI) [MON] Comboni Missionaries, La Grange Park, IL
Lokpo, Rev. Koudjo K, *MCCJ* (CHI) St. John XXIII, Evanston, IL
Lokuhettige, Rev. Sasika, *S.B.D.* (NEW) Don Bosco Preparatory High School (Salesians of St. John Bosco), Ramsey, NJ; [MON] Don Bosco Prep Salesian Residence, Ramsey, NJ (>NY) [RTR] Don Bosco Retreat Center and Marian Shrine, Stony Point, NY; (>NY) [RTR] Marian Shrine, Stony Point, NY
Lomasiewicz, Rev. Donald E., '62 (GR) Retired. Sacred Heart of Jesus, Grand Rapids, MI
Lomax, Rev. Mark, '80 (NO) Retired.
Lombardi, Rev. Gary, '69 (SR) Retired.
Lombardi, Rev. John J., '92 (BAL) St. Peter's, Hancock, MD
Lombardi, Rev. Joseph L., *S.J.* '75 (PH) [MIS] Jesuit Fathers, , ; [MON] Jesuit Community at St. Joseph's University, Merion Station, PA
Lombardi, Rev. Michael, '21 (RVC) St. Patrick, Smithtown, NY
Lombardi, Rev. Miguel, *IVE* '01 (SJ) Our Lady of Peace, Santa Clara, CA; [MON] The Institute of the Incarnate Word (IVE), Santa Clara, CA
Lombardi, Rev. Nicholas D, *S.J.* '72 (NY) [MON] Jesuit Community at Fordham University, New York, NY
Lombardo, Rev. Claude, *MC* (SD)
Lombardo, Rev. Francis, *O.F.M.Conv.* '71 (BUF) Retired. [MON] St. Francis of Assisi Friary, Hamburg, NY
Lombardo, Rev. Joseph A., '85 (TUC) Retired.
Lombardo, Rev. Michael D., '78 (PAT) Our Lady of Consolation, Wayne, NJ
Lombardo, Rev. Nicholas E., *O.P.* '04 (WDC) [COL] Catholic University of America, The, Washington, DC; [SEM] Dominican House of Studies, Washington, DC
Lomeli, Rev. Juan Carlos Garcia, *MSE* '19 (LA) St. Gerard Majella, Los Angeles, CA
Lomibao, Rev. Conrado, (RNO) Chap, St Mary's Hosp, Reno
Lomica, Rev. Frank A., '02 (DEN) On Duty Outside Diocese.
Lomnitzer, Rev. Colin, '22 (BGP) St. Mary's Corporation, Ridgefield, CT
LoMonaco, Rev. Lawrence M., '02 (CHL) St. Aloysius, Hickory, NC
Loncar, Rev. Stephen, *O.F.M.Conv.* '88 (GRY) St. Thomas Aquinas, Knox, IN
Lonchyna, Very Rev. Taras, '77 (PHU) Curia: Leadership; Offices and Directors
Lonchyna, Rev. Taras R., '77 (PHU) St. Josaphat's, Trenton, NJ
Loncle, Rev. John, '05 (ROC) Blessed Sacrament, Rochester, NY; St. Boniface, Rochester, NY; St. Mary, Rochester, NY
Londono, Rev. Carlos L., '20 (MIL) Our Lady of Divine Providence Congregation, Milwaukee, WI; SS. Peter and Paul, Milwaukee, WI; St. Mary's Congregation, Milwaukee, WI; Three Holy Women Congregation, Milwaukee, WI
Londono, Rev. Fernando, '16 (DEN) On Duty Outside Diocese. (>PH) St. Michael, Philadelphia, PA
Londono, Rev. Hugo A., '11 (MIL) St. Anthonys Congregation, Milwaukee, WI; St. Hyacinth's Congregation, Milwaukee, WI
Londono, Rev. Oscar, (GR) St. Edward, Lake Odessa, MI
Londono, Rev. Wilder A., '14 (PAT) [HOS] St. Joseph's University Medical Center, Paterson, NJ
Londoño, Rev. Yonhatan, '19 (MIA) St. Katharine Drexel, Weston, FL
Londono Zuluaga, Rev. Edwin Albeiro, '07 (SJN) Curia: Offices and Directors San Francisco de Sales, Catano, PR
Lonek, Rev. Stephen C., '76 (WIL) Our Lady of Good Counsel, Secretary, MD; St. Mary Refuge of Sinners, Cambridge, MD
Lonergan, Rev. James Barry, '66 (ALB) Retired.
Lonergan, Rev. Lester, *M.H.M.* '62 (NY) Retired. [MON] Mill Hill Fathers Residence, Hartsdale, NY
Lonergan, Rev. Michael J., '93 (PH) Retired. Our Lady of Fatima, Secane, PA
Lonfo, Rev. Yacob Fopa, '19 (STV) [MIS] Miscellaneous Organizations, Charlotte Amalie, VI
Lonfo, Rev. Yacob Fopa, '18 (STV) Church of the Holy Cross, Christiansted, VI
Long, Rev. Anthony Vu Khac, '92 (RCK) On Special Assignment. Curia: Offices and Directors St. Mary, DeKalb, IL
Long, Rev. Daniel, '94 (CHI) Cristo Rey Parish, Chicago, IL
Long, Rev. Daniel, (NOR) St. Mary Church of the Visitation, Clinton, CT
Long, Rev. David P., '02 (PAT) On Leave.
Long, Rev. Dominic, *S.S.S.* (SP) St. Vincent De Paul, Holiday, FL
Long, Rev. Garrett J., *S.M.* '76 (RVC) [MON] Provincial Residence and Novitiate, Mineola, NY
Long, Rev. J. William, '89 (R) Retired.
Long, Rev. James T., '63 (BEL) Retired.
Long, Rev. John, '78 (STP) Retired.
Long, Rev. John, '61 (JC) Retired.
Long, Rev. John Paul, '68 (BGP) Retired. [MON] The Catherine Dennis Keefe Queen of the Clergy Retired Priests' Residence, Stamford, CT
Long, Rev. John R., '89 (SUP) St. Bridget, Wilson, WI; St. John, Clear Lake, WI; St. John the Baptist, Glenwood City, WI
Long, Rev. Joseph J., *C.S.C.* '59 (ORL) [MON] Congregation of Holy Cross, United States Province, Cocoa Beach, FL
Long, Rev. Joseph J., *C.S.C.* '59 (SCR) Retired.
Long, Rev. Mark J., '07 (TUC) Curia: Consultative Bodies; Leadership Saint Ambrose Roman Catholic Parish - Tucson, Tucson, AZ
Long, Very Rev. Matthew T., '09 (SHP) Curia: Leadership; Offices and Directors St. Joseph, Shreveport, LA
Long, Rev. Melvin, '66 (SAL) Retired.
Long, Rev. Nathan, '08 (LKC) Curia: Advisory Boards, Commissions, Committees, and Councils St. Louis Catholic High School, Lake Charles, LA; St. Margaret, Lake Charles, LA
Long, Rev. Nguyen Phi, *C.Ss.R.* '03 (LA) [MON] Vietnamese Redemptorist Mission, Baldwin Park, CA
Long, Rev. Richard E., '90 (BRK) St. Mary Mother of Jesus, Brooklyn, NY; [CAM] Campus Ministers and Ministry Centers (Newman Apostolate, Inc.), Brooklyn, NY
Long, Very Rev. Thomas, '91 (GB) Curia: Advisory Boards, Commissions, Committees, and Councils
Long, Rev. Thomas E., *C.S.V.* '69 (CHI) [MON] Viatorian Province Center-Clerics of St. Viator, Arlington Heights, IL
Long, Rev. Vincent P., '69 (SY) Chap, Marcy Corr Fac; Mohawk Corr Fac, Oneida St. Leo & St. Ann, Holland Patent, NY
Long, Rev. W. Thomas, '91 (GB) St. Mary, Omro, WI; St. Mary, Winneconne, WI; St. Raphael the Archangel, Oshkosh, WI
Longalong, Rev. Patrick H., '08 (BRK) Curia: Consultative Bodies Our Lady of Lourdes, Queens Village, NY; [CCH] Filipino Ministry, ,
Longanga, Very Rev. Emery, '94 (SP) Curia: Pastoral Services Holy Cross, St. Petersburg, FL
Longbucco, Rev. John L., '90 (MAR) Retired.
Longe, Rev. James W., '07 (SPR) On Leave.
Longenecker, Rev. Dwight, '06 (CHR) Our Lady of the Rosary, Greenville, SC
Longo, Rev. Kirby, '17 (HEL) Christ the King Parish: Series 638, LLC, Missoula, MT
Longo, Rev. Robert, *O.F.M.Cap.* '85 (CAM) Retired.
Longobucco, Very Rev. Robert, '98 (ALB) On Special Assignment. Curia: Leadership; Offices and Directors St. Kateri Tekakwitha Parish, Schenectady, NY
Longoria, Rev. Jose Delacruz, *M.N.M.* '96 (ELP) Christ the King, Pecos, TX; Santa Rosa de Lima, Pecos, TX; St. Catherine, Pecos, TX
Longtin, Rev. Lucien, *S.J.* (PH) Retired. [MON] Jesuit Community at St. Joseph's University, Merion Station, PA
Lonzo, Rev. Anthony P., '05 (COL) Church of the Blessed Sacrament, Newark, OH
Looby, Rev. Christopher J., '01 (OG) Our Lady of Lourdes Church, Schroon Lake, NY, Schroon Lake, NY; St. Mary's Church, Ticonderoga, NY, Ticonderoga, NY
Looby, Rev. John J., '66 (OG) Retired.
Loomis, Rev. Sean A., '13 (PH) Curia: Evangelization Annunciation B.V.M., Havertown, PA
Loomis, Very Rev. Thomas A., '92 (WIN) Curia: Advisory Boards, Commissions, Committees, and Councils; Deaneries Holy Spirit, Rochester, MN; St. Bernard's, Stewartville, MN; St. Bridget's, Rochester, MN
Looney, Rev. Daniel A., '71 (SAC) Retired.
Looney, Rev. Edward L., '15 (GB) St. Francis & St. Mary Parish, Brussels, WI; St. Peter and St. Hubert, Casco, WI
Looney, Rev. Joseph E., '11 (HRT) Retired.
Looney, Rev. Thomas P., *C.S.C.* '87 (SCR) [COL] King's College, Wilkes-Barre, PA
Loos, Rev. Frederick C., '63 (SAG) Retired. On Duty Outside Diocese. Linden Square Assisted Living, Saline
Lopatesky, Rev. Msgr. Raymond M., '75 (PAT) Retired. [MIS] Nazareth Village, Chester, NJ
Lope, Rev. Elvio Baldeon, (CHI) St. Mary of the Lake and Our Lady of Lourdes Parish, Chicago, IL
Lopera, Rev. Carlos Mario, '86 (STA) Basilica of the Immaculate Conception, Jacksonville, FL
Lopes, Rev. Richard, *O.F.M.Cap.* '82 (SFR) [MON] Capuchin Provincial House, Burlingame, CA
Lopes, Rev. Richard A., *O.F.M.Cap* '82 (MO) Curia: Offices and Directors
Lopes, Rev. Thomas C., '65 (FR) Retired. Curia: Leadership
Lopez, Rev. Abel, '56 (SJ) Retired.
Lopez, Rev. Agustin, (WDC) St. Matthew Cathedral, Washington, DC
Lopez, Rev. Alfred A., *OP* '84 (CHI) [MON] Dominican Community of St. Martin de Porres, Oak Park, IL
Lopez, Rev. Alvaro M., '86 (STO) St. Jude Church (Pastor of), Ceres, CA
Lopez, Rev. Amador, (SAT) Retired. [NUR] Oblate Madonna Residence, San Antonio, TX
Lopez, Rev. Anthony, '08 (NSH) Our Lady of Lourdes, Springfield, TN
Lopez, Rev. Antonio, *F.S.C.B.* '95 (WDC) [MIS] Priestly Fraternity of the Missionaries of St. Charles Borromeo, Inc., Bethesda, MD
Lopez, Rev. Antony, *O.C.D.* '96 (PMB) St. Mark the Evangelist, Fort Pierce, FL

Lopez, Rev. Armando, *O.F.M.* '88 (LA) Our Lady of Victory, Los Angeles, CA
Lopez, Rev. Armando, *OFM* (OAK) [MON] Franciscan Friars of California (Province of St. Barbara), Oakland, CA
Lopez, Rev. Arturo, *OFM* (LA) Assumption, Los Angeles, CA
Lopez, Rev. Augustine, (WDC) On Duty Outside Diocese. St Louis, MO
Lopez, Rev. Basker, (KAL) St. Mary of the Assumption, Three Oaks, MI; St. Mary of the Lake, New Buffalo, MI
Lopez, Rev. Brandon Robert, '21 (ORG) St. Kilian, Mission Viejo, CA
Lopez, Rev. Camilo, '93 (NEW) Saint Michael the Archangel, Union, NJ
Lopez, Rev. Carlos, *O.S.B.* '02 (LA) [MON] St. Andrew's Abbey (Benedictine Monks), Valyermo, CA
Lopez, Rev. Carlos A., (ARE) On Duty Outside Diocese. Boston, MA
Lopez, Rev. Carlos A., (BO) On Leave.
Lopez, Rev. Daniel, '22 (LA) St. John Chrysostom, Inglewood, CA
Lopez, Rev. Msgr. Daniel, '63 (FRS) Retired.
Lopez, Rev. David, '19 (FRS) Our Lady of Perpetual Help, Bakersfield, CA
Lopez, Rev. David, *FSSP* '22 (ALN) St. Stephen of Hungary, Allentown, PA
Lopez, Rev. Eddy E., (PRO) On Leave.
Lopez, Rev. Edgar, *O.Carm.* '13 (TUC) Saint Cyril of Alexandria Roman Catholic Parish - Tucson, Tucson, AZ
Lopez, Rev. Edilberto Beto, '97 (ELP) San Juan Bautista, El Paso, TX; St. Joseph Mission, Ft. Davis, TX; St. Pius X, El Paso, TX
Lopez, Rev. Eli, '15 (GAL) Christ Our Light, Navasota, TX
Lopez, Rev. Elias, (GAL) All Saints, Houston, TX
Lopez, Rev. Elpidio, '96 (TYL) San Pedro the Fisherman, Tatum, TX
Lopez, Rev. Emmanuel Garduno, (KC) St. John Francis Regis, Kansas City, MO
Lopez, Rev. Ernesto, '06 (LUB) Curia: Leadership; Offices and Directors St. Philip Benizi, Shallowater, TX
Lopez, Rev. Fernando, *O.S.A.* '13 (LA) St. Thomas Aquinas, Ojai, CA
Lopez, Rev. Fernando, (NSH) Our Lady of Guadalupe, Antioch, TN
Lopez, Rev. Frank, '93 (ELP) St. Matthew, El Paso, TX
Lopez, Rev. Msgr. Gerard M., '91 (SB) Curia: Advisory Boards, Commissions, Committees, and Councils; Leadership [CEM] Our Lady Queen of Peace Catholic Cemetery, Colton, CA; [MIS] Diocese of San Bernardino Cemetery Corp., Inc., San Bernardino, CA
Lopez, Rev. Gustavo, *O.S.J.* '09 (FRS) Shrine of Our Lady of Guadalupe, Co-Patroness of the Unborn, Bakersfield, CA
Lopez, Rev. Gustavo, '95 (LFT) All Saints, Logansport, IN; St. Charles Borromeo, Peru, IN
Lopez, Rev. Gustavo, '90 (HRT) North American Martyrs Parish Corporation, East Hartford, CT
Lopez, Rev. Gustavo C., *C.S.V.* '16 (CHI) [MON] Viatorian Province Center-Clerics of St. Viator, Arlington Heights, IL
Lopez, Rev. Hector, '10 (FRS) St. Philip the Apostle, Bakersfield, CA
Lopez, Rev. Inigo, '01 (DAL) Sacred Heart Catholic Parish, Rowlett, TX
Lopez, Very Rev. Jairo, '94 (AUS) Curia: Leadership St. John the Evangelist, San Marcos, TX
Lopez, Rev. James F., '04 (DET) St. Sabina Parish Dearborn Heights, Dearborn Heights, MI
Lopez, Rev. Joel N., '03 (RCK) Holy Trinity, Scales Mound, IL; St. Mary, Galena, IL; St. Michael, Galena, IL
Lopez, Rev. Johnson, '11 (RCK) St. Edward, Rockford, IL
Lopez, Rev. Jorge, '17 (WCH) Our Lady of Guadalupe, Newton, KS
Lopez, Rev. Jorge Jesus, (LA) [COL] Thomas Aquinas College, Santa Paula, CA
Lopez, Rev. Jose, '94 (JKS) Retired.
Lopez, Rev. Jose, (GB) SS. Peter and Paul Catholic Congregation, Green Bay, WI
Lopez, Rev. Jose, '11 (PAT) On Leave.
Lopez, Rev. Jose E., '94 (BRK) Holy Spirit, Brooklyn, NY
Lopez, Rev. Jose Carlos Miguel, *G.H.M.* '21 (R) St. Joan of Arc, Plymouth, NC
Lopez, Rev. Joseph, '02 (CC) Curia: Leadership Most Precious Blood, Corpus Christi, TX; [MIS] Journey to Damascus, Inc., Corpus Christi, TX
Lopez, Rev. Juan, '18 (BRK) St. Joseph Patron of the Universal Church, Brooklyn, NY
Lopez, Rev. Juan C., (SB) St. Catherine of Alexandria, Temecula, CA
Lopez, Rev. Juan Carlos, '03 (AUS) St. Elizabeth, Pflugerville, TX
Lopez, Rev. Juan J., '89 (ARE) On Duty Outside Diocese. Sunrise, FL
Lopez, Rev. Juan M., '62 (MIA) Retired.
Lopez, Rev. Juan Manuel, '08 (SFR) Church of the Assumption, Tomales, CA
Lopez, Rev. Julius, '89 (ORL) Most Precious Blood Catholic Church, Oviedo, FL
Lopez, Rev. Karlogs, (CGS) Nuestra Senora del Carmen, Cidra, PR; [MIS] Movimiento Juan XXIII, Caguas, PR
Lopez, Rev. Leonardo, '11 (PAT) Sacred Heart Church and Our Lady Queen of the Most Holy Rosary, Dover, NJ
Lopez, Rev. Lionel, '96 (MIA) Belen Jesuit Preparatory School, Inc., Miami, FL
Lopez, Rev. Lionel, '96 (BWN) On Duty Outside Diocese. Arch. Miami (Belen Jesuit Preparatory School, Miami, FL)
Lopez, Rev. Luis, '16 (OAK) Corpus Christi, Fremont, CA
Lopez, Rev. Luis E., *C.S.V.* '95 (CHI) [MON] Viatorian Province Center-Clerics of St. Viator, Arlington Heights, IL
Lopez, Rev. Luis Rene, (AMA) St. Vincent de Paul, Pampa, TX
Lopez, Rev. Manny, (STA) Santa Maria Del Mar, Flagler Beach, FL
Lopez, Rev. Manuel, '10 (ORG) Mission Basilica - San Juan Capistrano, San Juan Capistrano, CA
Lopez, Rev. Marco T., '97 (SLC) Saint Bridget LLC 217, Milford, UT
Lopez, Rev. Mariano H., '11 (ELP) San Antonio, El Paso, TX
Lopez, Rev. Mario, *O.Carm* '76 (SAC) Retired. Pastor of Our Lady of Mount Carmel Parish, Fairfield, a Corporation Sole, Fairfield, CA
Lopez, Rev. Mario A., '10 (ATL) St. Francis of Assisi Catholic Church, Blairsville, Inc., Blairsville, GA
Lopez, Rev. Mauricio A., '92 (SAT) On Leave.
Lopez, Rev. Nahum, '10 (LUB) St. Francis of Assisi Mission, Wolfforth, TX; St. Theresa's, Lubbock, TX
Lopez, Rev. Nathan, '19 (SFE) San Juan Bautista, Ohkay Owingeh, NM
Lopez, Rev. Nestor, '99 (JOL) St. Dominic, Bolingbrook, IL
Lopez, Rev. Oscar A. Sanchez, (FAJ) Curia: Offices and Directors Cristo Rey, Palmer, PR
Lopez, Rev. Pedro J., '81 (LA) Our Lady of Guadalupe, Santa Barbara, CA
Lopez, Rev. Ramon A., '08 (NY) Our Lady of Esperanza, New York, NY; St. Rose of Lima, New York, NY; [MIS] St. Joseph's Cursillo Center, Bronx, NY
Lopez, Rev. Raul Martinez, (FWT) On Leave.
Lopez, Rev. Renato, *P.S.S.* '86 (BAL) [MIS] St. Mary's Seminary & University, Baltimore, MD; [MON] Society of St. Sulpice, Province of the United States, Baltimore, MD
Lopez, Rev. Renato, *P.S.S.* (SAT) Curia: Leadership [SEM] The Seminary of the Assumption of the Blessed Virgin Mary-St. John of San Antonio, TX (Assumption-St. John's Seminary), San Antonio, TX
Lopez, Rev. Msgr. Richard J., '73 (ATL) Retired.
Lopez, Rev. Roger, *O.F.M.* '16 (CIN) Roger Bacon High School, Cincinnati, OH; [MON] Brother Juniper Friary, Cincinnati, OH
Lopez, Rev. Sergio, '98 (OAK) Curia: Offices and Directors St. John the Baptist, San Lorenzo, CA
Lopez, Rev. Stephen Maria, *O.P.* '10 (OAK) [MON] Order of Preachers (Province of the Most Holy Name of Jesus - Western Dominican Province), Oakland, CA
Lopez, Rev. Vincent, *OP* '56 (LA) St. Dominic, Los Angeles, CA
López, Rev. Edgardo, '83 (MGZ) Church of San Isidro, Sabana Grande, PR
Lopez Alvarez, Rev. Jose Enrique, '19 (MIA) On Special Assignment. Doctoral Studies, Catholic University of America
Lopez Arias, Rev. Jose Jesus, '08 (PHX) Curia: Leadership Holy Trinity Newman Center, A Quasi-Parish, Flagstaff, AZ; St. Vincent de Paul Roman Catholic Parish, Phoenix, AZ
Lopez Camarena, Friar Francisco Javier, *OFM* '94 (ELP) [SEM] Roger Bacon College, El Paso, TX
Lopez Cardinale, Rev. Alejandro, '91 (BO) Sacred Hearts, Malden, MA; St. Benedict, Somerville, MA
Lopez Cortes, Rev. Juan, *MSP* '13 (SAN) St. Joseph, San Angelo, TX
Lopez Cruz, Rev. Serapio, '82 (STV) Cathedral of SS. Peter and Paul, Charlotte Amalie, VI
Lopez Cruz, Rev. Victor Bruno, (PCE) Retired. On Leave.
Lopez Figueroa, Rev. Msgr. Alberto, '87 (SJN) Catalina de Siena, Bayamon, PR
Lopez Galarza, Rev. Luis Alfredo, *C.P.* '91 (NY) [MON] The Congregation of the Passion - St. Paul of the Cross Province, Jamaica, NY
Lopez Ortiz, Rev. Feliciano, *O.M.I.* '15 (LA) St. Ferdinand, San Fernando, CA
Lopez Solis, Rev. Marciano, *AA* '19 (ELP) St. Francis Xavier, El Paso, TX
Lopez Vega, Rev. Jose Antonio, '92 (PCE) Curia: Leadership; Offices and Directors Academia Cristo Rey Inc., Ponce, PR; Cristo Rey, Ponce, PR
Lopez-Betanzos, Very Rev. Gabriel A., '15 (MAD) Curia: Offices and Directors St. Peter Catholic Church, Madison, WI
Lopez-Cardinale, Rev. Alejandro, '91 (NEW) Curia: Organizations (affiliated, inter-Diocesan, miscellaneous/ other) Blessed Sacrament, Elizabeth, NJ
Lopez-Flores, Rev. Antonio, '02 (ORG) Our Lady of Fatima, San Clemente, CA
Lopez-Galarza, Rev. Luis Alfredo, *C.P.* '91 (ATL) St. Paul of the Cross Catholic Church, Atlanta, Inc., Atlanta, GA
Lopez-Lopez, Rev. Ramon, *O.F.M.Cap.* '76 (SJN) San Francisco de Asis, San Juan, PR
Lopez-Restrepo, Rev. Eugenio, '84 (SAC) Retired.
Lopez-Romo, Rev. Eduardo, '03 (TUC) Immaculate Heart of Mary Roman Catholic Parish - Somerton, Somerton, AZ
López-Sanchez, Rev. Angel, *C.Ss.R.* (CGS) Church of Tres Santos Reyes, Aguas Buenas, PR
Lopina, Rev. Justin L., '14 (MIL) Curia: Leadership Sacred Heart Congregation, Horicon, WI; St. Matthew's Congregation, Neosho, WI
LoPinto, Rev. Msgr. Alfred P., '70 (BRK) Curia: Leadership; Pastoral Services St. Charles Borromeo, Brooklyn, NY; [CCH] Catholic Charities Neighborhood Services, Inc., Brooklyn, NY; [CCH] Catholic Charities, Diocese of Brooklyn, Brooklyn, NY; [CCH] Housing Development and Management Services, Brooklyn, NY; [SPF] Saints Joachim and Anne Nursing and Rehabilitation Center, Brooklyn, NY
LoPinto, Rev. Msgr. Alfred P., (BRK) Curia: Consultative Bodies [CCH] Catholic Charities Progress of Peoples Development Corporation, Brooklyn, NY; [CCH] Progress of Peoples Management Corporation, Brooklyn, NY
Lopoke, Rev. Symphorien O., '94 (DAV) St. Mary Church of Iowa City, Iowa, Iowa City, IA
LoPresti, Rev. Carl, '97 (PEO) Retired.
Lopresti, Rev. Marcelo R., *I.V.E.* '02 (BGP) On Duty Outside Diocese. Re-assigned by I.V.E.
Lorance, Very Rev. Archpriest Douglas, '84 (SJP) Curia: Leadership; Offices and Directors St. Michael, Lyndora, PA
Lorcha, Rev. Ronie R., *C.R.M.* (CHR) St. Anne and St. Jude, Sumter, SC
Lord, Rev. David, *M.I.C.* '91 (SPR) [MON] Congregation of Marian Fathers of The Immaculate Conception of the Most Blessed Virgin Mary, Stockbridge, MA
Lord, Rev. Laurence J., '64 (SY) Retired.
Lorden, Rev. Demetrio, '70 (SP) Retired.
Lorei, Rev. Brian T., '09 (ATL) St. Stephen the Martyr Catholic Church, Lilburn, Inc., Lilburn, GA
Lorens, Rev. Grzegorz, '14 (CHI) St. Monica and St. Rosalie Parish, Chicago, IL
Lorente, Rev. Jose, '65 (MET) Retired. Our Lady of Mt. Carmel, New Brunswick, NJ; [MON] Society of Jesus Christ the Priest, Stewartsville, NJ
Lorentsen, Friar Michael, *O.F.M.Conv.* (TR) St. Junipero Serra, Seaside Park, Seaside Park, NJ
Lorenz, Rev. Bernard A., '85 (LIN) Curia: Leadership St. Patrick, McCook, NE
Lorenz, Rev. Matthais E., '69 (CHI) Retired.
Lorenzana Fernandez, Rev. Elias, *O.de.M.* '55 (SJN) Colegio Nuestra Senora de La Merced, Hato Rey, PR; Ntra. Sra. de Fatima, San Juan, PR
Lorenzetti, Rev. Msgr. Dino J., '53 (BUF) Retired. [MON] O'Hara Residence, Tonawanda, NY
Lorenzo, Rev. Eduardo, '66 (LAN) Retired.
Lorenzo, Rev. Joseph, *O.F.M.* (NY) [MON] Franciscan Province of the Immaculate Conception, New York, NY; [MON] Padua Friary, New York, NY
Lorenzo, Rev. Juan, '97 (VEN) St. Michael Parish in Wauchula, Inc., Wauchula, FL
Lorenzoni, Rev. Larry, *S.D.B.* '51 (SFR) Retired.
Lorenzo-Puga, Rev. Andy, '03 (MIA) [MIS] Catholic Hospice, Inc., Miami, FL
Loresca, Rev. Victorino, (ELP) Our Lady of Peace, Alpine, TX; St. Joseph, Fort Davis, TX

Lorge, Rev. Felix P., '50 (SPK) Retired.
Lorig, Rev. Jeffrey P., '04 (OM) On Leave.
Lorilla, Rev. Ron, '17 (SFD) Chap, Jacksonville Corr Ctr Sacred Heart of Jesus, Franklin, IL; Sacred Heart of Mary, New Berlin, IL; St. Sebastian, Waverly, IL; Visitation B.V.M., Alexander, IL
Lorrain, Rev. Matthew P., '86 (BR) Congregation Of Holy Rosary Roman Catholic Church, St. Amant, Ascension Parish, Louisiana, St. Amant, LA
Lorsung, Rev. Kevin, '21 (FAR) St. James Basilica of Jamestown, Jamestown, ND; St. Margaret Church of Buchanan, Buchanan, ND; St. Mathias Church of Windsor, Windsor, ND
LosBanes, Rev. Hermes, '86 (MO) Curia: Offices and Directors
Loseke, Rev. Jeffery S., '00 (OM) Curia: Offices and Directors St. Charles Borromeo, Gretna, NE
Loskot, Rev. Donald, *S.D.S.* '76 (MIL) Retired. [MIS] Salvatorians - Jordan Hall, Milwaukee, WI
Losoya, Rev. Jose E., *C.O.* '91 (BWN) Curia: Advisory Boards, Commissions, Committees, and Councils; Leadership Oratory Academy of St. Philip Neri, Pharr, TX; Oratory Athenaeum for University Preparation, Pharr, TX; St. Jude Thaddeus, Pharr, TX; [MON] Pharr Oratory of St. Philip Neri of Pontifical Right, Pharr, TX
Lostritto, Rev. Paul, *O.F.M.* '96 (NY) (>PH) [MON] Order of Friars Minor of the Province of the Most Holy Name, Philadelphia, PA
Loterte, Rev. Samuel, (HON) St. Theresa, Mountain View, HI
Loterte, Rev. Samuel E., *S.S.S.* '91 (HON) Holy Rosary, Keaau, HI
Lotha, Rev. Abraham, '89 (MET) Transfiguration of the Lord Parish, Highland Park, NJ
Lotz, Rev. Ezekiel, *O.S.B.* '00 (B) [MON] Monastery of the Ascension, Jerome, ID
Loua, Rev. Pascal, (BO) [MON] Alberto Hurtado House, Boston, MA
Loubriel, Rev. Harry, '05 (MIA) Mary Help of Christians Church, Parkland, FL
Louchs, Rev. Thomas, (B) St. Mary Station, Potlatch, ID
Loucks, Rev. Thomas J., '77 (B) Retired.
Loughery, Rev. Robert L., *C.S.C.* '89 (FTW) (>P) [MON] Priests of Holy Cross in Oregon, Inc., Portland, OR
Loughman, Rev. Msgr. Kenneth M., '58 (NY) Retired.
Loughnane, Rev. John B., '88 (MAN) Chap, Sullivan Cty House of Corrections All Saints Parish, Charlestown, NH; [CEM] St. Catherine Cemetery, Charlestown, NH; [CEM] St. Peter Cemetery, Walpole, NH
Loughney, Rev. Gregory F., '11 (SCR) On Administrative Leave.
Loughran, Rev. James L., *S.A.* '89 (NY) [MON] Atonement Friars, New York, NY; [MON] Franciscan Friars of the Atonement, Minister General Office, Garrison, NY; [MON] Graymoor Ecumenical and Interreligious Institute, New York, NY
Loughran, Rev. John, *OSFS* (LAN) [MON] Oblate Fathers of St. Francis De Sales, Inc., Brooklyn, MI; [RTR] Lake Vineyard Camps, Inc., (De Sales Center), Brooklyn, MI
Loughran, Very Rev. John J., *O.S.F.S.* '80 (TOL) [MON] Oblate Residences, Toledo, OH; [MON] Oblates of St. Francis de Sales, Toledo, OH
Louis, Rev. Arlin J., *O.M.I.* '13 (CHI) St. Andrew, Chicago, IL
Louis, Rev. Feliere, *C.S.* (MIA) St. Mary Star of the Sea Basilica, Key West, FL
Louis, Rev. Jean Woady, '91 (VEN) St. Margaret Parish in Clewiston, Inc., Clewiston, FL
Louis, Rev. Kevin C., '89 (LC) On Leave.
Louis, Rev. Misser, *C.M* (SJN) San Vicente de Paul, San Juan, PR
Louis, Rev. Olin Pierre, '09 (SJN) Chap, Hospital Del Nino San Jorge, Santurce San Mateo, San Juan, PR; [HOS] San Jorge's Children Hospital, San Juan, PR
Louis, Rev. Olin Pierre, (SJN) Nuestra Senora de la Providencia, San Juan, PR
Louis, Rev. Pascal, '83 (BRK) Co-Cathedral of Saint Joseph – Saint Teresa of Avila, Brooklyn, NY
Lourdhuraj Durairaj, Rev. Jude, *H.G.N.* (SB) St. Mary, Fontana, CA
Lourdu, Rev. Xavier, '06 (LA) Corpus Christi, Pacific Palisades, CA
Lourdusamy, Rev. Inbaraj, *H.G.N.* (PT) Baptist Hosp, Pensacola Little Flower, Pensacola, FL
Lourdusamy, Rev. Joseph, '95 (TYL) St. Leo the Great, Centerville, TX
Louzon, Rev. Bede, *O.F.M.Cap.* '85 (DET) [MON] St. Bonaventure Monastery, Detroit, MI
Lovas, Rev. Donald J., '63 (WIN) Retired.
Love, Rev. John W., '90 (LA) Curia: (>MO) Offices and Directors Santa Clara, Oxnard, CA
Love, Rev. Lawrence L., '14 (TYL) Curia: Advisory Boards, Commissions, Committees, and Councils St. Peter the Apostle, Mineola, TX
Love, Rev. Lester E., *S.J.* '91 (OAK) [MON] Jesuit Fathers and Brothers, Oakland, CA
Lovell, Rev. Allen B., '02 (CAM) Church of St. Rose, Haddon Heights, N.J., Haddon Heights, NJ
Lovell, Rev. John P, '07 (RCK) On Administrative Leave.
Loverita, Rev. Jonathan, (SP) Corpus Christi, Temple Terrace, FL
Lovska, Rev. Taras, (PSC) St. Ann, Harrisburg, PA
Low, Rev. Corwin, *O.P.* (P) (>SFR) St. Raymond, Menlo Park, CA
Lowchy, Rev. Gregory, '01 (R) St. Patrick, Fayetteville, NC
Lowe, Rev. Adam, '19 (HPM) St. Thomas the Apostle, Gilbert, AZ
Lowe, Rev. Adam, (PHX) Chap, St Joseph's Hosp, Phoenix
Lowe, Rev. Bryan K., '01 (BIR) Curia: Leadership; Offices and Directors St. John the Baptist Catholic Parish, Madison, Madison, AL; [CAM] Campus Ministry - University of Alabama in Huntsville, Madison, AL; [EFT] St. John's Columbarium Perpetual Care Fund, Madison, AL
Lowe, Rev. Christopher L., '15 (BO) Curia: Consultative Bodies St. Michael, Lowell, MA
Lowe, Rev. Frank E., '85 (SB) Retired.
Lowe, Rev. James, *C.C.* '11 (DET) St. Scholastica Parish Detroit, Detroit, MI
Lowe, Rev. Philip J., '82 (PH) On Special Assignment. Faculty - Neumann College, SS Simon & Jude Rec, West Chester SS. Simon and Jude, West Chester, PA
Lowe, Rev. William C.B., '07 (LA) [HOS] St. John's Pleasant Valley Hospital, Camarillo, CA
Lowery, Rev. Martin J., *M.M.* '68 (NY) [MON] Maryknoll Fathers and Brothers (Catholic Foreign Mission Society of America, Inc.), Ossining, NY
Lowery, Rev. Stephen, *C.O.* '09 (PIT) [CAM] Chatham College, Pittsburgh, PA; [CAM] University of Pittsburgh, Pittsburgh, PA; [MON] Congregation of the Oratory of St. Philip Neri, Pittsburgh, PA
Lowrey, Rev. Robert, *O.M.V.* '78 (BO) [MIS] St. Clement Archdiocesan Eucharistic Shrine, Boston, MA
Lowry, Rev. Matthew, '08 (PHX) Curia: Leadership; Offices and Directors Holy Trinity Newman Center, A Quasi-Parish, Flagstaff, AZ; [CAM] Holy Trinity Newman Center, A Quasi-Parish, Flagstaff, AZ
Lowry, Rev. Nolan T., '10 (TYL) Curia: Deaneries St. Edward Church, Athens, TX
Loya, Rev. John F., '74 (CLV) Retired. St. John of the Cross, Euclid, OH
Loya, Rev. Joseph, *O.S.A.* '79 (PH) Our Mother of Good Counsel, Bryn Mawr, PA; [COL] Villanova University, Villanova, PA; [MON] Augustinians Friars (O.S.A.), Bryn Mawr, PA; [MON] Saxony Hall, Rosemont, PA
Loya, Rev. Mario, *O.Carm.* '04 (JOL) [MON] Carmelite Provincial Office, Darien, IL
Loya, Very Rev. Thomas, '82 (PRM) Curia: Advisory Boards, Commissions, Committees, and Councils; Leadership Annunciation Byzantine Catholic Church, Homer Glen, IL; [MIS] Byzantine Catholic Outreach of Iowa, Muscatine, IA; [MIS] Byzantine Catholic Outreach of Omaha & Lincoln, Ralston, NE
Loyson, Rev. Michael, '92 (DET) Curia: Tribunal
Lozada, Rev. Edwin, (YAK) Our Lady of Fatima, Moses Lake, WA
Lozano, Rev. Bernardo, '01 (CHI) St. Albert the Great, Burbank, IL
Lozier, Rev. Donald G., *O.M.I.* '60 (BO) Retired. Holy Family, Lowell, MA; [NUR] Immaculate Heart of Mary Residence, Tewksbury, MA
Lozinski, Rev. Msgr. Eugene L., '72 (NU) On Special Assignment. Curia: Leadership; Offices and Directors; Organizations (affiliated, inter-Diocesan, miscellaneous/other) St. Brendan, Green Isle, MN; St. John-Assumption, Belle Plaine, MN; St. Joseph, Henderson, MN; St. Mary, Arlington, MN; St. Michael, Gaylord, MN; St. Thomas (Oratory), Henderson, MN
Lozinski, Rev. Robert W., *C.S.C.* '73 (PSC) Curia: Advisory Boards, Commissions, Committees, and Councils St. Michael, Dunmore, PA
Lozinskyy, Rev. Hryhoriy, (PSC) St. John the Baptist, Trumbull, CT
Lu, Rev. Kangqiang, (BRK) Our Lady of Perpetual Help Basilica, Brooklyn, NY
Luamanu, Rev. Setefano T., '92 (SPP) Curia: Offices and Directors
Luan, Rev. Felix, *CMC* (SB) [MON] Shrine of Presentation, Corona, CA
Luan, Rev. Nguyen Truong, '98 (LA) [MON] Vietnamese Redemptorist Mission, Baldwin Park, CA
Lubanga, Rev. Nathaniel O., *S.J.* '19 (MIL) [MON] Arrupe House Jesuit Community, Milwaukee, WI
Lubatti, Rev. Joseph, (FRS) Chap, Pathways Girls Rehab; State Prison, Wasco
Lubecke, Rev. Christopher B., '13 (L) Curia: Leadership St. Peter the Apostle Parish, Louisville, KY
Luberti, Rev. Richard, *C.Ss.R.* '79 (SEA) Sacred Heart of Jesus, Seattle, WA; [MON] The Redemptorist Society of Washington, Seattle, WA
Lubic, Rev. Robert T., '96 (GBG) On Leave.
Lubinsky, Rev. Michael, '78 (SAV) Retired.
Lubiv, Rev. Yoan, *O.S.B.M.* '05 (STF) St. George, New York, NY
Lubowa, Rev. Francis Mutesaasira, '02 (SP) Curia: Leadership Holy Family, St. Petersburg, FL
Luboyera, Rev. Martin, '13 (CHI) St. Joseph, Libertyville, IL
Lubrano, Rev. Joseph, *S.D.S.* '74 (BIR) St. Joseph, Huntsville, AL
Lubrano, Rev. Robert, '85 (RVC) Retired. [MON] St Pius X Residence for Retired Priests LLC, Ronkonkoma, NY
Lucas, Rev. James W., '00 (GB) Curia: Advisory Boards, Commissions, Committees, and Councils St. John the Baptist Congregation, Howard, WI
Lucas, Rev. Jayaseelanraj, '96 (TYL) Our Lady of Sorrows, Jacksonville, TX
Lucas, Rev. Jeffery J., '81 (E) The Epiphany of the Lord, Meadville, PA
Lucas, Rev. Jeffrey, '81 (E) St. Hippolyte, Guys MIlls, PA; [CAM] Allegheny College, Meadville, PA
Lucas, Rev. John P., '68 (CHI) Curia: Tribunal Ascension and St. Edmund Parish, Oak Park, IL
Lucas, Rev. John P., '66 (STN) Curia: Offices and Directors St. Michael's, Chicago, IL
Lucas, Rev. Kyle, '14 (PEO) Curia: Organizations (affiliated, inter-Diocesan, miscellaneous/other) [CAM] St. John Paul II Catholic Newman Center, St. Robert Bellarmine Chapel, Normal, IL
Lucas, Rev. Robert D., *C.M.* '74 (CHI) [MON] Vincentian Community, Congregation of the Mission, Western Province, Chicago, IL; [NUR] Franciscan Communities, Inc. (Franciscan Village), Lemont, IL
Lucas, Rev. Robert F., '02 (PH) St. Cecilia, Philadelphia, PA
Lucas, Rev. Selvaraj, *MSC* (PH) St. John the Baptist, Ottsville, PA
Lucas, Rev. Theodore, '84 (CLV) On Administrative Leave.
Lucas, Rev. Thomas M., *S.J.* '85 (SEA) [MON] Arrupe Jesuit Community at Seattle University, Seattle, WA
Lucas, Rev. Thomas M., *S.J.* '85 (SAC) Pastor of St. Ignatius Loyola Parish, Sacramento, a corporation sole, Sacramento, CA; [MON] Sacramento Jesuit Community, Carmichael, CA
Lucas, Rev. William P., '90 (BIR) Curia: Leadership Our Lady of the Lake Catholic Parish, Pell City, Cropwell, AL
Lucasinsky, Rev. Raymond, *C.M.M.* '62 (DET) [MON] Mariannhill Mission Society, Dearborn Heights, MI
Lucatero, Rev. Heliodoro, '86 (SAT) St. Joan of Arc, San Antonio, TX
Lucchetti, Rev. Luis R., '97 (LA) St. Malachy, Los Angeles, CA
Lucero, Rev. Edward F., '08 (TUC) Curia: Advisory Boards, Commissions, Committees, and Councils; Consultative Bodies; Leadership; Organizations (affiliated, inter-Diocesan, miscellaneous/other) Roman Catholic Church of Saint Elizabeth Ann Seton - Tucson, Tucson, AZ; [EFT] Catholic Foundation for the Diocese of Tucson Stewardship and Charitable Giving, Tucson, AZ; [EFT] Parish Pooled Investment Trust, Tucson, AZ; [MIS] The Roman Catholic Diocese of Tucson Our Faith, Our Hope, Our Future, Tucson, AZ
Lucero, Rev. Emanuel, (WDC) St. Rose of Lima, Gaithersburg, MD
Lucero, Rev. Jose, *S.D.B.* (LAR) Curia: Leadership
Lucero, Rev. Jose F., (LAR) San Luis Rey, Laredo, TX
Lucht, Rev. Shannon G., '01 (BIS) Curia: Leadership St. Mary, Hague, ND; St. Michael, Linton, ND; Sts. Peter and Paul, Strasburg, ND
Lucia, Rev. Pedro, *Sch.P.* '08 (LA) [MON] Piarist Fathers, Los Angeles, CA
Luciana, Rev. Msgr. Lawrence J., '63 (WH) Retired.
Luciano, Rev. Edmund A., '09 (MET) Parish of the Visitation, New Brunswick, NJ
Luciano, Rev. William J., '83 (NY) Blessed Sacrament, New Rochelle, NY
Luciano-Gonzalez, Rev. Carmelo, *cmf* (CGS) Inmaculado Corazon de Maria, Caguas, PR; [MON]

Misioneros Hijos del Inmaculado Corazon de Maria (Claretianos), Caguas, PR
Lucila, Rev. Raner, (RIC) Good Shepherd, South Hill, VA; St. Paschal Baylon, South Boston, VA
Lucila, Rev. Raner Ombao, (RIC) St. Catherine of Siena, Clarksville, VA
Lucjan, Rev. Szymanski, '91 (BRK) St. Adalbert, Elmhurst, NY
Luckett, Rev. Charles E., '14 (WDC) Curia: Pastoral Services
Luczak, Rev. Andrew E., '70 (CHI) Retired.
Luczak, Rev. Jay R., '92 (TUC) Our Lady of Grace Roman Catholic Parish - Maricopa, Maricopa, AZ
Luczak, Rev. Pawel, (SFD) St. Mary, Ste. Marie, IL; St. Thomas the Apostle, Newton, IL
Luczak, Rev. Thomas, *O.F.M.* '70 (BWN) Holy Family, Edinburg, TX
Ludanha, Rev. John, (DEN) Blessed Sacrament Catholic Parish in Denver, Denver, CO
Ludeke, Rev. Bruce J., '06 (RCK) On Special Assignment. Newman Central Catholic High School, Sterling, IL; Sacred Heart, Sterling, IL
Ludescher, Rev. Kenneth F., '61 (STP) Retired.
Ludvik, Rev. John L., '71 (SEA) Retired. St. Bernadette, Seattle, WA
Ludwick, Rev. Edmond, '97 (CI) Assumption of the Blessed Virgin Mary, Chuuk, FM
Ludwicki, Rev. Tomasz, *SCH* (CHI) St. Ladislaus, Chicago, IL
Ludwig, Rev. David R., '16 (COV) On Leave.
Ludwig, Rev. Eugene M., *O.F.M.Cap.* '71 (SFR) Our Lady of Angels, Burlingame, CA
Ludwig, Rev. John P., '74 (DM) Retired. Curia: Offices and Directors
Ludwig, Rev. Peter Joseph, '22 (LAN) St. Thomas Aquinas Parish East Lansing, East Lansing, MI
Ludwig, Rev. Thomas, '87 (KC) Curia: (>MO) Offices and Directors
Ludwig, Rev. Thomas K., '87 (KC) St. Munchin, Cameron, MO
Ludwikoski, Rev. James, (MI) Blessed Sacrament, Kwajalein, MH
Ludwikoski, Rev. James E., '73 (KCK) Retired.
Lueckenotte, Rev. Daniel I.J., '90 (JC) Holy Cross, Cuba, MO; St. Francis Caracciolo, Bourbon, MO; St. Michael, Steelville, MO
Luedtke, Rev. Mark, *S.J.* '10 (CHI) St. Ignatius Jesuit Community, Chicago, IL
Luedtke, Rev. Mark W., *S.J.* '10 (DET) Loyola Work Experience Program, Inc., ,
Luemba, Rev. Albert Lelo, *C.I.C.M.* '96 (SAT) St. Philip Benizi, Poteet, TX
Lueras, Rev. Charles R., *C.R.I.C.* '81 (LA) Retired. [CON] Convent, Santa Paula, CA; [MON] Canons Regular of the Immaculate Conception, Santa Paula, CA
Luerman, Rev. John H., '56 (IND) Retired.
Luevano, Rev. Andres Rafael J., '81 (ORG) On Special Assignment. Curia: Leadership [CAM] Chapman University, Orange, CA
Luft, Rev. Matthew, *O.S.B* '05 (SCL) Church of Saint Boniface, Cold Spring, MN; SS. Peter and Paul, Richmond, MN; St. James, Cold Spring, MN; [MON] St. John's Abbey, of the Order of St. Benedict, Collegeville, MN; [NUR] Assumption Home, Inc., Cold Spring, MN
Lugemwa, Rev. John Mary, *O.S.B.* '12 (RIC) [MON] Mary Mother of the Church Abbey, Richmond, VA
Luger, Rev. Greg, (BIS) Curia: Leadership St. James, Sherwood, ND; St. Jerome, Mohall, ND; St. John's Church of Lansford, Lansford, ND
Lugge, Rev. Thomas, '22 (BEL) St. Nicholas, O'Fallon, IL
Lugger, Rev. William R., '89 (LAN) Retired. St. Mary Cathedral Lansing, Lansing, MI
Lugo, Rev. Camillo, '70 (RVC) St. Luke, Brentwood, NY
Lugo, Rev. Joseph W., '62 (PAT) Retired.
Lugo, Rt. Rev. Martin, *O.S.B.* '62 (OKL) [MON] St. Gregory's Abbey (Benedictine Fathers of Sacred Heart Mission, Inc.), Shawnee, OK
Lugo Perez, Rev. Orlando, '10 (PCE) Curia: Leadership Santisimo Sacramento, Ponce, PR
Lugonja, Rev. John Bosco, (BO) St. Mary, Waltham, MA
Lugo-Silva, Rev. Edwin, '89 (MGZ) San German de Auxerre, San German, PR
Lui, Rev. Gabriel, '79 (LA) Retired.
Lui, Rev. Tovia, (LA) St. John Baptist de la Salle, Granada Hills, CA
Luis, Rev. Raimundo, *O.Carm.* '18 (WDC) [SEM] Whitefriars Hall, Washington, DC
Luisi, Rev. Joseph G., '83 (PIT) Chap, Jefferson Hospital, Jefferson Hills Triumph of the Holy Cross, Jefferson Hills, PA
Luiten, Rev. Gary, '92 (FAR) Blessed Sacrament Church of West Fargo, West Fargo, ND; [MIS] Beginning Experience Apostolate, Fargo, ND
Lukas, Rev. Martin C., *O.S.F.S.* '80 (TOL) Gesu, Toledo, OH; [MIS] Gesu Parish, Toledo, OH; [MIS] St. Pius X, Toledo, OH
Lukaszewski, Rev. Stanley P., '79 (TR) Retired. [MON] Villa Vianney, Trenton, NJ
Lukavenko, Rev. Yaroslav, '13 (PHU) Holy Ghost, West Easton, PA
Luke, Rev. Francis Nampiaparambil, '78 (NY) Chap, St Barnabas Hosp, Bronx St. Martin of Tours, Bronx, NY
Lukenge, Rev. Augustine, '87 (RIC) Sacred Heart, Covington, VA; St. Joseph, Clifton Forge, VA; The Shrine of the Sacred Heart, Hot Springs, VA
Lukong, Rev. Kenneth, '22 (BAL) St. Francis of Assisi, Fulton, MD; St. Louis, Clarksville, MD
Lukose, Rev. Abraham, '07 (MCE) Curia: Advisory Boards, Commissions, Committees, and Councils; Offices and Directors
Lukosevicius, Rev. Vaidas, *S.J.* '08 (CHI) Blessed Jurgis Matulaitis Mission, Lemont, IL; St. Ignatius Jesuit Community, Chicago, IL
Lukosevicius, Rev. Vaidas, *S.J.* (LIT) Curia: Clergy and Religious Services
Lukyamuzi, Very Rev. Joseph Mary, '81 (RIC) Curia: Deaneries Catholic Church of the Holy Comforter, Charlottesville, VA
Lule, Rev. Mugagga, '95 (LAV) Prince of Peace, Las Vegas, NV
Lulf, Rev. Ken, '99 (SFS) Sacred Heart Parish of Marshall County, Eden, SD; Saint Joseph Parish of Day County, Grenville, SD
Lully, Rev. Jeremy, '21 (MIA) St. Anthony, Fort Lauderdale, FL
Lum, Rev. Donald, '79 (STA) Baptist Hosp, Jacksonville
Lumbre, Rev. Roger S., '86 (WCH) Sacred Heart, Cunningham, KS; St. John, Zenda, KS; St. Leo the Great, Nashville, KS; St. Peter, Spivey, KS
Lumpkin, Rev. Thomas, '64 (DET) Retired. [CCH] Manna Community Meal, Detroit, MI
Lumsden, Rev. Patrick L., '96 (DAV) Retired.
Luna, Rev. Jesus Trujillo, '98 (ATL) On Leave.
Luna, Rev. Msgr. Lambert J., '78 (SFE) Curia: Finance; Leadership; Offices and Directors St. Joseph on the Rio Grande, Albuquerque, NM
Luna-Barrera, Very Rev. Luis, *M.S.A.* '87 (NOR) [MON] Society of the Missionaries of the Holy Apostles, Cromwell, CT
Lundberg, Rev. Bjorn C., '06 (ARL) Sacred Heart of Jesus, Winchester, VA
Lundberg, Rev. Jan, *O.C.D.* (SEA) St. Cecilia, Stanwood, WA
Lundberg, Rev. John W., '60 (TLS) Retired.
Lundgren, Rev. Eric, (SCL) Holy Cross, Kimball, MN; Mary of the Immaculate Conception, Rockville, MN; St. Wendelin's, St. Cloud, MN
Lundgren, Rev. Erik, '12 (SCL) St. Mary Help of Christians, St. Augusta, MN
Lundgren, Rev. Erik Carl Martin, '10 (STP) On Duty Outside Diocese. Diocese of St. Cloud, MN [CEM] St. Mary of the Purification Cemetery, Shakopee, MN
Lundrigan, Rev. Stephen E., '15 (WOR) Curia: Leadership; Offices and Directors Annunciation Parish, Gardner, MA
Lungay, Rev. Jose Roel G., '84 (NO) On Special Assignment. Chaplain, Roquette Lodge
Lungren, Rev. Bryce, '18 (CHY) St. Matthew's, Gillette, WY
Lunimbu, Rev. Pierre Claver, *S.V.D.* '15 (TR) St. Ann, Browns Mills, NJ
Luniw, Rev. Paul, '82 (STF) Curia: Leadership St. Michael, Terryville, CT
Lunness, Rev. John A., '04 (WIL) St. Francis De Sales, Salisbury, MD; St. Luke-St. Andrew, Ocean City, MD
Lunney, Rev. William H., '94 (SPR) St. Joseph's, Shelburne Falls, MA
Lunsford, Rev. Keith, '92 (KCK) On Sick Leave.
Lunsford, Rev. Msgr. Robert D., '60 (LAN) Retired.
Luong, Rev. (Francis Xavier M.) Tri Van, *CRM* '83 (SPC) [MON] Congregation of the Mother of the Redeemer, Carthage, MO
Luong, Rev. Anthony Duy, *CMF* '19 (CHI) Our Lady of Guadalupe, Chicago, IL
Luong, Rev. Dat, '13 (SJ) St. Maria Goretti, San Jose, CA
Luong, Rev. John, *O.M.V.* (BO) [MIS] St. Clement Archdiocesan Eucharistic Shrine, Boston, MA; [SEM] Our Lady of Grace Seminary, Boston, MA
Luong, Rev. Tri M., '94 (HBG) St. Anne, Lancaster, PA
Luong, Rev. Vuong "Vic", '18 (OKL) St. Patrick's, Anadarko, OK; St. Richard, Carnegie, OK
Luongo, Rev. Anthony V., (BO) Ave Maria Parish, Lynnfield, MA
Luoni, Rev. Christopher, '05 (Y) St. Joan of Arc, Streetsboro, OH
Lupa, Rev. Gerard, '77 (SY) Retired.
Lupercio, Rev. Benjamin, (CHI) SS. Viator and Wenceslaus Parish, Chicago, IL
Lupico, Rev. Samuel, '65 (BAL) Retired. St. Mary of the Assumption, Baltimore, MD
Lupo, Rev. David, *SS.CC.* '91 (FR) Our Lady of the Assumption, New Bedford, MA; [MIS] Congregation of the Sacred Hearts - United States Province (Sacred Hearts Fathers; Sacred Hearts Missions), Fairhaven, MA
Lupo, Rev. Robert L., '08 (PRT) Our Lady of the Snows Parish, Dexter, ME; St. Agnes, Pittsfield, ME
Lupton, Rev. Brendan P., '05 (CHI) [SEM] University of Saint Mary of the Lake/Mundelein Seminary, Mundelein, IL
Lurochkin, Rev. Valentin, (KNX) [CAM] Newman Foundation of Chattanooga, Inc., Chattanooga, TN
Luschen, Rev. Timothy D., '88 (OKL) Curia: Consultative Bodies St. Charles Borromeo, Oklahoma City, OK
Lusk, Rev. Craig, '08 (KAL) St. Mary, Marshall, MI
Lusk, Rev. Craig, '08 (KAL) St. John the Evangelist, Albion, MI
Lussier, Rev. Bonaventure, *O.C.D.* '75 (MIL) [MON] Washington Province of Discalced Carmelite Friars, Inc., Milwaukee, WI
Lussier, Rev. Louis, *M.I.* (MIL) [MON] St. Camillus Communities, Inc., Wauwatosa, WI
Lussier, Rev. Louis, *O.S.Cam.* '90 (SAV) Our Lady of the Assumption, Sylvania, GA
Lusson, Rev. David R., '80 (SUP) Retired.
Lustan, Rev. Ariel G., '94 (TUC) Curia: Consultative Bodies; Leadership; Tribunal Saint Anthony of Padua Roman Catholic Parish - Casa Grande, Casa Grande, AZ
Lustig, Rev. Joseph V, '18 (B) Good Shepherd Catholic Community, Soda Springs, ID
Lutz, Rev. Bernard A., '63 (EVN) Retired.
Lutz, Rev. Frederick J., '73 (SPC) Retired.
Lutz, Rev. Gerald J., '56 (PIT) Retired.
Lutz, Rev. Msgr. James M., '58 (SY) Retired.
Lutz, Rev. Kevin F., '78 (COL) On Administrative Leave.
Lutz, Rev. Thomas P., (NY) Our Lady of Loretto, Cold Spring, NY
Luu, Rev. Khien Mai (John), *S.V.D.* (STL) Resurrection of Our Lord Catholic Church, St. Louis, MO
Luu, Rev. Vinh Dinh, '03 (NO) Curia: Leadership; Offices and Directors St. Agnes, Jefferson, LA
Lux, Rev. Joseph W., *S.J.* '71 (NY) [MON] Murray-Weigel Hall (A Jesuit Community at Murray-Weigel Hall and Kohlmann Hall), Bronx, NY
Lux, Rev. Thomas J., '85 (LIN) Curia: Offices and Directors St. James, Cortland, NE
Luxama, Rev. Juan, '15 (BRK) St. Bernadette, Brooklyn, NY
Luyet, Rev. Gregory T., '95 (LR) Curia: Leadership
Luyet, Rev. Gregory T., '95 (LR) Curia: Offices and Directors Our Lady of Good Counsel, Little Rock, AR
Luzi, Rev. Alexis, *O.F.M.Cap.* (GB) Retired.
Lwande, Rev. Teilo, *A.J.* '13 (PHX) St. Andrew the Apostle Roman Catholic Parish, Chandler, AZ
Lwin, Rev. Benjamin, '90 (OKL) SS. Peter and Paul, Kingfisher, OK
Lwin, Rev. David, (BEA) Our Lady of the Pines, Woodville, TX; St. Michael, Jasper, TX
Lwin, Rev. Paw, '02 (ORG) St. Pius V, Buena Park, CA
Lwin, Rev. Robert Zaw, *M.S.* '09 (ATL) St. Ann Catholic Church, Marietta, Inc., Marietta, GA
Ly, Rev. Toulee (Peter), '17 (STP) Curia: Leadership Presentation of the Blessed Virgin Mary, Maplewood, MN
Ly, Rev. Wayne, (GAL) St. Martha, Porter, TX
Lybarger, Rev. Curtis F., '77 (STP) Retired.
Lydon, Rev. Daniel J., *C.S.V.* '15 (CHI) St. Viator High School, Arlington Heights, IL; [MON] Viatorian Province Center-Clerics of St. Viator, Arlington Heights, IL
Lydon, Friar John, *O.P.* '99 (MEM) St. Peter Church, Memphis, TN; [MIS] The Dominican Friars of Memphis, Inc. (St. Peter Dominican Community), Memphis, TN
Lydon, Rev. Michael, '74 (SP) Retired.
Lydon, Rev. Michael J., '84 (STL) Sacred Heart Catholic Church, Troy, Troy, MO
Lyimo, Rev. Reginald, *O.F.M.Cap.* (PIT) Chap, Western Pennsylvania Hosp, Allegheny Cty
Lyle, Rev. Msgr. Dennis J., '91 (CHI) St. Mary Magdalene Parish, Blue Island, IL

Lyle, Rev. John W., *O.S.F.S.* '85 (WIL) [MON] Wilmington-Philadelphia Province of the Oblates of St. Francis de Sales, Wilmington, DE
Lyman, Rev. Edward P., '67 (SCR) Retired. [MON] Villa St. Joseph, Dunmore, PA
Lynam, Rev. Michael John, (PIT) St. Hilary, Washington, PA
Lynam, Rev. Robert G., '84 (MET) St. Augustine of Canterbury, Kendall Park, NJ
Lynch, Rev. Brian T., '06 (STP) Transfiguration, Oakdale, MN; [CEM] Sacred Heart Cemetery, Belle Plaine, MN; [CEM] Saint Peter and Paul Cemetery, Belle Plaine, MN
Lynch, Rev. Daniel, *S.M.A.* '73 (NEW) Retired.
Lynch, Rev. Dennis J., '68 (LC) Retired.
Lynch, Rev. E. Patrick, *C.Ss.R.* '69 (STV) Church of the Holy Cross, Christiansted, VI
Lynch, Rev. Gerard, *O.SS.T.* '74 (BAL) [MON] Holy Trinity Monastery, Sykesville, MD
Lynch, Rev. Gregory Alfred, *S.J.* '03 (MIL) [MON] Jesuit Community at Marquette University (Marquette Jesuit Associates, Inc.), Milwaukee, WI
Lynch, Rev. James M., *M.M.* '74 (NY) [MON] Maryknoll Fathers and Brothers (Catholic Foreign Mission Society of America, Inc.), Ossining, NY
Lynch, Rev. Jeremiah, *SJ* '03 (CHI) St. Ignatius Jesuit Community, Chicago, IL
Lynch, Rev. John E., *C.S.P.* '51 (WDC) Retired. [SEM] Paulist Washington Community, Washington, DC
Lynch, Rev. John W., (NY) St. Augustine, Highland, NY
Lynch, Very Rev. Michael, '88 (BRK) Curia: Pastoral Services Our Lady of the Cenacle, Richmond Hill, NY; Saint Athanasius - Saint Dominic, Brooklyn, NY
Lynch, Rev. Michael, '89 (MIA) Retired.
Lynch, Rev. Michael J., '82 (TR) Retired.
Lynch, Very Rev. Michael J., '88 (BRK) Curia: Leadership; Pastoral Services
Lynch, Rev. Patrick Edward, *C.Ss.R.* (STV) Curia: Leadership Sacred Heart Chapel, Christiansted, VI; [MIS] Miscellaneous Organizations, Charlotte Amalie, VI
Lynch, Rev. Patrick J., *S.J.* '72 (BUF) [MON] The Canisius Jesuit Community, Inc., Buffalo, NY
Lynch, Rev. Reginald, *O.P.* '13 (WDC) [SEM] Dominican House of Studies, Washington, DC
Lynch, Rev. Shane M., '01 (OG) Curia: Consultative Bodies Saint Andrew's Church, Norwood, Norwood, NY; St. Patrick, Brasher Falls, NY; The Parish of the Visitation and St. Raymond, Norfolk, NY
Lynch, Rev. Stephen P., '77 (BRK) Retired. Mary, Mother of the Church, Brooklyn, NY
Lynch, Rev. Thomas F., '71 (BGP) Retired.
Lynch, Rev. Thomas P., *O.P.* '86 (CHI) St. Pius V, Chicago, IL; [MON] St. Pius V Priory, Chicago, IL
Lynch, Rev. Timothy, '16 (COL) St. Brigid of Kildare, Dublin, OH
Lynes, Rev. James F., '79 (GAL) St. Jerome, Clute, TX
Lynes, Rev. John G., '87 (MOB) Little Flower Parish, Mobile, Mobile, AL
Lyness, Rev. Stephen J., '98 (ATL) St. George Catholic Church, Newnan, Inc., Newnan, GA
Lyon, Rev. Henry D, '20 (CHI) St. Emily, Mt. Prospect, IL
Lyons, Rev. Denis, '58 (ORG) Retired.
Lyons, Rev. James A., '94 (PH) Our Lady of Charity, Brookhaven, PA
Lyons, Rev. Msgr. James M., '88 (HBG) Curia: Offices and Directors St. Joseph, Hanover, PA
Lyons, Rev. John, *FSSP* '84 (SD) Pastor of Saint Anne Catholic Parish, San Diego, a corporation sole, San Diego, CA; [MIS] Saint Anne Catholic Parish in San Diego, CA Real Property Support Corporation, San Diego, CA
Lyons, Rev. John, '73 (CLV) On Administrative Leave.
Lyons, Rev. John J., '80 (SAV) Retired.
Lyons, Rev. Msgr. John P., '88 (TUC) On Special Assignment. Curia: Tribunal Saint Thomas the Apostle Roman Catholic Parish - Tucson, Tucson, AZ
Lyons, Rev. John R., *M.S.A.* '05 (NOR) Retired.
Lyons, Rev. John T., '74 (PH) Retired. St. Genevieve, Flourtown, PA
Lyons, Rev. Michael, '96 (VIC) Retired.
Lyons, Rev. Michael J., '70 (DUL) Retired. St. Mary, Silver Bay, MN
Lyons, Rev. Michael P., '96 (BGP) Notre Dame of Easton Roman Catholic Church Corporation, Easton, CT
Lyons, Rev. Patrick M., '70 (CHI) Retired.
Lyons, Rev. Peter, *T.O.R.* '66 (ALT) [MON] St. Bonaventure Hall, Loretto, PA
Lyons, Rev. Richard, (HBG) Annunciation of the Blessed Virgin Mary, McSherrystown, PA
Lyons, Rev. Richard, (HBG) Corpus Christi, Chambersburg, PA
Lyons, Rev. Msgr. Richard J., '74 (MET) Retired. Curia: Tribunal St. Joseph, North Plainfield, NJ
Lyons, Rev. Robert, *S.J.* '77 (SPK) [COL] Gonzaga University, Spokane, WA
Lyons, Rev. Timothy, *O.F.M. Conv.* '81 (R) Blessed Sacrament, Graham, NC
Lyons, Rev. Timothy, *O.F.M.Conv.* '81 (HRT) [MIS] St. Paul Friary (St. Paul Parish Corporation), Kensington, CT
Lyons, Friar Timothy, *OFM Conv* (ALB) [MON] Immaculate Conception Friary - Order of Friars Minor Conventual, Rensselaer, NY; [SHR] The National Shrine of Saint Kateri Tekakwitha and Friary, Fonda, NY
Lyons, Rev. Timothy V., *C.M.* '86 (PH) [ASN] The Central Association of the Miraculous Medal, Philadelphia, PA; [MON] Congregation of the Mission, Philadelphia, PA; [SEM] St. Vincent's Seminary, Philadelphia, PA
Ma, Rev. Matthew, *S.J.* (SEA) [MON] Arrupe Jesuit Community at Seattle University, Seattle, WA
Ma, Rev. Matthew, *S.J.* (STL) [MON] Jesuit Community Corporation at Saint Louis University - Jesuit Hall, St. Louis, MO
Ma, Rev. Peter, (BRK) Mary's Nativity-Saint Ann Roman Catholic Church, Flushing, NY
Maalouf, Rev. Joseph, '17 (MIA) St. Jerome, Fort Lauderdale, FL
Maambo, Rev. Choobe, *S.J.* '13 (CHI) [COL] Jesuit Community at Loyola University Chicago, Chicago, IL
Maas, Rev. Philip James, '21 (ALN) St. Francis de Sales, Robesonia, PA; St. Ignatius Loyola, West Lawn, PA
Mabango, Rev. Ashiono Anthony, '95 (PAT) On Leave.
Mabee, Rev. Andrew Ryan, '20 (DET) St. Damien of Molokai Parish Pontiac, Pontiac, MI
Mabee, Rev. Zachary M., '15 (LAN) St. Joseph Shrine Parish Brooklyn, Brooklyn, MI
Mac Mahon, Rev. Michael, '66 (BIR) Curia: Leadership Holy Spirit Catholic Parish, Huntsville, Huntsville, AL
Macabalo, Rev. Ponciano, *ofm* '77 (GB) [MON] Assumption of B.V.M. Friary, Pulaski, WI
Macadaeg, Very Rev. Brandon, '13 (OAK) Curia: Leadership; Offices and Directors Our Lady of Lourdes, Oakland, CA
Macadaeg, Rev. Brandon E., (OAK) Cathedral Parish of Christ the Light, Oakland, CA
Macalinao, Rev. Jimmy, (OAK) Curia: Leadership; Offices and Directors St. Perpetua, Lafayette, CA
Macatangay, Rev. Francis M., '99 (GAL) St. Cecilia, Houston, TX
MacAulay, Rev. Gerard, '59 (OKL) Retired.
Macaulay, Rev. Neil, *O.M.I.* '63 (SJN) Colegio Nuestra Senora de Guadalupe, San Juan, PR
Macaya, Rev. Miguel, '65 (LSC) Retired.
MacCarthy, Rev. John P., *O. Praem.* '69 (GB) St. Willebrord, Green Bay, WI; [MON] St. Norbert Abbey, De Pere, WI
MacCarthy, Rev. Joseph T., '97 (BO) St. John the Evangelist, Cambridge, MA
MacCarthy, Rev. Justin H., '64 (ORG) Retired.
MacCarthy, Rev. Liam J., '68 (SAC) Retired.
MacDonald, Rev. Adam, *S.V.D.* '00 (DUB) [SEM] Divine Word College, Epworth, IA
MacDonald, Rev. Msgr. Arthur F., '52 (GLP) Retired.
MacDonald, Rev. Eben, '12 (LA) Curia: Pastoral Services San Salvador Mission, Piru, CA; St. Cyril, Encino, CA
MacDonald, Rev. Fabian, '77 (SEA) Retired.
MacDonald, Rev. Hugh J., '64 (HRT) Retired. The Church of the Resurrection, Wallingford, CT
MacDonald, Rev. James H., '67 (SFR) Retired.
MacDonald, Rev. Kevin, *C.Ss.R.* '91 (ORL) Sacred Heart, New Smyrna Beach, FL
MacDonald, Rev. Matthew, '14 (NY) St. Joseph, Somers, NY; St. Mary, Washingtonville, NY
MacDonald, Rev. Richard J., *S.C.J.* '65 (MIL) Retired. [MON] Sacred Heart at Monastery Lake, Franklin, WI
Macdonald, Rev. Thomas, (BO) [SEM] Saint John's Seminary, Brighton, MA
MacDonald, Rev. Timothy E., '00 (LAN) Chap, Egeler Corr Fac Curia: Leadership Queen of the Miraculous Medal Parish Jackson, Jackson, MI; St. Catherine Parish Concord, Concord, MI
MacDonald, Rev. Timothy I., *S.A.* '67 (NY) [MON] Franciscan Friars of the Atonement, Minister General Office, Garrison, NY
MacDonough, Rev. Richard B., *P.S.S.* '60 (BAL) Retired.
MacDougall, Rev. James, *OSA* '59 (PH) [MON] St. Thomas Monastery, Villanova, PA
Macedo, Rev. Stephen A., '93 (HON) Immaculate Heart of Mary, Papaikou, HI; St. Anthony, Laupahoehoe, HI
MacElrath, Rev. Ian, (E) [CAM] Penn State Erie, The Behrend College, Erie, PA
Macfarlane, Rev. Msgr. John F., '66 (WDC) Retired. St. Elizabeth, Rockville, MD
Machado, Rev. Dayan, '10 (SP) St. Mary, Tampa, FL
Machado, Rev. Johnson, '05 (BUF) St. John Neumann, Strykersville, NY
Machado, Rev. Jose, '93 (WCH) Curia: Offices and Directors
Machado, Rev. Larry, '19 (STO) Curia: Leadership Cathedral of the Annunciation (Pastor of), Stockton, CA
Machado, Rev. Ronald, '96 (MET) Most Holy Name of Jesus Parish, Perth Amboy, NJ
Machain, Rev. David B., '52 (PH) Retired.
Machalski, Rev. Msgr. Thomas C., '85 (BRK) Curia: Leadership; Pastoral Services Sacred Heart of Jesus, Bayside, NY
Machar, Rev. Jerome J., *O.C.S.O.* '75 (ROC) [MON] Abbey of the Genesee, Inc., Piffard, NY
Machayi, Rev. Patrick, *SMA* '14 (NEW) [MON] Society of African Missions, Provincialate, S.M.A. Fathers, Tenafly, NJ
Macherla, Rev. Raju, (JKS) Immaculate Conception, Clarksdale, MS; St. Elizabeth, Clarksdale, MS; St. Mary, Shelby, MS
Machiki, Rev. Daniel, '83 (NY) Parish of St. Mary/Holy Name of Jesus and St. Peter, Kingston, NY
Machila, Rev. Timothy, *O.F.M. Conv.* '16 (GB) St. Francis Solanus, Gresham, WI
Machiorlatti, Rev. John, (MO) Curia: Offices and Directors
Machira, Rev. Paul, (SY) Immaculate Conception, Greene, NY; St. Thomas Aquinas, Binghamton, NY
Machnik, Rev. Theodore F., '91 (COL) St. Joseph, Circleville, OH
Maciag, Rev. Waldemar, '97 (ORL) St. Lawrence, Bushnell, FL
Macias, Rev. Byron, *C.M.F.* (FRS) St. Paul Catholic Newman Center, Fresno, CA
Macias, Rev. Frank, '94 (SAT) St. Leo, San Antonio, TX
Macias, Rev. Gabino Oliva, (BO) St. Stephen, Framingham, MA
Macias, Rev. Salvador, '82 (OAK) On Leave. Curia: Offices and Directors
Macias, Rev. Tobias, *O.S.M.* '94 (ELP) St. Ignatius of Loyola, El Paso, TX
Macias Zakoda, Rev. Alonso, (BO) St. Patrick, Lawrence, MA
Maciej, Rev. David, '80 (SCL) Retired. Curia: Leadership; Offices and Directors
Maciejewski, Rev. Jaroslaw, '15 (CHI) Sacred Heart, Palos Hills, IL
Maciejewski, Rev. Norbert F., '69 (DET) Retired.
Maciejewski, Rev. Tadeusz, *C.M.* '88 (HRT) The St. Joseph Church Corporation of Ansonia, Ansonia, CT; [MON] St. Joseph Rectory, Ansonia, CT
MacInnis, Rev. John E., (BO) Retired. St. Pius Fifth, Lynn, MA
MacInnis, Rev. Michael, '00 (BO) [SEM] Saint John's Seminary, Brighton, MA
MacIntyre, Rev. Frederick H., '92 (WDC) Retired. St. Patrick, Washington, DC
Macioce, Rev. Dominic, '16 (DET) Curia: Consultative Bodies St. Elizabeth Ann Seton Parish Troy, Troy, MI
Mack, Rev. John P., '85 (MIL) [SEM] Sacred Heart Seminary and School of Theology, Franklin, WI
Mack, Rev. John P., '85 (BUF) On Duty Outside Diocese. Sacred Heart Seminary, Wisconsin
Mack, Rev. Joseph W., '89 (CHL) St. Paul the Apostle, Greensboro, NC
Mack, Msgr. Thomas, '78 (PEO) Curia: Consultative Bodies; Deaneries; Offices and Directors Immaculate Conception, Monmouth, IL
Macke, Rev. Paul, (CIN) [MON] Jesuit Community at St. Xavier High School, Cincinnati, OH
MacKenzie, Very Rev. John B., '00 (MAN) Our Lady of Lourdes, Pittsfield, NH; [CEM] Mount Calvary Cemetery, Pittsfield, NH
Mackey, Rev. Alan C., '00 (BIR) Our Lady, Help of Christians, Huntsville, AL
Mackey, Rev. Geoffrey, '19 (PBR) St. George the Great Martyr, Aliquippa, PA; St. Mary's, Ambridge, PA
Mackey, Rev. James M., '61 (ALB) Retired. St. Michael the Archangel, Troy, NY
Mackin, Very Rev. Eamon, *C.H.S.* '70 (LA) Retired.
Mackin, Rev. Kevin, *O.F.M.* '64 (SP) [MON] St. Anthony Friary (St. Petersburg) Franciscan Friars-Holy Name Province, Inc., St. Petersburg, FL
MacKinnon, Rev. Donald, *CSSR* (BR) Retired. [MON] St. Gerard Residence, Baton Rouge, LA
MacKinnon, Rev. Donald, *C.Ss.R.* '59 (BR) Retired.

Congregation Of St. Gerard Majella Roman Catholic Church, Parish Of East Baton Rouge, Louisiana, Baton Rouge, LA; [MIS] Redemptorist Fathers of Baton Rouge, Inc., Baton Rouge, LA
Mackle, Rev. Daniel E., '80 (PH) [SEM] Theological Seminary of St. Charles Borromeo, Wynnewood, PA
Mackowicz, Rev. Jakub, '20 (ORG) Our Lady of Guadalupe, La Habra, CA
MacLean, Rev. Thomas S., '02 (LIN) Chap, Nebraska Penal Complex, Lincoln
MacLellan, Rev. Iain G., *O.S.B.* '87 (MAN) [MON] St. Anselm Abbey, Manchester, NH
MacLennan, Rev. Donald B., '67 (DET) Retired.
MacMahon, Rev. Craig, *O.M.V.* '90 (LA) (>BO) [MON] Oblate Residence (St. Joseph House), Milton, MA
MacMahon, Rev. Patrick, '69 (SPK) Retired.
MacMaster, Rev. Thomas A., *O.C.S.O.* '57 (DUB) [MON] New Melleray Abbey, Order of Cistercians of the Strict Observance (Corporation of New Melleray), Peosta, IA
MacMillan, Rev. Donald A., *S.J.* '72 (BO) [MON] Bellarmine House, Cohasset, MA
MacMillan, Rev. Leonard, (B) St. Pius X, Coeur d'Alene, ID
Macnab, Friar Jeff, (OAK) Retired.
MacNeil, Rev. Paul D., '89 (CHR) Precious Blood of Christ, Pawleys Island, SC; St. Elizabeth Ann Seton Catholic School, Myrtle Beach, SC
MacNeill, Rev. Joseph L., '21 (HRT) On Special Assignment. Theological Studies
Maco, Rev. Stephen L., '76 (ALN) Retired. Our Lady of Good Counsel, Bangor, PA
Macoy, Rev. Jose, '86 (HON) Curia: Consultative Bodies Holy Rosary, Paia, HI
MacPherson, Rev. Damian, *S.A.* '78 (NY) [MON] Franciscan Friars of the Atonement, Minister General Office, Garrison, NY
MacPherson, Rev. Stephen E.C., '86 (SR) Retired.
MacQuarrie, Rev. John D., '78 (CIN) St. Bernard, Springfield, OH; St. Charles Borromeo, South Charleston, OH; St. Joseph, Springfield, OH; St. Raphael, Springfield, OH; St. Teresa of the Child Jesus, Springfield, OH
Macsherry, Rev. Hugh, *O.F.M.* '09 (R) Immaculate Conception, Durham, NC
Mactal, Rev. Joseph, '21 (PAT) St. James of the Marches, Totowa, NJ
Mactutis, Rev. Peter, '06 (SEA) St. Mary, Marysville, WA
Macul, Rev. Joel, *O.S.B.* '76 (OM) [EFT] St. Benedict Center Endowment Fund, Schuyler, NE; [MON] Benedictine Mission House - Christ the King Priory, Schuyler, NE
Macul, Rt. Rev. Joel P., *O.S.B.* '76 (PAT) [MON] St. Paul's Abbey (Order of St. Benedict, Congregation of St. Ottilien), Newton, NJ
MacVeigh, Rev. Donal, *S.J.* '72 (NY) [MON] Murray-Weigel Hall (A Jesuit Community at Murray-Weigel Hall and Kohlmann Hall), Bronx, NY
Maczkiewicz, Rev. Keith, *S.J.* '18 (BGP) [CAM] Fairfield University, Fairfield, CT
Maczkiewicz, Rev. Keith A., (BGP) [MON] The Fairfield Jesuit Community-Fairfield University, Fairfield, CT
Madaki, Rev. Ferdinand, (NY) Parish of Our Lady of Perpetual Help and St. Catharine, Pelham Manor, NY
Madani, Rev. Vijay Kumar, '07 (SUP) SS. Peter and Paul, Gilman, WI; St. John the Apostle, Sheldon, WI; St. Michael, Jump River, WI; St. Stanislaus, Lublin, WI
Madanu, Rev. Anthony, *M.F.* '09 (OAK) Chap, Kaiser Permanente Fremont Med Ctr; Washington Hosp...
Madanu, Rev. Arogyaiah, (B) St. George's, Post Falls, ID
Madanu, Rev. Francis, '10 (LR) Immaculate Conception, Blytheville, AR; St. Matthew, Osceola, AR; St. Norbert, Marked Tree, AR
Madanu, Rev. Ignatius, (CIN) Incarnation, Centerville, OH
Madanu, Rev. John Paul, '08 (ELP) Blessed Sacrament, El Paso, TX
Madanu, Rev. Jojappa, '11 (SUP) Assumption of the Blessed Virgin Mary, Osceola, WI; St. Anne, Somerset, WI; St. Joseph, Osceola, WI
Madanu, Rev. Karunakar, '08 (SUP) St. Ann, Cable, WI; St. Francis of Solanus, Stone Lake, WI; St. Ignatius, New Post, WI; St. Joseph's Congregation, Hayward, WI; St. Philip Catholic Congregation, Stone Lake, WI
Madanu, Rev. Lourdu R., *M.F.* '02 (GB) Immaculate Conception, Florence, WI; St. Joan of Arc, Goodman, WI; St. Stanislaus Kostka, Armstrong Creek, WI (>OAK) [MON] Missionaries of Faith-India Inc., Fremont, CA
Madanu, Rev. Lourduraju, '05 (SUP) St. John the Baptist, Prentice, WI; St. Paul the Apostle, Catawba, WI; St. Therese of Lisieux, Phillips, WI
Madanu, Rev. Sleeva Raju, (B) [MIS] St. Joseph, Spirit Lake, ID; [MIS] St. Stanislaus, Rathdrum, ID
Madanu, Rev. Sleeva Raju, (B) St. George's, Post Falls, ID
Madarang, Rev. Edgar, '15 (MET) Cathedral of St. Francis of Assisi, Metuchen, NJ
Madathilpambil-Thomas, Rev. Babu, (CHI) [MIS] St. Mary's Malankara Catholic Church,
Madathilparambil, Rev. Babu, '04 (MCE) Curia: Advisory Boards, Commissions, Committees, and Councils; Offices and Directors St. Jude Malankara Catholic Church, Bensalem, PA
Madathiparambil, Rev. Babu, (PH) Curia: Evangelization
Maddaloni, Rev. Steve, '16 (RVC) St. Rosalie's, Hampton Bays, NY
Madden, Rev. Benjamin, *O.F.M. Cap.* '58 (PIT) [MON] St. Augustine Friary, Pittsburgh, PA
Madden, Rev. Daniel, *O.S.A.* (BO) [COL] Merrimack College, North Andover, MA
Madden, Rev. James P., *C.S.C.* '57 (FTW) [MIS] Holy Cross House, Notre Dame, IN
Madden, Rev. John F., '84 (WOR) St. John's, Worcester, MA
Madden, Rev. John J., *S.J.* '69 (BAL) Retired. [MIS] Colombiere Jesuit Community, Baltimore, MD
Madden, Rev. John R., '70 (SAV) Retired.
Madden, Rev. Mark R, (STL) St. Gabriel the Archangel Catholic Church, St. Louis, MO
Madden, Rev. P. J., (HT) Curia: Administration
Madden, Rev. Patrick J., '74 (SHP) Retired. [CAM] Student Center, Grambling, LA
Madden, Rev. Patrick J., '83 (MOB) St. Maurice Parish, Brewton, Brewton, AL
Madden, Rev. Patrick J., '04 (HT) Retired.
Madden, Rev. Stephen J., '88 (BO) Curia: Advisory Boards, Commissions, Committees, and Councils Incarnation of Our Lord and Savior Jesus Christ, Melrose, MA; Most Blessed Sacrament, Wakefield, MA
Madden, Rev. Thomas F., '76 (NY) Curia: Leadership Parish of St. Peter and St. Mary of the Assumption, Haverstraw, NY; St. Mary of the Assumption, Haverstraw, NY
Madden, Rev. Msgr. Thomas G., '55 (NEW) Retired. Queen of Peace, North Arlington, NJ; [MIS] New Jersey Caritas Corporation, Inc., Newark, NJ; [MON] St. John Vianney Residence for Retired Priests, Rutherford, NJ
Madden, Rev. Thomas L., '81 (SP) St. Mary, Our Lady of Sorrows, Masaryktown, FL
Madden, Rev. William T., *M.M.* '58 (NY) Retired. [MON] Maryknoll Fathers and Brothers (Catholic Foreign Mission Society of America, Inc.), Ossining, NY
Maddhichetty, Rev. Christuraj, '11 (OKL) St. Peter's, Woodward, OK
Maddock, Rev. Jay T., '75 (FR) Curia: Tribunal
Maddock, Rev. Thomas, '21 (KCK) Christ the King, Topeka, KS; Hayden High School, Topeka, KS
Maddu, Rev. Jaya Rao, *M.C.L.* '03 (PHX) Holy Cross Roman Catholic Parish, Mesa, AZ
Madej, Rev. Paul D., '90 (SY) On Leave.
Madejski, Rev. David, '18 (HRT) Saint Luke Parish Corporation, Southington, CT
Mader, Rev. Stanley P., '92 (STP) Curia: Consultative Bodies; Leadership St. Joseph Catholic Community, Waconia, MN; [CEM] St. Joseph Cemetery, Waconia, MN
Madero, Rev. Martin, *Sch.P.* '02 (LA) St. Francis Xavier, Pico Rivera, CA; St. Lorenzo Ruiz, Walnut, CA
Madeya, Rev. Gregory, '08 (SJP) Curia: Offices and Directors St. Demetrius, Jeannette, PA; St. John the Baptist, McKeesport, PA
Madhichetty Irudayaraj, Rev. Arokiasamy, (LR) St. Joseph, Tontitown, AR
Madigan, Rev. Arthur R., *S.J.* '77 (BO) [MON] Campion Health & Wellness, Inc., Weston, MA
Madigan, Rev. Daniel, '64 (SAC) Retired. Pastor of St. Joseph Parish, Clarksburg, a corporation sole, Clarksburg, CA
Madigan, Rev. Daniel A., *S.J.* '83 (WDC) [COL] Georgetown University, Washington, DC
Madigan, Rev. John C., '74 (SEA) Retired.
Madigan, Rev. John R., *O.M.I.* '77 (BEL) Retired. [MON] Shrine of Our Lady of the Snows, Belleville, IL; [NUR] Apartment Community of Our Lady of the Snows (Benedictine Living Community | At The Shrine), Belleville, IL
Madigan, Rev. Kevin V., '70 (NY) Parish of Our Lady of Good Counsel and St. Thomas More, New York, NY; St. Thomas More, New York, NY
Madigan, Rev. Michael, *S.P.S.* '87 (CHI) [MON] St. Patrick's Missionary Society, Chicago, IL
Madi-Okin, Rev. Charles, '07 (BO) Most Precious Blood, Boston, MA; St. Anne, Boston, MA; St. Pius Tenth, Milton, MA
Madison, Rev. Martin, *S.A.* '62 (NY) Retired.
Mado, Rev. Jacob, *OSA* (BEA) Our Lady of Guadalupe, Port Arthur, TX
Madori, Rev. Peter J., '69 (NY) St. Joseph, Wurtsboro, NY
Madrid, Rev. Jhon, (MO) Curia: Offices and Directors
Madrid, Rev. Jhon Edisson, '12 (PAT) On Duty Outside Diocese.
Madrid Maureira, Rev. Juan Manuel, '20 (DEN) Frassati Catholic Academy, Thornton, CO; Holy Cross Catholic Parish in Thornton, Thornton, CO
Madrigal, Rev. Ernesto, '13 (STO) Our Lady of Fatima Church (Pastor of), Modesto, CA
Madrigal, Rev. Ernesto, '13 (STO) Curia: Leadership
Madrigal, Rev. Hector, '87 (AMA) Curia: Advisory Boards, Commissions, Committees, and Councils; Consultative Bodies; Leadership; Offices and Directors; Organizations (affiliated, inter-Diocesan, miscellaneous/other) St. Joseph's, Amarillo, TX
Madrigal, Friar Teresiano, (NY) (>SFE) [MON] Community of the Franciscans of the Renewal San Juan Diego Friary, Albuquerque, NM
Madsen, Rev. Msgr. John W., '66 (BUF) Retired.
Madu, Rev. Ambrose, '96 (NY) Christ the King, Bronx, NY; Parish of St. Brendan and St. Ann, Bronx, NY
Madu, Rev. Anthony, (BUR) Chap, Veterans Administration Hosp
Madu, Rev. Anthony, '93 (MO) Curia: Offices and Directors
Madu, Rev. Innocent, (NY) St. Mary, Washingtonville, NY
Madu, Rev. Innocent, (FAJ) San Jose, Luquillo, PR
Maduba, Rev. Nazarus, '99 (LR) Immaculate Heart of Mary, Walnut Ridge, AR; St. Mary, Paragould, AR
Madubuko, Rev. Celestine Chukwunonso, (PH) Curia: Evangelization St. Gabriel, Norwood, PA
Madumere, Rev. Ignatius, *O.P.* (MO) Curia: Offices and Directors
Maduri, Rev. John, '87 (BRK) Curia: Consultative Bodies; Organizations (affiliated, inter-Diocesan, miscellaneous/other) Most Precious Blood – Ss. Simon and Jude, Brooklyn, NY
Maduro, Rev. Gabriel, '59 (ARE) Retired.
Madus, Rev. Msgr. Peter P., '68 (SCR) Retired. Sacred Heart of Jesus, Peckville, PA
Maduzia, Very Rev. Norbert J., '82 (GAL) Curia: Leadership; Offices and Directors St. Ignatius of Loyola, Spring, TX
Maekawa, Rev. Steve, *O.P.* '98 (AJ) Holy Family Old Cathedral, Anchorage, AK
Maes, Rev. Allen J., *O.M.I.* '68 (BEL) [MON] Missionary Oblates of Mary Immaculate - St. Henry's Oblate Residence, Belleville, IL
Maes, Very Rev. Clarence, '87 (SFE) Curia: Offices and Directors Our Lady of Sorrows-Bernalillo, Bernalillo, NM
Maes, Rev. John J., '67 (DOD) Retired.
Maese, Rev. Hugo O., *MSpS* (SAT) Curia: Administration St. Vincent de Paul, San Antonio, TX
Maestri, Rev. William F., '77 (NO) Retired.
Maffeo, Rev. Michael T., '91 (RVC) Curia: Leadership St. Edward Confessor, Syosset, NY
Mafikiri, Rev. Pastor, '99 (SP) St. Michael the Archangel, Hudson, FL
Mafuta, Rev. Ange Masuta, *C.I.C.M.* (ARL) St. Ann, Arlington, VA
Magaldi, Rev. Sean T., '15 (RVC) Curia: Offices and Directors
Magallanes, Rev. Manuel, *O.S.B.* '76 (OKL) [MON] St. Gregory's Abbey (Benedictine Fathers of Sacred Heart Mission, Inc.), Shawnee, OK
Magallon, Rev. Cesar, '13 (LA) Our Lady of Sorrows, Santa Barbara, CA
Magallon, Rev. Ernesto, '98 (BWN) Hosp Ministry Immaculate Heart of Mary, Harlingen, TX
Magallon, Rev. Hector, (SB) St. Edward, Corona, CA; [MIS] Confraternity of Operarios Del Reino De Cristo, C.O.R.C., Corona, CA
Magana, Rev. Edgar, '02 (FRS) St. Brigid, Hanford, CA
Magana, Rev. Emilio A., '07 (SD) Pastor of Saint Charles Catholic Parish, San Diego, a corporation sole, San Diego, CA; [MIS] Saint Charles Catholic Parish in San Diego, CA Real Property Support Corporation, San Diego, CA
Magana, Rev. Jose, '98 (LA) Curia: Advisory Boards, Commissions, Committees, and Councils; Pastoral Services St. Charles Borromeo, North Hollywood, CA
Magary, Rev. Thomas A., '66 (STU) Retired.
Magaso, Rev. Herbert, (GF) Our Lady of Ransom, Hingham, MT; St. Mary, Chester, MT

Magat, Rev. Geronimo A., '02 (ARL) On Duty Outside Diocese. Pontifical Canadian College, Rome, Italy
Magat, Rev. Geronimo A., *P.S.S.* '02 (BAL) [MIS] St. Mary's Seminary & University, Baltimore, MD; [MON] Society of St. Sulpice, Province of the United States, Baltimore, MD
Magat, Rev. Jerome, *PSS* (SAT) [SEM] The Seminary of the Assumption of the Blessed Virgin Mary-St. John of San Antonio, TX (Assumption-St. John's Seminary), San Antonio, TX
Magdaleno, Rev. Ricardo, '89 (FRS) Retired.
Magdaong, Rev. Joseph, '98 (LA) St. Stephen Martyr, Monterey Park, CA
Magdaraog, Rev. Vicente, (TR) St. James, Red Bank, NJ
Magdaraog, Rev. Vicente, '96 (TR) St. Isaac Jogues, Marlton, NJ
Magee, Rev. James J., '17 (R) Curia: Leadership; Offices and Directors St. Peter's, Greenville, NC; [MIS] Vocations Office, Raleigh, NC
Magee, Rev. Msgr. Michael K., '91 (PH) On Special Assignment. Dean School of Theol Studies, St Charles Borromeo Sem Overb... Curia: Advisory Boards, Commissions, Committees, and Councils [SEM] Theological Seminary of St. Charles Borromeo, Wynnewood, PA
Magee, Rev. Patrick F., '70 (TR) Retired.
Magee, Rev. Raphael Maria, *M.M.A.* '98 (SAM) [MON] Maronite Monks of Adoration - Most Holy Trinity Monastery, Petersham, MA
Mager, Rev. Martin J., *O.S.B.* '63 (SFR) Curia: Offices and Directors [MON] Woodside Priory, Portola Valley, CA
Magesa, Rev. Christopher, '01 (PEO) Saint John Paul II Parish, Kewanee, IL; St. John's, Galva, IL; St. John's, Woodhull, IL
Maghinay, Rev. Jose, '74 (STO) Presentation Church (Pastor of), Stockton, CA
Maghsoudi, Rev. Aron M., '06 (ALT) Chap, Sacr Min, State Corr Inst, Laurel Highlands, Somerset
Maghsoudi, Rev. Aron M., '06 (ALT) All Saints, Boswell, PA; Holy Family, Hooversville, PA; Our Lady Queen of Angels, Central City, PA
Magiera, Rev. Michael, *F.S.S.P* (JOL) St. Joseph Church, Rockdale, IL
Maginot, Rev. Michael L., '83 (GRY) St. Stephen, Martyr, Merrillville, IN
Magnan, Rev. Oscar, *S.J.* '63 (NY) [MON] Murray-Weigel Hall (A Jesuit Community at Murray-Weigel Hall and Kohlmann Hall), Bronx, NY
Magnano, Rev. Paul A., '67 (SEA) Retired.
Magnano, Very Rev. Paul A., '67 (SEA) Immaculate Conception, Mount Vernon, WA; Immaculate Heart of Mary, Sedro Woolley, WA; Sacred Heart, La Conner, WA; St. Charles, Burlington, WA
Magnaye, Rev. Carlo Benjamin, *M.F.* '96 (AUS) Sacred Heart Catholic Church - Waco, Texas, Waco, TX
Magner, Rev. Kevin P., '03 (STP) St. Timothy, Maple Lake, MN; The Church of St. Ignatius of Annandale, Minnesota, Annandale, MN
Magner, Rev. Richard P., *S.J.* '12 (FBK) Curia: Leadership Blessed Sacrament Catholic Church Scammon Bay, Scammon Bay, AK; Little Flower of Jesus Catholic Church Hooper Bay, Hooper Bay, AK; Sacred Heart Catholic Church Chevak, Chevak, AK; [MIS] Brother Joe Prince Jesuit Community, Bethel, AK
Magni, Rev. Daniel M., '78 (BO) Retired.
Magnor, Rev. Patrick J., '20 (MIL) St. Alphonsus Congregation, Greendale, WI
Magnuson, Rev. Jake, '22 (BIS) Cathedral of the Holy Spirit, Bismarck, ND
Magnuson, Rev. Sean R., '06 (STP) On Duty Outside Diocese. Active Duty Military
Magnuson, Rev. Thomas J., '87 (OM) On Special Assignment. In Res at St John Vianney Res
Mago, Very Rev. Israel E., '07 (MIA) Curia: Clergy and Religious Services; Leadership Our Lady of Guadalupe, Doral, FL
Magraw, Rev. Msgr. Daniel, (E) Holy Trinity, Erie, PA
Magraw, Rev. Msgr. Daniel E., '75 (E) Curia: Offices and Directors St. Stanislaus, Erie, PA
Magree, Rev. Michael, (BO) [MON] The Jesuit Community at Boston College, Chestnut Hill, MA
Maguire, Rev. Daniel J., '69 (SFR) Retired.
Maguire, Rev. Robert, *O.Cist.* '76 (DAL) [MON] Our Lady of Dallas Cistercian Abbey, Irving, TX
Maguire, Rev. William, *C.P.* '02 (NY) Yale-New Haven Hosp, New Haven, CT [MON] The Congregation of the Passion - St. Paul of the Cross Province, Jamaica, NY
Magwaza, Rev. Thulani D., '89 (CHI) St. Sabina, Chicago, IL
Mahalic, Rev. Philip A., '83 (LFT) Chap, Fort Sam Houston, TX Curia: (>MO) Offices and Directors
Mahan, Rev. Daniel J., '88 (IND) All Saints Catholic Church, Dearborn, Inc., Guilford, IN; St. Lawrence Catholic Church, Lawrenceburg, Inc., Lawrenceburg, IN; St. Mary Immaculate Conception Catholic Church, Aurora, Inc., Aurora, IN; St. Teresa Benedicta of the Cross, Bright, Indiana, Lawrenceburg, IN
Mahaney, Rev. Hilary F., '69 (CHI) St. Mary of the Angels, Chicago, IL; [MIS] Midtown Residence, Chicago, IL
Mahaney, Rev. Hilary F., '69 (POD) Curia: Clergy and Religious Services
Mahar, Rev. Christopher M., '04 (PRO) On Duty Outside Diocese. Rome, Italy
Mahar, Rev. Raymond J., '58 (BUF) Retired.
Mahar, Rev. Ryan P., '20 (SAC) Pastor of St. Joseph Parish, Redding, a corporation sole, Redding, CA
Mahas, Rev. George W., '15 (TOL) St. Francis Xavier, Willard, OH
Maher, Rev. Charles E., '60 (PRO) Retired.
Maher, Rev. Daniel J., '62 (ALB) Retired.
Maher, Rev. Edward J., '81 (CAM) St. Thomas' Catholic Church, Brigantine, N.J., Brigantine, NJ
Maher, Rev. James J., *C.M.* '90 (BUF) [COL] Niagara University, Niagara University, NY; [MON] Vincentian Community at Niagara University (Congregation of the Mission of St. Vincent de Paul), Niagara University, NY
Maher, Rev. James Joseph, '92 (LA) Retired.
Maher, Rev. Jim, (LA) Retired.
Maher, Rev. John Thomas, *CM* '81 (PH) [MON] Congregation of the Mission, Philadelphia, PA; [SEM] St. Vincent's Seminary, Philadelphia, PA
Maher, Rev. Joseph Braden, '16 (SFD) St. Charles Borromeo, Charleston, IL; [CAM] Eastern Illinois University Newman Catholic Center, Charleston, IL
Maher, Rev. Michael N., *SS.CC* '63 (LA) Retired. [MON] Congregation of the Sacred Hearts of Jesus and Mary, La Verne, CA
Maher, Rev. Michael W., *S.J.* '86 (MIL) [MON] Jesuit Community at Marquette University (Marquette Jesuit Associates, Inc.), Milwaukee, WI
Maher, Rev. P. Brent, '11 (BR) The Congregation of St. Agnes Roman Catholic Church, Baton Rouge, LA
Maher, Rev. Patrick, '71 (LUB) Retired.
Maher, Rev. Ryan, *SJ* '87 (ATL) [MON] Atlanta Jesuit Community, Inc., Decatur, GA
Maher, Very Rev. Ryan L., '05 (COV) Curia: Advisory Boards, Commissions, Committees, and Councils; Leadership Cathedral, Basilica of the Assumption (St. Mary's Cathedral), Covington, KY; Covington Latin School, Covington, KY
Maher, Rev. Sean M., '09 (BO) Curia: Leadership Our Lady of Grace, Pepperell, MA; St. John the Evangelist, Townsend, MA
Maher, Rev. T. Patrick, '02 (GLD) Cross in the Woods Catholic Shrine of Indian River, Indian River, MI
Maher, Rev. Thomas F., '94 (TR) St. William the Abbot, Howell, NJ
Mahler, Rev. Clyde, '99 (HT) Curia: Organizations (affiliated, inter-Diocesan, miscellaneous/other) St. Mary's Nativity, Raceland, LA
Mahlmann, Rev. Raymond, '85 (GLP) Retired. On Leave.
Mahon, Rev. Msgr. Dennis, '70 (NEW) Retired. [COL] Seton Hall University, South Orange, NJ
Mahon, Rev. Msgr. Gerald A., '71 (WIN) Co-Cathedral of St. John the Evangelist, Rochester, MN
Mahon, Rev. Joseph F., *C.S.P.* '56 (NY) Retired.
Mahon, Rev. M. Shawn, '88 (BAL) On Administrative Leave.
Mahone, Very Rev. Casey B., '89 (WH) Curia: Leadership; Offices and Directors Immaculate Conception, Clarksburg, WV
Mahone, Rev. Michael, '80 (RNO) Retired. Curia: Offices and Directors
Mahoney, Rev. Brian E., '95 (BO) Curia: Leadership St. John the Evangelist, Chelmsford, MA; St. Margaret of Scotland, Lowell, MA; St. Mary, Chelmsford, MA
Mahoney, Rev. Daniel, '21 (PRO) Our Lady of Mercy, Greenwich, Rhode Island, East Greenwich, RI
Mahoney, Rev. Daniel C., '70 (GBG) Curia: Advisory Boards, Commissions, Committees, and Councils St. Rose, Latrobe, PA
Mahoney, Rev. Daniel J., '56 (BO) Retired. St. Francis de Sales, Boston, MA
Mahoney, Rev. James M., '92 (BO) Curia: Consultative Bodies Saint Veronica Parish, Burlington, MA
Mahoney, Rev. Msgr. James T., (PAT) Retired. Curia: Leadership Corpus Christi, Chatham, NJ; [MIS] Consortium of Catholic Schools of the Roman Catholic Diocese of Paterson, Inc., Catholic Academy of Passaic County, Clifton, NJ; [MIS] Morris Catholic High School, Inc., Denville, NJ
Mahoney, Rev. John J., '90 (MAN) St. Joseph, Lincoln, NH
Mahoney, Rev. Joseph, '75 (DET) Chap, St John Hosp, Detroit
Mahoney, Rev. Kevin J., '81 (STL) Retired.
Mahoney, Rev. Mark A., '86 (BO) St. Julia, Weston, MA
Mahoney, Rev. Michael, *O.F.M.Cap.* '74 (SFR) Curia: Leadership Our Lady of Angels, Burlingame, CA
Mahoney, Rev. Msgr. Neil J., '70 (NEW) Retired.
Mahoney, Rev. Peter, '61 (BRK) Retired. On Administrative Leave.
Mahoney, Rev. Richard J., '58 (STP) Retired. St. Agatha, Rosemount, MN; [CEM] St. Agatha Cemetery, Rosemount, MN
Mahoney, Rev. Robert J., '55 (KC) Retired.
Mahoney, Rev. Shaun L., '91 (PH) On Special Assignment. Newman Chap, Temple Univ, Catholic Ctr for Young Adults, Ph... [CAM] Temple University, Philadelphia, PA
Mahoney, Rev. Thomas A., '98 (BO) St. Joseph, Belmont, MA; St. Luke, Belmont, MA
Mahoney, Rev. Thomas D., '65 (CLV) Retired.
Mahoney, Rev. Thomas E., '68 (WOR) Retired. On Administrative Leave.
Mahoney, Rev. Thomas M., '15 (BUF) Infant of Prague, Cheektowaga, NY; St. Andrew, Sloan, NY; [MIS] St. Bernard Church, Youngstown, NY
Mahonge, Rev. Augustine, '09 (CHI) St. Colette, Rolling Meadows, IL
Mahowald, Rev. Christopher, *FSSP* (SCR) St. Michael's, Scranton, PA
Mai, Rev. Dan, (SPK) [COL] Gonzaga University, Spokane, WA
Mai, Rev. San H. *S.J.* (SPK) [COL] Gonzaga University, Spokane, WA (>P) [MON] Colombiere Jesuit Community, Portland, OR
Mai, Rev. Trung, *S.V.D.* '05 (SB) St. George, Ontario, CA
Mai, Rev. Tuan, (NOR) [SEM] Holy Apostles College and Seminary, Cromwell, CT
Mai, Rev. Tuan Anh Dinh, '14 (HRT) Saint Andrew Dung-Lac Parish Corporation, West Hartford, CT; [CAM] University of Hartford Newman Center, Hartford, CT
Maichiki, Rev. Daniel, (NY) Chap, Health Alliance Hosp, Kingston
Maichrowicz, Rev. Dominic, *O.P.* (SEA) Blessed Sacrament, Seattle, WA
Maida, Rev. Thaddeus S., '58 (PIT) Retired.
Maier, Rev. Ionel, (ROM) Curia: Offices and Directors
Maier, Rev. Paul, '70 (RIC) Retired.
Maigamo, Rev. Bitrus, (PHX) St. Paul Roman Catholic Parish, Phoenix, AZ
Maikowski, Very Rev. Thomas, (GLP) Immaculate Heart School, Page, AZ
Maikowski, Very Rev. Thomas R., '76 (GLP) Curia: Leadership
Maikowski, Very Rev. Thomas R., '76 (GLP) Immaculate Heart of Mary, Page, AZ
Mailadiyil, Rev. Augustine, '75 (SP) Prince of Peace, Sun City Center, FL
Maillet, Rev. Paul A., *P.S.S.* '01 (BAL) [MON] Society of St. Sulpice, Province of the United States, Baltimore, MD; [SEM] St. Mary's Seminary and University, Baltimore, MD
Mainzer, Rev. James S., '87 (WCH) Retired.
Maione, Rev. Francis T., '65 (NEW) Retired.
Mair, Rev. Robert G., '65 (CHI) Retired.
Maisano, Rev. Richard J., '69 (PH) Retired.
Maisog, Rev. Alberic, *O.C.S.O.* '00 (DUB) [MON] New Melleray Abbey, Order of Cistercians of the Strict Observance (Corporation of New Melleray), Peosta, IA
Maisog, Rev. Alberic, *O.C.S.O.* '00 (SPC) [MON] Assumption Abbey (O.Cist), Ava, MO; [SEM] Assumption Novitiate (Trappists), Ava, MO
Maison, Rev. Gabriel, '78 (VIC) Curia: Leadership Assumption of the Blessed Virgin Mary Catholic Church, Flatonia, TX; St. Joseph's, Moulton, TX
Maison, Rev. John Bosco, '96 (ORL) Ascension, Melbourne, FL
Maivelett, Rev. Bruce, (BO) [MON] Campion Health & Wellness, Inc., Weston, MA
Maivelett, Rev. Bruce A., *S.J.* '88 (BAL) Retired.
Maj, Rev. Jerzy, *O.S.P.P.E.* (PH) [MON] The Order of Saint Paul, First Hermit - The Pauline Fathers, Doylestown, PA
Majano, Rev. Mario A., '12 (WDC) Curia: Clergy and Religious Services Our Lady of Sorrows, Takoma Park, MD
Majano, Rev. Rafael R., '16 (OM) St. Joseph, Omaha, NE

Majarucon, Rev. Msgr. Jon F., '84 (LA) St. Raphael, Santa Barbara, CA
Majcher, Rev. Zbigniew, *S.D.B.* (CAM) [CON] Little Servant Sisters of the Immaculate Conception, Cherry Hill, NJ
Majewski, Rev. Edmund W., *S.J.* '83 (NEW) [MON] Jesuits of Saint Peter College, Inc., Jersey City, NJ
Majewski, Rev. Joseph B., '67 (RIC) Retired.
Majewski, Rev. Mariusz, '08 (B) Curia: Leadership; Offices and Directors Cathedral of St. John the Evangelist, Boise, ID
Majikas, Rev. David J., '97 (CLV) Chap, Summa Barberton Citizens Hosps, Barberton St. Augustine, Barberton, OH
Majka, Rev. Frank A., *S.J.* '74 (MIL) [MON] St. Camillus Jesuit Community (Society of Jesus, USA Midwest Province), Wauwatosa, WI
Majka, Rev. Philip S., '65 (ARL) Retired.
Major, Rev. Peter, *M.H.M.* '68 (NY) [MON] Mill Hill Fathers Residence, Hartsdale, NY
Major, Rev. Steven P., '87 (LIN) Sacred Heart, Hebron, NE
Major, Rev. Thomas J., '91 (SCR) Immaculate Heart of Mary Parish, Mildred, PA
Majoros, Rev. Msgr. George A., '79 (PH) Sacred Heart, Clifton Heights, PA; St. Charles Borromeo, Drexel Hill, PA
Majstorovic, Rev. Ivica, *O.F.M.* '00 (CHI) St. Jerome (Croatian), Chicago, IL
Maka, Rev. Tomasz, '01 (DET) On Duty Outside Diocese. Archdiocese for Military Service Curia: (>MO) Offices and Directors
Makacinas, Rev. Stanley, *O.Carm.* '70 (JOL) Retired. [MON] Carmelite Provincial Office, Darien, IL
Makar, Rev. Paul J., '10 (PHU) Holy Ghost, West Easton, PA; St. Josaphat's, Bethlehem, PA
Makarewicz, Rev. Msgr. Marion J., '87 (JC) Curia: Deaneries Mary Immaculate, Kirksville, MO; [CAM] Catholic Newman Center, Truman State University, Kirksville, MO
Makarow, Rev. Jason J., '15 (NEW) Curia: Leadership; Offices and Directors
Makhle-Ghorr, Rev. Emmanuel, (OLL) Holy Family Maronite Catholic Church, Mendota Heights, MN
Maki, Rev. George S., '88 (MAR) Retired.
Makos, Rev. Jason M., '05 (BO) Blessed Sacrament, Saugus, MA; St. Margaret, Saugus, MA
Makothakat, Rev. John M., '62 (SAT) Retired.
Makovo, Rev. Isaac, (BAL) St. Agnes, Baltimore, MD; St. William of York, Baltimore, MD
Makowski, Rev. Lee J., *O.S.A.* '80 (PH) [COL] Villanova University, Villanova, PA; [MON] St. Thomas Monastery, Villanova, PA
Makowski, Rev. Tomasz, '93 (PMB) Mary Immaculate, West Palm Beach, FL
Makranyi, Rev. Steven F., '69 (LAN) Retired.
Maksvytis, Rev. Jerome J., '74 (MAD) Retired.
Maksym, Rev. John, '18 (DET) On Academic Leave. Catholic Univ of America, Washington St. Louis Parish Clinton Township, Clinton Township, MI
Maksym, Rev. John A., '18 (DET) St. Peter Parish Mount Clemens, Mount Clemens, MI
Maksymowicz, Rev. Msgr. John H., '70 (BRK) Retired.
Makwinja, Rev. Francis S., '97 (SC) [NUR] Holy Spirit Retirement Home, Sioux City, IA
Malacari, Rev. Carmen, '93 (CHL) Holy Spirit, Denver, NC
Malagon, Rev. Eduardo, '00 (GRY) Curia: Offices and Directors All Saints, Hammond, IN; St. Casimir, Hammond, IN
Malagreca, Rev. Msgr. Joseph P., '76 (BRK) Curia: Organizations (affiliated, inter-Diocesan, miscellaneous/ other) Holy Cross, Brooklyn, NY
Malain, Rev. Msgr. Dan, '86 (BEA) Retired. Monsignor Kelly Catholic High School, Beaumont, TX; St. Elizabeth, Port Neches, TX
Malaiyappan, Rev. Amalanathan, '04 (LC) Holy Rosary, Wisconsin Rapids, WI; St. James, Vesper, WI; St. Joachim, Pittsville, WI; [EFT] St. Joachim's Parish Endowment Trust, Pittsville, WI
Malaka, Rev. Srinivasa, (EVN) St. John the Baptist, Newburgh, IN
Malana, Rev. Marcelino Marquino, '85 (STO) St. Bernard Church (Pastor of), Tracy, CA
Malancheruvil, Rev. Biju, (RNO) Sacred Heart, Carlin, NV
Malancheruvil, Rev. Varghese, '95 (RNO) St. Brendan's, Eureka, NV; St. Joseph's, Elko, NV; St. Thomas Aquinas, Wells, NV
Malanyaon, Rev. Joven V., (TOL) Retired.
Malapady, Rev. Arokiaraj, '00 (AMA) Curia: Advisory Boards, Commissions, Committees, and Councils; Consultative Bodies; Leadership Immaculate Conception, Dimmitt, TX
Malapolu, Rev. Bhaskararao, (LR) Our Lady of the Holy Souls, Little Rock, AR
Malarz, Rev. Andrew, '92 (VEN) Retired.
Malatesta, Rev. Christopher A., '93 (SPR) St. Agnes, Dalton, MA; [PRE] Holy Cross Camp Grounds, Goshen, MA
Malave, Rev. Will-Roger, '86 (HRT) Retired. On Administrative Leave.
Malaver, Rev. Daniel, (LA) [HOS] Emanate Health Medical Center, West Covina, CA
Malaver, Rev. Daniel, '03 (WDC) On Duty Outside Diocese. Valinda, CA
Malavolti, Rev. Nathan, *T.O.R.* '05 (STU) [COL] Franciscan University of Steubenville, Steubenville, OH; [MON] Holy Spirit Friary, Steubenville, OH
Malczuk, Rev. Dariusz, (SAC) Pastor of Our Lady of Lourdes Parish, Sacramento, a corporation sole, Sacramento, CA
Maldonado, Rev. Angel M., *O.S.M.* '79 (ELP) Sts. Peter and Paul, El Paso, TX
Maldonado, Rev. Fernando, (SD) Pastor of Saint Richard Catholic Parish, Borrego Springs, a corporation sole, Borrego Springs, CA; [MIS] Saint Richard Catholic Parish in Borrego Springs, CA Real Property Support Corporation, Borrego Springs, CA
Maldonado, Rev. Francisco, '90 (TUC) Curia: Leadership Most Holy Nativity of Our Lord Jesus Christ Roman Catholic Parish - Rio Rico, Rio Rico, AZ; Our Lady of the Valley Roman Catholic Parish - Green Valley, Green Valley, AZ
Maldonado, Rev. Jaime, '20 (HRT) Saint Teresa of Calcutta Parish Corporation, Manchester, CT
Maldonado, Rev. Jose A. Rivera, (FAJ) Curia: Offices and Directors Nuestra Senora del Pilar, Canovanas, PR
Maldonado, Rev. Jose Jaime, (SPK) St. Patrick, Pasco, WA
Maldonado, Rev. Juan, '16 (FRS) Curia: Advisory Boards, Commissions, Committees, and Councils Sacred Heart, Merced, CA
Maldonado, Rev. Leonardo, '64 (RCK) Retired.
Maldonado Orozco, Rev. Candido, *M.N.M.* '86 (ARE) Our Lady of Monserrate, Camuy, PR
Maldonado Plaza, Rev. Edward, *OFM Cap.* '83 (ARE) San Miguel Arcangel, Utuado, PR
Maldonado Rivas, Friar Jose David, *O.F.M.Cap.* '17 (SJN) San Francisco de Asis, San Juan, PR
Maldonado Vazquez, Rev. Jose, *O.Carm.* (SJN) Santa Teresita del Nino Jesus, San Juan, PR
Maldonado-Aviles, Rev. Jaime G., (HRT) Curia: Offices and Directors
Maldonado-Pacheco, Rev. Jairo A., '20 (R) St. Ann, Edenton, NC
Male, Rev. Anthony, '08 (SAT) Curia: Administration St. Anthony – Saspamco, Elmendorf, TX; St. Anthony's, Runge, TX
Malek, Rev. Matthew, '13 (STP) Church of the Risen Savior, Burnsville, MN
Malene, Rev. Msgr. Robert M., '72 (E) Retired.
Maleszyk, Rev. Mieczyslaw Mitch, '00 (SAC) Pastor of St. Anthony Parish, Sacramento, a corporation sole, Sacramento, CA
Maletta, Rev. Sammie L., '80 (GRY) Curia: Leadership; Offices and Directors St. John the Evangelist, Saint John, IN
Maletz, Rev. Leo J., '73 (ALN) Retired.
Malewski, Rev. Christian J., '09 (KC) Our Lady of Guadalupe, St. Joseph, MO
Mali, Rev. Joseph, (ALB) On Special Assignment. Chap, St Peter's Hospital, Albany Parish of Our Lady of Hope, Copake Falls, NY
Malia, Rev. Thomas R., '84 (BAL) St. Charles Borromeo, Pikesville, MD; [HOS] Mercy Health Services Inc., Baltimore, MD
Maliakkal, Rev. Varghese, '85 (IND) Saint Thomas Aquinas Catholic Church, Indianapolis, Inc., Indianapolis, IN
Malick, Rev. Kevin M., '07 (NY) St. Peter, Rosendale, NY
Malin, Rev. Msgr. Delbert J., '58 (LC) Retired.
Malin, Rev. Donald P., '03 (PBL) Curia: Offices and Directors Our Lady of Mt. Carmel, Pueblo, CO
Malin, Rev. Gary J., '86 (CLV) St. Joan of Arc, Chagrin Falls, OH
Malingumu, Rev. Daniel J., (RIC) Church of the Ascension, Virginia Beach, VA
Malinowski, Rev. Msgr. John C., '63 (AUS) Retired.
Malins, Rev. Donald, '13 (POC) Retired.
Mallak, Rev. Mark S., '88 (NU) Curia: Leadership
Mallam, Rev. Paul, (DAL) St. Pius X Catholic Parish, Dallas, TX
Mallanga, Rev. Stephen, (NY) Blessed Sacrament, Bronx, NY; Parish of Holy Family, Blessed Sacrament, and St. John Vianney, Bronx, NY
Mallar, Rev. Esteban, (SAV) St. Francis Xavier, Brunswick, GA
Mallari, Rev. Arturo O., '07 (RCK) Retired.
Mallavarapu, Rev. Thomasaiah, (MET) Our Lady of Fatima, Perth Amboy, NJ
Mallet, Rev. Msgr. Charles J., '55 (LAF) Retired.
Mallet, Msgr. W. Curtis, (LAF) Curia: Leadership; Tribunal
Mallet, Msgr. William Curtis, '92 (LAF) On Special Assignment. Curia: Advisory Boards, Commissions, Committees, and Councils; Leadership
Mallett, Rev. James K., '66 (NSH) Retired.
Mallett, Rev. Raymond, *OFM Conv.* '76 (OAK) Our Lady of Grace, Castro Valley, CA
Mallett, Rev. Raymond, *O.F.M.Conv.* '76 (TOL) [ASN] Franciscan Mission Association, Carey, OH
Malley, Rev. Kenneth, '97 (SP) On Duty Outside Diocese. Spiritual Director - Pontifical North American College, Rome
Malley, Rev. Vernon, *O.Carm.* '59 (TUC) Retired.
Mallia, Rev. Joseph, '92 (DET) St. Kieran Parish Shelby Township, Shelby Twp., MI
Mallick, Rev. Andrew, '83 (ORL) Retired.
Mallick, Rev. Marcus, (DEN) On Duty Outside Diocese.
Mallick, Rev. Marcus Marcus, (NTN)
Mallin, Rev. Peter, *O.F.M.Conv.* '90 (LA) Our Lady of Guadalupe, Hermosa Beach, CA; [HOS] Providence Little Company of Mary Medical Center, Torrance, CA; [HOS] Providence Little Company of Mary Medical Center San Pedro, San Pedro, CA
Mallo, Rev. Walter D., *I.V.E.* '90 (CHI) St. Francis of Assisi, Chicago, IL
Mallon, Rev. Elias, *S.A.* '71 (NY) St. Joseph Church - Yorkville, New York, NY
Mallon, Rev. Elias D., *S.A.* '71 (NY) [MON] Franciscan Friars of the Atonement, Minister General Office, Garrison, NY
Mallory, Rev. Dale E, '22 (DAV) Church of St. Mary of the Visitation, Ottumwa, IA
Malloy, Rev. Edward A., *C.S.C.* '70 (FTW) [COL] University of Notre Dame Du Lac, Notre Dame, IN; [MON] Holy Cross Community, Corby Hall, University of Notre Dame, Notre Dame, IN
Malloy, Rev. Francis X., '85 (MIL) On Duty Outside Diocese. Bay Pines VA Med Ctr, Bay Pines FL, 33744
Malloy, Rev. Michael B., '76 (OM) Retired.
Malloy, Rev. Richard, *S.J.* (BAL) [COL] Jesuit Community of Loyola University, Inc., Baltimore, MD; [MON] Jesuit Community of Loyola University Maryland, Inc., Baltimore, MD
Malloy, Rev. Stephen J., '96 (BO) On Special Assignment.
Mallya, Rev. Sabas, *A.L.C.P.* '91 (PMB) St. Sebastian, Sebastian, FL
Mallya, Rev. Sabas Ntimia, *A.L.C.P.* '91 (PMB) Our Lady of Guadalupe Mission, Fellsmere, FL
Malm, Rev. Raymond B., '76 (PRO) Retired.
Malnar, Rev. Stan, '72 (HEL) Retired.
Malo, Rev. Richard C., '87 (PRT) Retired. [MIS] Sacred Heart, Winn, ME; [MIS] St. Anne, Danforth, ME; [MIS] St. Leo the Great, Howland, ME; [MIS] St. Mary of Lourdes, Lincoln, ME
Malonda Nyimi, Rev. Roger, '94 (R) St. Joseph Catholic Parish of Burgaw, Burgaw, NC; St. Stanislaus Catholic Parish of Castle Hayne, Castle Hayne, NC
Malone, Rev. Msgr. Alan, '59 (PHX) Retired.
Malone, Rev. Daniel L., '07 (MAR) Guardian Angels, Crystal Falls, MI; St. Rose, Channing, MI
Malone, Rev. Edward T., (BO) Retired.
Malone, Rev. H. Patrick, '69 (WCH) Retired. Chap, Veterans Administration Hosp
Malone, Rev. John M., '67 (STP) Retired.
Malone, Rev. Matthew F., *S.J.* '12 (NY) [MIS] America Media, New York, NY; [MON] America; Residence and Publication Office of the America Press, New York, NY
Malone, Rev. Msgr. Richard, '62 (PH) Retired.
Maloney, Rev. Bernard, *O.F.M.Cap.* '69 (ROC) The Parish of Mary, Mother of Mercy, Seneca County, NY, Interlaken, NY; [MON] St. Fidelis Friary, Interlaken, NY
Maloney, Rt. Rev. Daniel, *O.S.B.* '68 (BIS) Curia: Leadership [MON] Assumption Abbey, Richardton, ND
Maloney, Rev. Edward J., '55 (CHI) Retired.
Maloney, Rev. Msgr. J. Christopher, '66 (NY) Retired.
Maloney, Rev. James G., '71 (CLV) Retired. St. Andrew the Apostle, Norton, OH
Maloney, Rev. John P., '66 (BRK) Retired.
Maloney, Rev. Msgr. John W., '75 (BRK) St. Anselm, Brooklyn, NY
Maloney, Rev. Joseph L., '91 (PH) St. Aloysius, Pottstown, PA

Maloney, Rev. Kevin, '05 (SY) St. Charles - St. Ann, Syracuse, NY; St. Patrick-St. Brigid, Syracuse, NY
Maloney, Rev. Richard, *S.D.S.* '69 (WDC) [SEM] Salvatorian Community, Silver Spring, MD
Maloney, Rev. Robert P., *C.M.* '66 (PH) [MON] Congregation of the Mission, Philadelphia, PA
Maloney, Rev. Msgr. Thomas F., '68 (BUF) Retired.
Maloney, Rev. Thomas J., '65 (SCR) Retired.
Maloney, Rev. Wilfred F., '55 (PH) Retired.
Malovetz, Rev. Msgr. Gregory E. S., '83 (MET) St. Charles Borromeo, Skillman, NJ
Maltese, Rev. James L., '65 (RVC) Retired.
Malthaner, Very Rev. John P., '93 (E) Our Mother of Sorrows, Erie, PA; St. Luke, Erie, PA
Malucha, Rev. Michael J., '21 (MIL) Holy Family Congregation, Fond du Lac, WI
Malvey, Rev. Killian, *O.S.B.* '73 (SEA) [COL] Saint Martin's University (Order of St. Benedict Master's Comprehensive University), Lacey, WA; [MON] St. Martin's Abbey, Lacey, WA
Malyarchuk, Archpriest Roman, (STF) St. Nicholas, Brooklyn, NY
Malyarchuk, Rev. Archpriest Roman, '95 (STF) Curia: Offices and Directors
Mamangun, Rev. William, (AGN) Dulce Nombre de Maria Cathedral - Basilica, Agana, GU
Mamba, Rev. Maurice, (SEA) Our Lady, Queen of Heaven, Tacoma, WA
Mambrakatt, Rev. Kuriakose, '93 (RNO) St. John the Baptist, Lovelock, NV
Mambrakatt, Rev. Kuriakose, (RNO) Curia: Offices and Directors
Mamich, Rev. Joseph R., '06 (CLV) Curia: Advisory Boards, Commissions, Committees, and Councils St. Joseph, Strongsville, OH
Mamo, Rev. Nathan, '78 (HON) On Duty Outside Diocese. Diocese of Reno
Mamo, Rev. Nathan, '78 (RNO) Retired. Curia: Offices and Directors [CAM] University of Nevada, Newman Community, Reno, NV
Mampill, Rev. Joy, (NY) Curia: Offices and Directors
Mampilly, Rev. Joy, '84 (NY) Our Lady Star of the Sea, Staten Island, NY
Manahan, Rev. Christopher J, *S.J.* '03 (CHI) St. Ignatius Jesuit Community, Chicago, IL; [MIS] USA Midwest Province of the Society of Jesus, Inc., Chicago, IL
Manahan, Rev. Reynaldo, '95 (SD) Curia: Advisory Boards, Commissions, Committees, and Councils Pastor of Holy Trinity Catholic Parish, El Cajon, a corporation sole, El Cajon, CA
Manahan, Rev. Thomas C, *S.J.* '95 (CIN) [MON] Jesuit Community at St. Xavier High School, Cincinnati, OH
Manalastas, Rev. Michael, *S.J.* '22 (LA) Blessed Sacrament, Los Angeles, CA; [MON] Colombiere House (Jesuit Fathers), Los Angeles, CA
Manalo, Rev. Rosendo R., '94 (OAK) St. Patrick, Rodeo, CA
Manalo, Rev. Vincent P., *C.S.P.* (NY) [MON] Paulist Fathers' Motherhouse, New York, NY
Manango, Rev. Ronnie, '16 (STO) St. Anne Church (Pastor of), Lodi, CA
Manano, Rev. Grace, '96 (CAM) St. Clare of Assisi Parish, Gibbstown, N.J., Gibbstown, NJ
Manapuram, Rev. Joseph, (GAL) Sacred Heart, Conroe, TX
Manarchuck, Rev. Joseph J., '78 (SCR) Curia: Leadership St. Joseph, Matamoras, PA; St. Patrick, Milford, PA
Manatt, Rev. Timothy T., *S.J.* '07 (MIL) Curia: Leadership Our Lady of Guadalupe Congregation, Milwaukee, WI; St. Patricks Congregation, Milwaukee, WI; [MON] Jesuit Community at Marquette University (Marquette Jesuit Associates, Inc.), Milwaukee, WI
Mancha, Rev. George, '88 (SJ) Retired.
Manchas, Rev. Lawrence L., '78 (GBG) Curia: Advisory Boards, Commissions, Committees, and Councils; Leadership; Offices and Directors St. Bruno, Greensburg, PA; St. Paul, Greensburg, PA
Manchester, Rev. Roman R., '05 (PRO) On Leave.
Mancia Calderon, Rev. Miguel A., '01 (FRS) St. John the Evangelist, Wasco, CA; [MIS] Our Lady of the Assumption, Pixley, CA
Mancia Calderon, Rev. Miguel Angel, (FRS) St. John the Evangelist, Tipton, CA
Mancini, Rev. Msgr. Anthony, '78 (PRO) SS. Peter and Paul's Church, Providence, RI
Mancini, Rev. John, *O.S.F.S.* '80 (SAG) Saint Francis de Sales Parish of Bridgeport, Saginaw, MI
Mancini, Rev. Joseph A., '01 (NEW) Curia: Offices and Directors; Organizations (affiliated, inter-Diocesan, miscellaneous/other) Cathedral Basilica of the Sacred Heart, Newark, NJ; St. Stephen, Kearny, NJ
Mancini, Rev. Marc A., '92 (PAT) Curia: Leadership St. James of the Marches, Totowa, NJ
Mancini, Rev. Marc A., (PAT) Curia: Leadership
Mancini, Rev. Nicholas, '75 (Y) Retired.
Mancini, Rev. Nicholas J., '75 (Y) Retired.
Mancini, Rev. Robert, *O.S.F.S.* (WIL) Salesianum School, Wilmington, DE
Mancini, Rev. Robert, *O.S.F.S.* '77 (PH) [MON] Villa de Sales Oblate Residence, Wyndmoor, PA
Mancuso, Rev. Anthony, '83 (SJ) On Special Assignment. Curia: Offices and Directors
Mancuso, Rev. Anthony J., '83 (SJ) Retired. Curia: Offices and Directors Saint Francis High School, Mountain View, CA
Mancuso, Rev. Dennis J., '96 (BUF) Curia: Consultative Bodies Our Lady of Peace, Salamanca, NY
Mancuso, Rev. Henry, '75 (LKC) Retired.
Mancuso, Rev. Luke, *O.S.B.* '83 (SCL) [MON] St. John's Abbey, of the Order of St. Benedict, Collegeville, MN
Mandac, Rev. Elmer, '96 (SD) Curia: Advisory Boards, Commissions, Committees, and Councils Pastor of Saint Martin of Tours Catholic Parish, La Mesa, a corporation sole, La Mesa, CA
Mandagiri, Rev. Balaswamy, (OKL) St. Mary's, Clinton, OK
Mandamuna, Rev. Denis, (DEN) St. Therese Catholic Parish in Aurora, Aurora, CO
Mandamuna, Rev. Denis, '12 (WDC) Chap, MedStar Washington Hosp Ctr, Washington St. Luke, Washington, DC
Mandamuna, Rev. Denis M., *C.F.I.C.* '02 (MO) Curia: Offices and Directors
Mandato, Rev. Pio, *F.M.H.J.* '85 (SCR) [MON] Franciscan Missionary Hermits of St. Joseph, Laceyville, PA
Mandel, Rev. Brian L., '94 (NU) Church of Our Lady, Grove City, MN; St. John, Darwin, MN; St. Philip, Litchfield, MN
Mandel, Rev. Subhashisa, *CM* '09 (BUF) [MON] Vincentian Community at Niagara University (Congregation of the Mission of St. Vincent de Paul), Niagara University, NY
Mandelas, Very Rev. Michael, (PHX) Curia: (>HPM) Offices and Directors
Mandelas, Rev. Michael, '13 (HPM) Curia: Leadership; Offices and Directors St. John Chrysostom, Seattle, WA
Manderfield, Rev. Paul G., '60 (MAR) Retired.
Mandez Izquierdo, Rev. Jose Carmen, '02 (CHI) St. Oscar Romero Parish, Chicago, IL
Manding, Rev. Benito O., '64 (SJ) Retired.
Mandock, Rev. Patrick H., '72 (GBG) Retired.
Mandziuk, Rev. Paul, *M.S.* (FR) Our Lady of the Cape, Brewster, MA
Manerowski, Rev. Joseph, '95 (ALB) Retired.
Manfred, Rev. Donald J., '67 (OG) St. Francis Solanus Church, Harrisville, New York, Harrisville, NY; St. Stephen's Church, Croghan, NY, Croghan, NY; [CEM] St. Stephen's Cemetery Association, Inc., Croghan, NY
Manfredonia, Rev. Ignatius, *F.I.* (IND) [MON] Marian Friary of Our Lady Coredemptrix, Franciscans of the Immaculate, Bloomington, IN
Manfredonia, Rev. Ignatius, (NOR) [MON] Marian Friary of Our Lady of Guadalupe, Griswold, CT
Mang, Rev. Hau Hawm John, (IND) St. Mark the Evangelist Catholic Church, Indianapolis, Inc., Indianapolis, IN; St. Pius X Catholic Church, Indianapolis, Inc., Indianapolis, IN
Mangalath, Rev. Msgr. Augustine Abraham, '79 (MCE) St. Peter's Malankara Catholic Church, Blauvelt, NY
Mangalath, Rev. Jaison, *SVD* (GAL) St. Mary of the Purification, Houston, TX
Mangampo, Rev. Gil, '91 (GLP) St. Bonaventure, Crownpoint, NM; St. Paul, Crownpoint, NM
Mangan, Rev. Msgr. Charles, '89 (SFS) [CON] Monastery of Our Mother of Mercy and St. Joseph Discalced Carmelite Nuns, Alexandria, SD
Manganello, Rev. Msgr. Salvatore, '82 (BUF) Curia: Leadership St. Louis, Buffalo, NY
Mangano, Rev. Charles, (RVC) Our Lady of Lourdes, West Islip, NY
Mangattu Mathai, Rev. Thomas, *VC* '08 (SYM) St. George Syro-Malabar Catholic Church, Paterson, NJ
Manger, Rev. Daniel, *O.S.B.Cam.* '85 (MRY) [MON] Monastery of the Risen Christ, San Luis Obispo, CA
Mangesho, Rev. Paulinus, *A.L.C.P.* (P) Immaculate Heart of Mary, Portland, OR
Mangiafico, Rev. Paul J., '70 (HRT) Retired.
Mangiaracina, Rev. Cayet N., *O.P.* '64 (BR) Congregation Of Holy Ghost Roman Catholic Church, Hammond, Louisiana, Hammond, LA
Mangiaracina, Rev. George, *O.C.D.* '93 (MIL) [MON] Discalced Carmelite Friars of Holy Hill, Inc., Hubertus, WI
Mangieri, Rev. Thomas P., '01 (PAT) Retired.
Mangini, Rev. Richard A., '67 (OAK) Retired.
Manglaviti, Rev. Leo M., *S.J.* '99 (NY) [MON] Murray-Weigel Hall (A Jesuit Community at Murray-Weigel Hall and Kohlmann Hall), Bronx, NY
Mangubat, Very Rev. Marlon, '95 (NO) Curia: Leadership; Offices and Directors Our Lady of Prompt Succor, Chalmette, LA
Mangum, Very Rev. Peter B., '90 (SHP) Curia: Leadership; Offices and Directors St. John Berchmans Cathedral, Shreveport, LA
Maniangat, Rev. Joseph, '64 (STA) Retired.
Maniangattu, Rev. George, (BIR) St. Francis of Assisi, Livingston, AL; St. Leo, Demopolis, AL; [CAM] University of West Alabama Campus Ministry - St. Francis-Livingston, Livingston, AL
Manickam, Rev. Peter M., '81 (LC) St. Maximilian Maria Kolbe, Almond, WI; [EFT] St. Maximilian Kolbe Church Endowment Trust, Almond, WI
Manickam, Rev. Suresh, *H.G.N.* '10 (SB) Saint John XXIII Catholic Community, Inc., Fontana, CA
Manikuttiyil, Rev. Kurian, (PT) Our Lady of the Rosary, Panama City, FL
Manikyalarao, Rev. Penumaka, *H.G.N.* '09 (WH) Sacred Heart Mission, Point Pleasant, WV; St. Matthew, Ravenswood, WV
Manimala, Rev. Thomas, '95 (SAN) Retired.
Maniscalco, Rev. Msgr. Francis J., '71 (RVC) St. Thomas, the Apostle, West Hempstead, NY
Manista, Rev. Clemens D., '74 (WIL) Our Mother of Sorrows, Centreville, MD
Maniyangat, Rev. Jose, '75 (STA) Retired.
Manjadi, Rev. George, '67 (WH) Retired.
Manjakunnel, Rev. Jose, (CAM) St. Stephen's R.C. Church, Pennsauken Township, N.J., Pennsauken, NJ
Manjaly, Rev. Thomas, *S.A.C.* '85 (MIL) St. Vincent Pallotti Congregation, Milwaukee, WI; [MON] Pallotti House, Milwaukee, WI
Manjarrez, Rev. Juan, '12 (LR) Curia: Leadership St. Edward, Little Rock, AR
Manjooran, Rev. Simon Joseph Chummar, *S.B.D.* (KAL) Blessed Sacrament, Allegan, MI; St. Margaret, Otsego, MI
Mankowski, Rev. Canon Maciej, '01 (Y) Saint Mary, Massillon, OH; St. Joseph, Massillon, OH
Mankowski, Rev. Canon Matthew, '01 (Y) Holy Family Parish, Navarre, OH; St. Barbara, Massillon, OH; [SHR] National Shrine of St. Dymphna, Massillon, OH
Mann, Rev. Francis, '79 (BRK) Retired.
Mann, Rev. Kevin, *S.J.C.* '14 (CHI) [MIS] Canons Regular of Saint John Cantius, Chicago, IL
Mann, Rev. Kevin, *S.J.C.* '14 (SFD) St. Katharine Drexel, Springfield, IL
Mann, Rev. Quentin A., *C.D.L.* '06 (GB) Sacred Heart, Aurora, WI; St. Anthony, Niagara, WI; St. Margaret, Pembine, WI
Mann, Rev. Ryan J., '14 (CLV) St. Basil the Great, Brecksville, OH; [MIS] Retrouvaille of Cleveland, Inc., Solon, OH
Mannam, Rev. Sudhakar, *MOP* (SR) Pastor of St. Bernard Catholic Church of Eureka, A Corporation Sole, Eureka, CA
Mannara, Rev. Frederick R., '63 (SY) Most Holy Rosary, Syracuse, NY
Mannara, Rev. Kevin, *C.S.B.* '17 (ROC) [CAM] St. John Fisher College, Rochester, NY; [MON] Basilian Fathers, Rochester, NY
Mannebach, Rev. Thomas M., '99 (CIN) St. Ignatius of Loyola, Cincinnati, OH
Mannerino, Rev. Christopher J., '15 (PIT) Sts. Martha and Mary, Allison Park, PA
Manning, Rev. Brian F., '74 (BO) St. Mary, Franklin, MA
Manning, Rev. Christopher, '13 (KNX) Notre Dame High School, Chattanooga, TN; St. Stephen, Chattanooga, TN
Manning, Rev. James, *S.M.M.* '58 (RVC) Retired. [MON] Montfort Missionaries, Bay Shore, NY
Manning, Rev. James J., '75 (CIN) Retired. Our Lady of Good Hope, Miamisburg, OH; St. Henry, Dayton, OH; St. Mary of the Assumption, Springboro, OH
Manning, Rev. John E., '72 (CLV) Retired.
Manning, Rev. Michael, '97 (TR) Church of the Holy Cross of Sea Bright, NJ, Rumson, NJ
Manning, Rev. Patrick, (CLV) [SEM] Saint Mary Seminary and Graduate School of Theology, Wickliffe, OH
Manning, Rev. Paul R., '59 (NEW) Retired.
Manning, Rev. Paul S., '85 (PAT) Curia: Administration; Leadership [MIS] St. Paul Inside The Walls: The Catholic Center for Evangelization at Bayley-Ellard, Madison, NJ
Manning, Rev. Robert A., '83 (E) St. Columbkille,

Stoneboro, PA
Mannion, Rev. James P., '81 (RVC) Curia: Leadership St. James, Setauket, NY
Mannion, Rev. John H., (LFT) Retired.
Mannion, Rev. Msgr. M. Francis, '73 (SLC) Retired. Saint Vincent de Paul LLC 250, Salt Lake City, UT
Mannion, Rev. Mark, '95 (POD) Curia: Clergy and Religious Services
Mannion, Rev. Mark, (LA) [MIS] Tilden Study Center, Los Angeles, CA
Mannion, Rev. Msgr. Martin J., '62 (CAM) Retired.
Mannion, Rev. Martin K., '66 (STL) Retired.
Mannion, Rev. Msgr. Michael T., '71 (CAM) Retired.
Manno, Rev. John D., '01 (SY) Curia: Leadership; Offices and Directors Church of the Holy Family, Syracuse, NY
Manno, Rev. Kyle A., '16 (RCK) On Administrative Leave.
Mannoorvadakkethil, Rev. Mathai, '94 (WDC) Syro-Malankara Mission, Landover Hills, MD
Manolev, Rev. Cyril, (STF) Curia: Offices and Directors
Manolev, Rev. Kiril, '01 (STF) Curia: Leadership St. John the Baptist, Glastonbury, CT; St. Mary Dormition, Colchester, CT
Manos, Rev. James M., '96 (NEW) Curia: Organizations (affiliated, inter-Diocesan, miscellaneous/other) St. Luke, Ho Ho Kus, NJ
Manosalvas, Rev. Patricio, *C.P.* '04 (BIR) St. Joseph Catholic Parish, Birmingham, Birmingham, AL
Manrique, Rev. Msgr. Wilfredo S., '88 (SJ) On Special Assignment. St. John the Baptist, Milpitas, CA
Manriquez, Rev. Raymundo, '00 (LUB) Curia: Leadership St. Joseph's, Lubbock, TX
Mansfield, Rev. Scott, '00 (SFE) St. John Vianney Church, Rio Rancho, NM
Mansford, Rev. Emmanuel Mary, *C.F.R.* '07 (PAT) [MIS] Saint Michael's Friary (Franciscan Friars of the Renewal), Paterson, NJ
Manship, Rev. D. Joseph, '76 (PRT) Retired.
Manship, Rev. James C., '98 (HRT) Trustees of St. Roses Ch. Meriden, Connecticut, Meriden, CT
Mansini, Rev. Guy, *O.S.B.* '77 (IND) [MON] St. Meinrad Archabbey, St. Meinrad, IN
Manso, Rev. Bobby, '00 (SPC) On Leave.
Manson, Rev. Sean A., '99 (NEW) Curia: Offices and Directors Our Lady Mother of the Church, Woodcliff Lake, NJ
Manternach, Rev. Neil J., '85 (DUB) Curia: Leadership Epiphany Parish, Mason City, Iowa, Mason City, IA; Newman Catholic School System, Mason City, IA; Sacred Heart Church, Manly, Iowa, Manly, IA
Manthey, Rev. Kevin M., '14 (STP) On Duty Outside Diocese. Emmanuel School of Mission, NY
Mantia, Rev. Armand, '85 (NEW) Curia: Offices and Directors Holy Spirit, Union, NJ; St. Genevieve, Elizabeth, NJ
Mantilla Ramírez, Rev. Jorge Iván, *O.SS.T.* (ARE) Our Lady of Mount Carmel, Isabela, PR
Mantovani, Rev. Firmo, *C.S.* '73 (LA) St. Peter, Los Angeles, CA
Manuel, Rev. Gerdenio S., *S.J.* '79 (SFR) [MON] Loyola House Jesuit Community, San Francisco, CA
Manuel, Rev. Herman, *S.V.D.* '04 (SD) Pastor of Saint Kateri Tekakwitha National Indian Parish, Lakeside, CA
Manuel, Rev. Lukose, *O.S.H.* '02 (GAL) [MON] The Society of the Oblates of Sacred Heart, Missouri City, TX
Manuele, Rev. Christopher, '06 (NTN) St. Joseph Catholic Church, Inc., Scranton, PA
Manuel-Lopez, Rev. Eleazar, *OMI* '20 (SAT) [MON] Missionary Oblates of Mary Immaculate of Texas, Southern Province (San Antonio USP Support Office), San Antonio, TX
Manuppella, Rev. Anthony J., '76 (CAM) Curia: Leadership; Tribunal St. Gianna Beretta Molla Parish, Northfield, N.J., Northfield, NJ
Manyama, Rev. Augustine, *A.J.* '02 (P) [HOS] Providence Health & Services-Oregon (Providence Portland Medical Center), Portland, OR
Manz, Rev. Michael J., '79 (NY) [MIS] Personal Prelature, ,
Manz, Rev. Michael J., '79 (POD) Curia: Clergy and Religious Services
Manzano, Very Rev. Eurel, '11 (GAL) [SEM] St. Mary's Seminary, Houston, TX
Manzano, Rev. Eurel S. P., '11 (GAL) Curia: Offices and Directors
Manzo, Rev. Louis A., *C.S.C.* '65 (ORL) Retired. (>FTW) [MON] Congregation of Holy Cross, United States Province of Priests and Brothers, Notre Dame, IN
Manzo Madrigal, Rev. Jesus Antonio, '20 (ATL) San Felipe de Jesus, Forest Park, GA
Mapara, Rev. Ildefonce, *O.S.B.* '00 (BAK) [MIS] St. Maurus Hanga Abbey, Klamath Falls, OR
Maples, Rev. Frederic A., *S.J.* '72 (BO) [MON] Campion Health & Wellness, Inc., Weston, MA
Maples, Rev. Michael R., '05 (KNX) St. John Neumann, Farragut, TN
Mappilamattel, Rev. Joseph, (RVC) Notre Dame, New Hyde Park, NY
Mapunda, Rev. Christopher A., *S.J.* '17 (CIN) [MON] Cincinnati Jesuit Community, Cincinnati, OH
Maquinana, Rev. Ronald, '06 (GBG) St. Mary, Yatesboro, PA; St. Mary, Our Lady of Guadalupe, Kittanning, PA
Marable, Rev. Gerard C., '88 (CAM) Our Lady of Perpetual Help, Galloway, NJ
Maram Reddy, Rev. Louis Reddy, '89 (SUP) St. Augustine, Harrison, WI; St. Francis of Assisi, Tripoli, WI; St. Mary, Tomahawk, WI
Maramot, Rev. Faustino, '74 (MEM) Chap, Federal Corr Inst at Memphis
Marandi, Rev. Paulus, *C.M.F.* '16 (MET) St. Thomas the Apostle, Old Bridge, NJ
Marandu, Rev. Nicolaus, *A.L.C.P.* '82 (P) St. Frederic Catholic Church, St. Helens, OR
Marangone, Rev. Mark, *S.X.* '84 (PAT) [MON] Xaverian Missionary Fathers, Wayne, NJ
Marano, Rev. Fred, '91 (BRK) Sacred Heart of Jesus Church, Glendale, NY
Marano, Rev. Zaya, '92 (EST) Retired.
Maranowski, Rev. Michael J, (PIT) Our Lady of Mount Carmel, Pittsburgh, PA
Maranto, Rev. Samuel C., *C.Ss.R.* '72 (BR) [MIS] Redemptorist Fathers of Baton Rouge, Inc., Baton Rouge, LA
Maranto, Rev. Samuel C., *C.Ss.R.* '72 (BR) [MON] St. Gerard Residence, Baton Rouge, LA
Marascalco, Rev. Michael A., '12 (BLX) St. Francis Xavier, Wiggins, MS
Marat, Rev. Wojciech A., '88 (CHI) Our Lady of the Wayside, Arlington Heights, IL
Maravi, Rev. Raul, *O.Carm.* '97 (JOL) [MON] Carmelite Provincial Office, Darien, IL
Maraya, Rev. Felipe, '62 (ELP) On Leave.
Marbury, Rev. Christopher, '20 (DEN) On Academic Leave. Pontifical Univ of St Thomas Aquinas, Rome St. Thomas More Catholic Parish in Centennial, Centennial, CO
Marca Mansilla, Rev. Alejandro Jesus, *O.C.D.* '94 (CHI) Our Lady of Ransom, Niles, IL
Marcaccio, Rev. Msgr. Anthony J., '91 (CHL) St. Pius the Tenth, Greensboro, NC
Marcaida, Rev. Epifanio, '83 (NY) Resurrection, Rye, NY
Marcantonio, Rev. Clement, '59 (PBL) Retired.
Marcell, Rev. Robert G., '56 (BR) Retired.
Marcelli, Rev. Anthony, '21 (CIN) St. Margaret - St. John Parish, Cincinnati, OH
Marcelli, Rev. Anthony, '21 (CIN) St. Anthony Church, Cincinnati, OH; St. Cecilia, Cincinnati, OH; St. Mary, Cincinnati, OH
Marcelli, Rev. Michael, '11 (Y) On Duty Outside Diocese. Curia: (>MO) Offices and Directors
Marcello, Rev. Albert P., '09 (PRO) Chap, Rhode Island Hosp, Providence Curia: Leadership St. Martha's Church Corporation, East Providence, East Providence, RI
Marcello, Rev. Albert Peter, (BGP) Curia: Tribunal
Marcello, Rev. Joseph A., '03 (BGP) Curia: Clergy and Religious Services; Consultative Bodies Saint Catherine of Siena Corporation, Trumbull, CT
Marcelo, Rev. Florante, (CHY) St. Joseph's, Rawlins, WY
Marcelo, Rev. Jeronimo, (MRY) St. Jude Parish Community, Marina, CA
March, Rev. John W., (CAM) Our Lady of Hope Parish, Blackwood, N.J., Blackwood, NJ
March, Rev. Nathan D., '07 (PRT) Curia: Consultative Bodies Saint Brendan the Navigator Parish, Camden, ME; St. Michael Parish, Augusta, ME
March, Rev. Nicholas B., '04 (DUB) LaSalle Catholic, Cedar Rapids, Iowa, Cedar Rapids, IA; St. Jude Church, Cedar Rapids, Iowa, Cedar Rapids, IA; [CEM] St. Joseph's Cemetery Association, Clinton Township, Linn County, Iowa, Cedar Rapids, IA
Marcham, Rev. David S., '05 (BO) On Duty Outside Diocese.
Marchand, Rev. Gerald A., '54 (NEW) Retired.
Marchand, Rev. Steven, (BUR) St. Ambrose, Bristol, VT; St. Peter, Vergennes, VT
Marchesani, Rev. Gino, *F.D.P.* '56 (BO) [NUR] Don Orione Nursing Home, East Boston, MA
Marchese, Rev. Adam, '20 (ORL) St. Margaret Mary, Winter Park, FL
Marchese, Rev. Adam, (MO) Curia: Offices and Directors
Marchese, Rev. Joseph P., '69 (SPR) Retired.
Marchese, Rev. Msgr. Richard E., '70 (BRK) Retired. On Duty Outside Diocese. Apostolic Nunciature, Washington DC Sacred Heart of Jesus Church, Glendale, NY
Marchessault, Rev. Edward, *C.S.Sp.* '64 (SB) Retired.
Marchetti, Rev. Michael H., '82 (SCR) Retired.
Marchetto, Rev. Ezio, *C.S.* '82 (NY) Our Lady of Pompeii, New York, NY; [MON] Scalabrinian Missionaries (The Pious Society of the Missionaries of St. Charles Boromeo, Inc.), New York, NY
Marchewka, Rev. Jacek, '00 (NEW) Immaculate Heart of Mary, Mahwah, NJ
Marchionda, Rev. James, *O.P.* (NY) [EFT] St. Thomas Aquinas Foundation of the Dominican Fathers of the United States (STAF), New York, NY
Marchionda, Rev. James V., *O.P.* '73 (CHI) [EFT] St. Thomas Aquinas Priory, Chicago, IL; [MON] Dominicans (Provincial Office), Chicago, IL
Marchionda, Rev. James V., *O.P.* '73 (STL) [MIS] Dominican Studentate, St. Louis, MO
Marchwiany, Rev. Robert, (CHI) Our Lady of the Woods, Orland Park, IL
Marciano, Rev. Robert L., '83 (PRO) Bishop Hendricken High School, Warwick, RI; St. Benedict's Church, Conimicut, Warwick, RI; St. Kevin's Church Corporation, Warwick, Warwick, RI
Marciniak, Rev. Bartlomiej, *O.S.P.P.E.* '93 (PH) [MON] The Order of Saint Paul, First Hermit - The Pauline Fathers, Doylestown, PA
Marciniak, Rev. Canon Felix R., '79 (NEW) Most Sacred Heart of Jesus, Wallington, NJ
Marciniak, Rev. Stanislaw P., '86 (SAT) St. Cornelius, Karnes City, TX
Marciniak, Rev. Thomas R., *S.J.* (BAL) [MIS] Colombiere Jesuit Community, Baltimore, MD
Marco, Rev. Alfredo, '60 (LKC) Retired.
Marco, Rev. Jason, '07 (CHY) Chap, Wyoming State Penitentiary, Rawlins Holy Rosary, Lander, WY
Marco, Rev. Michael J., *S.J.* '96 (MIL) Marquette University High School, Milwaukee, WI; [MON] Jesuit Community at Marquette University (Marquette Jesuit Associates, Inc.), Milwaukee, WI
Marcoe, Very Rev. Timothy D., '07 (HBG) Curia: Offices and Directors St. Joseph, Danville, PA
Marcone, Rev. Eugene F., '64 (NEW) Retired.
Marconi, Rev. John, '93 (LR) [MON] St. John Manor, Little Rock, AR
Marconi, Rev. Joseph P., '01 (LR) Good Shepherd, Fordyce, AR; Holy Cross, Sheridan, AR; St. Joseph, Pine Bluff, AR
Marcotte, Rev. David P., *S.J.* '92 (NY) [MON] Jesuit Community at Fordham University, New York, NY
Marcotte, Very Rev. Douglas W., '13 (IND) Curia: Leadership; Offices and Directors St. Simon the Apostle Catholic Church, Indianapolis, Inc., Indianapolis, IN; [MIS] Indianapolis North Deanery, Indianapolis, IN
Marcoux, Rev. Joseph, (MO) Curia: Offices and Directors
Marcoux, Rev. Joseph W., '01 (ROC) St. Catherine of Siena, Ithaca, NY
Marcoux, Rev. Stephen, '93 (MAN) Sacred Heart Parish, Manchester, NH
Marcucci, Rev. John A., '68 (PIT) Retired. Curia: Consultative Bodies
Marcy, Rev. Bede, *O.S.B.* '09 (BIR) [MON] St. Bernard Abbey, Cullman, AL
Marczewski, Rev. Robert, '95 (LA) [COL] Thomas Aquinas College, Santa Paula, CA
Marczewski, Rev. Robert, '95 (PH) On Duty Outside Diocese. Thomas Aquinas College, Santa Paula, CA
Marczewski, Rev. Msgr. Ronald J., '74 (NEW) St. Anne, Garwood, NJ
Marczuk, Rev. Msgr. Scott L., '81 (LR) St. Stephen, Bentonville, AR
Marczuk, Msgr. Scott L., '81 (LR) Curia: Leadership
Marecki, Rev. Ronald, '83 (SP) Retired.
Mareedu, Rev. Vijaya, *SAC* (FWT) Holy Rosary, Cisco, TX; St. Francis Xavier, Eastland, TX; St. John, Strawn, TX; St. Rita, Ranger, TX
Marek, Rev. Dean V., '65 (MIL) Retired.
Marek, Rev. Libor, '05 (DET) SS. Cyril and Methodius (Slovak) Parish Sterling Heights, Sterling Heights, MI
Marek, Rev. Pawel, (JOL) Divine Mercy Parish, Lombard, IL
Marek, Rev. Raymond John, *OMI* '89 (OAK) [MON] Missionary Oblates of Mary Immaculate Western, Oakland, CA
Mares, Rev. Luis E., (LAR) Divine Mercy, Laredo, TX
Maresca, Rev. Msgr. Ralph J., '78 (BRK) St. Francis of

Assisi, Astoria, NY
Maresh, Rev. Mark, '94 (GI) St. Josaphat's, Loup City, NE
Marfori, Rev. Antonio, '78 (SCL) On Special Assignment.
Margalef, Rev. Josep M., *Sch.P.* '67 (LA) Santa Teresita, Los Angeles, CA; St. Lucy, Los Angeles, CA; [MON] Piarist Fathers, Los Angeles, CA
Margallo, Rev. Roy, *O.S.A.* '00 (MRY) St. John's, Felton, CA
Margevicius, Rev. Thomas, '99 (STP) Curia: Offices and Directors Church of St. Henry, Le Sueur, MN; Church of the Nativity, Cleveland, MN; Immaculate Conception of Marysburg, Madison Lake, MN; St. Mary, Le Center, MN
Marggraf, Rev. Brian, *SS.CC.* '55 (FR) Retired.
Margherio, Rev. Ronald L., *O.S.B.* '78 (PEO) St. Bede Academy (Benedictine Fathers and Brothers), Peru, IL; [SEM] St. Bede Abbey (Benedictine Society of St. Bede, Benedictine Fathers and Brothers), Peru, IL
Marginean, Very Rev. Ovidiu Ioan, '06 (ROM) Curia: Leadership; Offices and Directors St. George Cathedral, Canton, OH
Maria, Rev. John C, (ALN) St. Mary, Kutztown, PA; [CAM] Kutztown University (Kutztown), Kutztown, PA
Maria Augustin, Rev. David Milton, *HGN* (BLX) St. Ann, Gulfport, MS
Maria Francis, Rev. Jerome Patric, '97 (LC) St. Vincent de Paul, Wisconsin Rapids, WI; [EFT] St. Vincent de Paul Parish, Wisconsin Rapids Endowment Trust, Wisconsin Rapids, WI
Maria Susai, Rev. Barnabas, *I.M.S.* '90 (LR) St. Bernard of Clairvaux, Bella Vista, AR
Mariadoss, Rev. Saleth, '06 (MOB) St. Peter, Montgomery, AL
Mariani, Rev. Paul P., *S.J.* '02 (SJ) [MON] Jesuit Community at Santa Clara University, Inc., Santa Clara, CA
Mariano, Rev. John R., '13 (HRT) Retired. Corporation of the Church of the Immaculate Conception, Waterbury, Connecticut, Waterbury, CT
Mariano, Rev. Remigio Miguel, '94 (TUC) Saint Odilia Roman Catholic Community - Tucson, Oro Valley, AZ
Mariano, Rev. Remigio "Miguel", '94 (TUC) Curia: Advisory Boards, Commissions, Committees, and Councils
Mariappan, Rev. Arivu, (LC) Guardian Angels, Black River Falls, WI
Mariasamy, Rev. Peter Raj, '05 (LC) St. James, Camp Douglas, WI; St. Michael, Tomah, WI; St. Paul, New Lisbon, WI
Mariasoosai, Rev. Benjamin, '84 (BUF) St. Joseph, Holland, NY
Mariasoosai, Rev. Pragasam, (CHL) St. Joseph of the Hills, Eden, NC
Mariastanislaus, Rev. Jerold, '90 (CAM) Chap, Cooper Med Ctr
Mariasusai, Rev. Arockia Sabastian, *SVD* (LAF) Immaculate Heart of Mary, Lafayette, LA
Marich, Rev. Paul, *O.P.* '22 (COL) St. Patrick, Columbus, OH
Marick, Rev. Thomas D., '97 (STN) Retired.
Maridas, Rev. Francis, (TOL) St. Richard, Swanton, OH
Marien, Rev. Roy C., '85 (PT) Chap, Okaloosa Corr Fac Our Lady of Victory, Crestview, FL
Marien, Rev. Roy C., '85 (PT) Curia: Leadership
Marigliano, Rev. Michael, *O.F.M.Cap.* '84 (NY) Parish of Holy Cross and St. John the Baptist, New York, NY
Marin, Rev. Alberto, '09 (SAT) Curia: Administration St. Jude, San Antonio, TX
Marin, Rev. Jonathan, (BO) [MON] Isaac Jogues House, Brighton, MA
Marin, Rev. Jose, '95 (TYL) Sacred Heart, Nacogdoches, TX
Marin, Rev. Juan Carlos, '14 (DAL) Immaculate Conception Catholic Parish - Corsicana, Corsicana, TX
Marin, Rev. Martin Garcia, '99 (STO) St. George Church (Pastor of), Stockton, CA
Marin, Rev. Miguel, '78 (ELP) On Leave.
Marin, Rev. Romulo, '15 (BRK) All Saints – Our Lady of the Rosary of Pompeii, Brooklyn, NY
Marin Morales, Rev. Fabio, *C.Ss.R.* (CHL) St. James, Concord, NC
Marina, Rev. Joseph, *S.J* '12 (SCR) [COL] The University of Scranton, Scranton, PA
Marinak, Rev. Andrew P., '56 (HBG) Retired.
Marine, Rev. Msgr. John C., '76 (PH) On Special Assignment. Dean, Deanery 10, St Bede The Venerable Rectory, Holland Curia: Deaneries St. Bede the Venerable, Holland, PA
Marinelli, Rev. Matthew, '19 (MET) St. Magdalen de Pazzi, Flemington, NJ
Marini, Rev. Francis J., '95 (ROM) Curia: Offices and Directors
Marini, Rev. Msgr. Francis J., '95 (SAM) Curia: Leadership; Offices and Directors
Marini, Rev. Michael, '72 (MRY) Retired.
Marin-Leon, Rev. Rafael, '78 (LA) Retired. St. Joseph, Carpinteria, CA
Marino, Very Rev. Christopher B., '93 (MIA) Curia: Leadership; Pastoral Services St. Mary's Cathedral, Miami, FL
Marino, Rev. John J., *O.F.M.* '88 (SP) [MON] St. Anthony Friary (St. Petersburg) Franciscan Friars-Holy Name Province, Inc., St. Petersburg, FL
Marino, Rev. Msgr. Joseph T., '75 (PH) Retired.
Marino, Rev. Msgr. Ronald T., '73 (BRK) Retired. St. Rosalia-Regina Pacis, Brooklyn, NY
Marino, Rev. Shia Reh, (PHX) St. Clement of Rome Roman Catholic Parish, Sun City, AZ
Mario, Rev. Clemente Felix, *M.S.* '06 (ATL) St. Thomas the Apostle Catholic Church, Smyrna, Inc., Smyrna, GA
Marion, Rev. Craig F., '16 (DET) St. Anne Parish Ortonville, Ortonville, MI
Mariscal, Rev. Jesus, '18 (YAK) St. Paul Cathedral, Yakima, WA
Mariscal, Very Rev. Jose De Jesus, '18 (YAK) Curia: Leadership; Offices and Directors
Mariscal Chavez, Rev. Felipe Maria, *O.S.M.* '72 (ELP) Our Lady of Sorrows, El Paso, TX
Maristany, Rev. Edward G., '80 (POD) Curia: Clergy and Religious Services
Maristela, Rev. Victor T., '87 (SD) Pastor of Saint Michael Catholic Parish, Poway, a corporation sole, Poway, CA
Mark, Rev. John K., '01 (STV) Our Lady of Perpetual Help, Charlotte Amalie, VI; [MIS] Sons of Mary and Joseph - OLPH, ,
Mark, Rev. John Kennedy, '01 (STV) [MIS] Miscellaneous Organizations, Charlotte Amalie, VI
Mark, Rev. Urey P., *S.V.D.* '07 (ATL) [CAM] Catholic Center Georgia State University, Atlanta, GA; [CAM] Clark Atlanta, Atlanta, GA; [CAM] Morehouse College, Atlanta, GA; [CAM] Spellman College, Atlanta, GA
Markellos, Rev. Christopher M., '06 (CAM) On Duty Outside Diocese.
Markellos, Rev. Christopher M., *O.Praem.* (WIL) Cathedral of St. Peter, Wilmington, DE
Markellos, Rev. Christopher M., (WIL) St. Mary of the Immaculate Conception, Wilmington, DE; St. Patrick, Wilmington, DE
Markelz, Rev. Carl J., *O.Carm.* '91 (JOL) [MIS] The League of the Miraculous Infant Jesus of Prague, Darien, IL; [MON] Carmelite Provincial Office, Darien, IL; [MON] St. Simon Stock Priory, Darien, IL
Markelz, Rev. Carl J., *O.Carm.* '91 (CHI) [MON] Sant'Angelo Community at St. Cyril Priory, Chicago, IL
Markert, Rev. Leo F., '62 (ALB) Retired. St. Gabriel the Archangel, Schenectady, NY
Markewych, Rev. Archpriest Uriy, '65 (PHU) Retired.
Markey, Rev. Earle L., *S.J.* '63 (WOR) [MON] Jesuits of the Holy Cross, Inc., Worcester, MA
Markey, Rev. Greg J., '99 (BGP) On Duty Outside Diocese. Thomas Aquinas College, Northfield, MA
Markey, Rev. John J., *O.P.* '93 (SAT) [COL] Oblate School of Theology, San Antonio, TX; [CON] Dominican Community of San Juan Macias (San Juan Macias Community), San Antonio, TX
Markham, Rev. John C., '03 (SAV) Retired.
Markiewicz, Rev. Michal, (DAL) Curia: Administration [SEM] The Redemptoris Mater House of Formation (Redemptoris Mater Seminary), Dallas, TX
Markiewicz, Rev. Mikolaj, *S.D.S* '03 (GRY) [MON] Salvatorian Fathers (Society of the Divine Savior), Merrillville, IN
Markman, Rev. Christopher J., '11 (FAR) St. Thomas Aquinas Newman Center of Grand Forks, Grand Forks, ND; [CAM] St. Thomas Aquinas Newman Church of Grand Forks, Grand Forks, ND
Marko, Rev. Andrew, '98 (SJP) Retired. Curia: Offices and Directors
Markovic, Rev. Viktor, '10 (NEW) On Duty Outside Diocese. Rooma Katoliku Kirk Kogudas, Tartu
Marks, Rev. Kevin E., '04 (PBR) Curia: Leadership; Offices and Directors St. Michael, Campbell, OH; St. Michael, Hermitage, PA
Marks, Rev. Thomas C, '79 (LR) [MON] St. John Manor, Little Rock, AR
Marks, Rev. William G., '92 (IND) Curia: Leadership; Offices and Directors St. Mary-of-the-Knobs Catholic Church, Floyds Knobs, Inc., Floyds Knobs, IN
Markulak, Rev. Grzegorz M., *C.M.* '98 (BRK) St. Stanislaus Kostka, Brooklyn, NY
Markunas, Rev. Robert, '76 (ORL) Retired.
Markus, Rev. Anthony L., '80 (CHI) Retired.
Markwell, Rev. Benjamin, *O.F.M. Cap.* (SP) [MON] Missionaries of Africa, St. Petersburg, FL
Markwell, Rev. George, *M.Afr.* '65 (SP) [MON] Missionaries of Africa, St. Petersburg, FL
Marley, Rev. John, *S.S.C.* '50 (OM) Retired. [MON] Missionary Society of St. Columban, St. Columbans, NE
Marley, Rev. John, *S.S.C.* '50 (PRO) Retired. [MON] St. Columban's Retirement House (St. Columban's Foreign Mission Society), Bristol, RI
Marlovits, Rev. Kenneth W., '14 (PIT) Curia: Clergy and Religious Services
Marneni, Rev. Ignatius, '69 (PH) Retired.
Marneni, Rev. Prabhakar, '03 (FAR) St. Anthony of Padua's Church of Fargo, Fargo, ND
Marneni, Rev. Vijay, *PIME* '04 (NY) Parish of St. Ann and St. Lucy, New York, NY; St. Lucy, New York, NY
Marney, Rev. Matthew D., (WCH) Church of the Holy Spirit, Goddard, KS
Maro, Rev. Robert G., '15 (WDC) St. Francis Xavier, Leonardtown, MD
Maroney, Rev. Frank, '92 (DEN) Retired.
Maroney, Rev. Maurice J., '67 (HRT) Retired.
Maroney, Rev. Nicholas, (CHY) [MON] Monks of the Most Blessed Virgin Mary of Mt. Carmel (Carmelite Monks), Meeteetse, WY
Maroney, Rev. Simon Mary, *M.Carm.* (CHY) On Special Assignment. In Res, Monks of the Most Blessed Virgin Mary of Mt Carme...
Maroon, Rev. Donald M., '67 (COL) Retired.
Maroun, Chorbishop Sharbel, '89 (OLL) Curia: Leadership; Offices and Directors St. Maron Maronite Catholic Church, Minneapolis, MN
Marquard, Rev. Elmer E., '66 (CLV) Retired.
Marquard, Rev. Luke C., '13 (STP) Good Shepherd, Golden Valley, MN
Marquart, Rev. Ernest J., '70 (SPC) Retired.
Marques, Very Rev. Anthony E., '06 (RIC) Curia: Deaneries Cathedral of the Sacred Heart, Richmond, VA; [CAM] Catholic Campus Ministry, Virginia Commonwealth University, Richmond, VA
Marques, Rev. Jose E., (BO) Immaculate Conception, Stoughton, MA; St. James, Stoughton, MA
Marquez, Rev. Angelo, '16 (SFE) La Santisima Trinidad, Arroyo Seco, NM
Marquez, Rev. Celso, *M.Sp.S.* (LA) Our Lady of Guadalupe Parish, Oxnard, CA
Marquez, Rev. Esteban, '95 (LA) St. Augustine, Culver City, CA; St. Mary, Palmdale, CA
Marquez, Rev. Fabian, '04 (ELP) Curia: Offices and Directors St. Joseph's, El Paso, TX
Marquez, Rev. Fausto, '97 (ATL) St. Michael the Archangel Catholic Church, Woodstock, Inc., Woodstock, GA
Marquez, Rev. Gregory, '03 (ORG) Curia: Leadership
Marquez, Rev. Gregory Pablo, (ORG) Immaculate Heart of Mary, Santa Ana, CA
Marquez, Rev. Jose, '99 (GF) Mary Queen of Peace, Billings, MT
Marquez, Rev. Jose E., '99 (NEW) On Duty Outside Diocese. Mary, Queen of Peace, Billings, MT
Marquez, Rev. Miguel, *M.Sp.S.* (SEA) St. Elizabeth Ann Seton, Mill Creek, WA
Marquez, Rev. Raul O., '10 (P) St. Peter, Portland, OR
Marquez, Rev. Raymond, '10 (LA) [SEM] St. John's Seminary, Camarillo, CA
Marquez, Rev. Robert, '21 (ORL) St. Charles Borromeo, Orlando, FL
Marquez Salvador, Rev. Nelson Adan, (RVC) St. Hugh of Lincoln, Huntington Station, NY
Marquez-Munoz, Rev. Salvador, '03 (LR) St. Mary, Siloam Springs, AR
Marquis, Rev. Bill, '03 (CC) Our Lady of Refuge, Refugio, TX; St. James the Apostle, Refugio, TX; St. Therese, The Little Flower, Woodsboro, TX
Marquis, Rev. Joseph, '06 (PRM) Sacred Heart, Livonia, MI
Marquis, Rev. Paul, (PRT) Parish of the Holy Eucharist, Falmouth, ME
Marr, Rev. Andrew D., '17 (DUB) St. Boniface Church, Garner, Iowa, Garner, IA; St. James Catholic Church, Forest City, Iowa, Forest City, IA; St. Patrick Church, Britt, Iowa, Britt, IA; St. Patrick's Church, Buffalo Center, Iowa, Buffalo Center, IA; St. Patrick's Church, Lake Mills, Iowa, Lake Mills, IA; St. Wenceslaus Church, Duncan, Iowa, Britt, IA
Marr, Rev. Thomas P., '70 (MAD) Retired. St. John Vianney Cure of Ars, Janesville, WI
Marrano, Rev. Richard, '14 (NY) St. John Chrysostom, Bronx, NY; St. Rose of Lima, New York, NY; St.

Stephen, Warwick, NY
Marreddy, Rev. Allam, '79 (CHR) Our Lady of Peace Mission, Bonneau, SC; St. Philip Benizi, Moncks Corner, SC
Marrell, Rev. Dennis P., '78 (LA) St. Ambrose, West Hollywood, CA
Marren, Rev. Msgr. Hugh M., '76 (ATL) All Saints Catholic Church, Dunwoody, Inc., Dunwoody, GA
Marren, Rev. Martin T., '84 (CHI) St. John Fisher, Chicago, IL
Marrero, Rev. Adan, *S.D.B.* '97 (SJN) Prenoviciado Salesiano, Catano, PR
Marrero, Rev. Angel A., '13 (BAL) St. John the Evangelist, Frederick, MD; St. Joseph-on-Carrollton Manor, Frederick, MD
Marrero Berrios, Rev. Adan Luis, *S.D.B.* (ARE) San Juan Bautista, Orocovis, PR
Marrodan, Rev. Francisco J., *C.M.* (SJN) [HOS] Hospital Auxilio Mutuo, Hato Rey, PR; [SPF] Centro Medico de P.R., San Juan, PR
Marron, Rev. Msgr. Patrick L., '67 (SAT) Retired. [NUR] Casa De Padres, San Antonio, TX
Marroquin, Rev. Felipe de Jesus, *C.S.J.* (LAR) [MON] Congregation of St. John, Laredo, TX
Marroquin, Rev. Marco T., '12 (NEW) On Duty Outside Diocese. Our Lady of Divine Providence RC Mission, Providenciales
Marroquin-Monroy, Rev. Jose Raul, *F.M.* '21 (FTW) St. Anthony of Padua, Angola, IN; St. Joseph, LaGrange, IN; St. Paul Chapel, Fremont, IN
Marrufo, Rev. Ramon R., '76 (SD) Retired.
Marrufo Del Toro, Rev. Juan Pablo, *S.J.* (PHX) Brophy College Preparatory (Jesuit Fathers), Phoenix, AZ
Marrujo, Rev. Leonard, '13 (OAK) St. Anne, Walnut Creek, CA
Marsal, Rev. Armando, *D.C.J.M.* (ARL) Our Lady of Angels, Woodbridge, VA
Marsalek, Rev. Peter, *S.O.L.T.* '05 (CC) Curia: Leadership [MON] Society of Our Lady of the Most Holy Trinity, Corpus Christi, TX
Marse, Rev. John J., '81 (NO) St. Peter, Reserve, LA
Marsh, Rev. Ivan C., *O.Carm.* '80 (TUC) Retired.
Marshall, Rev. Anthony J., *S.S.S.* '11 (CLV) St. Christopher, Rocky River, OH
Marshall, Rev. Dean J., '19 (SAC) Pastor of St. John the Baptist Parish, Chico, a corporation sole, Chico, CA
Marshall, Very Rev. James, '04 (SFE) Curia: Offices and Directors San Clemente, Los Lunas, NM
Marshall, Very Rev. James E., '04 (SFE) Curia: Finance
Marshall, Rev. John Douglas, '13 (P) Curia: Offices and Directors St. John the Baptist, Milwaukie, OR
Marshall, Rev. Matthew N., '14 (LC) On Leave.
Marshall, Rev. Patrick M., '79 (CHI) Blessed Carlo Acutis Parish, Chicago, IL
Marshall, Rev. Peter, '09 (IND) St. Jude Catholic Church, Indianapolis, Inc., Indianapolis, IN
Marshall, Rev. Peter A., '09 (IND) Curia: Leadership; Offices and Directors
Marsicek, Rev. Robert, *S.D.S.* '68 (MIL) Retired. [MIS] Holy Apostles House of Formation, Milwauke, WI
Marsick, Rev. James J., '72 (CLV) Retired.
Marsolle, Rev. Karl, *F.S.S.P.* (PAT) Our Lady of Fatima Chapel (Tridentine), Pequannock, NJ
Marsolle, Rev. Karl, (RIC) St. Joseph, North Chesterfield, VA
Marstall, Rev. David, '04 (WCH) Curia: Offices and Directors St. Anne, Wichita, KS
Marszal, Rev. Theodore, '68 (CLV) St. Monica, Garfield Heights, OH
Marta, Rev. Msgr. Raul, '72 (FRS) Retired.
Martel, Rev. C. James, '70 (PRT) Retired.
Martel, Rev. Christopher M., '09 (MAN) Curia: Clergy and Religious Services St. Catherine of Siena, Manchester, NH
Martel, Rev. Leo E., '63 (BO) Retired.
Martel, Rev. Luc, *A.A.* (BO) (>WOR) St. Anne and St. Patrick, Fiskdale, MA
Martel, Rev. Marcel I., '79 (MAN) Curia: Consultative Bodies St. Mary, Hillsborough, NH; St. Theresa, Henniker, NH
Martell, Rev. James J., '88 (MEM) Curia: Advisory Boards, Commissions, Committees, and Councils; Leadership St. Philip the Apostle, Somerville, TN
Martello, Rev. Ernest, *O.S.C.* '70 (SCL) [MON] Crosier Priory, Onamia, MN
Martello, Rev. Lawrence N., '74 (CLV) Retired.
Martensen, Rev. Carsten, (BO) [MON] Campion Center, Inc., Weston, MA
Marthaler, Rev. Andrew, '90 (SCL) Retired.
Marti, Rev. Antonio (Tony), *O.F.M.Cap.* '96 (LA) St. Francis High School of La Canada-Flintridge, La Canada Flintridge, CA
Marti, Rev. Thomas J., *M.M.* '65 (NY) Retired. [MON] Maryknoll Fathers and Brothers (Catholic Foreign Mission Society of America, Inc.), Ossining, NY
Marti, Rev. Thomas J., *M.M.* '65 (SJ) Retired.
Martignetti, Rev. Richard, *O.F.M.* '97 (NY) [MON] Franciscan Province of the Immaculate Conception, New York, NY
Martignon, Rev. John E., '84 (MAR) Curia: Advisory Boards, Commissions, Committees, and Councils Holy Family, South Range, MI; St. Ignatius Loyola, Houghton, MI
Martin, Rev. Benjamin, '75 (DOD) Retired.
Martin, Rev. Benjamin, '20 (GLD) Saint Mary of the Assumption of Lake Leelanau, Lake Leelanau, MI; St. Mary School, Lake Leelanau, MI
Martin, Rev. C. Lou, '76 (BAL) Retired.
Martin, Rev. Charles A., *C.S.P.* '65 (BRK) Retired.
Martin, Rev. Charles A., *C.S.P.* '65 (BO) Retired. [MON] Missionary Society of St. Paul the Apostle in Massachusetts, Boston, MA
Martin, Rev. Chris, (WCH) [NUR] Catholic Care Center, Inc., Bel Aire, KS
Martin, Rev. Chris, (WCH) Curia: Leadership; Offices and Directors
Martin, Rev. Christopher M., '06 (STL) Curia: Leadership St. Clare of Assisi Catholic Church, Ellisville, MO; [COL] Cardinal Glennon College, ,
Martin, Rev. Clifford A., '76 (SFR) Retired.
Martin, Rev. Cristobal, *M. Id* (RVC) St. Luke, Brentwood, NY
Martin, Rev. Daniel P., '13 (MIA) [SEM] St. John Vianney College Seminary, Inc., Miami, FL
Martin, Rev. David, '76 (EVN) Retired.
Martin, Rev. David L., '73 (ARL) Retired.
Martin, Rev. Dennis A., '75 (E) Chap, St Vincent's Health Ctr, Erie
Martin, Rev. Dennis C., '67 (DAV) Retired.
Martin, Rev. Doug, '19 (PT) St. Peter, Mary Esther, FL
Martin, Rev. Edward, '77 (VEN) Curia: (>MO) Offices and Directors St. Isabel Parish in Sanibel, Inc., Sanibel, FL
Martin, Rev. Edwin J., '16 (BR) Assumption of the Blessed Virgin Mary (The Congregation Of The Assumption Roman Catholic Church Of Plattenville), Napoleonville, LA; Congregation of St. Anne Roman Catholic Church, Napoleonville, LA; The Congregation Of Saint Philomena Roman Catholic Church, Labadieville, LA
Martin, Very Rev. Elijah, *O.C.D.* '01 (MIL) St. Florian's Congregation, West Milwaukee, WI; [MON] Washington Province of Discalced Carmelite Friars, Inc., Milwaukee, WI
Martin, Rev. Msgr. Emilio, '52 (MIA) Retired.
Martin, Rev. Gerard R., '73 (BR) Curia: Administration; Canonical Services The Congregation Of St. John The Evangelist Roman Catholic Church, Prairieville, LA
Martin, Rev. Gilmer J., '74 (NO) Retired.
Martin, Rev. Hilary, *O.P.* '55 (OAK) [MON] Order of Preachers (Province of the Most Holy Name of Jesus - Western Dominican Province), Oakland, CA
Martin, Rev. Jacob, *SJ* (OM) [MON] Jesuit Community at Creighton University, Omaha, NE
Martin, Rev. James, *C.S.C.* '93 (AUS) Retired.
Martin, Rev. James J., *S.J.* '99 (NY) [MON] America; Residence and Publication Office of the America Press, New York, NY
Martin, Rev. Jeffrey D., '05 (LFT) St. Boniface, Lafayette, IN; St. Lawrence, Lafayette, IN
Martin, Rev. Joel W., *O.S.B.* '91 (BIR) St. Bernard Preparatory School, Cullman, AL; [MON] St. Bernard Abbey, Cullman, AL
Martin, Rev. John, *S.J.* '91 (PH) [MIS] Jesuit Fathers, ,
Martin, Rev. John, '17 (FWT) St. Thomas Aquinas, Pilot Point, TX
Martin, Rev. John B., '65 (NEW) Retired. [MON] The Rev. Msgr. James F. Kelley Residence for Retired Priests, Caldwell, NJ
Martin, Rev. Msgr. John J., '72 (ALN) Retired.
Martin, Rev. John J., '65 (SR) Retired.
Martin, Rev. John P., *M.M.* '66 (NY) Retired. [MON] Maryknoll Fathers and Brothers (Catholic Foreign Mission Society of America, Inc.), Ossining, NY
Martin, Rev. Msgr. John P., '61 (RVC) Retired.
Martin, Rev. Jon C., '65 (BO) Retired.
Martin, Rev. Msgr. Joseph, '67 (NY) Retired. St. James the Apostle, Carmel, NY
Martin, Rev. Kevin J., '03 (PRT) St. Agnes, Island Falls, ME; St. Mary of the Visitation, Houlton, ME
Martin, Rev. Lance S., '16 (WIL) St. Luke-St. Andrew, Ocean City, MD
Martin, Rev. Leon J., *S.A.C.* '75 (MIL) [MON] Pallotti House, Milwaukee, WI
Martin, Rev. Leonard A., *S.J.* '73 (SCR) [COL] The University of Scranton, Scranton, PA
Martin, Rev. Leonard A., *S.J.* '73 (PSC) St. John the Baptist, Scranton, PA; St. Mary's, Olean, NY; St. Mary's, Scranton, PA
Martin, Rev. Mark, '21 (LAN) St. Gerard Parish Lansing, Lansing, MI
Martin, Rev. Michael, (L) Holy Rosary-Manton, Springfield, KY
Martin, Rev. Michael, (L) Holy Rosary, Springfield, KY; Holy Trinity, Springfield, KY
Martin, Rev. Michael J., *C.S.P.* '77 (PMB) [MON] Paulist Fathers Residence, Vero Beach, FL
Martin, Very Rev. Michael T., *OFM Conv.* '89 (ATL) Curia: Leadership
Martin, Rev. Oscar, '01 (NEW) St. Anthony of Padua, Elizabeth, NJ
Martin, Rev. Patrick A., '78 (NOR) Retired.
Martin, Rev. Msgr. Ralph L., '65 (WIL) Retired.
Martin, Rev. Reginald, *O.P.* '74 (SFR) St. Raymond, Menlo Park, CA
Martin, Rev. Roosevelt, '88 (GAL) Retired.
Martin, Very Rev. Samuel A., '99 (LC) Curia: Leadership; Offices and Directors Holy Name of Jesus, Wausau, WI
Martin, Very Rev. Sean, '81 (DAL) Curia: Administration
Martin, Rev. Sean Charles, '81 (DAL) Our Lady of the Lake Catholic Parish, Rockwall, TX
Martin, Rev. Msgr. Stephen E., '98 (MOB) Holy Name of Jesus Parish, Semmes, Semmes, AL
Martin, Rev. Thomas, *O.C.D.* '61 (MIL) [MON] Washington Province of Discalced Carmelite Friars, Inc., Milwaukee, WI
Martin, Rev. Msgr. Thomas, '79 (KAL) Curia: Consultative Bodies; Tribunal St. Martin of Tours, Vicksburg, MI
Martin, Rev. Msgr. Thomas, '79 (KAL) Curia: Consultative Bodies; Leadership St. Edward, Mendon, MI
Martin, Rev. Thomas V., '13 (SFR) St. Pius, Redwood City, CA
Martin, Rev. Victor T., '80 (BGP) St. Thomas Church Fairfield Connecticut, Fairfield, CT
Martin, Rev. Vincente, '74 (VEN) Retired.
Martin, Rev. William F., '63 (NY) Retired.
Martin, Rev. William F., '78 (STP) Retired.
Martin Pinillos, Very Rev. Ricardo, '03 (MIL) Curia: Leadership Sacred Heart Congregation, Racine, WI; [MIS] Community of St. Paul, Inc., Racine, WI
Martin Rodriguez, Rev. Santiago, *F.M.* '79 (PH) [MIS] Franciscans of Mary, Coatesville, PA
Martina, Rev. Joseph A., '89 (SHP) Curia: Leadership; Offices and Directors Sacred Heart, Rayville, LA; St. Matthew, Monroe, LA
Martine, Rev. Michael T., '97 (NY) Curia: Leadership Holy Rosary, Staten Island, NY
Martinez, Rev. Adam, '85 (AUS) Retired.
Martinez, Rev. Agustin, '16 (KCK) St. Paul, Olathe, KS
Martinez, Rev. Alfredo, (CGS) Retired.
Martinez, Friar Andrew, (SAT) Immaculate Conception, San Antonio, TX; Our Lady of Guadalupe, San Antonio, TX; St. Alphonsus, San Antonio, TX; [MON] San Damiano Friary, San Antonio, TX; [SEM] San Damiano Friary, Initial House of Formation, San Antonio, TX
Martinez, Rev. Armando Morales, '05 (CHI) Immaculate Conception and St. Michael, Chicago, IL
Martinez, Rev. Carlos, '16 (SB) St. Martha, Murrieta, CA
Martinez, Rev. Carlos, *ICC* (STA) [SHR] Mission Nombre de Dios and Shrine of Our Lady of La Leche, St. Augustine, FL
Martinez, Very Rev. Carlos, *O.F.M.* '80 (LSC) Curia: Leadership St. Peter Parish, Inc., Roswell, NM
Martinez, Rev. Cesar, '15 (STO) Curia: Leadership; Offices and Directors [MIS] St. John Vianney House of Formation, Stockton, CA
Martinez, Rev. Christopher A., '18 (SFE) Holy Family-St. Joseph, Roy, NM; Santa Clara, Wagon Mound, NM
Martinez, Rev. Claudio Rogelio, *O.F.M.* '03 (SAT) San Jose y San Miguel, San Antonio, TX
Martinez, Rev. Daniel M., '04 (LA) St. Didacus, Sylmar, CA
Martinez, Rev. Danilo, '03 (SJN) Santa Cecilia, San Juan, PR
Martinez, Rev. Eduardo, (SAT) St. Joseph - Honey Creek, Spring Branch, TX
Martinez, Rev. Efrain, '04 (FRS) Immaculate Heart of Mary, Hanford, CA
Martinez, Rev. Ephrem, *O.S.B.* '20 (P) [MON] Mt. Angel Abbey, Saint Benedict, OR
Martinez, Rev. Eusebio, '03 (BWN) Hosp Ministry St.

Joseph, Brownsville, TX
Martinez, Rev. Felipe Antonio, '96 (TUC) On Administrative Leave.
Martinez, Rev. Frank X., (CC) Our Lady of Perpetual Help, Corpus Christi, TX
Martinez, Friar Gamalier, *O.F.M.Cap.* '21 (SJN) San Antonio de Padua, San Juan, PR; [MON] Fraternidad San Antonio, San Juan, PR; [MON] The Custody of Saint John the Baptist, Puerto Rico, of the Order Friars Minor Capuchin, San Juan, PR
Martinez, Rev. Gilbert S., *C.S.P.* '95 (NY) [MIS] The Missionary Society of St. Paul the Apostle in the State of California, New York, NY
Martinez, Rev. Gilbert S., *C.S.P.* '95 (LA) St. Paul the Apostle, Los Angeles, CA
Martinez, Rev. Gilberto, *S.S.P.* '75 (LA) [MON] The Society of St. Paul, Los Angeles, CA
Martinez, Rev. Guillermo Avila, (PHX) St. Vincent de Paul Roman Catholic Parish, Phoenix, AZ
Martinez, Rev. Herbert Sebastian, '22 (DAL) St. Augustine Catholic Parish, Dallas, TX
Martinez, Rev. Ignacio, '93 (MRY) Chap, Correctional Training Facility
Martinez, Rev. Jesse, (AUS) Santa Cruz, Buda, TX
Martinez, Rev. Jesus, (SP) St. Cecelia, Clearwater, FL
Martinez, Rev. Jesus M., '67 (GAL) Retired.
Martinez, Rev. Joaquin O., *S.J.* (SD) Mater Dei Catholic High School, Chula Vista, CA
Martinez, Rev. John, '18 (BAL) Prince of Peace, Edgewood, MD; St. Francis de Sales, Abingdon, MD
Martinez, Rev. Jose Luis, *O.A.R.* '64 (NY) [MIS] St. Joseph's Center, Bronx, NY; [RTR] St. Joseph's Center, Bronx, NY
Martinez, Rev. Joyle T., '91 (SAC) Curia: Organizations (affiliated, inter-Diocesan, miscellaneous/other) Pastor of St. Paul Parish, Sacramento, a corporation sole, Sacramento, CA
Martinez, Rev. Julio A., *O.F.M. Conv.* '82 (R) St. Julia Catholic Parish of Siler City, Siler City, NC; [MON] Our Lady of Guadalupe Friary, Pittsboro, NC
Martinez, Rev. Leonel, *O.S.A.* '74 (LAR) St. Vincent de Paul, Laredo, TX
Martinez, Rev. Macario, *O.S.B.* '14 (KC) [MON] Conception Abbey (Benedictine Monks), Conception, MO
Martinez, Rev. Macario J., *O.S.B.* '14 (MIL) [MON] St. Benedict's Abbey (Benedictine Monks of Wisconsin, Inc.), Benet Lake, WI; [RTR] St. Benedict's Retreat Center (Benedictine Monks of Wisconsin, Inc.), Benet Lake, WI
Martinez, Rev. Marco Tulio, *SJ* '96 (OAK) [MON] Jesuit Fathers and Brothers, Berkeley, CA
Martinez, Rev. Msgr. Marcos, '59 (CC) Retired.
Martinez, Rev. Mark, '96 (LA) St. Elizabeth Ann Seton, Rowland Heights, CA
Martinez, Rev. Martin S., '93 (TUC) Curia: Consultative Bodies Roman Catholic Parish of San Martin De Porres - Sahuarita, Sahuarita, AZ
Martinez, Rev. Matthias, *O.S.B.* '08 (GBG) [MON] Saint Vincent Archabbey, Latrobe, PA
Martinez, Rev. Michael, '89 (TUC) Curia: Consultative Bodies; Leadership; (>MO) Offices and Directors Our Lady of the Mountains Roman Catholic Parish - Sierra Vista, Sierra Vista, AZ
Martinez, Rev. Miguel Angel, '01 (CHI) Santa Maria Del Popolo, Mundelein, IL
Martinez, Rev. Nestor A., (BRK) Queen of Angels, Long Island City, NY
Martinez, Rev. Oscar Daniel, (LA) La Purisima Concepcion, Lompoc, CA
Martinez, Rev. Pablo A., '09 (NEW) On Duty Outside Diocese. Diocese of Gaylord, Gaylord, MI St. Mary, Plainfield, NJ
Martinez, Rev. Pedro Javier, '20 (FWT) Curia: Miscellaneous / Other Offices St. Peter the Apostle, Fort Worth, TX
Martinez, Rev. Peter G., '04 (CC) Bishop Garriga Middle Preparatory School, Corpus Christi, TX; Most Precious Blood, Corpus Christi, TX; St. John Paul II High School, Corpus Christi, TX; St. Thomas More Parish, Corpus Christi, TX
Martinez, Rev. Roberto, *O.F.M.Cap.* '96 (SJN) [MON] The Capuchin Formation Trust of Puerto Rico, San Juan, PR
Martinez, Rev. Rodolfo, *M.Sp.S.* (LA) Our Lady of Guadalupe Parish, Oxnard, CA
Martinez, Rev. Samuel, '21 (DAL) St. Ann Catholic Parish - Coppell, Coppell, TX
Martinez, Rev. Samuel, '12 (LAV) Curia: Catholic Charities; Tribunal St. Peter the Apostle, Henderson, NV
Martinez, Very Rev. Timothy A., '90 (SFE) Curia: Offices and Directors
Martinez, Rev. Virgilio, '65 (SJN) Colegio Santa Rosa, Bayamon, PR
Martinez, Rev. Vito Santiago, *O.F.M. Cap.* '18 (DET) [MIS] Provincialate, Detroit, MI; [RTR] Capuchin Retreat, Washington, MI
Martinez, Rev. Walter, '21 (FRS) St. Helen, Fresno, CA
Martinez Daimiel, Rev. Celedonio, *O.C.D.* '01 (MIL) [MON] Discalced Carmelite Friars of Holy Hill, Inc., Hubertus, WI
Martinez Negron, Rev. Roy F., '85 (ARE) Curia: Leadership Our Lady of Mercy, Florida, PR; [MIS] Chapel Divina Providencia, Ciales, PR; [MIS] Chapel Perpetuo Socorro, Ciales, PR; [MIS] Chapel Sagrada Familia, Ciales, PR; [MIS] Chapel San Jose, Ciales, PR
Martinez Pastoriza, Rev. William, (ARE) Nuestra Senora del Monte Carmelo, Utuado, PR
Martinez Patino, Rev. Daniel, '15 (BLX) Curia: Advisory Boards, Commissions, Committees, and Councils; Miscellaneous / Other Offices Blessed Francis Xavier Seelos, Biloxi, MS; Our Lady of Fatima, Biloxi, MS; Our Mother of Sorrows, Biloxi, MS
Martinez Rivera, Rev. Roberto, *OFM Cap* '96 (PCE) Santa Teresita del Nino Jesus, Ponce, PR
Martinez Santos Gallego, Rev. Jose Vicente, *cmf* (PCE) Nuestra Senora del Carmen, Ponce, PR
Martinez Tobon, Rev. Jose Dario, '87 (SJN) Ntra. Sra. de la Candelaria, Toa Baja, PR
Martinez y Alire, Rev. Msgr. Jerome, '76 (SFE) Retired. Curia: Offices and Directors Nuestra Senora de Guadalupe del Valle de Pojoaque, Santa Fe, NM
Martinez-Callejas, Rev. Edwin, *S.J.* '62 (SFR) [MON] Loyola House Jesuit Community, San Francisco, CA
Martinez-Escobar, Rev. Adolfo, '03 (TUC) Saint Jude Thaddeus Roman Catholic Parish - San Luis, San Luis, AZ
Martinez-Espronceda, Rev. Jesus, *O.A.R.* (ELP) Guardian Angel, El Paso, TX
Martinez-Santos Gallego, Rev. José Vicente, *CMF* (PCE) Curia: Leadership
Martini, Rev. Jason, (SAT) St. James, Gonzales, TX
Martini, Rev. Msgr. Richard, '80 (LA) St. Joseph, Carpinteria, CA
Martinosky, Rev. Joseph A., '57 (STU) Retired.
Martins, Rev. Celso, *C.Ss.R.* '06 (NEW) St. James, Newark, NJ
Martins, Rev. Vander Sebastiao, '03 (PRO) Saint Elizabeth's Church of Bristol, Bristol, RI
Martiny, Rev. Martin, *O.P.* (L) St. Louis Bertrand, Louisville, KY
Martocchio, Rev. Msgr. Peter T., '57 (BO) Retired.
Marton, Rev. Bernard, *O.Cist.* '67 (DAL) [MON] Our Lady of Dallas Cistercian Abbey, Irving, TX
Martorano, Rev. Nicholas, *O.S.A.* '77 (PH) Annunciation B.V.M., Philadelphia, PA; St. Nicholas of Tolentine, Philadelphia, PA; [MON] Augustinian Community (O.S.A.), Philadelphia, PA
Martos, Rev. Rafael, (SP) St. Clement, Plant City, FL
Martos, Rev. Rafael E., '96 (SP) Curia: Faith Formation
Martuscello, Rev. Joseph, '20 (ROC) Curia: Clergy and Religious Services Holy Cross, Rochester, NY; Our Mother of Sorrows, Rochester, NY
Martyniuk, Rev. Pawlo, '92 (STF) Curia: Offices and Directors St. Michael, Hartford, CT
Maruca, Rev. Dominic, *S.J.* '58 (PH) Retired.
Maruca, Rev. Dominic W., *S.J.* (PH) Retired.
Marucci, Rev. Msgr. Louis A., '87 (CAM) Curia: Leadership St. Andrew the Apostle R.C. Church, Gibbsboro, N.J., Gibbsboro, NJ
Marulanda, Rev. Martin, (CHI) Mother of the Americas Parish, Chicago, IL
Marullo, Rev. Lawrence E., '75 (OG) Church of the Nativity, B.M.V, West Leyden, NY; St. Martin, Port Leyden, NY; St. Mary's Catholic Church, Constableville, Constableville, NY
Marusceac, Rev. Canon Vladimir, '88 (STF) SS. Peter and Paul, Cohoes, NY
Marut, Rev. Thomas, '74 (STU) St. Mary, Martins Ferry, OH
Maruthukunnel Thomas, Rev. James, *C.M.I.* '77 (SAL) Immaculate Conception of the Blessed Virgin Mary Parish, Grinnell, Inc., Grinnell, KS; Sacred Heart Parish, Park, Inc., Park, KS; St. Agnes Parish, Grainfield, Inc., Grainfield, KS
Marva, Rev. Robert, *O.F.M. Cap.* '97 (PIT) [MON] The Capuchin Franciscan Friars Province of Saint Augustine, Pittsburgh, PA
Marva, Rev. Robert, *O.F.M.Cap.* '97 (CLV) (>PIT) [MON] St. Augustine Friary, Pittsburgh, PA
Marwa, Rev. Joseph Chacha, *SMA* '05 (BO) Immaculate Conception, Everett, MA (>NEW) [MON] Society of African Missions, Provincialate, S.M.A. Fathers, Tenafly, NJ
Mary Oniwe, Rev. Bernard, (HBG) St. Peter, Elizabethtown, PA; [CAM] Elizabethtown College, Elizabethtown, PA
Marzan, Rev. Michael, (OG) Holy Cross Parish, Plattsburgh, NY
Marziani, Rev. Nicholas, '12 (POC) Retired.
Marzonie, Rev. Nathan, (VEN) San Pedro Parish in North Port, Inc., North Port, FL
Marzynski, Rev. Janusz, '04 (LIN) St. Joseph's, York, NE
Mas, Rev. Leandro Nicolas Torres, '13 (NEW) Curia: Offices and Directors
Masabakhwa, Rev. Raphael, '95 (DM) St. Anne, Logan, IA; St. Patrick, Missouri Valley, IA
Masalu, Rev. Yohana Shija, (PIT) Archangel Gabriel, McKees Rocks, PA
Masar, Rev. Joseph, '89 (SD) Pastor of All Hallows Catholic Parish, La Jolla, a corporation sole, La Jolla, CA
Mascardo, Rev. Editho, '83 (STO) Stanislaus Co Hosps Our Lady of Fatima Church (Pastor of), Modesto, CA
Mascarenghas, Rev. Maschio, '94 (CR) St. Francis de Sales, Moorhead, MN
Mascarenhas, Rev. Gilbert, *S.A.C.* (TOL) St. Anthony, Milan, OH; St. Mary, Mother of the Redeemer, Norwalk, OH; [MIS] Saint Thomas Aquinas Campus, ,
Mascarenhas, Rev. James, *M.S.F.S.* '99 (TUC) Roman Catholic Church of Saint Elizabeth Ann Seton - Tucson, Tucson, AZ
Mascari, Rev. Michael, *OP* (STL) [SEM] Aquinas Institute of Theology, St. Louis, MO
Mascari, Rev. Michael A., *O.P.* '87 (STL) [MON] St. Dominic Priory, St. Louis, MO
Masello, Rev. David W., '78 (WOR) Curia: Leadership
Mash, Rev. Wesley M., '90 (PBR) St. Anne, Clymer, PA; St. Mary's Holy Protection, Homer City, PA
Mashak, Rev. Eric J, '21 (LC) Church of the Resurrection, Wausau, WI; St. Michael, Wausau, WI
Mashurano, Rev. Gilbert, '12 (CHI) Our Lady of the Wayside, Arlington Heights, IL
Masi, Rev. Louis, (NY) St. Augustine, Larchmont, NY
Masi, Rev. Louis P., '18 (NY) SS. John and Paul, Larchmont, NY
Masich, Rev. Michael P., *O.F.M. Cap.* '98 (PIT) [MON] St. Augustine Friary, Pittsburgh, PA
Masiello, Rev. Msgr. Joseph P., '69 (NEW) Retired.
Masih, Rev. Shafique, '93 (DET) St. Mary, Cause of Our Joy Parish Westland, Westland, MI
Masilamani, Rev. Gaspar, *C.M.F.* '91 (PHX) Sacred Heart Roman Catholic Parish Prescott, Prescott, AZ
Masillamony, Very Rev. Devdas, '94 (SD) Curia: Advisory Boards, Commissions, Committees, and Councils Pastor of Saint Therese Catholic Parish, San Diego, a corporation sole, San Diego, CA
Masinde, Rev. Steven, '00 (NY) SS. Philip and James, Bronx, NY
Maskal, Rev. Nathan, '18 (FTW) Curia: Leadership St. John the Baptist, New Haven, IN
Masla, Rev. Christopher, (RIC) St. Andrew, Roanoke, VA
Maslach, Rev. Paul, *O.F.M.* '62 (CHI) [MON] Croatian Franciscan Fathers, Chicago, IL
Maslak, Rev. Gregory, '72 (PHU) Retired.
Maslejak, Rev. Andrzej, (JOL) Divine Mercy Parish, Lombard, IL
Maslowski, Rev. Krzysztof K., '88 (NEW) Curia: Organizations (affiliated, inter-Diocesan, miscellaneous/other) St. Joseph the Carpenter (Sisters of St. Joseph, Chestnut Hill), Roselle, NJ
Maslowsky, Rev. Michael, '86 (P) [NUR] Assumption Village (activity of St. Anthony Village Enterprise), Portland, OR; [NUR] St. Anthony Village (activity of St. Anthony Village Enterprise), Portland, OR
Masluk, Rev. Alexander, '79 (PH) Retired. Immaculate Conception, Jenkintown, PA; Saint Martha, Philadelphia, PA
Masnicki, Rev. Marek, '92 (NOR) Curia: Leadership Guardian Angels Parish, Colchester, CT
Maso, Rev. Dario, *S.X.* '82 (PAT) [MON] Xaverian Missionary Fathers, Wayne, NJ
Mason, Rev. Brian G., '93 (MIL) On Special Assignment. Released for study - Center City, MN
Mason, Rev. Carl Louis, *O.P.* '64 (WDC) St. Dominic Church & Priory, Washington, DC; [MON] Center for Assisted Living, Washington, DC
Mason, Rev. Charlon O., '79 (GR) Retired.
Mason, Rev. Edward J., '87 (BRK) Curia: Consultative Bodies Mary, Mother of the Church, Brooklyn, NY
Mason, Rev. James, (STL) [SEM] Kenrick School of Theology, ,
Mason, Rev. Mark E., '75 (OKL) Curia: Consultative Bodies St. Francis Xavier, Enid, OK
Mason, Rev. Matthew J., '09 (MAN) Curia: Clergy and Religious Services St. Mary Church, Newmarket, NH;

St. Michael Parish, Exeter, NH
Mason, Rev. William, *O.M.I.* '71 (OAK) (>WDC) [MON] Oblate Community, Washington, DC
Mass, Rev. Ronald J., '70 (CHI) Retired.
Massa, Rev. Mark S., *S.J.* '80 (BO) [MON] The Jesuit Community at Boston College, Chestnut Hill, MA; [SEM] The Ecclesiastical Faculty at Boston College, Newton, MA
Massad, Rev. Tony, '10 (OLL) Curia: Offices and Directors St. Maron Maronite Catholic Church, Youngstown, OH; [MIS] National Maronite Young Adult Organization - National MYA, Youngstown, OH
Massaro, Rev. Gabriel, *OFM Cap* (NY) [MON] St. Clare Friary (Capuchin Franciscan Friars, Province of St. Mary), Yonkers, NY
Massaro, Rev. Thomas J., '93 (NY) [MON] Jesuit Community at Fordham University, New York, NY
Massart, Rev. James P., '66 (GB) Retired.
Massawe, Rev. Emmanuel, *A.J.* '12 (KNX) St. Dominic, Kingsport, TN
Massengill, Friar Peter, (LSC) [RTR] Holy Cross Retreat and Friary (Franciscan Fathers), Mesilla Park, NM
Massett, Rev. Msgr. Robert D., '66 (NO) Retired. Curia: Miscellaneous / Other Offices
Massetti, Rev. Philip V., *O.S.J.* '76 (SAC) Pastor of St. Joseph Marello Parish, Granite Bay, a corporation sole, Granite Bay, CA; [SEM] Mount St. Joseph Novitiate and Seminary (Novitiate of Oblates of St. Joseph), Loomis, CA
Massi, Rev. Anthony, '84 (MIA) Retired.
Massie, Rev. Msgr. Guy A., '81 (BRK) Curia: Pastoral Services Sacred Hearts of Jesus and Mary and St. Stephen, Brooklyn, NY
Massie, Rev. William, (LAF) St. Ann, Mamou, LA
Massieu, Rev. Carlos, (MIA) [MIS] House of the Divine Will, Inc., Coral Gables, FL
Massillon, Rev. Nazaire, '00 (ORL) St. Catherine of Siena, Kissimmee, FL
Massimino, Rev. Jerome, *O.F.M.* '77 (SP) Retired. [MON] St. Anthony Friary (St. Petersburg) Franciscan Friars-Holy Name Province, Inc., St. Petersburg, FL
Massingale, Rev. Bryan N., '83 (MIL) On Duty Outside Diocese. Faculty, Bronx, NY
Masson, Rev. John P., '12 (PH) Curia: Advisory Boards, Commissions, Committees, and Councils Cardinal O'Hara High School, Springfield, PA; St. Bernadette, Drexel Hill, PA
Massucci, Rev. Joseph D., '70 (STU) Retired.
Mast, Rev. Christian, '20 (DEN) Our Lady of the Valley Catholic Parish in Windsor, Windsor, CO
Mast, Rev. Paul, '72 (WIL) Retired.
Masteller, Rev. Michael, '21 (LA) St. Helen, South Gate, CA
Masters, Rev. Burke, '02 (JOL) St. Isaac Jogues, Hinsdale, IL
Masters, Rev. Gerard G., '66 (HRT) Retired.
Mastey, Rev. Gregory, '95 (SCL) Church of All Saints, Holdingford, MN; Immaculate Conception, Avon, MN
Mastey, Rev. Gregory John, '95 (SCL) St. Columbkille's, Avon, MN
Mastin, Rev. Mark, *SCJ* '07 (SFS) Immaculate Conception Parish of Hyde County, Stephan, SD; Saint Catherine Parish of Hughes County, Big Bend, SD
Mastrangelo, Rev. David, *SJ* '87 (RC) [MON] Holy Rosary Mission Jesuit Community, Pine Ridge, SD
Mastrangelo, Rev. Nicholas, '64 (PIT) Retired. St. Thomas the Apostle, Homestead, PA
Mastrian, Rev. Mark J, '87 (E) St. Joseph, Force, PA
Mastroeni, Rev. Anthony, (BAL) [MIS] Reparation Society of the Immaculate Heart of Mary, Inc., Ruxton, MD
Mastroeni, Rev. Anthony J., '72 (PAT) Retired. Curia: Leadership [MIS] Cor Jesu Mission Fund Inc, Hardyston, NJ
Mastrolia, Rev. Arthur, '87 (NY) Curia: Leadership; Offices and Directors St. Clare, Staten Island, NY
Masur, Rev. Joseph, (SD) [MIS] All Hallows Catholic Parish in La Jolla, CA Real Property Support Corporation, La Jolla, CA
Masutti, Rev. Federico, (PHX) Mater Misericordiae Catholic Church, Phoenix, AZ
Mata, Rev. Luke, '06 (LA) [MIS] Prelature of the Holy Cross and Opus Dei, Los Angeles, CA
Mata, Very Rev. Luke J., '06 (POD) Curia: Leadership
Mata Martinez, Rev. Jesus, *S.V.D.* (CHI) St. Joseph the Worker, Wheeling, IL
Mataafa, Rev. Mikaele, (LA) St. Philomena, Carson, CA
Matas, Rev. Msgr. Juan, '65 (LA) Retired.
Mateja, Rev. Steven J., '12 (DET) St. John Fisher Chapel University Parish Auburn Hills, Auburn Hills, MI; St. Joseph Parish Lake Orion, Lake Orion, MI
Mateo, Rev. Victor Santiago, *S.T.* (FAJ) Curia: Leadership
Mateo-Ayala, Rev. Agustin, '90 (WDC) St. Rose of Lima, Gaithersburg, MD
Matera, Rev. Msgr. Frank J., (HRT) Retired.
Materu, Rev. Paul, *A.L.C.P.* '98 (P) St. Boniface, Sublimity, OR; St. Mary - Shaw, Aumsville, OR
Mateus, Rev. Norberto, '81 (ATL) Retired.
Mateus-Ariza, Rev. Hector, '09 (BAL) Church of the Annunciation, Baltimore, MD; St. Clement Mary Hofbauer, Baltimore, MD; St. Michael, Baltimore, MD
Mathabela, Rev. Sipho, '01 (B) Our Lady of Limerick Station, Glenns Ferry, ID
Mathai, Rev. Mani T., '80 (TYL) St. Ann Catholic Church, Winnsboro, TX
Mathais, Rev. Rajain, (KAL) St. Barbara, Colon, MI; St. Clare, Centreville, MI
Mathangi, Rev. Suresh, (LAF) Sts. Peter and Paul, Scott, LA
Matheny, Rev. William K., '96 (WH) Immaculate Conception, New Cumberland, WV; Sacred Heart, Chester, WV
Matherne, Rev. John David, (HT) Curia: Administration; Clergy and Religious Services
Mathers, Rev. Msgr. Douglas J., '85 (NY) Curia: Leadership Our Lady of Peace, New York, NY; Parish of St. John the Evangelist and Our Lady of Peace, New York, NY
Mathesius, Rev. William P., '76 (WIL) Retired.
Matheus, Rev. Canon Heitor, '16 (LC) [MIS] St. Mary's Roman Catholic Oratory, Wausau, WI
Mathew, Rev. Abraham P., '97 (BRK) Retired. St. Nicholas of Tolentine, Jamaica, NY
Mathew, Rev. Aneesh, *CM* '11 (BRK) [MON] Reverend John B. Murray, C.M. House, Jamaica, NY
Mathew, Rev. Antony, (DM) All Saints, Stuart, IA; St. John, Adair, IA
Mathew, Rev. Augustine Laiju Kandanattuthara, (GLP) Curia: Leadership San Mateo, San Mateo, NM; St. Vivian, Milan, NM
Mathew, Rev. Benny, *M.S.T.* '98 (MAR) St. Bruno, Nadeau, MI; St. John Neumann, Spalding, MI
Mathew, Rev. Bibin, *C.M.F.* '14 (SPC) Curia: Offices and Directors Sacred Heart, Springfield, MO; [CAM] Catholic Campus Ministry O'Reilly Catholic Student Center, Missouri State University, Drury University, Ozarks Technical Community College, Springfield, MO; [MON] Claretians Missionaries' Residence-Villa Claret, Springfield, MO
Mathew, Rev. Biju, '98 (STP) St. Boniface, Minneapolis, MN
Mathew, Rev. Biju, *C.F.I.C.* '98 (STP) Chap, St Joseph's-HealthEast Hosp
Mathew, Rev. Binu, '98 (IND) Immaculate Conception Catholic Church, Millhousen, Inc., Greensburg, IN; St. John the Baptist Catholic Church, Osgood, Inc., Osgood, IN
Mathew, Rev. Jaison, *HGN* (CC) St. Patrick Church, Corpus Christi, TX
Mathew, Rev. Jerry, '16 (MCE) On Duty Outside Diocese. Doctoral studies in Rome Curia: Advisory Boards, Commissions, Committees, and Councils; Offices and Directors St. Mary's Malankara Catholic Church, Evanston, IL
Mathew, Rev. Jins, *MCBS* '09 (MEM) St. Louis, Memphis, TN
Mathew, Rev. Joby Kaniyamparambil, *H.G.N.* '09 (LKC) Sacred Heart of Jesus, Lake Charles, LA
Mathew, Rev. Joseph, '96 (NY) Parish of St. John the Baptist and Most Holy Trinity, Yonkers, NY
Mathew, Rev. Joshy, '05 (SAC) Pastor of St. Joseph Parish, Vacaville, a corporation sole, Vacaville, CA
Mathew, Rev. Joshy, (CR) Holy Rosary, Hallock, MN; Saint Patrick's Catholic Parish, Hallock, MN; St. Francis of Assisi, Fisher, MN
Mathew, Rev. Pius T., '90 (AUS) Retired.
Mathew, Rev. Sanish, *HGN* '09 (CC) St. Theresa of the Infant Jesus, Premont, TX
Mathew, Rev. Sebastian, *C.M.I.* '05 (NY) Christ the King, Yonkers, NY
Mathew, Rev. Shinto, '04 (WH) Christ Our Hope Mission, Pennsboro, WV; St. John, St. Marys, WV
Mathew, Rev. Suneesh, *H.G.N.* (OWN) Curia: Advisory Boards, Commissions, Committees, and Councils
Mathew, Rev. Sunny, '99 (NY) Parish of St. Brendan and St. Ann, Bronx, NY
Mathew, Rev. T. Shane, '05 (E) Curia: Miscellaneous / Other Offices
Mathew, Rev. T. Shane, (E) Our Lady of Peace, Erie, PA; St. Jude the Apostle, Erie, PA; [COL] Gannon University, Erie, PA
Mathew Pattasseril, Rev. Biju, '98 (SYM) St. Paul Knanaya Catholic Mission, Minnesota, Minneapolis, MN
Mathews, Rev. James D., '62 (SY) St. Lucy, Syracuse, NY
Mathews, Rev. James R., '75 (ALX) Retired.
Mathews, Rev. Michael C., *C.S.C.* '99 (FTW) [COL] University of Notre Dame Du Lac, Notre Dame, IN; [SEM] Moreau Seminary, Notre Dame, IN
Mathewson, Rev. Dean, '73 (COL) On Administrative Leave.
Mathias, Rev. Arularasu, '90 (CC) On Special Assignment.
Mathias, Rev. Edwin J., '67 (TR) Retired.
Mathias, Rev. Gregory A., '91 (FR) Our Lady of the Assumption, Osterville, MA; Our Lady of Victory, Centerville, MA
Mathias, Rev. R., *MSFS* '95 (KAL) Curia: Consultative Bodies; Deaneries Immaculate Conception, Three Rivers, MI
Mathie, Rev. D. Edward, *S.J.* '68 (MIL) [MON] Jesuit Community at Marquette University (Marquette Jesuit Associates, Inc.), Milwaukee, WI
Mathieu, Rev. Msgr. Rene T., '77 (PRT) Retired. Curia: Consultative Bodies
Mathis, Rev. R. Paul, '72 (SY) Retired.
Mathur, Rev. Keith A., '09 (ALN) Curia: Leadership Holy Infancy, Bethlehem, PA
Matijevic, Rev. Andrew W, '21 (CHI) Holy Name Cathedral, Chicago, IL
Matiru, Rev. Francis, *FMH* '18 (MOB) St. Ignatius Parish, Mobile, Mobile, AL
Matitu, Rev. Joseph, *SSS* '97 (PBL) Our Lady of Guadalupe / St. Patrick Parish, La Junta, CO; St. Mary, Las Animas, CO
Matlak, Rev. Joseph, '15 (CHL) Holy Trinity Catholic Middle School, Charlotte, NC
Matlak, Rev. Joseph, '15 (SJP) Curia: Offices and Directors Dormition of the Mother of God Mission, Greer, SC; Holy Cross Mission, Blythewood, SC; St. Basil the Great, Charlotte, NC
Matlob, Rev. Fadi, '15 (OLD) Saint Ephrem Syriac Church, Jacksonville, FL
Matonti, Rev. Charles J., '60 (BRK) Retired.
Matos, Rev. Angel R., '97 (WOR) Curia: Offices and Directors St. Francis of Assisi, Fitchburg, MA
Matro, Rev. Justin M., *O.S.B.* '89 (GBG) St. Bartholomew, Crabtree, PA; [MON] Saint Vincent Archabbey, Latrobe, PA
Matt, Rev. Erwin H., '56 (MIL) Retired.
Matt, Rev. Joseph H., '74 (KC) Retired.
Matta, Rt. Rev. Nassir, '78 (NTN) Retired.
Matta, Rev. Pablo, '90 (ELP) Our Lady of Peace, Alpine, TX; St. Joseph, Fort Davis, TX; St. Mary's, Marfa, TX
Matta, Rev. Pablo, '90 (ELP) Sacred Heart Mission, Marfa, TX
Matta, Rev. Ramesh Babu, (SFD) St. Aloysius, Springfield, IL; St. Frances Cabrini, Springfield, IL
Mattaliano, Rev. James R., *S.J.* '90 (BO) (>FR) St. Pius X, South Yarmouth, MA
Mattathilani, Rev. George, '86 (MAN) Saint John XXIII Parish, Nashua, NH
Mattathilanickal, Rev. Cyriac, '99 (ATL) St. Oliver Plunkett Catholic Church, Snellville, Inc., Snellville, GA
Mattern, Rev. Joseph A., '59 (GB) Retired.
Matthew, Rev. Ron, (AMA) On Special Assignment. In Residence of the Diocese of Amarillo, Hartly, Texas
Matthew, Rev. Sunny, (CAM) St. Gianna Beretta Molla Parish, Northfield, N.J., Northfield, NJ
Matthews, Rev. Andre, '84 (ROM) On Administrative Leave.
Matthews, Rev. Steve, (ALB) Curia: Offices and Directors Church of St. Joseph, Stuyvesant, NY; St. James, Chatham, NY; St. John the Baptist, Valatie, NY
Matthias, Rev. Mark, (CAM) St. Joseph the Worker Parish, Haddon Township, N.J., Haddonfield, NJ
Matthias, Rev. Mark A., '15 (BRK) On Duty Outside Diocese. St. Joseph the Worker Church, Haddonfield, NJ
Matthys, Rev. Donald R., *S.J.* '68 (MIL) [MON] St. Camillus Jesuit Community (Society of Jesus, USA Midwest Province), Wauwatosa, WI
Matti, Rev. Wisam, '97 (EST) St. Thomas Chaldean Catholic Parish, West Bloomfield, MI
Mattimore, Rev. Jack, *S.J.* (CHR) [MON] Mepkin Abbey, Moncks Corner, SC
Mattimore, Rev. John, *S.J.* (NY) Chap, George Vierno Ctr, East Elmhurst
Mattina, Rev. Louis A., '95 (MET) Curia: (>MO) Offices and Directors Our Lady of Mount Virgin, Middlesex, NJ
Mattingly, Rev. Andrew, '15 (KC) On Special Assignment. Our Lady of Good Counsel, Kansas City, MO; [CAM] University of Missouri - Kansas City

Newman Center at JPII Commons, Kansas City, MO
Mattingly, Rev. Ryan, '18 (PEO) Curia: Clergy and Religious Services St. Joseph, Roanoke, IL; St. Luke, Eureka, IL; [CAM] Salve Regina Newman Foundation, Eureka, IL
Mattingly, Rev. Thomas E., '97 (RIC) St. Olaf, Patron of Norway, Williamsburg, VA
Mattison, Rev. Thomas V., '73 (BUR) Curia: Leadership Holy Cross, Colchester, VT; Our Lady of Grace, Colchester, VT
Mattler, Rev. Albert A., '56 (STL) Retired.
Mattox, Rev. Arthur W., '17 (MIL) St. Alphonsus's Congregation, New Munster, WI; St. John the Evangelist Congregation, Twin Lakes, WI
Mattox, Rev. Randall, '01 (ATL) St. Anna Catholic Church, Monroe, Inc., Monroe, GA
Mattox, Rev. Richard, *O.F.M.Cap.* (NY) NY VA; NY Harbor
Mattox, Rev. Richard, *OFM Cap.* '13 (BRK) [MON] St. Michael Friary, Brooklyn, NY
Mattox, Rev. Richard F., (MO) Curia: Offices and Directors
Mattox, Rev. Richard F., *O.F.M.Cap.* (BRK) Chap, Veterans Affairs NY Harbor System, Brooklyn
Mattson, Rev. Steven M., '05 (LAN) Curia: Leadership Resurrection Parish Lansing, Lansing, MI
Mattson, Rev. Tyler, (SFS) Saint Christina Parish of Turner County, Parker, SD; Saint Nicholas Parish of Lincoln County, Tea, SD
Mattulke, Rev. Arthur E., '97 (BUF) St. Teresa of Avila, Akron, NY
Matulewicz, Rev. Ronald G., '59 (ALB) Retired.
Matunog, Rev. Reynaldo B., '91 (LA) Curia: Offices and Directors Sacred Heart, Los Angeles, CA
Matus, Rev. José, '98 (ATL) Holy Cross Catholic Church, Atlanta, Inc., Atlanta, GA
Matus, Rev. Thomas, *O.S.B.Conv.* '70 (MRY) [MON] New Camaldoli Hermitage (Camaldolese Hermits of America), Big Sur, CA
Matusz, Rev. Michael A., '89 (CLV) Our Lady of Victory, Tallmadge, OH
Matveenko, Rev. Michael J., '82 (CAM) The Church of St. Charles Borromeo, Washington Township, N.J., Sicklerville, NJ
Matya, Rev. Robert A., '95 (LIN) Curia: Leadership; Offices and Directors St. Thomas Aquinas, Lincoln, NE; [CAM] University of Nebraska, Newman Club, Lincoln, NE
Matysik, Rev. Robert B., '84 (CAM) The Parish of Saint Monica, Atlantic City, NJ
Matysik, Rev. Robert T., '84 (CAM) Chap, AtlantiCare Rgnl Med Ctr City Div; AtlantiCare Rgnl...
Matz, Rev. David, *C.PP.S.* '95 (LA) St. Agnes, Los Angeles, CA
Matz, Rev. David, *C.PP.S.* '95 (OAK) [MON] Society of the Precious Blood, Berkeley, CA
Matz, Rev. Msgr. Michael J., '84 (PH) Curia: Deaneries St. John Neumann, Bryn Mawr, PA
Matzko, Rev. David, *S.J.* '75 (OM) [MON] Jesuit Community at Creighton University, Omaha, NE
Mau, Rev. Nguyen Duc, *C.Ss.R.* '70 (LA) [MON] Vietnamese Redemptorist Mission, Baldwin Park, CA
Mauch, Rev. Ted J., '10 (GRY) Curia: Offices and Directors Holy Martyrs, Merrillville, IN; Our Lady of Consolation, Merrillville, IN
Mauck, Rev. George A., '77 (BEL) St. Mary, Carlyle, IL; St. Teresa of Avila, Carlyle, IL
Maughan, Rev. Richard N., '72 (NO) Retired.
Maul, Rev. Samuel, (FWT) St. John the Apostle, North Richland Hills, TX
Maullon, Rev. Alberto A., '82 (GAL) Curia: Leadership
Mauman, Rev. Adam G., '10 (LFT) Auxiliary Civilian Chap, Grissom AFB, St Michael's Chapel All Saints, Logansport, IN; St. Charles Borromeo, Peru, IN
Maung, Rev. Chrysostom Ah, '74 (WCH) Retired.
Maurel, Rev. Bruno, (WDC) St. Anthony of Padua, Washington, DC
Maurer, Rev. Carl R., '01 (SAT) Retired. [NUR] Casa De Padres, San Antonio, TX
Maurer, Rev. Daniel J., '97 (PIT) St. Catherine Laboure, Pittsburgh, PA
Maurer, Rev. Jacob M., '09 (SEA) St. Mark, Shoreline, WA
Maurer, Rev. Jeffrey J., '05 (NY) Church of the Good Shepherd, Rhinebeck, NY; Parish of St. Christopher and St. Sylvia, Red Hook, NY
Mauricci, Rev. Bruno, '90 (LAV) Curia: Advisory Boards, Commissions, Committees, and Councils Christ of the Desert Catholic Church, Amargosa Valley, NV; Our Lady of the Valley, Pahrump, NV
Maurice, Rev. Francis, '88 (NY) Holy Name of Jesus, New Rochelle, NY
Maurici, Rev. Joseph, '21 (ROC) Our Lady of the Snow, Auburn, NY; Saints Mary and Martha Roman Catholic Parish Cayuga County, NY, Auburn, NY; St. Mary, Auburn, NY
Mauriello, Rev. Matthew R., '88 (BGP) [HOS] St. Camillus Health Center, Stamford, CT
Mauritzen, Rev. Joseph H., '96 (FR) Retired.
Maurizio, Rev. Joseph D., '87 (ALT) On Leave.
Maus, Rev. Adam, (BIS) Our Lady of Grace, Minot, ND
Maus, Rev. Adam J., '02 (BIS) Curia: Leadership
Maus, Rev. Christopher P., '93 (DET) Curia: Administration; Consultative Bodies St. Thomas a'Becket Parish Canton, Canton, MI
Maus, Rev. Le Roy, '66 (SCL) Retired.
Mavelil, Rev. Joshua, (DAL) Holy Family of Nazareth Catholic Parish, Irving, TX
Mawn, Rev. Francis X., '85 (BO) Retired. St. Mary of the Assumption, Lawrence, MA
Mawusi, Rev. Anselmus, (BRK) St. Therese of Lisieux, Brooklyn, NY
Mawusi, Rev. Peter Justice, (BRK) St. Catherine of Genoa, Brooklyn, NY
Maxfield, Rev. Edward A., '14 (STU) On Duty Outside Diocese. Casa Santa Maria, Rome Curia: Deaneries Basilica of St. Mary of the Assumption, Marietta, OH; St. Henry, Lower Salem, OH
Maxim, Rev. Craig, '91 (KCK) St. Ann, Prairie Village, KS
Maxon, Rev. Mark, '12 (FRS) Holy Family, Kingsburg, CA
Maxwell, Rev. Brian, '13 (NOR) Curia: Offices and Directors Sacred Heart, Groton, CT; St. Mary Mother of the Redeemer, Groton, CT
Maxwell, Rev. Daniel J., '09 (BAK) Our Lady of Angels, Hermiston, OR
Maxwell, Rev. Maximillian (Mark), *O.S.B.* '13 (GBG) [MON] Saint Vincent Archabbey, Latrobe, PA
May, Rev. Darrin, (WCH) Curia: Leadership; Offices and Directors
May, Rev. Douglas E., *M.M.* '86 (NY) Retired. [MON] Maryknoll Fathers and Brothers (Catholic Foreign Mission Society of America, Inc.), Ossining, NY
May, Rev. Gregory, *C.Ss.R.* '88 (CHI) [MIS] Redemptorist Apostolic Works, Chicago, IL; [MON] The Redemptorist Fathers of Chicago, Chicago, IL; [MON] The Redemptorists/Denver Province, Chicago, IL
May, Rev. Gregory, *C.Ss.R.* '88 (STL) [MON] Liguori Mission House/Redemptorists, Liguori, MO
May, Rev. Gregory, *C.Ss.R.* '88 (OAK) [MIS] Redemptorist Vice Province Initiative, Oakland, CA
May, Rev. James, '98 (STA) Retired.
May, Rev. Michael K., *S.J.* '93 (STL) [COL] Saint Louis University, St. Louis, MO; [MON] Jesuit Community Corporation at Saint Louis University - Jesuit Hall, St. Louis, MO
May, Rev. Patrick, (SAV) Curia: Offices and Directors
May, Rev. Raymond, '93 (KCK) Holy Cross, Overland Park, KS
May, Rev. Ronald P., '86 (HRT) Retired.
May, Rev. Thomas P., '83 (CHI) Curia: Leadership St. Paul VI, Riverside, IL
May Correa, Rev. Carlos, *M.G* (LA) Our Lady of Guadalupe, El Monte, CA
Mayaka, Rev. Valentine, (BEA) St. Jude Thaddeus, Beaumont, TX
Mayakuntla, Rev. Joseph Kumar, '11 (SUP) Assumption of the Blessed Virgin Mary, Osceola, WI; St. Anne, Somerset, WI; St. Joseph, Osceola, WI
Mayall, Rev. Msgr. Daniel G., '77 (CHI) Retired.
Maybrier, Rev. Michael J., '86 (WCH) St. Anthony/St. Rose, Wellington, KS; St. Teresa, Hutchinson, KS
Mayefske, Rev. Thomas J., '62 (SFE) Retired. Curia: Offices and Directors
Mayefske, Rev. Thomas J., '62 (GB) Retired.
Mayer, Rev. Cory A., '09 (VEN) St. Francis of Assisi Parish in Grove City, Inc., Englewood, FL
Mayer, Rev. Douglas J., '86 (GRY) Curia: Leadership St. Paul, Valparaiso, IN
Mayer, Rev. Gary A., '09 (DUB) Sacred Heart Church, Walker, Iowa, Walker, IA; St. Elizabeth Ann Seton Church, Hiawatha, Iowa, Hiawatha, IA; St. Mary Church, Vinton, Iowa, Vinton, IA; St. Mary's Church, Urbana, Iowa, Urbana, IA; Xavier High School, Cedar Rapids, Iowa, Cedar Rapids, IA
Mayer, Rev. James, *O.de.M.* '93 (CLV) St. Rocco, Cleveland, OH; [MON] Mercedarians (Fathers of Our Lady of Mercy, Inc. / Order of the B.V.M. of Mercy / Mercedarian Friars USA), Cleveland, OH
Mayer, Rev. John L., '64 (STL) Retired.
Mayer, Very Rev. Joshua, '15 (GLP) Curia: Leadership; Offices and Directors St. Francis of Assisi, Gallup, NM
Mayer, Rev. Michael, '98 (ROC) Marianne Cope Roman Catholic Parish, Monroe County NY, Rochester, NY
Mayer, Rev. Philip, '19 (POC) St. James Catholic Church, Jacksonville, FL
Mayer, Rev. Msgr. Richard G., '61 (E) Retired.
Mayer, Rev. Walter W., '59 (OAK) Retired.
Mayers, Rev. Gregory, *C.Ss.R.* '70 (STL) Retired. [MON] St. Clement Health Care Center, Liguori, MO
Mayfield, Rev. Olin, '96 (LA) Holy Redeemer, Montrose, CA; St. Clare, Santa Clarita, CA; St. James the Less, La Crescenta, CA
Mayfield, Rev. Phillip, *PIME* '78 (DET) [MON] PIME Missionaries, Detroit, MI
Mayhew, Rev. John A., *C.J.* '65 (LA) St. Louis de Montfort, Santa Maria, CA
Mayilkunnel, Rev. Sanil, *S.J.* (BAL) [COL] Jesuit Community of Loyola University, Inc., Baltimore, MD; [MON] Jesuit Community of Loyola University Maryland, Inc., Baltimore, MD
Mayilkunnel, Rev. Sanil, *S.J.* (SFR) [MON] Loyola House Jesuit Community, San Francisco, CA
Maynard, Rev. Lewis H., '69 (BRK) Retired. Our Lady of Perpetual Help, South Ozone Park, NY
Maynard, Rev. Richard C., '56 (PRO) Retired. [MON] St. John Vianney Residence, Providence, RI
Mayne, Rev. Kenneth, '94 (LAF) St. Peter, Pine Prairie, LA
Maynigo-Arenas, Rev. Joseph Victor, '70 (NY) Retired. St. Patrick, Staten Island, NY
Mayo, Rev. James, '76 (P) Retired.
Mayo, Rev. Msgr. Joseph M., '73 (SLC) Retired. Curia: Offices and Directors
Mayo, Rev. Msgr. Reid C., '63 (BUR) Retired.
Mayorga, Rev. J. Guadalupe, '01 (AMA) St. Hyacinth's, Amarillo, TX
Mayorga, Rev. Juan Carlos Castillo, (SAV) St. Anthony of Padua Catholic Church, Ray City, GA
Mayorga, Rev. Victor, '95 (AUS) Santa Teresa, Bryan, TX
Mayorga Landeros, Rev. Rodrigo, '22 (DM) St. Anthony's, Des Moines, IA
Mayorga-Fonseca, Rev. Joaquin, '89 (SJN) Nuestra Senora de la Medalla Milagrosa, Toa Alta, PR
Mayovsky, Rev. David L., '97 (SEA) St. John Vianney, Vashon, WA
Mayovsky, Rev. Frederick P., *S.J.* '75 (SEA) Bellarmine Preparatory School, Tacoma, WA
Mayovsky, Rev. Gerald L., '59 (SEA) Retired.
Mayworm, Rev. James A., '66 (DET) Retired. St. Benedict Parish Waterford, Waterford, MI
Mayzik, Rev. James, (NY) Epiphany, New York, NY; [MON] Xavier Jesuit Community, New York, NY
Mazanec, Rev. James F., '81 (CLV) Retired.
Mazanowski, Rev. Ignatius, *F.H.S.* '11 (PHX) Curia: Offices and Directors St. John Vianney Roman Catholic Parish, Sedona, AZ; [MIS] Chapel of the Holy Cross, Sedona, AZ
Mazich, Rev. Edward M., *O.S.B.* '01 (GBG) [MON] Saint Vincent Archabbey, Latrobe, PA; [SEM] St. Vincent Seminary, Latrobe, PA
Mazouch, Rev. Charles J., '73 (DOD) Retired.
Mazuelos, Rev. Paulino, '54 (MGZ) Cathedral of Our Lady of Purification, Mayaguez, PR
Mazur, Rev. Francis X., '76 (BUF) Erie Cty Med Ctr Curia: Offices and Directors St. Rose of Lima, Buffalo, NY
Mazur, Rev. Jacek, '01 (VEN) Our Lady of the Miraculous Medal Parish in Bokeelia, Inc., Bokeelia, FL
Mazur, Rev. Jacek P., '04 (BUF) Divine Mercy, Niagara Falls, NY; St. Mary of the Cataract, Niagara Falls, NY
Mazur, Rev. Kenneth, *PIME* '82 (DET) [MON] PIME Missionaries, Detroit, MI
Mazur, Rev. Msgr. Robert C., '76 (ALT) On Leave.
Mazurek, Rev. James K., '73 (PIT) Retired. St. Matthew, Pittsburgh, PA
Mazurkiewicz, Rev. Tony, *O.Carm.* '09 (CHI) [MON] Sant'Angelo Community at St. Cyril Priory, Chicago, IL
Mazurowski, Rev. Rafal, '05 (STA) St. Mary (Mother of God, St. Mary Parish), Bunnell, FL
Mazuryk, Rev. Ivan, '94 (STF) Curia: Leadership Protection of B.V.M., Bridgeport, CT
Mazuski, Rev. Edward, *OSB* (PRO) [MON] Abbey of St. Gregory the Great (Order of St. Benedict in Portsmouth, Rhode Island, Benedictines of the English Congregation), Portsmouth, RI
Mazza, Rev. Mark G., '80 (SFR) Immaculate Heart of Mary, Belmont, CA
Mazzarella, Rev. Cadmus D., '85 (CAM) Notre Dame de la Mer Parish, Wildwood, N.J., Wildwood, NJ
Mazzarella, Rev. Cadmus D., '85 (CAM) Curia: Parish Services; Tribunal Christ the Redeemer Parish, Atco, N.J., Atco, NJ; Wildwood Catholic High School, North

Wildwood, NJ
Mazzone, Rev. James S., '99 (WOR) Curia: Advisory Boards, Commissions, Committees, and Councils; Leadership; Offices and Directors
Mazzone, Rev. James S., '99 (WOR) St. John the Guardian of Our Lady, Clinton, MA
Mazzone, Rev. Joseph M., (BO) Curia: Consultative Bodies Most Precious Blood, Boston, MA; St. Anne, Boston, MA; St. Pius Tenth, Milton, MA
Mbaegbu, Rev. Anthony, '92 (LA) [HOS] Providence Saint John's Health Center, Santa Monica, CA
Mbaegbu, Rev. Innocent, '92 (RVC) St. James, Seaford, NY
Mbaegbu, Rev. Theodore, (MAN) St. Anthony of Padua, Manchester, NH
Mbaegbu, Rev. Theodore, (MAN) Chap, Elliott Hosp; Hanover Hill Health Care Ctr
Mbagwu, Rev. Brendan O., '95 (LFT) Curia: (>MO) Offices and Directors
Mbagwu, Rev. Paschal, (SCR) St. Maximilian Kolbe, Pocono Pines, PA
MBah, Rev. Emmanuel, (KAL) St. Joseph, St. Joseph, MI
Mbala, Rev. Felicien, '84 (DEN) St. Andrew the Apostle Catholic Parish in Wray, Wray, CO; St. John the Evangelist Catholic Parish in Yuma, Yuma, CO
Mbam, Rev. Emmanuel, (BEA) Our Mother of Mercy, Ames, TX; Sacred Heart, Raywood, TX
Mbamalu, Rev. Vitus, (RVC) St. Joseph, Ronkonkoma, NY
Mbamobi, Rev. Bruno, *SMMM* '07 (B) St. Catherine of Siena, Kamiah, ID; St. Theresa of the Little Flower, Orofino, ID
Mbanefo, Rev. Anthony, *MSP* (GAL) St. Martin de Porres, Barrett Station, TX
Mbanu, Rev. Celestine, '78 (SB) Chap, Cmty Hosp of San Bernardino, San Bernardino
Mbanude, Rev. Ebuka, (BAL) (>WDC) [MIS] African Conference of Catholic Clergy & Religious in the United States, Inc., Washington, DC
Mbassi, Rev. Jean Claude, *SCJ* '09 (RC) Lower Brule Reservation, Lower Brule, SD; St. Mary's, Lower Brule, SD; St. Mary's, Reliance, SD; St. Michael's, Kennebec, SD; [MON] SCJ Community House, Lower Brule, SD
Mbatna Taiwe, Rev. Thomas D., *S.J.* '12 (MIL) [MON] Jesuit Community at Marquette University (Marquette Jesuit Associates, Inc.), Milwaukee, WI
Mbazuigwe, Rev. Patrick, '93 (LA) All Souls, Alhambra, CA
Mbidoaka, Rev. Eusebius C., (BEL) St. Aloysius/Sacred Heart, Royalton, IL; St. John the Baptist, West Frankfort, IL
Mbiere, Rev. Fredrick Chima, (SFD) Resurrection Parish (Visitation Parish), Illiopolis, IL; St. John Vianney, Sherman, IL
Mbinkar, Rev. Andrew, *Sch.P.* '09 (PH) Devon Preparatory School (Piarist Fathers), Devon, PA
Mbinkar, Rev. Ghenghan B., '12 (ARL) St. Mark, Vienna, VA
Mboe, Rev. Loius M., (CHI) Our Lady of the Blessed Sacrament, Elk Grove Village, IL
Mbogu, Rev. Christopher, (PIT) Chap, Mercy Health Sys of Pittsburgh-Pittsburgh Mercy Hosp,...
Mbonyumugenzi, Rev. Deogratias, (CHI) St. Procopius, Chicago, IL
Mboudou Abina, Rev. Mathieu, (CHI) Queen of Martyrs and St. Bernadette Parish, Evergreen Park, IL
Mbuk, Rev. Emmanuel, (GAL) St. Anne de Beaupre, Houston, TX
Mburu, Rev. Michael, (NY) Parish of Holy Family, Blessed Sacrament, and St. John Vianney, Bronx, NY
Mbuzi, Rev. Dean, '14 (SEA) St. Benedict, Seattle, WA; St. Catherine of Siena, Seattle, WA
Mbuzi, Rev. Wankie-Dean, (MO) Curia: Offices and Directors
Mc Grath, Rev. Lancelot, (MET) Nativity of Our Lord, Monroe Township, NJ
Mc Kee, Rev. Henry, (PH) St. Francis of Assisi, Springfield, PA
McAfee, Rev. Franklyn M., '71 (ARL) Retired.
McAleenan, Rev. Aidan, '05 (OAK) St. Columba, Oakland, CA
McAleer, Rev. Brendan J., *CSC* (FTW) [COL] University of Notre Dame Du Lac, Notre Dame, IN; [MON] Holy Cross Community, Corby Hall, University of Notre Dame, Notre Dame, IN
McAleer, Rev. Robert T., '71 (DAV) Retired.
McAlister, Rev. Richard A., *O.P.* '61 (PRO) [MON] St. Thomas Aquinas Priory at Providence College, Providence, RI
McAllister, Rev. Brian B., '15 (ARL) St. John the Evangelist, Warrenton, VA
McAllister, Rev. Donald, '71 (MAN) Retired. [NUR] St. Ann Rehabilitation and Nursing Center, Dover, NH
McAloon, Rev. Francis X., *S.J.* '92 (NY) [MON] Jesuit Community at Fordham University, New York, NY
McAlpin, Rev. Andrew, *O.P.* '10 (MAD) Blessed Sacrament, Madison, WI
McAndrew, Rev. John P., '86 (ORG) On Administrative Leave.
McAndrew, Rev. Michael, *C.Ss.R.* '73 (KC) Our Lady of Perpetual Help, Kansas City, MO; [MON] Redemptorists Fathers of Kansas City, Missouri, Kansas City, MO
McAndrew, Rev. Michael T., '19 (DUB) St. Joseph Church, Chelsea, Iowa, Chelsea, IA; St. Michael Church, Belle Plaine, Iowa, Belle Plaine, IA; St. Patrick's Church, Tama, Iowa, Tama, IA
McAndrews, Rev. James, *S.J.* '62 (PH) Retired. [MON] Jesuit Community at St. Joseph's University, Merion Station, PA
McAnerney, Rev. Brendan, *O.P.* '88 (OAK) [MON] Order of Preachers (Province of the Most Holy Name of Jesus - Western Dominican Province), Oakland, CA
McAniff, Rev. Bernard F., *S.J.* '03 (CLV) [COL] John Carroll Jesuit Community, University Heights, OH
McAree, Rev. Msgr. Francis J., '75 (NY) Curia: Leadership St. Catharine, Blauvelt, NY
McArthur, Rev. Msgr. John B., '74 (MEM) Retired.
McAteer, Rev. James, *I.C.* '64 (SP) Retired. St. Theresa, Spring Hill, FL
McAteer, Rev. Msgr. Kenneth P., '73 (PH) Retired. Saint Martha, Philadelphia, PA
McAteer, Rev. Patrick J., *S.J.* '73 (MIL) [MON] St. Camillus Jesuit Community (Society of Jesus, USA Midwest Province), Wauwatosa, WI
McAughan, Rev. Andrew, *O.C.S.O.* '92 (L) [MON] Abbey of Our Lady of Gethsemani, of the Order of Cistercians of the Strict Observance, Trappist, KY
McAuley, Rev. Edward J., '06 (BGP) Retired.
McAuley, Rev. James D., *M.M.* '80 (SJ) Retired. (>NY) [MON] Maryknoll Fathers and Brothers (Catholic Foreign Mission Society of America, Inc.), Ossining, NY
McAuley, Rev. John J., *M.M.* '81 (NY) Retired. [MON] Maryknoll Fathers and Brothers (Catholic Foreign Mission Society of America, Inc.), Ossining, NY
McAuliff, Rev. Richard, *S.J.* (CI) Curia: Leadership
McAuliff, Rev. Robert Richard, *S.J.* '92 (CI) Mindszenty High School, Koror, PW; Yap Catholic High School, Yap, FM; [MON] Jesuit Community of Yap, Yap, FM
McAuliffe, Rev. Msgr. Kevin W., '90 (HPM) Curia: Leadership; Tribunal [MIS] Holy Protection of Mary Byzantine Catholic Eparchy of Phoenix, Phoenix, AZ; [MIS] Holy Protection of Mary Facilities Corporation, Phoenix, AZ
McAuliffe, Rev. Msgr. Kevin W., '90 (LAV) On Duty Outside Diocese. Curia: (>HPM) Tribunal
McAvoy, Rev. Msgr. C. John, '63 (OG) Retired.
McAvoy, Rt. Rev. Clare Frances, *osc* (BO) [CON] Franciscan Monastery of St. Clare, The, Boston, MA
McBeth, Rev. Jeffrey R., '06 (TOL) Curia: Advisory Boards, Commissions, Committees, and Councils; Deaneries St. Peter, Huron, OH
McBrady, Rev. Lawrence P., '71 (CHI) Retired.
McBrearity, Rev. Gerald D., *P.S.S.* '73 (WDC) [COL] Catholic University of America, The, Washington, DC
McBrearity, Rev. Gerald D., *P.S.S.* '73 (BAL) Retired. [MON] Society of St. Sulpice, Province of the United States, Baltimore, MD
McBriar, Rev. David, *O.F.M.* '64 (NY) Retired.
McBride, Rev. Alfred A., *O. Praem.* '53 (GB) Retired.
McBride, Rev. Brendan, (WDC) [MIS] Irish Apostolate USA, Inc., Upper Marlboro, MD
McBride, Rev. Brendan, '75 (SFR) Curia: Offices and Directors St. Philip the Apostle, San Francisco, CA
McBride, Rev. Daniel, '95 (PHX) Curia: Leadership; Offices and Directors St. Mary Roman Catholic Parish Chandler, Chandler, AZ
McBride, Rev. Msgr. James P., '56 (PH) Retired.
McBride, Rev. Larry, '87 (OWN) Curia: Advisory Boards, Commissions, Committees, and Councils Holy Name of Jesus, Henderson, KY
McBride, Rev. Msgr. Peter A., '60 (PAT) Retired.
McBride, Rev. Robert G., '72 (NEW) Retired. Curia: Offices and Directors
McBride, Rev. Ronald Lynn, *M.I.C.* '12 (SPR) [MON] Congregation of Marian Fathers of The Immaculate Conception of the Most Blessed Virgin Mary, Stockbridge, MA
McBrien, Rev. Kevin F., '86 (BRK) Our Lady of the Snows, Floral Park, NY
McBurney, Rev. James D., *O.S.A.* '84 (PH) [MON] St. Thomas Monastery, Villanova, PA
McCabe, Rev. Charles J., '92 (MOB) Retired.
McCabe, Rev. Edward D., '68 (BO) Retired.
McCabe, Rev. James, *C.PP.S.* '58 (CIN) Retired. [MON] St. Charles, Celina, OH
McCabe, Rev. James T., '71 (PH) Retired.
McCabe, Rev. John H., '55 (RVC) Retired.
McCabe, Rev. Joseph V., *M.M.* '77 (NY) [MON] Maryknoll Fathers and Brothers (Catholic Foreign Mission Society of America, Inc.), Ossining, NY
McCabe, Rev. Kevin P., '03 (PH) St. Matthew, Philadelphia, PA
McCabe, Rev. Lou, *S.J.* '71 (LAF) [RTR] Our Lady of the Oaks Retreat House, Grand Coteau, LA
McCabe, Rev. Michael G., '89 (LIN) Curia: Leadership St. Joseph, Lincoln, NE
McCabe, Rev. Patrick A., '61 (CAM) Retired.
McCabe, Rev. Msgr. Robert J., '64 (NY) Retired.
McCabe, Rev. Robert J., '95 (DET) Divine Child Parish Dearborn, Dearborn, MI
McCabe, Rev. Thomas E., '92 (STP) The Church of the Holy Trinity, Goodhue, MN
McCabe, Rev. Timothy, *S.J.* '15 (DET) [MIS] Pope Francis Center, Detroit, MI; [MON] Jesuit Community at the University of Detroit Mercy, Detroit, MI
McCafferty, Rev. David L., '64 (CLV) Retired.
McCafferty, Rev. James B., *S.M.* '70 (WDC) Retired. [MON] Marist Center (The Marist Finance Center of the Atlanta Province of the Society of Mary, Marist Fathers and Brothers), Washington, DC
McCafferty, Rev. James B., *S.M.* '70 (WH) Retired.
McCafferty, Rev. Michael F., '67 (CHR) Retired.
McCaffery, Rev. Sean P., '11 (KC) St. John LaLande Catholic Church, Blue Springs, MO, Blue Springs, MO
McCaffrey, Rev. Brian, '21 (SAL) Sacred Heart Junior-Senior High School, Salina, KS; St. Mary, Queen of the Universe Parish, Salina, Inc., Salina, KS
McCaffrey, Rev. Daniel, '58 (OKL) On Special Assignment. Natural Family Planning Outreach, Oklahoma City
McCaffrey, Rev. Msgr. John A., '76 (AUS) Retired. [EFT] St. Joseph Memorial Endowment Fund, Bryan, TX; [EFT] St. Joseph's School Memorial Endowment Fund, Bryan, TX
McCaffrey, Rev. Joseph C., '99 (PH) Our Lady of Peace, Milmont Park, PA
McCaffrey, Rev. Joseph P., '77 (ROC) Nativity of the Blessed Virgin Mary, Brockport, NY; [CAM] State University College at Brockport, the Newman Oratory of Brockport, Brockport, NY
McCaffrey, Rev. Joseph R., '87 (PIT) Curia: Consultative Bodies Holy Spirit, New Castle, PA
McCaffrey, Rev. Kevin, '02 (Y) SS. Philip and James, Canal Fulton, OH
McCaffrey, Rev. Kilian, '07 (PHX) Curia: Leadership St. Elizabeth Seton Roman Catholic Parish, Sun City, AZ
McCaffrey, Rev. Msgr. William J., '72 (PRO) Retired.
McCahill, Rev. Msgr. Patrick P., '68 (NY) Retired. Parish of Our Lady of Good Counsel and St. Thomas More, New York, NY; St. Elizabeth of Hungary, New York, NY; [MIS] Deaf Apostolate, , ; [MIS] Deaf Catholic Center, New York, NY; [SPF] New York Catholic Deaf Center, New York, NY
McCahon, Rev. Msgr. Joseph F., '75 (SP) Retired.
McCain, Rev. Patrick, '21 (POC) The Cathedral of Our Lady of Walsingham, Houston, TX
McCain, Rev. William H., '86 (SFR) St. Finn Barr, San Francisco, CA
McCalister, Rev. Drake, '19 (STU) Holy Family, Steubenville, OH
McCallister, Rev. Richard, '91 (SEA) Immaculate Conception, Seattle, WA; St. Therese, Seattle, WA
McCallum, Rev. Dougald, '97 (HEL) Anaconda Catholic Community: Series 204, LLC, Anaconda, MT
McCallum, Rev. Gregory P., '97 (GLD) Saint Francis Xavier of Petoskey, Petoskey, MI
McCambridge, Rev. Paul, *FSSP* (LR) St. John the Baptist Catholic Church, Cabot, AR; [MON] Priestly Fraternity of St. Peter, Cabot, AR
McCandless, Rev. Michael P., '08 (CLV) Holy Family, Stow, OH
McCandless, Rev. Ryan, '17 (SAL) Seven Dolors of the Blessed Virgin Mary Parish, Manhattan, KS; St. Patrick Parish, Ogden, Inc., Ogden, KS
McCanless, Rev. David R., (CHL) Our Lady of Mercy, Winston-Salem, NC
McCann, Rev. Charles, '69 (WDC) Retired.
McCann, Rev. James M., (CIN) [MON] Cincinnati Jesuit Community, Cincinnati, OH
McCann, Rev. John, *S.M.M.* (RVC) Retired. [MON] Montfort Missionaries, Bay Shore, NY
McCann, Rev. Msgr. John B., '85 (ALN) Immaculate Conception, Douglassville, PA
McCann, Rev. Robert J., '81 (OAK) St. Theresa of the Infant Jesus (The Little Flower), Oakland, CA; [SEM] Jesuit School of Theology of Santa Clara University

(Berkeley, California Campus), Berkeley, CA
McCann, Rev. Thomas, *C.P.* '66 (NY) [MON] The Congregation of the Passion - St. Paul of the Cross Province, Jamaica, NY
McCann, Rev. Thomas, *C.P.* '66 (SCR) [MON] Saint Ann's Passionist Monastery of Scranton PA, Scranton, PA
McCann, Rev. Thomas M., '98 (NO) Chap, Ochsner Foundation Hosp, Jefferson St. Agnes, Jefferson, LA
McCann, Rev. Thomas W., '68 (CLV) Retired.
McCann, Rev. William, '94 (LSC) Retired. (>B) [CON] Marymount Hermitage, Inc., Hermit Sisters of Mary, Mesa, ID
McCarren, Rev. Msgr. Gerard H., '91 (NEW) Curia: Organizations (affiliated, inter-Diocesan, miscellaneous/ other) [COL] Seton Hall University, South Orange, NJ; [SEM] Immaculate Conception Seminary School of Theology, South Orange, NJ
McCarren, Rev. Paul J., *S.J.* '74 (WDC) [RTR] Loyola Retreat House, Faulkner, MD
McCarren, Rev. Paul J., *S.J.* (BAL) [MIS] Colombiere Jesuit Community, Baltimore, MD
McCarrick, Rev. Brendan, *S.A.C.* '16 (DET) St. Vincent Pallotti Parish Wyandotte, Wyandotte, MI; [MIS] Pallottine Missionary Center (Irish Province), Wyandotte, MI
McCarrick, Rev. Brendan Joseph, *S.A.C.* '16 (DET) [MON] Society of the Catholic Apostolate (Pallottine Fathers), Wyandotte, MI
McCarron, Rev. Msgr. Michael D., '77 (RIC) St. Thomas More, Lynchburg, VA
McCarthy, Rev. Anthony T., '71 (MIL) Retired.
McCarthy, Very Rev. Brian P., '75 (NY) Parish of St. Margaret of Cortona and St. Gabriel, Bronx, NY; St. Gabriel, Bronx, NY
McCarthy, Rev. C. Ryan, (IND) Our Lady of the Most Holy Rosary Catholic Church, Indianapolis, Inc., Indianapolis, IN
McCarthy, Rev. Carl, '95 (OWN) Curia: Advisory Boards, Commissions, Committees, and Councils Christ the King, Madisonville, KY
McCarthy, Rev. Charles, *OFM* (GLP) San Esteban, Acoma Catholic Indian Mission, Pueblo of Acoma, NM; St. Joseph, Laguna, NM
McCarthy, Rev. Charles, *O.F.M.Conv.* '79 (L) [EFT] The Franciscan Foundation, Inc., Louisville, KY
McCarthy, Rev. Daniel, *O.S.B.* '91 (KCK) [MON] St. Benedict's Abbey, Atchison, KS
McCarthy, Rev. Daniel P., '67 (CHI) Retired. St. Elizabeth of the Trinity, Chicago, IL
McCarthy, Rev. David J., '60 (CLV) Retired. SS. Peter and Paul, Doylestown, OH; St. Joseph, Cuyahoga Falls, OH
McCarthy, Rev. Dennis J., '17 (NTN) St. Ann, Waterford, CT
McCarthy, Rev. Edward, '71 (ORL) Retired.
McCarthy, Rev. Emmanuel Charles, '81 (NTN) Retired.
McCarthy, Rev. George B., '56 (PRO) Retired.
McCarthy, Rev. James J., '64 (BO) Retired.
McCarthy, Rev. Msgr. Jeremiah, (SAT) [COL] Oblate School of Theology, San Antonio, TX
McCarthy, Rev. Jeremiah, '78 (SAV) Retired.
McCarthy, Rev. Jeremiah J., '66 (BO) Retired.
McCarthy, Rev. Msgr. Jeremiah J., '72 (TUC) On Leave.
McCarthy, Rev. John D., '08 (RVC) St. Agnes Cathedral, Rockville Centre, NY
McCarthy, Rev. Msgr. John F., (HEL) On Duty Outside Diocese.
McCarthy, Rev. Msgr. John F., '55 (LC) Retired. [MIS] Society of the Oblates of Wisdom, Eastman, WI
McCarthy, Rev. Msgr. John F., *P.A.* '55 (STL) Retired.
McCarthy, Rev. Msgr. John J., (HRT) Retired. Curia: Tribunal
McCarthy, Rev. John M., (BO) Curia: Pastoral Services
McCarthy, Rev. Joseph Jerome, *O.Carm.* '60 (VEN) [MON] Carmel at Mission Valley, Nokomis, FL
McCarthy, Rev. Joseph S., '96 (BO) Retired. Our Lady of the Angels Parish, Hanover, MA
McCarthy, Rev. Kevin P., '89 (GRY) Curia: Leadership Nativity of Our Savior, Portage, IN
McCarthy, Rev. Msgr. Leo F., '59 (BUF) Retired.
McCarthy, Rev. Matthew, *F.S.S.P.* (LIN) Curia: Leadership
McCarthy, Rev. Matthew John, *FSSP* '11 (DEN) Our Lady of Mount Carmel Catholic Parish in Littleton, Littleton, CO
McCarthy, Rev. Michael, (BO) [MON] Francis Xavier House, Brighton, MA
McCarthy, Rev. Michael C., *S.J.* '96 (NY) [MON] Cardinal Spellman Hall, Jesuit Community, Bronx, NY
McCarthy, Rev. Patrick J., '08 (NY) St. John the Evangelist, Mahopac, NY
McCarthy, Rev. Paul, '84 (FTW) Retired.
McCarthy, Rt. Rev. Peter, *O.C.S.O.* '82 (P) [MON] The Cistercian (Trappist) Abbey of Our Lady of Guadalupe (Order of Cistercians of the Strict Observance), Carlton, OR
McCarthy, Rev. Scott, '74 (MRY) Retired.
McCarthy, Rev. Sean M., '91 (BO) On Special Assignment.
McCarthy, Rev. Terrence A., '74 (CHI) Retired.
McCarthy, Rev. Thomas, '61 (Y) Retired.
McCarthy, Rev. Thomas H., '07 (CIN) Holy Trinity, Batavia, OH; St. Ann, Williamsburg, OH; St. Louis, Owensville, OH; St. Philomena, Owensville, OH
McCarthy, Rev. Thomas J., '61 (Y) Retired.
McCarthy, Rev. Thomas R., *O.S.A.* '94 (CHI) [MON] St. Rita Monastery, Chicago, IL
McCarthy, Rev. Vincent, *S.S.C.* '64 (OM) Retired. [MON] Missionary Society of St. Columban, St. Columbans, NE
McCarthy, Rev. Vincent, *S.S.C.* '64 (BUF) Retired. [NUR] St. Columbans on the Lake, Home for the Aged, Silver Creek, NY
McCarthy, Rev. Msgr. William, '63 (PAT) Retired.
McCarthy, Rev. William A., '03 (SC) Sacred Heart, Ida Grove, IA; St. Mary's, Danbury, IA; St. Mary's, Mapleton, IA
McCarthy, Rev. William E., *M.M.* '58 (RVC) Retired.
McCarthy, Rev. William E., *M.M.* '58 (NY) Retired. [MON] Maryknoll Fathers and Brothers (Catholic Foreign Mission Society of America, Inc.), Ossining, NY
McCartney, Rev. James, '84 (LUB) Curia: Leadership St. John Neumann, Lubbock, TX
McCartney, Rev. James J., *O.S.A.* '70 (PH) [MON] Saxony Hall, Rosemont, PA; [MON] St. Thomas Monastery, Villanova, PA
McCartney, Rev. John J., '99 (RVC) Curia: Leadership Our Lady of Mercy, Hicksville, NY
McCarty, Rev. Bruce, '89 (OWN) St. Agnes, Uniontown, KY
McCarty, Rev. Francis, *O.S.B.* '20 (MAN) [MON] St. Anselm Abbey, Manchester, NH
McCarty, Rev. Joshua A., '09 (OWN) Curia: Advisory Boards, Commissions, Committees, and Councils St. Leo, Murray, KY
McCarty, Rev. Lawrence L., '63 (SC) Retired.
McCarty, Rev. Robert, *S.J.* '67 (NY) [MON] Murray-Weigel Hall (A Jesuit Community at Murray-Weigel Hall and Kohlmann Hall), Bronx, NY
McCarty, Rev. Samuel C., '20 (LC) Aquinas Middle School, La Crosse, WI; Blessed Sacrament Parish, La Crosse, WI; Roncalli Newman Parish, La Crosse, WI; [CAM] Roncalli Newman Parish, La Crosse, WI
McCaslin, Very Rev. John P., '02 (IND) Chap, Indianapolis Fire Department Curia: Leadership St. Monica Catholic Church, Indianapolis, Inc., Indianapolis, IN; [MIS] Indianapolis West Deanery, Indianapolis, IN
McCaslin, Rev. R. Patrick, '61 (OM) Retired.
McCaughey, Rev. Matthew E., '12 (BR) Curia: Administration Our Lady Of Peace Roman Catholic Church, Vacherie, LA; The Congregation Of Saint James Roman Catholic Church, St. James, LA; The Congregation Of Saint Philip Roman Catholic Church, Vacherie, LA
McCawley, Rev. Scott M., '93 (JOL) On Administrative Leave. Curia: Leadership [NUR] St. John Vianney Villa, Naperville, IL
McChesney, Rev. Robert, *S.J.* '81 (WDC) [MON] The Jesuit Community at Georgetown University, Washington, DC
McClain, Rev. Matthew R., '02 (PIT) St. Clare of Assisi, Chicora, PA; St. Francis of Assisi, Cabot, PA
McClanahan, Rev. Robert P., '84 (PT) Retired.
McClane, Rev. Michael T., '06 (TR) St. Dominic, Brick, NJ
McClellan, Rev. Keith J., '79 (GRY) Notre Dame, Michigan City, IN
McClellan, Rev. Robert J., '81 (RCK) Retired.
McClintock, Very Rev. James D., '86 (BEA) Curia: Advisory Boards, Commissions, Committees, and Councils; Leadership St. Elizabeth, Port Neches, TX
McCloskey, Rev. C. John, '81 (POD) Retired. Curia: Clergy and Religious Services
McCloskey, Rev. Gary N., *O.S.A.* '77 (BO) Curia: Clergy and Religious Services
McCloskey, Rev. Gary N., *O.S.A.* '77 (PH) [MON] St. Thomas Monastery, Villanova, PA
McCloskey, Rev. James P., *C.S.Sp.* (PIT) [COL] Duquesne University of the Holy Spirit, Pittsburgh, PA
McCloskey, Rev. James P., *C.S.Sp.* '80 (PH) [MON] Congregation of the Holy Spirit, Bensalem, PA
McCloskey, Friar John, *O.F.M. Cap.* '98 (PH) St. John the Evangelist, Philadelphia, PA
McCloskey, Rev. Patrick, *O.F.M.* '75 (CIN) [MON] St. Clare Friary, Cincinnati, OH; [MON] St. Francis Seraph Friary, Cincinnati, OH
McClure, Rev. Jack, *C.PP.S.* '76 (OAK) Retired.
McClure, Rev. Jack, *C.PP.S.* '76 (SFR) (>CIN) [MON] Society of the Precious Blood, United States Province, Inc., Dayton, OH
McClure, Rev. Jason, '03 (OWN) Curia: Advisory Boards, Commissions, Committees, and Councils; Leadership
McClure, Rev. Jason Wayne, '03 (OWN) Curia: Advisory Boards, Commissions, Committees, and Councils [CAM] St. Thomas Aquinas Catholic Campus Center at Western Kentucky University, Bowling Green, KY
McCollum, Rev. Paul, '98 (RNO) Curia: Offices and Directors St. Therese of the Little Flower Catholic Church, Reno, NV
McComiskey, Rev. Joseph C., '70 (RVC) Retired.
McConaghy, Rev. Robert J., '75 (ALN) Retired.
McConnell, Rev. James J., *SMA* '72 (NEW) Retired. [MON] Society of African Missions, Provincialate, S.M.A. Fathers, Tenafly, NJ
McConnell, Very Rev. Patrick J. A., '12 (SUP) Curia: Leadership; Offices and Directors Good Shepherd Catholic Church, Rib Lake, WI; Our Lady of Perpetual Help, Medford, WI; Our Lady of the Holy Rosary, Medford, WI; Sacred Heart of Jesus, Stetsonville, WI
McConnell, Rev. Sean, (PHX) St. John the Baptist, Laveen, AZ
McConvey, Rev. Michael, '79 (GLP) On Leave.
McConville, Rev. James P., '90 (STP) Curia: Tribunal St. Agnes, St. Paul, MN
McConville, Rev. William Edward, *OFM* '73 (SP) Retired. [MON] St. Anthony Friary (St. Petersburg) Franciscan Friars-Holy Name Province, Inc., St. Petersburg, FL
McConway, Rev. Jordan, '87 (TR) St. Mary, Middletown, NJ
McCoog, Rev. Thomas M., *S.J.* (BAL) [MIS] Colombiere Jesuit Community, Baltimore, MD
McCool, Rev. Naos, *C.S.Sp.* (PIT) Retired. [COL] Duquesne University of the Holy Spirit, Pittsburgh, PA
McCord, Rev. Kent G., '81 (MET) Retired. On Leave.
McCorkell, Rev. Patrick M., *S.J.* '74 (STP) [RTR] Jesuit Retreat House, Lake Elmo, MN
McCormac, Rev. Msgr. Michael P., '80 (PH) St. Frances Cabrini, Fairless Hills, PA
McCormack, Rev. James, *MIC* '10 (WDC) [EFT] Friends of John Paul II Foundation, Washington, DC
McCormack, Rev. James, *M.I.C.* '10 (WDC) [MIS] Divine Mercy Chapel, Brookeville, MD; [SEM] Marian Fathers Scholasticate and Novitiate, Washington, DC
McCormack, Rev. James, *M.I.C.* '10 (SPR) [MON] Congregation of Marian Fathers of The Immaculate Conception of the Most Blessed Virgin Mary, Stockbridge, MA
McCormack, Rev. John, '61 (KC) Retired.
McCormack, Rev. Michael J., *O.P.* '87 (WDC) [SEM] Dominican House of Studies, Washington, DC
McCormick, Rev. Brian J., '66 (TR) Retired. [MON] Villa Vianney, Trenton, NJ
McCormick, Rev. James P., '82 (E) St. James, Erie, PA; [MIS] St. James Place Erie, Erie, PA
McCormick, Rev. Jeffrey, '96 (MIA) St. Maximilian Kolbe, Pembroke Pines, FL
McCormick, Rev. Jerry, '73 (MRY) Retired.
McCormick, Rev. John, '99 (SR) Retired.
McCormick, Rev. Joseph, *O.S.A.* (JOL) St. Bernard, Homer Glen, IL
McCormick, Rev. Kieran J., '64 (SFR) Retired.
McCormick, Rev. Louis M., *O.F.M.* '65 (BUF) [CAM] St. Bonaventure University, St. Bonaventure, NY; [RTR] Mount Irenaeus, Franciscan Mountain Retreat & Holy Peace Friary (Order of Friars Minor Holy Name Province), West Clarksville, NY
McCormick, Rev. Mark, (RC) Rapid City Catholic School System, Rapid City, SD; [CAM] Rapid City Catholic Newman Center, Rapid City, SD
McCormick, Rev. Mark, '91 (RC) Curia: Leadership; Offices and Directors
McCormick, Rev. Msgr. Maurice M., '58 (SFR) Retired.
McCormick, Rev. Michael S., '85 (SCR) Our Lady of Lourdes, Montoursville, PA
McCormick, Rev. Patrick J., '68 (ATL) Retired.
McCormick, Rev. Msgr. Patrick Joseph, '75 (FRS) Curia: Leadership Holy Spirit, Fresno, CA
McCormick, Rev. Msgr. Patrick Joseph, '75 (FRS) Curia: Leadership
McCormick, Rev. Paul, *O.Cist.* '97 (DAL) C Preparatory (Cistercian Preparatory School), Irving, TX; [MON] Our Lady of Dallas Cistercian Abbey, Irving, TX
McCormick, Rev. Peter M., *C.S.C.* '07 (FTW) [COL]

University of Notre Dame Du Lac, Notre Dame, IN; [MON] Holy Cross Community, Corby Hall, University of Notre Dame, Notre Dame, IN
McCormick, Rev. Thomas, '59 (DEN) Retired.
McCouch, Rev. Richard S., *S.J.* '93 (PH) [MON] Arrupe Jesuit Community, Merion Station, PA
McCoy, Rev. Charles, *C.S.C.* '09 (P) (>FTW) [SEM] Moreau Seminary, Notre Dame, IN
McCoy, Rev. Daniel P., '03 (BO) Sacred Hearts, Haverhill, MA
McCoy, Rev. Msgr. James P., '63 (PH) Retired.
McCoy, Rev. John J., '93 (STU) St. John Fisher, Richmond, OH; St. Joseph, Amsterdam, OH; [MIS] Boy Scouts, Richmond, OH
McCoy, Rev. Msgr. Kevin C., '81 (SC) Chap, Fort Dodge Corr Fac Curia: Leadership; Offices and Directors Holy Trinity Parish of Webster County, Fort Dodge, IA; [CEM] Holy Trinity Parish Cemetery Improvement Society, Fort Dodge, IA; [EFT] Holy Trinity Parish Foundation of Webster County, Fort Dodge, IA
McCoy, Rev. Ryan M., '11 (BLX) Curia: Advisory Boards, Commissions, Committees, and Councils St. James, Gulfport, MS
McCracken, Rev. John E., '79 (GLD) Retired. (>ORL) St. Vincent de Paul, Wildwood, FL
McCracken, Rev. Kevin P., *C.M.* '82 (STL) [ASN] Association of the Miraculous Medal, Perryville, MO; [EFT] Congregation of the Mission International Fund, St. Louis, MO; [EFT] Lazarist Trust Fund, St. Louis, MO; [MON] Congregation of the Mission Vincentian Fathers Lazarist Residence, St. Louis, MO; [MON] Congregation of the Mission Western Province (Vincentians), St. Louis, MO
McCrane, Rev. Gerard T., *M.M.* '59 (NY) Retired.
McCrate, Rev. D. Stephen, (BEA) Curia: Leadership
McCrate, Rev. Stephen, '89 (BEA) St. Anne, Beaumont, TX
McCray, Rev. Kevin, '13 (CHI) St. Elizabeth Seton, Orland Hills, IL
McCreanor, Rev. James, '78 (MIA) Retired.
McCreary, Rev. Glenn E., '95 (SCR) Chap, Muncy Prison Curia: Leadership St. Boniface, Williamsport, PA; St. Lawrence, Williamsport, PA
McCreary, Rev. Robert L., *O.F.M. Cap.* '59 (PIT) [MON] St. Augustine Friary, Pittsburgh, PA
McCreedy, Rev. Harry E., '72 (PH) St. Paul, East Norriton, PA
McCreedy, Rev. Justin D., *O.S.B.* '70 (SEA) [MON] St. Martin's Abbey, Lacey, WA
McCreesh, Rev. Thomas P., *O.P.* '72 (PRO) [MON] St. Thomas Aquinas Priory at Providence College, Providence, RI
McCreight, Rev. James H., '68 (CLV) Retired. St. Michael the Archangel, Cleveland, OH
McCrimmon, Rev. Jason, '18 (POC) Incarnation Catholic Church, Orlando, FL
McCrone, Rev. John, '82 (NEW) Curia: Offices and Directors
McCrone, Rev. John M., '82 (NEW) Curia: Advisory Boards, Commissions, Committees, and Councils; Offices and Directors (>CHI) [MIS] National Organization for Continuing Education of Roman Catholic Clergy, Inc., Chicago, IL
McCue, Rev. Michael J., *O.S.F.S.* '90 (CAM) [MIS] DeSales Service Works Inc., Camden, NJ
McCue, Very Rev. Scott E., '01 (R) Curia: Leadership St. Thomas More, Chapel Hill, NC
McCulken, Rev. Msgr. Michael T., '76 (PH) On Special Assignment. St. Eleanor, Collegeville, PA; [CAM] Ursinus College, Collegeville, PA
McCulloch, Rev. Lawrence F., *M.M.* '70 (NY) Retired. [MON] Maryknoll Fathers and Brothers (Catholic Foreign Mission Society of America, Inc.), Ossining, NY
McCullough, Rev. Alexander C., '16 (CIN) Our Lady of the Rosary, Cincinnati, OH; Our Lady of the Valley Parish, Reading, OH; St. James of the Valley, Wyoming, OH; St. Matthias, Cincinnati, OH
McCullough, Rev. Edmund, *O.P.* '17 (BAL) (>PRO) [CAM] Brown University (Brown-RISD Catholic Community), Providence, RI
McCullough, Rev. Michael P., '73 (LA) Retired.
McCumber, Rev. Msgr. William W., '83 (STL) Assumption Catholic Church, O'Fallon, O'Fallon, MO
McCurry, Rev. James, *OFM Conv.* (SPR) Our Lady of the Cross, Holyoke, MA
McCusker, Rev. John, *O.S.B.* '15 (STL) [MON] The Abbey of St. Mary and St. Louis, St. Louis, MO
McDade, Rev. Msgr. Thomas J., '74 (NEW) Retired. Curia: Leadership; Offices and Directors
McDaid, Rev. Henry, '63 (BIR) Retired.
McDaid, Rev. Msgr. J. Anthony, '75 (DEN) Retired.
McDaid, Rev. Patrick, (SAT) [MON] Woodlawn Marianist Community, San Antonio, TX
McDaniel, Rev. George W., '70 (DAV) Retired.
McDaniel, Rev. Isaac, '82 (L) Retired. [COL] Bellarmine University, Louisville, KY
McDaniel, Rev. Jacob, '20 (GRY) Curia: Offices and Directors [CAM] St. Teresa of Avila Catholic Student Center, Valparaiso, IN
McDaniel, Rev. Jacob, '20 (GRY) Curia: Offices and Directors
McDaniel, Rev. John W., *S.J.* '71 (PH) Retired.
McDaniel, Very Rev. Raymond, '07 (FWT) Curia: Advisory Boards, Commissions, Committees, and Councils; Leadership St. Philip the Apostle, Flower Mound, TX
McDaniel, Very Rev. Raymond, '07 (FWT) Curia: Advisory Boards, Commissions, Committees, and Councils; Leadership
McDaniel, Rev. Ryan, (MO) Curia: Offices and Directors
McDermott, Rev. Aidan, *O.S.B.* '15 (STL) Most Holy Trinity Catholic Church, St. Louis, MO; St. Anselm Catholic Church, St. Louis, MO; [MON] The Abbey of St. Mary and St. Louis, St. Louis, MO
McDermott, Rev. Brian O., *S.J.* '68 (WDC) [MON] The Jesuit Community at Georgetown University, Washington, DC
McDermott, Rev. Charles B., '73 (NEW) Retired. Saint Michael the Archangel, Union, NJ
McDermott, Rev. Christopher H., *C.S.Sp.* '81 (PH) [MON] Congregation of the Holy Spirit, Bensalem, PA
McDermott, Rev. J. Patrick, '67 (SEA) Retired.
McDermott, Rev. James, *S.J.* '03 (LA) [MON] Jesuit Community, Los Angeles, CA (>NY) [MON] Xavier Jesuit Community, New York, NY
McDermott, Rev. Msgr. John J., '89 (BUR) Curia: Leadership
McDermott, Rev. Msgr. John J., '89 (BUR) Curia: Leadership; Offices and Directors [CAM] University of Vermont-The Catholic Center at UVM, Burlington, VT
McDermott, Rev. Joseph, *S.V.D.* '52 (DUB) [SEM] Divine Word College, Epworth, IA
McDermott, Rev. Joseph M., '95 (PH) St. Eugene, Primos, PA
McDermott, Rev. Joseph P., '62 (BO) Retired.
McDermott, Rev. Michael, (BAL) Saint John's Catholic Preparatory, Buckeystown, MD
McDermott, Rev. Michael F., '79 (GI) Retired. Curia: Tribunal
McDermott, Rev. Michael J., '65 (SEA) Curia: Leadership St. Charles Borromeo, Tacoma, WA
McDermott, Rev. Robert, '81 (STA) Retired.
McDermott, Rev. Robert B., '90 (PH) St. John Fisher, Boothwyn, PA
McDermott, Rev. Robert T., '81 (MIL) Our Lady of Mount Carmel, Kenosha, WI; St. Therese Congregation, Kenosha, WI
McDermott, Rev. Stephen C., '03 (PH) On Duty Outside Diocese. Curia: (>MO) Offices and Directors
McDermott, Rev. Thomas, *O.P.* (LFT) St. Thomas Aquinas, West Lafayette, IN; [CAM] St. Thomas Aquinas Parish and Foundation for Catholic Students Attending Purdue University, West Lafayette, IN
McDermott, Rev. Thomas, *O.P.* (LFT) Curia: Miscellaneous / Other Offices
McDermott, Rev. Thomas J., '97 (DUB) On Special Assignment. Spiritual Dir, St Pius X Seminary, Dubuque St. Columbkille Church, Dubuque, Iowa, Dubuque, IA; [CEM] Mount Olivet Cemetery Association, Dubuque, IA; [SEM] Seminary of St. Pius X, Dubuque, IA
McDermott, Rev. William, '98 (FAR) Retired.
McDevitt, Rev. Edward P., *C.O.* '71 (CHR) Retired. All Saints Parish, Lake Wylie, SC; [MON] Oratory of St. Philip Neri, Congregation of the Oratory of Pontifical Rite, Rock Hill, SC
McDevitt, Rev. James A., '90 (BGP) Retired.
McDevitt, Rev. Michael V., '71 (SPC) Retired. Chap, US Med Ctr, Springfield Curia: Offices and Directors
McDevitt, Rev. Patrick J, *CM* '86 (STL) [MON] Congregation of the Mission Western Province (Vincentians), St. Louis, MO
McDevitt, Rev. Patrick J., (CHI) (>STL) [MON] Congregation of the Mission Vincentian Fathers Lazarist Residence, St. Louis, MO
McDole, Rev. Ian Patrick, '10 (COV) On Duty Outside Diocese.
McDonagh, Rev. Ed, (RNO) Retired.
McDonagh, Rev. Edward C., '62 (BO) Retired.
McDonagh, Rev. John, '81 (NY) Retired.
McDonagh, Rev. John P., '82 (SPR) Curia: Offices and Directors; Tribunal SS. Patrick and Raphael, Williamstown, MA; [CAM] American International College, Springfield, MA; [CAM] Newman Apostolates and Campus Ministries, Springfield, MA; [CAM] Williams College, Williamstown, MA
McDonald, Rev. Alan Paul, '11 (DAL) [SEM] The Redemptoris Mater House of Formation (Redemptoris Mater Seminary), Dallas, TX
McDonald, Rev. Bernard J., '59 (NY) Retired.
McDonald, Rev. C. Alexander, '91 (CHR) St. John Neumann, Columbia, SC
McDonald, Rev. Charles P., *C.Ss.R.* (PH) St. Peter the Apostle, Philadelphia, PA; Visitation B.V.M., Philadelphia, PA
McDonald, Rev. Daniel, (CHI) [MIS] USA Midwest Province of the Society of Jesus, Inc., Chicago, IL
McDonald, Rev. James E., *C.S.C.* '84 (FTW) [COL] University of Notre Dame Du Lac, Notre Dame, IN; [MON] Holy Cross Community, Corby Hall, University of Notre Dame, Notre Dame, IN
McDonald, Rev. James R., *C.Ss.R.* '90 (NEW) [CON] St. Michael Villa (Sisters of St. Joseph of Peace), Englewood Cliffs, NJ
McDonald, Rev. John G., '07 (BIR) Curia: Leadership Sacred Heart of Jesus, Anniston, AL
McDonald, Rev. Joseph F., '87 (B) Curia: Leadership St. Mary's, Moscow, ID; St. Mary's Station, Genesee, ID
McDonald, Rev. Joseph F., '87 (B) Curia: Leadership
McDonald, Rev. Kenneth, '57 (LAN) Retired.
McDonald, Rev. Malcolm, '85 (PIT) State Corr Inst at Greene, Greene Cty [MON] St. John Vianney Manor, Pittsburgh, PA
McDonald, Rev. Martin, '62 (MRY) Retired.
McDonald, Rev. Michael D., '85 (GI) Curia: Offices and Directors Christ the King, Gering, NE; St. Theresa's, Mitchell, NE
McDonald, Rev. Perry, *O.F.M.Cap.* '67 (MIL) St. Francis of Assisi, Milwaukee, WI
McDonald, Rev. Richard J., '99 (KCK) Curia: Leadership Holy Angels, Basehor, KS
McDonald, Rev. William, '89 (STO) Curia: Leadership; Offices and Directors Presentation Church (Pastor of), Stockton, CA
McDonald, Rev. William, (NEW) [COL] Seton Hall University, South Orange, NJ
McDonell, Rev. Clint W., '08 (DET) On Special Assignment. Sacred Heart Major Seminary, Detroit [SEM] The College of Liberal Arts, ,
McDonnell, Rev. Anthony, '70 (LA) Retired.
McDonnell, Rev. Brian, (DAL) Mater Dei Personal Parish, Irving, TX
McDonnell, Rev. David, '72 (PAT) Curia: Leadership Our Lady of the Lake, Sparta, NJ
McDonnell, Rev. Joseph, '04 (STA) Retired.
McDonnell, Rev. Msgr. Martin, '68 (PAT) Retired. Curia: Leadership
McDonnell, Rev. Michael, *O.F.M.* '65 (NY) Parish of Holy Name of Jesus and St. Gregory the Great, New York, NY
McDonnell, Rev. Patrick J., '73 (TR) Retired.
McDonnell, Rev. Paul, *O.S.J.* (SCR) Curia: Leadership
McDonnell, Rev. Paul, *O.S.J.* '91 (MRY) [MIS] Shrine of St. Joseph, ,
McDonnell, Rev. Paul A., *O.S.J.* '91 (SCR) Our Lady of the Eucharist Parish, Pittston, PA; [MON] Holy Spouses Province of the Oblates of St. Joseph, Pittston, PA; [SEM] St. Joseph's Oblate Seminary, Pittston, PA
McDonnell, Rev. Sean, '88 (PAT) [NUR] St. Joseph's Home for the Elderly, Totowa, NJ
McDonnell, Rev. Thomas, (BAL) Retired. [MIS] Colombiere Jesuit Community, Baltimore, MD
McDonnell, Rev. Thomas P., *M.M.* '65 (NY) Retired.
McDonough, Rev. James E., *SS.CC.* '68 (FR) [MIS] Damien Residence Retirement Home, , ; [NUR] Our Lady's Haven of Fairhaven Inc., Fairhaven, MA
McDonough, Rev. James P., '84 (PIT) Curia: Tribunal St. Raphael the Archangel, Carnegie, PA
McDonough, Rev. John P., '95 (WH) Curia: (>MO) Offices and Directors St. Mary, Morgantown, WV
McDonough, Rev. John T., '00 (PHX) Ascension Roman Catholic Parish, Fountain Hills, AZ
McDonough, Rev. Kevin M., '80 (STP) Church of the Incarnation, Minneapolis, MN; [MIS] Sagrado Corazon de Jesus, Minneapolis, MN
McDonough, Rev. Roger F., '76 (BGP) Retired.
McDonough, Rev. Thomas R., '89 (STP) Retired.
McDonough, Rev. Vincent, *S.J.* '62 (NY) [MON] Murray-Weigel Hall (A Jesuit Community at Murray-Weigel Hall and Kohlmann Hall), Bronx, NY
McDougal, Rev. Jon, '79 (LR) Retired.
McDougall, Rev. James G., '75 (LAN) Retired.
McDougall, Rev. Jeff, *S.J.* (SEA) Seattle Nativity School, Seattle, WA; [MON] Jesuit House, Seattle, Seattle, WA
McDougall, Rev. Russell, *C.S.C.* (SCR) Curia:

Leadership
McDougall, Rev. Russell K., *C.S.C.* '91 (FTW) (>SCR) [COL] King's College, Wilkes-Barre, PA
McDowell, Rev. John, *O.F.M.* '77 (SP) Retired. [MON] St. Anthony Friary (St. Petersburg) Franciscan Friars-Holy Name Province, Inc., St. Petersburg, FL
McDowell, Rev. Leo G., '94 (GF) Curia: Offices and Directors St. Margaret, Clyde Park, MT; St. Patrick Co-Cathedral, Billings, MT; St. William, Gardiner, MT
McDowell, Rev. Patrick D., '68 (SCR) Retired. Sacred Heart, Weston, PA
McDuffie, Rev. Paul A., '95 (BR) Congregation Of St. Joseph's Roman Catholic Church Ponchatoula, LA, Ponchatoula, LA
McEachern, Rev. Bernard, *C.P.* '64 (NY) [MON] The Congregation of the Passion - St. Paul of the Cross Province, Jamaica, NY
McEachin, Rev. Donald J., *C.S.Sp.* (BAL) [MON] Congregation of the Holy Spirit, Baltimore, MD
McEachin, Rev. Donald J., *C.S.Sp.* '81 (PIT) [MON] Congregation of the Holy Spirit Province of the United States, Bethel Park, PA; [MON] Holy Spirit Fathers and Brothers Provincialate, Bethel Park, PA
McElhone, Rev. Jonathan, '12 (STU) [COL] Franciscan University of Steubenville, Steubenville, OH; [MON] Holy Spirit Friary, Steubenville, OH
McElligott, Rev. Thomas, '69 (OAK) Retired. [COL] Saint Mary's College of California (Saint Mary's College of California, Brothers of the Christian Schools, District of San Francisco), Moraga, CA
McElligott, Rev. Thomas J., '69 (SFR) Retired.
McElrath, Rev. Ian R., '18 (E) Mercyhurst Preparatory School, Erie, PA; Our Lady of Mt. Carmel, Erie, PA
McElroy, Rev. Charles J., '64 (PH) Retired. St. Joseph, Ambler, PA
McElroy, Rev. Damian J., '88 (TR) Curia: Leadership St. Catharine-St. Margaret, Spring Lake, NJ
McElroy, Rev. David R., *O. Praem.* '02 (GB) [MON] St. Norbert Abbey, De Pere, WI
McElroy, Rev. John W., '56 (BO) Retired.
McElwee, Rev. Robert W., '83 (WCH) Retired.
McEnhill, Rev. Gerald A., '72 (DET) Retired. Curia: Consultative Bodies
McEvilly, Rev. Msgr. John W., '64 (BEL) Retired.
McEvoy, Rev. David, *O.Carm.* '88 (JOL) [MON] Carmelite Provincial Office, Darien, IL; [MON] St. Simon Stock Priory, Darien, IL
McEvoy, Very Rev. John F., '76 (SP) Curia: Organizations (affiliated, inter-Diocesan, miscellaneous/other); Pastoral Services St. Anne, Ruskin, FL
McEvoy, Rev. William, '87 (KCK) St. Joseph-St. Lawrence, Easton, KS
McEwan, Rev. Kevin D., '02 (OG) Holy Cross Parish, Plattsburgh, NY; [CEM] Mount Carmel Cemetery, Plattsburgh, NY
McFadden, Rev. J. Michael, '74 (HBG) Retired.
McFadden, Rev. John, '21 (RCK) St. Peter, Geneva, IL
McFadden, Rev. John, (TLS) [MON] Our Lady of the Annunciation of Clear Creek Abbey, Hulbert, OK
McFadden, Rev. John R., '62 (PH) Retired.
McFadden, Rev. Michael, '61 (SAC) Retired. Pastor of St. Mary Parish, Vacaville, a Corporation Sole, Vacaville, CA
McFadden, Rev. Michael, *O.S.A.* '67 (SD) Retired. [MON] Augustinian Community, San Diego, CA
McFadden, Rev. Richard K., '05 (PH) On Academic Leave. Pontifical Univ of the Holy Cross, Rome Curia: Advisory Boards, Commissions, Committees, and Councils St. Philip Neri, Lafayette Hill, PA
McFadden, Rev. Richard K., (PH) Curia: Leadership
McFadden, Rev. William C., *S.J.* (BAL) Retired. [MIS] Colombiere Jesuit Community, Baltimore, MD
McFadden, Rev. William C., *S.J.* '59 (WDC) [COL] Georgetown University, Washington, DC
McFadin, Rev. Marcus, '92 (ELP) Curia: Advisory Boards, Commissions, Committees, and Councils; Offices and Directors Holy Family, El Paso, TX; St. Patrick Cathedral, El Paso, TX
McFall, Rev. Norman, '16 (LR) Sacred Heart, Charleston, AR; St. Anthony, Ratcliff, AR
McFarland, Rev. Anthony, '19 (BEA) Monsignor Kelly Catholic High School, Beaumont, TX; St. Anthony Cathedral Basilica, Beaumont, TX
McFarland, Rev. Michael C., *S.J.* '84 (WDC) [EFT] Gregorian University Foundation, Washington, DC; [MON] The Jesuit Community at Georgetown University, Washington, DC
McFarland, Rev. Tim, *C.PP.S.* '83 (GRY) [COL] Calumet College of St. Joseph, Whiting, IN
McGahagan, Rev. James E., '68 (SCR) Retired. Curia: Offices and Directors St. Andrew Parish, Wilkes-Barre, PA
McGahee, Rev. Thomas, *SDB* (SP) Retired. [RTR] Mary Help of Christians Center, Tampa, FL
McGahren, Rev. Joseph J., *M.M.* '51 (NY) Retired.
McGann, Rev. Thomas, *C.M.F.* '76 (CHI) [MON] Claretian Missionaries U.S.A.-Canada Province, Inc., Chicago, IL
McGarry, Rev. John, *S.J.* '93 (SAC) [MON] Sacramento Jesuit Community, Carmichael, CA
McGarry, Rev. John P., *S.J.* '93 (SAC) On Special Assignment. President, Jesuit High School, Carmichael
McGarry, Rev. Michael B., *C.S.P.* '75 (BO) [MIS] Chapel of the Holy Spirit, Boston, MA; [MIS] Paulist Center, Boston, MA; [MON] Missionary Society of St. Paul the Apostle in Massachusetts, Boston, MA
McGarry, Rev. Peter, *O.Carm.* '69 (JOL) [MON] Titus Brandsma Priory (Society of Mount Carmel), Darien, IL
McGarty, Rev. Msgr. Bernard O., '49 (LC) Retired.
McGaugh, Rev. Philip E., '78 (BO) St. Mary, Randolph, MA
McGeary, Rev. Mark, '19 (DM) SS. John and Paul, Altoona, IA
McGee, Very Rev. John E., *O.S.F.S.* '82 (R) Curia: Leadership Immaculate Conception, Wilmington, NC
McGee, Rev. Michael J., '78 (BRK) Retired.
McGee, Rev. Thomas J., *O.S.F.S.* '71 (WIL) Retired. Salesianum School, Wilmington, DE
McGee, Rev. Msgr. Timothy H., '87 (CR) Curia: Leadership; Offices and Directors
McGeean, Rev. John T., '86 (JOL) Retired. Sts. Peter and Paul, Naperville, IL
McGeory, Rev. Peter, '76 (NY) St. Joseph, Bronxville, NY
McGeough, Rev. Martin F., '76 (PH) [MON] Congregation of the Mission, Philadelphia, PA
McGerity, Rev. Francis X., '84 (CC) On Duty Outside Diocese.
McGhee, Rev. Msgr. William P., '82 (BEL) St. Augustine of Canterbury, Belleville, IL
McGillicuddy, Rev. Sean J., *C.Ss.R.* '86 (NY) Immaculate Conception, Bronx, NY; Nativity, New York, NY
McGilloway, Rev. Joseph, '03 (AJ) Our Lady of the Lake Church, Big Lake, AK; Sacred Heart, Wasilla, AK; St. Bernard, Talkeetna, AK
McGing, Rev. Thomas, '71 (JKS) Retired. Curia: Canonical Services; Consultative Bodies Holy Savior, Clinton, MS
McGinn, Rev. Anthony F., *S.J.* '77 (NO) Immaculate Conception, New Orleans, LA; [MON] Loyola Jesuit Community, New Orleans, LA
McGinn, Rev. Daniel, *S.S.C.* '53 (PRO) Retired. [MON] St. Columban's Retirement House (St. Columban's Foreign Mission Society), Bristol, RI
McGinness, Rev. Matthew C., '89 (WCH) Curia: Leadership St. Thomas Aquinas, Wichita, KS
McGinnis, Rev. Charles E., '06 (WH) On Leave.
McGinnis, Rev. Connor Thomas Z, '22 (STP) St. Michael, St. Michael, MN
McGinnis, Rev. J. Donald, *M.M.* '53 (NY) Retired.
McGinnis, Rev. Jay W., '76 (BUF) Retired. St. Francis of Assisi, Tonawanda, NY
McGinnis, Rev. John Arthur, '04 (FAR) Retired.
McGinnis, Rev. John P., '63 (GAL) Retired.
McGinnity, Rev. John, '75 (RIC) Retired.
McGinty, Rev. John P., '83 (BO) On Leave.
McGivern, Rev. John W., '91 (CHI)
McGivney, Rev. Thomas, '90 (JOL) Retired.
McGlinn, Rev. Robert J., '55 (CHI) Retired.
McGlone, Rev. Gerard J., *S.J.* '87 (WDC) [MON] The Jesuit Community at Georgetown University, Washington, DC
McGlone, Rev. Gerard M., '84 (SCR) Queen of Angels Parish, Jessup, PA
McGlynn, Rev. Msgr. Daniel J., '82 (WIL) Retired. Holy Cross, Dover, DE
McGlynn, Rev. Thomas E., '84 (FR) Curia: Tribunal
McGlynn, Rev. Thomas E., (FR) Curia: Tribunal
McGoldrick, Rev. John J., '79 (PH) St. Richard, Philadelphia, PA
McGonagle, Rev. Douglas, '00 (SPR) Most Holy Redeemer, Hadley, MA; Our Lady of Grace Parish, Hatfield, MA
McGough, Rev. Msgr. James P., '57 (BLX) Retired. Curia: Tribunal
McGough, Rev. Msgr. Stephen D., '68 (SCR) Retired.
McGough, Rev. William J., '57 (NO) Retired.
McGourn, Rev. Francis T., *M.M.* '64 (NY) Retired. [MON] Maryknoll House (Catholic Foreign Mission Society of America, Inc.), New York, NY
McGovern, Rev. Eugene, '56 (BRK) Retired. [MON] Bishop Mugavero Residence, Douglaston, NY
McGovern, Rev. Msgr. Lawrence, '67 (STO) Retired.
McGovern, Rev. Robert C., *M.Afr.* '63 (WDC) Retired. [MON] Society of Missionaries of Africa, Washington, DC
McGovern, Rev. Walter J., '64 (BAL) Retired.
McGowan, Rev. Dennis M., *O.S.A.* '83 (PH) [MON] St. Thomas Monastery, Villanova, PA
McGowan, Rev. James, '02 (SFE) San Ysidro, Corrales, NM
McGowan, Rev. Jeffrey A., '89 (STA) Retired.
McGowan, Rev. John, *C.Ss.R.* '62 (TR) [RTR] San Alfonso Retreat House, Long Branch, NJ
McGowan, Rev. Joseph, *O.Carm.* '62 (JOL) Retired.
McGowan, Rev. Joseph O., *S.J.* '74 (SEA) Bellarmine Preparatory School, Tacoma, WA
McGowan, Rev. Richard, *S.J.* (BAL) [COL] Jesuit Community of Loyola University, Inc., Baltimore, MD; [EFT] Maryland Province of the Society of Jesus Aged and Infirm Trust, Towson, MD; [EFT] Maryland Province of the Society of Jesus Formation Trust, Towson, MD; [MIS] Jesuit Jamshedpur Mission Society, Inc., Towson, MD; [MIS] Jesuit Mission Bureau, Maryland Province Inc., Towson, MD; [MIS] Jesuit Seminary Guild, Maryland Province, Inc., Towson, MD; [MON] Jesuit Community of Loyola University Maryland, Inc., Baltimore, MD; [MON] Maryland Province of the Society of Jesus, Towson, MD (>BO) [MON] The Society of Jesus of New England, Weston, MA
McGowan, Rev. Richard A, *S.J.* (NY) [MON] St. Ignatius Loyola Residence, New York, NY
McGowan, Rev. Robert, '17 (LA) Holy Innocents, Long Beach, CA
McGowan, Rev. Msgr. Seamus, '57 (CC) Retired. St. Mary, Corpus Christi, TX
McGowan, Rev. Timothy, '79 (LA) Visitation, Los Angeles, CA
McGrail, Rev. Charles A., '80 (NOR) Retired.
McGrann, Rev. John, '67 (P) Retired.
McGrath, Rev. Brian F., '92 (SPR) St. Mary's, Lee, MA
McGrath, Rev. Msgr. Conor, '74 (SAT) St. Elizabeth Ann Seton, San Antonio, TX
McGrath, Rev. Edward F., '80 (WIN) Curia: Advisory Boards, Commissions, Committees, and Councils Assumption, Canton, MN; Nativity of the Blessed Virgin Mary, Harmony, MN; St. Columban, Preston, MN; St. Mary, Chatfield, MN; St. Olaf, Mabel, MN; St. Patrick, Lanesboro, MN
McGrath, Rev. Msgr. Frank C., '70 (BGP) Retired. Ave Maria School of Law Naples, FL
McGrath, Rev. Msgr. John R., '82 (BLX) Retired. Curia: Advisory Boards, Commissions, Committees, and Councils; Leadership; Tribunal
McGrath, Rev. Jordan A., *O.P.* '59 (CHI) Retired.
McGrath, Rev. Joseph, '85 (LKC) Retired.
McGrath, Rev. Joseph, *O.F.M.* (NO) Retired.
McGrath, Rev. Kevin Anthony, *O.P.* '96 (L) Curia: Leadership St. Rose, Springfield, KY
McGrath, Rev. Msgr. Laurence W., '57 (BO) Retired.
McGrath, Rev. Noel, '80 (PMB) Curia: Leadership St. Joseph, Stuart, FL
McGrath, Rev. Patrick E., *S.J.* '06 (CHI) Loyola Academy, Wilmette, IL; Old St. Patrick's, Chicago, IL; St. Ignatius Jesuit Community, Chicago, IL; [MIS] Loyola Recreational Facility Corp., Wilmette, IL
McGrath, Rev. Msgr. Roger E., '67 (CAM) Retired. Curia: Tribunal
McGrath, Rev. Msgr. Roger E., '71 (CAM) Retired. Curia: Advisory Boards, Commissions, Committees, and Councils
McGrath, Rev. Sean J., '91 (DEN) Shrine of St. Anne Catholic Parish in Arvada, Arvada, CO
McGrath, Rev. Thomas, (PAT) Retired.
McGrath, Rev. Thomas B., *S.J.* '64 (AGN) Dulce Nombre de Maria Cathedral - Basilica, Agana, GU; [MON] Society of Jesus Micronesia, Tamuning, GU
McGrath, Rev. Thomas E., '77 (JC) Retired.
McGrath, Rev. Thomas J., '59 (SY) Retired.
McGrath, Rev. William, '00 (ROC) Church of the Assumption, Fairport, NY; Church of the Resurrection, Fairport, NY; [MIS] Catholic Committee on Scouting, Rochester, NY
McGratty, Rev. John J., '71 (RVC) Retired.
McGraw, Rev. Msgr. John T., '56 (SY) Retired.
McGraw, Rev. Robert H., '76 (LAN) Retired.
McGraw, Rev. Stephen F., '01 (ARL) On Duty Outside Diocese. Dominican Republic San Francisco de Asis, Banica, Arlington, VA; San Jose, Pedro Santana, Arlington, VA
McGraw, Rev. W. Howard, '62 (PH) [MON] St. Thomas Monastery, Villanova, PA
McGready, Rev. Msgr. Oliver W., '62 (WDC) Retired. St. Peter, Waldorf, MD
McGuffey, Rev. James W., '95 (MET) Immaculate Conception, Spotswood, NJ

McGuffie, Rev. Jacques A., '13 (BO) Retired.

McGuigan, Rev. David, *SM* '01 (CAM) [RTR] Marianist Family Retreat Center, Cape May Point, NJ

McGuigan, Rev. Hugh, *O.S.F.S.* '97 (VEN) Curia: Leadership

McGuigan, Rev. Hugh J., *O.S.F.S.* '97 (VEN) Our Lady of Light Parish in Fort Myers, Inc., Fort Myers, FL

McGuill, Rev. Martin, '64 (ARL) Retired.

McGuill, Rev. Martin F, '64 (ARL) (>SAT) [NUR] Missionary Servants of St. Anthony (Padua Place), San Antonio, TX

McGuine, Rev. Peter M., '90 (SD) Pastor of Mission San Diego de Alcala Catholic Parish, San Diego, a corporation sole, San Diego, CA; [MIS] Mission San Diego De Alcala Catholic Parish in San Diego, CA Real Property Support Corporation, San Diego, CA

McGuiness, Rev. Edward J., '61 (SB) Retired.

McGuinn, Rev. James T., '88 (PH) On Special Assignment. Rector, St Joseph's-in-the-Hills Retreat House, Malvern

McGuinn, Rev. James T., '88 (PH) [RTR] St. Joseph's-in-the-Hills, Malvern, PA

McGuinness, Rev. David, '77 (ATL) Retired.

McGuinness, Rev. Fergal, '86 (SR) Curia: Leadership Pastor of St. Apollinaris Catholic Church of Napa, A Corporation Sole, Napa, CA

McGuire, Rev. Anthony E., '65 (SFR) Retired.

McGuire, Rev. Brendan, '00 (SJ) Chap, Notre Dame Club of San Jose/Silicon Valley Curia: Leadership St. Simon, Los Altos, CA

McGuire, Rev. David V., '88 (RIC) Military Chap Curia: (>MO) Offices and Directors

McGuire, Rev. John, *O.P.* '79 (NY) [CAM] Pace University, New York, NY

McGuire, Rev. John, (RNO) Retired.

McGuire, Rev. John F., '76 (P) Retired.

McGuire, Rev. John Patrick, *O.P.* '73 (NY) St. Catherine of Siena, New York, NY

McGuire, Rev. Patrick N., *S.M.A.* '87 (GLP) Curia: Offices and Directors Good Shepherd Catholic Mission, Pinehaven, NM; San Lorenzo, Ramah, NM; St. Anthony, Zuni, NM; St. Patrick, Vanderwagen, NM

McGuire, Rev. Thaddeus M., '99 (PHX) Curia: Leadership St. Daniel the Prophet Roman Catholic Parish, Scottsdale, AZ

McGuire, Rev. Thomas D., '81 (LIN) Curia: Offices and Directors St. Andrew's, Tecumseh, NE

McGuire, Rev. Timothy P., '84 (STU) Retired.

McGuirk, Rev. William C., '82 (GBG) Retired.

McGuirl, Rev. Msgr. John A., '72 (BRK) Retired. Our Lady of Mercy, Forest Hills, NY

McGurn, Rev. Richard H., *S.J.* '75 (CHI) [RTR] Bellarmine Jesuit Retreat House, Inc., Barrington, IL

McHale, Rev. Daniel, (ALB) St. Matthew, Voorheesville, NY; St. Thomas the Apostle (St. Thomas' Church of Delmar, N.Y.), Delmar, NY

McHale, Rev. John F., '04 (SCR) Retired.

McHenry, Rev. Craig, '14 (Y) On Leave.

McHenry, Rev. Raymond, '00 (DM) Retired.

McHenry, Rev. Msgr. Stephen P., '73 (PH) St. Anthony of Padua, Ambler, PA

McHugh, Rev. Adrian, '92 (RVC) St. Aidan's Church, Williston Park, NY

McHugh, Rev. Alphonsus, *SS.CC.* (FR) Our Lady of the Assumption, New Bedford, MA; [NUR] Sacred Heart Home, New Bedford, MA

McHugh, Rev. Brian J., '88 (BO) Curia: Advisory Boards, Commissions, Committees, and Councils; Consultative Bodies; Leadership Saints Louis and Zelie Martin Parish, Somerville, MA; St. Ann, Somerville, MA; St. Catherine of Genoa, Somerville, MA; St. Joseph, Somerville, MA

McHugh, Rev. Connell A., '72 (SCR) Retired.

McHugh, Rev. Donald, '57 (P) Retired.

McHugh, Rev. Francis, '97 (SAT) On Leave.

McHugh, Rev. Francis M., *O.F.M.* '76 (PAT) Retired.

McHugh, Rev. James, *O.S.F.S.* '77 (LAN) Chap, Gus Harrison Rgnl Fac; Cotton Fac; Fed Corr Inst

McHugh, Rev. John, *O.F.M.Cap.* '69 (NY) Roman Catholic Church of the Sacred Heart, Yonkers, NY

McHugh, Rev. John W., '76 (HRT) Retired.

McHugh, Rev. Michael J., '80 (BRK) Our Lady of Mount Carmel, Long Island City, NY

McHugh, Rev. Msgr. Peter J., '65 (PAT) Retired. [MIS] Nazareth Village, Chester, NJ

McIlhenney, Rev. Gregory M. V., '14 (BRK) St. Andrew Avellino, Flushing, NY

McIlhenny, Rev. Bernard R., *S.J.* '56 (SCR) [COL] The University of Scranton, Scranton, PA

McIlhone, Rev. James P., '74 (CHI) Retired. St. Edward, Chicago, IL

McInerney, Rev. Blaise, *O.Carm.* '54 (JOL) Retired.

McInerney, Rev. Henry B., '77 (BLX) Curia: Advisory Boards, Commissions, Committees, and Councils Our Lady of Fatima, Biloxi, MS

McInerny, Rev. Msgr. Lawrence B., '79 (CHR) Stella Maris, Sullivan's Island, SC

McInerny, Rev. Msgr. Paul B., '72 (BO) On Special Assignment.

McIntire, Rev. Timothy M., *O.S.F.S.* (WIL) Curia: Education St. Thomas More Oratory, Newark, DE; [CAM] Catholic Campus Ministry, University of Delaware, Newark, DE

McIntire, Rev. William J., *M.M.* '67 (NY) Retired. [MON] Maryknoll Fathers and Brothers (Catholic Foreign Mission Society of America, Inc.), Ossining, NY

McIntosh, Rev. Carl, '15 (BGP) The St. Roch's Church Corporation of Greenwich, Greenwich, CT

McIntyre, Rev. Garrett K., '11 (LAF) St. Bernard, Breaux Bridge, LA

McIntyre, Rev. Msgr. Thomas J., '66 (CAM) Retired.

McIntyre, Rev. William, *O.F.M.* '95 (SAV) St. Peter Claver, Macon, GA

McKale, Rev. Harold B., '10 (PH) On Special Assignment. Chap, St John Neumann Ctr for Rehab & Healthcare, Resurrect… Resurrection of Our Lord, Philadelphia, PA

McKamy, Rev. Eldon J., '63 (OM) Retired.

McKane, Rev. Paul, '88 (WDC) Retired. [MON] St. Anselm's Abbey, Washington, DC

McKarns, Rev. James E., '62 (Y) Retired. St. Paul, North Canton, OH

McKay, Rev. Douglas M., '82 (PH) On Special Assignment. Chap, Our House of Ministries, Philadelphia

McKay, Rev. Msgr. James P., '56 (SFR) Retired.

McKay, Rev. John F., '73 (WDC) Retired.

McKay, Rev. Robert, '70 (SJ) Curia: Offices and Directors

McKay, Friar Simon, *O.F.M.* (WDC) [MON] Franciscan Monastery USA Inc., Washington, DC

McKeaney, Rev. James J., '69 (PH) Retired. St. Matthew, Conshohocken, PA

McKearney, Rev. James, *P.S.S.* '97 (WDC) [SEM] Theological College of the Catholic University of America, Washington, DC

McKearney, Rev. James L., *P.S.S.* '97 (HRT) On Duty Outside Diocese. Theological College, D.C.

McKearney, Rev. James L., *P.S.S.* '97 (BAL) [MON] Society of St. Sulpice, Province of the United States, Baltimore, MD

McKee, Rev. Francis X., '66 (PH) Retired.

McKee, Rev. Henry J., '72 (PH) Retired.

McKee, Rev. Jay R., '02 (WIL) Church of the Good Shepherd, Perryville, MD

McKee, Rev. Roderick D., '66 (WDC) Retired. St. Patrick, Washington, DC

McKee, Rev. Scott, '12 (SFE) St. Thomas Aquinas, Rio Rancho, NM

McKee, Rev. William, '83 (SEA) St. John the Baptist, Covington, WA

McKeefry, Rev. Brendan, '67 (SAC) Retired. Curia: Offices and Directors Pastor of Our Lady of the Assumption Parish, Carmichael, a corporation sole, Carmichael, CA

McKenna, Rev. Brian, *O.F.M.Cap.* '66 (SFR) Our Lady of Angels, Burlingame, CA

McKenna, Rev. Msgr. Enda, '64 (SAT) Retired. [NUR] Casa De Padres, San Antonio, TX

McKenna, Rev. Eugene J., '63 (PRO) Retired.

McKenna, Rev. Jerome, *C.P.* '68 (NY) [MON] The Congregation of the Passion - St. Paul of the Cross Province, Jamaica, NY

McKenna, Rev. Jerome, *C.P.* '58 (ATL) St. Paul of the Cross Catholic Church, Atlanta, Inc., Atlanta, GA

McKenna, Rev. John, *C.Ss.R.* '77 (BAL) St. Mary, Annapolis, MD

McKenna, Rev. John L., '88 (PIT) St. Aidan, Wexford, PA

McKenna, Rev. Joseph R., '57 (PRT) Retired.

McKenna, Rev. Kenneth N., *O.S.F.S.* '85 (LAN) [MON] Oblate Fathers of St. Francis De Sales, Inc., Brooklyn, MI; [RTR] Lake Vineyard Camps, Inc., (De Sales Center), Brooklyn, MI

McKenna, Rev. Kevin E., '77 (ROC) St. Theodore, Rochester, NY

McKenna, Rev. Peter, '57 (SAT) Retired.

McKenna, Rev. Thomas F., *C.M.* '70 (PH) [MON] Congregation of the Mission, Philadelphia, PA; [SEM] St. Vincent's Seminary, Philadelphia, PA

McKenna, Rev. Timothy, '79 (SEA) Retired.

McKenzie, Rev. John, '19 (DET) Christ the King Parish Detroit, Detroit, MI; St. Suzanne - Our Lady Gate of Heaven Parish Detroit, Detroit, MI

McKenzie, Rev. John, '85 (CC) Holy Family, Taft, TX; Immaculate Conception, Taft, TX

McKenzie, Rev. John H., *O.S.B.* '85 (MO) Curia: Offices and Directors

McKenzie, Rev. John J., *O.S.A.* '65 (PH) [MON] Saxony Hall, Rosemont, PA; [MON] St. Thomas Monastery, Villanova, PA

McKenzie, Rev. Thomas J., '15 (STP) Curia: Leadership Frassati Catholic Academy, White Bear Lake, MN; St. Pius X, White Bear Lake, MN

McKenzie, Rev. William L., '82 (KNX) Retired.

McKeon, Rev. Gerard R., *S.J.* '86 (SY) [MON] Jesuits at LeMoyne, Inc., Syracuse, NY

McKeon, Rev. Raymond T., '63 (NEW) Retired.

McKeon, Rev. Robert F., '90 (NY) Curia: Leadership St. Francis of Assisi, West Nyack, NY

McKeown, Very Rev. Timothy P., '97 (SAV) Curia: Leadership St. Francis Xavier, Brunswick, GA

McKercher, Rev. Mark J., '97 (OM) St. Robert Bellarmine, Omaha, NE

McKiernan, Rev. Msgr. J. Michael, '91 (ORG) Mission Basilica - San Juan Capistrano, San Juan Capistrano, CA

McKiernan, Rev. Vincent W., *C.S.P.* '57 (COL) (>NY) [MON] Paulist Fathers - Generalate, New York, NY

McKinley, Rev. Michael, (LFT) St. Maria Goretti, Westfield, IN

McKinley, Rev. Stephen, *O.F.M.Conv.* '94 (PEO) St. Ann Parish, Toluca, IL; St. John the Baptist, Lostant, IL; St. Mary's, Wenona, IL; St. Patrick's, Minonk, IL

McKinney, Rev. Michael A., '93 (LFT) Curia: Leadership Sorrowful Mother, Wheatfield, IN; St. Augusta, Lake Village, IN; St. Cecilia, De Motte, IN

McKinney, Rev. Ronald H., *S.J.* '83 (SCR) [COL] The University of Scranton, Scranton, PA

McKitrick, Rev. James V., '58 (RCK) Retired.

McKnight, Rev. James, '59 (SAC) Retired.

McKnight, Rev. Kevin F., '94 (PIT) On Sick Leave.

McKone, Rev. Jack, '08 (FWT) Curia: Advisory Boards, Commissions, Committees, and Councils St. John the Apostle, North Richland Hills, TX

McKone, Rev. John, '08 (FWT) Curia: Leadership

McKuskey, Rev. Kris, '05 (DUL) Chap, Moose Lake State Hosp; Challenge Incarceration Prog…

McKusky, Rev. Kristoffer T., '05 (DUL) Curia: (>MO) Offices and Directors Our Lady of Hope, Aurora, MN

McLafferty, Very Rev. Joseph M., '00 (NY) Curia: Leadership Saint Kateri Tekakwitha, LaGrangeville, NY; St. Margaret Mary, Staten Island, NY

McLagan, Very Rev. Joseph, '15 (DEN) Curia: Deaneries St. Bernadette Catholic Parish in Lakewood, Lakewood, CO

McLaughlin, Rev. Anthony, (LEX) Curia: Leadership

McLaughlin, Rev. Anthony K. W., '97 (TYL) On Duty Outside Diocese. (>LEX) SS. Peter & Paul, Danville, KY

McLaughlin, Rev. Brett, (BO) [MON] The Jesuit Community at Boston College, Chestnut Hill, MA

McLaughlin, Rev. Daniel, *S.T.* '63 (WDC) [MON] Father Judge Missionary Cenacle, Adelphi, MD

McLaughlin, Rev. Daniel, *O.S.A.* '83 (PH) St. Rita of Cascia, Philadelphia, PA; [MIS] National Shrine of Saint Rita of Cascia, Philadelphia, PA; [MON] Augustinian Community (O.S.A.), Philadelphia, PA

McLaughlin, Rev. Daniel F., *M.M.* '61 (NY) Retired.

McLaughlin, Rev. David S., '96 (NEW) Retired. [HOS] Saint Michael Medical Center, Newark, NJ

McLaughlin, Rev. Don E., '81 (JOL) Retired.

McLaughlin, Rev. Edward, '59 (CHI) Retired. St. Michael, Orland Park, IL

McLaughlin, Rev. Farrell E., '71 (PRO) Retired. [MON] St. John Vianney Residence, Providence, RI

McLaughlin, Rev. Gerard, *S.J.* (BO) [MON] Campion Health & Wellness, Inc., Weston, MA

McLaughlin, Rev. Gregory, '85 (AUS) Sacred Heart, Lott, TX; St. Joseph, Marlin, TX

McLaughlin, Rev. James, '73 (SB) St. Francis of Assisi, La Quinta, CA

McLaughlin, Rev. John, '61 (SEA) Retired.

McLaughlin, Rev. John E., '62 (BO) Retired.

McLaughlin, Rev. Msgr. John R., '95 (BO) On Duty Outside Diocese.

McLaughlin, Rev. Joseph, *S.M.* '66 (SFR) Retired. Notre Dame des Victoires, San Francisco, CA

McLaughlin, Rev. Joseph J., '66 (PH) Retired. St. Vincent de Paul, Richboro, PA

McLaughlin, Rev. Joseph P., *O.Praem.* '70 (WIL) Archmere Academy, Claymont, DE

McLaughlin, Rev. Joseph P., *O.Praem.* '70 (PH) [MON] Daylesford Abbey, Inc., Paoli, PA

McLaughlin, Rev. Michael R., '82 (DM) Retired. Chap

McLaughlin, Rev. Mitchell, '22 (SFS) Sacred Heart Parish of Brown County, Aberdeen, SD; Saint Mary Parish of Brown County, Aberdeen, SD; [CAM] Saint

Thomas Aquinas Newman Center, Aberdeen, SD

McLaughlin, Rev. Neil, *S.J.* '59 (PH) Retired.

McLaughlin, Rev. Neil R., '66 (BAL) Retired.

McLaughlin, Rev. Patrick A., '03 (OM) Curia: Leadership; Offices and Directors Sacred Heart Church of Norfolk, Norfolk, NE; St. Leonard of Port Maurice, Madison, NE; St. Patrick's, Battle Creek, NE; St. Peter, Stanton, NE

McLaughlin, Rev. Patrick J., '61 (BO) Retired. St. Agatha, Milton, MA

McLaughlin, Rev. Patrick J., '74 (SCR) Immaculate Conception, Scranton, PA

McLaughlin, Rev. Paul F., '71 (VEN) Retired.

McLaughlin, Rev. Peter, '78 (PT) Chap, Naval Air Station Pensacola

McLaughlin, Rev. Peter, (MO) Curia: Offices and Directors

McLaughlin, Rev. Peter A., '78 (CAM) On Duty Outside Diocese. Pace, FL

McLaughlin, Rev. Richard C., '74 (PRT) Retired.

McLaughlin, Rev. Richard P., '68 (BO) Retired.

McLaughlin, Rev. Robert P., '11 (NEW) Chap, Univ Hosp, Newark

McLaughlin, Rev. Msgr. William, '58 (ORG) Retired.

McLaughlin, Rev. William A., '92 (BRK) Immaculate Conception, Astoria, NY; St. Raphael, Long Island City, NY

McLaughlin, Rev. William H., '68 (BO) Retired. Immaculate Conception, Newburyport, MA

McLean, Rev. William, '69 (LA) Retired.

McLearen, Rev. Daniel J., '92 (HRT) Curia: Deaneries The St. Margaret's Church Corporation of Madison, Connecticut, Madison, CT

McLellan, Rev. Daniel, *O.F.M.* '76 (CHR) St. Andrew, Clemson, SC; [CAM] Clemson University, Southern Wesleyan University, and TriCounty Technical College, Clemson, SC

McLellan, Rev. James R., '70 (FR) Retired.

McLelland, Rev. James R., '00 (SHP) Retired. Curia: Leadership

McLinden, Rev. James E., *S.S.J.* '62 (WDC) [SEM] Josephite Pastoral Center, Washington, DC

McLinden, Rev. James E., *S.S.J.* '71 (BAL) Retired.

McLoud, Rev. Steven J., '94 (SC) Divine Mercy Catholic Parish, Algona, IA

McLoughlin, Rev. Brendan, '70 (PAT) Retired.

McLoughlin, Rev. Msgr. James W., '65 (RCK) Retired.

McLoughlin, Rev. John, *C.Ss.R.* '92 (TOL) St. Mary, Bluffton, OH

McLoughlin, Rev. John T., '73 (NY) Retired. St. Theresa, Briarcliff Manor, NY

McLoughlin, Rev. Luke, '66 (STA) Retired.

McLoughlin, Rev. Michael P., '81 (NY) St. Columba, Hopewell Junction, NY

McLoughlin, Rev. Nicholas, '66 (VEN) Retired.

McLoughlin, Rev. Paul J., '71 (SPC) Retired. Curia: Advisory Boards, Commissions, Committees, and Councils

McMackin, Rev. Thomas P., '63 (ORL) Retired.

McMahon, Rev. Bartholomew R., *O.F.M.* '62 (PAT) Retired. [MON] St. Anthony Friary (Order of Friars Minor), Butler, NJ

McMahon, Rev. Brian, '80 (BO) St. Gregory, Boston, MA

McMahon, Rev. Donald, *O.M.I.* '75 (NO) Chap, Tulane Med Ctr, New Orleans Our Lady of Guadalupe/ International Shrine of St. Jude, New Orleans, LA

McMahon, Rev. Francis X., *S.S.E.* '54 (BUR) Retired.

McMahon, Rev. Msgr. John, '66 (PMB) Retired.

McMahon, Rev. Joseph R., '71 (WIL) Retired.

McMahon, Rev. Joseph S., '68 (P) Retired.

McMahon, Rev. Joseph V., '84 (NSH) Curia: Leadership Holy Family, Brentwood, TN

McMahon, Rev. Msgr. Kevin T., '75 (WIL) Retired.

McMahon, Rev. Kieran M., '65 (SAC) Retired.

McMahon, Rev. Michael, '18 (JOL) Sts. Peter and Paul, Naperville, IL

McMahon, Rev. Michael J., '04 (PRO) Our Lady of Good Help (Eglise de Notre Dame de Bonsecours), Mapleville, RI; St. Philip's Church Greenville Rhode Island, Greenville, RI

McMahon, Rev. Timothy, *SJ* (STL) St. Matthew, Apostle Catholic Church, St. Louis, MO

McMahon, Rev. Timothy, *S.J.* '87 (STL) [MON] Jesuit Community Corporation at Saint Louis University - Jesuit Hall, St. Louis, MO

McMahon, Rev. Walter M., '73 (SJ) Retired.

McManaman, Rev. Kevin P., '11 (MIL) Curia: Leadership St. Alphonsus Congregation, Greendale, WI

McManamon, Rev. John M., *S.J.* '80 (CHI) [COL] Jesuit Community at Loyola University Chicago, Chicago, IL

McManus, Rev. Dennis, (OAK) Cathedral Parish of Christ the Light, Oakland, CA

McManus, Rev. Dennis D., '05 (MOB) On Duty Outside Diocese. Cathedral of Christ the Light, Oakland, CA (>BAL) [SEM] Mount St. Mary's Seminary, Emmitsburg, MD; (>SFR) [SEM] St. Patrick's Seminary and University (The Roman Catholic Seminary of San Francisco), Menlo Park, CA

McManus, Rev. Eamon, '54 (WDC) Retired.

McManus, Rev. Msgr. Gerald D., '79 (PH) On Duty Outside Diocese. US Air Force, Rapid City, SD Curia: (>MO) Offices and Directors

McManus, Rev. Msgr. Gerald D., '79 (MO) Curia: Offices and Directors

McManus, Rev. Msgr. Hugh F., '61 (NY) Retired.

McManus, Rev. Michael K., '85 (FR) St. Mary's, Mansfield, MA

McManus, Rev. Paul C., '65 (DUB) Retired.

McManus, Rev. Paul G., '87 (BO) Immaculate Conception, Salem, MA; St. John the Baptist, Peabody, MA; St. Thomas the Apostle, Peabody, MA

McManus, Rev. PJ, (DM) Christ the King, Des Moines, IA

McManus, Rev. Richard, *O.F.M.* '83 (OAK) [MON] Franciscan Friars of California (Province of St. Barbara), Oakland, CA

McMaster, Rev. Brian L., '01 (AUS) St. Vincent de Paul, Austin, TX

McMenamy, Rev. Alvin, (SAT) [MON] Marianist Residence, San Antonio, TX

McMichael, Rev. Steven J., *O.F.M.Conv.* '02 (STP) [RTR] Franciscan Retreats and Spirituality Center, Prior Lake, MN

McMichael, Rev. Steven J., *O.F.M.Conv.* '02 (STP) [MON] St. Joseph Cupertino Friary, Prior Lake, MN

McMichael, Rev. Thomas, '09 (SEA) Immaculate Conception, Mount Vernon, WA; Immaculate Heart of Mary, Sedro Woolley, WA; Sacred Heart, La Conner, WA; St. Charles, Burlington, WA

McMillan, Rev. Adam, (MO) Curia: Offices and Directors

McMillan, Rev. Adam J., '13 (WIN) On Duty Outside Diocese. Archdiocese for the Military Services

McMillan, Rev. Cliff J., '90 (DEN) Retired.

McMillan, Rev. John, *C.P.* '56 (NY) [MON] The Congregation of the Passion - St. Paul of the Cross Province, Jamaica, NY

McMillan, Rev. John F., *C.P.* '56 (PIT) Retired. [MON] St. Paul of the Cross Monastery, Pittsburgh, PA

McMillin, Rev. Charles, '02 (LKC) Retired.

McMillin, Rev. Charles, (AUS) Retired.

McMillin, Rev. Ryan, '19 (CHI) St. James, Arlington Heights, IL

McMorrow, Rev. Matthew J., '05 (RCK) Curia: Leadership St. Joseph, Aurora, IL

McMullan, Rev. John, '61 (SEA) Retired.

McMullen, Rev. Canice, *OSB* (PIT) Mary, Queen of Saints, Aliquippa, PA

McMullen, Rev. Francis R., '51 (RVC) Retired.

McMullen, Rev. John, *O.S.B.* '66 (SFS) [EFT] Blue Cloud Abbey Retirement Trust, Milbank, SD

McMullen, Rev. John, *O.S.B.* '66 (IND) [MON] St. Meinrad Archabbey, St. Meinrad, IN

McMullin, Rev. Daniel, '81 (ROC) [CAM] The Catholic Community of Ithaca College, Ithaca, NY; [CAM] The Cornell Catholic Community, Inc. (Ithaca), Ithaca, NY

McMurray, Rev. Thomas D., *S.J.* '79 (WOR) [MON] Jesuits of the Holy Cross, Inc., Worcester, MA

McMurry, Rev. John E., *S.S.* '56 (NSH) Retired.

McMurry, Rev. John E., *P.S.S.* '56 (BAL) Retired. [MON] Society of St. Sulpice, Province of the United States, Baltimore, MD

McMurry, Rev. Vincent deP., *P.S.S.* '49 (BAL) Retired.

McNair, Rev. Andrew, '97 (PHX) Curia: Offices and Directors

McNair, Rev. M. Andrew, '97 (R) On Duty Outside Diocese. Diocese of Phoenix

McNair, Rev. Marvin, (PHX) St. Josephine Bakhita Roman Catholic Mission Phoenix, Phoenix, AZ

McNalis, Rev. John P., '76 (CHI) Retired. Curia: Offices and Directors

McNally, Rev. Lawrence R., '77 (CHI) Retired.

McNally, Rev. Michael J., '73 (PMB) Retired. Curia: Leadership

McNally, Rev. Richard, *SS.CC.* '75 (HON) St. Ann, Kaneohe, HI

McNally, Rev. Thomas, '13 (KAL) Curia: Consultative Bodies

McNally, Rev. Thomas F., *C.S.C.* '59 (FTW) [MIS] Holy Cross House, Notre Dame, IN

McNamara, Rev. Anthony, *O.Carm.* '69 (JOL) Retired.

McNamara, Rev. Msgr. Brian J., '84 (RVC) Our Lady of Lourdes, West Islip, NY

McNamara, Rev. Brian J., '84 (RVC) Curia: (>MO) Offices and Directors

McNamara, Rev. Dennis L., *S.J.* '76 (WDC) [COL] Georgetown University, Washington, DC; [MON] The Jesuit Community at Georgetown University, Washington, DC

McNamara, Rev. Donald P., '61 (PH) Retired. St. John Chrysostom, Wallingford, PA

McNamara, Rev. Msgr. James M., (RVC) Our Lady of the Miraculous Medal, Point Lookout, NY

McNamara, Rev. John P., '15 (RCK) St. Catherine of Siena, West Dundee, IL; St. Mary's of Gilberts, Gilberts, IL

McNamara, Rev. Michael J., '80 (BO) Resurrection of Our Lord and Savior Jesus Christ, Hingham, MA; St. Paul, Hingham, MA

McNamara, Rev. Msgr. Patrick V., '60 (NY) Retired.

McNamara, Rev. Msgr. Robert J., '69 (LA) Retired.

McNamara, Very Rev. Msgr. Stephen E., '67 (VEN) Curia: Advisory Boards, Commissions, Committees, and Councils; Leadership Church of the Resurrection of Our Lord Catholic Parish in Fort Myers, Inc., Fort Myers, FL

McNamara, Rev. Thomas, *O.F.M.Cap.* '07 (NY) Our Lady of Sorrows, New York, NY

McNamara, Rev. Thomas J., '82 (SAG) Retired. Curia: Offices and Directors

McNamara, Rev. William, '65 (SAT) Retired. [NUR] Missionary Servants of St. Anthony (Padua Place), San Antonio, TX

McNamee, Rev. Msgr. Francis G., '95 (ATL) Cathedral of Christ the King Catholic Church, Atlanta, Inc., Atlanta, GA

McNamee, Rev. John P., '59 (PH) Retired.

McNamee, Rev. Patrick, '70 (P) Retired. Curia: Offices and Directors

McNamee, Rev. Paul, '85 (SAC) Chap, Sutter General Hosp, Sacramento

McNavish, Rev. Brian, '18 (ATL) [CAM] University of Georgia - Catholic Student Center, Athens, GA; [MIS] Catholic Student Center at The University of Georgia, Athens, GA

McNea, Very Rev. Mark C., '89 (WIN) Curia: Advisory Boards, Commissions, Committees, and Councils; Deaneries; Offices and Directors Cathedral of the Sacred Heart, Winona, MN; St. Casimir, Winona, MN

McNeeley, Rev. William J., '07 (KNX) Holy Ghost, Knoxville, TN

McNeely, Rev. Matthew, *F.S.S.P.* (PAT) Our Lady of Fatima Chapel (Tridentine), Pequannock, NJ

McNeese, Rev. Robert J., '98 (SPK) Retired. St. Joseph, Rockford, WA

McNeil, Rev. Bryan, '17 (NTN) Curia: Consultative Bodies Our Lady of Perpetual Help, Worcester, MA

McNeil, Rev. Dennis, (CLV) Immaculate Conception Parish, Willoughby, OH

McNeil, Rev. Joel, (DM) Holy Family, Mondamin, IA; Sacred Heart, Woodbine, IA; St. Patrick, Dunlap, IA

McNeil, Rev. Lawrence J., '73 (HBG) Retired. St. Joseph, Hanover, PA

McNeillie, Rev. Richard, '15 (GAL) Curia: Offices and Directors

McNeilly, Rev. Dennis, *S.J.* (CHI) (>OM) [MON] Jesuit Community at Creighton University, Omaha, NE

McNeilly, Rev. Dennis P., *S.J.* '85 (OM) [MON] Jesuit Residence at Creighton Prep, Omaha, NE

McNelis, Rev. Paul D., *S.J.* '77 (NY) [MON] Jesuit Community at Fordham University, New York, NY

McNellis, Rev. Paul, *S.J.* '87 (BO) [MON] The Jesuit Community at Boston College, Chestnut Hill, MA

McNew, Rev. Dwayne A., '95 (COL) SS. Simon and Jude, West Jefferson, OH

McNicholas, Rev. Declan, '19 (GRY) St. John the Evangelist, Saint John, IN

McNicholas, Rev. Declan, '19 (GRY) Curia: Leadership

McNichols, Rev. William, '79 (SFE) St. Joseph on the Rio Grande, Albuquerque, NM

McNulty, Rev. Edward, '93 (SD) Curia: Leadership Pastor of Saint Mary Magdalene Catholic Parish in San Diego, California, a Corporation Sole, San Diego, CA

McNulty, Rev. Francis J., '52 (NEW) Retired. [MON] The Rev. Msgr. James F. Kelley Residence for Retired Priests, Caldwell, NJ

McNulty, Rev. Gerard J., '67 (LA) Retired.

McNulty, Rev. James, '03 (DET) St. Edith Parish Livonia, Livonia, MI

McNulty, Rev. John P., '73 (CLV) Communion of Saints Parish, Cleveland Heights, OH

McNulty, Rev. John T., '74 (PRO) Retired.

McNulty, Rev. Joseph D., '69 (CLV) Retired.

McNulty, Rev. Martin J., '03 (BO) Holy Name, Boston, MA

McNulty, Rev. Paul, '14 (CHL) St. John the Evangelist, Waynesville, NC

McNulty, Rev. T. Michael, *S.J.* '73 (MIL) [MON] Jesuit

Community at Marquette University (Marquette Jesuit Associates, Inc.), Milwaukee, WI
McNulty, Rev. William J., '64 (NOR) Retired.
McPartland, Rev. Patrick, '08 (TR) Church of Saint Catharine, Holmdel, NJ
McPartland, Rev. Paul G., '57 (BO) Retired.
McPeak, Rev. Jude, *OP* (STP) Curia: Leadership St. Albert the Great, Minneapolis, MN; [MON] St. Albert the Great Priory, Minneapolis, MN
McPhail, Rev. J. Stuart, *O.P.* '69 (PRO) [COL] Providence College, Providence, RI; [MON] St. Thomas Aquinas Priory at Providence College, Providence, RI
McPhillips, Rev. James G., '83 (CLV) Chap, Geauga Cmty Hosp, Chardon St. Helen, Newbury, OH
McPhillips, Rev. Jay, (CLV) Chap, Geauga Cty Youth Ctr; Geauga Cty Jail, Chardon
McProud, Rev. Bryce, '11 (P) Retired.
McQuade, Rev. James F., *C.S.P.* '56 (NY) Retired. Roosevelt Hosp [MON] Paulist Fathers' Motherhouse, New York, NY
McQuade, Rev. Richard E., '57 (BO) Retired.
McQuaid, Rev. Thomas W., '79 (CHI) Retired.
McQuaide, Very Rev. Joseph W., '11 (WIL) Curia: Administration; Advisory Boards, Commissions, Committees, and Councils Cathedral of St. Peter, Wilmington, DE; St. Mary of the Immaculate Conception, Wilmington, DE; St. Patrick, Wilmington, DE
McQuaide, Very Rev. Joseph W., (WIL) Curia: Education; Offices and Directors
McQuaide, Very Rev. Joseph W., '11 (WIL) Curia: Administration; Leadership; Tribunal [MIS] Catholic Diocese of Wilmington, Inc., Wilmington, DE
McQuesten, Rev. Mark A., '87 (MAR) Retired. Immaculate Conception of the Blessed Virgin Mary, Iron Mountain, MI
McQuillan, Rev. Cornelius T., *C.S.Sp.* '75 (SB) Our Lady of the Valley, Hemet, CA
McQuinn, Rev. Peter B., '91 (CHI) Our Lady of the Holy Family, Chicago, IL
McQuone, Rev. Kevin, (PMB) [SEM] St. Vincent de Paul Regional Seminary, Boynton Beach, FL
McQuone, Rev. Kevin, '10 (PT) On Duty Outside Diocese. St. Vincent de Paul Seminary, Boynton Beach Curia: Leadership
McRae, Rev. Msgr. Cornelius M., '67 (BO) Retired.
McShane, Rev. Daniel Patrick, '19 (PEO) Peoria Notre Dame High School, Peoria, IL; St. Jude, Peoria, IL
McShane, Rev. John B., '74 (LAV) Retired.
McShane, Rev. Joseph, (FR) [MON] Marian Friary of Our Lady, Queen of the Seraphic Order, New Bedford, MA
McShane, Rev. Joseph M., *S.J.* '77 (NY) [MON] Cardinal Spellman Hall, Jesuit Community, Bronx, NY
McSherry, Rev. Patrick, *O.F.M.Cap.* '78 (DET) [MON] St. Bonaventure Monastery, Detroit, MI
McShurley, Rev. Peter M., '20 (ARL) Bishop Denis J. O'Connell High School, Arlington, VA
McShurley, Rev. Peter Michael, '20 (ARL) St. James, Falls Church, VA
McSweeney, Rev. Brian T., '88 (NY) St. Augustine, Ossining, NY
McSweeney, Rev. Msgr. Jeremiah F., '72 (WH) Retired.
McSweeney, Rev. Msgr. John J., '74 (CHL) Retired.
McSweeney, Rev. Joseph, *S.S.C.* '58 (PRO) Retired. [MON] St. Columban's Retirement House (St. Columban's Foreign Mission Society), Bristol, RI
McSweeney, Rev. Liam P., '63 (SAC) Retired.
McSweeney, Rev. Msgr. Thomas J., '71 (E) Retired.
McTeigue, Rev. Robert, *S.J* '97 (OAK) St. Edward, Newark, CA
McTeigue, Rev. Robert J, '97 (SFR) [MON] Loyola House Jesuit Community, San Francisco, CA
McVean, Rev. John J., *O.F.M.* '67 (NY) Retired.
McVoy, Rev. John C., '10 (WIL) Chap, Wilmington Hosp; Christiana Care Health Services...
McWeeney, Rev. Brian E., '73 (NY) Curia: Offices and Directors
McWhirter, Rev. Alan, *FSSP* '20 (SAC) Pastor of St. Stephen the First Martyr Parish, Sacramento, a corporation sole, Sacramento, CA
Mead, Rev. Gary M., '97 (NY) Holy Trinity, New York, NY; [MIS] Instructional Television, Yonkers, NY
Meade, Rev. Hershal Dale, '15 (ALX) Sacred Heart, Pineville, LA
Meade, Rev. James W., '81 (CIN) Retired.
Meade, Rev. Pachomius, *OSB* '09 (KC) [SEM] Conception Seminary College, Conception, MO
Meade, Rev. Pachomius, *O.S.B.* '09 (KC) [MON] Conception Abbey (Benedictine Monks), Conception, MO
Meagher, Rt. Rev. Cletus D., *O.S.B.* '71 (BIR) St. Michael, Florence, AL; [MON] St. Bernard Abbey, Cullman, AL
Meagher, Rev. Msgr. Frank J., '60 (COL) Retired.
Meagher, Rev. Joseph R., '92 (NEW) Curia: Organizations (affiliated, inter-Diocesan, miscellaneous/other) St. Antoninus, Newark, NJ
Meagher, Rev. Msgr. Michael T., '65 (SY) Curia: Offices and Directors Saints John & Andrew, Binghamton, NY
Meagher, Rev. Thomas L., '64 (DET) St. Patrick Parish White Lake, White Lake, MI; St. Perpetua Parish Waterford, Waterford, MI
Mealey, Rev. Mark S., *O.S.F.S.* '79 (WIL) [MON] Retirement and Assisted Care Facility, Childs, MD
Meaney, Rev. Brendan J., '65 (CAM) Retired.
Meaney, Rev. Patrick, '87 (CC) [MON] Catholic Solitudes, Benavides, TX
Means, Rev. David A., '81 (STL) On Duty Outside Diocese. Chamois, MO
Means, Rev. David A., '81 (STL) On Duty Outside Diocese. Serving in the Diocese of Jefferson City. (>JC) Assumption, Morrison, MO; (>JC) Most Pure Heart of Mary, Chamois, MO
Meany, Rev. John J., *OP* '87 (CHI) St. Vincent Ferrer, River Forest, IL; [MON] Dominicans (Provincial Office), Chicago, IL
Meany, Rev. Michael G., '80 (CHI) St. Patricia, Hickory Hills, IL
Meares, Rev. Clyde Timberlake, '02 (R) Our Lady of Perpetual Help, Rocky Mount, NC
Meaux, Rev. Glenn, '80 (LAF) On Special Assignment. SOLT Haiti Mission
Mecca, Rev. Gregg D., '96 (BGP) St. Peter's Corporate Society, Danbury, CT
Meccia, Rev. Francis S., *M.M.* '66 (NY) Retired. [MON] Maryknoll Fathers and Brothers (Catholic Foreign Mission Society of America, Inc.), Ossining, NY
Mech, Rev. John J., '95 (DET) Most Blessed Sacrament Cathedral Parish Detroit, Detroit, MI
Meconi, Rev. David V., *S.J.* '03 (STL) [COL] Saint Louis University, St. Louis, MO
Mecum, Rev. Travis, '20 (KCK) Holy Trinity, Lenexa, KS
Medairos, Rev. Anthony J., '73 (BO) Retired.
Medaki, Rev. Ferdinand, (NY) Chap, Montefiore Med Ctr, Henry and Lucy Moses Div, Bronx
Medas, Rev. Michael B., '88 (BO) Curia: (>MO) Offices and Directors St. Patrick, Watertown, MA; [ASN] KOLBE Association, Inc., Braintree, MA; [CAM] Massachusetts Institute of Technology - Tech Catholic Community, Cambridge, MA
Medeiros, Very Rev. Antonio F., '93 (BO) [SEM] Redemptoris Mater Archdiocesan Missionary Seminary, Chestnut Hill, MA
Medeiros, Rev. Arnold R., '75 (FR) Retired.
Medeiros, Rev. Benjamin, (ALT) [MON] St. Francis Friary at Mount Assisi, Loretto, PA
Medeiros, Rev. Leonel S., '04 (BGP) Curia: Consultative Bodies; Leadership Our Lady of Aparecida Corporation, Danbury, CT; St. Peter's Corporate Society, Danbury, CT
Medelin, Rev. Hugo, *CM* (CHL) Our Lady of Guadalupe Church, Charlotte, NC
Mederos, Rev. Delvis, (ORL) Our Lady of Guadalupe, Wahneta, FL
Mediana, Rev. Gil, (DAL) Divine Mercy of Our Lord Catholic Parish, Mesquite, TX
Medina, Rev. David, '02 (TLS) San Juan Diego Mission, Stilwell, OK; St. Brigid, Tahlequah, OK
Medina, Rev. Eduardo, '04 (PMB) Our Lady of Lourdes, Boca Raton, FL
Medina, Rev. Fabio E., '83 (SFR) St. Anthony, Menlo Park, CA
Medina, Rev. George A., '87 (TR) Retired. Curia: Leadership
Medina, Rev. Gilbert, '07 (ORL) St. Peter Church, DeLand, FL; [CAM] Catholic Campus Ministry at Stetson University, Deland, FL
Medina, Rev. Hector, '84 (FWT) Retired.
Medina, Rev. Ignazio C., '78 (JC) Retired.
Medina, Rev. Jesus S. (Jets), '10 (MIA) Curia: Pastoral Services St. Peter Catholic Church, Big Pine Key, FL
Medina, Rev. Joel G., *S.J.* '11 (DET) [MON] Jesuit Community at the University of Detroit Mercy, Detroit, MI
Medina, Rev. Jose, *F.S.C.B.* '01 (WDC) [MIS] Priestly Fraternity of the Missionaries of St. Charles Borromeo, Inc., Bethesda, MD
Medina, Rev. Jose, (NY) [MIS] The Human Adventure Corp., New York, NY
Medina, Rev. Julian, '73 (SAC) Retired. Pastor of St. Peter and All Hallows Parish, Sacramento, a corporation sole, Sacramento, CA
Medina, Rev. Leonardo, '07 (TLS) Curia: Offices and Directors Holy Rosary, Hartshorne, OK
Medina, Rev. Mauricio, '64 (B) Retired.
Medina, Rev. Odel, (SAV) Our Lady of Lourdes, Columbus, GA
Medina, Rev. Raymont, '15 (LA) Curia: Leadership Cathedral of Our Lady of the Angels, Los Angeles, CA
Medina, Rev. Roberto, '16 (FAJ) San Antonio de Padua, Ceiba, PR
Medina, Rev. Rolando, '71 (MIA) Retired.
Medina Radesco, Rev. Roberto, (FAJ) Curia: Offices and Directors
Medina Zermeno, Rev. Oscar Saul, '20 (FRS) St. Joseph, Los Banos, CA
Medina-Algaba, Rev. Felix, '04 (DEN) Queen of Peace Catholic Parish in Aurora, Aurora, CO
Medina-Leon, Rev. Marcos J., *M.S.P.* (SB) St. John the Evangelist, Riverside, CA
Medina-Santos, Rev. Msgr. Francisco, '89 (SJN) Curia: Offices and Directors Francisca Javiera Cabrini, San Juan, PR
Medio, Rev. Joseph Paul, *F.P.O.* '99 (BO) [MON] Franciscans of Primitive Observance, Lawrence, MA
Medley, Rev. Msgr. Robert W., '90 (MET) On Leave.
Medley, Rev. Samuel, *S.O.L.T.* '08 (CC) [MON] Society of Our Lady of the Most Holy Trinity, Corpus Christi, TX; [RTR] Our Lady of Corpus Christi Retreat Center, Corpus Christi, TX
Medlin, Rev. Bryan W., '13 (GLD) On Administrative Leave.
Medlin, Rev. Douglas S., '02 (ATL) Retired.
Medlock, Rev. Scott, '96 (AJ) Holy Family, Glennallen, AK; Sacred Heart, Seward, AK; St. Elizabeth Ann Seton, Anchorage, AK
Medow, Rev. David, '01 (JOL) [NUR] Franciscan Communities, Inc. (Marian Village), Homer Glen, IL
Medrano-Matos, Rev. Angel, '08 (BRK) Presentation of the Blessed Virgin Mary, Jamaica, NY
Mee, Rev. Msgr. Brian, '78 (SPK) St. Augustine, Spokane, WA
Meehan, Rev. Gabriel, '59 (CHL) Retired.
Meehan, Rev. Msgr. John T., '64 (NY) Retired.
Meehan, Rev. Joseph J., '61 (PH) Retired. St. Francis of Assisi, Springfield, PA
Meehan, Rev. Kenneth, *S.J.* '71 (BAL) Retired. [MIS] Colombiere Jesuit Community, Baltimore, MD
Meehan, Rev. Terence A., '67 (CIN) Retired.
Meehan, Rev. Thomas J., '72 (ATL) Retired.
Meehan, Rev. Timothy A., '59 (HRT) Retired.
Meehan LC, Rev. Kevin, *L.C.* (LA) [MON] Legionaries of Christ, Pasadena, CA
Meeks, Rev. Edward, '12 (POC) Christ the King Catholic Church, Towson, MD
Meeuwsen, Rev. Jeffrey, '07 (P) Curia: Offices and Directors; Tribunal St. Elizabeth Ann Seton, Aloha, OR
Mefrige, Rev. John, '02 (NTN) Curia: (>SAT) Administration; Pastoral Services (>NO) St. Nicholas of Myra Byzantine Catholic Mission, New Orleans, LA; (>PBR) St. Nicholas of Myra Byzantine Catholic Mission, New Orleans, LA
Mefrige, Rev. John, (SAT) Curia: Administration
Mego Diaz, Rev. Idelmo, (WIL) St. Michael the Archangel, Georgetown, DE
Megyery, Rev. Stefan, (WDC) Epiphany, Washington, DC
Mehan, Rev. Joseph A., '96 (DAL) St. Michael the Archangel Catholic Parish - Garland, Garland, TX
Mehanna, Rev. Andre, (OLL) St. Rafka Maronite Catholic Church, Lakewood, CO
Mehok, Rev. Edward E., (CLV) Retired.
Meidl, Rev. Gerald, '74 (NU) St. George, New Ulm, MN; St. John the Baptist, New Ulm, MN; St. Mary, New Ulm, MN
Meidl, Rev. Gerald Stanley, (NU) Cathedral of the Holy Trinity, New Ulm, MN
Meier, Rev. Denis, '63 (SFS) Retired.
Meier, Rev. Emeric, *O.F.M.* '68 (BO) Retired. [MIS] St. Anthony Shrine, Boston, MA
Meier, Rev. Gerald A., '66 (STL) Retired. Holy Spirit Catholic Church, Maryland Heights, MO
Meier, Rev. Timothy J, *SJ* '91 (LA) [MON] Colombiere House (Jesuit Fathers), Los Angeles, CA
Meiklejohn, Rev. Norman, *A.A.* '54 (WOR) Retired. [MON] Assumptionists (Augustinians of the Assumption), Worcester, MA
Meiman, Rev. Louis J., '87 (L) St. Frances of Rome, Louisville, KY; St. Leonard, Louisville, KY
Meinen, Rev. Dennis W., '87 (SC) Retired.
Meiners, Rev. Andrew, *C.Ss.R.* '70 (GAL) Holy Ghost, Houston, TX
Meinert, Rev. Thomas, '22 (HBG) St. Leo the Great, Lancaster, PA
Meinhart, Rev. Michael Joseph, '20 (SFD) St. Louis, Nokomis, IL

Meinholz, Rev. John M., '77 (MAD) Retired.
Meininger, Rev. William A., '15 (FTW) St. Mary of the Lake, Culver, IN
Meinzen, Rev. David, (MO) Curia: Offices and Directors
Meinzen, Rev. David L., '00 (STN) Chap Curia: (>MO) Offices and Directors
Meinzen, Rev. David L., (FTW) Chap, Veterans Administration Hosp, Fort Wayne
Meismer, Rev. Paul J., '69 (PEO) Retired.
Meissen, Rev. Randall, *LC* (ORL) [CAM] Catholic Campus Ministry at Florida Institute of Technology, Melbourne, FL
Meissner, Rev. Robert J., '69 (SAG) Retired.
Mejia, Rev. Jorge, (KNX) All Saints Catholic Church, Knoxville, TN
Mejia, Rev. Luis Alonso, '15 (DM) Curia: Leadership St. Patrick, Perry, IA
Mejia, Rev. Manuel J., *M.M.* '63 (NY) Retired.
Mejia, Rev. Miguel, '00 (SPK) Curia: Leadership; Offices and Directors Our Lady of Fatima, Spokane, WA
Mejia, Rev. Rodolfo P., '04 (GBG) St. John the Baptist, Perryopolis, PA
Mejia Gonzalez, Rev. Jose, (LA) On Administrative Leave.
Mekala, Rev. Krishnarao, *M.F.* (GB) Holy Cross, Kaukauna, WI; St. Katharine Drexel, Kaukauna, WI (>OAK) [MON] Missionaries of Faith-India Inc., Fremont, CA
Mekala, Rev. Sleeva Reddy, '07 (JKS) Immaculate Conception, Indianola, MS; St. Benedict the Moor, Indianola, MS; St. James, Leland, MS
Mekonnen, Rev. Addisalem T., '15 (PH) St. Martin De Porres, Philadelphia, PA; [MIS] Philadelphia Senatus of the Legion of Mary, Philadelphia, PA
Melaba, Rev. Daniel Ter, '91 (SAV) St. Joseph's, Waycross, GA
Melaku, Rev. Ben, (STL) Christ the Savior Catholic Church, Perryville, MO; Our Lady of Victory Catholic Church, Perryville, MO; St. Rose of Lima Catholic Church, Silver Lake, Perryville, MO; St. Vincent De Paul Catholic Church, Perryville, Perryville, MO; [MON] Congregation of the Mission, Perryville, MO
Melancon, Rev. Aaron, '97 (LAF) St. Benedict the Moor, Duson, LA; St. Theresa of the Child Jesus, Duson, LA
Melancon, Rev. Andre, '11 (HT) Curia: Administration St. Bernadette Soubirous Church, Houma, LA
Melancon, Rev. Bill John, '93 (LAF) St. Elizabeth, St. Martinville, LA; St. Rita, St. Martinville, LA
Melancon, Rev. Msgr. Louis J., '63 (LAF) Retired.
Melanson, Rev. Michael P., (ALB) St. Patrick, Athens, NY; St. Patrick, Catskill, NY
Melapuram, Rev. John, (RVC) Holy Name of Jesus, Woodbury, NY
Melcher, Rev. Luke A., '05 (ALX) On Duty Outside Diocese. Secretariat, ICEL, Washington DC
Melchior, Rev. Gerald P., '90 (OM) On Special Assignment. Mass Supply
Melchior, Rev. Thomas, '65 (KCK) Retired.
Meldrum, Rev. Brian J., '15 (DET) On Academic Leave. Catholic Univ of America, Washington
Mele, Rev. Joseph M., '73 (PIT) Retired. Divine Redeemer, Sewickley, PA; [MIS] The Ark and the Dove, Inc., Gibsonia, PA
Meledom, Rev. Joseph, '68 (FWT) Retired.
Melendez, Rev. Elberto, '04 (RNO) St. Michael's, Reno, NV
Melendez, Rev. Hector, '80 (PAT) Retired. Our Lady of Lourdes, Paterson, NJ
Melendez, Rev. Jose, (RIC) On Leave.
Melendez Vazquez, Rev. Alberto, '22 (PCE) Nuestra Senora del Carmen, Villalba, PR
Melepuram, Rev. John P, '78 (SYM) St. Mary Syro Malabar, Old Bethpage, New York, Old Bethpage, NY
Melfi, Rev. F. Patrick, '06 (BUF) Holy Name of Mary RC Church Society Ellicottville NY, Ellicottville, NY; Our Lady of the Angels Roman Catholic Church Society of Cuba, New York, Cuba, NY; St. Patrick's Roman Catholic Church Society of Belfast, New York, Belfast, NY; St. Patrick's Roman Catholic Church Society of Fillmore, New York, Fillmore, NY; St. Philomena's Roman Catholic Church Society of Franklinville, NY, Franklinville, NY
Melgarejo, Rev. Paul, (SAT) St. Matthew Catholic Church, San Antonio, TX
Melillo, Rev. William J., '66 (NEW) Retired. Seton Hall Preparatory School, West Orange, NJ
Melka, Rev. John, *O.C.D.* '64 (P) [MON] Discalced Carmelite Friars (O.C.D.), Mount Angel, OR
Melkias, Rev. Selvan, '12 (TYL) Immaculate Conception, Jefferson, TX; St. Joseph, Marshall, TX
Mellein, Rev. John Thomas, *O.P.* '07 (OAK) [MON] Order of Preachers (Province of the Most Holy Name of Jesus - Western Dominican Province), Oakland, CA
Mello, Rev. Jay, '07 (FR) St. Joseph, Fall River, MA; St. Michael, Fall River, MA
Mello, Very Rev. Matthew, '87 (ORL) Curia: Advisory Boards, Commissions, Committees, and Councils; Deaneries Our Lady of Hope, Port Orange, FL
Mellone, Rev. Msgr. Michael J., '76 (WDC) Curia: Consultative Bodies Annunciation, Washington, DC; St. Mary, Laurel, MD
Mellone, Rev. Vincent P., '65 (BO) Retired.
Melloria, Rev. Roselo, (GBG) St. Joseph, New Kensington, PA; St. Margaret Mary, Lower Burrell, PA; St. Mary of Czestochowa, New Kensington, PA
Melmer, Rev. John H., '91 (ARL) St. John the Beloved, McLean, VA
Melnic, Rev. Msgr. James T., '78 (PHU) Retired.
Melnick, Rev. John E., '86 (SCR) Retired. On Duty Outside Diocese. Mary-St Anthony Parish, Kansas City, KS
Melnick, Very Rev. John P., '00 (HRT) Curia: Advisory Boards, Commissions, Committees, and Councils; Clergy and Religious Services St. Joseph's Cathedral, Hartford, Connecticut, Hartford, CT
Melnick, Rev. William D., '75 (WIL) Retired. Immaculate Heart of Mary, Wilmington, DE
Melo, Rev. Fidel C., '96 (CHL) St. James, Hamlet, NC
Melo, Rev. Nicholas P., '83 (HRT) Curia: Advisory Boards, Commissions, Committees, and Councils Christ the King Parish Corporation, Wethersfield, CT
Melocoton, Rev. Carlos L., '09 (WH) Curia: Leadership St. Michael, Wheeling, WV
Melone, Rt. Rev. Mark E., '78 (NTN) Curia: Consultative Bodies Holy Transfiguration, McLean, VA
Melvin, Rev. Msgr. Thomas P., '01 (WIN) Immaculate Conception, Kellogg, MN; St. Joachim's, Plainview, MN
Mema, Rev. Robert, '17 (BRK) St. Kevin, Flushing, NY
Mena, Rev. Abel, '02 (SR) Curia: Leadership Pastor of St. Thomas Aquinas Catholic Church of Napa, A Corporation Sole, Napa, CA
Mena, Rev. Antonio, '81 (ELP) San Felipe de Jesus, Socorro, TX
Mena, Rev. J. Roberto, *S.T.* '01 (WDC) [MON] Holy Spirit Missionary Cenacle, Riverdale, MD
Mena, Rev. Jesus M., *O.A.R.* '86 (LSC) St. Anthony Parish, Anthony, Inc., Anthony, NM; [MON] Augustinian Recollect Fathers, Anthony, NM
Mena, Rev. Jose, (AUS) St. Louis, Austin, TX
Mena, Rev. Roberto, *S.T.* (LA) Our Lady of Victory, Compton, CA
Mena, Rev. Victor, (BAK) Curia: Leadership
Mena Martinez, Rev. Victor Manuel, '17 (BAK) St. Patrick, Madras, OR
Mena-Mena, Rev. Sergio, '10 (CHI) St. Oscar Romero Parish, Chicago, IL
Menard, Rev. Bernard, (SY) St. Peter's Church, Rome, NY
Menard, Rev. Gary, (KC) [MON] St. Peter Claver Jesuit Community, Kansas City, MO
Menard, Rev. Gilbert B., '55 (OG) Retired.
Menard, Rev. J. Godden, *C.M.* '55 (STL) Retired.
Menard, Rev. Robert J., *O.F.M.* '72 (CHR) Retired. St. Andrew, Clemson, SC
Menasco, Rev. Edward T., '90 (OKL) On Special Assignment. Priest Consultant Permanent Diaconate Program, Oklahoma City St. Joseph's, Hennessey, OK
Menchaca, Rev. Gerardo, '95 (SJ) On Special Assignment. Curia: Leadership; Offices and Directors Our Lady of Guadalupe, San Jose, CA
Menchu, Rev. Armando, *O.S.B.* (RCK) [MON] Marmion Abbey, Aurora, IL
Mencias, Rev. Jaime, '90 (AJ) St. John the Baptist, Homer, AK
Mencsik, Rev. John, *C.PP.S.* '74 (CIN) Retired. [MON] Society of the Precious Blood, United States Province, Inc., Dayton, OH
Mendem, Rev. Marianand, '93 (KCK) Sacred Heart-St. Casimir, Leavenworth, KS
Mendes, Rev. Joseph, *MSFS* '63 (ATL) Retired. [MON] The Missionaries of St. Francis de Sales - MSFS USA Vice Province, Loganville, GA
Mendez, Rev. Francisco, '60 (ARL) Retired.
Mendez, Rev. Juan, '73 (SFE) Retired. Curia: Offices and Directors
Mendez, Rev. Luis A., '95 (ARE) Pontificia Universidad Catolica de Puerto Rico, Recinto de Arecibo, Arecibo, PR
Mendez, Rev. Oscar, *OFM* (SD) Pastor of Mission San Luis Rey Catholic Parish, Oceanside, a corporation sole, Oceanside, CA; [MIS] Mission San Luis Rey Catholic Parish in Oceanside, CA Real Property Support Corporation, Oceanside, CA; [MON] Old Mission San Luis Rey, Oceanside, CA
Mendez, Rev. Rafael A, '93 (MGZ) St. Rose of Lima, Rincon, PR
Mendez, Rev. Robert, (B) St. Paul's, Nampa, ID
Mendez, Rev. Yerick, '12 (SPR) Cathedral of St. Michael the Archangel, Springfield, MA
Mendez Acevedo, Rev. Luis Antonio David, *S.E.M.V.* '95 (ARE) Our Lady of Guadalupe, Hatillo, PR
Mendez Silvagnoli, Rev. Winston R., '03 (PCE) La Resurreccion, Ponce, PR
Mendez-Cobos, Rev. Manuel, '94 (MAD) Good Shepherd Parish, Madison, WI
Mendez-Hernandez, Rev. Rafael, *P.B.R.O.* '94 (SJN) San Andres, Carolina, PR
Mendieta Lacayo, Rev. Ramses Abian, '17 (LR) St. Barbara, De Queen, AR
Mendieta Lacyo, Rev. Ramses Abian, '17 (LR) St. Juan Diego, Wickes, AR
Mendieta Rodas, Rev. Marlon A., '18 (R) St. John the Baptist, Roanoke Rapids, NC
Mendiola Arroyo, Rev. Gaston, '18 (ORG) La Purisima, Orange, CA
Mendis, Rev. Linus, (BO) St. Joseph, Medway, MA
Mendis, Rev. Ruwandana, '97 (NY) St. Charles, Staten Island, NY
Mendl, Rev. Michael, *SDB* (NY) [MON] Salesian Provincial House, New Rochelle, NY
Mendonca, Rev. Francisco Maria Cordeiro, (NEW) Our Lady of Peace, New Providence, NJ; St. Philomena, Livingston, NJ
Mendonca, Rev. John, '79 (BRK) Retired. Corpus Christi, Woodside, NY
Mendonca, Rev. Johnny, (RVC) St. Christopher's Parish, Baldwin, NY
Mendonca, Rev. Norbert C., '89 (CHR) On Duty Outside Diocese. Studying Abroad
Mendonca, Rev. Robert, '00 (OAK) Curia: Offices and Directors
Mendoza, Very Rev. Diodoro, (PHX) Curia: (>HPM) Offices and Directors
Mendoza, Very Rev. Diodoro, '11 (HPM) Curia: Leadership; Offices and Directors; Tribunal St. Stephen Cathedral, Phoenix, AZ; [EFT] Holy Angels, San Diego Charitable Trust, Phoenix, AZ; [NUR] St. Stephen Senior Citizen Apartments, Phoenix, AZ
Mendoza, Rev. Francis, '04 (LA) St. Finbar, Burbank, CA
Mendoza, Rev. Gerardo, '88 (SB) St. Mel, Norco, CA
Mendoza, Rev. Jacob, '17 (VIC) Curia: Leadership; Offices and Directors Our Lady of Guadalupe, Cuero, TX; SS. Peter & Paul, Meyersville, TX; St. Michael, Cuero, TX
Mendoza, Rev. Jose, '99 (OM) On Administrative Leave.
Mendoza, Rev. Jose Eduardo, '84 (SFR) St. Anthony, Menlo Park, CA
Mendoza, Rev. Lawrence, (SR) Pastor of St. Joseph Catholic Church of Middletown, A Corporation Sole, Middletown, CA
Mendoza, Very Rev. R. Anthony, '99 (LAR) Curia: Leadership; Offices and Directors St. Patrick, Laredo, TX
Mendoza Floyd, Rev. Andres, '12 (HRT) Most Holy Trinity Parish Corporation, Wallingford, CT
Mendyuk, Archpriest Yaroslav, '93 (STN) Chap Curia: Offices and Directors Immaculate Conception Ukrainian Catholic Church, Palatine, IL
Menegatti, Rev. Mark, *O.S.A.* '13 (LA) Our Mother of Good Counsel, Los Angeles, CA
Menegay, Rev. Gregory, '98 (PHX) St Clare of Assisi Roman Catholic Parish Surprise, Surprise, AZ
Menendez, Rev. Adolph J., *S.X.* '68 (BO) [MIS] Our Lady of Fatima Shrine, Holliston, MA; [MON] Xaverian Missionaries, Holliston, MA
Menendez, Rev. Jose Luis, '77 (MIA) Curia: Pastoral Services Corpus Christi, Miami, FL
Meneses, Rev. Isaque, '10 (FRS) Holy Rosary, Hilmar, CA
Meneses, Rev. Miguel, '61 (ELP) Retired.
Menezes, Rev. Gervan, '14 (NSH) Curia: Offices and Directors St. Thomas Aquinas, Cookeville, TN
Menezes, Rev. Mark, '59 (JOL) Retired.
Menezes, Rev. Wade, *C.P.M.* '00 (OWN) [MON] Fathers of Mercy, Auburn, KY
Meng, Rev. Andrew, '21 (WCH) St. Francis of Assisi, Wichita, KS
Meng, Rev. David P., '89 (ARL) St. Timothy, Chantilly, VA
Mengel, Rev. Mark, *S.S.C.* '71 (OM) Retired. [MON] Missionary Society of St. Columban, St. Columbans, NE
Mengelle, Rev. Ervens, *I.V.E.* (COL) [SEM] Pontifical College Josephinum, Columbus, OH
Mengon, Rev. Albert, *S.D.B.* '66 (SFR) SS. Peter and Paul, San Francisco, CA

Menjivar, Rev. Jose Arisitides, *O.Carm.* '21 (JOL) Our Lady of Mount Carmel, Joliet, IL
Menjivar, Rev. Miguel Angel, '03 (LA) St. Joseph, La Puente, CA
Menjivar-Ayala, Rev. Evelio, '04 (WDC) Curia: Deaneries
Menjivar-Ayala, Very Rev. Evelio, (WDC) Curia: Consultative Bodies
Menke, Rev. Andrew V., '99 (LIN) On Duty Outside Diocese. Washington, DC
Menkhaus, Rev. Joseph, '22 (CLV) St. Bernadette, Westlake, OH
Menna, Rev. Fiorelli Dominic, '58 (BO) Retired.
Menner, Rev. Michael L., '93 (PEO) St. Lawrence's, Penfield, IL; [MIS] The Order of the Legion of Little Souls of the Merciful Heart of Jesus, Moline, IL
Menniti, Rev. Diego, '15 (LA) Curia: Offices and Directors
Menolickal, Rev. Royston, *OFM Cap.* (NY) Good Shepherd, New York, NY
Menor, Rev. Lester T., '99 (SAC) Curia: Leadership Pastor of St. Anthony Parish, Mount Shasta, a corporation sole, Mt. Shasta, CA; Pastor of St. Joseph Parish, McCloud, a corporation sole, McCloud, CA
Mens, Rev. Theodore J., (GRY) Retired.
Mensa, Rev. Emmanuel, (RVC) St. Christopher's Parish, Baldwin, NY
Mensah, Rev. Emmanuel Tobi, '92 (RIC) On Special Assignment. Shrine of the Infant of Prague, Wakefield & St. Jude, Frankl St. Jude, Franklin, VA
Mensah, Rev. Francis, '10 (DAV) Curia: Leadership St. Mary Church of Oxford, Iowa, Oxford, IA; St. Peter Church of Cosgrove, Iowa, Oxford, IA
Mensah, Rev. Gabriel, '01 (DUB) Basilica of St. Francis Xavier, Dyersville, Iowa, Dyersville, IA; S.S. Peter and Paul Church, Petersburg, Iowa, Dyersville, IA; St. Boniface Church of New Vienna, New Vienna, Iowa, New Vienna, IA; St. Joseph's Church, Earlville, Iowa, Earlville, IA; St. Paul Church, Worthington, Iowa, Worthington, IA
Mensah, Rev. Gabriel J., '90 (VIC) Retired. St. Peter's, Blessing, TX
Mensah, Rev. Isaac, (NY) Chap, James F Peters Med Ctr, Bronx Sacred Heart, Bronx, NY
Mensah, Rev. Isaac Ebo, '81 (MO) Curia: Offices and Directors
Mensah, Rev. Robert, (NY) St. Frances de Chantal, Bronx, NY
Mensah, Rev. Tony K., '83 (NY) Chap, James F Peters Med Ctr, Bronx
Mensah, Rev. Tony Kyere, (MO) Curia: Offices and Directors
Menty, Rev. Ron, '69 (ALB) Retired.
Menzel, Rev. William G., '67 (LC) Retired. Curia: Leadership
Meoska, Rev. John, *O.S.B.* '82 (SCL) [MON] St. John's Abbey, of the Order of St. Benedict, Collegeville, MN
Mera-Vallejos, Rev. Jose E., '09 (HBG) St. Benedict the Abbot, Lebanon, PA
Meraz, Rev. Roque, '15 (GRY) St. Paul, Valparaiso, IN
Mercado, Rev. Heriberto, '06 (LUB) Curia: Offices and Directors St. Mary Magdalen, Earth, TX; St. William, Denver City, TX
Mercado, Rev. Jose Angel, '06 (HRT) Curia: Advisory Boards, Commissions, Committees, and Councils; Deaneries Saint John XXIII Parish Corporation, West Haven, CT
Mercado, Rev. Juan, (LAR) Christ the King, Laredo, TX
Mercado, Rev. Miguel, (ARE) Retired. [MIS] Chapel La Milagrosa, Arecibo, PR; [MIS] Chapel La Providencia, Arecibo, PR
Mercado, Rev. Pedro, (LAR) San Martin de Porres, Laredo, TX
Mercado, Rev. Ronaldo, '15 (FWT) St. Joseph, Arlington, TX
Mercado Rivera, Rev. Miguel, '83 (ARE) Church of Santa Teresita, Arecibo, PR
Merced, Rev. Roberto, *O.P.* '06 (BR) (>NO) [MON] Dominican Friars, Southern Dominican Province of St. Martin de Porres, New Orleans, LA
Merced, Rev. Roberto, *O.P.* '06 (NO) (>NY) [EFT] St. Thomas Aquinas Foundation of the Dominican Fathers of the United States (STAF), New York, NY
Mercer, Rev. David, '87 (SJ) Retired. On Duty Outside Diocese. Mission Work, Diocese of Las Cruces
Mercer, Rev. David, (LSC) St. Joseph Parish, Mescalero, Inc., Mescalero, NM
Mercer, Rev. Robert, *S.A.* '82 (NY) Retired. [MON] Franciscan Friars of the Atonement, Minister General Office, Garrison, NY
Mercier, Rev. Msgr. Joseph, '55 (BLX) Retired.
Mercieri, Rev. Dennis, (NOR) Chap, Lawrence and Mem Hosps, New London
Mercieri, Rev. Dennis J., '05 (NOR) Curia: (>MO) Offices and Directors; Offices and Directors
Mercure, Rev. Jerome, '79 (BUR) Curia: Leadership St. Patrick, Fairfield, VT
Merdian, Rev. Msgr. Mark J., '93 (PEO) Curia: Consultative Bodies; Deaneries St. Columba, Ottawa, IL; St. Francis of Assisi, Ottawa, IL; St. Patrick's, Ottawa, IL
Merdinger, Rev. Philip E., *B.H.* '64 (BO) On Duty Outside Diocese.
Meredith, Rev. Richard C., '78 (OWN) Curia: Advisory Boards, Commissions, Committees, and Councils SS. Peter and Paul, Hopkinsville, KY
Mergen, Rev. Timothy, '19 (MAD) St. Paul University Parish, Madison, WI
Mericantante, Rev. John J., '75 (PMB) Retired.
Merino, Rev. Jesus Carlo Leonardo, '17 (NEW) Church of the Presentation, Upper Saddle River, NJ
Merino Merino, Rev. Msgr. Baudilio, '48 (SJN) Curia: Offices and Directors
Merino Merino, Rev. Baudilio, '48 (SJN) Retired.
Meriwether, Rev. Stephen A., '83 (SFR) On Special Assignment.
Merkel, Rev. James, '73 (SP) Retired.
Merkel, Rev. Thomas, '20 (MAR) St. Albert the Great University Parish, Houghton, MI; St. Anne, Chassell, MI; [CAM] St. Albert the Great University Parish (Catholic Campus Ministry at Michigan Tech), Houghton, MI
Merkel, Rev. Thomas, *S.J.* '97 (OM) [MON] Jesuit Community at Creighton University, Omaha, NE
Merkelis, Rev. John D., *O.S.A.* '85 (JOL) Providence Catholic High School, New Lenox, IL; [MON] Augustinian Friary, New Lenox, IL
Merkle, Rev. Charles W., '88 (ARL) Corpus Christi, Aldie, VA
Merkt, Rev. Joseph T., '66 (L) Retired.
Merkt, Very Rev. Michael F., '81 (MIL) St. John, The Evangelist, Congregation, Greenfield, WI
Merlino, Rev. Darrin, *CMF* '00 (LA) [MON] Tepeyac House, Los Angeles, CA
Merold, Rev. James E., '71 (CHI) Retired. St. Francis de Sales, Lake Zurich, IL
Meroni, Rev. Fabrizio, *P.I.M.E.* (WDC) St. Patrick, Washington, DC
Merrick, Rev. Andrew J., '08 (BR) Curia: Clergy and Religious Services [CAM] Christ the King Parish and Catholic Center (Congregation of Christ the King Roman Catholic Church of the Diocese of Baton Rouge), Baton Rouge, LA
Merrick, Rev. Andrew J., '08 (BR) Congregation of Christ the King Roman Catholic Church of the Diocese of Baton Rouge, Baton Rouge, LA
Merrill, Rev. Charles, '13 (BIR) Annunciation of the Lord Catholic Parish, Decatur (St. Ann Catholic Church), Decatur, AL
Merrill, Rev. Thomas, *O.F.M.Conv.* '79 (TOL) Our Lady of Consolation, Carey, OH; [SHR] Basilica and National Shrine of Our Lady of Consolation, Carey, OH
Merritt, Rev. Jeffrey, '22 (NO) St. Dominic, New Orleans, LA
Merritt, Rev. Michael, '17 (ROC) Catholic Community of the Blessed Trinity, Clyde, NY; St. Joseph the Worker Roman Catholic Parish, Wayne County, Clyde, NY; St. Michael, Newark, NY
Mersmann, Rev. Anthony, '20 (KCK) Bishop Miege High School, Shawnee Mission, KS; Good Shepherd, Shawnee, KS
Merta, Rev. Lawrence, '02 (PHX) Holy Cross Roman Catholic Parish, Mesa, AZ
Mertes, Rev. Mark, '87 (KCK) Curia: Advisory Boards, Commissions, Committees, and Councils; Leadership St. Patrick's, Kansas City, KS
Mertes, Rev. Robert, *S.V.D.* '78 (CHI) Retired. [MON] Divine Word Residence, Techny, IL
Mervil, Rev. Ronald, (IND) St. John Paul II Catholic Church, Sellersburg, Inc., Sellersburg, IN
Merz, Very Rev. Daniel J., '98 (JC) Curia: Administration; Advisory Boards, Commissions, Committees, and Councils; Offices and Directors St. Thomas More Newman Center, University of Missouri, Columbia, MO; [CAM] St. Thomas More Newman Center, Columbia, MO
Merzweiler, Rev. David W., '77 (Y) Our Lady of the Lakes Parish, St. Catherine Church, Lake Milton, OH; Our Lady of the Lakes Parish, St. James Church, North Jackson, OH; St. Mary and St. Joseph Parish, Newton Falls, OH
Merzweiler, Rev. Jeremy D., '15 (CLV) St. Francis de Sales, Akron, OH
Mesa, Rev. Carlos, (LA) Holy Family, Wilmington, CA
Mesa, Rev. Jose A., *S.J.* '92 (CHI) [COL] Jesuit Community at Loyola University Chicago, Chicago, IL
Mesa, Rev. Jose Luis, *S.J.* '77 (MOB) [MON] Jesuits of Mobile, Inc., Mobile, AL
Mesa, Rev. Msgr. Luis, '00 (STL) On Duty Outside Diocese.
Mesa, Rev. Michael Samuel, '20 (LA) Holy Family, Glendale, CA
Mese, Rev. Prasanna Kumar, '10 (SAT) St. Paul, San Antonio, TX
Mesh, Rev. Moises, *C.S.V.* '11 (JOL) Maternity of the Blessed Virgin Mary, Bourbonnais, IL
Mesh, Rev. Moises L., *C.S.V.* '11 (CHI) [MON] Viatorian Province Center-Clerics of St. Viator, Arlington Heights, IL
Mesi, Friar Vincent, *O.F.M.* '72 (SD) Pastor of Immaculate Conception Catholic Parish, San Diego, a corporation sole, San Diego, CA
Mesley, Rev. Jerome T., '73 (GLP) Retired.
Messier, Rev. Gerard, *A.A.* (BO) Retired. [MON] Augustinians of the Assumption, Inc., Boston, MA
Messina, Very Rev. D. Andrew, '09 (PRO) Curia: Leadership Saint Catherine's Roman Catholic Church of Warwick, Rhode Island, Warwick, RI; Saint Francis Church Corporation, Hillsgrove, Warwick, RI; Sts. Rose & Clement, Warwick, RI
Messina, Rev. Joseph, '72 (CAM) Retired.
Messina, Rev. Samuel, '65 (JKS) Retired.
Messina, Rev. Victor G., '74 (BR) Retired.
Messner, Rev. Michael E., '98 (HBG) Mary, Gate of Heaven, Myerstown, PA
Mestas, Rev. Leonard, '81 (SB) Chap, Jerry L Pettis Mem Veterans Hosp, Loma Linda
Mestas, Rev. Leonard J., '81 (BWN) Retired. On Duty Outside Diocese. Living in Diocese of San Bernardino (in California)
Mestriparampil, Rev. Thomas, '89 (NY) Prison Chaplain, New York, NY Cardinal Hayes High School, Bronx, NY
Mesure, Rev. Msgr. Gerard C., '84 (PH) [SEM] Theological Seminary of St. Charles Borromeo, Wynnewood, PA
Mesure, Rev. Msgr. Gerard C., '84 (PH) On Special Assignment. Chancellor, St Matthias Rectory, Bala Cynwyd
Meszaros, Rev. Aaron, *C.Ss.R.* '16 (STP) (>CHI) [MON] The Redemptorists/Denver Province, Chicago, IL
Meszaros, Rev. Aaron, *C.Ss.R.* '16 (NO) (>CHI) [MON] The Redemptorist Fathers of Chicago, Chicago, IL
Meszaros, Rev. James J., '69 (BRK) Retired.
Metal, Rev. Gerald Glorioso, (MO) Curia: Offices and Directors
Metcalf, Rev. Andrew, '86 (SR) Retired.
Metellus, Rev. Jean Kesnel, *C.S.* '15 (VEN) Curia: Leadership Our Lady of Guadalupe Parish in Immokalee, Inc., Immokalee, FL
Metha, Rev. Msgr. Ronald W., '95 (YAK) Retired. On Duty Outside Diocese. Dept of the Air Force, 56FW/HC, Luke Afb, AZ Curia: (>MO) Offices and Directors
Metro, Rev. LeRoy, '63 (SAL) Retired.
Metz, Rev. Bradley J., *C.S.C.* '02 (FR) Holy Cross, South Easton, MA
Metz, Rev. David, '97 (SAL) Our Lady of Perpetual Help Parish, Concordia, Inc., Concordia, KS; St. Peter Parish, Aurora, Inc., Aurora, KS
Metz, Rev. John Michael, '18 (ATL) On Duty Outside Diocese. Active Duty Curia: (>MO) Offices and Directors
Metz, Rev. Kenneth J., '65 (MIL) Retired.
Metzgar, Rev. Michael, (HBG) Sacred Heart of Jesus, Lancaster, PA
Metzger, Rev. Msgr. Dennis M., '74 (TOL) Retired. Curia: Advisory Boards, Commissions, Committees, and Councils
Metzger, Rev. Kyle P., '15 (FAR) On Special Assignment. Curia: Offices and Directors St. John Paul II Catholic Schools Network (Blessed John Paul II Catholic Schools, Fargo Catholic Schools Network), Fargo, ND; Sts. Anne & Joachim Church of Fargo, Fargo, ND
Metzger, Rev. Richard L., '67 (COL) Retired.
Metzger, Rev. Stephen A., '70 (COL) Retired.
Metzger, Rev. Thomas H., '82 (LFT) St. Ambrose, Anderson, IN; St. Mary, Alexandria, IN; St. Mary, Anderson, IN
Metzger, Rev. William A., '78 (COL) Chap, Franklin Corr Med Ctr Our Lady of Victory, Columbus, OH
Metzger, Rev. William J., *O.S.F.S.* '71 (ARL) Retired. Our Lady of Good Counsel, Vienna, VA
Metzinger, Rev. John R., '82 (OKL) Curia: Consultative Bodies St. John Nepomuk, Yukon, OK
Metzler, Rev. Brett, (FWT) Curia: Miscellaneous / Other Offices

Metzler, Rev. William R., '72 (HRT) Retired.

Meulemans, Rev. Carl P., *M.M.* '60 (NY) Retired. [MON] Maryknoll Fathers and Brothers (Catholic Foreign Mission Society of America, Inc.), Ossining, NY

Meulemans, Rev. Dennis T., '61 (SUP) Retired.

Meulemans, Rev. Msgr. Ed, '60 (PHX) St. Peter School, ,

Meurer, Rev. Timothy J., '19 (SFE) San Jose-Anton Chico, Anton Chico, NM; St. Mary, Vaughn, NM

Mevissen, Rev. Richard, *C.Ss.R.* '66 (MIL) Retired. (>STL) [MON] St. Clement Health Care Center, Liguori, MO

Meyer, Rev. Bernard A., '59 (SFD) Retired.

Meyer, Rev. Christopher, (GAL) St. Faustina Catholic Church, Fulshear, TX

Meyer, Rev. Daniel J, '82 (CIN) Retired. St. Albert the Great, Kettering, OH

Meyer, Rev. Dennis J., *M.S.* '70 (STL) [MON] Missionaries of LaSalette, Province of Mary, Mother of the Americas, St. Louis, MO

Meyer, Rev. Earl, *O.F.M.Cap.* '60 (SAL) Retired. [MON] St. Fidelis Friary, Victoria, KS

Meyer, Rev. Eric, *C.P.* '66 (L) [MON] Sacred Heart Retreat, Louisville, KY

Meyer, Rev. Frederick C., '56 (STP) Retired.

Meyer, Rev. Gerald J., '96 (PEO) Retired.

Meyer, Rev. Harry J., '64 (CIN) Retired.

Meyer, Rev. Jacob A., '12 (FTW) Curia: Offices and Directors; (>MO) Offices and Directors

Meyer, Rev. James, '60 (DET) Retired.

Meyer, Rev. James, '94 (FAR) Holy Family Church of Grand Forks, Grand Forks, ND

Meyer, Rev. John A., '82 (IND) St. Charles Catholic Church, Milan, Inc., Milan, IN; St. Maurice Catholic Church, Napoleon, Inc., Napoleon, IN

Meyer, Rev. John A., (IND) St. Mary Catholic Church, Greensburg, Inc., Greensburg, IN; St. Vincent De Paul Catholic Church, Shelby County, Inc., Shelbyville, IN

Meyer, Rev. John D., '08 (STP) St. Timothy, Maple Lake, MN; The Church of St. Ignatius of Annandale, Minnesota, Annandale, MN; [CEM] St. Ignatius Cemetery, Annandale, MN; [CEM] St. Timothy Cemetery, Maple Lake, MN

Meyer, Rev. John R., '89 (LA) [MIS] Prelature of the Holy Cross and Opus Dei, Los Angeles, CA

Meyer, Rev. John R., '89 (POD) Curia: Clergy and Religious Services

Meyer, Rev. Jonathan P., '03 (IND) Curia: Leadership; Offices and Directors All Saints Catholic Church, Dearborn, Inc., Guilford, IN; St. Lawrence Catholic Church, Lawrenceburg, Inc., Lawrenceburg, IN; St. Mary Immaculate Conception Catholic Church, Aurora, Inc., Aurora, IN; St. Teresa Benedicta of the Cross, Bright, Indiana, Lawrenceburg, IN

Meyer, Rev. Jonathon, '15 (LA) On Academic Leave.

Meyer, Rev. Leo A., '65 (NO) Retired.

Meyer, Rev. Luke D., '06 (FAR) Sts. Anne & Joachim Church of Fargo, Fargo, ND

Meyer, Rev. Michael W., '93 (LA) Retired.

Meyer, Rev. Msgr. Robert G., '74 (WIN) Retired.

Meyer, Rev. Robert J., '64 (PIT) Retired. [MON] St. John Vianney Manor, Pittsburgh, PA

Meyer, Rev. Msgr. Robert S., '88 (NEW) Saint Teresa of Avila, Summit, NJ

Meyer, Rev. Ronald J., *OMI* '71 (BO) [MIS] St. Joseph the Worker Shrine, Lowell, MA; [MON] Missionary Oblates of Mary Immaculate Northern Province, Lowell, MA

Meyer, Rev. Stephen L., '79 (DUB) Retired.

Meyer, Rev. Steven, '90 (FAR) St. Joseph Church of Tolna, Tolna, ND; St. Lawrence O'Toole's Church of Michigan, Michigan, ND; St. Mary's Church of Lakota, Lakota, ND

Meyer, Rev. Thomas C., '98 (SFD) Blessed Sacrament, Quincy, IL

Meyer, Rev. William, *S.M.* '79 (SAT) [COL] St. Mary's University of San Antonio, Texas, San Antonio, TX

Meyer, Rev. William J., *S.M.* '79 (SAT) [MON] Ligustrum Marianist Community, San Antonio, TX

Meyers, Rev. James P., '70 (WDC) Retired.

Meyers, Rev. Msgr. Michael W., '77 (LA) Curia: Pastoral Services St. James, Redondo Beach, CA

Meyers, Rev. Nathaniel, '10 (STP) Curia: Leadership St. Francis Xavier, Buffalo, MN; [CEM] Saint Francis Xavier Cemetery, Buffalo, MN; [CEM] St. Mark's Cemetery, Buffalo, MN

Meyers, Rev. Robert V., '87 (MET) Curia: Tribunal Our Lady of Fatima, Piscataway, NJ

Meystrik, Very Rev. Gregory C., '90 (JC) Curia: Advisory Boards, Commissions, Committees, and Councils; Deaneries Immaculate Conception, St. James, MO; St. Anthony, Rosati, MO; St. Patrick, Rolla, MO; [CAM] Catholic Newman Center, Missouri University of Science and Technology, Rolla, MO

Meza, Rev. Msgr. Arturo, '88 (AMA) Elizabeth Ann Seton, Turkey, TX; Our Lady of Loretto, Silverton, TX

Meza, Rev. Fernando, (SAC) Pastor of St. Francis of Assisi Parish, Burney, a corporation sole, Burney, CA

Mezquida, Rev. Ramon, '58 (PCE) Retired. On Leave.

Mezydlo, Rev. James A., '77 (CHI) Retired. Curia: Leadership

Mfesao, Rev. Francis, *CICM* '06 (ARL) [MON] Missionhurst, C.I.C.M.-Central House and Provincialate (American I.H.M. Province, Inc., Immaculate Heart Missions, Inc., Missionhurst, Inc.), Arlington, VA

Mganga, Rev. Claudius Mpuya, '93 (SP) Our Lady of Fatima, Inverness, FL

Mgbaramuko, Rev. Modestus, (OAK) Curia: Offices and Directors

Mgbeajuo, Rev. Donatus, *M.S.P.* '97 (BEA) Chap, Baptist Hosp

Mgendwa, Rev. Felice Peter, '03 (SFE) Nuestra Senora De Guadalupe-Taos, Taos, NM

Mgimba, Rev. Thadeo E., '08 (CHI) St. Agatha and St. Martin De Porres Parish, Chicago, IL

Mgonja, Rev. Godfrey, *C.S.Sp.* (DET) St. Mary Parish Detroit, Detroit, MI

Miah, Rev. Gabriel, '77 (RVC) Our Lady of Grace, West Babylon, NY

Miara, Rev. James L., '01 (NY) Holy Innocents, New York, NY

Micale, Rev. Christopher, '14 (BUR) Curia: Leadership; Offices and Directors Holy Angels, St. Albans, VT; Immaculate Conception, St. Albans, VT

Micaphitak, Rev. Chakrit, *C.Ss.R.* '06 (MIL) St. Michael's Congregation, Milwaukee, WI; The Congregation of St. Rose, Milwaukee, WI

Micarelli, Rev. Edmond C., '59 (PRO) Retired.

Micca, Rev. Louis F., *S.A.C.* '66 (WDC) [SEM] Pallottine Seminary at Green Hill, West Hyattsville, MD

Micciulla, Rev. Angelo J., '05 (NY) Holy Family, Staten Island, NY

Micele, Rev. Philip, (NEW) Our Lady of Grace and Saint Joseph Parish, Hoboken, NJ

Miceli, Rev. John P., '94 (CLV) On Leave.

Miceli, Rev. Michael A., '97 (BR) Curia: Administration Congregation Of St. Patrick Roman Catholic Church, Baton Rouge, LA

Miceli, Rev. Paul E., '72 (BO) [SEM] Pope Saint John XXIII National Seminary, Weston, MA

Miceli, Rev. Ross R., '10 (E) St. Jude the Apostle, Erie, PA

Miceli, Rev. Vincent F., '91 (BRK) St. Frances Cabrini, Brooklyn, NY

Mich, Rev. Kenneth A., '70 (MIL) Retired.

Michael, Rev. Antony Samy, *HGN* '13 (FAR) Seven Dolors of Fort Totten, Fort Totten, ND

Michael, Rev. Carles Raj, *O.C.D.* (ELP) St. Thomas & St. Joseph, Kermit, TX

Michael, Rev. David, *H.G.N.* '10 (SAL) Immaculate Heart of Mary Parish, Hays, Inc., Hays, KS

Michael, Rev. David, '96 (CHR) Our Lady Star of the Sea, North Myrtle Beach, SC

Michael, Rev. David, (WCH) St. John, Iola, KS; St. Joseph, Yates Center, KS

Michael, Rev. David C., '86 (BO) Curia: Pastoral Services St. John the Evangelist, Beverly, MA; St. Margaret, Beverly, MA; St. Mary Star of the Sea, Beverly, MA

Michael, Rev. George, *V.C.* '95 (SCL) Church of Saint Henry, Perham, Perham, MN; Church of the Sacred Heart, Dent, MN; Holy Cross, Butler, MN; St. Lawrence, Perham, MN

Michael, Rev. Msgr. Kenneth, '65 (OLL) Retired.

Michael, Rev. Lawrence, (SAM) Retired.

Michael, Rev. Soosairaj, '15 (NY) St. Gregory the Great, Harrison, NY

Michael, Rev. Tukura Pius, *O.P.* (HBG) Chap, Selinsgrove Ctr [CAM] Susquehanna University Catholic Campus Ministry, Selinsgrove, PA

Michael Pandi, Rev. Arockiaraj (Raj), (P) St. Mary, Eugene, OR

Michaels, Rev. Dana P., '82 (OAK) Retired.

Michaels, Rev. Patrick T., '82 (SFR) Our Lady of Mt. Carmel, Mill Valley, CA

Michaelsamy, Rev. Francis, '88 (NY) St. Ursula, Mount Vernon, NY

Michaelson, Rev. Sean D., *S.J.* '06 (WDC) [EFT] Jesuit Health Trust, Washington, DC; [MIS] Jesuit Conference, Inc., Washington, DC; [MIS] Jesuit Missions, Inc., Washington, DC; [MON] Leonard Neale House, Washington, DC; [MON] The Jesuit Community of St. Aloysius Gonzaga, Washington, DC

Michalak, Rev. Jan, *O.S.P.P.E.* '81 (PH) [MON] The Order of Saint Paul, First Hermit - The Pauline Fathers, Doylestown, PA

Michalak, Rev. Jaromir, '91 (CAM) St. Joseph's Church, Somers Point, N.J., Somers Point, NJ

Michalak, Rev. Marcin, '13 (JOL) St. Joseph, Bradley, IL

Michalchuk, Rev. Jack H., '01 (ALX) On Leave.

Michalczak, Rev. John T., '70 (NEW) Retired. Curia: Organizations (affiliated, inter-Diocesan, miscellaneous/ other) [HOS] Trinitas Regional Medical Center (Sisters of Charity of Saint Elizabeth and Elizabethtown Healthcare Foundation), Elizabeth, NJ

Michalek, Rev. Msgr. George C., '78 (LAN) Curia: Leadership; Offices and Directors St. Mary Parish Morrice, Morrice, MI

Michalek, Rev. Stanislaw, (DEN) St. Joseph Polish Catholic Parish in Denver, Denver, CO

Michalenko, Rev. Alexei, '68 (HPM) Retired.

Michalik, Rev. Anthony, *C.Ss.R.* '15 (BO) Our Lady of Perpetual Help, Boston, MA

Michalik, Rev. Anthony, *C.Ss.R.* '15 (BO) Curia: Consultative Bodies

Michalik, Rev. Gary, '80 (DET) St. Colette Parish Livonia, Livonia, MI

Michalowski, Rev. John, *S.J.* '81 (CHL) St. Peter, Charlotte, NC; [MON] St. Peter Jesuit Community, Charlotte, NC

Michalowski, Rev. Marcin, '11 (PAT) Curia: Leadership Our Lady of the Mountain, Long Valley, NJ; St. Mark the Evangelist, Long Valley, NJ

Michalowski, Rev. Pawel, *SDB* '03 (MET) Blessed Sacrament, Martinsville, NJ

Michalski, Rev. Edward, '80 (WOR) Our Lady of Czestochowa, Worcester, MA

Michalski, Rev. Jan, *TChr* '86 (DET) Our Lady of Czestochowa (Polish) Parish Sterling Heights, Sterling Heights, MI

Michalski, Rev. Michael F., '76 (MIL) Retired.

Michalski, Rev. Simon-Felix, *OP* '08 (IND) St. Paul Catholic Center, Bloomington, Inc., Bloomington, IN

Michatek, Rev. William C., '66 (ROC) Retired.

Michaud, Rev. Gregory A., '09 (LC) St. Mary, Neillsville, WI; [EFT] The St. Mary's Catholic Church Endowment Trust, Neillsville, WI

Michayel, Rev. Thomas E., *R.C.J.* '12 (FRS) St. Anthony of Padua, Reedley, CA

Michelini, Rev. Edward L., '05 (SCR) Retired. Our Lady of Perpetual Help Parish, Wyalusing, PA

Michelini, Rev. Michael S., '71 (CHI) Retired.

Michell, Rev. Timothy, *O.C.S.O.* '65 (P) [MON] The Cistercian (Trappist) Abbey of Our Lady of Guadalupe (Order of Cistercians of the Strict Observance), Carlton, OR

Michels, Rev. Andrew J., '85 (NU) Curia: Organizations (affiliated, inter-Diocesan, miscellaneous/other) Holy Redeemer, Marshall, MN; St. Mary, Cottonwood, MN; St. Mary, Tracy, MN; St. Michael, Milroy, MN

Michelson, Rev. Chris, '80 (KNX) Saint Joseph School of Knoxville, Knoxville, TN; St. Albert the Great Church, Knoxville, TN

Michiels, Rev. Kenneth J., '91 (ALX) Curia: Miscellaneous / Other Offices St. Michael, Leesville, LA

Michiels, Rev. Philip F., '69 (SHP) Retired. Curia: Leadership

Michini, Rev. F. Joseph, *S.J.* '80 (BAL) Retired. [MIS] Colombiere Jesuit Community, Baltimore, MD

Michka, Rev. Aaron, *CSC* (FTW) [COL] University of Notre Dame Du Lac, Notre Dame, IN; [MON] Holy Cross Community, Corby Hall, University of Notre Dame, Notre Dame, IN

Michler, Rev. James R., '75 (STL) On Duty Outside Diocese. La Paz St. Cecilia Catholic Church, St. Louis, MO

Michlik, Very Rev. Val, (PIT) Curia: Tribunal

Michlik, Rev. Valerian M., '00 (PBR) Curia: Leadership St. Gregory Nazianzus, Upper St. Clair, PA

Michniewicz, Rev. Martin E., '86 (CHI) St. Alexander, Palos Heights, IL

Michniuk, Rev. John J., '12 (COV) On Administrative Leave.

Mick, Rev. Lawrence E., '72 (CIN) Retired. [MIS] St. Leonard Faith Community, Centerville, OH

Mickey, Rev. Richard L., '88 (MEM) Curia: Organizations (affiliated, inter-Diocesan, miscellaneous/ other) [MON] Villa Vianney Senior Priests Residence, Cordova, TN

Mickiewicz, Rev. David, '84 (ALB) Curia: Offices and Directors St. Mary, Albany, NY; St. Mary, Oneonta, NY

Miclot, Rev. Brian, '74 (DAV) Retired.

Midor, Rev. Adam, '91 (TR) Capital Health Sys - Mercer & Fuld Campuses St. Vincent de Paul, Trenton, NJ

Midzak, Archpriest Ihor, '90 (STF) Curia: Leadership; Offices and Directors St. Vladimir Cathedral, Stamford, CT
Mien, Rev. Francis, '65 (SEA) Retired.
Mierenfeld, Rev. Lawrence E., '73 (CIN) Retired.
Mierzwa, Rev. Ronald B., '76 (BUF) Retired. On Administrative Leave.
Mierzwa, Rev. Tadeusz, '92 (NEW) St. Theresa of the Child Jesus, Linden, NJ
Mifsud, Rev. Carmelo, '59 (OAK) Retired.
Migac, Rev. Stefan, '14 (RIC) St. Patrick, Lexington, VA; [CAM] Catholic Campus Ministry, Washington & Lee Univ. & VMI (Lexington Catholic Campus Ministry), Lexington, VA
Migone, Very Rev. Pablo, '09 (SAV) Curia: Leadership; Offices and Directors Our Lady of Lourdes, Port Wentworth, GA
Miguel, Rev. Matthew, '21 (LA) Our Lady of the Assumption, Ventura, CA
Miguelez, Rev. Msgr. Valeriano, '66 (SJN) Curia: Offices and Directors Colegio Espiritu Santo, San Juan, PR; Espiritu Santo, Hato Rey, PR; [HOS] Hospital Pavia, Hato Rey, PR; [SPF] Centro Medico de P.R., San Juan, PR
Miguez, Rev. Raul G., '99 (NY) Parish of St. Brendan and St. Ann, Bronx, NY; St. Ann, Bronx, NY
Mihalak, Rev. James J., '76 (ALN) Retired.
Mihalco, Rev. John J., '83 (PBR) SS. Cyril and Methodius, Girard, PA; SS. Peter and Paul, Erie, PA
Mihalic, Rev. Peter M., '76 (CLV) Retired.
Mihalik, Rev. Msgr. Alexis E., '64 (PBR) Retired.
Mijas, Rev. Paul, (ALB) Cathedral of the Immaculate Conception, Albany, NY; Sacred Heart, Margaretville, NY
Mijinke, Rev. Chrysotom, *O.P.* (SEA) [CAM] University of Washington, Catholic Newman Center, Seattle, WA
Mikalajunas, Rev. Canon John E., '69 (SY) Holy Trinity, Utica, NY
Mikalofsky, Rev. Hilarion A., '75 (MIL) Retired.
Mikalonis, Rev. Estanislao, '05 (SJ) St. Thomas Aquinas, Palo Alto, CA
Mikes, Rev. Pavel, '90 (FAR) On Duty Outside Diocese. Austria
Mikesch, Rev. Msgr. Gregory R., '75 (STL) Cathedral Basilica of Saint Louis Catholic Church, St. Louis, MO; [MIS] Archdiocesan Stewardship Education Committee, St. Louis, MO; [RTR] Vision of Peace Ministries, Pevely, MO; [SEM] Kenrick School of Theology, ,
Mikhael, Rev. Elie, '95 (SAM) Saint Anthony Maronite Catholic Church, Inc., Lawrence, MA
Mikkelson, Rev. Scott, '82 (AUS) Retired.
Mikobi, Rev. Alidor, (LA) St. Cyprian, Long Beach, CA
Mikolajczyk, Rev. Edward M., '73 (CHI) Retired. Curia: Leadership Our Lady of the Woods, Orland Park, IL
Mikolajewski, Rev. Daniel, '22 (MAN) Parish of the Assumption, Dover, NH
Mikonis, Rev. Gerald S., '74 (PIT) Retired. Chap, Mon Valley Hosp, Washington Cty St. Andrew the Apostle, Donora, PA
Miksch, Rev. Joseph A., '66 (OM) St. Isidore, Columbus, NE
Mikulanis, Very Rev. Msgr. Dennis, '77 (SD) Curia: Advisory Boards, Commissions, Committees, and Councils; Offices and Directors Pastor of San Rafael Catholic Parish, San Diego, a corporation sole, San Diego, CA; [CEM] Holy Cross Cemetery and Mausoleum, San Diego, CA; [MIS] Catholic Cemeteries of San Diego and Imperial Counties, San Diego, CA
Mikulcik, Rev. Ken, '98 (OWN) Sacred Heart, Russellville, KY; St. Francis of Assisi Catholic Church, Guthrie, KY
Mikulcik, Rev. Kenneth J., '98 (OWN) Curia: Organizations (affiliated, inter-Diocesan, miscellaneous/ other)
Mikulski, Rev. Marcim, (CHI)
Mikulski, Rev. Marcin, (PH) [MON] The Order of Saint Paul, First Hermit - The Pauline Fathers, Doylestown, PA
Mikwabe, Rev. Peter, (HEL) Saint Francis Parish: Series 352, LLC, Valier, MT; Saint Margaret Parish: Series 322, LLC, Cut Bank, MT; Saint William Parish: Series 346, LLC, Shelby, MT
Milanese, Rev. John M., '74 (BUR) Retired. [CAM] Vermont Technical College, Randolph, VT
Milani, Rev. Olmes, *C.S.* (PMB) Our Lady Queen of Peace, Delray Beach, FL
Milano, Rev. Cleo J., '83 (BR) Congregation Of Our Lady Of Mercy Roman Catholic Church, Baton Rouge, LA
Milanowski, Rev. Paul, '65 (GR) Retired.
Milbauer, Rev. Msgr. Robert L., '66 (LA) Retired. St. John Baptist de la Salle, Granada Hills, CA
Milby, Rev. Larry, (BUF) Retired. [MON] Bishop Head Residence, Lackawanna, NY
Milby, Rev. Lawrence M., '65 (BUF) Retired.
Milek, Rev. Richard, (CHI) St. Francis Xavier, La Grange, IL
Miles, Rev. Andrew, *O.S.B.* '60 (SFE) On Duty Outside Diocese. [MON] Our Lady of Guadalupe Abbey, Pecos, NM
Miles, Very Rev. C. Thomas, '99 (CHR) Curia: Advisory Boards, Commissions, Committees, and Councils; Tribunal St. Elizabeth Ann Seton, Simpsonville, SC
Miles, Rev. Michael Taras, (STN) Retired.
Miles, Rev. Richard M., '84 (NO) Retired.
Mileski, Rev. Christopher M., '13 (TOL) Most Pure Heart of Mary, Shelby, OH; St. Joseph, Plymouth, OH
Milewski, Rev. Casimir, '69 (TR) Retired.
Milewski, Rev. Douglas J., '89 (NEW) [SEM] Immaculate Conception Seminary School of Theology, South Orange, NJ
Milewski, Rev. John, (RIC) Military Chap
Miley, Rev. Eamon, '73 (MOB) Retired. St. Bridget, Whistler, AL
Miley, Rev. Mark H., '13 (LAF) Curia: Leadership Our Lady of the Holy Rosary, Kaplan, LA
Miliauskas, Rev. Tomas, (DET) On Special Assignment. Divine Providence Church, Springfield, MI Divine Providence (Lithuanian) Parish Southfield, Southfield, MI
Milich, Rev. Nicholas A., '01 (YAK) Retired.
Milik, Rev. Adrian A., '12 (BO) Curia: Clergy and Religious Services Holy Ghost, Whitman, MA; St. Bridget, Abington, MA
Milimo, Rev. Humphrey, *OMI* (SAT) Holy Family, San Antonio, TX
Millan, Rev. Jose Luis, '00 (SPK) St. Joseph, Otis Orchards, WA
Millane, Rev. Msgr. Thomas J., '63 (TUC) Retired.
Millar, Rev. Alexander, '15 (PEO) St. John's Catholic Chapel, Champaign, IL; [CAM] Newman Foundation at the University of IL (St. John's Catholic Newman Center), Champaign, IL
Millbourn, Rev. Richard, *S.J.* '01 (CIN) [MON] Jesuit Community at St. Xavier High School, Cincinnati, OH
Millea, Rev. Thomas V., '57 (CHI) Retired.
Millea, Rev. Msgr. William V., '80 (BGP) On Duty Outside Diocese. Rome
Miller, Rev. Abraham, (SEA) Chap, Veterans Admin Med Ctr
Miller, Rev. Abraham, (STN) Curia: (>MO) Offices and Directors
Miller, Rev. Abraham, '79 (STN) Curia: Offices and Directors Our Lady of Zarvanycia, Seattle, WA
Miller, Rev. Bert, '91 (FAR) St. Luke's Church of Veseleyville, Grafton, ND; St. Mary Church of Park River, Park River, ND
Miller, Rev. Bertin, *O.F.M.* '64 (STL) [MON] Franciscan Friars Province of the Sacred Heart, Dittmer, MO; [RTR] Il Ritiro-The Little Retreat (Il Ritiro Franciscan Retreat Center), Dittmer, MO
Miller, Rev. Brian M., '10 (ALN) Curia: Leadership St. Catharine of Siena, Reading, PA
Miller, Rev. Msgr. Bruce, '77 (NO) Retired.
Miller, Rev. Byron J., *C.Ss.R.* '90 (STL) [MIS] Redemptorist Fathers, Liguori, MO; [MON] St. Clement Health Care Center, Liguori, MO
Miller, Rev. Charles, *O.F.M.* (WDC) Retired. [SEM] Holy Name College, Silver Spring, MD
Miller, Rev. Charles Anthony, '80 (HBG) St. Aloysius, Littlestown, PA
Miller, Rev. Charles J., '72 (NEW) Retired.
Miller, Rev. Charles M., '91 (SB) Queen of Angels, Idyllwild, CA
Miller, Rev. Christopher J., '08 (LIN) St. Patrick's, Lincoln, NE
Miller, Rev. Christopher T., '93 (LFT) Our Lady of the Lakes, Monticello, IN; St. Joseph, Delphi, IN; St. Joseph, Reynolds, IN
Miller, Rev. Curtis, '16 (BUR) Most Holy Trinity, Barton, VT; [CAM] Lyndon State College, St. Johnsbury, VT
Miller, Rev. Msgr. D. Bruce, '77 (ALX) Retired. (>NO) [SEM] Saint Joseph Seminary College, Saint Benedict, LA
Miller, Rev. David L., '81 (SPC) Retired.
Miller, Rev. David L., '19 (R) Curia: Offices and Directors St. Mildred, Swansboro, NC
Miller, Rev. David P., '10 (CHL) St. Dorothy, Lincolnton, NC
Miller, Rev. Dennis W., '02 (DUB) St. Patrick Church, Cedar Rapids, Iowa, Cedar Rapids, IA
Miller, Rev. Francis, *O.C.D.* '49 (WDC) Retired.
Miller, Rev. Franklin, '89 (FAR) Curia: Leadership Our Lady of Mt. Carmel Church of Balta, Balta, ND; St. Mary's Church of Knox, Knox, ND; St. Theresa, Little Flower Church of Rugby, Rugby, ND
Miller, Rev. Frederick L., '72 (NEW) Curia: Organizations (affiliated, inter-Diocesan, miscellaneous/ other) [COL] Seton Hall University, South Orange, NJ; [SEM] College Seminary of the Immaculate Conception (Saint Andrew's Hall), South Orange, NJ
Miller, Rev. George, '78 (DET) Retired.
Miller, Rev. Gregory, *O.S.B.* '73 (SCL) Seven Dolors, Albany, MN; St. Anthony Catholic Church, Albany, MN; St. Benedict's, Avon, MN; St. Martin, St. Martin, MN; [MON] St. John's Abbey, of the Order of St. Benedict, Collegeville, MN
Miller, Rev. Jake, '01 (FAR) Holy Spirit Church of Nortonville, Nortonville, ND; Transfiguration Church of Edgeley, Edgeley, ND
Miller, Rev. James, *C.PP.S.* '54 (CIN) Retired.
Miller, Rev. Msgr. James L., '76 (DUB) Retired. Curia: Leadership
Miller, Rev. James Norman, '59 (NSH) Retired.
Miller, Rev. James P., (SAT) Retired. [NUR] Oblate Madonna Residence, San Antonio, TX
Miller, Rev. James W., '67 (CHI) [EFT] Divine Word Techny Community Corporation, Techny, IL
Miller, Rev. Jayson, '17 (FAR) On Special Assignment. Curia: Leadership; Offices and Directors
Miller, Rev. Jeremy P., '13 (TOL) Corpus Christi (University of Toledo), Toledo, OH
Miller, Rev. John A., '08 (TOL) Regina Coeli, Toledo, OH; St. Mary of the Snows, Mansfield, OH; St. Peter, Mansfield, OH
Miller, Rev. John C., '95 (BRK) On Leave.
Miller, Rev. John L., '09 (E) St. Joseph, Oil City, PA; [CAM] Clarion State University of PA - Venango Campus, Oil City, PA
Miller, Rev. John L., '09 (E) Chap, Polk Ctr
Miller, Rev. Joseph A., '89 (BRK) On Leave.
Miller, Rev. Joseph K., '57 (SAG) Retired.
Miller, Rev. Joshua, '10 (JOL) Assumption of the Blessed Virgin Mary, Coal City, IL; Immaculate Conception, Braidwood, IL
Miller, Rev. Justin D., '16 (ROC) St. John the Evangelist, Spencerport, NY
Miller, Rev. Msgr. Kenneth E, '77 (Y) Retired.
Miller, Rev. Msgr. Kenneth E., '77 (Y) Retired.
Miller, Rev. Kevin M., '21 (SCR) Curia: Leadership Most Holy Trinity Parish, Susquehanna, PA; Saint Brigid Parish, Friendsville, PA
Miller, Rev. Msgr. Lawrence J., '69 (NEW) Retired.
Miller, Rev. Mardean E., '94 (PH) St. Anne, Philadelphia, PA
Miller, Rev. Mark, '69 (ROC) Retired.
Miller, Rev. Mark, *C.PP.S.* '71 (KC) [MON] Society of the Precious Blood, Liberty, MO
Miller, Rev. Mark A., '15 (LC) Immaculate Conception, Custer, WI; Sacred Heart, Custer, WI; [EFT] Sacred Heart School, Polonia Endowment Trust, Custer, WI
Miller, Rev. Mark O., '05 (PEO) St. Patrick's, Sheffield, IL
Miller, Rev. Mark W., '12 (MAD) St. Francis of Assisi, Belleville, WI
Miller, Rev. Martin J., '02 (PIT) [MIS] Prelature of the Holy Cross and Opus Dei, Pittsburgh, PA
Miller, Rev. Martin John, '02 (POD) Curia: Clergy and Religious Services
Miller, Rev. Martin Joseph, '94 (POD) Curia: Clergy and Religious Services
Miller, Rev. Matthew, '20 (DUL) St. Francis, Brainerd, MN
Miller, Rev. Matthew, '20 (DUL) All Saints, Brainerd, MN; St. Thomas, Brainerd, MN
Miller, Rev. Meinrad, *O.S.B.* '94 (KCK) St. Benedict, Atchison, KS; [COL] Benedictine College, Atchison, KS; [MON] St. Benedict's Abbey, Atchison, KS
Miller, Rev. Michael J., '72 (MRY) On Special Assignment. St Margaret Mary Church, Chino
Miller, Rev. Michael J., '96 (STP) St. Patrick of Cedar Lake Township, Jordan, MN; [CEM] Saint Catherine Cemetery, Jordan, MN; [CEM] Saint Patrick Cemetery, Jordan, MN
Miller, Rev. Peter, *O.S.B.* '15 (TLS) [MON] Our Lady of the Annunciation of Clear Creek Abbey, Hulbert, OK
Miller, Rev. Philip, '77 (Y) Retired. Corpus Christi Parish, Conneaut, OH; St. Andrew Bobola, Kingsville, OH
Miller, Rev. Robert J., '76 (CHI) Retired.
Miller, Rev. Robert J., (PIT) Curia: Consultative Bodies
Miller, Rev. Robert J., '80 (PIT) Curia: Consultative Bodies Our Lady of Mount Carmel, Pittsburgh, PA
Miller, Rev. Robert M., '92 (PIT) St. John XXIII, McMurray, PA
Miller, Rev. Robert M., '02 (Y) Retired.
Miller, Rev. Scott Jeffrey, '21 (SFS) Saint Michael Parish of Minnehaha County, Sioux Falls, SD

Miller, Rev. Theodore J., '75 (TOL) Retired.

Miller, Rev. Thomas C., '93 (STL) Immaculate Heart of Mary Catholic Church, New Melle, New Melle, MO

Miller, Rev. Thomas R., '77 (PIT) Christ the Divine Shepherd, Monroeville, PA

Miller, Rev. Vincent, '98 (CR) Curia: Offices and Directors St. Joseph's, Moorhead, MN

Miller, Rev. Walter, *S.V.D.* '69 (CHI) [MON] Divine Word Residence, Techny, IL

Miller, Rev. Whitney, '80 (LKC) Curia: Advisory Boards, Commissions, Committees, and Councils Immaculate Conception of the B.V.M., Sulphur, LA

Miller, Rev. William, *C.PP.S.* '63 (CIN) Retired. [MON] St. Charles, Celina, OH

Miller, Rev. William, '91 (LKC) St. Lawrence, Jennings, LA

Miller, Rev. William T., '84 (PEO) Sacred Heart, Peoria, IL; St. Bernard's, Peoria, IL; St. Joseph, Peoria, IL; St. Mary's Cathedral, Peoria, IL; [ASN] St. Joseph's Cemetery Association of Galesburg, IL, Galesburg, IL; [MIS] Family Resource Center, Peoria, IL

Miller, Rev. Zachary K., '15 (SY) Christ the King, Liverpool, NY; Pope John XXIII RC Church, Liverpool, NY

Milless, Rev. Marcus F., '14 (STP) St. Helena, Minneapolis, MN

Millette, Rev. R. Lucien (Luke), '12 (GAL) Curia: Leadership

Milliken, Rev. Damian J., *O.S.B.* '58 (PAT) [MON] St. Paul's Abbey (Order of St. Benedict, Congregation of St. Ottilien), Newton, NJ

Milliken, Rev. David W., '77 (NEW) Retired.

Milling, Rev. Robert T., '04 (BO) Retired.

Millisor, Rev. Daniel J., '86 (COL) [COL] Ohio Dominican University, Columbus, OH

Millott, Rev. Thirburse F., '75 (WOR) Retired.

Mills, Rev. Alexander, '80 (TUC) Retired.

Mills, Rev. Brad, *SJ* (SD) Pastor of Our Lady of Guadalupe Catholic Parish, San Diego, a corporation sole, San Diego, CA

Mills, Rev. Elias, (NOR) [MON] Marian Friary of Our Lady of Guadalupe, Griswold, CT

Mills, Rev. Gabriel V, '20 (MOB) Christ the King Parish, Daphne, Daphne, AL

Mills, Rev. Steven A., '13 (LIN) On Academic Leave. Benedictine College, Atchison, KS Pius X Catholic High School, Lincoln, NE; St. John the Apostle, Lincoln, NE

Miloscia, Rev. David, (MO) Curia: Offices and Directors

Miloscia, Rev. David M., '15 (STL) Military Chap

Miloscia, Rev. Samuel, (KC) St. Margaret of Scotland Catholic Church, Lees Summit, MO

Milosz, Rev. Bogdan, '81 (DET) St. Faustina Parish Warren, Warren, MI

Milota, Rev. Thomas, '92 (JOL) St. Petronille, Glen Ellyn, IL

Milsted, Rev. Gordon N., '63 (MOB) Retired.

Milton, Rev. Anton y, (DET) [RTR] Capuchin Retreat, Washington, MI

Milton, Rev. David, *H.G.N.* (BLX) Our Lady of Chartres, Gulfport, MS

Milton, Rev. Hilary, *O.Carm.* '63 (NEW) St. Cecilia, Englewood, NJ

Milunski, Rev. Brad A., *O.F.M.Conv.* '93 (SPR) St. Stanislaus Basilica, Chicopee, MA

Mimnaugh, Rev. Stephen D, (BUF) [CAM] St. Bonaventure University, St. Bonaventure, NY

Mina, Rev. John L., '89 (PBR) Ascension of Our Lord, Clairton, PA

Minardi, Rev. Antony, *O.S.B.* '18 (RCK) [MON] Marmion Abbey, Aurora, IL

Minasian, Rev. Asadur, '21 (OLN) St. Mark's Armenian Catholic, Wynnewood, PA

Minch, Rev. Richard, '69 (SAV) Retired.

Minde, Rev. John, (LAV) St. Francis of Assisi, Henderson, NV

Mindling, Rev. Daniel, *O.F.M.Cap.* '80 (WDC) [SEM] St. Francis Friary-Capuchin College, Washington, DC

Mindling, Rev. J. Daniel, *O.F.M.Cap.* '80 (BAL) [SEM] Mount St. Mary's Seminary, Emmitsburg, MD

Mindling, Rev. Joseph, *O.F.M.Cap.* '66 (WDC) (>PIT) [MON] St. Augustine Friary, Pittsburgh, PA

Mingollo, Rev. Rodrigo, (GF) Curia: Offices and Directors St. Mark the Evangelist, Belt, MT

Minh, Rev. Vu Duc, '80 (TLS) On Duty Outside Diocese. Holy Martyrs, Colorado Springs, CO

Minh Vu, Rev. Joseph P., '80 (COS) The Vietnamese Holy Martyrs Parish, Colorado Springs, CO

Miniatt, Rev. Nathaniel J., '14 (MIL) Curia: Leadership Sons of Zebedee: Ss. James and John Congregation, Fond du Lac, WI; St. Mary's Congregation, Lomira, WI

Minifie, Rev. Michael, (BEA) Cristo Rey, Beaumont, TX

Minigan, Rev. William J., '86 (BO) St. Joseph, Malden, MA

Minimo, Rev. Lauro, '14 (SD) Curia: Advisory Boards, Commissions, Committees, and Councils Pastor of Our Lady of Grace Catholic Parish in El Cajon, CA, a corporation sole, El Cajon, CA; [MIS] Our Lady of Grace Catholic Parish in El Cajon, CA Real Property Support Corporation, El Cajon, CA

Minj, Rev. Nutan S., *I.M.S.* '97 (BR) The Congregation of St. Aloysius Roman Catholic Church, Baton Rouge, LA

Mink, Rev. John J., '85 (WIL) Chap, Delaware Air National Guard, New Castle Curia: Advisory Boards, Commissions, Committees, and Councils; (>MO) Offices and Directors St. Ann, Wilmington, DE

Minkel, Rev. William J., *O.F.M.* '05 (TUC) Curia: Consultative Bodies; Leadership San Solano Missions Roman Catholic Parish - Topawa, Topawa, AZ; [MON] San Francisco Solano Friary, Topawa, AZ

Minn, Rev. Augustine, *KMS* (AJ) St. John by the Sea, Klawock, AK

Minner, Rev. Ronald J., '01 (ALN) Chap, Luther Ridge Immaculate Conception, Jim Thorpe, PA

Minniti, Rev. Anthony L., '70 (CAM) Retired.

Minniti, Rev. David V., '72 (CAM) Retired.

Mino, Rev. Simon, '19 (Y) Holy Spirit, Uniontown, OH; St. Paul, North Canton, OH

Minogue, Rev. Michael J., '81 (PHX) Retired.

Mintah Mensah, Rev. Johnny, (RIC) Good Shepherd, South Hill, VA; St. Catherine of Siena, Clarksville, VA; St. Paschal Baylon, South Boston, VA

Minuth, Rev. Joseph M, *O.P.* '10 (SLC) Holy Family LLC 205, Ogden, UT

Minyati, Rev. Simon, (GB) St. Mary, Bear Creek, WI; St. Rose, Clintonville, WI

Minz, Rev. Arvind, (LKC) St. Peter the Apostle, Hackberry, LA

Miola, Rev. Luigi C., '77 (CLV) St. Benedict Catholic School, Garfield Heights, OH; St. Martin of Tours, Maple Heights, OH

Miquilena, Very Rev. Iden J. Bello, '05 (LAR) Curia: Leadership; Offices and Directors

Mira Alvarez, Rev. Victor Hugo, *SS.CC.* (SJN) Sagrados Corazones, Guaynabo, PR

Mirabelli, Rev. Daniel J., *C.S.V.* '60 (CHI) [MON] Viatorian Province Center-Clerics of St. Viator, Arlington Heights, IL

Mirabelli, Rev. Daniel J., *C.S.V.* '60 (PEO) Alleman High School, Rock Island, IL

Miracky, Rev. James J., *S.J.* '88 (NY) St. Francis Xavier, New York, NY; [MON] America; Residence and Publication Office of the America Press, New York, NY; [MON] Xavier Jesuit Community, New York, NY

Miracle, Rev. Jean Gustave, (BO) St. Angela Merici, Boston, MA

Miramontes, Rev. Francisco, '91 (SJ) St. Mary, Gilroy, CA

Miramontes, Rev. Jorge A., '11 (MAD) Holy Family Parish, Waterloo, WI

Miranda, Rev. Albert, '14 (TUC) Holy Angels Roman Catholic Church - Tucson, Globe, AZ

Miranda, Rev. John, '09 (LR) SS. Peter and Paul, Morrison Bluff, AR; St. Ignatius, Scranton, AR; St. Meinrad Church, Prairie View, AR

Miranda, Rev. Msgr. Lorenzo, '91 (LA) Curia: Offices and Directors

Miranda, Rev. Luis, *O.Carm.* '84 (SJN) Colegio Sagrada Familia, San Juan, PR

Miranda, Rev. Luke, '55 (FWT) Retired.

Miranda, Rev. R. Dario, '82 (LA) St. Rose of Lima, Maywood, CA

Miranda, Rev. Rohan, *O.C.D.* '06 (DEN) St. Thomas More Catholic Parish in Centennial, Centennial, CO

Miranda Perez, Rev. Yamil Alejandro, '15 (MIA) All Saints, Sunrise, FL

Miriyala, Rev. Balachandra Reddy, '02 (KCK) St. Francis de Sales, Lansing, KS

Miro Madariaga, Rev. Borja, (BO) [MON] Isaac Jogues House, Brighton, MA

Mirro, Rev. Joseph, '76 (RVC) Curia: Offices and Directors

Mirro, Rev. Msgr. Joseph A., '76 (RVC) Retired. Curia: Leadership St. Anthony of Padua, East Northport, NY

Mirsberger, Rev. Richard E., '66 (MIL) Retired.

Mirsel, Rev. Robert, *S.V.D.* (BRK) [CCH] Indonesian Ministry, ,

Mirto, Rev. Gregory, (GAL) St. Theresa, Sugar Land, TX

Misbrener, Rev. David M., '95 (Y) Our Lady of Lourdes, East Palestine, OH; St. Jude, Columbiana, OH

Miscamble, Rev. Wilson D., *C.S.C.* '88 (FTW) [COL] University of Notre Dame Du Lac, Notre Dame, IN; [MON] Congregation of Holy Cross, United States Province of Priests and Brothers, Notre Dame, IN

Mischke, Rev. Gerald, '64 (SCL) Retired.

Mischkowiuski, Rev. Henry B., '65 (LR) Retired.

Mischler, Rev. Thomas E., '81 (GRY) Curia: Leadership; Offices and Directors Holy Spirit, Crown Point, IN; St. Helen, Hebron, IN

Mischler, Rev. Thomas E., (GRY) St. Mary, Kouts, IN

Misenko, Rev. John A., '78 (CLV) Retired.

Miserendino, Rev. Richard A., '15 (ARL) St. Bernadette, Springfield, VA

Mishek, Rev. Nicholas A., '17 (OM) St. Rose of Lima, Hooper, NE

Misiuk, Rev. Bogumil, '16 (NEW) Seton Hall Preparatory School, West Orange, NJ; St. Catharine, Glen Rock, NJ

Miskell, Rev. Robert, '13 (SPR) St. Joseph's, Pittsfield, MA; [CAM] University of Massachusetts, Amherst, MA

Miskella, Rev. Richard, '65 (LA) Retired.

Miskin, Rev. Jon, (LR) St. Cecilia, Newport, AR; St. Mary, Batesville, AR; [CAM] Lyons College Catholic Campus Ministry, Batesville, AR

Misko, Very Rev. James A., '07 (AUS) Curia: Leadership

Missihoun, Rev. Jacques A., *O.S.B.* '10 (OM) [MON] Benedictine Mission House - Christ the King Priory, Schuyler, NE

Missimi, Rev. Msgr. Anthony N., '62 (COL) Retired.

Missler, Rev. John C., '78 (TOL) Immaculate Conception, Port Clinton, OH

Mistor, Rev. Todd C., '04 (DET) On Leave.

Misurda, Rev. Matthew, '77 (ALT) On Leave.

Mitas, Rev. Msgr. Matthew M., '79 (STL) St. Angela Merici Catholic Church, Florissant, MO

Mitchell, Rev. Charles I., '84 (ORL) St. Mary Magdalen, Altamonte Springs, FL

Mitchell, Rev. Colm B, '22 (CHI) St. Alexander, Palos Heights, IL

Mitchell, Rev. Darell J., '98 (YAK) Curia: Offices and Directors

Mitchell, Rev. Douglas J., '01 (SFE) Retired.

Mitchell, Rt. Rev. Eugene, *B.S.O.* '92 (NTN) Curia: Consultative Bodies St. Joseph, Akron, OH

Mitchell, Rev. Jason, '11 (E) [COL] Gannon University, Erie, PA

Mitchell, Rev. John, *S.J.* '72 (SFR) Chap, San Francisco Fire Department St. Ignatius College Preparatory (Coed), San Francisco, CA; [MON] Jesuit Community at St. Ignatius College Preparatory, San Francisco, CA

Mitchell, Rev. John J., '96 (STP) Curia: Leadership St Pascal Regional Catholic School, St. Paul, MN; St. Pascal Baylon, St. Paul, MN

Mitchell, Rev. John Paul, '16 (POD) Curia: Clergy and Religious Services

Mitchell, Rev. John Paul C., '13 (MIL) [SEM] Saint Francis de Sales Seminary, St. Francis, WI

Mitchell, Rev. Joseph, *C.P.* '81 (L) [MON] Sacred Heart Retreat, Louisville, KY

Mitchell, Rev. Joseph, '79 (SEA) Retired.

Mitchell, Rev. Mark E., '76 (GR) Retired.

Mitchell, Rev. Michael, *L.C.* '11 (CHI) [MON] Legion of Christ, Hickory Hills, IL

Mitchell, Rev. Michael, '05 (NO) Curia: Miscellaneous / Other Offices Our Lady of Divine Providence Roman Catholic Church, Metairie, Louisiana, Metairie, LA

Mitchell, Rev. Msgr. Michael J., '65 (SJ) Retired. [MIS] St. Joseph Cupertino Retirement Residence, Cupertino, CA

Mitchell, Rev. Mike, (CHL) St. Gabriel, Charlotte, NC

Mitchell, Rev. Peter, '78 (ORL) Retired.

Mitchell, Rev. Robert J., '85 (PAT) St. Patrick's, Chatham, NJ

Mitchell, Rev. Robert W., '73 (ORL) Retired.

Mitchican, Rev. Jonathan, '18 (POC) (>GAL) St. John XXIII College Preparatory, Katy, TX

Mitchko, Rev. James, '77 (PSC) On Leave.

Mitera, Rev. Andrzej, '94 (STA) Annunciation School, Middleburg, FL; St. Catherine of Siena, Orange Park, FL

Miti, Rev. Peter, '07 (HON) Curia: Consultative Bodies; Offices and Directors Resurrection of the Lord, Waipahu, HI

Mitka, Rev. John J., '66 (BUF) Retired. [MON] Msgr. Conniff Residence, Depew, NY

Mitolo, Rev. Frank, '68 (PIT) Chap, Villa St Joseph, Baden [CON] Sisters of St. Joseph, Baden, PA

Mitolo, Rev. Frank A., '68 (PIT) Retired.

Mitro, Rev. Lukas, (PRM) Curia: Advisory Boards, Commissions, Committees, and Councils Holy Resurrection Church, Euclid, OH

Mitten, Rev. Stephen F., *S.J.* '95 (CHI) [COL] Jesuit Community at Loyola University Chicago, Chicago, IL

Mitulski, Rev. James M., '72 (STL) St. Norbert Catholic Church, Florissant, MO
Mitzel, Rev. Daniel C., '81 (HBG) St. Francis Xavier, Gettysburg, PA
Miyares, Rev. Carlos, '81 (MIA) Retired.
Mizengo, Rev. Frederic, *C.I.C.M.* '13 (SAT) Curia: Administration Sacred Heart, San Antonio, TX
Mizeur, Rev. Thomas, '73 (PEO) Retired.
Mizicko, Rev. Carroll, *O.F.M.* '68 (BEL) Immaculate Conception, East Saint Louis, IL; St. Augustine of Hippo, East Saint Louis, IL; [MON] St. Benedict the Black Friary, East Saint Louis, IL
Miziuk, Rev. Vasyl, (STN) Holy Wisdom, Citrus Heights, CA; St. Andrew the Apostle, Sacramento, CA
Mizzi-Gill, Rev. Anthony, (NY) Holy Trinity, Poughkeepsie, NY
Mlaker, Rev. Jacob A., (CHL) Holy Cross, Kernersville, NC
Mlay, Rev. Mark, *A.L.C.P.* '84 (PMB) St. Clare, North Palm Beach, FL; [MIS] Adorer Missionary Sisters of the Poor, Port St. Lucie, FL
Mlelwa, Rev. Constantine, *OSA* (PIT) Archangel Gabriel, McKees Rocks, PA
Mleziva, Rev. Mark, (GB) Curia: Clergy and Religious Services
Mlsna, Rev. Todd A., '98 (LC) St. Stephen, Stevens Point, WI
Mlsna, Rev. Todd A., '98 (LC) Holy Spirit Parish, Stevens Point, WI; Pacelli Catholic High School, , ; Pacelli Catholic Middle School, Stevens Point, WI; St. Joseph, Stevens Point, WI; St. Peter, Stevens Point, WI
Mma, Rev. Nathaniel, (TUC) Holy Cross Roman Catholic Church - Morenci, Morenci, AZ; Sacred Heart Roman Catholic Church and St. Mary's Mission - Clifton, Clifton, AZ
Mmaduekwe, Rev. Charles, (DET) SS. Andrew and Benedict Parish Detroit, Detroit, MI
Moala, Rev. Saimone, '83 (SFR) Curia: Offices and Directors
Moat, Rev. Charles, *SVD* '19 (SD) [MIS] Saint John the Evangelist Catholic Parish San Diego in San Diego, CA Real Property Support Corporation, San Diego, CA
Moat, Rev. Charles A., (SD) Pastor of Saint John the Evangelist Catholic Parish, San Diego, a corporation sole, San Diego, CA
Moccia, Rev. Bonaventure, *C.P.* '52 (BRK) Retired.
Moccia, Rev. Bonaventure, *C.P.* '62 (NY) Retired.
Mocherla, Rev. Kondayya, *H.G.N.* '13 (STO) St. Patrick Church of Ripon (Pastor of), Ripon, CA
Mocio, Rev. Stephen J., '76 (DAL) St. Patrick Catholic Parish - Denison, Denison, TX; [CEM] St. Patrick Parish-Calvary Cemetery, Denison, TX
Mock, Rev. Robert M., '84 (BUF) Retired. South Buffalo Catholic School (Notre Dame Academy), Buffalo, NY
Mockaitis, Rev. Timothy J., '78 (P) Chap, Oregon State Corr Inst, Salem Curia: Offices and Directors Queen of Peace, Salem, OR
Mockel, Rev. George E., '75 (OAK) Curia: Leadership; Offices and Directors Santa Maria, Orinda, CA; [MIS] Catholic Management Services (CMS), Pleasanton, CA
Mockler, Rev. Patrick, (MO) Curia: Offices and Directors
Mockler, Rev. Patrick, '79 (JKS) Curia: Consultative Bodies
Mockler, Rev. Patrick J., '79 (BLX) Curia: Advisory Boards, Commissions, Committees, and Councils
Mockler, Rev. Patrick J., '79 (BLX) Chap, Naval Construction Battalion Ctr Curia: Advisory Boards, Commissions, Committees, and Councils Most Holy Trinity Parish, Pass Christian, MS
Moczulski, Rev. David, *O.F.M.* '93 (PIT) [CON] Sisters of Charity of Nazareth, Pittsburgh, PA; [MON] Holy Family Friary, Pittsburgh, PA
Moczydlowski, Rev. Msgr. Chester M., '73 (CHR) Retired.
Moczydlowski, Rev. Stanley M., '02 (ALN) St. Elizabeth of Hungary, Whitehall, PA
Modde, Rev. Bradley E., '97 (STL) St. Simon the Apostle Catholic Church, St. Louis, MO
Mode, Rev. Daniel L., '92 (ARL) On Duty Outside Diocese. Curia: (>MO) Offices and Directors Our Lady of Lourdes, Arlington, VA
Modebei, Rev. Sylvester, '03 (PHX) St. Mary Magdalene Roman Catholic Parish, Gilbert, AZ
Modeen, Rev. James, '81 (TUC) Retired.
Modlin, Rev. William F., '96 (PRT) Retired.
Modrys, Rev. Walter F., *S.J.* '78 (PH) (>NEW) [MON] Jesuits of Saint Peter College, Inc., Jersey City, NJ
Moebius, Rev. Kevin D., '20 (TOL) St. Mary of the Snows, Mansfield, OH; St. Peter, Mansfield, OH
Moeglein, Rev. James, *O.S.C.* '70 (SCL) [MON] Crosier Priory, Onamia, MN
Moellenberndt, Rev. Msgr. Duane R., '76 (MAD) Retired. Curia: Organizations (affiliated, inter-Diocesan, miscellaneous/other)
Moeller, Rev. Msgr. George B., '62 (BAL) Retired.
Moen, Rev. Brian, '03 (FAR) Curia: Leadership Sacred Heart Church of Minto, Minto, ND; St. Stanislaus Church of Warsaw, Warsaw, ND
Moenkedick, Rev. Leo, '86 (SCL) St. Gall, Tintah, MN; St. Mary of the Presentation, Breckenridge, MN; St. Thomas, Kent, MN; [NUR] St. Francis Home, Breckenridge, MN
Moerman, Rev. Stephen A., '94 (PH) Curia: Advisory Boards, Commissions, Committees, and Councils St. Isaac Jogues, Wayne, PA
Moeslein, Rev. Msgr. Francis R., '58 (R) Retired. St. Egbert, Morehead City, NC
Moffatt, Rev. Charles, *S.S.J.* (BAL) Retired.
Mohammed, Rev. Nigel R., '01 (NEW) St. Anne, Jersey City, NJ
Mohan, Rev. Bernard N., '61 (NEW) Retired.
Mohan, Rev. Brian, '05 (PBL) St. Mary's Med Center, Grand Junction, CO
Mohan, Rev. Kevin J., '13 (CAM) The Parish of Saint Monica, Atlantic City, NJ
Mohl, Rev. Andrew S., '84 (BAL) Retired.
Mohler, Rev. Jeremy J., '15 (PIT) Christ the Divine Shepherd, Monroeville, PA; [MIS] Christ Child Society of Pittsburgh, Pittsburgh, PA
Mohnickey, Rev. Ronald, *T.O.R.* '71 (FWT) Good Shepherd, Colleyville, TX
Mohr, Rev. J. Patrick, *S.J.* '75 (SCR) [COL] The University of Scranton, Scranton, PA
Mohrman, Rt. Rev. Gregory, *O.S.B.* '86 (STL) [MON] The Abbey of St. Mary and St. Louis, St. Louis, MO
Mohrman, Rev. J. Gregory, *O.S.B.* '86 (STL) St. Louis Priory School, Creve Coeur, MO
Moimoi, Rev. Salesi, '19 (SPP) Church of the Immaculate Conception, Pago Pago, AS
Moineau, Rev. John A., '87 (GBG) Curia: Offices and Directors Immaculate Conception, Irwin, PA; St. Elizabeth Ann Seton, North Huntingdon, PA
Moisant, Rev. William C., '01 (P) Chap, Coffee Creek Corr Fac, Wilsonville Resurrection Catholic Church, Tualatin, OR
Moisin, Very Rev. Michael, '88 (ROM) Curia: Offices and Directors Romanian Catholic Mission of Boston, Rockport, MA
Mojica, Rev. Luis A, '15 (MGZ) Ascension, Mayaguez, PR
Mojica Paez, Rev. Abelardo, (SJN) Ntra. Sra. del Rosario, Bayamon, PR
Mokluk, Rev. John M., *O.S.F.S.* '70 (WIL) Retired. [MON] Retirement and Assisted Care Facility, Childs, MD
Mol, Rev. Joseph C., '77 (CHI) Retired. Curia: Tribunal St. Albert the Great, Burbank, IL
Molano, Rev. Isaiah Mary, *O.P.* '10 (SFR) (>LA) St. Dominic, Los Angeles, CA
Moleke Akanang, Rev. Peter-Elvis, '12 (ATL) St. John Vianney Catholic Church, Lithia Springs, Inc., Lithia Springs, GA
Molengi, Rev. Prosper, '98 (SJ) Cathedral Basilica of St. Joseph, San Jose, CA
Molewski, Rev. Andrew, '82 (WIL) St. Hedwig, Wilmington, DE
Molewski, Rev. Pawel, '86 (NEW) Our Lady of Czestochowa, Harrison, NJ
Moley, Rev. Kevin, *C.Ss.R.* (HBG) [MON] St. Clement's Mission House, Ephrata, PA
Molgano, Rev. James, '03 (PMB) Retired.
Molina, Rev. Alfredo Valdez, '02 (PHX) La Santisima Trinidad Mission, A Quasi-Parish, Scenic, AZ
Molina, Rev. Angel, '94 (CGS) Curia: Leadership Inmaculada Concepcion, Juncos, PR
Molina, Rev. Arturo, '83 (LEX) Church of Jesus Our Savior, Morehead, KY; [CAM] Catholic Student Center-Morehead State University, Morehead, KY
Molina, Rev. Bolivar G., (CHI) Curia: (>MO) Offices and Directors
Molina, Rev. Joe, '95 (ELP) Curia: Advisory Boards, Commissions, Committees, and Councils St. Stephen, Deacon and Martyr, El Paso, TX
Molina, Rev. John, (HON) Sacred Heart, Pahoa, HI
Molina, Rev. John, *CRS* (HON) Curia: Consultative Bodies; Offices and Directors
Molina, Rev. Jonathan B., '04 (SAC) Curia: Offices and Directors Pastor of Holy Rosary Parish, Woodland, a corporation sole, Woodland, CA; Pastor of St. Paul Parish, Knights Landing, a corporation sole, Knights Landing, CA
Molina, Rev. Jorge Flores, (SEA) St. Francis Xavier, Toledo, WA; St. Joseph, Chehalis, WA; St. Mary, Centralia, WA
Molina, Rev. Jose, *I.V.E.* (PH) St. Veronica, Philadelphia, PA
Molina, Rev. Jose Ramon, (AMA) San Jose, Hereford, TX
Molina, Rev. Juan, '99 (SAT) [COL] The Mexican American Catholic College, San Antonio, TX; [MIS] Asociacion Nacional de Sacerdotes Hispanos, EEUU (Inc.), San Antonio, TX
Molina, Rev. Juan Francisco, '90 (TOL) SS. Peter and Paul, Toledo, OH
Molina, Rev. Rodel, (GBG) Mt. St. Peter, New Kensington, PA; St. Rose, Latrobe, PA
Molina, Rev. Rogelio, '19 (LAV) St. Francis de Sales, Las Vegas, NV
Molina, Rev. Seraphim, *S.T.* (PAT) [MON] Shrine of St. Joseph, Stirling, NJ
Molina Restrepo, Rev. Fernando, '99 (ATL) St. Thomas Aquinas Catholic Church, Alpharetta, Inc., Alpharetta, GA
Molina Torres, Rev. Robeth O., '08 (CHI) Curia: Tribunal
Molina-Juarez, Rev. Jaime, *M.N.M.* '88 (ATL) St. Thomas the Apostle Catholic Church, Smyrna, Inc., Smyrna, GA
Molina-Ramirez, Rev. Bolivar G., '06 (CHI) Our Lady of Mercy, Chicago, IL
Molina-Restrepo, Rev. Fernando, '99 (ATL) St. Thomas Aquinas Catholic Church, Alpharetta, Inc., Alpharetta, GA
Molinari, Rev. Todd, '95 (P) Curia: Offices and Directors
Molinaro, Rev. Kenneth M., *C.S.C.* '76 (COS) (>FTW) [MIS] Holy Cross House, Notre Dame, IN
Molinelli, Rev. Louis, (NY) [MON] Salesian Provincial House, New Rochelle, NY
Molini, Very Rev. Thomas M., '85 (STL) Curia: Leadership Ascension Catholic Church, Chesterfield, Chesterfield, MO; [SEM] Kenrick School of Theology, ,
Molka, Rev. Victor J., '78 (PIT) Chap, Ellwood City Hosp, Lawrence Cty; Jameson Care Ctr
Moll, Very Rev. Daniel J., '07 (MAR) Curia: Offices and Directors St. Christopher, Marquette, MI
Moll, Rev. Walter J., '85 (ALT) Retired.
Mollenhauer, Very Rev. Arthur C., '97 (BGP) Curia: Consultative Bodies; Leadership; Tribunal The Cathedral Parish, Bridgeport, CT
Molling, Rev. Mark L., '80 (MIL) Retired. St. Peters Congregation, East Troy, WI
Mollner, Rev. Jeffrey J., '08 (OM) St. Bernadette, Bellevue, NE
Molloy, Rev. Joseph M., '83 (SFD) St. Joseph the Worker, Chatham, IL
Molloy, Rev. Msgr. Thomas E., '70 (RVC) Retired.
Molnar, Rev. Michael, '76 (DET) Retired.
Molochko, Rev. Daniel, '19 (RIC) Incarnation Catholic Church, Charlottesville, VA
Molokie, Rev. Jerome M., *O.Praem.* '95 (ORG) [MON] Norbertine Fathers of Orange, Inc., Silverado, CA
Moloney, Rev. Daniel P., '10 (BO) On Duty Outside Diocese. Curia: Pastoral Services
Moloney, Rev. Msgr. James A., '56 (DET) Curia: Organizations (affiliated, inter-Diocesan, miscellaneous/other) St. Anselm Parish Dearborn Heights, Dearborn Heights, MI
Moloney, Rev. John, '72 (LA) Retired. On Sick Leave. St. Rose of Lima, Simi Valley, CA
Moloney, Rev. John C., '91 (PH) St. Kevin, Springfield, PA
Moloney, Rev. Michael, '12 (FWT) St. Boniface, Windthorst, TX; St. Mary, Windthorst, TX
Moloney, Rev. Patrick W., '77 (NTN) Retired.
Moloney, Rev. Msgr. Stephan J., '82 (COL) Curia: Consultative Bodies; Leadership St. Andrew, Columbus, OH
Molter, Rev. Richard J., '64 (MIL) Retired.
Molyn, Rev. John A., '81 (ALB) Retired.
Molyneux, Rev. John, *CMF* '97 (LA) San Gabriel Mission, San Gabriel, CA
Mominee, Rev. Joseph, (TOL) St. Joseph, Sylvania, OH
Monaco, Rev. David, *C.P.* '90 (NY) [MIS] New Jersey Friends of Mandeville Inc., Rye Brook, NY; [MON] The Congregation of the Passion - St. Paul of the Cross Province, Jamaica, NY; [SEM] St. Joseph's Seminary, Yonkers, NY
Monaco, Rev. David, *C.P.* (BRK) [MIS] St. Paul's Benevolent, Educational and Missionary Institute, Inc. (Congregation of the Passion - St. Paul of the Cross Province), Jamaica, NY
Monaco, Rev. James M., '85 (BUF) St. John Kanty, Buffalo, NY; St. Katharine Drexel, Buffalo, NY
Monagel, Rev. Robert, (MO) Curia: Offices and Directors
Monaghan, Rev. Fergus, '72 (SPC) Retired. Curia:

Advisory Boards, Commissions, Committees, and Councils
Monaghan, Rev. Robert T., '62 (STP) Retired.
Monaghan, Rev. Thomas J., '70 (MAD) Retired.
Monagle, Rev. Robert J., '91 (BO) Curia: (>MO) Offices and Directors
Monahan, Rev. Gabriel, *C.F.R.* '19 (NY) [MON] St. Joseph's Friary, New York, NY
Monahan, Rev. John, (MO) Curia: Offices and Directors
Monahan, Rev. John C., *S.J.* '99 (BO) [MON] The Jesuit Community at Boston College, Chestnut Hill, MA
Monahan, Rev. Joseph, *T.O.R.* '90 (CAM) Chap, Dir Pastoral Care, Virtua at Our Lady Lourdes Med Ctr
Monahan, Rev. Joseph E., '77 (DEN) Retired.
Monahan, Rev. Paul, '60 (DM) Retired.
Monahan, Rev. Shawn, *O.M.V.* (VEN) [RTR] Our Lady of Perpetual Help Retreat and Spirituality Center, Inc., Venice, FL
Monahan, Rev. Timothy F., '09 (CHI) Curia: Offices and Directors
Monahan, Rev. William J., '07 (PH) Curia: Advisory Boards, Commissions, Committees, and Councils St. John the Evangelist, Morrisville, PA
Monastere, Rev. Bony, '07 (BRK) St. Therese of Lisieux, Brooklyn, NY
Moncada, Rev. Fabian, (DM) Our Lady of the Americas, Des Moines, IA
Moncada Laguado, Rev. Cayetano, '96 (NEW) Shrine of Divine Mercy St. Francis Xavier, Newark, NJ
Monco, Rev. Nicholas, *OP* '13 (GR) St. Francis de Sales, Holland, MI
Mondesir, Rev. Emmery, (MGZ) San Vicente, Mayaguez, PR
Mondiek, Rev. Stephen J., '03 (CIN) Holy Angels, Sidney, OH; Sacred Heart of Jesus, Anna, OH
Mondji, Rev. Jean-Marie, '08 (PBL) Colo. Dept. of Corrections, Canon City, CO
Mondragon, Rev. Antonio, '63 (SFE) Retired.
Mondragon, Rev. Ezequiel, '62 (DET) On Leave.
Mondragon, Rev. Fidel, (SHP) Christ the King, Bossier City, LA
Moneck, Rev. George J., '89 (PIT) On Sick Leave.
Monestero, Rev. John, '75 (ORG) Retired. Curia: Offices and Directors St. Justin Martyr, Anaheim, CA
Monestime, Rev. Perard C, *SJ* '85 (ATL) [MON] Atlanta Jesuit Community, Inc., Decatur, GA
Monette, Rev. Michael R., '99 (MAN) St. Joachim, Sunapee, NH; St. Kathryn, Hudson, NH
Moneypenny, Rev. John W., '98 (ORG) St. Norbert, Orange, CA
Monfette, Rev. Edmond, (MRY) On Special Assignment. Hospital Chap, Ave Maria Senior Living, Monterey
Mongelluzzo, Rev. Msgr. James, '74 (BO) [SEM] Pope Saint John XXIII National Seminary, Weston, MA
Mongelluzzo, Rev. Msgr. James A., '74 (WOR) On Duty Outside Diocese. Pope St John XXIII Seminary, Weston
Mongeon, Rev. Peter M., '83 (NO) Retired.
Mongeon, Rev. Peter M., '83 (NO) On Sick Leave.
Mongiello, Rev. Anthony P., '80 (ALN) Curia: Leadership; Organizations (affiliated, inter-Diocesan, miscellaneous/other) St. Anne, Bethlehem, PA
Mongrain, Rev. Dennis, '77 (LA) St. Denis, Diamond Bar, CA
Monica, Rev. Louis J., (PH) Our Lady of Calvary, Philadelphia, PA
Monico Soltero, Rev. Gilberto, '02 (LA) On Administrative Leave.
Moniuk, Rev. Evhen, '92 (PHU) St. Michael's, Cherry Hill, NJ
Moniuk, Rev. Evhen, '92 (PHU) St. Nicholas, Millville, NJ
Moniz, Rev. Joseph V., '64 (LA) Retired.
Monn, Rev. Dominic, *O.F.M.* '71 (WDC) [MIS] Missionaries of the Kingship of Christ, Bethesda, MD
Monnig, Rev. Matthew, *S.J.* (BO) [MON] Noel Chabanel House, Brighton, MA
Monogue, Rev. Michael G., '85 (STP) Chap, United Hosps, Inc St Paul; Children's Hosp, St Paul
Monreal, Rev. Melchisedech, '95 (SD) Pastor of Saint Michael Catholic Parish, Poway, a corporation sole, Poway, CA
Monreal Pujante, Rev. Jesus, *O.Carm.* '69 (ARE) Curia: Leadership
Monreal Pujante, Rev. Jesús, *O. Carm* '69 (ARE) Nuestra Senora del Carmen, Morovis, PR
Monroe, Rev. Charles F., '75 (WOR) Curia: Advisory Boards, Commissions, Committees, and Councils; Clergy and Religious Services
Monroig Colón, Rev. Carlos Guillermo, '13 (ARE) La Milagrosa, Bajadero, PR
Monsalve, Rev. Carlos A., '88 (RCK) St. Mary, Sterling, IL
Monsalve, Rev. Diego, '22 (PAT) St. Peter the Apostle, Parsippany, NJ
Monshau, Rev. Michael, *OP* (STP) [MON] St. Albert the Great Priory, Minneapolis, MN
Monsieur, Rev. Lamartine P., '80 (BRK) Retired.
Montag, Rev. John, *S.J.* (LA) St. Mary Magdalen, Los Angeles, CA
Montagna, Rev. Matteo Dal Bianco, (BAL) Our Lady of Pompei, Baltimore, MD
Montagne, Rev. Pierre Henri, '03 (WDC) Church of St. Louis, Washington, DC
Montague, Rev. George, *S.M.* (SAT) [NUR] Marianist Residence: Skilled Nursing, San Antonio, TX
Montague, Rev. George, '58 (SAT) Retired.
Montague, Rev. George, *S.M.* (SAT) Retired.
Montague, Rev. George T., *S.M.* '58 (SAT) St. Mary Magdalen, San Antonio, TX
Montalvan, Rev. Asdruval Antonio Astudillo, '97 (NY) Parish of St. John and Visitation, Bronx, NY
Montalvo, Rev. Wilian, (VEN) St. Peter the Apostle Parish in Naples, Inc., Naples, FL
Montalvo-Aviles, Rev. Javier, *C.P.* '18 (SJN) Santa Gema Galgani Parish Sanctuary, Carolina, PR
Montana, Rev. Edwin, '11 (WOR) Immaculate Conception, Worcester, MA
Montanaro, Rev. Guido G., '69 (BGP) Retired. [MON] The Catherine Dennis Keefe Queen of the Clergy Retired Priests' Residence, Stamford, CT
Montanez, Rev. Gustavo, '08 (SAT) Military Chap St. Jude, San Antonio, TX
Montanez, Rev. Gustavo, (MO) Curia: Offices and Directors
Montanez, Rev. Melvin, '06 (CGS) Espiritu Santo, Aguas Buenas, PR
Montanez Lopez, Rev. Jose Ramon, *C.P.* '95 (NY) [MON] The Congregation of the Passion - St. Paul of the Cross Province, Jamaica, NY
Montano, Rev. Angel, '92 (CC) Curia: Leadership
Montavon, Rev. Thomas G., '61 (CLV) Retired. St. Colette, Brunswick, OH; St. Monica, Garfield Heights, OH
Montecalvo, Rev. Msgr. Carlo F., '73 (PRO) Retired.
Montecalvo, Rev. Roger Brigente, *CICM* '21 (SAT) St. James the Apostle, San Antonio, TX
Monteiro, Very Rev. Alfredo, '73 (NY) Retired. Sacred Heart, Mount Vernon, NY
Monteiro, Rev. Ivan, *O.C.D.* '01 (DEN) St. Thomas More Catholic Parish in Centennial, Centennial, CO
Monteiro, Rev. Ternan, *S.J.* '11 (CHI) [COL] Jesuit Community at Loyola University Chicago, Chicago, IL
Monteiro De Souza, Rev. Mateus, '15 (WOR) Our Lady Immaculate, Athol, MA; St. Francis, Athol, MA; St. Peter, Petersham, MA
Montejano, Rev. John, '94 (LA) Bishop Amat Memorial High School, La Puente, CA; St. Joseph, Pomona, CA
Montelaro, Rev. Thomas, '75 (LAF) Retired.
Monteleone, Rev. David, '13 (PAT) St. Philip the Apostle, Clifton, NJ
Monteleone, Rev. Jacob, '75 (SP) Retired.
Montelongo, Rev. Ivan A, (ELP) Curia: Tribunal
Montelongo, Rev. Ivan A., '20 (ELP) On Academic Leave. St. Stephen, Deacon and Martyr, El Paso, TX
Montemayor, Rev. Ted, *S.D.B.* '83 (LA) St. John Bosco High School, Bellflower, CA
Montenegro, Rev. Blas, *O.A.R.* '49 (NEW) St. Augustine, Union City, NJ
Montero, Rev. Alvaro, *DCJM* '04 (ARL) Our Lady of Angels, Woodbridge, VA
Montero, Rev. Eduardo G., '83 (PH) On Special Assignment. Asst Judicial Vicar, Ofc Met Trib, Presentation BVM Rect, W… Curia: Leadership Presentation B.V.M., Wynnewood, PA
Montero, Rev. Romulo, '98 (BUF) Christ Our Hope, Clymer, NY
Montero Pazimo, Rev. Hugo L., '92 (STP) Retired.
Monteron, Rev. Sherwin C., '05 (MOB) Holy Spirit Parish, Montgomery, Montgomery, AL; [CAM] Auburn University Montgomery Campus Ministry, Montgomery, AL
Monterosso, Rev. Jorge, *O. Carm.* '19 (PHX) St. Agnes Roman Catholic Parish, Phoenix, AZ
Montes, Rev. Francisco J., '03 (MRY) On Leave.
Montes, Rev. Jesse, (SFR) Corpus Christi, San Francisco, CA
Montes, Rev. Jesse, *S.D.B.* '79 (LA) St. Dominic Savio, Bellflower, CA; St. Mary, Los Angeles, CA
Montes, Rev. Jose Felipe, *C.S.V.* '01 (CHI) [MON] Viatorian Province Center-Clerics of St. Viator, Arlington Heights, IL
Montes Colon, Rev. Flavio, (MIA) Our Lady of the Lakes, Miami Lakes, FL
Montesanti, Rev. Steven G., (SPR) Sacred Heart, Pittsfield, MA
Montez, Rev. Jerome, *O.S.B.* '97 (B) St. Alphonsus, Wallace, ID; St. Mary Immaculate, St. Maries, ID; St. Rita's, Kellogg, ID; [MON] Monastery of the Ascension, Jerome, ID
Montez, Rev. Steven, *OMI* '21 (SD) Retired. (>SAT) San Juan De Los Lagos Shrine, San Antonio, TX
Montgomery, Rev. Angelus Immaculata, *C.F.R.* '18 (NY) [MON] St. Joseph's Friary, New York, NY
Montgomery, Rev. Innocent Mariae, *C.F.R.* '16 (NY) [MON] St. Joseph's Friary, New York, NY
Montgomery, Rev. Patrick, '20 (LSC) Our Lady of the Light, La Luz, Inc., La Luz, NM; St. Francis de Paula Parish, Inc., Tularosa, NM
Montgomery, Rev. William L., '79 (WDC) Retired. Nativity, Washington, DC
Monti, Rev. Dominic, *OFM* '71 (NY) [ASN] Lay Women's Association/Secular Institute of the Missionaries of the Kingship of Christ, New York, NY
Monti, Rev. Dominic V., *O.F.M.* '71 (BUF) Retired. [MON] St. Bonaventure Friary, St. Bonaventure, NY
Monticello, Rev. Msgr. Robert V., '51 (DET) Retired.
Montiel, Rev. Jose, '57 (FRS) Retired.
Montiel Romero, Rev. Vicente, (PHX) Sacred Heart Roman Catholic Parish Prescott, Prescott, AZ
Montminy, Rev. Msgr. Marc R., '77 (MAN) Curia: Consultative Bodies Saints Mary and Joseph, Salem, NH
Montminy, Rev. Paul D., '78 (MAN) Retired. Immaculate Conception, Nashua, NH
Montoro, Rev. Roberto, '01 (SLC) Sacred Heart LLC 210, Salt Lake City, UT
Montoya, Rev. Armando Rodriguez, (CAM) The Parish of the Holy Cross, Bridgeton, N.J., Bridgeton, NJ
Montoya, Rev. Hector, '09 (SAC) Pastor of St. Peter Parish, Dixon, a corporation sole, Dixon, CA
Montoya, Rev. Jose, '86 (BGP) On Duty Outside Diocese. Went back to Diocese in Columbia
Montoya, Rev. Juan Camilo, '10 (LSC) On Leave.
Montoya, Rev. Michael, *M.J.* '94 (LA) [MON] Missionaries of Jesus, Inc., Los Angeles, CA
Montoya, Rev. Msgr. Paul M., '73 (LA) Retired.
Monturo, Rev. Christopher W., '03 (NY) Parish of Sacred Heart and Our Lady of Pompeii, Dobbs Ferry, NY
Montz, Rev. Jeffrey A., '08 (NO) On Special Assignment. Archbishop Chapelle HS, Metairie [SEM] Notre Dame Seminary Graduate School of Theology, New Orleans, LA
Moodie, Rev. Michael, *S.J.* '79 (SJ) Bellarmine College Preparatory, San Jose, CA
Moody, Rev. Kenneth J., *M.M.* '70 (NY) Retired. [MON] Maryknoll Fathers and Brothers (Catholic Foreign Mission Society of America, Inc.), Ossining, NY
Moody, Rev. Kenneth John, *M.M.* (ELP) St. Patrick, Canutillo, TX
Moody, Rev. Paul, '16 (PT) St. Theresa, Sunny Hills, FL
Moody, Rev. Quentin E., '85 (NO) Retired.
Moolachalil, Rev. Roy Varkey, '04 (SYM) Our Lady of Perpetual Help Syro-Malabar Catholic Parish of Greater Washington Inc. of St. Thomas Syro Malabar Diocese of Chicago, Gaithersburg, MD
Moon, Rev. Maurice, (FWT) Curia: Miscellaneous / Other Offices St. Patrick Cathedral, Fort Worth, TX
Moon, Rev. Maurice, (FWT) Nolan Catholic High School, Fort Worth, TX
Moon, Rev. Michael C., '04 (NY) Sacred Heart, Hartsdale, NY; St John Nam, Bronx, NY
Moon, Rev. Michael E., '02 (MAD) Retired.
Mooney, Rev. Dennis M., '77 (PH) St. Mark, Bristol, PA
Mooney, Rev. Geoffrey, *CSC* '21 (FTW) Christ the King, South Bend, IN; Saint Joseph High School, South Bend, IN
Mooney, Rev. Msgr. Michael P., '63 (PT) Retired.
Mooney, Rev. Patrick, '66 (BGP) Retired.
Mooney, Rev. Richard, (RIC) Retired.
Mooney, Rev. William, '68 (STA) Retired. San Sebastian, St. Augustine, FL
Mooney, Rev. William J., '68 (PAT) Retired.
Moonjung, Rev. Kim, *I.M.C.* (SB) St. Francis de Sales, Riverside, CA
Moonnanappallil, Rev. Joseph, '92 (HRT) Curia: Advisory Boards, Commissions, Committees, and Councils Our Lady of Perpetual Help Parish Corporation, Washington Depot, CT
Moonnanappillil, Rev. Tomichan, (SAT) St. Francis of Assisi, San Antonio, TX
Moons, Rev. Joseph, *C.P.* '77 (CHI) [MON] Passionist Provincial Office (The Congregation of the Passion, Holy Cross Province), Park Ridge, IL
Moons, Rev. Joseph, *C.P.* '77 (SAC) [MON] Christ the King Passionist Retreat Center, Inc. (The Passionists (Chicago, IL)), Citrus Heights, CA
Mooradd, Rev. Paul, '84 (SAM) Retired.
Moorby, Rev. William A., '82 (ROC) Good Shepherd Catholic Community, Aurora, NY; [CAM] Wells

College, c/o Good Shepherd Catholic Community, Aurora, NY
Moore, Rev. Andrew R., '97 (BEA) Holy Spirit Mission, Kountze, TX; Infant Jesus, Lumberton, TX; St. Mark the Evangelist, Silsbee, TX
Moore, Rev. Brian R., '83 (DOD) Retired.
Moore, Rev. Christopher, (BAL) [MIS] Catholic Daughters of the Americas, Woodstock, MD
Moore, Rev. Christopher P., '77 (BAL) Retired. Curia: Tribunal
Moore, Very Rev. Daniel F., *P.S.S.* '84 (BAL) [EFT] Society of St. Sulpice Foundation US, Inc., Baltimore, MD; [MON] Society of St. Sulpice, Province of the United States, Baltimore, MD
Moore, Rev. Edward F., *M.M.* '58 (NY) Retired.
Moore, Rev. Ethan M., '15 (CIN) Annunciation of the Blessed Virgin Mary, Cincinnati, OH; Holy Name, Cincinnati, OH; St. Monica-St. George Parish Newman Center, Cincinnati, OH; [CAM] University of Cincinnati Newman Center, Cincinnati, OH
Moore, Rev. Frederick Thomas, '75 (STA) Retired.
Moore, Rev. James J., *O.P.* '08 (SFR) [MON] St. Dominic Priory, San Francisco, CA
Moore, Rev. Msgr. James R., '71 (NY) Retired.
Moore, Rev. James W., *S.J.* '59 (PH) Retired.
Moore, Rev. Jason, *OFM Cap.* '21 (DEN) [MON] San Antonio Friary, Denver, CO
Moore, Rev. Jeffery, '10 (IND) Good Shepherd Roman Catholic Church, Indianapolis, Inc., Indianapolis, IN; [HOS] Franciscan Health, Indianapolis, IN
Moore, Very Rev. Jeffrey, (SEA) Curia: Leadership Assumption, Bellingham, WA
Moore, Rev. John R., '64 (RVC) Retired. [MON] St Pius X Residence for Retired Priests LLC, Ronkonkoma, NY
Moore, Rev. Jon H., *O.Carm.* '81 (WIN) [MON] Annunciation Hermitage, North American Province of St. Elias, Carmelites, Austin, MN
Moore, Rev. Lawrence, *S.J.* '77 (NO) [COL] Loyola University New Orleans, New Orleans, LA; [MON] Loyola Jesuit Community, New Orleans, LA
Moore, Rev. Mark A., '03 (STU) Curia: Deaneries Christ the King University Parish, Athens, OH; Holy Cross, Glouster, OH; Sacred Heart, Pomeroy, OH; St. Paul Church, Athens, OH; [CAM] Christ the King University Parish - Ohio University, Athens, OH; [CAM] Hocking Technical College, Athens, OH
Moore, Rev. Mark J., '03 (STU) Curia: Deaneries
Moore, Rev. Michael, (FRS) St. Peter Prince of Apostles, Lemoore, CA
Moore, Rev. Michael, *S.P.S.* '84 (CHI) [MON] St. Patrick's Missionary Society, Chicago, IL
Moore, Rev. Michael, (FRS) Curia: Advisory Boards, Commissions, Committees, and Councils St. Frances Cabrini, Huron, CA
Moore, Rev. Neil, '60 (P) Retired.
Moore, Rev. Raymond H., '81 (WDC) Curia: Deaneries St. Thomas More, Washington, DC
Moore, Rev. Msgr. Terence M., '67 (SLC) Retired. Saint John the Baptist LLC 252, Draper, UT
Moore, Rev. Ward P., '72 (NEW) Retired. [MON] The Rev. Msgr. James F. Kelley Residence for Retired Priests, Caldwell, NJ
Moore, Rev. William C., *SS.CC.* '75 (LA) [MON] Congregation of the Sacred Hearts of Jesus and Mary, La Verne, CA
Moore, Rev. Msgr. William C., '68 (STO) Retired.
Moore, Rev. William F., '69 (CAM) Retired.
Moore Irizarry, Rev. Kenneth Daniel, '09 (ARE) [MIS] Chapel Perpetuo Socorro, Vega Alta, PR; [MIS] Chapel San Martin de Porres, Corozal, PR; [MIS] Chapel San Rafael Arcangel, Corozal, PR
Moore Irizarry, Rev. Kenneth D., '09 (ARE) Our Lady of the Seven Sorrows, Corozal, PR
Moorman, Rev. William J., *O.SS.T.* '79 (BAL) Resurrection of Our Lord, Laurel, MD; [MON] Holy Trinity Monastery, Sykesville, MD
Moorse, Rev. Dunstan, *O.S.B.* '78 (SCL) [MON] St. John's Abbey, of the Order of St. Benedict, Collegeville, MN
Mora, Rev. Daniel, *S.J.* '21 (ELP) Sacred Heart, El Paso, TX
Mora, Rev. Guillermo, '96 (NEW) SS. Joseph and Michael, Union City, NJ
Mora, Rev. Ismael, '02 (SR) Pastor of St. John the Baptist Catholic Church of Napa, A Corporation Sole, Napa, CA
Mora, Rev. Sergio, '93 (OAK) Curia: Leadership St. Cornelius, Richmond, CA
Mora Bello, Rev. Juan Francisco, *F.M.* '21 (PH) Our Lady of the Rosary, Coatesville, PA
Mora Duarte, Rev. Luis Alejandro, *SS.CC.* (SJN) Inmaculado Corazon de Maria, San Juan, PR
Mora Gomez, Rev. Guillermo Leon, (MO) Curia: Offices and Directors
Morabito, Rev. Vincent R., '87 (PH) Retired. On Sick Leave.
Moraga, Rev. Cecilio, '84 (SD) On Duty Outside Diocese. Missionary Work in Peru
Morales, Very Rev. Antonio, '18 (SD) Curia: Advisory Boards, Commissions, Committees, and Councils Pastor of Saint Patrick Catholic Parish, Calipatria, a corporation sole, Calipatria, CA
Morales, Rev. Carlos, *O.F.M.Conv.* '90 (LA) Our Lady of Guadalupe, Hermosa Beach, CA (>OAK) [MON] Conventual Franciscans (Province of St. Joseph Cupertino) Provincial Center, Castro Valley, CA
Morales, Rev. Carlos Gallardo, '11 (COS) St. Catherine of Siena, Burlington, CO; St. Charles Borromeo, Stratton, CO
Morales, Rev. Eduardo D., '96 (SAT) Sacred Heart, Uvalde, TX
Morales, Rev. Fabio De Jesus Marin, *C.Ss.R.* (CHL) St. Joseph Church, Kannapolis, NC
Morales, Rev. Gabriel, '13 (B) Presentation of the Lord, American Falls, ID
Morales, Rev. Hugo, '06 (CHI) St. John Vianney, Cure of Ars, Northlake, IL
Morales, Rev. Ignacio, '09 (ATL) Curia: Leadership Prince of Peace Catholic Church, Flowery Branch, Inc., Flowery Branch, GA
Morales, Rev. Ignacio Jimenez, '11 (BLX) Chap, South Mississippi Corr Inst
Morales, Rev. Isaac, *O.P.* (PRO) [MON] St. Thomas Aquinas Priory at Providence College, Providence, RI
Morales, Rev. Jorge Luis Caro, '89 (MGZ) Curia: Leadership
Morales, Rev. Jorge Luis Caro, (MGZ) [COL] Nuestra Senora de la Monserrate College, Moca, PR
Morales, Rev. Jose A., '10 (ELP) Curia: Advisory Boards, Commissions, Committees, and Councils St. Mark, El Paso, TX; [SEM] St. Anthony's School of Theology, El Paso, TX
Morales, Rev. Leonardo, '21 (TLS) Curia: Offices and Directors St. Thomas More, Tulsa, OK
Morales, Rev. Raul, '88 (CGS) San Andres Apostol, Comerio, PR
Morales, Rev. Raymond D., '81 (LA) On Administrative Leave.
Morales, Rev. Ricardo Hernandez, '98 (SJN) San Jose, Guaynabo, PR
Morales, Rev. Robert P., '66 (BRK) Retired.
Morales, Rev. Roberto, *Sch.P.* '96 (LA) St. Lucy, Los Angeles, CA; [MON] Piarist Fathers, Los Angeles, CA
Morales, Rev. Salomon J., '68 (ARE) Retired.
Morales Bermudez Buse, Rev. Remigo, *S.V.C.* (PH) St. Agatha-St. James, Philadelphia, PA
Morales Rivera, Rev. Jorge Yamil, '10 (ARE) Curia: Leadership; Offices and Directors Holy Rosary, Vega Baja, PR
Morales Rodriguez, Rev. Msgr. Elias S., '91 (PCE) Curia: Leadership; Offices and Directors [SEM] Seminario Mayor Interdiocesano Maria, Madre de la Divina Providencia, Ponce, PR
Morales Villarrubia, Rev. Milton, '18 (MGZ) Church of the Resurrection, Mayaguez, PR
Morales-Morfin, Rev. Ruben, '04 (OAK) Curia: Leadership St. Mark, Richmond, CA
Moran, Rev. Allen B., *O.P.* '07 (NO) [EFT] International Dominican Foundation, U.S.A., Metairie, LA
Moran, Rev. Charles, '67 (STU) Retired.
Moran, Rev. Edward, '89 (RIC) Retired.
Moran, Rev. Edward M., '76 (HRT) Saint Teresa of Calcutta Parish Corporation, Manchester, CT
Moran, Rev. Edwin, *C.P.* '61 (NY) Retired. [MON] The Congregation of the Passion - St. Paul of the Cross Province, Jamaica, NY
Moran, Rev. Edwin, *C.P.* (BRK) [MON] Immaculate Conception Monastery, Jamaica, NY
Moran, Rev. Gerard K., '71 (OAK) Retired. Christ the King, Pleasant Hill, CA
Moran, Rev. Msgr. J. Thomas, '57 (BUF) Retired. [MON] O'Hara Residence, Tonawanda, NY
Moran, Rev. James, *C.O.* '89 (SHP) Mary, Queen of Peace, Bossier City, LA
Moran, Rev. James F., '71 (BO) Retired.
Moran, Rev. Msgr. James P., '72 (MET) Retired.
Moran, Rev. John, *S.S.C.* '50 (PRO) Retired. [MON] St. Columban's Retirement House (St. Columban's Foreign Mission Society), Bristol, RI
Moran, Rev. John J., *M.M.* '66 (NY) Retired. [MON] Maryknoll Fathers and Brothers (Catholic Foreign Mission Society of America, Inc.), Ossining, NY
Moran, Rev. Kevin, '65 (SEA) Retired.
Moran, Rev. Martin O., (BAL) [COL] Mount Saint Mary's University, Emmitsburg, MD
Moran, Rev. Archpriest Michael, '63 (HPM) Retired.
Moran, Rev. Michael F., '82 (MIL) Retired.
Moran, Rev. Michael P., *SMA* '81 (NEW) [MON] Society of African Missions, Provincialate, S.M.A. Fathers, Tenafly, NJ
Moran, Rev. Michael P., *S.M.A.* '81 (WDC) St. Margaret, Seat Pleasant, MD
Moran, Rev. Owen B., '91 (PAT) St. Luke, Long Valley, NJ
Moran, Rev. Msgr. Peter C., '65 (LA) Retired.
Moran, Rev. Richard S., '61 (BO) Retired.
Moran, Rev. Robert, '64 (SJ) Retired.
Moran, Rev. Robert E., '69 (LFT) Retired.
Moran, Rev. Stephen P., '92 (CLV) Chap, Village Network, Smithville; Wayne Cty Jail, Wooster St. Mary of the Immaculate Conception, Wooster, OH; [CCH] St. Mary of the Immaculate Conception, Wooster, OH
Moran, Rev. Terence J., '90 (BO) On Leave.
Moran, Rev. Thomas A., '71 (CHI) Retired.
Moran, Rev. Msgr. Timothy J., '76 (BO) Our Lady, Star of the Sea, Marblehead, MA
Moran-Rosero, Rev. Norman H., '05 (CHI) St. Basil/ Visitation, Chicago, IL
Morard, Rev. Alexandre, (BRK) Saint Paul and Saint Agnes Roman Catholic Church, Brooklyn, NY
Moras, Rev. Leo, '89 (MO) Curia: Offices and Directors
Moratelli, Rev. Ronald J., '69 (HBG) Retired.
Moratin, Rev. Victor Antonio, *CPM* '18 (COL) [SEM] Pontifical College Josephinum, Columbus, OH
Mora-Torres, Rev. Everardo, (BLX) Sacred Heart, Pascagoula, MS
Moravitz, Rev. Brandon, '12 (DUL) Curia: Leadership Holy Spirit, Virginia, MN
Moravitz, Rev. Ryan, '08 (DUL) On Leave.
Morawiec, Rev. Zbigniew, *S.C.J.* '90 (MIL) [MON] Sacred Heart Monastery, Hales Corners, WI
Morawski, Rev. Stefan, *O.F.M.Conv.* '68 (BGP) The Church of St. Michael, Archangel Bridgeport, Bridgeport, CT
Morciniec, Rev. Peter J., '70 (SPC) Retired.
Morcone, Rev. Nicholas J., *O.S.B.* '69 (BO) [MON] Glastonbury Abbey, Hingham, MA
Mordalski, Rev. Jerzy, *S.C.J.* (GAL) Our Lady of Guadalupe, Houston, TX
More, Rev. Jonathan, (GAL) Immaculate Conception, Sealy, TX
Moreau, Rev. Canon Jean Marie, (LKC) [MIS] Saint Francis de Sales Oratory, Sulphur, LA
Moreau, Rev. Maurice, *OFM Cap* (BUR) Our Lady of Good Help (St. Mary), Brandon, VT
Moreau, Rev. Maurice, *OFM Cap* (BUR) St. Alphonsus Liguori, Pittsford, VT
Moreau, Very Rev. Paul, '02 (ATL) Curia: Leadership St. Catherine Laboure Catholic Church, Jefferson, Inc., Jefferson, GA; St. Joseph Catholic Church, Athens, Inc., Athens, GA
Moreau, Rev. Randy, '87 (LAF) Our Lady of Fatima, Lafayette, LA
Moreau, Rev. Raymond J., '85 (OG) Curia: Canonical Services; Consultative Bodies St. Mary's Church, Brushton, NY; The Roman Catholic Church of St. Augustine in North Bangor, NY, North Bangor, NY
Moreeuw, Rev. LeRoy, *C.PP.S.* '68 (CIN) [MON] Society of the Precious Blood, United States Province, Inc., Dayton, OH
Moreeuw, Rev. LeRoy, *C.S.Sp.* (DET) St. Mary Parish Detroit, Detroit, MI
Moreeuw, Rev. LeRoy, *C.PP.S.* '68 (CIN) Retired.
Morehead, Very Rev. Samuel, '12 (DEN) Curia: Deaneries Cathedral Basilica of the Immaculate Conception Catholic Parish in Denver, Denver, CO
Moreira, Rev. Adelson Silvestre, '03 (MIA) Corpus Christi, Miami, FL
Moreira, Rev. Leonardo C., (BO) St. Mary of the Assumption, Lawrence, MA
Moreira, Rev. Nelson A., *S.S.J.* '72 (BAL) [MIS] Friends of Ijebu-Ode Diocese, Inc., Glen Burnie, MD; [MON] St. Joseph Society of the Sacred Heart House of Central Administration, Baltimore, MD
Moreira de Sales, Rev. Lucas, '22 (DAL) Prince of Peace Catholic Parish, Plano, TX
Moreland, Rev. J. Gordon, *S.J.* '64 (SJ) [MON] Sacred Heart Jesuit Center, Los Gatos, CA
Morell, Rev. Fernando, '87 (ARE) Curia: Offices and Directors
Morell Dominguez, Rev. Fernando, (ARE) Cathedral of San Felipe Apostol, Arecibo, PR
Morelli, Rev. Attilio, '98 (NEW) On Duty Outside Diocese. Diocese of Hamilton in Bermuda, Hamilton
Morelli, Rev. Gary, (DET) Chap, Beaumont Hosp
Morelli, Rev. Matthew, '18 (HBG) Delone Catholic High School, McSherrystown, PA; St. Joseph, Hanover, PA
Morelli, Rev. Matthew Christopher, '18 (HBG) St.

Anthony of Padua, Lancaster, PA
Morelli, Rev. Matthew J., '13 (GBG) Curia: Leadership; Miscellaneous / Other Offices Church of the Good Shepherd, Kent, PA
Morello, Rev. Carl, '83 (CHI) Curia: Leadership St. Catherine of Siena-St. Lucy and St. Giles Parish, Oak Park, IL
Morello, Rev. Gustavo, *S.J.* '97 (BO) [MON] The Jesuit Community at Boston College, Chestnut Hill, MA
Morello, Rev. Peter, '78 (GLP) Retired.
Morello, Rev. Peter, '78 (ROC) Retired.
Morello, Friar Sam Anthony, *OCD* '62 (SAT) Basilica of the National Shrine of the Little Flower, Our Lady of Mt. Carmel and St. Therese Parish, San Antonio, TX; [MON] Discalced Carmelite Fathers of San Antonio, San Antonio, TX
Moren, Rev. Floi, *AM* (ORG) [CAM] California State University Fullerton, Titan Catholic Newman Club, Fullerton, CA
Morency, Rev. Raymond P., '87 (PRT) Retired.
Moreno, Rev. Andres, (KC) Curia: Leadership Our Lady of Peace, Kansas City, MO; St. Anthony, Kansas City, MO
Moreno, Rev. Benito, (BO) St. Patrick, Brockton, MA
Moreno, Rev. Daniel E., '15 (WOR) St. Anthony, Dudley, MA
Moreno, Rev. David, *S.D.B.* (NY) Parish of St. John Bosco, Port Chester, NY
Moreno, Rev. David, *SDB* '79 (NY) [MON] Salesian Provincial House, New Rochelle, NY
Moreno, Rev. Hector C., '05 (LC) On Leave.
Moreno, Rev. James, '76 (DEN) Retired.
Moreno, Rev. Jorge, '63 (SD) Retired.
Moreno, Rev. Jose Alfredo, '87 (SD) Pastor of Saint Joseph Catholic Parish, Holtville, a corporation sole, Holtville, CA
Moreno, Rev. Joseph George, '21 (FWT) Christ the King, Iowa Park, TX; St. Jude Thaddeus, Burkburnett, TX; St. Paul, Electra, TX
Moreno, Rev. Juan, '60 (LSC) Retired. St. Genevieve Parish, Inc., Las Cruces, NM
Moreno, Rev. Martin, (TUC) On Leave.
Moreno, Rev. Miguel, (SAT) St. Gregory's, San Antonio, TX
Moreno, Rev. Robert, '93 (STF) St. Nicholas, Buffalo, NY
Moreno, Rev. Robert, '20 (BWN) The Parish of the Lord of Divine Mercy, Brownsville, TX
Moreno-Urzua, Rev. Moises, '10 (KNX) St. Mary, Gatlinburg, TN
Moretta, Rev. Msgr. John T., '68 (LA) Curia: Pastoral Services Resurrection, Los Angeles, CA
Moretti, Rev. Mark E., '95 (ARL) Christ the Redeemer, Sterling, VA
Morey, Rev. Joshua, *O.S.B.* '09 (TLS) [MON] Our Lady of the Annunciation of Clear Creek Abbey, Hulbert, OK
Morey, Rev. Lawrence, (L) [MON] Abbey of Our Lady of Gethsemani, of the Order of Cistercians of the Strict Observance, Trappist, KY
Morey, Rev. Noah C., '15 (ARL) Basilica of St. Mary, Alexandria, VA; Bishop Ireton High School, Alexandria, VA
Morey, Rev. Robert E., '96 (BAL) Retired.
Morfin, Rev. John N., '67 (GAL) Retired.
Morgan, Rev. Brendan P., '64 (NO) Retired.
Morgan, Rev. Charles J., '79 (ALX) Retired.
Morgan, Rev. Drew P., *C.O.* '85 (PIT) Most Sacred Heart of Jesus, Moon Township, PA
Morgan, Rev. James P., '01 (SFS) Curia: Leadership Cathedral of Saint Joseph Parish, Sioux Falls, SD
Morgan, Rev. Jerome L., '62 (SAL) Retired. Curia: Organizations (affiliated, inter-Diocesan, miscellaneous/ other)
Morgan, Rev. Joachim J., *O.S.B.* '18 (PIT) Mary, Queen of Saints, Aliquippa, PA
Morgan, Rev. John Michael, *M.M.J.M.J.* '17 (OLL) [MON] Oblates of Jesus, Mary & Joseph, Beaverton, OR; [MON] Sacred Heart Maronite Monastery, Beaverton, OR
Morgan, Rev. Joseph A., '81 (OG) Curia: Canonical Services; Consultative Bodies; Leadership St. Mary's Church, Ogdensburg, Ogdensburg, NY
Morgan, Rev. K. Scott, '21 (CIN) St. Teresa of Avila, Cincinnati, OH; St. William, Cincinnati, OH
Morgan, Rev. Martin J., '70 (TLS) Retired.
Morgan, Rev. Msgr. Michael P., '01 (STA) On Duty Outside Diocese. Apostolic Nunciature to the United States, Washington, DC
Morgan, Rev. Roger James, '15 (CHR) St. Andrew, Myrtle Beach, SC
Morgan, Rev. Thomas, '84 (SP) St. Jerome, Largo, FL; [PRE] St. Jerome Early Childhood Center, Largo, FL
Morgan, Rev. Msgr. Thomas J., '65 (CAM) Retired.
Morgan, Rev. W. Donald, '07 (SJ) Retired.
Morgewicz, Rev. Robert A., '09 (HRT) Annunciation Parish Corporation, Newington, CT
Morgia, Rev. Robustiano D., '76 (NO) St. John the Baptist, Edgard, LA
Moriarity, Rev. Thomas, Curia: (>RVC) Leadership
Moriarity, Rev. William J., '66 (CHI) Retired. Holy Name Cathedral, Chicago, IL; St. John the Evangelist, Streamwood, IL
Moriarty, Rev. John, '91 (LEX) Cathedral of Christ the King, Lexington, KY
Moriarty, Very Rev. Joseph B., '93 (IND) Curia: Offices and Directors [SEM] Bishop Simon Bruté College Seminary, Inc., Indianapolis, IN
Moriarty, Rev. Mark D., '99 (STP) Curia: Leadership St. Agnes, St. Paul, MN
Moriarty, Rev. Michael, *L.C.* '12 (CHI) [MON] Legion of Christ, Hickory Hills, IL
Moriarty, Rev. Thomas, '92 (RVC) Our Lady of Good Counsel, Inwood, NY; St. Joachim, Cedarhurst, NY; St. Joseph's, Hewlett, NY
Moriarty, Rev. Timothy J., '03 (HEL) Curia: Leadership Saint Mary Catholic Community: Series 402, LLC, Helena, MT
Moriconi, Rev. Christopher C., '14 (PH) On Duty Outside Diocese.
Morin, Rev. Brad, '14 (PRT) Saint Kateri Tekakwitha Parish, Calais, ME
Morin, Rev. Eddy, '99 (PRT) Retired.
Morin, Rev. Francis P., '73 (PRT) Retired.
Morin, Rev. George E., '70 (BO) Retired. Immaculate Conception, Newburyport, MA
Morin, Rev. Joseph, *C.Ss.R.* '64 (STL) Retired. [MON] St. Clement Health Care Center, Liguori, MO
Morin, Rev. Michael J., '88 (LIN) Curia: Offices and Directors Blessed Sacrament, Lincoln, NE; St. Wenceslaus School, Wahoo, NE
Morin, Rev. Robert, *OMI* '69 (BEL) [MON] Missionary Oblates of Mary Immaculate - St. Henry's Oblate Residence, Belleville, IL
Morinelli, Rev. Emmanuel, *O.C.S.O.* '14 (WOR) [MON] St. Joseph's Abbey (Cistercian Abbey of Spencer, Inc., Cistercian Order of the Strict Observance (Trappists)), Spencer, MA; [RTR] St. Joseph Abbey, Spencer, MA
Moris, Rev. Daniel Lee, '10 (SFS) Retired.
Morisette, Rev. Richard P., '61 (SY) Retired.
Morkunas, Rev. Andrew, (CLV) Our Lady of Peace, Cleveland, OH
Morkunas, Rev. Andrew, (CLV) Chap, Rainbow Babies and Children's Hosp; Univ Hosps
Morkunas, Rev. Andrew M., '09 (WDC) On Leave.
Morley, Rev. Craig, '01 (SP) Curia: Leadership; Pastoral Services St. Paul, Tampa, FL; [PRE] St. Paul Catholic Preschool, Tampa, FL
Morley, Rev. James B., '15 (GBG) Curia: Advisory Boards, Commissions, Committees, and Councils; Leadership; Offices and Directors Church of the Resurrection, Clymer, PA
Morley, Rev. John J., '04 (MET) On Sick Leave.
Morlino, Rev. Paschal A., *O.S.B.* '66 (BAL) St. Benedict, Baltimore, MD; [MIS] The Benedictine Society of Baltimore, Inc., Baltimore, MD
Morlino, Rev. Paschal A., *O.S.B.* '66 (GBG) [MON] Saint Vincent Archabbey, Latrobe, PA
Morman, Rev. David G., '89 (BIS) On Duty Outside Diocese. Missionary, Kisii, Kenya, East Africa
Morman, Rev. James, *T.O.R.* '92 (FWT) (>TOL) St. John the Baptist, Toledo, OH
Morman, Rev. Msgr. Kenneth G., '73 (TOL) Curia: Advisory Boards, Commissions, Committees, and Councils; Deaneries
Morocho, Rev. Gonzalo, *S.D.B.* '01 (NY) Chap, Westchester Cty Jail, Valhalla; Manhattan Det Ctr
Moroda, Rev. Dawit T., (BRK) Chap, St John's Episcopal Hosp St. Mary Star of the Sea and St. Gertrude, Far Rockaway, NY
Moroney, Rev. Msgr. James P., '80 (WOR) Curia: Advisory Boards, Commissions, Committees, and Councils; Offices and Directors St. Cecilia, Leominster, MA
Moroney, Rev. Martin J., '67 (SAC) Retired. Pastor of St. John Vianney Parish, Rancho Cordova, a Corporation Sole, Rancho Cordova, CA
Moroney, Rev. Michael J., '71 (BR) Curia: Canonical Services; Pastoral Services Congregation Of St. Alphonsus Liguori Roman Catholic Church, Greenwell Springs, LA
Moronta, Rev. Andris Alexis, '02 (BGP) The St. George's Lithuanian Roman Catholic Church, Bridgeport, CT
Morozowich, Rev. Mark, *S.E.O.D.* (WDC) [COL] Catholic University of America, The, Washington, DC
Morozowich, Rev. Mark, '91 (SJP) On Duty Outside Diocese. Washington, DC Curia: Offices and Directors
Morrette, Rev. Thomas, '05 (ALB) Our Lady of Victory, Troy, NY; Parish of Our Lady of the Snow, Grafton, NY; [MIS] University Parish of Christ Sun of Justice, Troy, NY
Morris, Rev. Alan E., '92 (PIT) Archangel Gabriel, McKees Rocks, PA
Morris, Rev. Anthony W., '94 (RIC) Curia: Deaneries Church of the Holy Angels, Portsmouth, VA; Church of the Resurrection, Portsmouth, VA; St. Paul, Portsmouth, VA
Morris, Rev. Anthony William, '94 (RIC) St. Mary, Chesapeake, VA
Morris, Rev. Brian J., (PRO) Curia: Clergy and Religious Services
Morris, Rev. Msgr. C. Eugene, '96 (STL) Oratory of Saint Gregory and Saint Augustine, Richmond Heights, MO
Morris, Rev. Charles M., '83 (DET) Retired.
Morris, Rev. Daniel, '15 (KCK) Curia: Offices and Directors [CAM] St. Lawrence Catholic Campus Center at the University of Kansas and Residence, Lawrence, KS
Morris, Rev. Denton, (LIN) St. Joseph's, Harvard, NE
Morris, Rev. Denton R., '15 (LIN) Curia: Leadership; Offices and Directors
Morris, Rev. Donald, '22 (STL) Our Lady of Lourdes Catholic Church, Washington, Washington, MO
Morris, Rev. Gerald R., '70 (MIA) Retired.
Morris, Rev. James, '93 (STF) Curia: Leadership; Offices and Directors St. John the Baptist, Salem, MA
Morris, Rev. John, *O.P.* '66 (OAK) [COL] Saint Mary's College of California (Saint Mary's College of California, Brothers of the Christian Schools, District of San Francisco), Moraga, CA
Morris, Rev. John S., '62 (BO) Retired.
Morris, Rev. Jonathan, '02 (NY) [CAM] Columbia University, New York, NY
Morris, Rev. Joseph E., '96 (ATL) Immaculate Conception Catholic Church, Atlanta, Inc., Atlanta, GA; [CAM] Kennesaw State University, Kennesaw, GA
Morris, Rev. Loyd, '95 (DAL) Retired.
Morris, Rev. Matthew B., '13 (COL) St. Catharine, Columbus, OH
Morris, Rev. Michael, '89 (NY) Regina Coeli, Hyde Park, NY
Morris, Rev. Peter, (CLV) SS. Peter and Paul, Doylestown, OH; St. Anne, Rittman, OH
Morris, Rev. Msgr. Philip D., '62 (NEW) Retired. St. John the Baptist, Hillsdale, NJ
Morris, Rev. Placid, *O.C.S.O.* '13 (SAC) [SEM] Abbey of New Clairvaux, Trappist Seminary, Vina, CA
Morris, Rev. Msgr. Robert, '91 (SP) St. Catherine of Siena, Clearwater, FL
Morris, Rev. Msgr. Robert F., '91 (SP) Curia: Administration; Leadership; Miscellaneous / Other Offices; Organizations (affiliated, inter-Diocesan, miscellaneous/other); Pastoral Services [CCH] Catholic Charities Community Dev. Corp., St. Petersburg, FL; [CCH] Catholic Charities Housing, Inc., St. Petersburg, FL; [CCH] Catholic Charities, Diocese of St. Petersburg, Inc., St. Petersburg, FL
Morris, Rev. Robert J., '04 (NY) St. Bernard, White Plains, NY
Morris, Rev. Sean, *O.M.V.* '09 (VEN) (>BO) [MIS] St. Clement Archdiocesan Eucharistic Shrine, Boston, MA
Morris, Rev. Wayne E., '01 (STU) St. Ann, Chesapeake, OH; St. Joseph Parish, Ironton, OH; St. Lawrence Parish, Ironton, OH; St. Mary, Ironton, OH; [SHR] Our Lady of Fatima Shrine, Ironton, OH
Morris, Rev. William T., '69 (MET) Retired.
Morris, Rev. William T., '69 (NEW) Retired.
Morrisey, Friar Paul F., *O.S.A.* '67 (PH) St. Augustine, Philadelphia, PA
Morrison, Rev. Craig, *O.Carm.* '87 (JOL) [MON] Carmelite Provincial Office, Darien, IL
Morrison, Rev. Craig, *O.Carm.* '87 (WDC) [SEM] Whitefriars Hall, Washington, DC
Morrison, Rev. Msgr. David J., '54 (ALN) Retired. Curia: Leadership
Morrison, Rev. Douglas A., '56 (HRT) Retired.
Morrison, Rev. Jack, '92 (SAM) Retired. Curia: Offices and Directors
Morrison, Rev. James, '20 (WDC) Our Lady of Lourdes, Bethesda, MD
Morrison, Rev. James N., '10 (MOB) Curia: Leadership St. Patrick Parish, Robertsdale, Robertsdale, AL
Morrison, Rev. Larry, '79 (RNO) Our Lady of Tahoe, Zephyr Cove, NV
Morrison, Rev. Thomas F., '76 (CHR) Retired.
Morrissey, Rev. Daniel W., *O.P.* '62 (CHI) Retired. [MON] St. Pius V Priory, Chicago, IL

Morrissey, Rev. John, '63 (PMB) Our Lady of Guadalupe Mission, Fellsmere, FL; St. Sebastian, Sebastian, FL
Morrissey, Rev. Joseph G, *O.S.F.S.* '77 (WIL) [EFT] Salesianum School Endowment Trust I, Wilmington, DE; [EFT] Salesianum School Endowment Trust II, Wilmington, DE
Morrissey, Rev. Joseph G., *O.S.F.S.* '77 (WIL) Salesianum School, Wilmington, DE
Morrissey, Rev. Joseph G., *O.S.F.S.* '77 (WIL) [EFT] Nativity Preparatory School of Wilmington Trust, Wilmington, DE
Morrissey, Rev. Michael E., '86 (RCK) Holy Cross, Stockton, IL
Morrissey, Rev. Mike, '78 (P) Retired.
Morrissey, Rev. Paul, *S.M.* '75 (WDC) Retired.
Morrissey, Rev. Msgr. Robert O., '83 (RVC) Curia: Leadership St. Agnes Cathedral, Rockville Centre, NY
Morrissy, Rev. Dennis M., '06 (RCK) St. Mary's Church of Pecatonica, Pecatonica, IL
Morrone, Rev. Louis S., *O.P.* '92 (DEN) St. Dominic Parish, Denver, CO; [MON] Dominican Friars, St. Dominic Priory, Denver, Inc., Denver, CO
Morrow, Rev. Brian S., '82 (DEN) Retired.
Morrow, Rev. Michael D., '86 (NY) St. Paul the Apostle, Yonkers, NY
Morrow, Rev. Thomas G., '82 (WDC) Retired. St. Raphael, Rockville, MD; [MIS] The Blue Army, Archdiocese of Washington Division, Silver Spring, MD
Morse, Rev. Fred, '95 (PRT) Holy Spirit Parish, Wells, ME
Morse, Rev. James H., '67 (FR) Retired.
Morse, Rev. Jonathan, '88 (WIL) Chap, Veterans Admin
Morse, Very Rev. Jonathan K., '88 (STN) Chap Curia: (>MO) Offices and Directors
Morton, Rev. Jake, *S.J.* '75 (SPK) Sacred Heart Mission, Nespelem, WA; St. Joseph, Omak, WA; St. Mary's Mission, Omak, WA; St. Michael's Mission, Inchelium, WA; St. Rose of Lima, Keller, WA
Morton, Rev. Vincent, '86 (SP) Retired.
Morton, Rev. William, *S.S.C.* '85 (OM) [MON] Missionary Society of St. Columban, St. Columbans, NE
Morugudi, Rev. Bhaskar, '99 (MO) Curia: Offices and Directors
Mosbrucker, Rev. Jacob A., '66 (P) Retired.
Moscaritolo, Rev. Mario, '64 (KC) Retired.
Moschetto, Rev. Joseph, '20 (ARL) St. Luke, McLean, VA
Moscinski, Rev. Fidelis, *C.F.R.* '01 (NY) [MON] Franciscan Friars of the Renewal, Bronx, NY; [MON] St. Leopold's Friary, Yonkers, NY
Moser, Very Rev. John A., '86 (DUB) On Special Assignment. Dean of the Decorah Deanery St. Mary's Church, Dorchester, Iowa, Dorchester, IA; St. Mary's Church, Hanover, Iowa, Waukon, IA; St. Patrick's Church, Waukon, Iowa, Waukon, IA
Moser, Rev. Patrick E., '18 (OM) St. Columbkille, Papillion, NE
Moser, Rev. Thomas W., '94 (KNX) St. Catherine Laboure, Copperhill, TN
Moses, Rev. David Michael, (GAL) Christ the Good Shepherd, Spring, TX
Moses, Rev. Patrick A., '03 (ORG) St. Timothy, Laguna Niguel, CA
Moses, Rev. Thomas, '19 (NTN) St. Basil, Utica, NY
Mosher, Rev. Gabriel T., *O.P.* '15 (SLC) Saint Catherine of Siena Catholic Newman Center LLC 218, Salt Lake City, UT
Mosher, Rev. Robert, *S.S.C.* '82 (OM) [MON] Missionary Society of St. Columban, St. Columbans, NE
Mosher, Rev. Thomas L., '81 (BUR) Annunciation of the Blessed Virgin Mary, Ludlow, VT
Mosier, Rev. John Andrew, '19 (B) Curia: Leadership St. Charles, Salmon, ID
Mosimann, Rev. John P., '97 (ARL) St. Mary of the Immaculate Conception, Fredericksburg, VA
Moskal, Rev. Joseph E., '65 (SY) Retired. Holy Trinity, Utica, NY
Moskus, Rev. John T., '63 (HRT) Retired.
Mosley, Rev. Charles A., '85 (GRY) Curia: Leadership Our Lady of Perpetual Help, Hammond, IN
Mosley, Rev. Daniel E., '77 (STL) Ste. Genevieve Du Bois Catholic Church, Warson Woods, Warson Woods, MO
Mosley, Rev. Msgr. Godfrey T., '79 (WDC) St. Ann, Washington, DC
Mosley, Rev. Joseph, (SCR) Our Lady of Mt. Carmel, Carbondale, PA; St. Rose of Lima, Carbondale, PA
Moslosky, Rev. Robert W., *C.S.B.* '74 (DET) Retired. Detroit Catholic Central High School, Novi, MI
Moss, Rev. Andrew, '10 (CIN) [SEM] Mount St. Mary's Seminary of the West, Cincinnati, OH
Moss, Rev. Darius G. C., '97 (HBG) Retired. Queen of Peace, Millersburg, PA
Moss, Rev. Donald, (AUS) On Duty Outside Diocese. Curia: (>MO) Offices and Directors
Moss, Rev. James, (PAT) Retired.
Moss, Rev. James, '82 (STA) On Leave.
Moss, Rev. Raymond B., '86 (CHY) St. Anthony's, Guernsey, WY; St. Leo's, Lusk, WY; St. Rose, Torrington, WY
Moss, Rev. Robert H., *C.S.C.* '74 (FTW) [SEM] Moreau Seminary, Notre Dame, IN
Mossa, Rev. Mark S., *S.J.* '08 (NO) [COL] Loyola University New Orleans, New Orleans, LA; [MON] Loyola Jesuit Community, New Orleans, LA
Mossi, Rev. John P., *S.J.* '73 (SJ) [MON] Jesuit Community at Santa Clara University, Inc., Santa Clara, CA
Mostardi, Rev. Joseph, (CHI) [MON] St. Augustine Friary, Chicago, IL
Mostardi, Rev. Joseph S., *O.S.A.* '75 (CAM) [MON] Augustinian Friars, Ocean City, NJ
Mostardi, Rev. Joseph S., *O.S.A.* '75 (PH) Curia: Advisory Boards, Commissions, Committees, and Councils Our Mother of Good Counsel, Bryn Mawr, PA; [MON] Augustinians Friars (O.S.A.), Bryn Mawr, PA
Moster, Rev. Humbert, *O.F.M.* '57 (CIN) Retired.
Moster, Rev. James E., *O.F.M.Cap.* '76 (SAL) St. Ann Parish, Walker, Inc., Walker, KS; St. Boniface Parish, Vincent, Inc., Victoria, KS; The Basilica of St. Fidelis, Victoria, KS; [MON] St. Fidelis Friary, Victoria, KS
Moster, Rev. James E., (MO) Curia: Offices and Directors
Moszur, Rev. Edward J., '71 (GRY) Retired.
Motsay, Rev. Joseph R., '78 (SCR) Retired.
Motsay, Rev. Russell E., '72 (SCR) On Administrative Leave.
Mott, Very Rev. Allen P., '03 (MAR) Holy Name of Mary, Sault Sainte Marie, MI; Sacred Heart, Sugar Island, MI
Mott, Rev. David, (RIC) St. George, Scottsville, VA; St. Thomas Aquinas, Charlottesville, VA
Mott, Rev. James A., *O.S.A.* '65 (LA) Our Mother of Good Counsel, Los Angeles, CA
Motta, Rev. Anthony, '63 (ALB) Retired.
Motta, Rev. Michael J., '72 (HRT) Retired.
Motte, Rev. Albert Jerome, '21 (TYL) St. Boniface, Chandler, TX
Mottola, Very Rev. Peter B., '13 (ROC) Curia: Leadership; Tribunal Peace of Christ Roman Catholic Parish of Rochester, NY, Rochester, NY
Motyka, Rev. Matthew J., *S.J.* '10 (SFR) [MON] Loyola House Jesuit Community, San Francisco, CA
Moualeu, Friar Antonio, *OFM Conv.* (BUF) [MON] St. Francis of Assisi Friary, Hamburg, NY
Mouannes, Rev. Nabil, '84 (OLL) Our Lady of Lebanon Maronite Mission, Norman, OK
Mouawad, Rev. Paul, '69 (SAM) Retired.
Mouch, Rev. Msgr. Frank M., '58 (VEN) Retired.
Mould, Rev. Christopher J., '88 (ARL) On Leave.
Mould, Rev. Daniel, *FSSP* (STP) All Saints, Minneapolis, MN
Mount, Rev. Maurus B., *O.S.B.* '06 (GBG) [MON] Saint Vincent Archabbey, Latrobe, PA
Mouser, Rev. Joseph Irvin, '65 (L) Retired.
Moussallem, Rev. Jebrael, '17 (SAM) St. George, Dover, NH
Moussier, Rev. Howard R., *O.S.B.* '65 (BIR) Retired.
Mouton, Rev. Timothy, *C.S.C.* (FR) [COL] Holy Cross Fathers Religious, North Easton, MA
Mower, Rev. Russell, '15 (DAL) [SEM] Holy Trinity Seminary, Irving, TX
Mower, Rev. Scott M., '97 (PRT) Curia: Consultative Bodies Parish of the Ascension of the Lord, Kittery, ME
Mowery, Rev. Richard, '16 (HBG) Our Lady of Lourdes, Enola, PA
Mowry, Rev. David, (CHI) [SEM] University of Saint Mary of the Lake/Mundelein Seminary, Mundelein, IL
Mowry, Rev. David, '13 (JOL) On Duty Outside Diocese. St Mary of the Lake Seminary, Mundelein
Moya Montero, Rev. Bernardo, *O.F.M.* '15 (MIL) [MIS] General Secretariat of the Franciscan Missions, Inc., Burlington, WI
Moyer, Rev. Joseph M., *C.S.C.* '94 (NO) Holy Cross School, New Orleans, LA
Moyer, Rev. Joseph M., *C.S.C.* '94 (NO) Holy Cross School, New Orleans, LA
Moyer, Rev. Msgr. Richard W., '64 (PHX) Retired. St. Mary Roman Catholic Parish Chandler, Chandler, AZ
Moyher, Rev. Francis, *T.O.R.* '63 (ALT) [MON] St. Francis Friary at Mount Assisi, Loretto, PA
Moyna, Rev. John L., '73 (ALB) Retired. Curia: Leadership
Moyna, Rev. John L., '73 (ALB) Curia: Offices and Directors
Moynahan, Rev. Joseph, '21 (MAN) Good Shepherd, Berlin, NH; Holy Family, Gorham, NH
Moynahan, Rev. Michael, *SJ* '73 (P) St. Ignatius, Portland, OR; [MON] Colombiere Jesuit Community, Portland, OR
Moynihan, Rev. John C., *M.M.* '67 (NY) [MON] Maryknoll Fathers and Brothers (Catholic Foreign Mission Society of America, Inc.), Ossining, NY
Moys, Rev. Msgr. Gregory, '64 (P) Retired.
Mozer, Very Rev. Joseph F., '97 (BO) Curia: Leadership St. Martha, Plainville, MA; St. Mary, Wrentham, MA
Mozie, Rev. Leonard, (RVC) St. Patrick's, Glen Cove, NY
Mpagi, Rev. Anthony, '06 (WOR) Curia: Leadership Our Lady of Hope Parish Grafton, North Grafton, MA; [CAM] Fitchburg State College (Fitchburg), Fitchburg, MA
Mpanda, Rev. Apo T., '88 (DAV) Church of the Visitation of Camanche, Iowa, Camanche, IA; Our Lady of the River Church of Le Claire-Princeton, Iowa, LeClaire, IA
Mpeka, Rev. Rogatus, '82 (TR) St. Vincent de Paul, Trenton, NJ
Mpungu, Rev. Anthony, '05 (RIC) Catholic Church of St. Mark, Virginia Beach, VA
Mraz, Rev. Robert J., '74 (NU) Retired.
Mrosso, Rev. Bartholomew, *M.Afr.* '02 (BRK) Our Lady of Light Roman Catholic Church, St. Albans, NY
Mrosso, Rev. Dennis, *A.J.* '82 (CLV) Marymount Hospital [HOS] Marymount Hospital, Inc., Garfield Heights, OH
Mroz, Rev. Richard J., '92 (NEW) Retired. St. Cecilia, Kearny, NJ; St. Mary, Closter, NJ
Mrozek, Rev. John Robert, '17 (DEN) St. Clare of Assisi Catholic Parish in Edwards, Edwards, CO
Msigala, Rev. Marino, *OFM Cap.* (PIT) Our Lady of the Angels, Pittsburgh, PA; [MON] Our Lady of the Angels Friary, Pittsburgh, PA
Msinge, Rev. Nicetas, *ALCP/OSS* (HEL) Saint John Paul II Parish: Series 506, LLC, Bigfork, MT
Msinge, Rev. Nicetus, (HEL)
Mtenga, Rev. Dominic, '92 (P) [HOS] Providence Health & Services-Oregon (Providence Portland Medical Center), Portland, OR
Mtseka, Rev. Servasio, (STL) Chap, Barnes - Jewish Hosp
Mucci, Rev. Robert V., '09 (BRK) Curia: Consultative Bodies; Leadership Saint Mark – Saint Margaret Mary, Brooklyn, NY
Mucha, Rev. John, '81 (STU) Curia: Deaneries St. Anthony of Padua, Bridgeport, OH; St. Joseph, Bridgeport, OH
Mucowski, Rev. Richard, *O.F.M.* (PAT) Curia: Leadership
Mucowski, Rev. Richard J., *O.F.M.* '71 (NEW) Assumption of Our Blessed Lady, Wood Ridge, NJ
Muda, Rev. Adam, '09 (PAT) On Duty Outside Diocese. Military Chaplain Curia: (>MO) Offices and Directors
Mudakodil, Rev. Siju Kuriakose, '04 (SYM) St. Pius X Syro-Malabar Knanaya Catholic Church, Montebello, CA
Mudakodil, Rev. Siju Kuriakose, '04 (SYM) St. Stephen's Syro-Malabar Knanaya Catholic Mission, Las Vegas, Las Vegas, NV
Mudakodiyil, Rev. Jose Thomas, '02 (BAK) Curia: Offices and Directors St. Francis of Assisi Catholic Church of Bend, Inc., Bend, OR
Mudd, Rev. Gerald R., *O.F.M.* '66 (PAT) Retired. [MON] St. Anthony Friary (Order of Friars Minor), Butler, NJ
Mudd, Rev. James T., '64 (L) Retired.
Mudd, Rev. Joachim, (FR) [MON] Marian Friary of Our Lady, Queen of the Seraphic Order, New Bedford, MA
Mudd, Rev. John, '69 (WDC) Retired. Archbishop Carroll High School, Washington, DC
Mudd, Rev. Nathan, *CPM* '20 (OWN) [MON] Fathers of Mercy, Auburn, KY
Muddu, Rev. Alexander, (RIC) St. Mary of the Annunciation, Ruther Glen, VA
Mudrak, Rev. Lloyd, '62 (DUL) Retired.
Mueller, Rev. Eric L., '09 (TOL) Epiphany of the Lord Parish, Toledo, OH; St. John the Evangelist, Defiance, OH
Mueller, Rev. Hans, (P) St. Juan Diego Catholic Church, Portland, OR
Mueller, Rev. James, *O.Carm.* '69 (PHX) [MON] St. Therese Priory, Phoenix, AZ
Mueller, Rev. Jerome D., '73 (SFE) Retired.

Mueller, Rev. Joseph, *SJ* '93 (OAK) [MON] Jesuit Fathers and Brothers, Berkeley, CA; [SEM] Jesuit School of Theology of Santa Clara University (Berkeley, California Campus), Berkeley, CA
Mueller, Rev. Joseph G., *S.J.* '93 (SJ) [COL] Santa Clara University, Santa Clara, CA
Mueller, Rev. Kevin A., '92 (BAL) Our Lady of Hope, Baltimore, MD; St. Luke, Edgemere, MD
Mueller, Rev. Noel, *O.S.B.* '68 (IND) [MON] St. Meinrad Archabbey, St. Meinrad, IN
Mueller, Rev. Roman, *S.D.S.* '74 (MIL) [MIS] Salvatorians - Jordan Hall, Milwaukee, WI
Muema, Rev. Simon, *SDS* '22 (MIL) [MON] Salvatorian Provincial Offices (Society of the Divine Savior), Milwaukee, WI
Muench, Very Rev. Msgr. R. Francis, '81 (RIC) Curia: Administration; Deaneries St. Bridget, Richmond, VA
Muench, Rev. William, '59 (SY) Retired. Church of the Holy Family, Syracuse, NY
Muench, Rev. William G., '59 (OG) Retired.
Muenks, Rev. Nicholas J., '06 (STL) Curia: Leadership St. Ferdinand Catholic Church, Florissant, MO
Muer, Rev. Christopher, '18 (DET) St. Peter Parish Mount Clemens, Mount Clemens, MI
Mues, Rev. Kevin Joseph, '19 (SHP) St. Benedict the Black, Grambling, LA; St. Thomas Aquinas, Ruston, LA; [CAM] E. Donn Piatt Catholic Student Center at Louisiana Tech University, Ruston, LA
Muga, Rev. Geoffrey Omondi, *F.M.H.* '13 (NO) New Orleans East Hosp, New Orleans Resurrection of Our Lord Roman Catholic Church, New Orleans, Louisiana (St. Nicholas of Myra Mission), New Orleans, LA
Mugabi, Rev. Gerard, *A.J.* (SJN) San Jose, Toa Alta, PR
Mugabo, Rev. Bernardin, '96 (SAC) Pastor of St. John the Evangelist Parish, Carmichael, a corporation sole, Carmichael, CA
Mugasha, Rev. Chrisanth, *A.J.* '99 (NY) St. Columba, New York, NY
Mugavero, Rev. Anthony P., '81 (ROC) Holy Apostles, Rochester, NY
Muggli, Rev. Boniface, *O.S.B.* '90 (BIS) [MON] Assumption Abbey, Richardton, ND
Muggli, Rev. Odo, *O.S.B.* '66 (BIS) [MIS] Sacred Heart Mission, Richardton, ND; [MON] Assumption Abbey, Richardton, ND
Mugisha, Rev. Fortunatus, (RVC) Holy Family, Hicksville, NY
Mugisho, Rev. Patrick, *S.J.* '21 (CHI) St. Ignatius Jesuit Community, Chicago, IL
Mugomba, Rev. Michael, '82 (RIC) Holy Infant, Elkton, VA; Shepherd of the Hills, Ruckersville, VA
Muguerza, Rev. Octavio, (SAT) Church of the Good Shepherd, Schertz, TX
Muguerza, Rev. Octavio A., '92 (SAT) Immaculate Conception, Marion, TX
Muha, Rev. Joseph, '60 (B) Retired.
Muha, Rev. Peter J., '88 (GRY) Curia: Leadership St. Joseph, Dyer, IN
Muhero, Rev. Christon, (CR) St. Charles Catholic Church of Pennington, Pennington, MN; St. Philip's, Bemidji, MN
Muhlen, Rev. Micah, *O.F.M.* '91 (PHX) St. Mary's Roman Catholic Basilica, Phoenix, AZ
Muhlenkamp, Rev. Benjamin J., '12 (FTW) On Leave. On Personal Leave
Muhlenkamp, Rev. Robert K., '10 (CIN) Holy Rosary, St. Marys, OH; Immaculate Conception of the Blessed Virgin Mary, Celina, OH; St. Patrick, St. Marys, OH; St. Teresa, Rockford, OH
Muhr, Rev. Msgr. Michael G., '83 (SP) Curia: Pastoral Services St. Lawrence, Tampa, FL; [NUR] St. Lawrence Housing II, Inc., Tampa, FL
Muir, Rev. John, '07 (PHX) Curia: Leadership; Offices and Directors St. Thomas Aquinas Roman Catholic Parish, Avondale, AZ
Mujaeropiro, Rev. Joseph, *AJ* (P) St. Anne, Grants Pass, OR
Mujule, Rev. Michael Christopher, '78 (BEL) St. Patrick, Cairo, IL; St. Rose of Lima, Metropolis, IL
Mujuni, Rev. John Bosco, '97 (PEO) Immaculate Conception, Lacon, IL; St. John XXIII, Henry, IL
Muka, Rev. Patrick J., (PH) St. Robert Bellarmine, Warrington, PA
Mukamba, Rev. Benoit, *C.S.Sp.* '92 (PIT) [MON] Congregation of the Holy Spirit Province of the United States, Bethel Park, PA
Mukamba, Rev. Benoit, *C.S.Sp.* (CIN) Our Lady of Grace Parish, Dayton, OH
Mukamba, Rev. Benoit, *CSSp* '92 (CIN) Queen of Martyrs, Dayton, OH
Mukasa, Rev. Paul, (BO) St. Charles Borromeo, Woburn, MA
Mukasa, Rev. Vincent, '94 (BEL) St. Joseph, Elizabethtown, IL; St. Kateri Tekakwitha, Ridgway, IL
Mukiibi, Rev. Leonard, '05 (JC) St. Cecilia, Meta, MO; St. Thomas the Apostle, St. Thomas, MO
Mukkoot, Rev. Saji, '92 (PH) St. Katherine of Siena, Philadelphia, PA
Mukkoot, Very Rev. Saji G., '92 (MCE) Curia: Administration; Advisory Boards, Commissions, Committees, and Councils; Offices and Directors; Tribunal Atlanta Syro-Malankara Catholic Mission, Lawrenceville, GA; St. Jude Malankara Catholic Church, Bensalem, PA; Syro-Malankara Catholic Mission, Albany, NY; Syro-Malankara Catholic Mission, Phoenix, AZ, Elmont, NY
Mukoka, Rev. Jean-Marie, *OSC* '20 (PHX) [MON] Crosier Community of Phoenix (Canons Regular of the Order of the Holy Cross) (Conventual Priory of the Holy Cross), Phoenix, AZ
Mukuka, Very Rev. George S., '11 (HRT) Curia: Administration; Advisory Boards, Commissions, Committees, and Councils; Tribunal
Mukuna, Rev. Joseph N., *SCJ* '07 (MIL) [MON] Sacred Heart Novitiate, Franksville, WI
Mukundi, Rev. Samson Ngatia, '03 (CHI) Jesus, Bread of Life Parish, Chicago, IL
Mulackal, Rev. Binny Thomas, '98 (WH) Sacred Heart, Powhatan, WV; St. Peter, Welch, WV; [MIS] Holy Cross Chapel, Pineville, WV; [MIS] Our Lady of Victory Chapel, Gary, WV
Mulakaleti, Rev. Yesu, '04 (SAN) St. Ann's, Midland, TX
Mulanjanany, Rev. Augustine, '69 (LKC) Retired.
Mulavanal, Rev. Msgr. Thomas, '90 (SYM) Curia: Administration; Leadership St. Mary's Syro-Malabar Knanaya Catholic Parish (Morton Grove), Morton Grove, IL
Mulcahey, Rev. Andrew T., '96 (RCK) St. Laurence, Elgin, IL
Mulcahey, Rev. Timothy P., '97 (RCK) Our Lady of Good Counsel, Aurora, IL
Mulcahy, Rev. Bernard, *O.P.* '03 (COL) St. Patrick, Columbus, OH; [SEM] Pontifical College Josephinum, Columbus, OH
Mulcahy, Rev. Brian, *O.P.* '90 (MAN) [MON] Order of Preachers, Hanover, NH
Mulcahy, Rev. Daniel R., '79 (WOR) Assumption, Millbury, MA; St. Brigid, Millbury, MA
Mulcahy, Rev. Louis, *O.S.B.* '89 (IND) [MON] St. Meinrad Archabbey, St. Meinrad, IN
Mulcahy, Rev. Patrick J., '95 (SD) Pastor of Mary, Star of the Sea Catholic Parish, La Jolla, a corporation sole, La Jolla, CA; [MIS] Mary, Star of the Sea Catholic Parish in La Jolla, CA Real Property Support Corporation, La Jolla, CA
Mulcahy, Rev. Patrick M., '06 (JOL) St. Mary Immaculate, Plainfield, IL
Mulcahy, Rev. Sean, '62 (MIA) Retired.
Mulcrone, Rev. Joseph A., '71 (CHI) Retired. Curia: Social Services St. Francis Borgia, Chicago, IL; [SPF] Catholic Office of the Deaf, Chicago, IL
Mulcrone, Rev. Thomas A., '77 (CHI) Retired. [SPF] St. Mary of Providence, Chicago, IL
Mulderink, Rev. Robert C., '19 (GR) St. Luke University Parish, Jenison, MI; [CAM] St. Luke University Parish and Catholic Campus Ministry, Jenison, MI
Mulderry, Rev. Anthony, '67 (MIA) Retired.
Muldoon, Rev. Msgr. Brendan, '64 (SP) Retired. St. Jerome, Largo, FL
Muldoon, Rev. P. Christopher, '71 (PAT) Our Lady Star of the Sea, Lake Hopatcong, NJ
Muldoon, Rev. Ryan, '19 (NY) St. Patrick, Yorktown Heights, NY; [SEM] St. Joseph's Seminary, Yonkers, NY
Muldowney, Rev. Thomas M., '03 (SCR) St. Catherine of Siena, Moscow, PA; [MIS] Aid to the Church in Russia, Scranton, PA
Mulenda, Rev. Ignatius, '90 (PEO) Holy Family, Danville, IL; St. Anthony Church, Hoopeston, IL
Mulenga, Rev. Emmanuel, *O.M.I.* '12 (NO) Our Lady of Guadalupe/International Shrine of St. Jude, New Orleans, LA; St. Augustine, New Orleans, LA
Mulenga, Rev. Emmanuel, *OMI* (WDC) [MON] Missionary Oblates of Mary Immaculate, Washington, DC
Mulenga, Rev. Michael, (NO) Chap, St Tammany Hosp, Covington
Mulewski, Rev. Patrick M., '79 (NEW) Retired. Corpus Christi, Hasbrouck Heights, NJ
Mulgrew, Rev. John E., '56 (PH) Retired.
Mulhall, Rev. Colin J., '16 (GR) On Special Assignment. On Academic Leave
Mulhall, Rev. Michael, *O.Carm.* '67 (JOL) Retired.
Mulhauser, Rev. Daniel J., *S.J.* '60 (SY) Retired. (>NY) [MON] Murray-Weigel Hall (A Jesuit Community at Murray-Weigel Hall and Kohlmann Hall), Bronx, NY
Mulhearn, Rev. Michael, *C.M.* '68 (STL) [MON] Congregation of the Mission Vincentian Fathers Lazarist Residence, St. Louis, MO
Mulhern, Rev. Kevin P., '76 (SCR) Retired. Our Lady of Mount Carmel Parish, Dunmore, PA
Mulhollan, Rev. John, '16 (CLV) St. Francis Xavier, Medina, OH
Mulholland, Rev. David T., '02 (SEA) Holy Cross, Tacoma, WA; St. Patrick, Tacoma, WA
Muli, Rev. Killian, '01 (CHY) Curia: (>MO) Offices and Directors
Mull, Rev. Thomas P., '76 (ROC) Our Lady of Peace Roman Catholic Church of Geneva, NY, Geneva, NY; [CAM] Hobart and William Smith College, Geneva, NY; [MIS] Apostleship of Prayer, Rochester, NY
Mullady, Rev. Brian T.B., *O.P.* '72 (P) [MON] Holy Rosary Priory, Portland, OR
Mullah, Rev. Nixon, *S.S.J* (WDC) [SEM] St. Joseph's Seminary, Washington, DC
Mullakkara, Rev. Joseph, *MSFS* '75 (ATL) Good Shepherd Catholic Church, Cumming, Inc., Cumming, GA; [MON] The Missionaries of St. Francis de Sales - MSFS USA Vice Province, Loganville, GA
Mullally, Rev. Thomas A., *S.V.D.* '70 (JKS) Retired. Sacred Heart, Greenville, MS
Mullan, Rev. Glen F., '94 (CC) Our Lady of Guadalupe, Sinton, TX
Mullan, Rev. Msgr. Raymund A., '62 (FWT) Retired.
Mullan, Rev. William F., *M.M.* '62 (SJ) Retired.
Mullan, Rev. William F., *M.M.* '62 (NY) Retired.
Mullane, Rev. Thomas, '68 (MIA) Retired.
Mullaney, Rev. Gregory C., '90 (NOR) Saint Matthias Church Corporation, East Lyme, CT; St. Agnes, Niantic, CT
Mullaney, Rev. Larry, (RIC) Retired.
Mullaney, Rev. Mark, '03 (ARL) St. Louis, Alexandria, VA
Mullarkey, Rev. John T., '64 (GB) Retired.
Mullee, Rev. John J., '12 (CLV) St. Monica, Garfield Heights, OH
Mullelly, Rev. Msgr. Thomas J., '80 (TR) Curia: Clergy and Religious Services; Leadership St. James, Pennington, NJ
Mullen, Rev. Charles, *C.PP.S.* '64 (CIN) Retired. [MON] St. Charles, Celina, OH
Mullen, Rev. David J., '82 (BO) St. Brendan, Bellingham, MA
Mullen, Rev. Dennis M., '70 (SUP) Retired.
Mullen, Rev. Godfrey, *OSB* '94 (BEL) Cathedral of St. Peter, Belleville, IL
Mullen, Rev. Godfrey, *O.S.B.* '94 (IND) [MON] St. Meinrad Archabbey, St. Meinrad, IN
Mullen, Very Rev. Godfrey, *O.S.B.* '94 (EVN) Curia: Leadership
Mullen, Rev. Kevin, (PRO) [MIS] Poverello Corporation, Warwick, RI
Mullen, Rev. Kevin, *O.F.M.* '80 (NY) [EFT] Foundation of the Order of Friars Minor of the Province of the Most Holy Name, New York, NY; [EFT] Franciscans of Holy Name Province Benevolence Trust, Inc., New York, NY; [EFT] Franciscans of Holy Name Province Sick, Aged and Retired Trust, New York, NY
Mullen, Rev. Canon Kevin J., *O.F.M.* '80 (NY) [MON] Franciscan Friars, Holy Name Province (The Order of Friars Minor of the Province of the Most Holy Name), New York, NY
Mullen, Rev. Kevin J., *O.F.M.* (PAT) [MON] Order of Friars Minor of the Province of the Most Holy Name (Franciscan Friars-Holy Name Province (NJ), Inc.), Butler, NJ
Mullen, Rev. Michael, '75 (VEN) Retired.
Mullen, Rev. Msgr. Michael, '62 (KCK) Retired.
Mullen, Rev. Patrick, '85 (LA) St. Junipero Serra, Camarillo, CA
Mullen, Rev. Paul M., '73 (SCR) Retired. St. Vincent de Paul, Milford, PA
Muller, Rev. Earl C., *S.J.* '77 (NO) [MON] Loyola Jesuit Community, New Orleans, LA; [SEM] Notre Dame Seminary Graduate School of Theology, New Orleans, LA
Muller, Rev. Joseph T., *M.S.C.* '58 (ALN) [MON] Sacred Heart Villa, Missionaries of the Sacred Heart, Center Valley, PA
Muller, Rev. Msgr. Martin M., '57 (BIR) Curia: Leadership Our Lady of Sorrows Catholic Parish, Birmingham, Birmingham, AL; [EFT] Our Lady of Sorrows Educational School Foundation, Birmingham, AL
Muller, Rev. Peter, *O.Praem.* '93 (SFE) Curia: Offices and Directors St. Edwin, Albuquerque, NM; [MON] Santa Maria de la Vid Abbey, Albuquerque, NM

Muller, Rev. Stephen, *O.C.S.O.* '06 (ROC) [MON] Abbey of the Genesee, Inc., Piffard, NY
Muller, Rev. William H., *S.J.* '73 (WDC) [MON] Leonard Neale House, Washington, DC
Muller, Rev. William H., *S.J.* '73 (PHX) Brophy College Preparatory (Jesuit Fathers), Phoenix, AZ
Mullet, Rev. John, '56 (SAG) On Duty Outside Diocese. Saint Petersburg, FL
Mullett, Rev. Msgr. Gene W., '76 (STU) Retired.
Mulligan, Rev. Brian, (WIN) All Saints, New Richland, MN; St. Ann, Janesville, MN; St. Joseph, Waldorf, MN
Mulligan, Rev. Brian M., '18 (WIN) Curia: Offices and Directors
Mulligan, Rev. George B, *CSC* '82 (ORL) [MON] Congregation of Holy Cross, United States Province, Cocoa Beach, FL
Mulligan, Rev. James, *SOLT* (SFE) St. Gertrude the Great, Mora, NM
Mulligan, Rev. John M., '64 (ROC) Retired. Curia: Tribunal Holy Trinity, Webster, NY
Mulligan, Rev. Joseph V., '75 (CHL) Retired.
Mulligan, Rev. Kevin T., '15 (PH) Nativity of the Blessed Virgin Mary, Media, PA
Mulligan, Rev. Robert G., *O.S.F.S.* '85 (PH) Our Mother of Consolation, Philadelphia, PA
Mulligan, Rev. Sean P., '13 (FAR) St. Boniface Church of Wimbledon, Wimbledon, ND; St. John's Church of Kensal, Kensal, ND; St. Mary's Church of Dazey, Dazey, ND
Mullin, Rev. Douglas, *O.S.B.* '07 (SCL) [MON] St. John's Abbey, of the Order of St. Benedict, Collegeville, MN
Mullin, Rev. Douglas L., (MO) Curia: Offices and Directors
Mullin, Rev. Jay M., '69 (BO) Retired.
Mullin, Rev. John A., *S.J.* '75 (NEW) [MIS] Jesuit Community, Jersey City, NJ; [MON] Jesuits of Saint Peter College, Inc., Jersey City, NJ
Mullin, Rev. Patrick, (STL) [MON] Congregation of the Mission, Perryville, MO
Mullin, Rev. Msgr. Thomas M., '75 (PH) Saint Elizabeth, Chester Springs, PA
Mullins, Rev. Kevin, *S.S.C.* '78 (OM) [MON] Missionary Society of St. Columban, St. Columbans, NE
Mullins, Rev. Kevin C., *OSA* '90 (CHI) [MON] Federation of Augustinians of North America, Chicago, IL
Mullins, Rev. Kevin C., *O.S.A.* '90 (CHI) [MON] Federation of Augustinians of North America, Chicago, IL
Mullins, Rev. Michael E., '05 (ALN) St. Paul, Allentown, PA
Mullins, Rev. Richard A., '95 (WDC) St. Thomas Apostle, Washington, DC
Mullins, Rev. Richard A., '95 (ARL) On Duty Outside Diocese. St Thomas the Apostle Church, Washington, DC
Mullonkal, Rev. George, '71 (SJP) On Leave. Curia: Offices and Directors
Mulloth, Rev. Albi, '98 (ALX) St. John the Baptist, Deville, LA
Mullowney, Rev. Edward J., *S.S.J.* '55 (BAL) Retired.
Mullowney, Rev. Thomas E., '55 (GI) Retired.
Mulloy, Rev. James, *S.D.B.* '85 (NEW) Don Bosco Preparatory High School (Salesians of St. John Bosco), Ramsey, NJ; [MON] Don Bosco Prep Salesian Residence, Ramsey, NJ
Mulloy, Rev. John F., '70 (BO) Retired.
Mulloy, Rev. Michel, '79 (RC) On Administrative Leave. Without Faculties
Mulqueen, Rev. John D., '62 (Y) Retired.
Mulqueen, Rev. Msgr. Joseph C., '57 (BRK) Retired. Curia: Leadership
Mulranen, Rev. Francis J., '82 (PH) On Special Assignment. Chap, St Martha Ctr Rehab & Healthcare, St Joseph Rec Downi… Visitation B.V.M., Norristown, PA
Mulreany, Rev. John P., (BGP) [MON] The Fairfield Jesuit Community-Fairfield University, Fairfield, CT
Mulroney, Rev. Joseph G., '93 (MO) Curia: Offices and Directors
Mulroney, Rev. Joseph G., '93 (R) Sacred Heart Parish of Dunn, Dunn, NC
Mulrooney, Rev. Conan P., *O. Praem.* '67 (GB) Retired.
Mulroy, Rev. Timothy, *S.S.C.* '95 (CHI) [MON] Columban Fathers Theologate, Chicago, IL
Mulu, Rev. Sebastian, *OSM* (ORG) St. Philip Benizi, Fullerton, CA
Mulu, Rev. Sebastian, *OSM* (ORG) [MON] Servite Fathers and Brothers, Buena Park, CA
Mulvaney, Rev. Francis, *C.Ss.R.* '08 (PH) Visitation B.V.M., Philadelphia, PA
Mulvany, Rev. Michael, '88 (KCK) Holy Family, Eudora, KS
Mulvehill, Rev. John R., '57 (BO) Retired.
Mulvey, Rev. Gerard, *O.F.M.Cap.* (BRK) St. Michael - Saint Malachy, Brooklyn, NY; [MON] St. Michael Friary, Brooklyn, NY
Mulvihill, Rev. John E., '64 (CHI) Retired.
Mulvihill, Rev. Martin J., '83 (STL) Retired.
Mulyata, Rev. Neal M. N., '01 (BAL) [MON] Society of St. Sulpice, Province of the United States, Baltimore, MD
Muma, Rev. Sama, '07 (DET) SS. Peter and Paul Parish North Branch, North Branch, MI; St. Mary Burnside Parish North Branch, North Branch, MI
Mummadi, Rev. Lourdu, *S.J.* '14 (SPK) St. Patrick, Walla Walla, WA
Mumper, Rev. Edward, '63 (JOL) Retired.
Mundackal, Rev. Kevin, '18 (SYM) Curia: Offices and Directors
Mundackal, Rev. Sebastian, *O.S.B.* '91 (STL) Our Lady of Sorrows Catholic Church, St. Louis, MO
Mundakal, Rev. Joseph, *C.M.I.* '83 (NSH) St. Elizabeth Ann Seton, Tennessee Ridge, TN; St. Francis of Assisi, Dover, TN
Mundanmani, Rev. Paulson, '91 (OAK) Curia: Leadership Christ the King, Pleasant Hill, CA; St. Stephen, Walnut Creek, CA; [MIS] Catholic Professional & Business Breakfast Club of the Diocese of Oakland, Danville, CA
Mundattuchundayil, Rev. Elijah, *F.S.S.P.* '21 (TLS) Most Precious Blood Parish, Tulsa, OK
Mundumoozhikkaranirappel, Rev. Paul, *C.S.T.* (WH) Central Catholic High School, Wheeling, WV; Corpus Christi, Wheeling, WV
Mundwiller, Rev. Edmund, *O.F.M.* '81 (STL) [MON] Franciscan Friary of St. Anthony of Padua, St. Louis, MO
Mungai, Rev. Samuel, '21 (NSH) Holy Family, Lafayette, TN
Mungovan, Rev. Reed C., *S.D.S.* '09 (MIL) Mother of Good Counsel Congregation, Milwaukee, WI; [MON] Salvatorian Provincial Offices (Society of the Divine Savior), Milwaukee, WI
Mungujakisa, Rev. Alfred, '94 (CAM) Infant Jesus Parish, Woodbury Heights, N.J., Woodbury Heights, NJ
Munishi, Rev. Honest, (GAL) [MON] US Foundation for the Congregation of the Holy Ghost and the Immaculate Heart of Mary, Inc., Houston, TX
Muniz, Rev. Orlando Rosas, '97 (MGZ) Curia: Offices and Directors
Muniz Borrero, Rev. Alberto, (PCE) Retired.
Munjanath, Rev. Mathews Kurian, '92 (SYM) St. Thomas Apostle Syro-Malabar Catholic Church (Santa Ana), Santa Ana, CA
Munjanattu, Rev. George, *O.F.M.Conv* '00 (SYM) Divine Mercy Syro-Malabar Catholic Mission Louisville, Kentucky, Louisville, KY
Munjanattu, Rev. George, (L) Holy Family, Louisville, KY
Munkelt, Rev. Richard A., '01 (SCR) Retired. On Duty Outside Diocese. West Orange, NJ
Munoz, Rev. Antonio, (CGS) Retired.
Munoz, Rev. Chris, '15 (SAT) Blessed Sacrament, San Antonio, TX
Munoz, Rev. Elbano, '05 (VEN) Curia: Leadership Sacred Heart Parish in Bradenton, Inc., Bradenton, FL
Munoz, Rev. Esney, (MIA) St. Michael the Archangel, Miami, FL
Munoz, Rev. Feiser Elliott, '13 (ATL) On Leave.
Munoz, Rev. Francisco I. Ortega, '05 (CHI) Sacred Heart and St. Eulalia, Melrose Park, IL
Munoz, Rev. Javier, '96 (ATL) St. Pius X Catholic Church, Conyers, Inc., Conyers, GA
Munoz, Rev. Jesus M., '01 (ARE) On Duty Outside Diocese. Military Service
Munoz, Rev. Jose, '96 (ORL) Curia: Evangelization St. Catherine of Siena, Kissimmee, FL
Munoz, Rev. Juan, (FR) Cathedral of St. Mary of the Assumption, Fall River, MA; Parish of the Good Shepherd, Fall River, MA; St. Stanislaus, Fall River, MA
Munoz, Rev. Juan Carlos, (FR) Curia: Offices and Directors
Munoz, Rev. Manuel, '98 (ELP) On Leave.
Munoz, Rev. Martin, *M.D.M.* '10 (PHX) Holy Family Roman Catholic Parish, Phoenix, AZ; St. Martin de Porres Roman Catholic Parish, Phoenix, AZ
Munoz, Rev. Matthew, '02 (ORG) On Administrative Leave.
Munoz, Rev. Mauricio, '12 (YAK) St. Joseph Parish, Yakima, WA
Munoz, Rev. Nelson D., '15 (TYL) Curia: Advisory Boards, Commissions, Committees, and Councils; Miscellaneous / Other Offices St. Therese of Lisieux, Center, TX
Munoz, Rev. Rafael, '60 (PCE) Retired.
Munoz, Rev. Ruben D., '05 (GLD) Saint Joseph of Onekama, Onekama, MI; Saint Raphael of Copemish, Copemish, MI
Munoz, Rev. Wellington M., '10 (PH) St. Charles Borromeo, Philadelphia, PA
Munoz Escamilla, Rev. Martin, '19 (MIA) St. Elizabeth of Hungary Catholic Church, Pompano Beach, FL
Munoz Garcia, Rev. Francisco Javier, '96 (ATL) On Special Assignment. Archdiocesan Priest in Residence
Munoz Munoz, Rev. Pedro Manuel, *O.F.M.Cap.* '03 (R) Infant of Prague, Church of the Holy Spirit, Jacksonville, NC
Muñoz-Martinez, Rev. Oscar M., *MSP* (SB) St. Charles Borromeo, Bloomington, CA
Munro, Rev. Donald, '87 (PMB) Retired.
Munsch, Rev. Nathan J., *O.S.B.* '91 (GBG) Retired. [MON] Saint Vincent Archabbey, Latrobe, PA
Muntean, Very Rev. Iuliu-Vasile, '97 (ROM) Curia: Leadership; Offices and Directors St. Theodore, Alliance, OH
Munyaneza, Rev. Elias, *A.J.* '91 (ALN) Our Lady of Mercy Parish, Easton, PA
Munz, Rev. Ted, *S.J.* '83 (DET) (>CHI) [MON] Canisius House Jesuit Community, Evanston, IL
Muodiaju, Rev. Samuel, *C.S.Sp.* '85 (MIA) St. Monica, Miami Gardens, FL; [MIS] Congregation of the Holy Spirit Province of Nigeria South East, Inc., Miami Gardens, FL
Muoghalu, Rev. Adolphus, (MO) Curia: Offices and Directors
Muojekwu, Rev. Peter E., '01 (CHI) St. Josephine Bakhita Parish, Chicago, IL
Muoneke, Rev. Romanus, (GAL) St. Vincent de Paul, Houston, TX
Muorah, Rev. Charles, '91 (TR) Parish of the Sacred Heart, Trenton, N.J., Trenton, NJ
Mupparathara, Rev. Abraham J., *M.C.B.S.* '94 (MAR) Curia: Advisory Boards, Commissions, Committees, and Councils Holy Redeemer, Menominee, MI; Holy Spirit, Menominee, MI
Mur, Rev. Msgr. Rogelio, *O.Carm.* '56 (MGZ) Curia: Leadership; Offices and Directors
Murasso, Rev. Jeremiah N., (HRT) Saint Pio of Pietrelcina Parish Corporation, East Haven, CT
Muraya, Rev. Anthony, '12 (CHI) On Duty Outside Diocese. Maximilian Church, Pembroke, FL
Muraya, Rev. Anthony, '12 (CHI) [SEM] University of Saint Mary of the Lake/Mundelein Seminary, Mundelein, IL
Murd, Rev. Francis A., '76 (TOL) Retired.
Murhammer, Rev. Francis J., '88 (PIT) Retired.
Murillo, Rev. Rafael A., '96 (SLC) San Rafael, Huntington, UT; St. Marguerite LLC 235, Tooele, UT
Murillo Ferro, Rev. Jose de Jesus, '13 (DEN) St. Clare of Assisi Catholic Parish in Edwards, Edwards, CO
Muringayil, Rev. Raju D., *O.Praem* (BO) Immaculate Conception, Lowell, MA
Murnan, Rev. Sean, *O.F.M.* '73 (SFE) Retired. [MON] The Province of Our Lady of Guadalupe of the Order of Friars Minor, Inc., Albuquerque, NM
Muro, Rev. Jose Luis, '01 (SD) [MIS] Saint John of the Cross Catholic Parish in Lemon Grove, CA Real Property Support Corporation, Lemon Grove, CA
Muro, Rev. Jose Luis, '01 (SD) Pastor of Saint John of the Cross Catholic Parish, Lemon Grove, a corporation sole, Lemon Grove, CA
Muro, Rev. Msgr. Victor S., '66 (CAM) Retired.
Murori, Rev. Lawrence, '13 (NO) St. Angela Merici Roman Catholic Church, Metairie, Louisiana, Metairie, LA
Murphy, Rev. Athanasius, *O.P.* '16 (NY) [MON] St. Vincent Ferrer Priory, New York, NY
Murphy, Rev. Austin, '03 (BAL) Christ the King Roman Catholic Congregation, Inc., Glen Burnie, MD; [EFT] The Church of the Good Shepherd Parish Endowment Trust, Glen Burnie, MD
Murphy, Rt. Rev. Austin G., *O.S.B.* '04 (JOL) [MON] St. Procopius Abbey, Lisle, IL
Murphy, Rev. Bartholomew J., *S.J.* '72 (SJ) [MON] USA West Province, Society of Jesus, Los Gatos, CA
Murphy, Rev. Brendan, *SVD* '73 (FWT) Retired.
Murphy, Rev. Brendan, *O.P.* '99 (PRO) St. Jude's Church, Lincoln, Lincoln, RI
Murphy, Rev. Msgr. Charles M., '61 (PRT) Retired.
Murphy, Rev. Charles R., '91 (OKL) Retired.
Murphy, Rev. Christopher D., '96 (ARL) St. Stephen the Martyr, Middleburg, VA
Murphy, Rev. Christopher J., '12 (PRO) Curia: Advisory Boards, Commissions, Committees, and Councils; Clergy and Religious Services [SEM] Seminary of Our Lady of Providence, Providence, RI

Murphy, Rev. Christopher M., (PRO) Curia: Clergy and Religious Services
Murphy, Rev. Conrad, (WDC) Univ of Maryland St. Matthew Cathedral, Washington, DC; [CAM] University of Maryland Catholic Student Center, College Park, MD
Murphy, Rev. D. Brendan, *O.P.* '00 (MAN) [MON] Order of Preachers, Hanover, NH
Murphy, Rev. Daniel J., (PAT) Retired.
Murphy, Rev. Daniel S., '70 (BRK) Retired. St. Saviour, Brooklyn, NY
Murphy, Rev. Daniel S., '61 (BRK) Retired.
Murphy, Rev. Daniel T., '62 (MIL) Retired.
Murphy, Rev. David F., '87 (WIL) Chap, Delaware Air National Guard, New Castle St. Mary of the Assumption, Hockessin, DE
Murphy, Rev. Dennis, '75 (ALB) Retired.
Murphy, Rev. Dominic Savio Mary, *F.I.* '03 (NOR) [MON] Marian Friary of Our Lady of Guadalupe, Griswold, CT
Murphy, Rev. Edward A., '98 (FR) Curia: Advisory Boards, Commissions, Committees, and Councils Saint Andrew the Apostle Parish, Taunton, MA
Murphy, Rev. Edward F., *C.M.* '79 (STL) St. Vincent De Paul Catholic Church, St. Louis, St. Louis, MO
Murphy, Rev. Edward W., '92 (STA) Curia: Evangelization; Social Services
Murphy, Rev. Emmet, *OFM* '52 (PAT) Retired. [MON] St. Anthony Friary (Order of Friars Minor), Butler, NJ
Murphy, Rev. Eugene A., '10 (SUP) Retired.
Murphy, Rev. Francis J., *C.S.C.* '86 (FTW) [COL] University of Notre Dame Du Lac, Notre Dame, IN; [MON] Holy Cross Community, Corby Hall, University of Notre Dame, Notre Dame, IN
Murphy, Rev. Msgr. Frederick J., '57 (BO) Retired.
Murphy, Rev. G. Ronald, *S.J.* '69 (WDC) [COL] Georgetown University, Washington, DC; [MON] The Jesuit Community at Georgetown University, Washington, DC
Murphy, Rev. George E., '66 (BLX) Retired. Curia: Advisory Boards, Commissions, Committees, and Councils
Murphy, Rev. George R., *S.J.* '71 (OAK) [MON] Jesuit Fathers and Brothers, Berkeley, CA; [SEM] Jesuit School of Theology of Santa Clara University (Berkeley, California Campus), Berkeley, CA
Murphy, Rev. Harold B., '68 (CHI) Retired. Holy Child Jesus, Chicago, IL
Murphy, Rev. Hugh P., '71 (PAT) Our Lady of the Lake, Mount Arlington, NJ
Murphy, Rev. J. Patrick, *C.M.* '76 (CHI) [MON] Vincentian Community, Congregation of the Mission, Western Province, Chicago, IL
Murphy, Rev. James, '78 (JOL) St. Isidore, Bloomingdale, IL
Murphy, Rev. James, *C.S.C.* (FTW) [MIS] Holy Cross House, Notre Dame, IN
Murphy, Rev. James F., *C.S.B.* '01 (GAL) St. Thomas High School, Houston, TX; [MON] Keon House, Houston, TX
Murphy, Rev. James F., '70 (PIT) Retired. Chap, VA Med Ctr Butler
Murphy, Rev. James G., *S.J.* '83 (CHI) [COL] Jesuit Community at Loyola University Chicago, Chicago, IL
Murphy, Rev. James H., '81 (MAD) Saints Anthony and Philip Parish, Highland, WI; St. Thomas, Montfort, WI
Murphy, Rev. Msgr. James T., '68 (SAC) Retired. Curia: Organizations (affiliated, inter-Diocesan, miscellaneous/other)
Murphy, Rev. Jerry, (SFR) St. Sebastian, Greenbrae, CA
Murphy, Rev. John, *SJ* (SPK) [MON] Regis Community, Spokane, WA; [SEM] Bishop White Seminary, Spokane, WA
Murphy, Rev. John, '94 (ATL) Curia: Leadership Holy Trinity Catholic Church, Peachtree City, Inc., Peachtree City, GA
Murphy, Rev. John, '68 (DEN) Retired.
Murphy, Rev. John C., '65 (SP) Retired.
Murphy, Rev. John F., '59 (CLV) Retired.
Murphy, Rev. Msgr. John P., '64 (ALN) Retired. Curia: Leadership; Organizations (affiliated, inter-Diocesan, miscellaneous/other) St. Thomas More, Allentown, PA
Murphy, Rev. Msgr. John R., '73 (OG) Retired. Curia: Canonical Services
Murphy, Rev. John V., *S.J.* '52 (SPK) Retired. Curia: Leadership
Murphy, Rev. Joseph E., '61 (PAT) Retired. [MIS] Nazareth Village, Chester, NJ
Murphy, Rev. Joseph H., '61 (NEW) Retired.
Murphy, Rev. Kenneth R., '86 (MET) St. Stanislaus Kostka, Sayreville, NJ
Murphy, Rev. Laurence T., *M.M.* '54 (NY) Retired.
Murphy, Rev. Louis, *S.T.* '60 (WDC) [MON] Father Judge Missionary Cenacle, Adelphi, MD
Murphy, Rev. Mark D., '14 (DUB) On Special Assignment. Voc Dir, St Stephen Witness Catholic Stud Ctr, Cedar Falls Curia: Offices and Directors [CAM] Catholic Student Center of Cedar Falls, Iowa, Cedar Falls, IA
Murphy, Rev. Mark W., '11 (BO) On Leave.
Murphy, Rev. Michael A., '92 (BAL) St. Joseph Passionist Monastery Parish, Baltimore, MD
Murphy, Rev. Msgr. Michael D., '66 (LAN) Retired.
Murphy, Rev. Michael D., '77 (PH) St. Dorothy, Drexel Hill, PA
Murphy, Rev. Michael F., '83 (SD) Curia: Advisory Boards, Commissions, Committees, and Councils Pastor of Sacred Heart Catholic Parish, Coronado, a corporation sole, Coronado, CA; [MIS] Sacred Heart Catholic Parish Coronado in Coronado, CA Real Property Support Corporation, Coronado, CA
Murphy, Rev. Michael G., '87 (STL) St. Ferdinand Catholic Church, Florissant, MO
Murphy, Rev. Michael P., '89 (JC) St. Jude, Richland, MO; St. Robert Bellarmine, St. Robert, MO
Murphy, Rev. Myles P., '90 (NY) Parish of Our Lady of Victory and St. Andrew, New York, NY; St. Andrew, New York, NY
Murphy, Rev. Patrick, '04 (JOL) St. Francis of Assisi, Bolingbrook, IL
Murphy, Rev. Patrick E., '85 (MAR) On Duty Outside Diocese. Dept of Veterans Affairs Med Ctr Curia: (>MO) Offices and Directors
Murphy, Rev. Patrick F., '67 (LIN) Retired.
Murphy, Rev. Patrick J., '97 (SD) Pastor of Saint Gabriel Catholic Parish, Poway, a corporation sole, Poway, CA
Murphy, Rev. Paul G., '94 (BGP) Curia: Clergy and Religious Services; Consultative Bodies The Saint Thomas More Roman Catholic Church Corporation, Darien, CT
Murphy, Rev. Paul P., '78 (MRY) [MIS] Blessed Sacrament, ,
Murphy, Rev. Paul Patrick, (MRY) San Carlos Borromeo Basilica, Carmel, CA
Murphy, Rev. Peter P., '68 (PIT) Retired.
Murphy, Rev. Richard, '80 (Y) Curia: Leadership St. Mary, Mineral Ridge, OH; St. Stephen, Niles, OH; Ursuline High School, Youngstown, OH
Murphy, Rev. Richard D., '96 (BGP) The Saint Michael Roman Catholic Church Corporation, Greenwich, CT
Murphy, Rev. Msgr. Richard J., '73 (BAL) Retired.
Murphy, Rev. Robert, '93 (VEN) St. Raphael Parish in Englewood, Inc., Englewood, FL
Murphy, Rev. Msgr. Robert, '74 (KC) Retired.
Murphy, Rev. Robert, (BUR) St. Monica, Barre, VT
Murphy, Rev. Robert E., *S.J.* '14 (STL) [COL] Saint Louis University, St. Louis, MO
Murphy, Rev. Ronan B., '00 (CAM) On Duty Outside Diocese. Pope John Paul II House of Discernment, Brooklyn, NY
Murphy, Rev. Scott, (L) St. Edward, Louisville, KY
Murphy, Rev. T. Austin, '03 (BAL) St. Bernadette, Severn, MD
Murphy, Rev. T. Joseph, (WDC) Curia: Clergy and Religious Services
Murphy, Rev. Thomas, *O.F.M.Cap.* '71 (NY) [HOS] St. Joseph's Medical Center, Yonkers, NY
Murphy, Rev. Thomas, *L.C.* (GRY) Sacred Heart Apostolic School, Inc., Rolling Prairie, IN
Murphy, Rev. Thomas, '99 (BO) [MON] The Jesuit Community at Boston College, Chestnut Hill, MA
Murphy, Rev. Thomas J., '87 (SAV) St. Christopher, Claxton, GA
Murphy, Rev. Thomas K., *O.F.M.* '58 (SP) Retired. [MON] St. Anthony Friary (St. Petersburg) Franciscan Friars-Holy Name Province, Inc., St. Petersburg, FL
Murphy, Rev. Thomas P., *C.S.P.* '62 (NY) Retired.
Murphy, Rev. Thomas R.E., *S.J.* '99 (SEA) [COL] Seattle University, Seattle, WA; [MON] Arrupe Jesuit Community at Seattle University, Seattle, WA
Murphy, Rev. Timothy, '67 (P) Central Catholic High School, Portland, OR
Murphy, Rev. Timothy, '93 (JKS) Curia: Canonical Services; Consultative Bodies St. Francis of Assisi, Booneville, MS; St. James, Tupelo, MS; [CAM] Northeast Mississippi Community College Catholic Student Center, Booneville, MS
Murphy, Rev. Timothy J., '74 (SPR) Retired.
Murphy, Rev. William, *C.P.* '73 (BRK) Immaculate Conception, Jamaica, NY; [MIS] St. Paul's Benevolent, Educational and Missionary Institute, Inc. (Congregation of the Passion - St. Paul of the Cross Province), Jamaica, NY; [MON] Immaculate Conception Monastery, Jamaica, NY
Murphy, Rev. William, *C.P.* '73 (NY) [MIS] New Jersey Friends of Mandeville Inc., Rye Brook, NY; [MON] The Congregation of the Passion - St. Paul of the Cross Province, Jamaica, NY
Murphy, Rev. William F., '88 (BO) [SEM] Pope Saint John XXIII National Seminary, Weston, MA
Murphy, Rev. William J., '96 (SUP) Retired.
Murphy, Rev. William J., *S.J.* '57 (DET) Retired.
Murphy, Rev. William P., '86 (SPR) Saint Teresa of Calcutta Parish, Housatonic, MA; St. Peter Parish, Great Barrington, MA
Murray, Rev. Brendan J., '68 (PAT) Retired. [MIS] Nazareth Village, Chester, NJ
Murray, Rev. Eamon G., '11 (BRK) Visitation of the Blessed Virgin Mary, Brooklyn, NY; [MIS] Federation of Oases of Koinonia John the Baptist, Brooklyn, NY
Murray, Rev. Eugene, '65 (SC) Retired.
Murray, Rev. Frank J., '81 (PRT) Retired.
Murray, Rev. Gerald E., '84 (NY) Holy Family, New York, NY
Murray, Rev. Msgr. Ignatius L., '57 (PH) Retired.
Murray, Rev. John, '60 (CHY) Retired.
Murray, Rev. John, '69 (ORL) Retired.
Murray, Rev. John, '73 (BRK) Our Lady of Perpetual Help Basilica, Brooklyn, NY
Murray, Rev. John, *C.Ss.R.* (HBG) Our Mother of Perpetual Help, Ephrata, PA; [MON] St. Clement's Mission House, Ephrata, PA
Murray, Rev. John A., '62 (BO) Retired.
Murray, Rev. John E., '63 (HEL) Retired.
Murray, Rev. John Francis, *C.Ss.R.* '73 (BAL) Retired. [SPF] St. John Neuman Residence, Timonium, MD
Murray, Rev. John M., '98 (FR) St. Mary's, Our Lady of the Isle, Nantucket, MA
Murray, Rev. John M., '98 (FR) [MIS] Diocesan Facilities Self-Insurance Group, Inc., Fall River, MA
Murray, Rev. John P., *S.J.* (BGP) [MON] The Fairfield Jesuit Community-Fairfield University, Fairfield, CT
Murray, Rev. John W., '68 (CHI) Retired.
Murray, Rev. Joseph Aloysius, *O.S.A.* '16 (NY) St. Nicholas of Tolentine, Bronx, NY
Murray, Rev. Kevin P., '77 (PH) St. Hilary of Poitiers, Rydal, PA
Murray, Rev. Matthew, (OAK) Curia: Leadership
Murray, Rev. Matthew, '17 (OAK) St. Isidore, Danville, CA
Murray, Rev. Michael, '76 (WDC) Our Lady of Grace, Silver Spring, MD
Murray, Rev. Michael A., '16 (LAN) St. Martha Parish Okemos, Okemos, MI
Murray, Rev. Msgr. Michael J., '76 (WDC) On Special Assignment.
Murray, Rev. Michael S., *O.S.F.S.* '86 (WIL) [MIS] OSFS Endowment Trust, Wilmington, DE; [MON] De Sales Spirituality Services, Wilmington, DE
Murray, Rev. Michael S., (ARL) St. John Neumann, Reston, VA
Murray, Rev. Paul G., '09 (PRT) Retired.
Murray, Rev. Robert, *O.S.A.* '83 (CAM) St. Augustine Preparatory School, Richland, NJ
Murray, Rev. Robert W., '88 (BO) Mary, Queen of the Apostles Parish, Salem, MA
Murray, Rev. Russel, *O.F.M.* '98 (WDC) [SEM] Holy Name College, Silver Spring, MD
Murray, Rev. Archmandrite Seoirse (Tomas), '22 (ROM) [MON] Holy Resurrection Monastery, St. Nazianz, WI
Murray, Rev. Steven J., '00 (PBL) Curia: Leadership; Offices and Directors St. Joseph, Pueblo, CO; St. Therese, Pueblo, CO
Murray, Rev. Steven M., '88 (OG) Saint Andre Bessette Roman Catholic Parish, Malone, NY, Malone, NY; [CEM] Notre Dame Cemetery of Malone, N.Y., Inc., Malone, NY; [CEM] St. Joseph's Cemetery of Malone, N.Y., Inc., Malone, NY
Murray, Rev. Msgr. Thomas A., '68 (PH) Retired. Curia: Advisory Boards, Commissions, Committees, and Councils St. Eleanor, Collegeville, PA
Murray, Rev. Thomas P., '81 (RVC) St. Therese of Lisieux, Montauk, NY; [MON] St Pius X Residence for Retired Priests LLC, Ronkonkoma, NY
Murrin, Rev. Raymond J., '57 (BIR) Retired.
Murrman, Rev. Warren D., *O.S.B.* '65 (GBG) [MON] Saint Vincent Archabbey, Latrobe, PA
Murry, Rev. Trevor K., '01 (BEL) On Leave.
Murtagh, Rev. Henry Paul, *SS.CC.* '67 (LA) Retired. [MON] Congregation of the Sacred Hearts of Jesus and Mary, La Verne, CA
Murtagh, Rev. James, '66 (PMB) Retired.
Murtaugh, Rev. William A., '72 (STP) Pax Christi, Eden Prairie, MN
Murtha, Rev. Chester, '93 (SFS) Epiphany Parish of Hanson County, Epiphany, SD; Saint Agatha Parish of Miner County, Howard, SD; Saint William of Vercelli

Parish of Lake County, Ramona, SD
Musa, Rev. Antonio, *O.F.M.* (CHI) St. Jerome (Croatian), Chicago, IL
Musabe, Rev. Godfrey, (BO) Holy Family, Lynn, MA; St. Pius Fifth, Lynn, MA
Muscalino, Rev. Daniel C., '78 (SY) St. Francis Xavier, Marcellus, NY
Muscolino, Rev. Frank J., '68 (BIR) Retired.
Musgrave, Rev. Daniel, '12 (FAR) Sacred Heart Church of Cando, Cando, ND; St. Vincent de Paul Church of Leeds, Leeds, ND
Mushauko, Rev. Ignatius, (BO) Our Lady of the Assumption, Boston, MA
Mushe, Rev. Aphram, (OLD) Saints Behnam and Sarah Mission, Phoenix, AZ
Mushe, Rev. Raad, (PHX) St. Mary's Roman Catholic Basilica, Phoenix, AZ
Mushi, Very Rev. Peter, *A.J.* '87 (NY) Curia: Leadership Holy Agony, New York, NY; Parish of St. Cecilia and Holy Agony, New York, NY; St. John Vianney, Cure of Ars, Bronx, NY
Mushobozi, Rev. Leopold, '08 (PEO) Holy Cross, Champaign, IL
Musial, Rev. George, *O.F.M.* '67 (CHI) [MON] St. Peter's Friary, Chicago, IL
Musico, Rev. Edwin, '85 (STO) St. Mary of the Assumption Church (Pastor of), Stockton, CA
Musielak, Rev. Adam, '21 (DAL) St. Patrick Catholic Parish - Dallas, Dallas, TX
Musiimenta, Rev. Samuel, '05 (SFR) St. Charles, San Carlos, CA; St. Matthias, Redwood City, CA
Musinguzi, Rev. John Bosco, '00 (MO) Curia: Offices and Directors
Musinguzi, Rev. Justus, '01 (STP) Holy Cross, Minneapolis, MN
Musiol, Rev. Josef, *S.D.S.* '72 (SAT) [MON] Salvatorian Fathers Community of Texas, Falls City, TX
Musiol, Rev. Jozef, *S.D.S.* '72 (AUS) Curia: Tribunal (>GRY) [MON] Salvatorian Fathers (Society of the Divine Savior), Merrillville, IN
Musolooza, Very Rev. Francis Xavier, '98 (RIC) Curia: Deaneries St. John the Evangelist, Waynesboro, VA
Mussett, Rev. Peter, '06 (DEN) St. Thomas Aquinas University Catholic Parish in Boulder, Boulder, CO
Musso, Rev. David D., *S.M.* '98 (ATL) Marist School, Atlanta, GA
Musula, Rev. Charles E., '07 (CHI) Chap, Watertown, NY
Musumbu, Rev. Gilbert Malu, '88 (TUC) Saint Monica Roman Catholic Parish - Tucson, Tucson, AZ
Musuubire, Rev. Gerald F., '06 (RIC) St. Timothy, Tappahannock, VA
Muszkiewicz, Rev. Joseph, (GLD) Saint Mary of Hannah, Kingsley, MI
Muszkiewicz, Rev. Joseph, '08 (GLD) Curia: Advisory Boards, Commissions, Committees, and Councils; Leadership
Mutajuka, Rev. Delphinus, (NSH) Sacred Heart, Loretto, TN; St. Joseph, St.Joseph, TN
Muteru, Rev. Gabriel, (ARL) [CAM] Marymount University, Arlington, VA; [COL] Marymount University, Arlington, VA
Muth, Rev. Joseph L., '74 (BAL) St. Mary of the Assumption, Baltimore, MD; [CAM] Notre Dame of Maryland University, Baltimore, MD; [EFT] St. Matthew's Parish Endowment Trust, Baltimore, MD; [MIS] Immigration Outreach Services Center, Inc., ,
Muth, Rev. Stephen, '82 (PRM) Retired. On Leave.
Muthengi, Rev. John, *C.P.* '96 (NY) [MON] The Congregation of the Passion - St. Paul of the Cross Province, Jamaica, NY
Muthoottil, Rev. Chacko, *M.F.* '88 (HON) St. Rita, Haiku, HI (>OAK) [MON] Missionaries of Faith-India Inc., Fremont, CA
Muthu, Rev. Antony Savari, '90 (CAM) Holy Child Parish, Runnemede, N.J., Runnemede, NJ
Muthu Vijayan, Rev. John, '05 (LC) St. Joseph, Menomonie, WI; [CAM] Newman Center at University of Wisconsin - Stout, Menomonie, WI; [EFT] The St. Joseph School at Menomonie Endowment Trust, Menomonie, WI
Muthukattil, Rev. Thomas, '66 (BRK) Retired.
Muthukattil, Rev. Thomas, '66 (BRK) Retired.
Mutie, Rev. Stephen Muli, *SAC* '88 (DET) St. Vincent Pallotti Parish Wyandotte, Wyandotte, MI; [MON] Society of the Catholic Apostolate (Pallottine Fathers), Wyandotte, MI
Mutiso, Rev. Lawrence, '92 (SR) Pastor of St. James Catholic Church of Petaluma, A Corporation Sole, Petaluma, CA
Mutka, Rev. Vasyl, '08 (HPM) St. Irene Byzantine Catholic Church, Portland, OR
Muttathottil, Rev. Shajii, (CAM) Our Lady of Peace Parish, Monroe Township, N.J., Williamstown, NJ
Mutuku, Rev. Anthony, (NSH) Good Shepherd, Decherd, TN
Muweesi, Rev. John Vianney, *S.D.S.* '86 (MIL) [MON] Salvatorian Provincial Offices (Society of the Divine Savior), Milwaukee, WI
Muwonge, Rev. Expedito, '89 (L) Chap, Norton Hosps
Mux, Rev. Juan Francisco Peren, *O.S.B.* '07 (RCK) [MON] Marmion Abbey, Aurora, IL
Muyimbwa, Rev. Paul, '00 (RIC) Sacred Heart, Norfolk, VA
Muzas, Rev. Brian Keenan, '03 (NEW) [COL] Seton Hall University, South Orange, NJ
Muzzey, Rev. Charles H., '65 (WDC) Retired.
Mvondo, Rev. Laurent, '81 (SAN) Our Lady of Mt. Carmel, Winters, TX; Sacred Heart, Coleman, TX
Mvukiyehe, Rev. Jean Baptiste, *S.A.C.* '07 (CAM) Bishop Eustace Prep School, Pennsauken, NJ
Mwaba, Rev. Thomson, (BAL) [MON] Society of St. Sulpice, Province of the United States, Baltimore, MD
Mwageni, Rev. Honoratus C., '07 (CHI)
Mwamba, Rev. Elvis, *OMI* (BEL) [MON] Shrine of Our Lady of the Snows, Belleville, IL
Mwampela, Rev. Ayub, (GF) [HOS] St. Vincent Healthcare, Billings, MT
Mwanamwambwa, Rev. Victor, *P.S.S.* '05 (BAL) [MIS] St. Mary's Seminary & University, Baltimore, MD; [MON] Society of St. Sulpice, Province of the United States, Baltimore, MD
Mwangi, Rev. Martin, '14 (DAL) St. Michael the Archangel Catholic Parish - Garland, Garland, TX
Mwansa, Rev. Godfrey, (SAT) [NUR] Oblate Madonna Residence, San Antonio, TX; [SEM] Blessed Mario Borzaga Formation Community, San Antonio, TX
Mwanza, Rev. Eugene H., *P.S.S.* '04 (BAL) [MIS] St. Mary's Seminary & University, Baltimore, MD; [MON] Society of St. Sulpice, Province of the United States, Baltimore, MD
Mwape, Rev. Wilbroad, '95 (CHR) St. Anthony of Padua, Greenville, SC
Mwaura, Rev. Peter James, '03 (CHY) Curia: Consultative Bodies Our Lady of Peace, Pinedale, WY
Mwenze, Rev. Jean-Marie, '00 (DEN) Holy Family Catholic Parish in Ft. Collins, Fort Collins, CO
Mwepya, Rev. Edward M., '11 (BAL) [MIS] St. Mary's Seminary & University, Baltimore, MD
Mwesiga, Rev. Derick T, (PEO) St. Vincent De Paul, Peoria, IL
Mwesigye, Rev. Elias, '19 (CIN) St. Susanna, Mason, OH
Mwisheni, Rev. Richard A, *SMA* '06 (BO) [MON] Society of African Missions, Dedham, MA (>NEW) [MON] Society of African Missions, Provincialate, S.M.A. Fathers, Tenafly, NJ
Mwongyera, Rev. Martin, '96 (PEO) St. Edward, Chillicothe, IL
Myers, Rev. Christopher P., *S.O.L.T.* '90 (MO) Curia: Offices and Directors
Myers, Rev. Edward T., *O.P.* '65 (PRO) [MON] St. Thomas Aquinas Priory at Providence College, Providence, RI
Myers, Rev. Gabriel, *O.S.B.* '99 (WDC) [MON] St. Anselm's Abbey, Washington, DC
Myers, Rev. Gerald, '94 (FAR) Retired.
Myers, Rev. James, *P.S.S.* '80 (SAT) Curia: Leadership [SEM] The Seminary of the Assumption of the Blessed Virgin Mary-St. John of San Antonio, TX (Assumption-St. John's Seminary), San Antonio, TX
Myers, Rev. James E., '80 (PEO) On Duty Outside Diocese.
Myers, Rev. James E., *P.S.S.* '80 (BAL) [MON] Society of St. Sulpice, Province of the United States, Baltimore, MD
Myers, Rev. Jeremy B., '84 (DAL) On Administrative Leave.
Myett, Rev. Damian, *O.P.* (PRO) [MON] St. Thomas Aquinas Priory at Providence College, Providence, RI
Myett, Rev. Robert D., *O.P.* '60 (PRO) [MON] St. Thomas Aquinas Priory at Providence College, Providence, RI
Mykyta, Rev. Myron, '97 (STN) On Leave.
Mykytchyn, Rev. Ostap, (PHU) Curia: Offices and Directors
Mykytchyn, Rev. Ostap, (PHU) St. Michael the Archangel, Jenkintown, PA
Myladiyil, Rev. Sebastian, *SVD* '99 (JKS) Sacred Heart, Greenville, MS; Sacred Heart, Rosedale, MS; St. Francis of Assisi, Shaw, MS
Myler, Rev. Msgr. John T., '82 (BEL) Retired. Curia: Leadership; Offices and Directors [MIS] World Apostolate of Fatima, The Blue Army, U.S.A., Belleville, IL
Myles, Rev. John J., '64 (SAC) Retired. Pastor of Sacred Heart Parish, Maxwell, a corporation sole, Williams, CA
Mylet, Rev. James J., *M.M.* '75 (NY) [MON] Maryknoll Fathers and Brothers (Catholic Foreign Mission Society of America, Inc.), Ossining, NY
Myronyuk, Rev. Myron, (PHU) SS. Peter and Paul, Wilkes-Barre, PA; St. Vladimir's, Scranton, PA
Myshchuk, Rev. Mikhail, '94 (STF) Curia: Leadership; Offices and Directors Protection of B.V.M., Troy, NY; St. Nicholas Ukrainian Catholic Church, Watervliet, NY
Myslinski, Rev. Augustine, *O.C.S.O.* '11 (ATL) [MON] The Monastery of the Holy Spirit, Conyers, GA; [RTR] Monastery of the Holy Spirit, Conyers, GA
Myslinski, Rev. Msgr. John F., '80 (WDC) Retired.
Mysliwiec, Rev. Haldane, '70 (CHI) Retired.
Mysliwiec, Rev. Jan J., *S.D.S.* '62 (NEW) [MON] The Salvatorian Fathers, Verona, NJ
MyViet Tran, Rev. (Timothy M.), *C.R.M.* '11 (SPC) Curia: Offices and Directors Cathedral of St. Agnes, Springfield, MO; [MON] Congregation of the Mother of the Redeemer, Carthage, MO
Naah, Rev. Peter, (RIC) St. Matthew, Virginia Beach, VA
Nacarino, Rev. Raymond L., *SJS* '85 (MET) Our Lady of Mt. Carmel, New Brunswick, NJ; [MON] Society of Jesus Christ the Priest, Stewartsville, NJ
Nacciarone, Rev. Ugo R., *S.J.* '64 (NY) [MON] Murray-Weigel Hall (A Jesuit Community at Murray-Weigel Hall and Kohlmann Hall), Bronx, NY
Nacey, Rev. Paul Matthew, '21 (ATL) St. Jude the Apostle Catholic Church, Sandy Springs, Inc., Sandy Springs, GA
Nacino, Rev. Raynald, (CHR) St. Mary Magdalene, Simpsonville, SC
Nacius, Rev. Michael A., '89 (CHI) Curia: Leadership St. Mary, Lake Forest, IL
Nacke, Rev. Xavier, *O.S.B.* '63 (KC) [MON] Conception Abbey (Benedictine Monks), Conception, MO; [SEM] Conception Seminary College, Conception, MO
Nacorda, Rev. Cirilo A., '92 (CLV) Chap, Cleveland Clinic Foundation St. Vitus, Cleveland, OH
Nadeau, Rev. James L., '88 (PRT) Christ the King Parish, Skowhegan, ME
Nadeau, Rev. Lance P., *M.M.* '90 (NY) [MON] Maryknoll Fathers and Brothers (Catholic Foreign Mission Society of America, Inc.), Ossining, NY
Nadeau, Rev. Roland, *M.S.* '69 (ORL) Blessed Trinity, Orlando, FL
Nadeau, Rev. Roland P., '00 (PRT) Retired.
Nadeau, Rev. Roland S., *M.S.* '69 (HRT) [MON] Missionaries of La Salette Province of Mary, Mother of the Americas (The Missionaries of La Salette Corporation., MLS Religious Trust), Hartford, CT
Nadeau, Rev. Timothy J., '91 (PRT) Good Shepherd Parish, Saco, ME; [CAM] University of New England, Biddeford, ME
Nadeau, Rev. William, '68 (RNO) Retired.
Nader, Rev. Marwan Abi, *M.L.M.* (OLL) [MON] The Congregation of Maronite Lebanese Missionaries, Houston, TX
Nadicksbernd, Rev. Elmer, *SVD* '64 (CHI) Retired. [MON] Divine Word Residence, Techny, IL
Nadine, Rev. Jerome E., '58 (BRK) Retired.
Nadolny, Rev. Edmund S., '59 (HRT) Retired.
Nadolski, Rev. Kevin M., *O.S.F.S.* '97 (ALN) [COL] DeSales University, Center Valley, PA; [MON] Oblates of St. Francis de Sales, Center Valley, PA
Nadolski, Rev. Timothy E., '15 (ATL) St. Clare of Assisi Catholic Church, Acworth, Inc., Acworth, GA
Nadooparambil, Rev. Kuriakose, *M.F.* (HON) (>OAK) [MON] Missionaries of Faith-India Inc., Fremont, CA
Nadres, Rev. Sergio O., '91 (NEW) St. Vincent de Paul, Bayonne, NJ
Naduviledath, Rev. Sathyan, *O.I.C.* (RVC) Blessed Sacrament, Valley Stream, NY
Naduviledathu, Rev. Thomas, *S.D.V.* '08 (MET) St. James, Woodbridge, NJ
Naduvilekoot, Rev. Augustine, '71 (NOR) Retired.
Naegele, Rev. Gary P., '79 (WH) Good Shepherd, Glenville, WV; St. Boniface, Camden, WV
Naegele, Rev. Zacchaeus Maria, *O.S.B.Cam.* '98 (MRY) [MON] New Camaldoli Hermitage (Camaldolese Hermits of America), Big Sur, CA
Naessens, Rev. Philip, *O.F.M.Cap.* '86 (DET) [MON] St. Bonaventure Monastery, Detroit, MI
Naffate, Rev. Lenin, '00 (SAT) Saint Jose Luis Sanchez Del Rio Catholic Parish, San Antonio, TX
Nagel, Rev. Kurt, '97 (SEA) Curia: Leadership Sacred Heart, Bellevue, WA; St. Monica, Mercer Island, WA
Nagel, Rev. Rick, '07 (IND) Indiana Univ - Purdue Univ Indianapolis St. John the Evangelist Catholic Church, Indianapolis, Inc., Indianapolis, IN

Nagengast, Rev. Maynard G., *O.S.B.* '62 (NEW) [MON] Benedictine Abbey of Newark, Newark, NJ
Nagipogu, Rev. Balachandra, '07 (SAN) St. Margaret of Cortona, Big Lake, TX
Nagle, Rev. Gerald J., *M.M.* '57 (NY) Retired.
Nagle, Rev. Matthew, '15 (KCK) St. Mary, Hartford, KS; [CAM] Didde Catholic Campus Center, Emporia State University, Emporia, KS
Nagle, Rev. Walter M., '99 (NOR) Curia: Leadership; Offices and Directors Christ the King, Old Lyme, CT
Nagothu, Rev. Amarnath, *M.S.F.S.* '09 (STA) Curia: Evangelization Holy Spirit, Jacksonville, FL
Nagozi, Rev. A., (BRK) Sacred Hearts of Jesus and Mary and St. Stephen, Brooklyn, NY
Nagrant, Rev. Andrew, '14 (PRM) St. Nicholas, Lorain, OH
Naguit, Rev. Glenn A., '05 (OAK) Curia: Leadership St. Margaret Mary, Oakland, CA
Nagy, Rev. Martin, '21 (STN) St. Demetrius, Belfield, ND; St. John the Baptist, Belfield, ND
Nah, Rev. McDonald, '03 (STL) St. Nicholas Catholic Church, St. Louis, MO
Nahal, Rev. John, *M.L.M.* '93 (OLL) Curia: Offices and Directors St. Raymond - St. Elizabeth Maronite Catholic Church, Crestwood, MO; St. Raymond Maronite Catholic Cathedral, St. Louis, MO; [MIS] Caritas Lebanon, St. Louis, MO
Nahal, Rev. John, '93 (OLL) Curia: Leadership; Offices and Directors
Nahas, Rev. Joseph A., '06 (NY) On Sick Leave.
Nahman, Rev. Richard, *OSA* '65 (PH) [MON] St. Thomas Monastery, Villanova, PA
Nahoe, Rev. Francisco, *O.F.M.Conv.* '94 (OAK) Our Lady of Grace, Castro Valley, CA
Naill, Rev. Joseph P., '97 (RCK) St. Mary, Oregon, IL; St. Mary Church, Polo, IL
Nairn, Rev. Thomas, *O.F.M.* '75 (STL) [MON] Franciscan Friary of St. Anthony of Padua, St. Louis, MO
Najera, Rev. Arthur, '09 (SAC) On Leave. (>LA) St. Anthony, Oxnard, CA
Najim, Rev. Michael J., '01 (PRO) St. Pius X Parish Corporation, Westerly, Westerly, RI
Najim, Chorbishop Philip, (SD) Curia: Tribunal
Najjar, Rev. Samuel A., '84 (SAM) Retired.
Najmowski, Rev. James, *M.M.* '76 (NY) [MON] Maryknoll Fathers and Brothers (Catholic Foreign Mission Society of America, Inc.), Ossining, NY
Nakireru, Rev. Omoviekovwa, '77 (R) Chaplain at Duke University Hospital
Nakkeeran, Rev. Denis N., '20 (BO) On Special Assignment. Holy Name, Boston, MA
Nakooparambil, Rev. Kuriakose, *MF* (HON) Maria Lanakila (Victorious Mary), Lahaina, HI
Nakvasil, Rev. Richard, '05 (DEN) All Souls Catholic Parish in Englewood, Englewood, CO
Nakwah, Rev. Joseph C., '90 (LC) Sacred Heart, Marathon, WI; St. Patrick, Mosinee, WI
Nale, Rev. Joseph C, '98 (ALT) St. John the Baptist, Summerhill, PA
Nale, Rev. Joseph C., '03 (ALT) St. Bartholomew, Wilmore, PA
Nale, Rev. Joseph C., '03 (ALT) Immaculate Conception, , ; Most Holy Trinity, South Fork, PA
Nalepa, Rev. Richard, *C.P.* '70 (NY) [MON] The Congregation of the Passion - St. Paul of the Cross Province, Jamaica, NY
Nalepa, Rev. Richard A., *C.P.* '70 (PIT) [MON] St. Paul of the Cross Monastery, Pittsburgh, PA
Nall, Rev. Brent, '93 (SAC) Chap, Mercy General Hosp, Sacramento
Nall, Very Rev. James, '87 (BEL) Curia: Leadership Holy Trinity Catholic Church, Fairview Heights, IL
Nall, Rev. James M., '87 (BEL) Curia: Leadership
Nalley, Rev. Robert W., '75 (GLD) Retired.
Nalty, Rev. Msgr. Christopher, '99 (NO) Good Shepherd Roman Catholic Church, New Orleans, Louisiana, New Orleans, LA
Nalty, Rev. Msgr. Christopher, '99 (NO) [SEM] Notre Dame Seminary Graduate School of Theology, New Orleans, LA
Nalugon, Rev. Nilo, '94 (SAN) Curia: Advisory Boards, Commissions, Committees, and Councils Holy Spirit Parish, Sweetwater, TX
Nalysnyk, Rev. Bohdan, '95 (STN) Curia: Offices and Directors St. Joseph, Chicago, IL
Nalysnyk, Archpriest Yaroslav P, '90 (STF) Christ the King, Jamaica Plain, MA
Nam, Rev. Heebong, '97 (BRK) St. Paul Chong Ha-Sang Roman Catholic Chapel, Flushing, NY
Nam, Rev. Simon, '76 (NY) Retired.
Nambatac, Rev. Alner U., '96 (SFR) St. Luke, Foster City, CA; St. Timothy, San Mateo, CA
Nambusseril, Rev. Thankachan (John), *C.M.I.* '93 (HT) Curia: Administration Our Lady of Prompt Succor, Golden Meadow, LA
Namiotka, Rev. Edward F., '87 (CAM) The Church of St. Thomas More, Cherry Hill, New Jersey, Cherry Hill, NJ
Namocatcat, Rev. Felix S., '62 (SFR) Retired.
Nance, Rev. J. Todd, (TLS) Curia: Leadership Immaculate Conception, Hugo, OK; St. Agnes, Antlers, OK
Nance, Rev. Todd J., '13 (TLS) St. Jude, Boswell, OK
Nangachiveettil, Rev. George Joseph, (SYM) St. Mother Teresa of Calcutta Syro-Malabar Catholic Church, Henderson, NV
Nangachiveettil, Rev. George Joseph, '83 (IND) Retired.
Nangle, Rev. Thomas R., '70 (CHI) Retired.
Nannam, Rev. Ratna Swamy, *MSFS* '07 (KCK) Sacred Heart, Paxico, KS; [CAM] Catholic Campus Center at Washburn University, Topeka, KS
Nanz, Rev. John D., '71 (PIT) Retired. Chap, Canon House; Horizon Senior Care; Rest Haven Personal…
Napier, Rev. Malachy, *C.F.R.* '20 (NY) [MON] St. Crispin Friary, Bronx, NY
Napieralski, Rev. Maciej, '83 (FBK) Curia: (>MO) Offices and Directors
Napiere, Rev. Eliseo, *M.S.P.* '91 (SB) St. James, Perris, CA
Napierkowski, Rev. Peter, '98 (BUF) Our Lady of Czestochowa, Buffalo, NY
Naples, Rev. Timothy P., '09 (BUR) Curia: Offices and Directors
Naples, Rev. Timothy P., '09 (BUR) Curia: Leadership St. John Vianney, South Burlington, VT
Napolitano, Rev. Joseph V. Carmel, '76 (HRT) Holy Disciples Parish Corporation, Watertown, CT
Napolitano, Rev. Nicholas J., '17 (MOB) Our Lady of Bon Secour Parish, Bon Secour, AL; St. John the Baptist, Foley, AL
Napora, Rev. Jacek J., '06 (NEW) St. Philomena, Livingston, NJ
Nappier, Rev. Nicholas, '21 (TYL) Cathedral of the Immaculate Conception, Tyler, TX; [CAM] John Paul the Great Catholic Campus Ministry, Tyler, TX
Napuli, Rev. Raymond Philip, (SD) Pastor of Mission San Diego de Alcala Catholic Parish, San Diego, a corporation sole, San Diego, CA
Naquin, Rev. Roch, '62 (HT) Retired.
Naralely, Rev. José, *O.SS.T.* '81 (BAL) Resurrection of Our Lord, Laurel, MD; St. Lawrence Martyr, Hanover, MD
Naranjo, Rev. Francisco, '95 (STO) Retired.
Naranjo, Rev. Peter, '12 (SPR) Chap, Berkshire Med Ctr
Narciso, Rev. Richard A., '07 (PRO) St. Robert Bellarmine Church Corporation, Johnston, Johnston, RI
Nardoianni, Rev. Antonio, *O.F.M./I.C.* (NY) [MON] Franciscan Province of the Immaculate Conception, New York, NY
Narez, Rev. Juan, '93 (ELP) On Leave.
Narichetti, Rev. Jesuprathap, '92 (CHR) St. Mary, Yonges Island, SC; Sts. Frederick & Stephen Mission, Edisto Island, SC
Narikunnel, Rev. Regi Augustine, (SYM) St. Teresa of Calcutta Syro-Malabar Mission, Nashville, TN, Nashville, TN
Naripogula, Rev. Prakasham Babu, (LSC) Holy Family Parish, Inc., Deming, NM
Narisetti, Rev. Rayanna, '98 (OKL) St. Ann, Elgin, OK
Narla, Rev. Lourdeswamy Dhanraj, (SHP) St. John Berchmans Cathedral, Shreveport, LA
Narog, Rev. Joseph L., *O.S.A.* '05 (PH) [MON] Bellesini Friary, Ardmore, PA; [MON] Provincial Offices of the Order of St. Augustine, Province of St. Thomas of Villanova, Villanova, PA
Narra, Rev. Showri Raju, '10 (TUC) St Mary's Hosp, Tucson Saints Peter and Paul Roman Catholic Parish - Tucson, Tucson, AZ
Nartker, Rev. Michael F., *S.M.* '96 (CIN) [MIS] Marianist Network for the Arts, Dayton, OH
Nartker, Rev. Michael Francis, *S.M.* '96 (CIN) St. Francis de Sales, Cincinnati, OH
Narvaez, Rev. Alexander, (MIA) Our Lady of Guadalupe, Doral, FL
Nasada, Rev. Samuel, *OFM* (SD) Pastor of Mission San Luis Rey Catholic Parish, Oceanside, a corporation sole, Oceanside, CA; [MON] Old Mission San Luis Rey, Oceanside, CA
Nasar, Rev. Ayub, '85 (GR) St. Jude, Grand Rapids, MI
Nascimento, Rev. Daniel, '98 (SFR) St. Anne, San Francisco, CA
Naseman, Rev. Alfred, *C.PP.S.* '67 (CIN) [MON] St. Charles, Celina, OH
Nash, Rev. Dom Daniel Stephen, *Can.Reg.* '97 (RVC) Curia: Leadership St. Rocco, Glen Cove, NY
Nash, Rev. Francis J., *S.J.* '69 (SY) [MON] Jesuits at LeMoyne, Inc., Syracuse, NY
Nash, Rev. James, '94 (WIL) Curia: Advisory Boards, Commissions, Committees, and Councils SS. Peter and Paul, Easton, MD
Nash, Rev. James R., '89 (SCR) Retired. Our Lady of Mount Carmel, Hunlock Creek, PA; Saint Faustina Kowalska Parish, Nanticoke, PA
Nash, Rev. Matthew, '17 (GI) Curia: Offices and Directors St. Mary's, Mullen, NE
Naskar, Rev. Lawrence (Subroto), '98 (NY) Chap, St Vincent's Hospital; Mamaron, NY Parish of St. John Bosco, Port Chester, NY
Nasr, Rev. Toufic M., '97 (OLL) Curia: Leadership St. Ephrem Maronite Catholic Church, El Cajon, CA
Nasry, Rev. Wafik H., *S.J.* (SJ) [MON] USA West Province, Society of Jesus, Los Gatos, CA
Nassal, Rev. Joseph, *C.PP.S.* (OAK) [MON] Society of the Precious Blood, Berkeley, CA
Nassal, Rev. Joseph, *C.PP.S.* '82 (KC) (>CIN) [MON] Society of the Precious Blood, United States Province, Inc., Dayton, OH
Nassaney, Rev. Daniel, *O.M.I.* (BO) [NUR] Immaculate Heart of Mary Residence, Tewksbury, MA
Nassaney, Rev. Daniel, *O.M.I.* '74 (CR) St. Benedict, , ; St. Theodore, ,
Nassetta, Rev. Peter, *Y.A.* (RIC) Chap, James Madison Univ
Nassetta, Rev. Peter W., *Y.A.* '89 (ARL) On Duty Outside Diocese. Campus Min, JMU Campus Ministry, Harrisonburg
Nassr, Rev. Martin B., '67 (TOL) Retired.
Nasta, Rev. Thomas A., '82 (PH) Our Lady of Grace, Penndel, PA (>Y) [MIS] Conference of Slovak Clergy, Youngstown, OH
Natad, Rev. Diosmar, '04 (ATL) Good Shepherd Catholic Church, Cumming, Inc., Cumming, GA
Natale, Rev. Frank, *M.S.C.* '13 (OG) Our Lady of the Sacred Heart, Watertown, NY; St. Mary's Roman Catholic Church of Evans Mills, NY, Evans Mills, NY; St. Paul's Church, Black River, NY; [CEM] Calvary Cemetery Association of Watertown, N.Y., Watertown, NY; [MON] Missionaries of the Sacred Heart, Watertown, NY
Natale, Rev. Samuel, '79 (RIC) Retired.
Natalizia, Rev. Louis T., '80 (PRO) Retired.
Natha, Rev. Simon, '09 (EVN) Holy Name, Bloomfield, IN; St. Peter, Linton, IN
Nathan, Rev. Aro, '83 (NEW) SS. Joseph and Michael, Union City, NJ
Nathan, Rev. Matthew, '09 (JOL) On Special Assignment. Benedictine College, KS
Nathan, Rev. Pangiraj Jabamalai, (KAL) Our Lady of the Lake, Edwardsburg, MI; St. Ann, Cassopolis, MI
Nathan, Rev. Sahayanathan, '04 (MIA) Curia: Clergy and Religious Services St. Gabriel, Pompano Beach, FL
Nathe, Rev. Thomas, '04 (SEA) Holy Redeemer, Vancouver, WA
Nations, Rev. David G., *C.M.* '97 (STL) [MIS] Vincentian Marian Youth, U.S.A., St. Louis, MO
Nations, Rev. David G., *C.M.* '97 (LA) St. Vincent De Paul, Los Angeles, CA
Nau, Rev. Dale, '78 (DUL) Retired.
Nau, Rev. Thomas R., '78 (STU) Retired.
Naucke, Rev. Alfred E., *S.J.* '65 (SJ) [MON] Sacred Heart Jesuit Center, Los Gatos, CA
Naughton, Rev. Michael, *O.S.B.* '66 (SCL) [MON] St. John's Abbey, of the Order of St. Benedict, Collegeville, MN
Naughton, Rev. Patrick J., '91 (MIA) St. John the Baptist Catholic Church, Fort Lauderdale, FL
Naughton, Rev. Msgr. William M., '72 (PAT) Retired.
Naugle, Rev. John F., (PIT) St. Monica, Beaver Falls, PA
Nava, Rev. Rufino Carlos, *O.M.I.* '99 (LA) St. Bridget of Sweden, Lake Balboa, CA; St. Joseph the Worker, Winnetka, CA
Naval, Rev. Thomas Paul K., '89 (ORG) Santiago de Compostela, Lake Forest, CA
Navalo, Rev. Hector M., *C.M.F.* '03 (CHI) Our Lady of Guadalupe, Chicago, IL
Navaratne, Rev. Louis-Marie, *O.S.B.* '76 (PAT) [MON] Holy Face of Jesus Monastery (Sylvestrine Benedictine Monks), Clifton, NJ
Navarra, Rev. Peter, '81 (SD) Pastor of Saint Joseph Cathedral Catholic Parish, San Diego, a corporation sole, San Diego, CA
Navarrete, Rev. Fredi, *M.S.F.S.* '08 (ATL) St. John Neumann Catholic Church, Lilburn, Inc., Lilburn, GA; [MON] The Missionaries of St. Francis de Sales - MSFS USA Vice Province, Loganville, GA
Navarrete, Rev. Jesus, '87 (MO) Curia: Offices and

Directors
Navarro, Rev. Alex, *S.J.S.* '09 (MAD) On Administrative Leave.
Navarro, Rev. Allen, '09 (SJ) St. Victor, San Jose, CA
Navarro, Rev. Christopher, *M.S.* (SB) St. Christopher, Moreno Valley, CA; [MON] The Pacific Region Missionaries of Our Lady of La Salette, MS, Moreno Valley, CA
Navarro, Rev. Edison, *C.R.L.* '04 (NY) Our Lady Queen of Martyrs, New York, NY; St. Teresa of Avila, Sleepy Hollow, NY
Navarro, Very Rev. Luis, '08 (STO) Curia: Leadership Cathedral of the Annunciation (Pastor of), Stockton, CA
Navarro, Rev. Moises, (CHI) St. Mother Theodore Guerin, Elmwood Park, IL
Navarro, Msgr. Pablo A., '78 (MIA) Curia: Leadership [SEM] St. John Vianney College Seminary, Inc., Miami, FL
Navarro, Rev. Pedro, '63 (NEW) Retired.
Navarro Quintana, Rev. Nicolas, *SDB* (SJN) Maria Auxiliadora, San Juan, PR
Navarro Sanchez, Rev. Giovanny A, (CHI) Little Flower Parish, Waukegan, IL
Navarro-Sanchez, Rev. Juan, '05 (ORG) Christ Cathedral Parish, Garden Grove, CA
Nave, Rev. Arthur, '08 (PHX) St. Mary Magdalene Roman Catholic Parish, Gilbert, AZ
Navin, Rev. Timothy M., '79 (VEN) San Marco Parish in Marco Island, Inc., Marco Island, FL
Navit, Rev. Zachary W., '94 (PH) On Special Assignment. Chap, St Mary Ctr Rehab & Healthcare, St Stanislaus Rec, La… St. Stanislaus, Lansdale, PA
Navoy, Rev. Ronald W., '71 (CHI) Retired.
Naw, Rev. Paul Hta I, '06 (DUB) Sacred Heart Church, Waterloo, Iowa, Waterloo, IA
Nawalaniec, Rev. Mariusz J., '93 (CHI) St. Albert the Great, Burbank, IL
Nawarskas, Rev. Msgr. Frederick, '67 (SAN) Curia: Advisory Boards, Commissions, Committees, and Councils Holy Family, Abilene, TX
Nawodylo, Rev. Charles, *OCD* '16 (SJ) [MON] Carmelite Monastery, Novitiate, San Jose, CA
Nawrocki, Rev. Norman D., '82 (DET) Retired. Curia: Tribunal
Nayagam, Rev. Selva, *H.G.N.* (LUB) Curia: Leadership
Nayak, Rev. Christudas, '68 (ALX) Retired.
Nayak, Rev. Felix, '96 (GF) St. Margaret, Clyde Park, MT; St. Mary, Malta, MT; St. William, Gardiner, MT; [EFT] St. Mary's Catholic Education Trust, Malta, MT
Nayak, Rev. Kumud Chandra, *C.J.D.* '20 (MAD) St. Joseph, Rio, WI; St. Thomas, Poynette, WI
Nayak, Rev. Mahesh, *S.J.* (OM) [MON] Jesuit Community at Creighton University, Omaha, NE
Nayak, Rev. Manoj Kumar, *SS.CC.* '11 (BWN) Sacred Heart, Edinburg, TX; [CAM] Newman Center - Edinburg, Edinburg, TX
Nayak, Rev. Sudhir Christodas, *SS.CC.* '06 (FR) St. Gabriel the Archangel, New Bedford, MA
Naylor, Rev. David W., '00 (L) St. Charles, Lebanon, KY; St. Francis Xavier Church, Raywick, KY
Nazareth, Rev. Andrew, '87 (FTW) St. Martin de Porres, Syracuse, IN
Nazimek, Rev. David, (GBG) Holy Family, West Newton, PA; St. Anne, Rostraver Township, PA
Nazzaro, Rev. Alfonse, '03 (DAL) Mary Immaculate Catholic Parish, Dallas, TX; [CEM] Mary Immaculate Church - Columbarium, Farmers Branch, TX
Ndayisenga, Rev. Egide, *SJ* '11 (OAK) [MON] Jesuit Fathers and Brothers, Berkeley, CA
Ndeanaefo, Rev. Aloysius Okey, '05 (SFD) Sacred Heart, Villa Grove, IL; St. Michael, Hume, IL
Ndebilie, Rev. Valentine, '05 (TLS) St. Frances of Rome, Langley, OK; St. Mark's, Pryor, OK
Ndi, Rev. William Kingsley, '17 (BRK) On Academic Leave.
Ndikum, Rev. Desmond, '21 (DAL) Holy Family Catholic Parish, Van Alstyne, TX; St. Michael Catholic Parish - McKinney, McKinney, TX
Ndiokwere, Rev. Msgr. Nathaniel, (FRS) Retired.
Ndugbu, Rev. Polycarp E., '73 (SAC) On Special Assignment. Supply Priest
Nduka, Rev. Emmanuel-Lugard, '99 (TLS) On Special Assignment. Cimarron Corr Fac, Cushing Immaculate Conception, Pawhuska, OK
Ndulaka, Rev. Matthias, '78 (NY) St. Joseph, Wurtsboro, NY
Ndumbi, Rev. Charles, *S.V.D.* (NO) St. Paul the Apostle, New Orleans, LA
Ndung'u, Rev. Wanjiru, (SAT) St. Rose of Lima, San Antonio, TX
Ndunguru, Rev. Petro, '03 (FAR) Holy Family Church of Grand Forks, Grand Forks, ND
Ndyamukama, Rev. Justus, '01 (BUF) Curia: Offices and Directors St. Anthony of Padua, Buffalo, NY
Neal, Rev. Mark, '06 (DM) Holy Trinity, Des Moines, IA
Neary, Rev. Mark, '83 (SJ) Retired.
Neary, Rev. Pat, (P) Holy Redeemer, Portland, OR
Nebangongnjoh, Rev. Ernest, (CHL) St. Patrick Cathedral, Charlotte, NC
Nebesnyk, Rev. Oleksiy, '08 (PSC) St. Anne's, New Port Richey, FL
Nebrida, Rev. Dexter, *A.M.* (CAM) Paul VI High School, Haddon Township, N.J., Haddonfield, NJ
Nebrida, Rev. Dexter, *A.M.* (CAM) Saint Simon Stock Parish, Berlin, N.J., Berlin, NJ
Necaise, Rev. Braxton, '19 (BLX) Curia: Miscellaneous / Other Offices St. Thomas Aquinas, Hattiesburg, MS
Necaise, Rev. Braxton, '19 (BLX) Curia: Advisory Boards, Commissions, Committees, and Councils
Neculaesi, Rev. Claudiu Gabriel, '16 (BGP) The St. Theresa's Roman Catholic Church Corporation, Trumbull, CT
Nedder, Rev. Edward T., '87 (SAM) Retired.
Nediakala, Rev. Kuriakose, *M.C.B.S.* '78 (DUL) St. Charles, Cass Lake, MN; St. Joseph, Deer River, MN; St. Mary, Deer River, MN
Nedumankuzhiyil, Rev. Joseph, '99 (RVC) St. John Chrysostom Malankara Mission, Hempstead, NY
Nedumankuzhiyil, Rev. Joseph, '99 (DAL) UT SW Med Ctr; Zale Lipsky Hosp; WP Clements Jr Univ Hosp St. Joseph Catholic Parish - Richardson, Richardson, TX
Nedumaruthumchalil, Rev. George K., '78 (NY) St. Joseph, Kingston, NY
Nedumcheril, Rev. John, '91 (DET) St. Aloysius Parish Romulus, Romulus, MI
Nedungadan, Rev. Johnson, *C.M.* '91 (BRK) Chap, Flushing Hosp and Med Ctr; New York Presbyterian/ Qns St. Gregory the Great, Bellerose, NY
Nee, Rev. Robert E., '71 (BO) Retired.
Neeck, Rev. Jordan S., *O. Praem.* '19 (GB) [MON] St. Norbert Abbey, De Pere, WI
Needles, Rev. Brian X., '06 (NEW) Curia: Advisory Boards, Commissions, Committees, and Councils Our Lady of Sorrows, South Orange, NJ; [COL] Seton Hall University, South Orange, NJ
Neeley, Rev. Peter, *S.J.* '81 (TUC) [MIS] Kino Border Initiative, Nogales, AZ
Neely, Rev. Bradley, '03 (B) Our Lady of the Lake, McCall, ID; [CAM] Lewis Clark State College, Lewiston, ID
Neely, Rev. Jayd, '12 (NSH) St. Mary of the Seven Sorrows, Nashville, TN
Neely, Rev. Jayd, '12 (NSH) Curia: Leadership
Neenan, Rt. Rev. Benedict, *O.S.B.* (KC) [MON] Conception Abbey (Benedictine Monks), Conception, MO
Neenan, Rev. Benedict, *O.S.B.* '88 (KC) [EFT] The St. Benedict Education Foundation, Conception, MO; [SEM] Conception Seminary College, Conception, MO
Neff, Rev. Eugene J., '71 (BEL) Curia: Offices and Directors
Neff, Rev. Steven V., '05 (PIT) Curia: Clergy and Religious Services
Negley, Rev. Phil (Skip), (GAL) Curia: Offices and Directors
Negparanon, Rev. Nixon, '05 (RIC) Holy Name of Mary, Bedford, VA; Resurrection, Moneta, VA
Negrete, Rev. Wayne R., *S.J.* '91 (LA) Curia: Offices and Directors
Negro, Rev. Fernando, *Sch.P.* '72 (WDC) [MON] Piarist Fathers, Province of the U.S.A. and Puerto Rico, Washington, DC; [SEM] Queen of Pious Schools, Inc., Washington, DC
Negron, Rev. Juan Luis, '89 (CGS) Curia: Leadership Catedral Dulce Nombre de Jesus, Caguas, PR
Negron, Friar Ramon Hiram, *O.F.M.Cap.* (SJN) Colegio San Antonio, San Juan, PR; [MON] The Custody of Saint John the Baptist, Puerto Rico, of the Order Friars Minor Capuchin, San Juan, PR
Negrón, Rev. Juan Luis, (CGS) Curia: Leadership
Negron Cruz, Friar Ramon Hiram, *O.F.M.Cap.* (SJN) San Antonio de Padua, San Juan, PR; San Antonio de Padua School, San Juan, PR; [EFT] Capuchin Health and Retirement Trust of Puerto Rico, San Juan, PR; [MIS] Hogar Padre Venard, Inc., San Juan, PR; [MON] Fraternidad San Antonio, San Juan, PR
Negron Delgado, Rev. Juan Luis, '89 (PCE) [COL] The Pontifical Catholic University of Puerto Rico, Ponce, PR
Negron Martinez, Rev. Roy, '85 (ARE) Ntra. Sra. Madre del Redentor, Ciales, PR
Nehnevaj, Rev. Joshua T., '22 (SEA) St. Louise, Bellevue, WA
Nehrig, Rev. Robert V., *M.M.* '54 (NY) Retired. [MON] Maryknoll Fathers and Brothers (Catholic Foreign Mission Society of America, Inc.), Ossining, NY
Neihoff, Rev. Kevin, (CHI) [EFT] St. Jude Legacy Fund, ,
Neilson, Rev. James P., *O. Praem.* '93 (GB) [MON] St. Norbert Abbey, De Pere, WI; [RTR] Norbertine Center for Spirituality, De Pere, WI
Neiman, Rev. John, '86 (LA) Retired.
Neira, Rev. Juan Carlos, (FAJ) Nuestra Senora del Rosario, Naguabo, PR
Neitzke, Rev. Ron P., '89 (JOL) Curia: (>MO) Offices and Directors Sacred Heart, Bonfield, IL; St. James the Apostle, Irwin, IL; St. Margaret Mary, Herscher, IL
Neitzke, Rev. Thomas W., *S.J.* (CHI) [COL] Jesuit Community at Loyola University Chicago, Chicago, IL
Nelan, Rev. Msgr. Kevin J., '77 (NY) Curia: Leadership Immaculate Conception, New York, NY; Parish of St. Patrick's Old Cathedral and Most Precious Blood, New York, NY; St. Benedict the Moor, New York, NY; [MIS] Apostleship of the Sea, New York, NY
Nelen, Very Rev. Louis M., '12 (JC) Curia: Deaneries Cathedral of St. Joseph, Jefferson City, MO
Nellikunnel, Rev. George Philip, *S.A.C.* '77 (SFD) St. Aloysius, Springfield, IL; St. Frances Cabrini, Springfield, IL
Nellis, Rev. Thomas, (SAV) Retired.
Nellis, Rev. Thomas F., '66 (ROC) Retired.
Nellissery, Rev. Johnson, *I.S.P.* (AUS) St. Paul, Austin, TX
Nellissery, Rev. Johnson, *I.S.P.* '97 (AUS) [MON] Schoenstatt Fathers, Austin, TX
Nellissery, Rev. Joy Thomas, '88 (BIR) St. Mary of the Visitation, Huntsville, AL
Nelson, Rev. Andrew, '13 (MAN) Curia: Consultative Bodies Saint Ignatius of Loyola, Somersworth, NH; St. Mary, Rollinsford, NH
Nelson, Rev. Brian D, (WCH) Curia: Leadership
Nelson, Rev. Brian D., '03 (WCH) St. Mark, Colwich, KS
Nelson, Rev. Brian D., '03 (WCH) Curia: Leadership
Nelson, Rev. Caye A., '88 (BR) Curia: Administration The Congregation Of St. Jude The Apostle Roman Catholic Church Of Baton Rouge, Baton Rouge, LA
Nelson, Rev. Corey M., '13 (BIS) Curia: Leadership St. James, Powers Lake, ND; St. Michael, Ray, ND; St. Thomas, Tioga, ND
Nelson, Rev. Daniel C., *O.F.M.* '77 (ALB) [COL] Siena College, Loudonville, NY
Nelson, Rev. Dennis (Dan), '08 (STA) Retired.
Nelson, Rev. Frank M., '88 (RVC) Maria Regina, Seaford, NY
Nelson, Rev. Garrett, (GF) St. Mary, Livingston, MT
Nelson, Rev. Garrett J., '14 (GF) Curia: Leadership St. Joseph, Big Timber, MT; [PRE] Thieltges-St. Thomas Camp, Great Falls, MT
Nelson, Rev. Msgr. Glenn L., '93 (RCK) On Special Assignment. Curia: Leadership; Offices and Directors [MIS] Catholic Office of the Deaf, Rockford, IL
Nelson, Rev. Gregory, '97 (PEO) Curia: Consultative Bodies St. Mary's, Bloomington, IL
Nelson, Rev. Jadyn E., '12 (BIS) Bishop Ryan Catholic School, Minot, ND; St. Leo, Minot, ND; St. Mary, Foxholm, ND; St. Philomena, Glenburn, ND
Nelson, Rev. Joe, *O.F.M.* '64 (IND) Holy Family Catholic Church, Oldenburg, Inc., Oldenburg, IN
Nelson, Rev. Justin, (L) Curia: Leadership St. Agnes, Louisville, KY; [MON] Sacred Heart Retreat, Louisville, KY
Nelson, Rev. Kevin C., '00 (PMB) Curia: Leadership St. Jude, Tequesta, FL
Nelson, Rev. M. Dominique-Savio, *O.C.S.O.* '15 (P) [MON] The Cistercian (Trappist) Abbey of Our Lady of Guadalupe (Order of Cistercians of the Strict Observance), Carlton, OR
Nelson, Rev. Martin Lester, '97 (BEA) Retired. Curia: Administration; Advisory Boards, Commissions, Committees, and Councils
Nelson, Rev. Nicholas, '13 (DUL) Queen of Peace, Cloquet, MN
Nelson, Rev. Nicholas, '13 (DUL) Holy Family, Cloquet, MN
Nelson, Rev. Nicholas, '13 (DUL) [EFT] Educational Endowment Trust, Queen of Peace Church, Cloquet, MN
Nelson, Rev. Nicholas, '13 (DUL) Curia: Offices and Directors
Nelson, Rev. Patrick, *S.D.S.* '09 (MIL) St. Margaret Mary Congregation, Milwaukee, WI; [MON] Salvatorian Provincial Offices (Society of the Divine Savior), Milwaukee, WI
Nelson, Rev. Ronald, '07 (P) St. Catherine of Siena, Veneta, OR; St. Mary, Eugene, OR
Nelson, Rev. Ronald, '07 (P) Curia: Offices and

Directors
Nelson, Rev. Thomas, *O.Praem.* '81 (CHI) [MIS] Institute on Religious Life, Mundelein, IL
Nelson, Rev. Thomas, '12 (RNO) St. Ann, Dayton, NV; St. Mary's in the Mountains, Virginia City, NV
Nelson, Rev. Thomas A., '14 (STU) Curia: Deaneries Corpus Christi, Belle Valley, OH; Immaculate Conception, Caldwell, OH; St. Michael, Caldwell, OH; St. Stephen, Caldwell, OH
Nelson, Rev. Thomas W., *O.Praem.* '81 (ORG) [MON] Norbertine Fathers of Orange, Inc., Silverado, CA; [SEM] St. Michael's Norbertine Postulancy, Novitiate and Juniorate, Silverado, CA
Nelson, Rev. Timothy A., '00 (LAN) Chap, Parnall Facility Curia: Leadership St. Mary Star of the Sea Parish Jackson, Jackson, MI
Nelvy, Rev. Junot, '14 (ATL) Christ Our Hope Catholic Church, Lithonia, Inc., Lithonia, GA
Nelvy, Rev. Junot, (MO) Curia: Offices and Directors
Nemaisa, Rev. Abraham, (FBK) Holy Family Catholic Church Newtok, Newtok, AK; Immaculate Conception Catholic Church Bethel, Bethel, AK; Immaculate Heart of Mary Catholic Church Marshall, Marshall, AK; St. Catherine of Siena Catholic Church Chefornak, Chefornak, AK
Nemchausky, Rev. Matthew, '09 (CHI) St. Paul VI, Riverside, IL
Nemec, Rev. Msgr. Joseph J., '84 (LIN) Retired.
Nemecek, Rev. M. Cyril, '60 (CHI) Retired.
Nemergut, Rev. Robert S., '77 (EVN) Retired.
Nemeth, Rev. Ambrose, '22 (STN) [MON] Holy Protection Monastery, Eagle Harbor, MI
Nemeth, Rev. Edward G., '08 (STL) Ste. Genevieve Catholic Church, Ste. Genevieve, Ste. Genevieve, MO
Nemeth, Rev. Maurus B., *O.S.B.* '72 (SFR) [MIS] St. Stephen Hungarian Catholic Mission, Portola Valley, CA; [MON] Woodside Priory, Portola Valley, CA
Nemmers, Rev. Mark R., '66 (DUB) Retired.
Neneman, Rev. John, '00 (ORG) San Antonio de Padua Del Canon Church, Anaheim, CA
Nenneau, Rev. Thomas D., '81 (LAN) Retired.
Nepil, Rev. John, '11 (DEN) [SEM] Saint John Vianney Theological Seminary, Denver, CO
Nerbun, Rev. David D., '11 (CHR) Curia: Offices and Directors
Nero, Rev. James, '71 (SP) [MON] St. Anthony Friary (St. Petersburg) Franciscan Friars-Holy Name Province, Inc., St. Petersburg, FL
Nesbit, Rev. Jason, *C.S.V.* '11 (JOL) Maternity of the Blessed Virgin Mary, Bourbonnais, IL
Nesbit, Rev. Jason P., *C.S.V.* '11 (CHI) [MON] Viatorian Province Center-Clerics of St. Viator, Arlington Heights, IL
Nesbit, Rev. Robert, *O.S.B.* (TLS) [MON] Our Lady of the Annunciation of Clear Creek Abbey, Hulbert, OK
Neske, Rev. Mark I., '83 (MOB) Holy Family Parish, Mobile, Mobile, AL
Neske, Rev. Robert, (TUC) Sacred Heart of Jesus Roman Catholic Parish - Tombstone, Tombstone, AZ
Neske, Rev. Robert, (TUC) Saint Andrew the Apostle Roman Catholic Parish - Sierra Vista, Sierra Vista, AZ
Nesrsta, Very Rev. Stephen, '95 (AUS) Curia: Leadership Holy Trinity Catholic Church - Corn Hill, Texas, Jarrell, TX
Nessel, Rev. William, *O.S.F.S.* (WIL) [MON] Retirement and Assisted Care Facility, Childs, MD
Nessel, Rev. William, *O.S.F.S.* '56 (PH) Retired.
Nesti, Rev. Donald S., *C.Ss.P.* '63 (GAL) St. Cecilia, Houston, TX
Nestico, Rev. Jonathan, '20 (LA) Our Lady of Perpetual Help, Santa Clarita, CA
Nestler, Rev. David, (CLV) Holy Spirit Parish, Garfield Heights, OH
Nestler, Rev. W., *O.F.M. Cap.* '89 (CLV) [MON] St. Paul Friary, Cleveland, OH
Nestor, Rev. Robert P., '70 (NEW) Retired. [COL] Seton Hall University, South Orange, NJ
Nestor, Rev. Thomas F., '81 (BO) Curia: Clergy and Religious Services; Leadership Resurrection of Our Lord and Savior Jesus Christ, Hingham, MA; St. Paul, Hingham, MA
Nesvadba, Rev. Msgr. Reggie R., '66 (GAL) Retired.
Neterer, Rev. Kyle, '16 (LFT) All Saints, Logansport, IN; St. Charles Borromeo, Peru, IN
Netlas, Rev. Edwin, *CMF* '05 (LEX) St. Andrew, Harrodsburg, KY
Nett, Rev. Aaron, '14 (NU) Church of St. Anthony, Watkins, MN
Nett, Rev. Aaron, '14 (SCL) The Church of the Assumption, Eden Valley, MN
Nettekoven, Rev. Joseph M., '75 (ORG) Retired.
Nettem, Rev. Joseph, '01 (OKL) St. Mary's, Medford, OK
Neu, Rev. Joshua M., '15 (TYL) On Duty Outside Diocese. (>NO) [SEM] Notre Dame Seminary Graduate School of Theology, New Orleans, LA
Neubecker, Rev. William, *O.M.V.* (BO) [MON] Oblate Residence (St. Joseph House), Milton, MA
Neuhaus, Rev. Msgr. William B., '83 (COV) Retired. Curia: Clergy and Religious Services; Offices and Directors; Tribunal
Neuman, Rev. James L., '71 (SFD) Retired.
Neuman, Rev. Matthias, *O.S.B.* '67 (IND) [MON] St. Meinrad Archabbey, St. Meinrad, IN
Neumann, Rev. Aloysius J., '60 (RCK) Retired.
Neumann, Rev. Richard J., '65 (HRT) Retired.
Neumann, Rev. William J., '75 (ORL) Retired.
Neumeier, Rev. Larry, '95 (LA) Corpus Christi, Pacific Palisades, CA
Neusch, Rev. Antony C, '04 (AMA) St. Mary's Cathedral, Amarillo, TX
Neusch, Rev. Antony Carl, '04 (AMA) Curia: Advisory Boards, Commissions, Committees, and Councils
Neusch, Rev. Tony, '04 (AMA) Curia: Advisory Boards, Commissions, Committees, and Councils; Consultative Bodies; Leadership; Offices and Directors
Neuschwander, Rev. David L., '14 (SUP) Curia: Offices and Directors St. Ann, Cable, WI; St. Francis of Solanus, Stone Lake, WI; St. Ignatius, New Post, WI; St. Joseph's Congregation, Hayward, WI; St. Philip Catholic Congregation, Stone Lake, WI
Neuzil, Rev. Gregory, '67 (KNX) Retired. (>CLV) St. Richard, North Olmsted, OH
Nevels, Rev. Thomas A., '99 (CIN) St. Albert the Great, Kettering, OH; St. Charles Borromeo, Kettering, OH
Neville, Rt. Rev. Gary J., *O. Praem.* '78 (GB) Holy Cross, Green Bay, WI; [MIS] Norbertine Generalate, Inc., De Pere, WI; [MON] St. Norbert Abbey, De Pere, WI
Nevin, Rev. Msgr. Emmet R., '77 (NY) Curia: Leadership St. Aedan, Pearl River, NY
Nevins, Rev. Donald J., '75 (CHI) Curia: Leadership St. Agnes of Bohemia, Chicago, IL
Nevins, Rev. Troy A., '96 (GR) Curia: Clergy and Religious Services; Leadership Immaculate Heart of Mary, Grand Rapids, MI
Nevitt, Rev. Alex, '19 (PAT) Notre Dame of Mt. Carmel, Cedar Knolls, NJ
Nevitt, Rev. Joshua, (CAM) Retired. Curia: Leadership
Newcomb, Rev. Matthew C., '05 (NY) On Leave. (>ORL) Holy Name of Jesus, Indialantic, FL
Newland, Rev. Msgr. Ronald, '67 (BRK) Blessed Trinity Roman Catholic Church, Rockaway Point, NY
Newland, Rev. Msgr. Ronald A., '67 (NEW) Retired.
Newman, Rev. Brian, *O.F.M. Cap.* '61 (PIT) [MON] St. Augustine Friary, Pittsburgh, PA
Newman, Very Rev. Jay Scott, '93 (CHR) Curia: Advisory Boards, Commissions, Committees, and Councils; Deaneries; Tribunal San Sebastian Mission, Greenville, SC; St. Mary, Greenville, SC
Newman, Rev. Joseph, *O.S.F.S.* '13 (TOL) [EFT] St. Francis de Sales High School Foundation, Inc., Toledo, OH; [MON] Oblates of St. Francis de Sales, Toledo, OH
Newman, Rev. Mark L., *C.J.* '60 (LA) Retired. [MON] St. Joseph Seminary (Josephite Fathers' Novitiate), Santa Maria, CA
Newman, Rev. Michael, *OSFS* (TOL) [MON] Provincial Offices, ,
Newman, Rev. Michael, *OSFS* (LAN) Holy Family Parish Adrian, Adrian, MI
Newns, Rev. John J., '74 (PH) St. Ann, Phoenixville, PA
Newton, Rev. Arockiya, (SCL) St. Andrew's, Greenwald, MN; St. John's, Melrose, MN; St. Mary's, Melrose, MN; St. Michael's, Melrose, MN
Newton, Rev. David J., '88 (LFT) St. Elizabeth Seton, Carmel, IN
Newton, Very Rev. Joseph L., '08 (IND) Curia: Offices and Directors SS. Peter and Paul Cathedral, Indianapolis, Inc., Indianapolis, IN
Newton, Rev. Nicholas, '22 (SPC) Our Lady of the Lake, Branson, MO; Our Lady of the Ozarks, Forsyth, MO
Newton, Rev. Stephen P., *C.S.C.* '89 (FTW) [COL] University of Notre Dame Du Lac, Notre Dame, IN; [MON] Holy Cross Community, Corby Hall, University of Notre Dame, Notre Dame, IN (>CHI) [ASN] Association of U.S. Catholic Priests, Forest Park, IL
Newton, Rev. Thomas A., '88 (CAM) Curia: Clergy and Religious Services; Leadership; Tribunal Saint Damien Parish, Ocean City, N.J., Ocean City, NJ
Newton-Williamraj, Rev. Valanarasu, (BO) St. Clare, Braintree, MA; St. Francis of Assisi, Braintree, MA
Neyland, Rev. Malcolm, '73 (LUB) Retired.
Neyoh, Rev. Daniel, (RVC) St. Patrick's, Huntington, NY
Ng, Rev. Andrew, *S.D.B.* '97 (LA) St. Dominic Savio, Bellflower, CA
Ng, Rev. Francis, '09 (ORG) St. Angela Merici, Brea, CA
Ngageno, Rev. Robert, '97 (PH) St. Jerome, Philadelphia, PA
Ngah, Rev. Edwin, *C.F.I.C.* (STP) Hennepin Co Med Ctr, Minneapolis [MON] Congregation of the Sons of the Immaculate Conception, Bloomington, MN
Ngah Dzenjo, Rev. Eugene L., (ARL) All Saints, Manassas, VA
Ngandu, Rev. Leon, *SVD* (LR) Mount St. Mary Academy, Little Rock, AR; St. Augustine, North Little Rock, AR; St. Bartholomew, Little Rock, AR
Ng'ang'a, Rev. Patrick, *SJ* '18 (OAK) [MON] Jesuit Fathers and Brothers, Berkeley, CA
Ngema, Rev. Wilson E, '10 (OAK) St. Theresa of the Infant Jesus (The Little Flower), Oakland, CA
Ngnintedem, Rev. Robert Kenfack, '98 (STV) Holy Family Parish, St. Thomas, VI
Ngo, Rev. (John Damascene M.) Vuong Duc, *CRM* '91 (SPC) [MON] Congregation of the Mother of the Redeemer, Carthage, MO
Ngo, Rev. Anthony, '94 (RIC) Retired.
Ngo, Rev. Chi V., *S.J.* '00 (SJ) [RTR] Jesuit Retreat Center of Los Altos, Los Altos, CA
Ngo, Rev. Francis Huan Ton, '89 (GAL) Retired.
Ngo, Rev. Huan D., '16 (BO) St. Mary, Dedham, MA
Ngo, Rev. John Hieu, '17 (STO) Curia: Leadership St. Bernard Church (Pastor of), Tracy, CA
Ngo, Rev. John Baptist Duong Khac, *SDD* '21 (P) Our Lady of Lavang, Happy Valley, OR
Ngo, Rev. Joseph Thong, *C.Ss.R.* '07 (NY) Immaculate Conception, Bronx, NY
Ngo, Rev. Joseph Phuong, *O. Carm.* '12 (ALB) St. Joseph, Troy, NY
Ngo, Rev. Khan D., '11 (SB) St. Elizabeth of Hungary, Desert Hot Springs, CA
Ngo, Rev. Lan, *S.J.* '04 (LA) [MON] Jesuit Community, Los Angeles, CA
Ngo, Rev. Martin, *S.J.* '21 (LA) [MON] Jesuit Community, Los Angeles, CA
Ngo, Rev. Peter Dung Duc, '08 (OAK) St. Felicitas, San Leandro, CA
Ngo, Rev. Peter T.D., *C.Ss.R.* '62 (LA) Retired.
Ngo, Rev. Peter Thang C., '93 (LA) St. Michael, Los Angeles, CA
Ngo, Rev. Tammylee, (OAK) [MON] Conventual Franciscans (Province of St. Joseph Cupertino) Provincial Center, Castro Valley, CA; [MON] Conventual Franciscans (Province of St. Joseph of Cupertino), Castro Valley, CA
Ngo, Rev. Thinh Cuong, *SVD* (DUB) [SEM] Divine Word College, Epworth, IA
N'go, Rev. Anthony Chinh, '94 (L) St. John Vianney, Louisville, KY
Ngoc Dinh, Rev. Vincent Thao, (ARL) Holy Martyrs of Vietnam Catholic Church, Arlington, VA
Ngoka, Rev. Michael, (RVC) St. Barnabas the Apostle, Bellmore, NY
Ngondwe, Rev. Ponsiano, (BO) [MON] The Jesuit Community at Boston College, Chestnut Hill, MA
Ngosa, Rev. Alick-George, '11 (BAL) [MON] Society of St. Sulpice, Province of the United States, Baltimore, MD
Nguyen, Rev. (Dominic M.) Thien Toan, *CRM* '15 (SPC) [MON] Congregation of the Mother of the Redeemer, Carthage, MO
Nguyen, Rev. Andrew, '20 (JKS) Immaculate Heart of Mary, Greenwood, MS
Nguyen, Rev. Andrew C., '11 (SJ) On Special Assignment. Curia: Offices and Directors St. Thomas of Canterbury, San Jose, CA
Nguyen, Rev. Andrew Chien, '97 (ORL) On Special Assignment.
Nguyen, Rev. Andrew Dzung An, *O.S.B.* '90 (SFE) [MON] Monastery of Christ in the Desert, Abiquiu, NM
Nguyen, Rev. Andrew V., '09 (SJ) Curia: Offices and Directors Holy Family (Roman Catholic Bishop of San Jose, a Corporation Sole), San Jose, CA
Nguyen, Rev. Anh, (PHX) Vietnamese Martyrs Parish Roman Catholic Parish, Phoenix, AZ
Nguyen, Rev. Anh-Tuan D., '07 (LA) Our Lady of Loretto, Los Angeles, CA; St. Columban, Los Angeles, CA
Nguyen, Rev. Anthony Cong, *S.V.D.* '08 (DUB) [SEM] Divine Word College, Epworth, IA
Nguyen, Rev. Anthony Phuc, *C.Ss.R.* '92 (TUC) (>CHI) [MON] The Redemptorist Fathers of Chicago, Chicago, IL; (>CHI) [MON] The Redemptorists/Denver Province, Chicago, IL
Nguyen, Rev. Anthony Tan, (SJ) Our Lady of Refuge, San Jose, CA

Nguyen, Rev. Anthony Tin, '06 (PT) SS. Peter & Paul Parish, Panama City, FL
Nguyen, Rev. Anthony Tuong, (SJ) St. Joseph of Cupertino, Cupertino, CA
Nguyen, Rev. Augustine, '12 (BGP) Curia: Clergy and Religious Services; Consultative Bodies; Leadership St. Francis of Assisi, Weston, CT
Nguyen, Rev. Augustine Trung T., *CRM* '17 (SPC) [MON] Congregation of the Mother of the Redeemer, Carthage, MO
Nguyen, Rev. Bang Cong, *S.V.D.* '00 (CHI) [SEM] Divine Word Theologate, Chicago, IL
Nguyen, Rev. Bao, *S.J.* (BAL) [COL] Jesuit Community of Loyola University, Inc., Baltimore, MD; [MON] Jesuit Community of Loyola University Maryland, Inc., Baltimore, MD
Nguyen, Very Rev. Basil, *O.Cist.* '10 (SPC) [MON] Assumption Abbey (O.Cist), Ava, MO; [RTR] Assumption Abbey, Ava, MO
Nguyen, Rev. Basil, *OCist* '10 (SPC) [SEM] Assumption Novitiate (Trappists), Ava, MO
Nguyen, Rev. Benjamin N., '05 (WCH) St. Anthony, Wichita, KS
Nguyen, Rev. Bich N., '03 (OAK) Curia: Leadership; Offices and Directors Cathedral Parish of Christ the Light, Oakland, CA
Nguyen, Rev. Bieu Van, '00 (MOB) Christ the King, Andalusia, AL; St. Elizabeth, Greenville, AL
Nguyen, Rev. Binh, *C.M.* '82 (STL) [MON] Congregation of the Mission, Perryville, MO
Nguyen, Rev. Binh Chau, '14 (JKS) Immaculate Conception, West Point, MS
Nguyen, Rev. Binh T., '01 (ORG) Curia: Leadership St. Irenaeus, Cypress, CA
Nguyen, Rev. Binh Thanh, *S.V.D.* '02 (WDC) [MON] Society of the Divine Word/Divine Word House, Washington, DC
Nguyen, Rev. Bonaventure, *O.S.B.* '19 (SFE) [MON] Monastery of Christ in the Desert, Abiquiu, NM
Nguyen, Rev. Brandon, (MEM) Sacred Heart Church, Memphis, TN
Nguyen, Rev. Brandon Bay, *C.S.Sp.* '00 (GAL) St. Benedict the Abbot, Houston, TX
Nguyen, Rev. Chau J., '89 (ORL) Curia: Evangelization St. Philip Phan Van Minh Catholic Church, Orlando, FL
Nguyen, Rev. Chau Van, (FWT) Christ the King, Fort Worth, TX
Nguyen, Rev. Chinh, '94 (SR) [MIS] Pastor of Vietnamese Martyrs Catholic Church of Santa Rosa, A Corporation Sole, Santa Rosa, CA
Nguyen, Rev. Christopher T, *S.J.* (SD) [CAM] University of California at San Diego (Campus Ministry), San Diego, CA
Nguyen, Rev. Cuong H., *M.M.* '98 (NY) [MON] Maryknoll Fathers and Brothers (Catholic Foreign Mission Society of America, Inc.), Ossining, NY
Nguyen, Rev. Cuong Hung, '00 (SC) St. Mary's, Hawarden, IA; St. Patrick, Akron, IA
Nguyen, Rev. Cuong Van, '22 (MAN) Parish of the Holy Spirit, Keene, NH
Nguyen, Rev. Dam D., '93 (PIT) Curia: Consultative Bodies Christ Our Savior, Pittsburgh, PA
Nguyen, Rev. Danh, *M.S.A.* (NOR) [SEM] Holy Apostles College and Seminary, Cromwell, CT
Nguyen, Rev. Daokim, '93 (GAL) St. Joseph, New Waverly, TX
Nguyen, Rev. Dat, '18 (MRY) [CAM] Cabrillo College, Santa Cruz, CA; [CAM] University of California at Santa Cruz, Santa Cruz, CA
Nguyen, Rev. Dat Tan, *C.Ss.R.* '13 (LA) [MON] Vietnamese Redemptorist Mission, Baldwin Park, CA
Nguyen, Rev. Dinh Chin, '21 (BRK) St. Luke, Whitestone, NY
Nguyen, Rev. Doan Paul, '21 (PRO) SS. John and Paul Parish Corporation, Coventry, Coventry, RI
Nguyen, Rev. Dominic, *C.R.M.* (KNX) Church of Divine Mercy, Knoxville, TN
Nguyen, Rev. Dominic Dung Anh, *SVD* '98 (FTW) St. Patrick, Fort Wayne, IN
Nguyen, Rev. Dominic Hoan, '09 (HON) [MIS] Vietnamese Holy Martyrs Community, ,
Nguyen, Rev. Dominic Trung, '03 (VIC) Curia: Offices and Directors
Nguyen, Rev. Dovan, '93 (TLS) St. Joseph Church, Tulsa, OK
Nguyen, Rev. Du Truong Hai, *M.F.* '21 (OAK) [MON] Missionaries of Faith-India Inc., Fremont, CA
Nguyen, Rev. Duc, '09 (KC) St. Paul the Apostle, Tarkio, MO
Nguyen, Rev. Duc Cong, '06 (SEA) Our Lady of Sorrows, Snoqualmie, WA
Nguyen, Rev. Dung, '02 (ATL) Sacred Heart Catholic Church, Milledgeville, Inc., Milledgeville, GA
Nguyen, Rev. Duong, '12 (VEN) On Duty Outside Diocese. Diocese of San Jose
Nguyen, Rev. Duong, (SB) Our Lady of the Rosary Cathedral, San Bernardino, CA
Nguyen, Rev. Duong, '12 (SJ) St. Elizabeth, Milpitas, CA
Nguyen, Rev. Duy, *S.C.J.* '11 (MIL) [MON] Sacred Heart Monastery, Hales Corners, WI
Nguyen, Rev. Duy, (TLS) Curia: Leadership; Offices and Directors Bishop Kelley High School, Inc., Tulsa, OK
Nguyen, Rev. Francis, *S.D.D.* '15 (NO) Our Lady of Lavang Roman Catholic Church, New Orleans, Louisiana, New Orleans, LA
Nguyen, Rev. Francis, *S.J.* (SJ) Most Holy Trinity, San Jose, CA
Nguyen, Rev. Francis, (BR) [MON] Incarnatio Consecratio Missio, Baton Rouge, LA
Nguyen, Rev. Francis Khoi, '90 (DOD) Retired.
Nguyen, Rev. Francis Nhi, (WDC) Chap, Children's National Med Ctr, Washington
Nguyen, Rev. Francis T., '02 (OKL) Curia: Tribunal St. Andrew the Apostle Catholic Church, Moore, OK
Nguyen, Rev. Francis Tam, '15 (VIC) Holy Cross, Yorktown, TX
Nguyen, Rev. Gan, *C.Ss.R.* '98 (STL) [MON] St. Clement Health Care Center, Liguori, MO
Nguyen, Rev. Giovanni, '00 (GAL) St. Stanislaus, Anderson, TX
Nguyen, Rev. Gregory, '98 (OKL) St. Andrew Dung-Lac, Oklahoma City, OK
Nguyen, Rev. Hai D., '15 (AUS) St. Helen, Georgetown, TX
Nguyen, Rev. Hai Du Truong, *MF* (OAK) Our Lady of Guadalupe, Fremont, CA
Nguyen, Rev. Msgr. Hien Minh, '85 (SJ) On Leave.
Nguyen, Rev. Hien Paul, '00 (WCH) All Saints, Wichita, KS
Nguyen, Rev. Hiep, '20 (PRO) Curia: Leadership Saint Francis Xavier's Church, East Providence, RI
Nguyen, Rev. Hiep, '15 (CHY) Mary Queen of Heaven, Chugwater, WY
Nguyen, Rev. Hiep X., '15 (CHY) St. Patrick's, Wheatland, WY
Nguyen, Rev. Hieu, '07 (GAL) St. Ambrose, Houston, TX
Nguyen, Rev. Hieu Trong, *S.V.D.* '06 (SB) [RTR] Divine Word Province/ Retreat Center, Riverside, CA
Nguyen, Rev. Hieu Quang, *I.M.S.* (BR) Curia: Pastoral Services
Nguyen, Rev. Hilary Khanh Hai, *C.R.M.* (CLV) Curia: Parish Services
Nguyen, Rev. Hilary Khanh, '94 (CLV) St. Boniface, Cleveland, OH
Nguyen, Very Rev. Hoa, '98 (FWT) Curia: Leadership Holy Family, Fort Worth, TX
Nguyen, Rev. Hoa Van, '76 (HBG) St. Patrick Parish York Charitable Trust, York, PA
Nguyen, Rev. Hoan N., *C.M.* '99 (LA) [MON] Congregation of the Mission Western Province (DePaul Center Residence), Montebello, CA
Nguyen, Rev. Hoang Dinh, '05 (STP) Curia: Leadership St. Columba, St. Paul, MN
Nguyen, Rev. Hoang H., '04 (CHI) Chap, Hckiam AB, Hickam AFB, HI
Nguyen, Rev. Hoang Peter, (ORG) Curia: (>MO) Offices and Directors
Nguyen, Rev. Hung, *OFM Cap* (OAK) [MON] Capuchin Franciscan Friars, Berkeley, CA
Nguyen, Rev. Hung Joseph, '94 (STO) St. Anne Church (Pastor of), Lodi, CA
Nguyen, Rev. Hung T, *S.J.* '21 (ELP) Sacred Heart, El Paso, TX
Nguyen, Rev. Hung T., *S.J.* '21 (SD) Pastor of Our Lady of Guadalupe Catholic Parish, San Diego, a corporation sole, San Diego, CA
Nguyen, Rev. Hung T., '94 (SEA)
Nguyen, Rev. Hung Van, *S.O.L.T.* '02 (MO) Curia: Offices and Directors
Nguyen, Rev. Hung Viet, *I.C.M.* '69 (BR) [MIS] St. Michael's Home, Baton Rouge, LA; [MON] Incarnatio Consecratio Missio, Baton Rouge, LA
Nguyen, Rev. Huy H., '09 (BO) Immaculate Conception, Weymouth, MA; St. Jerome, Weymouth, MA
Nguyen, Rev. Huy Nhat, '95 (LA) St. Gregory the Great Church, Whittier, CA
Nguyen, Rev. Huyen T., *C.Ss.R.* '21 (PH) St. Peter the Apostle, Philadelphia, PA; Visitation B.V.M., Philadelphia, PA
Nguyen, Rev. Hy, *P.S.S.* '97 (OAK) On Duty Outside Diocese.
Nguyen, Rev. Hy K., *P.S.S.* '97 (BAL) [MON] Society of St. Sulpice, Province of the United States, Baltimore, MD
Nguyen, Rev. J. Christopher C., '08 (GAL) St. Matthias the Apostle, Magnolia, TX
Nguyen, Rev. J.B. Duc Minh, *O.P.* '09 (PHX) Vietnamese Martyrs Parish Roman Catholic Parish, Phoenix, AZ
Nguyen, Rev. James B., '01 (LAF) Saint Andrew Dung-Lac Roman Catholic Church, Abbeville, LA; St. Marcellus, New Iberia, LA
Nguyen, Rev. Joe, *SDB* (OAK) Salesian College Preparatory (Salesians of St. John Bosco), Richmond, CA
Nguyen, Rev. Joe Van Anh, '68 (AUS) Retired.
Nguyen, Rev. John Baptist, (SY) Curia: Offices and Directors
Nguyen, Rev. John C., '99 (PH) St. Maria Goretti, Hatfield, PA
Nguyen, Rev. John Doanh Phong, *S.J.* '01 (SJ) Church of the Resurrection, Sunnyvale, CA
Nguyen, Rev. John Duy, '14 (ORG) Holy Spirit, Fountain Valley, CA
Nguyen, Rev. John Luat, *O.F.M.* '94 (SFR) St. Boniface, San Francisco, CA
Nguyen, Rev. John Tung, '07 (WDC) Our Lady's, Leonardtown, MD; Shrine of St. Jude, Rockville, MD
Nguyen, Rev. John Baptist Khoi, (RIC) Church of the Vietnamese Martyrs, Richmond, VA; Our Lady of Vietnam Chapel, Norfolk, VA
Nguyen, Rev. John Tran, (SJ) Our Lady of La Vang Parish, San Jose, CA
Nguyen, Rev. Joseph, '90 (LIN) St. Andrew Dung Lac and Companions Catholic Church of Lincoln, Lincoln, NE
Nguyen, Rev. Joseph, *O.S.B.* '03 (P) [MON] Mt. Angel Abbey, Saint Benedict, OR
Nguyen, Rev. Joseph, *CM* (CHL) St. Mary, Greensboro, NC
Nguyen, Rev. Joseph An, '92 (CAM) Most Precious Blood Parish, Collingswood, N.J., Collingswood, NJ
Nguyen, Rev. Joseph C., *SVD* '08 (JKS) St. Joseph, Port Gibson, MS; St. Mary, Vicksburg, MS
Nguyen, Rev. Joseph D., '85 (BO) St. Mary, Waltham, MA
Nguyen, Rev. Joseph Dang Kim, '93 (LA) Nativity, El Monte, CA
Nguyen, Rev. Joseph Dau Van, '84 (NO) Retired.
Nguyen, Rev. Joseph H., *S.J.* '07 (SFR) [MON] Loyola House Jesuit Community, San Francisco, CA
Nguyen, Rev. Joseph Hau Duc, '69 (P) Retired.
Nguyen, Rev. Joseph Hoan, '22 (STP) St. John the Baptist, New Brighton, MN
Nguyen, Rev. Joseph Huyen Van, '95 (SAC) Curia: Offices and Directors
Nguyen, Rev. Joseph Long, '64 (MIA) Curia: Pastoral Services Our Lady of La Vang Vietnamese Catholic Mission, Hallandale Beach, FL
Nguyen, Rev. Joseph Luan, '90 (ORG) Immaculate Heart of Mary, Santa Ana, CA; Our Lady of La Vang, Santa Ana, CA
Nguyen, Rev. Joseph Minh, '61 (NEW) Curia: Offices and Directors St. Michael Parish, Jersey City, NJ
Nguyen, Rev. Joseph Nguyen Van, '02 (NO) [MIS] Chapel of the Vietnamese Martyrs, New Orleans, LA
Nguyen, Rev. Joseph Phien, '92 (RIC) Our Lady of Lavang, Norfolk, VA; Our Lady of Vietnam Chapel, Norfolk, VA
Nguyen, Rev. Joseph Phong, '11 (GAL) St. Justin Martyr, Houston, TX
Nguyen, Rev. Joseph Q., '05 (LA) St. Joan of Arc, Los Angeles, CA
Nguyen, Rev. Joseph Quoc-Tuan, '22 (SJ) Cathedral Basilica of St. Joseph, San Jose, CA
Nguyen, Rev. Joseph Son, '17 (STO) Cathedral of the Annunciation (Pastor of), Stockton, CA
Nguyen, Rev. Joseph Son Thai, '89 (ORG) Holy Family, Seal Beach, CA
Nguyen, Rev. Joseph T., '10 (DAV) On Duty Outside Diocese. Temple Terrace, FL
Nguyen, Rev. Joseph T., '05 (OAK) St. Leo the Great, Oakland, CA
Nguyen, Rev. Joseph T., '11 (CC) St. Paul the Apostle, Corpus Christi, TX
Nguyen, Rev. Joseph Thai, '95 (CHI) On Duty Outside Diocese. Vietnamese Catholic Ctr, Santa Ana, CA
Nguyen, Rev. Joseph Thai, (ORG) Our Lady of La Vang, Santa Ana, CA
Nguyen, Rev. Joseph Trong, '69 (LAV) Retired. St. Thomas More, Henderson, NV
Nguyen, Rev. Joseph Tuoc, *S.J.* '89 (DEN) [MON] Regis Jesuit Community (The Jesuits at Regis University), Denver, CO
Nguyen, Rev. Joseph Van Tao, '15 (SFE) San Juan Nepomuceno, El Rito, NM; St. Mary, Ojo Caliente, ,

Nguyen, Rev. Justin M., '09 (AUS) St. Martin de Porres, Dripping Springs, TX
Nguyen, Rev. Khanh D., '06 (SEA) St. Matthew, Seattle, WA
Nguyen, Rev. Khanh Pham, '97 (HON) SS Peter and Paul, Honolulu, HI
Nguyen, Rev. Khanh (Hilary M.) Hai, *CRM* '94 (SPC) [MON] Congregation of the Mother of the Redeemer, Carthage, MO
Nguyen, Rev. Kheim, (FWT) Immaculate Conception, Denton, TX
Nguyen, Very Rev. Khiet T., '96 (TLS) On Special Assignment. Oklahoma State Peneitentiary, McAlester Jackie Bannon Cor... Curia: Leadership
Nguyen, Rev. Khoa, *O.F.M.* (SFR) [SEM] St. Patrick's Seminary and University (The Roman Catholic Seminary of San Francisco), Menlo Park, CA
Nguyen, Rev. Kien, (L) Curia: Offices and Directors St. Gregory, Cox's Creek, KY
Nguyen, Rev. Kim Son, '87 (SAV) Sts. Peter and Paul, Savannah, GA
Nguyen, Rev. Lam, '08 (STA) Memorial Hosp, Jacksonville Prince of Peace, Jacksonville, FL
Nguyen, Rev. Lawrence Hy, *CRM* '09 (SPC) [MON] Congregation of the Mother of the Redeemer, Carthage, MO
Nguyen, Rev. Leo Tien, *OCist* (SAC) [MON] Our Lady of Sacramento Monastery, Walnut Grove, CA
Nguyen, Rev. Lich Van, '84 (NO) St. Martha Roman Catholic Church, Harvey, Louisiana, Harvey, LA
Nguyen, Rev. Liem, '99 (ATL) St. James Catholic Church, Madison, Inc., Madison, GA
Nguyen, Rev. Liem, *c.s.* '18 (SD) Pastor of Our Lady of Guadalupe Catholic Parish, Chula Vista, a corporation sole, Chula Vista, CA; [MIS] Our Lady of Guadalupe Catholic Parish Chula Vista in Chula Vista, CA Real Property Support Corporation, Chula Vista, CA
Nguyen, Rev. Linh, (FWT) St. Elizabeth Ann Seton, Keller, TX
Nguyen, Rev. Linh, '97 (LEX) Curia: Leadership SS. Francis & John Catholic Church, Georgetown, KY
Nguyen, Rev. Linh N., '06 (GAL) St. Rose of Lima, Houston, TX
Nguyen, Rev. Linh T., '00 (BO) St. Ambrose, Boston, MA; St. Mark, Boston, MA
Nguyen, Rev. Long, '08 (LA) St. Margaret Mary Alacoque, Lomita, CA
Nguyen, Rev. Long Phi, *S.V.D.* '07 (DUB) [SEM] Divine Word College, Epworth, IA
Nguyen, Rev. Luan D., '08 (P) Immaculate Conception, Stayton, OR; Our Lady of Lourdes, Scio, OR
Nguyen, Rev. Luke H., '02 (NO) St. Anthony, Lafitte, LA
Nguyen, Rev. Luong (Dominic M.) Hoan, *CRM* '09 (SPC) [MON] Congregation of the Mother of the Redeemer, Carthage, MO
Nguyen, Rev. M. Antony Sang H, *O. Cist.* (SB) [MON] The Cistercian Congregation of the Holy Family, St. Joseph Monastery, Lucerne Valley, CA
Nguyen, Rt. Rev. Marion (Qui-Thac), '04 (SEA) [COL] Saint Martin's University (Order of St. Benedict Master's Comprehensive University), Lacey, WA; [MON] St. Martin's Abbey, Lacey, WA
Nguyen, Rev. Martin, '16 (ORL) Holy Family, Orlando, FL
Nguyen, Rev. Martin Hiep, '05 (ORG) Curia: Leadership La Purisima, Orange, CA
Nguyen, Rev. Martin Lam, *C.S.C.* '89 (FTW) [COL] University of Notre Dame Du Lac, Notre Dame, IN; [MON] Holy Cross Community, Corby Hall, University of Notre Dame, Notre Dame, IN
Nguyen, Rev. Martin Thanh, *I.C.M.* '97 (BR) [MON] Incarnatio Consecratio Missio, Baton Rouge, LA
Nguyen, Rev. Martino Ba Thong, '04 (SAV) St. Boniface Church, Springfield, GA
Nguyen, Rev. Mendie, '13 (SJ) St. Joseph of Cupertino, Cupertino, CA
Nguyen, Rev. Michael D., '19 (ORG) On Academic Leave.
Nguyen, Rev. Michael Duc, '19 (ORG) Curia: Leadership St. Cecilia, Tustin, CA
Nguyen, Rev. Michael Nam Hoang, '93 (NO) Christ the King, Terrytown, LA
Nguyen, Rev. Minh, *c.s.* (GAL) St. John Neumann, Houston, TX
Nguyen, Rev. Minh Trieu, *SJ* '13 (OAK) [MON] Jesuit Fathers and Brothers, Berkeley, CA
Nguyen, Rev. Minh Van, *SDD* '10 (DAL) [MIS] Domus Dei Clerical Society of Apostolic Life, Kaufman, TX
Nguyen, Rev. Nghia, '16 (FWT) Curia: Miscellaneous / Other Offices St. George, Fort Worth, TX
Nguyen, Rev. Nghiem Van, '89 (NO) Curia: Offices and Directors Mary, Queen of Vietnam Roman Catholic Church, New Orleans, Louisiana, New Orleans, LA; [MIS] Chapel of the Vietnamese Martyrs, New Orleans, LA
Nguyen, Rev. Nick Hien, *SVD* '00 (JKS) Holy Ghost, Jackson, MS; [CAM] Tougaloo College Newman Center, Jackson, MS
Nguyen, Rev. Nicolas Toan, (ORG) St. Polycarp, Stanton, CA
Nguyen, Rev. Pascal B., *O.Praem.* '94 (ORG) St. John the Baptist, Costa Mesa, CA; [MON] Norbertine Fathers of Orange, Inc., Silverado, CA
Nguyen, Rev. Patrick M. Ngoc, *CRM* '12 (SPC) [MON] Congregation of the Mother of the Redeemer, Carthage, MO
Nguyen, Rev. Paul, '13 (VEN) St. Patrick Catholic Parish in Sarasota, Inc., Sarasota, FL
Nguyen, Rev. Paul, *O.M.V.* '18 (SFD) (>DEN) Holy Ghost Catholic Parish in Denver, Denver, CO
Nguyen, Rev. Paul, *C.Ss.R.* '06 (DAL) All Saints Catholic Parish, Dallas, TX
Nguyen, Rev. Paul, '14 (NSH) Immaculate Conception, Clarksville, TN
Nguyen, Rev. Paul Dean, '07 (WDC) St. George, Valley Lee, MD
Nguyen, Rev. Paul Hai, *C.Ss.R.* '97 (DAL) Mother of Perpetual Help Catholic Parish, Garland, TX; [CEM] Mother of Perpetual Help Church - Columbarium, Garland, TX
Nguyen, Rev. Paul Hai Dang, *O.P.* (GAL) Our Lady of Lavang Church, Houston, TX
Nguyen, Rev. Paul Tuan, *O.P.* '08 (RIC) Church of the Vietnamese Martyrs, Richmond, VA
Nguyen, Rev. Paul Van Tung, '79 (NO) Retired. On Duty Outside Diocese. St. Rita Catholic Church, New Orleans, LA
Nguyen, Rev. Peter, *C.S.J.B.* '03 (BRK) St. Francis of Assisi, Astoria, NY
Nguyen, Rev. Peter, '17 (MEM) Our Lady of Perpetual Help, Germantown, TN
Nguyen, Rev. Peter Duc Hung, '97 (SC) Holy Cross Catholic Parish, Sioux City, IA
Nguyen, Rev. Peter H., (BRK) [CCH] Vietnamese Ministry, ,
Nguyen, Rev. Peter Hai, '05 (BUF) On Sick Leave.
Nguyen, Rev. Peter Hieu Quang, *IMS* '18 (BR) Congregation Of St. Anthony Of Padua And Le Van Phung Roman Catholic Church, Baton Rouge, Louisiana, Baton Rouge, LA
Nguyen, Rev. Peter Hoai T., '06 (NO) Assumption of Mary Roman Catholic Church, Avondale, Louisiana, Avondale, LA
Nguyen, Rev. Peter Hung, (SAV) St. Michael Mission Catholic Church, Montezuma, GA
Nguyen, Rev. Peter P., *S.J.* '08 (OM) [MON] Jesuit Community at Creighton University, Omaha, NE
Nguyen, Rev. Peter Phong, *SVD* (BEA) St. Anne Mission, Dayton, TX; St. Joseph the Worker, Dayton, TX; [CEM] St. Anne Cemetery, Dayton, TX
Nguyen, Rev. Peter Phuong Dinh, *O.P.* (ARL) Holy Martyrs of Vietnam Catholic Church, Arlington, VA
Nguyen, Rev. Msgr. Peter Quang, '90 (DEN) All Saints Catholic Parish in Denver, Denver, CO
Nguyen, Rev. Peter Tu, '15 (OAK) On Leave.
Nguyen, Rev. Phi H., '06 (CHI) Curia: Leadership; Parish Services Holy Child Jesus, Chicago, IL
Nguyen, Rev. Phillip Hieu Van, '69 (SC) Retired.
Nguyen, Rev. Phuong, (ORG) St. Nicholas, Laguna Woods, CA
Nguyen, Rev. Polycarp M. DucThuan, *CRM* '91 (SPC) [MON] Congregation of the Mother of the Redeemer, Carthage, MO
Nguyen, Rev. Quan, '21 (L) St. Boniface, Louisville, KY; St. Patrick, Louisville, KY
Nguyen, Rev. Quang Minh, '14 (LA) [MON] Vietnamese Redemptorist Mission, Baldwin Park, CA
Nguyen, Rev. Quoc, *O.F.M.Cap.* '02 (SFR) [SEM] Capuchin Franciscan Order San Buenaventura Friary, San Francisco, CA
Nguyen, Rev. Quyen, *CMF* '07 (LA) [MON] Tepeyac House, Los Angeles, CA
Nguyen, Rev. Quyen, *CMF* (LA) St. Camillus de Lellis, Los Angeles, CA
Nguyen, Rev. Raymond Thu M., *CRM* '87 (SPC) [MON] Congregation of the Mother of the Redeemer, Carthage, MO
Nguyen, Rev. Ryan, '22 (PH) St. Bede the Venerable, Holland, PA
Nguyen, Rev. Scott C., '97 (WCH) On Duty Outside Diocese.
Nguyen, Rev. Son, *S.V.D.* '03 (MO) Curia: Offices and Directors
Nguyen, Rev. Son Anh, '03 (WOR) On Special Assignment. Chap, St Vincent Hosp Our Lady of Vilna, Worcester, MA
Nguyen, Rev. Son Thai, *SCJ* '20 (MIL) St. Martin of Tours Congregation, Franklin, WI; [MON] St. Joseph's at Monastery Lake (Priests of the Sacred Heart), Franklin, WI
Nguyen, Rev. Stephen Kha, *S.V.D.* '06 (DUB) [SEM] Divine Word College, Epworth, IA
Nguyen, Rev. Steve, (HON) Curia: Tribunal Blessed Sacrament, Honolulu, HI
Nguyen, Rev. Sy Uy, '91 (ORG) Curia: Leadership Holy Family Catholic Church, Orange, CA
Nguyen, Rev. Tai, '10 (SLC) Our Lady of Perpetual Help LLC 261, Kearns, UT
Nguyen, Rev. Tam, '18 (KCK) Cure of Ars, Leawood, KS
Nguyen, Rev. Tam V., *CMR* (OM) Our Lady of Fatima Catholic Community, Omaha, NE
Nguyen, Rev. Tan Viet, *S.V.D.* '03 (CHI) [MON] Divine Word Residence, Techny, IL
Nguyen, Rev. Te Van, '86 (SFR) Curia: Offices and Directors
Nguyen, Rev. Thach, (DAL) [MON] St. John Neumann Formation House, Dallas, TX
Nguyen, Rev. Thai Hung, '09 (SAG) Chap, Anointing Min, Covenant and Assumption St Mary Hosps [NUR] St. Francis Home of Saginaw, Saginaw, MI
Nguyen, Rev. Thang Thiet, *S.D.D.* '03 (NO) [MIS] Domus Dei Clerical Society of Apostolic Life, U.S.A., Inc., New Orleans, LA
Nguyen, Rev. Thanh, *C.Ss.R.* '14 (KC) Church of the Holy Martyrs, Kansas City, MO; Our Lady of Perpetual Help, Kansas City, MO; [MON] Redemptorists Fathers of Kansas City, Missouri, Kansas City, MO
Nguyen, Rev. Thanh, '67 (PRT) Retired.
Nguyen, Rev. Thanh Dac, (SAC) [MON] Our Lady of Sacramento Monastery, Walnut Grove, CA
Nguyen, Rev. Thanh N., '94 (R) Sacred Heart, Southport, NC
Nguyen, Rev. Thanh Van, '00 (OKL) Cathedral of Our Lady of Perpetual Help, Oklahoma City, OK
Nguyen, Rev. Thanh-Tai P., '12 (ORG) Curia: Offices and Directors Christ Our Savior Catholic Parish, Santa Ana, CA; St. Joseph, Santa Ana, CA
Nguyen, Rev. That Son Ngoc, '90 (WH) St. Francis Xavier, Moundsville, WV; [MIS] St. Martin of Tours Chapel, Cameron, WV
Nguyen, Rev. Thien, *SDB* (MRY) [MON] Saint Francis Salesian Community, ,
Nguyen, Rev. Thien, '18 (NO) Mary, Queen of Vietnam Roman Catholic Church, New Orleans, Louisiana, New Orleans, LA
Nguyen, Rev. Thien Van, '89 (WIN) St. Ann's, Slayton, MN; St. Columba's, Iona, MN; St. Mary, Lake Wilson, MN
Nguyen, Rev. Thien Duc, *S.V.D.* '16 (WH) Risen Lord Mission, Maysel, WV; St. Thomas, Gassaway, WV
Nguyen, Rev. Thinh, *SDB* (MRY) Our Lady Help of Christians, Watsonville, CA; [MON] Salesians of St. John Bosco, Watsonville, CA
Nguyen, Rev. Thomas, '16 (ARL) St. Leo the Great, Fairfax, VA
Nguyen, Rev. Thomas De, '82 (ORG) La Purisima, Orange, CA
Nguyen, Rev. Thomas Tuan Van, *C.M.C.* '04 (LIN) Immaculate Heart of Mary, Lincoln, NE
Nguyen, Rev. Thu, '92 (FWT) Curia: Miscellaneous / Other Offices St. Paul the Apostle, Fort Worth, TX
Nguyen, Rev. Thu Ngoc, '93 (GAL) Curia: Leadership Christ, The Incarnate Word, Houston, TX
Nguyen, Rev. Thuan, '93 (LA) St. Joseph the Worker, Winnetka, CA
Nguyen, Rev. Thuc H., '20 (GAL) St. Thomas More, Houston, TX
Nguyen, Rev. Thuong Hoai, '91 (OAK) St. John the Baptist, El Cerrito, CA
Nguyen, Rev. Thuy Quang, '98 (GAL) Guardian Angel, Wallis, TX; St. Mary, Frydek, TX
Nguyen, Rev. Thuy Quang, '98 (GAL) Curia: Leadership
Nguyen, Rev. Tien-Tri, '96 (SFE) St. Jude Thaddeus, Albuquerque, NM
Nguyen, Rev. Timothy, '08 (ORG) On Administrative Leave.
Nguyen, Rev. Tinh Van, '98 (BO) On Special Assignment.
Nguyen, Rev. Toan X., '96 (SFR) St. Catherine of Siena, Burlingame, CA
Nguyen, Rev. Tom, *OFM Cap.* (DET) [MON] St. Mary's Friary, Detroit, MI
Nguyen, Rev. Ton Thai, (CHI) Holy Name Cathedral, Chicago, IL
Nguyen, Rev. Tony Huu Khanh, *S.J.* (BO) [MON] Francis Xavier House, Brighton, MA

Nguyen, Rev. Tri John-Bosco, '12 (ATL) Our Lady of the Mountains Catholic Church, Jasper, Inc., Jasper, GA

Nguyen, Very Rev. Trung V., '94 (GAL) Curia: Leadership; Offices and Directors Sacred Heart of Jesus, Manvel, TX

Nguyen, Rev. Truong, (GAL) St. Laurence, Sugar Land, TX

Nguyen, Rev. Truyen, '03 (SJ) Chap, Det Min for Juveniles; Vietnamese Eucharis… Curia: Offices and Directors Sacred Heart of Jesus, San Jose, CA

Nguyen, Rev. Tu T., '07 (SAT) St. Matthew's, Jourdanton, TX

Nguyen, Rev. Tuan, *O.F.M.Conv.* '03 (OAK) St. Paul, San Pablo, CA

Nguyen, Rev. Tuan, '92 (SEA) Curia: Leadership St. Ann, Tacoma, WA

Nguyen, Rev. Tuan A., *C.Ss.R.* '09 (SEA) Our Lady of Hope, Everett, WA

Nguyen, Rev. Tuan Anh, *C.Ss.R.* '09 (SEA) Sacred Heart of Jesus, Seattle, WA; [MON] The Redemptorist Society of Washington, Seattle, WA

Nguyen, Rev. Tuan John, (ORG) San Antonio de Padua Del Canon Church, Anaheim, CA

Nguyen, Rev. Tuan Van, '86 (JOL) St. Mary, Minooka, IL

Nguyen, Rev. Tuan (Andrew M.) Van, *CRM* '08 (SPC) [MON] Congregation of the Mother of the Redeemer, Carthage, MO

Nguyen, Rev. Tuan (Bonaventure M.) Van, *CRM* '16 (SPC) St. Elizabeth of Hungary, El Dorado Springs, MO; [MON] Congregation of the Mother of the Redeemer, Carthage, MO

Nguyen, Rev. Tuoi (John) V., '08 (SY) Historic Old St. John's Church, Utica, NY; Our Lady of Pompei/St. Peter, Syracuse, NY

Nguyen, Rev. Tuyen, '87 (ORG) Curia: Leadership

Nguyen, Rev. Ty Van, '85 (HT) Retired.

Nguyen, Rev. Van, '08 (TLS) Curia: Offices and Directors

Nguyen, Rev. Van S, *CS* (CHI) St. Charles Borromeo, Melrose Park, IL

Nguyen, Rev. Vandennis, '90 (YAK) Retired. Christ the King, Richland, WA

Nguyen, Rev. vanThanh, *S.V.D.* '97 (CHI) [SEM] Catholic Theological Union, Chicago, IL; [SEM] Divine Word Theologate, Chicago, IL

Nguyen, Very Rev. Vien, *S.C.J.* '04 (MIL) [MON] Priests of the Sacred Heart, Hales Corners, WI; [MON] St. Joseph's at Monastery Lake (Priests of the Sacred Heart), Franklin, WI

Nguyen, Rev. Vien The, '89 (NO) On Duty Outside Diocese.

Nguyen, Rev. Viet, '18 (KCK) Church of the Ascension, Overland Park, KS

Nguyen, Rev. Viet, '20 (DAL) [MON] St. John Neumann Formation House, Dallas, TX

Nguyen, Rev. Viet Chau, *S.S.S.* '77 (NO) Retired.

Nguyen, Rev. Vihn "Daniel", *SVD* (SB) St. Anthony, San Bernardino, CA

Nguyen, Rev. Vincent, *C.S.J.B.* '03 (BRK) St. John Vianney, Flushing, NY; [MON] Congregation of St. John the Baptist of China, Elmhurst, NY

Nguyen, Rev. Vincent, '18 (NO) Our Lady of the Lake Roman Catholic Church, Mandeville, LA

Nguyen, Rev. Vincent Kien, '89 (HON) Retired.

Nguyen, Rev. Vincent Liem, *O.S.B.* '94 (P) [MON] Mt. Angel Abbey, Saint Benedict, OR

Nguyen, Rev. Vincent T., '14 (COL) Corpus Christi, Columbus, OH; St. Ladislas, Columbus, OH; St. Mary, Columbus, OH

Nguyen, Rev. Vincent Tranh, '97 (AUS) On Special Assignment. Hospital Ministry St. Luke, Temple, TX

Nguyen, Rev. Vincent Van Dao, '05 (SPK) Curia: Offices and Directors St. Anthony, Spokane, WA; [MIS] Our Lady of La Vang Center, Spokane, WA

Nguyen, Rev. Vincent Vuong-Quoc, '99 (GAL) St. Clare of Assisi, Houston, TX

Nguyen, Rev. Vinh Quang, '86 (NEW) Retired.

Nguyen, Rev. Vinh Van, *S.D.D.* '15 (NO) [MIS] Domus Dei Clerical Society of Apostolic Life, U.S.A., Inc., New Orleans, LA

Nguyen, Rev. Vinhson, '18 (PHX) Our Lady of Fatima Mission, Phoenix, AZ; St. Anthony of Padua Roman Catholic Parish, Wickenburg, AZ

Nguyen Chi, Rev. Ai, *AA* '15 (WOR) [MON] Augustinians of the Assumption at Assumption University, Worcester, MA (>BO) [MON] Augustinians of the Assumption, Inc., Boston, MA

Nguyen Hong An, Rev. Andrew M., *CRM* '87 (SPC) [MON] Congregation of the Mother of the Redeemer, Carthage, MO

Ngwa, Rev. Gregory Cheo, (GAL) St. Christopher, Houston, TX

Ngwaogu, Rev. Alphonsus, '03 (SB) St. Martha, Murrieta, CA

Ngwenya, Rev. Mark, *SJ* '18 (OAK) [MON] Jesuit Fathers and Brothers, Berkeley, CA

Ngwila, Rev. Filbert, '11 (CHI) Curia: (>MO) Offices and Directors St. Mother Theodore Guerin, Elmwood Park, IL

Ngwu, Rev. Modestus, *O.P.* (HBG) Chap, Penn State Milton S Hershey Med Ctr, Hershey St. Joan of Arc, Hershey, PA

Ni Ni, Rev. Robert, *MF* (HON) Maria Lanakila (Victorious Mary), Lahaina, HI

Nicastro, Rev. Thomas D., '90 (NEW) St. Mary, Nutley, NJ

Niccolls, Rev. Edward D., '74 (WOR) Curia: Clergy and Religious Services St. George, Worcester, MA

Nicholas, Rev. Gerald, *O.S.A.* '66 (JOL) Providence Catholic High School, New Lenox, IL; [MON] Augustinian Friary, New Lenox, IL

Nicholl, Rev. Msgr. Rex, '67 (AMA) Curia: Advisory Boards, Commissions, Committees, and Councils St. Martin De Porres Mission, Amarillo, TX

Nicholls, Rev. Trevor, '90 (NY) Retired. St. Catharine, Pelham, NY

Nichols, Rev. Aquinas, '80 (DM) Basilica of Saint John, Des Moines, IA

Nichols, Rev. Harry E., '73 (PIT) Retired.

Nichols, Rev. Henry P., '70 (BO) Retired.

Nichols, Rev. Irby C., '01 (SFE) St. Anne-Albuquerque, Albuquerque, NM

Nichols, Rev. John J., '62 (BO) Retired.

Nichols, Rev. Louis J., '60 (SY) Retired. On Duty Outside Diocese.

Nichols, Rev. Neal, '01 (RIC) St. Benedict, Chesapeake, VA

Nichols, Rev. Richard, *S.J.* '19 (WDC) [MON] The Jesuit Community at Georgetown University, Washington, DC

Nichols, Rev. Msgr. Timothy E., '73 (LA) Curia: Pastoral Services St. John Vianney, Hacienda Heights, CA

Nickle, Rev. Fred, *O.F.M.Cap.* '65 (NY) [MON] The Province of St. Mary of the Capuchin Order, White Plains, NY; [PRE] Capuchin Youth and Family Ministries, Garrison, NY

Nickol, Rev. G. Eugene, '73 (BAL) Retired.

Nickol, Rev. Gene, '73 (BAL) Our Lady, Queen of Peace, Middle River, MD

Nickolai, Rev. John C., '13 (STL) St. Rose Philippine Duchesne Catholic Church, Florissant, MO

Nicks, Rev. Matthew, '08 (SPK) Curia: Leadership Assumption Elementary School, Walla Walla, WA; Assumption of the Blessed Virgin Mary, Walla Walla, WA; Walla Walla Catholic School System (DeSales Catholic High School), Walla Walla, WA

Nicolas, Rev. Jean Vanes, (PMB) St. Ann, West Palm Beach, FL

Nicolas, Rev. Jeffrey Scott, '93 (L) Curia: Leadership; (>MO) Offices and Directors St. Bernadette Parish, Prospect, KY

Nicolat Herrera, Rev. Alejandro, '20 (ORG) St. Justin Martyr, Anaheim, CA

Nicolau, Rev. Msgr. Juan, '60 (BWN) Retired.

Nicolicchia, Rev. J. Andrew, *O.P.* '65 (WDC) St. Dominic Church & Priory, Washington, DC

Nicolo, Rev. Msgr. Joseph J., '74 (PH) On Special Assignment. Dean, Deanery 5, St Helena Rectory, Blue Bell St. Helena, Blue Bell, PA; St. Titus, East Norriton, PA; [CAM] Montgomery County Community College, Blue Bell, PA

Nicolosi, Rev. Joseph P, '97 (RCK) On Administrative Leave.

Nicolosi, Rev. Mark Ronald, *O.S.B.* '67 (BUR) [MON] The Benedictine Foundation of the State of Vermont, Inc., Weston, VT

Nidulaka, Rev. Matthias, (NY) Chap, Woodbourne Corr Fac

Nieberding, Rev. Robert H., '56 (LEX) Retired. Curia: Leadership

Nieblas, Rev. James, *SDB* '86 (LA) Santa Isabel, Los Angeles, CA; [MON] Dominic Savio Salesian Residence, Los Angeles, CA

Nieblas, Rev. Jim, *SDB* (LA) Bishop Mora Salesian High School (Salesians of Don Bosco), Los Angeles, CA

Niebrzydowski, Rev. Msgr. Walter J., '59 (NY) Retired. St. Columba, New York, NY

Niehaus, Rev. Mark J., *I.S.P.* '03 (MIL) [MIS] Secular Institute of Schoenstatt Fathers, Waukesha, WI

Niehaus, Rev. Thomas M., '08 (STP) Most Holy Redeemer, Montgomery, MN; St. Patrick, Shieldsville, Faribault, MN; [CEM] Calvary Cemetery, Montgomery, MN; [CEM] St. Canice Cemetery, Montgomery, MN; [CEM] St. John's Cemetery, Montgomery, MN; [CEM] St. Patrick Cemetery, Faribault, MN

Niehoff, Very Rev. Kevin W., *O.P.* '93 (GR) Curia: Leadership

Niehoff, Rev. Robert, (SEA) Bellarmine Preparatory School, Tacoma, WA (>SJ) [MON] USA West Province, Society of Jesus, Los Gatos, CA

Niehoff, Rev. Robert J., *S.J.* '82 (P) [MON] Colombiere Jesuit Community, Portland, OR

Niekamp, Rev. Philip E., '05 (JC) Church of the Risen Savior, Rhineland, MO; Immaculate Conception, Owensville, MO; St. Alexander, Belle, MO; St. George Catholic Church, Hermann, MO

Nields, Rev. Patrick, (OM) St. Francis of Assisi Catholic Church, Neligh, NE

Nields, Rev. Patrick K., '16 (OM) Our Lady of Mt. Carmel, Tilden, NE

Nieli, Rev. Bruce, (AUS) St. Austin, Austin, TX

Nielsen, Rev. Eric, '05 (NY) Parish of St. Peter and St. Denis, Yonkers, NY; [MON] Legionaries of Christ, Rye, NY

Nielsen, Rev. Eric H., '95 (MAD) St. Paul University Parish, Madison, WI; [EFT] St. Paul University Catholic Foundation, Inc., Madison, WI

Nielson, Rev. Ken, (AUS) Retired.

Nielson, Rev. Kenneth W., '99 (NY) Catholic Chapel of the Most Holy Trinity, West Point, NY

Niemann, Rev. Paul, '80 (PRM) St. Louis Mission, St. Louis, MO

Niemann, Very Rev. Paul J., '80 (STL) Curia: Leadership St. Pius V Catholic Church, St. Louis, MO

Niemczak, Rev. Michael, '16 (SFE) Curia: Offices and Directors

Niemczak, Rev. Michael, '16 (SFE) Sacred Heart-Clovis, Clovis, NM

Niemczyk, Rev. Stefan J., '87 (SPR) Divine Mercy Parish, Three Rivers, MA

Nieme, Rev. Lambert K., (BO) St. Martha, Plainville, MA; St. Mary, Wrentham, MA

Niemeier, Rev. Dennis A., '73 (CIN) Retired.

Niemiec, Rev. Christopher Antoninus, *O.P.* '01 (WDC) [SEM] Dominican House of Studies, Washington, DC

Niemira, Rev. Thomas, '65 (AUS) Retired.

Niemira, Rev. Thomas, '65 (JKS) Retired.

Nienaber, Rev. Msgr. Robert H., '63 (OM) Retired.

Nienhaus, Rev. Ivan R., '89 (DUB) St. Patrick's Church, Cedar Falls, Iowa, Cedar Falls, IA

Niese, Rev. Larry, '95 (ATL) St. Michael the Archangel Catholic Church, Woodstock, Inc., Woodstock, GA

Niespolo, Rev. Aelred, *O.S.B.* '05 (LA) [MON] St. Andrew's Abbey (Benedictine Monks), Valyermo, CA; [SEM] St. John's Seminary, Camarillo, CA

Nietfeld, Rev. Fred, (CIN) [MON] St. Charles, Celina, OH

Nietfeld, Rev. Fred J., '46 (TOL) Retired.

Nieto, Rev. Jose, *C.M.F.* '66 (SJN) Casa Mision Claret, Bayamon, PR; San Jose, Bayamon, PR

Nieto Restrepo, Rev. Jose Mario, '14 (MIL) Congregation of St. Richard, Racine, WI; St. Edward's Congregation, Racine, WI; St. Patrick's Congregation, Racine, WI

Nieto-Ruiz, Rev. Jesus, '94 (OAK) Our Lady of the Rosary, Union City, CA

Nietzke, Rev. Tom, *S.J.* (CHI) [COL] Arrupe College, Chicago, IL

Nieva, Rev. Javier, *D.C.J.M.* '00 (DEN) St. Mary Catholic Parish in Littleton, Littleton, CO; [MON] Disciples of the Hearts of Jesus and Mary, Littleton, CO

Nieves, Rev. Carlos, '86 (PCE) Retired.

Nieves, Rev. Encarnacion, '83 (CGS) Curia: Leadership San Esteban Protomartir, Cayey, PR

Nieves, Rev. Pablo, *S.X.* '99 (PAT) [MON] Xaverian Missionary Fathers, Wayne, NJ

Niewiadomski, Rev. Arthur J., '94 (TOL) Holy Family, North Baltimore, OH; Immaculate Conception, Deshler, OH

Niezer, Rev. Daniel, (FTW) St. Dominic, Bremen, IN

Niggel, Rev. Clement, '03 (SFE) Our Lady of Belen, Belen, NM

Niggemeyer, Rev. Matthew J., '15 (OM) Assumption B.V.M., West Point, NE; St. Aloysius, West Point, NE; St. Anthony, St. Charles, NE; St. Boniface, Monterey, NE

Nightingale, Rev. Maxmilian Jacob, '17 (KAL) Curia: Tribunal St. Monica, Kalamazoo, MI

Nigli, Rev. Francis A., '97 (OM) On Administrative Leave.

Nijem, Rev. Msgr. Fred J., '68 (SAV) Retired. Sacred Heart, Warner Robins, GA

Nikodem, Rev. Ronald, *S.M.* '94 (DET) Notre Dame Preparatory School and Marist Academy, Pontiac, MI

Nikolas, Rev. Patric, *SDS* '18 (SAC) Divine Savior,

Orangevale, CA
Nikolic, Very Rev. Dennis A., '02 (NY) Curia: Leadership St. Joseph, Middletown, NY
Nilles, Rev. Roger G., '59 (MAD) Retired.
Nillo, Rev. Mark, '14 (TR) Curia: Pastoral Services St. Mary, Middletown, NJ; [CAM] Catholic Center at Monmouth University, West Long Branch, NJ
Nilo, Rev. Oliver D., '15 (NEW) St. John the Evangelist, Bergenfield, NJ
Nimako, Rev. John, (BRK) St. Clare, Rosedale, NY
Nimerichter, Rev. Dean, '92 (DM) Retired.
Nimo, Rev. Peter, (VIC) Our Lady of Sorrows, Victoria, TX
Nimocks, Rev. Michael F., '96 (COL) Retired.
Nimwesiga, Rev. Ignitius, '16 (JC) Fr. Augustine Tolton Regional Catholic High School, Columbia, MO; St. Thomas More Newman Center, University of Missouri, Columbia, MO; [CAM] St. Thomas More Newman Center, Columbia, MO
Ninemire, Rev. Kerry, '75 (SAL) Saints Peter and Paul Parish, Clay Center, Inc., Clay Center, KS; St. Anthony Parish, Miltonvale, Inc., Miltonvale, KS
Ninh, Rev. Lawrence Tu Toan, *OP* (OAK) [MON] Order of Preachers (Province of the Most Holy Name of Jesus - Western Dominican Province), Oakland, CA
Nirappel, Rev. James, '90 (SYM) St. Thomas the Apostle Syro-Malabar Forane Catholic Church, Dallas/Garland, Texas, Garland, TX
Nirappel, Rev. Thomas, *MSFS* '92 (LC) St. Adalbert, Rosholt, WI; St. Mary (Immaculate Conception), Stevens Point, WI
Nisari, Rev. Joseph, '68 (AUS) Retired.
Nischan, Rev. James R., '83 (PCE) Retired.
Nishimura, Rev. Bryce T., *M.M.* '56 (SJ) Retired. (>NY) [MON] Maryknoll Fathers and Brothers (Catholic Foreign Mission Society of America, Inc.), Ossining, NY
Niskanen, Rev. Stephen, *CMF* '90 (CHI) [SHR] National Shrine of St. Jude, ,
Niskanon, Rev. Steve, *C.M.F.* '90 (CHI) Our Lady of Guadalupe, Chicago, IL
Nithiyaselvam, Rev. Arokiaselvam, *MSFS* (DET) St. Ephrem Parish Sterling Heights, Sterling Heights, MI
Nitz, Rev. Eliot, *S.D.S.* '68 (WDC) [SEM] Salvatorian Community, Silver Spring, MD
Niven, Rev. Timothy L., '98 (ROC) St. Rita, Webster, NY
Nix, Rev. Albert P., '73 (PAT) Retired.
Nix, Rev. David, '10 (DEN) On Duty Outside Diocese.
Nix, Rev. Julian, *O.S.B.* '87 (BIS) Retired. [MON] Assumption Abbey, Richardton, ND
Nixon, Rev. George K., '11 (PRO) On Leave.
Nixon, Rev. Michael J., '10 (PT) Curia: Leadership St. Dominic, Panama City, FL; [MIS] St. Dominic Media Production Center, Panama City, FL
Niyokwizera, Rev. Jean Bosco, (BO) [MON] Walter Ciszek House, Brighton, MA
Njau, Rev. Francis, *A.J.* '98 (P) [HOS] Providence Health & Services-Oregon (Providence St. Vincent Medical Center), Portland, OR
Njoalu, Rev. Martin S., '11 (SFR) St. Augustine, South San Francisco, CA
Njobam, Rev. Gilles D., *C.M.F.* '12 (MET) Our Lady of Fatima, Perth Amboy, NJ
Njoh, Rev. Moses Nikume, '13 (CHL) [CAM] High Point University, High Point, NC
Njoku, Rev. Andrew J., '12 (NEW) Christ the King, Hillside, NJ
Njoku, Rev. Camillus Okechukwu, '01 (PIT) Chap, Washington Hosp, Washington Cty; Humbert Lane Health…
Njoku, Rev. Canice Chukwuemeka, *C.S.Sp.* '12 (FAJ) Resurreccion del Senor, Canovanas, PR
Njoku, Rev. Francis, '97 (SAN) Our Lady of Guadalupe, Fort Stockton, TX; St. James Church, Sanderson, TX
Njoku, Rev. Innocent E., *C.S.Sp* '85 (MO) Curia: Offices and Directors
Njopmo, Rev. Jules Norbert, '06 (LR) St. John the Baptist, Hot Springs, AR
Njoroge, Rev. Richard Githang'a, *MHM* '04 (NY) Our Lady of Mount Carmel, White Plains, NY; Parish of St. John the Evangelist and Our Lady of Mount Carmel, White Plains, NY; [MON] Mill Hill Fathers Residence, Hartsdale, NY
Njuguna, Rev. Simon Waweru, (BO) [MON] Augustinians of the Assumption, Inc., Boston, MA
Nkachukwu, Rev. Michael C., '80 (DET) Our Lady Queen of Heaven - Good Shepherd Parish Detroit, Detroit, MI; St. Jude Parish Detroit, Detroit, MI; St. Raymond - Our Lady of Good Counsel Parish Detroit, Detroit, MI
Nkafu, Rev. Felix, (CHL) St. Leo the Great, Winston-Salem, NC
Nkardzedze, Rev. Eugen, (BEA) St. Charles Borromeo, Nederland, TX
Nketiah, Rev. Anthony Boahen, '03 (DUB) Sacred Heart Church (LaPorte City, Iowa), La Porte City, IA; St. Mary's Church, Eagle Center, Iowa, Waterloo, IA; St. Paul Church, Traer, Iowa, Traer, IA
Nkrumah, Rev. Benjamin, '08 (DUB) St. Athanasius Church, Jesup, Iowa, Jesup, IA; St. Francis Church, Barclay, Iowa, Dunkerton, IA
Nkrumah, Rev. David, (DM) Holy Trinity, Exira, IA; St. Patrick, Audubon, IA
Nkulu, Rev. Marc, *SMA* '15 (NEW) [MON] Society of African Missions, Provincialate, S.M.A. Fathers, Tenafly, NJ
Nkwasibwe, Rev. Frederick, '96 (P) [HOS] Providence Health & Services-Oregon (Providence Portland Medical Center), Portland, OR
Nkwocha, Rev. Levi UC, '00 (FTW) St. Thomas the Apostle, Elkhart, IN
Nlandu, Rev. Jean-Oscar, (SAT) St. Bonaventure, San Antonio, TX
Nna, Rev. Anayo, *C.Ss.R.* '03 (PH) St. Athanasius, Philadelphia, PA
Nnabuife, Rev. Bindel-Mary, *C.M.* '18 (PH) Saint John Paul II Parish, Philadelphia, PA; St. Vincent de Paul, Philadelphia, PA
Nnabuife, Rev. Charles, (BAK) Curia: Leadership
Nnabuife, Very Rev. Charles Chika, '05 (BAK) Curia: Leadership St. Francis of Assisi, Milton Freewater, OR
Nnadibuagha, Rev. Jude, '20 (OG) St. Mary's Church, Ogdensburg, Ogdensburg, NY
Nnadozie, Rev. Edmund, *MSP* '97 (LAV) St. Thomas More, Henderson, NV
Nnadozie, Friar Emmanuel Javert, *O.C.D.* '81 (SAT) Basilica of the National Shrine of the Little Flower, Our Lady of Mt. Carmel and St. Therese Parish, San Antonio, TX; [MON] Discalced Carmelite Fathers of San Antonio, San Antonio, TX
Nnaso, Rev. Sylvester A., '02 (RCK) St. Charles Borromeo, Hampshire, IL
Nnaukwu, Rev. Alex C., '93 (SB) Chap, Ironwood State Prison, Blythe
Nnonyelu, Rev. Christopher, '01 (SFE) St. Anthony of Padua-Pecos, Pecos, NM
Nobiletti, Rev. Raymond J., *M.M.* '69 (NY) Retired. Parish of Transfiguration and St. James/St. Joseph, New York, NY; St. James, New York, NY; St. Joseph, New York, NY
Noble, Rev. Jeffery J., '86 (E) Queen of the World, St. Marys, PA
Noble, Rev. Paul A., '81 (COL) Bishop Watterson High School, Columbus, OH
Noblefranca, Rev. Dexter, (MEM) St. Benedict at Auburndale High School, Cordova, TN
Nobles, Very Rev. James Martin, *O.P.* '21 (MEM) St. Peter Church, Memphis, TN; [MIS] The Dominican Friars of Memphis, Inc. (St. Peter Dominican Community), Memphis, TN; [SHR] St. Martin de Porres National Shrine & Institute, Memphis, TN
Nobrega, Rev. Kenneth, '08 (OAK) Curia: Leadership; Offices and Directors St. Barnabas, Alameda, CA
Nocchi, Rev. Martin S., '04 (BAL) On Academic Leave.
Noche, Rev. Joselito M., '07 (TR) Our Lady Queen of Peace, Hainesport, NJ
Nock, Rev. James J., '64 (HRT) Retired.
Noda, Rev. Jorge, '84 (MIA) Retired.
Noe, Rev. Martin S., '14 (NOR) Saint Pio Parish, Old Saybrook, CT
Noe, Rev. William A, *SJ* '13 (ATL) [MON] Atlanta Jesuit Community, Inc., Decatur, GA; [RTR] Ignatius House Jesuit Retreat Center, Sandy Springs, GA
Noel, Rev. Brian W., '10 (PIT) Divine Redeemer, Sewickley, PA; [SEM] Saint Paul Seminary, Pittsburgh, PA
Noel, Rev. Emile G. (Buddy), '12 (NO) Curia: Offices and Directors Our Lady of Prompt Succor Church, Westwego, LA
Noel, Rev. George E., '13 (CR) Curia: Offices and Directors Blessed Sacrament, Greenbush, MN; St. Edward the Confessor (Karlstad), Karlstad, MN; St. Joseph, Husband of Mary (Middle River), Middle River, MN
Noel, Rev. Guyma, '97 (ATL) Holy Trinity Catholic Church, Peachtree City, Inc., Peachtree City, GA
Noel, Rev. Marc A., '98 (ALX) St. Martin, Lecompte, LA
Noelke, Rev. Dennis Paul, *CSB* '81 (DET) Detroit Catholic Central High School, Novi, MI
Noelker, Rev. Timothy J., '10 (STL) St. Cecilia Catholic Church, St. Louis, MO
Noesen, Rev. Thomas, '76 (SFE) Retired.
Noga, Rev. Edward P., '76 (Y) Retired.
Noga, Very Rev. Gregory J., '79 (PSC) Curia: Advisory Boards, Commissions, Committees, and Councils; Leadership SS. Peter and Paul, Minersville, PA; St. John the Baptist Church, Hazleton, PA; St. Mary's, Minersville, PA
Noga, Rev. Henryk, *S.V.D.* '96 (OAK) St. Joachim, Hayward, CA
Noga, Rev. John T., '99 (CHI) Retired.
Nogaro, Rev. Paul M., '71 (BUF) Retired. [MON] Bishop Head Residence, Lackawanna, NY
Noguera, Rev. Ronald, '81 (MIA) Retired.
Nohs, Rev. Joseph E., '93 (RVC) St. Bernard, Levittown, NY; [MON] St Pius X Residence for Retired Priests LLC, Ronkonkoma, NY
Noiseux, Rev. Donald A., '84 (SPR) Retired.
Nolan, Rev. Brian J., '91 (MET) Blessed Sacrament, Martinsville, NJ
Nolan, Rev. Brian P., '01 (BAL) St. Isaac Jogues, Baltimore, MD
Nolan, Rev. Daniel, (DEN) Our Lady of Mount Carmel Catholic Parish in Littleton, Littleton, CO
Nolan, Rev. Daniel T, *CSV* '83 (LAV) Retired.
Nolan, Rev. Daniel T., *C.S.V.* '83 (CHI) [MON] Viatorian Province Center-Clerics of St. Viator, Arlington Heights, IL
Nolan, Rev. David E., '95 (NY) Blessed Sacrament, New York, NY
Nolan, Rev. Emmet J., *C.M.* '92 (BRK) [MON] Our Lady of Good Counsel, Brooklyn, NY
Nolan, Rev. Eugene A., *S.J.* '71 (SCR) [COL] The University of Scranton, Scranton, PA
Nolan, Rev. Jerome M., '74 (TR) Retired.
Nolan, Rev. John, '12 (SAT) Curia: Administration St. Francis Xavier, Stonewall, TX; St. Mary's, Fredericksburg, TX
Nolan, Rev. John H., '77 (SFD) Retired. St. Joseph the Worker, Chatham, IL
Nolan, Rev. Justin, *O.S.B.* '55 (GBG) [MON] Saint Vincent Archabbey, Latrobe, PA
Nolan, Rev. Kevin L., '90 (LA) Holy Trinity, San Pedro, CA
Nolan, Rev. Michael, '87 (KNX) Curia: Leadership; Offices and Directors St. Therese of Lisieux, Cleveland, TN
Nolan, Rev. Michael E., '84 (WCH) Curia: Leadership; (>MO) Offices and Directors; Offices and Directors
Nolan, Rev. Michael L., '00 (BO) St. Mary, Waltham, MA; [CAM] Bridgewater State College Catholic Center, Bridgewater, MA
Nolan, Rev. Michael L., (BO) Curia: Consultative Bodies
Nolan, Rev. Niall, '80 (GAL) St. Catherine of Siena, Houston, TX
Nolan, Rev. Paul J., '57 (NEW) Retired. Chap, Essex Cty Logan Hall, Newark; Delaney Hall Assessm…
Nolan, Rev. Peter P., *C.S.Sp.* '59 (BO) Retired.
Nolan, Rev. Robert, *S.A.C.* '70 (CAM) Bishop Eustace Prep School, Pennsauken, NJ
Nolan, Rev. Scott T., '13 (GR) St. Stephen Catholic Church, East Grand Rapids, MI
Nolan, Rev. Msgr. Timothy, '92 (PEO) Curia: Clergy and Religious Services; Offices and Directors St. Mary's, Canton, IL; St. Matthew's, Farmington, IL
Nolan, Rev. Timothy M., '02 (WIL) Holy Spirit, New Castle, DE; St. Peter the Apostle, New Castle, DE; [CON] Caterina Benincasa Dominican Monastery, Inc., New Castle, DE
Nolan, Rev. Msgr. Walter E., '69 (TR) Retired. Curia: Canonical Services
Nolan, Rev. William A., '85 (MAD) Retired.
Nolette, Rev. Mark P., '87 (PRT) Retired. Curia: Offices and Directors
Nolker, Rev. Thomas C., '72 (CIN) Retired.
Noll, Rev. Daniel J., '76 (LEX) Curia: Leadership; Offices and Directors
Nollette, Rev. Louis A., '75 (GI) Retired. Curia: Offices and Directors
Nollette, Rev. Neal P., '80 (GI) Retired.
Nolt, Very Rev. Timothy S., '13 (AUS) Curia: Leadership
Nolte, Rev. James, '12 (SPR) St. Patrick's, South Hadley, MA
Nolte, Rev. Mark J., '02 (OM) St. Gerald, Ralston, NE
Nolte, Rev. Walter L., '03 (OM) Curia: Leadership; Offices and Directors St. Patrick, Fremont, NE; St. Rose of Lima, Hooper, NE
Nondorf, Rev. Tim, (MRY) Our Lady Star of the Sea, Santa Cruz, CA
Nontol, Rev. Lucio M., *T.O.R.* '06 (NEW) Immaculate Heart of Mary, Newark, NJ; [CON] Missionary Sisters of the Most Blessed Sacrament and Mary Immaculate, Newark, NJ
Noonan, Rev. Bradford J., '99 (COS) Chap, Fire Department; Police Department

Noonan, Rev. Guy, '76 (STA) Our Lady of Good Counsel, St. Augustine, FL
Noonan, Rev. James P., *M.M.* '60 (NY) Retired.
Noonan, Rev. Joseph T., '95 (CHI) St. Damian, Oak Forest, IL
Noonan, Rev. Mark J., '07 (BUF) St. Elizabeth Ann Seton, Dunkirk, NY
Noonan, Rev. Mark L., '59 (BO) Retired.
Noone, Rev. Charles J., '67 (PH) Retired. St. Timothy, Philadelphia, PA
Noone, Rev. David E., '66 (ALB) Retired.
Noone, Rev. John T., '67 (BLX) Retired.
Noone, Rev. John T., '67 (BLX) Retired.
Noone, Rev. Msgr. Kevin B., '70 (BRK) Retired. Curia: Consultative Bodies St. Mel, Flushing, NY
Norba, Rev. Zaldy, *S.S.S.* '11 (PBL) St. Pius X, Pueblo, CO
Norbert, Rev. Keliher, *O.P.* (WDC) St. Dominic Church & Priory, Washington, DC
Nord, Very Rev. Aaron P., '06 (STL) Curia: Leadership
Nord, Rev. Alexander M., '15 (STL) St. Joseph Catholic Church, Cottleville, St. Charles, MO
Nord, Rev. Paul, *O.S.B.* '07 (IND) [MON] St. Meinrad Archabbey, St. Meinrad, IN
Nordeman, Rev. John J., '01 (PH) Sacred Heart, Havertown, PA
Nordenbrock, Rev. William, *C.PP.S.* '83 (CIN) [EFT] Community Support Charitable Trust, Dayton, OH; [MON] Society of the Precious Blood, Cincinnati Province, Inc., Dayton, OH; [MON] Society of the Precious Blood, United States Province, Inc., Dayton, OH (>KC) [MIS] St. Gaspar Society, Liberty, MO
Nordick, Rev. Jack (John) A., '90 (NU) Retired.
Nordquist, Rev. Theodore A., '80 (GRY) Curia: Offices and Directors
Norena, Rev. Nicholas, '94 (MET) Most Holy Name of Jesus Parish, Perth Amboy, NJ
Norena, Rev. Nicolas F, (MET) [MIS] La Asuncion Church, ,
Norfolk, Rev. Jeffrey Thomas, '09 (SFS) On Duty Outside Diocese. (>STP) [SEM] St. John Vianney Seminary, St. Paul, MN
Norick, Rev. Daniel J., '97 (DEN) Church of the Ascension Catholic Parish in Denver, Denver, CO
Noriega, Rev. Arnoldo, '75 (TUC) Retired.
Noriega, Rev. Jose, *D.C.J.M.* '90 (DEN) St. Mary Catholic Parish in Littleton, Littleton, CO; [MON] Disciples of the Hearts of Jesus and Mary, Littleton, CO
Noriega Muniz, Rev. Gil Abad, *O.F.M.* '13 (MIL) [MIS] General Secretariat of the Franciscan Missions, Inc., Burlington, WI
Norman, Rev. Canon Benjamin, '18 (OAK) St. Margaret Mary, Oakland, CA
Norman, Rev. Charles J., *O.S.F.S.* '65 (PH) Our Mother of Consolation, Philadelphia, PA; [MON] Villa de Sales Oblate Residence, Wyndmoor, PA
Norman, Rev. Gary, (PHX) Sacred Heart Roman Catholic Parish Prescott, Prescott, AZ
Norman, Rev. Gary, '94 (YAK) Retired.
Norman, Rev. John E., '79 (SLC) Curia: Offices and Directors [EFT] Catholic Foundation of Utah, Salt Lake City, UT
Norman, Rev. John M., '13 (OM) Pope John XXIII Central Catholic High School at Elgin, Elgin, NE; St. Bonaventure's Church of Raeville (Nebraska Non-Profit Corporation), Raeville, NE; St. Boniface Church of Elgin (Nebraska Non-Profit Corporation), Elgin, NE; St. John the Baptist, Clearwater, NE; St. John the Baptists' Church of Petersburg (Nebraska Non-Profit Corporation), Petersburg, NE; St. Peter de Alcantara, Ewing, NE; [EFT] St. Bonaventure's Church of Raeville Cemetery Endowment Trust Fund, Elgin, NE
Norman, Rev. Paul, '19 (SPR) All Saints, Ware, MA; St. John Paul II Parish, Adams, MA; St. Mary of the Assumption, Cheshire, MA
Norman, Rev. Reginald D., '09 (BGP) Curia: Clergy and Religious Services; Consultative Bodies; Leadership Our Lady of Fatima Roman Catholic Church Corporation of Wilton, Wilton, CT
Norrell, Rev. Brian, '22 (PBR) St. John the Baptist, Avella, PA; St. Mary's, Weirton, WV
Norris, Rev. David J., '74 (FRS) Retired.
Norris, Rev. Patrick F., *O.P.* '89 (MAD) [HOS] SSM Health St. Mary's Hospital-Madison, Madison, WI
Norris, Rev. Robert J., '80 (NY) Our Lady of Mt. Carmel, Elmsford, NY
Norris, Rev. Thomas P., *O.S.F.S.* '73 (CHL) Immaculate Heart of Mary, High Point, NC
Norris, Rev. Timothy L., '94 (STP) St. George, Long Lake, MN; The Church of Saint Stephen-Holy Rosary, Minneapolis, MN
Norsworthy, Rev. Richard, '85 (SHP) Curia: Leadership St. Elizabeth Ann Seton, Shreveport, LA
Northenscold, Rev. Matthew J., '16 (STP) Curia: Tribunal Cathedral of Saint Paul, St. Paul, MN
Northrop, Rev. James W., (SEA) St. Thomas, Tukwila, WA
Norton, Rev. Andrew, *O.S.B.* '14 (TLS) [MON] Our Lady of the Annunciation of Clear Creek Abbey, Hulbert, OK
Norton, Rev. Bryan Y., *S.J.* '19 (STL) [MON] Jesuit Community Corporation at Saint Louis University - Jesuit Hall, St. Louis, MO
Norton, Rev. Jonathan, '15 (FTW) Curia: Offices and Directors Sacred Heart, Warsaw, IN
Norton, Rev. Michael B., '13 (COV) On Leave.
Norton, Rev. Robert, *O.F.M.* (NEW) Assumption of Our Blessed Lady, Wood Ridge, NJ
Norton, Rev. Robert A., '72 (PIT) Retired.
Norton, Rev. Robert J, *O.F.M.* '74 (PAT) Retired. St. Bonaventure, Paterson, NJ
Norton, Rev. Stephen P., '01 (NY) Curia: Leadership Parish of St. John the Baptist and Most Holy Trinity, Yonkers, NY; St. Ann, Yonkers, NY
Norton, Rev. Thomas, '63 (NEW) Retired.
Nortz, Rev. Robert, *M.M.A.* '07 (SAM) [MON] Maronite Monks of Adoration - Most Holy Trinity Monastery, Petersham, MA
Norwood, Rev. Matthew, '20 (BO) Resurrection of Our Lord and Savior Jesus Christ, Hingham, MA; St. Paul, Hingham, MA
Nosbush, Rev. Peter C., '70 (NU) Retired.
Nosser, Rev. Msgr. John C., '64 (RVC) Retired. St. Patrick's, Bay Shore, NY
Notabartolo, Very Rev. Charles E., '77 (PMB) Curia: Leadership [EFT] Diocese of Palm Beach Health Plan Trust, , ; [EFT] Diocese of Palm Beach Pension Plan Trust, ,
Notebaart, Rev. James C., '71 (STP) Retired.
Notter, Rev. Richard E., '63 (TOL) Retired.
Nouck, Rev. Peter, '16 (CHL) Holy Angels, Mt. Airy, NC
Nourie, Rev. Paul, (SAT) Retired. [NUR] Oblate Madonna Residence, San Antonio, TX
Novack, Rev. Kevin F., '81 (PBL) St. Columba, Durango, CO
Novajosky, Rev. Michael P., '10 (BGP) (>WDC) St. Bernadette, Silver Spring, MD
Novak, Rev. David A., '77 (STL) Retired.
Novak, Rev. David A., '79 (CLV) [NUR] The Village at St. Edward, Fairlawn, OH
Novak, Very Rev. William L., '97 (OKL) Curia: Administration; Advisory Boards, Commissions, Committees, and Councils; Consultative Bodies; Leadership St. Francis of Assisi, Oklahoma City, OK
Novelly, Rev. Duane R., '79 (DET) St. Matthew Parish Detroit, Detroit, MI
Novick, Rev. Michael, '01 (CHI) St. Cletus, La Grange, IL
Novielli, Rev. John Joseph, *O. Praem.* '74 (PH) [MON] Daylesford Abbey, Inc., Paoli, PA
Novitzky, Rev. Martin, '11 (WOR) Curia: (>MO) Offices and Directors
Novoa, Rev. Jose Marino, *CMF* (SPC) St. Ann, Carthage, MO
Novotny, Rev. James F., (OM) Retired.
Novotny, Rev. Richard, '81 (RC) On Leave.
Novotny, Rev. Vaclav, *S.J.* (BO) [MON] Walter Ciszek House, Brighton, MA
Nowacki, Rev. Jaroslaw, (LSC) Curia: Leadership Assumption Parish Inc., Roswell, NM
Nowak, Rev. Adam, '19 (DET) St. Hugo of the Hills Parish Bloomfield Hills, Bloomfield Hills, MI
Nowak, Rev. Andrew, *OFM Cap* (NY) [MON] St. Clare Friary (Capuchin Franciscan Friars, Province of St. Mary), Yonkers, NY
Nowak, Rev. Bernard U., '74 (BUF) Curia: Leadership Holy Trinity, Medina, NY; Our Lady of the Lake, Barker, NY
Nowak, Rev. Christopher, '97 (RVC) Curia: Leadership Our Holy Redeemer, Freeport, NY
Nowak, Rev. David G., '85 (GRY) Retired.
Nowak, Rev. Eugene J., '70 (CHI) Retired. St. Gilbert, Grayslake, IL
Nowak, Rev. Jeffrey L., '12 (BUF) On Administrative Leave.
Nowak, Rev. Krzysztof, '05 (DET) St. Gerald Parish Farmington, Farmington, MI
Nowak, Rev. Mark A., '75 (E) Chap, Cambridge Springs Correction Inst St. Anthony of Padua, Cambridge Springs, PA
Nowak, Rev. Przemyslaw, '13 (PAT) On Duty Outside Diocese. Orchard Lake, MI
Nowak, Rev. Przemyslaw J., (MO) Curia: Offices and Directors
Nowel, Rev. Mark D., *O.P.* '86 (PRO) [COL] Providence College, Providence, RI; [MON] St. Thomas Aquinas Priory at Providence College, Providence, RI
Nowicki, Rt. Rev. Douglas R., *O.S.B.* '72 (GBG) Retired. [MON] Saint Vincent Archabbey, Latrobe, PA
Nowicki, Rev. Gary D., '96 (MIL) Retired.
Nowicki, Rev. Marcin, '11 (WOR) Chap, US Archdiocese Military Services, Fayetteville, NC
Nsambu, Rev. Jean-Marie, (HT) Holy Savior, Lockport, LA
Nsame, Rev. Colleens Dinladzer, *S.J.* (SEA) [MON] Arrupe Jesuit Community at Seattle University, Seattle, WA
Nsionu, Rev. Patrick N., '85 (NY) Holy Family, New Rochelle, NY
Nsongolo, Rev. Gaston, *C.P.* '91 (NY) [MON] The Congregation of the Passion - St. Paul of the Cross Province, Jamaica, NY
Nsubuga, Rev. Francis, '09 (RC) St. Therese the Little Flower, Rapid City, SD
Nsubuga, Rev. Lutakome, '10 (SPK) Holy Rosary, Tonasket, WA; Immaculate Conception, Oroville, WA; Our Lady of the Valley, Okanogan, WA
Nsuguba JJuuko, Rev. Herman Joseph, '93 (DEN) St. Anthony of Padua Catholic Parish in Julesburg, Julesburg, CO
Ntaiyia, Rev. Symon Peter, '80 (ROC) St. Maximilian Kolbe, Ontario, NY; The Parish of St. Katharine Drexel, Macedon, NY
Ntakarutimana, Rev. Dieudonne, (LAN) St. John the Evangelist Parish Davison, Davison, MI
Ntawugashira, Rev. Jean Bosco, *CMM* '06 (IND) St. Rita Catholic Church, Indianapolis, Inc., Indianapolis, IN
Ntawugashira, Rev. John, *CMM* (IND) Holy Angels Catholic Church, Indianapolis, Inc., Indianapolis, IN
Ntegerej'Imana, Rev. Vian, (RVC) St. Agnes Cathedral, Rockville Centre, NY
Ntsiful-Amissah, Rev. Kofi, '79 (ALB) Chap, Stratton Veterans' Administration Med Ctr Curia: Offices and Directors St. Joan of Arc, Menands, NY
Ntungu, Rev. Rodrigue Bamenga, *S.J.* '16 (WDC) [MON] The Jesuit Community of St. Aloysius Gonzaga, Washington, DC
Ntuwa, Rev. Msgr. Joseph K., '88 (R) Curia: Offices and Directors All Saints Catholic Parish of Hampstead, Hampstead, NC
Nuanez, Rev. Anthony, '79 (LA) Retired.
Nuelle, Rev. John, *M.S.* '64 (STL) Retired.
Nuelle, Rev. John R., *M.S.* '64 (FR) [MON] La Salette Shrine & Retreat Center, Attleboro, MA
Nufable, Rev. Michael Figura, '15 (OAK) St. Catherine of Siena, Martinez, CA
Nugent, Rev. Anthony A., '72 (JOL) Retired.
Nugent, Rev. John R., *S.J.* '15 (DEN) Arrupe Jesuit High School, Denver, CO; [MON] Regis Jesuit Community (The Jesuits at Regis University), Denver, CO
Nugent, Rev. Msgr. Peter D., '62 (LA) Retired.
Nunes, Rev. Aldrin, *C.Ss.R.* '99 (ORL) Sacred Heart, New Smyrna Beach, FL
Nunes, Rev. Brian, '08 (LA) Curia: Advisory Boards, Commissions, Committees, and Councils; Leadership Cathedral of Our Lady of the Angels, Los Angeles, CA; [MIS] Archdiocesan Catholic Center, Los Angeles, CA; [MIS] The Cardinal McIntyre Fund for Charity, Los Angeles, CA
Nunes, Rev. Daniel, (FR) Annunciation of the Lord, Taunton, MA; St. Nicholas of Myra Parish, North Dighton, MA
Nunes de Silva, Rev. Christiano, '14 (NSH) Curia: Leadership St. Rose of Lima, Murfreesboro, TN
Nunez, Rev. Baltazar, '88 (CGS) Curia: Leadership Santos Angeles Cutodios, Yabucoa, PR; [RTR] Casa Charlie Rodriguez, San Lorenzo, PR
Nunez, Rev. Damian de la Cruz, *C.R.* '05 (PBL) Holy Name of Mary, Del Norte, CO; St. Francis Jerome, Center, CO; St. Joseph, Monte Vista, CO
Nunez, Rev. Msgr. Edward H., '76 (PBL) Retired. Curia: Offices and Directors
Nunez, Rev. Felix, (CGS) [MIS] Seminario Pablo VI - Theological, Naranjito, PR
Nunez, Rev. Felix, '99 (CGS) Curia: Leadership; Offices and Directors San Miguel Arcangel, Naranjito, PR; [MIS] Diocesan Tribunal of Caguas, Caguas, PR
Nunez, Rev. Giovannie B., *C.R.M.* '11 (CHR) St. Anne and St. Jude, Sumter, SC
Nunez, Rev. Jose, *C.M.F.* (SJN) Santa Maria, Bayamon, PR
Nunez, Rev. Pedro Felix, '77 (NO) Retired.
Nunez, Rev. Roldan, (SD) Pastor of Saint Rose of Lima Catholic Parish, Chula Vista, a corporation sole, Chula Vista, CA
Nuñez, Rev. Jose Felix, *C.M.F.* (SJN) Casa Mision

Claret, Bayamon, PR
Nuñez Carrion, Rev. Phillip, (SJN) Corazon de Jesus, Guaynabo, PR
Nunez-Carrion, Rev. Phillip, '88 (SJN) Curia: Leadership
Nunez-Renteria, Rev. Lazaro, '90 (BRK) St. Martin of Tours-Our Lady of Lourdes, Brooklyn, NY
Nungari, Rev. Joseph, *F.M.H.* (RVC) Chap, St Francis Hosp
Nunning, Rev. David, '69 (EVN) Retired.
Nunning, Rev. David H., '69 (EVN) Retired. Curia: Leadership
Nuño Gorbea, Rev. Rafael, '69 (ARE) Our Lady of Hope, Arecibo, PR
Nuota, Rev. Juraj, (DET) SS. Cyril and Methodius (Slovak) Parish Sterling Heights, Sterling Heights, MI
Nurek, Rev. Marcin, (PAT) On Leave.
Nursey, Rev. Bradley, (GLD) Saint Ann of Cadillac, Cadillac, MI; Saint Edward of Harrietta, Harrietta, MI; Saint Stephen of Lake City, Lake City, MI; Saint Theresa of Manton, Manton, MI
Nursey, Rev. George, (PMB) [SEM] St. Vincent de Paul Regional Seminary, Boynton Beach, FL
Nursey, Rev. George A., '13 (ORL) On Duty Outside Diocese.
Nusbaum, Rev. Daniel C., '61 (ALB) Retired.
Nusi, Rev. Francies, '05 (GB) Curia: Advisory Boards, Commissions, Committees, and Councils
Nusi, Rev. Francis, (GB) Holy Trinity, Oconto, WI; St. Maximilian Kolbe, Sobieski, WI
Nusi, Rev. Konda Reddy, *MSFS* '02 (KCK) St. Patrick, Osage City, KS; St. Patrick, Scranton, KS
Nuss, Rev. David W., '93 (TOL) Christ the King, Toledo, OH; Little Flower of Jesus, Toledo, OH
Nuthulapati, Rev. Jayababu, *C.PP.S.* (GRY) Curia: Leadership
Nutt, Rev. Maurice J., *C.Ss.R.* '89 (NO) St. Alphonsus, New Orleans, LA
Nutter, Rev. Nicholas John, '89 (BR) Retired.
Nuyen, Rev. Paul, (AMA) Our Lady of Vietnam, Amarillo, TX
Nuzzi, Rev. Ronald, '84 (Y) On Duty Outside Diocese.
Nwabueze, Rev. Raymond, *O.P.* '06 (WDC) Chap, Children's National Med Ctr, Washington [MIS] Dominican Fathers & Brothers, Province of Nigeria, Mount Rainier, MD
Nwabueze, Rev. Victor, *O.M.V.* (BO) [MIS] St. Clement Archdiocesan Eucharistic Shrine, Boston, MA
Nwachukwu, Rev. Bruno, '15 (STP) St. Joseph, West St. Paul, MN
Nwachukwu, Rev. Innocent, '06 (NY) St. Joachim - St. John the Evangelist, Beacon, NY
Nwachukwu, Rev. Jude, *S.M.M.M.* (STA) On Special Assignment. Chaplain, Ascension - St. Vincent Medical Center
Nwachukwu, Rev. Lawrence, (TLS) St. Francis Xavier, Sallisaw, OK
Nwachukwu, Rev. Oliver, '82 (BEL) St. Michael the Archangel, Radom, IL
Nwachukwu, Rev. Oliver, '82 (BEL) St. Charles Borromeo, Dubois, IL
Nwachukwu, Rev. Patrick, (FR) St. Patrick's, Wareham, MA
Nwachukwu, Rev. Peter C., '86 (TUC) Immaculate Conception Roman Catholic Church - Ajo, Ajo, AZ; Saint Francis of Assisi Roman Catholic Parish - Superior, Superior, AZ
Nwachukwu, Rev. Raymond, '87 (BWN) St. Margaret Mary, Pharr, TX
Nwachukwu, Rev. Simon, (NY) St. Joseph, Middletown, NY
Nwachukwu, Rev. Thomas Kizito, '82 (CC) On Special Assignment. [HOS] CHRISTUS Spohn Hospital Corpus Christi - South, Corpus Christi, TX
Nwachukwu-Udaku, Rev. Benedict C., '02 (SB) Sacred Heart, Rancho Cucamonga, CA
Nwafor, Rev. Bartholomew Onyeka, '14 (DAL) St. Francis of Assisi Catholic Parish - Frisco, Frisco, TX
Nwafor, Rev. Gerald, '03 (SJ) St. Justin, Santa Clara, CA
Nwafor, Rev. Matthew, '20 (R) St. Catherine of Siena, Wake Forest, NC
Nwagbara, Rev. Augustine, *S.M.M.M.* (STA) Chaplain, University of Florida Shands Hospital
Nwagwu, Rev. Alexander, (MO) Curia: Offices and Directors
Nwagwu, Rev. Deniskingsley, *SDV* (MET) St. Cecelia, Iselin, NJ
Nwagwu, Rev. Nicholas, '98 (NY) Chap, St John's Riverside Hosp, Yonkers
Nwaiwu, Rev. Matthias, *CMF* '88 (LA) [MON] Dominguez Seminary Inc., Rancho Dominguez, CA
Nwajagu, Rev. Hilary, (RVC) St. Joseph's, Garden City, NY
Nwakile, Rev. Francis Chidi, *F.J.S.* '11 (MIA) St. Mary Magdalen, Sunny Isles Beach, FL
Nwakuna, Rev. Anselm, '93 (LA) [HOS] Tarzana Medical Center, LLC (Providence Cedars-Sinai Tarzana Medical Center), Tarzana, CA
Nwanekezie, Rev. Peter, '89 (SR) [HOS] Providence Santa Rosa Memorial Hospital, Santa Rosa, CA
Nwankwo, Rev. Fidelis, *C.S.Sp.* '94 (MIA) Curia: Pastoral Services St. Philip Neri Catholic Church, Miami Gardens, FL
Nwankwo, Rev. Moses, '04 (SFE) Our Lady of Guadalupe-Villanueva, Villanueva, NM; San Miguel Del Vado, Ribera, NM
Nwankwo, Rev. Simeon, (DAL) St. Jude Catholic Parish, Allen, TX
Nwanonenyi, Rev. Benjamin, '97 (PH) St. Francis de Sales, Philadelphia, PA
Nwaorgu, Rev. Msgr. Anselm I., '92 (NEW) Blessed Sacrament-St. Charles Borromeo, Newark, NJ
Nwaru, Rev. Romanus N., '95 (MIL) Curia: Leadership Blessed Savior Congregation, Milwaukee, WI
Nwatarali, Rev. Linus, (WIN) Chap, Mayo Clinic, Rochester
Nwauzor, Rev. Reginald, '80 (B) St. Catherine's, Priest River, ID
Nwegede, Rev. Raymond, (NY) Chap, Mount Vernon Hosp, Mount Vernon; Westchester Med Ctr… Sacred Heart Church, Monroe, NY
Nweke, Rev. Paulinus Emeka, (BO) St. Barbara, Woburn, MA
Nwele, Rev. Chrysogonus, '95 (PBL) Immaculate Heart of Mary, Grand Junction, CO
Nwiyi, Rev. Pius C, (CHI) St. Gertrude, Chicago, IL
Nwizu, Rev. Canice, (SB) Christ the Good Shepherd, Adelanto, CA
Nwoga, Rev. Laserian, '95 (CAM) On Duty Outside Diocese. CH MAJ, USAF, APO AE Curia: (>MO) Offices and Directors
Nwohu, Rev. Msgr. Ambrose O., '66 (TUC) Saint Helen Roman Catholic Parish - Oracle, Oracle, AZ
Nwokeogu, Rev. Patrick, (IND) Chap, Indiana Univ Health Methodist Hosp
Nwoko, Rev. Kingsley, '19 (GAL) St. Luke the Evangelist, Houston, TX
Nwokocha, Rev. Michael O., '99 (WH) [HOS] Wheeling Hospital, Wheeling, WV
Nwokocha, Rev. Rowland, '97 (SLC) Saint Joseph LLC 229, Monticello, UT; Saint Pius X LLC 244, Moab, UT
Nwokocha, Rev. Solomon, (LA) St. Raymond, Downey, CA
Nwokorie, Rev. Fabian, (SR) Pastor of Christ the King Catholic Church of McKinleyville, A Corporation Sole, McKinleyville, CA; Pastor of St. Kateri Tekakwitha Catholic Mission of Hoopa, A Corporation Sole, Hoopa, CA; Pastor of St. Mary Catholic Church of Arcata, A Corporation Sole, Arcata, CA; [CAM] Cal Poly Humboldt Newman Center, Arcata, CA
Nwokorie, Rev. Fabian, '90 (BAK) Retired.
Nwokoye, Rev. Patrick I., '02 (SPC) Curia: Advisory Boards, Commissions, Committees, and Councils; Consultative Bodies; Deaneries; Education; Offices and Directors Holy Trinity, Springfield, MO
Nwokoye, Rev. Peter, (MO) Curia: Offices and Directors
Nworah, Rev. Valentine Onyeka, (SPR) Curia: Offices and Directors Holy Trinity, Greenfield, MA; [CAM] Smith College, Northampton, MA
Nwosu, Rev. Abuchi, '08 (PAT) Our Lady of Mt. Carmel, Swartswood, NJ
Nwosu, Rev. Benjamin E., '01 (JC) St. Ann, Warsaw, MO; St. Bernadette, Hermitage, MO
Nwosu, Rev. Celestine, (RVC) St. Edward Confessor, Syosset, NY
Nwosu, Rev. Ekene (Alex), '19 (MIL) Blessed Sacrament Congregation, Milwaukee, WI
Nwosu, Rev. Eloo Malachy, '93 (ROC) St. Christopher, North Chili, NY; [CAM] Roberts Wesleyan College c/o St. Christopher Church, North Chili, NY
Nwosu, Rev. Raphael Chinedu, '11 (LSC) Immaculate Conception Parish, Dexter, Inc., Dexter, NM
Nwudah, Rev. Anthony, '90 (SC) [HOS] MercyOne Siouxland Medical Center, Sioux City, IA
Nyache, Rev. Collins Kisaka, '11 (CHI) St. Alphonsus and St. Patrick Parish, Lemont, IL
Nyamai, Rev. Anthony, '17 (JOL) St. Ambrose, Crest Hill, IL; St. Anne, Crest Hill, IL
Nyambe, Rev. Felix, *OMI* '18 (BUF) Holy Cross, Buffalo, NY; Our Lady of Hope, Buffalo, NY
Nyambe, Rev. Shoba, *P.S.S.* '03 (BAL) [MIS] St. Mary's Seminary & University, Baltimore, MD; [MON] Society of St. Sulpice, Province of the United States, Baltimore, MD
Nyardy, Rev. Jeffrey, *O.S.B.* '90 (GBG) [MON] Saint Vincent Archabbey, Latrobe, PA
Nyce, Rev. William, (ARL) Curia: Tribunal St. William of York, Stafford, VA
Nycz, Rev. Matt Mieczyslaw, '94 (BUF) Ss. Peter and Paul Roman Catholic Church Society of Williamsville, NY, Williamsville, NY
Nydegger, Rev. Msgr. Thomas P., '92 (NEW) Curia: Organizations (affiliated, inter-Diocesan, miscellaneous/other) St. Helen, Westfield, NJ; [COL] Seton Hall University, South Orange, NJ; [MIS] New Jersey Caritas Corporation, Inc., Newark, NJ
Nygaard, Rev. Robert C., '64 (STP) Retired.
Nyirenda, Rev. Boyd Kapyunga, *SJ* '03 (OAK) [MON] Jesuit Fathers and Brothers, Berkeley, CA
Nyman, Rev. Vincent R., '99 (STL) Our Lady of the Holy Cross Catholic Church, St. Louis, MO
Nyo, Rev. Anton, (HON) Our Lady Queen of the Angels, Kula, HI
Nyong, Rev. Anthony, *CM* '05 (SP) St. John Vianney, St. Pete Beach, FL; [HOS] St. Anthony's Hospital, Inc., St. Petersburg, FL
Nyong, Rev. Eugene, '97 (FWT) St. Mary, Graham, TX; St. Theresa, Olney, TX
Nyoni, Rev. Erasto, (CHI) St. Mary, Star of the Sea, Chicago, IL
Nyorko, Rev. Modi Abel, '71 (LA) [MIS] Comboni Mission Center, Covina, CA
Nzabhayanga, Rev. Sebastian, '93 (ORL) St. Joseph's, Winter Haven, FL
Nzabonimpa, Rev. Boniface Kasiita, '02 (JC) St. Boniface, Brunswick, MO; St. Joseph, Salisbury, MO; St. Mary of the Angels, Wien, MO
Nzeabalu, Rev. Cosmas, '01 (BRK) Curia: (>MO) Offices and Directors St. Mary Magdalene, Springfield Gardens, NY; [CCH] Nigerian Ministry, ,
Nzeh, Rev. Albert, (NEW) Blessed Sacrament-St. Charles Borromeo, Newark, NJ
Nzeh, Rev. Godwin O., *C.M.F.* (LAF) Our Lady of Victory, Loreauville, LA; St. Joseph, Loreauville, LA
Nzewuji, Rev. Innocent, '06 (GLP) St. Anthony, Zuni, NM
N'Zilamba, Rev. Norbert, *O. Praem.* '87 (GB) [MON] St. Norbert Abbey, De Pere, WI
O'Brien, Rev. Peter, (P) St. Edward, Lebanon, OR
O'Connor, Rev. Christopher, (BO) Curia: Pastoral Services
O'Loughlin, Rev. Patrick, *LC* '18 (ATL) [MON] Legionaries of Christ, Incorporated, Cumming, GA
O'Malley, Rev. Kenneth, (L) [MON] Sacred Heart Retreat, Louisville, KY
Oajaca-Lopez, Rev. Gonzalo, '08 (RVC) Curia: Leadership Church of the Resurrection, Farmingville, NY
Oakes, Rev. Eathan, '03 (BEA) St. Martin de Porres Mission, Beaumont, TX; St. Mary, Beaumont, TX
Oakham, Rev. Ronald, '77 (PHX) Retired. [MON] St. Therese Priory, Phoenix, AZ
Oakland, Very Rev. Matthew T., '10 (SEA) Curia: Leadership Holy Rosary, Seattle, WA
Oates, Rev. Thomas F., '63 (BO) Retired.
Obada, Rev. Taiye Anthony, '07 (SR) Pastor of St. Aloysius Catholic Church of Point Arena, A Corporation Sole, Point Arena, CA
Obasi, Rev. Augustine, (SB) (>GAL) Sacred Heart of Jesus, Manvel, TX
Obayashi, Rev. Hal N., '02 (BO) On Special Assignment.
Obaza, Rev. Theodore L., '61 (SCR) Retired.
Obel, Rev. Andrew, '04 (CR) Curia: Offices and Directors Sacred Heart, Baudette, MN; St. Mary's, Warroad, MN
Obele, Very Rev. Oliver, '95 (LSC) Curia: Clergy and Religious Services; Leadership St. Vincent de Paul Parish, Inc., Silver City, NM
O'Bell, Rev. John C., '91 (SCR) On Administrative Leave.
Obeng, Rev. Martin, '14 (DUB) Holy Family Church, New Melleray, Peosta, Iowa, Peosta, IA; St. Joseph's Church, Key West, Iowa, Dubuque, IA
Obeng-Yeboah-Asuamah, Rev. George, '03 (NY) Blessed Sacrament, New Rochelle, NY
Ober, Rev. Lawrence, *S.J.* '97 (STP) [SEM] Jesuit Novitiate of St. Alberto Hurtado, St. Paul, MN
Oberle, Rev. Gerard, *C.Ss.R.* '55 (NEW) St. James, Newark, NJ
Oberle, Rev. James P., *S.S.* '87 (WDC) On Duty Outside Diocese. Univ of Dallas, Irving, TX
Oberle, Rev. James P., *P.S.S.* '87 (BAL) Retired. [MON] Society of St. Sulpice, Province of the United States, Baltimore, MD
Obermeyer, Rev. Robert A., '61 (CIN) Retired.
Obermiller, Rev. Edwin, *C.S.C.* '96 (P) [MON] Priests of Holy Cross in Oregon, Inc., Portland, OR

Obero, Rev. Eduardo, '93 (SJ) St. Joseph, Mountain View, CA
Obersteiner, Rev. Ernest, '77 (GLP) On Leave.
Oberto, Rev. Msgr. Peter, '78 (MAR) Retired.
Oberts, Rev. David P., '69 (SUP) Retired.
Obeten, Rev. Mark C., '13 (MIL) St. Jude Congregation, Wauwatosa, WI
Obi, Rev. Casmir, '96 (RVC) Chap, Mt Sinai South Nassau Communities Hosp
Obi, Rev. Vincent J., '02 (BEL) St. Patrick, Enfield, IL; St. Polycarp (German), Carmi, IL
Obiaeri, Rev. John Paul, (BRK) Holy Child Jesus, Richmond Hill, NY
Obiansi, Rev. Livinus, (NY) Chap, Montefiore Med Ctr, Henry and Lucy Moses Div, Bronx
Obidiagha, Rev. Collins, *SJ* '19 (NY) [MON] Jesuit Community at Fordham University, New York, NY
Obidiegwu, Rev. Celestine, '04 (TLS) St. Augustine's, Tulsa, OK; St. Monica's, Tulsa, OK
Obiekwe, Rev. Kenneth, '93 (ALX) St. Louis, Glenmora, LA
Obijekwu, Rev. Francis, *S.M.M.M.* '06 (BAK) Curia: Leadership St. Augustine Catholic Church of Merrill, Inc., Merrill, OR
Obikwelu, Rev. Uche Evaristus, '09 (AUS) Our Lady of the Lake, Horseshoe Bay, TX; St. Charles Borromeo Catholic Church - Kingsland, Texas, Kingsland, TX
Obinwa, Rev. Charles, '95 (TOL) St. Joseph, Fort Jennings, OH; [HOS] Mercy Health - St. Rita's Medical Center LLC, Lima, OH
Obirieze, Rev. Louis C., '00 (TLS) Sacred Heart, Sapulpa, OK
Obiske, Rev. Bonaventure, (SPK) Chap
Obiudu, Rev. Alfred U., '05 (WH) St. Leo, Inwood, WV
O'Blaney, Rev. James, *C.Ss.R.* '58 (HBG) St. James, Lititz, PA
O'Blaney, Rev. James, *C.Ss.R.* (BAL) St. Mary, Annapolis, MD
Obloj, Rev. Stanley, '93 (DET) St. Mark Parish Warren, Warren, MI
Obloy, Rev. Leonard G., (CLV) Retired.
Obniski, Rev. Jeffrey, *I.V.E.* '07 (NY) St. Thomas Aquinas, Bronx, NY
Obotama, Rev. Raphael, (BIS) Holy Trinity, Hettinger, ND; Sacred Heart, Reeder, ND; Sacred Heart, Scranton, ND
Obour, Rev. Augustine Twum, (VEN) St. Francis Xavier Parish in Fort Myers, Inc., Fort Myers, FL
Obour, Rev. Dominic, (SD) Chap, Scripps Mercy Hosp, Chula Vista Pastor of Saint Michael Catholic Parish, Poway, a corporation sole, Poway, CA
Obregon, Rev. Jorge, *L.C.* '09 (NY) [MON] Legionaries of Christ, Rye, NY
Obregon, Rev. Jorge, *L.C.* '09 (ATL) [MIS] New Fire Evangelization Inc., Roswell, GA
Obrien, Rev. Sean, (TLS) Immaculate Conception, Poteau, OK
O'Brien, Rev. Andru, '18 (PEO) High School of St. Thomas More, Champaign, IL; Saint Matthew Roman Catholic Congregation of Champaign, Champaign, IL; St. Boniface, Seymour, IL; [MIS] The High School of St. Thomas More of Champaign, Inc., Champaign, IL
O'Brien, Rev. Brandon, '13 (RVC) On Duty Outside Diocese.
O'Brien, Rev. Brian D., '07 (TLS) St. Francis Xavier Catholic Church, Stillwater, OK
O'Brien, Rev. Daniel P., '85 (HBG) Retired.
O'Brien, Rev. David, (PH) Lansdale Catholic High School, Lansdale, PA; Our Lady of Mount Carmel, Doylestown, PA
O'Brien, Rev. Dennis J., '81 (PT) Retired. Curia: Leadership
O'Brien, Rev. Edmund M., '57 (HRT) Retired.
O'Brien, Rev. Edward, (HRT) [NUR] The Home for the Aged of the Little Sisters of the Poor, Enfield, CT
O'Brien, Rev. Elias, *O.Carm.* (JOL) [MON] Carmelite Provincial Office, Darien, IL
O'Brien, Rev. Elias, *O.Carm.* '86 (WDC) [SEM] Whitefriars Hall, Washington, DC
O'Brien, Rev. Francis P., '85 (BO) St. Matthias, Marlborough, MA
O'Brien, Rev. Garrett M., '12 (NO) St. John the Baptist, New Orleans, LA; St. Patrick, New Orleans, LA
O'Brien, Rev. Gerard, '95 (LA) Our Lady of Refuge, Long Beach, CA
O'Brien, Rev. James, *S.J.* '60 (BAL) [MIS] Colombiere Jesuit Community, Baltimore, MD
O'Brien, Rev. James C., *S.J.* '61 (BO) [MON] Campion Health & Wellness, Inc., Weston, MA
O'Brien, Rev. James J., *M.A.* '60 (CHI) Retired. Queen of Peace Parish, Chicago, IL
O'Brien, Rev. James R., '66 (HBG) Retired.
O'Brien, Rev. Msgr. James T., '70 (SY) Retired.
O'Brien, Rev. John, '55 (GB) Retired.
O'Brien, Rev. John, '96 (ALX) Curia: Miscellaneous / Other Offices St. Anthony of Padua, Natchitoches, LA
O'Brien, Rev. Msgr. John F., '61 (PH) Retired.
O'Brien, Rev. John J., '07 (STL) On Duty Outside Diocese. Saint John Seminary, Archdiocese of Los Angeles
O'Brien, Rev. John Joseph, '07 (LA) [SEM] St. John's Seminary, Camarillo, CA
O'Brien, Rev. John M., *O.C.S.O.* '81 (ATL) [MON] The Monastery of the Holy Spirit, Conyers, GA
O'Brien, Rev. John W., '67 (BO) Retired.
O'Brien, Rev. John W., '82 (PRO) Saint Lucy's Church Corp., Middletown, RI; [MIS] Charismatic Renewal, Middletown, RI
O'Brien, Rev. Joseph, '91 (ALB) Curia: Leadership; Offices and Directors St. Mary, Coxsackie, NY; St. Patrick, Ravena, NY
O'Brien, Rev. Joseph, *O.P.* '78 (LAV) Curia: Advisory Boards, Commissions, Committees, and Councils [MIS] Saint Therese Center, Henderson, NV; [MON] Dominican Rectory, Fra Angelico House, Las Vegas, NV
O'Brien, Rev. Joseph P., *O.Carm.* (JOL) [MON] Carmelite Provincial Office, Darien, IL
O'Brien, Rev. Joseph P., *O.Carm.* '63 (NEW) St. Cecilia, Englewood, NJ; [MIS] Carmelite Missions, Englewood, NJ
O'Brien, Rev. Kevin F., (BGP) [MON] The Fairfield Jesuit Community-Fairfield University, Fairfield, CT
O'Brien, Rev. Kevin J., '81 (OG) Curia: Administration; Consultative Bodies SS. Philip and James, Lisbon, NY; St. Raphael's, Heuvelton, NY
O'Brien, Rev. Kevin J., '79 (RIC) Curia: Administration Church of St. Therese of Lisieux, Chesapeake, VA
O'Brien, Rev. Msgr. Kevin P., '73 (NY) Retired. Sacred Heart, Bronx, NY; [EFT] New York Catholic Foundation, Inc., New York, NY
O'Brien, Rev. Leo P., '56 (ALB) Retired. St. Vincent de Paul, Albany, NY
O'Brien, Rev. Maurice, '68 (SAC) Retired.
O'Brien, Rev. Michael, *M.S.C.* '69 (SAT) [MON] Missionaries of the Sacred Heart, San Antonio, TX; [NUR] Missionary Servants of St. Anthony (Padua Place), San Antonio, TX
O'Brien, Rev. Michael, '05 (LAN) St. Paul Parish Owosso, Owosso, MI
O'Brien, Rev. Michael, '72 (JKS) Retired. Curia: Consultative Bodies
O'Brien, Rev. Michael J., '00 (DEN) On Leave.
O'Brien, Rev. Nicholas J., '83 (ORL) St. Matthew, Winter Haven, FL
O'Brien, Rev. Patrick, '69 (SAV) Retired.
O'Brien, Rev. Patrick, '89 (SAT) Curia: Administration St. Pius X, San Antonio, TX
O'Brien, Rev. Paul B., '91 (BO) Lawrence Catholic Academy of Lawrence, Massachusetts, Inc., Lawrence, MA; St. Patrick, Lawrence, MA
O'Brien, Rev. Peter, '05 (P) St. Bernard, Scio, OR
O'Brien, Rev. Raymond C., '75 (WDC) On Special Assignment. [COL] Catholic University of America, The, Washington, DC
O'Brien, Rev. Richard M., '92 (BO) Sacred Hearts, Haverhill, MA
O'Brien, Rev. Roger, '61 (SEA) Retired.
O'Brien, Rev. Scott, *OP* (STL) [MON] St. Dominic Priory, St. Louis, MO
O'Brien, Rev. Seamus, '76 (MRY) San Agustin, Scotts Valley, CA
O'Brien, Rev. Sean, (TLS) Curia: Leadership; Offices and Directors St. Elizabeth Seton, Spiro, OK; St. Joseph, Stigler, OK
O'Brien, Rev. Sean, *O.F.M.* '98 (ALB) [COL] Siena College, Loudonville, NY
O'Brien, Rev. Sean, (ALB) St. Francis of Assisi Parish, Albany, NY
O'Brien, Rev. Sean, '93 (SY) Curia: Leadership St. Peter's Church, Rome, NY
O'Brien, Rev. Thomas J., *M.M.* '74 (NY) [MON] Maryknoll Fathers and Brothers (Catholic Foreign Mission Society of America, Inc.), Ossining, NY
O'Brien, Rev. Timothy, *S.J.* (BAL) [COL] Jesuit Community of Loyola University, Inc., Baltimore, MD; [MON] Jesuit Community of Loyola University Maryland, Inc., Baltimore, MD
O'Brien, Rev. Timothy A., '94 (HRT) Mary, Gate of Heaven Parish Corporation, Windsor Locks, CT
O'Brien, Rev. Timothy J., '69 (MIL) On Special Assignment. Faculty, Marquette Univ, Washington, DC
O'Brien, Rev. Timothy P., *F.S.S.P.* (SEA) St. Joseph, Tacoma, WA
O'Brien, Rev. William, '61 (NEW) Retired.
O'Brien, Rev. William, '88 (HPM) SS. Cyril & Methodius, Spokane Valley, WA
O'Brien, Very Rev. William, '90 (GB) Retired. Curia: Administration; Advisory Boards, Commissions, Committees, and Councils; Leadership
O'Brien, Rev. William J., *C.M.* '67 (PH) [MON] Congregation of the Mission, Philadelphia, PA
O'Brien, Rev. William J., '78 (BAL) Retired.
O'Brien, Rev. William J., '80 (E) St. Callistus, Kane, PA
O'Brien, Rev. William M., *S.J.* (STP) [SEM] Jesuit Novitiate of St. Alberto Hurtado, St. Paul, MN
Obrigewitch, Rev. Logan, '22 (BIS) Church of Corpus Christi, Bismarck, ND
O'Bryan, Rev. James, *S.T.* '56 (WDC) [MON] Father Judge Missionary Cenacle, Adelphi, MD
O'Bryan, Rev. Michael, '06 (NSH) Retired.
Obu-Mends, Rev. Francis, *C.S.Sp.* (BRK) Chap, Maimonides Med Ctr of Brooklyn; The Brooklyn Hosp Immaculate Heart of Mary, Brooklyn, NY
O'Byrne, Rev. Patrick J., '60 (LIN) Retired.
O'Callaghan, Rev. John J., *S.J.* '62 (CHI) [COL] Jesuit Community at Loyola University Chicago, Chicago, IL
O'Callaghan, Rev. Thomas, '54 (SEA) Retired.
Ocampo, Rev. Alfredo, *C.P.* '11 (CHI) [MON] Passionist Community of St. Vincent Strambi, Chicago, IL; [MON] Passionist Provincial Office (The Congregation of the Passion, Holy Cross Province), Park Ridge, IL
Ocampo Lopez, Friar Roque, (AUS) Our Lady of Guadalupe, Austin, TX
Ocariz, Rev. Msgr. Fernando, '71 (POD) Curia: Leadership
Ocasio, Rev. Edgardo Acosta, '83 (MGZ) Curia: Offices and Directors
Ocasio, Rev. Jose L, '20 (MGZ) De la Merced Parish, Lajas, PR
Occeno, Rev. Adolfo, (NY) Church of St. Mary, Mother of the Church, Fishkill, NY
Occhiuto, Rev. Joseph L., '79 (MRY) Retired.
Ochalek, Rev. Arkadiusz, '99 (BAL) On Special Assignment. Chaplain, Archdiocese of Military Services Curia: (>MO) Offices and Directors
Ochetti, Rev. Jerome, '02 (SB) Retired.
Ochigbo, Rev. Emmanuel, '08 (SD) Curia: (>MO) Offices and Directors Pastor of Sacred Heart Catholic Parish, San Diego, a corporation sole, San Diego, CA; [HOS] Scripps Mercy Chula Vista, Chula Vista, CA
Ochoa, Rev. Anthony B., '10 (STL) All Souls Catholic Church, Overland, MO
Ochoa, Rev. Carlos, '09 (WIL) Curia: Offices and Directors St. John the Baptist-Holy Angels, Newark, DE
Ochoa, Rev. David, '72 (LA) Retired. St. Emydius, Lynwood, CA
Ochoa, Rev. Einer, '85 (SAT) Retired.
Ochoa, Rev. Guillermo J., '11 (WOR) On Administrative Leave.
Ochoa, Rev. Jorge, *M.C.C.J.* '96 (LA) [MIS] Comboni Mission Center, Covina, CA
Ochoa, Rev. Juan Jose, '14 (LA) Curia: Offices and Directors Christ the King, Los Angeles, CA
Ochs, Rev. Bryan A., '11 (SEA) Immaculate Heart of Mary, Kelso, WA; St. Mary, Castle Rock, WA; St. Rose de Viterbo, Longview, WA
Ochs, Rev. Daniel L., '76 (COL) Retired.
Ochu, Rev. Austin Charles, *S.M.A.* '92 (WDC) St. Margaret, Seat Pleasant, MD (>NEW) [MON] Society of African Missions, Provincialate, S.M.A. Fathers, Tenafly, NJ
Ochu, Rev. Austin Charles, *S.M.A.* '92 (MO) Curia: Offices and Directors
O'Cinnsealaigh, Rev. Benedict, '93 (CIN) St. Dominic, Cincinnati, OH
O'Cinnsealaigh, Rev. Benedict D., '93 (CIN) Curia: Administration Our Lady of Victory, Cincinnati, OH; St. Aloysius-on-the-Ohio, Cincinnati, OH; St. Vincent de Paul, Cincinnati, OH
O'Connell, Rev. Brendan M., *M.M.* '63 (NY) Retired.
O'Connell, Rev. Cuthbert R., '86 (BLX) Curia: Education; Leadership St. Thomas the Apostle, Long Beach, MS
O'Connell, Rev. Damian, *S.J.* '75 (NY) [MON] America; Residence and Publication Office of the America Press, New York, NY
O'Connell, Rev. Daniel C., '83 (BO) Corpus Christi - St. Bernard, Newton, MA
O'Connell, Rev. James, *O.F.M.* '82 (NY) Chap, New York Presbyterian Hosp, Manhattan
O'Connell, Rev. John R., '73 (NEW) Retired. Sacred Heart, Haworth, NJ
O'Connell, Rev. Michael W., '83 (CHI) Our Lady of the Rosary Parish, Chicago, IL
O'Connell, Rev. Neil, *O.F.M.* '64 (SP) Retired.
O'Connell, Rev. Neil J., *O.F.M.* '64 (NY) St. Joseph of the Holy Family, New York, NY

O'Connell, Rev. Paul A., '03 (SAV) St. Paul's, Douglas, GA
O'Connell, Rev. Paul T., '60 (WOR) Curia: Leadership; Offices and Directors St. Anne, Shrewsbury, MA
O'Connell, Rev. Terry, '92 (P) Retired.
O'Connell, Rev. Thomas P., '63 (KNX) Retired.
O'Connell, Rev. Timothy, (COS) Ave Maria, Parker, CO
O'Connell, Rev. Msgr. Timothy P., '63 (LA) Retired. Annunciation, Arcadia, CA
O'Connell, Rev. Walter T., *O.P.* '58 (CHI) [MON] St. Pius V Priory, Chicago, IL
O'Connell, Rev. William A., '55 (SFR) Retired.
O'Connor, Rev. Msgr. Albert G., '67 (SAC) Retired.
O'Connor, Rev. Andrew, '87 (STL) On Special Assignment. Chap, Nazareth Living Ctr, Saint Louis [NUR] Nazareth Living Center, St. Louis, MO
O'Connor, Rev. Andrew, '96 (NY) St. Mary, New York, NY
O'Connor, Rev. Brian, '15 (COL) Curia: Offices and Directors St. John XXIII (Pope John XXIII), Canal Winchester, OH
O'Connor, Rev. Charles John, *OFM* '73 (BO) [MIS] St. Anthony Shrine, Boston, MA
O'Connor, Rev. Charles T., '83 (MET) Curia: Consultative Bodies; Tribunal St. Cecilia, Monmouth Junction, NJ
O'Connor, Rev. Christopher, *L.C.* '07 (HRT) [MON] Legionaries of Christ, Cheshire, CT; [SEM] Novitiate of the Legion of Christ, Cheshire, CT
O'Connor, Rev. Christopher K., '98 (BO) Saint Michael the Archangel Parish, Winthrop, MA; [MIS] Our Lady of the Airways Chapel, Boston, MA
O'Connor, Rev. Christopher M., '99 (BRK) Curia: Consultative Bodies Blessed Virgin Mary, Help of Christians, Woodside, NY
O'Connor, Rev. Daniel, '90 (ALX) St. Joseph's, Marksville, LA
O'Connor, Rev. David, '64 (JKS) Retired.
O'Connor, Very Rev. David H., '86 (DUB) On Special Assignment. Dean of the Cedar Rapids Deanery St. Joseph Church, Marion, Iowa, Marion, IA; [EFT] Xavier High School Foundation, Cedar Rapids, IA
O'Connor, Rev. Dennis, '98 (SD) Retired.
O'Connor, Rev. Msgr. Desmond, '80 (NY) Curia: Leadership St. Joseph, Kingston, NY
O'Connor, Rev. Edward D., *C.S.C.* '48 (FTW) [MIS] Holy Cross House, Notre Dame, IN
O'Connor, Rev. Francis, '62 (ALB) Blessed Sacrament, Albany, NY
O'Connor, Rev. Francis, (BO) [MON] Campion Health & Wellness, Inc., Weston, MA
O'Connor, Rev. Frank, '62 (ALB) Retired.
O'Connor, Rev. Msgr. Fred P., '52 (GAL) Retired.
O'Connor, Rev. Gerald V., *S.J.* '76 (WDC) Gonzaga College High School, Washington, DC
O'Connor, Rev. Msgr. Gerard, (P) Cathedral of the Immaculate Conception, Portland, OR
O'Connor, Msgr. Gerard, (P) Curia: Offices and Directors
O'Connor, Rev. Msgr. Gerard P., (FR) On Duty Outside Diocese. Ofc Divine Worship, Archdiocese of Portland, c/o St Rose of...
O'Connor, Rev. James, '82 (WH) St. Brendan, Elkins, WV; St. Patrick, Coalton, WV; [CAM] Alderson-Broaddus College Newman Center, Philippi, WV
O'Connor, Rev. Msgr. James, '70 (LUB) Retired.
O'Connor, Rev. James C., '71 (BUF) Retired. St. Andrew, Sloan, NY
O'Connor, Rev. Javier, *DCJM* (DEN) St. Mary Catholic Parish in Littleton, Littleton, CO; [MON] Disciples of the Hearts of Jesus and Mary, Littleton, CO
O'Connor, Rev. Msgr. Jay, '74 (BAL) Curia: Leadership St. Ursula, Baltimore, MD
O'Connor, Rev. Canon John, '16 (RCK) St. Mary Oratory, Rockford, IL
O'Connor, Rev. John F., *O.F.M.* '73 (ARL) St. Francis of Assisi, Triangle, VA
O'Connor, Rev. John H., (PAT) Retired.
O'Connor, Rev. Msgr. John Philip, '61 (NEW) Retired.
O'Connor, Rev. Joseph, '05 (SY) Curia: Leadership; Offices and Directors St. Elizabeth Ann Seton, Baldwinsville, NY
O'Connor, Rev. Kent, '03 (KCK) Good Shepherd, Shawnee, KS
O'Connor, Rev. Kyle, (RIC) College of William & Mary
O'Connor, Rev. Kyle, (RIC) [CAM] Catholic Campus Ministry, College of William & Mary, Williamsburg, VA
O'Connor, Rev. Matthew J., '71 (MOB) Christ the King Parish, Daphne, Daphne, AL
O'Connor, Rev. Michael, (SD) Pastor of Saint John of the Cross Catholic Parish, Lemon Grove, a corporation sole, Lemon Grove, CA
O'Connor, Rev. Michael, '85 (AUS) On Sick Leave.
O'Connor, Rev. Michael, *O.P.* '12 (WDC) [SEM] Dominican House of Studies, Washington, DC
O'Connor, Rev. Michael D., *O.P.* '12 (PRO) [MON] St. Thomas Aquinas Priory at Providence College, Providence, RI (>WDC) [SEM] Dominican House of Studies, Washington, DC
O'Connor, Rev. Michael J., *O.S.A.* '71 (CHI) [MON] Austin Friary, Matteson, IL; [MON] St. John Stone Friary, Chicago, IL
O'Connor, Rev. Michael J., '72 (TR) Retired.
O'Connor, Rev. Michael P., '05 (BLX) Curia: Advisory Boards, Commissions, Committees, and Councils; Leadership Our Lady of the Gulf, Bay St. Louis, MS
O'Connor, Rev. Neil D., '69 (CLV) Retired.
O'Connor, Rev. Patrick C., '78 (SAG) Retired.
O'Connor, Rev. Patrick F., '22 (BO) Saint Michael the Archangel Parish, Winthrop, MA
O'Connor, Rev. Patrick J., '58 (SAC) Retired.
O'Connor, Rev. Patrick T., *O.S.F.S.* '97 (VEN) Jesus the Worker Parish in Fort Myers, Inc. (Jesus Obrero), Fort Myers, FL
O'Connor, Rev. Paul F., *O.S.B.* '70 (NY) Chap, Veterans Administration Hosp, Bronx
O'Connor, Rev. Paul F., *C.S.B.* '70 (GAL) Retired. [MON] The Basilian Fathers of Dillon House, Houston, TX
O'Connor, Rev. Pio, *O.F.M.* (GLP) Curia: Offices and Directors St. Michael, St. Michaels, AZ
O'Connor, Rev. Roc, *S.J.* (CHI) [RTR] Bellarmine Jesuit Retreat House, Inc., Barrington, IL
O'Connor, Rev. Shaun, '82 (SPR) St. Mary, Orange, MA
O'Connor, Rev. Terrence P., '01 (PIT) Mary, Mother of God, White Oak, PA
O'Connor, Rev. Thomas J., '93 (BO) [MON] Glastonbury Abbey, Hingham, MA
O'Connor, Rev. Timothy J., '75 (CLV) Nativity of Blessed Virgin Mary, South Amherst, OH; St. Joseph, Amherst, OH
O'Connor, Rev. Timothy L., *C.S.C.* '91 (FTW) [COL] University of Notre Dame Du Lac, Notre Dame, IN; [MON] Holy Cross Community, Corby Hall, University of Notre Dame, Notre Dame, IN; [NUR] Holy Cross Village at Notre Dame, Notre Dame, IN
Ocran, Rev. Joseph O., (ARL) St. Lawrence, Alexandria, VA
Ocran, Rev. Michael, '86 (MAR) Holy Rosary Church, Grand Marais, MI; Sacred Heart, Munising, MI
Ocul, Rev. Charles, *A.J.* (HBG) Chap, York Hosp Immaculate Conception of the Blessed Virgin Mary, York, PA
Ocun, Rev. Godfred, *A.J.* '96 (P) [CON] Sisters of St. Mary of Oregon, Beaverton, OR; [HOS] Providence Health & Services-Oregon (Providence St. Vincent Medical Center), Portland, OR
Odartey-Lamptey, Rev. Michael, (VIC) SS. Cyril and Methodius, Shiner, TX
Odbert, Rev. Jerome K., *S.J.* '69 (DET) [MON] Colombiere Center, Clarkston, MI
Oddo, Rev. Peter A., '61 (NEW) Retired.
O'Dell, Rev. Kevin, '00 (SFS) Saint Therese Parish of Minnehaha County, Sioux Falls, SD; [EFT] Little Flower of Jesus School Foundation, Inc., Sioux Falls, SD
O'Dell, Rev. Paul, (SFR) Our Lady of the Wayside, Portola Valley, CA
O'Dell, Rev. W. Paul, '93 (SFR) St. Denis, Menlo Park, CA
Odermann, Rev. Valerian, *O.S.B.* '73 (BIS) [MON] Assumption Abbey, Richardton, ND
Odey, Rev. Thomas E., (TOL) Retired.
Odien, Rev. Terry M., '73 (CAM) Retired.
Odikanoro, Rev. Vincent, '83 (NY) Chap, Bon Secours Cmty Hosp, Port Jervis
Odima, Rev. Anthony Reginald, '18 (SAN) On Special Assignment.
Odima, Rev. Reginald Anthony, (SAN) Curia: Advisory Boards, Commissions, Committees, and Councils
Odinukwe, Rev. Solomon Obiechina, (RVC) St. Aidan's Church, Williston Park, NY
Odinwankpa, Rev. Fausta, (MEM) St. John's, Memphis, TN
Odiong, Rev. Anthony, '93 (NO) St. Anthony of Padua, Luling, LA
Odoemenam, Rev. Vincent, *SDV* (BRK) St. Clement Pope, South Ozone Park, NY
Odoguje, Rev. Mark Alewo, *SVD* (LAF) St. Theresa, Crowley, LA
Odoh, Rev. Malachy E., '01 (NEW) Chap (Adjunct), Saint Barnabas Med Ctr, Livingston
O'Doherty, Rev. Gerard, *S.V.D.* '74 (CHI) Retired. [MON] Divine Word Residence, Techny, IL
O'Doherty, Rev. Msgr. Jude, '65 (MIA) Retired.
O'Doherty, Rev. Kevin, *C.M.M.* '62 (DET) [MON] Mariannhill Mission Society, Dearborn Heights, MI
O'Doherty, Rev. Liam, *OSA* (ALB) St. Mary of the Assumption, Waterford, NY
O'Doherty, Rev. Liam T., *O.S.A.* '76 (PH) (>ALB) St. Augustine, Lansingburgh, NY
O'Doherty, Rev. Patrick J., '70 (ORL) Queen of Peace, Ocala, FL
O'Donald, Rev. Thomas D., '16 (PH) Epiphany of Our Lord, Plymouth Meeting, PA
O'Donnell, Rev. Brian, *S.J.* (BAL) St. Alphonsus Rodriguez, Woodstock, MD
O'Donnell, Rev. Brian J., '09 (BUR) On Special Assignment. St Philip Neri Latin Mass Chaplaincy, South Burlington
O'Donnell, Rev. Dennis, '83 (GR) Retired.
O'Donnell, Rev. Dennis J.W., '74 (PH) Retired. On Special Assignment. Holy Redeemer Wellness Center, Huntingdon Valley [CON] Sisters of the Redeemer - Redeemer Community (Province Center), Meadowbrook, PA
O'Donnell, Rev. Edmond Ned, '64 (SB) Retired.
O'Donnell, Rev. Edward, *S.J.* (BAL) Retired.
O'Donnell, Rev. Msgr. Edward D., '54 (NY) Retired.
O'Donnell, Rev. Edward T., *S.J.* '74 (PH) [MON] Jesuit Community at St. Joseph's University, Merion Station, PA
O'Donnell, Rev. Msgr. Eugene P., '73 (SJ) Retired.
O'Donnell, Rev. Gabriel, *O.P.* '70 (WDC) St. Dominic Church & Priory, Washington, DC; [SEM] Dominican House of Studies, Washington, DC
O'Donnell, Rev. Msgr. Hugh A., '54 (NEW) Retired.
O'Donnell, Rev. Hugh F, *CM* (CHI) [MON] DePaul Vincentian Residence, Chicago, IL
O'Donnell, Rev. James, *O.S.B.* '52 (PAT) Retired. [MON] St. Mary's Abbey, Morristown, NJ
O'Donnell, Rev. James P., '56 (CLV) Retired. [MIS] Community of Little Brothers and Sisters of the Eucharist, Inc., Cleveland, OH
O'Donnell, Rev. John, *O.S.B.* '98 (BIR) [MON] St. Bernard Abbey, Cullman, AL
O'Donnell, Rev. John, '72 (DUL) Retired.
O'Donnell, Rev. Joseph P., '76 (CLV) Our Lady of Mount Carmel, Wickliffe, OH
O'Donnell, Rev. Mark D., '85 (NOR) Curia: Leadership; Offices and Directors Our Lady of Grace, New London, CT; St. Brendan the Navigator Parish, New London, CT
O'Donnell, Rev. Matthew, '95 (STO) Curia: Leadership St. Mary of the Annunciation Church (Pastor of), Oakdale, CA
O'Donnell, Rev. Matthew, '12 (CHI) Curia: Leadership St. Moses the Black Parish, Chicago, IL
O'Donnell, Rev. Paul, '93 (LA) Retired. On Duty Outside Diocese. Pastor of St. Mark Church in Boise, ID (>B) St. Mark's, Boise, ID
O'Donnell, Rev. Paul J., '02 (PH) Archbishop Wood Catholic High School, Warminster, PA; St. Monica, Berwyn, PA
O'Donnell, Rev. Peter, '10 (SAL) Curia: Tribunal St. Andrew Parish, Abilene, Inc., Abilene, KS; St. Michael Parish, Chapman, Inc., Chapman, KS
O'Donnell, Rev. Msgr. Peter C., '58 (NY) Retired. [MON] John Cardinal O'Connor Residence, Bronx, NY
O'Donnell, Rev. Ralph B., '97 (OM) Curia: Leadership; Offices and Directors St. Margaret Mary, Omaha, NE
O'Donnell, Rev. Robert J., *CSP* '74 (KNX) Retired. Saint John XXIII University Parish/Catholic Center, Knoxville, TN; [CAM] UT-Knoxville, Newman Foundation, Inc., Knoxville, TN; [MON] Paulist Fathers (Missionary Society of St. Paul the Apostle), Knoxville, TN
O'Donnell, Rev. Thomas M., '61 (HEL) Retired.
O'Donnell, Rev. Thomas V., '67 (CLV) Retired.
O'Donnell, Rev. Walter, *S.T.* '55 (WDC) [MON] Father Judge Missionary Cenacle, Adelphi, MD
O'Donnell, Rev. William, *O.M.I.* '70 (BO) [NUR] Immaculate Heart of Mary Residence, Tewksbury, MA
O'Donnell, Rev. William, *C.PP.S.* '77 (CIN) Retired.
O'Donnell, Rev. William, *C.PP.S* '77 (CLV) St. Augustine, Cleveland, OH
O'Donnell, Rev. William, '22 (FR) St. Mary's, South Dartmouth, MA
O'Donnell, Rev. William J., '66 (NO) Retired.
O'Donoghue, Rev. Neil Xavier, '00 (NEW) On Duty Outside Diocese. Holy Redeemer Parochial House, Dundalk
O'Donoghue, Rev. Patrick, '61 (BIR) Retired.
O'Donohue, Rev. John M., '00 (ARL) Holy Spirit, Annandale, VA
O'Donohue, Rev. Neville, (SAT) Holy Rosary, San

Antonio, TX; [MON] Holy Rosary Marianist Community, San Antonio, TX
O'Donovan, Rev. Msgr. Dennis, '69 (P) Retired.
O'Donovan, Rev. Leo J., *S.J.* '66 (NY) [MON] America; Residence and Publication Office of the America Press, New York, NY; [MON] Murray-Weigel Hall (A Jesuit Community at Murray-Weigel Hall and Kohlmann Hall), Bronx, NY
O'Donovan, Rev. Martin E., '78 (CHI) Curia: Leadership SS. Faith, Hope and Charity, Winnetka, IL
O'Donovan, Rev. Patrick G., '72 (PAT) Notre Dame of Mt. Carmel, Cedar Knolls, NJ
Odorizzi, Rev. Thomas A., *C.O.* '92 (MET) Curia: Family Life The Catholic Church of St. Ann, Raritan, NJ; [MON] The Raritan Congregation of the Oratory of St. Philip Neri, Raritan, NJ
O'Dowd, Rev. Francis, '01 (TYL) Curia: Deaneries Our Lady Queen of Angels, Overton, TX; St. Theresa of the Infant Jesus, Gladewater, TX
Odozor, Rev. Paulinus I., *C.S.Sp.* (FTW) [COL] University of Notre Dame Du Lac, Notre Dame, IN
O'Driscoll, Rev. James, (BO) Holy Family Parish, Rockland, MA
O'Duill, Rev. Fergal, *L.C.* (DAL) [MON] Legionaries of Christ, Irving, TX
Oduor, Rev. John Leo, '21 (SY) Christ the Good Shepherd, Oswego, NY
Oduro, Rev. Charles Akoto, '89 (BRK) On Leave. [CCH] Ghanaian Ministry, ,
O'Dwyer, Rev. Dominick, '66 (MIA) Retired.
O'Dwyer, Rev. Michael, *S.A.C.* '61 (LUB) Retired.
O'Dwyer, Rev. Ronald R., *S.J.* '15 (STL) [COL] Saint Louis University, St. Louis, MO; [MON] Jesuit Community Corporation at Saint Louis University - Jesuit Hall, St. Louis, MO
O'Dwyer, Rev. Thomas, '70 (MIA) Retired.
Oen, Rev. Edward, (CIN) [MON] St. Charles, Celina, OH
Oenbrink, Rev. Michael J., '99 (CHR) Curia: Offices and Directors St. Francis By the Sea, Hilton Head Island, SC
Oestreich, Rev. Brian W., '93 (NU) Holy Rosary, Graceville, MN; St. John, Ortonville, MN; St. Joseph, Bellingham, MN; St. Michael, Madison, MN
Oetjen, Rev. Steven G., (ARL) St. Agnes, Arlington, VA
Ofalsa, Rev. Rheo, (HON) Curia: Consultative Bodies Holy Family, Honolulu, HI
O'Farrell, Rev. John F., (ARL) St. Theresa, Ashburn, VA
O'Farrell, Rev. John V., '02 (RVC) Retired. Our Lady of Victory, Floral Park, NY
Offia, Rev. Francis, '16 (NO) St. Bonaventure Roman Catholic Church, Avondale, Louisiana, Avondale, LA
Offiong, Rev. Cyril, *SDV* (MET) St. Cecelia, Iselin, NJ
Offiong, Rev. Emmanuel, (DM) St. Catherine of Siena Catholic Student Center, Des Moines, IA; [MIS] City Hospital Chaplaincy Service, Des Moines, IA
Offor, Rev. John, (SJ) St. Victor, San Jose, CA
Offor, Rev. Oliver, '73 (NY) Parish of Our Lady of Perpetual Help and St. Catharine, Pelham Manor, NY
Offutt, Rev. Msgr. Bradley S., '86 (KC) Visitation of the Blessed Virgin Mary, Kansas City, MO
O'Flaherty, Rev. Michael, '75 (PMB) Retired.
O'Flanagan, Rev. Thomas P., '95 (PMB) Curia: (>MO) Offices and Directors
O'Flynn, Rev. Seamus, '59 (STA) Retired.
Ofodum, Rev. Anselm I., '95 (LAF) On Special Assignment. Chap, Our Lady of Lourdes Rgnl Med Ctr, Lafayette Our Lady of Perpetual Help, New Iberia, LA
Ofoha, Rev. Paul, *M.S.P.* (BEA) Chap, Baptist Hosp Blessed Sacrament, Beaumont, TX; [CEM] Blessed Sacrament Cemetery, Beaumont, TX
Ofomata, Rev. Valentine, (RVC) St. Anthony of Padua, East Northport, NY
Oforchukwu, Rev. Joachim, *C.S.Sp.* '90 (FTW) Chap, Memorial Hosp of South Bend, South Bend
Ofori, Rev. Maximillian, (NSH) On Special Assignment.
Ofori, Rev. Rudolf, (TUC) Saint Joseph the Worker Roman Catholic Parish - Wellton, Wellton, AZ
Ofori-Domah, Rev. John, '81 (LC) St. John the Baptist, Wilton, WI; St. Joseph, Kendall, WI; St. Patrick, Elroy, WI
Oforka, Rev. Francis I., (MO) Curia: Offices and Directors
Oganda, Rev. Joseph, '10 (BEL) St. Luke, Belleville, IL; St. Teresa of the Child Jesus, Belleville, IL
Ogar, Rev. Augustine, *M.S.P.* (GAL) St. Mary Magdalene, Humble, TX
O'Gara, Rev. Stephen R., '71 (STP) Retired.
Ogaro, Rev. Stephen Nyamweya, (SY) St. Patrick, Binghamton, NY; St. Thomas Aquinas, Binghamton, NY
Ogba, Rev. Isaac, (GLP) Curia: Offices and Directors
Ogbeifun, Rev. Daniel E., '15 (BUF) All Saints Roman Catholic Parish of Lockport, New York, Lockport, NY; St. John the Baptist Roman Catholic Congregation, Lockport, NY
Ogbemure, Rev. Raymond, '74 (OAK) St. Cornelius, Richmond, CA
Ogboe, Msgr. M. Parker, '79 (MIA) [NUR] St. Catherine's West Rehabilitation Hospital, Hialeah, FL; [NUR] Villa Maria West Skilled Nursing Facility, Hialeah, FL
Ogbonna, Rev. Christian Iheanyichukwu, '79 (ALX) St. John the Baptist, Cloutierville, LA
Ogbonna, Rev. Fredrick, (NY) (>PHX) St. Steven Roman Catholic Parish, Sun Lakes, AZ
Ogbonna, Rev. Joseph, '02 (SAN) Our Lady of Lourdes, Andrews, TX
Ogbonna, Rev. Leonard, '93 (BEA) [HOS] CHRISTUS Southeast Texas Health System - St. Elizabeth, Beaumont, TX
Ogbonna, Rev. Stanislaus, *C.S.Sp.* '73 (NY) Chap, Sullivan Corr Fac, Fallsburg; Sullivan Cty Jail St. Peter, Monticello, NY
Ogbonnaya, Rev. Emmanuel, '94 (FRS) Curia: Pastoral Services
Ogbuagu, Rev. Chidiebere, (Y) (>MIA) [HOS] Mercy Hospital, Inc., Miami, FL
Ogbuji, Rev. Kingsley, *S.S.J.* (NO) Corpus Christi-Epiphany, New Orleans, LA
Ogbuji, Rev. Kingsley, *S.S.J.* '18 (WDC) Our Lady of Perpetual Help, Washington, DC
Ogden, Rev. Edward F., *O.S.F.S.* '13 (WIL) Curia: Deaneries St. Margaret of Scotland, Newark, DE
Ogg, Rev. Thomas, '68 (CHY) Retired.
Oggero, Rev. Roy Joseph, *C.S.B.* '61 (GAL) Retired. [MON] The Basilian Fathers of Dillon House, Houston, TX
Oghenerukevwe, Rev. Daniel, '08 (TYL) [HOS] CHRISTUS Trinity Mother Frances Health System, Tyler, TX
Ogle, Rev. Msgr. Sean G., '77 (BRK) Curia: Consultative Bodies; Leadership; Pastoral Services Co-Cathedral of Saint Joseph – Saint Teresa of Avila, Brooklyn, NY
Ogonwa, Rev. Stephen, '01 (ORL) Immaculate Heart of Mary, Ocala, FL
Ogorevc, Rev. Metod, *O.F.M.* '92 (CHI) Slovenian Catholic Mission, Lemont, IL; [MON] The Slovene Franciscan Fathers, Order of Friars Minor, Commissariat of the Holy Cross, Lemont, IL; [RTR] St. Mary's Retreat House, Lemont, IL
O'Gorman, Rev. Eamon, (ORG) Retired. St. Joseph, Placentia, CA
O'Gorman, Rev. Eamon T., '67 (ORG) Retired.
O'Gorman, Rev. Msgr. Michael B., '64 (SAT) Retired.
O'Grady, Rev. Dennis R., '61 (CLV) Retired. St. Michael the Archangel, Cleveland, OH; [CCH] St. Michael, Cleveland, OH
O'Grady, Rev. Frank, (PAT) Retired.
O'Grady, Rev. John F., '66 (ALB) Retired.
O'Grady, Rev. Msgr. Robert A., '72 (HRT) Retired.
O'Grady, Rev. Robert M., '78 (BO) Curia: Communications
Ogrodowski, Rev. Msgr. William M., '75 (PIT) [MON] St. John Vianney Manor, Pittsburgh, PA
Ogrowdowski, Rev. Msgr. William M., (PIT) Retired.
Ogu, Rev. Cyriacus, (SB) St. Andrew Newman Center, Riverside, CA; [CAM] St. Andrew Newman Center, Riverside, CA
O'Guinn, Rev. Jon, '93 (BEL) On Leave.
Ogumelo, Rev. Bartholomew, (MAN) Ste. Marie, Manchester, NH
Ogumere, Rev. Augustine, *C.S.Sp.* '87 (PHX) Our Lady of Lourdes Roman Catholic Parish, Sun City West, AZ
Ogumoro, Rev. Isidro T., '89 (CHK) Curia: Faith Formation San Roque Parish, Saipan, MP
Ogwuegbu, Rev. Nelson, *S.M.M.M.* '01 (MO) Curia: Offices and Directors
Ogwuegbu, Rev. Nelson, '01 (NO) On Duty Outside Diocese. Archdiocese of the Military Services
Oh, Rev. Justin, '20 (LA) St. Gertrude, Bell Gardens, CA
Oh, Rev. Paul Saewan, '83 (OM) Retired. St. Andrew Kim Taegon Catholic Community, Omaha, NE
Oh, Rev. Seungsoo, (DET) St. Andrew Kim (Korean) Parish Northville, Northville, MI
O'Hala, Rev. Steven, '88 (MIA) Saint David, Davie, FL
O'Hallaran, Rev. John, *S.S.J.* '85 (BAL) Retired.
O'Halloran, Rev. Edward P., '78 (NY) St. John and St. Mary, Chappaqua, NY; St. Joseph, New Rochelle, NY
O'Halloran, Rev. Nathan, *S.J.* (NO) [COL] Loyola University New Orleans, New Orleans, LA; [MON] Loyola Jesuit Community, New Orleans, LA
Ohanaka, Rev. Nonso, (NSH) Our Lady of the Lake, Hendersonville, TN
Ohanga, Rev. Benedict Oduor, *MHM* '15 (NY) [MON] Mill Hill Fathers Residence, Hartsdale, NY
O'Hanlon, Rev. Brian, (BO) Sacred Heart, Lynn, MA; Saint Mary of the Sacred Heart Parish, Lynn, MA; St. Mary, Lynn, MA
O'Hanlon, Rev. Michael A., '57 (GF) Retired.
O'Hara, Rev. Charles R., '70 (PH) St. Joseph, Spring City, PA
O'Hara, Rev. Daniel J., '87 (SY) Epiphany Parish, Liverpool, NY; Immaculate Heart of Mary, Liverpool, NY; St. Joseph the Worker, Liverpool, NY
O'Hara, Rev. Emmet, *S.A.C* '02 (FWT) St. Stephen, Weatherford, TX (>DET) [MON] Society of the Catholic Apostolate (Pallottine Fathers), Wyandotte, MI
O'Hara, Rev. Eugene, *OFM Cap* (NY) Retired. [MON] St. Clare Friary (Capuchin Franciscan Friars, Province of St. Mary), Yonkers, NY
O'Hara, Rev. Francis W., '59 (PRO) Retired.
O'Hara, Rev. John, '71 (PRT) Retired.
O'Hara, Rev. Joseph M., '01 (LC) On Leave.
O'Hara, Rev. Michael, *O.M.I.* '76 (BO) St. Mary, Georgetown, MA
O'Hara, Rev. Michael D., '60 (BUF) Retired.
O'Hara, Rev. Thomas J., *C.S.C.* '78 (FTW) (>SCR) [COL] King's College, Wilkes-Barre, PA
O'Hare, Rev. Daniel G., *S.J.* '79 (NY) Retired. [MON] St. Ignatius Loyola Residence, New York, NY
O'Hare, Rev. Daniel M., '65 (NY) Church of the Assumption, Maybrook, NY
O'Hare, Rev. Keith M., '02 (ARL) St. Louis, Alexandria, VA
O'Hare, Rev. Robert V., *S.J.* '95 (NEW) [MIS] Jesuit Community, Jersey City, NJ; [MON] Jesuits of Saint Peter College, Inc., Jersey City, NJ
O'Hearn, Rev. Michael J., '95 (FR) [NUR] Catholic Memorial Home Inc., Fall River, MA
O'Hern, Rev. Mark, '02 (E) Sacred Heart, Erie, PA; St. Andrew, Erie, PA; St. Paul, Erie, PA
Ohlig, Rev. John M., '95 (LUB) St. Anthony's, Brownfield, TX
Ohm, Rev. Edward U., '92 (PEO) St. Mary's, Champaign, IL; [HOS] OSF HealthCare Heart of Mary Medical Center (Presence Central and Suburban Hospitals Network), Urbana, IL
Ohmann, Rev. Daniel, *M.M.* '55 (NY) Retired. [MON] Maryknoll Fathers and Brothers (Catholic Foreign Mission Society of America, Inc.), Ossining, NY
Ohner, Rev. John M., *O.S.A.* '74 (JOL) St. Jude, New Lenox, IL
Ohno, Rev. Ignatius, (SJ) [MON] USA West Province, Society of Jesus, Los Gatos, CA
Ohno, Rev. Ignatius F., *S.J.* '92 (SEA) [COL] Seattle University, Seattle, WA; [MON] Arrupe Jesuit Community at Seattle University, Seattle, WA
O'Hotto, Rev. Kenneth L., '80 (STP) St. Mary, Waverly, MN; [CEM] St. Mary Cemetery, Waverly, MN
Ohuche, Rev. Evaristus C., '02 (NY) St. Catherine of Genoa, New York, NY
Oiland, Rev. Kevin, '09 (SPK) St. John Vianney, Spokane Valley, WA; St. Paschal, Spokane Valley, WA
Ojachor, Rev. Alex G., '96 (CHI) St. Pius X and St. Leonard Parish, Berwyn, IL
Ojeda, Rev. Francisco, '21 (ORL) St. John Vianney, Orlando, FL
Ojedeji, Rev. Patrick, '00 (BIS) St. John the Baptist, Portal, ND; St. Luke, Noonan, ND; St. Patrick, Crosby, ND
Oji, Rev. Joseph Kalu, *C.S.Sp.* '95 (R) St. Michael the Archangel Catholic Church, Cary, NC
Ojike, Rev. Celestine, '96 (SFE) Sangre de Cristo, Albuquerque, NM
Ojomah, Rev. Elias A., (BO) Sacred Heart, Boston, MA
Ojuok, Rev. John Kennedy, '21 (OG) Holy Cross Parish, Plattsburgh, NY
Okafor, Rev. Chinedu Daniel, '17 (NO) St. Peter, Covington, LA
Okafor, Rev. Gabriel, (MRY) St. Timothy, Morro Bay, CA
Okafor, Rev. Gabriel, '99 (DEN) [HOS] Saint Joseph Hospital, Denver, CO
Okafor, Rev. Gregory, '88 (TUC) Immaculate Conception & Guadalupe Missions Roman Catholic Parish & Guadalupe Mission - Yuma, Yuma, AZ
Okafor, Rev. James, '02 (SJ) Curia: Leadership; Offices and Directors St. Frances Cabrini, San Jose, CA
Okafor, Rev. Jude, '96 (SAC) Chap, California State Prison, Solano, Vacaville
Okafor, Rev. Kevin C, '20 (PH) St. Katherine of Siena, Philadelphia, PA
Okafor, Rev. Michael, *S.M.M.M.* (SB) St. Joseph,

Barstow, CA; St. Philip Neri (Lenwood), Barstow, CA

Okafor, Rev. Theophine, (LSC) Curia: Leadership St. Genevieve Parish, Inc., Las Cruces, NM

Okagbue, Rev. Ikenna, '17 (BRK) Mary Queen of Heaven, Brooklyn, NY

Okajima, Rev. Peter, '20 (BRK) Our Lady of the Snows, Floral Park, NY

O'Kane, Rev. John, '04 (ALB) Blessed Sacrament, Bolton Landing, NY; Parish of St. Isaac Jogues, Chestertown, NY; St. James, North Creek, NY

O'Kane, Rev. John J., '08 (MET) Immaculate Conception, Spotswood, NJ

Okapal, Rev. Maximilian C., *O.Praem.* '12 (ORG) [MON] Norbertine Fathers of Orange, Inc., Silverado, CA; [SEM] St. Michael's Norbertine Postulancy, Novitiate and Juniorate, Silverado, CA

Okarma, Rev. Grzegorz, *CSMA* (SJN) Nuestra Senora de Lourdes, San Juan, PR

Okarma, Rev. Grzegorz, *C.S.M.A.* (SJN) Epifania del Senor, Carolina, PR

Okata, Rev. Michael, (MEM) St. Louis, Memphis, TN

Okeahialam, Very Rev. Timothy, '02 (PBL) Curia: Leadership; Offices and Directors Most Holy Trinity, Trinidad, CO

Okeahialam, Rev. Uju Patrick, *C.S.Sp.* (BAL) New All Saints, Baltimore, MD; St. Edward, Baltimore, MD; St. Gregory the Great, Baltimore, MD

Okechukwu, Rev. Michael, *S.S.J.* '11 (LA) St. Brigid, Los Angeles, CA

O'Keefe, Rev. Daniel Paul, *O.S.B.* '93 (GBG) [MON] Saint Vincent Archabbey, Latrobe, PA

O'Keefe, Rev. E. Joseph, *S.J.* '13 (P) (>SJ) [MON] Sacred Heart Jesuit Center, Los Gatos, CA

O'Keefe, Rev. J. Kevin, '95 (ARL) Saint Jude, Fredericksburg, VA

O'Keefe, Very Rev. Joseph, *S.J.* '86 (NY) [MIS] Jesuit Seminary and Mission Bureau, Inc., New York, NY; [MIS] The Jesuit Collaborative, New York, NY; [MON] Society of Jesus, New York Province, New York, NY; [MON] St. Ignatius Loyola Residence, New York, NY; [MON] The Society of Jesus of New England, New York, NY; [MON] USA East Province of the Society of Jesus, Inc., New York, NY; [MON] USA Northeast Province of the Society of Jesus, Inc., New York, NY

O'Keefe, Very Rev. Kevin, '13 (SAV) Curia: Offices and Directors Sacred Heart of Jesus, Savannah, GA

O'Keefe, Rev. Lawrence, '70 (GLP) Retired.

O'Keefe, Rev. Lawrence, (PHX) Christ the King Roman Catholic Parish, Mesa, AZ

O'Keefe, Rev. Mark, *O.S.B.* '83 (IND) [MON] St. Meinrad Archabbey, St. Meinrad, IN

O'Keefe, Rev. Patrick T., '96 (BUF) On Leave. St. Andrew, Kenmore, NY

O'Keefe, Rev. Msgr. William Joseph, '59 (LA) Retired.

O'Keeffe, Rev. Dennis J., '84 (LFT) Cathedral of St. Mary of the Immaculate Conception, Lafayette, IN; St. Ann, Lafayette, IN

O'Keeffe, Rev. Donal, *LC* (LA) [MON] Legionaries of Christ, Pasadena, CA

O'Keeffe, Rev. Jeremiah E., '66 (LA) Retired. Our Lady of Lourdes, Northridge, CA

O'Keeffe, Rev. Michael, '68 (SAV) Retired.

Okeiyi, Rev. Athanasius, (AUS) On Special Assignment.

Okeiyi, Rev. Emmanuel, *C.C.C.E.* (MO) Curia: Offices and Directors

Okeke, Rev. Chimezie Patrick, (FRS) Chap, Clovis Cmty Med Ctr

Okeke, Rev. Chimezie Patrick, '07 (FRS) Our Lady of Perpetual Help, Clovis, CA

Okeke, Rev. Cornelius, '93 (DET) St. André Bessette Parish Ecorse, Ecorse, MI

Okeke, Rev. Stephen, '96 (NY) Chap, NY Univ Med Ctr, New York; Hosp for Joint Disease

O'Kelly, Rev. P. Colm, '64 (SAC) Retired.

Okeny, Rev. Mark, (PHX) St. Helen Roman Catholic Parish, Glendale, AZ

Okeoma, Rev. Jude, (OWN) SS. Peter and Paul, Hopkinsville, KY

Okere, Rev. Bartholomew, '90 (KNX) St. Henry, Rogersville, TN; St. James the Apostle, Sneedville, TN

Okere, Rev. Cornelius A, '03 (GLP) Cathedral of the Sacred Heart, Gallup, NM

Okere, Rev. Cyprian, (GLP) Our Lady of Guadalupe, Holbrook, AZ; St. Joseph's Indian Mission, Keams Canyon, AZ

Okere, Rev. Erasmus, (NEW) Curia: Offices and Directors Blessed Sacrament-St. Charles Borromeo, Newark, NJ

Okere, Rev. Michael C., '91 (CHR) Curia: Offices and Directors Saint Martin de Porres, Columbia, SC

Okere, Rev. Remigius C., *C.S.Sp.* '94 (DM) St. John, Adel, IA

Okeyikam, Rev. Faustinus, *MSP* (LAV) St. Bridget Roman Catholic Church, Las Vegas, NV

Okhifo, Rev. Innocent, (GAL) St. Elizabeth Ann Seton, Houston, TX

Okhuoya, Rev. Kizito R., '96 (OM) Curia: (>MO) Offices and Directors

Okih, Rev. Peter Francis, *C.S.Sp.* (FAJ) Curia: Leadership

Okiria, Rev. Richard, (NOR) Chap, Connecticut Valley Hosp, Middletown

Okiria, Rev. Richard, (HRT) Retired.

Okitakatshi, Rev. Laurent, '17 (SPC) Cathedral of St. Mary of the Annunciation, Cape Girardeau, MO; [CAM] Catholic Campus Ministry Southeast Missouri State University, Newman Center, Cape Girardeau, MO

Okochi, Rev. Chux, '88 (NY) Chap, Dir Pastoral Svcs, Calvary Hosp, Bronx [HOS] Calvary Hospital, Bronx, NY

Okochi, Rev. Chux, '88 (RVC) St. Pius X, Plainview, NY

Okoh, Rev. Philemon, (MO) Curia: Offices and Directors

Okoh, Rev. Sylvester, '08 (DM) Sacred Heart, Bedford, IA; St. Clare, Clarinda, IA; St. Joseph, Villisca, IA

Okojie, Rev. Julius, '09 (FTW) St. Therese, Little Flower (Little Flower Catholic Church), South Bend, IN

Okojie, Rev. Peter, '18 (SP) St. Paul, Tampa, FL

Okola, Rev. Peter, *AJ* '98 (PEO) Holy Trinity, Bloomington, IL; St. Patrick, Bloomington, IL

Okoli, Rev. Christopher, '92 (BUF) St. Lawrence, Buffalo, NY

Okoli, Very Rev. Eugene, '93 (DAL) Curia: Administration Holy Spirit Catholic Parish, Duncanville, TX

Okoli, Rev. Francis, '00 (NY) Chap, Bellevue Hosp, New York Curia: (>MO) Offices and Directors St. Columba, New York, NY

Okoli, Rev. Gerald C., '10 (GLD) Saint Patrick of Traverse City, Traverse City, MI

Okoli, Rev. Jovita, '96 (DAL) All Saints Catholic Parish, Dallas, TX

Okolo, Rev. Anthony, (RVC) Our Lady of Peace, Lynbrook, NY

Okolo, Rev. Anthony O., *C.S.Sp.* '03 (PHX) Curia: Leadership; Offices and Directors Our Lady of the Lake Roman Catholic Parish, Lake Havasu City, AZ

Okon, Rev. Alan J., '98 (PH) St. Francis de Sales, Lenni, PA

Okondu-Ugba, Rev. Alexander Chukwuemeka, '06 (LA) Holy Family, Glendale, CA

Okonkwo, Rev. Bartholomew I., '98 (MAN) St. Mary Church, Newmarket, NH; St. Michael Parish, Exeter, NH

Okonkwo, Rev. Charles Osita, (RVC) Mary Immaculate, Bellport, NY

Okonkwo, Rev. Emmanuel, (RVC) Our Lady of Perpetual Help, Lindenhurst, NY

Okonkwo, Rev. Jovita, '97 (TLS) St. John, McAlester, OK

Okonkwo, Rev. Jude, '06 (FRS)

Okonkwo, Rev. Jude M., '03 (LSC) Curia: Leadership St. Joseph Parish, Lordsburg, Inc., Lordsburg, NM

Okonkwo, Rev. Marcel, '07 (LSC) Curia: Leadership St. Jude Parish, Inc., Alamogordo, NM

Okonkwo, Rev. Martin, (LSC) Our Lady of Fatima Parish, Inc., Bayard, NM

Okonkwo, Rev. Peter, '09 (LSC) Hospital chaplain St. Genevieve Parish, Inc., Las Cruces, NM

Okonma, Rev. Houston Ekene, '21 (GAL) St. Vincent de Paul, Houston, TX

Okonski, Rev. Joseph F., '90 (PH) Curia: Advisory Boards, Commissions, Committees, and Councils St. Athanasius, Philadelphia, PA

O'Konsky, Rev. Stanley J., *S.J.* '72 (NY) Fordham Preparatory School, Bronx, NY; [MON] Jesuit Community at Fordham University, New York, NY

Okorie, Rev. Onyema, '99 (FRS) On Duty Outside Diocese. Curia: (>MO) Offices and Directors

Okoro, Rev. Bonaventure, '02 (RCK) St. James, Lee, IL

Okoro, Rev. Bonaventure Chukwunomso, '20 (FRS) Catholic Community of St. Jude and Our Lady of the Assumption, Easton, CA

Okoro, Rev. Cyriacus, (SB) Chap, Kaiser Permanente, Riverside

Okoro, Rev. Franklin O., (WIN) Chap, Mayo Clinic, Rochester

Okoro, Rev. George, '94 (STO) On Special Assignment. St. Joseph Catholic Hosp St. Mary of the Assumption Church (Pastor of), Stockton, CA

Okoro, Rev. John, '95 (OWN) St. Ambrose, Morganfield, KY; St. William, Marion, KY

Okoro, Rev. John C., '95 (OWN) St. Francis Borgia, Sturgis, KY

Okoro, Rev. Martin, (MO) Curia: Offices and Directors

Okoro, Rev. Martin, (SP) St. Patrick, Largo, FL

Okoroafor, Rev. Augustine, '90 (BGP) Chap, Bridgeport Hosp

Okoroanyanwu, Rev. Julian Chikezie, '02 (SB) St. Elizabeth Ann Seton, Ontario, CA

Okoroichi, Rev. Chinonso, (SFR) Our Lady of Lourdes, San Francisco, CA

Okoroichi, Rev. Chinonso, (SFR) St. Paul of the Shipwreck, San Francisco, CA

Okoroji, Rev. Callistus, '02 (JC) Queen of Peace, Ewing, MO; St. Joseph, Canton, MO

Okoroji, Rev. Ignatius, *SDV* '04 (PAT) [RTR] Sanctuary of Mary-Our Lady of the Holy Spirit (Vocationist Fathers), Branchville, NJ

Okoroji, Rev. Ignatius, *SDV* '04 (PAT) [MON] Father Justin Vocationary (Vocationist Fathers), Florham Park, NJ; [RTR] Vocationist Fathers Retreat Center, Florham Park, NJ

Okoroudo, Rev. Kenneth I., (SB) St. Anthony, Upland, CA

Okorougo, Rev. Charles, '87 (LKC) Our Lady Queen of Heaven, Lake Charles, LA; [HOS] CHRISTUS Health Southwestern Louisiana, Lake Charles, LA

Okot, Rev. William, *A.J.* '99 (PHX) St. James Roman Catholic Parish, Glendale, AZ

Okoth, Rev. Crispin, '90 (SEA) St. John the Evangelist, Seattle, WA

Okoth, Rev. George, '89 (MO) Curia: Offices and Directors

Okoye, Rev. Charles, '92 (RVC) St. Patrick, Smithtown, NY

Okoye, Rev. Charles, (RVC) Chap, Stony Brook Univ Hosp

Okoye, Rev. Emmanuel O., (LSC) Immaculate Conception Parish, Alamogordo, Inc., Alamogordo, NM

Okoye, Rev. Ignatius, *OFM Cap.* '17 (BAL) St. Ambrose, Baltimore, MD; [MON] St. Ambrose Friary, Baltimore, MD

Okoye, Rev. James C., (PIT) [COL] Duquesne University of the Holy Spirit, Pittsburgh, PA

Okoye, Rev. Jude, (BAL) St. John, Westminster, MD; St. Joseph, Taneytown, MD

Okoye, Rev. Luke, '01 (FTW) St. Elizabeth Ann Seton, Fort Wayne, IN

Okoye, Rev. Sebastine, '13 (GAL) St. Mary: Star of the Sea, Freeport, TX

Okpala, Rev. Paulinus Chikelue, '01 (SAV) St. Theresa, Cordele, GA

Okpalauwaekwe, Rev. Emmanuel, '91 (NY) Chap, Harlem Hosp, New York Cardinal Hayes High School, Bronx, NY

Okpara, Rev. Benson Claret, '91 (Y) Curia: Leadership St. Michael the Archangel, Canton, OH

Okpara, Rev. Theophilus, '96 (BO) Saint Matthew the Evangelist Parish, Billerica, MA; St. Andrew, Billerica, MA

Okpara, Rev. Theophilus T., (MO) Curia: Offices and Directors

Okpogba, Rev. Desmond, '89 (TLS) Church of the Madalene, Tulsa, OK

Okpu, Rev. Edward, '11 (SFE) Our Lady of Fatima, Albuquerque, NM

Okuhara, Friar Hajime, *O.F.M.* (TUC) [MON] Filial Houses, Elfrida, AZ

Okum, Rev. Anthony, *S.S.J.* (NO) [MIS] The Josephite Faculty House of St. Augustine High School, ,

Okumu, Rev. Richard U., '81 (DAV) St. Mary Church of Mechanicsville, Iowa, Mechanicsville, IA; St. Mary Church of Tipton, Iowa, Tipton, IA

Okumu, Rev. Stephen, '86 (SEA) St. Thomas More, Lynnwood, WA

Okure, Rev. Athanasius, (FRS) St. Ann, Riverdale, CA

Okure, Rev. Athanasius, (FRS) Shrine of Our Lady of Fatima, Laton, CA

Okwalo, Rev. Protas Opondo, *S.J.* (DM) [CAM] St. Catherine of Siena Catholic Student Center, Des Moines, IA

Okwara, Rev. Marcel, *C.Ss.R.* '07 (STP) St. Bridget, Minneapolis, MN; [MON] Redemptorist Fathers of Hennepin County, Brooklyn Center, MN

Okwaraocha, Rev. Emmanuel, (MO) Curia: Offices and Directors

Okwum, Rev. Anthony, *S.S.J.* (JKS) Holy Family, Natchez, MS; St. Anne, Fayette, MS

Okwunka, Rev. Godfrey, (CHY) [COL] Wyoming Catholic College, Lander, WY

Okwuonu, Rev. Ignatius, (RVC) Maria Regina, Seaford, NY

Okwuosa, Rev. Emeka, (NEW) Curia: Offices and Directors

Okwuzu, Rev. Augustine, *SMMM* '04 (P) [HOS]

Providence Health & Services-Oregon (Providence Portland Medical Center), Portland, OR

Olaleye, Rev. Patrick, '02 (DAL) St. Martin of Tours Catholic Parish, Forney, TX

Olamolu, Very Rev. Stephen, *V.C.* '99 (PBL) Curia: Leadership; Offices and Directors St. Anne, Pueblo, CO

Olaso, Rev. Demosthenes, (GB) St. Benedict, Suamico, WI; St. Pius, Little Suamico, WI

O'Laughlin, Rev. Msgr. Patrick J., '67 (STL) Retired.

Olayo-Mendez, Rev. Alejandro, (BO) [MON] The Jesuit Community at Boston College, Chestnut Hill, MA

Olbrys, Rev. Mariusz, '07 (BGP) St. Cecilia-St. Gabriel Parish Corporation, Stamford, CT

Olczak, Rev. Joseph, (PH) [MON] The Order of Saint Paul, First Hermit - The Pauline Fathers, Doylestown, PA

Oldenski, Rev. Kenneth E., '66 (PIT) Retired.

Oldershaw, Rev. Robert H., '62 (CHI) Retired.

Oldfield, Rev. John, *O.A.R.* '63 (NY) [SEM] Tagaste Monastery, Suffern, NY

Oldham, Rev. David A., '03 (LIN) St. Ann's, Doniphan, NE

Olds, Rev. Steven, '88 (ORL) On Duty Outside Diocese. (>PMB) [SEM] St. Vincent de Paul Regional Seminary, Boynton Beach, FL

O'Leary, Rev. Andrew, '22 (SPK) Cathedral of Our Lady of Lourdes, Spokane, WA

O'Leary, Rev. David M., '85 (BO) Good Shepherd Parish, Wayland, MA

O'Leary, Rev. Hilary, *O.S.B.* '68 (PAT) [MON] St. Mary's Abbey, Morristown, NJ

O'Leary, Rev. James E., '68 (BO) Retired.

O'Leary, Rev. James J., *S.J.* '65 (MIL) [MON] St. Camillus Jesuit Community (Society of Jesus, USA Midwest Province), Wauwatosa, WI

O'Leary, Rev. James M., *S.J.* '91 (STL) [COL] Saint Louis University, St. Louis, MO

O'Leary, Rev. James S., '61 (KAL) Retired.

O'Leary, Rev. John, '67 (MIA) Retired. Corpus Christi, Miami, FL

O'Leary, Rev. John, *S.J.* '60 (SPK) Retired.

O'Leary, Rev. John A., '78 (CAM) Retired.

O'Leary, Rev. Msgr. Kevin J., '95 (BO) Cathedral of the Holy Cross, Boston, MA

O'Leary, Rev. Matthew L., '03 (SEA) Holy Rosary, Edmonds, WA

O'Leary, Rev. Niall Finbarr, '60 (LA) Retired.

O'Leary, Rev. Patrick B., *S.J.* '61 (SJ) [MON] Sacred Heart Jesuit Center, Los Gatos, CA

O'Leary, Rev. Richard, *O.S.A.* (PH) [MON] St. Thomas Monastery, Villanova, PA

O'Leary, Rev. Sean R., '61 (SAC) Retired.

Olek, Rev. Ralph F., *S.M.* '74 (ATL) Marist School, Atlanta, GA

Oleksiak, Rev. Donald P., '89 (CLV) Curia: Advisory Boards, Commissions, Committees, and Councils; Leadership Cathedral of St. John the Evangelist, Cleveland, OH

Oleksy, Rev. Kazimierz, *S.D.S.* '92 (SAT) St. Ignatius, Christine, TX

Oleksy, Rev. Wojciech Jan, '11 (CHI) Our Lady of Hope Mission, Rosemont, IL; St. Brigid, Wadsworth, IL

Olenowski, Rev. Mark, '85 (PAT) St. Pius X, Montville, NJ

Oleru, Rev. Bernard, *MSP* (CHL) St. Therese, Mooresville, NC

Olesik, Rev. William J., '72 (NOR) St. Maurice, Bolton, CT

Olguin, Rev. Jacinto, '74 (LAR) Retired. St. Patrick, Laredo, TX

Olguin, Rev. Luis, '92 (SY) Chap, Walsh Rgnl Med Unit, Rome Historic Old St. John's Church, Utica, NY; St. Mary of Mt. Carmel/Blessed Sacrament, Utica, NY

Oligschlaeger, Very Rev. P. Gregory, '93 (JC) Curia: Deaneries Holy Rosary, Monroe City, MO; St. Stephen Catholic Church, Indian Creek, MO

Oliinyk, Rev. Roman, (PHU) St. Mary's, McAdoo, PA; St. Michael's, Hazleton, PA

Olikenyi, Rev. Gregory, *C.S.Sp.* (PIT) [COL] Duquesne University of the Holy Spirit, Pittsburgh, PA

Olikkara, Rev. Joseph, *M.S.T.* '87 (MO) Curia: Offices and Directors

Olinger, Rev. Gerard J., *CSC* (FTW) [COL] University of Notre Dame Du Lac, Notre Dame, IN; [MON] Holy Cross Community, Corby Hall, University of Notre Dame, Notre Dame, IN

Oliva, Rev. George (Max), (SPK) [MON] Regis Community, Spokane, WA

Olivares, Rev. Robinson, '21 (BRK) St. Matthias, Ridgewood, NY

Olivas, Rev. J. Alfredo, '81 (ELP) On Leave.

Olivas, Rev. Jose Abel, (LSC) St. John Parish, Inc., Roswell, NM

Olive, Rev. Rodney, *C.Ss.R.* '86 (STL) St. Alphonsus Liguori Catholic Church, St. Louis, MO; [MON] Redemptorist Fathers, St. Louis, MO

Oliveira, Rev. Derrick K., '12 (OAK) On Leave.

Oliveira, Rev. Edivaldo daSilva, '09 (AGN) On Duty Outside Diocese.

Oliveira, Rev. Gastao A., '72 (FR) Retired.

Oliveira, Rev. Msgr. John J., '67 (FR) Curia: Offices and Directors

Oliveira, Rev. John J., '77 (FR) Curia: Offices and Directors

Oliveira, Rev. Msgr. John J., '67 (FR) Retired.

Oliveira, Rev. Manoel J., '04 (NEW) St. Mary, Plainfield, NJ

Oliveira, Rev. Robert A., '77 (FR) Holy Trinity, Fall River, MA

Oliveira, Rev. Vanderley, '02 (ATL) St. Jude the Apostle Catholic Church, Sandy Springs, Inc., Sandy Springs, GA

Oliveira, Rev. Wellington, (BO) Immaculate Conception, Revere, MA; St. Joseph, Lynn, MA

Olivencia Velez, Rev. Ramon V., '97 (ARE) Our Lady of Mt. Carmel, Hatillo, PR

Olivencia Velez, Rev. Ramon V., '97 (ARE) [MIS] Chapel Nuestra Senora del Perpetuo Socorro, Hatillo, PR; [MIS] Chapel Sagrada Familia, Hatillo, PR; [MIS] Chapel Sagrado Corazon de Jesus, Hatillo, PR; [MIS] Chapel San Pio X, Hatillo, PR; [MIS] Chapel Santa Rosa de Lima, Hatillo, PR

Oliver, Rev. James M., '88 (PH) On Duty Outside Diocese. Congregation for the Clergy, Rome, Italy

Oliver, Rev. John, '82 (STA) On Leave.

Oliver, Rev. Marc, '89 (NY) Retired.

Oliver, Rev. Marc K., '89 (NY) [CAM] Culinary Institute of America, Kingston, NY; [CAM] Dutchess Community College, Kingston, NY; [MIS] Hyde Park, P.J. Kenedy Memorial Chapel of Our Lady of the Way, Hyde Park, NY

Oliver, Rev. Msgr. Robert W., *B.H.* '00 (BO) Curia: Tribunal

Oliver, Rev. Williams A., '77 (GAL) Retired.

Olivera, Rev. Carlos Alberto, '84 (SJ) San Jose Chinese Catholic Mission, Santa Clara, CA; St. Clare, Santa Clara, CA

Olivera, Rev. Evaristo R., '88 (FTW) St. Henry, Fort Wayne, IN; St. Therese, Fort Wayne, IN

Oliveras, Rev. Gerardo Enrique, '19 (SJN) San Juan M. Vianney, San Juan, PR

Olivere, Rev. Michael S., '94 (PH) St. Bartholomew, Philadelphia, PA; St. Timothy, Philadelphia, PA

Oliveri, Rev. Armand, *S.D.B.* '50 (SFR) Retired. SS. Peter and Paul, San Francisco, CA

Oliveros, Rev. Jesus, '18 (JOL) St. Alexis, Bensenville, IL

Oliviera, Rev. Humbert, '77 (MAN) Retired.

Olkowski, Rev. Brian, '16 (HBG) Assumption of the Blessed Virgin Mary, Lancaster, PA

Olmer, Rev. Vernon, *OFM* '62 (GB) [MON] Blessed Giles Friary, Manitowoc, WI

Olmo, Very Rev. Ivan, '13 (ORL) Curia: Advisory Boards, Commissions, Committees, and Councils; Deaneries Annunciation, Altamonte Springs, FL

Olmo, Rev. Luis S., *O.F.M.* '85 (SJN) Santa Clara de Asis, Carolina, PR

Olmos, Rev. Pedro, '78 (FRS) Retired.

Olmos-Marcelo, Rev. Alfredo, *M.S.P* (SB) St. Joseph, Fontana, CA

Olmstead, Rev. Daryl, '75 (SAL) St. Aloysius Gonzaga Parish, Osborne, Inc., Osborne, KS; St. Boniface Parish, Tipton, Inc., Tipton, KS; St. Mary Parish, Downs, Inc., Downs, KS

Olnhausen, Rev. James Robert, '70 (AUS) Retired.

Olofson, Rev. James, (JOL) On Special Assignment. Studying in Rome

O'Loghlen, Rev. Martin, *SS.CC.* '61 (SB) [MON] Congregation of the Sacred Hearts of Jesus and Mary, SS.CC., Hemet, CA

O'Loghlen, Rev. Martin P., *SS.CC.* '61 (LA) [MON] Congregation of the Sacred Hearts of Jesus and Mary, La Verne, CA

Olokunboro, Rev. Fidelis A., '06 (PH) Mother of Divine Providence, King of Prussia, PA

Olona, Rev. Msgr. Richard, '70 (SFE) Retired.

O'Loughlin, Rev. Ben, *LC* (DAL) [MON] Legionaries of Christ, Irving, TX

O'Loughlin, Very Rev. Francis A., '80 (PRO) Newport Hosp Curia: Leadership Church of Jesus-Saviour, Newport, Newport, RI

O'Loughlin, Rev. Frank, '65 (PMB) Retired.

O'Loughlin, Very Rev. Michael, (PHX) Curia: (>HPM) Offices and Directors

O'Loughlin, Rev. Michael, '05 (HPM) Curia: Leadership; Offices and Directors St. Mary Proto-Cathedral, Sherman Oaks, CA

O'Loughlin, Rev. Patrick, *LC* '19 (ATL) Pinecrest Academy, Inc., Cumming, GA

O'Loughlin, Rev. Patrick J., '99 (MIL) St. Marys Congregation, Racine, WI; St. Matthews Congregation, Oak Creek, WI

Olowin, Rev. Msgr. Jan C., '68 (E) Retired.

Oloyede, Rev. Samuel, *O.P.* (MO) Curia: Offices and Directors

Ols, Rev. James R., '75 (CLV) Retired.

Olsavsky, Rev. John R., '62 (CLV) Retired. St. Joan of Arc, Chagrin Falls, OH

Olsem, Rev. Andrew D., '67 (WIN) Retired.

Olsen, Rev. Charles R., *S.J.* '68 (SJ) [MON] Sacred Heart Jesuit Center, Los Gatos, CA

Olsen, Rev. Eric F., '09 (STL) Our Lady of Guadalupe Catholic Church, St. Louis, MO

Olsen, Rev. Eric S., '01 (OM) Holy Family, Lindsay, NE; St. Mary, Leigh, NE; St. Michael, Tarnov, NE; [MIS] Immaculate Conception Church, St. Helena, NE; [MIS] Sacred Heart Church, Wynot, NE; [MIS] Ss. Peter and Paul Church, Bow Valley, NE

Olsen, Rev. Kenneth, '73 (P) Retired.

Olson, Very Rev. David P., '98 (LC) Curia: Leadership [EFT] The St. Francis Parish Endowment Trust, Ellsworth, WI

Olson, Rev. Drew Gregory, '18 (MAD) St. Patrick, Janesville, WI

Olson, Rev. Eric E., '84 (MAR) Retired.

Olson, Rev. Eric S., *Rev.* '02 (OM) St. Francis, Humphrey, NE

Olson, Rev. Hans M., '83 (SEA) Curia: Leadership St. Mary Magdalen, Everett, WA

Olson, Rev. James P., '88 (PH) Saint John Paul II Parish, Philadelphia, PA

Olson, Rev. John E., '07 (WIL) St. Paul's, Wilmington, DE

Olson, Rev. Michael, '15 (CHI) St. Damian, Oak Forest, IL

Olson, Rev. Michael P., '94 (GR) Retired.

Olson, Rev. Randy G., '90 (LC) On Leave.

Olson, Rev. Ronald, *O.F.M.Conv.* '58 (SUP) Retired.

Olson, Rev. Stephen, '14 (PT) Curia: Leadership St. Paul, Pensacola, FL

Olson, Rev. Theodore, '72 (ORG) Retired.

Olson, Rev. Thomas, '73 (SCL) Retired. Curia: Leadership

Olson, Rev. Thomas M., '16 (BO) On Leave.

Olsovsky, Rev. George J., '56 (GAL) Retired.

Olszamowski, Rev. Leon M., *S.M.* '76 (DET) Notre Dame Preparatory School and Marist Academy, Pontiac, MI

Olszewski, Rev. Alexander, '22 (BRK) St. Thomas Aquinas, Brooklyn, NY

Olszewski, Rev. Gregory J., '06 (CLV) On Sick Leave. Mater Dei Academy, Wickliffe, OH; Our Lady of Mount Carmel, Wickliffe, OH

Olszewski, Rev. Laurence, *C.S.C.* '64 (ORL) [MON] Congregation of Holy Cross, United States Province, Cocoa Beach, FL

Olszewski, Rev. Michal, '13 (SAC) Curia: Leadership

Olszewski, Rev. Michal, '03 (SAC) Curia: Offices and Directors Pastor of St. Joseph Parish, Marysville, a corporation sole, Marysville, CA

Olszewski, Rev. Paul A., '93 (CAM) St. Mary's R.C. Church, Delaware Township, N.J., Cherry Hill, NJ

Olszewski, Rev. Ronald W. E., *O.S.F.S.* '74 (TOL) [MON] Oblates of St. Francis de Sales, Toledo, OH

Olugbami, Rev. Godwin, (STL) Chap, St Luke's Hosp

Oluoha, Rev. Tobechukwu P., *OSA* '94 (SFE) Our Lady of Sorrows-La Joya, La Joya, NM

Olvera, Rev. Daniel, '17 (COL) St. Paul the Apostle, Westerville, OH

Olvera, Rev. Ignacio, '16 (DAL) St. Cecilia Catholic Parish, Dallas, TX

Olvida, Rev. Victor A., '82 (SEA) Retired.

Olzacki, Rev. Bogdan, (PH) [MON] The Order of Saint Paul, First Hermit - The Pauline Fathers, Doylestown, PA

Olzacki, Rev. Tadeusz, (PH) [MON] The Order of Saint Paul, First Hermit - The Pauline Fathers, Doylestown, PA

Omachi, Rev. Michael, (NY) Our Lady of Fatima, Plattekill, NY

O'Madagain, Rev. Murchadh, '98 (VEN) St. Vincent de Paul Parish in Fort Myers, Inc., Fort Myers, FL; [NUR] St. Vincent de Paul Housing, Inc. (Villa Vincente), Fort Myers, FL

O'Mahony, Rev. Maurice K., '67 (LA) Retired. Our Lady of Mount Carmel, Santa Barbara, CA

O'Malley, Rev. John J., *O.P.* '59 (CHI) St. Vincent Ferrer, River Forest, IL; [MON] St. Pius V Priory, Chicago, IL

O'Malley, Rev. John W., *S.J.* '57 (WDC) [COL] Georgetown University, Washington, DC
O'Malley, Rev. Leonard F., '74 (BO) St. Peter, Cambridge, MA
O'Malley, Rev. Paul, *S.S.C.* '57 (PRO) Retired. [MON] St. Columban's Retirement House (St. Columban's Foreign Mission Society), Bristol, RI
O'Malley, Rev. Timothy J., '97 (CHI) Curia: Leadership Most Blessed Trinity, Waukegan, IL
O'Malley, Rev. Vincent J., *C.M.* '73 (BUF) [MON] Vincentian Community at Niagara University (Congregation of the Mission of St. Vincent de Paul), Niagara University, NY
O'Malley, Rev. William, (BO) [MON] Campion Health & Wellness, Inc., Weston, MA
Oman, Rev. Brandon, '15 (MAR) On Duty Outside Diocese. Archdiocese for the Military Services, USA
Oman, Rev. Brandon W., (MO) Curia: Offices and Directors
Omana, Rev. Max B., '79 (MO) Curia: Offices and Directors
O'Mannion, Rev. Sean, '08 (SPR) Our Lady of Czestochowa, Turners Falls, MA
O'Mara, Rev. Dennis, *S.S.C.* '61 (OM) Retired. [MON] Missionary Society of St. Columban, St. Columbans, NE
O'Mara, Rev. Francis D., *S.S.C.* (PRO) [MON] St. Columban's Retirement House (St. Columban's Foreign Mission Society), Bristol, RI
O'Mara, Rev. Michael E., '88 (IND) Holy Spirit Catholic Church, Indianapolis, Inc., Indianapolis, IN
O'Mara, Rev. William T., '58 (CHI) Retired. St. Elizabeth Seton, Orland Hills, IL
Omboga, Rev. Johna Orenge, '04 (ROC) All Saints, Corning, NY
Omeaku, Rev. Fidelis C., '08 (LA) St. Anselm, Los Angeles, CA
O'Meara, Rev. Gregory J., *S.J.* '02 (MIL) [MON] Jesuit Community at Marquette University (Marquette Jesuit Associates, Inc.), Milwaukee, WI
O'Meara, Rev. Joseph M., '67 (BAL) Retired.
O'Meara, Rev. Joseph P., '53 (NY) Retired.
O'Meara, Rev. Noel P., *C.S.Sp.* '65 (BRK) [MIS] World Compassion Link, Long Island City, NY
O'Mearain, Rev. Msgr. Ciaran P., '60 (CAM) Retired.
O'Melia, Rev. Edward A., '77 (DAV) Retired.
Omenihu, Rev. Anthony O., '96 (NY) Curia: Leadership
Omenihu, Rev. Anthony O., (NY) Curia: Leadership
Omernick, Rev. Kenneth E., '74 (MIL) St. Charles Congregation, Hartland, WI
Omode, Rev. Cletus Oluwafemi, '12 (MIA) St. Lawrence, North Miami Beach, FL
Omogo, Rev. Peter O., '04 (GR) Our Lady of the Assumption, Rothbury, MI; St. James, Montague, MI
Omolo, Rev. Charles, '14 (WOR) St. Boniface, Lunenburg, MA
Omolo, Rev. Gilbert, '07 (RVC) Chap, Northwell North Shore Univ Hosp, Manhasset
Omolo, Rev. Gilbert, *C.P.* (MO) Curia: Offices and Directors
Omolo, Rev. Gilbert Otieno, *C.P.* '07 (BRK) [MON] Immaculate Conception Monastery, Jamaica, NY
Omolo, Rev. Gilbert Otieno, *C.P.* '07 (NY) [MON] The Congregation of the Passion - St. Paul of the Cross Province, Jamaica, NY
Omondi, Rev. Benard, *S.J.* '17 (DET) University of Detroit Jesuit High School and Academy, Detroit, MI
O'Mullane, Rev. Daniel P., '10 (PAT) Curia: Leadership Our Lady of Mount Carmel, Boonton, NJ
Onaiwu, Rev. Osas A., *CRS* '16 (GAL) Assumption, Houston, TX
Onate-Melendez, Very Rev. Refugio, '00 (ATL) Curia: Leadership St. Joseph Catholic Church, Dalton, Inc., Dalton, GA
Onate-Vargas, Rev. Francisco Javier, '19 (CHR) Our Lady of Lourdes, Greenwood, SC
Ondeck, Rev. Douglas A., '07 (WH) St. Patrick, Weston, WV
Ondrey, Rev. Stephen, '21 (COL) Seton Parish, Pickerington, OH
O'Neal, Rev. James E., '80 (STA) Retired.
O'Neal, Rev. Patrick, '90 (PEO) St. Joseph's, Ivesdale, IL; St. Patrick, Tolono, IL
O'Neal, Rev. Shawn, '00 (CHL) Sacred Heart, Brevard, NC
Onegiu, Rev. Benedict, *A.J.* '93 (PHX) St. James Roman Catholic Parish, Glendale, AZ
O'Neil, Rev. James, '85 (GF) Curia: Leadership
O'Neil, Rev. Jim, '85 (GF) St. Matthew, Sidney, MT
O'Neil, Rev. Joseph, *m.s.* '93 (HRT) Our Lady of Sorrows Church Corporation of Parkville, Hartford, Hartford, CT; [MON] Our Lady of Sorrows Rectory, Hartford, CT
O'Neil, Rev. Kevin J., *C.Ss.R.* '81 (TR) [RTR] San Alfonso Retreat House, Long Branch, NJ
O'Neil, Rev. Michael, '59 (SEA) Retired.
O'Neil, Rev. Michael, (PHX) All Saints Roman Catholic Parish, Mesa, AZ
O'Neil, Rev. Patrick, *O.P.* '95 (SFR) Retired. St. Raymond, Menlo Park, CA; [RTR] Vallombrosa Center, Conference and Retreat Center of the Archdiocese of San Francisco, Menlo Park, CA
O'Neil, Rev. Robert J., *M.H.M.* '65 (NY) [MON] Mill Hill Fathers Residence, Hartsdale, NY
O'Neil, Rev. Thomas D., '69 (PIT) Retired.
O'Neill, Rev. Anthony, '11 (STP) Faithful Shepherd Catholic School, Eagan, MN; St. John Neumann, Eagan, MN; [CEM] Our Lady of the Lake Cemetery, Mound, MN
O'Neill, Rev. Brian E., '68 (CAM) Retired.
O'Neill, Rev. Daniel, *O.Carm.* '69 (NEW) St. Cecilia, Englewood, NJ
O'Neill, Rev. Edward J., '63 (NY) Retired. [MON] Our Lady of Consolation Residence, Bronx, NY
O'Neill, Rev. Msgr. Edward M., '71 (MET) Retired. [MON] Maria Regina Residence, Somerset, NJ
O'Neill, Rev. George F., '97 (BGP) St. Joseph's Church Brookfield, Brookfield, CT
O'Neill, Rev. James, '07 (TR) St. John, Lakehurst, NJ
O'Neill, Rev. James, '57 (ALB) Retired.
O'Neill, Rev. John, '99 (NSH) Christ the Redeemer, Centerville, TN; Holy Trinity, Hohenwald, TN; St. Cecilia, Waynesboro, TN
O'Neill, Rev. John, '16 (TLS) St. James, Bartlesville, OK; St. John's, Bartlesville, OK
O'Neill, Rev. John, '00 (NY) [SEM] St. Joseph's Seminary, Yonkers, NY
O'Neill, Rev. John, '00 (BRK) Corpus Christi, Woodside, NY
O'Neill, Rev. John J., '67 (SFR) Retired.
O'Neill, Rev. Keith, *O.F.M.Conv.* '66 (SAV) St. Joseph, Jesup, GA
O'Neill, Rev. Kevin, *F.S.S.P.* '12 (ELP) Immaculate Conception, El Paso, TX
O'Neill, Rev. Msgr. Kevin S., '77 (HEL) Curia: Leadership Cathedral of Saint Helena Parish: Series 401, LLC, Helena, MT; Saint Thomas the Apostle Parish: Series 434, LLC, Helmville, MT
O'Neill, Rev. Msgr. Kevin S., (HEL) Curia: Leadership
O'Neill, Rev. Michael F., '76 (NO) Retired.
O'Neill, Rev. Patrick, '67 (MIA) Retired. Curia: Administration
O'Neill, Rev. Patrick J., '90 (CHI) Retired.
O'Neill, Rev. Philip, (MO) Curia: Offices and Directors
O'Neill, Rev. Philip T., *P.V.* '16 (HRT) On Duty Outside Diocese. Military Chaplain S. Korea
O'Neill, Rev. Sean F., '03 (PH) Our Lady of Consolation, Parkesburg, PA
O'Neill, Rev. Thomas D., '68 (PRO) Retired. [NUR] St. Clare Home, Newport, RI
O'Neill, Rev. Thomas H., *S.J.* '90 (SAC) Jesuit High School, Carmichael, CA; Pastor of St. Ignatius Loyola Parish, Sacramento, a corporation sole, Sacramento, CA; [MON] Sacramento Jesuit Community, Carmichael, CA
O'Neill, Rev. William J., '65 (PRO) Retired.
O'Neill, Rev. Msgr. William O., '67 (SAV) Retired.
O'Neill, Rev. William R., *S.J.* '81 (OAK) [SEM] Jesuit School of Theology of Santa Clara University (Berkeley, California Campus), Berkeley, CA
O'Neill, Rev. William R., *S.J.* '81 (SJ) [MON] USA West Province, Society of Jesus, Los Gatos, CA
Oneissy, Rev. Edgard (Neemtallah), '12 (SAM) Saint Anthony Maronite Catholic Church, Inc., Lawrence, MA
Oneko, Rev. Chrispin, '90 (OWN) St. Charles, Bardwell, KY; St. Denis, Fancy Farm, KY
Onjefu, Rev. Boniface, '98 (AUS) Good Shepherd, Lometa, TX; St. Mary of the Immaculate Conception, Lampasas, TX
Ono, Rev. Ioane, (OAK) St. Mary Magdalen, Berkeley, CA
Onofre Salazar, Rev. Jorge, '09 (LA) Nativity, Los Angeles, CA; Presentation of Mary, Los Angeles, CA
Onoko, Rev. Anthony A., '13 (GBG) St. Raymond of the Mountains, Donegal, PA
Onubogu, Rev. Charles, '88 (SFR) Curia: Offices and Directors Our Lady of the Pillar, Half Moon Bay, CA
Onuegbu, Rev. Patrick, (RVC) Chap, The Long Island Home Specialty Healthcare System; St...
Onuegbu, Rev. Rowland, '10 (BRK) Our Lady of Solace, Brooklyn, NY
Onuh, Rev. Innocent, (WIN) Chap, Mayo Clinic, Rochester
Onuh, Rev. Lazarus, '07 (PRO) Chap, Eleanor Slater Hosp; Dept of Corrections, Providence Curia: Social Services Church of the Holy Name of Jesus at Providence, Rhode Island, Providence, RI
Onumah, Rev. Callistus, (SFD) St. John Vianney, Sherman, IL
Onunkwo, Rev. Vincent, (FTW) Chaplain, Luther Hospital Fort Wayne
Onuoha, Rev. Augustine, '21 (FTW) Saint Joseph High School, South Bend, IN; St. Pius X, Granger, IN
Onuoha, Rev. Christopher, (MO) Curia: Offices and Directors
Onuoha, Rev. Christopher N., '06 (OM) Chaplain at VA Medical Center in Buffalo, NY
Onuoha, Rev. Silas, (CC) [HOS] CHRISTUS Spohn Hospital Corpus Christi - Shoreline, Corpus Christi, TX
Onuoha, Rev. Silas, '91 (CC) On Special Assignment.
Onuora, Rev. Felix A., *C.S.Sp.* '79 (DM) Retired.
Onwere, Rev. Callistus O. C., '82 (STA) Prince of Peace, Jacksonville, FL
Onwubiko, Rev. Augustus, (NY) Parish of Our Lady of the Assumption - St. Mary Star of the Sea, Bronx, NY; St. Mary Star of the Sea, Bronx, NY
Onwuegbule, Rev. Stanley I., '93 (SB) San Secondo d'Asti, Ontario, CA
Onwuegbuzie, Rev. Mike O., '86 (IND) Retired.
Onwuemelie, Rev. Michael, *C.S.Sp.* (SB) Holy Spirit, Hemet, CA; [MON] Congregation of the Holy Spirit, Hemet, CA
Onwuka, Rev. Chidi, *MSSCC* '10 (HBG) Immaculate Conception of the Blessed Virgin Mary, Fairfield, PA
Onwuka, Rev. Chidi, *MSSCC* '10 (HBG) St. Rita, Blue Ridge Summit, PA
Onwumelui, Rev. Benjamin O., '94 (SFE) Univ of New Mexico Hosp Sacred Heart-Albuquerque, Albuquerque, NM
Onwumere, Rev. Leonard, '90 (AUS) On Special Assignment.
Onwumere, Rev. Leonard, *J.P.* '90 (MO) Curia: Offices and Directors
Onyeabor, Rev. Ukachukwu, '86 (PH) Chap, Veterans Administration Med Ctr, Philadelphia
Onyeama, Rev. Vitalis, *SMMM* '81 (B) Holy Apostles, Meridian, ID
Onyegu, Rev. Lawrence, '12 (RVC) Curia: Leadership Blessed Sacrament, Valley Stream, NY
Onyegwara, Rev. Casmir, (WDC) [HOS] Holy Cross Health, Inc., Silver Spring, MD
Onyeihe, Rev. Anthony, '14 (JC) Immaculate Conception, Jefferson City, MO
Onyejegbu, Rev. Cyriacus N., '03 (GAL) Curia: (>MO) Offices and Directors
Onyejiuwa, Rev. Dilio A., '98 (MO) Curia: Offices and Directors
Onyeke, Rev. Donatus, *C.S.S.P.* '98 (SFE) Christus St Vincent Rgnl Med Ctr St. Anne Catholic Church, Santa Fe, NM
Onyekozuru, Rev. Francis, '13 (SAN) Curia: Advisory Boards, Commissions, Committees, and Councils St. Mary's, Brownwood, TX
Onyekuru, Rev. Michael U., '00 (ATL) Curia: Offices and Directors St. John the Evangelist Catholic Church, Hapeville, Inc., Hapeville, GA
Onyekwe, Rev. Anthony, '95 (MEM) St. Andrew the Apostle, Lexington, TN
Onyekwere, Rev. Godfrey C., '03 (GR) Curia: Offices and Directors Prince of Peace Parish North Muskegon, North Muskegon, MI
Onyekwere, Rev. Michael, *SDV* '95 (BRK) St. Clement Pope, South Ozone Park, NY
Onyemaobi, Rev. Nnaemeka A., '09 (NEW) St. Valentine, Bloomfield, NJ
Onyenagubo, Rev. Innocent, (SY) Chap, Upstate Univ Hosp, Syracuse Transfiguration, Syracuse, NY
Onyeneke, Rev. Charles, (ALB) Blessed Sacrament, Albany, NY
Onyeneke, Rev. Christopher, *M.SS.CC.* '11 (HBG) St. Andrew, Waynesboro, PA
Onyenobi, Rev. Christopher, '83 (LA) St. Anne, Santa Monica, CA
Onyeocha, Rev. Anthony Claret, (JKS) St. Joseph, Woodville, MS
Onyeocha, Rev. Chinemere Raphael, '08 (ALT) On Leave.
Onyigbuo, Rev. Cornelius, (GLP) Curia: Leadership Immaculate Conception, Cuba, NM; St. Francis of Assisi, Lumberton, NM
O'Nymawaro, Rev. Richard, *A.J.* '91 (ALN) [MIS] Apostles of Jesus, Northampton, PA
Oonnoonny, Rev. George, '91 (NY) Parish of St. Christopher and St. Patrick, Buchanan, NY; St. Patrick, Verplanck, NY
Oonnoony, Rev. George, (MCE) Curia: Administration; Tribunal

Opalalic, Rev. Agustin, '77 (SD) Curia: Tribunal Pastor of Church of the Nativity Catholic Parish, Rancho Santa Fe, a corporation sole, Rancho Santa Fe, CA; [MIS] Church of the Nativity Catholic Parish in Rancho Santa Fe, CA Real Property Support Corporation, Rancho Santa Fe, CA
Opalda, Rev. Jose, (BAL) Curia: Tribunal St. Mary of the Assumption, Baltimore, MD; St. Pius X, Baltimore, MD
Opara, Rev. Augustine, (GLP) St. John Vianney, Gallup, NM
Opara, Rev. Benedict M, '85 (MO) Curia: Offices and Directors
Opara, Rev. Isaac, '88 (MO) Curia: Offices and Directors
Opara, Rev. John, (NEW) Chap (Adjunct), Bergen Rgnl Med Ctr, Paramus Saint Joseph Parish, East Orange, NJ; [HOS] Holy Name Medical Center (Peace Ministries, Inc.), Teaneck, NJ
Opara, Rev. Peter Ben, '88 (DET) [HOS] Trinity Health Livonia, Livonia, MI
Opara, Rev. Peter C., *M.I.* '04 (MIL) [MON] St. Camillus Communities, Inc., Wauwatosa, WI
Oparaji, Rev. Lawrence K., '20 (MAD) St. Augustine, Footville, WI
Opeil, Rev. Cyril, *S.J.* '94 (BO) [MON] The Jesuit Community at Boston College, Chestnut Hill, MA
Ophals, Rev. Donald J., '61 (ALB) Retired.
Opoka, Rev. Lloyd E., '68 (KC) Retired.
Opoki, Rev. Michael, *A.J.* (HBG) Our Lady Help of Christians, Lykens, PA; Sacred Heart of Jesus, Williamstown, PA
Opoku-Mensah, Rev. Daniel, '14 (RVC) Holy Trinity Diocesan High School, Hicksville, NY
Opondo-Owora, Rev. Charles, '93 (SY) St. James, Johnson City, NY
Oppl, Rev. Ludwig M., *O.R.C.* '04 (STU) [MON] Opus Angelorum, Inc., Carrollton, OH; [MON] Order of the Holy Cross, Inc., Carrollton, OH
Oppong, Rev. Fidelis H., *S.T.D.* (NY) Parish of Sacred Heart and Our Lady of Pompeii, Dobbs Ferry, NY
Oppong, Rev. Samuel, (SJ) Chap, Stanford Med Ctr
Oppong, Rev. Sebastian, '12 (MAR) St. Anthony, Gwinn, MI
Oppong Afriyie, Rev. George, (RVC) St. Kilian, Farmingdale, NY
Opris, Rev. Gheorghe, '71 (ROM) Retired.
Oprych, Rev. Piotr, '22 (FBK) Sacred Heart Cathedral Catholic Church Fairbanks, Fairbanks, AK; St. Mark University Catholic Parish Fairbanks, Fairbanks, AK; [MON] St. Ignatius Residence, Fairbanks, AK
Opsahl, Rev. Andy, *OP* '19 (AJ) Holy Family Old Cathedral, Anchorage, AK
Orabuche, Rev. Ethelbert C., (MAN) Saint John XXIII Parish, Nashua, NH
Oracion, Rev. Samuel B., '82 (LUB) St. Michael, Ralls, TX
Orain, Rev. Renante, (CAM) Curia: Pastoral Services The Church of Saint Katharine Drexel, McKee City, New Jersey, Egg Harbor Township, NJ
Orama, Rev. Raymond, '08 (PAT) Curia: Administration Blessed Sacrament, Paterson, NJ
Oranefo, Rev. Francis, '94 (CAM) Chap, Virtua at Our Lady of Lourdes Med Ctr Church of Christ the King, Haddonfield, N.J., Haddonfield, NJ
Oranefo, Rev. Francis, (PIT) Chap, UPMC Univ of Pittsburgh Med Ctr, Allegheny Cty
Orapankal, Rev. Abraham, '83 (MET) St. Matthias, Somerset, NJ
Orathel, Rev. Sunil, *SDB* (OAK) St. Joseph Basilica, Alameda, CA
Oravetz, Rev. Robert F., '97 (PBR) Curia: Offices and Directors Holy Trinity, Conemaugh, PA; St. Nicholas, Nanty-Glo, PA
Orbih, Rev. William Ikhianosimhe, (FTW) St. Therese, Little Flower (Little Flower Catholic Church), South Bend, IN
Orchik, Rev. Michael J., '73 (BAL) [CON] Little Sisters of the Poor, Baltimore Province, Inc., Baltimore, MD; [MIS] Catholic War Veterans USA, Inc., Perry Hall, MD; [NUR] St. Martin's Home for Aged, Little Sisters of the Poor, Baltimore Inc., Baltimore, MD
Orci, Rev. Ernesto, '09 (SJ) On Special Assignment. Curia: Leadership; Offices and Directors Cathedral Basilica of St. Joseph, San Jose, CA; [CAM] SJSU Catholic Newman Center, San Jose, CA; [EFT] San Jose Cathedral Foundation, San Jose, CA
Ordonez, Rev. Jose Naul, (CC) Our Lady of Pilar, Corpus Christi, TX
Ordonez, Rev. Mario (Ricky) V., '08 (TUC) Saints Peter and Paul Roman Catholic Parish - Tucson, Tucson, AZ
Ordoveza, Rev. Justin, '22 (LA) St. Raymond, Downey, CA
O'Reilly, Rev. Aidan, '60 (SAC) Retired.
O'Reilly, Rev. Andrew, *C.PP.S.* '73 (CIN) [MON] St. Charles, Celina, OH
O'Reilly, Rev. Barnabas, *OSB* '22 (GBG) [MON] Saint Vincent Archabbey, Latrobe, PA
O'Reilly, Rev. Bernard M., '69 (PRO) Retired.
O'Reilly, Rev. Daniel, '03 (NY) St. Philip Neri, Bronx, NY; [CAM] Columbia University, New York, NY
O'Reilly, Rev. Desmond T., '90 (SAC) Pastor of St. Mel Parish, Fair Oaks, a corporation sole, Fair Oaks, CA
O'Reilly, Rev. Edward M., '68 (NY) Retired. Military Chap
O'Reilly, Rev. Gerald K., '85 (CHI) Mary, Mother of Martyrs, Des Plaines, IL
O'Reilly, Rev. James P., (RIC) St. Bridget, Richmond, VA
O'Reilly, Rev. Kevin P., '84 (WDC) St. Mary Church and Shrine of Our Lady of Fatima, Barnesville, MD
O'Reilly, Rev. Martin, '94 (TR) Parish of Mary, Mother of the Church, Bordentown N.J., Bordentown, NJ
O'Reilly, Rev. Michael, '96 (SAC) Curia: Offices and Directors Pastor of Cathedral of the Blessed Sacrament Parish, Sacramento, a corporation sole, Sacramento, CA; Pastor of St. Elizabeth Parish, Sacramento, a corporation sole, Sacramento, CA
O'Reilly, Rev. Msgr. Peter A., '61 (LA) Retired. St. Lawrence Martyr, Redondo Beach, CA
O'Reilly, Rev. Vincent P., '62 (SAC) Retired.
Orejuela, Rev. Fernando, *A.I.C.* '97 (MIA) St. Boniface, Pembroke Pines, FL
Orekie, Rev. Aloysius, (LSC) St. Ann Parish, Inc., Deming, NM
Orellana, Rev. Jose, '03 (BRK) St. Catharine of Alexandria, Brooklyn, NY
Orellana, Rev. Roberto, '01 (ATL) St. Augustine Catholic Church, Covington, Inc., Covington, GA
Orellana Diaz, Rev. Onildo, *MFM* '00 (MIL) Congregation of the Holy Family, Reeseville, WI; St. Columbkille, Columbus, WI; St. John's Congregation, Clyman, WI; St. Katharine Drexel Parish, Beaver Dam, WI
Orengo, Rev. Msgr. Juan Rodriguez, '79 (PCE) Curia: Offices and Directors
Organiza, Rev. Rogelio, (BUR) Holy Family Parish, Springfield, VT; [MIS] St. Amadeus Church (Alburgh, VT), Alburgh, VT; [MIS] St. Joseph Church (Isle La Motte), Isle La Motte, VT; [MIS] St. Rose of Lima Church (South Hero, VT), ,
Orian, Rev. Remus Anghel, '21 (ROM) St. Michael, Aurora, IL
Orians, Rev. Thomas, *S.A.* '92 (NY) [MON] Franciscan Friars of the Atonement, Garrison, NY; [MON] Franciscan Friars of the Atonement, Minister General Office, Garrison, NY
O'Riley, Rev. Dennis H., '59 (PEO) Retired.
Orimaco, Rev. Domingo, '72 (SFR) Our Lady of Mercy, Daly City, CA
Oriole, Rev. Philip M., '70 (E) Retired. Curia: Clergy and Religious Services; Finance
O'Riordan, Rev. Niall, (P) St. Henry, Gresham, OR
O'Riordan, Rev. William, '85 (NO) St. Ann Roman Catholic Church and Shrine, Metairie, Louisiana, Metairie, LA; [SHR] St. Ann National Shrine, Metairie, LA
Orique, Rev. David T., *O.P.* '01 (PRO) [MON] St. Thomas Aquinas Priory at Providence College, Providence, RI
Orji, Rev. Cletus, '18 (NO) St. Edward the Confessor Roman Catholic Church, Metairie, Louisiana, Metairie, LA
Orjianioke, Rev. Martin M., '95 (MEM) Holy Cross, Paris, TN
Orjikwe, Rev. Isidore, '01 (DEN) Light of the World Roman Catholic Parish in Littleton, Littleton, CO
Orlandi, Rev. Joseph J., '73 (PAT) Retired.
Orlandi, Rev. Nazareno, '61 (NEW) Retired. Our Lady of Mount Carmel, Lyndhurst, NJ
Orlando, Rev. Tom, '17 (STO) Curia: Leadership; Offices and Directors Pastor of All Saints University Church, Turlock, CA
Orlik, Rev. Dale A., '67 (SAG) Saint Jude Thaddeus Parish of Essexville, Essexville, MI
Orlowski, Rev. Robert J., '97 (BUF) Our Mother of Good Counsel, Blasdell, NY; Queen of Angels, Lackawanna, NY
Orlowsky, Rev. Michael T., '93 (ARL) St. Francis de Sales, Kilmarnock, VA
Ormin, Rev. Martin Bosco, *V.C.* (TUC) Saint Jude Thaddeus Roman Catholic Parish - Pearce Sunsites, Pearce, AZ
Orndorff, Rev. Christopher M., '97 (TUC) Curia: Consultative Bodies; Leadership Corpus Christi Roman Catholic Parish - Tucson, Tucson, AZ
Orndorff, Rev. Jared P., '08 (CLV) Chap, Summa Western Reserve, Cuyahoga Falls St. Joseph, Cuyahoga Falls, OH
Ornowski, Rev. Gerald Stanley, *M.I.C.* '62 (SPR) [MON] Congregation of Marian Fathers of The Immaculate Conception of the Most Blessed Virgin Mary, Stockbridge, MA
Oroffa, Rev. Francis A., (NY) Parish of St. Frances of Rome, St. Francis of Assisi, St. Anthony, and Our Lady of Grace, Bronx, NY
Oropel, Rev. James F. Gayta, '07 (SB) St. Frances of Rome, Wildomar, CA
O'Rorke, Rev. Msgr. James H., '61 (PAT) Retired.
Oros, Rev. Yuriy, (PSC) Curia: Leadership St. Mary, Trenton, NJ; St. Nicholas, Roebling, NJ
Orosa, Rev. Agustin R., *M.I.* '95 (MIL) [EFT] Order of St. Camillus Foundation, Inc., Wauwatosa, WI; [MIS] St. Camillus Health System, Inc., Wauwatosa, WI; [MIS] St. Camillus Ministries, Inc., Wauwatosa, WI; [MON] St. Camillus Communities, Inc., Wauwatosa, WI; [NUR] St. Camillus, Wauwatosa, WI; [NUR] St. Camillus Health Center, Inc., Wauwatosa, WI
Orosco, Rev. James P., '81 (DAL) Terrell State Hosp St. John the Apostle Catholic Parish, Terrell, TX
O'Rourke, Rev. Daniel, '88 (GF) Retired.
O'Rourke, Rev. David K., *O.P.* '62 (OAK) Curia: Offices and Directors Our Lady of Mercy, Point Richmond, CA; [MON] Order of Preachers (Province of the Most Holy Name of Jesus - Western Dominican Province), Oakland, CA
O'Rourke, Rev. Francis J., '75 (CHL) Retired.
O'Rourke, Very Rev. Francis J., '75 (CHL) Retired.
O'Rourke, Rev. James E., (ALB) St. Paul the Apostle, Hancock, NY
O'Rourke, Friar Michael James, *OP* '96 (BR) [CAM] St. Albert the Great Catholic Student Center, Hammond, LA
O'Rourke, Rev. P. Gerard, '50 (SFR) Retired.
O'Rourke, Rev. Peter J., '99 (SCR) Retired. On Special Assignment. St. Patrick, White Haven, PA
O'Rourke, Very Rev. Richard, *M.S.C.* '65 (AUS) Curia: Leadership St. Paul Chong Hasang, Harker Heights, TX
O'Rourke, Rev. Robert, *S.S.C.* '58 (PRO) Retired. [MON] St. Columban's Retirement House (St. Columban's Foreign Mission Society), Bristol, RI
O'Rourke, Rev. Thomas J., '64 (HRT) Retired.
Orozco, Very Rev. Argemiro, '92 (YAK) Curia: Leadership Holy Apostles, East Wenatchee, WA; [CCH] Holy Apostles Parish, East Wenatchee, WA
Orozco, Rev. Ariel F., '22 (MIL) St. Charles Congregation, Hartland, WI
Orozco, Rev. Edicson, (BGP) St. Joseph and St. Ladislaus Parish Corporation, Norwalk, CT
Orozco, Rev. Francis, *O.P.* '15 (DAL) [MON] Dominican Priory of St. Albert the Great and Novitiate, Irving, TX
Orozco, Rev. Francisco, *O.C.D.* '90 (DAL) St. Anthony Catholic Parish - Wylie, Wylie, TX
Orozco, Rev. Isaac, '07 (FWT) On Leave.
Orozco, Rev. J. Carlos, (SEA) Holy Spirit Parish, Kent, WA
Orozco, Rev. Jose A., '16 (SB) Holy Family Parish, Hesperia, CA
Orozco, Rev. Juan Pablo, *CC* '22 (GAL) [MIS] Catholic Charismatic Center, Houston, TX
Orozco Ortigosa, Rev. Jose Francisco, *C.M.* '95 (CHI) [MON] DePaul Vincentian Residence, Chicago, IL
Orpilla, Rev. Julito R., '06 (SAC) Pastor of St. Joseph Parish, Elk Grove, a corporation sole, Elk Grove, CA
Orr, Rev. James R., '79 (PIT) Immaculate Heart of Mary, Pittsburgh, PA; Most Holy Name of Jesus, Pittsburgh, PA; St. Nicholas, Pittsburgh, PA; St. Patrick-St. Stanislaus Kostka, Pittsburgh, PA
Orr, Rev. John Arthur, '01 (KNX) Curia: Leadership St. Mary, Athens, TN
Orr, Rev. Joseph, '82 (ALT) [CAM] Lock Haven University (Lock Haven), Lock Haven, PA
Orr, Rev. Joseph T., '82 (ALT) Curia: Offices and Directors Holy Spirit, Lock Haven, PA; St. Joseph, Renovo, PA
Orr, Rev. Sherman A., '91 (WCH) St. Elizabeth Ann Seton, Wichita, KS
Orr, Rev. Msgr. Stephen, '74 (DM) Retired. Curia:

Leadership
Orr, Rev. Msgr. Stephen L., '74 (DM) Retired. Curia: Offices and Directors
Orrigo, Rev. Mario J., '96 (BO) St. Patrick, Stoneham, MA
Orris, Rev. Daniel, '20 (GR) Our Lady of Consolation, Rockford, MI
Orsak, Rev. David Michael, '14 (MEM) St. Jude Catholic Church, Martin, TN
Orsborn, Very Rev. Bruce J., '81 (SD) Curia: Advisory Boards, Commissions, Committees, and Councils Pastor of Saint Mark Catholic Parish in San Marcos A Corporation Sole, San Marcos, CA
Orsi, Rev. Michael, '76 (VEN) St. Agnes Parish in Naples, Inc., Naples, FL; St. John Neumann Catholic High School, Inc., Naples, FL
Orsi, Rev. Michael P., '76 (CAM) Retired.
Orsini, Rev. James, '74 (HON) Retired.
Orsino, Rev. Jerry, *OMI* (LAR) Our Lady of Refuge, Eagle Pass, TX
Orso, Rev. Clair Antonio, *C.S.* (GAL) St. John Neumann, Houston, TX
Orsolin, Rev. Vilmar, (PRO) Saint Bartholomew's Church Corporation, Providence, RI
Orsolin, Rev. Vilmar, '80 (ATL) San Felipe de Jesus, Forest Park, GA
Orsot, Rev. Samuel, '18 (LKC) On Leave. Non-Active
Orsulak, Rev. Msgr. Thomas J., '90 (ALN) St. Peter the Apostle, Reading, PA
Orsy, Rev. Ladislas, *S.J.* '51 (WDC) [COL] Georgetown University, Washington, DC
Orsy, Rev. Ladislaus, (BAL) Retired. [MIS] Colombiere Jesuit Community, Baltimore, MD
Orszulak, Rev. Henry A., '67 (BUF) Retired. St. Anthony, Lackawanna, NY
Ortega, Rev. Alberto, '97 (R) Basilica Shrine of Saint Mary, Wilmington, NC
Ortega, Rev. Alejandro, (SAT) St. Monica, Converse, TX
Ortega, Rev. Carlos, '99 (SR) Pastor of Our Lady of Guadalupe Catholic Church of Windsor, A Corporation Sole, Windsor, CA
Ortega, Rev. Carlos G., (ATL) St. Clement Catholic Church, Calhoun, Inc., Calhoun, GA
Ortega, Rev. Eduardo, '95 (BWN) Curia: Leadership Immaculate Conception, Rio Grande City, TX; [EFT] El Rosario Charitable Trust, Mission, TX; [EFT] La Merced Charitable Trust, Mercedes, TX
Ortega, Rev. Fernando, '08 (STP) SS. Cyril and Methodius, Minneapolis, MN
Ortega, Rev. Gustavo, (LAR) Curia: Leadership St. Patrick, Batesvillle, TX
Ortega, Rev. Jose Felix, '01 (NY) Our Lady of Mt. Carmel, Bronx, NY; [PRE] Youth and Family Encounter, Inc., Thornwood, NY
Ortega, Rev. Juan Alexander, (NEW) St. Patrick Pro-Cathedral, Newark, NJ
Ortega, Rev. Leo, '08 (LA) [SEM] St. John's Seminary, Camarillo, CA
Ortega, Rev. Liberato, (GBG) Curia: Advisory Boards, Commissions, Committees, and Councils SS. Cyril and Methodius, Fairchance, PA; St. Hubert, Point Marion, PA
Ortega, Rev. Marco Antonio, '93 (NY) St. Philip Neri, Bronx, NY
Ortega, Rev. Miguel Angel, '09 (BWN) Mother Cabrini Parish, Pharr, TX
Ortega, Rev. Ricardo, '11 (PAT) Annunciation, Wayne, NJ
Ortega, Rev. Russell, *O.S.A.* '86 (PH) St. Maximilian Kolbe, West Chester, PA; [MON] St. Thomas Monastery, Villanova, PA; [MON] St. Thomas of Villanova Friary, Villanova, PA
Ortega, Rev. Santos L., '96 (SB) St. Frances Xavier Cabrini, Yucaipa, CA
Ortega de la Fuente, Very Rev. Jose Felix, (NY) Curia: Leadership
Ortega y Ortiz, Rev. Adam Lee, '92 (SFE) On Leave.
Ortega-Mancha, Rev. Oscar, '18 (BWN) St. John the Baptist, San Juan, TX
Ortega-Ruiz, Rev. Agustin, '93 (JOL) Divine Savior, Downers Grove, IL
Ortese, Rev. Oliver U., (SFR) St. Gregory, San Mateo, CA
Orthel, Rev. Joseph A., '89 (SPC) Sacred Heart, Springfield, MO
Orthmann, Rev. James, *O.C.S.O.* '94 (ARL) [RTR] Retreat House, Holy Cross Abbey, Berryville, VA
Ortigas, Rev. Jose Ignacio A., '09 (BGP) Saint Matthew's Roman Catholic Church Corporation, Norwalk, CT
Ortiz, Rev. Adrian Jimenez, '87 (ARE) Curia: Leadership
Ortiz, Rev. Angel, '87 (MGZ) Our Lady of Monserrate, Moca, PR
Ortiz, Rev. Antonio, '78 (GAL) Prince of Peace, Houston, TX
Ortiz, Rev. Arnold, '72 (HON) St. Elizabeth, Aiea, HI
Ortiz, Rev. Aurelio, (MRY) Christ the King, Salinas, CA
Ortiz, Rev. Claro, (SD) Pastor of Sacred Heart Catholic Parish, Brawley, a corporation sole, Brawley, CA; Pastor of Saint Joseph Catholic Parish, Westmorland, a corporation sole, Westmorland, CA; Pastor of Saint Margaret Mary Catholic Parish, Brawley, a corporation sole, Brawley, CA
Ortiz, Rev. Edwin A, '19 (BRK) Saint Athanasius - Saint Dominic, Brooklyn, NY
Ortiz, Rev. Emerito, '96 (WOR) Retired.
Ortiz, Friar Federico, *OFM, Cap.* (FWT) Our Lady of Guadalupe, Fort Worth, TX
Ortiz, Rev. Jaime Luis, (SJN) Santisima Trinidad, Levittown, PR
Ortiz, Rev. Jose A, (CGS) San Miguel Arcangel, Naranjito, PR
Ortiz, Rev. Jose A., '15 (NEW) St. Mary, Plainfield, NJ
Ortiz, Rev. Jose Arturo, '15 (NEW) St. Benedict, Newark, NJ
Ortiz, Rev. Jose Juan, *C.O.* '05 (BWN) Oratory Academy of St. Philip Neri, Pharr, TX; Oratory Athenaeum for University Preparation, Pharr, TX; St. Jude Thaddeus, Pharr, TX; [MON] Pharr Oratory of St. Philip Neri of Pontifical Right, Pharr, TX
Ortiz, Rev. Jose Manuel Sanchez, *MCCJ* '99 (CHI) St. John XXIII, Evanston, IL; [MON] Comboni Missionaries, La Grange Park, IL
Ortiz, Rev. Juan Alejandro, *OFM Cap.* (DAL) [MON] Capuchin Franciscan Friars, Custody Mexico - Texas, Dallas, TX
Ortiz, Rev. Juan Alexander, (NEW) St. John, Newark, NJ
Ortiz, Rev. Leo W., '00 (SFE) Church of the Incarnation, Rio Rancho, NM
Ortiz, Rev. Leonidas Abreu, (FAJ) Santiago Apostol e Inmaculada Concepcion, Vieques, PR
Ortiz, Rev. Marco Antonio, '00 (LA) St. Robert Bellarmine, Burbank, CA
Ortiz, Rev. Marco Antonio, *O.M.I.* '08 (GAL) Immaculate Conception, Houston, TX
Ortiz, Rev. Michael, '56 (SD) Retired.
Ortiz, Rev. Miguel Angel, *O.F.M.Cap.* '86 (SFR) [MON] Capuchin Provincial House, Burlingame, CA
Ortiz, Rev. Pedro, '82 (CGS) San Pablo Apostol, Caguas, PR
Ortiz, Rev. Ramon Alfredo, '91 (ORL) San Jose Mission, Pierson, FL
Ortiz, Rev. Richie, (CHI) Queen of Martyrs and St. Bernadette Parish, Evergreen Park, IL
Ortiz, Rev. Roberto, '09 (NEW) [SEM] Immaculate Conception Seminary School of Theology, South Orange, NJ
Ortiz, Rev. Robinson, '18 (CHI) St. Augustine Parish, Midlothian, IL
Ortiz, Rev. Victor R., '86 (CGS) Retired.
Ortiz Alvarez, Rev. Luis Enrique, *cmf* '19 (PCE) Nuestra Senora del Carmen, Ponce, PR
Ortiz Alvarez, Rev. Luis Enrique, *C.M.F.* (SJN) Casa Mision Claret, Bayamon, PR
Ortiz Dominicci, Rev. Arnaldo, '10 (PCE) On Duty Outside Diocese.
Ortiz-Cruz, Rev. Jaime Luis, (SJN) Curia: Leadership; Offices and Directors
Ortiz-Guzman, Rev. George, '13 (POC) Retired.
Ortiz-Montelongo, Rev. Ruben, '07 (WCH) On Duty Outside Diocese.
Ortiz-Montelongo, Rev. Ruben, (DAL) St. Paul the Apostle Catholic Parish, Richardson, TX
Oruko, Rev. William, (P) Curia: Offices and Directors St. Mary, Star of the Sea, Astoria, OR
O'Ryan, Rev. Colm, '55 (LA) Retired. Good Shepherd, Beverly Hills, CA
Orzech, Rev. Eric S., '93 (CLV) St. Casimir, Cleveland, OH; St. Stanislaus, Cleveland, OH
Orzechowski, Rev. Jacek, *O.F.M.* '02 (R) Immaculate Conception, Durham, NC
Orzel, Rev. David J., '79 (SY) Retired.
Osario Carmona, Rev. Pablo Julio, (SJN) [SPF] Casa de Ninos Manuel Fernandez Juncos, San Juan, PR
Osasona, Rev. Felix I., *M.S.P.* '00 (GAL) Curia: Offices and Directors St. Mary Magdalene, Humble, TX
Osbahr, Rev. Theodore W., '67 (NEW) Retired.
Osborn, Rev. Douglas, '68 (LAN) Retired.
Osborn, Rev. Msgr. Michael, '92 (KAL) Curia: Consultative Bodies; Leadership; Offices and Directors; Tribunal
Osborn, Rev. William, '66 (SFS) Retired.
Osborne, Rev. Kenan, *O.F.M.* '55 (LA) [MON] Franciscan Friary, Order of Friars Minor (Old Mission), Santa Barbara, CA
Osborne, Rev. Paul, *OFM* '64 (PAT) Retired. [MON] St. Anthony Friary (Order of Friars Minor), Butler, NJ
Osborne, Rev. R. Benjamin, *S.J.* '09 (MIL) Gesu Parish, Milwaukee, WI; [MON] Arrupe House Jesuit Community, Milwaukee, WI
Osborne, Rev. Robert E., '54 (L) Retired. Curia: Leadership St. Patrick, Louisville, KY
Osburg, Rev. Frank C., '60 (LEX) Retired. Curia: Leadership
Osburg, Rev. Gregory E., '77 (COV) Curia: Tribunal St. John the Baptist, Wilder, KY
Osebold, Rev. Richard A., '60 (DET) Retired.
Osei-Fosu, Rev. Paul, (BRK) St. Joan of Arc, Jackson Heights, NY
Osei-Nyarko, Msgr. Francis, (SY) Christ Our Light, Pulaski, NY; St. Anne, Mother of Mary, Mexico, NY
Osei-Poku, Rev. Patrick, '95 (RVC) St. Joseph's, Kings Park, NY
Osendorf, Rev. James R, *C.M.* '80 (STL) [MON] Congregation of the Mission, Perryville, MO
Oser, Rev. Ronald E., '92 (ORL) Retired.
O'Shaughnessy, Rev. Denis, '08 (STA) Retired.
O'Shaughnessy, Rev. Gerard, *S.S.C.* '60 (OM) [MON] Missionary Society of St. Columban, St. Columbans, NE
O'Shaughnessy, Rev. Gerard, *S.S.C.* '60 (LA) St. Hilary, Pico Rivera, CA
O'Shaughnessy, Rev. James J., '68 (NY) Retired. Cardinal Spellman High School, Bronx, NY
O'Shaughnessy, Rev. Patrick, '68 (BLX) Retired.
O'Shaughnessy, Rev. Thomas Brian, '16 (SAV) Christ the King Church, Pine Mountain, GA
O'Shea, Rev. Daniel, *S.A.* '64 (NY) Retired.
O'Shea, Rev. David T., '61 (PT) Retired.
O'Shea, Rev. James, *C.P.* (BRK) [MIS] St. Paul's Benevolent, Educational and Missionary Institute, Inc. (Congregation of the Passion - St. Paul of the Cross Province), Jamaica, NY; [MON] Immaculate Conception Monastery, Jamaica, NY
O'Shea, Rev. James, *C.P.* '89 (NY) [MIS] New Jersey Friends of Mandeville Inc., Rye Brook, NY; [MON] Passionist Residence Riverdale, Bronx, NY; [MON] St. Vincent Strambi Residence (The Passionists), Pelham Manor, NY; [MON] The Congregation of the Passion - St. Paul of the Cross Province, Jamaica, NY
O'Shea, Rev. James B., '65 (WOR) Retired.
O'Shea, Rev. Msgr. James D., '64 (SFD) Retired. St. Thomas the Apostle, Decatur, IL
O'Shea, Rev. Jeremiah T., '64 (PIT) Retired.
O'Shea, Rev. Jeremy, (GBG) Retired. [NUR] Neumann House, Greensburg, PA
O'Shea, Rev. John G., '60 (YAK) Retired. Holy Spirit, Kennewick, WA
O'Shea, Rev. William D., '62 (PMB) St. Clare, North Palm Beach, FL
O'Shea, Rev. William J., '63 (JOL) Retired.
O'Shea-Creal, Rev. Liam, '22 (LIN) St. Michael's, Hastings, NE
Osiander, Rev. Alfons M., '73 (BUF) St. Jude Roman Catholic Church Society of Sardinia, New York, Sardinia, NY
Osias, Rev. Jean Max, '94 (NEW) Holy Spirit-Our Lady Help of Christians, East Orange, NJ
Osigwe, Rev. Emmanuel, (DEN) Sacred Heart of Mary Catholic Parish in Boulder, Boulder, CO
Ositimehin, Rev. Stephen, (BAL) St. Veronica, Baltimore, MD
Osorio, Rev. Abel, *C.M.* '08 (PH) [MON] Congregation of the Mission, Philadelphia, PA
Osorio, Rev. Ambiorix, '16 (BRK) Queen of Angels, Long Island City, NY; St. Sebastian, Woodside, NY
Osorio, Rev. Carlos, '15 (BAL) On Leave.
Osorio, Rev. Celimo, '81 (ELP) Our Lady of Guadalupe, Fabens, TX
Osorio, Rev. Francisco J., '86 (PMB) Curia: Leadership; Organizations (affiliated, inter-Diocesan, miscellaneous/ other) Holy Cross, Indiantown, FL
Osorio, Rev. Francisco J., '86 (PMB) Curia: Leadership
Osorio, Rev. Louis S., '00 (CHL) On Duty Outside Diocese.
Osorio, Rev. Luis, '00 (ORL) Holy Spirit, Lake Wales, FL
Osorio, Rev. Pablo, *T.C.* (SJN) [SPF] Politecnico Amigo, Santurce, PR
Osorio Agudelo, Rev. Edison Adolfo, *C.S.* '00 (NY) [MON] Scalabrinian Missionaries (The Pious Society of the Missionaries of St. Charles Boromeo, Inc.), New York, NY
Osorio Hernandez, Rev. German, (MO) Curia: Offices and Directors
Osorno, Rev. Juan, '17 (ORL) Curia: Advisory Boards,

Commissions, Committees, and Councils St. Mary Catholic Church, Rockledge, FL

Ospina, Rev. Diego F., '05 (RCK) On Special Assignment. Curia: Offices and Directors St. Mary, Freeport, IL

Ospina-Briceno, Rev. Walter, '02 (R) On Leave.

Ospino, Rev. Nadin Williams, '21 (PBL) St. Joseph, Grand Junction, CO

Ossa, Rev. Pedro N., '63 (BRK) Retired. St. Martin of Tours-Our Lady of Lourdes, Brooklyn, NY

Ossola, Rev. Msgr. John R., '38 (SFD) Retired. Little Flower, Springfield, IL

Ostaszewski, Rev. Andrzej, '84 (NEW) Curia: Offices and Directors St. Casimir, Newark, NJ

Ostdiek, Rev. Gilbert, *O.F.M.* '60 (CHI) [MON] Holy Spirit Friary, Order of Friars Minor, Chicago, IL; [SEM] Catholic Theological Union, Chicago, IL

Ostdiek, Rev. Gregory J., *S.J.* '19 (CHI) [MON] Canisius House Jesuit Community, Evanston, IL

Osterhaus, Very Rev. Mark, '85 (DUB) On Special Assignment. Dean of the Dyersville Deanery St. Matthias Parish, Cascade, Iowa, Cascade, IA; St. Patrick Church, Garryowen, Bernard, Iowa, Bernard, IA; St. Peter's Church, Temple Hill, Cascade, Iowa, Cascade, IA; The Sacred Heart Church, Fillmore, Iowa, Bernard, IA

Osterhout, Rev. Conrad, *CFR* '83 (NY) [MON] St. Leopold's Friary, Yonkers, NY

Osterman, Rev. Gerald J., '67 (BO) Retired. Curia: Consultative Bodies; Leadership St. Peter, Boston, MA; [MIS] Pontifical Mission Societies in the Archdiocese of Boston (The Propagation of the Faith of Boston, Inc.), Braintree, MA

Osterman, Rev. Richard, '69 (GF) Retired.

Ostini, Rev. Anthony H., *S.J.* '72 (LAF) [MON] St. Charles College, Grand Coteau, LA; [RTR] Jesuit Spirituality Center (St. Charles College), Grand Coteau, LA

Ostler, Rev. David M., '87 (PHX) Prince of Peace Roman Catholic Parish Sun City West, Sun City West, AZ

Ostrander, Rev. Gary L., '71 (OM) Retired. St. Patrick (Elkhorn), Elkhorn, NE

Ostrowski, Rev. David T., '89 (STP) St. William, Fridley, MN

Ostrowski, Rev. Msgr. Eugene S., '77 (WH) Curia: Leadership; Offices and Directors [NUR] Welty Home for the Aged, Inc., Wheeling, WV

Ostrowski, Rev. John T., '98 (CLV) Chap, Casa Parroquial San Pedro Teotepeque

Ostrowski, Rev. Mark, '19 (KCK) St. James Catholic Academy, Inc., Lenexa, KS; St. Joseph, Shawnee, KS

Ostrowski, Rev. Ted, '81 (CHI) [HOS] Franciscan Health Olympia Fields (Franciscan Alliance, Inc.), Olympia Fields, IL

Ostrowski, Rev. Walter, *S.V.D.* '65 (MIL) [MON] Divine Word Missionaries, East Troy, WI

Ostrowski, Rev. Walter, *S.V.D.* '65 (PIT) [MON] Society of The Divine Word, Pittsburgh, PA

Osuafor, Rev. Boniface, (B) St. Paul's, Nampa, ID

Osuagwu, Rev. Anthony, '83 (RVC) Chap, Komanoff Ctr; S Point Plaza Nursing & Rehab Ctr; Gr… Our Lady of the Miraculous Medal, Point Lookout, NY; St. Mary of the Isle, Long Beach, NY

Osuagwu, Rev. Gerald, '08 (LA) Sacred Heart, Lancaster, CA

Osuagwu, Rev. Virginus, *S.D.S.* '19 (MIL) [MON] Salvatorian Provincial Offices (Society of the Divine Savior), Milwaukee, WI

Osuch, Rev. Michal, *C.R.* '80 (SB) Our Lady of the Lake, Lake Arrowhead, CA; St. Anne in the Mountains, Running Springs, CA; [MIS] Congregation of the Resurrection, Lake Arrowhead, CA

Osuchukwu, Rev. Simon, '03 (PHX) St. Bernard of Clairvaux Roman Catholic Parish, Scottsdale, AZ

Osuegbu, Rev. Cyprian C., '03 (WH) [HOS] Wheeling Hospital, Wheeling, WV

Osuji, Rev. Cletus, (P) Retired. [EFT] Mercy Foundation, Inc., Roseburg, OR

Osuji, Rev. Ngozi, '81 (BRK) Chap, Metropolitan Detention Ctr, Brooklyn

Osuji, Rev. Nigozi, (NY) Chap, Federal Corr Inst, Otisville

Osuji, Rev. Peter I., (PIT) [COL] Duquesne University of the Holy Spirit, Pittsburgh, PA

Osuji, Rev. Urban, *C.M.* '86 (BEL) Curia: Leadership St. Andrew, Christopher, IL; St. Joseph, Benton, IL; St. Mary, Sesser, IL

O'Sullivan, Rev. Brendan, *S.S.C.* '70 (OM) [MON] Missionary Society of St. Columban, St. Columbans, NE

O'Sullivan, Rev. Cyril J., '80 (SFR) Curia: Leadership St. Isabella, San Rafael, CA

O'Sullivan, Rev. Daniel, '60 (DET) Retired.

O'Sullivan, Rev. Daniel A., '63 (LA) Retired. Sacred Heart, Ventura, CA

O'Sullivan, Rev. Denis A., '72 (SR) Retired.

O'Sullivan, Rev. Msgr. John V., '68 (PT) Retired.

O'Sullivan, Rev. Msgr. John V., '68 (PT) Retired.

O'Sullivan, Very Rev. Michael T., *S.A.C.* '86 (FWT) (>DET) [MON] Society of the Catholic Apostolate (Pallottine Fathers), Wyandotte, MI

O'Sullivan, Rev. Raymond S., '68 (BO) Retired.

O'Sullivan, Rev. Sean, *S.J.* (SJN) San Ignacio de Loyola, San Juan, PR

O'Sullivan, Rev. Sean, '64 (MIA) Retired.

O'Sullivan, Rev. Sean A., *S.J.* '99 (MIL) [MON] St. Camillus Jesuit Community (Society of Jesus, USA Midwest Province), Wauwatosa, WI

O'Sullivan, Rev. Timothy, (PH) St. Ephrem, Bensalem, PA

Osuna, Rev. E. Donald, '63 (OAK) Retired.

Osunkwo, Rev. Jude Thaddeus, '90 (BO) Curia: Pastoral Services Saint Isidore Parish, Middleborough, MA

Osunwa, Rev. Malachy, *CMF* '94 (ATL) Corpus Christi Catholic Church, Stone Mountain, Inc., Stone Mountain, GA

Oswald, Rev. John, '61 (LR) Retired. [MON] St. John Manor, Little Rock, AR

Oswald, Rev. Leo P., '78 (PH) St. George, Glenolden, PA

Oswald, Rev. Norman R., '72 (MIL) Retired.

Oswald, Rev. Randall J., '97 (CHY) St. Mary's Cathedral, Cheyenne, WY

Oswald, Rev. Msgr. Richard S., '65 (LR) Retired. [MON] St. John Manor, Little Rock, AR

Oswald, Rev. Robert, '02 (STO) St. Anne Church (Pastor of), Lodi, CA

Oswalt, Rev. M. Price, '13 (OKL) On Special Assignment. Oklahoma City

Otaolaurruchi, Rev. Jose Manuel, (SAT) Sacred Heart, Del Rio, TX

Otellini, Rev. Msgr. Steven D., '78 (SFR) Chap, Knights of Malta Curia: Leadership Church of the Nativity, Menlo Park, CA

Otero, Rev. Jose Colon, (FAJ) Nuestra Senora del Carmen, Punta Santiago, PR

Otero, Rev. Lino, *L.C.* '04 (ATL) [MIS] Home and Family, Incorporated, Roswell, GA; [MON] Legionaries of Christ, Incorporated, Cumming, GA

Otiaba, Rev. Emanuel, (MO) Curia: Offices and Directors

Otieno, Rev. Chrispine, '13 (P) Our Lady of Sorrows, Portland, OR

Otieno, Rev. Clive, (MO) Curia: Offices and Directors

Otieno, Rev. Clive, '15 (JOL) St. Irene, Warrenville, IL

Otieno, Rev. Polycarp, *F.M.H.* (BEA) Curia: Advisory Boards, Commissions, Committees, and Councils Our Lady of Sorrows, China, TX; Our Lady of Victory, Sour Lake, TX

O'Toole, Rev. Brian P., '86 (WOR) Our Lady of Lourdes (Roman Catholic Bishop of Worcester, Corporation Sole), Worcester, MA

O'Toole, Rev. Matthew L., (STL) St. Peter Catholic Church, Kirkwood, Kirkwood, MO

O'Toole, Rev. Timothy, '89 (PMB) Retired.

O'Toole, Rev. William F., '96 (GRY) [HOS] Franciscan Health Michigan City, Michigan City, IN

Otor, Rev. Patrick A., *M.S.P.* '92 (SAV) St. Benedict the Moor Catholic Church, Columbus, GA

Otsiwah, Very Rev. Charles Elvis, '85 (VIC) Curia: Leadership; Offices and Directors [MIS] Cemetery Office, ,

Otsiwah, Very Rev. Charles Elvis, '85 (VIC) Holy Cross, East Bernard, TX

Ott, Rev. Jeffery, *O.P.* '02 (ATL) Our Lady of Lourdes Catholic Church, Atlanta, Inc., Atlanta, GA; [MON] Augustine House, Dominicans Friars of Atlanta (The Monastery on the Hill), Atlanta, GA

Ott, Rev. Mark S., '01 (CLV) [SEM] Saint Mary Seminary and Graduate School of Theology, Wickliffe, OH

Ottagan, Rev. Anthoni, '03 (OWN) St. Alphonsus, Owensboro, KY

Otting, Rev. Paul J., '66 (DUB) Retired.

Otto, Rev. Brent H, *S.J.* (SFR) [MON] Loyola House Jesuit Community, San Francisco, CA

Otto, Rev. David, '16 (ORG) St. Mary's, Fullerton, CA

Otto, Rev. James C., '97 (PH) Sacred Heart of Jesus, Philadelphia, PA

Otto, Rev. Thomas, '13 (PEO) Shrine of Queen of the Holy Rosary, LaSalle, IL; St. Hyacinth, LaSalle, IL; St. Patrick, LaSalle, IL; [HOS] OSF HealthCare Holy Family Medical Center, Monmouth, IL

Otuma, Rev. George, *A.J.* (L) St. Bernard, Liberty, KY

Otuwurunne, Rev. Onyedika Michael, '96 (NEW) Chap, Bergen Cty Corr Fac, Hackensack St. Margaret of Cortona, Little Ferry, NJ

Oubre, Rev. Carroll L., '91 (ARL) Holy Spirit, Annandale, VA

Oubre, Very Rev. Sinclair, '86 (BEA) Curia: Administration; Leadership; Offices and Directors St. Francis of Assisi, Orange, TX; [MIS] Apostleship of the Sea of the United States of America (AOSUSA), Port Arthur, TX

Ouda, Rev. Lukas O., (CHI) St. Elizabeth of the Trinity, Chicago, IL

Oudenhoven, Rev. Daniel E., '12 (LC) Newman Community, Eau Claire, WI; [CAM] Newman Parish, Eau Claire, WI

Oudenhoven, Rev. Timothy L., '10 (LC) St. Bernard, Abbotsford, WI; St. Louis, Dorchester, WI

Ouedraogo, Rev. Evariste, '93 (NY) All Saints, New York, NY

Ouedraogo, Rev. T. Basile, *SJ* '22 (OAK) [MON] Jesuit Fathers and Brothers, Berkeley, CA

Ouellette, Rev. Anthony, '06 (KCK) Curia: Advisory Boards, Commissions, Committees, and Councils Holy Name of Jesus Parish, Kansas City, KS

Ouellette, Rev. Donald C., '90 (WOR) Curia: Spiritual Life Our Lady of the Sacred Heart, West Brookfield, MA; St. John the Baptist, East Brookfield, MA; St. Joseph, North Brookfield, MA

Ouellette, Rev. John C., '95 (CC) Retired.

Ouellette, Rev. John Paul, *C.F.R.* '11 (NY) [MON] St. Crispin Friary, Bronx, NY

Ouellette, Rev. John Paul, (NY) [MON] Franciscan Friars of the Renewal, Bronx, NY

Ouellette, Rev. Kent R., '05 (PRT) Notre Dame du Mont Carmel Parish, Madawaska, ME; Our Lady of the Valley, St. Agatha, ME; Saint Peter Chanel Parish, Van Buren, ME; St. Paul, Patten, ME

Ouellette, Rev. Richard T., *M.M.* '63 (NY) Retired.

Oulds, Rev. John V., '68 (PH) Retired.

Ouma, Rev. Francis, '15 (BAL) St. Patrick's, Havre de Grace, MD

Ouma, Rev. Mark, '17 (LEX) Curia: Leadership Queen of All Saints, Beattyville, KY

Ouper, Rev. John J., '84 (JOL) St. Daniel the Prophet Church, Wheaton, IL

Ours, Rev. Donald J., *C.M.* (LA) [NUR] St. John of God Retirement and Care Center, Los Angeles, CA

Ouseph, Rev. Kuriakose P., '87 (SAT) St. Joseph's, Nixon, TX; St. Philip Benizi, Smiley, TX

Ouseph, Rev. Raphael Ambadan, '87 (SYM) Holy Family Syro-Malabar Catholic Church, Rockland, New York, Inc. of St. Thomas Syro Malabar Diocese of Chicago, Wesley Hills, NY

Outschoorn, Rev. Cryton, '02 (LC) St. Mary, Lyndon Station, WI

Ovalle, Rev. Thomas, *OMI* '77 (SAT) [MON] Oblate Benson Residence, San Antonio, TX

Ovando, Rev. Sergio, '93 (SJ) Curia: Leadership; Offices and Directors St. Catherine of Alexandria, Morgan Hill, CA

Overbaugh, Rev. Msgr. Hugh A., '61 (HBG) Retired.

Overbeck, Rev. Kenneth C., '97 (BO) St. Bonaventure, Plymouth, MA

Overbeck, Rev. T. Jerome, *S.J.* '74 (CHI) [COL] Jesuit Community at Loyola University Chicago, Chicago, IL

Overberg, Rev. Kenneth R., *S.J.* '73 (CIN) [MON] Cincinnati Jesuit Community, Cincinnati, OH

Overmyer, Rev. John, '97 (FTW) [MIS] Saint Anne Home & Retirement Community, Fort Wayne, IN

Overton, Rev. Troy, '89 (L) St. Thomas More, Louisville, KY

Overton, Rev. Troy D., '89 (L) Our Lady of Mount Carmel, Louisville, KY

Oviedo, Rev. Isaac, '22 (TYL) Immaculate Conception, Jefferson, TX; St. Joseph, Marshall, TX

Ovienloba, Rev. Andrew, '95 (NY) St. Ann, Bronx, NY

Ovsak, Rev. William, '99 (FAR) Retired.

Owczarczak, Rev. Robert J, '19 (BUF) Holy Trinity, Dunkirk, NY; Northern Chautauqua Catholic School, Dunkirk, NY

Owen, Rev. Leslie Mark, *C.Ss.R.* '85 (BAL) Sacred Heart of Jesus-Sagrado Corazon de Jesus, Baltimore, MD

Owen, Rev. Michael, (SP) Incarnation Catholic Church, Tampa, FL

Owen, Rev. Phillip T., '11 (CHI) St. John Vianney, Cure of Ars, Northlake, IL

Owens, Rev. Bernard, *S.J.* '72 (DET) [MON] Jesuit Community at the University of Detroit Mercy, Detroit, MI

Owens, Rev. Coady, (LFT) St. Francis of Assisi, Muncie, IN; St. Lawrence, Muncie, IN; St. Mary, Muncie, IN; [CAM] Newman Foundation-Ball State University, Muncie, IN

Owens, Very Rev. Douglas, '11 (KNX) Curia: Leadership; Offices and Directors All Saints Catholic Church, Knoxville, TN
Owens, Rev. Edward, *OSST* (SAT) [COL] The Mexican American Catholic College, San Antonio, TX
Owens, Rt. Rev. Elijah, *O.S.B.* '95 (LR) [MON] Subiaco Abbey, Subiaco, AR
Owens, Rev. J. Edward, *O.SS.T.* '80 (SAT) [MON] Holy Trinity Fathers, San Antonio, TX
Owens, Rev. J. Edward, *O.SS.T.* '80 (BAL) [MON] Holy Trinity Monastery, Sykesville, MD
Owens, Rev. Joseph V., *S.J.* '71 (BO) [MON] Campion Center, Inc., Weston, MA
Owens, Rev. Leroy E., '64 (BO) St. Linus, Natick, MA
Owens, Rev. Michael J., '84 (HON) Retired.
Owens, Rev. Richard, *OFM, Cap* (GBG) St. Bernard of Clairvaux, Indiana, PA; St. Thomas More University Parish, Indiana, PA (>PIT) [MON] The Capuchin Franciscan Friars Province of Saint Augustine, Pittsburgh, PA
Owera, Rev. Ramon Macoy, '98 (COL) Chap, Hospital Ministry Community of Holy Rosary and St. John, Columbus, OH; St. Dominic, Columbus, OH
Owuamanam, Rev. Remigius, *SMMM* (SB) St. Joseph, Barstow, CA; St. Philip Neri (Lenwood), Barstow, CA
Owusu, Rev. Augustine, '01 (DOD) St. Alphonsus Catholic Church of Satanta, Kansas, Satanta, KS; St. Anthony of Padua Catholic Church of Liberal, Kansas, Liberal, KS
Owusu, Rev. Benjamin, *OFM* '02 (WDC) [MON] Franciscan Monastery USA Inc., Washington, DC
Owusu, Rev. Clement, (DM) St. Michael, Harlan, IA
Owusu, Rev. Samuel, (VIC) St. Philip the Apostle, El Campo, TX
Owusu, Rev. Samuel Kwadwo, '99 (COV) St. Timothy, Union, KY
Owusu, Rev. Seth Nana Kwame, '01 (DM) St. Mary, Mediatrix of All Graces, Avoca, IA; St. Patrick, Walnut, IA
Owusu-Achiaw, Rev. John, *C.S.Sp.* (DET) St. Mary Parish Detroit, Detroit, MI
Owusu-Ansah, Rev. Edward, '18 (NO) St. Philip Neri, Metairie, LA
Owusu-Ansah, Rev. Edward Kofi, '94 (NO) Mary, Queen of Peace Roman Catholic Church, Mandeville, Louisiana, Mandeville, LA
Owusu-Ansah, Rev. Edward Kofi, (NY) Chap, New York Presbyterian (Downtown Hosp), New York
Owusu-Boateng, Rev. Johnson, '85 (VIC) St. John Bosco, Vanderbilt, TX
Owusu-Peprah, Rev. Anthony Augustine, (VIC) St. Robert Bellarmine, El Campo, TX
Oxley, Rev. Walter R., '03 (TOL) Curia: Advisory Boards, Commissions, Committees, and Councils; Clergy and Religious Services
Oya, Rev. Martial F., '12 (GAL) St. Matthew the Evangelist, Houston, TX
Oyama, Rev. Daniel Herve, '09 (BWN) St. Mary, Santa Rosa, TX
Oyarzo, Rev. Luis Alfredo, *S.D.B.* '98 (LA) Santa Isabel, Los Angeles, CA
Oye, Rev. Paul, '94 (LAV) Curia: (>MO) Offices and Directors
Oye, Very Rev. Paul Bola, *O.P.* '94 (HBG) Chap, Penn State Milton S Hershey Med Ctr, Hershey
Oyenugba, Rev. Peter, *M.S.P.* '99 (SAV) Our Divine Saviour, Tifton, GA
Oyola, Rev. Nelson, '14 (NEW) St. Joseph of the Palisades, West New York, NJ
Ozella, Rev. John, '07 (PBL) Retired.
Ozimek, Rev. Adam Z., '94 (ATL) Chap, Prison Apostolate
Ozminkowski, Rev. Clyde, *O.Carm.* '54 (JOL) Retired.
Ozoufuanya, Rev. Victor, '95 (LA) St. Anthony, Long Beach, CA
Paala, Rev. Jonathan, '75 (SFR) Retired.
Pabatao, Very Rev. Florecito P.J., *O.F.M.* (GLP) Curia: Leadership Our Lady of Fatima, Chinle, AZ; St. Berard, Navajo, NM; St. Isabel, Lukachukai, AZ; St. Mary of the Rosary, Pinon, AZ; St. Michael, St. Michaels, AZ
Pabin, Rev. Chester J., '92 (STU) Retired.
Pable, Rev. Martin, (GB) Retired.
Pablo, Rev. Calixto Alex, '83 (SEA) St. James Cathedral, Seattle, WA
Pabon, Rev. Danny Alexis, '16 (NEW) St. Anastasia, Teaneck, NJ
Pabst, Rev. Peter G., *S.J.* '86 (SJ) Cristo Rey San Jose Jesuit High School, San Jose, CA; [MON] Casa San Inigo, Jesuit Residence, Santa Clara, CA; [MON] Jesuit Community at Santa Clara University, Inc., Santa Clara, CA
Pacanza, Rev. Zani, (P) Chap, Federal Corr Inst, Sheridan St. James, McMinnville, OR
Pacciana, Rev. Marco, '11 (BGP) On Duty Outside Diocese. Called back to his Diocese in Newark, NJ
Pacciana, Rev. Marco, '11 (NEW) On Duty Outside Diocese. Remdemptoris Mater Missionary Seminary, Stamford, CT St. Mary, Plainfield, NJ
Pace, Rev. Paul J., '66 (HRT) Retired.
Pace, Very Rev. Woodrow H., '95 (LC) Curia: Leadership; Offices and Directors [MIS] Father Joseph Walijewski Legacy Guild, Inc., La Crosse, WI; [MIS] Holy Cross (Seminary) Diocesan Center, La Crosse, WI
Pacelli, Rev. Pier-Giorgio, *O.C.D.* '21 (MIL) [MON] Discalced Carmelite Friars of Holy Hill, Inc., Hubertus, WI
Pacer, Rev. Nathan, '22 (RCK) St. Patrick, St. Charles, IL
Pacheco, Rev. Alexandre, '68 (STO) Retired.
Pacheco, Rev. Andrew, '16 (SR) Pastor of Our Lady of Good Counsel Catholic Church, A Corporation Sole, Fort Bragg, CA
Pacheco, Rev. John, '09 (FWT) St. Mary, Gainesville, TX
Pacheco, Rev. Lionel, *C.P.* '96 (NY) [MON] The Congregation of the Passion - St. Paul of the Cross Province, Jamaica, NY
Pacheco, Rev. Lionel, *C.P.* (BRK) Immaculate Conception, Jamaica, NY; [MON] Immaculate Conception Monastery, Jamaica, NY
Pacheco, Rev. Luis, '00 (VEN) St. Paul Parish in Arcadia, Inc., Arcadia, FL
Pacheco, Rev. Luis Hurtado, '00 (VEN) Curia: Leadership; Organizations (affiliated, inter-Diocesan, miscellaneous/other)
Pacheco, Rev. Norbert a., *M.M.* '79 (NY) [MON] Maryknoll Fathers and Brothers (Catholic Foreign Mission Society of America, Inc.), Ossining, NY
Pacheco-Sanchez, Rev. Luis, '79 (MIL) Retired.
Pachence, Rev. Ronald A., '74 (SAV) On Duty Outside Diocese.
Pachla, Rev. Stanley L., '83 (DET) St. Veronica Parish Eastpointe, Eastpointe, MI
Pacholczyk, Rev. Tadeusz, '99 (PH) [MIS] The National Catholic Bioethics Center, Broomall, PA
Pacholczyk, Rev. Tadeusz, '99 (FR) On Duty Outside Diocese. Philadelphia, PA
Pacholczyk, Rev. Tadeusz, '99 (PH) Annunciation B.V.M., Havertown, PA
Pacholec, Rev. Daniel S., '96 (SPR) Curia: Offices and Directors Our Lady of the Blessed Sacrament, Westfield, MA
Pacini, Rev. Peter, *C.S.C.* '00 (FTW) St. Bavo, Mishawaka, IN
Pacitti, Rev. Gary T., '89 (PH) St. Basil the Great, Phoenixville, PA
Packard, Rev. Walter E., '71 (E) Retired. St. Luke, Erie, PA
Packuvettithara, Rev. George, '94 (MIA) St. Rose of Lima, Miami Shores, FL
Pacocha, Rev. Edwin D., '62 (CHI) Retired. St. Elizabeth of the Trinity, Chicago, IL
Pacquing, Very Rev. Joseph L., '83 (LSC) Curia: Leadership; Tribunal St. Helena Parish, Inc., Hobbs, NM
Pacwa, Rev. Mitchell C., *S.J.* '76 (CHI) [COL] Jesuit Community at Loyola University Chicago, Chicago, IL
Paczkowski, Rev. Vincent, *S.D.B.* '86 (NEW) [MON] The Salesian Community, Orange, NJ
Padamattummal, Rev. Bosco, '92 (LAN) St. Mary Parish Manchester, Manchester, MI
Padavick, Rev. William B., '63 (CLV) Retired.
Padazinski, Rev. Msgr. C. Michael, '88 (SFR) Curia: Offices and Directors
Padazinski, Rev. Msgr. C. Michael, '88 (SFR) On Special Assignment. Curia: Leadership
Padazinski, Rev. Msgr. C. Michael, '88 (SFR) St. Patrick, Larkspur, CA
Paddack, Rev. Msgr. John N., '84 (NY) Retired. On Leave.
Paddock, Rev. Joseph, '17 (HEL) Curia: Leadership Resurrection Parish: Series 158, LLC, Bozeman, MT
Padelli, Rev. Emilio P., '62 (HRT) Retired.
Paderon, Rev. Gerardo B., '94 (MET) Curia: Family Life Queenship of Mary, Plainsboro, NJ
Padget, Rev. Leo L., '01 (SFE) Retired.
Padgett, Rev. Gary T., '99 (L) Curia: Leadership St. Brigid, Louisville, KY; St. James, Louisville, KY; [MIS] Perpetual Eucharistic Adoration, Louisville, KY
Padickal Thomas, Rev. Mathew, '17 (MIA) St. Paul the Apostle, Lighthouse Point, FL
Padilla, Rev. Adrian Alicea, '90 (FAJ) Curia: Offices and Directors Nuestra Senora del Carmen, Rio Grande, PR
Padilla, Rev. Alex, '16 (SP) On Duty Outside Diocese. Faculty - St. Vincent de Paul Regional Seminary
Padilla, Rev. Alexander T., '16 (SP) Curia: Leadership
Padilla, Rev. Alexander Tadeo, (PMB) [SEM] St. Vincent de Paul Regional Seminary, Boynton Beach, FL
Padilla, Rev. Aquino, '60 (SFR) Retired.
Padilla, Rev. Christopher, '15 (MAD) Corpus Christi Parish, Boscobel, WI, Boscobel, WI
Padilla, Rev. Gerardo, (LA) St. Gerard Majella, Los Angeles, CA
Padilla, Rev. Jose David, *O.P.* '04 (MIA) [COL] Barry University, Miami, FL; [MON] Dominican Fathers of Miami, Inc., Miami, FL
Padilla, Rev. Jose Manuel, '03 (TUC) San Felipe de Jesus Roman Catholic Parish - Nogales, Nogales, AZ
Padilla, Rev. Luis Marrero, '12 (SJN) San Miguel Arcangel, Bayamon, PR
Padilla, Rev. Roberto C, '10 (TR) St. Mary Cathedral, Trenton, NJ
Padilla Cruz, Friar Luis Oscar, *O.F.M.Cap.* (SJN) [MON] Fraternidad Santa Maria de Los Angeles, Rio Piedras, PR
Padilla Cruz, Rev. Norberto, *C.M.F.* (SJN) Casa Mision Claret, Bayamon, PR; Santa Maria, Bayamon, PR
Padilla II, Rev. Alexander, (PMB) Curia: Leadership
Padilla Valdes, Rev. Rafael, '03 (AUS) Immaculate Heart of Mary, Martindale, TX; St. Michael, Uhland, TX
Padinjaredath, Rev. Sibi, *C.P.* '98 (NY) [MON] The Congregation of the Passion - St. Paul of the Cross Province, Jamaica, NY
Padinjaredath, Rev. Sibi, *C.P.* '98 (SCR) St. Ann's Basilica Parish, Scranton, PA
Padinjaredathu, Rev. Shinto, *C.M.I.* (NSH) St. Henry, Nashville, TN
Padinjarekkara, Rev. Suni Thomas, '03 (SYM) St. Mary's Syro-Malabar Knanaya Catholic Church of Houston, Missouri City, TX
Pado, Rev. Thomas, '75 (ORG) Retired.
Padovani, Rev. Martin, *S.V.D.* '60 (TR) Retired.
Padrnos, Rev. Scott Daniel, '22 (DUL) All Saints, Brainerd, MN
Padron-Hernandez, Rev. Rafael, *C.R.M.* (CHR) Jesus, Our Risen Savior, Spartanburg, SC
Padula, Rev. Armand, *O.F.M.* '56 (NY) [RTR] Mt. Alvernia Retreat House, Wappingers Falls, NY
Paek, Rev. Joseph, *O.S.B.* '03 (SP) St. Ignatius of Antioch, Tarpon Springs, FL; [MON] St. Leo Abbey, Saint Leo, FL
Paffel, Rev. Gregory, '01 (SCL) Our Lady of the Angels, Sauk Centre, MN; SS. Peter and Paul, Sauk Centre, MN; St. Alexius, West Union, MN; St. Donatus, Sauk Centre, MN; St. Francis De Sales, Belgrade, MN; St. Paul's, Sauk Centre, MN
Pagan, Rev. Miguel, '04 (WOR) St. George, Worcester, MA
Pagano, Rev. Richard, '13 (STA) St. John Paul II Catholic Church, Ponte Vedra, FL
Pagan-Torres, Rev. Angel, (SJN) Curia: Leadership
Page, Rev. Anthony J., '69 (LA) Retired. Beatitudes of Our Lord, La Mirada, CA
Page, Rev. Bryan E., '06 (NEW) Our Lady of Czestochowa, Jersey City, NJ
Page, Rev. Msgr. David, '58 (ORL) Retired. Holy Name of Jesus, Indialantic, FL
Page, Rev. Edmund, *O.Praem.* '20 (ORG) [MON] Norbertine Fathers of Orange, Inc., Silverado, CA
Page, Rev. Joseph, '05 (SJ) Our Lady of La Vang Parish, San Jose, CA
Page, Rev. Leon J., '56 (DET) Retired.
Page, Rev. Stephen C., '87 (DAV) SS. Philip and James Church of Grand Mound, Iowa, Grand Mound, IA; St. Joseph Church of DeWitt, Iowa, DeWitt, IA
Page, Rev. Thomas P., '79 (GR) Retired. Curia: Leadership
Pagel, Rev. John M., '80 (CHL) Retired.
Pagliari, Rev. Robert M., *C.Ss.R.* '75 (NY) Parish of Most Holy Redeemer and Nativity, New York, NY
Pagnotta, Rev. James V., '69 (NEW) Retired.
Pagones, Rev. Peter N., '68 (ALB) Retired.
Paguaga, Rev. Juan Carlos, '00 (MIA) St. Agnes, Key Biscayne, FL
Pahamtang, Rev. Leonardo, '77 (LUB) Retired. Immaculate Conception, Muleshoe, TX
Pahl, Rev. John E., '10 (HRT) Retired.
Pahler, Rev. Robert E., '57 (CLV) Retired. Queen of Heaven, Uniontown, OH
Paider, Rev. Paul J., '92 (GB) Immaculate Conception, De Pere, WI; St. Joseph, Oneida, WI
Paillacho, Rev. Jose J., '87 (MOB) St. Columba Parish, Dothan, Dothan, AL
Painadath, Rev. Devassy, *R.C.J.* '00 (FRS) Retired.
Pais, Rev. Rohwin, *O.F.M.* '89 (NY) [MON] Franciscan Province of the Immaculate Conception, New York, NY

Paisley, Rev. James J., '85 (SCR) St. Frances Cabrini, Wyoming, PA; St. Therese, Shavertown, PA
Paiz, Rev. William, *CMF* '79 (LA) Retired. [MON] Tepeyac House, Los Angeles, CA
Pajarillo, Rev. Cesar C, '03 (RCK) On Administrative Leave.
Pajerski, Rev. Daniel, *L.C.* '04 (WDC) [MON] Legionaries of Christ, Potomac, MD; [RTR] Alpha Omega, Inc. (Our Lady of Bethesda), Bethesda, MD
Pajor, Rev. Robert M., '07 (CHI) St. Gerald, Oak Lawn, IL
Pakianather, Rev. Aloysius, '78 (RVC) St. Frances de Chantal, Wantagh, NY
Pakula, Rev. Michael G., '73 (PEO) Retired.
Pal, Rev. Daniel, *O.F.M.Conv.* '00 (PMB) St. Lucie, Port St. Lucie, FL
Palacio, Rev. Jorge M., *O.S.M.* '79 (ELP) St. Ignatius of Loyola, El Paso, TX
Palacios, Rev. Antonio, *O.A.R.* '71 (NY) St. Roch, Bronx, NY
Palacios, Rev. Joseph Martin, '87 (LA) St. Agatha, Los Angeles, CA
Palacios, Rev. Luis, *O.F.M.Conv.* '18 (ATL) Chap, Hartsfield Jackson International Airport, Atlanta
Palacios-Rodriguez, Rev. Luis, *O.F.M. Conv.* '18 (R) St. Julia Catholic Parish of Siler City, Siler City, NC
Palackal, Rev. Joseph, *C.M.I.* '79 (BRK) St. Margaret, Middle Village, NY
Palacpac, Rev. Luello N., '87 (SFR) St. Raphael, San Rafael, CA
Paladino, Rev. John J., '91 (NEW) Curia: Advisory Boards, Commissions, Committees, and Councils St. Bartholomew, Scotch Plains, NJ
Palakkattuchira, Rev. Abraham, *CMI* '88 (ALX) St. Genevieve, Marksville, LA
Palakudy, Rev. James, *S.A.C.* '78 (MIL) [MON] Pallotti House, Milwaukee, WI
Palakudy, Rev. James, *S.A.C.* '78 (SFD) Holy Cross, Auburn, IL; Sacred Heart, Virden, IL; St. Patrick, Girard, IL
Palanca, Rev. Mario, (HON) St. Philomena, Honolulu, HI
Palanca, Rev. Mario, (MO) Curia: Offices and Directors
Palang, Rev. Mansueto P., '77 (BR) Retired.
Palardy, Rev. William B., '85 (BO) Curia: Advisory Boards, Commissions, Committees, and Councils; Consultative Bodies; Leadership St. Agatha, Milton, MA
Palas, Rev. Sean, '10 (BEL) On Leave.
Palatty, Rev. Jomon, *M.S.F.S.* '10 (KCK) Curia: Leadership Annunciation, Baldwin City, KS; St. Francis of Assisi, Overbrook, KS
Palatty, Rev. Roy, *C.M.I.* '05 (NSH) [RTR] Carmel Center of Spirituality, Liberty, TN
Palatty Koonathan, Rev. Rojo Anthony, *H.G.N.* '08 (LKC) Christ the King, Lake Charles, LA
Palatty Koonathan, Very Rev. Rojo Antony, *H.G.N.* '08 (LKC) Curia: Advisory Boards, Commissions, Committees, and Councils; Leadership
Palatucci, Rev. John F., '04 (NY) St. Aedan, Pearl River, NY; St. John the Evangelist, St. Charles Borromeo, Pawling, NY
Palazzo, Rev. Michael L., '87 (NY) Holy Cross, Middletown, NY; Holy Name of Jesus, Otisville, NY
Palazzolo, Rev. Anthony P., '93 (STA) Retired. Curia: Evangelization
Palazzolo, Rev. Salvatore, '12 (DET) On Academic Leave. Catholic Univ of America, Washington Curia: Tribunal
Palcisko, Rev. Raymond, '58 (CR) Retired.
Palecko, Rev. Roman Dominic, *C.O.* '98 (NY) Parish of St. Paul and St. Ann, Congers, NY; [MIS] New York Oratory of St. Philip Neri, Inc., Sparkill, NY
Palermo, Rev. Jason P., '07 (BR) St. Stephen the Martyr (Congregation Of St. Stephen's Roman Catholic Church Of Whitehall), Maurepas, LA; The Congregation Of Saint Joseph Roman Catholic Church Of The Parish Of Livingston, State Of Louisiana, French Settlement, LA
Palermo, Rev. Joseph S., '94 (NO) Curia: Miscellaneous / Other Offices St. Francis Xavier, Metairie, LA
Palick, Rev. George J., '58 (PIT) Retired.
Paligutan, Rev. Alvin, *O.S.A.* '07 (LA) Our Mother of Good Counsel, Los Angeles, CA; [MIS] Serra Institute, Los Angeles, CA
Palimattam, Rev. Augustine, (JKS) Curia: Consultative Bodies
Palimattam Poulose, Rev. Augustine, '04 (JKS) Curia: Consultative Bodies St. Joseph, Meridian, MS; St. Patrick, Meridian, MS
Paliwoda, Rev. Canon Steven, '94 (SJP) Curia: Leadership; Offices and Directors St. John the Baptist, Lorain, OH; St. Michael, Rossford, OH
Palka, Rev. Bernard, *S.A.* '72 (NY) [MON] Franciscan Friars of the Atonement, Minister General Office, Garrison, NY
Palka, Rev. Edwin, '96 (SP) Epiphany of Our Lord, Tampa, FL
Palkowski, Rev. Jan, '76 (PH) Curia: Evangelization Saint John Paul II Parish, Philadelphia, PA
Palkowski, Rev. Matthew, *O.F.M.Cap.* '05 (PH) (>PIT) [MON] St. Augustine Friary, Pittsburgh, PA
Palladino, Rev. W. Chris, '05 (BO) Curia: Tribunal Saint Martin de Porres Parish, Boston, MA; St. Ann, Boston, MA; St. Brendan, Boston, MA
Pallardy, Rev. James G., '87 (PEO) St. Anne, East Moline, IL
Palliparambil, Rev. Jose Simon, '62 (RVC) Retired.
Pallipparambil, Rev. Binochan, '02 (ALX) Curia: Miscellaneous / Other Offices Sts. Francis and Anne Catholic Church, Deville, LA
Pallipurath, Rev. Jose, '01 (ALX) Holy Cross, Natchitoches, LA; [CAM] Northwestern State University, Natchitoches, LA
Palluck, Rev. M. Charles, '66 (SEA) Retired.
Pallurathil, Rev. Mathai Naveen, *M.I.* '97 (MIL) [MON] St. Camillus Communities, Inc., Wauwatosa, WI
Pally, Rev. Dilip, *M.S.F.S.* (STA) San Juan Del Rio, St. John, FL
Palmares, Rev. Gerard-Jonas, *O.C.S.O.* (CHR) [MON] Mepkin Abbey, Moncks Corner, SC
Palmer, Rev. Frank S., '62 (DM) Retired.
Palmer, Rev. John, '14 (LA) St. Denis, Diamond Bar, CA; St. Margaret Mary Alacoque, Lomita, CA
Palmer, Rev. John M., *C.S.V.* '71 (CHI) [MON] Viatorian Province Center-Clerics of St. Viator, Arlington Heights, IL
Palmer, Rev. Justin, (SAL) Chaplain at Salina Regional Health Center, Salina, KS
Palmer, Rev. Michael, (MO) Curia: Offices and Directors
Palmer, Rev. Michael C., '63 (BGP) Retired. [MON] The Catherine Dennis Keefe Queen of the Clergy Retired Priests' Residence, Stamford, CT
Palmer, Rev. Msgr. Thomas, '58 (SAT) Retired. [NUR] Missionary Servants of St. Anthony (Padua Place), San Antonio, TX
Palmer, Rev. William E., '03 (TYL) On Duty Outside Diocese. St. Mary of the Cenacle, New Boston, TX
Palmieri, Rev. Frank, *C.R.M.* '62 (CHR) Retired. Immaculate Conception, Goose Creek, SC
Palmieri, Rev. Louis R., '93 (BO) Divine Mercy Parish, Quincy, MA
Palmieri, Rev. Luigi, '67 (ALN) Retired.
Palmigiano, Rev. James, *O.C.S.O.* '88 (WOR) [MON] St. Joseph's Abbey (Cistercian Abbey of Spencer, Inc., Cistercian Order of the Strict Observance (Trappists)), Spencer, MA
Palmisano, Rev. Peter J., '93 (NEW) Our Lady of Mt. Virgin, Garfield, NJ
Palombi, Rev. Francesco, (BO) [SEM] Redemptoris Mater Archdiocesan Missionary Seminary, Chestnut Hill, MA
Palombo, Rev. Anthony, '20 (NEW) Our Lady of Mount Carmel, Ridgewood, NJ
Palomino, Rev. Humberto, *P.E.S.* (STP) St. Mark, St. Paul, MN (>SAC) [MIS] Pro Ecclesia Sancta of California, Vacaville, CA
Palomino, Rev. Ignacio, '85 (HBG) Retired. St. Vincent de Paul, Hanover, PA
Palomo Casares, Friar Benigno, *O.S.A.* (SJN) Santa Rita de Casia, Bayamon, PR
Paloso, Rev. Nicasio G., '75 (SFR) Retired.
Palsa, Rev. Steven M., '79 (PIT) Chap, Forbes Rd Nursing Ctr; Hamilton Hills Personal Care… St. Jude, Pittsburgh, PA; St. Paul Cathedral, Pittsburgh, PA
Palthasar, Rev. Arockia Doss, *HGN* (LAF) Immaculate Conception, Morse, LA; St. John the Baptist, Crowley, LA
Paluch, Rev. Brandon, *S.M.* '20 (SAT) Holy Rosary, San Antonio, TX; [MON] Holy Rosary Marianist Community, San Antonio, TX
Paluch, Rev. Krzysztof, '05 (CHI) St. Veronica, Flossmoor, IL
Palud, Very Rev. Msgr. Michael, *C.O.* (MRY) [EFT] Newman Institute for Historical and Religious Studies/ Domus Patris Foundation, Monterey, CA; [MON] Oratorian Community-Congregation of the Oratory of Pontifical Right, Monterey, CA
Paluku, Rev. Godefroid M., *C.R.M.* (CHR) Jesus, Our Risen Savior, Spartanburg, SC
Palumbos, Rev. Edward L., '72 (ROC) Retired. Blessed Sacrament, Rochester, NY; St. Boniface, Rochester, NY; St. Mary, Rochester, NY
Palys, Rev. Daniel J., '69 (BUF) Retired. On Administrative Leave.
Pambello, Rev. Louis, '81 (NEW) Retired.
Pamintuan, Rev. Edison, *M.S.* '02 (HON) Immaculate Conception, Lihue, HI
Pamisetti, Rev. Praveen, '11 (GB) St. Ambrose, Wabeno, WI; St. Mary of the Lake, Lakewood, WI
Pamment, Rev. Duaine H., '64 (LAN) Retired.
Pampara, Rev. Michael, '94 (GI) Curia: Offices and Directors Christ the King, Cozad, NE
Pamplaniyil, Rev. Mathew V., '76 (FAR) Assumption Church of Starkweather, Starkweather, ND; St. Mary Church of Munich, Munich, ND
Pamula, Rev. Robert, '87 (MO) Curia: Offices and Directors
Panackachira, Rev. Mathew, *M.C.B.S.* '00 (MEM) Church of the Holy Spirit, Memphis, TN
Panackal, Rev. James, *C.M.I.* '84 (NSH) St. Frances Cabrini, Lebanon, TN; [RTR] Carmel Center of Spirituality, Liberty, TN
Panackal, Rev. Philip, '89 (CC) Saint Patrick Mission, San Patricio, TX; St. Thomas the Apostle, Robstown, TX
Panadarathikudiyil, Rev. Sebastian, (NY) Holy Rosary, Hawthorne, NY
Panagia, Rev. Sal J., '73 (PAT) Retired.
Panagoplos, Rev. Christopher, *T.O.R.* '76 (ALT) Chap, UMPC Altoona, Altoona [MON] St. Joseph Friary, Hollidaysburg, PA
Panakal, Rev. Paulson, '00 (CC) Our Lady of Good Counsel, Kingsville, TX; St. Joseph, Kingsville, TX
Panaligan, Rev. Vicente, '77 (LAV) St. Francis of Assisi, Henderson, NV
Panameno, Rev. Kevin E., '21 (NY) St. Joseph, Middletown, NY
Pancoast, Rev. Alexander W., '19 (PH) St. Andrew, Newtown, PA
Panczuk, Rev. Bernard Joseph, *O.S.B.M* '63 (STF) Retired. Holy Cross, Long Island City, NY
Pandarathikudiyil, Rev. Sebastian, *V.C.* '88 (NY) Parish of Holy Rosary and Nativity of Our Blessed Lady, Bronx, NY
Pandzic, Rev. Stjepan, *O.F.M.* '75 (STL) St. Joseph Croatian Catholic Church, St. Louis, MO
Panek, Rev. Andrzej, '83 (CLV) Immaculate Heart of Mary, Cleveland, OH
Pangan, Rev. Anthony, *SSS* (HON) Annunciation, Waimea, HI
Pangan, Rev. Honorio, '20 (AGN) Curia: Consultative Bodies; Spiritual Life St. Anthony and St. Victor, Tamuning, GU
Panganiban, Rev. Liam Reza, *C.R.M.* '07 (CHR) Jesus, Our Risen Savior, Spartanburg, SC
Pangilinan, Rev. Alfie A., '11 (NEW) St. Henry, Bayonne, NJ
Paniagua, Rev. Jaime, (SAT) Curia: Leadership Our Lady of Guadalupe, Del Rio, TX; St. Joseph, Del Rio, TX
Paniagua, Rev. Jose L., '62 (MIA) Retired.
Panicali, Rev. Michael, '17 (BRK) Saint Mark – Saint Margaret Mary, Brooklyn, NY; St. Helen, Howard Beach, NY
Panickomveli, Rev. Jose, (GF) St. Peter, Wibaux, MT
Pankanin, Rev. Krzysztof T., '02 (CHI) St. Gertrude, Franklin Park, IL
Panke, Rev. Msgr. Robert J., '96 (WDC) Curia: Consultative Bodies [SEM] Saint John Paul II Seminary, Washington, DC
Pankiewicz, Rev. James, '10 (PEO) St. Mary of Kickapoo, Kickapoo, IL; St. Patrick's, Elmwood, IL
Pankiraj, Rev. Theesmas, '90 (NEW) Curia: Offices and Directors Sacred Heart, Lyndhurst, NJ
Pankratz, Rev. John, '21 (GF) Curia: Leadership St. Patrick Co-Cathedral, Billings, MT
Pankratz, Rev. Richard, *S.S.C.* '74 (OM) Retired. [MON] Missionary Society of St. Columban, St. Columbans, NE
Pankratz, Rev. Richard L., *S.S.C.* '74 (PRO) Retired. [MON] St. Columban's Retirement House (St. Columban's Foreign Mission Society), Bristol, RI
Panlasigui, Rev. Renato, *R.C.J.* '88 (LA) [MON] Congregation of Rogationists, Inc., Van Nuys, CA
Panlilio, Rev. Christopher, '91 (NEW) St. Francis of Assisi, Hoboken, NJ
Panlilo, Rev. Christopher M., (NEW) Curia: Organizations (affiliated, inter-Diocesan, miscellaneous/ other)
Panneer Selvan, Rev. Johnson Sacreties, *HGN* '14 (PRT) Saint Peter the Fisherman Parish, Machias, ME; [CAM] University of Maine at Machias, Machias, ME
Panneerselvam, Very Rev. Arokiya Soosaidhas, *HGN* '16 (PBL) Curia: Leadership; Offices and Directors St. Margaret Mary, Cortez, CO; St. Rita of Cascia, Mancos, CO
Pannerselvam, Rev. Abil Raj, *H.G.N.* (SB) St. Margaret Mary, Chino, CA

Panqueva, Rev. Alvaro, '98 (DEN) Church of the Ascension Catholic Parish in Denver, Denver, CO
Pansza, Rev. Gilbert, '00 (FWT) Retired.
Panthalanickal, Rev. Abraham, '88 (NSH) St. Christopher, Dickson, TN
Panthananickal, Rev. George, *C.M.I.* '83 (NSH) Immaculate Conception, Pulaski, TN; St. Anthony, Fayetteville, TN
Panthaplamthottiyil, Rev. Jose, *C.M.I.* '75 (STA) St. Elizabeth Ann Seton, Palm Coast, FL
Pantiru, Friar Paul, *OFM Conv.* (SAV) (>ATL) St. Philip Benizi Catholic Church, Jonesboro, Inc., Jonesboro, GA
Pantoja, Rev. Lucas, '05 (MRY) San Miguel, San Miguel, CA
Panuvel, Rev. Pathrose, (DET) St. Michael Parish Livonia, Livonia, MI
Panuvel, Rev. Pathrose, '00 (MCE) Curia: Advisory Boards, Commissions, Committees, and Councils St. Joseph's Malankara Catholic Church, Warren, MI
Panza, Rev. Paulo Sergio, *O.S.B.* '03 (GBG) [MON] Saint Vincent Archabbey, Latrobe, PA
Panzer, Rev. Joel, '94 (LIN) On Duty Outside Diocese. Curia: (>MO) Offices and Directors
Paolino, Rev. Stephen H., '07 (PH) St. Vincent de Paul, Richboro, PA
Papa, Rev. Christopher J., '89 (PH) St. Maximilian Kolbe, West Chester, PA
Papa, Rev. Dominic, *C.P.* '60 (BRK) Retired.
Papa, Rev. Francesco, *CRSP* '66 (BUF) [SEM] St. Anthony M. Zaccaria Seminary, Youngstown, NY; [SHR] Basilica of the National Shrine of Our Lady of Fatima, Inc., Youngstown, NY
Papaj, Rev. Joseph J., *S.J.* '70 (NEW) (>NY) [MON] Murray-Weigel Hall (A Jesuit Community at Murray-Weigel Hall and Kohlmann Hall), Bronx, NY
Papalia, Rev. Pasquale A., '74 (TR) Retired. Church of St. Elizabeth Ann Seton, Whiting, NJ
Papania, Rev. Bernard J., '99 (BLX) Curia: Advisory Boards, Commissions, Committees, and Councils St. Charles Borromeo, Picayune, MS
Pape, Rev. William H., '70 (ALB) Retired. [MIS] The Cathedral Restoration Corp., Albany, NY
Papera, Rev. Msgr. Lewis V., '67 (NEW) Retired.
Paperini, Rev. Msgr. J. Richard, '77 (P) Retired.
Papes, Rev. Joseph M., '01 (PMB) Curia: Offices and Directors
Papes, Rev. Rudy, *C.Ss.R.* '65 (STL) Retired. [MON] St. Clement Health Care Center, Liguori, MO
Papesh, Rev. Michael L., '83 (PBL) Retired.
Papiez, Rev. Andrzej, *SDB* (CHI) St. John Bosco, Chicago, IL
Papineau, Rev. Andre, *S.D.S.* '65 (MIL) [MIS] Salvatorians - Jordan Hall, Milwaukee, WI
Papineau, Rev. Daniel R., '98 (CHR) St. Joseph the Worker Mission, Darlington, SC; St. Mary the Virgin Mother, Hartsville, SC
Papka, Rev. Ihor, '92 (STF) Protection of B.V.M., Manchester, NH
Pappan, Rev. Shibi, *OIC* '05 (RVC) St. Ignatius Loyola, Hicksville, NY
Pappu, Rev. Johny Injacka, (BR) The Congregation Of St. John The Baptist Roman Catholic Church, Brusly, LA
Pappu, Rev. Msgr. Xavier, '81 (TYL) St. Matthew Catholic Church, Longview, TX
Paquet, Rev. Hubert J., '55 (PRT) Retired.
Paquette, Rev. Joseph, '78 (PRO) Retired.
Parackkukizhakkethil, Rev. Daniel, '94 (TOL) St. John the Baptist, Delphos, OH
Paraday, Rev. Mark, *O.P.* '83 (CHI) St. Pius V, Chicago, IL; [MON] St. Pius V Priory, Chicago, IL
Paradayil, Rev. Joseph M., *S.D.B.* '91 (MRY) [MON] Salesians of St. John Bosco, Watsonville, CA
Paradis, Friar James, *O.S.A.* (PH) St. Augustine, Philadelphia, PA
Paradis, Rev. Steve, '10 (TYL) Curia: Advisory Boards, Commissions, Committees, and Councils St. William of Vercelli, Carthage, TX
Parafina, Rev. Rafael Alexander, '02 (RCK) St. Rita of Cascia, Aurora, IL
Parafiniuk, Rev. Emil, '08 (B) Holy Spirit Catholic Community, Pocatello, ID
Parafiniuk, Rev. Emil, (BRK) Our Lady of Hope, Middle Village, NY
Paraiso, Rev. Oscar, '81 (RIC) Our Lady of the Blessed Sacrament, West Point, VA
Parakkalayil, Rev. Biju, (DET) [RTR] Capuchin Retreat, Washington, MI
Parambil, Rev. Paul, *OCD* '78 (ORL) Queen of Peace, Ocala, FL
Parambukattil, Rev. Jacob Christy, '90 (SYM) St. Alphons Syro Malabar Catholic Church (Coppell), Coppell, TX
Parampil, Rev. Biju Paul, '98 (WH) Sacred Heart, Williamson, WV; St. Francis of Assisi, Logan, WV; [MIS] St. Edmund, Man, WV
Parangan, Rev. Maynard U., '06 (GAL) Our Lady of Grace, South Houston, TX
Paraniuk, Rev. Michael A., '81 (CIN) Holy Trinity, West Union, OH; St. Benignus, Greenfield, OH; St. Mary Catholic Church, Hillsboro, OH; St. Mary Queen of Heaven, Peebles, OH
Parapilly, Rev. Sojan, *O.F.M.Cap.* '07 (DEN) [MON] Capuchin Province of Mid-America, Inc. (Capuchin Province of St. Conrad), Denver, CO
Parappanattu, Rev. Aneesh, *MSFS* '10 (DOD) Curia: Offices and Directors Prince of Peace Catholic Church of Great Bend, Kansas, Great Bend, KS; [EFT] The Holy Family Grade School Education Endowment Fund, Great Bend, KS
Parappilly Xavier, Rev. Sojan, (MO) Curia: Offices and Directors
Parathanal, Rev. Jose, (PRO) Curia: Leadership Church of Saint Teresa of the Child Jesus, Nasonville, Harrisville, RI; St. Patrick's Church, Burrillville, Rhode Island, Harrisville, RI
Paratore, Rev. Matthew R., '09 (MET) Curia: Tribunal Our Lady of Peace, Edison, NJ
Parayill, Rev. Roy, *M.S.* (NOR) St. James, Danielson, CT
Parayno, Rev. Martin, *O.S.B.* '94 (SAT) Curia: Administration Senyor Santo Nino de Cebu, San Antonio, TX
Parcher, Rt. Rev. Adrian, *O.S.B.* '59 (SPK) Retired.
Parcon, Rev. Joemarie M., (NEW) Retired. Curia: Organizations (affiliated, inter-Diocesan, miscellaneous/other)
Parcon, Rev. Jose M., '89 (NEW) Curia: Organizations (affiliated, inter-Diocesan, miscellaneous/other)
Pardue, Rev. John, '88 (ALX) Curia: Miscellaneous / Other Offices St. Patrick, Ferriday, LA
Pare, Rev. Paul, *OFM* (GB) Retired. [MON] Blessed Giles Friary, Manitowoc, WI
Paredes, Rev. Jesus E., '12 (BWN) On Leave.
Paredes, Rev. Rodrigo, (MRY) Our Lady of Refuge, Castroville, CA
Paredes, Rev. Walter, '92 (LA) Mary Immaculate, Pacoima, CA
Paredes Beltran, Rev. Jorge A., '95 (ARE) San Juan Bosco, Arecibo, PR
Paredes Carrera, Rev. Hernan, *S.J.* '95 (NY) Parish of Our Lady of Mount Carmel-St. Benedicta and St. Mary of the Assumption, Staten Island, NY; St. Mary of the Assumption, Staten Island, NY
Parent, Rev. Basil R., '86 (NTN) On Duty Outside Diocese. Byzantine Catholic Association of Maine
Parent, Rev. Gregory, (GB) St. Patrick, Lena, WI; [MIS] Catholic Youth Expeditions, Inc., Baileys Harbor, WI
Parent, Rev. Philip, (BO) [MIS] Chapel of Our Lady of Lourdes, Boston, MA; [MIS] Lourdes Bureau, Boston, MA; [MON] Marist Fathers Lourdes Residence, Boston, MA
Parent, Rev. Rene, *M.S.* '76 (SPR) Holy Trinity, Westfield, MA
Parent, Rev. Robert A., '86 (PRT) Curia: Offices and Directors
Parent, Rev. Msgr. Wilfrid, (WDC) Curia: Consultative Bodies
Paretsky, Rev. J. Albert, *O.P.* '81 (NY) [MON] St. Vincent Ferrer Priory, New York, NY
Parfienczyk, Rev. Msgr. Stanislaw, '68 (BO) On Special Assignment.
Parinas, Rev. Joemin, '20 (PAT) St. Pius X, Montville, NJ
Paris, Rev. Benedetto J.J., '95 (MAR) Curia: Offices and Directors St. Francis de Sales, Manistique, MI
Paris, Rev. Benedetto J.J., (GLD) Curia: Offices and Directors
Paris, Rev. John, *S.J.* '69 (BO) Retired. [MON] Campion Health & Wellness, Inc., Weston, MA
Paris, Rev. John U., '50 (BO) Retired. St. Sebastian's School, Inc., Needham, MA
Paris, Rev. Michael S., '11 (WDC) On Leave.
Paris, Rev. Michael-Joseph, *O.C.D.* (MIL) [MON] Discalced Carmelite Friars of Holy Hill, Inc., Hubertus, WI
Parise, Rev. Michael, '79 (BO) On Leave.
Parisi, Rev. Joseph L., '74 (STL) Retired.
Parisi, Rev. Michael J., '82 (PAT) Curia: Leadership St. Catherine of Siena, Mountain Lakes, NJ
Park, Rev. Andrew J., (NEW) Church of Korean Martyrs, Saddle Brook, NJ
Park, Rev. Brian J., '13 (STP) St. Michael, St. Michael, MN
Park, Rev. Byoung-Ok, '08 (NO) Curia: Organizations (affiliated, inter-Diocesan, miscellaneous/other) Hanmaum Korean Catholic Chapel, Metairie, LA
Park, Rev. Don Bosco, (NEW) Parish of St. Joseph, Demarest, NJ
Park, Rev. Francisco, (BIR) Holy Spirit Catholic Parish, Huntsville, Huntsville, AL
Park, Rev. Hongshik Don Bosco, '01 (NEW) Curia: Organizations (affiliated, inter-Diocesan, miscellaneous/other)
Park, Rev. Hyosick John, '17 (BRK) St. Paul Chong Ha-Sang Roman Catholic Chapel, Flushing, NY
Park, Rev. Hyunwoung, '01 (NY) [MIS] Korean Catholic Apostolate of Staten Island, Inc., Staten Island, NY
Park, Rev. Jin Seung Pius, (IND) St. Lawrence Catholic Church, Lawrence, Inc., Indianapolis, IN
Park, Rev. Joseph Ho-Sung, (AJ) Corp. of St. Andrew Kim Parish of the Korean Community, Anchorage, AK
Park, Rev. Min Seo, (WDC) [CAM] Gallaudet University Catholic Community, Washington, DC
Park, Rev. Rakkun, *STM* '06 (OKL) Korean Martyrs, Oklahoma City, OK
Park, Rev. Robert G., '57 (WH) Curia: Offices and Directors Cathedral of St. Joseph, Wheeling, WV
Park, Rev. Soo Young, *S.J.* '17 (ATL) St. Andrew Kim Korean Catholic Church, Norcross, Inc., Duluth, GA
Park, Rev. Tony Key, (ORG) Our Lady Queen of Angels, Newport Beach, CA
Park, Rev. Val, (SEA) All Saints, Puyallup, WA; St. Martin of Tours, Fife, WA
Parker, Rev. Charles, '71 (PHX) Retired.
Parker, Rev. Frank J., *S.J.* '73 (BO) [MON] Campion Health & Wellness, Inc., Weston, MA
Parker, Rev. Glenn, (CHL) St. James, Concord, NC
Parker, Rev. James W., '03 (RCK) On Administrative Leave.
Parker, Rev. John W., '70 (CHI) Retired.
Parker, Rev. Kenneth, '65 (R) Retired.
Parker, Rev. Larry, '84 (WCH) Retired. Mother of God, Oswego, KS
Parker, Rev. Larry J., (WCH) Retired.
Parker, Rev. Michael J., '83 (BUF) St. John the Baptist, Buffalo, NY
Parker, Rev. Nicholas, '08 (SAL) Immaculate Heart of Mary Parish, Hays, Inc., Hays, KS
Parker, Rev. Paul R., '82 (BO) Retired.
Parker, Rev. Ross, '13 (DM) On Special Assignment. Diocesan Dir Seminarians & Vocations Curia: Leadership; Offices and Directors Corpus Christi, Council Bluffs, IA; [MIS] St. Thomas More Center, Panora, IA
Parker, Rev. Theodore K., (MO) Curia: Offices and Directors
Parker, Rev. Theodore K., '72 (DET) Curia: Consultative Bodies St. Charles Lwanga Parish Detroit, Detroit, MI
Parkerson, Rev. Paul, '98 (R) Our Lady of Perpetual Help, Rocky Mount, NC
Parkes, Rev. Joseph P., *S.J.* '76 (NY) Cristo Rey New York High School, Inc., New York, NY; [EFT] Fordham Prep Formation Foundation Trust, Bronx, NY; [MON] America; Residence and Publication Office of the America Press, New York, NY
Parkos, Rev. John F., '64 (STP) Retired.
Parks, Rev. John, '10 (PHX) St. Theresa Roman Catholic Parish, Phoenix, AZ
Parks, Rev. Patrick, '16 (FAR) St. Patrick Church of Fullerton, Fullerton, ND
Parks, Rev. Patrick, '16 (FAR) St. Helena's Church of Ellendale, Ellendale, ND
Parks, Rev. Richard L., *C.P.* '70 (L) [MON] Sacred Heart Retreat, Louisville, KY
Parlet, Rev. Stephen J., '97 (COS) Chap, Diocesan Prison Curia: Tribunal St. Rose of Lima, Buena Vista, CO
Parnell, Rev. Dennis R., *S.J.* '93 (SJ) [MON] Jesuit Community at Santa Clara University, Inc., Santa Clara, CA
Parr, Rev. John L., '78 (LC) Retired. [MIS] Holy Cross (Seminary) Diocesan Center, La Crosse, WI
Parra, Rev. Gerson, '18 (STL) St. Patrick Catholic Church, Wentzville, MO
Parra, Rev. Juan, '22 (WOR) Curia: Offices and Directors St. Paul Cathedral, Worcester, MA
Parrish, Very Rev. Bryan K., '88 (BO) Curia: Advisory Boards, Commissions, Committees, and Councils; Leadership St. Joseph, Needham, MA
Parrish, Rev. Bryan K., '88 (BO) Curia: Advisory Boards, Commissions, Committees, and Councils; Consultative Bodies
Parrish, Rev. Colin, (SEA) St. Anne, Seattle, WA
Parrish, Rev. Dan, *C.S.C.* '04 (P) [MON] Priests of Holy Cross in Oregon, Inc., Portland, OR
Parrish, Rev. Logan, '21 (FTW) St. John the Evangelist,

Goshen, IN
Parrott, Rev. Gregory W., '09 (WIN) Curia: Advisory Boards, Commissions, Committees, and Councils Holy Family, Fairmont, MN; SS. Peter and Paul's, Blue Earth, MN; St. John Vianney, Fairmont, MN; St. Mary's, Winnebago, MN
Parry, Rev. Msgr. Charles J., '81 (WDC) St. Patrick, Rockville, MD
Parsch, Rev. David L., '80 (SAG) Retired.
Parsons, Very Rev. Vincent L., '01 (GI) Curia: Leadership; Offices and Directors; Tribunal SS. Peter and Paul, St. Paul, NE
Partain, Rev. Chad A., '03 (ALX) Curia: Leadership; Miscellaneous / Other Offices St. Frances Xavier Cabrini, Alexandria, LA; [CEM] Maryhill Cemetery for Clergy, Pineville, LA
Parthie, Rev. Ralph, *O.F.M.* '75 (STL) [MON] Franciscan Friary of St. Anthony of Padua, St. Louis, MO
Partida, Rev. Cesar Uriel, '12 (BWN) Sacred Heart, Elsa, TX
Partida, Rev. Rafael A., '82 (SB) Curia: Offices and Directors
Partida, Very Rev. Rafael A., '86 (SB) Curia: Advisory Boards, Commissions, Committees, and Councils; Leadership
Partin, Rev. Lamar, *C.Ss.R.* '01 (TUC) (>BR) Congregation Of St. Gerard Majella Roman Catholic Church, Parish Of East Baton Rouge, Louisiana, Baton Rouge, LA; (>BR) [MIS] Redemptorist Fathers of Baton Rouge, Inc., Baton Rouge, LA; (>BR) [MON] St. Gerard Residence, Baton Rouge, LA
Partin, Rev. Lamar, *CsSR* (BR) The Congregation Of St. John The Evangelist Roman Catholic Church, Prairieville, LA
Parungao, Rev. Arnold P., '13 (SAC) Curia: Offices and Directors Pastor of Sacred Heart Parish, Susanville, a corporation sole, Susanville, CA
Parzynski, Rev. Jason M., '15 (TR) Curia: Offices and Directors
Parzynski, Rev. Tomasz P., '10 (SPR) On Leave.
Pasadilla, Rev. Nicolas O., '72 (GAL) Retired.
Pasala, Rev. Dharmendra, '13 (WIN) Christ the King, Medford, MN; Church of the Sacred Heart, Owatonna, MN; St. Joseph, Owatonna, MN
Pasala, Very Rev. Hriday K., (LSC) Curia: Consultative Bodies; Leadership Our Lady of Grace, Loving, NM; St. Edward Parish, Inc., Carlsbad, NM
Pasala, Rev. Johnpaul, *HGN* '09 (STO) St. Patrick Church of Angels Camp (Pastor of), Angels Camp, CA
Pasala, Rev. Joseph, (FR) Curia: Offices and Directors
Pasala, Rev. Joseph Kumar, '14 (CIN) Holy Trinity, Coldwater, OH; Mary Help of Christians, Fort Recovery, OH; St. Anthony, Fort Recovery, OH; St. Mary, Coldwater, OH; St. Paul, Fort Recovery, OH
Pasala, Rev. Joseph Anil Kumar, *SCJ* '14 (SUP) Immaculate Conception, Hammond, WI; St. Bridget, River Falls, WI
Pasala, Rev. Lourdu, '80 (GRY) Curia: Leadership Assumption of the Blessed Virgin Mary, Hobart, IN
Pasala, Rev. Maria Raju, (CIN) St. Margaret of York, Loveland, OH
Pasala, Rev. Showri Jojappa, '04 (SUP) St. Anne, Boulder Junction, WI; St. Mary, Sayner, WI; St. Rita, Presque Isle, WI
Pasala, Rev. Sleevaraj, '06 (STO) St. Stanislaus Church (Pastor of), Modesto, CA
Pasalic, Rev. Nikola, *O.F.M.* (NY) SS. Cyril and Methodius - St. Raphael, New York, NY
Pascazi, Rev. Louis F., '80 (PIT) St. Clare of Assisi, Chicora, PA; St. Francis of Assisi, Cabot, PA
Pasciak, Rev. Marcel J., '74 (CHI) Retired.
Pascual, Rev. Manuel, '46 (FRS) Retired.
Pascual de La Parte, Rev. Lope, *SJS* '82 (MET) [MON] Society of Jesus Christ the Priest, Stewartsville, NJ
Pashley, Rev. Msgr. Wilfred J., '63 (PH) St. Barbara, Philadelphia, PA
Pasicznyk, Rev. Walter, '14 (PHU) SS. Peter and Paul, Plymouth, PA; Transfiguration of Our Lord, Nanticoke, PA
Pasieczny, Rev. Roman, '80 (DET) St. Lawrence Parish Utica, Utica, MI
Paskert, Rev. Justin, '13 (SP) Curia: Pastoral Services Our Lady of the Rosary, Land O' Lakes, FL; [PRE] Our Lady of the Rosary Early Childhood Center - Mary's House - ECC, Land O' Lakes, FL
Pasley, Rev. Robert C., '82 (CAM) [MIS] Mater Ecclesiae Mission, Berlin, NJ
Pasqualetto, Rev. Vicente, *S.T.* '70 (FAJ) Sagrado Corazon de Jesus, Canovanas, PR
Pasquinelli, Rev. Msgr. Frederick A., '52 (STU) Retired.
Passauer, Rev. Gregory P., '86 (E) All Saints, Waterford, PA
Passenant, Rev. Francis J., '79 (BRK) Our Lady Queen of Martyrs, Forest Hills, NY
Passero, Rev. Ernest F., *S.J.* '70 (BO) [MON] Campion Health & Wellness, Inc., Weston, MA
Passo, Rev. Joshua, *FSSP* (LR) Our Lady of Sorrows Catholic Church, Springdale, AR
Passo, Rev. Michael, *F.S.S.P.* '13 (PHX) Mater Misericordiae Catholic Church, Phoenix, AZ
Passos, Rev. Preston P., '08 (LA) St. Mary Magdalen, Camarillo, CA
Pastores, Rev. Jerome Bose, '86 (OG) St. Regis Mission, Hogansburg, NY
Pastorius, Rev. Thomas M., '03 (STL) St. Joseph Catholic Church, Manchester, Manchester, MO
Pastors, Very Rev. Jerome P., '98 (GB) Most Blessed Sacrament, Oshkosh, WI
Pastrana, Rev. Ronal Vega, '22 (MET) Our Lady of Perpetual Help, Bernardsville, NJ
Pastro, Rev. Vincent, '78 (SEA) Retired.
Pastuszczak, Rev. Jan, *SVD* (TR) The Parish of Our Lady of Guadalupe, Lakewood, NJ
Patalano, Rev. Anthony, *OP* '86 (OAK) (>LA) St. Dominic, Los Angeles, CA
Patauave, Rev. George, '04 (DET) On Duty Outside Diocese. Archdiocese for Military Service
Patauave, Rev. George, (MO) Curia: Offices and Directors
Patella, Rev. Michael, *O.S.B.* '90 (SCL) [MON] St. John's Abbey, of the Order of St. Benedict, Collegeville, MN; [SEM] St. John's School of Theology and Seminary, Collegeville, MN
Patenaude, Rev. Andre A., *M.S.* (FR) [MON] La Salette Shrine & Retreat Center, Attleboro, MA
Pateno, Rev. Pelagio Calambia, *S.V.D.* (TR) The Parish of Our Lady of Guadalupe, Lakewood, NJ
Pater, Rev. Aurel, '90 (ROM) Retired.
Pater, Rev. Daniel R., '79 (CIN) On Administrative Leave.
Paternostro, Rev. David C., *S.J.* '18 (STL) [MON] Jesuit Community Corporation at Saint Louis University - Jesuit Hall, St. Louis, MO
Pates, Rev. Marlon Libres, '10 (GBG) Saint Francis of Assisi, Masontown, PA
Pathiala, Rev. Christy, (BIS) Curia: Leadership St. Agnes, Kenmare, ND; St. Joseph (Bowbells), Bowbells, ND
Pathiyamoola, Rev. Jolly, '02 (GF) St. David, Broadus, MT
Pathiyamoola, Rev. Jolly Ouseph, (GF) Sacred Heart, Miles City, MT; St. David, Broadus, MT
Pathiyil, Rev. Joseph, *M.F.* '88 (OAK) St. Philip Neri-St. Albert the Great, Alameda, CA; [MON] Missionaries of Faith-India Inc., Fremont, CA
Pathmarajah, Rev. T. Pius, '72 (ROC) Curia: Tribunal St. Charles Borromeo, Rochester, NY
Pathrose, Rev. Sales, *O.F.M.Cap.* '09 (DEN) [MON] St. Anthony of Padua Friary, Denver, CO
Patilla, Rev. John Michael, '16 (TR) St. Joan of Arc, Marlton, NJ
Patin, Rev. Paul B., *S.J.* '73 (COS) [MON] Sacred Heart Jesuit Community, Sedalia, CO
Patino, Rev. Artemio, (DAL) Santa Clara of Assisi Catholic Parish, Dallas, TX
Patino, Rev. Carlos, (FR) St. Mary's, Our Lady of the Isle, Nantucket, MA
Patino, Rev. Eliecer, (VIC) St. Anthony's, Palacios, TX
Patino, Very Rev. Ruben M., *C.S.P.* '79 (AUS) Curia: Leadership St. Paul the Apostle, Horseshoe Bay, TX
Patino Montoya, Rev. Fredy, '10 (NY) Immaculate Conception, Staten Island, NY
Patino Villa, Rev. Carlos, '00 (FR) Curia: Offices and Directors
Patras, Rev. Adam, *O.S.B.* '94 (OM) [MON] Benedictine Mission House - Christ the King Priory, Schuyler, NE
Patricio-Silva, Rev. Victor Manuel, *OMI* (SAT) [MIS] Oblate Vocation Office, San Antonio, TX; [SEM] Blessed Mario Borzaga Formation Community, San Antonio, TX
Patricio-Silva, Rev. Victor Manuel, *OMI* (BUF) [MIS] Oblate Vocation Office, Northeast Area, Buffalo, NY
Patrick, Rev. Msgr. John E., '67 (MAR) Retired.
Patrick, Rev. Onuegbu C., (RVC) Our Lady of Lourdes, Malverne, NY
Patrick, Rev. William J., '58 (CLV) Retired.
Patrizio, Rev. Anthony, '66 (CAM) Retired.
Patron, Rev. Charles A., '62 (SB) Retired.
Patros, Rev. Peter, (SPA) St. Matthew's Assyrian-Chaldean Catholic Church, Ceres, CA; St. Thomas Assyrian-Chaldean Parish, Turlock, CA
Pattamparambil, Rev. Dijan Michael, '14 (DET) [MON] St. Bonaventure Monastery, Detroit, MI
Pattasseril, Rev. Biju, *CFIC* (STP) [MIS] Francophone African Chaplaincy, Minneapolis, MN
Patte, Rev. Steven W., '69 (CHI) Retired.
Pattee, Rev. Daniel, *TOR* '87 (FWT) St. Andrew, Fort Worth, TX
Patterson, Rev. Alfred, *O.S.B.* '90 (GBG) [MON] Saint Vincent Archabbey, Latrobe, PA
Patterson, Rev. Bruce A., '86 (ORG) Curia: Leadership St. Angela Merici, Brea, CA
Patterson, Rev. Bryan D., '98 (BRK) The Cathedral-Basilica of St. James, Brooklyn, NY
Patterson, Rev. Frank, '67 (SAV) Retired.
Patterson, Rev. John M., *S.O.L.T.* (CC) St. Anthony, Robstown, TX; [MON] Society of Our Lady of the Most Holy Trinity, Corpus Christi, TX
Patterson, Rev. Patrick, *C.PP.S.* '65 (CIN) Retired. [MON] St. Charles, Celina, OH
Patterson, Rev. Randall P., '70 (ALB) Curia: Offices and Directors Notre Dame-Visitation, Schuylerville, NY
Patterson, Rev. Terrence R., '66 (OG) Retired.
Patti, Very Rev. Angelo J., '82 (ALT) Curia: Deaneries; Offices and Directors St. Peter, Somerset, PA
Patti, Rev. Steven, *OFM* '01 (NY) St. Francis of Assisi, New York, NY
Pattock, Rev. Mark, *O.F.M.Cap.* '13 (ALT) Curia: Offices and Directors St. John the Baptist, New Baltimore, PA; [RTR] St. John The Baptist Retreat Center, New Baltimore, PA
Patton, Rev. Emmanuel, '13 (CHI) [COL] Jesuit Community at Loyola University Chicago, Chicago, IL
Patton, Rev. Patrick G., '78 (HEL) Retired.
Pattugalan, Rev. Giancarlo T., '12 (BRK) On Leave. LAICIZED
Patullo, Rev. Michael, '02 (DUL) Holy Family, McGregor, MN; Our Lady of Fatima, McGrath, MN; St. James, Aitkin, MN
Pau, Rev. Tang Titus, (OKL) Corpus Christi, Oklahoma City, OK
Paul, Rev. Arunprakash, (VEN) Ss. Peter and Paul the Apostles Parish in Bradenton, Inc., Bradenton, FL
Paul, Rev. Benedict, '84 (NY) St. Michael, Bronx, NY
Paul, Rev. Dennis, '93 (JOL) St. Anthony, Frankfort, IL
Paul, Rev. Gregory, *C.P.* '58 (NY) Retired.
Paul, Rev. Leonard, '64 (GLD) Retired. Saint Gertrude The Great Of Northport, Northport, MI; Saint Michael the Archangel of Suttons Bay, Suttons Bay, MI
Paul, Rev. Melvin M., '20 (SYM) St. Joseph Syro-Malabar Catholic Church, Missouri City, TX
Paul, Rev. Pinto, *C.S.C.* '99 (FR) [COL] Holy Cross Fathers Religious, North Easton, MA; [MIS] Holy Cross Family Ministries, North Easton, MA
Paul, Rev. Sahaya, (BUR) Blessed Sacrament, Stowe, VT; Most Holy Name of Jesus Parish, Morrisville, VT
Paul, Very Rev. Thomas, '77 (JOL) Curia: Leadership Immaculate Conception, Elmhurst, IL
Paul, Rev. Thomas Elmus, '07 (ALX) St. Anthony of Padua, Natchitoches, LA; St. Francis of Assisi, Powhatan, LA
Paul, Rev. Vincent, '85 (NY) St. Mary of the Assumption, Katonah, NY
Paul, Rev. Wilkin, *S.D.S.* '19 (TUC) Most Holy Trinity Roman Catholic Parish - Tucson, Tucson, AZ
Paul Puthussery, Rev. Baiju, *O.S.F.S.* (CHL) Immaculate Heart of Mary, High Point, NC
Paulin, Rev. Jeremy, (SFD) (>BO) [MON] Oblate Residence (St. Joseph House), Milton, MA
Paulino, Rev. Alfredo Rosario, (SCR) Saint John Neumann Parish, Scranton, PA
Paulino, Rev. Felino, '77 (SEA) Retired.
Paulish, Rev. W. Jeffrey, '88 (SCR) On Administrative Leave.
Paulissen, Rev. Richard E., *M.M.* '63 (NY) Retired. [MON] Maryknoll Fathers and Brothers (Catholic Foreign Mission Society of America, Inc.), Ossining, NY
Paulli, Rev. Kenneth, *O.F.M.* '90 (ALB) [COL] Siena College, Loudonville, NY
Paulose, Rev. Antony, *C.M.I.* '97 (BEA) St. Mary, Orange, TX; St. Therese, Orange, TX
Paulose, Rev. Wilson Kidangan, '88 (CAM) St. Peter's Catholic Church, Merchantville, N.J., Merchantville, NJ
Paulraj, Rev. Chandrasekar Cellian, '05 (STO) St. Anthony Church of Hughson (Pastor of), Hughson, CA
Paulsen, Rev. Timothy, *O.M.I.* '97 (GAL) Immaculate Heart of Mary, Houston, TX
Paulson, Rev. Brian G., *S.J.* '92 (WDC) [MIS] Jesuit Conference, Inc., Washington, DC; [MON] The Jesuit Community of St. Aloysius Gonzaga, Washington, DC
Paulson, Rev. Jerome E., '76 (NU) Retired.
Paur, Rev. Roman, *O.S.B.* '66 (SCL) [MON] St. John's Abbey, of the Order of St. Benedict, Collegeville, MN
Paurazas, Rev. Peter P., '55 (CHI) Retired. Two Holy Martyrs Parish, Chicago, IL
Pausche, Rev. Frederick F., '78 (CLV) St. Anthony of

Padua, Fairport Harbor, OH; St. Gabriel, Concord Twp., OH
Pauselli, Rev. Francis L., '75 (SCR) Divine Mercy, Scranton, PA
Paustian, Friar Carl, *O.P.* '18 (NO) [MON] Dominican Friars, Southern Dominican Province of St. Martin de Porres, New Orleans, LA
Paustian, Rev. Carl, *O.P.* '18 (LUB) [MON] Southern Dominican Fathers of Lubbock, Lubbock, TX
Pautler, Rev. Msgr. Mark F., '74 (SPK) Retired. Curia: Leadership
Pautler, Rev. Steven, '18 (BEL) Curia: Offices and Directors St. Lawrence, Sandoval, IL; St. Mary, Centralia, IL; [MIS] Diocesan Council of Catholic Women, Belleville, IL
Paveglio, Rev. Jeffrey, (MO) Curia: Offices and Directors
Paveglio, Rev. Jeffrey A., '14 (MAN) On Duty Outside Diocese.
Paveglio, Rev. Marc V., '14 (STP) Saint Rose of Lima, Roseville, MN
Pavela, Rev. Wayne, (OM) Retired.
Pavelin, Rev. Branimir, '20 (DAL) Nuestra Senora del Pilar, Dallas, TX
Pavelis, Rev. Harold, '51 (SCL) Retired.
Pavia, Rev. Nicholas S., '00 (BGP) Curia: Pastoral Services The St. Roch's Church Corporation of Greenwich, Greenwich, CT
Pavich, Rev. Jason, '12 (MET) Curia: Family Life St. Peter the Apostle, New Brunswick, NJ; [CAM] Catholic Center at Rutgers University, New Brunswick, NJ
Pavich, Rev. Philip, *O.F.M.* '57 (CHI) [MON] St. Anthony's Friary, ,
Pavino, Rev. Romeo, '98 (RCK) Church of the Holy Spirit, Roscoe, IL; St. Peter, South Beloit, IL
Pavkovic, Rev. Miljenko, '08 (DEN) Immaculate Heart of Mary Catholic Parish in Northglenn, Northglenn, CO; St. Anthony of Padua Catholic Parish in Denver, Denver, CO
Pavlak, Rev. Andrew J., '00 (SFE) Curia: Offices and Directors Our Lady of Most Holy Rosary, Albuquerque, NM
Pavlak, Rev. Mark D., '16 (STP) Curia: Leadership Saint Thomas Academy, Mendota Heights, MN
Pavlakovich, Rev. Michael, '87 (DEN) On Duty Outside Diocese. Hospital Chap, Univ Hosp & Children's Hosp, Aurora
Pavlicek, Rev. Edward A., '83 (SAT) On Leave.
Pavlicek, Rev. Msgr. Louis, '71 (AUS) Retired.
Pavlick, Rev. Charles C., (ARL) St. Timothy, Chantilly, VA
Pavlick, Rev. Raymond A., '71 (PAT) Retired.
Pavlik, Rev. David P., '78 (CHI) Retired.
Pavlik, Rev. John A., *O.F.M. Cap.* (GBG) Curia: Advisory Boards, Commissions, Committees, and Councils
Pavlik, Rev. John A., *O.F.M. Cap.* (GBG) Our Lady of the Assumption, Coral, PA
Pavlik, Rev. Mark L., '03 (STP) The Catholic Church of Mary Queen of Peace, Rogers, MN
Pavlovsky, Rev. Wencil C., '91 (GAL) Curia: Leadership St. Paul the Apostle, Houston, TX
Pavon, Rev. Luis, '17 (MIA) Curia: Pastoral Services St. Agatha, Miami, FL
Pavur, Rev. Claude, *S.J.* '84 (BO) [MON] The Jesuit Community at Boston College, Chestnut Hill, MA
Pawelk, Rev. Steve, '89 (CIN) [MON] Headquarters of Glenmary Home Missioners (The Home Missioners of America), Fairfield, OH
Pawelko, Rev. Michael J., '10 (PH) Our Lady of the Sacred Heart, Hilltown, PA
Pawell, Rev. Robert, '66 (CHI) [MON] Holy Evangelists Friary, Chicago, IL
Pawlaczyk, Rev. Miroslaw, '92 (NY) Immaculate Conception, Kingston, NY
Pawlicki, Rev. James, *S.V.D.* '73 (BLX) [MON] Media Production Center "In A Word", Bay St. Louis, MS
Pawlicki, Rev. James A., *S.V.D.* (BLX) [MON] St. Augustine's Residence, Bay St. Louis, MS
Pawlikowski, Rev. John M., *O.S.M.* '67 (CHI) Assumption of the Blessed Virgin Mary, Chicago, IL; [MON] Assumption Priory, Chicago, IL; [SEM] Catholic Theological Union, Chicago, IL
Pawlikowski, Rev. Matthew, '97 (NEW) Chap, Lawton, OK
Pawlikowski, Rev. Matthew, (MO) Curia: Offices and Directors
Pawliszko, Rev. Pawel, '21 (B) St. Edward the Confessor, Twin Falls, ID; [CAM] College of Southern Idaho, Twin Falls, ID
Pawlowicz, Rev. Michael, '13 (JOL) On Duty Outside Diocese. Diplomatic Corps, Rome
Pawlowski, Rev. Charles H., '12 (MAN) Curia: Clergy and Religious Services; Consultative Bodies Sacred Heart, Lebanon, NH; St. Helena, Enfield, NH
Pawlowski, Rev. Joseph M., '73 (GRY) Retired. Curia: Leadership; Offices and Directors
Pawlowski, Rev. Krzysztof, (SAT) St. Jerome, San Antonio, TX
Pawlus, Rev. Piotr, '10 (SPR) St. Mary's, Ware, MA; [CEM] Our Lady of Mt. Carmel Cemetery, , ; [CEM] St. William Cemetery, ,
Pawson, Rev. Msgr. Robert J., '66 (BRK) Retired. Our Lady of Lourdes, Queens Village, NY
Paxton, Rev. Phil, *C.P.* (BIR) Holy Family, Birmingham, AL; [MIS] Congregation of the Passion: Holy Family Community, Inc., Birmingham, AL; [MIS] Tuxedo Junction Catholic Community, Inc., Birmingham, AL
Paxton, Rev. Philip, *C.P.* '95 (CHI) [MON] Passionist Provincial Office (The Congregation of the Passion, Holy Cross Province), Park Ridge, IL
Payea, Rev. Gerald, *O.Carm.* '70 (JOL) [MON] Carmelite Provincial Office, Darien, IL
Payer, Rev. Emil S., '71 (GBG) Retired. [NUR] Neumann House, Greensburg, PA
Payne, Rev. Charles E., *O.F.M.* '72 (CHI) [MON] Holy Spirit Friary, Order of Friars Minor, Chicago, IL
Payne, Rev. Jeremiah L., '07 (ORL) Curia: Consultative Bodies All Souls, Sanford, FL
Payne, Rev. John, (LKC) Curia: Leadership St. John Vianney, Bell City, LA
Payne, Rev. John J., '01 (NO) On Duty Outside Diocese. St. John Vianney Church, Bell City, LA 70603
Payne, Rev. John R., *S.J.* '70 (LAF) [MON] St. Charles College, Grand Coteau, LA; [RTR] Jesuit Spirituality Center (St. Charles College), Grand Coteau, LA
Payne, Very Rev. Mark C., '94 (MIL) Curia: Leadership Our Lady of Lourdes Congregation, Milwaukee, WI; St. Eugene Congregation, Fox Point, WI; St. Monica's Congregation, Whitefish Bay, WI
Payne, Rev. Nathaniel, '10 (CHI) St. John the Evangelist, Streamwood, IL
Payne, Rev. Stephen J., '71 (GAL) Holy Family, Galveston, TX; St. Mary's Cathedral Basilica, Galveston, TX
Payne, Rev. Steven, *O.C.D.* '82 (WDC) [MIS] Carmelite Institute of North America, Washington, DC; [SEM] Discalced Carmelite Friars, Inc., Washington, DC
Paysse, Rev. Wayne C., '87 (NO) St. Dominic, New Orleans, LA
Payyappilly, Friar Leo, *OFM Conv.* '03 (L) St. Paul, Louisville, KY
Paz, Friar David, *O.F.M.* (TUC) San Xavier Mission Roman Catholic Parish - Tucson, Tucson, AZ; [MON] San Xavier Mission Friary, Tucson, AZ
Paz, Rev. Jesus, *O.Carm.* (JOL) [MON] Carmelite Provincial Office, Darien, IL
Pazdan, Rev. Benedykt M., '06 (CHI) Queen of Martyrs and St. Bernadette Parish, Evergreen Park, IL
Pazhevetti, Rev. Jose, *M.S.T.* '97 (LA) [HOS] St. Mary Medical Center, Long Beach, CA
Pazhukkathara, Rev. Shaji Joseph, '02 (SUP) Immaculate Conception, Butternut, WI; St. Anthony of Padua, Park Falls, WI; St. Francis of Assisi, Fifield, WI
Pazmany, Rev. Geza, *Sch.P.* '61 (PH) Retired. Devon Preparatory School (Piarist Fathers), Devon, PA; [MON] Piarist Fathers (Order of the Pious Schools), Devon, PA
Pduti, Rev. Doug, *S.J.* (SEA) [MON] Arrupe Jesuit Community at Seattle University, Seattle, WA
Peach, Rev. Patrick Peter, *O.Carm.* '06 (STP) [MON] Carmelite Hermitage of the Blessed Virgin Mary, Lake Elmo, MN
Peacher, Rev. Ignatius, *O.Cist.* '11 (DAL) [MON] Our Lady of Dallas Cistercian Abbey, Irving, TX
Peacock, Rev. Mark E., '07 (GR) Holy Spirit, Grand Rapids, MI
Peak, Rev. James, '07 (SPK) Chap, US Army Curia: (>MO) Offices and Directors St. Anthony, Newport, WA; St. Bernard, Ione, WA; St. Joseph, Metaline Falls, WA; St. Jude, Usk, WA
Pearce, Rev. Joseph Francis, *C.O.* '99 (CHR) St. Anne, Rock Hill, SC; St. Anne Catholic School, Rock Hill, SC; [MON] Oratory of St. Philip Neri, Congregation of the Oratory of Pontifical Rite, Rock Hill, SC
Pearsall, Rev. William T., '53 (BO) Retired.
Pearson, Rev. Everett, '91 (WDC) Church of the Holy Spirit, Forestville, MD; Mt. Calvary, Forestville, MD
Pearson, Rev. John A., '66 (NU) Retired.
Pearson, Rev. John H., *C.S.C.* '73 (PHX) [MON] Holy Cross Congregation/Casa Santa Cruz, Phoenix, AZ
Pearson, Rev. Matthew Gregory, '22 (MAD) St. John Vianney Cure of Ars, Janesville, WI; St. Mary's Congregation, Janesville, WI
Pearson, Rev. Msgr. Robert A., '65 (SPK) Retired. Cathedral of Our Lady of Lourdes, Spokane, WA
Pease, Rev. Barrent C., (SPR) Holy Name, Springfield, MA
Peatee, Rev. Gregory L., '92 (TOL) St. Charles Borromeo, Toledo, OH; St. Hyacinth, Toledo, OH
Pecaric, Rev. Alfred F., '82 (BGP) The Holy Cross Church Corporation of Bridgeport, Fairfield, CT
Peccatiello, Rev. Robert, '13 (SFE) On Leave.
Pecchie, Rev. Paul, '95 (SP) St. Anthony the Abbot, Brooksville, FL
Pecevich, Rev. Conrad S., '77 (WOR) Retired.
Pecharroman, Rev. Ovidio, '65 (WDC) [SEM] Diocesan Laborer Priests, House of Studies, Washington, DC
Peck, Rev. David A., '94 (RCK) St. John Neumann, St. Charles, IL
Peck, Rev. John, *O.S.B.* '89 (GBG) [MON] Saint Vincent Archabbey, Latrobe, PA
Peck, Rev. John, *S.J.* '15 (STL) [MON] Jesuit Community Corporation at Saint Louis University - Jesuit Hall, St. Louis, MO
Peck, Rev. Lawrence, '15 (STA) St. Patrick Church, Gainesville, FL; St. Patrick School, Gainesville, FL
Peck, Rev. Michael R., '11 (PIT) St. Hilary, Washington, PA; St. James, Washington, PA; St. Katharine Drexel Parish, Bentleyville, PA; [CAM] Westminster College, New Castle, PA
Peckman, Rev. R. William, '97 (JC) Immaculate Conception, Macon, MO; St. Mary, Shelbina, MO; St. Patrick, Clarence, MO
Pecoraro, Rev. Robert, *S.J.* '10 (PRT) Cheverus High School, Portland, ME
Peddicord, Rev. Richard A., *O.P.* '86 (CHI) Fenwick High School, Oak Park, IL
Peddoju, Rev. Vijaya, *HGN* (LKC) Sacred Heart, Oakdale, LA
Pedersen, Rev. Bryan J. B., '03 (STP) Sacred Heart, Robbinsdale, MN
Pedersen, Very Rev. Gregg, '11 (DEN) Our Lady of the Valley Catholic Parish in Windsor, Windsor, CO; St. Mary in Ault, Ault, CO
Pedersen, Rev. Mark Joseph, *CSC* (FTW) [COL] University of Notre Dame Du Lac, Notre Dame, IN; [MON] Holy Cross Community, Corby Hall, University of Notre Dame, Notre Dame, IN
Pedigo, Rev. Jon, *S.T.L.* '91 (SJ) On Special Assignment. [CCH] Advocacy & Community Engagement, San Jose, CA; [CCH] Catholic Charities of Santa Clara County, San Jose, CA
Pedone, Rev. Msgr. F. Stephen, '78 (WOR) Curia: Leadership; Offices and Directors Our Lady of Mt. Carmel and Our Lady of Loreto Parish, Worcester, MA
Pedrano, Rev. Stephanos, *O.S.B.* '91 (SD) [MON] Prince of Peace Abbey, Oceanside, CA
Pedrasa, Rev. Peter, '20 (TUC) Saint Anthony of Padua Roman Catholic Parish - Casa Grande, Casa Grande, AZ
Pedrera, Rev. Gerald, '11 (OAK) St. Anne, Union City, CA
Pedroni, Rev. Michele Mario, '17 (NEW) St. Theresa, Kenilworth, NJ
Pedroza, Rev. Peeter, *C.M.F.* '11 (ATL) Divine Mercy Mission, Brookhaven, GA
Pedroza, Rev. Salvador, '81 (LAR) St. John Neumann, Laredo, TX
Pedzich, Rev. Henry J., '72 (SY) Retired. Curia: Offices and Directors
Pee Thuruthel, Rev. Joseph, '01 (PHX) St. Vincent de Paul Roman Catholic Parish, Phoenix, AZ
Peek, Rev. Kevin T., '98 (ATL) On Special Assignment. Airport Ministry, Prison Apostolate Curia: (>MO) Offices and Directors
Peelo, Rev. Adrian, *O.F.M.* '83 (LA) [MON] Franciscan Friary, Order of Friars Minor (Old Mission), Santa Barbara, CA
Peeters, Rev. John N., *C.S.V.* '83 (CHI) [MON] Viatorian Province Center-Clerics of St. Viator, Arlington Heights, IL
Peeters, Rev. John N., *C.S.V.* '83 (JOL) St. Patrick, Kankakee, IL
Peffley, Rev. Francis J., '90 (ARL) St. Mary of Sorrows, Fairfax, VA
Pehl, Rev. Jeff, (SAT) Our Lady of Perpetual Help, Selma, TX
Pehler, Rev. Gerald, (CHI) [MON] St. Clare Friary, Chicago, IL
Pehrsson, Rev. Alfred R., *C.M.* '58 (PH) [MON] Congregation of the Mission, Philadelphia, PA
Peiffer, Rev. James E., '67 (TOL) Retired.
Peinado, Rev. Louis A., *S.J.* '60 (SJ) [MON] Sacred Heart Jesuit Center, Los Gatos, CA
Peirano, Rev. Charles, '21 (SPC) Immaculate Conception, Springfield, MO; Springfield Catholic High School, Springfield, MO

Peirano, Rev. Juan Daniel, '04 (TR) St. Thomas More, Manalapan, NJ
Pekar, Rev. Msgr. Joseph W., '57 (BGP) Retired. [MON] The Catherine Dennis Keefe Queen of the Clergy Retired Priests' Residence, Stamford, CT
Peklo, Rev. Edward, *S.V.D.* '69 (MIL) [MON] Divine Word Missionaries, East Troy, WI
Pekola, Rev. David J., (MET) Our Lady of Fatima, Piscataway, NJ
Pekola, Rev. David J., '86 (MET) Our Lady of Victories, Sayreville, NJ
Pekron, Rev. Zane, '19 (RC) Immaculate Conception, Winner, SD; St. Isidore, Colome, SD; St. Paul, Belle Fourche, SD
Pelak, Rev. Anthony M., '03 (GR) Assumption of the Blessed Virgin Mary, Belmont, MI
Pelavendran, Rev. Chinnappan, '08 (LC) St. John the Baptist, Bloomer, WI; St. Paul, Bloomer, WI
Pelayo Corona, Rev. Mario H., (CHI) St. Ansgar, Hanover Park, IL
Pelc, Rev. Timothy R., '74 (DET) St. Ambrose Parish Grosse Pointe Park, Grosse Pointe Park, MI
Pelczar, Rev. Edward A., '62 (PH) Retired.
Pelczar, Rev. Krzysztof, '12 (MEM) On Leave.
Pelczarski, Rev. Wojciech, '00 (PBL) Sacred Heart, Paonia, CO
Pele Alu, Rev. Dimas Alexander, *O.Carm.* '16 (WDC) [SEM] Whitefriars Hall, Washington, DC
Peles, Rev. David S., '84 (ALT) St. Benedict, Johnstown, PA
Pellazar, Rev. Albert, *O.A.R.* (CHK) Curia: Consultative Bodies; Faith Formation
Pellegrini, Rev. Frederick J., *S.J.* '84 (NY) St. Aloysius, New York, NY; [MON] Murray-Weigel Hall (A Jesuit Community at Murray-Weigel Hall and Kohlmann Hall), Bronx, NY
Pellegrino, Rev. Msgr. Joseph A., '77 (SP) Curia: Administration
Pellerin, Very Rev. Keith, '98 (LKC) Curia: Advisory Boards, Commissions, Committees, and Councils; Leadership Our Lady Help of Christians, Jennings, LA
Pellessier, Rev. Rene J., (MO) Curia: Offices and Directors
Pellessier, Rev. Stephen, '18 (LAF) Our Lady of Wisdom, University of Louisiana, Lafayette, LA; [CAM] Our Lady of Wisdom Catholic Student Center, Lafayette, LA
Pelletier, Rev. Emile C. "Bud", '94 (PHX) Curia: Offices and Directors St. Clement of Rome Roman Catholic Parish, Sun City, AZ; [RTR] Mount Claret Roman Catholic Retreat Center, Phoenix, AZ
Pelletier, Rev. Norman, (SAT) St. Joseph, San Antonio, TX
Pelletier, Rev. Norman, *S.S.S.* '69 (NY) St. Jean Baptiste, New York, NY
Pelletier, Rev. Walter R., *S.J.* '60 (BO) [MON] Campion Health & Wellness, Inc., Weston, MA
Pelletier, Rev. Walter R., *S.J.* '60 (BGP) Retired.
Pellican, Rev. David, (DET) Divine Child Parish Dearborn, Dearborn, MI
Pellissier, Rev. Francois, *G.H.M.* '81 (CIN) [MON] Headquarters of Glenmary Home Missioners (The Home Missioners of America), Fairfield, OH
Peloso, Rev. John P., '96 (MIA) Retired.
Pelous, Rev. Donald, '77 (LAF) Retired.
Pelrine, Rev. Edward S., '01 (CHI) St. James, Arlington Heights, IL; [SEM] University of Saint Mary of the Lake/Mundelein Seminary, Mundelein, IL
Pelster, Rev. Christopher, *FSSP* (STP) All Saints, Minneapolis, MN
Peltzer, Rev. Michael, '80 (WCH) Retired.
Peluse, Rev. Dominic, *S.C.J.* '74 (MIL) [MON] St. Francis Residence, Franklin, WI
Pelzel, Very Rev. Bradley C., '02 (SC) Curia: Leadership; Offices and Directors Mater Dei Catholic Parish, Sioux City, IA; [CEM] Calvary Cemetery, Sioux City, IA
Pemberton, Rev. Msgr. Joseph, '77 (FWT) Most Blessed Sacrament, Arlington, TX
Pena, Rev. Cesar, (BRK) St. Bartholomew, Elmhurst, NY
Pena, Rev. Cesar E., '08 (MIA) On Leave.
Pena, Rev. Giovanni de Jesus, '10 (MIA) Prince of Peace, Miami, FL
Pena, Rev. Luis C., '97 (TYL) Christ the King, Kilgore, TX
Pena Berrios, Rev. Juan Javier, '12 (CGS) Santisimo Sacramento, Caguas, PR
Pena Jimenez, Rev. Rodrigo, (CHI) Holy Guardian Angels, Brookfield, IL
Pena Portillo, Rev. Marcos Tullio, (BO) All Saints, Haverhill, MA
Penafiel, Rev. Fausto, '83 (PHX) Curia: Offices and Directors St. Mark Roman Catholic Parish, Phoenix, AZ
Penafiel, Rev. Romel P., '10 (BRK) St. Andrew Avellino, Flushing, NY
Peñalba, Rev. Vicente, *C.M.F.* (SJN) Casa Mision Claret, Bayamon, PR
Penalosa, Rev. Lorenzo, *OSB* '20 (IND) [MON] St. Meinrad Archabbey, St. Meinrad, IN
Penaloza, Rev. Luis M., '99 (SR) Pastor of St. Elizabeth Catholic Church of Guerneville, A Corporation Sole, Guerneville, CA
Pena-Moredo, Rev. Msgr. Wilfredo, '74 (SJN) Curia: Offices and Directors Santa Bernardita Soubirous, San Juan, PR
Penascoza, Rev. Demetrio, '86 (CHY) Our Lady of the Mountains, Jackson, WY
Pendergraft, Rev. Gregory, *F.S.S.P.* '05 (ALN) Curia: Leadership St. Stephen of Hungary, Allentown, PA
Pendergraft, Rev. Michael, '81 (STA) Curia: Clergy and Religious Services; Leadership Annunciation School, Middleburg, FL; Sacred Heart, Fleming Island, FL
Pendzick, Rev. John S., '97 (ALN) St. Thomas More, Allentown, PA
Penez, Rev. Francisco, '00 (AMA) Curia: Leadership
Pengiperambil, Rev. Benni, *CMI* (L) Saint Teresa of Calcutta Parish, Fairdale, KY
Penhallurick, Rev. Robert, '96 (COL) St. Brendan, Hilliard, OH
Penkalski, Rev. Kevin, '20 (PHX) Saint Henry Roman Catholic Parish, Buckeye, AZ
Penn, Rev. Churchill, '96 (BGP) The Roman Catholic Church of St. Charles, Bridgeport, CT
Penn, Rev. Connor, '20 (SP) St. Catherine of Siena, Clearwater, FL
Penn, Rev. Michael W., '03 (JC) Curia: Organizations (affiliated, inter-Diocesan, miscellaneous/other) Our Lady of the Lake, Lake Ozark, MO
Penna, Rev. Anthony, '70 (BO) Curia: Pastoral Services
Pennati, Rev. Riccardo, '64 (RC) Retired. On Duty Outside Diocese. Incardination to Diocese of Brescia pending.
Pennett, Rev. Frederick J., '71 (MAN) On Leave.
Pennings, Rev. Gary, '01 (KCK) Curia: Advisory Boards, Commissions, Committees, and Councils Church of the Ascension, Overland Park, KS
Pennington, Rev. Matthew, '88 (MRY) Nativity of Our Lady, San Luis Obispo, CA
Pennock, Rev. Michael, '95 (JOL) On Duty Outside Diocese. Florida St. Luke, Carol Stream, IL
Penta, Rev. Leo J., '78 (BRK) On Duty Outside Diocese. Catholic University of Applied Sciences, Germany
Pentareddy, Rev. Balta Raju Reddy, '95 (BIR) St. Barnabas Catholic Parish, Birmingham, Birmingham, AL
Pentecost, Rev. Denver B., '69 (NO) Retired.
Pentello, Rev. Richard J., '79 (Y) St. Patrick's, Kent, OH; University Parish Newman Center, Kent, OH; [CAM] Kent State University Newman Center, Kent, OH
Penton, Rev. Edward, *S.J.* (WDC) [MON] The Jesuit Community of St. Aloysius Gonzaga, Washington, DC
Penton, Rev. Peter J., '14 (BRK) Good Shepherd, Brooklyn, NY
Penton, Rev. Ted, (WDC) [MIS] Jesuit Social and International Ministries-National Office, Washington, DC
Pepin, Rev. Darryl J., '78 (MAR) St. Elizabeth Ann Seton, Bark River, MI
Pepka, Rev. Edward P., '77 (SAC) Retired.
Peplowski, Rev. Sigmund, (PAT) Curia: Leadership
Peplowski, Rev. Sigmund A., '75 (PAT) Divine Mercy Academy, Inc., Rockaway, NJ; St. Cecilia's, Rockaway, NJ
Peppard, Rev. Patrick, (DET) [MON] Colombiere Center, Clarkston, MI
Pepper, Rev. Stephen, (FTW) [SEM] Moreau Seminary, Notre Dame, IN
Peprah, Rev. Dominic, (BRK) Chap, NY Presbyterian Brooklyn Methodist; SUNY Downstate Med St. Jude Shrine Church, Brooklyn, NY
Peprah, Rev. Owusu, (RIC) Holy Apostles Community Virginia Beach
Peprah, Rev. Msgr. Raphael A. Owusu, (RIC) Church of the Holy Apostles, Virginia Beach, VA; St. Luke, Virginia Beach, VA; [MIS] San Lorenzo Spiritual Center, Virginia Beach, VA
Perales, Rev. Jorge, '78 (MIA) [SEM] St. John Vianney College Seminary, Inc., Miami, FL
Peralta, Rev. Jesus, '13 (PAT) Saint Brendan and Saint George, Clifton, NJ
Perata, Rev. Msgr. Stephen, '58 (SJ) Retired.
Peraza, Rev. Pedro Bautista, '04 (SPK) St. Genevieve, Twisp, WA
Percell, Rev. Lawrence, '03 (SJ) Retired.
Percic, Rev. Janez, *S.J.* '94 (WOR) [MON] Jesuits of the Holy Cross, Inc., Worcester, MA
Perdue, Rev. John, *M.SS.CC.* '90 (CAM) Chap, Shore Med Ctr [MON] Villa Pieta. Missionaries of the Sacred Hearts of Jesus & Mary, Linwood, NJ
Perea, Rev. Jaime, '12 (GRY) St. Francis Xavier, Lake Station, IN
Perea, Rev. Michael U., *O.Praem.* '90 (LA) SS. Peter and Paul, Wilmington, CA
Perea, Rev. Michael U., *O.Praem.* '90 (ORG) [MON] Norbertine Fathers of Orange, Inc., Silverado, CA
Pereda, Rev. Msgr. James F., '81 (RVC) St. Paul the Apostle, Brookville, NY
Perehubka, Rev. Jozef, '84 (HEL) Saint Ann Parish: Series 607, LLC, Bonner, MT
Pereia, Rev. George E., '74 (PH) Our Lady of Grace, Penndel, PA
Pereida, Rev. Alex, '08 (SAT) St. John Neumann, San Antonio, TX
Pereira, Rev. Carlos P., *S.F.X.* '96 (CHI) All Saints Parish, Niles, IL
Pereira, Rev. Carlos Paulo, *sfx* '96 (CHI) [MON] Society of the Missionaries of St. Francis Xavier, Niles, IL
Pereira, Rev. Cyril F., '54 (ALB) Retired.
Pereira, Rev. Erik, '22 (SAC) Pastor of St. Isidore Parish, Yuba City, a corporation sole, Yuba City, CA
Pereira, Rev. Flavio, *C.M.* '96 (PH) [MON] Congregation of the Mission, Philadelphia, PA
Pereira, Rev. Manuel, *M.S.* '95 (HRT) [MIS] Missionaries of LaSalette, Hartford, CT
Pereira, Rev. Manuel C., *M.S.* '95 (FR) Retired.
Pereira, Rev. Sergio Jeair, *O.S.S.T.* (SJN) Espiritu Santo, Bayamon, PR
Pereira, Rev. Sunil, *I.M.S.* (BGP) The Saint Thomas More Roman Catholic Church Corporation, Darien, CT
Perera, Rev. Denzil M., '58 (NO) Retired. Curia: Miscellaneous / Other Offices
Perera, Rev. Kurt, '13 (PHX) Curia: Offices and Directors
Perera, Rev. L.J. Asantha Jude, *T.O.R.* '07 (WH) St. Anthony, Follansbee, WV; [CAM] West Liberty State College, St. Thomas Aquinas Campus Ministry, West Liberty, WV
Peres, Rev. Ignacio, '06 (ATL) Curia: Offices and Directors
Peres, Rev. Mark R., *C.PP.S.* (GRY) St. Adalbert, Whiting, IN; St. John the Baptist, Whiting, IN
Peretti, Rev. Peter L., '73 (GBG) [NUR] Neumann House, Greensburg, PA
Perez, Rev. Alberto A., '14 (OAK) St. Joseph the Worker, Berkeley, CA
Perez, Rev. Alvaro, *P.E.S.* '15 (SAC) Pastor of St. Lawrence Parish, North Highlands, a corporation sole, North Highlands, CA
Perez, Rev. Antonio, '90 (VIC) Curia: Leadership Our Lady of Mt. Carmel, Wharton, TX
Perez, Rev. Armando S., '02 (SEA) St. Edward, Seattle, WA; St. George, Seattle, WA; St. Paul, Seattle, WA; St. Peter, Seattle, WA
Perez, Rev. Aurelio H., '86 (MIL) Curia: Leadership
Perez, Rev. Carlos, '92 (B) On Academic Leave.
Perez, Rev. David, '87 (MGZ) Our Lady of Monserrate, Moca, PR
Perez, Rev. Edwin E., '01 (ARL) Our Lady of the Valley, Luray, VA
Perez, Rev. Eleazar, (PHX) St. Matthew Roman Catholic Parish, Phoenix, AZ
Perez, Very Rev. Francisco, '00 (AMA) Curia: Advisory Boards, Commissions, Committees, and Councils; Consultative Bodies; Leadership; Offices and Directors St. Vincent de Paul, Pampa, TX; [EFT] Roman Catholic Diocese of Amarillo Deposit and Loan Fund, Amarillo, TX
Perez, Rev. Freddy, '18 (SAN) Curia: Advisory Boards, Commissions, Committees, and Councils; Organizations (affiliated, inter-Diocesan, miscellaneous/other) [CAM] Catholic Newman Center, San Angelo, TX
Perez, Rev. George, *CJM* '20 (SD) Pastor of Saint James Catholic Parish, Solana Beach, a corporation sole, Solana Beach, CA
Perez, Rev. German, '97 (KAL) Immaculate Conception, Hartford, MI
Perez, Rev. Gustavo, (WDC) St. Mark, Hyattsville, MD
Perez, Rev. Hector, '00 (MIA) Our Lady of the Lakes, Miami Lakes, FL
Perez, Rev. Hector A., '07 (MIA) St. John the Apostle, Hialeah, FL
Perez, Rev. Canon Hector R.G., '81 (PT) Curia: Offices and Directors St. Stephen, Pensacola, FL
Perez, Rev. Horacio, *S.X.* '03 (PAT) [MON] Xaverian Missionary Fathers, Wayne, NJ

Perez, Rev. Isidro Marcelino, '81 (MIA) Retired.
Perez, Rev. Israel, '01 (BRK) Co-Cathedral of Saint Joseph – Saint Teresa of Avila, Brooklyn, NY; Holy Child Jesus, Richmond Hill, NY; St. Benedict Joseph Labre, South Richmond Hill, NY
Perez, Rev. Jairo A., *CMF* (CGS) Inmaculado Corazon de Maria, Caguas, PR; [MON] Misioneros Hijos del Inmaculado Corazon de Maria (Claretianos), Caguas, PR
Perez, Rev. Jesse L., '74 (PBL) St. Michael, Canon City, CO
Perez, Rev. Joel, '11 (LAR) Santo Nino de Atocha Catholic Church, Laredo, TX
Perez, Rev. John Jairo, '03 (BGP) Curia: Clergy and Religious Services; Consultative Bodies
Perez, Rev. Jonathan, '21 (MEM) St. John's Church, Brownsville, TN; St. Mary's Church, Jackson, TN
Perez, Rev. Jonathan, '20 (CGS) Sagrado Corazon de Jesus y 12 Apostoles, San Lorenzo, PR; [SHR] Diocesan Shrine Our Lady of Mount Carmel, San Lorenzo, PR
Perez, Rev. Jorge, '15 (MIL) St. John Neumann, Catholic Community of Waukesha, Waukesha, WI; St. Joseph, Catholic Community of Waukesha, Waukesha, WI; St. Mary, Catholic Community of Waukesha, Waukesha, WI; St. William, Catholic Community of Waukesha, Waukesha, WI
Perez, Rev. Jose, '99 (BRK) On Leave.
Perez, Rev. Juan C., '96 (SJN) Curia: (>MO) Offices and Directors
Perez, Rev. Leon, '60 (ARE) Retired.
Perez, Rev. Leopoldo, (WDC) [MON] Missionary Oblates of Mary Immaculate, Washington, DC; [MON] Oblate Community, Washington, DC
Perez, Rev. Luis A., '95 (MIA) San Lazaro, Hialeah, FL
Perez, Rev. Manuel, '05 (KNX) Curia: Leadership St. Stephen, Chattanooga, TN
Perez, Rev. Miguel, (GAL) Queen of Peace, Houston, TX; St. Martha, Porter, TX
Perez, Rev. Miguel, '19 (ELP) Holy Spirit, Horizon City, TX
Perez, Rev. Modesto Lewis, '84 (LA) St. Elizabeth of Hungary, Altadena, CA
Perez, Rev. Oscar A., '03 (OM) On Duty Outside Diocese. Archdiocese of Miami
Perez, Rev. Preston D., '20 (NEW) St. Francis de Sales Church, Lodi, NJ
Perez, Rev. Rafael, *O.S.B.* '79 (FAJ) [MON] San Antonio Abad Abbey of the Order of St. Benedict, Humacao, PR
Perez, Rev. Rafael J., '15 (BRK) Curia: Consultative Bodies Holy Family-Saint Thomas Aquinas, Brooklyn, NY; [CON] Convent, Brooklyn, NY
Perez, Rev. Raymond, (LA) Mary Star of the Sea, San Pedro, CA
Perez, Rev. Raymond, *O.Praem.* '88 (ORG) [MON] Norbertine Fathers of Orange, Inc., Silverado, CA
Perez, Rev. Rene, '03 (LUB) Curia: Offices and Directors St. Philip Benizi, Idalou, TX
Perez, Rev. Restituto, *O.P.* '60 (MIA) [MON] Dominican Fathers of Miami, Inc., Miami, FL
Perez, Rev. Ricardo, (BRK) Our Lady of Fatima, Jackson Heights, NY
Perez, Rev. Robert, (NEW) [MON] Capuchin Friars - Province of the Sacred Stigmata of St. Francis, Union City, NJ
Perez, Rev. Robert, '86 (CHI) Retired.
Perez, Rev. Roberto, *O.F.M. Cap.* '02 (NY) Chap, Montefiore Med Ctr, Henry and Lucy Moses Div, Bronx [MON] St. Albert's Priory, Middletown, NY
Perez, Rev. Rommel, *O.F.M.* (WDC) [SEM] Holy Name College, Silver Spring, MD
Perez, Rev. Ronald P., '08 (NY) Parish of St. Mary-St. Joseph and Our Lady of Mount Carmel, Poughkeepsie, NY
Perez, Very Rev. Samuel, '03 (TLS) Curia: Leadership Sacred Heart, Miami, OK
Perez, Rev. Samuel F., '01 (NU) Curia: Leadership St. Mary, Sleepy Eye, MN; St. Michael, Morgan, MN; St. Paul, Comfrey, MN
Perez, Rev. Victor C., '11 (GAL) Curia: Offices and Directors
Perez, Rev. Victor C., '11 (GAL) St. Joseph Church, Houston, TX
Perez, Rev. Victor Manuel, (MOB) St. Joseph Parish Holy Trinity, Fort Mitchell, AL; St. Patrick Parish, Phenix City, Phenix City, AL; [MON] St. Joseph Cenacle, Fort Mitchell, AL
Perez, Rev. Viktor, *O.F.M.Conv.* '89 (FRS) St. Paul the Apostle, Coalinga, CA
Perez Alzate, Rev. Jose Gustavo, (RVC) Our Lady of the Assumption, Copiague, NY
Perez Brown, Rev. Angel, '18 (DEN) St. Nicholas Catholic Parish in Platteville, Platteville, CO
Perez Cruz, Rev. Benjamin Antonio, (SJN) Curia: Offices and Directors
Perez Cruz, Rev. Benjamin Antonio, '10 (SJN) Curia: Leadership; Offices and Directors Catedral de San Juan Bautista, San Juan, PR; [MIS] Santa Ana Chapel, San Juan, PR
Perez Flores, Rev. Rommel, *OFM* '11 (JOL) St. John the Baptist, Joliet, IL; [MON] St. John the Baptist Friary, Joliet, IL
Perez Gonzalez, Rev. Osvaldo, *C.S.Sp.* '88 (ARE) Our Lady of Mt. Carmel, Vega Alta, PR
Perez Lopez, Rev. Israel, (DEN) St. Cajetan Catholic Parish in Denver, Denver, CO
Perez Lopez, Rev. Nicolas, '03 (PCE) Nuestra Senora de la Divina Providencia, Orocovis, PR
Perez Martell, Friar Samuel, *S.F.M.* (SJN) Nuestra Senora del Pilar, San Juan, PR
Perez Perez, Rev. Ovidio, '01 (ARE) On Duty Outside Diocese. Ponce, PR
Perez Perez, Rev. Ovidio, (PCE) Curia: Offices and Directors Nuestra Senora de la Merced, Ponce, PR
Perez Silva, Rev. Alvaro Daniel, *PES* '15 (SAC) [MIS] Pro Ecclesia Sancta of California, Vacaville, CA
Perez Vazquez, Rev. Juan De La Cruz, '96 (SJN) Chap, Army
Perez-Brown, Very Rev. Angel, (DEN) Curia: Deaneries St. John the Baptist Catholic Parish in Johnstown, Johnstown, CO
Perez-Cobo, Rev. Raul, '06 (CR) St. John, Georgetown, MN
Perez-Diaz, Rev. German, '97 (KAL) Curia: Offices and Directors
Perez-Diaz, Very Rev. German, '97 (KAL) Curia: Consultative Bodies; Deaneries
Perez-Dudamel, Rev. Oscar, (MIA) St. Augustine, Coral Gables, FL
Perez-Lopez, Very Rev. Angel, '05 (DEN) Curia: Leadership
Perez-Martinez, Rev. Jose Ramon, '80 (SAT) Curia: Leadership Our Lady of Sorrows, San Antonio, TX
Perez-Rodriguez, Rev. Arturo, '72 (CHI) Retired.
Perez-Sencion, Rev. Pedro, (SJ) St. Julie Billiart, San Jose, CA
Perez-Tellez, Rev. Clemente, *O de M* (SB) St. Anthony, Riverside, CA
Perfetto, Rev. Richard A., '66 (DET) Retired. Curia: Consultative Bodies
Pergjini, Rev. Nikolin, '99 (NY) On Duty Outside Diocese. Lajgia Pavaresia, Rruga David Selenicasi 229401, Vlora KP... St. Benedict, Bronx, NY
Perham, Rev. Arnold E., *C.S.V.* '56 (CHI) [MON] Viatorian Province Center-Clerics of St. Viator, Arlington Heights, IL
Peri, Rev. Paul, '71 (P) Retired.
Peries, Rev. Angelito, '74 (SR) Retired. Pastor of St. Sebastian Catholic Church of Sebastopol, A Corporation Sole, Sebastopol, CA
Perikala, Rev. Alfhones, '02 (LR) St. Mary Church, McCrory, AR; St. Peter, Wynne, AR
Perikomalayil, Rev. John, *H.G.N.* '04 (FWT) St. Mary of the Assumption, Fort Worth, TX; [MON] Heralds of Good News Mother Theresa Province, Inc., Munday, TX
Perino, Rev. John M., '79 (NO) Our Lady of the Angels Roman Catholic Church, Waggaman, Louisiana, Waggaman, LA
Perissinotto, Rev. Rodrigo, *O.S.B.* '04 (KCK) [MON] St. Benedict's Abbey, Atchison, KS
Perkin, Rev. David, '78 (NSH) Retired.
Perkins, Rev. Bernard, *O.C.D.* '82 (LA) St. Therese, Alhambra, CA
Perkins, Rev. Charles J., (HT) Retired.
Perkins, Rev. Dennis M., '95 (NOR) Curia: Leadership; Offices and Directors St. Michael's Church, Pawcatuck Parish, Pawcatuck, CT
Perkins, Rev. Joseph F., '68 (WDC) Retired. Holy Cross, Garrett Park, MD
Perkins, Rev. Msgr. Robert M., '71 (RIC) Retired.
Perkins, Rev. Msgr. Timothy P., '12 (POC) Curia: Leadership
Perkinton, Rev. Msgr. John J., '85 (LIN) Curia: Offices and Directors Pius X Catholic High School, Lincoln, NE; [RTR] Our Lady of Good Counsel Retreat House, Waverly, NE; [SPF] Villa Marie School and Home for the Educable Mentally Handicapped, Waverly, NE
Perkl, Rev. James M., '84 (STP) Mary, Mother of the Church, Burnsville, MN
Perko, Rev. Richard, '04 (STA) Retired.
Perozich, Rev. Richard L., '92 (SD) Retired.
Perrault, Rev. Joseph E., '75 (CAM) Curia: Advisory Boards, Commissions, Committees, and Councils
Perreault, Rev. Joseph A., '75 (CAM) Retired.
Perrella, Rev. Christopher J., '14 (BGP) St. Thomas Church Fairfield Connecticut, Fairfield, CT
Perretta, Rev. Andrew T., '75 (PAT) Retired. Sacred Heart, Clifton, NJ
Perri, Rev. Dean P., '02 (PRO) Curia: Leadership Saint Rita's Church Corporation, Oakland Beach, Warwick, RI; Saint Timothy's Church Corporation, Warwick, Warwick, RI
Perri, Rev. Dean P., (STL) Curia: Leadership
Perri, Rev. Rogerio, (BGP) Our Lady of Fatima Inc., Bridgeport, CT
Perricone, Rev. Charles A., '74 (PAT) Retired.
Perriello, Rev. Robert A., '76 (WH) Retired.
Perrin, Rev. Thomas, '97 (IND) [HOS] Franciscan Health, Indianapolis, IN
Perrin, Rev. Thomas, *S.D.S.* '97 (MIL) [MIS] SASC, Inc., Milwaukee, WI; [MON] Salvatorian Provincial Offices (Society of the Divine Savior), Milwaukee, WI; [NUR] St. Anne's Home for the Elderly, Milwaukee, Inc. (Sisters of the Divine Savior), Milwaukee, WI
Perrins, Rev. Samuel T., '86 (SCR) On Administrative Leave.
Perron, Rev. Gary, *A.A.* '66 (BO) [MON] Augustinians of the Assumption, Inc., Boston, MA
Perrone, Rev. Eduard, '78 (DET) On Leave.
Perrone, Rev. Vito J., '01 (SFR) Mater Dolorosa, South San Francisco, CA; [MIS] The Contemplatives of Saint Joseph, South San Francisco, CA; [SEM] St. Patrick's Seminary and University (The Roman Catholic Seminary of San Francisco), Menlo Park, CA
Perronie, Rev. Matthew, '22 (IND) St. Monica Catholic Church, Indianapolis, Inc., Indianapolis, IN
Perrotta, Rev. Jonathan P., '11 (LAN) Curia: Leadership Good Shepherd Parish Montrose, Montrose, MI; St. Robert Bellarmine Parish Flushing, Flushing, MI
Perry, Rev. Carmen J., '77 (SCR) [CON] Mercy Center (Convent), Dallas, PA
Perry, Rev. David A., '01 (E) St. Mary of the Assumption, Frenchville, PA
Perry, Rev. Francis, '98 (R) Retired.
Perry, Rev. Msgr. John A., '63 (FR) Retired.
Perry, Rev. Michael, (ALB) [COL] Siena College, Loudonville, NY
Perry, Rev. Michael, *O.F.M.* (CHI) [MON] St. Peter's Friary, Chicago, IL
Perry, Rev. Michael A., '71 (BRK) Retired.
Perry, Rev. Michael E., *O.de.M.* '85 (SP) [MON] St. Peter Nolasco Residence, St. Petersburg, FL
Perry, Rev. Paul E., '67 (SFR) Retired.
Perry, Rev. Richard, *S.J.* '70 (SJ) [MON] Sacred Heart Jesuit Center, Los Gatos, CA
Perry, Rev. Robert U., *O.P.* '59 (LUB) Retired. St. Elizabeth University Parish, Lubbock, TX; [MON] Southern Dominican Fathers of Lubbock, Lubbock, TX
Perry, Rev. Ronald V., (BGP) [MON] The Fairfield Jesuit Community-Fairfield University, Fairfield, CT
Perry, Rev. Scott, (TOL) St. John the Evangelist, Delphos, OH; St. Patrick, Spencerville, OH
Pers, Rev. Thomas J., '04 (RVC) St. Lawrence the Martyr, Sayville, NY
Persha, Rev. Gerald J., *M.M.* '70 (NY) Retired. [MON] Maryknoll Fathers and Brothers (Catholic Foreign Mission Society of America, Inc.), Ossining, NY
Persha, Rev. Gerald J., *M.M.* '70 (LA) Retired. [MON] Maryknoll Fathers and Brothers, Los Angeles, CA
Persich, Rev. Roy A., *C.M.* '60 (LA) Retired.
Persing, Rev. Charles L., '88 (HBG) Curia: Offices and Directors St. Elizabeth Ann Seton, Mechanicsburg, PA
Pertinã, Rev. Ivan, (WDC) On Special Assignment. American Univ
Pertine, Rev. Ivan, (WDC) [CAM] American University Catholic Community, ,
Perucho, Rev. Michael, '11 (LA) Curia: Offices and Directors
Perumanamcheril, Rev. Binny Isaac, *S.D.B* '90 (HRT) The Church of St. Vincent Ferrer of Naugatuck Corporation, Naugatuck, CT
Perumpil, Rev. Mathew, *M.I.* '94 (MIL) Mother of Perpetual Help Congregation, West Allis, WI; [MON] St. Camillus Communities, Inc., Wauwatosa, WI
Pesarchick, Rev. Robert A., '91 (PH) On Special Assignment. VP Acad Affairs, Systematic Theology, St Charles Borromeo S... Curia: Advisory Boards, Commissions, Committees, and Councils [SEM] Theological Seminary of St. Charles Borromeo, Wynnewood, PA
Pesaresi, Rev. Thomas, *M.M.* '85 (MO) Curia: Offices and Directors
Pesaresi, Rev. Thomas E., *M.M.* '85 (NY) [MON] Maryknoll Fathers and Brothers (Catholic Foreign Mission Society of America, Inc.), Ossining, NY
Pescatello, Rev. Joseph, (PRO) [CAM] Bryant

University, Smithfield, RI

Pescatello, Rev. Joseph A., '89 (PRO) Saint John Baptist Mary Vianney Church Corporation, Diamond Hill, Cumberland, RI

Pesch, Rev. Elroy, *O.F.M.Cap.* '63 (MIL) Retired. [MON] St. Lawrence Friary, Mount Calvary, WI

Peschel, Rev. Christopher M, (FR) Our Lady of Mt. Carmel, New Bedford, MA

Peschel, Rev. Roland A., '60 (OM) Retired. On Administrative Leave.

Pesci, Rev. Thomas A., *S.J.* '79 (PH) (>KC) [MON] St. Peter Claver Jesuit Community, Kansas City, MO

Pesek, Rev. Fred, '89 (CHI) St. Catherine of Alexandria, Oak Lawn, IL

Peshu, Rev. Kombo L., '01 (CHI) [EFT] Mughamba Scholarship Foundation, Chicago, IL

Pesongco, Rev. Rudy, '82 (RVC) Good Shepherd, Holbrook, NY

Pestano, Rev. Leonardo, '94 (SEA) Our Lady of Lourdes, Vancouver, WA

Pestun, Rev. Aloysius J., *S.D.B.* '54 (SFR) Corpus Christi, San Francisco, CA

Petan, Very Rev. Dominic C., '12 (LFT) Curia: Clergy and Religious Services; Leadership; Miscellaneous / Other Offices

Pete, Rev. Joseph P., '76 (WIN) Retired. Curia: Advisory Boards, Commissions, Committees, and Councils

Petekiewicz, Rev. Robert P., '91 (LAV) On Administrative Leave.

Peter, Rev. Arul Rajan, '84 (NOR) Saint Teresa of Calcutta Parish, Essex, CT

Peter, Rev. Augustine, (SC) [HOS] MercyOne Siouxland Medical Center, Sioux City, IA

Peter, Rev. Biju, *C.M.I.* '02 (NY) Blessed Sacrament, New Rochelle, NY

Peter, Rev. Francis Okih, (FAJ) Curia: Clergy and Religious Services San Jose, Luquillo, PR

Peter, Rev. Jegan, '09 (IND) St. Mary of the Assumption Catholic Church, Mitchell, Inc., Mitchell, IN; St. Vincent de Paul Catholic Church, Bedford, Inc., Bedford, IN

Peter, Rev. Jos R., *MSC* (SB) Our Lady of Guadalupe, Palm Springs, CA; Our Lady of Solitude, Palm Springs, CA

Peter, Rev. Martin A., '67 (IND) Retired.

Peter, Rev. Patrick N., '75 (BEL) St. Dominic, Breese, IL; [CEM] St. Dominic Roman Catholic Cemetery of Breese, Breese, IL

Peter, Rev. Roji, *H.G.N.* '08 (SAT) Resurrection of the Lord, San Antonio, TX

Peter, Rev. Sahaya Rubiston, *C.M.F.* '16 (CHI) [MON] Claret House (Formation Residence), Chicago, IL

Petering, Rev. Michael, '99 (VIC) Curia: Offices and Directors St. Agnes, Edna, TX

Peterka, Rev. Dale C., '68 (CIN) Retired.

Peterka, Rev. Sylvester, *C.M.* '76 (PH) St. Vincent de Paul, Philadelphia, PA

Peterman, Rev. Derik E., '19 (DET) Our Lady of Sorrows Parish Farmington, Farmington, MI

Peterman, Rev. Thomas J., '57 (WIL) Retired.

Petermeier, Rev. Virgil, *O.S.C.* '77 (PHX) [MON] Crosier Community of Phoenix (Canons Regular of the Order of the Holy Cross) (Conventual Priory of the Holy Cross), Phoenix, AZ

Peters, Rev. Aaron, *O.S.B.* '77 (KCK) [MON] St. Benedict's Abbey, Atchison, KS

Peters, Rev. Daniel E., '89 (RCK) Retired.

Peters, Rev. Msgr. David L., '58 (SFD) Retired. Curia: Leadership St. Paul, Highland, IL

Peters, Rev. Eric, '80 (SP) St. Thomas Aquinas, New Port Richey, FL; [PRE] St. Thomas Aquinas Early Childhood Center, New Port Richey, FL

Peters, Rev. Msgr. John C., '74 (VIC) Curia: Leadership; Offices and Directors Sacred Heart, Hallettsville, TX; St. John the Baptist, Schulenburg, TX; St. Mary, Hallettsville, TX

Peters, Rev. Joshua, *SJ* '20 (CHI) St. Ignatius Jesuit Community, Chicago, IL

Peters, Rev. Jude, *O.C.D.* '89 (MIL) St. Mary's of the Hill Congregation, Hubertus, WI; [CON] Carmel of the Mother of God (Discalced Carmelite Nuns of Milwaukee), Pewaukee, WI; [MON] Discalced Carmelite Friars of Holy Hill, Inc., Hubertus, WI

Peters, Rev. Julian, *O.S.B.* '88 (IND) [MON] St. Meinrad Archabbey, St. Meinrad, IN

Peters, Rev. Kenan, *C.P.* '60 (BRK) Retired. [MON] Immaculate Conception Monastery, Jamaica, NY

Peters, Rev. Kenan, *C.P.* '60 (NY) [MON] The Congregation of the Passion - St. Paul of the Cross Province, Jamaica, NY

Peters, Rev. Kevin, '90 (Y) Saint Angela Merici Parish, Youngstown, OH; St. Patrick, Youngstown, OH

Peters, Rev. Michael G., '88 (DM) Retired.

Peters, Rev. Paul R., '62 (DUB) Retired.

Peters, Rev. Timothy, '03 (LA) [SEM] St. John's Seminary, Camarillo, CA

Peters, Rev. Timothy J., '03 (ORG) On Duty Outside Diocese.

Petersen, Rev. Michael C., '92 (MIL) St. Rita's Congregation, Racine, WI

Petersen, Rev. Todd J., '99 (NU) St. Edward, Minneota, MN; St. Eloi, Ghent, MN

Peterson, Rev. Bradley L., *O. Carm.* '92 (PHX) St. Agnes Roman Catholic Parish, Phoenix, AZ; [MON] St. Therese Priory, Phoenix, AZ

Peterson, Rev. C. Vincent, '74 (SEA) Retired.

Peterson, Rev. Daniel Raymond, '16 (NEW) St. Catherine of Siena, Cedar Grove, NJ

Peterson, Rev. Dennis M., '06 (MRY) Mission San Antonio de Padua, Jolon, CA; St. William's, Atascadero, CA

Peterson, Rev. Frederick, *O.S.B.* '95 (ROM) St. George, Aurora, IL

Peterson, Rev. Frederick, *O.S.B.* '95 (RCK) [MON] Marmion Abbey, Aurora, IL

Peterson, Rev. Gerald, '56 (CIN) Retired. [MON] Headquarters of Glenmary Home Missioners (The Home Missioners of America), Fairfield, OH

Peterson, Rev. James E., '13 (STP) Immaculate Conception, Columbia Heights, MN

Peterson, Rev. Jay H., '78 (GF) Retired. Curia: Leadership

Peterson, Rev. John S., *O.P.* '62 (PRO) [MON] St. Thomas Aquinas Priory at Providence College, Providence, RI

Peterson, Rev. Msgr. Joseph L., '75 (WH) Retired. Curia: Leadership; Offices and Directors

Peterson, Rev. Leonard N., '67 (PH) Retired.

Peterson, Rev. Louis P., '74 (BEL) Retired.

Peterson, Rev. Maurice F., '87 (YAK) Retired.

Peterson, Rev. Michael, '11 (KCK) St. Bernard, Wamego, KS; St. Joseph, St. George, KS

Peterson, Rev. Michael, *O.S.B.* (SCL) [MON] St. John's Abbey, of the Order of St. Benedict, Collegeville, MN

Peterson, Rev. Paul, *S.J.* (DET) [MON] Colombiere Center, Clarkston, MI

Peterson, Rev. Steven J., '94 (WIN) Retired.

Peterson, Rev. Trevor, '21 (DUL) Cathedral of Our Lady of the Rosary, Duluth, MN; St. Mary Star of the Sea, Duluth, MN

Peterson, Rev. William, *C.Ss.R.* '67 (STP) St. Alphonsus, Brooklyn Center, MN; [MON] Redemptorist Fathers of Hennepin County, Brooklyn Center, MN

Peterson, Rev. Zachary D., '11 (NU) Curia: Offices and Directors Holy Redeemer, Renville, MN; St. Aloysius, Olivia, MN; St. Mary, Bird Island, MN

Petilla, Rev. Antonio G., '61 (SFR) Retired. Holy Angels, Colma, CA

Petilla, Rev. Msgr. Cesar, '77 (SP) St. Joseph Catholic Church, Zephyrhills, FL

Petit, Rev. Lamartine, '10 (BRK) SS. Joachim and Anne, Queens Village, NY

Petkash, Rev. Donald J., *S.J.* '71 (CLV) Walsh Jesuit High School, Cuyahoga Falls, OH

Petkosek, Rev. Michael, (CLV) St. Albert the Great, North Royalton, OH

Petracca, Rev. Anthony, '85 (ALT) On Leave.

Petras, Rev. Archpriest David, '67 (PRM) Retired.

Petras, Rev. David M., (HPM) Curia: Offices and Directors

Petri, Very Rev. Jacob Thomas, *O.P.* '09 (WDC) [SEM] Dominican House of Studies, Washington, DC

Petrica, Very Rev. Stephen C., '13 (MAD) St. Bernadette, Ridgeway, WI

Petrich, Rev. John C., '83 (DUL) Chap, St Luke's Hosp; Northeast Rgnl Corr Inst St. Joseph, Duluth, MN

Petrie, Rev. Michael J., '87 (MIL) St. Bonifacius Congregation, Germantown, WI

Petrie, Rev. William F., *SS.CC.* '69 (HON) [MON] St. Patrick's Monastery, Honolulu, HI

Petrikovic, Rev. John, *O.F.M. Cap.* '81 (PIT) [MON] St. Fidelis Friary, Beaver, PA; [MON] The Capuchin Franciscan Friars Province of Saint Augustine, Pittsburgh, PA

Petrillo, Rev. Msgr. Thomas F., '83 (NY) Parish of Our Lady of Perpetual Help and St. Catharine, Pelham Manor, NY

Petrillo, Rev. Thomas J., '59 (NEW) Retired.

Petringa, Rev. Gerard, (BO) Retired. St. Timothy, Norwood, MA

Petriv, Rev. Vasyl, '92 (SJP) On Duty Outside Diocese. Curia: Offices and Directors

Petriv, Rev. Volodymyr, '89 (STN) Curia: Offices and Directors Our Lady of Perpetual Help, Dearborn Heights, MI

Petro, Rev. Thomas J., '00 (SCR) Curia: Leadership Sacred Heart of Jesus, Dupont, PA

Petro, Rev. Thomas J., '00 (MO) Curia: Offices and Directors

Petro, Rev. William, '68 (WH) Retired.

Petroff, Rev. Alberto, (MIA) St. Timothy, Miami, FL

Petroff, Rev. Steven J., *C.S.P.* '17 (NY) [MON] Paulist Fathers - Generalate, New York, NY

Petrone, Rev. Joseph, '20 (E) The Epiphany of the Lord, Meadville, PA

Petronek, Rev. Msgr. Thomas C., '65 (STU) Retired.

Petronio, Rev. Rolando C., '77 (STO) Sacred Heart Church of Turlock (Pastor of), Turlock, CA

Petroske, Rev. Peter, '84 (DET) On Leave.

Petroski, Rev. Michael A., '00 (LAN) Retired.

Petrovsky, Rev. Felix, *O.F.M.Cap.* '55 (SAL) Retired. [MON] St. Fidelis Friary, Victoria, KS

Petrovsky, Rev. James F., '68 (GBG) St. Joan of Arc, Farmington, PA

Petroy, Rev. Dominic J., *O.S.B.* '87 (GBG) Assoc Chap, Excela Health - Latrobe Area Hosp, Latrobe [MON] Saint Vincent Archabbey, Latrobe, PA

Petrucci, Rev. Raymond K., '73 (BGP) Retired.

Petruska, Rev. William M., '73 (SCR) Retired.

Petry, Rev. Thomas G., '78 (COL) Saint Anthony, Columbus, OH

Petryshak, Rev. Roman, '02 (PHU) SS. Cyril and Methodius, Berwick, PA; St. Nicholas, Glen Lyon, PA

Petrytsya, Rev. Volodymyr, '13 (SJP) Curia: Offices and Directors Protection of the Mother of God, Conyers, GA

Petsche, Rev. Daniel, *O.S.B.* '67 (KC) [MON] Conception Abbey (Benedictine Monks), Conception, MO (>MIL) [MON] St. Benedict's Abbey (Benedictine Monks of Wisconsin, Inc.), Benet Lake, WI; (>MIL) [RTR] St. Benedict's Retreat Center (Benedictine Monks of Wisconsin, Inc.), Benet Lake, WI

Petta, Rev. Phil D, (FWT) St. Mary, Quanah, TX

Petta, Rev. Phil D, '10 (FWT) St. Joseph, Crowell, TX

Petta, Rev. Philip, '11 (FWT) Holy Family of Nazareth, Vernon, TX

Pettei, Rev. Thomas G., '89 (BRK) Curia: Consultative Bodies Resurrection Ascension - Our Lady of the Angelus Roman Catholic Church, Rego Park, NY

Petter, Rev. Msgr. Henry V., '76 (DAL) Retired.

Pettigrew, Rev. Jason, '18 (SFE) San Diego Mission, Jemez Pueblo, NM

Pettingill, Rev. David M., '62 (SFR) Retired. St. Emydius, San Francisco, CA

Pettit, Rev. Joseph H., '56 (HRT) Retired.

Pettit, Rev. Neil, '13 (LAF) St. Landry, Opelousas, LA

Petty, Rev. Benjamin, (WDC) [CAM] George Washington University Newman Center, Washington, DC

Peyton, Rev. Mark J., '77 (CLV) St. Francis de Sales, Parma, OH

Peyton, Rev. Thomas A., *M.M.* '58 (NY) Retired. [MON] Maryknoll Fathers and Brothers (Catholic Foreign Mission Society of America, Inc.), Ossining, NY

Peyton, Rev. Thomas J., '74 (SAV) Retired. Cathedral Basilica of St. John the Baptist, Savannah, GA

Pezhathinal, Rev. Jaison Thomas, *M.S.F.S.* '00 (GAL) St. Laurence, Sugar Land, TX

Pezzi, Rev. John Paolo, *M.C.C.J.* '68 (NEW) [MON] Comboni Missionaries of the Heart of Jesus (Verona Fathers), Newark, NJ

Pezzullo, Rev. Angelo B., '62 (BRK) Retired.

Pezzulo, Rev. Neil, *GHM* (KNX) Saint John Paul II Catholic Mission, Rutledge, TN

Pezzulo, Rev. Neil, *G.H.M.* '99 (CIN) (>KNX) Saint Teresa of Kolkata Church, Maynardville, TN

Pfab, Rev. Cletus H., *S.J.* '69 (DET) [MON] Colombiere Center, Clarkston, MI

Pfaff, Rev. Aaron J., '96 (IND) St. Bernard Catholic Church, Frenchtown, Inc., Depauw, IN; St. Joseph Catholic Church, Marengo, Inc., Marengo, IN; St. Michael Catholic Church, Bradford, Inc., Greenville, IN

Pfalzer, Rev. Miles, *O.F.M.* (CIN) Retired.

Pfander, Rev. Timothy, '04 (BIR) Good Shepherd Catholic Parish, Huntsville, Huntsville, AL; [EFT] Good Shepherd Parish Endowment Fund, Huntsville, AL

Pfannenstiel, Rev. Donald F., '75 (SAL) Retired.

Pfannenstiel, Rev. John, *O.F.M. Cap.* '82 (PIT) [MON] St. Augustine Friary, Pittsburgh, PA; [MON] The Capuchin Franciscan Friars Province of Saint Augustine, Pittsburgh, PA

Pfau, Rev. Bernard, '65 (FAR) Retired.

Pfeifer, Rev. Frederick, '93 (NEW) Holy Name of Jesus, East Orange, NJ

Pfeifer, Rev. Frederick A., '93 (NEW) Curia: Advisory Boards, Commissions, Committees, and Councils

Pfeifer, Rev. John M., '65 (BIS) Retired.

Pfeifer, Rev. John M., '07 (CLV) St. Patrick, Cleveland, OH; St. Vincent de Paul, Cleveland, OH
Pfeifer, Rev. Neil J., '11 (FAR) Curia: Offices and Directors St. James Basilica of Jamestown, Jamestown, ND; St. Margaret Church of Buchanan, Buchanan, ND; St. Mathias Church of Windsor, Windsor, ND; [CAM] University of Jamestown, Jamestown, ND
Pfeiffer, Rev. David L., *M.M.* '66 (NY) Retired. [MON] Maryknoll Fathers and Brothers (Catholic Foreign Mission Society of America, Inc.), Ossining, NY
Pfeiffer, Rev. Msgr. Joseph C., '58 (BRK) Retired.
Pfeiffer, Rev. Mark S., '82 (LIN) St. Mary Catholic Church of Nebraska City, Nebraska City, NE
Pfeiffer, Rev. Matthew E., '09 (CLV) Curia: Advisory Boards, Commissions, Committees, and Councils St. Paul, Akron, OH
Pfeiffer, Rev. Robert F., '61 (CLV) Retired.
Pfeister, Rev. Jeremy, *FGBC* '14 (CLV) [HOS] Marymount Hospital, Inc., Garfield Heights, OH
Pfister, Rev. John, (EVN) St. Isidore the Farmer, Celestine, IN; St. Joan of Arc, Sullivan, IN; St. Mary, Sullivan, IN
Pfister, Rev. Neal A., '90 (DEN) Retired.
Pfleger, Rev. Matthew J., '12 (TR) Holy Family, Union Beach, NJ
Pfleger, Rev. Phillip C., '79 (TR) Curia: Leadership St. Isaac Jogues, Marlton, NJ; St. John Neumann, Mount Laurel, NJ
Pflomm, Rev. Msgr. Peter J, (RVC) Maria Regina, Seaford, NY
Pfundstein, Rev. George A., '63 (BRK) Retired. Mary's Nativity-Saint Ann Roman Catholic Church, Flushing, NY
Phalen, Rev. John L., '59 (DET) Retired.
Pham, Rev. Andrew T., (CAM) The Parish of Saint Monica, Atlantic City, NJ
Pham, Rev. Ansgar, *S.D.D.* '03 (P) Our Lady of Lavang, Happy Valley, OR; Southeast Asian Vicariate, Portland, OR
Pham, Rev. Bernardo Son, *S.D.D.* '63 (NO) Retired. [MIS] Domus Dei Clerical Society of Apostolic Life, U.S.A., Inc., New Orleans, LA
Pham, Rev. Bryan, (SPK) [COL] Gonzaga University, Spokane, WA
Pham, Rev. Charles S., *CRM* (BO) St. Bernadette, Randolph, MA
Pham, Rev. Chau, *S.V.D.* '95 (CIN) [MIS] Vietnamese Catholic Community of Our Lady of Lavang, Cincinnati, OH
Pham, Rev. Christopher, '07 (ORG) Blessed Sacrament, Westminster, CA
Pham, Rev. Msgr. Cuong M., '01 (BRK) Our Lady of Mount Carmel, Long Island City, NY
Pham, Rev. Danh, *SVD* (SB) [MIS] Ministerio Biblico Verbo Divino (MBVD), San Bernardino, CA
Pham, Rev. Dat Huu, *S.D.D.* '03 (NO) [MIS] Domus Dei Clerical Society of Apostolic Life, U.S.A., Inc., New Orleans, LA
Pham, Rev. Doan The, '98 (LA) Cathedral Chapel of St. Vibiana, Los Angeles, CA
Pham, Rev. Dominic, *C.Ss.R.* '05 (LA) [MON] Vietnamese Redemptorist Mission, Baldwin Park, CA
Pham, Rev. Dominic, '04 (BLX) Curia: Advisory Boards, Commissions, Committees, and Councils Sacred Heart, D'Iberville, MS
Pham, Rev. Dominic Chinh, *I.C.M.* (KCK) Chap, KU Med Ctr and Chapel; Cathedral of St Peter
Pham, Rev. Dominic Phuc, *C.Ss.R.* '05 (DAL) Sacred Heart of Jesus Christ Catholic Parish, Carrollton, TX
Pham, Rev. Dominic Thao, '98 (ALN) St. Joseph, Sheppton, PA; St. Mary, Ringtown, PA
Pham, Rev. Ducanh, *O.F.M.* (IND) Sacred Heart of Jesus Catholic Church, Indianapolis, Inc., Indianapolis, IN
Pham, Rev. Francis, '19 (BO) Our Lady, Comforter of the Afflicted, Waltham, MA
Pham, Rev. Francis Hau, *C.Ss.R.* '93 (KC) Church of the Holy Martyrs, Kansas City, MO; Our Lady of Perpetual Help, Kansas City, MO; [MON] Redemptorists Fathers of Kansas City, Missouri, Kansas City, MO
Pham, Rev. Hai Hgoc, *SVD* (LAF) Holy Ghost, Opelousas, LA
Pham, Rev. Hanh D., *S.J.* '08 (COS) [MON] Sacred Heart Jesuit Community, Sedalia, CO (>LAF) [SEM] Jesuit Novitiate of St. Stanislaus Kostka at St. Charles College, Grand Coteau, LA
Pham, Rev. Hien, *S.V.D.* '16 (SB) St. George, Ontario, CA
Pham, Rev. Hung, '19 (NSH) Curia: Offices and Directors St. Pius X, Nashville, TN
Pham, Rev. Hung T, *S.J.* '06 (DEN) [MON] Xavier Jesuit Center, Denver, CO
Pham, Rev. Hung T., *S.J.* '06 (STL) [MON] USA Central & Southern Province, Society of Jesus, St. Louis, MO (>DEN) [MON] Regis Jesuit Community (The Jesuits at Regis University), Denver, CO
Pham, Rev. Huong, *O.P.* '85 (GAL) [MON] Vietnamese Dominican Vicariate of St. Vincent Liem, Houston, TX
Pham, Rev. John, '02 (PEO) On Leave.
Pham, Rev. Joseph C., '01 (CAM) Catholic Community of the Holy Spirit, Mullica Hill, N.J., Mullica Hill, NJ
Pham, Rev. Joseph Luong, '98 (CAM) Infant Jesus Parish, Woodbury Heights, N.J., Woodbury Heights, NJ
Pham, Rev. Joseph Tuan, '88 (ORG) St. Barbara Catholic Church, Santa Ana, CA
Pham, Rev. Josephtan, '70 (BRK) Retired. Our Lady of Mount Carmel, Long Island City, NY
Pham, Rev. Khiet Huu Manh, *S.J.* '12 (MIA) St. Thomas Aquinas High School, Inc., Fort Lauderdale, FL
Pham, Rev. Khoi, '94 (STO) St. Jude Church (Pastor of), Ceres, CA
Pham, Rev. Lau, *C.PP.S.* '89 (KC) Saint Francis Xavier Catholic Church, St. Joseph, MO; [MIS] St. Gaspar Society, Liberty, MO
Pham, Rev. Le-Minh, '93 (AUS) Holy Vietnamese Martyrs Catholic Church - Austin, Texas, Austin, TX; [EFT] Diocese of Austin Pension Plan and Trust, Austin, TX
Pham, Rev. Linh, *S.V.D.* '09 (DUB) [SEM] Divine Word College, Epworth, IA
Pham, Rev. Loi D., '20 (L) St. James, Elizabethtown, KY
Pham, Rev. Louis Ha, *CRM* '94 (STP) Church of St. Anne - St. Joseph Hien, Minneapolis, MN
Pham, Rev. M. Anthony Hanh Si, *O.Cist.* '04 (SB) [MON] The Cistercian Congregation of the Holy Family, St. Joseph Monastery, Lucerne Valley, CA
Pham, Rev. M. Peter-Binh Quynh Dang, *O.Cist.* (SB) [MON] The Cistercian Congregation of the Holy Family, St. Joseph Monastery, Lucerne Valley, CA
Pham, Rev. Marty, '04 (GAL) St. Michael, Needville, TX; Sts. Cyril and Methodius, Damon, TX
Pham, Rev. Michael, *CRM* '06 (ORL) St. Philip Phan Van Minh Catholic Church, Orlando, FL
Pham, Rev. Michael, '14 (OAK) St. Jerome Church, El Cerrito, CA
Pham, Very Rev. Michael, '99 (SD) Curia: Advisory Boards, Commissions, Committees, and Councils; Leadership; Offices and Directors Pastor of Good Shepherd Catholic Parish, San Diego, a corporation sole, San Diego, CA; [MIS] Good Shepherd Catholic Parish in San Diego, CA Real Property Support Corporation, San Diego, CA
Pham, Rev. Michel, *O.S.B.* '10 (SD) [MON] Prince of Peace Abbey, Oceanside, CA
Pham, Rev. Minh J., *C.M.* '91 (DAL) St. Peter Vietnamese Catholic Parish, Dallas, TX; [MON] Congregation of the Mission, Western Province, Dallas, TX
Pham, Rev. Peter T., '98 (CHL) St. John Neumann, Charlotte, NC
Pham, Rev. Phong, (GR) Holy Redeemer, Jenison, MI
Pham, Rev. Msgr. Phuong Van, '66 (ATL) Retired.
Pham, Rev. Quang D., *C.O.* (CHR) St. Anne, Rock Hill, SC; [MON] Oratory of St. Philip Neri, Congregation of the Oratory of Pontifical Rite, Rock Hill, SC
Pham, Rev. Quy K, '18 (PH) St. Albert the Great, Huntingdon Valley, PA
Pham, Rev. Quyet A., '04 (ALN) St. Joseph, Reading, PA; St. Paul, Reading, PA
Pham, Rev. Tai, '18 (SFE) Curia: Offices and Directors Saint John XXIII Catholic Community, Albuquerque, NM
Pham, Rev. Tan Robert, *S.J.* '04 (ATL) Our Lady of Vietnam Catholic Church, Riverdale, Inc., Riverdale, GA
Pham, Rev. Thang John, '07 (BLX) Curia: Miscellaneous / Other Offices Vietnamese Martyrs Church, Biloxi, MS
Pham, Rev. Thang M., '10 (ATL) St. Mary Catholic Church, Toccoa, Inc., Toccoa, GA
Pham, Rev. Thanh Q., '07 (CAM) Church of the Holy Family, Washington Township, Sewell, NJ
Pham, Rev. Thinh Duc, '01 (LA) [SEM] St. John's Seminary, Camarillo, CA
Pham, Rev. Thomas T., *C.Ss.R.* '09 (MO) Curia: Offices and Directors
Pham, Rev. Thomas T., *C.Ss.R.* '09 (SAT) [MON] The Redemptorists/San Antonio, San Antonio, TX
Pham, Rev. Tin Cosmas Kim, '95 (GAL) St. Joseph on the Brazos, Brazoria, TX
Pham, Rev. Toan, (SB) St. Mother Teresa of Calcutta Catholic Community, Inc., Winchester, CA
Pham, Rev. Tri Tang, '04 (PMB) Holy Family, Port St. Lucie, FL
Pham, Rev. Trung, *S.J.* '12 (SEA) [COL] Seattle University, Seattle, WA; [MON] Arrupe Jesuit Community at Seattle University, Seattle, WA
Pham, Rev. Truong, '21 (NO) St. Matthew the Apostle, River Ridge, LA
Pham, Rev. Tuan, *OMI* '02 (BUF) Coronation of the Blessed Virgin Mary, Buffalo, NY; Our Lady of Hope, Buffalo, NY
Pham, Rev. Tuan, *C.Ss.R.* '99 (LA) St. Mary of the Assumption, Whittier, CA; [MON] Redemptorists of Whittier, Whittier, CA
Pham, Rev. Tuan, '06 (ATL) St. Joseph Catholic Church, Dalton, Inc., Dalton, GA
Pham, Rev. Tuan Anh, '99 (NO) St. John of the Cross Roman Catholic Church, Lacombe, Louisiana, Lacombe, LA
Pham, Rev. Msgr. Tuan Joseph, '94 (ORG) Curia: Leadership
Pham, Rev. Msgr. Tuan Joseph, '94 (ORG) St. Columban, Garden Grove, CA
Pham, Rev. Tuan Joseph, '88 (ORG) St. Kilian, Mission Viejo, CA
Pham, Rev. Vincent, '97 (ORG) Curia: Leadership; Offices and Directors
Pham, Rev. Vincent Don, '95 (NO) Retired.
Pham, Rev. Vinh, *L.C.* (WDC) [MON] Legionaries of Christ, Potomac, MD
Pham, Rev. Xuan Hien, *S.V.D.* '99 (DUB) [SEM] Divine Word College, Epworth, IA
Phan, Rev. Allan, '19 (LIN) Curia: Leadership
Phan, Rev. Allan N., '19 (LIN) Sacred Heart, Crete, NE
Phan, Rev. Andy, '06 (OM) All Saints Church of Northeast Nebraska, Fordyce, NE; Holy Family Parish of Cedar County, Fordyce, NE; St. Rose of Lima, Crofton, NE
Phan, Rev. Anh Tuan, '18 (NSH) Cathedral of the Incarnation, Nashville, TN
Phan, Rev. Anton Ba, '01 (NO) Chap, Univ Med Ctr, New Orleans
Phan, Rev. Cho Dinh Peter, '72 (DAL) On Duty Outside Diocese.
Phan, Rev. David Q., *O.F.M.* '10 (CHR) Curia: Offices and Directors Our Lady of La Vang, Greer, SC
Phan, Rev. Dominic T.H., '09 (LIN) St. Cecilia's, Hastings, NE
Phan, Rev. Duc, *OFM* (IND) St. Patrick Catholic Church, Indianapolis, Inc., Indianapolis, IN
Phan, Rev. James, (OAK) Our Lady of Grace, Castro Valley, CA; [MON] Conventual Franciscans (Province of St. Joseph of Cupertino), Castro Valley, CA
Phan, Rev. John, '05 (JOL) Curia: (>MO) Offices and Directors Holy Family, Shorewood, IL
Phan, Rev. Joseph Duong, '93 (OAK) Retired. Curia: Offices and Directors Divine Mercy Parish, Oakland, CA
Phan, Rev. Joseph Son Thanh, '03 (GAL) St. Francis de Sales, Houston, TX
Phan, Rev. Khoi Tan, '09 (ORG) Curia: Leadership St. Cecilia, Tustin, CA
Phan, Rev. Loc Joseph, (GAL) Vietnamese Martyrs, Houston, TX
Phan, Rev. Long N., '09 (OKL) St. Wenceslaus, National Shrine of the Infant Jesus of Prague, Prague, OK; [SHR] National Shrine of the Infant Jesus of Prague, Prague, OK
Phan, Rev. Minh, '97 (NO) [SEM] Notre Dame Seminary Graduate School of Theology, New Orleans, LA
Phan, Rev. Nghia, *O.F.M.* '14 (OAK) [MON] Franciscan Friars of California (Province of St. Barbara), Oakland, CA
Phan, Rev. Ngoan V., '07 (SFR) St. Cecilia, Lagunitas, CA
Phan, Rev. Paul, (LA) Our Lady of the Assumption, Claremont, CA
Phan, Rev. Peter, '10 (SB) Holy Innocents, Victorville, CA
Phan, Rev. Peter P., *C.Ss.R.* (LA) Retired.
Phan, Rev. Peter-Luc, '90 (SJ) St. Martin, Sunnyvale, CA
Phan, Rev. Philip Lahn, (BGP) Our Lady of Fatima Inc., Bridgeport, CT; Our Lady of Fatima Roman Catholic Church Corporation of Wilton, Wilton, CT
Phan, Rev. Vincent, '95 (NO) St. John the Baptist, Folsom, LA
Phelan, Rev. Cornelius Noel, '59 (LA) Retired.
Phelan, Rev. Edward, '63 (SFR) Retired.
Phelan, Rev. Matthew H, *O. de. M* (BUF) (>PH) [MON] Monastery of Our Lady of Mercy (Fathers of Our Lady of Mercy, Inc. / Order of the B.V.M. of Mercy (Mercedarian Friars)), Philadelphia, PA
Phelan, Rev. Matthew H., *O.de.M* '02 (PH) Our Lady of Lourdes, Philadelphia, PA
Phelan, Rev. Thomas E., '76 (BEA) Retired.
Phelps, Rev. Brian W., '14 (CIN) Incarnation,

Centerville, OH; St. Francis of Assisi, Centerville, OH
Phelps, Rev. Joel, '12 (PEO) Curia: Clergy and Religious Services; Deaneries St. Elizabeth of Hungary, Thomasboro, IL; St. Malachy R.C. Congregation, Rantoul, IL
Phelps, Rev. John, *C.Ss.R.* '68 (CHI) [MON] The Redemptorist Fathers of Chicago, Chicago, IL
Phelps, Rev. John, *C.Ss.R.* '68 (DET) St. Peter Claver Parish Detroit, Detroit, MI; [MON] St. Paul of the Cross Community, Congregation of the Passion, Detroit, MI
Philen, Rev. James Michael, (DEN) Retired.
Philip, Rev. Anish, *O.S.H* (BAK) St. Bridget of Kildare, Nyssa, OR
Philip, Rev. Binny, (GAL) St. Thomas More, Houston, TX
Philip, Rev. Binny, '07 (MCE) St. Peter's Malankara Catholic Church, Stafford, TX
Philip, Rev. Binny, '07 (MCE) Curia: Advisory Boards, Commissions, Committees, and Councils; Offices and Directors
Philip, Rev. Fadi, (EST) Sacred Heart Chaldean Parish, Warren, MI
Philip, Rev. Fadi, '04 (EST) Curia: Offices and Directors
Philip, Very Rev. Msgr. Gigi, '91 (MCE) Curia: Administration; Advisory Boards, Commissions, Committees, and Councils
Philip, Rev. Rajeev Valiyaveettil, '18 (SYM) St. Mary's Syro-Malabar Catholic Church Charlotte, North Carolina, Inc. of St. Thomas Syro-Malabar Catholic Diocese of Chicago, Charlotte, NC
Philip, Rev. Stephan, *M.S.F.S.* (KAL) St. Rose of Lima, Hastings, MI
Philip, Rev. Thomas, *O.S.H.* (BAK) St. Patrick Catholic Church of Lakeview, Inc., Lakeview, OR
Philip, Rev. Thomas, (CHI) SS. Faith, Hope and Charity, Winnetka, IL
Philiposki, Rev. Richard, '79 (LAV) Retired.
Philippe, Rev. Jean-Rony, '99 (BGP) Chap, Danbury Hospital The Church of the Sacred Heart of Jesus, Danbury, Danbury, CT; [MIS] Haitian American Catholic Center, Stamford, CT
Philipsen, Rev. Todd K., '89 (GI) Curia: Offices and Directors St. Patrick's, Chadron, NE
Philius, Rev. Vilaire, '09 (ORL) Our Lady of Grace, Palm Bay, FL
Phillippino, Rev. Michael L., '79 (NOR) Good Shepherd Parish (Church of the Holy Family of Hebron, Incorporated), Columbia, CT
Phillippino, Rev. Michael L., '90 (NOR) Curia: Leadership; Offices and Directors
Phillips, Rev. Ambrose K., *T.O.R.* '71 (WDC) [MON] Franciscan Monastery USA Inc., Washington, DC
Phillips, Rev. Benet C., *O.S.B.* '92 (MAN) [MON] St. Anselm Abbey, Manchester, NH
Phillips, Rev. Brian, '17 (AUS) Sacred Heart of Jesus, La Grange, TX
Phillips, Rev. C.R. Frank, *C.R.* '77 (CHI) [MIS] Canons Regular of Saint John Cantius, Chicago, IL
Phillips, Rev. Christopher G., '83 (SAT) Retired.
Phillips, Rev. Clyde, *M.M.* '78 (NY) Retired. [MON] Maryknoll Fathers and Brothers (Catholic Foreign Mission Society of America, Inc.), Ossining, NY
Phillips, Rev. Edward J., *M.M.* '74 (NY) [EFT] Maryknoll Fathers and Brothers Apostolic Trust, Maryknoll, NY; [MON] Maryknoll Fathers and Brothers (Catholic Foreign Mission Society of America, Inc.), Ossining, NY
Phillips, Rev. Glenn, *O.F.M.* '66 (CHI) [MON] St. Peter's Friary, Chicago, IL
Phillips, Rev. Glenn, *O.F.M.* '66 (STL) [MON] Franciscan Friary of St. Anthony of Padua, St. Louis, MO
Phillips, Rev. Gregory, *O.S.B.* '01 (WOR) [MIS] St. Mary and St. Scholastica Church, Inc., Petersham, MA; [MON] St. Mary's Monastery, Petersham, MA
Phillips, Rev. Jonathan, '16 (LUB) Curia: Leadership St. Michael's, Levelland, TX
Phillips, Rev. Joseph H., '68 (SY) Retired.
Phillips, Rev. Kenneth, '91 (BIS) St. Therese the Little Flower, Minot, ND
Phillips, Rev. Louis J., '81 (PRT) Curia: Leadership St. Anthony of Padua Parish, Westbrook, ME; [CAM] University of Southern Maine, Gorham, ME
Phillips, Rev. Msgr. Michael J., '60 (BRK) Retired. St. Anselm, Brooklyn, NY
Phillips, Rev. Michael T., '69 (DAV) Retired.
Phillips, Rev. Randall, '83 (DET) St. Blase Parish Sterling Heights, Sterling Heights, MI
Phillips, Rev. Randy, '97 (SFS) Saint Liborius Parish of Hand County, Polo, SD; Saint Thomas the Apostle Parish of Faulk County, Faulkton, SD
Phillips, Rev. Robert, *S.J.* '72 (BAL) Retired.
Phillips, Rev. Robert, *SJ* (BO) [MON] Campion Health & Wellness, Inc., Weston, MA
Phillips, Rev. Robert A., '20 (SAV) St. John the Evangelist, Valdosta, GA
Phillips, Rev. Msgr. Thomas L., '71 (BAL) St. Gabriel, Windsor Mill, MD
Phillipson, Rev. David, '03 (SFE) On Leave.
Philogene, Rev. Luc, *O.F.M.Cap.* (WDC) Shrine of the Sacred Heart, Washington, DC
Philominsamy, Rev. Michaelraj, '91 (SR) Curia: Leadership Pastor of St. Rose of Lima Catholic Church of Santa Rosa, A Corporation Sole, Santa Rosa, CA
Phipps, Rev. Charles T., *S.J.* '59 (SJ) [MON] Sacred Heart Jesuit Center, Los Gatos, CA
Phipps, Rev. Ricardo M., '02 (JKS) On Leave.
Phongo, Rev. Jean-Marie Mvumbi, '03 (ARL) [MON] Missionhurst, C.I.C.M.-Central House and Provincialate (American I.H.M. Province, Inc., Immaculate Heart Missions, Inc., Missionhurst, Inc.), Arlington, VA
Phuc, Rev. Tran Dinh, *C.Ss.R.* '56 (LA) [MON] Vietnamese Redemptorist Mission, Baldwin Park, CA
Phung, Rev. Chi Peter, '90 (TLS) Retired.
Phung, Rev. Joseph P. V., '00 (DAV) Holy Family Parish of Fort Madison, Iowa, Fort Madison, IA; St. Joseph Church of Montrose, Iowa, Montrose, IA
Phung, Rev. Vincent, '96 (DEN) Curia: Tribunal Mother of God Catholic Parish in Denver, Denver, CO
Phuoc Hoa, Rev. Dang, *C.Ss.R.* '03 (LA) [MON] Vietnamese Redemptorist Mission, Baldwin Park, CA
Piasecki, Rev. Timothy, '73 (RCK) Retired.
Piasta, Rev. Krystian J., *O.F.M.* '95 (BRK) Our Lady of the Skies Chapel, Jamaica, NY; St. Joseph, Jamaica, NY
Piatkowski, Rev. Mariusz, '00 (BRK) St. Aloysius, Ridgewood, NY
Piatt, Rev. Charley, *S.T.* (TUC) Saint Kateri Tekakwitha Roman Catholic Missions Parish - Tucson, Tucson, AZ
Piatt, Rev. Gregory A., '14 (DET) St. John XXIII Parish Redford Charter Township, Redford, MI
Pica, Rev. Michael, '16 (PEO) Shrine of Queen of the Holy Rosary, LaSalle, IL; St. Hyacinth, LaSalle, IL; St. Patrick, LaSalle, IL
Picard, Rev. Daniel, '79 (LAF) Retired.
Picard, Rev. Michael, *L.C.* '11 (DAL) [MON] Legionaries of Christ, Irving, TX
Picard, Rev. Msgr. Michael C., '66 (PH) St. Andrew, Newtown, PA
Picard, Rev. Raymond, '65 (PRT) Retired.
Picarella, Rev. Dale, '84 (BAL) Catholic Community of Ascension and St. Augustine Roman Catholic Congregation, Inc., Elkridge, MD
Picazo, Rev. Luis, *S.F.* '72 (WDC) [SEM] Holy Family Seminary, Silver Spring, MD
Picchioni, Rev. Thomas F., '16 (COV) Curia: Advisory Boards, Commissions, Committees, and Councils St. John the Evangelist, Carrollton, KY
Piccinini, Rev. Claudio, *C.P.* '72 (NY) [MON] The Congregation of the Passion - St. Paul of the Cross Province, Jamaica, NY
Piccinino, Rev. Corey V., '86 (BGP) Curia: Consultative Bodies St. Mary's Church Corporation Bethel Connecticut, Bethel, CT
Piccola, Rev. Michael, (SCR) St. Patrick, White Haven, PA
Piccola, Rev. Michael J., '78 (SCR) Curia: Leadership SS. Cyril & Methodius, Hazleton, Hazleton, PA
Piccolo, Rev. Bruno, *PIME* '65 (DET) [MON] PIME Missionaries, Detroit, MI
Piccolongo, Rev. Claudio, (BAL) Our Lady of Pompei, Baltimore, MD; St. Clement, Lansdowne, MD
Pichard, Rev. Msgr. Lawrence, '73 (DAL) Retired.
Pichardo, Rev. Juan Angel, '96 (BRK) Blessed Sacrament, Jackson Heights, NY; Blessed Sacrament - Saint Sylvester, Brooklyn, NY
Piche, Rev. Donald J., '77 (STP) Retired.
Picinic, Rev. John P., '05 (CAM) Curia: Advisory Boards, Commissions, Committees, and Councils; Clergy and Religious Services; Tribunal The Catholic Community of Christ Our Light, Cherry Hill, N.J., Cherry Hill, NJ
Pick, Rev. Anthony, '67 (SC) Retired.
Pick, Very Rev. Timothy A., '19 (SC) Curia: Leadership; Offices and Directors Holy Name, Marcus, IA; St. Mary's, Remsen, IA
Pickard, Rev. William B., '76 (SCR) Retired.
Pickens, Rev. David, '09 (PAT) St. Peter the Apostle, Parsippany, NJ
Pickett, Rev. James B., '61 (OAK) Retired. St. Philip Neri-St. Albert the Great, Alameda, CA
Pickett, Rev. Thomas Aquinas, *O.P.* '18 (WDC) [SEM] Dominican House of Studies, Washington, DC
Picollo, Rev. Christopher P., '11 (TR) Curia: Leadership Church of the Nativity, Fair Haven, NJ
Picone, Rev. Alfonso, '00 (NEW) On Duty Outside Diocese. Sacred Heart Church, Stamford, CT
Picone, Rev. Alfonso, '00 (BGP) The Church of the Sacred Heart Corporation, Stamford, Stamford, CT
Picos, Rev. Oscar Martin, '06 (SLC) Saint Mary LLC 237, West Haven, UT
Picou, Rev. Gary, '14 (FWT) On Leave.
Picton, Rev. James, '75 (SEA) Retired.
Picton, Rev. Thomas D., *C.Ss.R.* '72 (SEA) Sacred Heart of Jesus, Seattle, WA; [MON] The Redemptorist Society of Washington, Seattle, WA
Pictorius, Rev. Victorius, *O.F.M.Cap.* (NY) [EFT] Capuchin Friars International, Inc., White Plains, NY
Piczon, Rev. Eric, (SJ) St. Maria Goretti, San Jose, CA
Piderit, Rev. John, (BO) [MON] The Jesuit Community at Boston College, Chestnut Hill, MA
Pidgeon, Rev. John J., '87 (PH) On Administrative Leave. Saint Teresa of Calcutta, Schwenksville, PA; [MIS] State Correctional Institution, Collegeville, PA
Pieber, Rev. Carl L., *C.M.* '80 (PH) [MON] Congregation of the Mission, Philadelphia, PA
Piechocki, Rev. Msgr. Bruce, '84 (FTW) Curia: Offices and Directors St. Aloysius, Yoder, IN
Piechota, Rev. Msgr. Lech, '89 (SFR) On Duty Outside Diocese.
Pieczara, Rev. Stanislaw, *S.D.S.* (GRY) [MON] Salvatorian Fathers (Society of the Divine Savior), Merrillville, IN
Piedra, Rev. Ruskin, *C.Ss.R.* '60 (BRK) Our Lady of Perpetual Help Basilica, Brooklyn, NY
Piedrahita, Rev. Carlos, '13 (TYL) Curia: Pastoral Services
Piedrahita, Rev. Carlos A., '13 (HRT) On Duty Outside Diocese. Lindale, TX
Piedrahita, Rev. Jose Gabriel, '86 (NY) Holy Spirit, Bronx, NY
Piega, Rev. Paul-Michael, (AUS) St. Patrick, Hutto, TX
Piekarczyk, Rev. Marian, *S.D.S.* '80 (SAT) Chap, Audie Murphy VA Hosp, San Antonio Our Lady of Sorrows, San Antonio, TX; [MON] Salvatorian Fathers Community of Texas, Falls City, TX
Piekarczyk, Rev. Marian A., *S.D.S.* '80 (MO) Curia: Offices and Directors
Piekarski, Very Rev. Joseph J., '86 (WIL) Curia: Deaneries St. John the Beloved, Wilmington, DE
Pieper, Rev. Msgr. James E., '57 (STL) Retired.
Pierce, Rev. Brian, *O.P.* '88 (DAL) [MON] Dominican Priory of St. Albert the Great and Novitiate, Irving, TX
Pierce, Rev. Edward J., '72 (SFS) Retired.
Pierce, Rev. James L., *S.J.* '77 (NY) [MON] Xavier Jesuit Community, New York, NY
Pierce, Rev. Joseph B., (WDC) St. John Vianney, Prince Frederick, MD
Pierce, Rev. Msgr. Mark R., '81 (LC) On Administrative Leave.
Pierce, Rev. Paul, '21 (MIA) St. Hugh, Miami, FL
Pierce, Rev. William M., '71 (CAM) Retired.
Pierini, Rev. Raymond G., *M.M.* '87 (NY) Chap, P/T Spiritual Counselor, Calvary Hosp, Bronx [MON] Maryknoll Fathers and Brothers (Catholic Foreign Mission Society of America, Inc.), Ossining, NY
Pierino, Rev. Vicente, '64 (SJN) On Duty Outside Diocese. Caguas, FL
Pierjok, Rev. Peter Augustine, *O.S.B.* '88 (GBG) St. Bruno, Greensburg, PA; St. Paul, Greensburg, PA; [MON] Saint Vincent Archabbey, Latrobe, PA
Pieroni, Rev. Edward L., '85 (PRO) Chap, Miriam Hosp, Providence Saint Raymond's Church Corporation, Providence, RI
Pierre, Rev. Darren, *O.P.* '04 (CIN) St. Gertrude, Cincinnati, OH; [MON] St. Gertrude Priory, Cincinnati, OH
Pierre, Rev. Gilbert T., '18 (MOB) St. Mary of the Mission Parish, Opelika, Opelika, AL
Pierre, Msgr. Jean, '88 (MIA) Retired.
Pierre, Rev. Jean Odny, '07 (BRK) Most Precious Blood – Ss. Simon and Jude, Brooklyn, NY; Our Lady of Sorrows, Corona, NY
Pierre, Rev. Jean Yvon, '85 (BRK) Curia: Consultative Bodies St. Jerome, Brooklyn, NY; [MIS] National Center of the Haitian Apostolate, Brooklyn, NY
Pierre, Rev. Joseph, (BRK) Most Precious Blood – Ss. Simon and Jude, Brooklyn, NY
Pierre, Rev. Kenneth J., '63 (STP) Retired.
Pierre, Rev. Lucien Eugene, '07 (MIA) Curia: Clergy and Religious Services St. Helen, Lauderdale Lakes, FL
Pierre, Rev. Pierre Andre, (BRK) St. Matthew, Brooklyn, NY
Pierre Louis, Rev. Michel, (BRK) Holy Innocents, Brooklyn, NY; Our Lady of Refuge, Brooklyn, NY
Pierre-Jules, Rev. Oswald, *S.S.J.* '06 (NO) St. David,

New Orleans, LA
Pierre-Louis, Rev. Andre Dumarsais, (PMB) St. Elizabeth Ann Seton, Port St. Lucie, FL
Pierre-Louis, Rev. Robert, '14 (BRK) On Duty Outside Diocese. 454 Rene-Levesque Blvd. W., Montreal, PQ Canada H2Z 1A7
Pierrilus, Rev. Killick, '13 (BRK) Incarnation, Queens Village, NY; Nativity of the Blessed Virgin Mary-Saint Stanislaus Bishop and Martyr Roman Catholic Church, Ozone Park, NY; St. Gerard Majella, Hollis, NY
Pierro, Rev. Sebastian C., '82 (BUF) St. Amelia's Roman Catholic Church Society of the Town of Tonawanda, N.Y., Tonawanda, NY
Pierson, Rev. Dominic Bernard, '14 (SFE) Sacred Heart-Espanola, Espanola, NM
Pierz, Rev. Michael, '13 (SPR) Curia: Tribunal Blessed Trinity Parish, Greenfield, MA; Holy Trinity, Greenfield, MA
Pierzak, Rev. Sylwester, (PAT) St. Peter the Apostle, Parsippany, NJ
Pierzchala, Rev. Ireneusz, '08 (NEW) St. Theresa of the Child Jesus, Linden, NJ
Pietramale, Rev. John L., '92 (OM) Christ the King, Omaha, NE
Pietrocarlo, Rev. Ryan, *C.S.C.* (FTW) Curia: Offices and Directors St. Adalbert, South Bend, IN; St. Casimir, South Bend, IN
Pietropaoli, Rev. John, (HRT) [MON] Legionaries of Christ, Cheshire, CT; [SEM] Novitiate of the Legion of Christ, Cheshire, CT
Pietrowski, Rev. Stephen J., '92 (RVC) Curia: Offices and Directors Our Lady Queen of Martyrs, Centerport, NY
Pietrucha, Rev. Edward S., *C.S.P.* '57 (NY) Retired. [MON] Paulist Fathers' Motherhouse, New York, NY
Pietruszka, Rev. John, (OAK) St. Michael, Livermore, CA
Pietryga, Rev. Jan, (WDC) Our Lady Help of Christians, Waldorf, MD; St. John the Evangelist, Silver Spring, MD
Pietrzak, Rev. Bernard J., '81 (CHI) St. Anne, Barrington, IL
Pietrzak, Rev. Tomasz, *SChr* '06 (DET) St. Florian Parish, Hamtramck, Hamtramck, MI
Pietrzyk, Rev. Pius, *O.P.* (MO) Curia: Offices and Directors
Pifher, Rev. William A., '94 (TOL) St. Mary, Leipsic, OH
Piga, Rev. Stephen M., '02 (TR) St. Maximilian Kolbe, Toms River, NJ
Piggford, Rev. George, *C.S.C.* '05 (FR) [COL] Holy Cross Fathers Religious, North Easton, MA; [COL] Stonehill College, North Easton, MA
Pighini, Rev. Richard J., *C.S.V.* '85 (CHI) [MON] Viatorian Province Center-Clerics of St. Viator, Arlington Heights, IL
Pignato, Very Rev. David A., '01 (FR) Curia: Leadership St. Julie Billiart, North Dartmouth, MA
Pignato, Rev. Salvatore A., '68 (PSC) Curia: Leadership Holy Dormition, Ormond Beach, FL; St. Basil, Miami, FL; St. Nicholas of Myra, Orlando, FL
Pigon, Rev. Judah S., *M.F.* '03 (GB) St. Patrick Congregation, Menasha, WI
Pikulinski, Rev. Jerzy, (MO) Curia: Offices and Directors
Pikulski, Rev. John F., '60 (BGP) Retired.
Pikus, Rev. Karl A., *F.S.S.P* '92 (FWT) (>SFD) St. Rose of Lima Parish, Quincy, IL; (>SFD) [MIS] Priestly Fraternity of St. Peter, Quincy, IL
Pilato, Rev. Msgr. Sabato "Sal" A., '92 (LA) St. Anthony of Padua, Gardena, CA
Pilcher, Rev. John, '99 (KCK) Mater Dei, Topeka, KS
Pileggi, Rev. Anthony J., '81 (KC) On Special Assignment.
Pileggi, Rev. Anthony M., '07 (WIL) St. Paul's, Wilmington, DE
Pileggi, Rev. Francis J., *O.S.F.S.* '61 (WIL) Salesianum School, Wilmington, DE
Piletic, Rev. William R, (CHI) [MON] DePaul Vincentian Residence, Chicago, IL
Pilger, Rev. G. Richard, *I.C.* '79 (SP) Blessed Sacrament, Seminole, FL
Pilipie, Rev. John P., '16 (PAT) Retired.
Pilizue, Rev. Alou, *SMA* '11 (PEO) Saint Matthew Roman Catholic Congregation of Champaign, Champaign, IL; St. Boniface, Seymour, IL
Pilla, Rev. P. Carl, '54 (SY) Retired.
Pilla, Rev. Raju, '91 (PH) Our Lady of Grace, Penndel, PA
Pillai, Rev. Joseph Anthony, *C.Ss.R.* '93 (CHI) Ascension and St. Edmund Parish, Oak Park, IL
Pillai, Rev. Paul Jeyamani, (P) Curia: Offices and Directors
Pillai PJ, Rev. Chanda, *I.M.S.* (LR) Christ the King, Little Rock, AR; St. Francis of Assisi Church, Roland, AR
Pillarelli, Rev. Alfred M., '16 (GLD) Saint Francis of Assisi of Lewiston, Lewiston, MI
Pilola, Rev. Joseph, '87 (HT) Maria Immacolata, Houma, LA
Pilon, Rev. Msgr. Daniel J., '76 (FAR) Retired. Curia: Leadership St. Michael's Church of Grand Forks, Grand Forks, ND
Pilon, Rev. James F., '67 (HRT) Retired.
Pilon, Rev. Jean-Pierre G., '02 (SCR) On Duty Outside Diocese. Campbellford, ON
Pilon, Rev. Peter A., '00 (PEO) Holy Cross, Mendota, IL; SS. Peter and Paul, Mendota, IL; St. Theresa Parish, Earlville, IL
Pilones, Rev. Loji, '86 (FRS) St. Mary of the Miraculous Medal, Delano, CA
Pilotin, Rev. Joseph Christian, *M.S.* '12 (SB) St. Paul the Apostle, Chino Hills, CA; [MON] The Pacific Region Missionaries of Our Lady of La Salette, MS, Moreno Valley, CA
Pilsner, Rev. Peter R., '89 (NY) Cardinal Spellman High School, Bronx, NY; St. Lucy, Bronx, NY
Pilus, Rev. Jaroslaw, '98 (DET) SS. Peter and Paul (Westside) Parish Detroit, Detroit, MI
Pina, Rev. Martin, '93 (LUB) Curia: Offices and Directors Our Lady of Guadalupe, Lubbock, TX
Pina, Rev. Salomon Covarrubias, '91 (YAK) Curia: Leadership; Offices and Directors
Pinacue, Rev. Alexander, '15 (BRK) Blessed Sacrament, Jackson Heights, NY; St. Joan of Arc, Jackson Heights, NY
Pinaire, Rev. Zachary G.B., '15 (WCH) St. Andrew, Independence, KS; St. Francis Xavier, Cherryvale, KS
Pinarkayil, Rev. Saji Kurian, '99 (SYM) St. Mary's Syro-Malabar Knanaya Catholic Church of San Jose, San Jose, CA
Pince, Rev. Alexander W., '21 (VEN) Epiphany Cathedral Catholic Parish in Venice, Inc., Venice, FL
Pincelli, Rev. Thomas L., '70 (BWN) Retired.
Pinchock, Rev. Joseph, '72 (PT) Retired. St. Dominic, Panama City, FL
Pinchock, Rev. Joseph, '72 (ORL) Retired.
Pinciaro, Rev. Albert G., '84 (BGP) The Church of the Holy Name of Jesus, Stratford, Stratford, CT
Pincince, Rev. Gerald P., '65 (PRO) Retired.
Pinczewski, Rev. Phillip, '87 (E) Blessed Sacrament, Erie, PA
Pineda, Rev. Juan G., '90 (GAL) St. Theresa, Sugar Land, TX
Pineda, Rev. Juan G., '90 (BGP) On Duty Outside Diocese. St Ambrose Church, Houston, TX
Pineda, Rev. Ricardo, *C.P.M.* '13 (OWN) [MON] Fathers of Mercy, Auburn, KY
Pineda, Rev. Ryan I., '16 (WDC) Holy Redeemer, Kensington, MD; St. Peter, Olney, MD
Pineda, Rev. Vincent, '05 (SJ) St. Cyprian, Sunnyvale, CA
Pineda Avellanada, Rev. Reybert, '14 (ATL) Curia: Leadership; Offices and Directors
Pinette, Rev. Stuart H., '95 (HRT) Saint Louis de Montfort Parish Corporation, Litchfield, CT
Pingol, Rev. Rogelio, (SD) Pastor of Saint Mary Catholic Parish, National City, a corporation sole, National City, CA
Pinheiro, Rev. Jackson, *O.S.J.* '98 (SCR) St. Joseph Marello Parish, Pittston, PA
Pinheiro, Rev. Samuel, *OSB* '22 (GBG) [MON] Saint Vincent Archabbey, Latrobe, PA
Pinheiro, Rev. Samuel, *OSB* (GBG) Our Lady of Grace, Greensburg, PA; St. Benedict, Greensburg, PA
Pinheiro Bede, Rev. Cristiano, (BRK) Divine Mercy Roman Catholic Church, Brooklyn, NY
Pinhero, Rev. Jackson, (SCR) St. John the Evangelist, Pittston, PA
Pinizzotto, Rev. Anthony J., '78 (ARL) Retired. St. Agnes, Arlington, VA
Pinninti, Rev. Babu, '01 (WCH) St. Joan of Arc, Harper, KS
Pinnisi, Rev. Robert, '18 (MET) On Administrative Leave.
Pino, Rev. Justin P., '07 (E) Curia: Offices and Directors St. Leo Magnus, Ridgway, PA
Pins, Rev. Herbert J., '71 (HEL) Retired.
Pins, Rev. Joseph, (DM) Curia: Leadership; Offices and Directors St. Francis of Assisi, West Des Moines, IA; [EFT] St. Francis of Assisi Roman Catholic School Foundation, West Des Moines, IA
Pintabone, Rev. Canon John A., '79 (NY) On Sick Leave.
Pintacura, Rev. Michael, '76 (STO) Retired.
Pinti, Rev. Msgr. Domencio, '85 (TUC) [EFT] Catholic Foundation for the Diocese of Tucson Stewardship and Charitable Giving, Tucson, AZ
Pinti, Rev. Msgr. Domencio C., '85 (TUC) Retired. On Special Assignment. Curia: Leadership; Organizations (affiliated, inter-Diocesan, miscellaneous/other) Saint George Roman Catholic Parish - Apache Junction, Apache Junction, AZ
Pinto, Rev. Alex D., '69 (NEW) Retired.
Pinto, Rev. David, '20 (KAL) St. Ann, Augusta, MI
Pinto, Rev. Franco, *S.D.B.* (SP) Cristo Rey Tampa Salesian High School, Tampa, FL; [CAM] Mary Help of Christians Camp, Tampa, FL; [MON] Salesians of Don Bosco, Tampa, FL; [RTR] Mary Help of Christians Center, Tampa, FL
Pinto, Rev. Henry, '17 (PAT) Curia: Leadership St. Paul's, Prospect Park, NJ
Pinto, Rev. P. Francis, *S.D.B.* '97 (NEW) [MIS] Salesians of Don Bosco, South Orange, NJ
Pinto, Rev. Raphael C., (BO) St. Charles Borromeo, Woburn, MA
Pinuela, Rev. Freddie, *MJ* '95 (LA) Precious Blood, Los Angeles, CA
Pinuela, Rev. Freddie B, *MJ* '95 (LA) St. Kevin, Los Angeles, CA
Pinyan, Rev. Charles, '92 (NEW) Curia: Advisory Boards, Commissions, Committees, and Councils; Leadership; Offices and Directors Church of St. Thomas the Apostle, Bloomfield, NJ
Pinzon, Rev. Carlos Eduardo, '02 (SAV) St. Juliana's Catholic Church, Fort Valley, GA
Pinzon, Rev. Steven V., '05 (CAM) Our Lady of Guadalupe Parish, Lindenwold, N.J., Lindenwold, NJ
Pinzon Palacio, Rev. Fredy Hernán, '12 (KCK) Blessed Sacrament Church, Kansas City, KS; Our Lady of Unity, Kansas City, KS
Pinzon-Umana, Rev. Eduardo, *S.J.* '60 (CHI) Retired.
Pio Van Elshout, Rev. Johannes, *C.S.J.* (LAR) On Special Assignment. [MON] Congregation of St. John, Laredo, TX; [RTR] Holy Spirit Retreat and Conference Center, Laredo, TX
Piontkowski, Rev. Richard L., '82 (GI) Curia: Tribunal Our Lady of Lourdes, Ravenna, NE; St. Josaphat's, Loup City, NE
Piotrowski, Rev. Krzysztof, (VEN) St. Agnes Parish in Naples, Inc., Naples, FL
Piotrowski, Rev. Leonard G., '93 (SP) Curia: Pastoral Services Espiritu Santo, Safety Harbor, FL
Pipa, Rev. Krzysztof, *S.V.D.* '98 (TR) St. Ann, Browns Mills, NJ
Piper, Rev. Alan, *O.P.* (PRO) [MON] St. Thomas Aquinas Priory at Providence College, Providence, RI
Piper, Rev. Joseph, (WDC) [CAM] American University Catholic Community, ,
Pipp, Rev. Thomas Joseph, (CLV) [COL] John Carroll Jesuit Community, University Heights, OH
Pipta, Very Rev. Robert M., '94 (PBR) Curia: Offices and Directors [SEM] Byzantine Catholic Seminary of SS. Cyril and Methodius, Pittsburgh, PA
Pipta, Rev. Robert M., '94 (HPM) On Special Assignment. Curia: Offices and Directors
Piquado, Rev. Thomas G., *S.J.* '72 (SJ) [MON] Sacred Heart Jesuit Center, Los Gatos, CA
Piraro, Rev. Don, '67 (LKC) Retired.
Pirateque Serrano, Rev. César, '22 (CAM) Notre Dame de la Mer Parish, Wildwood, N.J., Wildwood, NJ
Pires, Rev. Francisco, '84 (SLC) Curia: Offices and Directors Saint Henry LLC 225, Brigham City, UT
Piro, Rev. Gerald J., '79 (BRK) On Leave.
Pirrone, Rev. Roberto, '88 (LA) St. Anthony of Padua, Gardena, CA; St. Teresa of Avila, Los Angeles, CA
Piruwa, Rev. Clement L., (SEA) Sacred Heart of Jesus, Lacey, WA
Pisaneschi, Rev. Joseph J., '01 (SCR) Curia: Leadership St. Elizabeth Ann Seton Parish, Swoyersville, PA
Pisano, Rev. Joseph Daniel, '07 (WH) Epiphany of the Lord, Moorefield, WV; St. Elizabeth Ann Seton, Franklin, WV; St. Mary, Petersburg, Petersburg, WV
Pisano, Rev. Mario, *O.M.* '68 (LA) All Saints, Los Angeles, CA; [MON] Minim Fathers, Los Angeles, CA
Pisarcik, Rev. John G., (PAT) Retired.
Piscitello, Rev. Primo, (ALB) St. Anthony of Padua, Troy, NY
Pisegna, Rev. Cedric, *C.P.* '91 (GAL) [MON] Congregation of the Passion, Holy Name Passionist Community and Retreat Center, Houston, TX
Pish, Rev. Robert H., '05 (STP) On Leave.
Piso, Rev. Volodymyr, '73 (STF) Retired.
Pisors, Rev. John A., *C.S.V.* '66 (CHI) [MON] Viatorian Province Center-Clerics of St. Viator, Arlington Heights, IL
Pistacchio, Rev. Gene, *O.F.M.* '89 (BO) [MIS] St. Anthony Shrine, Boston, MA
Pistone, Rev. Benardo, '73 (HBG) Retired.
Pisut, Rev. Christopher, '02 (DM) Curia: Offices and

Directors St. Augustin's, Des Moines, IA
Piszker, Rev. James, '91 (E) [CAM] Mercyhurst University, Erie, PA; [COL] Mercyhurst University, Erie, PA
Pitchai, Rev. Lourduraj, *O. Praem.* '89 (BGP) On Duty Outside Diocese. Returned to ministry in India
Pitchai-Savari, Rev. Mariapackiam, '10 (LC) St. Bartholomew, Stevens Point, WI; St. Michael, Junction City, WI; St. Wenceslaus, Milladore, WI
Pitol, Rev. Petrus, *C.S.* (BRK) St. Joseph Patron of the Universal Church, Brooklyn, NY
Pitre, Rev. Benjamin, (MO) Curia: Offices and Directors
Pitstick, Rev. Martin John, '08 (COV) Divine Mercy, Bellevue, KY; St. Bernard, Dayton, KY
Pitstick, Rev. Rory, '94 (SPK) Sacred Heart Catholic Parish - Wilbur, Wilbur, WA; St. Agnes Catholic Parish - Ritzville, Ritzville, WA; St. Joseph Catholic Parish - Odessa, Odessa, WA
Pitstick, Rev. Rory, (MO) Curia: Offices and Directors
Pitstick, Rev. Rory K., '94 (SPK) Curia: Leadership; (>MO) Offices and Directors
Pittappillil, Rev. Antony, (SYM) Divine Mercy Syro-Malabar Catholic Church (Edinburg), Texas, Edinburg, TX
Pittappilly, Rev. Antony, *S.D.V.* '91 (BUR) [CAM] Castleton State College, Fair Haven, VT
Pittard, Rev. Wayne M., '83 (GF) Retired.
Pittman, Rev. Robert, *s.s.s.* (CLV) Retired.
Pitts, Rev. Stephen, *SJ* '17 (STP) [MON] Markoe House Jesuit Community, Minneapolis, MN
Pitts, Rev. William L., '70 (R) Retired.
Pitula, Very Rev. Roman, '98 (PHU) Immaculate Conception of Blessed Virgin Mary, Cathedral, Philadelphia, PA
Pivarnik, Rev. R. Gabriel, *O.P.* '97 (PRO) [COL] Providence College, Providence, RI; [MON] St. Thomas Aquinas Priory at Providence College, Providence, RI
Pivonka, Rev. Dave, *TOR* '96 (STU) Curia: Deaneries [COL] Franciscan University of Steubenville, Steubenville, OH; [MON] Holy Spirit Friary, Steubenville, OH
Pivonka, Rev. Msgr. Leonard, '77 (CC) Retired.
Pizmoht, Rev. Louis A., '66 (CLV) Retired.
Pizzamiglio, Rev. Msgr. Ernest E., '66 (PEO) Retired.
Pizzamiglio, Rev. Msgr. Ernest E., '66 (PEO) Retired.
Pizzarelli, Rev. Francis, *S.M.M.* '79 (RVC) Curia: Leadership Most Precious Blood, Davis Park, NY; [MON] Montfort Missionaries, Bay Shore, NY
Pizzo, Very Rev. Anthony B., *O.S.A.* '84 (CHI) [MON] Federation of Augustinians of North America, Chicago, IL; [MON] The Augustinians-Provincialate, Chicago, IL
Pizzo, Rev. Philip J., '77 (BRK) Retired.
Pizzonia, Rev. Domenico, '05 (GF) St. Rose of Lima, Stanford, MT
Placa, Rev. Msgr. Alan J., '70 (RVC) Retired.
Place, Rev. Michael D., '70 (CHI) On Special Assignment. Northbrook Curia: Leadership
Placette, Rev. David D., '04 (BEA) Retired.
Plaisted, Rev. Eugene D., *O.S.C.* '61 (SCL) Retired. [MON] Crosier Priory, Onamia, MN
Plakut, Rev. Peter, *O.C.S.O.* '58 (P) [MON] The Cistercian (Trappist) Abbey of Our Lady of Guadalupe (Order of Cistercians of the Strict Observance), Carlton, OR
Plammoottil, Rev. Sunny Joseph, *O.S.H.* '93 (GAL) Holy Family, Missouri City, TX; [MON] The Society of the Oblates of Sacred Heart, Missouri City, TX
Plamondon, Rev. Donald J., '72 (DUB) Retired. Curia: Administration
Plancencia-Puntiel, Rev. Samuel De Jesus, *OFM Cap.* '16 (MGZ) Santuario Protomártires de la Inmaculada Concepción, Aguada, PR
Plancher, Rev. Christian, '66 (PT) St. Rose of Lima, Milton, FL
Plank, Rev. Stephen J., *O.S.B.* '94 (OM) Mount Michael Benedictine School, Elkhorn, NE; [MON] Mount Michael Benedictine Abbey, Elkhorn, NE
Planning, Rev. Stephen W., *S.J.* '99 (WDC) Gonzaga College High School, Washington, DC; [MON] The Jesuit Community at Georgetown University, Washington, DC
Plant, Rev. Christopher M., '08 (GAL) St. Vincent de Paul, Houston, TX
Plante, Rev. Msgr. Jacques L., '82 (PRO) Curia: Advisory Boards, Commissions, Committees, and Councils St. Aidan Church Corporation, Cumberland, Cumberland, RI
Plante, Rev. Pierre J., '78 (PRO) [CON] Convent, Warwick, RI
Planty, Rev. Donald J., '93 (ARL) St. Charles Borromeo, Arlington, VA
Plasencia, Rev. Antonio, (SAC) Pastor of Our Lady of Guadalupe Parish, Sacramento, a corporation sole, Sacramento, CA
Plass, Rev. John, (SR) Cardinal Newman High School, Santa Rosa, CA; Pastor of St. Joseph Catholic Church of Cotati, A Corporation Sole, Cotati, CA; [EFT] Angela Merici and John Henry Newman Foundation, Inc., Santa Rosa, CA
Platania, Rev. James, '13 (PAT) On Duty Outside Diocese.
Platania, Rev. James P., '13 (NEW) [SEM] Immaculate Conception Seminary School of Theology, South Orange, NJ
Plate, Rev. Brian, (MO) Curia: Offices and Directors
Plathe, Rev. Anthony H., '63 (NU) Retired.
Plathottam, Rev. Mathew, '67 (PHX) Retired.
Platt, Rev. William F., '88 (BGP) St. Catherine of Siena and St. Agnes Parish Corporation, Riverside, CT
Plavac, Rev. Timothy J., '86 (CLV) St. Bede the Venerable, Mentor, OH
Plavcan, Very Rev. Jon J., '94 (GRY) Curia: Leadership; Offices and Directors St. Ann, Beverly Shores, IN; St. Patrick, Chesterton, IN
Plawecki, Rev. Joseph A., '83 (DET) SS. Simon and Jude Parish Westland, Westland, MI
Plazewski, Very Rev. Leonard, '91 (SP) Curia: Pastoral Services Christ the King, Tampa, FL; [MIS] Renew Haiti, Inc., Tampa, FL
Pleban, Rev. Alexander L., '57 (GBG) Retired. [NUR] Neumann House, Greensburg, PA
Pleho, Rev. Anthony J., '79 (NY) Parish of Holy Rosary and Nativity of Our Blessed Lady, Bronx, NY
Pleier, Rev. David J., '75 (GB) St. Peter the Fisherman, Two Rivers, WI
Pleiman, Rev. Kenneth, *C.PP.S.* '70 (CIN) Retired. [MON] Society of the Precious Blood, United States Province, Inc., Dayton, OH
Pleiman, Rev. Kenneth, *C.PP.S.* '70 (CIN) Retired.
Pleiman, Rev. Kenneth F., *C.PP.S.* '70 (CIN) Retired.
Pleiness, Rev. Gregg, '81 (LAN) St. Augustine Parish Howell, Howell, MI
Pleitez, Rev. Kevin P., (BO) Immaculate Conception, Marlborough, MA
Plessala, Rev. Connor R., '20 (MOB) St. Bede the Venerable Catholic Church, Montgomery, AL
Plessala, Rev. Peyton, '20 (MOB) St. Michael, Auburn, AL
Pleus, Rev. Adrian C.H., '99 (ATL) St. Vincent De Paul Catholic Church, Dallas, Inc., Dallas, GA
Pleva, Rev. Michael, '21 (ALT) St. Joseph, Bellwood, PA; St. Matthew, Tyrone, PA
Plewka, Rev. Msgr. Mark, '76 (PBL) Curia: Leadership; Offices and Directors
Plishka, Rev. Andrew, '06 (STN) On Leave.
Plishka, Rev. Richard, '08 (PRM) On Leave.
Ploch, Rev. Jacek, '08 (PRO) Church of Our Lady of Czenstochowa, Coventry, RI; Church of Saint Vincent de Paul, Anthony, Rhode Island, Coventry, RI
Ploch, Rev. Robert J., (SAT) Our Lady Queen of Peace, Kenedy, TX
Ploch, Rev. Timothy, *SDB* (NY) Salesian High School, New Rochelle, NY
Plocharczyk, Rev. Msgr. Daniel J., '74 (HRT) Church Corporation of the Sacred Heart of Jesus of New Britain, New Britain, CT
Plodari, Rev. Angelo, *C.S.* '04 (NY) Our Lady of Pompeii, New York, NY; [EFT] Trust for the Center for Migration Studies in New York, New York, NY; [MON] Scalabrinian Missionaries (The Pious Society of the Missionaries of St. Charles Boromeo, Inc.), New York, NY
Plohimon, Rev. Nelson S., *OAR* '15 (CHK) San Francisco de Borja Parish, Rota, MP; San Isidro Parish, Rota, MP
Plona, Rev. Michael, '17 (RVC) St. John the Evangelist, Center Moriches, NY
Plona, Rev. Michael, (MO) Curia: Offices and Directors
Plona, Rev. Michael, (RVC) Curia: Leadership
Ploof, Rev. Gerald, '75 (LAN) Retired.
Ploof, Rev. Jeremy, '12 (SCL) Our Lady of the Runestone, Kensington, MN; St. Charles, Herman, MN; St. Olaf, Elbow Lake, MN
Ploplis, Rev. Theodore, '77 (CHI) Retired.
Plotkowski, Rev. Jerome A., '65 (SFE) Retired. Curia: Offices and Directors
Plotkowski, Rev. Jerome A., '65 (SFE) Retired. Curia: Offices and Directors
Plotkowski, Rev. John S., '74 (CHI) Retired.
Plourde, Rev. James S., '82 (PRT) Retired.
Plow, Rev. Gregory, *TOR* (STU) [MON] Holy Spirit Friary, Steubenville, OH
Plow, Rev. Gregory, *T.O.R.* '08 (STU) [COL] Franciscan University of Steubenville, Steubenville, OH
Pluciennik, Rev. Marcin P., '09 (HRT) Curia: Deaneries Saint Teresa of Calcutta Parish Corporation, Manchester, CT
Plummer, Rev. Samuel Isaac, '13 (WDC) St. Mary's Church of Piscataway, Clinton, MD
Plunkett, Rev. Craig, '06 (FRS) Retired.
Plunkett, Rev. Msgr. Joseph P., '60 (NEW) Retired. Our Lady of Czestochowa, Harrison, NJ
Pluth, Rev. Paul R., '96 (SEA) Curia: Tribunal
Po, Rev. Fernando R., '84 (NEW) Retired.
Poblocki, Rev. Richard M., '83 (BUF) Retired.
Pocernich, Rev. Eugene S., '74 (MIL) Retired.
Pocetto, Rev. Alexander T., *O.S.F.S.* (WIL) Salesianum School, Wilmington, DE
Poche, Rev. Daniel M., '78 (HT) Retired.
Poche, Rev. Leon, '19 (NO) On Special Assignment. Ursuline Academy St. Matthew the Apostle, River Ridge, LA
Pochelti, Rev. Angelo, '67 (NEW) Holy Redeemer, West New York, NJ
Podhajsky, Rev. Christopher R., '01 (DUB) Basilica of St. Francis Xavier, Dyersville, Iowa, Dyersville, IA; Beckman Catholic High School, Dyersville, Iowa, Dyersville, IA; S.S. Peter and Paul Church, Petersburg, Iowa, Dyersville, IA; St. Boniface Church of New Vienna, New Vienna, Iowa, New Vienna, IA; St. Francis Xavier School, Dyersville, Iowa, Dyersville, IA; St. Joseph's Church, Earlville, Iowa, Earlville, IA; St. Paul Church, Worthington, Iowa, Worthington, IA
Podlesny, Rev. James F., *O.S.B.* '80 (GBG) Curia: Advisory Boards, Commissions, Committees, and Councils; Offices and Directors Sacred Heart, Youngstown, PA; St. Cecilia, Whitney, PA; [MON] Saint Vincent Archabbey, Latrobe, PA
Podraza, Rev. Timothy, '97 (OM) St. Wenceslaus, Omaha, NE
Podsiadlo, Rev. Grzegorz, *S.D.S.* '01 (MET) Ss. Peter and Paul, Great Meadows, NJ
Podwysocki, Very Rev. Grzegorz, '08 (JOL) Curia: Leadership Our Mother of Good Counsel, Homer Glen, IL
Podwysocki, Very Rev. Grzegorz, (CHI) Curia: Tribunal
Podymniak, Rev. Miroslaw, *O.F.M.Conv.* '92 (BRK) St. Adalbert, Elmhurst, NY
Poecking, Very Rev. David G., '96 (PIT) Curia: Consultative Bodies; Leadership
Poecking, Rev. Kevin G., '04 (PIT) Holy Family, Pittsburgh, PA
Poehlmann, Rev. Edward J., '67 (DEN) Presentation of Our Lady Catholic Parish in Denver, Denver, CO
Poerio, Rev. John, '59 (LKC) Retired.
Poettgen, Rev. Edward L., '80 (ORG) St. Boniface, Anaheim, CA
Pogatchnik, Rev. Scott, '10 (SCL) St. Augustine, St. Cloud, MN; St. Mary's Cathedral of St. Cloud, St. Cloud, MN
Poggemeyer, Rev. Joseph T., '97 (TOL) Curia: Advisory Boards, Commissions, Committees, and Councils; Deaneries Divine Mercy Parish, Paulding, OH
Pogorelc, Rev. Anthony J., *P.S.S.* '88 (BAL) [MON] Society of St. Sulpice, Province of the United States, Baltimore, MD
Pogorzelski, Rev. Andrzej, '77 (HRT) Retired. The Church of S.S. Cyril & Methodius of Hartford, Connecticut, Hartford, CT
Pogue, Rev. Sean V., '11 (LFT) Sacred Heart of Jesus, Cicero, IN
Pohlman, Rev. Stephen J., '84 (SFD) Retired.
Pohlmeier, Rev. Loren G., '82 (GI) Retired.
Pohto, Rev. J. Thomas, *O.S.A.* '67 (PH) Our Mother of Good Counsel, Bryn Mawr, PA; [MON] Augustinians Friars (O.S.A.), Bryn Mawr, PA
Poirier, Rev. David, *S.A.* '77 (NY) [MON] Franciscan Friars of the Atonement, Minister General Office, Garrison, NY
Poirier, Rev. Ralph J., *C.S.Sp.* '63 (PIT) [RTR] The Spiritan Center, Bethel Park, PA
Poirier, Rev. Robert, *SJ* '77 (MOB) Curia: Leadership [MON] Jesuits of Mobile, Inc., Mobile, AL
Poirot, Rev. Jeff, '01 (FWT) On Leave.
Poirrier, Rev. Connor, (LAF) St. Pius X, Lafayette, LA
Poissant, Rev. Msgr. Leeward J., '63 (OG) Retired.
Poisson, Rev. Thomas L., '78 (MAR) Retired.
Poje, Rev. Kyle, '22 (SEA) St. Michael, Olympia, WA
Pokrzewinski, Rev. Justus Marcel, *OP* '60 (IND) Retired. St. Paul Catholic Center, Bloomington, Inc., Bloomington, IN
Pol, Friar Mateus Maria, *OSM* '18 (ELP) Our Lady of Sorrows, El Paso, TX
Polak, Rev. Jozef, *S.J.* '97 (CHI) [MIS] Jan Beyzym Society, Inc., Chicago, IL; [MON] Sacred Heart Mission House (The Polish Messenger of The Sacred Heart, Inc.), Chicago, IL
Polamarasetty, Rev. Vijaya, (SP) St. Anne, Ruskin, FL

Polanco, Rev. Dennis, *S.A.* '74 (WDC) [SEM] Atonement Seminary-Franciscan Friars of the Atonement, Washington, DC

Polanco, Rev. Dennis, *S.A.* '74 (NY) [MON] Franciscan Friars of the Atonement, Minister General Office, Garrison, NY; [MON] St. Christopher's Inn, Garrison, NY; [SPF] St. Christopher's Inn (Atonement Friars), Garrison, NY

Polando, Rev. Peter M., '80 (Y) Curia: Leadership St. Patrick, Leetonia, OH; St. Paul, Salem, OH

Polansky, Rev. Lawrence E., '09 (CAM) Curia: Clergy and Religious Services Parish of St. Michael the Archangel, Franklinville, N.J., Clayton, NJ

Polasek, Rev. Jeffrey S., '91 (TLS) St. Clement of Rome, Bixby, OK

Polce, Rev. Jonathon, *S.J.* '22 (BO) (>NO) [MON] Loyola Jesuit Community, New Orleans, LA

Polczyk, Rev. Stanislaus, '82 (TR) Retired.

Polczynski, Rev. Alan N., '07 (GBG) [MIS] Clairvaux Commons, Indiana, PA

Polednak, Rev. John V., '76 (SCR) Curia: Leadership; Offices and Directors St. Peter's Cathedral, Scranton, PA

Polek, Rev. David, *C.Ss.R.* '62 (STL) Retired. [MON] St. Clement Health Care Center, Liguori, MO

Polek, Rev. Richard W., '93 (WOR) Curia: Leadership; Offices and Directors Our Lady of Czestochowa, Worcester, MA

Polenz, Rev. Gordon, '82 (ALB) Retired.

Poliafico, Rev. David A., '95 (COL) St. Timothy, Columbus, OH

Policetti, Rev. Julian, (FRS) St. Mary of the Desert, Rosamond, CA

Policetty, Rev. Balaraju, '96 (SUP) St. Anthony of Padua, Gordon, WI; St. Mary, Minong, WI; St. Pius X, Solon Springs, WI

Polich, Rev. David J., '76 (DM) Retired. Curia: Offices and Directors

Polichnowski, Rev. Nicholas, '77 (STU) [COL] Franciscan University of Steubenville, Steubenville, OH; [MON] Holy Spirit Friary, Steubenville, OH

Polifka, Rev. Charles J., *O.F.M.Cap.* '71 (DEN) Annunciation Catholic Parish in Denver, Denver, CO; [MON] San Antonio Friary, Denver, CO

Polimetla, Rev. Thomas, (BAK) Our Lady of Mount Carmel Catholic Church of Chiloquin, Inc., Chiloquin, OR

Polinek, Rev. Michael C., '10 (E) St. Joseph, Lucinda, PA; St. Michael, Fryburg, PA

Polinski, Rev. Nathanael R., *O.S.B.* '12 (GBG) [MON] Saint Vincent Archabbey, Latrobe, PA

Polishetty, Rev. Jayaraju, '09 (AUS) Our Lady of Lourdes Catholic Church - Gatesville, Texas, Gatesville, TX; St. Thomas Catholic Church - Hamilton, Texas, Hamilton, TX

Polito, Rev. Martin F., '76 (CLV) Holy Redeemer, Cleveland, OH

Polizzi, Rev. Msgr. Salvatore E., '56 (STL) St. Roch Catholic Church, St. Louis, MO

Poljicak, Rev. Vlatko, '65 (LA) Retired.

Polk, Rev. Page, (PHX) Our Lady of the Angels Conventual Church, Scottsdale, AZ

Poll, Rev. Jeffrey A., '05 (LAN) Light of Christ Parish Deerfield, Deerfield, MI

Pollard, Rev. Christopher J., '98 (ARL) St. John the Beloved, McLean, VA

Pollard, Rev. Msgr. John, '74 (CHI) Retired.

Pollard, Rev. Marcus, (ARL) [COL] Christendom College, Front Royal, VA

Pollard, Rev. Msgr. Patrick J., '72 (CHI) Retired. Curia: Leadership

Pollard, Rev. Roy F., '66 (WIL) Retired.

Pollette, Rev. Cameron, '21 (SFR) St. Veronica, South San Francisco, CA

Pollman, Rev. Kent M., '16 (STL) Ascension Catholic Church, Chesterfield, Chesterfield, MO

Pollock, Rev. Jonah F., *O.P.* '09 (NY) Chap, Mem Sloan Kettering Cancer Ctr, New York; New York P… St. Catherine of Siena, New York, NY; [MON] St. Catherine of Siena Priory, New York, NY

Polman, Rev. Shawn, '20 (NU) St. Mary, Tracy, MN

Polmounter, Rev. Richard J., '78 (SCR) Curia: Leadership St. John Bosco, Conyngham, PA

Polo, Rev. Peter, *C.S.* '68 (PRO) [NUR] Scalabrini Villa Inc., North Kingstown, RI

Poloche, Rev. Pedro, '98 (ATL) Curia: Leadership; Offices and Directors St. Patrick Catholic Church, Norcross, Inc., Norcross, GA

Polosky, Very Rev. Archpriest Michael, '91 (SJP) Curia: Leadership; Offices and Directors Assumption of the Blessed Virgin Mary, Latrobe, PA; Ss. Peter and Paul, Aliquippa, PA; Ss. Peter and Paul, Ambridge, PA

Polselli, Rev. Leo, *C.S.C.* '70 (FR) [COL] Holy Cross Fathers Religious, North Easton, MA

Polson, Rev. Mikel Anthony, '02 (LAF) St. Michael Archangel, Crowley, LA

Poltorak, Rev. George, *S.A.C.* '90 (BRK) St. Aloysius, Ridgewood, NY

Poltorak, Rev. Stanley T., '82 (SAC) Pastor of Presentation of the Blessed Virgin Mary Parish, Sacramento, a corporation sole, Sacramento, CA

Polumari, Rev. Anil, (GB) St. Hubert Mission, Newald, WI; St. Leonard, Laona, WI; St. Norbert, Long Lake, WI

Polyak, Rev. John V., '69 (MET) Retired.

Polyak, Very Rev. Vasyl, '03 (PBR) Curia: Leadership Sts. Peter and Paul, Tarentum, PA

Polycarpe, Rev. Pierre G., '99 (RCK) [HOS] Saint Anthony Medical Center (OSF Saint Anthony Medical Center), Rockford, IL

Polynice, Rev. Wilgintz, *S.D.B.* '17 (NO) Archbishop Shaw High School (Salesians of St. John Bosco), Marrero, LA; St. John Bosco Roman Catholic Church, Harvey, Louisiana, Harvey, LA

Pomeisl, Rev. Jeffrey, (NY) St. Charles, Staten Island, NY

Pomerleau, Rev. Claude, *C.S.C.* '65 (P) Retired.

Pomerleau, Rev. William A., '79 (SPR) Retired.

Pomeroy, Rev. Thomas, '93 (GB) Holy Family, Brillion, WI

Pomposello, Rev. Peter, '04 (NY) Military Chap, Fort Campbell, KY

Pomposello, Rev. Peter A., '04 (NY) Curia: (>MO) Offices and Directors

Ponce, Rev. Antonio, *O.M.I.* '09 (SAT) [COL] Oblate School of Theology, San Antonio, TX; [SEM] Blessed Mario Borzaga Formation Community, San Antonio, TX

Ponce, Rev. Demetrio, '88 (ELP) On Leave.

Ponce, Rev. Gerardo M, '20 (CC) Holy Family Church, Corpus Christi, TX

Ponce, Rev. Jaime, (LAV) Curia: Tribunal

Ponce, Rev. Jaimes, '01 (COS) Curia: Leadership; Tribunal

Ponce, Rev. Jose Antonio, *O.M.I.* '09 (WDC) [MON] Missionary Oblates of Mary Immaculate, Washington, DC

Poncette, Rev. Marion, *C.M.* '03 (SJN) Chap, Hospital Pavia-Santurce, Santurce

Poncette, Rev. Marion, *C.M.* (ARE) Sagrada Familia, Manati, PR

Poncini, Rev. John, '05 (SJ) St. Nicholas and St. William Catholic Parish, Los Altos, CA

Pondo, Rev. Stanley, '98 (IND) St. Anthony of Padua Catholic Church, Morris, Inc., Morris, IN; St. Louis Catholic Church, Batesville, Inc., Batesville, IN

Ponessa, Rev. Joseph, '74 (GF) Curia: Leadership St. Francis Xavier, Circle, MT

Pongantung, Rev. Herman, *MSC* '93 (ALN) Cathedral of St. Catharine of Siena, Allentown, PA

Ponisciak, Rev. Daniel, *C.S.C.* '15 (FTW) [MON] Congregation of Holy Cross, United States Province of Priests and Brothers, Notre Dame, IN

Ponnaiyan, Rev. Arul, '13 (MIL) Congregation of the Holy Apostles, New Berlin, WI

Ponnapati, Rev. Balireddy, '98 (OKL) St. Monica, Edmond, OK

Ponnet, Rev. Christopher, '83 (LA) [MIS] Catholic HIV/AIDS Office, , ; [MIS] Catholic Ministry with Lesbian & Gay Persons, , ; [MIS] Catholics Against the Death Penalty Center, , ; [MIS] Consistent Life Ethics Institute, , ; [MIS] Pax Christi Los Angeles, ,

Ponnet, Rev. Christopher D., '83 (LA) Chap, Los Angeles Cty-Univ of Southern Calif Med Ctr Curia: Advisory Boards, Commissions, Committees, and Councils; Offices and Directors St. Camillus de Lellis, Los Angeles, CA

Pons, Rev. Ramon, '88 (SR) On Duty Outside Diocese. Archdiocese of Los Angeles

Pontarelli, Rev. Michael M., *O.S.M.* '82 (ORG) Curia: Leadership St. Juliana Falconieri, Fullerton, CA; [MON] Servite Fathers and Brothers, Fullerton, CA

Pontes, Rev. Scott D., '04 (PRO) Saint Joseph's Church of Newport, Rhode Island, Newport, RI; [COL] Salve Regina University (Salve Regina University, Sisters of Mercy of the Americas), Newport, RI

Ponton, Rev. Evan, '20 (BAL) St. John the Evangelist, Severna Park, MD

Pontzer, Rev. Stephen, '07 (SAV) Curia: Leadership

Pontzer, Rev. Stephen J., '07 (SAV) Curia: Leadership Sacred Heart, Warner Robins, GA

Ponzini, Rev. Thomas V., '96 (GAL) Prince of Peace, Houston, TX

Poochakkattil Baby, Rev. Joby, '06 (SYM) St. Stephen's Knanaya Catholic Mission Orlando, Inc., Orlando, FL

Pool, Rev. Jefferson, *SVD* '92 (MIL) [MON] Divine Word Missionaries, East Troy, WI

Poole, Rev. Michael, (HEL) Retired.

Poole, Rev. Richard C., '94 (SPK) Chap, US Air Force Curia: (>MO) Offices and Directors

Poole, Rev. Stafford, *C.M.* '56 (LA) Retired.

Poole, Rev. Steven F., '96 (BEL) Retired.

Poonely, Rev. George, '01 (LUB) Curia: Leadership Sacred Heart, Plainview, TX; St. Alice, Plainview, TX; St. Peter the Apostle, Olton, TX

Poonoly, Rev. Peter, (BRK) St. Patrick, Brooklyn, NY

Poorman, Rev. Mark L., *C.S.C.* '82 (FTW) [COL] University of Notre Dame Du Lac, Notre Dame, IN; [MON] Holy Cross Community, Corby Hall, University of Notre Dame, Notre Dame, IN

Poovakulam, Rev. Antony P., '63 (TR) Retired.

Poovathumkudy, Rev. Sunny, *MS* '04 (ORL) Good Shepherd, Orlando, FL

Poovathumoottil, Rev. Baiju Antony, (SYM) [MIS] Vincentian House, Divine Mercy Prayer House, Plant City, FL

Popadick, Rev. Msgr. Peter J., '70 (BUF) St. Aloysius Gonzaga, Cheektowaga, NY

Pope, Rev. Msgr. Charles E., '89 (WDC) Curia: Consultative Bodies; Deaneries Holy Comforter - St. Cyprian, Washington, DC

Pope, Rev. L. Michael, *S.J.* '81 (SJ) [MON] Sacred Heart Jesuit Center, Los Gatos, CA

Pope, Rev. Nicholas F., *S.J.* '72 (MIL) [MON] St. Camillus Jesuit Community (Society of Jesus, USA Midwest Province), Wauwatosa, WI

Pope, Rev. Robert, (PMB) St. Mark the Evangelist, Fort Pierce, FL

Pope, Very Rev. Robert L., '16 (PMB) Curia: Leadership

Popik, Rev. Cameron D., '21 (CLV) St. Hilary, Fairlawn, OH

Popish, Rev. Edward, *SS.CC.* (FR) [MIS] Congregation of the Sacred Hearts - United States Province (Sacred Hearts Fathers; Sacred Hearts Missions), Fairhaven, MA

Popish, Rev. Edward, *SS.CC.* '90 (HON) St. Ann, Kaneohe, HI; [MON] St. Patrick's Monastery, Honolulu, HI

Popivchak, Rev. Msgr. Ronald P., '67 (PHU) SS. Peter and Paul, Bridgeport, PA

Poplawski, Rev. John F., '74 (SCR) Retired.

Popov, Rev. Pavlo, '09 (STN) St. Sophia Ukrainian Catholic Church, The Colony, TX

Popovich, Rev. Peter, '85 (NY) Church of Our Lady of Shkodra, Hartsdale, NY

Popovich, Rev. Stephen E., '81 (Y) On Sick Leave.

Popovici, Rev. Olvian, '98 (STF) Curia: Offices and Directors Holy Family, Lindenhurst, NY

Popp, Rev. Kenneth, '83 (SCL) St. Joseph's, Pierz, MN; St. Michael's, Pierz, MN

Poppish, Rev. Ephrem, *O.C.S.O.* '13 (DUB) [MON] New Melleray Abbey, Order of Cistercians of the Strict Observance (Corporation of New Melleray), Peosta, IA

Popson, Rev. Michael G., '87 (PSC) Curia: Advisory Boards, Commissions, Committees, and Councils

Popyk, Rev. Volodymyr, '97 (PHU) St. Stephen's, Toms River, NJ

Porada, Rev. Marcin, '08 (BUF) Curia: Consultative Bodies Our Lady Help of Christians, Cheektowaga, NY; Resurrection, Cheektowaga, NY; St. Josaphat, Cheektowaga, NY

Porkorsky, Rev. Jerry, '90 (ARL) St. Catherine of Siena, Great Falls, VA

Porpiglia, Rev. Joseph D., '86 (BUF) Curia: Offices and Directors Blessed Sacrament, Buffalo, NY

Porpora, Rev. Robert D., '90 (NY) St. Peter, Monticello, NY

Porras, Very Rev. Adrian, '01 (CHL) St. Barnabas, Arden, NC

Porras, Rev. Alfredo Raul, '19 (WOR) Curia: Offices and Directors

Port, Rev. Dennis R., '74 (STL) St. Matthias Catholic Church, St. Louis, MO

Portalatin, Rev. Antonio, (PCE) [MIS] Santuario de Schoenstatt, Juana Diaz, PR

Portalatin, Rev. Antonio, '91 (ARE) On Duty Outside Diocese. Prof, Washington DC

Portelli, Rev. Joseph Marcel, '11 (SAG) Sacred Heart Parish of Gladwin, Gladwin, MI; Saint Athanasius Parish of Harrison, Harrison, MI

Porter, Rev. John E., '56 (CIN) Retired.

Porter, Rev. Lawrence B., '74 (NEW) Retired. Curia: Organizations (affiliated, inter-Diocesan, miscellaneous/other) [COL] Seton Hall University, South Orange, NJ

Porter, Rev. Paul, '20 (ATL) St. Peter Chanel Catholic Church, Roswell, Inc., Roswell, GA

Porter, Rev. Robert G., '81 (HEL) Retired. [HOS] St. James Healthcare, Butte, MT

Porter, Rev. Rocco, '97 (DEN) Christ the King Catholic

Parish in Denver, Denver, CO

Porter, Rev. Stephen C., '81 (SB) Saint Kateri Tekakwitha Catholic Community, Inc., Beaumont, CA

Porter, Rev. William, '80 (KCK) St. Agnes, Roeland Park, KS

Porterfield, Rev. David J., *C.S.C.* '79 (FTW) Retired. [MON] Congregation of Holy Cross, United States Province of Priests and Brothers, Notre Dame, IN

Portillo, Rev. Maurico, (ARL) Christ the Redeemer, Sterling, VA

Portland, Rev. Paul, *S.D.S.* '76 (MIL) St. Pius Congregation, Wauwatosa, WI; [MIS] Holy Apostles House of Formation, Milwauke, WI

Portorreal, Rev. David, (VEN) Bishop Verot Catholic High School, Fort Myers, FL; St. Leo Parish in Bonita Springs, Inc., Bonita Springs, FL

Portula, Rev. Ramel O., *C.I.C.M.* '00 (ARL) St. Ann, Arlington, VA

Portzer, Rev. Joseph, *FSSP* (PHX) Mater Misericordiae Catholic Church, Phoenix, AZ

Poser, Rev. Gregory, *O.S.C.* '75 (SCL) [MON] Crosier Priory, Onamia, MN

Posey, Very Rev. Patrick L., '91 (ARL) Curia: Offices and Directors Cathedral of St. Thomas More, Arlington, VA

Posiewala, Rev. John, *S.A.C.* '76 (BUF) [MON] Society of the Catholic Apostolate, North Tonawanda, NY; [SHR] Shrine of the Infant Jesus, North Tonawanda, NY

Post, Very Rev. Joseph S., '07 (STL) Curia: Leadership Immaculate Conception Catholic Church, Union, Union, MO

Post, Rev. Robert J., '82 (BGP) Retired. [MON] The Catherine Dennis Keefe Queen of the Clergy Retired Priests' Residence, Stamford, CT

Poster, Very Rev. James M., '03 (MAD) St. Joseph, Baraboo, WI

Poston, Rev. J. Collin, '03 (BAL) St. Bartholomew, Manchester, MD

Postrano, Rev. Anastacio, '84 (HON) St. Ann, Waihee, HI

Potaczek, Very Rev. John A., '99 (LC) Curia: Leadership St. Patrick, Mauston, WI; [EFT] St. Patrick's Congregation Trust, Mauston, WI

Potencio, Rev. Aldo, *O.S.A* '17 (PH) [MON] Provincial Offices of the Order of St. Augustine, Province of St. Thomas of Villanova, Villanova, PA; [MON] St. Augustine Friary, Villanova, PA

Poth, Rev. Thomas, *S.M.M.* '83 (RVC) [MON] Montfort Missionaries, Bay Shore, NY

Pothier, Rt. Rev. Archmandrite Glen J., '95 (PMB) Curia: Leadership

Pothier, Rt. Rev. Archmandrite Glen J., '95 (PMB) Curia: Leadership St. Edward, Palm Beach, FL

Pothireddy, Rev. Chinnappa, '79 (WIN) Holy Trinity, Rollingstone, MN; St. Joseph, Rushford, MN; St. Rose of Lima, Lewiston, MN

Pothireddy, Very Rev. Marreddy, '94 (WIN) Curia: Advisory Boards, Commissions, Committees, and Councils; Deaneries

Pothireddy, Rev. Marreddy, '94 (WIN) St. Finbarr's, Grand Meadow, MN; St. Ignatius, Spring Valley, MN; St. Patrick's, LeRoy, MN

Pothireddy, Rev. Ray, '94 (AUS) St. Catherine of Siena, Austin, TX

Pothireddy, Rev. Swaminatha R., '93 (WIN) Curia: Advisory Boards, Commissions, Committees, and Councils Church of the Sacred Heart, Owatonna, MN

Pottemmel, Rev. Joseph, *M.S.F.S.* '76 (GAL) St. Thomas Aquinas, Sugar Land, TX

Pottemmel, Rev. Joseph, *M.S.F.S.* '76 (ATL) [MIS] Fransalian House, Loganville, GA

Potter, Rev. Adam C., '16 (PIT) Curia: Consultative Bodies Mary, Mother of God, White Oak, PA

Potter, Rev. Msgr. Joseph D., '54 (BGP) Retired.

Potthoff, Rev. Scott, '13 (PEO) Parish of the Nativity of Our Lord Roman Catholic Congregation, Spring Valley, IL

Potts, Rev. Richard M., *C.Ss.R.* '91 (STL) [MON] St. Clement Health Care Center, Liguori, MO

Potts, Rev. Robert J., '64 (ALN) Retired. St. Elizabeth of Hungary, Whitehall, PA

Potts, Rev. Ronald A., '89 (WDC) Curia: Pastoral Services Blessed Sacrament, Shrine of the Most, Washington, DC; Sacred Heart, Bowie, MD

Potts, Rev. Thomas, *S.V.D.* '61 (BLX) [MIS] Province Development Office, Bay St. Louis, MS

Potvin, Rev. Leo F., '64 (ALB) Retired. Blessed Sacrament, Mohawk, NY; St. Francis de Sales, Herkimer, NY

Potvin, Rev. Raymond J., '80 (MAN) Retired. [CEM] Calvary Cemetery, Penacook, NH

Poulin, Rev. Arthur, *O.S.B.Cam.* '81 (OAK) [MON] Incarnation Monastery, Camaldolese Benedictines, Berkeley, CA

Pouliot, Rev. Eugene A., '70 (STP) Retired.

Poulose, Rev. Alexandar, '01 (BAK) Saint Thomas Catholic Church of Redmond, Inc., Redmond, OR

Poulose, Rev. Augustine Palimattam, (JKS) Chap, East Mississippi State Hosp

Poulose, Rev. Jeo, *M.C.B.S.* (MEM) Holy Rosary, Memphis, TN

Poulose, Rev. Sibi, '09 (BAK) St. Edward the Martyr, Sisters, OR

Poulsen, Rev. James N., '68 (SD) Retired.

Povero, Rev. Andrea, '18 (BO) Our Lady of Lourdes, Boston, MA; St. Mary of the Angels, Boston, MA; St. Thomas Aquinas, Boston, MA

Povis, Rev. Zachary D., '15 (STL) Cathedral Basilica of Saint Louis Catholic Church, St. Louis, MO

Powell, Rev. Daniel F.X., (HBG) Curia: Offices and Directors St. John Neumann, Lancaster, PA

Powell, Rev. Msgr. Eric S., '90 (PEO) Curia: Tribunal Epiphany, Normal, IL

Powell, Rev. Jacob Jacob, '17 (LUB) Curia: Offices and Directors Holy Cross, Post, TX

Powell, Rev. Joseph, *O.F.M.* (MAN) St. Thomas Aquinas, Derry, NH

Powell, Rev. Marc L., '03 (SEA) St. Benedict, Seattle, WA; St. Catherine of Siena, Seattle, WA

Powell, Rev. Mario M., *S.J.* '14 (BRK) Brooklyn Jesuit Prep, Brooklyn, NY; [MON] Carroll Street Jesuit Community, Brooklyn, NY

Powell, Rev. Matthew D., *O.P.* '75 (PRO) [MON] St. Thomas Aquinas Priory at Providence College, Providence, RI

Powell, Rev. Michael, *O.M.I.* '02 (STP) (>WDC) [MON] Oblate Community, Washington, DC

Powell, Rev. Michael, '89 (JOL) St. Edmund, Watseka, IL; St. Mary, Beaverville, IL

Powell, Rev. Philip Neri, *OP* '05 (DAL) [MON] Dominican Priory of St. Albert the Great and Novitiate, Irving, TX

Powell, Rev. Ray, '15 (KNX) Curia: Leadership St. Thomas the Apostle, Lenoir City, TN; [MIS] Diocesan Council of Catholic Women, Knoxville, TN

Powell, Rev. Robert J., '76 (FR) Retired.

Powell, Rev. Msgr. Robert J., '74 (PH) St. Cyril of Jerusalem, Jamison, PA

Power, Rev. Gerard, *O.Carm.* '99 (JOL) [MON] Carmelite Provincial Office, Darien, IL

Power, Rev. James P., '16 (E) Chap, State Corr Inst-Forest Cty, Marienville St. Mary, Leeper, PA

Powers, Rev. Msgr. Bernard, '52 (OWN) Retired. Curia: Organizations (affiliated, inter-Diocesan, miscellaneous/ other)

Powers, Rev. Bruce J., '73 (RVC) St. Anthony of Padua, East Northport, NY

Powers, Rev. David B., *Sch.P.* (NY) St. Helena, Bronx, NY

Powers, Rev. Glenn E., '87 (MIL) On Special Assignment. Dir, Form Svcs, St Francis de Sales Seminary, St Francis Blessed Sacrament Congregation, Milwaukee, WI; [SEM] Saint Francis de Sales Seminary, St. Francis, WI

Powers, Rev. J. Daniel, *S.J.* '68 (SJ) [MON] Sacred Heart Jesuit Center, Los Gatos, CA

Powers, Rev. John, '15 (STP) Bethlehem Academy, Faribault, MN; Holy Trinity, Waterville, MN; St. Andrew, Elysian, MN

Powers, Rev. John, *C.P.* '77 (NY) [MON] The Congregation of the Passion - St. Paul of the Cross Province, Jamaica, NY

Powers, Rev. John, *C.P.* '77 (BRK) [MON] Immaculate Conception Monastery, Jamaica, NY

Powers, Rev. Joseph, '79 (KC) St. Mark, Independence, MO

Powers, Rev. Luke, '21 (MAD) St. Joseph, Baraboo, WI

Powers, Rev. Richard, '59 (OWN) Retired.

Powers, Rev. Robert M., '92 (BRK) St. Patrick, Long Island City, NY

Powers, Rev. Thomas F., '66 (BO) Retired.

Powers, Rev. Msgr. Thomas W., '97 (BGP) On Duty Outside Diocese. Rector - Pontifical North American College, Rome, Italy

Powhida, Rev. Robert, '78 (ALB) Retired.

Powroznik, Rev. Tomasz, '22 (BLX) Sacred Heart, Hattiesburg, MS

Pozas Perez, Rev. Emiliano, *MSC* '95 (LA) San Miguel, Los Angeles, CA

Pozhathuparambil, Rev. John, *O.F.M.Conv.* '01 (L) Holy Family, Louisville, KY

Pozza, Rev. Aldo, *M.C.C.J.* '66 (LA) [MIS] Comboni Mission Center, Covina, CA

Prabell, Rev. Paul, '72 (LEX) Curia: Leadership

Prachar, Rev. Andrew M., '90 (NEW) Curia: Advisory Boards, Commissions, Committees, and Councils Church of the Little Flower, Berkeley Heights, NJ

Pracz, Rev. Ted, (PEO) Retired.

Prada, Rev. John J., '09 (NEW) Chap, Hackensack Univ Med Ctr

Prada, Rev. Mario, '07 (CR) Retired. Curia: Offices and Directors

Prada, Rev. Pedro, '17 (NO) St. Anselm, Madisonville, LA

Prado, Rev. Amilcar B., '04 (NEW) Saint Teresa of Calcutta Parish, Montclair, NJ

Prado, Rev. George, '06 (RIC) St. Jerome, Newport News, VA

Prado, Rev. Luis, *I.V.E.* '17 (DAL) Chap, City Hosp at White Rock, Dallas St. Bernard of Clairvaux Catholic Parish, Dallas, TX

Prado, Rev. Victor M., '01 (MRY) Our Lady of the Assumption, Royal Oaks, CA

Prado-Reyes, Rev. Daniel, *O de M* (SB) Our Lady of Guadalupe Shrine, Riverside, CA

Pragasam, Rev. John Peter, '05 (STO) St. Anthony Church of Manteca (Pastor of), Manteca, CA

Prager, Rev. John Patrick, *C.M.* '82 (PH) [MON] Congregation of the Mission, Philadelphia, PA

Pramod, Rev. Philip, *SMM* (RVC) [MON] Montfort Missionaries, Bay Shore, NY

Pranaitis, Rev. Mark S., *C.M.* '93 (STL) [MIS] VIMS, St. Louis, MO; [MON] Congregation of the Mission Vincentian Fathers Lazarist Residence, St. Louis, MO

Pranzo, Rev. Joseph, *C.S.* '71 (PRO) Saint Bartholomew's Church Corporation, Providence, RI

Prathipati, Rev. Dasu, *OFM Cap.* (NY) Immaculate Conception, Bronx, NY

Pratico, Rev. Msgr. Patrick J., '79 (SCR) Curia: (>SAM) Leadership; Leadership Visitation of the Blessed Virgin Mary, Dickson City, PA

Pratscher, Very Rev. Matthew, '08 (JOL) Curia: Leadership St. John Paul II Parish, Kankakee, IL

Pratt, Rev. Edward T., '08 (CIN) Ascension, Kettering, OH; St. Albert the Great, Kettering, OH; St. Charles Borromeo, Kettering, OH

Pratt, Rev. Jerry, (EVN) Curia: Leadership Resurrection, Evansville, IN

Pratt, Rev. Michael, (TLS) [EFT] Saint John Vianney Seminary Trust, Broken Arrow, OK

Pratt, Rev. Michael, (TLS) Curia: Leadership

Pratt, Rev. Michael, '11 (TLS) Curia: Offices and Directors

Pratt, Rev. Oscar J., '96 (BO) Holy Name, Boston, MA; St. Katharine Drexel, Boston, MA

Pravetz, Rev. Matthew A., *O.F.M.* '79 (NY) Parish of Holy Name of Jesus and St. Gregory the Great, New York, NY

Prazak, Rev. Artur, '19 (PAT) St. Patrick's, Chatham, NJ

Prebendowski, Rev. Leslaw, (JOL) St. Petronille, Glen Ellyn, IL

Prechtl, Rev. Ronald G., '80 (WH) Holy Redeemer, Spencer, WV; St. Elizabeth of Hungary, Elizabeth, WV

Preciado, Very Rev. Fernando, '10 (FWT) Curia: Leadership St. Frances Cabrini, Granbury, TX; St. Rose of Lima, Glen Rose, TX

Preciado, Rev. Rudolph, '69 (ORG) Retired.

Preciado, Rev. Rudolph J., '69 (ORG) Retired. Christ Our Savior Catholic Parish, Santa Ana, CA

Precourt, Rev. Peter, *A.A.* (ELP) St. Francis Xavier, El Paso, TX (>BO) [MON] Augustinians of the Assumption, Inc., Boston, MA

Predelus, Rev. Dessier, (NY) St. Catherine of Genoa, New York, NY

Predmone, Rev. John A., *S.J.* '05 (BO) Boston College High School, Boston, MA

Pregana, Rev. Craig A., '89 (FR) Curia: Offices and Directors St. John the Evangelist, Attleboro, MA

Prehn, Rev. James S., *S.J.* '99 (CHI) [COL] Jesuit Community at Loyola University Chicago, Chicago, IL; [MIS] President's Office, Chicago, IL

Prendergast, Rev. Edmond, '73 (MIA) St. Bonaventure, Davie, FL

Prendergast, Rev. Noel, '58 (JKS) Retired.

Prendergast, Rev. Richard J., '79 (CHI) St. Gertrude, Chicago, IL

Prendiville, Rev. Kerry, '84 (RC) Curia: Leadership St. John the Evangelist, New Underwood, SD; St. Therese the Little Flower, Rapid City, SD

Prendiville, Rev. Thomas, *S.D.B.* '56 (SFR) [MON] Salesian Provincial Residence, San Francisco, CA

Prengaman, Rev. Leo P., *S.J.* '93 (LA) [MON] Colombiere House (Jesuit Fathers), Los Angeles, CA

Prensa, Rev. Pedro Velez, '04 (PHX) Blessed Sacrament Roman Catholic Parish, Tolleson, AZ

Prentice, Rev. Ted, '04 (P) Church of St. Joseph the Worker, Portland, OR

Presenti, Rev. Richard, *S.D.B.* '68 (SFR) [MON] Salesian Provincial Residence, San Francisco, CA
Preskenis, Rev. James T., *C.S.C.* '75 (ORL) [MON] Congregation of Holy Cross, United States Province, Cocoa Beach, FL
Presmanes, Rev. Jorge L., *O.P.* '91 (MIA) [COL] Barry University, Miami, FL; [MON] Dominican Fathers of Miami, Inc., Miami, FL
Presta, Rev. James, '86 (CHI) St. Emily, Mt. Prospect, IL
Preston, Rev. Michael A., (WIL) Curia: Administration St. John the Beloved, Wilmington, DE
Presutti, Rev. Robert, *L.C.* '98 (WDC) [MON] Legionaries of Christ, Potomac, MD
Presutti, Rev. Zachariah, *S.J.* '21 (NY) [MIS] Thrive For Life Prison Project, New York, NY; [MON] Xavier Jesuit Community, New York, NY
Pretto-Ferro, Rev. Franklin D., '72 (SFE) Curia: Offices and Directors Nuestra Senora de Guadalupe del Valle de Pojoaque, Santa Fe, NM
Preuss, Rev. David, *O.F.M.Cap.* '79 (DET) [MON] St. Bonaventure Monastery, Detroit, MI
Previte, Rev. Joseph, '07 (CLV) Holy Rosary, Cleveland, OH
Prevosto, Rev. Paul, '96 (NEW) Holy Trinity, Hackensack, NJ
Pribek, Rev. James M., *S.J.* '99 (MIL) [MON] Jesuit Community at Marquette University (Marquette Jesuit Associates, Inc.), Milwaukee, WI
Pribonic, Rev. Phillip, '67 (PIT) Retired.
Pribula, Rev. Duane, '70 (CR) Retired.
Pribyl, Rev. Ross T., *S.J.* '99 (MIL) [MON] Jesuit Community at Marquette University (Marquette Jesuit Associates, Inc.), Milwaukee, WI
Pricco, Rev. Msgr. Richard A., '62 (PEO) Retired.
Price, Rev. Bede, (NSH) Assumption, Nashville, TN
Price, Rev. Daniel, '16 (TR) On Duty Outside Diocese. Texas
Price, Rev. Daniel, '16 (WH) Annunciation of Our Lord, Fort Ashby, WV; St. Anthony, Ridgeley, WV
Price, Rev. David Ramsey, '10 (COS) Curia: Tribunal St. Mary's Cathedral, Colorado Springs, CO
Price, Rev. James, *C.P.* (BRK) [MIS] St. Paul's Benevolent, Educational and Missionary Institute, Inc. (Congregation of the Passion - St. Paul of the Cross Province), Jamaica, NY; [MON] Immaculate Conception Monastery, Jamaica, NY
Price, Rev. James, *C.P.* '94 (NY) [MIS] New Jersey Friends of Mandeville Inc., Rye Brook, NY; [MON] The Congregation of the Passion - St. Paul of the Cross Province, Jamaica, NY
Price, Rev. John R., '66 (CHI) Retired.
Price, Very Rev. Rothell, '88 (SHP) Curia: Canonical Services; Leadership; Offices and Directors St. Elizabeth Ann Seton, Shreveport, LA
Prichard, Rev. Adam, '15 (SFD) On Special Assignment. [HOS] St. Anthony's Memorial Hospital, Effingham, IL
Priebe, Rev. Msgr. Norman F., '67 (LA) Retired. St. Dorothy, Glendora, CA
Prieto, Rev. Frank, '64 (SFE) Retired.
Prieto, Rev. Harry, '17 (BGP) St. Mary's Church Corporation Bethel Connecticut, Bethel, CT
Prietto, Rev. Mario J., *S.J.* '73 (SJ) Curia: Leadership Bellarmine College Preparatory, San Jose, CA
Prill, Rev. Mark P., '08 (DET) St. Joseph Parish Erie, Erie, MI
Primavera, Rev. Mauro, '09 (NEW) Curia: Offices and Directors Holy Family, Nutley, NJ; St. John the Apostle, Linden, NJ
Primich, Rev. John, '95 (MET) Chap, Hunterdon Med Ctr [CON] The Carmel of Mary Immaculate and St. Mary Magdalen, Flemington, NJ
Prince, Rev. Joseph A., '71 (BGP) Retired. The Saint Elizabeth Seton Roman Catholic Church Corporation, Ridgefield, CT
Prince, Rev. Michael J., '98 (DET) On Leave.
Prince, Very Rev. Sean M., '12 (RIC) Curia: Advisory Boards, Commissions, Committees, and Councils; Deaneries St. Pius X, Norfolk, VA
Prindiville, Rev. Gerard T., (NEW) Retired.
Prindle, Rev. Richard, '78 (LA) American Martyrs, Manhattan Beach, CA
Pringle, Rev. John R., '72 (MET) Retired. [MON] Maria Regina Residence, Somerset, NJ
Pringle, Rev. Tom, '20 (ORL) Holy Family, Orlando, FL
Prior, Rev. Msgr. Joseph G., '90 (PH) Curia: Advisory Boards, Commissions, Committees, and Councils; Deaneries Our Lady of Grace, Penndel, PA
Prior, Rev. Richard P., '01 (SY) Our Lady of Sorrows, Vestal, NY; Sacred Heart, Cicero, NY
Priscaro, Rev. Jerry S., '93 (E) Chap, Soldiers and Sailors Home Curia: Miscellaneous / Other Offices Our Mother of Sorrows, Erie, PA
Prisk, Rev. Stephen, '15 (PAT) Curia: Leadership Holy Spirit, Pequannock, NJ
Prist, Rev. Msgr. Wayne F., '67 (CHI) Retired. Queen of All Saints Basilica, Chicago, IL
Prive, Rev. Francis R., '69 (BUR) Retired. [CAM] Johnson State College (Johnson), ,
Privett, Rev. John, *S.J.* '72 (SJ) [MON] Sacred Heart Jesuit Center, Los Gatos, CA
Proanos, Rev. Miguel E., (WIN) St. Mary's, Worthington, MN
Probst, Rev. R. Dean, '81 (SFD) St. Mary, Ste. Marie, IL; St. Thomas the Apostle, Newton, IL
Procaccini, Rev. David C., '93 (PRO) Curia: Advisory Boards, Commissions, Committees, and Councils St. Francis de Sales Church Corporation, North Kingstown, North Kingstown, RI
Prochaska, Rev. John, '93 (OAK) On Duty Outside Diocese. Curia: Leadership St. Ambrose, Berkeley, CA; St. Joseph the Worker, Berkeley, CA
Procyk, Rev. Marijan, '80 (STF) Curia: Offices and Directors St. Nicholas, Buffalo, NY
Prodanets, Rev. Mykhaylo, '01 (PSC) St. John's, Wilkes-Barre, PA; St. Mary's, Kingston, PA
Prodehl, Rev. Richard B., '66 (JOL) Retired.
Proehl, Rev. Douglas, '74 (CLV) Retired.
Proffitt, Rev. James D., '91 (BAL) Curia: Clergy and Religious Services
Promesso, Rev. William J., '89 (DET) Curia: Administration; Consultative Bodies Christ the Redeemer Parish Lake Orion, Lake Orion, MI
Promis, Rev. Christopher, *CSSp* '72 (PIT) Retired. [RTR] The Spiritan Center, Bethel Park, PA
Pronesti, Rev. Salvatore J., '67 (PH) Retired.
Propst, Rev. Sergius, *O.P.* '73 (OAK) [MON] Order of Preachers (Province of the Most Holy Name of Jesus - Western Dominican Province), Oakland, CA
Prosper, Friar Cadelin, *O.F.M.Cap.* '15 (ARE) San Miguel Arcangel, Utuado, PR
Prost, Rev. Charles E., *C.M.* '78 (STL) St. Catherine Laboure Catholic Church, St. Louis, MO; [MON] Congregation of the Mission Vincentian Fathers Lazarist Residence, St. Louis, MO
Protano, Rev. Joseph, '63 (PRO) Saint Andrew's Church Corporation, Block Island, Block Island, RI
Proulx, Very Rev. Arthur, '70 (SP) Curia: Leadership
Proulx, Very Rev. Arthur J., '80 (SP) Curia: Pastoral Services Cathedral of St. Jude the Apostle, St. Petersburg, FL
Proulx, Rev. Bertrand L., '22 (BO) St. Mary, Foxborough, MA
Prout, Rev. Thomas S., *S.J.* '92 (NY) [MON] Murray-Weigel Hall (A Jesuit Community at Murray-Weigel Hall and Kohlmann Hall), Bronx, NY
Provenza, Rev. Msgr. Earl V., '64 (SHP) Retired. Curia: Leadership
Provinsal, Rev. Thomas G., *S.J.* '75 (FBK) Our Lady of Perpetual Help, Nightmute, AK; St. Joseph Catholic Church Tununak, Tununak, AK; St. Peter the Fisherman, Toksook Bay, AK; [MIS] Brother Joe Prince Jesuit Community, Bethel, AK
Provost, Rev. John T., '73 (ALB) Retired. Curia: Offices and Directors
Proxell, Rev. Leo J., '77 (HEL) Curia: Leadership Holy Rosary Parish: Series 109, LLC, Bozeman, MT
Pruess, Rev. Ryan J., '12 (MIL) Holy Family Congregation, Fond du Lac, WI; [CEM] St. Charles Cemetery, Taycheedah, WI
Pruett, Rev. Bill H., '79 (OKL) Curia: Consultative Bodies; Organizations (affiliated, inter-Diocesan, miscellaneous/other); Tribunal St. James the Greater, Oklahoma City, OK
Prus, Rev. Edward J., '61 (DET) Retired.
Prus, Rev. Msgr. Eugene, '64 (MET) Retired. Curia: Consultative Bodies
Prusaitis, Rev. John P., '78 (BO) Retired.
Prusakowski, Rev. Gerald, *O.F.M.* (GB) Retired. [CON] Holy Family Convent of Franciscan Sisters of Christian Charity, Manitowoc, WI
Prusakowski, Rev. Gerald A., *O.F.M.* '65 (GB) Retired. [MON] Assumption of B.V.M. Friary, Pulaski, WI
Pruss, Rev. Rodney Lee A., (PHX) St. Thomas Aquinas Roman Catholic Parish, Avondale, AZ
Pruss, Rev. Rodney Lee A., '69 (GI) Retired.
Pruszynski, Rev. Konstanty J., '83 (PH) St. John Cantius, Philadelphia, PA
Pruys, Rev. George L., '75 (STN) SS. Peter and Paul, Wilton, ND
Pryor, Rev. Richard P., (SY) Curia: Leadership
Przepiora, Rev. Mieczyslaw, '90 (AMA) Curia: Evangelization Immaculate Conception, Vega, TX; [CON] Disciples of the Lord Jesus Christ, Prayer Town, TX
Przybilla, Rev. Troy D., '05 (STP) St. Charles Borromeo, St. Anthony, MN; [EFT] St. Charles Borromeo Endowment Fund Trust, St. Anthony, MN
Przybocki, Rev. Msgr. Bernard A., '58 (ALT) Retired.
Przybyl, Rev. Tomasz, *SVD* '10 (BGP) St. Rose's Church Newtown, Newtown, CT
Przybyla, Rev. Philip J., '70 (PIT) Retired. [MON] St. John Vianney Manor, Pittsburgh, PA
Przybylski, Rev. Donald L., '74 (LC) Retired.
Przybysz, Rev. Mark C., '90 (GR) Curia: Clergy and Religious Services St. Anthony of Padua, Grand Rapids, MI
Przygocki, Rev. Edward, *M.S.A.* '81 (NOR) [MON] Society of the Missionaries of the Holy Apostles, Cromwell, CT
Przystasz, Rev. Wojciech, '98 (LAR) Curia: Leadership Blessed Sacrament, Laredo, TX
Przywara, Rev. Artur, '10 (CHR) St. Ann, Kingstree, SC; St. Patrick Mission, Johnsonville, SC; St. Philip the Apostle, Lake City, SC
Przywara, Rev. Gerald A., '67 (RIC) Retired.
Ptak, Rev. Slawomir, '03 (BEL) St. John the Baptist, McLeansboro, IL
Ptak, Rev. Canon Walter J., '87 (DET) Our Lady of Sorrows Parish Farmington, Farmington, MI
Ptaszynski, Rev. Thomas E., '73 (HRT) Retired.
Puaauli, Rev. Kelemete L., '01 (SPP) Sacred Heart of Jesus Parish, Pago Pago, AS
Pua'auli, Rev. Kelemete L., '01 (SPP) Curia: Offices and Directors Church of the Holy Cross, Pago Pago, AS; Sts. Peter & Paul, Pago Pago, AS
Pucciarelli, Rev. George, '74 (WH) Retired.
Pucciarelli, Rev. George W., '74 (BO) On Special Assignment.
Puccinelli, Rev. Alfred, *S.M.* '66 (SFR) Retired. [MON] Marist Center of the West, San Francisco, CA
Puccini, Rev. Paolo, *C.S.P.* (AUS) St. Austin, Austin, TX
Puchakattil Baby, Rev. Joby, '07 (SYM) Sacred Heart Syro-Malabar Knanaya Catholic Church, Tampa, Brandon, FL
Puchner, Rev. Augustine R., *O.Praem.* '97 (ORG) [MON] Norbertine Fathers of Orange, Inc., Silverado, CA
Pucke, Rev. Michael U., '73 (CIN) Retired.
Pudhota, Rev. Paul, (SPC) Holy Trinity, Aurora, MO; SS. Peter and Paul, Pulaskifield, MO
Pudichery, Rev. Joseph P., '62 (PIT) Retired.
Pudota, Rev. Bala Raju, '05 (OKL) St. Rose of Lima, Perry, OK
Pudota, Rev. Joseph Sundar Raju, '82 (OKL) St. Paul, Apostle, Del City, OK
Pudota, Rev. Rayanna, '01 (FRS) St. Joseph, Firebaugh, CA
Pudota, Rev. Shouraiah, '79 (SFR) St. James, San Francisco, CA
Puello, Rev. Alejandro, '12 (LR) Curia: Offices and Directors St. Anne, North Little Rock, AR
Puentas, Rev. Elias, *S.J.* (SEA) Sacred Heart, Tacoma, WA
Puente, Rev. Benjamin, '07 (STO) St. Linus Church (Pastor of), Stockton, CA
Puentes, Rev. Elias, *S.J.* (SEA) St. Leo the Great, Tacoma, WA
Puentes Mejia, Rev. Abraham, '94 (AUS) San Francisco Javier, Austin, TX; San Juan Diego - Stony Point, Austin, TX
Puerta, Rev. Jorge I., '89 (MIA) Retired.
Puetz, Rev. Richard W., '45 (LFT) Retired.
Puga, Rev. Gerardo, (DEN) Holy Family in Meeker, Meeker, CO; St. Ignatius of Antioch in Rangely, Rangely, CO; St. Michael Catholic Parish in Craig, Craig, CO
Pugliese, Rev. Steven, *S.J.* (PAT) [RTR] Loyola Jesuit Center, Morristown, NJ
Puglisi, Rev. James F., *S.A.* '73 (NY) [MON] Franciscan Friars of the Atonement, Minister General Office, Garrison, NY
Puhak, Rev. Msgr. Nicholas I., '57 (PSC) Retired.
Puhlman, Rev. Robert W., '84 (LAV) St. Anthony of Padua, Las Vegas, NV
Puigbo, Rev. Juan, (ARL) St. Leo the Great, Fairfax, VA
Pujals, Rev. Msgr. Antoni, '85 (POD) Curia: Leadership
Pujante, Rev. Jesus Monreal, (ARE) Curia: Leadership
Pujante, Rev. P. Jesus Monreal, *O.Carm.* '69 (ARE) Curia: Leadership
Pujdak, Rev. Steve, *S.C.J.* '69 (SP) Retired. [MON] Priests of the Sacred Heart, Pinellas Park, FL
Pujol, Rev. Christopher James, '01 (GBG) Blessed Sacrament Cathedral, Greensburg, PA
Pukayev, Rev. Vitaliy, '15 (PSC) St. George the Great Martyr, Linden, NJ
Pukhayev, Rev. Vitaliy, (PSC) Curia: Advisory Boards,

Commissions, Committees, and Councils St. Elias, Carteret, NJ
Puleo, Rev. Augustus C., '05 (PH) [SEM] Theological Seminary of St. Charles Borromeo, Wynnewood, PA
Puleo, Rev. Derek J., '10 (PRO) On Leave.
Puleo, Rev. Msgr. Edward C., '88 (MET) Curia: Clergy and Religious Services; Consultative Bodies St. Elizabeth - St. Brigid, Peapack, NJ
Pulgarin, Rev. Rene Mauricio, '04 (TR) Parish of Our Lady of Fatima, Keyport, N.J., Keyport, NJ
Pulickal, Rev. Sony G., '83 (OG) Curia: Consultative Bodies Church of St. James Major, Lake Pleasant, Hamilton County, Lake Pleasant, NY; St. Ann's, Wells, NY
Pulickal, Rev. Thomas, (PMB) [SEM] St. Vincent de Paul Regional Seminary, Boynton Beach, FL
Pulido, Very Rev. Felipe, '02 (YAK) Curia: Leadership; Offices and Directors St Joseph Parish, Kennewick, WA
Pulido, Rev. Luis, '96 (NY) St. Gregory, New York, NY
Pulido, Rev. V. Felipe, '14 (YAK) [CCH] St. Joseph Parish Conference, Kennewick, WA
Pulikal, Rev. Antony, '01 (PMB) Holy Name of Jesus, West Palm Beach, FL
Pulikal, Rev. Thomas, *O.Praem.* '03 (SFE) [MON] Santa Maria de la Vid Abbey, Albuquerque, NM
Pulimoottil, Rev. Gracious Joseph, *M.C.B.S.* '09 (MAR) Our Lady of Peace, Ahmeek, MI; Sacred Heart, Calumet, MI; St. Paul the Apostle, Calumet, MI
Puling, Rev. Tarsisius, *svd* '08 (PT) St. Francis of Assisi, Blountstown, FL
Puliyan, Rev. Tomy J., *MSFS* '94 (ATL) St. Marguerite d'Youville Catholic Church, Lawrenceville, Inc., Lawrenceville, GA; [MON] The Missionaries of St. Francis de Sales - MSFS USA Vice Province, Loganville, GA
Puljic-Vlahic, Rev. Marko, *OFM* '81 (CHI) [MON] Croatian Franciscan Custody of the Holy Family, Chicago, IL
Pullambrayil, Very Rev. George, '93 (FWT) Curia: Leadership
Pullikattil, Rev. Joseph, '00 (SYM) St. Thomas Syro-Malabar Catholic Church, West Hartford, CT, Inc. of St. Thomas Syro-Malabar Catholic Diocese of Chicago, West Hartford, CT
Pullikattil, Rev. Joseph, '00 (HRT) Annunciation Parish Corporation, Newington, CT
Pullis, Rev. Stephen, '11 (DET)
Pullukattu, Rev. Antony Xavier, '98 (SYM) St. Thomas Syro-Malabar Catholic Church Inc. (East Millstone), Somerset, NJ
Pulskamp, Rev. Msgr. James E., '67 (SR) Pastor of Star of the Valley Catholic Church of Santa Rosa, A Corporation Sole, Santa Rosa, CA
Punakkattu, Rev. Sojan, '00 (SP) Curia: Pastoral Services St. Elizabeth Ann Seton, Citrus Springs, FL
Punch, Rev. Nicholas W., *O.P.* '66 (SUP) [MIS] Thomas More Center for Preaching and Prayer, Inc., Webster, WI
Punderson, Rev. Msgr. Joseph R., '76 (TR) Retired. [MON] Villa Vianney, Trenton, NJ
Pung, Rev. Karl L., '97 (LAN) Curia: Leadership; Offices and Directors St. Mary Cathedral Lansing, Lansing, MI
Punganoor, Rev. Amal Raju, (LR) St. Mary of the Mount, Horseshoe Bend, AR; St. Michael, Cherokee Village, AR
Punnackal, Rev. Antony, *C.M.I.* '92 (KNX) On Administrative Leave.
Punnakunnel, Rev. John, '79 (BGP) Retired. On Duty Outside Diocese. In India
Punnakuziyil, Rev. Sunny Joseph, *M.S.F.S.* '94 (ATL) St. John Neumann Catholic Church, Lilburn, Inc., Lilburn, GA; [MON] The Missionaries of St. Francis de Sales - MSFS USA Vice Province, Loganville, GA
Punnolil, Rev. Reji Joseph, *CMI* (BIR) [CAM] Talladega College Catholic Campus Ministry, Talladega, AL
Punnoose, Rev. Siby, '98 (SC) St. Andrew's, Sibley, IA; St. Patrick's, Sheldon, IA
Puntal, Rev. Peter, '82 (ORL) St. Vincent de Paul, Wildwood, FL
Puntel, Rev. Adam D., '11 (CIN) Holy Cross-Immaculata, Cincinnati, OH; Our Lord, Christ the King, Cincinnati, OH; St. Rose of Lima, Cincinnati, OH
Punti, Rev. George, '55 (RVC) Retired.
Puntino, Rev. John, (OAK) Salesian College Preparatory (Salesians of St. John Bosco), Richmond, CA
Punzalan, Rev. Manolo, '92 (NEW) Immaculate Conception, Mahwah, NJ
Puodziunas, Rev. John, *O.F.M.* '87 (MIL) [MON] Francis and Clare Friary, Franklin, WI
Puopolo, Rev. Rocco N., *S.X.* '77 (BO) [MIS] Our Lady of Fatima Shrine, Holliston, MA; [MON] Xaverian Missionaries, Holliston, MA
Purcaro, Rev. Arthur P., *O.S.A.* '75 (PH) [COL] Villanova University, Villanova, PA
Purcell, Rev. Msgr. Lawrence M., '65 (SD) Retired.
Purpura, Rev. Peter J., '07 (BRK) Curia: Leadership Our Lady of Hope, Middle Village, NY
Purta, Rev. Jerome J., *O.S.B.* '61 (GBG) [MON] Saint Vincent Archabbey, Latrobe, PA
Pusateri, Rev. Joseph M., *S.M.* '66 (WDC) Retired. [MON] Marist Center (The Marist Finance Center of the Atlanta Province of the Society of Mary, Marist Fathers and Brothers), Washington, DC
Pushpanathan, Rev. Zacharias, '81 (HRT) Christ the King Parish Corporation, Wethersfield, CT
Pushparaj, Rev. Augustine, *S.J.* '07 (CHI) [COL] Jesuit Community at Loyola University Chicago, Chicago, IL
Pusic, Rev. Dragan, (BRK) St. Gabriel, East Elmhurst, NY
Putano, Rev. Msgr. John P., '70 (SY) Holy Trinity, Binghamton, NY; Immaculate Conception, Greene, NY; SS. Cyril and Method, Binghamton, NY; St. Joseph, Oxford, NY; St. Patrick, Binghamton, NY; St. Thomas Aquinas, Binghamton, NY; [MIS] The Robert L. McDevitt, K.S.G., K.C.H.S. and Catherine H. McDevitt, L.C.H.S. Fund of St. Patrick's Catholic Church of Binghamton, N.Y., Binghamton, NY; [MIS] The Robert H. McDevitt, K.S.G., K.C.H.S. and Catherine H. McDevitt, L.C.H.S. Fund of St. Thomas Aquinas Church, Binghamton, NY
Putchakayala, Rev. Sundar Bala, *MSFS* (SR) Pastor of St. Eugene Cathedral of Santa Rosa, A Corporation Sole, Santa Rosa, CA
Putera, Rev. Vasyl, '96 (PHU) Assumption B.V.M., Bayonne, NJ; SS. Peter and Paul, Jersey City, NJ
Puthanpura, Rev. Augusty, (MOB) St. Lawrence Parish, Fairhope, Fairhope, AL
Puthen, Rev. Pradeep Joseph, (CC) Sacred Heart, Falfurrias, TX
Puthenkulathil, Rev. Joseph, '76 (SFS) Retired.
Puthenpeedika, Rev. George, '79 (LAN) St. Peter Parish Eaton Rapids, Eaton Rapids, MI
Puthenpurackal, Rev. Jegin, *H.G.N.* '04 (OWN) St. Charles Borromeo, Livemore, KY; St. Sebastian, Calhoun, KY
Puthoff, Rev. Elijah R., '21 (CIN) St. Bernard, Springfield, OH; St. Charles Borromeo, South Charleston, OH; St. Joseph, Springfield, OH; St. Raphael, Springfield, OH; St. Teresa of the Child Jesus, Springfield, OH
Puthota, Rev. Charles, '89 (SFR) Curia: Advisory Boards, Commissions, Committees, and Councils St. Elizabeth, San Francisco, CA
Puthumayil, Rev. Chacko, '71 (GAL) Retired. Curia: Leadership St. Frances Cabrini, Houston, TX
Puthuparambil, Rev. Jacob P., *O.S.B.* '77 (LUB) Our Lady of Guadalupe, Slaton, TX; St. Joseph's, Slaton, TX
Puthusseril, Msgr. George, '79 (MIA) Visitation, Miami, FL
Puthussery, Rev. Anil Thomas, '07 (BIR) Holy Spirit, Winfield, AL
Puthussery, Rev. Joby Abraham, '99 (IND) Sacred Heart Church, Clinton, Inc., Clinton, IN; St. Joseph Catholic Church, Rockville, Inc., Rockville, IN
Puthussery, Rev. Jojo, *M.F.* '02 (SR) Pastor of St. Leo the Great Catholic Church of Boyes Hot Springs, A Corporation Sole, Sonoma, CA (>OAK) [MON] Missionaries of Faith-India Inc., Fremont, CA
Puthussery, Rev. Justin, (PHX) Chap, Maricopa Med Ctr, Phoenix
Puthussery, Rev. Justin Ouseph, '96 (SYM) St. Thomas Syro-Malabar Catholic Church, Detroit, Southfield, MI
Puthussery, Rev. Shaju, *O.F.M. Conv* (L) Incarnation, Louisville, KY
Puthussery, Friar Shaju, *O.F.M.Conv.* '01 (L) St. Paul, Louisville, KY
Putka, Rev. John, *S.M.* '69 (SJ) [MON] The Marianist Center, Cupertino, CA
Putnam, Very Rev. John T., '92 (CHL) Curia: Consultative Bodies; Leadership St. Mark, Huntersville, NC
Putnam, Rev. Richard J., *S.D.B.* '89 (NY) [RTR] Don Bosco Retreat Center and Marian Shrine, Stony Point, NY; [RTR] Marian Shrine, Stony Point, NY
Puttananickal, Rev. Jimmy Mathew, *C.F.I.C.* '07 (STP) Blessed Sacrament, St. Paul, MN; [MON] Congregation of the Sons of the Immaculate Conception, Bloomington, MN
Putthoff, Rev. Jeffrey P., *S.J.* '98 (STL) [MON] Sacred Heart Jesuit Community, St. Louis, MO
Putti, Rev. Jayaraj, (NY) Curia: Leadership
Putz, Rev. Kenneth G., '73 (PH) Retired.
Putzer, Rev. Msgr. John D., '10 (MAD) On Duty Outside Diocese. Diplomatic Service of the Holy See, Switzerland
Puyic, Rev. Iliya, *O.F.M.* (NY) SS. Cyril and Methodius - St. Raphael, New York, NY
Puzio, Rev. Thomas, '70 (DET) Retired.
Puznakoski, Rev. Gilbert Z., '75 (PIT) Chap, Kane Rgnl Ctr - Scott, Allegheny Cty; St Clair Mem…
Pyka, Rev. Lukasz, (CHI) St. Ferdinand, Chicago, IL
Pynadath, Rev. Sinoj E., *HGN* '12 (OWN) St. John the Evangelist, Sunfish, KY; St. Joseph, Leitchfield, KY; [MIS] Heralds of Good News of St. Paul, Inc., Owensboro, KY
Pyo, Rev. Edward J., '85 (PBR) Retired.
Pyrc, Rev. Matthew T., *S.J.* (SEA) St. Joseph, Seattle, WA
Pyrchla, Rev. Rafal, (SFD) St. Francis Solanus, Quincy, IL
Quach, Rev. Binh T., *C.S.Sp.* '91 (PIT) [MON] Congregation of the Holy Spirit Province of the United States, Bethel Park, PA
Quach, Rev. Binh T., *C.S.Sp.* '91 (GAL) [MON] US Foundation for the Congregation of the Holy Ghost and the Immaculate Heart of Mary, Inc., Houston, TX
Quail, Rev. Matthew, (STP) Sts. Joachim and Anne, Shakopee, MN
Quaine, Rev. Michael W., '85 (DET) St. Michael Parish Sterling Heights, Sterling Heights, MI
Quaini, Rev. Luiz, *S.A.C.* '69 (NEW) Our Lady of Grace, Fairview, NJ
Quainoo, Rev. Clement, '82 (VIC) Retired. Curia: Leadership
Qualizza, Rev. Franco, *S.X.* '71 (PAT) [MON] Xaverian Missionary Fathers, Wayne, NJ
Quan, Rev. Aristotle, (ORG) San Francisco Solano Catholic Church, Rancho Santa Margarita, CA
Quan, Rev. Sang Ky, '15 (AUS) Christ the King, Belton, TX
Quang, Rev. John, '70 (SAV) Retired.
Quang Do, Rev. Michael, *CRM* '93 (SPC) Cathedral of St. Agnes, Springfield, MO
Quang Le, Rev. Peter, '79 (LR) Sacred Heart of Mary, Barling, AR
Quanz, Rev. Paul E., '84 (GRY) Curia: Leadership Our Lady of Sorrows, Valparaiso, IN; Sacred Heart, Wanatah, IN; St. Mary, Otis, IN
Quarato, Rev. Robert A., '91 (NY) Saint Elizabeth Ann Seton, Shrub Oak, NY
Quartier, Rev. Msgr. Neal E., '76 (SY) On Special Assignment. Curia: Offices and Directors The Cathedral of the Immaculate Conception, Syracuse, NY
Que, Rev. Dinh Ngoc, *C.Ss.R.* '56 (LA) [MON] Vietnamese Redemptorist Mission, Baldwin Park, CA
Queally, Rev. Kevin, *T.O.R.* '77 (ALT) [MON] Saint Elizabeth Friary, Loretto, PA
Quebedeaux, Rev. Carl, *CMF* '82 (ELP) El Buen Pastor Mission, El Paso, TX
Queen, Rev. James T., '66 (SY) Retired.
Queimado, Rev. Jose Luis, *C.Ss.R.* '12 (PH) St. Martin of Tours, Philadelphia, PA
Quejadas, Rev. Mario S., '00 (JOL) St. Walter, Roselle, IL
Quenneville, Rev. Gregory K., (FR) St. Julie Billiart, North Dartmouth, MA
Quera, Rev. Jose Maria, '10 (DEN) St. Clare of Assisi Catholic Parish in Edwards, Edwards, CO; St. Patrick Catholic Parish in Minturn, Minturn, CO
Querijero, Rev. Andres, '97 (SR) Pastor of Our Lady of Perpetual Help Catholic Church of Calistoga, A Corporation Sole, Calistoga, CA
Querobin, Rev. Rafael, *SCJ* (GAL) Our Lady of Guadalupe, Houston, TX
Quesada, Rev. Manuel, (RVC) Retired.
Quesea, Rev. Roy, '16 (MET) Curia: Leadership; Offices and Directors; Tribunal Cathedral of St. Francis of Assisi, Metuchen, NJ
Quevedo Rodriguez, Rev. Hernan, '97 (ATL) St. Joseph Catholic Church, Marietta, Inc., Marietta, GA
Quezada, Rev. Francisco, '88 (COS) Curia: Offices and Directors St. Patrick, Colorado Springs, CO
Quezada, Rev. Joel, *M.Sp.S.* (SAT) St. Luke, San Antonio, TX
Quezada Covarrubias, Rev. Fernando, (SAT) Our Lady of Good Counsel, San Antonio, TX; St. Martin de Porres, San Antonio, TX
Quezada Covarrubias, Rev. Fernando, *MNM* (SAT) St. Gabriel, San Antonio, TX
Quezada-Avila, Rev. Alfredo, (BIR) Prince of Peace Catholic Parish, Birmingham, Birmingham, AL
Quiamjot, Rev. William, (HON) St. Michael the Archangel, Kailua-Kona, HI
Quic, Rev. Cristobal Coche, *O.S.B.* '92 (RCK) [MON] Marmion Abbey, Aurora, IL
Quiceno, Rev. Walter Andre, '12 (TR) St. Mary, Barnegat, NJ

Quigley, Rev. John, *O.F.M.* '72 (CIN) [MIS] Franciscans Network, Cincinnati, OH; [MON] Pleasant Street Friary, Cincinnati, OH
Quigley, Rev. William G., *C.I.C.M.* '74 (ARL) [MIS] Mount Tabor Society, Inc., Vienna, VA; [MON] Missionhurst, C.I.C.M.-Central House and Provincialate (American I.H.M. Province, Inc., Immaculate Heart Missions, Inc., Missionhurst, Inc.), Arlington, VA
Quijano, Rev. Antonio, '92 (RNO) St. Patrick, Fallon, NV
Quijano, Rev. Carlos, *S.J.* '98 (BRK) St. Paul the Apostle, Corona, NY
Quijano, Rev. Carlos, *O.P.* '02 (Y) St. Dominic, Youngstown, OH
Quijano, Rev. Jose Juan, '73 (MIA) Retired.
Quijano, Rev. Regino, '84 (FRS) St. Anthony of Padua, Fresno, CA
Quilcate, Rev. Jose P., (CHR) Holy Family, Hilton Head Island, SC; St. Francis By the Sea, Hilton Head Island, SC
Quill, Rev. James E., '53 (COV) Retired.
Quill, Rev. John A., '74 (NEW) Retired. [MON] The Rev. Msgr. James F. Kelley Residence for Retired Priests, Caldwell, NJ
Quill, Rev. Msgr. John A.; (NEW) Retired.
Quilligan, Rev. Michael, '71 (MIA) Retired.
Quimno, Rev. Matias M., '10 (E) Chap, DuBois Rgnl Hosp, Du Bois [NUR] Christ the King Manor, Inc., Du Bois, PA
Quindlen, Rev. Joseph J., '73 (PH) Retired. Nativity of Our Lord, Warminster, PA
Quindlen, Rev. Joseph J., (PH) Retired.
Quinkert, Rev. Denis, *O.S.B.* '76 (IND) [MON] St. Meinrad Archabbey, St. Meinrad, IN
Quinlan, Very Rev. Edward J., '78 (HBG) Curia: Offices and Directors Holy Name of Jesus, Harrisburg, PA; [EFT] The Neumann Scholarship Foundation, Harrisburg, PA
Quinlan, Rev. Jack, '97 (DET) On Leave.
Quinlan, Rev. James V., '76 (CHI) Retired.
Quinlan, Rev. Joseph M., '52 (TR) Retired.
Quinlan, Rev. Joseph M., (NEW) Curia: Organizations (affiliated, inter-Diocesan, miscellaneous/other)
Quinlan, Rev. William M., '99 (BGP) Curia: Tribunal St. John's R.C. Church Corporation, Darien, CT
Quinlivan, Rev. Thomas J., '72 (BUF) Retired.
Quinlivan, Rev. William J., '95 (BUF) Our Lady of Charity, Buffalo, NY; St. Martin of Tours, Buffalo, NY; St. Teresa, Buffalo, NY; St. Thomas Aquinas, Buffalo, NY
Quinn, Rev. Bernard, *C.M.* '72 (STL) [MON] Congregation of the Mission Vincentian Fathers Lazarist Residence, St. Louis, MO
Quinn, Rev. Brendan, '74 (NEW) Chap, Trinitas Rgnl Med Ctr, Elizabeth Immaculate Conception, Elizabeth, NJ; [HOS] Trinitas Regional Medical Center (Sisters of Charity of Saint Elizabeth and Elizabethtown Healthcare Foundation), Elizabeth, NJ
Quinn, Rev. Brian P., '10 (PAT) Curia: Leadership St. Matthew the Apostle, Randolph, NJ; [MIS] Nazareth Village, Chester, NJ
Quinn, Rev. Charles P., '66 (PRO) Retired.
Quinn, Rev. Daniel J., '12 (ALB) Curia: Leadership Blessed Sacrament, Albany, NY
Quinn, Rev. Edward J., *M.M.* '51 (NY) Retired.
Quinn, Rev. Gavin, *O.Carm.* '65 (JOL) [MON] St. Simon Stock Priory, Darien, IL
Quinn, Rev. J. Patrick, *T.O.R.* '84 (ORL) Our Lady Star of the Sea, New Smyrna Beach, FL
Quinn, Rev. James A., '67 (MIA) Retired. [HOS] Holy Cross Hospital, Inc., Fort Lauderdale, FL
Quinn, Rev. Jarlath, '96 (NY) Our Lady of the Rosary, New York, NY; Parish of Saint Peter and Our Lady of the Rosary, New York, NY
Quinn, Rev. Jarlath, '15 (TR) The Church of Our Lady of Perpetual Help-Saint Agnes, Atlantic Highlands, N.J., Atlantic Highlands, NJ
Quinn, Rev. Joe, *O.F.M.* '86 (BO) [MIS] St. Anthony Shrine, Boston, MA
Quinn, Rev. John L., '62 (NY) Retired.
Quinn, Rev. Msgr. John P., '68 (MAN) St. Elizabeth Seton, Bedford, NH
Quinn, Rev. Msgr. Joseph G., '85 (SCR) Chap, Keystone College, Clarks Summit Curia: Leadership Our Lady of the Snows, Clarks Summit, PA; Saint Paul of the Cross, Scranton, Scranton, PA
Quinn, Rev. Msgr. Joseph G., '85 (SAM) Curia: Leadership
Quinn, Rev. Kenneth, '71 (BO) Retired.
Quinn, Rev. Liam T., '83 (MIA) Retired.
Quinn, Rev. Michael F., '70 (JC) Retired. Curia: Tribunal
Quinn, Rev. Michael F., '09 (SFR) Chap, San Francisco Police Department Saint Brendan the Navigator Church, San Francisco, CA; St. Mary Star of the Sea, Sausalito, CA
Quinn, Rev. Michael P., *C.Ss.R.* '72 (STL) Retired. [MON] St. Clement Health Care Center, Liguori, MO
Quinn, Rev. Patrick T, *S.J.* '88 (DEN) St. Ignatius Loyola Catholic Parish in Denver, Denver, CO; [MON] Society of Jesus - St. Ignatius Loyola Jesuit Community, Denver, CO
Quinn, Rev. Peter N., '75 (PH) Retired.
Quinn, Rev. Richard, *C.Ss.R.* '62 (STL) Retired. [MON] St. Clement Health Care Center, Liguori, MO
Quinn, Rev. Richard, *C.Ss.R* '62 (KC) Retired.
Quinn, Rev. Richard J., *M.M.* '54 (NY) Retired.
Quinn, Rev. Thomas, '62 (SEA) Retired.
Quinn, Rev. Thomas Patrick, '05 (NEW) Curia: Advisory Boards, Commissions, Committees, and Councils St. Michael Parish, Jersey City, NJ
Quinn, Rev. Thomas P. THE, (NEW) St. Mary of the Assumption, Elizabeth, NJ
Quinn, Rev. Msgr. William, '62 (CAM) Retired.
Quinnan, Rev. Edward J., *S.J.* '87 (NY) (>CI) [MON] Jesuit Community of Palau, Manresa Jesuit House, Koror, PW
Quinnan, Rev. Edward J., *S.J.* '87 (CHK) (>AGN) [MON] Society of Jesus Micronesia, Tamuning, GU
Quinnan, Rev. Michael F., '86 (SCR) Curia: Leadership St. Luke, Stroudsburg, PA
Quinones, Rev. Cesar, (NEW) Curia: Offices and Directors
Quinones, Rev. Luis, '97 (ARL) All Saints, Manassas, VA
Quiñones Menjura, Rev. Eder Tufay, *S.T.* (SB) Sanctuary of Our Lady of Guadalupe, Mecca, CA
Quiñones Tirú, Rev. German, *O.F.M.Cap.* '11 (WDC) [SEM] St. Francis Friary-Capuchin College, Washington, DC
Quinonez, Rev. Alonso, '15 (LSC) On Duty Outside Diocese. Mexico Our Lady of Health Parish, Inc., Las Cruces, NM
Quint, Very Rev. Dennis J., '96 (DUB) Holy Family Catholic Schools, Dubuque, Iowa, Dubuque, IA; St. Patrick's Church, Dubuque, Iowa, Dubuque, IA; St. Raphael's Cathedral Church, Dubuque, Iowa, Dubuque, IA
Quintana, Rev. Jose Luis, '96 (GR) Curia: Offices and Directors St. Joseph the Worker, Wyoming, MI
Quintana Puente, Rev. Msgr. Carlos, (SJN) Nuestra Senora de la Providencia, Rio Piedras, PR
Quintela, Rev. Preston, '16 (GAL) Our Lady of Perpetual Help, Sweeny, TX
Quinter, Rev. Paul S., '82 (PH) Maternity B.V.M., Philadelphia, PA
Quintero, Rev. Carlos, '84 (ATL) Mision del Divino Nino Jesus, Duluth, GA
Quintero, Rev. Ever, '00 (LA) Curia: Pastoral Services Nativity, Los Angeles, CA; St. Columbkille, Los Angeles, CA
Quintero, Rev. Gilberto, '88 (SP) Our Lady of Guadalupe Mission, Wimauma, FL
Quintero, Rev. Gustavo, '80 (STO) St. Jude Church (Pastor of), Ceres, CA
Quintero, Rev. Haider, '11 (AMA) St. Laurence Church, Amarillo, TX
Quintero, Rev. Manuel, '81 (LAV) [SHR] Shrine of the Most Holy Redeemer, Las Vegas, NV
Quintero-Angueira, Rev. Jose Francisco, '89 (SJN) [HOS] Hospital del Maestro, Rio Piedras, PR
Quinteros, Rev. Ruben, '10 (LR) Immaculate Heart of Mary, North Little Rock, AR; St. Mary, North Little Rock, AR
Quinto, Rev. Jupeter, *R.C.J.* '99 (LA) St. Jane Frances de Chantal, North Hollywood, CA; [MON] Congregation of Rogationists, Inc., Van Nuys, CA
Quintos, Rev. Nico, '20 (PAT) St. Philip the Apostle, Clifton, NJ
Quiogue, Rev. Roy, *C.I.C.M.* '82 (SAT) Chap, Santa Rosa Hosp System, San Antonio Sacred Heart, San Antonio, TX
Quirk, Rev. Msgr. Kevin Michael, '93 (WH) Curia: Leadership Holy Rosary Mission, Sistersville, WV; Mater Dolorosa, Paden City, WV; St. Joseph, Proctor, WV; St. Vincent de Paul, New Martinsville, WV
Quirk, Rev. Richard J., '78 (STL) St. James the Greater Catholic Church, St. Louis, MO
Quirk, Rev. Thomas, (TUC) Saint Philip the Apostle Roman Catholic Church - Payson, Payson, AZ
Quiroga Ceballos, Rev. Edgar, '20 (YAK) Christ the King, Richland, WA
Quiroz, Very Rev. Francisco M., '14 (LAR) Curia: Leadership; Offices and Directors Immaculate Conception, Asherton, TX
Quiroz, Rev. Salvador, (OAK) St. Peter, Martyr of Verona, Pittsburg, CA
Quitalig, Rev. Angel N., '98 (SFR) On Special Assignment. St. Mark, Belmont, CA; [MIS] Catholic Charismatic Renewal (CCR), San Francisco, CA
Quito, Rev. Ian, '20 (SFR) Our Lady of Mount Carmel, Redwood City, CA
Quitugua, Rev. Msgr. David C, '84 (PH) Blessed Virgin Mary, Darby, PA
Quitugua, Rev. Msgr. David C., '84 (AGN) On Duty Outside Diocese.
Quitugua, Rev. Msgr. David I.A., '64 (AGN) Retired.
Qureshi, Rev. Aaron, (PHX) All Saints Roman Catholic Newman Center, Tempe, AZ
Qureshi, Rev. Aaron M., '14 (WDC) St. Catherine of Alexandria, Port Tobacco, MD
Quy Duy Pham, Rev. (Benedict M.), *CRM* '22 (SPC) [MON] Congregation of the Mother of the Redeemer, Carthage, MO
Quyen, Rev. Peter Pham Kim, *M.I.* '18 (MIL) [MON] St. Camillus Communities, Inc., Wauwatosa, WI
Quyet, Rev. Anthony, '83 (JKS) Retired.
Raab, Rev. Christian, *O.S.B.* '09 (IND) [MON] St. Meinrad Archabbey, St. Meinrad, IN (>EVN) St. Joseph, Jasper, IN
Raab, Rev. John, *CMF* '76 (LA) [MON] Dominguez Seminary Inc., Rancho Dominguez, CA
Raaser, Rev. Eric P., '85 (NY) St. Margaret of Antioch, Pearl River, NY
Raaz, Rev. Paul A., '70 (SAT) Retired. Sacred Heart, Gonzales, TX
Rabalais, Rev. Rusty P., '97 (ALX) Curia: Miscellaneous / Other Offices Our Lady of Prompt Succor, Alexandria, LA
Rabayda, Rev. Lewis, '16 (PSC) Curia: Advisory Boards, Commissions, Committees, and Councils Epiphany of Our Lord Byzantine Catholic Church, Roswell, GA
Racanelli, Rev. Vincent, '20 (MAD) St. John Vianney Cure of Ars, Janesville, WI; St. Mary's Congregation, Janesville, WI
Racco, Rev. Philip G., '77 (CLV) Curia: Advisory Boards, Commissions, Committees, and Councils St. Bernadette, Westlake, OH
Racela, Rev. Antonio B., '13 (SAC) Curia: Offices and Directors; Organizations (affiliated, inter-Diocesan, miscellaneous/other) Pastor of St. James Parish, Davis, a corporation sole, Davis, CA
Rach, Rev. Gabriel, (RVC) St. Patrick's, Glen Cove, NY
Rached Herrera, Rev. Jose J., *C.Ss.R.* '70 (PCE) San Antonio de Padua, Guayama, PR
Rachford, Rev. Nicholas, '71 (PRM) Retired.
Racho, Rev. Mario, '19 (BUF) St. Vincent de Paul (St.Leo/Prince of Peace), Niagara Falls, NY
Rachwalski, Rev. Jakub, '15 (BGP) The Church of the Holy Name of Jesus, Stamford, CT
Racine, Rev. Michael S., '95 (FR) Curia: Advisory Boards, Commissions, Committees, and Councils St. Francis of Assisi, New Bedford, MA
Racine, Rev. Michael Scott, '95 (FR) St. Lawrence Martyr, New Bedford, MA
Racine, Rev. Michael Scott, '95 (FR) Holy Name of the Sacred Heart of Jesus, New Bedford, MA
Racos, Rev. Irinel, '02 (RVC) Curia: Organizations (affiliated, inter-Diocesan, miscellaneous/other) St. Elizabeth of Hungary, Melville, NY
Racos, Rev. Irinel, '02 (RVC) Curia: Leadership; Offices and Directors
Raczka, Rt. Rev. Philip, '80 (NTN) Curia: Administration; Consultative Bodies Annunciation Cathedral Melkite Catholic Church Inc., West Roxbury, MA
Raczkowski, Rev. Andrew, '16 (KAL) Curia: Consultative Bodies Holy Angels, Sturgis, MI; St. Joseph, White Pigeon, MI
Raczynski, Rev. Paul L., '72 (MIL) Retired.
Radano, Rev. Msgr. John A., '65 (NEW) Retired. [COL] Seton Hall University, South Orange, NJ
Radecki, Rt. Rev. Dane J., *O. Praem.* '77 (GB) [MIS] NORBERT & CO., De Pere, WI; [MIS] Norbertine Generalate, Inc., De Pere, WI; [MON] St. Norbert Abbey, De Pere, WI; [RTR] Norbertine Center for Spirituality, De Pere, WI
Radek, Rev. James, (JOL) St. Joan of Arc, Lisle, IL
Radek, Rev. James, '89 (JOL) [NUR] St. John Vianney Villa, Naperville, IL
Rademacher, Rev. Germain P., '58 (NU) Retired. Curia: Leadership
Rademacher, Rev. John R., '70 (GI) Retired.
Rader, Rev. Matthew R., '10 (TOL) Central Catholic High School, Toledo, OH; St. Mary, Tiffin, OH
Radermacher, Rev. Michael, '06 (SEA) All Saints, Puyallup, WA; St. Martin of Tours, Fife, WA
Radetski, Rev. John J., '77 (MIL) Annunciation

Congregation, Fox Lake, WI; St. Josephs Congregation, Waupun, WI

Radetski, Rev. Paul J., '82 (GB) Retired.

Radice, Rev. Lawrence D., *M.M.* '85 (NY) [MON] Maryknoll Fathers and Brothers (Catholic Foreign Mission Society of America, Inc.), Ossining, NY

Radko, Rev. Volodymyr, (PHU) Curia: Offices and Directors

Radloff, Rev. Nicholas R, '20 (DUB) Assumption Church, Little Turkey, Lawler, Iowa, Lawler, IA; Holy Trinity Church, Protivin, Iowa, Protivin, IA; Our Lady of Mt. Carmel Church, Lawler, Iowa, Lawler, IA; St. John Church, Fort Atkinson, Iowa, Fort Atkinson, IA; St. Luke's Church, St. Lucas, Iowa, St. Lucas, IA; St. Mary Church, Waucoma, Iowa, Waucoma, IA; Trinity Catholic School, Protivin, Iowa, Protivin, IA

Radocha, Rev. Msgr. Stephen J., '77 (ALN) Curia: Leadership St. Jane Frances de Chantal, Easton, PA

Radomski, Rev. Joseph A., '62 (TR) Retired.

Radosevich, Rev. Eugene A., '90 (PEO) St. Augustine, St. Augustine, IL; St. Bernard, Bushnell, IL

Radosevich, Rev. George, '68 (SFD) Retired. Sacred Heart, Livingston, IL; St. Michael the Archangel, Staunton, IL

Radowicz, Rev. Michael R., '05 (MAD) St. Bernard, Madison, WI

Radtke, Rev. Fred, *O.F.M.* '67 (BEL) Retired.

Radwan, Rev. John Z., '05 (NEW) St. Joseph, New Milford, NJ

Raef, Rev. Scott, '94 (AMA) Curia: Advisory Boards, Commissions, Committees, and Councils St. Ann's, Canyon, TX

Raeke, Rev. Joseph K., '80 (BO) Curia: Advisory Boards, Commissions, Committees, and Councils Mary, Queen of Martyrs Parish, Plymouth, MA

Raether, Rev. Philip H., '04 (SEA) Our Lady of Fatima, Seattle, WA

Rafaj, Very Rev. Elias L., '99 (PBR) Curia: Leadership St. Basil the Great, Irving, TX

Rafferty, Rev. Brian M., '94 (RIC) Retired.

Rafferty, Rev. James, '72 (SD) Retired.

Rafferty, Rev. James A., (OM) On Special Assignment.

Rafferty, Rev. James F., '63 (BO) Retired.

Rafferty, Rev. James R., '01 (DET) St. Mary, Our Lady of the Annunciation Parish Rockwood, Rockwood, MI

Rafferty, Rev. John Michael, *O.A.R.* '03 (LA) [MON] Order of Augustinian Recollects (O.A.R.), St. Augustine Priory, Oxnard, CA

Rafferty, Rev. John Michael, *OAR* '03 (NY) Sacred Heart, Suffern, NY

Rafferty, Rev. Michael, (NY) [SEM] Tagaste Monastery, Suffern, NY

Rafferty, Rev. Michael J., '57 (SCR) Retired. [MON] Villa St. Joseph, Dunmore, PA

Rafferty, Rev. Oliver P., *S.J.* '87 (BO) [MON] The Jesuit Community at Boston College, Chestnut Hill, MA

Rafferty, Rev. Raymond M., '66 (NY) Retired.

Rafferty, Rev. Thomas F., '83 (GAL) Curia: Leadership; Offices and Directors St. Michael, Houston, TX

Rafferty, Rev. Thomas S., '05 (BO) Saint Oscar Romero Parish, Canton, MA

Raffo, Rev. Cesar, '85 (LA) Peter Pitchess Detention Ctr (Wayside Honor Ranch), Castaic

Raffo, Rev. Frank M., '98 (R) Retired.

Raftery, Rev. Paul, *O.P.* '84 (LA) (>P) Holy Rosary Parish Dominican, Portland, OR; (>P) [MON] Holy Rosary Priory, Portland, OR

Raftis, Rev. Sean, '12 (HEL) Curia: Leadership Saint Charles Borromeo Parish: Series 553, LLC, Whitefish, MT; Saint Richard Parish: Series 520, LLC, Columbia Falls, MT

Raga, Rev. Gemechu Y, *C.M.* (BAL) Immaculate Conception, Baltimore, MD; St. Cecilia, Baltimore, MD

Ragan, Rev. Gerald, '79 (SAV) St. Michael's Catholic Church, Tybee Island, GA

Ragan, Rev. James A., '98 (PBR) Dormition of the Mother of God, Clarence, PA; St. John the Baptist, Hawk Run, PA; State College PA Byzantine Catholic Community, State College, PA

Ragas, Rev. Roy, *S.J.* (SJ) [MON] Jesuit Community at Santa Clara University, Inc., Santa Clara, CA

Ragsdale, Rev. Msgr. Patrick J., *V.U.* '72 (SAT) Curia: Administration

Ragsdale, Rev. Msgr. Patrick J., *VU* '72 (SAT) Shrine of St. Padre Pio of Pietrelcina, San Antonio, TX

Ragusa, Rev. Salvatore, *S.D.S.* '88 (OAK) [CAM] Holy Names University Campus Ministry, Oakland, CA; [COL] Holy Names University (Sisters of the Holy Names of Jesus and Mary, A Corporation, Holy Names University, A Corporation, Sisters of the Holy Names of Jesus and Mary), Oakland, CA

Raharjo, Rev. Johanes Teguh, *C.I.C.M.* '06 (SAT) St. Patrick, San Antonio, TX

Rahill, Rev. Patrick, '68 (SP) Retired.

Rahilly, Rev. Msgr. Paul F., '81 (RVC) Retired.

Rahmat, Rev. Paulus, (BRK) Queen of Angels, Long Island City, NY

Rahmeh, Rev. Manuel Bassam, '19 (SAM) Our Lady of Lebanon, Miami, FL

Rai, Rev. Kevin, '74 (AUS) Retired.

Raia, Rev. Jonathan, (AUS) [CAM] University Catholic Center, Austin, TX

Raila, Rev. Donald, *O.S.B.* '83 (GBG) [MON] Saint Vincent Archabbey, Latrobe, PA

Raines, Rev. Justin N., '13 (NSH) Curia: Offices and Directors St. Matthew, Franklin, TN

Rainville, Rev. Marcel R., *S.S.E.* '71 (BUR) [COL] St. Michael's College, Colchester, VT; [MIS] Society of St. Edmund, ,

Rainville, Rev. Mark, '13 (WOR) Curia: Advisory Boards, Commissions, Committees, and Councils Our Lady of the Angels, Worcester, MA

Rainville, Rev. Paul G., *M.S.* '65 (ATL) (>HRT) [MIS] Missionaries of LaSalette, Hartford, CT

Rainwater, Rev. Trevor J., *S.J.* (DET) University of Detroit Jesuit High School and Academy, Detroit, MI

Raj, Rev. Amrit, *I.M.S.* '91 (BR) The Congregation Of Immaculate Conception Roman Catholic Church, Lakeland, LA

Raj, Rev. Baltha, (SAG) Saint Cyril Parish of Bannister, Bannister, MI; Saint Peter Parish of Chesaning, Chesaning, MI

Raj, Rev. Joseph Anthu, (PT) St. Elizabeth Ann Seton, Crawfordville, FL

Raj, Rev. Justin, *I.M.S.* '04 (BGP) St. Mary's Corporation, Ridgefield, CT

Raj, Rev. Martin, *OSB* (STA) St. Mary, Mother of Mercy, Macclenny, FL

Raj, Rev. Mohan, *HGN* '10 (GF) Immaculate Conception, Fort Benton, MT

Raj, Rev. Percy Joseph, '74 (NY) Chap, Staten Island Univ Hosp South and North, Staten Island

Raj, Rev. Roland Antony, *M.M.I.* '02 (NY) Blessed Sacrament, Staten Island, NY; St. George-St. Francis, Jeffersonville, NY

Raj, Rev. Victor, *HGN* '15 (PBL) Sacred Heart, Avondale, CO; St. Leander, Pueblo, CO

Raj, Rev. Vijan Kiran Anthony, (PRO) The Church of the Blessed Sacrament in Providence, Rhode Island, Providence, RI

Raj Samala, Rev. Arokia, '02 (AMA) Immaculate Heart of Mary, Groom, TX; St. Mary's, Clarendon, TX

Raja, Rev. Prince, (WIN) St. Agnes, Kellogg, MN; St. Felix, Wabasha, MN

Raja, Rev. Tiburtius Anthony, (HBG) [CAM] Dickinson College, Carlisle, PA

Rajaian, Rev. Suresh, *S.A.C.* (DET) St. Pius X Parish Southgate, Southgate, MI

Rajaian, Rev. Suresh, *S.A.C.* '00 (DET) St. Vincent Pallotti Parish Wyandotte, Wyandotte, MI

Rajan, Rev. Charles Michael, *O.C.D.* (ELP) San Juan Bautista, El Paso, TX

Rajayan, Rev. Antony W., (MO) Curia: Offices and Directors

Rajesh, Rev. Antony, '10 (KAL) Curia: Consultative Bodies St. Joseph, Kalamazoo, MI

Raji, Rev. Arokiadoss, '10 (NEW) St. Joseph, East Rutherford, NJ (>STP) Church of St. Bernard, St. Paul, MN

Raji, Rev. Francis Olalekan, *MSP* (CHL) St. Vincent de Paul, Charlotte, NC

Rajski, Rev. Daniel K., '11 (BRK) Holy Cross, Maspeth, NY; Saint Camillus-Saint Virgilius, Rockaway Park, NY

Raju, Rev. Arogya, (NY) Parish of St. Paul and St. Ann, Congers, NY

Raju, Rev. Jay, (VEN) Curia: Leadership

Raju, Rev. Jayabalan, '99 (VEN) Epiphany Cathedral Catholic Parish in Venice, Inc., Venice, FL

Raju Yanamala, Rev. Anthony, (AMA) Sacred Heart, Spearman, TX

Rakotovoavy, Rev. Ralainirina Francois, *M.S.F.* '00 (SAT) Holy Family, New Braunfels, TX

Rakowicz, Rev. William, *S.J.* '80 (WDC) [RTR] Loyola Retreat House, Faulkner, MD

Ralko, Rev. Martin J., '84 (COL) St. Nicholas, Zanesville, OH; [EFT] St. Nicholas Foundation, Zanesville, OH

Rallanka, Rev. Ryan, *S.J.* (SEA) [MON] Jesuit House, Seattle, Seattle, WA

Ralph, Rev. Francis, *O.P.* '72 (L) Retired.

Ralph, Rev. Sean P., '09 (CLV) Cathedral of St. John the Evangelist, Cleveland, OH; [EFT] St. John Cathedral Endowment Trust, Cleveland, OH

Ralston, Rev. Timothy W., '10 (CIN) St. Bernadette, Amelia, OH; St. Mary, Bethel, OH; St. Peter, New Richmond, OH; St. Thomas More, Cincinnati, OH

Rama, Rev. Edward, '12 (PAT) Curia: Administration; Leadership

Ramacciotti, Rev. Msgr. James J., '85 (STL) Curia: Leadership [SEM] Kenrick School of Theology, ,

Ramaekers, Rev. Timothy, '82 (ORG) Corpus Christi, Aliso Viejo, CA

Ramat, Rev. Martin J., '07 (SAC) Pastor of Our Divine Savior Parish, Chico, a corporation sole, Chico, CA; Pastor of St. Thomas More Parish, Paradise, a corporation sole, Paradise, CA

Ramatowski, Rev. Edward F., (MO) Curia: Offices and Directors

Ramatowski, Rev. Edward F., '03 (STL) Military Chap

Ramelow, Rev. Anselm, *O.P.* '03 (OAK) [SEM] Dominican School of Philosophy and Theology, Berkeley, CA

Ramelow, Rev. Anselm, *O.P.* '03 (SFR) Curia: Offices and Directors [MON] St. Dominic Priory, San Francisco, CA

Ramen, Rev. Paul F., '60 (NOR) Retired.

Ramer, Rev. Msgr. James K., '86 (PEO) Retired.

Raminedi, Rev. Shravankumar, (LIN) St. Vincent de Paul, Seward, NE

Ramirez, Rev. Alfredo, *O.F.M.* '99 (ELP) [SEM] St. Anthony's School of Theology, El Paso, TX

Ramirez, Rev. Charles J., '87 (LA) Our Lady of the Assumption, Claremont, CA

Ramirez, Rev. David, (DAL) Mater Dei Personal Parish, Irving, TX

Ramirez, Rev. David, '01 (NSH) Curia: Offices and Directors

Ramirez, Rev. David Anthony, '18 (MRY) St. Michael's, Boulder Creek, CA

Ramirez, Rev. Edgar, *FSSP* '22 (LR) Our Lady of Sorrows Catholic Church, Springdale, AR

Ramirez, Rev. Erialdo, (ORG) St. Cecilia, Tustin, CA

Ramirez, Rev. Eric, *S.J.* (DEN) [MON] Regis High Jesuit Community, Centennial, CO

Ramirez, Rev. Evelio, '13 (KAL) SS. Cyril and Methodius, Wayland, MI; St. Therese of Lisieux, Wayland, MI

Ramirez, Rev. Fernando, '78 (SD) Curia: Advisory Boards, Commissions, Committees, and Councils

Ramirez, Friar Francisco, *OFM, Cap* (SAT) St. Joseph Spouse of the Virgin Mary, San Antonio, TX

Ramirez, Rev. Francisco X., '79 (LA) Retired.

Ramirez, Rev. Guillermo, '13 (SAC) On Leave.

Ramirez, Rev. Gustavo, *SDB* '19 (STO) Curia: Leadership St. Luke Church of Stockton (Pastor of), Stockton, CA

Ramirez, Rev. Henry, '17 (WOR) Immaculate Heart of Mary, Winchendon, MA

Ramirez, Rev. Israel, *MSP* '15 (LA) Our Lady of Solitude, Los Angeles, CA

Ramirez, Rev. Ivan D., '03 (HRT) Curia: Advisory Boards, Commissions, Committees, and Councils; Deaneries St. Joseph's Church, Bristol, Connecticut, Bristol, CT

Ramirez, Rev. Jacob, (GAL) Sacred Heart, Conroe, TX

Ramirez, Rev. Javier, '19 (OAK) St. Cornelius, Richmond, CA

Ramirez, Rev. Javier D, *FN* '11 (DAL) Good Shepherd Catholic Parish, Garland, TX

Ramirez, Rev. Jorge I., '16 (ROC) All Saints, Lansing, NY; Holy Cross, Freeville, NY; St. Anthony, Groton, NY

Ramirez, Rev. Jose, *S.M.* '69 (STL) Retired. [MON] Marianist Province of the United States (Society of Mary), St. Louis, MO

Ramirez, Rev. Jose Alfredo, *O.F.M.* '99 (ELP) St. Francis of Assisi, El Paso, TX

Ramirez, Rev. Jose Nieves, '79 (ELP) On Leave.

Ramirez, Rev. Jose T., '10 (B) Curia: Offices and Directors Our Lady of the Valley, Caldwell, ID; [CAM] The College of Idaho, Caldwell, ID

Ramirez, Rev. Juan, '15 (WOR) St. Anthony of Padua, Fitchburg, MA

Ramirez, Rev. Juan, '19 (EVN) Our Lady of Hope, Washington, IN

Ramirez, Rev. Juan Carlos, '07 (LSC) Curia: Leadership San Jose Parish, Carlsbad, Inc., Carlsbad, NM

Ramirez, Rev. Luis Ariel, *C.M.* '94 (STO) Sacred Heart Church of Patterson (Pastor of), Patterson, CA

Ramirez, Rev. Nicolas, '16 (GAL) St. Frances Cabrini, Houston, TX

Ramirez, Rev. Msgr. Pedro, '74 (SPK) Retired. St. Patrick, Pasco, WA

Ramirez, Rev. Rafael M., *S.S.D.* (DAL) Our Lady of Perpetual Help Catholic Parish, Dallas, TX

Ramirez, Rev. Renel, (MGZ) Our Lady of Monserrate, Moca, PR; Sacred Heart, Mayaguez, PR

Ramirez, Very Rev. Ricardo, '20 (SAT) Curia: Administration; Leadership St. Ann, San Antonio, TX
Ramirez, Rev. Roland B., '08 (SAC) Pastor of Sacred Heart Parish, Gridley, a corporation sole, Gridley, CA
Ramirez, Rev. Salvador, '04 (BWN) St. Helen, Rio Hondo, TX
Ramirez, Friar Sergio, *S.F.M.* (SJN) Nuestra Senora del Pilar, San Juan, PR
Ramirez, Rev. Theilo, '09 (PHX) Curia: Leadership; Offices and Directors St. Anne Roman Catholic Mission, A Quasi-Parish, Ashfork, AZ; St. Francis Roman Catholic Parish, Seligman, AZ; St. Joseph Roman Catholic Parish, Williams, AZ
Ramirez, Rev. Tulio E., *M.X.Y.* '90 (NY) Church of Our Saviour, Bronx, NY; [MON] Yarumal Mission Society, Inc., Bronx, NY
Ramirez Briseno, Rev. Jose Maria, (SEA) Immaculate Conception, Mount Vernon, WA; Immaculate Heart of Mary, Sedro Woolley, WA; St. Charles, Burlington, WA
Ramirez de Paz, Rev. Noe, '19 (R) On Duty Outside Diocese.
Ramirez La Cruz, Rev. Darwin Daniel, '11 (MIA) SS. Peter and Paul, Miami, FL
Ramirez López, Rev. Oran de Jesús, (ARE) Church of Christ the King, Arecibo, PR
Ramirez Moreno, Rev. Teofilo, *C.S.* '15 (VEN) Curia: Leadership Our Lady of Guadalupe Parish in Immokalee, Inc., Immokalee, FL
Ramirez Sanchez, Rev. Jorge Alberto, *C.O.R.C.* (SJN) Ntra. Sra. de los Dolores, Bayamon, PR
Ramirez Soler, Rev. Henry, *C.M.F.* '01 (NEW) St. Joseph, Jersey City, NJ
Ramirez Torres, Rev. Gerardo, '91 (PCE) Curia: Leadership; Offices and Directors Colegio Del Sagrado Corazon De Jesus de Ponce, Inc., Ponce, PR; Nuestra Senora de la Monserrate, Jayuya, PR
Ramirez-Portugal, Rev. Daniel, '91 (LAR) Curia: Leadership; Offices and Directors Our Lady of Lourdes, Zapata, TX
Ramirez-Siller, Rev. Gonzalo, '17 (FRS) St. Catherine of Siena, Dinuba, CA
Ramji, Rev. Shouraiah, '78 (ALX) Little Flower, Evergreen, LA
Ramler, Rev. Michael J., '74 (LEX) Curia: Leadership St. Jude, Louisa, KY
Ramon, Rev. Edilberto, (SR) Pastor of St. Joseph Catholic Church of Fortuna, a Corporation Sole, Fortuna, CA
Ramon, Rev. Edildberto, '04 (SR) St. Patrick, Loleta, CA
Ramon, Rev. Gustavo J., '92 (LA) San Antonio de Padua, Los Angeles, CA
Ramon-Cabrera, Rev. Rodolfo, *OFM* '01 (SAV) St. Peter Claver, Macon, GA
Ramon-Landry, Rev. Kenneth, '87 (BLX) Curia: Advisory Boards, Commissions, Committees, and Councils Holy Rosary, Hattiesburg, MS; Sacred Heart, Hattiesburg, MS
Ramos, Rev. A.W., '94 (SFS) Retired.
Ramos, Rev. Alexander, (MO) Curia: Offices and Directors
Ramos, Rev. Amado, '16 (AUS) Our Lady of Guadalupe Catholic Church - Temple, Texas, Temple, TX
Ramos, Rev. Andre, '88 (SD) Pastor of Guardian Angels Catholic Parish, Santee, a corporation sole, Santee, CA
Ramos, Rev. Angel Roman, '90 (MGZ) St. Rose of Lima, Rincon, PR
Ramos, Rev. Daniel, (LR) St. John, Russellville, AR
Ramos, Rev. Daniel, '18 (LR) St. Leo the Great University Parish, Russellville, AR; [CAM] St. Leo the Great University Parish, Russellville, AR; [EFT] St. John's Educational Trust, ,
Ramos, Rev. Danilo, '79 (DAL) Retired.
Ramos, Rev. German Plaza, '18 (SAC) Pastor of St. Thomas the Apostle Parish, Oroville, a corporation sole, Oroville, CA
Ramos, Rev. Israel, (CGS) Curia: Leadership
Ramos, Rev. Jose C., *A.M.* '03 (NY) St. Pius X, Scarsdale, NY
Ramos, Rev. Joselito C., *A.M.* '03 (CAM) The Church of Saint Katharine Drexel, McKee City, New Jersey, Egg Harbor Township, NJ
Ramos, Rev. Juancho Choy, (CLV) St. Paschal Baylon, Highland Heights, OH
Ramos, Rev. June N., '10 (SFE) Our Lady of Sorrows-Bernalillo, Bernalillo, NM
Ramos, Rev. Justin S., *O.Praem.* '95 (ORG) [MON] Norbertine Fathers of Orange, Inc., Silverado, CA
Ramos, Rev. Manuel, '20 (LA) St. Joseph, Carpinteria, CA
Ramos, Rev. Marcos, (SAT) Purisima Concepcion, San Antonio, TX; [CON] Dominican Community of San Juan Macias (San Juan Macias Community), San Antonio, TX; [SEM] The Seminary of the Assumption of the Blessed Virgin Mary-St. John of San Antonio, TX (Assumption-St. John's Seminary), San Antonio, TX
Ramos, Rev. Martel, (MRY) St. John the Baptist, King City, CA
Ramos, Rev. Michael, *O.F.M.Cap.* '13 (NY) Good Shepherd, New York, NY; [MON] St. Joseph Friary (Capuchin Franciscans, Province of St. Mary), New Paltz, NY
Ramos, Rev. Osman Guzman, *F.M.* '16 (FTW) St. Anthony of Padua, Angola, IN; St. Joseph, LaGrange, IN; St. Paul Chapel, Fremont, IN
Ramos, Rev. Sergio, '99 (ORG) St. Justin Martyr, Anaheim, CA
Ramos, Rev. Victor Raul, '84 (LA) Sagrado Corazon, Sacred Heart, Compton, CA
Ramos, Rev. Victoriano, '54 (SJN) Retired.
Ramos, Rev. Wilmar, '16 (WOR) Curia: Offices and Directors St. Joan of Arc, Worcester, MA
Ramos Cintron, Rev. Israel, '08 (CGS) Curia: Leadership Sagrado Corazon de Jesus y 12 Apostoles, San Lorenzo, PR
Ramos Medina, Rev. Juan Ramón, *C.M.V.* '01 (ARE) Nuestra Senora de Fatima, Sabana Hoyos, PR
Ramos Ortega, Rev. Julio Cesar, *M.G.* '01 (LA) Our Lady of Guadalupe, El Monte, CA; St. Martha, Huntington Park, CA
Ramos Ramos, Rev. Arturo, '15 (PCE) On Leave.
Ramos Rodriguez, Rev. Rafael, (ARE) On Duty Outside Diocese. New York
Ramoso, Rev. Rene R., '89 (SFR) St. Cecilia, San Francisco, CA
Ramos-Valdes, Rev. Agapito Antonio, *M.SS.CC.* (SJN) Curia: Leadership Santiago Apostol, Bayamon, PR
Rampino, Rev. Joseph M., '16 (ARL) St. Ambrose, Annandale, VA
Ramsak, Rev. Finbar, *O.S.B* '11 (CLV) Benedictine High School, Cleveland, OH; [MIS] Assumption Church, Broadview Heights, OH
Ramsey, Rev. James Boniface, '73 (NY) St. Joseph Church - Yorkville, New York, NY
Ramsey, Rev. John David, '10 (RIC) Saint Benedict, Richmond, VA
Ramson, Rev. Ronald W., *C.M.* '59 (STL) [MON] Congregation of the Mission, Perryville, MO
Ranallo, Rev. Albert A., '07 (PRO) Dir Catholic Chaplaincy Curia: Social Services St. Francis of Assisi, Wakefield, RI
Ranallo, Rev. Albert D., '07 (PRO) Saint Ann's Catholic Church of Providence, Rhode Island, Providence, RI
Randall, Rev. Jude D., *O.S.B.* '60 (JOL) Retired.
Randall, Rev. Msgr. Kevin S., '92 (NOR) On Duty Outside Diocese. Washington, DC
Randall, Rev. Robert J., '51 (PRO) Retired.
Randazzo, Rev. Anthony J., '86 (NEW) Holy Trinity, Westfield, NJ; [CCH] St. Joseph Social Service Center, Elizabeth, NJ
Randl, Rev. Ewald, '98 (NEW) On Duty Outside Diocese. Pfarre St Ruprecht, Klagenfurt
Ranek, Rev. Jerome, '91 (SFS) Saint Agnes Parish of Clay County, Vermillion, SD
Rangel, Rev. Carlos, '98 (TYL) On Duty Outside Diocese. Mexico
Rangel, Rev. Hector G., '16 (HRT) Our Lady of Guadalupe Parish Corporation, New Haven, CT; Saint Anthony Parish Corporation, New Haven, CT
Rangel, Rev. Marco, '10 (DAL) St. Michael the Archangel Catholic Parish - Grand Prairie, Grand Prairie, TX; [CEM] Calvary Catholic Cemetery, Corsicana, TX
Rangel Calderon, Rev. Jesus Alberto, '05 (PCE) Santos Apostoles Pedro y Pablo, Guayama, PR
Ranges, Rev. Charles H., *S.S.E.* '72 (BUR) Holy Family-St. Lawrence, Essex Junction, VT; St. Pius X, Essex Junction, VT
Ranieri, Rev. John J., '82 (NEW) [COL] Seton Hall University, South Orange, NJ
Ranieri, Rev. Msgr. Joseph A., '57 (WDC) Retired. On Special Assignment. Curia: Clergy and Religious Services; Consultative Bodies
Rank, Rev. Robert F., '68 (GB) Retired.
Rank OFM CAP, Friar Donald, *OFM Cap* '20 (SAT) Our Lady of the Angels, San Antonio, TX
Rankin, Rev. Dominic, '18 (SFD) On Special Assignment. Cathedral of the Immaculate Conception, Springfield, IL
Rankin, Rev. Dominic J., '18 (SFD) On Special Assignment. Curia: Leadership
Rankin, Rev. Joseph M., '79 (L) Retired. St. Luke, Louisville, KY; St. Rita, Louisville, KY
Rankin, Very Rev. Robert, (PHX) Curia: (>HPM) Offices and Directors
Rankin, Rev. Robert, '80 (HPM) Curia: Leadership St. Melany, Tucson, AZ
Rannazzisi, Rev. Gregory, (RVC) St. Gerard Majella, Port Jefferson Station, NY
Ransom, Rev. Donald B., '64 (NEW) Retired.
Ranzino, Very Rev. Thomas C., '78 (BR) Curia: Administration; Clergy and Religious Services; Leadership Congregation of St. Jean Vianney Roman Catholic Church, Baton Rouge, LA; [MIS] Baton Rouge Chancery Office, Baton Rouge, LA
Rapaglia, Rev. Eric, '00 (NY) St. Joseph-St. Thomas St. John Neumann Parish, Staten Island, NY
Rapcia, Rev. Piotr, (CHI) St. Zachary, Des Plaines, IL
Raphael, Rev. John, '96 (NSH) Curia: Offices and Directors
Raphael, Rev. Mark S., '98 (NO) St. Louis King of France, Metairie, LA; [SEM] Notre Dame Seminary Graduate School of Theology, New Orleans, LA
Rapheal, Rev. Innasi, *H.G.N.* '00 (SR) Pastor of St. Rose of Lima Catholic Church of Santa Rosa, A Corporation Sole, Santa Rosa, CA
Raphel, Rev. James, *CMF* '94 (NEW) St. Joseph, Jersey City, NJ
Raphel, Rev. Tomy, (SAT) Chap, Baptist Hosp Sys, San Antonio; San Antonio State Hosp… Curia: (>MO) Offices and Directors
Rapisarda, Rev. Gregory, '10 (BAL) Our Lady of Hope, Baltimore, MD; St. Luke, Edgemere, MD; [EFT] St. Luke Parish Education Endowment Trust, Baltimore, MD
Rapisarda, Rev. John C., '08 (BAL) St. Joseph, Baltimore, MD
Rapoport, Rev. Andrew, *FSSP* '18 (ATL) St. Francis de Sales Catholic Church, Mableton, Inc., Mableton, GA
Rapose, Rev. Mario D., '00 (OM) On Leave.
Raposo, Rev. John A., '77 (FR) St. Gabriel the Archangel, New Bedford, MA
Rapozo, Rev. Anthony W., '11 (HON) Curia: Consultative Bodies; Offices and Directors St. John Apostle and Evangelist, Mililani Town, HI
Rapp, Rev. Michael, '10 (DEN) Cathedral Basilica of the Immaculate Conception Catholic Parish in Denver, Denver, CO
Rappl, Rev. Matthew, (GB) Curia: Advisory Boards, Commissions, Committees, and Councils Sacred Heart, Manawa, WI; SS. Peter and Paul, Weyauwega, WI
Rappold, Rev. Norbert F., '99 (LR) Curia: Leadership; Offices and Directors St. Peter the Fisherman, Mountain Home, AR
Rapposelli, Rev. Stephen J., '98 (CAM) The Church of Saints Peter and Paul, Washington Township, Gloucester County, N.J., Turnersville, NJ
Rappu, Rev. Mathew, '78 (SAC) Curia: Leadership; Offices and Directors Pastor of Our Lady of Grace Parish, West Sacramento, a corporation sole, West Sacramento, CA
Raptosh, Very Rev. R. Joseph, '87 (PBR) Curia: Leadership St. Michael, Canonsburg, PA
Raquepo, Rev. Mario, '79 (HON) St. Stephen, Honolulu, HI
Rareshide, Rev. Msgr. Lanaux J., '61 (NO) Retired. Curia: Miscellaneous / Other Offices St. Anthony, Gretna, LA; St. Joseph Church and Shrine on the Westbank, Gretna, LA
Rasaian, Rev. Lawrence, '97 (TYL) Curia: Advisory Boards, Commissions, Committees, and Councils; Tribunal
Raschko, Rev. Michael, '75 (SEA) Retired.
Rashford, Rev. John, *S.J.* '71 (SEA) [MON] Jesuit House, Seattle, Seattle, WA
Rashford, Rev. Nicholas J., *S.J.* '71 (PH) Retired. [MIS] Jesuit Fathers, , ; [MON] Jesuit Community at St. Joseph's University, Merion Station, PA
Rask, Rev. Phillip J., '72 (STP) Retired.
Rasmussen, Rev. John, '69 (SFS) Retired.
Rasner, Very Rev. David L., '82 (LFT) Curia: Leadership; Miscellaneous / Other Offices; Tribunal St. Francis Xavier, Attica, IN; St. Joseph, Covington, IN
Raso, Rev. Anthony F., '75 (BRK) Our Lady of Guadalupe, Brooklyn, NY
Rasonabe, Rev. Mario Roberto, *SVD* '95 (JKS) Holy Family, Jackson, MS
Rassmussen, Rev. Terrence, '79 (STP) St. Joseph, New Hope, MN; [CEM] St. Joseph Cemetery, New Hope, MN
Raszeja, Rev. Norbert, *C.R.* '72 (JOL) St. Scholastica, Woodridge, IL
Rata, Rev. Jovito D., '07 (SAC) Curia: Leadership; Offices and Directors Pastor of St. Peter and All Hallows Parish, Sacramento, a corporation sole, Sacramento, CA
Ratajczak, Rev. Mateusz, '19 (DEN) On Special Assignment.

Ratermann, Rev. Jerome B., '57 (BEL) Retired. On Administrative Leave.
Rath, Rev. Jeff, *OSA* '21 (JOL) St. Jude, New Lenox, IL
Rath, Rev. Richard J., '88 (STL) Curia: (>MO) Offices and Directors Immaculate Conception Catholic Church, Old Monroe, Old Monroe, MO
Rathgeb, Rev. Msgr. William R., '67 (GBG) Curia: Leadership; Offices and Directors [MIS] Sisters of Charity of Seton Hill, United States Province, Ennis Hall, Greensburg, PA
Rathinam, Rev. John Stephen, *I.M.S.* '97 (LUB) Curia: Leadership St. Pius X, O'Donnell, TX
Rathke, Rev. Zachary, *CSC* '20 (FTW) St. Adalbert, South Bend, IN; St. Casimir, South Bend, IN
Rathschmidt, Rev. John, *O.F.M.Cap.* '69 (NY) [MON] The Province of St. Mary of the Capuchin Order, White Plains, NY
Ratigan, Rev. Patrick A., '83 (OG) Retired.
Rativá, Very Rev. Jorge, *O.P.* '10 (NO) [MON] Dominican Friars, Southern Dominican Province of St. Martin de Porres, New Orleans, LA
Ratterman, Rev. Kevin J., '94 (OKL) Curia: Deaneries St. Mary, Ardmore, OK
Ratuiste, Rev. Kyle, '15 (SPK) Curia: Offices and Directors [MIS] Serra Club of Spokane, Spokane Valley, WA; [SEM] Bishop White Seminary, Spokane, WA
Ratzenburger, Rev. Raymond, (TUC) Retired.
Ratzmann, Rev. George, '87 (VEN) Curia: Leadership St. William Parish in Naples, Inc., Naples, FL
Ratzmann, Rev. George, '87 (VEN) Curia: Leadership
Ratzmann, Rev. George, '81 (VEN) Curia: Leadership
Rau, Rev. Msgr. Peter J., '85 (ATL) St. Peter Chanel Catholic Church, Roswell, Inc., Roswell, GA
Rauch, Rev. David E., '70 (STL) Retired.
Rauch, Rev. Edward L., *O.S.F.S.* '64 (PH) Retired.
Rauck, Rev. Trenton, *SJC* (CHI) St. John Cantius, Chicago, IL; [MIS] Canons Regular of Saint John Cantius, Chicago, IL
Raudes, Rev. Santiago E., '02 (SAC) Curia: Offices and Directors Pastor of St. Joseph Parish, Clarksburg, a corporation sole, Clarksburg, CA
Rauenbuehler, Rev. Andrew, '21 (DAV) Our Lady of Victory Church of Davenport, Iowa, Davenport, IA
Raum, Friar Michael, *OFM* (WDC) [MON] Franciscan Monastery USA Inc., Washington, DC
Raun, Rev. Msgr. Douglas A., '82 (SFE) St. Thomas Aquinas, Rio Rancho, NM
Rausch, Rev. Clyde, *OMI* '68 (SAT) (>BEL) [MON] Missionary Oblates of Mary Immaculate - St. Henry's Oblate Residence, Belleville, IL
Rausch, Rev. Dennis, '80 (MIA) Retired.
Rausch, Rev. John, *OFM* (GB) Retired.
Rausch, Rev. Thomas P., *S.J.* '72 (LA) [MON] Jesuit Community, Los Angeles, CA
Rauscher, Rev. Donald, *S.J.* '68 (MIL) [MON] St. Camillus Jesuit Community (Society of Jesus, USA Midwest Province), Wauwatosa, WI
Rauscher, Rev. Russell G., '75 (CLV) Retired.
Rauschuber, Rev. Anthony, *SJ* '05 (FWT) [RTR] Montserrat Jesuit Retreat House, Lake Dallas, TX
Russeo Gomez, Rev. Jose Gregorio, '07 (SLC) Saint Patrick LLC 257, Eureka, UT; San Andres LLC 212, Payson, UT
Rautenberg, Rev. Joseph F., '73 (IND) Retired.
Rauth, Rev. Philip J., '59 (LIN) Retired.
Raux, Rev. Redmond P., '82 (BO) Curia: (>MO) Offices and Directors
Ravenkamp, Rev. Michael, *S.J.* (SAT) Curia: Leadership
Ravenkamp, Rev. Michael, *S.J.* '96 (SD) Curia: Tribunal
Ravert, Rev. Charles J., '14 (PH) St. Ambrose, Philadelphia, PA
Ravizza, Rev. Mark A., *S.J.* '99 (SJ) [MON] USA West Province, Society of Jesus, Los Gatos, CA
Rawicki, Rev. Luke, *L.C.* '22 (R) Cardinal Gibbons High School, Raleigh, NC
Rawson, Rev. Matthew E., '18 (SY) Christ Our Hope Parish, Boonville, NY
Ray, Rev. Brian, '13 (POC) Military Chap Curia: (>MO) Offices and Directors
Ray, Rev. Charles, '12 (ALX) Curia: Miscellaneous / Other Offices St. Augustine's, Natchez, LA
Ray, Rev. Daniel, *L.C.* '06 (NY) [MON] Legionaries of Christ, Rye, NY
Ray, Rev. David, '22 (BAL) St. Joseph, Cockeysville, MD
Ray, Rev. Douglas, *SJ* (CHL) (>PH) [MON] Arrupe Jesuit Community, Merion Station, PA
Ray, Rev. Robert E., '69 (L) Retired.
Rayapati, Rev. Bala Prabhakar, (LAF) St. Ann, Mamou, LA
Rayappan, Rev. Amalraj, '99 (P) Curia: Offices and Directors Sacred Heart Parish, Newport, OR
Rayappan, Rev. Amalraj, (P) Curia: Tribunal
Rayappan, Rev. Francis, '15 (CHI) Our Lady of Africa Parish, Chicago, IL; [MON] Divine Word Residence, Techny, IL
Rayappan, Rev. Murali Anand, '11 (LC) Nativity of the Blessed Virgin Mary, Auburndale, WI; St. Kilian, Blenker, WI; St. Michael, Hewitt, WI; [EFT] St. Mary Education Endowment Trust, Auburndale, WI
Rayappan, Rev. Philip S., '98 (SCR) Holy Name of Mary, Montrose, PA
Rayappan, Very Rev. Ranees Anbukumar, *SMA* '04 (NEW) [MON] Society of African Missions, Provincialate, S.M.A. Fathers, Tenafly, NJ
Rayar, Rev. Thomas, '93 (STP) St. Margaret Mary, Golden Valley, MN
Rayder, Rev. Peter J., '02 (BRK) American Martyrs, Oakland Gardens, NY
Rayer, Rev. Daniel J., '99 (LIN) Curia: Leadership; Offices and Directors
Rayes, Rev. Emanuel, '54 (EST) Retired.
Raymond, Rev. David R., '03 (PRT) Curia: Consultative Bodies Parish of the Precious Blood, Caribou, ME; [CAM] University of Maine at Presque Isle, Presque Isle, ME
Raymond, Rev. Tyler C, '19 (DUB) Holy Cross Church, Holy Cross, Iowa, Holy Cross, IA; Holy Trinity Church, Luxemburg, Iowa, Luxemburg, IA; LaSalle Elementary Schools, Holy Cross, Iowa, Holy Cross, IA; S.S. Peter and Paul Church, Sherrill, Iowa, Sherrill, IA; St. Francis Church, Balltown, Iowa, Balltown, IA; St. Joseph Church, Rickardsville, Iowa, Durango, IA
Raymond, Rev. Wilfred, *C.S.C.* '71 (FR) [MIS] Holy Cross Family Ministries, North Easton, MA
Raymond, Rev. Wilfred, *C.S.C.* (ALB) [MIS] Crusade for Family Prayer, Inc. (Holy Cross Family Ministries Foundation), Albany, NY; [MIS] Family Theater Ministries, Albany, NY; [MIS] The Family Rosary, Inc., Albany, NY
Raymond, Rev. Wilfred J., *C.S.C.* '71 (FR) [COL] Holy Cross Fathers Religious, North Easton, MA
Raymundo, Rev. Anthony, '19 (PH) St. Laurence, Upper Darby, PA
Rayson, Rev. Robert, '99 (PEO) St. John, Benson, IL; St. Mary's, El Paso, IL
Razafimahafaly, Rev. Patric R, *S.J.* '14 (SFR) [MON] Loyola House Jesuit Community, San Francisco, CA
Razo, Rev. Manuel Alfredo, '11 (BWN) San Felipe de Jesus, Brownsville, TX
Razzouk, Rev. Rami, (OLL) Our Lady of Lebanon Maronite Catholic Church, Millbrae, CA
Read, Rev. Jeffrey W., '12 (EVN) Curia: Leadership Holy Family, Jasper, IN
Reade, Rev. John M., '09 (COL) Retired.
Reader, Rev. Daniel B., '11 (ORG) Curia: Leadership; Offices and Directors Christ Cathedral Parish, Garden Grove, CA
Reading, Rev. Edward, '72 (PAT) Retired.
Reagan, Rev. Msgr. Dennis, (RVC) Retired. [MON] St Pius X Residence for Retired Priests LLC, Ronkonkoma, NY
Reagan, Rev. Thomas, (GB) [SHR] The National Shrine of Our Lady of Good Help, Inc., New Franken, WI
Real-Linares, Rev. Romulo, '05 (KCK) Our Lady of Guadalupe, Topeka, KS
Reamer, Very Rev. Mark G., *O.F.M.* '91 (ALB) On Special Assignment. Guardian Siena College Friary, Loudonville Curia: Leadership; Offices and Directors [COL] Siena College, Loudonville, NY; [MIS] St. Francis Chapel (Albany), Franciscan Friars-Holy Name Province, Inc., Albany, NY
Reamer, Rev. William G., '87 (OG) University of Vermont Health Network, CVPH, Plattsburgh
Reamsnyder, Rev. David M., '12 (LAN) St. Anthony Parish Hillsdale, Hillsdale, MI
Rearden, Rev. Patrick R., *O.P.* '60 (CHI) [MON] St. Pius V Priory, Chicago, IL
Reardon, Rev. Daniel, '97 (KC) Our Lady of Lourdes Catholic Church, Harrisonville, Harrisonville, MO
Reardon, Rev. Dennis A., '72 (PRO) Retired.
Reardon, Rev. Francis, '78 (PMB) Retired. Our Lady of Lourdes, Boca Raton, FL
Reardon, Rev. John F., '76 (BO) Retired.
Reardon, Rev. Jonathan, '08 (SPR) Curia: Offices and Directors Holy Name, Springfield, MA
Reardon, Rev. Michael, *S.D.V.* '99 (NEW) St. Michael, Newark, NJ
Reardon, Rev. Michael, '74 (LA) Retired.
Reaume, Rev. Michael R., *S.M.* '69 (STL) [MON] Marianist Province of the United States (Society of Mary), St. Louis, MO
Reaves, Rev. Phillip A., '94 (LR) Curia: Offices and Directors
Rebacz, Rev. Boguslaw, (DEN) St. Mary Catholic Parish in Breckenridge, Breckenridge, CO
Rebacz, Rev. Jerzy, '96 (LC) St. James, Amherst, WI; St. Mary of Mount Carmel, Amherst, WI
Rebamontan, Rev. Marito F., '70 (ORG) Retired.
Rebanal, Rev. Msgr. Jeremias R., '55 (NEW) Retired. St. Mary of the Assumption, Elizabeth, NJ
Rebatzki, Rev. George M., '64 (MIL) Retired.
Rebeck, Rev. Msgr. Eugene M., '65 (TR) Retired. Curia: Canonical Services
Rebeggiani, Rev. Daniele, '15 (WDC) On Special Assignment. Shrine of St. Jude, Rockville, MD
Rebel, Rev. Patrick M., '85 (SP) Saint Joan of Arc, Spring Hill, FL
Rebello, Rev. Hendrico, *S.A.C.* '06 (DET) St. Anne Parish Monroe, Monroe, MI
Rebello, Rev. Hendrico, *SAC* '06 (DET) [MON] Society of the Catholic Apostolate-Indian Province of the State of Michigan, Redford, MI
Rebello, Rev. Henry, *S.A.C.* '06 (DET) St. Charles Borromeo Parish Newport, Newport, MI
Rebello, Rev. Valentine D., '89 (RVC) St. Pius X, Plainview, NY
Rebeta, Rev. James, (NY) St. Augustine, Larchmont, NY
Rebeyro, Rev. Lloyd, '70 (ALB) Retired.
Reboli, Rev. John P., *S.J.* '70 (WOR) [MON] Jesuits of the Holy Cross, Inc., Worcester, MA
Reboli, Rev. John P., *S.J.* '70 (BO) [MON] Campion Health & Wellness, Inc., Weston, MA
Rebolledo, Rev. Cesar A, '97 (CAM) Saint Mary of Mount Carmel Parish, Hammonton, N.J., Hammonton, NJ
Rebosura, Rev. Sabino (Benny), '87 (HT) Curia: Administration
Rebuldela, Rev. Alfred, '72 (HON) Retired.
Reburiano, Rev. V. Mark P., '05 (SFR) St. Gregory, San Mateo, CA
Recana, Rev. Brando, *C.P.* '97 (NY) [MON] The Congregation of the Passion - St. Paul of the Cross Province, Jamaica, NY
Receconi, Rev. Edward R., *O.S.B.* '79 (SEA) Retired. [MON] St. Martin's Abbey, Lacey, WA
Recera, Rev. Manuel, '85 (MRY) Holy Cross, Santa Cruz, CA
Recio, Rev. Dennis C., *S.J.* '04 (SFR) [MON] Loyola House Jesuit Community, San Francisco, CA
Recker, Rev. Anthony L., '09 (TOL) All Saints, Rossford, OH; St. Paul, Norwalk, OH
Recker, Rev. Odo, *O.S.B.* '78 (P) [MON] Mt. Angel Abbey, Saint Benedict, OR; [SEM] Mount Angel Seminary, Saint Benedict, OR
Recker, Rev. Philip F., '59 (DUB) Retired.
Recker, Rev. Ralph, *O.S.B.* '09 (P) St. Mary, Mount Angel, OR; [MON] Mt. Angel Abbey, Saint Benedict, OR
Reckers, Rev. Andrew M, '20 (CIN) Holy Angels, Sidney, OH; Sacred Heart of Jesus, Anna, OH
Reckker, Rev. Stephen C., '63 (DET) St. Clement of Rome Parish Romeo, Romeo, MI
Rector, Rev. Warren, *OFM* '68 (GB) Retired. [MON] Assumption of B.V.M. Friary, Pulaski, WI
Rector, Rev. Warren, *OFM* (MIL) [MON] Queen of Peace Friary (Franciscan Friars of the Assumption B.V.M. Province), Burlington, WI
Reczek, Rev. Paul, *OFM* '72 (FTW) [CON] Our Lady of the Angels Convent, Mishawaka, IN
Redcay, Rev. Christopher, '89 (PH) St. Patrick, Malvern, PA
Reddick, Rev. E. Peter, '72 (SY) Retired.
Reddimasu, Rev. Sraven Kumar, (WH) Our Lady of Perpetual Help, Stonewood, WV
Reddy, Rev. Pentareddy Baltha, '95 (BIR) Holy Rosary, Birmingham, AL; [EFT] St. Barnabas Catholic Education Foundation, Birmingham, AL
Redfern, Rev. D. Joseph, '06 (LC) St. Mary Help of Christians, Colby, WI; [EFT] St. Mary's Catholic School, Colby Endowment Trust, Colby, WI
Reding, Rev. Michael A., '97 (STP) Carondelet Catholic School, Minneapolis, MN; St. Thomas the Apostle, Minneapolis, MN
Redington, Rev. James D., *S.J.* '78 (SCR) [COL] The University of Scranton, Scranton, PA
Redito, Rev. Benedict, '91 (PMB) St. John Fisher, West Palm Beach, FL
Redmond, Rev. Nicholas E., '18 (RIC) St. John the Evangelist, Highland Springs, VA
Redmond, Rev. Nicholas E., '18 (RIC) Chap, College of William & Mary St. Patrick, Richmond, VA; St. Peter, Richmond, VA
Redmond, Rev. Paul, (KAL) St. Thomas More Student Parish, Kalamazoo, MI; [CAM] Western Michigan University, Kalamazoo College, Kalamazoo Valley Community College, Kalamazoo, MI
Redolad, Rev. Esteve, '96 (MIL) [MIS] Community of St.

Paul, Inc., Racine, WI
Redstone, Rev. James, '90 (NEW) Retired.
Redulla, Rev. Msgr. Arsenio C., '74 (LUB) Retired. St. Elizabeth's, Snyder, TX
Redulla, Rev. Msgr. Arsenio C., (LUB) St. John, Hermleigh, TX
Redulla, Rev. Flordito, *S.V.D.* '83 (FRS) Chap, North Kern State Prison, Delano
Redwanski, Rev. Dale H., *O.S.C.* '71 (DET) Retired.
Reece, Rev. Richard T., *O.S.F.S.* '65 (PH) [MON] Villa de Sales Oblate Residence, Wyndmoor, PA
Reed, Rev. Bradley, (SP) Sacred Heart, Pinellas Park, FL
Reed, Rev. Daniel J., '84 (CLV) St. Martin of Tours, Valley City, OH; [CCH] Parishes with Ministry to Spanish Speaking: St. Bernard, Akron, OH
Reed, Rev. David, '05 (FRS) Retired.
Reed, Rev. Msgr. Douglas, '71 (R) Retired.
Reed, Rev. Joseph, '07 (KNX) Curia: Leadership St. John Neumann, Farragut, TN
Reed, Rev. Msgr. Michael V., '84 (PT) Chap, Blackwater Corr Inst Curia: Leadership St. Rose of Lima, Milton, FL
Reed, Rev. Msgr. Michael V., '84 (PT) Curia: Leadership; Offices and Directors
Reed, Rev. William C., '74 (NEW) Retired.
Reedy, Rev. Brian, *S.J.* (MO) Curia: Offices and Directors
Reehil, Rev. Daniel J., '14 (NSH) Curia: Leadership St. Catherine, Columbia, TN
Rees, Rev. Clement, *O.S.B.* '15 (SP) [MON] St. Leo Abbey, Saint Leo, FL
Reese, Rev. David J., '08 (RCK) St. Ambrose, Erie, IL; St. Catherine, Prophetstown, IL
Reese, Rev. Edward, *S.J.* '73 (SFR) [MON] Jesuit Community at St. Ignatius College Preparatory, San Francisco, CA
Reese, Rev. Edward A., *S.J.* '73 (SFR) Chap, San Francisco Fire Department St. Ignatius College Preparatory (Coed), San Francisco, CA
Reese, Rev. Matthew A., '02 (ALT) Our Lady of the Alleghenies, Lilly, PA
Reese, Rev. Philip Neri, *O.P.* '15 (PRO) [MON] St. Thomas Aquinas Priory at Providence College, Providence, RI
Reese, Rev. Robert P., '89 (ALT) St. Joan of Arc, Fallentimber, PA; St. Thomas Aquinas, Ashville, PA
Reese, Rev. Thomas J., *S.J.* '74 (WDC) [MON] Leonard Neale House, Washington, DC; [MON] The Jesuit Community of St. Aloysius Gonzaga, Washington, DC
Reesman, Very Rev. Nathan D., '06 (MIL) Curia: Leadership Congregation of the Immaculate Conception, West Bend, WI; St. Frances Cabrini Congregation, West Bend, WI
Reeson, Rev. David G., '80 (OM) [EFT] Saint Robert Bellarmine Parish Foundation, Omaha, NE
Reeson, Rev. David G., '80 (OM) St. Robert Bellarmine, Omaha, NE
Reeve, Rev. Christopher A., *C.R.I.C.* '17 (LA) [MON] Canons Regular of the Immaculate Conception, Santa Paula, CA
Reeves, Rev. Joseph, '76 (BAK) Retired.
Reeves, Rev. Marc, *S.J.* '05 (LA) Curia: Advisory Boards, Commissions, Committees, and Councils; Offices and Directors [MON] Jesuit Community, Los Angeles, CA
Reeves, Rev. Mark Thomas, '02 (MIA) Retired.
Reeves, Rev. Steven, '19 (L) St. Monica, Bardstown, KY; St. Thomas, Bardstown, KY
Reeves, Rev. Thomas, *OCD* '08 (SJ) [MON] Carmelite Monastery, Novitiate, San Jose, CA
Refermat, Rev. Thomas G., (CHI) St. Benedict, Chicago, IL
Reffner, Rev. Joseph, (MO) Curia: Offices and Directors
Reffner, Rev. Joseph, (POC) Military Chap
Refosco, Very Rev. Fabio, *C.O.* '04 (CHR) Curia: Advisory Boards, Commissions, Committees, and Councils; Deaneries St. Anne Catholic School, Rock Hill, SC; St. Philip Neri, Fort Mill, SC; [MON] Oratory of St. Philip Neri, Congregation of the Oratory of Pontifical Rite, Rock Hill, SC
Regalado, Rev. Ramiro, '19 (CC) Most Precious Blood, Corpus Christi, TX
Regalado, Rev. Ricardo, '21 (DAL) St. Mark the Evangelist Catholic Parish, Plano, TX
Regales, Rev. Oriol, '01 (MIL) St. Andrew's Congregation, Delavan, WI; St. Catherine's Congregation, Sharon, WI; St. Patrick's Congregation, Elkhorn, WI
Regan, Rev. David, (RVC) Holy Name of Mary, Valley Stream, NY; St. Gertrude's, Bayville, NY
Regan, Rev. Msgr. Dennis M., '64 (RVC) Retired.
Regan, Rev. John, '89 (JOL) St. Mary Immaculate, Plainfield, IL
Regan, Rev. Kevin J., '08 (WDC) On Special Assignment. Curia: Clergy and Religious Services Holy Family, Hillcrest Heights, MD
Regan, Rt. Rev. Patrick, *O.S.B.* '65 (NO) Retired.
Regan, Rev. Richard J., '85 (SAN) Retired.
Regan, Rev. Robert, '15 (CHI) Two Holy Martyrs Parish, Chicago, IL
Regan, Rev. Terrence P., '68 (GF) Retired.
Regan, Rev. Thomas, *S.J.* (NY) [MON] Jesuit Community at Fordham University, New York, NY
Regan, Rev. Timothy J., '91 (DAV) Chap, Univ of Iowa Hosps and Clinics
Reger, Rev. George L., '69 (BUF) Retired.
Reginato, Rev. Julian, '64 (GR) Retired.
Reginato, Rev. Julian, (PHX) Prince of Peace Roman Catholic Parish Sun City West, Sun City West, AZ
Regojo, Rev. Oscar, '10 (FTW) [MIS] Prelature of the Holy Cross and Opus Dei, South Bend, IN
Regojo, Rev. Oscar, '10 (POD) Curia: Clergy and Religious Services
Regojo, Rev. Oscar, *OP Dei* '18 (PMB) [MIS] Prelature of the Holy Cross and Opus Dei, Delray Beach, FL
Regoli, Rev. Msgr. John A., '61 (GBG) Retired. [NUR] St. Anne Home, Greensburg, PA
Regotti, Rev. Benjamin R., *O.F.M.Cap.* '79 (PH) Chap, Philadelphia Fed Detention Ctr St. John the Evangelist, Philadelphia, PA
Regula, Rev. Gary R., '00 (PHX) Curia: Leadership; Offices and Directors St. Jerome Roman Catholic Parish, Phoenix, AZ
Regula, Rev. Ronald R., '57 (NEW) Retired.
Regynski, Rev. Larry, '95 (SFS) Holy Trinity Parish of Beadle County, Huron, SD
Rehagen, Rev. Christopher, *C.S.C.* '15 (FTW) [COL] University of Notre Dame Du Lac, Notre Dame, IN; [MON] Holy Cross Community, Corby Hall, University of Notre Dame, Notre Dame, IN
Rehrauer, Rev. Matthew J., '92 (SPC) St. Agnes, Sarcoxie, MO; St. Mary, Pierce City, MO
Rehrauer, Rev. Stephen, *C.Ss.R.* '80 (CHI) (>TUC) [MON] Redemptorist Society of Arizona Desert House of Prayer Residence, Tucson, AZ; (>TUC) [RTR] Desert House of Prayer Retreat House, Tucson, AZ; (>TUC) [RTR] Redemptorist Society of Arizona Redemptorist Renewal Center, Tucson, AZ
Reich, Rev. Paul A., *S.M.* '57 (CIN) Retired.
Reichardt, Rev. Jack, '20 (RCK) On Special Assignment. Dir., Vocations Office, Curia Curia: Clergy and Religious Services St. Bridget, Loves Park, IL
Reichenbacher, Rev. Charles, *O.S.B.* '67 (RCK) [MON] Marmion Abbey, Aurora, IL
Reicher, Rev. A. Paul, '62 (CHI) Retired. Our Lady of the Holy Family, Chicago, IL
Reichert, Rev. Msgr. James J., '71 (ALN) Retired. Curia: Leadership St. Rocco, Martins Creek, PA
Reichert, Rev. Kenneth, *O.S.B.* '59 (KC) [MON] Conception Abbey (Benedictine Monks), Conception, MO
Reichlen, Rev. Gregory A., '08 (SCR) St. John's Church, East Stroudsburg, PA
Reichling, Rev. David, *O.F.M.Cap.* '67 (GF) St. Bernard, Billings, MT
Reichling, Rev. Paul, (GB) Retired.
Reicks, Rev. Allan, '76 (SC) Retired.
Reid, Rev. Adam R., '05 (WOR) Curia: Leadership; Offices and Directors Sacred Heart of Jesus, Webster, MA
Reid, Rev. David, *SS.CC.* '66 (WDC) St. Margaret, Seat Pleasant, MD
Reid, Rev. Henry W., '06 (RVC) Curia: Leadership Our Lady of Mt. Carmel, Patchogue, NY
Reid, Rev. Malcolm, '57 (CHY) Retired.
Reid, Rev. Mark R, (ALT) [CAM] Juniata College, Huntington, PA
Reid, Rev. Mark R., '07 (ALT) Immaculate Conception, Dudley, PA; Most Holy Trinity, Huntingdon, PA
Reid, Rev. Msgr. Michael J., '78 (BRK) Curia: Leadership; Organizations (affiliated, inter-Diocesan, miscellaneous/other) [CEM] Saint John's Cemetery, Middle Village, NY; [CEM] St. Mary Star of the Sea Cemetery, Far Rockaway, NY; [EFT] Compostela Corporation of the Roman Catholic Diocese of Brooklyn, New York, Brooklyn, NY; [EFT] Good Shepherd Charitable Trust, Brooklyn, NY; [EFT] Parish Assistance Charitable Trust Fund, Brooklyn, NY; [EFT] Saint Vincent DePaul Charitable Trust, Brooklyn, NY; [EFT] St. Elizabeth Ann Seton Charitable Trust, Brooklyn, NY; [EFT] St. John Vianney Fund Charitable Trust, Brooklyn, NY; [EFT] The Roman Catholic Diocese of Brooklyn, New York Group Medical Insurance Trust, Brooklyn, NY
Reid, Rev. Michael P., '00 (HBG) St. Vincent de Paul, Hanover, PA
Reid, Rev. Nicholas J., '11 (JC) On Duty Outside Diocese. Service in the Archdiocese for the Military Services Curia: (>MO) Offices and Directors
Reid, Rev. R. Michael, '69 (RVC) Retired. Chap, Holly Patterson Geriatric Ctr
Reid, Rev. R. Michael, '67 (RVC) [MON] St Pius X Residence for Retired Priests LLC, Ronkonkoma, NY
Reid, Very Rev. Timothy S., '04 (CHL) Curia: Leadership St. Ann Catholic Church, Charlotte, NC
Reidy, Rev. James E., '56 (STP) Retired.
Reidy, Rev. Richard F., '94 (WOR) Curia: Offices and Directors
Reidy, Rev. Richard F., '94 (WOR) Curia: Advisory Boards, Commissions, Committees, and Councils; Finance; Leadership; Offices and Directors Christ the King, Worcester, MA; St. Paul, Warren, MA; St. Stanislaus, West Warren, MA
Reidy, Rev. Msgr. Robert, '62 (Y) Retired.
Reidy, Rev. Robert J., '75 (CLV) Mary, Queen of the Apostles Parish, Brook Park, OH; [CCH] Hispanic Parishes: Iglesia La Sagrada Familia, Cleveland, OH
Reidy, Rev. Msgr. Thomas E., '67 (SPC) Chap, US Med Ctr, Springfield Curia: Consultative Bodies Immaculate Conception, Springfield, MO
Reif, Rev. Bryan T., '01 (CIN) St. Ann, Cincinnati, OH; St. Bernard, Cincinnati, OH; St. James the Greater, Cincinnati, OH
Reif, Rev. John, '65 (ROC) Retired.
Reifenberg, Very Rev. Philip D., '79 (MIL) Congregation of St. John the Baptist, Plymouth, WI; St. Thomas Aquinas Congregation, Elkhart Lake, WI; [MIS] The Sheboygan County Catholic Fund, Inc., Sheboygan, WI
Reiff, Rev. Dennis E., '81 (NEW) Retired.
Reigle, Rev. Gordon P., '05 (LAN) St. Thomas Aquinas Parish East Lansing, East Lansing, MI
Reigler, Rev. Frederick J., (PH) Retired.
Reiker, Rev. John, '78 (STL) St. Anthony Catholic Church, High Ridge, High Ridge, MO
Reiker, Rev. Robert J., '73 (STL) St. Bernadette Catholic Church, Lemay, MO; St. Raphael the Archangel Catholic Church, St. Louis, MO
Reiley, Rev. Robert J., *M.M.* '59 (NY) Retired. [MON] Maryknoll Fathers and Brothers (Catholic Foreign Mission Society of America, Inc.), Ossining, NY
Reilley, Rev. Patrick R., '10 (WCH) Curia: Leadership
Reilly, Rev. Msgr. Bernard, '73 (LAN) Retired.
Reilly, Rev. David F., '75 (CIN) Retired.
Reilly, Rev. Denis, (OAK) Retired.
Reilly, Rev. Donald F., *O.S.A.* '74 (PH) Malvern Preparatory School for Boys, Malvern, PA; [MON] Augustinian Friars (O.S.A.), Malvern, PA
Reilly, Rev. Francis E., '80 (SPR) [CEM] St. Jerome Cemetery, ,
Reilly, Rev. Francis Eugene, '80 (SPR) St. Jerome, Holyoke, MA
Reilly, Rev. George M., '60 (NEW) Retired. Our Lady of Mt. Virgin, Garfield, NJ
Reilly, Rev. James, '68 (NEW) Retired.
Reilly, Rev. James J., '68 (NEW) Retired. [MON] St. John Vianney Residence for Retired Priests, Rutherford, NJ
Reilly, Rev. Msgr. Joseph R., '91 (NEW) [COL] Seton Hall University, South Orange, NJ
Reilly, Rev. Kevin M., '03 (NOR) Curia: Offices and Directors St. Patrick, Mystic, CT
Reilly, Rt. Rev. Lambert, *O.S.B.* '59 (IND) [MON] St. Meinrad Archabbey, St. Meinrad, IN
Reilly, Very Rev. Lawrence, '64 (YAK) Retired. Curia: Leadership St Joseph Parish, Kennewick, WA
Reilly, Rev. Mark R., '97 (OG) Curia: Consultative Bodies St. Peter's Parish, Massena, NY
Reilly, Rev. Michael J., '01 (PH) St. Jerome, Philadelphia, PA
Reilly, Rev. Michael P., '92 (NY) St. Joseph by the Sea, High School, Staten Island, NY
Reilly, Rev. Msgr. Philip J., '60 (BRK) Retired.
Reilly, Rev. Steven, *L.C.* '94 (ATL) [MON] Legionaries of Christ, Incorporated, Cumming, GA
Reilly, Rev. Thomas J., '00 (BO) St. Florence, Wakefield, MA
Reilly, Rev. Thomas W., *M.Afr.* '78 (WDC) Retired. (>SP) [MON] Missionaries of Africa, St. Petersburg, FL
Reilly, Rev. Timothy D., '03 (PRO) [CON] St. Clare Convent, Cutting Memorial (The Saint Clare Home), Providence, RI
Reilly, Rev. Timothy D., '03 (PRO) Saint Luke's Church Corporation, Barrington, Barrington, RI
Reilly, Rev. Timothy D., '03 (PRO) Curia: Advisory Boards, Commissions, Committees, and Councils; Leadership Church of Our Lady of Charity of Providence, Providence, RI; Church of St. Maron in Providence, Providence, RI; Holy Angel's Church

Corporation, Barrington, RI; [MIS] Miscellaneous Listings for the Diocese of Providence, Providence, RI
Reilly, Rev. Msgr. William J., '65 (NEW) Most Holy Name, Garfield, NJ
Reilman, Rev. Thomas J., '61 (DAV) Retired.
Reim, Rev. Daniel, (CLV) St. Ignatius High School, Cleveland, OH
Reiman, Rev. Matthew W., '15 (NY) Parish of Holy Name of Mary - Assumption, Montgomery, NY; St. Francis Xavier, Bronx, NY
Reimer, Rev. Lawrence H., (DAL) On Administrative Leave.
Reina, Rev. Nicholas, *S.B.D.* '78 (SFR) [MON] Salesian Provincial Residence, San Francisco, CA
Reina, Rev. Richard A., '70 (BUF) Retired.
Reinbold, Rev. Charles, '56 (NEW) Retired.
Reinders, Rev. David H., '97 (TUC) On Leave.
Reinders, Rev. David H., (ARL) St. Peter, Washington, VA
Reinersman, Rev. Msgr. Gerald L., '79 (COV) Curia: Advisory Boards, Commissions, Committees, and Councils; Leadership Bishop Brossart High School, Alexandria, KY; St. Joseph, Cold Spring, KY
Reinert, Rev. Duane F., *O.F.M.Cap.* '76 (KC) [SEM] Conception Seminary College, Conception, MO
Reinert, Rev. Duane F., *O.F.M.Cap.* '76 (KCK) [MON] St. Conrad Friary, Lawrence, KS
Reinhardt, Rev. Leo J., '78 (ROC) Our Lady of the Lakes Catholic Community, Penn Yan, NY; [CAM] Keuka College c/o Our Lady of the Lakes, Penn Yan, NY
Reinhardt, Rev. Michael Fredrik, '21 (STP) All Saints, Lakeville, MN
Reinhart, Rev. James M., '10 (L) Retired. On Duty Outside Diocese. Chicago Ridge, IL
Reinhart, Rev. Robert J., '61 (TOL) Retired.
Reinke, Rev. Robert J., '49 (COV) Retired.
Reinoso, Rev. Carlos Ernesto, '01 (MAD) Queen of All Saints, Fennimore, WI
Reis, Rev. Daniel O., '75 (FR) Retired.
Reis, Rev. Lancelot, '67 (PAT) Retired.
Reis, Very Rev. Timothy P., '86 (FR) Curia: Leadership St. Mary's, Norton, MA
Reisenauer, Rev. Augustine, *O.P.* (PRO) [MON] St. Thomas Aquinas Priory at Providence College, Providence, RI
Reiser, Rev. Anastasius, *osb* '99 (OM) [MON] Benedictine Mission House - Christ the King Priory, Schuyler, NE
Reiser, Rev. Richard J., '80 (OM) St. John Vianney, Omaha, NE
Reiser, Rev. Robert E., *S.J.* '77 (WDC) [MIS] Jesuit Schools Network, Washington, DC; [MON] The Jesuit Community of St. Aloysius Gonzaga, Washington, DC
Reiser, Rev. William E., *S.J.* '72 (WOR) Curia: Offices and Directors [MON] Jesuits of the Holy Cross, Inc., Worcester, MA
Reisert, Rev. Gregory, *OFMCap* '64 (NY) [MON] The Province of St. Mary of the Capuchin Order, White Plains, NY
Reising, Rev. Christopher, (DM) Curia: Offices and Directors St. Anthony's, Des Moines, IA
Reiter, Rev. Edard, *M.S.A.* '79 (NOR) Retired. [MON] Society of the Missionaries of the Holy Apostles, Cromwell, CT
Reith, Very Rev. David H., '76 (MIL) Curia: Leadership [CCH] Catholic Charities of the Archdiocese of Milwaukee, Inc., St. Francis, WI; [MIS] Catholic Charities Foundation, Inc., St. Francis, WI
Reither, Rev. Timothy M., '21 (LC) Holy Rosary, Durand, WI; Sacred Heart of Jesus, Mondovi, WI; St. Mary's Assumption, Durand, WI; [EFT] St. Mary Catholic School Endowment Trust, Durand, WI
Reitmeyer, Rev. Thomas, '15 (AUS) Curia: Tribunal St. Vincent de Paul, Austin, TX; [EFT] Diocese of Austin Pension Plan and Trust, Austin, TX
Reitter, Rev. Frank, '84 (AJ) St. Francis Xavier, Valdez, AK
Reitz, Rev. Andrew, *O.F.M.* '71 (TR) St. Francis of Assisi, Long Beach Township, NJ
Reitz, Rev. Glenn, (STL) [HOS] SSM Health De Paul Hospital - St. Louis, Bridgeton, MO
Reitz, Rev. Louis M., *P.S.S.* '55 (BAL) Retired. [MON] Society of St. Sulpice, Province of the United States, Baltimore, MD
Reker, Rev. Timothy, '82 (WIN) [CEM] Calvary Cemetery Association, Mankato, MN
Reker, Rev. Timothy T., '82 (WIN) Curia: Advisory Boards, Commissions, Committees, and Councils Holy Family, Lake Crystal, MN; St. Joseph the Worker, Mankato, MN
Rekiel, Rev. Thomas, (PAT) Curia: Leadership Holy Family, Florham Park, NJ
Relihan, Rev. Thomas, '47 (SAC) Retired. Pastor of St. Katharine Drexel Parish, Martell, a corporation sole, Jackson, CA
Rella, Very Rev. Francis J., '12 (PSC) Curia: Leadership; (>MO) Offices and Directors Our Lady of Perpetual Help, Toms River, NJ
Reller, Rev. Gary W., '71 (HEL) Retired. Curia: Leadership
Relles, Rev. Arnold, '94 (RCK) St. Patrick, St. Charles, IL
Remick, Rev. Todd M., '06 (BUF) Curia: Leadership; Offices and Directors Holy Apostles, Jamestown, NY; St. James, Jamestown, NY
Remillard, Rev. Andre N., '70 (WOR) Retired.
Remington, Rev. Leo, '65 (P) Retired.
Remke, Rev. Raymond J., '88 (BIR) Curia: Offices and Directors St. Peter the Apostle Catholic Parish, Birmingham, Birmingham, AL
Remm, Rev. George F., '60 (PEO) Retired.
Remmerswaal, Rev. James H., *O.S.C.* '65 (SCL) [MON] Crosier Priory, Onamia, MN
Remmes, Rev. Richard R., '62 (SC) Retired.
Remo, Rev. Allan Roy, (SFR) Holy Name of Jesus, San Francisco, CA
Remo, Rev. Roy, (SFR) Curia: Offices and Directors
Remski, Rev. Howard, *F.S.S.P.* (IND) Oratory of SS. Philomena and Cecilia Catholic Church, Brookville, Inc., Brookville, IN
Remy, Rev. David P., '67 (DUB) Retired.
Remy, Rev. Dickens, '02 (SD) Pastor of Holy Spirit Catholic Parish, San Diego, a corporation sole, San Diego, CA; [MIS] Holy Spirit Catholic Parish in San Diego, CA Real Property Support Corporation, San Diego, CA
Renard, Rev. Eugene C., *S.J.* '60 (STL) [RTR] Retreat House, ,
Renard, Rev. John F., '65 (NEW) Retired.
Renard, Rev. Peter J., *O. Praem.* '68 (GB) [MON] St. Norbert Abbey, De Pere, WI
Renaud, Rev. Daniel, *OMI* '03 (SAT) [COL] Oblate School of Theology, San Antonio, TX; [MON] Missionary Oblates of Mary Immaculate of Texas, San Antonio, TX
Render, Rev. Patrick, *C.S.V.* '68 (JOL) Retired. St. Patrick, Kankakee, IL
Render, Rev. Patrick W., *C.S.V.* '68 (CHI) [MON] Viatorian Province Center-Clerics of St. Viator, Arlington Heights, IL
Rendon, Rev. Daniel, '16 (DAL) San Juan Diego Catholic Parish, Dallas, TX; [SEM] The Redemptoris Mater House of Formation (Redemptoris Mater Seminary), Dallas, TX
Rendon, Rev. Matthias, *OFM* (ALT) SS. Peter and Paul, Philipsburg, PA
Rendon, Rev. Msgr. Nicolas, '76 (LUB) Retired.
Rendon, Rev. Samuel, '92 (LA) On Sick Leave.
Renggli, Rev. John J., '68 (SEA) Retired.
Reniva, Rev. Cary, '09 (P) On Academic Leave. Curia: Offices and Directors
Reniva, Rev. Raphael, '19 (MRY) Old Mission Church (Mission San Luis Obispo de Tolosa), San Luis Obispo, CA
Renken, Rev. Msgr. John, '79 (SFD) On Duty Outside Diocese. Ottawa, ON
Renne, Rev. David M., '13 (E) On Duty Outside Diocese. The Catholic University of America, Washington D.C. Curia: Clergy and Religious Services [COL] Gannon University, Erie, PA; [SEM] St. Mark Seminary, Erie, PA
Renner, Very Rev. Christopher A., '91 (DEN) Curia: Deaneries Spirit of Christ Catholic Parish in Arvada, Arvada, CO
Renner, Rev. Frank G., '81 (EVN) Blessed Sacrament, Oakland City, IN; SS. Peter and Paul, Petersburg, IN
Renner, Rev. Robert, (ARL) St. Mary of the Immaculate Conception, Fredericksburg, VA
Rennier, Rev. Michael, '16 (STL) Epiphany of Our Lord Catholic Church, St. Louis, MO
Renninger, Very Rev. Michael A., '93 (RIC) Curia: Deaneries St. Mary, Richmond, VA
Rensburg, Rev. Charles, *OMI* '06 (CHI) [EFT] Oblates for International Pastoral (Oblate International Pastoral Investment Trust), Chicago, IL
Rensch, Rev. Matthew, (BUR) Chap, State Hosp St. Andrew, Waterbury, VT
Renteria, Rev. Javier, *Sch.P.* '83 (PH) [MON] Piarist Fathers (Order of the Pious Schools), Devon, PA
Rentner, Rev. Randall C, (COS) Sacred Heart, Colorado Springs, CO
Rento, Rev. Richard G., '58 (PAT) Retired.
Renz, Rev. Christopher J., *O.P.* '97 (OAK) [MON] Order of Preachers (Province of the Most Holy Name of Jesus - Western Dominican Province), Oakland, CA; [SEM] Dominican School of Philosophy and Theology, Berkeley, CA
Renz, Very Rev. Timothy J., '11 (MAD) St. Joseph, Fort Atkinson, WI
Repko, Rev. Cyril, *O.F.M. Cap.* '62 (PIT) [MON] St. Augustine Friary, Pittsburgh, PA
Repko, Rev. Joseph, '95 (PRM) Curia: Advisory Boards, Commissions, Committees, and Councils; (>MO) Offices and Directors St. Mary, Marblehead, OH
Replogle, Rev. John, *S.J.* (NY) Xavier High School, New York, NY
Replogle, Rev. John F., *S.J.* '64 (NY) [MON] Murray-Weigel Hall (A Jesuit Community at Murray-Weigel Hall and Kohlmann Hall), Bronx, NY
Repollet, Rev. Pedro, '14 (NEW) Curia: Advisory Boards, Commissions, Committees, and Councils Our Lady of Mt. Carmel, Jersey City, NJ
Reque, Rev. Francis M., *O.S.B.* '00 (BIR) [MON] St. Bernard Abbey, Cullman, AL
Resen, Rev. W. Patrick, '07 (KNX) Retired.
Resila, Rev. Nathaniel, (ALB) Parish of Our Lady of the Snow, Grafton, NY
Resinto, Rev. E.J., '16 (HON) Curia: Consultative Bodies
Resinto, Rev. EJ, '16 (HON) Sacred Heart, Honolulu, HI
Reskey, Rev. George A., '73 (MOB) Retired.
Resop, Rev. Michael A., '79 (MAD) Our Lady of the Assumption, Beloit, WI
Ressler, Rev. Clint C., '93 (GAL) St. Mary of the Miraculous Medal, Texas City, TX
Ressler, Rev. Mark A., '76 (DUB) Retired. [CON] Mt. Loretto Convent, Dubuque, IA
Restituyo, Rev. Elvi J, *OSA* '14 (MGZ) St. Francis of Assisi, Aguada, PR
Restrepo, Rev. Adriano H., (BRK) St. Rita, Long Island City, NY
Restrepo, Rev. Francisco, '88 (DET) St. Matthias Parish Sterling Heights, Sterling Heights, MI
Restrepo, Rev. Jaime, (SCR) Curia: Offices and Directors Most Holy Trinity Parish, Cresco, PA; St. Matthew, East Stroudsburg, PA
Restrepo, Rev. Jairo, '92 (B) On Duty Outside Diocese.
Restrepo, Rev. John, *OP* '04 (LUB) St. Elizabeth University Parish, Lubbock, TX
Restrepo, Rev. Juan Camilo, '12 (NEW) Corpus Christi, Hasbrouck Heights, NJ
Restrepo, Rev. Nelson, '01 (SP) St. Joseph, Tampa, FL
Restrepo, Rev. Ruben D., *C.M.* '97 (LA) St. Matthias, Huntington Park, CA
Restrepo, Rev. Steven, '22 (BO) St. Thomas Aquinas, Bridgewater, MA
Restrepo Prisco, Rev. Jose Luis, (LAR) San Agustin Cathedral, Laredo, TX
Restreppo, Rev. Martin, (BRK) Saint Athanasius - Saint Dominic, Brooklyn, NY
Restrick, Rev. Jacob, *O.P.* '89 (WDC) St. Dominic Church & Priory, Washington, DC
Restrick, Friar Jacob, *OP* (NY) [CON] Motherhouse & Novitiate of the Sisters of St. Dominic, Congregation of St. Rose of Lima, Hawthorne, NY; [MON] St. Vincent Ferrer Priory, New York, NY
Reszel, Rev. Marc W., '88 (CHI) St. John of the Cross, Western Springs, IL
Retar, Rev. John C., '03 (CLV) Curia: Advisory Boards, Commissions, Committees, and Councils St. Vitus, Cleveland, OH; [MIS] Joseph House of Cleveland, Inc., Cleveland, OH; [MIS] St. Vitus Development Corporation, Cleveland, OH
Rettger, Rev. Thaddeus E., *O.S.B.* '74 (ALT) St. Bernard, Hastings, PA
Rettger, Rev. Thaddeus E., *O.S.B.* '74 (GBG) [MON] Saint Vincent Archabbey, Latrobe, PA
Rettig, Rev. Donald R., '71 (CIN) Retired. St. Vincent de Paul, Cincinnati, OH
Rettig, Rev. Kevin E., '84 (LA) Holy Angels, Arcadia, CA
Retzner, Rev. James, *O.S.A.* '95 (SD) Retired. [MON] Augustinian Community, San Diego, CA
Retzner, Rev. James P, *O.S.A.* '95 (SD) Retired.
Reuse, Rev. Patrick, *S.J.* '73 (SJ) [MON] Sacred Heart Jesuit Center, Los Gatos, CA
Reusing, Rev. James M., '94 (BAL) Retired.
Reutemann, Rev. John F., '10 (WDC) Chap, USAF Curia: (>MO) Offices and Directors
Reuter, Rev. John F., '67 (GB) Retired.
Reutter, Rev. James, '04 (CIN) Holy Family, Versailles, OH; Immaculate Conception, Bradford, OH; St. Denis, Versailles, OH; St. Louis, North Star, OH; St. Mary, Greenville, OH; St. Nicholas, Osgood, OH; St. Remy, Russia, OH
Reuwer, Rev. Daniel S., (ARL) All Saints, Manassas, VA
Revello, Rev. James K.I., '73 (DEN) Retired.

Revilla, Rev. Lazaro, '10 (LA) St. Mariana de Paredes, Pico Rivera, CA
Revilla, Rev. Leonard Mary, *M.F.V.A.* '12 (BIR) [MON] Franciscan Missionaries of the Eternal Word, A Public Clerical Association of the Christian Faithful, Irondale, AL
Revilla, Rev. Nicholas J., (OG) St. Peter's Parish, Massena, NY
Revuelto, Rev. Manuel, '59 (NEW) Retired.
Rewak, Rev. William J., *S.J.* '64 (SJ) [MON] Sacred Heart Jesuit Center, Los Gatos, CA
Rewtiuk, Rev. Msgr. Michael, '69 (SJP) Retired.
Rexroat, Rev. Benjamin, '16 (GLD) Curia: Offices and Directors Saint Joseph of Mapleton, Traverse City, MI
Reycraft, Rev. Robert J., '75 (DEN) Retired.
Reyes, Rev. Alejandro, '12 (LSC) Curia: Leadership Immaculate Heart of Mary Cathedral Parish, Inc., Las Cruces, NM; [MIS] Magnificat-Our Lady of the Cross Chapter, Inc., Mesilla, NM
Reyes, Rev. Andres J., '70 (NEW) Retired.
Reyes, Rev. Carlos Andres, *CS* (MIA) St. Vincent, Margate, FL
Reyes, Rev. Eider, '05 (PAT) St. Anthony's, Paterson, NJ
Reyes, Rev. Elky, '09 (NEW) St. Aloysius, Newark, NJ; St. Benedict, Newark, NJ
Reyes, Friar Emanuel, *S.F.M.* (SJN) Nuestra Senora del Pilar, San Juan, PR
Reyes, Rev. Emilio, *S.V.D.* '85 (LA) (>OAK) St. Joachim, Hayward, CA
Reyes, Rev. Felino, '89 (BRK) Blessed Sacrament - Saint Sylvester, Brooklyn, NY
Reyes, Rev. Felino, '89 (NY) Immaculate Conception, Yonkers, NY
Reyes, Rev. Felix, *C.R.L.* '09 (NY) St. Teresa of Avila, Sleepy Hollow, NY
Reyes, Rev. Francisco Javier, *C.M.F.* '09 (CHI) [MON] Claret House (Formation Residence), Chicago, IL
Reyes, Rev. Jaime, *O.S.B.* '64 (FAJ) [MON] San Antonio Abad Abbey of the Order of St. Benedict, Humacao, PR
Reyes, Rev. Jesse A., (CHK) Curia: Consultative Bodies
Reyes, Rev. Jesse T., '07 (CHK) Curia: Faith Formation San Vicente Parish, Saipan, MP
Reyes, Rev. Jesus, *C.S.* '93 (CHI) [MON] Scalabrini House of Theology, Chicago, IL
Reyes, Rev. Jorge A., *O.S.A.* (ALB) On Special Assignment. Chap Spanish Apostolate, St Mary's, Waterford
Reyes, Rev. Julio Herman, '20 (RIC) Our Lady of Perpetual Help, Salem, VA; St. Gerard, Roanoke, VA
Reyes, Rev. Louie, '20 (LA) St. Philip Neri, Lynwood, CA
Reyes, Rev. Marco D., '85 (LA) Sacred Heart, Ventura, CA; St. Linus, Norwalk, CA
Reyes, Rev. Michael, *OFM* '16 (BUF) St. Bonaventure, Allegany, NY; [MON] St. Bonaventure Friary, St. Bonaventure, NY
Reyes, Rev. Noel Beltran, '05 (CHI) St. Jerome, Chicago, IL
Reyes, Rev. Orlando, *O.F.M.Cap.* '12 (HBG) Holy Family, Harrisburg, PA; St. Francis of Assisi, Harrisburg, PA (>WDC) Shrine of the Sacred Heart, Washington, DC
Reyes, Rev. Ramiro, (LEX) Mary, Queen of the Holy Rosary, Lexington, KY
Reyes, Rev. Ramon, '22 (LA) Incarnation, Glendale, CA
Reyes, Friar Raul, *OCD* '69 (SAT) Basilica of the National Shrine of the Little Flower, Our Lady of Mt. Carmel and St. Therese Parish, San Antonio, TX; [MON] Discalced Carmelite Fathers of San Antonio, San Antonio, TX
Reyes, Rev. Raymond, (SFR) Curia: Offices and Directors
Reyes, Rev. Raymund M., '88 (SFR) Curia: Advisory Boards, Commissions, Committees, and Councils St. Augustine, South San Francisco, CA; [MIS] Catholic Charismatic Renewal (CCR), San Francisco, CA
Reyes, Rev. Victor J., '94 (ATL) On Sick Leave.
Reyes, Rev. Xamie M., '00 (CHI) Little Flower Parish, Waukegan, IL
Reyes, Rev. Yean, '20 (CGS) Santo Cristo de la Salud, Comerio, PR
Reyes Alba, Rev. Felix Antonio, *C.R.L.* (NY) Our Lady Queen of Martyrs, New York, NY; St. Jude, New York, NY
Reyes Cedillo, Rev. Jose, *C.O.R.C.* (SB) [MIS] Confraternity of Operarios Del Reino De Cristo, C.O.R.C., Corona, CA
Reyes Paulino, Rev. Luis Alberto, (ARE) San Juan Bautista, Orocovis, PR
Reyes Reyes, Rev. Erik, '22 (R) Holy Name of Jesus Cathedral, Raleigh, NC
Reyes-Cedillo, Rev. Jose, *C.O.R.C* (SB) Our Lady of Guadalupe, San Bernardino, CA
Reyes-Garced, Rev. Wilberto, *L.D.* '93 (NY) [MIS] Lumen Dei, New York, NY
Reyes-Lebron, Rev. Pedro L., '90 (SJN) San Jorge, San Juan, PR
Reyes-Lebron, Rev. Pedro Luis, '90 (SJN) Curia: Leadership
Reyes-Mata, Rev. Ricardo, '22 (DAL) St. Jude Catholic Parish, Allen, TX
Reyling, Very Rev. Mark D., '98 (BEL) Curia: Leadership Church of the Holy Spirit, Carterville, IL; Our Lady of Mount Carmel, Herrin, IL
Reynaga, Rev. J. Jesus, '04 (FRS) San Clemente Mission Parish, Bakersfield, CA; St. Joseph, Bakersfield, CA
Reynebeau, Rev. Thomas J., '87 (GB) Resurrection, Green Bay, WI
Reynierse, Rev. Peter, '95 (WDC) Retired.
Reynolds, Rev. Brad, *S.J.* '77 (SPK) [COL] Gonzaga University, Spokane, WA
Reynolds, Rev. George, '97 (LA) St. Cornelius, Long Beach, CA
Reynolds, Rev. J. Patrick, '80 (OWN) Curia: Advisory Boards, Commissions, Committees, and Councils; Leadership Our Lady of Lourdes, Owensboro, KY; [MIS] Owensboro Catholic Consolidated School System, Owensboro, KY
Reynolds, Rev. James J., '84 (BRK) Retired. [MON] Bishop Mugavero Residence, Douglaston, NY
Reynolds, Rev. John R., '83 (STA) On Special Assignment. Tribunal Judge
Reynolds, Rev. Kirk R., *S.J.* '79 (PAT) (>RVC) St. Anthony, Oceanside, NY
Reynolds, Friar Nicholas, *O.P.* '19 (GAL) Holy Rosary, Houston, TX
Reynolds, Rev. Rubin R., '79 (BR) Congregation Of St. Mark Roman Catholic Church, Gonzales, LA
Reynolds, Rev. Stephen B., '89 (GAL) Curia: Offices and Directors St. Elizabeth Ann Seton, Houston, TX
Reynolds, Rev. Taylor, '14 (ALX) Curia: Miscellaneous / Other Offices St. Joseph, St. Joseph, LA
Reynolds, Rev. Thomas, *S.S.C.* '61 (OM) [MON] Missionary Society of St. Columban, St. Columbans, NE
Reynolds, Rev. Thomas, *S.S.C.* '61 (LA) St. Hilary, Pico Rivera, CA
Reynolds, Rev. William E., '81 (DAV) Retired. Curia: Leadership
Reynoso, Rev. Ernesto, '07 (PHX) Curia: Leadership; Offices and Directors Our Lady of Perpetual Help Roman Catholic Parish, Glendale, AZ
Reynoso, Rev. Juan Carlos, '22 (FRS) St. Joseph, Bakersfield, CA
Reynoso, Rev. Marco Antonio, '11 (BWN) Saint Juan Diego Cuauhtlatoatzin, McAllen, TX
Rezac, Rev. Keith D., '87 (OM) St. Charles Borromeo, North Bend, NE; St. Leo, Snyder, NE
Rezende, Rev. Vinicius de Queiroz, '08 (KCK) [MON] St. Benedict's Abbey, Atchison, KS
Rezula, Rev. Leon J., '69 (CHI) Retired.
Rhinehart, Rev. Richard E., '18 (SUP) St. Albert, Land O'Lakes, WI; St. Kunegunda of Poland, Sugar Camp, WI; St. Mary, Phelps, WI; St. Peter the Fisherman, Eagle River, WI; St. Theresa, Three Lakes, WI
Rhinehart, Rev. William, *C.M.* '79 (STL) [MON] Congregation of the Mission, Perryville, MO
Rhodes, Rev. Christopher S., '12 (L) Curia: Leadership Christ the King, Louisville, KY; Immaculate Heart of Mary, Louisville, KY; St. Augustine, Louisville, KY
Rhodes, Rev. Msgr. David W., '65 (Y) Retired.
Ribbens, Rev. William H., *O. Praem.* '62 (GB) [MON] St. Norbert Abbey, De Pere, WI
Ribits, Rev. Thomas, *O.S.F.S.* '82 (BUF) [MIS] Salesian Studios, Buffalo, NY
Ricafort, Rev. Jovencio D., '82 (SD) Pastor of Mater Dei Catholic Parish, Chula Vista, a corporation sole, Chula Vista, CA; [MIS] Mater Dei Catholic Parish in Chula Vista, CA Real Property Support Corporation, Chula Vista, CA
Ricafranca, Rev. Joel R, (CHI) St. Jerome, Chicago, IL
Ricard, Rev. David F., '69 (PRO) Retired. St. Gregory the Great Church Corporation, Warwick, Warwick, RI
Ricard, Rev. Richard J., '98 (NOR) Curia: Leadership; Offices and Directors Blessed Sacrament Parish, Rockville, CT
Ricard, Rev. Rodney Anthony, '95 (NO) On Special Assignment. St. Augustine HS St. Gabriel the Archangel, New Orleans, LA
Ricarte, Rev. Antonio L., '98 (NEW) Our Lady Queen of Peace, Maywood, NJ
Ricaud, Rev. Fernando, (AUS) [CAM] University Catholic Center, Austin, TX
Ricca, Rev. Francis, '05 (MAR) Immaculate Conception, Moran, MI; St. Ignatius Loyola, St. Ignace, MI
Riccardi, Rev. Salvatore, *C.P.* '62 (NY) Retired. Parish of Annunciation-Our Lady of Fatima, Crestwood, NY; [MON] The Congregation of the Passion - St. Paul of the Cross Province, Jamaica, NY
Riccardo, Rev. John, '96 (DET) [MIS] Acts XXIX - Mobilizing for Mission, Detroit, MI
Riccardo, Rev. Msgr. Joseph J., '75 (E) SS. Cosmas and Damian, Punxsutawney, PA; [CAM] Indiana University of PA - Punxsutawney Campus, Punxsutawney, PA
Ricchini, Rev. Joseph, *O.F.M.* '64 (CIN) [MON] St. John the Baptist Friary, Cincinnati, OH
Ricci, Rev. Alfred V., '80 (PRO) St. Gregory the Great Church Corporation, Warwick, Warwick, RI
Ricci, Rev. Andrew P., '97 (SUP) Curia: Leadership; Offices and Directors Cathedral of Christ the King, Superior, WI; Holy Assumption, Superior, WI; St. Anthony, Superior, WI; St. Anthony Catholic Church, Lake Nebagamon, WI; St. Michael, Iron River, WI; St. William, Foxboro, WI
Ricci, Rev. Lorenzo, '06 (DEN) On Duty Outside Diocese.
Ricci, Rev. Nathan J., '16 (PRO) Curia: Clergy and Religious Services; Leadership; Offices and Directors [MIS] Bishop McVinney Auditorium, Providence, RI
Ricci, Rev. Msgr. Philip C., '65 (PH) Retired.
Ricciardelli, Rev. Albert, '84 (TR) Retired. [MON] Villa Vianney, Trenton, NJ
Ricciardi, Rev. August A., '83 (SCR) Curia: Leadership; Offices and Directors Prince of Peace Parish, Old Forge, Old Forge, PA
Riccio, Rev. Antonio, *O.F.M.* '70 (NY) [MON] Franciscan Province of the Immaculate Conception, New York, NY
Riccio, Rev. Fred, '77 (OAK) St. Mary, Walnut Creek, CA
Riccio, Rev. Fred A., '77 (OAK) Curia: Offices and Directors
Riccio, Rev. Salvatore M., '66 (PH) Retired.
Riccitelli, Rev. Dennis, '85 (PHX) Retired. St. Anne Roman Catholic Parish, Gilbert, AZ
Rice, Rev. Anthony, *S.J.C.* '08 (CHI) St. John Cantius, Chicago, IL; [MIS] Canons Regular of Saint John Cantius, Chicago, IL
Rice, Rev. Daniel A., (ARL) Holy Family, Dale City, VA
Rice, Rev. G. Nicholas, '67 (L) Retired.
Rice, Rev. John, '03 (WH) Curia: Offices and Directors Parkersburg Catholic Junior-Senior High School, Parkersburg, WV; St. Francis Xavier, Parkersburg, WV; St. Monica Mission, Lubeck, WV
Rice, Rev. Jonathan G., '19 (PH) St. Stanislaus, Lansdale, PA
Rice, Rev. Joseph, '16 (WOR) Our Lady of the Sacred Heart, West Brookfield, MA; St. John the Baptist, East Brookfield, MA; St. Joseph, North Brookfield, MA
Rice, Rev. Larry, *C.S.P.* '89 (NY) [MON] Paulist Fathers - Generalate, New York, NY
Rice, Rev. Lawrence, *CSP* (ALB) [CAM] The Rensselaer Newman Foundation, Troy, NY
Rice, Rev. Michael D., '64 (KC) Retired.
Rice, Rev. Patrick, (ALB) St. Jude the Apostle, Wynantskill, NY; St. Michael the Archangel, Troy, NY
Rice, Rev. Richard P., '60 (PRT) Retired.
Rice, Rev. Msgr. Thomas G., '77 (DET) St. Thomas More Parish, Troy, MI
Rice, Rev. William A., '63 (E) Retired.
Rich, Rev. John A., *M.M.* (MO) Curia: Offices and Directors
Rich, Rev. John A., *M.M.* '58 (NY) Retired. [MON] Maryknoll Fathers and Brothers (Catholic Foreign Mission Society of America, Inc.), Ossining, NY
Rich, Rev. Joseph, '74 (SJ) Retired.
Richard, Very Rev. Edward J., *M.S.* '91 (LKC) Curia: Advisory Boards, Commissions, Committees, and Councils; Leadership Our Lady of Prompt Succor, Sulphur, LA; [MIS] Catholic Daughters of America, Baton Rouge, LA
Richard, Rev. Joseph E., '58 (SFR) Retired.
Richard, Very Rev. Louis J., '81 (LAF) Curia: Leadership St. Mary Magdalen, Abbeville, LA
Richard, Rev. Michael, '16 (LAF) Curia: Tribunal
Richard, Rev. Normand P., '72 (PRT) Retired.
Richard, Rev. Philion, *OMI* (SAT) [NUR] Oblate Madonna Residence, San Antonio, TX
Richard, Rev. Rusty P., '97 (LAF) On Administrative Leave.
Richard, Rev. Terga, *CICM* '72 (ARL) Retired. [MON] Missionhurst, C.I.C.M.-Central House and Provincialate (American I.H.M. Province, Inc., Immaculate Heart Missions, Inc., Missionhurst, Inc.), Arlington, VA
Richards, Rev. Damian, '92 (SAL) Curia: Consultative

Bodies St. Francis of Assisi Parish, Munjor, Inc., Munjor, KS; St. Nicholas of Myra Parish, Hays, Inc., Hays, KS; Thomas More Prep-Marian High Inc., Hays, KS
Richards, Rev. David I., '10 (BUF) Assumption, Buffalo, NY; Holy Spirit, Buffalo, NY; St. Margaret, Buffalo, NY; St. Mark, Buffalo, NY
Richards, Rev. George, (NOR) St. John, Middletown, CT
Richards, Rev. George J., '95 (NOR) Curia: Tribunal
Richards, Rev. Joseph, '90 (CR) Curia: Leadership; Offices and Directors St. Mary's (Two Inlets), Park Rapids, MN; St. Peter the Apostle, Park Rapids, MN
Richards, Rev. Joseph M., '20 (LC) Annunciation of the Blessed Virgin Mary, Viroqua, WI; St. Mary, Coon Valley, WI; [EFT] St. Mary's Parish Viroqua Endowment Trust, Viroqua, WI
Richards, Rev. Lawrence R., '89 (E) Curia: Miscellaneous / Other Offices St. Joseph, Erie, PA
Richards, Very Rev. Mark, (OAK) Curia: Leadership
Richards, Very Rev. Mark R., '93 (SAC) Curia: Leadership; Offices and Directors Pastor of Sacred Heart Parish, Sacramento, a corporation sole, Sacramento, CA
Richards, Rev. Peter M., '98 (STP) Our Lady of the Lake, Mound, MN; [CEM] St. Albert Cemetery, Albertville, MN; [CEM] St. Michael Cemetery, St. Michael, MN
Richards, Rev. Ronald, '04 (DET) On Duty Outside Diocese. Archdiocese of Agana Our Lady of Refuge Parish Orchard Lake, Orchard Lake, MI
Richardson, Rev. David P., '03 (PEO) Curia: Consultative Bodies St. Philomena, Peoria, IL
Richardson, Rev. Donald, '57 (GLP) Retired.
Richardson, Rev. Francis X., '93 (ATL) Retired.
Richardson, Rev. James, '06 (KAL) Curia: Consultative Bodies St. Ambrose, Delton, MI; St. Philip, Battle Creek, MI
Richardson, Rev. John T., *C.M.* '49 (STL) Retired.
Richardson, Rev. M. Paul, '91 (ARL) Retired.
Richardson, Rev. Robert C., '71 (WDC) Retired.
Richardson, Rev. Msgr. Ronald A., '61 (RVC) Retired.
Richardson, Rev. Ryan, *LC* (ATL) [MIS] Catholic Worldview Fellowship, Inc., Roswell, GA
Richardson, Rev. Ryan, *LC* '16 (DAL) [MON] Legionaries of Christ, Irving, TX
Richardson, Rev. Ryan, *L.C.* (KCK) On Special Assignment. Chaplain, Benedictine College, Atchison [COL] Benedictine College, Atchison, KS
Richardson, Rev. Vincent, (LAN) Cristo Rey Parish Lansing, Lansing, MI
Richardson, Rev. Msgr. William M., '72 (HBG) Retired. Immaculate Heart of Mary, Abbottstown, PA
Richardt, Rev. J. Lawrence, '62 (IND) Retired.
Richart, Rev. Msgr. Paul F., '61 (IND) Retired.
Richetta, Rev. John J., '55 (MIL) Retired.
Richmeier, Rev. Garry, *C.PP.S.* '83 (KC) St. James, Kansas City, MO; [MON] Society of the Precious Blood, Liberty, MO; [SEM] Gaspar Mission House, Kansas City, MO
Richmond, Rev. Leonard Paul, *O. Carm.* '20 (NY) Our Lady of Mt. Carmel, Middletown, NY
Richmond, Rev. Troy A., '03 (DAV) St. Mary Church of Oskaloosa, Iowa, Oskaloosa, IA; St. Mary Church of Pella, Iowa, Pella, IA
Richstatter, Rev. Thomas, *O.F.M.* '66 (CIN) Retired. [SHR] St. Anthony Shrine, Cincinnati, OH
Richter, Rev. David, '00 (BIS) Curia: Leadership; Offices and Directors
Richter, Rev. David A., '00 (BIS) St. John the Apostle, Minot, ND
Richter, Rev. Helmut W., '94 (OAK) Retired.
Richter, Rev. Msgr. John A., '64 (NU) Retired.
Richter, Rev. Kevin M., '88 (SC) St. John Paul II Catholic Parish, Carroll, IA
Richter, Rev. Robert J., '67 (MIL) Retired.
Richter, Rev. Robert J., '67 (ARL) Our Lady, Queen of Peace, Arlington, VA
Richter, Rev. Msgr. Thomas J., '96 (BIS) Queen of Peace Church, Dickinson, ND; [MIS] Bismarck Guild, Mandan, ND
Richter, Rev. Tony, (DET) Guardian Angels Parish Clawson, Clawson, MI; St. Lucy (Croatian) Parish Troy, Troy, MI
Richtsteig, Rev. Erik J., (SLC) Saint Ambrose LLC 214, Salt Lake City, UT
Rickels, Rev. Raymond, *OFM* '82 (GB) [MON] Blessed Giles Friary, Manitowoc, WI
Rickey, Rev. James E., '69 (PEO) Retired.
Rickles, Rev. Gary A., '96 (GAL) Retired.
Rico, Rev. Dairo Antonio, '03 (ATL) St. Benedict Catholic Church, Johns Creek, Inc., Johns Creek, GA
Rico, Rev. Jose Luis, (FRS) St. Therese, Shafter, CA
Rider, Rev. David, '14 (NY) Sacred Heart Church, Monroe, NY
Ridgeway, Rev. Kenneth, *S.M.* '69 (SP) Our Lady of Perpetual Help, Tampa, FL
Ridgway, Rev. John, *S.J.* '82 (SJ) [MON] Sacred Heart Jesuit Center, Los Gatos, CA
Ridore, Rev. Danis, '67 (PMB) Curia: Organizations (affiliated, inter-Diocesan, miscellaneous/other) St. Vincent Ferrer, Delray Beach, FL
Riebe, Very Rev. Bruce, '85 (PRM) On Leave.
Riedemann, Rev. Kenneth, '64 (SCL) Retired.
Rieder, Rev. Michael J., '94 (RVC) St. Joseph, Ronkonkoma, NY
Rieder, Rev. Ronald, (GB) Retired. [MON] St. Fidelis Friary, Appleton, WI
Riedman, Rev. John, '62 (SFS) Retired.
Riedman, Rev. Msgr. Joseph G., '56 (IND) Retired.
Rieger, Rev. Alan J., *O.C.D.* '61 (MIL) [MON] Washington Province of Discalced Carmelite Friars, Inc., Milwaukee, WI
Rieger, Rev. Karl Josef, '92 (WDC) Nativity of the Blessed Virgin (German Mission), McLean, VA; [MIS] German Speaking Catholic Mission, Washington DC, McLean, VA
Riegger, Rev. Patrick M., '01 (RVC) Curia: Leadership; Offices and Directors Infant Jesus, Port Jefferson, NY
Riegler, Rev. Frederick J., '67 (PH) Retired.
Riegler, Rev. Frederick J., (SCR) Retired.
Riegler, Rev. Frederick J., (SCR) Retired. St. Rita, Gouldsboro, PA
Riehle, Rev. James J., '14 (CIN) St. Maximilian Kolbe, Liberty Township, OH
Rielage, Rev. Joseph, '21 (COV) St. Pius X, Edgewood, KY
Riello, Rev. Kenneth, '13 (NY) St. Mary and St. Andrew, Ellenville, NY
Riemer, Rev. Lawrence H., '95 (DAL) On Duty Outside Diocese.
Rien, Rev. Robert K., '74 (OAK) St. Ignatius of Antioch, Antioch, CA
Riendeau, Rev. Alfred A., '98 (BGP) Retired.
Riendeau, Rev. Richard A., '57 (SPR) Retired.
Ries, Rev. Carl A., '70 (DUB) Retired.
Ries, Rev. Stephen, '15 (NY) Curia: Leadership
Riesenberg, Rev. John J., '60 (COV) Retired. [NUR] Madonna Manor, Villa Hills, KY
Riffle, Rev. David, '67 (B) Retired.
Riffle, Rev. Henry J., '70 (SP) Retired. St. Anthony of Padua, San Antonio, FL
Riffle, Rev. Patrick J., '08 (WDC) Military Chap Curia: (>MO) Offices and Directors
Riffle, Rev. Msgr. Raymond E., '79 (GBG) Curia: Administration; Advisory Boards, Commissions, Committees, and Councils; Leadership; Miscellaneous / Other Offices; Offices and Directors Blessed Sacrament Cathedral, Greensburg, PA
Rigatuso, Rev. Leo A., '94 (OM) St. Matthew the Evangelist Church of Bellevue, Bellevue, NE
Rigaud, Rev. Lucon, '13 (BRK) Holy Innocents, Brooklyn, NY; Our Lady of Refuge, Brooklyn, NY
Rigdon, Rev. Vincent J., '77 (WDC) Retired.
Rigert, Rev. James, *C.S.C.* '66 (P) Retired. [MON] Priests of Holy Cross in Oregon, Inc., Portland, OR
Rigney, Rev. Msgr. Dennis A., '66 (ALN) Retired.
Rigoli, Rev. Anthony, *O.M.I.* '72 (NO) Our Lady of Guadalupe/International Shrine of St. Jude, New Orleans, LA; [SHR] Shrine of St. Jude Thaddeus, New Orleans, LA
Riley, Rev. Benjamin A, (LR) Mary, Mother of God, Harrison, AR; St. Andrew Church, Yellville, AR
Riley, Rev. Blayne C., (SAT) On Leave.
Riley, Rev. Daniel J., '84 (BO) Immaculate Conception, Salem, MA; Our Lady Help of Christians, Newton, MA; Sacred Heart, Newton, MA; St. James, Salem, MA
Riley, Rev. Daniel P., *O.F.M.* '71 (BUF) [CAM] St. Bonaventure University, St. Bonaventure, NY; [RTR] Mount Irenaeus, Franciscan Mountain Retreat & Holy Peace Friary (Order of Friars Minor Holy Name Province), West Clarksville, NY
Riley, Rev. David J., '64 (BGP) Retired. St. Peter's Corporate Society, Danbury, CT
Riley, Rev. Edward H., *O.P.* '60 (CHI) [MON] St. Pius V Priory, Chicago, IL
Riley, Rev. Eric D., '98 (OWN) St. Joseph, Mayfield, KY
Riley, Rev. James H., '58 (BO) Retired.
Riley, Rev. John, '03 (KCK) Curia: Advisory Boards, Commissions, Committees, and Councils; Leadership Sacred Heart, Shawnee, KS; [MIS] Catholic Housing of Wyandotte County, Kansas City, KS
Riley, Rev. John J., '91 (ARL) Sacred Heart of Jesus, Winchester, VA
Riley, Very Rev. Kenneth A., '92 (KC) On Special Assignment. Curia: Leadership; Offices and Directors
Riley, Rev. Leo P., '82 (VEN) San Antonio Parish in Port Charlotte, Inc., Port Charlotte, FL
Riley, Rev. Mark J., '90 (BO) Retired.
Riley, Rev. Mark R., '95 (CLV) St. Michael the Archangel, Cleveland, OH; [CCH] St. Michael, Cleveland, OH
Riley, Rev. Miles O'Brien, '63 (SFR) Retired.
Riley, Rev. Ryan L., '16 (LAN) Curia: Leadership Father Gabriel Richard High School, Ann Arbor, MI
Riley, Rev. Walter J., '06 (WOR) St. Anne, Shrewsbury, MA
Rimelspach, Rev. Jeffrey J., '85 (COL) St. Margaret of Cortona, Columbus, OH
Rimonds, Rev. Clement, *H.G.N.* '07 (OG) St. Alphonsus - Holy Name of Jesus, Tupper Lake, NY; St. Henry, Long Lake, NY; St. Therese Church, Newcomb, NY, Newcomb, NY
Rinaldi, Rev. Dario, (HON) St. Catherine, Kapaa, HI
Rinaldi, Rev. Francis J., *O.S.F.S.* (WIL) St. Anthony of Padua, Wilmington, DE
Rinaldo, Rev. Anthony R., '13 (JC) Immaculate Conception, Loose Creek, MO; St. Louis of France, Bonnots Mill, MO
Riney, Rev. Jerry, '75 (OWN) Curia: Advisory Boards, Commissions, Committees, and Councils
Ring, Rev. Daniel J., '68 (TOL) Retired.
Ring, Rev. John K., '61 (SFR) Retired.
Ring, Rev. Joseph G, '88 (SFD) [CAM] Illinois College Newman Catholic Community, Jacksonville, IL
Ring, Rev. Joseph G., '88 (SFD) Our Saviour, Jacksonville, IL
Ring, Rev. Paul L., '95 (BO) St. Ann, West Bridgewater, MA; St. John the Evangelist, East Bridgewater, MA
Ring, Rev. Robert P., '82 (ROC) St. Leo, Hilton, NY
Ringenback, Rev. Msgr. Gerard A., '72 (RVC) Good Shepherd, Holbrook, NY; [MIS] Society of St. Vincent de Paul-Central Council, Bethpage, NY
Ringley, Rev. Frederick John, '01 (BGP) St. Mary's Church, Norwalk, Norwalk, CT
Rini, Rev. John, '67 (ELP) Retired.
Rinn, Rev. Richard A., *C.S.V.* '81 (LAV) St. Viator Catholic Community, Las Vegas, NV
Rinn, Rev. Richard A., *C.S.V.* '81 (CHI) [MON] Viatorian Province Center-Clerics of St. Viator, Arlington Heights, IL
Riordan, Rev. Msgr. Brendan P., '70 (RVC) Retired.
Riordan, Rev. John B., *O.F.M.Cap.* '71 (NY) Parish of Holy Cross and St. John the Baptist, New York, NY; St. John the Baptist, New York, NY
Riordan, Rev. Patrick M., '90 (PEO) Retired.
Rios, Friar Angel, *OFM. Cap* '19 (DAL) Our Lady of Lourdes Catholic Parish, Dallas, TX; [MON] Capuchin Franciscan Friars, Custody Mexico - Texas, Dallas, TX
Rios, Rev. Msgr. Francisco, '91 (SJ) St. Catherine of Alexandria, Morgan Hill, CA
Rios, Rev. Guadalupe, '09 (FRS) On Administrative Leave.
Rios, Rev. Jorge, '03 (GAL) St. Juan Diego, Pasadena, TX
Rios, Rev. Juan Carlos, '93 (MIA) On Special Assignment. faculty St Vincent de Paul Regional Seminary Boynton Beach (>PMB) [SEM] St. Vincent de Paul Regional Seminary, Boynton Beach, FL
Rios, Rev. Manuel D., '86 (NEW) St. Mary of the Assumption, Elizabeth, NJ
Rios, Rev. Moises, '01 (MGZ) Sacred Heart, Mayaguez, PR
Rios, Rev. Nabor, '12 (LA) Curia: Advisory Boards, Commissions, Committees, and Councils; Pastoral Services St. Gertrude, Bell Gardens, CA
Rios Matos, Rev. Angel Luis, (MGZ) Curia: Leadership
Rioux, Rev. Ray, '94 (SR) Retired.
Ripley, Rev. Kevin, (GB) St. Mary, Omro, WI; St. Raphael the Archangel, Oshkosh, WI
Ripperger, Rev. Chad, (DEN) [ASN] Societas Matris Dolorosissimae, Keenesburg, CO
Ripperger, Rev. Mark, *O.Cist.* '93 (DAL) [MON] Our Lady of Dallas Cistercian Abbey, Irving, TX
Rippinger, Rev. Joel, *O.S.B.* '74 (RCK) [MON] Marmion Abbey, Aurora, IL
Rippy, Very Rev. Robert J., '84 (ARL) Curia: Leadership; Tribunal
Riquelme, Rev. Alvaro, *C.Ss.R.* '97 (R) Our Lady of Guadalupe, Newton Grove, NC
Risacher, Rev. James E., '52 (TOL) Retired.
Risanto, Rev. Christoforus Bayu, *S.J.* '12 (TUC) [MON] Jesuit Community of the Vatican Observatory, Tucson, AZ
Risley, Rev. John C., *O.P.* '65 (MAD) [CON] Sinsinawa Dominican Congregation of the Most Holy Rosary., Sinsinawa, WI

Risse, Friar John M., *F.I.* (FR) [MON] Marian Friary of Our Lady, Queen of the Seraphic Order, New Bedford, MA
Rita, Rev. Thomas L., '70 (FR) Retired. Curia: Tribunal
Ritch, Rev. James, *O.P.* '22 (NY) [MON] St. Vincent Ferrer Priory, New York, NY
Ritchie, Rev. David L., '01 (TOL) Curia: Advisory Boards, Commissions, Committees, and Councils; Deaneries Our Lady of Perpetual Help, Toledo, OH
Ritchie, Rev. Msgr. Robert T., '71 (NY) Retired.
Ritchie, Rev. Vincent J., *S.J.* '81 (RVC) St. Dominic's, Oyster Bay, NY
Ritchie, Rev. Vincent J., *S.J.* '74 (NY) [MON] Murray-Weigel Hall (A Jesuit Community at Murray-Weigel Hall and Kohlmann Hall), Bronx, NY
Ritt, Rev. Paul E., '81 (BO) Curia: Leadership Ave Maria Parish, Lynnfield, MA
Ritter, Rev. Anthony, '19 (STL) St. Francis Borgia Catholic Church, Washington, MO
Ritter, Rev. Charles F., '67 (TOL) Retired.
Ritter, Rev. Charles F., '67 (TOL) Retired.
Ritter, Rev. Eric, '03 (SAT) St. Matthew Catholic Church, San Antonio, TX
Ritter, Rev. Michael D., '15 (SAC) Curia: Leadership Pastor of St. Robert Parish, Sacramento, A Corporation sole, Sacramento, CA
Ritz, Rev. Eugene P., '09 (ALN) Curia: Leadership
Riva, Rev. Gerald, '68 (JOL) Retired.
Rivard, Rev. Benjamin, '21 (MAR) St. Peter Cathedral, Marquette, MI
Rivard, Rev. Robert, *F.M.S.I.* '77 (BO) St. Jude, Norfolk, MA; [SEM] Sylva Maria, Framingham, MA
Rivas, Rev. Jose, '89 (NY) St. Athanasius, Bronx, NY
Rivas, Rev. Jose Luis, (SB) Our Lady of Guadalupe, Chino, CA
Rivas, Rev. Oscar, (IND) Saint Mary of the Immaculate Conception Catholic Church, Indianapolis, Inc., Indianapolis, IN
Rivas Guardado, Rev. Pedro De Jesús, *Sch. P.* '19 (PCE) Colegio Ponceno, Ponce, PR
Rivas Rivera, Rev. David, '85 (ARE) Parroquia de San Martin de Porres, Vega Baja, PR
Rivas Rivera, Rev. David, '85 (ARE) [MIS] Chapel Sagrado Corazon, Vega Baja, PR; [MIS] Chapel San Jose, Vega Baja, PR; [MIS] Chapel St. Anthony de Padua, Vega Baja, PR
Rivera, Rev. Adalin, '77 (PCE) Curia: Leadership
Rivera, Rev. Alexander, (MIA) On Special Assignment. Doctoral Studies, Rome, Italy
Rivera, Rev. Anastacio S., *S.J.* '74 (SJ) [MON] Sacred Heart Jesuit Center, Los Gatos, CA
Rivera, Rev. Andres, (SB) St. Peter & St. Paul, Alta Loma, CA
Rivera, Rev. Andres, *SDB* (SJN) Maria Auxiliadora, San Juan, PR
Rivera, Rev. Angel L, '19 (MGZ) Our Lady of Rosary, Rosario, PR
Rivera, Rev. Angel L., '19 (MGZ) On Special Assignment.
Rivera, Rev. Daniel, *M.Sp.S.* '16 (RVC) St. John of God, Central Islip, NY
Rivera, Rev. Daniel, (RVC) On Duty Outside Diocese.
Rivera, Rev. David, (CAM) Saint Mary of Mount Carmel Parish, Hammonton, N.J., Hammonton, NJ
Rivera, Rev. David, '10 (CAM) Curia: Tribunal
Rivera, Rev. Diego, (BAL) Christ the King Roman Catholic Congregation, Inc., Glen Burnie, MD; St. Bernadette, Severn, MD
Rivera, Rev. Edgar O., '13 (PAT) On Leave.
Rivera, Rev. Eduardo, (GAL) St. Anne, Houston, TX
Rivera, Rev. Elvin, '15 (NY) St. Ann, Ossining, NY; St. Raymond, Bronx, NY
Rivera, Rev. Guillermo, *O.P.* '76 (LSC) Curia: Leadership San Martin de Porres Parish, Inc., Sunland Park, NM
Rivera, Rev. Henry, '10 (FRS) Sacred Heart, Lindsay, CA
Rivera, Rev. Israel, '04 (HRT) Saint Joachim Parish Corporation, New Britain, CT
Rivera, Rev. Jaime, '07 (ATL) St. Thomas Aquinas Catholic Church, Alpharetta, Inc., Alpharetta, GA
Rivera, Rev. Jose Rolando, '94 (LAV) Prince of Peace, Las Vegas, NV
Rivera, Rev. Juan, (BO) [MON] The Jesuit Community at Boston College, Chestnut Hill, MA
Rivera, Rev. Juan Carlos, '11 (TYL) Holy Cross, Pittsburg, TX
Rivera, Rev. Luis, '83 (CGS) Nuestra Senora de la Asuncion, Cayey, PR
Rivera, Rev. Luis J., (ARE) [MIS] Chapel La Milagrosa, Lares, PR; [MIS] Chapel La Pasion, Lares, PR; [MIS] Chapel La Resurreccion, Lares, PR; [MIS] Chapel Nuestra Senora de la Divina Providencia, Lares, PR; [MIS] Chapel San Carlos, Lares, PR
Rivera, Rev. Luis R., '84 (MIA) St. Maurice at Resurrection, Dania, FL
Rivera, Rev. Nelson, '11 (WOR) St. Denis, Douglas, MA
Rivera, Rev. Oscar, '79 (CGS) Church of St. Anthony of Padua, Barranquitas, PR
Rivera, Rt. Rev. Oscar, *O.S.B.* '78 (FAJ) Colegio San Antonio Abad, Humacao, PR; [MON] San Antonio Abad Abbey of the Order of St. Benedict, Humacao, PR
Rivera, Rev. Pedro, '06 (SD) [CAM] Newman Center - SDSU, San Diego, CA
Rivera, Rev. Raimundo, '11 (PAT) Our Lady of Lourdes, Paterson, NJ; Our Lady of Victories, Paterson, NJ
Rivera, Rev. Ralph, *S.J.* '07 (BRK) [MON] Carroll Street Jesuit Community, Brooklyn, NY
Rivera, Rev. Ralph, *S.J.* '07 (NY) Xavier High School, New York, NY
Rivera, Friar Reynaldo, *O.S.A.* (SJN) Ntra. Sra. de la Monserrate, Bayamon, PR
Rivera, Rev. Ricardo, *Sch.P.* '19 (MIA) [MON] Piarist Fathers, Province of the USA & Puerto Rico, Miami, FL
Rivera, Rev. Richard, '22 (TUC) Roman Catholic Church of Saint Elizabeth Ann Seton - Tucson, Tucson, AZ
Rivera Borges, Rev. Miguel, *S.D.B.* (SJN) [HOS] Doctors' Community Hospital, San Juan, PR
Rivera Calderon, Rev. Miguel A., (ARE) Retired.
Rivera Maldonado, Rev. Jorge Maria, *O.Carm.* (SJN) Santa Teresita del Nino Jesus, San Juan, PR
Rivera Martinez, Rev. Jery, '00 (PCE) Retired.
Rivera Medina, Rev. Juan Carlos, (PCE) Curia: Offices and Directors
Rivera Medina, Rev. Juan Carlos, '10 (PCE) [SEM] Seminario Mayor Interdiocesano Maria, Madre de la Divina Providencia, Ponce, PR
Rivera Rivera, Rev. Felix A., *O.Carm.* (ARE) Holy Rosary, Ciales, PR
Rivera Rivera, Rev. Luis Javier, '06 (ARE) Curia: Leadership
Rivera Rivera, Rev. Luis Javier, '06 (ARE) St. Joseph, Lares, PR
Rivera Saez, Rev. Adalin, '77 (PCE) Inmaculada Concepcion, Guayanilla, PR
Rivera Sepulveda, Rev. Raymond L., '86 (PCE) San Martin de Porres, Yauco, PR
Rivera Soto, Rev. Orlando, '90 (PCE) Colegio Nuestra Senora del Perpetuo Socorro, Salinas, PR; Sagrado Corazon de Jesus, Aguirre, PR
Rivera Torres, Rev. Edgar Eloy, '15 (P) St. Helen, Junction City, OR; St. Rose of Lima, Monroe, OR
Rivera-Borges, Rev. Miguel, (SJN) Nuestra Senora de la Esperanza, San Juan, PR; Sagrado Corazon de Jesus, San Juan, PR
Rivera-Fals, Rev. Angel, *S.J.* '10 (SP) Jesuit High School of Tampa, Inc., Tampa, FL
Rivera-Martinez, Rev. Jonas, *C.S.Sp.* '98 (SJN) [SPF] Santuario del Espiritu Santo-Congregacion del Espiritu Santo, Dorado, PR
Rivera-Marzan, Rev. Eddie, '90 (SJN) San Fernando Rey, Toa Alta, PR
Rivera-Perez, Rev. Marco Antonio, '06 (SJN) San Luis Rey, San Juan, PR; Santa Maria de Los Angeles, San Juan, PR
Rivera-Perez, Rev. Marcos, (SJN) [SPF] Centro Medico de P.R., San Juan, PR
Rivera-Vigo, Rev. Milton Agustin, '05 (SJN) Espiritu Santo, Toa Baja, PR
Rivero, Rev. Carlos, '20 (SAV) Our Lady of Lourdes, Port Wentworth, GA; Sacred Heart, Warner Robins, GA
Rivero, Rev. Eduardo, *O.Carm.* '02 (JOL) [MON] Carmelite Provincial Office, Darien, IL
Rivero, Rev. Fidel V., (SB) Corpus Christi, Corona, CA
Rivero, Rev. Jordi S., '82 (MIA) Retired.
Rivero, Rev. Msgr. Juan, (FWT) Retired.
Rivero, Rev. Julio, *T.O.R.* '69 (ALT) [MON] St. Francis Friary at Mount Assisi, Loretto, PA
Rivero, Rev. Leonides, '78 (ELP) Retired.
Rivero, Rev. Luis Ardiel, '10 (MIA) Curia: Canonical Services [SEM] St. John Vianney College Seminary, Inc., Miami, FL
Rivero, Rev. Luis Felipe, *LC* '02 (MAD) Oaklawn Academy, Edgerton, WI; [MIS] Oaklawn Incorporated, Edgerton, WI; [MON] Koshkonong Pastoral Center, Edgerton, WI
Riveros, Rev. Belisario, (SP) Church of the Nativity, Brandon, FL
Riveros, Rev. Wilfredo, '97 (CGS) Nuestra Senora de la Merced, Cayey, PR
Rivers, Rev. Robert S., *C.S.P.* '68 (BO) Retired. [MON] Missionary Society of St. Paul the Apostle in Massachusetts, Boston, MA
Riviere, Rev. Patrick, '19 (HT) Our Lady of Prompt Succor, Thibodaux, LA
Rizk, Rev. Antoine, *B.S.O.* '96 (NTN) Curia: Consultative Bodies Church of the Virgin Mary, Brooklyn, NY
Rizo, Rev. Sergio, '89 (FWT) St. Joseph, Cleburne, TX
Rizzi, Rev. Carmine, '13 (NEW) Curia: Offices and Directors
Rizzo, Rev. Angelo, *S.J.* '17 (SCR) [COL] The University of Scranton, Scranton, PA
Rizzo, Rev. David R., '99 (ALT) On Leave.
Rizzo, Rev. Giovanni, '00 (NEW) Curia: Offices and Directors
Rizzo, Rev. Mario, (OAK) St. Joseph Basilica, Alameda, CA
Rizzo, Rev. Mario, '18 (OAK) Curia: Leadership
Rizzo, Rev. Matteo J., '73 (BRK) Retired.
Rizzo, Rev. Michael, '20 (ORG) Sts. Simon & Jude, Huntington Beach, CA
Rizzo, Rev. Patricio Montsalvas, *C.P.* (BIR) [MIS] Congregation of the Passion: Holy Family Community, Inc., Birmingham, AL
Rizzo, Rev. Robert C., '74 (CHI) Retired.
Ro, Rev. Matheus, *S.V.D.* '07 (CHI) [EFT] Divine Word Techny Community Corporation, Techny, IL; [MIS] Techny Land Investments, Techny, IL; [MON] Divine Word Residence, Techny, IL; [MON] Society of the Divine Word, Provincial Headquarters-Chicago Prov., Techny, IL
Roa, Rev. Daniel, (SR) Holy Family, ,
Roa, Rev. Daniel Enrique, '08 (SR) Pastor of St. Joan of Arc Catholic Church of Yountville, A Corporation Sole, Yountville, CA
Roach, Rev. Francis J., '73 (WOR) Chap, Univ of Mass Med Ctr Our Lady of Lourdes (Roman Catholic Bishop of Worcester, Corporation Sole), Worcester, MA
Roach, Rev. James, '88 (CLV) St. John Cantius, Cleveland, OH
Roach, Rev. John A., '58 (SPR) Retired. Curia: Clergy and Religious Services; Offices and Directors
Roach, Rev. Michael, '81 (KC) St. James, Liberty, MO
Roach, Rev. Michael J., '71 (BAL) [SEM] Mount St. Mary's Seminary, Emmitsburg, MD
Roach, Rev. Thomas, *S.J.* '70 (SY) [MIS] Saint Andrew Hall, Syracuse, NY
Roache, Rev. Dermot, *SMA* '07 (NEW) [MON] Society of African Missions, Provincialate, S.M.A. Fathers, Tenafly, NJ
Roache, Rev. John, *SS.CC* '83 (LA) Holy Name of Mary, San Dimas, CA
Roaldi, Rev. Francis Mary, *C.F.R.* '08 (NEW) [MON] Franciscan Friars of the Renewal (Most Blessed Sacrament Friary), Newark, NJ
Roark, Rev. Michael B., '70 (WIL) Retired.
Robak, Rev. Anthony G., '74 (NEW) Retired.
Robb, Rev. Dennis E., '74 (SEA) Retired.
Robb, Rev. Kevin D., *O.P.* '77 (PRO) [MON] St. Thomas Aquinas Priory at Providence College, Providence, RI
Robben, Rev. Matthew, (CIN) St. Aloysius Gonzaga, Cincinnati, OH
Robben, Rev. Matthew J., '12 (CIN) Our Lady of Lourdes, Cincinnati, OH; St. Antoninus, Cincinnati, OH
Robbins, Rev. Anthony M., '10 (LR) Curia: Leadership; Offices and Directors St. Joseph, Conway, AR; [MIS] Magnificat - Central Arkansas Chapter, Conway, AR
Robbins, Rev. Ian, '20 (SAT) Curia: Leadership Our Lady of Grace Catholic School, Pleasanton, TX; St. Andrew, Pleasanton, TX
Robbins, Rev. Robert J., '74 (NY) Chapel of the Sacred Hearts of Jesus and Mary, New York, NY; Christ the King, Yonkers, NY; Parish of Our Saviour and St. Stephen/Our Lady of the Scapular, New York, NY; St. Stephen and Our Lady of the Scapular, New York, NY
Robbins, Rev. Stephen, (CAM) Saint Damien Parish, Ocean City, N.J., Ocean City, NJ; The Parish of the Cathedral of the Immaculate Conception, Camden, N.J., Camden, NJ
Robbins, Rev. Thomas P., '74 (COV) Retired. Holy Cross High School, Covington, KY
Roberge, Rev. Francis A., '78 (WOR) St. Vincent De Paul, Baldwinville, MA
Roberge, Rev. Richard A., '85 (MAN) Chap, NH Prison for Men Christ the King Parish, Concord, NH
Roberson, Rev. Henry, '71 (OKL) Retired.
Roberson, Rev. Ronald G., *C.S.P.* '77 (WDC) [SEM] Paulist Washington Community, Washington, DC
Roberson, Rev. Shawn, *T.O.R.* '02 (STU) [COL] Franciscan University of Steubenville, Steubenville, OH; [MON] Holy Spirit Friary, Steubenville, OH
Robert, Rev. Darin T., '71 (LAN) Retired.
Roberts, Rev. Benjamin A., '09 (CHL) Curia:

Consultative Bodies Our Lady of Lourdes, Monroe, NC
Roberts, Rev. Bo, (BLX) Curia: Advisory Boards, Commissions, Committees, and Councils
Roberts, Rev. Don J., '78 (SFD) Blessed Trinity, Brussels, IL; St. Francis of Assisi, Hardin, IL
Roberts, Rev. Eugene J., '75 (TR) St. Gabriel, Marlboro, NJ
Roberts, Rev. G. Richard, '91 (LC) VA Med Ctr, Tomah Holy Trinity, La Crosse, WI; [EFT] Holy Trinity Catholic Church Endowment Trust, La Crosse, WI
Roberts, Rev. Guy R., '98 (IND) St. Barnabas Catholic Church, Indianapolis, Inc., Indianapolis, IN
Roberts, Rev. Joseph, '02 (ORL) Retired.
Roberts, Rev. Mark, (LAV) On Administrative Leave.
Roberts, Rev. Nathanael, *O.S.B.* '03 (RCK) [MON] Marmion Abbey, Aurora, IL
Roberts, Rev. Ralph O., '98 (GAL) St. Martha, Porter, TX
Roberts, Rev. Randall, *O.F.M.* '84 (MO) Curia: Offices and Directors
Roberts, Rev. Stephen, '07 (LEX) Holy Spirit Church - the Newman Center, Lexington, KY; [CAM] Holy Spirit Parish Newman Center, University of Kentucky, Lexington, KY
Robertson, Rev. Curtis L., '10 (WCH) Chap, Correctional Facility St. Patrick, Parsons, KS
Robertson, Very Rev. Douglas C., '96 (LC) Curia: Leadership Our Lady of Peace, Marshfield, WI; [EFT] The Our Lady of Peace Endowment Trust, Marshfield, WI
Robertson, Rev. Eugene G., '78 (STL) Immaculate Conception Catholic Church, Augusta, Augusta, MO
Robertson, Rev. James E., '77 (AUS) Retired.
Robertson, Rev. John W., '71 (HEL) Retired. On Special Assignment. Judicial Vicar, Helena Curia: Leadership
Robertson, Rev. John W., '71 (GF) Curia: Leadership
Robertson, Rev. Luke, *TOR* '99 (STU) [COL] Franciscan University of Steubenville, Steubenville, OH; [MON] Holy Spirit Friary, Steubenville, OH
Robertson, Rev. Thomas M., '65 (STL) Retired.
Robeson, Rev. Robert J., '03 (IND) Good Shepherd Roman Catholic Church, Indianapolis, Inc., Indianapolis, IN; Holy Name of Jesus Catholic Church, Indianapolis, Inc., Beech Grove, IN; Roncalli High School, Inc., Indianapolis, IN
Robeson, Rev. Steven P., '84 (STL) St. Ignatius Loyola Catholic Church, Marthasville, MO
Robey, Rev. Bradley, '21 (DM) St. Pius X, Urbandale, IA
Robichaux, Very Rev. Msgr. Robie E., '76 (LAF) On Administrative Leave.
Robideau, Rev. Jeffrey, '97 (LAN) [MIS] St. Gregory the Great Community, Lansing, MI
Robillard, Rev. Joseph, '84 (ORG) Christ Our Savior Catholic Parish, Santa Ana, CA
Robin, Rev. Richard A., *S.J.* '67 (LA) [MON] Jesuit Community, Los Angeles, CA
Robinchaud, Rev. Paul, (NY) [MON] Paulist Fathers' Motherhouse, New York, NY
Robine, Rev. Paul M., '59 (ALT) Retired.
Robins, Rev. Dean L., '87 (NO) Chap, St. Tammany Hospital, Covington
Robinson, Rev. Christopher S., *C.M.* '89 (CHI) [MON] Vincentian Community, Congregation of the Mission, Western Province, Chicago, IL
Robinson, Rev. David, *S.J.* (SFR) [SEM] St. Patrick's Seminary and University (The Roman Catholic Seminary of San Francisco), Menlo Park, CA
Robinson, Rev. David C., *S.J.* '92 (ORG) [MON] Manresa Jesuit Residence, Anaheim, CA
Robinson, Rev. Denis, *O.S.B.* '93 (IND) [MON] St. Meinrad Archabbey, St. Meinrad, IN; [SEM] Saint Meinrad School of Theology, St. Meinrad, IN
Robinson, Rev. Donald A., '80 (OG) Saint Andrew's Church, Sackets Harbor, Sackets Harbor, NY; The Roman Catholic Community of Brownville and Dexter, Brownville, NY
Robinson, Rev. Gerald, *S.J.* '77 (SJ) [MON] Jesuit Community at Santa Clara University, Inc., Santa Clara, CA
Robinson, Rev. Gerald, *S.J.* (MRY) [CAM] California State Polytechnic Institute/Cuesta College, San Luis Obispo, CA
Robinson, Rev. Jerome, '75 (NO) Retired.
Robinson, Rev. Joseph A., '64 (CIN) Retired.
Robinson, Rev. Joseph P., '68 (BO) Retired.
Robinson, Rev. Joseph P., '20 (CLV) Chap, Grafton Corr Inst St. Columbkille Parish, Parma, OH
Robinson, Rev. Kenneth, '92 (FWT) Retired.
Robinson, Rev. Michael, '96 (SD) Pastor of Saint Elizabeth Seton Catholic Parish, Carlsbad, a corporation sole, Carlsbad, CA; [MIS] Saint Elizabeth Seton Catholic Parish in Carlsbad, CA Real Property Support Corporation, Carlsbad, CA
Robinson, Rev. Patrick, '91 (PHX) Retired. St. Patrick Roman Catholic Parish, Scottsdale, AZ
Robinson, Rev. Paul, *O.Carm.* '67 (JOL) Retired.
Robinson, Rev. Richard J., '71 (MIL) Retired.
Robinson, Rev. Tyrone, '79 (DET) Our Lady Queen of Heaven - Good Shepherd Parish Detroit, Detroit, MI; St. Jude Parish Detroit, Detroit, MI; St. Raymond - Our Lady of Good Counsel Parish Detroit, Detroit, MI
Robinson, Rev. William, (MO) Curia: Offices and Directors
Robinson, Rev. William J., *O.F.M.Conv.* '74 (R) Newman Catholic Student Center, University of North Carolina, Chapel Hill, NC
Robisch, Rev. David C., '62 (CIN) Retired.
Robitaille, Rev. Jean Claude, *M.Afr.* (SP) [MON] Missionaries of Africa, St. Petersburg, FL
Robitaille, Rev. Raymond, '47 (LAF) Retired.
Robledo, Rev. Jaime, *P.S.S.* (WDC) [SEM] Theological College of the Catholic University of America, Washington, DC
Robledo, Rev. Jaime E., *P.S.S.* '90 (BAL) [MIS] St. Mary's Seminary & University, Baltimore, MD; [MON] Society of St. Sulpice, Province of the United States, Baltimore, MD
Robles, Rev. Ariel, '96 (TR) Our Lady of Good Counsel, West Trenton, NJ
Robles, Rev. Daniel, '01 (SPC) Curia: Deaneries Sacred Heart, Poplar Bluff, MO; St. Benedict, Doniphan, MO
Robles, Rev. Ismael R., '13 (LA) St. John the Baptist, Baldwin Park, CA
Robles, Rev. Juan Pablo, '07 (BWN) Our Heavenly Father Parish, Olmito, TX
Robles Cuevas, Rev. Jorge, '15 (FRS) Our Lady of Guadalupe, Mendota, CA
Robles-Cardenas, Rev. Sergio, *C.R.* '99 (PBL) Our Lady of Guadalupe, Conejos, CO
Roblez-Baltazar, Rev. Juan Pedro, '17 (LC) St. Bronislava, Plover, WI
Robu, Rev. Emil, '98 (MRY) On Leave.
Roby, Rev. Albin, (NY) Parish of St. Adalbert and St. Roch, Staten Island, NY
Roby, Rev. Brian, '96 (OWN) St. John the Baptist, Fordsville, KY; St. Mary of the Woods, Whitesville, KY
Roby, Rev. Brian J., '96 (OWN) Curia: Advisory Boards, Commissions, Committees, and Councils
Roby, Rev. Bruce, (BGP) [MON] The Catherine Dennis Keefe Queen of the Clergy Retired Priests' Residence, Stamford, CT
Roca, Rev. Albert L., '77 (MET) Retired.
Rocca, Rev. Peter, *C.S.C.* (KAL) St. Mark, Niles, MI
Rocca, Rev. Peter D., *C.S.C.* '74 (FTW) Curia: Offices and Directors [COL] University of Notre Dame Du Lac, Notre Dame, IN; [SEM] Moreau Seminary, Notre Dame, IN
Roccasalva, Rev. Joseph, *OSA* '21 (JOL) [MON] Augustinian Friary, New Lenox, IL
Rocchi, Rev. Frank J., '82 (NEW) Good Shepherd, Irvington, NJ
Rocco, Rev. Msgr. Remigio G., '66 (PAT) Retired.
Rocha, Rev. Antonio Nuno, '06 (NEW) Our Lady of Fatima, Elizabeth, NJ
Rocha, Rev. Constantino, '95 (FTW) Our Lady of Guadalupe, Warsaw, IN
Rocha, Rev. Msgr. Ivo D., '66 (STO) Retired.
Rocha, Rev. Jorge V., '16 (PRO) Saint Francis Xavier's Church, East Providence, RI
Rocha, Rev. Jose F., '04 (PRO) Retired.
Rocha, Rev. Leonardo, (SJ) Holy Cross, San Jose, CA
Rocha, Rev. Michael, '88 (LA) St. Paschal Baylon, Thousand Oaks, CA; [EFT] University Series Foundation, Inc., Thousand Oaks, CA
Rocha, Rev. Michael P., (SFR) Church of the Epiphany, San Francisco, CA; St. Monica - St. Thomas the Apostle Parish, San Francisco, CA
Rocha, Rev. Richard D., '02 (KC) St. Robert Bellarmine, Blue Springs, MO
Rocha, Rev. Ruben, '98 (LA) Holy Family, Wilmington, CA
Roche, Rev. Alex J., '12 (SCR) Curia: Offices and Directors St. Maria Goretti, Laflin, PA; [COL] Misericordia University, Dallas, PA
Roche, Rev. Amalraj, '98 (LC) Immaculate Conception, Eau Claire, WI; [HOS] St. Joseph's Hospital of the Hospital Sisters of the Third Order of St. Francis, Chippewa Falls, WI
Roche, Rev. David, '58 (PEO) Retired.
Roche, Rev. John, *SS.CC.* '82 (LA) [MON] Congregation of the Sacred Hearts of Jesus and Mary, La Verne, CA
Roche, Rev. Matthew F, *SJ* '81 (PH) (>NY) [MON] Murray-Weigel Hall (A Jesuit Community at Murray-Weigel Hall and Kohlmann Hall), Bronx, NY
Roche, Rev. Matthew F., *S.J.* '81 (NY) [RTR] Mount Manresa Jesuit Retreat House (Society of Jesus), Staten Island, NY
Roche, Rev. Michael J., '11 (PIT) Saint Luke the Evangelist, Sewickley, PA
Roche, Rev. Randall, *S.J.* '68 (LA) [MON] Jesuit Community, Los Angeles, CA
Rochford, Rev. Thomas, *S.J.* (DEN) [MON] Regis High Jesuit Community, Centennial, CO
Rochon, Rev. Robert A., '74 (PRO) Retired.
Rock, Rev. Richard, '73 (BRK) [MON] Reverend John B. Murray, C.M. House, Jamaica, NY
Rock, Rev. Msgr. Russell L., '62 (CAM) Retired.
Rock, Very Rev. Stephen B., '74 (BO) Curia: Clergy and Religious Services; Leadership Christ the King Parish, Reading, MA
Rock, Rev. William, *FSSP* '19 (GAL) Regina Caeli, Houston, TX
Rocker, Rev. Stephen, '79 (OG) Retired. On Duty Outside Diocese. Magdalen College of the Liberal Arts Warner, NH
Rockers, Rev. Alfred, '62 (KCK) Retired.
Rockers, Rev. Andrew, '15 (SAL) Sacred Heart Parish, Esbon, Inc., Esbon, KS; Saints Peter and Paul Parish, Cawker City, Inc., Cawker City, KS; St. John the Baptist Parish, Beloit, Inc., Beloit, KS; St. Theresa Parish, Mankato, Inc., Mankato, KS
Rocks, Rev. Jason T., '02 (CAM) Curia: Leadership; Tribunal Holy Eucharist Parish, Cherry Hill, N.J., Cherry Hill, NJ
Rocus, Rev. John George, '01 (LAN) Holy Spirit Parish Brighton, Brighton, MI
Rodak, Rev. Joseph, *C.PP.S.* (CLV) Retired.
Rodak, Rev. Michael, '07 (PAT) Curia: Administration; Leadership St. Jude the Apostle, Hardyston, NJ
Rodarte, Rev. Alex, (SB) St. Joseph, Upland, CA
Rodas, Rev. Mauro G., '65 (IND) Retired. Our Lady of the Greenwood Catholic Church, Inc., Greenwood, IN
Rodas Aguilar, Rev. Fabian F., *M.F.M.* '93 (MIL) Prince of Peace/Principe de Paz Congregation, Milwaukee, WI; St. Rafael the Archangel Congregation, Milwaukee, WI; The St. Vincent a Paulo Congregation, Milwaukee, WI
Rodas Grajales, Rev. Duberney, *OP* '06 (ORL) St. Mary Magdalen, Altamonte Springs, FL
Rodden, Rev. Kyle, '16 (IND) St. Joseph Catholic Church, Corydon, Inc., Corydon, IN; St. Mary Catholic Church, Lanesville, Inc., Lanesville, IN
Roden, Rev. Raymond, '81 (BRK) [SEM] Cathedral Seminary House of Formation, Douglaston, NY
Rodenfels, Rev. Jerome P., '74 (COL) Retired.
Roden-Lucero, Rev. Ed, '82 (SFE) Curia: Offices and Directors
Roden-Lucero, Rev. Ed, '82 (SFE) Curia: Offices and Directors
Roder, Rev. Terry A., '88 (SC) Good Shepherd Catholic Parish, Breda, IA
Rodgers, Rev. Msgr. Arthur E., '65 (PH) Retired. On Special Assignment. Dir, Society for the Propagation of the Faith, Philadelphia
Rodgers, Rev. Philip F., '81 (ALN) St. Patrick, Pottsville, PA
Rodgers, Rev. Robert, '14 (CHY) Curia: Consultative Bodies St. Francis, Thermopolis, WY; St. Mary Magdalen, Worland, WY
Rodia, Rev. James C., *O.Praem.* '72 (PH) St. Norbert, Paoli, PA; [MON] Daylesford Abbey, Inc., Paoli, PA
Rodoni, Rev. Rick, '91 (SJ) Curia: Leadership Presentation High School, San Jose, CA; St. Lucy, Campbell, CA
Rodrigalvarez, Rev. Jose Antonio, *O.A.R.* (NY) Parish of St. Anselm and St. Roch, Bronx, NY
Rodrigo, Rev. B.K. Akila Gayan, *T.O.R.* '10 (WH) Sacred Heart Mission, Salem, WV; St. Ann Catholic Church, Shinnston, WV; St. James the Apostle, Clarksburg, WV
Rodrigo, Rev. Niranjan, '99 (NY) The Infant Saviour, Pine Bush, NY
Rodrigo, Rev. Stephen, '75 (KAL) St. Mary's Visitation, Byron Center, MI; St. Stanislaus, Dorr, MI
Rodrigo Gil, Rev. Salvador, *O.Carm* '62 (ARE) Nuestra Senora del Carmen, Morovis, PR
Rodrigue, Rev. Jared, '17 (NO) St. Luke the Evangelist Roman Catholic Church, Slidell, Louisiana, Slidell, LA
Rodrigue, Very Rev. Joshua J., (HT) On Duty Outside Diocese. (>NO) [SEM] Notre Dame Seminary Graduate School of Theology, New Orleans, LA
Rodrigue, Rev. Raymond E., '97 (NEW) Our Lady of Good Counsel, Washington, NJ
Rodrigue, Rev. Rodlin, '13 (CHI) St. Raymond de Penafort, Mt. Prospect, IL
Rodrigues, Rev. Amancio J., '66 (P) Retired.
Rodrigues, Rev. Carlos, '95 (BGP) The Saint Clement's

Church Corporation, Stamford, CT
Rodrigues, Rev. Charles, *S.J.* '08 (CHI) [COL] Jesuit Community at Loyola University Chicago, Chicago, IL; [MIS] USA Midwest Province of the Society of Jesus, Inc., Chicago, IL
Rodrigues, Rev. Danny Santos, '16 (NEW) Our Lady of Mt. Carmel, Newark, NJ
Rodrigues, Rev. Ignatius H., '66 (SB) Retired. Chap, Patton State Hosp
Rodrigues, Rev. Jeremy J., '08 (PRO) Curia: Offices and Directors Saint Margaret's Church Corporation, East Providence Rhode Island, Rumford, RI; SS. Peter and Paul's Church, Providence, RI
Rodrigues, Rev. Joseph C., *S.D.S.* '93 (MIL) [MON] Salvatorian Provincial Offices (Society of the Divine Savior), Milwaukee, WI
Rodrigues, Rev. Navil, '93 (GF) Curia: Leadership; Offices and Directors St. Agnes, Red Lodge, MT; St. Mary, Columbus, MT
Rodrigues, Rev. Tommy, '69 (TOL) Retired.
Rodrigues, Rev. William M., '00 (FR)
Rodrigues deAraujo, Rev. Luis Carlos, '21 (NEW) St. Stephen, Kearny, NJ
Rodriguez, Rev. Alberto A., '81 (GAL) Retired.
Rodriguez, Rev. Alejandro, *SDB* '03 (OAK) [MON] Salesians of Don Bosco, Berkeley, CA
Rodriguez, Rev. Allen D., *S.T.* '07 (SB) On Special Assignment.
Rodriguez, Rev. Ambiorix, '97 (NY) St. Elizabeth, New York, NY
Rodriguez, Rev. Andrew, *S.J.* '16 (SJ) (>LA) [SEM] Ignatius House, The Novitiate of the U.S. West Province, Society of Jesus, Culver City, CA
Rodriguez, Rev. Anibal, *C.P.* '03 (SJN) Colegio Santa Gema, Carolina, PR; Santa Gema Galgani Parish Sanctuary, Carolina, PR (>BRK) [MIS] St. Paul's Benevolent, Educational and Missionary Institute, Inc. (Congregation of the Passion - St. Paul of the Cross Province), Jamaica, NY
Rodriguez, Rev. Anibal, *C.P.* '03 (NY) [MON] The Congregation of the Passion - St. Paul of the Cross Province, Jamaica, NY
Rodriguez, Rev. Anselm, *O. Praem.* '20 (LA) SS. Peter and Paul, Wilmington, CA
Rodriguez, Rev. Anselm, *O.Praem.* '20 (ORG) [MON] Norbertine Fathers of Orange, Inc., Silverado, CA
Rodriguez, Rev. Antonio, '93 (PAT) Holy Trinity, Passaic, NJ
Rodriguez, Rev. Asiel, (NEW) [MON] Benedictine Abbey of Newark, Newark, NJ
Rodriguez, Rev. Astor, *C.M.* '93 (BRK) St. John the Baptist, Brooklyn, NY
Rodriguez, Rev. Carlos, '10 (CHI) [SEM] University of Saint Mary of the Lake/Mundelein Seminary, Mundelein, IL
Rodriguez, Rev. Carlos, *O.C.S.O.* '70 (L) [MON] Abbey of Our Lady of Gethsemani, of the Order of Cistercians of the Strict Observance, Trappist, KY
Rodriguez, Rev. Carlos Felipe, '97 (SAN) St. Anthony, Odessa, TX; St. Joseph, Odessa, TX
Rodriguez, Rev. David, '89 (STL) [MON] Franciscan Friary of St. Anthony of Padua, St. Louis, MO
Rodriguez, Rev. David, *O.F.M.* '89 (CHI) Hales Franciscan High School, Inc., Chicago, IL; [MON] Holy Spirit Friary, Order of Friars Minor, Chicago, IL
Rodriguez, Rev. Domingo, *S.T.* (LA) Our Lady of Victory, Compton, CA
Rodriguez, Rev. Edgar, '03 (CHI) SS. Genevieve and Stanislaus Bishop and Martyr, Chicago, IL
Rodriguez, Rev. Edgar A. Carlo, '97 (MGZ) Santa Teresita, Mayaguez, PR
Rodriguez, Rev. Edgardo, (SFR) Holy Angels, Colma, CA
Rodriguez, Rev. Eduardo, *O.C.S.O.* '69 (ATL) [MON] The Monastery of the Holy Spirit, Conyers, GA
Rodriguez, Very Rev. Edvin, '07 (SAT) Curia: Administration St. Cecilia, San Antonio, TX
Rodriguez, Rev. Elmer, (TLS) Curia: Offices and Directors St. Francis Xavier Church and Diocesan Marian Shrine & Expiatory Temple of Our Lady of Guadalupe, Tulsa, OK
Rodriguez, Rev. Emilio, *O. Carm.* '05 (NEW) St. Cecilia, Englewood, NJ
Rodriguez, Rev. Fabian Rodriguez, *S.J.* (SJN) San Ignacio de Loyola, San Juan, PR; [SPF] Centro Medico de P.R., San Juan, PR
Rodriguez, Rev. Feliciano, '85 (CGS) Curia: Leadership; Offices and Directors Nuestra Senora de la Asuncion, Cayey, PR
Rodriguez, Rev. Felix, (YAK) St. Aloysius, Toppenish, WA
Rodriguez, Rev. Fidel, '97 (ORL) St. Thomas Aquinas Church, St. Cloud, FL
Rodriguez, Rev. Florencio, *T.O.R.* '80 (AUS) Our Lady of Guadalupe, Austin, TX
Rodriguez, Rev. Francis, *O.C.S.O.* '55 (WOR) [MON] St. Joseph's Abbey (Cistercian Abbey of Spencer, Inc., Cistercian Order of the Strict Observance (Trappists)), Spencer, MA
Rodriguez, Rev. Francisco, '15 (AUS) St. William, Round Rock, TX
Rodriguez, Very Rev. Francisco J., '10 (NEW) Curia: Advisory Boards, Commissions, Committees, and Councils; Offices and Directors St. Francis de Sales Church, Lodi, NJ
Rodriguez, Rev. Franklin, '64 (CGS) Retired.
Rodriguez, Rev. German, (MRY) St. John the Baptist, King City, CA
Rodriguez, Rev. Gilbert, '74 (SAN) Retired.
Rodriguez, Rev. Gilberto, *S.T.* (LA) Our Lady of Victory, Compton, CA
Rodriguez, Rev. Giovanni, '15 (PAT) St. Clement, Pope and Martyr, Dover, NJ
Rodriguez, Rev. Guillermo, '56 (SFR) Retired.
Rodriguez, Rev. Msgr. Guillermo A., '69 (LA) Retired.
Rodriguez, Rev. Hector M, '15 (FAJ) Curia: Communications; Leadership Colegio Nuestra Senora del Carmen, Rio Grande, PR; [PRE] Divine Child Jesus Children's Home of the Hermanas Hijas del Corazon Misericordioso de Maria, Luquillo, PR
Rodriguez, Rev. Hector William, '79 (LA) Our Lady of Guadalupe, Irwindale, CA
Rodriguez, Rev. Homero, (EVN) Curia: Leadership St. Joseph, Jasper, IN; Visitation of the Blessed Virgin Mary, Huntingburg, IN
Rodriguez, Rev. Israel J., '09 (BO) Curia: Clergy and Religious Services St. Joseph, Lynn, MA; St. Mary of the Assumption, Lawrence, MA
Rodriguez, Rev. Ivan Maximiliano, '14 (MIA) Curia: Leadership Our Lady Queen of Martyrs, Fort Lauderdale, FL
Rodriguez, Rev. Jaime A., *S.S.S.* (CGS) Church of St. Anthony of Padua, Barranquitas, PR
Rodriguez, Rev. James, '08 (BRK) St. Rose of Lima, Rockaway Beach, NY
Rodriguez, Rev. Jesus, *S.J.* '95 (NO) [MON] Jesuit Provincial Office (Catholic Society of Religious and Literary Education), New Orleans, LA
Rodriguez, Rev. Jesus, *C.S.J.* (NEW) Our Lady of Mt. Carmel, Orange, NJ
Rodriguez, Rev. Joaquin, '72 (MIA) St. Martin de Porres Catholic Church, Leisure City, FL
Rodriguez, Rev. Msgr. John F., '59 (SFR) Retired.
Rodriguez, Rev. Jorge, *S.D.B.* (NY) Parish of St. John Bosco, Port Chester, NY
Rodriguez, Rev. Jorge I., '86 (PAT) Assumption of the Blessed Virgin Mary, Passaic, NJ
Rodriguez, Rev. Jose A., '95 (WOR) Curia: Leadership; Offices and Directors Holy Family of Nazareth, Leominster, MA
Rodriguez, Rev. Msgr. Jose A., '64 (SFR) Retired. Our Lady of the Wayside, Portola Valley, CA; St. Peter, San Francisco, CA
Rodriguez, Rev. Jose Alberto, '05 (AGN) Our Lady of Mount Carmel, Hågat, GU
Rodriguez, Rev. Jose Alberto, '05 (AGN) Curia: Miscellaneous / Other Offices
Rodriguez, Rev. Jose deJesus, '12 (NEW) St. Nicholas, Jersey City, NJ
Rodriguez, Rev. Juan Edwardo, '21 (ALN) St. Peter the Apostle, Reading, PA
Rodriguez, Rev. Leonel, '16 (BWN) Curia: Advisory Boards, Commissions, Committees, and Councils; Leadership; Offices and Directors St. Benedict, San Benito, TX; The Parish of the Lord of Divine Mercy, Brownsville, TX
Rodriguez, Rev. Libardo, '17 (CGS) Church of St. Joseph, Aibonito, PR
Rodriguez, Rev. Luis, *S.J.* '65 (MIL) [MON] St. Camillus Jesuit Community (Society of Jesus, USA Midwest Province), Wauwatosa, WI
Rodriguez, Very Rev. Luis F., '01 (NO) Curia: Leadership St. Clement of Rome Roman Catholic Church, Metairie, Louisiana, Metairie, LA
Rodriguez, Rev. Luis R., '93 (HBG) Corpus Christi, Chambersburg, PA; Our Lady of Refuge Mission, Doylesburg, PA; San Juan Bautista Parish Lancaster Charitable Trust, Lancaster, PA
Rodriguez, Rev. Manuel A., '19 (SAC) Pastor of St. Charles Borromeo Parish, Sacramento, a corporation sole, Sacramento, CA
Rodriguez, Rev. Manuel de Jesus, '04 (BRK) Curia: Leadership Our Lady of Sorrows, Corona, NY
Rodriguez, Rev. Mario, *M.Sp.S* '00 (P) St. Matthew Catholic Church, Hillsboro, OR; [MON] Missionaries of the Holy Spirit, M.Sp.S., Hillsboro, OR
Rodriguez, Rev. Martin, (LA) St. Andrew, Pasadena, CA
Rodriguez, Rev. Martin, '13 (IND) On Special Assignment. Calle 11 Notre numero 30; Barrio de San Juan, Tecamachal...
Rodriguez, Rev. Matias, '66 (TYL) Retired.
Rodriguez, Rev. Michael Michael, '90 (SAN) St. Joseph's, Stanton, TX; [MIS] St. Vincent De Paul Society, Stanton, TX
Rodriguez, Rev. Miguel, '12 (MRY) St. Joseph, Nipomo, CA
Rodriguez, Very Rev. Nestor, '93 (PMB) Curia: Leadership St. Joan of Arc, Boca Raton, FL
Rodriguez, Rev. Orlando J., *Sch.P.* (NY) Annunciation, New York, NY
Rodriguez, Rev. Rafael, *S.J.* '84 (SJN) Curia: Offices and Directors [MIS] Centro Universitario Catolico, San Juan, PR
Rodriguez, Rev. Rafael G., '04 (MIL) St. Michael's Congregation, Milwaukee, WI; The Congregation of St. Rose, Milwaukee, WI
Rodriguez, Rev. Raguiel, (STA) St. Augustine Church and Catholic Student Center, Gainesville, FL
Rodriguez, Rev. Ray, '94 (CHY) Curia: Consultative Bodies [CAM] St. Francis Newman Center, Casper, WY
Rodriguez, Rev. Raymond P., '94 (CHY) St. Anthony of Padua, Casper, WY; [EFT] St. Anthony Tri-Parish Catholic School Foundation, Casper, WY
Rodriguez, Rev. Reyes G., '67 (SLC) Retired.
Rodriguez, Rev. Rigoberto, '89 (LA) St. Emydius, Lynwood, CA
Rodriguez, Rev. Robert, '14 (NY) St. Lucy, Bronx, NY
Rodriguez, Rev. Robert A., '08 (TUC) Saint Joseph Roman Catholic Parish - Tucson, Tucson, AZ; [MIS] Diocese of Tucson Catholic Committee on Scouting, Tucson, AZ; [MIS] Rachel's Vineyard Retreat Ministries Tucson and Southern Arizona, Inc., Hereford, AZ
Rodriguez, Rev. Roberto, *M.M.* '95 (SJ) [MON] Maryknoll, Los Altos, CA
Rodriguez, Rev. Rogelio, '95 (GBG) Holy Cross, Youngwood, PA
Rodriguez, Rev. Ruben Dario, '09 (MGZ) St. Anthony Abbot, Anasco, PR
Rodriguez, Rev. Santos, '70 (SFR) St. Raphael, San Rafael, CA
Rodriguez, Rev. Sergio, (JOL) St. Dominic, Bolingbrook, IL
Rodriguez, Rev. Sergio, '19 (MIL) Curia: Leadership Congregation of the Immaculate Conception (St. Mary), Burlington, WI; St. Charles Congregation, Burlington, WI; St. Joseph's Congregation, Lyons, WI
Rodriguez, Rev. Tobias, '02 (NEW) On Duty Outside Diocese. Most Holy Name of Jesus, Washington, DC
Rodriguez, Rev. Val Gabriel Roa, '98 (AGN) Curia: Advisory Boards, Commissions, Committees, and Councils; Consultative Bodies Immaculate Heart of Mary (Toto Church), Toto, GU
Rodriguez, Rev. William H., '02 (R) Sts. Mary and Edward, Roxboro, NC
Rodriguez, Rev. Wilson Montes, '06 (MGZ) St. Michael, Cabo Rojo, PR
Rodriguez, Rev. Wilson Montes, '06 (MGZ) Curia: Offices and Directors
Rodriguez, Rev. Zack, '20 (AUS) Curia: Tribunal St. Louis, Austin, TX
Rodriguez, Rev. Melquiades Rojas, '91 (ARE) Curia: Leadership
Rodriguez Artola, Rev. Alejandro J., '08 (MIA) Curia: Consultative Bodies; Leadership St. Thomas the Apostle Church, Miami, FL
Rodriguez de la Viuda, Rev. Jorge L., '01 (MIA) St. Bernard, Sunrise, FL
Rodriguez Ferra, Rev. Gilberto, '20 (PCE) Catedral Nuestra Senora de Guadalupe, Ponce, PR
Rodriguez Garnica, Rev. Luis Felipe, '97 (SJN) Cristo Salvador, Guaynabo, PR
Rodriguez Genao, Rev. Francisco Jose, *M.SS.CC.* (SJN) San Juan Bautista de la Salle, Bayamon, PR
Rodriguez Gomez, Rev. Alejandro, *S.X.* '07 (MIL) [SEM] Xaverian Missionary Fathers College Seminary, Franklin, WI
Rodriguez Goopio, Rev. Jose, *S.V.D.* (SB) St. Matthew, Corona, CA
Rodriguez Hernandez, Rev. Carlos Luis, *C.P.* '99 (NY) [MON] The Congregation of the Passion - St. Paul of the Cross Province, Jamaica, NY
Rodriguez Hernandez, Rev. Carlos Luis, *CP* (SJN) Nuestra Senora de la Piedad, Carolina, PR
Rodriguez Lopez, Friar Alberto, *O.P.* (GAL) Holy Rosary, Houston, TX
Rodriguez Martino, Rev. Jose Diego, '81 (PCE) San Jose Obrero, Ponce, PR

Rodriguez Muniz, Rev. Jesús Antonio, '93 (ARE) [MIS] Chapel La Milagrosa, Arecibo, PR; [MIS] Chapel San Jose, Arecibo, PR; [MIS] Chapel San Martin de Porres, Arecibo, PR; [MIS] Chapel San Pascual, Arecibo, PR; [MIS] Chapel Santisimo Sacramento, Arecibo, PR
Rodriguez Muniz, Rev. Jesús Antonio, '93 (ARE) Church of Santa Cecilia, Arecibo, PR
Rodriguez Orengo, Rev. Msgr. Juan, '79 (PCE) San Conrado, Ponce, PR; San Jose, Ponce, PR
Rodríguez Ramos, Rev. Rubén Darío, *O. Carm.* (ARE) Holy Rosary, Ciales, PR
Rodriguez Reyes, Rev. Jose Angel, (SJN) Curia: Offices and Directors San Antonio de Padua, Dorado, PR
rodriguez Roman, Friar Francsico Javier, *OFM* (ELP) All Saints, El Paso, TX
Rodriguez-Delgado, Rev. Emerson, *O.F.M.* (CHR) St. Andrew, Myrtle Beach, SC
Rodriguez-Fuentes, Rev. Rafael, '07 (LIN) Curia: Leadership; Offices and Directors
Rodriguez-Garibay, Rev. Gerardo, *CMF* '09 (FRS) St. Anthony Claret, Fresno, CA
Rodriguez-Hernandez, Rev. Edwin, '95 (ALX) St. Alphonsus, Hessmer, LA
Rodriguez-Jimenes, Rev. Msgr. Leonardo J., '90 (SJN) Curia: Leadership; Offices and Directors Maria Madre de la Misericordia, Guaynabo, PR
Rodriguez-Ochoa, Rev. Leonardo, (SJN) Resurreccion del Senor, San Juan, PR
Rodriguez-Otero, Rev. Msgr. Efrain, '74 (SJN) Curia: Leadership San Fernando, Carolina, PR
Rodriguez-Perez, Rev. Gustavo, '20 (MET) Curia: Family Life St. Joseph, North Plainfield, NJ
Rodriguez-Reyes, Rev. Jose De Jesus, (NEW) Holy Cross, Harrison, NJ
Rodriquez Villanueva, Rev. Hector M., '15 (FAJ) Curia: Offices and Directors Cathedral Santiago Apostol, Fajardo, PR
Roebert, Rev. Michael, '66 (LA) Retired.
Roedel, Rev. Jeff, *ISP* '20 (AUS) [MON] Schoenstatt Fathers, Austin, TX
Roedlach, Rev. Alexander, *S.V.D.* '90 (DUB) [SEM] Divine Word College, Epworth, IA
Roehrich, Rev. David, '84 (SFS) Good Shepherd Parish of Turner County, Centerville, SD; Saint Patrick Parish of Clay County, Wakonda, SD; St. Teresa of Avila Parish of Union County, Beresford, SD
Roehrig, Rev. Matthew, *S.S.P.* '84 (Y) [MIS] Society of St. Paul (Alba House Communications), Canfield, OH
Roehrig, Rev. Matthew, *S.S.P.* '84 (NY) [SEM] Society of St. Paul, Staten Island, NY
Roelant, Rev. Kevin, '16 (DET) St. Thecla Parish Clinton Township, Clinton Township, MI
Roemer, Rev. Richard, *C.F.R.* '98 (NY) [MIS] Franciscan Friars of the Renewal, Yonkers, NY
Roemmele, Rev. Michael P., '11 (TOL) St. Ann, Fremont, OH; St. Joseph, Fremont, OH
Roesch, Rev. David H., '67 (ALT) Retired.
Roeseler, Rev. Brian A, '11 (COS) Corpus Christi, Colorado Springs, CO
Roetzel, Rev. Robert E, *CSC* (FR) [COL] Holy Cross Fathers Religious, North Easton, MA
Roetzel, Rev. Robert E., (MO) Curia: Offices and Directors
Rog, Rev. Stanislaw, '93 (HEL) Curia: Leadership Risen Christ Parish: Series 536, LLC, Kalispell, MT; Saint Matthew Parish: Series 535, LLC, Kalispell, MT
Rogaczewski, Rev. Daniel, '00 (ATL) All Saints Catholic Church, Dunwoody, Inc., Dunwoody, GA
Rogala, Rev. Gerald E., '66 (CHI) Retired. St. Elizabeth of the Trinity, Chicago, IL
Roger-Ndzana, Rev. Jules, *O. de M.* (CGS) Nuestra Senora de la Merced, Cayey, PR
Rogers, Rev. Christopher B., '00 (PH) St. Patrick, Kennett Square, PA
Rogers, Rev. Dalton, '22 (FRS) Good Shepherd Catholic Parish, Visalia, CA
Rogers, Rev. Joel, *C.P.M.* '00 (OWN) [MON] Fathers of Mercy, Auburn, KY (>L) St. Helen, Glasgow, KY
Rogers, Rev. Joel C., *C.P.M.* (L) Curia: Leadership Emmanuel Catholic, Albany, KY
Rogers, Rev. Joseph E., '07 (WDC) On Leave. St. John Neumann, Gaithersburg, MD
Rogers, Rev. Joseph Everett, (MIA) On Special Assignment. Chaplain, Servants of the Pierced Hearts of Jesus and Mary [CON] Siervas de los Corazones Traspasados de Jesus y Maria, Inc. (Servants of the Pierced Hearts of Jesus and Mary), Miami, FL; [SEM] St. John Vianney College Seminary, Inc., Miami, FL
Rogers, Rev. Michael J., *S.J.* '13 (WOR) On Administrative Leave. married [MON] Jesuits of the Holy Cross, Inc., Worcester, MA
Rogers, Rev. Patrick D., *S.J.* '02 (SCR) (>SY) [COL] Le Moyne College, Syracuse, NY; (>SY) [MON] Jesuits at LeMoyne, Inc., Syracuse, NY
Rogers, Rev. Peter, *O.P.* '02 (OAK) (>LA) St. Dominic, Los Angeles, CA
Rogers, Rev. Philip E., '80 (Y) Christ Our Savior Parish, Struthers, OH
Rogers, Rev. Robert C., '92 (HT) St. Louis, Houma, LA
Rogers, Rev. Sean, '04 (SR) Curia: Leadership Pastor of St. John the Baptist Catholic Church of Healdsburg, A Corporation Sole, Healdsburg, CA
Rogers, Rev. Steven C., '06 (KC) Holy Trinity, Weston, MO; Twelve Apostles Parish, Platte City, MO
Rogers, Rt. Rev. Vincent, '10 (WOR) [MON] St. Joseph's Abbey (Cistercian Abbey of Spencer, Inc., Cistercian Order of the Strict Observance (Trappists)), Spencer, MA
Rogers, Rev. Vincent M., '93 (KC) St. Andrew the Apostle, Gladstone, MO
Rogliano, Rev. Joseph S., '85 (BUF) Curia: Consultative Bodies St. Martin de Porres, Buffalo, NY
Roh, Rev. Msgr. Robert A., '65 (LIN) Retired.
Rohen, Rev. Patrick J., '96 (TOL) Retired.
Rohleder, Rev. Earl, '63 (EVN) Retired.
Rohlfing, Rev. Cory J., '01 (STP) Divine Mercy Catholic Church, Faribault, MN; St. Michael, Kenyon, MN; [CEM] Calvary Cemetery, Faribault, MN; [CEM] St. Edwards of Richland, Kenyon, MN; [CEM] St. Lawrence Cemetery, Faribault, MN
Rohlfs, Rev. Msgr. Steven P., '76 (PEO) Retired. On Duty Outside Diocese. St Paul Seminary, St Paul, MN
Rohr, Rev. Jerry, (DEN) Catholic Parish of Saint Patrick in Holyoke, Holyoke, CO
Rohr, Rev. Richard, *O.F.M.* '70 (SFE) [MON] The Province of Our Lady of Guadalupe of the Order of Friars Minor, Inc., Albuquerque, NM
Rohrich, Rev. Robert R., *C.M.* '61 (CHI) [MON] DePaul Vincentian Residence, Chicago, IL
Roia, Rev. Martino, *S.X.* '82 (PAT) [MON] Xaverian Missionary Fathers, Wayne, NJ
Roide, Rev. Thomas, '18 (LA) On Administrative Leave.
Rojas, Rev. Arthur F., '06 (NY) Parish of Presentation of the Blessed Virgin Mary and Sacred Heart, Port Ewen, NY
Rojas, Rev. Arthur F., '06 (NY) On Sick Leave.
Rojas, Rev. Arthur Fernando, '06 (NY) [MIS] Presentation of the Blessed Virgin Mary, ,
Rojas, Rev. Carlos E., *Sch.P.* '98 (LA) Santa Teresita, Los Angeles, CA; [MON] Piarist Fathers, Los Angeles, CA
Rojas, Rev. Carlos J., '06 (SP) St. Rita, Dade City, FL
Rojas, Rev. Carlos Jose, '06 (SP) [MIS] Schoenstatt Tampa Bay, Inc., Tampa, FL
Rojas, Rev. Diego Cabrera, *S.S.C.* '95 (LA) St. Hilary, Pico Rivera, CA
Rojas, Rev. Hugo Marcel, '97 (SJ) Curia: Leadership; Offices and Directors Our Lady of Refuge, San Jose, CA
Rojas, Rev. Joaquin J., *M.N.M.* '02 (SAT) St. Gabriel, San Antonio, TX; St. Martin de Porres, San Antonio, TX
Rojas, Rev. Loreto Bong B., '00 (SAC) Pastor of Holy Spirit Parish, Sacramento, a corporation sole, Sacramento, CA
Rojas, Rev. Louis E., *S.A.C.* '97 (NSH) Retired.
Rojas, Rev. Richard, '13 (POC) On Duty Outside Diocese.
Rojas, Rev. Richard, (MO) Curia: Offices and Directors
Rojas, Rev. Roberto, '96 (SJ) On Leave.
Rojas, Rev. Tito Nels, '68 (ORL) Retired.
Rojas Fernandez, Rev. Joaquin J., (SAT) Our Lady of Good Counsel, San Antonio, TX
Rojas Rodriguez, Rev. Melquiades, '91 (ARE) Curia: Leadership [MIS] Chapel San Jose, Manati, PR; [MIS] Chapel San Martin de Porres, Manati, PR
Rojas Rodriguez, Rev. Melquiades, '91 (ARE) Our Savior, Manati, PR
Rojas Rodriguez, Rev. Victor, '85 (ARE) Immaculate Conception of Blessed Virgin Mary, Vega Alta, PR
Rojas Rodriguez, Rev. Victor, '85 (ARE) Curia: Leadership; Offices and Directors [MIS] Chapel Inmaculado Corazon de Maria, Vega Alta, PR; [MIS] Chapel Nuestra Senora de Lourdes, Vega Alta, PR; [MIS] Chapel Sagrado Corazon de Jesus, Vega Alta, PR; [MIS] Chapel Santa Ana, Vega Alta, PR
Rojas-Hernandez, Rev. Juan Gabriel, '13 (TR) On Duty Outside Diocese. Working in the Arch Diocese of Newark (>NEW) St. Helen, Westfield, NJ
Rojo, Rev. Ryan, '15 (SAN) Curia: Advisory Boards, Commissions, Committees, and Councils; Offices and Directors
Rokita, Rev. Lukasz Stanislaw, '12 (NEW) Church of St. Thomas the Apostle, Bloomfield, NJ; Sacred Heart, Bloomfield, NJ
Rokitka, Rev. Nick, *O.F.M.Conv.* (TR) St. Peter's, Point Pleasant Beach, NJ
Roland, Rev. Charles W., '67 (PT) Retired.
Roland, Rev. Glynn (Bud), '99 (AUS) Retired.
Roldan, Rev. Jorge, (SLC) Our Lady of Guadalupe LLC 208, Salt Lake City, UT
Roldan, Rev. Msgr. Joseph L., '02 (TR) St. Joseph, Trenton, NJ; St. Mary Cathedral, Trenton, NJ
Roldan, Rev. Jovito B., (SB) Chap, Marine Corps Base, Twentynine Palms
Roldan, Rev. Jovy, '98 (STO) On Duty Outside Diocese. Archdiocese of Military Services, Twentynine Palms Curia: (>MO) Offices and Directors
Roldan, Rev. Juan, '56 (SJN) On Duty Outside Diocese. Caguas, PR
Rolewicz, Rev. Richard S., *M.M.* '65 (NY) Retired. [MON] Maryknoll Fathers and Brothers (Catholic Foreign Mission Society of America, Inc.), Ossining, NY
Rolex, Rev. Jean, *CM* (SJN) Jesus Maestro, San Juan, PR
Rolfes, Rev. Robert E., '77 (SCL) Curia: Leadership; Offices and Directors
Rolheiser, Rev. Ronald, *O.M.I.* '72 (SAT) [COL] Oblate School of Theology, San Antonio, TX; [MON] Missionary Oblates of Mary Immaculate of Texas, San Antonio, TX
Rolland, Rev. Daniel, *O.P.* '93 (LAV) [CAM] St. Thomas Aquinas Catholic Newman Community at UNLV, Las Vegas, NV; [MON] Dominican Rectory, Fra Angelico House, Las Vegas, NV
Rolland, Rev. Michael, *OP* '88 (LAV) St. Christopher, North Las Vegas, NV
Rolland, Rev. Michael (Miguel), *O.P.* '88 (LAV) Curia: Advisory Boards, Commissions, Committees, and Councils
Roller, Rev. John W., '60 (CHI) Retired. St. Emily, Mt. Prospect, IL; St. Thomas Becket, Mt. Prospect, IL
Rolling, Rev. Brendan, *O.S.B.* '00 (KCK) [MON] St. Benedict's Abbey, Atchison, KS
Rolling, Rev. Matthew M., '10 (LIN) [SEM] St. Gregory the Great Seminary, Seward, NE
Rolon Ortiz, Rev. Alfredo A., '02 (MIA) St. Malachy, Tamarac, FL
Rolon Torres, Rev. Julio A., '93 (PCE) Curia: Leadership San Blas de Illescas, Coamo, PR
Rolph, Rev. James R., '14 (LAN) Curia: Leadership Immaculate Heart of Mary Parish Lansing, Lansing, MI
Rom, Rev. Gregory A., '75 (CHI) Retired.
Romaine, Rev. Robert G., '92 (SP) Holy Family, St. Petersburg, FL
Roman, Rev. David, '19 (BGP) St. Aloysius Church Corporation of Connecticut, New Canaan, CT
Roman, Rev. Jorge A., '81 (STO) St. Joseph Church of Mammoth Lakes, Mammoth Lakes, CA
Roman, Rev. Julio, '73 (LA) Retired.
Roman, Rev. Julio I., '00 (NEW) On Duty Outside Diocese. Archdiocese of Asuncion, Asuncion
Roman, Rev. Mitchel, '19 (GLD) Curia: Advisory Boards, Commissions, Committees, and Councils Holy Redeemer of Vanderbilt, Vanderbilt, MI; Saint Mary, Our Lady of Mt. Carmel Cathedral of Gaylord, Gaylord, MI; Saint Thomas Aquinas of Elmira, Elmira, MI
Roman, Rev. Paul, '99 (BWN) Hosp Ministry St. Anne, Mother of Mary, Pharr, TX
Roman, Rev. Stephen, '57 (SEA) Retired.
Roman, Rev. Thomas, '10 (BUF) Our Lady of Pompeii, Lancaster, NY; [MON] Brothers of Mercy of Mary Help of Christians, Inc., Clarence, NY
Roman, Rev. Victor, '84 (DET) On Leave.
Roman Toro, Rev. Carlos, '89 (PCE) Retired. On Duty Outside Diocese.
Romanek, Very Rev. Janusz, '07 (MAR) Curia: Advisory Boards, Commissions, Committees, and Councils St. Mary and St. Joseph, Iron Mountain, MI
Romanello, Rev. James S., '13 (CIN) Our Lady of Lourdes, Cincinnati, OH; St. Antoninus, Cincinnati, OH
Romankiv, Very Rev. Archpriest Andrii, '02 (SJP) Curia: Leadership; Offices and Directors Assumption of the Blessed Virgin Mary, Miami, FL
Romano, Rev. Blase, *T.O.R.* '89 (ORL) [MON] Franciscan Friars, TOR, New Smyrna Beach, FL; [MON] Villa Madonna Friary (Franciscan Friars TOR), New Smyrna Beach, FL
Romano, Rev. Charles, '79 (RVC) St. Raymond's, East Rockaway, NY
Romano, Rev. Joseph L., '63 (DET) Retired.
Romano, Rev. Nathaniel, '18 (BO) (>MIL) [MON] Jesuit Community at Marquette University (Marquette Jesuit Associates, Inc.), Milwaukee, WI
Romano, Rev. Philip, *O.F.M. Cap.* (NY) [MON] St.

Clare Friary (Capuchin Franciscan Friars, Province of St. Mary), Yonkers, NY
Romano, Rev. Msgr. Robert J., '77 (BRK) Our Lady of Guadalupe, Brooklyn, NY
Romano, Rev. Robert J., '77 (BRK) Curia: Pastoral Services
Romanoski, Rev. Jonathan, *FSSP* '08 (PRO) St. Mary's Church Providence Rhode Island, Providence, RI
Romanoski, Rev. Joseph V., '86 (CHR) Corpus Christi, Lexington, SC
Romanowski, Rev. Brian J., '03 (NOR) Curia: Leadership; Offices and Directors; Tribunal St. Patrick Cathedral, Norwich, CT
Romanowski, Rev. Slawomir, *C.Ss.R* '99 (MET) Saint John Paul II Parish, Perth Amboy, NJ
Romans, Rev. Jeffrey V., '03 (HRT) Curia: Advisory Boards, Commissions, Committees, and Councils; Deaneries; Development Saint Bridget of Sweden Parish Corporation, Cheshire, CT
Romanyuk, Rev. Ruslan, '09 (PHU) Curia: Leadership St. Vladimir's, Elizabeth, NJ
Rome, Rev. James, (HT) St. Bernadette Soubirous Church, Houma, LA
Romeo, Rev. Robert A., '87 (RVC) Curia: Leadership St. Mary's, Manhasset, NY
Romerde, Rev. Manuel R., '08 (NEW) On Duty Outside Diocese. Tagbilaran City, Bohol
Romero, Rev. Anthony E., '05 (SFE) Retired.
Romero, Rev. Arturo, '12 (P) St. Patrick, Canby, OR
Romero, Rev. Benjamin, *C.M.F.* (SAT) Immaculate Heart of Mary, San Antonio, TX
Romero, Rev. Domingo, *O.F.M.* '00 (ORG) Our Lady of Guadalupe, Delhi, Santa Ana, CA
Romero, Rev. Donald, '91 (DEN) Chap, Major Curia: (>MO) Offices and Directors
Romero, Rev. Elmer, '03 (CHI) St. Cletus, La Grange, IL; [SEM] University of Saint Mary of the Lake/ Mundelein Seminary, Mundelein, IL
Romero, Rev. Erasmo, *O.F.M.* '12 (SFE) [MON] The Province of Our Lady of Guadalupe of the Order of Friars Minor, Inc., Albuquerque, NM
Romero, Rev. Gilbert Claude, '61 (LA) Retired.
Romero, Rev. Msgr. J. Robert, '75 (LAF) Nativity of Our Lady, New Iberia, LA
Romero, Rev. Juan Antonio, *MSpS* (P) [MON] Missionaries of the Holy Spirit, M.Sp.S., Mount Angel, OR
Romero, Rev. Juan R., '64 (LA) Retired.
Romero, Rev. Juan R., '64 (SB) Retired.
Romero, Rev. Luis M., *M.Id* (RVC) Curia: Leadership Our Lady of Loretto, Hempstead, NY
Romero, Rev. Mario P., '90 (LAF) Holy Cross, Lafayette, LA
Romero, Rev. Miguel, (SD) Pastor of Saint Mark Catholic Parish in San Marcos A Corporation Sole, San Marcos, CA
Romero, Friar Pedro, *OFM Cap.* (DAL) Our Lady of Lourdes Catholic Parish, Dallas, TX; [MON] Capuchin Franciscan Friars, Custody Mexico - Texas, Dallas, TX
Romero, Rev. Ruben, '91 (LSC) Curia: Consultative Bodies; Evangelization Our Lady of Health Parish, Inc., Las Cruces, NM
Romero Morales, Rev. Jose Angel Santos, *M.C.C.J* '95 (LA) Holy Cross, Los Angeles, CA
Romero-Galan, Rev. Jesus, (CHI) Our Lady, the Mystical Rose Parish, Cicero, IL
Romito, Rev. Msgr. Donald, '74 (ORG) Retired. St. Joseph, Placentia, CA
Romke, Rev. Keith D., '11 (RCK) St. Elizabeth Ann Seton, Crystal Lake, IL
Romkema, Rev. Karl, *CSC* '19 (FTW) [MON] Holy Cross Community, Corby Hall, University of Notre Dame, Notre Dame, IN; [SEM] Moreau Seminary, Notre Dame, IN; [SEM] Old College, Notre Dame, IN
Romo, Rev. Sergio, '93 (CHI) St. Andrew, Chicago, IL
Romo-Romo, Rev. Antonio, *S.V.D.* '05 (MEM) [MON] Society of the Divine Word (Chicago Province), Memphis, TN
Romo-Romo, Rev. Juan Antonio, *S.V.D.* '05 (MEM) Curia: Leadership St. Joseph Catholic Church, Memphis, TN
Ronaghan, Rev. John J., '80 (BO) Saint Teresa of Calcutta Parish, Boston, MA
Ronan, Rev. Gerald C., '74 (PH) Retired.
Ronan, Rev. Msgr. Hugh F., '61 (TR) Retired. [MON] Villa Vianney, Trenton, NJ
Ronan, Rev. James J., '82 (BO) Retired. Curia: Leadership St. Mary - St. Catherine of Siena, Boston, MA
Ronayne, Rev. Michael, *O.F.M.* '96 (LA) St. Lawrence of Brindisi, Los Angeles, CA
Roncancio, Rev. Luis A., '95 (TYL) Retired.
Roncase, Rev. Robert A., '82 (PH) Retired. On Leave.
Rondael, Rev. Mariano, (CHI) SS. Peter and Lambert Parish, Skokie, IL
Rondeau, Rev. Lawrence J., '58 (BO) Retired. Immaculate Conception, Salem, MA; St. James, Salem, MA
Roodbeen, Rev. Henry W., '75 (DET) Retired.
Roof, Rev. Frank, '72 (OWN) Retired.
Rooney, Rev. Aidan R, *C.M.* '84 (BRK) [COL] St. John's University, Queens, NY (>NY) [COL] St. John's University Staten Island Campus, Staten Island, NY
Rooney, Rev. Donald J., '94 (ARL) Curia: Offices and Directors St. Bernadette, Springfield, VA
Rooney, Rev. Edward K., '62 (STA) Retired.
Rooney, Rev. John, *M.R.E.* '01 (GAL) St. Mary, League City, TX
Rooney, Rev. John C., '89 (LIN) Curia: Offices and Directors
Rooney, Rev. John Cletus, '89 (LIN) [SEM] St. Gregory the Great Seminary, Seward, NE
Rooney, Rev. Kevin E., '62 (BUR) Retired.
Rooney, Rt. Rev. Marcel, *O.S.B.* '63 (KC) Retired. [MON] Conception Abbey (Benedictine Monks), Conception, MO
Rooney, Very Rev. Martin, *M.S.A.* '93 (NOR) [MON] Society of the Missionaries of the Holy Apostles, Cromwell, CT
Rooney, Rev. Ryan, '11 (SPR) Our Lady of the Sacred Heart, Springfield, MA
Rooney, Rev. William, '20 (AUS) St. Joseph, Bryan, TX
Roos, Very Rev. Lee R., '90 (ARL) Curia: Tribunal All Saints, Manassas, VA
Roost, Rev. Joseph F., '89 (DAV) Retired.
Root, Rev. Msgr. James A., '84 (SAM) Curia: Offices and Directors St. Anthony of the Desert, Fall River, MA
Root, Rev. Richard, '90 (SPK) Retired.
Ropel, Rev. Mark A., '02 (BLX) Chap, Univ of Southern Mississippi Curia: Advisory Boards, Commissions, Committees, and Councils; Faith Formation; Leadership St. Thomas Aquinas, Hattiesburg, MS; [CAM] University of Southern Mississippi, Hattiesburg, MS
Roque, Rev. Reynaldo, '86 (SD) Pastor of Saint Didacus Catholic Parish, San Diego, a corporation sole, San Diego, CA; [MIS] Saint Didacus Catholic Parish in San Diego, CA Real Property Support Corporation, San Diego, CA
Rora, Rev. Michael S., '18 (BO) Curia: Consultative Bodies Mary, Queen of Martyrs Parish, Plymouth, MA
Roraff, Rev. Arthur, '15 (AJ) Curia: Offices and Directors St. Andrew, Eagle River, AK
Rosa, Rev. Michal, '05 (SFD) Sacred Heart, Effingham, IL
Rosado, Rev. Adaly, '11 (NY) St. Christopher and St. Margaret Mary, Staten Island, NY
Rosado, Rev. Adaly, (NY) Parish of Saint Joseph/Saint Boniface, Spring Valley, NY
Rosado, Rev. Anthony F., '14 (BRK) On Duty Outside Diocese. 46-02 Parsons Blvd., Flushing, NY 11355 Mary's Nativity-Saint Ann Roman Catholic Church, Flushing, NY; [CAM] Campus Ministers and Ministry Centers (Newman Apostolate, Inc.), Brooklyn, NY
Rosado, Rev. Benjamin, (SFR) St. Matthew, San Mateo, CA
Rosado, Rev. Efrain, *OSB* (SCL) [MON] St. John's Abbey, of the Order of St. Benedict, Collegeville, MN
Rosado, Rev. Rodney Algarin, '01 (SJN) Curia: Leadership
Rosaforte, Rev. Msgr. Anthony S., '70 (NOR) Curia: Leadership; Offices and Directors St. Patrick Cathedral, Norwich, CT
Rosal, Rev. Rey, (CHK) Cathedral of Our Lady of Mt. Carmel, Saipan, MP
Rosales, Rev. Deogracias, '82 (POD) Curia: Clergy and Religious Services
Rosales, Rev. Deogracias, '82 (CHI) [MIS] Midtown Residence, Chicago, IL
Rosales, Rev. Fredy B., '03 (LA) Presentation of Mary, Los Angeles, CA
Rosales, Rev. Martin Renzo, *S.J.* '98 (OM) [MON] Jesuit Community at Creighton University, Omaha, NE
Rosales, Rev. Ricardo, *L.C.* '97 (COS) St. Mary's Cathedral, Colorado Springs, CO
Rosales, Rev. Roberto, '18 (SAT) St. Elizabeth Ann Seton, San Antonio, TX
Rosales, Rev. Samuel, *S.J.* '73 (ELP) Sacred Heart, El Paso, TX
Rosalinas, Rev. Rogel, *S.O.L.T.* '94 (CC) St. Joseph, Corpus Christi, TX; [MON] Society of Our Lady of the Most Holy Trinity, Corpus Christi, TX
Rosario, Rev. George, *C.Ss.R.* (CHR) Our Lady of the Hills, Columbia, SC
Rosario, Rev. Mario, (B) [MIS] St. Mary's A.F.B., Mountain Home, ID
Rosario, Rev. Mario S., '90 (MO) Curia: Offices and Directors
Rosario, Rev. William D., '90 (OAK) St. John Vianney, Walnut Creek, CA
Rosario Mercado, Rev. Anibal, *O.F.M.Cap.* (SJN) San Francisco de Monte Alvernia, San Juan, PR
Rosario Prendes, Rev. Enzo, '22 (MIA) Immaculate Conception, Hialeah, FL
Rosas Flores, Rev. Salvador, *OFM* '11 (WDC) [MON] Franciscan Monastery USA Inc., Washington, DC
Rosca, Rev. Adrian V., '16 (ROM) Presentation of Mary Romanian Catholic Church, Sherman Oaks, CA
Rosca, Rev. Paschal, *O.de.M.* '63 (CLV) Retired. St. Rocco, Cleveland, OH; [MON] Mercedarians (Fathers of Our Lady of Mercy, Inc. / Order of the B.V.M. of Mercy / Mercedarian Friars USA), Cleveland, OH
Roscioli, Rev. Dominic J., '74 (MIL) Retired.
Rose, Rev. Frank, '90 (NEW) Curia: Offices and Directors St. Bernard of Clairvaux and St. Stanislaus Kostka, Plainfield, NJ
Rose, Rev. Geoffrey N., *O.S.F.S.* '02 (TOL) St. Francis de Sales School, Toledo, OH; [MON] Oblates of St. Francis de Sales, Toledo, OH
Rose, Rev. John F., '72 (SY) Retired.
Rose, Rev. Justin, '95 (NTN) Curia: Administration St. George Church, Birmingham, AL
Rose, Rev. Msgr. Michael F., '81 (WOR) St. Mary's, Shrewsbury, MA
Rose, Rev. William J., '96 (TOL) Curia: Advisory Boards, Commissions, Committees, and Councils; Deaneries
Rosebrough, Rev. Robert T., '69 (STL) Retired.
Roselada, Rev. Eulogio, *O.F.M.* '93 (STL) [MON] Franciscan Friary of St. Anthony of Padua, St. Louis, MO
Roselada, Rev. Eulogio, *O.F.M.* '93 (CHI) [MON] Holy Evangelists Friary, Chicago, IL
Roselli, Rev. Marc J., *S.J.* '85 (NY) Parish of Our Lady of Mount Carmel-St. Benedicta and St. Mary of the Assumption, Staten Island, NY
Rosen, Rev. Cyprian, *O.F.M.Cap.* '62 (WIL) [MON] Capuchin Franciscan Friars, St. Francis of Assisi Friary, Wilmington, DE
Rosenau, Rev. Alan, '88 (LR) Retired.
Rosenbaum, Rev. Mark, '07 (JOL) St. Alexander, Villa Park, IL; St. John the Apostle, Villa Park, IL
Rosenbaum, Rev. William E., '76 (ALT) St. Clement, Johnstown, PA
Rosenberg, Rev. David B., '11 (LAN) Retired.
Roser, Rev. Shawn, (VEN) Our Lady of the Angels Parish in Lakewood Ranch, Inc., Lakewood Ranch, FL
Roser, Rev. Shawn, '18 (VEN) Curia: Leadership
Rosera, Rev. Steve, '80 (SFE) Curia: Offices and Directors Immaculate Conception-Albuquerque, Albuquerque, NM
Rosero, Rev. Carlos, '09 (B) St. Anthony's, Wendell, ID; St. Elizabeth's, Gooding, ID; St. Peter's, Shoshone, ID
Roseswog, Rev. Kenneth, *O.F.M.* '57 (GB) Retired.
Rosette, Rev. Fabian Maria, *O.Carm.* '80 (SAN) [MON] Hermits of the Blessed Virgin Mary of Mount Carmel, Christoval, TX
Rosevear, Rev. Anthony R., *O.P.* '78 (SFR) [MON] St. Dominic Priory, San Francisco, CA
Rosie, Rev. Msgr. Joseph N., '90 (TR) Curia: Leadership St. James, Red Bank, NJ
Rosin, Rev. Richard F, (SP) Espiritu Santo, Safety Harbor, FL
Rosing, Rev. Paul J., '73 (CLV) Retired. Holy Family, Stow, OH
Rosinski, Rev. Adam, *S.J.* '19 (SY) [MIS] Saint Andrew Hall, Syracuse, NY
Rosinski, Rev. Richard A., '91 (RCK) St. Mary, Byron, IL
Rosolen, Rev. Emil, '86 (AMA) On Duty Outside Diocese.
Rosolen, Rev. Higinio, *I.V.E.* '03 (SP) (>NO) [SEM] Saint Joseph Seminary College, Saint Benedict, LA
Rosolowski, Rev. Romulus, *O.F.M.Conv.* '74 (BUF) Our Lady of Victory National Shrine and Basilica, Lackawanna, NY; [MON] St. Maximilian Kolbe Friary, Hamburg, NY
Rosonke, Rev. Steven J., '82 (DUB) St. Anthony Church (Dubuque, Iowa), Dubuque, IA; [MIS] St. Raphael Priest Fund Society of the Archdiocese of Dubuque, Dubuque, IA
Rosonke, Rev. Vince G., '75 (DM) Retired.
Rospond, Rev. Paul S, *CSP* '81 (NY) St. Paul the Apostle, New York, NY
Rospond, Rev. Paul S., *C.S.P.* '81 (NY) [MON] Paulist Fathers' Motherhouse, New York, NY
Ross, Rev. Benjamin J., '12 (GRY) Curia: Leadership; Offices and Directors St. Bridget, Hobart, IN

Ross, Rev. Cody, '16 (SEA) Sacred Heart, Bellingham, WA; [CAM] Western Washington University-Newman Center, Bellingham, WA
Ross, Rev. David M., '75 (TOL) St. John the Evangelist, Lima, OH; St. Rose of Lima, Lima, OH
Ross, Friar Gregory, *OCD* '95 (SAT) Basilica of the National Shrine of the Little Flower, Our Lady of Mt. Carmel and St. Therese Parish, San Antonio, TX; [MON] Discalced Carmelite Fathers of San Antonio, San Antonio, TX; [SHR] Basilica of the National Shrine of the Little Flower, San Antonio, TX
Ross, Rev. Mark J., '88 (SAV) Curia: Leadership St. Mary on the Hill, Augusta, GA
Ross, Rev. Richard, *S.J.* '10 (BO) [MON] The Jesuit Community at Boston College, Chestnut Hill, MA
Ross, Rev. Robert J., *S.J.* '72 (CIN) [MON] Cincinnati Jesuit Community, Cincinnati, OH
Ross, Rev. Theodore C., *S.J.* '67 (DET) [MON] Colombiere Center, Clarkston, MI
Rossell, Rev. Richard, *O.F.M.Conv.* '61 (TR) St. Peter's, Point Pleasant Beach, NJ
Rossetti, Rev. Msgr. Stephen, '84 (SY) On Duty Outside Diocese. Washington, DC
Rossetti, Rev. Msgr. Stephen J., '84 (WDC) [COL] Catholic University of America, The, Washington, DC
Rossey, Rev. Stephen J., *O. Praem.* '59 (GB) [MON] St. Norbert Abbey, De Pere, WI
Rossi, Rev. Anthony T., '09 (PH) St. Anselm, Philadelphia, PA
Rossi, Rev. Desmond, '92 (ALB) St. Gabriel the Archangel, Schenectady, NY; St. Madeleine Sophie, Schenectady, NY
Rossi, Rt. Rev. Domenic A., *O. Praem.* '74 (PH) [MON] Daylesford Abbey, Inc., Paoli, PA; [SEM] Daylesford Abbey (Norbertine Fathers, Inc.), Paoli, PA
Rossi, Rev. Msgr. Frank H., '83 (GAL) Retired.
Rossi, Rev. Gino P., '13 (RIC) St. Joseph, Petersburg, VA
Rossi, Rev. John A., '09 (CAM) Curia: Pastoral Services St. Bridget's Catholic Church, Glassboro, N.J. (St. Bridget University Parish), Glassboro, NJ; [CAM] Rowan University, Glassboro, NJ; [CEM] St. Bridget's Cemetery, Glassboro, NJ
Rossi, Rev. Joseph S., *S.J.* '80 (BAL) [COL] Jesuit Community of Loyola University, Inc., Baltimore, MD; [MON] Jesuit Community of Loyola University Maryland, Inc., Baltimore, MD
Rossi, Rev. Lucas C., '10 (CHL) St. Michael, Gastonia, NC
Rossi, Rev. Paul J., '74 (SFR) Retired.
Rossi, Rev. Philip J., *S.J.* '71 (MIL) [MON] St. Camillus Jesuit Community (Society of Jesus, USA Midwest Province), Wauwatosa, WI
Rossi, Rev. Robert J., *O.S.C.* '70 (PHX) [MON] Crosier Community of Phoenix (Canons Regular of the Order of the Holy Cross) (Conventual Priory of the Holy Cross), Phoenix, AZ
Rossi, Rt. Rev. Ronald J., *O. Praem.* '70 (PH) Retired. [MON] Daylesford Abbey, Inc., Paoli, PA; [SEM] Daylesford Abbey (Norbertine Fathers, Inc.), Paoli, PA
Rossi, Rev. Thomas, '83 (BO) On Leave. St. Angela Merici, Boston, MA
Rossi, Rev. Thomas J., *O.Praem.* '73 (PH) [MON] Daylesford Abbey, Inc., Paoli, PA
Rossi, Rev. Msgr. Walter R., '87 (SCR) On Duty Outside Diocese. (>WDC) [SHR] Basilica of the National Shrine of the Immaculate Conception, Washington, DC
Rossi, Rev. Msgr. Walter R., '87 (WDC) [COL] Catholic University of America, The, Washington, DC; [SHR] Basilica of the National Shrine of the Immaculate Conception, Washington, DC
Rossiter, Rev. Aidan Peter, *C.J.* '92 (LA) St. Louis de Montfort, Santa Maria, CA
Rossman, Rev. Christopher, '07 (KCK) On Leave.
Rossman, Rev. Dick, '71 (P) Curia: Offices and Directors
Rossman, Rev. Richard, '71 (P) Retired. St. Mary - Shaw, Aumsville, OR
Rosson, Rev. John P., '75 (ALB) Retired.
Rosson, Rev. John P., (ALB) (>MAN) St. Thomas More, Durham, NH
Rossotti, Rev. Pietro, *F.S.C.B.* (STP) St. Peter, North St. Paul, MN
Rosswog, Rev. Kenneth, *O.F.M.* '57 (GB) Retired. [MON] Blessed Giles Friary, Manitowoc, WI
Rost, Rev. Robert A., '74 (KC) Retired.
Rostro, Rev. Lino Rico, '98 (ARL) Good Shepherd, Alexandria, VA
Roten, Rev. Johan G., *S.M.* '69 (CIN) [COL] The University of Dayton, Dayton, OH; [MON] Marianist Community, Dayton, OH
Rotert, Rev. Matthew, '94 (KC) St. Peter's, Kansas City, MO
Roth, Rev. Kenneth, (HBG) Saint Joseph Catholic Church, Mechanicsburg, PA
Roth, Rev. Kenneth, (HBG) St. Joan of Arc, Hershey, PA
Roth, Rt. Rev. Neal G., *O.S.B.* '74 (SEA) Retired. [MON] St. Martin's Abbey, Lacey, WA
Roth, Rev. Stephen P., (BAL) Curia: Clergy and Religious Services Cathedral of Mary Our Queen, Baltimore, MD; [EFT] Serra Foundation, Baltimore, MD; [SEM] St. Mary's Seminary and University, Baltimore, MD
Roth, Rev. Timothy, *M.I.C.* '74 (NOR) Marianapolis Preparatory School, Thompson, CT; [MON] Marians of the Immaculate Conception of the B.V.M., Thompson, CT
Roth, Rev. Timothy J., '14 (CLV) Curia: Tribunal
Roth, Rev. Timothy J., *M.I.C.* '74 (NOR) [MIS] Congregation of Marian Fathers of the Immaculate Conception of the B.V.M., Thompson, CT
Rother, Rev. Michael, '07 (VIC) Curia: Leadership St. Andrew, El Campo, TX; St. Philip the Apostle, El Campo, TX
Rothermel, Rev. Paul L., '94 (ALN) Curia: Organizations (affiliated, inter-Diocesan, miscellaneous/ other)
Rothfuchs, Rev. Gregory, '95 (JOL) St. Joseph, Lockport, IL
Rothrock, Rev. Theodore D., '83 (LFT) St. Paul, Marion, IN
Rotola, Rev. Albert C., *S.J.* '68 (STL) [COL] Saint Louis University, St. Louis, MO
Rotondi, Rev. Paul, *O.F.M.* (NY) Retired.
Rott, Rev. Bernard E., '79 (MAD) Holy Ghost, Dickeyville, WI; Immaculate Conception, Kieler, WI
Rott, Rev. Jeffrey M., '09 (PH) [CAM] Delaware Valley College of Science and Agriculture, Chalfont, PA
Rottgers, Rev. Robert A., '09 (COV) St. Philip, Melbourne, KY
Rottman, Rev. Gary P., '03 (TYL) Retired.
Rouch, Very Rev. Nicholas J., '89 (E) Curia: Clergy and Religious Services; Leadership; Miscellaneous / Other Offices Our Lady of Mt. Carmel, Erie, PA; [MIS] Bishop Michael J. Murphy Residence for Retired Priests, Erie, PA
Rouech, Rev. Chris W., '96 (GR) Holy Trinity, Comstock Park, MI
Rougeau, Rev. Marc, *S.D.B.* '77 (STO) St. Luke Church of Stockton (Pastor of), Stockton, CA
Rouhana, Rev. Fadi, '09 (SAM) Mission of Sts. Peter & Paul, Tampa, FL
Rouleau, Rev. Francis, '00 (NOR) Curia: Offices and Directors
Rouleau, Rev. Francis C., '00 (NOR) On Duty Outside Diocese.
Rourke, Rev. John, '63 (VEN) Retired.
Rourke, Rev. Paul K., *S.J.* (BGP) [MON] The Fairfield Jesuit Community-Fairfield University, Fairfield, CT
Rourke, Rev. Paul K., *S.J.* '10 (WDC) [COL] Georgetown University, Washington, DC
Rouse, Rev. Carignan L., (BO) On Leave.
Rouse, Rev. Jacob D., '18 (DUB) Notre Dame Church, Cresco, Iowa, Cresco, IA
Rouse, Rev. Warren, *O.F.M.* '57 (LA) [RTR] Serra Retreat, Malibu, CA
Roush, Rev. Eric P., (CIN) Our Lord, Christ the King, Cincinnati, OH
Roush, Rev. William D., '15 (DAV) Holy Family Church of Riverside, Iowa, Riverside, IA
Rousseau, Rev. Stanley, (BO) Divine Mercy Parish, Quincy, MA
Rousseau, Rev. William C., '95 (SPR) Retired.
Routhier, Rev. Msgr. Peter A., '78 (BUR) Curia: Leadership; Offices and Directors Cathedral of St. Joseph, Burlington, VT
Roux, Very Rev. Christopher A., '01 (CHL) Curia: Leadership St. Patrick Cathedral, Charlotte, NC
Roux, Rev. G. Albert, '66 (PRT) Retired.
Roux, Rev. Philippe D., '73 (SPR) Retired.
Roverse, Rev. Michael E., '84 (SAV) St. Teresa of Avila, Grovetown, GA
Rowan, Rev. Msgr. John J., '61 (RVC) Retired.
Rowan, Rev. John M., '89 (BO) St. George, Framingham, MA
Rowan, Rev. Msgr. Mark P., '91 (RVC) St. Kilian, Farmingdale, NY
Rowan, Rev. Stephen, '70 (SEA) Retired.
Rowe, Very Rev. Charles N., '99 (KC) Curia: Leadership; Offices and Directors
Rowe, Very Rev. Charles N., '99 (KC) On Special Assignment. Curia: Leadership; Offices and Directors [MIS] Diocese of Kansas City-St. Joseph Real Estate Corporation, Kansas City, MO
Rowe, Rev. Michael, *C.P.* '11 (NY) [MON] The Congregation of the Passion - St. Paul of the Cross Province, Jamaica, NY
Rowe, Rev. William J., '64 (BEL) Retired.
Rowen, Rev. Cyrus, (LIN) St. Cecilia's Middle School/ High School, Hastings, NE
Rowgh, Rev. T. Mathew, '75 (WH) Retired.
Rowland, Rev. Anthony T., '11 (LFT) Curia: Leadership; Miscellaneous / Other Offices Cathedral of St. Mary of the Immaculate Conception, Lafayette, IN; St. Ann, Lafayette, IN
Rowland, Rev. Msgr. Charles H., '70 (CHR) Curia: Tribunal Holy Spirit, Johns Island, SC
Rowland, Rev. James M., '09 (TYL) Curia: Advisory Boards, Commissions, Committees, and Councils; Deaneries; Tribunal St. Mary Magdalene Church, Flint, TX
Rowland, Rev. William F., *CJM* '70 (SD) Retired.
Rowland, Rev. William F., *S.M.* '79 (ATL) Marist School, Atlanta, GA; [MON] Marist Provincial Office, Society of Mary - Atlanta Province, Atlanta, GA
Rowntree, Rev. Stephen C., *S.J.* '75 (NO) Holy Name of Jesus, New Orleans, LA; [MON] Loyola Jesuit Community, New Orleans, LA
Roxas, Rev. Rodolfo P., (SAV) Retired. [HOS] St. Joseph's Hospital, Inc., Savannah, GA
Roy, Rev. Msgr. Allen J., '54 (NO) Retired.
Roy, Rev. Donald J., '70 (BUR) Retired.
Roy, Rev. Duane, *O.S.B.* '67 (KCK) [MON] St. Benedict's Abbey, Atchison, KS
Roy, Rev. George, *O.M.I.* '73 (BO) St. William, Tewksbury, MA
Roy, Rev. James R., *M.M.* '61 (NY) Retired. [MON] Maryknoll Fathers and Brothers (Catholic Foreign Mission Society of America, Inc.), Ossining, NY
Roy, Rev. Maurice J., '73 (BUR) Retired. Curia: Leadership
Roy, Rev. Michael J., '75 (WOR) St. Ann, North Oxford, MA; St. Roch, Oxford, MA
Roy, Rev. Richard M., '75 (FR) Retired.
Roy, Rev. Robert P., '94 (HRT) The St. Michael's Church Corporation, N. Haven, Connecticut, New Haven, CT
Royal, Rev. Adam, (KNX) Our Lady of Fatima, Alcoa, TN
Royal, Rev. Msgr. Kevin T., '85 (BGP) St. Mary's Corporation, Ridgefield, CT
Royals, Rev. Andrew Francis, '06 (WDC) St. Joseph, Morganza, MD
Royer, Rev. Francis J., *S.S.C.* '57 (PRO) Retired. [MON] St. Columban's Retirement House (St. Columban's Foreign Mission Society), Bristol, RI
Royer, Rev. Msgr. Ronald, '58 (FRS) Retired.
Royer, Rev. Msgr. Ronald Edmund, '58 (LA) Retired.
Royer, Rev. Thomas J., '60 (PEO) Retired.
Royer, Rev. Yvon J., '90 (BUR) Curia: Leadership St. Francis Xavier, Winooski, VT
Royik, Very Rev. Ihor, (PHU) Curia: Leadership
Royik, Very Rev. Ihor, '92 (PHU) SS. Peter and Paul, Phoenixville, PA; St. Michael's, Pottstown, PA
Royston, Rev. Basil G., '81 (SJ) Retired.
Roza, Rev. Andrew J., '07 (OM) St. Vincent de Paul, Omaha, NE
Rozansky, Rev. Joseph, (CHI) [MON] St. Joseph Interprovincial Post-Novitiate Formation House, Chicago, IL
Rozario, Rev. Arun William, *OMI* '22 (SAT) [SEM] Blessed Mario Borzaga Formation Community, San Antonio, TX
Rozario, Rev. Mintu, '17 (BRK) Corpus Christi, Woodside, NY
Rozas, Rev. David, (LAF) Our Lady of the Sacred Heart, Church Point, LA; St. Joseph, Parks, LA
Rozborski, Rev. Grzegorz, '05 (LA) St. Anastasia, Los Angeles, CA
Rozek, Rev. Piotr, '88 (RVC) Curia: Leadership St. Hedwig's, Floral Park, NY
Rozembajgier, Rev. John M., '04 (MET) Curia: Tribunal St. Thomas the Apostle, Old Bridge, NJ
Rozier, Rev. Blake Edward, '14 (DUL) St. Augustine, Cohasset, MN; St. Joseph, Grand Rapids, MN
Rozier, Rev. Michael, *S.J.* '14 (STL) [MON] Jesuit Community Corporation at Saint Louis University - Jesuit Hall, St. Louis, MO
Rozman, Very Rev. Thomas J., '86 (HBG) Curia: Offices and Directors Saint Joseph Catholic Church, Mechanicsburg, PA
Rozmarynowycz, Rev. Mychail, '95 (PRM) Curia: Leadership St. Basil, Sterling Heights, MI
Rozniak, Rev. Msgr. Ronald J., '71 (NEW) Curia: Advisory Boards, Commissions, Committees, and Councils; Leadership Our Lady of Mount Carmel, Ridgewood, NJ
Rozum, Rev. George A., *C.S.C.* '68 (FTW) [COL] University of Notre Dame Du Lac, Notre Dame, IN;

[MON] Holy Cross Community, Corby Hall, University of Notre Dame, Notre Dame, IN
Rozycki, Rev. Msgr. Isidore, '68 (AUS) Retired.
Ruan, Rev. Joseph Guo Zhang, (NY) St. Teresa, New York, NY
Ruane, Rev. Edward, *O.P.* '69 (STL) [MON] St. Dominic Priory, St. Louis, MO
Ruane, Rev. George, '73 (NEW) Retired. Holy Rosary, Edgewater, NJ; Notre Dame, North Caldwell, NJ
Ruani, Rev. Pablo, (BRK) St. Leo, Corona, NY; St. Mary Star of the Sea and St. Gertrude, Far Rockaway, NY
Rubbelke, Rev. Ronald J., '64 (STL) Retired.
Rubeling, Rev. Michael, '16 (BAL) St. Margaret, Bel Air, MD
Rubey, Rev. Charles T., '66 (CHI) Retired. Curia: Offices and Directors [CCH] Catholic Charities of the Archdiocese of Chicago-Archdiocesan Offices, Chicago, IL
Rubiano, Rev. Cesar A., '96 (TR) Holy Innocents, Neptune, NJ
Rubie, Rev. Christopher M., '18 (STL) St. Gerard Majella Catholic Church, Kirkwood, MO
Rubino, Msgr. David A., '73 (E) [CON] Sisters of Mercy of the Americas - New York, Pennsylvania, Pacific West Community, Erie, PA
Rubino, Rev. Vincent P., *O.F.M.Conv.* '00 (R) Blessed Sacrament, Graham, NC; [MON] Conventual Franciscans, Elon, NC
Rubio, Rev. Alex, *M.Sp.S.* '15 (P) [EFT] Felix Rougier Religious Care Trust, Banks, OR; [MON] Missionaries of the Holy Spirit, M.Sp.S., Milwaukie, OR; [SEM] Felix Rougier House of Studies, Mount Angel, OR
Rubio, Rev. David Martinez, (JKS) [MIS] Parroquia De San Miguel Arcangel, Jackson, MS
Rubio, Rev. Jose, '80 (SJ) Retired. On Special Assignment. Dir Ecumenical & Interreligious Affairs & Delegate Easter... Curia: Offices and Directors St. Mary, Gilroy, CA
Rubio, Rev. Juan Pablo, *SDB* (CHI) St. John Bosco, Chicago, IL
Rubio, Rev. Nelson, (LR) St. James, Searcy, AR; St. Richard Church, Bald Knob, AR; St. Theresa, Little Rock, AR
Rubio, Rev. Santiago, '80 (NY) Retired.
Rubio-Boitel, Rev. Fernando, '75 (SFE) Retired.
Rubio-Boitel, Rev. Fernando, '75 (OAK) St. Francis of Assisi, Concord, CA
Ruby, Rev. David C., '91 (GB) On Leave.
Rucando, Rev. Anthony M., '70 (BRK) Retired. St. Anastasia, Douglaston, NY
Ruchgy, Rev. Canon Wayne J., '66 (STN) Curia: Offices and Directors St. Michael's, Dearborn, MI
Ruchinski, Rev. David, '07 (STA) Curia: Evangelization St. Augustine Church and Catholic Student Center, Gainesville, FL
Ruckel, Rev. Timothy, '14 (OKL) Our Lady of Sorrows, Chandler, OK
Rudd, Rev. Thad B., '91 (ATL) Retired.
Rudecki, Rev. Marek, *S.A.C.* '81 (NY) Our Lady of Mt. Carmel, Yonkers, NY; St. Casimir, Yonkers, NY
Rudjak, Rev. Joseph S., '00 (Y) Holy Apostles Parish, Youngstown, OH
Rudmann, Rev. Andrew, '19 (NO) On Special Assignment. Archbishop Chapelle High School, Metairie St. Clement of Rome Roman Catholic Church, Metairie, Louisiana, Metairie, LA; St. Philip Neri, Metairie, LA
Rudnick, Rev. Kenneth, *S.J.* '91 (LA) [MON] Jesuit Community, Los Angeles, CA
Rudnicki, Rev. Zbigniew A., '90 (PMB) Our Lady Queen of the Apostles, Royal Palm Beach, FL
Rudnik, Rev. John J., '61 (CHI) Retired.
Rudnik, Rev. Tadeusz, '55 (SY) Retired.
Rudolf, Rev. Rosendo, '07 (CI) Curia: Leadership Hall Islands Parish, Chuuk, FM; Mortlock Parish, Chuuk, FM; [COL] Caroline College and Pastoral Institute, Chuuk, FM; [MON] Vicariate Residence, Tunnuk, Chuuk, FM
Rudolph, Rev. Michael L., '05 (STP) Saint Nickolaus, Elko New Market, MN
Rudolph, Rev. Patrick N., '88 (ORG) St. Catherine of Siena, Laguna Beach, CA
Rudolphi, Rev. Stephen A., '79 (BEL) Retired.
Rudolphi, Rev. Timothy C., '89 (STP) Church of the Risen Savior, Burnsville, MN; Mary, Mother of the Church, Burnsville, MN
Rudy, Rev. Richard E., '76 (PH) On Leave. St. John the Evangelist, Morrisville, PA
Rudzewicz, Rev. Jan, '83 (OAK) Curia: Leadership Our Lady of Good Counsel, San Leandro, CA
Rudzik, Rev. Mateusz K., '12 (MOB) St. Joseph, Tuskegee Institute, AL; St. Vincent de Paul Parish, Tallassee, Tallassee, AL; [CAM] Tuskegee University Newman Center, Tuskegee Institute, AL
Rueb, Rev. Nathan, '19 (KC) On Special Assignment. Vocation Dir
Rueda Catetano, Rev. Roberto, '97 (LA) St. Joseph, Hawthorne, CA
Ruede, Rev. Ernest, '66 (R) Retired.
Ruedisueli, Rev. Robert A., '69 (DET) Retired.
Rueger, Rev. William J., '75 (BRK) Retired.
Ruelle, Rev. William A., '11 (BIS) Curia: Offices and Directors St. Patrick, Dickinson, ND
Ruetz, Rev. Edward J., '62 (FTW) Retired.
Ruff, Rev. Anthony, *O.S.B.* '93 (SCL) [MON] St. John's Abbey, of the Order of St. Benedict, Collegeville, MN
Ruff, Rev. Damien, *S.J.* '86 (PH) [MIS] Jesuit Fathers, ,
Ruff, Rev. Daniel M., *S.J.* '86 (PH) [MON] Arrupe Jesuit Community, Merion Station, PA
Ruff, Rev. Frank, '63 (CIN) Retired. [MON] Headquarters of Glenmary Home Missioners (The Home Missioners of America), Fairfield, OH
Ruffalo, Rev. Michael, (PIT) Chap, Ohio Valley Gen Hosp, Allegheny Cty
Ruffalo, Rev. Michael R., '08 (PIT) Curia: Leadership Immaculate Heart of Mary, Pittsburgh, PA; Most Holy Name of Jesus, Pittsburgh, PA; St. Nicholas, Pittsburgh, PA; St. Patrick-St. Stanislaus Kostka, Pittsburgh, PA
Ruffing, Rev. Norman, '63 (OAK) Retired.
Ruffo, Friar John, *OFM Conv.* (ALB) [MON] Franciscan Friars Conventual, Rensselaer, NY
Rufo, Rev. Henry, '01 (P) Chap, Shutter Creek Corr Inst, North Bend
Ruge, Rev. Paul, '97 (FAR) Retired.
Rugen, Rev. Patrick, (FWT) Retired.
Rugen, Rev. Patrick J., '76 (CHI) Retired.
Ruggere, Rev. Peter L., *M.M.* '68 (SJ) Retired. (>NY) [MON] Maryknoll Fathers and Brothers (Catholic Foreign Mission Society of America, Inc.), Ossining, NY
Ruggere, Rev. Peter L., *M.M.* '68 (NY) Retired.
Ruggeri, Rev. Joseph A., '65 (BO) Retired.
Ruggeri, Rev. Salvatore M., '99 (CLV) On Leave.
Ruggieri, Rev. James T., '95 (PRO) St. Michael's Providence, Rhode Island, Providence, RI; St. Patrick's Church, Providence, Rhode Island, Providence, RI
Ruggiero, Rev. Philip, '81 (TR) Retired.
Ruggles, Rev. Christopher V., '79 (TYL) Retired.
Ruhlin, Very Rev. James, '02 (SP) Curia: Pastoral Services St. Michael the Archangel, Hudson, FL
Ruhnke, Rev. Robert A., *C.Ss.R.* '66 (LA) [MON] Redemptorists of Whittier, Whittier, CA
Ruis Rebollo, Rev. German, (B) Our Lady of the Valley, Caldwell, ID
Ruisanchez, Rev. Joseph P., '86 (POD) Curia: Clergy and Religious Services
Ruiz, Rev. Albert Capello, '73 (AUS) Our Lady of San Juan Catholic Mission Church - Moody, Texas, Moody, TX; St. Eugene Catholic Church - McGregor, Texas, McGregor, TX
Ruiz, Rev. Alberto, *C.M.F.* '84 (MET) Our Lady of Fatima, Perth Amboy, NJ
Ruiz, Rev. Antonio A., '71 (TUC) Retired.
Ruiz, Rev. Armand Ramirez, (CHI) Most Blessed Trinity, Waukegan, IL
Ruiz, Rev. Carlos, '15 (WOR) Curia: Leadership St. Anna, Leominster, MA
Ruiz, Rev. Diego, *I.V.E.* (BAL) [CAM] Mount St. Mary's University, Emmitsburg, MD; [SEM] Mount St. Mary's Seminary, Emmitsburg, MD
Ruiz, Rev. Diego, *I.V.E.* (WDC) St. John Baptist de la Salle, Chillum, MD
Ruiz, Rev. Dominic, *O.S.B.* '83 (SCL) [MON] St. John's Abbey, of the Order of St. Benedict, Collegeville, MN
Ruiz, Rev. Eddie, '99 (SD) Retired.
Ruiz, Rev. Edgar, '01 (PAT) On Leave.
Ruiz, Rev. Edwin J., *C.S.V.* '16 (CHI) [MON] Viatorian Province Center-Clerics of St. Viator, Arlington Heights, IL
Ruiz, Rev. Efrain Medina, (MRY) Christ Child, Los Gatos, CA
Ruiz, Rev. Faustino, '91 (MAD) St. Norbert, Sauk City, WI
Ruiz, Rev. Gabriel, *CMF* '89 (LA) San Gabriel Mission, San Gabriel, CA
Ruiz, Rev. Jean-Pierre, '82 (BRK) St. Francis of Assisi-St. Blaise, Brooklyn, NY
Ruiz, Rev. John Martin, *O.P.* '08 (WDC) [SEM] Dominican House of Studies, Washington, DC
Ruiz, Rev. Jorge L., '12 (ARE) [MIS] Chapel Nuestra Senora del Carmen, Arecibo, PR
Ruiz, Rev. Juan, '99 (BRK) St. Martin of Tours-Our Lady of Lourdes, Brooklyn, NY
Ruiz, Rev. Juan Antonio, *C.M.* '65 (LA) [MON] Congregation of the Mission Western Province (DePaul Center Residence), Montebello, CA
Ruiz, Rev. Luis, '68 (SAT) Retired.
Ruiz, Rev. Mark S., '19 (OAK) Immaculate Heart of Mary, Brentwood, CA
Ruiz, Rev. Miguel A, *SVD* (SFR) St. Kevin, San Francisco, CA
Ruiz, Rev. Orlando, *OFM* '06 (BRK) Our Lady of Peace, Brooklyn, NY
Ruiz, Rev. Rick, '92 (ELP) On Leave.
Ruiz, Rev. Ruben, '13 (ORG) Curia: Offices and Directors St. Bonaventure, Huntington Beach, CA
Ruiz, Rev. Rudy, '79 (MRY) Retired.
Ruiz, Rev. Ryan, *S.L.D.* '08 (CIN) [SEM] Mount St. Mary's Seminary of the West, Cincinnati, OH
Ruiz, Rev. Ryan Thomas, '08 (CIN) [SEM] The Athenaeum of Ohio, Cincinnati, OH
Ruiz Andujo, Rev. Jose Alejandro, *S.J.* (SJN) San Ignacio de Loyola, San Juan, PR
Ruiz Lebron, Rev. Luis Manuel, '85 (FAJ) San Jose, Canovanas, PR
Ruiz Rivera, Rev. Jorge L., '12 (ARE) [MIS] Chapel Santuario Cristo de los Milagros, Arecibo, PR
Ruiz Rivera, Rev. Jorge L., '12 (ARE) Santa Ana, Arecibo, PR
Ruiz Santos, Rev. Carlos, '03 (SAL) Curia: Miscellaneous / Other Offices Holy Ghost Parish, Sharon Springs, Inc., Sharon Springs, KS; Our Lady of Perpetual Help Parish, Goodland, Inc., Goodland, KS
Ruiz-Aular, Rev. Pedro Javier, '22 (MIL) Holy Family Congregation, Fond du Lac, WI
Ruiz-Juarez, Rev. Miguel Gustavo, '06 (SPK) Curia: Leadership St. Paul the Apostle, Eltopia, WA; St. Vincent, Connell, WA
Ruiz-Marentes, Rev. Jose Hugo, '96 (CHR) Holy Spirit Mission, Laurens, SC; St. Boniface, Joanna, SC; St. Mark, Newberry, SC
Ruiz-Victoria, Rev. Lorenzo, *SDB* (CGS) Retired. [MON] Casa Salesiana de Retiros, Aibonito, PR
Rukuratwa Kiguta, Rev. Avitus L., '06 (CHI)
Rumback, Rev. Chris, '21 (WCH) Our Lady of Lourdes, Pittsburg, KS
Rumble, Rev. Clarence F., '86 (SY) Church of the Holy Family, Endwell, NY; Most Holy Rosary, Maine, NY
Ruminski, Rev. Michael A., '14 (HRT) Curia: Advisory Boards, Commissions, Committees, and Councils; Clergy and Religious Services; Offices and Directors Sacred Heart Church Corporation, Bloomfield, Bloomfield, CT
Rummell, Rev. Bonaventure, *C.F.R.* '13 (NY) [MIS] The Saint Padre Pio Shelter Corporation, Bronx, NY; [PRE] St. Francis Youth Center, Inc., Bronx, NY
Runde, Rev. Luis, *O.F.M.* '65 (STL) [MON] Franciscan Friars Province of the Sacred Heart, Dittmer, MO
Rundzio, Rev. Mark A., '81 (MAN) Retired.
Runnion, Rev. David A., '06 (CHR) Retired. St. Joseph, Anderson, SC
Runyon, Very Rev. Jacob, '09 (FTW) Curia: Leadership; Offices and Directors Cathedral of the Immaculate Conception, Fort Wayne, IN
Ruoff, Rev. Chuck, (VEN) San Marco Parish in Marco Island, Inc., Marco Island, FL
Rupert, Rev. Msgr. Dale R., '77 (SCR) St. Peter's Cathedral, Scranton, PA
Rupp, Rev. Daniel J., '98 (SC) Curia: Leadership Immaculate Conception, Cherokee, IA; Our Lady of Good Counsel, Holstein, IA
Rupp, Rev. Daniel N., '66 (MAR) Retired.
Rupp, Rev. William J., (PBR) SS. Peter and Paul's, Warren, OH; [NUR] Infant of Prague Manor, Warren, OH
Ruppert, Rev. Alan E., '78 (BEL) Retired.
Ruppert, Rev. David, '05 (FTW) St. Mary of the Assumption, Decatur, IN
Rurangirwa, Rev. Romain, (BO) Saint Matthew the Evangelist Parish, Billerica, MA
Rurangirwa, Rev. Romain, (MO) Curia: Offices and Directors
Rusay, Rev. Leonard F.A., '85 (MET) Our Lady of Lourdes, Whitehouse Station, NJ
Ruschman, Rev. Albert E., '53 (COV) Retired.
Rusconi, Rev. Msgr. Richard A., '72 (PAT) Retired.
Ruse, Rev. Fred R., '76 (ORL) Retired. Curia: Advisory Boards, Commissions, Committees, and Councils
Rush, Rev. Msgr. J. Kenneth, '71 (RIC) Retired.
Rush, Rev. Michael P., '73 (CAM) Retired.
Rush, Rev. Patrick J., '69 (KC) Retired.
Rush, Rev. Thomas, (SAT) Retired. [NUR] Oblate Madonna Residence, San Antonio, TX
Rushofsky, Rev. John R., '79 (PIT) Our Lady of Mount Carmel, Pittsburgh, PA
Rusin, Rev. Christopher, '07 (MEM) On Leave.
Rusk, Rev. Richard M., '90 (MET) Curia: Consultative Bodies

Rusk, Rev. Richard M., '90 (MET) St. John Neumann, Califon, NJ; [MIS] The Anawim Community, Oxford, NJ
Rusk, Rev. Ron L., '68 (SB) Retired.
Ruskamp, Rev. Robert L., '85 (ARL) St. John Bosco, Woodstock, VA
Ruskoski, Rev. William Paul, '74 (LAF) Retired.
Rusnak, Rev. Anton, *O.C.S.O.* '03 (L) [MON] Abbey of Our Lady of Gethsemani, of the Order of Cistercians of the Strict Observance, Trappist, KY
Rusnak, Rev. Melvin E., '70 (Y) Retired.
Rusnak, Rev. Tadeusz, *S. Ch.* '85 (SFR) Nativity, San Francisco, CA
Rusnak, Rev. Tadeusz, (GAL) Our Lady of Czestochowa, Houston, TX
Rusnak, Rev. Tadeusz, *S.Ch.* '85 (SFR) Curia: Offices and Directors
Russeau, Rev. Kevin M., *C.S.C.* '01 (FTW) (>BUR) Sacred Heart St. Francis de Sales Parish Charitable Trust, Bennington, VT; (>BUR) St. John the Baptist, North Bennington, VT
Russell, Rev. Cassian, *OCSO* '19 (ATL) [MON] The Monastery of the Holy Spirit, Conyers, GA
Russell, Rev. David, '64 (MIA) Retired.
Russell, Rev. David P., '81 (WDC) Retired.
Russell, Rev. Dean E., '00 (RCK) St. Mary, DeKalb, IL
Russell, Very Rev. Edward K., '83 (NY) Curia: Leadership Incarnation, New York, NY
Russell, Rev. James A., *S.M.* '64 (CIN) [COL] The University of Dayton, Dayton, OH; [MON] Marianist Community, Dayton, OH
Russell, Very Rev. James D., '60 (WIN) Retired. Curia: Offices and Directors
Russell, Rev. John, '17 (PRM) St. Stephen, Allen Park, MI
Russell, Rev. Nock W., '08 (AUS) Retired.
Russell, Rev. Patrick, '19 (STL) Assumption Catholic Church, O'Fallon, O'Fallon, MO
Russell, Rev. Patrick Mary, *M.F.V.A.* '12 (BIR) [MON] Franciscan Missionaries of the Eternal Word, A Public Clerical Association of the Christian Faithful, Irondale, AL
Russell, Rev. Samuel, *O.S.B.* '94 (KC) [MON] Conception Abbey (Benedictine Monks), Conception, MO
Russell, Rev. Msgr. Stanley J., '61 (WIL) St. Helena, Wilmington, DE
Russell, Rev. Travis Dean, *SJ* '19 (LA) Verbum Dei Jesuit High School, Los Angeles, CA
Russell, Rev. William C., *S.J.* '65 (BO) [MON] Campion Health & Wellness, Inc., Weston, MA
Russick, Rev. Matthew, *T.O.R.* (ARL) St. Joseph, Herndon, VA
Russo, Rev. Anthony, *C.Ss.R.* '65 (BAL) Retired. [SPF] St. John Neuman Residence, Timonium, MD
Russo, Rev. Anthony J., '00 (BR) Retired.
Russo, Rev. Anthony P., *S.C.J.* '66 (MIL) Retired. [MON] Sacred Heart at Monastery Lake, Franklin, WI
Russo, Rev. Anthony S., '00 (GR) St. Robert of Newminster, Ada, MI
Russo, Rev. Msgr. Caesar, '74 (STA) Retired. (>OLD) Saint Ephrem Syriac Church, Jacksonville, FL
Russo, Chorbishop Caesar, (OLD) Curia: Leadership
Russo, Rev. Lawrence J., '80 (BO) On Leave.
Russo, Rev. Michael, '89 (LAF) St. Anne, Youngsville, LA; St. Thomas More High School, Lafayette, LA
Russo, Rev. Michael A., '19 (WDC) Sacred Heart, Bowie, MD
Russo, Rev. Michael A., (NEW) Retired.
Russo, Rev. Michael A., '71 (OAK) On Duty Outside Diocese. Monterey, CA
Russo, Rev. Ricardo, *O.F.M.* '74 (CIN) Retired. [MON] St. Francis Seraph Friary, Cincinnati, OH
Russo, Rev. Richard M., '82 (RCK) St. Andrew, Rock Falls, IL; St. Mary, Tampico, IL
Russo, Rt. Rev. Romanos, (NTN) Retired.
Rusyn, Rev. Ivan, '09 (PBR) SS. Peter and Paul, Jerome, PA; St. Mary (Dormition) Church, Windber, PA
Ruszel, Rev. Henry A., *C.R.* '54 (SB) Retired. Our Lady of the Desert, Apple Valley, CA; [MON] Congregation of the Resurrection, CR, Needles, CA
Ruteaga, Rev. Rogelio Martinez, *OFM* (SAT) San Juan Capistrano, San Antonio, TX
Ruth, Rev. John C., '85 (SCR) Curia: Offices and Directors Sacred Hearts of Jesus & Mary, Jermyn, Jermyn, PA
Ruthenberg, Rev. Michael B., *O.P.* '88 (CHI) [MON] St. Pius V Priory, Chicago, IL
Rutherford, Rev. Donald L., '81 (ALB) Curia: Offices and Directors Immaculate Heart of Mary, Watervliet, NY
Rutherford, Very Rev. Mark, (MO) Curia: Offices and Directors
Rutherford, Rev. Mark J., '09 (LAN) On Duty Outside Diocese.
Rutherford, Rev. Richard, *C.S.C.* '64 (P) Retired. [MON] Priests of Holy Cross in Oregon, Inc., Portland, OR
Rutkowski, Rev. Jim, (SAT) [NUR] Incarnate Word Retirement Community (The Village at Incarnate Word), San Antonio, TX
Rutkowski, Rev. William J., '87 (SAG) Christ the Good Shepherd Parish of Saginaw, Saginaw, MI; Saint John Paul II Parish of Carrollton, Carrollton, MI
Rutkowski, Rev. William J., '87 (SAG) Curia: Leadership; Offices and Directors
Rutledge, Rev. Robert M., *O.S.F.S.* '89 (R) Holy Infant Catholic Parish, Durham, NC
Rutler, Rev. George W., '81 (NY) Retired.
Rutten, Rev. Erich, '05 (STP) Curia: Consultative Bodies St. Odilia, Shoreview, MN
Rutten, Rev. John, '12 (SFS) [CAM] Saint Thomas More Newman Center, Vermillion, SD
Rutten, Rev. Paul A., '02 (SFS) Curia: Leadership; Offices and Directors Immaculate Heart of Mary Parish of Minnehaha County, Sioux Falls, SD
Rutter, Rev. George W., '81 (NY) Retired.
Ruttle, Rev. Paul, *C.P.* '80 (NY) [MON] The Congregation of the Passion - St. Paul of the Cross Province, Jamaica, NY
Ruttle, Rev. Paul, *C.P.* '80 (PMB) [MON] Our Lady of Florida Spiritual Center, North Palm Beach, FL
Rutz, Rev. Msgr. Gilbert J., '66 (PHX) Retired. [RTR] Mount Claret Roman Catholic Retreat Center, Phoenix, AZ
Rutz, Rev. Msgr. Gilbert J., '66 (COV) Retired.
Ruvalcaba, Rev. Victor J., '96 (LA) St. Basil's Roman Catholic Church, Los Angeles, CA
Ruwaainenyi, Rev. Deogratias M., '06 (CLV) Chap. Fairview Gen Hosp St. Clement, Lakewood, OH
Ruwe, Rev. Paul A., '05 (CIN) St. John the Baptist, Harrison, OH
Ruyechan, Rev. Matthew J., '80 (E) Our Lady of Fatima, Farrell, PA; St. Anthony, Sharon, PA
Ruygt, Rev. Hans P., '85 (PHX) St Clare of Assisi Roman Catholic Parish Surprise, Surprise, AZ
Ruzicka, Very Rev. Gary, '76 (CHY) Retired.
Ruzicka, Rev. Gary J., '76 (CHY) Retired. [EFT] The Wyoming Catholic Ministries Foundation, Cheyenne, WY
Ruzicka, Rev. Jonathan R., '21 (STL) St. Joseph Catholic Church, Imperial, Imperial, MO
Rwandekwe, Rev. Abdon, *S.J.* (SFR) [MON] Loyola House Jesuit Community, San Francisco, CA
Rwechungura, Rev. Siffredus B., '99 (NEW) Our Lady Mother of the Church, Woodcliff Lake, NJ
Rwegasira, Rev. Deogratias, *A.J.* (HBG) St. Joseph Church, Lancaster, PA
Rweyemamu, Rev. Justinian B., '93 (NOR) On Leave.
Rwezahura, Rev. Gosbert, '11 (CHI) Christ Our Savior, South Holland, IL
Ryan, Rev. Adam, *O.S.B.* '90 (KC) [MON] Conception Abbey (Benedictine Monks), Conception, MO
Ryan, Rev. Brogan C., *C.S.C.* '19 (FTW) (>SCR) [COL] King's College, Wilkes-Barre, PA
Ryan, Rev. C. Duane, '54 (KC) Retired.
Ryan, Rev. Charles, *F.S.S.P.* '94 (LIN) [SEM] Our Lady of Guadalupe Seminary, Inc., Denton, NE
Ryan, Rev. Daniel P., '10 (ALB) On Leave.
Ryan, Rev. Denis, *C.Ss.R.* '06 (SEA) Retired. (>STL) [MON] St. Clement Health Care Center, Liguori, MO
Ryan, Rev. Denis, *C.Ss.R.* '06 (LA) Retired.
Ryan, Very Rev. Dennis, (GB) Prince of Peace, Green Bay, WI
Ryan, Very Rev. Dennis M., '74 (GB) Retired. Curia: Advisory Boards, Commissions, Committees, and Councils
Ryan, Rev. Donald P., '63 (L) Retired.
Ryan, Rev. Msgr. Edward J., '71 (BRK) Retired.
Ryan, Rev. Edward M., '74 (WOR) Retired. St. Paul, Warren, MA; St. Stanislaus, West Warren, MA
Ryan, Rev. Francis J., *S.J.* '56 (BO) [MON] Campion Health & Wellness, Inc., Weston, MA
Ryan, Rev. Msgr. George J., '62 (BRK) Retired. St. Anastasia, Douglaston, NY
Ryan, Rev. J. Patrick, '76 (PAT) Retired.
Ryan, Rev. John, *CSC* (ALB) [MIS] Holy Cross International, Inc., Albany, NY
Ryan, Rev. John A., '70 (SFR) St. Catherine of Siena, Burlingame, CA
Ryan, Rev. John David, '10 (RVC) St. Jude, Mastic Beach, NY
Ryan, Rev. John J., '71 (ORL) Retired.
Ryan, Rev. Msgr. John M., '55 (BUF) Retired. [MON] O'Hara Residence, Tonawanda, NY
Ryan, Rev. John M., '64 (CHI) Retired. Little Flower Parish, Waukegan, IL
Ryan, Rev. John P., '63 (NEW) Retired.
Ryan, Rev. Joseph, *O.S.A.* '83 (PH) [COL] Villanova University, Villanova, PA
Ryan, Rev. Joseph G., *O.S.A.* '87 (PH) [MON] St. Thomas Monastery, Villanova, PA
Ryan, Rev. Justin, (SEA) Curia: Offices and Directors
Ryan, Rev. Msgr. Kevin E., '70 (SAT) St. Mark the Evangelist, San Antonio, TX
Ryan, Rev. Lawrence D., '12 (BRK) Holy Name, Brooklyn, NY
Ryan, Rev. Lawrence David, *S.J.* '77 (BO) [MON] Campion Health & Wellness, Inc., Weston, MA
Ryan, Rev. Msgr. Martin P., '76 (BGP) Our Lady of Grace Parish, Stratford, CT
Ryan, Very Rev. Michael G., '66 (SEA) Christ Our Hope Parish, Seattle, WA; St. James Cathedral, Seattle, WA; [MIS] L'Arche Noah Sealth of Seattle, Seattle, WA; [MIS] St. Patrick, Seattle, WA
Ryan, Rev. Michael J., '74 (PH) Retired.
Ryan, Rev. Michael J., '72 (PH) Retired. St. Jerome, Philadelphia, PA
Ryan, Rev. Milton, *C.M.* (DAL) Holy Trinity Catholic Parish, Dallas, TX; [MON] Congregation of the Mission, Western Province, Dallas, TX
Ryan, Rev. Milton F., *C.M.* '91 (STL) [EFT] St. Vincent de Paul Educational Foundation, Perryville, MO
Ryan, Rev. Patrick, '70 (STL) Retired.
Ryan, Rev. Patrick J., *S.J.* '59 (BO) [MON] Campion Health & Wellness, Inc., Weston, MA
Ryan, Rev. Patrick J., '58 (STP) Retired.
Ryan, Rev. Patrick J., *S.J.* '68 (NY) [MON] Cardinal Spellman Hall, Jesuit Community, Bronx, NY
Ryan, Rev. Msgr. Paul T., '58 (BO) Retired.
Ryan, Rev. Peter, *S.J.* (DET) St. Therese of Lisieux Parish Shelby Township, Shelby Twp., MI; [SEM] The College of Liberal Arts, ,
Ryan, Rev. Philip V., '57 (DAV) Retired.
Ryan, Rev. Regis J., '66 (PIT) Retired. Curia: Consultative Bodies Archangel Gabriel, McKees Rocks, PA
Ryan, Rev. Richard, '77 (PHX) Retired. Our Lady of Lourdes Roman Catholic Parish, Sun City West, AZ
Ryan, Rev. Msgr. Richard, '73 (STO) Curia: Leadership
Ryan, Rev. Msgr. Richard J., '73 (STO) Retired. St. Michael Church of Stockton (Pastor of), Stockton, CA
Ryan, Rev. Robert S., '21 (CHI) SS. Joseph and Francis Xavier, Wilmette, IL
Ryan, Rev. Robin, *C.P.* '84 (CHI) [MON] Passionist Community of St. Vincent Strambi, Chicago, IL
Ryan, Rev. Robin, *C.P.* '84 (NY) [MON] The Congregation of the Passion - St. Paul of the Cross Province, Jamaica, NY
Ryan, Rev. Robin, *CP* (CHI) [SEM] Catholic Theological Union, Chicago, IL
Ryan, Rev. Stephen C., *S.D.B.* '92 (NO) Archbishop Shaw High School (Salesians of St. John Bosco), Marrero, LA
Ryan, Rev. Stephen Desmond, *O.P.* '93 (WDC) [SEM] Dominican House of Studies, Washington, DC
Ryan, Rev. Steve, *S.D.B.* '92 (NEW) [MIS] Salesians of Don Bosco, South Orange, NJ
Ryan, Rev. Msgr. T. Peter, '62 (RVC) Retired. [MON] St Pius X Residence for Retired Priests LLC, Ronkonkoma, NY
Ryan, Rev. Terrance, *C.S.P.* '77 (SFR) Old St. Mary's Cathedral & Chinese Mission, San Francisco, CA
Ryan, Rev. Thomas, (BO) [MON] Missionary Society of St. Paul the Apostle in Massachusetts, Boston, MA
Ryan, Rev. Thomas, '73 (BAL) Retired.
Ryan, Rev. Thomas A., '64 (GI) Retired.
Ryan, Rev. Thomas F., '93 (MET) Holy Family Parish, New Brunswick, NJ
Ryan, Rev. Thomas J., '79 (SY) Immaculate Conception, Fayetteville, NY
Ryan, Rev. Timothy E, '12 (HRT) North American Martyrs Parish Corporation, East Hartford, CT
Ryan, Rev. William, '68 (SAC) Chap, Carmelite Monastery, Georgetown
Ryan, Rev. William, '68 (STO) Retired.
Ryan, Rev. William A., '80 (WDC) On Duty Outside Diocese. Togo, West Africa [MON] The Jesuit Community at Georgetown University, Washington, DC
Ryba, Rev. Charles J., '69 (CLV) Retired.
Ryba, Rev. Tomasz, *O.F.M. Conv.* '94 (RCK) St. Margaret Mary, Algonquin, IL
Ryba, Rev. Tomasz, *OFM, Conv* '94 (BRK) Most Holy Trinity - Saint Mary, Brooklyn, NY
Rybacki, Rev. Czeslaw, *S.Ch.* '85 (SD) Pastor of Saint Maximilian Kolbe Mission, a corporation sole, San Diego, CA
Rybchuk, Rev. Bogdan, '12 (STN) Retired. St. Vladimir's Ukrainian Catholic Church, Flint, MI

Rybicki, Rev. Daryl, '79 (FTW) Corpus Christi, South Bend, IN
Rybicki, Rev. David G., '09 (LC) Retired.
Rybinski, Rev. Michal, (PAT) Our Lady of the Mountain, Long Valley, NJ; St. Mark the Evangelist, Long Valley, NJ
Rybolt, Rev. John E., *C.M.* '67 (CHI) [MON] DePaul Vincentian Residence, Chicago, IL
Rydzon, Rev. Walter G., '73 (PIT) Retired.
Rye, Rev. Gary, *O.S.A.* '65 (LA) Retired.
Rykala, Rev. Jan, (VEN) St. Martha Parish in Sarasota, Inc., Sarasota, FL
Rykwalder, Rev. David L., '85 (GI) Retired.
Ryle, Rev. Gerald J., '68 (SAC) Retired. Pastor of St. Philomene Parish, Sacramento, a corporation sole, Sacramento, CA
Rymdeika, Rev. Joseph F., '82 (PH) St. Catherine of Siena, Horsham, PA
Rynda, Rev. Reynold, *O.F.M.Cap.* '54 (GB) Retired.
Rynearson, Rev. Benjamin J., '14 (LIN) Immaculate Conception, Rulo, NE
Ryska, Rev. Leo M., *O.S.B.* '59 (RCK) [MON] Marmion Abbey, Aurora, IL
Rywalt, Rev. Lawrence, *C.P.* '92 (NY) [MON] The Congregation of the Passion - St. Paul of the Cross Province, Jamaica, NY
Rzadca, Rev. Janusz, '95 (PAT) St. Joseph's, Paterson, NJ
Rzasowski, Rev. Jerzy, '85 (MO) Curia: Offices and Directors
Rzeczkowski, Rev. Matthew, *O.P.* '69 (WDC) St. Dominic Church & Priory, Washington, DC
Rzepiela, Rev. Thomas R., '72 (CHI) Retired.
Rzonca, Rev. Michael W., '73 (PH) Retired.
Sa, Rev. Dominic Phan, '88 (PT) Retired.
Saab, Rev. Antoine, (SAM) St. George, Cranston, RI
Saad, Chorbishop Richard D., '72 (OLL) St. Elias Maronite Catholic Church, Birmingham, AL
Saade, Rev. Bassam M., '92 (SAM) Curia: Offices and Directors St. Anthony, Springfield, MA
Saah-Buckman, Rev. Michael, *S.S.J.* '93 (GAL) St. Francis Xavier, Houston, TX
Saah-Buckman, Very Rev. Michael K., *S.S.J.* (BAL) [MON] St. Joseph Society of the Sacred Heart House of Central Administration, Baltimore, MD
Saato, Rev. Fred, '67 (NTN) On Leave.
Saavedra, Rev. Daniel, *O.S.B.* '18 (BUR) [MON] The Benedictine Foundation of the State of Vermont, Inc., Weston, VT
Saavedra, Rev. Ramon, (MO) Curia: Offices and Directors
Sabak, Rev. James, *O.F.M.* '99 (R) Curia: Leadership; Offices and Directors Saint Francis of Assisi Catholic Parish of Raleigh, Raleigh, NC
Saballo, Rev. Carlito, *S.O.L.T.* '96 (KC) Guardian Angels, Kansas City, MO; St. Louis Catholic Church, Kansas City, MO; [MON] Society of Our Lady of the Most Holy Trinity, Kansas City, MO
Saban, Rev. Michael J., '89 (PH) St. Anthony of Padua, Ambler, PA
Sabando, Rev. Manuel, '92 (DAL) Hutchins State Jail, Dallas Corpus Christi Catholic Parish, Ferris, TX
Sabatini, Rev. Francis J., '63 (PH) Retired.
Sabatos, Rev. Daniel C., '62 (BRK) Retired.
Sabbagh, Rev. Choukri, '14 (NTN) St. Demetrius, Cliffside Park, NJ
Sabbatte, Rev. Frank, *C.S.P.* '80 (NY) [MON] Paulist Fathers' Motherhouse, New York, NY
Sabel, Rev. David, '09 (PEO) Curia: Deaneries St. Joseph's, Chenoa, IL; St. Mary's, Pontiac, IL
Sabella, Rev. Charles A., '94 (MET) St. Patrick, Belvidere, NJ; St. Rose of Lima, Oxford, NJ
Sabia, Rev. Msgr. John B., '64 (BGP) Retired. [MON] The Catherine Dennis Keefe Queen of the Clergy Retired Priests' Residence, Stamford, CT
Sabio, Rev. Lennard, '97 (RVC) St. Anthony of Padua, Rocky Point, NY
Sable, Rev. Msgr. Robert M., '74 (DET) On Duty Outside Diocese. Prelate Auditor of the Roman Rota, Vatican
Sabo, Rev. Paul P., '69 (BUF) Retired. Curia: Offices and Directors
Sabo, Rev. Steven, '03 (RCK) St. Katharine Drexel Parish, Sugar Grove, IL
Sabol, Rev. George, *O.F.M. Conv.* '71 (NY) [MON] St. Francis Friary, Staten Island, NY
Sabourin, Rev. Msgr. Gerard O., '60 (PRO) Retired. Saint Kateri Tekakwitha Catholic Community, Exeter, RI
Sabourin, Rev. Leo F., '58 (DET) St. Constance Parish Taylor, Taylor, MI
Sabugo, Rev. Jeremy, *SS.CC.* '17 (FR) St. Mary's, Fairhaven, MA; [MIS] Congregation of the Sacred Hearts - United States Province (Sacred Hearts Fathers; Sacred Hearts Missions), Fairhaven, MA
Saburo, Rev. Rusk, '88 (CI) Curia: Leadership
Saburo, Rev. Rusk R., '93 (CI) Sacred Heart, Koror, PW; [MON] Vicariate Residence, Koror, PW
Sacca, Rev. Raymond, '79 (OAK) Curia: Leadership St. Joan of Arc, San Ramon, CA
Saccacio, Rev. Msgr. Robert J., '61 (RVC) Retired.
Sacha, Rev. David, '22 (GR) Basilica of St. Adalbert, Grand Rapids, MI; St. Mary, Grand Rapids, MI
Sack, Rev. Juan Carlos, (VEN) Our Lady Queen of Heaven Parish in LaBelle, Inc., LaBelle, FL
Sacks, Rev. Msgr. Edward R., '64 (ALN) Retired. Our Lady of Perpetual Help, Bethlehem, PA
Sacks, Rev. Francis W., *C.M.* '67 (PH) [MON] Congregation of the Mission, Philadelphia, PA
Sacus, Rev. Msgr. Samuel S., '66 (WH) Retired. Curia: Offices and Directors
Sadaba Sarobe, Rev. Martin Jose, '83 (ARE) Curia: Leadership [MIS] Chapel Madre Dolorosa, Quebradillas, PR; [MIS] Chapel Nuestra Senora del Perpetuo Socorro, Quebradillas, PR; [MIS] Chapel San Miguel Arcangel, Quebradillas, PR
Sadaba Sarobe, Rev. Martin Jose, '83 (ARE) Santuario Diocesano Virgen del Perpetuo Socorro, Quebradillas, PR
Sada-Coeto, Rev. Enrique, (AUS) St. Elizabeth, Pflugerville, TX
Sadhanala, Rev. Sriram, *H.G.N.* '10 (ROC) Holy Spirit, Webster, NY; St. Joseph, Penfield, NY
Sadie, Rev. Msgr. P. Edward, '57 (WH) Retired.
Sadlack, Rev. Robert J., '70 (BRK) St. Gabriel, East Elmhurst, NY
Sadlowski, Rev. Ronald F., '72 (SPR) Holy Family Parish, Russell, MA
Sadowski, Rev. Izydor, *S.D.B.* (NOR) [NUR] Matulaitis Nursing Home Inc., Putnam, CT
Sadowski, Rev. Marek, *C.M.* '94 (HRT) St. Michael the Archangel (The St. Michael's Church of Derby), Derby, CT
Sadusky, Rev. Msgr. Joseph F., '70 (WDC) Retired. Curia: Tribunal St. Peter, Washington, DC
Saenz, Rev. Alonso, '97 (PHX) St. Catherine of Siena Roman Catholic Parish, Phoenix, AZ
Saenz, Rev. Christian A., *S.J.* '11 (MIA) Belen Jesuit Preparatory School, Inc., Miami, FL; [EFT] Father Amando Llorente, S.J. Foundation, Inc., Miami, FL; [MIS] Agrupacion Catolica Universitaria, Inc., Miami, FL; [MIS] Jesus Maestro, Inc., Miami, FL
Saenz, Rev. Fernando, (AUS) St. Joseph, Waco, TX
Saenz, Rev. Gerald, *S.S.C.* '00 (OM) [MON] Missionary Society of St. Columban, St. Columbans, NE
Saenz, Rev. Jorge, (SJN) [HOS] Hospital Hima San Pablo, Bayamon, PR; [SPF] Centro Medico de P.R., San Juan, PR
Saenz, Rev. Jose, '04 (DEN) St. Augustine Catholic Parish in Brighton, Brighton, CO; St. Therese Catholic Parish in Aurora, Aurora, CO
Saenz, Rev. Nestor, '90 (CHI) Our Lady of Fatima and St. Pancratius, Chicago, IL
Saenz-Ramirez, Rev. Urbano, *O.S.A.* (BEA) Our Lady of Guadalupe, Port Arthur, TX
Saenz-Ramos, Rev. Jorge Luis, (SJN) Curia: Leadership
Saez, Rev. Jesus, *O M* (SJN) Nuestra Senora de la Merced, San Juan, PR
Saez Castrillo, Rev. Jesus, (SJN) Ntra. Sra. de Fatima, San Juan, PR
Saffron, Rev. Stephen A., '12 (BRK) St. Josaphat, Bayside, NY
Safranek, Rev. William J., '96 (OM) St. Bridget-St. Rose Church of Omaha, Omaha, NE; St. Francis Assisi, Omaha, NE
Safraniec, Rev. Joseph N., '76 (STU) Retired.
Sagili Jesudas, Rev. Balraj, '08 (OKL) Sacred Heart, Alva, OK; [CAM] Northwestern Oklahoma State College, Alva, OK
Sagorski, Rev. Peter A., '95 (ORL) Retired.
Saguin, Rev. Marinello, '15 (LA) Our Lady of Grace, Encino, CA
Saguin, Rev. Marinello, '15 (LA) St. Margaret Mary Alacoque, Lomita, CA
Sagum, Rev. Ronald, '21 (LEX) Holy Family, Ashland, KY; [CAM] Holy Spirit Parish Newman Center, University of Kentucky, Lexington, KY
Saharic, Rev. Michael C., '88 (MET) Curia: Family Life St. Ann, Hampton, NJ
Sahayam, Rev. Jude Meril, '16 (IND) St. Ann Catholic Church, Indianapolis, Inc., Indianapolis, IN; St. Thomas More Catholic Church, Mooresville, Inc., Mooresville, IN
Sahd, Rev. Christopher S., '01 (SCR) On Leave. Discerning vocation to consecrated life
Sahd, Rev. Kyle S., '14 (HBG) Curia: Offices and Directors St. Theresa of the Infant Jesus, New Cumberland, PA
Sahd, Rev. Timothy J., '18 (HBG) Seven Sorrows of the Blessed Virgin Mary, Middletown, PA; Trinity High School, Camp Hill, PA
Saiki, Rev. Anthony, '14 (KCK) Curia: Tribunal Cathedral of St. Peter the Apostle, Kansas City, KS
Saint Jean, Rev. Kidney M., '92 (MIA) Our Lady Queen of Heaven, North Lauderdale, FL
Saint Louis, Rev. Roneld, '22 (PH) Holy Innocents, Philadelphia, PA
Sainte-Marie, Rev. Francois, (LAF) St. Theresa of the Child Jesus, Abbeville, LA
Saint-Hilaire, Rev. Emmanuel, '16 (VEN) St. Maximilian Kolbe Parish in Port Charlotte, Inc., Port Charlotte, FL
Saint-Jean, Rev. Fenly E., '14 (MIA) St. Elizabeth of Hungary Catholic Church, Pompano Beach, FL
Saiz, Rev. Rafael, *SDB* (MRY) Our Lady Help of Christians, Watsonville, CA; [MON] Salesians of St. John Bosco, Watsonville, CA
Sajda, Rev. Michael, (PMB) St. Mark, Boynton Beach, FL
Sajdak, Rev. David, *SDB* (CHI) St. John Bosco, Chicago, IL
Sajdak, Rev. Ronald P., '96 (BUF) Curia: Leadership Nativity of the Blessed Virgin Mary, Williamsville, NY
Sakala, Rev. Boniface, (HON) St. Jude, Kapolei, HI
Sakano, Rev. Msgr. Donald, '71 (NY) Retired. Most Precious Blood, New York, NY
Sakowicz, Rev. Gregory, '79 (CHI) Holy Name Cathedral, Chicago, IL
Sakowski, Rev. Derek J., '03 (LC) St. Mary, Altoona, WI; St. Raymond of Penafort, Fall Creek, WI; [CEM] Calvary Cemetery Association, Eau Claire, WI; [EFT] St. Mary Parish Endowment Trust, Altoona, WI
Sala, Rev. Michael J., *S.J.* '77 (NY) Chap, Metropolitan Hosp, New York [MON] St. Ignatius Loyola Residence, New York, NY
Salah, Rev. Michael A., '91 (WDC) St. Raphael, Rockville, MD
Salamanca, Rev. Uriel, '87 (BEL) St. Joseph, Cobden, IL; St. Mary, Anna, IL
Salameh, Rev. Adib, '20 (SAM) St. Anthony & St. George, Wilkes-Barre, PA
Salamone, Rev. Charles E., '75 (BO) Retired. Sacred Heart, Watertown, MA
Salamoni, Rev. Vincent, *M.S.A.* '84 (NOR) [MON] Society of the Missionaries of the Holy Apostles, Cromwell, CT
Salanitro, Rev. Carl A., '70 (OM) Holy Cross, Omaha, NE
Salapata, Rev. Andrzej, '97 (SJ) On Special Assignment. Church of the Resurrection, Sunnyvale, CA
Salas, Rev. Benjamin, *O.Carm.* (JOL) [MON] Carmelite Provincial Office, Darien, IL
Salas, Rev. Juan, (DOD) Curia: Leadership; Offices and Directors
Salas, Rev. Mark N.P., '11 (ELP) Curia: Advisory Boards, Commissions, Committees, and Councils; Tribunal Our Lady of Assumption, El Paso, TX
Salas, Rev. Raimundo, *S.J.* '80 (WDC) [MON] The Jesuit Community at Georgetown University, Washington, DC
Salas, Rev. Raul, *O.M.I.* (BEL) [MON] Shrine of Our Lady of the Snows, Belleville, IL
Salas, Rev. Yasid, '18 (PAT) St. Therese, Paterson, NJ
Salas Alanis, Rev. Juan Manuel, '16 (DOD) St. Alphonsus Catholic Church of Satanta, Kansas, Satanta, KS; St. Anthony of Padua Catholic Church of Liberal, Kansas, Liberal, KS; [EFT] St. Anthony School Endowment Fund, Liberal, KS
Salas Hinojosa, Rev. Vicente Oswaldo, *S.J.S.* '13 (MAD) On Duty Outside Diocese. Serves in Chile
Salata, Rev. Gregory J., '94 (MEM) On Leave.
Salatino, Rev. John C., '94 (SPR) St. Mary's, Westfield, MA
Salazar, Rev. Msgr. Alejandro, '91 (LAR) Curia: Offices and Directors San Martin de Porres, Laredo, TX
Salazar, Rev. Eusebio C. Fernandez, '71 (SJN) Santa Catalina Laboure, San Juan, PR
Salazar, Rev. George, '67 (SFE) Retired. State Hosp
Salazar, Rev. Jose A., (NY) Chap, New York City Veterans Administration Hosp, New York
Salazar, Rev. Jose Luis S., *S.J.* '01 (NY) [MON] Jesuit Community at Fordham University, New York, NY
Salazar, Rev. Juan, (BO) [MON] Edmund Campion House, Brighton, MA
Salazar, Rev. Juan Manuel, '13 (BWN) Curia: Advisory Boards, Commissions, Committees, and Councils Immaculate Conception, Edinburg, TX; St. Isidore, San Isidro, TX
Salazar, Rev. Luis, '16 (ORL) Holy Redeemer, Kissimmee, FL

Salazar, Rev. Msgr. Mario P., '61 (YAK) Retired. Curia: Leadership
Salazar Castano, Rev. Jairo, (SJN) Nuestra Senora de Covadonga, Toa Baja, PR
Salazar Gomez, Rev. Juan Carlos, (MIA) St. Martha, Miami Shores, FL
Salazar-Valero, Rev. Rogelio, '08 (SJN) Colegio Angeles Custodios, San Juan, PR; San Jose Obrero, San Juan, PR; Santismo Sacramento, Rio Piedras, PR
Salcedo, Rev. Osiris, *S.D.B.* '97 (NY) St. Luke, Bronx, NY
Saldana, Rev. Jesus, '82 (MIA) St. Kevin, Miami, FL
Saldana, Rev. Luis, '99 (NY) Immaculate Conception, Bronx, NY; [SEM] St. Joseph's Seminary, Yonkers, NY
Saldaña Sarmiento, Rev. Wilson, (ARE) Santa Ana, Vega Alta, PR
Saldanha, Rev. Derek, '19 (ORL) Curia: Advisory Boards, Commissions, Committees, and Councils St. Thomas Aquinas Church, St. Cloud, FL
Saldanha, Rev. Reginald, '97 (KCK) Sacred Heart, Baileyville, KS; St. Mary's Catholic Church, St. Benedict, KS
Salditos, Rev. Henry P., '89 (LAV) St. John the Evangelist, Logandale, NV
Salditos, Rev. Rey, '83 (LAV) Retired.
Saldua, Rev. Clarence Gesbert, *M.S.* '13 (SB) Our Lady of Lourdes, Montclair, CA; [MON] The Pacific Region Missionaries of Our Lady of La Salette, MS, Moreno Valley, CA
Saldua, Rev. Max E., '78 (LA) Chap, Veterans Administration Los Angeles Health System
Salemi, Rev. Msgr. Cajetan P., '61 (NEW) Retired. Our Lady Mother of the Church, Woodcliff Lake, NJ
Salemi, Rev. Cajetan P., '61 (NEW) Retired.
Salemi, Rev. Paul S., '00 (BUF) On Administrative Leave.
Salen, Rev. Enrique V., '90 (GAL) St. Francis de Sales, Houston, TX; [MIS] The Catholic Chaplain Corps, Houston, TX
Salera, Rev. Alfredo J., '77 (CHI) Retired.
Salerno, Rev. Emilio J., '59 (BRK) Retired.
Salerno, Rev. Joseph A., '80 (SY) Mary, Mother of Our Savior, New Hartford, NY; [MIS] Christ Child Society of Utica, Utica, NY
Sales, Rev. Kenneth L., '04 (OAK) Curia: Leadership; Offices and Directors Holy Spirit, Fremont, CA
Saleth, Rev. Joseph Albert, '08 (LC) St. Therese of the Child Jesus, Rothschild, WI; [EFT] St. Therese Catholic Church Endowment Fund, Schofield, WI
Saleth-Pitchai, Rev. Sebastian S., '07 (LC) St. Bartholomew, Trempealeau, WI; St. Mary, Galesville, WI
Saletrik, Rev. E. George, '96 (GBG) Curia: Offices and Directors
Salgado, Rev. Gerardo Francisco, *O.F.M.* '99 (ELP) [SEM] St. Anthony's School of Theology, El Paso, TX
Salgado Benitez, Rev. Manuel E., *O.SS.T.* '96 (PCE) San Jose, Penuelas, PR
Salgado Pabon, Rev. Salvador, *C.M.F.* (SJN) Casa Mision Claret, Bayamon, PR
Salgado Pabón, Rev. Salvador, *cmf* '87 (PCE) Nuestra Senora del Carmen, Ponce, PR
Saliba, Rev. Anthony, '01 (RVC) The Roman Catholic Church of Saint Rose of Lima, Massapequa, NY
Saliba, Rev. Dimitrios, *BCO* (NTN) St. Anne Melkite Co-Cathedral, North Hollywood, CA
Saliba, Rev. John A., *S.J.* '65 (DET) [MON] Colombiere Center, Clarkston, MI
Salibindla, Rev. Pratap Reddy, *O.F.M.* '91 (WIN) Sacred Heart, Brewster, MN; Sacred Heart, Heron Lake, MN; St. Francis Xavier Church, Windom, MN
Saliga, Rev. Christopher, (CHI) St. Vincent Ferrer, River Forest, IL
Saligumba, Rev. Ma Carlos Datu, *S.O.L.T.* '91 (RCK) Christ the King, Wonder Lake, IL
Salim, Rev. Anthony, '74 (OLL) Retired.
Salinas, Rev. Andres, '93 (RCK) Curia: Offices and Directors St. Joseph, Harvard, IL
Salinas, Rev. Jesus, *LC* '19 (CIN) Royalmont Academy, Mason, OH
Salinas, Rev. Juan Jose, (SJN) [MIS] Opus Dei, Guaynabo, PR
Salinas, Rev. Juan Jose, (POD) Curia: Clergy and Religious Services
Salinas, Rev. Octavio, *O.F.M.* '83 (BRK) Our Lady of Peace, Brooklyn, NY
Salinas, Rev. Rodolfo A., '11 (WDC) Christ the King, Silver Spring, MD; Most Holy Rosary, Upper Marlboro, MD
Salinas, Rev. Romeo, '00 (CC) St. George Catholic Church, George West, TX
Salinas Hernandez, Rev. Jesus Erasmo, *C.S.* '10 (NY) [MON] Scalabrinian Missionaries (The Pious Society of the Missionaries of St. Charles Boromeo, Inc.), New York, NY
Salisbury, Rev. Keith R., '06 (NU) Retired. Curia: Offices and Directors St. Leo, St. Leo, MN; St. Peter, Canby, MN
Salisbury, Rev. Paschal Donald, *O.P.* '67 (P) Retired. [MON] Holy Rosary Priory, Portland, OR
Salisbury, Rev. Ryan L., '15 (LIN) St. Paulinus, Syracuse, NE
Saliva Gonzalez, Rev. Juan Jose, '90 (PCE) Curia: Leadership San Ramon Nonato, Juana Diaz, PR
Saliva Gonzalez, Rev. Juan Jose, '90 (PCE) Curia: Offices and Directors
Salkovski, Rev. Basil, *O.S.B.M.* (STF) Curia: Offices and Directors
Salkovski, Rev. Varcilio Basil, *O.S.B.M.* '88 (STF) Curia: Leadership [MON] Provincialate of the Basilian Order of St. Josaphat, Locust Valley, NY
Salla, Rev. Mano, (WIL) St. Edmond, Rehoboth Beach, DE
Sallese, Rev. Albert J., '66 (BO) Retired.
Sallot, Rev. Steven, '80 (ORG) Curia: Offices and Directors Our Lady Queen of Angels, Newport Beach, CA
Salmani, Rev. Frank S., '82 (PRO) St. Agnes Church, Providence, RI
Salmi, Rev. Richard Patrick, *S.J.* '82 (CHI) [COL] Jesuit Community at Loyola University Chicago, Chicago, IL
Salmon, Rev. Edward P., '59 (CHI) Retired. St. Catherine of Siena-St. Lucy and St. Giles Parish, Oak Park, IL
Salmon, Rev. James F., *S.J.* '64 (BAL) [MIS] Colombiere Jesuit Community, Baltimore, MD
Salmon, Rev. William F., '65 (BO) Retired. Our Lady of the Angels Parish, Hanover, MA
Salnicky, Very Rev. Michael J., '93 (PSC) Curia: Advisory Boards, Commissions, Committees, and Councils
Salnicky, Very Rev. Michael J., '93 (PSC) Curia: Advisory Boards, Commissions, Committees, and Councils; Leadership St. Nicholas, Pocono Summit, PA; [SHR] Carpathian Village, Cresco, PA
Salocks, Rev. Stephen E., '80 (BO) [SEM] Saint John's Seminary, Brighton, MA
Salomon, Rev. Victor, '98 (WDC) [SEM] Diocesan Laborer Priests, House of Studies, Washington, DC
Salomon, Rev. Victor, (BIR) Holy Spirit, Tuscaloosa, AL
Salomone, Rev. Gregory, *O.P.* (NEW) [CON] Monastery of Our Lady of the Rosary, Summit, NJ
Salonek, Rev. Josh Jacob, '21 (STP) St. John Neumann, Eagan, MN
Salonga, Rev. Juan S., '10 (MET) On Duty Outside Diocese. Archdiocese for the Military Services, USA Curia: (>MO) Offices and Directors
Saloy, Rev. Thomas, '88 (RVC) Retired.
Saltar Arocho, Rev. William, *S.F.M.* '08 (MGZ) Our Lady of Mt. Carmel, Mayaguez, PR
Saltarin, Rev. Jose C., '67 (NEW) Retired. [MON] St. John Vianney Residence for Retired Priests, Rutherford, NJ
Salus, Rev. Jude S., *O.S.B.* '75 (PAT) [MON] St. Mary's Abbey, Morristown, NJ
Salvador, Rev. Stephen B., '74 (FR) Retired.
Salvagna, Rev. Micahel, *C.P.* '69 (SCR) [MON] Saint Ann's Passionist Monastery of Scranton PA, Scranton, PA
Salvagna, Rev. Michael, *C.P.* '69 (PIT) [RTR] St. Paul of the Cross Retreat Center, Pittsburgh, PA
Salvagna, Rev. Michael J., *C.P.* '69 (NY) [MON] The Congregation of the Passion - St. Paul of the Cross Province, Jamaica, NY
Salvania, Rev. Leopoldo S., '11 (MET) Assumption of the Blessed Virgin Mary, Hackettstown, NJ
Salvatierra, Rev. Calixto, *OMF Conv.* '04 (ATL) St. Philip Benizi Catholic Church, Jonesboro, Inc., Jonesboro, GA
Salvatori, Rev. Christopher, *S.A.C.* '00 (NY) [MON] Pallottine Fathers, New York, NY
Salvidar, Rev. Roberto, *M.Sp.S.* (SEA) St. Pius X, Mountlake Terrace, WA
Salvo, Very Rev. Enrique, '10 (NY) Curia: Leadership Cathedral of St. Patrick, New York, NY
Salwowski, Rev. Andrzej, '86 (BRK) Holy Cross, Maspeth, NY
Saly, Rev. Msgr. Robert J., '85 (ALT) St. Catherine of Siena, Duncansville, PA
Salzmann, Rev. George S., *O.S.F.S.* '77 (BO) St. Paul, Cambridge, MA; [CAM] Harvard Catholic Center, Cambridge, MA
Sama, Rev. Cassian Kenneth, *O.P.* '11 (STP) M Health Fairview Univ of Minnesota Med Ctr [MON] St. Albert the Great Priory, Minneapolis, MN
Samaan, Rev. Rezkallah, '86 (NTN) St. John the Baptist, Northlake, IL
Samaha, Rev. Jeffrey F., '78 (WDC) Chap, Hosp & Nursing Home Min, MedStar Southern Maryland Ho… Church of the Holy Spirit, Forestville, MD
Samaha, Rt. Rev. Victor, *B.C.O.* (NTN) Retired.
Samaila, Rev. Ishaya S., '97 (PHX) St. Paul Roman Catholic Parish, Phoenix, AZ
Samala, Rev. Savio J., '89 (GB) [MIS] Society for Faith and Children's Education, Inc., Green Bay, WI
Samala, Rev. Suresh, '88 (SPC) St. Michael the Archangel, Fredericktown, MO
Samaniego, Rev. Eduardo, *S.J.* (SD) Curia: Offices and Directors
Samaniego, Rev. Tarsicio, *L.C.* '67 (HRT) Retired.
Samboni, Rev. Apolinar, '14 (ELP) St. Paul the Apostle, El Paso, TX
Sambor, Rev. David R., '78 (SY) Retired.
Samborski, Rev. Piotr, '15 (CHI) St. Daniel the Prophet, Chicago, IL
Sambu, Rev. Jean Olivier M., '02 (BWN) Curia: Leadership Our Lady of Mercy, Mercedes, TX
Samele, Rev. Christopher J., '03 (BGP) St. Thomas Church Fairfield Connecticut, Fairfield, CT
Samide, Rev. Daniel, (CLV) St. Anthony of Padua, Parma, OH
Samide, Rev. Richard, (CLV) St. Mary of the Immaculate Conception, Wooster, OH
Sammarco, Rev. Bruno S., '08 (NEW) Retired.
Sammons, Rev. Charles, *OFMCap* '07 (NY) [MON] The Province of St. Mary of the Capuchin Order, White Plains, NY
Sammut, Rev. George, '99 (PT) Retired.
Samour, Rev. Richard, '12 (SAT) St. Clare, San Antonio, TX
Samoylo, Rev. Francis, (NY) St. Columbanus, Cortlandt Manor, NY
Samperi, Rev. Charles J., '96 (GAL) St. James the Apostle, Spring, TX
Sample, Rev. Clark, (GAL) St. Thomas More, Houston, TX; [EFT] The St. Thomas More Parish School Endowment Foundation, Houston, TX
Samples, Rev. Zachary, '22 (SFD) St. Peter, Quincy, IL
Sampson, Rev. Elric, *O.F.M.* '85 (CHI) [MON] St. Peter's Friary, Chicago, IL
Sampson, Rev. Kenneth, '08 (P) Curia: Offices and Directors Sacred Heart of Jesus, Medford, OR
Sampungi, Rev. Didier, *CMM* '21 (IND) St. Jude Catholic Church, Indianapolis, Inc., Indianapolis, IN
Samra, Rev. Basil, '86 (NTN) Retired.
Samsa, Rev. John F., (GB) Retired. [MON] St. Fidelis Friary, Appleton, WI
Samson, Rev. Arokiaswamy, (NEW) Chap, (Adjunct), Hackensack Univ Med Ctr
Samson, Rev. Charles K., '13 (STL) Basilica of St. Louis, King of France Catholic Church, St. Louis, MO; St. Mary of Victories Catholic Church and St. Stephen of Hungary Chapel, St. Louis, MO; [SEM] Kenrick School of Theology, ,
Samson, Rev. Jordan, '11 (SFS) Curia: Leadership; Offices and Directors Christ the King Parish of Minnehaha County, Sioux Falls, SD
Samson, Rev. Robert J., '79 (STL) St. Joseph Catholic Church, Josephville, Wentzville, MO
Samuel, Rev. Francis A., *O.C.I.* '72 (RVC) St. Ignatius Loyola, Hicksville, NY; St. Joseph, Babylon, NY
Samuel, Rev. John, (GAL) St. Rose of Lima, Houston, TX
Samuels, Rev. Reginald W., '03 (GAL) Curia: Leadership St. Hyacinth, Deer Park, TX
Samway, Rev. Patrick H., *S.J.* '69 (PH) [MIS] Jesuit Fathers, ,
Samway, Rev. Patrick H., *S.J.* '69 (PH) [MON] Jesuit Community at St. Joseph's University, Merion Station, PA
Samy, Rev. Agnel, *H.G.N.* (BUR) Our Lady of Mercy, Townshend, VT; St. Charles, Bellows Falls, VT
Samy, Rev. Alwin, *H.G.N.* (BLX) Holy Trinity, Columbia, MS
Samy, Rev. Antoninus, *O.P.* (WDC) St. Dominic Church & Priory, Washington, DC
Samy, Rev. Antony, '13 (FAR) Christ the King - Tokio, Tokio, ND; Christ the King Church of Tokio, Fort Totten, ND; Seven Dolors Indian Mission, Fort Totten, ND; St. Jerome - Crow Hill, Oberon, ND; St. Jerome's Church of Crow Hill, Oberon, ND
Samy, Rev. Ed, '67 (SJ) Retired.
San Llorente Puente, Rev. Ricardo, (ARE) Retired.
San Nicolas, Rev. Jeffrey C., '97 (AGN) Curia: Administration; Family Life; Leadership
San Nicolas, Rev. Jeffrey C., '97 (AGN) Curia: Consultative Bodies St. Anthony and St. Victor, Tamuning, GU

Sanaghan, Rev. John J., '72 (CHI) Retired.
Sanahuja, Rev. Manuel, *Sch.P.* (SD) Pastor of Our Lady of Guadalupe Catholic Parish, Calexico, a corporation sole, Calexico, CA
Sanahuja, Rev. Manuel, *Sch.P.* '67 (LA) Our Lady Help of Christians (Maria Auxiliadora), Los Angeles, CA
Sanches, Rev. Joseph Anthony, '70 (ATL) Retired.
Sanchez, Rev. Adalberto, '11 (RCK) SS. Peter and Paul, Rockford, IL
Sanchez, Rev. Adrian, *O.Praem* '95 (LA) SS. Peter and Paul, Wilmington, CA
Sanchez, Rev. Adrian, *O.Praem.* '95 (ORG) [MON] Norbertine Fathers of Orange, Inc., Silverado, CA
Sanchez, Rev. Alan, (LAR) Our Lady of Lourdes, Zapata, TX
Sanchez, Rev. Alejandro, '93 (STV) On Duty Outside Diocese.
Sanchez, Rev. Angel, '90 (PCE) Curia: (>MO) Offices and Directors
Sanchez, Rev. Antero, *M.S.C.* '65 (FRS) St. Elizabeth, McFarland, CA
Sanchez, Rev. Antero, *M.S.C.* '65 (LA) [MON] Misioneros del Sagrado Corazon y Santa Maria de Guadalupe, Cudahy, CA
Sanchez, Rev. Antonio, '90 (MRY) Christ the King, Salinas, CA
Sanchez, Rev. Ariel, (FWT) St. Matthew, Arlington, TX
Sanchez, Rev. Baltazar, *Sch.P.* '96 (NY) [MON] Calasanzian Fathers (Piarists), New York, NY
Sanchez, Rev. Carlos, '15 (ROC) Chap, Strong Health System, Rochester Our Lady of Peace Roman Catholic Church of Geneva, NY, Geneva, NY
Sanchez, Rev. Cesar, '20 (JKS) St. James, Tupelo, MS
Sanchez, Rev. David, '02 (L) Annunciation of the Blessed Virgin Mary, Shelbyville, KY
Sanchez, Rev. Edward Joseph, '20 (MIL) Holy Family Congregation, Fond du Lac, WI
Sanchez, Rev. Erik, *CM* (CHL) St. Mary, Greensboro, NC
Sanchez, Rev. Ernesto Esqueda, (DAL) St. Luke Catholic Parish, Irving, TX
Sanchez, Rev. Esequiel, '95 (CHI) Curia: Leadership St. Paul Chong Hasang, Des Plaines, IL; [MIS] Shrine of Our Lady of Guadalupe, Des Plaines, IL
Sanchez, Rev. Felix, '96 (BRK) St. Pius V, Jamaica, NY
Sanchez, Rev. Fernando, *O.C.D.* (CGS) San Jose, Caguas, PR
Sanchez, Rev. Francisco, *M.Id* (NY) [MON] Idente Missionaries - Santa Maria Residence, Bronx, NY
Sanchez, Rev. Francisco, *M.Id* (NY) [EFT] Foundation of Christ the Redeemer, Bronx, NY
Sanchez, Rev. Francisco Nicomedes S., '94 (HON) Diocesan Hospital Chap Dir St. Anthony, Honolulu, HI
Sanchez, Rev. Fredy, '12 (NEW) Blessed Sacrament, Elizabeth, NJ
Sanchez, Rev. Gabriel, '22 (SR) Pastor of St. Eugene Cathedral of Santa Rosa, A Corporation Sole, Santa Rosa, CA
Sanchez, Rev. Gerardo, *M.C.M.* '04 (BWN) St. Ignatius of Loyola Parish, San Benito, TX
Sanchez, Rev. German, '90 (LA) St. Sebastian, Los Angeles, CA
Sanchez, Rev. Hever, *C.Ss.R.* (BAL) St. Mary, Annapolis, MD
Sanchez, Rev. Hugo D., *M.C.M.* '20 (BWN) St. Ignatius of Loyola Parish, San Benito, TX
Sanchez, Rev. Humberto Aristizabal, *C.M.* '98 (AJ) Cathedral of Our Lady of Guadalupe, Anchorage, AK
Sanchez, Rev. Israel, *O.S.B.* '21 (P) [MON] Mt. Angel Abbey, Saint Benedict, OR
Sanchez, Rev. James, '01 (SFE) St. John the Baptist-Santa Fe, Santa Fe, NM
Sanchez, Rev. Jordan, '21 (SFE) St. Alice, Mountainair, NM
Sanchez, Rev. Jose, *C.M.F.* '95 (CHI) [MON] Claretian Missionaries U.S.A.-Canada Province, Inc., Chicago, IL
Sanchez, Rev. Jose, *CMF* '95 (FRS) St. Anthony Claret, Fresno, CA
Sanchez, Rev. Jose de Jesus, '14 (JKS) Curia: Consultative Bodies St. Joseph, Greenville, MS
Sanchez, Rev. Jose M., '58 (GAL) Retired.
Sanchez, Rev. Jose de Jesus, *M.Sp.S.* (SEA) St. Elizabeth Ann Seton, Mill Creek, WA
Sanchez, Rev. Juan Luis, '84 (MIA) Retired. SS. Peter and Paul, Miami, FL
Sanchez, Rev. Juan Miguel, (CHL) St. Matthew, Charlotte, NC
Sanchez, Rev. Luis Fernando, '10 (BWN) Curia: Leadership St. Pius X, Weslaco, TX
Sanchez, Rev. Marco, *S.T.* '92 (JKS) St. Anne, Carthage, MS; St. Therese, Kosciusko, MS
Sanchez, Rev. Mauro, '16 (SC) Christ the King, Sioux Center, IA; St. Mary's, Rock Valley, IA
Sanchez, Rev. Miguel Angel, '98 (ELP) Curia: Advisory Boards, Commissions, Committees, and Councils San Judas Tadeo, El Paso, TX
Sanchez, Rev. Miguel Angel, (ELP) Curia: Advisory Boards, Commissions, Committees, and Councils Santa Teresita, El Paso, TX
Sanchez, Rev. Nestor, '19 (JOL) Sts. Peter and Paul, Naperville, IL
Sanchez, Rev. Nicolas, '91 (LA) St. Patrick, North Hollywood, CA
Sanchez, Rev. Raul, '02 (OKL) Good Shepherd, Marietta, OK
Sanchez, Rev. Raul N., '74 (GLP) On Leave.
Sanchez, Rev. Ricardo, '99 (CHL) Our Lady of the Americas, Biscoe, NC
Sanchez, Rev. Salvador, (DEN) St. Mary of the Crown Catholic Parish in Carbondale, Carbondale, CO; St. Vincent Catholic Parish in Basalt, Basalt, CO
Sanchez, Friar Stephen, *O.C.D.* '92 (LR) [SEM] Discalced Carmelite Friars of St. Therese, Little Rock, Little Rock, AR
Sanchez, Rev. William, '83 (SFE) St. Joseph-Cerrillos, Cerrillos, NM
Sanchez Alonzo, Rev. Baltazar, (BRK) Curia: Consultative Bodies
Sanchez Chan, Rev. Ramiro, *C.S.* '03 (KCK) Curia: Offices and Directors
Sanchez Chan, Rev. Ramiro, *C.S.* (KC) Holy Rosary, Kansas City, MO
Sanchez Chan, Rev. Ramiro V., *C.S.* '03 (LA) [MON] Scalabrini House of Discernment, Sun Valley, CA
Sanchez Guzman, Rev. Juan-Sebastian, '18 (WOR) St. Richard of Chichester, Sterling, MA
Sanchez Hernandez, Rev. Angel M., '90 (PCE) Military Chap Parroquia Santiago Apostol, Santa Isabel, PR
Sanchez Leandro, Rev. Juan Alfredo, '92 (MIA) [SEM] The Redemptoris Mater Seminary Archdiocese of Miami, Inc., Hialeah, FL
Sanchez Malagon, Rev. Julio Cesar, '09 (AGN) On Duty Outside Diocese.
Sanchez Mares, Rev. Cruz, '16 (NY) Parish of St. Gabriel and St. Joseph, New Rochelle, NY
Sanchez Muniz, Rev. Victor Rene, '10 (PCE) Nuestra Senora de Fatima, Yauco, PR; Nuestra Senora de la Monserrate, Yauco, PR; Sagrado Corazon, Yauco, PR; San Jose, Yauco, PR; San Juan Macias, Yauco, PR; San Martin de Porres, Yauco, PR; Santa Rosa de Lima, Yauco, PR; Santa Teresita, Yauco, PR
Sanchez Muniz, Rev. Victor Rene, '10 (PCE) Santo Domingo de Guzman, Yauco, PR
Sanchez Olvera, Rev. Oscar, *CORC* (FWT) Immaculate Heart of Mary, Fort Worth, TX
Sanchez Romero, Rev. Edwin L, '15 (P) On Leave.
Sanchez Velez, Rev. Victor, '90 (ARE) Inmaculado Corazon de Maria, Sabana Hoyos, PR
Sanchez Velez, Rev. Victor, '90 (ARE) Curia: Offices and Directors
Sanchez-Munoz, Rev. Alejandro, '66 (STV) On Duty Outside Diocese. Curia: (>MO) Offices and Directors
Sancho, Rev. Jesus, *O.C.D.* '64 (OKL) Our Lady of Mount Carmel and St. Therese Little Flower, Oklahoma City, OK; [MON] Monastery of Our Lady of Mount Carmel and Little Flower, Oklahoma City, OK
Sand, Rev. James, (TOL) St. John's Jesuit High School and Academy, Toledo, OH; [MON] St. John's Jesuit High School Jesuit Community, Holland, OH
Sandberg, Rev. Kevin J., *C.S.C.* '05 (FTW) [COL] University of Notre Dame Du Lac, Notre Dame, IN; [MON] Holy Cross Community, Corby Hall, University of Notre Dame, Notre Dame, IN
Sandberg, Rev. Stuart, '68 (NY) [MIS] Company of St. Paul, White Plains, NY
Sandbothe, Rev. Aaron J., (SAM) St. George, Uniontown, PA
Sander, Rev. Reginald, *O.S.B.* '63 (KC) [MON] Conception Abbey (Benedictine Monks), Conception, MO
Sanderfoot, Rev. Brian P., '04 (WDC) St. Francis de Sales, Washington, DC
Sanders, Rev. Daniel J., '78 (MIL) Retired.
Sanders, Rev. Edwin, *S.J.* '59 (PH) Retired.
Sanders, Very Rev. Gary, *O.S.A.* (CHI) [MON] Federation of Augustinians of North America, Chicago, IL
Sanders, Rev. Gary, *O.S.A.* '75 (SD) [EFT] The Bellesini Foundation, San Diego, CA; [EFT] The Tagaste Foundation, San Diego, CA; [MIS] St. Augustine High School Chapel, San Diego, CA; [MON] Augustinian Community, San Diego, CA
Sanders, Rev. George W., '13 (LR) St. John the Baptist, Hot Springs, AR; [HOS] CHI St. Vincent Hot Springs, Hot Springs, AR
Sanders, Rev. Kyle J., '12 (NO) Holy Family Roman Catholic Church, Franklinton, Louisiana, Franklinton, LA
Sanders, Rev. Lawrence E., *C.Ss.R.* '93 (CHI) St. Michael in Old Town, Chicago, IL; [MON] The Redemptorist Fathers of Chicago, Chicago, IL
Sanders, Rev. Nathaniel A., '22 (BO) St. Columbkille, Brighton, MA
Sanders, Rev. Paul, *C.PP.S.* '62 (KC) Retired. [MON] Society of the Precious Blood, Liberty, MO
Sanders, Rev. Philip A., '05 (NEW) Curia: Advisory Boards, Commissions, Committees, and Councils; Organizations (affiliated, inter-Diocesan, miscellaneous/ other) The Parish of Blessed Miriam Teresa Demjanovich Church, Bayonne, NJ
Sanders, Rev. William F., '75 (WOR) Retired. Curia: Leadership
Sandersfeld, Rev. Msgr. John, '66 (SJ) Retired.
Sanderson, Rev. Joseph, (BUR) Our Lady of the Lake, South Hero, VT
Sanderson, Rev. William E., '83 (OM) Holy Ghost, Omaha, NE; St. Stanislaus, Omaha, NE
Sandhage, Rev. Martin J., '86 (LFT) St. Ambrose, Anderson, IN; St. Mary, Alexandria, IN; St. Mary, Anderson, IN
Sandi, Rev. Msgr. Thomas P., '73 (NY) Curia: Offices and Directors Holy Trinity, New York, NY
Sandman, Rev. Gregory, '80 (MRY) Madonna Del Sasso, Salinas, CA
Sandor, Rev. Albert, *O.F.M.Cap.* '82 (DET) [MON] St. Bonaventure Monastery, Detroit, MI
Sandoval, Very Rev. Clarence J., '87 (SLC) Curia: Offices and Directors
Sandoval, Rev. Eliecer, *SMA* '09 (NEW) [MON] Society of African Missions, Provincialate, S.M.A. Fathers, Tenafly, NJ
Sandoval, Rev. Ismael, '03 (CHI) Curia: Parish Services Blessed Sacrament, Chicago, IL
Sandoval, Rev. Lazaro, *O.F.M.Conv.* '07 (OAK) St. Paul, San Pablo, CA
Sandoval, Rev. Luis, '74 (SAT) On Leave.
Sandoval, Rev. Norberto, '05 (MIL) Congregation of the Holy Name, Sheboygan, WI; St. Clement's Congregation, Sheboygan, WI; St. Dominic Congregation, Sheboygan, WI; [MIS] The Sheboygan County Catholic Fund, Inc., Sheboygan, WI
Sandoval, Rev. Oswaldo, '12 (KCK) Curia: Advisory Boards, Commissions, Committees, and Councils Holy Cross, Overland Park, KS
Sandoval, Rev. Parker, '15 (LA) Curia: Advisory Boards, Commissions, Committees, and Councils; Offices and Directors Incarnation, Glendale, CA
Sandoval Duron, Rev. Adan, (CHI) St. Procopius, Chicago, IL
Sandoval Pliego, Rev. Jairo, (AUS) San Jose, Austin, TX
Sandoval-Ochoa, Rev. Juan M., (SB) St. Christopher, Moreno Valley, CA
Sandoz, Rev. Robert, (ALB) [COL] Siena College, Loudonville, NY
Sandquist, Rev. Tim, '17 (STP) Chesterton Academy, Hopkins, MN
Sandquist, Rev. Timothy David, '17 (STP) Holy Family, St. Louis Park, MN
Sandrick, Rev. Philip Patrick, *OSBM* '84 (STF) [SEM] Basilian Fathers Novitiate of the Order of St. Basil the Great (St. Josaphat Monastery), Glen Cove, NY
Sands, Rev. Joseph C., *S.J.* '92 (SY) (>SCR) [COL] The University of Scranton, Scranton, PA
Sands, Rev. Maurice Henry, '05 (DET) On Duty Outside Diocese. United States Conference of Catholic Bishops
Sandstrom, Rev. Philip, '62 (NY) Retired. [MIS] St. Ansgar Scandinavian Catholic League, New York, NY
Sandval, Rev. Francisco, *OAR* (ORG) Our Lady of the Pillar, Santa Ana, CA
Sandweg, Rev. Michael J., '79 (STL) Retired.
Sane, Rev. Barwende, *S.J.* '13 (SFR) [MON] Loyola House Jesuit Community, San Francisco, CA
Sanez, Rev. Hilario S., (BO) St. Rose of Lima, Chelsea, MA
Sanford, Rev. James R., '86 (TOL) Retired. St. Patrick of Heatherdowns, Toledo, OH
Sanford, Rev. L. Harold, *S.J.* '75 (DET) [MON] Colombiere Center, Clarkston, MI
Sanford, Rev. Stephen J., *S.J.* '94 (BO) [MON] Campion Health & Wellness, Inc., Weston, MA
Sanford, Rev. Taylor, '21 (BR) Congregation Of The Immaculate Conception Roman Catholic Church, Denham Springs, Louisiana, Denham Springs, LA
Sang, Rev. Francis D., '73 (RVC) Retired. SS. Cyril and Methodius, Deer Park, NY
Sangabathini, Rev. John Sudhatar, '16 (AMA) Holy

Angels, Childress, TX; Our Mother of Mercy, Wellington, TX; Sacred Heart, Memphis, TX
Sangermano, Rev. Msgr. Charles L., '78 (PH) Curia: Deaneries Holy Saviour, Norristown, PA
Sanggaria, Rev. Leoyd, *CICM* (SAT) Our Lady of Grace, LaCoste, TX
Sang-Nguyen, Rev. Francis, (RVC) Retired.
Sangu, Rev. James E., (BO) Immaculate Conception, Malden, MA
Sanka, Rev. Matthew, *S.A.C.* '02 (FWT) Our Lady of Guadalupe, DeLeon, TX; Sacred Heart, Comanche, TX; St. Brendan, Stephenville, TX; St. Mary, Dublin, TX (>DET) [MON] Society of the Catholic Apostolate (Pallottine Fathers), Wyandotte, MI
Sankar, Rev. Paul, '91 (BGP) Saint Matthew's Roman Catholic Church Corporation, Norwalk, CT
Sankoorikal, Rev. George S., '71 (BGP) Retired.
Sanks, Rev. T. Howland, *S.J.* '65 (BAL) Retired.
Sanks, Rev. T. Howland, *S.J.* '65 (BAL) Retired. [MIS] Colombiere Jesuit Community, Baltimore, MD
Sanks, Rev. T. Howland, *S.J.* '65 (BAL) Retired.
Sannella, Rev. Nicholas A., (BO) Holy Family, Lowell, MA; Holy Trinity, Lowell, MA; Immaculate Conception, Lowell, MA; St. Anthony of Padua, Lowell, MA
Sanner, Rev. Msgr. James E., '59 (E) Retired.
Sansevere, Rev. Stephen, (TR) St. Alphonsus, Hopewell, NJ; St. George, Titusville, NJ; St. James, Pennington, NJ
Sanson, Rev. Robert J., '67 (CLV) Retired.
Sansone, Rev. Anthony J., '80 (BRK) Our Lady of the Miraculous Medal, Ridgewood, NY
Sant, Rev. Ivan, '08 (NEW) On Duty Outside Diocese. Archdioces of St Paul & Minneapolis, St Paul, MN
Santa, Rev. Thomas, *C.Ss.R.* '78 (GR) St. Alphonsus, Grand Rapids, MI; [MIS] The Society of the Redemptorists of the City of Grand Rapids, Grand Rapids, MI
Santa Cruz, Rev. Ramon, '99 (SEA) Saint Teresa of Calcutta, Woodinville, WA
Santamaria Belda, Rev. Manuel, *SJ* '22 (OAK) [MON] Jesuit Fathers and Brothers, Berkeley, CA
Santana Cardoso, Rev. Hugo, *C.S.* (MIA) St. Vincent, Margate, FL
Santana-Figueroa, Rev. Ramón, (CGS) Maria Madre de la Iglesia, Caguas, PR
Santandreu, Rev. Peter, '18 (BUF) (>WDC) St. Bernadette, Silver Spring, MD
Santangelo, Rev. Christopher, *SS.CC.* '99 (LA) Holy Name of Mary, San Dimas, CA; [MON] Congregation of the Sacred Hearts of Jesus and Mary, La Verne, CA
Santangelo, Rev. Michael A., '95 (TR) Curia: Pastoral Services Epiphany, Brick, NJ
Santarosa, Rev. Scott, *SJ* (SD) Pastor of Our Lady of Guadalupe Catholic Parish, San Diego, a corporation sole, San Diego, CA; [MIS] Our Lady of Guadalupe Catholic Parish San Diego in San Diego, CA Real Property Support Corporation, San Diego, CA
Santen, Rev. Thomas J., '70 (STL) Retired. St. Simon the Apostle Catholic Church, St. Louis, MO
Santerre, Rev. Richard R., '82 (BO) Retired.
Santhiyagu, Rev. Arockiasmy, *H.G.N.* '07 (PRT) Prince of Peace Parish, Lewiston, ME; [HOS] St. Mary's Regional Medical Center, Lewiston, ME; [NUR] St. Mary's d'Youville Pavilion, Lewiston, ME
Santhouse, Rev. William M., '15 (SP) St. Scholastica, Lecanto, FL
Santiago, Rev. Bernard Shaw, '04 (LA) St. Barnabas, Long Beach, CA
Santiago, Rev. Bruno, (NU) St. Andrew, Fairfax, MN; St. Francis de Sales, Winthrop, MN; St. Willibrord, Gibbon, MN
Santiago, Rev. Felipe, *C.Ss.R.* (CGS) Nuestra Senora de la Mercedes, San Lorenzo, PR
Santiago, Rev. Florentino, '78 (HT) Retired.
Santiago, Rev. Hiriam, *S.B.D.* '92 (SJN) Colegio San Juan Bosco, San Juan, PR
Santiago, Rev. Jorge, *SDB* (SJN) Maria Auxiliadora, San Juan, PR
Santiago, Rev. Jose Antonio, (SJN) Maria Reina del Mundo, San Juan, PR
Santiago, Rev. Jose Antonio, (SJN) Ntra. Sra. de Guadalupe, San Juan, PR
Santiago, Rev. Leoncia, '73 (CHI) Retired.
Santiago, Rev. Leoncio S., '73 (CHI) Retired.
Santiago, Rev. Michael A., '13 (HRT) Chap. North Haven Police Dept. Curia: Advisory Boards, Commissions, Committees, and Councils; Clergy and Religious Services Saint Elizabeth of the Trinity Parish Corporation, North Haven, CT
Santiago, Rev. Xavier, '07 (GB) St. Mary Magdalene, Waupaca, WI
Santiago De Jesus, Rev. Samuel, '76 (PCE) Curia: Offices and Directors Nuestra Senora de la Monserrate, Salinas, PR
Santiago Hernandez, Rev. Manuel A., '85 (PCE) Curia: Leadership; Offices and Directors Nuestra Senora del Carmen, Ponce, PR
Santiago Mateo, Rev. Victor, *S.T.* '82 (FAJ) Concathedral Dulce Nombre de Jesus, Humacao, PR; [MON] Siervos Misioneros de la Santisima Trinidad, Loiza, PR
Santiago Ramirez, Rev. Carlos Rafael, (SJN) Curia: Offices and Directors
Santiago Ramirez, Rev. Carlos Rafael, (SJN) Santa Teresa de Jesus, Bayamon, PR
Santiago Roman, Friar Jose, *O.P.* '93 (SJN) [COL] Universidad Central de Bayamon, Inc., Bayamon, PR
Santiago Torres, Rev. Francisco, (PCE) Inmaculado Corazon de Maria, Patillas, PR
Santiago-Ramirez, Rev. Carlos Rafael, '15 (SJN) Curia: Leadership
Santin, Rev. Ricardo, '07 (CGS) Curia: Leadership; Offices and Directors Nuestra Senora del Carmen, Cidra, PR; [MIS] Diocesan Tribunal of Caguas, Caguas, PR
Santin, Rev. Ricardo A., (CGS) Curia: Leadership
Santin-Flores, Rev. Ricardo, *P.B.R.O.* '07 (SJN) [COL] Universidad Central de Bayamon, Inc., Bayamon, PR
Santo Tomas, Rev. Darren, (NEW) St. Peter, Belleville, NJ
Santoianni, Rev. Rolando, '90 (SJ) St. Thomas Aquinas, Palo Alto, CA
Santone, Rev. John M., *C.S.C.* '00 (FTW) Holy Cross, South Bend, IN; [COL] University of Notre Dame Du Lac, Notre Dame, IN
Santor, Rev. John E., '65 (E) Retired.
Santora, Rev. Alexander M., '82 (NEW) Our Lady of Grace and Saint Joseph Parish, Hoboken, NJ
Santoro, Rev. David J., *O.P* '77 (DET) [CON] Monastery of the Blessed Sacrament, Farmington Hills, MI
Santos, Rev. David C., '12 (NEW) Curia: Advisory Boards, Commissions, Committees, and Councils St. Bartholomew, Scotch Plains, NJ
Santos, Rev. Msgr. Francisco Medina, '89 (SJN) San Pablo, Puerto Nuevo, PR; [COL] ISTEPA (Instituto Superior de Teologia y Pastoral - Luis Cardenal Aponte Martinez), Bayamon, PR
Santos, Rev. Fredy L., *C.S.V.* '12 (CHI) [MON] Viatorian Province Center-Clerics of St. Viator, Arlington Heights, IL
Santos, Rev. Jose Carlos, *O.F.M.* '00 (FRS) [NUR] New Bethany Residential Care and Skilled Nursing Community, Los Banos, CA
Santos, Rev. Jose Emilio (Joshua), (SLC) Curia: Offices and Directors
Santos, Rev. Jose Matinez, (SJN) Colegio Sagrado Corazon de Jesus, San Juan, PR
Santos, Rev. Joshua Maria, (SLC) Saint Joseph LLC 230, Ogden, UT; [CAM] Utah State University (Saint Jerome Newman Center), Logan, UT
Santos, Rev. Joy Lawrence, '91 (LA) St. Genevieve, Panorama City, CA
Santos, Rev. Nicholas J., *S.J.* '00 (OM) [MON] Jesuit Community at Creighton University, Omaha, NE
Santos, Rev. Tomas, '95 (ARE) Curia: Leadership [MIS] Chapel Espiritu Santo, Orocovis, PR; [MIS] Chapel Nuestra Senora del Perpetuo Socorro, Orocovis, PR; [MIS] Chapel San Martin de Porres, Orocovis, PR; [MIS] Chapel Santo Cristo de la Salud, Orocovis, PR; [MIS] Chapel Virgen de los Dolores, Orocovis, PR
Santos Garcia, Rev. Uriel, '22 (CIN) Holy Angels, Dayton, OH; Our Lady of the Immaculate Conception, Dayton, OH; St. Mary, Dayton, OH
Santos Rodriguez, Rev. Tomas, '95 (ARE) Our Lady of Fatima, Orocovis, PR
Santos Romero, Rev. Cesar Edgardo, (SJN) Ntra. Sra. de la Providencia, Toa Alta, PR
Santos Santos, Rev. Angel M., '77 (ARE) La Milagrosa, Corozal, PR
Santoso, Rev. Fransiskus, *S.V.D.* (SB) Our Lady of the Rosary Cathedral, San Bernardino, CA
Santucci, Rev. Francis, *O.M.I.* '76 (SAT) [SEM] Blessed Mario Borzaga Formation Community, San Antonio, TX
Santucci, Rev. Frank, *OMI* (SAT) [COL] Oblate School of Theology, San Antonio, TX
Sanvicente, Rev. Noel, '85 (SJ) On Special Assignment. Adjutant Judicial Vicar, Judicial Vicariate Curia: Leadership; Offices and Directors St. Joseph, Mountain View, CA
Sanz, Rev. Florentino, '65 (SJN) Retired.
Sanz, Rev. Jose, *D.L.P.* '73 (WDC) On Duty Outside Diocese. California
Saporito, Rev. Peter M., '77 (CAM) Retired.
Sappenfield, Rev. John P., '98 (NSH) On Administrative Leave.
Sappenfield, Rev. Mark, '08 (NSH) Christ the King, Nashville, TN
Sappington, Rev. Paul, (KC) St. Thomas More, Kansas City, MO
Saprano, Rev. Samuel, '71 (STU) Retired.
Sarabia, Rev. Ritche Malacas, (RIC) Blessed Sacrament, Harrisonburg, VA
Saran, Rev. Dennis J., '15 (MIL) St Dominic's Congregation, Brookfield, WI
Sarasin, Rev. Aloysius, *O.S.B.* (MAN) [MON] St. Anselm Abbey, Manchester, NH
Sardina, Rev. John J., '60 (BUF) Retired. [MON] Msgr. Conniff Residence, Depew, NY
Sardinas, Rev. Juan Carlos, '98 (TYL) St. Bernard of Clairvaux, Fairfield, TX
Sare, Rev. Rajesh Sagar, '11 (SUP) Holy Family, Bayfield, WI; St. Ann, Cornucopia, WI; St. Francis, Red Cliff, WI; St. Joseph, La Pointe, WI; St. Louis, Washburn, WI
Sargado, Rev. Hermogenes, *SDV* '11 (ORL) St. Patrick's, Mount Dora, FL
Sarge, Rev. John S., '73 (SAG) Retired. Our Lady of Peace Parish of Bay City, Bay City, MI
Sargent, Rev. Anthony G., *O.S.B.* '02 (PAT) [MON] St. Mary's Abbey, Morristown, NJ
Sariego, Rev. Francis, *O.F.M.Cap.* '69 (WIL) [CON] Monastery of St. Veronica Giuliani, Wilmington, DE; [MON] Capuchin Franciscan Friars, St. Francis of Assisi Friary, Wilmington, DE
Sarker, Rev. Paschal, *CSC* (FTW) [SEM] Moreau Seminary, Notre Dame, IN
Sarmiento, Rev. Jhonatan, '18 (RCK) On Special Assignment. Curia: Tribunal St. James, Rockford, IL
Sarmiento, Rev. Reynaldo, '14 (SJ) Church of the Ascension, Saratoga, CA
Sarnecki, Rev. Thomas G., '02 (SCR) Retired.
Sarnicki, Rev. Piotr, *O.F.M.Conv.* '94 (RCK) (>PEO) St. Pius X, Rock Island, IL
Sarniewicz, Rev. Marek, *S.D.S.* '95 (ORL) Blessed Sacrament, Cocoa, FL
Sarno, Rev. Msgr. Robert J., '73 (BRK) Retired. Curia: Leadership Our Lady of Grace, Howard Beach, NY (>NY) [SEM] St. Joseph's Seminary, Yonkers, NY
Saroki, Rev. Anthony, '05 (SD) Pastor of Our Lady of Mt. Carmel Catholic Parish, San Diego, a corporation sole, San Diego, CA
Sarpong, Rev. Francis Sam, (RVC) Holy Family, Hicksville, NY; St. James, Seaford, NY
Sarpong, Rev. Peter, (RVC) Sacred Heart, North Merrick, NY
Sarrazin, Rev. Edward, *O.F.M.* '07 (PHX) St. Mary's Roman Catholic Basilica, Phoenix, AZ
Sartori, Rev. Michael L., '16 (MAN) St. Patrick, Newport, NH; [CEM] St. Patrick Cemetery, Newport, NH
Sas, Rev. Thomas J., '76 (HRT) The Church of St. John Fisher of Marlborough Corporation, Marlborough, CT
Sas, Rev. Yurii, '09 (STN) St. John the Baptizer, La Mesa, CA
Sasa Nganomo Babisayone, Rev. Sebastien, (SLC) Saints Peter and Paul LLC 243, West Valley City, UT
Sasin, Rev. Jan, '77 (NEW) Curia: Advisory Boards, Commissions, Committees, and Councils Shrine of Divine Mercy St. Francis Xavier, Newark, NJ
Saso, Rev. Michael, *SJ* (LA) Retired. Immaculate Conception, Los Angeles, CA
Saso, Rev. Michael, '61 (SJ) Retired.
Sass, Rev. Pawel, '09 (WDC) Curia: Consultative Bodies; Deaneries Our Lady Queen of Peace, Washington, DC
Sassano, Rev. Rock, '63 (P) Retired.
Sasse, Rev. Alec J., '20 (LIN) Curia: Offices and Directors
Sasse, Rev. Alec J., (LIN) St. Thomas Aquinas, Lincoln, NE; [CAM] University of Nebraska, Newman Club, Lincoln, NE
Sasse, Rev. Alex J., '20 Curia: (>LIN) Leadership
Sasse, Rev. John J., '02 (MAD) On Administrative Leave.
Sasso, Rev. Frank M., '73 (CHI) Retired.
Sasso, Rev. Joseph M., '58 (ROC) Retired.
Sasway, Rev. Msgr. John R., '62 (ALT) Retired.
Sateesh, Rev. Narisetti, *H.G.N.* '12 (WH) Curia: Leadership Cathedral of St. Joseph, Wheeling, WV
Sato, Rev. Toshio, *CM* '13 (STL) [MON] Congregation of the Mission Vincentian Fathers Lazarist Residence, St. Louis, MO
Satoun, Rev. Arbogaste, '99 (SCR) Our Lady of the Abingtons, Dalton, PA; St. Mary of the Lake, Lake Winola, PA; St. Patrick, Nicholson, PA
Sattler, Rev. Brian, '14 (SPK) St. Anthony, Spokane, WA; St. Joseph, Spokane, WA

Sattler, Rev. Henry E., *C.Ss.R.* '76 (BRK) [MON] Redemptorist Fathers of New York, Inc.-Baltimore Province, Brooklyn, NY
Sattler, Rev. Wayne V., '97 (BIS) Saint Anne, Bismarck, ND
Sauber, Rev. Arnold M., '69 (STP) Retired.
Saucedo, Rev. Pedro, '18 (LA) Curia: Offices and Directors Cathedral of Our Lady of the Angels, Los Angeles, CA
Saucier, Rev. Thomas, *O.P.* (STL) [MON] Dominican Community of St. Louis, St. Louis, MO
Saucier, Very Rev. William P, '01 (MOB) Curia: Leadership St. Bridget, Whistler, AL; St. Thomas the Apostle, Chickasaw, AL
Sauer, Rev. Anthony P., *S.J.* '71 (PHX) [MON] Society of Jesus, Phoenix, AZ
Sauer, Friar Bonaventure, *O.C.D.* '92 (LR) [SEM] Discalced Carmelite Friars of St. Therese, Little Rock, Little Rock, AR
Sauer, Rev. Gerard J., '01 (BRK) St. Patrick, Brooklyn, NY
Sauer, Rev. Gregory, '19 (SCL) Holy Cross, North Prairie, MN; Holy Trinity, Royalton, MN; Immaculate Conception, Rice, MN; Our Lady of Mt. Carmel, Holdingford, MN; St. Stanislaus Kostka, Bowlus, MN
Sauer, Rev. James, '77 (EVN) Retired.
Sauer, Rev. John M., '85 (WIN) Curia: Advisory Boards, Commissions, Committees, and Councils Pax Christi, Rochester, MN; SS. Peter and Paul, Mazeppa, MN
Sauer, Rev. Timothy J., '76 (SEA) Retired.
Saumell, Rev. Amaro, '92 (SB) Retired.
Saunders, Rev. Allan L., '86 (SPC) Curia: Advisory Boards, Commissions, Committees, and Councils; Consultative Bodies; Deaneries Cathedral of St. Mary of the Annunciation, Cape Girardeau, MO
Saunders, Rev. Donald E., *S.J.* '84 (LAF) [RTR] Our Lady of the Oaks Retreat House, Grand Coteau, LA
Saunders, Rev. Ryan, '20 (MIA) Curia: Leadership
Saunders, Rev. Thomas C., *M.M.* '65 (NY) Retired.
Saunders, Very Rev. William P., '84 (ARL) Curia: Leadership; Offices and Directors St. Agnes, Arlington, VA
Sauppe, Rev. Timothy J., '92 (PEO) St. Isaac Jogues, Georgetown, IL; St. Mary's, Westville, IL
Sauriol, Rev. Mark A., '99 (PRO) Curia: Advisory Boards, Commissions, Committees, and Councils St. Mary's, Newport, Rhode Island, Newport, RI
Sauser, Rev. Steven J., '10 (AUS) St. John the Baptist, Fayetteville, TX; St. Martin Catholic Church - Warrenton, Texas, Round Top, TX; St. Mary, Ellinger, TX; St. Mary Catholic Church, Ellinger, TX
Sauter, Rev. David A., *S.J.* '72 (WDC) Georgetown Preparatory School, North Bethesda, MD; [MON] The Jesuit Community at Georgetown University, Washington, DC
Sauter, Rev. John, '85 (GLP) Our Lady of Sorrows, Ceboyeta, NM; San Mateo, San Mateo, NM; San Rafael, San Rafael, NM; St. Teresa of Avila, Grants, NM; St. Vivian, Milan, NM
Sautner, Rev. Scott, '00 (FAR) St. Aloysius Church of Lisbon, Lisbon, ND; St. Vincent's Church of Gwinner, Lisbon, ND
Savadera, Rev. Frank B., *S.J.* '09 (SEA) [COL] Seattle University, Seattle, WA; [MON] Arrupe Jesuit Community at Seattle University, Seattle, WA
Savage, Rev. James W., '70 (BO) Retired.
Savage, Rev. Roger A., '77 (MIL) Retired.
Savage, Rev. Warren J., '79 (SPR) Curia: Offices and Directors St. Peter and St. Casimir, Westfield, MA; [CAM] Amherst College, Amherst, MA; [CAM] Mount Holyoke College, South Hadley, MA; [CAM] Westfield State University, Westfield, MA
Savarayia, Rev. Nehru Stephen, *H.G.N.* '13 (PRT) Curia: Consultative Bodies St. Michael Parish, Augusta, ME
Savard, Rev. John D., (BGP) [MON] The Fairfield Jesuit Community-Fairfield University, Fairfield, CT
Savard, Rev. John D., *S.J.* '91 (BAL) [COL] Jesuit Community of Loyola University, Inc., Baltimore, MD; [MON] Jesuit Community of Loyola University Maryland, Inc., Baltimore, MD
Savarimuthu, Rev. Alphonse, *M.S.F.S.* (KAL) Retired.
Savarimuthu, Rev. Amalraj, *IMS* '97 (BR) Congregation Of The Most Blessed Sacrament Parish, Baton Rouge, LA
Savarimuthu, Rev. Aruldoss, '07 (LC) Immaculate Conception, Fountain City, WI; St. Boniface, Waumandee, WI; St. Lawrence, Alma, WI; [EFT] St. Boniface Parish Catholic School Endowment Trust Fund, Waumandee, WI
Savarimuthu, Rev. Eugene, (MO) Curia: Offices and Directors
Savarimuthu, Rev. Kulandairajan, (RVC) Church of Saint Brigid, Inc., Westbury, NY
Savarimuthu, Rev. Kulandairajan, (RVC) St. Anthony of Padua, East Northport, NY
Savarimuthu, Rev. Pancras, '80 (TYL) Retired.
Savarimuthu, Rev. Rajasekar, *H.G.N.* '01 (SEA) St. Thomas Aquinas, Camas, WA
Savarimuthu, Rev. Sebastian Vincent, *HGN* '15 (PBL) Most Holy Trinity, Trinidad, CO
Savarimuthu, Rev. Stephen, *H.G.N.* (MAN) Good Shepherd, Berlin, NH; Holy Family, Gorham, NH
Savchyn, Rev. Vasyl, '79 (STN) St. Michaels, Milwaukee, WI
Savela, Rev. Erwin M., *C.S.V.* '71 (CHI) [MON] Viatorian Province Center-Clerics of St. Viator, Arlington Heights, IL
Savelesky, Rev. Michael, '73 (SPK) Retired. Curia: Leadership
Savelesky, Rev. Michael J., '73 (SPK) Curia: Leadership Holy Rosary, Rosalia, WA
Savickas, Rev. Michael G., '74 (DET) St. William Parish Walled Lake, Walled Lake, MI
Savidge, Rev. Peter M., '89 (KC) St. Mary, Nevada, MO
Savilla, Rev. Edmund, '77 (SFE) Church of the Ascension, Albuquerque, NM
Savino, Rev. Michael A., '82 (CIN) Retired.
Savinski, Rev. Msgr. John M., '71 (PH) Retired. On Special Assignment. Master Ceremonies, St Charles Borromeo Sem Overbrook, Wynne...
Savinski, Rev. Msgr. John M., '71 (PH) Retired. Cathedral Basilica of Saints Peter and Paul and the Shrine of Saint Katharine Drexel, Philadelphia, PA; [SEM] Theological Seminary of St. Charles Borromeo, Wynnewood, PA
Savio, Rev. Arokia, '83 (JKS) St. John, Charleston, MS; St. Peter, Grenada, MS
Savio, Rev. Dominic, *H.G.N.* '03 (PRT) Christ the Divine Mercy Parish, East Millinocket, ME; St. Benedict's, Benedicta, ME
Savior, Rev. Jose, (DET) [MON] St. Bonaventure Monastery, Detroit, MI
Savoie, Rev. Dominic, *FSSP* '16 (FTW) Sacred Heart, Fort Wayne, IN
Savoie, Rev. Garrett, '13 (LAF) Our Lady of Perpetual Help, New Iberia, LA
Savoie, Rev. Johnny S., '95 (MOB) Curia: Leadership St. Pius X Parish, Mobile, Mobile, AL
Saw Lone, Rev. Henry, '94 (SAL) Assumption of Mary Parish, Herndon, Inc., Herndon, KS; Sacred Heart Parish, Atwood, Inc., Atwood, KS
Sawicki, Rev. John A., *C.S.Sp.* '86 (PIT) [COL] Duquesne University of the Holy Spirit, Pittsburgh, PA; [MON] Congregation of the Holy Spirit Province of the United States, Bethel Park, PA
Sawicki, Rev. Jonathan P., '09 (HBG) Curia: Offices and Directors Prince of Peace, Steelton, PA
Sawicki, Rev. Mitchell, *O.F.M.Conv.* '05 (BAL)
Sawuaan, Rev. Stephen, (MIA) Little Flower, Coral Gables, FL
Sawyer, Rev. Benjamin S., '09 (WCH) On Duty Outside Diocese.
Sawyer, Chorbishop Donald, '74 (OLL) Curia: Offices and Directors
Sawyer, Chorbishop Donald, (OLL) Curia: Leadership
Sawyer, Rev. Msgr. Donald J., '74 (OLL) Curia: Offices and Directors Our Lady's Maronite Parish, Austin, TX
Sawyer, Rev. Samuel, (NY) [MON] America; Residence and Publication Office of the America Press, New York, NY
Sax, Rev. Joseph, (MEM) St. Louis, Memphis, TN
Say, Rev. James K., '60 (TOL) Retired.
Sayegh, Rt. Rev. Fouad, '79 (NTN)
Sayegh, Rev. George, '22 (NTN) Annunciation Melkite Catholic Church Inc., Covina, CA; St. Anne Melkite Co-Cathedral, North Hollywood, CA
Sayers, Very Rev. B. LaMounte, '86 (E) Immaculate Conception, Clarion, PA; [CAM] Clarion University of Pennsylvania, Clarion, PA
Sayers, Rev. Raymond J., '64 (DET) Retired.
Saylor, Rev. Barry P., '18 (LC) Christ the King, Spencer, WI
Saylor, Rev. Brian R., '99 (ALT) St. John the Evangelist, Bellefonte, PA; St. Kateri Tekakwitha, Spring Mills, PA
Sayuk, Rev. Thomas, '74 (SJP) Retired.
Sazama, Rev. Warren, *S.J.* '77 (STP) [MON] Markoe House Jesuit Community, Minneapolis, MN
Sbarbati, Rev. Sauro, '15 (BRK) Visitation of the Blessed Virgin Mary, Brooklyn, NY; [MIS] Federation of Oases of Koinonia John the Baptist, Brooklyn, NY
Sbordone, Rev. Gaetano J., '83 (BRK) Our Lady of Grace, Brooklyn, NY
Scafidi, Rev. William A., *M.Ss.A.* '83 (NY) Parish of St. Mary/Holy Name of Jesus and St. Peter, Kingston, NY
Scaglione, Rev. Paul A., '73 (L) Retired.
Scahill, Rev. James J., '74 (SPR) Retired.
Scalco, Rev. Joseph, *CSJ* '79 (CLV) St. Jude, Elyria, OH; [MON] Congregation of St. Joseph, Avon, OH
Scalco, Rev. Joseph, *C.S.J.* '79 (LA) St. Peter, San Pedro, CA
Scalese, Rev. Mark P., *S.J.* (CHI) [COL] Jesuit Community at Loyola University Chicago, Chicago, IL
Scalf, Rev. Kevin, *CPPS* '09 (CIN) Archbishop McNicholas High School, Cincinnati, OH; The Cathedral Basilica of St. Peter in Chains, Cincinnati, OH
Scalia, Very Rev. Paul D., '96 (ARL) Curia: Consultative Bodies; Leadership; Offices and Directors
Scalia, Rev. Paul David, '96 (ARL) St. James, Falls Church, VA
Scalo, Rev. Christian, '21 (NEW) St. Joseph, New Milford, NJ
Scanlan, Rev. Eric, '13 (VEN) Cardinal Mooney Catholic High School, Inc., Sarasota, FL; Incarnation Parish in Sarasota, Inc., Sarasota, FL
Scanlin, Rev. Joseph T., '89 (HBG) Curia: Offices and Directors Queen of the Most Holy Rosary, Elysburg, PA
Scanlon, Rev. Francis P., '83 (NY) Parish of St. Mary-Our Lady of Mt. Carmel, Mount Vernon, NY; St. Ann, Bronx, NY
Scannell, Rev. Timothy J., '69 (NY) Retired. [SEM] St. Joseph's Seminary, Yonkers, NY
Scantlin, Rev. Msgr. Joseph S., '59 (FWT) Retired. Most Blessed Sacrament, Arlington, TX
Scarangella, Rev. Joseph A., '92 (NEW) Curia: Advisory Boards, Commissions, Committees, and Councils Cathedral Basilica of the Sacred Heart, Newark, NJ
Scarcella, Rev. Philip J., '77 (CHL) Our Lady of the Assumption, Charlotte, NC
Scarcia, Rev. John J., '74 (PH) Retired.
Scardella, Rev. Joseph E., (SY) Curia: Leadership Church of the Holy Trinity, Fulton, NY; St. Stephen, Phoenix, NY
Scaria, Rev. Nipin, (DM) St. Ambrose Cathedral, Des Moines, IA
Scarmozzino, Rev. Steven, '97 (ALB) (>BUR) St. Raphael, Poultney, VT
Scarmozzino, Rev. Steven, (BUR) Our Lady of Seven Dolors, Fair Haven, VT; St. Bridget, West Rutland, VT; St. Dominic, Proctor, VT; St. John the Baptist, Castleton, VT; St. Paul, Orwell, VT; St. Stanislaus Kostka, West Rutland, VT
Scarpetta, Rev. Milhton, '01 (SEA) St. Francis Xavier, Toledo, WA; St. Joseph, Chehalis, WA; St. Mary, Centralia, WA
Scepaniak, Rev. Russell G., '93 (WIN) St. Pius X, Rochester, MN
Sceski, Rev. Alfred P., (HBG) St. Joan of Arc, Hershey, PA
Scesney, Rev. Everard, *O.F.M.* '68 (GB) [MON] Assumption of B.V.M. Friary, Pulaski, WI
Schaab, Rev. Dennis, *C.PP.S.* '68 (KCK) [CON] Motherhouse of the Sisters of Charity of Leavenworth, Leavenworth, KS
Schaab, Rev. Dennis, *C.PP.S.* '68 (KC) (>CIN) [MON] Society of the Precious Blood, United States Province, Inc., Dayton, OH
Schaab, Rev. R. Michael, '71 (PEO) Retired.
Schaarschmidt, Rev. Mark, (NY) Chap, Mid-Hudson Psychiatric Ctr, New Hampton
Schabowski, Rev. Henry F., '60 (TR) Retired.
Schack, Rev. Stephen, '99 (PHX) Santa Teresita Roman Catholic Parish, El Mirage, AZ
Schad, Rev. Joseph J., *S.J.* (BGP) [MON] The Fairfield Jesuit Community-Fairfield University, Fairfield, CT
Schad, Rev. Marco Federico, '08 (WDC) Curia: Tribunal Immaculate Heart of Mary, Lexington Park, MD
Schaedel, Rev. Msgr. Joseph F., '82 (IND) Saint Luke Catholic Church, Indianapolis, Inc., Indianapolis, IN
Schaefer, Rev. Msgr. Dennis R., '75 (BEL) Curia: Leadership St. John the Baptist, Red Bud, IL; St. Patrick, Red Bud, IL
Schaefer, Rev. Edward F., '75 (BEL) Curia: Offices and Directors St. Felicitas, Carlyle, IL; St. Rose, St. Rose, IL
Schaefer, Rev. James F., '61 (LC) Retired.
Schaefer, Rev. James W., '56 (STL) Sacred Heart Catholic Church, Ozoro, St. Mary, MO
Schaefer, Rev. Martin T., '92 (WIN) Curia: Advisory Boards, Commissions, Committees, and Councils [SEM] Immaculate Heart of Mary Seminary, Winona, MN
Schaeffer, Rev. Bradley M., *S.J.* '77 (CHI) (>DET) [MON] Colombiere Center, Clarkston, MI
Schaeffer, Rev. Eugene W., (STL) Holy Redeemer Catholic Church, Webster Groves, MO

Schaeffer, Rev. Richard C., '83 (MAR) Retired.
Schaeper, Rev. James P., '16 (COV) Mary, Queen of Heaven, Erlanger, KY
Schaeper, Rev. Lawrence A., '09 (COV) Curia: Pastoral Services Sts. Boniface and James, Ludlow, KY
Schafer, Rev. Dennis, *O.F.M.* '80 (IND) Sacred Heart of Jesus Catholic Church, Indianapolis, Inc., Indianapolis, IN; St. Patrick Catholic Church, Indianapolis, Inc., Indianapolis, IN
Schafer, Rev. Dennis R., '89 (BIS) St. Elizabeth, Lefor, ND; St. Mary, New England, ND
Schafer, Rev. Patrick, *O.F.M.* '08 (SFE) Curia: Offices and Directors Holy Family-Albuquerque, Albuquerque, NM; [MON] The Province of Our Lady of Guadalupe of the Order of Friars Minor, Inc., Albuquerque, NM
Schafer, Rev. Peter C., '05 (GR) All Saints, Fremont, MI; St. Bartholomew, Newaygo, MI; St. Joseph, White Cloud, MI; St. Michael, Fremont, MI
Schafer, Rev. Raymond E., '89 (IND) Retired.
Schaff, Rev. Tyrone J., '73 (SPK) Retired. Curia: Leadership; Offices and Directors
Schaffer, Rev. Darrell, '90 (DEN) Retired. Sts. Peter & Paul Catholic Parish in Wheat Ridge, Wheat Ridge, CO
Schaffer, Rev. Gregory J., '94 (STP) On Duty Outside Diocese. Jesucristo Resucitado, Puerto Ordaz
Schaffner, Rev. Mark, *O.Carm.* '89 (VEN) St. William Parish in Naples, Inc., Naples, FL
Schaffner, Rev. Mark, *O.CARM* '89 (JOL) Retired.
Schaftlein, Rev. Steven, '78 (IND) On Leave.
Schaicoski, Rev. Daniel, *O.S.B.M.* '95 (STN) Curia: Offices and Directors Immaculate Conception Ukrainian Catholic Church, Hamtramck, MI
Schalk, Rev. David A., '08 (COL) Curia: Offices and Directors Christ the King, Columbus, OH; St. Thomas the Apostle, Columbus, OH; [SEM] Pontifical College Josephinum, Columbus, OH
Schallberger, Rev. Meinrad, *O.S.B.* '64 (B) Chap, Monastery of St Gertrude, Cottonwood [CON] Monastery of St. Gertrude, Motherhouse and Novitiate, Cottonwood, ID; [HOS] St. Mary's Hospital, Cottonwood, ID; [MON] Monastery of the Ascension, Jerome, ID
Schaller, Very Rev. Robert A., '87 (LC) Curia: Leadership SS. Peter and Paul, Wisconsin Rapids, WI
Schamber, Rev. Richard Lee, '07 (PT) On Academic Leave. Augustinianum, Rome
Schambough, Rev. William, '12 (LAF) St. Joseph, Milton, LA
Schamoun, Rev. Roni, (SPA) St. George Chaldean Catholic Church, Santa Ana, CA
Schanberger, Rev. J. Lawrence, *M.M.* '49 (NY) Retired.
Schaner, Rev. Rafael, *O.Cist.* '19 (DAL) [MON] Our Lady of Dallas Cistercian Abbey, Irving, TX
Schappler, Rev. Norbert, *O.S.B.* '52 (KC) [MON] Conception Abbey (Benedictine Monks), Conception, MO
Scharbach, Rev. Albert, '13 (POC) Retired. Mount Calvary Church, Baltimore, MD
Schardt, Rev. William B., '75 (ARL) Curia: Tribunal St. Thomas a Becket, Reston, VA
Schartz, Rev. Kenneth E., '84 (CIN) St. Anthony Church, Cincinnati, OH; St. Cecilia, Cincinnati, OH; St. Mary, Cincinnati, OH
Schatteman, Rev. Rene J., '60 (POD) Curia: Clergy and Religious Services
Schatz, Very Rev. David A., '00 (DUB) On Special Assignment. Rector, St Pius X Seminary, Dubuque St. Columbkille Church, Dubuque, Iowa, Dubuque, IA; [SEM] Seminary of St. Pius X, Dubuque, IA
Schatzel, Rev. John E., '61 (BO) Retired.
Schatzle, Rev. Michael J., '74 (BR) Retired.
Schaukowitch, Rev. James, *S.J.* '79 (SJ) [MON] Sacred Heart Jesuit Center, Los Gatos, CA
Schaut, Rev. Gregory F., '85 (CLV) Chap, Tri Point Med Ctr, Concord; Lake Health Hosp, Willoug… Our Lady of Mount Carmel, Wickliffe, OH
Schavitz, Rev. Peter, *C.Ss.R.* '76 (STL) St. Alphonsus Liguori Catholic Church, St. Louis, MO; [MON] Redemptorist Fathers, St. Louis, MO
Schawe, Rev. Wesley W., '04 (DOD) Curia: Leadership; Offices and Directors Cathedral of Our Lady of Guadalupe Catholic Church of Dodge City, Kansas, Dodge City, KS; [EFT] Sacred Heart Cathedral School Endowment Fund, Dodge City, KS
Scheaffer, Rev. Msgr. Walter T., '66 (ALN) Retired.
Schebera, Rev. Richard, *S.M.M.* (RVC) [MON] Montfort Missionaries, Bay Shore, NY
Scheckel, Rev. Msgr. Roger J., '84 (LC) St. Mary (Assumption of B.V.M.), Richland Center, WI; [EFT] The Assumption of the Blessed Virgin Mary Parish Endowment Trust, Richland Center, WI
Scheckenback, Rev. Robert, '89 (RVC) St. James, Setauket, NY
Scheckenback, Rev. Robert C., '89 (RVC) Christ the King, Commack, NY
Schecker, Rev. Robert J.W., '71 (TR) Retired.
Scheel, Rev. Msgr. Daniel L., '69 (GAL) Curia: Leadership; Offices and Directors
Scheeler, Rev. Jeffrey, *O.F.M.* (DET) Church of the Transfiguration Parish Southfield, Southfield, MI
Scheer, Rev. John R., *S.A.C.* '70 (MIL) [RTR] St. Vincent Pallotti Center, Elkhorn, WI
Scheetz, Rev. Daniel L., '65 (SAL) Retired. Curia: Tribunal
Schefers, Rev. Eberhard, '64 (SCL) Retired.
Scheff, Rev. Philip, '01 (VEN) Curia: Advisory Boards, Commissions, Committees, and Councils
Scheff, Rev. Philip J., '01 (VEN) St. Charles Borromeo Parish in Port Charlotte, Inc., Port Charlotte, FL
Scheffer, Rev. Peter, (FR) St. John the Baptist, Westport, MA
Scheffer, Rev. Peter R., '21 (FR) Our Lady of Grace, Westport, MA; St. George's, Westport, MA
Scheffler, Rev. Mark, *C.Ss.R.* '70 (LA) [MON] Redemptorists of Whittier, Whittier, CA
Schehr, Rev. Timothy P., '73 (CIN) Retired. [SEM] Mount St. Mary's Seminary of the West, Cincinnati, OH
Scheib, Rev. Joseph C., '76 (PIT) Retired. Curia: Tribunal
Scheib, Rev. Joseph Charles, '76 (PIT) St. Philip, Pittsburgh, PA
Scheible, Rev. Michael, '63 (EVN) Retired.
Scheiblhofer, Rev. Robert, '13 (POC) Retired. St. Barnabas Church of the Personal Ordinariate of the Chair of St. Peter, Omaha, NE
Scheich, Rev. Eugene, '66 (L) Retired.
Scheick, Rev. James C., '63 (DET) Retired.
Scheiderer, Rev. Scott L., '16 (STL) St. Paul Catholic Church, Fenton, Fenton, MO
Scheidt, Rev. Daniel, '01 (FTW) Curia: Offices and Directors St. Vincent de Paul, Fort Wayne, IN
Scheierl, Rev. LeRoy, '91 (SCL) St. Paul, St. Cloud, MN; St. Peter, St. Cloud, MN
Scheinost, Rev. Douglas P., '92 (OM) Retired.
Scheip, Rev. Michael A., '94 (VEN) Retired.
Schellenberg, Rev. James E., '77 (SAT) Retired.
Schemm, Rev. Michael, '93 (WCH) Church of the Resurrection, Wichita, KS
Schempp, Rev. Albert, *M.I.* '04 (PIT) Chap, Mercy Health Sys of Pittsburgh-Pittsburgh Mercy Hosp,…
Schempp, Rev. Albert, (MIL) [MON] St. Camillus Communities, Inc., Wauwatosa, WI
Schenck, Rev. Paul CB, (HBG) On Duty Outside Diocese.
Schenden, Rev. Gregory A., *S.J.* '08 (WDC) [MON] The Jesuit Community at Georgetown University, Washington, DC
Schenk, Rev. Francis, '55 (CIN) Retired.
Schenkel, Rev. Dennis L., '08 (MEM) Curia: Advisory Boards, Commissions, Committees, and Councils; Offices and Directors Church of the Ascension, Memphis, TN
Schenning, Rev. Msgr. Kevin T., '81 (BAL) St. Margaret, Bel Air, MD
Scherba, Rev. Raymond M., '82 (BGP) Asst Chap, Danbury Hosp The Church of the Sacred Heart of Jesus, Danbury, Danbury, CT
Scherer, Rev. Albert, *OFM Conv.* '85 (SPR) Our Lady of the Cross, Holyoke, MA
Scherer, Rev. John, *OFM Cap.* (CHI) [MON] St. Clare Friary, Chicago, IL
Scherer, Rev. Thomas, '19 (DEN) Curia: Offices and Directors
Scherger, Rev. Herman F., '58 (TOL) Retired.
Scherrer, Rev. Msgr. Carl E., '73 (BEL) Retired.
Scherrer, Rev. Steven S., *M.M.* '72 (NY) Retired. [MON] Maryknoll Fathers and Brothers (Catholic Foreign Mission Society of America, Inc.), Ossining, NY
Scherschel, Rev. Michael G., '07 (CHI) St. Hubert, Hoffman Estates, IL; [MIS] The Catholic Kolping Society of Chicago, Chicago, IL
Schetelick, Rev. Msgr. Paul D., '76 (NEW) Retired. Our Lady of the Visitation, Paramus, NJ
Schetter, Rev. Jerome A., '11 (TOL) Immaculate Conception, Ottoville, OH; St. Barbara, Cloverdale, OH
Schexnayder, Rev. Gary, '69 (LAF) Retired.
Schexnayder, Rev. James, '64 (OAK) Retired. Our Lady of Lourdes, Oakland, CA
Scheyd, Rev. Msgr. William J., '65 (BGP) Retired. Curia: Consultative Bodies; Leadership [MON] The Catherine Dennis Keefe Queen of the Clergy Retired Priests' Residence, Stamford, CT
Schiavo, Rev. Sylvan, *C.S.J.* '63 (LA) St. Junipero Serra, Lancaster, CA
Schiavone, Rev. John, '73 (LA) St. Maria Goretti, Long Beach, CA
Schiavone, Rev. Robert W., '69 (GB) Retired.
Schibi, Rev. James M., (WCH) Holy Name, Coffeyville, KS
Schiblin, Rev. Richard, *C.Ss.R.* '61 (STL) Retired. [MON] St. Clement Health Care Center, Liguori, MO
Schichtel, Rev. Kenneth H., '62 (GR) Retired.
Schieber, Rev. Brian, '99 (KCK) Curia: Advisory Boards, Commissions, Committees, and Councils; Leadership St. Michael the Archangel, Overland Park, KS
Schiele, Rev. John D., '93 (PH) Corpus Christi, Lansdale, PA
Schierer, Rev. Nicholas J., '18 (ARL) St. Rita, Alexandria, VA
Schierer, Rev. William B., '11 (ARL) St. Patrick, Fredericksburg, VA
Schifano, Rev. Msgr. Albert I., '01 (TUC) Retired. Curia: Consultative Bodies
Schifano, Rev. Vincent, '00 (RVC) St. Martin of Tours, Bethpage, NY
Schiferl, Rev. David E., '01 (P) St. Alexander, Cornelius, OR
Schiffelbein, Rev. Matthew, '09 (KCK) Christ the King, Topeka, KS
Schik, Rev. Jerome, *O.S.C.* '75 (SCL) Church of St. Rita of Hillman, Hillman, MN; Sacred Heart, Wahkon, MN; St. Therese, Onamia, MN; The Church of the Holy Cross of Onamia, Onamia, MN; [MON] Crosier Priory, Onamia, MN
Schik, Rev. LeRoy, '03 (SCL) Church of Saint James at Maine, Underwood, MN; Church of St. Edward of Henning, Henning, MN; Our Lady of the Lake, Battle Lake, MN
Schikora, Rev. Robert, '11 (SAG) Retired. On Duty Outside Diocese. Plymouth
Schild, Rev. Eric P., '07 (TOL) St. Jerome, Walbridge, OH; St. Kateri Catholic Schools, Oregon, OH
Schilereff, Rev. Fabio, *I.V.E.* (PHX) Immaculate Heart of Mary Roman Catholic Parish, Phoenix, AZ; St. Anthony Roman Catholic Parish, Phoenix, AZ
Schilken, Rev. Karl W., '79 (FWT) St. Bartholomew, Fort Worth, TX
Schill, Rev. Frederick J., '57 (TOL) Retired.
Schill, Rev. Gerald F. (Damien), '87 (FAR) Curia: (>MO) Offices and Directors
Schiller, Rev. Francis E., '65 (NEW) Retired. [EFT] St. Patrick and Assumption All Saints Foundation, Jersey City, NJ
Schilli, Rev. Richard J., '77 (STL) Our Lady of Providence Catholic Church, St. Louis, MO
Schillinger, Rev. Msgr. James A., '84 (ATL) On Special Assignment. St. Joseph Catholic Church, Marietta, Inc., Marietta, GA
Schilmoeller, Rev. Scott A., '17 (OM) Curia: Offices and Directors St. John Paul II Newman Center, Inc., Omaha, NE
Schimelpfening, Rev. James, *S.M.* '80 (STL) [MON] Marianist Province of the United States (Society of Mary), St. Louis, MO
Schimmel, Rev. Eric, *CSC* (FTW) [COL] University of Notre Dame Du Lac, Notre Dame, IN; [MON] Holy Cross Community, Corby Hall, University of Notre Dame, Notre Dame, IN; [SEM] Moreau Seminary, Notre Dame, IN
Schindler, Rev. Carl, *C.Ss.R.* '63 (STL) Retired. [MON] St. Clement Health Care Center, Liguori, MO
Schindler-McGraw, Rev. Kevin, *O.F.M.Conv.* '84 (OAK) Curia: Leadership; Offices and Directors [MON] Conventual Franciscans (Province of St. Joseph of Cupertino), Castro Valley, CA
Schineller, Rev. J. Peter, *S.J.* '70 (NY) [MIS] Catholic Medical Mission Board, Inc., New York, NY; [MON] Murray-Weigel Hall (A Jesuit Community at Murray-Weigel Hall and Kohlmann Hall), Bronx, NY
Schinelli, Rev. A. Giles, *T.O.R.* (ALT) [MON] St. Bernardine Monastery, Hollidaysburg, PA
Schinstock, Very Rev. Victor, *O.S.B.* '13 (KC) [MON] Conception Abbey (Benedictine Monks), Conception, MO; [SEM] Conception Seminary College, Conception, MO
Schipp, Rev. John, '64 (EVN) Retired.
Schipp, Rev. Ralph, '65 (EVN) Retired.
Schipper, Rev. Carl A., '68 (SFR) Retired.
Schipper, Rev. William, (WOR) Curia: Leadership; Offices and Directors Mary, Queen of the Rosary, Spencer, MA
Schladen, Rev. Robert, '59 (PEO) Retired.
Schlafer, Rev. Joseph M., '75 (RVC) St. John Nepomucene, Bohemia, NY
Schlag, Rev. Martin, '96 (POD) Curia: Clergy and Religious Services
Schlageter, Rev. Robert, *O.F.M.Conv.* (TR) St. Peter's,

Point Pleasant Beach, NJ
Schlaline, Rev. Dwight D., '10 (HBG) Basilica of the Sacred Heart of Jesus, Hanover, PA; [CAM] Shippensburg University, Shippensburg, PA
Schlangen, Rev. Louis, '57 (SFD) Retired.
Schlarb, Rev. Gregory J., '97 (PHX) Curia: Leadership; Offices and Directors Our Lady of Perpetual Help Roman Catholic Parish, Scottsdale, AZ
Schlax, Rev. Charles H., '66 (CHI) Retired.
Schlegel, Rev. Daniel F., '88 (CLV) Curia: Advisory Boards, Commissions, Committees, and Councils; Clergy and Religious Services; Leadership Cathedral of St. John the Evangelist, Cleveland, OH; [CCH] Pastoral Care Services, Cleveland, OH
Schlegel, Rev. Laurence, *O.S.B.* '54 (MAN) Retired.
Schlesselmann, Rev. Msgr. Gregory J., '93 (FAR) Curia: Leadership; Offices and Directors Holy Spirit Church of Fargo, Fargo, ND; St. Paul's Newman Church of Fargo, Fargo, ND; [CAM] St. Paul's Newman Church of Fargo, Fargo, ND
Schleter, Rev. Edward J., '67 (TOL) Retired. St. Mary, Clyde, OH; [CON] St. Bernardine Home, Fremont, OH
Schleupner, Rev. Msgr. G. Michael, '72 (BAL) Retired.
Schlichte, Rev. Carl, *O.P.* '98 (SAC) St. Dominic, Benicia, CA
Schliessmann, Rev. Thomas L., (IND) Chaplain of Scouts St. Joan of Arc Catholic Church, Indianapolis, Inc., Indianapolis, IN
Schlimm, Rev. Chrysostom V., *O.S.B.* '61 (GBG) [MON] Saint Vincent Archabbey, Latrobe, PA
Schlitt, Rev. Dale M., *OMI* (BEL) [MON] Missionary Oblates of Mary Immaculate - St. Henry's Oblate Residence, Belleville, IL
Schloemer, Rev. Bernard J., '60 (STL) Retired.
Schloemer, Rev. Leo, '56 (CIN) Retired.
Schloemer, Friar Paul Gregory, *OFM Conv.* '04 (L) [EFT] The Franciscan Foundation, Inc., Louisville, KY
Schloemer, Rev. Thomas N., *S.J.* '68 (MIL) [MON] St. Camillus Jesuit Community (Society of Jesus, USA Midwest Province), Wauwatosa, WI
Schloesser, Rev. Stephen, *S.J.* '92 (CHI) [COL] Jesuit Community at Loyola University Chicago, Chicago, IL (>NY) [MON] Jesuit Community at Fordham University, New York, NY
Schlosser, Rt. Rev. Leo R., '59 (PBR) [MON] Holy Trinity Monastery, Pittsburgh, PA
Schlosser, Rev. Richard, '74 (GF) Retired.
Schloth, Rev. Brian, *M.S.* (FR) [MON] La Salette Shrine & Retreat Center, Attleboro, MA
Schloth, Rev. Brian, *M.S.* '89 (WDC) [MON] Missionaries of La Salette Corporation, Washington, DC
Schludecker, Rev. Andre, *O.F.M.* '64 (GB) Retired.
Schluep, Rev. Thomas G., (PIT) On Duty Outside Diocese.
Schmalhofer, Rev. John D., '74 (HBG) Retired.
Schmeckel, Rev. Jonathon A., '19 (MIL) Blessed Trinity Congregation, Sheboygan Falls, WI; St. John Evangelist Congregation, Kohler, WI; [MIS] The Sheboygan County Catholic Fund, Inc., Sheboygan, WI
Schmeidler, Rev. John, '97 (SAL) Saints Philip and James Parish, Phillipsburg, Inc., Phillipsburg, KS; St. John the Evangelist Parish, Logan, Inc., Logan, KS; St. Mary Parish, Smith Center, Inc., Smith Center, KS
Schmid, Rev. Robert L., '15 (R) St. Charles Borromeo, Ahoskie, NC
Schmid, Rev. Wayne L., '68 (WCH) Retired.
Schmid, Rev. William, '09 (PHX) Chap, Flagstaff Med Ctr Curia: Leadership; Offices and Directors San Francisco de Asis Roman Catholic Parish, Flagstaff, AZ
Schmidt, Rev. Darin, '15 (SFS) Saint Anthony Parish of Potter County, Hoven, SD; Saint Augustine Parish of Edmunds County, Bowdle, SD
Schmidt, Rev. David, '77 (SFD) On Leave.
Schmidt, Rev. David C., (PIT) Regina Coeli, Pittsburgh, PA
Schmidt, Rev. David R, (GB) St. Marys Congregation, Crivitz, WI
Schmidt, Rev. David R., '81 (GB) St. Agnes, Amberg, WI; St. Augustine, Wausaukee, WI
Schmidt, Rev. Dennis C., '80 (STL) Our Lady, Queen of Peace Catholic Church, House Springs, MO
Schmidt, Rev. Donald A., '73 (MIL) Retired.
Schmidt, Rev. Ed, (CIN) St. Robert Bellarmine, Cincinnati, OH
Schmidt, Rev. Edward W., *S.J.* '73 (CIN) [MON] Cincinnati Jesuit Community, Cincinnati, OH
Schmidt, Rev. Edward W., *S.J.* '73 (NY) [MON] America; Residence and Publication Office of the America Press, New York, NY
Schmidt, Rev. Francis J., '58 (MAD) Retired.
Schmidt, Rev. Msgr. Francis X., '57 (PH) Retired.
Schmidt, Rev. Msgr. Gregory L., '61 (STL) Retired.
Schmidt, Very Rev. Jan Kevin, '90 (CIN) Curia: Pastoral Services The Cathedral Basilica of St. Peter in Chains, Cincinnati, OH
Schmidt, Rev. John, *C.Ss.R.* '89 (STP) St. Alphonsus, Brooklyn Center, MN; [MON] Redemptorist Fathers of Hennepin County, Brooklyn Center, MN
Schmidt, Rev. Jordan Joseph, *O.P.* '12 (WDC) [SEM] Dominican House of Studies, Washington, DC
Schmidt, Rev. Joseph F., '66 (B) Retired.
Schmidt, Rev. Kenneth, '81 (KAL) Curia: Clergy and Religious Services; Consultative Bodies; Offices and Directors; Tribunal St. Jerome, Battle Creek, MI
Schmidt, Rev. Les, *GHM* '61 (CIN) [MON] Headquarters of Glenmary Home Missioners (The Home Missioners of America), Fairfield, OH
Schmidt, Rev. Paul, *SVD* (SB) [RTR] Divine Word Province/ Retreat Center, Riverside, CA
Schmidt, Rev. Paul J., '64 (OAK) Retired. St. Philip Neri-St. Albert the Great, Alameda, CA
Schmidt, Rev. Peter, *O.C.S.O.* '75 (WOR) [MON] St. Joseph's Abbey (Cistercian Abbey of Spencer, Inc., Cistercian Order of the Strict Observance (Trappists)), Spencer, MA
Schmidt, Rev. Raymond F., '84 (WDC) St. John Francis Regis, Hollywood, MD
Schmidt, Rev. Raymond F., '60 (BRK) Retired. [MON] Bishop Mugavero Residence, Douglaston, NY
Schmidt, Rev. Teofilo Pale, '06 (SPP) Co-Cathedral of St. Joseph the Worker, Pago Pago, AS
Schmidt, Rev. William T., '76 (BO) [MIS] Our Lady of the Airways Chapel, Boston, MA
Schmied, Rev. Msgr. Michael S., '71 (RIC) Retired.
Schmit, Rev. Frederick, *O.Praem.* '21 (ORG) Archangel Institute (St. Michael's Preparatory School), Silverado, CA; [MON] Norbertine Fathers of Orange, Inc., Silverado, CA
Schmit, Rev. George V., '68 (NU) Curia: Advisory Boards, Commissions, Committees, and Councils; Offices and Directors Holy Redeemer, Renville, MN; St. Aloysius, Olivia, MN; St. Mary, Bird Island, MN
Schmit, Rev. Msgr. Jerome L., '57 (LA) Retired.
Schmit, Rev. Kenneth A., '79 (ORG) Our Lady of Mount Carmel, Newport Beach, CA
Schmit, Rev. Louis, *C.PP.S.* '63 (CIN) Retired. [MON] St. Charles, Celina, OH
Schmit, Rev. Roger, *O.S.B.* '62 (KC) [MON] Conception Abbey (Benedictine Monks), Conception, MO
Schmit, Rev. Ronald G., '85 (OAK) St. Anne, Byron, CA
Schmit, Rev. Ryan M., '11 (COL) St. Ann, Dresden, OH
Schmit, Rev. Stanley T., '94 (OM) Holy Trinity, Clarkson, NE; SS. Peter and Paul, Howells, NE; St. John Nepomucene, Howells, NE
Schmitmeyer, Rev. Daniel J., '06 (CIN) Curia: Offices and Directors [SEM] Mount St. Mary's Seminary of the West, Cincinnati, OH
Schmitmeyer, Rev. James, '81 (AMA) Curia: Offices and Directors
Schmitt, Rev. Adam, '57 (FTW) Retired. [NUR] Saint Anne Home at Randallia Place (Saint Anne Home of the Diocese of Fort Wayne-South Bend, Inc.), ,
Schmitt, Rev. Bowan M., (MO) Curia: Offices and Directors
Schmitt, Rev. Bowan M., '97 (PEO) Church of St. Patrick, Ransom, IL; St. Patrick's, Seneca, IL
Schmitt, Rev. Carl E., '05 (GB) Curia: Advisory Boards, Commissions, Committees, and Councils Holy Spirit, Kimberly, WI
Schmitt, Rev. Msgr. Carl L., '61 (DUB) Retired. Curia: Leadership
Schmitt, Rev. Charles R., '59 (E) Retired.
Schmitt, Rev. Christopher, '60 (GAL) [MIS] Opus Dei, Houston, TX
Schmitt, Rev. Christopher, '61 (POD) Curia: Clergy and Religious Services
Schmitt, Rev. Conrad, (WDC) [MON] Father Judge Missionary Cenacle, Adelphi, MD
Schmitt, Rev. David J., '67 (WH) Retired.
Schmitt, Rev. Eugene R., '00 (EVN) St. Benedict Cathedral, Evansville, IN; Sts. Mary & John, Evansville, IN
Schmitt, Rev. Gregory, *C.Ss.R.* '69 (KC) Our Lady of Perpetual Help, Kansas City, MO; [MON] Redemptorists Fathers of Kansas City, Missouri, Kansas City, MO
Schmitt, Rev. James C., '66 (GI) Retired.
Schmitt, Rev. Kent A., '73 (MAD) Retired.
Schmitt, Rev. Levi J., '20 (LC) Regis High School, Eau Claire, WI; Regis Middle School, Eau Claire, WI; St. Mary, Altoona, WI; St. Raymond of Penafort, Fall Creek, WI
Schmitt, Rev. Michael T., '71 (ALB) Retired.
Schmittgens, Rev. Kevin V., '83 (STL) Holy Redeemer Catholic Church, Webster Groves, MO
Schmitz, Rev. Msgr. Bernard A., '74 (DEN) Retired.
Schmitz, Very Rev. Donald J., '80 (WIN) Retired. Curia: Offices and Directors
Schmitz, Rev. George R., '69 (CIN) Retired.
Schmitz, Rev. Msgr. Gerard G., '68 (HRT) Retired. Curia: Advisory Boards, Commissions, Committees, and Councils; Clergy and Religious Services
Schmitz, Rev. James P., '86 (CLV) St. Leo the Great, Cleveland, OH
Schmitz, Rev. John J., '91 (JC) St. Patrick, Laurie, MO
Schmitz, Rev. Matthew, *LC* '13 (SJ) Canyon Heights Academy, Inc., Campbell, CA
Schmitz, Rev. Matthew, (CR) Curia: Offices and Directors Holy Trinity Catholic (Tabor), Angus, MN; Sacred Heart, East Grand Forks, MN; St. Francis of Assisi, Fisher, MN
Schmitz, Rev. Michael, '03 (DUL) Curia: Offices and Directors [CAM] Newman Catholic Campus Ministry, Duluth, MN
Schmitz, Rev. Michael D., '96 (OM) Retired.
Schmitz, Rev. Quentin, '13 (KCK) Curia: Organizations (affiliated, inter-Diocesan, miscellaneous/other) St. Gregory, Marysville, KS; St. Malachy, Beattie, KS
Schmitz, Rev. Msgr. R. Michael, '82 (CHI) [MON] Institute of Christ the King Sovereign Priest, Chicago, IL (>DET) [MON] Institute of Christ the King Sovereign Priest, Inc., Detroit, MI
Schmitz, Rev. Robert E., '75 (CIN) Retired.
Schmoll, Rev. John, *Obl. O.S.B. Cam.* '85 (FRS) St. Joseph, Los Banos, CA
Schmolt, Rev. Johnathan P., '08 (E) Curia: Miscellaneous / Other Offices St. Joseph, Oil City, PA; St. Michael, Emlenton, PA
Schnakenberg, Very Rev. Gregory, *O.P.* '09 (WDC) [SEM] Dominican House of Studies, Washington, DC
Schneck, Rev. Richard J., *S.J.* (SJ) [MON] USA West Province, Society of Jesus, Los Gatos, CA
Schneibel, Rev. Jeffrey, *C.S.C.* '85 (P) [MON] Priests of Holy Cross in Oregon, Inc., Portland, OR
Schneible, Rev. Peter, *O.F.M.* '89 (BUF) Archbishop Walsh High School, Olean, NY; [CAM] St. Bonaventure University, St. Bonaventure, NY; [MON] St. Bonaventure Friary, St. Bonaventure, NY
Schneider, Rev. Bernard R., '67 (FAR) Retired.
Schneider, Rev. Brandon C., '22 (BUR) Our Lady of the Angels, Randolph, VT; Our Lady of the Valley Parish, Bethel, VT; [CAM] Norwich Newman Apostolate, Northfield, VT
Schneider, Rev. Daniel Mary, *M.Carm.* '98 (CHY) On Special Assignment. Prior, In Res, Monks of the Most Blessed Virgin Mary of Mt… [MON] Monks of the Most Blessed Virgin Mary of Mt. Carmel (Carmelite Monks), Meeteetse, WY
Schneider, Rev. Eric, '14 (KC) St. Ann's, Plattsburg, MO; St. Joseph's, Easton, MO
Schneider, Rev. Msgr. Ernest, '77 (GR) Retired.
Schneider, Rev. Msgr. Francis J., '83 (RVC) Curia: Leadership St. John Baptist, Wading River, NY; St. Mark, Shoreham, NY
Schneider, Rev. Harold F., '74 (KCK) Retired.
Schneider, Rev. Jacob, (DOD) Curia: Leadership St. Mary Catholic Church of Garden City, Kansas, Garden City, KS; [EFT] St. Mary Catholic Education Endowment Fund, Garden City, KS
Schneider, Rev. John, '83 (CHL) On Leave.
Schneider, Rev. John H., '68 (STL) Retired.
Schneider, Rev. John J., '11 (CLV) SS. Peter and Paul, Garfield Heights, OH; St. Therese, Garfield Heights, OH
Schneider, Rev. Joseph M., '74 (DUB) Retired.
Schneider, Rev. Kevin C., *S.J.* '94 (OM) [MON] Jesuit Community at Creighton University, Omaha, NE
Schneider, Rev. Lance J., '08 (MAD) On Leave.
Schneider, Rev. Leo J., '83 (STP) Holy Name, Minneapolis, MN; St. Leonard of Port Maurice, Minneapolis, MN
Schneider, Rev. Michael, '81 (SFS) Retired.
Schneider, Rev. Michael, '94 (GF) Curia: Leadership; Offices and Directors St. Gabriel, Chinook, MT; St. Paul's Indian Mission, Hays, MT
Schneider, Rev. Nick L., '09 (BIS) Curia: Offices and Directors St. Vincent, Crown Butte, ND
Schneider, Rev. Ric, *OFM* (CIN) Retired. [MON] St. Clement Friary, Cincinnati, OH
Schneider, Rev. Robert J., '78 (WIN) Curia: Advisory Boards, Commissions, Committees, and Councils All Saints, Madison Lake, MN; Immaculate Conception, St. Clair, MN
Schneider, Rev. Robert J., '81 (SP) Curia: Faith Formation; Pastoral Services St. Cecelia, Clearwater, FL

Schneider, Rev. Ronald, '75 (GB) On Sick Leave.
Schneider, Rev. Samuel, '17 (SUP) On Duty Outside Diocese. Military Arch-Diocese, Navy Chaplain
Schneider, Rev. Samuel F., (MO) Curia: Offices and Directors
Schneider, Rev. Terrance L., '79 (CIN) Retired.
Schneider, Rev. Todd, '85 (SCL) Assumption of the Blessed Virgin Mary, Morris, MN
Schneller, Very Rev. Michael J., '72 (NO) Curia: Leadership St. Francis of Assisi, New Orleans, LA
Schnipke, Rev. Ken, *C.PP.S.* '90 (CIN) Holy Redeemer, New Bremen, OH
Schnipke, Rev. Kenneth, *C.PP.S.* '90 (CIN) Most Precious Blood, Chickasaw, OH; Nativity of the Blessed Virgin Mary, Maria Stein, OH; St. Augustine, Minster, OH; St. John the Baptist, Maria Stein, OH; St. Joseph, Minster, OH; St. Rose, Maria Stein, OH; St. Sebastian, Celina, OH
Schnippel, Rev. Kyle E., '04 (CIN) Holy Cross, Dayton, OH; Our Lady of the Rosary, Dayton, OH; St. John the Baptist, Tipp City, OH; St. Peter, Huber Heights, OH
Schnipple, Rev. Kyle, (CIN) St. Christopher, Vandalia, OH
Schnobrich, Rev. Jon, '07 (BUR) Blessed Sacrament, Stowe, VT; Most Holy Name of Jesus Parish, Morrisville, VT
Schnobrich, Rev. Jon, (BUR) Curia: Leadership
Schnur, Very Rev. Edward C., '91 (EVN) Curia: Leadership St. Francis Xavier, Poseyville, IN; St. Wendel, Evansville, IN
Schober, Rev. Robert J, '77 (BUF) Retired.
Schock, Rev. Ronald A., '96 (TOL) St. Alphonsus Liguori, Monroeville, OH; St. Joseph, Monroeville, OH
Schoeberle, Rev. Bradford C., *CSP* (CHI) Old St. Mary, Chicago, IL
Schoenauer, Rev. Msgr. Francis P., '73 (ALN) Retired. St. Thomas More, Allentown, PA
Schoenberger, Rev. James T., '57 (STP) Retired.
Schoenhofen, Rev. Darr F., '82 (SY) Retired.
Schoenig, Rev. Steven A., *S.J.* '01 (STL) [COL] Saint Louis University, St. Louis, MO; [MON] Bellarmine House of Studies, St. Louis, MO
Schoenstene, Rev. Robert, (CHI) Retired. [SEM] University of Saint Mary of the Lake/Mundelein Seminary, Mundelein, IL
Schoenstene, Rev. Robert L., '75 (JOL) Retired. On Duty Outside Diocese. St Mary of the Lake Seminary, Mundelein
Schoettelkotte, Rev. Lawrence, (CIN) [MIS] Marianist Community, Cincinnati, OH; [MON] Siena Woods Marianist Community, Dayton, OH
Scholla, Rev. Robert W., *S.J.* '86 (SJ) [MON] Jesuit Community at Santa Clara University, Inc., Santa Clara, CA
Scholz, Rev. Mark A., '02 (KNX) Our Lady of Lourdes, South Pittsburg, TN; Shepherd of the Valley, Dunlap, TN
Schomaker, Very Rev. Daniel L., '08 (COV) Curia: Advisory Boards, Commissions, Committees, and Councils; Offices and Directors St. Augustine, Covington, KY
Schommer, Rev. Michael, '93 (FAR) St. Cecilia's Church of Towner, Towner, ND
Schon, Rev. Randy L., '88 (SC) Curia: Offices and Directors Immaculate Conception, Moville, IA; St. Joseph's, Anthon, IA; St. Michael's, Kingsley, IA
Schonberger, Rev. Micah, *O.C.S.O.* '05 (DEN) [MON] St. Benedict's Monastery, Snowmass, CO
Schoofs, Rev. Robert, (KC) [MON] Conception Abbey (Benedictine Monks), Conception, MO
Schooler, Rev. Msgr. William C., '74 (FTW) Curia: Offices and Directors St. Pius X, Granger, IN
Schopfer, Rev. John C., '69 (SY) Retired. Chap, Justice Ctr, Syracuse The Cathedral of the Immaculate Conception, Syracuse, NY; [MIS] Brady Faith Center, Inc., Syracuse, NY
Schopp, Rev. George, (GRY) [HOS] Franciscan Health Michigan City, Michigan City, IN
Schopp, Rev. George L., '74 (CHI) Retired.
Schork, Rev. John, *C.P.* '76 (CHI) [MIS] Province Finance Office, , (>GAL) [MON] Congregation of the Passion, Holy Name Passionist Community and Retreat Center, Houston, TX
Schorp, Rev. W. Franz, *S.M.* '64 (SAT) [COL] St. Mary's University of San Antonio, Texas, San Antonio, TX; [MON] Marianist Residence, San Antonio, TX
Schott, Rev. James E., '61 (NO) Retired.
Schott, Rev. Kevin J., '90 (NEW) Curia: Advisory Boards, Commissions, Committees, and Councils Sacred Heart, Cliffside Park, NJ
Schott, Rev. Timothy R., '70 (SC) Retired.
Schotzko, Rev. Philip M., '77 (NU) Retired. On Special Assignment. Curia: Leadership; Offices and Directors
Schouler, Rt. Rev. Leo, (PBR) Retired.
Schouten, Rev. Francis L., '55 (CHI) Retired.
Schrad, Rev. Merlin J., '77 (SC) Retired. Curia: Leadership; Offices and Directors
Schrader, Rev. Dylan, '10 (JC) Curia: Faith Formation St. Anthony of Padua, Folk, MO; St. Joseph, Westphalia, MO
Schrader, Rev. James, *C.PP.S.* '56 (CIN) Retired.
Schrader, Very Rev. John M., '15 (FR) Curia: Leadership; Offices and Directors St. John Neumann, East Freetown, MA
Schrader, Rev. Robert J., '78 (ROC) Retired. Holy Cross, Rochester, NY; Our Mother of Sorrows, Rochester, NY
Schrader, Rev. Thomas, *O.Carm.* '01 (JOL) [ASN] Association of Our Lady of Mount Carmel, Darien, IL; [MIS] National Shrine Museum of St. Therese of Lisieux, Darien, IL; [MIS] Society of the Little Flower, Darien, IL; [MIS] The League of the Miraculous Infant Jesus of Prague, Darien, IL; [MON] Carmelite Provincial Office, Darien, IL; [MON] St. Simon Stock Priory, Darien, IL
Schrage, Rev. Carl, '20 (BEL) Immaculate Conception, Tamaroa, IL; Sacred Heart of Jesus, Du Quoin, IL; St. Bruno, Pinckneyville, IL; St. Mary Magdalen, Pinckneyville, IL
Schramm, Rev. Charles H., '71 (MIL) Retired.
Schramm, Rev. Msgr. Donald C., '67 (STL) Retired.
Schratz, Friar Martin, *O.F.M.Cap.* '83 (NEW) St. Francis of Assisi, Hackensack, NJ
Schratz, Friar Martiz, *OFM Cap.* '83 (NEW) [MON] Capuchin Friars - Province of the Sacred Stigmata of St. Francis, Union City, NJ
Schraufnagel, Rev. Steven, '02 (SAV) On Leave.
Schray, Rev. Karl, '65 (P) Retired. All Souls Catholic Church, Myrtle Creek, OR
Schreck, Rev. Msgr. Christopher J., '77 (SAV) On Duty Outside Diocese. Pontifical College Josephinum, Columbus, OH St. William, St. Simons Island, GA
Schreck, Very Rev. J. Gerard, '83 (SAV) Curia: Leadership Cathedral Basilica of St. John the Baptist, Savannah, GA
Schreck, Rev. Kim J., '07 (PIT) St. Blaise, Midland, PA; St. Monica, Beaver Falls, PA; [CAM] Geneva College, New Brighton, PA
Schreiber, Rev. Francis, '02 (GF) Curia: Leadership; Offices and Directors Sacred Heart, Glendive, MT
Schreiber, Rev. Francis A., '02 (GF) Curia: Leadership
Schreiber, Rev. Stephen J., '99 (E) Chap, Warren State Hosp Holy Redeemer, Warren, PA
Schreiber, Rev. William A., '79 (SC) Curia: Leadership Holy Family, Emmetsburg, IA; Immaculate Conception, Graettinger, IA
Schreiner, Rev. Robert, '89 (CR) St. Joseph, Red Lake Falls, MN; St. Joseph (Church of Brooks), Red Lake Falls, MN
Schreiter, Rev. John P., '69 (MIL) Retired.
Schreitmueller, Rev. Henry, '56 (NEW) Retired.
Schremmer, Rev. Robert A., '76 (DOD) Retired. Curia: Offices and Directors
Schrenk, Rev. Aleksandr, '17 (PIT) St. Raphael the Archangel, Carnegie, PA
Schriber, Rev. Robert T., '96 (R) Retired.
Schroedel, Rev. Lawrence, *CFR* '07 (NY) [MON] St. Leopold's Friary, Yonkers, NY
Schroeder, Rev. Eugene A., '79 (EVN) Curia: Offices and Directors St. Joseph, Evansville, IN
Schroeder, Rev. Msgr. George, '62 (DEN) Retired.
Schroeder, Rev. Msgr. George, '62 (PHX) Blessed Sacrament Roman Catholic Parish, Scottsdale, AZ
Schroeder, Rev. James, *S.C.J.* '70 (MIL) Retired. [MON] Sacred Heart at Monastery Lake, Franklin, WI
Schroeder, Rev. Jerome, *OFM Cap.* (MIL) [MIS] Capuchin Community Services, Milwaukee, WI
Schroeder, Rev. Kenneth J., *C.PP.S.* '65 (CIN) Retired. [MON] St. Charles, Celina, OH
Schroeder, Rev. Kevin, (STL) Incarnate Word Catholic Church, Chesterfield, MO
Schroeder, Rev. Matthew, '02 (SJP) Curia: Offices and Directors
Schroeder, Rev. Roger P., *S.V.D.* '79 (CHI) [SEM] Catholic Theological Union, Chicago, IL; [SEM] Divine Word Theologate, Chicago, IL
Schroeder, Rev. Stephen L., '01 (TOL) Retired.
Schroeder, Rev. Tait C., '02 (MAD) On Duty Outside Diocese. Dicastery for the Doctrine of the Faith, Rome
Schroeder, Rev. Timothy, '88 (FAR) Curia: Offices and Directors St. Charles Church of Oakes, Oakes, ND; St. Mary Church of Forman, Forman, ND
Schroer, Rev. Thomas A., *S.M.* '72 (CIN) [MON] Siena Woods Marianist Community, Dayton, OH
Schroer, Rev. Thomas A., *S.M.* '72 (CIN) Queen of Apostles, Beavercreek, OH; [MIS] Change and Be Changed, Inc., Dayton, OH
Schuckman, Rev. Kenneth J., '92 (WCH) Chap, Correctional Facility St. Mary's, Oxford, KS
Schudde, Rev. Derk, '89 (ORL) Saints Peter and Paul, Winter Park, FL
Schuele, Rev. John, '76 (KC) Retired.
Schuelkens, Very Rev. Dennis R., '06 (WH) Curia: Leadership; Offices and Directors Madonna High School, Weirton, WV; Sacred Heart of Mary, Weirton, WV; St. Joseph the Worker, Weirton, WV
Schueller, Rev. Michael G., '97 (DUB) Saint Joseph's Church, Farley, Iowa, Farley, IA; Seton Catholic Schools, Farley, Iowa, Peosta, IA; St. Clement Church, Bankston, Iowa, Epworth, IA; St. John Church, Placid, Epworth, Iowa, Epworth, IA; St. John the Baptist Church of Peosta, Iowa, Peosta, IA; St. Patrick Church, Epworth, Iowa, Epworth, IA
Schuerger, Rev. Anthony J., '77 (CLV) On Administrative Leave.
Schuessler, Rev. Peter, *S.D.S.* '80 (MIL) [MON] Salvatorian Provincial Offices (Society of the Divine Savior), Milwaukee, WI
Schuessler, Rev. William R., '67 (RCK) Retired. St. James, Belvidere, IL
Schuetz, Very Rev. Michael G., '16 (R) Curia: Leadership Mother of Mercy, Washington, NC
Schuh, Rev. Msgr. John H., '65 (GB) Retired.
Schuh, Rev. Karl Christopher, '09 (NOR) On Leave.
Schukei, Rev. Tony, '22 (LIN) St. Mary's, David City, NE
Schuler, Rev. Msgr. A. John, '74 (STL) St. Cronan Catholic Church, St. Louis, MO
Schuler, Rev. Emett, *O.F.M.Cap.* '69 (WDC) [NUR] Sacred Heart Home Inc., Hyattsville, MD; [SEM] St. Francis Friary-Capuchin College, Washington, DC
Schuler, Rev. Stephen, *SVD* '79 (TR) St. Raphael-Holy Angels Parish, Hamilton, NJ
Schulte, Rev. Francisco, *O.S.B.* '79 (SCL) [MON] St. John's Abbey, of the Order of St. Benedict, Collegeville, MN
Schulte, Rev. Gary W., '72 (DET) On Leave.
Schulte, Rev. Jeffrey, '21 (SFS) Sacred Heart Parish of Brown County, Aberdeen, SD; Saint Mary Parish of Brown County, Aberdeen, SD
Schulte, Rev. Msgr. John R., '77 (COV) Retired. Curia: Tribunal
Schulte, Rev. Mark A., '97 (SFD) St. Mark, Winchester, IL; St. Mary, Pittsfield, IL
Schulte, Rev. Msgr. Robert C., '75 (FTW) Curia: Offices and Directors St. Jude, Fort Wayne, IN
Schultenover, Rev. David G., *S.J.* '69 (MIL) [MON] Jesuit Community at Marquette University (Marquette Jesuit Associates, Inc.), Milwaukee, WI
Schultes, Rev. Thomas J., '12 (LIN) St. Mary Catholic Church of Nebraska City, Nebraska City, NE
Schultz, Rev. Brian, '82 (DUL) Retired.
Schultz, Rev. Bruce, *O.P.* '88 (ATL) [MON] Augustine House, Dominicans Friars of Atlanta (The Monastery on the Hill), Atlanta, GA
Schultz, Rev. C. Raymond, '91 (BEL) Retired.
Schultz, Rev. Charles F., '80 (SB) Retired.
Schultz, Rev. Dustin P., '08 (PEO) Curia: Deaneries St. Mary's, Downs, IL; St. Patrick Church of Merna, Bloomington, IL
Schultz, Rev. James A., '11 (SY) Church of the Holy Trinity, Fulton, NY; Transfiguration, Syracuse, NY; [SHR] St. Mary's Parish & Shrine, Oswego, NY
Schultz, Rev. John A., '65 (LC) Retired. [HOS] HSHS Sacred Heart Hospital, Eau Claire, WI; [HOS] St. Joseph's Hospital of the Hospital Sisters of the Third Order of St. Francis, Chippewa Falls, WI
Schultz, Rev. Matthew, (MAN) [CEM] St. Matthew Cemetery, Whitefield, NH
Schultz, Rev. Matthew, (MAN) Our Lady of the Holy Rosary, Rochester, NH; St. Leo, Gonic, NH
Schultz, Rev. Patrick R., '16 (CLV) Sacred Heart of Jesus, Wadsworth, OH
Schultz, Rev. Robert, '01 (CHI) Holy Virgin Martyrs: St. Beatrice and St. Maria Goretti Parish, Schiller Park, IL
Schultz, Very Rev. Stephen, '99 (SFE) Curia: Offices and Directors
Schultz, Very Rev. Stephen C., '99 (SFE) Curia: Leadership; Offices and Directors Our Lady of Fatima, Albuquerque, NM
Schultz, Rev. Stephen J., '09 (ARL) Corpus Christi, Aldie, VA; Saint Paul VI Catholic High School, Chantilly, VA
Schulz, Rev. Ronald, '68 (PMB) Retired.
Schulze, Rev. Philip R., '16 (HRT) Saint Francis de Sales Parish Corporation, Bristol, CT
Schulzi, Rev. James W., *S.J.* '77 (CHI) (>DET) [MON] Colombiere Center, Clarkston, MI
Schumacher, Rev. Andrew, (LAF) St. John the

Evangelist, Mermentau, LA
Schumacher, Rev. Msgr. Andrew, '59 (B) Retired. Curia: Leadership; Offices and Directors
Schumacher, Rev. James, '95 (CHY) St. Barbara, Powell, WY
Schumacher, Rev. Msgr. Patrick A., '93 (BIS) Curia: Offices and Directors Church of Corpus Christi, Bismarck, ND
Schumacher, Rev. Paul A., '62 (NU) Retired.
Schumacher, Rev. Stephen, '19 (STL) Ascension Catholic Church, Chesterfield, Chesterfield, MO
Schumaker, Rev. Daniel P., '16 (GR) On Sick Leave. Medical Leave St. Gregory-Our Lady of Fatima, Hart, MI
Schumaker, Rev. Philip J., '13 (MIL) Sacred Heart of Jesus Congregation, St. Francis, WI; St. Augustinus Congregation, Milwaukee, WI; The Congregation of the Immaculate Conception, Milwaukee, WI
Schumaker, Rev. Timothy R., '21 (MIL) St Dominic's Congregation, Brookfield, WI
Schumer, Rev. Jason J., '10 (STL) [SEM] Kenrick School of Theology, ,
Schumm, Rev. Nicholas, '06 (PT) Curia: Offices and Directors St. Thomas More, Pensacola, FL
Schunk, Rev. David A., '10 (SFR) On Duty Outside Diocese. Pontifical College of North America, Rome
Schuster, Rev. Daniel J., '08 (GB) Curia: Advisory Boards, Commissions, Committees, and Councils Holy Trinity, Casco, WI; Immaculate Conception (St. Mary Parish), Luxemburg, WI
Schuster, Rev. Mark, '19 (KNX) Curia: Leadership St. Alphonsus, Crossville, TN
Schuster, Rev. Matthew, *S.J.C.* (CHI) St. John Cantius, Chicago, IL; [MIS] Canons Regular of Saint John Cantius, Chicago, IL
Schuster, Rev. Paul, '93 (FAR) St. Michael's Church of St. Michael, St. Michael, ND
Schuster, Rev. Paul R., '93 (FAR) Curia: Offices and Directors St. Michael's Church of St. Michael, St. Michael, ND
Schuster, Rev. Peter L., '95 (WIN) Curia: Advisory Boards, Commissions, Committees, and Councils; Offices and Directors Resurrection, Rochester, MN
Schuster, Rev. Raymond, '93 (SAT) Retired. [NUR] Missionary Servants of St. Anthony (Padua Place), San Antonio, TX
Schuster, Rev. Robert C., '95 (DET) On Leave.
Schute, Rev. Arthur B., '67 (NEW) Retired.
Schute, Rev. Bruce J., *S.A.C.* '60 (MIL) [MON] Pallotti House, Milwaukee, WI
Schutte, Rev. James R., '79 (CIN) Retired.
Schwab, Rev. Elijah, *O.Carm.* '17 (STP) [MON] Carmelite Hermitage of the Blessed Virgin Mary, Lake Elmo, MN
Schwab, Rev. Elwin, '60 (P) Retired.
Schwab, Rev. James, '81 (JOL) St. Mary of Gostyn, Downers Grove, IL; [EFT] Diocese of Joliet Priests' Pension Plan, Crest Hill, IL; [EFT] Diocese of Joliet Retired Priests' Other Benefits Plan, Crest Hill, IL
Schwab, Rev. Joseph, *O.F.M.* '08 (PHX) Our Lady of the Angels Conventual Church, Scottsdale, AZ; [RTR] Franciscan Renewal Center, Inc. (Casa de Paz Y Bien), Scottsdale, AZ
Schwab, Rev. Steven C., '90 (IND) Retired. Chap, Indianapolis Metropolitan Police Department
Schwall, Rev. John J., '06 (SLC) Retired.
Schwan, Rt. Rev. Paul Mark, *O.C.S.O.* '88 (SAC) [MON] Abbey of New Clairvaux, Trappist (Cistercian Abbey, Cistercians of the Strict Observance), Vina, CA; [SEM] Abbey of New Clairvaux, Trappist Seminary, Vina, CA
Schwanger, Msgr. Kenneth K., '90 (MIA) Curia: Administration; Canonical Services; Clergy and Religious Services Our Lady of Lourdes, Miami, FL; [MIS] Hospitalite de Miami, LLC, Miami Shores, FL
Schwantes, Rev. John A., *S.J.* '69 (MIL) [MON] Jesuit Community at Marquette University (Marquette Jesuit Associates, Inc.), Milwaukee, WI
Schwartz, Rev. Charles J., '13 (GR) Curia: Leadership St. Patrick - St. Anthony, Grand Haven, MI
Schwartz, Rev. Charles M., '99 (TR) Sacred Heart, Riverton, NJ
Schwartz, Rt. Rev. Christopher, *O.S.B.* '74 (CLV) Retired.
Schwartz, Very Rev. James A., '68 (ROC) Curia: Deaneries Holy Spirit, Webster, NY; St. Joseph, Penfield, NY
Schwartz, Rev. Norman R., '69 (MIL) Retired.
Schwartz, Rev. Robert M., '67 (STP) Retired.
Schwartz, Rev. Rodney A., '92 (SFD) Sacred Heart, Oconee, IL; St. Patrick, Pana, IL
Schwartz, Rev. Msgr. William H., '68 (RCK) Retired.
Schwartz, Rev. William J., '68 (PIT) Retired. Chap, Friendship Ridge Skilled Nursing, Beaver Cty
Schwarz, Rev. Frank L., '01 (BRK) Our Lady of Mercy, Forest Hills, NY
Schwarz, Rev. Joseph Patrick, '08 (OKL) St. Benedict, Shawnee, OK
Schwarz, Rev. Thomas J. E., *S.J.* '01 (MIL) [MON] Jesuit Community at Marquette University (Marquette Jesuit Associates, Inc.), Milwaukee, WI
Schwarzkopf, Rev. Rudi O., *O.S.F.S.* '13 (TOL) Immaculate Conception, Toledo, OH; [MON] Oblates of St. Francis de Sales, Toledo, OH
Schwebs, Rev. Daniel L., *O.S.J.* '86 (SCR) Retired.
Schweda, Rev. Phillip, '79 (LAN) Retired.
Schweda, Rev. Phillip, '79 (VEN) Curia: Leadership St. Bernard Parish in Holmes Beach, Inc., Holmes Beach, FL
Schweers, Rev. Gregory, *O.Cist.* '81 (DAL) [MON] Our Lady of Dallas Cistercian Abbey, Irving, TX
Schweiger, Rev. Troy J., '95 (LIN) Curia: Offices and Directors
Schweiger, Rev. Troy J., '95 (LIN) St. Patrick's, Lincoln, NE (>OM) [MIS] Marianna, Inc., Omaha, NE
Schweitzer, Rev. Gerald H., '71 (GRY) Retired.
Schweitzer, Rev. Thomas, '82 (LA) Holy Angels Parish of the Deaf, Vernon, CA
Schweizer, Rev. Paul, *O.Carm.* '62 (NEW) Retired.
Schwendeman, Rev. Daniel, '01 (LEX) Curia: Offices and Directors
Schwendeman, Rev. Daniel P., '01 (LEX) Curia: Leadership
Schwenka, Rev. Andrew, (LIN) St. Wenceslaus, Wahoo, NE
Schwenka, Rev. Andrew, '19 (LIN) Curia: Leadership
Schwenka, Rev. Christian, (LIN) St. Teresa Catholic Church, Lincoln, NE
Schwenke, Rev. Andrew, *O.S.B.* '14 (P) [MON] Mt. Angel Abbey, Saint Benedict, OR
Schwertner, Rev. Msgr. Timothy, '65 (LUB) Retired. San Ramon, Lubbock, TX
Schwet, Rev. Edward N., '82 (CLV) Retired.
Schwind, Rev. Christopher, '13 (AMA) Retired.
Schwind, Rev. Christopher, (AMA) [MIS] Project Solidarity, Amarillo, TX
Schwinghamer, Rev. David J., *M.M.* '73 (SJ) Retired. [MON] Maryknoll, Los Altos, CA
Schwinghamer, Rev. David J., *M.M.* '73 (WDC) [SEM] Maryknoll Fathers and Brothers, Washington, DC
Sciacca, Rev. Guy F., '10 (BO) Curia: Clergy and Religious Services St. Margaret, Beverly, MA; St. Mary Star of the Sea, Beverly, MA
Scianna, Rev. Bernard C., *O.S.A.* (PH) [COL] Villanova University, Villanova, PA
Scianna, Rev. Bernard C., *O.S.A.* '93 (CHI) [MON] St. Rita Monastery, Chicago, IL (>PH) [MON] Fray de Leon Community, Villanova, PA
Sciarappa, Rev. Anthony R., '16 (PIT) Curia: Consultative Bodies St. Michael the Archangel, Pittsburgh, PA
Scibbior, Rev. Mikolaj L., (MO) Curia: Offices and Directors
Sciberras, Rev. Ivan, '99 (NEW) Curia: Advisory Boards, Commissions, Committees, and Councils St. Peter, Belleville, NJ
Sciberras, Rev. Michael J., '67 (GBG) Christ the King, Leechburg, PA; St. Gertrude, Vandergrift, PA
Scibilia, Rev. Santi, *RCJ* '04 (LA) St. Jane Frances de Chantal, North Hollywood, CA; [MON] Congregation of Rogationists, Inc., Van Nuys, CA
Sciera, Msgr. Ronald P., '61 (BUF) Retired. On Administrative Leave.
Scillieri, Rev. Charles P., '73 (MET) Retired.
Scioli, Rev. Richard A., *C.S.S.* '79 (WOR) Sacred Heart of Jesus, Milford, MA
Scirghi, Rev. Thomas J., *S.J.* '86 (NY) [MON] Jesuit Community at Fordham University, New York, NY
Sciumbato, Rev. Michael R., '94 (SLC) Retired.
Sciurba, Rev. Salvatore, *O.C.D.* '71 (WDC) [SEM] Discalced Carmelite Friars, Inc., Washington, DC
Scocco, Rev. Victor J., *O.SS.T.* '81 (BAL) Resurrection of Our Lord, Laurel, MD; St. Lawrence Martyr, Hanover, MD; [MON] Holy Trinity Monastery, Sykesville, MD
Scolaro, Rev. Joseph, '14 (RVC) Curia: Leadership Notre Dame, New Hyde Park, NY
Scollen, Rev. Msgr. Francis J., '71 (WOR) Curia: Leadership; Offices and Directors; Spiritual Life St. Andrew the Apostle, Worcester, MA; St. Peter, Worcester, MA; [CAM] Clark University, Worcester, MA
Scornaienchi, Rev. Frank, *T.O.R.* '79 (ALT) Our Lady of Mt. Carmel, Altoona, PA
Scornaienchi, Rev. Frank A, *TOR* (ALT) Our Lady of the Assumption, Altoona, PA
Scotchie, Rev. David, '93 (ORL) Church of the Nativity, Longwood, FL
Scott, Rev. Alexander, (MO) Curia: Offices and Directors
Scott, Rev. Alexander B., '15 (WDC) Military Chap Blessed Sacrament, Shrine of the Most, Washington, DC
Scott, Rev. Alfonso A., '59 (LA) Retired.
Scott, Rev. Brendan T., *S.J.* '78 (NY) [MON] Murray-Weigel Hall (A Jesuit Community at Murray-Weigel Hall and Kohlmann Hall), Bronx, NY
Scott, Rev. Daniel J., *M.S.* '73 (HRT) [MIS] Missionaries of LaSalette, Hartford, CT
Scott, Very Rev. Derrek D., '01 (PBL) Curia: Leadership; Offices and Directors Cathedral of the Sacred Heart, Pueblo, CO
Scott, Rev. John V., '69 (GRY) Retired.
Scott, Rev. Joseph, *C.S.P.* '73 (SFR) Old St. Mary's Cathedral & Chinese Mission, San Francisco, CA
Scott, Rev. Msgr. Leonard G., '64 (CAM) Retired.
Scott, Rev. Mark A., *O.C.S.O.* '87 (DUB) Retired.
Scott, Very Rev. Michael Craig, '96 (ALX) Curia: Leadership; Miscellaneous / Other Offices St. James Memorial, Alexandria, LA
Scott, Rev. Msgr. Patrick J., '60 (PAT) Retired. St. Andrew the Apostle, Clifton, NJ
Scott, Rev. Philip, '89 (SP) On Duty Outside Diocese.
Scott, Rev. Samuel V., '95 (BGP) Curia: Clergy and Religious Services; Consultative Bodies; Leadership The St. Joseph's Church, Danbury, Danbury, CT
Scott, Rev. Timothy, *O.C.S.O.* '05 (WOR) [MON] St. Joseph's Abbey (Cistercian Abbey of Spencer, Inc., Cistercian Order of the Strict Observance (Trappists)), Spencer, MA
Scott, Rev. Vincent J., '75 (OAK) Retired.
Scotti, Rev. Paschal P., *O.S.B.* '89 (PRO) [MON] Abbey of St. Gregory the Great (Order of St. Benedict in Portsmouth, Rhode Island, Benedictines of the English Congregation), Portsmouth, RI
Scuderi, Rev. Carmen, *OFM* '83 (GB) St. Casimir Congregation, Krakow, WI; [MON] Assumption of B.V.M. Friary, Pulaski, WI
Scullin, Rev. Robert J., *S.J.* '76 (DET) [RTR] Manresa Jesuit Retreat House, Bloomfield Hills, MI
Scullion, Rev. James, (ARL) St. Francis of Assisi, Triangle, VA
Scully, Rev. Michael, *O.F.M.Cap.* '65 (KCK) [CAM] Haskell Catholic Campus Center, Lawrence, KS; [MON] St. Conrad Friary, Lawrence, KS
Scully, Rev. Michael G., *S.J.* '86 (HON) (>SJ) [MON] Sacred Heart Jesuit Center, Los Gatos, CA
Scully, Rev. Patrick A., '56 (SHP) Retired.
Scully, Rev. Robert E., *S.J.* '96 (SY) [MON] Jesuits at LeMoyne, Inc., Syracuse, NY
Scurti, Rev. Louis J., '73 (PAT) Retired.
Seabo, Rev. Frank J., '00 (CHL) Holy Infant, Reidsville, NC
Seabold, Rev. John P., '88 (CLV) Our Lady Queen of Peace Parish, Grafton, OH
Seabridge, Rev. Thomas L., '88 (SAC) Retired.
Seagriff, Rev. Edward M., '81 (RVC) St. Gertrude's, Bayville, NY; [MON] St Pius X Residence for Retired Priests LLC, Ronkonkoma, NY
Seaman, Rev. Paul G., '85 (CHI) St. George, Tinley Park, IL
Searby, Rev. James R., '05 (ARL) St. Timothy, Chantilly, VA
Searles, Rev. Lawrence, *S.J.* '87 (R) St. Raphael the Archangel, Raleigh, NC; [MON] Jesuit Community, Raleigh, NC
Searles, Rev. Mark R., '14 (ALN) Curia: Leadership Holy Infancy, Bethlehem, PA; [CAM] Lehigh University (Bethlehem), Bethlehem, PA
Sears, Rev. G. David, '63 (SY) St. Thomas, New Hartford, NY
Sears, Rev. George, (NY) Curia: Offices and Directors Parish of Holy Name of Jesus and St. Gregory the Great, New York, NY
Sears, Rev. Robert T., *S.J.* '66 (CHI) (>DET) [MON] Colombiere Center, Clarkston, MI
Seaver, Rev. Paul E., *O.P.* '59 (PRO) [MON] St. Thomas Aquinas Priory at Providence College, Providence, RI
Seavey, Rev. Michael J., '86 (PRT) On Leave.
Seay, Friar Robert, *O.F.M.* (NO) Retired.
Seay, Friar Robert, *O.F.M.* (NO) Retired.
Seba, Rev. Andrew, '13 (EST) Holy Cross Chaldean Catholic Church, Farmington Hills, MI
Sebaali, Rev. Msgr. George M., '83 (SAM) Curia: Offices and Directors Our Lady of Lebanon Maronite Church, Washington, DC
Sebahar, Rev. John, '58 (JOL) Retired. [NUR] St. John Vianney Villa, Naperville, IL
Sebamalai, Rev. Anthony, (RVC) Maria Regina,

Seaford, NY
Sebamalai, Rev. Anthony, '87 (NY) Our Lady of Good Counsel, Staten Island, NY
Sebamalai, Rev. Emmanuel, (NY) Our Lady of Solace, Bronx, NY
Sebamalai, Rev. Emmanuel, (NY) St. Dominic, Bronx, NY
Sebasthiyan, Rev. Agustin, *HGN* '11 (PRT) Notre Dame du Mont Carmel Parish, Madawaska, ME; Our Lady of the Valley, St. Agatha, ME; Saint Peter Chanel Parish, Van Buren, ME
Sebastian, Rev. Angelos, '01 (ORG) Curia: Leadership; Offices and Directors St. Kilian, Mission Viejo, CA
Sebastian, Rev. Benny, *CST* '05 (SFE) San Juan Bautista, Ohkay Owingeh, NM
Sebastian, Rev. Binu, *M.C.B.S.* '09 (WH) St. Paul, Weirton, WV
Sebastian, Rev. Dileep, *RCJ* '14 (LA) St. Elizabeth, Van Nuys, CA
Sebastian, Rev. Francis, *M.S.T.* '88 (CC) St. Mary, Freer, TX
Sebastian, Rev. Henry K., (SP) Blessed Sacrament, Seminole, FL
Sebastian, Rev. Jolly, *MCBS* (MEM) Our Lady of Perpetual Help, Germantown, TN
Sebastian, Rev. Jolly, *M.C.B.S.* '00 (MEM) Curia: Advisory Boards, Commissions, Committees, and Councils
Sebastian, Rev. Joseph, *C.M.I.* '08 (SAC) Curia: Offices and Directors Pastor of St. Theresa Parish, South Lake Tahoe, a Corporation Sole, South Lake Tahoe, CA
Sebastian, Rev. Joseph Henry, (HT) Sacred Heart of Jesus, Morgan City, LA
Sebastian, Rev. Joseph Pradeep, *MCBS* '06 (MIL) Divine Mercy Congregation, South Milwaukee, WI
Sebastian, Rev. Jospeh A., *S.V.D.* (SB) St. Matthew, Corona, CA
Sebastian, Rev. Pradeep Joseph, *M.C.B.S.* '06 (MIL) [CEM] Holy Sepulcher, Cudahy, WI; [MON] Missionary Congregation of the Blessed Sacrament, Inc., Zion Province, Cudahy, WI
Sebastian, Rev. Shinto, *R.C.J.* '09 (LA) St. Elizabeth, Van Nuys, CA; [MON] Congregation of Rogationists, Inc., Van Nuys, CA
Sebastian, Rev. Siby, *MST* '01 (SYM) St. Mary's Syro-Malabar Catholic Church (Orlando), Sanford, FL
Sebastian, Rev. Soney, *S.V.D.* '92 (SB) [MIS] Wordnet, Inc., San Bernardino, CA
Sebastian, Rev. Soney, *S.V.D.* (SD) Curia: Miscellaneous / Other Offices; Offices and Directors
Sebastian, Rev. Thomas A., *C.S.T.* '91 (WH) Assumption, Keyser, WV; Our Lady of Grace, Romney, WV
Sebastiar, Rev. Amal, *M.S.F.S.* '05 (TUC) Saint Patrick Roman Catholic Parish - Bisbee, Bisbee, AZ
Sebastin, Rev. Ravi Earnest, (GAL) [MIS] The Catholic Chaplain Corps, Houston, TX
Sebastin, Rev. RaviEarnest, *SSS* (GAL) Corpus Christi, Houston, TX
Sebasty, Rev. Joseph, '85 (P) St. Augustine, Lincoln City, OR
Sebescak, Rev. Gary, '94 (BEL) On Leave.
Sebesta, Rev. James A., *S.J.* '70 (STL) [COL] Saint Louis University, St. Louis, MO
Sebra, Rev. Anthony G., '72 (STA) Retired.
Secor, Very Rev. Msgr. Gary L., '77 (HON) Curia: Consultative Bodies
Secor, Rev. Msgr. Gary L., '77 (HON) Curia: Administration; Advisory Boards, Commissions, Committees, and Councils; Consultative Bodies
Secora, Very Rev. James L., '75 (DUB) On Special Assignment. Dean of the Marshalltown Deanery
Secrist, Rev. Jeremy A., '04 (JC) Curia: Organizations (affiliated, inter-Diocesan, miscellaneous/other) St. Peters Church Parish, Jefferson City, MO
Seculoff, Rev. James F., '62 (FTW) Retired.
Seda, Rev. Jon M., '88 (DUB) St. Pius and St. Elizabeth Ann Seton Schools, Cedar Rapids, Iowa, Cedar Rapids, IA; St. Pius the X Church, Cedar Rapids, Iowa, Cedar Rapids, IA
Sedar, Very Rev. Adam C., '98 (ALN) Curia: Leadership St. Nicholas, Walnutport, PA; [EFT] Clergy Third Age Charitable Trust, Allentown, PA; [MON] Holy Family Villa, Bethlehem, PA
Sede, Rev. Basile, (CHL) Our Lady of Consolation, Charlotte, NC
Sedita, Rev. Msgr. Vincent, '72 (LKC) Retired.
Sedlacek, Rev. Daniel J., '16 (LC) Aquinas High School, La Crosse, WI; St. Charles Borromeo, Genoa, WI
Sedlacek, Rev. Richard D., '79 (YAK) Our Lady of Lourdes, Selah, WA
Sedlak, Rev. John A., '82 (GBG) Curia: Miscellaneous / Other Offices St. Florian, United, PA; [MIS] Ladies of Charity, United, PA
Sedley, Rev. Joseph, *C.P.* '69 (NY) [MON] The Congregation of the Passion - St. Paul of the Cross Province, Jamaica, NY
Sedley, Rev. Joseph, *C.P.* '69 (PIT) [MON] St. Paul of the Cross Monastery, Pittsburgh, PA
Sedlmayer, Rev. Lauro Colen, '85 (MET) Retired.
Sedor, Very Rev. Michael S., '12 (PIT) Curia: Consultative Bodies; Leadership; Tribunal Corpus Christi, Bridgeville, PA
Seebauer, Rev. Joseph G., '11 (CLV) Our Lady of Hope, Bedford, OH; St. Mary, Bedford, OH
Seed, Rev. Michael, *S.A.* '86 (NY) [MON] Franciscan Friars of the Atonement, Minister General Office, Garrison, NY
Seegar, Rev. Kenneth M., '87 (SCR) Holy Name of Jesus Parish, West Hazleton, PA; Holy Rosary, Hazleton, PA
Seeman, Rev. Robert L., '79 (PIT) Most Sacred Heart of Jesus, Moon Township, PA; [CAM] Slippery Rock University, Newman Center (Slippery Rock), Slippery Rock, PA
Seethaler, Rev. Scott, *O.F.M. Cap.* '69 (PIT) [MON] St. Augustine Friary, Pittsburgh, PA
Seeton, Rev. Philip M., '91 (OKL) Curia: Consultative Bodies; Deaneries Holy Family, Lawton, OK; [CAM] Cameron University, Lawton, OK
Sefcik, Rev. Dennis L., '65 (SC) Retired.
Segatta, Rev. Bruno, '74 (B) Retired.
Seger, Rev. Oscar H., '70 (CIN) Retired.
Segerblom, Very Rev. Kevin L., '07 (RIC) Curia: Deaneries St. Andrew, Roanoke, VA
Segotta, Rev. Vincent, *C.P.* '65 (BRK) Retired.
Segotta, Rev. Vincent, *C.P.* '65 (NY) Retired.
Segovia, Rev. Cesar, (E) St. Stephen, Erie, PA
Segovia, Rev. Norman, '67 (SJ) Retired.
Segovia, Rev. Normandy, '06 (SJ) On Leave.
Segura, Very Rev. Anastacio Jun, '00 (ALB) Curia: Leadership St. Francis of Assisi, Northville, NY; St. Joseph's Church, Broadalbin, NY
Segura, Rev. Darrell, '22 (SFE) Santa Maria de la Paz Catholic Community, Santa Fe, NM
Segura, Rev. Luis A., (SB) St. Catherine of Alexandria, Riverside, CA
Segura, Rev. Luis G., *O.F.M.* '09 (ORG) St. Polycarp, Stanton, CA
Segura, Rev. Ralph, '13 (BGP) St. Thomas the Apostle Roman Catholic Church Corporation, Norwalk, CT
Seh, Rev. Edwin, (ARL) Sacred Heart, Manassas, VA
Seher, Rev. Philip O., '65 (CIN) Retired.
Sehler, Rev. Michael E., *S.J.* '73 (NY) [MON] America; Residence and Publication Office of the America Press, New York, NY
Sehr, Rev. Bernard J., '10 (RCK) St. Paul the Apostle, Sandwich, IL
Seibt, Rev. Christopher, '13 (SY) Curia: Leadership; Offices and Directors Divine Mercy, Central Square, NY; St. Mary of the Assumption Oratory, Cleveland, NY
Seid, Rev. David K., *O.P.* '08 (NO) St. Anthony of Padua, New Orleans, LA; [SEM] Saint Joseph Seminary College, Saint Benedict, LA
Seidel, Rev. Curtis, '14 (SPK) Assumption Elementary School, Walla Walla, WA; St. Francis of Assisi, Walla Walla, WA; Walla Walla Catholic School System (DeSales Catholic High School), Walla Walla, WA
Seidel, Rev. George J., *O.S.B.* '58 (SEA) [COL] Saint Martin's University (Order of St. Benedict Master's Comprehensive University), Lacey, WA; [MON] St. Martin's Abbey, Lacey, WA
Seidel, Rev. Victor, *S.T.* '61 (WDC) [MON] Father Judge Missionary Cenacle, Adelphi, MD
Seidl, Rev. Larry J., '75 (GB) Curia: Advisory Boards, Commissions, Committees, and Councils
Seifert, Rev. Michael D., '84 (Y) Retired.
Seifert, Rev. William, *S.V.D.* '67 (CHI) Retired. [MON] Divine Word Residence, Techny, IL
Seifert, Rev. William N., '81 (ALN) Retired.
Seifried, Rev. Msgr. Kenneth A., '63 (SC) Retired. Our Lady of Good Counsel, Holstein, IA
Seigel, Rev. Timothy J., '91 (RCK) SS. Peter & Paul, Cary, IL
Seiker, Rev. Leo V., '91 (LIN) St. Joseph's, Friend, NE
Seil, Rev. Paul D., '89 (BUF) Buffalo Fire Dept; Erie Cty Emergency Svcs Our Lady of Perpetual Help, Buffalo, NY
Seiler, Rev. Andrew J., '88 (WCH) St. Anthony of Padua, Strong City, KS; St. Rose of Lima, Council Grove, KS
Seiler, Rev. Brian, '15 (ALX) Our Lady of Sorrows, Moreauville, LA; Sacred Heart, Moreauville, LA
Seiler, Rev. Christopher M., '13 (STL) On Duty Outside Diocese. Rome
Seiler, Very Rev. Gerald L., '90 (NO) Curia: Leadership; Offices and Directors St. Genevieve Roman Catholic Church, Slidell, Louisiana, Slidell, LA
Seimas, Rev. Peter, '02 (SJ) On Leave.
Seipp, Rev. Joel, '20 (BEL) Curia: Offices and Directors St. Andrew, Murphysboro, IL; St. Ann, Jacob, IL
Seiter, Rev. Joseph A., *C.S.Sp.* '62 (PIT) [RTR] The Spiritan Center, Bethel Park, PA
Seith, Rev. Christopher J., '14 (WDC) On Special Assignment. Curia: Clergy and Religious Services
Seitz, Rev. Eric, '20 (FAR) Holy Cross Church of West Fargo, West Fargo, ND
Seitz, Rev. Patrick K., '92 (BWN) St. Theresa of the Infant Jesus, Edcouch, TX
Seitz, Rev. Wolfgang, *O.R.C.* '02 (STU) [MON] Opus Angelorum, Inc., Carrollton, OH; [MON] Order of the Holy Cross, Inc., Carrollton, OH
Seiwert, Rev. Charles, '99 (DOD) Curia: Leadership; Offices and Directors Mary, Queen of Peace Catholic Church of Ulysses, Kansas, Ulysses, KS; St. Bernadette Catholic Church of Johnson, Kansas, Johnson, KS
Seiwert, Rev. James K., '09 (SAT) On Leave.
Seixas-Nunes, Rev. Afonso, *S.J.* '10 (STL) [MON] Jesuit Community Corporation at Saint Louis University - Jesuit Hall, St. Louis, MO
Sejba, Rev. Anthony F., '99 (CLV) St. Francis Xavier, Medina, OH
Seleccion, Very Rev. Romeo N., *M.S.* '82 (SB) Curia: Leadership St. Christopher, Moreno Valley, CA; [MON] The Pacific Region Missionaries of Our Lady of La Salette, MS, Moreno Valley, CA
Selenski, Rev. Michael Patrick, '22 (STP) St. Vincent de Paul, Brooklyn Park, MN
Selinger, Rev. Joseph, *O.P.* (OAK) (>P) Holy Rosary Parish Dominican, Portland, OR; (>P) [MON] Holy Rosary Priory, Portland, OR
Selker, Rev. Raymond C., *O.F.M.* '04 (BO) [MIS] St. Anthony Shrine, Boston, MA
Sell, Rev. Msgr. Robert L., '78 (LFT) Curia: Miscellaneous / Other Offices
Selladurai, Rev. Selvaraj, '85 (GRY) Retired. Sacred Heart, Whiting, IN
Selladurai, Rev. Selvaraj, '85 (GRY) Retired.
Sellas, Rev. Joseph, (KCK) Holy Trinity, Paola, KS
Sellers, Rev. Steven, '13 (POC) Retired.
Selvam, Rev. Panneer, '81 (P) St. John the Apostle, Reedsport, OR; St. Mary, Our Lady of the Dunes, Florence, OR
Selvam, Rev. Raja, '07 (GB) St. Joseph, Appleton, WI
Selvam, Rev. Raja, '07 (LA) [MIS] Apostleship of the Sea, Catholic Maritime Ministry, San Pedro, CA
Selvam, Rev. Tamil, (SP) St. Paul, Tampa, FL
Selvanayakam, Rev. Darnis, (JKS) Holy Cross, Philadelphia, MS; Sacred Heart, Louisville, MS
Selvaraj, Rev. Arockiaraj Kunipaku, *HGN* '83 (PT) Good Shepherd, Tallahassee, FL
Selvaraj, Rev. Balappa, '86 (ATL) On Duty Outside Diocese. Diocese of Chikmagalur
Selvaraj, Rev. Bose Raja, '73 (BGP) Retired. [MON] The Catherine Dennis Keefe Queen of the Clergy Retired Priests' Residence, Stamford, CT
Selvaraj, Rev. Paul Dass, *OMI* (SD) Pastor of Most Precious Blood Catholic Parish, Chula Vista, a corporation sole, Chula Vista, CA; [MIS] Most Precious Blood Catholic Parish in Chula Vista, CA Real Property Support Corporation, Chula Vista, CA
Selvaraj, Rev. Rakshaganathan, '94 (AUS) San Salvador, Caldwell, TX; St. Anthony, Bryan, TX
Selvaraj, Rev. Santhiago, *HGN* (LUB) Curia: Leadership St. Joseph, Rotan, TX
Selvaraj, Rev. Selladurai, '85 (GRY) [HOS] Franciscan Health Dyer, Dyer, IN
Selvaraj, Rev. Thomas, (GF) St. Mary, Custer, MT
Selvester, Rev. Guy W., '97 (MET) Curia: Family Life St. Joseph, Washington, NJ
Selvin, Rev. Suganthan, *HGN* '13 (SPC) St. Joseph, Billings, MO; St. Susanne, Mount Vernon, MO
Semancik, Rev. Msgr. Joseph F., '53 (GRY) Retired.
Semar, Rev. Mitchel, '12 (HT) Curia: Administration; Clergy and Religious Services; Faith Formation St. Thomas Aquinas, Thibodaux, LA
Sember, Very Rev. Joel A., '07 (GB) Curia: Advisory Boards, Commissions, Committees, and Councils SS. James-Stanislaus, White Lake, WI; SS. Mary & Hyacinth, Antigo, WI; St. John, Antigo, WI; St. Wenceslaus, Deerbrook, WI; [RTR] Teens Encounter Christ (TEC), Green Bay Chapter, Green Bay, WI
Semeniuk, Rev. Gregory J., *C.M.* '89 (PH) [SEM] Vincentian Theologate-DeAndreis House, Philadelphia, PA
Semeniuk, Rev. Gregory J., *CM* '89 (BUF) [MON] Vincentian Community at Niagara University (Congregation of the Mission of St. Vincent de Paul), Niagara University, NY
Semik, Rev. Leszek, '94 (LA) St. Anastasia, Los Angeles,

CA
Seminara, Rev. Ronald S., *S.J.* '74 (RC) Curia: Leadership St. Francis Mission, St. Francis, SD; St. Thomas the Apostle, Mission, SD; [MON] Holy Rosary Mission Jesuit Community, Pine Ridge, SD; [MON] Kino Jesuit Community, Mission, SD
Seminatore, Rev. Joseph, '69 (CLV) Retired.
Semler, Rev. Albert J., '67 (PIT) Retired.
Semler, Rev. Albert J., '67 (PIT) Retired.
Semler, Rev. Andrew V., '00 (DAL) St. Jude Catholic Parish, Allen, TX; [CEM] St. Jude Parish Columbarium, Allen, TX; [EFT] St. Jude Parish Building Trust, Allen, TX
Semmer, Rev. Dean F., '79 (CHI) Retired.
Semonin, Rev. James R., '71 (CLV) Retired. Queen of Heaven, Uniontown, OH
Sempa, Rev. Msgr. John J., '80 (SCR) Corpus Christi Parish, West Pittston, PA; Saint Barbara Parish, Exeter, PA
Semple, Rev. Richard, '00 (SPK) Chesterton Academy of Notre Dame, Spokane, WA; St. Patrick, Spokane, WA
Semple, Rev. Richard, (SPK) St. Francis Xavier, Spokane, WA
Sena, Rev. Charles A., '92 (PBL) Retired.
Sena, Rev. Neftali Feliz, (SCR) Queen of Heaven, Hazleton, Hazelton, PA
Sena, Rev. Sotero, '81 (SFE) Retired.
Senay, Rev. Andrew, *O.S.B.* (STL) [MON] The Abbey of St. Mary and St. Louis, St. Louis, MO
Sendlein, Rev. Thomas A., *C.M.* '72 (PH) [MON] Congregation of the Mission, Philadelphia, PA
Senechal, Rev. Vincent, (SFR) [MIS] American Auxiliary of Paris Foreign Missions, San Francisco, CA
Senetsky, Rev. Msgr. Robert, '60 (PSC) Saints Peter and Paul's Byzantine Catholic Church, Peekskill, NY
Senetsky, Rev. Msgr. Robert, '60 (PSC) Retired. Curia: Leadership Saints Peter and Paul's Byzantine Catholic Church, Peekskill, NY
Sengol, Rev. Rajan, '85 (LA) St. Bridget of Sweden, Lake Balboa, CA; St. Raphael, Santa Barbara, CA
Sengol Bazil, Rev. Xavier, *H.G.N.* (SEA) St. Anthony, Renton, WA
Sengolraj, Rev. Jeyaseelan W., '08 (IND) St. Francis Catholic Church, Henryville, Inc., Henryville, IN; St. Michael Catholic Church, Charlestown, Inc., Charlestown, IN
Seniw, Very Rev. John, '82 (PHU) Retired.
Senk, Rev. Christopher, '76 (VEN) On Leave.
Sennik, Rev. Thomas W., '76 (NOR) On Leave.
Sensat, Rev. Clinton M., '09 (LAF) Our Lady of Lourdes, Erath, LA; St. Thomas More, Eunice, LA
Sensenig, Very Rev. Andrew, *OMI* (CC) Curia: Leadership Our Lady of Guadalupe, Riviera, TX; Our Lady of Guadalupe, Sarita, TX; [RTR] Oblate La Parra Center, Sarita, TX
Sensenig, Rev. Andy, *OMI* (CC) Our Lady of Consolation, Riviera, TX
Senyah, Rev. Anthony O., '04 (RIC) Sacred Heart, Danville, VA
Senz, Rev. Augustine, *O.S.B.* '07 (WOR) [MON] Benedictine Monks, St. Benedict Abbey, Still River, MA
Seo, Rev. Daniel, (ORG) [MIS] Our Lady of Peace Korean Catholic Center, Irvine, CA
Seo, Rev. Hyunjin, '06 (P) Korean Martyrs Catholic Church, Portland, OR
Seo, Rev. Patrick J., '17 (NEW) Our Lady of Mercy, Park Ridge, NJ
Sepe, Rev. Kevin M., '86 (BO) St. Francis of Assisi, Dracut, MA
Seper, Rev. John M., '83 (STL) Curia: Leadership St. Peter Catholic Church, St. Charles, St. Charles, MO
Sepich, Rev. Lawrence, '74 (MIL) Retired.
Sepulveda, Rev. Miguel A., '02 (MIA) St. Brendan, Miami, FL
Sequeira, Rev. Canon Adrian, *I.C.R.S.S.* (DET) St. Joseph Shrine Parish Detroit (St. Joseph Roman Catholic Church), Detroit, MI
Sequeira, Rev. Eustace, *S.J.* '75 (DEN) [MON] Regis Jesuit Community (The Jesuits at Regis University), Denver, CO
Sequeira, Rev. Marcos, '91 (NEW) Immaculate Conception, Newark, NJ; Our Lady of Good Counsel, Newark, NJ
Sequeira, Rev. Michael, '66 (NOR) Retired.
Sequeira, Rev. Ronald, (DEN) St. Frances Cabrini Catholic Parish in Littleton, Littleton, CO
Sequeira-Treminio, Rev. Franklin, '15 (DEN) On Duty Outside Diocese.
Sera, Rev. Enrique, '78 (ORG) Curia: Leadership
Sera, Rev. Enrique J., '78 (ORG) St. Mary's, Fullerton, CA
Serafica, Rev. Macias Wency D., (BAL) Church of the Annunciation, Baltimore, MD; St. Clement Mary Hofbauer, Baltimore, MD; St. Michael, Baltimore, MD
Serafin, Rev. Thomas J., '93 (MET) St. Elizabeth Ann Seton, Three Bridges, NJ
Serafini, Rev. Augustine, '62 (GB) Retired. [MON] Community of Our Lady, Oshkosh, WI
Seraiah, Rev. Chori, (POC) Saint George Catholic Church, Republic, MO
Seran, Rev. Agustinus, *S.V.D.* (SP) St. Peter Claver, Tampa, FL
Serano, Rev. Joseph A., *O.Praem.* '69 (PH) [MON] Daylesford Abbey, Inc., Paoli, PA; [SEM] Daylesford Abbey (Norbertine Fathers, Inc.), Paoli, PA
Serban, Rev. Ron, '93 (SR) Pastor of Holy Spirit Catholic Church of Santa Rosa, A Corporation Sole, Santa Rosa, CA
Serbicki, Rev. Daniel J., '11 (BUF) St. John the Baptist, Alden, NY; St. Maximilian Kolbe Parish, Corfu, NY
Seremchuk, Rev. Oleh, '10 (PBR) St. John the Baptist, Scottdale, PA; St. Nicholas, Perryopolis, PA
Sereno, Rev. David, '86 (SD) Pastor of Our Lady of the Valley Catholic Parish in El Centro, a corporation sole, El Centro, CA
Serfino, Rev. Jude, (MO) Curia: Offices and Directors
Sergi, Rev. Michael, *C.Ss.R.* (TOL) St. Gerard, Lima, OH
Sergott, Rev. Joseph, *OP* '96 (LAV) [MIS] Saint Therese Center, Henderson, NV; [MON] Dominican Rectory, Fra Angelico House, Las Vegas, NV
Sergott, Rev. Lawrence J., '01 (GLD) On Duty Outside Diocese. Brothers of the Beloved Disciple, Archdiocese of San Antonio
Sergott, Rev. Lawrence Jerome, *BBD* '01 (SAT) [MIS] Brothers of the Beloved Disciple, San Antonio, TX
Serna, Rev. Alfonso, (NTN) On Special Assignment. Melkite Eparchy of Mexico
Serna, Rev. Juan, *S.T.L.* '00 (STO) On Leave. Curia: Offices and Directors
Serna-Ocampo, Rev. Andres, '12 (TR) Church of the Precious Blood, Monmouth Beach, NJ; St. Dorothea, Eatontown, NJ
Sernett, Rev. Msgr. Michael D., '70 (SC) Retired. Curia: Leadership
Serour, Rev. George J., '59 (SAG) Retired.
Serowik, Rev. James P., '87 (SY) Curia: Leadership Immaculate Conception, Greene, NY; St. John the Evangelist, Bainbridge, NY; St. Joseph, Deposit, NY; St. Joseph, Port Crane, NY; St. Mary, Kirkwood, NY; St. Vincent de Paul-Blessed Sacrament, Vestal, NY; The Catholic Community of St. Stephen-St. Patrick, Whitney Point, NY
Serpa, Rev. Vincent, *O.P.* '68 (SAC) Retired. St. Dominic, Benicia, CA
Serra, Rev. Dominic, '72 (NY) Retired.
Serra, Rev. Dominic F., '72 (WDC) [COL] Catholic University of America, The, Washington, DC
Serraino, Rev. Fred, *C.S.C.* (FTW) [MIS] Holy Cross House, Notre Dame, IN
Serrano, Rev. Carlos, '11 (FRS) Our Lady of Mt. Carmel, Fresno, CA; St. Alphonsus, Fresno, CA
Serrano, Rev. Edgar, '87 (SD) Chap, Metropolitan Correction Ctr, San Diego
Serrano, Rev. Heriberto, '67 (LA) Santa Rosa, San Fernando, CA
Serrano, Rev. Jose A., '95 (NY) St. Anthony, Bronx, NY
Serrano, Friar Mario, *OFM Conv.* '04 (L) St. Paul, Louisville, KY
Serrano, Friar Mario L., *OFM Conv.* (ELP) Our Lady of Mt. Carmel, El Paso, TX; [CAM] Catholic Campus Ministry at University of Texas at El Paso, El Paso, TX
Serrano, Friar Mario L., *O.F.M. Conv.* (IND) [MON] Provincial Headquarters, Our Lady of Consolation Province, Conventual Franciscans (Province of Our Lady of Consolation), Mount St. Francis, IN
Serrano, Rev. Roberto, (ALB) [COL] Siena College, Loudonville, NY
Serrano, Rev. Rodrigo, '01 (FWT) On Leave.
Serrano, Rev. Sergio, *O.P.* '07 (NO) Curia: Offices and Directors
Serrano Ardila, Rev. Orlando, *MXY/IMEY* (CHR) St. Mary Help of Christians, Aiken, SC
Serrano Figueroa, Rev. Carmelo J., '15 (PCE) Santa Teresita del Nino Jesus, Juana Diaz, PR
Serrano-Rivera, Rev. Ivan R., (SJN) San Judas Tadeo, Trujillo Alto, PR
Serrao, Rev. Ronald, '92 (SUP) Curia: Leadership St. Albert, Land O'Lakes, WI; St. Kunegunda of Poland, Sugar Camp, WI; St. Mary, Phelps, WI; St. Peter the Fisherman, Eagle River, WI; St. Theresa, Three Lakes, WI
Sertich, Rev. Nicholas Charles, '20 (NEW) On Duty Outside Diocese. Casa Santa Maria, Rome
Serva, Rev. Donald, *S.J.* (CLV) [COL] John Carroll Jesuit Community, University Heights, OH
Servatius, Rev. Thomas, (SY) Curia: Leadership; Offices and Directors Historic Old St. John's Church, Utica, NY
Servatius, Rev. Thomas R., '03 (SY) Curia: Leadership St. Joseph and St. Patrick, Utica, NY; St. Peter, Utica, NY
Servinsky, Rev. Msgr. Michael E., '70 (ALT) Retired.
Serwa, Rev. Gregory P., *S.A.C.* '70 (BAL) [MIS] Union of Catholic Apostolate USA, Inc., Baltimore, MD
Serwa, Rev. Gregory P., *S.A.C.* '70 (MIL) [MON] Pallotti House, Milwaukee, WI
Sescon, Rev. Albert C., '86 (KNX) St. Augustine, Signal Mountain, TN
Sescon, Rev. Esteban, '77 (ELP) San Judas Tadeo, El Paso, TX
Sessions, Rev. Phillip D., '80 (LAN) Retired.
Sestito, Rev. Joseph N., '59 (OG) Retired.
Setelik, Rev. James, '84 (RNO) Curia: Offices and Directors Corpus Christi, Carson City, NV
Setiawan, Rev. Charles, (WDC) [SEM] Whitefriars Hall, Washington, DC
Setter, Rev. H. Jay, '88 (WCH) Immaculate Conception (St. Mary, Aleppo), Garden Plain, KS; St. Anthony, Garden Plain, KS
Settle, Rev. Harry A., '14 (COV) St. Cecilia, Independence, KY
Settle, Rev. Matthew W., '04 (GB) Holy Family-St. William, Wittenberg, WI; St. Anthony, Tigerton, WI; St. Mary, Marion, WI
Setto, Rev. Patrick, (EST) St. Joseph Chaldean Parish, Troy, MI
Setubi, Rev. Armel, *S.J.* '19 (WDC) [MON] The Jesuit Community at Georgetown University, Washington, DC
Seubert, Rev. August, *O.F.M.Cap.* '57 (GB) Retired. [MON] St. Fidelis Friary, Appleton, WI
Seubert, Rev. Xavier John, *OFM* '71 (BUF) [MON] St. Bonaventure Friary, St. Bonaventure, NY
Seuferling, Rev. George, '56 (KCK) Retired. On Leave. Inactive
Sevcik, Rev. Joseph J, '20 (DUB) Immaculate Conception Church, Wexford, Iowa, Lansing, IA; St. Ann-St. Joseph Church, Harpers Ferry, Iowa, Harpers Ferry, IA; St. Joseph Church, New Albin, Iowa, New Albin, IA; The Immaculate Conception Church, Lansing, Iowa, Lansing, IA
Severson, Rev. David, '11 (HEL) Chap, Montana National Guard Curia: (>MO) Offices and Directors Saint John the Baptist Parish: Series 630, LLC, Frenchtown, MT; Saint Mary Mission Parish: Series 647, LLC, Stevensville, MT
Severt, Rev. William H., '74 (CLV) Retired.
Sevigny, Rev. Michael E., *O.F.M.Cap.* '78 (PRT) Curia: Offices and Directors
Sevilla, Rev. Dennis, '69 (SEA) Retired. Our Lady, Star of the Sea, Bremerton, WA; [HOS] St. Joseph Medical Center, Tacoma, WA
Sevola, Rev. Frank, (BO) [MIS] St. Anthony Shrine, Boston, MA
Sewell, Rev. Jack K., '78 (ORG) Retired.
Sexton, Rev. Msgr. Michael F., '61 (BIR) Retired.
Sexton, Rev. William, '17 (BO) St. Mary of the Assumption, Hull, MA
Sexton, Rev. William P., (BO) St. Anthony of Padua, Cohasset, MA
Seyd, Rev. Samuel, '00 (MAN) Chap, Dartmouth-Hitchcock Med Ctr
Seyer, Rev. Lawrence, '97 (LA) Curia: Pastoral Services Our Lady of Mount Carmel, Santa Barbara, CA
Seyler, Rev. Kyle, (E) On Sick Leave.
Seymour, Rev. James W., '87 (OG) Curia: Offices and Directors Saint James Church of Gouverneur, Gouverneur, NY; The Roman Catholic Church of Saint Hubert in Star Lake, NY, Star Lake, NY
Seymour, Rev. Scott R., '99 (OG) Curia: Consultative Bodies Saint Augustine's Church, Peru, NY, Peru, NY; St. James Church, Cadyville, NY, Cadyville, NY; The Roman Catholic Community of St. Alexander and St. Joseph, Morrisonville, NY
Sezzi, Rev. Michael J., '96 (LA) St. Peter Claver, Simi Valley, CA
Sfeir, Rev. Abda, (OLL) Saints Peter and Paul Maronite Catholic Church, Simi Valley, CA
Shaba, Rev. Daniel, '18 (SPA) St. Peter Chaldean Cathedral, El Cajon, CA; [MIS] Chaldean Media Center, El Cajon, CA
Shaba, Rev. Peter, *S.M.A.* '10 (PRT) All Saints Parish, Brunswick, ME
Shabi, Rev. Felix, (SD) (>SPA) Mar Auraha Chaldean Catholic Parish (The Chaldean Catholic Church of Arizona Corporation), Scottsdale, AZ

Shackelford, Rev. Christopher, '91 (GAL) St. Andrew, Channelview, TX
Shackett, Rev. Bryan, (DET) St. Anthony Parish Belleville, Belleville, MI
Shackil, Rev. Richard, '17 (OLN) Sacred Heart, Little Falls, NJ
Shadwell, Rev. Damian, '90 (WDC) On Leave.
Shadwell, Rev. Steven, (PAT) Our Lady of the Magnificat, Kinnelon, NJ
Shafer, Rev. Msgr. Drake R., '73 (DAV) Retired.
Shafer, Rev. Eric L., (ARL) St. Elizabeth of Hungary, Colonial Beach, VA
Shafer, Rev. James, '75 (FTW) Curia: Offices and Directors
Shafer, Rev. James A., '75 (FTW) St. Joseph, Garrett, IN; [MIS] Saint Anne Home & Retirement Community, Fort Wayne, IN
Shaffer, Rev. G. Scott, '89 (TR) St. Joseph, Toms River, NJ
Shaffer, Rev. Gregory W., '06 (WDC) Our Lady of the Visitation, Darnestown, MD
Shaffer, Rev. Gregory William, (WDC) Church of the Assumption of the Blessed Virgin Mary, Washington, DC
Shafran, Rev. Steve, (NY) [RTR] Don Bosco Retreat Center and Marian Shrine, Stony Point, NY; [RTR] Marian Shrine, Stony Point, NY
Shaghel, Rev. Nicodemus, *V.C.* (TUC) Our Lady of Guadalupe Roman Catholic Parish - Solomon, Solomon, AZ; Saint Rose of Lima Roman Catholic Parish - Safford, Safford, AZ; [CAM] Eastern Arizona College - Newman Center, Thatcher, AZ
Shaji, Rev. Jose, '92 (SFR) St. Bartholomew, San Mateo, CA; St. Mary Magdalene, Bolinas, CA
Shaldone, Rev. Robert, (CC) [MON] Society of Our Lady of the Most Holy Trinity, Corpus Christi, TX
Shallbetter, Rev. Martin, '69 (STP) Retired.
Shallow, Rev. Edmund J., '81 (MET) Curia: Leadership Divine Mercy Parish, Carteret, NJ
Shallow, Rev. Zachary, (PHX) Corpus Christi Roman Catholic Parish, Phoenix, AZ
Shallow, Rev. Zachary of the Mother of God, *SOLT* '04 (CC) [MON] Society of Our Lady of the Most Holy Trinity, Corpus Christi, TX
Shami, Rev. Michael, (FTW) [SEM] Moreau Seminary, Notre Dame, IN
Shami, Rev. Michael, '20 (OLL) On Special Assignment. Doctoral Student, Rome Curia: Offices and Directors
Shamleffer, Rev. Msgr. John B., '83 (STL) Curia: Leadership St. Gabriel the Archangel Catholic Church, St. Louis, MO
Shammami, Rev. Marcus, (EST) Holy Martyrs Chaldean Catholic Church, Sterling Heights, MI
Shanahan, Rev. John, *T.O.R.* '08 (FWT) St. Andrew, Fort Worth, TX
Shanahan, Rev. Kevin, *M.S.C.* '86 (SAT) St. Anthony of Padua, San Antonio, TX; [MON] Missionaries of the Sacred Heart, San Antonio, TX
Shanahan, Rev. Michael, *SS.CC.* '62 (FR) [MIS] Damien Residence Retirement Home, ,
Shanahan, Rev. Michael J., (CHI) Our Lady of the Rosary Parish, Chicago, IL
Shanahan, Rev. Thomas J., *S.J.* '67 (OM) (>MIL) [MON] St. Camillus Jesuit Community (Society of Jesus, USA Midwest Province), Wauwatosa, WI
Shane, Rev. Donald W., '69 (OM) Retired.
Shanfelt, Rev. Thomas G., '78 (ALN) Retired.
Shanley, Rev. Brian J, *O.P.* (NY) [COL] St. John's University Staten Island Campus, Staten Island, NY
Shanley, Rev. Brian J, *O.P.* (BRK) [COL] St. John's University, Queens, NY
Shanley, Rev. Brian J., *O.P.* '87 (PRO) [MON] St. Thomas Aquinas Priory at Providence College, Providence, RI
Shanley, Rev. Msgr. James A., '80 (HRT) Curia: Administration; Advisory Boards, Commissions, Committees, and Councils; Clergy and Religious Services; Offices and Directors [ASN] The Benevolent Association for Priests of The Archdiocese of Hartford, Incorporated, Hartford, CT; [MIS] The Catholic Mission Aid Society of Hartford, Inc., Bloomfield, CT
Shanley, Rev. Matthias, *SS.CC.* '65 (FR) [MIS] Damien Residence Retirement Home, ,
Shanley, Rev. Owen F., '53 (ALB) Retired.
Shanmugam, Rev. Anbalagan, '09 (LC) Sacred Heart, Elmwood, WI; Sacred Heart of Jesus, Spring Valley, WI
Shannon, Rev. Francis T., '88 (BRK) St. Mary Star of the Sea and St. Gertrude, Far Rockaway, NY
Shannon, Rev. John, *F.S.S.P.* (SEA) North American Martyrs Personal Parish, Edmonds, WA
Shannon, Rev. Michael, '93 (ATL) St. Brendan Catholic Church, Cumming, Inc., Cumming, GA; [MON] Legionaries of Christ, Incorporated, Cumming, GA
Shannon, Rev. Richard J., '59 (CHI) Retired. St. Alphonsus and St. Patrick Parish, Lemont, IL
Shannon, Rev. Timothy J., '75 (STU) Retired.
Shannon, Rev. William, '71 (HON) Retired.
Shantillo, Rev. Gerald W., '09 (SCR) Curia: Leadership; Offices and Directors St. Peter's Cathedral, Scranton, PA
Shantiraj, Rev. Joseph, '88 (LR) All Saints Church, Mount Ida, AR; St. Agnes, Mena, AR
Shao, Rev. Caroli Borromeo, *A.J.* (CLV) St. Colman, Cleveland, OH; St. Stephen, Cleveland, OH
Shapiro, Rev. Matthew, *O.S.B.* '86 (TLS) [MON] Our Lady of the Annunciation of Clear Creek Abbey, Hulbert, OK
Sharbaugh, Rev. Jason, '10 (LR) Curia: Leadership; Offices and Directors St. Thomas Aquinas University Parish, Fayetteville, AR; [CAM] University of Arkansas, St. Thomas Aquinas University Parish, Fayetteville, AR
Sharbel, Rev. Joseph M., '85 (KC) Holy Spirit, Lees Summit, MO; St. Margaret of Scotland Catholic Church, Lees Summit, MO
Sharkey, Rev. Peter E., *S.J.* '74 (MIL) [MON] St. Camillus Jesuit Community (Society of Jesus, USA Midwest Province), Wauwatosa, WI
Sharkey, Rev. Philip J., '98 (HRT) Retired.
Sharland, Rev. David M., *Y.A.* '99 (RIC) On Administrative Leave.
Sharman, Rev. Robert F., '84 (HBG) Curia: Offices and Directors St. Bernard, New Bloomfield, PA; [HOS] Holy Spirit Corporation, Camp Hill, PA; [HOS] Holy Spirit Hospital of the Sisters of Christian Charity, Camp Hill, PA; [HOS] Spirit Physician Services, Inc., Camp Hill, PA
Sharon, Rev. Charles J., *S.A.* '72 (NY) [MON] Atonement Friars, New York, NY; [MON] Franciscan Friars of the Atonement, Minister General Office, Garrison, NY; [MON] St. Francis of Assisi Novitiate, ,
Sharp, Rev. David L., *C.S.B.* '70 (LSC) [MON] The Basilian Fathers of Las Cruces, Las Cruces, NM
Sharp, Rev. Donald B., *S.J.* '71 (SJ) Retired. [MON] Sacred Heart Jesuit Center, Los Gatos, CA
Sharp, Rev. George F., '89 (NEW) Retired. Chap, Elizabeth Fed Detention Ctr St. Matthew, Ridgefield, NJ
Sharp, Rev. James, '84 (DAL) Retired.
Sharp, Rev. Patrick, (COS) [HOS] St. Francis Medical Center, Colorado, CO
Sharpe, Rev. Peter, '09 (FAR) St. Francis de Sales Church of Steele, Steele, ND; St. Mary's Church of Medina, Medina, ND; St. Paul of Tappen, Tappen, ND
Sharrett, Rev. Victor F., '65 (PH) Retired.
Shaughnessy, Very Rev. Daniel G., '12 (STL) St. Joseph Catholic Church, Imperial, Imperial, MO
Shaughnessy, Rev. James, '73 (KCK) Holy Family, Summerfield, KS; St. Michael, Axtell, KS
Shaughnessy, Rev. James M., *S.J.* '79 (BO) [MON] Loyola House, Boston, MA
Shaughnessy, Rev. Martin G., *S.J.* '63 (BO) Boston College High School, Boston, MA; [MON] Campion Health & Wellness, Inc., Weston, MA
Shaughnessy, Rev. Thomas, *S.S.C.* '66 (OM) Retired. [MON] Missionary Society of St. Columban, St. Columbans, NE
Shaughnessy, Rev. William, *OP Dei* (PMB) [MIS] Prelature of the Holy Cross and Opus Dei, Delray Beach, FL
Shaughnessy, Friar William, *O.F.M.* (OAK) [MON] Franciscan Friars of California (Province of St. Barbara), Oakland, CA; [RTR] San Damiano Retreat, Danville, CA
Shaughnessy, Rev. William, '92 (POD) Curia: Clergy and Religious Services (>MIA) [MIS] Prelature of the Holy Cross and Opus Dei, Miami, FL
Shaunessey, Rev. Paul, *S.J.* '77 (WOR) St. Cecilia, Leominster, MA
Shaute, Rev. Joseph, '01 (ATL) St. Theresa of the Child Jesus Catholic Church, Douglasville, Inc., Douglasville, GA
Shaver, Rev. James, '89 (LAN) Retired.
Shaw, Rev. David, '06 (P) (>STP) St. Peter, Richfield, MN; (>STP) St. Richard, Richfield, MN
Shaw, Rev. David, '06 (P) (>STP) The Church of the Assumption/La Iglesia de La Asuncion, Richfield, MN
Shaw, Rev. John M., '57 (YAK) Retired.
Shaw, Rev. Kenneth, *S.D.B.* '78 (NY) [RTR] Don Bosco Retreat Center and Marian Shrine, Stony Point, NY; [RTR] Marian Shrine, Stony Point, NY
Shaw, Rev. Peter J., '12 (CHL) St. Joseph, Bryson City, NC
Shaw, Rev. Richard D., '68 (ALB) Retired.
Shaw, Rev. Thomas, '01 (PEO) Immaculate Conception Church, Ohio, IL; St. John the Evangelist, Walnut, IL
Shay, Rev. Michael, *S.D.S.* '73 (MIL) [MIS] Salvatorians - Jordan Hall, Milwaukee, WI
Shayo, Rev. Barnabas, *A.J.* '98 (ALN) St. Patrick, Pottsville, PA
Shayo, Rev. Jude, *A.J.* (SAV) Holy Redeemer, McRae, GA; Immaculate Conception, Dublin, GA; St. Mark, Eastman, GA
Shayo, Rev. Yovin, (HEL) Saint John the Evangelist Parish: Series 329, LLC, Fairfield, MT; Saint Joseph Parish: Series 319, LLC, Choteau, MT
Shea, Rev. Daniel B., '69 (HEL) Retired. Our Lady of the Valley Parish: Series 460, LLC, Helena, MT
Shea, Rev. Edward, *O.F.M.* '87 (CHI) [MON] St. Peter's Friary, Chicago, IL
Shea, Rev. Henry, (BO) [MON] The Jesuit Community at Boston College, Chestnut Hill, MA
Shea, Rev. James E., *C.Ss.R.* '65 (TUC) [MON] Redemptorist Society of Arizona Desert House of Prayer Residence, Tucson, AZ; [RTR] Redemptorist Society of Arizona Redemptorist Renewal Center, Tucson, AZ
Shea, Rev. James J., *Sch.P.* '92 (PH) Devon Preparatory School (Piarist Fathers), Devon, PA; [MON] Piarist Fathers (Order of the Pious Schools), Devon, PA
Shea, Rev. James M., '65 (BUR) Retired.
Shea, Rev. James Matthew, *S.J.* '75 (WDC) [MON] The Jesuit Community at Georgetown University, Washington, DC
Shea, Rev. Msgr. James P., '02 (BIS) [COL] University of Mary, Bismarck, ND
Shea, Rev. James R., *S.J.* (CHI) (>GB) [RTR] Jesuit Retreat House, Oshkosh, WI
Shea, Rev. John F., *S.J.* '14 (OM) [MON] Jesuit Community at Creighton University, Omaha, NE
Shea, Rev. John J., *S.J.* '75 (NY) [MON] Jesuit Community at Fordham University, New York, NY
Shea, Rev. John Paul, '13 (TUC) St. Charles Roman Catholic Community - San Carlos (San Carlos Apache Community), San Carlos, AZ
Shea, Rev. Joseph P., '78 (LA) St. Rose of Lima, Simi Valley, CA
Shea, Rev. Leo B., *M.M.* '66 (NY) Retired. [MON] Maryknoll Fathers and Brothers (Catholic Foreign Mission Society of America, Inc.), Ossining, NY
Shea, Very Rev. Louis M., '12 (CHY) Curia: Consultative Bodies St. Margaret's, Riverton, WY
Shea, Rev. Michael J., *C.M.* '70 (PH) [MON] Congregation of the Mission, Philadelphia, PA
Shea, Rev. Michael J., '76 (SFE) Prince of Peace Catholic Community, Albuquerque, NM
Shea, Rev. Msgr. Richard J., '61 (BGP) Retired.
Shea, Rev. Robert P., '13 (BIS) St. Wenceslaus, Dickinson, ND
Shea, Rev. Thomas M., '66 (SPR) Retired. Curia: Clergy and Religious Services; Offices and Directors Blessed Sacrament, Holyoke, MA
Shea, Rev. Timothy J., '61 (BO) Retired. St. Barbara, Woburn, MA
Shea, Rev. William, *S.V.D.* '64 (DUB) [SEM] Divine Word College, Epworth, IA
Sheaffer, Rev. John K., '93 (SPR) St. Thomas the Apostle, West Springfield, MA
Sheaffer, Rev. John K., '93 (SPR) St. Thomas the Apostle School, West Springfield, MA; [CEM] St. Thomas the Apostle Cemetery, ,
Sheahan, Rev. Msgr. Donal C., '60 (SD) Retired. Pastor of Sacred Heart Catholic Parish, Coronado, a corporation sole, Coronado, CA
Sheahan, Rev. Msgr. Richard D., '69 (PRO) Retired.
Sheahan, Rev. William T., *S.J.* (NY) [MIS] Ciszek Hall Jesuit Residential College, Bronx, NY
Shearer, Rev. John D, (FRS) St. Joachim, Madera, CA
Shearer, Rev. John D., *O.S.J.* '13 (SCR) [SEM] St. Joseph's Oblate Seminary, Pittston, PA
Shearer, Rev. Thomas M., '78 (CIN) Retired.
Sheckells, Rev. Marc, *OFM* (CLV) [MON] St. Anthony of Padua Friary, Brooklyn, OH
Shecterle, Rev. Msgr. Ross A., '86 (MIL) St. Anthony's Congregation, Menomonee Falls, WI; St. Mary's Congregation, Menomonee Falls, WI
Shedlock, Rev. John, '94 (SFE) Retired.
Sheedy, Rev. Edward J., '72 (BUF) Retired.
Sheedy, Rev. Msgr. Patrick J., '65 (ORL) Blessed Trinity, Ocala, FL
Sheedy, Rev. Timothy J., '76 (DAV) Retired.
Sheehan, Rev. Donald P., '68 (NEW) Retired.
Sheehan, Rev. Edward, *S.M.* '61 (ATL) Retired. Our Lady of the Assumption Catholic Church, Brookhaven, Inc., Brookhaven, GA
Sheehan, Rev. Eugene, *OFM Cap* (NY) Retired. [MON] St. Clare Friary (Capuchin Franciscan Friars, Province of St. Mary), Yonkers, NY
Sheehan, Rev. Msgr. George F., '61 (SY) Retired.
Sheehan, Rev. Gerard J., *S.O.L.T.* '85 (CC) Curia:

Leadership St. Anthony, Robstown, TX; [MON] Society of Our Lady of the Most Holy Trinity, Corpus Christi, TX
Sheehan, Rev. James, '79 (NY) Cardinal Hayes High School, Bronx, NY
Sheehan, Rev. James C., '79 (NY) St. Elizabeth of Hungary, New York, NY
Sheehan, Rev. John P., '89 (NY) St. Peter, Monticello, NY
Sheehan, Rev. Joseph, *O.Carm.* '63 (SFS) [COL] Presentation College, Aberdeen, SD (>ALB) St. Joseph, Troy, NY
Sheehan, Rev. Joseph A., '59 (ALN) Retired.
Sheehan, Rev. Justin R., *O.C.S.O.* '91 (ROC) [MON] Abbey of the Genesee, Inc., Piffard, NY
Sheehan, Rev. Michael J., '78 (NEW) St. Peter the Apostle, River Edge, NJ
Sheehan, Rev. Myles, *SJ* '94 (WDC) [MON] The Jesuit Community at Georgetown University, Washington, DC
Sheehan, Rev. Peter J., '04 (PRO) On Leave.
Sheehan, Rev. Thomas J., *S.J.* '97 (BO) [MON] Campion Health & Wellness, Inc., Weston, MA
Sheehan, Rev. Thomas J., *S.J.* '99 (WOR) Chap, Memorial Hosp
Sheehan, Rev. William, *O.M.I.* '65 (BO) [MON] Missionary Oblates of Mary Immaculate Northern Province, Lowell, MA
Sheehan, Rev. William John, *C.S.B.* '66 (GAL) Retired.
Sheehy, Rev. Michael, *C.M.M.* '64 (DET) [MON] Mariannhill Mission Society, Dearborn Heights, MI
Sheehy, Rev. Sean O., '70 (BR) Retired.
Sheehy, Rev. Vincent J., '61 (VEN) Retired.
Sheehy, Rev. Yvon, *S.C.J.* '78 (MIL) [MON] Sacred Heart Monastery, Hales Corners, WI
Sheekey, Rev. Philip P., '64 (WIL) Retired.
Sheeran, Rev. Desmond (Fintan), *SS.CC.* '55 (FR) [MIS] Damien Residence Retirement Home, ,
Sheeran, Rev. Fintan, *SS.CC.* '56 (WDC) St. Margaret, Seat Pleasant, MD
Sheeran, Rev. Michael, *S.J.* (KC) [MON] St. Peter Claver Jesuit Community, Kansas City, MO
Sheeran, Rev. Michael J., *S.J.* '70 (WDC) [MON] Leonard Neale House, Washington, DC
Sheeran, Rev. Robert, (NEW) Retired.
Sheeran, Rev. Msgr. Robert T., '70 (SFR) Retired. (>NEW) [COL] Seton Hall University, South Orange, NJ
Sheeran, Rev. Msgr. Robert T., (NEW) Retired.
Sheerin, Rev. Philip F., *M.M.* '55 (SJ) Retired.
Sheets, Rev. James P., '75 (SAC) Retired.
Sheets, Rev. Joseph B., '57 (IND) Retired.
Sheider, Rev. Ric, *O.F.M.* '59 (CIN) Retired.
Sheil, Rev. James E., '66 (CLV) Retired.
Shekar, Rev. Y. Vijaya, (NY) St. Mary and St. Andrew, Ellenville, NY
Shelander, Rev. Donald E., '70 (CIN) Retired.
Shelby, Rev. Charles F., *C.M.* '68 (STL) [MON] Congregation of the Mission, Perryville, MO
Shell, Rev. Jonas, '12 (STU) Curia: Deaneries Our Lady of Mercy, Carrollton, OH; St. Mary, Waynesburg, OH
Sheller, Rev. Paul, *O.S.B.* '13 (KC) [MON] Conception Abbey (Benedictine Monks), Conception, MO; [SEM] Conception Seminary College, Conception, MO
Shellito, Rev. Edward, (SJ) Curia: Leadership
Shelly, Rev. Roy, '78 (MRY) Retired.
Shelton, Rev. Brent A., (KNX) Curia: Leadership; Offices and Directors
Shelton, Rev. Henry, '69 (JKS) Retired.
Shelton, Rev. James Brent, '01 (KNX) St. Mary, Oak Ridge, TN
Shelton, Rev. Joey, '18 (COV) St. Augustine, Augusta, KY; St. James, Brooksville, KY
Shelton, Rev. Lawrence, '66 (LA) Retired.
Shelton, Rev. Paul, *S.J.* (CHI) [COL] Jesuit Community at Loyola University Chicago, Chicago, IL
Shema, Rev. Rene, (BO) [MON] Francis Xavier House, Brighton, MA
Shemuga, Rev. Kevin C., '83 (CLV) Our Lady of Guadalupe, Macedonia, OH
Shen, Rev. Peter H., (BO) Mary, Queen of Peace Parish, Medford, MA
Shenosky, Rev. Joseph T., '00 (PH) Curia: Deaneries Church of the Sacred Heart, Oxford, PA
Shepanzyk, Rev. Thomas, '08 (BRK) On Duty Outside Diocese. St. John the Baptist Church, Front Royal, VA
Shepanzyk, Rev. Thomas K., (ARL) St. John the Baptist, Front Royal, VA
Shepard, Rev. Thomas B., '77 (HRT) The Church of St. Thomas the Apostle of Oxford, Oxford, CT
Shepherd, Rev. Todd, '18 (WCH) Cathedral of the Immaculate Conception, Wichita, KS
Sherbo, Rev. Albert, '87 (DM) Retired.
Sherbourne, Rev. Gerald, '13 (POC) Military Chap Curia: (>MO) Offices and Directors
Sherdel, Rev. Lawrence W., '81 (HBG) St. Philip the Apostle, Lancaster, PA
Sheridan, Rev. Brian R., *M.S.* '83 (ATL) St. Thomas the Apostle Catholic Church, Smyrna, Inc., Smyrna, GA
Sheridan, Rev. Edward J., '63 (CHL) Retired.
Sheridan, Rev. Edward M., '07 (RVC) Our Lady of the Magnificat, Ocean Beach, NY; St. Aidan's Church, Williston Park, NY
Sheridan, Rev. James J., (CHI) [MON] St. John Stone Friary, Chicago, IL
Sheridan, Very Rev. John E., '10 (Y) Basilica of Saint John the Baptist, Canton, OH; St. Peter, Canton, OH
Sheridan, Rev. John E., '90 (BO) Curia: Leadership
Sheridan, Rev. John J., *O.S.A.* (PH) [MON] St. Thomas Monastery, Villanova, PA
Sheridan, Rev. Michael, (WOR) Retired.
Sheridan, Rev. Patrick, *O.S.B.* '11 (LA) [MON] St. Andrew's Abbey (Benedictine Monks), Valyermo, CA; [RTR] St. Andrew's Abbey Retreat Center, Valyermo, CA
Sheridan, Rev. Philip A., '51 (HRT) Retired.
Sheridan, Rev. William J., '72 (CHI) Retired.
Sheridan, Rev. William P., '89 (NEW) St. Agnes, Clark, NJ; [CAM] Kean University, Union, NJ
Sherlock, Rev. James C., '64 (PH) Retired.
Sherlock, Rev. John P., '69 (WCH) Retired. Curia: Leadership
Sherlock, Rev. R. Marc, '79 (CIN) Retired. Curia: Administration
Sherman, Rev. Msgr. Anthony F., '70 (BRK) Retired. St. Anastasia, Douglaston, NY
Sherman, Rt. Rev. Kenneth, '80 (NTN) Curia: Administration; Consultative Bodies St. Ann, Woodland Park, NJ
Sherman, Rev. Richard T., '00 (SLC) Retired. Saint Christopher LLC 219, Kanab, UT
Sherman, Rev. Thomas P, *S.J.* '87 (SJ) [MON] USA West Province, Society of Jesus, Los Gatos, CA
Sherrard, Rev. Patrick, '16 (SEA) Holy Innocents, Duvall, WA; St. Jude, Redmond, WA
Sherrer, Rev. Charles D., *C.S.C.* '61 (P) Retired.
Sherry, Rev. Frank, *C.P.M.* '89 (LEX) [NUR] Taylor Manor, Versailles, KY
Sherry, Rev. Robert N., '66 (RCK) Retired.
Shershanovich, Rev. Msgr. Michael, '74 (SPR) St. Joseph's, Pittsfield, MA
Sherwood, Rev. Stephen, *CMF* '71 (LA) Retired. [MON] Dominguez Seminary Inc., Rancho Dominguez, CA
Sherwood, Rev. Timothy H., '93 (SP) St. Brendan, Clearwater, FL
Shestak, Rev. Eduard, (SCR) Curia: Leadership
Shestak, Very Rev. Eduard, '06 (PSC) Curia: Leadership St. Mary's, Old Forge, PA; St. Nicholas, Old Forge, PA
Sheto, Rev. Yousif, (OLD) Christ the King Church, Troy, MI
Shevchuk, Very Rev. Archpriest Vsevolod, '11 (SJP) Curia: Offices and Directors Holy Ghost, Akron, OH
Shevchuk, Rev. Vsevolod, '11 (SJP) Curia: Leadership; Offices and Directors Protection of the Blessed Virgin Mary, Solon, OH
Shields, Rev. David M., *S.J.* '73 (MIL) [MON] Arrupe House Jesuit Community, Milwaukee, WI; [RTR] Casa Romero Renewal Center, Inc., Milwaukee, WI
Shields, Rev. Msgr. Hugh Joseph, '72 (PH) Retired. Curia: Advisory Boards, Commissions, Committees, and Councils St. John the Baptist, Philadelphia, PA
Shields, Rev. Michael, '79 (AJ) St. Michael, Palmer, AK
Shields, Rev. Stephen L., '74 (CLV) St. Thomas the Apostle, Sheffield Lake, OH
Shields, Rev. W. Bry, '84 (MOB) McGill-Toolen Catholic High School, Mobile, AL; St. Ignatius Parish, Mobile, Mobile, AL
Shihadeh, Rev. Musil Kamil, (NTN) Christ the Savior Church, Yonkers, NY
Shikany, Rev. Paul M., (IND) Curia: Offices and Directors St. Christopher Catholic Church, Indianapolis, Inc., Indianapolis, IN
Shikaputo, Rev. Victor S., *P.S.S.* '94 (BAL) [MON] Society of St. Sulpice, Province of the United States, Baltimore, MD
Shikina, Rev. Edward, '18 (COL) Immaculate Conception, Kenton, OH; Our Lady of Lourdes, Ada, OH
Shillcox, Rev. Timothy D., *O.Praem.* '87 (GB) [MON] St. Norbert Abbey, De Pere, WI
Shimek, Rev. Joseph J., '07 (MIL) On Sick Leave.
Shimkus, Rev. John Martin, *O.S.B.* '03 (DET) [MON] St. Benedict Monastery, Oxford, MI; [SEM] St. Benedict Monastery, House of Formation, Oxford, MI
Shimotsu, Rev. John M., '94 (ORG) St. Anne Church, Seal Beach, CA
Shin, Rev. Ignatius Mary, *C.F.R.* (NY) [MIS] St. Anthony Shelter for Renewal, Bronx, NY; [MON] St. Crispin Friary, Bronx, NY
Shin, Rev. Stephen, *O.F.M.Cap.* '90 (ALT) Chap, Sacramental Min, State Corr Inst, Somerset SS. Philip and James, Meyersdale, PA; St. John the Baptist, New Baltimore, PA
Shine, Rev. Daniel P., '15 (LFT) St. Ann, Kewanna, IN; St. Anne, Monterey, IN; St. Francis Solano, Francesville, IN; St. Joseph, Rochester, IN; St. Joseph, Star City, IN; St. Peter, Winamac, IN
Shine, Rev. Edward J., '57 (CIN) Retired. St. John the Baptist, Harrison, OH
Shine, Rev. John V., *C.M.* '63 (STL) Retired. [MON] Congregation of the Mission, Perryville, MO
Shinney, Rev. Robert J., *S.J.* '68 (SJ) Bellarmine College Preparatory, San Jose, CA; [MON] Sacred Heart Jesuit Center, Los Gatos, CA
Shinseki, Rev. Kyle, (LAN) St. Mary Student Parish Ann Arbor, Ann Arbor, MI; [CAM] St. Mary Student Parish, Ann Arbor, MI; [MON] USA Midwest Province of the Society of Jesus - Jesuit Residence, Ann Arbor, MI
Shinsky, Friar Felix, *O.F.M.Cap.* (COS) [MON] Our Lady of the Angels Friary, Colorado Springs, CO
Shipp, Rev. Edmund N., '61 (SFR) Retired.
Shipps, Rev. Bede, *O.P.* '85 (WDC) St. Dominic Church & Priory, Washington, DC
Shireman, Rev. Matthew, '18 (STP) Sacred Heart, Rush City, MN; St. Gregory the Great, North Branch, MN
Shirima, Rev. Chrispin, *O.F.M.Cap.* '16 (MIL) [MON] St. Lawrence Friary, Mount Calvary, WI; [SEM] St. Lawrence Seminary High School, Mount Calvary, WI
Shirley, Rev. Msgr. Richard, '67 (CC) Retired.
Shirley, Rev. Ron, '73 (MRY) Retired. Cathedral of San Carlos Borromeo, Monterey, CA
Shirley, Rev. Ronald, '73 (MRY) Retired.
Shiverski, Rev. John J., '68 (MAR) Retired. Curia: Offices and Directors
Shkumbatyuk, Rev. Ivan, '09 (STN) St. Constantine, Minneapolis, MN
Shkumbatyuk, Rev. Ivan, '09 (STN) Curia: Offices and Directors
Shkyndya, Rev. Mykhaylo, (PRM) St. Athanasius Church, Indianapolis, IN
Shmaruk, Rev. Richard J., '65 (BO) Retired.
Shnob, Rev. Alan D., '78 (OG) Retired. Curia: Canonical Services The Church of Saint Mary of Champlain, Champlain, NY
Shoback, Rev. Thomas P., '77 (SCR) On Administrative Leave.
Shockey, Rev. Benjamin D., '04 (WCH) St. Bridget of Sweden, Lindsborg, KS; St. Joseph, McPherson, KS
Shocklee, Very Rev. Christopher R., '09 (LFT) Curia: Leadership; Miscellaneous / Other Offices St. Joan of Arc, Kokomo, IN; St. Patrick, Kokomo, IN; [MIS] Hamilton County Catholic High School Corporation (St. Theodore Guerin High School; Guerin Catholic High School), Noblesville, IN
Shoemaker, Very Rev. David M., '00 (MOB) Ventress Corr Inst & Bullock Cty Corr Fac, Eufaula Curia: Leadership Holy Redeemer Parish, Eufaula, Eufaula, AL; St. Pius X Parish, Union Springs, AL
Shoemaker, Rev. Thomas, '90 (FTW) Curia: Offices and Directors St. Charles Borromeo, Fort Wayne, IN
Shoemaker, Rev. Victor, *C.S.J.* '03 (LAR) [MON] Congregation of St. John, Laredo, TX
Shoffner, Rev. Mark H, '19 (JKS) Curia: (>BLX) Advisory Boards, Commissions, Committees, and Councils St. John the Evangelist, Oxford, MS; [CAM] Ole Miss Campus Ministries, Oxford, MS
Shofner, Rev. Christopher L., '05 (STP) St. Anne, Le Sueur, MN; [CEM] Calvary Cemetery, Le Sueur, MN; [CEM] St. Anne Cemetery, Le Sueur, MN; [CEM] St. Thomas Cemetery, Le Sueur, MN
Sholander, Rev. Anthony E., *S.J.* '84 (SJ) [MON] Jesuit Community at Santa Clara University, Inc., Santa Clara, CA; [MON] USA West Province, Society of Jesus, Los Gatos, CA
Shoni, Rev. Bassim, '05 (OLD) On Leave.
Shonis, Rev. Anthony J., '71 (OWN) Retired. Curia: Advisory Boards, Commissions, Committees, and Councils
Shooner, Rev. Jeffrey P., '04 (L) Curia: Leadership; Offices and Directors St. Boniface, Louisville, KY; St. Patrick, Louisville, KY
Short, Rev. John W., '99 (SFS) All Saints Parish of Spink County, Mellette, SD; Saint Bernard Parish of Spink County, Redfield, SD
Short, Very Rev. Peter M., '82 (GLP) Curia: Leadership; Offices and Directors Madre de Dios, Winslow, AZ; St. Joseph's, Winslow, AZ
Shorter, Rev. Melvin, *C.P.* '86 (PMB) [MON] Our Lady

of Florida Spiritual Center, North Palm Beach, FL
Shorter, Rev. Melvin, *C.P.* '86 (NY) [MON] The Congregation of the Passion - St. Paul of the Cross Province, Jamaica, NY
Shott, Rev. Stephen E., *O.S.F.S.* (PH) St. Thomas the Apostle, Glen Mills, PA
Shoup, Rev. Steven L., '84 (CIN) St. Boniface, Piqua, OH; St. Patrick, Troy, OH; St. Teresa of the Infant Jesus, Covington, OH; Transfiguration, West Milton, OH
Shovelain, Rev. Paul J., '14 (STP) Curia: Leadership St. John the Baptist, New Brighton, MN; [CEM] St. John the Baptist Cemetery, New Brighton, MN
Showalter, Rev. Msgr. Paul E., '66 (PEO) Retired. Curia: Consultative Bodies
Showers, Rev. Andrew J., '17 (MAD) All Saints Catholic Congregation, Berlin, WI
Showers, Rev. Robert G., *O.F.M.Conv.* '16 (FTW) (>IND) St. Joseph University Parish, Terre Haute, IN
Showfety, Rev. Msgr. Joseph, '55 (CHL) Retired.
Showraiah, Rev. Bala, *OFM* (NSH) St. Catherine, McMinnville, TN
Shreenan, Rev. Timothy J., *O.F.M.* '84 (HRT) St. Patrick and St. Anthony Roman Catholic Church Corporation, Hartford, CT; [MON] St. Patrick-St. Anthony Friary (Franciscan Friars), Hartford, CT
Shreve, Rev. Msgr. Thomas F., '61 (RIC) Retired. Chap, St Francis Hosp, Midlothian
Shroff, Rev. Gaurav Manu, '13 (ATL) Our Lady of Perpetual Help Catholic Church, Carrollton, Inc., Carrollton, GA; [CAM] University of West Georgia, Carrollton, GA
Shrum, Rev. Jack D., '08 (SEA) (>P) [MON] Mt. Angel Abbey, Saint Benedict, OR
Shubeck, Rev. Thomas, '21 (PSC) St. Thomas the Apostle, Rahway, NJ
Shuda, Rev. Paul R., '60 (HBG) Retired. Curia: Offices and Directors
Shuey, Very Rev. Archpriest Mark, '07 (SJP) Curia: Leadership; Offices and Directors St. John the Theologian Ukrainian Catholic Mission, Martinez, GA; St. Sophia Ukrainian Catholic Church, Garner, NC
Shugrue, Rev. Msgr. Michael P., '66 (R) Retired.
Shugrue, Rev. Msgr. Timothy J., '73 (NEW) Curia: Advisory Boards, Commissions, Committees, and Councils St. Michael, Cranford, NJ
Shuler, Rev. Thomas Benjamin, '13 (ATL) Retired.
Shuley, Rev. Keith, *C.C.* '92 (CC) Command Chap, US Merchant Marine Acad, Kings Point, NY (>SD) Pastor of Sacred Heart Catholic Parish, San Diego, a corporation sole, San Diego, CA
Shuping, Rev. Kenneth J., '03 (RIC) St. Bridget, Richmond, VA
Shurtleff, Rev. F. James, '66 (OG) Retired. St. Mary's Church, Ogdensburg, Ogdensburg, NY
Shuter, Very Rev. Alex, '91 (PSC) Curia: Leadership Ascension of Our Lord, Williamsburg, VA
Shutt, Rev. Paul-Alexander, *O.S.B.* '98 (GBG) [MON] Saint Vincent Archabbey, Latrobe, PA
Shutt OSB, Rev. Paul-Alexander, *O.S.B.* '98 (PBR) Curia: Leadership St. Mary, Latrobe, PA
Shuttleworth, Very Rev. Edward J., '90 (LC) Curia: Leadership St. Bronislava, Plover, WI; [EFT] St. Bronislava Parish, Plover Endowment Trust, Plover, WI
Shuyaka, Rev. Albert, '11 (WDC) [HOS] Medstar Georgetown University Hospital, Washington, DC
Shyshka, Rev. Peter, '12 (STF) Curia: Leadership; Offices and Directors St. George, New York, NY
Sia, Rev. Joseph M., '08 (DAV) St. Patrick Church of Iowa City, Iowa, Iowa City, IA
Sia, Rev. Joshua, '17 (SAC) Curia: Leadership Pastor of Our Lady of the Snows Parish, Lake Almanor, a corporation sole, Lake Almanor, CA
Sialo, Rev. Christopher Matumbai, *F.M.H.* '16 (MOB) Prince of Peace Parish, Mobile, Mobile, AL
Sianturi, Rev. Kosman, *OSC* '04 (PHX) [MON] Crosier Community of Phoenix (Canons Regular of the Order of the Holy Cross) (Conventual Priory of the Holy Cross), Phoenix, AZ
Siasa, Friar Andrew, *ALCP/OSS* (PIT) St. James, Washington, PA
Sibel, Rev. John J., '72 (PH) Retired. Chap, Southeastern Pennsylvania Veterans Ctr, Spring City
Sibenik, Rev. Simeon B., '81 (PBR) Retired.
Siberski, Rev. John R., *S.J.* '07 (BO) [MON] The Jesuit Community at Boston College, Chestnut Hill, MA
Sibilano, Rev. Joseph D., *O.S.J.* '65 (SCR) [SEM] St. Joseph's Oblate Seminary, Pittston, PA
Sibirnyy, Rev. Volodymyr, (NY) St. Michael Chapel, New York, NY
Sibley, Rev. Bryce, '00 (LAF) (>NO) [SEM] Notre Dame Seminary Graduate School of Theology, New Orleans, LA
Sibugan, Rev. Ronald, *A.A.* (ELP) St. Francis Xavier, El Paso, TX
Sicard, Rev. Kenneth, *O.P.* '90 (PRO) [COL] Providence College, Providence, RI; [MON] St. Thomas Aquinas Priory at Providence College, Providence, RI
Sicari, Rev. Msgr. Joseph J., '82 (BUF) Retired. [MON] O'Hara Residence, Tonawanda, NY
Siceloff, Rev. John C., '04 (MET) Our Lady of Perpetual Help, Bernardsville, NJ
Sichko, Rev. James W., '98 (LEX) On Special Assignment. Papal Missionary of Mercy/Evangelization
Siciliano, Rev. Donald E., '93 (CIN) Our Lady of the Visitation, Cincinnati, OH; St. Joseph, North Bend, OH; St. Jude the Apostle, Cincinnati, OH
Siciliano, Rev. Jude, *O.P.* '69 (DAL) [MON] Dominican Priory of St. Albert the Great and Novitiate, Irving, TX
Sickler, Rev. Robert, *M.S.A.* '87 (NOR) [MON] Society of the Missionaries of the Holy Apostles, Cromwell, CT; [SEM] Holy Apostles College and Seminary, Cromwell, CT
Sickler, Rev. Thomas, *M.S.* '73 (NOR) Retired. St. James, Danielson, CT
Sickler, Rev. Thomas G., *M.S.* '73 (HRT) [MIS] Missionaries of LaSalette, Hartford, CT
Siconolfi, Rev. Msgr. Constantine V., '59 (SCR) Retired.
Siconolfi, Rev. Thomas, *C.Ss.R.* '70 (HBG) [MON] St. Clement's Mission House, Ephrata, PA
Sida, Rev. Ramon, '20 (JOL) St. Mary Immaculate, Plainfield, IL
Sidawi, Rev. Ramzi, *OFM* '02 (WDC) [MON] Commissariat of the Holy Land, Franciscan Monastery - Mount St. Sepulchre, Washington, DC; [MON] Franciscan Monastery USA Inc., Washington, DC
Sidler, Rev. Jack, '14 (LR) Christ the King, Fort Smith, AR
Sidney, Rev. Walter, *S.J.* '78 (LAF) [MON] St. Charles College, Grand Coteau, LA; [RTR] Jesuit Spirituality Center (St. Charles College), Grand Coteau, LA
Sidney, Rev. Walter T., *S.J.* '78 (STL) De Smet Jesuit High School, Creve Coeur, MO
Siebenaler, Rev. John M., '61 (STP) Retired.
Siebenaler, Rev. Martin, '59 (STP) Retired.
Siebenand, Rev. Paul Alcuin, '60 (LA) Retired.
Sieber, Rev. Patrick K, *OFM* '71 (PH) [MON] Order of Friars Minor of the Province of the Most Holy Name, Philadelphia, PA
Siebert, Rev. Edward J., *S.J.* '97 (LA) [MIS] Loyola Productions, Inc., Los Angeles, CA; [MON] Jesuit Community, Los Angeles, CA
Siebert, Rev. Paul S., '86 (E) St. Mark, Emporium, PA
Siebert, Rev. Stephen A., '94 (DEN) Our Lady of Peace Silverthorne, Silverthorne, CO
Siebert, Rev. William P., '81 (DET) Retired.
Siebold, Rev. Martin, (LR) Curia: Leadership; Offices and Directors St. Jude the Apostle, Jacksonville, AR
Sieczynski, Rev. Jerzy, '00 (SAT) Retired.
Siedlarz, Rev. Jozef K, *SCH* (CHI) St. Ladislaus, Chicago, IL
Siefer, Rev. Msgr. Richard, (E) [CAM] Penn State University - DuBois Campus, DuBois, PA
Siefer, Rev. Msgr. Richard R., '75 (E) Curia: Leadership Assumption of Blessed Virgin Mary, Sykesville, PA; St. Bernard, Falls Creek, PA; St. Catherine of Siena, Du Bois, PA; St. Mary, Reynoldsville, PA; St. Michael, Du Bois, PA
Sieg, Rev. Leslie, '76 (P) Retired.
Sieg, Friar Robert Charles, *OFM* '75 (STL) [MIS] The Franciscan Connection, St. Louis, MO
Sieg, Rev. Thomas H., '71 (STP) Retired.
Siegert, Rev. Johannes S.A.G., '08 (BRK) Visitation of the Blessed Virgin Mary, Brooklyn, NY; [MIS] Federation of Oases of Koinonia John the Baptist, Brooklyn, NY
Siegman, Rev. Matthew, '19 (WCH) Church of Blessed Sacrament, Wichita, KS
Siekierski, Msgr. John J., '67 (GRY) Retired. Curia: Leadership St. Stanislaus Roman Catholic Church, East Chicago, IN
Sielicki, Rev. Tomasz, '78 (JOL) Holy Cross, Joliet, IL; St. Mary Nativity, Joliet, IL
Siemianowski, Rev. John S., '89 (CHI) Curia: Offices and Directors St. Juliana, Chicago, IL
Siendo, Rev. Ralph D., '97 (NEW) Our Lady of Victories, Jersey City, NJ
Siepka, Rev. Msgr. Richard W., '82 (BUF) Blessed Mother Teresa of Calcutta (dba Saint Mother Teresa of Calcutta), Depew, NY; Our Lady of Pompeii, Lancaster, NY; St. Mary of the Assumption, Lancaster, NY; St. Philip the Apostle, Cheektowaga, NY; [SEM] Christ the King Seminary, East Aurora, NY
Siepker, Rev. Daniel E., '93 (DM) Our Lady of the Holy Rosary, Glenwood, IA
Sierotowicz, Rev. Felicjan, '90 (ROC) Catholic Community of the Blessed Trinity, Clyde, NY; St. Joseph the Worker Roman Catholic Parish, Wayne County, Clyde, NY; St. Michael, Newark, NY
Sierra, Rev. Angel, '80 (SFD) Forty Martyrs, Tuscola, IL; St. John the Baptist, Arcola, IL
Sierra, Rev. Elkin, '19 (MIA) St. Louis, Pinecrest, FL
Sierra, Rev. Luis Fermin, '03 (DAL) Immaculate Conception Catholic Parish - Grand Prairie, Grand Prairie, TX
Sierra, Rev. Rolando A., '99 (LA) Our Lady of Guadalupe, Guadalupe, CA; St. John Neumann, Santa Maria, CA
Sierra, Rev. Victor A., '18 (WOR) Curia: Offices and Directors St. Mary of the Assumption, Milford, MA
Sierra-Posada, Rev. Pedro J., '76 (ALX) Retired.
Sierra-Ruiz, Rev. Daniel, '15 (ROC) Roman Catholic Parish of St. Frances Xavier Cabrini, Rochester, NY
Sievel, Rev. Thomas A., '78 (HRT) On Administrative Leave.
Siewiera, Rev. Bogdan, '98 (COS) St. Mary of the Rockies, Bailey, CO
Siffert, Rev. Etienne, *S.M.* '58 (SFR) Retired. [MON] Marist Center of the West, San Francisco, CA
Siffrin, Very Rev. Msgr. Robert J., '79 (Y) Curia: Leadership; Miscellaneous / Other Offices St. Columba Parish, Youngstown, OH; St. Edward, Youngstown, OH; [MIS] Conference of Slovak Clergy, Youngstown, OH
Sigarara, Rev. Ioane I., *M.S.C.* '91 (ALN) [MON] Sacred Heart Villa, Missionaries of the Sacred Heart, Center Valley, PA
Sigler, Rev. Gary, '79 (FTW) Retired.
Sigler, Rev. Gary L., '79 (FTW) Retired.
Sigler, Rev. John, *F.S.P.* '94 (LA) Chap, Hospital Chaplain, Cedars Sinai Med Ctr, Los Angeles
Sigman, Rev. Ambrose, *O.P.* '13 (OAK) [MON] Order of Preachers (Province of the Most Holy Name of Jesus - Western Dominican Province), Oakland, CA; [SEM] Dominican School of Philosophy and Theology, Berkeley, CA
Sigmund, Rev. Andrew J., '64 (STL) Retired. Our Lady of Sorrows Catholic Church, St. Louis, MO
Signalness, Rev. Jason R., '11 (BIS) Queen of the Most Holy Rosary, Stanley, ND; St. Ann, Berthold, ND
Signorelli, Rev. Francis, *S.X.* '59 (BO) [MIS] Our Lady of Fatima Shrine, Holliston, MA; [MON] Xaverian Missionaries, Holliston, MA
Siguenza, Rev. Edmundo Nachor, (GB) SS. Joseph & Edward, Porterfield, WI; St. Mary, Peshtigo, WI
Sigulenza, Rev. Francisco, *O.A.R.* '56 (NEW) [MON] Augustinian Recollects, St. Nicholas of Tolentine Monastery, Union City, NJ
Sigur, Rev. Joseph R, (BEA) Curia: Leadership St. Joseph, Port Arthur, TX
Siket, Rev. Bruce, '07 (PRT) Saint Paul the Apostle Parish, Bangor, ME
Sikon, Rev. Michael P., '96 (GBG) Curia: Offices and Directors St. Barbara, Harrison City, PA
Sikora, Rev. James, '67 (GF) Retired.
Sikora, Rev. Thomas More, *O.S.B.* '97 (GBG) [MON] Saint Vincent Archabbey, Latrobe, PA
Sikora, Rev. Thomas More, *O.S.B.* '97 (PIT) (>E) St. Mary, St. Marys, PA
Sikora, Rev. Thomas More, *OSB* '97 (GBG) [MON] Saint Vincent Archabbey, Latrobe, PA
Sikorski, Rev. Allan, '08 (RVC) St. Elizabeth Ann Seton, Lake Ronkonkoma, NY
Sikorski, Rev. Jeffery P., '73 (TOL) Retired.
Sikorski, Rev. Leszek, '97 (VEN) On Duty Outside Diocese. Chaplain, US Navy Curia: (>MO) Offices and Directors
Sikorski, Rev. Louis S., '64 (GAL) Retired.
Sikorsky, Rev. Charles, *L.C.* '02 (ARL) [COL] Divine Mercy University, Arlington, VA
Sila, Rev. Alexander, *S.V.D.* (SB) Queen of Angels, Riverside, CA
Sila, Rev. Alexander, *S.V.D.* '09 (LA) St. John the Evangelist, Los Angeles, CA
Silcox, Rev. John D., '95 (PH) Retired.
Sileika, Rev. Jonas, *O.F.M.* '06 (LIT) Curia: Clergy and Religious Services; Organizations (affiliated, inter-Diocesan, miscellaneous/other)
Sileo, Rev. Joseph R., '71 (WDC) Retired.
Siler, Rev. James, (GLD) Jesus the Good Shepherd of Atlanta, Atlanta, MI; Saint Augustine of Hillman, Hillman, MI
Siler, Rev. Paschal, *O.F.M.Cap.* '60 (GB) Retired.
Siler, Rev. Msgr. Robert M., '01 (YAK) Curia: Leadership; Offices and Directors
Siliako, Rev. Petelo, '86 (SPP) St. Peter Chanel-Sa'ilele, Pago Pago, AS
Siliako, Rev. Petelo, '86 (SPP) Church of St. Peter and

Paul, Pago Pago, AS
Silipigni, Rev. Stephan, (MO) Curia: Offices and Directors
Silipigni, Rev. Stephan A., '81 (PRO) Saint Madeleine's Church Corporation of Tiverton, Tiverton, RI; St. Catherine's Church Corporation, Little Compton, Little Compton, RI
Sill, Rev. Theodore K., '89 (COL) St. Matthew the Apostle Catholic Church & School, Gahanna, OH
Silloway, Very Rev. Michael, '10 (ATL) Curia: Leadership Christ Our King and Savior Catholic Church, Greensboro, Inc., Greensboro, GA
Silos, Rev. Gerardo, '07 (LAR) Sacred Heart, Crystal City, TX
Siluvai Rayan, Rev. Antony Jeya, (PRO) Chap, Rhode Island Hosp, Providence Saint Ann's Catholic Church of Providence, Rhode Island, Providence, RI
Siluvai Rayan, Rev. Christopher, '04 (P) St. Joseph, Salem, OR
Silva, Rev. Alvaro, (POD) Retired. Curia: Clergy and Religious Services
Silva, Rev. Bryan, *O.M.I.* '85 (SAT) [COL] Oblate School of Theology, San Antonio, TX; [MON] De Mazenod House, San Antonio, TX
Silva, Rev. Caesar, '74 (HT) Retired.
Silva, Rev. Eleazar, (SLC) St. Francis of Assisi LLC 221, Orem, UT
Silva, Rev. Eric, (BGP) High School Chaplain St. Pius X Corporation, Fairfield, CT
Silva, Rev. Eusebio F., '66 (MAN) Retired.
Silva, Rev. Francisco C. Martins, (BO) St. Anthony of Padua, Boston, MA
Silva, Very Rev. Frank J., '76 (BO) Curia: Leadership Holy Family, Concord, MA; St. Irene, Carlisle, MA; St. Margaret of Antioch, Burlington, MA
Silva, Rev. Frank J., '76 (BO) Curia: Clergy and Religious Services
Silva, Rev. Hilary, '89 (FRS) Sacred Heart, Fresno, CA
Silva, Rev. Ismael, '79 (ORG) Retired. La Purisima, Orange, CA
Silva, Very Rev. John A., '04 (MAD) All Saints Catholic Congregation, Berlin, WI; Our Lady of the Lake, Green Lake, WI
Silva, Rev. Juan, '92 (LA) St. Odilia, Los Angeles, CA
Silva, Very Rev. Langes J., '95 (SLC) Curia: Leadership; Offices and Directors
Silva, Rev. Luis, '98 (CR) On Duty Outside Diocese.
Silva, Rev. Martin O., *SJ* '15 (SJ) Most Holy Trinity, San Jose, CA
Silva, Rev. Miguel J., '84 (SAC) Pastor of St. Christopher Parish, Galt, a corporation sole, Galt, CA
Silva, Rev. Nalaka, *O.M.I.* '03 (MET) Nativity of Our Lord, Monroe Township, NJ
Silva, Rev. Paul, *L.C.* (GRY) Sacred Heart Apostolic School, Inc., Rolling Prairie, IN
Silva, Rev. Raul, '06 (NEW) On Duty Outside Diocese. Queen of Angels Church, Austin, MN
Silva, Rev. Raul, *MSC* '79 (LA) Sagrado Corazon y Santa Maria de Guadalupe, Cudahy, CA
Silva, Very Rev. Raul I., '06 (WIN) Curia: Advisory Boards, Commissions, Committees, and Councils; Offices and Directors Queen of Angels, Austin, MN; [CEM] Calvary Cemetery, Austin, MN
Silva, Rev. Msgr. Robert J., '65 (STO) Retired. Our Lady of Fatima Church (Pastor of), Modesto, CA
Silva, Rev. Rolando, '06 (GLD) Saint Ignatius of Loyola of Rogers City, Rogers City, MI
Silva, Rev. Shaji, '08 (PH) Curia: Evangelization Corpus Christi, Lansdale, PA
Silva, Rev. Thiago Ferreira, *O.S.B.* (KCK) [MON] St. Benedict's Abbey, Atchison, KS
Silva, Rev. Victor T., '07 (PRO) On Administrative Leave. Church of Christ the King, West Warwick, West Warwick, RI; Saint Anthony's Church Corporation, River Point, West Warwick, RI
Silva Cervantes, Rev. Luis, '20 (NY) St. Raymond, Bronx, NY
Silva González, Rev. Jaime, (PCE) Nuestra Senora de la Monserrate, Jayuya, PR
Silva Ortega, Rev. Jesus, *CMH* '87 (LA) St. Mary of the Assumption, Santa Maria, CA
Silva_Bisbal, Friar Pedro Juan, *OFM Cap* '75 (SJN) [MON] Fraternidad San Antonio, San Juan, PR
Silvadasan, Rev. Xavier, *H.G.N.* '10 (FWT) Our Lady of Guadalupe, Morgan, TX; Our Lady of Guadalupe, Wichita Falls, TX
Silveira, Rev. Antonio, '13 (SJ) Five Wounds Portuguese National Church, San Jose, CA
Silveira, Rev. Eduino T., '87 (SAC) Pastor of Our Lady of the Assumption Parish, Carmichael, a corporation sole, Carmichael, CA
Silver, Rev. Jeffrey P., '84 (CIN) Queen of Peace, Hamilton, OH; St. Aloysius, Hamilton, OH
Silveri, Rev. Donato P., '64 (PH) Retired. St. Joseph, Spring City, PA
Silvey, Rev. Canon Bryan, *I.C.R.S.S.* '21 (TUC) [MIS] The Oratory of St. Gianna, Tucson, AZ
Silvey, Rev. Canon David, *I.C.* '16 (COL) [MIS] St. Leo the Great Oratory (Institute of Christ the King Sovereign Priest, Inc.), Columbus, OH
Silvia, Rev. Kenneth J., *CSC* (FTW) Retired. [MIS] Holy Cross House, Notre Dame, IN
Silvio Woo, Rev. Yong Kook, (WIL) Curia: Offices and Directors
Simango, Rev. Lucas K., '87 (CHY) Curia: Consultative Bodies St. James, Douglas, WY; St. Louis Catholic Church, Glenrock, WY
Simas, Very Rev. Jason, '15 (MRY) Curia: Deaneries
Simas, Rev. Jason J., '15 (MRY) St. Patrick, Watsonville, CA
Simas, Rev. Msgr. Manuel C., '61 (OAK) St. Joseph (Old Mission San Jose), Fremont, CA
Simas, Rev. Ryan J., '15 (PRO) Curia: Advisory Boards, Commissions, Committees, and Councils All Saints Parish, Woonsocket, RI; Saint Joseph's Church, Woonsocket, Woonsocket, RI; St. Charles Borromeo's Church, Woonsocket, RI, Woonsocket, RI; St. Raphael Academy, Pawtucket, RI
Simbula, Rev. Luca, '14 (DAL) Federal Corr Inst Seagoville, Seagoville St. Augustine Catholic Parish, Dallas, TX
Simburger, Rev. R. Joseph, '79 (SFD) Retired.
Simchock, Rev. Shawn M., '20 (SCR) Saint Faustina Kowalska Parish, Nanticoke, PA; St. Ignatius Loyola, Kingston, Kingston, PA
Simeon, Rev. Wisman, (PMB) St. Joseph, Stuart, FL
Simeon Raj, Rev. Vinner Raj, *H.G.N.* '12 (SEA) St. Joseph, Frances, WA; St. Lawrence, Raymond, WA; St. Mary, Seaview, WA
Simeone, Rev. Msgr. Gary F., '75 (HRT) Retired.
Simeone, Rev. Msgr. Ronald P., '82 (PRO) Curia: Leadership Saint Anthony's Church, Woonsocket, RI, Woonsocket, RI
Simien, Rev. Gregory M., '99 (LAF) Our Lady of Mercy, Opelousas, LA
Simington, Rev. Evan, (POC) Saint John Henry Newman, Irvine, CA
Simington, Rev. Msgr. Ralph P., '62 (DUB) Retired.
Simisky, Rev. Thomas M, *S.J.* '03 (R) St. Raphael the Archangel, Raleigh, NC; [MON] Jesuit Community, Raleigh, NC
Simko, Rev. James G., '91 (VEN) St. Joseph Parish in Bradenton, Inc., Bradenton, FL
Simmons, Rev. Jerome S., '68 (E) Retired. Sacred Heart, Erie, PA; [CON] Sisters of Saint Joseph of Northwestern Pennsylvania, Erie, PA
Simmons, Rev. Mark, '07 (BRK) Our Lady of Angels, Brooklyn, NY
Simmons, Rev. Matthew P., '03 (JKS) Curia: Canonical Services; Leadership St. Joseph, Gluckstadt, MS
Simo, Rev. Philip, *O.S.B.* '97 (WDC) Chap, Hosp & Nursing Home Min, Little Sisters of the Poor… [MON] St. Anselm's Abbey, Washington, DC
Simoes, Rev. Pedro Camilo, *S.A.C.* (SP) St. Luke the Evangelist, Palm Harbor, FL
Simon, Rev. Akan S., '98 (RCK) Holy Family, Rockford, IL
Simon, Rev. Brian, '96 (SFS) Sacred Heart Parish of Potter County, Gettysburg, SD; Saint Pius X Parish of Sully County, Onida, SD
Simon, Rev. Carl, '71 (LAN) Retired.
Simon, Rev. Msgr. Joseph M., '71 (STL) St. Gabriel the Archangel Catholic Church, St. Louis, MO
Simon, Rev. Richard T., '75 (CHI) Retired.
Simon, Rev. Robert J., '90 (SCR) Our Lady Queen of Peace, Gilbert, PA
Simon, Rev. Thomas, *M.S.A.* '79 (NOR) [MON] Society of the Missionaries of the Holy Apostles, Cromwell, CT
Simonar, Very Rev. Mathew J., '97 (GB) Curia: Advisory Boards, Commissions, Committees, and Councils Nativity of Our Lord, Green Bay, WI
Simonds, Rev. Donald D., *M.S.* '63 (HRT) [MIS] Missionaries of LaSalette, Hartford, CT
Simonds, Rev. Thomas A., *S.J.* '99 (OM) [MON] Jesuit Community at Creighton University, Omaha, NE
Simone, Rev. Anthony, (CLV) St. Aloysius - St. Agatha, Cleveland, OH; St. Jerome, Cleveland, OH
Simone, Rev. Earl Francis, '77 (CIN) Retired.
Simone, Rev. Michael, *S.J.* '07 (BO) (>CHI) [COL] Jesuit Community at Loyola University Chicago, Chicago, IL
Simone, Rev. Michael R, *SJ* (CHI) Old St. Patrick's, Chicago, IL
Simoneau, Rev. Norman J., '67 (MAN) Retired.
Simoneau, Rev. Roland L., '78 (PRO) Retired.
Simoneaux, Rev. Jody, '82 (LAF) On Administrative Leave.
Simonetti, Rev. David J., '05 (CHI) Christ Our Light Parish, Chicago, IL
Simons, Rev. Derek, *S.V.D.* '70 (CHI) [MON] Divine Word Residence, Techny, IL
Simons, Rev. James L., '00 (CIN) Retired.
Simons, Friar Matthew, *T.O.R.* '20 (ALT) [MON] Sacred Heart Friary, Loretto, PA
Simons, Rev. Thomas G., '77 (GR) Retired.
Simonsen, Rev. Troy K., '13 (FAR) St. Arnold's Church of Milnor, Milnor, ND; St. John the Baptist Church of Wyndmere, Wyndmere, ND
Simpson, Rev. Brian L., '72 (CHI) Retired.
Simpson, Rev. David, *O.Carm.* '70 (KCK) Retired. St. Boniface, Garnett, KS; St. Therese, Richmond, KS
Simpson, Rev. Gary, (LEX) [CAM] St. Clare Church-Berea College, Berea, KY
Simpson, Rev. Gary, '13 (LEX) St. Clare, Berea, KY
Simpson, Rev. Kenneth C., '78 (CHI) Curia: Offices and Directors
Simpson, Rev. Mark, '19 (NSH) Holy Family, Brentwood, TN
Simpson, Rev. Robert, '65 (RNO) Retired.
Sims, Rev. John Dominic, *O.P.* '04 (NO) (>MEM) St. Peter Church, Memphis, TN
Sims, Friar John Dominic, *O.P.* '04 (MEM) [MIS] The Dominican Friars of Memphis, Inc. (St. Peter Dominican Community), Memphis, TN
Sims, Rev. Robert W., '71 (IND) Curia: Offices and Directors Immaculate Heart of Mary Catholic Church, Indianapolis, Inc., Indianapolis, IN
Simutonga, Rev. Victor, *P.S.S.* (BAL) [MON] Society of St. Sulpice, Province of the United States, Baltimore, MD
Simutowe, Rev. Patrick, *P.S.S.* '96 (BAL) [MON] Society of St. Sulpice, Province of the United States, Baltimore, MD
Sina, Rev. Scott, '14 (ARL) St. Mary of the Immaculate Conception, Fredericksburg, VA
Sinaga, Rev. Masco S., *S.J.* '12 (CI) St. Joseph, Colonia, Yap, FM
Sinatra, Rev. Robert L., '04 (CAM) Curia: Leadership; Tribunal St. Padre Pio Parish, Vineland, N.J., Vineland, NJ
Sinatra, Rev. William D., '64 (DET) Retired.
Singarayar, Rev. James, (BR) Congregation Of Holy Family Roman Catholic Church, Port Allen, LA
Singarayar, Rev. Philip, *O.M.I.* '64 (OAK) Sacred Heart, Oakland, CA
Singareddy, Rev. Prabhakar, '12 (MAD) St. Stephen, Clinton, WI
Singareddy, Rev. Shobhan, (BIR) St. Francis of Assisi, Talladega, AL; St. Jude, Sylacauga, AL
Singelyn, Rev. Robert K., '60 (DET) Retired.
Singer, Rev. Christopher J., (E) [SEM] St. Mark Seminary, Erie, PA
Singer, Rev. Christopher J., '03 (E) Curia: Clergy and Religious Services; Leadership; Miscellaneous / Other Offices; Offices and Directors [ASN] St. Thomas More Society, Erie, PA; [MIS] Bishop Michael J. Murphy Residence for Retired Priests, Erie, PA
Singler, Rev. Msgr. Charles E., '84 (TOL) Holy Family, Miller City, OH; St. Nicholas, Miller City, OH; St. Rose, Perrysburg, OH
Singler, Rev. James E., '82 (CLV) Immaculate Heart of Mary, Cuyahoga Falls, OH
Singler, Rev. John P., '82 (CLV) St. Mary, Berea, OH
Singleton, Rev. Jeremiah, '65 (MIA) Retired.
Singson, Rev. Celso, (SJ) Queen of Apostles, San Jose, CA
Sinisi, Rev. Daniel, (ALT) [MON] St. Francis Friary at Mount Assisi, Loretto, PA
Sinkler, Rev. Michael, '81 (LR) Retired.
Sinnappan, Rev. Selvaraj, '97 (TYL) St. Francis of the Tejas, Crockett, TX
Sinnott, Rev. Andrew R., '99 (SCR) Retired.
Sinor, Rev. Michael, '88 (SD) Curia: Advisory Boards, Commissions, Committees, and Councils; Offices and Directors [SEM] The Roman Catholic Seminary of San Diego, San Diego, CA
Siok, Rev. Slawomir, *SAC* '90 (COL) St. Aloysius, Columbus, OH; St. Mary Magdalene, Columbus, OH
Sioleti, Rev. Andrew, *I.V.Dei.* '84 (MO) Curia: Offices and Directors
Sioleti, Rev. Andrew, *I.V.Dei.* '05 (NY) Military Chap - NY Harbor Heathcare-NYC and Brooklyn
Siordia, Rev. Oscar O., '06 (BWN) St. Joseph, Brownsville, TX; [MIS] Movimiento Familiar Cristiano: Federacion Brownsville, Brownsville, TX
Sipe, Rev. Robert J., '59 (STP) Retired.
Sipitowski, Rev. James A., (SPR) Retired.
Siple, Rev. Donald M., *O.S.M.* '92 (CHI) [MON] Order of Friar Servants of Mary (Servites) United States of America Province, Inc., Chicago, IL

Siple, Rev. William P., '92 (PIT) Christ the King, Pittsburgh, PA
Sipo, Rev. Ankido, '15 (SPA) Curia: Leadership
Sippel, Rev. Bernard S., '65 (MIL) Retired. Curia: Leadership
Sippel, Rev. Edward F., '47 (MIL) Retired.
Siqueira, Rev. Leandro Freitas, '21 (MIA) St. Augustine, Coral Gables, FL
Siracuse, Rev. Guy F., '67 (BUF) Retired.
Siranni, Rev. Anthony, '89 (MET) Curia: Consultative Bodies
Sirba, Rev. Joseph A., '87 (DUL) Curia: Leadership St. Luke, Sandstone, MN; St. Patrick, Hinckley, MN
Sirianni, Rev. Anthony M., '89 (MET) Curia: Consultative Bodies St. Helena, Edison, NJ
Sirianni, Rev. Klaus J., '78 (WDC) Chap, Hosp & Nursing Home Ministry, George Washington Univ... St. Stephen Martyr, Washington, DC
Sirianni, Rev. Louis A., '74 (ROC) Curia: Tribunal St. Mark, Rochester, NY
Sirianni, Rev. Richard, '78 (P) Retired.
Sirianni, Rev. Msgr. Sam A., '84 (TR) Curia: Leadership Co-Cathedral of St. Robert Bellarmine, Freehold, NJ
Sirico, Rev. Robert A., '89 (GR) Retired. Sacred Heart of Jesus, Grand Rapids, MI
Sirvent, Rev. Francisco, '88 (PCE) Retired. On Leave.
Sisam, Rev. Kaster, '16 (CI) Immaculate Heart of Mary Cathedral, Chuuk, FM; [MON] Vicariate Residence, Tunnuk, Chuuk, FM
Sisco, Rev. Michael A., '97 (PRO) Saint Mary's Church, Cranston, Cranston, RI
Sisneros, Rev. Adrian, '22 (SFE) Estancia Valley Catholic Parish, Moriarty, NM
Sison, Rev. Alden J., '87 (LA) St. Euphrasia, Granada Hills, CA
Sison, Rev. Antonio, *C.P.P.S.* (CHI) [SEM] Catholic Theological Union, Chicago, IL
Sison, Rev. Dave Thomas N., '04 (NEW) St. Anthony of Padua, Newark, NJ
Sison, Rev. Ronnie, '03 (VEN) Our Lady of Grace Parish in Avon Park, Inc., Avon Park, FL
Sistare, Rev. Brian M., '03 (PRO) The Church of St. John the Baptist of Pawtucket Rhode Island, Pawtucket, RI; The Church of the Immaculate Conception of Pawtucket, Rhode Island, Pawtucket, RI
Sistare, Rev. John A., (PRO) On Leave.
Sisul, Rev. Paul, *C.M.* '72 (STL) [MON] Congregation of the Mission Vincentian Fathers Lazarist Residence, St. Louis, MO
Sitko, Rev. Joseph S., '68 (SCR) Retired. On Special Assignment. St. Mary, Waymart, PA
Sitto, Rev. Bashar, '12 (EST) Curia: Leadership; Offices and Directors
Sitzmann, Rev. Eugene E., '62 (SC) Retired. Immaculate Conception, Cherokee, IA
Sitzmann, Rev. Richard A., '62 (SC) Retired.
Siu, Rev. Peter K., *S.J.* (SJ) [MON] USA West Province, Society of Jesus, Los Gatos, CA
Siva, Rev. Renier C., '11 (SAC) Curia: Leadership Pastor of St. John the Baptist Parish, Folsom, a corporation sole, Folsom, CA
Sivalon, Rev. John C., *M.M.* '75 (NY) Retired. [MON] Maryknoll Fathers and Brothers (Catholic Foreign Mission Society of America, Inc.), Ossining, NY
Sivinskyi, Rev. Vasyl, '92 (PHU) SS. Peter and Paul, Baltimore, MD; St. Michael's, Baltimore, MD
Siwek, Rev. Daniel S., '73 (CHI) Retired. [SEM] University of Saint Mary of the Lake/Mundelein Seminary, Mundelein, IL
Siwinski, Rev. Norbert M., *O.F.M.Conv.* '04 (BGP) The Church of St. Michael, Archangel Bridgeport, Bridgeport, CT
Sixon, Rev. Noel, (RVC) St. Patrick's, Huntington, NY
Sixtus, Rev. Chudy Peter, '13 (LSC) Our Lady of Perpetual Help, Mesquite, NM
Sizemore, Rev. David, (COL) St. Francis de Sales, Newark, OH
Sjoquist, Rev. Bradley S., '15 (MAR) Curia: Advisory Boards, Commissions, Committees, and Councils; Offices and Directors St. Joseph, Sault Sainte Marie, MI; [CAM] Lake Superior State University, Newman Center, Sault Sainte Marie, MI
Skagen, Rev. Robert, '70 (PHX) Retired.
Skaja, Rev. Thomas, (SCL) Church of Saint Henry, Perham, Perham, MN; Church of the Sacred Heart, Dent, MN; Holy Cross, Butler, MN; St. Lawrence, Perham, MN
Skalsky, Rev. Ted A., '72 (DOD) Retired. Curia: Offices and Directors St. Joseph Catholic Church of Greensburg, Kansas, Greensburg, KS
Skamai, Rev. Thomas, *C.O.* '22 (PIT) [CAM] Carnegie-Mellon University, Pittsburgh, PA; [CAM] Chatham College, Pittsburgh, PA; [CAM] University of Pittsburgh, Pittsburgh, PA; [MON] Congregation of the Oratory of St. Philip Neri, Pittsburgh, PA
Skaria, Rev. Antony, *C.F.I.C.* '96 (SYM) St. Alphonsa Syro-Malabar Catholic Church Minnesota, Richfield, MN
Skaria, Rev. Antony, *C.F.I.C.* '96 (STP) Curia: Leadership St. John Vianney, South St. Paul, MN; St. Matthew, St. Paul, MN; [MON] Congregation of the Sons of the Immaculate Conception, Bloomington, MN
Skehan, Rev. John A., '52 (PMB) Retired.
Skeldon, Very Rev. John Robert, '00 (FWT) Curia: Leadership St. Patrick Cathedral, Fort Worth, TX
Skelly, Rev. Francis, *C.Ss.R.* '72 (BRK) Our Lady of Perpetual Help Basilica, Brooklyn, NY
Skenderovic, Rev. Ivan, '76 (BUF) St. Raphael, Niagara Falls, NY
Skeris, Rev. Robert A., '61 (MIL) Retired.
Skerl, Rev. Alphonse, '55 (GRY) Retired.
Skerry, Rev. Donald, *SVD* (CHI) Retired.
Skillman, Rev. David P., '09 (STL) St. Patrick Catholic Church, Wentzville, MO
Skindeleski, Rev. Canon Thomas J., '71 (PMB) Curia: Organizations (affiliated, inter-Diocesan, miscellaneous/other)
Skirtich, Rev. John W., '90 (PIT) Curia: Consultative Bodies Our Lady of Hope, Bethel Park, PA
Sklar, Rev. Louis E., '01 (ALX) St. Michael, Kleinwood, LA; St. Peter, Bordelonville, LA
Skluzacek, Rev. Michael C., '80 (STP) St. Wenceslaus, New Prague, MN
Skoblow, Rev. David V., '15 (MET) Curia: Family Life Our Lady of Mount Virgin, Middlesex, NJ
Skoneki, Rev. Msgr. William J., '87 (MOB) Cathedral-Basilica of the Immaculate Conception Parish, Mobile, Mobile, AL; [MIS] Camp Cullen, Inc., Mobile, AL
Skoneki, Rev. Msgr. William J., '87 (MOB) Curia: Leadership; Offices and Directors; Organizations (affiliated, inter-Diocesan, miscellaneous/other) [MIS] The Portier House, Mobile, AL
Skonezny, Rev. Raymond, '61 (ORG) Retired.
Skonseng, Rev. Msgr. Dennis A., '82 (FAR) Curia: Leadership St. Rose of Lima's Church of Hillsboro, Hillsboro, ND; St. William's Church of Argusville, Argusville, ND
Skorka, Rev. Terence, *C.P.* (NY) [MON] The Congregation of the Passion - St. Paul of the Cross Province, Jamaica, NY
Skorup, Rev. Ildephonse, *OFM* (GB) Retired.
Skotek, Rev. Thomas D., (SCR) On Administrative Leave.
Skowera, Rev. Dennis, (SPR) St. Anne's, Chicopee, MA
Skowron, Rev. Greg, '89 (JOL) St. Mary, Park Forest, IL
Skowron, Rev. Thomas, *OFM Cap* '22 (MIL) St. Francis of Assisi, Milwaukee, WI
Skrobutt, Rev. Andrew T., '06 (RCK) St. Ann, Warren, IL; St. Joseph, Apple River, IL; St. Joseph, Lena, IL
Skrocki, Rt. Rev. Michael K., '00 (NTN) Curia: Administration; Consultative Bodies St. Ignatios of Antioch, Augusta, GA
Skrypek, Rev. Gregory A., '70 (STP) Retired.
Skrzynski, Rev. Gerard, '18 (BUF) St. John the Baptist, Boston, NY
Skrzypek, Rev. Jaroslaw, (HON) St. John the Baptist, Honolulu, HI
Skrzypek, Rev. Jaroslaw Z., '04 (SPC) On Leave.
Skrzypiec, Rev. Andrej, '82 (SLC) Curia: Offices and Directors
Skrzypiec, Rev. Andrzej, '82 (SLC) Saint Olaf LLC 239, Bountiful, UT
Skublics, Rev. Mat, '09 (NEW) On Duty Outside Diocese. Szechenyi
Skudlarek, Rev. William, *O.S.B.* '64 (SCL) [MIS] Dialogue Interreligieux Monastique (Monastic Interreligious Dialogue) (DIMMID), Collegeville, MN; [MON] St. John's Abbey, of the Order of St. Benedict, Collegeville, MN
Skura, Rev. Mark David, *O.F.M.Conv.* '82 (BUF) [MON] St. Francis of Assisi Friary, Hamburg, NY
Slaby, Rev. Joseph, *M.M.* '66 (NY) Retired. [MON] Maryknoll Fathers and Brothers (Catholic Foreign Mission Society of America, Inc.), Ossining, NY
Slaby, Rev. Stanislaw, *C.Ss.R.* '99 (MET) Christ the Redeemer Parish, Manville, NJ
Sladek, Rev. Kyle, (GB) Sacred Heart of Jesus, Poy Sippi, WI; St. Mark, Redgranite, WI; St. Paul, Plainfield, WI
Sladicka, Rev. Phillip J., '76 (SCR) Curia: Offices and Directors Queen of the Apostles Parish, Avoca, PA
Slater, Rev. Isaac, *O.C.S.O.* '12 (ROC) [MON] Abbey of the Genesee, Inc., Piffard, NY
Slaton, Rev. Robert J., '12 (DET) St. Anthony Parish Temperance, Temperance, MI
Slattery, Rev. Joseph A., '66 (RIC) Retired.
Slattery, Rev. Kevin, (BLX) Curia: Tribunal
Slattery, Rev. Kevin, '86 (JKS) Curia: (>BLX) Advisory Boards, Commissions, Committees, and Councils; Canonical Services; Consultative Bodies St. Stephen, Magee, MS; St. Therese, Jackson, MS
Slattery, Rev. Kirk, '08 (COS) St. Gabriel the Archangel, Colorado Springs, CO
Slattery, Rev. Msgr. Michael J., '62 (LA) Retired. St. Kateri Tekakwitha, Santa Clarita, CA
Slattery, Rev. William, '15 (FAR) Chap, Shanley/ Sullivan Catholic Schools St. John Paul II Catholic Schools Network (Blessed John Paul II Catholic Schools, Fargo Catholic Schools Network), Fargo, ND; Sts. Anne & Joachim Church of Fargo, Fargo, ND
Slattum, Friar Scott William, *O.F.M.* (PHX) St. Mary's Roman Catholic Basilica, Phoenix, AZ
Slaughter, Rev. Msgr. Martin, '85 (LA) Retired.
Slavinskas, Rev. Jonathan J., '12 (WOR) Our Lady of Providence Parish, Worcester, MA
Sledesky, Rev. Stephen M., '93 (HRT) The St. Mary's Church Corporation of Simsbury, Simsbury, CT
Sledz, Rev. Stanley V., '69 (STP) Retired. Church of Gichitwaa Kateri, Minneapolis, MN
Sleiman, Rev. Elias, *M.L.M.* '98 (OLL) Curia: Leadership Our Lady of Mt. Lebanon-St. Peter Maronite Catholic Cathedral, Los Angeles, CA; [MIS] The Congregation of Maronite Lebanese Missionaries, Los Angeles, CA; [MON] The Congregation of Maronite Lebanese Missionaries, Houston, TX
Sleiman, Rev. Elias, *M.L.M.* '98 (OLL) Curia: Leadership; Offices and Directors
Slesinski, Rev. Robert F., '76 (PSC) Retired.
Slevin, Rev. Henry, '62 (WDC) St. Francis de Sales, Washington, DC
Slezak, Rev. Brian K., '14 (ALB) Holy Family, Little Falls, NY; St. Joseph, Dolgeville, NY
Slight, Rev. William, *M.S.* '65 (ORL) Blessed Trinity, Orlando, FL
Slimak, Rev. Krzystof, '18 (PAT) Sacred Heart, Clifton, NJ
Sliney, Rev. Michael, *L.C.* (WDC) [MON] Legionaries of Christ, Potomac, MD
Slipe, Rev. Msgr. Robert H., '73 (NEW) St. Catherine of Siena, Cedar Grove, NJ
Slisz, Rev. Charles E., '71 (BUF) Retired. Curia: Leadership
Sliwa, Rev. Ryan T., '15 (SPR) Our Lady of the Valley, Easthampton, MA
Sliwinski, Rev. Phillip A., '97 (GR) Curia: Leadership; Offices and Directors St. Gregory-Our Lady of Fatima, Hart, MI; St. Joseph, Hart, MI
Sliwinski, Rev. Richard, '95 (NOR) St. Mary of Czestochowa, Middletown, CT
Sloan, Rev. Anthony, '00 (SAN) Retired.
Sloan, Rev. Daniel, '82 (MET) Retired. [MON] Maria Regina Residence, Somerset, NJ
Slobig, Rev. John, '90 (PHX) Retired. St. Gabriel Roman Catholic Parish, Cave Creek, AZ
Slobogin, Rev. Roland D., '73 (PH) Our Lady of Fatima, Secane, PA
Slomba, Rev. Eugene S., '64 (BUF) Retired.
Slon, Rev. Thomas R., *S.J.* '90 (BUF) Curia: Consultative Bodies [MON] The Canisius Jesuit Community, Inc., Buffalo, NY
Sloneker, Rev. Patrick L., '97 (CIN) Church of the Resurrection - Bond Hill, Cincinnati, OH; Holy Trinity Church, Cincinnati, OH; Nativity of Our Lord, Cincinnati, OH; St. John the Evangelist, Cincinnati, OH; St. Saviour, Cincinnati, OH
Slovak, Rev. Michael, *SOLT* '14 (FAR) St. Ann, Belcourt, ND; St. Ann's Church of Belcourt, Belcourt, ND; St. Anthony, Belcourt, ND; St. Anthony Church of Alcide, Alcide, ND; St. Michael the Archangel Dunseith, Dunseith, ND
Slovikovski, Rev. John, (ALT) Visitation of the B.V.M., Johnstown, PA
Slowiak, Rev. Allan L., '73 (LC) St. Mark, Rothschild, WI; [EFT] The St. Mark Catholic Parish Endowment Trust, Rothschild, WI
Slowik, Rev. Joseph S., '72 (RIC) Retired.
Slowinski, Rev. Jerome, '90 (DET) Retired.
Slowinski, Rev. Thomas F., '81 (DET) St. Paul Parish Grosse Pointe Farms, Grosse Pointe Farms, MI
Slusser, Rev. Michael S., '66 (STP) Retired.
Sly, Rev. Randolph, '12 (KC) On Special Assignment. St. Therese Parish, Kansas City, MO
Sly, Rev. Randy, '12 (KC) St. Michael the Archangel Catholic High School, Lees Summit, MO
Smalarz, Rev. James A., '04 (DET) Our Lady Queen of Martyrs Parish Beverly Hills, Beverly Hills, MI
Small, Rev. Andrew, *O.M.I.* '99 (WDC) [MON] Oblate Community, Washington, DC

Small, Rev. Andrew, *O.M.I.* (NY) [MIS] Propagation of the Faith National Office, New York, NY
Small, Rev. Bryan D., '02 (ATL) Curia: Leadership Sts. Peter and Paul Catholic Church, Decatur, Inc., Decatur, GA
Small, Rev. Jeffery A., '93 (PEO) St. Joseph's, Peru, IL; St. Mary, Peru, IL; St. Valentine, Peru, IL
Smart, Rev. John, (NY) St. Barnabas, Bronx, NY
Smart, Rev. Raymond W., '70 (PH) Retired.
Smay, Rev. Martin, '18 (WH) Curia: Offices and Directors Our Lady of Mercy Mission, Parsons, WV; St. Thomas Aquinas, Thomas, WV
Smedile, Rev. Anselm, *O.S.B* '03 (MAN) St. Raphael, Manchester, NH; [MON] St. Anselm Abbey, Manchester, NH
Smegelsky, Rev. John J., '66 (SY) Retired. Christ the Good Shepherd, Oswego, NY
Smela, Rev. Anthony, (LAN) Powers Catholic High School, Flint, MI; St. John Vianney Parish Flint, Flint, MI
Smeltzer, Rev. Stuart M., '96 (WCH) Curia: Leadership Sacred Heart, Fredonia, KS; St. Ignatius, Neodesha, KS
Smerauskas, Rev. Nerijus, '10 (LIT) Curia: Organizations (affiliated, inter-Diocesan, miscellaneous/other)
Smereka, Rev. John, '83 (SJP) Curia: Offices and Directors Holy Trinity Ukrainian Catholic Church, Carnegie, PA
Smetanka, Rev. Msgr. Gary T., '82 (DET) Our Lady Star of the Sea Parish Grosse Pointe Woods, Grosse Pointe Woods, MI
Smialek, Rev. Jeffery, *O.Carm.* '07 (JOL) Our Lady of Mount Carmel, Darien, IL
Smialowski, Rev. Raymond S., '82 (HRT) The Church of Our Lady of Mercy Corporation, Plainville, CT
Smiga, Rev. George, '75 (CLV) Holy Angels, Chagrin Falls, OH; [SEM] Saint Mary Seminary and Graduate School of Theology, Wickliffe, OH
Smilanic, Rev. Daniel, '73 (CHI) Retired.
Smilanic, Rev. Daniel A., (GLD) Curia: Offices and Directors
Smiley, Rev. Douglas J., '00 (R) Retired.
Smith, Rev. Alexander Xavier, '21 (LR) SS. Peter and Paul Catholic Church, Lincoln, AR; St. Joseph, Fayetteville, AR
Smith, Rt. Rev. Alexei, '87 (NTN) Curia: Administration; Consultative Bodies St. Paul, El Segundo, CA
Smith, Rt. Rev. Alexei R., '87 (LA) Curia: Offices and Directors St. Andrew, El Segundo, CA
Smith, Rev. Msgr. Alfred E., '56 (BAL) Retired.
Smith, Rev. Andrew, '18 (CIN) St. Christopher, Vandalia, OH; St. John the Baptist, Tipp City, OH; St. Peter, Huber Heights, OH
Smith, Rev. Andrew, (LR) Retired.
Smith, Rev. Andrew T., *O.S.B.* '64 (PAT) Retired. [MON] St. Mary's Abbey, Morristown, NJ
Smith, Rev. Anthony J., '11 (HRT) Curia: Advisory Boards, Commissions, Committees, and Councils Holy Disciples Parish Corporation, Watertown, CT; [CON] St. John the Evangelist Convent, Watertown, CT
Smith, Very Rev. Brent, '18 (LAF) Curia: Leadership Notre Dame High School of Acadia Parish, Crowley, LA; St. Joseph, Rayne, LA
Smith, Rev. Brian C., '21 (Y) Curia: Catholic Charities
Smith, Rev. Charles, *S.V.D.* '88 (IND) Chap, Veterans' Administration Hosp
Smith, Rev. Charles C., '06 (ARL) St. John the Evangelist, Warrenton, VA
Smith, Rev. Charles F., *S.V.D.* '88 (MO) Curia: Offices and Directors
Smith, Rev. Chris, (AUS) St. Mary, College Station, TX
Smith, Rev. Christian, (BIS) Dickinson Catholic Schools (Trinity Catholic Schools), Dickinson, ND; St. Patrick, Dickinson, ND; Trinity High School, Dickinson, ND
Smith, Rev. Christopher, '05 (CHR) Curia: Advisory Boards, Commissions, Committees, and Councils Prince of Peace, Taylors, SC
Smith, Rev. Christopher D., '20 (STL) Holy Infant Catholic Church, Ballwin, MO
Smith, Rev. Christopher H., '78 (ORG) Curia: Leadership [MIS] Christ Catholic Cathedral Corporation, Garden Grove, CA
Smith, Rev. Clifford G., '96 (DAL) Retired.
Smith, Very Rev. Craig, '05 (PT) Curia: Leadership
Smith, Very Rev. Craig, '05 (PT) St. Paul, Pensacola, FL
Smith, Rev. D. Stephen, '73 (MAD) Retired.
Smith, Rev. Daniel H., '10 (SFS) Blessed Sacrament Parish of Codington County, Florence, SD; Saint Henry Parish of Codington County, Henry, SD; Saint Michael Parish of Clark County, Clark, SD
Smith, Rev. David, *MIC* '20 (WDC) [SEM] Marian Fathers Scholasticate and Novitiate, Washington, DC
Smith, Rev. David, (PHX) Saint John Vianney Roman Catholic Parish, Goodyear, AZ
Smith, Rev. David A., *M.M.* '85 (NY) [MON] Maryknoll Fathers and Brothers (Catholic Foreign Mission Society of America, Inc.), Ossining, NY
Smith, Rev. David W., *CSC* (FTW) St. Joseph, South Bend, IN
Smith, Rev. Dean M., '99 (RCK) Holy Angels, Aurora, IL
Smith, Rev. Dennis, '75 (FWT) Retired.
Smith, Rev. Dominic, *O.S.A.* '22 (SD) [MON] Augustinian Community, San Diego, CA
Smith, Rev. Edmund, *O.S.B.* '65 (P) Retired. [MON] Mt. Angel Abbey, Saint Benedict, OR
Smith, Rev. Edward, *O.Praem.* (WIL) [MON] Immaculate Conception Priory of the Canons Regular of Premontre, Middletown, DE
Smith, Rev. Edward J., '01 (CLV) St. Anthony of Padua, Lorain, OH; St. Teresa of Avila, Sheffield Village, OH
Smith, Rev. Edward J., '65 (BRK) Retired.
Smith, Rev. Edward P., '82 (CIN) St. Columban, Loveland, OH; St. Margaret of York, Loveland, OH; St. Stephen, Cincinnati, OH
Smith, Rev. Eugene M., *O.S.M.* '88 (CHI) [MIS] Monastery of Our Lady of Sorrows, , ; [MIS] Order of Friar Servants of Mary United States of America Province, Inc., Chicago, IL
Smith, Rev. Eugene M., *O.S.M.* '84 (CHI) [MON] Order of Friar Servants of Mary (Servites) United States of America Province, Inc., Chicago, IL
Smith, Rev. Gabriel J., '82 (CHR) Retired.
Smith, Rev. Gary N., *S.J.* '71 (P) Retired. Chap, Multnomah Cty Detention Ctr, Portland [MON] Colombiere Jesuit Community, Portland, OR
Smith, Rev. Gene F., '84 (CHI) Retired. Our Lady of the Ridge and St. Linus Parish, Oak Lawn, IL
Smith, Rev. Geoffrey C., '74 (HRT) Retired.
Smith, Rev. George T., *C.S.B.* '89 (ROC) [MON] Basilian Fathers, Rochester, NY
Smith, Rev. Howard C., *S.M.* '72 (WDC) Retired. [MON] Marist Center (The Marist Finance Center of the Atlanta Province of the Society of Mary, Marist Fathers and Brothers), Washington, DC
Smith, Rev. Hyland, '13 (SFD) Holy Ghost, Jerseyville, IL; St. Mary, Fieldon, IL
Smith, Rev. Ignatius, *O.F.M.* '56 (ALB) [COL] Siena College, Loudonville, NY
Smith, Rev. Innoncent, *O.P.* (BAL) SS. Philip and James, Baltimore, MD; [SEM] St. Mary's Seminary and University, Baltimore, MD
Smith, Rev. Jacob Mathew, *O.F.M.* (BLX) St. Clare, Waveland, MS (>WDC) [MON] Franciscan Monastery USA Inc., Washington, DC
Smith, Rev. James, (HBG) Curia: Offices and Directors
Smith, Rev. James, '18 (TR) St. Aloysius, Jackson, NJ
Smith, Rev. James, *C.PP.S.* (OAK) [MON] Society of the Precious Blood, Berkeley, CA
Smith, Rev. James B., '85 (WIL) Retired.
Smith, Rev. James G., *O.Praem.* '77 (ORG) [MON] Norbertine Fathers of Orange, Inc., Silverado, CA
Smith, Rev. James Michael, '15 (BLX) Our Lady of the Gulf, Bay St. Louis, MS
Smith, Rev. Jeffery J., '16 (TOL) Sacred Heart of Jesus, Shelby, OH; St. Joseph, Crestline, OH
Smith, Rev. Jeremy, (BAL) Church of the Immaculate Conception, Towson, MD
Smith, Rev. John, *S.S.C.* (CHI) [MON] Korean Catholic Center, Chicago, IL
Smith, Rev. Johnnie B., '10 (MEM) Retired.
Smith, Rev. Jonathan M., (ARL) St. Andrew the Apostle, Clifton, VA
Smith, Rev. Joseph A., '96 (SAV) [HOS] St. Joseph's Hospital, Inc., Savannah, GA
Smith, Rev. Msgr. Joseph P.T., '60 (ALN) Retired. St. Joseph the Worker, Orefield, PA
Smith, Rev. Msgr. K. Bartholomew, '98 (WDC) St. Bernadette, Silver Spring, MD
Smith, Rev. Kareem R., (NY) Saint Elizabeth Ann Seton, Shrub Oak, NY; St. Michael, Bronx, NY
Smith, Rev. Kenneth, '16 (NO) Our Lady of Lourdes Roman Catholic Church, Violet, Louisiana, Violet, LA
Smith, Rev. Kenneth, '16 (NO) St. Mary Magdalen, Metairie, LA
Smith, Rev. Kenneth G., '84 (HBG) Saint Katharine Drexel, Mechanicsburg, PA
Smith, Rev. Kenneth J., '64 (NY) Retired.
Smith, Rev. Kevin M., '88 (RVC) Chap Curia: Leadership; Offices and Directors Our Lady of the Snow, Blue Point, NY
Smith, Rev. Kyle, '14 (SP) Curia: Pastoral Services St. Mary, Tampa, FL
Smith, Rev. Lawrence C., *S.J.* '82 (WDC) [MON] The Jesuit Community at Georgetown University, Washington, DC
Smith, Rev. Lawrence R., '76 (PIT) Retired. On Leave.
Smith, Rev. Leo, '06 (VEN) St. Finbarr Parish in Naples, Inc., Naples, FL
Smith, Rev. Leonard A., '91 (WH) Curia: Leadership; Offices and Directors St. Francis De Sales, Beckley, WV
Smith, Rev. LeRoy J., '78 (BRK) Retired.
Smith, Rev. Lester E., '75 (SY) Retired. St. John the Baptist/Holy Trinity, Syracuse, NY
Smith, Rev. M. Christopher, '83 (KC) Retired.
Smith, Rev. Mark L., '05 (WDC) Curia: Clergy and Religious Services; Consultative Bodies
Smith, Rev. Mark Leo, '05 (WDC) Holy Redeemer, College Park, MD; St. Bartholomew, Bethesda, MD
Smith, Rev. Mark S., '96 (JC) SS. Peter and Paul, Boonville, MO; St. Joseph, Pilot Grove, MO; [MIS] St. Joseph, ,
Smith, Rev. Martin, '15 (SFD) St. Francis Xavier, Jerseyville, IL; St. Patrick, Grafton, IL
Smith, Rev. Martin L., *O.S.A.* '77 (PH) [MON] St. Thomas Monastery, Villanova, PA
Smith, Rev. Michael B., '74 (CLV) Retired.
Smith, Rev. Michael R., '00 (SP) Church of the Nativity, Brandon, FL; [MIS] Partners with La Victoria, Inc., Brandon, FL
Smith, Rev. Michael S., '92 (NOR) On Leave.
Smith, Rev. Nicholas, '22 (DM) Our Lady's Immaculate Heart, Ankeny, IA
Smith, Rev. Nicholas P., '65 (PRO) Retired. [MON] St. John Vianney Residence, Providence, RI
Smith, Rev. Nicholas W., '94 (STL) Curia: Offices and Directors Basilica of St. Louis, King of France Catholic Church, St. Louis, MO
Smith, Rev. Patrick A., '90 (WDC) St. Augustine, Washington, DC
Smith, Rev. Paul, '59 (ALB) Retired. St. Lucy/St. Bernadette, Altamont, NY
Smith, Rev. Paul, *C.R.* '10 (SB) St. Joseph, Big Bear Lake, CA; [MIS] Congregation of the Resurrection, Big Bear City, CA
Smith, Rev. Paul, '62 (HON) Retired.
Smith, Rev. Philip A., '11 (TOL) Curia: Clergy and Religious Services
Smith, Rev. Philip A., '11 (TOL) St. Joseph, Sylvania, OH
Smith, Rev. Philip Innocent, *O.P.* '15 (NY) St. Catherine of Siena, New York, NY
Smith, Rev. Philip T., '84 (ORG) St. Edward the Confessor, Dana Point, CA
Smith, Rev. R. Douglas, *O.S.F.S.* '62 (WIL) Retired. [MON] Retirement and Assisted Care Facility, Childs, MD
Smith, Rev. Raymond, *C.M.F.* '12 (SPC) Sacred Heart, Springfield, MO; [MON] Claretians Missionaries' Residence-Villa Claret, Springfield, MO
Smith, Rev. Richard, '98 (FRS) Retired.
Smith, Rev. Richard G., '97 (NY) Curia: Leadership St. Joachim - St. John the Evangelist, Beacon, NY; [SEM] St. Joseph's Seminary, Yonkers, NY
Smith, Rev. Richard J., '09 (PH) St. Francis of Assisi, Norristown, PA
Smith, Very Rev. Richard L., '76 (JOL) Curia: Leadership [EFT] Diocese of Joliet Parish Deposit & Loan Trust, Crest Hill, IL
Smith, Rev. Richard P., *M.M.* '76 (NY) Retired. [MON] Maryknoll Fathers and Brothers (Catholic Foreign Mission Society of America, Inc.), Ossining, NY
Smith, Rev. Robert F., '97 (FAR) Our Lady of Peace Church of Mayville, Mayville, ND; St. Agnes Church of Hunter, Hunter, ND
Smith, Rev. Msgr. Robert J., '70 (E) Retired.
Smith, Rev. Robert J., '83 (RVC) Curia: Leadership; Offices and Directors St. Hugh of Lincoln, Huntington Station, NY
Smith, Rev. Robert V., '61 (CAM) Retired.
Smith, Very Rev. Msgr. Roger R., '76 (CC) Curia: Leadership St. Patrick Church, Corpus Christi, TX
Smith, Rev. Romeo John, '00 (SD) Chap, Tri City Hosp, Oceanside
Smith, Rev. Ronald, (GB) Retired.
Smith, Rev. Ronald T., '73 (HRT) Retired.
Smith, Rev. Russell E., '80 (RIC) Retired.
Smith, Rev. S. Douglas, *C.S.C.* '76 (FTW) [MON] Holy Cross Community, Corby Hall, University of Notre Dame, Notre Dame, IN
Smith, Rev. Sean, '20 (DUB) St. John's Church, Coggon, Iowa, Coggon, IA; St. Joseph's Church, Prairieburg, Iowa, Prairieburg, IA; St. Patrick's Church, Anamosa, Iowa, Anamosa, IA; St. Stephen's Church, Central City, Iowa, Central City, IA
Smith, Rev. Simon E., *S.J.* '61 (BO) [MON] Campion Health & Wellness, Inc., Weston, MA

Smith, Rev. Stephen, '16 (COL) Church of the Ascension, Johnstown, OH
Smith, Rev. T. Anthony, (L) Retired. St. Patrick, Louisville, KY
Smith, Rev. Terrence T., *T.O.R.* '73 (ALT) Retired. [MON] St. Bernardine Monastery, Hollidaysburg, PA
Smith, Rev. Theodore R., *O.Praem.* '91 (ORG) [MON] Norbertine Fathers of Orange, Inc., Silverado, CA
Smith, Rev. Thomas A., *O.F.M.Conv.* '79 (LSC) [RTR] Holy Cross Retreat and Friary (Franciscan Fathers), Mesilla Park, NM
Smith, Rev. Thomas A., '83 (L) Retired.
Smith, Rev. Thomas E., *S.J.* '74 (NY) [MON] Murray-Weigel Hall (A Jesuit Community at Murray-Weigel Hall and Kohlmann Hall), Bronx, NY
Smith, Rev. Thomas F., *O.C.S.O.* '58 (ATL) [MON] The Monastery of the Holy Spirit, Conyers, GA
Smith, Rev. Thomas J., '82 (NOR) Retired.
Smith, Rev. Vernon, (DM) Retired.
Smith, Rev. Walter J., *S.J.* '72 (BO) [MON] The Jesuit Community at Boston College, Chestnut Hill, MA
Smith, Rev. William, *CSSp.* '74 (PIT) Retired. [RTR] The Spiritan Center, Bethel Park, PA
Smith, Rev. William A., '03 (CLV) Our Lady of Grace, Hinckley, OH
Smith, Rev. William G., '80 (BRK) St. Charles Borromeo, Brooklyn, NY
Smith, Rev. William J., '81 (MET) St. Anthony of Padua, Port Reading, NJ
Smith, Rev. Wilton S., '58 (SFR) Retired.
Smithson, Rev. Thomas, *SSS* '01 (GAL) Corpus Christi, Houston, TX
Smits, Rev. Joseph, *C.I.C.M.* '56 (ARL) Retired.
Smolarski, Rev. Dennis C., *S.J.* '79 (SJ) [MON] Jesuit Community at Santa Clara University, Inc., Santa Clara, CA
Smolenski, Rev. Stanley, '68 (HRT) Retired.
Smolenski, Rev. Stanley, *S.P.M.A.* '68 (CHR) Curia: Offices and Directors [SHR] Shrine of Our Lady of South Carolina-Our Lady of Joyful Hope, Kingstree, SC
Smolich, Rev. Thomas H., *S.J.* (SJ) [MON] USA West Province, Society of Jesus, Los Gatos, CA
Smolik, Rev. Peter K., '02 (BGP) Our Lady, Star of the Sea Corporation, Stamford, CT
Smolka, Rev. Marek Maciej, '14 (CHI) Curia: Parish Services St. Francis Borgia, Chicago, IL
Smuda, Rev. Alfred J., *O.S.F.S.* '66 (R) Our Lady of the Seas, Buxton, NC
Smutelovic, Rev. Msgr. Peter, (NEW) St. John the Baptist, Hillsdale, NJ
Smyth, Rev. Joseph, (SY) Chap, Min, Univ Hosp at Cmty Campus Hosp, Syracuse
Sneck, Rev. William, *S.J.* '71 (PH) Retired. [MON] Jesuit Community at St. Joseph's University, Merion Station, PA
Sneck, Rev. William J., *S.J.* (PH) Retired.
Snedeker, Rev. Arthur, '74 (CLV) Retired.
Snell, Rev. Francis, '91 (HRT) Saint Francis Xavier Parish Corporation, New Milford, CT
Snell, Rev. Roger K., '72 (FAR) Retired.
Sneyd, Rev. Derrick, (CHR) Blessed Sacrament, Charleston, SC
Sneyd, Rev. Derrick, '70 (FTW) Retired.
Snider, Rev. Harold, *O.F.M.Cap.* '89 (SFR) [SEM] Capuchin Franciscan Order San Buenaventura Friary, San Francisco, CA
Snider, Rev. Michael T., '08 (TYL) Holy Spirit, Holly Lake Ranch, TX
Snider, Rev. Scott A., '12 (SFD) Curia: Leadership St. Brigid, Liberty, IL; St. Edward, Mendon, IL; St. Joseph, Quincy, IL
Snieg, Rev. Peter, '93 (RCK) St. Thomas Aquinas, Freeport, IL
Snieg, Rev. Peter, '93 (CHI) On Duty Outside Diocese. Diocese of Rockford
Snieg, Very Rev. Peter, '93 (RCK) Curia: Leadership
Sniezyk, Rev. Msgr. Richard S., '62 (SPR) Retired.
Sniosek, Rev. Jaroslaw (Jarek), '98 (VEN) Curia: Leadership St. Leo Parish in Bonita Springs, Inc., Bonita Springs, FL
Snipes, Rev. Roy Lee, *O.M.I.* '80 (BWN) Our Lady of Guadalupe, Mission, TX
Sniscak, Rev. Stephen, '10 (PAT) Chap, St Clare's Hosp Sacred Heart, Rockaway, NJ
Snitily, Rev. Steven P., '09 (LIN) Curia: Leadership Holy Trinity, Brainard, NE; [SHR] St. Luke's Czech Catholic Shrine, Loma, NE
Snodgrass, Rev. Thomas A., '76 (CIN) Retired.
Snow, Rev. Glenn, *O.Carm.* '89 (KCK) Immaculate Conception-St. Joseph, Leavenworth, KS
Snow, Rev. Lorn J., *S.J.* '99 (OM) (>DET) Gesu Parish Detroit, Detroit, MI
Snyder, Rev. Alexander, '59 (OAK) Retired. [NUR] Mercy Retirement and Care Center, Oakland, CA
Snyder, Rev. Ben G., '22 (DAV) Our Lady of Lourdes Church of Bettendorf, Iowa, Bettendorf, IA
Snyder, Rev. Chester P., '77 (HBG) Retired.
Snyder, Rev. Donald E., '73 (CLV) St. Ladislas, Westlake, OH
Snyder, Rev. Gary B., '74 (SC) Retired.
Snyder, Rev. George T., '07 (SAC) St. Clare, Roseville, CA
Snyder, Rev. Larry, (STP) Retired.
Snyder, Rev. Michael E., '97 (BLX) Curia: Advisory Boards, Commissions, Committees, and Councils St. Alphonsus, Ocean Springs, MS
Snyder, Rev. Michael E., (BLX) Curia: Leadership
Snyder, Rev. Michael J., *M.M.* '79 (NY) [CON] Maryknoll Communities, Inc., Maryknoll, NY; [MON] Maryknoll Fathers and Brothers (Catholic Foreign Mission Society of America, Inc.), Ossining, NY
Snyder, Rev. Paul M., '12 (DET) St. Mary Parish Royal Oak, Royal Oak, MI
Snyders, Rev. William J., *S.J.* '66 (LAF) [MON] St. Charles College, Grand Coteau, LA
Snyderwine, Rev. Msgr. L. Thomas, '68 (E) Retired.
Soares, Rev. John P., '92 (PRO) Curia: Advisory Boards, Commissions, Committees, and Councils Corporation of the Church of the Holy Cross, Providence, RI; St. Thomas' Church of Manton Rhode Island, Providence, RI
Soares, Rev. Msgr. Nicholas J., '64 (NY) Retired.
Soares, Rev. Stephen P., '97 (BUF) Our Lady of the Lake, Barker, NY
Sobczak, Rev. Marek, *CM* '74 (HRT) St. Michael the Archangel (The St. Michael's Church of Derby), Derby, CT; [MON] DePaul Provincial Residence (The New England Province of the Congregation of the Mission Incorporated, Congregation of the Mission, New England Province), Manchester, CT
Sobczyk, Rev. Patryk, '19 (BUF) On Administrative Leave. St. John the Baptist, Alden, NY
Soberal, Rev. Jose D., '60 (ARE) Retired.
Sobiech, Rev. Slawomir, '01 (BRK) Nativity of the Blessed Virgin Mary-Saint Stanislaus Bishop and Martyr Roman Catholic Church, Ozone Park, NY
Sobiecki, Rev. Peter S., '66 (HRT) Retired.
Sobierajski, Rev. Joseph A., *S.J.* (BAL) Retired. [MIS] Colombiere Jesuit Community, Baltimore, MD
Sobiesiak, Rev. Msgr. Joseph, (SP) Retired.
Sobiesiak, Rev. Msgr. Joseph R., '76 (ALN) Retired.
Sobolewski, Rev. Wlodzimierz, *C.R.* (BO) Curia: Tribunal
Sobolik, Rev. Joseph T., '09 (DUL) Mary Immaculate, Coleraine, MN; St. Cecilia's, Nashwauk, MN
Sobus, Rev. James M., '86 (WH) On Leave.
Socha, Rev. Bronislaw F., *O.C.D.* '89 (GRY) [MON] Discalced Carmelite Fathers Monastery, Munster, IN
Socha, Rev. Mikolaj, *O.S.P.P.E.* '93 (PH) (>RVC) St. Isidore, Riverhead, NY
Sochacki, Rev. Walter L., '68 (STP) Retired.
Socualaya, Rev. Bladi J., '01 (NY) Parish of St. Patrick and St. Mary, Newburgh, NY
Sodanango, Rev. Yos, *SVD* '13 (SD) Pastor of Blessed Sacrament Catholic Parish, San Diego, a corporation sole, San Diego, CA; [MIS] Blessed Sacrament Catholic Parish in San Diego, CA Real Property Support Corporation, San Diego, CA
Sodano, Rev. Thomas M., '91 (PH) St. Joseph, Collingdale, PA
Sodini, Rev. Pierre G., '68 (PIT) Retired. UPMC Shadyside Hosp, Allegheny Cty Our Lady of the Angels, Pittsburgh, PA; St. Maria Goretti Parish, Pittsburgh, PA
Sodoro, Rev. Carl F., (OM) Retired.
Soehner, Rev. Mark, *O.F.M.* '87 (CIN) [MON] Pleasant Street Friary, Cincinnati, OH; [MON] St. Francis Seraph Friary, Cincinnati, OH
Sofie, Rev. J. Francis, '94 (MOB) Retired. St. Dominic Parish, Mobile, Mobile, AL
Sogliuzzo, Rev. Louis P., *S.J.* '87 (SY) [MON] Jesuits at LeMoyne, Inc., Syracuse, NY
Soha, Rev. Roderick N., *T.O.R.* '95 (ALT) SS. Cyril and Methodius, Windber, PA; St. Anthony of Padua, Windber, PA; St. Elizabeth Ann Seton, Windber, PA
Sohe, Rev. Stephen, *SSJ* '14 (WDC) Incarnation, Washington, DC
Sohm, Rev. Andrew L., '05 (OM) Curia: Leadership; Offices and Directors St. Joseph, Ponca, NE; St. Patrick, Jackson, NE; St. Peter, Newcastle, NE; [EFT] St. Joseph's Church of Ponca South Creek Cemetery Endowment Fund, Ponca, NE
Sohm, Rev. John E., '58 (SFD) Retired. St. Columcille, Sullivan, IL
Sojka, Rev. Louis L., *O.S.B.* '90 (OM) Mount Michael Benedictine School, Elkhorn, NE; [EFT] Mount Michael Foundation, Elkhorn, NE; [MON] Mount Michael Benedictine Abbey, Elkhorn, NE
Sokol, Rev. Nathaniel J., '04 (LAN) Curia: Offices and Directors St. Agnes Parish Fowlerville, Fowlerville, MI
Sokolovych, Rev. Vasyl, (PSC) Saints Cyril and Methodius Byzantine Catholic Church, Cary, NC
Sokolowski, Rev. Msgr. Robert S., '65 (HRT) On Duty Outside Diocese. Catholic Univ of America, Washington, DC (>WDC) [COL] Catholic University of America, The, Washington, DC
Sokolowski, Rev. Waclaw, *O.F.M.Conv.* (PAT) St. John Kanty, Clifton, NJ
Sokolowski, Rev. William R., '65 (HRT) Retired.
Soku, Rev. Jerome - Nerio Missay, *MCCJ* '11 (CHI) [MON] Comboni Missionaries, La Grange Park, IL
Solan, Rev. Lawrence T., '80 (COS) Chap, Memorial Hosp
Solano, Rev. Julio R., '93 (MIA) Mary Help of Christians Church, Parkland, FL
Solano-Uribe, Rev. Jose Maria, '96 (SJN) Corpus Christi, San Juan, PR
Solari, Rev. James K., '55 (CHL) Retired.
Solari, Rt. Rev. Placid, *O.S.B.* '80 (RIC) [MON] Mary Mother of the Church Abbey, Richmond, VA
Solari, Rt. Rev. Placid D., *O.S.B.* '80 (CHL) [COL] Belmont Abbey College, Belmont, NC; [MON] Belmont Abbey (Southern Benedictine Society of North Carolina, Inc.), Belmont, NC
Solarski, Rev. John E., '76 (DAL) [MIS] Opus Dei, Irving, TX
Solazzo, Rev. Michael J., '76 (CHI) Retired.
Solcia, Rev. Louis M., *C.R.S.P.* '57 (SD) Pastor of Our Lady of the Rosary Catholic Parish, San Diego, a corporation sole, San Diego, CA
Soler, Rev. Esteban F., *I.V.E.* '04 (SPK) St. Charles, Spokane, WA
Soler, Rev. Jean-Paul, '07 (NY) St. Clement, Staten Island, NY
Soley, Rev. Roger A., '78 (WDC) Retired.
Solianyk, Rev. Mykhailo, (PRM) St. Nicholas, Clinton Township, MI
Soliman, Rev. Lynx, (NEW) St. Aloysius, Caldwell, NJ
Solis, Rev. Francisco J., '06 (BWN) St. Joan of Arc, Weslaco, TX
Solis, Rev. Marco, '97 (LA) Our Lady of Guadalupe, Los Angeles, CA
Solis, Rev. Olman, '97 (OAK) Curia: Offices and Directors Most Holy Rosary, Antioch, CA
Solis, Rev. Ralph, '93 (ELP) Curia: Advisory Boards, Commissions, Committees, and Councils Corpus Christi, El Paso, TX
Solis, Rev. Sergio, '00 (CHI) St. Anthony of Padua, Cicero, IL
Solis, Rev. Victor Ommar, (MRY) Cathedral of San Carlos Borromeo, Monterey, CA
Solis, Rev. Victor Ommar, '15 (MRY) On Special Assignment. Dir of Vocations, Monterey
Solitario, Rev. John Mark, *O.P.* (WDC) St. Dominic Church & Priory, Washington, DC
Solitario, Rev. John Mark, *O.P.* '19 (CIN) St. Gertrude, Cincinnati, OH; [MON] St. Gertrude Priory, Cincinnati, OH
Solivan, Rev. Roberto, '81 (CGS) Sagrado Corazon de Jesus, Caguas, PR
Soliven, Rev. Brian J., '11 (SAC) Pastor of St. Mary Parish, Vacaville, a Corporation Sole, Vacaville, CA
Solma, Rev. Martin, *sm* '78 (HON) [MIS] Mystical Rose Oratory, , ; [MON] Center Marianist Community, ,
Solomon, Rev. Benedict, *O.Praem.* '10 (ORG) St. John the Baptist, Costa Mesa, CA; [MON] Norbertine Fathers of Orange, Inc., Silverado, CA
Solomon, Rev. Fernando V., '21 (OG) Saint Andre Bessette Roman Catholic Parish, Malone, NY, Malone, NY
Solomon, Very Rev. John T., '11 (WIL) Curia: Advisory Boards, Commissions, Committees, and Councils; Deaneries St. Mary, Star of the Sea, Ocean City, MD
Solomon, Rev. Marc J., '06 (E) St. Lawrence the Martyr, Albion, PA; [MIS] Parish Office, Lucinda, PA
Solorio, Rev. Cesar, '16 (FRS) Our Lady of Lourdes, Corcoran, CA
Solorio, Rev. Rafael, *O.M.V.* (DEN) Holy Ghost Catholic Parish in Denver, Denver, CO

Solorzano, Rev. Mario, '06 (JKS) St. James the Less, Corinth, MS
Solorzano, Rev. Miguel A., '93 (GAL) Curia: Leadership St. Bartholomew the Apostle, Katy, TX
Soltis, Rev. John, *M.M.* '63 (SJ) Retired. [MON] Maryknoll, Los Altos, CA
Soltys, Rev. Daniel F., '68 (OM) Retired.
Soltys, Rev. Raymond A., '79 (SPR) Christ the King, Ludlow, MA
Solyntjes, Rev. Matthew, '17 (SC) Divine Mercy Catholic Parish, Algona, IA
Somarriba, Very Rev. Marcos A., '93 (MIA) Curia: Leadership; Pastoral Services St. Agatha, Miami, FL
Sombilon, Rev. Edmundo, '93 (NEW) Holy Trinity, Fort Lee, NJ
Somera, Rev. Romelo B., '99 (MO) Curia: Offices and Directors
Somers, Rev. Michael, (BLX) [MON] Southern Province of St. Augustine - Provincial Offices, Bay St. Louis, MS; [MON] St. Augustine's Residence, Bay St. Louis, MS
Somerville, Rev. Alvin, *O.F.M.Conv.* '58 (ALB) Retired. [MON] Immaculate Conception Friary - Order of Friars Minor Conventual, Rensselaer, NY
Sommer, Rev. Anton, (RNO) Retired.
Sommer, Rev. Msgr. Ralph, '83 (RVC) St. Bernard, Levittown, NY
Sommermeyer, Rev. Gary H., '91 (BRK) Retired. St. Teresa, Woodside, NY
Son, Rev. Doan Trong, *C.Ss.R.* '99 (LA) [MON] Vietnamese Redemptorist Mission, Baldwin Park, CA
Song, Rev. Jae Heon, (AGN) St. Andrew Kim, Dededo, GU
Song, Rev. Jaehun, '91 (LA) Holy Trinity, Los Angeles, CA
Song, Rev. Simeon, '15 (LA) On Administrative Leave.
Songy, Rev. David, *O.F.M.Cap.* '87 (WDC) [EFT] St. Luke Institute Foundation, Silver Spring, MD; [SPF] Saint Luke Institute, Inc., Silver Spring, MD (>DEN) [MON] St. Francis of Assisi Friary, Denver, CO
Sonnier, Rev. Cedric, '97 (LAF) Curia: Miscellaneous / Other Offices St. Mary Mother of the Church, Lafayette, LA
Soo-Gil Chae, Rev. Cyril, '04 (ATL) St. Patrick Catholic Church, Norcross, Inc., Norcross, GA
Soon-Jin, Rev. Joseph Kim, (PH) Curia: Evangelization
Soosai, Rev. Sahaya Kennedy Reelan, '14 (BLX) St. Alphonsus, Ocean Springs, MS
Soosai, Rev. Sebastian Kumar, *MF* '05 (HON) St. Roch, Kahuku, HI
Soosai, Rev. Selvanathan, *HGN* '09 (PBL) Immaculate Heart of Mary, Grand Junction, CO
Soosai Antony, Rev. Reehan, *SAC* '08 (FWT) St. Ann, Burleson, TX
Soper, Rev. Paul, (BO) St. Denis, Westwood, MA; St. Margaret Mary, Westwood, MA
Soper, Rev. Paul R., '90 (BO) Curia: Advisory Boards, Commissions, Committees, and Councils; Consultative Bodies; Pastoral Services
Sopiak, Rev. Donald A., '78 (DET) Retired.
Soprano, Rev. Ernest R., '79 (CAM) The Parish of Saint John Neumann, North Cape May, N.J., North Cape May, NJ
Soranno, Rev. Joseph M., '74 (SPR) Retired.
Sordillo, Rev. Ronald, '74 (PAT) Retired. [MIS] Nazareth Village, Chester, NJ
Soreng, Rev. Birendra, '96 (BGP) Curia: Clergy and Religious Services; Consultative Bodies St. Mark Roman Catholic Church, Stratford, CT
Soreng, Rev. Dilip, *SVD* (LAF) Holy Ghost, Opelousas, LA
Sorensen, Rev. Bryan, '88 (RC) Curia: Leadership Blessed Sacrament, Bison, SD; St. Anthony, Buffalo, SD
Sorensen, Rev. Jonathan D., '09 (GI) Curia: Leadership; Offices and Directors; Tribunal St. Patrick, North Platte, NE
Sorenson, Rev. Kris, '08 (FRS) Our Lady of Lourdes, California City, CA
Sorgie, Rev. Anthony D., '82 (NY) Assumption, Tuckahoe, NY; Parish of Immaculate Conception and Assumption, Tuckahoe, NY
Soria, Rev. Manuel B., '81 (SAC) Retired.
Soriano, Rev. Arnel, *M.S.* '04 (HON) St. Theresa, Kihei, HI
Soriano, Rev. Danilo, '78 (JOL) Retired. [NUR] St. John Vianney Villa, Naperville, IL
Soriano, Rev. Erasmus B., '93 (LA) St. Linus, Norwalk, CA; St. Paul, Los Angeles, CA
Soriano, Rev. Jesus T., '70 (SAC) Retired.
Soriano, Rev. Mamerto, (RVC) Retired.
Soriano, Rev. Rosanno, (FR) [MON] La Salette Shrine & Retreat Center, Attleboro, MA
Sork, Rev. Msgr. David A., '70 (LA) St. John Fisher, Rancho Palos Verdes, CA
Sormani, Rev. Daniel, *C.S.Sp.* (PH) Holy Ghost Preparatory School, Bensalem, PA
Sorra, Rev. James L., '06 (BAL) On Leave.
Sosa, Rev. Elio, *I.V.E.* (BGP) Our Lady of Guadalupe Roman Catholic Church Corporation, Danbury, CT
Sosa, Rev. Emilio, '06 (SAN) Curia: Advisory Boards, Commissions, Committees, and Councils St. Vincent Pallotti, Abilene, TX
Sosa, Rev. Jose A., *Sch.P.* '04 (SD) Pastor of Our Lady of Guadalupe Catholic Parish, Calexico, a corporation sole, Calexico, CA; [MIS] Our Lady of Guadalupe Catholic Parish Calexico in Calexico, CA Real Property Support Corporation, Calexico, CA
Sosa, Rev. Juan J., '72 (MIA) Curia: Leadership; Pastoral Services St. Joseph, Miami Beach, FL
Sosa, Rev. Mauricio, *M.N.M.* '11 (DAL) St. James Catholic Church, Dallas, TX
Sosa, Rev. Pedro A., (BGP) Our Lady of Guadalupe Roman Catholic Church Corporation, Danbury, CT
Sosa, Rev. Philip, *M.S.F.* (STL) St. Wenceslaus Catholic Church, St. Louis, MO
Sosa, Rev. Philip, *M.S.F.* '68 (STL) [EFT] Missionaries of the Holy Family Retirement Trust Fund, St. Louis, MO
Sosio, Rev. Mirco, *A.V.I.* (STL) [SEM] Kenrick School of Theology, ,
Sosio, Rev. Mirco, '11 (KCK) On Duty Outside Diocese. Diocese of Como, Italy
Sosnowski, Very Rev. Ted, '97 (PT) Curia: Leadership St. Bernadette, Panama City Beach, FL
Sotak, Rev. John, (JOL) St. Jude, New Lenox, IL
Sotelo, Rev. Msgr. Antonio, '58 (PHX) Retired. On Special Assignment. Prison Chap, Phoenix Immaculate Heart of Mary Roman Catholic Parish, Phoenix, AZ
Sotiroff, Rev. Stephen T., '81 (SFD) On Special Assignment. [CON] St. Francis Convent, Alton, IL; [HOS] OSF HealthCare Saint Anthony's Health Center, Alton, IL
Soto, Rev. Angel Leonides, '92 (MGZ) Iglesia Diocesana de La Inmaculada Concepcion Hospital La Concepcion, San German, PR; [HOS] Hospital of the Immaculate Conception, San Germán, PR
Soto, Rev. Athanasius, *O.S.B.* '19 (STL) [MON] The Abbey of St. Mary and St. Louis, St. Louis, MO
Soto, Rev. Charles, *O.F.M.* '70 (NY) Retired. [MON] Franciscan Province of the Immaculate Conception, New York, NY
Soto, Rev. Charles, *O.F.M.* (PIT) Chap, VA Pittsburgh Health Care System
Soto, Rev. Enrique Omar, *M.N.M* (ELP) San Lorenzo, Clint, TX
Soto, Rev. Marvin, '22 (PHX) Immaculate Conception Roman Catholic Parish, Cottonwood, AZ
Soto Maldonado, Rev. Angel L., (ARE) [MIS] Chapel Nuestra Senora de los Dolores, Lares, PR; [MIS] Chapel Nuestra Senora del Perpetuo Socorro, Lares, PR; [MIS] Chapel Sagrada Familia, Lares, PR
Soto Maldonado, Rev. Angel L., '14 (ARE) St. Judas Tadeos, Lares, PR
Soto Montoya, Rev. Everardo, (LA) St. Joseph, Pomona, CA
Soto Silvera, Rev. Calixto, '85 (SJN) San Pedro Apostol, Toa Baja, PR
Soto Torres, Rev. Omar Omi, '12 (PCE) Curia: Leadership [SEM] Seminario Mayor Interdiocesano Maria, Madre de la Divina Providencia, Ponce, PR
Sotomayor, Rev. Emilio, *Sch.P.* (WDC) [MON] Piarist Fathers, Province of the U.S.A. and Puerto Rico, Washington, DC
Soto-Tanon, Rev. Carmelo, '89 (SJN) Ntra. Sra. Reina de Los Angeles, Carolina, PR
Sottocornola, Rev. Frank, *S.X.* '59 (PAT) [MON] Xaverian Missionary Fathers, Wayne, NJ
Soubrier, Rev. Miguel Angel, (DEN) Holy Name Catholic Parish in Steamboat Springs, Steamboat Springs, CO
Souckar, Msgr. Michael A., '88 (MIA) Curia: Canonical Services; Leadership St. Andrew, Coral Springs, FL
Soucy, Rev. A. Francis, (HRT) St. Patrick and St. Anthony Roman Catholic Church Corporation, Hartford, CT; [MON] St. Patrick-St. Anthony Friary (Franciscan Friars), Hartford, CT
Soucy, Rev. Robert P., '62 (BO) Retired.
Soukup, Rev. Paul A., *S.J.* '79 (SJ) Chap, Catholic Scouting [MON] Jesuit Community at Santa Clara University, Inc., Santa Clara, CA
Soule, Rev. W. Becket, *OP* (CHL) St. Margaret of Scotland, Maggie Valley, NC
Sounou, Rev. Cocou Cyriaque, *SVD* '17 (GAL) Holy Name, Houston, TX
Sounou, Rev. Cocou Cyriaque, *SVD* (LAF) Notre Dame de Perpetuel Secours, St. Martinville, LA
Sousa, Rev. Edward A., '03 (PRO) Church of Saint Sebastian, Providence, RI; St. Joseph's Church Providence Rhode Island, Providence, RI
Sousa, Rev. Eugene, *O.P.* (OAK) [MON] Order of Preachers (Province of the Most Holy Name of Jesus - Western Dominican Province), Oakland, CA
Sousa, Rev. Eugene W., *O.P.* '58 (SFR) Retired.
Sousa, Rev. Manuel F., '80 (STO) Our Lady of the Assumption of the Portuguese Church (Pastor of), Turlock, CA
Sousa, Rev. Peter E., *C.Ss.R.* '78 (CHR) Curia: Advisory Boards, Commissions, Committees, and Councils Our Lady of the Hills, Columbia, SC
Southard, Rev. Ethan, '16 (LA) St. John Eudes, Chatsworth, CA
Soutus, Rev. Anibal, '06 (SJP) Curia: Offices and Directors
Soutus, Very Rev. Hugo C., '94 (STN) Curia: (>MO) Offices and Directors; Offices and Directors Dormition of the Mother of God, Phoenix, AZ
Soutuyo, Rev. Raul S., '93 (MIA) Retired. St. Agatha, Miami, FL
Souza, Rev. Gerald A., '13 (BO) Curia: Consultative Bodies Ascension of Our Lord and Savior Jesus Christ Parish, Sudbury, MA
Souza, Rev. Jason, '98 (LA) On Duty Outside Diocese.
Sowa, Rev. Artur J., '06 (CHI) St. Francis of Assisi, Orland Park, IL
Sowada, Rev. Arlie, '73 (SCL) Retired.
Spacek, Rev. Frank W., '97 (BRK) Christ the King High School, Middle Village, NY; St. Saviour, Brooklyn, NY
Spacht, Rev. Andres, *C.Ss.R.* '61 (CGS) Nuestra Senora de la Mercedes, San Lorenzo, PR
Spadaro, Rev. Msgr. Thomas L., '64 (RVC) Retired. Good Shepherd, Holbrook, NY
Spahn, Rev. James, *OP* (SJN) Invencion de la Santa Cruz, Bayamon, PR
Spahn, Very Rev. James S., '00 (DEN) Curia: Deaneries
Spahn, Rev. Stephen F., *S.J.* (BAL) [COL] Jesuit Community of Loyola University, Inc., Baltimore, MD; [MON] Jesuit Community of Loyola University Maryland, Inc., Baltimore, MD
Spahr, Very Rev. Matthew D., '92 (SD) Curia: Advisory Boards, Commissions, Committees, and Councils; Offices and Directors Pastor of The Immaculata Catholic Parish, San Diego, a corporation sole, San Diego, CA; [MIS] The Immaculata Catholic Parish in San Diego, CA Real Property Support Corporation, San Diego, CA; [SEM] The Roman Catholic Seminary of San Diego, San Diego, CA
Spalding, Rev. Leon C., '59 (L) Retired.
Spanel, Rev. Hubert J., '59 (GI) Retired.
Spangenberg, Rev. George J., *C.S.Sp.* '76 (PIT) [COL] Duquesne University of the Holy Spirit, Pittsburgh, PA; [RTR] The Spiritan Center, Bethel Park, PA
Spanier, Rev. Marian, '81 (NEW) St. Stanislaus, Newark, NJ
Spanley, Rev. Anthony L., '68 (GRY) Holy Cross, Hamlet, IN
Spannagel, Rev. Luke A., '03 (PEO) Peoria Notre Dame High School, Peoria, IL; Sacred Heart, Peoria, IL; St. Bernard's, Peoria, IL; St. Joseph, Peoria, IL; St. Mary's Cathedral, Peoria, IL; St. Philomena, Peoria, IL
Spano, Rev. Philip F., '82 (BR) Retired.
Sparacino, Rev. Thomas A., '98 (PIT) Curia: Clergy and Religious Services; Consultative Bodies [SEM] Saint Paul Seminary, Pittsburgh, PA
Sparklin, Rev. Paul, '91 (BAL) St. Michael, Mount Airy, MD
Sparks, Rev. Kenneth A., '95 (PIT) Blessed Trinity, Pittsburgh, PA
Sparks, Rev. Nathan, '11 (RC) On Duty Outside Diocese. Released to Jesuits.
Sparks, Rev. Richard, (PMB) [MON] Paulist Fathers Residence, Vero Beach, FL
Sparling, Rev. Adam M., '13 (LIN) St. Anne, Campbell, NE
Sparough, Rev. J. Michael, *S.J.* '78 (CHI) [RTR] Bellarmine Jesuit Retreat House, Inc., Barrington, IL
Sparrow, Rev. Tyler Austin, '21 (R) St. Patrick, Fayetteville, NC
Spaulding, Very Rev. Robert, '09 (CHY) Curia: Clergy and Religious Services; Consultative Bodies St. Paul's Newman Center, Laramie, WY; [CAM] St. Paul's Newman Center, University Catholic Community (University of Wyoming), Laramie, WY
Speaks, Rev. Sidney, '99 (NO) St. Joseph the Worker, Marrero, LA
Specht, Rev. Terry W., '96 (ARL) Retired.
Speck, Rev. Gregory, *S.C.J.* '76 (SP) [MON] Priests of the Sacred Heart, Pinellas Park, FL
Speckman, Rev. Harry, *OFM* (GB) Retired.
Speedy, Rev. Antonio Maria, *pgsm* (HT) Holy Family,

Dulac, LA; St. Eloi, Theriot, LA

Speicher, Rev. Charles W., '75 (PIT) Retired. Our Lady of Hope, Bethel Park, PA

Speicher, Rev. David J., '86 (LAN) Retired. St. Jude Parish DeWitt, DeWitt, MI

Speier, Rev. Francis, '75 (TOL) St. Catherine of Siena, Toledo, OH; St. Clement, Toledo, OH

Speier, Rev. Thomas, *O.F.M.* '58 (CIN) Retired. [MON] St. Clement Friary, Cincinnati, OH; [MON] St. Francis Seraph Friary, Cincinnati, OH

Speitel, Very Rev. Mark M., '08 (HBG) Curia: Leadership; Offices and Directors [EFT] Roman Catholic Diocese of Harrisburg Charitable Trust, Harrisburg, PA

Spellman, Rev. John P., *O.S.F.S.* '66 (WIL) [MON] Retirement and Assisted Care Facility, Childs, MD

Spencer, Rev. Evan, (RIC) Chap, Salem VA Med Ctr

Spencer, Rev. Gregory D., '89 (R) Christ the King, Riegelwood, NC; St. Mark Catholic Parish of Wilmington, Wilmington, NC

Spencer, Rev. John P., *S.J.* '79 (BO) Curia: Pastoral Services [MON] Campion Health & Wellness, Inc., Weston, MA; [MON] Loyola House, Boston, MA

Spencer, Rev. Matthew Daniel, *O.S.J.* '09 (MRY) [MON] Oblates of St. Joseph Provincial House and Shrine, Santa Cruz, CA; [SHR] Shrine of St. Joseph Guardian of the Redeemer, Santa Cruz, CA

Spencer, Rev. Robert A., '98 (CHR) Christ Our King, Mount Pleasant, SC

Spencer, Rev. Robert K, '85 (WCH) Sacred Heart, Caney, KS; St. Mary's, Moline, KS; St. Robert Bellarmine, Sedan, KS

Spencer, Rev. Robert M., '82 (RIC) Saint Kateri Tekakwitha, Yorktown, VA

Spencer, Rev. Stephen, '18 (SAC) [SEM] Mount St. Joseph Novitiate and Seminary (Novitiate of Oblates of St. Joseph), Loomis, CA

Spencer, Rev. William, *OFM* (BEL) [MON] St. Benedict the Black Friary, East Saint Louis, IL

Spencer, Rev. William W., '07 (SAG) Retired. On Duty Outside Diocese. Ann Arbor

Spengler, Rev. Msgr. James F., '68 (BRK) Retired. [MON] Bishop Mugavero Residence, Douglaston, NY

Spenik, Rev. Alexander C., '21 (CLV) St. Mary, Painesville, OH

Spenner, Rev. Jerome I., '64 (OM) Retired.

Spera, Rev. James F., '77 (NEW) Assumption, Roselle Park, NJ

Sperger, Rev. Herbert J., '79 (PH) [SEM] Theological Seminary of St. Charles Borromeo, Wynnewood, PA

Spexarth, Rev. Aaron, '08 (WCH) Chap, Kansas State Industrial Reformatory Church of the Holy Cross, Hutchinson, KS; Holy Trinity, Little River, KS

Spexarth, Rev. Daniel J., '84 (WCH) St. Catherine of Siena, Wichita, KS

Spexarth, Rev. Jerome J., '01 (WCH) Our Lady of Lourdes, Pittsburg, KS

Spezia, Rev. Leo J., '76 (STL) Most Sacred Heart Catholic Church, Eureka, Eureka, MO

Spezia, Rev. Robert R., '96 (DET) Curia: Consultative Bodies; Offices and Directors [EFT] Archdiocese of Detroit Priests' Pension Plan, Inc., Detroit, MI

Speziale, Rev. Michael G., '09 (PH) St. Ephrem, Bensalem, PA

Spicer, Rev. Kevin P., *C.S.C.* '92 (FR) [COL] Holy Cross Fathers Religious, North Easton, MA; [COL] Stonehill College, North Easton, MA

Spicer, Rev. Patrick A., '12 (CLV) St. Columbkille Parish, Parma, OH

Spiegel, Rev. John D., '76 (DAV) Retired.

Spiegel, Rev. Msgr. Robert H., '66 (DAV) Retired.

Spiegel, Rev. Thomas J., '67 (DAV) Retired.

Spiekermeier, Rev. Michael J., '69 (DAV) Retired. [MON] St. Vincent Center, Davenport, IA

Spielman, Rev. Paul J., '61 (STL) Retired.

Spiering, Rev. Samuel, '12 (GF) Curia: Leadership; Offices and Directors St. Leo, Lewistown, MT; [EFT] St. Leo's Catholic Education Trust, Lewistown, MT

Spies, Rev. Dennis, *S.T.L.* '02 (CHI) [SEM] University of Saint Mary of the Lake/Mundelein Seminary, Mundelein, IL

Spies, Very Rev. Dennis, '02 (JOL) On Duty Outside Diocese. St Mary of the Lake Seminary, Mundelein

Spiess, Rev. Kevin J., '86 (CHI) On Duty Outside Diocese. Hinsdale

Spilka, Very Rev. Anthony Francis, '69 (ALT) Curia: Leadership St. Francis of Assisi, Johnstown, PA

Spillett, Rev. Thomas, '64 (SP) Retired.

Spilly, Rev. William V., '74 (ROC) Retired.

Spina, Rev. Douglas, (PHX) St. Bernadette Roman Catholic Parish, Scottsdale, AZ

Spina, Rev. Douglas J., '76 (PRO) Retired.

Spinale, Rev. Kevin, *S.J.* '16 (WOR) [MON] Jesuits of the Holy Cross, Inc., Worcester, MA

Spinale, Rev. Kevin, *SJ* '16 (NY) [MON] Jesuit Community at Fordham University, New York, NY

Spinhirene, Rev. Canon Grant, (AMA) Curia: Pastoral Services

Spinhirne, Rev. Grant, '17 (AMA) St. Anthony's, Hereford, TX; [CAM] Catholic Student Center at West Texas A & M University, Canyon, TX

Spino, Rev. John J., '90 (NEW) Retired.

Spinosa, Chorbishop Anthony, '83 (OLL) Curia: Leadership; Offices and Directors [MON] Father Tobia Retirement Home, North Jackson, OH; [SHR] Basilica & National Shrine of Our Lady of Lebanon, North Jackson, OH

Spirko, Rev. Nicholas A., '72 (PIT) Retired.

Spishak, Rev. Carl A., '59 (ALT) Retired. St. Rose of Lima, Altoona, PA

Spiteri, Rev. Msgr. Laurence, (ATL) [EFT] The Sanctuary of Culture Foundation, Inc., Atlanta, GA; [MIS] Treasures of History, Inc., Atlanta, GA

Spiteri, Rev. Msgr. Laurence J., '78 (LA) On Duty Outside Diocese.

Spitz, Rev. Gregory M., '67 (MIL) Retired.

Spitz, Rev. Simeon Z., *O.S.B.* '14 (OKL) [MON] St. Gregory's Abbey (Benedictine Fathers of Sacred Heart Mission, Inc.), Shawnee, OK

Spitzer, Rev. Robert J., *S.J.* '83 (ORG) [MIS] Magis Institute, Garden Grove, CA; [RTR] House of Prayer for Priests, Orange, CA

Spitzley, Rev. Denis R., '75 (LAN) Retired.

Splain, Rev. Thomas E., *S.J.* '71 (SJ) [MON] Sacred Heart Jesuit Center, Los Gatos, CA

Splawski, Rev. Bernerd, *O.F.M.* '63 (SP) Retired.

Spodnik, Rev. A. Leo, '48 (HRT) Retired.

Spohrer, Rev. Dennis, '03 (PEO) [HOS] OSF HealthCare Saint Francis Medical Center, East Peoria, IL

Spolny, Rev. Joseph R., '78 (CLV) Holy Family, Parma, OH

Sponder, Rev. John, '93 (JOL) Holy Spirit Catholic Community, Naperville, IL

Spong, Rev. William, '79 (FWT) Retired.

Spong, Rev. William, (ROC) Retired.

Spontak, Very Rev. James A., '75 (PBR) Curia: Leadership SS. Peter and Paul, Dunlo, PA; SS. Peter and Paul, Portage, PA; St. Mary's, Beaverdale, PA

Spoto, Rev. Giuseppe, (DAL) Our Lady of Perpetual Help Catholic Parish, Dallas, TX

Spotswood, Rev. Cecil R., '97 (MOB) St. Joan of Arc Parish, Mobile, Mobile, AL; St. Mary Parish, Mobile, Mobile, AL

Spotts, Rev. Matthew, *S.J.* (OM) Creighton Preparatory School, Omaha, NE; [MON] Jesuit Community at Creighton University, Omaha, NE

Sprauer, Rev. Michael, '72 (P) Retired.

Spriggs, Rev. Robert W., '65 (SFD) Retired.

Sprigler, Rev. William A., '75 (NU) Retired.

Springer, Rev. Lawrence F., '59 (CHI) Retired. St. Zachary, Des Plaines, IL

Springer, Rev. William A., '72 (SD) Pastor of Mission San Diego de Alcala Catholic Parish, San Diego, a corporation sole, San Diego, CA

Springman, Rev. Donald W., '67 (L) Retired.

Springuel, Rev. Samuel, *O.S.B.* '19 (WDC) St. Anselm's Abbey School, Inc, Washington, DC; [MON] St. Anselm's Abbey, Washington, DC

Spruill, Rev. Mark T., *O.B.S.B.* '07 (BIR) St. William, Guntersville, AL

Spuhler, Friar Gregory, *OFM Conv.* (ALB) [MON] Franciscan Friars Conventual, Rensselaer, NY

Spyrow, Rev. Andrew P., '14 (SFR) On Special Assignment. Curia: Advisory Boards, Commissions, Committees, and Councils; Leadership St. Gabriel, San Francisco, CA; St. Monica - St. Thomas the Apostle Parish, San Francisco, CA

Squeo, Rev. Eugene P., '71 (NEW) Retired. Chap, Hudson Cty Corr Ctr, South Kearny [MIS] St. Patrick Housing Corp., Jersey City, NJ

Squillacioti, Rev. Joseph Vincent, (ORG) St. Edward the Confessor, Dana Point, CA

Srambickal, Rev. Varghese, (CAM) St. Joseph Catholic Church, East Camden, N.J. (Pro-Cathedral), Camden, NJ

Srayil Kurian, Rev. Santhosh, (SAC) St. Clare, Roseville, CA

Sreboth, Rev. Michael J., '86 (MOB) Frank Lee Corr Fac, Deatsville Holy Spirit Parish, Montgomery, Montgomery, AL

Srenn, Rev. Thomas E., '77 (CHI) Retired.

Srion, Rev. Charles, '78 (RVC) Retired.

Srivokoral, Rev. Mathee, (NY) Immaculate Conception, Bronx, NY

Sroka, Rev. Gerald A., '60 (GRY) Retired.

Srsich, Rev. Peter, '21 (DEN) On Special Assignment. Studying Biblical Theology at Pontifical University

Ssamba, Rev. Deogratias, *A.J.* (L) Good Shepherd, Louisville, KY

Ssebalamu, Very Rev. Charles, '96 (RIC) St. Stephen, Martyr, Chesapeake, VA

Ssebbowa, Rev. Polycarp, '97 (LR) St. Stephen, Bentonville, AR

Ssebina, Rev. Raymond, '19 (LAF) St. Anthony of Padua, Eunice, LA; St. Mathilda, Eunice, LA

Ssegawa, Rev. John R., *A.J.* '94 (PHX) Curia: Leadership; Offices and Directors St. Helen Roman Catholic Parish, Glendale, AZ

Ssekabembe, Rev. Albert Mutebi, '03 (SFE) Our Lady of Belen, Belen, NM

Ssekannyo, Rev. Denis, (MO) Curia: Offices and Directors

Ssekiranda, Rev. Remigious, '98 (VEN) St. Paul Parish in Arcadia, Inc., Arcadia, FL

Ssekitto, Rev. Cornelius, *AJ* '96 (P) [HOS] Providence Health & Services-Oregon (Providence St. Vincent Medical Center), Portland, OR

Ssekkomo, Rev. John Bosco, '13 (GR) Sacred Heart of Jesus, Grand Rapids, MI

Ssekyole, Rev. Patrick, '09 (WOR) Holy Cross, Templeton, MA; St. Martin Mission, Otter River, MA

Ssemakula, Rev. Joseph, (WDC) [SEM] St. Joseph's Seminary, Washington, DC

Ssemakula, Rev. Luke, '97 (OAK) The Catholic Community of Pleasanton, Pleasanton, CA

Ssemakula, Rev. Yozefu B., '93 (PT) On Duty Outside Diocese. Washington DC

Ssembajja, Rev. Arthur Joseph, (FTW) St. Anthony de Padua, South Bend, IN

Ssenfuma, Rev. Michael D., (BO) Incarnation of Our Lord and Savior Jesus Christ, Melrose, MA; Most Blessed Sacrament, Wakefield, MA

Ssensamba, Rev. Aloysius G., '99 (SEA) St. Alphonsus, Seattle, WA

Ssentamu, Rev. David Martin, (RIC) Ss. Peter & Paul, Palmyra, VA; St. Joseph's/Shrine of St. Katharine Drexel, Columbia, VA

Ssenyonjo, Rev. Leonard, '93 (RC) Cathedral of Our Lady of Perpetual Help, Rapid City, SD; St. Michael's, Hermosa, SD

Sseriiso, Rev. Henry M., *I.M.C.* '06 (SB) St. Peter & St. Paul, Alta Loma, CA

Ssmugabe, Rev. John Baptist, *O.P.* '13 (WDC) [SEM] Dominican House of Studies, Washington, DC

Ssozi, Rev. William, '92 (MAR) St. Charles Borromeo, Rapid River, MI; St. Joseph, Perkins, MI; St. Rita, Trenary, MI

St. Amand, Rev. Kenneth J., '69 (NEW) Retired.

St. Andre, Rev. Jonathan, *TOR* '06 (STU) [COL] Franciscan University of Steubenville, Steubenville, OH

St. Fort, Rev. Elifete, '08 (PMB) Holy Spirit, Lantana, FL

St. George, Rev. Peter J., (ARL) Blessed Sacrament, Alexandria, VA

St. George, Rev. Peter T., '95 (CIN) Corpus Christi, Cincinnati, OH; St. John Neumann, Cincinnati, OH; St. John the Baptist, Cincinnati, OH

St. Germain, Rev. Andre, '96 (NTN) Retired.

St. Germain, Rev. Brian, '88 (PRM) On Leave.

St. Hilaire, Rev. Andrew, (HBG) St. Francis Xavier, Gettysburg, PA; [CAM] Gettysburg College, Gettysburg, PA

St. Hilaire, Rev. Kenneth, (SPK) Immaculate Conception, Colville, WA; Immaculate Conception, Republic, WA; Pure Heart of Mary, Northport, WA; Sacred Heart, Springdale, WA; Sacred Heart of Jesus, Kettle Falls, WA; St. Mary of the Rosary, Chewelah, WA; St. Patrick Mission, Curlew, WA; [SEM] Bishop White Seminary, Spokane, WA

St. Jean, Rev. Marcel, '96 (BGP) Chaplain at Norwalk Hospital The Church of Our Lady of the Assumption, Fairfield, CT

St. John, Rev. George, (ALB) Curia: Offices and Directors

St. Jules, Very Rev. Stephen, '79 (RCK) On Special Assignment. Dean, Aurora Deanery Curia: Leadership; Offices and Directors St. Katharine Drexel Parish, Sugar Grove, IL

St. Laurent, Rev. Daniel A., '71 (MAN) Retired.

St. Louis, Rev. Richard E., '00 (MAN) On Leave.

St. Louis, Rev. Spenser, '19 (FTW) Queen of Angels, Fort Wayne, IN

St. Marie, Rev. Michael, '93 (B) Curia: Leadership

St. Marie, Rev. Michael A., '93 (B) All Saints Catholic Parish, Lewiston, ID

St. Martin, Rev. Jeremy P., '02 (BO) Curia: Consultative Bodies St. Jude, Waltham, MA

St. Martin, Rev. Robert, *O.F.M.Conv.* '77 (IND) St. Anthony of Padua Catholic Church, Clarksville, Inc.,

Clarksville, IN; St. Benedict Catholic Church, Terre Haute, Inc., Terre Haute, IN; St. Joseph University Parish, Terre Haute, IN
St. Paul, Rev. Michael, '05 (ORG) Holy Trinity, Ladera Ranch, CA
St. Peter, Rev. Dallas T., '07 (BUR) Curia: Leadership Our Lady of Grace, Colchester, VT; St. Mark's, Burlington, VT
St. Pierre, Rev. Ronald L., (BO) Holy Family, Amesbury, MA; Star of the Sea, Amesbury, MA
St. Preux Dabel, Rev. Andre F., '03 (BRK) Chap, Jamaica Hosp - Trump Pavilion Our Lady of the Cenacle, Richmond Hill, NY
St. Romain, Rev. Irion, '10 (ALX) Immaculate Conception, Natchitoches, LA
St. Vil, Rev. Romane, *M.M.* '03 (NY) [MON] Maryknoll Fathers and Brothers (Catholic Foreign Mission Society of America, Inc.), Ossining, NY
Staal, Rev. David E., '90 (OAK) Curia: Offices and Directors St. Michael, Livermore, CA
Staar, Rev. Robert J., '77 (NY) Retired. Christ the King, Yonkers, NY
Stabile, Very Rev. Thomas, *T.O.R.* '87 (ALT) Holy Family, Portage, PA
Stabile, Very Rev. Thomas F., *T.O.R.* '87 (ALT) Curia: Deaneries
Stachacz, Rev. James T., '98 (RVC) Curia: Offices and Directors
Stacherczak, Rev. Idzi, '75 (CHI) Retired. [MIS] Catholic League for Religious Assistance to Poland, Chicago, IL
Stachnik, Rev. Kenneth R., '86 (GLD) Saint Philip Neri of Empire, Empire, MI; Saint Rita-Saint Joseph of Maple City, Maple City, MI
Stachowiak, Rev. Conrad P., '74 (BUF) Retired. [MON] Msgr. Conniff Residence, Depew, NY
Stachowiak, Rev. Kamil, '15 (PAT) Our Lady Queen of Peace, Hewitt, NJ
Stachura, Rev. Thaddeus X., '64 (WOR) Retired.
Stachura, Rev. Wojciech, *SAC* '95 (COL) St. Christopher, Columbus, OH
Stachurski, Rev. Miroslaw, '03 (BGP) St. Thomas the Apostle Roman Catholic Church Corporation, Norwalk, CT
Stachyra, Rev. Kenneth J., '01 (RCK) St. Bernadette, Rockford, IL
Stack, Rev. Msgr. Daniel, '82 (ATL) Retired.
Stack, Rev. Gabriel D., *O.Praem.* '82 (ORG) [MON] Norbertine Fathers of Orange, Inc., Silverado, CA
Stack, Rev. James M., '86 (WDC) St. Anthony's, North Beach, MD
Stack, Rev. Jerome P., *C.PP.S.* '72 (CIN) Retired. [MON] St. Charles, Celina, OH
Stack, Rev. John J., '88 (DAV) Holy Family Parish of Fort Madison, Iowa, Fort Madison, IA
Stack, Rev. Padraic, (OM) St. Patrick (Elkhorn), Elkhorn, NE
Stacy, Rev. Brian, *O.F.M.Cap.* '16 (WDC) [SEM] St. Francis Friary-Capuchin College, Washington, DC
Stacy, Rev. Brian, *OFM Cap* '16 (PIT) [MON] The Capuchin Franciscan Friars Province of Saint Augustine, Pittsburgh, PA
Stadmeyer, Rev. Raymond, *O.F.M. Cap* (GB) [MON] St. Joseph Church, Appleton, WI
Stadtmueller, Rev. Roman, *S.D.S.* '54 (WDC) Retired. [SEM] Salvatorian Community, Silver Spring, MD
Staehler, Rev. Adrian, *O.F.M.Cap.* '67 (MIL)
Stafford, Rev. Dennis, '91 (CHI) Retired.
Stagg, Rev. Robert B., '75 (NEW) Church of the Presentation, Upper Saddle River, NJ
Stagnaro, Rev. John J., '76 (BO) Retired.
Stahl, Rev. Allen M., '75 (ORL) Retired.
Stahl, Rev. David A., '91 (DEN) Retired.
Stahmer, Rev. Andrew J., '05 (HBG) Holy Angels, Kulpmont, PA; Our Lady of Lourdes Regional School, Coal Township, PA
Stahura, Rev. Joseph L., '81 (HBG) Retired.
Staib, Rev. Msgr. Donald F., '61 (R) Retired. St. Mary Magdalene, Apex, NC
Staigers, Rev. P. Del, '87 (CIN) St. Andrew, Milford, OH; St. Elizabeth Ann Seton, Milford, OH; St. Veronica, Cincinnati, OH
Stainbrook, Rev. Christopher, '12 (POC) Church of St. Mary the Virgin, Arlington, TX
Stainwall, Rev. Bernal, '80 (NY) Holy Rosary, Staten Island, NY; Parish of St. John the Evangelist and Our Lady of Peace, New York, NY
Stajkowski, Rev. Leo S., '66 (ALN) Retired.
Stake, Rev. Ronald P., '85 (CHI) St. Elizabeth of the Trinity, Chicago, IL
Stakem, Rev. Ward, *O.F.M.Cap.* '78 (PIT) St. Clare of Assisi, Chicora, PA; St. Francis of Assisi, Cabot, PA; St. John the Evangelist, Fenelton, PA; St. Mary of the Assumption, Butler, PA; [MON] St. Mary's Friary, Butler, PA
Staley, Rev. George, '19 (STL) St. Francis of Assisi Catholic Church, Oakville, St. Louis, MO
Staley, Rev. Robert P., '95 (R) St. Matthew, Durham, NC
Stalla, Rev. Michael J., '03 (CLV) SS. Cosmas and Damian, Twinsburg, OH
Stamm, Rev. Peter L., '15 (BO) [SEM] Saint John's Seminary, Brighton, MA
Stampiglia, Very Rev. Fausto, *S.A.C.* '60 (VEN) Retired. Curia: Advisory Boards, Commissions, Committees, and Councils; Leadership
Stamschror, Rev. Robert P., '61 (WIN) Retired.
Stanberry, Rev. Stephen L., '80 (TOL) Our Lady of Mercy, Fayette, OH; St. Peter, Archbold, OH
Stanchik, Rev. Dennis P., '59 (LC) Retired. St. Bartholomew, Stevens Point, WI
Stander, Rev. Charles, *SM* (STL) [MON] Marianist Province of the United States (Society of Mary), St. Louis, MO
Stander, Rev. Charles J., *S.M.* '81 (CIN) [COL] The University of Dayton, Dayton, OH; [SEM] Marianist Community, Dayton, OH
Stander, Rev. Edwin L., '63 (LIN) Retired.
Stanfield, Rev. William L., '76 (MIL) Retired.
Stanfill, Rev. David J., '10 (RIC) Retired.
Stang, Rev. John Albert, '22 (DOD) Cathedral of Our Lady of Guadalupe Catholic Church of Dodge City, Kansas, Dodge City, KS
Stang, Rev. Mark, '90 (SCL) Curia: Leadership [HOS] St. Cloud Hospital, St. Cloud, MN
Stang, Rev. William, *C.PP.S.* '77 (CIN) [MON] Society of the Precious Blood, United States Province, Inc., Dayton, OH
Stanganelli, Rev. Anthony M., '79 (RVC) Church of Saint Brigid, Inc., Westbury, NY
Stanger, Rev. Edward J., '91 (STL) Holy Infant Catholic Church, Ballwin, MO
Stanger, Rev. Harold B., '77 (CHI) Retired.
Stangricki, Rev. Peter, *M.S.* '05 (MIL) [MON] La Salette Missionaries, Twin Lakes, WI
Stanibula, Rev. Christopher, '95 (FR) St. Anthony's, Mattapoisett, MA; St. Rita's, Marion, MA
Stanichar, Rt. Rev. Joseph, '68 (HPM) Curia: Leadership; Offices and Directors
Stanish, Very Rev. Christopher M., '14 (GRY) Curia: Leadership; Offices and Directors
Staniskis, Rev. Daniel, '84 (WIL) Holy Name of Jesus, Pocomoke City, MD
Stankard, Rev. Albert H., '59 (BO) Retired.
Stanley, Rev. Charles R., '71 (BO) Retired. Immaculate Conception, Newburyport, MA
Stanley, Rev. Cory D., '11 (OKL) Curia: Clergy and Religious Services Holy Trinity, Okarche, OK
Stanley, Rev. James Colm, *S.S.C.* '69 (OM) Retired. [MON] Missionary Society of St. Columban, St. Columbans, NE
Stanley, Rev. Matthew D., '91 (SJ) Curia: Offices and Directors St. Francis of Assisi, San Jose, CA
Stanley, Rev. Richard J., *S.J.* '74 (BO) [MON] Campion Health & Wellness, Inc., Weston, MA; [RTR] Eastern Point Retreat House, Gloucester, MA
Stano, Rev. Luke M, *O.S.M.* (CHI) [MIS] Monastery of Our Lady of Sorrows, ,
Stano, Rev. Nicholas H., '22 (BO) Holy Family, Concord, MA; St. Irene, Carlisle, MA
Stanosz, Rev. Paul A., '84 (MIL) On Sick Leave.
Stanowski, Rev. Bartlomiej, *O.C.D.* '06 (GRY) [MON] Discalced Carmelite Fathers Monastery, Munster, IN
Stanowski, Rev. Piotr, *S.J.* (BO) [MON] Alberto Hurtado House, Boston, MA
Stansberry, Rev. Richard D., '92 (OKL) Curia: Advisory Boards, Commissions, Committees, and Councils; Organizations (affiliated, inter-Diocesan, miscellaneous/ other); Tribunal Cathedral of Our Lady of Perpetual Help, Oklahoma City, OK
Stansley, Rev. Msgr. Ralph W., '73 (TR) Retired. Curia: Canonical Services [MON] Villa Vianney, Trenton, NJ
Stanton, Rev. Finbarr P., '67 (SAV) Retired.
Stanton, Rev. Francis M., '51 (COL) Retired.
Stanton, Rev. John E., '13 (BUF) Saint John XXIII, West Seneca, NY
Stanton, Very Rev. Kyle F., '11 (MAN) Chap, Northern New Hampshire Corr Fac Curia: Consultative Bodies Good Shepherd, Berlin, NH; Holy Family, Gorham, NH
Stanton, Rev. Thomas J., '91 (BO) St. Agatha, Milton, MA
Stapenhorst, Rev. Verne P., '61 (SC) Retired.
Staples, Rev. Terrence R., '95 (ARL) St. Isidore the Farmer, Orange, VA
Stapleton, Rev. Gerard P., '85 (NO) St. Patrick, Port Sulphur, LA
Stapleton, Rev. John, '21 (DEN) St. John the Baptist Catholic Parish in Longmont, Longmont, CO
Starasinich, Rev. James, (WIN) Christ the King, Medford, MN; St. Joseph, Owatonna, MN
Starasinich, Rev. James E., '99 (NEW) On Duty Outside Diocese. St Joseph, Owatonna, MN
Starbuck, Rev. James, '48 (OAK) Retired.
Starbuck, Rev. James, (PHX) St. Rose Philippine Duchesne Roman Catholic Parish, Anthem, AZ
Starcher, Rev. Gilbert, '20 (MET) St. Philip & St. James, Phillipsburg, NJ
Starczewski, Very Rev. John Francis, '04 (CHL) St. John Neumann, Charlotte, NC
Stark, Rt. Rev. Matthew, *O.S.B.* '63 (PRO) Retired. [MON] Abbey of St. Gregory the Great (Order of St. Benedict in Portsmouth, Rhode Island, Benedictines of the English Congregation), Portsmouth, RI
Stark, Rev. Nicholas, (DM) Christ the King, Des Moines, IA
Stark, Rev. Robert, *S.S.S.* '77 (HON) Curia: Advisory Boards, Commissions, Committees, and Councils; Community Services Mary, Star of the Sea, Honolulu, HI
Stark, Rev. Ronald, *OFM* '66 (SP) Retired. [MON] St. Anthony Friary (St. Petersburg) Franciscan Friars-Holy Name Province, Inc., St. Petersburg, FL
Stark, Rev. Ronald P., *O.F.M.* '66 (NY) [MIS] Franciscan Missionary Charities, Inc., New York, NY
Starkovich, Rev. Jeffery Paul, '11 (LKC) Curia: Advisory Boards, Commissions, Committees, and Councils; Leadership St. Pius X Catholic Church, Ragley, LA
Starks, Rev. Ryan, '14 (GB) St. Therese, Appleton, WI
Starman, Rev. Bernard G, (OM) [RTR] Niobrara Valley House of Renewal, Lynch, NE
Starman, Rev. Bernard G., '06 (OM) Curia: Leadership; Offices and Directors Sacred Heart Parish of Boyd County, Butte, NE; St. Boniface, Stuart, NE; St. Joseph, Atkinson, NE; St. Patrick, O'Neill, NE
Starr, Rev. Bradley A., '17 (ATL) Good Samaritan Catholic Church, Ellijay, Inc., Ellijay, GA
Starr, Rev. Mark, '12 (ATL) Curia: Advisory Boards, Commissions, Committees, and Councils Our Lady of LaSalette Catholic Church, Canton, Inc., Canton, GA
Starzynski, Rev. Stefan P., '96 (ARL) St. Michael, Annandale, VA
Stash, Rev. Robert, '82 (PRM) St. Michael the Archangel, Oregon, OH
Stashek, Rev. Brian E., '02 (LC) On Leave.
Stashkevych, Rev. Vitalii, '18 (PBR) SS. Peter and Paul, Braddock, PA; St. Elias, Munhall, PA
Stasiak, Rev. Grzegorz, '99 (BRK) St. Rose of Lima, Brooklyn, NY; [CCH] Polish Ministry, ,
Stasiak, Rt. Rev. Kurt, *O.S.B.* '80 (IND) Retired. [MON] St. Meinrad Archabbey, St. Meinrad, IN
Stasiowski, Rev. John, '65 (FWT) Retired.
Stasker, Rev. Msgr. R. Louis, '65 (GR) Retired.
Stasyszen, Rt. Rev. Lawrence R., *O.S.B.* '94 (OKL) [MON] St. Gregory's Abbey (Benedictine Fathers of Sacred Heart Mission, Inc.), Shawnee, OK
Staszewski, Rev. Joseph P., '64 (E) Retired.
Staszewski, Rev. Robert M., '72 (PIT) Retired.
Stattmiller, Rev. John E., '66 (COL) Retired.
Statz, Rev. James, '84 (SCL) Church of Saint Anne, Kimball, MN; St. Nicholas, Watkins, MN
Statz, Rev. Jeffrey P., '05 (MAN) St. Francis of Assisi, Litchfield, NH; St. Joseph Cathedral, Manchester, NH
Staublin, Very Rev. Daniel J., '82 (IND) Curia: Leadership St. Agnes Catholic Church, Nashville, Inc., Nashville, IN; St. Ambrose Catholic Church, Seymour, Inc., Seymour, IN; [MIS] Seymour Deanery, Indianapolis, IN
Staudenmaier, Rev. John M., *S.J.* '70 (DET) [MON] Colombiere Center, Clarkston, MI
Staudinger, Rev. Gregory, '81 (GF) St. Pius X, Billings, MT
Staudt, Rev. Msgr. Joseph W., '78 (RVC) Our Lady of Ostrabrama, Cutchogue, NY; Sacred Heart, Cutchogue, NY
Staunton, Rev. Msgr. Patrick Joseph, '60 (LA) Retired.
Stavarz, Rev. David, (CLV) St. Gabriel, Concord Twp., OH
Stavoy, Rev. Stephen J., '79 (SCR) Retired.
Stawarczyk, Rev. Pawel, '96 (PHX) St. Luke Roman Catholic Parish, Phoenix, AZ
Stawasz, Rev. David, *S.D.C.* '04 (LAN) [PRE] St. Louis Center for Exceptional Children & Adults, Chelsea, MI
Stawiarski, Rev. Waldemar, '03 (CHI) SS. Cyril and Methodius, Lemont, IL; St. James at Sag Bridge Mission, Lemont, IL
Stayer, Rev. Jayme, *S.J.* (CHI) [COL] Jesuit Community at Loyola University Chicago, Chicago, IL

Staysniak, Rev. Dale W., '75 (CLV) St. Anthony of Padua, Parma, OH
Stearns, Rev. John David, '14 (COS) Chap, Fire Department; Police Department St. Dominic, Security, CO
Stearns, Rev. Msgr. Joseph E., '72 (VEN) Retired.
Steber, Rev. Msgr. Michael J., '86 (MAR) Curia: Advisory Boards, Commissions, Committees, and Councils; Organizations (affiliated, inter-Diocesan, miscellaneous/other) St. Peter Cathedral, Marquette, MI
Stec, Rev. John, '74 (MET) St. Mary of Czestochowa, Bound Brook, NJ
Stec, Very Rev. Mark D., '88 (BEL) Curia: Leadership Holy Cross, Newton, IL; St. Joseph, Olney, IL; St. Lawrence, Lawrenceville, IL
Stec, Rev. Michael S., '94 (LIN) Curia: Offices and Directors Immaculate Conception, Ulysses, NE
Stec, Rev. Robert G., '88 (CLV) St. Ambrose, Brunswick, OH
Stecher, Rev. John E., '72 (DAV) Retired. [MON] St. Vincent Center, Davenport, IA
Stechmann, Rev. Michael, *O.A.R.* '08 (LA) Cristo Rey, Los Angeles, CA
Stechschulte, Rev. Barry J., '09 (CIN) St. Susanna, Mason, OH
Steck, Rev. Christopher W., *S.J.* '94 (WDC) [COL] Georgetown University, Washington, DC; [MIS] Theological Studies, Inc., Washington, DC; [MON] The Jesuit Community at Georgetown University, Washington, DC
Steckel, Rev. Gregory A., '81 (DAV) Retired.
Stecklein, Rev. Warren L., '90 (DOD) Curia: Offices and Directors St. Dominic Catholic Church of Garden City, Kansas, Garden City, KS; St. Stanislaus Catholic Church of Ingalls, Kansas, Ingalls, KS
Steckler, Rev. Kenneth, '96 (EVN) On Leave.
Stecz, Rev. Jeffrey M., '99 (PH) St. Agnes, Sellersville, PA
Stecz, Rev. Rafal, '13 (CHI) St. Daniel the Prophet, Chicago, IL
Steele, Rev. Daniel O., '16 (YAK) Holy Family, Yakima, WA
Steele, Rev. Jeffrey, *OSB* '07 (SFE) [MON] Monastery of Christ in the Desert, Abiquiu, NM
Steele, Rev. John, *C.S.C.* '97 (FTW) Blessed Sacrament, Albion, IN; Immaculate Conception, Kendallville, IN
Steele, Rev. Joseph S., '97 (LIN) [MIS] Madonna Rehabilitation Hospitals, Lincoln, NE
Steele, Rev. Michael L., '77 (BO) Retired.
Stefancin, Rev. Joseph, '20 (SUP) Curia: Offices and Directors Immaculate Conception, Hammond, WI; St. Bridget, River Falls, WI; [CAM] St. Thomas More Newman Center, River Falls, WI
Stefanko, Rev. Msgr. Paul F., '76 (PRT) Retired. Curia: Clergy and Religious Services; Consultative Bodies; Leadership; Offices and Directors
Stefanowski, Rev. Mariusz P., '04 (CHI) Our Lady of the Rosary Parish, Chicago, IL; St. Ferdinand, Chicago, IL
Steffen, Rev. Jonathan, '12 (PEO) St. Monica Church, East Peoria, IL; St. Patrick's, Washington, IL
Steffen, Rev. Msgr. Kenneth Charles, '84 (SFD) Retired.
Steffens, Rev. Terrence J., '82 (GRY) Holy Trinity, East Chicago, IN
Steffensmeier, Rev. Msgr. Ralph J., (OM) Retired.
Steffes, Rev. James P., '93 (WIN) St. Augustine's, Austin, MN; St. Edward's, Austin, MN; [CEM] Calvary Cemetery, Austin, MN
Steffes, Rev. LuVerne W., '95 (OM) Retired.
Steffes, Rev. Raymond, *O.S.C.* '58 (SCL) [MON] Crosier Priory, Onamia, MN
Steffl, Rev. Mark S., '05 (NU) On Special Assignment. Curia: Leadership; Offices and Directors Church of the Japanese Martyrs, Sleepy Eye, MN; St. Mary, Sleepy Eye, MN; St. Michael, Morgan, MN; St. Paul, Comfrey, MN
Stefula, Rev. Salvator, *T.O.R.* (SP) St. Patrick, Tampa, FL; [NUR] St. Patrick's Housing Corporation (Patrician Arms), Tampa, FL; [NUR] St. Patrick's Housing Corporation II (Patrician Arms II), Tampa, FL
Stegbauer, Rev. Jeffrey, '19 (CIN) Our Lady of the Rosary, Cincinnati, OH; Our Lady of the Valley Parish, Reading, OH; St. James of the Valley, Wyoming, OH; St. Matthias, Cincinnati, OH
Steggert, Rev. Bruce A., *S.J.* '93 (BAL) [COL] Jesuit Community of Loyola University, Inc., Baltimore, MD; [MON] Jesuit Community of Loyola University Maryland, Inc., Baltimore, MD
Stegman, Rev. Thomas D., *S.J.* '95 (BO) [COL] The School of Theology and Ministry, , ; [MON] Campion Health & Wellness, Inc., Weston, MA; [MON] Walter Ciszek House, Brighton, MA
Stegmann, Rev. Robert, '95 (GB) SS. Peter and Paul, Sturgeon Bay, WI; St. Joseph, Sturgeon Bay, WI
Stehlik, Rev. Thomas J., *C.M.* '96 (NO) St. Joseph Roman Catholic, New Orleans, LA; [MON] Congregation of the Mission Western Province (Vincentians) (DePaul Residence), New Orleans, LA
Stehling, Rev. Larry, '88 (AUS) Santa Rosa, Florence, TX
Stehling, Rev. Matthew, '14 (TYL) Sacred Heart, Nacogdoches, TX; St. Boniface Catholic Classical High School, Nacogdoches, TX
Stehly, Rev. Msgr. Dennis R., '77 (STL) Curia: Leadership
Stehly, Rev. James, '61 (LA) St. Jude, Westlake Village, CA
Steier, Rev. Charles, '73 (SAL) Christ the King Parish, WaKeeney, Inc., WaKeeney, KS; St. Michael Parish, Collyer, Inc., Collyer, KS
Steimel, Rev. Craig E., '89 (DUB) Immaculate Conception Church, Van Horne, Iowa, Van Horne, IA; St. John's Church, Blairstown, Iowa, Blairstown, IA; St. Michael Church, Norway, Iowa, Norway, IA; St. Patrick Church, Watkins, Iowa, Watkins, IA; St. Paul's Church, Newhall, Iowa, Newhall, IA
Stein, Rev. John, *OFM* (CIN) [MON] St. Clement Friary, Cincinnati, OH
Stein, Rev. John, *O. F. M.* '85 (CIN) St. Clement, Cincinnati, OH
Stein, Rev. Mark J., '02 (TUC) Assumption of the Blessed Virgin Mary Roman Catholic Parish - Florence, Florence, AZ; Sacred Heart of Jesus Roman Catholic Church - Willcox, Willcox, AZ
Steinacker, Rev. Anthony, '06 (FTW) SS. Peter and Paul, Huntington, IN
Steinbacher, Rev. Wil, '62 (CIN) Retired. [MON] Headquarters of Glenmary Home Missioners (The Home Missioners of America), Fairfield, OH
Steinbauer, Rev. Joseph R., '79 (TOL) [EFT] Sandusky Central Catholic Educational Foundation, Inc., Sandusky, OH
Steinbeisser, Rev. Joseph A., '86 (NU) Curia: Advisory Boards, Commissions, Committees, and Councils Holy Redeemer, Renville, MN; St. Aloysius, Olivia, MN; St. Mary, Bird Island, MN
Steinbrunner, Rev. Jerome, *C.PP.S.* '74 (CIN) [MON] Society of the Precious Blood, United States Province, Inc., Dayton, OH
Steinbrunner, Rev. Jerome R., *C.PP.S.* '74 (MO) Curia: Offices and Directors
Steiner, Rev. Bernard J., '61 (NU) Retired.
Steiner, Rev. Daniel J., '16 (NSH) Curia: Leadership Holy Rosary, Nashville, TN
Steiner, Rev. Daniel R., '79 (CHI) On Special Assignment. [NUR] Ascension Living Casa Scalabrini Village (Ascension Senior Services-Chicagoland; Casa San Carlo Retirement Community), Northlake, IL
Steiner, Rev. Edward F., '82 (NSH) Curia: Leadership St. Philip, Franklin, TN
Steiner, Rev. Msgr. John, '69 (SPK) Retired. Curia: Leadership
Steiner, Rev. Msgr. John M., '69 (SPK) Retired.
Steingraeber, Rev. John, *C.Ss.R.* '74 (CHI) [MON] The Redemptorist Fathers of Chicago, Chicago, IL; [MON] The Redemptorists/Denver Province, Chicago, IL
Steinhauser, Rev. Kenneth B., '70 (JC) Retired.
Steinle, Rev. David G., '79 (DAV) Retired.
Steinmetz, Rev. Thomas P., (MAN) Chap, Veterans Administration Med Ctr
Steinmetz, Rev. Thomas P., (MO) Curia: Offices and Directors
Steinmetz, Very Rev. Archpriest Thomas P., '02 (NTN) Curia: Administration; Consultative Bodies; (>MO) Offices and Directors; Pastoral Services Our Lady of the Cedars, Manchester, NH
Steinmiller, Rev. Alex, *CP* '70 (DET) [MON] St. Paul of the Cross Community, Congregation of the Passion, Detroit, MI
Steinwachs, Rev. David, *O.S.B.* '58 (SP) [MON] St. Leo Abbey, Saint Leo, FL
Steller, Rev. Paul W., '65 (BUF) Retired.
Stellini, Rev. Robert J., '07 (MEM) Retired.
Stelmach, Rev. Dawid, (MO) Curia: Offices and Directors
Stelmach, Rev. Jerome J., '80 (BUF) Retired.
Stelmach, Rev. Maciej, '14 (JOL) St. Andrew the Apostle, Romeoville, IL
Stelmach, Rev. Canon Michael, (STN) Retired.
Stelmaszczyk, Rev. Miroslaw, '77 (PIT) St. Matthew, Pittsburgh, PA; [MON] St. John Vianney Manor, Pittsburgh, PA
Steltenkamp, Rev. Michael, *SJ* (SAG) Saint John XXIII Parish of Hemlock and Merrill, Hemlock, MI
Stelter, Rev. Richard T., '80 (RVC) Our Lady of Peace, Lynbrook, NY
Stelzer, Rev. Eric, '19 (STA) Assumption, Jacksonville, FL; Our Lady Star of the Sea, Ponte Vedra Beach, FL
Stelzer, Rev. Mark S., '83 (SPR) Curia: Leadership; Offices and Directors Saint Mary's Parish, Hampden, Hampden, MA; [CAM] College of Our Lady of the Elms College, Chicopee, MA
Stembler, Very Rev. James G., '89 (CC) Curia: Administration; Leadership; Organizations (affiliated, inter-Diocesan, miscellaneous/other)
Stemmann, Rev. Joseph, '63 (LAF) Retired.
Stemn, Rev. Paul G., '09 (CHI) St. John Newman, Evanston, IL
Stempora, Rev. Daniel F., '60 (JOL) Retired. [NUR] St. John Vianney Villa, Naperville, IL
Stempsey, Rev. William E., *S.J.* '92 (WOR) [MON] Jesuits of the Holy Cross, Inc., Worcester, MA
Stengel, Rev. Mark, *O.S.B.* '72 (LR) St. Benedict, Subiaco, AR; St. Scholastica, New Blaine, AR; [MON] Subiaco Abbey, Subiaco, AR; [RTR] Hesychia House of Prayer, New Blaine, AR
Stenger, Rev. James R., '81 (CLV) Mary, Queen of the Apostles Parish, Brook Park, OH
Stenger, Very Rev. Ryan L., '14 (COV) Curia: Advisory Boards, Commissions, Committees, and Councils; Tribunal St. Joseph, Camp Springs, KY
Stenson, Rev. Patrick, (SAT) [MON] Missionaries of the Sacred Heart, San Antonio, TX
Stenson, Rev. Patrick J., *M.S.C.* '63 (CHR) Retired.
Stenson, Rev. Paul, (PH) Retired. Sacred Heart, Clifton Heights, PA
Stenzel, Rev. Eugene F., '67 (WIN) Retired.
Stenzel, Rev. William J., '75 (CHI) Retired.
Stepanski, Rev. Thomas K., '62 (IND) Retired.
Stephan, Rev. Jeeson V., *MCBS* (SYM) St. Mary Syro-Malabar Catholic Mission Pittsburgh, PA, Pittsburgh, PA
Stephan, Rev. Jeeson Venattu, '09 (WH) Our Lady of Seven Dolors Mission, Triadelphia, WV; St. Vincent de Paul, Wheeling, WV
Stephan, Rev. M. Jeffrey, '01 (KC) St. Sabina Catholic Church, Belton, Belton, MO
Stephan, Rev. Matthew J., '83 (CC) Retired.
Stephanz, Rev. Jonathan, '16 (SP) St. Raphael, St. Petersburg, FL
Stephen, Rev. Ashok, *O.M.I.* '00 (SAC) Pastor of Sacred Heart Parish, Alturas, a corporation sole, Alturas, CA
Stephen, Rev. Emmanuel Eche, '16 (LSC) St. Eleanor Parish, Inc., Ruidoso, NM
Stephens, Rev. Anthony M., *C.P.M.* '05 (OWN) [MON] Fathers of Mercy, Auburn, KY
Stephens, Rev. Kevin, *OP* (STL) [SEM] Aquinas Institute of Theology, St. Louis, MO
Stephens, Rev. Kevin, *O.P.* '08 (STL) [MON] St. Dominic Priory, St. Louis, MO
Stephens, Rev. Timothy J., *SJ* (CHL) St. Peter, Charlotte, NC; [MON] St. Peter Jesuit Community, Charlotte, NC
Stephens, Rev. Tony, *C.P.M.* '05 (SFD) [CAM] Newman Connection, Inc., Teutopolis, IL
Stephens, Rev. Travis R., '12 (LFT) Curia: Miscellaneous / Other Offices St. Alphonsus Liguori, Zionsville, IN
Stephenson, Rev. Alphonse J., '75 (PAT) Retired.
Sterling, Rev. John J., '96 (COV) St. Barbara, Erlanger, KY
Stern, Rev. Msgr. Robert L., '58 (NY) Retired.
Sternberg, Rev. Eric G., '05 (MAD) Saint Cecilia, Wisconsin Dells, WI
Sternemann, Rev. Reinhard J., *O.S.A.* '66 (CHI) [MON] St. John Stone Friary, Chicago, IL
Sternhagen, Rev. Dominic, (SLC) Curia: Offices and Directors Saint Ann LLC 215, Salt Lake City, UT
Sterowski, Rev. Scott P., '91 (SCR) Curia: Offices and Directors Blessed Sacrament Parish, Throop, PA; Holy Cross Parish, Olyphant, PA; St. Francis of Assisi, Scranton, PA
Stettler, Rev. Aaron, *SSJ* (P) Church of St. Michael the Archangel, Portland, OR
Stetz, Rev. Allan, *O.S.B.* '87 (KC) [MON] Conception Abbey (Benedictine Monks), Conception, MO
Steuterman, Rev. James M., '75 (WOR) Retired.
Steven, Rev. Frenier, *OFM Conv* (SY) Retired.
Stevens, Rev. Barton K., '10 (GF) Curia: Leadership St. Anthony, Laurel, MT
Stevens, Rev. David, '98 (SFS) Sacred Heart Parish of Hutchinson County, Parkston, SD; Saints Peter and Paul Parish of Hutchinson County, Dimock, SD
Stevens, Rev. Gladstone H., *S.S.* '00 (L) On Duty Outside Diocese. St. Mary's Seminary, Baltimore MD
Stevens, Rev. Gladstone H., *P.S.S.* '00 (BAL) [MIS] St. Mary's Seminary & University, Baltimore, MD; [MON] Society of St. Sulpice, Province of the United States, Baltimore, MD; [SEM] St. Mary's Seminary and University, Baltimore, MD

Stevens, Rev. Joshua R., (MO) Curia: Offices and Directors
Stevens, Rev. Shane, (SFS) Curia: Offices and Directors Saint Mary Parish of Minnehaha County, Dell Rapids, SD
Stevensky, Rev. Msgr. Mitred John P., '63 (SJP) Retired. Curia: Offices and Directors
Stevenson, Rev. R. Francis, '92 (SAC) Pastor of Corpus Christi Parish, Tahoe City, a corporation sole, Tahoe City, CA
Stevenson, Rev. William, '86 (SD) Retired.
Stevenson, Rev. William J., '82 (LAN) Retired.
Stewart, Rev. Anthony, '18 (NSH) Mother Teresa, Nolensville, TN
Stewart, Rev. August, '94 (COS) St. Joseph's, Colorado Springs, CO
Stewart, Rev. Claudio, *I.V.E.* '90 (VEN) Curia: Leadership; Organizations (affiliated, inter-Diocesan, miscellaneous/other)
Stewart, Rev. Columba, *O.S.B.* '90 (SCL) [MON] St. John's Abbey, of the Order of St. Benedict, Collegeville, MN
Stewart, Rev. Edward R., '89 (BRK) On Duty Outside Diocese.
Stewart, Rev. George R., '94 (NY) St. Augustine Our Lady of Victory, Bronx, NY
Stewart, Very Rev. J. Keith, '93 (MEM) Curia: Leadership St. Louis, Memphis, TN
Stewart, Rev. Matthew C., *S.J.* '20 (STL) [MON] Saint Jean de Brebeuf Jesuit Community, St. Louis, MO
Stewart, Rev. Patrick F., '78 (LEX) Pax Christi Catholic Church, Lexington, KY
Stewart, Rev. Paul, '73 (PT) Retired. Curia: (>MO) Offices and Directors
Stewart, Rev. Msgr. Terrence L., '70 (GR) Holy Family, Sparta, MI
Sticco, Rev. Peter T., *S.A.C.* '69 (NEW) Our Lady of Grace, Fairview, NJ; [MIS] The Pallottines of South Orange, Inc., South Orange, NJ; [MON] Pallottine Fathers & Brothers, South Orange, NJ
Sticco, Rev. Peter T., *S.A.C.* '69 (BAL) [EFT] Pallottine Charitable, Educational and Apostolic Ministry Trust, Baltimore, MD; [MIS] St. Jude Shrine Corporation, Baltimore, MD; [MON] Pallottine Center for Apostolic Causes, Baltimore, MD
Stice, Rev. Randy, '07 (KNX) Curia: Offices and Directors
Sticha, Rev. Cory D., '08 (GF) Curia: Leadership; Offices and Directors St. Ann, Fort Shaw, MT
Stiegeler, Rev. A. Francis, *S.J.* '78 (SFR) [MON] Jesuit Community at St. Ignatius College Preparatory, San Francisco, CA
Stiene, Rev. Paul, *I.C.* (SP) St. Theresa, Spring Hill, FL
Stikel, Rev. Roman, '88 (MIL) St. Mary's Congregation, Kenosha, WI
Stiles, Rev. J. Roy, '63 (L) Retired.
Stiles, Rev. James J., '15 (STP) Curia: Consultative Bodies The Church of Saint Stephen-Holy Rosary, Minneapolis, MN; [CEM] Calvary Cemetery, Le Center, MN; [CEM] Marysburg Cemetery, Madison Lake, MN; [CEM] St. Mary's Calvary Cemetery, Le Center, MN
Stillmunks, Rev. Steven, (STA) Retired. Blessed Trinity, Jacksonville, FL
Stilson, Rev. Sean, (SAT) St. Philip of Jesus, San Antonio, TX; [MIS] Brothers of the Beloved Disciple, San Antonio, TX
Stilwell, Rev. Dennis R., '71 (GLD) Retired. Curia: Leadership Saint Augustine of Boyne Falls, Boyne Falls, MI; Saint John Nepomucene of Praga, East Jordan, MI; Saint Matthew of Boyne City, Boyne City, MI
Stimpson, Rev. Adam, '09 (PEO) Curia: Deaneries St. Paul's, Macomb, IL; St. Rose, Rushville, IL; [CAM] St. Francis of Assisi Newman Center, Macomb, IL
Stine, Rev. Robert F., '73 (BR) Retired.
Stinea, Rev. Petru, '01 (ROM) St. Helena, Cleveland, OH
Stingel, Rev. Louis F., '60 (MET) Retired. [MON] Maria Regina Residence, Somerset, NJ
Stinson, Rev. Cassidy, (RIC) St. Jude, Christiansburg, VA; [CAM] Catholic Campus Ministry, Radford University, Radford, VA
Stinson, Rev. Michael, (PHX) Mater Misericordiae Catholic Church, Phoenix, AZ
Stirniman, Rev. Jeffrey D., '95 (PEO) Holy Trinity, Bloomington, IL; St. Patrick, Bloomington, IL; [ASN] Bloomington-Normal Catholic Cemetery Association, Bloomington, IL
Stirpe, Rev. Carlo C., '65 (SY) Retired.
Stiteler, Rev. Francis Michael, *O.C.S.O.* '83 (ATL) [MON] The Monastery of the Holy Spirit, Conyers, GA; [RTR] Monastery of the Holy Spirit, Conyers, GA
Stites, Rev. John F., '76 (TOL) Retired.
Stitt, Rev. Bryan D., '03 (OG) Curia: Administration; Offices and Directors The Roman Catholic Church of St. Mary in Canton, NY, Canton, NY
Stluka, Rev. Jerome D., '69 (COL) Retired.
Stober, Rev. Msgr. William P., '73 (PAT) Retired.
Stobie, Rev. Stephen A., '81 (P) Retired. On Leave.
Stochmal, Rev. Marek, '95 (DET) On Leave.
Stock, Rev. Maximo, *S.S.J.* '12 (P) [CAM] Newman Center at Oregon State University (Corvallis), Corvallis, OR; [MON] Saint John Society, Corvallis, OR
Stock, Rev. Thomas E., '98 (CLV) St. Mary, Berea, OH
Stock, Rev. Wayne, (SFD) On Leave.
Stockbridge, Rev. Kevin J., '09 (MEM) On Leave.
Stockdale, Rev. Bret, *S.J.* '13 (RVC) St. Anthony, Oceanside, NY
Stockelman, Rev. William R., '78 (CIN) Retired.
Stockton, Rev. Marc A., '02 (E) Curia: Offices and Directors St. Boniface, Erie, PA
Stodola, Rev. Francisco, '89 (LAR) Nuestra Senora del Rosario, Laredo, TX
Stoeckig, Rev. Robert E., '94 (LAV) Curia: Catholic Charities
Stoeckig, Rev. Robert E., '94 (LAV) Guardian Angel Cathedral, Las Vegas, NV
Stoecklein, Rev. Ted D., '01 (DOD) Curia: Leadership; Offices and Directors
Stoecklein, Rev. Ted Dean, '01 (DOD) St. Andrew Catholic Church of Wright, Kansas, Wright, KS
Stoeger, Rev. James A., *S.J.* '75 (CHI) (>DET) [MON] Colombiere Center, Clarkston, MI
Stoeger, Rev. Msgr. John D., '72 (LA) Curia: Offices and Directors
Stoeppel, Rev. Anthony J., '10 (TYL) On Duty Outside Diocese. (>SFR) [SEM] St. Patrick's Seminary and University (The Roman Catholic Seminary of San Francisco) Menlo Park, CA
Stoetzel, Rev. Msgr. Charles D., '80 (LC) Holy Family Parish, Prairie Du Chien, WI; [EFT] The St. Gabriel's Endowment Trust, Prairie du Chien, WI; [EFT] The St. John's Endowment Trust, Prairie du Chien, WI
Stoffel, Very Rev. Richard J., '79 (MIL) Congregation of the Resurrection, Allenton, WI; St. Lawrence Congregation, Hartford, WI; St. Peter's Congregation, Slinger, WI
Stoffer, Rev. Patrick, *OFM, Conv.* '97 (DET) St. Linus Parish Dearborn Heights, Dearborn Heights, MI
Stoia, Rev. Aurelius E., '09 (AGN) On Duty Outside Diocese.
Stokely, Rev. John P., '13 (PH) On Duty Outside Diocese.
Stokes, Rev. David L., '02 (PRO) Retired.
Stokes, Rev. Harry J., '10 (WDC) St. Joseph, Pomfret, MD
Stokes, Rev. Jason F., '11 (ALN) Chap, Manor Care Holy Family Parish, Minersville, PA
Stoley, Rev. Christopher, '15 (LIN) Sacred Heart, Crete, NE
Stoley, Rev. Christopher E., '15 (LIN) Curia: Leadership
Stoley, Rev. Lawrence J., '91 (LIN) Curia: Leadership; Offices and Directors SS. Peter and Paul, Falls City, NE; [EFT] Falls City Sacred Heart Catholic School Foundation, Falls City, NE
Stolinski, Rev. Robert A., '70 (BUF) Retired. [MON] O'Hara Residence, Tonawanda, NY
Stoll, Rev. Mark J., '92 (SC) Curia: Leadership; Offices and Directors Mater Dei Catholic Parish, Sioux City, IA
Stollenwerk, Rev. Charles J., '73 (CLV) Retired.
Stolowski, Rev. Stephen, '79 (NSH) Retired.
Stolt, Rev. Kevin, (WIN) SS. Peter and Paul Catholic Church, Mankato, MN
Stoltz, Rev. John J., '90 (L) Curia: Leadership St. Aloysius, Pewee Valley, KY
Stoltz, Rev. Richard L., '74 (STL) St. Alban Roe Catholic Church, Wildwood, MO
Stolzman, Rev. William F., '71 (STP) Retired.
Stone, Rev. Bob, '01 (CR) Retired.
Stone, Rev. Jason, '10 (JOL) Immaculate Conception of the Blessed Virgin Mary, Morris, IL
Stone, Rev. Jason P., '15 (SFD) Curia: Leadership Our Lady of the Holy Spirit, Mt. Zion, IL; St. Isidore, Bethany, IL
Stone, Rev. Jeffrey E., '05 (SFD) Fed Corr Inst, Greenville St. Lawrence, Greenville, IL
Stone, Rev. Robert, '90 (KC) Nativity of Mary Parish, Independence, MO; St. Bernadette Catholic Church, Kansas City, MO
Stone, Rev. Robert L., '01 (ORG) Retired. St. Elizabeth Ann Seton, Irvine, CA
Stone, Rev. Ronald, '01 (KNX) Holy Cross, Pigeon Forge, TN
Stone, Rev. Ronald, '01 (SFE) On Duty Outside Diocese.
Stoneberg, Rev. Jeffery, '90 (JOL) Christ the King, Lombard, IL
Stoner, Rev. Timothy L., '96 (GI) All Souls, Bridgeport, NE
Stookey, Rev. Gerald, *OP* '78 (CHI) [EFT] St. Dominic's Mission Society of the Dominican Fathers of the Province of St. Albert the Great, ,
Stookey, Rev. Gerald, *O.P.* (STL) [MON] Dominican Community of St. Louis, St. Louis, MO
Stoppel-Wasinger, Rev. Mark Shane, '94 (STP) St. George, Long Lake, MN; [CEM] Calvary Cemetery, Rush City, MN; [CEM] St. Joseph Cemetery, North Branch, MN
Storey, Rev. Mark D., '14 (BO) Retired. On Leave.
Storey, Rev. Richard, '04 (KCK) Cure of Ars, Leawood, KS
Stormes, Rev. James R., *S.J.* '79 (WOR) [MON] Jesuits of the Holy Cross, Inc., Worcester, MA (>ATL) [MON] Atlanta Jesuit Community, Inc., Decatur, GA
Stout, Rev. William, *O.F.M.* '00 (MIL) [MIS] Provincial Offices of the Franciscan Friars, Assumption BVM Province, Inc., , ; [MON] Queen of Peace Friary (Franciscan Friars of the Assumption B.V.M. Province), Burlington, WI
Stover, Rev. Daniel, '15 (KCK) Curia: Leadership Holy Angels, Garnett, KS; St. John the Baptist, Greeley, KS
Stoverink, Rev. Joseph, (SPC) Curia: Advisory Boards, Commissions, Committees, and Councils Sacred Heart, Willow Springs, MO; St. John Vianney, Mountain View, MO
Stoviak, Rev. Leonard W., (GBG) [NUR] Neumann House, Greensburg, PA
Stowe, Rev. Gregory P., '06 (PRO) Curia: Advisory Boards, Commissions, Committees, and Councils St. Joseph's Church, Natick RI, West Warwick, RI
Stoyle, Rev. James, '91 (FTW) Retired.
Strabala, Rev. Matthew, *OP* '00 (CHI) Fenwick High School, Oak Park, IL
Strachota, Rev. Michael D., '79 (MIL) St. Catherine's Congregation, Oconomowoc, WI; St. Joan of Arc Congregation, Nashotah, WI
Strader, Rev. Mark A., '91 (LA) St. Bartholomew, Long Beach, CA
Stradinger, Rev. Stephen J., '74 (MIL) Retired.
Stradomski, Rev. Ryszard, '83 (SP) St. Benedict, Crystal River, FL
Stradomski, Rev. Zbigniew, '91 (ORL) Blessed Trinity, Ocala, FL
Straley, Rev. Michael, '83 (PHX) St. Bernard of Clairvaux Roman Catholic Parish, Scottsdale, AZ
Strand, Rev. Jacob A., '12 (MIL) Holy Trinity Congregation, Kewaskum, WI; St. Michaels' Congregation, Kewaskum, WI
Strand, Very Rev. Luke N., '09 (MIL) Curia: Leadership [SEM] Saint Francis de Sales Seminary, St. Francis, WI
Strand, Rev. Tyler A., '15 (PSC) Retired.
Strand, Rev. Vincent L., *S.J.* '16 (FTW) (>WDC) [MON] The Jesuit Community at Georgetown University, Washington, DC
Strange, Rev. Gerard Jerry, '11 (NSH) Church of the Nativity, Thompsons Station, TN
Strange, Rev. J. Michael, *P.S.S.* '65 (BAL) Retired. [MON] Society of St. Sulpice, Province of the United States, Baltimore, MD
Strange, Rev. J. Michael, *P.S.S.* '65 (SFR) Retired.
Strange, Rev. Michael, *P.S.S.* '65 (SFR) St. Vincent de Paul, San Francisco, CA
Strange, Rev. Todd O., '09 (SEA) St. Joseph, Issaquah, WA
Stransky, Rev. Thomas F., *C.S.P.* '57 (NY) Retired.
Strassburger, Rev. Brian A., *S.J.* '21 (BWN) San Felipe de Jesus, Brownsville, TX
Strasser, Rev. John R., '76 (DOD) Retired.
Strasz, Rev. James, *S.M.* '80 (DET) Notre Dame Preparatory School and Marist Academy, Pontiac, MI
Straten, Rev. William, '09 (AUS) St. Mary, College Station, TX
Stratman, Rev. Thomas F., '50 (DAV) Retired. [MON] St. Vincent Center, Davenport, IA
Straub, Rev. Msgr. Edward F., '65 (NY) Retired.
Straub, Rev. Jacob E., '13 (COV) St. Matthew, Morning View, KY
Straughn, Rev. Daniel T., '04 (PIT) On Administrative Leave.
Straus, Rev. Brian, '18 (SPC) Curia: Offices and Directors McAuley Catholic High School, Joplin, MO; St. Peter the Apostle, Joplin, MO; [CAM] Catholic Campus Ministry, Missouri Southern State University, Joplin, MO
Straus, Rev. Brian, '18 (SPC) Curia: Consultative Bodies
Strausser, Rev. George L., '77 (PH) On Special Assignment. Chap, Univ City Hosps, St Francis De Sales Rec, Philadelphia St. Francis de Sales, Philadelphia, PA
Stravinskas, Rev. Peter M.J., '77 (B) On Duty Outside

Diocese.
Strazicich, Rev. Mel, '07 (SEA) St. Mary, Anacortes, WA; St. Paul, La Conner, WA
Strebler, Rev. Charles, (PRM) Curia: Leadership
Strebler, Rev. Charles F., '94 (CLV) Curia: Tribunal Holy Spirit, Avon Lake, OH
Strecok, Very Rev. Lubomir J., '98 (ALT) Curia: Deaneries Immaculate Conception, Altoona, PA; Sacred Heart, Altoona, PA
Streifel, Rev. John, (BAL) St. Clare, Baltimore, MD
Streifel, Rev. Keith N., '99 (BIS) Curia: Leadership Spirit of Life, Mandan, ND; St. Anthony, St. Anthony, ND; St. Martin, Huff, ND
Streit, Rev. David, *S.V.D.* '69 (CHI) [MON] Divine Word Residence, Techny, IL
Streit, Rev. Thomas G., *C.S.C.* '86 (FTW) [MON] Congregation of Holy Cross, United States Province of Priests and Brothers, Notre Dame, IN; [MON] Holy Cross Community, Corby Hall, University of Notre Dame, Notre Dame, IN
Streitenberger, Rev. Adam A., '07 (COL) Curia: Offices and Directors [CAM] St. Thomas More Newman Center at The Ohio State University, Columbus, OH
Strelecki, Rev. Msgr. Richard T., '69 (NEW) Retired. [MON] St. John Vianney Residence for Retired Priests, Rutherford, NJ
Stretton, Rev. Noel, '59 (DUL) Retired.
Strickenberger, Rev. Matthew J., '10 (E) St. Teresa of Avila, Union City, PA; St. Thomas the Apostle, Corry, PA
Strieder, Rev. Leon, '76 (GAL) [SEM] St. Mary's Seminary, Houston, TX
Strieder, Rev. Leon, '76 (AUS) (>GAL) All Saints, Houston, TX
Striedl, Rev. Max J., '96 (RCK) St. Gall, Elburn, IL
Stringini, Rev. John L., '79 (RCK) Retired.
Stripe, Rev. Keith A., '96 (TOL) Curia: Advisory Boards, Commissions, Committees, and Councils; Deaneries St. Joseph, Maumee, OH
Strittmatter, Rev. Robert, '66 (FWT) Retired.
Stroba, Rev. Marek, (SD) [MIS] Most Precious Blood Catholic Parish in Chula Vista, CA Real Property Support Corporation, Chula Vista, CA
Stroba, Rev. Marek, *OMI* '85 (SAT) [MON] Missionary Oblates of Mary Immaculate of Texas, Southern Province (San Antonio USP Support Office), San Antonio, TX
Strobl, Rev. Andrew, '09 (KCK) Curia: Advisory Boards, Commissions, Committees, and Councils Holy Spirit, Overland Park, KS
Strohmeyer, Rev. George E., '64 (E) Retired. [COL] Gannon University, Erie, PA
Stroik, Rev. Placid, *OFM* '63 (LC) On Special Assignment. Franciscans Downtown, Stevens Point
Stroik, Rev. Placid, *O.F.M.* '63 (GB) [CON] Holy Family Convent of Franciscan Sisters of Christian Charity, Manitowoc, WI; [MON] Assumption of B.V.M. Friary, Pulaski, WI
Strollo, Rev. Charles P., *C.M.* '73 (PH) [SEM] Vincentian Theologate-DeAndreis House, Philadelphia, PA
Strommer, Rev. James, *C.P.* '70 (CHI) [MON] Passionist Provincial Office (The Congregation of the Passion, Holy Cross Province), Park Ridge, IL
Strommer, Rev. James G., *C.P.* '70 (SAC) [MON] Christ the King Passionist Retreat Center, Inc. (The Passionists (Chicago, IL)), Citrus Heights, CA
Strommer, Rev. Paul, '16 (DUL) Our Lady of the Sacred Heart, Buhl, MN; St. Joseph, Chisholm, MN
Stronach, Rev. Jacob, *O.S.B.* '12 (P) [MON] Mt. Angel Abbey, Saint Benedict, OR
Stronach, Rev. Mark, (AJ) St. Mary's, Kodiak, AK
Strong, Rev. Ambrose, *O.Cist.* '11 (DAL) [MON] Our Lady of Dallas Cistercian Abbey, Irving, TX
Strong, Rev. Barry R., *O.S.F.S.* '84 (WIL) [MON] Wilmington-Philadelphia Province of the Oblates of St. Francis de Sales, Wilmington, DE
Strontsitskyy, Rev. Raphael, (STF) [SEM] Ukrainian Catholic Seminary Inc. St. Basil College - Seminary, Stamford, CT
Stroot, Rev. Thomas J., '70 (WCH) Retired.
Strother, Rev. Michael A., '05 (BEA) St. Helen, Orange, TX; St. Maurice, Orange, TX
Strouse, Rev. Anthony J., '10 (LAN) Curia: Offices and Directors St. Matthew, Flint, MI; St. Pius X Parish Flint, Flint, MI
Strupp, Rev. Joachim, *O.F.M.Cap.* '63 (MIL) Retired.
Struzik, Rev. Edward J., '85 (MET) Retired. [MON] Maria Regina Residence, Somerset, NJ
Stryker, Rev. Peter, *CPM* '98 (OWN) [MON] Fathers of Mercy, Auburn, KY
Strynkowski, Rev. Msgr. John J., '63 (BRK) Curia: Leadership; Pastoral Services
Strynkowski, Rev. Msgr. John J., '63 (BRK) Retired.
Strzadala, Rev. Wieslaw P., '90 (BRK) Curia: (>MO) Offices and Directors Our Lady of Consolation, Brooklyn, NY
Strzalkowski, Rev. Dariusz, '00 (DET) Our Lady of the Angels Parish Taylor, Taylor, MI
Strzebonski, Rev. Tomasz, (DEN) St. Peter Catholic Parish in Greeley, Greeley, CO
Strzelecki, Rev. Dariusz, '11 (BRK) St. Catharine of Alexandria, Brooklyn, NY
Strzelinski, Rev. Ernest J., (PIT) Our Lady of Perpetual Help, Glenshaw, PA
Strzok, Rev. James, *S.J.* '70 (CHI) (>DET) [MON] Colombiere Center, Clarkston, MI
Strzyz, Rev. Stanislaus, '68 (BAK) Curia: Offices and Directors St. Helen, Pilot Rock, OR
Stuart, Very Rev. George E., '89 (WDC) On Special Assignment. Curia: Leadership; Tribunal Little Flower, Bethesda, MD
Stuart, Very Rev. George E., '89 (WDC) Curia: Canonical Services
Stuart, Rev. Thomas Joseph, '20 (SR) Pastor of St. Vincent de Paul Catholic Church of Petaluma, A Corporation Sole, Petaluma, CA
Stubbs, Rev. Michael C., '78 (KCK) Retired.
Stubeda, Rev. Anthony J., '85 (NU) Curia: Leadership; Offices and Directors Holy Redeemer, Marshall, MN; St. Clotilde, Marshall, MN; St. Mary, Cottonwood, MN; St. Mary, Tracy, MN; St. Michael, Milroy, MN
Stubna, Rev. Kris D., '85 (PIT) St. Paul Cathedral, Pittsburgh, PA
Studeny, Rev. Colman, *OFM Cap.* '61 (PIT) [MON] St. Augustine Friary, Pittsburgh, PA
Studer, Rev. Louis, *O.M.I.* '76 (WDC) [MIS] Oblate Missionary Society, Inc., Washington, DC; [MON] Missionary Oblates of Mary Immaculate, Washington, DC; [MON] Oblate Community, Washington, DC (>BO) [MON] Missionary Oblates of Mary Immaculate Northern Province, Lowell, MA; (>SAT) [MON] Missionary Oblates of Mary Immaculate of Texas, Southern Province (San Antonio USP Support Office), San Antonio, TX
Studerus, Rev. Msgr. Gregory J., '80 (NEW) Curia: Deaneries
Studwell, Rev. Joachim, *O.F.M.* '87 (JKS) St. Francis of Assisi, Greenwood, MS; St. Thomas, Lexington, MS; [CAM] Holmes Community College Newman Center, Lexington, MS; [MON] St. Francis of Assisi Friary (Franciscan Friars - O.F.M.), Greenwood, MS
Studzinski, Rev. Raymond, *O.S.B.* '69 (WDC) [COL] Catholic University of America, The, Washington, DC
Studzinski, Rev. Raymond, *O.S.B.* '69 (IND) [MON] St. Meinrad Archabbey, St. Meinrad, IN
Stuempel, Rev. Robert L., '75 (L) Retired.
Stueve, Rev. Andrew B., '13 (STP) St. Charles, Bayport, MN
Stuever, Rev. Will, '21 (WCH) Church of the Holy Cross, Hutchinson, KS; Trinity Catholic High School, Hutchinson, KS
Stuglik, Rev. Robert, '03 (CHI) St. Stephen, Deacon and Martyr, Tinley Park, IL
Stuglik, Rev. Stanley, '10 (CHI) St. Gerald, Oak Lawn, IL
Stuhrenberg, Rev. James A., '06 (CHL) Holy Family, Winston-Salem, NC; St. Frances of Rome, Sparta, NC
Stull, Rev. Brent Luke, *OP* '19 (KCK) Church of the Ascension, Overland Park, KS
Stump, Rev. David X., *S.J.* (NY) [MON] Kolhmann Hall Jesuit Community, Bronx, NY
Stump, Rev. James, *O.F.M.Cap.* '88 (SFR) Our Lady of Angels, Burlingame, CA
Stumpf, Rev. Michael J., '01 (PIT) Mary, Queen of Peace, Pittsburgh, PA
Stumpf, Rev. Walter P., '06 (GB) St. Anthony, Oconto Falls, WI
Stumpf, Rev. Msgr. William F., '85 (IND) St. Matthew Catholic Church, Indianapolis, Inc., Indianapolis, IN
Stumpf, Very Rev. Msgr. William F., (IND) Curia: Leadership; Offices and Directors
Stunek, Rev. Leonard, *O.F.M.* '60 (MIL) [MON] Francis and Clare Friary, Franklin, WI
Sturm, Rev. Samuel L., '99 (KNX) Christ the King, Tazewell, TN; Our Lady of Perpetual Help, La Follette, TN; St. Jude Parish, Helenwood, TN
Sturn, Rev. Michael L., '77 (SB) Retired.
Stybor, Rev. Marek, *OFM Conv.* (TR) (>MRY) [MON] St. Francis of Assisi Friary & Novitiate, Arroyo Grande, CA
Styles, Rev. Kenneth A., *S.J.* '72 (CLV) Walsh Jesuit High School, Cuyahoga Falls, OH
Su, Rev. Dominic, (LA) St. Elizabeth Ann Seton, Rowland Heights, CA
Su Han, Rev. Deog, '91 (ORL) Curia: Evangelization St. Ignatius Kim Korean Mission, Orlando, FL
Suarez, Rev. Carlos D., '11 (BO) Curia: Clergy and Religious Services Immaculate Conception, Stoughton, MA; St. James, Stoughton, MA
Suarez, Rev. Edgar, *C.S.V.* '04 (CHI) [MON] Viatorian Province Center-Clerics of St. Viator, Arlington Heights, IL
Suarez, Rev. Gildardo, '92 (PRO) The Church of the Assumption, Providence, Rhode Island, Providence, RI
Suarez, Rev. Hamilton, '00 (STO) Curia: Leadership Sacred Heart Church of Turlock (Pastor of), Turlock, CA
Suarez, Rev. Jose, '91 (ORG) St. Anne, Santa Ana, CA
Suarez, Rev. Luis Felipe, (KC) Sacred Heart-Guadalupe, Kansas City, MO
Suarez, Rev. Luke P., '11 (BGP) The Holy Spirit Roman Catholic Church Corporation, Stamford, CT
Suarez, Rev. Michael F., *S.J.* '94 (NY) [MON] Cardinal Spellman Hall, Jesuit Community, Bronx, NY
Suarez, Rev. Miguel Angel, *S.B.D.* '13 (NEW) Our Lady of the Valley, Orange, NJ
Suarez, Rev. Pedro A., *S.J.* '72 (MIA) Belen Jesuit Preparatory School, Inc., Miami, FL; [MON] Villa Javier, Miami, FL
Suarez, Rev. Walter, '96 (SJ) Curia: Leadership St. Athanasius, Mountain View, CA
Suarez Barbosa, Rev. Roberto, '16 (ATL) Holy Spirit Catholic Church, Atlanta, Inc., Atlanta, GA
Suarez Saenz, Rev. Alexander, '19 (RCK) St. Nicholas, Aurora, IL
Suarez-Pasillas, Rev. Adolfo, '19 (JKS) Curia: Consultative Bodies St. Michael, Forest, MS; St. Michael, Paulding, MS
Suaybaguio, Rev. Evangelio R., '75 (NY) St. Joseph-St. Thomas St. John Neumann Parish, Staten Island, NY
Subaar, Rev. Emmanuel, '09 (BLX) St. Matthew the Apostle, Perkinston, MS
Subiza, Rev. Innocent, '01 (SAC) Pastor of Holy Family Parish, Portola, a corporation sole, Portola, CA
Subocz, Rev. Adam C., '86 (HRT) Retired.
Subosa, Rev. Cristobal, '01 (SB) St. Elizabeth Ann Seton, Ontario, CA
Suchan, Rev. Msgr. Aleksander, '88 (DUL) Immaculate Conception, Pine City, MN; St. Joseph, Beroun, MN
Sucharski, Rev. Michael M., *S.V.D.* '83 (LAF) St. Lawrence, Eunice, LA
Suchnicki, Rev. Michael, *O.F.M.Cap.* '88 (DEN) [MON] St. Francis of Assisi Friary, Denver, CO
Sucholet, Rev. James. J., '91 (NOR) St. Joseph, Norwich, CT
Suckiel, Rev. Sean, (BRK) Holy Family, Flushing, NY
Sudano, Rev. Glenn, *C.F.R.* '84 (NY) [MON] St. Joseph's Friary, New York, NY
Sudherson, Rev. Antony, (ALT) Chap, Conemaugh Health Sys Conemaugh Mem Med Ctr, Main Cam… St. Benedict, Johnstown, PA
Sudlik, Rev. Leonard A., '76 (GR) Retired. Curia: Leadership
Sudlik, Rev. Richard, (STP) [RTR] Christ the King Retreat Center, Buffalo, MN
Sudol, Rev. Andrzej, *SCJ* '96 (MIL) St. Martin of Tours Congregation, Franklin, WI; [MON] Sacred Heart Novitiate, Franksville, WI
Sudol, Rev. Ignatius, *O.H.* (LA) [EFT] St. Joseph's H. & RC Foundation, Ojai, CA; [MIS] Women's League of St. Joseph's Health & Retirement Center, Ojai, CA
Suehr, Rev. Philip, *O.S.C.* '66 (PHX) Retired.
Suellentrop, Rev. Anthony J., '73 (DOD) Retired.
Suenram, Friar John, *OCD* (DAL) Mount Carmel Center, Dallas, TX; [MON] Mt. Carmel Center (Discalced Carmelite Fathers of Dallas, Inc.), Dallas, TX
Sueper, Rev. Alban, *S.S.C.* '53 (PRO) Retired. [MON] St. Columban's Retirement House (St. Columban's Foreign Mission Society), Bristol, RI
Suero, Rev. Jason J., '19 (CHI) St. Francis of Assisi, Orland Park, IL
Sughroue, Rev. Adam M., '11 (LIN) Curia: Leadership Sacred Heart, Kenesaw, NE; St. Francis, David City, NE
Sughrue, Rev. Paul S., '70 (BO) Retired. St. Brigid, Lexington, MA
Suglia, Rev. Dennis, '11 (RVC) St. Sylvester, Medford, NY
Sugrue, Rev. Patrick, *O.C.D.* '64 (SJ) [MON] Carmelite Monastery, Novitiate, San Jose, CA
Suh, Rev. Daniel Sang-Bong, '95 (BRK) On Leave.
Suhaka, Rev. Peter, '86 (MET) [HOS] Saint Peter's University Hospital, New Brunswick, NJ
Suhoza, Rev. John E., '68 (PIT) Retired.
Suire, Rev. Jared G., (LAF) St. Leo the Great, Lafayette, LA
Suire, Very Rev. Jared G., '10 (LAF) On Special

Assignment. Curia: Advisory Boards, Commissions, Committees, and Councils; Leadership; Offices and Directors
Suit, Rev. Robert J., '74 (STL) All Saints Catholic Church, St. Peters, St. Peters, MO
Sulkowski, Rev. Anthony, '86 (DET) St. Jane Frances de Chantal Parish Sterling Heights, Sterling Heights, MI
Sullins, Rev. Paul, '02 (WDC) St. Mark, Hyattsville, MD; [COL] Catholic University of America, The, Washington, DC
Sullivan, Rev. Brian, '03 (PAT) Christ the King, New Vernon, NJ
Sullivan, Rev. Charles, (BO) [MON] Campion Health & Wellness, Inc., Weston, MA
Sullivan, Rev. Charles J., '66 (PH) Retired. Immaculate Conception, Jenkintown, PA
Sullivan, Rev. Christopher, (RVC) Curia: Leadership Holy Family, Hicksville, NY
Sullivan, Rev. Conor M., '14 (STL) On Special Assignment. Chap, St Agnes Home, St Louis Immacolata Catholic Church, Richmond Heights, MO; [NUR] St. Agnes Home for the Elderly, Kirkwood, MO
Sullivan, Rev. Daniel, (PHX) St. Francis Xavier Roman Catholic Parish, Phoenix, AZ
Sullivan, Rev. Daniel F., '57 (CHI) Retired.
Sullivan, Rev. Msgr. Daniel J., '77 (PH) On Special Assignment. Vicar for Clergy, Sisters of Mercy Convent, Merion Station Curia: Clergy and Religious Services
Sullivan, Rev. Daniel James, '63 (HRT) Retired.
Sullivan, Rev. Donal P., '64 (STA) Retired.
Sullivan, Rev. E. Paul, '63 (BO) Retired.
Sullivan, Rev. Emmanuel, *S.A.* '55 (NY) Retired.
Sullivan, Rev. Eugene P., '68 (BO) Retired. Sacred Heart, Boston, MA
Sullivan, Rev. Francis E., '88 (BO) Immaculate Conception, Malden, MA; Immaculate Conception, Salem, MA; St. James, Salem, MA
Sullivan, Rev. George R., *S.J.* '75 (MIL) [MON] St. Camillus Jesuit Community (Society of Jesus, USA Midwest Province), Wauwatosa, WI
Sullivan, Rev. J. Richard, '77 (L) Retired.
Sullivan, Rev. James, '06 (OAK) Bishop O'Dowd High School, Oakland, CA; St. Clement, Hayward, CA
Sullivan, Rev. James, (NY) Retired.
Sullivan, Rev. James F., '87 (PH) On Special Assignment. Chap, Holy Family Home, Philadelphia [NUR] Holy Family Home (Little Sisters of the Poor), Philadelphia, PA
Sullivan, Rev. James M., '66 (STL) Retired. Incarnate Word Catholic Church, Chesterfield, MO
Sullivan, Very Rev. James M., '14 (HRT) Curia: Deaneries Corporation of the Church of the Immaculate Conception, Waterbury, Connecticut, Waterbury, CT; St. Michael's Church of Waterville, Connecticut, Waterbury, CT; [MON] Basilica of the Immaculate Conception Rectory, Waterbury, CT
Sullivan, Rev. James Mary, *O.P.* '95 (PRO) Saint Pius V Church, Providence, Rhode Island, Providence, RI
Sullivan, Rev. James Mary, *O.P.* '95 (PRO) Curia: Advisory Boards, Commissions, Committees, and Councils; Clergy and Religious Services
Sullivan, Rev. Msgr. James P., '70 (NY) Retired.
Sullivan, Rev. Jan C., '91 (COL) St. Thomas Aquinas, Zanesville, OH
Sullivan, Rev. Jeffrey, *S.J.* '21 (OM) [MON] Jesuit Community at Creighton University, Omaha, NE
Sullivan, Rev. John, *O.C.D.* '68 (WDC) [SEM] Discalced Carmelite Friars, Inc., Washington, DC
Sullivan, Rev. John, *M.S.* (MAN) [MON] Shrine of Our Lady of La Salette (La Salette of Enfield, Inc.), Enfield, NH; [RTR] Shrine of Our Lady of La Salette (La Salette of Enfield, Inc), Enfield, NH
Sullivan, Rev. John D., '54 (JOL) Retired. St. Petronille, Glen Ellyn, IL
Sullivan, Rev. John J., '67 (CLV) Retired.
Sullivan, Rev. John J., *M.M.* '60 (NY) Retired.
Sullivan, Rev. John J., '66 (DET) Retired.
Sullivan, Rev. John J., '77 (CHI) Retired.
Sullivan, Rev. John L., '74 (BO) St. Mary, Franklin, MA
Sullivan, Rev. John M., '90 (FR) Holy Redeemer, Chatham, MA
Sullivan, Rev. John P., (HRT) Retired.
Sullivan, Rev. John P., '72 (SAC) Retired.
Sullivan, Rev. John R., '94 (LIN) Chap, Nebraska Penal Complex, Lincoln St. Joseph's, York, NE; [MIS] Madonna Rehabilitation Hospitals, Lincoln, NE
Sullivan, Rev. Joseph, '03 (SPK) Retired.
Sullivan, Rev. Joseph, '03 (SPK) Retired.
Sullivan, Rev. Kenneth J., *M.M.* '57 (NY) Retired. [MON] Maryknoll Fathers and Brothers (Catholic Foreign Mission Society of America, Inc.), Ossining, NY
Sullivan, Rev. Kevin B., '63 (SFD) Retired.
Sullivan, Rev. Msgr. Kevin L., '76 (NY) Curia: Offices and Directors Parish of Our Saviour and St. Stephen/ Our Lady of the Scapular, New York, NY; [CCH] Catholic Charities Alliance, New York, NY; [CCH] The Catholic Charities of the Archdiocese of New York, New York, NY; [EFT] Carmel Housing Development Fund Co., Inc., New York, NY; [EFT] Cor Mariae Development Fund Corporation, New York, NY; [EFT] Cor Mariae Housing Development Fund, Inc., New York, NY; [EFT] The Housing Fund of the Archdiocese of New York, New York, NY; [SPF] Catholic Charities Department of Housing, Housing Development Institute, Inc., New York, NY
Sullivan, Rev. Lawrence J., '92 (CHI) Curia: Finance Christ the King, Chicago, IL; [CEM] Central Office, Hillside, IL
Sullivan, Rev. Michael, *O.F.M.Cap.* '84 (DET) [RTR] Capuchin Retreat, Washington, MI
Sullivan, Rev. Michael, '81 (STP) St. Joseph the Worker, Maple Grove, MN
Sullivan, Rev. Michael B., *C.S.C.* '75 (FTW) Retired. [MON] Holy Cross Community, Corby Hall, University of Notre Dame, Notre Dame, IN
Sullivan, Rev. Michael D., '91 (TR) Church of the Precious Blood, Monmouth Beach, NJ; St. Dorothea, Eatontown, NJ
Sullivan, Rev. Michael P., *O.S.A.* '67 (PH) [MON] St. Thomas Monastery, Villanova, PA
Sullivan, Rev. Neil S., '97 (HBG) Curia: Offices and Directors Good Shepherd, Camp Hill, PA
Sullivan, Rev. Patrick, '82 (CR) Retired. Holy Family (Halstad), Halstad, MN; St. Joseph's, Ada, MN; St. William (Twin Valley), Twin Valley, MN
Sullivan, Rev. Patrick, '09 (KCK) Curia: Advisory Boards, Commissions, Committees, and Councils Sacred Heart, Shawnee, KS
Sullivan, Rev. Patrick J., *C.S.C.* '56 (FTW) [MIS] Holy Cross House, Notre Dame, IN
Sullivan, Rev. Patrick J., *S.J.* '50 (NY) [MON] Murray-Weigel Hall (A Jesuit Community at Murray-Weigel Hall and Kohlmann Hall), Bronx, NY
Sullivan, Rev. Patrick M., *O.S.B.* '87 (MAN) [MON] St. Anselm Abbey, Manchester, NH
Sullivan, Rev. Paul, *S.J.* '83 (PRT) Our Lady of Hope Parish, Portland, ME
Sullivan, Rev. Paul, '07 (PHX) Sacred Heart Roman Catholic Parish, Phoenix, AZ; St. Gregory Roman Catholic Parish, Phoenix, AZ
Sullivan, Rev. Paul V., (BO) Mary, Queen of Peace Parish, Medford, MA
Sullivan, Rev. Philip, *O.C.D.* '07 (LA) St. Therese, Alhambra, CA
Sullivan, Rev. R. William, *O.S.A.* '67 (JOL) St. Jude, New Lenox, IL
Sullivan, Rev. Robert D., '13 (MRY) Curia: Offices and Directors Our Lady Star of the Sea, Santa Cruz, CA
Sullivan, Rev. Robert E., '80 (BO) On Special Assignment.
Sullivan, Rev. Robert E., (FTW) [COL] University of Notre Dame Du Lac, Notre Dame, IN
Sullivan, Rev. Robert J., '63 (SY) Retired. Saints John & Andrew, Binghamton, NY
Sullivan, Very Rev. Robert J., '93 (BIR) Curia: Leadership; Offices and Directors John Carroll Catholic High School, Birmingham, AL; St. Mark the Evangelist Catholic Parish, Birmingham, Birmingham, AL; [EFT] Jack Miller Education Foundation, Birmingham, AL; [EFT] John Carroll Catholic High School Educational Foundation, Inc., Birmingham, AL; [EFT] John Carroll Catholic High School Endowed Choir Fund, Birmingham, AL; [EFT] John Carroll Catholic High School Endowment Scholarship Fund, Birmingham, AL; [EFT] Lee Fisher Memorial Award, Birmingham, AL; [EFT] St. Mark the Evangelist Columbarium Fund, Birmingham, AL; [EFT] Thomas Scott Messina Memorial Endowment, Birmingham, AL
Sullivan, Rev. Msgr. Terrence J., '64 (SJ) Retired.
Sullivan, Rev. Thomas, *C.Ss.R.* '72 (BAL) [SPF] St. John Neuman Residence, Timonium, MD
Sullivan, Rev. Msgr. Thomas J., '77 (WOR) Curia: Leadership; Offices and Directors Christ the King, Worcester, MA; [CAM] Worcester State College, Worcester, MA
Sullivan, Rev. Thomas K., '52 (STA) Retired.
Sullivan, Rev. Timothy, *C.S.P.* (KNX) Curia: Leadership Immaculate Conception, Knoxville, TN; [MIS] Ladies of Charity Knoxville, Knoxville, TN; [MON] Paulist Fathers (Missionary Society of St. Paul the Apostle), Knoxville, TN
Sullivan, Rev. Timothy, '90 (BUR) Chap, Univ of Vermont Med Ctr, Burlington St. Mark's, Burlington, VT
Sullivan, Rev. Vincent, '83 (ATL) Holy Family Catholic Church, Marietta, Inc., Marietta, GA
Sullivan, Rev. Vincent B., *S.J.* '76 (BRK) Our Lady of the Presentation-Our Lady of Mercy Roman Catholic Church, Brooklyn, NY; [MON] Carroll Street Jesuit Community, Brooklyn, NY
Sullivan, Rev. Msgr. W. Jerome, '61 (BUF) Retired. [MON] Msgr. Conniff Residence, Depew, NY
Sullivan, Rev. William, *O.SS.T.* '81 (BAL) [MON] Holy Trinity Monastery, Sykesville, MD
Sullivan, Rev. William, '72 (FTW) Retired. Curia: Offices and Directors
Sullivan, Rev. William F., *S.S.C.* '56 (PRO) Retired. [MON] St. Columban's Retirement House (St. Columban's Foreign Mission Society), Bristol, RI
Sumampong, Rev. Jed, *C.P.* '84 (NY) [MON] The Congregation of the Passion - St. Paul of the Cross Province, Jamaica, NY
Sumampong, Rev. Jed, *C.P.* '84 (BRK) Mary's Nativity-Saint Ann Roman Catholic Church, Flushing, NY
Sumanga, Rev. Oscar B., '95 (TR) Curia: Canonical Services St. Anthony of Padua, Hightstown, NJ
Summerhays, Rev. Patrick J., '15 (SFR) Curia: Advisory Boards, Commissions, Committees, and Councils; Communications; Leadership Cathedral of St. Mary (Assumption), San Francisco, CA
Summerlin, Rev. William, '19 (LFT) St. Boniface, Lafayette, IN; St. Lawrence, Lafayette, IN
Summers, Rev. Mark S., '10 (COL) St. Agatha, Columbus, OH
Summers, Rev. Randall R., '07 (IND) Our Lady of the Springs Catholic Church, French Lick, Inc., French Lick, IN; Our Lord Jesus Christ the King Catholic Church, Paoli, Inc., Paoli, IN
Summerson, Rev. Andrew, '15 (PRM) Assumption of the Blessed Virgin (St. Mary Byzantine Catholic Church), Whiting, IN
Summerson, Rev. Andrew, (HPM) Curia: Offices and Directors
Summerson, Rev. Andrew, '15 (PRM) Curia: Leadership (>STN) [MIS] Metropolitan Andrey Sheptytsky Institute of Eastern Christian Studies, Flagstaff, AZ
Sumpter, Rev. Gary, '79 (SR) Retired. Kolbe-Trinity, Napa, CA
Sumpter, Rev. Gary, (SR) Pastor of St. Thomas Aquinas Catholic Church of Napa, A Corporation Sole, Napa, CA
Sunberg, Rev. David A., '92 (CIN) Curia: Offices and Directors [SEM] Mount St. Mary's Seminary of the West, Cincinnati, OH
Sund, Rev. Joseph R., '16 (OM) St. Bonaventure's Church of Raeville (Nebraska Non-Profit Corporation), Raeville, NE; St. Boniface, Stuart, NE; St. Boniface Church of Elgin (Nebraska Non-Profit Corporation), Elgin, NE; St. John the Baptist, Clearwater, NE; St. John the Baptists' Church of Petersburg (Nebraska Non-Profit Corporation), Petersburg, NE; St. Peter de Alcantara, Ewing, NE
Sundaram, Rev. Manuel A., '90 (LA) [HOS] St. Mary Medical Center, Long Beach, CA
Sundborg, Rev. Stephen V., *S.J.* '74 (SEA) [MON] Arrupe Jesuit Community at Seattle University, Seattle, WA (>WDC) [MON] The Jesuit Community at Georgetown University, Washington, DC
Sundeme, Rev. Hughes, '14 (KCK) St. Ann, Effingham, KS; St. Louis, Good Intent, KS; St. Mary, Purcell, Lancaster, KS
Sundrup, Rev. Eric M., *S.J.* '14 (CIN) St. Robert Bellarmine, Cincinnati, OH; [COL] Xavier University, Cincinnati, OH; [MON] Cincinnati Jesuit Community, Cincinnati, OH
Sunds, Rev. Msgr. Elvin, '73 (JKS) Retired. Curia: Consultative Bodies St. Francis of Assisi, Madison, MS
Sung, Rev. Hyunsang, '06 (NY) Korean Catholic Apostolate of Staten Island, Staten Island, NY
Sung, Rev. Thomas, *C.S.J.B.* '51 (BRK) Retired.
Sungcad, Rev. Nemesio, '76 (SD) Pastor of Saint Mary Catholic Parish, National City, a corporation sole, National City, CA; [MIS] Saint Mary Catholic Parish National City in National City, CA Real Property Support Corporation, National City, CA
Sunghera, Rev. Gilbert, *S.J.* '02 (DET) [MON] Jesuit Community at the University of Detroit Mercy, Detroit, MI
Sunguti, Rev. Vincent, '01 (OM) Curia: Offices and Directors Holy Cross, Beemer, NE; St. Joseph, Wisner, NE
Suniga, Rev. Matthew Gilbert, '18 (GAL) [SEM] St. Mary's Seminary, Houston, TX
Sunkara, Rev. Hrudaya Raju, '95 (SUP) St. Ann, Saxon, WI; St. Mary of the Seven Dolors, Hurley, WI
Sunnenberg, Rev. Scott M., '02 (SPC) Curia: Deaneries; Offices and Directors Sacred Heart, Bolivar, MO
Sunwoo, Rev. Richard, '09 (LA) Curia: Offices and

Directors Our Savior Parish & U.S.C. Caruso Catholic Center, Los Angeles, CA
Supancheck, Rev. Norman A., '68 (LA) Retired. St. Matthew, Long Beach, CA
Suparman, Rev. Vincent, *S.C.J.* (SP) [MON] Priests of the Sacred Heart, Pinellas Park, FL
Super, Rev. David J., '80 (CR) Curia: Offices and Directors St. Joseph Parish (Beaulieu), Mahnomen, MN; St. Michael's Parish, Mahnomen, MN
Suppa, Rev. F. Thomas, '78 (E) Retired. Chap, Veterans Affairs Med Ctr
Supple, Rev. Richard A, *O. Carm.* '02 (NEW) Our Lady of Mount Carmel, Tenafly, NJ
Supranes, Rev. Renier, (RIC) St. Michael, Glen Allen, VA
Sure, Rev. Jayaraju, '12 (LR) St. Leo the Great University Parish, Russellville, AR
Sure, Rev. Jayarayu, (LR) St. John, Russellville, AR
Sureau, Rev. John, '11 (RVC) Curia: Leadership Our Lady, Queen of Apostles Regional School, Center Moriches, NY; St. John the Evangelist, Center Moriches, NY
Suresh, Rev. Britto Raja, '03 (MIL) St. John's Congregation, Rubicon, WI; St. Kilians Congregation, Hartford, WI
Suresh, Rev. Edward, (IND) Annunciation Catholic Church, Brazil, Inc., Brazil, IN; St. Paul the Apostle Catholic Church, Putnam County, Inc., Greencastle, IN
Suresh, Rev. Mathew, (COS) Ave Maria, Parker, CO
Surette, Rev. John E., *S.J.* '67 (BO) [MON] Campion Health & Wellness, Inc., Weston, MA
Surges, Rev. Robert F., '64 (MIL) Retired.
Suriani, Rev. Raymond N., '85 (PRO) Retired. St. Pius X Parish Corporation, Westerly, Westerly, RI
Suriano, Rev. Thomas M., '64 (MIL) Retired. Good Shepherd Congregation, Menomonee Falls, WI
Surma, Rev. Tomasz, (DEN) St. Nicholas Catholic Parish in Platteville, Platteville, CO
Surman, Rev. Darrell, '62 (YAK) Retired.
Surman, Rev. Stanley, '56 (SAG) Retired.
Surmeier, Rev. William J., '65 (SAL) Retired.
Surovick, Rev. Stephen, (PH) [MON] Arrupe Jesuit Community, Merion Station, PA
Surprenant, Rev. Paul W., '73 (WIN) Retired.
Surrency, Rev. D. Scott, *O.F.M. Cap.* (BO) [MON] San Lorenzo Friary, Boston, MA
Surufka, Rev. Michael, *O.F.M.* (GRY) SS. Monica-St. Luke, Gary, IN; St. Joseph the Worker, Gary, IN; [MON] Our Lady of Lourdes Friary, Cedar Lake, IN
Surufka, Rev. Michael, *OFM* (GRY) Cathedral of the Holy Angels, Gary, IN
Surwilo, Rev. Msgr. Edward R., '63 (BGP) Retired. [MON] The Catherine Dennis Keefe Queen of the Clergy Retired Priests' Residence, Stamford, CT
Susai Pragasam, Rev. Albert, *O.S.M* '98 (LA) Divine Saviour, Los Angeles, CA; St. Ann, Los Angeles, CA
Susairaj, Rev. Maria, (MAN) [CEM] St. Joseph Cemetery, Bath, NH
Susairaj, Rev. Sebastian, *H.G.N.* (MAN) Chap, Grafton Cty House of Correction Curia: Consultative Bodies St. Joseph, Claremont, NH; St. Mary, Claremont, NH
Suskey, Rev. Robert G., '90 (PH) Our Lady of Good Counsel, Southampton, PA
Suslenko, Rev. Mark S., '86 (HRT) Saints Isidore and Maria Parish Corporation, Glastonbury, CT
Suslowicz, Rev. Michael S., '80 (PIT) Our Lady of Hope, Bethel Park, PA
Suso, Rev. Anthony J., '09 (CLV) St. Columbkille Parish, Parma, OH
Suss, Rev. Thomas, (PHX) St. Helen Roman Catholic Parish, Glendale, AZ
Suss, Rev. Thomas J., '73 (SEA) Retired.
Sustar, Rev. Jernej, '16 (MAR) Sacred Heart, DeTour Village, MI; St. Stanislaus Kostka, Goetzville, MI
Sustayta, Rev. Paul A., '91 (LA) St. John Chrysostom, Inglewood, CA
Suszko, Rev. George, *S.A.C.* '89 (VEN) St. Martha Parish in Sarasota, Inc., Sarasota, FL; [EFT] St. Martha School Foundation, Sarasota, FL; [NUR] St. Martha's Housing II, Inc (Casa Santa Marta II), Sarasota, FL; [NUR] St. Martha's Housing, Inc. (Casa Santa Marta), Sarasota, FL
Suszko, Rev. Robert K., '02 (NEW) Curia: Offices and Directors [COL] Seton Hall University, South Orange, NJ; [SEM] Immaculate Conception Seminary School of Theology, South Orange, NJ
Suszynski, Rev. Edward F., '08 (CLV) Curia: Advisory Boards, Commissions, Committees, and Councils Our Lady Help of Christians Parish, Litchfield, OH
Suszynski, Rev. Michael, '86 (SP) Our Lady of Fatima, Inverness, FL
Sutachan, Rev. Alexander, '20 (SPC) Notre Dame Regional High School, Cape Girardeau, MO; St. Vincent de Paul, Cape Girardeau, MO
Sutherland, Rev. Juan Diego, *C.F.R.* '07 (SFE) [MON] Community of the Franciscans of the Renewal San Juan Diego Friary, Albuquerque, NM
Sutherland, Rev. Philip, *S.J.* '17 (MIL) [MON] Arrupe House Jesuit Community, Milwaukee, WI
Sutherland, Rev. Thomas J., '60 (DET) Retired.
Sutherland, Rev. William E., '83 (E) Chaplain at Nightingale Nursing & Rehab Center
Sutil, Rev. Florencio, '44 (SJN) Retired.
Sutman, Rev. Frank I., *O.P.* '85 (NY) Church of the Holy Innocents, Pleasantville, NY
Sutter, Rev. Conrad, *O.F.M.Conv.* '93 (TOL) [SHR] Basilica and National Shrine of Our Lady of Consolation, Carey, OH
Sutter, Rev. Raymond A., '73 (CLV) Retired.
Sutter, Rev. Richard Frank, (CHL) St. Gabriel, Charlotte, NC
Sutton, Rev Brian F., '06 (WIN) On Leave.
Sutton, Rev. Douglas B., '02 (WH) Retired.
Sutton, Rev. ST, (PAT) St. Joseph, Newton, NJ
Sutton, Rev. Stephen, '84 (BAL) Retired. St. Ignatius, Forest Hill, MD
Sutton, Rev. Thomas E., '73 (SAG) Curia: Offices and Directors Saint Gabriel Parish of Auburn, Auburn, MI
Suvakeen, Rev. John Melkies, '04 (CR) Curia: Offices and Directors St. Joseph, Bagley, MN; St. Mary's, Fosston, MN
Suvakkin, Rev. Masilamani, '01 (GF) Sacred Heart, Bridger, MT
Suwalsky, Rev. David, *S.J.* '95 (STL) [MON] Jesuit Community Corporation at Saint Louis University - Jesuit Hall, St. Louis, MO
Svarczkopf, Rev. Msgr. Mark, '74 (IND) Retired.
Sverdan, Rev. Roman, '13 (PHU) Nativity of Blessed Virgin Mary, Reading, PA
Svida, Rev. Wayne A., '02 (CHI) St. Christina, Chicago, IL
Svirchuk, Rev. Taras, *C.Ss.R.* '06 (PHU) Curia: Leadership St. John the Baptist, Newark, NJ
Svirdan, Rev. Roman, (PHU) Curia: Leadership St. Andrew the Apostle, Lancaster, PA
Swacha, Rev. Stanley, (E) Our Mother of Perpetual Help, Lewis Run, PA
Swai, Rev. Costance, *ALCP* '14 (B) Sacred Heart, Boise, ID
Swain, Rev. Kenneth J., '72 (ALB) Holy Mother and Child Parish, Corinth, NY
Swallows, Rev. Josh, '15 (ORL) Curia: Clergy and Religious Services Most Precious Blood Catholic Church, Oviedo, FL; [CAM] Catholic Campus Ministry at the University of Central Florida, Oviedo, FL
Swaminathan, Rev. John Peter, '93 (OKL) Our Lady of Victory, Purcell, OK
Swamy, Rev. Anthony, *M.S.S.C.C.* (CHR) Our Lady of the Valley, Gloverville, SC; St. Mary of the Immaculate Conception, Edgefield, SC
Swann, Rev. Nate, '21 (SAV) Most Blessed Sacrament, Savannah, GA
Swanson, Rev. Charles F., '66 (OM) Retired.
Swanson, Rev. Derek C, *C.M.* '03 (LA) (>DAL) [MON] Congregation of the Mission, Western Province, Dallas, TX
Swanson, Rev. James, *L.C.* '94 (ATL) [MIS] Legionaries of Christ, Atlanta, GA
Swantek, Rev. David S., '08 (TR) Curia: Leadership St. Martha, Point Pleasant, NJ
Swantek, Rev. Zachary, '14 (NEW) Curia: Organizations (affiliated, inter-Diocesan, miscellaneous/other) St. Theresa of the Child Jesus, Linden, NJ (>TR) [CAM] The Aquinas Institute for Catholic Life at Princeton University, Princeton, NJ
Swantek, Rev. Zachary, (TR) Curia: Pastoral Services
Swanton, Rev. Michael J., '05 (OM) St. Leo, Omaha, NE
Swarick, Rev. Joachim, *O.F.M.* '52 (GB) Retired. [MON] Friary, Pulaski, WI
Swartvagher, Rev. Marc E., '96 (BRK) Our Lady of Grace, Howard Beach, NY
Swartz, Rev. Daniel, '16 (COL) On Duty Outside Diocese. Archdiocese for Military Services
Swartz, Rev. Daniel, (MO) Curia: Offices and Directors
Sway, Rev. Amandus B., *A.J.* '01 (PRT) Chap, Maine Med Ctr, Portland; Mercy Hosp, Portland St. Louis, Portland, ME
Sweany, Rev. Thomas M., '80 (CLV) Retired.
Sweeney, Rev. Callan, '21 (AUS) St. Thomas More, Austin, TX
Sweeney, Rev. Daniel, *S.J.* '94 (SCR) [COL] The University of Scranton, Scranton, PA
Sweeney, Rev. Daniel, *S.J.* '94 (MO) Curia: Offices and Directors
Sweeney, Rev. E. Daniel, (PIT) St. Thomas the Apostle, Homestead, PA
Sweeney, Rev. Edward, '88 (AMA) Retired.
Sweeney, Rev. John, *L.C.* (WDC) [MON] Legionaries of Christ, Potomac, MD
Sweeney, Rev. John P., '73 (PIT) Curia: Consultative Bodies St. Jude, Pittsburgh, PA
Sweeney, Rev. John T., '70 (GBG) Retired. On Administrative Leave.
Sweeney, Rev. Kevin, '94 (ORG) Military Chap Curia: Leadership St. Vincent de Paul, Huntington Beach, CA
Sweeney, Rev. Msgr. Luke M., '01 (NY) Immaculate Heart of Mary, Scarsdale, NY
Sweeney, Rev. Michael, '79 (KNX) Blessed Sacrament, Harriman, TN; St. Ann, Lancing, TN; St. Christopher Catholic Church, Jamestown, TN
Sweeney, Rev. Michael, *O.P.* '79 (OAK) [MON] Order of Preachers (Province of the Most Holy Name of Jesus - Western Dominican Province), Oakland, CA
Sweeney, Rev. Msgr. Patrick E., '72 (PH) Holy Family, Philadelphia, PA
Sweeney, Rev. Peter T., '61 (WDC) Retired.
Sweeney, Rev. Msgr. Robert J., '69 (RCK) Retired.
Sweeney, Rev. Robert J., '82 (NY) Retired.
Sweeney, Rev. William, *S.S.C.* '75 (OM) Retired. [MON] Missionary Society of St. Columban, St. Columbans, NE
Sweeney, Rev. William F., '81 (BRK) St. Francis de Sales, Belle Harbor, NY
Sweeney, Rev. William F., *S.S.C.* '75 (PRO) [MON] St. Columban's Retirement House (St. Columban's Foreign Mission Society), Bristol, RI
Sweeny, Rev. Richard R., '86 (TR) Retired.
Sweet, Very Rev. Daniel J., '01 (PRO) Curia: Leadership Holy Trinity Parish Woonsocket, Woonsocket, RI
Sweetser, Rev. Thomas P., *S.J.* '70 (MIL) [MON] Arrupe House Jesuit Community, Milwaukee, WI
Sweitzer, Rev. Raymond, *SJ* '75 (BUF) St. Michael, Buffalo, NY
Sweitzer, Rev. Raymond M., *S.J.* '75 (NY) [MON] Cardinal Spellman Hall, Jesuit Community, Bronx, NY
Swencki, Rev. John T., '79 (BO) Retired. Mary, Queen of Peace Parish, Medford, MA
Swengros, Rev. William J., '91 (SP) Curia: Leadership St. Ignatius of Antioch, Tarpon Springs, FL; [PRE] St. Ignatius Early Childhood Center, Tarpon Springs, FL
Swetland, Rev. Msgr. Stuart, '91 (KCK) Our Lady and St. Rose, Kansas City, KS; [COL] Donnelly College, Kansas City, KS
Swetland, Rev. Msgr. Stuart W., '91 (PEO) On Duty Outside Diocese. Pres, Donnelly College, Kansas City, KS
Swetnam, Rev. James H., *S.J.* '58 (STL) Retired.
Swett, Rev. Charles J., '57 (TLS) Retired.
Swett, Rev. Msgr. Ronald, '67 (FRS) Retired.
Swiader, Rev. Msgr. James P., '75 (RVC) Curia: Leadership; Offices and Directors St. Joseph's, Garden City, NY
Swiat, Rev. James R., '67 (LAN) Retired.
Swiatek, Rev. Emil P., '65 (BUF) Retired. [MON] Msgr. Conniff Residence, Depew, NY
Swichtenberg, Rev. William, (GB) St. Mary Congregation, Appleton, WI
Swickard, Rev. John L., '74 (COL) Retired.
Swiderski, Rev. Jan, '94 (NOR) Our Lady of Mercy Parish, Durham, CT
Swiderski, Rev. Jan, '94 (NOR) Curia: Leadership
Swiderski, Rev. Stan, '63 (LR) Retired.
Swierczynski, Very Rev. Krzysztof, '12 (CHI) Curia: Tribunal St. Luke and St. Bernardine Parish, River Forest, IL
Swierz, Rev. Michael, '85 (Y) St. Joseph the Provider Catholic School, Youngstown, OH; St. Patrick, Hubbard, OH
Swierzbiolek, Rev. Waclaw, *S.D.B.* '62 (NY) [RTR] Don Bosco Retreat Center and Marian Shrine, Stony Point, NY; [RTR] Marian Shrine, Stony Point, NY
Swift, Very Rev. Daniel F., '89 (TR) Curia: Leadership; Offices and Directors St. Mary of the Lakes, Medford, NJ
Swinerton, Rev. Scott, '22 (CLV) St. Mary, Hudson, OH
Swing, Rev. R. John, '70 (LC) Sacred Heart of Jesus, Nekoosa, WI; St. Alexander, Port Edwards, WI; [EFT] St. Alexander's Church, Port Edwards Endowment Trust, Port Edwards, WI
Swink, Rev. Larry, (WDC) [CAM] St. Mary's College Campus Ministry, St. Mary's City, MD
Swink, Rev. Lawrence C., '06 (WDC) Sacred Heart, La Plata, MD; St. Cecilia, St. Mary's City, MD; [MIS] Sodality Union, Bowie, MD
Swisshelm, Rev. Germain, *O.S.B.* '60 (IND) [MON] St. Meinrad Archabbey, St. Meinrad, IN
Swistovich, Rev. John, '98 (FWT) Retired.
Switzer, Rev. Andrew M., '11 (WH) St. Agnes,

Shepherdstown, WV
Switzer, Rev. Peter, (POC) Retired.
Swoger, Rev. Msgr. John W., '63 (E) Retired.
Swope, Rev. John W, *S.J.* (NY) [MON] St. Ignatius Loyola Residence, New York, NY
Swope, Rev. Msgr. Timothy J., '66 (ALT) Retired.
Syberg, Rev. Andrew W., '15 (IND) [SEM] Bishop Simon Bruté College Seminary, Inc., Indianapolis, IN
Syberg, Very Rev. Benjamin D., '14 (IND) Curia: Leadership Sacred Heart of Jesus Catholic Church, Terre Haute, Inc., Terre Haute, IN; St. Margaret Mary Catholic Church, Terre Haute, Inc., Terre Haute, IN; St. Mary-of-the-Woods Catholic Church, Inc., St. Mary of the Woods, IN; St. Patrick Catholic Church, Terre Haute, Inc., Terre Haute, IN; [MIS] Terre Haute Deanery, Indianapolis, IN; [MIS] Terre Haute Deanery Pastoral Center, Terre Haute, IN
Sybertz, Rev. Donald F., *M.M.* '55 (NY) Retired.
Sydorovych, Very Rev. Roman, '00 (STF) Curia: Leadership Ukrainian Catholic Church of Epiphany, Rochester, NY
Syjueco, Rev. Michael, '13 (SJ) St. Joseph of Cupertino, Cupertino, CA
Sylva, Rev. Msgr. Eugene R., '93 (PAT) Curia: Leadership Cathedral of St. John the Baptist, Paterson, NJ
Sylva, Rev. Msgr. Geno, (PAT) Curia: Leadership
Sylvain, Rev. Rubens, *CS* '10 (NY) [MON] Scalabrinian Missionaries (The Pious Society of the Missionaries of St. Charles Boromeo, Inc.), New York, NY
Sylvester, Rev. Emmanuel, '88 (CR) St. Mary, ,
Sylvester, Rev. Emmanuel, *CMF* '88 (LA) San Gabriel Mission, San Gabriel, CA; St. John the Baptist, Baldwin Park, CA
Sylvester, Rev. Jose, (PHX) Immaculate Heart of Mary Roman Catholic Parish, Phoenix, AZ
Sylvia, Rev. Edmund, *C.S.C.* '77 (ORL) [MON] Congregation of Holy Cross, United States Province, Cocoa Beach, FL
Symolon, Rev. Lawrence S., '75 (HRT) Curia: Advisory Boards, Commissions, Committees, and Councils; Facilities
Symyon, Very Rev. Vasyl, '14 (PBR) St. John the Baptist, Uniontown, PA
Synek, Rev. Roger A., '98 (BIS) St. Anthony, Mandaree, ND; St. Anthony, New Town, ND
Syracuse, Rev. Ross, *O.F.M.Conv.* '78 (MO) Curia: Offices and Directors
Syracuse, Rev. Ross M., *O.F.M.Conv.* '78 (BUF) Buffalo Police Dept; Erie Cty Sheriff's Dept St. Francis of Assisi, Hamburg, NY; [MON] St. Maximilian Kolbe Friary, Hamburg, NY
Syring, Rev. Andrew J., '11 (OM) On Administrative Leave.
Syse, Rev. Luke, '17 (MAD) Our Lady of Fatima Congregation, Lafayette County, WI, Inc., Darlington, WI
Syslo, Rev. Alan M., *C.S.V.* '66 (CHI) [MON] Viatorian Province Center-Clerics of St. Viator, Arlington Heights, IL
Szabo, Rev. Marcel, '71 (PSC) Retired.
Szabo, Rev. Phillip R., '21 (WH) St. John University, Morgantown, WV
Szada, Rev. John A., '78 (HBG) Chap, State Hosp, Danville Curia: Offices and Directors
Szafarski, Rev. Krzysztof, '12 (AGN)
Szakaly, Rev. Anthony V., *C.S.C.* '92 (FR) Curia: Offices and Directors [COL] Holy Cross Fathers Religious, North Easton, MA; [COL] Stonehill College, North Easton, MA
Szakaly, Rev. Anthony V., *C.S.C.* (FTW) [EFT] Blessed Basil Moreau Endowment Trust, Notre Dame, IN
Szal, Rev. George, (LSC) Mesilla Valley Hospice
Szal, Rev. George, *S.M.* (BO) (>WDC) [MON] Marist Center (The Marist Finance Center of the Atlanta Province of the Society of Mary, Marist Fathers and Brothers), Washington, DC
Szamocki, Rev. Piotr, '91 (CAM) Curia: Leadership St. Joachim Parish, Bellmawr, N.J., Bellmawr, NJ
Szamreta, Rev. John, (RIC) Military Chap
Szantyr, Rev. Eugene R., '78 (BGP) Retired.
Szanyi, Rev. Mark, *O.F.M.Conv.* '78 (PMB) St. Lucie, Port St. Lucie, FL
Szarek, Rev. Eugene, *C.R.* '67 (CHI) Blessed Carlo Acutis Parish, Chicago, IL
Szaroleta, Rev. Msgr. Andrew L., '77 (MET) St. Bernadette, Parlin, NJ
Szatkowski, Rev. David, *SCJ* (JKS) Christ the King, Southaven, MS; Good Shepherd Catholic Church, Robinsonville, MS; Holy Spirit, Hernando, MS; Queen of Peace, Olive Branch, MS; St. Gregory the Great, Senatobia, MS; St. Joseph, Holly Springs, MS; [MON] St. Michael Community House, Nesbit, MS
Szatkowski, Rev. David, *S.C.J.* '02 (JKS) Curia: Canonical Services; Consultative Bodies
Szatkowski, Rev. John, '10 (DAL) Med City Dallas Hosp, Dallas St. Paul the Apostle Catholic Parish, Richardson, TX; [EFT] St. Paul Parish Endowment Trust Fund, Richardson, TX
Szczapa, Rev. Stanley J., '71 (NOR) Retired.
Szczawinski, Rev. Sebastian, (VEN) Our Lady of the Angels Parish in Lakewood Ranch, Inc., Lakewood Ranch, FL
Szczechowski, Rev. Glen, '05 (CHY) Curia: Consultative Bodies Church of the Sacred Heart, Greybull, WY; St. Joseph's, Lovell, WY
Szczechura, Very Rev. Robert, '12 (MEM) Curia: Advisory Boards, Commissions, Committees, and Councils; Leadership; Offices and Directors Cathedral of the Immaculate Conception, Memphis, TN
Szczepanik, Rev. John, '88 (MET) St. Stephen Protomartyr, South River, NJ
Szczepankiewicz, Rev. Gary J., '75 (BUF) Our Lady of Czestochowa, North Tonawanda, NY
Szczesniak, Rev. Harry F., '72 (BUF) Retired. [MON] Bishop Head Residence, Lackawanna, NY
Szczesnowicz, Rev. Andrzej, '03 (COS) Our Lady of the Pines-Black Forest, Colorado Springs, CO; Pax Christi Catholic Church, Littleton, CO
Szczesny, Rev. Walter J., '90 (BUF) Curia: Consultative Bodies; Leadership Our Lady of Peace, Clarence, NY
Szczotka, Rev. Krzysztof, '88 (NEW) Saint Adalbert and Saints Peter & Paul, Elizabeth, NJ
Szczurek, Rev. Victor S., *O.Praem.* '00 (ORG) [MON] Norbertine Fathers of Orange, Inc., Silverado, CA; [SEM] St. Michael's Norbertine Postulancy, Novitiate and Juniorate, Silverado, CA
Szczykutowicz, Rev. Msgr. Francis S., '58 (PT) Retired.
Szczypula, Rev. Marcin D., '08 (CHI) St. Francis Borgia, Chicago, IL
Szebenyi, Rev. Andrew, *S.J.* '61 (NY) [MON] Murray-Weigel Hall (A Jesuit Community at Murray-Weigel Hall and Kohlmann Hall), Bronx, NY
Szeman, Rev. Stephen J., '53 (SEA) Retired.
Szendrey, Rev. J. Edward, *M.M.* '00 (NY) [CON] Maryknoll Sisters Charitable Trust, Maryknoll, NY; [MON] Maryknoll Fathers and Brothers (Catholic Foreign Mission Society of America, Inc.), Ossining, NY
Szeraszewicz, Rev. Jaroslaw, '16 (BRK) Our Lady of the Miraculous Medal, Ridgewood, NY
Szews, Rev. George R., '78 (LC) Retired.
Szidik, Rev. Nathaniel, *OSB* '22 (IND) [MON] St. Meinrad Archabbey, St. Meinrad, IN
Szkredka, Rev. Slawomir, '02 (LA) [SEM] St. John's Seminary, Camarillo, CA
Szmyd, Rev. John S., '96 (CHI) Our Lady of Ransom, Niles, IL
Szobonya, Rev. James, *C.Ss.R.* (HBG) Our Mother of Perpetual Help, Ephrata, PA; [MON] St. Clement's Mission House, Ephrata, PA
Szolack, Rev. Joseph T., '88 (CAM) Curia: Advisory Boards, Commissions, Committees, and Councils; Leadership; Tribunal Our Lady of Hope Parish, Blackwood, N.J., Blackwood, NJ
Szparagowski, Rev. George J., '02 (PH) On Special Assignment. Dean of Men, Coll Div, St Charles Borromeo Sem, Overbrook… St. Philip Neri, Lafayette Hill, PA
Szpilski, Rev. Joseph, *C.M.* '56 (BRK) St. Stanislaus Kostka, Brooklyn, NY
Sztorc, Rev. Richard E., '69 (CHI) Retired. St. Mary, Buffalo Grove, IL
Sztuber, Rev. Tomasz, '80 (HRT) The St. Stanislaus Church Corporation of Bristol, Bristol, CT
Sztybel, Rev. Jaroslaw, '97 (ORL) St. John Neumann, Lakeland, FL
Szucki, Rev. Slawomir, *C.M.* (BRK) SS. Cyril and Methodius, Brooklyn, NY; St. Stanislaus Kostka, Brooklyn, NY
Szudera, Rev. Theodore, '77 (GF) Retired.
Szufel, Rev. Adam, *O.F.M.* '64 (SP) [MON] St. Anthony Friary (St. Petersburg) Franciscan Friars-Holy Name Province, Inc., St. Petersburg, FL
Szukalski, Rev. John, *S.V.D.* '97 (DUB) [SEM] Divine Word College, Epworth, IA
Szura, Rev. John, *O.S.A.* '66 (CHI) [MON] St. John Stone Friary, Chicago, IL
Szura, Rev. Thomas, *C.M.M.* '78 (DET) [MON] Mariannhill Mission Society, Dearborn Heights, MI
Szurek, Rev. Pawel F., '05 (PAT) St. Catherine of Bologna, Ringwood, NJ
Szwarc, Rev. Michal J., '16 (PAT) Corpus Christi, Chatham, NJ
Szybka, Rev. Stanley S., '80 (TOL) St. Mary of the Assumption, Van Wert, OH
Szyda, Rev. Arkadiusz, '98 (MO) Curia: Offices and Directors
Szydlik, Rev. Thomas R., '03 (PEO) Schlarman Academy, Danville, IL; St. Paul's, Danville, IL; [MIS] Schlarman Academy of Danville, Inc., Danville, IL
Szydlowski, Rev. Joel, *O.F.M.* '67 (MIL) [MON] Francis and Clare Friary, Franklin, WI
Szylar, Rev. Jan, (BRK) SS. Cyril and Methodius, Brooklyn, NY
Szymakowski, Rev. Andrew, '04 (BAK) Curia: Leadership
Szymanski, Rev. Edward S., '99 (BAL) Retired.
Szymanski, Rev. Lucjan, (RCK) (>SPR) St. Stanislaus Basilica, Chicopee, MA
Szymanski, Rev. Marcin, *O.P.* '11 (SEA) [CAM] University of Washington, Catholic Newman Center, Seattle, WA
Szymaszek, Rev. Leszek P., '97 (BGP) St. Paul's Church of Glenville Connecticut, Greenwich, CT
Szymczyk, Rev. Tomasz, *S.J.* '09 (CHI) [MIS] Jan Beyzym Society, Inc., Chicago, IL; [MON] Sacred Heart Mission House (The Polish Messenger of The Sacred Heart, Inc.), Chicago, IL
Szymkowiak, Rev. Gerard J., *C.Ss.R.* '68 (HBG) [MON] St. Clement's Mission House, Ephrata, PA
Szynal, Rev. Miroslaw, '90 (MAD) Sacred Hearts of Jesus and Mary, Sun Prairie, WI
Szyszka, Rev. Michal, '11 (VEN) St. Raphael Parish in Lehigh, Inc., Lehigh Acres, FL
Ta, Rev. Binh, *C.Ss.R.* '93 (GAL) Holy Ghost, Houston, TX
Ta, Rev. Kiet A., '10 (ORG) St. Thomas More, Irvine, CA
Ta, Rev. Tien Van, *Lm.* (FWT) Christ the King, Fort Worth, TX
Tabak, Rev. Thaddeus, *SDS* (AUS) Blessed Virgin Mary, Washington, TX; St. Ann, Somerville, TX; St. Stanislaus Catholic Church, Chappell Hill, TX
Tabalanza, Rev. Celso, (ARL) [MON] Missionhurst, C.I.C.M.-Central House and Provincialate (American I.H.M. Province, Inc., Immaculate Heart Missions, Inc., Missionhurst, Inc.), Arlington, VA
Tabares, Rev. Christian F., '10 (SAG) Saint Agnes Parish of Freeland, Freeland, MI
Tabbert, Rev. Robert D., '79 (VEN) St. John XXIII Catholic Parish in Fort Myers, Inc., Fort Myers, FL; [NUR] St. John XXIII Housing, Inc., Fort Myers, FL
Taber, Rev. Brian, (CHI) St. Ignatius Jesuit Community, Chicago, IL
Tabera-Vasquez, Rev. Mauricio, '16 (MET) Curia: Clergy and Religious Services St. Joseph, North Plainfield, NJ
Tabernero, Rev. Michael, '19 (MET) Parish of the Visitation, New Brunswick, NJ; St. Thomas Aquinas High School, Edison, NJ
Taberski, Rev. Richard M., '64 (HRT) Retired.
Tabigue, Rev. Joseph, *C.R.S.P.* '04 (SD) Pastor of Our Lady of the Rosary Catholic Parish, San Diego, a corporation sole, San Diego, CA; [MIS] Our Lady of the Rosary Catholic Parish in San Diego, CA Real Property Support Corporation, San Diego, CA
Tabo, Rev. Virgilio, '05 (TUC) Immaculate Conception Roman Catholic Parish - Douglas, Douglas, AZ; Saint Bernard Roman Catholic Church - Pirtleville, Pirtleville, AZ; Saint Luke Roman Catholic Church - Douglas, Douglas, AZ
Tabon, Rev. Raymond, *O.S.J.* '60 (SCR) [SEM] St. Joseph's Oblate Seminary, Pittston, PA
Tabor, Rev. Stanislaw, (TOL) St. Mary, Tiffin, OH; St. Michael the Archangel Church, Gibsonburg, OH
Tabujara, Rev. Oscar, '75 (SJ) Retired.
Tacaisan, Rev. Teodorico E., *M.S.P.* (SB) St. James, Perris, CA
Tacay, Rev. Archie, *C.I.C.M.* '08 (R) St. Eugene, Wendell, NC
Tacelli, Rev. Ronald K., *S.J.* '82 (BO) [MON] The Jesuit Community at Boston College, Chestnut Hill, MA
Tacito, Rev. Nicholas, (LA) Mary, Star of the Sea High School, San Pedro, CA
Tacito, Rev. Nicholas M., *O.Praem.* '96 (ORG) [MON] Norbertine Fathers of Orange, Inc., Silverado, CA
Tackney, Rev. John P., '74 (BO) Retired.
Tadak, Rev. Tacusz, (SAT) [MON] Salvatorian Fathers Community of Texas, Falls City, TX
Taddy, Rev. Jerome J., '60 (GB) Retired.
Taganahan, Rev. Jason, '21 (MRY) St. Rose of Lima Church, Paso Robles, CA
Taggart, Rev. Fred, *O.S.A.* (TLS) Retired.
Taggart, Rev. James, *O.M.I.* (CC) [RTR] Oblate La Parra Center, Sarita, TX
Tagle, Rev. Hugo, *I.S.P.* '95 (AUS) [MON] Schoenstatt Fathers, Austin, TX
Taglianetti, Rev. August A, (PH) St. Pius X, Broomall,

PA
Taglianetti, Rev. Bernard J., '05 (PH) St. Bridget, Philadelphia, PA
Tah, Rev. Canisius T., '14 (BAL) St. Charles Borromeo, Pikesville, MD
Tah, Rev. Philip P., (MO) Curia: Offices and Directors
Taheny, Rev. Mark V., '95 (SFR) Star of the Sea, San Francisco, CA
Taillon, Rev. Marcel L., '94 (PRO) St. Thomas More, Narragansett, RI
Tairo, Rev. Gilbert, *C.S.Sp.* '10 (LR) St. Andrew, Marianna, AR; St. Francis of Assisi, Forrest City, AR; St. John the Baptist, Brinkley, AR; St. Mary, Helena, AR; St. Mary of the Lake Church, Horseshoe Lake, AR
Takuski, Rev. Walter J, '95 (CHI) St. John of the Cross, Western Springs, IL
Takyi-Asante, Rev. Matthew, '06 (NY) Assumption/St. Paul, Staten Island, NY; Parish of Sts. Peter and Paul and Assumption, Staten Island, NY
Takyi-Nketiah, Rev. Philbert, (SCR) Our Lady Help of Christians, Wapwallopen, PA; St. Jude, Mountain Top, PA
Talafous, Rev. Don, *O.S.B.* '52 (SCL) [MON] St. John's Abbey, of the Order of St. Benedict, Collegeville, MN
Talamo, Rev. John F., '98 (NO) St. Andrew the Apostle, New Orleans, LA
Talar, Rev. Charles J., '79 (GAL) St. John Vianney, Houston, TX; [SEM] St. Mary's Seminary, Houston, TX
Talar, Rev. Charles J.T., '79 (BGP) On Duty Outside Diocese. St Mary's Seminary, Houston, TX
Talari, Rev. Ravindranath Jose, '98 (KC) Church of the Annunciation, Kearney, MO
Talarico, Rev. Canon Matthew L., '07 (CHI) [MON] Institute of Christ the King Sovereign Priest, Chicago, IL (>DET) [MON] Institute of Christ the King Sovereign Priest, Inc., Detroit, MI
Talati, Rev. Samir, *S.J.* '95 (CHI) [COL] Jesuit Community at Loyola University Chicago, Chicago, IL
Talavera, Rev. Carlos, '97 (HT) St. Anthony of Padua, Houma, LA
Talbot, Rev. Christopher, '04 (DET) Curia: Administration; Consultative Bodies St. Francis of Assisi - St. Maximilian Kolbe Parish Ray Township, Ray Township, MI
Talbot, Rev. Ralph W., '04 (STP) Curia: Leadership Frassati Catholic Academy, White Bear Lake, MN; St. Mary of the Lake, White Bear Lake, MN; [CEM] St. Mary of the Lake Cemetery, White Bear Lake, MN
Talbott, Rev. Ron, (OAK) [MON] Capuchin Franciscan Friars, Berkeley, CA; [NUR] Mercy Retirement and Care Center, Oakland, CA
Talcott, Rev. Peter, '75 (SR) Retired.
Talentino, Rev. Bill, *OFM Cap.* (LA) [SEM] San Lorenzo Seminary - Novitiate, Santa Ynez, CA
Talento, Rev. Reynante P., (RCK) St. Catherine of Siena, West Dundee, IL
Talesfore, Rev. Msgr. John J., '89 (SFR) St. Matthew, San Mateo, CA
Taliercio, Rev. Pasquale, *M.S.A.* '92 (NOR) Retired.
Tallman, Rev. Gilmary, *O.F.M.Cap.* '60 (SAL) Retired. [MON] St. Fidelis Friary, Victoria, KS
Tallman, Rev. John, '88 (ALB) Chap, St Peter's Hosp
Talmelli, Rev. Raffaele, *sP* (STL) [MIS] Servants of the Paraclete Missouri Generalate Corporation, Dittmer, MO
Tamaiian, Very Rev. Calin, (ROM) St. John the Baptist Romanian Catholic Mission, Tustin, CA
Tamara, Rev. Eder, (LA) St. Mary, Palmdale, CA
Tamayo, Rev. Alberto W., (TR) St. Anthony Church, Red Bank, NJ
Tamayo, Rev. Alfredo L., '77 (SAC) Retired. Pastor of St. John Vianney Parish, Rancho Cordova, a Corporation Sole, Rancho Cordova, CA
Tamayo, Rev. Dante, '93 (OAK) St. Callistus, El Sobrante, CA
Tamayo, Rev. Eric, '18 (SD) Curia: Advisory Boards, Commissions, Committees, and Councils; Offices and Directors [SEM] The Roman Catholic Seminary of San Diego, San Diego, CA
Tamayo, Rev. Nolasco, '98 (PRO) Curia: Advisory Boards, Commissions, Committees, and Councils; Social Services
Tamayo, Rev. Sergio Rivas, (CHI) Cristo Rey Parish, Chicago, IL
Tambornino, Rev. James M., *S.O.L.T.* '91 (MIL) [CON] Carmelite Hermit of the Trinity - CHT, Slinger, WI
Tamburello, Rev. Dennis, *O.F.M.* '80 (ALB) [COL] Siena College, Loudonville, NY
Tamburro, Rev. Francis J., '74 (HBG) Retired.
Tamez, Rev. Benito, '02 (DAL) Blessed Sacrament Catholic Parish, Dallas, TX
Tamiian, Rev. Calin, '02 (ROM) Curia: Offices and Directors
Tamoro, Rev. Briccio, *S.V.D.* (SB) Our Lady of Guadalupe, Ontario, CA
Tancial, Rev. Nodius, '11 (BRK) Our Lady of Grace, Brooklyn, NY
Tancredi, Rev. Carl T., '67 (HBG) Retired.
Tandayu, Rev. Jonas, *MSC* '82 (ALN) Holy Family, Nazareth, PA
Tandoh, Rev. Francis, *C.S.Sp.* '93 (CIN) Our Lady of Grace Parish, Dayton, OH; Queen of Martyrs, Dayton, OH; St. Augustine, Germantown, OH; St. Benedict the Moor, Dayton, OH
Taneo, Rev. Teodulo G., '89 (YAK) St. Henry's, Grand Coulee, WA; St. Joseph's, Waterville, WA
Tanghe, Rev. Warren V., '11 (BAL) Retired.
Tangorra, Rev. Philip-Michael, '09 (PAT) Curia: Leadership Our Lady of Consolation, Wayne, NJ; Our Lady Queen of Peace, Branchville, NJ
Tanguay, Rev. William H., '69 (PRO) Retired.
Tank, Rev. Msgr. Thomas, '67 (KCK) Curia: Advisory Boards, Commissions, Committees, and Councils Holy Spirit, Overland Park, KS
Tanner, Rev. John, *S.J.* '18 (LA) [MON] Colombiere House (Jesuit Fathers), Los Angeles, CA
Tanner, Rev. John, *S.J.* '18 (LA) Blessed Sacrament, Los Angeles, CA
Tanu, Rev. Emanuel, *S.V.D.* '04 (NO) Our Lady Star of the Sea, New Orleans, LA
Tanzini, Rev. Paolo, '08 (NEW) On Duty Outside Diocese. Archdiocese of Detroit, MI
Tanzola, Rev. Josh, (SY) Chap, St Joseph's Hosp Health Ctr, Syracuse
Taormina, Rev. Msgr. Andrew C., '62 (NO) Retired. Curia: Offices and Directors
Taosan, Rev. John Kare, '96 (GAL) Curia: Leadership St. John the Baptist, Alvin, TX
Tapel, Rev. Rene O., '84 (RVC) St. Aloysius, Great Neck, NY
Tapella, Very Rev. Joseph J., '78 (JOL) Retired.
Taphorn, Rev. Joseph, (STP) [COL] University of St. Thomas, St. Paul, MN; [SEM] The Saint Paul Seminary, St. Paul, MN
Taphorn, Rev. Joseph C., '97 (OM) On Duty Outside Diocese. Rector at St. Paul Seminary
Tapia, Rev. Benjamin, '12 (P) St. Anthony of Padua, Forest Grove, OR
Tapia, Rev. Gilberto Mora, '88 (SEA) St. Philomena, Des Moines, WA; St. Theresa, Federal Way, WA
Tapia, Rev. Ignacio, '04 (BWN) Curia: Advisory Boards, Commissions, Committees, and Councils San Cristobal Magallanes & Companions, Mission, TX
Taponi, Rev. Selwan, (EST) Holy Martyrs Chaldean Catholic Church, Sterling Heights, MI
Taponi, Rev. Selwan, (EST) Curia: Offices and Directors
Taponi, Rev. Selwan Sulaiman, '94 (OLD) On Leave.
Tapp, Rev. John G., '84 (SP) Curia: Leadership; Pastoral Services Our Lady of Lourdes, Dunedin, FL
Tappe, Rev. Walter J., '85 (WDC) Curia: Deaneries Saint Hugh of Grenoble, Greenbelt, MD
Tarabay, Rev. Paul, *O.M.M.* '06 (OLL) [MON] Maronite Order of the Blessed Virgin Mary, Ann Arbor, MI
Taran, Rev. Peter, '60 (NY) Retired.
Tarantino, Rev. John F., '78 (PAT) Resurrection, Randolph, NJ
Taranto, Rev. James, '81 (KC) Holy Rosary, Clinton, MO
Tarazona, Rev. Ramiro, '08 (AUS) Ascension Catholic Church, Bastrop, TX
Targonski, Rev. Conrad, *OFM* '75 (LC) [COL] Viterbo University, La Crosse, WI
Targonski, Rev. George, '02 (MET) St. Matthew the Apostle, Edison, NJ
Tarigopula, Rev. Joseph Michael, '94 (MAD) Congregation of St. Mary-St. Paul, Mineral Point, WI; St. Philomena, Belmont, WI
Tarnacki, Rev. Tymoteusz, *O.S.P.P.E.* '16 (PH) [MON] The Order of Saint Paul, First Hermit - The Pauline Fathers, Doylestown, PA
Tarnawski, Rev. Wiktor, '81 (ARE) [MIS] Chapel Inmaculado Corazon de Maria, Barceloneta, PR; [MIS] Chapel Nuestra Senora de Fatima, Barceloneta, PR; [MIS] Chapel San Jose Obrero, Barceloneta, PR; [MIS] Chapel San Juan Bautista, Barceloneta, PR
Tarnawski, Rev. Wiktor, '81 (ARE) Our Lady of Victory, Barceloneta, PR
Tarraza, Rev. William Hector, (RVC) St. Joseph the Worker, East Patchogue, NY (>BO) [MON] San Lorenzo Friary, Boston, MA
Tartaglia, Rev. Paul P., '58 (ALB) Retired.
Taschetta, Rev. Anthony, '71 (JOL) Retired. [EFT] Diocese of Joliet Priests' Pension Plan, Crest Hill, IL; [EFT] Diocese of Joliet Retired Priests' Other Benefits Plan, Crest Hill, IL
Tashibelit, Rev. Moses, '09 (CI) St. Mary's, Colonia, Yap, FM; [MON] Vicariate Residence, Yap, FM
Tassini, Rev. Peter F., '16 (SY) On Leave. Transfiguration, Syracuse, NY
Tassone, Rev. Salvatore A., *S.J.* '63 (SJ) [MON] Jesuit Community at Santa Clara University, Inc., Santa Clara, CA
Tassone, Rev. Thomas W., '08 (RVC) St. Joseph's, Kings Park, NY
Tasto, Rev. Harold J., '68 (STP) Retired.
Tasto, Rev. John P., *O.S.A.* '67 (CHI) [MON] St. Rita Monastery, Chicago, IL
Tate, Rev. David, '15 (GLP) On Leave. Curia: Leadership St. Francis of Assisi, Gallup, NM
Tatel, Rev. Orlando G., '65 (STP) Retired.
Tati, Rev. Zacharie Lukielo, '92 (R) St. Francis De Sales Catholic Parish of Lumberton, Lumberton, NC
Tatino, Rev. Tagaloa, '91 (SPP) Christ the King, Pago Pago, AS
Tatino, Rev. Tagaloa, '91 (SPP) Our Lady of the Rosary Parish, Pago Pago, AS
Tatman, Rev. Robert, '03 (VEN) St. Jude Parish in Sarasota, Inc., Sarasota, FL
Tatro, Rev. Joseph, '00 (WCH) St. John, Viola, KS
Tatro, Rev. Kenneth J., '76 (SPR) Retired. Mary Mother of Hope Parish, Springfield, MA
Tattegrain, Rev. Jean, '10 (LA) St. Joseph, La Puente, CA
Tatum, Rev. Gregory T., *O.P.* '89 (OAK) [MON] Order of Preachers (Province of the Most Holy Name of Jesus - Western Dominican Province), Oakland, CA
Tatyrek, Rev. Matthew, (FWT) Curia: Miscellaneous / Other Offices Immaculate Conception, Denton, TX
Taube, Rev. Sylvester, '64 (DET) Retired.
Tauber, Rev. Jerome A., '02 (ALN) St. Anne, Bethlehem, PA
Taugher, Rev. Timothy J., '78 (SY) St. Francis of Assisi, Binghamton, NY
Taurasi, Rev. David, '88 (CC) On Duty Outside Diocese.
Tauscher, Rev. Donald, *O.S.B.* '65 (SCL) [MON] St. John's Abbey, of the Order of St. Benedict, Collegeville, MN
Tavares-Hernandez, Rev. Martin, '14 (P) Chap, Federal Corr Inst, Sheridan Curia: Offices and Directors St. Peter, Newberg, OR
Tavarez, Rev. Demuel, *CMF* '06 (SJN) San Antonio Maria Claret, Bayamon, PR
Tavella, Rev. Thomas A., *C.S.P.* '81 (SFR) Retired. Old St. Mary's Cathedral & Chinese Mission, San Francisco, CA
Taveras De Leon, Friar Jose Aridio, *O.S.A.* (SJN) Ntra. Sra. de la Monserrate, San Juan, PR
Tavete, Rev. Sagato, '18 (SPP) Christ the King, Pago Pago, AS
Tavis, Rev. Gordon, *O.S.B.* '58 (SCL) [MON] St. John's Abbey, of the Order of St. Benedict, Collegeville, MN
Tawiah, Rev. Msgr. Francis Boachie, '90 (FWT) St. Philip the Apostle, Flower Mound, TX
Tawiah, Rev. Gabriel Oduro, '97 (VIC) St. John Nepomucene, El Campo, TX
Tay, Rev. Msgr. Peter P., '54 (PBR) Retired.
Tayag, Rev. Aldrin, '19 (LEX) St. Luke, Nicholasville, KY
Tayag, Very Rev. Edison, '08 (ROC) Curia: Deaneries St. Patrick, Victor, NY
Taylor, Rev. Brian, '06 (LAF) St. Genevieve, Lafayette, LA
Taylor, Rev. Brian, (NY) On Special Assignment. Service to the Holy See
Taylor, Rev. Britt A., '19 (CHL) St. Leo the Great, Winston-Salem, NC
Taylor, Rev. Daniel, '75 (TUC) On Administrative Leave.
Taylor, Rev. Danny, '20 (LEX) Curia: Leadership St. Mildred, Somerset, KY; St. Peter, Monticello, KY
Taylor, Rev. David H., '74 (PIT) Retired. Curia: Consultative Bodies St. Benedict the Moor Parish, Pittsburgh, PA; St. Mary Magdalene, Pittsburgh, PA
Taylor, Rev. Douglas D., '97 (TOL) Our Lady of Lourdes, New London, OH; St. John the Baptist, Delphos, OH; St. Patrick, Spencerville, OH
Taylor, Rev. Emmanuel, (P) [CAM] University of Oregon (Eugene), Eugene, OR (>TUC) Saint Thomas More Roman Catholic Newman Parish - Tucson, Tucson, AZ
Taylor, Rev. Emmanuel, *O.P.* '12 (TUC) [CAM] University of Arizona Newman Center, Tucson, AZ
Taylor, Rev. John, *M.H.M* '66 (PHX) Retired.
Taylor, Rev. Jon, '64 (LAN) Retired.
Taylor, Rev. Joseph C., '53 (CHI) Retired. St. Edward, Chicago, IL
Taylor, Rev. Mel, *O.S.B.* '67 (SCL) [MON] St. John's

Abbey, of the Order of St. Benedict, Collegeville, MN
Taylor, Very Rev. Michael G., '93 (ARL) Corpus Christi, Aldie, VA
Taylor, Very Rev. Michael S., '97 (MAN) Curia: Consultative Bodies; Tribunal Divine Mercy Parish, Peterborough, NH; [CEM] Mount Calvary Cemetery, Bennington, NH; [CEM] St. Denis, Harrisville, NH; [CEM] St. Peter Cemetery (new), Peterborough, NH; [CEM] St. Peter Churchyard Cemetery (old), Peterborough, NH
Taylor, Rev. Paul R., *O.S.B.* '92 (GBG) [MON] Saint Vincent Archabbey, Latrobe, PA
Taylor, Rev. Paul R., *O.S.B.* (GBG) [COL] Saint Vincent College Corporation, Latrobe, PA
Taylor, Rev. Reynaldo S., '07 (CIN) Children's Hosp, VA Hosp Curia: (>MO) Offices and Directors St. Ann, Cincinnati, OH; St. Bernard, Cincinnati, OH; St. James the Greater, Cincinnati, OH
Taylor, Rev. Samuel, (NY) Retired.
Taylor, Rev. Senan, *O.F.M.Cap.* '70 (NY) [MON] St. Clare Friary (Capuchin Franciscan Friars, Province of St. Mary), Yonkers, NY
Taylor, Rev. Thomas, '83 (PEO) Retired.
Taylor, Rev. William, '64 (B) Retired.
Tcheou, Rev. Pang S., '06 (HBG) St. Joseph Church, Lancaster, PA
Tchingui, Rev. Antonio Jorge, '97 (HRT) The Our Lady of Fatima Roman Catholic Church Corporation of Hartford, Hartford, CT
Te, Rev. Angelo, '11 (P) St. Joseph, Cloverdale, OR
Te, Rev. Jesus Angelo, '11 (P) Sacred Heart, Tillamook, OR
Te, Rev. Jose Alvin, *O.F.M.* '10 (NY) [MON] Franciscan Province of the Immaculate Conception, New York, NY
Te, Rev. Jose Alvin, *OFM* (NY) [MON] Franciscan Mission Associates (Province of the Immaculate Conception), Mount Vernon, NY
Teague, Rev. Bruce, '80 (SPR) Retired.
Teague, Rev. Bruce, (MO) Curia: Offices and Directors
Teague, Rev. James B., '87 (NY) On Leave.
Teall, Rev. Richard, *C.S.C.* '50 (FTW) Retired.
Teater, Rev. Kristian C., '00 (STL) Immaculate Heart of Mary Catholic Church, St. Louis, St. Louis, MO; [SEM] Kenrick School of Theology, ,
Tebalt, Rev. Timothy D., '04 (CHR) Stella Maris, Sullivan's Island, SC
Tebbe, Rev. Francis, *O.F.M.* '75 (GRY) [HOS] Franciscan Health Munster, Munster, IN
Tebbe, Rev. Francis S., *O.F.M.* '75 (CIN) [MON] St. Francis Seraph Friary, Cincinnati, OH
Tedesche, Rev. David, '13 (ROC) Chap, Highland Hosp, Rochester; Park Ridge Hosp/Unity Healt… Blessed Sacrament, Rochester, NY; St. Boniface, Rochester, NY; St. Mary, Rochester, NY
Tedesco, Rev. Joseph, *O.C.S.O.* '79 (CHR) [MON] Mepkin Abbey, Moncks Corner, SC
Tedone, Rev. Michael G., '91 (BRK) Curia: Consultative Bodies St. Bernard of Clairvaux, Brooklyn, NY; [CAM] Campus Ministers and Ministry Centers (Newman Apostolate, Inc.), Brooklyn, NY
Tegamaisho, Rev. Achilleus R, '96 (PEO) St. Thomas, Peoria Heights, IL
Tegha Afuhwi, Rev. Nji, (FTW) St. Mary of the Annunciation, Bristol, IN
Teichert, Rev. Isaiah, *O.S.B.Cam.* '90 (MRY) [MON] New Camaldoli Hermitage (Camaldolese Hermits of America), Big Sur, CA
Tejada, Rev. Francisco, (NY) Incarnation, New York, NY
Tejada, Rev. Jose, '92 (SP) St. Frances Xavier Cabrini, Spring Hill, FL
Tejada, Rev. Juan Carlos, '16 (SAT) Curia: Administration
Tejada, Rev. Juan Carlos, '16 (SAT) St. Timothy's, San Antonio, TX
Tejada Henriquez, Rev. Francisco, (ARE) On Duty Outside Diocese. New York
Tejano, Rev. Carlo Paul G., '13 (SAC) Pastor of St. Joseph Parish, Auburn, a corporation sole, Auburn, CA
Tejeda, Rev. Pedro, (SJ) St. Maria Goretti, San Jose, CA
Teklemariam, Rev. Begashaw, *O.F.M. Cap.* '10 (CHI) [MON] St. Clare Friary, Chicago, IL
Telagani, Rev. Suresh Kumar, '04 (BAK) Cathedral of St. Francis De Sales, Baker City, OR
Telken, Rev. Paul E., '73 (STL) St. Anthony Catholic Church, Sullivan, Sullivan, MO
Teller, Rev. Jonah, *O.P.* '20 (WDC) St. Dominic Church & Priory, Washington, DC
Telles, Rev. John, '75 (ELP) Curia: Faith Formation; Offices and Directors [SEM] St. Charles Seminary, El Paso, TX
Tellez, Rev. Eric, '86 (PHX) St. Patrick Roman Catholic Parish, Scottsdale, AZ
Tellez, Rev. Jairo A., '62 (SAT) Chap, Major, USAF, Air Police CMR 480, APO Europe
Tellez, Rev. Jorge, (SB) St. Elizabeth Ann Seton, Ontario, CA
Tello-Curiel, Rev. Oscar, '12 (SAT) Our Lady Queen of Heaven, Atascosa, TX; Sacred Heart, Von Ormy, TX
Telnack, Rev. Methodius, *O.C.S.O.* '57 (ATL) [MON] The Monastery of the Holy Spirit, Conyers, GA
Tembo, Rev. Edward, *C.I.C.M.* '20 (R) Maria, Reina De Las Americas, Mount Olive, NC
Tempel, Rev. Theodore, '64 (EVN) Retired.
Temple, Rev. Matthew, *O.Carm.* '82 (ROC) [MON] Whitefriars Priory, Rochester, NY
Templeton, Rev. Msgr. Robert E., '88 (NEW) Retired.
Temu, Rev. Augustine, (PIT) St. Mary Magdalene, Pittsburgh, PA
Tenas, Rev. Jose Luis, (RVC) Holy Name of Mary, Valley Stream, NY; St. Kilian, Farmingdale, NY
Tenbarge, Rev. Timothy, '73 (EVN) Retired.
Tenbarge, Rev. Tyler, '16 (EVN) Corpus Christi, Evansville, IN
Tenbarge, Rev. Tyler R., '16 (EVN) On Special Assignment. Curia: Offices and Directors
Teneti, Rev. Yesupadam, (LA) St. Genevieve, Panorama City, CA
Teneza, Rev. Vicente C., '01 (SAC) Pastor of St. Vincent Ferrer Parish of Vallejo, a Corporation Sole, Vallejo, CA
Tennant, Rev. Kyle, '19 (COL) St. Cecilia, Columbus, OH
Tenorio, Rev. Michael C., *O.F.M.Cap.* '99 (MO) Curia: Offices and Directors
Tensi, Rev. Lawrence R., '79 (CIN) St. Columban, Loveland, OH; St. Margaret of York, Loveland, OH
Teodoro, Rev. George, *S.J.* '16 (PHX) St. Francis Xavier Roman Catholic Parish, Phoenix, AZ
Teodoro, Rev. George, (LA)
Teran Sanchez, Rev. Juan Jose, '11 (ATL) On Duty Outside Diocese.
Terdine, Rev. Richard G., '65 (PIT) Retired. [MON] St. John Vianney Manor, Pittsburgh, PA
Terembula, Rev. Tadeusz, '96 (SJ) St. Anthony, San Jose, CA
Teresa, Rev. Carlo Santa, (CAM) St. Joseph's Church, Somers Point, N.J., Somers Point, NJ
Terhes, Rev. Chris, '06 (ROM) On Administrative Leave.
Terico, Rev. Nicholas R., *O.Praem.* '89 (PH) [MON] Daylesford Abbey, Inc., Paoli, PA
Terlecky, Rt. Rev. Mitred Msgr. John, '76 (STF) St. Peter & Paul Ukrainian Catholic Church, Spring Valley, NY
Terlecky, Rt. Rev. Mitred Msgr. John, '76 (STF) Curia: Offices and Directors
Termyna, Rev. James J., '70 (PAT) Retired.
Ternes, Rev. Gary, '79 (SFS) Retired.
Ternullo, Rev. Joseph P., '73 (SAC) Retired. On Special Assignment. Chaplain, Sacramento PD & Fire Departments, Sacramento
Tero, Rev. Richard, '74 (AJ) Retired. Sacred Heart, Seward, AK
Terra, Rev. Joseph, (B) St. Joan of Arc, Post Falls, ID
Terra, Rev. Msgr. Russell G., '62 (SAC) Retired. Pastor of St. Joseph Parish, Redding, a corporation sole, Redding, CA
Terranova, Rev. Robert, (PH) Annunciation B.V.M., Philadelphia, PA; St. Nicholas of Tolentine, Philadelphia, PA; [MON] Augustinian Community (O.S.A.), Philadelphia, PA
Terrazas, Rev. Vicente, (SAV) St. Christopher, Claxton, GA
Terrebonne, Rev. Burnick J., '77 (NO) Retired.
Terrera, Rev. Carlos Bernardo, '89 (SCR) On Administrative Leave.
Terrien, Rev. Lawrence B., *P.S.S.* '72 (BAL) Retired. [MON] Society of St. Sulpice, Province of the United States, Baltimore, MD; [SEM] St. Mary's Seminary and University, Baltimore, MD
Terrien, Rev. Lawrence B., *S.S.* '72 (ARL) On Duty Outside Diocese. Dir Spiritual Life Progs, Systematic Theology, St Mary's Se…
Terrill, Rev. Gabriel, '20 (PHX) Queen of Peace Roman Catholic Parish, Mesa, AZ
Terriquez, Rev. Enrique, '63 (B) Retired. Curia: Leadership
Terry, Rev. Brian F., *S.A.* '97 (NY) [MON] Atonement Friars, New York, NY; [MON] Franciscan Friars of the Atonement, Minister General Office, Garrison, NY
Terry, Rev. John S., '75 (SCR) Our Lady of Hope Parish, Wilkes-Barre, PA; [PRE] Catholic Youth Center, Wilkes-Barre, PA
Terza, Rev. William R., '69 (PIT) Retired. Triumph of the Holy Cross, Jefferson Hills, PA
Terzano, Rev. John D., '74 (CLV) Retired.
Testa, Rev. John J., '11 (TR) Curia: Miscellaneous / Other Offices Corpus Christi, Willingboro, NJ
Testa, Rev. Richard, '67 (ALB) Retired.
Testa, Rev. Msgr. Steve J., '64 (ALX) Retired. Curia: Miscellaneous / Other Offices
Tesvich, Rev. Daniel J., *S.J.* '12 (KC) [MON] St. Peter Claver Jesuit Community, Kansas City, MO
Teter, Rev. Patrick A., '92 (SPC) The Assumption of the Blessed Virgin Mary, Lamar, MO
Teti, Rev. James V., '97 (NEW) On Duty Outside Diocese. Curia: Offices and Directors Annunciation, Paramus, NJ (>OG) St. Alphonsus - Holy Name of Jesus, Tupper Lake, NY; (>OG) St. Henry, Long Lake, NY; (>OG) St. Therese Church, Newcomb, NY, Newcomb, NY
Tetlow, Rev. John H., '84 (STA) Curia: Clergy and Religious Services Cathedral - Basilica of St. Augustine, St. Augustine, FL
Tetlow, Rev. Joseph A., *S.J.* (FWT) [RTR] Montserrat Jesuit Retreat House, Lake Dallas, TX
Tetrault, Rev. Raymond L., '60 (PRO) Retired.
Tetreault, Rev. Maynard, *O.F.M.* '60 (CIN) [MON] St. John the Baptist Friary, Cincinnati, OH
Tetreault, Rev. Raymond A., '71 (PRO) Retired.
Tettedji, Rev. Daniel M., (PH) Our Lady of Hope, Philadelphia, PA
Tetteh, Rev. Edward, *SVD* (WH) Holy Rosary, Buckhannon, WV; [CAM] West Virginia Wesleyan College Newman Center, Buckhannon, WV; [MIS] Sacred Heart Chapel, Pickens, WV
Tettekpoe, Rev. Messan K, *SVD* (CHI) St. Joseph the Worker, Wheeling, IL
Teverzczuk, Rev. William J., '73 (PH) Retired.
Tezone, Rev. Adriano, (BO) St. Anthony of Padua, Everett, MA
Thachara, Rev. Joseph, '21 (SYM) St. Mary's Syro-Malabar Knanaya Catholic Church of Houston, Missouri City, TX
Thachil, Rev. Joy A., *S.A.C.* '88 (MIL) St. Agnes Congregation, Butler, WI; [MON] Pallotti House, Milwaukee, WI
Thadathil, Rev. Chacko, '94 (LUB) St. Margaret Mary, Lamesa, TX
Thadathil, Rev. Francis, *MSFS* '81 (LC) Immaculate Conception, Eau Claire, WI
Thadathil, Rev. George, *C.M.I.* '88 (SAC) St. Francis Catholic High School, Sacramento, CA
Thaden, Rev. Roy W., *S.J.* '73 (SJ) [MON] Sacred Heart Jesuit Center, Los Gatos, CA
Thaden, Rev. William A., '88 (CLV) Curia: Advisory Boards, Commissions, Committees, and Councils Sacred Heart Chapel, Lorain, OH; [MIS] Sacred Heart Chapel, Lorain, OH
Thai, Rev. Bao Q., '03 (ORG) Curia: Leadership Christ Cathedral Parish, Garden Grove, CA
Thai, Rev. Nicolaus Duy, '16 (ORG) Curia: Offices and Directors St. Martin de Porres, Yorba Linda, CA
Thai, Rev. Thomas V., '54 (LEX) Retired.
Thai Do, Rev. (Bartholomew M.) Hoa, *CRM* '77 (SPC) [MON] Congregation of the Mother of the Redeemer, Carthage, MO
Thai Tran, Rev. Joseph, (SAT) St. Joseph, San Antonio, TX
Thaikoottathil, Rev. James, '84 (NOR) Curia: Offices and Directors St. John, Middletown, CT; St. Sebastian, Middletown, CT
Thainase, Very Rev. Irudayanathan, '03 (LC) Curia: Leadership Nativity of the Blessed Virgin Mary, Richland Center, WI; Sacred Heart, Lone Rock, WI; St. Anthony de Padua, Cazenovia, WI
Thakadipuram, Rev. Tom, (DM) St. Mary, Shenandoah, IA
Thalakkottur, Rev. Nicholas A., (ARL) St. Andrew the Apostle, Clifton, VA
Thalakkottur Anthony, Rev. Nicholas, *S.D.B.* '08 (SYM) St. Jude Syro-Malabar Catholic Church, Northern Virginia of St. Thomas Syro-Malabar Catholic Diocese, Chantilly, VA
Thalakulam, Rev. Cherian, *C.M.I.* '76 (CHR) St. Edward, Murphy Village, SC
Thaler, Rev. Joseph L., *M.M.* '77 (NY) [MON] Maryknoll Fathers and Brothers (Catholic Foreign Mission Society of America, Inc.), Ossining, NY
Thames, Rev. Robert, '64 (FWT) Retired. On Duty Outside Diocese. Santa Cruz
Thampi, Rev. Aby, *C.M.I.* (COV) St. Henry, Elsmere, KY
Than, Rev. M. Timothy Qui Van, *O.Cist.* '75 (SB) [MON] The Cistercian Congregation of the Holy Family, St. Joseph Monastery, Lucerne Valley, CA
Thanavelil, Rev. Joseph, '81 (LUB) St. Patrick, Lubbock,

TX
Thandiackal, Rev. Seejo, *C.M.I.* (L) St. Martha, Louisville, KY
Thang, Rev. Eustace, (IND) St. Barnabas Catholic Church, Indianapolis, Inc., Indianapolis, IN; St. Pius X Catholic Church, Indianapolis, Inc., Indianapolis, IN
Thangavel, Rev. JeganMari, *HGN* '15 (PBL) Christ the King, Pueblo, CO
Thang'wa, Rev. Michael, *F.M.H.* '10 (SHP) Jesus the Good Shepherd, Monroe, LA; St. Joseph, Bastrop, LA
Thang'wa, Very Rev. Michael, (SHP) Curia: Leadership
Thanippilly, Rev. T. John, (SAT) On Special Assignment. Hospital Min, San Antonio
Thanippilly, Rev. Teji John, (MO) Curia: Offices and Directors
Thaniyel, Rev. Raja, *HGN* '15 (PRT) Prince of Peace Parish, Lewiston, ME
Thankickal, Rev. Aby, *CMI* '01 (NSH) St. Thomas Aquinas, Cookeville, TN
Thannickal, Rev. Abraham, *OIC* '11 (RVC) St. Patrick, Smithtown, NY
Thannickal, Rev. Ruban, '94 (SYM) Infant Jesus Syro Malabar Catholic Church, Sacramento, CA of St. Thomas Syro Malabar Catholic Diocese of Chicago, Sacramento, CA
Thanugundla, Rev. Balajoji, '94 (CHI) St. Anne, Barrington, IL
Thanugundla, Rev. Manohar, (JKS) St. Francis of Assisi, Brookhaven, MS; [CAM] Lincoln Junior College Newman Center, Brookhaven, MS
Thapwa, Rev. Stephen M., '76 (WCH) Retired.
Tharackal, Rev. Joseph, (BRK) Chap, Kingsboro Psychiatric Ctr; Hosp Menonita St. Gerard Majella, Hollis, NY
Tharackal, Rev. Joseph, '83 (SYM) Brooklyn Queens Long Island Knanaya Catholic Mission Inc. (St. Stephen's Knanaya Catholic Forane Church), Hempstead, NY
Tharakal, Rev. Joseph, (BRK) Chap, Woodhull Med & Mental Health Ctr
Tharakunnel Scaria, Rev. Sijo, '08 (SYM) St. Teresa of Calcutta Syro-Malabar Catholic Church, San Francisco, California of St. Thomas Syro-Malabar Catholic Diocese of Chicago, Livermore, CA
Tharayil, Rev. Bipy Mathew, '04 (SYM) St. Joseph's Syro-Malabar Knanaya Catholic Mission of Westchester, NY, Yonkers, NY; St. Mary's Syro-Malabar Knanaya Catholic Church, Rockland, NY, Haverstraw, NY
Tharayil, Rev. Jose J., '70 (GAL) St. Theresa, Sugar Land, TX
Tharp, Rev. Larry R., '77 (CIN) Sacred Heart of Jesus, Fairfield, OH; St. Ann, Hamilton, OH
Thayer, Rev. Brent, (NSH) St. Edward, Nashville, TN
Thayer, Rev. David D., *P.S.S.* '75 (BAL) Retired. [MON] Society of St. Sulpice, Province of the United States, Baltimore, MD
Thayer, Rev. David D., *S.S.* '75 (HRT) On Duty Outside Diocese. Theological College Catholic Univ. of America, Washington
Thayer, Rev. David D., *P.S.S.* '75 (WDC) [COL] Catholic University of America, The, Washington, DC
Thayil, Rev. Mathew, '67 (ATL) Retired. [MON] The Missionaries of St. Francis de Sales - MSFS USA Vice Province, Loganville, GA
Thayil, Rev. Mathew, *M.S.F.S.* '67 (GAL) Retired.
Thayilkuzhithottu, Rev. George Kutty, *M.S.F.S.* '97 (LC) SS. Peter and Paul, Independence, WI; St. John the Apostle, Whitehall, WI; [EFT] St. John Parish Endowment Trust, Whitehall, WI; [EFT] The SS. Peter & Paul Parish-Independence Education Endowment Trust, Independence, WI
The Nguyen, Rev. Joseph Hieu, *C.S.* '19 (GAL) St. Leo the Great, Houston, TX
The Pham, Rev. Vincent Tung, '85 (PH) Holy Innocents, Philadelphia, PA
Theby, Rev. James D., '08 (STL) Our Lady of Lourdes Catholic Church, Washington, Washington, MO
Theby, Rev. James D., '08 (PRM) St. Louis Mission, St. Louis, MO
Theetla, Rev. Francis, '97 (SPC) Holy Trinity, Marshfield, MO
Theetla, Rev. Francis, (SPC) Chap, Ozark Corr Ctr, Fordland
Thein, Rev. Msgr. Edward, '79 (ATL) Retired.
Theis, Rev. Gerard, *S.V.D.* '60 (CHI) Retired. [MON] Divine Word Residence, Techny, IL
Theis, Rev. Jeremy, '14 (SCL) Our Lady of the Angels, Sauk Centre, MN; SS. Peter and Paul, Sauk Centre, MN; St. Alexius, West Union, MN; St. Donatus, Sauk Centre, MN; St. Francis De Sales, Belgrade, MN; St. Paul's, Sauk Centre, MN
Theisen, Rev. Brandon M., (STP) Church of St. Joseph, Red Wing, MN
Theisen, Rev. Eugene A., *M.M.* '53 (NY) Retired.
Theisen, Rev. Eugene J., '99 (STP) Curia: Leadership St. Wenceslaus, New Prague, MN; [CEM] St. Benedict Cemetery, New Prague, MN; [CEM] St. John the Evangelist Cemetery, New Prague, MN; [CEM] St. Joseph Cemetery, New Prague, MN; [CEM] St. Scholastica Cemetery, New Prague, MN; [CEM] St. Wenceslaus Cemetery, New Prague, MN
Theisen, Rev. Kenneth, *O.S.B.* '84 (RCK) [MON] Marmion Abbey, Aurora, IL
Theisen, Rev. Wilfred, *O.S.B.* '56 (SCL) [MON] St. John's Abbey, of the Order of St. Benedict, Collegeville, MN
Thekkan, Rev. Pauly, *C.M.I.* '89 (MET) Chap, Robert Wood Johnson Univ Hosp
Thekkanath, Rev. Antony, *VC* (SPC) St. John, Leopold, MO
Thekkedam, Rev. Sebastian, *C.M.I.* '84 (NSH) [RTR] Carmel Center of Spirituality, Liberty, TN
Thekkedath, Rev. Sebastian, *CMI* '99 (BLX) Annunciation, Kiln, MS
Thekkekara, Rev. Antony, '91 (GI) Curia: Leadership; Offices and Directors St. Michael's, Spalding, NE
Thekkineth, Rev. Soju, (SYM) Blessed Kunjachan Syro-Malabar Catholic Mission, Staten Island, NY, Staten Island, NY
Thekku, Rev. George, '90 (PT) Curia: Leadership St. Jude Thaddeus, Cantonment, FL
Thelander, Rev. Scott, *S.J.C.* '12 (CHI) St. John Cantius, Chicago, IL; [MIS] Canons Regular of Saint John Cantius, Chicago, IL
Thelappilly, Rev. Babu, '08 (PAT) Our Lady of Fatima, Highland Lakes, NJ
Thelen, Rev. Albert R., *SJ* '68 (MIL) [MON] St. Camillus Jesuit Community (Society of Jesus, USA Midwest Province), Wauwatosa, WI
Thelen, Rev. Daniel L., '15 (LC) Curia: Leadership St. John the Baptist, Marshfield, WI; [EFT] St. John the Baptist Educational Endowment Trust, Marshfield, WI; [EFT] St. John the Baptist Maintenance Endowment Trust, Marshfield, WI
Thelen, Rev. Frederick L., '80 (LAN) Retired.
Thelen, Rev. Mathias D., '10 (LAN) Curia: Leadership St. Patrick Parish Brighton, Brighton, MI
Thelen, Rev. Noah, '21 (GR) Curia: Leadership St. Francis de Sales, Holland, MI
Thelen, Rev. Msgr. Robert, '70 (NY) [SEM] St. Joseph's Seminary, Yonkers, NY
Thelen, Rev. Msgr. Robert J., '70 (BRK) Retired. St. Margaret, Middle Village, NY
Thelly, Rev. Matthew, '71 (TR) Retired.
Then de la Cruz, Friar Antonio, *O.S.A.* (SJN) Ntra. Sra. de la Monserrate, Bayamon, PR; San Agustin, Bayamon, PR
Thenan, Rev. Peter, '98 (CC) Sacred Heart, Mathis, TX; St. Pius X Mission - Sandia, Mathis, TX
Theneth, Rev. Thomas, *CMI* (JOL) St. Joseph Catholic Church, Manteno, IL
Theobald, Rev. Charles, '58 (NEW) Retired.
Theodat, Rev. Ralph, (BRK) St. Matthew, Brooklyn, NY
Theodor, Rev. Dominic, (CI) Holy Cross Parish, Chuuk, FM
Theophilus, Rev. Malachy, *O.S.A.* (SFR) Chap, Kaiser & Sequoia Hosp
Theoret, Rev. Glenn J., '99 (MAR) Retired.
Therese, Rev. John, *CSJ* (DEN) All Souls Catholic Parish in Englewood, Englewood, CO
Theroux, Rev. Bertrand L., '67 (PRO) Retired.
Theroux, Rev. David J., *S.S.E.* '74 (BUR) [COL] St. Michael's College, Colchester, VT
Theroux, Rev. Denis B., '88 (DET) Our Lady of Victory Parish Northville, Northville, MI
Theroux, Rev. Msgr. Paul D., '77 (PRO) Curia: Clergy and Religious Services; Leadership
Theroux, Rev. Raymond C., '65 (PRO) Retired. [NUR] St. Clare Home, Newport, RI
Therrien, Rev. Shawn M., '87 (MAN) Curia: Clergy and Religious Services; Consultative Bodies; Leadership St. Anne-St. Augustin, Manchester, NH; [CEM] St. Mary Cemetery, Claremont, NH
Thesing, Rev. Gilbert Jerome, *OP* '75 (STP) [MON] St. Albert the Great Priory, Minneapolis, MN
Thesing, Rev. Mark B., *C.S.C.* '86 (FTW) [COL] University of Notre Dame Du Lac, Notre Dame, IN; [MIS] Holy Cross House, Notre Dame, IN; [MON] Holy Cross Community, Corby Hall, University of Notre Dame, Notre Dame, IN
Thesing, Rev. Robert J., *S.J.* '76 (CIN) [MON] Jesuit Community at St. Xavier High School, Cincinnati, OH
Thess, Very Rev. William C., '00 (STL) Curia: Leadership St. Catherine of Alexandria, Ste. Genevieve, MO; St. Joseph Catholic Church, Farmington, Farmington, MO
Thessing, Rev. Charles, '88 (LR) Sacred Heart Church, Crawfordsville, AR; St. Michael, West Memphis, AR
Theuerer, Rev. Ulrich Maria, *O.S.B.* '01 (TLS) [MON] Our Lady of the Annunciation of Clear Creek Abbey, Hulbert, OK
Thevenin, Rev. Donelson, '05 (BRK) Chap, USS BOXER, Chaplain Department, FPO AP 96661-1663 Curia: (>MO) Offices and Directors
Thi, Rev. Andrew, '85 (NY) Retired. Parish of St. Patrick's Old Cathedral and Most Precious Blood, New York, NY
Thibault, Rev. Todd E., '16 (OG) Curia: Consultative Bodies St. Mary's Church, Copenhagen, NY, Copenhagen, NY; The Society of St. Jame's Church Carthage, Carthage, NY; [CEM] St. James Cemetery Corporation, Carthage, NY
Thibodeau, Rev. Kenneth, *S.M.* '68 (WDC) Retired. [MON] Marist Center (The Marist Finance Center of the Atlanta Province of the Society of Mary, Marist Fathers and Brothers), Washington, DC
Thibodeau, Rev. Kenneth A., *S.M.* '68 (BO) Retired.
Thibodeau, Rev. Raynold, *OFM Cap* (NY) Retired. [MON] St. Clare Friary (Capuchin Franciscan Friars, Province of St. Mary), Yonkers, NY
Thibodeau, Rev. Raynold, *O.F.M.Cap.* '85 (NOR) Retired.
Thibodeau, Rev. Scott A., '98 (DET) Curia: Consultative Bodies Our Lady of the Lakes Parish Waterford, Waterford, MI
Thibodeaux, Rev. Mark Edward, *S.J.* '01 (NO) Holy Name of Jesus, New Orleans, LA; [MON] Loyola Jesuit Community, New Orleans, LA
Thiede, Rev. John S., *S.J.* '03 (MIL) [MON] Jesuit Community at Marquette University (Marquette Jesuit Associates, Inc.), Milwaukee, WI
Thiel, Rev. Michael, '16 (GB) St. Denis, Shiocton, WI; St. Patrick, Stephenville, WI
Thielen, Rev. Jeffrey M., '74 (MIL) Retired.
Thielen, Rev. Luke, '16 (SAL) St. Joseph Parish, Oakley, Inc., Oakley, KS; St. Paul Parish, Angelus, Inc., Angelus, KS
Thielman, Rev. Kenneth, '55 (SCL) Retired.
Thieman, Rev. Donald J., *C.PP.S.* '53 (CIN) Retired. [MON] St. Charles, Celina, OH
Thien, Rev. Bruno Chi, *O.Cist* '17 (SPC) [MON] Assumption Abbey (O.Cist), Ava, MO
Thien-Dinh, Rev. Joseph, *S.C.J.* '02 (MIL) [MON] Sacred Heart Monastery, Hales Corners, WI
Thierry, Rev. Jude W., '09 (LAF) St. Joseph, Iota, LA
Thiers, Rev. Georges G., *C.O.* '70 (PH) St. Francis Xavier, Philadelphia, PA; [MON] The Philadelphia Congregation of The Oratory of St. Philip Neri, Philadelphia, PA
Thieryoung, Rev. John, '96 (PEO) Saint Mary Magdalene Roman Catholic Congregation of Aledo, Aledo, IL; St. Anthony's Church, Matherville, IL; St. Catherine's Church, Aledo, IL
Thies, Rev. Grant, '18 (MAD) St. Jerome, Columbus, WI; St. Patrick, Doylestown, WI
Thiess, Rev. Daniel R., *C.M.* '90 (STL) [MON] Congregation of the Mission Vincentian Fathers Lazarist Residence, St. Louis, MO
Thiessen, Rev. Dennis D., *S.D.S.* '78 (MIL) [MIS] Salvatorians - Jordan Hall, Milwaukee, WI
Thimm, Rev. Donald H., '76 (MIL) Retired. Congregation of Our Lady of the Lakes, Random Lake, WI; Divine Savior Congregation, Fredonia, WI; [MIS] Works of Mercy Ministry, Inc., Cedarburg, WI
Thirumalareddy, Rev. Anthony, '08 (MAD) All Saints Catholic Congregation, Berlin, WI; Our Lady of the Lake, Green Lake, WI
Thirumalareddy, Rev. Joji Reddy, '96 (MAD) Holy Family Parish, Markesan, WI; St. Faustina Congregation, Pardeeville, WI
Thirumalareddy, Rev. Pradeep Kumar, '07 (JKS) St. Mary, Batesville, MS
Thirumalareddy, Rev. Rayapu, (SR) Pastor of St. Mary of the Angels Catholic Church of Ukiah, a Corporation Sole, Ukiah, CA
Thirumalareddy, Rev. Showreddy, '97 (FRS) St. Jude, Wofford Heights, CA
Thirumalareddy, Rev. Sudhakar Reddy, *C.F.I.C.* '15 (COL) St. Elizabeth, Columbus, OH
Thirumalareddy, Rev. Suresh Reddy, '04 (JKS) Curia: Consultative Bodies St. Alphonsus, McComb, MS; St. James the Greater Catholic Parish, Magnolia, MS
ThirumangalaM, Rev. George, *CMI* (SHP) St. Lucy, Hodge, LA
Thirunelliparamabil, Rev. Lukose, '92 (CC) Our Lady of Victory, Beeville, TX; Sacred Heart Mission, Pettus, TX
Thirunelliparambil, Rev. Lukose, (CC) St. James, Bishop,

TX
Thoa, Rev. Ngo Dinh, *C.Ss.R.* '62 (LA) [MON] Vietnamese Redemptorist Mission, Baldwin Park, CA
Thodukulan, Rev. Thomas Anthony, *S.D.B.* '00 (SFR) Corpus Christi, San Francisco, CA
Tholitho, Rev. Tholitho, (MET) St. Bernard of Clairvaux, Bridgewater, NJ
Thoma, Rev. Steven, *CR* (BEL) Immaculate Conception of the B.V.M., Columbia, IL
Thoma, Rev. Steven, *C.R.* '91 (LA) [SEM] St. John's Seminary, Camarillo, CA
Thoman, Rev. Dwayne J., '76 (DUB) Retired.
Thomas, Rev. Abraham, (MCE) Curia: Advisory Boards, Commissions, Committees, and Councils; Offices and Directors; Tribunal St. Mary's Malankara Catholic Church, Mesquite, TX
Thomas, Rev. Akhil, (SB) [MIS] Wordnet, Inc., San Bernardino, CA
Thomas, Rev. Alan E, '92 (ALT) [MIS] Diocese of Altoona-Johnstown, Altoona, PA
Thomas, Very Rev. Alan E., '92 (ALT) Curia: Leadership; Offices and Directors St. Mary, Hollidaysburg, PA; St. Michael the Archangel, Hollidaysburg, PA; [CAM] Penn State University, Altoona, Altoona, PA; [MIS] Office of Ongoing Formation of Clergy, Altoona, PA; [NUR] Dmitri Manor Priests' Residence, Hollidaysburg, PA
Thomas, Rev. Andrew, '19 (EVN) SS. Peter and Paul, Haubstadt, IN; St. James, Haubstadt, IN
Thomas, Rev. Andrew R., '05 (P) St. Philip Neri, Portland, OR
Thomas, Rev. Anil, *SVD* (BLX) St. Rose De Lima, Bay St. Louis, MS
Thomas, Rev. Antony Primal, '10 (MIL) St. Patrick's Congregation, Whitewater, WI
Thomas, Rev. Biju, '00 (EVN) Visitation of the Blessed Virgin Mary, Huntingburg, IN
Thomas, Rev. Biju Mandapathil, *S.V.D.* (SB) [MIS] Wordnet, Inc., San Bernardino, CA
Thomas, Rev. Boby, '02 (SYM) St. Anthony Syro-Malabar Knanaya Catholic Church (San Antonio), San Antonio, TX
Thomas, Rev. Ciya, *C.Ss.R.* (NY) Immaculate Conception, Bronx, NY
Thomas, Rev. Curtis R., '87 (NO) Retired.
Thomas, Rev. Delroy, (MGZ) Curia: Offices and Directors
Thomas, Rev. Delroy E., '86 (MGZ) St. Charles Borromeo, Aguadilla, PR
Thomas, Rev. Demetrius M., *O.S.B.* '17 (PAT) [MON] St. Mary's Abbey, Morristown, NJ
Thomas, Rev. Dijo, *M.S.F.S.* (HBG) Our Lady of Good Counsel, Marysville, PA
Thomas, Rev. Dominic, (NY) Our Lady, Queen of Peace, Staten Island, NY
Thomas, Rev. Dominic, (NY) (>MIL) [MON] Missionary Congregation of the Blessed Sacrament, Inc., Zion Province, Cudahy, WI
Thomas, Rev. Gary, '83 (SJ) (>SFR) [SEM] St. Patrick's Seminary and University (The Roman Catholic Seminary of San Francisco), Menlo Park, CA
Thomas, Rev. Gary R., '83 (SJ) Curia: Leadership
Thomas, Rev. Jacob, (KAL) St. Jerome, Battle Creek, MI; St. Joseph, Battle Creek, MI
Thomas, Rev. Jacob, (NY) St. Clare, Staten Island, NY
Thomas, Rev. Jacob, '76 (ALX) Retired.
Thomas, Rev. James J., '76 (ALN) Retired. On Duty Outside Diocese. Belleville, IL
Thomas, Rev. Jeremy, (CHI) Church of the Holy Spirit, Schaumburg, IL
Thomas, Rev. Jesudoss, '02 (TYL) Curia: Advisory Boards, Commissions, Committees, and Councils St. Therese, Canton, TX
Thomas, Rev. Jobin, (MCE) Curia: Administration; Advisory Boards, Commissions, Committees, and Councils; Miscellaneous / Other Offices; Offices and Directors; Tribunal St. Thomas Malankara Catholic Church, Elizabeth, NJ
Thomas, Rev. Joby C., '98 (TYL) St. Andrew, Lufkin, TX
Thomas, Rev. Joby Parakkacharuvil, '00 (JC) St. Pius X, Moberly, MO
Thomas, Rev. John, (MIA) Curia: Pastoral Services
Thomas, Rev. John M., '93 (OWN) Curia: Advisory Boards, Commissions, Committees, and Councils St. Stephen Cathedral, Owensboro, KY
Thomas, Rev. John M., '66 (SC) Retired.
Thomas, Rev. Jon P., '10 (CAM) Curia: Advisory Boards, Commissions, Committees, and Councils Church of Christ the King, Haddonfield, N.J., Haddonfield, NJ
Thomas, Rev. Jose, *mcbs* '09 (AJ) St. Catherine of Siena, Petersburg, AK; St. Rose of Lima, Wrangell, AK
Thomas, Rev. Jose, (EVN) Divine Mercy, St. Anthony, IN
Thomas, Rev. Joseph, (TR) [MIS] Opus Dei, Princeton, NJ
Thomas, Rev. Joseph, *C.M.I.* (L) Christ the Healer, Edmonton, KY
Thomas, Rev. Joseph, '11 (DAL) [MIS] Opus Dei, Irving, TX
Thomas, Rev. Joseph, *B.S.O.* '71 (NTN) Retired.
Thomas, Rev. Joseph P., '11 (POD) Curia: Clergy and Religious Services
Thomas, Rev. Joseph P., '09 (BAK) Curia: Offices and Directors
Thomas, Rev. Joseph Puthiyath, '09 (BAK) Blessed Sacrament, Ontario, OR
Thomas, Rev. Joseph S., '52 (CHI) Retired.
Thomas, Rev. Joy, *M.S.F.S.* (GAL) St. Angela Merici, Missouri City, TX
Thomas, Rev. Justin, *H.G.N.* '11 (OG) Catholic Community of St. Philip of Jesus and St. Joseph of Willsboro, New York, Willsboro, NY; The St. Elizabeth Roman Catholic Church, Elizabethtown, NY; The St. Philip of Neri Roman Catholic Church, at Westport, NY, Westport, NY
Thomas, Rev. Kevin, '88 (DET) St. Aidan Parish Livonia, Livonia, MI
Thomas, Rev. LaVerne Pike, '86 (SHP) Retired.
Thomas, Rev. Lijo, '14 (HRT) Precious Blood Parish Corporation, Milford, CT
Thomas, Rev. Liju, '08 (MCE) St. Mary's Malankara Catholic Church, Yonkers, NY
Thomas, Rev. Liju, '08 (MCE) Curia: Advisory Boards, Commissions, Committees, and Councils; Offices and Directors
Thomas, Rev. Litto, (DM) Sacred Heart, West Des Moines, IA
Thomas, Rev. Louis H., '13 (CLV) St. Andrew the Apostle, Norton, OH
Thomas, Rev. Mark A., '96 (PIT) On Leave.
Thomas, Rev. Mark Edward, '15 (ATL) Our Lady of the Mount Catholic Church, Lookout Mountain, Inc., Lookout Mountain, GA
Thomas, Rev. Mark L., '93 (PIT) Divine Grace, Cranberry Township, PA
Thomas, Chorbishop Michael G., '83 (SAM) Curia: Leadership; Offices and Directors Heart of Jesus Catholic Church, Fort Lauderdale, FL; [EFT] Bishops Retirement Trust Fund, Brooklyn, NY; [EFT] Disability Fund Trust, Brooklyn, NY; [EFT] Endowment Fund Trust, Brooklyn, NY; [EFT] Priest Retirement Trust Fund, Brooklyn, NY; [EFT] Seminary Endowment Trust, Brooklyn, NY; [MIS] Tele Lumiere and Noursat USA, Brooklyn, NY; [MON] Bishop's Residence, Brooklyn, NY
Thomas, Chorbishop Michael G., '83 (MIA) Curia: Canonical Services
Thomas, Rev. Milton, *O.Praem.* (SFE) St. Augustine, Isleta Pueblo, NM; [MON] Santa Maria de la Vid Abbey, Albuquerque, NM; [SHR] Shrine of Saint Kateri Tekakwitha (St. Augustine Parish), Isleta Pueblo, NM
Thomas, Rev. Navykumar, (SEA) Our Lady of Good Help, Hoquiam, WA; St. Jerome, Ocean Shores, WA; St. Joseph, Elma, WA; St. Mary, Aberdeen, WA
Thomas, Rev. Noby, '01 (BAK) Our Lady of the Valley, La Grande, OR; Sacred Heart, Union, OR; St. Mary, Elgin, OR
Thomas, Rev. Norman P., '55 (DET) Sacred Heart (African American) Parish Detroit, Detroit, MI; St. Elizabeth Parish Detroit, Detroit, MI
Thomas, Rev. P. George, '97 (CC) Santa Rosa de Lima, Benavides, TX
Thomas, Rev. Paul, *O.S.B.* '82 (P) [MON] Mt. Angel Abbey, Saint Benedict, OR
Thomas, Rev. Paul K., '63 (BAL) Retired.
Thomas, Rev. Phillip, *O.C.D.* '79 (MIL) [MON] Discalced Carmelite Friars of Holy Hill, Inc., Hubertus, WI
Thomas, Rev. Ralph W., '65 (CLV) Retired. Immaculate Heart of Mary, Cuyahoga Falls, OH
Thomas, Rev. Raymond J., '72 (Y) Corpus Christi Parish, Conneaut, OH; Our Lady of Peace Parish, Ashtabula, OH; St. Andrew Bobola, Kingsville, OH
Thomas, Rev. Richard L., '66 (GB) Retired.
Thomas, Rev. Robert W., '61 (BO) Retired.
Thomas, Rev. Saji K., '05 (BAK) Curia: Leadership
Thomas, Rev. Santhosh, '11 (MIA) [NUR] St. John's Rehabilitation Hospital and Nursing Center, Inc., Lauderdale Lakes, FL
Thomas, Rev. Santhosh, (MCE) Curia: Advisory Boards, Commissions, Committees, and Councils St. Mary's Malankara Catholic Church, Fort Lauderdale, FL
Thomas, Rev. Scott, '10 (JKS) On Leave.
Thomas, Rev. Sebastian, *C.R.M.* (CHR) Immaculate Conception, Goose Creek, SC; St. Francis Caracciolo Mission, Goose Creek, SC
Thomas, Rev. Shaiju, (OWN) St. Anthony, Hardinsburg, KY; St. Mary-of-the-Woods, Hardinsburg, KY
Thomas, Rev. Shaji, (BAK) St. Bernard, Jordan Valley, OR
Thomas, Rev. Shaji Jacob, '97 (WH) Sacred Heart, Huntington, WV; St. Peter Claver, Huntington, WV
Thomas, Rev. Shenoy, *MC* '97 (ORL) Holy Family, Orlando, FL; St. Margaret Mary, Winter Park, FL
Thomas, Rev. Sibi, (NY) St. John the Evangelist, St. Charles Borromeo, Pawling, NY
Thomas, Rev. Siby, *CMI* (NY) Parish of Sacred Heart and Our Lady of Pompeii, Dobbs Ferry, NY
Thomas, Friar Sojan, *CFIC* '08 (STP) M Health Fairview Southdale Hosp [MON] Congregation of the Sons of the Immaculate Conception, Bloomington, MN
Thomas, Rev. Subi Pootharayil, *MCBS* '09 (MIL) Immaculate Conception Congregation, Sheboygan, WI; St. Peter Claver Congregation, Sheboygan, WI; Sts. Cyril and Methodius' Congregation, Sheboygan, WI; [MIS] The Sheboygan County Catholic Fund, Inc., Sheboygan, WI; [MON] Missionary Congregation of the Blessed Sacrament, Inc., Zion Province, Cudahy, WI
Thomas, Rev. Sunoj, *O.S.B.* '02 (KC) St Charles Borromeo Catholic Church Kansas City, Kansas City, MO
Thomas, Rev. Thomas P., '64 (MEM) Retired. St. Anne's, Memphis, TN
Thomas, Rev. Tomi, *I.M.S.* '94 (BGP) On Duty Outside Diocese. Holy Rosary Catholic Church, Amant, LA
Thomas, Rev. Tomi, *IMS* '94 (BR) St. Elizabeth Interparochial School, Inc., Paincourtville, LA; The Congregation Of Saint Elizabeth Roman Catholic Church, Paincourtville, LA; The Congregation Of St. Jules Roman Catholic Church, Belle Rose, LA
Thomas, Rev. Tomson, '13 (DM) St. Bernard, Osceola, IA; St. Joseph, Mt. Ayr, IA; St. Patrick, Grand River, IA
Thomas, Rev. Tomy O., '82 (CAM) The Church of Saints Peter and Paul, Washington Township, Gloucester County, N.J., Turnersville, NJ
Thomas, Rev. Wilbur N., '73 (CHL) Retired.
Thomas, Rev. Zacharias (Freddie), (SFR) St. Gabriel, San Francisco, CA
Thomas (Thachara), Rev. John, '94 (SYM) Our Lady of Health Syro-Malabar Catholic Church, Coral Springs, FL, Inc. of St. Thomas Syro-Malabar Catholic Diocese of Chicago, Coral Springs, FL; St. George Syro-Malabar Catholic Mission, Miami FL, Coral Springs, FL
Thomas Reddy, Rev. Gopu, '08 (BIR) St. John the Apostle, Alexander City, AL
Thome, Rev. Derek, '18 (WCH) [CAM] St. Pius X Catholic Student Center (Pittsburg State University), Pittsburg, KS
Thomlison, Rev. Steven, (MO) Curia: Offices and Directors
Thompson, Rev. Andrew, *C.Ss.R.* '81 (KC) Our Lady of Perpetual Help, Kansas City, MO; [MON] Redemptorists Fathers of Kansas City, Missouri, Kansas City, MO
Thompson, Rev. Brian D., '14 (SEA) St. Columban, Yelm, WA
Thompson, Rev. Clayton D., '13 (LFT) Curia: Miscellaneous / Other Offices Our Lady of Grace, Noblesville, IN
Thompson, Very Rev. D. Timothy, '82 (FWT) Curia: Miscellaneous / Other Offices All Saints, Fort Worth, TX
Thompson, Rev. D. B., '12 (LKC) On Duty Outside Diocese. Diocese of Tyler
Thompson, Rev. D.B., '12 (LKC) Immaculate Heart of Mary, Lake Charles, LA
Thompson, Rev. Dean Brian, (LKC) On Duty Outside Diocese. Diocese of Tyler
Thompson, Rev. Dennis S., '89 (STP) Retired.
Thompson, Rev. Gregory S., '06 (ARL) St. Louis, Alexandria, VA
Thompson, Very Rev. James D, *O.P.* '03 (OAK) [MON] Order of Preachers (Province of the Most Holy Name of Jesus - Western Dominican Province), Oakland, CA
Thompson, Rev. James G., *O.S.A.* '71 (CHI) [MON] St. Augustine Friary, Chicago, IL
Thompson, Rev. Jeffrey, *M.S.A.* '15 (NOR) [MON] Society of the Missionaries of the Holy Apostles, Cromwell, CT
Thompson, Rev. Jerald Wayne, '94 (LA) Retired.
Thompson, Rev. Jerald (Jerry) W., '94 (GLP) Our Lady of the Assumption, Overgaard, AZ
Thompson, Rev. Jerome H., '60 (LA) Retired.
Thompson, Rev. John, *S.M.* '99 (SAT) [COL] St. Mary's University of San Antonio, Texas, San Antonio, TX;

[MON] Ligustrum Marianist Community, San Antonio, TX
Thompson, Rev. Kevin, *O.F.M. Cap* '97 (PH) [MON] Padre Pio Friary, Province of St. Augustine, Philadelphia, PA
Thompson, Rev. Kevin, '11 (RVC) Our Lady of Lourdes, Massapequa Park, NY; Sacred Heart, North Merrick, NY
Thompson, Rev. Levi, '20 (LKC) Our Lady Queen of Heaven, Lake Charles, LA
Thompson, Rev. Michael, '96 (STA) On Leave.
Thompson, Rev. Michael Leon, *S.S.J.* '04 (WDC) Our Lady of Perpetual Help, Washington, DC
Thompson, Rev. Nicholas, (VEN) St. John the Evangelist Parish in Naples, Inc., Naples, FL
Thompson, Rev. Nicholas Ryan, '11 (MAR) On Duty Outside Diocese. Diocese of Venice, FL
Thompson, Rev. Philip E., '78 (DUB) Retired. Curia: Leadership
Thompson, Rev. Richard B., '95 (P) St. John Fisher, Portland, OR
Thompson, Rev. Richard B., '69 (MAN) Retired. St. Andre Bessette, Laconia, NH; St. Joseph, Belmont, NH
Thompson, Rev. Richard J., '96 (PIT) Chap, UPMC East; West Penn Allegheny Health Sys-Forbes Rgnl… All Saints, Butler, PA
Thompson, Rev. Stephen A., '10 (SFD) Holy Family, Granite City, IL; St. Mary and St. Mark, Madison, IL; [ASN] Calvary Cemetery Association, Granite City, IL; [CEM] Mt. Sterling Catholic Cemetery, Mt. Sterling, IL
Thompson, Rev. Thomas A., *S.M.* '68 (CIN) [MIS] The Marian Library/International Marian Research Institute (IMRI), , ; [MON] Siena Woods Marianist Community, Dayton, OH
Thompson, Rev. Thomas E., '92 (SUP) Curia: Leadership; Offices and Directors Sacred Heart of Jesus Church, Almena, WI; St. Ann, Turtle Lake, WI; St. Anthony Abbot, Cumberland, WI
Thompson, Rev. Thomas W., '64 (LAN) Retired.
Thompson, Very Rev. William D., '08 (WIN) Curia: Advisory Boards, Commissions, Committees, and Councils; Offices and Directors
Thompson, Rev. William R., '14 (OWN) Curia: Leadership St. Augustine, Reed, KY; St. Peter of Alcantara, Owensboro, KY
Thomsen, Rev. Benjamin, '22 (ATL) St. Benedict Catholic Church, Johns Creek, Inc., Johns Creek, GA
Thomson, Rev. Elijiah, '22 (DAL) St. Monica Catholic Parish, Dallas, TX
Thomson, Rev. Sean, '04 (SPK) Curia: Leadership Immaculate Conception, Davenport, WA; Our Lady of Lourdes, Fruitland, WA; Our Lady of Sorrows, Cusick, WA; Sacred Heart, Wellpinit, WA; St. Francis of Assisi, Harrington, WA; St. Philip Benizi, Ford, WA
Thon, Rev. Andrew J., *S.J.* '74 (MIL) [MON] Jesuit Community at Marquette University (Marquette Jesuit Associates, Inc.), Milwaukee, WI
Thondappa, Rev. Paulraj, *HGN* '07 (FAR) Holy Rosary Church of Bisbee, Bisbee, ND; Notre Dame de la Victoire Church of Willow City, Willow City, ND; Sacred Heart Church of Rolette, Rolette, ND
Thooft, Rev. Tanner, '22 (NU) St. Mary, Sleepy Eye, MN; St. Paul, Comfrey, MN
Thoompunkal, Rev. Biju Joseph, (CC) Our Lady of Guadalupe, Alice, TX
Thoonkuzhy, Rev. Joseph, '58 (TLS) Retired.
Thorburn, Rev. Msgr. Timothy J., '83 (LIN) Curia: Leadership; Offices and Directors Sacred Heart, Lincoln, NE; [CEM] Calvary Cemetery and Mausoleum, Lincoln, NE; [MIS] Ecclesial Carmelite Movement, Lincoln, NE (>OM) [MIS] Marianna, Inc., Omaha, NE
Thorn, Rev. Robert C., '99 (LC) Retired.
Thorne, Rev. Stephen D., '98 (PH) Nativity of the Blessed Virgin Mary, Media, PA
Thorne, Rev. Thomas P., '76 (BGP) Retired. [MIS] Saint Charles Brazilian Children, Bridgeport, CT
Thornton, Rev. Andrew, '21 (LFT) Holy Spirit Church, Fishers, IN; St. John Vianney Parish, Fishers, IN
Thornton, Rev. James W., *C.S.C.* '64 (PHX) Retired. [MON] Holy Cross Congregation/Casa Santa Cruz, Phoenix, AZ
Thornton, Rev. Msgr. Michael, '69 (JKS) Curia: Consultative Bodies
Thornton, Rev. Msgr. Michael J., '69 (BLX) Retired. Curia: Advisory Boards, Commissions, Committees, and Councils; Leadership; Tribunal
Thornton, Rev. Ryan, *O.F.M.* '15 (LA) Curia: Offices and Directors St. Mark University Parish, Isla Vista, CA
Thornton, Rev. William H., '09 (SFR) St. Sebastian, Greenbrae, CA
Thorpe, Rev. Leland, *OMV* (SFD) St. Mary's, Alton, IL
Thorsen, Rev. Jon, (GB) Good Shepherd, Chilton, WI
Thotankara, Rev. Santtosh, (HON) Our Lady of Good Counsel, Pearl City, HI
Thottankara, Rev. Raju, (MO) Curia: Offices and Directors
Thottankara, Very Rev. Raju, '95 (CC) Curia: Administration; Leadership St. Peter, Prince of Apostles, Corpus Christi, TX
Thottankara, Very Rev. Raju, (MO) Curia: Offices and Directors
Thottukadavil, Rev. Joseph Lawrence, *OCD* '81 (FRS) St. Francis of Assisi, Bakersfield, CA
Thottungal, Rev. Thomas, '70 (NEW) Saint Paul the Apostle, Jersey City, NJ
Thottyil, Rev. Mathew, *MSFS* '78 (GAL) St. Anthony of Padua, The Woodlands, TX
Thrasher, Rev. Robert W., '62 (SPR) Retired.
Thuerauf, Rev. Jason M., '99 (DEN) St. Jude Catholic Parish in Lakewood, Lakewood, CO
Thuerauf, Rev. Jeffrey P., '89 (TUC) On Leave.
Thuma, Rev. Clifton M., '96 (BO) On Leave. [CAM] The Catholic Center at Boston University, Boston, MA
Thumbi, Rev. Francis, '87 (SEA) St. Joseph, Ferndale, WA
Thumma, Rev. Aloysius, '80 (NY) St. Mary of the Assumption, Katonah, NY
Thumma, Rev. Jacob, '93 (NY) St. Ann, Staten Island, NY; St. Sylvester, Staten Island, NY
Thumma, Rev. Naveen, (SAT) Our Lady of Guadalupe, Del Rio, TX; St. Joseph, Del Rio, TX
Thumma, Rev. Prathap Reddy, (SAT) St. Monica, Converse, TX
Thumma, Rev. Prem S., '11 (SAN) St. Lawrence, Garden City, TX
Thumma, Rev. Rayappa Reddy, '86 (NY) Immaculate Heart of Mary, Scarsdale, NY
Thumma, Rev. Sunil Kumar, '09 (SUP) Sacred Heart, Radisson, WI; St. Peter, Winter, WI
Thundathil, Rev. Antony, '91 (SYM) [MIS] Missionary Society of St. Thomas the Apostle, M.S.T., Glenview, IL
Thundathil, Rev. Mathew, '78 (MIA) Curia: Canonical Services
Thurber, Rev. David G., '08 (PRO) Curia: (>MO) Offices and Directors St. Barnabas Church Corporation, Portsmouth, Portsmouth, RI
Thuringer, Rev. Andrew, (SFS) Bishop O'Gorman Catholic Schools (Sioux Falls Catholic Schools), Sioux Falls, SD; Saint Ann Parish of Minnehaha County, Humboldt, SD; St. George Parish of Minnehaha County, Hartford, SD
Thurman, Rev. Shannon, (DEN) St. Clare of Assisi Catholic Parish in Edwards, Edwards, CO; St. John the Evangelist Catholic Parish in Loveland, Loveland, CO
Thurston, Rev. Anthony, '82 (WH) Sacred Heart of Mary, Weirton, WV
Thurston, Rev. Anthony, '82 (OAK) On Duty Outside Diocese.
Thuruthiyil, Rev. Shiju, '06 (BAK) Curia: Leadership St. Pius X, Klamath Falls, OR
Thury, Rev. Gerald, '67 (SFS) Retired.
Tian, Rev. Justin Liu Zhen, '99 (LA) St. Thomas Aquinas, Monterey Park, CA
Tiano, Rev. Christopher M., '89 (HRT) Saint Paul VI Parish Corporation, Hamden, CT
Tibai, Rev. Mark, '20 (DET) St. Fabian Parish Farmington Hills, Farmington Hills, MI
Tibaldo, Rev. Mariano, *M.C.C.J* '82 (LA) Holy Cross, Los Angeles, CA
Tibay, Rev. Ernesto, '76 (NEW) Retired. Curia: Offices and Directors St. Joseph of the Palisades, West New York, NJ
Tibbetts, Rev. Richard K., '98 (ATL) Retired.
Tiboni, Rev. Msgr. Vito, '69 (NEW) Retired.
Tiburcio, Rev. Leo, *CM* (CHL) Our Lady of Guadalupe Church, Charlotte, NC
Tice, Rev. Cecil, '81 (CHL) On Leave.
Tichacek, Rev. Charles P., '94 (STL) Sacred Heart Catholic Church, Elsberry, Elsberry, MO; St. Alphonsus Catholic Church, Millwood, Silex, MO
Tickerhoof, Rev. Bernard, *T.O.R.* '78 (PIT) [MON] Franciscan Friars, T.O.R. (Queen of Peace Friary), Pittsburgh, PA
Ticllasuca, Rev. Rolando, '94 (RVC) Infant Jesus, Port Jefferson, NY
Ticona, Rev. Fidel, *C.S.C.* '00 (SCR) Our Lady of Fatima Parish, Wilkes-Barre, PA; St. Nicholas, Wilkes-Barre, PA
Tidd, Rev. Michael, *O.S.B.* '13 (PAT) Delbarton School, Morristown, NJ; [MON] St. Mary's Abbey, Morristown, NJ
Tiegs, Rev. James R., '74 (OM) Retired.
Tiell, Rev. Florian, *O.F.M.Conv.* '68 (IND) St. Anthony of Padua Catholic Church, Clarksville, Inc., Clarksville, IN
Tierney, Rev. Gary M., '67 (DET) Retired.
Tierney, Rev. Joseph P., '86 (NY) Cardinal Hayes High School, Bronx, NY; Parish of St. Vito and Most Holy Trinity, Mamaroneck, NY; St. Gregory the Great, Harrison, NY
Tierney, Rev. Msgr. Michael J., '67 (RCK) Retired.
Tierney, Rev. Patrick J., '69 (BIR) Retired.
Tierrablanca, Rev. Nicolas Battas, (SB) Our Lady of Guadalupe Shrine, Riverside, CA
Tietjen, Rev. Michael E., '06 (WDC) Immaculate Conception, Mechanicsville, MD
Tietz, Rev. Kyle T, '21 (DUB) St. Francis of Assisi Parish, Marshalltown, Iowa, Marshalltown, IA
Tiffany, Rev. Eugene W., '72 (STP) Retired.
Tigatiga, Rev. John, *SDS* '15 (MIL) [MON] Salvatorian Provincial Offices (Society of the Divine Savior), Milwaukee, WI
Tigga, Rev. Alexander, *M.S.F.S.* '99 (TUC) Saint Therese of Lisieux Roman Catholic Parish - Patagonia, Patagonia, AZ
Tigga, Rev. Basil, '92 (JC) Holy Guardian Angels, Brinktown, MO; St. Aloysius, Argyle, MO; Visitation of the Blessed Virgin Mary, Vienna, MO
Tigga, Rev. Luis, *HGN* '05 (LKC) Our Lady of La Salette, DeQuincy, LA
Tigges, Rev. James J., '71 (SC) Retired. Curia: Offices and Directors
Tighe, Rev. James L., '70 (BRK) Retired. Queen of Peace, Flushing, NY
Tighe, Rev. Leonard J., '73 (BO) Retired.
Tighe, Rev. Timothy P., *C.S.P.* '69 (NY) Retired. [MON] Paulist Fathers' Motherhouse, New York, NY
Tignoua, Rev. Touchard G., '15 (STV) Curia: Offices and Directors Church of St. Patrick, Frederiksted, VI
Tignoua, Rev. Touchard Goula, '15 (STV) [MIS] Miscellaneous Organizations, Charlotte Amalie, VI
Tigyer, Rev. Jeffrey E., '00 (COL) Our Lady of Lourdes, Ada, OH
Tijerina, Rev. Richard, (AUS) Church of the Resurrection, Emmaus, Lakeway, TX
Tillekeratne, Rev. Eugene, *S.S.S.* '00 (TYL) Our Lady of Fatima, Daingerfield, TX
Tilley, Rev. Stephen, (SLC) Saint John the Baptist LLC 252, Draper, UT
Tilley, Rev. Stephen M., (SLC) Curia: Offices and Directors
Tillman, Rev. Msgr. Richard H., '65 (BAL) Retired. Church of the Immaculate Conception, Towson, MD
Tillman, Rev. Richard J., '65 (STL) Retired.
Tillman, Rev. Robert J., *S.J.* '77 (OM) Creighton Preparatory School, Omaha, NE; [MON] Jesuit Community at Creighton University, Omaha, NE
Tillotson, Rev. Frederick, *O.Carm.* '69 (VEN) Retired.
Tillrock, Rev. Raymond J., '69 (CHI) Retired. St. Barnabas, Chicago, IL
Tillya, Rev. Ephrem R., (SFR) St. Isabella, San Rafael, CA
Tillyer, Rev. Msgr. Herbert K., '68 (PAT) Retired. Curia: Administration; Leadership St. Peter the Apostle, Parsippany, NJ; [MIS] Martin de Porres Village Corporation, Paterson, NJ; [MIS] Riese Corporation, Bloomfield, NJ
Timko, Rev. Philip S., *O.S.B.* '69 (JOL) Retired. [MON] St. Procopius Abbey, Lisle, IL
Timlin, Rev. John P., *CM* (CHL) St. Mary, Greensboro, NC
Timlin, Rev. Philip, '16 (STA) Mary, Queen of Heaven, Jacksonville, FL
Timmel, Rev. Gerald L., '56 (L) Retired.
Timmerman, Rev. Bart D., '01 (MAD) St. Thomas Aquinas, Madison, WI
Timmerman, Rev. Craig A., '05 (NU) On Special Assignment. Curia: Leadership; Offices and Directors Church of St. Peter, St. Peter, MN; St. Paul, Nicollet, MN
Timmerman, Rev. David W., '87 (MAD) St. Pius X, Cambridge, WI
Timmerman, Rev. Paul D., '07 (NU) Curia: Offices and Directors St. Andrew, Granite Falls, MN; St. James, Dawson, MN; St. Joseph, Montevideo, MN
Timmerman, Very Rev. Randy J., '93 (MAD) Saint Dennis Congregation, Madison, WI
Timmerman, Rev. Sean M., '03 (LIN) Church of the Holy Spirit, Plattsmouth, NE; [EFT] Aquinas High School Endowment Fund, David City, NE
Timmers, Rev. Jozef, *OFM Cap.* '99 (GF) St. Labre, Ashland, MT
Timock, Rev. Ronald K., '83 (MAR) Retired.
Timone, Rev. Donald, (NY) Retired.
Timoney, Rev. Brian, '56 (OAK) Retired. Christ the King, Pleasant Hill, CA
Timothy, Rev. Bernard, *O.P.* '13 (L) St. Louis Bertrand,

Louisville, KY; [MON] St. Louis Bertrand Priory, Louisville, KY
Tinajero, Rev. Frank, *SVD* '88 (LA) St. John the Evangelist, Los Angeles, CA
Tinajero, Rev. Luis Roberto, '12 (BWN) On Leave.
Tindall, Rev. Msgr. William, '89 (DET) Curia: Consultative Bodies St. Michael Parish Livonia, Livonia, MI
Tinh, Rev. Joseph Nguyen, '57 (SJ) Retired.
Tinh Tran, Rev. John M., *CRM* (FWT) Church of the Vietnamese Martyrs, Arlington, TX
Tinker, Rev. Antony, *F.H.S.* '13 (PHX) Curia: Offices and Directors St. John the Baptist, Laveen, AZ; St. Peter, Bapchule, AZ
Tino, Rev. John, '01 (BRK) Nativity of the Blessed Virgin Mary-Saint Stanislaus Bishop and Martyr Roman Catholic Church, Ozone Park, NY
Tino, Rev. Robert, (PHX) St Clare of Assisi Roman Catholic Parish Surprise, Surprise, AZ
Tino, Rev. Robert F., '71 (MIL) Retired.
Tintle, Rev. Raymond, *O.F.M.* '69 (LA) Retired. [RTR] Serra Retreat, Malibu, CA
Tiongson, Rev. Joselito S., '92 (MO) Curia: Offices and Directors
Tipton, Rev. Christopher F., (ARL) Holy Family, Dale City, VA; Saint John Paul the Great Catholic High School, Potomac Shores, VA
Tipton, Rev. Gregory, (POC) St. Aelred Catholic Community, Bishop, GA
Tipton, Rev. Prentice, '08 (SAG) Cathedral of Mary of the Assumption Parish of Saginaw, Saginaw, MI; Holy Family Parish of Saginaw, Saginaw, MI
Tirado, Rev. Ramon Orlando, '86 (SJN) Curia: (>MO) Offices and Directors San Lucas, San Juan, PR
Tissera, Rev. Christie, '89 (BAK) Saint Elizabeth of Hungary Catholic Church, John Day, OR
Tito, Rev. Joseph, '88 (NOR) Sacred Heart, Taftville, CT; St. Joseph, Versailles, CT; St. Mary of the Immaculate Conception, Baltic, CT
Tito, Rev. Joseph P., '96 (CHI) Our Lady of Mercy, Chicago, IL
Titonea, Rev. Radu, (BRK) Chap, Northwell Health Forest Hills Hosp, Forest Hills, NY
Titonea, Rev. Radu, (ROM) St. Mary Romanian Catholic Mission, Astoria, NY
Titonea, Rev. Radu N., '09 (ROM) Curia: Offices and Directors
Titus, Rev. Austin E., '92 (NY) Epiphany, New York, NY
Titus, Rev. Fernando, '05 (CI) Immaculate Heart of Mary Cathedral, Chuuk, FM; Sacred Heart Parish, Chuuk, FM; [MON] Vicariate Residence, Tunnuk, Chuuk, FM
Titus, Very Rev. John M., '89 (SFD) Curia: Deaneries Immaculate Conception, Mattoon, IL; St. Columcille, Sullivan, IL
Titus, Rev. Steven, '08 (CHY) St. Matthew's, Gillette, WY
Tiu, Rev. Jim, '00 (FAR) [CON] Carmel of Mary, Wahpeton, ND
Tivadar, Rev. Vasile, '95 (STF) Blessed Nicholas Chernetsky, ,
Tivadar, Rev. Vasile, '95 (STF) St. Mary Protectress, Ozone Park, NY
Tivenan, Rev. John J., '72 (BRK) Retired.
Tivnan, Rev. Paul J., '63 (BO) Retired.
Tivy, Rev. Gerald, '64 (JOL) Retired.
Tix, Very Rev. Michael, '92 (STP) Curia: Leadership Academy of Holy Angels, Richfield, MN; St. John the Baptist, Vermillion, MN; St. Mary, Hampton, MN; St. Mathias, Hampton, MN; [MIS] Regina Healthcare, Inc., Hastings, MN
Tizio, Rev. John, *C.Ss.R.* '85 (ORL) Sacred Heart, New Smyrna Beach, FL
Tizio, Rev. Joseph, *C.Ss.R.* (BO) Our Lady of Perpetual Help, Boston, MA
Tkachuk, Rev. William, '81 (CHI) St. Francis Xavier, La Grange, IL
Tkocz, Rev. Peter, '01 (ALB) Holy Cross, Salem, NY; Immaculate Conception, Hoosick Falls, NY; Sacred Heart, Lake George, NY; St. Patrick, Cambridge, NY
Tlae, Rev. Reginald Damian, *O.F.M.Cap.* (HBG) Chap, Cmty Gen Pinnacle Health Hosp, Harrisburg; Pinna...
Tlucek, Rev. Edward, *O.F.M.* '78 (MIL) St. Clare Congregation, Wind Lake, WI; St. Thomas Aquinas Congregation, Waterford, WI; [MIS] Provincial Offices of the Franciscan Friars, Assumption BVM Province, Inc., , ; [MON] Queen of Peace Friary (Franciscan Friars of the Assumption B.V.M. Province), Burlington, WI
Toale, Rev. Msgr. Thomas E., '81 (DUB) On Special Assignment. Curia: Administration; Advisory Boards, Commissions, Committees, and Councils; Leadership Holy Family Church, New Melleray, Peosta, Iowa, Peosta, IA; St. Joseph's Church, Key West, Iowa, Dubuque, IA; [EFT] Catholic Charities Foundation (St. Mary's Home), Dubuque, IA; [MIS] St. Raphael Priest Fund Society of the Archdiocese of Dubuque, Dubuque, IA
Toalepai, Rev. Etuale, '98 (SPP) Sacred Heart Parish-Pago Pago, Pago Pago, AS
To'alepai, Rev. Etuale, '98 (SPP) Curia: Offices and Directors
Tobias, Rev. Joseph F., *M.S.C.* '66 (ALN) Retired. [MON] Sacred Heart Villa, Missionaries of the Sacred Heart, Center Valley, PA
Tobin, Rev. Charles P., '68 (KC) Retired.
Tobin, Rev. James, *S.M.* '69 (SAT) [MON] Casa Maria Marianist Community, San Antonio, TX
Tobin, Rev. Jeremy, *O. Praem.* '69 (GB) [MON] St. Norbert Abbey, De Pere, WI
Tobin, Rev. Mark, '21 (PH) Mary, Mother of the Redeemer, North Wales, PA
Tobin, Rev. Patrick, *OP* (DEN) [MON] Dominican Friars, St. Dominic Priory, Denver, Inc., Denver, CO
Tobin, Rev. T. Michael, '93 (L) St. Luke, Louisville, KY
Tobin, Rev. T. Michael, (L) St. Rita, Louisville, KY
Tobin, Rev. Thomas, '59 (GF) Retired.
Tobolski, Very Rev. James F., '84 (SUP) Curia: Leadership; Offices and Directors Our Lady of Perpetual Help, Danbury, WI; Sacred Hearts of Jesus and Mary, Webster, WI; St. Francis Xavier, Superior, WI; St. John the Baptist, Webster, WI
Tobon, Rev. John J., '95 (BRK) On Leave.
Toborowsky, Very Rev. Jonathan S., '98 (MET) Curia: Consultative Bodies; Evangelization; Leadership; Offices and Directors
Toboso, Rev. Richard, *G.H.M.* '19 (R) St. Joan of Arc, Plymouth, NC
Tocci, Rev. Laurence M., '14 (BO) St. Michael, Hudson, MA
Tochtrop, Rev. Randolph G., '96 (SPC) Immaculate Conception, Jackson, MO
Todd, Rev. Canon Andrew, *ICRSS* (KC) Oratory of Old St. Patrick (Institute of Christ the King), Kansas City, MO
Todd, Rev. Andrew, '14 (NO) (>BGP) The Slovak Roman Catholic Church of Saints Cyril and Methodius, Bridgeport, CT
Todd, Rev. Richard J., *C.M.F.* '55 (CHI) Retired.
Todd, Rev. Wilmer, '63 (HT) Retired.
Todd, Rev. Wilmer, '50 (HT) Curia: Administration
Toepfer, Rev. John, *O.F.M.Cap.* '86 (COS) Curia: Leadership Our Lady of Guadalupe, Colorado Springs, CO; [MON] Solanus Casey Friary, Colorado Springs, CO
Togni, Rev. Peter J., *S.J.* '85 (SJ) [MON] Sacred Heart Jesuit Center, Los Gatos, CA
Toilolo, Rt. Rev. Damien, *O.S.B.* '05 (LA) [MON] St. Andrew's Abbey (Benedictine Monks), Valyermo, CA
Tokarczyk, Rev. Joseph M., '79 (NY) Sacred Heart of Jesus, Highland Falls, NY
Tokarski, Rev. Gregory, '95 (DET) Mother of Divine Mercy Parish Detroit, Detroit, MI
Tokarski, Rev. Stan, '93 (DET) St. Joseph Parish South Lyon, South Lyon, MI
Tokarz, Rev. David J., '91 (MOB) Curia: Leadership Our Savior Parish, Mobile, Mobile, AL
Tokarz, Rev. Thomas M., '77 (WOR) St. Joseph the Good Provider, Berlin, MA
Tokashiki, Rev. Adam, *P.E.S.* '16 (SAC) Curia: Offices and Directors Pastor of St. Lawrence Parish, North Highlands, a corporation sole, North Highlands, CA
Tokasz, Rev. Joseph, (BUF) St. Gregory the Great, Williamsville, NY
Tokaz, Rev. John, *O.F.M. Cap* (BUR) St. Peter, Rutland, VT
Toland, Rev. Eugene W., *M.M.* '64 (NY) Retired. [MON] Maryknoll Fathers and Brothers (Catholic Foreign Mission Society of America, Inc.), Ossining, NY
Tolang, Rev. Jaime, '58 (SEA) Retired.
Toledo, Rev. Ivan, '02 (MIA) St. Joachim, Miami, FL
Toledo, Rev. Joseph, '09 (DEN) St. Elizabeth Ann Seton Catholic Parish in Ft. Collins, Fort Collins, CO
Toledo, Rev. Nelson, (PT) Chap, Eglin Air Force Base
Toledo, Rev. Nelson T., '72 (MO) Curia: Offices and Directors
Toledo, Rev. Nicholas Rafael, *D.* '21 (MIA) St. John Neumann, Miami, FL
Toledo, Rev. Pedro, '14 (POC) Retired.
Toledo, Rev. Pedro, (MIA) [HOS] Mercy Hospital, Inc., Miami, FL
Toledo Ramirez, Rev. Emmanuel, (SJN) Maria Madre de la Misericordia, Guaynabo, PR; Nuestra Senora de la Milagrosa, Bayamon, PR
Tolentino, Rev. Msgr. Eddie E., '84 (WDC) Curia: Consultative Bodies St. Michael, Silver Spring, MD
Tolentino, Rev. Eric N., '06 (ALN) Chap, Schuylkill Cty Prison Annunciation B.V.M.-St. Mary's, Catasauqua, PA
Tolentino, Rev. Michael, (HON) St. Joseph, Makawao, HI
Tolentino, Rev. Rommel P., '05 (LKC) Curia: Advisory Boards, Commissions, Committees, and Councils Immaculate Heart of Mary, Lake Charles, LA
Tolentino, Rev. Virgilio T., '82 (MET) On Leave.
Tolentino de la Rosa, Rev. Lorenzo Maria, *O.Cart.* '92 (BUR) [MON] Carthusian Foundation in America, Inc., Charterhouse of the Transfiguration, Arlington, VT
Tolg, Rev. Killian, *O.S.B.* '04 (NO) [MON] St. Joseph Abbey, St. Benedict, LA
Tollefson, Rev. Rolf R., '01 (STP) St. Hubert, Chanhassen, MN; [CEM] St. Hubert Cemetery, Chanhassen, MN
Tolleson, Rev. Bart, (HEL) [RTR] Sycamore Tree Catholic Retreat: Series 680, LLC, Swan Lake, MT
Tolleson, Rev. Bart, '07 (HEL) Curia: Leadership; Offices and Directors St. John the Evangelist, Boulder Valley, MT
Tolosa, Rev. Armando, '10 (MIA) St. Catherine of Siena, Miami, FL
Tolve, Rev. Paul, *I.V.Dei* '92 (NY) Chap, Westchester Cty Jail, Valhalla
Toma, Rev. Zuhair G., '00 (LA) (>ORG) St. George (Chaldean Catholic), Santa Ana, CA
Tomas, Rev. Efren A., *M.S.* '81 (HON) St. Joseph, Waipahu, HI
Tomaselli, Rev. Msgr. Samuel J., '59 (ALT) Retired.
Tomasiewicz, Rev. Frank, '65 (SCL) Retired.
Tomasiewicz, Rev. Mark A., '91 (OM) St. Anthony, Cedar Rapids, NE; St. Michael, Albion, NE
Tomasko, Rev. Andrew J., '91 (DET) On Leave.
Tomaskovic, Rev. Emil, *S.A.* '71 (NY) [MON] Franciscan Friars of the Atonement, Garrison, NY; [MON] Franciscan Friars of the Atonement, Minister General Office, Garrison, NY
Tomasone, Rev. Richard C., '80 (E) St. Joseph, Warren, PA
Tomasso, Very Rev. Paul J., '81 (ROC) Curia: Clergy and Religious Services; Leadership [CON] Sisters St. Joseph of Rochester, Rochester, NY; [MIS] Family Rosary For Peace, Inc., Rochester, NY
Tomasz, Rev. Puslecki, (CHI) St. George, Tinley Park, IL
Tomaszewski, Rev. Slawomir, '16 (PAT) Holy Rosary, Passaic, NJ
Tomaszycki, Rev. David M., '16 (DET) Curia: Administration
Tomczak, Rev. Peter A., '05 (SCR) Saint Monica Parish, West Wyoming, PA
Tomczyk, Rev. Paul, (PAT) On Duty Outside Diocese. [CAM] William Paterson University of New Jersey, Haledon, NJ
Tomczyk, Rev. Pawel, (NEW) [SEM] Immaculate Conception Seminary School of Theology, South Orange, NJ
Tomczyk, Rev. Pawel, '15 (PAT) On Duty Outside Diocese. Archdiocese of Newark, NJ Curia: Leadership
Tomczyk, Rev. Przemyslaw, (CHI) St. Mary of Vernon, Indian Creek, IL
Tomeny, Rev. Matthew, *MIC* '21 (SPR) [MON] Congregation of Marian Fathers of The Immaculate Conception of the Most Blessed Virgin Mary, Stockbridge, MA
Tomic, Rev. Tomislav, (DEN) Sacred Heart of Jesus Catholic Parish in Boulder, Boulder, CO
Tomiczek, Rev. Damian, *S.D.S.* '82 (MET) St. Theodore, Port Murray, NJ
Tomiczek, Rev. Damian, *S.D.S.* '82 (NEW) [MON] The Salvatorian Fathers, Verona, NJ
Tomkeka, Rev. Albert, (SAT) SS. Peter and Paul, New Braunfels, TX
Tomkosky, Rev. Richard B., '00 (ALT) Seven Dolors B.V.M., Clearville, PA; St. Thomas the Apostle, Bedford, PA
Tomlinson, Rev. Richard B., '09 (CHR) Prince of Peace, Taylors, SC
Tomo, Rev. Ferdinand, *SSS* (HON) St. Joseph, Hilo, HI
Tomonto, Rev. Andrew James, '20 (MIA) Little Flower, Coral Gables, FL
Tompkins, Rev. John Mary, *O.S.B.* '93 (GBG) [MON] Saint Vincent Archabbey, Latrobe, PA; [SEM] St. Vincent Seminary, Latrobe, PA
Tompkins, Rev. Terry, '82 (OAK) Retired. On Duty Outside Diocese.
Tomson, Rev. Lucas E., '07 (SPK) Curia: Leadership; Offices and Directors [SEM] Bishop White Seminary, Spokane, WA
Tomson, Rev. Lucas Ethan, '07 (SPK) Curia: Leadership

St. Peter, Spokane, WA
Tomson, Rev. Tyron J., '11 (COL) St. Bernadette, Lancaster, OH; St. Mary, Bremen, OH; William V. Fisher Catholic High School, Lancaster, OH
Tonary, Rev. David, *M.S.F.* '81 (SAT) Our Lady of Guadalupe, Seguin, TX
Tonelli, Rev. Robert F., '72 (CHI) Retired.
Tonelotto, Rev. Walter, (ATL) San Felipe de Jesus, Forest Park, GA
Tonelotto, Rev. Walter, *C.S.* '74 (BRK) [MIS] Friends of RADIO MARIA, Inc., Ridgewood, NY
Toner, Rev. Oliver, '71 (VEN) Church of the Resurrection of Our Lord Catholic Parish in Fort Myers, Inc., Fort Myers, FL
Toner, Rev. Patrick A., '75 (COL) Retired. St. Patrick, London, OH
Tong, Rev. Peter, *O.C.S.O.* '68 (L) [MON] Abbey of Our Lady of Gethsemani, of the Order of Cistercians of the Strict Observance, Trappist, KY
Toniazzo, Very Rev. Marcio, *C.S.* (BO) St. Tarcisius, Framingham, MA
Tonkin, Rev. John W., '05 (CIN) Holy Rosary, St. Marys, OH; Immaculate Conception of the Blessed Virgin Mary, Celina, OH; Our Lady of Guadalupe, Montezuma, OH; St. Patrick, St. Marys, OH; St. Teresa, Rockford, OH
Tonos, Rev. Joseph, '94 (JKS) Curia: Canonical Services; Consultative Bodies St. Richard of Chichester, Jackson, MS
Tonry, Rev. Patrick, (CIN) (>SJ) [MON] The Marianist Center, Cupertino, CA
Toof, Rev. Daniel R., '94 (ATL) Retired.
Toohey, Rev. Richard J., '01 (E) Our Lady of Peace, Erie, PA
Toohey, Rev. Timothy, (SPC) Retired.
Toohey, Rev. Timothy J., '65 (STL) Retired.
Toole, Rev. Arthur A., '58 (ALB) Retired.
Toole, Rev. Lawrence E., '67 (PRO) Retired.
Tooman, Rev. Robert E., '77 (NEW) Retired. Christ, the King, Jersey City, NJ
Toomey, Rev. Daniel A., '03 (SCR) Epiphany Parish, Sayre, PA
Topel, Rev. L. John, *S.J.* '65 (SEA) [COL] Seattle University, Seattle, WA; [MON] Arrupe Jesuit Community at Seattle University, Seattle, WA
Topf, Rev. Thomas J., '63 (SC) Retired.
Topolewski, Rev. Jaroslaw P., '00 (OKL) St. Anthony's, Okeene, OK
Topper, Rev. Charles J., '68 (HBG) Retired.
Topper, Rev. John, *OSM* (P) Retired. [MON] The Grotto, The National Sanctuary of Our Sorrowful Mother, Portland, OR
Toppo, Rev. Rawel, (SCR) Our Lady of the Immaculate Conception, Freeland, PA
Toppo, Rev. Sudhir, (SCR) St. John Bosco, Conyngham, PA
Torba, Rev. Zdzislaw J., '91 (CHI) St. John Brebeuf, Niles, IL
Torchia, Rev. Joseph, *O.P.* '01 (PRO) [MON] St. Thomas Aquinas Priory at Providence College, Providence, RI
Torczynski, Rev. Robert, '97 (SR) Pastor of St. Anthony Catholic Church of Mendocino, a Corporation Sole, Mendocino, CA
Torgerson, Rev. Msgr. Lloyd A., '65 (LA) St. Monica, Santa Monica, CA
Torm, Rev. Agustin, (CHR) St. Peter, Beaufort, SC
Torma, Rev. Andrew, *M.S.C.* '76 (ALN) [MON] Sacred Heart Villa, Missionaries of the Sacred Heart, Center Valley, PA
Tormey, Rev. Daniel, '55 (ROC) Retired.
Tormey, Rev. James D., '78 (SY) Retired. Chap, Dir, Our Lady of Lourdes Mem Hosp, Binghamton
Tornes, Rev. Dale F., '70 (STU) Retired. Curia: Deaneries
Toro, Rev. Carlos Perez, '88 (SJN) Santa Rosa de Lima, San Juan, PR
Toro, Rev. Carlos Roman, (WDC) Chap, Armed Forces Retirement Home, Washington
Torok, Rev. George J., *C.O.* '58 (NY) Retired. [MIS] Hallel Institute, Sparkill, NY; [MIS] New York Oratory of St. Philip Neri, Inc., Sparkill, NY
Toro-Rivas, Rev. Gabriel, '02 (BRK) Blessed Sacrament, Jackson Heights, NY
Torpey, Rev. Charles L., '69 (GI) Retired. Curia: Tribunal
Torpey, Rev. James M., '83 (ALN) Retired.
Torpey, Rev. Matt G., *O.C.S.O.* '56 (ATL) [MON] The Monastery of the Holy Spirit, Conyers, GA
Torpey, Rev. Michael J., '68 (RVC) Retired.
Torquato, Rev. James R., '89 (PIT) St. Philip, Pittsburgh, PA
Torrens, Rev. James, (SPK) [MON] Regis Community, Spokane, WA (>SJ) [MON] Sacred Heart Jesuit Center, Los Gatos, CA
Torrente, Rev. Lorenzo, '75 (RNO) Retired.
Torres, Rev. Adrian, '75 (PMB) Retired.
Torres, Rev. Agustino Miguel, *C.F.R.* '08 (NY) [MIS] Casa Juan Diego, Inc., Yonkers, NY; [MIS] Corazon Puro, Bronx, NY
Torres, Rev. Agustino Miguel, *C.F.R.* '08 (PAT) Chap, William Paterson College [MIS] Casa Guadalupe, Inc., Clifton, NJ; [MIS] Saint Michael's Friary (Franciscan Friars of the Renewal), Paterson, NJ
Torres, Rev. Andres Ernesto, (SD) Pastor of Saint Pius X Catholic Parish, Chula Vista, a corporation sole, Chula Vista, CA
Torres, Rev. Angel, '22 (PAT) St. Lawrence the Martyr, Chester, NJ
Torres, Rev. Angel Pagan, '80 (SJN) Curia: Leadership Ntra. Sra. de La Salud, Dorado, PR
Torres, Rev. Arthur, (KNX) Curia: Offices and Directors
Torres, Rev. Bernardo, *L.C.* '08 (NO) (>HRT) [MON] Legionaries of Christ, Cheshire, CT; (>HRT) [SEM] Novitiate of the Legion of Christ, Cheshire, CT
Torres, Rev. Cristobal, *O.P.* '14 (MIA) Curia: Pastoral Services [COL] Barry University, Miami, FL; [MON] Dominican Fathers of Miami, Inc., Miami, FL
Torres, Rev. Msgr. Daniel A., '96 (LKC) Curia: Advisory Boards, Commissions, Committees, and Councils; Leadership Our Lady Queen of Heaven, Lake Charles, LA; [MIS] Society of Roman Catholic Church of the Dioceses of Lake Charles, Lake Charles, LA
Torres, Rev. Elvin L., '21 (BRK) St. Sebastian, Woodside, NY
Torres, Rev. Emmanuel, '21 (LR) Immaculate Heart of Mary, North Little Rock, AR; St. Mary, North Little Rock, AR
Torres, Rev. Ernesto, '72 (DAL) Retired.
Torres, Rev. Fernando, *L.C.* '06 (PIT) Curia: Consultative Bodies St. Teresa of Kolkata, Pittsburgh, PA
Torres, Rev. Henry, '17 (BRK) Mary of Nazareth, Brooklyn, NY
Torres, Rev. Heriberto, *C.R.* '05 (PBL) Curia: Offices and Directors Sacred Heart, Durango, CO
Torres, Rev. Hipolito, '85 (CGS) [MIS] Movimiento Juan XXIII, Caguas, PR
Torres, Rev. Ignacio, *sx* (MIL) [SEM] Xaverian Missionary Fathers College Seminary, Franklin, WI
Torres, Rev. Ivan J., '88 (SJN) Curia: (>MO) Offices and Directors
Torres, Rev. Jonathan, (CHL) St. Matthew, Charlotte, NC
Torres, Friar Jose Feliciano, *O.F.M.Cap.* '01 (FWT) Our Lady of Guadalupe, Fort Worth, TX
Torres, Rev. Jose Gustavo, '12 (MGZ) Curia: Offices and Directors St. Rose of Lima, Rincon, PR
Torres, Friar Joshua, *S.F.M.* (SJN) Nuestra Senora del Pilar, San Juan, PR
Torres, Friar Juan M., *OP* (GAL) Holy Rosary, Houston, TX
Torres, Rev. Juan R., '21 (DAL) San Juan Diego Catholic Parish, Dallas, TX
Torres, Rev. Mario, '96 (LA) St. Thomas the Apostle, Los Angeles, CA
Torres, Rev. Mario A., *S.J.* '01 (SJN) San Ignacio de Loyola, San Juan, PR
Torres, Rev. Mario Ivan, '20 (LSC) Our Lord of Mercy Parish, Inc., Hatch, NM
Torres, Rev. Mark, '98 (LA) Dolores Mission, Los Angeles, CA
Torres, Rev. Nohe, (CHL) Basilica of St. Lawrence, Asheville, NC
Torres, Rev. Pablo, *sx* (MIL) [SEM] Xaverian Missionary Fathers College Seminary, Franklin, WI
Torres, Rev. Patrick, *M.C.* '01 (LA) St. Francis Xavier, Pico Rivera, CA
Torres, Rev. Rendell, (ALB) St. Joseph the Worker, West Winfield, NY
Torres, Rev. Rendell R., '10 (ALB) Chapel of the Assumption, Huletts Landing, NY
Torres, Rev. Rolando, '07 (BGP) St. Mary's Roman Catholic Church Corporation, Inc. (Bridgeport), Bridgeport, CT
Torres, Rev. Ronald, '13 (SAC) All Saints, Happy Camp, CA; Immaculate Conception, Hawkinsville, CA; St. Joseph, Sawyers Bar, CA; St. Mary's, Etna, CA; [MIS] Catechetical Center, Yreka, CA
Torres, Rev. Ronald V., '13 (SAC) Curia: Offices and Directors Pastor of Sacred Heart Parish, Fort Jones, a corporation sole, Fort Jones, CA; Pastor of St. Joseph Parish, Yreka, a corporation sole, Yreka, CA
Torres Barona, Rev. Arthur, '13 (KNX) Our Lady of Perpetual Help, Chattanooga, TN
Torres Germoso, Rev. Emilio Jose, *S.D.B.* (ARE) San Juan Bautista, Orocovis, PR
Torres Graciani, Rev. Ivan, '88 (SJN) On Duty Outside Diocese. Rochester, NY
Torres Hernandez, Rev. Carlos Alonso, *O.SS.T.* '07 (PCE) Santisima Trinidad, Ponce, PR
Torres Martinez, Rev. Cesar, '93 (R) St. Mark Catholic Parish of Wilmington, Wilmington, NC
Torres Montejo, Rev. Julio Cesar, '14 (P) St. John the Evangelist, Yamhill, OR
Torres Moreno, Rev. Eduardo, (ARE) Curia: Offices and Directors
Torres Pagan, Rev. William, (SJN) Santisima Trinidad, Carolina, PR
Torres Reyes, Rev. Juan Alberto, '96 (PCE) Nuestra Senora del Carmen, Arroyo, PR
Torres Rivera, Rev. Jorge Ernesto, (SJN) Curia: Offices and Directors
Torres Samudio, Rev. Pedro, (MIA) Saint John XXIII Church, Miramar, FL
Torres Santos, Rev. George Antonio, '22 (PCE) Inmaculado Corazon de Maria, Patillas, PR
Torres Torres, Friar Macario, *OFM* (SAT) San Francisco de la Espada, San Antonio, TX
Torres-Acosta, Rev. Gonzalo de Jesús, *O.F.M.* '08 (R) Immaculate Conception, Durham, NC
Torres-Cesneros, Rev. Victor Modesto, (SJN) San Luis Gonzaga, San Juan, PR
Torres-Fuentes, Rev. Jesus, (CHI) St. Joseph, Libertyville, IL
Torres-Madrigal, Rev. Miguel, (SB) Sacred Heart, Jurupa Valley, CA
Torres-Ortiz, Rev. Anibal Rafael, '00 (SJN) Curia: Leadership; Offices and Directors Nuestra Senora del Rosario, Bayamon, PR; [COL] ISTEPA (Instituto Superior de Teologia y Pastoral - Luis Cardenal Aponte Martinez), Bayamon, PR
Torres-Pagan, Rev. William, '91 (SJN) Curia: Leadership
Torres-Pinzon, Rev. Cesar, (STA) St. John the Evangelist, Chiefland, FL
Torres-Rico, Rev. Rafael, '07 (COS) Holy Family Parish, Leadville, CO
Torres-Rico, Rev. Rafael, Chap, Diocesan Prison
Torres-Santos, Rev. Edgar Luis, *CSsR* (CGS) [RTR] Casa Cristo Redentor, Aguas Buenas, PR
Torres-Santos, Rev. Edgar Luis, *C.Ss.R.* (CGS) Church of Tres Santos Reyes, Aguas Buenas, PR
Torretta, Rev. Gabriel J., *O.P.* '15 (CHI) [MON] St. Pius V Priory, Chicago, IL
Torretto, Rev. Joseph, '75 (RIC) Retired.
Torrey, Rev. Nathan, *LC* (HRT) [MON] Legionaries of Christ, Cheshire, CT; [SEM] Novitiate of the Legion of Christ, Cheshire, CT
Torrez, Rev. Basil, '56 (SAL) Retired.
Torrez, Rev. John, '98 (KCK) Curia: Leadership St. Matthew Catholic Church Topeka, Topeka, KS
Torson, Rev. Daniel, (CHI) (>CIN) [MON] Society of the Precious Blood, United States Province, Inc., Dayton, OH
Tortora, Rev. James F., '72 (NEW) Retired.
Tortorelli, Rev. Kevin, *O.F.M.* '73 (NY) Parish of Holy Name of Jesus and St. Gregory the Great, New York, NY
Tortorelli, Rev. Kevin, (SP) [MON] St. Anthony Friary (St. Petersburg) Franciscan Friars-Holy Name Province, Inc., St. Petersburg, FL
Torwoe, Rev. Severinus, '20 (OG) St. Peter's Parish, Massena, NY
Toscano, Rev. Gerardo, *C.J.* '21 (LA) St. Louis de Montfort, Santa Maria, CA; [MON] St. Joseph Seminary (Josephite Fathers' Novitiate), Santa Maria, CA
Toscano, Rev. Javier, '06 (AUS) St. Mary, San Saba, TX; St. Peter, Mission of St. Mary, San Saba, Goldthwaite, TX
Toschi, Rev. Larry, *O.S.J.* '76 (FRS) Shrine of Our Lady of Guadalupe, Co-Patroness of the Unborn, Bakersfield, CA
Tosello, Rev. Matthew, '62 (PIT) Retired.
Tosti, Rev. Msgr. Ronald A., '62 (FR) Retired.
Tosto, Rev. Louis F., '97 (RCK) Retired.
Totaro, Rev. Dominic J., *S.J.* '67 (BAL) Retired. [MIS] Colombiere Jesuit Community, Baltimore, MD
Toth, Rev. Stephen J., '02 (NEW) Chap, Valley Hosp, Ridgewood Our Lady of Mount Carmel, Ridgewood, NJ
Tottle, Rev. Gregg, '91 (SP) Retired. [MIS] Water 4 Mercy, Inc., Clearwater, FL
Totton, Rev. Joseph, '04 (KC) Curia: (>MO) Offices and Directors St. James, St. Joseph, MO
Totzke, Rev. Andrzej, *S.Ch.* '00 (CHI) Holy Trinity Mission, Chicago, IL

Tou, Rev. Ivan, *C.S.P.* '02 (OAK) Holy Spirit Parish/ Newman Hall, Berkeley, CA

Tougas, Rev. Paul J., '64 (WOR) Retired.

Toups, Rev. Msgr. David, (NO) Curia: Miscellaneous / Other Offices

Toups, Rev. Mark, '01 (HT) Curia: Administration; Leadership

Toups, Rev. Mark Anthony, '01 (HT) Curia: Clergy and Religious Services Our Lady of the Isle, Grand Isle, LA

Tourigny, Rev. William A., '80 (SPR) Holy Name of Jesus, Chicopee, MA; St. Rose de Lima, Chicopee, MA

Tourville, Rev. David E., '09 (BUF) St. Dominic, Westfield, NY; St. Mary of Lourdes (St. Mary's of Mayville and Our Lady of Lourdes of Bemus Point), Bemus Point, NY

Touzeau, Rev. James F., '19 (CHR) St. Mary, Our Lady of Ransom, Georgetown, SC

Tovar, Rev. Francisco M., '06 (LSC) St. John Paul II Parish, Inc., Santa Teresa, NM

Tovar, Rev. Francisco Manuel, '06 (WDC) On Duty Outside Diocese. Las Cruces, NM

Tovar, Rev. Ireneo Lopez, '50 (CAM) Retired.

Tovar, Rev. Mauricio M, '20 (OM) Assumption of the Blessed Virgin Mary-Our Lady of Guadalupe Church of Omaha, Omaha, NE; St. Mary, Omaha, NE; Sts. Peter and Paul Church of Omaha, Omaha, NE

Towle, Rev. Joseph W., *M.M.* '65 (NY) Retired. [MON] Maryknoll Fathers and Brothers (Catholic Foreign Mission Society of America, Inc.), Ossining, NY

Townsend, Rev. Joe C., '88 (TLS) St. Patrick's, Sand Springs, OK

Townsend, Rev. Joseph B., (ARL) Basilica of St. Mary, Alexandria, VA

Towsley, Rev. Peter J., '91 (BGP) Curia: Evangelization Our Lady of Peace Roman Catholic Church Corporation, Stratford, CT

Toyinbo, Rev. Andrew, *MSP* (BEA) [CEM] Our Mother of Mercy Cemetery, Liberty, TX

Toyinbo, Rev. Andrew A, *MSP* (BR) St. Benedict the Moor, Napoleonville, LA

Tozzi, Rev. Chris, (SD) Pastor of Saint Therese of Carmel Catholic Parish, San Diego, a corporation sole, San Diego, CA

Tozzi, Rev. Ross, '01 (FBK) Curia: Leadership; Offices and Directors Sacred Heart Cathedral Catholic Church Fairbanks, Fairbanks, AK; St. Mark University Catholic Parish Fairbanks, Fairbanks, AK; [MON] St. Ignatius Residence, Fairbanks, AK

Tracey, Rev. Bernard M., *C.M.* '74 (BRK) [MON] Reverend John B. Murray, C.M. House, Jamaica, NY

Tracey, Rev. Michael, '72 (BLX) Retired.

Tracy, Rev. David W., '63 (BGP) Retired.

Tracy, Rev. Eugene, '91 (SPK) Retired. Curia: Leadership Cathedral of Our Lady of Lourdes, Spokane, WA

Tracy, Rev. James, (SCR) Retired.

Tracy, Rev. Msgr. James R., '60 (CAM) Retired. Mary, Mother of Mercy Parish, Glassboro, N.J., Glassboro, NJ

Tracy, Rev. Msgr. Joseph A., '92 (PH) Our Lady of Good Counsel, Southampton, PA

Tracy, Rev. Mark, (MO) Curia: Offices and Directors

Tracy, Rev. Mark, (SFD) Holy Family, Decatur, IL

Tracy, Rev. Philip A., '88 (PRT) Curia: Leadership All Saints Parish, Brunswick, ME

Tracy, Rev. Philip A., '88 (PRT) Curia: Consultative Bodies

Tracy, Rev. Philip Michael, '60 (PRT) Retired.

Traczyk, Rev. Edward W., *S.Chr.* '78 (MIL) S.S. Cyril and Method's Congregation, Milwaukee, WI

Trader, Friar William, *O.Praem.* (WIL) [MON] Immaculate Conception Priory of the Canons Regular of Premontre, Middletown, DE; [MON] Norbertine Fathers of Delaware, Inc., Middletown, DE

Trahan, Rev. Charles N., '81 (LAF) Retired.

Trahan, Rev. Clint James, '08 (LAF) Sacred Heart of Jesus, Port Barre, LA; St. Mary, Port Barre, LA

Trahan, Rev. David, '12 (AUS) St. Thomas More, Austin, TX

Trahan, Rev. Harold, '69 (LAF) Retired.

Trail, Rev. Michael, '16 (CHI) St. Thomas Apostle, Chicago, IL

Trainor, Rev. Henry J., '73 (SFR) Retired.

Trainor, Rev. Michael S. P., '07 (NEW) Curia: Advisory Boards, Commissions, Committees, and Councils Immaculate Conception (St. Mary's), Hackensack, NJ

Trainor, Rev. Richard F., '75 (WOR) Curia: Clergy and Religious Services

Trainor, Rev. Wade, '22 (PAT) Our Lady of Mount Carmel, Boonton, NJ

Trajano, Rev. Danilo B., '96 (AGN) Assumption of Our Lady, Piti, GU

Tralies, Rev. Matthew J., '10 (PH) St. Francis of Assisi, Springfield, PA

Trambley, Rev. John B., '10 (SFE) Our Lady of Fatima, Albuquerque, NM; Queen of Heaven, Albuquerque, NM; St. Pius X High School, Inc., Albuquerque, NM

Tran, Rev. (Patrick M.) Mac The, *CRM* '12 (SPC) [MON] Congregation of the Mother of the Redeemer, Carthage, MO

Tran, Rev. Alfonso, '12 (GAL) St. Jerome, Houston, TX

Tran, Rev. Andrew P., *O.Praem.* '06 (ORG) St. John the Baptist, Costa Mesa, CA; [MON] Norbertine Fathers of Orange, Inc., Silverado, CA

Tran, Rev. Anh, (FWT) St. John the Apostle, North Richland Hills, TX

Tran, Rev. Anh, '90 (FWT) Curia: Miscellaneous / Other Offices

Tran, Rev. Anh Q., *S.J.* '05 (OAK) [MON] Jesuit Fathers and Brothers, Berkeley, CA; [SEM] Jesuit School of Theology of Santa Clara University (Berkeley, California Campus), Berkeley, CA

Tran, Rev. Anthony Doan, '88 (BLX) Retired.

Tran, Friar Anthony Hung N., *O.P.* '92 (GAL) Holy Rosary, Houston, TX

Tran, Rev. Anthony Lan, '70 (SEA) Retired.

Tran, Rev. Anthony Phuc, *C.Ss.R.* '05 (LA) Retired.

Tran, Rev. Augustine, '98 (ATL) St. Monica Catholic Church, Duluth, Inc., Duluth, GA

Tran, Rev. Augustine M., '04 (ARL) St. John Bosco, Woodstock, VA

Tran, Rev. Benjamin, '06 (ORG) Our Lady of Fatima, San Clemente, CA

Tran, Rev. Binh K., '92 (PEO) Holy Trinity, Cherry, IL; St. Patrick's, Arlington, IL; St. Thomas More, Dalzell, IL

Tran, Rev. Charles, '14 (ORG) Holy Trinity, Ladera Ranch, CA

Tran, Rev. Chinh Quang, *SVD* (STL) Resurrection of Our Lord Catholic Church, St. Louis, MO

Tran, Rev. Chinh Quang Joseph, *S.V.D.* '15 (WH) Sacred Heart, Rainelle, WV; St. Patrick, Hinton, WV

Tran, Rev. Chung, *C.Ss.R.* '19 (GR) St. Alphonsus, Grand Rapids, MI; [MIS] The Society of the Redemptorists of the City of Grand Rapids, Grand Rapids, MI

Tran, Rev. Dat, *C.S.P.* '11 (NY) Curia: (>GR) Leadership (>GR) Cathedral of St. Andrew, Grand Rapids, MI; (>GR) [MIS] Catholic Information Center, Grand Rapids, MI

Tran, Rev. Dat T., *S.J.* '09 (SJ) [MON] Jesuit Community at Santa Clara University, Inc., Santa Clara, CA

Tran, Rev. Dieu Van, *SDD* '01 (DAL) [MIS] Domus Dei Clerical Society of Apostolic Life, Kaufman, TX

Tran, Rev. Dominic, *S.D.B.* '03 (NEW) [MON] The Salesian Community, Orange, NJ

Tran, Rev. Dominic, '09 (ATL) Holy Vietnamese Martyrs Catholic Church, Norcross, Inc., Norcross, GA

Tran, Rev. Dominic Dahn Cong, *S.D.B.* '03 (NY) [MON] Salesian Office of Vocations, New Rochelle, NY; [MON] Salesian Provincial House, New Rochelle, NY

Tran, Rev. Dominic Dat, '99 (PT) St. Margaret, Monticello, FL; St. Vincent de Paul, Madison, FL

Tran, Rt. Rev. Dominic Hung, *OCist.* '97 (SAC) [MON] Our Lady of Sacramento Monastery, Walnut Grove, CA

Tran, Rev. Dominic Toan, '11 (PMB) St. John the Evangelist, Boca Raton, FL

Tran, Rev. Dominic Bao Quoc, *C.Ss.R.* '90 (NO) St. Alphonsus, New Orleans, LA; St. Mary's Assumption, New Orleans, LA; [MIS] St. Mary's Chapel, New Orleans, LA

Tran, Rev. Duy John, *S.V.D.* '11 (SB) St. Catherine of Siena, Rialto, CA

Tran, Rev. Francis, '97 (ATL) Curia: Leadership

Tran, Rev. Francis Dien, *CSsR* '08 (TUC) Our Lady of LaVang Roman Catholic Parish - Tucson, Tucson, AZ

Tran, Rev. Francis Vu, *SCJ* '05 (MIL) [MON] St. Joseph's at Monastery Lake (Priests of the Sacred Heart), Franklin, WI

Tran, Rev. Hap, *C.S.* '20 (DAL) St. Luke Catholic Parish, Irving, TX

Tran, Rev. Hieu Chi, '08 (LA) Sacred Heart, Lancaster, CA

Tran, Rev. Hoa, (ORG) St. Bonaventure, Huntington Beach, CA

Tran, Rev. Hoi, '01 (SFE) Curia: Offices and Directors Our Lady of Lavang, Albuquerque, NM

Tran, Rev. Hung Ba, '98 (LA) Nativity, Torrance, CA

Tran, Rev. Hung Sy, '21 (BRK) Our Lady of Mount Carmel, Long Island City, NY

Tran, Rev. Huy, *O. Carm.* (NY) Transfiguration, Tarrytown, NY

Tran, Rev. James Taiviet, *S.J.* '04 (SEA) [MON] Arrupe Jesuit Community at Seattle University, Seattle, WA

Tran, Rev. John, '04 (KAL) St. John Bosco, Mattawan, MI

Tran, Rev. John, (MO) Curia: Offices and Directors

Tran, Rev. John Hue, *S.V.D.* '96 (WH) Holy Rosary, Buckhannon, WV

Tran, Rev. John Kha, '89 (GAL) Vietnamese Martyrs, Houston, TX

Tran, Rev. John Lan, *S.J.* '08 (LAF) [MON] St. Charles College, Grand Coteau, LA; [RTR] Jesuit Spirituality Center (St. Charles College), Grand Coteau, LA

Tran, Rev. John Quy V., '05 (LA) Retired. St. Lucy, Long Beach, CA

Tran, Rev. John Son, *C.Ss.R.* '18 (STP) St. Alphonsus, Brooklyn Center, MN; [MON] Redemptorist Fathers of Hennepin County, Brooklyn Center, MN

Tran, Rev. John-Nhan, '92 (NO) Curia: Offices and Directors

Tran, Rev. Jon Bennet, '08 (STP) Church of St. Stephen, Anoka, MN; [CEM] Calvary Cemetery/Church of St. Stephen, Anoka, MN; [EFT] Church of St. Stephen of Anoka Building Fund Trust, Anoka, MN

Tran, Rev. Joseph, '95 (NY) St. Nicholas of Tolentine, Bronx, NY

Tran, Rev. Joseph, '22 (ORL) Church of the Resurrection, Lakeland, FL

Tran, Rev. Joseph, '05 (HRT) [CON] St. Lucian's Residence, New Britain, CT; [NUR] St. Lucian's Residence, Inc. (Daughters of Mary of the Immaculate Conception), New Britain, CT

Tran, Very Rev. Joseph, '04 (DEN) Curia: Deaneries St. Joseph Catholic Parish in Golden, Golden, CO

Tran, Rev. Joseph, '02 (OAK) Chap, John Muir Med Ctr; Contra Costa Rgnl Med Ctr Curia: (>MO) Offices and Directors St. John the Baptist, El Cerrito, CA

Tran, Rev. Joseph, (GF) Curia: Leadership; Offices and Directors St. Margaret Mary, Big Sandy, MT

Tran, Rev. Joseph Chuc, *M.M.* (BAL) Our Lady of La Vang, Baltimore, MD

Tran, Rev. Joseph Hung Ducq, *C.Ss.R.* '14 (BRK) Our Lady of Perpetual Help Basilica, Brooklyn, NY

Tran, Rev. Joseph M. Duykim N., '90 (NEW) On Duty Outside Diocese. c/o Most Rev Joseph Nguyen Van Yen, Bishop of Phat Diem,...

Tran, Rev. Joseph Man, '95 (NO) St. Edward the Confessor Roman Catholic Church, Metairie, Louisiana, Metairie, LA

Tran, Rev. Joseph Sai, *S.V.D.* '03 (LAF) St. Joseph, Maurice, LA; St. Jules, Lafayette, LA

Tran, Rev. Joseph Thang Dinh, '96 (NO) St. Joseph Roman Catholic Church, Algiers, Louisiana, New Orleans, LA

Tran, Rev. Joseph Thuong, '05 (ORG) Curia: Leadership Holy Spirit, Fountain Valley, CA

Tran, Rev. Joseph Mary, *OCD* '22 (SR) [MON] Carmelite House of Prayer, Oakville, CA; [RTR] Carmelite House of Prayer, Oakville, CA

Tran, Rev. Kha Philip, *C.R.M.* (BEA) Queen of Vietnam, Port Arthur, TX

Tran, Rev. Khoi, (MO) Curia: Offices and Directors

Tran, Rev. Kiem Van, '91 (ORG) [CCH] Vietnamese Catholic Center, Santa Ana, CA

Tran, Rev. Liem Trung, *O.P.* (GAL) Our Lady of Lavang Church, Houston, TX; Our Lady of Lourdes, Houston, TX

Tran, Rev. Luan Q., '94 (P) Curia: Offices and Directors St. Agatha, Portland, OR

Tran, Rev. Luke Duc, '01 (NEW) Christ the King, Hillside, NJ

Tran, Rev. Martin Duc, '90 (ORG) St. Pius V, Buena Park, CA

Tran, Rev. Mayeal Thu Van, *O.S.B.* '61 (SFE) [MON] Monastery of Christ in the Desert, Abiquiu, NM

Tran, Rev. Michael X., '93 (SD) Retired.

Tran, Rev. Mike, '02 (HT) Curia: Administration Holy Cross, Morgan City, LA

Tran, Rev. Minh, '22 (OM) St. Patrick, Fremont, NE

Tran, Rev. Nhan, *C.M.* '10 (STO) Sacred Heart Church of Patterson (Pastor of), Patterson, CA

Tran, Rev. Nhan, *S.V.D.* '00 (CHI) [EFT] Blessed Arnold Religious Charitable Trust, Techny, IL; [EFT] Divine Word Techny Community Corporation, Techny, IL; [MIS] Techny Land Corporation, NFP, Techny, IL; [MON] Divine Word Residence, Techny, IL

Tran, Rev. Nhi Dinh, '71 (ARL) Retired.

Tran, Rev. Nick, (KNX) Basilica of Sts. Peter and Paul, Chattanooga, TN

Tran, Rev. Nicola N.H., '12 (HRT) On Duty Outside Diocese. Chattanooga, TN

Tran, Rev. Paul Hung, *S.D.B.* '95 (STO) St. Luke Church of Stockton (Pastor of), Stockton, CA

Tran, Rev. Paul M. Tai, *CRM* '05 (SPC) [MON] Congregation of the Mother of the Redeemer, Carthage,

MO
Tran, Rev. Paul Tam X., '00 (WDC) Our Lady of Vietnam, Silver Spring, MD
Tran, Rev. Peter, '73 (RIC) Retired. Our Lady of Mount Carmel, Newport News, VA
Tran, Rev. Peter, '99 (MET) Curia: Family Life Our Lady of Czestochowa, South Plainfield, NJ
Tran, Rev. Peter M. Khuong, *CRM* '10 (SPC) [MON] Congregation of the Mother of the Redeemer, Carthage, MO
Tran, Rev. Peter Nam Van, '84 (NO) St. Agnes Le Thi Thanh Roman Catholic Church, Marrero, Louisiana, Marrero, LA
Tran, Rev. Peter Trong, '04 (DOD) Curia: Leadership; Offices and Directors Christ the King Catholic Church of Deerfield, Kansas, Deerfield, KS; St. Anthony of Padua Catholic Church of Lakin, Kansas, Lakin, KS; St. Raphael Catholic Church of Syracuse, Kansas, Syracuse, KS
Tran, Rev. Philip, '92 (NY) On Sick Leave.
Tran, Rev. Phillip, (BEA) Our Lady of Light, Anahuac, TX; St. Louis, Winnie, TX
Tran, Rev. Phillip H., '15 (MIA) On Leave. ministry in Diocese of Beaumont
Tran, Rev. Phuc Trong, (SJ) Christ the King (Parroquia Cristo Rey), San Jose, CA
Tran, Rev. Quan, *S.J.* (SPK) [COL] Gonzaga University, Spokane, WA
Tran, Rev. Quan Dinh, '11 (ORG) St. Hedwig, Los Alamitos, CA
Tran, Rev. Quan H., '96 (PH) Immaculate Heart of Mary, Philadelphia, PA
Tran, Rev. Quynh Dinh, '93 (SPR) On Leave. Holy Cross, Springfield, MA
Tran, Rev. Raymond Son Thai, (CAM) Most Precious Blood Parish, Collingswood, N.J., Collingswood, NJ
Tran, Rev. Sang V., '92 (LA) Maria Regina, Gardena, CA
Tran, Rev. Steven Son, '15 (GAL) Co-Cathedral of the Sacred Heart, Houston, TX
Tran, Rev. Thinh Van, *OFM* '13 (FBK) Our Lady of Snows Catholic Church Nulato, Nulato, AK; St. Patrick Catholic Church, Koyukuk, AK
Tran, Rev. Thomas, *S.V.D.* '00 (ORG) Our Lady Queen of Angels, Newport Beach, CA
Tran, Rev. Thomas, (SEA) St. John Bosco, Lakewood, WA
Tran, Rev. Thomas Thien-An, *O.P.* '09 (GAL) Our Lady of Lavang Church, Houston, TX
Tran, Rev. Tien, '09 (NSH) St. Matthew, Franklin, TN
Tran, Rev. Tuan Quoc, '97 (ATL) Curia: Leadership Holy Vietnamese Martyrs Catholic Church, Norcross, Inc., Norcross, GA
Tran, Rev. Tung T., '03 (CC) St. Peter's Parish, Rockport, TX
Tran, Rev. Vang Cong, *C.Ss.R.* '83 (BAL) St. Mary, Annapolis, MD
Tran, Rev. Vincent Vu, '07 (GAL) Christ the Redeemer, Houston, TX; St. Albert of Trapani, Houston, TX
Tran, Rev. Vinh-Thinh Nguyen, '20 (STP) Church of St. Stephen, Anoka, MN
Tran, Rev. Vu Phong, '04 (SEA) St. Aloysius, Buckley, WA; St. John Mary Vianney, Kirkland, WA
Tran Liem, Rev. Aloysius M., *CRM* '96 (SPC) [MON] Congregation of the Mother of the Redeemer, Carthage, MO
Tran Ngoc Thoai, Rev. (Aloysius M.), *CRM* '92 (SPC) [MON] Congregation of the Mother of the Redeemer, Carthage, MO
Tran Van Ban, Rev. Martin M., *C.R.M.* '94 (R) Our Lady of La Vang Parish, Raleigh, NC
Trancone, Rev. Gerard A., '69 (WDC) Retired. [NUR] Cardinal O'Boyle Residence for Priests, Washington, DC
Tranel, Rev. Don, *G.H.M.* (NSH)
Tranel, Rev. Don, '88 (CIN) [MON] Headquarters of Glenmary Home Missioners (The Home Missioners of America), Fairfield, OH
Trapp, Rev. Andrew, '07 (CHR) Holy Cross Mission, Saint Helena Island, SC; St. Peter, Beaufort, SC
Trapp, Rev. Msgr. Daniel J., '84 (DET) Nativity of Our Lord Parish Detroit, Detroit, MI; St. Augustine and St. Monica Parish Detroit, Detroit, MI; St. Charles Borromeo Parish Detroit, Detroit, MI
Trapp, Rev. Msgr. Daniel J., '84 (DET)
Trapp, Rev. Joseph J., '96 (COL) Chap, Sacr Min, Corr Reception Ctr: Ohio Reformatory… Saint Joseph Catholic Church, Plain City, OH
Trask, Rev. David R., '86 (CLV) Chap, Mercy Health-Allen Hosp, Oberlin; Lorain Corr Inst Sacred Heart of Jesus Catholic Church, Oberlin, OH; St. Patrick, Wellington, OH; [EFT] St. Patrick Endowment Trust, Wellington, OH
Trask, Rev. John Paul, '15 (RC) All Saints, Eagle Butte, SD; Cheyenne River Reservation, Eagle Butte, SD
Traudt, Rev. Robert, (JOL) [MON] St. Simon Stock Priory, Darien, IL
Traufler, Rev. John F., '57 (WIN) Retired.
Traupman, Rev. Robert, '69 (ORL) Retired.
Travaglione, Rev. Michael, *O.F.M.* '66 (NY) [MON] Franciscan Province of the Immaculate Conception, New York, NY
Travassos, Rev. Horace J., '73 (FR) Retired.
Travers, Rev. Alan, '83 (NY) Retired.
Travers, Rev. Patrick, *SS.CC.* '62 (SB) [MON] Congregation of the Sacred Hearts of Jesus and Mary, SS.CC., Hemet, CA
Travers, Rev. Patrick, *SS.CC.* '62 (LA) Retired. [EFT] Picpus Charitable Trust, La Verne, CA; [MON] Congregation of the Sacred Hearts of Jesus and Mary, La Verne, CA
Travers, Rev. Patrick, '92 (AJ) Curia: Leadership Holy Cross, Anchorage, AK
Travers, Rev. Thomas, *C.Ss.R.* '62 (ROC) [RTR] Notre Dame Retreat House, Canandaigua, NY
Travers, Rev. Thomas J., *C.Ss.R.* '62 (NY) [RTR] Redemptorist Community at Esopus (Redemptorist Fathers and Brothers), Ulster Park, NY
Traverso Feliciano, Rev. Francisco, (ARE) On Duty Outside Diocese. Spain
Travis, Rev. Adam Frederick, '07 (ALX) On Leave. Curia: (>MO) Offices and Directors
Travis, Rev. Robert, '07 (MRY) Santa Margarita de Cortona, Santa Margarita, CA
Trawick, Rev. Gregory G., '85 (OWN) St. Henry, Hardin, KY; St. Stephen, Cadiz, KY
Traylor, Rev. William, '76 (EVN) Retired.
Traynor, Rev. Roarke, '22 (MAN) St. John the Baptist, Suncook, NH; St. Peter, Auburn, NH
Traynor, Rev. Scott, (SFS) [CAM] Dakota State University, Madison, SD
Traynor, Rev. Scott, '00 (SFS) Curia: Leadership
Traynor, Rev. Scott S., '00 (SFS) [RTR] Broom Tree Retreat and Conference Center, Irene, SD
Treacy, Rev. John R., *S.J.* '90 (SJ) [COL] Santa Clara University, Santa Clara, CA
Treacy, Rev. Paul C., '06 (STP) Assumption, St. Paul, MN
Trefney, Rev. Joshua F., '19 (CLV) St. Albert the Great, North Royalton, OH
Treglio, Rev. Vincent, (PAT) On Leave.
Tregre, Rev. Joseph, (HT) St. Genevieve, Thibodaux, LA
Trejo-Estrada, Very Rev. Alejandro, '03 (YAK) Curia: Offices and Directors St. Andrew's, Ellensburg, WA
Trejo-Flores, Rev. Octavio, *S.D.S.* '19 (MIL) [MON] Salvatorian Provincial Offices (Society of the Divine Savior), Milwaukee, WI
Trela, Rev. Jan, '98 (BUF) Blessed Mary Angela Parish, Dunkirk, NY
Trela, Rev. Norman J., '66 (CHI) Retired.
Trela, Rev. Tadeusz, '82 (NEW) Sacred Heart of Jesus, Irvington, NJ
Treloar, Rev. John L., *S.J.* '70 (GB) [RTR] Jesuit Retreat House, Oshkosh, WI
Tremari, Rev. Albert, *S.J.C.* '03 (CHI) St. John Cantius, Chicago, IL; [MIS] Canons Regular of Saint John Cantius, Chicago, IL
Tremblay, Rev. Alan C., '12 (MAN) Chap, Cheshire Cty House of Corrections Parish of the Holy Spirit, Keene, NH
Tremblay, Rev. Albert J., '97 (MAN) St. Luke the Evangelist Parish, Plaistow, NH
Tremblay, Rev. Eugene, *O.M.I.* '74 (BO) [MIS] St. Joseph the Worker Shrine, Lowell, MA
Tremblay, Rev. Marc P., '80 (FR) Holy Trinity, West Harwich, MA
Tremblay, Rev. Nellis, '54 (ALB) Retired. Sacred Heart, Lake George, NY
Tremblay, Rev. Peter C., *O.F.M.Conv.* '12 (R) Blessed Sacrament, Graham, NC; [CAM] Elon University, Elon, NC
Tremel, Rt. Rev. Jerome G., *O. Praem.* '54 (GB) [MON] St. Norbert Abbey, De Pere, WI
Tremie, Rev. Eugene R., '71 (LAF) Retired.
Treml, Rev. Richard L., '99 (DET) SS. Peter and Paul Parish North Branch, North Branch, MI; St. Mary Burnside Parish North Branch, North Branch, MI
Tremmel, Rev. Benjamin, *O.S.B.* '66 (KCK) [MON] St. Benedict's Abbey, Atchison, KS
Trempe, Rev. James, (PHX) [RTR] Mount Claret Roman Catholic Retreat Center, Phoenix, AZ
Trempe, Rev. James F., '96 (LC) St. Francis Xavier, Mosinee, WI; St. John the Baptist, Mosinee, WI
Trenchera, Rev. Manuel (Jun), '80 (AGN) Curia: Advisory Boards, Commissions, Committees, and Councils; Consultative Bodies; Organizations (affiliated, inter-Diocesan, miscellaneous/other) Nuestra Senora de las Aguas, Mongmong, GU
Trenta, Rev. Christopher J., '09 (CLV) [SEM] Saint Mary Seminary and Graduate School of Theology, Wickliffe, OH
Treppa, Rev. Terence, '67 (DET) Retired.
Tressic, Rev. David L., '96 (ALB) On Leave.
Tressler, Rev. Msgr. David L., (SCR) St. Ignatius Loyola, Kingston, Kingston, PA
Treston, Rev. Msgr. James A., '60 (ALN) Retired. St. Ignatius Loyola, West Lawn, PA
Treston, Rev. Kevin, *O.F.M.* '81 (WDC) [MON] Franciscan Monastery USA Inc., Washington, DC
Trevino, Rev. Alberto, (SAT) Retired. [CON] Cordi-Marian Missionary Sisters, San Antonio, TX
Trevino, Rev. Guillermo, '15 (DAV) St. Joseph Church of Columbus Junction, Iowa, Columbus Junction, IA; St. Joseph Church of West Liberty, Iowa, West Liberty, IA
Trevino, Rev. Raciel, (PMB) St. Matthew, Lake Worth, FL
Trevizo, Rev. Msgr. Raul P., '88 (TUC) On Special Assignment. Curia: Consultative Bodies; Leadership Saint John the Evangelist Roman Catholic Parish - Tucson, Tucson, AZ
Treyes, Rev. Reynaldo B., '78 (JOL) St. Isidore, Bloomingdale, IL
Tri Tran, Rev. Francis, *SVD* (GAL) St. Mary of the Purification, Houston, TX
Tria, Rev. Maximino E., '87 (CHR) St. Francis By the Sea, Hilton Head Island, SC
Tria, Rev. Noel, (CHR) St. Denis, Bennettsville, SC; St. Ernest, Pageland, SC; St. Peter, Cheraw, SC
Triana Beltran, Rev. John Fredy, *C.O.* '20 (MET) [MON] Clairvaux House, Raritan, NJ; [MON] The Raritan Congregation of the Oratory of St. Philip Neri, Raritan, NJ; [SHR] Shrine Chapel of the Blessed Sacrament, Raritan, NJ
Trigilio, Rev. John P., (BAL) [SEM] Mount St. Mary's Seminary, Emmitsburg, MD
Trigilio, Rev. John P., '88 (HBG) On Duty Outside Diocese. Mount St Mary's Seminary, Emmitsburg, MD
Trigueros, Rev. Raul, '69 (ELP) Retired.
Trimbur, Rev. John S., '74 (Y) Retired.
Trinh, Rev. Danh Ngoc, '05 (ORG) St. Barbara Catholic Church, Santa Ana, CA
Trinh, Rev. Ephrem Duc Van, *OCist.* (SAC) Retired. [MON] Our Lady of Sacramento Monastery, Walnut Grove, CA
Trinh, Rev. Hoang T., *O.F.M.* '01 (SFR) St. Boniface, San Francisco, CA
Trinh, Rev. Huy The, *O.P.* (GAL) Our Lady of Lourdes, Houston, TX
Trinh, Rev. Joseph Hoa Duc, '93 (DAL) St. Francis of Assisi Catholic Parish - Lancaster, Lancaster, TX
Trinh, Rev. Msgr. Joseph T., '91 (PH) On Special Assignment. Coord, Vietnamese Apostolate, St Helena Rec, Philadelphia Curia: Evangelization St. Helena, Philadelphia, PA
Trinh, Rev. Loc Q., '92 (GR) Sacred Heart, Evart, MI; St. Agnes, Marion, MI; St. Philip Neri, Reed City, MI
Trinh, Rev. Paul, (ORG) St. Elizabeth Ann Seton, Irvine, CA
Trinh, Rev. Quan M., '02 (PH) On Special Assignment. Chap, Vietnamese Apostolate, Delaware Cty, St Laurence Rec… Divine Mercy Parish, Philadelphia, PA
Trinh, Rev. Sinh, (SPR) Holy Name, Springfield, MA
Trinh, Rev. Sinh, '20 (SPR) St. Paul the Apostle, Springfield, MA
Trinh, Rev. Truong Quang, '99 (BLX) St. Ann, Bay St. Louis, MS
Trinh, Rev. Vinh T., *S.V.D.* (SB) [RTR] Divine Word Province/ Retreat Center, Riverside, CA
Trinidad, Rev. Mel, *S.D.B.* '85 (SFR) [MON] Salesian Provincial Residence, San Francisco, CA
Trinidad, Rev. Nelson, '86 (LA) Our Lady of Guadalupe, Los Angeles, CA
Trinidad, Rev. Victor, '19 (SJ) St. Clare, Santa Clara, CA
Trinidad-Fonseca, Rev. Miguel Angel, '00 (SJN) Curia: Offices and Directors
Triplett, Rev. Michael S., '07 (BAL) Our Lady of Perpetual Help, Ellicott City, MD
Tripole, Rev. Martin R., *S.J.* '67 (PH) [MON] Jesuit Community at St. Joseph's University, Merion Station, PA
Tripp, Rev. Tyler, '15 (SB) Curia: Advisory Boards, Commissions, Committees, and Councils Sacred Heart, Palm Desert, CA
Trisco, Rev. Msgr. Robert F., '54 (CHI) Retired. On Duty Outside Diocese. Curley Hall, Catholic Univ of America, Washington, DC
Trocchio, Rev. Thomas, '15 (E) Mount Calvary, Erie,

PA; St. Mark the Evangelist, Erie, PA
Trocha, Rev. Lukasz, '00 (BRK) St. Edmund, Brooklyn, NY
Troche, Rev. Hector, (MIA) St. Louis, Pinecrest, FL
Troha, Rev. Michael J., '80 (CLV) Curia: Clergy and Religious Services Our Lady of Mount Carmel, Wickliffe, OH
Troha, Rev. Michael James, '80 (CLV) Immaculate Conception Parish, Willoughby, OH
Troiano, Rev. Msgr. Leonard F., '79 (TR) Retired. Curia: Leadership
Troiano, Rev. Louis, *O.F.M.* '57 (NY) Retired. [MON] Padua Friary, New York, NY
Trojanowski, Rev. Leszek, '14 (VEN) Holy Cross Parish in Palmetto, Inc., Palmetto, FL; [NUR] Holy Cross Manor II, Inc., Palmetto, FL; [NUR] Holy Cross Manor, Inc., Palmetto, FL
Trombetta, Rev. Duane C., '18 (SHP) Holy Trinity, Shreveport, LA; Our Lady of the Blessed Sacrament, Shreveport, LA
Troncale, Rev. Msgr. F. Charles, '65 (MOB) Retired. Our Lady of Guadalupe Parish, Wetumpka, Wetumpka, AL
Troncoso Martin, Rev. Jose Felix, *OAR* (ORG) Our Lady of Guadalupe, Santa Ana, CA; [MON] Augustinian Recollects, Santa Ana, CA
Trong, Rev. John T.B., '71 (ARL) Retired.
Trosley, Rev. Anthony J., '78 (PEO) Immaculate Conception, Carthage, IL; Sacred Heart, Warsaw, IL; SS. Peter and Paul, Nauvoo, IL
Trouille, Rev. Alan P., '97 (LKC) Curia: Leadership St. Philip Neri, Kinder, LA
Trout, Rev. John, *S.P.S.* '89 (CHI) St. Joseph, Libertyville, IL
Trout, Very Rev. Richard W., '85 (ORL) Curia: Leadership Corpus Christi, Celebration, FL
Trowbridge, Rev. Jeremy A., '10 (RCK) On Special Assignment. Curia: Offices and Directors SS. Peter & Paul, Cary, IL
Troxell, Rev. Christopher, '92 (LA) On Sick Leave.
Troyan, Very Rev. Archpriest Daniel, '82 (PHU) Holy Myrrh-Bearers Ukrainian Catholic Church, Swarthmore, PA
Trudel, Rev. Guy Albert, *O.P.* '94 (WDC) [SEM] Dominican House of Studies, Washington, DC
Truhan, Rev. Luke, *O.C.S.O.* '82 (WOR) [MON] St. Joseph's Abbey (Cistercian Abbey of Spencer, Inc., Cistercian Order of the Strict Observance (Trappists)), Spencer, MA
Trujillo, Rev. Ariel, '71 (NY) Saint Joseph and Saint Mary Immaculate, Staten Island, NY
Trujillo, Rev. David, '15 (SLC) Saint James the Just LLC 226, Ogden, UT
Trujillo, Rev. Ivan R., '85 (BUF) Attica Corr Fac Curia: Offices and Directors; (>MO) Offices and Directors Resurrection, Batavia, NY
Trujillo, Rev. Mauro, (ORG) St. Irenaeus, Cypress, CA
Trujillo, Rev. Robert, '07 (STA) St. Elizabeth Ann Seton, Palm Coast, FL
Trujillo, Rev. Teofilo, '89 (CHR) Curia: Advisory Boards, Commissions, Committees, and Councils; Offices and Directors St. Mary Magdalene, Simpsonville, SC
Trujillo, Rev. Vincent, *O.S.B.* '82 (P) Retired. [MON] Mt. Angel Abbey, Saint Benedict, OR
Trujillo-Gonzalez, Rev. Francisco de Asis, '05 (NEW) On Duty Outside Diocese. Cadiz
Trull, Rev. Jason, '02 (STA) Curia: Leadership Assumption, Jacksonville, FL; [PRE] Assumption Early Learning Center, Jacksonville, FL
Trull, Rev. Jeremy, '20 (LUB) Curia: Leadership; Offices and Directors
Trullols, Rev. Charles, (WDC) [MIS] Prelature of the Holy Cross and Opus Dei, Washington, DC; [RTR] Catholic Information Center, Washington, DC
Trullols, Rev. Charles, '06 (POD) Curia: Clergy and Religious Services
Trummer, Rev. Christopher A., '21 (SFD) Curia: Leadership St. Agnes, Springfield, IL
Trummer, Rev. Michael, '20 (SFD) St. Boniface, Edwardsville, IL; [CAM] Millikin University Newman Catholic Community, Decatur, IL
Trung, Rev. Nguyen Dinh, *C.Ss.R.* '03 (LA) [MON] Vietnamese Redemptorist Mission, Baldwin Park, CA
Truong, Rev. Dien, *C.PP.S.* '97 (LA) St. Agnes, Los Angeles, CA
Truong, Rev. Joseph Ngu Cong, '12 (ORG) St. Boniface, Anaheim, CA
Truong, Rev. Martin, *C.R.M.* '14 (ROC) The Parish of the Holy Family, Monroe County, NY, Rochester, NY
Truong, Rev. Peter, '99 (PMB) St. Francis of Assisi, Riviera Beach, FL
Truong, Rev. Quyen, '16 (ORG) Christ Cathedral Parish, Garden Grove, CA
Truong, Rev. Tri Vinh, '08 (CHL) St. Joseph Church, Charlotte, NC
Trupkovich, Rev. Thomas S., '97 (GBG) Retired.
Truss, Rev. Ryan W., '21 (STL) Sacred Heart Catholic Church, Valley Park, Valley Park, MO
Trzecieski, Rev. Stephen P., *C.M.* '60 (PH) [MON] Congregation of the Mission, Philadelphia, PA
Tsada, Rev. Tesfaldet Tekie, '97 (LA) Sacred Heart, Los Angeles, CA
Tsanga, Rev. Francois, *S.C.J.* '05 (BWN) Our Lady, Queen of the Universe, San Benito, TX
Tschakert, Rev. Gregory, '82 (SFS) Curia: Offices and Directors Saint Elizabeth Ann Seton Parish of Brown County, Groton, SD; Saint Joseph Parish of Spink County, Turton, SD
Tschakert, Rev. Gregory, '82 (SFS) Curia: Leadership
Tseu, Rev. Msgr. Andrew Stanislaus, '56 (LA) Retired.
Tshibambe, Very Rev. Henri, '81 (DEN) Our Lady of Fatima Catholic Parish in Lakewood, Lakewood, CO
Tshuma, Rev. Alvin, (AMA) Holy Name of Jesus, Happy, TX; St. Mary's, Umbarger, TX
Tu, Rev. Qiang (Keon), *O.F.M.Cap.* '22 (WDC) [SEM] St. Francis Friary-Capuchin College, Washington, DC
Tuan, Rev. Bui Quang, *C.Ss.R.* '97 (LA) [MON] Vietnamese Redemptorist Mission, Baldwin Park, CA
Tubana, Rev. Leonardo, (HON) Cathedral Basilica of Our Lady of Peace, Honolulu, HI
Tucci, Rev. Matthew, '16 (IND) On Leave.
Tucker, Rev. James A., '01 (ARL) On Leave.
Tucker, Rev. James Gregory, '06 (MET) Our Lady of Peace, Edison, NJ
Tucker, Rev. James S., *P.S.S.* '69 (BAL) Retired.
Tucker, Rev. Mark E., '89 (WDC) On Special Assignment. Curia: Tribunal Holy Redeemer, Kensington, MD; Nativity, Washington, DC
Tucker, Rev. Patrick M., '74 (CHI) Retired.
Tucker, Rev. Robert F., '70 (HRT) Retired.
Tucker, Rev. Msgr. Robert G., '89 (LIN) Curia: Leadership St. Vincent de Paul, Seward, NE
Tucker, Rev. Thomas J., *O.S.F.S.* '66 (WIL) Retired. [MON] Retirement and Assisted Care Facility, Childs, MD
Tucker, Rev. Zachary T., (OM) St. Stephen the Martyr, Omaha, NE
Tuckerman, Rev. Dale, '14 (SPK) St. Anne, Medical Lake, WA; St. Michael, Reardan, WA; St. Patrick, Walla Walla, WA
Tudgay, Rev. Jeffrey D., '12 (SCR) Curia: Leadership St. Peter's Cathedral, Scranton, PA
Tudu, Rev. Sushil William, *T.O.R.* '06 (FWT) St. Catherine of Siena, Carrollton, TX; [MON] Third Order Regular of St. Francis, Province of St. Thomas, Carrollton, TX
Tufaro, Rev. Douglas, '83 (BGP) Retired.
Tufford, Rev. Corey, '16 (SD) Pastor of Santa Sophia Catholic Parish, Spring Valley, a corporation sole, Spring Valley, CA
Tugwell, Rev. Msgr. Michael W., '75 (PT) Retired.
Tui, Rev. Ese'ese, '21 (HON) St. Anthony of Padua, Wailuku, HI
Tuisea, Rev. Setefano, '92 (SPP) Cathedral of the Holy Family, Pago Pago, AS
Tuite, Rev. Daniel, (NY) St. Anthony, Yonkers, NY
Tuite, Rev. Thomas, (RVC) St. Mark, Shoreham, NY
Tuite, Rev. Thomas P., '86 (RVC) Chap, LI State Veterans' Home
Tukidia, Rev. Patrick, *sscc* (HON) St. Ann, Kaneohe, HI
Tulko, Rev. Richard, *O.F.M.* '64 (MIL) [MON] Queen of Peace Friary (Franciscan Friars of the Assumption B.V.M. Province), Burlington, WI
Tully, Rev. Eugene D., '68 (BO) Retired.
Tully, Rev. Eugene M., '73 (PH) St. Joseph, Ambler, PA
Tully, Rev. Gerard, *C.S.P.* '94 (LA) St. Paul the Apostle, Los Angeles, CA
Tully, Rev. Henry F., '77 (IND) Retired.
Tully, Rev. Ignatius, *OSB Cam.* '18 (MRY) [MON] New Camaldoli Hermitage (Camaldolese Hermits of America), Big Sur, CA
Tully, Rev. Thomas S., '85 (R) Saint Peter the Fisherman, Oriental, NC; St. Paul, New Bern, NC
Tulua, Rev. William, '18 (HON) Holy Rosary, Pahala, HI; Sacred Heart, Naalehu, HI
Tumaca, Rev. Delfin, '03 (STO) St. Bernadette Church (Pastor of), Stockton, CA
Tumicki, Rev. Ted F., '97 (NOR) Curia: Leadership; Offices and Directors; Tribunal St. Catherine of Siena, Preston, CT; St. Mary, Jewett City, CT; St. Thomas the Apostle, Voluntown, CT
Tumino, Rev. Frank C., '98 (BRK) St. Francis Xavier, Brooklyn, NY
Tumosa, Rev. John Joseph, '69 (CAM) Retired.
Tumuhereze, Rev. Tarasisio, *A.J.* '03 (MO) Curia: Offices and Directors
Tumusiime, Rev. Dominic, *AJ* '93 (PRT) St. Anthony of Padua Parish, Westbrook, ME
Tumwekwase, Rev. Robert, *A.J.* '88 (PRT) Saint Paul the Apostle Parish, Bangor, ME; [HOS] St. Joseph Hospital, Bangor, ME
Tumwesigye, Rev. Alfred, '05 (SFD) St. Elizabeth, Granite City, IL
Tunarosa, Rev. Rafael, '98 (RCK) On Administrative Leave.
Tunarosa, Rev. William, '06 (RCK) St. Thomas the Apostle, Crystal Lake, IL
Tuner, Rev. Robert D., (SEA) Curia: Tribunal
Tung, Rev. Thanh Tran, (MO) Curia: Offices and Directors
Tungol, Rev. Eugene D., '75 (SFR) On Special Assignment. Curia: Leadership; Offices and Directors Church of the Epiphany, San Francisco, CA
Tunink, Rev. Shawn, '08 (KCK) On Leave.
Tunney, Rev. Michael F, *S.J.* (NY) [MON] St. Ignatius Loyola Residence, New York, NY
Tunnicliff, Rev. Jeffrey, '07 (ROC) St. Benedict, Watkins Glen, NY; St. Mary of the Lake, Watkins Glen, NY
Tuoc, Rev. Ignatius, '71 (SP) Retired. Epiphany of Our Lord, Tampa, FL
Tuohey, Rev. John F., '81 (SPR) Holy Cross, Springfield, MA
Tuong, Rev. Hoang Minh, '01 (NO) St. Bernard, St. Bernard, LA
Tuong, Rev. Peter, *SSS* (GAL) Corpus Christi, Houston, TX
Tupa, Rev. Allan, '97 (SP) St. Joseph Catholic Church, Zephyrhills, FL
Tupa, Rev. Jerome, *O.S.B.* '82 (SCL) [MON] St. John's Abbey, of the Order of St. Benedict, Collegeville, MN
Tupiza, Rev. Juan Antonio, '09 (MIA) Curia: Canonical Services; Leadership St. Rose of Lima, Miami Shores, FL
Tupper, Rev. Dale E., '67 (WIN) Retired.
Tupuola, Rev. Iosefo V., '99 (SPP) Curia: Leadership; Offices and Directors Cathedral of the Holy Family, Pago Pago, AS
Turba, Rev. Johnathan F., *O. Praem.* '22 (GB) [MON] St. Norbert Abbey, De Pere, WI
Turcios, Rev. Juan, *OFM* '21 (GRY) SS. Monica-St. Luke, Gary, IN
Turcotte, Rev. Louis, '18 (SP) St. Raphael, St. Petersburg, FL
Turcotte, Rev. Louis, '18 (SP) Curia: Pastoral Services
Turczany, Rev. Christopher J., '83 (BRK) St. Mary, Long Island City, NY
Turek, Very Rev. Michael E., '76 (STL) Curia: Leadership Christ the King Catholic Church, University City, MO; St. Rita Catholic Church, St. Louis, MO
Turek, Rev. Ronald J., '74 (CLV) Chap, Aultman-Orville Hosp, Orrville St. Agnes, Orrville, OH
Tureman, Rev. Thomas, *S.D.S.* '88 (TUC) Most Holy Trinity Roman Catholic Parish - Tucson, Tucson, AZ
Tureman, Rev. Thomas, *S.D.S.* '88 (MIL) [MON] Salvatorian Provincial Offices (Society of the Divine Savior), Milwaukee, WI
Turi, Rev. John J., '55 (SCR) Retired. [MON] Villa St. Joseph, Dunmore, PA
Turiano, Rev. Santiago, (GB) St. James, Cooperstown, WI; St. Joseph, Kellnersville, WI
Turillo, Rev. B. Samuel, '46 (PRO) Retired.
Turley, Rev. Sean F., '71 (WIL) Retired.
Turlick, Rev. Donald A., (BGP) Retired. [MON] The Catherine Dennis Keefe Queen of the Clergy Retired Priests' Residence, Stamford, CT
Turner, Rev. Andrew B., '06 (CLV) [SEM] Saint Mary Seminary and Graduate School of Theology, Wickliffe, OH
Turner, Rev. Bernard R., '77 (ALB) On Leave.
Turner, Rev. Christopher, (WH) Sacred Heart Mission, Salem, WV; St. Ann Catholic Church, Shinnston, WV; St. James the Apostle, Clarksburg, WV
Turner, Rev. David, *O.S.B.* '63 (JOL) Retired. [MIS] Founders Woods, Ltd., Lisle, IL; [MON] St. Procopius Abbey, Lisle, IL
Turner, Rev. James, '84 (PHX) Curia: Offices and Directors St. Thomas More Roman Catholic Parish, Glendale, AZ
Turner, Rev. Jerome R., '64 (MAD) Retired.
Turner, Rev. Luke, *O.S.B.* '19 (KCK) On Duty Outside Diocese. Diocese of Dallas - St. Thomas Aquinas Church, Dallas, TX [MON] St. Benedict's Abbey, Atchison, KS
Turner, Rev. Luke, *OSB* (DAL) St. Thomas Aquinas Catholic Parish, Dallas, TX
Turner, Rev. Paul, '79 (KC) On Special Assignment. Curia: Offices and Directors Cathedral of Immaculate

Conception, Kansas City, MO; Sacred Heart-Guadalupe, Kansas City, MO
Turner, Rev. Richard M., '80 (SPR) St. Thomas the Apostle, Palmer, MA
Turner, Rev. Richard W., '91 (R) Retired.
Turner, Rev. Robert D., '82 (SPK) St. Patrick, Pasco, WA
Turner, Rev. Robert D., '88 (MIL) Retired.
Turner, Rev. Robert L., '11 (HRT) Saint Ambrose Parish Corporation, North Branford, CT
Turner, Rev. William J., '75 (IND) Retired. St. Maurice Catholic Church, Napoleon, Inc., Napoleon, IN
Turner, Rev. William J., '79 (LAN) Chap, Camp Cassidy Lake St. Mary Parish Chelsea, Chelsea, MI
Turpin, Rev. Alexander, '19 (RVC) On Duty Outside Diocese.
Turro, Rev. Msgr. James C., '48 (NEW) Retired. [COL] Seton Hall University, South Orange, NJ
Turyk, Rev. Ivan, '03 (PHU) Curia: Leadership; Offices and Directors Assumption of B.V.M., Perth Amboy, NJ
Tuscan, Rev. Joseph, *O.F.M. Cap.* (PIT) [MON] St. Augustine Friary, Pittsburgh, PA
Tuscano, Rev. Walter E., *S.A.C.* (TOL) Curia: Advisory Boards, Commissions, Committees, and Councils St. Louis, Custar, OH; St. Patrick, Grand Rapids, OH
Tuskiewiecz, Rev. Joseph, (DET) St. Priscilla Parish Livonia, Livonia, MI
Tusky, Rev. Richard J., '73 (PIT) Retired. Our Lady of Hope, Bethel Park, PA
Tustin, Rev. Joseph E., *O.S.F.S.* '67 (WIL) Retired. [MON] Retirement and Assisted Care Facility, Childs, MD
Tutone, Rev. Msgr. John J., '71 (RVC) Sacred Heart, Island Park, NY
Tutor, Rev. Edwin, '97 (SD) Curia: Advisory Boards, Commissions, Committees, and Councils Pastor of Ascension Catholic Parish, San Diego, a corporation sole, San Diego, CA; [MIS] Ascension Catholic Parish in San Diego, CA Real Property Support Corporation, San Diego, CA
Tuttle, Rev. Arthur, *C.Ss.R.* (HBG) Retired. [MON] St. Clement's Mission House, Ephrata, PA
Tuttle, Rev. Charles W., '74 (BEL) Mater Dei High School, Breese, IL; St. Anthony, Beckemeyer, IL; St. Augustine, Breese, IL
Tuttle, Rev. Christopher, '18 (COL) St. Peter, Columbus, OH
Tuttle, Rev. Patrick Edwin, *OFM* '94 (SAV) Holy Spirit, Macon, GA
Tuttle, Rev. Richard J., '76 (STU) Retired.
Tutuwan, Rev. Henry, (MO) Curia: Offices and Directors
Tutuwan, Rev. Henry, (CHL) St. Benedict the Moor, Winston-Salem, NC
Tuwekwase, Rev. Robert, *A.J.* Chap, St Joseph Healthcare Foundation, Bangor
Tuyor, Rev. Exsequel, '94 (HON) St. Anthony of Padua School, Kailua, HI
Tuzeneu, Rev. Msgr. Kenard J., '79 (TR) St. Mary, Barnegat, NJ
Tuzik, Rev. Robert L., '73 (CHI) Retired.
Tveit, Rev. Jon, '16 (NY) St. Mary, Wappingers Falls, NY
Tviet, Rev. Jon, '16 (NY) Resurrection, Rye, NY
Tvrdik, Rev. Roy, *S.M.M.* '93 (RVC) [MIS] Magnificat - Suffolk County NY Chapter, Eastport, NY; [MON] Montfort Missionaries, Bay Shore, NY
Tvrdy, Rev. Julius P., '73 (LIN) Retired.
Twaddell, Rev. Msgr. Gerald E., '67 (COV) Curia: Pastoral Services; Tribunal [COL] Thomas More University, Crestview Hills, KY; [CON] Monastery of the Sacred Passion, Erlanger, KY
Twaibu, Rev. Boniface-Blanchard M., '14 (STV) Chapel of St. Anne, Carenage, VI
Twardzik, Rev. Michael W., '70 (ROC) Retired.
Twardzik, Rev. Michael W.T., '70 (SPR) Retired.
Twaruzek, Rev. Canon Michal, '15 (JOL) St. Charles Borromeo, Bensenville, IL
Twele, Rev. Robert, *O.F.M. Conv.* '81 (BAL) [MIS] Catholic Relief Services Foundation, Inc., Baltimore, MD
Twenty, Rev. Jared, '14 (RCK) On Special Assignment. Curia: Offices and Directors Holy Cross, Batavia, IL
Twilliger, Rev. Derek, '16 (SD) Pastor of Our Lady of Perpetual Help Catholic Parish Lakeside in Lakeside California, A Corporation Sole, Lakeside, CA
Twinomujuni, Rev. John, '01 (PEO) [HOS] OSF HealthCare Saint Francis Medical Center, East Peoria, IL
Twohig, Rev. Michael J., '83 (SPR) St. Theresa of Lisieux, South Hadley, MA
Twohig, Rev. Richard H., *S.J.* '65 (DET) [MON] Colombiere Center, Clarkston, MI
Twohy, Rev. Patrick J., *S.J.* '70 (SEA) [MON] Arrupe Jesuit Community at Seattle University, Seattle, WA
Twumasi, Rev. Felix, '04 (VIC) Queen of the Holy Rosary, La Grange, TX; SS. Peter and Paul, La Grange, TX
Ty, Rev. Apolinario, *SSS* (HON) St. Joseph, Hilo, HI
Ty, Rev. Jesus "Jess" G., '98 (PHX) Our Lady of Joy Roman Catholic Parish, Carefree, AZ
Tyburski, Rev. Zbigniew, '73 (PAT) Retired.
Tyhovych, Rev. Evon, (NY) Chap, USVA Med Ctr, Manhattan
Tyhovych, Rev. Ivan, '94 (STF) Curia: (>MO) Offices and Directors Holy Ghost, Brooklyn, NY
Tyl, Rev. Dominique, *S.J.* '75 (CI) [MON] Jesuit Community of Palau, Manresa Jesuit House, Koror, PW
Tyler, Rev. Bernard L., '61 (GLD) Retired. Saint Hubert of Higgins Lake, Higgins Lake, MI; Saint James the Greater of Houghton Lake, Houghton Lake, MI
Tyler, Rev. Jason, '05 (LR) Curia: Offices and Directors SS. Peter and Paul Catholic Church, Lincoln, AR; St. John the Evangelist, Huntsville, AR; St. Joseph, Fayetteville, AR
Tyler, Rev. Thomas L., '79 (E) Holy Cross, Fairview, PA
Tyman, Rev. Gary L., '86 (ROC) Our Lady of Lourdes, Rochester, NY; St. Anne, Rochester, NY; St. George, Rochester, NY; [CAM] Monroe Community College c/o Our Lady of Lourdes / St. Anne, Rochester, NY
Tymchyshyn, Archpriest Bohdan, (STF) [SEM] Ukrainian Catholic Seminary Inc. St. Basil College - Seminary, Stamford, CT
Tymchyshyn, Rev. Bohdan, (STF) Curia: Leadership; Offices and Directors
Tymchyshyn, Very Rev. Bohdan, (STF) Curia: Leadership; Offices and Directors
Tymko, Rev. Piotr, *O.F.M. Conv.* '94 (R) Blessed Sacrament, Graham, NC
Tynan, Rev. Desmond A., '67 (BO) Retired.
Tynan, Rev. Peter, *O.S.B.* '11 (SEA) [CAM] Saint Martin's University (Lacey), Lacey, WA; [COL] Saint Martin's University (Order of St. Benedict Master's Comprehensive University), Lacey, WA; [MON] St. Martin's Abbey, Lacey, WA
Tyochemba, Rev. Raymond, (SFR) Saint Brendan the Navigator Church, San Francisco, CA
Tyohemba, Rev. Raymond, (SFR) St. James, San Francisco, CA
Tyohemba, Rev. Raymond D., *VC* (SFR) Chap, Laguna Honda Home St. Finn Barr, San Francisco, CA
Tyowua, Rev. Celestine, (SFR) Saint Brendan the Navigator Church, San Francisco, CA
Tyrrell, Rev. Bernard, (SJ) [MON] Sacred Heart Jesuit Center, Los Gatos, CA
Tyrrell, Rev. Joseph J., '89 (NY) Roman Catholic Church of Sacred Heart and Saint Francis of Assisi, Newburgh, NY; St. Patrick, Highland Mills, NY
Tyrrell, Rev. Michael, (OAK) [MON] Jesuit Fathers and Brothers, Berkeley, CA
Tyrrell, Rev. William, *S.A.* (NY) [CAM] Manhattanville College, Purchase, NY
Tyrtania, Rev. Joachim B., '83 (RCK) St. John the Evangelist, Hanover, IL; St. Mary, Elizabeth, IL
Tyson, Rev. David T., *C.S.C.* '75 (FTW) [MON] Holy Cross Community, Corby Hall, University of Notre Dame, Notre Dame, IN
Tywoniak, Rev. Robert F., '83 (MIA) Blessed Sacrament, Oakland Park, FL
Tzul Lacan, Rev. Dionicio Maximo, (SB) Immaculate Conception, Colton, CA
Uba, Rev. Alban, '99 (SAC) Mercy San Juan Hosp, Carmichael Pastor of St. John the Evangelist Parish, Carmichael, a corporation sole, Carmichael, CA
Uba, Rev. Chike Emmanuel, '00 (SFE) Nativity of the Blessed Virgin Mary, Albuquerque, NM
Uba, Rev. Emmanuel Chike, '00 (SFE) Curia: Offices and Directors
Ubalde, Rev. Ulysses L., '93 (NEW) Curia: (>MO) Offices and Directors
Ubalde, Rev. Ulysses L., '93 (NEW) Chap, Camp Lejeune, NC
Ubben, Rev. Michael Luke, *OFM* (GB) Retired.
Ubel, Rev. John L., '89 (STP) Curia: Consultative Bodies Cathedral of Saint Paul, St. Paul, MN
Ubiparipovic, Rev. Sinisa, '15 (BO) Curia: (>MO) Offices and Directors St. Thomas the Apostle, Millis, MA
Ucerler, Rev. Antoni J., *S.J.* '94 (SFR) [MIS] The Ricci Institute for Chinese-Western Cultural History, San Francisco, CA
Ucerler, Rev. M. Antoni, (BO) [MON] The Jesuit Community at Boston College, Chestnut Hill, MA
Uche, Rev. Jude, '85 (LA) St. John the Baptist, Baldwin Park, CA
Uche, Rev. Jude, *M.S.P.* (AUS) St. Stephen, Salado, TX; [MON] Missionary Society of St. Paul, MSP, Salado, TX
Udagandla, Rev. Kumar, '94 (BAK) St. Mary, Pendleton, OR
Udayar, Very Rev. Santiago D., '89 (SAN) Curia: Advisory Boards, Commissions, Committees, and Councils; Canonical Services; Leadership Holy Angels, San Angelo, TX
Udeagu, Rev. Leo, *S.S.J.* '12 (WDC) [SEM] St. Joseph's Seminary, Washington, DC
Udechukwu, Rev. Bedemoore, '98 (MO) Curia: Offices and Directors
Udegbunam, Rev. Michael, '81 (SAN) Curia: Advisory Boards, Commissions, Committees, and Councils St. Ann's, Colorado City, TX
Udeh, Rev. Elias, *C.S.Sp.* '12 (COL) St. Joseph Cathedral, Columbus, OH
Udemgba, Rev. Simon, '96 (ALB) St. Joseph, Greenfield Center, NY
Udeolisa, Rev. Ferdinand, '05 (FRS) Good Shepherd Catholic Parish, Visalia, CA
Udeze, Rev. Joseph, (MO) Curia: Offices and Directors
Udeze, Rev. Kieran, (BRK) Sacred Heart of Jesus, Bayside, NY; St. Thomas Aquinas, Brooklyn, NY
Udobi, Rev. Matthew, (RVC) Infant Jesus, Port Jefferson, NY
Udobi, Rev. Matthew, (RVC) Chap, Mather Mem Hosp
Udoh, Rev. Chrysanthus, (DET) Chap, John D Dingell Veterans Admin Med Ctr, Detroit
Udoh, Rev. Chrysanthus F., (DAL) Chap., Dallas VA Medical Center
Udoh, Rev. Chrysanthus F., *M.S.P.* '90 (MO) Curia: Offices and Directors
Udoh, Rev. Emmanuel, '14 (OWN) Curia: Advisory Boards, Commissions, Committees, and Councils Rosary Chapel, Paducah, KY; St. Mary, LaCenter, KY; [CEM] Mt. Carmel Cemetery, Inc., Paducah, KY
Udoh, Rev. Ernest P., (BAL) Our Lady of Mount Carmel, Essex, MD; [HOS] Mercy Health Services Inc., Baltimore, MD
Udoh, Rev. Ike, *S.J.* '15 (OAK) [MON] Jesuit Fathers and Brothers, Oakland, CA
Udoh, Rev. Michael, (BRK) St. Margaret, Middle Village, NY
Udoh, Rev. Tony, *MSP* (LAV) Holy Family, Las Vegas, NV
Udoji, Rev. Ambrose, (LA) St. Linus, Norwalk, CA
Udokang, Rev. Charles, (NY) Our Lady of Grace, Bronx, NY
Udouj, Rev. Reginald, *OSB* '18 (LR) St. Joseph, Paris, AR; St. Mary, Altus, AR; [MON] Subiaco Abbey, Subiaco, AR
Udovic, Rev. Edward R., *C.M.* '84 (CHI) [MON] Vincentian Community, Congregation of the Mission, Western Province, Chicago, IL
Udulutsch, Rev. Robert, *O.F.M.Cap.* '56 (GB) Retired.
Udumka, Rev. Kenny, *C.S.Sp.* (BAL) New All Saints, Baltimore, MD; St. Edward, Baltimore, MD; St. Gregory the Great, Baltimore, MD
Uebler, Rev. Luke P., '17 (BUF) St. Mary, Swormville, NY
Uecker, Rev. Joseph, *C.PP.S.* '68 (KC) (>CIN) [MON] Society of the Precious Blood, United States Province, Inc., Dayton, OH
Uecker, Rev. Joseph, *CPPS* '68 (SAN) Retired.
Uftring, Rev. Richard A., '76 (BO) Retired. Curia: Pastoral Services
Ugalde, Rev. Jose, *M.Sp.S.* '09 (SEA) (>P) [MON] Missionaries of the Holy Spirit, M.Sp.S., Milwaukie, OR
Ugbor, Rev. Michael, (BRK) Queen of Peace, Flushing, NY
Ugbor, Rev. Michael O., '17 (BRK) Chap, Long Island Jewish Hosp
Ugo, Rev. Charles Chidindu, '06 (ALT) Chap, Alamogordo, NM Curia: (>MO) Offices and Directors
Ugobueze, Rev. John, '05 (GAL) Curia: (>MO) Offices and Directors
Ugochukwu, Rev. Charles, '96 (SFE) Risen Savior Catholic Community, Albuquerque, NM
Ugochukwu, Rev. Eric, *SDV* (BRK) St. Clement Pope, South Ozone Park, NY
Ugochukwu, Rev. Eric I., *S.D.V.* '04 (NEW) St. Michael, Newark, NJ
Ugochukwu, Rev. John, (BLX) Memorial Hospital at Gulfport Chaplain
Ugochukwu, Rev. Nicholas, (NY) Chap, Lincoln Med and Mental Health Ctr, Bronx
Ugochukwu, Rev. Sebastian A., '79 (MO) Curia: Offices and Directors
Ugwejeh, Rev. Emmanuel, *S.J.* '01 (MIL) [MON] Jesuit Community at Marquette University (Marquette Jesuit Associates, Inc.), Milwaukee, WI

Ugwoegbu, Rev. Edmund U., (BO) St. Anthony of Padua, Woburn, MA; St. Barbara, Woburn, MA
Ugwoji, Rev. Matthew, '92 (NY) Chap, Sing Sing Corr Fac, Ossining; Edgecombe Corr Fac, NY Parish of St. Christopher and St. Patrick, Buchanan, NY
Ugwu, Rev. Amaechi M., *S.J.* '07 (LA) [MON] Jesuit Community, Los Angeles, CA
Ugwu, Rev. Charles, (FRS) Chap, California State Prison, Corcoran
Ugwu, Rev. Georginus Esiofor, *M.S.P.* '00 (NY) Our Lady of Grace, Bronx, NY; Parish of St. Frances of Rome, St. Francis of Assisi, St. Anthony, and Our Lady of Grace, Bronx, NY; St. Anthony, Bronx, NY; St. Francis of Assisi, Bronx, NY
Ugwu, Rev. Kenneth C., *S.S.J.* '10 (LA) Holy Name of Jesus, Los Angeles, CA
Ugwu, Rev. Stephen Chibunda, '02 (LAF) St. John the Evangelist, Melville, LA
Ugwuanya, Rev. Valentine C., '94 (NEW) Curia: (>MO) Offices and Directors Immaculate Heart of Mary, Scotch Plains, NJ
Ugwuegbu, Rev. Ambrose O., '87 (SAC) Pastor of St. Basil Parish, Vallejo, a corporation sole, Vallejo, CA
Ugwuegbulem, Rev. Longinus N., '93 (NEW) Blessed Sacrament-St. Charles Borromeo, Newark, NJ
Uhen, Rev. Timothy J., (NY) [MIS] Prelature of the Holy Cross and Opus Dei, New York, NY
Uhen, Rev. Timothy J., '96 (POD) Curia: Clergy and Religious Services
Uhlenkott, Rev. Benjamin R., '06 (B) Curia: Offices and Directors Risen Christ Catholic Community, Boise, ID
Uhlenkott, Rev. Gary, *S.J.* '80 (SJ) [MON] Sacred Heart Jesuit Center, Los Gatos, CA
Uhlenkott, Rev. Mark, '16 (B) St. John Paul II Parish, Idaho Falls, ID
Uhlman, Rev. Laurence, *T.O.R.* (SP) St. Mary Our Lady of Grace, St. Petersburg, FL
Uhrig, Rev. A. Gregory, '73 (MET) Retired. [MON] Maria Regina Residence, Somerset, NJ
Uju, Rev. Eliseus, '03 (SB) Blessed Sacrament, Twentynine Palms, CA
Ukaegbu, Rev. Jon O., '79 (BRK) St. Rose of Lima, Brooklyn, NY
Ukaegbu-Onuoha, Rev. Emmanuel, '95 (SB) [SEM] Saint Junipero Serra House of Formation, Grand Terrace, CA
Ukanide, Rev. Anietie, (GF) Our Lady of Lourdes, Poplar, MT
Uko, Rev. Fidelis, (MIA) Little Flower, Coral Gables, FL
Uko, Rev. Joseph, (GRY) [HOS] Franciscan Health Michigan City, Michigan City, IN
Uko, Rev. Joseph M., '88 (BLX) Curia: Advisory Boards, Commissions, Committees, and Councils; Leadership St. Joseph Catholic Church, Gulfport, MS
Ukoh, Rev. Sebastian, *C.M.* '08 (BEL) Divine Maternity of the B.V.M., Ellis Grove, IL; St. Joseph, Prairie du Rocher, IL; St. Mary Help of Christians, Chester, IL
Ukwueze, Rev. Ernest, '17 (BWN) Holy Spirit, McAllen, TX
Ulak, Rev. Robert T., '70 (NEW) Our Lady of Mercy, Park Ridge, NJ
Ulam, Rev. Richard, *O.S.B.* '82 (GBG) St. Vincent Basilica, Latrobe, PA; [MON] Saint Vincent Archabbey, Latrobe, PA
Ulaski, Rev. Michał, (FBK) Church of the Holy Angels Catholic Church Unalakleet, Unalakleet, AK; St. Ann Catholic Church Teller, Nome, AK; St. Bernard Catholic Church Stebbins, Stebbins, AK; St. Francis Xavier Catholic Church Kotzebue, Kotzebue, AK; St. Joseph Catholic Church Nome, Nome, AK; St. Michael Catholic Church St. Michael, St. Michael, AK
Uline, Rev. Cyprian, *OFMConv* '70 (IND) St. Joseph University Catholic Church, Terre Haute, Inc., Terre Haute, IN; St. Joseph University Parish, Terre Haute, IN
Ulinzwenimana, Rev. Lambert, (MO) Curia: Offices and Directors
Ulishney, Rev. Daniel J., '13 (GBG) Curia: Leadership St. John Baptist de La Salle, Delmont, PA; St. Mary, Export, PA
Ullmer, Rev. James, *O.S.B.* '09 (TLS) [MON] Our Lady of the Annunciation of Clear Creek Abbey, Hulbert, OK
Ulloa, Rev. Daniel, *O.P.* '70 (NY) Parish of St. John the Baptist and Most Holy Trinity, Yonkers, NY
Ulloa-Chavarry, Rev. Rodrigo, *M.M.* '11 (NY) [MON] Maryknoll Fathers and Brothers (Catholic Foreign Mission Society of America, Inc.), Ossining, NY
Ullrich, Rev. David, *O.M.I.* (CC) [RTR] Oblate La Parra Center, Sarita, TX
Ullrich, Very Rev. Msgr. Mark C., '78 (STL) Curia: Leadership Sacred Heart Catholic Church, Florissant, Florissant, MO
Ullrich, Rev. Peter, *O.S.B.* '87 (KC) St Columba Catholic Church Conception Junction, MO, Conception Junction, MO; St. Joseph's, Parnell, MO; [MON] Conception Abbey (Benedictine Monks), Conception, MO
Ulm, Rev. John F., '58 (GAL) Retired.
Ulman, Rev. Stanley A., '73 (DET) Curia: Consultative Bodies; Offices and Directors St. Mary of the Hills, Rochester Hills, Rochester Hills, MI
Ulmer, Rev. Daniel R., '21 (BUF) St. Gregory the Great, Williamsville, NY
Ulrich, Rev. Eugene P., '74 (BUF) Church of the Annunciation, Elma, NY
Ulrich, Rev. John M., *S.M.* '86 (ATL) Our Lady of the Assumption Catholic Church, Brookhaven, Inc., Brookhaven, GA
Ulrick, Rev. Jonathan, *OFM Cap.* '17 (PIT) Our Lady of the Angels, Pittsburgh, PA; St. Maria Goretti Parish, Pittsburgh, PA; [MON] Our Lady of the Angels Friary, Pittsburgh, PA
Ulrick, Rev. Saint-Louis, *O. Carm.* (FAJ) Maria, Madre del Redentor, Luquillo, PR
Ulrick, Rev. Stephen D., '82 (STP) Holy Name of Jesus, Wayzata, MN; [CEM] Holy Name of Jesus Cemetery, Wayzata, MN
Ulshafer, Rev. Thomas, *P.S.S.* '70 (WDC) Retired.
Ulshafer, Rev. Thomas R., *P.S.S.* '70 (BAL) Retired. [MON] Society of St. Sulpice, Province of the United States, Baltimore, MD
Ulto, Rev. Victor A., '80 (PMB) St. Bernadette, Port St. Lucie, FL
Umana, Rev. Pedro, (FRS) Our Lady of Sorrows (Nuestra Señora de Los Dolores), Parlier, CA
Umaña, Rev. Rafael, *I.V.E.* '14 (PHX) Our Lady of Guadalupe Roman Catholic Parish, Guadalupe, AZ
Umberg, Rev. Andrew J., '91 (CIN) Church of the Assumption, Cincinnati, OH; Mother of Christ, Cincinnati, OH; St. Bartholomew, Cincinnati, OH; St. Bernard, Cincinnati, OH; St. Clare, Cincinnati, OH; St. Vivian, Cincinnati, OH
Umbras, Rev. Thomas, *SVD* '81 (CHI) [MON] Divine Word Residence, Techny, IL
Ume, Rev. Michael, '93 (LA) Assumption of the Blessed Virgin Mary, Pasadena, CA
Umeobi, Rev. Jude, '97 (LA) St. Eugene, Los Angeles, CA
Umeokeke, Rev. Damian, (RVC) St. Thomas, the Apostle, West Hempstead, NY
Umeokeke, Rev. Damian, (RVC) Chap, NYU Winthrop Univ Hosp
Umeyor, Rev. Eugene, *C.M.F.* (RVC) Chap, Northwell at Valley Stream (Formerly Franklin); North…
Umeyor, Rev. Eugene Chi Jioke, (RVC) Our Lady of Lourdes, Malverne, NY
Umingli, Rev. Tetzel, '16 (P) St. Rita, Portland, OR
Umoenoh, Rev. Clement, '96 (NY) Chap, New York Presbyterian-Columbia Med Ctr, New York
Umoren, Rev. Linus, *C.M.* '97 (BEL) SS. Peter and Paul, Waterloo, IL; St. Augustine of Canterbury, Hecker, IL
Umoren, Rev. Linus Aniekan, *C.M.* '97 (BEL) [MON] Vincentian Community (Province of Nigeria), Waterloo, IL
Umouyo, Rev. Sebastian, *MSP* (CHL) Our Lady of the Rosary, Lexington, NC
Umukoro, Rev. Fidelis, *O.P.* (WDC) Chap, MedStar National Rehab Hosp, Washington; MedStar…
Umul Chopox, Rev. Alejandro, *M.F.M.* '07 (MIL) Prince of Peace/Principe de Paz Congregation, Milwaukee, WI; St. Rafael the Archangel Congregation, Milwaukee, WI; The St. Vincent a Paulo Congregation, Milwaukee, WI
Umunnakwe, Rev. Eze Venantius, *C.S.Sp.* (DM) Holy Trinity Church of Southeast Warren County, Lacona, IA; Immaculate Conception, St. Marys, IA
Unachukwu, Rev. Arthur, '11 (DAL) Curia: Administration; Offices and Directors Holy Cross Catholic Parish, Dallas, TX; St. Anthony Catholic Parish - Dallas, Dallas, TX
Unachukwu, Rev. Benjamin, *OMV* (SFD) St. Mary's, Alton, IL
Unachukwu, Rev. Christian, *M.S.P.* (AUS) St. Mary, Wimberley, TX
Unakalamba, Rev. Oscar, (SP) St. Anthony of Padua, San Antonio, FL
Underdahl, Rev. Mark J., '96 (STP) St. Francis of Assisi, Lake St. Croix Beach, MN
Underwood, Very Rev. Eric C., '06 (LFT) Curia: Leadership; Miscellaneous / Other Offices St. Francis of Assisi, Muncie, IN; St. Lawrence, Muncie, IN; St. Mary, Muncie, IN
Underwood, Rev. Scott J., *O.S.B.* '76 (NO) [MON] St. Joseph Abbey, St. Benedict, LA
Undralla, Rev. Deva, '97 (OKL) St. Teresa of Avila, Harrah, OK
Ungashick, Rev. Thomas, '76 (Y) Retired.
Unger, Rev. Robert P., '99 (FAR) Retired.
Unger, Rev. Todd, '82 (BAK) Curia: Leadership; Offices and Directors Saint Thomas Catholic Church of Redmond, Inc., Redmond, OR; [ASN] The Health and Retirement Association of the Diocese of Baker, Oregon, Redmond, OR
Universal, Rev. Patrick J., (GLP) (>BO) St. Stephen, Boston, MA
Unlayao, Rev. Jose, *C.J.D.* (LAV) Holy Spirit Catholic Church, Las Vegas, NV
Unni, Rev. John J., '92 (BO) St. Cecilia, Boston, MA
Unoenoh, Rev. Clement, (NY) Chap, Good Samaritan Hosp, Suffern
Unser, Friar Timothy, *O.F.M.Conv.* (SAT) [SEM] San Damiano Friary, Initial House of Formation, San Antonio, TX
Unsworth, Rev. John E., '76 (PRO) Retired.
Untereiner, Rev. Harry P., '72 (PSC) Retired.
Unterreiner, Rev. James J., '70 (SPC) Retired. St. Joseph, Pomona, MO
Unverdorben, Rev. Ernest, *O.C.D.* '66 (MIL) [MON] Discalced Carmelite Friars of Holy Hill, Inc., Hubertus, WI
Unverferth, Rev. Steven R., '89 (BEL) On Leave.
Unz, Rev. Thomas E., '83 (CHI) Retired.
Uong, Rev. Luong, *C.Ss.R.* '95 (SAT) [MON] The Redemptorists/San Antonio, San Antonio, TX
Uong, Rev. Luong, *C.Ss.R.* (SAT) Vietnamese Martyrs Catholic Center, San Antonio, TX
Upah, Rev. Andrew J, '18 (DUB) Mazzuchelli Catholic Middle School, Dubuque, IA; The Church of the Nativity, Dubuque, Iowa, Dubuque, IA; Wahlert High School, Dubuque, IA
Upah, Rev. William J., '98 (R) St. Therese Catholic Parish of Wrightsville, Wrightsville Beach, NC
Upham, Rev. Kevin, '18 (PRT) Cathedral of the Immaculate Conception, Portland, ME; Sacred Heart/ St. Dominic, Portland, ME; St. Christopher's, Peaks Island, ME; St. Louis, Portland, ME; St. Peter's, Portland, ME
Uppena, Rev. Msgr. James J., '68 (MAD) Retired.
Upson, Rev. Michael, '76 (ROC) Retired.
Upton, Rev. Edward F., '69 (CHI) Retired. St. Francis of Assisi, Orland Park, IL
Upton, Rev. Joseph R., '10 (PRO) Church of Saint Mary of the Bay, Warren, RI; Saint Alexander's Church Corporation, Warren, Warren, RI
Urarte Aberasturi, Rev. Carmelo, '59 (ARE) San Raphael, Quebradillas, PR
Urassa, Rev. Edward, (PHX) St. Andrew the Apostle Roman Catholic Parish, Chandler, AZ
Urassa, Rev. Rogatian, '83 (BAK) Curia: Leadership; Offices and Directors Sacred Heart, Klamath Falls, OR
Urban, Rev. Anthony, '11 (SFS) Saint Thomas Aquinas Parish of Lake County, Madison, SD
Urban, Rev. Anthony M., '73 (SCR) Retired.
Urban, Rev. Joseph, '72 (NEW) St. Anthony of Padua, Jersey City, NJ
Urban, Rev. Msgr. Lonnie A., '67 (AUS) Retired.
Urban, Rev. Peter, '58 (DEN) Retired. St. Anthony of Padua Catholic Parish in Denver, Denver, CO; [MIS] Miguel Pro Mission, Denver, CO
Urban, Rev. Reginald A., '77 (DOD) Retired.
Urban, Rev. Thomas E., '02 (DET) Curia: Tribunal
Urbaniak, Rev. Adam, '14 (BLX) Curia: Advisory Boards, Commissions, Committees, and Councils; Miscellaneous / Other Offices Our Lady of Victories, Pascagoula, MS
Urbaniak, Rev. Msgr. Bernard J., '68 (E) Retired. [MIS] St. Hedwig, Erie, PA
Urbaniak, Rev. Lawrence M., '61 (RCK) Retired.
Urbanski, Rev. Louis, '69 (P) Retired.
Urbanski, Rev. Louis, (P) Retired.
Urbina, Rev. Carlos, *O.S.A.* '04 (NY) St. Nicholas of Tolentine, Bronx, NY
Urbina, Rev. Ramon, '22 (OAK) St. Bonaventure, Concord, CA
Urcia, Rev. Daniel C., '89 (SJ) St. Athanasius, Mountain View, CA
Ureel, Rev. Wayne G., '90 (DET) Holy Spirit Parish Highland, Highland, MI
Urell, Rev. Msgr. John, '78 (ORG) Curia: Leadership St. Timothy, Laguna Niguel, CA
Uriarte, Rev. Jose Martin, '15 (TUC) Immaculate Conception & Guadalupe Missions Roman Catholic Parish & Guadalupe Mission - Yuma, Yuma, AZ
Uribe, Rev. Arturo, *C.Ss.R.* '95 (SD) Pastor of Saint Peter the Apostle Catholic Parish, Fallbrook, a corporation sole, Fallbrook, CA
Uribe, Rev. David, *OMI* '14 (WDC) [MIS] Oblate

Missionary Society, Inc., Washington, DC; [MON] Missionary Oblates of Mary Immaculate, Washington, DC
Uribe, Rev. David, *OMI* '14 (BEL) [MON] Missionary Association of Mary Immaculate- USA (MAMI-USA), Belleville, IL; [MON] Shrine of Our Lady of the Snows, Belleville, IL
Uribe, Rev. David Paul, *OMI* '14 (SAT) [MIS] Missionary Oblates of Mary Immaculate - USA (MAMI-USA), San Antonio, TX; [MON] Oblate Benson Residence, San Antonio, TX; [SHR] Oblate Lourdes Grotto Shrine of the Southwest, Tepeyac de San Antonio, San Antonio, TX
Uribe, Rev. Gerardo, (AUS) St. Joseph, Killeen, TX
Uribe, Rev. Rolands, '13 (PAT) Our Lady of Fatima and Saint Nicholas, Passaic, NJ
Urizalqui, Rev. Msgr. Richard, '77 (FRS) St. Aloysius, Tulare, CA
Urmston, Rev. Benjamin J., *S.J.* (DET) [MON] Colombiere Center, Clarkston, MI
Urnick, Rev. Charles B., '74 (NEW) On Duty Outside Diocese. St John the Baptist, Laughlin, NV
Urnick, Rev. Charles B., '74 (LAV) Curia: Advisory Boards, Commissions, Committees, and Councils; Deaneries St. John the Baptist Catholic Church, Laughlin, NV
Urrabazo, Rev. Rosendo, *C.M.F.* '78 (CHI) [MON] Claretian Missionaries U.S.A.-Canada Province, Inc., Chicago, IL
Urrabazo, Rev. Rosendo, *CMF* '78 (LA) [MIS] Claretian Teaching Ministry, Temple CIty, CA; [MIS] Educational and Renewal Center, Inc., ,
Urrea, Rev. Miguel A., '87 (SB) Chap, Arrowhead Rgnl Med Ctr, Colton
Urrego, Rev. Luis F., '01 (SAC) Pastor of Immaculate Conception Parish, Sacramento, a corporation sole, Sacramento, CA
Urrego Restrepo, Rev. Edisson, '17 (R) St. Elizabeth of Hungary, Raeford, NC
Urumolug, Rev. Kenneth, *S.J.* '02 (CI) Curia: Leadership [MON] Jesuit Community of Pohnpei, Kolonia, FM
Usandivaras, Rev. Silvana, (NY) Curia: Leadership
Useche, Rev. Teofilo, '84 (VEN) St. Maximilian Kolbe Parish in Port Charlotte, Inc., Port Charlotte, FL
Usselmann, Rev. Gregory, *LC* '10 (DAL) [MON] Legionaries of Christ, Irving, TX
Ussher, Rev. Henry, '99 (JC) St. Clement, St. Clement, MO; St. Joseph, Louisiana, MO
Ustaski, Rev. William B., *C.R.I.C.* '77 (LA) Retired. [MON] Canons Regular of the Immaculate Conception, Santa Paula, CA
Ustick, Rev. Anthony J., '15 (SP) St. Stephen, Riverview, FL
Utecht, Rev. John Joseph, '22 (STP) Our Lady of Grace, Edina, MN
Uter, Rev. Frank M., '69 (BR) Retired. Curia: Canonical Services
Uthuppu, Rev. Augustine, *M.S.* '88 (HON) Christ the King, Kahului, HI
Utrup, Rev. Eugene E., '59 (STL) Retired.
Utz, Rev. Raymond M., '63 (PIT) Retired. [MON] St. John Vianney Manor, Pittsburgh, PA
Utzig, Rev. Albert, *S.S.C.* '83 (OM) [MON] Missionary Society of St. Columban, St. Columbans, NE
Utzig, Rev. Albert R., *S.S.C.* '83 (SB) St. Mary, Fontana, CA
Uwamungu, Rev. Jean Bosco, '06 (SHP) St. Patrick, Lake Providence, LA
Uwamungu, Rev. Jean Bosco, '06 (SHP) Sacred Heart, Oak Grove, LA
Uwandu, Rev. Anthony, '02 (NEW) Saint Joseph Parish, East Orange, NJ
Uwandu, Rev. Marcellinus U., (MO) Curia: Offices and Directors
Uwasomba, Rev. Benet, (RVC) St. Matthew, Dix Hills, NY
Uy, Rev. Anthony, *F.S.S.P.* '13 (LIN) [SEM] Our Lady of Guadalupe Seminary, Inc., Denton, NE
Uytingco, Rev. Anthony, '12 (SJ) St. Lawrence, the Martyr, Santa Clara, CA
Uzar, Rev. Joseph, '21 (PIT) St. Andrew the Apostle, Donora, PA
Uzondu, Rev. Gabriel C., '01 (TYL) St. Kateri Tekakwitha Church, Buffalo, TX
Uzoukwu, Rev. Samuel, (BAL) [HOS] University of Maryland St. Joseph Medical Center, Towson, MD
Uzuegbu, Rev. Kelechi, '09 (JC) St. Francis Xavier, Taos, MO
Uzuegbunam, Rev. Benjamin, '92 (RVC) Chap, Northwell at Plainview
Uzukwu, Rev. Eugene, *C.S.Sp.* (PIT) [COL] Duquesne University of the Holy Spirit, Pittsburgh, PA
Uzzilio, Rev. Robert A., '65 (BGP) Retired.
Vacca, Rev. Daniel L., '95 (WCH) On Duty Outside Diocese. (>JC) St. Anthony, Camdenton, MO
Vaccarella, Rev. Samuel, *T.O.R.* '77 (ALT) [MON] St. Francis Friary at Mount Assisi, Loretto, PA
Vaccari, Rev. Msgr. Andrew J., '86 (BRK) Curia: Consultative Bodies St. Mary Mother of Jesus, Brooklyn, NY
Vaccari, Rev. Msgr. Peter I., '77 (BRK) On Duty Outside Diocese. 201 Seminary Ave., Yonkers, 10704 (>NY) [MIS] Catholic Near East Welfare Association (CNEWA), New York, NY
Vaccari, Rev. Msgr. Peter I., '77 (RVC) Curia: Leadership
Vaccaro, Rev. Christopher T., '08 (ARL) Curia: Offices and Directors [CAM] University of Mary Washington, Fredericksburg, VA
Vaccaro, Rev. Stephen M., (ARL) Sacred Heart of Jesus, Winchester, VA
Vacek, Rev. Carl, *T.O.R.* '79 (ALT) Our Lady of Mt. Carmel, Altoona, PA
Vacek, Rev. Carl E., *T.O.R.* '79 (MO) Curia: Offices and Directors
Vacek, Rev. Edward, *S.J.* '73 (NO) [COL] Loyola University New Orleans, New Orleans, LA; [MON] Loyola Jesuit Community, New Orleans, LA
Vacek, Rev. Stephen, '17 (VIC) Holy Cross, Bay City, TX
Vadakara, Rev. Antony, *CMI* (BIR) St. John the Baptist Catholic Parish, Madison, Madison, AL
Vadakemuriyil, Rev. Thomas John, *CMI* '92 (NY) [NUR] Cabrini of Westchester, Dobbs Ferry, NY
Vadakemury, Rev. Thomas, *CMI* '92 (PBL) [HOS] Centura Health-St. Mary-Corwin Medical Center, Pueblo, CO
Vadakkedath, Rev. Clement, *C.Ss.R.* '90 (BAL) St. Mary, Annapolis, MD
Vadakkekara, Rev. J. Philip, '69 (MET) Retired.
Vadakkumcherry, Rev. Johnson, (PHX) Corpus Christi Roman Catholic Parish, Phoenix, AZ
Vadakumkara, Rev. Shijo, '04 (OWN) St. Lawrence, Philpot, KY; St. William, Philpot, KY
Vadakumpadan, Rev. Saju M., *C.M.I.* '92 (L) Curia: Leadership Our Lady of Perpetual Help, Campbellsville, KY; Our Lady of the Hills, Finley, KY
Vadana, Rev. Kuriakose Chacko, *M.S.T.* '81 (SYM) Lourdes Matha Syro-Malabar Catholic Church, Raleigh/Durham, North Carolina of St. Thomas Malabar Catholic Diocese of Chicago, Apex, NC
Vaeth, Rev. Paul, *C.P.* (NY) Retired. [MON] The Congregation of the Passion - St. Paul of the Cross Province, Jamaica, NY
Vaeth, Rev. Paul, *C.P.* '68 (BRK) Retired. [MON] Immaculate Conception Monastery, Jamaica, NY
Vagenas, Rev. William, '12 (JOL) On Leave.
Vaghetto, Rev. Benedetto P., '78 (PIT) Curia: Consultative Bodies; Tribunal
Vaghi, Rev. Msgr. Peter J., '85 (WDC) Curia: Consultative Bodies Little Flower, Bethesda, MD; [COL] Catholic University of America, The, Washington, DC; [MIS] The John Carroll Society, Glen Echo, MD
Vaglienty, Rev. Felipe, '00 (CHI) Most Blessed Trinity, Waukegan, IL
Vahi, Rev. Salvador, '85 (POD) Curia: Clergy and Religious Services
Vahi, Rev. Salvador S., '85 (WDC) [MIS] Prelature of the Holy Cross and Opus Dei, Washington, DC
Vahling, Rev. Dominic B., '20 (SFD) On Special Assignment. Cathedral of the Immaculate Conception, Springfield, IL
Vaillancourt, Rev. Mark G., '94 (NY) Curia: Leadership John F. Kennedy Catholic High School (Diocesan Priests, Sisters of the Divine Compassion), Somers, NY; St. Mary of the Assumption, Katonah, NY; [SEM] St. Joseph's Seminary, Yonkers, NY
Vaillancourt, Rev. Raymond, *M.S.* '89 (FR) Retired. [MON] La Salette Shrine & Retreat Center, Attleboro, MA
Vaillant, Rev. Luc-Marie, *C.B.* (DEN) St. Catherine of Siena Catholic Parish in Denver, Denver, CO
Vainavicz, Rev. Anthony C., '61 (GR) Retired.
Vakapadath Xavier, Rev. Junesh, (PMB) St. Joan of Arc, Boca Raton, FL
Vakayil, Rev. Joseph Varghese, '78 (CC) Retired.
Vala, Rev. Thomas M., '09 (TR) St. Clement, Matawan, NJ
Valabazzi, Rev. Ashok, *HGN* (IND) Holy Trinity Catholic Church, Edinburgh, Inc., Edinburgh, IN; Our Lady of the Greenwood Catholic Church, Inc., Greenwood, IN
Valadao, Rev. Marc, (SFR) [SEM] St. Patrick's Seminary and University (The Roman Catholic Seminary of San Francisco), Menlo Park, CA
Valadez, Rev. Arturo, '88 (LA) Holy Spirit, Los Angeles, CA
Valadez, Very Rev. Eli, '14 (SFE) Curia: Offices and Directors Our Lady of Guadalupe-Clovis, Clovis, NM
Valayath, Rev. Jacob John, '99 (CC) St. James, Beeville, TX; [HOS] CHRISTUS Spohn Hospital Beeville, Beeville, TX
Valbuena, Rev. Luis, (SAT) Retired. [NUR] Oblate Madonna Residence, San Antonio, TX
Valcin, Rev. Fritzner, '99 (COL) St. Francis of Assisi, Columbus, OH; [MIS] Haitian Catholic Coalition of Ohio, Columbus, OH
Valdazo, Rev. Stephen, '58 (BRK) Retired. St. Joan of Arc, Jackson Heights, NY
Valdepenas, Rev. Danilo, '88 (SD) Chap, Kaiser Permanente Med Ctr; Sharp Grossmont Hosp Pastor of Saint Anthony of Padua Catholic Parish, Imperial, a corporation sole, Imperial, CA; [MIS] Saint Anthony of Padua Catholic Parish Imperial in Imperial, CA Real Property Support Corporation, Imperial, CA
Valderrama, Rev. Viliulfo, '96 (TUC) Our Lady of Fatima Roman Catholic Parish - Tucson, Tucson, AZ
Valdes, Rev. Juan Jose, '91 (IND) St. Anthony Catholic Church, Indianapolis, Inc., Indianapolis, IN
Valdez, Rev. Alfredo, (SLC) Cathedral of the Madeleine LLC 202, Salt Lake City, UT
Valdez, Rev. John, '91 (AMA) Curia: Advisory Boards, Commissions, Committees, and Councils; Consultative Bodies; Offices and Directors St. Thomas the Apostle, Amarillo, TX
Valdez, Rev. Jose, *MSC* '95 (FRS) St. Jude Thaddeus, Earlimart, CA
Valdez, Rev. Pat, *C.R.* '75 (PBL) On Leave.
Valdez, Rev. Paul R., '82 (MRY) Retired. Curia: Advisory Boards, Commissions, Committees, and Councils
Valdez, Rev. Pedro, (LA) St. Paschal Baylon, Thousand Oaks, CA
Valdez, Rev. Pedro, (LA) St. Pius X, Santa Fe Springs, CA
Valdez, Rev. Raul Adrian, '04 (ORL) St. Jude Catholic Community, Ocala, FL
Valdez, Rev. Victor, '14 (SAT) St. Rose of Lima, San Antonio, TX
Valdez Vargas, Rev. Jaime, (DEN) Immaculate Conception Catholic Parish in Lafayette, Lafayette, CO
Valdivia, Rev. Msgr. Antonio, '63 (OAK) Retired. St. Cornelius, Richmond, CA
Valencheck, Rev. John A., '98 (CLV) St. Sebastian, Akron, OH
Valencia, Rev. Alan, '15 (TUC) Saint Augustine Cathedral Roman Catholic Parish - Tucson, Tucson, AZ; [EFT] Catholic Foundation for the Diocese of Tucson Stewardship and Charitable Giving, Tucson, AZ
Valencia, Rev. Ariel A., '03 (RCK) On Special Assignment. Curia: Offices and Directors St. Patrick, Rockford, IL
Valencia, Rev. Braulio, '87 (MRY) Sacred Heart/St. Benedict Catholic Community, Hollister, CA
Valencia, Rev. Cesar, *PES* (SFS) Holy Family Parish of Davison County, Mitchell, SD; Holy Spirit Parish of Davison County, Mitchell, SD
Valencia, Rev. Gerardo Barajas, '22 (MRY) Madonna Del Sasso, Salinas, CA
Valencia, Rev. Jose R., '14 (NEW) Holy Spirit, Union, NJ
Valencia, Rev. Junee, (AGN) Our Lady of the Purification, Maina, GU
Valencia, Rev. Mario, '10 (SR) Pastor of St. Sebastian Catholic Church of Sebastopol, A Corporation Sole, Sebastopol, CA
Valencia, Rev. Mario, '10 (SR) Curia: Offices and Directors
Valencia, Rev. Raul Posada, (BIR) Sacred Heart of Jesus Catholic Parish, Cullman, Cullman, AL
Valencia, Rev. Victor, '93 (STP) St. Jerome, Maplewood, MN
Valencia Obando, Rev. Sebastian, '18 (NEW) St. Michael, Cranford, NJ
Valentine, Rev. Benjamin P, '22 (DUB) St. Boniface Church, Garner, Iowa, Garner, IA; St. James Catholic Church, Forest City, Iowa, Forest City, IA; St. Patrick Church, Britt, Iowa, Britt, IA; St. Patrick's Church, Buffalo Center, Iowa, Buffalo Center, IA; St. Patrick's Church, Lake Mills, Iowa, Lake Mills, IA; St. Wenceslaus Church, Duncan, Iowa, Britt, IA
Valentine, Rev. Joseph, *FSSP* '93 (TYL) St. Joseph the Worker Catholic Church, Tyler, TX
Valentine, Rev. Richard A., '74 (PRO) St. Michael's Church, Georgiaville, Rhode Island, Smithfield, RI
Valentine, Rev. Msgr. Timothy, (RVC) St. Mary's, Roslyn, NY

Valentini, Rev. Marco, '94 (MIL) St. John Vianney Congregation, Brookfield, WI
Valentino, Rev. Msgr. Frederick A., '50 (TR) Retired.
Valenton, Rev. Randy S., '06 (SJ) Chap, Santa Clara Valley Med Ctr; O'Connor Hosp
Valentyn, Rev. Scott, '16 (GB) Sacred Heart Parish, Shawano, WI; St. Martin of Tours Catholic Parish, Cecil, WI
Valenzuela, Rev. Cristian, *S.J.S.* '19 (MAD) Corpus Christi Parish, Boscobel, WI, Boscobel, WI; [MIS] St. John Nepomuc, Muscoda, WI; [MIS] St. Lawrence O'Toole, Mount Hope, WI; [MIS] St. Mary, ,
Valenzuela, Very Rev. James Paul, '05 (PT) Curia: Leadership Cathedral of the Sacred Heart, Pensacola, FL; St. Anthony of Padua, Pensacola, FL
Valenzuela, Rev. John F., *C.R.S.* (CHR) St. John, North Charleston, SC
Valenzuela Salazar, Rev. Ismael, (SB) Holy Innocents, Victorville, CA
Valera, Very Rev. Edmundo, '02 (PBL) Curia: Leadership; Offices and Directors St. Paul the Apostle, Pueblo West, CO
Valera, Rev. Ramon G., '75 (LA) St. John Baptist de la Salle, Granada Hills, CA
Valerio Romero, Rev. Luis, '10 (CHI) Jesus, Shepherd of Souls, Calumet City, IL
Valero Castillo, Rev. Ysidro Giber, (SJN) Retired.
Valit, Rev. Robert L., '61 (STP) Retired.
Valiyaparampil, Rev. Sebastian, (SYM) Bl. Chavara Syro-Malabar Catholic Mission (Bakersfield), San Fernando, CA; St. Alphonsa Syro-Malabar Catholic Church of Los Angeles, San Fernando, CA
Valko, Rev. Msgr. George J., '77 (ALT) Retired.
Vallabhaneni, Rev. Mariadas, '03 (SUP) St. Francis Xavier, Merrill, WI; St. John the Baptist, Gleason, WI
Valladares, Rev. Alejandro E., '00 (MOB) Curia: Leadership St. Bede the Venerable Catholic Church, Montgomery, AL
Vallamattam, Rev. George Johnson, '98 (CC) St. Joseph, Port Aransas, TX
Vallayil, Rev. Abraham, *C.M.I.* '76 (NY) St. Catharine, Blauvelt, NY
Valle, Rev. Angel, '08 (MGZ) Church of San Isidro, Sabana Grande, PR
Valle, Rev. Miguel, '95 (TR) St. Paul, Princeton, NJ
Valle, Rev. Miguel A., (ARL) St. Anthony, Falls Church, VA
Valle Alvarez, Rev. Jose de Jesus, *MSC* '99 (FRS) St. Jude Thaddeus, Earlimart, CA
Valle Diaz, Rev. Kevin Esau, '17 (NEW) On Duty Outside Diocese. Casa Santa Marta, Roma
Vallecillo, Rev. Tony S., '14 (SFR) Our Lady of Loretto, Novato, CA
Vallee, Rev. Robert, '87 (MIA) Carrollton School of the Sacred Heart, Miami, FL
Vallejo, Rev. Msgr. Arquimedes, '89 (RCK) On Special Assignment. Curia: Leadership; Offices and Directors; Tribunal St. Joseph, Elgin, IL
Vallejo, Rev. Gilberto, '02 (SAT) Curia: Leadership St. Brigid, San Antonio, TX
Vallejo, Rev. Jorge Mario, (BRK) Blessed Sacrament - Saint Sylvester, Brooklyn, NY; Holy Child Jesus, Richmond Hill, NY
Vallejo, Rev. William E., '96 (RCK) St. Monica, Carpentersville, IL
Vallejo Garcia, Rev. Amado, '10 (FWT) On Leave.
Vallelonga, Very Rev. J. Stephen, '90 (WH) Curia: Leadership; Offices and Directors Parkersburg Catholic Elementary School, Parkersburg, WV; St. Margaret Mary, Parkersburg, WV
Valle-Reyes, Rev. Tomas Del, '79 (NY) [MIS] Descubriendo El Siglo XXI, Inc. (Discovering XXI Century Inc.), New York, NY
Valliamthadathil, Rev. George, *M.S.F.S.* (NY) St. Paul the Apostle, Yonkers, NY
Vallier, Rev. John F., '87 (GR) Curia: Leadership St. John Vianney, Wyoming, MI
Valliere, Rev. Laurent, (FR) Our Lady of the Assumption, Osterville, MA; Our Lady of Victory, Centerville, MA
Valliparambil, Rev. Jose, '83 (GF) St. Raphael, Glasgow, MT
Vallone, Rev. Louis F., '73 (PIT) Retired. Curia: Consultative Bodies Archangel Gabriel, McKees Rocks, PA
Valls, Rev. Richard, '57 (KAL) Retired.
Valmorida, Rev. Mario, '83 (SAC) Pastor of Holy Family Parish, Weed, a corporation sole, Weed, CA; Pastor of St. John the Evangelist Parish, Dunsmuir, a corporation sole, Mount Shasta, CA
Valomchalil, Rev. Augusty, *MSSCC* '96 (OWN) St. Mary Magdalene, Owensboro, KY
Valone, Rev. Fred W., '94 (GAL) St. Thomas the Apostle, Huntsville, TX
Valoret, Rev. Joseph, '83 (MIA) Retired.
Val-Serra, Rev. Andres, *S.J.* (SJN) San Ignacio de Loyola, San Juan, PR
Valvano, Rt. Rev. Melvin J., *O.S.B.* '65 (NEW) [MON] Benedictine Abbey of Newark, Newark, NJ
Valverde, Rev. German, (ARE) Christ the King, Corozal, PR
Valverde, Rev. William, (SB) Retired.
Vamos, Rev. Joseph E., '66 (GRY) Retired.
Van Abel, Rev. John W., '72 (MIL) Retired.
Van Alstine, Very Rev. Mark N., '05 (SAV) Curia: Leadership Aquinas High School, Augusta, GA; St. Joseph, Augusta, GA
Van Alstyne, Rev. Donald J., *M.I.C.* '81 (MO) Curia: Offices and Directors
Van Alstyne, Rev. Robert, '19 (BO) [MON] The Jesuit Community at Boston College, Chestnut Hill, MA
Van Assche, Rev. Jacob A., '15 (DET) St. Damien of Molokai Parish Pontiac, Pontiac, MI
Van Beek, Rev. Alois, '73 (MIL) Retired.
Van Beek, Rev. Dennis E., '69 (MIL) Retired.
Van Dam, Rev. Luis, (LAV) St. Elizabeth Ann Seton, Las Vegas, NV; [MON] Canons Regular of Jesus the Lord of Nevada, Inc., Las Vegas, NV
Van Damme, Rev. Larry P., '93 (MAR) Curia: Advisory Boards, Commissions, Committees, and Councils; Organizations (affiliated, inter-Diocesan, miscellaneous/ other) St. Anthony, Gwinn, MI; St. Paul, Negaunee, MI; [EFT] Negaunee St. Paul Endowment Fund, Negaunee, MI
Van Daniker, Rev. Derek, *S.D.B.* '09 (NEW) [MON] The Salesian Community, Orange, NJ
Van Dau, Rev. Peter Minh, *O.F.M.* (CHI) [MON] St. Peter's Friary, Chicago, IL
van de Crommert, Rev. Paul H., '88 (NU) Holy Rosary, North Mankato, MN
Van De Loo, Rev. Willard J., '55 (GB) Retired.
Van De Moortell, Rev. Raymond, '76 (BO) St. Adelaide, Peabody, MA; St. Ann, Peabody, MA
Van de Paer, Rev. John, *C.I.C.M.* '47 (ARL) Retired.
Van De Water, Rev. Richard, (SFR) Curia: Offices and Directors St. Thomas More, San Francisco, CA
Van Del, Rev. Curtis E., *S.J.* '65 (STL) Retired.
Van der Woerd, Rev. Albert, (LA) St. Mark, Venice, CA
Van Deuren, Rev. John H., '59 (GB) Retired.
Van Do, Rev. (Michael M.) Quang, *CRM* '93 (SPC) [MON] Congregation of the Mother of the Redeemer, Carthage, MO
Van Dorn, Rev. James, *O.F.M.Conv.* '67 (STP) [MON] St. Joseph Cupertino Friary, Prior Lake, MN; [RTR] Franciscan Retreats and Spirituality Center, Prior Lake, MN
Van Dyke, Rev. James, *SJ* '93 (WDC) Georgetown Preparatory School, North Bethesda, MD; [MON] The Jesuit Community at Georgetown University, Washington, DC
Van Dynhoven, Rev. William J., '12 (GB) On Sick Leave.
Van Fossen, Rev. Brian F., '05 (SCR) Chap, Lycoming College, Williamsport Our Lady of Mount Carmel, Hunlock Creek, PA
Van Guilder, Rev. Alphonse, *OFM Conv.* '64 (MRY) St. Paul the Apostle, Pismo Beach, CA
Van Haight, Rev. Christopher C., *O.F.M.* '08 (PAT) [MON] St. Anthony Friary (Order of Friars Minor), Butler, NJ
Van Haverbeke, Rev. Kenneth S., '91 (WCH) St. Vincent de Paul, Andover, KS
Van Heusen, Rev. Ian C., '15 (R) St. Peter's, Greenville, NC; [CAM] Campbell University Catholic Campus Ministry, Raleigh, NC; [CAM] Newman Catholic Student Center at East Carolina University, Greenville, NC
Van House, Rev. Joseph, *O.Cist.* '09 (DAL) [MON] Our Lady of Dallas Cistercian Abbey, Irving, TX
Van Kempen, Rev. Robert, '93 (FTW) St. Mary of the Annunciation, Bristol, IN
Van Kuren, Rev. Corey S., '86 (SY) Retired. Chap & Dir, UHS, Binghamton Gen Hosp; Wilson Mem Hosp, John… The Catholic Community of St. Stephen-St. Patrick, Whitney Point, NY
Van Lian, Rev. Michael, '10 (KCK) St. Patrick's, Kansas City, KS
Van Loon, Rev. Msgr. Neil J., '79 (SCR) Curia: Leadership
Van Loon, Rev. Msgr. Neil J., '79 (SCR) St. Paul, Scranton, PA
Van Massenhove, Rev. David L., '83 (SLC) Retired.
Van Minh Pham, Rev. Bartholomew M., *CRM* '77 (SPC) [MON] Congregation of the Mother of the Redeemer, Carthage, MO
Van Nguyen, Rev. Joseph Son, '82 (DAL) Immaculate Conception Catholic Parish - Grand Prairie, Grand Prairie, TX
Van Nguyen, Rev. Long, *SVD* (SB) [RTR] Divine Word Province/ Retreat Center, Riverside, CA
Van Nguyen, Rev. Stephan Hoa, *O.Cist.* (SB) [MON] The Cistercian Congregation of the Holy Family, St. Joseph Monastery, Lucerne Valley, CA
Van Nguyen, Rev. Te, (SFR) Retired. St. Monica - St. Thomas the Apostle Parish, San Francisco, CA
Van Nguyen, Rev. Tuyen, '87 (ORG) Blessed Sacrament, Westminster, CA
Van Oosbree, Rev. Christian J., '92 (SC) On Leave.
Van Oss, Rev. James R., '64 (BEL) Retired.
Van Overbeek, Rev. Gerald J., *O.S.A.* '65 (CHI) [MON] St. Rita Monastery, Chicago, IL
Van Pham, Rev. Hanh, '92 (CC) Curia: Leadership Saint Andrew By the Sea Parish, Corpus Christi, TX
Van Pham, Rev. Phien, '77 (SD) Pastor of Holy Spirit Catholic Parish, San Diego, a corporation sole, San Diego, CA
Van Phuong, Rev. Msgr. Francis Pham, '66 (ATL) Retired.
Van Sloun, Rev. Michael, '95 (STP) Retired. Curia: Clergy and Religious Services
Van Smoorenburg, Rev. Matthew, *L.C.* '94 (ATL) St. Brendan Catholic Church, Cumming, Inc., Cumming, GA; [MON] Legionaries of Christ, Incorporated, Cumming, GA
Van Tassell, Rev. Malachi, *T.O.R.* '04 (ALT) [MIS] American Parish Youth Center, Inc., Loretto, PA
Van Tassell, Rev. Malachi, *T.O.R.* '04 (ALT) [COL] St. Francis University, Loretto, PA; [MON] Sacred Heart Friary, Loretto, PA
Van Thanh, Rev. Louis M., '94 (NY) Holy Innocents, New York, NY
Van Thien, Rev. James Nguyen, *C.M.C.* '08 (HT) Thanh Gia, Morgan City, LA
Van Tran, Rev. Thinh, *O.F.M.* (FBK) Curia: Leadership
Van Tran, Rev. Tri, '02 (JOL) Queenship of Mary, Glen Ellyn, IL; Resurrection Catholic Church, Wayne, IL
Van Vlaenderen, Rev. Leonard S., '88 (MIL) Retired.
Van Vliet, Rev. Charles, *F.S.S.P.* (GAL) Regina Caeli, Houston, TX
Van Vurst, Rev. James, *O.F.M.* '61 (CIN) Retired.
Van Wagner, Rev. Bill, '19 (MAD) St. Joseph, Dodgeville, WI
Van Wiel, Rev. John E., *C.S.V.* '66 (CHI) [MON] Viatorian Province Center-Clerics of St. Viator, Arlington Heights, IL
Van Winkle, Rev. Charles, *C.S.C.* '78 (AUS) Retired.
Van Winkle, Rev. Charles E., *CSC* (FTW) Retired. [MIS] Holy Cross House, Notre Dame, IN
Van Wormer, Rev. Giles, *O.F.M.Conv.* '57 (ALB) [MON] Immaculate Conception Friary - Order of Friars Minor Conventual, Rensselaer, NY
Vanasse, Rev. Bernard, '78 (FR) Retired. [NUR] Marian Manor Inc., Taunton, MA
VanBerkum, Rev. Anthony, *OP* '20 (PRO) Curia: Leadership Saint Pius V Church, Providence, Rhode Island, Providence, RI
VanBerkum, Rev. Anthony, *O.P.* '20 (WDC) St. Dominic Church & Priory, Washington, DC
Vance, Rev. Msgr. Charles P., '70 (PH) Retired. On Special Assignment. Dean, Deanery 7, St Philip Neri Rectory, Lafayette Hill St. Philip Neri, Lafayette Hill, PA
Vance, Rev. James L., '63 (SFE) Retired.
Vandehey, Rev. Kelly M., *J.C.L.* '96 (MRY) Sacred Heart, Salinas, CA
Vanden Boogard, Rev. Steven J., *O. Praem.* '65 (GB) Retired. [MON] St. Norbert Abbey, De Pere, WI
Vanden Branden, Rev. Bradley R., *O. Praem.* '16 (GB) [MIS] NORBERT & CO., De Pere, WI; [MON] St. Norbert Abbey, De Pere, WI; [RTR] Norbertine Center for Spirituality, De Pere, WI
Vanden Hogen, Rev. Msgr. James, '64 (GB) Retired.
Vanden Hogen, Rev. Paul, '54 (GB) Retired.
Vandenakker, Rev. Roger, (GAL) [MON] The Companions of The Cross, Houston, TX
Vandenberg, Rev. Thomas L., '62 (SEA) Retired. Curia: Leadership
VanDenBroeke, Rev. Nicholas William, (STP) Holy Cross Catholic School, Webster, MN
VanDenBroeke, Rev. Nicholas William, '12 (STP) Immaculate Conception, Lonsdale, MN; [CEM] Calvary Cemetery, Lonsdale, MN
Vander Heyden, Rev. William F., '70 (GB) Retired.
Vander Laan, Rev. James R., '13 (GR) Curia: Leadership Christ the King-St. Francis de Sales, Howard City, MI
Vander Steeg, Rev. Mark P., '99 (GB) St. Bernard, Green Bay, WI
Vander Werff, Rev. William R., '15 (GR) Curia: Leadership; Offices and Directors St. Mary, Spring

Lake, MI
Vander Woude, Rev. Thomas P., '92 (ARL) Holy Trinity, Gainesville, VA
Vanderbeek, Rev. Michael, *LC* (CHI) Everest Academy of Lemont, Inc., Lemont, IL
Vanderberg, Rev. Joseph, '89 (SCL) Sacred Heart, Glenwood, MN; St. Bartholomew's, Glenwood, MN; St. John Nepomuk Catholic Church (Lake Reno), Lowry, MN
Vanderholt, Rev. Msgr. James, '57 (BEA) Retired.
Vanderkolk, Rev. Peter J., '83 (LFT) Sacred Heart of Jesus, Fowler, IN; St. Charles, Otterbein, IN; St. John the Baptist, Earl Park, IN; St. Mary, Ambia, IN; St. Patrick, Oxford, IN
VanderLaan, Rev. James, (GR) St. Bernadette of Lourdes-St. Margaret Mary Alacoque, Stanton, MI
Vanderlin, Rev. Philip, *O.S.B.* '70 (CHY) Our Lady of the Mountains, Jackson, WY
VanderLoop, Rev. Tony, '03 (STP) Guardian Angels, Chaska, MN; St. Nicholas, Carver, MN; [CEM] Church of Saint Henry Cemetery, Monticello, MN
VanDerveer, Rev. Scott, '13 (ALB) Curia: Offices and Directors St. Mary, Glens Falls, NY
VanderWeyst, Rev. Peter, '07 (SCL) Church of St. Ann, Brandon, MN; Church of St. William, Parkers Prairie, MN; Sacred Heart, Parkers Prairie, MN; Seven Dolors, Brandon, MN
Vandewalle, Rev. Matthew J., '00 (LIN) St. John Nepomucene, Weston, NE
VanDoan, Rev. Vincent, '86 (LAN) Curia: (>MO) Offices and Directors Immaculate Conception Parish Milan, Milan, MI
Vandorpe, Rev. John, '22 (ATL) [MIS] Legionaries of Christ, Atlanta, GA
Vanecko, Rev. William, '65 (CHI) Retired.
Vanegas, Rev. Albeyro, *C.S.V.* '90 (CHI) [MON] Viatorian Province Center-Clerics of St. Viator, Arlington Heights, IL
VanFossen, Rev. Brian, (SCR) Curia: Leadership
VanHoose, Rev. Chad, (STP) St. Jude of the Lake, Mahtomedi, MN
Vanin, Rev. Dino, *PIME* '72 (DET) San Francesco (Italian) Parish Clinton Township, Clinton Township, MI
Vaniyapurackal, Rev. George, (STA) St. Paul's, Jacksonville, FL
VanKuren, Rev. Corey, (SY) Retired.
VanLente, Rev. Richard, '66 (GR) Retired.
VanLieshout, Very Rev. Peter D., '14 (ROC) Curia: Clergy and Religious Services Sacred Heart Cathedral, Rochester, NY
Vannicola, Rev. Michael C., *O.S.F.S.* (WIL) [MON] Wilmington-Philadelphia Province of the Oblates of St. Francis de Sales, Wilmington, DE
Vanorny, Rev. Ed, '98 (RC) Retired. Cathedral of Our Lady of Perpetual Help, Rapid City, SD
vanRooyen, Rev. Pieter, '10 (LAN) St. Joseph Parish Ypsilanti, Ypsilanti, MI
Vanthu, Rev. Joseph N., '71 (SJ) Retired. On Special Assignment. [MIS] Vietnamese Catholic Center, San Jose, CA; [MIS] Vietnamese Ministry, San Jose, CA
Vanyo, Rev. Dan, '12 (PHX) Curia: Offices and Directors San Francisco de Asis Roman Catholic Parish, Flagstaff, AZ
Vanzillotta, Rev. Gino, *O.M.* '54 (LA) [MON] Minim Fathers, Los Angeles, CA
Vap, Rev. Msgr. Ivan F., '54 (LIN) Retired.
Varano, Rev. Andrew R., '58 (BRK) Retired.
Varaparla, Rev. Kishore Babu, *H.G.N.* '13 (WH) Immaculate Conception, Fairmont, WV
Varela, Rev. Enrique, (CHI) [MON] Sant'Angelo Community at St. Cyril Priory, Chicago, IL
Varela, Rev. Mariano O., *I.V.E.* (FR) Curia: Offices and Directors Our Lady of the Immaculate Conception, New Bedford, MA; St. Anthony of Padua's, New Bedford, MA
Varela Delgadillo, Rev. Francisco J., (SB) Our Lady of Guadalupe, San Bernardino, CA
Varela-Nungaray, Rev. Enrique, *O.Carm.* '08 (JOL) Our Lady of Mount Carmel, Joliet, IL
Varettoni, Rev. Msgr. Julian B., '55 (PAT) Retired.
Varga, Rev. Wayne F., '74 (PAT) St. James the Greater, Montague, NJ; St. Thomas the Apostle, Sandyston, NJ
Vargas, Rev. Agapito Antonio, *M.SS.CC.* (SJN) Curia: Offices and Directors
Vargas, Rev. Alberto E., (SAG) Curia: Offices and Directors Saint Francis of Assisi Parish of Saginaw, Saginaw, MI
Vargas, Rev. Alex J., '02 (PMB) St. Thomas More, Boynton Beach, FL
Vargas, Rev. Alfredo, *CMF* '94 (LA) St. Athanasius, Long Beach, CA
Vargas, Rev. Carlos E., '10 (ATL) St. John Paul II Catholic Mission, Gainesville, GA
Vargas, Rev. David, '02 (ORL) Holy Redeemer, Kissimmee, FL
Vargas, Rev. Dennis, '01 (RCK) Nativity of the Blessed Virgin Mary, Menominee, IL; St. Mary, East Dubuque, IL
Vargas, Rev. Guadalupe, '16 (FRS) St. Brigid, Hanford, CA
Vargas, Rev. John C., *C.Ss.R.* '78 (BR) Retired. Congregation Of St. Gerard Majella Roman Catholic Church, Parish Of East Baton Rouge, Louisiana, Baton Rouge, LA; [MIS] Redemptorist Fathers of Baton Rouge, Inc., Baton Rouge, LA; [MON] St. Gerard Residence, Baton Rouge, LA
Vargas, Rev. Leonel M., '91 (ORG) Our Lady of Guadalupe, La Habra, CA
Vargas, Rev. Luis, '98 (SJ) Sacred Heart of Jesus, San Jose, CA
Vargas, Rev. Luis, '01 (WIN) St. Francis of Assisi, Rochester, MN
Vargas, Rev. Luis A., *T.O.R.* '98 (NEW) Immaculate Heart of Mary, Newark, NJ
Vargas, Rev. Osmin, '03 (BRK) Our Lady of Sorrows, Corona, NY
Vargas Acevedo, Rev. German A., *C.S.* (BO) St. Tarcisius, Framingham, MA
Vargas Cruz, Friar Gerardo Antonio, *O.F.M.* (SJN) Curia: Leadership San Jose Obrero, Toa Baja, PR
Vargas La Rosa, Rev. Jorge Santiago, (LSC) Our Lady of Guadalupe Parish, Inc., Hobbs, NM
Vargas Oliveras, Rev. Jose Carlos, '92 (PCE) Curia: Offices and Directors
Vargas Oliveras, Rev. Jose Carlos, (PCE) Curia: Leadership La Milagrosa, Ponce, PR
Vargas Oliveras, Rev. José Carlos, (PCE) El Buen Pastor, Ponce, PR
Vargas-Castro, Rev. Bernardo, *M.M.A.* '19 (SAM) [MON] Maronite Monks of Adoration - Most Holy Trinity Monastery, Petersham, MA
Vargese, Rev. Joseph, '12 (LFT) Our Lady of Mount Carmel, Carmel, IN
Varghese, Rev. Abihlash, *O.F.M.Cap.* '19 (WDC) [SEM] St. Francis Friary-Capuchin College, Washington, DC
Varghese, Rev. Abraham, '03 (ALX) Holy Ghost Catholic Church, Marksville, LA
Varghese, Rev. Aji, (MCE) Curia: Advisory Boards, Commissions, Committees, and Councils
Varghese, Rev. Antony Chooravady, *C.F.I.C.* '96 (COL) St. Elizabeth, Columbus, OH
Varghese, Rev. Biju, '04 (MCE) Curia: Advisory Boards, Commissions, Committees, and Councils St. Jude Malankara Catholic Church, Saratoga, CA
Varghese, Rev. Biju, '04 (SJ) Sacred Heart, Saratoga, CA
Varghese, Rev. Binu, *O.Praem* (JOL) St. Philip the Apostle, Addison, IL
Varghese, Rev. C. P., '94 (GI) St. Patrick's, Sidney, NE
Varghese, Rev. Christhudasan, *H.G.N.* '11 (STO) Holy Family Church (Pastor of), Modesto, CA
Varghese, Rev. Jacob, *V.C.* '92 (COV) Curia: Advisory Boards, Commissions, Committees, and Councils Sts. Peter and Paul, California, KY
Varghese, Rev. Jimson, *S.D.V.* '16 (ORL) St. Patrick's, Mount Dora, FL
Varghese, Rev. Josekutty, '92 (HT) St. John the Evangelist, Thibodaux, LA
Varghese, Rev. Kurian N., '91 (SYM) Curia: Administration; Leadership
Varghese, Rev. Mathew, '02 (MIA) St. Elizabeth Ann Seton, Coral Springs, FL
Varghese, Rev. Peter, *C.M.I.* '91 (BLX) St. Joseph, Moss Point, MS
Varghese, Rev. Roshan, (SYM) St. Chavara Syro-Malabar Catholic Church - Cincinnati, Cincinnati, OH
Varghese, Rev. Sebastian, *CMI* (BO) St. John the Baptist, Quincy, MA
Varghese, Rev. Stephen K., '96 (MIL) Curia: Leadership St. John Nepomucene Congregation, Racine, WI; St. Joseph's Congregation, Racine, WI
Varghese, Rev. Thomas, (TOL) St. Charles Borromeo, Lima, OH
Varghese, Rev. TJ, '95 (PRO) Mary, Mother of Mankind Church Corporation, North Providence, North Providence, RI
Varkey, Rev. George, *M.S.T.* '90 (SP) St. Thomas Aquinas, New Port Richey, FL
Varkey, Rev. George, (MO) Curia: Offices and Directors
Varkey, Rev. George P., *M.S.F.S.* (CLV) Chap, Veterans Med Ctr, Louis Stokes VA, Cleveland
Varkey, Rev. Thomas, *SAC* '06 (MIL) St. Therese Congregation, Milwaukee, WI; [MON] Pallotti House, Milwaukee, WI
Varnabas, Rev. Arokiaraj, (TUC) Saint Kateri Tekakwitha Roman Catholic Missions Parish - Tucson, Tucson, AZ
Varner, Rev. Rick M., '10 (SAG) On Duty Outside Diocese. Epiphany Cathedral Parish, Venice, FL
Varner, Rev. Ricky, '10 (VEN) St. Katharine Drexel Parish in Cape Coral, Inc., Cape Coral, FL
Varno, Rev. John, '66 (ALB) Retired.
Varno, Rev. John J., '66 (ALB) Retired.
Varon, Rev. Nestor A., *AIC* (GRY) St. Mary, East Chicago, IN
Varone, Rev. Msgr. Normand G., '75 (SPC) Retired.
Varuvel, Rev. Paul L., '72 (BUF) Retired. [MON] O'Hara Residence, Tonawanda, NY
Vas, Rev. Henry, *O.F.M.Cap.* '98 (RVC) Chap, St Charles Hosp, Port Jefferson, New York Infant Jesus, Port Jefferson, NY; St. Joseph the Worker, East Patchogue, NY
Vasconcelos, Friar Emanuel, *O.F.M.Conv.* (SAV) Curia: Offices and Directors
Vasek, Rev. Craig J., '10 (CR) On Duty Outside Diocese.
Vashon, Rev. Msgr. Randall J., '00 (MET) Curia: Consultative Bodies St. Bernard of Clairvaux, Bridgewater, NJ
Vasile, Rev. Louis, '72 (ROC) Retired.
Vaske, Rev. Philip J, '06 (CHY) St. Anthony of Padua, Casper, WY
Vasko, Rev. Msgr. Christopher P., '83 (TOL) Historic Church of Saint Patrick, Toledo, OH; Immaculate Conception, Toledo, OH
Vaskov, Rev. Nicholas, (PIT) St. Nicholas, Pittsburgh, PA
Vaskov, Rev. Nicholas S., '09 (PIT) Curia: Consultative Bodies Christ Our Savior, Pittsburgh, PA; Immaculate Heart of Mary, Pittsburgh, PA; Most Holy Name of Jesus, Pittsburgh, PA; St. Patrick-St. Stanislaus Kostka, Pittsburgh, PA; [CAM] Art Institute of Pittsburgh, Pittsburgh, PA; [CAM] Point Park College, Pittsburgh, PA
Vasquez, Rev. Alfonso Ponchie, *O.F.M.* '99 (TUC) San Xavier Mission Roman Catholic Parish - Tucson, Tucson, AZ; [MON] San Xavier Mission Friary, Tucson, AZ
Vasquez, Rev. Hector, (SB) St. Patrick, Moreno Valley, CA
Vasquez, Rev. James, '06 (CC) SS. Cyril and Methodius, Corpus Christi, TX
Vasquez, Rev. Javier Garcia, (CHI) Transfiguration, Wauconda, IL
Vasquez, Rev. Jose Abelardo, (BGP) Curia: Clergy and Religious Services The Roman Catholic Church of St. Charles, Bridgeport, CT
Vasquez, Rev. Oscar, *S.M.* '05 (STL) [MON] Marianist Province of the United States (Society of Mary), St. Louis, MO
Vasquez, Rev. Paul L., '98 (OM) On Leave.
Vasquez, Rev. Raul A., *S.T.* '16 (MOB) St. Joseph Parish Holy Trinity, Fort Mitchell, AL; St. Patrick Parish, Phenix City, Phenix City, AL; [MON] St. Joseph Cenacle, Fort Mitchell, AL
Vasquez, Rev. Rodolfo D., '03 (CC) Saint John the Baptist, Corpus Christi, TX
Vasquez, Rev. Tomas, '04 (YAK) On Duty Outside Diocese. On Sabbatical, Continuing Studies in the Holy Land
Vass, Rev. Robert, *S.D.V.* (PAT) St. Gerard Majella, Paterson, NJ
Vassalotti, Rev. Thomas F., '07 (BRK) Divine Mercy Roman Catholic Church, Brooklyn, NY
Vassar, Rev. Paul R., (OAK) Curia: Leadership
Vathappallil, Rev. Thomas, *M.C.B.S.* '01 (MIL) St. Lucy Congregation, Racine, WI; St. Sebastian Congregation, Sturtevant, WI; [MON] Missionary Congregation of the Blessed Sacrament, Inc., Zion Province, Cudahy, WI
Vattakudiyil, Rev. Francis P., '63 (RVC) Retired. St. Joseph's, Kings Park, NY
Vattakunnel, Rev. James, (BGP) [MON] The Catherine Dennis Keefe Queen of the Clergy Retired Priests' Residence, Stamford, CT
Vattakunnel, Rev. James, *V.C.* '88 (SYM) Our Lady of the Assumption Syro-Malabar Catholic Church Norwalk, CT Inc., Stamford, CT
Vattakunnel, Rev. James C., *V.C.* '88 (BGP) Chap, Stamford Hosp
Vattakunnel, Rev. Jose, *M.C.* '90 (LKC) Curia: Leadership St. Joseph's, Elton, LA; St. Paul, Elton, LA
Vattampurath, Rev. Boby, '02 (SYM) Holy Family Syro-Malabar Knanaya Catholic Church (Atlanta), Loganville, GA
Vattaparambil, Rev. Antony V., *O.F.M.Conv.* (TOL) Transfiguration of the Lord, Upper Sandusky, OH
Vatter, Rev. Joseph E., '78 (BUF) Retired.
Vatti, Rev. Albeenreddy, '00 (JKS) St. Francis of Assisi,

Madison, MS
Vattothu, Rev. Jossy G., *C.M.I.* '09 (SAC) Pastor of Immaculate Conception Parish, Downieville, a corporation sole, Downieville, CA; Pastor of St. Canice Parish, Nevada City, a corporation sole, Nevada City, CA; Pastor of St. Patrick Parish, Grass Valley, a corporation sole, Grass Valley, CA
Vaughan, Rev. Msgr. Gregory D., '72 (TR) Retired. [MON] Villa Vianney, Trenton, NJ
Vaughan, Rev. Msgr. John J., '67 (MIA) Retired.
Vaughan, Rev. John R., '74 (OWN) Curia: Leadership The Immaculate, Owensboro, KY
Vaughan, Rev. John R., '74 (OWN) Curia: Advisory Boards, Commissions, Committees, and Councils
Vaughan, Rev. Michael D., '04 (SAC) Pastor of Good Shepherd Parish, Elk Grove, a corporation sole, Elk Grove, CA
Vaughan, Rev. Thomas, *S.S.C.* (PRO) [MON] St. Columban's Retirement House (St. Columban's Foreign Mission Society), Bristol, RI
Vaughn, Rev. Roland G., '71 (LKC) Retired.
Vaverek, Rev. Gavin N., '90 (TYL) Curia: Advisory Boards, Commissions, Committees, and Councils; Tribunal Our Lady of Victory, Paris, TX; St. Joseph, Clarksville, TX
Vaverek, Rev. Timothy V., '85 (AUS) St. Mary's Church of the Assumption, West, TX
Vavonese, Rev. Charles S., '73 (SY) Retired.
Vavrak, Rev. Martin, (MO) Curia: Offices and Directors
Vavrak, Rev. Martin, '03 (PSC) St. Michael, Perth Amboy, NJ; St. Nicholas, Perth Amboy, NJ
Vavrick, Rev. Eugene B., '93 (TR) St. Anselm, Tinton Falls, NJ
Vavrina, Rev. Kenneth P., '62 (OM) Retired.
Vayalikarottu, Rev. Antony, '03 (MIA) [MIS] St. Joseph Residence, Inc., Lauderdale Lakes, FL; [NUR] St. John's Rehabilitation Hospital and Nursing Center, Inc., Lauderdale Lakes, FL
Vazhakkoottahil John, Rev. Shinu, (SCR) Epiphany Parish, Sayre, PA
Vazhappilly, Rev. Anthony, '82 (OAK) Curia: Leadership St. James the Apostle, Fremont, CA
Vazhappilly, Rev. Jeejo K., *Sch.P.* '07 (LA) Santa Rosa, San Fernando, CA; [MON] Piarist Fathers, Los Angeles, CA
Vazquez, Rev. Adrian, '08 (B) St. Jerome's, Jerome, ID
Vazquez, Rev. Albert, *CMF* '55 (LA) Retired. [MON] Dominguez Seminary Inc., Rancho Dominguez, CA
Vazquez, Rev. Carlos J., (CGS) Curia: Leadership [MIS] Casa del Apostol San Andres, ,
Vazquez, Rev. Felipe R., '99 (RVC) Our Lady of Loretto, Hempstead, NY
Vazquez, Rev. Jose Luis, '87 (MAD) Cathedral Parish of St. Raphael, Madison, WI
Vazquez, Rev. Salvador, (LA) Holy Family, Wilmington, CA
Vazquez Colon, Rev. Msgr. Antonio Jose, '90 (SJN) Chap, Ashford Presbyterian Cmty Hosp, Santurce Stella Maris, Condado, San Juan, PR; [SPF] Centro Medico de P.R., San Juan, PR
Vazquez Gonzalez, Rev. J. Guadalupe, (SAC) Pastor of Holy Rosary Parish, Woodland, a corporation sole, Woodland, CA
Vazquez Saad, Rev. Hector, '08 (ORL) St. Clare, Deltona, FL
Vazquez Santos, Rev. Luis Ángel, '90 (ARE) Perpetuo Socorro, Vega Baja, PR
Vazquez Vega, Rev. Edwin Cleofe, '95 (PCE) On Leave.
Vazquez-Martinez, Rev. Jose Alberto, '02 (MRY) St. Patrick, Arroyo Grande, CA
Vazquez-Rubio, Rev. Juan, *O.SS.T.* '99 (BAL) St. Timothy, Walkersville, MD
Vead, Rev. Victor P., '92 (ALX) On Duty Outside Diocese. Federal Corr Complex, Beaumont, TX
Vebelun, Rev. Edward, *O.S.B.* '04 (SCL) Seven Dolors, Albany, MN; St. Anthony Catholic Church, Albany, MN; St. Benedict's, Avon, MN; St. Martin, St. Martin, MN
Vecellio, Rev. Peter Mary, *O.C.D* (P) [MON] Discalced Carmelite Friars (O.C.D.), Mount Angel, OR
Vecina, Rev. Albino, *C.R.S.P.* '14 (SD) Pastor of Our Lady of the Rosary Catholic Parish, San Diego, a corporation sole, San Diego, CA
Vedanayagam, Rev. John, *M.S.F.S.* '09 (R) St. Isidore, Fayetteville, NC
Vega, Rev. Aglayde Rafael, '06 (BWN) Curia: Advisory Boards, Commissions, Committees, and Councils; Leadership Church of the Good Shepherd, Brownsville, TX
Vega, Rev. Carlos, '89 (MIA) St. Timothy, Miami, FL
Vega, Rev. Daniel, '22 (LA) St. Dorothy, Glendora, CA
Vega, Rev. Hector, *I.S.P.* '74 (AUS) Retired. St. Paul, Austin, TX; [MON] Schoenstatt Fathers, Austin, TX
Vega, Rev. John Michael, '74 (CC) Retired.
Vega, Rev. Jose L., *O.M.* '69 (LA) Retired. All Saints, Los Angeles, CA; [MON] Minim Fathers, Los Angeles, CA
Vega, Rev. Richard, '83 (LA) St. Frances of Rome, Azusa, CA
Vega, Rev. Roberto, '87 (ARE) [MIS] Chapel Nuestra Senora de Fatima, Barceloneta, PR; [MIS] Chapel Nuestra Senora del Mar, Barceloneta, PR; [MIS] Chapel San Antonio de Padua, Barceloneta, PR
Vega, Rev. Saturnino Juan, (MGZ) St. Rose of Lima, San German, PR
Vega Caraballo, Rev. Roberto, (ARE) Church of Our Lady of Mt. Carmel, Barceloneta, PR
Vega Graniela, Rev. Javier, '18 (PCE) San Conrado, Ponce, PR
Vega Graniela, Rev. Javier, '18 (PCE) Curia: Offices and Directors
Vega Mendoza, Rev. Cesar, '08 (YAK) Holy Family, Yakima, WA
Vega-Alvarenga, Rev. Salvador, '01 (LR) Curia: Offices and Directors Our Lady of Guadalupe Church, Glenwood, AR; St. Martin Church, Nashville, AR
Veguilla, Rev. Antonio Cartagena, (ARE) (>CGS) Colegio San Juan Apostol y Evangelista, Caguas, PR
Veigas, Rev. Albert, '80 (CLV) Retired.
Veik, Rev. Alan D., *O.F.M.Cap.* '67 (MIL) Curia: Leadership [MIS] Capuchin Community Services, Milwaukee, WI; [MIS] Works of Mercy Ministry, Inc., Cedarburg, WI
Veit, Rev. David J., '98 (JC) St. Brendan, Mexico, MO
Veith, Rev. William E., '70 (CHI) Retired.
Vela, Rev. Edison, '91 (DAL) St. Edward Catholic Parish, Dallas, TX
Velasco, Rev. Arturo, '86 (LA) St. Joseph, Hawthorne, CA
Velasco, Rev. Romeo "Billy", '98 (HT) Our Lady of the Most Holy Rosary, Houma, LA
Velasco-Perez, Rev. Daniel, (LR) Our Lady of the Holy Souls, Little Rock, AR
Velasquez, Rev. Bernardo, (PAT) Retired.
Velasquez, Rev. Carlos C, '14 (BRK) St. Brigid, Brooklyn, NY
Velasquez, Rev. Carlos C., '14 (BRK) Curia: Pastoral Services (>NY) [SEM] St. Joseph's Seminary, Yonkers, NY
Velasquez, Rev. Eric J., (BO) Immaculate Conception, Revere, MA
Velasquez, Rev. Marcos, '89 (TUC) Sacred Heart of Jesus Roman Catholic Parish - Nogales, Nogales, AZ
Velasquez, Rev. Rafael, (NEW) On Duty Outside Diocese. Holy Cross Mission, Grand Turks & Caicos Island
Velasquez, Rev. Roger, '19 (RVC) St. Patrick's, Bay Shore, NY
Velasquez-Ducayin, Rev. Juan Carlos, (NEW) St. Cecilia, Kearny, NJ
Velasquez-Ducayin, Rev. Juan Carlos, (NEW) Our Lady of Sorrows, Kearny, NJ
Velasquez-Serrano, Rev. Samuel, (SJN) On Academic Leave. Rome, Italy
Velazco Ornelas, Rev. Ismael, *MSP* '19 (SAN) Holy Redeemer, Odessa, TX
Velazquez, Rev. Carlos B., '90 (SAT) Curia: Administration
Velazquez, Rev. Eduardo, *M.S.P.* '99 (COL) St. Agnes, Columbus, OH
Velazquez, Rev. Francisco, '90 (SAC) Curia: Leadership
Velazquez, Rev. Yamil A., '05 (CGS) Curia: Leadership; Offices and Directors Inmaculada Concepcion, Las Piedras, PR
Velazquez Ramirez, Rev. Alfredo M., (SEA) St. John the Evangelist, Vancouver, WA
Velez, Rev. Angel Ortiz, '87 (MGZ) Our Lady of the Purification, Lajas, PR
Velez, Rev. Daniel Hernandez, (MGZ) Curia: Leadership
Velez, Rev. Juan, (PMB) [MIS] Prelature of the Holy Cross and Opus Dei, Delray Beach, FL
Velez, Rev. Juan R., '98 (CHI) [MIS] Northview University Center, Chicago, IL (>MIA) [MIS] Prelature of the Holy Cross and Opus Dei, Miami, FL
Velez, Rev. Juan R., '98 (POD) Curia: Clergy and Religious Services
Velez, Rev. Ramon Olivencia, '97 (ARE) Curia: Leadership; Offices and Directors
Velez, Rev. Victor Sanchez, '91 (ARE) Curia: Leadership
Velez Nieves, Rev. Miguel Jose, '17 (ARE) Our Lady of Angels, Ángeles, PR; Our Lady of Sorrows, Utuado, PR
Velez-Cardona, Rev. Miguel, '08 (KNX) St. Patrick, Morristown, TN
Vella, Rev. Edward, *C.Ss.R.* (CHI) [MON] The Redemptorist Fathers of Chicago, Chicago, IL
Vella, Rev. Edward, *C.Ss.R.* '85 (MIL) (>CHI) St. Michael in Old Town, Chicago, IL
Vella, Rev. Joseph, '68 (BRK) Retired.
Vellaplackil, Rev. George, '98 (HRT) Saint John Bosco Parish Corporation, Branford, CT
Vellappallil, Rev. Thomas, *M.S.* '94 (HRT) [MIS] North American La Salette Mission Center, Hartford, CT; [MIS] North American La Salette Mission Center, Inc., Hartford, CT
Vellappallil, Rev. Thomas, *M.S.* '94 (STL) [MON] Missionaries of LaSalette, Province of Mary, Mother of the Americas, St. Louis, MO
Vellenga, Rev. R. Stephen, '81 (CLV) Curia: Offices and Directors St. Mary, Painesville, OH; [CCH] St. Mary's - Painesville, Painesville, OH
Velliyedathu, Rev. Tom John, *CMI* (BIR) St. Paul's, Athens, AL
Velloorattil, Rev. George, '78 (CHI) Our Lady at St. Germaine, Oak Lawn, IL
Vells, Rev. Biju, '12 (MIA) St. Bernadette, Hollywood, FL
Velo, Rev. Msgr. Kenneth, '73 (CHI) On Duty Outside Diocese. DePaul Univ, Chicago
Velos, Rev. Romeo, *C.S.* '92 (SD) Pastor of Saint Agnes Catholic Parish, San Diego, a corporation sole, San Diego, CA; [MIS] Saint Agnes Catholic Parish in San Diego, CA Real Property Support Corporation, San Diego, CA
Velpula, Rev. Anthony Xavier, (AUS) Curia: Tribunal St. Margaret Mary, Cedar Park, TX
Veluz, Rev. Edward T., '64 (NEW) Chap, Holy Name Med Ctr, Teaneck
Veluz, Rev. Edwardo, '89 (NEW) [HOS] Holy Name Medical Center (Peace Ministries, Inc.), Teaneck, NJ
Vendredy, Rev. Charlince, (RVC) St. Anne's, Brentwood, NY
Venegas, Rev. Dennis, (SAT) El Carmen Catholic Church, San Antonio, TX
Venegas, Rev. Miguel, (CHI) Immaculate Conception and Five Holy Martyrs, Chicago, IL
Venegas, Rev. Rafael, '07 (LA) On Administrative Leave.
Veneklase, Rev. Gregory L., '93 (MAR) [MIS] Companions of Christ the Lamb, Paradise, MI
Veneroso, Rev. Joseph R., *M.M.* '78 (NY) Retired. [MON] Maryknoll Fathers and Brothers (Catholic Foreign Mission Society of America, Inc.), Ossining, NY
Veneroso, Rev. Joseph R., *M.M.* '74 (BRK) St. Paul Chong Ha-Sang Roman Catholic Chapel, Flushing, NY
Venette, Rev. Howard J., '84 (OG) Clinton Correctional Facility, Dannemora Curia: Consultative Bodies
Venezia, Rev. Arthur, '71 (PMB) Retired.
Vengayil, Rev. Thomas, '59 (PMB) Retired.
Venker, Rev. Josef V., *S.J.* '87 (SEA) [COL] Seattle University, Seattle, WA; [MON] Arrupe Jesuit Community at Seattle University, Seattle, WA
Venne, Rev. R. Thomas, '62 (MIL) Retired.
Venneri, Rev. Michael D., '82 (SPK) Retired. St. Peter, Spokane, WA
Vennetti, Rev. Robert, *M.I.C.* '06 (SPR) [MON] Congregation of Marian Fathers of The Immaculate Conception of the Most Blessed Virgin Mary, Stockbridge, MA
Vennitti, Rev. Thomas A., '73 (STU) Curia: Deaneries St. Francis of Assisi, Toronto, OH; St. Joseph's, Toronto, OH
Venters, Rev. Darrell, '89 (OWN) Curia: Advisory Boards, Commissions, Committees, and Councils St. Jerome, Fancy Farm, KY
Ventiquattro, Rev. Jude, (PIT) [MON] Franciscan Friars, T.O.R. (Queen of Peace Friary), Pittsburgh, PA
Ventline, Rev. Lawrence M., '76 (DET) Retired.
Ventre, Rev. Michael A., '14 (LIN) Curia: Leadership Aquinas/St. Mary's Schools, David City, NE; Presentation, Bellwood, NE; St. Bernard's, Julian, NE
Ventura, Rev. Nicola, '15 (COL) St. Cecilia, Columbus, OH
Ventura, Rev. Raul, *S.T.* (PAT) [MON] Shrine of St. Joseph, Stirling, NJ
Venuti, Rev. Matthew A, '12 (MOB) Retired.
Venuti, Rev. Matthew A., '12 (POC) Retired.
Venza, Rev. Felix F., '72 (TR) Retired.
Venzor, Rev. Jesse C., '80 (FRS) St. Frances Cabrini, Woodlake, CA
Ver, Rev. Alexander, '67 (NEW) Curia: Organizations (affiliated, inter-Diocesan, miscellaneous/other) St. Nicholas, Jersey City, NJ
Vera, Rev. Francisco, '07 (GAL) Holy Cross Chapel, Houston, TX; [MIS] Opus Dei, Houston, TX
Vera, Rev. Francisco, '07 (POD) Curia: Clergy and

Religious Services
Vera, Rev. Jude, '89 (SP) Retired.
Vera, Rev. Julio, (FAJ) Cathedral Santiago Apostol, Fajardo, PR
Vera, Rev. Luis A., *O.S.A.* '96 (NY) St. Nicholas of Tolentine, Bronx, NY
Vera, Rev. Roberto, '01 (MRY) On Special Assignment. Chap, St Clare's Retreat, Soquel
Vera, Rev. Vicente Antonio, '85 (TOL) St. John the Evangelist, Delphos, OH
Vera Gonzalez, Rev. Julio Angel, '98 (MGZ) Curia: (>MO) Offices and Directors El Salvador, Hormigueros, PR
Veras, Rev. Richard, '96 (NY) [MIS] Patrons of the Arts in Vatican Museums, New York, NY; [SEM] St. Joseph's Seminary, Yonkers, NY
Verber, Rev. Thomas G, *O.S.A.* '99 (SD) Retired.
Verberg, Rev. Richard R., '71 (MIL) Retired.
Verbest, Rev. Stephen, *O.C.S.O.* '98 (DUB) [MON] New Melleray Abbey, Order of Cistercians of the Strict Observance (Corporation of New Melleray), Peosta, IA
Verbryke, Rev. William, *S.J.* '83 (IND) Brebeuf Jesuit Preparatory School, Inc. (Society of Jesus Community), Indianapolis, IN
Verbsky, Rev. David, '22 (CLV) St. Francis de Sales, Akron, OH
Vercellone, Rev. Anthony, '80 (RNO) Retired.
Verdelotti, Rev. Anthony W., '86 (PRO) Saint Mark's Church Corporation of Cranston, Cranston, RI
Verdelotti, Rev. James J., '78 (PRO) Retired.
Verdi, Rev. Ralph, *C.PP.S.* '71 (CIN) Retired.
Verdia Nay, Rev. Carlos, '85 (SJN) Ntra. Sra. de la Medalla Milagrosa, San Juan, PR
Vereb, Rev. Jerome, *C.P.* '72 (PIT) Retired.
Vereecke, Rev. Robert, (BO) [MON] Campion Center, Inc., Weston, MA
Vereeth, Rev. Babu Nalkara, '99 (BR) Congregation Of St. Ann Roman Catholic Church Of Morganza, Morganza, LA
Verespy, Rev. Joseph D., '79 (SCR) Curia: Leadership Our Lady of Fatima Parish, Wilkes-Barre, PA; St. Nicholas, Wilkes-Barre, PA
Vergara, Rev. Arlon, *OSA* '90 (RNO) St. Therese of the Little Flower Catholic Church, Reno, NV
Vergara, Rev. Armando, '73 (STO) Retired.
Vergara, Rev. Heriberto, '86 (STA) San Sebastian, St. Augustine, FL
Vergara, Rev. Msgr. Romulo A., '82 (SFR) On Special Assignment. Curia: Advisory Boards, Commissions, Committees, and Councils; Offices and Directors Our Lady of Mount Carmel, Redwood City, CA
Verhalen, Rt. Rev. Peter, *O.Cist.* '81 (DAL) [EFT] Cistercian Abbey Foundation, Irving, TX; [EFT] Cistercian Prep Foundation, Irving, TX; [MIS] CREC, Irving, TX; [MON] Our Lady of Dallas Cistercian Abbey, Irving, TX
Verhelst, Rev. Steven J., '90 (NU) On Special Assignment. Curia: Leadership; Offices and Directors Our Lady of the Lakes, Spicer, MN; St. Clara, Clara City, MN; St. Mary, Willmar, MN
Verley, Rev. Jude, *O.S.C.* '79 (PHX) [MON] Crosier Community of Phoenix (Canons Regular of the Order of the Holy Cross) (Conventual Priory of the Holy Cross), Phoenix, AZ
Vermiglio, Rev. Thomas Michael, *MCCJ* '72 (CIN) Retired. [MON] Comboni Missionaries (Verona Fathers)-Comboni Mission Center, Cincinnati, OH
Verner, Rev. Dominic M., *O.P.* '16 (PRO) [MON] St. Thomas Aquinas Priory at Providence College, Providence, RI
Vernon, Rev. William F., '97 (MAD) St. Clement, Lancaster, WI
Verona, Rev. Adam M., '11 (PIT) St. Faustina, Slippery Rock, PA
Veronesi, Rev. Giulio, *S.J.E.* '75 (GAL) Assumption, Houston, TX
Verrier, Rev. John M., '95 (PEO) St. Joseph's, Brimfield, IL
Verrill, Rev. O. Wendell, '63 (BO) Retired.
Verruni, Rev. Samuel A., '86 (PH) St. Joseph, Downingtown, PA
Verschaeve, Rev. C. Michael, '77 (DET) Retired.
Verschaeve, Rev. Michael, (GLD) Retired. Saint Aloysius of Fife Lake, Fife Lake, MI; Saint Mary of the Woods of Kalkaska, Kalkaska, MI
Verstreaken, Rev. Alfred, *C.J.* '73 (LA) St. Louis de Montfort, Santa Maria, CA
Vesey, Rev. John E., '68 (BRK) Retired. Presentation of the Blessed Virgin Mary, Jamaica, NY
Vesga, Rev. Mario, '62 (SD) Retired.
Vethamanickam, Rev. Joseph Xavier, '92 (ALX) Our Lady of Lourdes, Vidalia, LA
Vethanayagam, Rev. Sengole V., '95 (LC) St. Andrew, Stratford, WI; St. Joseph, Stratford, WI; [EFT] St. Joseph Parish Endowment Trust, Stratford, WI
Vetrano, Rev. Michael A., '79 (RVC) Curia: Leadership Basilica Church of Sacred Hearts of Jesus and Mary, Southampton, NY
Vettathu, Rev. Jacob Thomas, *MS* '95 (PHX) St Clare of Assisi Roman Catholic Parish Surprise, Surprise, AZ
Vetter, Rev. Nicholas, '21 (BIS) St. Mary, Bismarck, ND
Vettese, Rev. Donald, (DET) [MON] Jesuit Community at the University of Detroit Mercy, Detroit, MI
Vettickal, Rev. Sebastian, *C.M.I.* '91 (LA) St. Francis Xavier, Burbank, CA
Vevik, Rev. Paul, '77 (SPK) Curia: Leadership Mary Queen, Spokane, WA; [SEM] Bishop White Seminary, Spokane, WA
Vi Tran, Rev. Gregory, *C.R.M.* (SB) St. Mary Magdalene, Corona, CA; [MON] Shrine of Presentation, Corona, CA
Via, Rev. Anthony P., *S.J.* '60 (SJ) [MON] Sacred Heart Jesuit Center, Los Gatos, CA
Vialpando, Very Rev. Kenneth L., '91 (SLC) Chap, Utah State Prison Curia: Leadership; Offices and Directors
Vianney, Rev. John M., '88 (LA) Our Lady of the Miraculous Medal, Montebello, CA
Vicari, Rev. Marc A., '97 (NEW) St. Cassian, Upper Montclair, NJ
Vicens Vicens, Rev. Hipolito, *C.Ss.R.* (PCE) San Antonio de Padua, Guayama, PR
Vicente, Rev. Julio, '08 (B) St. Edward the Confessor, Twin Falls, ID
Vicente, Rev. Julio, '08 (B) Curia: Leadership [CAM] College of Southern Idaho, Twin Falls, ID
Vicente, Rev. Saulo S., '12 (WDC) On Special Assignment. Vice Rec, Redemptoris Mater Seminary Curia: Consultative Bodies St. Michael, Silver Spring, MD; [SEM] Redemptoris Mater Archdiocesan Missionary Seminary, Hyattsville, MD
Vicente Martinez-Santos, Rev. Jose, *C.M.F.* (SJN) Casa Mision Claret, Bayamon, PR
Vichich, Rev. Michael T., '74 (MAR) Retired.
Vicini, Rev. Andrea, *S.J.* '96 (BO) [MON] The Jesuit Community at Boston College, Chestnut Hill, MA
Vick, Rev. James L., '99 (KNX) St. Bridget, Dayton, TN
Victor, Rev. John, *O.M.I.* '08 (RVC) St. Boniface, Elmont, NY
Victor, Rev. Ponnuswamy R., '88 (CC) Our Lady of Guadalupe, Tivoli, TX
Victor, Rev. Ronald, '78 (DET) St. Isidore Parish Macomb Township, Macomb, MI
Victor, Rev. Wesbee, '21 (NY) Parish of Holy Name of Jesus and St. Gregory the Great, New York, NY
Victoria, Rev. John J., '08 (SCR) Retired.
Victoria, Rev. Jose Helber, '07 (NEW) St. Joseph of the Palisades, West New York, NJ; St. Mary Parish, Jersey City, NJ
Victorino, Rev. Florentino, *M.S.C.* '01 (LA) Immaculate Heart of Mary, Los Angeles, CA
Vidad, Rev. Gerald, '97 (SB) St. Anthony, Upland, CA
Vidal, Rev. David, (VEN) Ave Maria Parish, Inc., Ave Maria, FL
Vidal, Rev. Gustavo, '97 (SLC) Curia: Offices and Directors Saint Rose of Lima LLC 245, Layton, UT
Vidal, Rev. Jesus Hernandez, '94 (OAK) St. Peter, Martyr of Verona, Pittsburg, CA
Vidal, Rev. John, (POC) Saint Luke, Fort Washington, MD
Vidal, Rev. John, (CC) St. Anselm Anglican Use Community, Corpus Christi, TX
Vidal, Rev. Robert S., '66 (ORG) Retired. St. Anne Church, Seal Beach, CA
Vidal, Rev. Tomas, (YAK) Immaculate Conception, Mabton, WA; Our Lady of Guadalupe, Granger, WA
Vidarte, Rev. Jose Luis, '08 (TYL) St. Anthony, Longview, TX
Vidmar, Rev. John C., *O.P.* '80 (PRO) [MON] St. Thomas Aquinas Priory at Providence College, Providence, RI
Vidor, Rev. Jakov, (BGP) Curia: Clergy and Religious Services
Vidrine, Rev. Jason, '06 (LAF) St. Martin de Tours, St. Martinville, LA
Vidrine, Rev. Richard, '95 (LAF) Retired.
Vidro, Rev. Floyd Mercado, '03 (FAJ) Curia: Offices and Directors La Sagrada Familia Parish, Humacao, PR
Viego, Rev. Carlos M., '98 (NEW) Curia: Organizations (affiliated, inter-Diocesan, miscellaneous/other)
Viego, Rev. Carlos M., '98 (NEW) St. Leo, Irvington, NJ
Vieira, Rev. Joseph, '13 (POC) The Catholic Church of Holy Nativity, Payson, AZ
Vieira, Rev. Msgr. Victor M., '67 (PRO) Retired.
Vien, Rev. John Rogers, '93 (STL) St. Margaret of Scotland Catholic Church, St. Louis, MO; [MIS] Archdiocesan Stewardship Education Committee, St. Louis, MO
Viera, Rev. Manuel, *O.F.M.* '82 (CIN) [MON] St. Francis Seraph Friary, Cincinnati, OH
Viera, Rev. Manuel, *O.F.M.* '82 (TUC) Curia: Consultative Bodies; Leadership; Tribunal San Xavier Mission Roman Catholic Parish - Tucson, Tucson, AZ; [MON] San Xavier Mission Friary, Tucson, AZ
Vierra, Rev. Theodore A., '60 (LA) Retired. St. Paul the Apostle, Los Angeles, CA
Viet Tran, Rev. Bac-Hai, '84 (NO) St. Agnes, Jefferson, LA
Vietor, Rev. Oliver, '10 (PHX) St. Joan of Arc Roman Catholic Parish, Phoenix, AZ
Vieyra, Rev. Eladio, (B) St. Therese Little Flower, Burley, ID
Vieyra, Rev. Eladio, '08 (B) Curia: Offices and Directors
Vigil, Rev. Joseph A., '07 (PBL) Retired. Curia: Leadership; Offices and Directors (>SFE) The Cathedral Basilica of St. Francis of Assisi, Santa Fe, NM
Vigil, Rev. Michael A., '85 (GLP) On Leave.
Vigil, Rev. Paul E., '91 (LA) St. Anthony, El Segundo, CA
Vigil Reyes, Rev. Erik, '15 (DEN) St. Helena Catholic Parish in Ft. Morgan, Fort Morgan, CO
Vignato, Rev. Joe, *S.X.* '93 (PAT) [MON] Xaverian Missionary Fathers, Wayne, NJ
Vigneron, Rev. Philippe, '15 (STP) Holy Childhood, St. Paul, MN; Maternity of the Blessed Virgin, St. Paul, MN
Vigneron, Rev. Philippe Bernard Marie, *EC* '15 (NY) [MIS] Emmanuel School of Mission, Inc., Bronx, NY
Vignone, Rev. John J., '75 (CAM) Retired.
Vigoa, Rev. Richard J., '08 (MIA) Curia: Leadership; Pastoral Services St. Augustine, Coral Gables, FL
Vigueras, Rev. Arturo, '21 (LC) Holy Family, Arcadia, WI; Most Sacred Heart, Dodge, WI
Vigues, Rev. Gabriel, '93 (MIA) Curia: Consultative Bodies St. Louis, Pinecrest, FL
Vila, Rev. Carlos, (CHK) Curia: Tribunal
Vila, Rev. Carlos S., '83 (AGN) Curia: Leadership; Tribunal Nuestra Senora de la Paz y Buen Viaje, Hagatna, GU
Vila, Rev. Richard C, '02 (TR) St. Ann, Keansburg, NJ
Viladesau, Rev. Richard R., '69 (RVC) Our Lady Star of the Sea, Mission Chapel, Saltaire, NY; St. John Nepomucene, Bohemia, NY
Vilanculo, Rev. Tiago, *CMM* '19 (IND) St. Christopher Catholic Church, Indianapolis, Inc., Indianapolis, IN
Vilano, Rev. Tony, '96 (SAT) Curia: Administration; Leadership St. Francis of Assisi, San Antonio, TX
Vilchez, Rev. Pedro E., '11 (NEW) On Duty Outside Diocese. Grand Turk
Vileo, Rev. Stephen L., '87 (DET) On Leave.
Vilkauskas, Rev. Edward, *CSSp* '73 (PIT) Retired. [RTR] The Spiritan Center, Bethel Park, PA
Vill, Rev. Andrew A., '14 (BGP) On Duty Outside Diocese. Calle Isla Canarias, 142, 28905 Getafe (Madrid), Spain
Villa, Rev. Eduardo, '80 (BWN) Retired.
Villa, Rev. Erick, (OAK) Chap, Federal Prison Corrections Inst
Villa, Rev. James, *O.F.M.* '69 (NY) [MON] St. Bernardine of Siena Friary (Franciscan Friars, Province of Immaculate Conception), Mount Vernon, NY
Villa, Rev. John Erick, '16 (OAK) Curia: Leadership St. Raymond, Dublin, CA
Villa, Rev. Leonard F., '86 (NY) St. Paul the Apostle, Yonkers, NY
Villa, Rev. Richard, *S.M.* '08 (SAT) [MON] Ligustrum Marianist Community, San Antonio, TX
Villa, Rev. Robert, '02 (HRT) Chap, Cheshire Corr Inst; Willard-Cybulski Corr Inst, Enf… Saint Jeanne Jugan Parish Corporation, Enfield, CT
Villa, Rev. William, (STA) St. John the Baptist, Crescent City, FL
Villabon, Rev. German, *O.S.A.* '54 (RVC) St. Agnes Cathedral, Rockville Centre, NY
Villaescusa, Rev. Gregory, '03 (SR) Pastor of St. Joseph Catholic Church of Crescent City, A Corporation Sole, Crescent City, CA
Villafan, Rev. Ignacio, (FRS) St. John's Cathedral, Fresno, CA
Villagomez, Rev. Jose G., *O.F.M.Cap.* '74 (AGN) Curia: Miscellaneous / Other Offices; Tribunal [MON] St. Fidelis Friary, Agana Heights, GU
Villagomez, Rev. Juan, *SOLT* '14 (CC) [MON] Society of Our Lady of the Most Holy Trinity, Corpus Christi, TX
Villa-Holguin, Rev. John F., '06 (CHI) Mary, Mother of Mercy, Chicago, IL
Villalobos, Rev. Alberto, '85 (LA) St. Joseph the Worker,

Winnetka, CA
Villalobos, Rev. Daniel, '21 (CHI) St. Michael, Orland Park, IL
Villalobos, Rev. Efrain, *MSP* '11 (LA) Our Lady of Solitude, Los Angeles, CA
Villalobos, Rev. Efrain, *MSP* (COL) Saint Stephen the Martyr, Columbus, OH
Villalobos, Rev. Lucio, *M.Sp.S.* (SEA) St. Elizabeth Ann Seton, Mill Creek, WA
Villalobos, Rev. Manuel, *C.M.F.* '04 (CHI) [MON] Claretian Missionaries U.S.A.-Canada Province, Inc., Chicago, IL
Villalon, Rev. Jose M., '89 (BWN) St. Theresa, San Benito, TX; [MIS] Catholic Engaged Encounter, San Juan, TX
Villalon-Rivera, Rev. Ruben, '17 (MEM) Our Lady of Sorrows, Memphis, TN
Villalta, Friar Moises, *O.F.M.Cap.* '95 (SJN) San Francisco de Asis, San Juan, PR; [MIS] Hogar Padre Venard, Inc., San Juan, PR
Villaluz, Rev. Carlo, '97 (GB) St. Joseph, Champion, WI; St. Kilian, New Franken, WI; St. Thomas the Apostle, Luxemburg, WI
Villamide, Rev. Msgr. Aniceto, (BGP) Retired. [MON] The Catherine Dennis Keefe Queen of the Clergy Retired Priests' Residence, Stamford, CT
Villamide, Rev. Msgr. Aniceto, '67 (BGP) Retired.
Villamil, Rev. Francisco (Paco) Gordillo, '15 (SPC) Curia: Organizations (affiliated, inter-Diocesan, miscellaneous/other) McAuley Catholic High School, Joplin, MO; Sacred Heart, Webb City, MO; St. Ann, Carthage, MO
Villamizar, Rev. Duberney, '16 (PAT) Holy Cross, Wayne, NJ; St. Margaret of Scotland, Morristown, NJ
Villamthanam, Rev. George, *C.S.T.* '81 (NOR) St. Luke, Ellington, CT
Villano, Rev. Mark, *C.S.P.* '88 (LA) St. Paul the Apostle, Los Angeles, CA
Villanova, Rev. Richard A., '67 (NEW) Retired.
Villanueva, Rev. Edgar, '08 (RNO) St. Peter Canisius, Sun Valley, NV
Villanueva, Rev. Efrain, '04 (AUS) St. Julia, Austin, TX
Villanueva, Rev. Gary T., '04 (WDC) St. Columba, Oxon Hill, MD
Villanueva, Rev. Jose Antonio, '63 (SAT) Retired. [NUR] Casa De Padres, San Antonio, TX
Villanueva, Rev. Marcos, (SEA) Our Lady of Good Help, Hoquiam, WA; St. Mary, Aberdeen, WA
Villanueva, Rev. Maximo, '93 (NY) St. John the Evangelist, Mahopac, NY
Villapaz, Rev. Junabe Villaflor, '10 (LC) St. John the Baptist, Plum City, WI; St. Joseph, Arkansaw, WI
Villaran, Friar Jose Antonio, *O.F.M.Cap.* '05 (SJN) [MON] Fraternidad Santa Maria de Los Angeles, Rio Piedras, PR
Villariza, Rev. Theodbriel, (OAK) St. Michael, Livermore, CA
Villarreal, Rev. Alfredo, (CC) [MIS] St. Thomas Aquinas Newman Center and Chapel (Texas A&M University Kingsville), Kingsville, TX
Villarreal, Rev. Daniel E., (SAT) On Leave.
Villarreal, Rev. Daniel Edduardo, (SAT) On Leave.
Villarreal, Rev. L. Alfredo, (CC) St. Martin, Kingsville, TX
Villarreal, Rev. Louis, *O.M.I.* '65 (WDC) [MON] Oblate Community, Washington, DC
Villarreal, Rev. Manuel, (SAT) Retired. [NUR] Oblate Madonna Residence, San Antonio, TX
Villarreal, Rev. Manuel, '08 (SD) Retired.
Villarreal, Very Rev. Ricardo A., '98 (YAK) Curia: Offices and Directors
Villarreal, Very Rev. Ruben, '15 (LKC) St. Louis Catholic High School, Lake Charles, LA
Villarreal, Very Rev. Ruben, '15 (LKC) Our Lady Queen of Heaven, Lake Charles, LA; [MIS] Society of Roman Catholic Church of the Dioceses of Lake Charles, Lake Charles, LA
Villarreal, Very Rev. Ruben, '15 (LKC) Curia: Leadership
Villarrubia, Rev. Roger, '99 (HT) Retired.
Villarson, Rev. Albert Gardy, *O.M.I.* '86 (PH) St. Helena, Philadelphia, PA
Villaruel, Rev. Alvin, '94 (SR) Curia: Leadership Pastor of St. Francis Solano Catholic Church of Sonoma, A Corporation Sole, Sonoma, CA
Villaruel, Rev. Alvin M., '94 (SR) Curia: Leadership; Offices and Directors
Villasano, Rev. Carlos, (LA) Santa Clara, Oxnard, CA
Villaseca, Rev. Gonzalo, '19 (AUS) [MON] Schoenstatt Fathers, Austin, TX
Villaverde, Rev. Tirso S., '96 (CHI) Saint Julie Billiart, Tinley Park, IL
Villavicencio, Rev. Juan Carlos, *P.E.S.* '18 (SAC) Pastor of St. Anthony Parish, Walnut Grove, a corporation sole, Walnut Grove, CA; Pastor of St. Therese Parish, Isleton, a corporation sole, Isleton, CA
Villegas, Rev. Diego, '74 (BRK) St. Leo, Corona, NY
Villegas, Rev. Gonzalo J., '92 (TUC) Sacred Heart Roman Catholic Parish - Tucson, Tucson, AZ
Villegas, Rev. Robert, (AUS) Retired.
Villela-Huerta, Rev. Hector, '05 (SJ) Our Lady, Star of the Sea, Alviso, CA
Villeneuve, Rev. Max, *O.S.A.* (SD) [EFT] The Bellesini Foundation, San Diego, CA; [EFT] The St. Augustine Foundation, San Diego, CA; [EFT] The Tagaste Foundation, San Diego, CA
Villeneuve, Rev. Maxime, *O.S.A.* '18 (SD) St. Augustine High School, San Diego, CA; [MON] Augustinian Community, San Diego, CA
Villero, Rev. Melchor N., *M.J.* '76 (BWN) Saint Anne, Penitas, TX
Villosillo, Rev. Alberto, '95 (NO) On Special Assignment. Chaplain, Place DuBourg
Villote, Rev. Augusto E., '03 (SFR) Our Lady of Perpetual Help, Daly City, CA
Vima, Rev. Benjamin A., '71 (TLS) Retired.
Vincent, Rev. David P., '64 (CIN) Retired.
Vincent, Rev. Jean-Marie, '00 (WDC) Chap, Hospital & Nursing Home Ministry, Adventist HealthCar...
Vincent, Rev. John, *O.S.C.* '58 (SCL) [MON] Crosier Priory, Onamia, MN
Vincent, Rev. Joji, *O.S.B.* '06 (SPC) On Special Assignment. Tucson, AZ St. Joseph the Worker, Ozark, MO
Vincent, Rev. Michael A., *S.J.* '82 (CLV) Gesu, University Heights, OH; [COL] John Carroll Jesuit Community, University Heights, OH
Vincent, Rev. Paul, '04 (PMB) St. Joseph, Stuart, FL
Vincent, Rev. Roy Russel, '14 (JKS) St. Paul, Vicksburg, MS
Vincent, Rev. Rusty, '14 (JKS) Curia: Consultative Bodies
Vincenzo, Rev. Dennis J., '91 (HRT) Retired. [MON] Basilica of the Immaculate Conception Rectory, Waterbury, CT
Vinci, Rev. Msgr. Guy, '59 (NY) Retired.
Vinci, Rev. Terzo, *S.A.C.* '58 (NY) [MON] Pallottine Fathers, New York, NY
Vinjoe, Rev. Ben, (NOR) Our Lady of La Salette, Brooklyn, CT
Vinsko, Rev. John J., *M.M.* '62 (NY) Retired.
Vinslauski, Rev. Robert B., '71 (SFS) Retired.
Vinson, Rev. Anthony, *O.S.B.* '05 (IND) St. Boniface Catholic Church, Fulda, Inc., Fulda, IN; St. Meinrad Catholic Church, Inc., St. Meinrad, IN; [MON] St. Meinrad Archabbey, St. Meinrad, IN
Vinton, Rev. John, (LAN) St. Francis of Assisi Parish Ann Arbor, Ann Arbor, MI
Vintson, Rev. Wyman, '16 (BIR) Curia: Leadership; Offices and Directors St. Elizabeth Ann Seton, Gardendale, AL
Viola, Rev. William L., '84 (BAL) Retired.
Violi, Rev. David, '16 (FTW) Curia: Offices and Directors St. Joseph, Bluffton, IN
Viray, Rev. Eric, (ORG) St. Pius V, Buena Park, CA
Virella, Rev. Miguel, *S.V.D.* '96 (TR) The Church of Mother of Mercy, Asbury Park, N.J., Asbury Park, NJ
Virella Vazquez, Rev. Jorge L., '97 (ARE) Curia: Leadership Church of Sagrado Corazon de Jesus, Arecibo, PR
Virella Vazquez, Rev. Jorge Luis, '97 (ARE) Curia: Leadership
Virgen, Rev. Javier G., '93 (SLC) Curia: Offices and Directors Saint Joseph the Worker LLC 232, West Jordan, UT
Virginia, Rev. Stephen G., '79 (COL) Retired.
Virnig, Rev. Laurn, '63 (SCL) Retired. Curia: Offices and Directors
Virrey, Rev. Armando, '03 (ORG) Immaculate Heart of Mary, Santa Ana, CA
Virus, Rev. Keith, (GRY) St. Ann, Gary, IN
Virus, Rev. Keith M., '92 (GRY) St. Mary, Griffith, IN
Viruthakulangara, Rev. Alex Thomas, (LAV) St. Patrick, Tonopah, NV
Viscardi, Rev. Christopher J., *S.J.* '76 (MOB) [MON] Jesuits of Mobile, Inc., Mobile, AL
Visnovsky, Mitred Archpriest Marek, '04 (PRM) Curia: Advisory Boards, Commissions, Committees, and Councils; Leadership Dormition of the Theotoko, Cleveland, OH; St. John the Baptist, Solon, OH; St. Joseph, Brecksville, OH
Visperas, Rev. Joseph, '86 (LA) St. Paul of the Cross, La Mirada, CA; St. Timothy, Los Angeles, CA
Vistal, Rev. Felix, '87 (P) Chap, US Veterans Affairs Domiciliary, White City
Visuvasam, Rev. Arul Joseph, '78 (LC) St. Casimir (Township of Hull), Stevens Point, WI; St. Peter, Stevens Point, WI
Vit, Rev. William J., '05 (MO) On Duty Outside Diocese. Archdiocese for the Military Services, USA Curia: Offices and Directors
Vit, Rev. William J., '05 (SC) On Duty Outside Diocese. Chaplain, US Air Force
Vitaglione, Rev. Robert P., '76 (BRK) Retired. St. Rita, Brooklyn, NY
Vitale, Rev. Louis, *O.F.M.* '63 (OAK) [MON] Franciscan Friars of California (Province of St. Barbara), Oakland, CA; [NUR] Mercy Retirement and Care Center, Oakland, CA
Vitali, Rev. Theodore, *C.P.* '69 (NY) [MON] The Congregation of the Passion - St. Paul of the Cross Province, Jamaica, NY
Vitali, Rev. Theodore, *C. P.* '69 (STL) [COL] Arts and Sciences, College of, ,
Vitaliano, Rev. Dominic, '91 (MIL) Chap, Veterans Administration Med Ctr, Wood
Vitaliano, Rev. Dominic J., '91 (PEO) On Duty Outside Diocese. Military; Veteran's Administration, WI Curia: (>MO) Offices and Directors
Vitela, Rev. Francisco Pineda, '68 (LA) Retired.
Viteri, Rev. Juan Carlos Villota, '22 (ATL) Cathedral of Christ the King Catholic Church, Atlanta, Inc., Atlanta, GA
Vithanage, Rev. Denzil J., '93 (TYL) Curia: Deaneries St. Patrick, Lufkin, TX; [EFT] St. Patrick School Foundation, Lufkin, TX
Vitillo, Rev. Msgr. Robert J., '72 (PAT) On Duty Outside Diocese. Geneva, Switzerland
Vito, Rev. Michael, '98 (SPP) Sacred Heart Parish-Pago Pago, Pago Pago, AS
Vitro, Rev. Thomas J., '66 (CHI) Retired.
Vitturino, Rev. Saverio T., '67 (WDC) Retired.
Vitug II, Rev. Victor Luna, (STV) Church of St. Joseph, Frederiksted, VI
Viuya, Rev. Melanio, *M.J.* '95 (LA) [MON] Missionaries of Jesus, Inc., Los Angeles, CA
Vivacqua, Rev. Francis, (ALB) St. Mary, Ballston Spa, NY
Vivas, Rev. Fernando J., (BO) St. Mary, Waltham, MA
Viveiros, Rev. Joseph F., '74 (FR) Retired.
Vivero, Rev. David P., '90 (ORL) Retired.
Viveros, Rev. Ricardo Henry, '08 (LA) Holy Trinity, Los Angeles, CA
Vives, Rev. Felipe, '21 (DAL) St. Joseph Catholic Parish - Richardson, Richardson, TX
Vives, Rev. Leopoldo M., *D.C.J.M.* '92 (ARL) Our Lady of Angels, Woodbridge, VA
Viviano, Rev. Anthony J., '12 (JC) Annunciation, California, MO; St. Andrew, Tipton, MO
Viviano, Rev. Benedict T., *O.P.* '66 (CHI) [MON] St. Pius V Priory, Chicago, IL
Viviano, Rev. Charles, '89 (ORL) Saint Frances Xavier Cabrini Catholic Church, St. Cloud, FL
Viviano, Rev. Thomas A., '13 (PH) On Duty Outside Diocese.
Vizcaino, Rev. Mario, *Sch.P.* '60 (MIA) [MON] Piarist Fathers, Province of the USA & Puerto Rico, Miami, FL
Vizcara, Rev. Armando, '20 (PAT) Christ the King, New Vernon, NJ
Vladyka, Rev. Vasyl, (PHU) Immaculate Conception, Hillside, NJ; St. Mary's, Carteret, NJ
Vlasz, Rev. Melvyn J., '63 (RCK) Retired.
Vlaun, Rev. Msgr. James C., '88 (RVC) Curia: Offices and Directors St. Agnes Cathedral, Rockville Centre, NY; [MIS] Catholic Faith Network, Uniondale, NY
Vo, Rev. Cong Chi, (ELP) On Academic Leave. St. Patrick Cathedral, El Paso, TX
Vo, Rev. Dong (Derek) P, *S.J.* '14 (DAL) [MON] St. Aloysius Gonzaga Jesuit Community, Dallas, TX
Vo, Rev. Khoa Phi, '07 (BLX) Sacred Heart, Pass Christian, MS
Vo, Rev. Peter Phong Cao, (NEW) Retired.
Vo, Rev. Peter Son, '06 (OAK) Military Chap Curia: (>MO) Offices and Directors
Vo, Rev. Peter Phong C., '88 (SPC) Retired.
Vo, Rev. Quy, '10 (ALB) Curia: Offices and Directors Holy Spirit, East Greenbush, NY
Vo, Rev. Thanh Dinh, *SDD* '16 (P) Our Lady of Lavang, Happy Valley, OR
Vo, Rev. Thanh Dinh, *S.D.D.* '16 (NO) [MIS] Domus Dei Clerical Society of Apostolic Life, U.S.A., Inc., New Orleans, LA
Vo Tran Gia, Rev. Dihn, *AA* '11 (WOR) [MON] Assumptionists (Augustinians of the Assumption), Worcester, MA
Vodoklys, Rev. Edward, *SJ* (BO) [MON] Campion Health & Wellness, Inc., Weston, MA
Vodoklys, Rev. Edward J., *S.J.* '91 (WOR) [MON] Jesuits

of the Holy Cross, Inc., Worcester, MA
Voegeli, Rev. Philip John (P.J.), '15 (WCH) Curia: Leadership St. James the Greater, Augusta, KS
Voelker, Rev. David A., '74 (BEL) Retired.
Voelker, Rev. Harold H., '54 (STL) Retired.
Voelker, Rev. James A., '69 (BEL) Retired. St. Michael, Waterloo, IL
Voelker, Rev. Nicholas A., '02 (WCH) St. Mary, Newton, KS
Voelker, Rev. Peter H., *C.Ss.R.* '61 (GAL) Retired. Holy Ghost, Houston, TX
Vogal, Rev. Caleb, (B) Curia: Leadership
Vogan, Rev. Howard L., '69 (DET) Retired.
Vogan, Rev. Msgr. Robert C., '70 (PH) Retired. St. Denis, Havertown, PA
Vogel, Rev. Andrew P., '10 (WIN) Curia: Offices and Directors St. Joseph, Good Thunder, MN; St. Matthew, Vernon Center, MN; St. Teresa Church, Mapleton, MN; St. Thomas More Catholic Newman Center Parish of Mankato, Minnesota, Mankato, MN
Vogel, Rev. Bill, *S.J.* '75 (YAK) St. Joseph Parish, Yakima, WA
Vogel, Rev. Caleb, '04 (B) Curia: Leadership
Vogel, Rev. Curt, '15 (KC) St. Bridget Catholic Church, Pleasant Hill, Pleasant Hill, MO; St. Patrick's, Holden, MO
Vogel, Rev. David M, '06 (RCK) On Administrative Leave.
Vogel, Rev. Joseph, '87 (SFS) Saint Joseph Parish of Union County, Elk Point, SD; Saint Peter Parish of Union County, Jefferson, SD; Saint Teresa of Calcutta of Union County, Dakota Dunes, SD
Vogel, Rev. Kevin W., '11 (OM) St. Jane Frances de Chantal, Randolph, NE; St. Joseph, Pierce, NE; St. Mary of the Seven Dolors, Osmond, NE
Vogel, Rev. Marcel, '89 (GF) Retired.
Vogel, Rev. Walter J., '58 (MIL) Retired. St. Alphonsus Congregation, Greendale, WI
Vogel, Rev. William, *S.J.* '75 (YAK) Resurrection, Zillah, WA (>P) [MON] Colombiere Jesuit Community, Portland, OR
Vogelpohl, Rev. Msgr. Daniel J., '75 (COV) Retired. Curia: Clergy and Religious Services
Vogelsang, Rev. Clifford R., '63 (IND) Retired.
Vogl, Rev. John C., '00 (YAK) St. Frances Xavier Cabrini, Benton City, WA
Vogler, Rev. J. Edward, '65 (STL) Retired. St. Elizabeth, Mother of John the Baptist Catholic Church, St. Louis, MO
Vogler, Rev. Jean, '70 (EVN) Retired.
Vogt, Rev. Emmerich W., *O.P.* '78 (OAK) (>SFR) [MIS] Shrine of St. Jude Thaddeus, San Francisco, CA; (>SFR) [MON] St. Dominic Priory, San Francisco, CA
Vogt, Rev. Eric, *O.S.B.* '79 (GBG) [MON] Saint Vincent Archabbey, Latrobe, PA
Voiland, Rev. Robert, '21 (DET) Our Lady of the Lakes Parish Waterford, Waterford, MI
Voiss, Rev. James, *S.J.* '88 (MIL) [CAM] Marquette University/Campus Ministry, Milwaukee, WI; [COL] Marquette University, Milwaukee, WI; [MON] Jesuit Community at Marquette University (Marquette Jesuit Associates, Inc.), Milwaukee, WI
Voithofer, Rev. Michael B., '10 (OM) St. Benedict the Moor, Omaha, NE; [MIS] Ablaze Ministries, Inc., Springfield, NE
Voitus, Rev. Joshua A., '11 (CHL) St. Vincent de Paul, Charlotte, NC
Voity, Rev. Msgr. Maurice, '79 (SAN) Retired.
Volavola, Rev. Simione, *M.S.C.* '01 (ALN) Our Lady of Good Counsel, Bangor, PA
Volertas, Rev. Vytautas, '93 (BRK) Retired. [CCH] Lithuanian Ministry, ,
Volk, Rev. Msgr. Marvin C., '74 (BEL) St. James, Millstadt, IL
Volk, Very Rev. Michael, '92 (MRY) Curia: Deaneries St. Joseph, Spreckels, CA
Volk, Rev. Norman, *OMI* '74 (BEL) Retired. [MON] Shrine of Our Lady of the Snows, Belleville, IL; [NUR] Apartment Community of Our Lady of the Snows (Benedictine Living Community | At The Shrine), Belleville, IL
Volkert, Rev. Daniel P., '01 (MIL) St. Bruno's Congregation, Dousman, WI; St. Paul's Catholic Church, Waukesha, WI
Volkert, Very Rev. James T., '90 (MIL) Congregation of the Immaculate Conception (St. Mary), Burlington, WI; St. Charles Congregation, Burlington, WI; St. Joseph's Congregation, Lyons, WI
Volkmer, Rev. Michael, *C.PP.S.* (KC) Retired. St. James, Liberty, MO; [MON] Precious Blood Center, Liberty, MO; [MON] Society of the Precious Blood, Liberty, MO
Voll, Rev. Walter Urban, *O.P.* '49 (PRO) [MON] St. Thomas Aquinas Priory at Providence College, Providence, RI
Vollmer, Rev. Daniel, '02 (PHX) Curia: Leadership; Offices and Directors St. Margaret Mary Roman Catholic Parish, Bullhead City, AZ
Vollmer, Rev. William J., '97 (CHI) St. Alexander, Palos Heights, IL
Vollmer-Konig, Rev. Josef, '21 (DAL) Retired. St. Patrick Catholic Parish - Dallas, Dallas, TX
Volmi, Rev. Dennis G., '75 (WIL) Retired.
Voltaggio, Rev. Joseph, *O.S.B.* '17 (PAT) [MON] St. Mary's Abbey, Morristown, NJ; [RTR] St. Mary's Abbey Retreat Center, Morristown, NJ
Voltz, Rev. Gus, '17 (ALX) Nativity of the Blessed Virgin Mary, Campti, LA
Volz, Rev. Msgr. Anthony R., '85 (IND) Christ The King Catholic Church, Indianapolis, Inc., Indianapolis, IN
Volz, Rev. Edward Raymond, *O.S.P.P.E.* '88 (GBG) [MON] Pauline Fathers Monastery, Kittanning, PA
Volz, Rev. Gerald, '92 (KCK) Corpus Christi, Lawrence, KS
Volz, Rev. Peter, (NEW) St. John the Apostle, Linden, NJ
von Behren, Rev. Thomas, *C.S.V.* (LAV) Cristo Rey St. Viator Las Vegas Preparatory, Inc., North Las Vegas, NV
von Behren, Rev. Thomas R., *C.S.V.* '83 (CHI) [MON] Viatorian Province Center-Clerics of St. Viator, Arlington Heights, IL
Von Braunsburg, Rev. Kit, (RVC) Chap, Mercy Med Ctr
von Duerbeck, Rev. Julian, *O.S.B.* '76 (JOL) Retired. [MON] St. Procopius Abbey, Lisle, IL
Von Essen, Rev. Pacificus, *S.A.* '53 (NY) Retired.
Von Handorf, Rev. Jay, '75 (LEX) St. Mildred, Somerset, KY
Von Kaenel, Rev. George, (DET) [MON] Colombiere Center, Clarkston, MI
Von Lehmen, Rev. Jeffrey D., '85 (COV) Holy Cross High School, Covington, KY; St. Patrick, Taylor Mill, KY
von Maluski, Rev. Kris M., '01 (PRO) Saint Augustin's Church of Newport, Newport, RI
von Nell, Rev. Boniface, *O.S.B.* '91 (WDC) [MON] St. Anselm's Abbey, Washington, DC
Vona, Rev. Michael S., '68 (TR) Retired.
Vonderhaar, Rev. Eugene F., '59 (CIN) Retired.
Vondou, Rev. Augustin, (BO) St. Mary, Winchester, MA
Voor, Rev. Joseph H., '50 (L) Retired.
Voorhes, Rev. Msgr. Fred R., '71 (BUF) Retired.
Voorhies, Rev. Msgr. Bennett J., '83 (SFE) Our Lady of the Annunciation, Albuquerque, NM
Voorhies, Very Rev. Thomas P., '90 (LAF) Curia: Leadership Sacred Heart of Jesus, Ville Platte, LA; St. Joseph, Ville Platte, LA
Voors, Rev. David W., '81 (FTW) Curia: Offices and Directors St. Mary of the Assumption, Avilla, IN
Vorderlandwehr, Rev. Adrian R., *O.S.B.* '67 (OKL) Retired. [MON] St. Gregory's Abbey (Benedictine Fathers of Sacred Heart Mission, Inc.), Shawnee, OK
Vordtriede, Rev. Thomas A., '14 (STL) Holy Rosary Catholic Church, Warrenton, MO
Voris, Rev. Francis, *OFM Cap.* (DET) [MON] St. Bonaventure Monastery, Detroit, MI
Voris, Rev. Francis, *O.F.M.Cap.* '73 (SAG) Saint Joseph Parish of Saginaw, Saginaw, MI
Vorontsov, Rev. Ihor, '10 (PSC) Blessed Basil Hopko Byzantine Catholic Mission, Conway, SC; Holy Spirit, Mahwah, NJ; St. Nicholas of Myra, White Plains, NY
Vorwald, Rev. Aloysius J., '64 (DUB) Retired.
Vorwoldt, Rev. James, *S.J.* (MIL) [MON] St. Camillus Jesuit Community (Society of Jesus, USA Midwest Province), Wauwatosa, WI
Vos, Rev. Jude, '96 (FAR) Retired.
Vos, Rev. William, '64 (SCL) Retired. Curia: Offices and Directors
Vosko, Rev. Richard, '69 (ALB) Retired.
Voss, Rev. David M., '12 (WCH) On Duty Outside Diocese. Active Duty Archdiocese for Military Services Curia: (>MO) Offices and Directors
Voss, Rev. Dennis F., '64 (BEL) Retired.
Voss, Rev. Donald J., '93 (PBR) St. Nicholas, McKeesport, PA
Voss, Rt. Rev. Marcus J., *O.S.B.* '71 (BIR) [EFT] Clairvaux Society Foundation, Cullman, AL; [EFT] St. Bernard Abbey Foundation, Cullman, AL; [EFT] St. Bernard Preparatory School Educational Foundation, Cullman, AL; [MON] St. Bernard Abbey, Cullman, AL
Voss, Rev. Robert D., *S.J.* '72 (STL) Retired.
Voss, Rev. Robert J., '70 (PHX) Retired. St. Bridget Roman Catholic Parish, Mesa, AZ
Vossler, Rev. Brian E., '91 (E) St. George, Erie, PA
Votraw, Rev. Wilbur J., '55 (SY) Retired.
Votruba, Rev. Joshua, '21 (TLS) Curia: Offices and Directors Holy Family Cathedral, Tulsa, OK
Vottola, Rev. Pio, '18 (ORG) [MON] Norbertine Fathers of Orange, Inc., Silverado, CA
Vowells, Rev. John J., *S.J.* '90 (STL) [MON] Bellarmine House of Studies, St. Louis, MO
Voyt, Very Rev. Stephen A., '85 (PT) Curia: Leadership Holy Name of Jesus, Niceville, FL
Voytek, Rev. Leonard E., '74 (ALT) Saint Mary's Church, Nanty-Glo, PA
Vozzo, Rev. Gregory G., '10 (BO) St. Edward the Confessor, Medfield, MA; St. James, Salem, MA; St. Jude, Norfolk, MA
Vrabel, Rev. George A., '87 (CLV) Retired.
Vrazel, Rev. Edward, '58 (SAT) [NUR] Oblate Madonna Residence, San Antonio, TX
Vrazel, Very Rev. Stephen G., '11 (MOB) Curia: Leadership St. Joan of Arc Parish, Mobile, Mobile, AL; St. Mary Parish, Mobile, Mobile, AL; [MIS] Catholic Scouting - Boy Scouts, Mobile, AL
Vrba, Rev. James J., '77 (DAV) Retired.
Vricella, Rev. Archmandrite Michele, (BRK) Our Lady of Mount Carmel - Annunciation of the Blessed Virgin Mary, Brooklyn, NY
Vu, Rev. Andy Dinh, *S.V.D.* '07 (BEA) St. Mary, Cleveland, TX
Vu, Rev. Anh Ngoc Quoc, '22 (BGP) Saint Leo Roman Catholic Church Corporation, Stamford, CT
Vu, Rev. Anthony Hien, '09 (ORG) St. Barbara Catholic Church, Santa Ana, CA
Vu, Rev. Anthony Minh, '18 (L) Curia: Leadership
Vu, Rev. Benoit Trieu Van, '15 (SFE) Holy Angels, Angel Fire, NM; Our Lady of Mt Carmel Mission, , ; San Antonio, , ; San Isidro Mission, , ; St. Mel, Eagle Nest, NM
Vu, Rev. Benoit Trieu Van, '15 (SFE) Immaculate Conception Church-Cimarron, Cimarron, NM; St. Joseph, Springer, NM
Vu, Rev. Dat, '04 (B) Our Lady of the Rosary, Boise, ID
Vu, Rev. Dominic, '16 (SB) St. Francis of Assisi, La Quinta, CA
Vu, Rev. Douglas Michael, '12 (BIR) Our Lady of La Vang Parish @ St. John Bosco Church, Birmingham, AL
Vu, Rev. Duc, *S.J.* '02 (SJ) Curia: Leadership Most Holy Trinity, San Jose, CA
Vu, Rev. Dustin L., '04 (DUB) [COL] Clarke University of Dubuque, Iowa, Dubuque, IA; [COL] Loras College, Dubuque, IA
Vu, Rev. Francis Nam, *OCist.* (SAC) [MON] Our Lady of Sacramento Monastery, Walnut Grove, CA
Vu, Rev. Hau Q., '16 (SB) Curia: Offices and Directors
Vu, Rev. Hoai Phong, *S.D.B.* '11 (LA) Our Lady of Peace, North Hills, CA
Vu, Rev. Hung, (SJ) Our Lady of La Vang Parish, San Jose, CA
Vu, Rev. Huy, *C.Ss.R.* (TUC) Santa Catalina Roman Catholic Parish - Tucson, Tucson, AZ
Vu, Rev. Huy, *C.Ss.R.* '20 (STP) (>TUC) [MON] Redemptorist Society of Arizona Desert House of Prayer Residence, Tucson, AZ; (>TUC) [RTR] Redemptorist Society of Arizona Redemptorist Renewal Center, Tucson, AZ
Vu, Rev. Ignatius, '94 (NY) Retired.
Vu, Rev. Jack, '02 (LR) St. Patrick Catholic Church, North Little Rock, AR
Vu, Rev. John Cuong Ba, *C.Ss.R.* '14 (LA) [MON] Vietnamese Redemptorist Mission, Baldwin Park, CA
Vu, Rev. John Francis, *S.J.* '97 (ORG) Curia: Leadership [CAM] University Catholic Community at UCI, Irvine, CA; [MON] Manresa Jesuit Residence, Anaheim, CA
Vu, Rev. Joseph, '90 (BRK) Retired.
Vu, Very Rev. Joseph Dang, *S.D.D.* '02 (NO) [MIS] Domus Dei Clerical Society of Apostolic Life, U.S.A., Inc., New Orleans, LA
Vu, Rev. Joseph Dang Hai, *S.D.D.* (MO) Curia: Offices and Directors
Vu, Rev. Joseph Khai Dinh, (NEW) Retired.
Vu, Rev. Joseph Q., '06 (ARL) St. James, Falls Church, VA
Vu, Rev. Joseph Thanh, '75 (GAL) Retired.
Vu, Rev. Joseph Toan Du, *C.R.M.* (VEN) St. Martha Parish in Sarasota, Inc., Sarasota, FL
Vu, Rev. Joseph Van, '09 (LA) St. Lucy, Long Beach, CA
Vu, Rev. Joseph Dang Hai, *S.D.D.* (SEA) Our Lady of Lourdes, Seattle, WA
Vu, Rev. Joseph Tien Minh, *O.P.* '06 (ARL) Holy Martyrs of Vietnam Catholic Church, Arlington, VA
Vu, Rev. Ken T., '16 (SB) Our Lady of Hope Catholic Community, Inc., San Bernardino, CA
Vu, Rev. Khoa, '17 (SJ) St. Christopher, San Jose, CA
Vu, Rev. Leo, *CRM* (PT) Our Lady Queen of Martyrs,

Pensacola, FL
Vu, Rev. Lieu, '91 (SJ) St. Francis of Assisi, San Jose, CA
Vu, Rev. Linh, '21 (CHY) Church of the Holy Trinity, Cheyenne, WY
Vu, Rev. Long Ngoc, '06 (ORG) On Administrative Leave.
Vu, Rev. Martin, '19 (ORG) Santiago de Compostela, Lake Forest, CA
Vu, Rev. Martin Tu Quoc, (ARL) Our Lady, Queen of Peace, Arlington, VA
Vu, Rev. Michael Long, *SVD* (MOB) St. Margaret Parish, Bayou La Batre, Bayou La Batre, AL
Vu, Rev. Minh, (L) St. Athanasius, Louisville, KY
Vu, Rev. Minh, '94 (STP) St. Adalbert, St. Paul, MN
Vu, Rev. Nam, *S.V.D.* '12 (FTW) St. Patrick, Fort Wayne, IN
Vu, Rev. Paul H., *S.J.* '11 (LA) [MON] Jesuit Community, Los Angeles, CA
Vu, Rev. Paul Hoa Duy, '12 (ORG) On Duty Outside Diocese. Curia: Leadership St. Columban, Garden Grove, CA
Vu, Rev. Paul Thien, *SD* '03 (DAL) Retired. [MIS] Domus Dei Clerical Society of Apostolic Life, Kaufman, TX
Vu, Rev. Peter Duc, '96 (ATL) Our Lady of Vietnam Catholic Church, Riverdale, Inc., Riverdale, GA
Vu, Rev. Peter G., '97 (GR) St. Mary Magdalen, Kentwood, MI
Vu, Rev. Richard Anh, '13 (ATL) St. Gabriel Catholic Church, Fayetteville, Inc., Fayetteville, GA
Vu, Rev. Thanh Khan, *C.S.* '19 (SJ) Holy Cross, San Jose, CA
Vu, Rev. Tho, *SJ* (OM) (>CHI) [COL] Jesuit Community at Loyola University Chicago, Chicago, IL
Vu, Rev. Thomas, *CRM* '12 (STP) (>GAL) St. Elizabeth Ann Seton, Houston, TX
Vu, Rev. Thomas, '01 (SPC) Retired. [MON] Congregation of the Mother of the Redeemer, Carthage, MO
Vu, Rev. Tung Duc, *C.Ss.R.* '07 (LA) [MON] Vietnamese Redemptorist Mission, Baldwin Park, CA
Vu, Rev. Tung Duc, *S.D.D.* '07 (NO) [MIS] Domus Dei Clerical Society of Apostolic Life, U.S.A., Inc., New Orleans, LA
Vu, Rev. Vincent, (HON) Curia: Consultative Bodies St. John Vianney, Kailua, HI
Vu, Rev. Vinh Van, *C.M.C.* '00 (FWT) Our Lady of Fatima, Fort Worth, TX
Vu Viet, Rev. Nguyen, (SP) Holy Martyrs of Vietnam Parish, St. Petersburg, FL
Vuelvas-Arias, Rev. David, '75 (ORG) Retired.
Vujs, Rev. Joseph E., '57 (HRT) Retired.
Vujs, Rev. Robert, *M.M.* (HRT) Retired.
Vujs, Rev. Robert, *M.M.* (NOR) Curia: Offices and Directors
Vujs, Rev. Robert W., *M.M.* '61 (NY) Retired. [MON] Maryknoll Fathers and Brothers (Catholic Foreign Mission Society of America, Inc.), Ossining, NY
Vuky, Rev. Michael, '05 (P) Curia: Offices and Directors; Tribunal St. Edward, North Plains, OR; St. Francis of Assisi Catholic Church, Banks, Oregon, Banks, OR; Visitation B.V.M., Forest Grove, OR
Vular, Rev. Robert J., '01 (PIT) Sts. Martha and Mary, Allison Park, PA
Vuong, Rev. Joseph-Quoc T., '07 (STP) On Leave.
Vuong, Rev. Paulavang, *O.S.B.* '14 (DAL) [MON] Benedictine Monastery of Thien Tam, Kerens, TX
Vuoso, Rev. Pasquale, *C.R.I.C.* '87 (LA) St. Sebastian, Santa Paula, CA; [MON] Canons Regular of the Immaculate Conception, Santa Paula, CA
Vuturo, Rev. Paul V., '73 (MIA) Retired.
Vyverman, Rev. Mark, '93 (KAL) Curia: Consultative Bodies; Offices and Directors St. Catherine of Siena, Portage, MI
Waalkes, Rev. James F., (ARL) St. Anthony, Falls Church, VA
Wachdorf, Rev. Paul H., '75 (CHI) Retired.
Wachowiak, Rev. Duane A., '98 (GLD) Curia: Advisory Boards, Commissions, Committees, and Councils; Leadership Assumption of the Blessed Virgin Mary of Burt Lake, Brutus, MI; Sacred Heart of Riggsville, Cheboygan, MI; Saint Clement of Pellston, Pellston, MI; Saint Mary-Saint Charles of Cheboygan, Cheboygan, MI
Wachowicz, Rev. John, '17 (RVC) Curia: Leadership
Wachter, Rev. Robert B., '76 (WCH) Retired.
Wack, Very Rev. Neil, *C.S.C.* '04 (FR) Immaculate Conception, North Easton, MA; [CEM] Immaculate Conception, North Easton, MA; [COL] Holy Cross Fathers Religious, North Easton, MA
Wackerman, Rev. John F., '98 (PH) St. Luke the Evangelist, Glenside, PA
Waclawik, Rev. Leszek J., (LAR) Our Lady of Guadalupe, Laredo, TX
Waclawik, Rev. Leszek J., '84 (LAR) Curia: Leadership
Wadas, Rev. Raymond J., '72 (WDC) Retired. Our Lady of Sorrows, Takoma Park, MD
Waddell, Rev. Paul M., '84 (NY) Parish of Immaculate Conception and Assumption, Tuckahoe, NY; St. Theresa, Briarcliff Manor, NY
Waddill, Rev. Dale T., '64 (P) Retired.
Wade, Rev. Edward C., '72 (CAM) Retired.
Wade, Rev. Gerald T., *S.J.* '68 (SJ) Bellarmine College Preparatory, San Jose, CA
Wadelton, Rev. Christopher, '09 (IND) Curia: Leadership; Offices and Directors St. Bartholomew Catholic Church, Columbus, IN, Columbus, IN
Wadeson, Rev. John, (AGN) On Duty Outside Diocese. Itinerant Catechist, CA
Wadowski, Rev. Stanislaw, '97 (RVC) St. Anne's, Brentwood, NY
Wagenhoffer, Rev. Josef A., '65 (CAM) Retired.
Waggoner, Rev. Ross E., '12 (BEA) Our Lady of Lourdes, Vidor, TX
Wagner, Rev. Alan, *S.D.S.* '76 (MIL) [MIS] Salvatorians - Jordan Hall, Milwaukee, WI
Wagner, Rev. Braden, '11 (DEN) [SEM] Saint John Vianney Theological Seminary, Denver, CO
Wagner, Rev. Christopher, *SJ* '17 (WDC) [MON] The Jesuit Community at Georgetown University, Washington, DC
Wagner, Rev. Donald, '87 (SCL) Curia: Leadership Christ the King, Cambridge, MN; St. Elizabeth Ann Seton, Isanti, MN; St. Peter & Paul, Braham, MN
Wagner, Rev. Eric, *CR* (BEL) Immaculate Conception of the B.V.M., Columbia, IL
Wagner, Rev. John F., '64 (SB) Retired.
Wagner, Rev. John J., '87 (RIC) Holy Rosary, Richmond, VA
Wagner, Rev. John P., '62 (SY) Retired.
Wagner, Rev. Msgr. Joseph, '65 (SFS) Retired.
Wagner, Rev. Joseph, '22 (ATL) Cathedral of Christ the King Catholic Church, Atlanta, Inc., Atlanta, GA
Wagner, Rev. Joseph F., *S.J.* '98 (LAN) St. Mary Student Parish Ann Arbor, Ann Arbor, MI; [CAM] St. Mary Student Parish, Ann Arbor, MI; [MON] USA Midwest Province of the Society of Jesus - Jesuit Residence, Ann Arbor, MI
Wagner, Rev. Mark, '88 (STO) Curia: Leadership Presentation Church (Pastor of), Stockton, CA
Wagner, Rev. Matthew, (WIN) St. Mary, Caledonia, MN
Wagner, Rev. Matthew R., '19 (WIN) St. Patrick's, Brownsville, MN
Wagner, Rev. Robert, (ARL) St. Andrew the Apostle, Clifton, VA
Wagner, Rev. Ronald F., '79 (SAG) Curia: Offices and Directors [MIS] St. Joseph Church, Alger, MI
Wagner, Rev. Ronald F., *Fr.* '79 (SAG) Resurrection of the Lord Parish of Standish, Standish, MI
Wagner, Rev. Thomas A., '83 (PIT) St. Joachim and Anne, Elizabeth, PA
Wagner, Rev. Walter C., (RIC) St. George, Scottsville, VA; St. Thomas Aquinas, Charlottesville, VA
Wagner, Rev. Walter Cornelius, *O.P.* '93 (NY) St. Catherine of Siena, New York, NY; [MON] St. Catherine of Siena Priory, New York, NY
Wagner, Rev. William, *O.R.C.* '77 (STU) [MON] Order of the Holy Cross, Inc., Carrollton, OH
Wagner, Rev. William C., '73 (CIN) St. Mary, Bethel, OH; St. Peter, New Richmond, OH; St. Thomas More, Cincinnati, OH
Wah, Rev. Joseph C., '05 (LA) Retired.
Wahal, Rev. Stephen J., '00 (PBR) Assumption of the Blessed Virgin, Monessen, PA; Holy Ghost, Charleroi, PA; St. Michael, Donora, PA
Wahl, Rev. Richard, *CSB* '73 (GAL) [MON] The Basilian Fathers of Dillon House, Houston, TX
Wahl, Rev. Richard A., *C.S.B.* '73 (GAL) Curia: Leadership
Wahl, Rev. Richard A., *C.S.B.* '73 (GAL) Curia: Leadership
Wahl, Rev. Thomas, *O.S.B.* '58 (SCL) [MON] St. John's Abbey, of the Order of St. Benedict, Collegeville, MN
Wahlmeier, Rev. Joseph, '20 (LIN) Curia: Leadership North American Martyrs, Lincoln, NE
Wahyudianto, Rev. Agung, (NEW) St. Cecilia, Englewood, NJ
Waibel, Rev. Philip, *O.S.B.* '83 (P) [MON] Mt. Angel Abbey, Saint Benedict, OR
Wainwright, Rev. Walter L., '65 (ROC) Retired.
Waiss, Rev. John R., '87 (CHI) Curia: Leadership St. Mary of the Angels, Chicago, IL; [MIS] Midtown Residence, Chicago, IL
Waiss, Rev. John R., '87 (POD) Curia: Clergy and Religious Services
Wait, Rev. Dennis, '72 (KCK) Retired.
Waite, Rev. James A., '04 (BUF) On Leave. Curia: Consultative Bodies
Waitekus, Rev. Christopher J., '91 (SPR) St. Mary's, Longmeadow, MA; [CAM] Bay Path University, Longmeadow, MA
Waithaka, Rev. Paul Maina, '02 (CHI) [SEM] University of Saint Mary of the Lake/Mundelein Seminary, Mundelein, IL
Waiwood, Rev. Richard, '73 (ELP) Retired.
Wajda, Rev. Mark R., '08 (ORL) Blessed Sacrament, Clermont, FL
Wajdzik, Rev. Tomasz, (CHI) Sacred Heart and St. Eulalia, Melrose Park, IL
Wake, Rev. John F., '74 (TR) Retired.
Wakefield, Rev. Alan, '75 (LAN) Retired.
Wakefield, Rev. Michael, '81 (LA) St. Francis de Sales, Sherman Oaks, CA
Wakim, Rev. Rodolph, '96 (SAM) Saint Stephen Maronite Catholic Church, Waxhaw, NC
Wakube, Rev. John, *A.J.* '02 (LR) Immaculate Conception, North Little Rock, AR
Wakulich, Rev. Kerry J., '10 (TLS) St. John the Evangelist Parish and Catholic Student Center, Stillwater, OK; [CAM] St. John's University Parish and Catholic Student Center, Stillwater, OK
Wakuma, Rev. Fufa Ensermu, (LA) St. Catherine of Siena, Reseda, CA
Walas, Rev. Joseph, '59 (RVC) Retired.
Walczyk, Rev. Rafal, *O.S.P.P.E.* '05 (PH) [MON] The Order of Saint Paul, First Hermit - The Pauline Fathers, Doylestown, PA; [RTR] National Shrine of Our Lady of Czestochowa, Doylestown, PA
Wald, Rev. Conrad Wald, *OSB* '19 (CLV) [MON] Benedictine Order of Cleveland (St. Andrew Abbey), Cleveland, OH
Walden, Rev. Msgr. Ellsworth R., '71 (RVC) St. Patrick, Smithtown, NY
Walden, Rev. Thomas R., '12 (ORL) Our Lady of Lourdes, Melbourne, FL
Walder, Rev. Keith A., '03 (PEO) St. Mary, Pesotum, IL; St. Thomas, Philo, IL
Waldman, Rev. Noah A., '08 (STL) St. Martin of Tours Catholic Church, Lemay, MO
Waldmann, Rev. Pablo, *I.V.E.* '97 (NY) Holy Rosary, New York, NY; Parish of St. Paul and Holy Rosary, New York, NY
Waldrep, Rev. Jeffrey, (JKS) Curia: Canonical Services; Consultative Bodies; Leadership Annunciation, Columbus, MS; [CAM] Mississippi University for Women Student Center, Columbus, MS
Waldrop, Rev. Gregory S., *S.J.* '99 (NO) [COL] Loyola University New Orleans, New Orleans, LA; [MON] Loyola Jesuit Community, New Orleans, LA
Waldschmidt, Rev. Valens J., *O.F.M.* '47 (CIN) Retired.
Walega, Rev. Stanley J., '64 (MET) Retired.
Walk, Rev. Edward J., '78 (E) Assumption of Blessed Virgin Mary, Sykesville, PA; St. Bernard, Falls Creek, PA; St. Mary, Reynoldsville, PA
Walka, Rev. Marcin, '09 (PAT) On Leave.
Walker, Rev. Ako, *C.Ss.R.* (BAL) Sacred Heart of Jesus-Sagrado Corazon de Jesus, Baltimore, MD
Walker, Rev. Brian G., *O.P.* '86 (CHI) [MON] St. Pius V Priory, Chicago, IL
Walker, Rev. Charles, (L) St. Bernard, Louisville, KY
Walker, Rev. Msgr. David M., '64 (HRT) Retired. Saint John Bosco Parish Corporation, Branford, CT
Walker, Rev. Dennis, '21 (SY) Curia: Leadership St. Anthony of Padua, Cortland, NY; St. Margaret, Homer, NY; St. Mary, Cortland, NY; St. Patrick, Truxton, NY
Walker, Rev. Douglas, '99 (FRS) Santa Rosa, Lone Pine, CA
Walker, Rev. Francisco J., '87 (BRK) St. Thomas Apostle, Woodhaven, NY
Walker, Rev. Gerard T., '80 (BRK) Retired.
Walker, Rev. Henry B., *O.M.I.* '85 (GAL) Immaculate Conception, Houston, TX
Walker, Very Rev. J. Kenneth, '81 (EVN) On Special Assignment. Curia: Leadership; Offices and Directors
Walker, Rev. J. Patrick, '88 (STO) Curia: Leadership Sacred Heart Church of Turlock (Pastor of), Turlock, CA
Walker, Rev. J. Kenneth, '81 (EVN) Curia: Leadership St. John, Loogootee, IN
Walker, Rev. James E., '99 (GLP) Retired.
Walker, Rev. James P., '77 (Y) Retired.
Walker, Rev. Jeffery, '13 (TOL) Holy Angels, Sandusky, OH; St. Mary's, Sandusky, OH; [CAM] Bowling Green State University Campus Ministry, Bowling Green, OH
Walker, Rev. Jeffrey, (TOL) SS. Peter and Paul, Sandusky, OH
Walker, Rev. John Paul, *O.P.* '02 (CIN) St. Gertrude,

Cincinnati, OH; [MON] St. Gertrude Priory, Cincinnati, OH
Walker, Rev. Kent A., '89 (ORL) On Leave.
Walker, Rev. Michael, '62 (KC) Retired.
Walker, Rev. Michael, '99 (P) Chap, Federal Corr Inst, Sheridan Curia: Offices and Directors St. Cecilia, Beaverton, OR
Walker, Rev. Mike, '99 (P) Good Shepherd, Sheridan, OR; St. Michael, Grand Ronde, OR
Walker, Friar Pachomius, *O.P.* '22 (WDC) (>PH) St. Patrick, Philadelphia, PA
Walker, Rev. Steven R., '14 (ARL) On Duty Outside Diocese. Our Lady of Lourdes, Arlington, VA
Walker, Rev. Steven R., (MO) Curia: Offices and Directors
Walker, Rev. Thomas J., '89 (MIL) Retired.
Walker, Rev. Thomas J., '90 (STP) Church of St. Michael of Prior Lake, Prior Lake, MN; [CEM] St. Michael Cemetery, Prior Lake, MN
Wall, Rev. Augustine, *SVD* '91 (LAF) Immaculate Heart of Mary, Lafayette, LA
Wall, Rev. Msgr. Barry W., '62 (FR) Retired.
Wall, Rev. Damian, *C.Ss.R.* (SJN) San Agustin, San Juan, PR
Wall, Rev. Msgr. G. Warren, '76 (MOB) Retired.
Wall, Rev. Msgr. James E., '63 (BUF) Retired. St. George, West Falls, NY; [MON] Bishop Head Residence, Lackawanna, NY
Wall, Rev. Msgr. John A., '60 (R) Retired. St. Michael the Archangel Catholic Church, Cary, NC
Wall, Rev. John J., '68 (CHI) [MIS] The Catholic Church Extension Society of the United States of America, Chicago, IL
Wall, Rev. Sherman B., *O.M.I.* (BEL) [MON] Missionary Oblates of Mary Immaculate - St. Henry's Oblate Residence, Belleville, IL
Wall, Rev. Sherman B., *O.M.I.* '57 (SPC) Retired.
Wall, Rev. Terence Damian, *C.Ss.R.* '65 (SJN) [MIS] Casa San Clemente, San Juan, PR
Wallace, Rev. Cavana, '92 (SD) Pastor of Saint Timothy Catholic Parish, Escondido, a corporation sole, Escondido, CA
Wallace, Rev. Christopher W., '13 (BO) Curia: Consultative Bodies All Saints, Haverhill, MA
Wallace, Rev. Donald, (SAT) [NUR] Marianist Residence: Skilled Nursing, San Antonio, TX
Wallace, Rev. Donald L., '62 (JC) Retired.
Wallace, Rev. James, *C.Ss.R.* '70 (BRK) [MON] Redemptorist Fathers of New York, Inc.-Baltimore Province, Brooklyn, NY
Wallace, Rev. James, '20 (AJ) Holy Name, Ketchikan, AK
Wallace, Rev. James, '12 (CHI) Curia: Leadership St. Paul of the Cross, Park Ridge, IL
Wallace, Rev. Jason, '04 (DEN) Curia: Offices and Directors
Wallace, Rev. Kenneth F., '00 (CLV) Holy Family, Parma, OH
Wallace, Rev. William, *O.S.A.* '74 (NOR) [CAM] Wesleyan University-The University Ministry, Middletown, CT
Wallace, Rev. William J., *O.S.A.* '74 (NY) St. Nicholas of Tolentine, Bronx, NY
Wallack, Very Rev. Michael, (TR) Curia: Leadership St. John, Allentown, NJ
Wallenfelsz, Rev. Scott, *S.D.S.* '69 (MIL) [EFT] Society of the Divine Savior Ongoing Community Support Trust, Milwaukee, WI; [MIS] Salvatorian Institute of Philosophy and Theology, Inc., Milwaukee, WI; [MON] Salvatorian Provincial Offices (Society of the Divine Savior), Milwaukee, WI
Wallenfelsz, Rev. Scott, *SDS* (MIL) (>SJ) [EFT] Our Lady of Fatima Villa Foundation, Saratoga, CA
Waller, Rev. Charles J., '73 (PAT) Retired.
Waller, Rev. Robert C., '75 (CIN) Retired.
Wallin, Rev. Msgr. Kevin W., '84 (BGP) Retired.
Walling, Rev. James, (MO) Curia: Offices and Directors
Walling, Rev. Richard W., '78 (CIN) Queen of Peace, Hamilton, OH; St. Aloysius, Hamilton, OH; St. Joseph, Hamilton, OH; St. Julie Billiart, Hamilton, OH; St. Peter in Chains, Hamilton, OH; [MIS] St. Marys Deanery Center, Celina, OH
Wallis, Very Rev. Jonathan, '07 (FWT) Curia: Advisory Boards, Commissions, Committees, and Councils; Leadership; Miscellaneous / Other Offices
Wallisch, Rev. Scott, '10 (KCK) St. Joseph, Shawnee, KS
Walmsley, Rev. John, (SEA) Retired.
Walsh, Rev. Aidan J., '70 (BO) Retired.
Walsh, Rev. Andrew J, '14 (WCH) Curia: Leadership St. Patrick, Kingman, KS
Walsh, Rev. Arthur, '85 (CC) Retired.
Walsh, Rev. Brendan J., '93 (LAN) St. Joseph Parish Dexter, Dexter, MI
Walsh, Rev. Broderick Matthew, *CSP* '92 (NY) St. Paul the Apostle, New York, NY; [MON] Paulist Fathers' Motherhouse, New York, NY
Walsh, Rev. Christopher, (ALB) Curia: Offices and Directors
Walsh, Rev. Msgr. Christopher J., '87 (BGP) Retired. Curia: Canonical Services
Walsh, Rev. Christopher M., '99 (PH) Curia: Advisory Boards, Commissions, Committees, and Councils St. Cecilia, Philadelphia, PA; [MIS] Pro-Life Union of Greater Philadelphia, Oreland, PA
Walsh, Rev. Daniel L., *C.S.Sp.* '91 (PIT) Curia: Consultative Bodies St. Paul Cathedral, Pittsburgh, PA; [CAM] Duquesne University, Pittsburgh, PA; [COL] Duquesne University of the Holy Spirit, Pittsburgh, PA
Walsh, Rev. Daniel P., '68 (BUF) Retired. Curia: Consultative Bodies
Walsh, Rev. Dennis, *S.O.L.T.* '04 (DET) Curia: Consultative Bodies Holy Redeemer Parish Detroit, Detroit, MI; St. Cunegunda Parish Detroit, Detroit, MI
Walsh, Rev. Dennis, *SOLT* (CC) (>DET) St. Gabriel Parish Detroit, Detroit, MI
Walsh, Rev. Dennis G., '92 (TOL) Curia: Advisory Boards, Commissions, Committees, and Councils; Deaneries St. John the Baptist, Delphos, OH; St. John the Evangelist, Delphos, OH; St. Patrick, Spencerville, OH; [EFT] St. John Parish Foundation, Inc., Delphos, OH
Walsh, Rev. Msgr. Francis E., '66 (SPR) Retired.
Walsh, Rev. Francis M., '67 (WDC) On Duty Outside Diocese. Holy Name, Washington, DC
Walsh, Rev. Francis P., '57 (CLV) Retired.
Walsh, Rev. Gerald G., '95 (CHI) Prince of Peace, Lake Villa, IL
Walsh, Rev. James B., '65 (SAC) Retired.
Walsh, Rev. James F., *S.J.* '72 (BO) [MON] Campion Center, Inc., Weston, MA
Walsh, Rev. James J., '73 (SCR) Retired.
Walsh, Rev. James J., '68 (CIN) St. Dominic, Cincinnati, OH
Walsh, Rev. James J., '93 (ALB) Curia: Leadership St. Pius X, Loudonville, NY
Walsh, Rev. James J., (SAM) Curia: Leadership
Walsh, Rev. Jeffrey J., '94 (SCR) On Duty Outside Diocese. Named Bishop of Gaylord, Michigan
Walsh, Rev. Jerome, '69 (DET) Retired.
Walsh, Rev. John A., '80 (E) Retired. On Sick Leave.
Walsh, Rev. John Daly, *M.M.* '56 (NY) Retired.
Walsh, Rev. John F., '76 (PIT) Retired.
Walsh, Rev. John Joseph, *S.J.* '71 (BO) [MON] Campion Health & Wellness, Inc., Weston, MA
Walsh, Rev. Msgr. John P., '77 (ATL) Curia: Leadership St. Joseph Catholic Church, Marietta, Inc., Marietta, GA
Walsh, Rev. Joseph, (RNO) St. Joseph's, Elko, NV
Walsh, Rev. Joseph, (RNO) Curia: Leadership; Offices and Directors
Walsh, Rev. Joseph M., '86 (LIN) Curia: Leadership St. Mary, Lincoln, NE
Walsh, Rev. Joseph R., '64 (SFR) Retired.
Walsh, Very Rev. Kevin B., '92 (ARL) Curia: Consultative Bodies Precious Blood, Culpeper, VA
Walsh, Rev. Kevin V., *O.C.S.O* '78 (CHR) [MON] Mepkin Abbey, Moncks Corner, SC
Walsh, Rev. Leo A., '94 (AJ) Curia: Tribunal St. Patrick, Anchorage, AK
Walsh, Rev. Martin, *O.P.* '69 (OAK) (>SFR) [MON] St. Dominic Priory, San Francisco, CA
Walsh, Rev. Matthew S., *S.J.* '09 (OM) St. John's at Creighton University Parish - Omaha, Omaha, NE; [MON] Jesuit Community at Creighton University, Omaha, NE
Walsh, Rev. Msgr. Michael J., '73 (TR) Retired,
Walsh, Rev. Michael P., *M.M.* '88 (NY) [MON] Maryknoll Fathers and Brothers (Catholic Foreign Mission Society of America, Inc.), Ossining, NY
Walsh, Rev. Miles D., '80 (BR) Curia: Administration
Walsh, Rev. Patrick, '69 (SC) Retired.
Walsh, Rev. Peter, *C.S.C.* '89 (AUS) (>P) [MON] Priests of Holy Cross in Oregon, Inc., Portland, OR
Walsh, Rev. Msgr. Richard, '68 (ORL) Curia: Advisory Boards, Commissions, Committees, and Councils; Leadership St. Margaret Mary, Winter Park, FL; [CAM] Catholic Campus Ministry at Rollins College, Winter Park, FL
Walsh, Rev. Robert E., '06 (WDC) Our Lady of Lourdes, Bethesda, MD
Walsh, Rev. Ronald J., '54 (NY) Retired.
Walsh, Rev. Seamus, '66 (DUL) Retired.
Walsh, Rev. Terrence P., '04 (BGP) Sacred Heart and Saint Patrick Parish Corporation, Redding Ridge, CT
Walsh, Rev. Thomas, (LIN) St. James, Curtis, NE
Walsh, Rev. Thomas, *O.Carm.* '50 (JOL) Retired.
Walsh, Rev. Thomas J., '67 (BO) Retired.
Walsh, Rev. Thomas J., *C.O.* '94 (MET) Curia: Consultative Bodies
Walsh, Rev. Thomas J., '94 (MET) St. Bartholomew, East Brunswick, NJ
Walsh, Rev. Thomas J., '89 (HRT) Saint Augustine Parish Corporation, Hartford, CT
Walsh, Rev. Thomas P., '72 (STA) Retired. San Sebastian, St. Augustine, FL
Walsh, Rev. Timothy, *L.C.* (HRT) [MON] Legionaries of Christ, Cheshire, CT; [SEM] Novitiate of the Legion of Christ, Cheshire, CT
Walsh, Rev. William F., *O.S.F.S.* '68 (R) Holy Redeemer by the Sea, Kitty Hawk, NC
Walshe, Rev. Sebastian A., *O.Praem.* '05 (ORG) [MON] Norbertine Fathers of Orange, Inc., Silverado, CA; [SEM] St. Michael's Norbertine Postulancy, Novitiate and Juniorate, Silverado, CA
Walter, Rev. Andrew M., '00 (BGP) Retired.
Walter, Rev. James A., '69 (BUF) Retired.
Walter, Rev. Msgr. James A., '62 (COL) Retired.
Walter, Rev. Joseph, '98 (BUF) St. Anthony, Fredonia, NY; St. Joseph, Fredonia, NY
Walter, Rev. Mark J., '88 (CHI) Our Lady of the Ridge and St. Linus Parish, Oak Lawn, IL
Walter, Rev. Mathew J, '19 (ROC) St. Benedict Roman Catholic Parish Ontario County, NY, Canandaigua, NY
Walter, Rev. Steven P., '77 (CIN) Retired.
Walter, Rev. William, *C.PP.S.* '61 (KC) Saint Francis Xavier Catholic Church, St. Joseph, MO; [MON] Society of the Precious Blood, Liberty, MO
Walters, Rev. Frederick, '87 (PAT) Retired. Holy Family, Florham Park, NJ
Walters, Rev. Gary R., '79 (TOL) Retired. St. Pius X, Tiffin, OH
Walters, Rev. Graham, (OKL) Retired.
Walters, Rev. James, *S.C.J.* '78 (MIL) [EFT] Congregation of the Priests of the Sacred Heart Support and Maintenance Trust, Hales Corners, WI; [MON] Sacred Heart at Monastery Lake, Franklin, WI
Walters, Rev. Neil, (CLV) St. Frances Xavier Cabrini Parish (St. John the Baptist, St. Vitus, Saints Cyril and Methodius), Lorain, OH
Walters, Rev. Neil, '89 (CLV) St. Vincent de Paul, Elyria, OH
Walters, Very Rev. Ronald, *O.F.M.* '78 (SFE) Curia: Offices and Directors [MON] The Province of Our Lady of Guadalupe of the Order of Friars Minor, Inc., Albuquerque, NM
Walterscheid, Rev. Kyle, '02 (FWT) Curia: Leadership; Miscellaneous / Other Offices St. John Paul II Parish, Denton, TX
Walther, Rev. James, *O.M.V.* '95 (BO) [EFT] Lanteri Charitable Trust, Boston, MA; [SEM] Oblate Provincialate, Boston, MA
Walther, Rev. James, *O.M.V.* '95 (BO) [MIS] St. Clement Archdiocesan Eucharistic Shrine, Boston, MA
Walton, Rev. James, *O.F.M.* '91 (CHI) [MON] St. Gratian Friary, Franciscan Friars, Countryside, IL
Walton, Rev. Msgr. Robert P., '74 (SAC) Retired. Curia: Leadership
Waltz, Rev. Joshua, '07 (BIS) St. Joseph, Mandan, ND
Waltz, Rev. Justin P., '08 (BIS) Curia: Offices and Directors; (>MO) Offices and Directors SS. Peter and Paul, New Hradec, ND; St. Joseph, Dickinson, ND
Walugembe, Rev. John Bosco, '06 (RIC) Prince of Peace, Chesapeake, VA
Walz, Rev. Daniel, '03 (SCL) Immaculate Conception, New Munich, MN; Sacred Heart, Freeport, MN; St. Rose of Lima, Freeport, MN
Walz, Rev. Gabriel, '15 (SCL) Sacred Heart, Staples, MN; St. Ann's, Wadena, MN; St. Frederick, Verndale, MN; St. Hubert, Sebeka, MN; St. John the Baptist, Bluffton, MN; St. Joseph, Bertha, MN; St. Michael, Motley, MN; The Church of the Assumption of Our Lady of Menahga, Menahga, MN
Walz, Rev. Richard, *O.S.B.* '67 (LR) [MON] Subiaco Abbey, Subiaco, AR
Walz, Rev. Msgr. W. Dean, '53 (DUB) Retired.
Wamala, Rev. Joseph, '04 (RIC) Christ the King, Norfolk, VA; St. Francis of Assisi, Staunton, VA
Wamala, Rev. Matthias M., '06 (COV) St. Joseph, Cold Spring, KY
Wamayose, Rev. Bernard, *A.J.* (HBG) Divine Redeemer, Mount Carmel, PA
Wambua, Rev. Cosmus Mutie, (CHR) Church of the Resurrection, Loris, SC; Our Lady Star of the Sea, North Myrtle Beach, SC
Wambua, Rev. Mathias, (SFR) Star of the Sea, San Francisco, CA
Wampach, Rev. Frank J., '84 (STP) Retired.

Wanat, Rev. Mitchell, *C.M.* '71 (HRT) The St. Joseph Church Corporation of Ansonia, Ansonia, CT
Wanaurny, Rev. John, *S.S.C.* '59 (OM) Retired. [MON] Missionary Society of St. Columban, St. Columbans, NE
Wanaurny, Rev. John Q., *S.S.C.* '59 (PRO) Retired. [MON] St. Columban's Retirement House (St. Columban's Foreign Mission Society), Bristol, RI
Wanda, Rev. Michael J., '91 (CHI) St. Theresa, Palatine, IL
Wander, Rev. Paul H., '90 (B) Curia: Leadership Assumption, Ferdinand, ID; St. Anthony's, Greencreek, ID; St. Mary's, Cottonwood, ID
Wandera, Rev. Kenneth, *GHM* '21 (KNX) St. Michael the Archangel Catholic Church, Erwin, TN
Wang, Rev. John, '54 (HEL) Retired.
Wangler, Rev. Msgr. William O., '63 (BUF) Retired. [MON] Bishop Head Residence, Lackawanna, NY
Wangwe, Rev. Fred, *A.J.* '00 (HBG) St. Monica Parish Sunbury Charitable Trust, Sunbury, PA
Wanish, Rev. David A., '02 (MAD) St. Joseph, Edgerton, WI; St. Mary, Milton, WI
Wankar, Rev. Gabriel, '04 (SFR) Immaculate Heart of Mary, Belmont, CA; Our Lady of Mercy, Daly City, CA
Wankerl, Rev. Gary A., '80 (MAD) Holy Mother of Consolation, Oregon, WI
Wanner, Rev. Benjamin, '22 (BIS) SS. Peter and Paul, New Hradec, ND; St. Joseph, Dickinson, ND
Wanser, Rev. George, *S.J.* (SJ) [MON] Sacred Heart Jesuit Center, Los Gatos, CA
Wanser, Rev. George, *S.J.* (PHX) [MON] Society of Jesus, Phoenix, AZ
Wanta, Rev. Michael, '21 (MAD) St. Bernard, Watertown, WI; St. Henry, Watertown, WI
Wantland, Rev. Thomas A., '67 (MAR) Retired.
Wapen, Rev. Francis A., '70 (SY) St. Patrick, Taberg, NY
Wapenski, Rev. Robert, '05 (FAR) Assumption Church of Pembina, Pembina, ND; St. Edward's Church of Drayton, Drayton, ND
Waraksa, Rev. Alex, '90 (KNX) Curia: Leadership
Waraska, Rev. Alex, (KNX) St. Jude, Chattanooga, TN
Warburton, Rev. John, *O.S.J.* '80 (FRS) St. Joachim, Madera, CA
Warchola, Rev. Brian Lee, '11 (ALT) Chap, Sacramental Min, State Corr Inst, Somerset Holy Name, Ebensburg, PA
Ward, Rev. Daniel, *O.S.B.* '71 (SCL) [MON] St. John's Abbey, of the Order of St. Benedict, Collegeville, MN
Ward, Rev. Edward, *O.Carm.* '73 (JOL) Our Lady of Mount Carmel, Joliet, IL; [MON] St. Elias Carmelites, Joliet, IL
Ward, Rev. Msgr. Gerald T., '79 (PEO) Blessed Sacrament, Morton, IL
Ward, Rev. James G, (STL) [MON] Congregation of the Mission, Perryville, MO
Ward, Rev. James J., '73 (ALN) Retired. Curia: Organizations (affiliated, inter-Diocesan, miscellaneous/other) Immaculate Conception, Jim Thorpe, PA
Ward, Rev. Jerome A., '67 (CHR) Retired.
Ward, Rev. John B., '86 (MO) Curia: Offices and Directors
Ward, Rev. John B., '86 (BAL) Curia: Tribunal Our Lady of the Fields, Millersville, MD
Ward, Rev. John P., '65 (CAM) Retired.
Ward, Rev. Justin, '19 (BIR) Curia: Offices and Directors
Ward, Rev. Mark, *C.P.* (NY) [MON] The Congregation of the Passion - St. Paul of the Cross Province, Jamaica, NY
Ward, Rev. Mark G., *C.P.* '76 (PIT) (>NY) [MON] The Congregation of the Passion - St. Paul of the Cross Province, Jamaica, NY
Ward, Rev. Mark G., *C.P.* (SCR) [MON] Saint Ann's Passionist Monastery of Scranton PA, Scranton, PA
Ward, Rev. Michael G., '97 (NEW) Curia: Offices and Directors Immaculate Heart of Mary, Scotch Plains, NJ
Ward, Rev. Nicholas Scott, '20 (STU) Curia: Deaneries St. Ann, Chesapeake, OH; St. Joseph Parish, Ironton, OH; St. Lawrence Parish, Ironton, OH; St. Mary, Ironton, OH
Ward, Rev. Paul, '04 (DET) Holy Family (Italian) Parish Detroit, Detroit, MI
Ward, Rev. Richard E., '68 (PIT) Retired.
Ward, Rev. Richard J., '93 (SEA) Retired.
Ward, Rev. Samuel, (LA) St. Raymond, Downey, CA
Ward, Rev. Thomas I, '97 (SY) St. Daniel, Syracuse, NY
Ward, Rev. Msgr. William P., '57 (SCR) Retired. St. Vincent de Paul, Milford, PA; [MON] Villa St. Joseph, Dunmore, PA
Wardanski, Rev. Msgr. Joseph V., '67 (E) Retired.
Warden, Rev. Daniel L., '66 (GAL) Retired.
Warden, Rev. Michael J., '13 (GB) St. Mary, Greenville, WI
Wardenski, Rev. Robert W., '72 (BUF) Immaculate Conception, East Aurora, NY; St. George, West Falls, NY
Ware, Rev. Brandon M., '07 (STO) Curia: Leadership St. Anne Church (Pastor of), Lodi, CA; [EFT] Bishop Ministry Appeal Trust, Stockton, CA; [EFT] St. Anne's Endowment, Lodi, CA
Ware, Rev. Donald, *C.P.* '72 (NY) [MON] The Congregation of the Passion - St. Paul of the Cross Province, Jamaica, NY
Ware, Rev. Donald, *C.P.* '72 (PIT) [MON] St. Paul of the Cross Monastery, Pittsburgh, PA; [RTR] St. Paul of the Cross Retreat Center, Pittsburgh, PA
Ware, Rev. Nicholas, '22 (LAF) St. Anthony of Padua, Eunice, LA
Ware, Rev. Nick, (LAF) St. Mathilda, Eunice, LA
Wargacki, Rev. Joseph, (HPM) Saint Nicholas of Myra, Anchorage, AK
Wargo, Rev. Msgr. Robert J., '72 (ALN) Retired.
Wargovich, Rev. James P., (BO) St. Margaret, Beverly, MA; St. Mary Star of the Sea, Beverly, MA
Waris, Rev. Gerald R., '67 (KC) Retired.
Warkulwiz, Rev. Victor P., *M.S.S.* '91 (PH) [MON] Missionaries of the Blessed Sacrament (M.S.S.), Bensalem, PA
Warman, Rev. William C., '64 (BAL) Retired.
Warmuz, Rev. Grzegorz, '94 (CHI) St. Fabian, Bridgeview, IL
Warnakulasooriya, Rev. Joseph Xavier, (FRS) Our Lady of the Snows, Frazier Park, CA
Warnakulasuriya, Rev. Prasanna Costa, (RVC) St. Joseph's, Garden City, NY
Warner, Rev. James P., '69 (GI) Retired.
Warner, Rev. Joseph A., '03 (CLV) Blessed Trinity, Akron, OH
Warnisher, Rev. Maximilian M., *F.I.* '94 (FR) [MON] Marian Friary of Our Lady, Queen of the Seraphic Order, New Bedford, MA
Warosh, Rev. James B., *S.J.* '67 (MIL) [MON] St. Camillus Jesuit Community (Society of Jesus, USA Midwest Province), Wauwatosa, WI
Warren, Rev. Anthony, *SSP* '85 (Y) [MIS] Society of St. Paul (Alba House Communications), Canfield, OH
Warren, Rev. Charles, '19 (RCK) On Special Assignment. Curia: Clergy and Religious Services Marian Central Catholic High School, Woodstock, IL
Warren, Rev. Lance A., '15 (OKL) Sacred Heart, El Reno, OK; St. Joseph's, Union City, OK
Warren, Rev. Michael, *O.M.V.* (BO) [MIS] St. Francis Chapel, Boston, MA; [MON] Oblate Residence (St. Joseph House), Milton, MA
Warren, Rev. Paul F., '78 (SFR) Retired. Saint Brendan the Navigator Church, San Francisco, CA
Warren, Rev. Robert, *S.A.* '81 (NY) [MON] Franciscan Friars of the Atonement, Garrison, NY; [MON] Franciscan Friars of the Atonement, Minister General Office, Garrison, NY; [MON] St. Christopher's Inn Friary, Garrison, NY
Warshak, Rev. Joshua Trey, *O.SS.T.* '20 (BAL) [MON] Holy Trinity Monastery, Sykesville, MD
Waruszewski, Rev. Daniel, (PIT) St. Aidan, Wexford, PA
Waruszewski, Rev. Stephen, *TOR* '20 (ALT) [CAM] St. Francis University (Loretto), Loretto, PA; [MON] Sacred Heart Friary, Loretto, PA
Washabaugh, Rev. Robert, '78 (NOR) Curia: Offices and Directors
Washabaugh, Rev. Robert, '78 (NOR) SS. Peter and Paul, Norwich, CT; [CAM] Connecticut College, New London, CT
Washabaugh, Rev. Robert J., '78 (NOR) St. Mary, Norwich, CT
Washburn, Very Rev. Thomas, '00 (FR) Curia: Offices and Directors Cathedral of St. Mary of the Assumption, Fall River, MA; Parish of the Good Shepherd, Fall River, MA; St. Stanislaus, Fall River, MA
Washington, Msgr. Christopher T., '06 (SCR) On Special Assignment. Diplomatic Service, Rome, Italy (Vatican)
Washington, Rev. Freddy, *CSSp* '92 (PIT) [RTR] The Spiritan Center, Bethel Park, PA
Washington, Rev. Maria Antony H., (BO) St. Anthony of Padua, Revere, MA
Washko, Rt. Rev. Mitred Archpriest Stephen, (PHX) Curia: (>HPM) Offices and Directors
Washko, Rt. Rev. Stephen G., '78 (HPM) Curia: Leadership; Offices and Directors Annunciation, Anaheim, CA
Wasiecko, Rev. Allan, *O.F.M. Cap.* '68 (PIT) [MON] St. Augustine Friary, Pittsburgh, PA
Wasielewski, Rev. Henry R., '64 (PHX) Retired.
Wasikowski, Rev. Ronald S., '75 (OM) Retired.
Wasilewski, Rev. John D., (CAM) Christ the Good Shepherd Parish, Vineland, N.J., Vineland, NJ
Wasilewski, Rev. John D., '97 (CAM) Chap, Inspira Med Ctr; Mem Hosp of Salem Cty
Wasilewski, Rev. Kenneth, '03 (RCK) On Sick Leave.
Wasilewski, Rev. Marek, *M.Id.* '13 (SCR) On Administrative Leave.
Wasilewski, Rev. Rafal, *C.R.* '12 (JOL) Holy Trinity, Westmont, IL
Wasilewski, Rev. Thomas, '10 (LAN) St. Patrick Parish Ann Arbor, Ann Arbor, MI
Wasko, Rev. Andrzej, *S.D.S.* (BRK) Our Lady of Consolation, Brooklyn, NY
Waskowiak, Rev. Harlan D. P., '98 (LIN) St. Joseph's, Geneva, NE
Waslo, Rev. Msgr. Peter D., '86 (PHU) Curia: Leadership; Offices and Directors
Waslo, Msgr. Peter D., '86 (PHU) Curia: Leadership
Wasnie, Rev. Blane, *O.S.B.* '66 (SCL) [MON] St. John's Abbey, of the Order of St. Benedict, Collegeville, MN
Wasnock, Rev. Seth D., '15 (SCR) Curia: Leadership Our Lady of Mt. Carmel, Carbondale, PA; St. Rose of Lima, Carbondale, PA
Wassef, Rev. Msgr. Pafnouti, '79 (MET) Chap, John F Kennedy Med Ctr St. Anthony of Padua, Port Reading, NJ; St. Joseph, Carteret, NJ
Wassell, Rev. John E., '97 (NEW) Our Lady of Sorrows, Kearny, NJ; St. Cecilia, Kearny, NJ
Wassie, Rev. Stephen M., '79 (Y) St. George, Lisbon, OH; St. John, Summitville, OH; St. Philip Neri, Hanoverton, OH
Wassmuth, Rev. Msgr. Dennis, '73 (B) Retired.
Wasswa, Rev. Joseph, '21 (CHL) Our Lady of Grace, Greensboro, NC
Waszczenko, Rev. Andrzej, *S.D.S.* '89 (SAT) Holy Trinity, Falls City, TX; St. Boniface, Hobson, TX; [MON] Salvatorian Fathers Community of Texas, Falls City, TX
Watanabe, Rev. Msgr. Terrence A.M., '77 (HON) Curia: Consultative Bodies; Offices and Directors St. Anthony of Padua, Wailuku, HI
Waterman, Rev. Alain, '21 (PMB) St. Joseph, Stuart, FL
Waterman, Rev. Gerald, *O,F,M.Conv.* (SY) Assumption B.V.M., Syracuse, NY; [CAM] Syracuse University Catholic Center & St. Thomas More Foundation, Inc., Syracuse, NY
Waters, Rev. David, '14 (PH) Curia: Evangelization
Waters, Rev. David A., '14 (PH) Curia: Evangelization St. Martin of Tours, Philadelphia, PA
Waters, Rev. Edward, '77 (ORL) Retired. Curia: Advisory Boards, Commissions, Committees, and Councils
Waters, Rev. John J., *S.J.* '64 (STL) Retired.
Waters, Very Rev. Joseph L., '87 (VEN) Curia: Leadership
Waters, Very Rev. Joseph L., '87 (SP) Curia: Leadership; Pastoral Services
Waters, Very Rev. Joseph L., '87 (SP) Curia: Leadership; Pastoral Services St. John Vianney, St. Pete Beach, FL
Waters, Rev. Kevin, (SJ) [MON] Sacred Heart Jesuit Center, Los Gatos, CA
Waters, Rev. Mark S., '90 (STA) Retired.
Waters, Rev. Philip J., *O.S.B.* '72 (NEW) St. Mary of the Immaculate Conception, Newark, NJ; [MON] Benedictine Abbey of Newark, Newark, NJ
Waters, Rev. Robert E., '69 (BUF) Resurrection, Batavia, NY
Waters, Friar William F., *O.S.A.* '71 (PH) St. Augustine, Philadelphia, PA
Wathen, Msgr. Daniel J., '06 (GF) Curia: Leadership; Offices and Directors St. Jude Thaddeus, Havre, MT
Wathen, Rev. David, *O.F.M.* '99 (WDC) [MON] Franciscan Monastery USA Inc., Washington, DC
Wathier, Rev. Douglas O., '84 (DUB) St. Mary's Church, Waverly, Iowa, Waverly, IA
Watikha, Rev. Patrick, *AJ* '93 (COL) Holy Redeemer, Portsmouth, OH; St. Mary, Portsmouth, OH; St. Peter, Wheelersburg, OH
Watin, Rev. Nestor, (RVC) St. Peter of Alcantara, Port Washington, NY
Watkins, Rev. Charles W., '03 (CHI) Retired.
Watkins, Rev. Donald R, '19 (BUF) St. Patrick, Randolph, NY
Watkins, Rev. Msgr. James D., '89 (WDC) Curia: Deaneries
Watkins, Rev. Mark T., '91 (CIN) St. Lawrence, Cincinnati, OH
Watkins, Rev. Thomas, '64 (R) On Leave.
Watson, Rev. David E., *SJ* '92 (CIN) [MON] Jesuit Community at St. Xavier High School, Cincinnati, OH
Watson, Rev. Eric J., *S.J.* '09 (SEA) [COL] Seattle University, Seattle, WA; [MON] Arrupe Jesuit

Community at Seattle University, Seattle, WA
Watson, Rev. James, *OFM Cap* '17 (CLV) St. Agnes - Our Lady of Fatima, Cleveland, OH
Watson, Rev. Joseph G., '92 (PH) Nativity of Our Lord, Warminster, PA
Watson, Very Rev. Mark, '96 (SHP) Curia: Leadership
Watson, Rev. Mark Andrew, '96 (SHP) St. Mary of the Pines, Shreveport, LA
Watson, Rev. Michael B., '86 (COL) Our Lady of Perpetual Help, Grove City, OH
Watson, Rev. Richard, '11 (LEX) Curia: Leadership; Offices and Directors St. Paul, Lexington, KY
Watson, Rev. Stephen, *O.C.D.* (TUC) Curia: Consultative Bodies; Leadership Santa Cruz Roman Catholic Parish - Tucson, Tucson, AZ
Watson, Rev. Timothy, *C.Ss.R.* '90 (BR) Congregation Of St. Gerard Majella Roman Catholic Church, Parish Of East Baton Rouge, Louisiana, Baton Rouge, LA; [MIS] Redemptorist Fathers of Baton Rouge, Inc., Baton Rouge, LA; [MON] St. Gerard Residence, Baton Rouge, LA
Watson, Rev. William M., *S.J.* '85 (SEA) [MIS] Sacred Story Institute, Seattle, WA; [MON] Arrupe Jesuit Community at Seattle University, Seattle, WA
Watt, Rev. Gerald, *C.R.* '67 (JOL) Immaculate Conception of the Blessed Virgin Mary, Morris, IL
Watters, Rev. Timothy J., '71 (CHR) Retired.
Watters, Rev. William, *S.J.* (BAL) The Loyola School, Inc., Baltimore, MD
Watters, Rev. William J., *S.J.* '65 (BAL) St. Ignatius Church, Baltimore, MD; [MIS] Colombiere Jesuit Community, Baltimore, MD
Watterson, Rev. John E., '62 (PRO) Retired.
Watts, Rev. Franklin, (MO) Curia: Offices and Directors
Watts, Rev. Wayne F., '90 (CHI) Curia: Leadership SS. Joseph and Francis Xavier, Wilmette, IL; [CCH] Catholic Charities of the Archdiocese of Chicago-Archdiocesan Offices, Chicago, IL
Waturuocha, Rev. Anthony C., '08 (SB) Christ the Redeemer, Grand Terrace, CA
Watzke, Rev. James N, *CSC* (FTW) [MIS] Holy Cross House, Notre Dame, IN
Waugh, Rev. Jarrod, *C.S.C.* (SCR) Holy Family, Luzerne, PA
Waugh, Rev. Jarrod, *csc* '13 (COS) Sacred Heart, Colorado Springs, CO
Waugh, Rev. John G., '55 (PEO) IL Industrial School for Boys; Sheridan Correctional Center St. Joseph's, Wedron, IL
Waugh, Rev. Luke, *O.S.B.* '15 (IND) Curia: Offices and Directors St. Isidore the Farmer Catholic Church, Bristow, Inc., Bristow, IN; [MON] St. Meinrad Archabbey, St. Meinrad, IN
Waun, Rev. William, '14 (POC) Curia: (>MO) Offices and Directors Our Lady of Good Counsel Community, Jacksonville, NC
Wawerski, Rev. Msgr. Edward, '61 (RVC) Retired. St. Hedwig's, Floral Park, NY
Waweru, Rev. Gabriel, '07 (DUL) St. Andrew, Brainerd, MN; St. Mathias, Fort Ripley, MN
Wawryszuk, Rev. Zdzislaw F., '85 (RCK) St. Catherine of Genoa, Genoa, IL
Wawrzycki, Rev. Andrew, '70 (ORL) Retired.
Wawrzyn, Rev. Andrew, '10 (CHI) [CAM] University of Chicago Calvert House, Chicago, IL
Way, Rev. Steven, *SDB* '04 (LA) [MON] Dominic Savio Salesian Residence, Los Angeles, CA
Waymel, Very Rev. Kevin, (LSC) Curia: Consultative Bodies; Evangelization; Leadership St. Albert the Great Newman Parish, Inc., Las Cruces, NM
Wea, Rev. Raymundus, *S.V.D.* '82 (SD) Sharp Hospital and Rady Children's Hosp, San Diego Curia: Advisory Boards, Commissions, Committees, and Councils
Weare, Rev. Kenneth M., '01 (SFR) St. Rita, Fairfax, CA
Wearsch, Rev. Ronald, '92 (CLV) St. Joseph, Avon Lake, OH
Weary, Rev. William M., '84 (HBG) Curia: Offices and Directors Sacred Heart of Jesus, Lewistown, PA; St. Jude, Mifflintown, PA
Weaver, Rev. Cyprian, *O.S.B.* '72 (SCL) [MON] St. John's Abbey, of the Order of St. Benedict, Collegeville, MN
Weaver, Rev. John G., '70 (HRT) Retired.
Weaver, Rev. Mark, *O.F.M.Conv.* '77 (IND) St. Anthony of Padua Catholic Church, Clarksville, Inc., Clarksville, IN; St. Mary of the Annunciation Catholic Church, New Albany, Inc., New Albany, IN
Webb, Rev. David, (TLS) On Special Assignment. St Philip Neri Newman Ctr, Tulsa, OK Curia: Offices and Directors
Webb, Rev. David Michael, '17 (TLS) [CAM] St. Philip Neri University Parish, Tulsa, OK
Webb, Rev. Raymond J., '67 (CHI) Retired. [SEM] University of Saint Mary of the Lake/Mundelein Seminary, Mundelein, IL
Webb, Rev. Zachary, '12 (DAL) Curia: Offices and Directors [SEM] Holy Trinity Seminary, Irving, TX
Webber, Rev. Donald, *C.P.* '73 (CHI) [MON] Passionist Community of St. Vincent Strambi, Chicago, IL
Webber, Rev. Msgr. Donald S., '62 (SB) Retired.
Webber, Rev. Lawrence, *OFMCap* '80 (MIL) St. Francis of Assisi, Milwaukee, WI
Weber, Rev. Alan, '84 (SP) All Saints, Clearwater, FL
Weber, Rev. Casey C., '21 (MEM) Cathedral of the Immaculate Conception, Memphis, TN
Weber, Rev. Christopher, '17 (DAV) SS. Mary and Mathias Church of Muscatine, Iowa, Muscatine, IA
Weber, Rev. Christopher H., '02 (CLV) Guardian Angels, Copley, OH
Weber, Rev. Dennis M., *S.D.C.* '97 (PH) [MON] Servants of Charity (SdC), Ridley Park, PA; [PRE] St. Edmond's Home for Children, Rosemont, PA; [SPF] Communities of Don Guanella and Divine Providence, Norwood, PA
Weber, Rev. Donald E., '58 (GR) Retired.
Weber, Rev. Eric C., '01 (LAN) Most Holy Trinity Parish Fowler, Fowler, MI; St. Mary Parish Westphalia, Westphalia, MI
Weber, Rev. Msgr. Francis J., '59 (LA) Retired.
Weber, Rev. Herbert F., '74 (TOL) Saint John XXIII, Perrysburg, OH
Weber, Rev. James P., '04 (CIN) St. Anthony Church, Cincinnati, OH; St. Cecilia, Cincinnati, OH; St. Margaret - St. John Parish, Cincinnati, OH; St. Mary, Cincinnati, OH
Weber, Rev. Jason, '10 (ARL) On Duty Outside Diocese. Banica Mission, Dominican Republic
Weber, Rev. John R., '09 (PH) Queen of the Universe, Levittown, PA
Weber, Rev. Joseph A., '76 (STL) St. John Bosco Catholic Church, Maryland Heights, MO; St. Monica Catholic Church, Creve Coeur, MO
Weber, Rev. Joseph A., '76 (PRM) St. Louis Mission, St. Louis, MO
Weber, Rev. Justin, '20 (MIL) Holy Family Congregation, Fond du Lac, WI
Weber, Rev. Keith, '83 (SAL) Curia: Advisory Boards, Commissions, Committees, and Councils; Consultative Bodies St. Elizabeth Ann Seton Parish, Salina, Inc., Salina, KS
Weber, Rev. Kevin, '93 (SAL) Curia: Consultative Bodies Sacred Heart Junior-Senior High School, Salina, KS; St. Mary, Queen of the Universe Parish, Salina, Inc., Salina, KS
Weber, Rev. Leo F., *S.J.* '56 (STL) Retired.
Weber, Rev. Logan, '22 (GR) St. Robert of Newminster, Ada, MI
Weber, Rev. Mark Edward, *S.V.D.* '82 (CHI) [SEM] Divine Word Theologate, Chicago, IL
Weber, Rev. Matthew, '90 (CAM) The Parish of the Holy Cross, Bridgeton, N.J., Bridgeton, NJ
Weber, Rev. Michael J., *O. Praem.* '77 (GB) [MON] St. Norbert Abbey, De Pere, WI
Weber, Rev. Randall D., '91 (SAL) Curia: Tribunal Seven Dolors of the Blessed Virgin Mary Parish, Manhattan, KS
Weber, Rev. Reese, '12 (FAR) St. John's Church of New Rockford, New Rockford, ND; Sts. Peter & Paul Church of McHenry, McHenry, ND
Weber, Rev. Robert C., '81 (SY) On Special Assignment. St. Mary, Clinton, NY; St. Patrick-St. Anthony, Chadwicks, NY
Weber, Rev. Robert P., '65 (CAM) Retired.
Weber, Rev. Ronald J., '12 (BEL) Retired.
Weber, Rev. Samuel, *O.S.B.* '96 (IND) [MON] St. Meinrad Archabbey, St. Meinrad, IN
Weber, Rev. Samuel F., *O.S.B.* '96 (SFR) [SEM] St. Patrick's Seminary and University (The Roman Catholic Seminary of San Francisco), Menlo Park, CA
Weber, Rev. Terry, '85 (SFS) Saint John Parish of Aurora County, Plankinton, SD; Saint Mary Parish of Aurora County, Stickney, SD; Saint Peter Parish of Aurora County, White Lake, SD
Weber, Rev. Thomas L., '74 (CLV) Retired.
Weber, Rev. Zachary, (GB) On Special Assignment. Dir, Newman Ctr, Oshkosh Curia: Faith Formation
Weberg, Rev. M. Paul, *O.S.B.* '03 (MO) Curia: Offices and Directors
Weberg, Rev. Paul, *O.S.B.* '03 (RCK) [MON] Marmion Abbey, Aurora, IL
Webster, Rev. Cole T., '17 (BUF) Curia: Consultative Bodies St. Peter, Lewiston, NY
Webster, Rev. Robert E., '86 (ORL) Retired.
Weckert, Rev. Paul M., *O.S.B.* '99 (SEA) Curia: Leadership [MON] St. Martin's Abbey, Lacey, WA
Wedeking, Rev. Patrick, '88 (GLP) Christ the King, Shiprock, NM; Sacred Heart, Waterflow, NM
Wedig, Rev. James M., '93 (CIN) St. Ann, Cincinnati, OH; St. Bernard, Cincinnati, OH; St. James the Greater, Cincinnati, OH; St. Margaret Mary, Cincinnati, OH
Wedig, Rev. Mark, *O.P.* '86 (STL) [MON] St. Dominic Priory, St. Louis, MO
Wedig, Rev. Mark, *OP* (STL) [SEM] Aquinas Institute of Theology, St. Louis, MO
Wedow, Rev. Robert L., '01 (DEN) St. Scholastica Catholic Parish in Erie, Erie, CO; [MIS] Our Lady of Tenderness, Poustinia, Estes Park, CO
Wee, Rev. Damien, (OM) St. Francis Borgia, Blair, NE
Weed, Rev. Timothy, (P) [CAM] University of Portland, Portland, OR; [MIS] Christ The Teacher, University of Portland, Portland, OR; [MON] Priests of Holy Cross in Oregon, Inc., Portland, OR
Weeder, Rev. James M., '11 (OM) Assumption B.V.M., West Point, NE; Guardian Angels Central Catholic, West Point, NE; St. Aloysius, West Point, NE; St. Anthony, St. Charles, NE; St. Boniface, Monterey, NE
Weekly, Rev. Christopher, *S.J.* '98 (SJ) [MON] USA West Province, Society of Jesus, Los Gatos, CA
Weekly, Rev. Christopher S., *S.J.* '98 (P) [MON] Colombiere Jesuit Community, Portland, OR
Weeks, Rev. Sean M., '04 (P) St. Pius X, Portland, OR
Weerasinghe, Rev. Felix M., '64 (RVC) Retired.
Weezorak, Rev. Dennis R., '86 (MET) Curia: Consultative Bodies St. Mary, South Amboy, NJ
Wegenka, Rev. Michael, *S.J.* (GAL) (>DEN) [MON] Regis Jesuit Community (The Jesuits at Regis University), Denver, CO
Weger, Rev. Daniel, '19 (KCK) On Leave.
Wegner, Rev. Gary, *O.F.M. Cap.* (DET) [CCH] Capuchin Soup Kitchen, Detroit, MI; [MON] St. Bonaventure Monastery, Detroit, MI
Wego, Rev. Benignus, *SVD* (LR) [CON] Holy Angels Convent-Motherhouse (Olivetan Benedictine Sisters), Jonesboro, AR
Wehby, Rev. Albert, *B.A.O.* '63 (NTN) Retired.
Wehman, Rev. Jack W., '80 (CIN) The Community of the Good Shepherd, Cincinnati, OH
Wehmann, Rev. Mark H., '03 (STP) St. Olaf, Minneapolis, MN
Wehn, Rev. Timothy, '79 (LAV) Retired.
Wehner, Rev. Eugene C., *O.C.D.* '75 (WDC) [SEM] Discalced Carmelite Friars, Inc., Washington, DC
Wehner, Rev. James A., '95 (PIT) Divine Grace, Cranberry Township, PA
Wehner, Rev. James A., '95 (NO) Curia: Leadership
Wehnert, Rev. Donald R., *C.S.V.* '63 (JOL) Retired. St. Patrick, Kankakee, IL
Wehnert, Rev. Donald R., *C.S.V.* '63 (CHI) [MON] Viatorian Province Center-Clerics of St. Viator, Arlington Heights, IL
Wehr, Rev. Arthur J., *S.J.* '90 (SAC) Pastor of St. Ignatius Loyola Parish, Sacramento, a corporation sole, Sacramento, CA; [MON] Sacramento Jesuit Community, Carmichael, CA
Wehr, Rev. Zachary R., '19 (ALN) St. Francis de Sales, Robesonia, PA; St. Ignatius Loyola, West Lawn, PA
Wehrle, Rev. Peter G., '99 (NEW) Our Lady of the Lake, Verona, NJ
Wehrlin, Rev. Leo J., '93 (Y) Curia: Leadership Holy Trinity Parish, East Liverpool, OH
Wehrs, Rev. Kenneth J., '10 (LIN) Curia: Leadership St. John's, Cambridge, NE
Wei, Rev. Luke, '60 (BRK) Retired.
Weibl, Rev. Nicholas, '64 (TOL) Retired.
Weibley, Rev. Michael, *O.P.* (BAL) SS. Philip and James, Baltimore, MD
Weidenbenner, Rev. Joseph, '07 (SPC) Curia: Consultative Bodies; Deaneries McAuley Catholic High School, Joplin, MO; St. Mary, Joplin, MO; St. Mary, Seneca, MO
Weider, Rev. Gregory S., '63 (ALB) Retired.
Weidner, Rev. Larry, (PHX) St. Joan of Arc Roman Catholic Parish, Phoenix, AZ
Weidner, Rev. S. Anthony, '05 (OM) St. Michael, South Sioux City, NE
Weigand, Rev. Peter, *O.S.B.* '70 (WDC) [MON] St. Anselm's Abbey, Washington, DC
Weighner, Rev. James C., '07 (LC) St. Elizabeth Ann Seton, Holmen, WI
Weighner, Very Rev. Robert J., '99 (MIL) Curia: Leadership Congregation of St. Anne, Pleasant Prairie, WI
Weigman, Rev. Joseph A., '91 (TOL) Retired.
Weik, Rev. Terence P., '80 (PH) St. Jude, Chalfont, PA
Weikart, Rev. G. David, '03 (Y) St. Joseph, Alliance, OH
Weikart, Rev. G. David, (Y) Regina Coeli (Queen of

Heaven), Alliance, OH; St. Ann, Sebring, OH
Weiksnar, Rev. William J., *O.F.M.* '94 (BUF) SS. Columba-Brigid, Buffalo, NY
Weil, Rev. Frank, *O.Carm.* '67 (JOL) [MON] Carmelite Provincial Office, Darien, IL
Weiler, Rev. Michael F, *S.J.* '88 (P) [MON] Colombiere Jesuit Community, Portland, OR
Weinandy, Rev. Thomas, *O.F.M.Cap.* '72 (WDC) [SEM] St. Francis Friary-Capuchin College, Washington, DC
Weiner, Mitred Archpriest Philip, '91 (STF) St. Josaphat, Rochester, NY
Weiner, Rt. Rev. Mitred Archpriest Philip Canon, (STF) Curia: Offices and Directors
Weinert, Rev. Allen, *C.Ss.R.* '72 (NO) St. Alphonsus, New Orleans, LA; St. Mary's Assumption, New Orleans, LA; [MIS] St. Mary's Chapel, New Orleans, LA
Weingartner, Rev. Derrick, *S.J.* (KC) [MON] St. Peter Claver Jesuit Community, Kansas City, MO
Weingartz, Rev. Francis A., '54 (DET) Retired.
Weir, Rev. Bernard E., '86 (DAV) St. James Church of Washington, Iowa, Washington, IA
Weis, Rev. Anthony J., '10 (BIR) St. Patrick's, Adamsville, AL; St. Stanislaus, Birmingham, AL; [EFT] St. Michael Cemetery Fund, Adamsville, AL
Weis, Rev. Denis P., '63 (MIL) Retired.
Weis, Rev. Eugene R., '62 (ROC) Retired.
Weisbeck, Rev. Paul, '70 (SJ) Retired.
Weisbecker, Rev. Thomas W., '96 (OM) St. James, Omaha, NE
Weise, Rev. Thomas D., '62 (MOB) Retired.
Weisenberger, Rev. Gary, '77 (SEA) Retired.
Weisenberger, Rev. Leon, *M.S.C.* '59 (ALN) [MON] Sacred Heart Villa, Missionaries of the Sacred Heart, Center Valley, PA
Weisenberger, Rev. Richard J., '79 (LFT) Sacred Heart of Jesus, Fowler, IN; St. Charles, Otterbein, IN; St. John the Baptist, Earl Park, IN; St. Joseph, Kentland, IN; St. Mary, Ambia, IN; St. Patrick, Oxford, IN
Weiser, Rev. Charles B., '66 (TR) Retired. Curia: Canonical Services St. Catharine-St. Margaret, Spring Lake, NJ
Weishaar, Rev. Leo G., '84 (MOB) Retired.
Weiske, Rev. Daniel, '12 (DUL) Curia: Leadership Blessed Sacrament, Hibbing, MN; [EFT] Hibbing Catholic Schools Endowment Fund, Hibbing, MN
Weisman, Rev. Raymond F., '76 (WIL) Retired. St. Francis De Sales, Salisbury, MD
Weiss, Rev. Erich J., '10 (MIL) On Duty Outside Diocese. United States Navy, Camp Pendleton, CA Curia: (>MO) Offices and Directors
Weiss, Rev. Jerome P., '77 (DUL) Retired.
Weiss, Rev. Joseph, *S.J.* '85 (BO) [MON] The Jesuit Community at Boston College, Chestnut Hill, MA
Weiss, Rev. Mark E., '04 (HBG) Curia: Offices and Directors St. Joseph, Dallastown, PA
Weiss, Rev. Robert, *C.P.* '65 (L) [MON] Sacred Heart Retreat, Louisville, KY
Weiss, Rev. Robert, *CP* (BIR) Holy Family, Birmingham, AL; [MIS] Congregation of the Passion: Holy Family Community, Inc., Birmingham, AL
Weiss, Rev. Msgr. Robert E., '73 (BGP) Curia: Clergy and Religious Services; Consultative Bodies St. Rose's Church Newtown, Newtown, CT
Weissbeck, Rev. Reinhold, '72 (DEN) Retired.
Weist, Rev. Edward F., '69 (CLV) Retired.
Weitensteiner, Rev. Joseph M., '66 (SPK) Retired.
Weitzel, Rev. Stephen D., '90 (HBG) St. Richard, Manheim, PA
Weitzel, Rev. Theodore, '68 (JOL) Retired.
Wejnerowski, Rev. Dawid, '12 (MET) St. Mary, Alpha, NJ
Wekerle, Rev. Ronald, '90 (B) Our Lady of the Snows, Sun Valley, ID; St. Charles Borromeo, Hailey, ID
Wekesa, Rev. Pius S., '95 (R) Holy Cross, Durham, NC
Welbers, Rev. Msgr. Thomas, '68 (LA) Retired.
Welch, Rev. Bernard J., '81 (PRT) Retired.
Welch, Rev. Christopher, '94 (ALB) Curia: Offices and Directors Sacred Heart, Tribes Hill, NY; St. Cecilia, Fonda, NY; St. Paul the Apostle, Hancock, NY
Welch, Rev. D. Michael, '70 (IND) Retired. Curia: Leadership; Offices and Directors
Welch, Rev. Gregory T., '67 (STP) Retired.
Welch, Rev. John, *O.Carm.* '65 (JOL) Retired. [MON] St. Elias Carmelites, Joliet, IL
Welch, Rev. John, *MS* (LKC) Our Lady of LaSalette, Sulphur, LA
Welch, Rev. John E., *M.S.* '60 (NOR) Retired. St. James, Danielson, CT
Weldgen, Rev. Msgr. Francis G., '59 (BUF) Retired.
Welding, Rev. Brian J., '91 (PIT) St. Michael the Archangel, Pittsburgh, PA
Weldishofer, Rev. Bernard J., '92 (CIN) St. Augustine, Waynesville, OH; St. Columbkille, Wilmington, OH; [CAM] Wilmington College Campus Ministry, Wilmington, OH
Weldon, Rev. Eric M., '00 (WCH) Our Lady of Guadalupe, South Hutchinson, KS
Weldon, Rev. James F., '98 (WCH) Curia: Leadership St. Patrick, Wichita, KS
Weldon, Rev. Michael, *O.F.M.* '81 (PHX) St. Mary's Roman Catholic Basilica, Phoenix, AZ
Weldu, Rev. Awte, *O. Cist* '80 (PHX) Curia: Leadership St. Louis the King Roman Catholic Parish, Glendale, AZ; St. Thomas the Apostle Roman Catholic Parish, Phoenix, AZ
Weling, Rev. John B., '81 (ORG) On Sick Leave.
Welk, Rev. Thomas, *C.PP.S.* '69 (KC) (>CIN) [MON] Society of the Precious Blood, United States Province, Inc., Dayton, OH
Welk, Rev. Thomas, *C.P.P.S.* '69 (WCH) [CON] Adorers of the Blood of Christ U.S. Region, Wichita, KS
Wellar, Rev. Thomas, '80 (CC) Retired.
Welle, Rev. Tony, '07 (ORL) St. Luke, Barefoot Bay, FL
Weller, Rev. Andre, (GB) Retired. [MON] St. Fidelis Friary, Appleton, WI
Weller, Rev. Steven J., '22 (LC) Assumption High School, Wisconsin Rapids, WI; Assumption Middle School, Wisconsin Rapids, WI; Our Lady, Queen of Heaven, Wisconsin Rapids, WI
Welles, Rev. Timothy J., '06 (LC) St. Joseph, Elk Mound, WI; St. Joseph, Mondovi, WI
Wellington, Rev. Ajith, (NY) Holy Trinity, Poughkeepsie, NY
Wellman, Rev. Msgr. Dale, '64 (PEO) Retired.
Wellman, Rev. Msgr. Dale L., '64 (PEO) Retired. Curia: Advisory Boards, Commissions, Committees, and Councils
Wells, Rev. David G., '10 (WDC) Curia: Consultative Bodies; Tribunal St. Martin of Tours, Gaithersburg, MD
Wells, Rev. James, *O.F.M.* '82 (NY) [MON] Franciscan Province of the Immaculate Conception, New York, NY
Wells, Rev. Msgr. Patrick R., '93 (GAL) Retired.
Wells, Rev. Peter VB., '84 (PAT) Curia: Finance Holy Cross, Wayne, NJ; Our Lady of the Valley, Wayne, NJ
Wells, Rev. Philip J., '83 (SAC) Retired.
Wells, Rev. Thomas, '20 (PBR) St. John Chrysostom, Houston, TX
Welsch, Rev. Gerard R., '66 (STL) Retired.
Welsh, Rev. Christopher B., '86 (GLD) Retired. Saint Ann of Frankfort, Frankfort, MI
Welsh, Rev. Garry, '01 (SP) St. Anthony of Padua, San Antonio, FL
Welsh, Rev. Patrick J., '00 (PH) St. Matthew, Philadelphia, PA
Welsh, Rev. Patrick J., '98 (CIN) Retired.
Welsh, Rev. Peter J., '80 (PH) St. Helena, Philadelphia, PA
Welsh, Rev. Richard C., '60 (DET) Retired.
Welter, Rev. Brian, (OM) St. Margaret Mary, Omaha, NE
Welter, Rev. Brian T., '05 (CHI) On Duty Outside Diocese. (>OM) [MIS] Institute for Priestly Formation, Omaha, NE
Weltin, Rev. Richard W., '83 (SFD) Retired. Our Lady of Lourdes, Decatur, IL; St. Thomas the Apostle, Decatur, IL
Welzbacher, Rev. George, '51 (STP) Retired.
Wen, Rev. Colin C., '13 (SAC) Curia: Offices and Directors Pastor of St. Katharine Drexel Parish, Martell, a corporation sole, Jackson, CA
Wendel, Rev. Alfred W., '78 (ATL) Retired.
Wendel, Rev. Arthur, *C.Ss.R.* '59 (BAL) [SPF] St. John Neuman Residence, Timonium, MD
Wendel, Rev. Daniel, '22 (LR) St. Raphael, Springdale, AR
Wendel, Rev. Fred, '78 (ATL) [CAM] University of Georgia - Catholic Student Center, Athens, GA
Wendell, Rev. Richard C., '06 (MIL) On Sick Leave.
Wenderoth, Rev. Joseph R., '62 (BAL) Retired.
Wendler, Rev. Patrick J., '08 (MAD) Sacred Heart, Reedsburg, WI
Wendling, Rev. Mark, *S.O.L.T.* '03 (DET) Holy Redeemer Parish Detroit, Detroit, MI
Wendt, Rev. George, (ROM) Most Holy Trinity, Chesterland, OH
Wendt, Rev. Nathan, *S.J.* '14 (CIN) Xavier Jesuit Academy, Cincinnati, OH; [MON] Cincinnati Jesuit Community, Cincinnati, OH
Wendt, Rev. Patrick R., '79 (MIL) St. John XXIII Congregation, Port Washington, WI
Wenke, Rev. Leonard C., '79 (CIN) Holy Angels, Dayton, OH; Our Lady of the Immaculate Conception, Dayton, OH; St. Mary, Dayton, OH
Wensing, Rev. Michael, '76 (SFS) [EFT] Holy Name Foundation, Inc., Watertown, SD
Wentink, Rev. William R., '70 (RCK) Retired.
Wentz, Rev. Aelred W., *O.C.S.O.* '85 (ROC) [MON] Abbey of the Genesee, Inc., Piffard, NY
Wenz, Rev. Robert F., '82 (CLV) Retired.
Wenzel, Rev. James, *OSA* '56 (PH) [MON] St. Thomas Monastery, Villanova, PA
Wenzel, Rev. Timothy, '66 (SCL) Retired.
Wenzinger, Rev. Mark, *OSB* '95 (RIC) St. Gregory the Great, Virginia Beach, VA
Wenzinger, Rev. Mark Edward, *O.S.B.* '95 (GBG) Assoc Chap [MON] Saint Vincent Archabbey, Latrobe, PA
Wenzinger, Rev. Msgr. Robert D., '82 (FRS) San Joaquin Memorial High School, Fresno, CA; St. Anthony of Padua, Fresno, CA
Weria, Rev. Theobald, *A.L.C.P.* '98 (SP) St. Cecelia, Clearwater, FL
Werkhoven, Rev. Michael E., '02 (MEM) Curia: Advisory Boards, Commissions, Committees, and Councils Church of the Incarnation, Collierville, TN
Werley, Rev. Paul, (SAG) Nativity of the Lord Parish of Alma and St. Louis, Alma, MI
Werling, Rev. Wolf V.K., '99 (JOL) [SPF] Good Shepherd Manor, Momence, IL
Werner, Rev. Gerald, *OCD* (SB) [RTR] El Carmelo Retreat House, Redlands, CA
Werner, Rev. John, (CAM) Chap, Virtua at Our Lady of Lourdes Med Ctr
Werner, Rev. John J., '00 (MET) On Duty Outside Diocese.
Werner, Rev. Jon, '82 (SY) Curia: Offices and Directors St. Mary of the Assumption, Binghamton, NY; St. Paul, Binghamton, NY
Werner, Rev. Jon K., (SY) Curia: Offices and Directors
Werner, Rev. Justin, '58 (GB) Retired.
Werner, Rev. Steven, '98 (SPK) Curia: Leadership Holy Rosary, Pomeroy, WA; St. Joseph, Dayton, WA; St. Mark, Waitsburg, WA; [EFT] Holy Rosary Catholic Church Foundation of Garfield County, Pomeroy, WA; [EFT] St. Mark Waitsburg and St. Joseph Dayton Catholic Parish Foundation, Dayton, WA; [MIS] Project Timothy: Christian Service Center, Dayton, WA
Wertanen, Rev. Steven A., '97 (DET) St. Anastasia Parish Troy, Troy, MI
Werth, Rev. Alvin, '59 (SAL) Retired.
Werth, Rev. Frederick H., '07 (CHL) St. Andrew the Apostle, Mars Hill, NC
Werth, Rev. Joshua, '09 (SAL) Curia: Miscellaneous / Other Offices St. Bernard Parish, Ellsworth, Inc., Ellsworth, KS; St. Ignatius Loyola Parish, Kanopolis, Inc., Kanopolis, KS; [MIS] Vocatio of Salina, Salina, KS
Werth, Rev. Robert Thomas, '79 (ROC) Roman Catholic Parish of St. Frances Xavier Cabrini, Rochester, NY
Wertin, Rev. Carl, '15 (PBL) Curia: Offices and Directors Christ the King, Pueblo, CO
Wertin, Very Rev. Henry James, '16 (PBL) Curia: Leadership; Offices and Directors St. Joseph, Grand Junction, CO
Wertin, Rev. Matthew, '06 (PBL) St. Mary, Montrose, CO
Wertz, Rev. Jerry, *S.D.B.* '88 (SFR) [MON] Salesian Provincial Residence, San Francisco, CA
Wesely, Rev. Mark, '93 (SAL) Immaculate Conception of the Blessed Virgin Mary Parish, Minneapolis, Inc., Minneapolis, KS; St. Mary Parish, Glasco, Inc., Glasco, KS; St. Patrick Parish, Lincoln, Inc., Lincoln, KS
Wesley, Rev. Andrew, '80 (DET) St. John Paul II Parish Detroit, Detroit, MI
Wesley, Rev. Shaun C., '05 (LR) SS. Cyril and Methodius, Stuttgart, AR; St. Rose of Lima Church, Carlisle, AR
Wesnofske, Rev. Donald Philip, (RVC) St. Joseph the Worker, East Patchogue, NY
Wesnofske, Rev. Matthias, *O.F.M., Cap.* '67 (NOR) Retired. St. Pius X, Middletown, CT
Wesoloski, Rev. Richard J., '72 (PIT) Retired.
Wesolowski, Rev. Anthony, *O.S.B.* '72 (GBG) [MON] Saint Vincent Archabbey, Latrobe, PA
Wesolowski, Rev. Jacek, *SChr* (DAL) St. Peter the Apostle Catholic Parish, Dallas, TX
Wesonga, Rev. Pius, *A.J.* (SJN) San Judas Tadeo, Toa Alta, PR
Wessel, Rev. John F., '57 (CLV) Retired.
Wesselsky, Rev. Msgr. Emil J., '56 (SAT) Retired. [NUR] Casa De Padres, San Antonio, TX
Wessman, Rev. R. Aaron, (CIN) [MON] Headquarters of Glenmary Home Missioners (The Home Missioners of America), Fairfield, OH
West, Rev. Don J., '90 (CIN) Corpus Christi, Cincinnati, OH; St. John Neumann, Cincinnati, OH; St. John the Baptist, Cincinnati, OH

West, Rev. H. Gregory, '91 (CHR) Curia: Tribunal St. Clare of Assisi, Daniel Island, SC

West, Rev. James Renaurd, '13 (CHR) Bishop England High School, Charleston, SC; Sacred Heart, Charleston, SC; [CAM] The Citadel, Catholic Campus Ministry, Charleston, SC

West, Rev. Joseph, *O.F.M.Conv.* '92 (IND) St. John the Baptist Catholic Church, Starlight, Inc., Floyds Knobs, IN; St. Mary of the Annunciation Catholic Church, Navilleton, Inc., Floyds Knobs, IN

West, Rev. Joshua, *L.C.* '09 (R) Sacred Heart, Whiteville, NC

West, Rev. Joshua, *L.C.* '09 (CHI) [MON] Legion of Christ, Hickory Hills, IL

West, Rev. Msgr. Mauricio W., '79 (CHL) On Leave.

West, Rev. Patrick J., '81 (BRK) St. Sebastian, Woodside, NY

West, Rev. Paul R. Varchola, '20 (PSC) Holy Trinity, Philadelphia, PA; Our Lady of Perpetual Help, Levittown, PA

West, Rev. Peter, '91 (NEW) St. John, Orange, NJ

West, Rev. Samuel G., '09 (STO) Curia: Leadership St. Joseph Church of Modesto (Pastor of), Modesto, CA

West, Rev. Thomas, *O.F.M.* '86 (OAK) [MON] Franciscan Friars of California (Province of St. Barbara), Oakland, CA

West, Rev. Thomas B., *OFM* (SFR) St. Boniface, San Francisco, CA

Westcott, Very Rev. Matthew J., '07 (BO) Curia: (>MO) Offices and Directors Christ the King, Brockton, MA; Our Lady of Lourdes, Brockton, MA; St. Edith Stein, Brockton, MA

Wester, Rev. Donald R., '78 (STL) All Saints Catholic Church, St. Peters, MO

Westerhoff, Rev. Ralph A., '62 (CIN) Retired.

Westermann, Rev. Daniel J., '14 (LAN) St. John the Baptist Parish Ypsilanti, Ypsilanti, MI

Westfall, Rev. Joseph, (NY) Chap, VA Hudson Valley Healthcare, Castle Point

Westfall, Rev. Joseph B., '93 (LFT) On Duty Outside Diocese. Putnam Valley, NY Curia: (>MO) Offices and Directors

Westhoff, Rev. Dane, (STL) St. Joseph Catholic Church, Cottleville, St. Charles, MO

Westhoff, Rev. Dane, (MO) Curia: Offices and Directors

Westhoven, Rev. Thomas, *S.C.J.* '66 (MIL) Retired. [MON] Sacred Heart at Monastery Lake, Franklin, WI

Weston, Rev. Michael D., '02 (ARL) On Duty Outside Diocese. Basilica of the National Shrine of the Immaculate Concept... Curia: Offices and Directors Cathedral of St. Thomas More, Arlington, VA (>WDC) [SHR] Basilica of the National Shrine of the Immaculate Conception, Washington, DC

Weston, Rev. Thomas C., *S.J.* '78 (OAK) [MON] Jesuit Fathers and Brothers, Oakland, CA

Westphal, Rev. Adam, '13 (DM) St. Thomas Aquinas, Indianola, IA

Wetovick, Rev. Michael E., '14 (GI) St. Pius X, Ainsworth, NE

Wetsel, Rev. Matthew, '10 (ALB) Church of the Holy Spirit, Gloversville, NY; Holy Trinity Parish, Johnstown, NY

Wetta, Rev. Augustine, *O.S.B.* '03 (STL) St. Louis Priory School, Creve Coeur, MO; [MON] The Abbey of St. Mary and St. Louis, St. Louis, MO

Wetter, Rev. Msgr. Richard L., '57 (BUF) Retired.

Wetterer, Rev. Msgr. Edward V., '64 (BRK) Retired. St. Joan of Arc, Jackson Heights, NY

Wetzel, Rev. Christopher, *O.P.* '17 (SFR) St. Dominic's Catholic Church, San Francisco, CA; [MON] St. Dominic Priory, San Francisco, CA

Wetzel, Rev. Estevan, '20 (PHX) St. John Paul II Roman Catholic High School, Avondale, AZ; St. Thomas Aquinas Roman Catholic Parish, Avondale, AZ

Wevita, Rev. Bede, '91 (LAV) On Sick Leave. Curia: Advisory Boards, Commissions, Committees, and Councils

Wewers, Rev. William, *O.S.B.* '67 (LR) Holy Redeemer, Clarksville, AR; [MON] Subiaco Abbey, Subiaco, AR

Weyker, Rev. James, *S.D.S.* (MIL) [MIS] Holy Apostles House of Formation, Milwauke, WI

Weymes, Rev. Gerald, '74 (ARL) Retired. [MIS] Divine Mercy Care, Fairfax, VA

Weyrens, Rev. Ronald, '82 (SCL) St. Francis Xavier, Sartell, MN; St. Stephen's, St. Stephen, MN

Wezner, Rev. Timothy J., '16 (DET) Curia: Offices and Directors

Whalen, Rev. David M., *O.S.F.S.* '71 (TOL) St. Pius X, Toledo, OH; [MIS] St. Pius X, Toledo, OH

Whalen, Rev. Joseph, '99 (STP) St. Timothy's, Blaine, MN

Whalen, Rev. Joseph T., '71 (ALN) Retired. St. Richard, Barnesville, PA

Whalen, Rev. Timothy F., '78 (PIT) Our Lady of Perpetual Help, Glenshaw, PA

Whalen, Rev. William, '60 (MIL) Retired.

Wharff, Rev. Arian, '15 (TR) On Leave.

Wharton, Rev. Alan Bernardine, *F.I.* (FR) [MON] Marian Friary of Our Lady, Queen of the Seraphic Order, New Bedford, MA

Wharton, Rev. Paul J., '82 (WH) Curia: Offices and Directors Blessed Sacrament, South Charleston, WV

Whatley, Rev. Francis, (MIA) [NUR] St. Anne's Nursing Center, St. Anne's Residence, Inc., Miami, FL

Whatley, Rev. Frank, *O.SS.T.* '88 (BAL) [MON] Holy Trinity Monastery, Sykesville, MD

Whealen, Rev. Martin J., *S.J.* '62 (STL) Retired.

Wheatley, Rev. Herbert, '67 (P) Retired.

Wheaton, Rev. William F., '92 (SLC) Retired.

Whedbee, Rev. Dominic, *O.C.S.O.* '77 (WOR) [MON] St. Joseph's Abbey (Cistercian Abbey of Spencer, Inc., Cistercian Order of the Strict Observance (Trappists)), Spencer, MA

Wheelahan, Rev. Michael, '80 (OKL) Holy Name of Jesus Catholic Church, Chickasha, OK; [CAM] University of Science & Arts of Oklahoma, Chickasha, OK

Wheelan, Rev. Mark, *S.O.L.T.* '04 (CC) St. John Nepomucene, Robstown, TX; [MON] Society of Our Lady of the Most Holy Trinity, Corpus Christi, TX

Wheeler, Rev. Arthur F., *C.S.C.* '84 (P) [MON] Priests of Holy Cross in Oregon, Inc., Portland, OR

Wheeler, Rev. Charles, '79 (JOL) Retired.

Wheeler, Rev. Christopher A., '22 (E) St. Eulalia, Coudersport, PA; St. Gabriel the Archangel, Port Allegany, PA

Wheeler, Rev. Daniel F., '75 (LAN) St. Elizabeth Parish Tecumseh, Tecumseh, MI

Wheeler, Rev. David, (LEX) Cathedral of Christ the King, Lexington, KY

Wheeler, Rev. James, *O.F.M.* '66 (SFD) [MON] Holy Cross Friary (Quincy University Friary), Quincy, IL

Wheeler, Rev. James J., *S.J.* '68 (RVC) [RTR] St. Joseph's Prayer Center, Patchogue, NY

Wheeler, Rev. Thomas F.X., *S.J.* '62 (PH) Retired.

Wheeler, Rev. Wayne B., '79 (GR) Curia: Leadership St. Simon, Ludington, MI

Wheeler, Rev. William Matthew, '18 (LA) Visitation, Los Angeles, CA

Whelan, Rev. Msgr. Bill S., '57 (OM) Retired. [MIS] Cor Unum Family Inc., Omaha, NE

Whelan, Rev. Daniel, '04 (L) On Duty Outside Diocese. Fort Wayne, IN

Whelan, Rev. Daniel, '04 (FTW) Our Lady of Good Hope, Fort Wayne, IN

Whelan, Rev. Dennis J., '65 (RVC) Retired.

Whelan, Rev. Edward J., *M.M.* '61 (NY) Retired. [MON] Maryknoll Fathers and Brothers (Catholic Foreign Mission Society of America, Inc.), Ossining, NY

Whelan, Rev. James P., '93 (NEW) Retired.

Whelan, Rev. John F., '58 (RVC) Retired.

Whelan, Rev. Robert J., '83 (BRK) Our Lady of the Blessed Sacrament, Bayside, NY

Whelan, Rev. Steven, *S.D.B.* '69 (OAK) Retired.

Whelan, Rev. Thomas J., '81 (BO) On Leave.

Whelton, Rev. Msgr. Daniel P., '70 (SR) Curia: Leadership

Whelton, Rev. Msgr. Daniel P., '70 (SR) Retired. Pastor of St. Vincent de Paul Catholic Church of Petaluma, A Corporation Sole, Petaluma, CA

Wherley, Rev. Charles, *C.Ss.R.* '01 (BRK) [MON] Redemptorist Fathers of New York, Inc.-Baltimore Province, Brooklyn, NY

Whewell, Rev. Glenn, '01 (CHY) Curia: Consultative Bodies Holy Name, Sheridan, WY

Whistle, Rev. Brad, '81 (OWN) St. Thomas More, Paducah, KY; [CEM] Mt. Carmel Cemetery, Inc., Paducah, KY

White, Rev. Bernard L., '77 (ALT) Retired.

White, Rev. Charles, '09 (DET) St. Mary Queen of Creation Parish New Baltimore, New Baltimore, MI

White, Rev. Charles H., '65 (BRK) Retired.

White, Rev. Daniel E., '04 (ROC) Curia: Administration; Consultative Bodies Sacred Heart Cathedral, Rochester, NY

White, Rev. Daniel L., '19 (ROC) Curia: Clergy and Religious Services St. Maximilian Kolbe, Ontario, NY; The Parish of St. Katharine Drexel, Macedon, NY

White, Rev. Daniel P., *S.J.* '01 (STL) St. Francis Xavier Catholic Church, St. Louis, MO; [COL] Saint Louis University, St. Louis, MO; [MON] Sacred Heart Jesuit Community, St. Louis, MO

White, Rev. Edward Goodwin, '05 (SEA) St. Stephen the Martyr, Renton, WA

White, Rev. James, *C.Ss.R.* '81 (KC) Our Lady of Perpetual Help, Kansas City, MO; [MON] Redemptorists Fathers of Kansas City, Missouri, Kansas City, MO

White, Rev. Msgr. James E., '83 (NY) On Leave.

White, Rev. James J., *S.J.* '71 (KC) [MON] St. Peter Claver Jesuit Community, Kansas City, MO

White, Rev. James R., '80 (NEW) Seton Hall Preparatory School, West Orange, NJ; St. Joseph, West Orange, NJ

White, Rev. Joseph, (GAL) St. John Vianney, Houston, TX

White, Rev. Joseph M., '91 (BO) Curia: Consultative Bodies St. Joseph, Boston, MA

White, Rev. Kenneth R., '68 (PIT) Retired.

White, Rev. Kevin R., (BO) [MON] Campion Center, Inc., Weston, MA

White, Rev. Kyle, '18 (LAF) St. Leo the Great, Lafayette, LA

White, Rev. Msgr. Lawrence E., '70 (CC) Retired.

White, Rev. Mark, '19 (ATL) Queen of Angels Catholic Church, Thomson, Inc., Thomson, GA; St. Joseph Catholic Church, Washington, Inc., Washington, GA

White, Rev. Michael, '84 (BAL) Church of the Nativity, Timonium, MD

White, Rev. Michael, *C.S.Sp.* '83 (SD) [COL] University of San Diego, San Diego, CA

White, Rev. Morgan M., '02 (TYL) On Duty Outside Diocese. D. Ferns, Ireland

White, Rev. Paul C., '89 (RCK) On Special Assignment. Sr. Priest Advocate Church of Holy Apostles, McHenry, IL

White, Rev. Paul T., '83 (PT) Retired. Curia: Leadership

White, Rev. Peter H., '62 (WOR) Retired.

White, Rev. Philip, *OFM Cap.* '18 (HBG) Holy Family, Harrisburg, PA; St. Francis of Assisi, Harrisburg, PA

White, Rev. Robert, '70 (SD) Retired.

White, Rev. Robert Kevin, '61 (SFR) Retired.

White, Rev. Robert L., '74 (STP) St. Victoria, Victoria, MN; [CEM] St. Victoria Cemetery, Victoria, MN

White, Rev. Robert S., *C.S.S.* '73 (SPR) Our Lady of Mt. Carmel, Springfield, MA

White, Very Rev. Rodney, '03 (SAN) Curia: Advisory Boards, Commissions, Committees, and Councils; Canonical Services St. Stephen's, Midland, TX

White, Rev. Roger, *O.F.M.Cap.* '65 (PH) St. John the Evangelist, Philadelphia, PA

White, Rev. Sebastian, *O.P.* (NY) [CAM] New York University, New York, NY (>WDC) [SEM] Dominican House of Studies, Washington, DC

White, Rev. Thomas, '64 (BLX) Retired.

White, Rev. William A., '90 (NY) Retired.

White OFM Cap, Rev. Philip, *OFM Cap* (GBG) Church of the Resurrection, Clymer, PA

Whited, Rev. Msgr. Walter M., '66 (STL) Retired.

Whiteford, Rev. David, (E) Our Lady of Peace, Erie, PA

Whitehead, Rev. Joseph, '84 (STA) On Leave.

Whitehead, Rev. Matthew, (POC) Military Chap

Whitehead, Rev. Matthew, (MO) Curia: Offices and Directors

Whiteing, Rev. Richard J., '80 (OM) Retired.

Whiteside, Rev. Daniel R., '92 (CHI) St. Mary, Buffalo Grove, IL

Whiteside, Rev. David, '97 (PEO) St. Mary Parish, Lewistown, IL; St. Patrick's, Havana, IL

Whitestone, Rev. David A., '89 (ARL) St. Anthony, Falls Church, VA

Whitfield, Rev. Joshua, '12 (DAL) Curia: Administration St. Rita Catholic Parish, Dallas, TX

Whiting, Rev. Andrew, *IVE* (WIN) SS. Peter and Paul Catholic Church, Mankato, MN

Whitley, Rev. Rufus, *O.M.I.* '76 (WDC) [MON] Missionary Oblates of Mary Immaculate, Washington, DC; [MON] Oblate Community, Washington, DC

Whitley, Rev. Rufus J., *O.M.I.* '76 (CHI) [EFT] Oblates for International Pastoral (Oblate International Pastoral Investment Trust), Chicago, IL

Whitlock, Rev. John J., '13 (LAN) Curia: Offices and Directors St. Martha Parish Okemos, Okemos, MI

Whitman, Rev. Dan G., '83 (KNX) Retired. Curia: Offices and Directors [MIS] Diocesan Council of Catholic Women, Knoxville, TN

Whitman, Rev. David R., '05 (CHR) Curia: Offices and Directors St. Paul the Apostle, Spartanburg, SC

Whitman, Rev. Glenn R., '75 (E) Good Shepherd, West Middlesex, PA

Whitman, Rev. Mark, '95 (STL) St. Cletus, St. Charles, MO; St. Robert Bellarmine Catholic Church, St. Charles, MO

Whitman, Rev. Thomas J., '87 (E) St. Joseph, Sharon, PA; [CAM] Penn State University - Shenango Valley Campus, Sharon, PA

Whitmore, Rev. Msgr. Paul E., '54 (OG) Retired. The Church of the Holy Family, Watertown, NY

Whitney, Rev. John, *S.J.* '94 (SEA) [MON] Jesuit House,

Seattle, Seattle, WA
Whitney, Rev. John D., *S.J.* (SFR) St. Ignatius, San Francisco, CA; [MON] Loyola House Jesuit Community, San Francisco, CA
Whitney, Rev. Patrick J., '68 (RVC) St. Francis de Sales, Patchogue, NY
Whitney, Rev. Richard, *CSP* '21 (KNX) Saint John XXIII University Parish/Catholic Center, Knoxville, TN; [CAM] UT-Knoxville, Newman Foundation, Inc., Knoxville, TN; [MON] Paulist Fathers (Missionary Society of St. Paul the Apostle), Knoxville, TN
Whitney, Rev. Robert, (AJ) Our Lady of Perpetual Help, Soldotna, AK
Whitney, Rev. Robert, (AJ) Our Lady of the Angels, Kenai, AK
Whitt, Rev. D. Reginald, *O.P.* (BAL) Curia: Tribunal
Whitt, Rev. D. Reginald, *O.P.* (BAL) SS. Philip and James, Baltimore, MD
Whittaker, Very Rev. Kenneth D., '77 (MIA) Curia: Canonical Services; Leadership Our Lady of Mercy, Deerfield Beach, FL
Whittier, Rev. William O., '61 (STP) Retired.
Whittingham, Rev. Thomas P., '12 (PH) Curia: Advisory Boards, Commissions, Committees, and Councils; Deaneries St. Laurence, Upper Darby, PA; [CAM] Widener University, Chester, PA
Whittington, Rev. Justin, *S.J.* '99 (TUC) [MON] Jesuit Community of the Vatican Observatory, Tucson, AZ
Whittington, Rev. Kenneth L., '88 (CHL) St. Charles Borromeo, Morganton, NC
Whittington, Rev. Paul de Porres, *O.P.* '97 (CHI) St. Katharine Drexel, Chicago, IL
Whittington, Rev. Shaun P., '05 (IND) St. Charles Catholic Church, Milan, Inc., Milan, IN; St. Nicholas Catholic Church, Sunman, Inc., Sunman, IN
Whittington, Rev. Taryn, '16 (LR) Christ the King, Little Rock, AR; St. Boniface, Bigelow, AR
Whittle, Rev. Patrick, (WDC) [MON] St. Louis Friary, Washington, DC
Whorton, Rev. Jeffrey T., '08 (SFE) On Duty Outside Diocese. Curia: (>MO) Offices and Directors
Whyte, Rev. Michael G., '03 (HRT) Curia: Advisory Boards, Commissions, Committees, and Councils; Education The Church of St. Catherine of Siena of Simsbury Corporation, West Simsbury, CT; [SEM] St. Thomas Seminary, Bloomfield, CT
Wiatrowski, Rev. Ralph E., '74 (CLV) On Sick Leave. St. Barnabas, Northfield, OH
Wible, Rev. Charles M., '96 (BAL) St. Peter the Apostle, Union Bridge, MD
Wichert, Very Rev. Nicholas F., '10 (SEA) Curia: Leadership St. Brendan, Bothell, WA
Wichlan, Rev. David L., '57 (STL) Retired.
Wichman, Rev. Edwin J., '80 (PIT) [CON] Divine Redeemer Motherhouse, Elizabeth, PA
Wicht, Rev. Robert, *S.D.S.* '67 (MIL) [MIS] Salvatorians - Jordan Hall, Milwaukee, WI
Wickenhauser, Rev. Gerald M., *M.M.* '62 (NY) Retired. [MON] Maryknoll Fathers and Brothers (Catholic Foreign Mission Society of America, Inc.), Ossining, NY
Wickersham, Rev. James A., '08 (OKL) St. Mary, Guthrie, OK
Wickowski, Rev. Leroy A., '66 (CHI) Retired. St. Luke and St. Bernardine Parish, River Forest, IL
Wickrematunge, Rev. Vernon P., '87 (NY) Chap, Hudson Valley Hospital, Cortlandt Manor Holy Spirit, Cortlandt Manor, NY
Wicks, Rev. Jared, (DET) [MON] Colombiere Center, Clarkston, MI
Widder, Rev. Matthew J., '10 (MIL) St. John Neumann, Catholic Community of Waukesha, Waukesha, WI; St. Joseph, Catholic Community of Waukesha, Waukesha, WI; St. Mary, Catholic Community of Waukesha, Waukesha, WI; St. William, Catholic Community of Waukesha, Waukesha, WI
Wideman, Rev. Brian, '14 (GB) St. Clare Parish Corporation, Greenleaf, WI
Wieber, Rev. Donald A., '57 (KAL) Retired.
Wiechmann, Rev. Derek, '17 (SCL) St. Kathryn's, Mora, MN; St. Louis Bertrand, Foreston, MN; St. Mary's, Mora, MN; The Church of St. Mary of Milaca, Milaca, MN
Wieck, Rev. Anthony J., *S.J.* '10 (STL) [MIS] Office, St. Louis, MO
Wieck, Rev. Shane, (AMA) St. John the Evangelist, Borger, TX
Wiedel, Rev. Thomas L., '90 (LIN) St. Patrick's, Manley, NE
Wiedenfeld, Rev. Kurtis, '12 (AUS) St. Mary Catholic Church, Temple, TX
Wiederholt, Rev. Clarence E., '55 (JC) Retired.
Wiederholt, Rev. Thomas W., '63 (KC) Retired.
Wiedner, Rev. Larry W., '80 (PHX) Retired.
Wiegand, Rev. William R., '05 (DAV) Retired.
Wieging, Rev. James F., '67 (DET) Retired.
Wieladek, Rev. Waldemar, *C.Ss.R* '92 (MET) Saint John Paul II Parish, Perth Amboy, NJ
Wieliczko, Rev. Andrzej, '99 (MET) Holy Trinity, Helmetta, NJ
Wielinski, Rev. Alan, '84 (SCL) Our Lady of Victory, Fergus Falls, MN; St. Elizabeth, Elizabeth, MN; St. Leonard's, Pelican Rapids, MN
Wielunski, Rev. Msgr. Gregory C., '78 (BRK) On Duty Outside Diocese. The Tribunal, Archdiocese of Miami,
Wielunski, Msgr. Gregory C., '78 (MIA) Curia: Canonical Services; Pastoral Services
Wienhoff, Rev. Paul R., '78 (BEL) Curia: Leadership Corpus Christi, Shiloh, IL; St. Joseph, Lebanon, IL
Wiera, Rev. Stefan, '68 (SAT) Retired.
Wierichs, Rev. Paul, *C.P.* '78 (NY) [MON] The Congregation of the Passion - St. Paul of the Cross Province, Jamaica, NY
Wierichs, Rev. Paul, *C.P.* (BRK) [MON] Immaculate Conception Monastery, Jamaica, NY
Wiering, Rev. Matthew J., '10 (NU) On Special Assignment. Curia: Offices and Directors Church of the Holy Family, Silver Lake, MN; Holy Trinity, Winsted, MN; St. Pius X, Glencoe, MN
Wierzba, Rev. Alan P., '01 (LC) Holy Family, Edgar, WI; St. John the Baptist, Edgar, WI
Wierzbicki, Rev. Kamil Peter, '14 (PAT) St. Jude's, Hopatcong, NJ
Wierzchowski, Rev. Marian, *S.A.C.* (NY) Our Lady of Mt. Carmel, New York, NY
Wierzowiecki, Rev. Gregory, *OFM Conv* (SPR) Our Lady of the Cross, Holyoke, MA
Wieseler, Rev. Larry, '69 (CR) Retired.
Wiesenbaugh, Rev. Robert D., *S.J.* (NY) [MON] Kolhmann Hall Jesuit Community, Bronx, NY
Wieser, Rev. Stanley, '68 (SCL) Retired.
Wieslaw, Rev. Strzadala, *S.D.S.* '90 (NEW) [MON] The Salvatorian Fathers, Verona, NJ
Wiesner, Rev. Mark, '95 (OAK) Curia: Leadership The Catholic Community of Pleasanton, Pleasanton, CA
Wiest, Rev. Gregory, *C.Ss.R.* '89 (STP) St. Alphonsus, Brooklyn Center, MN; [MON] Redemptorist Fathers of Hennepin County, Brooklyn Center, MN
Wigand, Rev. William J., '83 (STL) Retired.
Wiggins, Rev. Frank, '86 (RIC) Retired.
Wiggins, Rev. Mason, (STA) Holy Family, Jacksonville, FL
Wiggins, Rev. Mason Edward, (STA) St. Philip Neri Mission, Hawthorne, FL; St. William, Keystone Heights, FL
Wiggins, Rev. Timothy, (NY) The Magdalene, Sleepy Hollow, NY
Wigginton, Rev. Ellsworth T., '76 (FWT) Retired.
Wight, Rev. Jonathan C., '86 (TOL) Immaculate Conception, Bellevue, OH
Wightman, Rev. Paul, *OMI* (BEL) Retired. [MON] Missionary Oblates of Mary Immaculate - St. Henry's Oblate Residence, Belleville, IL
Wigton, Rev. Matthew, '01 (GLD) Holy Redeemer of Vanderbilt, Vanderbilt, MI; Saint Mary, Our Lady of Mt. Carmel Cathedral of Gaylord, Gaylord, MI; Saint Thomas Aquinas of Elmira, Elmira, MI
Wigton, Rev. Matthew A., '01 (GLD) Curia: Advisory Boards, Commissions, Committees, and Councils; Leadership; Offices and Directors
Wigton, Rev. Peter T., '12 (GLD) Holy Cross of Beaver Island, Beaver Island, MI; Saint Mary of the Assumption of Charlevoix, Charlevoix, MI
Wikarski, Rev. Tomasz, '06 (DEN) On Leave.
Wiktor, Rev. Marcin, '18 (BLX) St. Bernadette, Waynesboro, MS
Wiktor, Rev. Marcin S., '18 (BLX) Immaculate Conception, Laurel, MS
Wiktorek, Rev. Walter, (MET) Holy Family Parish, New Brunswick, NJ
Wilber, Rev. Stewart A., '92 (ATL) Retired.
Wilbers, Rev. Msgr. Michael T., '72 (JC) Retired.
Wilborn, Very Rev. Jeffrey, '00 (DEN) Our Lady of the Plains Catholic Parish in Byers, Byers, CO
Wilbricht, Rev. Stephen S., *C.S.C.* '97 (FR) [COL] Holy Cross Fathers Religious, North Easton, MA; [COL] Stonehill College, North Easton, MA
Wilbur, Rev. Joshua, '18 (HRT) St. Patricks Church Society of Farmington, Connecticut, Farmington, CT; St. Paul Catholic High School, Bristol, CT; The Star of the Sea Church Corporation of Unionville, Connecticut, Unionville, CT
Wilcox, Rev. Gino, *Rev.* '19 (LSC) Santa Rosa de Lima Parish, Inc., Las Cruces, NM
Wilcox, Rev. James, '13 (FWT) On Leave.
Wilczak, Rev. Adam, '14 (KCK) Curia: Leadership Divine Mercy, Gardner, KS
Wild, Rev. Alexander, '89 (DUB) Retired.
Wild, Rev. J. Jerome, '81 (PH) St. Teresa of Avila, Norristown, PA
Wild, Rev. Michael L., '84 (MIL) Retired.
Wild, Rev. Robert A., '70 (BUF) On Duty Outside Diocese. Madonna House, Combermere, ON
Wild, Rev. Robert A., *S.J.* '70 (MIL) [MON] St. Camillus Jesuit Community (Society of Jesus, USA Midwest Province), Wauwatosa, WI
Wilde, Rev. Adrian, *O.Carm.* '72 (VEN) Retired. [MON] Carmel at Mission Valley, Nokomis, FL
Wilde, Rev. Denis G., *O.S.A.* '70 (PH) [MON] St. Thomas Monastery, Villanova, PA
Wilder, Rev. Daniel J., '96 (PEO) On Duty Outside Diocese.
Wilder, Rev. Frank, *O.A.R* (ORG) Our Lady of the Pillar, Santa Ana, CA
Wilder, Rev. Frank T., *O.A.R.* '91 (LA) [MON] Order of Augustinian Recollects (O.A.R.), St. Augustine Priory, Oxnard, CA
Wilderotter, Rev. Paul C., '74 (CHL) On Duty Outside Diocese.
Wildes, Rev. Kevin, *S.J.* '86 (PH) [MON] Jesuit Community at St. Joseph's University, Merion Station, PA
Wiley, Rev. Leo A., '56 (OG) Retired. The Church of the Holy Family, Watertown, NY
Wiley, Rev. Nye, '19 (WH) Central Catholic High School, Wheeling, WV; St. Alphonsus, Wheeling, WV
Wilgenbusch, Rev. Luke, '19 (NSH) Curia: Leadership; Offices and Directors
Wilgenbusch, Rev. Msgr. Lyle L., '66 (DUB) Retired.
Wilhelm, Rev. Chad F., '94 (FAR) Curia: Leadership; Offices and Directors St. Joseph Church, Devils Lake, ND
Wilhelm, Rev. Dean, '88 (AUS) St. John Neumann, Westlake Hills, TX; [EFT] Diocese of Austin Pension Plan and Trust, Austin, TX
Wilhelm, Rev. H. Joseph, *S.M.* '59 (WH) Retired.
Wilhelm, Rev. H. Joseph, *S.M.* '59 (WDC) Retired. [MON] Marist Center (The Marist Finance Center of the Atlanta Province of the Society of Mary, Marist Fathers and Brothers), Washington, DC
Wilhelm, Rev. Patrick R.C., '71 (NEW) Retired. Our Lady of Sorrows, Kearny, NJ
Wilhelm, Rev. Paul, *O.M.I.* '68 (BWN) Our Lady of Refuge, Roma, TX
Wilhelm, Rev. Robert J., '59 (TOL) Retired.
Wilhite, Rev. Philip A., '90 (GAL) Curia: Leadership; Offices and Directors Sacred Heart, Conroe, TX
Wilisowski, Rev. Tomasz, *C.S.M.A.* '00 (DET) St. Genevieve - St. Maurice Parish Livonia, Livonia, MI; [MON] Congregation of St. Michael the Archangel - Michaelite Fathers, Grosse Pointe Park, MI
Wilk, Rev. Brian J., '03 (MAD) St. Bernard, Middleton, WI
Wilk, Rev. Mitchell S., '70 (SPC) Retired.
Wilk, Rev. Tomasz P., *O.S.P.P.E.* '05 (CHI) St. Monica and St. Rosalie Parish, Chicago, IL
Wilk, Rev. Tomasz Piotr, *O.S.P.P.E.* '05 (SPC) St. Augustine, Kelso, MO; St. Joseph, Scott City, MO
Wilke, Rev. Mark T., '13 (HBG) Curia: Offices and Directors
Wilken, Rev. Paul Timothy, *S.D.S.* '19 (MIL) [MON] Salvatorian Provincial Offices (Society of the Divine Savior), Milwaukee, WI
Wilkening, Rev. David F., '79 (DAV) St. Joseph Church of North English, Iowa, North English, IA; St. Mary Church of Williamsburg, Iowa, Williamsburg, IA; St. Patrick Church of Marengo, Iowa, Marengo, IA
Wilker, Rev. Austin J., '17 (DUB) St. Joseph's Church, Preston, Iowa, Preston, IA; St. Lawrence Church, Otter Creek, Iowa, Zwingle, IA; The Sacred Heart Church, Maquoketa, Iowa, Maquoketa, IA
Wilker, Rev. Ronald H., '71 (CIN) Retired.
Wilkerson, Rev. Wayne W., '99 (GAL) St. Michael, Houston, TX
Wilkes, Rev. Michael, '09 (DET) On Leave.
Wilkie, Rev. John J., '92 (SEA) Retired.
Wilkins, Rev. Bernard J., '61 (STL) Retired. St. Gertrude Catholic Church, Washington, MO
Wilkins, Rev. David P., '14 (GF) Curia: Leadership
Wilkinson, Rev. Bruce Wilmer, '81 (ATL) Retired.
Wilkinson, Rev. George A., '01 (WDC) Retired.
Wilkinson, Rev. Neal J., *S.J.* '00 (SD) Pastor of Our Lady of Guadalupe Catholic Parish, San Diego, a corporation sole, San Diego, CA
Wilkinson, Rev. Peter, '12 (POC) Retired.
Wilkinson, Rev. Richard S., *C.S.C.* '79 (FTW) [COL] University of Notre Dame Du Lac, Notre Dame, IN; [MON] Holy Cross Community, Corby Hall, University of Notre Dame, Notre Dame, IN

Wilkinson Brusda, Rev. Benjamin Andrew, (ARE) On Duty Outside Diocese. Spain
Will, Rev. Lowell, '68 (EVN) Retired.
Will, Rev. Ron, *C.PP.S.* (KC) Retired. [MIS] St. Gaspar Society, Liberty, MO; [MON] Precious Blood Center, Liberty, MO; [MON] Society of the Precious Blood, Liberty, MO (>CIN) [MON] Society of the Precious Blood, United States Province, Inc., Dayton, OH
Willard, Rev. Donald, *C.Ss.R.* '08 (SAT) St. Gerard Majella, San Antonio, TX; [MON] The Redemptorists/ San Antonio, San Antonio, TX
Willard, Rev. Jordan M., (ARL) Our Lady of Hope, Potomac Falls, VA
Willard, Rev. Stephen A., '93 (PEO) Curia: Consultative Bodies; Deaneries St. Vincent De Paul, Peoria, IL
Wille, Rev. Arthur H., *M.M.* '51 (NY) Retired.
Willemsen, Rev. Rolf, (JOL) [MON] Carmelite Provincial Office, Darien, IL
Willemsen, Rev. Rolf, *O.Carm.* '17 (WDC) [SEM] Whitefriars Hall, Washington, DC
Willenberg, Rev. Lukasz J., '08 (PRO) On Duty Outside Diocese. Archdiocese for the Military Services, USA Curia: (>MO) Offices and Directors
Willenborg, Rev. Daniel L., '05 (SFD) Chap, Graham Corr Ctr, Hillsboro Curia: Leadership Holy Family, Litchfield, IL; St. Agnes, Hillsboro, IL; [ASN] Holy Cross Cemetery Association, Litchfield, IL
Willett, Rev. Joseph, *O.S.B.*
Willette, Rev. Donald, '84 (DEN) Retired.
Willey, Rev. Dennis B., '94 (CHR) Our Lady of the Lake, Chapin, SC
Willger, Rev. Gerard I., '86 (SUP) On Administrative Leave.
Willhite, Rev. Msgr. Robert J., '63 (RCK) Retired. St. Joseph, Aurora, IL
William, Rev. John, '92 (GLD) Saint Anne of Harrisville, Harrisville, MI; Saint Catherine of Alexandria of Ossineke, Ossineke, MI; Saint Gabriel of Black River, Black River, MI; Saint Raphael of Mikado, Mikado, MI
William, Rev. John, (GLD) Curia: Offices and Directors
Williams, Rev. Aaron, (JKS) Curia: Consultative Bodies Assumption of the B.V.M., Natchez, MS; St. Mary Basilica, Natchez, MS
Williams, Rev. Andrew, '18 (SPC) McAuley Catholic High School, Joplin, MO; St. Mary, Joplin, MO; St. Mary, Seneca, MO
Williams, Rev. Anthony C., '83 (KCK) Retired.
Williams, Rev. Benjamin, (PAT) Curia: Leadership St. John Vianney, Stockholm, NJ; St. Thomas, the Apostle, Oak Ridge, NJ
Williams, Rev. Brady, *S.O.L.T.* '04 (CC) [MON] Society of Our Lady of the Most Holy Trinity, Corpus Christi, TX
Williams, Rev. Brandon, '10 (OWN) Curia: Advisory Boards, Commissions, Committees, and Councils St. Anthony, Clarkson, KY; St. Augustine, Clarkson, KY; St. Benedict, Wax, KY
Williams, Very Rev. Christopher E., '12 (LSC) Curia: Consultative Bodies; Leadership; Tribunal San Albino Parish, Inc., Mesilla, NM
Williams, Rev. Clarence, *C.PP.S.* '78 (CIN) [MON] Society of the Precious Blood, United States Province, Inc., Dayton, OH
Williams, Rev. Claude, *O. Praem.* '09 (LA) SS. Peter and Paul, Wilmington, CA
Williams, Rev. Claude A., *O.Praem.* '09 (ORG) [MON] Norbertine Fathers of Orange, Inc., Silverado, CA
Williams, Rev. Cody, '16 (HEL) Holy Cross Parish: Series 451, LLC, Townsend, MT; Saint Bartholomew Parish: Series 455, LLC, White Sulphur Springs, MT; Saint Joseph Parish: Series 432, LLC, Harlowton, MT
Williams, Rev. Daniel R., '20 (LC) Columbus Catholic High School, , ; Columbus Catholic Middle School, , ; St. John the Baptist, Marshfield, WI
Williams, Rev. David, '98 (AUS) Retired.
Williams, Rev. Dennis T., '91 (NY) Nativity of Our Blessed Lady, Bronx, NY; Parish of Holy Rosary and Nativity of Our Blessed Lady, Bronx, NY
Williams, Rev. Donald J., (SCR) St. Matthew, East Stroudsburg, PA
Williams, Rev. George, *SJ* (BO) [MON] Campion Health & Wellness, Inc., Weston, MA
Williams, Rev. George, *S.J.* '04 (OAK) [SEM] Jesuit School of Theology of Santa Clara University (Berkeley, California Campus), Berkeley, CA
Williams, Rev. George S., *S.J.* '72 (BAL) Retired.
Williams, Rev. George T., *S.J.* '04 (SFR) St. Agnes, San Francisco, CA; [MON] Loyola House Jesuit Community, San Francisco, CA
Williams, Rev. H. Brendan, '65 (TR) Retired. [MON] Villa Vianney, Trenton, NJ
Williams, Rev. Ian J., '96 (GRY) Retired. Holy Family, La Porte, IN
Williams, Rev. J. Gerald, *O.Carm.* '80 (KCK) St. Boniface, Garnett, KS; St. Therese, Richmond, KS
Williams, Rev. James, '65 (SEA) Retired.
Williams, Rev. James, (COS) Curia: Leadership
Williams, Rev. James J., '70 (MAR) Retired.
Williams, Rev. Jason A., '16 (CIN) Curia: Administration
Williams, Rev. Jim M., '97 (COS) Chap, Diocesan Prison Curia: Leadership St. Joseph, Salida, CO
Williams, Rev. Msgr. John, '78 (R) Retired. Curia: Leadership St. Anthony of Padua, Southern Pines, NC
Williams, Rev. John L., '91 (HRT) Retired.
Williams, Rev. Jonathan, *O.F.M. Cap.* '71 (PIT) [MON] St. Augustine Friary, Pittsburgh, PA
Williams, Rev. Joseph S, (CHI) St. Vincent de Paul, Chicago, IL; [MON] DePaul Vincentian Residence, Chicago, IL
Williams, Rev. Manuel B., *C.R.* '87 (MOB) Resurrection Catholic Church, Montgomery, AL; [MIS] Resurrection Catholic Missions, Montgomery, AL
Williams, Rev. Matthew, *OCD* '90 (SR) [RTR] Carmelite House of Prayer, Oakville, CA
Williams, Rev. Matthew, *OCD* (SR) [MON] Carmelite House of Prayer, Oakville, CA
Williams, Rev. Matthew M., '03 (BO) Curia: Consultative Bodies; Pastoral Services St. John the Baptist, Quincy, MA; St. Joseph, Quincy, MA
Williams, Rev. Michael, '97 (OWN) Curia: Advisory Boards, Commissions, Committees, and Councils
Williams, Rev. Michael A., *S.J.* '75 (MOB) [MON] Jesuits of Mobile, Inc., Mobile, AL
Williams, Rev. Michael E., '97 (OWN) SS. Joseph and Paul, Owensboro, KY; [COL] Brescia University, Owensboro, KY
Williams, Rev. Michael J., '09 (LSC) Curia: Consultative Bodies; Leadership Our Lady of Perpetual Help Parish, Inc., Truth or Consequences, NM; San Isidro Parish, Inc., Garfield, NM
Williams, Rev. Michael J., '95 (LAN) St. Joseph Parish St. Johns, St. Johns, MI
Williams, Rev. Michael S., '64 (STA) Retired.
Williams, Rev. Oliver F., *C.S.C.* '70 (FTW) [COL] University of Notre Dame Du Lac, Notre Dame, IN; [MON] Holy Cross Community, Corby Hall, University of Notre Dame, Notre Dame, IN
Williams, Very Rev. Patrick J., '93 (NO) Curia: Leadership; Offices and Directors St. Pius X, New Orleans, LA
Williams, Very Rev. Patrick J., '93 (NO) Curia: Leadership
Williams, Rev. Peter, '04 (STP) Saint Ambrose of Woodbury, Woodbury, MN; [MIS] The Companions of Christ, St. Paul, MN
Williams, Rev. Peter Y., '87 (BUR) Retired.
Williams, Rev. R.B., *O.P.* '71 (LUB) Retired. St. Elizabeth University Parish, Lubbock, TX; [MON] Southern Dominican Fathers of Lubbock, Lubbock, TX
Williams, Rev. Rhett Butler, '18 (CHR) Curia: Advisory Boards, Commissions, Committees, and Councils; Offices and Directors St. Thomas More, Columbia, SC; [CAM] University of South Carolina, Columbia, SC
Williams, Rev. Richard C., '65 (PH) Retired.
Williams, Very Rev. Riley J., '11 (FR) Curia: Advisory Boards, Commissions, Committees, and Councils; Leadership Holy Name, Fall River, MA
Williams, Rev. Robert, *O.F.M.Cap.* '09 (NEW) [MON] Capuchin Friars - Province of the Sacred Stigmata of St. Francis, Union City, NJ
Williams, Rev. Robert, (LFT) St. Lawrence, Muncie, IN
Williams, Rev. Robert, '71 (DAL) Retired. (>LUB) St. Ann, Morton, TX
Williams, Rev. Robert, '91 (LUB) Retired.
Williams, Rev. Robert, '91 (DAL) Retired. Our Lady of Fatima Catholic Parish, Quinlan, TX; St. William Catholic Parish, Greenville, TX
Williams, Rev. Robert Hayes, '82 (DET) Curia: Tribunal St. Justin - St. Mary Magdalen Parish Hazel Park, Hazel Park, MI
Williams, Rev. Robert L., '68 (LFT) Retired.
Williams, Rev. Scott, (BIR) Curia: Leadership
Williams, Rev. Steven T., '91 (MOB) Curia: Leadership St. Lawrence Parish, Fairhope, Fairhope, AL; [RTR] Holy Spirit Ministries, Inc., Fairhope, AL
Williams, Rev. W. Ray, '97 (CHL) On Leave.
Williams, Rev. William G., '69 (BO) Retired. Curia: Consultative Bodies
Williamson, Rev. G. Michael, '86 (CLV) St. Matthew, Akron, OH
Williamson, Rev. John A., '00 (BAL) St. John the Evangelist, Frederick, MD; St. Joseph-on-Carrollton Manor, Frederick, MD
Williamson, Rev. Msgr. Robert J., '62 (BUF) Retired.
Williamson, Rev. Thomas, '96 (CHL) On Leave.
Williford, Rev. Timothy, '18 (SP) St. Paul, Tampa, FL
Williford, Rev. Timothy, '18 (SP) Curia: Pastoral Services
Willig, Rev. Jacob, '18 (CIN) St. Mary Church, Oxford, OH
Willig, Rev. Jacob Edward, (CIN) Miami University [CAM] Miami University Catholic Campus Ministry, Oxford, OH
Willig, Rev. Michael A, '22 (CIN) Immaculate Conception, Botkins, OH; St. John, Wapakoneta, OH; St. Joseph, Wapakoneta, OH; St. Lawrence, Botkins, OH
Willingham, Rev. Charles W., *O.Praem.* '95 (ORG) [MON] Norbertine Fathers of Orange, Inc., Silverado, CA
Willis, Rev. Glen, *S.D.S.* '69 (WDC) [SEM] Salvatorian Community, Silver Spring, MD
Willis, Rev. Thomas S., '84 (STA) Curia: Offices and Directors [MIS] St. Mark the Evangelist Catholic Church, ,
Wills, Rev. Ed, '18 (POC) Our Lady of Hope Ordinariate Community, Kansas City, MO
Wills, Rev. Edward, '18 (KC) Retired.
Wills, Rev. Nathan D., *C.S.C.* '06 (FTW) [COL] University of Notre Dame Du Lac, Notre Dame, IN; [MON] Holy Cross Community, Corby Hall, University of Notre Dame, Notre Dame, IN
Wilmot, Rev. John P., '77 (WIN) Retired.
Wilmoth, Rev. James R., '65 (IND) Retired.
Wilmsen, Rev. Gerard P., *S.S.C.* '59 (PRO) Retired. [MON] St. Columban's Retirement House (St. Columban's Foreign Mission Society), Bristol, RI
Wilson, Rev. Alan, *O.F.M.Cap.* '69 (OAK) [NUR] Mercy Retirement and Care Center, Oakland, CA
Wilson, Rev. Alan, *O.F.M.Cap* '69 (SFR) [MON] San Buenaventura Friary, San Francisco, CA (>OAK) [MON] Capuchin Franciscan Friars, Berkeley, CA
Wilson, Rev. Albert L., '51 (L) Retired.
Wilson, Rev. Andrew, '19 (SPP) Sts. Peter & Paul, Pago Pago, AS
Wilson, Rev. Andrew, '19 (SPP) Church of the Holy Cross, Pago Pago, AS
Wilson, Rev. Bill D., '02 (SP) Light of Christ, Clearwater, FL
Wilson, Rev. Cedric M., *O.S.A.* '78 (ARL) Good Shepherd, Alexandria, VA
Wilson, Rev. David J., '88 (E) Holy Rosary, Johnsonburg, PA
Wilson, Rev. Dennis, *OFM* '92 (NY) [MON] Franciscan Friars, Holy Name Province (The Order of Friars Minor of the Province of the Most Holy Name), New York, NY
Wilson, Rev. Dennis M., *O.F.M.* '92 (NY) [MIS] The Migrant Center of New York, Inc., New York, NY
Wilson, Rev. Edward J., '01 (PRO) Immaculate Conception Church Corporation, Cranston, Cranston, RI
Wilson, Rev. Eugene C., '00 (PH) St. Gabriel of the Sorrowful Mother, Stowe, PA
Wilson, Rev. George B., *S.J.* (BAL) Retired. (>PH) [MON] Jesuit Community at St. Joseph's University, Merion Station, PA
Wilson, Very Rev. Gregory B., '01 (CHR) Curia: Advisory Boards, Commissions, Committees, and Councils; Deaneries St. Mary Help of Christians, Aiken, SC
Wilson, Rev. Guy, *S.T.* (JKS) Curia: Consultative Bodies Holy Child Jesus, Canton, MS; Sacred Heart, Camden, MS
Wilson, Rev. Jeffrey, '11 (STO) Curia: Leadership All Saints Church (Pastor of), Twain Harte, CA
Wilson, Rev. Joel R., '09 (TR) Curia: Leadership Our Lady of Perpetual Help, Maple Shade, NJ
Wilson, Rev. John, '16 (NY) Saint Kateri Tekakwitha, LaGrangeville, NY
Wilson, Rev. Jonathan F., '03 (COL) St. Paul the Apostle, Westerville, OH
Wilson, Rev. Joseph F., '86 (BRK) Parish of Transfiguration – Saint Stanislaus Kostka, Maspeth, NY
Wilson, Rev. Lawrence C., '09 (GAL) Shrine of the True Cross, Dickinson, TX
Wilson, Rev. Msgr. Michael, '75 (WDC) Retired. Curia: Consultative Bodies Our Lady Star of the Sea, Solomons, MD
Wilson, Rev. Nicolas, '21 (PEO) St. Columba, Ottawa, IL; St. Francis of Assisi, Ottawa, IL; St. Patrick's, Ottawa, IL
Wilson, Rev. R., '05 (VEN) Retired.
Wilson, Rev. Richard Charles, '15 (CHR) Our Lady of Peace, North Augusta, SC

Wilson, Rev. Robert K., '90 (NY) Parish of Immaculate Conception and St. Anthony, Amenia, NY; St. Anthony, Pine Plains, NY
Wilson, Rev. Samuel, *S.J.* (SJN) San Ignacio de Loyola, San Juan, PR
Wilson, Rev. Sean M., '16 (CIN) Immaculate Conception, Botkins, OH; St. John, Wapakoneta, OH; St. Joseph, Wapakoneta, OH; St. Lawrence, Botkins, OH
Wilson, Rev. Steven, *C.Ss.R.* '01 (SEA) Sacred Heart of Jesus, Seattle, WA; [MON] The Redemptorist Society of Washington, Seattle, WA
Wilson, Rev. Stuart T., '67 (BAL) Retired.
Wilson, Rev. Thomas W., '96 (STP) All Saints, Lakeville, MN; [CEM] All Saints Cemetery, Lakeville, MN
Wilson Smith, Rev. Stuart, *CSP* (CHI) Old St. Mary, Chicago, IL
Wilton, Rev. David, *C.P.M.* '93 (OWN) [MON] Fathers of Mercy, Auburn, KY
Wiltse, Rev. John, '16 (ALX) St. Mary Assumption, Cottonport, LA
Wilwerding, Rev. Glen, '04 (DM) On Sick Leave.
Wilwert, Rev. Kevin, '14 (DAL) [SEM] Holy Trinity Seminary, Irving, TX
Wimmer, Rev. Joseph F., *O.S.A.* '64 (WDC) St. Joseph, Beltsville, MD
Wimmershoff, Rev. Simeon F., '97 (SFE) Queen of Heaven, Albuquerque, NM
Wimsatt, Rev. Michael, (MO) Curia: Offices and Directors
Wimsatt, Rev. Michael T., '10 (L) Curia: Leadership St. James, Elizabethtown, KY
Wimsatt, Rev. Michael T., '10 (L) Curia: Leadership
Wimsett, Rev. Scott J., '88 (L) Our Lady of Lourdes, Louisville, KY
Winchel, Very Rev. Scott, '09 (SAV) Curia: Leadership St. Anne, Columbus, GA
Winchester, Rev. George P., *S.J.* '65 (BO) [MON] Campion Health & Wellness, Inc., Weston, MA
Wind, Rev. Jeremy J., '08 (SC) Cathedral of the Epiphany, Sioux City, IA
Windhaus, Rev. Edward A., '72 (PH) Retired.
Windholtz, Rev. Barry, '88 (LEX) Curia: Leadership
Windholtz, Rev. Barry M., '88 (COV) Curia: Tribunal
Windholtz, Rev. Barry M., '88 (CIN) Curia: Administration
Windle, Rev. Matthew, '16 (PH) St. David, Willow Grove, PA
Windschitl, Rev. Andrew, '15 (DM) St. Joseph, Earling, IA; St. Peter, Defiance, IA
Windsor, Rev. David, *CM* '74 (CHI) [MON] DePaul Vincentian Residence, Chicago, IL
Windsor, Rev. Keith, *O.F.M.Cap.* (DEN) [MON] San Antonio Friary, Denver, CO
Windy, Rev. Jeff, '96 (PEO) Holy Cross, Mendota, IL; St. Theresa Parish, Earlville, IL
Wingate, Rev. Arthur K., '57 (FR) Retired.
Wingerter, Rev. Peter, (NTN) Holy Transfiguration, McLean, VA
Winikates, Rev. Thomas, '70 (CHI) Retired.
Winings, Rev. James T., '21 (CLV) St. Raphael, Bay Village, OH
Winkel, Rev. Thomas J., '71 (CLV) Retired. Sacred Heart of Jesus Parish, South Euclid, OH
Winkelbauer, Rev. Phillip J., '75 (KCK) Retired.
Winkeljohn, Rev. Christian, '08 (PT) Curia: Leadership St. Mary, Pensacola, FL
Winkelmann, Rev. Luke E., '05 (CHI) St. John Vianney, Cure of Ars, Northlake, IL
Winkels, Rev. Michael A., *O.P.* '76 (CHI) [MON] Dominican Community of St. Martin de Porres, Oak Park, IL
Winker, Rev. Nicklaus E., '10 (STL) St. Ann Catholic Church, Normandy, Normandy, MO; [CAM] University of Missouri, St. Louis, Catholic Newman Center, St. Louis, MO
Winkler, Rev. Chauncey, '03 (PHX) St. Timothy Roman Catholic Parish, Mesa, AZ
Winkler, Rev. Edward J., '86 (VIC) Curia: Leadership Sacred Heart, Flatonia, TX; SS. Cyril and Methodius, Flatonia, TX
Winkowitsch, Rev. John, *O.P.* '20 (SFR) St. Raymond, Menlo Park, CA
Winne, Rev. George R., '83 (ALN) Curia: Organizations (affiliated, inter-Diocesan, miscellaneous/other) Immaculate Conception, Allentown, PA; Sacred Heart of Jesus, Allentown, PA
Winshman, Rev. Alfred O., *S.J.* '65 (BO) [MON] Campion Health & Wellness, Inc., Weston, MA
Winslow, Very Rev. Msgr. Patrick J., '99 (CHL) Curia: Consultative Bodies; Leadership [MIS] Catholic Diocese of Charlotte Housing Corp., Charlotte, NC
Winter, Rev. Evan, (LIN) Curia: Leadership
Winter, Rev. Harry, *O.M.I.* '64 (BO) St. Mary, Georgetown, MA
Winter, Rev. James E., '16 (LIN) Curia: Offices and Directors St. John the Baptist, Minden, NE
Winterer, Rev. Msgr. Michael J., '60 (SLC) Retired.
Wintering, Rev. Ian, '21 (PHX) San Francisco de Asis Roman Catholic Parish, Flagstaff, AZ
Winters, Rev. Darvin E., '99 (IND) Sacred Heart of Jesus Catholic Church, Terre Haute, Inc., Terre Haute, IN; St. Mary-of-the-Woods Catholic Church, Inc., St. Mary of the Woods, IN
Winters, Rev. Sean G., '87 (MET) Chap, Raritan Bay Med Ctr, Perth Amboy; Adult Diagnostic... Curia: Clergy and Religious Services St. Joseph, Carteret, NJ
Winters, Rev. Vaughn P., '93 (LA) St. Kateri Tekakwitha, Santa Clarita, CA; St. Mary, Palmdale, CA
Winters, Rev. William, *OFM Cap.* (NY) Retired. [MON] St. Clare Friary (Capuchin Franciscan Friars, Province of St. Mary), Yonkers, NY
Wintz, Rev. Jack R., *O.F.M.* '63 (CIN) Retired.
Winzenburg, Rev. George E., *S.J.* '74 (MIL) [MON] St. Camillus Jesuit Community (Society of Jesus, USA Midwest Province), Wauwatosa, WI
Wipf, Rev. Terry, '00 (BIS) Curia: Offices and Directors Sacred Heart, Plaza, ND; St. Bridget, Parshall, ND; St. Elizabeth, Makoti, ND
Wippel, Rev. Msgr. John, '60 (STU) On Duty Outside Diocese. Chevy Chase, MD (>WDC) [COL] Catholic University of America, The, Washington, DC
Wirkes, Rev. Stephen P., '80 (SY) St. Francis of Assisi, Bridgeport, NY; St. Mary, Minoa, NY; St. Matthew, East Syracuse, NY
Wirkowski, Rev. Mariusz, '04 (PBL) St. Patrick, Telluride, CO
Wironen, Rev. John, *C.S.C.* '79 (P) Retired.
Wirsiy, Rev. Anthanasius S., '03 (PRT) Parish of the Transfiguration, Bar Harbor, ME; St. Joseph, Ellsworth, ME; Stella Maris Parish, Bucksport, ME
Wirth, Rev. Brian, '20 (LIN) Curia: Offices and Directors Cristo Rey, Lincoln, NE; St. Peter, Lincoln, NE
Wirth, Rev. Brian R., '20 (LIN) Curia: Leadership
Wirth, Rev. Geoffrey D., '67 (RCK) Retired.
Wirth, Rev. Seraphim, *F.B.P.* '19 (STP) St. Jerome School, Maplewood, MN; [MIS] Franciscan Brothers of Peace, St. Paul, MN
Wirth, Rev. Steven, '16 (FAR) St. Augustine's Church of Fessenden, Fessenden, ND; St. Boniface Church of Esmond, Esmond, ND; St. William Church of Maddock, Maddock, ND
Wisdom, Rev. Andrew-Carl, *O.P.* '87 (CHI) [MON] Dominicans (Provincial Office), Chicago, IL
Wise, Rev. Mark B., *C.Ss.R.* '72 (R) Immaculate Conception, Clinton, NC; Our Lady of Guadalupe, Newton Grove, NC
Wise, Rev. Richard P., '81 (ATL) Retired.
Wiseman, Rev. Eric, '04 (AJ) Retired.
Wiseman, Rt. Rev. James A., *O.S.B.* '70 (WDC) [MON] St. Anselm's Abbey, Washington, DC
Wiseman, Rev. Robert A., *C.S.C.* '77 (BUR) (>ORL) [MON] Congregation of Holy Cross, United States Province, Cocoa Beach, FL
Wisnefski, Rev. Robert W., '80 (PAT) Chap, Chilton Mem Hosp, Pompton Plains Sacred Heart, Clifton, NJ
Wisneski, Rev. Edward, '67 (NOR) Retired.
Wisneski, Rev. Jonathan J., '98 (GBG) On Leave.
Wisniewski, Rev. Joseph, *C.M.* '65 (BRK) Retired. SS. Cyril and Methodius, Brooklyn, NY
Wisniewski, Rev. Lukasz M., '08 (BO) [SEM] Redemptoris Mater Archdiocesan Missionary Seminary, Chestnut Hill, MA
Wisniewski, Rev. Robert W., '89 (CLV) St. Bridget of Kildare, Parma, OH
Wisniewski, Rev. Thomas, '76 (MIA) Retired.
Wisniewski, Rev. Thomas S., '80 (NEW) St. Catharine, Glen Rock, NJ
Wissler, Rev. Thomas, '83 (STL) St. Joseph Catholic Church, Neier, Union, MO
Wissman, Rev. J. Patrick, '64 (SPC) Retired.
Wister, Rev. Msgr. Robert J., '68 (NEW) Retired. Curia: Organizations (affiliated, inter-Diocesan, miscellaneous/ other) [COL] Seton Hall University, South Orange, NJ
Wit, Rev. Mieczyslaw, *O.F.M.Conv.* '95 (RCK) St. Stanislaus Kostka, Rockford, IL
Witalec, Rev. Dennis J., '82 (PH) Retired.
Witczak, Rev. Michael G., '77 (MIL) On Duty Outside Diocese. Faculty, Washington, DC (>WDC) [COL] Catholic University of America, The, Washington, DC
Witek, Rev. Bernard, *S.D.S.* (DET) [SEM] SS. Cyril and Methodius Seminary, Orchard Lake, MI
With, Rev. William A., '72 (BRK) Resurrection, Brooklyn, NY
Witherup, Rev. Ronald, *P.S.S.* (E) On Duty Outside Diocese.
Witherup, Rev. Ronald D., *P.S.S.* '76 (BAL) [MON] Society of St. Sulpice, Province of the United States, Baltimore, MD
Witkowski, Rev. Phillip, '75 (MAR) Retired.
Witkowski, Rev. Phillip J., '75 (GR) Retired.
Witkowski, Rev. Robert J., '61 (DET) Retired.
Witmer, Rev. Joseph W., '67 (Y) Retired. Curia: Miscellaneous / Other Offices [NUR] Emmaus House, Louisville, OH
Witt, Rev. Alexander T., (CIN) Holy Trinity, Coldwater, OH; Mary Help of Christians, Fort Recovery, OH; St. Anthony, Fort Recovery, OH; St. Joseph, Fort Recovery, OH; St. Mary, Coldwater, OH; St. Paul, Fort Recovery, OH; St. Peter Catholic Church, Fort Recovery, OH
Witt, Rev. Ed, *S.J.* '91 (RC) Curia: Leadership St. Isaac Jogues, Rapid City, SD
Witt, Rev. George, *S.J.* '06 (SY) [MIS] Saint Andrew Hall, Syracuse, NY
Witt, Rev. Michael J., '90 (STL) All Saints Catholic Church, University City, University City, MO; [SEM] Kenrick School of Theology, ,
Witt, Rev. Msgr. Paul K., '71 (LIN) Retired. Curia: Offices and Directors
Witt, Rev. Stephen J., '12 (DAV) St. Mary Church of Iowa City, Iowa, Iowa City, IA
Witte, Rev. Mark G., '95 (COV) On Leave.
Witte, Rev. Steven D., '92 (BEL) On Leave.
Wittnebel, Rev. Benjamin, (STP) Saint Ambrose of Woodbury, Woodbury, MN
Wittouck, Rev. Frank, *S.C.J.* '65 (MIL) Retired. [MON] Sacred Heart Monastery, Hales Corners, WI
Wittrock, Rev. Daniel L., '93 (OM) St. Bernard, Omaha, NE
Wittstock, Rev. Joseph, *O.C.S.O.* '84 (ARL) [MON] Community of Cistercians of the Strict Observance, Inc., Berryville, VA
Witucki, Rev. Roy R., '05 (LC) Retired.
Witzemann, Rev. B. Gerald, '61 (COV) Retired.
Wlodarczyk, Rev. Marek S, (CHI) Our Lady, Mother of the Church Polish Mission, Willow Springs, IL
Wnuk, Rev. Lukasz, '18 (PAT) Assumption of the Blessed Virgin Mary, Morristown, NJ
Wocken, Very Rev. Jeffrey, *S.D.S.* '99 (MIL) [MON] Salvatorian Provincial Offices (Society of the Divine Savior), Milwaukee, WI
Wodecki, Rev. Filip P., '12 (CHR) On Duty Outside Diocese. US Air Force
Wodecki, Rev. Jeremi C., '07 (CHR) On Duty Outside Diocese. Military Chaplain, US Army Curia: (>MO) Offices and Directors
Wodziak, Rev. Jan, '12 (PAT) St. Monica, Sussex, NJ
Woempner, Rev. Michael A., '79 (MAR) Curia: Advisory Boards, Commissions, Committees, and Councils; Offices and Directors St. Mary Queen of Peace, Kingsford, MI
Woerter, Rev. Dennis C., *O.P.* (IND) St. Paul Catholic Center, Bloomington, Inc., Bloomington, IN
Woerth, Rev. Thomas, '66 (DEN) Retired.
Woestman, Rev. William H., *O.M.I.* '56 (CHI) Curia: Tribunal
Woestman, Rev. William H., *O.M.I.* (BEL) Retired. [MON] Shrine of Our Lady of the Snows, Belleville, IL; [NUR] Apartment Community of Our Lady of the Snows (Benedictine Living Community | At The Shrine), Belleville, IL
Wohlwend, Rev. Paul W., *C.PP.S.* '54 (CIN) Retired. [MON] St. Charles, Celina, OH
Wojcicki, Rev. Miroslaus A., '62 (PIT) Retired. St. Joachim and Anne, Elizabeth, PA
Wojcicki, Rev. Msgr. Ted L., '75 (STL) Immaculate Conception Catholic Church, Dardenne, Dardenne Prairie, MO
Wojcicki, Rev. Wojciech, '90 (DET) Retired.
Wojciechowski, Rev. Kevin, '21 (SAG) Holy Name of Mary Parish of Harbor Beach, Harbor Beach, MI
Wojciechowski, Friar Maximilian, *O.F.M.* (WDC) [MON] Franciscan Monastery USA Inc., Washington, DC
Wojciechowski, Rev. Thomas, *O.F.M.* '75 (MIL) [MON] Queen of Peace Friary (Franciscan Friars of the Assumption B.V.M. Province), Burlington, WI
Wojciechowski, Rev. Tomasz, *C.R.* '08 (CHI) Blessed Carlo Acutis Parish, Chicago, IL
Wojcik, Rev. Dominik, (FBK) Our Lady of Sorrows Catholic Church Delta Junction, Delta Junction, AK; St. Nicholas Catholic Church North Pole, North Pole, AK
Wojcik, Rev. Eugene H., '74 (BEL) Retired. Curia: Leadership
Wojcik, Rev. Grzegorz, (DEN) St. William Catholic

Parish in Ft. Lupton, Fort Lupton, CO
Wojcik, Rev. Grzegorz, '08 (CHI) St. Monica and St. Rosalie Parish, Chicago, IL
Wojcik, Rev. Joseph J., '69 (CHI) Retired.
Wojcik, Rev. Przemyslaw, '08 (CHI) St. Clement, Chicago, IL; [MIS] St. Bonaventure Oratory, Chicago, IL
Wojcinski, Rev. Anthony A., '85 (PBL) Retired.
Wojda, Very Rev. Peter, '17 (DEN) Curia: Deaneries St. Anne Catholic Parish in Grand Lake, Grand Lake, CO; St. Ignatius Catholic Parish in Walden, Walden, CO; St. Peter Catholic Parish in Kremmling, Kremmling, CO
Wojdelski, Rev. Mark, *F.S.S.P.* '05 (FTW) Sacred Heart, Fort Wayne, IN
Wojtan, Rev. Andrzej, '83 (ORL) Holy Spirit, Mims, FL
Wojtek, Rev. Robert, *C.Ss.R.* (NY) Immaculate Conception, Bronx, NY
Wojtun, Rev. Daniel, (HRT) Hosps of Central CT New Britain and MidState Meriden
Wolanski, Rev. Edward, *C.P.* '72 (PMB) [MON] Our Lady of Florida Spiritual Center, North Palm Beach, FL
Wolanski, Rev. Edward, *C.P.* '72 (NY) [MON] The Congregation of the Passion - St. Paul of the Cross Province, Jamaica, NY
Woldai, Rev. Ghebriel, '93 (OAK) Curia: Offices and Directors St. Anthony-Mary Help of Christians, Oakland, CA
Wolesky, Rev. John, '67 (SAL) Curia: Organizations (affiliated, inter-Diocesan, miscellaneous/other) Immaculate Conception of the Blessed Virgin Mary Parish, Solomon, Inc., Solomon, KS; St. Patrick Parish, Gypsum, KS
Wolf, Rev. Anthony J., '96 (LC) On Leave.
Wolf, Rev. Brandon, '19 (BIS) Bishop Ryan Catholic School, Minot, ND
Wolf, Rev. Donald J., '81 (OKL) Curia: Consultative Bodies Sacred Heart, Oklahoma City, OK
Wolf, Rev. Eugene J., '63 (LC) Retired. [MIS] Holy Cross (Seminary) Diocesan Center, La Crosse, WI
Wolf, Rev. Jarad, (BIS) [COL] University of Mary, Bismarck, ND
Wolf, Rev. John, *C.PP.S.* '69 (KC) Retired. [MIS] St. Gaspar Society, Liberty, MO; [MON] Society of the Precious Blood, Liberty, MO
Wolf, Rev. Joseph, (GB) Retired. [MON] St. Fidelis Friary, Appleton, WI
Wolf, Rev. Joseph D., '87 (BUF) St. Bernadette, Orchard Park, NY
Wolf, Rev. Joseph M., '94 (DAV) Curia: Leadership St. Ann Church of Long Grove, Iowa, Long Grove, IA
Wolf, Rev. Paul L., '83 (NU) Curia: Leadership Church of St. Anastasia, Hutchinson, MN; Church of St. Boniface, Stewart, MN
Wolf, Rev. Robert, '10 (P) St. Anne, Grants Pass, OR; St. Monica, Coos Bay, OR
Wolf, Rev. Stephen J., '97 (NSH) Retired. On Administrative Leave.
Wolfbauer, Rev. Michael, '10 (SCL) Church of St. John, Foley, MN; St. Patrick, Sauk Rapids, MN
Wolfe, Very Rev. Allan F., '92 (HBG) Curia: Offices and Directors
Wolfe, Rev. Keith, '16 (JOL) St. James the Apostle, Glen Ellyn, IL
Wolfe, Rev. Keith, (MO) Curia: Offices and Directors
Wolfe, Rev. Ken, (POC) Retired.
Wolfe, Rev. Michael, '16 (MIL) On Duty Outside Diocese. Parroquia la Resurreccion, Bogota [MIS] Community of St. Paul, Inc., Racine, WI
Wolfe, Rev. Michael A., '09 (ALT) Queen of Archangels, Clarence, PA
Wolfe, Rev. Robert L, '14 (BGP) St. Edward the Confessor, New Fairfield, CT
Wolfee, Rev. Robert, '98 (NEW) Curia: Offices and Directors Sacred Heart, Haworth, NJ; Saint Michael the Archangel, Union, NJ
Wolff, Rt. Rev. Theodore, *O.S.B.* '54 (OM) Retired. [MON] Mount Michael Benedictine Abbey, Elkhorn, NE
Wolfla, Friar Nicholas, *O.F.M.Conv.* '16 (IND) [RTR] Mount Saint Francis Friary and Retreat Center, Mount St. Francis, IN
Wolford, Rev. Donald L., '79 (SFD) Holy Angels, Wood River, IL
Wolford, Rev. Reginald, *OP* (IND) St. Paul Catholic Center, Bloomington, Inc., Bloomington, IN
Wolkovits, Rev. Paul Dennis, '93 (LA) Retired.
Wollering, Rev. Carl J., '66 (CIN) Retired.
Wolniakowski, Rev. Kolbe, *OSB* '22 (IND) St. Paul Catholic Church, Tell City, Inc., Tell City, IN; [MON] St. Meinrad Archabbey, St. Meinrad, IN
Wolnik, Rev. James G., '79 (STP) Retired.
Wolski, Rev. Mark J., '67 (BUF) Retired. On Administrative Leave.
Woltornist, Rev. Alexei, '21 (NTN) St. Joseph, Lansing, MI
Womack, Rev. Luke, (LR) Our Lady of Fatima, Benton, AR; St. Jude Church, Clinton, AR
Wonch, Rev. Charles, *S.C.J.* '02 (MIL) Retired. [MON] Sacred Heart at Monastery Lake, Franklin, WI
Wong, Rev. Ashton I.F., '22 (NEW) St. John the Evangelist, Bergenfield, NJ
Wong, Rev. David, (MAN) Immaculate Conception, Penacook, NH
Wong, Rev. Jules, *O.F.M.* '73 (Y) [MON] Mt. Alverna Friary, Youngstown, OH
Wonganant, Rev. Benedict, '13 (OAK) St. David of Wales, Richmond, CA
Wood, Rev. Brian, '12 (LUB) St. Isidore, Abernathy, TX
Wood, Rev. Charles A., '00 (P) St. Elizabeth of Hungary, Portland, OR
Wood, Rev. Chuck, (P) Curia: Offices and Directors
Wood, Rev. D. Mark, '87 (LR) Curia: Offices and Directors St. John the Baptist, Malvern, AR; St. Mary, Arkadelphia, AR; St. Theresa, Little Rock, AR
Wood, Rev. Eric M., '15 (CIN) [SEM] Mount St. Mary's Seminary of the West, Cincinnati, OH
Wood, Rev. Gregg D., *S.J.* '75 (FBK) Curia: Offices and Directors Holy Family Catholic Church Newtok, Newtok, AK; Immaculate Conception Catholic Church Bethel, Bethel, AK; Immaculate Heart of Mary Catholic Church Marshall, Marshall, AK; St. Catherine of Siena Catholic Church Chefornak, Chefornak, AK; [MIS] Brother Joe Prince Jesuit Community, Bethel, AK
Wood, Rev. James L., '72 (RVC) St. Margaret of Scotland, Selden, NY; [MON] St Pius X Residence for Retired Priests LLC, Ronkonkoma, NY
Wood, Rev. Michael J., '11 (SPR) Mary Mother of Hope Parish, Springfield, MA
Wood, Rev. Norbert J., *O.Praem.* '81 (ORG) [MON] Norbertine Fathers of Orange, Inc., Silverado, CA; [SEM] St. Michael's Norbertine Postulancy, Novitiate and Juniorate, Silverado, CA
Wood, Rev. Raymond B., '64 (SY) Retired.
Wood, Rev. Robert, *C.M.* '56 (STL) [MON] Congregation of the Mission, Perryville, MO
Wood, Rev. Robert T., '87 (OKL) Curia: Clergy and Religious Services; Consultative Bodies St. Philip Neri, Midwest City, OK
Wood, Rev. Steven J. W., '19 (SAC) Pastor of St. Vincent Ferrer Parish of Vallejo, a Corporation Sole, Vallejo, CA
Wood, Rev. Tyson, (HBG) Chap, Veterans Administration Med Ctr, Lebanon
Wood, Rev. Tyson J., '05 (BAL) On Duty Outside Diocese. Chaplain, V.A.
Wood, Rev. Tyson J., (MO) Curia: Offices and Directors
Wood, Rev. William Andrew, '73 (GAL) St. Laurence, Sugar Land, TX
Woodeshick, Rev. Martin E., '69 (PH) Retired.
Woodhouse, Rev. Thomas J., '13 (PRO) La Salle Academy (St. John Baptist de LaSalle Institute), Providence, RI; Saint Paul's Church of Edgewood, Cranston, RI
Woodke, Rev. Mark (Drew), '20 (SP) Curia: Pastoral Services St. Timothy, Lutz, FL
Woodland, Rev. Stephen, '88 (SEA) St. Philomena, Des Moines, WA
Woodman, Rev. Gerald, '78 (SEA) Retired.
Woodrow, Rev. Brian P., '06 (TR) St. Dominic, Brick, NJ
Woodruff, Rev. Mark, '72 (SAN) Sacred Heart, Menard, TX; St. Theresa of the Child Jesus, Junction, TX
Woodruff, Rev. William F., '82 (NY) Chap, St Luke's-Cornwall Hosp, Newburgh
Woods, Rev. Keith, '95 (WDC) Curia: Deaneries
Woods, Rev. Keith A., '54 (WDC) St. Peter, Waldorf, MD
Woods, Rev. Michael, '66 (KNX) St. Francis of Assisi, Fairfield Glade, TN
Woods, Rev. Patrick, *C.Ss.R.* '75 (BAL) St. Mary, Annapolis, MD
Woods, Rev. Samuel, '11 (STO) Retired. Curia: Leadership
Woods, Rev. Scott, '02 (WDC) Curia: Consultative Bodies St. Peter Claver, St. Inigoes, MD
Woods, Rev. Scott S., (TOL) Curia: Advisory Boards, Commissions, Committees, and Councils; Deaneries
Woods, Rev. Thomas F., '02 (BIR) St. Jude, Scottsboro, AL
Woods, Rev. Thomas Matthew, '05 (WDC) On Leave.
Woods, Rev. Walter J., '69 (BO) Retired.
Woody, Rev. William, *S.J.* (BO) [MON] The Jesuit Community at Boston College, Chestnut Hill, MA
Wooleyhan, Friar Jason, *T.O.R.* '17 (ALT) [MON] Sacred Heart Friary, Loretto, PA
Woolley, Rev. Michael J., '99 (PRO) SS. John and Paul Parish Corporation, Coventry, Coventry, RI
Woost, Rev. David G., '91 (CLV) Curia: Advisory Boards, Commissions, Committees, and Councils Divine Word, Kirtland, OH; [MIS] Joseph House of Cleveland, Inc., Cleveland, OH
Woost, Rev. Thomas G., '97 (CLV) St. Brendan, North Olmsted, OH; St. Richard, North Olmsted, OH
Wooten, Rev. Scott, (POC) St. John Vianney Catholic Church, Cleburne, TX
Wooton, Rev. Jerry A., '96 (ARL) Holy Spirit, Annandale, VA
Wopperer, Rev. Thomas J., '64 (BUF) Retired.
Wopperer, Rev. Thomas J., '64 (BUF) Retired. [MON] Msgr. Conniff Residence, Depew, NY
Worcester, Rev. Thomas, *SJ* '93 (BO) (>NY) [MON] Jesuit Community at Fordham University, New York, NY
Wordekemper, Rev. Thomas, *O.S.B.* '94 (BIS) St. Mary, Richardton, ND; St. Stephen, King of Hungary, Richardton, ND; St. Thomas the Apostle, Gladstone, ND; [MON] Assumption Abbey, Richardton, ND
Worgul, Rev. John, (BAL) St. Joseph, Sykesville, MD; [EFT] St. Joseph Catholic Community Endowment Trust, Sykesville, MD
Worgul, Rev. John, '13 (POC) St. Timothy Catholic Community, Sykesville, MD
Workman, Very Rev. Jamie R., '06 (ARL) Curia: Leadership St. Luke, McLean, VA; [EFT] Diocese of Arlington Scholarship Foundation, Inc., Arlington, VA; [EFT] The Foundation for the Catholic Diocese of Arlington, Inc., Arlington, VA; [MIS] Arlington Diocesan Investment and Loan Corp., Arlington, VA; [MIS] Rooted in Faith-Forward in Hope, Inc., Arlington, VA
Workman, Rev. Joseph G., '04 (CLV) Curia: Advisory Boards, Commissions, Committees, and Councils St. Clement, Lakewood, OH; St. James, Lakewood, OH
Worland, Rev. Christopher J., '01 (CIN) On Sick Leave. St. Columban, Loveland, OH; St. Margaret of York, Loveland, OH
Worley, Rev. Jason, '99 (BAL) St. Ursula, Baltimore, MD
Worm, Rev. Paul F., '88 (LR) St. Albert Church, Heber Springs, AR; St. Mary Church, Mountain View, AR
Wormek, Rev. Joseph E., '76 (STL) All Saints Catholic Church, St. Peters, St. Peters, MO
Worn, Rev. Peter, (SY) Retired.
Woroniewicz, Rev. Michael A., '85 (DET) Curia: Administration; Consultative Bodies
Woroniewicz, Rev. Michael Allen, (DET) Divine Grace Parish Carleton, Carleton, MI
Worry, Rev. Benedict M., *O.S.B.* '87 (PAT) Retired. [MON] St. Mary's Abbey, Morristown, NJ
Worschak, Rev. D. George, '78 (PHU) Curia: Offices and Directors
Worschak, Rev. D.George, '78 (PHU) Curia: Offices and Directors
Worsley, Rev. Msgr. Stephen C., '84 (R) Retired.
Worster, Rev. John R., '87 (B) Curia: Leadership St. Mary's, Boise, ID
Worster, Very Rev. John R., '87 (B) Curia: Leadership; (>MO) Offices and Directors
Worth, Rev. James, '01 (NEW) St. Joseph, Maplewood, NJ
Worthen, Rev. Matthew C., (MO) Curia: Offices and Directors
Worthen, Rev. Matthew Cameron, '11 (PT) On Leave.
Worthley, Rev. Jason W., '04 (BO) On Leave.
Worthley, Rev. John, '90 (RVC) Retired.
Worthy, Rev. Donald L., '62 (DET) Retired.
Woster, Rev. Msgr. Michael, '82 (RC) Curia: Leadership St. Paul, Belle Fourche, SD; [ASN] Priest Retirement and Aid Association/Pension Plan Board, Rapid City, SD
Wotypka, Rev. Robert, (DET) [CCH] Conner Kitchen, Detroit, MI; [MON] St. Bonaventure Monastery, Detroit, MI
Wouters, Rt. Rev. Jos, *O.Praem.* (GB) [MIS] Norbertine Generalate, Inc., De Pere, WI
Woy, Rev. Msgr. Richard W., '79 (BAL) St. Elizabeth Ann Seton, Crofton, MD
Woytavich, Rev. William, '15 (SFE) St. Patrick - St. Joseph, Raton, NM
Wozniak, Rev. Casimir, '68 (E) Our Lady of Mt. Carmel, Erie, PA; [COL] Gannon University, Erie, PA
Wozniak, Rev. James E., '97 (GRY) Curia: Offices and Directors St. Matthias, Crown Point, IN
Wozniak, Rev. Robert A., '88 (BUF) St. Pius X, Getzville, NY
Wozniak, Rev. Robert A., '72 (WIL) Immaculate Heart of Mary, Wilmington, DE
Wozniak, Rev. Timothy, '74 (STP) Benilde-St. Margaret's

School, St. Louis Park, MN; St. Thomas Becket, Eagan, MN
Woznicki, Rev. Donald C., '02 (CHI) St. Mary of the Lake and Our Lady of Lourdes Parish, Chicago, IL; [MIS] New Ethos, Lake Forest, IL
Wozny, Rev. Jacek, '88 (NY) St. Stanislaus Kostka, Staten Island, NY
Wratkowski, Rev. Timothy, '17 (STP) Holy Name of Jesus, Wayzata, MN
Wray, Rev. J. Thomas, '15 (CIN) Bethesda North Hosp All Saints, Cincinnati, OH; St. Vincent Ferrer, Cincinnati, OH
Wray, Rev. Joseph M., '96 (OM) St. Pius X, Omaha, NE
Wren, Rev. Bruce, *L.C.* '96 (CHI) [MON] Legion of Christ, Hickory Hills, IL (>ATL) [MIS] Legionaries of Christ, Atlanta, GA
Wrenn, Rev. Lawrence, '77 (WH) Retired.
Wrenn, Rev. Lawrence G., '53 (HRT) Retired.
Wright, Rev. Addison G., *P.S.S.* '57 (BAL) Retired.
Wright, Rev. Arthur F., '67 (BO) St. John the Baptist, Quincy, MA
Wright, Rev. Bryan B., '00 (SCR) Holy Child, Mansfield, PA
Wright, Rev. Charles, *O.S.B.* '70 (SD) Retired. [MON] Prince of Peace Abbey, Oceanside, CA
Wright, Rev. David F., *O.P.* '68 (DEN) St. Dominic Parish, Denver, CO; [MON] Dominican Friars, St. Dominic Priory, Denver, Inc., Denver, CO
Wright, Rev. Frank, *SMA* (HEL) (>NEW) [MON] Society of African Missions, Provincialate, S.M.A. Fathers, Tenafly, NJ
Wright, Rev. Frank A., *S.M.A.* '93 (WDC) [MIS] Archdiocese of Washington, Department of Special Needs Ministries, Landover Hills, MD
Wright, Rev. Gary R., *S.J.* '80 (DET) SS. Peter and Paul (Jesuit) Parish Detroit, Detroit, MI; [MON] Jesuit Community at the University of Detroit Mercy, Detroit, MI
Wright, Rev. Gerald, *O.M.V.* '80 (E) Chap, Erie Cty Prison
Wright, Rev. Gerald, *OMV* (LA) St. Peter Chanel, Hawaiian Gardens, CA
Wright, Rev. John, '12 (POC) Retired.
Wright, Rev. John, '16 (SAV) Sacred Heart, Waynesboro, GA
Wright, Rev. Michael, (SEA) Retired.
Wright, Rev. Michael Mary of the Trinity, *M.Carm.* '10 (CHY) On Special Assignment. In Res, Monks of the Most Blessed Virgin Mary of Mt Carme... [MON] Monks of the Most Blessed Virgin Mary of Mt. Carmel (Carmelite Monks), Meeteetse, WY
Wright, Rev. Ralph, *O.S.B.* '70 (STL) [MON] The Abbey of St. Mary and St. Louis, St. Louis, MO
Wright, Rev. Robert, *O.M.I.* '74 (SAT) [NUR] Oblate Madonna Residence, San Antonio, TX
Wright, Rev. Robert E., *O.M.I.* '74 (SAT) [COL] Oblate School of Theology, San Antonio, TX
Wright, Rev. Russell, *S.T.L.* '98 (VEN) St. Patrick Catholic Parish in Sarasota, Inc., Sarasota, FL
Wrightson, Rev. Mark J., *O.S.F.S.* '86 (WIL) St. Anthony of Padua, Wilmington, DE
Wrobel, Rev. Charles, '10 (MIL) St. John Neumann, Catholic Community of Waukesha, Waukesha, WI; St. Joseph, Catholic Community of Waukesha, Waukesha, WI; St. Mary, Catholic Community of Waukesha, Waukesha, WI; St. William, Catholic Community of Waukesha, Waukesha, WI
Wrobleski, Rev. Edward D., *C.S.P.* '62 (LA) Retired.
Wroblewski, Rev. Anthony, '95 (DUL) Curia: Leadership; Offices and Directors Cathedral of Our Lady of the Rosary, Duluth, MN; St. Mary Star of the Sea, Duluth, MN; [EFT] Holy Rosary Parish Endowment Fund, Duluth, MN
Wroblewski, Rev. Anthony, '95 (DUL) Curia: Offices and Directors
Wroblewski, Rev. Brendan, *O.F.M.* '55 (GB) [MON] Assumption of B.V.M. Friary, Pulaski, WI
Wroblewski, Rev. John J., '92 (NY) Parish of Our Lady of Pity and St. Anthony of Padua, Staten Island, NY; St. Anthony of Padua, Staten Island, NY
Wroblicky, Rev. Alexander, '15 (SJP) On Leave. Curia: Offices and Directors
Wrona, Rev. Jacek, '95 (CHI) Sacred Heart, Palos Hills, IL
Wronski, Rev. John, (NY) [MON] Xavier Jesuit Community, New York, NY
Wrozek, Rev. Timothy A., '88 (FTW) Retired. Curia: Offices and Directors
Wtorek, Rev. Krzysztof, '94 (CAM) [CAM] Rutgers University, Camden, NJ
Wtulich, Rev. John, '72 (BRK) Retired.
Wtyklo, Rev. Jacek S., '98 (MAR) Our Lady of Victory, Paradise, MI; St. Stephen, Naubinway, MI
Wtyklo, Rev. Jacek S., '98 (MAR) St. Gregory, Newberry, MI
Wu, Rev. Francis Xinfei, *O.P.* '17 (WDC) [SEM] Dominican House of Studies, Washington, DC
Wu, Rev. Jay, '07 (LA) Retired.
Wu, Rev. Michael Joseph, *O.Carm.* '12 (LA) St. Clement, Santa Monica, CA
Wu, Rev. Peter A., *M.M.* '61 (NY) Retired.
Wudarski, Rev. Dariusz P., '96 (SPR) Saint Elizabeth of Hungary Parish, North Adams, MA; [CAM] Massachusetts College of Liberal Arts, North Adams, MA
Wuenchel, Rev. William, (PIT) Chap, Butler Mem Hosp, Butler Cty; Autumn Grove Care Ctr…
Wuenschel, Rev. William D., '15 (PIT) St. Aidan, Wexford, PA
Wulinski, Rev. Stanley F., '80 (BRK) Retired.
Wunderlich, Rev. Dale P., '74 (STL) Shrine of St. Joseph, St. Louis, MO
Wunsch, Rev. Jason F., '14 (DEN) Saint Gianna Beretta Molla Catholic Parish, Denver, CO
Wurst, Rev. Wayne H., '80 (CHI) Chap, Oak Forest Hosp, Oak Forest
Wurth, Rev. Elmer P., *M.M.* '56 (NY) Retired.
Wurtz, Rev. Michael B., *CSC* (FTW) (>SCR) [COL] King's College, Wilkes-Barre, PA
Wurz, Rev. George E., '60 (SY) Retired. Oswego Cty Jail Christ the Good Shepherd, Oswego, NY
Wurzel, Rev. Richard T., '59 (TOL) Retired.
Wyciskalla, Rev. Timothy M., '14 (IND) Curia: Offices and Directors St. Mark the Evangelist Catholic Church, Indianapolis, Inc., Indianapolis, IN
Wydeven, Rev. John L., '79 (OAK) On Duty Outside Diocese.
Wylie, Rev. Justin, (LIN) (>TYL) Cathedral of the Immaculate Conception, Tyler, TX
Wymelenberg, Rev. M. John, *S.J.* '60 (MIL) [MON] St. Camillus Jesuit Community (Society of Jesus, USA Midwest Province), Wauwatosa, WI
Wymes, Rev. John F., *M.M.* '54 (NY) Retired.
Wyndaele, Rev. William, *C.I.C.M.* '59 (ARL) Retired. [MON] Missionhurst, C.I.C.M.-Central House and Provincialate (American I.H.M. Province, Inc., Immaculate Heart Missions, Inc., Missionhurst, Inc.), Arlington, VA
Wyndham, Rev. Thomas F., '69 (BO) Retired.
Wynne, Rev. Robert F., *M.M.* '68 (NY) Retired. [MON] Maryknoll Fathers and Brothers (Catholic Foreign Mission Society of America, Inc.), Ossining, NY
Wynnycky, Rev. John, '92 (DET) Holy Innocents - St. Barnabas Parish Roseville, Roseville, MI
Wyrostek, Rev. Andrzej, '00 (RC) Curia: Leadership Our Lady of the Black Hills, Piedmont, SD; Rapid City Catholic School System, Rapid City, SD
Wyrzykowski, Rev. Michael, '14 (CHI) St. Stephen, Deacon and Martyr, Tinley Park, IL
Wyse, Rev. James B., '87 (GR) St. Charles Borromeo, Greenville, MI; St. Joseph-St. Mary, Belding, MI
Wysochansky, Rev. Canon Walter, '64 (SJP) Retired. Curia: Offices and Directors Ss. Peter and Paul, Ambridge, PA
Wysocki, Rev. Marek B., '85 (NEW) St. Michael the Archangel, Lyndhurst, NJ; St. Pius X, Old Tappan, NJ
Wysocki, Rev. Paul, '64 (CLV) Retired.
Wysocki, Rev. Timothy, *LC* (DAL) [MON] Legionaries of Christ, Irving, TX
Wysoczanski, Friar Jaroslaw, *OFM Conv.* '86 (ELP) Our Lady of Mt. Carmel, El Paso, TX
Wyvill, Rev. Christopher, *O.S.B.* '65 (WDC) [MON] St. Anselm's Abbey, Washington, DC
Wyzykiewicz, Rev. Richard S., *Sch.P.* '91 (NY) St. Helena, Bronx, NY
Xavariapitchai, Rev. Udayakumar, '92 (BGP) Saint Luke's Roman Catholic Church Corporation, Westport, CT
Xavier, Rev. Jesuraj, '06 (JKS) St. Francis of Assisi, New Albany, MS
Xavier, Rev. Leo Joseph, *S.D.C.* (LAN) [MIS] The Pious Union of St. Joseph, Grass Lake, MI
Xavier, Rev. Sojan, '97 (WH) St. Francis of Assisi, St. Albans, WV
Xaviour, Rev. Jaisemon, '02 (STA) St. Luke, Middleburg, FL
Xaviour, Rev. John, '98 (CC) St. Philip the Apostle, Corpus Christi, TX
Xaviour(Punnolikunnel), Rev. Jaisemon, (SYM) St. Mary's Syro-Malabar Catholic Mission, Jacksonville, FL, Inc. of St. Thomas Syro-Malabar Catholic Diocese of Chicago, Jacksonville, FL
Xuereb, Rev. Msgr. Publius, '68 (FWT) Holy Redeemer Parish, Aledo, TX
Yabes, Rev. Arthur, *S.V.D.* '87 (SJ) Church of the Resurrection, Sunnyvale, CA
Yackanich, Rev. Archpriest Eugene P., '65 (PBR) Retired.
Yacobi, Rev. Francis X., *O.F.M.Cap.* '90 (PIT) [MIS] The Capuchin Franciscan Volunteer Corps, Inc. (Province of St. Augustine of the Capuchin Order), Pittsburgh, PA; [MON] St. Augustine Friary, Pittsburgh, PA; [MON] The Capuchin Franciscan Friars Province of Saint Augustine, Pittsburgh, PA
Yadao, Rev. Rolando R., '11 (NEW) Immaculate Conception, Secaucus, NJ
Yaddanapalli, Rev. Bala Jayanna, '11 (TLS) St. Henry, Owasso, OK
Yadron, Rev. Michael J., '83 (GRY) Curia: Leadership St. Thomas More, Munster, IN; [CEM] Saint John-Saint Joseph, Hammond, IN; [CEM] Saint Stanislaus, Michigan City, IN
Yadron, Rev. Raymond A., '63 (CHI) Retired. St. Thomas of Villanova, Palatine, IL
Yaeger, Rev. Joseph J., '89 (R) Holy Spirit Catholic Church, Kinston, NC
Yagappa Rajappa, Rev. Dominic Savio, '92 (FRS) Sacred Heart, Exeter, CA
Yagappan, Rev. Arulanantham, *M.S.F.S.* '97 (R) Good Shepherd Catholic Church, Hope Mills, NC
Yagaza, Rev. Severine, (SY) Chap, St Joseph's Hosp Health Ctr, Syracuse Blessed Sacrament, Syracuse, NY; St. Vincent de Paul, Syracuse, NY
Yaghi, Rev. Milad T., *M.L.M.* '88 (OLL) Curia: Leadership; Offices and Directors Our Lady of the Cedars Maronite Catholic Church, Houston, TX; [MON] The Congregation of Maronite Lebanese Missionaries, Houston, TX
Yainao, Rev. Edmund, *SJ* '13 (RC) St. Agnes, Manderson, SD; [MON] Holy Rosary Mission Jesuit Community, Pine Ridge, SD
Yakkel, Rev. Christopher M., '19 (COL) On Duty Outside Diocese. Curia: (>MO) Offices and Directors
Yaksich, Rev. George Robert, '15 (SFE) [MIS] Archdiocesan Priests Retirement Fund, Inc., Albuquerque, NM
Yaksich, Very Rev. Rob, '15 (SFE) Our Lady of Sorrows Church-Las Vegas, Las Vegas, NM
Yaksich, Very Rev. Rob, '15 (SFE) Curia: Offices and Directors Christ the King, El Llanito, , ; Holy Family, Variadero, , ; Nuestra Senora de Guadalupe, Sapello, , ; Our Lady of Sorrows, Tecolote, , ; San Antonio, El Porvenir, , ; San Antonio, Los Montoyas, , ; San Augustine, San Augustine, , ; San Geronimo, San Geronimo, , ; San Isidro, Trujillo, , ; San Jose, Upper Rociada, , ; San Rafael, Trementina, , ; Santo Nino, Gallinas, , ; Santo Nino, La Manga, , ; Santo Nino, Lower Rociada, ,
Yaksick, Rev. Michael L., '94 (PIT) Chap, Kindred Hosp Pittsburgh
Yakubu, Rev. Victor, '96 (PHX) St. Mary Roman Catholic Parish, Kingman, AZ
Yakubych, Rev. Vasyl, (PBR) St. Mary's, Herminie, PA; St. Stephen's, North Huntingdon, PA
Yallaly, Rev. David, *S.J.C.* (CHI) St. John Cantius, Chicago, IL; [MIS] Canons Regular of Saint John Cantius, Chicago, IL
Yalmadau, Rev. Kelly, '07 (CI) Curia: Leadership
Yalmadau, Rev. Kelly, '09 (CI) Curia: Leadership [MON] Vicariate Residence, Yap, FM
Yamanaka, Rev. Taiju, *SJ* '07 (NY) [MON] Jesuit Community at Fordham University, New York, NY
Yamaoka, Rev. Joseph, (MO) Curia: Offices and Directors
Yamauchi, Rev. James, '11 (DAL) St. Joseph Catholic Parish - Waxahachie, Waxahachie, TX
Yamoah, Rev. Dominic Afrifa, '09 (MAR) Holy Family Mission, Barbeau, MI; Saint Kateri Tekakwitha, Bay Mills, MI; St. Isaac Jogues Mission, Sault Sainte Marie, MI
Yanas, Rev. John, '84 (ALB) Curia: Offices and Directors Sacred Heart, Troy, NY
Yander, Rev. Steven L., '74 (ATL) Retired.
Yanez, Rev. Horacio V., '75 (SEA) Retired.
Yanez, Rev. Omar, '96 (MGZ) Nuestra Senora de Fatima, Mayaguez, PR
Yang, Rev. Anthony, *SVD* (SD) Pastor of Saint John the Evangelist Catholic Parish, San Diego, a corporation sole, San Diego, CA
Yang, Rev. Augustine (Pinyu), *OSB* '03 (GBG) [MON] Saint Vincent Archabbey, Latrobe, PA
Yang, Rev. Joseph, '96 (LA) St. Anthony, Long Beach, CA
Yang, Rev. Joseph, '96 (LA) Chap, Hospital Chaplain, Long Beach Mem Med Ctr, Long Beach
Yang, Rev. Taehyun Gregory, '90 (LA) Sung Sam Korean Catholic Center, Los Angeles, CA; [MIS] Korean Catholic Renewal Movement of Southern California, Los Angeles, CA
Yanju, Rev. Henry M., '96 (BO) Curia: (>MO) Offices

and Directors
Yankaukas, Rev. David, *O.M.V.* '88 (LA) St. Peter Chanel, Hawaiian Gardens, CA
Yankevitch, Rev. Robert, *S.J.* (BAL) Retired. [MIS] Colombiere Jesuit Community, Baltimore, MD
Yannam, Rev. Anthoni Reddy, '11 (SUP) Cathedral of Christ the King, Superior, WI; Holy Assumption, Superior, WI; St. Anthony, Superior, WI; St. Anthony Catholic Church, Lake Nebagamon, WI; St. Michael, Iron River, WI; St. William, Foxboro, WI
Yannarell, Rev. James J., *S.J.* '71 (NY) [MON] Murray-Weigel Hall (A Jesuit Community at Murray-Weigel Hall and Kohlmann Hall), Bronx, NY
Yanni, Rev. Brandon S, '22 (MAR) All Saints, Gladstone, MI; St. Andrew, Nahma, MI; St. John the Baptist, Garden, MI; St. Mary Magdalene, Cooks, MI
Yanos, Rev. Richard, (CHI) Queen of Peace Parish, Chicago, IL
Yanovsky, Rev. Stepan, (STF) Retired.
Yanta, Rev. Timothy J., '05 (STP) St. John the Baptist, Dayton, MN; [CEM] Old St. John the Baptist Cemetery, Dayton, MN; [CEM] St. John the Baptist Cemetery, Dayton, MN
Yanus, Rev. Gary, (PRM) Curia: Advisory Boards, Commissions, Committees, and Councils; Leadership
Yanus, Rev. Gary D., '81 (CLV) Curia: Canonical Services; Clergy and Religious Services; Leadership; Tribunal St. Mel, Cleveland, OH
Yara, Rev. Freddy Alexander, (MIA) St. Stephen, Miramar, FL
Yarce, Rev. Eugenio, '92 (SLC) Saint Francis Xavier LLC 222, Kearns, UT
Yargeau, Rev. Msgr. Ronald G., '73 (SPR) Retired.
Yarnell, Rev. Kevin, '16 (SP) Sacred Heart, Pinellas Park, FL
Yarno, Rev. Kenneth, *C.S.V.* '59 (JOL) Retired.
Yaroch, Rev. Kenneth E., '67 (SAG) Retired.
Yates, Rev. Anthony R., '10 (STL) St. Francis of Assisi Catholic Church, Oakville, St. Louis, MO
Yates, Rev. Mark V., *C.PP.S.* '12 (DAV) St. Mary Church of Albia, Iowa, Albia, IA; St. Patrick Church of Georgetown, Iowa, Albia, IA; St. Peter Church of Lovilia, Iowa, Lovilia, IA
Yatkauskas, Rev. Matthew, '89 (NY) St. Charles Borromeo, Gardiner, NY
Yavarone, Rev. Mark, *O.M.V.* (VEN) [RTR] Our Lady of Perpetual Help Retreat and Spirituality Center, Inc., Venice, FL
Yaya, Rev. Louis, '80 (NY) Chap, Health Alliance Hosp, Kingston
Yazbeck, Rev. Elias, (OLL) St. Maron Maronite Catholic Church, Independence, OH
Yazji, Rev. Talat, (OLD) Jesus Sacred Heart Church, North Hollywood, CA
Ybarra, Rev. Manuel, *O.F.M.* '86 (WDC) [MON] Franciscan Monastery USA Inc., Washington, DC
Ybarra, Rev. Paul, *CSC* (PHX) Curia: Leadership; Offices and Directors Saint John Vianney Roman Catholic Parish, Goodyear, AZ
Yeager, Rev. Vincent, (WDC) [MON] St. Louis Friary, Washington, DC
Yeakel, Rev. James R., *O.S.F.S.* '79 (WIL) Immaculate Conception, Elkton, MD
Yeazel, Rev. Msgr. J. Robert, '67 (SY) Retired.
Yeazel, Rev. Msgr. J. Robert, (SY) Church of the Holy Family, Syracuse, NY
Yeboah, Rev. James Owusu, *SMA* '99 (PEO) Sacred Heart, Farmer City, IL; St. John the Baptist Catholic Church, Clinton, IL; [ASN] St. Joseph Cemetery Association of Farmer City, IL, Farmer City, IL
Yeboah, Rev. Samuel, '15 (ALN) Holy Rosary, Reading, PA; Sacred Heart, West Reading, PA
Yeboah-Amanfo, Rev. Peter, '83 (VIC) Nativity of the Blessed Virgin Mary, Nada, TX
Yebra, Rev. Bernardino S., '88 (CHR) On Duty Outside Diocese. Military Chaplain, CH (Captain), US Army Curia: (>MO) Offices and Directors
Yedanapalli, Rev. Amulraj, (GF) St. Benedict, Roundup, MT
Yehl, Rev. Thomas M., *Y.A.* '12 (ARL) Blessed Sacrament, Alexandria, VA; [PRE] Youth Apostles Institute, An Association of Christian Faithful, McLean, VA
Yela, Rev. Jose Rodolfo, *OAR* '12 (LSC) St. Thomas More Parish, Inc., Chaparral, NM
Yelenc, Rev. Joseph, *T.O.R.* '71 (STU) (>ALT) [MON] St. Francis Friary at Mount Assisi, Loretto, PA
Yenkevich, Rev. Daniel J., '90 (SCR) Retired.
Yennock, Rev. Msgr. Eugene M., '50 (SY) Retired.
Yenushosky, Rev. Msgr. Daniel J., '77 (ALN) Curia: Leadership; Organizations (affiliated, inter-Diocesan, miscellaneous/other) Holy Trinity, Whitehall, PA
Yepes, Rev. Walter, '01 (CHI) Curia: Leadership Our Lady of Nazareth Parish, Chicago, IL
Yerasani, Rev. Savio, '09 (MAD) Good Shepherd, Westfield, WI; St. John the Baptist, Montello, WI
Yerpula, Rev. Kishor, *H.G.N.* '12 (STO) Our Lady of Fatima Church (Pastor of), Modesto, CA
Yerrnini, Rev. Chinnaiah, '90 (PRO) Church of Our Lady of Victory, Ashaway, Ashaway, RI
Yerrnini, Rev. Chinnaiah, '90 (PRO) Saint Joseph's Church, Hope Valley, Hope Valley, RI
Yeruva, Rev. Papi Reddy, '95 (SUP) Curia: Leadership Our Lady of Sorrows, Ladysmith, WI; SS. Peter and Paul, Weyerhaeuser, WI; St. Anthony de Padua, Tony, WI; St. Francis of Assisi, Holcombe, WI; St. Mary, Bruce, WI; St. Mary of Czestochowa, Hawkins, WI
Yeruva, Rev. Rajasekhar, '04 (GLP) Holy Trinity (St. Joseph Church), Flora Vista, NM; St. Joseph (Holy Trinity), Aztec, NM
Yesalonia, Rev. Dennis J., *S.J.* '85 (NY) St. Ignatius Loyola, New York, NY; [MON] St. Ignatius Loyola Residence, New York, NY
Yi, Rev. Ju Hyung (Paul), '08 (BR) Curia: Administration Congregation Of St. George Roman Catholic Church, Baton Rouge, Louisiana, Baton Rouge, LA
Yi, Rev. Seungyoung, (BGP) Church of Assumption, Westport, Connecticut, Westport, CT
Yiadom, Rev. Joseph Boakye, '98 (MAR) Resurrection, Menominee, MI
Yiftheg, Rev. Cuthbert, '89 (CI) St. Mary's, Colonia, Yap, FM; [MON] Vicariate Residence, Yap, FM
Yike, Rev. John, '20 (NO) St. Charles Borromeo, Destrehan, LA
Yildirmaz, Rev. Jeff, '15 (RVC) Curia: Leadership St. Barnabas the Apostle, Bellmore, NY
Yim, Rev. Louis H., '57 (HON) Retired.
Yim, Rev. Matthew, *S.J.* '22 (SAC) Pastor of St. Ignatius Loyola Parish, Sacramento, a corporation sole, Sacramento, CA; [MON] Sacramento Jesuit Community, Carmichael, CA
Yinah, Rev. Wilfred, *V.C.* (PHX) St. Steven Roman Catholic Parish, Sun Lakes, AZ
Yllana, Rev. Pio Antonio, '84 (RIC) Church of the Good Shepherd, Smithfield, VA
Ymson, Rev. Enrique, *M.J.* '75 (LA) [MON] Missionaries of Jesus, Inc., Los Angeles, CA
Yncierto, Rev. Frank, '75 (LAV) Retired.
Yoakam, Rev. Lee R., *O.S.B.* '01 (RIC) St. Gregory the Great, Virginia Beach, VA
Yoakam, Rev. Lee R., *O.S.B.* '01 (GBG) [MON] Saint Vincent Archabbey, Latrobe, PA
Yobu, Rev. Jeyaseelan, '04 (LC) St. Ansgar, Blair, WI; St. Bridget, Ettrick, WI; [EFT] The St. Ansgar Catholic Church Endowment Trust, Blair, WI
Yockey, Rev. Aelred, *O.S.B.* '93 (P) [MON] Mt. Angel Abbey, Saint Benedict, OR
Yoda, Very Rev. Wossoyam Elie, *SJ* '22 (OAK) [MON] Jesuit Fathers and Brothers, Berkeley, CA
Yohannan, Rev. Santhosh, (IND) Church of the American Martyrs, Scottsburg, Inc., Scottsburg, IN; St. Patrick Catholic Church, Salem, Inc., Salem, IN
Yohe, Rev. Paschal Mary, *M.F.V.A.* '13 (BIR) [MIS] Shrine of the Most Blessed Sacrament (Our Lady of the Angels Monastery in Hanceville, Alabama), Hanceville, AL
Yohe, Rev. Robert A., '89 (HBG) St. John the Baptist, New Freedom, PA
Yokum, Rev. Joseph T., '07 (COL) Our Lady of Perpetual Help, Grove City, OH
Yom, Rev. Yongsop, *S.J.* '97 (ATL) St. Andrew Kim Korean Catholic Church, Norcross, Inc., Duluth, GA
Yonas, Rev. Deebar, *S.V.D.* '07 (SB) St. George, Fontana, CA
Yonkovig, Rev. John R., '77 (OG) Curia: Canonical Services; Consultative Bodies Saint Agnes Church, Lake Placid, NY, Lake Placid, NY; Saint Brendan's Roman Catholic Church, Keene, NY
Yono, Rev. Kevin, (EST) St. George Chaldean Catholic Church, Shelby Twp., MI
Yonta, Rev. Maurice, (SFD) Holy Family, Athens, IL; St. Peter, Petersburg, IL
Yoo, Rev. Michael, (PH) Holy Mary Korean Catholic Church, Newtown Square, PA
Yoo, Rev. Michael Jung-Kyuto, (PH) Holy Angels, Philadelphia, PA
Yoo, Rev. SeungWon, '04 (JOL) Our Lady of Korean Martyrs Mission, Lockport, IL
Yoo, Rev. Seungwon John, (MIL) St. Mary Magdalen Congregation, Milwaukee, WI
Yoon, Rev. Jiwon, '14 (BO) Curia: Consultative Bodies St. Margaret of Antioch, Burlington, MA; St. Michael, North Andover, MA
York, Very Rev. Kenneth J., '88 (BEL) Curia: Leadership; Offices and Directors St. Henry, Belleville, IL
York, Rev. Patrick G., '90 (WCH) Curia: Leadership; Offices and Directors Sacred Heart, Colwich, KS
York, Rev. Richard, '73 (VEN) Retired.
York, Rev. Msgr. Vincent P., '68 (ALN) St. Elizabeth of Hungary, Pen Argyl, PA
Yorke, Rev. Anthony, '00 (NY) Our Lady of Loretto, Cold Spring, NY
Yossa, Rev. Kenneth F., '88 (ROM) On Administrative Leave.
Yost, Rev. Alan, (SEA) Bellarmine Preparatory School, Tacoma, WA
Yost, Rev. Herbert C., *C.S.C.* '75 (FTW) [MON] Congregation of Holy Cross, United States Province of Priests and Brothers, Notre Dame, IN
Youkhanna, Rev. Sanharib, '92 (EST) Curia: Offices and Directors Our Lady of Chaldeans Cathedral, Mother of God Chaldean Parish, Southfield, MI
Youn, Rev. Pius, *OP* '17 (TUC) (>P) St. Thomas More Catholic Church, Eugene, OR; (>P) [CAM] Lane Community College (St. Thomas More Catholic Church, Eugene, Newman Center), Eugene, OR
Younan, Rev. Andrew, '04 (SPA) Curia: Offices and Directors St. Peter Chaldean Cathedral, El Cajon, CA
Young, Rev. Adam A., '10 (PRO) On Leave.
Young, Rev. Andrew, '12 (SFS) Curia: Leadership; (>MO) Offices and Directors; Offices and Directors Risen Savior Parish of Minnehaha County, Brandon, SD
Young, Rev. Andrew, (PT) Military Chap
Young, Very Rev. Andrew L., '15 (COV) Curia: Leadership Holy Redeemer, Vanceburg, KY; St. Patrick, Maysville, KY; St. Patrick High School, Maysville, KY
Young, Rev. Msgr. Bill, '70 (GAL) Curia: Leadership
Young, Rev. Christopher R., '14 (DAV) Curia: Leadership Holy Family Church of Davenport, Iowa, Davenport, IA
Young, Rev. Daniel A., '95 (BUF) Good Shepherd, North Tonawanda, NY
Young, Rev. David E., '95 (COL) Retired. St. Sylvester, Zaleski, OH
Young, Rev. David H., '02 (SEA) St. Olaf, Poulsbo, WA
Young, Rev. David J., '04 (COL) St. Pius X, Reynoldsburg, OH
Young, Rev. Dennis M., '80 (STA) Retired.
Young, Rev. Dominic G., '79 (LFT) Retired.
Young, Rev. Archpriest Edward Canon, '83 (STF) Curia: Leadership; Offices and Directors SS. Peter and Paul, Ansonia, CT
Young, Rev. Frank, '70 (SY) Retired.
Young, Rev. Gary, *C.R.* '76 (L) On Special Assignment. [CON] Generalate, Motherhouse and Novitiate of the Sisters of Charity of Nazareth, Nazareth, KY
Young, Rev. Gerald A., '72 (LA) Retired.
Young, Rev. Gerard F., '63 (BR) Retired.
Young, Rev. Msgr. James E., '74 (TYL) Retired.
Young, Rev. John L., *C.S.C.* (FTW) [MIS] Holy Cross House, Notre Dame, IN
Young, Rev. John L., *C.S.C.* '71 (HRT)
Young, Rev. Kevin, '13 (TYL) On Duty Outside Diocese. Buffalo, NY
Young, Rev. Kurt, '12 (NO) On Special Assignment. Archbishop Rummel HS [SEM] Notre Dame Seminary Graduate School of Theology, New Orleans, LA
Young, Rev. Kurt, (MO) Curia: Offices and Directors
Young, Rev. Larry E., '81 (OAK) Curia: Leadership; Offices and Directors St. Patrick, Rodeo, CA; [SPF] St. Joseph's Center for Deaf and Hard of Hearing (St. Joseph's Center for the Deaf and Hard of Hearing, A Corporation), Fremont, CA
Young, Rev. Lawrence A., '03 (WDC) Curia: Consultative Bodies
Young, Rev. Michael, '22 (VEN) St. John XXIII Catholic Parish in Fort Myers, Inc., Fort Myers, FL
Young, Rev. Peter G., '59 (ALB) Retired.
Young, Rev. Richard, *O.S.A.* '95 (JOL) Providence Catholic High School, New Lenox, IL; [MON] Augustinian Friary, New Lenox, IL
Young, Rev. Richard, '95 (SAV) Retired.
Young, Rev. Samuel V., '90 (BAL) Church of the Holy Spirit, Joppa, MD; St. Stephen, Kingsville, MD
Young, Rev. Msgr. Terry W., '72 (ATL) Retired. St. James Catholic Church, McDonough, Inc., McDonough, GA
Young, Rev. Valentine, *O.F.M.* '50 (CIN) Retired.
Young, Rev. Vincent J., '78 (SCR) On Administrative Leave.
Young, Rev. William E., '90 (SFE) Retired.
Young, Rev. Msgr. William L., '70 (GAL) Curia: Offices and Directors St. Vincent de Paul, Houston, TX
Young, Rev. William W., '76 (SFR) Retired.
Youngberg, Rev. Vincent, *C.P.* (BRK) [MON]

Immaculate Conception Monastery, Jamaica, NY
Youngberg, Rev. Vincent, *C.P.* '67 (NY) Retired. [MON] The Congregation of the Passion - St. Paul of the Cross Province, Jamaica, NY
Youngkamp, Rev. Vincent, *S.S.C.* '59 (PRO) Retired. [MON] St. Columban's Retirement House (St. Columban's Foreign Mission Society), Bristol, RI
Youngman, Rev. Wayne M., '10 (MOB) St. Bartholomew Parish, Elberta, Elberta, AL
Youssef, Rev. Antoun, '16 (SAM) St. Ann, Scranton, PA
Youtz, Rev. Msgr. Richard A., '66 (HBG) Retired. Curia: Offices and Directors Sacred Heart of Jesus, Lancaster, PA
Yrlas, Rev. Raynaldo, '97 (CC) Curia: Administration Sacred Heart, Rockport, TX
Yrlas, Very Rev. Raynaldo, '97 (CC) Curia: Leadership [MIS] Stella Maris Chapel, Lamar, TX
Yslas, Rev. Martin, *O.S.B.* '87 (LA) [MON] St. Andrew's Abbey (Benedictine Monks), Valyermo, CA
Ysmael, Rev. Arturo, *S.D.S.* '15 (MIL) [MON] Salvatorian Provincial Offices (Society of the Divine Savior), Milwaukee, WI
Ytsen, Rev. Robert A., *S.J.* '82 (DET) University of Detroit Jesuit High School and Academy, Detroit, MI
Yu, Rev. Celso, *MF* '92 (AUS) St. Francis of Assisi, Franklin, TX; St. Mary, Bremond, TX; [MON] Clerical Congregation Missionaries of Faith, Bremond, TX
Yu, Rev. Reynaldo T., '83 (SEA) [MIS] St. Mary, Seattle, WA
Yu Ming, Rev. Vincent Lin, '01 (DAL) Sacred Heart of Jesus Catholic Parish - Plano, Plano, TX
Yuantoro, Rev. Franciscus Asisi Eka, *M.S.F.* '02 (BWN) St. Joseph, Donna, TX
Yuenger, Rev. Paul D., '00 (WH) Retired.
Yuhas, Rev. Edward L., '97 (PIT) St. James, Washington, PA; St. Katharine Drexel Parish, Bentleyville, PA
Yulfo-Hoffman, Rev. Msgr. Nestor, '92 (SJN) Colegio Maria Auxiliadora, Carolina, PR; Santo Cristo de los Milagros, Carolina, PR
Yumo, Rev. Mechesideck, (CHL) St. Mark, Huntersville, NC
Yungwirth, Friar Peter Martyr, *O.P.* (NY) [MON] St. Vincent Ferrer Priory, New York, NY
Yungwirth, Rev. Peter Martyr Joseph, *O.P.* '14 (PRO) [COL] Providence College, Providence, RI; [MON] St. Thomas Aquinas Priory at Providence College, Providence, RI
Yungwirth, Rev. Peter Martyr, *OP* (NY) Parish of St. Vincent Ferrer and St. Catherine of Siena, New York, NY
Yurchak, Rev. Thomas D., '76 (P) Retired.
Yurochko, Rev. Dennis P., (PBR) Curia: Leadership
Yurochko, Rev. Dennis P., '02 (PIT) Curia: Consultative Bodies; Tribunal Corpus Christi, Bridgeville, PA
Zaba, Rev. Artur P., '16 (PAT) St. Joseph's, Lincoln Park, NJ
Zabala, Rev. Efrain, (SJN) Curia: Offices and Directors
Zaballa, Rev. Pedro Luis, '57 (SJN) [SPF] Centro Medico de P.R., San Juan, PR
Zabarian, Rev. Georges, '72 (OLN) Curia: Leadership
Zabinski, Rev. Joseph Arthur, '16 (STP) St. Albert, Albertville, MN
Zabler, Rev. Charles G., '77 (MIL) Retired.
Zaborowski, Rev. Konrad Jozef, *S.D.S* '10 (MIA) [SEM] St. John Vianney College Seminary, Inc., Miami, FL
Zaborowski, Rev. Paul, *O.F.M.Cap.* '97 (BAL) St. Ambrose, Baltimore, MD; [MON] Our Lady of the Mountains Friary, Cumberland, MD; [MON] St. Ambrose Friary, Baltimore, MD
Zabrocki, Rev. Patrick, '88 (GF) Retired. Curia: Offices and Directors St. Patrick, Medicine Lake, MT
Zabrocki, Rev. Patrick R., '88 (GF) Retired. Curia: Offices and Directors
Zabrocki, Rev. Stephen J., '89 (GF) Curia: Leadership St. Thomas the Apostle, Billings, MT
Zabrocki, Rev. Stephen J., '89 (GF) Curia: Leadership; Offices and Directors
Zabusu, Very Rev. Jean Baptiste Magbia, (SAT) Curia: Administration St. John the Evangelist, San Antonio, TX
Zacarias, Rev. Carlos, *S.T.* '97 (LA) Our Lady of Victory, Compton, CA
Zacarias Palos, Rev. Anthony, *OAR* (ORG) [MON] Augustinian Recollects, Santa Ana, CA
Zaccagnini, Rev. Kenneth G., '82 (GBG) Curia: Advisory Boards, Commissions, Committees, and Councils; Leadership; Offices and Directors Mt. St. Peter, New Kensington, PA; St. Joseph, New Kensington, PA; St. Margaret Mary, Lower Burrell, PA; St. Mary of Czestochowa, New Kensington, PA
Zaccardo, Rev. Msgr. Peter J., '64 (NEW) Retired.
Zaccone, Rev. Paul, *SS.CC.* (HON) Curia: (>MO) Offices and Directors [MON] St. Patrick's Monastery, Honolulu, HI
Zaccone, Rev. Paul Carl, *SS.CC.* '87 (LA) [MON] Congregation of the Sacred Hearts of Jesus and Mary, La Verne, CA
Zachariadis, Rt. Rev. Archmandrite Nicholas, '87 (ROM) Retired. Curia: Offices and Directors [MON] Holy Resurrection Monastery, St. Nazianz, WI
Zachariah, Rev. Kurian, '85 (ALX) Our Lady of Lourdes, Marksville, LA; St. Martin of Tours, Hessmer, LA
Zachman, Rev. Clarence, *O.M.I.* '48 (BEL) [MON] Shrine of Our Lady of the Snows, Belleville, IL; [NUR] Apartment Community of Our Lady of the Snows (Benedictine Living Community | At The Shrine), Belleville, IL
Zacker, Rev. Mark, '96 (COS) Curia: Leadership St. Francis of Assisi, Castle Rock, CO
Zaczynski, Rev. Piotr F., '04 (BUF) Holy Spirit, North Collins, NY; Immaculate Conception, Eden, NY; Sacred Heart, Lakewood, NY
Zadora, Rev. Boleslaw, *S.D.S.* '74 (SAT) Annunciation of the Blessed Virgin Mary, St. Hedwig, TX; [MON] Salvatorian Fathers Community of Texas, Falls City, TX
Zadora, Rev. Charles J., '67 (BUF) Retired. [MON] Bishop Head Residence, Lackawanna, NY
Zadorozny, Rev. Tadeusz, '99 (NOR) Curia: Leadership St. Joseph, Rockville, CT
Zadroga, Rev. Jean-Luc C., *O.S.B.* '01 (GBG) [MON] Saint Vincent Archabbey, Latrobe, PA
Zagarella, Very Rev. John C., *O. Praem.* '86 (PH) [MON] Daylesford Abbey, Inc., Paoli, PA; [SEM] Daylesford Abbey (Norbertine Fathers, Inc.), Paoli, PA
Zagone, Rev. Frederick P., *S.J.* '93 (MIL) [MON] Jesuit Community at Marquette University (Marquette Jesuit Associates, Inc.), Milwaukee, WI
Zagorc, Rev. Francis D., *C.S.C.* '58 (FTW) [MON] Congregation of Holy Cross, United States Province of Priests and Brothers, Notre Dame, IN
Zagorski, Rev. Andrew, *M.S.* '88 (MIL) [MON] La Salette Missionaries, Twin Lakes, WI
Zagorski, Rev. Jan A., '02 (MOB) Retired.
Zahler, Rev. Paul J., *O.S.B.* '62 (OKL) [MON] St. Gregory's Abbey (Benedictine Fathers of Sacred Heart Mission, Inc.), Shawnee, OK
Zahuta, Rev. Thomas A., '10 (ATL) St. Peter the Rock Catholic Church, The Rock, Inc., Thomaston, GA
Zaiats, Rev. Volodymyr, '73 (STN) Retired.
Zajac, Rev. Adam A., '13 (CLV) Curia: Tribunal St. Mark, Cleveland, OH; St. Mel, Cleveland, OH
Zajac, Rev. Maciej Jan, '07 (NEW) Chap, Holy Name Med Ctr, Teaneck St. Hedwig, Elizabeth, NJ; [COL] School of Nursing, ,
Zajac, Rev. Richard E., '76 (BUF) Curia: Consultative Bodies; Offices and Directors
Zajchowski, Rev. Zbigniew, *O.F.M.Conv.* '94 (RCK) St. Margaret Mary, Algonquin, IL
Zajdel, Rev. Robert J., '80 (PIT) Retired.
Zajecki, Rev. Dawid, (PAT)
Zak, Rev. Daniel, '67 (TOL) Retired.
Zak, Rev. Elliot D, '21 (LFT) St. Joan of Arc, Kokomo, IN; St. Patrick, Kokomo, IN
Zak, Rev. Msgr. Steven B., '88 (LA) On Administrative Leave.
Zak, Rev. Timothy, *S.D.B.* '91 (NY) [MIS] Salesian Missions, Inc., New Rochelle, NY; [MON] Salesian Provincial House, New Rochelle, NY
Zake, Rev. Louis J., '60 (CHI) Retired.
Zalecki, Rev. Dennis M., '76 (CHI) Retired.
Zaleski, Rev. Daniel, '80 (DET) Retired.
Zaleski, Rev. Joseph S., '15 (PH) St. Katherine of Siena, Philadelphia, PA
Zalewski, Rev. Michal, (BO) [MON] Edmund Campion House, Brighton, MA
Zalewski, Rev. Peter, '97 (PT) Curia: Leadership; (>MO) Offices and Directors Blessed Sacrament, Tallahassee, FL
Zalewski, Rev. Thomas, *O.Carm.* '79 (NY) [MON] St. Albert's Priory, Middletown, NY
Zalewski, Rev. Tomasz, '06 (VEN) Curia: Leadership St. John the Evangelist Parish in Naples, Inc., Naples, FL
Zaloga, Rev. Daniel S., '67 (MAR) Retired. [MIS] Companions of Christ the Lamb, Paradise, MI
Zalubski, Rev. Czeslaw, '93 (MET) St. Catherine of Siena, Pittstown, NJ
Zamagni, Rev. Stefano, *FSCB* '21 (WDC) [MIS] Priestly Fraternity of the Missionaries of St. Charles Borromeo, Inc., Bethesda, MD
Zamarripa, Rev. Jesus, *S.V.D.* '01 (LA) Our Lady of Lourdes, Los Angeles, CA
Zamary, Rev. Joseph, '01 (Y) St. James, Waynesburg, OH
Zambakari, Rev. Elario, '12 (PHX) St. Mary Roman Catholic Parish Chandler, Chandler, AZ
Zambanini, Rev. Julian, *OFM Conv.* (ALB) [MON] Immaculate Conception Friary - Order of Friars Minor Conventual, Rensselaer, NY
Zambanini, Rev. Julian, *OFM Conv* (MRY) Retired.
Zamborsky, Rev. Bill, '74 (ORL) Our Lady of the Springs, Ocala, FL
Zambua, Rev. Innocent, (GLD) Saint Francis of Assisi of Traverse City, Traverse City, MI
Zammit, Rev. Francis X., '66 (ORL) Retired.
Zammit, Rev. Jimmy, *O.F.M.* '81 (NY) [MON] Franciscan Province of the Immaculate Conception, New York, NY
Zammit, Rev. Msgr. Joseph J., '56 (NY) Retired. Chap, New York Police Department
Zamora, Rev. Arnold, '86 (SFR) St. Robert, San Bruno, CA
Zamora, Rev. Bradley Angelo, '14 (CHI) [SEM] University of Saint Mary of the Lake/Mundelein Seminary, Mundelein, IL
Zamora, Rev. Clarence, (HON) Retired. St. Jude, Kapolei, HI
Zamora, Rev. Clarence S. A., '05 (OAK) Retired.
Zamora, Rev. Gaudioso, (PMB) Emmanuel, Delray Beach, FL
Zamora, Rev. Marcos, *C.S.P.* '90 (PMB) [MON] Paulist Fathers Residence, Vero Beach, FL
Zamora, Rev. Mateo, *O.S.B.* '07 (IND) [MON] St. Meinrad Archabbey, St. Meinrad, IN
Zamorano, Rev. Richard, '93 (ELP) On Leave.
Zamorski, Rev. Msgr. Robert J., '72 (MET) Retired. [MON] Maria Regina Residence, Somerset, NJ
Zanatta, Rev. Albert, *C.R.S.* '74 (GAL) Curia: Leadership; Offices and Directors
Zanatta, Rev. Remo, (MAN) Immaculate Conception, Nashua, NH; [PRE] Pine Haven Boys Center, Allenstown, NH
Zancan, Rev. Robert D., '82 (BUF) Retired.
Zandri, Rev. William A., '84 (RC) Retired.
Zandy, Rev. Edward J., '70 (SY) Retired.
Zanetti, Rev. Gordon, '05 (VEN) Curia: Leadership St. Thomas More Parish in Sarasota, Inc., Sarasota, FL
Zanetti, Very Rev. Jose Ricardo, '03 (AMA) Curia: Advisory Boards, Commissions, Committees, and Councils; Consultative Bodies; Offices and Directors
Zanetti, Rev. Jose Ricardo, *J.C.L.* '03 (AMA) St. Francis, Amarillo, TX
Zang, Rev. Richard P, *CSC* '69 (FTW) [MIS] Holy Cross House, Notre Dame, IN
Zaniolo, Rev. Michael G., '88 (CHI) Curia: Offices and Directors [MIS] Chicago Airports Catholic Chaplaincy, Chicago, IL
Zannetti, Rev. Gregory, '21 (MET) St. James, Basking Ridge, NJ
Zanni, Rev. Frank L., '90 (Y) Retired. Curia: Leadership
Zanon, Rev. Andrei, *C.S.* '19 (NY) Our Lady of Pompeii, New York, NY
Zanon, Rev. Romano A., '66 (BRK) [MON] Bishop Mugavero Residence, Douglaston, NY
Zanoni, Rev. Richard J., *S.J.* '75 (BUF) St. Michael, Buffalo, NY
Zanoni, Rev. Ron, (LAV) St. Andrew Catholic Community, Boulder City, NV
Zanoni, Very Rev. Ronald, '05 (LAV) Curia: Advisory Boards, Commissions, Committees, and Councils; Clergy and Religious Services
Zanotto, Rev. Luigi, *M.C.C.J.* '68 (NEW) Retired. [MON] Comboni Missionaries of the Heart of Jesus (Verona Fathers), Newark, NJ
Zaorski, Rev. Edward F., '90 (DET) Curia: Consultative Bodies St. James Parish Novi, Novi, MI
Zapalac, Rev. David J., *C.S.B.* '93 (GAL) St. Anne, Houston, TX
Zapalac, Rev. William E., *O.M.I.* '70 (SAT) Retired. [NUR] Oblate Madonna Residence, San Antonio, TX
Zapata, Rev. Antonio Jesus, '68 (ORG) Retired.
Zapata, Rev. Carlos, '88 (HRT) Curia: Spiritual Life Saint John Paul the Great Parish Corporation, Torrington, CT
Zapata, Rev. Carlos Alberto, '12 (MIL) St. Charles Borromeo Congregation, Milwaukee, WI; St. Roman Congregation, Milwaukee, WI; [MIS] Cursillos in Christianity, Milwaukee, WI
Zapata, Rev. Emiliano, *OP* '95 (LUB) St. Elizabeth University Parish, Lubbock, TX; [MON] Southern Dominican Fathers of Lubbock, Lubbock, TX
Zapata, Rev. Pedro, (SP) St. Clement, Plant City, FL
Zapata, Rev. Urian J. Perez, '97 (MGZ) De la Merced Parish, Lajas, PR
Zapata-Ramirez, Rev. Josegerman, '90 (MIL) St. Andrew's Congregation, Delavan, WI; St. Catherine's Congregation, Sharon, WI; St. Patrick's Congregation, Elkhorn, WI

Zapata-Torres, Rev. Jose Cruz, '14 (MEM) Church of the Nativity, Bartlett, TN

Zapf, Rev. Albert L., '80 (PIT) Retired.

Zapfel, Rev. Msgr. Robert E., '81 (BUF) Curia: Consultative Bodies; Leadership; Offices and Directors St. Andrew Kim, Tonawanda, NY; St. Benedict, Eggertsville, NY; St. Leo the Great, Amherst, NY

Zapp, Rev. John, '72 (Y) Retired.

Zappitelli, Rev. Francis, '62 (PHX) Retired.

Zarate, Rev. Juan, '08 (GB) St. Philip the Apostle, Green Bay, WI

Zarate-Suarez, Very Rev. Edmundo, '96 (SD) Curia: Advisory Boards, Commissions, Committees, and Councils Pastor of Saint Anthony of Padua Catholic Parish, National City, a corporation sole, National City, CA; Pastor of Saint Jude Shrine of the West Catholic Parish, San Diego, a corporation sole, San Diego, CA

Zarebski, Rev. Dariusz, *S.D.S* '90 (MIA) St. Ambrose, Deerfield Beach, FL

Zareski, Rev. Joseph, '80 (SY) Curia: Leadership St. Anthony of Padua, Cortland, NY; St. Margaret, Homer, NY; St. Mary, Cortland, NY; St. Patrick, Truxton, NY

Zarse, Rev. Jaime, '14 (KCK) Sacred Heart, Sabetha, KS; St. Augustine, Sabetha, KS; St. James, Wetmore, KS

Zarsky, Rev. Brion, '07 (AUS) Good Shepherd, Johnson City, TX; St. Ferdinand, Blanco, TX; St. Mary's Help of Christians, Twin Sisters, TX

Zas Friz de Col, Rev. Rossano, *SJ* '89 (OAK) [MON] Jesuit Fathers and Brothers, Berkeley, CA

Zasada, Rev. Hubert, *S.Ch.R.* '02 (MIA) Curia: Pastoral Services Our Lady of Czestochowa Mission, Pompano Beach, FL

Zasada, Rev. Marcin, '12 (CHI) St. Thomas of Villanova, Palatine, IL

Zas-Friz, Rev. Rossano, *S.J.* (OAK) [SEM] Jesuit School of Theology of Santa Clara University (Berkeley, California Campus), Berkeley, CA

Zaslona, Rev. Jerzy R., '04 (NEW) Holy Rosary, Jersey City, NJ

Zastrow, Rev. John A., '56 (LIN) Retired.

Zaucha, Rev. Finian, *ofm* '68 (GB) St. Mary of the Angels, Green Bay, WI

Zaucha, Rev. Finian, *OFM* '68 (GB) [MON] Assumption of B.V.M. Friary, Pulaski, WI

Zavackis, Rev. Christopher P., '15 (NO) Our Lady of Lourdes, Slidell, LA; St. Cletus Roman Catholic Church, Gretna, Louisiana, Gretna, LA

Zavage, Rev. Michael A., '09 (PIT) St. James, Washington, PA; St. Katharine Drexel Parish, Bentleyville, PA; [CAM] California University (California), California, PA; [CAM] Washington and Jefferson College (Washington), California, PA; [CAM] Waynesburg College (Waynesburg), California, PA

Zavala, Rev. Douglas, '09 (ORG) Blessed Sacrament, Westminster, CA

Zavala, Rev. Miguel, *I.V.E* (NY) St. Thomas Aquinas, Bronx, NY

Zavala, Rev. Octavio, '65 (STO) Retired.

Zavala Contreras, Rev. Victor Manuel, *MG* '91 (LA) [MON] Guadalupe Missioners Procure, Los Angeles, CA

Zavaski, Rev. William J., '69 (CHI) Retired. St. James, Arlington Heights, IL

Zawacki, Rev. Robert, *S.S.J.* '77 (BAL) Retired.

Zawadzki, Rev. Adam, '18 (SFD) Our Saviour, Jacksonville, IL

Zawadzki, Rev. Ryszard, *S.V.D.* (LAF) St. Joseph, Broussard, LA

Zborowski, Rev. Msgr. Richard M., '78 (CHI) Retired. St. Thomas More Mission, Chicago, IL

Zdancewicz, Rev. Carl, (PMB) St. Mark, Boynton Beach, FL

Zdancewicz, Rev. Carl S., *O.F.M.Conv.* (CHL) Our Lady of Fatima, Winston-Salem, NC

Zdebik, Rev. Daniel P., *O.F.M.Conv.* '07 (RCK) St. Margaret Mary, Algonquin, IL

Zdilla, Rev. Val, '96 (HEL) Our Lady of the Pines Parish: Series 163, LLC, West Yellowstone, MT

Zdilla, Rev. Valentine D., '96 (HEL) Curia: Leadership St. Joseph of Big Sky, Big Sky, MT

Zebrowski, Rev. Arnold, '73 (VEN) Retired.

Zebrowski, Rev. Jerzy, *O.F.M.Conv.* (BO) Our Lady of Czestochowa, Boston, MA

Zebrowski, Rev. Sebastian, '21 (CHI) Immaculate Conception and Five Holy Martyrs, Chicago, IL

Zec, Rev. John, (MET) Retired.

Zec, Rev. John, '70 (TR) Retired.

Zeck, Rev. George, '70 (DUL) Retired.

Zee, Rev. Louis C., '59 (DUB) Retired.

Zegar, Rev. David E., '79 (P) St. Andrew, Portland, OR

Zegeer, Rev. Eric D., '05 (MIA) On Leave. ministry in Archdiocese of Denver (>DEN) Sacred Heart Catholic Parish in Denver, Denver, CO

Zehler, Rev. Steven, '07 (STA) Curia: Offices and Directors St. Ambrose, Elkton, FL

Zehnle, Rev. Daren J., '05 (SFD) Curia: Leadership St. Alexius, Beardstown, IL; St. Augustine, Ashland, IL; St. Fidelis, Arenzville, IL; St. Luke, Virginia, IL

Zehr, Rev. Thomas, '18 (FTW) Curia: Offices and Directors St. Mary, Huntington, IN

Zehren, Rev. Dennis, '04 (STP) St. Vincent de Paul, Brooklyn Park, MN; [CEM] St. Vincent de Paul Cemetery, Brooklyn Park, MN

Zeid, Rev. Nadim Abou, *M.L.M.* '94 (OLL) St. Sharbel Maronite Catholic Mission, Las Vegas, NV; [MON] The Congregation of Maronite Lebanese Missionaries, Houston, TX

Zeigler, Rev. Stephen, '11 (Y) St. Paul the Apostle, New Middletown, OH

Zeiler, Rev. Donald, '01 (DAL) St. Gabriel the Archangel Catholic Parish, McKinney, TX

Zelaya, Rev. Cristians, '02 (TYL) Sacred Heart, Palestine, TX

Zelik, Rev. Richard J., *O.F.M.Cap.* '77 (PIT) Our Lady of the Angels, Pittsburgh, PA; [MON] Our Lady of the Angels Friary, Pittsburgh, PA

Zelinsk, Rev. James, *O.F.M.Cap.* '61 (GB) [MON] St. Fidelis Friary, Appleton, WI

Zelinski, Rev. Enan, '20 (MAD) St. Maria Goretti Congregation, Madison, WI

Zelinski, Rev. Thomas, *OFM Cap* '72 (MIL) [MON] St. Lawrence Friary, Mount Calvary, WI

Zelker, Rev. Thomas, '83 (ALB) Our Lady of Fatima, Delanson, NY; Parish of Our Lady of the Valley, Middleburgh, NY

Zeller, Rev. Leonard H., '73 (BAL) Retired.

Zelonis, Rev. Christopher M., '03 (ALN) Curia: Leadership SS. Peter and Paul, Lehighton, PA

Zemanik, Rev. Msgr. Edward S., '81 (ALN) St. Ambrose, Schuylkill Haven, PA

Zemczak, Rev. Pawel, '05 (CHI) Chap, Curia: (>MO) Offices and Directors

Zemelko, Rev. John J., '87 (GRY) Curia: Offices and Directors Sacred Heart, Wanatah, IN; St. Mary, Otis, IN

Zemlik, Rev. Edward, *S.C.J.* '01 (MIL) [MON] Sacred Heart Monastery, Hales Corners, WI

Zemula, Rev. Anthony, *S.A.C.* '79 (BRK) St. Frances de Chantal, Brooklyn, NY

Zender, Very Rev. Gary M., '86 (SEA) On Special Assignment. Vicar for Clergy, Seattle Curia: Leadership; Offices and Directors St. Louise, Bellevue, WA; St. Madeleine Sophie, Bellevue, WA

Zengierski, Rev. Patrick J., '91 (BUF) [CAM] SUNY Buffalo State Newman Center, Buffalo, NY

Zenthoefer, Very Rev. Alex J., '05 (EVN) On Special Assignment. Curia: Leadership; Offices and Directors St. Benedict Cathedral, Evansville, IN; Sts. Mary & John, Evansville, IN

Zenz, Rev. Msgr. John P., '78 (DET) Curia: Consultative Bodies Holy Name Parish Birmingham, Birmingham, MI; Marian High School for Young Women, Bloomfield Hills, MI; [MIS] Christ Child Society (Christ Child House), Detroit, MI

Zepecki, Rev. Ronald P., '95 (HRT) Saint Marianne Cope Parish Corporation, Broad Brook, CT

Zepeda, Rev. Alejandro, '06 (SPK) Sacred Heart, Othello, WA

Zepeda, Rev. Jose, *F.S.S.P.* (FRS) Curia: Organizations (affiliated, inter-Diocesan, miscellaneous/other)

Zeps, Rev. Michael J., *S.J.* '71 (MIL) [MON] Jesuit Community at Marquette University (Marquette Jesuit Associates, Inc.), Milwaukee, WI

Zercie, Rev. David, *M.S.A.* '69 (NOR) [MON] Society of the Missionaries of the Holy Apostles, Cromwell, CT

Zerkel, Rev. Donald F., '57 (MIL) Retired.

Zermeno, Rev. Joaquin, '11 (BWN) Curia: Advisory Boards, Commissions, Committees, and Councils; Offices and Directors Our Lady, Queen of Angels, La Joya, TX

Zermeno, Rev. Joseph, *O.F.M.* (TUC) Retired.

Zermeno-Martin, Rev. Felix, '00 (DEN) Our Lady of Grace Catholic Parish in Denver, Denver, CO

Zero, Rev. Frank, '11 (RVC) Curia: Leadership; Offices and Directors Our Lady of Perpetual Help, Lindenhurst, NY

Zerr, Rev. Dennis P., '03 (CC) St. Elizabeth of Hungary, Alice, TX

Zerr, Rev. Gary L., '97 (P) Chap, Santiam Corr Inst, Salem St. Edward, Keizer, OR

Zerr, Rev. Maurice J., *M.M.* '51 (NY) Retired.

Zerucha, Rev. Christopher J., '11 (CLV) St. Bernard Parish, Akron, OH; St. Mary, Akron, OH

Zerwas, Very Rev. Rick, '91 (SFE) Curia: Offices and Directors Shrine of St. Bernadette, Albuquerque, NM; [SHR] Shrine of St. Bernadette, Albuquerque, NM

Zeth, Rev. Allen, (ALT) St. Thomas More, Roaring Spring, PA

Zeth, Rev. Allen P., '86 (ALT) St. Patrick, Newry, PA

Zetouna, Rev. Matthew, '12 (EST) St. Thomas Chaldean Catholic Parish, West Bloomfield, MI

Zettel, Rev. David H., '66 (L) Retired.

Zeugner, Rev. Raymond L., '67 (MAR) Retired.

Zeyack, Rev. John, '65 (PSC) Retired.

Zgonc, Rev. Michael S., '14 (MAN) St. Mark the Evangelist, Londonderry, NH

Zgunda, Rev. Ronald S., '77 (EVN) Retired.

Zhai, Rev. Peter L., *S.V.D.* '06 (SFR) Curia: Offices and Directors St. Anne, San Francisco, CA

Zhanay, Rev. Jerry O., *S.J.S.* '14 (MAD) On Duty Outside Diocese. Serves in Spain

Zhang, Rev. Dehua, *C.S.J.B.* '76 (BRK) Retired.

Zhang, Rev. Joseph, *AA* (BO) St. James the Greater, Boston, MA

Zhang, Rev. Roger Shu-Xin, '00 (GAL) Ascension Chinese Mission, Houston, TX

Zhang, Rev. Yanjun, '08 (BRK) St. Michael, Flushing, NY

Zheng, Rev. Tiancang (Joseph), (BRK) St. John Vianney, Flushing, NY; [MON] Congregation of St. John the Baptist of China, Elmhurst, NY

Zhybak, Rev. Lubomir, '08 (SJP) Curia: Offices and Directors Holy Trinity, Youngstown, OH; St. Anne, Austintown, OH

Zibara, Rev. Roby, '08 (OLL) St. Maron Maronite Catholic Church, Detroit, MI

Ziccardi, Rev. Msgr. C. Anthony, '90 (NEW) Curia: Organizations (affiliated, inter-Diocesan, miscellaneous/other) [COL] Seton Hall University, South Orange, NJ; [SEM] Immaculate Conception Seminary School of Theology, South Orange, NJ

Zidak, Rev. Vincent, *O.S.B.* (GBG) St. James the Greater, Apollo, PA

Zidek, Rev. Vincent E., *O.S.B.* '91 (GBG) Our Lady, Queen of Peace, East Vandergrift, PA; [MON] Saint Vincent Archabbey, Latrobe, PA

Zieba, Rev. Jerzy, *C.R.* '92 (JOL) St. Pius X, Lombard, IL

Ziebacz, Rev. Wieslaw M., '92 (SCR) On Administrative Leave.

Ziebowicz, Rev. Dariusz, *S.D.S.* '88 (SAT) [MON] Salvatorian Fathers Community of Texas, Falls City, TX

Ziebowicz, Rev. Dariusz, *S.D.S.* '88 (AUS) Assumption of the Blessed Virgin Mary, String Prairie, TX; Sacred Heart, Bastrop, TX; St. Mary of the Assumption, Bastrop, TX

Ziegler, Rev. John A., '96 (ARL) St. Patrick, Fredericksburg, VA

Ziegler, Rev. Michael Tod, '01 (KCK) On Leave. Inactive

Ziegler, Rev. Thomas G., '69 (Y) Retired.

Zielenieski, Rev. Bryan J., '14 (BUF) Curia: Consultative Bodies; Leadership; Offices and Directors St. Mary, Swormville, NY

Zielinski, Rev. Carter, '18 (KCK) Sacred Heart, Emporia, KS

Zielinski, Rev. Francis A., '62 (DET) Retired.

Zielinski, Rev. Martin, '78 (CHI) Retired. [SEM] University of Saint Mary of the Lake/Mundelein Seminary, Mundelein, IL

Zielinski, Rev. Ryszard, '83 (CC) Sacred Heart, Three Rivers, TX

Zielinski, Rev. Zbigniew, (BGP) On Duty Outside Diocese. In North Carolina

Zielinski, Rev. Zbigniew, (MO) Curia: Offices and Directors

Zielke, Rev. Michael, *O.F.M.Conv.* '89 (CHI) (>WDC) [SEM] St. Bonaventure Friary, Silver Spring, MD

Zielonka, Msgr. Dariusz J., (MIA) Curia: Canonical Services; Leadership; Pastoral Services

Zielonka, Rev. Msgr. Dariusz J., '95 (BGP) On Duty Outside Diocese. Excardinated

Ziemba, Rev. Howard, '79 (Y) Retired.

Ziemkiewicz, Rev. Frank, *OSB* '84 (SAV) Benedictine Military School, Savannah, GA; [MON] The Benedictine Priory, Savannah, GA

Ziemkiewicz, Rev. Frank, *O.S.B.* '84 (GBG) [MON] Saint Vincent Archabbey, Latrobe, PA

Ziemnicki, Rev. Edward, (HRT) Saint Faustina Parish Corporation, Meriden, CT

Ziemniek, Rev. Jan, (LAR) Santa Rita de Casia, Rio Bravo, TX

Zientek, Rev. Msgr. Benedict, '58 (SAN) Retired.

Zientek, Rev. Msgr. Benedict Julian, '58 (AUS) Retired.

Zientek, Rev. Msgr. Boleslaus, '59 (GAL) Retired.

Zigmond, Rev. Kenneth, *O.S.B.* '57 (JOL) Retired. [MON] St. Procopius Abbey, Lisle, IL

Zignego, Rev. Canon Luke, (CHI) [MON] Institute of Christ the King Sovereign Priest, Chicago, IL
Zilimu, Rev. Johndamaseni, '95 (PEO) Curia: Clergy and Religious Services; Consultative Bodies; Deaneries Saint John Paul II Parish, Kewanee, IL; St. John's, Galva, IL; St. John's, Woodhull, IL; [HOS] OSF HealthCare Saint Luke Medical Center, Kewanee, IL
Ziminski, Rev. James C., '91 (MAR) Curia: Advisory Boards, Commissions, Committees, and Councils All Saints, Gladstone, MI; St. Andrew, Nahma, MI; St. John the Baptist, Garden, MI; St. Mary Magdalene, Cooks, MI
Zimmer, Rev. Anthony J., '86 (MIL) St. Anthony Congregation, Pewaukee, WI
Zimmer, Rev. David L., '88 (BIS) Retired. Curia: Leadership
Zimmer, Rev. Eric A., '94 (FTW) [COL] University of Saint Francis, Fort Wayne, IN
Zimmer, Rev. Matthew, '11 (LIN) Sts. Mary and Joseph's, Valparaiso, NE
Zimmer, Rev. Michael, (MO) Curia: Offices and Directors
Zimmer, Rev. Michael J., '12 (LIN) St. Mary's, Sutton, NE
Zimmer, Rev. William E., '91 (CHI) On Special Assignment. Cicero
Zimmerman, Rev. Donald, '73 (SAL) Curia: Organizations (affiliated, inter-Diocesan, miscellaneous/ other)
Zimmerman, Rev. Msgr. Donald F., '73 (DAL) Retired.
Zimmerman, Rev. John M., '03 (CHR) Curia: Advisory Boards, Commissions, Committees, and Councils; Organizations (affiliated, inter-Diocesan, miscellaneous/ other) Our Lady of Perpetual Help, Camden, SC
Zimmerman, Rev. Joseph, *O.F.M.* '62 (SFD) Retired. [MON] Holy Cross Friary (Quincy University Friary), Quincy, IL
Zimmerman, Rev. Michael, (BO) Curia: Clergy and Religious Services Sacred Heart, Watertown, MA
Zimmerman, Rev. Mitchel, '04 (KCK) [CAM] St. Lawrence Catholic Campus Center at the University of Kansas and Residence, Lawrence, KS
Zimmerman, Rev. Ralph G., '76 (SCL) Retired. Curia: Offices and Directors
Zimmerman, Rev. Rex A., '67 (LC) Retired.
Zimmermann, Rev. Dominic, *S.O.L.T.* '01 (CC) [MON] Society of Our Lady of the Most Holy Trinity, Corpus Christi, TX
Zimmerschied, Rev. Daniel, '97 (DEN) Guardian Angels Catholic Parish in Denver, Denver, CO
Zimodro, Rev. Slawomir, '08 (RCK) Immaculate Conception, Fulton, IL; St. Mary, Morrison, IL; St. Patrick, Albany, IL
Zimoha, Rev. Jude, '02 (BRK) Chap, NYC Health & Hospitals/Queens-Pastoral Care Office St. Elizabeth, Ozone Park, NY
Zina, Rev. George, '86 (SAM) St. Elias, Roanoke, VA
Zingales, Rev. A. Jonathan, '76 (CLV) Retired. Curia: Tribunal
Zingales, Rev. A. Jonathan, (PRM) Curia: Leadership
Zingales, Rev. A. Jonathan, '76 (CLV) St. Vitus, Cleveland, OH
Zinger, Rev. Daniel, (BO) St. Mary of the Annunciation, Cambridge, MA
Zink, Rev. David L., '90 (CIN) Retired. [MON] St. Charles, Celina, OH
Zink, Rev. William F., '68 (GR) Retired.
Zinno, Rev. Henry P., '82 (PRO) Church of Our Lady of Mount Carmel, Bristol, Bristol, RI
Zins, Rev. Charles A., '77 (BIS) Retired.
Zinser, Rev. Robert E., '68 (STL) Retired.
Zinthefer, Rev. Neil G., '69 (MIL) Retired.
Zinzer, Rev. Walter W., '64 (STL) Retired.
Ziolkowski, Rev. Adam, *OFM Conv.* '72 (SPR) Our Lady of the Cross, Holyoke, MA
Ziolkowski, Rev. Kamil, '22 (LA) St. Joseph, Hawthorne, CA
Ziomek, Rev. Dennis A., '78 (CHI) Curia: Leadership St. Catherine of Alexandria, Oak Lawn, IL
Zipay, Rev. Michael J., '68 (SCR) Retired. [MON] Villa St. Joseph, Dunmore, PA
Zipp, Rev. Andrew Herbert, '19 (STP) St. Mary of the Lake, Plymouth, MN; Totino-Grace High School, Fridley, MN
Zipple, Rev. Jeremy, (NY) [MON] America; Residence and Publication Office of the America Press, New York, NY
Zirilli, Rev. David A., '08 (MIA) On Leave. Sabbatical period
Zirimenya, Rev. Paul, '07 (SFR) St. Benedict Parish at St. Francis Xavier Church, San Francisco, CA; St. Gabriel, San Francisco, CA; [MIS] St. Benedict Parish for Deaf and Hearing Impaired at St. Francis Xavier Church, San Francisco, CA
Zirnheld, Rev. Matthew J., '93 (BUF) St. Andrew, Kenmore, NY
Zittle, Rev. Mark, *O.Carm* '12 (NY) [MON] Carmelite Friars (North American Province of St. Elias), Middletown, NY
Ziuraitis, Rev. Gary, *C.Ss.R.* '78 (KC) Our Lady of Perpetual Help, Kansas City, MO; [EFT] Our Lady of Perpetual Help Charitable Trust, Kansas City, MO; [MON] Redemptorists Fathers of Kansas City, Missouri, Kansas City, MO
Zkunaeziri, Rev. Joseph, (NY) St. Barnabas, Bronx, NY
Zlock, Rev. Charles, '03 (PH) St. Raymond of Penafort, Philadelphia, PA
Zlotkowski, Rev. Frank, *C.S.C.* '76 (AUS) On Special Assignment. Chaplain at Ascension Hospital
Zmuda, Rev. Christopher J., '01 (NOR) Sacred Heart, Taftville, CT; St. Joseph, Versailles, CT; St. Mary of the Immaculate Conception, Baltic, CT
Zobler, Rev. Alan D., *O.S.F.S.* '07 (TOL) [MON] Oblates of St. Francis de Sales, Toledo, OH
Zodrow, Rt. Rev. Nathan, *O.S.B.* '88 (P) Retired. [MON] Mt. Angel Abbey, Saint Benedict, OR
Zoellner, Rev. Michael, *O.S.B.* '80 (KCK) [MON] St. Benedict's Abbey, Atchison, KS
Zogbi, Rev. Peter John, '20 (OLL) St. Elias Maronite Catholic Church, Birmingham, AL
Zoghby, Rev. James F., '71 (MOB) Retired.
Zoghby, Very Rev. Paul G., '93 (MOB) Curia: Leadership St. Margaret Queen of Scotland, Foley, AL
Zohlen, Rev. Ray, '53 (SFR) Retired.
Zollinger, Rev. Msgr. Richard, '55 (GRY) Retired.
Zoma, Rev. Rudy, '09 (EST) Curia: Offices and Directors Our Lady of Perpetual Help Chaldean Catholic Church, Warren, MI
Zomaya, Rev. Anwar, '05 (PHX) St. Thomas Aquinas Roman Catholic Parish, Avondale, AZ
Zomerfeld, Rev. Zbigniew, '93 (DET) St. Mary Parish Port Huron, Port Huron, MI
Zondler, Rev. William, (SD) Pastor of Saint Mark Catholic Parish in San Marcos A Corporation Sole, San Marcos, CA
Zorjan, Rev. Peter, '07 (PEO) Our Lady of Guadalupe, Silvis, IL; St. Patrick's, Colona, IL
Zoubek, Rev. Ronald, '89 (BAL) Retired.
Zoucha, Rev. Carl J., '98 (OM) Holy Name, Omaha, NE
Zoufal, Rev. Michael L., '87 (CHI) St. Joseph, Round Lake, IL
Zowada, Rev. Stanislaw, *O.M.I.* (LAR) Our Lady of Refuge, Eagle Pass, TX
Zrallack, Rev. Nicholas Paul, '20 (PMB) St. Helen, Vero Beach, FL
Zubel, Rev. Kevin, *C.Ss.R.* '17 (JKS) On Special Assignment. Sr. Thea Bowman Cause for Canonization
Zubel, Rev. Kevin, *C.Ss.R.* '17 (BR) (>CHI) [MON] The Redemptorist Fathers of Chicago, Chicago, IL; (>CHI) [MON] The Redemptorists/Denver Province, Chicago, IL
Zuberbueler, Rev. Matthew H., '96 (ARL) St. Anthony, Falls Church, VA
Zubieta, Rev. Alejandro, (POD) Curia: Clergy and Religious Services
Zubieta Peniche, Rev. Francisco Alejandro, '96 (PCE) [MIS] Prelatura de la Santa Cruz y Opus Dei, Ponce, PR
Zubik, Rev. Rudolf, '64 (NEW) Retired. [MON] St. John Vianney Residence for Retired Priests, Rutherford, NJ
Zuccaro, Rev. James E., '06 (BUR) Our Lady of Mount Carmel, Charlotte, VT; St. Jude the Apostle, Hinesburg, VT
Zuchowski, Rev. Robert J., '72 (GLD) Sacred Heart of Elk Rapids, Elk Rapids, MI
Zuelch, Rev. Michael Christopher, '10 (DET) St. Mary Parish St. Clair, St. Clair, MI
Zuelke, Rev. Brian, *OP* (STP) St. Odilia, Shoreview, MN; [MON] St. Albert the Great Priory, Minneapolis, MN
Zuerlein, Rev. Damian, '81 (OM) Curia: Leadership; Offices and Directors St. Frances Cabrini, Omaha, NE
Zuerlein, Rev. Damian J., '81 (OM) Curia: Leadership [MIS] IXIM, Spirit of Solidarity, Omaha, NE
Zuffoletto, Rev. Michael P., '72 (BUF) Retired. St. Anthony of Padua, Buffalo, NY
Zugaj, Rev. Piotr W., '04 (VEN) On Leave.
Zugger, Rev. Christopher L., '81 (HPM) Retired. Our Lady of Perpetual Help, Albuquerque, NM
Zukas, Rev. Stephen P., '93 (BO) St. Edward the Confessor, Medfield, MA; St. Jude, Norfolk, MA
Zukowski, Rev. Nicholas, '82 (DET) St. Martin de Porres Parish Warren, Warren, MI
Zumbrum, Rev. Brian D., *O.S.F.S.* '13 (WIL) Salesianum School, Wilmington, DE
Zuniga, Rev. Carlos, '98 (BWN) On Leave.
Zuniga, Rev. Eric, '17 (HRT) All Saints Parish Corporation, Waterbury, CT
Zuniga, Rev. Jose M., '22 (PAT) St. Anthony of Padua, Passaic, NJ
Zuniga, Friar Juan, *OFM Conv.* '21 (ELP) Our Lady of Mt. Carmel, El Paso, TX
Zuñiga, Rev. Juan M., *M.M.* '88 (NY) [MON] Maryknoll Fathers and Brothers (Catholic Foreign Mission Society of America, Inc.), Ossining, NY
Zunini, Rev. Raul Acosta, *S.D.B.* '67 (SP) [RTR] Mary Help of Christians Center, Tampa, FL
Zunmas, Rev. Oby J., '00 (OKL) Curia: Consultative Bodies Holy Cross Church, Madill, OK
Zunno, Rev. Michael O., '53 (NY) Retired.
Zunun, Rev. Nicolas, *SCH.p* (SJN) Santisimo Salvador, San Juan, PR
Zupka, Rev. Anselm, *O.S.B.* '67 (CLV) Benedictine High School, Cleveland, OH; [MON] Benedictine Order of Cleveland (St. Andrew Abbey), Cleveland, OH
Zuraw, Very Rev. Msgr. John A., '87 (Y) Curia: Leadership; Pastoral Services
Zuraw, Very Rev. Msgr. John A., '87 (Y) Curia: Leadership; Offices and Directors St. Luke, Boardman, OH; [MIS] First Friday Club of Greater Youngstown, Youngstown, OH
Zuraw, Very Rev. Msgr. Msgr. John, '87 (Y) St. Charles Borromeo, Boardman, OH
Zurawski, Rev. Lawrence, '93 (DET) St. Thomas the Apostle Parish Garden City, Garden City, MI
Zurcher, Rev. Thomas K, *CSC* (FTW) Holy Cross, South Bend, IN; [MON] Congregation of Holy Cross, United States Province of Priests and Brothers, Notre Dame, IN
Zurek, Rev. John, '04 (CHI) St. Elizabeth Seton, Orland Hills, IL
Zurita, Rev. Simon, *F.S.S.P.* '15 (OKL) St. Damien of Molokai Church, Edmond, OK
Zuschmidt, Rev. Joseph, *O.S.F.S.* (WIL) [MON] Retirement and Assisted Care Facility, Childs, MD
Zuzarte, Rev. Manuel, (RVC) St. Andrew's, Sag Harbor, NY
Zuziak, Rev. Joseph R., *S.D.S.* '66 (GRY) Retired.
Zvarych, Rev. Petro, '00 (PHU) St. John the Baptist, Maizeville, PA; St. Michael's, Frackville, PA
Zwack, Rev. Jeffrey A., '84 (BIS) Saint Anne, Bismarck, ND
Zwilling, Rev. Matthew, '20 (Y) Christ the Good Shepherd Parish, Campbell, OH; St. Columba Parish, Youngstown, OH; St. Edward, Youngstown, OH
Zwilling, Rev. Robert J., '05 (BEL) Curia: Offices and Directors St. Mary, Mount Carmel, IL; St. Sebastian, Mount Carmel, IL
Zwirn, Rev. Ralph H., '85 (CHI) Curia: Leadership St. John Neumann, Homewood, IL
Zwolenkiewicz, Rev. Rapael, (BRK) Most Holy Trinity - Saint Mary, Brooklyn, NY
Zwosta, Rev. Joseph M., '12 (BRK) On Duty Outside Diocese. Pope St. John XXIII National Seminary, Weston MA St. Helen, Howard Beach, NY (>BO) [SEM] Pope Saint John XXIII National Seminary, Weston, MA
Zygadlo, Rev. Mitchell, '82 (ROC) St. Louis, Pittsford, NY
Zywan, Rev. Paul J, (PIT) Triumph of the Holy Cross, Jefferson Hills, PA

NECROLOGY

POPE

Benedict, XVI, His Holiness Pope Emeritus, Died: 2022

ARCHBISHOPS

Fiorenza, Most Rev. Joseph A., (GAL) Died: 2022
Weakland, Most Rev. Rembert G., O.S.B. (MIL) Died: 2022

BISHOPS

Bura, Most Rev. John, (PHU) Died: 2023
Casey, Most Rev. Luis M. (Aloysius), (STL) Died: 2022
Clark, Most Rev. Matthew Harvey, (ROC) Died: 2023
Maginnis, Most Rev. Robert P., (PH) Died: 2022
Melczek, Most Rev. Dale J., (GRY) Died: 2022
Moskal, Most Rev. Robert M., (SJP) Died: 2022
O'Connell, Most Rev. David G., (LA) Died: 2023
Sheridan, Most Rev. Michael J., (COS) Died: 2022
Swain, Most Rev. Paul J., (SFS) Died: 2022
Weitzel, Most Rev. John Q., M.M. (SPP) Died: 2022
Yanta, Most Rev. John W., (AMA) Died: 2022

PRIESTS

Abe, Rev. John Adam, (RIC) Died: 2022
Affelt, Rev. Francis, O.F.M. (FTW) Died: 2022 Alves, Rev. Jose D., (BGP) Died: 2022
Anthony, Rev. Julian, (PBR) Died: 2022
Antolini, Rev. Vincenzo, O.M.V. (LA) Died: 2022
Arcamo, Rev. Msgr. Floro B., (SFR) Died: 2022
Argent, Rev. Robert W., (STL) Died: 2022
Aubin, Rev. Msgr. Joseph G., (OG) Died: 2022 Aubry, Rev. Ronald J., (COL) Died: 2022
Auer, Rev. Msgr. John J., (BAL) Died: 2022
Babin, Rev. Albert C., c.ss.r. (STL) Died: 2022 Babjak, Rev. Marian, (Y) Died: 2022
Backiel, Rev. Bernard, m.i.c. (NOR) Died: 2022 Badia, Rev. Leonard F., (BRK) Died: 2022
Baek, Rev. Augustine, s.d.b. (NY) Died: 2022 Bakewell, Rev. Donald V., (DUB) Died: 2022 Baldonado, Rev. Luis, O.F.M. (PHX) Died: 2022 Banach, Rev. Henry S., (WOR) Died: 2023
Bantz, Rev. William, (Y) Died: 2022
Barachini, Rev. Nello, (BGP) Died: 2022
Baranowski, Rev. David J., (HRT) Died: 2022 Barclift, Rev. Richard L., (PEO) Died: 2022
Barrett, Rev. William, (ROC) Died: 2022
Bartlett, Rev. James, s.m. (CIN) Died: 2022
Barton, Rev. Msgr. Raymond A., (RIC) Died: 2022
Barwig, Rev. Regis N., (GB) Died: 2022
Beath, Rev. James D., (CHI) Died: 2022
Beckman, Rev. Richard J., (OKL) Died: 2022 Bednartz, Rev. Msgr. August C., (BRK) Died: 2022 Begin, Rev. Robert T., (CLV) Died: 2022
Behan, Rev. Hugh F., (JC) Died: 2022
Bell, Rev. Brian, (PHX) Died: 2022
Benoit, Rev. Lloyd F., (LAF) Died: 2022
Berg, Rev. Peter M., (OG) Died: 2022
Berner, Rev. Francis, (NO) Died: 2022
Bisson, Rev. Eddy N., (MAN) Died: 2022
Blaine, Rev. James E., (SLC) Died: 2022
Blanchard, Rev. David, O.Carm. (WDC) Died: 2022
Bleichner, Rev. Howard P., S.S. (PIT) Died: 2022
Block, Rev. John G., (PMB) Died: 2022
Bly, Rev. Walter J., (FTW) Died: 2023
Bolton, Rev. Paul J., (PRO) Died: 2022
Bonano, Rev. Salvatore, C.M.F. (LA) Died: 2022
Bond, Rev. B. Daniel, (RIC) Died: 2022
Bordeaux, Friar Henry, O.C.D. (SAT) Died: 2022
Borgesen, Rev. Kenneth G., o.ss.t. (TR) Died: 2022
Bormann, Rev. Charles P., (PHX) Died: 2022
Borsuk, Rev. Ronald Walter, (PBR) Died: 2022
Botello, Rev. Camillo, M.S.F. (SAT) Died: 2022
Bottino, Rev. Msgr. Edward J., (BRK) Died: 2022
Boucher, Rev. Gilmond, o.m.i. (BO) Died: 2022
Bouley, Rev. Allan, O.S.B. (SCL) Died: 2022
Boyle, Rev. Michael J., C.M. (PHX) Died: 2022
Boyle, Rev. Patrick J., S.J. (MIL) Died: 2022
Brady, Rev. Philip W., (BGP) Died: 2022
Brandes, Rev. John F., (STP) Died: 2023
Brantley, Rev. Mark, (DOD) Died: 2022
Breen, Rev. Joseph P., (NSH) Died: 2023
Breier, Rev. Donald P., (PIT) Died: 2022
Breindel, Rev. Charles L., (RIC) Died: 2022
Brenk, Rev. Frederick E., S.J. (MIL) Died: 2022
Brennan, Rev. Brian C., (NY) Died: 2022
Brinn, Rev. Msgr. John J., (NY) Died: 2022
Brown, Rev. Charles, (PSC) Died: 2022
Brunkan, Rev. Msgr. Walter L., (DUB) Died: 2022
Brunskill, Rev. Richard W., (PEO) Died: 2022
Bryan, Rev. Francis E., (IND) Died: 2022
Brylka, Rev. Vincent R., (OAK) Died: 2022
Buchanan, Rev. Donald E., (IND) Died: 2022
Buckley, Rev. Gerald J., (SY) Died: 2022
Bui, Rev. Joseph Tin Manh, (SFE) Died: 2022
Bulwith, Rev. Richard E., (CHI) Died: 2022
Burden, Rev. George W., s.s.j. (BAL) Died: 2022
Burke, Rev. Michael, (ORL) Died: 2022
Burns, Rev. John R., (PEO) Died: 2022
Burns, Rev. Michael J., (SJ) Died: 2022
Burns, Rev. Robert A., o.p. (TUC) Died: 2022
Byron, Rev. J. Michael, (STP) Died: 2022
Campbell, Rev. Stephen F., s.j. (MOB) Died: 2023
Campion, Rev. William T., (ALN) Died: 2022
Canez, Rev. Jorge, (PHX) Died: 2022
Carkenord, Rev. David, (FTW) Died: 2022
Carlsen, Rev. James F., (MOB) Died: 2022
Carroll, Rev. Brian, (JKS) Died: 2022
Carter, Rev. Francis T., (HRT) Died: 2023
Case, Rev. Lowell D., s.s.j. (BAL) Died: 2022
Celano, Rev. Leo J., O.Praem. (ORG) Died: 2022
Champlin, Rev. Michael A., O.P. (SUP) Died: 2022
Chretien, Rev. Richard L., (FR) Died: 2022
Cirillo, Rev. Nicholas A., (BGP) Died: 2022
Clancy, Rev. Raphael "Ray", (AUS) Died: 2022
Cleu, Rev. Paul, (OAK) Died: 2022
Coakley, Rev. John P., S.J. (DET) Died: 2022
Colella, Rev. David, o.ss.t. (BAL) Died: 2022
Coleman, Rev. John R., (PHX) Died: 2022
Collet, Rev. John, O.M.I. (SAT) Died: 2022
Collins, Rev. Bill, (SAT) Died: 2022
Collins, Rev. Chester L., (GLD) Died: 2023
Collins, Rev. James R., (CIN) Died: 2022
Concannon, Rev. Stephen F., (PRT) Died: 2022
Connolly, Rev. John T., (PAT) Died: 2022
Conway, Rev. Msgr. Jeffrey, (NY) Died: 2022
Conway, Rev. Msgr. John L., (GBG) Died: 2022
Cortese, Rev. Richard A., (MEM) Died: 2022
Cosgrove, Rev. Jerome P., (SC) Died: 2022
Costello, Rev. Msgr. John M., (STL) Died: 2022
Coulthard, Rev. Gregory, S.D.S. (MIL) Died: 2022
Cramer, Rev. Joseph, (KCK) Died: 2022
Cronin, Rev. Harry, c.s.c. (FTW) Died: 2022
Cummins, Rev. Robert L., (RIC) Died: 2022
Cunniff, Rev. Vincent, (P) Died: 2022
Curran, Rev. Msgr. Hugh D., (NY) Died: 2022
Currans, Rev. Clement W., (SC) Died: 2022
Dahlby, Rev. Charles, (SFD) Died: 2022
Daly, Rev. Bartholomew, M.H.M. (NY) Died: 2022
Damian, Rev. Ronald, (WOR) Died: 2022
Das Neves, Rev. Antonio C., (SB) Died: 2022
Davadilla, Rev. Patrick Joel, (FRS) Died: 2022
Davenport, Rev. Christopher M., (PRO) Died: 2022
Davignon, Rev. Charles P., (BUR) Died: 2022
de la Calle, Rev. Juan, (PMB) Died: 2022
DeCarolis, Rev. Vito C., (HRT) Died: 2022
Del Torro, Rev. Jose, t.o.r. (SP) Died: 2022
Demers, Rev. Gerard, s.m. (BO) Died: 2022
Desrosiers, Rev. Paul H., (NO) Died: 2022
Dietz, Rev. Donald, (BEL) Died: 2022
Donnelly, Rev. William, (JOL) Died: 2022
Dorson, Rev. James E., (RIC) Died: 2022
Dowling, Rev. Raymond, (GB) Died: 2022
Doyle, Rev. John, (DUL) Died: 2022
Duhaime, Rev. John N., (WH) Died: 2022
Dummer, Rev. Leo, O.M.I. (SAT) Died: 2022
Dunn, Rev. Gerald R., (MAN) Died: 2022
Dunn, Rev. Jerome, o.f.m. cap. (PIT) Died: 2022
DuPont, Rev. Arthur J., (HRT) Died: 2022
Duyka, Rev. Stephen J., (TYL) Died: 2022
Dvorak, Rev. Donald, o.p. (DAL) Died: 2022
Eagan, Rev. Joseph F., S.J. (MIL) Died: 2022
Eck, Rev. John E., C.S.V. (CHI) Died: 2022
Eichhoff, Rev. Paul E., (TLS) Died: 2022
Eschweiler, Rev. Edward R., (MIL) Died: 2022
Escobedo, Rev. Brian, (HPM) Died: 2022
Espinoza, Rev. Xavier, (DEN) Died: 2022
Evenson, Rev. Dennis D., (STP) Died: 2022
Fahey, Rev. John Peter, (LA) Died: 2022
Falk, Rev. Robert, s.d.b. (NY) Died: 2022
Fangmann, Rev. Frederick C., (DUB) Died: 2022
Fanrak, Rev. James M., (LR) Died: 2022
Faricy, Rev. Robert L., S.J. (MIL) Died: 2022
Farley, Rev. John, S.V.D. (CHI) Died: 2022
Farrell, Rev. Lawrence, (KAL) Died: 2022
Faustner, Rev. William J., (COL) Died: 2022
Feeley, Rev. Paul, O.Carm. (NY) Died: 2022
Fekete, Rev. George J., (GR) Died: 2023
Feltz, Rev. Thomas, (LA) Died: 2022
Feminelli, Rev. John, (CC) Died: 2023
Ferraioli, Rev. Joseph, o.m.i. (BEL) Died: 2023
Finn, Rev. Peter, (NY) Died: 2022
Fisher, Rev. Kyle, c.ss.r. (STL) Died: 2022
Ford, Rev. Michael F., s.j. (BO) Died: 2022
Fortier, Rev. Theodore L., a.a. (WOR) Died: 2022
Francez, Rev. James, m.c.c.j. (CIN) Died: 2022
Frechette, Rev. Leo L., (MAN) Died: 2022
Gaeke, Rev. Thomas M., (CIN) Died: 2022
Gagliardi, Rev. Richard, (OAK) Died: 2022
Gally, Rev. Lourduraj, (SLC) Died: 2022
Garcia Echevarria, Rev. Roberto, (PCE) Died: 2022
Gargotta, Rev. Anthony, (PIT) Died: 2022
Gariepy, Rev. Robert E., (WOR) Died: 2022
Gensler, Rev. Harry J, S.J. (MIL) Died: 2022
Getz, Rev. Joseph J., O.S.A. (PH) Died: 2022
Gigante, Rev. Louis R., (NY) Died: 2022
Gilles, Rev. Thomas C., (CLV) Died: 2022
Gingras, Rev. Dennis C., (HRT) Died: 2022
Glepko, Rev. Robert J., (CLV) Died: 2022

Gorski, Rev. Msgr. J. Donald, (CHR) Died: 2022
Gorski, Rev. John J., (CLV) Died: 2022
Graham, Rev. James D., (P) Died: 2022
Gregoire, Rev. Paul L., (MAN) Died: 2022
Gregoire, Rev. Wilfrid G., (PRO) Died: 2022
Gribble, Rev. G. Michael, (COL) Died: 2022
Groner, Rev. John W., (JC) Died: 2023
Guagliardo, Rev. Salvatore J., (RCK) Died: 2022
Gummersheimer, Rev. Gary P., (BEL) Died: 2023
Gurovich, Rev. Archpriest Daniel, (PHU) Died: 2022
Guzman, Rev. Julian, s.d.s. (NY) Died: 2022
Hackel, Rev. Robert, s.m. (SJ) Died: 2022
Halabura, Rev. Stephen J., (ALN) Died: 2023
Halbing, Rev. William J., (NEW) Died: 2022
Hall, Rev. Robert, (HEL) Died: 2022
Hardesty, Rev. Ernest L., (LR) Died: 2022
Harer, Rev. Eric K., (SY) Died: 2022
Harmon, Rev. John, (DM) Died: 2022
Harrington, Rev. Msgr. Joseph D., (HEL) Died: 2022
Hart, Rev. Paul S., (NO) Died: 2022
Hart, Rev. Rolland A., (OG) Died: 2022
Hartway, Rev. Alan, C.PP.S. (DEN) Died: 2022
Hartzer, Rev. John, (IND) Died: 2022
Hascall, Rev. John, (GB) Died: 2022
Haselhorst, Rev. Msgr. Vincent, (BEL) Died: 2022
Hawkins, Rev. Robert F., (PRO) Died: 2022
Hazel, Rev. Terrence J., (Y) Died: 2022
Heffernan, Rev. A. Joseph, (FRS) Died: 2022
Heffernan, Rev. Robert G., (HRT) Died: 2022
Hendricks, Rev. Clare, (GRY) Died: 2022
Heneghan, Rev. Jarlath, (SEA) Died: 2022
Henrick, Rev. John C., (NSH) Died: 2022
Herrero Mombiela, Rev. Jose Maria, (PCE) Died: 2022
Hilz, Rev. Robert, t.o.r. (ALT) Died: 2022
Himes, Rev. Michael J., (BRK) Died: 2022
Hinch, Rev. Msgr. Lawrence E., (BRK) Died: 2022
Hochstatter, Rev. Theodore, (PEO) Died: 2022
Hofstetter, Rev. Msgr. Robert J., (KNX) Died: 2022
Honold, Rev. Thomas G., (MIA) Died: 2022
Hoppe, Rev. Lawrence, (GBG) Died: 2022
Horanzy, Rev. Joseph M., (SCR) Died: 2022
Hosinski, Rev. Thomas E., c.s.c. (P) Died: 2022
Huber, Rev. Msgr. Dan, (PBL) Died: 2022
Hudgins, Rev. David W., (LAN) Died: 2022
Hulko, Rev. Joseph D., (ALN) Died: 2022
Hulsman, Rev. Paul E., (IND) Died: 2022
Hurley, Rev. George, (JOL) Died: 2022
Jackson, Rev. Richard W., (CHR) Died: 2022
Jaksina, Rev. Edward S., (HRT) Died: 2022
Jakubauskas, Rev. Richard A., (WOR) Died: 2022
Janeczek, Rev. Vladimir, (GRY) Died: 2022
Janze, Rev. John E., (ORG) Died: 2022
Jeanfreau, Rev. James J., (NO) Died: 2022
Johnson, Rev. Andrew L., (SFR) Died: 2022
Jones, Rev. Robert L, (PBR) Died: 2022
Kabat, Rev. Carl Kenneth, OMI (SAT) Died: 2022
Kain, Rev. Msgr. Peter V., (BRK) Died: 2022
Kappes, Rev. Joseph B., S.J. (DET) Died: 2022
Kapral, Rev. Richard J., (SY) Died: 2022
Karl, Rev. Robert John, (PBR) Died: 2022
Keefe, Rev. Bernard A., (BGP) Died: 2022
Kellerman, Rev. Raymond C., (CIN) Died: 2022
Kelly, Rev. Msgr. Raymond J., (BRK) Died: 2022
Kennelley, Rev. James J., (E) Died: 2022
Kenshol, Rev. Joseph, (GR) Died: 2022
Ketteler, Rev. Msgr. Ronald M., (COV) Died: 2022
Kettron, Rev. W. Michael, (LFT) Died: 2022
Kieltyka, Rev. Robert, (MOB) Died: 2022
Kilianski, Rev. Edward, S.C.J. (MIL) Died: 2022
Killeen, Rev. Msgr. John P., (CC) Died: 2022
King, Rev. Gregory C., (LA) Died: 2022
King, Rev. Thomas F., (LA) Died: 2022
Kirtz, Rev. Raymond R., o.m.i. (BEL) Died: 2022
Kizis, Rev. Kenneth G., (SCR) Died: 2022
Klaers, Rev. Marvin J., (STP) Died: 2022
Klees, Rev. Raymond F., (CHI) Died: 2022
Klemme, Rev. Dennis C., (MIL) Died: 2022
Klimczyk, Rev. Jan, (FTW) Died: 2022
Klingler, Rev. John, S.C.J. (MIL) Died: 2022
Koetter, Rev. Msgr. Paul D., (IND) Died: 2022
Kordas, Rev. Edward J., (CLV) Died: 2022
Kosse, Rev. Theodore C., (CIN) Died: 2022
Kostek, Rev. John S., (NY) Died: 2022
Kramer, Rev. William J., (CIN) Died: 2022
Krawontka, Rev. Stephen A., (SCR) Died: 2022
Krenzke, Rev. John, (DEN) Died: 2022
Krier, Rev. John P., (GF) Died: 2022
Kuczmanski, Rev. Gregory M., (BWN) Died: 2022
Kulik, Msgr. Alexander T., (SCR) Died: 2022
Kunkel, Rev. A. Henry, (BAL) Died: 2022
La Goe, Rev. John P., (GR) Died: 2022
Labita, Rev. Francis J., (BRK) Died: 2022
LaCorte, Rev. Richard, (FAR) Died: 2022
Lacson, Rev. Luis A., (WH) Died: 2022
Lahey, Rev. Piers M., (SFR) Died: 2022
Lamb, Rev. Bruce, O.F.M. Conv. (LA) Died: 2022
Larkin, Rev. Patrick, (WCH) Died: 2022
Lauerman, Rev. James P., (FAR) Died: 2022
Lavin, Rev. John, C.Ss.R. (BAL) Died: 2022
Le Mieux, Rev. Thomas A., (MIL) Died: 2022
Lebar, Rev. Ivan, t.o.r. (ALT) Died: 2022
Lehman, Very Rev. Msgr. Joseph P., (RIC) Died: 2022
Leisen, Rev. Richard, (SCL) Died: 2022
Lewandowski, Rev. Theodore V., (RCK) Died: 2022
Littlefield, Rt. Rev. Philaret, (NTN) Died: 2022
Lively, Rev. Jerome, a.a. (WOR) Died: 2022
Lively, Rev. Joseph A., (BUR) Died: 2022
Lonardo, Rev. Alfred C., (PRO) Died: 2022
Lowe, Rev. Russell P., (CLV) Died: 2022
Loya, Rev. Daniel J, (PBR) Died: 2022
Luca, Rev. Msgr. Joseph L., (BAL) Died: 2022
Lucey, Rev. Beatus T., O.S.B. (PAT) Died: 2022
Lynch, Rev. Kevin A., c.s.p. (NY) Died: 2022
MacGabhann, Rev. Kevin, (PMB) Died: 2022
Madden, Rev. J. Thomas, (SFR) Died: 2022
Magallanes, Rev. Alejandro, O.F.M. Cap. (LA) Died: 2022
Maguire, Rev. Thomas J., (SAC) Died: 2022
Maier, Rev. John, (DM) Died: 2022
Mainardi, Rev. Donald G., (ORL) Died: 2022
Malloy, Rev. William, (CHI) Died: 2022
Marani, Rev. Philip F., O.Carm. (NY) Died: 2022
Marchitelli, Rev. Msgr. Anthony D., (NY) Died: 2022
Marchulones, Rev. Kenneth L., (PEO) Died: 2022
Markalonis, Rev. Joseph, t.o.r. (ALT) Died: 2022
Martinez, Rev. Manuel, (SAT) Died: 2022
Marzetti, Rev. Raul Lopez, (PHX) Died: 2022
Mastrangelo, Rev. Mario, o.f.m. cap. (PCE) Died: 2022
Maty, Rev. Robert J., (BGP) Died: 2022
Maung, Rev. John S., (IND) Died: 2022
Maurer, Rev. Russell J., (PIT) Died: 2022
McAndrew, Rev. Joseph P., (NY) Died: 2022
McCarthy, Rev. Donal, SS.CC. (LA) Died: 2022
McCarthy, Rev. James H., (CHI) Died: 2022
McCauley, Rev. Msgr. James A., (WIN) Died: 2022
McCluskey, Rev. James F., (OM) Died: 2022
McCool, Rev. Patrick, O.S.B. (OKL) Died: 2022
McCormick, Rev. Frank, (HEL) Died: 2022
McCorry, Rev. Msgr. Edward J., (NY) Died: 2022
McDermott, Rev. Michael A., (PIT) Died: 2022
McDonnell, Rev. Kilian, O.S.B. (SCL) Died: 2022
McDonough, Rev. James A., o.p. (AUS) Died: 2022
McDonough, Rev. Patrick M., (WH) Died: 2022
McGinnis, Rev. Jack, (SB) Died: 2022
McGovern, Rev. Mark J., (DUB) Died: 2023
McGraw, Rev. Rene, O.S.B. (SCL) Died: 2022
McKenna, Rev. Philip A., (MOB) Died: 2022
McKernan, Rev. Leo J., (SCR) Died: 2022
McNally, Rev. Stephen, (RIC) Died: 2023
McNamee, Rev. James P., (LC) Died: 2022
Meier, Rev. Msgr. John P., (NY) Died: 2022
Merino, Rev. Santiago James, (LA) Died: 2022
Merkovsky, Rev. Paul W., (PIT) Died: 2022
Messina, Rev. Angelo, (ALX) Died: 2022
Meuret, Rev. Donald L., (LC) Died: 2022
Meyer, Rev. Frederick A., (STL) Died: 2022
Meyers, Rev. Msgr. John F., (DAL) Died: 2022
Micka, Rev. Alphonse, M.I.C. (JOL) Died: 2022
Miele, Rev. Joseph J., (TR) Died: 2022
Mikolajczyk, Rev. Bruno, (CC) Died: 2022
Milewski, Rev. Richard R., (TR) Died: 2022
Miller, Rev. William C., (E) Died: 2022
Milton, Rev. John W., C.S.V. (CHI) Died: 2022
Milton, Rev. Kevin, C.Ss.R. (BAL) Died: 2022
Mock, Rev. Timothy, c.m.m. (DET) Died: 2022
Moeggenberg, Rev. Raymond, (SAG) Died: 2022
Monsour, Rev. Raymond G., (STP) Died: 2022
Montgomery, Rev. Joseph T., (HRT) Died: 2022
Moore, Rev. Augustine J., (SFE) Died: 2022
Moreshead, Rev. Harold D., (PRT) Died: 2022
Mulkerin, Rev. Msgr. Terrence J., (BRK) Died: 2022
Murnane, Rev. Thomas M., O.S.A. (PH) Died: 2022
Murphy, Rev. Kevin P., (ROC) Died: 2022
Murphy, Rev. Patrick L., S.J. (MIL) Died: 2022
Murtagh, Rev. John J., (YAK) Died: 2022
Naumann, Rev. Paul S., S.J. (SY) Died: 2022
Neis, Rev. William P., (LC) Died: 2022
Nelson, Rev. Robert W., (LC) Died: 2022
Ness, Rev. Bernardine, O.S.B. (SCL) Died: 2022
Nguyen, Rev. Dominic Hanh, O.S.B. (DAL) Died: 2022
Nguyen, Rev. Peter, (GAL) Died: 2022
Noesen, Rev. Robert, (JOL) Died: 2022
Novak, Rev. Thomas, S.D.S. (MIL) Died: 2022
O'Brien, Rev. Donald J., (GI) Died: 2022
O'Callaghan, Rev. Tiernan, O.Carm. (PHX) Died: 2022
O'Connor, Rev. John L., (ROC) Died: 2022
O'Connor, Rev. Patrick, M.S.C. (SAT) Died: 2022
O'Kane, Rev. James D., (GI) Died: 2022
O'Keeffe, Rev. Msgr. William J., (LA) Died: 2022
O'Leary, Rev. Malcolm, S.V.D. (JKS) Died: 2022
O'Malley, Rev. John W., S.J. (BAL) Died: 2022
O'Neill, Rev. John J., M.S. (NOR) Died: 2022
O'Neill, Rev. William P., (CLV) Died: 2022
O'Rafferty, Rev. Patrick, (SAC) Died: 2022
Organ, Rev. Patrick C., (VEN) Died: 2022
Osborne, Rev. Thomas L., o.s.a. (JOL) Died: 2022
Paisley, Rev. John C., (DUB) Died: 2022
Pallo, Rev. Joseph L., (LR) Died: 2022
Paluck, Rev. Casimir S., (BIS) Died: 2023
Parenti, Rev. Thomas M., (SFR) Died: 2022
Park, Rev. Thomas R., (SEA) Died: 2022
Parrinello, Rev. Frank P., (OM) Died: 2023
Parrotta, Rev. Michael, (FAR) Died: 2022
Patrick, Rev. Michael, (P) Died: 2022

Pentony, Rev. Liam Francis, (JKS) Died: 2023
Pershe, Rev. Joseph N., S.J. (MIL) Died: 2022
Peterson, Rev. Eric, (MEM) Died: 2022
Petro, Archpriest John George, (PBR) Died: 2022
Phan, Rev. Paul-Cuong, (SJ) Died: 2022
Phelps, Rev. Lawrence J., O.S.B. (NO) Died: 2022
Philbin, Rev. Patrick B., s.m. (ORG) Died: 2022
Pleban, Rev. Leo, (Y) Died: 2022
Poff, Rev. Pius, O.F.M.Conv. (IND) Died: 2022
Porter, Rev. Msgr. John F., (GLD) Died: 2022
Pouliot, Rev. Francis A., (STP) Died: 2022
Preisinger, Rev. Robert F., (OM) Died: 2022
Pugat, Rev. Gaudencio G., (RIC) Died: 2022
Putrimas, Rev. Msgr. Edmond, (LIT) Died: 2022
Quigley, Rev. Joseph P., (BRK) Died: 2022
Quinn, Rev. Thomas J., S.J. (PBL) Died: 2022
Rable, Rev. Cyril J., (SCR) Died: 2022
Rahoy, Rev. Nicholas P., (CI) Died: 2022
Rascher, Rev. Joseph C., (BEL) Died: 2022
Rasquinha, Rev. G. Ignatius, (SB) Died: 2022
Rausch, Rev. John W., (MIL) Died: 2022
Ravey, Rev. Donald J., (BUR) Died: 2022
Recchuti, Rev. William, O.S.A. (PH) Died: 2022
Rehkemper, Rev. Msgr. Robert C., (DAL) Died: 2022
Reichert, Rev. James, O.S.B. (SCL) Died: 2022
Reid, Rev. David, (FR) Died: 2022
Repenshek, Rev. Jerome V., (MIL) Died: 2022
Rewtiuk, Rev. Msgr. Mitred Michael, (SJP) Died: 2022
Reymann, Rev. James J., (CLV) Died: 2022
Rhyner, Rev. Robert E., (GB) Died: 2022
Richey, Rev. Msgr. Terrence, (LA) Died: 2022
Riehl, Rev. Christopher M., (KNX) Died: 2022
Rightor, Rev. Harold W., (IND) Died: 2022
Riley, Rev. George F., O.S.A. (PH) Died: 2022
Ring, Rev. Vincent D., (SFR) Died: 2022
Rink, Rev. George, (SEA) Died: 2022
Ripperger, Rev. William, (IND) Died: 2022
Ritchie, Rev. Msgr. Gerald T., (E) Died: 2022
Rivard, Rev. Msgr. Roland J., (BUR) Died: 2023
Rock, Rev. William J., O.P. (Y) Died: 2022
Rodney, Rev. Joseph C., s.s.j. (BAL) Died: 2022
Rodrigues, Rev. Urbano, (NY) Died: 2022
Rodriguez, Rev. Msgr. Benigno Antonio, (LA) Died: 2022
Rolfs, Rev. Richard W., S.J. (LA) Died: 2022
Roll, Rev. Robert J., (CHI) Died: 2022
Rooney, Rev. Robert B., (GI) Died: 2022
Ross, Rev. Richard, (JOL) Died: 2022
Ruppert, Rev. Donald R., (VIC) Died: 2022
Russo, Rev. Francis X., o.f.m. cap. (WDC) Died: 2022
Ruther, Rev. William E., (LA) Died: 2022
Sabio, Rev. Msgr. Raymundo T., m.s.c. (MI) Died: 2022
Saglio, Rev. Charles A., (RIC) Died: 2022
Sakowski, Rev. John J., (SFR) Died: 2022
Sans, Rev. Pablo, (BRK) Died: 2022
Sarauskas, Rev. Msgr. George, (CHI) Died: 2022
Savundra, Rev. Edwin, (STP) Died: 2023
Sayuk, Rev. Msgr. Mitred Thomas A., (SJP) Died: 2022
Scanlan, Rev. Francis G., (CHI) Died: 2022
Scaramuzzo, Rev. Peter C., (NY) Died: 2022
Scaravelli, Rev. Volmar, C.S. (NY) Died: 2022
Schifano, Rev. James, S.C.J (MIL) Died: 2022
Schiltz, Rev. Roger J., (WIN) Died: 2022
Schlaver, Rev. David E, c.s.c. (FTW) Died: 2022
Schleicher, Rev. Edward R., (PIT) Died: 2022
Schlitt, Rev. Msgr. Harry G., (SFR) Died: 2022
Schmidt, Rev. Henry, (SFD) Died: 2022
Schmitt, Rev. Silverius, (SCL) Died: 2022
Schoemann, Rev. Robert L., (DM) Died: 2022
Schubeck, Rev. Thomas, (DET) Died: 2022
Schwartz, Rev. Hugh F., (OM) Died: 2023
Scott, Rev. Philip P., (PSC) Died: 2022
Scotto, Rev. Dominic, t.o.r. (ALT) Died: 2022
Scully, Rev. John J., (TR) Died: 2022
Sedlock, Rev. Stephen J., c.s.c. (PHX) Died: 2022
Semko, Rev. Edward, (PSC) Died: 2022
Senghas, Rev. Richard E., (PRT) Died: 2022
Senior, Rev. Donald P., C.P. (CHI) Died: 2022
Serrick, Rev. James K., S.J. (DET) Died: 2022
Shelley, Rev. Msgr. Thomas J., (NY) Died: 2022
Sherman, Rev. Edward, (FAR) Died: 2022
Sidoti, Rev. James R., O.Carm. (ALB) Died: 2022
Siebenaler, Rev. Leonard, (STP) Died: 2023
Sirolli, Rev. Francis A., O.S.A. (PH) Died: 2022
Skehan, Rev. John R., (PRT) Died: 2022
Smith, Rev. David, (MIA) Died: 2022
Smith, Rev. David W., (STP) Died: 2022
Smith, Rev. Francis, (ORL) Died: 2022
Smith, Rev. Roger J., (SEA) Died: 2022
Somers, Rev. Michael, (GB) Died: 2022
Souffrant, Rev. Claude, S.J. (DET) Died: 2022
Sperry, Rev. Scott M., (PHX) Died: 2022
Spexarth, Rev. Joachim, O.S.B. (OKL) Died: 2022
Stack, Rev. John P., O.S.A. (PH) Died: 2022
Stakem, Rev. Gary, o.f.m. cap. (PIT) Died: 2022
Stanis, Rev. Casimir M., (SCR) Died: 2022
Stankus, Rev. Gregory A., (BRK) Died: 2022
Stanley, Rev. Michael, O.S.A. (ALB) Died: 2022
Statt, Rev. Thomas R., (ROC) Died: 2022
Steffener, Rev. Gerard, IVDEI (BAL) Died: 2022
Stephenson, Rev. Patrick, (SR) Died: 2022
Stewart, Rev. Michael L., (MEM) Died: 2022
Stiefvater, Rev. Robert X., (MIL) Died: 2022
Straub, Rev. David R., (CHI) Died: 2022
Sullivan, Rev. Daniel Jeremiah, (HRT) Died: 2022
Sullivan, Rev. Michael P., (MIA) Died: 2022
Suntum, Rev. James, S.F. (SFE) Died: 2022
Suquilvide, Rev. Abel, (LA) Died: 2022
Susa, Rev. Robert P., (E) Died: 2022
Susann, Rev. Robert F., M.S. (ORL) Died: 2023
Tate, Rev. Joseph H., c.s.c. (FTW) Died: 2022
Telthorst, Rev. Msgr. James T., (STL) Died: 2022
Tewes, Rev. Msgr. Thomas J., (BAL) Died: 2022
Thanh Dinh, Rev. Isidore M. Bac, crm (SPC) Died: 2022
Theriault, Rev. H., (NY) Died: 2022
Thibeau, Rev. Richard, S.V.D. (CHI) Died: 2022
Thinnes, Rev. John M., (CHI) Died: 2022
Tietjen, Rev. Kenneth F., o.c.s.o. (DUB) Died: 2022
Tinney, Rev. Richard W., (BUR) Died: 2022
Tito, Rev. Rocco A., (E) Died: 2022
Tomich, Rev. Daniel M., (CHI) Died: 2022
Torres, Rev. Frank D., (GRY) Died: 2022
Tran, Rev. Joseph, (LAN) Died: 2022
Travis, Rev. Leo J., c.ss.r. (CHI) Died: 2022
Treacy, Rev. William, (SEA) Died: 2022
Trinkle, Rev. Clarence M., (ARL) Died: 2022
Twiggs, Rev. Matthew J., (PAT) Died: 2022
Uhler, Rev. Carl A., (CLV) Died: 2022
Urdiain, Rev. Angelo, C.R. (DEN) Died: 2022
Uvietta, Rev. Joseph, S.M. (SAT) Died: 2022
Valente, Rev. Michael, (JOL) Died: 2022
Valla, Rev. Dominic J., (HRT) Died: 2023
Varga, Rev. Msgr. Andrew G., (BGP) Died: 2022
Vesbit, Rev. Thomas, (GR) Died: 2022
Vesely, Rev. James J., (CLV) Died: 2022
Victoria, Rev. Robert, (LA) Died: 2022
Villanueva, Rev. Felix Oliveras, (CGS) Died: 2022
Vrana, Rev. John G., (CLV) Died: 2022
Wagner, Rev. Edward, o.ss.t. (BAL) Died: 2022
Walker, Rev. Gerald Bernard, (LA) Died: 2022
Wallace, Rev. Msgr. Francis T., (LA) Died: 2022
Wallen, Rev. Charles L., c.s.c. (FTW) Died: 2022
Walsh, Rev. Richard (Denis) L, (TYL) Died: 2023
Wang, Rev. Peter, (STP) Died: 2022
Warner, Rev. Richard V., c.s.c. (FTW) Died: 2022
Wawrzyniakowski, Rev. Edward J., (MIL) Died: 2022
Weber, Rev. Fidelis, t.o.r. (ALT) Died: 2022
Wechter, Rev. David, o.c.s.o. (DUB) Died: 2022
Wegher, Rev. William, (LAN) Died: 2022
Wehrlen, Rev. Msgr. John B., (PAT) Died: 2022
Weisensel, Rev. Cyril O., (MAD) Died: 2022
Wester, Rev. Charles H., (MIL) Died: 2022
Wetovick, Rev. Jerry P., (GI) Died: 2022
Wharff, Rev. Jonah, O.C.S.O. (DUB) Died: 2022
White, Rev. James D., (TLS) Died: 2022
Williamson, Rev. Christopher, (ATL) Died: 2022
Wolf, Rev. George C., (RNO) Died: 2022
Wolfe, Rev. William P., (LA) Died: 2022
Woodhall, Rev. Jonathan A., (R) Died: 2022
Yagesh, Rev. Richard C., (PIT) Died: 2022
Yakubich, Rev. Vasyl, (PBR) Died: 2022
Young, Rev. Otis W., (NO) Died: 2022
Zaccagnigno, Rev. Raffaele, (BRK) Died: 2022
Zaccarelli, Rev. Herman F., c.s.c. (FTW) Died: 2022
Zahn, Rev. George E., (RIC) Died: 2022
Zak, Rev. Stanislaw, (OAK) Died: 2023
Zampino, Rev. David, (MIL) Died: 2022
Zientek, Rev. Msgr. Boleslaus John, (AUS) Died: 2022
Zimmerman, Rev. David M., (GB) Died: 2022

Catholic Dioceses in the United States

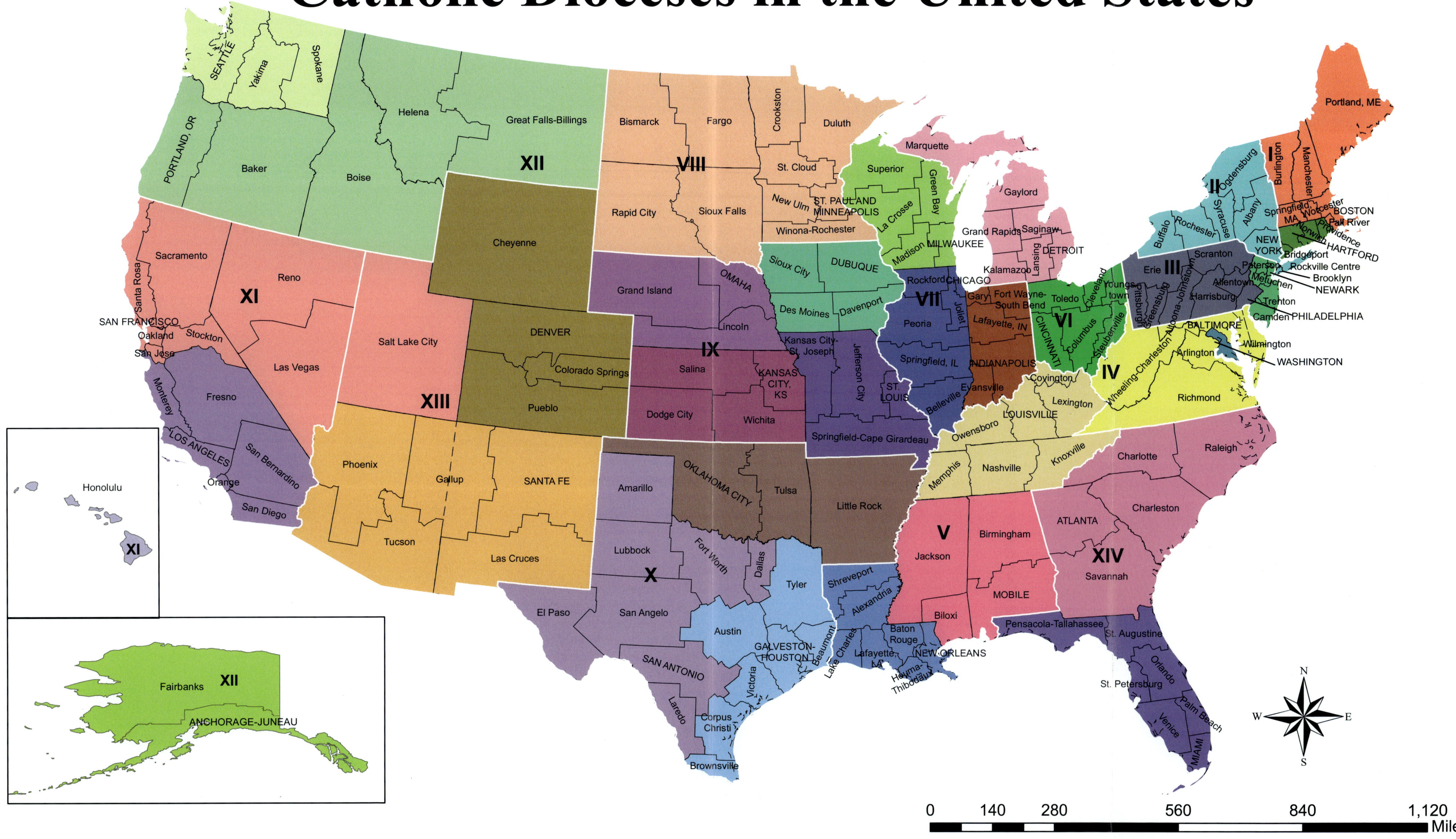

2300 Wisconsin Ave NW Suite 400A
Washington, DC 20007
cara.georgetown.edu

This map shows boundaries of the Latin Rite dioceses whose bishops belong to the United States Conference of Catholic Bishops (USCCB). Archdioceses are indicated by capital letters and Ecclesiastical Provinces are grouped by color. USCCB regions are shown within white lines and indicated by Roman numerals. Dashed lines show where dioceses cross state lines. This map does not show the Diocese of St. Thomas in the U.S. Virgin Islands, which is part of the Ecclesiastical Province of Washington, or the Archdiocese for the Military Services.

The Official Catholic Directory®

Products and Services Guide

Index to Advertisers

AUDIO & VIDEO—General

Cassettes, Audio & Video

HOLY CROSS
FAMILY MINISTRIES

Holy Cross Family Ministries
Family Rosary
Family Theater Productions
Father Peyton Family Institute
Catholic Mom
Museum of Family Prayer
518 Washington Street
North Easton, MA 02356
Tel: 508-238-4095
Fax: 508-238-3953
Website: www.hcfm.org

Type of Business:

Continuing the mission of our founder, Venerable Patrick Peyton. Holy Cross Family Ministries serves Jesus Christ and His Church throughout the world by promoting and supporting the spiritual well-being of the family through products, programs, events and media.

Personnel:

Father Fred Jenga, C.S.C. (President)
Father Pinto Paul, C.S.C. (International Director – HCFM)
Thomas Lyman (Director – Family Rosary USA)
Father David Guffey, C.S.C. (National Director – Family Theater Productions)
Susan Wallace (Chief Marketing & Communications Officer)

BUSINESS & FINANCE—General

United States Conference of Catholic Bishops
Office of National Collections
3211 Fourth Street, N.E.
Washington, DC 20017
Tel: 202-541-3000
Website: www.usccb.org/nationalcollections

Type of Business:

The national collections administered by the United States Conference of Catholic Bishops (USCCB) have been established by either the Holy Father or the bishops of the United States. The national collections support the Church's works of social justice, evangelization, and education, both domestically and around the globe.
Every Catholic participates in a global community of faith by contributing and acting as faithful stewards of the gifts God has given them. The national collections of the USCCB are a powerful way to express your solidarity with this community.

Computers & Software

Church Budget Envelope & Mailing Company
271 South Ellsworth Avenue
Salem, OH 44460
Tel: 800-446-9780; 877-393-3330 (myEoffering)
Fax: 330-337-5990
E-mail: info@churchbudget.com; info@myEoffering.com
Website: www.churchbudget.com; www.myEoffering.com

Type of Business:

Church Budget Envelope Company (CBE) is a premier offertory solutions provider specializing in full-color offertory envelopes, direct mail services and a complete line of electronic services. CBE has a proven history of impacting churches nationwide by increasing mass attendance, increasing offertory giving and reducing envelope costs by up to 40%. Founded in 1917, CBE is a 4th generation family-owned business headquartered in Salem, OH.

Offertory Products include:

Annual Boxed Sets, Periodic Mail Services, Mailback Return Booklets, Prestige Series Holy Day Envelopes, Children Collection Envelopes, Diocesan Mailing Services, Full Color Print Capability, Electronic Giving Services, Parish Growth Software, NCOA Services, 24/7 Emergency Customer Service

Office Equipment & Supplies

Institutional Commodity Services Corp. (ICS)
The Catholic Center
1011 First Avenue, 16th Floor
New York, NY 10022
Tel: 646-794-2600
E-mail: icsap@nyics.org
Website: www.nyics.org

Type of Business:

ICS is the recognized central purchasing agency for parishes, schools and Catholic institutions in the New York tri-state area. We help religious institutions save time and money by procuring for them quality products and services at extremely competitive prices; we also ensure timely delivery, provide outstanding customer service, and offer a full one-stop shop solution for both liturgical and non-liturgical products. We represent a vast array of products, including: clergy attire, altar bread, candles, chalices, liturgical publications, office furniture and supplies, appliances, electronics, maintenance/janitorial products and equipment. In addition, we have a copier lease program, can procure (school and coach) bus charters, and offer printing services – the list of products and services we represent is endless. ICS primarily serves the Arch/dioceses of New York, Newark, Albany, Bridgeport, Brooklyn and Camden, but welcome inquiries from all Catholic institutions.

CHURCH ART–General

Botti Studio of Architectural Arts, Inc.
2930 Central Street
Evanston, IL 60201
Tel: 800-524-7211; 847-869-5933; Fax: 847-869-5996
E-mail: botti@bottistudio.com
Website: www.bottistudio.com

Type of Business:

Since 1864, Botti Studio has specialized in serving the ecclesiastic environment through design, fabrication, delivery, and installation. Experts on staff in new design commissions, repair, restoration, conservation, and repair provide a source for experienced project management – from conception through completion. Services include: stained, faceted, sandblasted, carved and painted glass, wood / metal / stone frames / protective glazing, murals, marble, mosaics, bronze, statuary, gilding, painting and decorating, complete interiors, new and restorations, historic discovery, documentation and consultation to owner / architect.

Our staff of 45 includes internationally recognized ecclesiastic artists / designers working in conjunction with highly skilled craftspeople / artisans / conservators.

Locations: New York, NY / (212) 362-6085, LaPorte, IN / (219) 362-5934, Chicago, IL / (847) 869-5933, San Diego, CA / (760) 753-0705, Sarasota, FL / (941) 951-0978, Agropoli, Italy / (800) 524-7211.

Personnel:

Ettore Christopher Botti (President, Botti Studio of Architectural Arts Inc. est. 1864)
Megan Brady (Principal)

CONRAD SCHMITT STUDIOS, INC.
Excellence in Artistry Since 1889

Conrad Schmitt Studios, Inc. (CSS)
2405 S. 162nd Street
New Berlin, WI 53151
Tel: 800-969-3033; 262-786-3030; Fax: 262-786-9036
E-mail: studio@conradschmitt.com
Website: www.conradschmitt.com

Type of Business:

For over 130 years, CSS has advanced a tradition of excellence in artistry and craftsmanship. Studio artisans do more than paint walls or assemble windows – they create inspirational environments and enduring works of art. Our comprehensive scope of services allows us to be a single source for a variety of needs, creating the best projects in terms of function, longevity and aesthetics.

Decorative Painting/Restoration – Our experienced staff assists projects in the early stages to help assemble the master plan, communicate the vision and generate the enthusiasm/funding needed to make the plan a reality. Tools used to accomplish these goals include renderings, on-site samples, budgetary estimates and fundraising materials. Services include investigation/documentation of decorative schemes, gilding, glazing, marbleizing, stenciling, trompe l'oeil and faux finishing.

Stained Glass/Architectural Art Glass – Original stained-glass windows are created in a variety of styles by experienced artists/craftspeople. From the first idea to final installation, the best of traditional craft and new technology are combined to offer unparalleled quality in new design. CSS artisans also conserve/restore thousands of square feet of stained glass each year. Services include thematic development, design, cartoons, glass selection, sample panel, fabrication/installation, framing, storm glass and fundraising.

Gaspard, Inc.
200 N. Janacek Road
Brookfield, WI 53045
Tel: 800-784-6868 (toll free)
Fax: 800-784-7567
E-mail: customerservice@gaspardinc.com
Website: www.gaspardinc.com

Type of Business:

Experience the Gaspard Difference. For more than six decades customers have looked to Gaspard for their superb quality in handcrafted vestments and paraments that are made in the USA. Offerings include the exquisite Castle Craft® collection; wardrobe essentials such as albs, surplices, cassocks, robes, and clergy shirts; extensive metalware offerings, fair linens, altar accessories, and communion ware. Because your vestment and parament selections are made to order in our one and only location in Brookfield, Wisconsin, special sizes and custom designs are not a problem. One of our friendly Customer Service Representatives will be happy to help you find just the right size and style to enhance your spiritual expression. Please visit GASPARDINC.COM or call us to speak with one of our friendly and knowledgeable Customer Service Representatives to discover what GASPARD can do for you.

Personnel:

Jason R. Gaspard (President)

PSG Vestments
Plot No: 152 & 153 Gangaparameshwari Nagar, PhaseII
Tuticorin, TN, India 628002
Tel: 802-255-2045
E-mail: sale@psgvestments.com
Website: www.psgvestments.com

Type of Business:

PSG your source for quality made to measure vestments. Garments crafted in India to provide world-class production service and quality at an affordable price. We offer modern interpretations of traditional designs.

We offer Cassocks, Cloaks, Chasubles: Gothic, Semi Gothic, Roman styles, Boromean and Pugin. We create exceptional surplices in an English style as well as traditional lace trimmed models. We celebrate copes with Gothic and Roman styles. We can also create Greek and Roman Orthodox Vestments.

Our aim is to have what you need or can dream of available for your worship. We weave our own fabric and create designs on state-of-the-art embroidery machines. This ensures your made-to-measure vestments and paraments, antipendia and more are no problem. At our newly constructed campus and production hub, one of our knowledgeable customer care staff can assist you with your size needs and special design requests.

Please visit us online or call for a catalog.

Personnel:

Suhand Barnabas (Managing Director)

RAMBUSCH

Rambusch
160 Cornelison Avenue
Jersey City, NJ 07304
Tel: 201-333-2525
E-mail: info@rambusch.com
Website: www.rambusch.com

Type of Business:

For 123 years, Rambusch has excelled in the fields of lighting, church furnishings, stained glass, mosaics, and individual works of art. Our in-house design group provides the same attention to detail to all commissions, be it new work, renovations, or interior restorations. Our in-house lighting art-metal and stained glass workshops are under the direct supervision of a Rambusch family member.

Lighting: Rambusch custom-engineered lighting systems are the industry standard for church lighting. Utilizing LED technology and other sources, Rambusch designs and fabricates standard and custom lighting fixtures in keeping with the architectural style and requirements of the space.

Church Furnishings: In response to the voice of the parish community and the building, Rambusch designs and creates furnishings to serve all liturgical needs in nearly every medium and for all budgets.

Stained Glass: Rambusch creates and executes new traditional or contemporary designs and restores and conserves treasured older windows. On time and within budget.

Mosaic: Rambusch handles the logistics to produce small, and large-scale mosaic installation. We plan, design and cartoon in our facility. Fabrication, sectioning and projection are performed under our close supervision in Italy, or in other studios nearby.

Personnel:

Viggo B.A. Rambusch (Third Generation)
Edwin P. Rambusch (Fourth Generation)
Martin V. Rambusch (Fourth Generation)

Art, Statuary & Decorations

CONRAD SCHMITT STUDIOS, INC.
Excellence in Artistry Since 1889

Conrad Schmitt Studios, Inc. (CSS)
2405 S. 162nd Street
New Berlin, WI 53151
Tel: 800-969-3033; 262-786-3030; Fax: 262-786-9036
E-mail: studio@conradschmitt.com
Website: www.conradschmitt.com

Type of Business:

For over 130 years, CSS has advanced a tradition of excellence in artistry and craftsmanship. Studio artisans do more than paint walls or assemble windows – they create inspirational environments and enduring works of art. Our comprehensive scope of services allows us to be a single source for a variety of needs, creating the best projects in terms of function, longevity and aesthetics.

Decorative Painting/Restoration – Our experienced staff assists projects in the early stages to help assemble the master plan, communicate the vision and generate the enthusiasm/funding needed to make the plan a reality. Tools used to accomplish these goals include renderings, on-site samples, budgetary estimates and fundraising materials. Services include investigation/documentation of decorative schemes, gilding, glazing, marbleizing, stenciling, trompe l'oeil and faux finishing.

Stained Glass/Architectural Art Glass – Original stained-glass windows are created in a variety of styles by experienced artists/craftspeople. From the first idea to final installation, the best of traditional craft and new technology are combined to offer unparalleled quality in new design. CSS artisans also conserve/restore thousands of square feet of stained glass each year. Services include thematic development, design, cartoons, glass selection, sample panel, fabrication/installation, framing, storm glass and fundraising.

Gold Leafing & Painted Murals

ChurchWindowFilm.com/Bell Stained Glass
2016 Airport Boulevard
Mobile, AL 36606
Tel: 1-800-291-3739; Fax: 1-251-473-6865
E-mail: lewis@churchwindowfilm.com
Website: www.ChurchWindowFilm.com

Type of Business:

The look of priceless stained glass is here for a fraction of the cost. Our film is guaranteed for ***TEN*** years. Since 1989 our company Bell Stained Glass saw the need to offer magnificent stained glass art to churches for a reasonable price. Also, our designs are made to apply to your own glass. It's a low-cost substitute for a stained glass look that will add beauty to your sanctuary. In traditional Catholic, modern, and orthodox designs. It's easily installed by most anyone. See our short installation video or have someone professionally install it for you! Across America, ChurchWindowFilm has been the answer. This is peerless quality that you must see for yourself. Call for a sample. Our artists also produce custom designed Murals and Medallions of religious saints and scenes to enhance your church, school, or chapel.

- **A fraction of the cost of stained glass but looks the same**
- **Church's all over America enjoy our film**
- **10-Year Guarantee - Save carpets and pews from sun damage**
- **Custom sized ... made to your needs, Saints, emblems.**
- **Samples available ... colors to your taste**

CONRAD SCHMITT STUDIOS, INC.
Excellence in Artistry Since 1889

Conrad Schmitt Studios, Inc. (CSS)
2405 S. 162nd Street
New Berlin, WI 53151
Tel: 800-969-3033; 262-786-3030
Fax: 262-786-9036
E-mail: studio@conradschmitt.com
Website: www.conradschmitt.com

Type of Business:

For over 130 years, CSS has advanced a tradition of excellence in artistry and craftsmanship. Studio artisans do more than paint walls or assemble windows – they create inspirational environments and enduring works of art. Our comprehensive scope of services allows us to be a single source for a variety of needs, creating the best projects in terms of function, longevity and aesthetics.

Decorative Painting/Restoration – Our experienced staff assists projects in the early stages to help assemble the master plan, communicate the vision and generate the enthusiasm/funding needed to make the plan a reality. Tools used to accomplish these goals include renderings, on-site samples, budgetary estimates and fundraising materials. Services include investigation/documentation of decorative schemes, gilding, glazing, marbleizing, stenciling, trompe l'oeil and faux finishing.

Stained Glass/Architectural Art Glass – Original stained-glass windows are created in a variety of styles by experienced artists/craftspeople. From the first idea to final installation, the best of traditional craft and new technology are combined to offer unparalleled quality in new design. CSS artisans also conserve/restore thousands of square feet of stained glass each year. Services include thematic development, design, cartoons, glass selection, sample panel, fabrication/installation, framing, storm glass and fundraising.

Mosaics

Baker Liturgical Art, LLC
1210 Meriden Waterbury Road
Plantsville, CT 06479
Tel: 860-621-7471
Fax: 860-621-7607
E-mail: info@bakerart.net
Website: www.bakerliturgicalart.com

Type of Business:

Baker Liturgical Art, LLC offers a full range of construction and renovation services. These services encompass architectural specifications and liturgical design as well as sound system and lighting design.

Our liturgical design talents result in beautiful altar furnishings of hand-carved wood or of fine imported Italian marble. Stained glass and sacred artwork (painted, wood-carved or chiseled from marble) are the final accents to complete prayerful settings in every worship space from the smallest Chapel to the grandest Cathedral! Baker Liturgical Art, LLC prides itself in offering uncompromising quality in its products and services.

Our Services Include: Liturgical Design, Architectural Services, Liturgical Furnishings, Sculpture & Artwork, Flooring, Millwork, Multi-Media Systems, Stained Glass Fabrication & Restoration, Historical Painting & Decorating.

Additional location: 9427 S. Ocean Drive, Jensen Beach, FL 34957. Tel: 860-919-2119.

Personnel:

Brian T. Baker (President)

FRANZ MAYER OF MUNICH est. 1847
Stained Glass, Architectural Art Glass and Mosaic

Mayer of Munich
Mayer´sche Hofkunstanstalt GmbH
Seidlstrasse 25
80335 Munich, Germany
E-mail: m.mayer@mayer-of-munich.com
Website: www.mayer-of-munich.com

Type of Business:

Founded in 1847, Franz Mayer of Munich remains a family business in fifth generation, specializing in the development and production of international projects, spanning traditional to avantgarde artworks and techniques.

Around the turn of the 19th Century, the two sister companies Franz Mayer of Munich and F.X.Zettler belonged to the worldwide renown and appreciated stained glass studios. They produced stained glass windows of finest quality for more than 50 cathedrals and thousands of churches in America. Until today "Munich Style" and "Mayer Style" are synonymous for unique quality.

The Mayer studio is obliged to its tradition and heritage: in style, qualities and values. The crew of artists, glass painters and master craftsmen, take all efforts to meet the high standards, details and transparency of the traditional windows.

The "Munich Style" made Franz Mayer of Munich remain as one of the international leading studios for stained glass, architectural glass and mosaic.

RAMBUSCH

Rambusch
160 Cornelison Avenue, Jersey City, NJ 07304
Tel: 201-333-2525
E-mail: info@rambusch.com; Website: www.rambusch.com

Type of Business:

For 123 years, Rambusch has excelled in the fields of lighting, church furnishings, stained glass, mosaics, and individual works of art. Our in-house design group provides the same attention to detail to all commissions, be it new work, renovations, or interior restorations. Our in-house lighting art-metal and stained glass workshops are under the direct supervision of a Rambusch family member.

Lighting: Rambusch custom-engineered lighting systems are the industry standard for church lighting. Utilizing LED technology and other sources, Rambusch designs and fabricates standard and custom lighting fixtures in keeping with the architectural style and requirements of the space.

Church Furnishings: In response to the voice of the parish community and the building, Rambusch designs and creates furnishings to serve all liturgical needs in nearly every medium and for all budgets.

Stained Glass: Rambusch creates and executes new traditional or contemporary designs and restores and conserves treasured older windows. On time and within budget.

Mosaic: Rambusch handles the logistics to produce small, and large-scale mosaic installation. We plan, design and cartoon in our facility. Fabrication, sectioning and projection are performed under our close supervision in Italy, or in other studios nearby.

Personnel:

Viggo B.A. Rambusch (Third Generation)
Edwin P. Rambusch (Fourth Generation)
Martin V. Rambusch (Fourth Generation)

Sculpture

RAMBUSCH

Rambusch
160 Cornelison Avenue, Jersey City, NJ 07304
Tel: 201-333-2525
E-mail: info@rambusch.com; Website: www.rambusch.com

Type of Business:

For 123 years, Rambusch has excelled in the fields of lighting, church furnishings, stained glass, mosaics, and individual works of art. Our in-house design group provides the same attention to detail to all commissions, be it new work, renovations, or interior restorations. Our in-house lighting art-metal and stained glass workshops are under the direct supervision of a Rambusch family member.

Lighting: Rambusch custom-engineered lighting systems are the industry standard for church lighting. Utilizing LED technology and other sources, Rambusch designs and fabricates standard and custom lighting fixtures in keeping with the architectural style and requirements of the space.

Church Furnishings: In response to the voice of the parish community and the building, Rambusch designs and creates furnishings to serve all liturgical needs in nearly every medium and for all budgets.

Stained Glass: Rambusch creates and executes new traditional or contemporary designs and restores and conserves treasured older windows. On time and within budget.

Mosaic: Rambusch handles the logistics to produce small, and large-scale mosaic installation. We plan, design and cartoon in our facility. Fabrication, sectioning and projection are performed under our close supervision in Italy, or in other studios nearby.

Personnel:

Viggo B.A. Rambusch (Third Generation)
Edwin P. Rambusch (Fourth Generation)
Martin V. Rambusch (Fourth Generation)

CHURCH FURNISHINGS—General

Baker Liturgical Art, LLC
1210 Meriden Waterbury Road
Plantsville, CT 06479
Tel: 860-621-7471; Fax: 860-621-7607
E-mail: info@bakerart.net
Website: www.bakerliturgicalart.com

Type of Business:

Baker Liturgical Art, LLC offers a full range of construction and renovation services. These services encompass architectural specifications and liturgical design as well as sound system and lighting design.

Our liturgical design talents result in beautiful altar furnishings of hand-carved wood or of fine imported Italian marble. Stained glass and sacred artwork (painted, wood-carved or chiseled from marble) are the final accents to complete prayerful settings in every worship space from the smallest Chapel to the grandest Cathedral! Baker Liturgical Art, LLC prides itself in offering uncompromising quality in its products and services.

Our Services Include: Liturgical Design, Architectural Services, Liturgical Furnishings, Sculpture & Artwork, Flooring, Millwork, Multi-Media Systems, Stained Glass Fabrication & Restoration, Historical Painting & Decorating.

Additional location: 9427 S. Ocean Drive, Jensen Beach, FL 34957. Tel: 860-919-2119.

Personnel:

Brian T. Baker (President)

Institutional Commodity Services Corp. (ICS)
The Catholic Center
1011 First Avenue, 16th Floor
New York, NY 10022
Tel: 646-794-2600
E-mail: icsap@nyics.org
Website: www.nyics.org

Type of Business:

ICS is the recognized central purchasing agency for parishes, schools and Catholic institutions in the New York tri-state area. We help religious institutions save time and money by procuring for them quality products and services at extremely competitive prices; we also ensure timely delivery, provide outstanding customer service, and offer a full one-stop shop solution for both liturgical and non-liturgical products. We represent a vast array of products, including: clergy attire, altar bread, candles, chalices, liturgical publications, office furniture and supplies, appliances, electronics, maintenance/janitorial products and equipment. In addition, we have a copier lease program, can procure (school and coach) bus charters, and offer printing services – the list of products and services we represent is endless. ICS primarily serves the Arch/dioceses of New York, Newark, Albany, Bridgeport, Brooklyn and Camden, but welcome inquiries from all Catholic institutions.

PSG Vestments
Plot No: 152 & 153 Gangaparameshwari Nagar, Phasell
Tuticorin, TN, India 628002
Tel: 802-255-2045
E-mail: sale@psgvestments.com
Website: www.psgvestments.com

Type of Business:

PSG your source for quality made to measure vestments. Garments crafted in India to provide world-class production service and quality at an affordable price. We offer modern interpretations of traditional designs.

We offer Cassocks, Cloaks, Chasubles: Gothic, Semi Gothic, Roman styles, Boromean and Pugin. We create exceptional surplices in an English style as well as traditional lace trimmed models. We celebrate copes with Gothic and Roman styles. We can also create Greek and Roman Orthodox Vestments.

Our aim is to have what you need or can dream of available for your worship. We weave our own fabric and create designs on state-of-the-art embroidery machines. This ensures your made-to-measure vestments and paraments, antipendia and more are no problem. At our newly constructed campus and production hub, one of our knowledgeable customer care staff can assist you with your size needs and special design requests.

Please visit us online or call for a catalog.

Personnel:

Suhand Barnabas (Managing Director)

RAMBUSCH

Rambusch
160 Cornelison Avenue
Jersey City, NJ 07304
Tel: 201-333-2525
E-mail: info@rambusch.com
Website: www.rambusch.com

Type of Business:

For 123 years, Rambusch has excelled in the fields of lighting, church furnishings, stained glass, mosaics, and individual works of art. Our in-house design group provides the same attention to detail to all commissions, be it new work, renovations, or interior restorations. Our in-house lighting art-metal and stained glass workshops are under the direct supervision of a Rambusch family member.

Lighting: Rambusch custom-engineered lighting systems are the industry standard for church lighting. Utilizing LED technology and other sources, Rambusch designs and fabricates standard and custom lighting fixtures in keeping with the architectural style and requirements of the space.

Church Furnishings: In response to the voice of the parish community and the building, Rambusch designs and creates furnishings to serve all liturgical needs in nearly every medium and for all budgets.

Stained Glass: Rambusch creates and executes new traditional or contemporary designs and restores and conserves treasured older windows. On time and within budget.

Mosaic: Rambusch handles the logistics to produce small, and large-scale mosaic installation. We plan, design and cartoon in our facility. Fabrication, sectioning and projection are performed under our close supervision in Italy, or in other studios nearby.

Personnel:

Viggo B.A. Rambusch (Third Generation)
Edwin P. Rambusch (Fourth Generation)
Martin V. Rambusch (Fourth Generation)

Altars, Tabernacles, etc.

Institutional Commodity Services Corp. (ICS)
The Catholic Center
1011 First Avenue, 16th Floor
New York, NY 10022
Tel: 646-794-2600
E-mail: icsap@nyics.org
Website: www.nyics.org

Type of Business:

ICS is the recognized central purchasing agency for parishes, schools and Catholic institutions in the New York tri-state area. We help religious institutions save time and money by procuring for them quality products and services at extremely competitive prices; we also ensure timely delivery, provide outstanding customer service, and offer a full one-stop shop solution for both liturgical and non-liturgical products. We represent a vast array of products, including: clergy attire, altar bread, candles, chalices, liturgical publications, office furniture and supplies, appliances, electronics, maintenance/janitorial products and equipment. In addition, we have a copier lease program, can procure (school and coach) bus charters, and offer printing services – the list of products and services we represent is endless. ICS primarily serves the Arch/dioceses of New York, Newark, Albany, Bridgeport, Brooklyn and Camden, but welcome inquiries from all Catholic institutions.

RAMBUSCH

Rambusch
160 Cornelison Avenue
Jersey City, NJ 07304
Tel: 201-333-2525
E-mail: info@rambusch.com
Website: www.rambusch.com

Type of Business:

For 123 years, Rambusch has excelled in the fields of lighting, church furnishings, stained glass, mosaics, and individual works of art. Our in-house design group provides the same attention to detail to all commissions, be it new work, renovations, or interior restorations. Our in-house lighting art-metal and stained glass workshops are under the direct supervision of a Rambusch family member.

Lighting: Rambusch custom-engineered lighting systems are the industry standard for church lighting. Utilizing LED technology and other sources, Rambusch designs and fabricates standard and custom lighting fixtures in keeping with the architectural style and requirements of the space.

Church Furnishings: In response to the voice of the parish community and the building, Rambusch designs and creates furnishings to serve all liturgical needs in nearly every medium and for all budgets.

Stained Glass: Rambusch creates and executes new traditional or contemporary designs and restores and conserves treasured older windows. On time and within budget.

Mosaic: Rambusch handles the logistics to produce small, and large-scale mosaic installation. We plan, design and cartoon in our facility. Fabrication, sectioning and projection are performed under our close supervision in Italy, or in other studios nearby.

Personnel:

Viggo B.A. Rambusch (Third Generation)
Edwin P. Rambusch (Fourth Generation)
Martin V. Rambusch (Fourth Generation)

Baptismal Fonts

RAMBUSCH

Rambusch
160 Cornelison Avenue
Jersey City, NJ 07304
Tel: 201-333-2525
E-mail: info@rambusch.com
Website: www.rambusch.com

Type of Business:

For 123 years, Rambusch has excelled in the fields of lighting, church furnishings, stained glass, mosaics, and individual works of art. Our in-house design group provides the same attention to detail to all commissions, be it new work, renovations, or interior restorations. Our in-house lighting art-metal and stained glass workshops are under the direct supervision of a Rambusch family member.

Lighting: Rambusch custom-engineered lighting systems are the industry standard for church lighting. Utilizing LED technology and other sources, Rambusch designs and fabricates standard and custom lighting fixtures in keeping with the architectural style and requirements of the space.

Church Furnishings: In response to the voice of the parish community and the building, Rambusch designs and creates furnishings to serve all liturgical needs in nearly every medium and for all budgets.

Stained Glass: Rambusch creates and executes new traditional or contemporary designs and restores and conserves treasured older windows. On time and within budget.

Mosaic: Rambusch handles the logistics to produce small, and large-scale mosaic installation. We plan, design and cartoon in our facility. Fabrication, sectioning and projection are performed under our close supervision in Italy, or in other studios nearby.

Personnel:

Viggo B.A. Rambusch (Third Generation)
Edwin P. Rambusch (Fourth Generation)
Martin V. Rambusch (Fourth Generation)

Bells, Carillons, Etc.

The Verdin Company
444 Reading Road
Cincinnati, OH 45202
Tel: 800-543-0488; 513-241-4010
Fax: 888-298-0597
E-mail: info@verdin.com
Website: www.verdin.com

Type of Business:

Bells, Clocks, Carillons, Towers

Call the community to church with the inspiring, rich sound of cast bronze bells!

For more than 180 years, The Verdin Company has provided churches across the country with cast bronze bells, electronic carillon bells, and bell & clock towers. With more than 55,000 installations, Verdin today is led by the sixth generation of family ownership who remain committed to the spirit of artisanal craftsmanship and technological innovation that has guided the company since 1842.

Personnel:

Robert Verdin III (CEO)
Tim Verdin (President)

Interior Design/Restoration

Baker Liturgical Art, LLC
Church Restoration / Church Renovation

Baker Liturgical Art, LLC
1210 Meriden Waterbury Road
Plantsville, CT 06479
Tel: 860-621-7471
Fax: 860-621-7607
E-mail: info@bakerart.net
Website: www.bakerliturgicalart.com

Type of Business:

Baker Liturgical Art, LLC offers a full range of construction and renovation services. These services encompass architectural specifications and liturgical design as well as sound system and lighting design.

Our liturgical design talents result in beautiful altar furnishings of hand-carved wood or of fine imported Italian marble. Stained glass and sacred artwork (painted, wood-carved or chiseled from marble) are the final accents to complete prayerful settings in every worship space from the smallest Chapel to the grandest Cathedral! Baker Liturgical Art, LLC prides itself in offering uncompromising quality in its products and services.

Our Services Include: Liturgical Design, Architectural Services, Liturgical Furnishings, Sculpture & Artwork, Flooring, Millwork, Multi-Media Systems, Stained Glass Fabrication & Restoration, Historical Painting & Decorating.

Additional location: 9427 S. Ocean Drive, Jensen Beach, FL 34957. Tel: 860-919-2119.

Personnel:

Brian T. Baker (President)

CONRAD SCHMITT STUDIOS, INC.
Excellence in Artistry Since 1889

Conrad Schmitt Studios, Inc. (CSS)
2405 S. 162nd Street
New Berlin, WI 53151
Tel: 800-969-3033; 262-786-3030
Fax: 262-786-9036
E-mail: studio@conradschmitt.com
Website: www.conradschmitt.com

Type of Business:

For over 130 years, CSS has advanced a tradition of excellence in artistry and craftsmanship. Studio artisans do more than paint walls or assemble windows – they create inspirational environments and enduring works of art. Our comprehensive scope of services allows us to be a single source for a variety of needs, creating the best projects in terms of function, longevity and aesthetics.

Decorative Painting/Restoration – Our experienced staff assists projects in the early stages to help assemble the master plan, communicate the vision and generate the enthusiasm/funding needed to make the plan a reality. Tools used to accomplish these goals include renderings, on-site samples, budgetary estimates and fundraising materials. Services include investigation/documentation of decorative schemes, gilding, glazing, marbleizing, stenciling, trompe l'oeil and faux finishing.

Stained Glass/Architectural Art Glass – Original stained-glass windows are created in a variety of styles by experienced artists/craftspeople. From the first idea to final installation, the best of traditional craft and new technology are combined to offer unparalleled quality in new design. CSS artisans also conserve/restore thousands of square feet of stained glass each year. Services include thematic development, design, cartoons, glass selection, sample panel, fabrication/installation, framing, storm glass and fundraising.

RAMBUSCH

Rambusch
160 Cornelison Avenue
Jersey City, NJ 07304
Tel: 201-333-2525
E-mail: info@rambusch.com; Website: www.rambusch.com

Type of Business:

For 123 years, Rambusch has excelled in the fields of lighting, church furnishings, stained glass, mosaics, and individual works of art. Our in-house design group provides the same attention to detail to all commissions, be it new work, renovations, or interior restorations. Our in-house lighting art-metal and stained glass workshops are under the direct supervision of a Rambusch family member.

Lighting: Rambusch custom-engineered lighting systems are the industry standard for church lighting. Utilizing LED technology and other sources, Rambusch designs and fabricates standard and custom lighting fixtures in keeping with the architectural style and requirements of the space.

Church Furnishings: In response to the voice of the parish community and the building, Rambusch designs and creates furnishings to serve all liturgical needs in nearly every medium and for all budgets.

Stained Glass: Rambusch creates and executes new traditional or contemporary designs and restores and conserves treasured older windows. On time and within budget.

Mosaic: Rambusch handles the logistics to produce small, and large-scale mosaic installation. We plan, design and cartoon in our facility. Fabrication, sectioning and projection are performed under our close supervision in Italy, or in other studios nearby.

Personnel:

Viggo B.A. Rambusch (Third Generation)
Edwin P. Rambusch (Fourth Generation)
Martin V. Rambusch (Fourth Generation)

Lighting of Liturgical Space

RAMBUSCH

Rambusch
160 Cornelison Avenue
Jersey City, NJ 07304
Tel: 201-333-2525
E-mail: info@rambusch.com; Website: www.rambusch.com

Type of Business:

For 123 years, Rambusch has excelled in the fields of lighting, church furnishings, stained glass, mosaics, and individual works of art. Our in-house design group provides the same attention to detail to all commissions, be it new work, renovations, or interior restorations. Our in-house lighting art-metal and stained glass workshops are under the direct supervision of a Rambusch family member.

Lighting: Rambusch custom-engineered lighting systems are the industry standard for church lighting. Utilizing LED technology and other sources, Rambusch designs and fabricates standard and custom lighting fixtures in keeping with the architectural style and requirements of the space.

Church Furnishings: In response to the voice of the parish community and the building, Rambusch designs and creates furnishings to serve all liturgical needs in nearly every medium and for all budgets.

Stained Glass: Rambusch creates and executes new traditional or contemporary designs and restores and conserves treasured older windows. On time and within budget.

Mosaic: Rambusch handles the logistics to produce small, and large-scale mosaic installation. We plan, design and cartoon in our facility. Fabrication, sectioning and projection are performed under our close supervision in Italy, or in other studios nearby.

Personnel:

Viggo B.A. Rambusch (Third Generation)
Edwin P. Rambusch (Fourth Generation)
Martin V. Rambusch (Fourth Generation)

Liturgical Design

Baker Liturgical Art, LLC
1210 Meriden Waterbury Road
Plantsville, CT 06479
Tel: 860-621-7471
Fax: 860-621-7607
E-mail: info@bakerart.net
Website: www.bakerliturgicalart.com

Type of Business:

Baker Liturgical Art, LLC offers a full range of construction and renovation services. These services encompass architectural specifications and liturgical design as well as sound system and lighting design.

Our liturgical design talents result in beautiful altar furnishings of hand-carved wood or of fine imported Italian marble. Stained glass and sacred artwork (painted, wood-carved or chiseled from marble) are the final accents to complete prayerful settings in every worship space from the smallest Chapel to the grandest Cathedral! Baker Liturgical Art, LLC prides itself in offering uncompromising quality in its products and services.

Our Services Include: Liturgical Design, Architectural Services, Liturgical Furnishings, Sculpture & Artwork, Flooring, Millwork, Multi-Media Systems, Stained Glass Fabrication & Restoration, Historical Painting & Decorating.

Additional location: 9427 S. Ocean Drive, Jensen Beach, FL 34957. Tel: 860-919-2119.

Personnel:

Brian T. Baker (President)

RAMBUSCH

Rambusch
160 Cornelison Avenue
Jersey City, NJ 07304
Tel: 201-333-2525
E-mail: info@rambusch.com
Website: www.rambusch.com

Type of Business:

For 123 years, Rambusch has excelled in the fields of lighting, church furnishings, stained glass, mosaics, and individual works of art. Our in-house design group provides the same attention to detail to all commissions, be it new work, renovations, or interior restorations. Our in-house lighting art-metal and stained glass workshops are under the direct supervision of a Rambusch family member.

Lighting: Rambusch custom-engineered lighting systems are the industry standard for church lighting. Utilizing LED technology and other sources, Rambusch designs and fabricates standard and custom lighting fixtures in keeping with the architectural style and requirements of the space.

Church Furnishings: In response to the voice of the parish community and the building, Rambusch designs and creates furnishings to serve all liturgical needs in nearly every medium and for all budgets.

Stained Glass: Rambusch creates and executes new traditional or contemporary designs and restores and conserves treasured older windows. On time and within budget.

Mosaic: Rambusch handles the logistics to produce small, and large-scale mosaic installation. We plan, design and cartoon in our facility. Fabrication, sectioning and projection are performed under our close supervision in Italy, or in other studios nearby.

Personnel:

Viggo B.A. Rambusch (Third Generation)
Edwin P. Rambusch (Fourth Generation)
Martin V. Rambusch (Fourth Generation)

CHURCH GLASS–GENERAL

Associated Crafts® & Willet Hauser®
1685 Wilkie Drive
Winona, MN 55987
Tel: 800-533-3960
Fax: 877-495-9486
E-mail: info@willethauser.com
Website: www.willethauser.com

Type of Business:

A significant part of history involving art glass in the United States belongs to Associated Crafts® & Willet Hauser®. Today our windows can be found all throughout the United States and in 14 other countries. From religious institutions to commercial buildings we have created, repaired, and protected hundreds of thousands of stained glass windows.

Following are just a few notable examples of the institutions whose stained glass our artisans have restored and preserved over more than a century:

The National Cathedral, Washington, DC; The Church Center, United Nations, NY; The Cathedral of St. Mary of the Assumption, San Francisco, CA; Cathedral of Mary Our Queen, Baltimore, MD; Princeton University Chapel; The Cadet Chapel, United States Military Academy, West Point; Arlington National Cemetery Chapel

When you choose our studio to preserve your stained glass legacy, you are trusting your legacy to ours.

CONRAD SCHMITT STUDIOS, INC.
Excellence in Artistry Since 1889

Conrad Schmitt Studios, Inc. (CSS)
2405 S. 162nd Street
New Berlin, WI 53151
Tel: 800-969-3033; 262-786-3030; Fax: 262-786-9036
E-mail: studio@conradschmitt.com; Website: www.conradschmitt.com

Type of Business:

For over 130 years, CSS has advanced a tradition of excellence in artistry and craftsmanship. Studio artisans do more than paint walls or assemble windows – they create inspirational environments and enduring works of art. Our comprehensive scope of services allows us to be a single source for a variety of needs, creating the best projects in terms of function, longevity and aesthetics.

Decorative Painting/Restoration – Our experienced staff assists projects in the early stages to help assemble the master plan, communicate the vision and generate the enthusiasm/funding needed to make the plan a reality. Tools used to accomplish these goals include renderings, on-site samples, budgetary estimates and fundraising materials. Services include investigation/documentation of decorative schemes, gilding, glazing, marbleizing, stenciling, trompe l'oeil and faux finishing.

Stained Glass/Architectural Art Glass – Original stained-glass windows are created in a variety of styles by experienced artists/craftspeople. From the first idea to final installation, the best of traditional craft and new technology are combined to offer unparalleled quality in new design. CSS artisans also conserve/restore thousands of square feet of stained glass each year. Services include thematic development, design, cartoons, glass selection, sample panel, fabrication/installation, framing, storm glass and fundraising.

RAMBUSCH

Rambusch
160 Cornelison Avenue, Jersey City, NJ 07304
Tel: 201-333-2525
E-mail: info@rambusch.com; Website: www.rambusch.com

Type of Business:

For 123 years, Rambusch has excelled in the fields of lighting, church furnishings, stained glass, mosaics, and individual works of art. Our in-house design group provides the same attention to detail to all commissions, be it new work, renovations, or interior restorations. Our in-house lighting art-metal and stained glass workshops are under the direct supervision of a Rambusch family member.

Lighting: Rambusch custom-engineered lighting systems are the industry standard for church lighting. Utilizing LED technology and other sources, Rambusch designs and fabricates standard and custom lighting fixtures in keeping with the architectural style and requirements of the space.

Church Furnishings: In response to the voice of the parish community and the building, Rambusch designs and creates furnishings to serve all liturgical needs in nearly every medium and for all budgets.

Stained Glass: Rambusch creates and executes new traditional or contemporary designs and restores and conserves treasured older windows. On time and within budget.

Mosaic: Rambusch handles the logistics to produce small, and large-scale mosaic installation. We plan, design and cartoon in our facility. Fabrication, sectioning and projection are performed under our close supervision in Italy, or in other studios nearby.

Personnel:

Viggo B.A. Rambusch (Third Generation)
Edwin P. Rambusch (Fourth Generation)
Martin V. Rambusch (Fourth Generation)

Antiqued Stained Glass

Associated Crafts® & Willet Hauser®
1685 Wilkie Drive
Winona, MN 55987
Tel: 800-533-3960
Fax: 877-495-9486
E-mail: info@willethauser.com
Website: www.willethauser.com

Type of Business:

A significant part of history involving art glass in the United States belongs to Associated Crafts® & Willet Hauser®. Today our windows can be found all throughout the United States and in 14 other countries. From religious institutions to commercial buildings we have created, repaired, and protected hundreds of thousands of stained glass windows.

Following are just a few notable examples of the institutions whose stained glass our artisans have restored and preserved over more than a century:

The National Cathedral, Washington, DC; The Church Center, United Nations, NY; The Cathedral of St. Mary of the Assumption, San Francisco, CA; Cathedral of Mary Our Queen, Baltimore, MD; Princeton University Chapel; The Cadet Chapel, United States Military Academy, West Point; Arlington National Cemetery Chapel

When you choose our studio to preserve your stained glass legacy, you are trusting your legacy to ours.

Decorative/Religious Window Film

ChurchWindowFilm.com/Bell Stained Glass
2016 Airport Boulevard
Mobile, AL 36606
Tel: 1-800-291-3739; Fax: 1-251-473-6865
E-mail: lewis@churchwindowfilm.com
Website: www.ChurchWindowFilm.com

Type of Business:

The look of priceless stained glass is here for a fraction of the cost. Our film is guaranteed for ***TEN*** years. Since 1989 our company Bell Stained Glass saw the need to offer magnificent stained glass art to churches for a reasonable price. Also, our designs are made to apply to your own glass. It's a low-cost substitute for a stained glass look that will add beauty to your sanctuary. In traditional Catholic, modern, and orthodox designs. It's easily installed by most anyone. See our short installation video or have someone professionally install it for you! Across America, ChurchWindowFilm has been the answer. This is peerless quality that you must see for yourself. Call for a sample. Our artists also produce custom designed Murals and Medallions of religious saints and scenes to enhance your church, school, or chapel.

- **A fraction of the cost of stained glass but looks the same**
- **Church's all over America enjoy our film**
- **10-Year Guarantee - Save carpets and pews from sun damage**
- **Custom sized … made to your needs, Saints, emblems.**
- **Samples available ... colors to your taste**

Etched Glass

Associated Crafts® & Willet Hauser®
1685 Wilkie Drive
Winona, MN 55987
Tel: 800-533-3960
Fax: 877-495-9486
E-mail: info@willethauser.com
Website: www.willethauser.com

Type of Business:

A significant part of history involving art glass in the United States belongs to Associated Crafts® & Willet Hauser®. Today our windows can be found all throughout the United States and in 14 other countries. From religious institutions to commercial buildings we have created, repaired, and protected hundreds of thousands of stained glass windows.

Following are just a few notable examples of the institutions whose stained glass our artisans have restored and preserved over more than a century:

The National Cathedral, Washington, DC; The Church Center, United Nations, NY; The Cathedral of St. Mary of the Assumption, San Francisco, CA; Cathedral of Mary Our Queen, Baltimore, MD; Princeton University Chapel; The Cadet Chapel, United States Military Academy, West Point; Arlington National Cemetery Chapel

When you choose our studio to preserve your stained glass legacy, you are trusting your legacy to ours.

Faceted Glass

Associated Crafts® & Willet Hauser®
1685 Wilkie Drive
Winona, MN 55987
Tel: 800-533-3960
Fax: 877-495-9486
E-mail: info@willethauser.com
Website: www.willethauser.com

Type of Business:

A significant part of history involving art glass in the United States belongs to Associated Crafts® & Willet Hauser®. Today our windows can be found all throughout the United States and in 14 other countries. From religious institutions to commercial buildings we have created, repaired, and protected hundreds of thousands of stained glass windows.

Following are just a few notable examples of the institutions whose stained glass our artisans have restored and preserved over more than a century:

The National Cathedral, Washington, DC; The Church Center, United Nations, NY; The Cathedral of St. Mary of the Assumption, San Francisco, CA; Cathedral of Mary Our Queen, Baltimore, MD; Princeton University Chapel; The Cadet Chapel, United States Military Academy, West Point; Arlington National Cemetery Chapel

When you choose our studio to preserve your stained glass legacy, you are trusting your legacy to ours.

Stained Glass

Associated Crafts® & Willet Hauser®
1685 Wilkie Drive
Winona, MN 55987
Tel: 800-533-3960
Fax: 877-495-9486
E-mail: info@willethauser.com
Website: www.willethauser.com

Type of Business:

A significant part of history involving art glass in the United States belongs to Associated Crafts® & Willet Hauser®. Today our windows can be found all throughout the United States and in 14 other countries. From religious institutions to commercial buildings we have created, repaired, and protected hundreds of thousands of stained glass windows.

Following are just a few notable examples of the institutions whose stained glass our artisans have restored and preserved over more than a century:

The National Cathedral, Washington, DC; The Church Center, United Nations, NY; The Cathedral of St. Mary of the Assumption, San Francisco, CA; Cathedral of Mary Our Queen, Baltimore, MD; Princeton University Chapel; The Cadet Chapel, United States Military Academy, West Point; Arlington National Cemetery Chapel

When you choose our studio to preserve your stained glass legacy, you are trusting your legacy to ours.

Baker Liturgical Art, LLC
1210 Meriden Waterbury Road
Plantsville, CT 06479
Tel: 860-621-7471; Fax: 860-621-7607
E-mail: info@bakerart.net; Website: www.bakerliturgicalart.com

Type of Business:

Baker Liturgical Art, LLC offers a full range of construction and renovation services. These services encompass architectural specifications and liturgical design as well as sound system and lighting design.

Our liturgical design talents result in beautiful altar furnishings of hand-carved wood or of fine imported Italian marble. Stained glass and sacred artwork (painted, wood-carved or chiseled from marble) are the final accents to complete prayerful settings in every worship space from the smallest Chapel to the grandest Cathedral! Baker Liturgical Art, LLC prides itself in offering uncompromising quality in its products and services.

Our Services Include: Liturgical Design, Architectural Services, Liturgical Furnishings, Sculpture & Artwork, Flooring, Millwork, Multi-Media Systems, Stained Glass Fabrication & Restoration, Historical Painting & Decorating.

Additional location: 9427 S. Ocean Drive, Jensen Beach, FL 34957. Tel: 860-919-2119.

Personnel:

Brian T. Baker (President)

Botti Studio of Architectural Arts, Inc.
2930 Central Street
Evanston, IL 60201
Tel: 800-524-7211; 847-869-5933; Fax: 847-869-5996
E-mail: botti@bottistudio.com; Website: www.bottistudio.com

Type of Business:

Since 1864, Botti Studio has specialized in serving the ecclesiastic environment through design, fabrication, delivery, and installation. Experts on staff in new design commissions, repair, restoration, conservation, and repair provide a source for experienced project management – from conception through completion. Services include: stained, faceted, sandblasted, carved and painted glass, wood / metal / stone frames / protective glazing, murals, marble, mosaics, bronze, statuary, gilding, painting and decorating, complete interiors, new and restorations, historic discovery, documentation and consultation to owner / architect.

Our staff of 45 includes internationally recognized ecclesiastic artists / designers working in conjunction with highly skilled craftspeople / artisans / conservators.

Locations: New York, NY / (212) 362-6085, LaPorte, IN / (219) 362-5934, Chicago, IL / (847) 869-5933, San Diego, CA / (760) 753-0705, Sarasota, FL / (941) 951-0978, Agropoli, Italy / (800) 524-7211.

Personnel:

Ettore Christopher Botti (President, Botti Studio of Architectural Arts Inc. est. 1864)
Megan Brady (Principal)

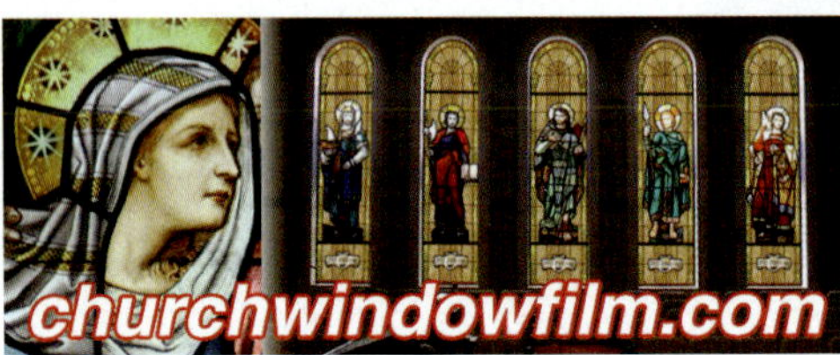

ChurchWindowFilm.com/Bell Stained Glass
2016 Airport Boulevard
Mobile, AL 36606
Tel: 1-800-291-3739; Fax: 1-251-473-6865
E-mail: lewis@churchwindowfilm.com
Website: www.ChurchWindowFilm.com

Type of Business:

The look of priceless stained glass is here for a fraction of the cost. Our film is guaranteed for ***TEN*** years. Since 1989 our company Bell Stained Glass saw the need to offer magnificent stained glass art to churches for a reasonable price. Also, our designs are made to apply to your own glass. It's a low-cost substitute for a stained glass look that will add beauty to your sanctuary. In traditional Catholic, modern, and orthodox designs. It's easily installed by most anyone. See our short installation video or have someone professionally install it for you! Across America, ChurchWindowFilm has been the answer. This is peerless quality that you must see for yourself. Call for a sample. Our artists also produce custom designed Murals and Medallions of religious saints and scenes to enhance your church, school, or chapel.

- **A fraction of the cost of stained glass but looks the same**
- **Church's all over America enjoy our film**
- **10-Year Guarantee - Save carpets and pews from sun damage**
- **Custom sized ... made to your needs, Saints, emblems.**
- **Samples available ... colors to your taste**

CONRAD SCHMITT STUDIOS, INC.
Excellence in Artistry Since 1889

Conrad Schmitt Studios, Inc. (CSS)
2405 S. 162nd Street
New Berlin, WI 53151
Tel: 800-969-3033; 262-786-3030
Fax: 262-786-9036
E-mail: studio@conradschmitt.com
Website: www.conradschmitt.com

Type of Business:

For over 130 years, CSS has advanced a tradition of excellence in artistry and craftsmanship. Studio artisans do more than paint walls or assemble windows – they create inspirational environments and enduring works of art. Our comprehensive scope of services allows us to be a single source for a variety of needs, creating the best projects in terms of function, longevity and aesthetics.

Decorative Painting/Restoration – Our experienced staff assists projects in the early stages to help assemble the master plan, communicate the vision and generate the enthusiasm/funding needed to make the plan a reality. Tools used to accomplish these goals include renderings, on-site samples, budgetary estimates and fundraising materials. Services include investigation/documentation of decorative schemes, gilding, glazing, marbleizing, stenciling, trompe l'oeil and faux finishing.

Stained Glass/Architectural Art Glass – Original stained-glass windows are created in a variety of styles by experienced artists/craftspeople. From the first idea to final installation, the best of traditional craft and new technology are combined to offer unparalleled quality in new design. CSS artisans also conserve/restore thousands of square feet of stained glass each year. Services include thematic development, design, cartoons, glass selection, sample panel, fabrication/installation, framing, storm glass and fundraising.

FRANZ MAYER OF MUNICH est. 1847
Stained Glass, Architectural Art Glass and Mosaic

Mayer of Munich
Mayer´sche Hofkunstanstalt GmbH
Seidlstrasse 25
80335 Munich, Germany
E-mail: m.mayer@mayer-of-munich.com
Website: www.mayer-of-munich.com

Type of Business:

Founded in 1847, Franz Mayer of Munich remains a family business in fifth generation, specializing in the development and production of international projects, spanning traditional to avantgarde artworks and techniques.

Around the turn of the 19th Century, the two sister companies Franz Mayer of Munich and F.X.Zettler belonged to the worldwide renown and appreciated stained glass studios. They produced stained glass windows of finest quality for more than 50 cathedrals and thousands of churches in America. Until today "Munich Style" and "Mayer Style" are synonymous for unique quality.

The Mayer studio is obliged to its tradition and heritage: in style, qualities and values. The crew of artists, glass painters and master craftsmen, take all efforts to meet the high standards, details and transparency of the traditional windows.

The "Munich Style" made Franz Mayer of Munich remain as one of the international leading studios for stained glass, architectural glass and mosaic.

Hiemer & Company Stained Glass Studio
141 Wabash Avenue
Clifton, NJ 07011
Tel: 973-772-5081
E-mail: clericalsupport@hiemco.com

Type of Business:

Premier restorers of stained glass experienced in all styles from American opalescent to European antique. Our permanent staff of artists and craftsmen expertly deal in sympathetic restorations retaining as much of the original fabric of a window as possible. We are highly experienced with large scale restorations, artistic replications and window renovations. Exercising only tried and true methods of restoration, we assure the longevity of beautiful works for generations to come. New works range from bold Liturgical statements to traditional Biblical portrayals executed in magnificent color schemes and created from the finest materials. Trained through a traditional apprenticeship program, the members of Hiemer & Company are dedicated to excellence in craft and the promotion of faith through art. Family owned and operated for four generations. Proposals submitted with no obligation.

RAMBUSCH

Rambusch
160 Cornelison Avenue
Jersey City, NJ 07304
Tel: 201-333-2525
E-mail: info@rambusch.com
Website: www.rambusch.com

Type of Business:

For 123 years, Rambusch has excelled in the fields of lighting, church furnishings, stained glass, mosaics, and individual works of art. Our in-house design group provides the same attention to detail to all commissions, be it new work, renovations, or interior restorations. Our in-house lighting art-metal and stained glass workshops are under the direct supervision of a Rambusch family member.

Lighting: Rambusch custom-engineered lighting systems are the industry standard for church lighting. Utilizing LED technology and other sources, Rambusch designs and fabricates standard and custom lighting fixtures in keeping with the architectural style and requirements of the space.

Church Furnishings: In response to the voice of the parish community and the building, Rambusch designs and creates furnishings to serve all liturgical needs in nearly every medium and for all budgets.

Stained Glass: Rambusch creates and executes new traditional or contemporary designs and restores and conserves treasured older windows. On time and within budget.

Mosaic: Rambusch handles the logistics to produce small, and large-scale mosaic installation. We plan, design and cartoon in our facility. Fabrication, sectioning and projection are performed under our close supervision in Italy, or in other studios nearby.

Personnel:

Viggo B.A. Rambusch (Third Generation)
Edwin P. Rambusch (Fourth Generation)
Martin V. Rambusch (Fourth Generation)

CLERICAL APPAREL–GENERAL

Gaspard, Inc.
200 N. Janacek Road
Brookfield, WI 53045
Tel: 800-784-6868 (toll free)
Fax: 800-784-7567
E-mail: customerservice@gaspardinc.com
Website: www.gaspardinc.com

Type of Business:

Experience the Gaspard Difference. For more than six decades customers have looked to Gaspard for their superb quality in handcrafted vestments and paraments that are made in the USA. Offerings include the exquisite Castle Craft® collection; wardrobe essentials such as albs, surplices, cassocks, robes, and clergy shirts; extensive metalware offerings, fair linens, altar accessories, and communion ware. Because your vestment and parament selections are made to order in our one and only location in Brookfield, Wisconsin, special sizes and custom designs are not a problem. One of our friendly Customer Service Representatives will be happy to help you find just the right size and style to enhance your spiritual expression. Please visit GASPARDINC.COM or call us to speak with one of our friendly and knowledgeable Customer Service Representatives to discover what GASPARD can do for you.

Personnel:

Jason R. Gaspard (President)

Institutional Commodity Services Corp. (ICS)
The Catholic Center
1011 First Avenue, 16th Floor
New York, NY 10022
Tel: 646-794-2600
E-mail: icsap@nyics.org
Website: www.nyics.org

Type of Business:

ICS is the recognized central purchasing agency for parishes, schools and Catholic institutions in the New York tri-state area. We help religious institutions save time and money by procuring for them quality products and services at extremely competitive prices; we also ensure timely delivery, provide outstanding customer service, and offer a full one-stop shop solution for both liturgical and non-liturgical products. We represent a vast array of products, including: clergy attire, altar bread, candles, chalices, liturgical publications, office furniture and supplies, appliances, electronics, maintenance/janitorial products and equipment. In addition, we have a copier lease program, can procure (school and coach) bus charters, and offer printing services – the list of products and services we represent is endless. ICS primarily serves the Arch/dioceses of New York, Newark, Albany, Bridgeport, Brooklyn and Camden, but welcome inquiries from all Catholic institutions.

PSG Vestments
Plot No: 152 & 153 Gangaparameshwari Nagar, PhaseII
Tuticorin, TN, India 628002
Tel: 802-255-2045
E-mail: sale@psgvestments.com
Website: www.psgvestments.com

Type of Business:

PSG your source for quality made to measure vestments. Garments crafted in India to provide world-class production service and quality at an affordable price. We offer modern interpretations of traditional designs.
We offer Cassocks, Cloaks, Chasubles: Gothic, Semi Gothic, Roman styles, Boromean and Pugin. We create exceptional surplices in an English style as well as traditional lace trimmed models. We celebrate copes with Gothic and Roman styles. We can also create Greek and Roman Orthodox Vestments.
Our aim is to have what you need or can dream of available for your worship. We weave our own fabric and create designs on state-of-the-art embroidery machines. This ensures your made-to-measure vestments and paraments, antipendia and more are no problem. At our newly constructed campus and production hub, one of our knowledgeable customer care staff can assist you with your size needs and special design requests.
Please visit us online or call for a catalog.

Personnel:

Suhand Barnabas (Managing Director)

CONSTRUCTION, MAINTENANCE & RENOVATION—GENERAL

Associated Crafts® & Willet Hauser®
1685 Wilkie Drive
Winona, MN 55987
Tel: 800-533-3960
Fax: 877-495-9486
E-mail: info@willethauser.com
Website: www.willethauser.com

Type of Business:

A significant part of history involving art glass in the United States belongs to Associated Crafts® & Willet Hauser®. Today our windows can be found all throughout the United States and in 14 other countries. From religious institutions to commercial buildings we have created, repaired, and protected hundreds of thousands of stained glass windows.

Following are just a few notable examples of the institutions whose stained glass our artisans have restored and preserved over more than a century:

The National Cathedral, Washington, DC; The Church Center, United Nations, NY; The Cathedral of St. Mary of the Assumption, San Francisco, CA; Cathedral of Mary Our Queen, Baltimore, MD; Princeton University Chapel; The Cadet Chapel, United States Military Academy, West Point; Arlington National Cemetery Chapel

When you choose our studio to preserve your stained glass legacy, you are trusting your legacy to ours.

Baker Liturgical Art, LLC
1210 Meriden Waterbury Road
Plantsville, CT 06479
Tel: 860-621-7471
Fax: 860-621-7607
E-mail: info@bakerart.net
Website: www.bakerliturgicalart.com

Type of Business:

Baker Liturgical Art, LLC offers a full range of construction and renovation services. These services encompass architectural specifications and liturgical design as well as sound system and lighting design.
Our liturgical design talents result in beautiful altar furnishings of hand-carved wood or of fine imported Italian marble. Stained glass and sacred artwork (painted, wood-carved or chiseled from marble) are the final accents to complete prayerful settings in every worship space from the smallest Chapel to the grandest Cathedral! Baker Liturgical Art, LLC prides itself in offering uncompromising quality in its products and services.
Our Services Include: Liturgical Design, Architectural Services, Liturgical Furnishings, Sculpture & Artwork, Flooring, Millwork, Multi-Media Systems, Stained Glass Fabrication & Restoration, Historical Painting & Decorating.
Additional location: 9427 S. Ocean Drive, Jensen Beach, FL 34957. Tel: 860-919-2119.

Personnel:

Brian T. Baker (President)

Artists & Decorators

Botti Studio of Architectural Arts, Inc.
2930 Central Street
Evanston, IL 60201
Tel: 800-524-7211; 847-869-5933 ; Fax: 847-869-5996
E-mail: botti@bottistudio.com
Website: www.bottistudio.com

Type of Business:

Since 1864, Botti Studio has specialized in serving the ecclesiastic environment through design, fabrication, delivery, and installation. Experts on staff in new design commissions, repair, restoration, conservation, and repair provide a source for experienced project management – from conception through completion. Services include: stained, faceted, sandblasted, carved and painted glass, wood / metal / stone frames / protective glazing, murals, marble, mosaics, bronze, statuary, gilding, painting and decorating, complete interiors, new and restorations, historic discovery, documentation and consultation to owner / architect.
Our staff of 45 includes internationally recognized ecclesiastic artists / designers working in conjunction with highly skilled craftspeople / artisans / conservators.
Locations: New York, NY / (212) 362-6085, LaPorte, IN / (219) 362-5934, Chicago, IL / (847) 869-5933, San Diego, CA / (760) 753-0705, Sarasota, FL / (941) 951-0978, Agropoli, Italy / (800) 524-7211.

Personnel:

Ettore Christopher Botti (President, Botti Studio of Architectural Arts Inc. est. 1864)
Megan Brady (Principal)

CONRAD SCHMITT STUDIOS, INC.
Excellence in Artistry Since 1889

Conrad Schmitt Studios, Inc. (CSS)
2405 S. 162nd Street
New Berlin, WI 53151
Tel: 800-969-3033; 262-786-3030; Fax: 262-786-9036
E-mail: studio@conradschmitt.com
Website: www.conradschmitt.com

Type of Business:

For over 130 years, CSS has advanced a tradition of excellence in artistry and craftsmanship. Studio artisans do more than paint walls or assemble windows – they create inspirational environments and enduring works of art. Our comprehensive scope of services allows us to be a single source for a variety of needs, creating the best projects in terms of function, longevity and aesthetics.

Decorative Painting/Restoration – Our experienced staff assists projects in the early stages to help assemble the master plan, communicate the vision and generate the enthusiasm/funding needed to make the plan a reality. Tools used to accomplish these goals include renderings, on-site samples, budgetary estimates and fundraising materials. Services include investigation/documentation of decorative schemes, gilding, glazing, marbleizing, stenciling, trompe l'oeil and faux finishing.

Stained Glass/Architectural Art Glass – Original stained-glass windows are created in a variety of styles by experienced artists/craftspeople. From the first idea to final installation, the best of traditional craft and new technology are combined to offer unparalleled quality in new design. CSS artisans also conserve/restore thousands of square feet of stained glass each year. Services include thematic development, design, cartoons, glass selection, sample panel, fabrication/installation, framing, storm glass and fundraising.

Restoration/Refinishing

Associated Crafts® & Willet Hauser®
1685 Wilkie Drive
Winona, MN 55987
Tel: 800-533-3960
Fax: 877-495-9486
E-mail: info@willethauser.com
Website: www.willethauser.com

Type of Business:

A significant part of history involving art glass in the United States belongs to Associated Crafts® & Willet Hauser®. Today our windows can be found all throughout the United States and in 14 other countries. From religious institutions to commercial buildings we have created, repaired, and protected hundreds of thousands of stained glass windows.

Following are just a few notable examples of the institutions whose stained glass our artisans have restored and preserved over more than a century:

The National Cathedral, Washington, DC; The Church Center, United Nations, NY; The Cathedral of St. Mary of the Assumption, San Francisco, CA; Cathedral of Mary Our Queen, Baltimore, MD; Princeton University Chapel; The Cadet Chapel, United States Military Academy, West Point; Arlington National Cemetery Chapel

When you choose our studio to preserve your stained glass legacy, you are trusting your legacy to ours.

Botti Studio of Architectural Arts, Inc.
2930 Central Street
Evanston, IL 60201
Tel: 800-524-7211; 847-869-5933; Fax: 847-869-5996
E-mail: botti@bottistudio.com; Website: www.bottistudio.com

Type of Business:

Since 1864, Botti Studio has specialized in serving the ecclesiastic environment through design, fabrication, delivery, and installation. Experts on staff in new design commissions, repair, restoration, conservation, and repair provide a source for experienced project management – from conception through completion. Services include: stained, faceted, sandblasted, carved and painted glass, wood / metal / stone frames / protective glazing, murals, marble, mosaics, bronze, statuary, gilding, painting and decorating, complete interiors, new and restorations, historic discovery, documentation and consultation to owner / architect.

Our staff of 45 includes internationally recognized ecclesiastic artists / designers working in conjunction with highly skilled craftspeople / artisans / conservators.

Locations: New York, NY / (212) 362-6085, LaPorte, IN / (219) 362-5934, Chicago, IL / (847) 869-5933, San Diego, CA / (760) 753-0705, Sarasota, FL / (941) 951-0978, Agropoli, Italy / (800) 524-7211.

Personnel:

Ettore Christopher Botti (President, Botti Studio of Architectural Arts Inc. est. 1864)
Megan Brady (Principal)

CONRAD SCHMITT STUDIOS, INC.
Excellence in Artistry Since 1889

Conrad Schmitt Studios, Inc. (CSS)
2405 S. 162nd Street
New Berlin, WI 53151
Tel: 800-969-3033; 262-786-3030; Fax: 262-786-9036
E-mail: studio@conradschmitt.com
Website: www.conradschmitt.com

Type of Business:

For over 130 years, CSS has advanced a tradition of excellence in artistry and craftsmanship. Studio artisans do more than paint walls or assemble windows – they create inspirational environments and enduring works of art. Our comprehensive scope of services allows us to be a single source for a variety of needs, creating the best projects in terms of function, longevity and aesthetics.

Decorative Painting/Restoration – Our experienced staff assists projects in the early stages to help assemble the master plan, communicate the vision and generate the enthusiasm/funding needed to make the plan a reality. Tools used to accomplish these goals include renderings, on-site samples, budgetary estimates and fundraising materials. Services include investigation/documentation of decorative schemes, gilding, glazing, marbleizing, stenciling, trompe l'oeil and faux finishing.

Stained Glass/Architectural Art Glass – Original stained-glass windows are created in a variety of styles by experienced artists/craftspeople. From the first idea to final installation, the best of traditional craft and new technology are combined to offer unparalleled quality in new design. CSS artisans also conserve/restore thousands of square feet of stained glass each year. Services include thematic development, design, cartoons, glass selection, sample panel, fabrication/installation, framing, storm glass and fundraising.

FRANZ MAYER OF MUNICH est. 1847
Stained Glass, Architectural Art Glass and Mosaic

Mayer of Munich
Mayer´sche Hofkunstanstalt GmbH
Seidlstrasse 25
80335 Munich, Germany
E-mail: m.mayer@mayer-of-munich.com
Website: www.mayer-of-munich.com

Type of Business:

Founded in 1847, Franz Mayer of Munich remains a family business in fifth generation, specializing in the development and production of international projects, spanning traditional to avantgarde artworks and techniques.

Around the turn of the 19th Century, the two sister companies Franz Mayer of Munich and F.X.Zettler belonged to the worldwide renown and appreciated stained glass studios. They produced stained glass windows of finest quality for more than 50 cathedrals and thousands of churches in America. Until today "Munich Style" and "Mayer Style" are synonymous for unique quality. The Mayer studio is obliged to its tradition and heritage: in style, qualities and values. The crew of artists, glass painters and master craftsmen, take all efforts to meet the high standards, details and transparency of the traditional windows.

The "Munich Style" made Franz Mayer of Munich remain as one of the international leading studios for stained glass, architectural glass and mosaic.

RAMBUSCH

Rambusch
160 Cornelison Avenue
Jersey City, NJ 07304
Tel: 201-333-2525
E-mail: info@rambusch.com
Website: www.rambusch.com

Type of Business:

For 123 years, Rambusch has excelled in the fields of lighting, church furnishings, stained glass, mosaics, and individual works of art. Our in-house design group provides the same attention to detail to all commissions, be it new work, renovations, or interior restorations. Our in-house lighting art-metal and stained glass workshops are under the direct supervision of a Rambusch family member.

Lighting: Rambusch custom-engineered lighting systems are the industry standard for church lighting. Utilizing LED technology and other sources, Rambusch designs and fabricates standard and custom lighting fixtures in keeping with the architectural style and requirements of the space.

Church Furnishings: In response to the voice of the parish community and the building, Rambusch designs and creates furnishings to serve all liturgical needs in nearly every medium and for all budgets.

Stained Glass: Rambusch creates and executes new traditional or contemporary designs and restores and conserves treasured older windows. On time and within budget.

Mosaic: Rambusch handles the logistics to produce small, and large-scale mosaic installation. We plan, design and cartoon in our facility. Fabrication, sectioning and projection are performed under our close supervision in Italy, or in other studios nearby.

Personnel:

Viggo B.A. Rambusch (Third Generation)
Edwin P. Rambusch (Fourth Generation)
Martin V. Rambusch (Fourth Generation)

EDUCATION–GENERAL

Educational Opportunities

Aquinas Institute of Theology
23 S. Spring Avenue
St. Louis, MO 63108
Tel: 314-256-8800; Fax: 1-833-213-6749
E-mail: info@ai.edu; Website: www.ai.edu

Type of Business:

As a Roman Catholic graduate school of theology and ministry, Aquinas Institute of Theology carries forward an 800-year-old Dominican tradition that serves the Dominican Family, local churches, and religious communities through its commitments to priestly and Catholic leadership formation, preaching education, and ecumenical and interreligious dialogue. Aquinas Institute teaches men and women, lay, religious, and ordained, to be hopeful about their faith, faithful to the Church, and servants to God's people in the world. Aquinas Institute is a generous innovator in collaborating with others to teach and to practice theology as a fruit of contemplation, a resource for life, and a ministry to the Church and wider world.

Impelled by the Catholic faith and the Dominican mission, Aquinas Institute of Theology educates men and women to preach, to teach, to minister, and to lead.

Personnel:

Rev. Mark E. Wedig, OP (President)
Rev. Michael A. Mascari, OP (Vice President & Academic Dean)
Rev. Patrick Baikauskas, OP (Vice President of Institutional Advancement)

Seton Hall University
Immaculate Conception Seminary School of Theology
400 South Orange Avenue
South Orange, NJ 07079
Tel: 973-761-9575; Fax: 973-761-9577
E-mail: theology@shu.edu
Website: www.shu.edu/theology/

Type of Business:

Immaculate Conception Seminary School of Theology (ICSST) is the school of theology of Seton Hall University and the major seminary of the Catholic Archdiocese of Newark. With nearly 160 years of preparing committed Catholics for service to the Church, ICSST admits both seminarians studying for the Catholic priesthood and lay students. ICSST offers three graduate degree programs—the Master of Arts in Theology, the Master of Arts in Pastoral Ministry and the Master of Arts in Divinity—in addition to a Bachelor of Arts in Catholic Theology. The School also offers a graduate Certificate in Catholic Evangelization and a graduate Certificate in Christian Spirituality. Since Fall 2011, the School's Center for Diaconal Formation has provided graduate-level intellectual formation for permanent diaconate candidates.

Personnel:

Msgr. Gerard H. McCarren, S.T.D. (Rector and Dean)
Rev. Robert K. Suszko, M.B.A., M.Div. (Vice Rector and Business Manager)
Rev. Christopher M. Ciccarino, S.S.L., S.T.D. (Associate Dean for Seminary and Academic Programs)
Dianne M. Traflet, J.D., S.T.D. (Associate Dean for Graduate Studies and Administration)
Msgr. C. Anthony Ziccardi, S.T.D., S.S.L. (Coordinator for Undergraduate Admissions and Retention)

Spiritual Enrichment

HOLY CROSS
FAMILY MINISTRIES

Holy Cross Family Ministries
Family Rosary
Family Theater Productions
Father Peyton Family Institute
Catholic Mom
Museum of Family Prayer
518 Washington Street
North Easton, MA 02356
Tel: 508-238-4095; Fax: 508-238-3953
Website: www.hcfm.org

Type of Business:

Continuing the mission of our founder, Venerable Patrick Peyton. Holy Cross Family Ministries serves Jesus Christ and His Church throughout the world by promoting and supporting the spiritual well-being of the family through products, programs, events and media.

Personnel:

Father Fred Jenga, C.S.C. (President)
Father Pinto Paul, C.S.C. (International Director – HCFM)
Thomas Lyman (Director – Family Rosary USA)
Father David Guffey, C.S.C. (National Director – Family Theater Productions)
Susan Wallace (Chief Marketing & Communications Officer)

"It's better to light one candle than to curse the darkness"

The Christophers
5 Hanover Square, 22nd Floor, New York, NY 10004
Tel: 888-298-4050, ext. 241; 212-759-4050, ext. 241; Fax: 212-838-5073
E-mail: mail@christophers.org; Website: www.christophers.org

Type of Business:

A non-profit founded in 1945 by Father James Keller, M.M., and grounded in Judeo-Christian principles, The Christophers encourage people to use their God-given talents to make a positive difference in the world. By sharing their gifts with others, each person becomes a Christ-bearer, a "Christopher" in the most fundamental sense of that word. The mission is best expressed in The Christophers' motto: "It's better to light one candle than to curse the darkness."

The Christophers' outreach includes: **Christopher News Notes**, motivational pamphlets; ***Christopher Closeup***, radio show/podcast and blog; **Christopher Awards** for TV, Films, and Books; **Christopher Leadership Courses**; ***Three Minutes a Day*** books; **Annual Poster Contest for High School Students**; **Annual Video Contest for College Students**; **Christopher Minutes**, syndicated radio PSAs; ***Light One Candle***, columns; **Honor and Memorial Cards**; **Military and Prison ministries**; **Donations of Christopher materials** to the needy; **Online ministry**, etc.

Personnel:

Robert V. Okulski (Chairman/Treasurer)
Mary Ellen Robinson (President/CEO)
Tony Rossi (Director of Communications)
Mark E. Jackson (Director of Donor Relations)
Yaneza Santos (Finance Manager)
Edward M. Dougherty, M.M. (Board Member)
Sr. Nancy Usselmann, F.S.P. (Board Member)

FUNDRAISING–GENERAL

Fundraising Counseling

CCS Fundraising
527 Madison Avenue, 5th Floor
New York, NY 10022
Tel: 212-695-1175
E-mail: info@ccsfundraising.com; Website: ccsfundraising.com

Type of Business:

For 75 years, CCS has played a vital role in helping Catholic institutions address critical pastoral, educational, and charitable priorities. As one of the largest and most widely recommended consulting firms for nonprofits, CCS provides fundraising counsel and management services to Catholic institutions worldwide. Our methodology, combined with an emphasis on the precepts and principles of stewardship, has helped to shape some of the most successful and complex fundraising campaigns in the history of Catholic fundraising. CCS successfully plans and manages campaigns and stewardship initiatives for dioceses, parishes, universities, colleges, high schools, hospitals, homes for the aged, social service agencies, seminaries, and religious communities. CCS offices are located around the world, including: Baltimore, Boston, Chicago, Dallas, Denver, Houston, Miami, New York, Philadelphia, San Francisco, Seattle, Southern California, St. Louis, Washington, D.C., as well as Dublin, London, Sydney, and Toronto. To learn more visit ccsfundraising.com, contact us at info@ccsfundraising.com, or call 212-695-1175.

GIFT & SPECIALTY SHOPS–GENERAL

PSG Vestments
Plot No: 152 & 153 Gangaparameshwari Nagar, PhaseII
Tuticorin, TN, India 628002
Tel: 802-255-2045
E-mail: sale@psgvestments.com
Website: www.psgvestments.com

Type of Business:

PSG your source for quality made to measure vestments. Garments crafted in India to provide world-class production service and quality at an affordable price. We offer modern interpretations of traditional designs.
We offer Cassocks, Cloaks, Chasubles: Gothic, Semi Gothic, Roman styles, Boromean and Pugin. We create exceptional surplices in an English style as well as traditional lace trimmed models. We celebrate copes with Gothic and Roman styles. We can also create Greek and Roman Orthodox Vestments.
Our aim is to have what you need or can dream of available for your worship.
We weave our own fabric and create designs on state-of-the-art embroidery machines. This ensures your made-to-measure vestments and paraments, antipendia and more are no problem. At our newly constructed campus and production hub, one of our knowledgeable customer care staff can assist you with your size needs and special design requests.
Please visit us online or call for a catalog.

Personnel:

Suhand Barnabas (Managing Director)

Paintings, Prints & Figurines

ChurchWindowFilm.com/Bell Stained Glass
2016 Airport Boulevard
Mobile, AL 36606
Tel: 1-800-291-3739; Fax: 1-251-473-6865
E-mail: lewis@churchwindowfilm.com
Website: www.ChurchWindowFilm.com

Type of Business:

The look of priceless stained glass is here for a fraction of the cost. Our film is guaranteed for ***TEN*** years. Since 1989 our company Bell Stained Glass saw the need to offer magnificent stained glass art to churches for a reasonable price. Also, our designs are made to apply to your own glass. It's a low-cost substitute for a stained glass look that will add beauty to your sanctuary. In traditional Catholic, modern, and orthodox designs. It's easily installed by most anyone. See our short installation video or have someone professionally install it for you! Across America, ChurchWindowFilm has been the answer. This is peerless quality that you must see for yourself. Call for a sample. Our artists also produce custom designed Murals and Medallions of religious saints and scenes to enhance your church, school, or chapel.

- **A fraction of the cost of stained glass but looks the same**
- **Church's all over America enjoy our film**
- **10-Year Guarantee - Save carpets and pews from sun damage**
- **Custom sized ... made to your needs, Saints, emblems.**
- **Samples available ... colors to your taste**

LITURGICAL & CHURCH GOODS–GENERAL

Church Budget Envelope & Mailing Company
271 South Ellsworth Avenue
Salem, OH 44460
Tel: 800-446-9780; 877-393-3330 (myEoffering)
Fax: 330-337-5990
E-mail: info@churchbudget.com; info@myEoffering.com
Website: www.churchbudget.com; www.myEoffering.com

Type of Business:

Church Budget Envelope Company (CBE) is a premier offertory solutions provider specializing in full-color offertory envelopes, direct mail services and a complete line of electronic services. CBE has a proven history of impacting churches nationwide by increasing mass attendance, increasing offertory giving and reducing envelope costs by up to 40%. Founded in 1917, CBE is a 4th generation family-owned business headquartered in Salem, OH.

Offertory Products include:

Annual Boxed Sets, Periodic Mail Services, Mailback Return Booklets, Prestige Series Holy Day Envelopes, Children Collection Envelopes, Diocesan Mailing Services, Full Color Print Capability, Electronic Giving Services, Parish Growth Software, NCOA Services, 24/7 Emergency Customer Service

Gaspard, Inc.
200 N. Janacek Road
Brookfield, WI 53045
Tel: 800-784-6868 (toll free)
Fax: 800-784-7567
E-mail: customerservice@gaspardinc.com
Website: www.gaspardinc.com

Type of Business:

Experience the Gaspard Difference. For more than six decades customers have looked to Gaspard for their superb quality in handcrafted vestments and paraments that are made in the USA. Offerings include the exquisite Castle Craft® collection; wardrobe essentials such as albs, surplices, cassocks, robes, and clergy shirts; extensive metalware offerings, fair linens, altar accessories, and communion ware. Because your vestment and parament selections are made to order in our one and only location in Brookfield, Wisconsin, special sizes and custom designs are not a problem. One of our friendly Customer Service Representatives will be happy to help you find just the right size and style to enhance your spiritual expression. Please visit GASPARDINC.COM or call us to speak with one of our friendly and knowledgeable Customer Service Representatives to discover what GASPARD can do for you.

Personnel:

Jason R. Gaspard (President)

Institutional Commodity Services Corp. (ICS)
The Catholic Center
1011 First Avenue, 16th Floor
New York, NY 10022
Tel: 646-794-2600
E-mail: icsap@nyics.org
Website: www.nyics.org

Type of Business:

ICS is the recognized central purchasing agency for parishes, schools and Catholic institutions in the New York tri-state area. We help religious institutions save time and money by procuring for them quality products and services at extremely competitive prices; we also ensure timely delivery, provide outstanding customer service, and offer a full one-stop shop solution for both liturgical and non-liturgical products. We represent a vast array of products, including: clergy attire, altar bread, candles, chalices, liturgical publications, office furniture and supplies, appliances, electronics, maintenance/janitorial products and equipment. In addition, we have a copier lease program, can procure (school and coach) bus charters, and offer printing services – the list of products and services we represent is endless. ICS primarily serves the Arch/dioceses of New York, Newark, Albany, Bridgeport, Brooklyn and Camden, but welcome inquiries from all Catholic institutions.

PSG Vestments
Plot No: 152 & 153 Gangaparameshwari Nagar, PhaseII
Tuticorin, TN, India 628002
Tel: 802-255-2045
E-mail: sale@psgvestments.com
Website: www.psgvestments.com

Type of Business:

PSG your source for quality made to measure vestments. Garments crafted in India to provide world-class production service and quality at an affordable price. We offer modern interpretations of traditional designs.
We offer Cassocks, Cloaks, Chasubles: Gothic, Semi Gothic, Roman styles, Boromean and Pugin. We create exceptional surplices in an English style as well as traditional lace trimmed models. We celebrate copes with Gothic and Roman styles. We can also create Greek and Roman Orthodox Vestments.
Our aim is to have what you need or can dream of available for your worship. We weave our own fabric and create designs on state-of-the-art embroidery machines. This ensures your made-to-measure vestments and paraments, antipendia and more are no problem. At our newly constructed campus and production hub, one of our knowledgeable customer care staff can assist you with your size needs and special design requests.
Please visit us online or call for a catalog.

Personnel:

Suhand Barnabas (Managing Director)

Bibles, Hymnals, Missalettes

Bibles.com – A Ministry of American Bible Society
101 North Independence Mall East, FL 8
Philadelphia, PA 19106
Tel: 1-215-309-0900
E-mail: abscast@americanbible.org
Website: www.bibles.com

Type of Business:

American Bible Society offers an affordable variety of English, Spanish and international language Bibles for Catholic readers, including the New American Bible Revised Edition (NABRE), the Good News Translation, the New Revised Standard Version, the New Jerusalem Bible, Dios Habla Hoy and more. There are outstanding resources for children, youth and adults, as well as multimedia and academic resources. Please visit www.Bibles.com to view our Scripture Resources.

Personnel:

John Greco (Managing Director)

Candles, Incense

Cathedral Candle Corp/eximious ®
Website: www.cathedralcandles.com

Type of Business:

Classical symbolism and expressive liturgical design in the luxurious hand decorated artistry of SCULPTWAX, created and mastercrafted here in the United States... exclusively at Cathedral Candle Co.
Now in stock at your nearest church goods dealer.

Institutional Commodity Services Corp. (ICS)
The Catholic Center
1011 First Avenue, 16th Floor
New York, NY 10022
Tel: 646-794-2600
E-mail: icsap@nyics.org
Website: www.nyics.org

Type of Business:

ICS is the recognized central purchasing agency for parishes, schools and Catholic institutions in the New York tri-state area. We help religious institutions save time and money by procuring for them quality products and services at extremely competitive prices; we also ensure timely delivery, provide outstanding customer service, and offer a full one-stop shop solution for both liturgical and non-liturgical products. We represent a vast array of products, including: clergy attire, altar bread, candles, chalices, liturgical publications, office furniture and supplies, appliances, electronics, maintenance/janitorial products and equipment. In addition, we have a copier lease program, can procure (school and coach) bus charters, and offer printing services – the list of products and services we represent is endless. ICS primarily serves the Arch/dioceses of New York, Newark, Albany, Bridgeport, Brooklyn and Camden, but welcome inquiries from all Catholic institutions.

Offering Envelopes

Church Budget Envelope & Mailing Company
271 South Ellsworth Avenue
Salem, OH 44460
Tel: 800-446-9780; 877-393-3330 (myEoffering)
Fax: 330-337-5990
E-mail: info@churchbudget.com; info@myEoffering.com
Website: www.churchbudget.com; www.myEoffering.com

Type of Business:

Church Budget Envelope Company (CBE) is a premier offertory solutions provider specializing in full-color offertory envelopes, direct mail services and a complete line of electronic services. CBE has a proven history of impacting churches nationwide by increasing mass attendance, increasing offertory giving and reducing envelope costs by up to 40%. Founded in 1917, CBE is a 4th generation family-owned business headquartered in Salem, OH.

Offertory Products include:

Annual Boxed Sets, Periodic Mail Services, Mailback Return Booklets, Prestige Series Holy Day Envelopes, Children Collection Envelopes, Diocesan Mailing Services, Full Color Print Capability, Electronic Giving Services, Parish Growth Software, NCOA Services, 24/7 Emergency Customer Service

PROFESSIONAL ASSOCIATIONS & ORGANIZATIONS–GENERAL

Food For The Poor
6401 Lyons Road
Coconut Creek, FL 33073
Tel: 954-427-2222
Website: www.FoodForThePoor.org

Type of Business:

Founded in 1982, Food For The Poor is one of the largest international relief and development organizations in the nation. The organization feeds hungry children and families living in poverty primarily in 17 countries of the Caribbean and Latin America. Food For The Poor has worked with dioceses and parishes across the United States to transform impoverished communities for more than 40 years. Thanks to faithful donors, the interdenominational Christian ministry's programs are providing housing, health care, education, access to water, emergency relief, micro-enterprise assistance and support for vulnerable children and the elderly, in addition to feeding hundreds of thousands of people each day. Since inception, donors have built more than 93,600 homes for families in need of safe shelter and provided more than $17.8 billion in aid. For more information, please visit www.FoodForThePoor.org.

Personnel:

Ed Raine (President/CEO)
Michael R. Chin Quee (Executive Vice President, Church Alliances)
Rev. Robert E. White (Manager, Catholic Clergy Speakers)

"It's better to light one candle than to curse the darkness"

The Christophers
5 Hanover Square, 22nd Floor
New York, NY 10004
Tel: 888-298-4050, ext. 241; 212-759-4050, ext. 241; Fax: 212-838-5073
E-mail: mail@christophers.org; Website: www.christophers.org

Type of Business:

A non-profit founded in 1945 by Father James Keller, M.M., and grounded in Judeo-Christian principles, The Christophers encourage people to use their God-given talents to make a positive difference in the world. By sharing their gifts with others, each person becomes a Christ-bearer, a "Christopher" in the most fundamental sense of that word. The mission is best expressed in The Christophers' motto: "It's better to light one candle than to curse the darkness." The Christophers' outreach includes: **Christopher News Notes**, motivational pamphlets; ***Christopher Closeup***, radio show/podcast and blog; **Christopher Awards** for TV, Films, and Books; **Christopher Leadership Courses**; ***Three Minutes a Day*** books; **Annual Poster Contest for High School Students**; **Annual Video Contest for College Students**; **Christopher Minutes**, syndicated radio PSAs; ***Light One Candle***, columns; **Honor and Memorial Cards**; **Military and Prison ministries**; **Donations of Christopher materials** to the needy; **Online ministry**, etc.

Personnel:

Robert V. Okulski (Chairman/Treasurer)
Mary Ellen Robinson (President/CEO)
Tony Rossi (Director of Communications)
Mark E. Jackson (Director of Donor Relations)
Yaneza Santos (Finance Manager)
Edward M. Dougherty, M.M. (Board Member)
Sr. Nancy Usselmann, F.S.P. (Board Member)

TRAVEL & TOURISM—GENERAL

The Leo House
332 West 23rd Street
New York, NY 10011
Tel: 212-929-1010
Fax: 212-366-6801

You can make your reservations below by:
Calling 212-929-1010, ext. 219
E-mail: lhreservations@332west23nyc.org
Book now on our website: leohousenyc.org

Type of Business:

The Leo House for German Catholic Emigrants, Inc. (the "Leo House") is a nonprofit Catholic guesthouse dedicated to offering affordable and temporary accommodations. People of all faiths are welcome, and we host a variety of guests including clergy and religious, persons visiting the sick and elderly, students, and travelers from the United States and abroad.

The Leo House is, indeed, unique as we are the only place where guests can sleep, go to morning Mass (in our in-house chapel and celebrated by our in-house chaplain) all under the same roof. Our convenient central location is easily accessed by subway, bus and rail. The Chelsea section of Manhattan is a lively and safe neighborhood. Full breakfast is complimentary Monday through Saturday.

Relax in our peaceful outdoor garden, or perhaps take a moment to reflect in our chapel. Free Wi-Fi throughout the property. Standard rates range from $189 to $409 per night. Non-refundable rates are also available on our website. **YOU CAN MAKE A RESERVATION IN ADVANCE.** We accept Visa, Mastercard and American Express. ***Cash, Travelers Checks, Personal Checks or Money Orders will not be accepted.***

Personnel:

Ashley Bryant (Assistant Executive Director)
Karina Cadle (Reservations)

PILGRIMAGES

REGINA TOURS

Regina Tours
545 Eighth Avenue, Suite 1030
New York, NY 10018
Tel: 800-CATHOLIC (800-228-4654)
Fax: 212-594-7073
E-mail: regina@groupist.com
Website: www.1800CATHOLIC.com

Type of Business:

Regina Tours has been the leader in Catholic Pilgrimages since 1984. Our pilgrimages include Fatima, Lourdes, the Shrines of Italy (Assisi, Florence, Rome, San Giovanni Rotondo – St. Padre Pio – Pompeii, & Sicily), Greece (following St. Paul), Mexico (Our Lady of Guadalupe), Poland (Our Lady of Czestochowa), Ireland (Our Lady of Knock) and the Holy Land. We also operate Canonizations, World Youth Day, Oberammergau, Eucharistic Congresses and many other church celebrations.

Pilgrimages offer opportunities to enhance our faith. Contact us for our free color brochure. Learn how you can travel for free and/or use travel as a fundraiser. For more information, visit our website or contact us today.

Personnel:

Nicholas Mancino (President)
Raymond Masillo (Senior Vice President)
Gregg Murasso (Operations Manager)
Dariusz Maciejewski (Sales Manager)
Sharon, Eddie, Kallie, Nick, Loretta, Harry, Fern & Larry (Travel Professionals)

The Leo House

America's only Catholic Guest House named after Pope Leo XIII.

The Leo House is a quiet, Catholic guest house with an old-world charm. We provide hospitality to travelers of all religions, both foreign and domestic. We offer Mass four mornings a week, in our in-house chapel, said by our in-house chaplain, as well as afternoon Rosary.

We offer peace and tranquility in the heart of Manhattan. Enjoy our outdoor garden area, or take a moment to reflect in our chapel. Breakfast is complimentary. We welcome you to be a part of our family. We are your home away from home.

We offer both standard and non-refundable rates, plus Hospital, Clergy and Heroes rate. A full listing is available on our website, where you can book your stay today! Standard rates range from $159 to $409 per night.

For Reservations:

- Please visit our newly revised website at www.leohousenyc.org
- Reservations can be made up to one year in advance.
- You can also email us at lhreservations@332west23nyc.org
- Call us at 212-929-1010 Ext. 219

"Not just another hotel, but a unique spot."

332 West 23rd Street, New York, NY 10011